THE FAMILY RECORD

CERTIFICATE OF MARRIAGE

THIS CERTIFIES THAT

_____

AND

_____

WERE UNITED IN

HOLY MATRIMONY

ON THE _____ DAY OF _____

IN THE YEAR OF OUR LORD _____

AT _____

_____

BY _____

WITNESS _____

WITNESS _____

FAMILY HISTORY

Husband's Family   Wife's Family

PARENTS

FATHER

PLACE OF BIRTH

DATE OF BIRTH

DATE OF DEATH

PLACE OF BURIAL

MOTHER

PLACE OF BIRTH

DATE OF BIRTH

DATE OF DEATH

PLACE OF BURIAL

"Honor thy father and thy mother."
— Exodus 20:12

CHILDREN

CHILD'S NAME

PLACE OF BIRTH   DATE

MARRIED TO

MARRIED AT   DATE

DATE OF DEATH

PLACE OF BURIAL

CHILD'S NAME

PLACE OF BIRTH   DATE

MARRIED TO

MARRIED AT   DATE

DATE OF DEATH

PLACE OF BURIAL

CHILD'S NAME

PLACE OF BIRTH   DATE

MARRIED TO

MARRIED AT   DATE

DATE OF DEATH

PLACE OF BURIAL

CHILDREN

CHILD'S NAME _____

PLACE OF BIRTH _____ DATE _____

MARRIED TO _____

MARRIED AT _____ DATE _____

DATE OF DEATH _____

PLACE OF BURIAL _____

CHILD'S NAME _____

PLACE OF BIRTH _____ DATE _____

MARRIED TO _____

MARRIED AT _____ DATE _____

DATE OF DEATH _____

PLACE OF BURIAL _____

CHILD'S NAME _____

PLACE OF BIRTH _____ DATE _____

MARRIED TO _____

MARRIED AT _____ DATE _____

DATE OF DEATH _____

PLACE OF BURIAL _____

THE KING JAMES BIBLE
RED LETTERED

LARGE PRINT

SPECIAL MARGIN EDITION

- ❖ HEBREW NAMES OF GOD INDICATED AND EXPLAINED
- ❖ SPECIAL WORD MEANINGS NOTED
- ❖ MAP SECTION WITH NEW ORIGINAL STUDY MAPS
- ❖ COMPLETE RED LETTER EDITION
  - OLD TESTAMENT — THE DIRECT WORDS OF GOD IN RED
  - NEW TESTAMENT — THE WORDS OF CHRIST IN RED
- ❖ TOPICAL CONCORDANCE, BOOK SUMMARIES, AND MANY OTHER HELPS
- ❖ OLD TESTAMENT REFERENCES TIED TO NEW TESTAMENT REFERENCES CONCERNING THE MESSIAH
- ❖ MARGIN STUDY GUIDE

The Publisher
P.O. Box 1273
Palm Beach, Florida 33480

THE KING JAMES BIBLE
RED LETTERED

LARGE PRINT

SPECIAL MARGIN EDITION:

✧ HEBREW NAMES OF GOD INDICATED AND EXPLAINED
✧ SPECIAL WORD MEANINGS NOTED
✧ MAP SECTION WITH NEW ORIGINAL STUDY MAPS
✧ COMPLETE RED LETTER EDITION —
  • OLD TESTAMENT — THE DIRECT WORDS OF GOD IN RED
  • NEW TESTAMENT — THE WORDS OF CHRIST IN RED
✧ TOPICAL CONCORDANCE, BOOK SUMMARIES, AND
  MANY OTHER HELPS
✧ OLD TESTAMENT REFERENCES TIED TO NEW
  TESTAMENT REFERENCES CONCERNING THE MESSIAH
✧ MARGIN STUDY GUIDE

The Publisher
P.O. Box 2273
Palm Beach, Florida 33480

022598

INTRODUCTION

The Bible is a book of books, the story of God. It is God's way of having people come to know Him, and His plan for mankind, His chosen and special people. It is not about organizations, but individuals, Old Testament and New Testament believers who by faith will form the true family of God throughout eternity.

The Bible reveals that God has existence from eternity past to eternity future . . . that He is supreme, knows all, is all knowing, all present, all powerful, and without any equal. This self-existing God is revealed to be a tri-unity, with the Father having created "In the beginning . . . the heavens and the earth." It is also revealed that in that same beginning, the Son "was the Word" and "the Word was with God," and "all things were made by Him" (John 1:1-3). The Holy Spirit likewise was present in that beginning, as "the Spirit of God moved upon the face of the waters" (Genesis 1:2). This same Spirit of God is the Comforter, the Spirit of Truth, who "dwells with you, and shall be in you," i.e., the One who lives within the heart of every believer. Being all-knowing, He knew of the angels, of the nature of man, and of sin from the beginning.

The Bible also tells of Lucifer (Satan), to whom it would seem that God in eternity past gave some degree of dominion over planet earth. Then Lucifer fell (Job 1:6-12; 2:1-7; Isaiah 14:12; Ezekiel 28:12-19).

The great message of the Bible is Christ, that He came to this earth to live a perfect sinless life, to teach us the truth, and then to die as the true Passover Lamb, as the innocent sacrificial atonement for our sins. Thus the Scriptures boldly proclaim in a thousand ways, "Believe on the Lord Jesus Christ, and thou shalt be saved, and thy house" (Acts 16:31).

The Bible at first may seem difficult for the average person to understand. As, however, the reader yields himself to the Holy Spirit, who will come to dwell within the believer, the Spirit of God will lead the reader first to Himself, and then to know God more fully and into the understanding of His master plan. The Holy Spirit will glorify Jesus and show the reader God's perfect love in the compassion of Christ and in His touching of needy lives by His holy and beautiful teachings and by His miracles. The reader's eyes will be opened and he or she will come to see the Jesus who fulfilled the Messianic prophecies of the Old Testament (John 14:21, 26; 15:26-27; 16:8-15).

Then the reader will also discover that the Old Testament is not dry reading, but it is the foundation for believing in Jesus, as He is seen in the ancient prophecies and types. This is true because "Christ is in the Old Testament concealed, and in the New Testament revealed." Christ is then seen in the New Testament as the true and sinless man, and as the true and faithful One, God the Son—our King, our Prophet, and our High Priest.

Because the Bible is God's sacred message of mankind, it is often referred to as God's Word. 2 Timothy 3:16 says that it is "inspired," that is theopneustos in the Greek original, "God breathed." Our Lord declared that "Scripture cannot be broken" (John 10:35). 2 Peter 1:21 affirms that the Bible is not really of human origin, but rather "Holy men of God spoke as they were moved by the Holy Ghost."

The depth of this message is so vast that, although the message of salvation from sin may be in its essence simple, yet for a greater comprehension of God and a closer walk with Him, many readings of the Bible are required with the Holy Spirit's guidance. It is thus the prayer of the publishers of this Bible that you will seek that deeper understanding by diligently reading and studying these sacred pages. May it bring new joy and blessing into your life.

Note also the margin markings that cover about 100 subjects divided in three sections. G for those verses relating to God and the many attributes of God the Father, Son and Holy Spirit. Also with God having a Plan, then the verses that are illustrating the Plan and to implement God's Plan, He uses man which then comes under the heading M.

At the end of each line there is a number which is the reference to a succeeding page for you to continue the study of the subject.

It is natural that there are many verses where there is a co-relationship one with the other and also it would be impossible to list all the verses and therefore, the listings are not conclusive but they will enable you to have a good knowledge of the subject by following through the subject to the succeeding pages so forth.

If by chance you find a verse that has been omitted and you would like to add it into your own Bible, then you can easily do so, either by marking it on the margin yourself or you can also, if you want to make a special study of some subject, you could develop your own reference on one of the blank pages that is in the back of the Bible.

We trust you will find this a very interesting subject and will enable you to further develop the different themes that are involved and your knowledge of Him, His Plan and Man, will be greatly enhanced.

Heaven or Hell?

TABLE OF CONTENTS

THE KING JAMES RED LETTER BIBLE
PREFACE

The King James Red Letter Bible is offered to the Christian public as a unique Bible study tool, providing a combination of helps hitherto found in no other Bible. The text, of course, is the beloved King James Version of 1611, with only some minor word changes in the case of clearly archaic words. These have been noted on a separate page entitled "Spelling Changes."

The Red lettering in this Bible is a first, in that it has been done throughout both the Old and New Testaments. While the publishers believe firmly that *ALL* of the Bible is God's Word and inerrant (2 Timothy 3:16), nevertheless the highlighting of *Christ's words in the New Testament* has proven to be a special help and blessing to countless people during the last few decades. Added to this, in this Bible, *throughout the entire Old Testament the direct words of God* have also been placed in red type. This added emphasis, it is hoped, will add blessing and clarity to Old Testament devotional reading and study.

The reader should be aware, however, that the red lettering is only "suggestive," and that in many instances both in the Old and New Testaments scholars, as well as ordinary people, will differ as to whether or not this or that particular verse or passage should have been colored red. Great effort, none-the-less, has gone into the effort to color code the text as soundly as possible, and this labor, it is trusted, will indeed bring to many greater enjoyment and understanding in their Bible reading.

Another unique feature of this Bible is the emphasis which has been placed upon providing the reader with indications of *the Hebrew names of God* used in many places in the Old Testament. A complete explanatory section of the names of God and the significance of each can be found on pages xi-xvi. These names of God, usually indicated at end of verse of the Old Testament will prove to be a continual source of added inspiration and blessing. The reader will need only to consult the explanatory pages for the basic meanings of each name of God a few times, and then he or she will soon find his Bible reading enriched on countless occasions as he sees the significance of the particular name of God chosen by the Holy Spirit for each passage. As each individual name of God emphasizes a different character trait of God the study of the one used in each verse further enlightens and illuminates every verse where a name of God appears. That the Hebrew often used *a combination of two names for God*, e.g., "the Lord-God," adds further interest and blessing to this fascinating and edifying study.

Due to the fact that some names of God are used over and over thousands of times in the Old Testament, in cases of repetition within a chapter—and occasionally due to oversight—periodically the Hebrew name of God may not be indicated at end of verse. The reader's indulgence is thus asked for in such cases of human limitation.

Underlined words are explained at the end of the verse in different typeface. When an underlined word occurs more than once per column, it is explained generally in the first and last occurrence in text column. The explanatory words are not necessarily to be understood as alternate translations, nor as corrective translations. These words, however, experience has proved, will often open up the meaning of a word or verse that often has been otherwise not understood or misunderstood.

Added to the above features, this Bible comes with its own entire *mini-library of special features* to help the sincere student of the Bible who is searching for greater knowledge and understanding, *viz.*,

At the opening of each of the sixty-six Bible books there appears a brief *introduction and outline of each book* in order to provide the reader with an instant overview and historical understanding of the book.

Historical outlines of varied length and detail are to be found both at the start of the Old and New Testaments and also at the back of the Bible amid the section entitled, *"A Treasury of Biblical Information."* The reader is urged to leaf through this section several times so as to become familiar with the wealth of information quickly available at his finger tips. *Articles* on the inspiration of Scriptures, how our Bible came to us, on the Intertestament 400 Years, on archaeology and the Bible, as well as on the Bible and Science...prophecy ...and on How to Witness all are contained in these pages to bring instruction, wisdom, and blessing to the reader.

A unique and *original set of maps* has been added also to give greater geographical insights.

Finally, the special *Topical Concordance* of Biblical words, found at the end of this volume, will provide countless aids for locating desired subjects and verses. These sections in themselves will often provide necessary and helpful outlines for Sunday School and other Biblical lessons.

The reader is therefore urged again to leaf through the entire Bible so as to familiarize himself with the wealth of helps available.

It is the sincere prayer of the publisher that this special edition of the Bible will bring glory to God and will prove over the years to be of help to those around the world of every tribe and kindred who seek to know Him better. May many find their Saviour because of these pages, and finding Him, may they continue in the years beyond in the joy, peace, and rest that only the Almighty One can give. Matthew 11:28-30.

Sincerely,

the Publisher

ABOUT THIS SPECIAL BIBLE

The Red Letter King James Bible uniquely uses the color red in the Old Testament to highlight where God Himself is speaking. Quotations of God's word by Biblical speakers or angels are encircled with a red line.

In the New Testament the traditional scheme is used, denoting the words of Christ in red. Here citations of the direct words of God from the Old Testament have been encircled in red (as in the case of many of the OT prophecies concerning the coming of Christ). Likewise, quotations of the words of God or of Christ by others have been encircled in red.

Readers are asked to realize that the red printing and encirclements are offered as a study help to the scriptures with the full realization and affirmation that all of the Bible in its entirety, be it here in red or black print, is indeed God's infallible Word (2 Timothy 3:16).

It is further to be understood that the editors have red-marked verses in both testaments in an attitude of prayerful study and dependance on God. Since neither the OT Hebrew nor the NT Greek manuscripts use quotation marks, it is often difficult to determine whether God or Christ is speaking directly.

Nevertheless, it is our prayer that these aids, including the marginal citations, reference material included at the end of the Bible, and the maps will better enable you to understand God's holy Word and to love and worship Him in all of His redemptive fullness.

THE NAMES AND ORDER OF ALL THE BOOKS OF THE OLD AND NEW TESTAMENT

A BASIC OUTLINE OF OLD TESTAMENT HISTORY

"?" to 2000 BC	Creation to Abraham.
2000	Abraham.
2000 to 1700	The Patriarchs.
1447	The Exodus from Egypt.
1447 to 1407	The Wilderness Wanderings.
1407 to 1400	Joshua's Conquest.
1350 to 1050	Period of the Judges.
1000	David is King.
931	Division of the Kingdom.
721	Northern Kingdom and Samaria fall to Assyrians.
701	Assyria attacks Southern Kingdom and Jerusalem.
612	Nineveh, capital of Assyria, falls.
606	Babylon (Nebuchadnezzar) defeats Egypt (Nacho) at Charchemish.
605	Nebuchadnezzar takes Jerusalem (Daniel taken to Babylon).
597	Nebuchadnezzar subdues Jerusalem second time.
586	Nebuchadnezzar subdues Jerusalem third time, destroys Solomon's Temple and takes the nation captive to Babylon.
539	Persians and allies conquer Babylon.
536	First return to Jerusalem, under Zerubbabel.
454	Second return to Jerusalem, under Ezra.
444	Third return to Jerusalem, under Nehemiah.
420	Old Testament closes with Malachi.

G. COHEN

THE NAMES AND ATTRIBUTES OF GOD

The Hebrew Old Testament names of God teach us concerning His character. The study which follows, if pursued, will amply reward and bless either individual or class. It is a worshipful experience to study the names and attributes of God. It molds both our own faith and character, and moves our heart. May this study lead each one to seek to follow Him closer and to love Him more.

I. The Single Names of God

Abbreviations: s.f. and p.f. Throughout the text of the Old Testament various notes will be found in the margins denoting the different Hebrew names of God which underlie our English translation. The abbreviations s.f. and p.f. indicate respectively SINGULAR FORM and PLURAL FORM for these Hebrew names of God. The fact that the Hebrew often uses a plural form for deity has been taken for centuries by Christians who accept the Bible as the inspired Word of God as an indication of the Tri-unity (three-in-one, hence "Trinity"). Explanations which suggest that this is merely the "plural of majesty" seem inadequate when sufficient Hebrew singular forms of God existed in the ancient world. The combination and alternations between *singular form (s.f.)* and *plural form (p.f.)* for the name of deity, at the barest minimum, harmonize well with the Trinity, which was always existent, but revealed fully in the New Testament. Bible readers, it is the hope of the publishers, will gain much additional understanding and blessing from the numerous indications of the names of God throughout this Bible. It is their prayer that these indicated names of God will show forth the Almighty's wonderful attributes as seen in the Scriptures, and that He will be more understood, worshipped, and loved because of His wonderful everlasting qualities.

Below is a listing of the more frequently used names for God with a brief explanation of each.

1. ĒL — "The Strong One"

This title, singular in form, occurs about 250 times. Ēl brings forth the character of *strength* and that God, Ēl, is the first-cause of all things, i.e., ". . . the most high God, the possessor of heaven and earth . . ." Gen. 14:22. The title is often connected with such Divine attributes as:

"Almighty—God"	Gen. 17:1
"Everlasting—God"	Gen. 21:33
"The living—God"	Josh. 3:10
"A faithful—God"	Deut. 7:9

2. ELOAH — "The Mighty One"

Another singular title occurring some 50 times is ELOAH. The word derives from AHLAH, meaning to worship, to adore. Thus presents God as the one supreme object of worship.

". . . Thou art a God ready to pardon, gracious and merciful . . ." Neh. 9:17

The term is found most frequently in the Book of Job, viz., Job 3:4, 23; 19:4; 37:15, 22; 39:17; 40:2.

3. ELOHIM — "The Almighty"

ELOHIM is a plural form of ELOAH occurring about 2,500 times. It is first used in Gen. 1:1: " . . . God created the heavens and the earth." The same form is used with the pronoun, "us," (plural) and "image" (singular) in Gen. 1:26: "Let us make man in our image," giving an early indication of the mystery of the "Tri-unity" of the Godhead.

4. JEHOVAH "HE IS" — "the Self-Existing One"

This is the most frequently used name (about 6,000 times) and is generally translated as "the *LORD*" and only occasionally as "Jehovah." The spelling as used here was formed in a later time period by inserting vowels to the Hebrew form YHWH to Yahweh, transliterated to Jehovah.

It is used first in connection with Elohim in Gen. 2:4: "The LORD God (Jehovah Elohim) made . . ."

In the name Jehovah three periods of existence come together in one word: the past, the present, and the future—He that always was, that always is, and that ever is to come, as is interpreted in Revelation 1:4.

This name parallels "Lord" as used of Jesus Christ in the New Testament.

5. ADŌN — "Lord"

This is a singular form meaning Lord, Master, Possessor, or Proprietor. It first appears in Ex. 23:17 as "Adōn Jehovah" and is found about 30 times.

6. ADONAHY — "Lord"

The plural form of ADŌN. Used as "Lord" or "Master" only in reference to a Divine title. Occurs about 290 times. "And Abram said, 'Adonahy Jehovah.' " Gen. 15:2.

Divine titles which are compound in form occur throughout the Old Testament by combining the above names with other titles. A total of thirteen are found and indicated in the paragraphs which follow. These are made up usually of two elements, each of which may occur countless times independently. Placed together in compounds, these elements form, in effect, "double" names of God. The double names provide us with a sense of the greatness and omnipotence of God, as He was known to the ancient Israelites through various titles in addition to The LORD (Jehovah) or God (Elohim).

II. The Combination Names of God

The double names of God will often be noted in the text by an underscoring of the name itself within the verse. The Hebrew form of the name will often be given at the end of the verse.

1. *Jehovah* [s.f.] *Adonahy* [p.f.] (Adonay). Translated "God the Lord" of "the Lord God." Meaning: JEHOVAH (IS) THE LORD.

> *Ps. 68:20*   "...And unto God the Lord belong the issues from death."
> See also: Ps. 109:21; 140:7; 141:8.
> *Hab. 3:19*   "The LORD God is my strength..."

2. *Jehovah*[s.f.] *Elohim*[p.f.] Translated: "The LORD God." Meaning: JEHOVAH IS GOD.

Gen. 2:4	"…in the day that the LORD God made the earth and the heavens…"
Gen. 3:9	"And the Lord God called unto Adam…"
2 Sam. 7:22	"Wherefore thou art great, O LORD God."
See also:	2 Kings 19:19
	1 Chron. 17:16; 22:1
	Ps. 72:18
	Jonah 4:6

3. *Jehovah Sabaoth*[s.f.] (Tsebaoth). Translated: "The LORD of Hosts." Meaning: JEHOVAH OF THE (HEAVENLY) ARMIES.

1 Sam. 1:3	"…and to sacrifice unto the LORD of hosts in Shiloh…"
Isaiah 31:4	"…So shall the LORD of hosts come down to fight for mount Zion.."
See also:	II Sam. 6:2, 18; 7:8, 26, 27.
	II Kings 3:14.
	Psalm 24:10; 46:7; 84:1, 3, 12.
	Jeremiah 6:6, 7:3, 30:8.
	Micah 4:4.
	Zephaniah 2:9, 10.

4. Jehovah Elohe Sabaoth[s.f.] (Tsebaoth). Translated: "The LORD God of Hosts." Meaning: JEHOVAH (IS) GOD OF (HEAVENLY) ARMIES.

II Sam. 5:10	"And David went on, and grew great, and the LORD God of hosts was with him."
I Kings 19:10	"And he said, 'I have been very jealous for the LORD God of hosts.'"
See also:	Psalms 59:5; 80:4, 19; 84:8; 89:8.
	Jeremiah 5:14; 15:16; 37:17; 44:7.
	Hosea 12:5.
	Amos 3:13; 4:13, 6:18, 14.

5. *Adonahy*[p.f.] (Adonay) *Jehovah Sabaoth* (Tsebaoth). Translated: "The Lord, the LORD of Hosts." Meaning: THE LORD, JEHOVAH OF THE (HEAVENLY) ARMIES.

Isaiah 1:24	"Therefore saith the Lord, the LORD of hosts…"
Isaiah 19:4	"And a fierce king shall rule over them, saith the Lord, the LORD of hosts"
See also:	Isa. 10:16, 33.

6. *Elohim*[p.f.] *Sabaoth* (Tsebaoth). Translated: "God of Hosts." Meaning: GOD OF THE (HEAVENLY) ARMIES.

Ps. 80:7	"Turn us again, O God of hosts, and cause Thy face to shine; and we shall be saved."
See also:	Ps. 80:14.

7. *Adonahy*[p.f.] (Adonahy) *Jehovah*. Translated: "Lord God." Meaning: THE LORD (IS) JEHOVAH.

Gen. 15:2	"And Abram said, 'Lord God, what wilt Thou give me...'"
Deut 3:24	"O Lord God, Thou hast begun to show Thy servant Thy greatness, and Thy mighty hand."
Ps. 73:28	"I have put my trust in the Lord God..."
See also:	Josh 7:7.
	Judg. 6:22; 16:28.
	I Kings 2:26.
	Micah 1:2.
	Zeph. 1:7.
	Is used frequently throughout Ezekiel.

8. *El Elyon.* Translated: "The most high God," or "the high God." Meaning: GOD (IS) THE HIGH ONE.

Gen. 14:18	"...and he was the priest of the most high God."
Ps. 78:35	"And they remembered that God was their rock, and the high God their redeemer."
See also:	Gen. 14:19, 20, 22.

9. *El Roi.* Translated: "God seest me." Meaning: GOD (IS) THE ONE WHO SEES ME. Occurs once in —

Gen. 16:13	"And she called the name of the LORD that spake unto her, 'Thou God seest me.'"

10. *El Shadday*[p.f.] (Shaddai). Translated: "The Almighty God," "God Almighty," or "The Almighty." Meaning: GOD (IS) THE ALL-POWERFUL ONE. The title is found 7 times in its full form and 41 times in the form "the Almighty." Found most in the Book of Job.

Gen. 17:1	"...said unto him. I (am) the Almighty God."
Gen 43:14	"God Almight give you mercy."
Job 8:5	"make thy supplication to the Almighty."

11. *El Olam.* Translated: "The everlasting God." Meaning: GOD (IS) THE ETERNAL ONE.

Gen. 21:33	"...and called there on the name of the LORD, the everlasting God."
See also:	Deut. 33:27; Ps. 146:10.

12. *El Gibbor.* Translated: "The mighty God." Meaning: GOD (IS) THE WARRIOR.

Isaiah 9:6	"And His name shall be called Wonderful, Counselor, The Mighty God ..."
Isaiah 10:21	"The remnant shall return, even the remnant of Jacob, unto the Mighty God."

13. *Elaha Illaya* (Aramaic). Translated: "The most high God." Aramaic equivalent to the Hebrew *El Elyon* (#8 above). Meaning: GOD (IS) THE HIGH ONE.

Dan. 3:26	"...ye servants of the Most high God, come forth, and come hither."
Dan. 5:18	"O thou king the Most high God gave Nebuchadnezzar."
Dan. 5:21	"...till he knew that the Most high God ruled in the kingdom of men ..."

III. Additional Descriptive Names of God
(A similar New Testament verse is indicated in parentheses for each name.)

1. Jehovah Nissi
   Ex 17:15
   "The Lord My Banner"
   (Heb 12:2)

2. Jehovah Rophi
   Ex 15:26
   "The Lord Who Heals You"
   (John 9:1-7)

3. Jehovah Jireth
   Gen 22:14
   "The Lord Who Provides"
   (Matt 6:33)

4. Jehovah Tzadekenu (Tsidikenu)
   Jer. 23:6
   "The Lord Our Righteousness"
   (Rom 4:6, 24)

5. Jehovah Shalom
   Judg. 6:24
   "The Lord Is Peace"
   (John 14:27)

6. Jehovah Rohi
   Ps. 23:1
   "The Lord My Shepherd"
   (John 10:14, 15)

7. El Chai (Hai)
   Deut 5:25
   "The Living God"
   (Rev 1:18)

8. El Kanna
   Ex 20:5
   "The Jealous God"
   (John 2:13-17)

9. El Hannun
   Deut 4:31
   "The Merciful God"
   (John 8:10, 11)

10. El Avraham Yitzak v-Yacov
    Ex 3:15
    "The God of Abraham, Isaac, and Jacob"
    (John 8:38, 39)

IV. The Attributes of God

His unity   Deut 6:4

A spirit   John 4:24

Invisible   Ex 33:20

True God   Jer 10:10

Living God   Dan 4:34

None beside Him   Deut 4:35

None with Him   Deut 32:39

None before Him   Isa 43:10

None like Him   Ex 8:10

Blessed   Ps 110:12

His name revered   Deut 5:11

His majesty   Hab 3:3

Incomprehensible   Job 11:7

His superiority to idols   Isa 40:12

Creator of all things   Neh 9:6

Governor of all things   Ps 135:6

His works unsearchable   Eccl 8:17

Our constant preserver   Acts 17:28

His immortality   Deut 33:27

His immutability   Ex 3:14, 15

His incorruptibility   Rom 1:23

His eternity   Ps 9:7

First and last   Isa 41:4

His omnipresence   1 Kg 8:27

Omniscience   1 Sam 2:3

His power   Gen 17:1

Wisdom   Rom 16:27

Perfection   Ex 15:7

Produces good from evil designs of men   Gen. 45:8

Disposes of things as He pleases from the beginning   1 Chr 29:12

His justice   Rev 15:3

Does not punish children for sins of parents   Deut 24:16

Often delays His judgments   Eccl 8:11

His chastisements to be borne   Heb 12:5

His mercy   2 Cor 1:2

His love to Christians   1 John 3:1

His love to the world   John 3:16

His goodness   Ps 86:5

His holiness   Isa 6:3

The One who heals   Ex 15:26

His truth and faithfulness   Isa 65:16

Exhorted to trust in Him   Ps 61

Promises to Israel kept   Josh 21:43

Sole object of worship   Ex 20:1

To be feared   Ps 33:8

To be loved   Mt 22:37

To be obeyed   Acts 5:29

Not to be tempted   Deut 6:16

Compared to light   1 John 1:5

His throne   Rev 4:2

His presence   Ezek 43:1

To be imitated   Eph 5:1

The mark of his children   John 13:35

DEFINITIONS OF BIBLICAL TERMS LITTLE USED TODAY

Ariv (Abib)   The first month of the Hebrew calendar, corresponding to the period from about mid-March to about mid-April. This month is also called Nisan.

Acacia   A flowering tree, a type of mimosa, with hard and durable wood.

Adar   The twelfth month of the Hebrew calendar, corresponding to the period from about mid-February to about mid-March.

Agate   A semiprecious stone of various colors, but usually white and brown.

Alabaster   A soft stone of usually light creamy color, from which vases and jars were made.

Aloes   A sweet-smelling substance, derived from a plant. It was used medicinally and as a perfume.

Amen   A Hebrew word which means "it is so" or "may it be so." It can be translated "certainly," "truly," or "surely." In Revelation 3:14 it is used as a title for Christ.

Amethyst   A semiprecious stone, usually purple or violet in color.

Anoint   To pour or rub olive oil on someone in order to honor him or to appoint him to some special work. The Israelite kings were anointed as a sign of their taking office, and so the king could be called "the anointed one." In a figurative sense, "The Anointed One" is the title of the one whom God chose and appointed as Savior and Lord.

Apostle   Principally one of the group of twelve men whom Jesus chose to be his special followers and helpers. It is also used in the New Testament to refer to Paul and other Christian workers. The word may have the sense of "messenger."

Areopagus   A hill in Athens where the city council used to meet. For this reason the council itself was called Areopagus, even after it no longer met on the hill. Acts 17:19

Ark   The wooden chest covered with gold, in which were kept the two stone tablets on which were written the Ten Commandments. It has traditionally been called the Ark of the Covenant.

Artemis   The Greek name of an ancient goddess of fertility, worshiped especially in Asia Minor.

Asherah   A goddess of fertility worshiped by the Canaanites; her male counterpart was Baal. After the Hebrews invaded Canaan, many of them began worshiping these two gods.

Astarte   A goddess of fertility and war who was widely worshiped in the ancient Near East.

Atonement, Day of   The most important of Israel's holy days, when the High Priest would offer sacrifice for the sins of the people of Israel (Leviticus 16). It was held on the 10th day of the seventh month of the Hebrew calendar (around October 1). The Jewish name for this day is Yom Kippur.

Baal   The god of fertility worshiped by the Canaanites; his female counterpart was Asherah. After the Hebrews invaded Canaan, many of them began worshiping these two gods.

Baal-of-the-Covenant   A name by which the god Baal was known by the people of Shechem.

Balsam   A tree from which sweet-smelling resin was obtained; the resin was used for perfume and medicine.

Barley   A cultivated grain similar to wheat, grown as a food crop.

Baalzebub   A New Testament name given in derision to the Devil as the chief of the evil spirits. In the Hebrew, literally, Baal-zevuv, "Lord-Baal of-the-fly"–hence Baal of garbage, where flies dwell. Matt 10:25; 12:24.

Beauty and Bands   (Zech 11:7, 10). In apocalyptic imagery, two shepherd sticks are named "Favor and Unity." God's breaking them symbolized His removal for a time of "Blessing and togetherness" from the Land of Israel because of her continual sins.

Beryl   A semiprecious stone, usually green or bluish green in color.

Book of Jashar   An ancient writing no longer existing, mentioned in Joshua 10:13 and 2 Sam. 1:18. These references imply that the book was well-known and respected. It probably contained songs and accounts of a national character. Literally, Jashar, or Yashar, means "straight."

Breastplate   Part of a soldier's armor, made of leather or metal; it covered the chest and sometimes the back as a protection against arrows and the blows of a sword.

Bul   The eighth month of the Hebrew calendar, corresponding to the period from about mid-October to about mid-November.

Burnt offering   A type of sacrifice in which all the parts of the animal were completely burned on the altar; in other sacrifices only certain parts of the animal were burned.

Caesar   The title given to the Roman Emperor.

Capital   The top part of a column supporting a roof.

Carnelian   A semiprecious stone, usually red in color.

Cassia   A spice made from the bark of a tree; it closely resembles cinnamon.

Chalcedony   A semiprecious stone, usually milky or gray in color.

Christ   The Greek equivalent of the Hebrew word "Messiah." It means "the Anointed One." Jesus was called the Christ because He was the one whom God chose and sent as Savior and Lord.

College   2 Kings 22:14, a district of Jerusalem in which Huldah the prophetess lived. Also referred to as the "second quarter."

Concubine   A servant wife of her master. She had some legal rights, and her master was referred to as her husband.

Coral   A brightly colored stony substance found in the sea; it was used as jewelry.

Council   The supreme religious court of the Jews, composed of seventy leaders of the Jewish people and presided over by the High Priest. It was also called the Sanhedran.

Covenant   An agreement, either between persons or between God and a person or a people. God made a covenant with Noah (Genesis 9:8-17) and with Abraham (Genesis 17:1-8), but in the Old Testament the term usually refers to the covenant made between God and the people of Israel at the time of Moses (Exodus 24:4-8).

Cummin   A small plant whose seeds are ground up and used for seasoning foods.

Cymbals   A pair of thin pieces of metal held in the hands and struck together rhythmically in music.

David's City   In the Old Testament the reference is generally to that part of the city of Jerusalem which was captured from the Jebusites by King David. In the New Testament the reference is to the town of Bethlehem, David's boyhood home, where Jesus was born.

Dedication, Festival of   The Jewish festival, lasting eight days, which celebrated the restoration and re-dedication in 165 B.C. of the Temple altar by the Jewish patriot Judas Maccabeus. The festival began on the 25th day of the month Kislev (around December 10). The Jewish name for this festival is Hannukah.

Defile   To make ritually unclean or impure. Certain foods and practices were prohibited by the law of Moses because they were thought to make a person ritually or ceremonially unclean. Such a person could not take part in the public worship until he had performed certain rituals which would remove the defilement.

Demon   An evil spirit with the power to harm people; it was a messenger and servant of the Devil.

Disciple   A person who follows and learns from someone else. In the New Testament the word is used of the followers of John the Baptist and especially of the followers of Jesus, particularly the twelve apostles.

Divination   The attempt to discover a message from God or the gods by examining such things as marked stones or the liver of a sacrificed animal.

Dragon   A legendary beast, thought to be like a huge lizard. It is also a serpent and appears as a figure of the Devil (Revelation 12:3-13:4; 20:2-3).

Elders   In the Old Testament this is a name given to certain respected leaders of a tribe, nation, or city. In the New Testament three different groups are called elders: (1) in the Gospels the elders are influential Jewish religious leaders, some of whom were members of the supreme Council; (2) in Acts 11-21 and the Letters the elders are Christian church officers who had general responsibility for the work of the church; (3) in Revelation the twenty-four elders are part of God's court in heaven, perhaps as representatives of God's people.

Elul   The sixth month of the Hebrew calendar, corresponding to the period from about mid-August to about mid-September.

Ephod   A close-fitting, armless outer vest, generally extending down to the hips in length. Used almost exclusively as a high priestly garment. It had an emblem upon it for each of the twelve tribes. Ex 28:6-13.

Epicureans   Those who followed the teaching of Epicurus (died 270 B.C.), a Greek philosopher who taught that happiness is the highest good in life.

Epileptic   A person who suffers from a nervous disease causing convulsions and fainting.

Ethanim   The seventh month of the Hebrew calendar, corresponding to the period from about mid-September to about mid-October; it was later called Tishri.

Eunuch   A man who has been made physically incapable of having sexual relations. Eunuchs were often important officials in the courts of ancient kings, and the term may have come to be used of such officials in general, regardless of their sexual condition.

Fast   To go without food for a while as a religious duty.

Fellowship offerings   A type of sacrifice offered to insure a right relationship with God. Only a portion of the animal was burned on the altar; the rest was eaten by the worshipers or the priests.

Flax A small cultivated plant; the fibers of its stem are spun into thread used in making linen cloth.

Flowers (Lev 15:33). Hebrew word means "to flow," an excretion; any impurity. Can be used for male or female. The singular form has quite a different meaning; e.g., "blossom" as in Job 15:33.

For three transgressions... (Amos 1:3; 2:1) A poetic way of saying "because of the many transgressions...this will happen."

Frankincense A valuable incense, made from the sap of a certain tree. This incense was probably imported from Arabia.

Garnet A semiprecious stone, usually red in color.

Gazelle A kind of antelope, known for its beauty and gracefulness.

Gentile A person who is not a Jew.

Giants in the earth Gen. 6:4, may have reference to men of unusual size or to a race of descendants from a union of angels and men.

Hades The Greek name used in the New Testament to refer to the world of the dead. Literally, in the Greek, "Not seen," hence, the unseen world.

Harrow A farm implement used to break up the ground and level it after plowing.

Harvest Festival The Israelite festival celebrating the wheat harvest, held in the latter part of May, fifty days after Passover. The Jewish name for this festival is Shavuoth (the Feast of Weeks). It has also been called Pentecost.

Hermes The name of a Greek god who served as messenger of the gods.

Herodians A political party in New Testament times composed of Jews who favored being ruled by one of the descendants of Herod the Great rather than by the Roman governor.

High Priest The priest who occupied the highest office in the Jewish priestly system and was president of the supreme Council of the Jews. Once a year (on the Day of Atonement) he would enter the Most Holy Place in the Temple and offer sacrifice for himself and for the sins of the people of Israel.

Hyssop A small bush plant, used in religious ceremonies to sprinkle liquids.

Incense Material which is burned in order to produce a pleasant smell. The Israelites used it in their worship.

Jackal A small wild animal resembling a fox. These travel in large packs.

Jasper A semiprecious stone of various colors. The jasper mentioned in the Bible was probably green, or else clear.

Javelin A short, light spear used by soldiers in ancient times.

Kislev The ninth month of the Hebrew calendar, corresponding to the period from about mid-November to about mid-December.

Law The name which the Jews applied to the first five books of the Old Testament, also called "The Books of Moses." Sometimes, however, the name is applied in a more general way to the entire Old Testament.

Leviathan An animal associated with water, in some passages identified by some as the crocodile; by others as a whale.

Levite (1) A member of the tribe of Levi; (2) a man who assisted the priest in the performance of religious duties.

Levitical priest A Hebrew priest descended from the tribe of Levi. All priests were supposed to be members of the tribe of Levi, but in later times not all members of the tribe of Levi were priests.

Living creatures (also referred to as "winged creatures" and traditionally called "cherubim") Symbols of God's majesty and associated with His presence. For a description of such creatures see Exodus 25:18-20; Ezekiel 1:5-13; 10; Revelation 4:6-9.

Lord In this translation represents the Hebrew name Yahweh (traditionally represented by Jehovah), corresponding either to the occurrence of the name itself or to a pronoun standing for the name.

Lyre A kind of harp.

Mandrake A small plant; it was believed that eating its root or fruit would make a woman more easily able to have children.

Manna A food eaten by the Israelites during their travels in the wilderness. It was white and flaky and looked like small seeds (Exodus 16:14-21; Numbers 11:7-9).

Medium A person who believes that he or she can communicate with the dead.

Messiah A Hebrew title (meaning "the Anointed One") given to the promised Savior, whose coming was foretold by the Hebrew prophets; the corresponding Greek word "the Christ" has the same meaning.

Milcom One of the gods of the ancient people of Canaan.

Mildew A fungus that appears on various objects, especially in damp weather.

Millet A cultivated grain that was grown as a food crop.

Most Holy Place The innermost room of the Tent of the Lord's presence or the Temple. The Ark was kept

there. Only the High Priest could enter the Most Holy Place, and he did so only once a year, on the Day of Atonement; the Holy of Holies.

Mustard   A large plant which grows from a very small seed. The seeds were ground into powder and used as spice on food.

Myrrh   A sweet-smelling resin that was highly prized. It served as a medicine (Mark 15:23) and was used by the Jews in preparing bodies for burial (John 19:39).

Myrtle   A kind of evergreen shrub or tree. Esther (Hadasseh, in Hebrew) means Myrtle.

Nard   An expensive perfume made from a plant.

Nazarene   Someone from the town of Nazareth. The name was used as a title for Jesus and also a name for the early Christians (Acts 24:5).

Nazarite   A person who took a special vow of self-dedication. Such a person was not to drink wine, cut his hair, or touch a dead body (Numbers 6:1-21). The vow could be taken for a certain period of time but some persons were dedicated to God as Nazarites from their birth.

New Moon Festival   A religious observance held by the Israelites on the day of each new moon.

New Year Festival   The Jewish name for this festival is "Rosh Hashana."

Nisan   The first month of the Hebrew calendar, corresponding to the period from about mid-March to mid-April. The month is also called Aviv.

Onyx   A semiprecious stone of various colors.

Orion   A group of prominent stars visible during winter evenings.

Outcasts   In the Gospels this name, which in many translations appears as "sinners," refers to those Jews who had been excluded from synagogue worship because they violated rules about foods that should not be eaten and about associating with people who were not Jews. Such outcasts were despised by many of their fellow Jews, and Jesus was criticized for associating with them (Mark 2:15-17; Luke 7:34; 15:1-2).

Parable   A story or proverb which teaches spiritual truth; it was often used by Jesus.

Paradise   A name for heaven (Luke 23:43; 2 Corinthians 12:3).

Paralytic   Someone who suffers from a disease that prevents him from moving part or all of his body.

Passover   The Israelite festival, on the 14th day of the month Nisan (around April 1), which celebrated the deliverance of the ancient Hebrews from their captivity in Egypt. The Angel of Death killed the first-born in the Egyptian homes but passed over the Hebrew homes (Exodus 12:23-27). The Jewish name for this festival is Pesach.

Pentecost, Day of   The Greek name for the Israelite festival of wheat harvest (see Harvest Festival). The name Pentecost (meaning "fiftieth") comes from the fact that the feast was held fifty days after Passover.

Pervert   One who commits unnatural sexual acts.

Pharisees   Literally, in Hebrew, "the Separated Ones." A Jewish religious party during the time of Jesus. They were strict in obeying the Law of Moses and other regulations which had been added to it through the centuries.

Pleiades   A small group of stars visible during winter evenings. This is a star cluster of several hundred stars located in Taurus the Bull. Seven are usually seen clearly.

Pomegranate   A reddish fruit about the size of a large apple; it has a hard rind and is full of tasty seeds.

Precepts   This refers to commandments, teachings, or words of instruction. Psa 119:15.

Preparation, Day of   The sixth day of the week (Friday), on which the Jews made the required preparations to observe the Sabbath (Friday evening to Saturday eve).

Prophet   A person who proclaims a message from God. The term usually refers to men in the Old Testament, but the New Testament speaks of prophets in the early church. John the Baptist was called a prophet.

Psaltery   An ancient three-stringed instrument similar to a lyre. The word "Psalter," however, always refers to the Book of Psalms.

Purim   The Jewish religious holiday held on the 14th day of the month Adar (around March 1), celebrating the deliverance of the Jews from Haman by Esther and Mordecai. The story is told in the book of Esther.

Phut and Lubim   The land and people of North Africa, west of Egypt, modern day Libya.

Quartz   A semiprecious stone of various colors, but usually clear.

Rabbi   A Hebrew teacher of the religious law.

Red Sea (in Hebrew literally "Sea of Reeds")   Evidently referred originally to (1) a series of lakes and marshes between the head of the Gulf of Suez and the Mediterranean, the region generally regarded as the site of the events described in Exodus 13, and was also used to designate (2) the Gulf of Suez, (3) the Gulf of Aqaba, and (4) the Red Sea proper.

Rephan   The name of an ancient god that was worshiped as the ruler of the planet Saturn.

Resin   A fragrant, gummy substance produced from the sap of certain trees and shrubs.

Restoration, Year of   The year, coming every fifty years, when the ancient Israelites returned to the original owner any property they were holding, freed their Israelite slaves, and did not cultivate their fields. This is also called, The Jubilee, and the Year of Jubilee.

Sabbath   The seventh day of the Jewish week (from sundown on Friday to sundown on Saturday), a holy day on which no work was permitted.

Sackcloth   A coarse cloth made of goats' hair, which was worn as a sign of mourning or distress.

Sadducees   Literally, in Hebrew, "the Righteous Ones." A small Jewish religious party in New Testament times, composed largely of priests. They based their beliefs primarily on the first five books of the Old Testament and differed in several matters of belief and practice from the larger party of the Pharisees.

Samaritan   A name used to refer to a native of Samaria, the region between Judea and Galilee. Because of differences in politics, race, customs, and religion (including especially the central place of worship), there was much bad feeling between the Jews and the Samaritans.

Sanhedran   See Council.

Sanctuary   A building dedicated to the worship of God. Sometimes the word refers to the central place of worship and not to the whole building.

Sapphire   A very valuable stone, usually blue in color.

Scepter   A short rod held by kings to symbolize their authority.

Scorpion   A small creature which has eight legs and a long tail with a poisonous sting. It can inflict a very painful, and sometimes fatal, wound, may also refer to a many thonged whip.

Scribe   A person who was a professional copier of Old Testament scrolls and whose business it was to write documents for others or to copy written material. Some scribes were employed by ancient kings to prepare official documents, and some of them became important officials.

Scriptures   In the New Testament the word refers to the collected body of Hebrew sacred writings known to Christians as the Old Testament. Various names are used: the Law (or the Law of Moses) and the prophets (Matthew 5:17; 7:12; Luke 2:22 24:44; Acts 13:15; 28:23); the Holy Scriptures (Romans 1:2; 2 Timothy 3:15); the old covenant (2 Corinthians 3:14). The singular "scripture" refers to a single passage of the Old Testament.

Sea monster or "jackal"   the same Heb. word is used for both. Context of passage dictates which is the correct meaning. See Lam 4:3.

Selah   This word means "lift up;" could therefore mean lifting up of voices in benediction, or lifting up of instruments in an interlude.

Serpent   A name given to the Devil, which appears in the New Testament as the dragon (Revelation 12:3-17; 20:2-3).

Seventh year   The year, coming every seventh year, when the ancient Israelites did not cultivate their fields and when debts were canceled.

Shevat   The eleventh month of the Hebrew calendar, corresponding to the period from about mid-January to about mid-February.

Sickle   A tool consisting of a curved metal blade and a wooden handle, used for cutting wheat and other crops.

Sivan   The third month of the Hebrew calendar corresponding to the period from about mid-May to about mid-June.

Silver cord   In Ecc 12:6 this expression seems to refer to the string that keeps us alive, especially to the spinal column and even more precisely to the spinal nerve cord. How much Solomon may or may not have known or realized about the spinal nerve cord is, of course not known at this time. Solomon, nevertheless, may have known this-even though such knowledge was later lost in the dark ages.

Snuffer   The Hebrew word translated "snuffer" apparently identifies an implement used to trim the oil lamps used in the Tent of the Lord's presence or the Temple.

Sons of God   This phrase usually refers to beings who form a "heavenly court" for Yahweh. In Gen. 6:4, it is not clear as to its meaning. Some say that it is here a reference to fallen spiritual beings who, like demons, entered human bodies, cohabited with human women, and corrupted the pre-Noah human race. Others take Gen. 6:4 to mean simply that the righteous people mixed and married the wicked.

Sorcerer   A person who works magic for evil purposes.

Stoics   Those who followed the teachings of the Greek philosopher Zeno (died 265 B.C.), who taught that happiness is to be found in being free from pleasure and pain.

Sulfur   In the Bible this refers to a sulfur compound which burns with great heat and produces an unpleasant smell.

Tabernacles, Festival of   A joyous festival celebrated by the Israelites in the fall after the completion of the harvest. In order to help them remember the years when their ancestors wandered through the wilderness, the Israelites constructed rough shelters to live in during the festival. The Jewish name for this festival is Sukkoth. It has been traditionally called the Feast of Tabernacles or the Feast of Booths.

Tamborine   A small drum with pieces of metal in the rim, held in the hand and shaken. In biblical times it was generally used by women.

Tassel   A group of threads or cords, fastened together at one end and loose at the other. The Israelites were commanded to wear these on their clothes (Numbers 15:37-41).

Teachers of the Law   Men who in New Testament times taught and interpreted the teachings of the Old Testament, especially the first five books.

Tevet   The tenth month of the Hebrew calendar, corresponding to the period from about mid-December to about mid-January.

Tenant   A man who grows crops on land owned by someone else, and turns over part of the harvest to the owner to pay for the use of his land.

Tent of the Lord's presence   The large tent described in detail in Exodus 26, where the Israelites worshiped God until Solomon built the Temple. It has traditionally been called the Tabernacle or Tent of meeting.

Tithe   A tenth part of a person's produce or income, given to God for religious purposes.

Topaz   A semiprecious stone, usually yellow in color.

Turban   A head covering worn by men, made of cloth wrapped around the head.

Turquoise   A semiprecious stone, blue or bluish green in color.

Unleavened Bread, Festival of   The Israelite festival, lasting seven days after Passover and part of the Passover week. It celebrated the deliverance of the ancient Hebrews from Egypt. The name came from the practice of not using leaven (yeast) in making bread during that week (Exodus 12:14-20). It was held from the 15th to the 22nd day of the month Nisan (around the first week of April).

Urim and Thummim   Urim means lights and Thummim, perfection. Divine judgment on a matter was made known to Israel in certain cases, using these stones. One stone signified yes and the other no-God guiding the High Priests' hands to draw or cast the correct one. These may have been kept in the High Priests' ephod.

Vow   A strong declaration or promise, usually made while calling upon God to punish the speaker if the statement should prove to be not true or if the promise were not kept.

Winged creatures   See living creatures.

Winnowing shovel   A tool like a shovel or a large fork, used to separate the wheat from the chaff.

Woe   Calamity, affliction, sorrow; a condition of deep suffering from misfortune or affliction.

Worm   Quoted in Mark 9:44 from Isaiah 66:24. A poetic and vivid description of the consequences of death in hell. It may refer to the agony of lingering memories.

Wreath-crown   Flowers or leaves arranged in a circle, to be placed on a persons' head. In ancient times a wreath of leaves was the prize given to winners in athletic contests.

Yeast   A substance, also called leaven, which is added to dough made from the flour of wheat or barley to make it rise before being baked into bread.

Yoke   A heavy bar of wood fitted over the necks of two oxen to make it possible for them to pull a plow or a cart. The word is used figuratively to describe the moral lessons that a teacher passes on to his pupils.

Zeus   The name of the supreme god of the Greeks.

Zion   Originally a designation for "David's City," the Jebusite stronghold captured by King David's forces. The term "Zion" was later extended in meaning to refer to the hill on which the Temple stood.

Ziv   The second month of the Hebrew calendar, corresponding to the period from about mid-April to about mid-May.

SCRIPTURE THEME STUDY GUIDE

GOD

ALL POWERFUL   ALL KNOWING   ALL PRESENT

(omnipotent)   (omniscient)   (omnipresent)

JEALOUS

GOD God wants us to know Him —   Father - Son - Spirit

PLAN To know His plan
The Bible tells us of Him
The Bible tells us of His Plan Eternity to Eternity
The Bible tells us of Man - his part of plan

MAN First — called — chosen — Israel
Now — Believers — obedient — followers — church

Follow the references — subject by subject — through the Bible

Make and mark your own special subject you want to know about

ALL COMES OF GOD — HIS WORD THE BIBLE

This booklet leads you through Bible studies by following the verse listing for a study of a particular theme.

This booklet covers only a partial listing of studies. It is broken down into three sections:

1) The **BIBLE** is **God's word** - God wants you to **know Him**

2) **God's plan** - God has a plan from eternity past to eternity future

3) **Man** - The Israel people and the Church today

You will see page number listings in the booklet after each verse. These apply only to the Special Edition Bible, and refer to the pages of the reference. However, the guide can be used with any Bible by using the scripture references.

GOD

Code	Title
G	God
G1	Wrath - Anger
G1A	God's Kingdom
G1D	Omniscience
G1E	Omnipotence
G1F	Omnipresence
G1G	Angels, Holy
G1H	Angels, Evil, Demons
G1L	God's Grace
G1N	God's Sovereignty
G1O	God's Heaven
G1P	God's Hell
G2	Trinity
G3	Father
G4	God - Son - Jesus
G4A	Saviour
G4B	Lord
G4C	Love
G4G	Worship of God the Son
G4H	Blessing
G4K	Judgment by the Son
G4L	Gifts & Crowns
G4N	Resurrection
G4O	God's Commands
G4R	Blood
G4T	Promises
G4U	Sacrifices
G5	Holy Spirit

Plan

Code	Title
P	Plan
P01	Bible
P02	Promises
P03	Covenants-Land
P04	Prophecy
P09	Satan
P09A	Antichrist
P09B	False Prophets
P11	Prayer
P12	Church
P13	Fellowship with God
P15	Man, Abram & Jews
P15A	Chosen-Called
P15B	History
P15C	Special Prophets
P16	Mysteries
P17	End Times
P18	Tribulation: 1st Half
P19	Tribulation: 2nd Half
P20	Rapture
P21	Great White Throne
P22	Lake of Fire
P25	Hades - Hell
P26	Paradise
P27	Millennium

Man

Code	Title
M	Man
M01	Foreknown
M03	Obedience
M05	Life
M06	Second Death
M07	Faith
M09	Future
M10	Sinful
M11	Disobedience
M13	Lying
M15	Baptism
M16	Salvation
M17	Temptation
M18	Grace-Rewards-Gifts
M19	Repentance
M20	Pride
M21	Selfishness
M22	Marriage
M23	Morality
M24	Patience
M25	Doubt
M26	Discipline
M27	Prayer
M28	Man-Anger
M29	Forgiveness
M30	Fellowship
M32	Justification
M33	Sanctification
M34	Glorification
M35	Humility
M36	Hope
M37	Purpose
M38	Law
M40	Work
M41	Believe
M42	To Love God
M44	To Love Man
M45	Truth
M46	Divorce
M47	Righteousness
M48	Wealth, Riches

Book	Chap	Verse	Page
ROM	13	:4	266
COL	3	:6	338
1TH	1	:10	343
HEB	3	:11	378
HEB	4	:3	378
REV	6	:16-17	434
REV	11	:18	439
REV	14	:10	442
REV	14	:19	443
REV	15	:1	443
REV	15	:7	443
REV	16	:1	443
REV	16	:19	444
REV	19	:15	448

G1A God's Kingdom

Book	Chap	Verse	Page
GEN	1	:16	3
GEN	2	:4-7	4
GEN	5	:2	8
GEN	17	:1-2	23
GEN	26	:24	40
GEN	28	:13	44
GEN	28	:15	44
EXO	31	:17	136
DEU	26	:15	324
1KG	8	:30	552
JOB	38	:4-11	833
PSA	2	:4	842
PSA	19	:1	852
PSA	23	:6	855
PSA	100	:3	910
PSA	124	:8	932
PRO	16	:4	963
ISA	33	:17	1043
ISA	40	:21-22	1051
ISA	43	:7	1055
ISA	45	:12	1059
ISA	64	:4	1079
JER	4	:23	1092
HAG	1	:1	1357
MATT	3	:2	6
MATT	5	:3	8
MATT	6	:9	11
MATT	6	:20	11
MATT	6	:33	12
MATT	7	:21	13
MATT	10	:7	17
MATT	11	:11-12	19
MATT	12	:28	22
MATT	13	:11	23
MATT	13	:24	24
MATT	13	:33	24
MATT	13	:44-47	25
MATT	16	:19	30
MATT	18	:3-4	32
MATT	18	:23	33
MATT	19	:14	34
MATT	19	:23-24	35
MATT	20	:1	35
MATT	21	:31	38
MATT	21	:43	39
MATT	22	:2	39
MATT	22	:32	41
MATT	25	:1	45
MATT	25	:14	46
MARK	10	:24	77
MARK	12	:34	81
MARK	16	:19	90
LUKE	9	:27	114
LUKE	9	:62	116
LUKE	12	:32	122
LUKE	13	:18	125
LUKE	13	:20	125
LUKE	14	:15	126
LUKE	17	:20-21	131
LUKE	23	:43	145
JOHN	1	:3	151
JOHN	3	:3	154
JOHN	3	:5	154
JOHN	8	:58	168
JOHN	14	:2	178
1CO	4	:20	278
1CO	15	:24	291
1CO	15	:50	292
COL	1	:16	336
TIT	1	:2	368
HEB	1	:2	376
2PT	3	:13	412
REV	1	:17-18	429
REV	4	:11	432
REV	8	:1	436
REV	10	:6	438

G1D Omniscience

Book	Chap	Verse	Page
EXO	3	:7	88
2CH	16	:9	703
PSA	44	:21	871
PSA	69	:5	886
PSA	103	:14	912
PSA	137	:4	936
PSA	139	:2	937
PSA	139	:4	937
PRO	15	:3	962
JER	1	:5	1086
JER	29	:11	1129
MATT	6	:32	12
MATT	10	:29-30	18
MATT	11	:21-27	20
JOHN	1	:1	151
JOHN	1	:4	151
JOHN	1	:48	153
JOHN	2	:25	154
JOHN	10	:14	171
JOHN	13	:1	177
JOHN	14	:6	179
JOHN	17	:5	183
2TM	2	:19	362
HEB	7	:24-27	382
HEB	13	:8	390

G1E Omnipotence

Book	Chap	Verse	Page
EXO	8	:22	97
NUM	11	:23	233
NUM	11	:25-26	233
NUM	14	:18	237
NUM	14	:27-35	238
PSA	145	:13	941
AMOS	9	:2	1322
MATT	18	:19-20	33
MATT	22	:29	41
MATT	28	:20	55
MARK	2	:10	60
MARK	2	:28	61
LUKE	1	:37	94
JOHN	5	:27	159
JOHN	5	:29	159
ROM	4	:21	255
EPH	3	:20	324
HEB	4	:12	379
JUDE	0	:24-25	425
REV	19	:6	448

G1F Omnipresence

Book	Chap	Verse	Page
PSA	139	:7-12	937
PRO	15	:3	962
MATT	4	:10	7
MATT	9	:2	15
MATT	9	:6	15
MATT	14	:31-33	27
MATT	28	:18	55
JOHN	5	:22	159
JOHN	5	:27	159
JOHN	11	:4	172
JOHN	11	:41-43	174
ACTS	17	:31	226
2TM	4	:1	364
HEB	1	:3	376

G1G Angels, Holy

Book	Chap	Verse	Page
GEN	16	:7-11	22
GEN	19	:13	27
GEN	19	:15	27
GEN	22	:11	31
GEN	28	:12	43
GEN	32	:1	51
GEN	48	:16	79
EXO	3	:2	88
EXO	14	:19	107
EXO	23	:20-23	121
EXO	32	:34	138
NUM	22	:23-24	253
JUDG	2	:1	388
JUDG	6	:11	395
JUDG	6	:21-22	396
JUDG	13	:9	409
JUDG	13	:13	410
JUDG	13	:16-18	410
JUDG	13	:21	410
2SAM	14	:20	511
1KG	19	:5-7	576
2KG	19	:35	622
JOB	2	:1-7	799
JOB	38	:7	834
PSA	8	:4-5	845
PSA	34	:7	862
PSA	68	:17	885
PSA	91	:11-13	905
PSA	103	:20	912
PSA	104	:4	912
PSA	104	:35	913
PSA	148	:2-5	943
ISA	6	:3	1012
ISA	37	:36	1048
DAN	3	:28	1275
DAN	6	:22	1281
DAN	8	:15-23	1285
DAN	9	:20-27	1287
DAN	10	:10	1288
DAN	10	:12-13	1288
DAN	10	:21	1289
DAN	12	:1	1292
ZEC	1	:9	1361
ZEC	1	:13-14	1361
ZEC	1	:19	1362
ZEC	6	:5	1365
MATT	1	:20	4
MATT	2	:13	5
MATT	2	:19-20	6
MATT	4	:11	7
MATT	13	:39-42	25
MATT	13	:49-50	25
MATT	18	:10	32
MATT	22	:29-30	41
MATT	24	:31	44
MATT	24	:36	45
MATT	25	:31-32	47
MATT	26	:53	50
MATT	28	:2-7	54
MARK	12	:25	81
MARK	16	:6-7	90
LUKE	1	:11-20	93
LUKE	1	:26-38	94
LUKE	2	:9-15	97
LUKE	4	:10	101
LUKE	12	:8-9	121
LUKE	15	:10	128
LUKE	16	:22	130
LUKE	20	:36	138
LUKE	22	:43	142
LUKE	24	:4-7	146
LUKE	24	:23	147
JOHN	1	:51	153
JOHN	5	:4	158
JOHN	20	:12-13	189
ACTS	1	:10	194
ACTS	5	:19	202
ACTS	6	:15	204

Book	Chap	Verse	Page
ACTS	7	:35	205
ACTS	8	:26	208
ACTS	10	:3	211
ACTS	10	:22	212
ACTS	12	:7-11	215
ACTS	12	:15	216
ACTS	12	:23	216
ACTS	27	:23-24	244
1CO	4	:9	277
1CO	6	:3	279
1CO	13	:1	288
GAL	3	:19	315
COL	1	:16	336
COL	2	:18	338
2TH	1	:7	349
1TM	3	:16	356
1TM	5	:21	358
HEB	1	:5-6	376
HEB	1	:13-14	376
HEB	2	:2	376
HEB	2	:7	377
HEB	12	:22	389
HEB	13	:2	390
1PT	1	:12	401
1PT	3	:22	404
2PT	2	:11	410
JUDE	0	:9	424
REV	1	:20	429
REV	2	:1	429
REV	2	:8	429
REV	2	:12	429
REV	3	:1	431
REV	3	:7	431
REV	3	:14	431
REV	5	:11	433
REV	7	:1-17	434
REV	8	:1-13	436
REV	9	:1-21	436
REV	10	:1-11	438
REV	11	:1-19	438
REV	12	:7	440
REV	14	:6	442
REV	14	:8	442
REV	14	:10	442
REV	15	:1	443
REV	15	:6	443
REV	16	:2-17	444
REV	18	:1	446
REV	19	:10	448
REV	21	:9	450
REV	22	:8-9	451

G1H Angels, Evil, Demons

Book	Chap	Verse	Page
GEN	6	:2	10
LEV	20	:27	191
1CH	21	:1	668
JOB	1	:6	798
JOB	1	:9-13	798
ISA	14	:12-19	1022
DAN	10	:13	1288
ZEC	3	:1-2	1363
MATT	4	:3	7
MATT	4	:5-6	7
MATT	4	:8-11	7
MATT	4	:24	8
MATT	7	:22	13
MATT	8	:16	14
MATT	8	:28-33	15
MATT	12	:26	21
MATT	12	:43-45	22
MATT	25	:41	47
MARK	1	:13	58
MARK	1	:23-24	59
MARK	3	:23	62
MARK	3	:26	62
MARK	4	:15	63
MARK	5	:1-18	65
LUKE	4	:34	102
LUKE	4	:41	103
LUKE	8	:30	112
LUKE	11	:18	119
LUKE	22	:3	140
JOHN	13	:27	178
ACTS	19	:15	229
EPH	6	:11-12	327
1TM	3	:6	356
JAM	2	:19	396
2PT	2	:4	410
JUDE	0	:6	424
JUDE	0	:9	424
REV	12	:7	440
REV	12	:9	440
REV	12	:12	440

G1L God's Grace

Book	Chap	Verse	Page
GEN	6	:8	10
2CH	7	:14	692
PSA	45	:2	871
PSA	51	:1	875
PRO	1	:9	947
PRO	3	:22	949
PRO	3	:34	950
ZEC	4	:7	1364
JOHN	1	:14	151
JOHN	1	:16-18	151
ACTS	4	:33	200
ACTS	11	:23	214
ACTS	14	:3	219
ROM	1	:7	250
ROM	3	:24	254
ROM	4	:4	254
ROM	5	:2	255
ROM	5	:20	256
ROM	6	:1	256
ROM	6	:14	257
ROM	11	:5-6	263
1CO	10	:30	285
2CO	8	:7	304
2CO	8	:9	304
2CO	9	:8	305
2CO	12	:9	308
GAL	1	:6	312
EPH	2	:8	322
EPH	2	:15	323
EPH	3	:8	323
EPH	6	:24	327
COL	3	:16	339
COL	4	:6	339
2TH	2	:16	350
1TM	1	:2	354
2TM	2	:1	362
HEB	4	:16	379
HEB	10	:29	386
HEB	12	:28	390
JAM	4	:6	397
1PT	3	:7	404
2PT	3	:18	412

G1N God's Sovereignty

Book	Chap	Verse	Page
EXO	15	:18	109
EXO	18	:11	113
DEU	4	:39	290
JOS	2	:11	343
PSA	93	:1	906
PSA	95	:3-5	907
PSA	96	:10	908
DAN	6	:26	1282
MATT	6	:10	11
MATT	6	:13	11
MATT	11	:25	20
ACTS	17	:24	226
ROM	14	:11	267
1TM	6	:15	359
REV	19	:6	448

G1O God's Heaven

Book	Chap	Verse	Page
EXO	29	:46	133
DEU	26	:15	324
1KG	8	:30	552
2CH	2	:6	684
PSA	2	:4	842
PSA	73	:24-25	890
ISA	33	:17	1043
MATT	3	:17	7
MATT	5	:3	8
MATT	6	:9	11
MATT	6	:20	11
MARK	16	:19	90
LUKE	10	:20	117
LUKE	23	:43	145
JOHN	14	:2-3	178
2CO	12	:4	308
1TH	4	:17	346
1PT	1	:3-4	401
2PT	3	:13	412

G1P God's Hell

Book	Chap	Verse	Page
JOB	11	:8	808
JOB	26	:6	821
PSA	9	:17	846
PSA	16	:10	849
PSA	55	:15	877
PSA	139	:8	937
PRO	5	:5	951
PRO	7	:27	954
PRO	15	:11	962
PRO	27	:20	976
ISA	5	:14	1011
ISA	14	:9	1021
ISA	28	:15	1036
ISA	33	:14	1042
EZE	31	:16	1234
EZE	32	:21	1236
HAB	2	:5	1348
MATT	5	:22	9
MATT	8	:12	14
MATT	10	:28	18
MATT	11	:23	20
MATT	13	:41-42	25
MATT	23	:15	42
MATT	25	:41	47
MARK	9	:43-44	75
LUKE	16	:22-24	130
ACTS	2	:31	197
2TH	1	:7-9	349
JAM	3	:6	396
2PT	2	:4	410
REV	1	:18	429
REV	19	:20	448
REV	20	:10	449
REV	20	:14-15	449
REV	21	:8	450

G2 Trinity

Book	Chap	Verse	Page
GEN	1	:26	4
GEN	3	:22	7
GEN	11	:7	16
EXO	20	:3	116
PRO	8	:27-30	955
MATT	28	:19	55
LUKE	3	:22	100
JOHN	3	:34	155
JOHN	14	:16	179
JOHN	15	:26	181
ACTS	2	:33	197
ACTS	5	:29-32	202
ROM	15	:30	269
1CO	12	:3	286
EPH	2	:18	323
1PT	1	:2	401
1JN	4	:13-14	418
1JN	5	:7	419

Book	Chap	Verse	Page
MARK	14	:61-62	87
LUKE	1	:46	95
LUKE	6	:46	107
LUKE	21	:27-28	139
JOHN	5	:39	160
JOHN	13	:13	177
JOHN	14	:1-7	178
ACTS	1	:11	194
ACTS	17	:24	226
ROM	11	:16	264
ROM	14	:8-9	267
ROM	14	:11	267
1CO	1	:31	275
1CO	3	:16-17	276
1CO	7	:32	281
1CO	12	:3	286
EPH	4	:8	324
PHI	2	:11	331
1TH	1	:10	343
1TM	6	:15	359
2TM	4	:8	364
HEB	11	:5	386
JUDE	0	:14	424
REV	4	:8	432
REV	4	:11	432
REV	17	:14	445
REV	19	:6	448

G4C Love

Book	Chap	Verse	Page
EXO	20	:6	116
DEU	7	:7-9	295
DEU	10	:15-16	300
DEU	23	:5	319
DEU	33	:3	337
DEU	33	:12	338
JOS	24	:19	381
2CH	7	:14	692
PSA	18	:1	850
PSA	33	:4	861
PSA	34	:15-17	862
PSA	42	:8	869
PSA	63	:3	882
PSA	91	:14-15	905
PRO	8	:17	954
ISA	54	:10	1069
ISA	65	:24	1081
JER	2	:2	1087
JER	31	:3	1132
JER	33	:3	1138
LAM	3	:22	1180
EZE	14	:14	1203
EZE	14	:20	1204
MATT	7	:8	12
MATT	21	:22	38
MATT	26	:38-42	49
MARK	12	:29-33	81
LUKE	6	:27-28	106
LUKE	11	:42	120
JOHN	3	:16	155
JOHN	13	:1	177

Book	Chap	Verse	Page
JOHN	14	:13-14	179
JOHN	14	:21-23	179
JOHN	15	:7	180
JOHN	16	:27	182
JOHN	17	:10	183
JOHN	17	:23	184
JOHN	17	:26	184
ROM	1	:7	250
ROM	5	:5	255
ROM	5	:8	255
ROM	8	:26	260
ROM	8	:31-32	260
ROM	8	:35	260
ROM	8	:38-39	260
1CO	1	:27	275
1CO	8	:3	282
1CO	16	:22	294
2CO	12	:9	308
EPH	2	:4	322
EPH	3	:19-20	324
EPH	5	:2	325
2TH	2	:16	350
2TH	3	:5	350
2TM	1	:7	361
TIT	3	:4-5	369
HEB	12	:6	389
1PT	1	:18-19	402
1JN	3	:1	417
1JN	3	:16	417
1JN	4	:5 21	418
1JN	5	:1-3	419
JUDE	0	:21	425
REV	1	:5	428

G4G Worship of God the Son

Book	Chap	Verse	Page
LEV	10	:3	170
2SAM	7	:26-29	500
2CH	29	:17	723
PSA	86	:9	901
MATT	18	:20	33
LUKE	4	:8	101
LUKE	24	:52	148
JOHN	11	:4	172
JOHN	12	:16	175
JOHN	13	:32	178
1PT	3	:15	404

G4H Blessing

Book	Chap	Verse	Page
GEN	6	:8	10
GEN	14	:18	20
GEN	28	:15	44
GEN	31	:24	49
GEN	32	:26-29	52
GEN	50	:17	82
EXO	19	:5-6	115
EXO	33	:12-14	139
EXO	34	:6-7	140
NUM	14	:19	237

Book	Chap	Verse	Page
NUM	21	:8	250
DEU	4	:31	290
DEU	11	:27	302
1SAM	1	:19	438
1SAM	3	:11-14	441
1SAM	25	:28	479
1KG	8	:36	553
1KG	8	:39	553
1KG	8	:45-46	553
1KG	9	:3	555
2KG	4	:42-44	593
2KG	13	:23	609
NEH	9	:17	771
PSA	17	:15	850
PSA	25	:9	856
PSA	48	:14	873
PSA	50	:7-15	874
PSA	50	:23	875
PSA	89	:33-37	903
PSA	103	:2-5	911
PSA	103	:17	912
PSA	107	:9	917
PSA	110	:4	920
PSA	112	:1-9	921
PSA	121	:4	931
PSA	132	:14-18	934
PRO	16	:7	963
PRO	21	:2	968
ISA	41	:10	1053
ISA	42	:16	1055
ISA	45	:21-25	1060
ISA	58	:11	1073
ISA	62	:11-12	1078
JER	18	:23	1114
ZEP	3	:15	1355
ZEP	3	:17	1355
MAL	4	:2	1379
LUKE	18	:29-30	133
JOHN	1	:16	151
JOHN	4	:13-14	156
ROM	3	:24	254
ROM	4	:13	255
ROM	5	:2	255
ROM	8	:32	260
ROM	9	:15-16	261
ROM	11	:5-6	263
2CO	2	:10	298
2CO	4	:14	300
EPH	2	:7-8	322
EPH	4	:32	325
COL	1	:11	336
COL	3	:13	339
2TM	1	:12	361
HEB	4	:16	379
HEB	8	:12	383
2PT	3	:9	411
1JN	1	:9	415
1JN	5	:7	419

G4K Judgment by the Son

Book	Chap	Verse	Page
EXO	32	:33	138
NUM	16	:44-50	243
NUM	20	:8-12	249
DEU	32	:35	336
1CH	16	:33	663
PSA	9	:7-8	846
PSA	50	:16-22	874
ECL	12	:14	995
JER	17	:10	1111
EZE	22	:30-31	1219
DAN	7	:9-10	1283
MATT	12	:36-37	22
MATT	25	:41	47
JOHN	5	:22	159
JOHN	9	:39	170
JOHN	12	:48	177
JOHN	16	:8	182
ACTS	10	:42	213
ROM	2	:5-16	251
ROM	14	:10	267
1CO	3	:13	276
1CO	4	:5	277
2CO	5	:10	301
2TM	4	:1	364
2TM	4	:8	364
1PT	4	:17	405
2PT	2	:4	410
2PT	2	:9	410
2PT	3	:7-12	411
REV	6	:15-17	434
REV	22	:12	452

G4L Gifts & Crowns

Book	Chap	Verse	Page
GEN	15	:6-7	21
2CH	16	:9	703
PSA	1	:1-3	842
PSA	24	:3-5	855
PSA	39	:4	867
PSA	84	:11	900
PRO	4	:18	950
PRO	8	:10-11	954
ISA	45	:3	1059
MATT	5	:6	8
MATT	11	:27	20
MATT	16	:16	30
MATT	16	:18-20	30
JOHN	6	:39-40	162
JOHN	6	:65	163
JOHN	14	:13-14	179
ROM	8	:28-30	260
ROM	12	:3-21	265
1CO	9	:25-27	283
2CO	5	:17	301
EPH	1	:17	321
EPH	2	:8-9	322
EPH	3	:17-19	323
COL	1	:12-15	336

Book	Chap	Verse	Page
ISA	48	:16	1063
ISA	59	:21	1075
ISA	61	:1	1076
ISA	63	:10-11	1078
ISA	63	:14	1079
JER	31	:33	1134
EZE	2	:2	1187
EZE	3	:14	1189
EZE	3	:24	1189
EZE	8	:3	1195
EZE	11	:1	1198
EZE	11	:5	1198
EZE	11	:24	1199
EZE	36	:27	1243
EZE	37	:1	1244
EZE	37	:14	1244
EZE	43	:5	1255
DAN	4	:8	1276
DAN	5	:11-14	1279
DAN	6	:3	1280
JOEL	2	:28-29	1311
MIC	2	:7	1334
MIC	3	:8	1335
HAG	2	:5	1358
ZEC	4	:6	1363
ZEC	7	:12	1366
ZEC	12	:10	1371
MATT	1	:18-20	4
MATT	3	:11-12	7
MATT	3	:16-17	7
MATT	10	:20	18
MATT	12	:18	21
MATT	12	:28	22
MATT	12	:31-32	22
MATT	28	:19	55
MARK	1	:10	58
MARK	1	:12	58
MARK	12	:36	82
LUKE	1	:15	93
LUKE	1	:35	94
LUKE	1	:41	95
LUKE	2	:26	97
LUKE	3	:22	100
LUKE	4	:18	101
LUKE	11	:13	119
LUKE	12	:10	121
LUKE	12	:12	121
LUKE	24	:49	148
JOHN	1	:32	152
JOHN	3	:5-6	154
JOHN	4	:24	157
JOHN	6	:63	163
JOHN	7	:39	165
JOHN	14	:16-17	180
JOHN	14	:26	179
JOHN	15	:26	181
JOHN	16	:7-8	181
JOHN	16	:13-15	182
JOHN	20	:22	189
ACTS	1	:5-8	194
ACTS	2	:2-4	195

Book	Chap	Verse	Page
ACTS	2	:17-18	196
ACTS	2	:38	197
ACTS	4	:8	199
ACTS	4	:31	200
ACTS	5	:3	201
ACTS	5	:32	202
ACTS	6	:10	203
ACTS	7	:51	206
ACTS	8	:15	208
ACTS	8	:17-19	208
ACTS	8	:29	208
ACTS	8	:39	209
ACTS	9	:31	210
ACTS	10	:19	212
ACTS	10	:44-45	213
ACTS	10	:47	213
ACTS	11	:15-16	214
ACTS	13	:2-4	216
ACTS	13	:9	217
ACTS	15	:8	221
ACTS	19	:2-6	228
ACTS	20	:28	232
ACTS	28	:25	246
ROM	1	:4	250
ROM	5	:5	255
ROM	8	:2	259
ROM	8	:9-11	259
ROM	8	:14-16	259
ROM	8	:26-27	260
1CO	2	:4	275
1CO	2	:10-14	275
1CO	3	:16	276
1CO	6	:11	279
1CO	12	:3	286
1CO	12	:7-11	287
1CO	12	:13	287
2CO	3	:17	299
2CO	13	:14	310
GAL	3	:2	314
GAL	4	:6	315
GAL	5	:16	317
GAL	5	:22-23	317
EPH	1	:13	321
EPH	3	:16	323
EPH	4	:3-4	324
EPH	4	:30	325
EPH	5	:18	326
1TH	4	:8	345
1TH	5	:19	347
1TM	4	:1	356
2TM	1	:14	361
TIT	3	:5	369
HEB	2	:4	377
HEB	3	:7	378
HEB	9	:14	384
HEB	10	:15-16	385
HEB	10	:29	386
1PT	1	:2	401
1PT	1	:12	401
1PT	3	:18	404
2PT	1	:21	410

Book	Chap	Verse	Page
1JN	4	:13	418
1JN	5	:6-7	419
JUDE	0	:19-20	425
REV	17	:3	445
REV	22	:17	452

P Plan

Book	Chap	Verse	Page
GEN	1	:1-31	3
GEN	2	:7-9	5
GEN	2	:15-22	5
GEN	45	:5-8	74
GEN	50	:19-20	83
EXO	16	:26	111
EXO	16	:33	112
EXO	24	:16	123
JOHN	1	:2-31	151
ACTS	23	:27	238

P01 Bible

Book	Chap	Verse	Page
EXO	17	:14	113
EXO	24	:7	122
DEU	4	:2	288
DEU	6	:6-25	293
DEU	8	:3	296
DEU	11	:18-26	302
DEU	17	:17-19	311
DEU	18	:18	313
DEU	30	:11-14	332
JOS	1	:8	342
JOS	8	:32	354
JOS	8	:34	354
JOS	23	:6	379
2CH	17	:9	704
NEH	8	:13	770
JOB	23	:12	820
PSA	12	:6	848
PSA	19	:7-11	852
PSA	40	:8	868
PSA	119	:9-12	924
PSA	119	:47-48	926
PSA	119	:50	926
PSA	119	:72	927
PSA	119	:82	927
PSA	119	:89	927
PSA	119	:97	928
PSA	119	:103-105	928
PSA	119	:130	929
PSA	119	:140	929
PRO	4	:2	950
PRO	30	:5-6	978
ISA	2	:3	1008
ISA	28	:9	1035
ISA	34	:16	1044
ISA	40	:8	1051
ISA	51	:16	1066
ISA	55	:8-11	1070
JER	5	:14	1093
JER	6	:19	1095
JER	15	:16	1109

Book	Chap	Verse	Page
JER	22	:29	1119
JER	23	:29	1121
JER	30	:2	1131
JER	36	:2-3	1142
EZE	3	:1	1188
DAN	9	:2	1286
DAN	10	:7-8	1288
DAN	10	:21	1289
AMOS	2	:4	1316
MATT	4	:4	7
MATT	5	:17	9
MATT	7	:24	13
MATT	7	:28	13
MATT	12	:3	20
MATT	12	:40-41	22
MATT	15	:4	27
MATT	15	:9	28
MATT	19	:4	34
MATT	22	:29	41
MATT	24	:35	45
MATT	26	:54	50
MATT	26	:56	50
MARK	1	:27	59
MARK	12	:24	81
MARK	13	:31	84
LUKE	4	:4	101
LUKE	4	:17	101
LUKE	8	:11	110
LUKE	11	:28	119
LUKE	16	:17	130
LUKE	24	:27	147
LUKE	24	:32	147
LUKE	24	:45	148
JOHN	1	:1	151
JOHN	1	:14	151
JOHN	2	:22	154
JOHN	3	:10	154
JOHN	5	:24	159
JOHN	5	:39-40	160
JOHN	5	:46-47	160
JOHN	7	:17	164
JOHN	8	:31	167
JOHN	10	:35	172
JOHN	12	:14	175
JOHN	12	:38	176
JOHN	12	:48	177
JOHN	15	:3	180
JOHN	17	:12	183
JOHN	17	:17	184
JOHN	19	:20	187
JOHN	19	:24	187
JOHN	19	:36	188
JOHN	20	:9	189
JOHN	20	:30-31	190
ACTS	1	:16	195
ACTS	2	:42	197
ACTS	7	:20	205
ACTS	8	:32	208
ACTS	15	:15	221
ACTS	17	:11	225
ACTS	18	:28	228

Book	Chap	Verse	Page
1CO	2	:7	275
1CO	15	:51-53	292
EPH	3	:3-6	323
COL	1	:26-27	337
1TH	4	:15-17	346
2TH	2	:7-9	350
1TM	3	:16	356
2PT	3	:15-16	412
REV	1	:20	429
REV	17	:1	445

P17 End Times

Book	Chap	Verse	Page
NUM	16	:28-33	242
ISA	11	:6-10	1019
ISA	11	:15	1019
ISA	13	:5	1020
ISA	13	:9-12	1020
ISA	13	:17-18	1021
ISA	19	:18	1027
ISA	19	:23-24	1027
ISA	26	:20-21	1034
ISA	34	:8	1044
ISA	35	:4	1044
ISA	51	:6	1066
ISA	60	:18-22	1076
ISA	61	:1-7	1076
ISA	65	:20	1081
ISA	65	:25	1081
ISA	66	:23-24	1083
JER	6	:22	1095
JER	9	:25-26	1101
JER	30	:7	1131
EZE	36	:26-28	1243
EZE	38	:1-23	1245
EZE	39	:1-29	1247
DAN	2	:26-45	1271
DAN	7	:17-28	1283
DAN	8	:23-25	1285
DAN	9	:24-27	1287
DAN	11	:36-39	1291
DAN	12	:1-13	1292
JOEL	1	:15	1309
JOEL	2	:1-11	1310
JOEL	2	:31	1312
JOEL	3	:2-21	1312
AMOS	2	:4	1316
AMOS	5	:18	1319
AMOS	5	:20	1319
AMOS	9	:9-15	1323
OBA	0	:15	1327
HAB	2	:2-3	1348
HAB	2	:14	1348
ZEP	1	:7-8	1352
ZEP	1	:14-15	1352
ZEP	1	:18	1353
ZEP	2	:2-3	1353
ZEP	3	:8-9	1354
ZEC	4	:12-14	1364
ZEC	8	:7-8	1367
ZEC	8	:20-23	1367

Book	Chap	Verse	Page
ZEC	10	:9-12	1369
ZEC	12	:1-14	1371
ZEC	13	:8-9	1372
ZEC	14	:1-4	1372
ZEC	14	:8-11	1373
MAL	4	:5	1379
MATT	13	:49-50	25
MATT	23	:35-36	43
MATT	24	:3-4	43
MATT	24	:14-36	44
MATT	24	:44	44
MATT	25	:31-46	47
MATT	27	:53	53
MARK	13	:14	83
MARK	13	:24-27	83
MARK	13	:31	84
LUKE	9	:26-27	114
LUKE	21	:8-9	139
LUKE	21	:25-26	139
LUKE	21	:32	140
LUKE	21	:35	140
JOHN	14	:1-4	178
ROM	11	:25	264
1CO	1	:7	274
1CO	15	:20	291
PHI	1	:3	330
1TH	4	:14-17	346
1TH	5	:3	346
2TH	1	:10	349
2TH	2	:3-4	349
2TH	2	:8-12	350
1TM	6	:14	359
TIT	2	:13	369
HEB	9	:28	384
HEB	12	:26	412
2PT	3	:10-14	412
1JN	2	:28	417
JUDE	0	:14	424
REV	3	:10	431
REV	6	:1-17	433
REV	8	:7-13	436
REV	9	:1-21	436
REV	11	:3-12	438
REV	11	:15	439
REV	12	:6-14	440
REV	13	:1-18	441
REV	15	:6-8	443
REV	16	:1-21	443
REV	19	:11-21	448
REV	20	:1-3	449
REV	20	:12	449
REV	21	:4	450

P18 Tribulation 1st Half

Book	Chap	Verse	Page
ZEC	14	:1-21	1372
1CO	15	:50-58	292
1TH	4	:15-17	346
REV	6	:2-17	433
REV	17	:1-6	445

P19 Tribulation 2nd Half

Book	Chap	Verse	Page
DAN	11	:40-45	1292
REV	8	:1-13	436
REV	9	:1-21	436
REV	12	:7-17	440
REV	13	:5	441

P20 Rapture

Book	Chap	Verse	Page
MATT	24	:36-37	45
MATT	24	:42	45
LUKE	17	:26	132
JOHN	5	:28-29	159
1CO	15	:50-58	292
1TH	4	:13-18	345
JUDE	0	:6	424

P21 Great White Throne

Book	Chap	Verse	Page
ACTS	17	:31	226
JUDE	0	:6	424
REV	20	:11-15	449

P22 Lake of Fire

Book	Chap	Verse	Page
MATT	13	:42	25
MATT	25	:46	47
LUKE	3	:17	99
REV	20	:7-10	449
REV	20	:14-15	449
REV	21	:8	450

P25 Hades-Hell

Book	Chap	Verse	Page
2SAM	22	:6	526
JOB	17	:13	814
JOB	26	:6	821
PSA	16	:10	849
PSA	30	:3	859
PSA	86	:13	901
PSA	139	:8	937
PRO	5	:5	951
PRO	23	:14	971
ISA	33	:14	1042
EZE	32	:21	1236
AMOS	9	:2	1322
HAB	2	:5	1348
MATT	13	:42	25
MATT	16	:18	30
MATT	25	:46	47
LUKE	3	:27	100
LUKE	16	:23-26	130
LUKE	16	:30	130
ACTS	2	:31	197
2PT	2	:4	410
JUDE	0	:6	424
REV	1	:18	429
REV	14	:10	442
REV	20	:2-3	449

P26 Paradise

Book	Chap	Verse	Page
PSA	49	:15	874
LUKE	16	:23	130
LUKE	16	:25-26	130
LUKE	23	:43	145
ACTS	2	:21	196

P27 Millennium

Book	Chap	Verse	Page
REV	16	:12-17	444
REV	19	:14-21	448

M Man

Book	Chap	Verse	Page
GEN	1	:26-28	4
GEN	2	:5	5
GEN	2	:7	5
GEN	2	:16-18	5
JOB	4	:17	801
JOB	7	:1	804
JOB	31	:15	826
JOB	32	:7-22	827
JOB	38	:1-41	833
JOB	39	:1-30	833
JOB	40	:6-24	835
JOB	41	:1-34	836
PSA	8	:4	845
PSA	49	:20	874
PSA	53	:1	876
PSA	144	:3	940
PRO	15	:14	962
PRO	16	:4	963
PRO	18	:13	965
ECL	12	:13	995
NAH	1	:7	1342
MATT	5	:14	9
JOHN	1	:18	151
ROM	7	:2-6	257
ROM	8	:15	259
1CO	2	:14-15	276
1CO	3	:1	276
1CO	13	:11	288
HEB	2	:6	377
REV	3	:20	432

M01 Foreknown

Book	Chap	Verse	Page
1SAM	16	:7	461
JOB	1	:21	799
JOHN	17	:6	183
JOHN	17	:11-12	183
JOHN	17	:20	184
JOHN	17	:24	184
ROM	3	:22-26	253
ROM	5	:1	255
ROM	5	:10	256
ROM	6	:1-10	256
ROM	8	:23	259
ROM	8	:29-30	260
1CO	1	:30	275

Book	Chap	Verse	Page
1CO	2	:11	275
1CO	3	:9-15	276
2CO	5	:18-19	301
GAL	3	:26	315
EPH	1	:4-7	321
EPH	2	:13	322
COL	1	:12-13	336
COL	2	:13-15	338
1TH	5	:24	347
HEB	10	:14	385
1PT	1	:2-3	401
1PT	1	:20	402

M03 Obedience

Book	Chap	Verse	Page
GEN	2	:16	5
GEN	7	:5	11
GEN	7	:16	11
GEN	8	:16-17	13
GEN	18	:19	25
GEN	22	:2-12	31
GEN	28	:1-7	43
GEN	42	:18	69
EXO	17	:6	112
EXO	18	:21	114
EXO	20	:22-26	117
LEV	19	:30	189
LEV	22	:31-33	194
DEU	4	:10	289
DEU	4	:30	290
DEU	5	:29	293
DEU	5	:33	293
DEU	6	:12	294
DEU	9	:4-6	298
DEU	10	:12	300
DEU	11	:19	302
DEU	11	:26-28	302
DEU	12	:32	305
DEU	27	:9-10	324
DEU	30	:2	331
JOS	11	:15	360
JOS	24	:14	381
JOS	24	:24	381
JUDG	10	:14-18	405
JUDG	11	:35-40	408
1SAM	12	:15	453
1SAM	12	:20	454
1SAM	12	:24	454
1SAM	16	:4	461
1KG	8	:43	553
1KG	12	:24	563
2KG	12	:2	607
2KG	17	:13	616
2KG	17	:39	617
2KG	18	:6	618
2KG	22	:2	625
2KG	23	:3	627
2KG	23	:25	629
1CH	16	:15	662
2CH	13	:10	700
2CH	14	:11-12	701

Book	Chap	Verse	Page
2CH	20	:32	710
2CH	29	:2	722
2CH	34	:3	732
2CH	34	:27	734
EZRA	9	:11-12	753
NEH	1	:9	758
JOB	1	:1	798
JOB	2	:3	799
JOB	10	:7	807
PSA	18	:30-31	851
PSA	25	:14	856
PSA	27	:8	857
PSA	27	:14	858
PSA	37	:22-27	865
PSA	40	:8	868
PSA	71	:3	888
PSA	111	:10	921
PSA	119	:2	924
PSA	119	:115	928
PSA	150	:6	944
PRO	4	:1	950
PRO	6	:20	952
PRO	14	:27	961
PRO	19	:1	966
PRO	22	:1	969
PRO	28	:26	977
ECL	12	:13	995
ISA	40	:31	1052
JER	7	:23	1097
JER	26	:13	1125
EZE	18	:9	1210
EZE	18	:21	1211
EZE	18	:28	1211
EZE	20	:19	1214
DAN	9	:4	1286
MATT	7	:24-29	13
MATT	16	:24	20
MATT	28	:19-20	55
MARK	16	:15-16	90
LUKE	14	:26-27	127
JOHN	15	:10-14	180
JOHN	21	:19	191
ACTS	5	:29-32	202
ACTS	9	:6	209
ACTS	9	:11	209
ACTS	26	:19	242
ROM	6	:16	257
ROM	8	:13	259
ROM	11	:4	263
ROM	13	:9	266
ROM	14	:17-23	267
ROM	15	:1	267
1CO	11	:24-25	286
1CO	11	:28	286
2CO	5	:20	301
COL	3	:22	339
TIT	2	:9	369
TIT	3	:1	369
1PT	1	:14	401
1PT	2	:17	403
1JN	3	:24	418

Book	Chap	Verse	Page
2JN	0	:5-6	421
REV	22	:14	452

M05 Life

Book	Chap	Verse	Page
GEN	2	:7	5
GEN	3	:22	7
NUM	23	:10	255
RUTH	1	:17	428
1SAM	20	:3	469
2SAM	14	:14	510
1CH	29	:15	681
JOB	5	:7	802
JOB	7	:17	804
JOB	11	:12	808
JOB	14	:1	810
JOB	25	:6	821
PSA	13	:3	848
PSA	39	:4	967
PSA	68	:20	885
PSA	90	:3	904
PSA	90	:9-10	904
PSA	103	:14-16	912
PSA	121	:8	931
PSA	144	:15	941
PRO	12	:2	958
ISA	25	:8	1033
ISA	51	:7	1066
JER	1	:5	1086
JER	10	:23	1102
JER	31	:22	1133
DAN	12	:2	1292
MATT	6	:24	11
MATT	16	:28	30
LUKE	2	:26	97
LUKE	12	:20	122
JOHN	3	:3	154
JOHN	3	:18	155
JOHN	3	:36	156
JOHN	5	:24	159
JOHN	5	:28-29	159
JOHN	8	:51	168
JOHN	11	:23-26	173
JOHN	20	:31	190
ROM	5	:10	256
ROM	6	:4	256
ROM	6	:9	257
ROM	6	:23	257
ROM	8	:5-24	259
1CO	2	:11	275
1CO	11	:8	285
2CO	4	:16	300
EPH	2	:5	322
2TM	1	:10	361
HEB	2	:9	377
HEB	2	:14-15	377
1JN	2	:17	416
1JN	2	:25	416
1JN	3	:14	417
1JN	5	:16	420
1JN	5	:20	420

Book	Chap	Verse	Page
REV	2	:10	429
REV	20	:12	449
REV	21	:4	450
REV	22	:1-5	451
REV	22	:17	452

M06 Second Death

Book	Chap	Verse	Page
GEN	2	:17	5
GEN	21	:16	30
DEU	16	:16	310
DEU	30	:15	332
1SAM	15	:31-33	461
1KG	19	:2	576
JOB	7	:15	804
JOB	34	:20	830
PSA	6	:5	844
PSA	23	:4	855
PSA	39	:13	867
PSA	48	:14	873
PSA	49	:15	874
PSA	89	:48	904
PSA	90	:9-10	905
PSA	116	:15	923
PRO	8	:36	955
PRO	14	:32	961
PRO	29	:25	978
ECL	7	:1	989
SOL	8	:6	1002
ISA	28	:15	1036
ISA	51	:12	1066
EZE	18	:32	1212
DAN	12	:2	1292
MATT	16	:16	30
LUKE	12	:20	122
JOHN	3	:18	155
JOHN	3	:36	156
JOHN	5	:28-29	159
JOHN	11	:25-26	173
ACTS	8	:1	207
ACTS	17	:31	226
ROM	1	:32	251
ROM	5	:12	256
ROM	5	:14	256
ROM	6	:23	257
ROM	7	:13	258
ROM	14	:7-8	267
1CO	15	:21-22	291
1CO	15	:55-57	293
EPH	2	:5	322
PHI	1	:21	331
1TH	4	:13-18	345
HEB	9	:27	384
JAM	1	:15	394
2PT	1	:10	409
REV	6	:8	434
REV	9	:6	437
REV	20	:5	449
REV	20	:11-15	449
REV	21	:4	450
REV	21	:8	450

Book	Chap	Verse	Page
EPH	1	:11	321
EPH	2	:8	322
COL	3	:3	338
1TM	4	:16	357
2TM	4	:18	364
TIT	2	:11-14	369
HEB	2	:3	376
HEB	7	:16	381
HEB	12	:2	388
HEB	12	:14	388
JAM	4	:14	397
2PT	1	:10	409
1JN	1	:2	415
1JN	1	:7	415
1JN	2	:16	416
1JN	3	:2	417
1JN	5	:11	419
REV	2	:10	429
REV	22	:1	451

M17 Temptation

Book	Chap	Verse	Page
GEN	3	:1-6	6
PRO	1	:10	947
MATT	6	:13	11
MATT	26	:41	49
LUKE	8	:13	111
1CO	1	:19-21	274
1CO	10	:13	284
GAL	4	:14	316
1TM	6	:9	358
JAM	1	:2	394
JAM	1	:12	394
1PT	1	:6	401
1PT	5	:8-9	406
2PT	2	:9	410

M18 Grace, Rewards, Gifts

Book	Chap	Verse	Page
EXO	20	:12	116
LEV	25	:18-19	198
DEU	4	:40	291
DEU	11	:26	302
1KG	3	:11-14	541
PSA	103	:2-5	911
PSA	122	:6	931
PSA	145	:15	941
PRO	3	:3-4	949
PRO	3	:9-10	949
PRO	3	:13-15	949
PRO	3	:27-35	949
ISA	3	:10	1008
ISA	40	:10	1051
DAN	6	:10	1281
MAL	3	:10	1378
MAL	4	:2	1379
MATT	5	:11-12	9
MATT	10	:32	18
MARK	9	:41	75
LUKE	6	:22-23	106

Book	Chap	Verse	Page
LUKE	18	:29-30	133
LUKE	24	:49	148
ACTS	20	:32	232
ROM	2	:10	252
1CO	2	:9	275
1CO	3	:18	277
1CO	9	:24-25	283
1CO	15	:35-40	292
2CO	9	:6	305
2CO	9	:8	305
GAL	6	:8	318
PHI	2	:16	332
COL	1	:11	336
COL	4	:5	339
1TH	2	:19	344
1TM	6	:19	359
HEB	6	:10	380
JAM	1	:17	394
1PT	4	:10	405
1PT	4	:13	405
1JN	1	:9	415
2JN	0	:8	421
REV	2	:10	429
REV	22	:12	452

M19 Repentance

Book	Chap	Verse	Page
2CH	7	:14	692
NEH	1	:9	758
JOB	33	:26-28	829
JOB	34	:31-32	830
PSA	34	:14	862
PSA	34	:18	862
PSA	51	:17	875
PRO	28	:13	977
ISA	55	:6-7	1070
LUKE	5	:32	104
LUKE	13	:2-3	124
LUKE	15	:7	127
LUKE	24	:47	148
ACTS	3	:19	198
ACTS	17	:30	226
1JN	1	:9	415

M20 Pride

Book	Chap	Verse	Page
GEN	10	:8-10	15
1SAM	2	:3-5	438
1SAM	18	:8	466
1KG	1	:5	535
2KG	5	:1	593
2CH	32	:25	729
PSA	10	:2-11	846
PSA	12	:3-4	847
PSA	73	:6-9	890
PSA	101	:5	910
PRO	8	:13	954
PRO	11	:2	957
PRO	16	:5	963
JER	9	:23-24	1101
MAL	4	:1	1379

Book	Chap	Verse	Page
MATT	23	:6-12	41
MARK	12	:38-39	82
LUKE	1	:51-52	95
ROM	12	:3	265
ROM	12	:16	265
1CO	1	:29	275
1CO	3	:18	277
1CO	4	:6-8	277
1CO	10	:12	284
2CO	10	:5	305
2CO	10	:12	306
2CO	10	:18	306
GAL	6	:3	318
1TM	2	:9	355
2TM	3	:2	363
JAM	4	:6	397
1PT	3	:3-4	403
1JN	2	:16	416
REV	3	:17-18	431

M21 Selfishness

Book	Chap	Verse	Page
GEN	25	:32	38
PRO	11	:26	958
PRO	18	:17	966
PRO	28	:27	977
EZE	34	:18	1240
MIC	3	:11	1335
HAG	1	:4-10	1357
MAL	1	:10	1376
MATT	19	:21-22	35
MATT	20	:12-15	36
ROM	14	:15	267
ROM	15	:1-2	267
1CO	3	:19	277
1CO	10	:24	284
2CO	5	:15	301
GAL	6	:2	318
PHI	2	:4	331
PHI	2	:20	332
2TM	3	:2-4	363
JAM	2	:15-16	396
1JN	3	:17	417

M22 Marriage

Book	Chap	Verse	Page
GEN	1	:28	4
GEN	20	:18	29
GEN	49	:25	81
NUM	30	:6-16	267
DEU	21	:11-13	316
DEU	22	:13-21	318
DEU	24	:1-5	320
1SAM	1	:5-6	437
PSA	127	:1	932
PSA	127	:3	933
ISA	44	:2	1057
ISA	49	:5	1063
ISA	66	:9	1082
MATT	19	:4-6	34
MATT	19	:10	34

Book	Chap	Verse	Page
MARK	10	:2-12	76
1CO	7	:1-40	280
1CO	11	:9-12	285
2CO	6	:14	302
2CO	11	:2	306
EPH	5	:21-33	326
1TM	3	:2	355
HEB	13	:4	390

M23 Morality

Book	Chap	Verse	Page
GEN	19	:32-36	28
GEN	35	:22	56
EXO	22	:16-17	120
LEV	18	:6-23	186
LEV	20	:10	190
LEV	20	:15-17	190
DEU	22	:22-30	318
DEU	27	:21	325
2SAM	11	:3-5	503
2SAM	12	:5-14	505
2SAM	13	:22	508
1KG	11	:1	558
1KG	14	:24	558
1KG	22	:46	567
PSA	91	:3-7	905
PRO	5	:3	951
PRO	5	:15-21	951
PRO	6	:24-29	952
PRO	6	:32-33	952
PRO	7	:4-27	953
AMOS	2	:7	1316
MATT	5	:27-28	9
MARK	7	:21	71
LUKE	12	:8-9	121
JOHN	8	:10-11	166
ROM	1	:24-27	251
1CO	5	:1	278
1CO	6	:9	279
1CO	6	:15-16	279
1CO	9	:27	283
EPH	5	:3	325
COL	3	:5	338
HEB	13	:4	390
JAM	4	:4	397
1JN	2	:16-17	416

M24 Patience

Book	Chap	Verse	Page
PSA	37	:7-8	864
PSA	40	:1	867
ECL	7	:8-9	990
ISA	33	:2	1042
JER	7	:24	1097
LAM	3	:26-27	1180
LUKE	21	:19	139
ACTS	1	:4	194
ROM	5	:3	255
ROM	8	:25	260
ROM	12	:12	265
ROM	15	:4	268

Book	Chap	Verse	Page
ACTS	16 :31	224
ROM	3 :22	253
ROM	3 :26	254
ROM	4 :5	254
ROM	4 :11	254
ROM	4 :24	255
ROM	6 :8-10	257
ROM	6 :14	257
ROM	10 :4	262
ROM	10 :10	262
1CO	10 :27	285
1CO	13 :7	288
2CO	4 :13	300
GAL	3 :22	315
PHI	1 :29	331
1TH	1 :7	343
1TH	4 :14	346
2TH	2 :11	350
1TM	4 :10	356
HEB	10 :39	386
HEB	11 :6	386
JAM	2 :19	396
1PT	2 :7	402
1JN	3 :23	418
1JN	4 :1	418
1JN	5 :5	419
1JN	5 :10	419

M42 To Love God

Book	Chap	Verse	Page
GEN	8 :21-22	13
EXO	20 :6	116
DEU	6 :5	293
DEU	7 :9	295
DEU	10 :12	300
PSA	18 :1-3	850
PSA	31 :23	860
PSA	67 :3	884
JER	2 :2	1087
MATT	26 :12	48
LUKE	11 :42	120
JOHN	16 :27	182
ACTS	2 :42	197
ACTS	2 :47	197
ACTS	11 :18	214
ROM	8 :28	260
ROM	11 :33	264
1CO	8 :3	282
1CO	16 :22	294
2TH	3 :5	350
2TM	1 :7	361
HEB	13 :15	390
1PT	2 :9	402
1JN	3 :17-18	417
1JN	4 :12	418
JUDE	0 :21	425

M44 To Love Man

Book	Chap	Verse	Page
LEV	19 :18	188
DEU	10 :19	300
PSA	133 :1-3	934
PRO	10 :12	956
PRO	17 :17	965
MARK	12 :31	81
JOHN	13 :14	179
JOHN	15 :12-13	180
ROM	12 :9-10	265
ROM	13 :8-10	266
GAL	5 :14	317
1TH	3 :12	345
1TH	4 :9	345
HEB	13 :1-2	390
JAM	2 :8	395
1PT	1 :22	402

M45 Truth

Book	Chap	Verse	Page
1KG	17 :24	573
PSA	25 :5	856
PSA	33 :4	861
PSA	43 :3	869
PSA	51 :6	875
PSA	100 :5	910
DAN	10 :21	1289
JOHN	1 :17	151
JOHN	8 :44	168
JOHN	14 :6	179
JOHN	14 :17	179
JOHN	16 :13	182
JOHN	17 :17	184
2CO	6 :7	302
EPH	1 :17	321
EPH	4 :15	324
EPH	4 :25	325
EPH	6 :14	327
2TH	2 :10-11	350
2TM	2 :15	362
1JN	3 :19	418
3JN	0 :4	422
3JN	0 :8	422

M46 Divorce

Book	Chap	Verse	Page
EXO	21 :10-11	118
LEV	21 :14	191
LEV	22 :13	193
DEU	24 :1-4	320
EZRA	10 :3	754
EZRA	10 :10-17	755
EZRA	10 :19	755
EZRA	10 :44	755
JER	3 :1	1089
JER	3 :8-9	1089
MAL	2 :14-16	1377
MATT	5 :31-32	10
MATT	19 :3-9	34
MARK	10 :2-9	76
LUKE	16 :18	120
1CO	7 :10-17	280

M47 Righteousness

Book	Chap	Verse	Page
GEN	7 :1	11
GEN	15 :6	21
PSA	1 :1-3	842
PSA	11 :7	847
PSA	24 :3-5	855
PSA	37 :21	865
PSA	37 :39-40	866
PSA	119 :142	929
PRO	10 :2	956
PRO	10 :25	957
PRO	10 :28-32	957
PRO	11 :28	958
PRO	14 :9	960
PRO	14 :34	961
PRO	15 :6	962
PRO	15 :9	962
EZE	3 :21	1189
EZE	13 :22	1202
EZE	33 :13	1237
MATT	5 :6	8
ROM	3 :22-25	253
1CO	1 :30	275
2CO	5 :17	301
COL	1 :12-13	336
2TM	2 :22	363
2TM	4 :8	364
2JN	0 :5-7	421
REV	22 :11	452

M48 Wealth, Riches

Book	Chap	Verse	Page
GEN	13 :2	18
GEN	24 :35	35
EXO	30 :15	134
DEU	8 :18	297
1SAM	2 :7	439
1CH	29 :12-14	681
JOB	36 :19	832
PSA	49 :6	873
PSA	49 :16	874
PSA	62 :10	881
PRO	8 :18-19	954
PRO	10 :4	956
PRO	10 :15	956
PRO	11 :4	957
PRO	11 :28	958
PRO	13 :7	959
PRO	16 :16	963
PRO	18 :11	965
PRO	23 :4	970
PRO	28 :20	977
PRO	28 :22	977
ECL	2 :8-11	985
ECL	5 :10	988
ECL	6 :2	989
JER	9 :23	1101
JER	17 :11	1111
EZE	7 :19	1194
ZEP	1 :18	1353

Book	Chap	Verse	Page
MATT	6 :19-21	11
MATT	19 :23-24	35
MATT	25 :14-30	46
MARK	10 :25	77
LUKE	6 :24	106
LUKE	12 :15-34	122
LUKE	18 :23-24	133
LUKE	21 :1-4	138
ROM	13 :10	266
1CO	4 :7	277
2CO	9 :6-7	305
PHI	4 :11	334
1TM	6 :8-10	358
1TM	6 :17	359
JAM	1 :11	394
JAM	5 :1-3	398
REV	3 :17	431

CHANGES IN SPELLING AND WORD USAGE

Old "KING JAMES" English to modern American English

Old English words are changed from "our" or "iour" endings to modern endings, for example
"behaviour-behavior," "endeavour-endeavor," "honour-honor," "Saviour-Savior"
Also English style of double "ll" 's to modern style of single "l"

From:	To:	From:	To:
astonied	astonished	neesing	sneezing
Balac	Balak	nigh	near
begat	fathered	Noe	Noah
behoved	behooved	Osee	Hosea
betwixt	between	payed	paid
brasen	brazen	pilled	peeled
broided	braided	publick	public
cloke	cloak	ribband	ribbon
drave	drove	rie	rye
duke	chief	sceptre	scepter
durst	dare	sepulchre	sepulcher
Elias	Elijah	serjeant	sergeant
cnsample	example	shew	show
ere	before	shewbread	showbread
fetch, etc.	bring, brought	Sion	Zion
forbad	forbade	spue	spew
forgat	forgot	subtil	subtle
furbushed	furbished	sycomore	sycamore
gat	got	Timotheus	Timothy
heretick	heretic	traffick	traffic
holpen	helped	vail	veil
Isaias	Isaiah	wist	knew, know
Jonas	Jonah	wit	for example
knop	knob	withs	withes
lentiles	lentils	wot	know
musick	music	wottech	knew
		Zacharias	Zachariah

CHANGES IN SPELLING AND WORD USAGE

Old King James' English to modern American English

Old English words are changed from 'our' or 'your' endings to modern endings, for example: 'behaviour-behavior,' 'endeavour-endeavor,' 'honour-honor,' 'Saviour-Savior.' Also English style phonetic 'll' to modern style of single 'l.'

Word	From	To	Word	From	To
astonied	astonished		sneezing	sneezing	
Balac	Balak		light	near	
begat	fathered		Noe	Noah	
behoved	behooved		Osee	Hosea	
betwixt	between		payed	paid	
brasen	brazen		pilled	peeled	
broided	braided		publick	public	
cloke	cloak		ribband	ribbon	
drave	drove		rie	rye	
duke	chief		secure	scepter	
dure	date		sepulchre	sepulcher	
Elijah	Elijah		scream	scream	
example	example		shew	show	
ere	before		shewbread	showbread	
fetch, etc.	bring, brought		sion	Zion	
forbad	forbade		spue	spew	
forsak	forsook		sithd	subtil	
furbished	furbished		sycomore	sycamore	
ear	plow		Timotheus	Timothy	
herdick	sheriffe		traffick	traffic	
holpen	helped		vail	veil	
Isaiah	Isaiah		wist	knew, know	
Jonah	Jonah		wit	for example	
Job	high		whps	willies	
lentils	lentils		wet	know	
music	Zacharias		wotteth	knew	

THE RED LETTER KING JAMES BIBLE

EASY READING EDITION

It has been said that the *King James Bible* has been used of God to convert and to edify more people than any other version in history. From our human standpoint, a list of the most used and blessed Bible versions in history would certainly include the *Latin Vulgate, Luther's German Bible,* and the *King James Version.* Of course, other nationalities would include their own beloved translation, especially those who could not read Latin, German, nor English.

The *Latin Vulgate Bible* was translated by Jerome in 397-404 AD in Palestine, much of the time out of a cave in Bethlehem. Jerome was a brilliant and pious scholar who felt that the Old Latin translation of 200 AD was not close enough in accuracy to the original Hebrew and Greek. *Luther's German Bible,* was translated first in the New Testament, 1520-21, when he was hidden in the Wartburg Castle, having been condemned by Charles V for his opposition to the sale of indulgences and then to the entire medieval doctrine that one could be saved by works. He then completed the Old Testament in 1537 AD. This Bible not only consolidated the Reformation in Northern Europe, but it also forged the style of the German language thereafter.

Much the same could be said of the beloved *King James Version.* The Puritans were not totally pleased at the accession of James VI of Scotland, son of Mary Queen of Scots, to the throne of England in 1603. They forced a meeting with him at Hampton Court and placed before him various demands, which he generally refused. One request, however, he agreed to honor, the making of a new English Bible. To this end three committees of 18 scholars each, 9 for the Old Testament and 9 for the New Testament, were appointed to work at Oxford, at Cambridge, and at Westminister Abbey. These 54 scholars were among the most learned and pious in the land, and from 1604 to 1611 they labored, producing the *King James Version* that we know today.

The KJV has been the beloved version of the English speaking world for almost 400 years, 1611 to the approach of 2011. For 300 of these years, from 1650 when it really gained the ascendancy, to 1950, at the beginning of the new wave of translations, it reigned as the absolute Queen of the English translations. Yet at the beginning it was attacked by many of the Puritans and other independent Protestants as being too favorable to the King, as being High Church, and because it had the *Apocrypha* as an addition until 1629. The Pilgrims who landed in 1620 on Plymouth Rock were from the Scrooby Congregation, and they carried with them the *Geneva Bible.*

To solidify the text and to correct various errors made in the early printing, there was a *Cambridge Revision of 1629,* and a *2nd Cambridge Revision of 1638.* Then in 1762 Dr. Thomas Paris, Fellow of Trinity College, led a committee which accomplished a *3rd Cambridge Revision.* This committee changed italicized words and modernized spelling and punctuation closer to the speech of that day. The *Oxford Revision of 1769,* chaired by Dr. Benjamin Blayney, the Regius Hebrew Professor at Oxford, is the KJV that we are most familiar with today, and the one used by almost every modern KJV printing.

The King James Red Letter Bible--Large Print Special Study Edition, the precursor to the present edition, was first published some twenty years ago. It was published in order (1) to more widely distribute God's Holy Word for evangelization and edification; (2) to provide the public with a large print easy-to-read Bible; (3) to provide a Bible at a reasonable cost; (4) to help the Bible Student by the placing in the Old Testament the words spoken directly by God in red, and words spoken directly by our Lord in the New Testament in red; (5) to assist the Bible Student by indicating in the OT at the end of the verse the Hebrew name(s) for God used in that verse; (6) to provide the reader at the end of each verse with a simple synonym of difficult, archaic, or hard to understand words or terms no longer in use, and (7) to enhance the study of the sacred page by various study notes and concordance in the back of the Bible.

This first edition of the *King James Red Letter Bible--Large Print Study Edition* has gone through various printings during the last twenty years, and has been blessed of God by its wide distribution, ready acceptance, and appreciation by many of God's people. It had been noted, however, that there were also two needs that were felt during this period, and these needs are behind the making of this present, RED LETTER KING JAMES BIBLE - EASY READING EDITION.

There is the need that many had who desired the *King James Bible*, but who were not familiar with and as comfortable with many of the *olde* English forms and words. The old English pronouns, which were plain speech in 1611 but which are no longer used, and which cause an added difficulty of understanding to some, are put into the English of today. Thus *thy* is translated as "your," *thine* is "yours," and *thee* and *thou* is "you." <u>When these forms reflect the name of deity, they begin with a capital.</u>

Along with the changes in spelling of the old English pronouns, a group of archaic words which cause some readers to stumble has also been changed to more understandable terms. A list of these words (provided on succeeding pages) was compiled, such as *has* for *hath*, a *tenth* for a *deal*, *know* for *wit*, *leather* for *leathern*, etc. Many of the changes are *shalt* to *shall*, and *wilt* to *will*, involving only the spelling of verb tenses, and not altering the tenses themselves at all. The *King James* translation is thus still presented in its verbal formal equivalence accuracy [i.e., a word for word translation, as opposed to a dynamic equivalence translation, more subjectively translating expression for expression.] One will scarcely realize the difference, except in an occasional improved understanding of God's Word here and there, unless he or she be a time traveler from Old England.

Good theological doctrine tells us that it is only the Hebrew and Greek autographs, the originals, which are inspired of God (2 Tim 3:16; 2 Pet 1:21)--not the copies, nor the translations. We believe, however, that God so preserved the manuscripts from the ancient world that we do indeed have the entire Bible, and that we have it accurately. That is what is here presented, with the sincere prayer to God and reliance on His promise that His sacred and holy Word will accomplish the change in hearts by the new birth, and the edifying and blessing of the saints for which He alone provided.   -- The Publishers,

> *So shall My word be that goes forth out of My mouth: it shall not return*
> *unto Me void, but it shall accomplish that which I please, and it shall*
> *prosper in the thing whereto I sent it* - Isaiah 55:11

Word Changes in New Edition of
EASY READING King James Red Letter Bible
Please check carefully this listing.
Please note that <u>no</u> word of <u>doctrine</u> has been changed.

A
abhorest - abhor
abhoreth - abhors
abideth - abides
aboundeth - abounds
accepteth - accepts
acknowledgeth -
    acknowledges
addeth - adds
advantageth - advantages
afore - before
aforetime - before
alloweth - allows
an hungered - hungry
answereth - answers
appeareth - appears
appertaineth - appertains
approvest - approve
ariseth - arises
art - are
asketh - ask/asks
availeth - avails

B
backbiteth - backbites
badest - bade
baptizeth - baptizes
bearest - bear
beareth - bears
beateth - beats
becometh - becomes
begat - fathered
beholdeth - beholds
believest - believe
believeth - believes
belongeth - belongs
bendeth - bends
blasphemeth - blasphemes
blessest - bless
blesseth - blesses
blindeth - blinds
boasteth - boasts
borroweth - borrows
bow - rainbow
brake - broke
breakest - break/broke
breaketh - breaks
bridleth - bridles
bringeth - brings
broke - break
broughest - brough
broughtest - brought
builded - built
burneth - burns
buyest - buy

C
calleth - calls
camest - came
canst - can
careth - cares
catcheth - catches
causeth - causes
ceaseth - ceases
challengeth - challenges
chasteneth - chastens
cherisheth - cherishes
cheweth - chews
cleanest - clings
cleanseth - cleanses
clove - split
comest - come
cometh - come/comes/came
commandeth - commands
commendeth - commend
committeth - commits
compasseth - compasses
compellest - compel
compoundeth - compounds
condemnest - condemn
condemneth - condemns
confirmeth - confirms
considercth - considers
continueth - continues
converteth - converts
coupleth - couples
covereth - covers
creepeth - creeps
criest - cry
crieth - cries
croucheth - crouches
crownedst - crowned
crownest - crown
curseth - curses

D
dasheth - dashes
deal - one tenth
dealest - deal
dealeth - deals
decayeth - decays
deceiveth - deceives
defiledst - defiled
defileth - defiles
delighteth - delights
delivereth - delivers
denieth - denies
departeth - departs
descendeth - descends
describeth - describes

desireth - desires
despisest - despise
despiseth - despises
devineth - devines
devoureth - devours
didst - did
diest - die
dieth - dies
differeth - differs
digged - dig
disanulleth - disanulls
discovereth - discovers
dishonorest - dishonor
dishonoreth - dishonors
divideth - divides
doest - do
doeth - does
dost - do
doth - does
doubteth - doubts
draweth - draws
dresseth - dresses
drieth - dries
drinketh - drinks
driveth - drives
drunken - drunk
duke(s) - chief(s)
dwellest - dwell
dwelleth - dwells
dwelt - dwelled

E
earneth - earns
eatest - eat
eateth - eats
encampeth - encamps
endureth - endures
entangleth - entangles
entereth - enters
enviest - envy
Esaias - Isaiah
establisheth - establishes
exaltest - exalt
exalteth - exalts
executeth - executes

F
fadeth - fades
faileth - fails
falleth - fall
fastest - fast
favorest - favor
feareth - fears
feedeth(-est) - feed(s)
fetch - bring

fighteth - fights
filleth - fills
findeth - finds
flattereth - flatters
fleeth - flees
floweth - flows
followedest - followed
followeth - follows
forbeareth - forbears
forgat - forgot
forgavest - forgave
forgeteth - forgets
frameth - frames

G
gat - got
gathereth - gathers
gavest - gave
giveth - gives
glorieth - glories
gnapheth - gnaphs
goest - go
goeth - goes/went
greeteth - greets
grieveth - grieves
groaneth - groans
groweth - grows

H
hadst - had
halted - leave
hangeth - hangs
happeneth - happens
hardeneth - hardens
hast - have
hasted - hurried
hateth - hates
hath - has
healeth - heals
heaped - heaps
heapeth - heaps
hearest - hear
heareth - hears
helpeth - helps
hence - from here
henceforth - hereafter
hereunto - hereto
hideth - hides
hither - here (before)
hitherto - previously
holden - helped
holpen - helped
howbeit - however
humbleth - humbles
hungered - hungry

hunteth - hunts

I
imagineth - imagines
imputeth - imputes
inhereteth - inherets
intendest - intend

J
judgest - judge
judgeth - judges
justifieth - justifies

K
keepeth - keeps
killedst - killed
killeth - kills
kindleth - kindles
knasheth - knashes
knewest - knew
knocketh - knocks
knowest - know
knoweth - knows

L
lacketh - lacks
languisheth - languishes
layest - lay
layeth - lay
leadeth - leads
leaveth - left/leaves
lest - less
letteth - lets
licketh - licks
liest - lay
lieth - ly/lay/lies
lifteth - lifts
lightest - light
lighteth - lights
limiteth - limits
lingereth - lingers
listeth - lists
livest - live
liveth - lives
loatheth - loathes
lodgest - lodge
looketh - looks
lovest - love
loveth - loves
lusteth - lusts

M
madest - made
makest - make
maketh - makes

mayest - may
meaneth - means
meeteth - meets
melteth - melts
mightest - might
mine - my
ministereth - ministers
mourneth - mourns
moveth - moves

N
nameth - names
needeth - needs
nought - nothing
nourisheth - nourishes
numberest - number

O
occupieth - occupies
offereth - offers
ofttimes - often
openeth - opens
opposeth - opposes
oppresseth - oppresses
ordaineth - ordains
ordereth - orders
ought - anything
oughtest - ought
over against - opposite
owest - owe
oweth - owes
owneth - ownes

P
panted - pants
panteth - pants
parteth - parts
passest - pass
passeth - passes
peradventure - perhaps
perisheth - perishes
pertaineth - pertains
perverteth - perverts
pilled - peeled
plantedst - planted
planteth - plants
pleaseth - pleases
plotted - plots
ploweth - plowes
pluckt - plucked
possesseth - possesses
prayest - pray
preachest - preach
preacheth - preaches
preparest - prepare
priseth - prises
proceedeth - proceeds
profiteth - profits
prophesieth - prophesies
publisheth - publishes
puffeth - puffs
purifieth - purifies
pursueth - pursues
puttest - put
putteth - puts

Q
quickeneth - makes alive

R
rammeth - rams
reacheth - reaches
rebuketh - rebukes
receiveth - receives
refuseth - refuses
regardeth - regards
remainest - remain
remaineth - remains
rememberest - remember
remembereth - remembers
renewest - renew
repentest - repent
repenteth - repents
repliest - reply
reproacheth - reproaches
requirest - require
requite - repay
reserveth - reserves
resisteth -resists
restest - rest
resteth -rests
revengeth - revenges
rideth - rides
ruleth -rules

S
sacrificeth - sacrifices
saidst - said/says
saith - said/says
saluteth - salutes
sanctifieth - sanctifies
savest - save
saveth - saves
sawest - saw
sayest - say
scattereth - scatters
scourgeth - scourges
searcheth - searches
seekest - seek
seeketh - seeks
seemeth - seems
seest - see
seeth - sees
selleth - sells
sendest - send
sendeth - sends
separateth - separates
serveth - serves
setteth - sets
shaketh - shakes
shalt - shall
sheddeth - sheds
sheweth - showed
shineth -shines
shouldest - should
showest - show
showeth - shows
signifieth - signifies
sinneth - sins/sinning
sittest - sit
sitteth - sits
slayeth - slays

sleepeth - sleeps
slippeth - slips
slumbereth - slumbers
smotest - smote
sojourns - sojurns
soundeth - sounds
soweth - sows
spake - spoke
spareth - spares
speakest - speak
speaketh - speaks
spreadeth - spreads
sprinkleth - sprinkles
standeth - stands
stayest - stay
stinketh - stinks
stoodest - stood
stoppeth - stops
straightway -immediately
strengtheneth - strengthens
striveth - strives
subdueth -subdues
suffer -allow/permit
sufficeth - suffices
supplieth - supplies
sware - swear
swarest - swear
swareth - swears

T
takest - take
taketh - take/took/takes
teachest - teach
teacheth - teaches
tellest - tell
telleth - tells
temptteth - tempts
testifieth - testifies
thee - you
thence - there/that place/
        from there
thence from - there
thenceforth - therefore
thine - yours/your
thinkest - think
thinketh - thinks
thirsteth - thirsts
thither -there
thitherward - aside there
thou - you
thresheth - threshes
thundereth - thunders
thy - your
thyself - yourself
tillest - till
tooketh - took
toucheth - touches
transgresseth -
transgresses
travalleth - travails
treadeth - treads
treasurest - treasure
trieth - tries
trode - trampled
troubleth - troubles
trusteth - trusts
turneth - turns

U
understandeth -
        understands
unto - to
upbraideth - upbraids
upholdeth - upholds
useth - uses

V
valuest - value
vanisheth - vanishes
visitest - visit
vomiteth - vomits
vowedst - vowed

W
waiteth - waits
waketh - wakes
walkest - walk
walketh - walks
wanteth - wants
warreth - goes to war
warted - warts
wast - were
watereth - waters
wavereth - wavers
waxeth - waxes
weareth - wears
wert - were
whence - where
whereunto - whereto
whicheth - which
whiles -while
whilst - until
whirleth -whirles
whither - where
whitersoever - wherever
willeth - wills
wilt - will
wist - knew
withal - with/meanwhile/
        besides/throughout
withereth - withers
withholdeth -withholds
within - inside
without - outside
worketh - works
wouldest - would
wrest - twist/turn
wroth - angry

X

Y
ye - you
yieldeth - yields

Z

THE
OLD TESTAMENT

GENESIS

OUTLINE

SURVEY

Genesis is properly described as the book of beginnings. It may be divided into two main parts. The first part is concerned with the early history of mankind (chs. 1-11). The second part deals with the history of the specific people whom God chose as His own (chs. 12-50).

The author presents the material in a very simple manner. He offers ten "stories," readily discerned from the outline of the book. Some of these "stories" are brief and much condensed, but they nonetheless help to round out the content. It is quite likely that the author of the book used sources, oral and written, for his accounts go back to the earliest history of mankind. Though much has been written on the subject of the possible literary sources (J,E,D,P) of Genesis, there are too many valid objections to accept the findings of source analysis.

The Book of Genesis emphasizes throughout its pages the unmerited grace of God. In the creation of the world, grace displays itself in the wonderful provision that God makes for His creatures. In the creation of man, the grace of God is represented as bestowing even God-likeness upon him. God's grace is in evidence even in the flood. Abraham is chosen not because he is worthy but rather because God is gracious. In all His dealings with the patriarchs, God displays great mercy: they always receive far more favor than any one of them could merit.

Another important feature of Genesis should not be overlooked, namely, the eminently satisfactory way in which it answers our questions about origins. Man will always want to know how the world as a whole came into being. He also will want to know how man originated. Moreover, he feels rather painfully that some major disorder has come upon the world, and would like to know what its nature is; in short, he is concerned to know how sin and all its dire consequences came about. And then man must know if a basic and sure hope of redemption exists for this world and its inhabitants, what that hope is, and how it came into the possession of man.

AUTHOR

No man can claim to know with absolute assurance who wrote the Book of Genesis. Since Genesis is a necessary foundation for Exodus to Deuteronomy, and since the available evidence indicates that Moses wrote these four books, Moses is likely the author of Genesis itself. The New Testament evidence points in the same direction (cf. especially Jn 5.46, 47; Lk 16.31; 24.44). In the tradition of the Church, Genesis has commonly been designated as the First Book of Moses. No evidence to the contrary has been able to invalidate this tradition.

H.C.L.

THE FIRST BOOK OF MOSES COMMONLY CALLED

GENESIS

"Beginnings " of the Universe, of God's People

CHAPTER 1

IN the beginning God created the heaven and the earth. ACTS 17:24 JOHN 1:1 Elohim p.f.

2 And the earth was without form, and void; and darkness *was* upon the face of the deep. And the Spirit of God moved upon the face of the waters. ie new beginning , recreation 2 PET. 3:5-6

3 And God said, Let there be light: and there was light. 2 COR. 4:6

4 And God saw the light, that *it was* good: and God divided the light from the darkness. 2 COR. 4:6 separated

5 And God called the light Day, and the darkness he called Night. And the evening and the morning were the first day. Elohim p.f.

6 And God said, Let there be a firmament in the midst of the waters, and let it divide the waters from the waters. 2 PET. 3:5 expanse

7 And God made the firmament, and divided the waters which *were* under the firmament from the waters which *were* above the firmament: and it was so. expanse - separated

8 And God called the firmament Heaven. And the evening and the morning were the second day.

9 And God said, Let the waters under the heaven be gathered together to one place, and let the dry *land* appear: and it was so. Elohim p.f.

10 And God called the dry *land* Earth; and the gathering together of the waters called He Seas: and God saw that *it was* good. Elohim p.f.

11 And God said, Let the earth bring forth grass, the herb yielding seed, *and* the fruit tree yielding fruit after its kind, whose seed *is* in itself, upon the earth: and it was so. 1 COR. 15:38 vegetation, plants

12 And the earth brought forth grass, *and* herb yielding seed after its kind, and the tree yielding fruit, whose seed *was* in itself, after its kind: and God saw that *it was* good.

13 And the evening and the morning were the third day.

14 And God said, Let there be lights in the firmament of the heaven to divide the day from the night; and let them be for signs, and for seasons, and for days, and years: Elohim p.f. lightbearers, sun, moon, stars - expanse

15 And let them be for lights in the firmament of the heaven to give light upon the earth: and it was so.

16 And God made two great lights; the greater light to rule the day, and the lesser light to rule the night: *He made* the stars also. sun - moon

17 And God set them in the firmament of the heaven to give light upon the earth, Elohim p.f.

18 And to rule over the day and over

the night, and to divide the light from the darkness: and God saw that *it was* good.   Elohim^p.f.

19 And the evening and the morning were the fourth day.

20 And God said, Let the waters bring forth abundantly the moving creature that has life, and fowl *that* may fly above the earth in the open firmament of heaven.   expanse

21 And God created great whales, and every living creature that moves, which the waters brought forth abundantly, after their kind, and every winged fowl after its kind: and God saw that *it was* good.

22 And God blessed them, saying, Be fruitful, and multiply, and fill the waters in the seas, and let fowl multiply in the earth.   Elohim^p.f.

23 And the evening and the morning were the fifth day.

24 And God said, Let the earth bring forth the living creature after its kind, cattle, and creeping thing, and beast of the earth after its kind: and it was so.

25 And God made the beast of the earth after its kind, and cattle after their kind, and every thing that creeps upon the earth after its kind: and God saw that *it was* good.   Elohim^p.f.

26 And God said, Let Us make man in Our image, after Our likeness: and let them have dominion over the fish of the sea, and over the fowl of the air, and over the cattle, and over all the earth, and over every creeping thing that creeps upon the earth.   MATT. 19:4   COL. 3:10   authority

27 So God created man in His *own* image, in the image of God created He him; male and female created He them.   MARK 10:6

28 And God blessed them, and God said to them, Be fruitful, and multiply, and replenish the earth, and subdue it: and have dominion over the fish of the sea, and over the fowl of the air, and over every living thing that moves upon the earth.   Elohim^p.f. - authority

29 And God said, Behold, I have given you every herb bearing seed, which *is* upon the face of all the earth, and every tree, in the which *is* the fruit of a tree yielding seed; to you it shall be for meat.   food

30 And to every beast of the earth, and to every fowl of the air, and to every thing that creeps upon the earth, wherein *there is* life, *I have given* every green herb for meat: and it was so.   breath of life

31 And God saw every thing that He had made, and, behold, *it was* very good. And the evening and the morning were the sixth day.

CHAPTER 2

THUS the heavens and the earth were finished, and all the host of them.

2 And on the seventh day God ended His work which He had made; and He rested on the seventh day from all His work which He had made.   HEB. 4:10   JOHN 5:17   Elohim^p.f.

3 And God blessed the seventh day, and sanctified it: because that in it He had rested from all His work which God created and made.   set apart

4 These *are* the generations of the

heavens and of the earth when they were created, in the day that the Lord God made the earth and the heavens,   Jehovah ^{s.f.} Elohim ^{p.f.}

5 And every plant of the field before it was in the earth, and every herb of the field before it grew: for the Lord God had not caused it to rain upon the earth, and *there was* not a man to till the ground.

6 But there went up a <u>mist</u> from the earth, and watered the whole <u>face</u> of the ground.   vapor - surface

7 And the Lord God formed man *of* the dust of the ground, and breathed into his nostrils the breath of life; and man became a living <u>soul</u>.   1 COR. 15:45 1 TIM. 2:13 Jehovah ^{s.f.} Elohim ^{p.f.} - from - being

8 And the Lord God planted a garden eastward in E`den; and there He put the man whom He had formed.

9 And out of the ground made the Lord God to grow every tree that is pleasant to the sight, and good for food; the tree of life also in the midst of the garden, and the tree of knowledge of good and evil.   REV. 2:7 REV. 22:2

10 And a river <u>went</u> out of E'den to water the garden; and from there it was parted, and became into four <u>heads</u>.   flowed - rivers

11 The name of the first *is* Pi`son: that *is* it which <u>compasses</u> the whole land of Hav`i-lah, where *there* is gold;   surrounds

12 And the gold of that land *is* good: there *is* bdellium and the onyx stone.

13 And the name of the second river *is* Gi`hon: the same *is* it that <u>compass-</u>es the whole land of E-thi-o`pi-a.   Cush

14 And the name of the third river *is* Hid`de-kel: that *is* it which goes toward the east of As-syr'i-a. And the fourth river *is* Eu-phra`tes.   Tigris

15 And the Lord God took <u>the man</u>, and put him into the garden of E'den to <u>dress</u> it and to keep it.   Jehovah ^{s.f.} Elohim ^{p.f.} - Adam - cultivate

16 And the Lord God commanded the man, saying, Of every tree of the garden you may freely eat:

17 But of the tree of the knowledge of good and evil, you shall not eat of it: for in the day that you eat thereof you shall surely die.

18 And the Lord God said, *It is* not good that the man should be alone; I will make him an help <u>meet</u> for him.   1 COR. 11:9 fit

19 And out of the ground the Lord God formed every beast of the field, and every fowl of the air; and brought *them* to Ad'am to see what he would call them: and whatsoever Ad'am called every living creature, that *was* the name thereof.

20 And Ad`am gave names to all cattle, and to the fowl of the air, and to every beast of the field; but for Ad'am there was not found an help <u>meet</u> for him.   fit

21 And the Lord God caused a deep sleep to fall upon Ad`am, and he slept: and He took one of his ribs, and closed up the flesh <u>instead thereof</u>;   1 COR. 11:8 Jehovah ^{s.f.} Elohim ^{p.f.} - in place of it

22 And the rib, which the Lord God had taken from man, made He a woman, and brought her to the man.

23 And Ad'am said, This *is* now bone of my bones, and flesh of my flesh: she shall be called <u>Woman</u>, because she was taken out of <u>Man</u>.   Isha (Heb.) - Ish (Heb.)

24 Therefore shall a man leave his father and his mother, and shall cling to his wife: and they shall be one flesh.

MARK 10:8   1 COR. 6:16   EPH. 5:31   MATT. 19:5

25 And they were both naked, the man and his wife, and were not ashamed.

CHAPTER 3

NOW the serpent was more subtle than any beast of the field which the <u>Lord God</u> had made. And <u>he</u> said to the woman, Yea, <u>has God</u> said, You shall not eat of every tree of the garden?   Jehovah ^{s.f.} Elohim ^{p.f.} - satan - because - Elohim ^{p.f.}

2 And the woman said to the serpent, We may eat of the fruit of the trees of the garden:

3 But of the fruit of the tree which *is* in the midst of the garden, <u>God</u> has said, You shall not eat of it, neither shall you touch it, <u>less you die</u>.

Elohim ^{p.f.} - i.e. spiritual death

4 And the serpent said to the woman, <u>You shall not surely die</u>:

2 COR. 11:3   i.e. physical death

5 For <u>God</u> does know that in the day you eat thereof, then your eyes shall be opened, and you shall be as god, knowing good and evil.

6 And when the woman saw that the tree *was* good for food, and that it *was* pleasant to the eyes, and a tree to be desired to make *one* wise, she took of the fruit thereof, and did eat, and gave also to her husband with her; and he did eat.   1 TIM 2:14

7 And the eyes of them both were opened, and they knew that they *were* naked; and they sewed fig leaves together, and made themselves <u>aprons</u>.

coverings

8 And they heard the voice of the <u>Lord God</u> walking in the garden in the cool of the day: and Ad'am and his wife hid themselves from the presence of the <u>Lord God</u> among the trees of the garden.   Jehovah ^{s.f.} Elohim ^{p.f.}

9 And the <u>Lord God</u> called to Ad'am, and said to him, Where *are* you?

10 And he said, I heard your voice in the garden, and I *was* afraid, because I was naked; and I hid myself.

11 And He said, Who told you that you *were* naked? Have you eaten of the tree, whereof I commanded you that you should not eat?

12 And the man said, The woman whom You gave *to be* with me, she gave me of the tree, and I did eat.

13 And the <u>Lord God</u> said to the woman, What *is* this *that* you have done? And the woman said, The serpent <u>beguiled</u> me, and I did eat.

tricked

14 And the <u>Lord God</u> said to the serpent, Because you have done this, you *are* cursed above all cattle, and above every beast of the field; upon your belly shall you go, and dust shall you eat all the days of your life: Jehovah ^{s.f.} Elohim ^{p.f.}

15 And I will put <u>enmity</u> between <u>you</u> and the woman, and between your <u>seed</u> and her <u>seed</u>; it shall <u>bruise your head</u>, and you shall <u>bruise his heel</u>.

REV. 12:9   ROM. 16:20   hostility - Satan - offspring - He - i.e., deadly wound - i.e., wound

16 To the woman He said, I will greatly multiply your sorrow and your <u>conception</u>; in sorrow you shall bring forth children; and your desire *shall be* <u>to</u> your husband, and he shall rule over you.   pain in childbirth - for

17 And to Ad'am He said, Because you have hearkened to the voice of your wife, and have eaten of the tree, of which I commanded you, saying, You shall not eat of it: cursed *is* the ground for your sake; in sorrow shall you eat *of* it all the days of your life;

18 Thorns also and thistles shall it bring forth to you; and you shall eat the herb of the field;

19 In the sweat of your face shall you eat bread, till you return to the ground; for out of it were you taken: for dust you *are*, and to dust shall you return.

20 And Ad'am called his wife's name <u>Eve</u>; because she was the mother of all living.   life/living

21 To Ad'am also and to his wife did the <u>Lord God</u> make <u>coats of skins</u>, and clothed them.

Jehovah s.f. Elohim p.f. - i.e., causing shed blood

22 And the <u>Lord God</u> said, Behold, the man is become as one of Us, to know good and evil: and now, less he put forth his hand, and take also of the tree of life, and eat, and live for ever:

23 Therefore the <u>Lord God</u> sent him forth from the garden of E'den, to till the ground from where he was taken.

which

24 So He drove out the man; and He placed at the east of the garden of E'den Cher'u-bims, and a flaming sword which turned every way, to keep the way of the tree of life.

CHAPTER 4

AND Ad'am <u>knew</u> Eve his wife; and she conceived, and <u>bare Cain</u>, and said, I have gotten a man from the <u>Lord</u>. i.e., had intercourse with - bore - i.e., gotten one - El s.f.

2 And she again <u>bare</u> his brother A'bel. And A'bel was a keeper of sheep, but Cain was a <u>tiller</u> of the ground.   one who cultivates/farmer

3 And in process of time it came to pass, that Cain brought of the fruit of the ground an offering to the Lord.

4 And A'bel, he also brought of the <u>first-lings</u> of his flock and of the fat thereof. And the Lord had respect to A'bel and to his offering: HEB. 11:4 firstborn

5 But to Cain and to his offering He had not respect. And Cain was very angry, and his countenance fell.

6 And the <u>Lord</u> said to Cain, Why are you angry? and why is your <u>countenance fallen</u>?   El s.f. - face downcast

7 If you do well, shall you not be accepted? and if you do not well, sin lies at the door. And to you *shall be* his desire, and you shall rule over him.

8 And Cain talked with A'bel his brother: and it came to pass, when they were in the field, that Cain rose up against A'bel his brother, and slew him.   HEB. 11:4

9 And the <u>Lord</u> said to Cain, Where *is* A'bel your brother? And he said, I know not: *Am* I my brother's keeper?

MATT. 23:35 1 JOHN 3:12 HEB. 12:24 El s.f.

10 And He said, What have you done? the voice of your brother's blood cries to Me from the ground.

11 And now *are* you cursed from the earth, which has opened its mouth to receive your brother's blood from your hand;

12 When you <u>till</u> the ground, it shall not hereafter yield to you its strength; a fugitive and a <u>vagabond</u> shall you be in the earth.

cultivate - wanderer

13 And Cain said to the Lord, My punishment *is* greater than I can bear.

14 Behold, you have driven me out this day from the face of the earth; and from Your face shall I be hid; and I shall be a fugitive and a <u>vagabond</u> in the earth; and it shall come to pass, that every one that finds me shall slay me.

15 And the Lord said to him, Therefore whosoever slays Cain, vengeance shall be taken on him sevenfold. And the Lord set a mark upon Cain, less any finding him should kill him.

El ^{s.f.}

16 And Cain went out from the presence of the Lord, and dwelt in the land of <u>Nod</u>, on the east of E'den.

i.e., Wandering

17 And Cain <u>knew</u> his wife; and she conceived, and <u>bare</u> <u>E'noch</u>: and he builded a city, and called the name of the city, after the name of his son, <u>E'noch</u>.

i.e., had intercourse with - bore - teacher

18 And to E'noch was born I'rad: and I'rad fathered Me-hu'ja-el: and Me-hu'ja-el fathered Me-thusa-el: and Me-thusa-el fathered La'mech.

19 And La'mech took to him two wives: the name of the one *was* A'dah, and the name of the other Zil'lah.

20 And A'dah bare Ja'bal: he was the father of such as dwell in tents, and *of such as have* <u>cattle</u>.

livestock

21 And his brother's name *was* Ju'bal: he was the father of all such as handle the harp and organ.

22 And Zil'lah, she also bare Tu'bal-cain, an <u>instructer</u> of every <u>artificer</u> in brass and iron: and the sister of Tu'bal-cain *was* Na'a-mah.

forger - implement

23 And La'mech said to his wives, A'dah and Zil'lah, Hear my voice; you wives of La'mech, hearken to my speech: for I have slain a man <u>to my wounding</u>, and a young man to my hurt.

for wounding me

24 If Cain shall be avenged sevenfold, truly La'mech seventy and sevenfold.

25 And Ad'am <u>knew</u> his wife again; and she bare a son, and called his name Seth: For <u>God</u>, *said she*, has appointed me another <u>seed</u> instead of A'bel, whom Cain slew.

i.e., had intercourse with - Elohim ^{p.f.} - offspring

26 And to Seth, to him also there was born a son; and he called his name E'nos: then began men to call upon the name of the Lord.

El ^{s.f.}

CHAPTER 5

THIS *is* the book of the generations of Ad'am. In the day that <u>God</u> created man, in the likeness of <u>God</u> made He him;

Elohim ^{p.f.}

2 Male and female created He them; and blessed them, and called their name Ad'am, in the day when they were created.

MATT. 19:4

3 And Ad'am lived an hundred and thirty years, and fathered a *son* in his own

likeness, after his image; and called his name Seth:

4 And the days of Ad'am after he had fathered Seth were eight hundred years: and he fathered sons and daughters:

5 And all the days that Ad'am lived were nine hundred and thirty years: and he died.

6 And Seth lived an hundred and five years, and fathered E'nos:

7 And Seth lived after he fathered E'nos eight hundred and seven years, and fathered sons and daughters:

8 And all the days of Seth were nine hundred and twelve years: and he died.

9 And E'nos lived ninety years, and fathered Ca-i'nan:

10 And E'nos lived after he fathered Ca-i'nan eight hundred and fifteen years, and fathered sons and daughters:

11 And all the days of E'nos were nine hundred and five years: and he died.

12 And Ca-i'nan lived seventy years, and fathered Ma-ha'la-le-el:

13 And Ca-i'nan lived after he fathered Ma-ha'la-le-el eight hundred and forty years, and fathered sons and daughters:

14 And all the days of Ca-i'nan were nine hundred and ten years: and he died.

15 And Ma-ha'la-le-el lived sixty and five years, and fathered Ja'red:

16 And Ma-ha'la-le-el lived after he fathered Ja'red eight hundred and thirty years, and fathered sons and daughters:

17 And all the days of Ma-ha'la-le-el were eight hundred ninety and five years: and he died.

18 And Ja'red lived an hundred sixty and two years, and he fathered E'noch:

19 And Ja'red lived after he fathered E'noch eight hundred years, and fathered sons and daughters:

20 And all the days of Ja'red were nine hundred sixty and two years: and he died.

21 And E'noch lived sixty and five years, and fathered Me-thu'se-lah:

22 And E'noch walked with <u>God</u> after he fathered Me-thu'se-lah three hundred years, and fathered sons and daughters:

23 And all the days of E'noch were three hundred sixty and five years:

24 And E'noch walked with <u>God</u>: and he was not; for <u>God</u> took him.

HEB. 11:5   Elohim p.f.

25 And Me-thu'se-lah lived an hundred eighty and seven years, and fathered La'mech:

26 And Me-thu'se-lah lived after he fathered La'mech seven hundred eighty and two years, and fathered sons and daughters:

27 And all the days of Me-thu'se-lah were nine hundred sixty and nine years: and he died.

28 And La'mech lived an hundred eighty and two years, and fathered a son:

29 And he called his name No'ah, saying, This *same* shall comfort us concerning our work and toil of our hands, because of the ground which the LORD has cursed.

30 And La'mech lived after he fathered No'ah five hundred ninety and five years, and fathered sons and daughters:

31 And all the days of La'mech were

seven hundred seventy and seven years: and he died.

32 And No'ah was five hundred years old: and No'ah fathered Shem, Ham, and Ja'pheth.

CHAPTER 6

AND it came to pass, when men began to multiply on the face of the earth, and daughters were born to them, 2 That the sons of God saw the daughters of men that they *were* fair; and they took them wives of all which they chose. 3 And the LORD said, My Spirit shall not always strive with man, for that he also *is* flesh: yet his days shall be an hundred and twenty years.   El ˢ·ᶠ· - contend

4 There were giants in the earth in those days; and also after that, when the sons of God came in to the daughters of men, and they bare *children* to them, the same *became* mighty men which *were* of old, men of renown.

5 And GOD saw that the wickedness of man *was* great in the earth, and *that* every imagination of the thoughts of his heart *was* only evil continually.   all the time

6 And it repented the LORD that He had made man on the earth, and it grieved Him at His heart.   grieved - El ˢ·ᶠ·

7 And the LORD said, I will destroy man whom I have created from the face of the earth; both man, and beast, and the creeping thing, and the fowls of the air; for it repents Me that I have made them.

8 But No'ah found grace in the eyes of the LORD.

9 These are the generations of No'ah: No'ah was a just man *and* perfect in his generations, *and* No'ah walked with God.   Elohim ᵖ·ᶠ·

10 And No'ah fathered three sons, Shem, Ham, and Ja'pheth.

11 The earth also was corrupt before God, and the earth was filled with violence.

12 And God looked upon the earth, and, behold, it was corrupt; for all flesh had corrupted its way upon the earth.

13 And God said to No'ah, The end of all flesh is come before Me; for the earth is filled with violence through them; and, behold, I will destroy them with the earth.   HEB. 11:7 Elohim ᵖ·ᶠ· - from

14 Make you an ark of gopher wood; rooms shall you make in the ark, and shall pitch it inside and outside with pitch.   i.e., sealed with tar

15 And this *is the fashion* which you shall make it *of*: The length of the ark *shall be* three hundred cubits, the breadth of it fifty cubits, and the height of it thirty cubits.

16 A window shall you make to the ark, and in a cubit shall you finish it above; and the door of the ark shall you set in the side thereof; with *lower*, second, and third *stories* shall you make it.   roof

17 And, behold, I, even I, do bring a flood of waters upon the earth, to destroy all flesh, wherein *is* the breath of life, from under heaven; *and* every thing that *is* in the earth shall die.   2 PET. 3:6

18 But with thee will I establish my covenant; and you shall come into the

ark, you, and your sons, and your wife, and your sons' wives with you. agreement
19 And of every living thing of all flesh, two of every *sort* shall you bring into the ark, to keep *them* alive with you; they shall be male and female.
20 Of fowls after their kind, and of cattle after their kind, of every creeping thing of the earth after its kind, two of every *sort* shall come to you, to keep them alive.
21 And take you to you of all food that is eaten, and you shall gather *it* to you; and it shall be for food for you, and for them.
22 Thus did No'ah; according to all that God commanded him, so did he. Elohim p.f.

CHAPTER 7

M47–21

AND the LORD said to No'ah, Come you and all your house into the ark; for you have I seen righteous before Me in this generation.
2 Of every clean beast you shall take to you by sevens, the male and his female: and of beasts that *are* not clean by two, the male and his female.
3 Of fowls also of the air by sevens, the male and the female; to keep seed alive upon the face of all the earth. descendants
4 For yet seven days, and I will cause it to rain upon the earth forty days and forty nights; and every living substance that I have made will I destroy from off the face of the earth. thing
M03–11
5 And No'ah did according to all that the LORD commanded him.
6 And No'ah *was* six hundred years old when the flood of waters was upon the earth. came
7 And No'ah went in, and his sons, and his wife, and his sons' wives with him, into the ark, because of the waters of the flood.
8 Of clean beasts, and of beasts that *are* not clean, and of fowls, and of every thing that creeps upon the earth,
9 There went in two and two to No'ah into the ark, the male and the female, as God had commanded No'ah. Elohim p.f.
10 And it came to pass after seven days, that the waters of the flood were upon the earth.
11 In the six hundredth year of No'ah's life, in the second month, the seventeenth day of the month, the same day were all the fountains of the great deep broken up, and the windows of heaven were opened.
12 And the rain was upon the earth forty days and forty nights. fell
13 In the selfsame day entered No'ah, and Shem, and Ham, and Ja'pheth, the sons of No'ah, and No'ah's wife, and the three wives of his sons with them, into the ark;
14 They, and every beast after its kind, and all the cattle after their kind, and every creeping thing that creeps upon the earth after its kind, and every fowl after its kind, every bird of every sort.
15 And they went in to No'ah into the ark, two and two of all flesh, wherein *is* the breath of life.
16 And they that went in, went in male and female of all flesh, as God

M03

had commanded him: and the LORD shut him in.   Elohim ^{p.f.}

17 And the flood <u>was</u> forty days upon the earth; and the waters increased, and <u>bare</u> up the ark, and it was lifted up above the earth.   came - lifted

18 And the waters prevailed, and were increased greatly upon the earth; and the ark <u>went</u> upon the face of the waters.   floated

19 And the waters prevailed exceedingly upon the earth; and all the high hills, that *were* under the whole heaven, were covered.

20 Fifteen cubits upward did the waters prevail; and the mountains were covered.

21 And all flesh died that moved upon the earth, both of fowl, and of cattle, and of beast, and of every creeping thing that creep upon the earth, and every man:

22 All in whose nostrils *was* the breath of life, of all that *was* in the dry *land*, died.

23 And every living substance was destroyed which was upon the face of the ground, both man, and cattle, and the creeping things, and the fowl of the heaven; and they were destroyed from the earth: and No'ah only remained *alive*, and they that *were* with him in the ark.

24 And the waters prevailed upon the earth an hundred and fifty days.

CHAPTER 8

A ND <u>God</u> remembered No'ah, and every living thing, and all the cattle that *was* with him in the ark: and <u>God</u> made a wind to pass over the earth, and the waters <u>assuaged</u>;   Elohim ^{p.f.} - subsided

2 The fountains also of the deep and the windows of heaven were stopped, and the rain from heaven was restrained;

3 And the waters <u>returned</u> from off the earth continually: and after the end of the hundred and fifty days the waters <u>were abated</u>.   receded - decreased

4 And the ark rested in the seventh month, on the seventeenth day of the month, upon the mountains of Ar'a-rat.

5 And the waters decreased continually until the tenth month: in the tenth *month*, on the first *day* of the month, were the tops of the mountains seen.

6 And it came to pass at the end of forty days, that No'ah opened the window of the ark which he had made:

7 And he sent forth a raven, which went forth to and fro, until the waters were dried up from off the earth.

8 Also he sent forth a dove from him, to see if the waters <u>were abated</u> from off the face of the ground;

9 But the dove found no rest for the sole of her foot, and she returned to him into the ark, for the waters *were* on the <u>face</u> of the whole earth: then he put forth his hand, and took her, and <u>pulled</u> her in to him into the ark.   surface - brought

10 And he <u>stayed</u> yet other seven days; and again he sent forth the dove out of the ark;   waited

11 And the dove came in to him in the evening; and, lo, in her mouth *was* an olive leaf plucked off: so No'ah knew that the waters <u>were abated</u> from off the earth.   decreased

12 And he <u>stayed</u> yet other seven days; and sent forth the dove; which returned not again to him any more.   waited

13 And it came to pass in the six hundredth and first year, in the first *month*, the *first* day of the month, the waters were dried up from off the earth: and No'ah removed the covering of the ark, and looked, and, behold, the face of the ground was dry.

14 And in the second month, on the seven and twentieth day of the month, was the earth dried.

15 And <u>God</u> spoke to No'ah, saying,   Elohim ᵖ·ᶠ·

16 Go forth of the ark, you, and your wife, and your sons, and your sons' wives with you.

17 Bring forth with you every living thing that *is* with you, of all flesh, *both* of fowl, and of cattle, and of every creeping thing that creeps upon the earth; that they may breed abundantly in the earth, and be fruitful, and multiply upon the earth.

18 And No'ah went forth, and his sons, and his wife, and his sons' wives with him: 2 PET. 2:5

19 Every beast, every creeping thing, and every fowl, *and* whatsoever creeps upon the earth, after their kinds, went forth out of the ark.

20 And No'ah builded an altar to the Lord; and took of every clean beast, and of every clean fowl, and offered burnt offerings on the altar.   El ˢ·ᶠ·

21 And the Lord smelled a <u>sweet savor</u>; and the Lord said in His heart, I will not again curse the ground any more for man's sake; <u>for</u> the imagination of man's heart *is* evil from his youth; neither will I again smite any more every thing living, as I have done.   El ˢ·ᶠ· - soothing aroma - though

22 <u>While</u> the earth remains, seedtime and harvest, and cold and heat, and summer and winter, and day and night shall not cease.   As long as

CHAPTER 9

AND <u>God</u> blessed No'ah and his sons, and said to them, Be fruitful, and multiply, and <u>replenish</u> the earth.   Elohim ᵖ·ᶠ·- fill

2 And the fear of you and the dread of you shall be upon every beast of the earth, and upon every fowl of the air, upon all that moves *upon* the earth, and upon all the fishes of the sea; into your hand are they delivered.

3 Every moving thing that lives shall be <u>meat</u> for you; even as the green herb have I given you all things.   food

4 But flesh with the life thereof, *which is* the blood thereof, shall you not eat.

5 And surely your blood of your lives will I require; at the hand of every beast will I require it, and at the hand of man; at the hand of every man's brother will I require the life of man.

6 Whoso sheds man's blood, by man shall his blood be shed: for in the image of <u>God</u> made He man.   MATT. 26.52 Elohim ᵖ·ᶠ·

7 And you, be you fruitful, and <u>multiply</u>; bring forth abundantly in the earth, and <u>multiply</u> therein.   increase

8 And <u>God</u> spoke to No'ah, and to his sons with him, saying,

9 And I, behold, I establish My <u>cov-</u>

enant with you, and with your <u>seed</u> after you;

agreement - descendants

10 And with every living creature that *is* with you, of the fowl, of the cattle, and of every beast of the earth with you; from all that go out of the ark, to every beast of the earth.

11 And I will establish My <u>covenant</u> with you; neither shall all flesh be cut off any more by the waters of a flood; neither shall there any more be a flood to destroy the earth.

12 And <u>God</u> said, This *is* the <u>token</u> of the <u>covenant</u> which I make between Me and you and every living creature that *is* with you, for perpetual generations:

Elohim ᵖˑᶠˑ *- sign*

13 I do set My <u>bow</u> in the cloud, and it shall be for a token of a <u>covenant</u> between Me and the earth.

rainbow

14 And it shall come to pass, when I bring a cloud over the earth, that the <u>bow</u> shall be seen in the cloud:

15 And I will remember My <u>covenant</u>, which *is* between Me and you and every living creature of all flesh; and the waters shall no more become a flood to destroy all flesh.

agreement

16 And the <u>bow</u> shall be in the cloud; and I will look upon it, that I may remember the everlasting <u>covenant</u> between <u>God</u> and every living creature of all flesh that *is* upon the earth.

Elohim ᵖˑᶠˑ

17 And <u>God</u> said to No'ah, This *is* the <u>token</u> of the <u>covenant</u>, which I have established between Me and all flesh that *is* upon the earth.

sign

18 And the sons of No'ah, that went forth of the ark, were Shem, and Ham, and Ja'pheth: and Ham *is* the father of Ca'naan.

19 These *are* the three sons of No'ah: and of them was the whole earth <u>overspread</u>.

populated

20 And No'ah began *to be* an <u>husbandman</u>, and he planted a vineyard:

farmer

21 And he drank of the wine, and was drunk; and he was uncovered inside his tent.

22 And Ham, the father of Ca'naan, saw the nakedness of his father, and told his two brethren outside.

23 And Shem and Ja'pheth took a garment, and laid *it* upon both their shoulders, and <u>went</u> backward, and covered the nakedness of their father; and their faces *were* <u>backward</u>, and they saw not their father's nakedness.

walked - turned away

24 And No'ah awoke from his wine, and knew what his younger son had done to him.

25 And he said, Cursed *be* Ca'naan; a servant of servants shall he be to his brethren.

26 And he said, Blessed *be* the L<small>ORD</small> God of Shem; and Ca'naan shall be his servant.

Jehovah ˢˑᶠˑ *Elohim* ᵖˑᶠˑ

27 <u>God</u> shall enlarge Ja'pheth, and he shall dwell in the tents of Shem; and Ca'naan shall be his servant.

Elohim ᵖˑᶠˑ

28 And No'ah lived after the flood three hundred and fifty years.

29 And all the days of No'ah were nine hundred and fifty years: and he died.

CHAPTER 10

NOW these *are* the generations of the sons of No'ah, Shem, Ham, and Ja'pheth: and to them were sons born after the flood.

2 The sons of Ja'pheth; Go'mer, and Ma'gog, and Mad'a-i, and Ja'van, and Tu'bal, and Me'shech, and Ti'ras.

3 And the sons of Go'mer; Ash'kenaz, and Ri'phath, and To-gar'mah.

4 And the sons of Ja'van; E-li'shah, and Tar'shish, Kit'tim, and Dod'a-nim.

5 By these were the isles of the Gentiles divided in their lands; every one after his tongue, after their families, in their nations. _{distant lands}

6 And the sons of Ham; Cush, and Miz'ra-im, and Phut, and Ca'naan.

7 And the sons of Cush; Se'ba, and Hav'i-lah, and Sab'tah, and Ra'a-mah, and Sab'te-chah: and the sons of Ra'a-mah; She'ba, and De'dan.

8 And Cush fathered Nim'rod: he began to be a mighty one in the earth.

9 He was a mighty hunter before the LORD: wherefore it is said, Even as Nim'rod the mighty hunter before the LORD.

10 And the beginning of his kingdom was Ba'bel, and E'rech, and Ac'cad, and Cal'neh, in the land of Shi'nar.

11 Out of that land went forth As'shur, and built Nin'e-veh, and the city Re-ho'both, and Ca'lah,

12 And Re'sen between Nin'e-veh and Ca'lah: the same *is* a great city.

13 And Miz'ra-im fathered Lu'dim, and An'a-mim, and Le'ha-bim, and Naph'tu-him,

14 And Path-ru'sim, and Cas'lu-him, (out of whom came Phi-lis'tim,) and Caph'to-rim.

15 And Ca'naan fathered Si'don his firstborn, and Heth,

16 And the Jub'u-site, and the Am'orite, and the Gir'ga-site,

17 And the Hi'vite, and the Ark'ite, and the Sin'ite,

18 And the Ar'vad-ite, and the Zem'a-rite, and the Ha'math-ite: and afterward were the families of the Ca'naan-ites spread abroad.

19 And the border of the Ca'naan-ites was from Si'don, as you come to Ge'rar, to Ga'za; as you go, to Sod'om, and Go-mor'rah, and Ad'mah, and Ze-bo'im, even to La'sha.

20 These *are* the sons of Ham, after their families, after their tongues, in their countries, *and* in their nations. _{according to - by}

21 To Shem also, the father of all the children of E'ber, the brother of Ja'pheth the elder, even to him were *children* born.

22 The children of Shem; E'lam, and As'shur, and Arphax'ad, and Lud, and A'ram.

23 And the children of A'ram; Uz, and Hul, and Ge'ther, and Mash.

24 And Arphax'ad fathered Sa'lah; and Sa'lah fathered E'ber.

25 And to E'ber were born two sons: the name of one *was* Pe'leg; for in his days was the earth divided; and his brother's name *was* Jok'tan.

26 And Jok'tan fathered Al-mo'dad, and She'leph, and Ha'zar-ma'veth, and Je'rah,

27 And Ha-do'ram, and U'zal, and Dik'lah,

28 And O'bal, and A-bim'a-el, and She'ba,

29 And O'phir, and Hav'i-lah, and Jo'bab: all these *were* the sons of Jok'tan.

30 And their <u>dwelling was</u> from Me'sha, as you go to Se'phar a mount of the east.   settlement extended

31 These *are* the sons of Shem, <u>after</u> their families, <u>after</u> their tongues, <u>in</u> their lands, after their nations.   according to - by

32 These *are* the families of the sons of No'ah, <u>after</u> their generations, in their nations: and by these were the nations divided in the earth after the flood.

CHAPTER 11

AND the whole earth was of one language, and of one speech.

2 And it came to pass, as they journeyed from the east, that they found a plain in the land of Shi'nar; and they dwelt there.

3 And they said one to another, <u>Go to</u>, let us make brick, and burn them throughly. And they had brick for stone, and slime had they for mortar.come

4 And they said, <u>Go to</u>, let us build us a city and a tower, whose top *may reach* to heaven; and let us make us a name, less we be scattered abroad upon the face of the whole earth.

5 And the Lord came down to see the city and the tower, which the children of men built.   El s.f.

6 And the Lord said, Behold, the people *is* one, and they have all one language; and this they begin to do: and now nothing will be restrained from them, which they have imagined to do.   El s.f. - are

7 <u>Go to</u>, let Us go down, and there <u>confound</u> their language, that they may not understand one another's speech.   come - confuse

8 So the Lord scattered them abroad from there upon the face of all the earth: and they left off to build the city.

9 Therefore is the name of it called <u>Ba'bel</u>; because the Lord did there confound the language of all the earth: and from there did the Lord scatter them abroad upon the face of all the earth.   Confusion - El s.f.

10 These *are* the generations of Shem: Shem *was* an hundred years old, and fathered Arphax'ad two years after the flood:

11 And Shem lived after he fathered Arphax'ad five hundred years, and fathered sons and daughters.

12 And Arphax'ad lived five and thirty years, and fathered Sa'lah:

13 And Arphax'ad lived after he fathered Sa'lah four hundred and three years, and fathered sons and daughters.

14 And Sa'lah lived thirty years, and fathered E'ber:

15 And Sa'lah lived after he fathered E'ber four hundred and three years, and fathered sons and daughters.

16 And E'ber lived four and thirty years, and fathered Pe'leg:

17 And E'ber lived after he fathered Pe'leg four hundred and thirty years, and fathered sons and daughters.

18 And Pe'leg lived thirty years, and fathered Re'u:

19 And Pe'leg lived after he fathered Re'u two hundred and nine years, and fathered sons and daughters.

20 And Re'u lived two and thirty years, and fathered Se'rug:

21 And Re'u lived after he fathered Se'rug two hundred and seven years, and fathered sons and daughters.

22 And Se'rug lived thirty years, and fathered Na'hor:

23 And Se'rug lived after he fathered Na'hor two hundred years, and fathered sons and daughters.

24 And Na'hor lived nine and twenty years, and fathered Te'rah:

25 And Na'hor lived after he fathered Te'rah an hundred and nineteen years, and fathered sons and daughters.

26 And Te'rah lived seventy years, and fathered A'bram, Na'hor, and Ha'ran.

27 Now these *are* the generations of Te'rah: Te'rah fathered A'bram, Na'hor, and Ha'ran; and Ha'ran fathered Lot.

28 And Ha'ran died <u>before</u> his father Te'rah in the land of his nativity, in Ur of the Chal'dees.   in the presence of

29 And A'bram and Na'hor took them wives: the name of A'bram's wife *was* Sa'rai; and the name of Na'hor's wife, Mil'cah, the daughter of Ha'ran, the father of Mil'cah, and the father of Is'cah.

30 But Sa'rai was barren; she *had* no child.

31 And Te'rah took A'bram his son, and Lot the son of Ha'ran his son's son, and Sa'rai his daughter in law, his son A'bram's wife; and they went forth with them from Ur of the Chal'dees, to go into the land of Ca'naan; and they came to Ha'ran, and dwelt there.   ACTS 7:2

32 And the days of Te'rah were two hundred and five years: and Te'rah died in Ha'ran.

CHAPTER 12

NOW the <u>Lord</u> had said to A'bram, Get you out of your country, and from your kindred, and from your father's house, to a land that I will show you: ACTS 7:3 El ˢ·ᶠ

2 And I will make of you a great nation, and I will bless you, and make your name great; and you shall be a blessing:

3 And I will bless them that bless you, and curse him that curses you: and in you shall all families of the earth be blessed.   GAL. 3:8

4 So A'bram departed, as the <u>Lord</u> had spoken to him; and Lot went with him: and A'bram *was* seventy and five years old when he departed out of Ha'ran.   HEB. 11:8

5 And A'bram took Sa'rai his wife, and Lot his brother's son, and all their <u>sub-stance</u> that they had gathered, and the <u>souls</u> that they had <u>gotten</u> in Ha'ran; and they went forth to go into the land of Ca'naan; and into the land of Ca'naan they came.   possessions - people - acquired

6 And A'bram passed through the land to the place of Si'chem, to the plain of Mo'reh. And the Ca'naan-ite *was* then in the land.

7 And the LORD appeared to A'bram, and said, To your <u>seed</u> will I give this land: and there built he an altar to the LORD, who appeared to him.

ACTS 7:5   Gal. 3:16   El ^{s.f.} - descendants

8 And he removed from there to a mountain on the east of Beth'-el, and pitched his tent, *having* Beth'-el on the west, and Ha'i on the east: and there he built an altar to the LORD, and <u>called upon</u> the name of the LORD.

prayed to

9 And A'bram journeyed, going on still toward the south.

10 And there was a famine in the land: and A'bram went down into E'gypt to <u>sojourn</u> there; for the famine *was* grievous in the land.

live

11 And it came to pass, when he was come near to enter into E'gypt, that he said to Sa'rai his wife, Behold now, I know that you *are* a fair woman to look upon:

12 Therefore it shall come to pass, when the E-gyptians shall see you, that they shall say, This *is* his wife: and they will kill me, but they will save you alive.

13 Say, I pray you, you *are* my sister: that it may be well with me for your sake; and <u>my soul</u> shall live because of you.

14 And it came to pass, that, when A'bram was come into E'gypt, the E-gyptians <u>beheld</u> the woman that she *was* very fair.

saw

15 The princes also of Pha'raoh saw her, and commended her before Pha'raoh: and the woman was taken into Pha'raoh's house.

16 And he <u>entreated</u> A'bram well for her sake: and he <u>had</u> sheep, and oxen, and he asses, and menservants, and maidservants, and she asses, and camels.

ACTS 7:5   treated - gave him

17 And the LORD plagued Pha'raoh and his house with great plagues because of Sa'rai A'bram's wife.

18 And Pha'raoh called A'bram, and said, What *is* this *that* you have done to me? why did you not tell me that she *was* your wife?

19 Why said you, She *is* my sister? so I might have taken *her* to me to wife: now therefore behold your wife, take her, and go your way.

20 And Pha'raoh commanded *his* men concerning him: and they sent him away, and his wife, and all that he had.

CHAPTER 13

AND A'bram went up out of E'gypt, he, and his wife, and all that he had, and Lot with him, into the <u>south</u>.

Negev

2 And A'bram *was* very rich in cattle, in silver, and in gold.

3 And he went on his journeys from the <u>south</u> even to Beth'-el, to the place where his tent had been at the beginning, between Beth'-el and Ha'i;

4 To the place of the altar, which he had made there at the first: and there A'bram called on the name of the LORD.

5 And Lot also, <u>which</u> went with A'bram, had flocks, and herds, and tents.

who

6 And the land was not able to <u>bear</u> them, that they might dwell together:

for their <u>substance</u> was great, so that they could not dwell together.

support - possessions

7 And there was a <u>strife</u> between the herdmen of A'bram's <u>cattle</u> and the herdmen of Lot's <u>cattle</u>: and the Ca'naan-ite and the Per'iz-zite dwelled then in the land.

quarreling - livestock

8 And A'bram said to Lot, Let there be no <u>strife</u>, I pray you, between me and you, and between my herdmen and your herdmen; for we *be* <u>brethren</u>.

related

9 *Is* not the whole land before you? separate yourself, I pray you, from me: if *you will take* the left hand, then I will go to the right; or if *you depart* to the right hand, then I will go to the left.

10 And Lot lifted up his eyes, and beheld all the <u>plain</u> of Jor'dan, that it *was* well watered every where, before the LORD destroyed Sod'om and Gomor'rah, *even* as the garden of the LORD, like the land of E'gypt, as you come to Zo'ar.

valley

11 Then Lot chose him all the <u>plain</u> of Jor'dan; and Lot journeyed east: and they separated themselves the one from the other.

12 A'bram dwelled in the land of Ca'naan, and Lot dwelled in the cities of the plain, and pitched *his* tent toward Sod'om.

13 But the men of Sod'om *were* wicked and sinners before the LORD exceedingly.

14 And the <u>LORD</u> said to A'bram, after that Lot was separated from him, Lift up now your eyes, and look from the place where you are northward, and southward, and eastward, and westward:

El ˢ·ᶠ·

15 For all the land which you see, to you will I give it, and to your <u>seed</u> for ever.

descendants

16 And I will make your <u>seed</u> as the dust of the earth: so that if a man can number the dust of the earth, *then* shall your <u>seed</u> also be numbered.

17 Arise, walk through the land in the length of it and in the breadth of it; for I will give it to you.

18 Then A'bram removed *his* tent, and came and dwelt <u>in the plain</u> of Mam're, which *is* in He'bron, and built there an altar to the LORD.

by the oaks

CHAPTER 14

AND it came to pass in the days of Am'ra-phel king of Shi'nar, A'rioch king of El'la-sar, Ched-or-la'o-mer king of E'lam, and Ti'dal king of nations;

2 *That these* made war with Be'ra king of Sod'om, and with Bir'sha king of Gomor'rah, Shi'nab king of Ad'mah, and Shem'e-ber king of Ze-boi'im, and the king of Be'la, which is Zo'ar.

3 All these were joined together in the <u>vale</u> of Sid'dim, which is the <u>salt</u> sea.

Valley - i.e. Dead

4 Twelve years they served Ched-or-la'o-mer, and in the thirteenth year they rebelled.

5 And in the fourteenth year came Ched-or-la'o-mer, and the kings that *were* with him, and <u>smote</u> the Reph'a-ims in Ash'te-roth Kar-na'im, and the Zu'zims in Ham, and the E'mims in Sha'veh Kir-i-a-tha'im,

defeated

6 And the Ho'rites in their mount Se'ir, <u>to</u> El-pa'ran, which *is* by the wilderness. as far as

7 And they returned, and came to En-mish'pat, which is Ka'desh, and <u>smote</u> all the country of the Am'a-lek-ites, and also the Am'or-ites, that dwelt in Haz'e-zon-ta'mar. conquered

8 And there went out the king of Sod'om, and the king of Go-mor'rah, and the king of Ad'mah, and the king of Ze-boi'im, and the king of Be'la (the same is Zo'ar;) and they joined battle with them in the <u>vale</u> of Sid'dim; valley

9 With Ched-or-la'o-mer the king of E'lam, and with Ti'dal king of nations, and Am'ra-phel king of Shi'nar, and A'ri-och king of El'la-sar; four kings <u>with</u> five. against

10 And the <u>vale</u> of Sid'dim *was full of* <u>slimepits</u>; and the kings of Sod'om and Go-mor'rah fled, and fell there; and they that remained fled to the mountain. tar pits

11 And they took all the goods of Sod'om and Go-mor'rah, and all their <u>victuals</u>, and went their way. food supply

12 And they took Lot, A'bram's brother's son, who dwelt in Sod'om, and his goods, and departed.

13 And there came one that had escaped, and told A'bram the He'brew; for he dwelt <u>in the plain</u> of Mam're the Am'or-ite, brother of Esh'col, and brother of A'ner: and these *were* <u>confederate</u> with A'bram. by the oaks - allies

14 And when A'bram heard that his brother was taken captive, he armed his trained *servants*, born in his own house,

three hundred and eighteen, and pursued *them* to Dan.

15 And he divided himself against them, he and his servants, by night, and <u>smote</u> them, and pursued them to Ho'bah, which *is* on the left hand of Da-mas'cus. defeated

16 And he brought back all the <u>goods</u>, and also brought again his brother Lot, and his goods, and the women also, and the people. possessions

17 And the king of Sod'om went out to meet him after his return from the slaughter of Ched-or-la'o-mer, and of the kings that *were* with him, at the valley of Sha'veh, which *is* the king's <u>dale</u>. HEB. 7:1-10 valley

18 And Mel-chiz'e-dek king of <u>Sa'lem</u> brought forth bread and wine: and he *was* the priest of the <u>Most High God</u>. i.e. Jerusalem - El Elyon ˢ·ᶠ·

19 And he blessed him, and said, Blessed *be* A'bram of the <u>Most High God</u>, possessor of heaven and earth:

20 And blessed be the <u>Most High God</u>, which has delivered your enemies into your hand. And he gave him tithes of all.

21 And the king of Sod'om said to A'bram, Give me the <u>persons</u>, and take the <u>goods</u> to yourself. people - things recovered

22 And A'bram said to the king of Sod'om, I have <u>lift up my hand</u> to the LORD, the <u>Most High God</u>, the possessor of heaven and earth, sworn - El Elyon ˢ·ᶠ·

23 That I will not *take* from a thread even to a <u>shoelatchet</u>, and that I will not take any thing that *is* yours, less you should say, I have made A'bram rich: sandal thong

24 Save only that which the young

men have eaten, and the portion of the men which went with me, A'ner, Esh'col, and Mam're; let them take their portion.

CHAPTER 15

AFTER these things the word of the LORD came to A'bram in a vision, saying, Fear not, A'bram: I *am* your shield, *and* your exceeding great reward.   El ^{s.f.} - provider

2 And A'bram said, Lord GOD, what will you give me, seeing I go childless, and the steward of my house *is* this E-li-e'zer of Da-mas'cus? Adonay ^{p.f.} Jehovah ^{s.f.} - remain

3 And A'bram said, Behold, to me You have given no seed: and, lo, one born in my house is my heir.

offspring - one of my servants

4 And, behold, the word of the LORD *came* to him, saying, This shall not be your heir; but he that shall come forth out of your own bowels shall be your heir.   body

5 And He brought him forth abroad, and said, Look now toward heaven, and tell the stars, if you be able to number them: and He said to him, So shall your seed be.   HEB. 11:12 count - descendants

6 And he believed in the LORD; and He counted it to him for righteousness.   ROM. 4:3 JAM. 2:23 El ^{s.f.}

7 And He said to him, I *am* the LORD that brought you out of Ur of the Chal'dees, to give you this land to inherit it.

8 And he said, Lord GOD, whereby shall I know that I shall inherit it?

9 And He said to him, Take Me an heifer of three years old, and a she goat of three years old, and a ram of three years old, and a turtledove, and a young pigeon.

10 And he took to him all these, and divided them in the midst, and laid each piece one against another: but the birds divided he not.   cut them in two

11 And when the fowls came down upon the carcases, A'bram drove them away.

12 And when the sun was going down, a deep sleep fell upon A'bram; and, lo, an horror of great darkness fell upon him.

13 And He said to A'bram, Know of a surety that your seed shall be a stranger in a land *that is* not theirs, and shall serve them; and they shall afflict them four hundred years;   ACTS 7:7 descendants - temporary resident -Egypt

14 And also that nation, whom they shall serve, will I judge: and afterward shall they come out with great substance.   ACTS 7:7 possessions

15 And You shall go to your fathers in peace; you shall be buried in a good old age.   die

16 But in the fourth generation they shall come here again: for the iniquity of the Am'or-ites *is* not yet full.

to this place - sin

17 And it came to pass, that, when the sun went down, and it was dark, behold a smoking furnace, and a burning lamp that passed between those pieces.   blazing torch

18 In the same day the LORD made a covenant with A'bram, saying, To your seed have I given this land, from

the river of E'gypt unto the great river, the river Eu-phra'tes: GAL. 3:17

El^s.f. - agreement - descendants

19 The Ken'ites, and the Ken'iz-zites, and the Kad'mon-ites,
20 And the Hit'tites, and the Per'iz-zites, and the Reph'a-ims,
21 And the Am'or-ites, and the Ca'naan-ites, and the Gir'ga-shites, and the Jeb'u-sites.

CHAPTER 16

NOW Sa'rai A'bram's wife bare him no children: and she had an handmaid, an E-gyp'tian, whose name *was* Ha'gar.
2 And Sa'rai said to A'bram, Behold now, the LORD has restrained me from bearing: I pray you, go in to my maid; it may be that I may obtain children by her. And A'bram hearkened to the voice of Sa'rai.   i.e. build a family through
3 And Sa'rai A'bram's wife took Ha'gar her maid the E-gyp'tian, after A'bram had dwelt ten years in the land of Ca'naan, and gave her to her husband A'bram to be his wife.
4 And he went in to Ha'gar, and she conceived: and when she saw that she had conceived, her mistress was de-spised in her eyes.
5 And Sa'rai said to A'bram, My wrong *be* upon you: I have given my maid into your bosom; and when she saw that she had conceived, I was de-spised in her eyes: the LORD judge be-tween me and you.   arms - El^s.f.
6 But A'bram said to Sa'rai, Behold, your maid *is* in your hand; do to her

as it pleases you. And when Sa'rai dealt hardly with her, she fled from her face.   harshly
7 And the angel of the LORD found her by a fountain of water in the wilder-ness, by the fountain in the way to Shur.   El^s.f.
8 And he said, Ha'gar, Sa'rai's maid, where came you? and where will you go? And she said, I flee from the face of my mistress Sa'rai.
9 And the angel of the LORD said to her, Return to your mistress, and submit yourself under her hands.   obey
10 And the angel of the LORD said to her, I will multiply your seed exceed-ingly, that it shall not be numbered for multitude.   descendants
11 And the angel of the LORD said to her, Behold, you *are* with child, and shall bear a son, and shall call his name Ish'ma-el; because the LORD has heard your affliction.   God hears
12 And he will be a wild man; his hand *will be* against every man, and every man's hand against him; and he shall dwell in the presence of all his brethren.   prosper
13 And she called the name of the LORD that spoke to her, You God see me: for she said, Have I also here looked after Him that sees me?   El Roi^s.f.
14 Wherefore the well was called Be'er-la-hai'-roi; behold, *it is* between Ka'desh and Be'red.   the living one who sees me
15 And Ha'gar bare A'bram a son: and A'bram called his son's name, which Ha'gar bare, Ish'ma-el.   GAL. 4:22
16 And A'bram *was* fourscore and six

years old, when Ha'gar bare Ish'ma-el to A'bram.

CHAPTER 17

AND when A'bram was ninety years old and nine, the Lord appeared to A'bram, and said to him, I *am* the Almighty God; walk before Me, and be you perfect. El^s.f. - El^s.f. Shaddai - blameless

2 And I will make My covenant between Me and you, and will multiply you exceedingly. agreement - increase

3 And A'bram fell on his face: and God talked with him, saying, Elohim^p.f.

4 As for Me, behold, My covenant *is* with you, and you shall be a father of many nations. ROM. 4:13 - a multitude of

5 Neither shall your name any more be called A'bram, but your name shall be A'bra-ham; for a father of many nations have I made you. ROM. 4:17

6 And I will make you exceeding fruitful, and I will make nations of you, and kings shall come out of you. many descendants

7 And I will establish My covenant between Me and you and your seed after you in their generations for an everlasting covenant, to be a God to you, and to your seed after you.

LUKE 1:55 agreement - descendants

8 And I will give to you, and to your seed after you, the land wherein you are a stranger, all the land of Ca'naan, for an everlasting possession; and I will be their God. temporary resident - Elohim^p.f.

9 And God said to A'bra-ham, You shall keep My covenant therefore, you, and your seed after you in their generations.

10 This *is* My covenant, which you shall keep, between Me and you and your seed after you; Every man child among you shall be circumcised. ACTS 7:8 ROM. 4:11 agreement - descendants

11 And you shall circumcise the flesh of your foreskin; and it shall be a token of the covenant between Me and you.

12 And he that is eight days old shall be circumcised among you, every man child in your generations, he that is born in the house, or bought with money of any stranger, which *is* not of your seed. LUKE 1:59 i.e. have one's foreskin removed

13 He that is born in your house, and he that is bought with your money, must needs be circumcised: and My covenant shall be in your flesh for an everlasting covenant. surely

14 And the uncircumcised man child whose flesh of his foreskin is not circumcised, that soul shall be cut off from his people; he has broken My covenant. person - agreement

15 And God said to A'bra-ham, As for Sa'rai your wife, you shall not call her name Sa'rai, but Sa'rah *shall* her name *be*. Elohim^p.f. -i.e. Princess

16 And I will bless her, and give you a son also of her: yea, I will bless her, and she shall be a *mother* of nations; kings of people shall be of her.

17 Then A'bra-ham fell upon his face, and laughed, and said in his heart, Shall a *child* be born to him that is an hundred years old? and shall Sa'rah, that is ninety years old, bear? ROM. 4:19

18 And A'bra-ham said to God, O that Ish'ma-el might live before you!

Elohim^p.f.

19 And God said, Sa'rah your wife shall bear you a son indeed; and you shall call his name I'saac: and I will establish My covenant with him for an everlasting covenant, *and* with his seed after him.   HEB. 11:11 Elohim[nf] - agreement descendants

20 And as for Ish'ma-el, I have heard you: Behold, I have blessed him, and will make him fruitful, and will multiply him exceedingly; twelve princes shall he father, and I will make him a great nation.

21 But My covenant will I establish with I'saac, which Sa'rah shall bear to you at this set time in the next year.

22 And He left off talking with him, and God went up from A'bra-ham.

23 And A'bra-ham took Ish'ma-el his son, and all that were born in his house, and all that were bought with his money, every male among the men of A'bra-ham's house; and circumcised the flesh of their foreskin in the selfsame day, as God had said to him.

24 And A'bra-ham *was* ninety years old and nine, when he was circumcised in the flesh of his foreskin.

25 And Ish'ma-el his son *was* thirteen years old, when he was circumcised in the flesh of his foreskin.

26 In the selfsame day was A'bra-ham circumcised, and Ish'ma-el his son.   same

27 And all the men of his house, born in the house, and bought with money of the stranger, were circumcised with him.

CHAPTER 18

AND the LORD appeared to him in the plains of Mam're: and he sat in the tent door in the heat of the day;   by the oaks

2 And he lift up his eyes and looked, and, lo, three men stood by him: and when he saw *them*, he ran to meet them from the tent door, and bowed himself toward the ground,   HEB. 13:2 humbled

3 And said, my Lord, if now I have found favor in your sight, pass not away, I pray you, from your servant: El[hf] - do not pass by

4 Let a little water, I pray you, be brought, and wash your feet, and rest yourselves under the tree:

5 And I will bring a morsel of bread, and comfort you your hearts; after that you shall pass on: for therefore are you come to your servant. And they said, So do, as you have said.

6 And A'bra-ham hastened into the tent to Sa'rah, and said, Make ready quickly three measures of fine meal, knead *it*, and make cakes upon the hearth.

7 And A'bra-ham ran to the herd, and brought a calf tender and good, and gave *it* to a young man; and he hasted to dress it.   prepare

8 And he took butter, and milk, and the calf which he had dressed, and set *it* before them; and he stood by them under the tree, and they did eat.

9 And they said to him, Where *is* Sa'rah your wife? And he said, Behold, in the tent.

10 And he said, I will certainly return to you according to the time of life;

and, lo, Sa'rah your wife shall have a son. And Sa'rah heard *it* in the tent door, which *was* behind him.   ROM. 9:9

11 Now A'bra-ham and Sa'rah *were* old *and* well stricken in age; *and* it ceased to be with Sa'rah after the manner of women.

12 Therefore Sa'rah laughed within herself, saying, After I am waxed old shall I have pleasure, my lord being old also?   1 PET. 3:6 have grown

13 And the LORD said to A'bra-ham, Wherefore did Sa'rah laugh, saying, Shall I of a surety bear a child, which am old?

14 Is any thing too hard for the LORD? At the time appointed I will return to you, according to the time of life, and Sa'rah shall have a son. LUKE 1:37 MATT. 19:26

15 Then Sa'rah denied, saying, I laughed not; for she was afraid. And he said, Nay; but you did laugh.

16 And the men rose up from there, and looked toward Sod'om: and A'bra-ham went with them to bring them on the way.

17 And the LORD said, Shall I hide from A'bra-ham that thing which I do;   El^{s.f.}

18 Seeing that A'bra-ham shall surely become a great and mighty nation, and all the nations of the earth shall be blessed in him?

19 For I know him, that he will command his children and his household after him, and they shall keep the way of the LORD, to do justice and judgment; that the LORD may bring upon A'bra-ham that which He has spoken of him.   family - El^{s.f.}

20 And the LORD said, Because the cry of Sod'om and Go-mor'rah is great, and because their sin is very grievous;   El^{s.f.} - bad

21 I will go down now, and see whether they have done altogether according to the cry of it, which is come to Me; and if not, I will know.

22 And the men turned their faces from there, and went toward Sod'om: but A'bra-ham stood yet before the LORD.

23 And A'bra-ham drew near, and said, Will You also destroy the righteous with the wicked?

24 Perhaps there be fifty righteous inside the city: will You also destroy and not spare the place for the fifty righteous that *are* therein?

25 That be far from You to do after this manner, to slay the righteous with the wicked: and that the righteous should be as the wicked, that be far from You: Shall not the Judge of all the earth do right?

26 And the LORD said, If I find in Sod'om fifty righteous inside the city, then I will spare all the place for their sakes.

27 And A'bra-ham answered and said, Behold now, I have taken upon me to speak to the Lord, which *am but* dust and ashes:

28 Perhaps there shall lack five of the fifty righteous: will You destroy all the city for *lack of* five? And He said, If I find there forty and five, I will not destroy *it*.

29 And he spoke to Him yet again, and said, Perhaps there shall be

forty found there. And He said, I will not do *it* for forty's sake.

30 And he said *to Him*, Oh let not the Lord be angry, and I will speak: Perhaps there shall thirty be found there. And He said, I will not do *it*, if I find thirty there.   EI^s.f.

31 And he said, Behold now, I have taken upon me to speak to the Lord: Perhaps there shall be twenty found there. And He said, I will not destroy *it* for twenty's sake.   been so bold

32 And he said, Oh let not the Lord be angry, and I will speak yet but this once: Perhaps ten shall be found there. And He said, I will not destroy *it* for ten's sake.

33 And the LORD went His way, as soon as He had left communing with A'bra-ham: and A'bra-ham returned to his place.

CHAPTER 19

AND there came two angels to Sod'om at even; and Lot sat in the gate of Sod'om: and Lot seeing *them* rose up to meet them; and he bowed himself with his face toward the ground;   messengers - in the evening

2 And he said, Behold now, my lords, turn in, I pray you, into your servant's house, and tarry all night, and wash your feet, and you shall rise up early, and go on your ways. And they said, Nay; but we will abide in the street all night.

3 And he pressed upon them greatly; and they turned in to him, and entered into his house; and he made them a feast, and did bake unleavened bread, and they did eat.   without yeast (contamination)

4 But before they lay down, the men of the city, *even* the men of Sod'om, compassed the house round, both old and young, all the people from every quarter: surrounded

5 And they called to Lot, and said to him, Where *are* the men which came in to you this night? bring them out to us, that we may know them.

6 And Lot went out at the door to them, and shut the door after him,

7 And said, I pray you, brethren, do not so wickedly.   JUDE 7

8 Behold now, I have two daughters which have not known man; let me, I pray you, bring them out to you, and do you to them as *is* good in your eyes: only to these men do nothing; for therefore came they under the shadow of my roof.

9 And they said, Stand back. And they said *again*, This one *fellow* came in to sojourn, and he will needs be a judge: now will we deal worse with you, than with them. And they pressed sore upon the man, *even* Lot, and came near to break the door.   i.e., temporarily - hard

10 But the men put forth their hand, and pulled Lot into the house to them, and shut to the door.

11 And they smote the men that *were* at the door of the house with blindness, both small and great: so that they wearied themselves to find the door.   struck

12 And the men said to Lot, Have you here any besides? son in law, and your sons, and your daughters, and whatsoever you have in the city, bring *them* out of this place:

13 For we will destroy this place, because the cry of them is <u>waxen</u> great before the face of the Lord; and the Lord has sent us to destroy it. has become - El^{s.f.}

14 And Lot went out, and spoke to his sons in law, which married his daughters, and said, Up, get you out of this place; for the Lord will destroy this city. But he seemed as one that <u>mocked</u> to his sons in law. joked

15 And when the morning arose, then the <u>angels</u> hastened Lot, saying, Arise, take your wife, and your two daughters, which are here; less you be <u>consumed</u> in the <u>iniquity</u> of the city. messengers - destroyed - punishment

16 And while he lingered, the men laid hold upon his hand, and upon the hand of his wife, and upon the hand of his two daughters; the Lord being merciful to him: and they brought him forth, and set him outside the city. 2 PET. 2:7

17 And it came to pass, when they had brought them forth abroad, that He said, Escape for your life; look not behind you, neither stay you in all the plain; escape to the mountain, less you be consumed.

18 And Lot said to them, Oh, not so, my <u>Lord</u>: El^{s.f.}

19 Behold now, your servant has found grace in your sight, and you have magnified your mercy, which you have showed to me in saving my life; and I cannot escape to the mountain, less some evil take me, and I die:

20 Behold now, this city *is* near to flee to, and it *is* a little one: Oh, let me escape there, (*is* it not a little one?) and my <u>soul shall live</u>. life shall be spared

21 And He said to him, See, I have accepted you concerning this thing also, that I will not overthrow this city, for the which you have spoken. grant you

22 Haste you, escape there; for I cannot do any thing till you be come there. Therefore the name of the city was called Zo'ar.

23 The sun was risen upon the earth when Lot entered into Zo'ar. i.e., small

24 Then the Lord rained upon Sod'om and upon Go-mor'rah brimstone and fire from the Lord out of heaven; 2 PET 2:6 El^{s.f.}

25 And He <u>overthrew</u> those cities, and all the plain, and all the inhabitants of the cities, and that which grew upon the ground. destroyed

26 But his wife looked back from behind him, and she became a pillar of salt. LUKE 17:32

27 And A'bra-ham got up early in the morning to the place where he stood before the Lord:

28 And he looked toward Sod'om and Go-mor'rah, and toward all the land of the plain, and beheld, and, lo, the smoke of the country went up as the smoke of a furnace.

29 And it came to pass, when God destroyed the cities of the plain, that <u>God</u> remembered A'bra-ham, and sent Lot out of the midst of the overthrow, when He overthrew the cities in the which Lot dwelt. Elohim^{p.f.}

30 And Lot went up out of Zo'ar,

and dwelt in the mountain, and his two daughters with him; for he feared to dwell in Zo'ar: and he dwelt in a cave, he and his two daughters.

31 And the firstborn said to the younger, Our father *is* old, and *there is* not a man in the earth to come in to us after the manner of all the earth:

32 Come, let us make our father drink wine, and we will lie with him, that we may preserve <u>seed of</u> our father.   <small>our family through</small>

33 And they made their father drink wine that night: and the firstborn went in, and lay with her father; and he perceived not when she lay down, nor when she arose.

34 And it came to pass on the morrow, that the firstborn said to the younger, Behold, I lay <u>yesternight</u> with my father: let us make him drink wine this night also; and go you in, *and* lie with him, that we may preserve <u>seed</u> of our father.   <small>last night</small>

35 And they made their father drink wine that night also: and the younger arose, and lay with him; and he perceived not when she lay down, nor when she arose.

36 Thus were both the daughters of Lot with child by their father.

37 And the firstborn bare a son, and called his name Mo'ab: the same *is* the father of the Mo'ab-ites to this day.

38 And the younger, she also bare a son, and called his name Ben-am'mi: the same *is* the father of the children of Am'mon to this day.

CHAPTER 20

AND A'bra-ham journeyed from there toward the south country, and dwelled between Ka'desh and Shur, and sojourned in Ge'rar.

2 And A'bra-ham said of Sa'rah his wife, She *is* my sister: and A-bim'e-lech king of Ge'rar sent, and took Sa'rah.

3 But <u>God</u> came to A-bim'e-lech in a dream by night, and said to him, Behold, you *are but* a dead man, for the woman which you have taken; for she *is* <u>a man's wife</u>.   <small>Elohim^{p.f.} - married</small>

4 But A-bim'e-lech had not come near her: and he said, Lord, will You slay also a righteous nation?

5 Said he not to me, She *is* my sister? and she, even she herself said, He *is* my brother: in the integrity of my heart and innocency of my hands have I done this.

6 And <u>God</u> said to him in a dream, Yea, I know that you did this in the integrity of your heart; for I also withheld you from sinning against Me: therefore allowed I you not to touch her.

7 Now therefore restore the man *his* wife; for he *is* a prophet, and he shall pray for you, and you shall live: and if you restore *her* not, know you that you shall surely die, you, and all that *are* yours.

8 Therefore A-bim'e-lech rose early in the morning, and called all his servants, and told all these things in their ears: and the men were <u>sore</u> afraid.   <small>greatly</small>

9 Then A-bim'e-lech called A'bra-ham, and said to him, What have

you done to us? and what have I offended you, that you have brought on me and on my kingdom a great sin? you have done deeds to me that ought not to be done.

10 And A-bim'e-lech said to A'bra-ham, What <u>saw you</u>, that you have done this thing?   have you encountered

11 And A'bra-ham said, Because I thought, Surely the <u>fear</u> of <u>God</u> *is* not in this place; and they will slay me for my wife's sake.   reverence - Elohim[p.f.]

12 And yet indeed *she is* my sister; she *is* the daughter of my father, but not the daughter of my mother; and she became my wife.

13 And it came to pass, when <u>God</u> caused me to wander from my father's house, that I said to her, This *is* your kindness which you shall show to me; at every place where we shall come, say of me, he *is* my brother.   Elohim[p.f.]

14 And A-bim'e-lech took sheep, and oxen, and menservants, and womenservants, and gave *them* to A'bra-ham, and restored him Sa'rah his wife.

15 And A-bim'e-lech said, Behold, my land *is* before you: dwell where it pleases you.

16 And to Sa'rah he said, Behold, I have given your brother a thousand *pieces* of silver: behold, he *is* to you a covering of the eyes, to all that *are* with you, and with all *other*: thus she was reproved.

17 So A'bra-ham prayed to God: and <u>God</u> healed A-bim'e-lech, and his wife, and his maidservants; and they bare *children*.   Elohim[p.f.]

18 For the <u>Lord</u> had fast closed up all the wombs of the house of A-bim'e-lech, because of Sa'rah A'bra-ham's wife.   El[s.f.]

CHAPTER 21

AND the <u>Lord</u> visited Sa'rah as He had said, and the <u>Lord</u> did to Sa'rah as He had spoken.

2 For Sa'rah conceived, and bare A'bra-ham a son in his old age, at the set time of which <u>God</u> had spoken to him.   Elohim[p.f.]

3 And A'bra-ham called the name of his son that was born to him, whom Sa'rah bare to him, <u>I'saac</u>.   i.e., he laughs

4 And A'bra-ham <u>circumcised</u> his son I'saac being eight days old, as <u>God</u> had commanded him.   i.e. removed the foreskin

5 And A'bra-ham was an hundred years old, when his son I'saac was born to him.

6 And Sa'rah said, <u>God</u> has made <u>me</u> <u>to laugh</u>, *so that* all that hear will laugh with me.   laughter for me

7 And she said, Who would have said to A'bra-ham, that Sa'rah should have <u>given children suck</u>? for I have born *him* a son in his old age.   nursed children

8 And the child grew, and was weaned: and A'bra-ham made a great feast the *same* day that I'saac was weaned.

9 And Sa'rah saw the son of Ha'gar the E-gyp'tian, which she had born to A'bra-ham, <u>mocking</u>.   ridiculing

10 Wherefore she said to A'bra-ham, Cast out this bondwoman and her son: for the son of this bondwoman

shall not be heir with my son, *even* with I'saac. GAL. 4:30

11 And the thing was very grievous in A'bra-ham's sight because of his son. distressing

12 And God said to A'bra-ham, Let it not be grievous in your sight because of the lad, and because of your bondwoman; in all that Sa'rah has said to you, hearken to her voice; for in I'saac shall your seed be called. ROM. 9:7 HEB 11:18 Elohim p.f.- descendants

13 And also of the son of the bond-woman will I make a nation, because he *is* your seed.

14 And A'bra-ham rose up early in the morning, and took bread, and a bottle of water, and gave *it* to Ha'gar, putting *it* on her shoulder, and the child, and sent her away: and she departed, and wandered in the wilderness of Be'er-she'ba. skin

15 And the water was spent in the bottle, and she cast the child under one of the shrubs. used up

16 And she went, and sat her down opposite *him* a good way off, as it were a bowshot: for she said, Let me not see the death of the child. And she sat opposite *him*, and lift up her voice, and wept.

17 And God heard the voice of the lad; and the angel of God called to Ha'gar out of heaven, and said to her, What ails you, Ha'gar? fear not; for God has heard the voice of the lad where he *is*. Elohim p.f. - messenger

18 Arise, lift up the lad, and hold him in your hand; for I will make him a great nation. take care of him

19 And God opened her eyes, and she saw a well of water; and she went, and filled the bottle with water, and gave the lad drink. Elohim p.f.

20 And God was with the lad; and he grew, and dwelt in the wilderness, and became an archer.

21 And he dwelt in the wilderness of Pa'ran: and his mother took him a wife out of the land of E'gypt.

22 And it came to pass at that time, that A-bim'e-lech and Phi'chol the chief captain of his host spoke to A'bra-ham, saying, God *is* with you in all that you do: Elohim p.f.

23 Now therefore swear to me here by God that you will not deal falsely with me, nor with my son, nor with my son's son: *but* according to the kindness that I have done to you, you shall do to me, and to the land wherein you have sojourned.
promise - offspring - descendants - lived

24 And A'bra-ham said, I will swear. promise

25 And A'bra-ham reproved A-bim'e-lech because of a well of water, which A-bim'e-lech's servants had violently taken away.

26 And A-bim'e-lech said, I know not who has done this thing: neither did you tell me, neither yet heard I *of it*, but to day.

27 And A'bra-ham took sheep and oxen, and gave them to A-bim'e-lech; and both of them made a covenant. agreement

28 And A'bra-ham set seven ewe lambs of the flock by themselves.

29 And A-bim'e-lech said to A'bra-ham, What *mean* these seven ewe lambs which you have set by themselves?

30 And he said, For *these* seven ewe lambs shall you take of my hand, that they may be a witness to me, that I have dug this well.

31 Wherefore he called that place Be'er-she'ba; because there they swear both of them.

32 Thus they made a <u>covenant</u> at Be'-er-she'ba: then A-bim'e-lech rose up, and Phi'chol the chief captain of his host, and they returned into the land of the Phi-lis'tines.   agreement

33 And A'bra-ham planted a grove in Be'er-she'ba, and called there on the name of the L<small>ORD</small>, the <u>everlasting God</u>.

El^{s.f.} - El Olam

34 And A'bra-ham <u>sojourned</u> in the Phi-lis'tines' land many days.   stayed

CHAPTER 22

AND it came to pass after these things, that God did <u>tempt</u> A'bra-ham, and said to him, A'bra-ham: and he said, Behold, *here* I *am*.   HEB. 11:17 test

2 And He said, Take now your son, your only *son* I'saac, whom you love, and get you into the land of Mo-ri'ah; and offer him there for a burnt offering upon one of the mountains which I will tell you of.

3 And A'bra-ham rose up early in the morning, and saddled his ass, and took two of his young men with him, and I'saac his son, and <u>clave</u> the wood for the burnt offering, and rose up, and went to the place of which God had told him.   split - Elohim^{p.f.}

4 Then on the third day A'bra-ham lifted up his eyes, and saw the place afar off.

5 And A'bra-ham said to his young men, Abide you here with the ass; and I and the lad will go yonder and worship, and come again to you.

6 And A'bra-ham took the wood of the burnt offering, and laid *it* upon I'saac his son; and he took the fire in his hand, and a knife; and they went both of them together.

7 And I'saac spoke to A'bra-ham his father, and said, My father: and he said, Here *am* I, my son. And he said, Behold the fire and the wood: but where *is* the lamb for a burnt offering?

8 And A'bra-ham said, my son, <u>God</u> will provide Himself a lamb for a burnt offering: so they went both of them together.   Elohim^{p.f.}

9 And they came to the place which <u>God</u> had told him of; and A'bra-ham built an altar there, and laid the wood in order, and bound I'saac his son, and laid him on the altar upon the wood.

10 And A'bra-ham stretched forth his hand, and took the knife to slay his son.

11 And the <u>angel</u> of the L<small>ORD</small> called to him out of heaven, and said, A'bra-ham, A'bra-ham: and he said, Here *am* I.   messenger

12 And He said, Lay not your hand upon the lad, neither do you any thing to him: for now I know that you <u>fear</u> <u>God</u>, seeing you have not withheld your son, your only *son* from Me.   JAMES 2:21 reverence - Elohim^{p.f.}

13 And A'bra-ham lifted up his eyes, and looked, and behold behind *him* a

ram caught in a thicket by its horns: and A'bra-ham went and took the <u>ram</u>, and offered him up for a burnt offering in the <u>stead</u> of his son.   <small>male goat - instead</small>

14 And A'bra-ham called the name of that place Je-ho'vah-ji'reh: as it is said *to* this day, In the mount of the L<small>ORD</small> it shall be <u>seen</u>.   <small>The LORD will provide - El^{s-f.} - provided</small>

15 And the <u>angel</u> of the L<small>ORD</small> called to A'bra-ham out of heaven the second time,   <small>messenger</small>

16 And said, By Myself have I sworn, says the L<small>ORD</small>, for because you have done this thing, and have not withheld your son, your only *son*:   <small>HEB. 6:14</small>

17 That in blessing I will bless you, and in multiplying I will multiply your <u>seed</u> as the stars of the heaven, and as the sand which *is* upon the sea shore; and your <u>seed</u> shall possess the gate of his enemies;   <small>HEB. 6:14 descendants</small>

18 And in your <u>seed</u> shall all the <u>nations</u> of the earth be blessed; because you have obeyed My voice. <small>ACTS 3:25 GAL. 3:8 people</small>

19 So A'bra-ham returned to his young men, and they rose up and went together to Be'er-she'ba; and A'bra-ham dwelt at Be'er-she'ba.

20 And it came to pass after these things, that it was told A'bra-ham, saying, Behold, Mil'cah, she has also born children to your brother Na'hor;

21 Huz his firstborn, and Buz his brother, and Ke-mu'el the father of A'ram,

22 And Che'sed, and Ha'zo, and Pil'dash, and Jid'laph, and Beth-u'el.

23 And Beth-u'el fathered Re-bek'ah: these eight Mil'cah did bear to Na'hor, A'bra-ham's brother.

24 And his concubine, whose name *was* Reu'mah, she bare also Te'bah, and Ga'ham, and Tha'hash, and Ma'a-chah.

CHAPTER 23

AND Sa'rah was an hundred and seven and twenty years old: *these were* the years of the life of Sa'rah.

2 And Sa'rah died in Kir'jath-ar'ba; the same *is* He'bron in the land of Ca'naan: and A'bra-ham came to mourn for Sa'rah, and to weep for her.

3 And A'bra-ham stood up from before his dead, and spoke to the sons of Heth, saying,

4 I *am* a stranger and a <u>sojourner</u> with you: give me a possession of a buryingplace with you, that I may bury my dead out of my sight.   <small>alien</small>

5 And the children of Heth answered A'bra-ham, saying to him,

6 Hear us, my lord: you *are* a <u>mighty prince</u> among us: in the choice of our <u>sepulchers</u> bury your dead; none of us shall withhold from you his <u>sepulcher</u>, but that you may bury your dead.   <small>prince of God - tombs</small>

7 And A'bra-ham stood up, and bowed himself to the people of the land, *even* to the children of Heth.

8 And he communed with them, saying, If it be your mind that I should bury my dead out of my sight; hear me, and intreat for me to E'phron the son of Zo'har,

9 That he may give me the cave of Mach-pe'lah, which he has, which *is* in the end of his field; for <u>as much money as it is worth</u> he shall give it me for a

possession of a buryingplace among you.   *the full price*

10 And E'phron dwelt among the children of Heth: and E'phron the Hit'tite answered A'bra-ham in the <u>audience</u> of the children of Heth, *even* of all that went in at the gate of his city, saying,   *hearing*

11 Nay, my lord, hear me: the field give I you, and the cave that *is* therein, I give it you; in the presence of the sons of my people give I it you: bury your dead.

12 And A'bra-ham bowed down himself before the people of the land.

13 And he spoke to E'phron in the <u>audience</u> of the people of the land, saying, But if you *will give it*, I pray you, hear me: I will give you money for the field; take *it* of me, and I will bury my dead there.

14 And E'phron answered A'bra-ham, saying to him,

15 My lord, hearken to me: the land *is worth* four hundred shekels of silver; what *is* that between me and you? bury therefore your dead.

16 And A'bra-ham hearkened to E'phron; and A'bra-ham weighed to E'phron the silver, which he had named in the <u>audience</u> of the sons of Heth, four hundred shekels of silver, current *money* with the merchant.   *hearing*

17 And the field of E'phron, which *was* in Mach-pe'lah, which *was* before Mam're, the field, and the cave which *was* therein, and all the trees that *were* in the field, that *were* in all the borders round about, were <u>made sure.</u>   *deeded over*

18 To A'bra-ham for a possession in the presence of the children of Heth, before all that went in at the gate of his city.

19 And after this, A'bra-ham buried Sa'rah his wife in the cave of the field of Mach-pe'lah before Mam're: the same *is* He'bron in the land of Ca'naan.

20 And the field, and the cave that *is* therein, were <u>made sure</u> to A'bra-ham for a possession of a buryingplace by the sons of Heth.   *deeded over*

CHAPTER 24

AND A'bra-ham was old, *and* well <u>stricken</u> in age: and the LORD had blessed A'bra-ham in all things.   *advanced*

2 And A'bra-ham said to his eldest servant of his house, that ruled over all that he had, Put, I pray you, your hand under my thigh:

3 And I will make you <u>swear</u> by the LORD, the <u>God</u> of heaven, and the <u>God</u> of the earth, that you shall not take a wife to my son of the daughters of the Ca'naan-ites, among whom I dwell: *promise - El[s.f.] - Elohim[p.f.]*

4 But you shall go to my country, and to my kindred, and take a wife to my son I'saac.

5 And the servant said to him, Perhaps the woman will not be willing to follow me to this land: must I <u>needs</u> bring your son again to the land from where you came?   *necessarily*

6 And A'bra-ham said to him, Beware you that you bring not my son there again.

G   35   P15A — 37

7 The LORD God of heaven, which took me from my father's house, and from the land of my kindred, and which spoke to me, and that swear to me, saying, To your seed will I give this land; He shall send His angel before you, and you shall take a wife to my son from there.　Jehovah^s.f. - Elohim^p.f. - descendants - messenger

8 And if the woman will not be willing to follow you, then you shall be clear from this my oath: only bring not my son there again.

9 And the servant put his hand under the thigh of A'bra-ham his master, and swear to him concerning that matter.

10 And the servant took ten camels of the camels of his master, and departed; for all the goods of his master *were* in his hand: and he arose, and went to Mes-o-po-ta'mi-a, to the city of Na'hor.　good things

11 And he made his camels to kneel down outside the city by a well of water at the time of the evening, *even* the time that women go out to draw *water*.

12 And he said, O LORD God of my master A'bra-ham, I pray You, send me good speed this day, and show kindness to my master A'bra-ham.

Jehovah^s.f. - Elohim^p.f. - grant me success

13 Behold, I stand *here* by the well of water; and the daughters of the men of the city come out to draw water:

14 And let it come to pass, that the damsel to whom I shall say, Let down your pitcher, I pray you, that I may drink; and she shall say, Drink, and I will give your camels drink also: *let the* same be she *that* You have appointed for Your servant I'saac; and thereby shall I know that You have showed kindness to my master.　young girl

15 And it came to pass, before he had done speaking, that, behold, Re-bek'ah came out, who was born to Beth-u'el, son of Mil'cah, the wife of Na'hor, A'bra-ham's brother, with her pitcher upon her shoulder.

16 And the damsel *was* very fair to look upon, a virgin, neither had any man known her: and she went down to the well, and filled her pitcher, and came up.　had relations with her

17 And the servant ran to meet her, and said, Let me, I pray you, drink a little water of your pitcher.

18 And she said, Drink, my lord: and she hasted, and let down her pitcher upon her hand, and gave him drink.

19 And when she had done giving him drink, she said, I will draw *water* for your camels also, until they have done drinking.

20 And she hasted, and emptied her pitcher into the trough, and ran again to the well to draw *water*, and drew for all his camels.

21 And the man wondering at her held his peace, that is whether the LORD had made his journey prosperous or not.

22 And it came to pass, as the camels had done drinking, that the man took a golden earring of half a shekel weight, and two bracelets for her hands of ten *shekels* weight of gold;ring

23 And said, Whose daughter *are* you? tell me, I pray you: is there room

in your father's house for us to lodge in?
24 And she said to him, I *am* the daughter of Beth-u'el the son of Mil'cah, which she bare to Na'hor.
25 She said moreover to him, We have both straw and <u>provender</u> enough, and room to lodge in.   feed
26 And the man bowed down his head, and worshiped the LORD.   El^{s.f.}
27 And he said, Blessed *be* the LORD <u>God</u> of my master A'bra-ham, who has not left destitute my master of His mercy and His truth: I *being* in the way, the LORD led me to the house of my master's brethren.   Jehovah^{s.f.} - Elohim^{p.f.}
28 And the <u>damsel</u> ran, and told *them of* her mother's house these things.   young girl
29 And Re-bek'ah had a brother, and his name *was* La'ban: and La'ban ran out to the man, to the well.
30 And it came to pass, when he saw the <u>earring</u> and bracelets upon his sister's hands, and when he heard the words of Re-bek'ah his sister, saying, Thus spoke the man to me; that he came to the man; and, behold, he stood by the camels at the well.   ring
31 And he said, Come in, you blessed of the LORD; wherefore stand you outside? for I have prepared the house, and room for the camels.   El^{s.f.}
32 And the man came into the house: and he <u>ungirded</u> his camels, and gave straw and <u>provender</u> for the camels, and water to wash his feet, and the men's feet that *were* with him.   unloaded - food
33 And there was set *meat* before him to eat: but he said, I will not eat, until I have told mine errand. And he said, Speak on.   food
34 And he said, I *am* A'bra-ham's servant.
35 And the LORD has blessed my master greatly; and he is become great: and He has given him flocks, and herds, and silver, and gold, and menservants, and maidservants, and camels, and asses.
36 And Sa'rah my master's wife bare a son to my master when she was old: and to him has he given all that he has.
37 And my master made me swear, saying, You shall not take a wife to my son of the daughters of the Ca'naan-ites, in whose land I dwell:
38 But you shall go to my father's house, and to my <u>kindred</u>, and take a wife to my son.   relatives
39 And I said to my master, Perhaps the woman will not follow me.
40 And he said to me, The LORD, before whom I walk, will send His <u>angel</u> with you, and prosper your way; and you shall take a wife for my son of my kindred, and of my father's house: El^{s.f.} - messenger
41 Then shall you be <u>clear</u> from *this* my oath, when you come to my kindred; and if they give not you *one*, you shall be <u>clear</u> from my oath.   free
42 And I came this day to the well, and said, O LORD God of my master A'braham, if now you do prosper my way which I go: Jehovah^{s.f.} Elohim^{p.f.}
43 Behold, I stand by the well of water; and it shall come to pass, that when

the virgin come forth to draw *water*, and I say to her, Give me, I pray you, a little water of your pitcher to drink;

44 And she say to me, Both drink you, and I will also draw for your camels: *let* the same *be* the woman whom the Lord has appointed out for my master's son.   El^{s.f.}

45 And before I had done speaking in my heart, behold, Re-bek'ah came forth with her pitcher on her shoulder; and she went down to the well, and drew *water*: and I said to her, Let me drink, I pray you.

46 And she made haste, and let down her pitcher from her *shoulder*, and said, Drink, and I will give your camels drink also: so I drank, and she made the camels drink also.

47 And I asked her, and said, Whose daughter *are* you? And she said, The daughter of Beth-u'el, Na'hor's son, whom Mil'cah bare to him: and I put the <u>earring upon her face</u>, and the brace-lets upon her hands.   ring in her nose

48 And I bowed down my head, and worshiped the Lord, and blessed the Lord God of my master A'bra-ham, which had led me in the right way to take my master's brother's daughter to his son.   El^{s.f.} - Jehovah^{s.f.} - Elohim^{p.f.}

49 And now if you will deal kindly and truly with my master, tell me: and if not, tell me; that I may turn to the right hand, or to the left.

50 Then La'ban and Beth-u'el an-swered and said, The thing proceeds from the Lord: we cannot speak to you bad or good.

51 Behold, Re-bek'ah *is* before you,

take *her*, and go, and let her be your master's son's wife, as the Lord has spoken.   El^{s.f.}

52 And it came to pass, that, when A'bra-ham's servant heard their words, he worshiped the Lord, *bow-ing himself* to the earth.

53 And the servant brought forth jewels of silver, and jewels of gold, and <u>rai-ment</u>, and gave *them* to Re-bek'ah: he gave also to her brother and to her mother precious things.   clothing

54 And they did eat and drink, he and the men that *were* with him, and tarried all night; and they rose up in the morning, and he said, Send me away to my master.

55 And her brother and her mother said, Let the <u>damsel</u> abide with us a *few* days, at the least ten; after that she shall go.   young girl

56 And he said to them, <u>Hinder me not</u>, seeing the Lord has prospered my way; send me away that I may go to my master.   Do not detain me

57 And they said, We will call the <u>damsel</u>, and <u>esquire at her mouth</u>.
    young girl - consult her wishes

58 And they called Re-bek'ah, and said to her, Will you go with this man? And she said, I will go.

59 And they sent away Re-bek'ah their sister, and her nurse, and A'bra-ham's servant, and his men.

60 And they blessed Re-bek'ah, and said to her, You *are* our sister, be you *the mother* of thousands of mil-lions, and let your <u>seed possess the gate of</u> those which hate them.

    descendants - be victorious over

61 And Re-bek'ah arose, and her <u>dam-sels</u>, and they rode upon the camels, and followed the man: and the servant took Re-bek'ah, and went his way.

62 And I'saac came from the way of the well La-hai'roi; for he dwelt in the south country.

63 And I'saac went out to meditate in the field at the <u>eventide</u>: and he lifted up his eyes, and saw, and, behold, the camels *were* coming. _{evening}

64 And Re-bek'ah lifted up her eyes, and when she saw I'saac, she <u>lighted</u> off the camel. _{dismounted}

65 For she *had* said to the servant, What man *is* this that walks in the field to meet us? And the servant *had* said, It *is* my master: therefore she took a veil, and covered herself.

66 And the servant told I'saac all things that he had done.

67 And I'saac brought her into his mother Sa'rah's tent, and took Re-bek'ah, and she became his wife; and he loved her: and I'saac was comforted after his mother's *death*.

CHAPTER 25

THEN again A'bra-ham took a wife, and her name *was* Ke-tu'rah.

2 And she bare him Zim'ran, and Jok'shan, and Me'dan, and Mid'i-an, and Ish'bak, and Shu'ah.

3 And Jok'shan fathered She'ba, and De'dan. And the sons of De'dan were As-shu'rim, and Le-tu'shim, and Le-um'mim.

4 And the sons of Mid'i-an; E'phah, and E'pher, and Ha'noch, and A-bi'-dah, and El'da-ah. All these *were* the children of Ke-tu'rah.

5 And A'bra-ham gave all that he had to I'saac.

6 But to the sons of the concubines, which A'bra-ham had, A'bra-ham gave gifts, and sent them away from I'saac his son, while he yet lived, eastward, to the east country.

7 And these *are* the days of the years of A'bra-ham's life which he lived, an <u>hundred threescore and fifteen</u> years. _{175 years old}

8 Then A'bra-ham gave up the ghost, and died in a good old age, an old man, and full of *years*; and was <u>gathered</u> to his people. _{buried}

9 And his sons I'saac and Ish'ma-el buried him in the cave of Mach-pe'lah, in the field of E'phron the son of Zo'har the Hit'tite, which *is* before Mam're;

10 The field which A'bra-ham purchased of the sons of Heth: there was A'bra-ham buried, and Sa'rah his wife.

11 And it came to pass after the death of A'bra-ham, that <u>God</u> blessed his son I'saac; and I'saac dwelt by the well La-hai'roi. _{Elohim^{p.f.}}

12 Now these *are* the <u>generations</u> of Ish'ma-el, A'bra-ham's son, whom Ha'gar the E-gyp'tian, Sa'rah's handmaid, bare to A'bra-ham: _{descendants}

13 And these *are* the names of the sons of Ish'ma-el, by their names, according to their generations: the firstborn of Ish'ma-el, Ne-ba'joth; and Ke'dar, and Ad'be-el, and Mib'sam,

14 And Mish'ma, and Du'mah, and Mas'sa,

15 Ha'dar, and Te'ma, Je'tur, Na'phish, and Ked'e-mah:

16 These *are* the sons of Ish'ma-el, and these *are* their names, by their towns, and by their <u>castles</u>; twelve princes according to their nations.   camps

17 And these *are* the years of the life of Ish'ma-el, an hundred and thirty and seven years: and he gave up the ghost and died; and was gathered to his people.

18 And they dwelt from Hav'i-lah to Shur, that *is* before E'gypt, as you go toward As-syr'i-a: *and* he died in the presence of all his brethren.

19 And these *are* the generations of I'saac, A'bra-ham's son: A'bra-ham fathered I'saac:

20 And I'saac was forty years old when he took Re-bek'ah to wife, the daughter of Beth-u'el the Syr'i-an of Pa'dan-a'ram, the sister to La'ban the Syr'i-an.

21 And I'saac <u>entreated</u> the LORD for his wife, because she *was* barren: and the LORD was entreated of him, and Re-bek'ah his wife conceived.   ROM. 9:10 prayed

22 And the children struggled together inside her; and she said, If *it be* so, why *am* I thus? And she went to enquire of the LORD.

23 And the LORD said to her, <u>Two nations</u> *are* in your womb, and two manner of people shall be separated from your <u>bowels;</u> and *the* one people shall be stronger than *the other* people; and the elder shall serve the younger.   ROM. 9:12 i.e. two families Esau and Jacob - body

24 And when her days to be deliv-

ered were fulfilled, behold, *there were* twins in her womb.

25 And the first came out red, all over like an hairy garment; and they called his name E'sau.

26 And after that came his brother out, and his hand took hold on E'sau's heel; and his name was called Ja'cob: and I'saac *was* <u>threescore</u> years old when she bare them.   60

27 And the boys grew: and E'sau was a cunning hunter, a man of the field; and Ja'cob *was* a plain man, dwelling in tents.

28 And I'saac loved E'sau, because he did eat of *his* venison: but Re-bek'ah loved Ja'cob.

29 And Ja'cob <u>sod pottage</u>: and E'sau came from the field, and he *was* faint: cooked stew

30 And E'sau said to Ja'cob, Feed me, I pray you, with that same red <u>pottage</u>; for I *am* faint: therefore was his name called <u>E'dom</u>.   means Red

31 And Ja'cob said, Sell me this day your birthright.

32 And E'sau said, Behold, I *am* <u>at the point</u> to die: and what profit shall this birthright do to me?   HEB. 12:16 about

33 And Ja'cob said, <u>Swear</u> to me this day; and he swear to him: and he sold his birthright to Ja'cob.   Promise

34 Then Ja'cob gave E'sau bread and pottage of lentils; and he did eat and drink, and rose up, and went his way: thus E'sau despised *his* birthright.

CHAPTER 26

AND there was a famine in the land, beside the first famine that was in

the days of A'bra-ham. And I'saac went to A-bim'e-lech king of the Phi-lis'tines to Ge'rar.

2 And the LORD appeared to him, and said, Go not down into E'gypt; dwell in the land which I shall tell you of:

3 <u>Sojourn</u> in this land, and I will be with you, and will bless you; for to you, and to your <u>seed</u>, I will give all these countries, and I will perform the oath which I swear to A'bra-ham your father; Stay temporarily - descendants

4 And I will make your <u>seed</u> to multiply as the stars of heaven, and will give to your <u>seed</u> all these countries; and in your *seed* shall all the nations of the earth be blessed;

5 Because that A'bra-ham obeyed My voice, and kept My charge, My commandments, My statutes, and My laws.

6 And I'saac dwelt in Ge'rar:

7 And the men of the place asked *him* of his wife; and he said, She *is* my sister: for he feared to say, *She is* my wife; lest, *said he*, the men of the place should kill me for Re-bek'ah; because she *was* fair to look upon.

8 And it came to pass, when he had been there a long time, that A-bim'e-lech king of the Phi-lis'tines looked out at a window, and saw, and, behold, I'saac *was* <u>sporting</u> with Re-bek'ah his wife. caressing

9 And A-bim'e-lech called I'saac, and said, Behold, <u>of a surety</u> she *is* your wife: and how said you, She *is* my sister? And I'saac said to him, Because I said, Less I die for her. certainly

10 And A-bim'e-lech said, What *is*

this you have done to us? one of the people might lightly have lien with your wife, and you should have brought guiltiness upon us.

11 And A-bim'e-lech charged all *his* people, saying, He that touches this man or his wife shall surely be put to death.

12 Then I'saac sowed in that land, and <u>received</u> in the same year an hundredfold: and the LORD blessed him. reaped - El

13 And the man <u>waxed great</u>, and <u>went forward</u>, and grew until he became very great: became rich - continued to grow

14 For he had possession of flocks, and possession of herds, and great store of servants: and the Phi-lis'tines envied him.

15 For all the wells which his father's servants had dug in the days of A'bra-ham his father, the Phi-lis'tines had stopped them, and filled them with earth.

16 And A-bim'e-lech said to I'saac, Go from us; for you are much mightier than we.

17 And I'saac departed there, and <u>pitched his tent</u> in the valley of Ge'rar, and dwelt there. camped

18 And I'saac dug again the wells of water, which they had dug in the days of A'bra-ham his father; for the Phi-lis'tines had stopped them after the death of A'bra-ham: and he called their names after the names by which his father had called them.

19 And I'saac's servants dug in the valley, and found there a well of <u>springing</u> water. flowing

20 And the herdmen of Ge'rar did <u>strive</u> with I'saac's herdmen, saying, The water *is* ours: and he called the name of the well E'sek; because they <u>strove</u> with him. <small>quarreled</small>

21 And they dug another well, and <u>strove</u> for that also: and he called the name of it <u>Sit'nah</u>. <small>Enmity</small>

22 And he removed from there, and dug another well; and for that they strove not: and he called the name of it Re-ho'both; and he said, For now the LORD has made room for us, and we shall be fruitful in the land.

23 And he went up from there to Be'er-she'ba.

24 And the LORD appeared to him the same night, and said, I *am* the God of A'bra-ham your father: fear not, for I *am* with you, and will bless you, and multiply your <u>seed</u> for My servant A'bra-ham's sake. <small>descendants</small>

25 And he built an altar there, and called upon the name of the LORD, and pitched his tent there: and there I'saac's servants dug a well.

26 Then A-bim'e-lech went to him from Ge'rar, and A-huz'zath one of his friends, and Phi'chol the chief captain of his army.

27 And I'saac said to them, Wherefore come you to me, seeing you <u>hate</u> me, and have sent me away from you? <small>despise</small>

28 And they said, We saw <u>certainly</u> that the LORD was with you: and we said, Let there be now an oath between us, *even* between us and you, and let us make a <u>covenant</u> with you; <small>plainly - agreement</small>

29 That you will do us no <u>hurt</u>, as we have not touched you, and as we have done to you nothing but good, and have sent you away in peace: you *are* now the blessed of the LORD. <small>harm - El^{s.f.}</small>

30 And he made them a feast, and they did eat and drink.

31 And they rose up <u>betimes</u> in the morning, and <u>swear</u> one to another: and I'saac sent them away, and they departed from him in peace. <small>early - exchanged oaths</small>

32 And it came to pass the same day, that I'saac's servants came, and told him concerning the well which they had dug, and said to him, We have found water.

33 And he called it <u>She'bah</u>: therefore the name of the city *is* <u>Be'er-she'ba</u> to this day. <small>an oath - the well of the oath</small>

34 And E'sau was forty years old when he took to wife Ju'dith the daughter of Be-e'ri the Hit'tite, and Bash'e-math the daughter of E'lon the Hit'tite:

35 Which <u>were a</u> grief of mind to I'saac and to Re-bek'ah. <small>brought</small>

CHAPTER 27

AND it came to pass, that when I'saac was old, and his eyes were dim, so that he could not see, he called E'sau his eldest son, and said to him, My son: and he said to him, Behold, *here am* I.

2 And he said, Behold now, I am old, I know not the day of my death:

3 Now therefore <u>take</u>, I pray you, your weapons, your quiver and your bow, and go out to the field, and <u>take</u> me *some* venison; <small>get</small>

4 And make me savory meat, such as I love, and bring *it* to me, that I may

eat; that my soul may bless you before I die.

5 And Re-bek'ah heard when I'saac spoke to E'sau his son. And E'sau went to the field to hunt *for* venison, *and* to bring *it*.

6 And Re-bek'ah spoke to Ja'cob her son, saying, Behold, I heard your father speak to E'sau your brother, saying,

7 Bring me venison, and make me savory meat, that I may eat, and bless you before the Lord before my death.   El^s.f.

8 Now therefore, my son, obey my voice according to that which I command you.

9 Go now to the flock, and bring me from there two good kids of the goats; and I will make them savory meat for your father, such as he loves:

10 And you shall bring *it* to your father, that he may eat, and that he may bless you before his death.

11 And Ja'cob said to Re-bek'ah his mother, Behold, E'sau my brother *is* a hairy man, and I *am* a smooth man:

12 My father perhaps will feel me, and I shall seem to him as a deceiver; and I shall bring a curse upon me, and not a blessing.

13 And his mother said to him, Upon me *be* your curse, my son: only obey my voice, and go bring me *them*.

14 And he went, and brought, and brought *them* to his mother: and his mother made savory meat, such as his father loved.

15 And Re-bek'ah took goodly raiment of her eldest son E'sau, which

were with her in the house, and put them upon Ja'cob her younger son:
_{clothing}

16 And she put the skins of the kids of the goats upon his hands, and upon the smooth of his neck:

17 And she gave the savory meat and the bread, which she had prepared, into the hand of her son Ja'cob.

18 And he came to his father, and said, My father: and he said, Here *am* I; who *are* you, my son?

19 And Ja'cob said to his father, I *am* E'sau your firstborn; I have done according as you bade me: arise, I pray you, sit and eat of my venison, that your soul may bless me.

20 And I'saac said to his son, How *is it* that you have found *it* so quickly, my son? And he said, Because the Lord your God brought *it* to me.   El^s.f. - Elohim^p.f.

21 And I'saac said to Ja'cob, Come near, I pray you, that I may feel you, my son, whether you *be* my very son E'sau or not.

22 And Ja'cob went near to I'saac his father; and he felt him, and said, The voice *is* Ja'cob's voice, but the hands *are* the hands of E'sau.

23 And he discerned him not, because his hands were hairy, as his brother E'sau's hands: so he blessed him.

24 And he said, *Are* you my very son E'sau? And he said, I *am*.

25 And he said, Bring *it* near to me, and I will eat of my son's venison, that my soul may bless you. And he brought *it* near to him, and he did eat:

and he brought him wine, and he drank.

26 And his father I'saac said to him, Come near now, and kiss me, my son.

27 And he came near, and kissed him: and he smelled the smell of his <u>raiment</u>, and blessed him, and said, See, the smell of my son *is* as the smell of a field which the LORD has blessed: clothing

28 Therefore <u>God</u> give you of the dew of heaven, and the fatness of the earth, and plenty of <u>corn</u> and wine: Elohim^{p.f.} - grain

29 Let people serve you, and nations bow down to you: be lord over your brethren, and let your mother's sons bow down to you: cursed *be* every one that curses you, and blessed *be* he that blesses you. HEB. 11:20

30 And it came to pass, as soon as I'saac had made an end of blessing Ja'cob, and Ja'cob was yet scarce gone out from the presence of I'saac his father, that E'sau his brother came in from his hunting.

31 And he also had made <u>savory</u> meat, and brought it to his father, and said to his father, Let my father arise, and eat of his son's venison, that your soul may bless me. tasty

32 And I'saac his father said to him, Who *are* you? And he said, I *am* your son, your firstborn E'sau.

33 And I'saac trembled very exceedingly, and said, Who? where is *he* that has <u>taken</u> venison, and brought *it* me, and I have eaten of all before you came, and have blessed him? yea, *and* he shall be blessed. hunted

34 And when E'sau heard the words of his father, he cried with a great and exceeding bitter cry, and said to his father, Bless me, *even* me also, O my father. HEB. 12:17

35 And he said, Your brother came with subtilty, and has taken away your blessing.

36 And he said, Is not he rightly named Ja'cob? for he has <u>supplanted</u> me these two times: he took away my birthright; and, behold, now he has taken away my blessing. And he said, Have you not reserved a blessing for me? deceived

37 And I'saac answered and said to E'sau, Behold, I have made him your lord, and all his brethren have I given to him for servants; and with <u>corn</u> and wine have I <u>sustained</u> him: and what shall I do now to you, my son? grain - supplied

38 And E'sau said to his father, Have you but one blessing, my father? bless me, *even* me also, O my father. And E'sau lifted up his voice, and wept.

39 And I'saac his father answered and said to him, Behold, your dwelling shall be the fatness of the earth, and of the dew of heaven from above;

40 And by your sword shall you live, and shalt serve your brother; and it shall come to pass when you shall have the dominion, that you shall break his yoke from off your neck.

41 And E'sau <u>hated</u> Ja'cob because of the blessing wherewith his father blessed him: and E'sau said in his

heart, The days of mourning for my father are at hand; then will I slay my brother Ja'cob.

held a grudge against

42 And these words of E'sau her elder son were told to Re-bek'ah: and she sent and called Ja'cob her younger son, and said to him, Behold, your brother E'sau, as touching you, does comfort himself, *purposing* to kill you.

concerning

43 Now therefore, my son, obey my voice; and arise, flee you to La'ban my brother to Ha'ran;

do what I say

44 And tarry with him a few days, until your brother's fury turn away;

stay

45 Until your brother's anger turn away from you, and he forget *that* which you have done to him: then I will send, and bring you from there: why should I be deprived also of you both in one day?

bereaved

46 And Re-bek'ah said to I'saac, I am weary of my life because of the daughters of Heth: if Ja'cob take a wife of the daughters of Heth, such as these *which are* of the daughters of the land, what good shall my life do me?

CHAPTER 28

AND I'saac called Ja'cob, and blessed him, and charged him, and said to him, You shall not take a wife of the daughters of Ca'naan.

commanded

2 Arise, go to Pa'dan-a'ram, to the house of Beth-u'el your mother's father; and take you a wife from there of the daughters of La'ban your mother's brother.

3 And God Almighty bless you, and make you fruitful, and multiply you, that you may be a multitude of people;

El s.f. Shaddai

4 And give you the blessing of A'bra-ham, to you, and to your seed with you; that you may inherit the land wherein you are a stranger, which God gave to A'bra-ham.

descendants - an alien - Elohim p.f.

5 And I'saac sent away Ja'cob: and he went to Pa'dan-a'ram to La'ban, son of Beth-u'el the Syr'i-an, the brother of Re-bek'ah, Ja'cob's and E'sau's mother.

6 When E'sau saw that I'saac had blessed Ja'cob, and sent him away to Pa'dan-a'ram, to take him a wife from there; and that as he blessed him he gave him a charge, saying, You shall not take a wife of the daughters of Ca'naan;

7 And that Ja'cob obeyed his father and his mother, and was gone to Pa'dan-a'ram;

8 And E'sau seeing that the daughters of Ca'naan pleased not I'saac his father;

9 Then went E'sau to Ish'ma-el, and took to the wives which he had Ma'ha-lath the daughter of Ish'ma-el A'bra-ham's son, the sister of Ne-ba'joth, to be his wife.

10 And Ja'cob went out from Be'er-she'ba, and went toward Ha'ran.

11 And he lighted upon a certain place, and tarried there all night, because the sun was set; and he took of the stones of that place, and put *them for* his pillows, and lay down in that place to sleep.

remained

12 And he dreamed, and behold a

<u>ladder</u> set up on the earth, and the top of it reached to heaven: and behold the <u>angels</u> of <u>God</u> ascending and descending on it.   JOHN 1:51   stairway - messengers - Elohim^{p.f.}

13 And, behold, the L<small>ORD</small> stood <u>above</u> it, and said, I *am* the L<small>ORD</small> <u>God</u> of A'bra-ham your father, and the <u>God</u> of I'saac: the land whereon you lie, to you will I give it, and to your <u>seed</u>;

El^{s.f.} - beside him - Jehovah^{s.f.} - Elohim^{p.f.}

14 And your <u>seed</u> shall be as the dust of the earth, and you shall spread abroad to the west, and to the east, and to the north, and to the south: and in you and in your <u>seed</u> shall all the families of the earth be blessed. descendants

15 And, behold, I *am* with you, and will <u>keep</u> you in all *places* wherever you go, and will bring you again into this land; for I will not leave you, until I have done *that* which I have spoken to you of.   watch over

16 And Ja'cob awaked out of his sleep, and he said, Surely the L<small>ORD</small> is in this place; and I knew *it* not.   El^{s.f.}

17 And he was afraid, and said, How <u>dreadful</u> *is* this place! this *is* none other but the house of <u>God</u>, and this *is* the gate of heaven.   awesome - Elohim^{p.f.}

18 And Ja'cob rose up early in the morning, and took the stone that he had put *for* his pillows, and set it up *for* a pillar, and poured oil upon the top of it.

19 And he called the name of that place <u>Beth'-el</u>: but the name of that city *was called* Luz at the first.   house of God

20 And Ja'cob vowed a vow, saying, If <u>God</u> will be with me, and will keep me in this way that I go, and will give me bread to eat, and <u>raiment</u> to put on,   clothing

21 So that I <u>come again</u> to my father's house in peace; then shall the L<small>ORD</small> be my <u>God</u>:   return - El^{s.f.} - Elohim^{p.f.}

22 And this stone, which I have set *for* a pillar, shall be <u>God's</u> house: and of all that you shall give me I will surely give the tenth to You.

CHAPTER 29

THEN Ja'cob went on his journey, and came into the land of the people of the east.

2 And he looked, and behold a well in the field, and, lo, there *were* three flocks of sheep lying by it; for out of that well they watered the flocks: and a great stone was upon the well's mouth.

3 And there were all the flocks gathered: and they rolled the stone from the well's mouth, and watered the sheep, and put the stone again upon the well's mouth in its place.

4 And Ja'cob said to them, My brethren, where *be* you? And they said, Of Ha'ran *are* we.

5 And he said to them, Know you La'ban the son of Na'hor? And they said, We know *him*.

6 And he said to them, *Is* he well? And they said, *He is* well: and, behold, Ra'chel his daughter comes with the sheep.

7 And he said, Lo, *it is* yet <u>high day</u>, neither *is it* time that the cattle should be gathered together: water you the sheep, and go *and* feed *them*. early in the day

8 And they said, We cannot, until all the flocks be gathered together, and *till*

they roll the stone from the well's mouth; then we water the sheep.

9 And while he yet spoke with them, Ra'chel came with her father's sheep: for she kept them.

10 And it came to pass, when Ja'cob saw Ra'chel the daughter of La'ban his mother's brother, and the sheep of La'ban his mother's brother, that Ja'cob went near, and rolled the stone from the well's mouth, and watered the flock of La'ban his mother's brother.

11 And Ja'cob kissed Ra'chel, and lifted up his voice, and wept.

12 And Ja'cob told Ra'chel that he *was* her father's brother, and that he *was* Re-bek'ah's son: and she ran and told her father.

13 And it came to pass, when La'ban heard the tidings of Ja'cob his sister's son, that he ran to meet him, and embraced him, and kissed him, and brought him to his house. And he told La'ban all these things.

14 And La'ban said to him, Surely you *are* my bone and my flesh. And he abode with him the space of a month.

15 And La'ban said to Ja'cob, Because you *are* my brother, should you therefore serve me for nothing? tell me, what *shall* your wages be?

16 And La'ban had two daughters: the name of the elder *was* Le'ah, and the name of the younger *was* Ra'chel.

17 Le'ah *was* <u>tender eyed</u>; but Ra'chel was beautiful and well favored.   weakeyed

18 And Ja'cob loved Ra'chel; and said, I will serve you seven years for Ra'chel your younger daughter.

19 And La'ban said, *It is* better that I give her to you, than that I should give her to another man: abide with me.

20 And Ja'cob served seven years for Ra'chel; and they seemed to him *but* a few days, for the love he had to her.

21 And Ja'cob said to La'ban, Give *me* my wife, for my days are fulfilled, that I may <u>go in to her</u>.   lie with her

22 And La'ban gathered together all the men of the place, and made a feast.

23 And it came to pass in the evening, that he took Le'ah his daughter, and brought her to him; and he went in to her.

24 And La'ban gave to his daughter Le'ah Zil'pah his maid *for* an handmaid.

25 And it came to pass, that in the morning, behold, it *was* Le'ah: and he said to La'ban, What *is* this you have done to me? did not I serve with you for Ra'chel? wherefore then have you <u>beguiled</u> me?   deceived

26 And La'ban said, <u>It must not be so done</u> in our country, to give the younger before the firstborn.   It is not the practice

27 Fulfil her week, and we will give you this also for the service which you shall serve with me yet seven other years.

28 And Ja'cob did so, and fulfilled her week: and he gave him Ra'chel his daughter to wife also.

29 And La'ban gave to Ra'chel his daughter Bil'hah his handmaid to be her maid.

30 And he went in also to Ra'chel, and he loved also Ra'chel more than Le'ah,

and served with him yet seven other years.

31 And when the LORD saw that Le'ah *was* <u>hated</u>, He <u>opened her womb</u>: but Ra'chel *was* barren. <small>unloved - enabled her to have children</small>

32 And Le'ah conceived, and bare a son, and she called his name Reu'ben: for she said, Surely the LORD has looked upon my affliction; now therefore my husband will love me.

33 And she conceived again, and bare a son; and said, Because the LORD has heard that I *was* <u>hated</u>, He has therefore given me this *son* also: and she called his name <u>Sim'e-on</u>. <small>unloved - Hearing</small>

34 And she conceived again, and bare a son; and said, Now this time will my husband be <u>joined to</u> me, because I have born him three sons: therefore was his name called Le'vi. <small>attached to</small>

35 And she conceived again, and bare a son: and she said, Now will I praise the LORD: therefore she called his name Ju'dah; and <u>left</u> bearing. <small>stopped</small>

CHAPTER 30

AND when Ra'chel saw that she bare Ja'cob no children, Ra'chel envied her sister; and said to Ja'cob, Give me children, or else I die.

2 And Ja'cob's anger was kindled against Ra'chel: and he said, *Am* I in <u>God's stead</u>, who has withheld from you the fruit of the womb? <small>in the place of God</small>

3 And she said, Behold my maid Bil'hah, go in to her; and she shall bear upon my knees, that I may also have children by her.

4 And she gave him Bil'hah her hand-maid to wife: and Ja'cob went in to her.

5 And Bil'hah conceived, and bare Ja'cob a son.

6 And Ra'chel said, <u>God</u> has judged me, and has also heard my voice, and has given me a son: therefore called she his name <u>Dan</u>. <small>Elohim^{p.f.} - Judging</small>

7 And Bil'hah Ra'chel's maid conceived again, and bare Ja'cob a second son.

8 And Ra'chel said, With great wrestlings have I wrestled with my sister, and I have prevailed: and she called his name Naph'ta-li.

9 When Le'ah saw that she had left bearing, she took Zil'pah her maid, and gave her Ja'cob to wife.

10 And Zil'pah Le'ah's maid bare Ja'cob a son.

11 And Le'ah said, A troop comes: and she called his name <u>Gad</u>. <small>Fortune</small>

12 And Zil'pah Le'ah's maid bare Ja'cob a second son.

13 And Le'ah said, Happy am I, for the daughters will call me blessed: and she called his name <u>Ash'er</u>. <small>Happy</small>

14 And Reu'ben went in the days of wheat harvest, and found mandrakes in the field, and brought them to his mother Le'ah. Then Ra'chel said to Le'ah, Give me, I pray you, of your son's <u>mandrakes</u>. <small>herb causing sexual desire</small>

15 And she said to her, *Is it* a small matter that you have taken my husband? and would you take away my son's mandrakes also? And Ra'chel said, Therefore he shall lie with you to night for your son's <u>mandrakes</u>.

16 And Ja'cob came out of the field in

the evening, and Le'ah went out to meet him, and said, You must come in to me; for surely I have hired you with my son's <u>mandrakes</u>. And he lay with her that night.   _{i.e. for causing sexual desire}

17 And <u>God</u> hearkened to Le'ah, and she conceived, and bare Ja'cob the fifth son.   Elohim^{p.f.}

18 And Le'ah said, <u>God</u> has given me my <u>hire</u>, because I have given my maiden to my husband: and she called his name Is'sa-char.   wages

19 And Le'ah conceived again, and bare Ja'cob the sixth son.

20 And Le'ah said, <u>God</u> has endued me *with* a good dowry; now will my husband dwell with me, because I have born him six sons: and she called his name Zeb'u-lun.

21 And afterwards she bare a daughter, and called her name Di'nah.

22 And <u>God</u> remembered Ra'chel, and God hearkened to her, and opened her womb.   Elohim^{p.f.}

23 And she conceived, and bare a son; and said, <u>God</u> has taken away my reproach:

24 And she called his name <u>Jo'seph</u>; and said, The Lord shall add to me another son.   Adding - El^{s.f.}

25 And it came to pass, when Ra'chel had born Jo'seph, that Ja'cob said to La'ban, Send me away, that I may go to my own place, and to my country.

26 Give *me* my wives and my children, for whom I have served you, and let me go: for you know my service which I have done you.

27 And La'ban said to him, I <u>pray</u> you, if I have found favor in your eyes, *tarry*: *for* I have learned by experience that the Lord has blessed me for your sake.   beg

28 And he said, <u>Appoint</u> me your wages, and I will give *it*.   Name

29 And he said to him, You know how I have served you, and how your cattle was with me.

30 For *it was* little which you had before I *came*, and it is *now* increased to a multitude; and the <u>Lord</u> has blessed you since my coming: and now when shall I provide for my own house also?   El^{s.f.}

31 And he said, What shall I give you? And Ja'cob said, You shall not give me any thing: if you will do this thing for me, I will again feed *and* keep your flock.

32 I will pass through all your flock to day, removing from there all the speckled and spotted cattle, and all the brown cattle among the sheep, and the spotted and speckled among the goats: and *of such* shall be my <u>hire</u>.   wages

33 So shall my righteousness answer for me in <u>time to come</u>, when it shall come for my <u>hire</u> before your face: every one that *is* not speckled and spotted among the goats, and brown among the sheep, that shall be counted stolen with me.   the future

34 And La'ban said, Behold, I would it might be according to your word.

35 And he removed that day the he goats that were ringstraked and spotted, and all the she goats that were speckled and spotted, *and* every one that had *some* white in it, and all the

brown among the sheep, and gave *them* into the hand of his sons.

36 And he set three days' journey between himself and Ja'cob: and Ja'cob fed the rest of La'ban's flocks.

37 And Ja'cob took him rods of green poplar, and of the hazel and chesnut tree; and peeled white <u>strakes</u> in them, and made the white appear which *was* in the rods. streaks

38 And he set the rods which he had peeled before the flocks in the gutters in the watering troughs when the flocks came to drink, that they should conceive when they came to drink.

39 And the flocks conceived before the rods, and brought forth cattle ringstraked, speckled, and spotted.

40 And Ja'cob did separate the lambs, and set the faces of the flocks toward the ringstraked, and all the brown in the flock of La'ban; and he put his own flocks by themselves, and put them not to La'ban's <u>cattle</u>. flock

41 And it came to pass, whensoever the stronger cattle did conceive, that Ja'cob laid the rods before the eyes of the cattle in the gutters, that they might conceive among the rods.

42 But when the cattle were feeble, he put *them* not in: so the feebler were La'ban's, and the stronger Ja'cob's.

43 And the man increased exceedingly, and had <u>much cattle</u>, and maidservants, and menservants, and camels, and asses. large flocks

CHAPTER 31

AND he heard the words of La'ban's sons, saying, Ja'cob has taken away all that *was* our father's; and of *that* which *was* our father's has he gotten all this <u>glory</u>. wealth

2 And Ja'cob beheld the countenance of La'ban, and, behold, it *was* not <u>toward</u> him as before. friendly to

3 And the Lord said to Ja'cob, Return to the land of your fathers, and to your kindred; and I will be with you. El s.f.

4 And Ja'cob sent and called Ra'chel and Le'ah to the field to his flock,

5 And said to them, I see your father's countenance, that it *is* not toward me as before; but the <u>God</u> of my father has been with me. Elohim p.f.

6 And you know that with all my <u>power</u> I have served your father. strength

7 And your father has deceived me, and changed my wages ten times; but <u>God</u> allowed him not to hurt me.

8 If he said thus, The speckled shall be your wages; then all the cattle bare speckled: and if he said thus, The <u>ringstraked</u> shall be your <u>hire</u>; then bare all the cattle <u>ringstraked</u>. striped - wages

9 Thus <u>God</u> has taken away the cattle of your father, and given *them* to me.

10 And it came to pass at the time that the cattle conceived, that I lifted up my eyes, and saw in a dream, and, behold, the rams which leaped upon the cattle *were* ringstraked, speckled, and grisled.

11 And the <u>angel</u> of <u>God</u> spoke to me in a dream, *saying*, Ja'cob: And I said, Here *am* I. messenger - Elohim p.f.

12 And He said, Lift up now your eyes, and see, all the rams which leap upon the cattle *are* ringstraked,

speckled, and grisled: for I have seen all that La'ban does to you.

13 I *am* the God of Beth'-el, where you anointed the pillar, *and* where you <u>vowed a vow</u> to Me: now arise, get you out from this land, and return to the land of your kindred. make a pledge

14 And Ra'chel and Le'ah answered and said to him, *Is there* yet any portion or inheritance for us in our father's house?

15 Are we not counted of him strangers? for he has sold us, and has quite <u>devoured</u> also our money. consumed

16 For all the riches which God has taken from our father, that *is* ours, and our children's: now then, whatsoever God has said to you, do. Elohim^{p.f.}

17 Then Ja'cob rose up, and set his sons and his wives upon camels;

18 And he carried away all his cattle, and all his goods which he had gotten, the cattle of his getting, which he had gotten in Pa'dan-a'ram, for to go to I'saac his father in the land of Ca'naan.

19 And La'ban went to shear his sheep: and Ra'chel had stolen the <u>images</u> that *were* her father's. household idols

20 And Ja'cob stole away unawares to La'ban the Syr'i-an, in that he told him not that he fled.

21 So he fled with all that he had; and he rose up, and passed over the river, and set his face *toward* the mount Gil'e-ad.

22 And it was told La'ban on the third day that Ja'cob was fled.

23 And he took his brethren with him, and pursued after him seven days' journey; and they overtook him in the mount Gil'e-ad.

24 And <u>God</u> came to La'ban the Syr'i-an in a dream by night, and said to him, Take heed that you speak not to Ja'cob either good or bad. Elohim^{p.f.}

25 Then La'ban overtook Ja'cob. Now Ja'cob had pitched his tent in the mount: and La'ban with his brethren <u>pitched</u> in the mount of Gil'e-ad. camped

26 And La'ban said to Ja'cob, What have you done, that you have stolen away unawares to me, and carried away my daughters, as captives *taken* with the sword?

27 Wherefore did you flee away secretly, and <u>steal away from me</u>; and did not tell me, that I might have sent you away with mirth, and with songs, with tabret, and with harp? deceive me

28 And has not allowed me to kiss my sons and my daughters? you have now done foolishly in *so* doing.

29 It is in the power of my hand to do you <u>hurt</u>: but the <u>God</u> of your father spoke to me yesternight, saying, Take you heed that you speak not to Ja'cob either good or bad. harm - Elohim^{p.f.}

30 And now, *though* you would needs be gone, because you <u>sore</u> long after your father's house, *yet* wherefore have you stolen my gods? greatly

31 And Ja'cob answered and said to La'ban, Because I was afraid: for I said, Perhaps you would take by force your daughters from me.

32 With whomsoever you find your gods, let him not live: before our brethren <u>discern you</u> what *is* yours with me,

M13-54

and take *it* to you. For Ja'cob knew not that Ra'chel had stolen them. point out

33 And La'ban went into Ja'cob's tent, and into Le'ah's tent, and into the two maidservants' tents; but he found *them* not. Then went he out of Le'ah's tent, and entered into Ra'chel's tent.

34 Now Ra'chel had taken the images, and put them in the camel's furniture, and sat upon them. And La'ban searched all the tent, but found *them* not. household idols - saddle

35 And she said to her father, Let it not displease my lord that I cannot rise up before you; for the custom of women *is* upon me. And he searched, but found not the images.

36 And Ja'cob was angry, and chode with La'ban: and Ja'cob answered and said to La'ban, What *is* my trespass? what *is* my sin, that you have so hotly pursued after me?

contended - transgression

37 Whereas you have searched all my stuff, what have you found of all your household stuff? set *it* here before my brethren and your brethren, that they may judge between us both. goods

38 This twenty years *have* I *been* with you; your ewes and your she goats have not cast their young, and the rams of your flock have I not eaten. These

39 That which was torn *of beasts* I brought not to you; I bare the loss of it; of my hand did you require it, *whether* stolen by day, or stolen by night.

40 *Thus* I was; in the day the drought consumed me, and the frost by night; and my sleep departed from my eyes.

41 Thus have I been twenty years in your house; I served you fourteen years for your two daughters, and six years for your cattle: and you have changed my wages ten times.

42 Except the God of my father, the God of A'bra-ham, and the fear of I'saac, had been with me, surely you had sent me away now empty. God has seen my affliction and the labor of my hands, and rebuked *you* yesternight. Elohim^{p.f} - respect - for

43 And La'ban answered and said to Ja'cob, *These* daughters *are* my daughters, and *these* children *are* my children, and *these* cattle *are* my cattle, and all that you see *is* mine: and what can I do this day to these my daughters, or to their children which they have born?

44 Now therefore come you, let us make a covenant, I and you; and let it be for a witness between me and you. agreement

45 And Ja'cob took a stone, and set it up *for* a pillar.

46 And Ja'cob said to his brethren, Gather stones; and they took stones, and made an heap: and they did eat there upon the heap.

47 And La'ban called it Je'gar-sa-ha-du'tha: but Ja'cob called it Gal'e-ed.

48 And La'ban said, This heap *is* a witness between me and you this day. Therefore was the name of it called Gal'e-ed;

49 And Miz'pah; for he said, The LORD watch between me and you, when we are absent one from another. El^{s.f}

50 If you shall <u>afflict</u> my daughters, or if you shall take *other* wives beside my daughters, no man *is* with us; see, <u>God</u> *is* witness between me and you.   mistreat - Elohim^{p.f.}

51 And La'ban said to Ja'cob, Behold this heap, and behold *this* pillar, which I have cast between me and you;

52 This heap *be* witness, and *this* pillar *be* witness, that I will not pass over this heap to you, and that you shall not pass over this heap and this pillar to me, for harm.

53 The <u>God</u> of A'bra-ham, and the <u>God</u> of Na'hor, the <u>God</u> of their father, judge between us. And Ja'cob <u>swear</u> by the <u>fear</u> of his father I'saac.

Elohim^{p.f.} - promised - reverence

54 Then Ja'cob offered sacrifice upon the mount, and called his brethren to eat bread: and they did eat bread, and tarried all night in the mount.

55 And early in the morning La'ban rose up, and kissed his sons and his daughters, and blessed them: and La'ban departed, and returned to his place.

CHAPTER 32

AND Ja'cob went on his way, and the <u>angels</u> of <u>God</u> met him.

messengers - Elohim^{p.f.}

2 And when Ja'cob saw them, he said, This *is* <u>God's</u> host: and he called the name of that place <u>Ma-ha-na'im</u>.   i.e. two camps

3 And Ja'cob sent messengers before him to E'sau his brother to the land of Se'ir, the country of E'dom.

4 And he commanded them, saying, Thus shall you speak to my lord E'sau; Your servant Ja'cob says thus, I have <u>sojourned</u> with La'ban, and stayed there until now: lived some time

5 And I have oxen, and asses, flocks, and menservants, and womenservants: and I have sent to <u>tell</u> my lord, that I may find grace in your sight.   greet

6 And the messengers returned to Ja'cob, saying, We came to your brother E'sau, and also he comes to meet you, and four hundred men with him.

7 Then Ja'cob was greatly afraid and distressed: and he divided the people that *was* with him, and the flocks, and herds, and the camels, into two bands;

8 And said, If E'sau come to the one company, and <u>smite</u> it, then the other company which is left shall escape. attacks

9 And Ja'cob said, O <u>God</u> of my father A'bra-ham, and <u>God</u> of my father I'saac, the LORD which said to me, Return to your country, and to your kindred, and I will deal well with you: Elohim^{p.f.}

10 I am not worthy of the least of all the mercies, and of all the truth, which you have showed to Your servant; for with my staff I passed over this Jor'dan; and now I am become two <u>bands</u>.   companies

11 Deliver me, I pray You, from the hand of my brother, from the hand of E'sau: for I fear him, less he will come and <u>smite</u> me, *and* the mother with the children.   attack

12 And You said, I will surely do you good, and make your <u>seed</u> as the sand of the sea, which cannot be numbered for multitude.   descendants

M07
M11
M27
798
M35
846
55
P15B
56
G1G
79
52

13 And he lodged there that same night; and took of that which <u>came to his hand a present</u> for E'sau his brother; ^{he had}

14 Two hundred she goats, and twenty he goats, two hundred ewes, and twenty rams,

15 Thirty <u>milch</u> camels with their colts, forty <u>kine</u>, and ten bulls, twenty she asses, and ten foals. ^{milk-cows}

16 And he delivered *them* into the hand of his servants, every drove by themselves; and said to his servants, Pass over before me, and put a space between drove and drove.

17 And he commanded the foremost, saying, When E'sau my brother meets you, and asks you, saying, Whose *are* you? and where go you? and whose *are* these before you?

18 Then you shall say, *They be* your servant Ja'cob's; it *is* a present sent to my lord E'sau: and, behold, also he *is* behind us.

19 And so commanded he the second, and the third, and all that followed the droves, saying, On this manner shall you speak to E'sau, when you find him.

20 And say you moreover, Behold, your servant Ja'cob *is* behind us. For he said, I will appease him with the present that goes before me, and afterward I will see his face; perhaps he will <u>accept</u> of me. ^{receive}

21 So went the present over before him: and himself lodged that night in the <u>company</u>. ^{camp}

22 And he rose up that night, and took his two wives, and his two women-servants, and his eleven sons, and passed over the ford Jab'bok.

23 And he took them, and sent them over the brook, and sent over <u>that</u> he had. ^{whatever}

24 And Ja'cob was left alone; and there wrestled a man with him until <u>the breaking of the day</u>. ^{dawn}

25 And when he saw that he prevailed not against him, he touched the hollow of his thigh; and the hollow of Ja'cob's thigh was out of joint, as he wrestled with him.

26 And He said, Let Me go, for the day breaks. And he said, I will not let You go, except You bless me.

27 And He said to him, What *is* your name? And he said, Ja'cob.

28 And He said, Your name shall be called no more Ja'cob, but <u>Is'ra-el</u>: for as a prince have you power with God and with men, and have <u>prevailed</u>. ^{a prince of God - overcome}

29 And Ja'cob asked *Him*, and said, Tell *me*, I pray You, Your name. And He said, Wherefore *is* it *that* you do ask after My name? And He blessed him there.

30 And Ja'cob called the name of the place <u>Pe-ni'el</u>: for I have seen <u>God</u> face to face, and my life is preserved. ^{The face of God - Elohim}

31 And as he passed over <u>Pe-nu'el</u> the sun rose upon him, and he <u>halted</u> upon his thigh. ^{limped}

32 Therefore the children of Is'ra-el eat not *of* the sinew which shrank, which *is* upon the hollow of the thigh, to this day: because He touched the

hollow of Ja'cob's thigh in the sinew that shrank.

CHAPTER 33

AND Ja'cob lifted up his eyes, and looked, and, behold, E'sau came, and with him four hundred men. And he divided the children to Le'ah, and to Ra'chel, and to the two handmaids.

2 And he put the handmaids and their children foremost, and Le'ah and her children after, and Ra'chel and Jo'seph <u>hindermost</u>.   last

3 And he passed over before them, and <u>bowed</u> himself to the ground seven times, until he came near to his brother.   i.e. showing respect

4 And E'sau ran to meet him, and embraced him, and fell on his neck, and kissed him: and they wept.

5 And he lifted up his eyes, and saw the women and the children; and said, Who *are* those with you? And he said, The children which <u>God</u> has graciously given your servant.   Elohim^p.f.

6 Then the handmaidens came near, they and their children, and they bowed themselves.

7 And Le'ah also with her children came near, and bowed themselves: and after came Jo'seph near and Ra'chel, and they bowed themselves.

8 And he said, What *means* you by all this drove which I met? And he said, *These are* to find <u>grace</u> in the sight of my lord.   favor

9 And E'sau said, I have enough, my brother; keep that you have to yourself.

10 And Ja'cob said, Nay, I pray you, if now I have found <u>grace</u> in your sight, then receive my present at my hand: for therefore I have seen your face, as though I had seen the face of <u>God</u>, and you were pleased with me.   favor

11 Take, I pray you, my blessing that is brought to you; because <u>God</u> has dealt graciously with me, and because I have enough. And he urged him, and he took *it*.   Elohim^p.f.

12 And he said, Let us take our journey, and let us go, and I will go before you.

13 And he said to him, My lord knows that the children *are* <u>tender</u>, and the flocks and herds with young *are* with me: and if men should overdrive them one day, all the flock will die.   frail

14 Let my lord, I pray you, pass over before his servant: and I will lead on <u>softly</u>, according as the cattle that goes before me and the children be able to endure, until I come to my lord to Se'ir.   leisurely

15 And E'sau said, Let me now leave with you *some* of the folk that *are* with me. And he said, What needs it? let me find grace in the sight of my lord.

16 So E'sau returned that day on his way to Se'ir.

17 And Ja'cob journeyed to Suc'coth, and built him an house, and made <u>booths</u> for his cattle: therefore the name of the place is called Suc'coth.   shelters

18 And Ja'cob came to Sha'lem, a city of Shechem, which *is* in the land of Ca'naan, when he came from Pa'dan-

a'ram; and pitched his tent before the city.

19 And he bought a parcel of a field, where he had spread his tent, at the hand of the children of Ha'mor, She'chem's father, for an hundred pieces of money.

20 And he erected there an altar, and called it El-e-lo'he-Is'ra-el.　Els.f. Elohimp.f.

CHAPTER 34

AND Di'nah the daughter of Le'ah, which she bare to Ja'cob, went out to see the daughters of the land.

2 And when Shechem the son of Ha'mor the Hi'vite, prince of the country, saw her, he took her, and lay with her, and <u>defiled</u> her.　violated

3 And his <u>soul</u> <u>cleave</u> to Di'nah the daughter of Ja'cob, and he loved the <u>damsel</u>, and spoke kindly to the <u>damsel</u>.　heart - was drawn - young girl

4 And Shechem spoke to his father Ha'mor, saying, Get me this <u>damsel</u> to wife.

5 And Ja'cob heard that he had <u>defiled</u> Di'nah his daughter: now his sons were with his cattle in the field: and Ja'cob held his peace until they were come.

6 And Ha'mor the father of Shechem went out to Ja'cob to <u>commune</u> with him.　speak

7 And the sons of Ja'cob came out of the field when they heard *it*: and the men were <u>grieved</u>, and they were very angry, because he had <u>wrought</u> <u>folly</u> in Is'ra-el in lying with Ja'cob's daughter; which thing ought not to be done.　offended - done a disgraceful thing

8 And Ha'mor <u>communed</u> with them, saying, The <u>soul</u> of my son Shechem longs for your daughter: I pray you give her him to wife.　spoke - heart

9 And make you marriages with us, *and* give your daughters to us, and take our daughters to you.

10 And you shall dwell with us: and the land shall be before you; dwell and trade you therein, and get you possessions therein.

11 And Shechem said to her father and to her brethren, Let me find <u>grace</u> in your eyes, and what you shall say to me I will give.　favor

12 Ask me never so much dowry and gift, and I will give according as you shall say to me: but give me the <u>damsel</u> to wife.　young girl

13 And the sons of Ja'cob answered Shechem and Ha'mor his father deceitfully, and said, because he had defiled Di'nah their sister:

14 And they said to them, We cannot do this thing, to give our sister to one that is uncircumcised; for that *were* a reproach to us:

15 But in this will we consent to you: If you will be as we *be*, that every male of you be circumcised;

16 Then will we give our daughters to you, and we will take your daughters to us, and we will dwell with you, and we will become one people.

17 But if you will not hearken to us, to be circumcised; then will we take our daughter, and we will be gone.

18 And their words pleased Ha'mor, and Shechem Ha'mor's son.

19 And the young man deferred not to do the thing, because he had delight in Ja'cob's daughter: and he *was* more honorable than all the house of his father.

20 And Ha'mor and Shechem his son came to the gate of their city, and <u>communed</u> with the men of their city, saying, _{spoke}

21 These men *are* peaceable with us; therefore let them dwell in the land, and trade therein; for the land, behold, *it is* large enough for them; let us take their daughters to us for wives, and let us give them our daughters.

22 Only <u>herein</u> will the men consent to us for to dwell with us, to be one people, if every male among us be circumcised, as they *are* circumcised. _{on this condition}

23 *Shall* not their cattle and their substance and every beast of theirs *be* ours? only let us consent to them, and they will dwell with us.

24 And to Ha'mor and to Shechem his son hearkened all that went out of the gate of his city; and every male was circumcised, all that went out of the gate of his city.

25 And it came to pass on the third day, when they were sore, that two of the sons of Ja'cob, Sim'e-on and Le'vi, Di'nah's brethren, took each man his sword, and came upon the city boldly, and slew all the males.

26 And they slew Ha'mor and She'chem his son with the edge of the sword, and took Di'nah out of She'chem's house, and went out.

27 The sons of Ja'cob came upon the slain, and <u>spoiled</u> the city, because they had defiled their sister. _{looted}

28 They took their sheep, and their oxen, and their asses, and that which *was* in the city, and that which *was* in the field,

29 And all their wealth, and all their little ones, and their wives took they captive, and <u>spoiled</u> even all that *was* in the house.

30 And Ja'cob said to Sim'e-on and Le'vi, You have troubled me to make me <u>to stink</u> among the inhabitants of the land, among the Ca'naan-ites and the Per'iz-zites: and I *being* few in number, they shall gather themselves together against me, and slay me; and I shall be destroyed, I and my house. _{odious}

31 And they said, Should he deal with our sister as with an harlot?

CHAPTER 35

AND God said to Ja'cob, Arise, go up to Beth'-el, and dwell there: and make there an altar to <u>God</u>, that appeared to you when you fled from the face of E'sau your brother. _{El s.f.}

2 Then Ja'cob said to his household, and to all that *were* with him, Put away the strange gods that *are* among you, and be clean, and change your garments:

3 And let us arise, and go up to Beth'-el; and I will make there an altar to <u>God</u>, who answered me in the day of my distress, and was with me in the way which I went.

4 And they gave to Ja'cob all the <u>strange</u> gods which *were* in their hand, and *all their* earrings which *were* in

their ears; and Ja'cob hid them under the oak which *was* by Shechem.   foreign

5 And they journeyed: and the terror of God was upon the cities that *were* round about them, and they did not pursue after the sons of Ja'cob.   Elohim p.f.

6 So Ja'cob came to Luz, which *is* in the land of Ca'naan, that *is*, Beth'-el, he and all the people that *were* with him.

7 And he built there an altar, and called the place El'bethel: because there God appeared to him, when he fled from the face of his brother.

The God of Bethel

8 But Deb'o-rah Re-bek'ah's nurse died, and she was buried beneath Beth'-el under an oak: and the name of it was called Al'lon-bach'uth.

i.e. Oak of weeping

9 And God appeared to Ja'cob again, when he came out of Pa'dan-a'ram, and blessed him.

10 And God said to him, Your name *is* Ja'cob: your name shall not be called any more Ja'cob, but Is'ra-el shall be your name: and He called his name Is'ra-el.

11 And God said to him, I *am* God Almighty: be fruitful and multiply; a nation and a company of nations shall be of you, and kings shall come out of your loins;   Elohim p.f. - El s.f. Shaddai - forth from you

12 And the land which I gave A'braham and I'saac, to you I will give it, and to your seed after you will I give the land.   descendants

13 And God went up from him in the place where He talked with him.   Elohim p.f.

14 And Ja'cob set up a pillar in the place where he talked with Him, *even* a pillar of stone: and he poured a drink offering thereon, and he poured oil thereon.

15 And Ja'cob called the name of the place where God spoke with him, Beth'-el.   Elohim p.f.

16 And they journeyed from Beth'-el; and there was but a little way to come to Eph'rath: and Ra'chel travailed, and she had hard labor.

17 And it came to pass, when she was in hard labor, that the midwife said to her, Fear not; you shall have this son also.

18 And it came to pass, as her soul was in departing, (for she died) that she called his name Ben-o'ni: but his father called him Ben'ja-min.

i.e. The son of the right hand

19 And Ra'chel died, and was buried in the way to Eph'rath, which *is* Beth'le-hem.

20 And Ja'cob set a pillar upon her grave: that *is* the pillar of Ra'chel's grave to this day.

21 And Is'ra-el journeyed, and spread his tent beyond the tower of E'dar.

22 And it came to pass, when Is'ra-el dwelt in that land, that Reu'ben went and lay with Bil'hah his father's concubine: and Is'ra-el heard *it*. Now the sons of Ja'cob were twelve:

23 The sons of Le'ah; Reu'ben, Ja'cob's firstborn, and Sim'e-on, and Le'vi, and Ju'dah, and Is'sa-char, and Zeb'u-lun:

24 The sons of Ra'chel; Jo'seph, and Ben'ja-min:

25 And the sons of Bil'hah, Ra'chel's handmaid; Dan, and Naph'ta-li:

26 And the sons of Zil'pah, Le'ah's handmaid; Gad, and Ash'er: these *are* the sons of Ja'cob, which were born to him in Pa'dan-a'ram.

27 And Ja'cob came to I'saac his father to Mam're, to the city of Ar'bah, which *is* He'bron, where A'bra-ham and I'saac sojourned.

28 And the days of I'saac were an hundred and fourscore years. 180

29 And I'saac gave up the ghost, and died, and was gathered to his people, *being* old and full of days: and his sons E'sau and Ja'cob buried him. breathed his last

CHAPTER 36

NOW these *are* the generations of E'sau, who *is* E'dom.

2 E'sau took his wives of the daughters of Ca'naan; A'dah the daughter of E'lon the Hit'tite, and A-ho-lib'a-mah the daughter of A'nah the daughter of Zib'e-on the Hi'vite;

3 And Bash'e-math Ish'ma-el's daughter, sister of Nc-ba'joth.

4 And A'dah barc to E'sau El'i-phaz; and Bash'e-math bare Reu'el;

5 And A-ho-lib'a-mah bare Je'ush, and Ja-a'lam, and Ko'rah: these *are* the sons of E'sau, which were born to him in the land of Ca'naan.

6 And E'sau took his wives, and his sons, and his daughters, and all the persons of his house, and his cattle, and all his beasts, and all his substance, which he had got in the land of Ca'naan; and went into the country from the face of his brother Ja'cob.

7 For their riches were more than that they might dwell together; and the land wherein they were strangers could not bear them because of their cattle. sustain

8 Thus dwelled E'sau in mount Se'ir: E'sau *is* E'dom.

9 And these *are* the generations of E'sau the father of the E'dom-ites in mount Se'ir:

10 These *are* the names of E'sau's sons; El'i-phaz the son of A'dah the wife of E'sau, Reu'el the son of Bash'e-math the wife of E'sau.

11 And the sons of El'i-phaz were Te'man, O'mar, Ze'pho, and Ga'tam, and Ke'naz.

12 And Tim'na was concubine to El'i-phaz E'sau's son; and she bare to El'i-phaz Am'a-lek: these *were* the sons of A'dah E'sau's wife.

13 And these *are* the sons of Reu'el; Na'hath, and Ze'rah, Sham'mah, and Miz'zah: these were the sons of Bash'e-math E'sau's wife.

14 And these were the sons of A-ho-lib'a-mah, the daughter of A'nah the daughter of Zib'e-on, E'sau's wife: and she bare to E'sau Je'ush, and Ja-a'lam, and Ko'rah.

15 These *were* chiefs of the sons of E'sau: the sons of El'i-phaz the first-born *son* of E'sau; chief Te'man, chief O'mar, chief Ze'pho, chief Ke'naz,

16 Chief Ko'rah, chief Ga'tam, *and* chief Am'a-lek: these *are* the chiefs *that came* of El'i-phaz in the land of E'dom; these *were* the sons of A'dah.

17 And these *are* the sons of Reu'el E'sau's son; chief Na'hath, chief Ze'rah, chief Sham'mah, chief Miz'zah:

these *are* the chiefs *that came* of Reu'el in the land of E'dom; these *are* the sons of Bash'e-math E'sau's wife.

18 And these *are* the sons of A-ho-lib'a-mah E'sau's wife; chief Je'ush, chief Ja-a'lam, chief Ko'rah: these *were* the chief *that came* of A-ho-lib'a-mah the daughter of A'nah, E'sau's wife.

19 These *are* the sons of E'sau, who *is* E'dom, and these *are* their chief.

20 These *are* the sons of Se'ir the Ho'rite, who inhabited the land; Lo'tan, and Sho'bal, and Zib'e-on, and A'nah,

21 And Di'shon, and E'zer, and Di'shan: these *are* the chiefs of the Ho'rites, the children of Se'ir in the land of E'dom.

22 And the children of Lo'tan were Ho'ri and He'mam; and Lo'tan's sister *was* Tim'na.

23 And the children of Sho'bal *were* these; Al'van, and Man'a-hath, and E'bal, She'pho, and O'nam.

24 And these *are* the children of Zib'e-on; both A'jah, and A'nah: this *was that* A'nah that found the mules in the wilderness, as he fed the asses of Zib'e-on his father. _{hot springs}

25 And the children of A'nah *were* these; Di'shon, and A-ho-lib'a-mah the daughter of A'nah.

26 And these *are* the children of Di'shon; Hemdan, and Esh'ban, and Ith'ran, and Che'ran.

27 The children of E'zer *are* these; Bil'han, and Za'a-van, and A'kan.

28 The children of Di'shan *are* these; Uz, and A'ran.

29 These *are* the chiefs *that came* of the Ho'rites; chief Lo'tan, chief Sho'bal, chief Zib'e-on, chief A'nah,

30 Chief Di'shon, chief E'zer, chief Di'shan: these *are* the chiefs *that came* of Ho'ri, among their chief in the land of Se'ir.

31 And these *are* the kings that reigned in the land of E'dom, before there reigned any king over the children of Is'ra-el.

32 And Be'la the son of Be'or reigned in E'dom: and the name of his city *was* Din'ha-bah.

33 And Be'la died, and Jo'bab the son of Ze'rah of Boz'rah reigned in his stead.

34 And Jo'bab died, and Hu'sham of the land of Tem'a-ni reigned in his stead.

35 And Hu'sham died, and Ha'dad the son of Be'dad, who smote Mid'i-an in the field of Mo'ab, reigned in his stead: and the name of his city *was* A'vith.

36 And Ha'dad died, and Sam'lah of Mas're-kah reigned in his stead.

37 And Sam'lah died, and Saul of Re-ho'both *by* the river reigned in his stead.

38 And Saul died, and Ba'al-ha'nan the son of Ach'bor reigned in his stead.

39 And Ba'al-ha'nan the son of Ach'bor died, and Ha'dar reigned in his stead: and the name of his city *was* Pa'u; and his wife's name *was* Me-het'a-bel, the daughter of Ma'tred, the daughter of Mez'a-hab.

40 And these *are* the names of the chiefs *that came* of E'sau, according to their families, after their places, by their

names; chief Tim'nah, chief Al'vah, chief Je'theth,

41 Chief A-ho-lib'a-mah, chief E'lah, chief Pi'non,

42 Chief Ke'naz, chief Te'man, chief Mib'zar,

43 Chief Mag'di-el, chief I'ram: these *be* the chiefs of E'dom, according to their habitations in the land of their possession: he *is* E'sau the father of the E'dom-ites.

CHAPTER 37

A ND Ja'cob dwelt in the land wherein his father was a <u>stranger</u>, in the land of Ca'naan.   alien

2 These *are* the generations of Ja'cob. Jo'seph, *being* seventeen years old, was feeding the flock with his brethren; and the lad *was* with the sons of Bil'hah, and with the sons of Zil'pah, his father's wives: and Jo'seph brought to his father their <u>evil</u> report.   a bad

3 Now Is'ra-el loved Jo'seph more than all his children, because he *was* the son of his old age: and he made him a coat of *many* colors.

4 And when his brethren saw that their father loved him more than all his brethren, they <u>hated</u> him, and could not speak peaceably to him.   despised

5 And Jo'seph dreamed a dream, and he told *it* his brethren: and they <u>hated</u> him yet the more.

6 And he said to them, Hear, I pray you, this dream which I have dreamed:

7 For, behold, we *were* binding sheaves in the field, and, lo, my sheaf arose, and also stood upright; and, be-hold, your sheaves stood round about, and <u>made obeisance</u> to my sheaf.   bowed down

8 And his brethren said to him, Shall you indeed reign over us? or shall you indeed have <u>dominion</u> over us? And they <u>hated</u> him yet the more for his dreams, and for his words.   rule - despise

9 And he dreamed yet another dream, and told it his brethren, and said, Be-hold, I have dreamed a dream more; and, behold, the sun and the moon and the eleven stars <u>made obeisance</u> to me.   bowed down

10 And he told *it* to his father, and to his brethren: and his father re-buked him, and said to him, What *is* this dream that you have dreamed? Shall I and your mother and your brethren indeed come to bow down ourselves to you to the earth?

11 And his brethren envied him; but his father <u>observed</u> the saying. remembered

12 And his brethren went to feed their father's flock in Shechem.

13 And Is'ra-el said to Jo'seph, Do not your brethren feed *the flock* in Shec-hem? come, and I will send you to them. And he said to him, Here *am I*.

14 And he said to him, Go, I pray you, see whether it be well with your breth-ren, and well with the flocks; and bring me word again. So he sent him out of the <u>vale</u> of He'bron, and he came to Shechem.   valley

15 And a certain man found him, and, behold, *he was* wandering in the field: and the man asked him, saying, What seek you?

16 And he said, I seek my brethren:

tell me, I pray you, where they feed *their flocks*.

17 And the man said, They are departed from here; for I heard them say, Let us go to Do'than. And Jo'seph went after his brethren, and found them in Do'than.

18 And when they saw him afar off, even before he came near to them, they conspired against him to slay him.

19 And they said one to another, Behold, this dreamer comes.

20 Come now therefore, and let us slay him, and cast him into some pit, and we will say, Some evil beast has devoured him: and we shall see what will become of his dreams.

21 And Reu'ben heard *it*, and he delivered him out of their hands; and said, Let us not kill him.

22 And Reu'ben said to them, Shed no blood, *but* cast him into this pit that *is* in the wilderness, and lay no hand upon him; that he might <u>rid</u> him out of their hands, to deliver him to his father again. _{rescue}

23 And it came to pass, when Jo'seph was come to his brethren, that they stripped Jo'seph out of his coat, *his* coat of *many* colors that *was* on him;

24 And they took him, and cast him into a pit: and the pit *was* empty, *there was* no water in it.

25 And they sat down to eat <u>bread</u>: and they lifted up their eyes and looked, and, behold, a company of Ish'me-el-ites came from Gil'e-ad with their camels bearing spicery and balm and myrrh, going to carry *it* down to E'gypt. _{a meal}

26 And Ju'dah said to his brethren, What profit *is it* if we slay our brother, and conceal his blood?

27 Come, and let us sell him to the Ish'me-el-ites, and let not our hand be upon him; for he *is* our brother *and* our flesh. And his brethren <u>were content</u>. _{agreed}

28 Then there passed by Mid'i-an-ites merchantmen; and they drew and lifted up Jo'seph out of the pit, and sold Jo'seph to the Ish'me-el-ites for twenty *pieces* of silver: and they brought Jo'seph into E'gypt.

29 And Reu'ben returned to the pit; and, behold, Jo'seph *was* not in the pit; and he <u>rent</u> his clothes. _{tore}

30 And he returned to his brethren, and said, The <u>child</u> *is* not; and I, where shall I go? _{boy}

31 And they took Jo'seph's coat, and killed a kid of the goats, and dipped the coat in the blood;

32 And they sent the coat of *many* colors, and they brought *it* to their father; and said, This have we found: know now whether it *be* your son's coat or <u>no</u>. _{not}

33 And he <u>knew</u> it, and said, *It is* my son's coat; an evil beast has devoured him; Jo'seph is without doubt <u>rent</u> in pieces. _{examined - torn}

34 And Ja'cob <u>rent</u> his clothes, and put sackcloth upon his loins, and mourned for his son many days. _{tore}

35 And all his sons and all his daughters rose up to comfort him; but he refused to be comforted; and he said, For I will go down into the grave to my

son mourning. Thus his father wept for him.

36 And the Mid'i-an-ites sold him into E'gypt to Pot'i-phar, an officer of Pha'raoh's, *and* captain of the guard.

CHAPTER 38

AND it came to pass at that time, that Ju'dah went down from his brethren, and turned in to a certain A-dul'lam-ite, whose name *was* Hi'rah.

2 And Ju'dah saw there a daughter of a certain Ca'naan-ite, whose name *was* Shu'ah; and he took her, and went in to her.

3 And she conceived, and bare a son; and he called his name Er.

4 And she conceived again, and bare a son; and she called his name O'nan.

5 And she yet again conceived, and bare a son; and called his name She'lah: and he was at Che'zib, when she bare him.

6 And Ju'dah took a wife for Er his firstborn, whose name *was* Ta'mar.

7 And Er, Ju'dah's firstborn, was <u>wicked</u> in the sight of the Lord; and the Lord <u>slew him</u>.   evil - took his life

8 And Ju'dah said to O'nan, Go in to your brother's wife, and marry her, and raise up <u>seed</u> to your brother.   offspring

9 And O'nan knew that the seed should not be his; and it came to pass, when he went in to his brother's wife, that he spilled *it* on the ground, less that he should give <u>seed</u> to his brother.

10 And the thing which he did displeased the Lord: wherefore He slew him also.

11 Then said Ju'dah to Ta'mar his daughter in law, Remain a widow at your father's house, till She'lah my son be grown: for he said, Less perhaps he die also, as his brethren *did*. And Ta'mar went and dwelt in her father's house.

12 And in process of time the daughter of Shu'ah Ju'dah's wife died; and was comforted, and went up to his sheepshearers to Tim'nath, he and his friend Hi'rah the A-dul'lam-ite.

13 And it was told Ta'mar, saying, Behold your father in law goes up to Tim'nath to shear his sheep.

14 And she put her widow's garments off from her, and covered her with a veil, and wrapped herself, and sat in an open placc, which *is* by the way to Tim'nath; for she saw that She'lah was grown, and she was not given to him to wife.

15 When Ju'dah saw her, he thought her *to be* an harlot; because she had covcred her face.

16 And he turned to her by the way, and said, <u>Go to</u>, I pray you, let me come in to you; (for he knew not that she *was* his daughter in law.) And she said, What will you give me, that you may come in to me?   Come now

17 And he said, I will send *you* a kid from the flock. And she said, Will you give *me* a pledge, till you send *it*?

18 And he said, What pledge shall I give you? And she said, Your <u>signet</u>, and your bracelets, and your staff that *is* in your hand. And he gave *it* her, and

came in to her, and she conceived by him.

19 And she arose, and went away, and laid by her veil from her, and put on the garments of her widowhood.

20 And Ju'dah sent the kid by the hand of his friend the A-dul'lam-ite, to receive *his* pledge from the woman's hand: but he found her not.

21 Then he asked the men of that place, saying, Where *is* the harlot, that *was* openly by the way side? And they said, There was no harlot in this *place*.

22 And he returned to Ju'dah, and said, I cannot find her; and also the men of the place said, *that* there was no harlot in this *place*.

23 And Ju'dah said, Let her take *it* to her, less we be shamed: behold, I sent this kid, and you have not found her.

24 And it came to pass about three months after, that it was told Ju'dah, saying, Ta'mar your daughter in law has played the harlot; and also, behold, she *is* with child by whoredom. And Ju'dah said, Bring her forth, and let her be burned.

25 When she *was* brought forth, she sent to her father in law, saying, By the man, whose these *are, am* I with child: and she said, Discern, I pray you, whose *are* these, the signet, and bracelets, and staff. seal-ring

26 And Ju'dah acknowledged *them*, and said, She has been more righteous than I; because that I gave her not to She'lah my son. And he knew her again no more.

27 And it came to pass in the time of her travail, that, behold, twins *were* in her womb.

28 And it came to pass, when she travailed, that *the one* put out *his* hand: and the midwife took and bound upon his hand a scarlet thread, saying, This came out first.

29 And it came to pass, as he drew back his hand, that, behold, his brother came out: and she said, How have you broken forth? *this* breach *be* upon you: therefore his name was called Pharez.

30 And afterward came out his brother, that had the scarlet thread upon his hand: and his name was called Za'rah.

CHAPTER 39

AND Jo'seph was brought down to E'gypt; and Pot'i-phar, an officer of Pha'raoh, captain of the guard, an E-gyp'tian, bought him of the hands of the Ish'me-el-ites, which had brought him down there.

2 And the LORD was with Jo'seph, and he was a prosperous man; and he was in the house of his master the E-gyp'tian. Elˢ·ᶠ - successful

3 And his master saw that the LORD *was* with him, and that the LORD made all that he did to prosper in his hand. succeed

4 And Jo'seph found grace in his sight, and he served him: and he made him overseer over his house, and all *that* he had he put into his hand. favor

5 And it came to pass from the time *that* he had made him overseer in his house, and over all that he had, that the LORD blessed the E-gyp'tian's house for

Jo'seph's sake; and the blessing of the LORD was upon all that he had in the house, and in the field.   Elʲᵗ

6 And he left all that he had in Jo'seph's hand; and he knew not anything he had, save the bread which he did eat. And Jo'seph was *a* goodly *person*, and well favored.

7 And it came to pass after these things, that his master's wife cast her eyes upon Jo'seph; and she said, Lie with me.

8 But he refused, and said to his master's wife, Behold, my master knew not what *is* with me in the house, and he has committed all that he has to my hand;

9 *There is* none greater in this house than I; neither has he kept back any thing from me but you, because you *are* his wife: how then can I do this great wickedness, and sin against God?   Elohimᵖᶠ

10 And it came to pass, as she spoke to Jo'seph day by day, that he hearkened not to her, to lie by her, *or* to be with her.

11 And it came to pass about this time, that *Joseph* went into the house to do his business; and *there was* none of the men of the house there inside.   work

12 And she caught him by his garment, saying, Lie with me: and he left his garment in her hand, and fled, and got him out.

13 And it came to pass, when she saw that he had left his garment in her hand, and was fled forth,

14 That she called to the men of her house, and spoke to them, saying,

See, he has brought in an He'brew to us to mock us; he came in to me to lie with me, and I cried with a loud voice:

15 And it came to pass, when he heard that I lifted up my voice and cried, that he left his garment with me, and fled, and got him out.   raised

16 And she laid up his garment by her, until his lord came home.

17 And she spoke to him according to these words, saying, The He'brew servant, which you have brought to us, came in to me to mock me:

18 And it came to pass, as I lifted up my voice and cried, that he left his garment with me, and fled out.

19 And it came to pass, when his master heard the words of his wife, which she spoke to him, saying, After this manner did your servant to me; that his anger was kindled.

20 And Jo'seph's master took him, and put him into the prison, a place where the king's prisoners *were* bound: and he was there in the prison.

21 But the LORD was with Jo'seph, and showed him mercy, and gave him favor in the sight of the keeper of the prison.   Elʲᵗ

22 And the keeper of the prison committed to Jo'seph's hand all the prisoners that *were* in the prison; and whatsoever they did there, he was the doer *of it*.   responsible for

23 The keeper of the prison looked not to any thing *that was* under his hand; because the LORD was with him, and *that* which he did, the LORD made *it* to prosper.

CHAPTER 40

AND it came to pass after these things, *that* the butler of the king of E'gypt and *his* baker had offended their <u>lord</u> the king of E'gypt.   master

2 And Pha'raoh was angry against two *of* his officers, against the chief of the butlers, and against the chief of the bakers.

3 And he put them in <u>ward</u> in the house of the captain of the guard, into the prison, the place where Jo'seph *was* <u>bound</u>.   confinement - imprisoned

4 And the captain of the guard charged Jo'seph with them, and he served them: and they continued a season in <u>ward</u>.

5 And they dreamed a dream both of them, each man his dream in one night, each man according to the interpretation of his dream, the butler and the baker of the king of E'gypt, which *were* bound in the prison.

6 And Jo'seph came in to them in the morning, and looked upon them, and, behold, they *were* <u>sad</u>.   dejected

7 And he asked Pha'raoh's officers that *were* with him in the <u>ward</u> of his <u>lord's</u> house, saying, Wherefore look you *so* sadly to day?   confinement - master's

8 And they said to him, We have dreamed a dream, and *there is* no interpreter of it. And Jo'seph said to them, *Do* not interpretations *belong* to God? tell me *them*, I pray you.

9 And the chief butler told his dream to Jo'seph, and said to him, In my dream, behold, a vine *was* before me;

10 And in the vine *were* three branches: and it *was* as though it budded, *and* her blossoms shot forth; and the clusters thereof brought forth ripe grapes:

11 And Pha'raoh's cup *was* in my hand: and I took the grapes, and pressed them into Pha'raoh's cup, and I gave the cup into Pha'raoh's hand.

12 And Jo'seph said to him, This *is* the <u>interpretation</u> of it: The three branches *are* three days: meaning

13 Yet within three days shall Pha'raoh lift up your head, and restore you to your <u>place</u>: and you shall deliver Pha'raoh's cup into his hand, after the former manner when you were his butler.   office

14 But <u>think</u> on me when it shall be well with you, and show kindness, I pray you, to me, and make mention of me to Pha'raoh, and bring me out of this house: remember

15 For indeed I was stolen away out of the land of the Hebrews: and here also have I done nothing that they should put me into the dungeon.

16 When the chief baker saw that the interpretation was good, he said to Jo'seph, I also *was* in my dream, and, behold, I *had* three white baskets on my head:

17 And in the uppermost basket *there was* of all manner of <u>bakemeats</u> for Pha'raoh; and the birds did eat them out of the basket upon my head.   baked goods

18 And Jo'seph answered and said, This *is* the interpretation thereof: The three baskets *are* three days:

19 Yet within three days shall Pha'raoh lift up your head from off you, and shall hang you on a tree; and the birds shall eat your flesh from off you.

20 And it came to pass the third day, *which was* Pha'raoh's birthday, that he made a feast to all his servants: and he lifted up the head of the chief butler and of the chief baker among his servants.

21 And he restored the chief butler to his butlership again; and he gave the cup into Pha'raoh's hand:

22 But he hanged the chief baker: as Jo'seph had interpreted to them.

23 Yet did not the chief butler remember Jo'seph, but forgot him.

CHAPTER 41

AND it came to pass at the end of two full years, that Pha'raoh dreamed: and, behold, he stood by the river. _{Nile}

2 And, behold, there came up out of the river seven well favored kine and fat fleshed; and they fed in a meadow. _{cows}

3 And, behold, seven other kine came up after them out of the river, ill favored and lean fleshed; and stood by the *other* kine upon the brink of the river. _{ugly}

4 And the ill favored and lean fleshed kine did eat up the seven well favored and fat kine. So Pha'raoh awoke.

5 And he slept and dreamed the second time: and, behold, seven ears of corn came up upon one stalk, rank and good. _{grain - plump}

6 And, behold, seven thin ears and blasted with the east wind sprung up after them.

7 And the seven thin ears devoured the seven rank and full ears. And Pha'raoh awoke, and, behold, *it was* a dream. _{plump}

8 And it came to pass in the morning that his spirit was troubled; and he sent and called for all the magicians of E'gypt, and all the wise men thereof: and Pha'raoh told them his dream; but *there was* none that could interpret them to Pha'raoh.

9 Then spoke the chief butler to Pha'raoh, saying, I do remember my faults this day:

10 Pha'raoh was angry with his servants, and put me in ward in the captain of the guard's house, *both* me and the chief baker: _{confinement}

11 And we dreamed a dream in one night, I and he; we dreamed each man according to the interpretation of his dream.

12 And *there was* there with us a young man, an He'brew, servant to the captain of the guard; and we told him, and he interpreted to us our dreams; to each man according to his dream he did interpret.

13 And it came to pass, as he interpreted to us, so it was; me he restored to my office, and him he hanged.

14 Then Pha'raoh sent and called Jo'seph, and they brought him hastily out of the dungeon: and he shaved *himself*, and changed his raiment, and came in to Pha'raoh. _{clothes}

15 And Pha'raoh said to Jo'seph, I have dreamed a dream, and *there is*

none that can interpret it: and I have heard say of you, *that* you can understand a dream to interpret it.

16 And Jo'seph answered Pha'raoh, saying, *It is* not in me: <u>God</u> shall give Pha'raoh an answer of peace.   Elohim^{p.f.}

17 And Pha'raoh said to Jo'seph, In my dream, behold, I stood upon the bank of the river:

18 And, behold, there came up out of the river seven <u>kine</u>, fat fleshed and well favored; and they fed in a meadow: cows

19 And, behold, seven other <u>kine</u> came up after them, poor and very <u>ill favored</u> and lean fleshed, such as I never saw in all the land of E'gypt for <u>badness</u>:   ugly - ugliness

20 And the lean and the <u>ill favored kine</u> did eat up the first seven fat <u>kine</u>:   cows

21 And when they had eaten them up, it could not be known that they had eaten them; but they *were* still <u>ill favored</u>, as at the beginning. So I awoke.

22 And I saw in my dream, and, behold, seven ears came up in one stalk, full and good:

23 And, behold, seven ears, withered, thin, *and* <u>blasted</u> with the east wind, sprung up after them: scorched

24 And the thin ears devoured the seven good ears: and I *told* this to the magicians; but *there was* none that could declare *it* to me.

25 And Jo'seph said to Pha'raoh, The dream of Pha'raoh *is* one: <u>God</u> has showed Pha'raoh what He *is* about to do.   Elohim^{p.f.}

26 The seven good <u>kine</u> *are* seven years; and the seven good ears *are* seven years: the dream *is* one.   cows

27 And the seven thin and <u>ill favored kine</u> that came up after them *are* seven years; and the seven empty ears <u>blasted</u> with the east wind shall be seven years of famine   ugly - scorched

28 This *is* the thing which I have spoken to Pha'raoh: What God *is* about to do He showed to Pha'raoh.

29 Behold, there come seven years of great plenty throughout all the land of E'gypt:

30 And there shall arise after them seven years of famine; and all the plenty shall be forgotten in the land of E'gypt; and the famine shall consume the land;

31 And the plenty shall not be known in the land by reason of that famine following; for it *shall be* very grievous.

32 And for that the dream was <u>doubled</u> to Pha'raoh twice; *it is* because the thing *is* <u>established</u> by <u>God</u>, and <u>God</u> will shortly bring it to pass.   given - determined - Elohim^{p.f.}

33 Now therefore let Pha'raoh look <u>out</u> a man <u>discreet</u> and wise, and set him over the land of E'gypt.   for - discerning

34 Let Pha'raoh do *this*, and let him appoint <u>officers</u> over the land, and take up the fifth part of the land of E'gypt in the seven plenteous years.   commissioners

35 And let them gather all the food of those good years that come, and lay up corn under the hand of Pha'raoh, and let them keep food in the cities.

36 And that food shall be for store to

the land against the seven years of famine, which shall be in the land of E'gypt; that the land perish not through the famine.

37 And the thing was good in the eyes of Pha'raoh, and in the eyes of all his servants.

38 And Pha'raoh said to his servants, Can we find *such a one* as this *is*, a man in whom the Spirit of God *is*?

39 And Pha'raoh said to Jo'seph, Forasmuch as <u>God</u> has showed you all this, *there is* none so discreet and wise as you *are*:   Elohim^p.f.

40 You shall be <u>over</u> my house, and according to your <u>word</u> shall all my people be ruled: only in the throne will I be greater than you.   in charge of - command

41 And Pha'raoh said to Jo'seph, See, I have set you over all the land of E'gypt.   ACTS 7:10

42 And Pha'raoh took off his ring from his hand, and put it upon Jo'seph's hand, and arrayed him in <u>vestures</u> of fine linen, and put a gold chain about his neck;   garments

43 And he made him to ride in the second chariot which he had; and they cried before him, Bow the knee: and he made him *ruler* over all the land of E'gypt.

44 And Pha'raoh said to Jo'seph, I *am* Pha'raoh, and without <u>you</u> shall no man lift up his hand or foot in all the land of E'gypt.   your permission

45 And Pha'raoh called Jo'seph's name Zaph'nath-pa-a-ne'ah; and he gave him to wife As'e-nath the daughter of Po-tiphe-rah priest of On. And Jo'seph went out over *all* the land of E'gypt.

46 And Jo'seph *was* thirty years old when he <u>stood before</u> Pha'raoh king of E'gypt. And Jo'seph went out from the presence of Pha'raoh, and went throughout all the land of E'gypt.   entered the service of

47 And in the seven plenteous years the earth brought forth <u>by handfuls</u>.   abundantly

48 And he gathered up all the food of the seven years, which were in the land of E'gypt, and laid up the food in the cities: the food of the field, which *was* round about every city, laid he up in the same.

49 And Jo'seph gathered <u>corn</u> as the sand of the sea, very much, until he left numbering; for *it was* without number.

50 And to Jo'seph were born two sons before the years of famine came, which As'e-nath the daughter of Po-tiphe-rah priest of On bare to him.

51 And Jo'seph called the name of the firstborn Ma-nas'seh: For <u>God</u>, *said he*, has made me forget all my toil, and all my father's house.   Elohim^p.f.

52 And the name of the second called He E'phra-im: For <u>God</u> has caused me to be fruitful in the land of my affliction.

53 And the seven years of plenteousness, that was in the land of E'gypt, were ended.

54 And the seven years of <u>dearth</u> began to come, according as Jo'seph had said: and the <u>dearth</u> was in all lands; but in all the land of E'gypt there was bread.   famine

55 And when all the land of E'gypt

was famished, the people cried to Pha'raoh for bread: and Pha'raoh said to all the E-gyptians, Go to Jo'seph; what he says to you, do.

56 And the famine was over all the face of the earth: and Jo'seph opened all the storehouses, and sold to the E-gyptians; and the famine <u>waxed sore</u> in the land of E'gypt.   was severe

57 And all countries came into E'gypt to Jo'seph for to buy <u>corn</u>; because that the famine was *so sore* in all lands.   grain - severe

CHAPTER 42

NOW when Ja'cob saw that there was <u>corn</u> in E'gypt, Ja'cob said to his sons, Why do you look one upon another?

2 And he said, Behold, I have heard that there is <u>corn</u> in E'gypt: get you down there, and buy for us from that place; that we may live, and not die.

3 And Jo'seph's ten brethren went down to buy <u>corn</u> in E'gypt.   grain

4 But Ben'ja-min, Jo'seph's brother, Ja'cob sent not with his brethren; for he said, Less perhaps mischief befall him.

5 And the sons of Is'ra-el came to buy *corn* among those that came: for the famine was in the land of Ca'naan.

6 And Jo'seph *was* the governor over the land, *and* he *it was* that sold to all the people of the land: and Jo'seph's brethren came, and bowed down themselves before him *with* their faces to the earth.

7 And Jo'seph saw his brethren, and he knew them, but made himself strange to them, and spoke <u>roughly</u> to them; and he said to them, Where come you? And they said, From the land of Ca'naan to buy food.   harshly

8 And Jo'seph knew his brethren, but they knew not him.

9 And Jo'seph remembered the dreams which he dreamed of them, and said to them, You *are* spies; to see the <u>nakedness</u> of the land you are come.   unprotected parts

10 And they said to him, Nay, my lord, but to buy food are your servants come.

11 We *are* all one man's sons; we *are* true *men*, your servants are no spies.

12 And he said to them, Nay, but to see the <u>nakedness</u> of the land you are come.

13 And they said, Your servants *are* twelve brethren, the sons of one man in the land of Ca'naan; and, behold, the youngest *is* this day with our father, and one *is* not.

14 And Jo'seph said to them, That *is it* that I spoke to you, saying, You *are* spies:

15 Hereby you shall be proved: By the life of Pha'raoh you shall not go forth from here, except your youngest brother come here.

16 Send one of you, and let him bring your brother, and you shall <u>be kept</u> in prison, that your words may be proved, whether *there be any* truth in you: or else by the life of Pha'raoh surely you *are* spies.   remain

17 And he put them all together into <u>ward</u> three days. confinement

18 And Jo'seph said to them the third day, This do, and live; *for* I <u>fear God</u>: revere - Elohim^p.f.

19 If *you be* true *men*, let one of your brethren be bound in the house of your prison: go you, carry <u>corn</u> for the famine of your houses: grain

20 But bring your youngest brother to me; so shall your words be verified, and you shall not die. And they did so.

21 And they said one to another, We *are* <u>verily</u> guilty concerning our brother, in that we saw the anguish of his soul, when he besought us, and we would not hear; therefore is this distress come upon us. truly

22 And Reu'ben answered them, saying, Spoke I not to you, saying, Do not sin against the <u>child</u>; and you would not hear? therefore, behold, also his blood is required. boy

23 And they knew not that Jo'seph understood *them*; for he spoke to them by an interpreter.

24 And he turned himself about from them, and wept; and returned to them again, and <u>communed</u> with them, and took from them Sim'e-on, and bound him before their eyes. spoke

25 Then Jo'seph commanded to fill their sacks with <u>corn</u>, and to restore every man's money into his sack, and to give them provision for the way: and thus did he to them. grain

26 And they <u>laded</u> their asses with the <u>corn</u>, and departed from there. loaded - grain

27 And as one of them opened his sack to give his ass <u>provender</u> in the inn, he <u>espied</u> his money; for, behold, it *was* in his sack's mouth. fodder - saw

28 And he said to his brethren, My money is restored; and, <u>lo</u>, *it is* even in my sack: and their heart failed *them*, and they were afraid, saying one to another, What *is* this *that* God has done to us? behold

29 And they came to Ja'cob their father to the land of Ca'naan, and told him all that befell to them; saying,

30 The man, *who* is the <u>lord</u> of the land, spoke <u>roughly</u> to us, and took us for spies of the country. head man - harshly

31 And we said to him, We *are* true *men*; we are no spies:

32 We *be* twelve brethren, sons of our father; one *is* not, and the youngest *is* this day with our father in the land of Ca'naan.

33 And the man, the <u>lord</u> of the country, said to us, Hereby shall I know that you *are* true *men*; leave one of your brethren *here* with me, and take *food for* the famine of your households, and be gone:

34 And bring your youngest brother to me: then shall I know that you *are* no spies, but *that* you *are* true *men*: *so* will I deliver you your brother, and you shall <u>traffic</u> in the land. trade

35 And it came to pass as they emptied their sacks, that, behold, every man's bundle of money *was* in his sack: and when *both* they and their father saw

the bundles of money, they were afraid.

36 And Ja'cob their father said to them, me have you bereaved *of my children*: Jo'seph *is* not, and Sim'e-on *is* not, and you will take Ben'ja-min *away*: all these things are against me.

37 And Reu'ben spoke to his father, saying, Slay my two sons, if I bring him not to you: deliver him into my hand, and I will bring him to you again.

38 And he said, My son shall not go down with you; for his brother is dead, and he is left alone: if mischief befall him by the way in the which you go, then shall you bring down my gray hairs with sorrow to the grave.   harm should

CHAPTER 43

AND the famine *was* sore in the land.   severe

2 And it came to pass, when they had eaten up the corn which they had brought out of E'gypt, their father said to them, Go again, buy us a little food.   grain

3 And Ju'dah spoke to him, saying, The man did solemnly protest to us, saying, You shall not see my face, except your brother *be* with you.

4 If you will send our brother with us, we will go down and buy you food:

5 But if you will not send *him*, we will not go down: for the man said to us, You shall not see my face, except your brother *be* with you.

6 And Is'ra-el said, Wherefore dealt you *so* ill with me, *as* to tell the man whether you had yet a brother?

7 And they said, The man asked us straitly of our state, and of our kindred, saying, *Is* your father yet alive? have you *another* brother? and we told him according to the tenor of these words: could we certainly know that he would say, Bring your brother down?   particularly - general idea

8 And Ju'dah said to Is'ra-el his father, Send the lad with me, and we will arise and go; that we may live, and not die, both we, and you, *and* also our little ones.

9 I will be surety for him; of my hand shall you require him: if I bring him not to you, and set him before you, then let me bear the blame for ever: guarantee

10 For except we had lingered, surely now we had returned this second time.

11 And their father Is'ra-el said to them, If *it must be* so now, do this; take of the best fruits in the land in your vessels, and carry down the man a present, a little balm, and a little honey, spices, and myrrh, nuts, and almonds:

12 And take double money in your hand; and the money that was brought again in the mouth of your sacks, carry *it* again in your hand; perhaps it *was* an oversight:

13 Take also your brother, and arise, go again to the man:

14 And God Almighty give you mercy before the man, that he may send away your other brother, and Ben'ja-min. If I be bereaved *of my children*, I am bereaved.   El s.t. Shaddai

15 And the men took that present, and they took double money in their

hand, and Ben'ja-min; and rose up, and went down to E'gypt, and stood before Jo'seph.

16 And when Jo'seph saw Ben'ja-min with them, he said to the ruler of his house, Bring *these* men home, and slay, and make ready; for *these* men shall dine with me at noon. kill an animal

17 And the man did as Jo'seph bade; and the man brought the men into Jo'seph's house. said

18 And the men were afraid, because they were brought into Jo'seph's house; and they said, Because of the money that was returned in our sacks at the first time are we brought in; that he may seek occasion against us, and fall upon us, and take us for bondmen, and our asses. slaves

19 And they came near to the steward of Jo'seph's house, and they communed with him at the door of the house, spoke

20 And said, O sir, we came indeed down at the first time to buy food:

21 And it came to pass, when we came to the inn, that we opened our sacks, and, behold, *every* man's money *was* in the mouth of his sack, our money in full weight: and we have brought it again in our hand.

22 And other money have we brought down in our hands to buy food: we cannot tell who put our money in our sacks.

23 And he said, Peace *be* to you, fear not: your God, and the God of your father, has given you treasure in your sacks: I had your money. And he brought Sim'e-on out to them. Elohim p.f.

24 And the man brought the men into Jo'seph's house, and gave *them* water, and they washed their feet; and he gave their asses provender. fodder

25 And they made ready the present against Jo'seph came at noon: for they heard that they should eat bread there.

26 And when Jo'seph came home, they brought him the present which *was* in their hand into the house, and bowed themselves to him to the earth. humbled

27 And he asked them of *their* welfare, and said, *Is* your father well, the old man of whom you spoke? *Is* he yet alive?

28 And they answered, Your servant our father *is* in good health, he *is* yet alive. And they bowed down their heads, and made obeisance. paid him honor

29 And he lifted up his eyes, and saw his brother Ben'ja-min, his mother's son, and said, *Is* this your younger brother, of whom you spoke to me? And he said, God be gracious to you, my son. Elohim p.f.

30 And Jo'seph made haste; for his bowels did yearn upon his brother: and he sought *where* to weep; and he entered into *his* chamber, and wept there. i.e. heart

31 And he washed his face, and went out, and refrained himself, and said, Set on bread.

32 And they set on for him by himself, and for them by themselves, and for the E-gyptians, which did eat with him, by themselves: because the E-gyptians might not eat bread with the He'brews; for that *is* an abomination to the E-gyptians. served - loathsome

33 And they sat before him, the first-

born according to his birthright, and the youngest according to his youth: and the men marvelled one at another. 34 And he took *and sent* messes to them from before him: but Ben'jamin's mess was five times so much as any of theirs. And they drank, and were merry with him.   portions

CHAPTER 44

AND he commanded the steward of his house, saying, Fill the men's sacks *with* food, as much as they can carry, and put every man's money in his sack's mouth.

2 And put my cup, the silver cup, in the sack's mouth of the youngest, and his corn money. And he did according to the word that Jo'seph had spoken.

3 As soon as the morning was light, the men were sent away, they and their asses.

4 *And* when they were gone out of the city, *and* not *yet* far off, Jo'seph said to his steward, Up, follow after the men; and when you do overtake them, say to them, Wherefore have you rewarded evil for good?   repaid

5 *Is* not this *it* in which my lord drinks, and whereby indeed he divines? you have done evil in so doing.   tells the future

6 And he overtook them, and he spoke to them these same words.

7 And they said to him, Wherefore says my lord these words? God forbid that your servants should do according to this thing:

8 Behold, the money, which we found in our sacks' mouths, we brought again to you out of the land of Ca'naan:

how then should we steal out of your lord's house silver or gold?

9 With whomsoever of your servants it be found, both let him die, and we also will be my lord's bondmen.   slaves

10 And he said, Now also *let* it *be* according to your words: he with whom it is found shall be my servant; and you shall be blameless.

11 Then they speedily took down every man his sack to the ground, and opened every man his sack.

12 And he searched, *and* began at the eldest, and left at the youngest: and the cup was found in Ben'jamin's sack.   ending with

13 Then they rent their clothes, and laded every man his ass, and returned to the city.   tore

14 And Ju'dah and his brethren came to Jo'seph's house; for he *was* yet there: and they fell before him on the ground.

15 And Jo'seph said to them, What deed *is* this that you have done? know you not that such a man as I can certainly divine?   foretell

16 And Ju'dah said, What shall we say to my lord? what shall we speak? or how shall we clear ourselves? God has found out the iniquity of your servants: behold, we *are* my lord's servants, both we, and *he* also with whom the cup is found.   Elohim^{p.f.}

17 And he said, God forbid that I should do so: *but* the man in whose hand the cup is found, he shall be my servant; and as for you, get you up in peace to your father.

18 Then Ju'dah came near to

him, and said, Oh my lord, let your servant, I pray you, speak a word in my lord's ears, and let not your anger burn against your servant: for you *are* even as Pha'raoh.

19 My lord asked his servants, saying, Have you a father, or a brother?

20 And we said to my lord, We have a father, an old man, and a child of his old age, a little one; and his brother is dead, and he alone is left of his mother, and his father loves him.

21 And you said to your servants, Bring him down to me, that I may set mine eyes upon him.

22 And we said to my lord, The lad cannot leave his father: for *if* he should leave his father, *his father* would die.

23 And you said to your servants, Except your youngest brother come down with you, you shall see my face no more.

24 And it came to pass when we came up to your servant my father, we told him the words of my lord.

25 And our father said, Go again, *and* buy us a little food.

26 And we said, We cannot go down: if our youngest brother be with us, then will we go down: for we may not see the man's face, except our youngest brother *be* with us.

27 And your servant my father said to us, You know that my wife <u>bare</u> me two *sons*:   bore

28 And the one went out from me, and I said, Surely he is torn in pieces; and I saw him not since:

29 And if you take this also from me, and mischief befall him, you shall bring down my gray hairs with sorrow to the grave.

30 Now therefore when I come to your servant my father, and the lad *be* not with us; seeing that his life is bound up in the lad's life;

31 It shall come to pass, when he sees that the lad *is* not *with us*, that he will die: and your servants shall bring down the gray hairs of your servant our father with sorrow to the grave.

32 For your servant became <u>surety</u> for the lad to my father, saying, If I bring him not to you, then I shall bear the blame to my father for ever.   guarantee

33 Now therefore, I pray you, let your servant <u>abide</u> instead of the lad a <u>bondman</u> to my lord; and let the lad go up with his brethren.   remain - slave

34 For how shall I go up to my father, and the lad *be* not with me? less perhaps I see the <u>evil</u> that shall <u>come on</u> my father.   misery - overtake

CHAPTER 45

THEN Jo'seph could not <u>refrain</u> himself before all them that stood by him; and he cried, Cause every man to go out from me. And there stood no man with him, while Jo'seph made himself known to his brethren.   control

2 And he wept aloud: and the E-gyptians and the house of Pha'raoh heard.

3 And Jo'seph said to his brethren, I *am* Jo'seph; does my father yet live? And his brethren could not answer him; for they were troubled at his presence.   ACTS 7:13

4 And Jo'seph said to his brethren,

Come near to me, I pray you. And they came near. And he said, I *am* Jo'seph your brother, whom you sold into E'gypt.

5 Now therefore be not grieved, nor angry with yourselves, that you sold me here: for God did send me before you to preserve life.   distressed - Elohim[p.f.]

6 For these two years *has* the famine *been* in the land: and yet *there* are five years, in the which *there shall* neither *be* earing nor harvest.   ploughing

7 And God sent me before you to preserve you a posterity in the earth, and to save your lives by a great deliverance.

8 So now *it was* not you *that* sent me here, but God: and He has made me a father to Pha'raoh, and lord of all his house, and a ruler throughout all the land of E'gypt.   Elohim[p.f.]

9 Haste you, and go up to my father, and say to him, Thus says your son Jo'seph, God has made me lord of all E'gypt: come down to me, tarry not: delay

10 And you shall dwell in the land of Go'shen, and you shall be near to me, you, and your children, and your children's children, and your flocks, and your herds, and all that you have:

11 And there will I nourish you ; for yet *there are* five years of famine; less you, and your household, and all that you have, come to poverty.

12 And, behold, your eyes see, and the eyes of my brother Ben'ja-min, that *it is* my mouth that speaks to you.

13 And you shall tell my father of all my glory in E'gypt, and of all that you have seen; and you shall haste and bring down my father here.

14 And he fell upon his brother Ben'ja-min's neck, and wept; and Ben'ja-min wept upon his neck.

15 Moreover he kissed all his brethren, and wept upon them: and after that his brethren talked with him.

16 And the fame thereof was heard in Pha'raoh's house, saying, Jo'seph's brethren are come: and it pleased Pha'raoh well, and his servants.   news

17 And Pha'raoh said to Jo'seph, Say to your brethren, This do you; lade your beasts, and go, get you to the land of Ca'naan;   load

18 And take your father and your households, and come to me: and I will give you the good of the land of E'gypt, and you shall eat the fat of the land.   best

19 Now you are commanded, this do you; take you wagons out of the land of E'gypt for your little ones, and for your wives, and bring your father, and come.

20 Also regard not your stuff; for the good of all the land of E'gypt *is* yours.

21 And the children of Is'ra-el did so: and Jo'seph gave them wagons, according to the commandment of Pha'raoh, and gave them provision for the way.

22 To all of them he gave each man changes of raiment; but to Ben'ja-min he gave three hundred *pieces* of silver, and five changes of raiment.   garments

23 And to his father he sent after this *manner*; ten asses laden with the good things of E'gypt, and ten she asses laden with corn and bread and meat for his father by the way.   loaded - grain

24 So he sent his brethren away, and they departed: and he said to them, See that you <u>fall not out by the way.</u>

quarrel not on

25 And they went up out of E'gypt, and came into the land of Ca'naan to Ja'cob their father,

26 And told him, saying, Jo'seph *is* yet alive, and he *is* governor over all the land of E'gypt. And Ja'cob's heart fainted, for he believed them not.

27 And they told him all the words of Jo'seph, which he had said to them: and when he saw the wagons which Jo'seph had sent to carry him, the <u>spirit</u> of Ja'cob their father revived:

hope

28 And Is'ra-el said, *It is* enough; Jo'seph my son *is* yet alive: I will go and see him before I die.

CHAPTER 46

AND Is'ra-el took his journey with all that he had, and came to Be'-er-she'ba, and offered sacrifices to the <u>God</u> of his father I'saac.

Elohim^p.f.

2 And God spoke to Is'ra-el in the visions of the night, and said, Ja'cob, Ja'cob. And he said, Here *am* I.

3 And He said, I *am* <u>God</u>, the <u>God</u> of your father: fear not to go down into E'gypt; for I will there make of you a great nation:

Elohim^p.f. - El^s.f.

4 I will go down with you into E'gypt; and I will also surely bring you up *again*: and Jo'seph shall <u>put his hand upon your</u> eyes.

close your

5 And Ja'cob rose up from Be'er-she'ba: and the sons of Is'ra-el carried Ja'cob their father, and their little ones, and their wives, in the wagons which Pha'raoh had sent to carry him.

6 And they took their cattle, and their goods, which they had gotten in the land of Ca'naan, and came into E'gypt, Ja'cob, and all his <u>seed</u> with him:

descendants

7 His sons, and his sons' sons with him, his daughters, and his sons' daughters, and all his <u>seed</u> brought he with him into E'gypt.

8 And these *are* the names of the children of Is'ra-el, which came into E'gypt, Ja'cob and his sons: Reu'ben, Ja'cob's firstborn.

9 And the sons of Reu'ben; Ha'noch, and Phal'lu, and Hez'ron, and Car'mi.

10 And the sons of Sim'e-on; Jemu'el, and Ja'min, and O'had, and Ja'chin, and Zo'har, and Sha'ul the son of a Ca'naan-it-ish woman.

11 And the sons of Le'vi; Ger'shon, Ko'hath, and Me-ra'ri.

12 And the sons of Ju'dah; Er, and O'nan, and She'lah, and Pha'rez, and Za'rah: but Er and O'nan died in the land of Ca'naan. And the sons of Pha'rez were Hez'ron and Ha'mul.

13 And the sons of Is'sa-char; To'la, and Phu'vah, and Job, and Shim'ron.

14 And the sons of Zeb'u-lun; Se'red, and E'lon, and Jah'le-el.

15 These *be* the sons of Le'ah, which she bare to Ja'cob in Pa'dan-a'ram, with his daughter Di'nah: all the souls of his sons and his daughters *were* thirty and three.

16 And the sons of Gad; Ziph'i-on, and Hag'gi, Shu'ni, and Ez'bon, E'ri, and Ar'o-di, and A-re'li.

17 And the sons of Ash'er; Jim'nah, and Ishu-ah, and Is'u-i, and Be-ri'ah, and Se'rah their sister: and the sons of Be-ri'ah; He'ber, and Mal'chiel.

18 These *are* the sons of Zil'pah, whom La'ban gave to Le'ah his daughter, and these she bare to Ja'cob, *even* sixteen souls.

19 The sons of Ra'chel Ja'cob's wife; Jo'seph, and Ben'ja-min.

20 And to Jo'seph in the land of E'gypt were born Ma-nas'seh and E'phra-im, which As'e-nath the daughter of Po-tiphe-rah priest of On bare to him.

21 And the sons of Ben'ja-min *were* Be'lah, and Be'cher, and Ash'bel, Ge'ra, and Na'a-man, E'hi, and Rosh, Mup'pim, and Hup'pim, and Ard.

22 These *are* the sons of Ra'chel, which were born to Ja'cob: all the souls *were* fourteen.

23 And the sons of Dan; Hu'shim.

24 And the sons of Naph'ta-li; Jah'ze-el, and Gu'ni, and Je'zer, and Shil'lem.

25 These *are* the sons of Bil'hah, which La'ban gave to Ra'chel his daughter, and she bare these to Ja'cob: all the souls *were* seven.

26 All the souls that came with Ja'cob into E'gypt, <u>which came out of his loins</u>, besides Ja'cob's sons' wives, all the souls *were* <u>threescore and six</u>;   *his direct descendants - 66*

27 And the sons of Jo'seph, which were born him in E'gypt, *were* two souls: all the souls of the house of Ja'cob, which came into E'gypt, *were* <u>threescore and ten</u>.   70

28 And he sent Ju'dah before him to Jo'seph, to direct his face to Go'shen; and they came into the land of Go'shen.

29 And Jo'seph <u>made ready</u> his chariot, and went up to meet Is'ra-el his father, to Go'shen, and presented himself to him; and he fell on his neck, and wept on his neck a good while.   *prepared*

30 And Is'ra-el said to Jo'seph, Now let me die, since I have seen your face, because you *are* yet alive.

31 And Jo'seph said to his brethren, and to his father's house, I will go up, and show Pha'raoh, and say to him, My brethren, and my father's house, which *were* in the land of Ca'naan, are come to me;

32 And the men *are* shepherds, for their trade has been <u>to feed cattle</u>; and they have brought their flocks, and their herds, and all that they have.   *as keepers of livestock*

33 And it shall come to pass, when Pha'raoh shall call you, and shall say, What *is* your occupation?

34 That you shall say, Your servants' trade has been about cattle from our youth even until now, both we, *and* also our fathers: that you may dwell in the land of Go'shen; for every shepherd *is* <u>an abomination</u> to the E-gyptians.   *loathsome*

M13

77

CHAPTER 47

THEN Jo'seph came and told Pha'raoh, and said, My father and my brethren, and their flocks, and their herds, and all that they have, are come out of the land of Ca'naan; and, behold, they *are* in the land of Go'shen.

2 And he took some of his brethren, *even* five men, and presented them to Pha'raoh.

3 And Pha'raoh said to his brethren, What *is* your occupation? And they said to Pha'raoh, Your servants *are* shepherds, both we, *and* also our fathers.

4 They said moreover to Pha'raoh, For to sojourn in the land are we come; for your servants have no pasture for their flocks; for the famine *is* sore in the land of Ca'naan: now therefore, we pray you, let your servants dwell in the land of Go'shen. _{live awhile - severe}

5 And Pha'raoh spoke to Jo'seph, saying, Your father and your brethren are come to you:

6 The land of E'gypt *is* before you; in the best of the land make your father and brethren to dwell; in the land of Go'shen let them dwell: and if you know *any* men of activity among them, then make them rulers over my cattle. _{capable men}

7 And Jo'seph brought in Ja'cob his father, and set him before Pha'raoh: and Ja'cob blessed Pha'raoh.

8 And Pha'raoh said to Ja'cob, How old *are* you?

9 And Ja'cob said to Pha'raoh, The days of the years of my pilgrimage *are* an hundred and thirty years: few and evil have the days of the years of my life been, and have not attained to the days of the years of the life of my fathers in the days of their pilgrimage. _{life}

10 And Ja'cob blessed Pha'raoh, and went out from before Pha'raoh.

11 And Jo'seph placed his father and his brethren, and gave them a possession in the land of E'gypt, in the best of the land, in the land of Ra-me'ses, as Pha'raoh had commanded.

12 And Jo'seph nourished his father, and his brethren, and all his father's household, with bread, according to *their* families.

13 And *there was* no bread in all the land; for the famine *was* very sore, so that the land of E'gypt and *all* the land of Ca'naan fainted by reason of the famine. _{severe}

14 And Jo'seph gathered up all the money that was found in the land of E'gypt, and in the land of Ca'naan, for the corn which they bought: and Jo'seph brought the money into Pha'raoh's house. _{grain}

15 And when money failed in the land of E'gypt, and in the land of Ca'naan, all the E-gyptians came to Jo'seph, and said, Give us bread: for why should we die in your presence? for the money fails.

16 And Jo'seph said, Give your cattle; and I will give you for your cattle, if money fail.

17 And they brought their cattle to Jo'seph: and Jo'seph gave them bread *in exchange* for horses, and for the

flocks, and for the cattle of the herds, and for the asses: and he <u>fed</u> them with <u>bread</u> for all their cattle for that year.   food - provided

18 When that year was ended, they came to him the second year, and said to him, We will not hide *it* from my lord, how that our money is spent; my lord also has our herds of cattle; there is not anything left in the sight of my lord, but our bodies, and our lands:

19 Wherefore shall we die before your eyes, both we and our land? buy us and our land for <u>bread</u>, and we and our land will be servants to Pha'raoh: and give *us* seed, that we may live, and not die, that the land be not desolate.

20 And Jo'seph bought all the land of E'gypt for Pha'raoh; for the E-gyptians sold every man his field, because the famine prevailed over them: so the land became Pha'raoh's.

21 And as for the people, he removed them to cities from *one* end of the borders of E'gypt even to the *other* end thereof.

22 Only the land of the priests bought he not; for the priests had a portion *assigned them* of Pha'raoh, and did eat their portion which Pha'raoh gave them: wherefore they sold not their lands.

23 Then Jo'seph said to the people, Behold, I have bought you this day and your land for Pha'raoh: lo, *here is* seed for you, and you shall sow the land.

24 And it shall come to pass in the increase, that you shall give the fifth *part*

to Pha'raoh, and four parts shall be your own, for seed of the field, and for your food, and for them of your households, and for food for your little ones.

25 And they said, You have saved our lives: let us find grace in the sight of my lord, and we will be Pha'raoh's servants.

26 And Jo'seph made it a law over the land of E'gypt to this day, *that* Pha'raoh should have the fifth *part*; except the land of the priests only, *which* became not Pha'raoh's.

27 And Is'ra-el dwelt in the land of E'gypt, in the country of Go'shen; and they had possessions therein, and grew, and multiplied exceedingly.

28 And Ja'cob lived in the land of E'gypt seventeen years: so the whole age of Ja'cob was an hundred forty and seven years.

29 And the time drew near that Is'ra-el must die: and he called his son Jo'seph, and said to him, If now I have found grace in your sight, put, I pray you, your hand under my thigh, and deal kindly and truly with me; bury me not, I pray you, in E'gypt:

30 But I will lie with my fathers, and you shall carry me out of E'gypt, and bury me in their buryingplace. And he said, I will do as you have said.

31 And he said, <u>Swear</u> to me. And he swear to him. And Is'ra-el bowed himself upon the bed's head.   Promise

CHAPTER 48

AND it came to pass after these things, that *one* told Jo'seph, Be-

hold, your father *is* sick: and he took with him his two sons, Ma-nas'seh and E'phra-im.

2 And *one* told Ja'cob, and said, Behold, your son Jo'seph comes to you: and Is'ra-el strengthened himself, and sat upon the bed.   rallied

3 And Ja'cob said to Jo'seph, God Almighty appeared to me at Luz in the land of Ca'naan, and blessed me,

El^{s.f.} Shaddai

4 And said to me, Behold, I will make you fruitful, and multiply you, and I will make of you a multitude of people; and will give this land to your seed after you *for* an everlasting possession.   descendants

5 And now your two sons, E'phra-im and Ma-nas'seh, which were born to you in the land of E'gypt before I came to you into E'gypt, *are* mine; as Reu'ben and Sim'e-on, they shall be mine.

6 And your issue, which you fathered after them, shall be yours, *and* shall be called after the name of their brethren in their inheritance.

7 And as for me, when I came from Pa'dan, Ra'chel died by me in the land of Ca'naan in the way, when yet *there was* but a little way to come to Eph'rath: and I buried her there in the way of Eph'rath; the same *is* Beth'-le-hem.   to my sorrow

8 And Is'ra-el beheld Jo'seph's sons, and said, Who *are* these?

9 And Jo'seph said to his father, They *are* my sons, whom God has given me in this *place*. And he said,

Bring them, I pray you, to me, and I will bless them.

10 Now the eyes of Is'ra-el were dim for age, *so that* he could not see. And he brought them near to him; and he kissed them, and embraced them.   failing

11 And Is'ra-el said to Jo'seph, I had not thought to see your face: and, lo, God has showed me also your seed.

Elohim^{p.f.} - children

12 And Jo'seph brought them out from between his knees, and he bowed himself with his face to the earth.

13 And Jo'seph took them both, E'phra-im in his right hand toward Is'ra-el's left hand, and Ma-nas'seh in his left hand toward Is'ra-el's right hand, and brought *them* near to him.

14 And Is'ra-el stretched out his right hand, and laid *it* upon E'phra-im's head, who *was* the younger, and his left hand upon Ma-nas'seh's head, guiding his hands wittingly; for Ma-nas'seh *was* the firstborn.   HEB. 11:21   crossing - intentionally

15 And he blessed Jo'seph, and said, God, before whom my fathers A'bra-ham and I'saac did walk, the God which fed me all my life long to this day,

16 The Angel which redeemed me from all evil, bless the lads; and let my name be named on them, and the name of my fathers A'bra-ham and I'saac; and let them grow into a multitude in the midst of the earth.

17 And when Jo'seph saw that his father laid his right hand upon the head of E'phra-im, it displeased him: and he held up his father's hand, to remove it

M27 from E'phra-im's head to Ma-nas'seh's head.

18 And Jo'seph said to his father, Not so, my father: for this *is* the firstborn; put your right hand upon his head.

19 And his father refused, and said, I know *it*, my son, I know *it*: he also shall become a people, and he also shall be great: but truly his younger brother shall be greater than he, and his <u>seed</u> shall become a multitude of nations.   descendants

20 And he blessed them that day, saying, In you shall Is'ra-el bless, saying, <u>God</u> make you as E'phra-im and as Ma-nas'seh: and he set E'phra-im before Ma-nas'seh.   Elohim^{p.f.}

21 And Is'ra-el said to Jo'seph, Behold, I die: but <u>God</u> shall be with you, and bring you again to the land of your fathers.

22 Moreover I have given to you one <u>por-tion</u> above your brethren, which I took out of the hand of the Am'or-ite with my sword and with my bow.   ridge of land

CHAPTER 49

M27 **A**ND Ja'cob called to his sons, and said, Gather yourselves together, that I may tell you *that* which shall befall you in the last days.

2 Gather yourselves together, and hear, you sons of Ja'cob; and hearken to Is'ra-el your father.

3 Reu'ben, you *are* my firstborn, my might, and the <u>beginning</u> of my strength, the excellency of dignity, and the excellency of power: first sign

4 Unstable as water, you shall not ex-cel; because you went up to your father's bed; then defiled you *it*: he went up to my couch.

5 Sim'e-on and Le'vi *are* brethren; <u>in-struments of cruelty *are in* their habita-tions</u>.   their swords are weapons of violence

6 O my soul, come not you into their secret; to their assembly, my honor, be not you united: for in their anger they slew a man, and in their selfwill they <u>dug down a wall</u>.   i.e., self destruction

7 Cursed *be* their anger, for *it was* fierce; and their wrath, for it was cruel: I will divide them in Ja'cob, and scatter them in Is'ra-el.

8 Ju'dah, you *are he* whom your brethren shall praise: your hand *shall be* in <u>the neck</u> of your enemies; your father's children shall bow down before you.   control over

9 Ju'dah *is* a lion's whelp: from the prey, my son, you are gone up: he stooped down, he couched as a lion, and as an old lion; who shall rouse him up?

10 The scepter shall not depart from Ju'dah, nor a lawgiver from between his feet, until Shi'loh come; and to him *shall* the <u>gathering</u> of the people *be*.   LUKE 1:33 obedience

11 Binding his foal to the vine, and his ass's colt to the choice vine; he washed his garments in wine, and his clothes in the blood of grapes:

12 His eyes *shall be* red with wine, and his teeth white with milk.

13 Zeb'u-lun shall dwell at the haven of the sea; and he *shall* be for an

haven of ships; and his border *shall be* unto Zi'don.

14 Is'sa-char *is* a strong ass couching down between two burdens:

15 And he saw that rest *was* good, and the land that *it was* pleasant; and bowed his shoulder to bear, and became a servant to tribute.

16 Dan shall judge his people, as one of the tribes of Is'ra-el.

17 Dan shall be a serpent by the way, an adder in the path, that bites the horse heels, so that his rider shall fall backward.

18 I have waited for your <u>salvation</u>, O LORD.   i.e. Heb. Jeshua

19 Gad, a troop shall overcome him: but he shall overcome at the last.

20 Out of Ash'er his bread *shall be* fat, and he shall yield royal dainties.

21 Naph'ta-li *is* a <u>hind</u> let loose: he gives <u>goodly</u> words.   doe   beautiful

22 Jo'seph *is* a fruitful bough, *even* a fruitful bough by a well; *whose* branches run over the wall:

23 The archers have <u>sorely grieved</u> him, and shot *at him*, and hated him: bitterly attacked

24 But his bow abode in strength, and the arms of his hands were made strong by the hands of the mighty *God* of Ja'cob; (from there *is* the shepherd, the <u>stone</u> of Is'ra-el:)   rock

25 *Even* by the <u>God</u> of your father, who shall help you; and by the Almighty, who shall bless you with blessings of heaven above, blessings of the deep that lies under, blessings of the breasts, and of the womb: El s.f.

26 The blessings of your father have prevailed above the blessings of my progenitors to the utmost bound of the everlasting hills: they shall be on the head of Jo'seph, and on the crown of the head of him that was separate from his brethren.

27 Ben'ja-min shall ravin *as* a wolf: in the morning he shall devour the prey, and at night he shall divide the spoil.

28 All these *are* the twelve tribes of Is'ra-el: and this *is it* that their father spoke to them, and blessed them; every one according to his blessing he blessed them.

29 And he charged them, and said to them, I am to be gathered to my people: bury me with my fathers in the cave that *is* in the field of E'phron the Hit'tite,

30 In the cave that *is* in the field of Mach-pe'lah, which *is* before Mam're, in the land of Ca'naan, which A'braham bought with the field of E'phron the Hit'tite for a possession of a buryingplace.

31 There they buried A'bra-ham and Sa'rah his wife; there they buried I'saac and Re-bek'ah his wife; and there I buried Le'ah.

32 The purchase of the field and of the cave that *is* therein *was* from the children of Heth.

33 And when Ja'cob had made an end of commanding his sons, he gathered up his feet into the bed, and <u>yielded up the ghost</u>, and was gathered to his people.   expired

CHAPTER 50

AND Jo'seph fell upon his father's face, and wept upon him, and kissed him.

2 And Jo'seph commanded his servants the physicians to embalm his father: and the physicians embalmed Is'ra-el.

3 And forty days were fulfilled for him; for so are fulfilled the days of those which are embalmed: and the E-gyptians mourned for him threescore and ten days.   wept - 70

4 And when the days of his mourning were past, Jo'seph spoke to the house of Pha'raoh, saying, If now I have found grace in your eyes, speak, I pray you, in the ears of Pha'raoh, saying,

5 My father made me swear, saying, Lo, I die: in my grave which I have dug for me in the land of Ca'naan, there shall you bury me. Now therefore let me go up, I pray you, and bury my father, and I will come again.   travel

6 And Pha'raoh said, Go up, and bury your father, according as he made you swear.

7 And Jo'seph went up to bury his father: and with him went up all the servants of Pha'raoh, the elders of his house, and all the elders of the land of E'gypt,

8 And all the house of Jo'seph, and his brethren, and his father's house: only their little ones, and their flocks, and their herds, they left in the land of Go'shen.

9 And there went up with him both chariots and horsemen: and it was a very great company.

10 And they came to the threshing floor of A'tad, which *is* beyond Jor'dan, and there they mourned with a great and very sore lamentation: and he made a mourning for his father seven days.

11 And when the inhabitants of the land, the Ca'naan-ites, saw the mourning in the floor of A'tad, they said, This *is* a grievous mourning to the E-gyptians: wherefore the name of it was called A'bel-miz'ra-im, which *is* beyond Jor'dan.   solemn ceremony

12 And his sons did to him according as he commanded them:

13 For his sons carried him into the land of Ca'naan, and buried him in the cave of the field of Mach-pe'lah, which A'bra-ham bought with the field for a possession of a buryingplace of E'phron the Hit'tite, before Mam're.

14 And Jo'seph returned into E'gypt, he, and his brethren, and all that went up with him to bury his father, after he had buried his father.

15 And when Jo'seph's brethren saw that their father was dead, they said, Jo'seph will perhaps hate us, and will certainly requite us all the evil which we did to him.   pay us back

16 And they sent a messenger to Jo'seph, saying, Your father did command before he died, saying,

17 So shall you say to Jo'seph, Forgive, I pray you now, the trespass of your brethren, and their sin; for they did to you evil: and now, we pray you, forgive the trespass of the servants of

the God of your father. And Jo'seph wept when they spoke to him.   Elohim^{p.f.}

18 And his brethren also went and fell down before his face; and they said, Behold, we *be* your servants.

19 And Jo'seph said to them, Fear not: for *am* I in the place of God? 20 But as for you, you thought evil against me; *but* God meant it to good, to bring to pass, as *it is* this day, to save much people alive.

21 Now therefore fear you not: I will nourish you, and your little ones. And he comforted them, and spoke kindly to them.   provide for

22 And Jo'seph dwelt in E'gypt, he, and his father's house: and Jo'seph lived an hundred and ten years.

23 And Jo'seph saw E'phra-im's children of the third *generation*: the children also of Ma'chir the son of Ma-nas'seh were brought up upon Jo'seph's knees.

24 And Jo'seph said to his brethren, I die: and God will surely visit you, and bring you out of this land to the land which He swear to A'bra-ham, to I'saac, and to Ja'cob.   Elohim^{p.f.}

25 And Jo'seph took an oath of the children of Is'ra-el, saying, God will surely visit you, and you shall carry up my bones from here.   come to your aid

26 So Jo'seph died, *being* an hundred and ten years old: and they embalmed him, and he was put in a coffin in E'gypt.

EXODUS

OUTLINE

OPPRESSION IN EGYPT 1.1—11.10
  Egyptian Servitude 1.1-22
  Preparation of the Deliverer 2.1—4.31
  Struggle with the Oppressor 5.1—11.10

REDEMPTION OUT OF EGYPT 12.1—14.31
  Redemption by Blood 12.1-51
    Institution of the Passover 12.1-28
    Tenth Plague—Death of the Firstborn 12.29-51
  Redemption by Power 13.1—14.31
    Consecration of the Firstborn 13.1-16
    Crossing of the Reed Sea 13.17—14.31

EDUCATION OF THE REDEEMED IN THE WILDERNESS 15.1—18.27
  Song of Triumph of the Redeemed 15.1-21
  Testing of the Redeemed 15.22—17.16
    Bitter Trial 15.22-27
    Hunger 16.1-36
    Thirst 17.1-7
    Conflict 17.8-16
  Government of the Redeemed 18.1-27

CONSECRATION OF THE REDEEMED AT SINAI 19.1—34.35
  Acceptance of the Law 19.1—31.18
    Directions to Moses 19.1-25
    The Moral Commandments 20.1-26
    The Social Ordinances 21.1—24.11
    The Religious Regulations 24.12—31.18
  Infraction of the Law 32.1-35
    The Golden Calf 32.1-14
    The Broken Tablets 32.15-35
  Restoration of the Law 33.1—34.35
    Renewed Vision 33.1-23
    The Second Tablets 34.1-35

WORSHIP OF THE REDEEMED IN TABERNACLE, PRIESTHOOD, AND RITUAL 35.1—40.38
  Gifts and Workmen for the Tabernacle 35.1-35
  Construction and Appointments of the Tabernacle 36.1—39.43
  Erection of the Tabernacle and Filling with the Divine Glory 40.1-38

SURVEY

As Genesis is the book of beginnings, Exodus is the book of redemption. The deliverance of the oppressed Israelites out of Egypt is the type of all redemption (1 Co 10.11). The rigors of bondage in Egypt (type of the world) and Pharaoh (a type of Satan) call forth the preparation of the deliverer Moses (2.1—4.31), a type of Christ. The contest with the oppressor (5.1—11.10) eventuates in the

departure (Greek *exodus,* "outgoing") of the Hebrews from Egypt. They are redeemed by the blood of the Passover lamb (12.1-28) and by the power of the Lord manifested in the passage through the Reed Sea (Heb. *Yam suf,* "Reed Sea") (13.1—14.31). The experience of redemption, celebrated by a triumphal ode of the redeemed (15.1-21), is followed by their testing in the wilderness (15.22—18.27). At Mount Sinai the redeemed nation accepts the law (19.1—31.18). Failure to rely upon grace leads to infraction and condemnation (32.1—34.35). God's grace triumphs, however, in the giving of the tabernacle, priesthood, and sacrifice, whereby the redeemed could worship and fellowship with their Redeemer (36.1—40.38).

AUTHOR

Although the Book of Exodus nowhere claims Mosaic authorship *in toto,* the entire body of Pentateuchal law, comprising principally the portion extending from Exodus 20 through the Book of Deuteronomy, in explicitly positive terms claims to be Mosaic. Moses is declared to be the writer of the Book of the Covenant (chs. 20—23), comprising the Ten Commandments and the accompanying judgments and ordinances (24.4, 7). The so-called Priest Code dealing with tabernacle ritual and priesthood contained in the rest of Exodus (except chs. 32—34) are declared to have been vouchsafed directly to Moses by the Lord (25.1, 23, 31; 26.1, and so on). The setting up of the tabernacle is represented as being "as Jehovah commanded. . ." This or similar terminology recurs many times in chapters 39 and 40. Mosaic authorship is also asserted of a prominent narrative section—Israel's victory over Amalek (17.4). In a citation from Exodus 3, Jesus calls the Pentateuch in general and Exodus in particular "the book of Moses" (Mk 12.26). Present-day conservative scholarship as well as tradition have maintained the Mosaic authorship. Critical theories offer no adequate substitute for Mosaic authenticity.

                                                                    M.F.U.

THE SECOND BOOK OF MOSES COMMONLY CALLED

EXODUS

CHAPTER 1

NOW these *are* the names of the children of Is'ra-el, which came into E'gypt; every man and his household came with Ja'cob.

2 Reu'ben, Sim'e-on, Le'vi, and Ju'dah,

3 Is'sa-char, Zeb'u-lun, and Ben'ja-min,

4 Dan, and Naph'ta-li, Gad, and Ash'er.

5 And all the souls that came out of the loins of Ja'cob were seventy souls: for Jo'seph was in E'gypt *already*.   persons

6 And Jo'seph died, and all his brethren, and all that generation.

7 And the children of Is'ra-el were fruitful, and increased abundantly, and multiplied, and waxed exceeding mighty; and the land was filled with them.   became

8 Now there arose up a new king over E'gypt, which knew not Jo'seph. ACTS 7:18

9 And he said to his people, Behold, the people of the children of Is'ra-el *are* more and mightier than we:

10 Come on, let us deal wisely with them; less they multiply, and it come to pass, that, when there falls out any war, they join also to our enemies, and fight against us, and *so* get them up out of the land.   war occurs

11 Therefore they did set over them taskmasters to afflict them with their burdens. And they built for Pha'raoh treasure cities, Pi'thom and Ra-am'ses.

12 But the more they afflicted them, the more they multiplied and grew. And they were grieved because of the children of Is'ra-el.

13 And the E-gyptians made the children of Is'ra-el to serve with rigor: harshness

14 And they made their lives bitter with hard bondage, in mortar, and in brick, and in all manner of service in the field: all their service, wherein they made them serve, *was* with rigor.

15 And the king of E'gypt spoke to the He'brew midwives, of which the name of the one *was* Shiphrah, and the name of the other Pu'ah:

16 And he said, When you do the office of a midwife to the He'brew women, and see *them* upon the stools; if it *be* a son, then you shall kill him: but if it *be* a daughter, then she shall live.   childbirth seat

17 But the midwives feared God, and did not as the king of E'gypt commanded them, but saved the men children alive.   revered - Elohim^p.f.

18 And the king of E'gypt called for the midwives, and said to them, Why have you done this thing, and have saved the men children alive?   male

19 And the midwives said to Pha'raoh, Because the He'brew women *are* not as the E-gyp'tian women; for they

are lively, and are delivered before the midwives come in to them.

20 Therefore <u>God</u> dealt well with the midwives: and the people multiplied, and <u>waxed</u> very mighty. Elohim^{p.f.} - grew

21 And it came to pass, because the midwives <u>feared</u> <u>God</u>, that He made them <u>houses</u>. revered - families

22 And Pha'raoh <u>charged</u> all his people, saying, Every son that is born you shall cast into the river, and every daughter you shall save alive. ordered

CHAPTER 2

AND there went a man of the house of Le'vi, and took *to wife* a daughter of Le'vi.

2 And the woman conceived, and bare a son: and when she saw him that he *was a* goodly *child*, she hid him three months. ACTS 7:20 HEB. 11:23

3 And when she could not longer hide him, she <u>took</u> for him an ark of bulrushes, and daubed it with <u>slime</u> and with <u>pitch</u>, and put the child therein; and she laid *it* in the <u>flags</u> by the river's brink. made - asphalt - tar -needs

4 And his sister stood afar off, to see what would be done to him.

5 And the daughter of Pha'raoh came down to wash *herself* at the river; and her maidens walked along by the river's side; and when she saw the ark among the flags, she sent her maid to bring it.

6 And when she had opened *it*, she saw the child: and, behold, the babe wept. And she had compassion on him, and said, This *is one* of the He'brews' children.

7 Then said his sister to Pha'raoh's daughter, Shall I go and call to you a nurse of the He'brew women, that she may nurse the child for you?

8 And Pha'raoh's daughter said to her, Go. And the maid went and called the child's mother.

9 And Pha'raoh's daughter said to her, Take this child away, and nurse it for me, and I will give *you* your wages. And the woman took the child, and nursed it.

10 And the child grew, and she brought him to Pha'raoh's daughter, and he became her son. And she called his name <u>Moses</u>: and she said, Because I drew him out of the water. meaning: to draw out

11 And it came to pass in those days, when Mo'ses was grown, that he went out to his brethren, and looked on their burdens: and he spied an E-gyp'tian <u>smiting</u> an He'brew, one of his brethren. fighting

12 And he looked this way and that way, and when he saw that *there was* no man, he slew the E-gyp'tian, and hid him in the sand.

13 And when he went out the second day, behold, two men of the Hebrews <u>strove</u> together: and he said to him that did the wrong, Wherefore smite you your fellow? struggled

14 And he said, Who made you a prince and a judge over us? intend you to kill me, as you killed the E-gyp'tian? And Mo'ses feared, and said, Surely this thing is known. ACTS 7:27

15 Now when Pha'raoh heard this thing, he sought to slay Mo'ses. But

Mo'ses fled from the <u>face</u> of Pha'raoh, and dwelt in the land of Mid'i-an: and he sat down by a well.   presence

16 Now the priest of Mid'i-an had seven daughters: and they came and drew *water*, and filled the troughs to water their father's flock.

17 And the shepherds came and drove them away: but Mo'ses stood up and helped them, and watered their flock.

18 And when they came to Reu'el their father, he said, How *is it that* you are come so soon to day?

19 And they said, An E-gyp'tian delivered us out of the hand of the shepherds, and also drew *water* enough for us, and watered the flock.

20 And he said to his daughters, And where *is* he? why *is* it *that* you have left the man? call him, that he may eat bread.

21 And Mo'ses was content to dwell with the man: and he gave Mo'ses Zip-po'rah his daughter.

22 And she <u>bare</u> *him* a son, and he called his name Ger'shom: for he said, I have been a stranger in a strange land.   gave birth to

23 And it came to pass in process of time, that the king of E'gypt died: and the children of Is'ra-el <u>sighed</u> by reason of the <u>bondage</u>, and they cried, and their cry came up to <u>God</u> by reason of the <u>bondage</u>.   JAMES 5:4   suffered - slavery - Elohim^{p.f.}

24 And <u>God</u> heard their groaning, and <u>God</u> remembered His <u>covenant</u> with A'bra-ham, with I'saac, and with Ja'cob.   agreement

25 And <u>God</u> looked upon the children of Is'ra-el, and <u>God</u> <u>had respect to</u> *them*.   Elohim^{p.f.} - paid attention to

CHAPTER 3

NOW Mo'ses kept the flock of Je'thro his father in law, the priest of Mid'i-an: and he led the flock to the backside of the desert, and came to the mountain of God, *even* to Ho'reb.

2 And the angel of the LORD appeared to him in a flame of fire out of the midst of a bush: and he looked, and, behold, the bush burned with fire, and the bush *was* not <u>consumed</u>.   destroyed

3 And Mo'ses said, I will now turn aside, and see this great sight, why the bush is not burned.   ACTS 7:31

4 And when the LORD saw that he turned aside to see, <u>God</u> called to him out of the midst of the bush, and said, Mo'ses, Mo'ses. And he said, Here *am* I.   Elohim^{p.f.}

5 And He said, Draw not near here: put off your shoes from off your feet, for the place whereon you stand *is* holy ground.

6 Moreover He said, I *am* the God of your father, the <u>God</u> of A'bra-ham, the <u>God</u> of I'saac, and the <u>God</u> of Ja'cob. And Mo'ses hid his face; for he was afraid to look upon <u>God</u>.   MATT. 22:32   MARK 12:26   LUKE 20:37

7 And the LORD said, I have surely seen the <u>affliction</u> of My people which *are* in E'gypt, and have heard their cry by reason of their taskmasters; for I know their <u>sorrows</u>;   suffering - troubles

8 And I am come down to deliver them out of the hand of the E-gyptians, and to bring them up out of that land to a good land and a large, to a

land flowing with milk and honey; to the place of the Ca'naan-ites, and the Hit'tites, and the Am'or-ites, and the Per'iz-zites, and the Hi'vites, and the Jeb'u-sites.

9 Now therefore, behold, the cry of the children of Is'ra-el is come to Me: and I have also seen the oppression wherewith the E-gyptians oppress them.

10 Come now therefore, and I will send you to Pha'raoh, that you may bring forth My people the children of Is'ra-el out of E'gypt.

11 And Mo'ses said to God, Who *am* I, that I should go to Pha'raoh, and that I should bring forth the children of Is'ra-el out of E'gypt?

12 And He said, Certainly I will be with you; and this *shall be* a token to you, that I have sent you: When you have brought forth the people out of E'gypt, you shall serve God upon this mountain.

sign - Elohim[p.f.]

13 And Mo'ses said to God, Behold, *when* I come to the children of Is'ra-el, and shall say to them, The God of your fathers has sent me to you; and they shall say to me, What *is* His name? what shall I say to them?

14 And God said to Mo'ses, I AM THAT I AM: and He said, Thus shall you say to the children of Is'ra-el, I AM has sent me to you.

REV. 1:8 Elohim[p.f.] - Heb. Ehyeh - Asher - Ehyeh "I cause"

15 And God said moreover to Mo'ses, Thus shall you say to the children of Is'ra-el, The LORD God of your fathers, the God of A'bra-ham, the God of I'saac, and the God of Ja'cob, has sent me to you: this *is* My name for ever, and this *is* My memorial to all generations.

ACTS 7:32 Elohim[p.f.]

16 Go, and gather the elders of Is'ra-el together, and say to them, The LORD God of your fathers, the God of A'bra-ham, of I'saac, and of Ja'cob, appeared to me, saying, I have surely visited you, and *seen* that which is done to you in E'gypt:

17 And I have said, I will bring you up out of the affliction of E'gypt to the land of the Ca'naan-ites, and the Hit'tites, and the Am'or-ites, and the Per'iz-zites, and the Hi'vites, and the Jeb'u-sites, to a land flowing with milk and honey.

suffering

18 And they shall hearken to your voice: and you shall come, you and the elders of Is'ra-el, to the king of E'gypt, and you shall say to him, The LORD God of the He'brews has met with us: and now let us go, we beseech you, three days' journey into the wilderness, that we may sacrifice to the LORD our God.

listen - implore

19 And I am sure that the king of E'gypt will not let you go, no, not by a mighty hand.

20 And I will stretch out My hand, and smite E'gypt with all My wonders which I will do in the midst thereof: and after that he will let you go.

strike

21 And I will give this people favor in the sight of the E-gyptians: and it shall come to pass, that, when you go, you shall not go empty:

JOHN 12:40

22 But every woman shall borrow of her neighbor, and of her that sojourn in her house, jewels of silver, and

jewels of gold, and <u>raiment</u>: and you shall put *them* upon your sons, and upon your daughters; and you shall <u>spoil</u> the E-gyptians.

lives - clothing - take the wealth of

CHAPTER 4

AND Mo'ses answered and said, But, behold, they will not believe me, nor hearken to my voice: for they will say, The LORD has not appeared to you.

2 And the LORD said to him, What *is* that in your hand? And he said, A rod.

3 And He said, Cast it on the ground. And he cast it on the ground, and it became a serpent; and Mo'ses fled from before it.

4 And the LORD said to Mo'ses, Put forth your hand, and take it by the tail. And he put forth his hand, and caught it, and it became a rod in his hand:

5 That they may believe that the LORD God of their fathers, the <u>God</u> of A'bra-ham, the <u>God</u> of I'saac, and the <u>God</u> of Ja'cob, has appeared to you.

Elohim^{p.f.}

6 And the LORD said furthermore to him, Put now your hand into your bosom. And he put his hand into his bosom: and when he took it out, behold, his hand *was* leprous as snow.

7 And He said, Put your hand into your bosom again. And he put his hand into his bosom again; and plucked it out of his bosom, and, behold, it was turned again as his *other* flesh.

8 And it shall come to pass, if they will not believe you, neither hearken to the voice of the first sign, that they will believe the voice of the latter sign.

9 And it shall come to pass, if they will not believe also these two signs, neither hearken to your voice, that you shall take of the water of the river, and pour *it* upon the dry *land*: and the water which you take out of the river shall become blood upon the dry *land*.

10 And Mo'ses said to the LORD, O my Lord, I *am* not eloquent, neither heretofore, nor since You have spoken to Your servant: but I *am* slow of speech, and <u>of a slow tongue</u>.   not eloquent

11 And the LORD said to him, Who has made man's mouth? or Who makes the dumb, or deaf, or the seeing, or the blind? have not I the LORD?

12 Now therefore go, and I will be with your mouth, and teach you what you shall say.

13 And he said, O my Lord, send, I pray You, by the hand *of him* whom You will send.   some other person

14 And the anger of the LORD was kindled against Mo'ses, and He said, *Is* not Aar'on the Le'vite your brother? I know that he can speak well. And also, behold, he comes forth to meet you: and when he sees you, he will be glad in his heart.

15 And you shall speak to him, and put words in his mouth: and I will be with your mouth, and with his mouth, and will teach you what you shall do.

16 And he shall be your spokesman to the people: and he shall be, *even* he shall be to you instead of a mouth, and you shall be to him <u>instead</u> of God.   as - Elohim^{p.f.}

P15A
P15B
272
140

17 And you shall take this rod in your hand, wherewith you shall do signs.

18 And Mo'ses went and returned to Je'thro his father in law, and said to him, Let me go, I pray you, and return to my brethren which *are* in E'gypt, and see whether they be yet alive. And Je'thro said to Mo'ses, Go in peace.

19 And the LORD said to Mo'ses in Mid'i-an, Go, return into E'gypt: for all the men are dead which sought your life.

20 And Mo'ses took his wife and his sons, and set them upon an ass, and he returned to the land of E'gypt: and Mo'ses took the rod of God in his hand.

21 And the LORD said to Mo'ses, When you go to return into E'gypt, see that you do all those <u>wonders</u> before Pha'raoh, which I have put in your hand: but I will harden his heart, that he shall not let the people go. miracles

P15
115

22 And you shall say to Pha'raoh, Thus says the LORD, Is'ra-el *is* My son, *even* My firstborn: MATT. 2:15

23 And I say to you, Let My son go, that he may serve Me: and if you refuse to let him go, behold, I will slay your son, *even* your firstborn.

24 And it came to pass by the way in the inn, that the LORD met him, and sought to kill him.

25 Then Zip-po'rah took a sharp stone, and cut off the foreskin of her son, and cast *it* at his feet, and said, Surely a bloody husband *are* you to me.

26 So He let him go: then she said, A bloody husband *you are*, because of the circumcision.

27 And the LORD said to Aar'on, Go into the wilderness to meet Mo'ses. And he went, and met him in the mount of <u>God</u>, and kissed him. Elohim^{p.f.}

28 And Mo'ses told Aar'on all the words of the LORD Who had sent him, and all the signs which He had commanded him.

29 And Mo'ses and Aar'on went and gathered together all the elders of the children of Is'ra-el:

30 And Aar'on spoke all the words which the LORD had spoken to Mo'ses, and did the signs in the sight of the people.

31 And the people believed: and when they heard that the LORD had visited the children of Is'ra-el, and that He had looked upon their affliction, then they bowed their heads and worshiped.

CHAPTER 5

AND afterward Mo'ses and Aar'on went in, and told Pha'raoh, Thus says the LORD God of Is'ra-el, Let My people go, that they may <u>hold</u> a feast to Me in the wilderness. celebrate

2 And Pha'raoh said, Who *is* the LORD, that I should obey His voice to let Is'ra-el go? I know not the LORD, neither will I let Is'ra-el go.

3 And they said, The <u>God</u> of the He'brews has met with us: let us go, we pray you, three days' journey into the desert, and sacrifice to the LORD our <u>God</u>; less He fall upon us with pestilence, or with the sword. Elohim^{p.f.}

4 And the king of E'gypt said to them, Wherefore do you, Mo'ses and Aar'on, <u>let</u> the people from their works? get <u>you to your burdens</u>.

<small>draw - get back to your labors</small>

5 And Pha'raoh said, Behold, the people of the land now *are* many, and you make them rest from their burdens.

6 And Pha'raoh commanded the same day the taskmasters of the people, and their officers, saying,

7 You shall no more give the people straw to make brick, as heretofore: let them go and gather straw for themselves.

8 And the <u>tale</u> of the bricks, which they did make heretofore, you shall lay upon them; you shall not diminish *any* thereof: for they *be* idle; therefore they cry, saying, Let us go *and* sacrifice to our <u>God</u>.

<small>number - Elohim^{p.f.}</small>

9 Let there more work be laid upon the men, that they may labor therein; and let them not regard <u>vain</u> words.

<small>false</small>

10 And the taskmasters of the people went out, and their officers, and they spoke to the people, saying, Thus says Pha'raoh, I will not give you straw.

11 Go you, get you straw where you can find it: yet not any of your work shall be diminished.

12 So the people were scattered abroad throughout all the land of E'gypt to gather stubble instead of straw.

13 And the taskmasters <u>hasted</u> *them*, saying, Fulfil your works, *your* daily tasks, as when there was straw.

<small>pressed</small>

14 And the officers of the children of Is'ra-el, which Pha'raoh's taskmasters had set over them, were beaten, *and* demanded, Wherefore have you not fulfilled your task in making brick both yesterday and to day, as heretofore?

15 Then the officers of the children of Is'ra-el came and cried to Pha'raoh, saying, Wherefore deal you thus with your servants?

16 There is no straw given to your servants, and they say to us, Make brick: and, behold, your servants *are* beaten; but the fault *is* in your own people.

17 But he said, You *are* idle, *you are* idle: therefore you say, Let us go *and* do sacrifice to the LORD.

18 Go therefore now, *and* work; for there shall no straw be given you, yet shall you deliver the <u>tale</u> of bricks.

<small>number</small>

19 And the officers of the children of Is'ra-el did see *that* they *were* in evil *case*, after it was said, You shall not <u>minish</u> *any* from your bricks of your daily task.

<small>reduce</small>

20 And they met Mo'ses and Aar'on, who stood in the way, as they came forth from Pha'raoh:

21 And they said to them, The LORD look upon you, and judge; because <u>you have made our savor to be abhorred</u> in the eyes of Pha'raoh, and in the eyes of his servants, to put a sword in their hand to slay us.

<small>you have made us offensive</small>

22 And Mo'ses returned to the LORD, and said, Lord, wherefore have You <u>so evil entreated</u> this people? why *is* it *that* you have sent me?

<small>brought harm to</small>

23 For since I came to Pha'raoh to speak in Your name, he has done evil to

this people; neither have You delivered Your people at all.

CHAPTER 6

THEN the LORD said to Mo'ses, Now shall you see what I will do to Pha'raoh: for with a strong hand shall he let them go, and with a strong hand shall he drive them out of his land.

ACTS 13:17

2 And God spoke to Mo'ses, and said to him, I *am* the LORD: Elohim[p.f.] - Jehovah

3 And I appeared to A'bra-ham, to I'saac, and to Ja'cob, by *the name of* God Almighty, but by My name JE-HO'VAH was I not known to them.   El[s.f.] Shadday - LORD (YAHWEH)

4 And I have also established My covenant with them, to give them the land of Ca'naan, the land of their pilgrimage, wherein they were strangers.   agreement - foreigners

5 And I have also heard the groaning of the children of Is'ra-el, whom the E-gyptians keep in bondage; and I have remembered My covenant.

6 Wherefore say to the children of Is'ra-el, I *am* the LORD, and I will bring you out from under the burdens of the E-gyptians, and I will rid you out of their bondage, and I will redeem you with a stretched out arm, and with great judgments: ACTS 13:17 displaying My power

7 And I will take you to Me for a people, and I will be to you a God: and you shall know that I *am* the LORD your God, which brings you out from under the burdens of the E-gyptians.

8 And I will bring you in to the land, concerning the which I did swear to give it to A'bra-ham, to I'saac, and to Ja'cob; and I will give it you for an heritage: I *am* the LORD.

9 And Mo'ses spoke so to the children of Is'ra-el: but they hearkened not to Mo'ses for anguish of spirit, and for cruel bondage.   impatience

10 And the LORD spoke to Mo'ses, saying,

11 Go in, speak to Pha'raoh king of E'gypt, that he let the children of Is'ra-el go out of his land.

12 And Mo'ses spoke before the LORD, saying, Behold, the children of Is'ra-el have not hearkened to me; how then shall Pha'raoh hear me, who *am* of uncircumcised lips?   a man

13 And the LORD spoke to Mo'ses and to Aar'on, and gave them a charge to the children of Is'ra-el, and to Pha'raoh king of E'gypt, to bring the children of Is'ra-el out of the land of E'gypt.   order

14 These *be* the heads of their fathers' houses: The sons of Reu'ben the firstborn of Is'ra-el; Ha'noch, and Pal'lu, Hez'ron, and Car'mi: these *be* the families of Reu'ben.

15 And the sons of Sim'e-on; Je-mu'el, and Ja'min, and O'had, and Ja'chin, and Zo'har, and Sha'ul the son of a Ca'naan-it-ish woman: these *are* the families of Sim'e-on.

16 And these *are* the names of the sons of Le'vi according to their generations; Ger'shon, and Ko'hath, and Me-ra'ri: and the years of the life of Le'vi *were* an hundred thirty and seven years.

17 The sons of Ger'shon; Lib'ni, and Shi'mi, according to their families.

18 And the sons of Ko'hath; Am'ram, and Iz'har, and He'bron, and Uz'zi-el: and the years of the life of Ko'hath *were* an hundred thirty and three years.

19 And the sons of Me-ra'ri; Ma'ha-li and Mu'shi: these *are* the families of Le'vi according to their <u>genera-tions</u>.

families

20 And Am'ram took him Joch'e-bed his father's sister to wife; and she bare him Aar'on and Mo'ses: and the years of the life of Am'ram *were* an hundred and thirty and seven years.

21 And the sons of Iz'har; Ko'rah, and Nepheg, and Zich'ri.

22 And the sons of Uz'zi-el; Mish'a-el, and El'za-phan, and Zith'ri.

23 And Aar'on took him E-lish'e-ba, daughter of Am-min'a-dab, sister of Na-ash'on, to wife; and she bare him Na'dab, and A-bi'hu, E-le-a'zar, and Ith'a-mar.

24 And the sons of Ko'rah; As'sir, and El'ka-nah, and A-bi'a-saph: these *are* the families of the Kor'hites.

25 And E-le-a'zar Aar'on's son took him *one* of the daughters of Pu'ti-el to wife; and she bare him Phin'e-has: these *are* the heads of the fathers of the Le'vites according to their families.

26 These *are* that Aar'on and Mo'ses, to whom the LORD said, Bring out the children of Is'ra-el from the land of E'gypt according to their armies.

27 These *are* they which spoke to Pha'raoh king of E'gypt, to bring out the children of Is'ra-el from E'gypt: these *are* that Mo'ses and Aar'on.

28 And it came to pass on the day *when* the LORD spoke to Mo'ses in the land of E'gypt,

29 That the LORD spoke to Mo'ses, saying, I *am* the LORD: speak you to Pha'raoh king of E'gypt all that I say to you.

30 And Mo'ses said before the LORD, Behold, I *am* of uncircumcised lips, and how shall Pha'raoh hearken to me?

CHAPTER 7

AND the LORD said to Mo'ses, See, I have made you a god to Pha'raoh: and Aar'on your brother shall be your prophet.

2 You shall speak all that I command you: and Aar'on your brother shall speak to Pha'raoh, that he send the children of Is'ra-el out of his land.

3 And I will harden Pha'raoh's heart, and multiply My signs and My wonders in the land of E'gypt.   ACTS 7:36

4 But Pha'raoh shall not hearken to you, that I may lay My hand upon E'gypt, and bring forth My armies, *and* My people the children of Is'ra-el, out of the land of E'gypt by great judgments.

5 And the E-gyptians shall know that I *am* the LORD, when I stretch forth My hand upon E'gypt, and bring out the children of Is'ra-el from among them.

6 And Mo'ses and Aar'on did as the LORD commanded them, so did they.

7 And Mo'ses *was* <u>fourscore</u> years old, and Aar'on <u>fourscore and three years</u> old, when they spoke to Pha'raoh.   83

8 And the LORD spoke to Mo'ses and to Aar'on, saying,

9 When Pha'raoh shall speak to you, saying, Show a miracle for you: then you shall say to Aar'on, Take your rod, and cast *it* before Pha'raoh, *and* it shall become a serpent.

10 And Mo'ses and Aar'on went in to Pha'raoh, and they did so as the LORD had commanded: and Aar'on cast down his rod before Pha'raoh, and before his servants, and it became a serpent.

11 Then Pha'raoh also called the wise men and the sorcerers: now the magicians of E'gypt, they also did in like manner with their enchantments.

12 For they cast down every man his rod, and they became serpents: but Aar'on's rod swallowed up their rods.

13 And He hardened Pha'raoh's heart, that he hearkened not to them; as the LORD had said.

14 And the LORD said to Mo'ses, Pha'raoh's heart *is* hardened, he refuses to let the people go.

15 Get you to Pha'raoh in the morning; lo, he goes out to the water; and you shall stand by the river's brink against he come; and the rod which was turned to a serpent shall you take in your hand. ^when

16 And you shall say to him, The LORD God of the He'brews has sent me to you, saying, Let My people go, that they may serve Me in the wilderness: and, behold, presently you would not hear. ^Jehovah Elohim^p.f.

17 Thus says the LORD, In this you shall know that I *am* the LORD: behold, I will smite with the rod that *is* in my hand upon the waters which *are* in the river, and they shall be turned to blood.

18 And the fish that *is* in the river shall die, and the river shall stink; and the E-gyptians shall loathe to drink of the water of the river. ^REV. 16:3 not desire

19 And the LORD spoke to Mo'ses, Say to Aar'on, Take your rod, and stretch out your hand upon the waters of E'gypt, upon their streams, upon their rivers, and upon their ponds, and upon all their pools of water, that they may become blood; and *that* there may be blood throughout all the land of E'gypt, both in *vessels of* wood, and in *vessels of* stone.

20 And Mo'ses and Aar'on did so, as the LORD commanded; and he lifted up the rod, and smote the waters that *were* in the river, in the sight of Pha'raoh, and in the sight of his servants; and all the waters that *were* in the river were turned to blood.

21 And the fish that *was* in the river died; and the river stank, and the E-gyptians could not drink of the water of the river; and there was blood throughout all the land of E'gypt.

22 And the magicians of E'gypt did so with their enchantments: and Pha'raoh's heart was hardened, neither did he hearken to them; as the LORD had said. ^secret arts

23 And Pha'raoh turned and went into his house, neither did he set his heart to this also. ^with no concern even for this

24 And all the E-gyptians dug round about the river for water to

drink; for they could not drink of the water of the river.   <small>i.e. either side</small>

25 And seven days were fulfilled, after that the LORD had smitten the river.

CHAPTER 8

AND the LORD spoke to Mo'ses, Go to Pha'raoh, and say to him, Thus says the LORD, Let My people go, that they may serve Me.

2 And if you refuse to let *them* go, behold, I will <u>smite</u> all your borders with frogs: <small>bring upon</small>

3 And the river shall bring forth frogs abundantly, which shall go up and come into your house, and into your bedchamber, and upon your bed, and into the house of your servants, and upon your people, and into your ovens, and into your kneading <u>troughs:</u><small>bowls</small>

4 And the frogs shall come up both on you, and upon your people, and upon all your servants.

5 And the LORD spoke to Mo'ses, Say to Aar'on, Stretch forth your hand with your rod over the streams, over the rivers, and over the ponds, and cause frogs to come up upon the land of E'gypt.

6 And Aar'on stretched out his hand over the waters of E'gypt; and the frogs came up, and covered the land of E'gypt.

7 And the magicians did so with their <u>enchantments</u>, and brought up frogs upon the land of E'gypt.   <small>secret arts</small>

8 Then Pha'raoh called for Mo'ses and Aar'on, and said, entreat the LORD, that He may take away the frogs from me, and from my people; and I will let the people go, that they may do sacrifice to the LORD.

9 And Mo'ses said to Pha'raoh, Glory over me: when shall I entreat for you, and for your servants, and for your people, to destroy the frogs from you and your houses, *that* they may remain in the river only?

10 And he said, To morrow. And he said, *Be it* according to your word: that you may know that *there is* none like to the LORD our <u>God</u>.   <small>Elohim^{p.f.}</small>

11 And the frogs shall depart from you, and from your houses, and from your servants, and from your people; they shall remain in the river only.

12 And Mo'ses and Aar'on went out from Pha'raoh: and Mo'ses cried to the LORD because of the frogs which He had brought against Pha'raoh.

13 And the LORD did according to the word of Mo'ses; and the frogs died out of the houses, out of the villages, and out of the fields.

14 And they gathered them together upon heaps: and the land stank.

15 But when Pha'raoh saw that there was <u>respite</u>, he hardened his heart, and <u>hearkened</u> not to them; as the LORD had said.   <small>relief - listened</small>

16 And the LORD said to Mo'ses, Say to Aar'on, Stretch out your rod, and smite the dust of the land, that it may become lice throughout all the land of E'gypt.

17 And they did so; for Aar'on stretched out his hand with his rod, and smote the dust of the earth, and it became <u>lice</u> <u>in</u> man, and <u>in</u> beast; all the

dust of the land became <u>lice</u> throughout all the land of E'gypt.   gnats - upon

18 And the magicians did so with their <u>enchantments</u> to bring forth <u>lice</u>, but they could not: so there were <u>lice</u> upon man, and upon beast.   secret arts

19 Then the magicians said to Pha'raoh, This *is* the finger of <u>God</u>: and Pha'raoh's heart was hardened, and he hearkened not to them; as the Lord had said.   Elohim^{p.f.}

20 And the Lord said to Mo'ses, Rise up early in the morning, and stand before Pha'raoh; lo, he comes forth to the water; and say to him, Thus says the Lord, Let My people go, that they may serve Me.

21 Else, if you will not let My people go, behold, I will send swarms *of flies* upon you, and upon your servants, and upon your people, and into your houses: and the houses of the E-gyptians shall be full of swarms *of flies*, and also the ground whereon they *are*.

22 And I will <u>sever</u> in that day the land of Go'shen, in which My people dwell, that no swarms *of flies* shall be there; to the end you may know that I *am* the Lord in the midst of the earth.   divide

23 And I will put a <u>division</u> between My people and your people: to-morrow shall this sign be.   distinction

24 And the Lord did so; and there came a grievous swarm *of flies* into the house of Pha'raoh, and *into* his servants' houses, and into all the land of E'gypt: the land was corrupted by reason of the swarm *of flies*.

25 And Pha'raoh called for Mo'ses and for Aar'on, and said, Go you, sacrifice to your <u>God</u> in the land. Elohim^{p.f.}

26 And Mo'ses said, It is not <u>meet</u> so to do; for we shall sacrifice the <u>abomination</u> of the E-gyptians to the Lord our <u>God</u>: lo, shall we sacrifice the <u>abomination</u> of the E-gyptians before their eyes, and will they not <u>stone</u> us?   fitting - detestable things - kill

27 We will go three days' journey into the wilderness, and sacrifice to the Lord our <u>God</u>, as He shall command us.

28 And Pha'raoh said, I will let you go, that you may sacrifice to the Lord your <u>God</u> in the wilderness; only you shall not go very far away: <u>entreat</u> for me.   intercede

29 And Mo'ses said, Behold, I go out from you, and I will <u>entreat</u> the Lord that the swarms *of flies* may depart from Pha'raoh, from his servants, and from his people, to-morrow: but let not Pha'raoh deal deceitfully any more in not letting the people go to sacrifice to the Lord.

30 And Mo'ses went out from Pha'raoh, and <u>entreated</u> the Lord.

31 And the Lord did according to the word of Mo'ses; and He removed the swarms *of flies* from Pha'raoh, from his servants, and from his people; there remained not one.

32 And Pha'raoh hardened his heart at this time also, neither would he let the people go.

CHAPTER 9

THEN the Lord said to Mo'ses, Go in to Pha'raoh, and tell him,

Thus says the Lord God of the He'brews, Let My people go, that they may serve Me.   Jehovah^{s.f.} Elohim^{p.f.}

2 For if you refuse to let *them* go, and will hold them still,

3 Behold, the hand of the Lord is upon your cattle which *is* in the field, upon the horses, upon the asses, upon the camels, upon the oxen, and upon the sheep: *there shall be* a very <u>grievous murrain</u>.   severe pestilence

4 And the Lord shall <u>sever</u> between the cattle of Is'ra-el and the cattle of E'gypt: and there shall nothing die of all *that is* the children's of Is'ra-el.   make a distinction

5 And the Lord appointed a set time, saying, To morrow the Lord shall do this thing in the land.

6 And the Lord did that thing on the morrow, and all the cattle of E'gypt died: but of the cattle of the children of Is'ra-el died not one.

7 And Pha'raoh sent, and, behold, there was not one of the cattle of the Is'ra-el-ites dead. And the heart of Pha'raoh was hardened, and he did not let the people go.

8 And the Lord said to Mo'ses and to Aar'on, Take to you handfuls of ashes of the furnace, and let Mo'ses sprinkle it toward the heaven in the sight of Pha'raoh.

9 And it shall become small dust in all the land of E'gypt, and shall be a boil breaking forth *with* <u>blains</u> upon man, and upon beast, throughout all the land of E'gypt.   sores

10 And they took ashes of the furnace, and stood before Pha'raoh; and Mo'ses sprinkled it up toward heaven; and it became a boil breaking forth *with* <u>blains</u> upon man, and upon beast.   sores

11 And the magicians could not stand before Mo'ses because of the boils; for the boil was upon the magicians, and upon all the E-gyptians.   REV. 16:2

12 And the Lord hardened the heart of Pha'raoh, and he hearkened not to them; as the Lord had spoken to Mo'ses.

13 And the Lord said to Mo'ses, Rise up early in the morning, and stand before Pha'raoh, and say to him, Thus says the Lord God of the Hebrews, Let My people go, that they may serve Me.   Jehovah^{s.f.} Elohim^{p.f.}

14 For I will at this time send all My plagues upon your heart, and upon your servants, and upon your people; that you may know that *there is* none like Me in all the earth.

15 For now I will stretch out My hand, that I may smite you and your people with pestilence; and you shall be cut off from the earth.

16 And in very deed for this *cause* have I raised you up, for to show in you My power; and that My name may be declared throughout all the earth.   ROM. 9:17

17 As yet exalt you yourself against My people, that you will not let them go?

18 Behold, to morrow about this time I will cause it to rain a very <u>grievous</u> hail, such as has not been in E'gypt since the foundation thereof even until now.   heavy

19 Send therefore now, *and* gather your

cattle, and all that you have in the field; *for upon* every man and beast which shall be found in the field, and shall not be brought home, the hail shall come down upon them, and they shall die.

20 He that <u>feared</u> the word of the LORD among the servants of Pha'raoh made his servants and his cattle flee into the houses: revered

21 And he that regarded not the word of the LORD left his servants and his cattle in the field.

22 And the LORD said to Mo'ses, Stretch forth your hand toward heaven, that there may be hail in all the land of E'gypt, upon man, and upon beast, and upon every herb of the field, throughout the land of E'gypt.

23 And Mo'ses stretched forth his rod toward heaven: and the LORD sent thunder and hail, and the fire ran along upon the ground; and the LORD rained hail upon the land of E'gypt. REV 16:21

24 So there was hail, and fire <u>mingled</u> with the hail, very grievous, such as there was none like it in all the land of E'gypt since it became a nation. flashing continually

25 And the hail <u>smote</u> throughout all the land of E'gypt all that *was* in the field, both man and beast; and the hail <u>smote</u> every herb of the field, and broke every tree of the field. struck

26 Only in the land of Go'shen, where the children of Is'ra-el *were*, was there no hail.

27 And Pha'raoh sent, and called for Mo'ses and Aar'on, and said to them, I have sinned this time: the LORD *is* righteous, and I and my people *are* wicked.

28 <u>Entreat</u> the LORD (for *it is* enough) that there be no *more* mighty thunderings and hail; and I will let you go, and you shall stay no longer. Intercede with

29 And Mo'ses said to him, As soon as I am gone out of the city, I will spread abroad my hands to the LORD; *and* the thunder shall cease, neither shall there be any more hail; that you may know how that the earth *is* the LORD's.

30 But as for you and your servants, I know that you will not yet <u>fear</u> the LORD God. reverence

31 And the flax and the barley was smitten: for the barley *was* in the ear, and the flax *was* <u>bolled</u>. in bud

32 But the wheat and the rye were not smitten: for they *were* not grown up.

33 And Mo'ses went out of the city from Pha'raoh, and spread abroad his hands to the LORD: and the thunders and hail ceased, and the rain was not poured upon the earth.

34 And when Pha'raoh saw that the rain and the hail and the thunders were ceased, he sinned yet more, and hardened his heart, he and his servants.

35 And the heart of Pha'raoh was hardened, neither would he let the children of Is'ra-el go; as the LORD had spoken by Mo'ses.

CHAPTER 10

AND the LORD said to Mo'ses, Go in to Pha'raoh: for I have hardened his heart, and the heart of his ser-

vants, that I might show these My signs before him:

2 And that you may tell in the ears of your son, and of your son's son, what things I have <u>wrought</u> in E'gypt, and My signs which I have done among them; that you may know how that I *am* the LORD. _{worked}

3 And Mo'ses and Aar'on came in to Pha'raoh, and said to him, Thus says the <u>LORD God</u> of the He'brews, How long will you refuse to humble yourself before Me? let My people go, that they may serve Me. _{Jehovah Elohim}p.f.

4 Else, if you refuse to let My people go, behold, to morrow will I bring the locusts into your <u>coast:</u> _{territory}

5 And they shall cover the face of the earth, that one cannot be able to see the earth: and they shall eat the residue of that which is escaped, which remains to you from the hail, and shall eat every tree which grows for you out of the field:

6 And they shall fill your houses, and the houses of all your servants, and the houses of all the E-gyptians; which neither your fathers, nor your fathers' fathers have seen, since the day that they were upon the earth to this day. And he turned himself, and went out from Pha'raoh.

7 And Pha'raoh's servants said to him, How long shall this man <u>be a snare to us</u>? let the men go, that they may serve the LORD their God: know you not yet that E'gypt is destroyed? _{bring us trouble}

8 And Mo'ses and Aar'on were brought again to Pha'raoh: and he said to them, Go, serve the LORD your <u>God</u>: *but* who *are* they that shall go? _{Elohim}p.f.

9 And Mo'ses said, We will go with our young and with our old, with our sons and with our daughters, with our flocks and with our herds will we go; for we *must hold* a feast to the LORD.

10 And he said to them, Let the LORD be so with you, as I will let you go, and your little ones: look *to it*; for evil *is* before you.

11 Not so: go now you *that are* men, and serve the LORD; for that you did desire. And they were <u>driven</u> out from Pha'raoh's presence. _{dismissed}

12 And the LORD said to Mo'ses, Stretch out your hand over the land of E'gypt for the locusts, that they may come up upon the land of E'gypt, and eat every herb of the land, *even* all that the hail has left.

13 And Mo'ses stretched forth his rod over the land of E'gypt, and the LORD brought an east wind upon the land all that day, and all *that* night; *and* when it was morning, the east wind brought the locusts.

14 And the locusts went up over all the land of E'gypt, and rested in all the <u>coasts</u> of E'gypt: very <u>grievous</u> *were they*; before them there were no such locusts as they, neither after them shall be such. _{territories - numerous}

15 For they covered the face of the whole earth, so that the land was darkened; and they did eat every <u>herb</u> of the land, and all the fruit of the trees which the hail had left: and there remained not any green thing in the trees, or in

the <u>herbs</u> of the field, through all the land of E'gypt. plant

16 Then Pha'raoh called for Mo'ses and Aar'on in haste; and he said, I have sinned against the Lord your <u>God</u>, and against you. Elohim^{p.f.}

17 Now therefore forgive, I pray you, my sin only this once, and <u>entreat</u> the Lord your <u>God</u>, that He may take away from me this death only. intercede

18 And he went out from Pha'raoh, and <u>entreated</u> the Lord.

19 And the Lord turned a mighty strong west wind, which took away the locusts, and cast them into the Red sea; there remained not one locust in all the <u>coasts</u> of E'gypt. territories

20 But the Lord hardened Pha'raoh's heart, so that he would not let the children of Is'ra-el go.

21 And the Lord said to Mo'ses, Stretch out your <u>hand</u> toward heaven, that there may be darkness over the land of E'gypt, even darkness *which* may be felt.

22 And Mo'ses stretched forth his hand toward heaven; and there was a thick darkness in all the land of E'gypt three days:

23 They saw not one another, neither rose any from his place for three days: but all the children of Is'ra-el had light in their dwellings.

24 And Pha'raoh called to Mo'ses, and said, Go you, serve the Lord; only let your flocks and your herds be <u>stayed</u>: let your little ones also go with you. detained

25 And Mo'ses said, You must give us also sacrifices and burnt offerings, that we may sacrifice to the Lord our <u>God</u>. Elohim^{p.f.}

26 Our cattle also shall go with us; there shall not an hoof be left behind; for thereof must we take to serve the Lord our <u>God</u>; and we know not with what we must serve the Lord, until we come there.

27 But the Lord hardened Pha'raoh's heart, and he would not let them go.

28 And Pha'raoh said to him, Get you from me, take heed to yourself, see my face no more; for in *that* day you see my face you shall die.

29 And Mo'ses said, You have spoken well, I will see your face again no more.

CHAPTER 11

AND the Lord said to Mo'ses, Yet will I bring one plague *more* upon Pha'raoh, and upon E'gypt; afterwards he will let you go from here: when he shall let *you* go, he shall surely thrust you out from here altogether.

2 Speak now in the ears of the people, and let every man <u>borrow</u> of his neighbor, and every woman of her neighbor, jewels of silver, and jewels of gold. ask

3 And the Lord gave the people favor in the sight of the E-gyptians. Moreover the man Mo'ses *was* very <u>great</u> in the land of E'gypt, in the sight of Pha'raoh's servants, and in the sight of the people. esteemed

4 And Mo'ses said, Thus says the Lord, About midnight will I go out into the midst of E'gypt:

5 And all the firstborn in the land of

E'gypt shall die, from the firstborn of Pha'raoh that sits upon his throne, even to the firstborn of the maidservant that *is* behind the mill; and all the firstborn of beasts.

6 And there shall be a great cry throughout all the land of E'gypt, such as there was none like it, nor shall be like it any more.

7 But against any of the children of Is'ra-el shall not a dog move his tongue, against man or beast: that you may know how that the LORD does put a difference between the E-gyptians and Is'ra-el.

8 And all these your servants shall come down to me, and bow down themselves to me, saying, Get you out, and all the people that follow you: and after that I will go out. And he went out from Pha'raoh in a great anger.

9 And the LORD said to Mo'ses, Pha'raoh shall not hearken to you; that My wonders may be multiplied in the land of E'gypt.

10 And Mo'ses and Aar'on did all these wonders before Pha'raoh: and the LORD hardened Pha'raoh's heart, so that he would not let the children of Is'ra-el go out of his land.

CHAPTER 12

AND the LORD spoke to Mo'ses and Aar'on in the land of E'gypt, saying,

2 This month *shall be* to you the beginning of months: it *shall be* the first month of the year to you.

3 Speak you to all the congrega-tion of Is'ra-el, saying, In the tenth *day* of this month they shall take to them every man a lamb, according to the house of *their* fathers, a lamb for an house:

4 And if the household be too little for the lamb, let him and his neighbor next to his house take *it* according to the number of the souls; every man according to his eating shall make your count for the lamb.   persons

5 Your lamb shall be without blemish, a male of the first year: you shall take *it* out from the sheep, or from the goats: defect

6 And you shall keep it up until the fourteenth day of the same month: and the whole assembly of the congregation of Is'ra-el shall kill it in the evening.

7 And they shall take of the blood, and strike *it* on the two side posts and on the upper door post of the houses, wherein they shall eat it.   lintel

8 And they shall eat the flesh in that night, roast with fire, and unleavened bread; *and* with bitter *herbs* they shall eat it.   i.e. without yeast (uncontaminated)

9 Eat not of it raw, nor sodden at all with water, but roast *with* fire; its head with its legs, and with the purtenance thereof.   boiled - entrails

10 And you shall let nothing of it remain until the morning; and that which remains of it until the morning you shall burn with fire.

11 And thus shall you eat it; *with* your loins girded, your shoes on your feet, and your staff in your hand; and you shall eat it in haste: it *is* the LORD's passover.

12 For I will pass through the land of E'gypt this night, and will smite all the firstborn in the land of E'gypt, both man and beast; and against all the gods of E'gypt I will execute judgment: I *am* the LORD. 13 And the blood shall be to you for a token upon the houses where you *are*: and when I see the blood, I will pass over you, and the plague shall not be upon you to destroy *you*, when I smite the land of E'gypt.　　　sign

14 And this day shall be to you for a memorial; and you shall keep it a feast to the LORD throughout your generations; you shall keep it a feast by an ordinance for ever.　　ceremony

15 Seven days shall you eat unleavened bread; even the first day you shall put away leaven out of your houses: for whosoever eats leavened bread from the first day until the seventh day, that soul shall be cut off from Is'ra-el.　i.e. without yeast (uncontaminated) - person - outlawed

16 And in the first day *there shall be* an holy convocation, and in the seventh day there shall be an holy convocation to you; no manner of work shall be done in them, save *that* which every man must eat, that only may be done of you.　　LUKE 23:56

17 And you shall observe the *feast of* unleavened bread; for in this selfsame day have I brought your armies out of the land of E'gypt: therefore shall you observe this day in your generations by an ordinance for ever.　masses of people - from generation to generation

18 In the first *month*, on the fourteenth day of the month at even, you shall eat unleavened bread, until the one and twentieth day of the month at even.　　i.e. without yeast - evening

19 Seven days shall there be no leaven found in your houses: for whosoever eats that which is leavened, even that soul shall be cut off from the congregation of Is'ra-el, whether he be a stranger, or born in the land. 1 COR. 5:8 yeast

20 You shall eat nothing leavened; in all your habitations shall you eat unleavened bread.

21 Then Mo'ses called for all the elders of Is'ra-el, and said to them, Draw out and take you a lamb according to your families, and kill the passover.　　HEB. 11:28

22 And you shall take a bunch of hyssop, and dip *it* in the blood that *is* in the basin, and strike the lintel and the two side posts with the blood that *is* in the basin; and none of you shall go out at the door of his house until the morning. upper door post

23 For the LORD will pass through to smite the E-gyptians; and when He sees the blood upon the lintel, and on the two side posts, the LORD will pass over the door, and will not allow the destroyer to come in to your houses to smite *you*.　　REV. 9:4

24 And you shall observe this thing for an ordinance to you and to your sons for ever.

25 And it shall come to pass, when you be come to the land which the LORD will give you, according as He has promised, that you shall keep this service.

26 And it shall come to pass, when

your children shall say to you, What mean you by this service?

27 That you shall say, It *is* the sacrifice of the LORD's passover, Who passed over the houses of the children of Is'ra-el in E'gypt, when He smote the E-gyptians, and delivered our houses. And the people bowed the head and worshiped.

28 And the children of Is'ra-el went away, and did as the LORD had commanded Mo'ses and Aar'on, so did they.

29 And it came to pass, that at midnight the LORD smote all the firstborn in the land of E'gypt, from the firstborn of Pha'raoh that sat on his throne to the firstborn of the captive that *was* in the dungeon; and all the firstborn of cattle.

30 And Pha'raoh rose up in the night, he, and all his servants, and all the E-gyptians; and there was a great cry in E'gypt; for *there was* not a house where *there was* not one dead.

31 And he called for Mo'ses and Aar'on by night, and said, Rise up, *and* get you forth from among my people, both you and the children of Is'ra-el; and go, serve the LORD, as you have said.

32 Also take your flocks and your herds, as you have said, and be gone; and <u>bless</u> me also.   pray for

33 And the E-gyptians were urgent upon the people, that they might send them out of the land in haste; for they said, We *be* all dead *men*.

34 And the people took their dough before it was <u>leavened</u>, their kneading troughs being bound up in their clothes upon their shoulders.   with yeast - bowls

35 And the children of Is'ra-el did according to the word of Mo'ses; and they borrowed of the E-gyptians jewels of silver, and jewels of gold, and <u>raiment</u>:   clothing

36 And the LORD gave the people favor in the sight of the E-gyptians, so that they <u>lent to them</u> *such things as they required*. And they spoiled the E-gyptians.   Heb. gave them

37 And the children of Is'ra-el journeyed from Ra-me'ses to Suc'coth, about six hundred thousand on foot *that were* men, beside children.

38 And a mixed multitude went up also with them; and flocks, and herds, *even* very much cattle.

39 And they baked <u>unleavened</u> cakes of the dough which they brought forth out of E'gypt, for it was not <u>leavened</u>; because they were thrust out of E'gypt, and could not tarry, neither had they prepared for themselves any <u>victual</u>.   i.e. without yeast - provisions

40 Now the <u>sojourning</u> of the children of Is'ra-el, who dwelt in E'gypt, *was* four hundred and thirty years.   GAL. 3:17 dwelling time

41 And it came to pass at the end of the four hundred and thirty years, even the selfsame day it came to pass, that all the hosts of the LORD went out from the land of E'gypt.

42 It *is* a night to be much observed to the LORD for bringing them out from the land of E'gypt: this *is* that night of the LORD to be observed of all

the children of Is'ra-el in their generations.

43 And the LORD said to Mo'ses and Aar'on, This *is* the ordinance of the passover: There shall no stranger eat thereof:

44 But every man's servant that is bought for money, when you have circumcised him, then shall he eat thereof.

45 A foreigner and an hired servant shall not eat thereof.

46 In one house shall it be eaten; you shall not carry forth any of the flesh abroad out of the house; neither shall you break a bone thereof.   JOHN 19:36

47 All the congregation of Is'ra-el shall <u>keep</u> it.   celebrate

48 And when a stranger shall <u>sojourn</u> with you, and will keep the passover to the LORD, let all his males be circumcised, and then let him come near and keep it; and he shall be as one that is born in the land: for no uncircumcised person shall eat thereof.   stay

49 One law shall be to him that is homeborn, and to the stranger that <u>sojourns</u> among you.

50 Thus did all the children of Is'ra-el; as the LORD commanded Mo'ses and Aar'on, so did they.

51 And it came to pass the selfsame day, *that* the LORD did bring the children of Is'ra-el out of the land of E'gypt by their <u>armies</u>.   hosts

CHAPTER 13

AND the LORD spoke to Mo'ses, saying,

2 <u>Sanctify</u> to Me all the firstborn, whatsoever opens the womb among the children of Is'ra-el, *both* of man and of beast: it *is* Mine.   dedicate

3 And Mo'ses said to the people, Remember this day, in which you came out from E'gypt, out of the house of <u>bondage</u>; for by strength of hand the LORD brought you out from this *place*: there shall no <u>leavened</u> bread be eaten.   slavery - i.e. with yeast

4 This day came you out in the month A'bib.

5 And it shall be when the LORD shall bring you into the land of the Ca'naan-ites, and the Hit'tites, and the Am'or-ites, and the Hi'vites, and the Jeb'u-sites, which he swear to your fathers to give you, a land flowing with milk and honey, that you shall keep this service in this month.

6 Seven days you shall eat <u>unleavened</u> bread, and in the seventh day *shall be* a feast to the LORD.   i.e. without yeast

7 <u>Unleavened</u> bread shall bc eaten seven days; and there shall no <u>leavened</u> bread be seen with you, neither shall there be <u>leaven</u> seen with you in all your quarters.

8 And you shall <u>show</u> your son in that day, saying, *This is done* because of that *which* the LORD did to me when I came forth out of E'gypt.   tell

9 And it shall be for a sign to you upon your hand, and for a memorial between your eyes, that the LORD's law may be in your mouth: for with a strong hand has the LORD brought you out of E'gypt.

10 You shall therefore keep this <u>ordinance</u> in its season from year to year.   rule

11 And it shall be when the LORD shall bring you into the land of the Ca'naan-ites, as He swear to you and to your fathers, and shall give it you,

12 That you shall set apart to the LORD all that opens the <u>matrix</u>, and every <u>firstling</u> that comes of a beast which you have; the males *shall be* the LORD's.   LUKE 2:23   womb - firstborn

13 And every <u>firstling</u> of an ass you shall redeem with a lamb; and if you will not redeem it, then you shall break its neck: and all the firstborn of man among your children shall you <u>redeem</u>   i.e. spare by offering a substitute

14 And it shall be when your son asks you in time to come, saying, What *is* this? that you shall say to him, By strength of hand the LORD brought us out from E'gypt, from the house of bondage:

15 And it came to pass, when Pha'raoh would hardly let us go, that the LORD slew all the firstborn in the land of E'gypt, both the firstborn of man, and the firstborn of beast: there-fore I sacrifice to the LORD all that opens the <u>matrix</u>, being males; but all the firstborn of my children I <u>redeem</u>.   womb - i.e., spare by offering a substitute

16 And it shall be for a <u>token</u> upon your hand, and for <u>frontlets</u> between your eyes: for by strength of hand the LORD brought us forth out of E'gypt.   sign - i.e. a type of forehead ornament

17 And it came to pass, when Pha'-raoh had let the people go, that God led them not *through* the way of the land of the Phi-lis'tines, although that *was* near; for God said, Less perhaps the people <u>repent</u> when they see war, and they return to E'gypt: by chance - change their minds

18 But God led the people about, *through* the way of the wilderness of the Red sea: and the children of Is'ra-el went <u>up harnessed</u> out of the land of E'gypt.   armed

19 And Mo'ses took the bones of Jo'seph with him: for he had <u>straitly</u> sworn the children of Is'ra-el, saying, God will surely <u>visit</u> you; and you shall carry up my bones away from here with you.   solemnly - take care of

20 And they took their journey from Suc'coth, and encamped in E'tham, in the edge of the wilderness.

21 And the LORD went before them by day in a pillar of a cloud, to lead them the way; and by night in a pil-lar of fire, to give them light; to go by day and night:

22 He took not away the pillar of the cloud by day, nor the pillar of fire by night, *from* before the people.

CHAPTER 14

AND the LORD spoke to Mo'ses, saying,

2 Speak to the children of Is'ra-el, that they turn and <u>encamp</u> before Pi-ha-hi'roth, between Mig'dol and the sea, over against Ba'al-ze'phon: before it shall you <u>encamp</u> by the sea.   camp

3 For Pha'raoh will say of the chil-dren of Is'ra-el, They *are* en-tangled in the land, the wilderness has shut them in.

4 And I will harden Pha'raoh's heart, that he shall follow after them; and I

will be honored upon Pha'raoh, and upon all his host; that the E-gyptians may know that I *am* the LORD. And they did so.

5 And it was told the king of E'gypt that the people fled: and the heart of Pha'raoh and of his servants was turned against the people, and they said, Why have we done this, that we have let Is'ra-el go from serving us?

6 And he <u>made ready</u> his chariot, and took his people with him: prepared

7 And he took six hundred chosen chariots, and all the chariots of E'gypt, and captains over every one of them.

8 And the LORD hardened the heart of Pha'raoh king of E'gypt, and he pursued after the children of Is'ra-el: and the children of Is'ra-el went out with an high hand.

9 But the E-gyptians pursued after them, all the horses *and* chariots of Pha'raoh, and his horsemen, and his army, and overtook them <u>encamping</u> by the sea, beside Pi-ha-hi'roth, before Ba'al-ze'phon. camping

10 And when Pha'raoh drew near, the children of Is'ra-el lifted up their eyes, and, behold, the E-gyptians marched after them; and they were <u>sore</u> afraid: and the children of Is'ra-el cried out to the LORD. very

11 And they said to Mo'ses, Because *there were* no graves in E'gypt, have you taken us away to die in the wilderness? wherefore have you dealt thus with us, to carry us forth out of E'gypt?

12 *Is* not this the word that we did tell you in E'gypt, saying, Let us alone, that we may serve the E-gyptians? For *it had been* better for us to serve the E-gyptians, than that we should die in the wilderness.

13 And Mo'ses said to the people, Fear you not, stand <u>still</u>, and see the <u>salvation</u> of the LORD, which He will show to you to day: for the E-gyptians whom you have seen to day, you shall see them again no more for ever. by - deliverance - Jeshua

14 The LORD shall fight for you, and you shall hold your peace.

15 And the LORD said to Mo'ses, Wherefore cry you to Me? speak to the children of Is'ra-el, that they go forward:

16 But lift you up your rod, and stretch out your hand over the sea, and divide it: and the children of Is'ra-el shall go on dry *ground* through the midst of the sea.

17 And I, behold, I will harden the hearts of the E-gyptians, and they shall follow them: and I will get Me honor upon Pha'raoh, and upon all his host, upon his chariots, and upon his horsemen.

18 And the E-gyptians shall know that I *am* the LORD, when I have gotten Me honor upon Pha'raoh, upon his chariots, and upon his horsemen.

19 And the <u>angel</u> of <u>God</u>, which went before the camp of Is'ra-el, removed and went behind them; and the pillar of the cloud went from before their face, and stood behind them: messenger - Elohim p-f

20 And it came between the camp of the E-gyptians and the camp of Is'ra-el; and it was a cloud and darkness *to*

them, but it gave light by night *to these*: so that the one came not near the other all the night.

21 And Mo'ses stretched out his hand over the sea; and the LORD caused the sea to go *back* by a strong east wind all that night, and made the sea dry *land*, and the waters were divided.

22 And the children of Is'ra-el went into the midst of the sea upon the dry *ground*: and the waters *were* a wall to them on their right hand, and on their left.

23 And the E-gyptians pursued, and went in after them to the midst of the sea, *even* all Pha'raoh's horses, his chariots, and his horsemen.

24 And it came to pass, that in the morning watch the LORD looked to the host of the E-gyptians through the pillar of fire and of the cloud, and troubled the host of the E-gyptians,   confused

25 And took off their chariot wheels, that they drove them heavily: so that the E-gyptians said, Let us flee from the face of Is'ra-el; for the LORD fights for them against the E-gyptians.   swerved

26 And the LORD said to Mo'ses, Stretch out your hand over the sea, that the waters may come again upon the E-gyptians, upon their chariots, and upon their horsemen.   HEB. 11:29

27 And Mo'ses stretched forth his hand over the sea, and the sea returned to its strength when the morning appeared; and the E-gyptians fled against it; and the LORD overthrew the E-gyptians in the midst of the sea.   flowed back - defeated

28 And the waters returned, and cov-ered the chariots, and the horsemen, *and* all the host of Pha'raoh that came into the sea after them; there remained not so much as one of them.

29 But the children of Is'ra-el walked upon dry *land* in the midst of the sea; and the waters *were* a wall to them on their right hand, and on their left.

30 Thus the LORD saved Is'ra-el that day out of the hand of the E-gyptians; and Is'ra-el saw the E-gyptians dead upon the sea shore.   delivered

31 And Is'ra-el saw that great work which the LORD did upon the E-gyptians: and the people feared the LORD, and believed the LORD, and His servant Mo'ses.   JOHN 2:11   revered

CHAPTER 15

THEN sang Mo'ses and the children of Is'ra-el this song to the LORD, and spoke, saying, I will sing to the LORD, for He has triumphed gloriously: the horse and its rider has He thrown into the sea.   REV. 15:3

2 The LORD *is* my strength and song, and He is become my salvation: He *is* my God, and I will prepare Him an habitation; my father's God, and I will exalt him. Jah - i.e., Heb. Jeshua - El$^{s.f.}$ - Elohim$^{p.f.}$

3 The LORD *is* a man of war: the LORD *is* His name.

4 Pha'raoh's chariots and his host has He cast into the sea: his chosen captains also are drowned in the Red sea.

5 The depths have covered them: they sank into the bottom as a stone.

6 Your right hand, O LORD, is become

glorious in power: Your right hand, O LORD, has dashed in pieces the enemy.

7 And in the greatness of your excellency You have overthrown them that rose up against You: You sent forth Your anger, *which* <u>consumed</u> them as stubble.   destroyed

8 And with the blast of Your nostrils the waters were gathered together, the floods stood upright as an heap, *and* the depths were <u>congealed</u> in the heart of the sea.   made firm

9 The enemy said, I will pursue, I will overtake, I will divide the spoil; my lust shall be satisfied upon them; I will draw my sword, my hand shall destroy them.

10 You did blow with your wind, the sea covered them: they sank as lead in the mighty waters.

11 Who *is* like to You, O LORD, among the gods? who *is* like You, glorious in holiness, fearful *in* praises, doing wonders?

12 You stretched out your right hand, the earth swallowed them.

13 You in Your mercy have led forth the people *which* You have redeemed: You have guided *them* in Your strength to Your holy habitation.

14 The people shall hear, *and* be afraid: <u>sorrow</u> shall take hold on the inhabitants of Pal-es-ti'na.   anguish

15 Then the chiefs of E'dom shall be amazed; the mighty men of Mo'ab, trembling shall take hold upon them; all the inhabitants of Ca'naan shall melt away.

16 Fear and dread shall fall upon them; by the greatness of Your arm they shall be *as* still as a stone; till Your people pass over, O LORD, till the people pass over, *which* You have purchased.

17 You shall bring them in, and plant them in the mountain of Your inheritance, *in* the place, O LORD, *which* You have made for You to dwell in, *in* the Sanctuary, O LORD, *which* Your hands have established.   Jehovah^s.f. - Adonay^p.f.

18 The LORD shall reign for ever and ever.

19 For the horse of Pha'raoh went in with his chariots and with his horsemen into the sea, and the LORD brought again the waters of the sea upon them; but the children of Is'ra-el went on dry *land* in the midst of the sea.

20 And Mir'i-am the prophetess, the sister of Aar'on, took a timbrel in her hand; and all the women went out after her with timbrels and with dances.

21 And Mir'i-am answered them, Sing you to the LORD, for He has triumphed gloriously; the horse and its rider has He thrown into the sea.

22 So Mo'ses brought Is'ra-el from the Red sea, and they went out into the wilderness of Shur; and they went three days in the wilderness, and found no water.

23 And when they came to <u>Ma'rah</u>, they could not drink of the waters of <u>Ma'rah</u>, for they *were* bitter: therefore the name of it was called <u>Ma'rah</u>.   i.e., bitterness

24 And the people <u>murmured</u> against Mo'ses, saying, What shall we drink?   grumbled

25 And he cried to the LORD; and

the LORD showed him a tree, *which* when he had cast into the waters, the waters were made sweet: there He made for them a statute and an ordinance, and there He proved them,   regulation - tested

26 And said, If you will diligently hearken to the voice of the LORD your God, and will do that which is right in His sight, and will give ear to His commandments, and keep all His statutes, I will put none of these diseases upon you, which I have brought upon the E-gyptians: for I *am* the LORD that heals you.   Elohim^p.f. - Jehovah Rophi

27 And they came to E'lim, where *were* twelve wells of water, and three-score and ten palm trees: and they encamped there by the waters.

CHAPTER 16

AND they took their journey from E'lim, and all the congregation of the children of Is'ra-el came to the wilderness of Sin, which *is* between E'lim and Si'nai, on the fifteenth day of the second month after their departing out of the land of E'gypt.

2 And the whole congregation of the children of Is'ra-el murmured against Mo'ses and Aar'on in the wilderness: grumbled

3 And the children of Is'ra-el said to them, Would to God we had died by the hand of the LORD in the land of E'gypt, when we sat by the flesh pots, *and* when we did eat bread to the full; for you have brought us forth into this wilderness, to kill this whole assembly with hunger.

4 Then said the LORD to Mo'ses, Behold, I will rain bread from heaven for you; and the people shall go out and gather a certain rate every day, that I may prove them, whether they will walk in My law, or no.   JOHN 6:31 test

5 And it shall come to pass, that on the sixth day they shall prepare *that* which they bring in; and it shall be twice as much as they gather daily.

6 And Mo'ses and Aar'on said to all the children of Is'ra-el, At even, then you shall know that the LORD has brought you out from the land of E'gypt:

7 And in the morning, then you shall see the glory of the LORD; for that He hears your murmurings against the LORD: and what *are* we, that you murmur against us?   grumblings

8 And Mo'ses said, *This shall be*, when the LORD shall give you in the evening flesh to eat, and in the morning bread to the full; for that the LORD hears your murmurings which you murmur against Him: and what *are* we? your murmurings *are* not against us, but against the LORD.

9 And Mo'ses spoke to Aar'on, Say to all the congregation of the children of Is'ra-el, Come near before the LORD: for He has heard your murmurings.   grumblings

10 And it came to pass, as Aar'on spoke to the whole congregation of the children of Is'ra-el, that they looked toward the wilderness, and, behold, the glory of the LORD appeared in the cloud.

11 And the LORD spoke to Mo'ses, saying,

12 I have heard the <u>murmurings</u> of the children of Is'ra-el: speak to them, saying, At even you shall eat flesh, and in the morning you shall be filled with bread; and you shall know that I *am* the LORD your God.   grumblings

13 And it came to pass, that at even the quails came up, and covered the camp: and in the morning the dew lay round about the host.

14 And when the dew that lay was gone up, behold, upon the face of the wilderness *there lay* a small round thing, *as* small as the hoar frost on the ground.

15 And when the children of Is'ra-el saw *it*, they said one to another, It *is* <u>manna</u>: for they knew not what it *was*. And Mo'ses said to them, This *is* the bread which the LORD has given you to eat.   1 COR. 10:3   what is it (Aram.)

16 This *is* the thing which the LORD has commanded, Gather of it every man according to his eating, an omer for every man, *according to* the number of your persons; take you every man for *them* which *are* in his tents.

17 And the children of Is'ra-el did so, and gathered, some more, some less.

18 And when they did <u>mete</u> *it* with an omer, he that gathered much had nothing over, and he that gathered little had no lack; they gathered every man according to his eating.   2 COR. 8:15   measure

19 And Mo'ses said, Let no man leave of it till the morning.

20 Notwithstanding they hearkened not to Mo'ses; but some of them left of it until the morning, and it bred worms, and stank: and Mo'ses was angry with them.

21 And they gathered it every morning, every man according to his eating: and when the sun <u>waxed</u> hot, it melted.   grew

22 And it came to pass, *that* on the sixth day they gathered twice as much bread, two omers for one *man*: and all the rulers of the congregation came and told Mo'ses.

23 And he said to them, This *is that* which the LORD has said, Tomorrow *is* the rest of the holy <u>sabbath</u> to the LORD: bake *that* which you will bake *today*, and <u>seethe</u> that you will <u>seethe</u>; and that which remains over lay up for you to be kept until the morning.   rest day - boil

24 And they laid it up till the morning, as Mo'ses bade: and it did not stink, neither was there any worm therein.

25 And Mo'ses said, Eat that to day; for to day *is* a <u>sabbath</u> to the LORD: to day you shall not find it in the field.

26 Six days you shall gather it; but on the seventh day, *which is* the <u>sabbath</u>, in it there shall be none.

27 And it came to pass, *that* there went out *some* of the people on the seventh day for to gather, and they found none.

28 And the LORD said to Mo'ses, How long refuse you to <u>keep</u> My commandments and My laws?   obey

29 See, for that the LORD has given you the <u>sabbath</u>, therefore He gives you on the sixth day the bread of two

days; abide you every man in his place, let no man go out of his place on the seventh day. _{rest day}

30 So the people rested on the seventh day.

31 And the house of Is'ra-el called the name thereof Manna: and it *was* like coriander seed, white; and the taste of it *was* like wafers *made* with honey.

32 And Mo'ses said, This *is* the thing which the LORD commands, Fill an omer of it to be kept for your generations; that they may see the bread wherewith I have fed you in the wilderness, when I brought you forth from the land of E'gypt.

P 33 And Mo'ses said to Aar'on, Take a pot, and put an omer full of manna therein, and lay it up before the LORD, to be kept for your generations. 123

34 As the LORD commanded Mo'ses, so Aar'on laid it up before the Testimony, to be kept.

35 And the children of Is'ra-el did eat manna forty years, until they came to a land inhabited; they did eat manna, until they came to the borders of the land of Ca'naan.

36 Now an omer *is* the tenth *part* of an ephah.

CHAPTER 17

AND all the congregation of the children of Is'ra-el journeyed from the wilderness of Sin, after their journeys, according to the commandment of the LORD, and pitched in Reph'i-dim: and *there was* no water for the people to drink. _{camped}

2 Wherefore the people did chide with Mo'ses, and said, Give us water that we may drink. And Mo'ses said to them, Why chide you with me? wherefore do you tempt the LORD? _{quarrel - test}

3 And the people thirsted there for water; and the people murmured against Mo'ses, and said, Wherefore *is* this *that* you have brought us up out of E'gypt, to kill us and our children and our cattle with thirst? _{grumbled}

4 And Mo'ses cried to the LORD, saying, What shall I do to this people? they be almost ready to stone me. _{JOHN 8:59}

5 And the LORD said to Mo'ses, Go on before the people, and take with you of the elders of Is'ra-el; and your rod, wherewith you smote the river, take in your hand, and go. _{Struck}

6 Behold, I will stand before you there upon the rock in Ho'reb; and you shall smite the rock, and there shall come water out of it, that the people may drink. And Mo'ses did so in the sight of the elders of Is'ra-el. _{1 COR. 10:4}

M03 — — — 114

7 And he called the name of the place Mas'sah, and Mer'i-bah, because of the chiding of the children of Is'ra-el, and because they tempted the LORD, saying, Is the LORD among us, or not? _{i.e., proof - i.e., contention}

8 Then came Am'a-lek, and fought with Is'ra-el in Reph'i-dim.

9 And Mo'ses said to Josh'u-a, Choose us out men, and go out, fight with Am'a-lek: to morrow I will stand on the top of the hill with the rod of God in my hand.

10 So Josh'u-a did as Mo'ses had said

to him, and fought with Am'a-lek: and Mo'ses, Aar'on, and Hur went up to the top of the hill.

11 And it came to pass, when Mo'ses held up his hand, that Is'ra-el <u>prevailed</u>: and when he let down his hand, Am'a-lek <u>prevailed</u>.   was victorious

12 But Mo'ses' hands *were* <u>heavy</u>; and they took a stone, and put *it* under him, and he sat thereon; and Aar'on and Hur <u>stayed</u> up his hands, the one on the one side, and the other on the other side; and his hands were <u>steady</u> until the going down of the sun.   tired - supported - firm

13 And Josh'u-a discomfited Am'a-lek and his people with the edge of the sword.

14 And the LORD said to Mo'ses, Write this *for* a memorial in a book, and re-hearse *it* in the ears of Josh'u-a: for I will utterly put out the remembrance of Am'a-lek from under heaven.

15 And Mo'ses built an altar, and called the name of it <u>Je-ho'vah-nis'si</u>:   The Lord is my banner

16 For he said, Because the LORD has sworn *that* the LORD *will have* war with Am'a-lek from generation to generation.

CHAPTER 18

WHEN Je'thro, the priest of Mid'i-an, Mo'ses' father in law, heard of all that <u>God</u> had done for Mo'ses, and for Is'ra-el His people, *and* that the LORD had brought Is'ra-el out of E'gypt;   Elohim^{p.f.}

2 Then Je'thro, Mo'ses' father in law, took Zip-po'rah, Mo'ses' wife, after he had sent her back,

3 And her two sons; of which the name of the one *was* Ger'shom; for he said, I have been an alien in a strange land:

4 And the name of the other *was* E-li-e'zer; for the <u>God</u> of my father, *said he, was* my help, and delivered me from the sword of Pha'raoh: Elohim^{p.f.}

5 And Je'thro, Mo'ses' father in law, came with his sons and his wife to Mo'ses into the wilderness, where he encamped at the mount of God:

6 And he said to Mo'ses, I your father in law Je'thro am come to you, and your wife, and her two sons with her.

7 And Mo'ses went out to meet his father in law, and did obeisance, and kissed him; and they asked each other of *their* welfare; and they came into the tent.

8 And Mo'ses told his father in law all that the LORD had done to Pha'raoh and to the E-gyptians for Is'ra-el's sake, *and* all the <u>travail</u> that had come upon them by the way, and *how* the LORD delivered them.   hardship

9 And Je'thro rejoiced for all the goodness which the LORD had done to Is'ra-el, whom He had delivered out of the hand of the E-gyptians.

10 And Je'thro said, Blessed *be* the LORD, Who has delivered you out of the hand of the E-gyptians, and out of the hand of Pha'raoh, Who has delivered the people from under the hand of the E-gyptians.

11 Now I know that the LORD *is* greater than all gods: for in the thing

G4B-187
GIN-290

wherein they dealt proudly *He was* above them.

12 And Je'thro, Mo'ses' father in law, took a burned offering and sacrifices for <u>God</u>: and Aar'on came, and all the elders of Is'ra-el, to eat <u>bread</u> with Mo'ses' father in law before <u>God</u>.   Elohim^{p.f.} - a meal

13 And it came to pass on the morrow, that Mo'ses sat to judge the people: and the people stood by Mo'ses from the morning to the evening.

14 And when Mo'ses' father in law saw all that he did to the people, he said, What *is* this thing that you do to the people? why sit you <u>yourself alone</u>, and all the people stand by you from morning to even?   alone as judge

15 And Mo'ses said to his father in law, Because the people come to me to enquire of <u>God</u>:   Elohim^{p.f.}

16 When they have a <u>matter</u>, they come to me; and I judge between one and another, and I do make *them* know the statutes of God, and His laws.   dispute

17 And Mo'ses' father in law said to him, The thing that you do *is* not good.

18 You will surely wear away, both you, and this people that *is* with you: for this thing *is* too heavy for you; you are not able to perform it yourself alone.

19 Hearken now to my voice, I will give you <u>counsel</u>, and <u>God</u> shall be with you: Be you for the people to God-ward, that you may bring the <u>causes</u> to <u>God</u>:   advice - Elohim^{p.f.} - disputes

20 And you shall teach them ordinances and laws, and shall show them the way wherein they must walk, and the work that they must do.

21 Moreover you shall provide out of all the people able men, such as <u>fear God</u>, men of truth, hating covetousness; and place *such* over them, *to be* rulers of thousands, *and* rulers of hundreds, rulers of fifties, and rulers of tens: ACTS 6:3 revere - Elohim^{p.f.}

M03

117

22 And let them judge the people at all <u>seasons</u>: and it shall be, *that* every great matter they shall bring to you, but every small matter they shall judge: so shall it be easier for yourself, and they shall bear *the burden* with you.   times

23 If you shall do this thing, and God command you *so*, then you shall be able to endure, and all this people shall also go to their place in peace.

24 So Mo'ses hearkened to the voice of his father in law, and did all that he had said.

25 And Mo'ses chose able men out of all Is'ra-el, and made them heads over the people, rulers of thousands, rulers of hundreds, rulers of fifties, and rulers of tens.

26 And they judged the people at all seasons: the hard <u>causes</u> they brought to Mo'ses, but every small matter they judged themselves.   disputes

27 And Mo'ses let his father in law depart; and he went his way into his own land.

CHAPTER 19

IN the third month, when the children of Is'ra-el were gone forth out of the land of E'gypt, the same day came they *into* the wilderness of Si'nai.

2 For they were departed from Reph'i-dim, and were come *to* the desert of Si'nai, and had pitched in the wilderness; and there Is'ra-el camped before the mount.

3 And Mo'ses went up to <u>God</u>, and the LORD called to him out of the mountain, saying, Thus shall you say to the house of Ja'cob, and tell the children of Is'ra-el;   Elohim^{p-f}

4 You have seen what I did to the E-gyptians, and *how* I <u>bare</u> you on eagles' wings, and brought you to Myself.   REV 12:14   bore

5 Now therefore, if you will obey My voice indeed, and keep My <u>covenant</u>, then you shall be a <u>peculiar</u> treasure to Me above all people: for all the earth *is* Mine: 2 PET. 2:5,9 1 PET. 2:5 agreement - special

6 And you shall be to Me a kingdom of priests, and an holy nation. These *are* the words which you shall speak to the children of Is'ra-el. REV. 1.6 REV. 5:10

7 And Mo'ses came and called for the elders of the people, and <u>laid</u> before their faces all these words which the LORD commanded him.   set

8 And all the people answered together, and said, All that the LORD has spoken we will do. And Mo'ses returned the words of the people to the LORD.

9 And the LORD said to Mo'ses, Lo, I come to you in a thick cloud, that the people may hear when I speak with you, and believe you for ever. And Mo'ses told the words of the people to the LORD.

10 And the LORD said to Mo'ses, Go to the people, and <u>sanctify</u> them to day and to morrow, and let them wash their clothes,   consecrate

11 And be ready against the third day: for the third day the LORD will come down in the sight of all the people upon mount Si'nai.

12 And you shall set bounds to the people round about, saying, Take heed to yourselves, *that you* go *not* up into the mount, or touch the border of it: whosoever touches the mount shall be surely put to death: HEB. 12:18

13 There shall not an hand touch it, but he shall surely be stoned, or shot through; whether *it be* beast or man, it shall not live: when the trumpet sounds long, they shall come up to the mount.   HEB. 12:20

14 And Mo'ses went down from the mount to the people, and <u>sanctified</u> the people; and they washed their clothes.   consecrated

15 And he said to the people, Be ready against the third day: come not at *your* wives.   1 COR. 7:5

16 And it came to pass on the third day in the morning, that there were thunders and lightnings, and a thick cloud upon the mount, and the voice of the trumpet exceeding loud; so that all the people that *was* in the camp trembled.

17 And Mo'ses brought forth the people out of the camp to meet with God; and they stood at the <u>nether</u> part of the mount.   lower

18 And mount Si'nai was altogether on a smoke, because the LORD descended upon it in fire: and the smoke

thereof ascended as the smoke of a furnace, and the whole mount quaked greatly.

19 And when the voice of the trumpet sounded long, and <u>waxed</u> louder and louder, Mo'ses spoke, and <u>God</u> answered him by a voice.   grew - Elohim^{p.f.}

20 And the LORD came down upon mount Si'nai, on the top of the mount: and the LORD called Mo'ses *up* to the top of the mount; and Mo'ses went up.

21 And the LORD said to Mo'ses, Go down, <u>charge</u> the people, less they break through to the LORD to gaze, and many of them perish.   warn

22 And let the priests also, which come near to the LORD, <u>sanctify</u> themselves, less the LORD break forth upon them.   consecrate

23 And Mo'ses said to the LORD, The people cannot come up to mount Si'nai: for You charged us, saying, Set bounds about the mount, and <u>sanctify</u> it.

24 And the LORD said to him, Away, get you down, and you shall come up, you, and Aar'on with you: but let not the priests and the people break through to come up to the LORD, less He break forth upon them.

25 So Mo'ses went down to the people, and spoke to them.   REV. 4:1

CHAPTER 20

AND God spoke all these words, saying,

2 I *am* the LORD your <u>God</u>, which have brought you out of the land of E'gypt, out of the house of <u>bondage</u>.   Elohim ^{p.f.} - slavery

3 You shall have no other gods before Me.

4 You shall not make to you any graven image, or any likeness *of any thing* that *is* in heaven above, or that *is* in the earth beneath, or that *is* in the water under the earth:

5 You shall not <u>bow down yourself to</u> them, nor serve them: for I the <u>LORD</u> your <u>God</u> *am* a jealous <u>God,</u> <u>v</u>isiting the iniquity of the fathers upon the children to the third and fourth *generation* of them that <u>hate</u> Me;   worship - Jehovah ^{s.f.} - Elohim^{p.f.} - El^{s.f.} - bringing - abhor

6 And showing mercy to thousands of them that love Me, and keep My commandments.

7 You shall not take the name of the LORD your God in vain; for the LORD will not hold him guiltless that takes His name in vain.

8 Remember the <u>sabbath</u> day, to keep it holy.   rest day

9 Six days shall you labor, and do all your work:

10 But the seventh day *is* the <u>sabbath</u> of the LORD your God: *in it* you shall not do any work, you, nor your son, nor your daughter, your manservant, nor your maidservant, nor your cattle, nor your stranger that *is* within your gates: LUKE 13:14

11 For *in* six days the LORD made heaven and earth, the sea, and all that in them *is*, and rested the seventh day: wherefore the LORD blessed the <u>sabbath</u> day, and hallowed it.   ACTS 14:15

12 Honor your father and your mother: that your days may be long upon the land which the LORD your God gives you.   MATT. 15:4 MARK 7:10 EPH. 6:2

G2-955
G40

M42---293
G4C—295

M40-121

G4
G

139
409 M18

198

13 You shall not kill. MATT. 5:21 ROM. 13:9

14 You shall not commit adultery.

15 You shall not steal. MATT. 5:27 MATT. 19:18

16 You shall not bear false witness against your neighbor. MARK 10:19

17 You shall not covet your neighbor's house, you shall not covet your neighbor's wife, nor his manservant, nor his maidservant, nor his ox, nor his ass, nor any thing that *is* your neighbor's. ROM. 7:7

18 And all the people saw the thunderings, and the lightnings, and the noise of the trumpet, and the mountain smoking: and when the people *saw it*, they removed, and stood afar off. moved away

19 And they said to Mo'ses, Speak you with us, and we will hear: but let not God speak with us, less we die. HEB. 12:25

20 And Mo'ses said to the people, Fear not: for God is come to prove you, and that His fear may be before your faces, that you sin not. test - that the reverence of Him

21 And the people stood afar off, and Mo'ses drew near to the thick darkness where God *was*. Elohimᵖ·ᶠ·

22 And the LORD said to Mo'ses, Thus you shall say to the children of Is'ra-el, You have seen that I have talked with you from heaven.

23 You shall not make Me gods of silver, neither shall you make to you gods of gold.

24 An altar of earth you shall make to Me, and shall sacrifice thereon your burned offerings, and your peace offerings, your sheep, and your oxen: in all places where I record My name I will come to you, and I will bless you. put

25 And if you will make Me an altar of stone, you shall not build it of hewn stone: for if you lift up your tool upon it, you have polluted it.

26 Neither shall you go up by steps to My altar, that your nakedness be not discovered thereon.

CHAPTER 21

NOW these *are* the judgments which you shall set before them. ordinances

2 If you buy an He'brew servant, six years he shall serve: and in the seventh he shall go out free for nothing.

3 If he came in by himself, he shall go out by himself: if he were married, then his wife shall go out with him.

4 If his master have given him a wife, and she have born him sons or daughters; the wife and her children shall be her master's, and he shall go out by himself.

5 And if the servant shall plainly say, I love my master, my wife, and my children; I will not go out free: as a free man

6 Then his master shall bring him to the judges; he shall also bring him to the door, or to the door post; and his master shall bore his ear through with an awl; and he shall serve him for ever.

7 And if a man sell his daughter to be a maidservant, she shall not go out as the menservants do.

8 If she please not her master, who has betrothed her to himself, then shall he let her be redeemed: to sell her to a strange nation he shall have no power, seeing he has dealt deceitfully with her. foreign

9 And if he have betrothed her to his son, he shall deal with her after the manner of daughters.

10 If he take him another *wife*; her food, her <u>raiment</u>, and her duty of marriage, shall he not diminish. clothes

11 And if he do not these three to her, then shall she go out free without money.

12 He that smites a man, so that he die, shall be surely put to death.

13 And if a man lie not in wait, but God deliver *him* into his hand; then I will appoint you a place where he shall flee.

14 But if a man come <u>presumptuously</u> upon his neighbor, to slay him with <u>guile</u>; you shall take him from My altar, that he may die. willfully - deceit

15 And he that smites his father, or his mother, shall be surely put to death.

16 And he that <u>steals</u> a man, and sells him, or if he be found in his hand, he shall surely be put to death. kidnaps

17 And he that curses his father, or his mother, shall surely be put to death. MATT 15:4 MARK 7:10

18 And if men strive together, and one smite another with a stone, or with *his* fist, and he die not, but keeps *his* bed:

19 If he rise again, and walk abroad upon his staff, then shall he that <u>smote</u> *him* <u>be quit</u>: only he shall pay *for* the loss of his time, and shall cause *him* to be thoroughly healed. struck - go unpunished

20 And if a man <u>smite</u> his servant, or his maid, with a rod, and he die under his hand; he shall be surely punished. strikes

21 Notwithstanding, if he continue a day or two, he shall not be punished: for he *is* his money.

22 If men strive, and hurt a woman with child, so that <u>her fruit depart</u> *from her*, and yet no mischief follow: he shall be surely punished, according as the woman's husband will lay upon him; and he shall pay as the judges *determine*. she suffers a miscarriage

23 And if *any* <u>mischief</u> follow, then you shall give life for life, further injury

24 Eye for eye, tooth for tooth, hand for hand, foot for foot, MATT. 5:38

25 Burning for burning, wound for wound, stripe for stripe.

26 And if a man <u>smite</u> the eye of his servant, or the eye of his maid, that it perish; he shall let him go free for his eye's sake. strike

27 And if he <u>smite</u> out his manservant's tooth, or his maidservant's tooth; he shall let him go free for his tooth's sake.

28 If an ox gore a man or a woman, that they die: then the ox shall be surely stoned, and its flesh shall not be eaten; but the owner of the ox *shall be* <u>quit</u>. free

29 But if the ox <u>were wont</u> to push with his horn in time past, and it has been testified to his owner, and he has not kept him in, but that he has killed a man or a woman; the ox shall be stoned, and its owner also shall be put to death. had a habit

30 If there be laid on him a sum of money, then he shall give for the ran-

som of his life whatsoever is laid upon him.

31 Whether he have gored a son, or have gored a daughter, according to this judgment shall it be done to him.

32 If the ox shall push a manservant or a maidservant; he shall give to their master thirty shekels of silver, and the ox shall be stoned. MATT. 26:15

33 And if a man shall open a pit, or if a man shall dig a pit, and not cover it, and an ox or an ass fall therein;

34 The owner of the pit shall make *it* good, *and* give money to the owner of them; and the dead *beast* shall be his.

35 And if one man's ox hurt another's, that he die; then they shall sell the live ox, and divide the money of it; and the dead *ox* also they shall divide.

36 Or if it be known that the ox has used to push in time past, and its owner has not kept him in; he shall surely pay ox for ox; and the dead shall be his own.

CHAPTER 22

IF a man shall steal an ox, or a sheep, and kill it, or sell it; he shall restore five oxen for an ox, and four sheep for a sheep.

2 If a thief be found breaking up, and be smitten that he die, *there shall* no blood *be shed* for him. in

3 If the sun be risen upon him, *there shall be* blood *shed* for him; *for* he should make full restitution; if he have nothing, then he shall be sold for his theft. i.e., as slave

4 If the theft be certainly found in his hand alive, whether it be ox, or ass, or sheep; he shall restore double.

5 If a man shall cause a field or vineyard to be eaten, and shall put in his beast, and shall feed in another man's field; of the best of his own field, and of the best of his own vineyard, shall he make restitution.

6 If fire break out, and catch in thorns, so that the stacks of corn, or the standing corn, or the field, be consumed *therewith*; he that kindled the fire shall surely make restitution. grain

7 If a man shall deliver to his neighbor money or stuff to keep, and it be stolen out of the man's house; if the thief be found, let him pay double.

8 If the thief be not found, then the master of the house shall be brought to the judges, *to see* whether he have put his hand to his neighbor's goods. laid his hand on

9 For all manner of trespass, *whether it be* for ox, for ass, for sheep, for raiment, *or* for any manner of lost thing, which *another* challenges to be his, the cause of both parties shall come before the judges; *and* whom the judges shall condemn, he shall pay double to his neighbor. clothing

10 If a man deliver to his neighbor an ass, or an ox, or a sheep, or any beast, to keep; and it die, or be hurt, or driven away, no man seeing *it*:

11 *Then* shall an oath of the LORD be between them both, that he has not put his hand to his neighbor's goods; and the owner of it shall accept *thereof*, and he shall not make *it* good.

12 And if it be stolen from him, he

shall make restitution to the owner thereof.

13 If it be torn in pieces, *then* let him bring it *for* witness, *and* he shall not make good that which was torn.

14 And if a man borrow anything of his neighbor, and it be hurt, or die, the owner thereof *being* not with it, he shall surely make *it* good.

15 *But* if the owner thereof *be* with it, he shall not make *it* good: if it *be* an hired *thing*, it came for his hire.

16 And if a man entice a maid that is not betrothed, and lie with her, he shall surely endow her to be his wife.

17 If her father utterly refuse to give her to him, he shall pay money according to the dowry of virgins.

18 You shall not allow a witch to live.

19 Whosoever lies with a beast shall surely be put to death.

20 He that sacrifices to *any* god, save to the LORD only, he shall be utterly destroyed.

21 You shall neither <u>vex</u> a <u>stranger</u>, nor oppress him: for you were <u>strangers</u> in the land of E'gypt.

trouble - foreigner

22 You shall not afflict any widow, or fatherless child.

23 If you afflict them in any <u>wise</u>, and they cry at all to Me, I will surely hear their cry;

way

24 And My wrath shall <u>wax hot</u>, and I will kill you with the sword; and your wives shall be widows, and your children fatherless.

be kindled

25 If you lend money to *any of* My people *that is* poor by you, you shall not be to him as an <u>usurer</u>, neither shall you lay upon him <u>usury.</u>

creditor - interest

26 If you at all take your neighbor's <u>raiment</u> to pledge, you shall deliver it to him by that the sun goes down:

cloak

27 For that *is* his covering only, it *is* his <u>raiment</u> for his skin: <u>wherein</u> shall he sleep? and it shall come to pass, when he cries to Me, that I will hear; for I *am* gracious.

in what else

28 You shall not revile <u>the gods</u>, nor curse the ruler of your people. ACTS 23:5 God

29 You shall not delay *to offer* the first of your ripe fruits, and of your liquors: the firstborn of your sons shall you give to Me.

30 Likewise shall you do with your oxen, *and* with your sheep: seven days it shall be with his <u>dam</u>; on the eighth day you shall give it Me.

mother

31 And you shall be <u>holy</u> men to Me: neither shall you eat *any* flesh *that is* torn of beasts in the field; you shall cast it to the dogs.

dedicated

CHAPTER 23

YOU shall not raise a false report: put not your hand with the wicked to be an unrighteous witness.

2 You shall not follow a multitude to *do* evil; neither shall you speak in a cause to <u>decline</u> after many to pervert *judgment*:

follow

3 Neither shall you <u>countenance</u> a poor man in his <u>cause</u>. *be partial to - dispute*

4 If you meet your enemy's ox or his ass going astray, you shall surely bring it back to him again.

5 If you see the ass of him that <u>hates</u>

you lying under his burden, and would forbear to help him, you shall surely help with him. despises - you refrain

6 You shall not pervert the judgment of your poor in his cause.

7 Keep you far from a false matter; and the innocent and righteous slay you not: for I will not justify the wicked.

8 And you shall take no gift: for the gift blinds the wise, and perverts the words of the righteous. bribe

9 Also you shall not oppress a stranger: for you know the heart of a stranger, seeing you were strangers in the land of E'gypt. foreigner

10 And six years you shall sow your land, and shall gather in the fruits thereof:

11 But the seventh *year* you shall let it rest and lie still; that the poor of your people may eat: and what they leave the beasts of the field shall eat. In like manner you shall deal with your vineyard, *and* with your oliveyard. olive grove

12 Six days you shall do your work, and on the seventh day you shall rest: that your ox and your ass may rest, and the son of your handmaid, and the stranger, may be refreshed. MARK 2:27

13 And in all *things* that I have said to you be circumspect: and make no mention of the name of other gods, neither let it be heard out of your mouth. on guard

14 Three times you shall keep a feast to Me in the year.

15 You shall keep the feast of unleavened bread: (you shall eat unleavened bread seven days, as I com-manded you, in the time appointed of the month A'bib; for in it you came out from E'gypt: and none shall appear before Me empty:) i.e., without yeast

16 And the feast of harvest, the firstfruits of your labors, which you have sown in the field: and the feast of ingathering, *which is* in the end of the year, when you have gathered in your labors out of the field.

17 Three times in the year all your males shall appear before the Lord God. Adon^{s.f.} Jehovah^{s.f.}

18 You shall not offer the blood of My sacrifice with leavened bread; neither shall the fat of My sacrifice remain until the morning. offering - feast

19 The first of the firstfruits of your land you shall bring into the house of the Lord your God. You shall not seethe a kid in his mother's milk. boil

20 Behold, I send an angel before you, to keep you in the way, and to bring you into the place which I have prepared.

21 Beware of him, and obey his voice, provoke him not; for he will not pardon your transgressions: for My name is in him.

22 But if you shall indeed obey his voice, and do all that I speak; then I will be an enemy to your enemies, and an adversary to your adversaries.

23 For My angel shall go before you, and bring you in to the Am'or-ites, and the Hit'tites, and the Per'iz-zites, and the Ca'naan-ites, and the Hi'vites, and the Jeb'u-sites: and I will cut them off.

24 You shall not bow down to their gods, nor serve them, nor do after their works: but you shall utterly overthrow them, and quite break down their images.

25 And you shall serve the LORD your God, and He shall bless your bread, and your water; and I will take sickness away from the midst of you.

26 There shall nothing cast their young, nor be barren, in your land: the number of your days I will fulfill.

27 I will send My fear before you, and will destroy all the people to whom you shall come, and I will make all your enemies turn their backs to you.

28 And I will send hornets before you, which shall drive out the Hi'vite, the Ca'naan-ite, and the Hit'tite, from before you.

29 I will not drive them out from before you in one year; less the land become desolate, and the beast of the field multiply against you.

30 By little and little I will drive them out from before you, until you be increased, and inherit the land.

31 And I will set your bounds from the Red sea even to the sea of the Phi-lis'tines, and from the desert to the river: for I will deliver the inhabitants of the land into your hand; and you shall drive them out before you.

boundries - i.e. Mediterranean

32 You shall make no covenant with them, nor with their gods.   *agreement*

33 They shall not dwell in your land, less they make you sin against Me: for if you serve their gods, it will surely be a snare to you.   *trap*

CHAPTER 24

AND He said to Mo'ses, Come up to the LORD, you, and Aar'on, Na'dab, and A-bi'hu, and seventy of the elders of Is'ra-el; and worship you afar off.

2 And Mo'ses alone shall come near the LORD: but they shall not come near; neither shall the people go up with him.

3 And Mo'ses came and told the people all the words of the LORD, and all the judgments: and all the people answered with one voice, and said, All the words which the LORD has said will we do.   *ordinances*

4 And Mo'ses wrote all the words of the LORD, and rose up early in the morning, and built an altar under the hill, and twelve pillars, according to the twelve tribes of Is'ra-el.

5 And he sent young men of the children of Is'ra-el, which offered burned offerings, and sacrificed peace offerings of oxen to the LORD.

6 And Mo'ses took half of the blood, and put *it* in basins; and half of the blood he sprinkled on the altar. HEB. 9:18

7 And he took the book of the covenant, and read in the audience of the people: and they said, All that the LORD has said will we do, and be obedient.   HEB. 9:19 *agreement - hearing*

8 And Mo'ses took the blood, and sprinkled *it* on the people, and said, Behold the blood of the covenant, which

the LORD has made with you concerning all these words.

MATT. 26:28 MARK 14:24 agreement

9 Then went up Mo'ses, and Aar'on, Na'dab, and A-bi'hu, and seventy of the elders of Is'ra-el:

10 And they saw the God of Is'ra-el: and *there was* under His feet as it were a paved work of a sapphire stone, and as it were the body of heaven in *its* clearness. Elohim[p.f.]

11 And upon the nobles of the children of Is'ra-el He laid not His hand: also they saw God, and did eat and drink.

12 And the LORD said to Mo'ses, Come up to Me into the mount, and be there: and I will give you tables of stone, and a law, and commandments which I have written; that you may teach them.

13 And Mo'ses rose up, and his minister Josh'u-a: and Mo'ses went up into the mount of God. servant

14 And he said to the elders, Tarry you here for us, until we come again to you: and, behold, Aar'on and Hur *are* with you: if any man have any matters to do, let him come to them.

15 And Mo'ses went up into the mount, and a cloud covered the mount.

16 And the glory of the LORD abode upon mount Si'nai, and the cloud covered it six days: and the seventh day He called to Mo'ses out of the midst of the cloud.

17 And the sight of the glory of the LORD *was* like devouring fire on the top of the mount in the eyes of the children of Is'ra-el.

18 And Mo'ses went into the midst of the cloud, and got him up into the mount: and Mo'ses was in the mount forty days and forty nights.

CHAPTER 25

AND the LORD spoke to Mo'ses, saying,

2 Speak to the children of Is'ra-el, that they bring Me an offering: of every man that gives it willingly with his heart you shall take My offering.

3 And this *is* the offering which you shall take of them; gold, and silver, and brass,

4 And blue, and purple, and scarlet, and fine linen, and goats' *hair*,

5 And rams' skins dyed red, and badgers' skins, and shittim wood,

6 Oil for the light, spices for anointing oil, and for sweet incense,

7 Onyx stones, and stones to be set in the ephod, and in the breastplate,

8 And let them make Me a sanctuary; that I may dwell among them.

9 According to all that I show you, *after* the pattern of the tabernacle, and the pattern of all the instruments thereof, even so shall you make *it*. furniture

10 And they shall make an ark *of* shittim wood: two cubits and a half *shall be* the length thereof, and a cubit and a half the breadth thereof, and a cubit and a half the height thereof.

11 And you shall overlay it with pure gold, inside and outside shall you overlay it, and shall make upon it a crown of gold round about. border

12 And you shall cast four rings of gold for it, and put *them* in the four corners thereof; and two rings *shall be* in

the one side of it, and two rings in the other side of it.   _{feet}

13 And you shall make <u>staves</u> *of* shittim wood, and overlay them with gold.   _{poles}

14 And you shall put the <u>staves</u> into the rings by the sides of the ark, that the ark may be borne with them.

15 The <u>staves</u> shall be in the rings of the ark: they shall not be taken from it.

16 And you shall put into the ark the testimony which I shall give you.

17 And you shall make a mercy seat *of* pure gold: two cubits and a half *shall be* the length thereof, and a cubit and a half the breadth thereof.

18 And you shall make two cherubims *of* gold, *of* beaten work shall you make them, in the two ends of the mercy seat.

19 And make one cherub on the one end, and the other cherub on the other end: *even* of the mercy seat shall you make the cherubims on the two ends thereof.

20 And the cherubims shall stretch forth *their* wings on high, covering the mercy seat with their wings, and their faces *shall look* one to another; toward the mercy seat shall the faces of the cherubims be.

21 And you shall put the mercy seat above upon the ark; and in the ark you shall put the testimony that I shall give you.

22 And there I will meet with you, and I will <u>commune</u> with you from above the mercy seat, from between the two cherubims which *are* upon the ark of the testimony, of all *things* which I

will give you in commandment to the children of Is'ra-el.   _{speak}

23 You shall also make a table *of* shittim wood: two cubits *shall be* the length thereof, and a cubit the breadth thereof, and a cubit and a half the height thereof.

24 And you shall overlay it with pure gold, and make thereto a <u>crown</u> of gold round about.   _{border}

25 And you shall make to it a border of an <u>hand breadth</u> round about, and you shall make a golden crown to the border thereof round about.   _{3 inches}

26 And you shall make for it four rings of gold, and put the rings in the four corners that *are* on the four feet thereof.

27 Over against the border shall the rings be for places of the <u>staves</u> to bear the table.   _{poles}

28 And you shall make the <u>staves</u> *of* shittim wood, and overlay them with gold, that the table may be borne with them.

29 And you shall make the dishes thereof, and spoons thereof, and covers thereof, and bowls thereof, to <u>cover</u> <u>withal</u>: *of* pure gold shall you make them.   _{pour with}

30 And you shall set upon the table showbread before Me alway.

31 And you shall make a candlestick *of* pure gold: *of* beaten work shall the candlestick be made: its shaft, and its branches, its bowls, its knobs, and his flowers, shall be of the same.

32 And six branches shall come out of the sides of it; three branches of the candlestick out of the one side, and

three branches of the candlestick out of the other side:

33 Three bowls made like to almonds, *with* a knob and a flower in one branch; and three bowls made like almonds in the other branch, *with* a knob and a flower: so in the six branches that come out of the candlestick.

34 And in the candlestick *shall be* four bowls made like to almonds, *with* their knobs and their flowers.

35 And *there shall* be a knob under two branches of the same, and a knob under two branches of the same, and a knob under two branches of the same, according to the six branches that proceed out of the candlestick.

36 Their knobs and their branches shall be of the same: all it *shall be* one beaten work *of* pure gold.

37 And you shall make the seven lamps thereof: and they shall light the lamps thereof, that they may give light opposite it.

38 And the <u>tongs</u> thereof, and the snuffdishes thereof, *shall be* of pure gold.   snuffers

39 *Of* a talent of pure gold shall he make it, with all these vessels.

40 And look that you make *them* after their pattern, which was showed you in the mount.   HEB. 8:5

CHAPTER 26

MOREOVER you shall make the tabernacle *with* ten curtains *of* fine twined linen, and blue, and purple, and scarlet: *with* cherubims of <u>cunning</u> work shall you make them.   skillful

2 The length of one curtain *shall be* eight and twenty cubits, and the breadth of one curtain four cubits: and every one of the curtains shall have one measure.

3 The five curtains shall be coupled together one to another; and *other* five curtains *shall be* coupled one to another.

4 And you shall make loops of blue upon the edge of the one curtain from the selvedge in the coupling; and likewise shall you make in the uttermost edge of *another* curtain, in the coupling of the second.

5 Fifty loops shall you make in the one curtain, and fifty loops shall you make in the edge of the curtain that *is* in the coupling of the second; that the loops may take hold one of another.

6 And you shall make fifty <u>taches</u> of gold, and couple the curtains together with the <u>taches</u>: and it shall be one tabernacle.   hooks

7 And you shall make curtains *of* goats' *hair* to be a covering upon the tabernacle: eleven curtains shall you make.

8 The length of one curtain *shall be* thirty cubits, and the breadth of one curtain four cubits: and the eleven curtains *shall be all* of one measure.

9 And you shall couple five curtains by themselves, and six curtains by themselves, and shall double the sixth curtain in the forefront of the tabernacle.

10 And you shall make fifty loops on the edge of the one curtain *that is* outmost in the coupling, and fifty loops in

the edge of the curtain which couples the second.

11 And you shall make fifty <u>taches</u> of brass, and put the <u>taches</u> into the loops, and couple the <u>tent</u> together, that it may be one.   <small>hooks - covering</small>

12 And the remnant that remains of the curtains of the tent, the half curtain that remains, shall hang over the backside of the tabernacle.

13 And a cubit on the one side, and a cubit on the other side of that which remains in the length of the curtains of the tent, it shall hang over the sides of the tabernacle on this side and on that side, to cover it.

14 And you shall make a covering for the tent *of* rams' skins dyed red, and a covering above *of* badgers' skins.

15 And you shall make boards for the tabernacle *of* shittim wood standing up.

16 Ten cubits *shall be* the length of a board, and a cubit and a half *shall be* the breadth of one board.

17 Two <u>tenons</u> *shall there be* in one board, set in order one against another: thus shall you make for all the boards of the tabernacle.   <small>clasps</small>

18 And you shall make the boards for the tabernacle, twenty boards on the south side southward.

19 And you shall make forty sockets of silver under the twenty boards; two sockets under one board for his two <u>tenons</u>, and two sockets under another board for his two <u>tenons</u>.   <small>clasps</small>

20 And for the second side of the tabernacle on the north side *there shall be* twenty boards:

21 And their forty sockets *of* silver; two sockets under one board, and two sockets under another board.

22 And for the sides of the tabernacle westward you shall make six boards.

23 And two boards shall you make for the corners of the tabernacle in the two sides.

24 And they shall be <u>coupled</u> together beneath, and they shall be <u>coupled</u> together above the head of it to one ring: thus shall it be for them both; they shall be for the two corners.   <small>joined</small>

25 And they shall be eight boards, and their sockets *of* silver, sixteen sockets; two sockets under one board, and two sockets under another board.

26 And you shall make bars *of* shittim wood; five for the boards of the one side of the tabernacle,

27 And five bars for the boards of the other side of the tabernacle, and five bars for the boards of the side of the tabernacle, for the two sides westward.

28 And the middle bar in the midst of the boards shall reach from end to end.

29 And you shall overlay the boards with gold, and make their rings *of* gold *for* <u>places</u> for the bars: and you shall overlay the bars with gold.   <small>holders</small>

30 And you shall <u>rear up</u> the tabernacle according to the fashion thereof which was showed you in the mount.   <small>erect</small>

31 And you shall make a veil *of* blue, and purple, and scarlet, and fine twined linen of cunning work: with cherubims shall it be made:

32 And you shall hang it upon four pillars of shittim *wood* overlaid with

gold: their hooks *shall be of* gold, upon the four sockets of silver.

33 And you shall hang up the veil under the taches, that you may bring in there within the veil the ark of the testimony: and the veil shall divide to you between the holy *place* and the most holy. HEB. 9:2 hooks

34 And you shall put the mercy seat upon the ark of the testimony in the most holy *place*.

35 And you shall set the table outside the veil, and the candlestick opposite the table on the side of the tabernacle toward the south: and you shall put the table on the north side.

36 And you shall make an hanging for the door of the tent, *of* blue, and purple, and scarlet, and fine twined linen, wrought with needlework. screen

37 And you shall make for the hanging five pillars *of* shittim *wood*, and overlay them with gold, *and* their hooks *shall be of* gold: and you shall cast five sockets of brass for them.

CHAPTER 27

AND you shall make an altar *of* shittim wood, five cubits long, and five cubits broad; the altar shall be foursquare: and the height thereof *shall be* three cubits.

2 And you shall make the horns of it upon the four corners thereof: its horns shall be of the same: and you shall overlay it with brass.

3 And you shall make its pans to receive its ashes, and its shovels, and its basins, and its fleshhooks, and its fire-pans: all the vessels thereof you shall make *of* brass.

4 And you shall make for it a grate of network *of* brass; and upon the net shall you make four brazen rings in the four corners thereof.

5 And you shall put it under the compass of the altar beneath, that the net may be even to the midst of the altar. ledge

6 And you shall make staves for the altar, staves *of* shittim wood, and overlay them with brass. poles

7 And the staves shall be put into the rings, and the staves shall be upon the two sides of the altar, to bear *it*.

8 Hollow with boards shall you make it: as it was showed you in the mount, so shall they make *it*.

9 And you shall make the court of the tabernacle: for the south side southward *there shall be* hangings for the court *of* fine twined linen of an hundred cubits long for one side:

10 And the twenty pillars thereof and their twenty sockets *shall be of* brass; the hooks of the pillars and their fillets *shall be* of silver. bands

11 And likewise for the north side in length *there shall be* hangings of an hundred *cubits* long, and its twenty pillars and their twenty sockets *of* brass; the hooks of the pillars and their fillets *of* silver.

12 And *for* the breadth of the court on the west side *shall be* hangings of fifty cubits: their pillars ten, and their sockets ten.

13 And the breadth of the court on

the east side eastward *shall be* fifty cubits.

14 The hangings of one side *of the gate shall be* fifteen cubits: their pillars three, and their sockets three.

15 And on the other side *shall be* hangings fifteen *cubits*: their pillars three, and their sockets three.

16 And for the gate of the court *shall be* an hanging of twenty cubits, *of* blue, and purple, and scarlet, and fine twined linen, wrought with needlework: *and* their pillars *shall be* four, and their sockets four.

17 All the pillars round about the court *shall be* filleted with silver; their hooks *shall be of* silver, and their sockets *of* brass.

18 The length of the court *shall be* an hundred cubits, and the breadth fifty every where, and the height five cubits *of* fine twined linen, and their sockets *of* brass.

19 All the <u>vessels</u> of the tabernacle in all the service thereof, and all the pins thereof, and all the pins of the court, *shall be of* brass. _{utensils}

20 And you shall command the children of Is'ra-el, that they bring you pure oil olive beaten for the light, to cause the lamp to burn always.

21 In the tabernacle of the congregation outside the veil, which *is* before the testimony, Aar'on and his sons shall <u>order</u> it from evening to morning before the LORD: *it shall be* a statute for ever to their generations on the behalf of the children of Is'ra-el. _{arrange}

CHAPTER 28

AND take you to you Aar'on your brother, and his sons with him, from among the children of Is'ra-el, that he may minister to Me in the priest's office, *even* Aar'on, Na'dab and A-bi'hu, E-le-a'zar and Ith'a-mar, Aar'on's sons.

2 And you shall make <u>holy</u> garments for Aar'on your brother for glory and for beauty. _{special}

3 And you shall speak to all *that are* <u>wise hearted</u>, whom I have filled with the spirit of wisdom, that they may make Aar'on's garments to consecrate him, that he may minister to Me in the priest's office. _{skillful}

4 And these *are* the garments which they shall make; a breastplate, and an <u>ephod</u>, and a robe, and a broidered coat, a <u>mitre</u>, and a girdle: and they shall make holy garments for Aar'on your brother, and his sons, that he may minister to Me in the priest's office. _{priestly garment - turban}

5 And they shall take gold, and blue, and purple, and scarlet, and fine linen.

6 And they shall make the <u>ephod</u> *of* gold, *of* blue, and *of* purple, *of* scarlet, and fine twined linen, with <u>cunning</u> work. _{artistic}

7 It shall have the two shoulderpieces thereof joined at the two edges thereof; and *so* it shall be joined together.

8 And the <u>curious</u> girdle of the <u>ephod</u>, which *is* upon it, shall be of the same, according to the work thereof; *even of* gold, *of* blue, and purple, and scarlet, and fine twined linen. _{embroidered}

9 And you shall take two onyx stones, and <u>grave</u> on them the names of the children of Is'ra-el: engrave

10 Six of their names on one stone, and *the other* six names of the rest on the other stone, according to their birth.

11 With the work of an engraver in stone, *like* the engravings of a <u>signet,</u> shall you engrave the two stones with the names of the children of Is'ra-el: you shall make them to be set in <u>ouches</u> of gold. seal - settings

12 And you shall put the two stones upon the shoulders of the <u>ephod</u> *for* stones of memorial to the children of Is'ra-el: and Aar'on shall bear their names before the LORD upon his two shoulders for a <u>memorial</u>. priestly garment - remembrance

13 And you shall make <u>ouches</u> *of* gold;

14 And two chains *of* pure gold at the ends; *of* <u>wreathen</u> work shall you make them, and fasten the <u>wreathen</u> chains to the <u>ouches</u>. braided - settings

15 And you shall make the breastplate of judgment with <u>cunning</u> work; after the work of the <u>ephod</u> you shall make it; *of* gold, *of* blue, and *of* purple, and *of* scarlet, and *of* fine twined linen, shall you make it. artistic - priestly garment

16 Foursquare it shall be *being* doubled; a <u>span</u> *shall be* the length thereof, and a <u>span</u> *shall be* the breadth thereof. 9 inches

17 And you shall set in it settings of stones, *even* four rows of stones: *the first* row *shall be* a sardius, a topaz, and a <u>carbuncle</u>: *this shall be* the first row. emerald

18 And the second row *shall be* an emerald, a sapphire, and a diamond.

19 And the third row a <u>ligure</u>, an agate, and an amethyst. jacinth

20 And the fourth row a beryl, and an onyx, and a jasper: they shall be set in gold in their <u>inclosings</u>. settings

21 And the stones shall be with the names of the children of Is'ra-el, twelve, according to their names, *like* the engravings of a <u>signet</u>; every one with his name shall they be according to the twelve tribes. seal

22 And you shall make upon the breastplate chains at the ends *of* <u>wreathen</u> work *of* pure gold. braided

23 And you shall make upon the breastplate two rings of gold, and shall put the two rings on the two ends of the breastplate.

24 And you shall put the two <u>wreathen</u> *chains* of gold in the two rings *which are* on the ends of the breastplate.

25 And *the other* two ends of the two <u>wreathen</u> *chains* you shall fasten in the two <u>ouches</u>, and put *them* on the shoulderpieces of the <u>ephod</u> before it. settings - priestly garment

26 And you shall make two rings of gold, and you shall put them upon the two ends of the breastplate in the border thereof, which *is* in the side of the <u>ephod</u> inward.

27 And two *other* rings of gold you shall make, and shall put them on the two sides of the <u>ephod</u> underneath, toward the forepart thereof, opposite the *other* coupling thereof, above the <u>curious</u> girdle of the <u>ephod</u>. embroidered

28 And they shall bind the breastplate by the rings thereof to the rings of the ephod with a lace of blue, that *it* may be above the curious girdle of the ephod, and that the breastplate be not loosed from the ephod.

priestly garment - embroidered

29 And Aar'on shall bear the names of the children of Is'ra-el in the breastplate of judgment upon his heart, when he goes in to the holy *place*, for a memorial before the LORD continually.

30 And you shall put in the breastplate of judgment the U'rim and the Thum'mim; and they shall be upon Aar'on's heart, when he goes in before the LORD: and Aar'on shall bear the judgment of the children of Is'ra-el upon his heart before the LORD continually.

i.e., Lights and the Perfections - carry

31 And you shall make the robe of the ephod all *of* blue.

32 And there shall be an hole in the top of it, in the midst thereof: it shall have a binding of woven work round about the hole of it, as it were the hole of an habergeon, that it be not rent.

JOHN 19:24 coat of mail

33 And *beneath* upon the hem of it you shall make pomegranates *of* blue, and *of* purple, and *of* scarlet, round about the hem thereof; and bells of gold between them round about:

34 A golden bell and a pomegranate, a golden bell and a pomegranate, upon the hem of the robe round about.

35 And it shall be upon Aar'on to minister: and his sound shall be heard when he goes in to the holy *place* before the LORD, and when he comes out, that he die not.

36 And you shall make a plate *of* pure gold, and grave upon it, *like* the engravings of a signet, HOLINESS TO THE LORD.

seal

37 And you shall put it on a blue lace, that it may be upon the mitre; upon the forefront of the mitre it shall be.

turban

38 And it shall be upon Aar'on's forehead, that Aar'on may bear the iniquity of the holy things, which the children of Is'ra-el shall hallow in all their holy gifts; and it shall be always upon his forehead, that they may be accepted before the LORD.

39 And you shall embroider the coat of fine linen, and you shall make the mitre *of* fine linen, and you shall make the girdle *of* needlework.

40 And for Aar'on's sons you shall make coats, and you shall make for them girdles, and bonnets shall you make for them, for glory and for beauty.

head pieces

41 And you shall put them upon Aar'on your brother, and his sons with him; and shall anoint them, and consecrate them, and sanctify them, that they may minister to Me in the priest's office.

42 And you shall make them linen breeches to cover their nakedness; from the loins even to the thighs they shall reach:

bare flesh

43 And they shall be upon Aar'on, and upon his sons, when they come in to the tabernacle of the congregation, or when they come near to the altar to minister in the holy *place*; that they bear not iniquity, and die: *it shall be* a

statute for ever to him and his <u>seed</u> after him.   <small>do not incur guilt - ordinance - descendants</small>

CHAPTER 29

AND this *is* the thing that you shall do to them to hallow them, to minister to Me in the priest's office: Take one young bullock, and two rams without blemish,

2 And <u>unleavened</u> bread, and cakes <u>unleavened</u> tempered with oil, and wafers <u>unleavened</u> anointed with oil: *of* wheaten flour shall you make them.

<small>i.e., without yeast</small>

3 And you shall put them into one basket, and bring them in the basket, with the bullock and the two rams.

4 And Aar'on and his sons you shall bring to the door of the <u>tabernacle</u> of the congregation, and shall wash them with water.   <small>tent</small>

5 And you shall take the garments, and put upon Aar'on the coat, and the robe of the <u>ephod</u>, and the <u>ephod</u>, and the breastplate, and gird him with the <u>curious</u> girdle of the <u>ephod</u>:

<small>priestly garment - embroidered</small>

6 And you shall put the <u>mitre</u> upon his head, and put the holy crown upon the <u>mitre</u>.   <small>turban</small>

7 Then shall you take the anointing oil, and pour *it* upon his head, and anoint him.

8 And you shall bring his sons, and put coats upon them.

9 And you shall gird them with girdles, Aar'on and his sons, and put the bonnets on them: and the priest's office shall be theirs for a perpetual statute:

and you shall consecrate Aar'on and his sons.

10 And you shall cause a bullock to be brought before the tabernacle of the congregation: and Aar'on and his sons shall put their hands upon the head of the bullock.

11 And you shall kill the bullock before the LORD, *by* the door of the tabernacle of the congregation.

12 And you shall take of the blood of the bullock, and put *it* upon the horns of the altar with your finger, and pour all the blood beside the bottom of the altar.

13 And you shall take all the fat that covers the inwards, and the <u>caul</u> *that is* above the liver, and the two kidneys, and the fat that *is* upon them, and burn *them* upon the altar.   <small>fatty appendage</small>

14 But the flesh of the bullock, and its skin, and its dung, shall you burn with fire outside the camp: it *is* a sin offering.

15 You shall also take one ram; and Aar'on and his sons shall put their hands upon the head of the ram.

16 And you shall slay the ram, and you shall take its blood, and sprinkle *it* round about upon the altar.

17 And you shall cut the ram in pieces, and wash the <u>inwards</u> of him, and its legs, and put *them* <u>to</u> its pieces, and to its head.   <small>entrails - upon</small>

18 And you shall burn the whole ram upon the altar: it *is* a burnt offering to the LORD: it *is* a <u>sweet savor</u>, an offering made by fire to the LORD.

<small>soothing aroma</small>

19 And you shall take the other

ram; and Aar'on and his sons shall put their hands upon the head of the ram.

20 Then shall you kill the ram, and take of its blood, and put *it* upon the tip of the right ear of Aar'on, and upon the tip of the right ear of his sons, and upon the thumb of their right hand, and upon the <u>great</u> toe of their right foot, and sprinkle the blood upon the altar round about. big

21 And you shall take of the blood that *is* upon the altar, and of the anointing oil, and sprinkle *it* upon Aar'on, and upon his garments, and upon his sons, and upon the garments of his sons with him: and he shall be hallowed, and his garments, and his sons, and his sons' garments with him.

22 Also you shall take of the ram the fat and the rump, and the fat that covers the inwards, and the <u>caul</u> *above* the liver, and the two kidneys, and the fat that *is* upon them, and the right <u>shoulder</u>; for it *is* a ram of consecration: fatty appendage - thigh

23 And one loaf of bread, and one cake of oiled bread, and one wafer out of the basket of the <u>unleavened</u> bread that *is* before the LORD: i.e. without yeast

24 And you shall put all in the hands of Aar'on, and in the hands of his sons; and shall wave them *for* a wave offering before the LORD.

25 And you shall receive them of their hands, and burn *them* upon the altar for a burnt offering, for a <u>sweet savor</u> before the LORD: it *is* an offering made by fire to the LORD.   soothing aroma

26 And you shall take the breast of the ram of Aar'on's consecration, and wave it *for* a wave offering before the LORD: and it shall be your part.

27 And you shall sanctify the breast of the wave offering, and the shoulder of the heave offering, which is waved, and which is heaved up, of the ram of the consecration, *even* of *that* which *is* for Aar'on, and of *that* which is for his sons:

28 And it shall be Aar'on's and his sons' <u>by a statute</u> for ever from the children of Is'ra-el: for it *is* an heave offering: and it shall be an heave offering from the children of Is'ra-el of the sacrifice of their peace offerings, *even* their heave offering to the LORD.   as their portion

29 And the holy garments of Aar'on shall be his sons' after him, to be anointed therein, and to be consecrated in them.

30 *And* that son that is priest in his stead shall put them on seven days, when he comes into the tabernacle of the congregation to minister in the holy *place*.

31 And you shall take the ram of the consecration, and <u>seethe</u> its flesh in the holy place.   boil

32 And Aar'on and his sons shall eat the flesh of the ram, and the bread that *is* in the basket, *by* the door of the tabernacle of the congregation.

33 And they shall eat those things wherewith the atonement was made, to consecrate *and* to sanctify them: but a stranger shall not eat *thereof,* because they *are* <u>holy</u>.   set aside

34 And if any of the flesh of the consecrations, or of the bread, remain to the morning, then you shall burn

the remainder with fire: it shall not be eaten, because it *is* holy.

35 And thus shall you do to Aar'on, and to his sons, according to all *things* which I have commanded you: seven days shall you consecrate them.

36 And you shall offer every day a bullock *for* a sin offering for atonement: and you shall cleanse the altar, when you have made an <u>atonement</u> for it, and you shall anoint it, to sanctify it.   special ceremony

37 Seven days you shall make an atonement for the altar, and sanctify it; and it shall be an altar most holy: whatsoever touches the altar shall be holy.

38 Now this *is that* which you shall offer upon the altar; two lambs of the first year day by day continually.

39 The one lamb you shall offer in the morning; and the other lamb you shall offer at <u>even</u>.   twilight

40 And with the one lamb a tenth deal of flour mingled with the fourth part of an hin of beaten oil; and the fourth part of an hin of wine *for* a drink offering.

41 And the other lamb you shall offer at <u>even</u>, and shall do thereto according to the <u>meat</u> offering of the morning, and according to the drink offering thereof, for a <u>sweet</u> <u>savor</u>, an offering made by fire to the LORD.   grain - soothing aroma

42 *This shall be* a continual burned offering throughout your generations *at* the door of the tabernacle of the congregation before the LORD: where I will meet you, to speak there to you.

43 And there I will meet with the children of Is'ra-el, and *the tabernacle* shall be sanctified by My glory.

44 And I will sanctify the tabernacle of the congregation, and the altar: I will sanctify also both Aar'on and his sons, to minister to Me in the priest's office.

45 And I will dwell among the children of Is'ra-el, and will be their <u>God</u>.   REV. 21:3

46 And they shall know that I *am* the LORD their <u>God</u>, that brought them forth out of the land of E'gypt, that I may dwell among them: I *am* the LORD their <u>God</u>.   Elohim^p.f.

GIO
—
324

CHAPTER 30

AND you shall make an altar to burn incense upon: *of* shittim wood shall you make it.

2 A cubit *shall be* the length thereof, and a cubit the breadth thereof; foursquare shall it be: and two cubits *shall be* the height thereof: the horns thereof *shall be* of the same.

3 And you shall overlay it with pure gold, the top thereof, and the sides thereof round about, and the horns thereof; and you shall make to it a <u>crown</u> of gold round about.   molding

4 And two golden rings shall you make to it under the <u>crown</u> of it, by the two corners thereof, upon the two sides of it shall you make *it*; and they shall be for places for the <u>staves</u> to bear it <u>withal</u>.   poles-with

5 And you shall make the st<u>aves</u> *of* shittim wood, and overlay them with gold.

6 And you shall put it before the veil

that *is* by the ark of the testimony, before the mercy seat that *is* over the testimony, where I will meet with you.

7 And Aar'on shall burn thereon sweet incense every morning: when he dressed the lamps, he shall burn incense upon it.

8 And when Aar'on lights the lamps at <u>even</u>, he shall burn incense upon it, a perpetual incense before the LORD throughout your generations. *twilight*

9 You shall offer no strange incense thereon, nor burned sacrifice, nor <u>meat</u> offering; neither shall you pour drink offering thereon. *meal*

10 And Aar'on shall make an atonement <u>upon</u> the horns of it once in a year with the blood of the sin offering of atonements: once in the year shall he make atonement upon it throughout your generations: it *is* most holy to the LORD. *for*

11 And the LORD spoke to Mo'ses, saying,

12 When you take the sum of the children of Is'ra-el after their number, then shall they give every man a ransom for <u>his soul</u> to the LORD, when you number them; that there be no plague among them, when *you* number them. *himself*

13 This they shall give, every one that passes among them that are numbered, half a shekel after the shekel of the sanctuary: (a shekel *is* twenty gerahs:) an half shekel *shall be* the offering of the LORD.

14 Every one that passes among them that are numbered, from twenty years old and above, shall give an <u>offering</u> to the LORD. *contribution*

15 The rich shall not give more, and the poor shall not give less than half a shekel, when *they* give an offering to the LORD, to make an atonement for <u>your souls</u>. *yourselves*

16 And you shall take the atonement money of the children of Is'ra-el, and shall appoint it for the service of the tabernacle of the congregation; that it may be a <u>memorial</u> to the children of Is'ra-el before the LORD, to make an atonement for your souls. *reminder*

17 And the LORD spoke to Mo'ses, saying,

18 You shall also make a <u>laver</u> *of* brass, and its foot *also of* brass, to wash *with*: and you shall put it between the tabernacle of the congregation and the altar, and you shall put water therein. *tub*

19 For Aar'on and his sons shall wash their hands and their feet thereat:

20 When they go into the tabernacle of the congregation, they shall wash with water, that they die not; or when they come near to the altar to minister, to burn offering made by fire to the LORD:

21 So they shall wash their hands and their feet, that they die not: and it shall be a <u>statute</u> for ever to them, *even* to him and to his <u>seed</u> throughout their generations. *rule - descendants*

22 Moreover the LORD spoke to Mo'ses, saying,

23 Take you also to your principal spices, of pure myrrh five hundred *shekels*, and of sweet cinnamon half so

much, *even* two hundred and fifty *shekels*, and of sweet calamus two hundred and fifty *shekels*,

24 And of cassia five hundred *shekels*, after the shekel of the sanctuary, and of oil olive <u>an hin</u>:

25 And you shall make it an oil of holy ointment, an ointment compound after the art of the <u>apothecary</u>: it shall be an holy anointing oil.   perfumer

26 And you shall anoint the tabernacle of the congregation therewith, and the ark of the testimony,

27 And the table and all its <u>vessels</u>, and the candlestick and its <u>vessels</u>, and the altar of incense,   utensils

28 And the altar of burned offering with all its vessels, and the laver and its foot.

29 And you shall <u>sanctify</u> them, that they may be most holy: whatsoever touches them shall be holy.   consecrate

30 And you shall anoint Aar'on and his sons, and consecrate them, that *they* may minister to Me in the priest's office.

31 And you shall speak to the children of Is'ra-el, saying, This shall be an holy anointing oil to Me throughout your generations.

32 Upon <u>man's flesh</u> shall it not be poured, neither shall you make *any other* like it, after the composition of it: it *is* holy, *and* it shall be holy to you.   anyone's body

33 Whosoever <u>compounds</u> *any* like it, or whosoever puts *any* of it upon a stranger, shall even be <u>cut off</u> from his people.   shall mix - destroyed

34 And the LORD said to Mo'ses, Take to you sweet spices, stacte, and onycha, and galbanum; *these* sweet spices with pure frankincense: of each shall there be a <u>like *weight*</u>:   equal part

35 And you shall make it a perfume, a confection after the art of the apothecary, tempered together, pure *and* holy:

36 And you shall beat *some* of it very small, and put of it before the testimony in the tabernacle of the congregation, where I will meet with you: it shall be to you most holy.

37 And *as for* the perfume which you shall make, you shall not make to yourselves according to the composition thereof: it shall be to you holy for the LORD.

38 Whosoever shall make like to that, to smell thereto, shall even be cut off from his people.

CHAPTER 31

AND the LORD spoke to Mo'ses, saying,

2 See, I have called by name Be-zal'e-el the son of U'ri, the son of Hur, of the tribe of Ju'dah:

3 And I have filled him with the Spirit of God, in wisdom, and in understanding, and in knowledge, and in all manner of workmanship,

4 To devise <u>cunning</u> works, to work in gold, and in silver, and in brass,   artistic

5 And in <u>cutting</u> of stones, to set *them*, and in carving of timber, to work in all manner of workmanship   .engraving

6 And I, behold, I have given with him A-ho'li-ab, the son of A-his'a-mach, of the tribe of Dan: and in the hearts of all that are <u>wise hearted</u> I

have put wisdom, that they may make all that I have commanded you;

good judgment

7 The tabernacle of the congregation, and the ark of the testimony, and the mercy seat that *is* thereupon, and all the furniture of the tabernacle,

8 And the table and its furniture, and the pure candlestick with all its furniture, and the altar of incense,

9 And the altar of burned offering with all its furniture, and the laver and its foot,

10 And the cloths of service, and the holy garments for Aar'on the priest, and the garments of his sons, to minister in the priest's office,

11 And the anointing oil, and sweet incense for the holy *place*: according to all that I have commanded you shall they do.

12 And the LORD spoke to Mo'ses, saying,

M33

13 Speak you also to the children of Is'ra-el, saying, Verily My sabbaths you shall keep: for it *is* a sign between Me and you throughout your generations; that *you* may know that I *am* the LORD that does sanctify you.

170

truly - rest days - observe - set you apart

14 You shall keep the sabbath therefore; for it *is* holy to you: every one that defiles it shall surely be put to death: for whosoever does *any* work therein, that soul shall be cut off from among his people.

profanes - person

15 Six days may work be done; but in the seventh *is* the sabbath of rest, holy to the LORD: whosoever does *any* work in the sabbath day, he shall surely be put to death.

rest

16 Wherefore the children of Is'ra-el shall keep the sabbath, to observe the sabbath throughout their generations, *for* a perpetual covenant.

agreement

17 It *is* a sign between Me and the children of Is'ra-el for ever: for *in* six days the LORD made heaven and earth, and on the seventh day He rested, and was refreshed.

GIA

324

18 And He gave to Mo'ses, when He had made an end of communing with him upon mount Si'nai, two tables of testimony, tables of stone, written with the finger of God.

Elohim[p.f.]

CHAPTER 32

AND when the people saw that Mo'ses delayed to come down out of the mount, the people gathered themselves together to Aar'on, and said to him, Up, make us gods, which shall go before us; for *as for* this Mo'ses, the man that brought us up out of the land of E'gypt, we know not what is become of him.

ACTS 7:40　a god

2 And Aar'on said to them, Break off the golden earrings, which *are* in the ears of your wives, of your sons, and of your daughters, and bring *them* to me.

3 And all the people brake off the golden earrings which *were* in their ears, and brought *them* to Aar'on.

4 And he received *them* at their hand, and fashioned it with a graving tool, after he had made it a molten calf: and they said, These *be* your gods, O Is'ra-el,

which brought you up out of the land of E'gypt.

5 And when Aar'on saw *it*, he built an altar before it; and Aar'on made proclamation, and said, To morrow *is* a feast to the LORD.

6 And they rose up early on the morrow, and offered burned offerings, and brought peace offerings; and the people sat down to eat and to drink, and rose up to play. ACTS 7:41 1 COR. 10:7

7 And the LORD said to Mo'ses, Go, get you down; for your people, which you brought out of the land of E'gypt, have <u>corrupted</u> *themselves*:   done wrong

8 They have turned aside quickly out of the way which I commanded them: they have made them a molten calf, and have worshiped it, and have sacrificed thereto, and said, These *be* your gods, O Is'ra-el, which have brought you up out of the land of E'gypt.

9 And the LORD said to Mo'ses, I have seen this people, and, behold, it *is* a <u>stiffnecked</u> people: obstinate

10 Now therefore let Me alone, that My wrath may <u>wax</u> hot against them, and that I may <u>consume</u> them: and I will make of you a great nation.   grow - destroy

11 And Mo'ses besought the LORD his <u>God</u>, and said, LORD, why does Your wrath <u>wax</u> hot against Your people, which You have brought forth out of the land of E'gypt with great power, and with a mighty hand?   Elohim^{p.f.}

12 Wherefore should the E-gyptians speak, and say, For <u>mischief</u> did He bring them out, to slay them in the mountains, and to consume them from the face of the earth? Turn from Your fierce wrath, and <u>repent</u> of this evil against Your people.   evil intent - grieve

13 Remember A'bra-ham, I'saac, and Is'ra-el, Your servants, to whom You <u>swear</u> by Your Own Self, and said to them, I will multiply your <u>seed</u> as the stars of heaven, and all this land that I have spoken of will I give to your <u>seed</u>, and they shall inherit *it* for ever.   did promise - descendants

14 And the LORD <u>repented</u> of the <u>evil</u> which He thought to do to His people.   grieved - harm

15 And Mo'ses turned, and went down from the mount, and the two tables of the testimony *were* in his hand: the tables *were* written on both their sides; on the one side and on the other *were* they written.

16 And the tables *were* the work of <u>God</u>, and the writing *was* the writing of <u>God</u>, graven upon the tables. Elohim^{p.f.}

17 And when Josh'u-a heard the noise of the people as they shouted, he said to Mo'ses, *There is* a noise of war in the camp.

18 And he said, *It is* not the voice of *them that* shout for mastery, neither *is it* the voice of *them that* cry for being overcome: *but* the noise of *them that* sing do I hear.

19 And it came to pass, as soon as he came near to the camp, that he saw the calf, and the dancing: and Mo'ses' anger <u>waxed</u> hot, and he cast the tables out of his hands, and broke them beneath the mount.   grew

20 And he took the calf which they

had made, and burned *it* in the fire, and ground *it* to powder, and spread *it* upon the water, and made the children of Is'ra-el drink *of it.*

21 And Mo'ses said to Aar'on, What did this people to you, that you have brought so great a sin upon them?

22 And Aar'on said, Let not the anger of my lord <u>wax</u> hot: you know the people, that they *are set* on mischief.   grow

23 For they said to me, Make us gods, which shall go before us: for *as for* this Mo'ses, the man that brought us up out of the land of E'gypt, we know not what is become of him.

24 And I said to them, Whosoever has any gold, let them break *it* off. So they gave *it* me: then I cast it into the fire, and there came out this calf.

25 And when Mo'ses saw that the people *were* naked; (for Aar'on had made them naked to *their* shame among their enemies:)

26 Then Mo'ses stood in the gate of the camp, and said, Who *is* on the LORD's side? *let him come* to me. And all the sons of Le'vi gathered themselves together to him.

27 And he said to them, Thus says the LORD God of Is'ra-el, Put every man his sword by his side, *and* go in and out from gate to gate throughout the camp, and slay every man his brother, and every man his companion, and every man his neighbor.

28 And the children of Le'vi did according to the word of Mo'ses: and there fell of the people that day about three thousand men.

29 For Mo'ses had said, Consecrate yourselves to day to the LORD, even every man upon his son, and upon his brother; that He may bestow upon you a blessing this day.

30 And it came to pass on the morrow, that Mo'ses said to the people, You have sinned a great sin: and now I will go up to the LORD; perhaps I shall make an atonement for your sin.

31 And Mo'ses returned to the LORD, and said, Oh, this people have sinned a great sin, and have made them gods of gold.

32 Yet now, if You will forgive their sin; and if not, blot me, I pray You, out of Your book which You have written.   LUKE 10:20 REV. 3:5

33 And the LORD said to Mo'ses, Whosoever has sinned against Me, him will I blot out of My book.

34 Therefore now go, lead the people to *the place* of which I have spoken to you: behold, My angel shall go before you: nevertheless in the day when I visit I will visit their sin upon them.

35 And the LORD <u>plagued</u> the people, because they made the calf, which Aar'on made.   smote

CHAPTER 33

AND the LORD said to Mo'ses, Depart, *and* go up from here, you and the people which you have brought up out of the land of E'gypt, to the land which I swear to A'bra-ham, to I'-

saac, and to Ja'cob, saying, To your seed will I give it: descendants
2 And I will send an angel before you; and I will drive out the Ca'naan-ite, the Am'or-ite, and the Hit'tite, and the Per'iz-zite, the Hi'vite, and the Jeb'u-site: messenger
3 To a land flowing with milk and honey: for I will not go up in the midst of you; for you *are* a stiffnecked people: less I consume you in the way. ACTS 7:51 obstinate
4 And when the people heard these evil tidings, they mourned: and no man did put on him his ornaments. were sorry
5 For the LORD had said to Mo'ses, Say to the children of Is'ra-el, You *are* a stiffnecked people: I will come up into the midst of you in a moment, and consume you: therefore now put off your ornaments from you, that I may know what to do to you. jewelry
6 And the children of Is'ra-el stripped themselves of their ornaments by the mount Ho'reb.
7 And Mo'ses took the tabernacle, and pitched it outside the camp, afar off from the camp, and called it the Tabernacle of the congregation. And it came to pass, *that* every one which sought the LORD went out to the tabernacle of the congregation, which was outside the camp.
8 And it came to pass, when Mo'ses went out to the tabernacle, *that* all the people rose up, and stood every man *at* his tent door, and looked after Mo'ses, until he was gone into the tabernacle.
9 And it came to pass, as Mo'ses en-

tered into the tabernacle, the cloudy pillar descended, and stood *at* the door of the tabernacle, and *the* LORD talked with Mo'ses.
10 And all the people saw the cloudy pillar stand *at* the tabernacle door: and all the people rose up and worshiped, every man *in* his tent door.
11 And the LORD spoke to Mo'ses face to face, as a man speaks to his friend. And he turned again into the camp: but his servant Josh'u-a, the son of Nun, a young man, departed not out of the tabernacle.
12 And Mo'ses said to the LORD, See, you say to me, Bring up this people: and You have not let me know whom You will send with me. Yet You have said, I know you by name, and you have also found grace in My sight.
13 Now therefore, I pray You, if I have found grace in Your sight, show me now your way, that I may know You, that I may find grace in Your sight: and consider that this nation *is* Your people.
14 And He said, My presence shall go *with you,* and I will give you rest. peace
15 And he said to Him, If your presence go not *with me,* carry us not up from here.
16 For wherein shall it be known here that I and Your people have found grace in Your sight? *is it* not in that You go with us? so shall we be separated, I and Your people, from all the people that *are* upon the face of the earth.
17 And the LORD said to Mo'ses, I will do this thing also that you have

spoken: for you have found grace in My sight, and I know you by name.

18 And he said, I <u>beseech</u> you, show me Your glory. beg

19 And He said, I will make all My goodness pass before you, and I will proclaim the name of the LORD before you; and will be gracious to whom I will be gracious, and will show mercy on whom I will show mercy. ROM. 9:15

20 And He said, You can not see My face: for there shall no man see Me, and live. JOHN 1:18

21 And the LORD said, Behold, *there is* a place by Me, and you shall stand upon a rock:

22 And it shall come to pass, while My glory passes by, that I will put you in a <u>clift</u> of the rock, and will cover you with My hand while I pass by: cleft

23 And I will take away My hand, and you shall see My back parts: but My face shall not be seen.

CHAPTER 34

AND the LORD said to Mo'ses, Hew you two tables of stone like to the first: and I will write upon *these* tables the words that were in the first tables, which you broke. cut out

2 And be ready in the morning, and come up in the morning to mount Si'nai, and present yourself there to Me in the top of the mount.

3 And no man shall come up with you, neither let any man be seen throughout all the mount; neither let the flocks nor herds feed before that mount.

4 And he <u>hewed</u> two tables of stone like to the first; and Mo'ses rose up early in the morning, and went up to mount Si'nai, as the LORD had commanded him, and took in his hand the two tables of stone. cut

5 And the LORD descended in the cloud, and stood with him there, and <u>proclaimed</u> the name of the LORD. made known

6 And the LORD passed by before him, and <u>proclaimed</u>, The <u>LORD</u>, The <u>LORD God</u>, merciful and gracious, longsuffering, and abundant in goodness and truth, Jehovah^{s.f.} - Jehovah^{s.f.} Elohim^{p.f.}

7 Keeping mercy for thousands, forgiving iniquity and transgression and sin, and that will by no means clear *the guilty*; visiting the iniquity of the fathers upon the children, and upon the children's children, to the third and to the fourth *generation*.

8 And Mo'ses made haste, and bowed his head toward the earth, and worshiped.

9 And he said, If now I have found grace in Your sight, O Lord, let my Lord, I pray You, go among us; for it *is* a <u>stiffnecked</u> people; and pardon our iniquity and our sin, and take us for Your inheritance. obstinate

10 And He said, Behold, I make a <u>covenant</u>: before all your people I will do marvels, such as have not been done in all the earth, nor in any nation: and all the people among which you *are* shall see the work of the LORD: for it *is* a <u>terrible</u> thing that I will do with you. agreement - fearful

11 Observe you that which I command you this day: behold, I drive out before you the Am'or-ite, and the Ca'-

naan-ite, and the Hit'tite, and the Per'iz-zite, and the Hi'vite, and the Jeb'u-site.

12 Take heed to yourself, less you make a <u>covenant</u> with the inhabitants of the land where you go, less it be for a <u>snare</u> in the midst of you:

agreement - trap

13 But you shall destroy their altars, break their <u>images</u>, and cut down their groves:

sacred pillars

14 For you shall worship no other god: for the L<small>ORD</small>, whose name *is* Jealous, *is* a jealous <u>God</u>:

Jehovah - El^{s.f.}

15 Less you make a <u>covenant</u> with the inhabitants of the land, and they go <u>a whoring after their gods</u>, and do sacrifice to their gods, and *one* call you, and you eat of his sacrifice;

1 COR. 8:4 loving other gods

16 And thou take of their daughters to your sons, and their daughters go <u>a whoring after their gods</u>, and make your sons go <u>a whoring after their gods</u>.

17 You shall make you no molten gods.

18 The feast of <u>unleavened</u> bread shall you keep. Seven days you shall eat <u>unleavened</u> bread, as I commanded you, in the time of the month A'bib: for in the month A'bib you came out from E'gypt.

i.e., without yeast

19 All that opens the <u>matrix</u> *is* Mine; and every firstling among your cattle, *whether* ox or sheep, *that is male*.

womb

20 But the firstling of an ass you shall redeem with a lamb: and if you redeem *him* not, then shall you break its neck. All the firstborn of your sons you shall redeem. And none shall appear before Me empty.

21 Six days you shall work, but on the seventh day you shall rest: in <u>earing</u> time and in harvest you shall rest.

ploughing

22 And you shall observe the feast of weeks, of the firstfruits of wheat harvest, and the feast of ingathering at the year's end.

23 Thrice in the year shall all your men children appear before the Lord G<small>OD</small>, the God of Is'ra-el.

24 For I will cast out the nations before you, and enlarge your borders: neither shall any man desire your land, when you shall go up to appear before the L<small>ORD</small> your God thrice in the year.

25 You shall not offer the blood of My sacrifice with <u>leaven</u>; neither shall the sacrifice of the feast of the passover be left to the morning.

yeast

26 The first of the firstfruits of your land you shall bring to the house of the L<small>ORD</small> your <u>God</u>. You shall not <u>seethe a kid</u> in its mother's milk.

Elohim^{p.f.} - boil a young goat

27 And the L<small>ORD</small> said to Mo'ses, Write you these words: for after the tenor of these words I have made a <u>covenant</u> with you and with Is'ra-el.

agreement

28 And he was there with the L<small>ORD</small> forty days and forty nights; he did neither eat bread, nor drink water. And he wrote upon the tables the words of the <u>covenant</u>, the ten commandments.

MATT. 4:2

29 And it came to pass, when Mo'ses came down from mount Si'nai with the two tables of testimony in Mo'ses' hand, when he came down from the

mount, that Mo'ses knew not that the skin of his face shone while he talked with Him. 　　　2 COR 3:7

30 And when Aar'on and all the children of Is'ra-el saw Mo'ses, behold, the skin of his face shone; and they were afraid to come near him.

31 And Mo'ses called to them; and Aar'on and all the rulers of the congregation returned to him: and Mo'ses talked with them.

32 And afterward all the children of Is'ra-el came near: and he gave them in commandment all that the LORD had spoken with him in mount Si'nai.

33 And *till* Mo'ses had done speaking with them, he put a veil on his face.

34 But when Mo'ses went in before the LORD to speak with Him, he took the veil off, until he came out. And he came out, and spoke to the children of Is'ra-el *that* which he was commanded.

35 And the children of Is'ra-el saw the face of Mo'ses, that the skin of Mo'ses' face shone: and Mo'ses put the veil upon his face again, until he went in to speak with Him.

CHAPTER 35

AND Mo'ses gathered all the congregation of the children of Is'ra-el together, and said to them, These *are* the words which the LORD has commanded, that *you* should do them.

2 Six days shall work be done, but on the seventh day there shall be to you an holy day, a sabbath of rest to the LORD: whosoever does work therein shall be put to death. 　　day

3 You shall kindle no fire throughout your habitations upon the sabbath day. 　　rest

4 And Mo'ses spoke to all the congregation of the children of Is'ra-el, saying, This *is* the thing which the LORD commanded, saying,

5 Take you from among you an offering to the LORD: whosoever *is* of a willing heart, let him bring it, an offering of the LORD; gold, and silver, and brass,

6 And blue, and purple, and scarlet, and fine linen, and goats' *hair*,

7 And rams' skins dyed red, and badgers' skins, and shittim wood,

8 And oil for the light, and spices for anointing oil, and for the sweet incense,

9 And onyx stones, and stones to be set for the ephod, and for the breastplate.

10 And every wise hearted among you shall come, and make all that the LORD has commanded; 　　skillful man

11 The tabernacle, its tent, and its covering, its taches, and its boards, its bars, its pillars, and its sockets, 　　hooks

12 The ark, and the staves thereof, *with* the mercy seat, and the veil of the covering, 　　poles

13 The table, and its staves, and all its vessels, and the showbread,

14 The candlestick also for the light, and its furniture, and its lamps, with the oil for the light, 　　utensils

15 And the incense altar, and its staves, and the anointing oil, and the sweet incense, and the hanging for the door at the entering in of the tabernacle,

16 The altar of burned offering, with its brazen grate, its <u>staves</u>, and all its vessels, the laver and its <u>foot</u>, poles - stand
17 The hangings of the court, its pillars, and their sockets, and the hanging for the door of the court,
18 The <u>pins</u> of the tabernacle, and the <u>pins</u> of the court, and their cords, pegs
19 The cloths of service, to do service in the holy *place*, the holy garments for Aar'on the priest, and the garments of his sons, to minister in the priest's office.
20 And all the congregation of the children of Is'ra-el departed from the presence of Mo'ses.
21 And they came, every one whose heart stirred him up, and every one whom his spirit made willing, *and* they brought the LORD's offering to the work of the tabernacle of the congregation, and for all his service, and for the holy garments.
22 And they came, both men and women, as many as were willing hearted, *and* brought bracelets, and earrings, and rings, and tablets, all jewels of gold: and every man that offered *offered* an offering of gold to the LORD.
23 And every man, with whom was found blue, and purple, and scarlet, and fine linen, and goats' *hair*, and red skins of rams, and badgers' skins, brought *them*.
24 Every one that did offer an offering of silver and brass brought the LORD's offering: and every man, with whom was found shittim wood for any work of the service, brought *it*.
25 And all the women that were <u>wise</u> hearted did spin with their hands, and brought that which they had spun, *both* of blue, and of purple, *and* of scarlet, and of fine linen. skilled
26 And all the women whose heart stirred them up in wisdom spun goats' *hair*.
27 And the rulers brought onyx stones, and stones to be set, for the <u>ephod</u>, and for the breastplate; priestly garment
28 And spice, and oil for the light, and for the anointing oil, and for the sweet incense.
29 The children of Is'ra-el brought a <u>willing</u> offering to the LORD, every man and woman, whose heart made them willing to bring for all manner of work, which the LORD had commanded to be made by the hand of Mo'ses. free will
30 And Mo'ses said to the children of Is'ra-el, See, the LORD has called by name Be-zal'e-el the son of U'ri, the son of Hur, of the tribe of Ju'dah;
31 And He has filled him with the Spirit of God, in wisdom, in understanding, and in knowledge, and in all manner of workmanship;
32 And to devise <u>curious</u> works, to work in gold, and in silver, and in brass, artistic
33 And in the cutting of stones, to set *them*, and in carving of wood, to make any manner of <u>cunning</u> work. inventive
34 And He has put in his heart that he may teach, *both* he, and A-ho'li-ab, the son of A-his'a-mach, of the tribe of Dan.
35 Them has He filled with wisdom of heart, to work all manner of work, of

the engraver, and of the cunning workman, and of the embroiderer, in blue, and in purple, in scarlet, and in fine linen, and of the weaver, *even* of them that do any work, and of those that devise <u>cunning</u> work.   skillful

CHAPTER 36

THEN wrought Be-zal'e-el and A-ho'li-ab, and every <u>wise hearted</u> man, in whom the LORD put wisdom and understanding to know how to work all manner of work for the service of the sanctuary, according to all that the LORD had commanded.   skillful
2 And Mo'ses called Be-zal'e-el and A-ho'li-ab, and every <u>wise hearted</u> man, in whose heart the LORD had put wisdom, *even* every one whose heart <u>stirred</u> him up to come to the work to do it: inwardly moved
3 And they received of Mo'ses all the offering, which the children of Is'ra-el had brought for the work of the service of the sanctuary, to make it *with*. And they brought yet to him free offerings every morning.
4 And all the wise men, that wrought all the work of the sanctuary, came every man from his work which they made;
5 And they spoke to Mo'ses, saying, The people bring much more than enough for the service of the work, which the LORD commanded to make.
6 And Mo'ses gave commandment, and they caused it to be proclaimed throughout the camp, saying, Let neither man nor woman make any more work for the offering of the sanctuary.

So the people were restrained from bringing.
7 For the stuff they had was sufficient for all the work to make it, and too much.
8 And every <u>wise hearted</u> man among them that wrought the work of the tabernacle made ten curtains *of* fine twined linen, and blue, and purple, and scarlet: *with* cherubims of <u>cunning</u> work made he them.   skillful - skillful
9 The length of one curtain *was* twenty and eight cubits, and the breadth of one curtain four cubits: the curtains *were* all of one size.
10 And he coupled the five curtains one to another: and *the other* five curtains he coupled one to another.
11 And he made loops of blue on the edge of one curtain from the selvedge in the coupling: likewise he made in the uttermost side of *another* curtain, in the coupling of the second.
12 Fifty loops made he in one curtain, and fifty loops made he in the edge of the curtain which *was* in the coupling of the second: the loops held one *curtain* to another.
13 And he made fifty <u>taches</u> of gold, and coupled the curtains one to another with the <u>taches</u>: so it became one tabernacle.   clasps
14 And he made curtains *of* goats' *hair* for the tent over the tabernacle: eleven curtains he made them.
15 The length of one curtain *was* thirty cubits, and four cubits *was* the breadth of one curtain: the eleven curtains *were* of one size.
16 And he coupled five curtains by

themselves, and six curtains by themselves.

17 And he made fifty loops upon the uttermost edge of the curtain in the <u>coupling</u>, and fifty loops made he upon the edge of the curtain which couples the second.   first set

18 And he made fifty <u>taches</u> *of* brass to couple the tent together, that it might be one.   clasps

19 And he made a covering for the tent *of* rams' skins dyed red, and a covering *of* badgers' skins above *that*.

20 And he made boards for the tabernacle *of* shittim wood, standing up.

21 The length of a board *was* ten cubits, and the breadth of a board one cubit and a half.

22 One board had two <u>tenons</u>, equally distant one from another: thus did he make for all the boards of the tabernacle.   pins

23 And he made boards for the tabernacle; twenty boards for the south side southward:

24 And forty sockets of silver he made under the twenty boards; two sockets under one board for his two <u>tenons</u>, and two sockets under another board for his two <u>tenons</u>.

25 And for the other side of the tabernacle, *which is* toward the north corner, he made twenty boards,

26 And their forty sockets of silver; two sockets under one board, and two sockets under another board.

27 And for the sides of the tabernacle westward he made six boards.

28 And two boards made he for the corners of the tabernacle in the two sides.

29 And they were <u>coupled</u> beneath, and <u>coupled</u> together at the <u>head</u> thereof, to one ring: thus he did to both of them in both the corners.   joined - top

30 And there were eight boards; and their sockets *were* sixteen sockets of silver, under every board two sockets.

31 And he made bars of shittim wood; five for the boards of the one side of the tabernacle,

32 And five bars for the boards of the other side of the tabernacle, and five bars for the boards of the tabernacle for the sides westward.

33 And he made the middle bar to <u>shoot</u> through the boards from the one end to the other.   pass

34 And he overlaid the boards with gold, and made their rings *of* gold *to be* places for the bars, and overlaid the bars with gold.

35 And he made a veil *of* blue, and purple, and scarlet, and fine twined linen: *with* cherubims made he it of cunning work.

36 And he made thereto four pillars *of* shittim *wood*, and overlaid them with gold: their hooks *were of* gold; and he cast for them four sockets of silver.

37 And he made an hanging for the tabernacle door *of* blue, and purple, and scarlet, and fine twined linen, of needlework;

38 And the five pillars of it with their hooks: and he overlaid their <u>chapiters</u> and their fillets with gold: but their five sockets *were of* brass.   tops

CHAPTER 37

AND Be-zal'e-el made the ark *of* shittim wood: two cubits and a half *was* the length of it, and a cubit and a half the breadth of it, and a cubit and a half the height of it:

2 And he overlaid it with pure gold inside and outside, and made a <u>crown</u> of gold to it round about.   moulding

3 And he cast for it four rings of gold, *to be set* by the four corners of it; even two rings upon the one side of it, and two rings upon the other side of it.

4 And he made <u>staves</u> *of* shittim wood, and overlaid them with gold.   poles

5 And he put the <u>staves</u> into the rings by the sides of the ark, to bear the ark.

6 And he made the mercy seat *of* pure gold: two cubits and a half *was* the length thereof, and one cubit and a half the breadth thereof.

7 And he made two cherubims *of* gold, beaten out of one piece made he them, on the two ends of the mercy seat;

8 One cherub on the end on this side, and another cherub on the *other* end on that side: out of the mercy seat made he the cherubims on the two ends thereof.

9 And the cherubims spread out *their* wings on high, *and* covered with their wings over the mercy seat, with their faces one to another; *even* to the mercy seatward were the faces of the cherubims.

10 And he made the table *of* shittim wood: two cubits *was* the length thereof, and a cubit the breadth thereof, and a cubit and a half the height thereof:

11 And he overlaid it with pure gold, and made thereto a <u>crown</u> of gold round about.   moulding

12 Also he made thereto a <u>border of an handbreadth</u> round about; and made a <u>crown</u> of gold for the <u>border</u> thereof round about.   3 inch rim

13 And he cast for it four rings of gold, and put the rings upon the four corners that *were* in the four feet thereof.

14 Opposite the border were the rings, the places for the <u>staves</u> to bear the table.   poles

15 And he made the <u>staves</u> *of* shittim wood, and overlaid them with gold, to bear the table.

16 And he made the vessels which *were* upon the table, its dishes, and its spoons, and its bowls, and its covers to cover <u>withal</u>, *of* pure gold.   everything

17 And he made the candlestick *of* pure gold: *of* beaten work made he the candlestick; its shaft, and its branch, its bowls, its knobs, and its flowers, were of the same:

18 And six branches going out of the sides thereof; three branches of the candlestick out of the one side thereof, and three branches of the candlestick out of the other side thereof:

19 Three bowls made after the fashion of <u>almonds</u> in one branch, a knob and a flower; and three bowls made like <u>almonds</u> in <u>another</u> branch, a knob and a flower: so throughout the six branches going out of the candlestick.   blossoms - one

20 And in the candlestick *were* four bowls made like almonds, its knobs, and its flowers:

21 And a knob under two branches of the same, and a knob under two branches of the same, and a knob under two branches of the same, according to the six branches going out of it.

22 Their knobs and their branches were of the same: all of it *was* one beaten work *of* pure gold.

23 And he made its seven lamps, and its snuffers, and its snuffdishes, *of* pure gold.

24 *Of* a talent of pure gold made he it, and all the vessels thereof.

25 And he made the incense altar *of* shittim wood: the length of it *was* a cubit, and the breadth of it a cubit; *it was* foursquare; and two cubits *was* the height of it; the horns thereof were of the same.

26 And he overlaid it with pure gold, *both* the top of it, and the sides thereof round about, and the horns of it: also he made to it a crown of gold round about.

27 And he made two rings of gold for it under the <u>crown</u> thereof, by the two corners of it, upon the two sides thereof, to be places for the <u>staves</u> to bear it with.   moulding - poles

28 And he made the <u>staves</u> *of* shittim wood, and overlaid them with gold.

29 And he made the holy anointing oil, and the pure incense of sweet spices, according to the work of the apothecary.

CHAPTER 38

AND he made the altar of burned offering *of* shittim wood: five cubits *was* the length thereof, and five cubits the breadth thereof; *it was* foursquare; and three cubits the height thereof.

2 And he made the horns thereof on the four corners of it; the horns thereof were of the same: and he overlaid it with brass.

3 And he made all the vessels of the altar, the pots, and the shovels, and the basins, *and* the fleshhooks, and the firepans: all the vessels thereof made he *of* brass.

4 And he made for the altar a brazen grate of network under the <u>compass</u> thereof beneath to the midst of it.   ledge

5 And he cast four rings for the four ends of the grate of brass, *to be* places for the <u>staves</u>.   poles

6 And he made the <u>staves</u> *of* shittim wood, and overlaid them with brass.

7 And he put the <u>staves</u> into the rings on the sides of the altar, to bear it with; he made the altar hollow with boards.

8 And he made the laver *of* brass, and the foot of it *of* brass, of the <u>looking glasses</u> of *the women* assembling, which assembled *at* the door of the tabernacle of the congregation.   mirrors

9 And he made the court: on the south side southward the hangings of the court *were of* fine twined linen, an hundred cubits:

10 Their pillars *were* twenty, and their brazen sockets twenty; the hooks of the pillars and their <u>fillets</u> *were of* silver.   bands

11 And for the north side *the hangings were* an hundred cubits, their pillars *were* twenty, and their sockets of brass twenty; the hooks of the pillars and their <u>fillets</u> *of* silver.   bands

12 And for the west side *were* hangings of fifty cubits, their pillars ten, and their sockets ten; the hooks of the pillars and their <u>fillets</u> *of* silver.

13 And for the east side eastward fifty cubits.

14 The hangings of the one side *of the gate were* fifteen cubits; their pillars three, and their sockets three.

15 And for the other side of the court gate, on this hand and that hand, *were* hangings of fifteen cubits; their pillars three, and their sockets three.

16 All the hangings of the court round about *were* of fine twined linen.

17 And the sockets for the pillars *were of* brass; the hooks of the pillars and their <u>fillets</u> *of* silver; and the overlaying of their <u>chapiters</u> *of* silver; and all the pillars of the court *were* <u>filleted</u> with silver.   bands - tops

18 And the hanging for the gate of the court *was* needlework, *of* blue, and purple, and scarlet, and fine twined linen: and twenty cubits *was* the length, and the height in the breadth *was* five cubits, answerable to the hangings of the court.

19 And their pillars *were* four, and their sockets *of* brass four; their hooks *of* silver, and the overlaying of their <u>chapiters</u> and their <u>fillets</u> *of* silver.

20 And all the pins of the tabernacle, and of the court round about, *were of* brass.

21 This is the sum of the tabernacle, *even* of the tabernacle of testimony, as it was counted, according to the commandment of Mo'ses, *for* the service of the Le'vites, by the hand of Ith'a-mar, son to Aar'on the priest.

22 And Be-zal'e-el the son of U'ri, the son of Hur, of the tribe of Ju'dah, made all that the LORD commanded Mo'ses.

23 And with him *was* A-ho'li-ab, son of A-his'a-mach, of the tribe of Dan, an <u>engraver</u>, and a <u>cunning</u> workman, and an embroiderer in blue, and in purple, and in scarlet, and fine linen.   craftsman - skillful

24 All the gold that was occupied for the work in all the work of the holy *place*, even the gold of the offering, was twenty and nine talents, and seven hundred and thirty shekels, after the shekel of the sanctuary.

25 And the silver of them that were numbered of the congregation *was* an hundred talents, and a thousand seven hundred and threescore and fifteen shekels, after the shekel of the sanctuary:

26 A bekah for every man, *that is*, half a shekel, after the shekel of the sanctuary, for every one that went to be numbered, from twenty years old and upward, for six hundred thousand and three thousand and five hundred and fifty *men*.

27 And of the hundred talents of silver were cast the sockets of the sanctuary, and the sockets of the veil; an hundred sockets of the hundred talents, a talent for a socket.

28 And of the thousand seven hun-

dred seventy and five *shekels* he made hooks for the pillars, and overlaid their chapiters, and filleted them. _{tops - banded}

29 And the brass of the offering *was* seventy talents, and two thousand and four hundred shekels.

30 And therewith he made the sockets to the door of the tabernacle of the congregation, and the brazen altar, and the brazen grate for it, and all the vessels of the altar,

31 And the sockets of the court round about, and the sockets of the court gate, and all the pins of the tabernacle, and all the pins of the court round about.

CHAPTER 39

AND of the blue, and purple, and scarlet, they made cloths of service, to do service in the holy *place*, and made the holy garments for Aar'on; as the LORD commanded Mo'ses.

2 And he made the ephod *of* gold, blue, and purple, and scarlet, and fine twined linen. _{priestly garment}

3 And they did beat the gold into thin plates, and cut *it into* wires, to work *it* in the blue, and in the purple, and in the scarlet, and in the fine linen, *with* cunning work. _{threads - skillful}

4 They made shoulderpieces for it, to couple *it* together: by the two edges was it coupled together.

5 And the curious girdle of his ephod, that *was* upon it, *was* of the same, according to the work thereof; *of* gold, blue, and purple, and scarlet, and fine twined linen; as the LORD commanded Mo'ses. _{skillfully woven band - priestly garment}

6 And they wrought onyx stones inclosed in ouches of gold, graven, as signets are graven, with the names of the children of Is'ra-el. _{settings - seals}

7 And he put them on the shoulders of the ephod, *that they should be* stones for a memorial to the children of Is'ra-el; as the LORD commanded Mo'ses. _{priestly garment}

8 And he made the breastplate *of* cunning work, like the work of the ephod; *of* gold, blue, and purple, and scarlet, and fine twined linen. _{skillful}

9 It was foursquare; they made the breastplate double: a span *was* the length thereof, and a span the breadth thereof, *being* doubled. _{9 inches}

10 And they set in it four rows of stones: *the first* row *was* a sardius, a topaz, and a carbuncle: this *was* the first row. _{ruby}

11 And the second row, an emerald, a sapphire, and a diamond.

12 And the third row, a ligure, an agate, and an amethyst. _{jacinth}

13 And the fourth row, a beryl, an onyx, and a jasper: *they were* enclosed in ouches of gold in their enclosings. _{settings}

14 And the stones *were* according to the names of the children of Is'ra-el, twelve, according to their names, *like* the engravings of a signet, every one with his name, according to the twelve tribes. _{seal}

15 And they made upon the breastplate chains at the ends, *of* wreathen work *of* pure gold. _{chains like cords - twisted}

16 And they made two ouches *of* gold, and two gold rings; and put the two rings in the two ends of the breastplate.

17 And they put the two <u>wreathen</u> chains of gold in the two rings on the ends of the breastplate. _{twisted}

18 And the two ends of the two <u>wreathen</u> chains they fastened in the two <u>ouches</u>, and put them on the shoulderpieces of the <u>ephod</u>, before it. _{settings - priestly garment}

19 And they made two rings of gold, and put *them* on the two ends of the breastplate, upon the border of it, which *was* on the side of the <u>ephod</u> inward.

20 And they made two *other* golden rings, and put them on the two sides of the <u>ephod</u> underneath, toward the forepart of it, opposite the *other* coupling thereof, above the <u>curious girdle</u> of the <u>ephod</u>. _{woven band - priestly garment}

21 And they did bind the breastplate by its rings to the rings of the <u>ephod</u> with a lace of blue, that it might be above the <u>curious girdle</u> of the <u>ephod</u>, and that the breastplate might not be loosed from the <u>ephod</u>; as the LORD commanded Mo'ses.

22 And he made the robe of the <u>ephod</u> *of* woven work, all *of* blue.

23 And *there was* an hole in the midst of the robe, as the hole of an <u>habergeon</u>, *with* a band round about the hole, that it should not rend. _{coat of mail}

24 And they made upon the hems of the robe pomegranates *of* blue, and purple, and scarlet, *and* twined *linen*.

25 And they made bells *of* pure gold, and put the bells between the pomegranates upon the hem of the robe, round about between the pomegranates;

26 A bell and a pomegranate, a bell and a pomegranate, round about the hem of the robe to <u>minister</u> *in*; as the LORD commanded Mo'ses. _{serve}

27 And they made coats *of* fine linen *of* woven work for Aar'on, and for his sons,

28 And a <u>mitre</u> *of* fine linen, and goodly bonnets *of* fine linen, and linen breeches *of* fine twined linen, _{turban}

29 And a girdle *of* fine twined linen, and blue, and purple, and scarlet, *of* needlework; as the LORD commanded Mo'ses.

30 And they made the plate of the holy crown *of* pure gold, and wrote upon it a writing, *like to* the engravings of a <u>signet</u>, **HOLINESS TO THE LORD**. _{seal}

31 And they tied to it a lace of blue, to fasten *it* on high upon the <u>mitre</u>; as the LORD commanded Mo'ses. _{turban}

32 Thus was all the work of the tabernacle of the tent of the congregation finished: and the children of Is'rael did according to all that the LORD commanded Mo'ses, so did they.

33 And they brought the tabernacle to Mo'ses, the tent, and all its furniture, its <u>taches</u>, its boards, its bars, and its pillars, and its sockets, _{clasps}

34 And the covering of rams' skins dyed red, and the covering of badgers' skins, and the veil of the <u>covering</u>, _{screen}

35 The ark of the testimony, and the <u>staves</u> thereof, and the mercy seat, _{poles}

36 The table, *and* all the vessels thereof, and the <u>showbread</u>, _{bread of the Presence}

37 The pure candlestick, *with* the lamps thereof, *even with* the lamps to be set in order, and all the vessels thereof, and the oil for light,

38 And the golden altar, and the anointing oil, and the <u>sweet incense</u>, and the hanging for the tabernacle door, fragrant spices

39 The brazen altar, and its grate of brass, its <u>staves</u>, and all its vessels, the laver and its <u>foot</u>, poles - stand

40 The hangings of the court, its pillars, and its sockets, and the hanging for the court gate, its cords, and its pins, and all the vessels of the service of the tabernacle, for the tent of the congregation,

41 The cloths of service to do service in the holy *place*, and the holy garments for Aar'on the priest, and his sons' garments, to <u>minister</u> in the priest's office. serve

42 According to all that the LORD commanded Mo'ses, so the children of Is'ra-el made all the work.

43 And Mo'ses did look upon all the work, and, behold, they had done it as the LORD had commanded, even so had they done it: and Mo'ses blessed them.

CHAPTER 40

A ND the LORD spoke to Mo'ses, saying,

2 On the first day of the first month shall you set up the tabernacle of the tent of the congregation.

3 And you shall put therein the <u>ark of the testimony</u>, and <u>cover</u> the ark with the veil. tables of the law - screen

4 And you shall bring in the table, and set in order the things that are to be set in order upon it; and you shall bring in the candlestick, and light the lamps thereof.

5 And you shall set the altar of gold for the incense before the ark of the testimony, and put the <u>hanging</u> of the door to the tabernacle. veil

6 And you shall set the altar of the burned offering before the door of the tabernacle of the tent of the congregation.

7 And you shall set the laver between the tent of the congregation and the altar, and shall put water therein.

8 And you shall set up the court round about, and hang up the <u>hanging</u> at the court gate. veil

9 And you shall take the anointing oil, and anoint the tabernacle, and all that *is* therein, and shall hallow it, and all the vessels thereof: and it shall be holy.

10 And you shall anoint the altar of the burned offering, and all its vessels, and <u>sanctify</u> the altar: and it shall be an altar <u>most holy</u>. consecrate - only for God

11 And you shall anoint the laver and its <u>foot</u>, and sanctify it. stand

12 And you shall bring Aar'on and his sons to the door of the tabernacle of the congregation, and wash them with water.

13 And you shall put upon Aar'on the holy garments, and anoint him, and <u>sanctify</u> him; that he may minister to Me in the priest's office.

14 And you shall bring his sons, and clothe them with coats:

15 And you shall anoint them, as

you did anoint their father, that they may minister to Me in the priest's office: for their anointing shall surely be an everlasting priesthood throughout their generations.

16 Thus did Mo'ses: according to all that the LORD commanded him, so did he.

17 And it came to pass in the first month in the second year, on the first *day* of the month, *that* the tabernacle was reared up.

18 And Mo'ses reared up the tabernacle, and fastened its sockets, and set up the boards thereof, and put in the bars thereof, and reared up its pillars.

19 And he spread abroad the tent over the tabernacle, and put the covering of the tent above upon it; as the LORD commanded Mo'ses.

20 And he took and put the testimony into the ark, and set the <u>staves</u> on the ark, and put the mercy seat above upon the ark: poles

21 And he brought the ark into the tabernacle, and set up the veil of the covering, and covered the ark of the testimony; as the LORD commanded Mo'ses.

22 And he put the table in the tent of the congregation, upon the side of the tabernacle northward, outside the veil.

23 And he set the bread in order upon it before the LORD; as the LORD had commanded Mo'ses.

24 And he put the candlestick in the tent of the congregation, opposite the table, on the side of the tabernacle southward.

25 And he lighted the lamps before the LORD; as the LORD commanded Mo'ses.

26 And he put the golden altar in the tent of the congregation before the veil:

27 And he burned sweet incense thereon; as the LORD commanded Mo'ses.

28 And he set up the hanging *at* the door of the tabernacle.

29 And he put the altar of burnt offering *by* the door of the tabernacle of the tent of the congregation, and offered upon it the burned offering and the meat offering; as the LORD commanded Mo'ses.

30 And he set the laver between the tent of the congregation and the altar, and put water there, to wash *with*.

31 And Mo'ses and Aar'on and his sons washed their hands and their feet thereat:

32 When they went into the tent of the congregation, and when they came near to the altar, they washed; as the LORD commanded Mo'ses.

33 And he reared up the court round about the tabernacle and the altar, and set up the hanging of the court gate. So Mo'ses finished the work.

34 Then a cloud covered the tent of the congregation, and the glory of the LORD filled the tabernacle.

35 And Mo'ses was not able to enter into the tent of the congregation, because the cloud abode thereon, and the glory of the LORD filled the tabernacle.

36 And when the cloud was taken up from over the tabernacle, the children

of Is'ra-el went onward in all their journeys:

37 But if the cloud were not taken up, then they journeyed not till the day that it was taken up.

38 For the cloud of the LORD *was* upon the tabernacle by day, and fire was on it by night, in the sight of all the house of Is'ra-el, throughout all their journeys.

LEVITICUS

OUTLINE

SURVEY

As indicated by its name "Leviticus," this third book of Moses stresses the function of Israel's priests, those members of the tribe of Levi whom God chose for service at His sanctuary (Dt 10.8). Many Christians accordingly think of Leviticus as a kind of technical manual for directing ancient priests in the details of ceremonies that are no longer observed by God's people; as a result Leviticus is today the least appreciated portion of the Pentateuch. Actually, however, its message was originally directed to all believers (Lv 1.2), and its truths are still of primary significance for God's people. For Leviticus constitutes the first detailed revelation of the living theme of the Great Book as a whole, namely, of the way by which God restores lost men to himself. Both the redemptive activity of God and the response of appropriation due from man are summed up in the key verse,

"Ye shall be holy unto me: for I the Lord am holy, and have severed you from other people, that ye should be mine" (20.26).

In order to accomplish salvation and to restore man to his Maker, a means of access to God must be provided. The first half of Leviticus (chs. 1-16) thus presents a series of religious actions that picture the way by which God redeems the lost, separating them from their sin and its consequences. The various sacrifices (chs. 1-7) were anticipations of the death of Christ on Calvary, where the Sinless One suffered the wrath of God in our place, that we might be ransomed from our guilt (2 Co 5.21; Mk 10.45). The Levitical priests (chs. 8-10) then foreshadowed Christ's faithful service in making reconciliation for the sins of the people (He 2.17). The laws of cleanness (chs. 11-15) were perpetual reminders of the repentance and separation from impurity that must characterize the redeemed (Lk 13.5); while the climactic day of atonement service (Lv 16) proclaimed God's forgiveness to those who should humble themselves in faithful commitment to the Christ, who would yet provide access to heaven itself (He 9.24).

But salvation is not only a separation *from* the wrong; it involves a positive union with what is right. Thus the second half of Leviticus (chs. 17-27) presents a series of practical standards to which men are to be conformed in holy living. These include expressions of devotion in matters of ceremony (ch. 17) and worship (chs. 23-25), but they center in matters of daily conduct (chs. 18-22). Christ himself summed up the divine law (Mt 22.37-40) by speaking of a wholehearted love for God, and by quoting from this section of Leviticus, "Thou shalt love thy neighbor as thyself" (19.18).

In its form, Leviticus exists primarily as legislation spoken by God: "And the Lord called unto Moses . . . saying, Speak unto the children of Israel, and say unto them . . ." (1.1,2). The two historical narratives (chs. 8-10 and 24.10-23) serve as a background for legislative matters; and the only other variation in form, Moses' concluding sermon of exhortation (ch. 26), is yet followed by an appendix of laws regulating such matters as are not in themselves obligatory (ch. 27).

AUTHOR

At over 50 points in its 27 chapters, Leviticus claims itself to be the God-directed words of Moses. The New Testament, too, introduces a quotation from the book by saying, "Moses writeth that . . ." (Ro 10.5, ASV). Critics who relegate Leviticus to a millennium after Moses do so at the expense of the integrity of the Biblical evidence. Scripture describes Leviticus as granted to Israel soon after their adoption as God's covenant people (Ex 19.5). They had been given the basic moral law, the Decalogue (Ex 20), and God's presence had come to dwell in the newly constructed tabernacle (Ex 29.43; 40.34). Then came Leviticus, even as God had promised (Ex 25.22), as a guide to life and worship before Him. Its legislation and events span but a few weeks in actual time, from Moses' erection of the tabernacle (Ex 20.17) to Israel's departure from Mount Sinai less than two months later (Nu 10.11), in May of 1445 B.C., as dated by most evangelical scholars.

J.B.P.

THE THIRD BOOK OF MOSES COMMONLY CALLED

LEVITICUS

"Pertaining to the Levites"
Holy Offerings & Days

CHAPTER 1

AND the LORD called to Mo'ses, and spoke to him out of the tabernacle of the congregation, saying, El s.f.

2 Speak to the children of Is'ra-el, and say to them, If any man of you bring an offering to the LORD, you shall bring your offering of the cattle, *even* of the herd, and of the flock.

3 If his offering *be* a burned sacrifice of the herd, let him offer a male without blemish: he shall offer it of his own voluntary will at the door of the tabernacle of the congregation before the LORD. EPH. 5:27

4 And he shall put his hand upon the head of the burned offering; and it shall be accepted for him to make atonement for him.

5 And he shall kill the bullock before the LORD: and the priests, Aar'on's sons, shall bring the blood, and sprinkle the blood round about upon the altar that *is by* the door of the tabernacle of the congregation. Jehovah s.f.

6 And he shall <u>flay</u> the burnt offering, and cut it into its pieces . skin

7 And the sons of Aar'on the priest shall put fire upon the altar, and lay the wood in order upon the fire:

8 And the priests, Aar'on's sons, shall lay the parts, the head, and the fat, in order upon the wood that *is* on the fire which is upon the altar:

9 But its <u>inwards</u> and its legs shall he wash in water: and the priest shall burn all on the altar, *to be* a burned sacrifice, an offering made by fire, of a <u>sweet savor</u> to the LORD. entrails - soothing aroma

10 And if his offering *be* of the flocks, *namely*, of the sheep, or of the goats, for a burned sacrifice; he shall bring it a male without blemish.

11 And he shall kill it on the side of the altar northward before the LORD: and the priests, Aar'on's sons, shall sprinkle its blood round about upon the altar. Jehovah s.f.

12 And he shall cut it into its pieces, with its head and its fat: and the priest shall lay them in order on the wood that *is* on the fire which *is* upon the altar:

13 But he shall wash the inwards and the legs with water: and the priest shall bring *it* all, and burn *it* upon the altar: it *is* a burned sacrifice, an offering made by fire, of a sweet savor to the LORD.

14 And if the burned sacrifice for his offering to the LORD *be* of fowls, then he shall bring his offering of turtledoves, or of young pigeons.

15 And the priest shall bring it to the altar, and wring off its head, and burn *it* on the altar; and the blood thereof shall be wrung out at the side of the altar:

16 And he shall pluck away its <u>crop</u> with its feathers, and cast it beside the

altar on the east part, by the place of the ashes: gullet

17 And he shall <u>cleave</u> it with the wings thereof, *but* shall not divide *it* <u>asunder</u>: and the priest shall burn it upon the altar, upon the wood that *is* upon the fire: it *is* a burnt sacrifice, an offering made by fire, of a sweet savor to the L<small>ORD</small>.   tear - in two - El^{s.f.}

CHAPTER 2

A<small>ND</small> when any will offer a <u>meat</u> offering to the L<small>ORD</small>, his offering shall be *of* fine flour; and he shall pour oil upon it, and put frankincense thereon: grain - Jehovah^{s.f.}

2 And he shall bring it to Aar'on's sons the priests: and he shall take thereout his handful of the flour thereof, and of the oil thereof, with all the frankincense thereof; and the priest shall burn the <u>memorial</u> of it upon the altar, *to be* an offering made by fire, of a sweet savor to the L<small>ORD</small>:   token part

3 And the remnant of the meat offering *shall be* Aar'on's and his sons': *it is* a thing most <u>holy</u> of the offerings of the L<small>ORD</small> made by fire.   set aside

4 And if you bring an <u>oblation</u> of a meat offering baken in the oven, it *shall be* <u>unleavened</u> cakes of fine flour mingled with oil, or <u>unleavened</u> wafers <u>anointed</u> with oil.   offering - without yeast - spread

5 And if your <u>oblation</u> *be* a meat offering *baken* in a pan, it shall be *of* fine flour <u>unleavened</u>, mingled with oil.

6 You shall part it in pieces, and pour oil thereon: it *is* a <u>meat</u> offering.   grain

7 And if your <u>oblation</u> *be* a <u>meat</u> offering *baken* in the fryingpan, it shall be made *of* fine flour with oil.   offering - grain

8 And you shall bring the meat offering that is made of these things to the L<small>ORD</small>: and when it is presented to the priest, he shall bring it to the altar.

9 And the priest shall take from the <u>meat</u> offering a <u>memorial</u> thereof, and shall burn *it* upon the altar: *it is* an offering made by fire, of a sweet savor to the L<small>ORD</small>.   grain - token part

10 And that which is left of the <u>meat</u> offering *shall be* Aar'on's and his sons': *it is* a thing most holy of the offerings of the L<small>ORD</small> made by fire.   Jehovah^{s.f.}

11 No <u>meat</u> offering, which you shall bring to the L<small>ORD</small>, shall be made with <u>leaven</u>: for you shall burn no <u>leaven</u>, nor any honey, in any offering of the L<small>ORD</small> made by fire.   yeast

12 As for the <u>oblation</u> of the firstfruits, you shall offer them to the L<small>ORD</small>: but they shall not be burned on the altar for a sweet savor.   offering

13 And every <u>oblation</u> of your <u>meat</u> offering shall you season with salt; neither shall you allow the <u>salt</u> of the <u>covenant</u> of your <u>God</u> to be lacking from your meat offering: with all your offerings you shall offer salt.   preservation - agreement - Elohim^{p.f.}

14 And if you offer a <u>meat</u> offering of your firstfruits to the L<small>ORD</small>, you shall offer for the <u>meat</u> offering of your firstfruits green ears of <u>corn</u> dried by the fire, *even* <u>corn</u> beaten out of full ears.   grain

15 And you shall put oil upon it, and

lay frankincense thereon: it *is* a <u>meat</u> offering. _{grain}

16 And the priest shall burn the <u>me-</u><u>morial</u> of it, *part* of the beaten corn thereof, and *part* of the oil thereof, with all the frankincense thereof: *it is* an offering made by fire to the Lord. _{token part}

CHAPTER 3

AND if his <u>oblation</u> *be* a sacrifice of peace offering, if he offer *it* of the herd; whether *it be* a <u>male</u> or female, he shall offer it without blemish before the Lord. _{offering}

2 And he shall lay his hand upon the head of his offering, and kill it *at* the door of the tabernacle of the congregation: and Aar'on's sons the priests shall sprinkle the blood upon the altar round about.

3 And he shall offer of the sacrifice of the peace offering an offering made by fire to the Lord; the <u>fat</u> that covers the <u>inwards</u>, and all the <u>fat</u> that *is* upon the <u>inwards</u>, _{suet - entrails}

4 And the two kidneys, and the fat that *is* on them, which *is* by the <u>flanks</u>, and the <u>caul</u> above the liver, with the kidneys, it shall he take away. _{loins - lobe}

5 And Aar'on's sons shall burn it on the altar upon the burned sacrifice, which *is* upon the wood that *is* on the fire: *it is* an offering made by fire, of a sweet savor to the Lord.

6 And if his offering for a sacrifice of peace offering to the Lord *be* of the flock; male or female, he shall offer it without blemish. _{Jehovah^{s.f.}}

7 If he offer a lamb for his offering, then shall he offer it before the Lord.

8 And he shall lay his hand upon the head of his offering, and kill it before the tabernacle of the congregation: and Aar'on's sons shall sprinkle the blood thereof round about upon the altar.

9 And he shall offer of the sacrifice of the peace offering an offering made by fire to the Lord; the fat thereof, *and* the whole rump, it shall he take off <u>hard</u> by the backbone; and the fat that covers the inwards, and all the fat that *is* upon the <u>inwards</u>, _{close - entrails}

10 And the two kidneys, and the fat that *is* upon them, which *is* by the flanks, and the <u>caul</u> above the liver, with the kidneys, it shall he take away. _{lobe}

11 And the priest shall burn it upon the altar: *it is* the food of the offering made by fire to the Lord.

12 And if his offering *be* a goat, then he shall offer it before the Lord.

13 And he shall lay his hand upon the head of it, and kill it before the tabernacle of the congregation: and the sons of Aar'on shall sprinkle the blood thereof upon the altar round about.

14 And he shall offer thereof his offering, *even* an offering made by fire to the Lord; the fat that covers the inwards, and all the fat that *is* upon the inwards,

15 And the two kidneys, and the fat that *is* upon them, which *is* by the <u>flanks</u>, and the <u>caul</u> above the liver, with the kidneys, it shall he take away.

16 And the priest shall burn them

upon the altar: *it is* the food of the offering made by fire for a sweet savor: all the fat *is* the Lord's. _{El s.f.}

17 *It shall be* a perpetual statute for your generations throughout all your dwellings, that you eat neither fat nor blood.

CHAPTER 4

AND the Lord spoke to Mo'ses, saying,

2 Speak to the children of Is'ra-el, saying, If a <u>soul</u> shall sin through ignorance against any of the commandments of the Lord *concerning things* which ought not to be done, and shall do against any of them: _{person}

3 If the priest that is <u>anointed</u> do sin according to the sin of the people; then let him bring for his sin, which he has sinned, a young bullock without blemish to the Lord for a sin offering. _{placed in office}

4 And he shall bring the bullock to the door of the tabernacle of the congregation before the Lord; and shall lay his hand upon the bullock's head, and kill the bullock <u>before</u> the Lord. _{as to}

5 And the priest that is anointed shall take of the bullock's blood, and bring it to the tabernacle of the congregation:

6 And the priest shall dip his finger in the blood, and sprinkle of the blood seven times before the Lord, before the veil of the sanctuary. _{Jehovah s.f.}

7 And the priest shall put *some* of the blood upon the horns of the altar of sweet incense before the Lord, which *is* in the tabernacle of the congregation;

and shall pour all the blood of the bullock at the bottom of the altar of the burned offering, which *is at* the door of the tabernacle of the congregation.

8 And he shall take off from it all the fat of the bullock for the sin offering; the fat that covers the inwards, and all the fat that *is* upon the inwards,

9 And the two kidneys, and the fat that *is* upon them, which *is* by the <u>flanks</u>, and the <u>caul</u> above the liver, with the kidneys, it shall he take away, _{loins - lobe}

10 As it was taken off from the bullock of the sacrifice of peace offerings: and the priest shall burn them upon the altar of the burned offering.

11 And the skin of the bullock, and all its flesh, with its head, and with its legs, and its inwards, and its dung,

12 Even the whole bullock shall he carry forth without the camp to a clean place, where the ashes are poured out, and burn it on the wood with fire: where the ashes are poured out shall it be burned.

13 And if the whole congregation of Is'ra-el sin through ignorance, and the <u>thing be hid from the eyes</u> of the assembly, and they have done *somewhat against* any of the commandments of the Lord *concerning things* which should not be done, and are guilty; _{matter escapes the notice}

14 When the sin, which they have sinned against it, <u>is</u> known, then the congregation shall offer a young bullock for the sin, and bring him before the tabernacle of the congregation. _{becomes}

15 And the elders of the congregation shall lay their hands upon the head of the bullock before the LORD: and the bullock shall be killed before the LORD.

16 And the priest that is anointed shall bring of the bullock's blood to the tabernacle of the congregation:

17 And the priest shall dip his finger *in some* of the blood, and sprinkle *it* seven times before the LORD, *even* before the veil.

18 And he shall put *some* of the blood upon the horns of the altar which *is* before the LORD, that *is* in the tabernacle of the congregation, and shall pour out all the blood at the bottom of the altar of the burned offering, which *is at* the door of the tabernacle of the congregation.

19 And he shall take all its fat from it, and burn *it* upon the altar.

20 And he shall do with the bullock as he did with the bullock for a sin offering, so shall he do with this: and the priest shall make an <u>atonement</u> for them, and it shall be forgiven them.

a reconciliation

21 And he shall carry forth the bullock outside the camp, and burn him as he burned the first bullock: it *is* a sin offering for the congregation.

22 When a <u>ruler</u> has sinned, and done *somewhat* through ignorance *against* any of the commandments of the LORD his God *concerning things* which should not be done, and is guilty;

a leader

23 Or if his sin, wherein he has sinned, <u>come to his knowledge</u>; he shall bring his offering, a kid of the goats, a male without blemish:

is made known to him

24 And he shall lay his hand upon the head of the goat, and kill it in the place where they kill the burned offering before the LORD: it *is* a sin offering.

25 And the priest shall take of the blood of the sin offering with his finger, and put *it* upon the horns of the altar of burned offering, and shall pour out its blood at the bottom of the altar of burned offering.

26 And he shall burn all its fat upon the altar, as the fat of the sacrifice of peace offerings: and the priest shall make an atonement for him as concerning his sin, and it shall be forgiven him.

27 And if any one of the common people sin through ignorance, while he does *somewhat against* any of the commandments of the LORD *concerning things* which ought not to be done, and be guilty;

28 Or if his sin, which he has sinned, come to his knowledge: then he shall bring his offering, a kid of the goats, a female without blemish, for his sin which he has sinned.

29 And he shall lay his hand upon the head of the sin offering, and slay the sin offering in the place of the burned offering.

30 And the priest shall take of the blood thereof with his finger, and put *it* upon the horns of the altar of burned offering, and shall pour out all the blood thereof at the bottom of the altar.

31 And he shall take away all the fat thereof, as the fat is taken away from off the sacrifice of peace offerings; and

the priest shall burn *it* upon the altar for a sweet savor to the LORD; and the priest shall make an atonement for him, and it shall be forgiven him.

32 And if he bring a lamb for a sin offering, he shall bring it a female without blemish.

33 And he shall lay his hand upon the head of the sin offering, and slay it for a sin offering in the place where they kill the burned offering.

34 And the priest shall take of the blood of the sin offering with his finger, and put *it* upon the horns of the altar of burned offering, and shall pour out all the blood thereof at the bottom of the altar:

35 And he shall take away all the fat thereof, as the fat of the lamb is taken away from the sacrifice of the peace offerings; and the priest shall burn them upon the altar, according to the offerings made by fire to the LORD: and the priest shall make an atonement for his sin that he has committed, and it shall be forgiven him.

CHAPTER 5

AND if a soul sin, and hear the voice of swearing, and *is* a witness, whether he has seen or known *of it*; if he do not utter *it*, then he shall bear his iniquity. _{person}

2 Or if a soul touch any unclean thing, whether *it be* a carcase of an unclean beast, or a carcase of unclean cattle, or the carcase of unclean creeping things, and *if it* be hidden from him; he also shall be unclean, and guilty. _{unfit}

3 Or if he touch the uncleanness of man, whatsoever uncleanness *it be* that a man shall be defiled with it, and it be hid from him; when he knows *of it*, then he shall be guilty. _{it is hidden}

4 Or if a soul swear, pronouncing with *his* lips to do evil, or to do good, whatsoever *it be* that a man shall pronounce with an oath, and it be hid from him; when he knows *of it*, then he shall be guilty in one of these. _{JAMES 5:12 person - makes a vow}

5 And it shall be, when he shall be guilty in one of these *things*, that he shall confess that he has sinned in that *thing*: _{responsible}

6 And he shall bring his trespass offering to the LORD for his sin which he has sinned, a female from the flock, a lamb or a kid of the goats, for a sin offering; and the priest shall make an atonement for him concerning his sin. _{guilt}

7 And if he be not able to bring a lamb, then he shall bring for his trespass, which he has committed, two turtledoves, or two young pigeons, to the LORD; one for a sin offering, and the other for a burned offering.

8 And he shall bring them to the priest, who shall offer *that* which *is* for the sin offering first, and wring off its head from its neck, but shall not divide *it* asunder:

9 And he shall sprinkle of the blood of the sin offering upon the side of the altar; and the rest of the blood shall be wrung out at the bottom of the altar: it *is* a sin offering.

10 And he shall offer the second *for* a

burnt offering, according to the manner: and the priest shall make an atonement for him for his sin which he has sinned, and it shall be forgiven him. law

11 But if he be not able to bring two turtledoves, or two young pigeons, then he that sinned shall bring for his offering the tenth part of an ephah of fine flour for a sin offering; he shall put no oil upon it, neither shall he put *any* frankincense thereon: for it *is* a sin offering.

12 Then shall he bring it to the priest, and the priest shall take his handful of it, *even* a memorial thereof, and burn *it* on the altar, according to the offerings made by fire to the LORD: it *is* a sin offering.

13 And the priest shall make an atonement for him as touching his sin that he has sinned in one of these, and it shall be forgiven him: and *the remnant* shall be the priest's, as a meat offering.

14 And the LORD spoke to Mo'ses, saying,

15 If a soul commit a trespass, and sin through ignorance, in the holy things of the LORD; then he shall bring for his trespass to the LORD a ram without blemish out of the flocks, with your estimation by shekels of silver, after the shekel of the sanctuary, for a trespass offering: person

16 And he shall make amends for the harm that he has done in the holy thing, and shall add the fifth part thereto, and give it to the priest: and the priest shall make an atonement for him with the ram of the trespass offering, and it shall be forgiven him.

17 And if a soul sin, and commit any of these things which are forbidden to be done by the commandments of the LORD; though he knew *it* not, yet is he guilty, and shall bear his iniquity. person - Jehovah^s.f. - punishment

18 And he shall bring a ram without blemish out of the flock, with your estimation, for a trespass offering, to the priest: and the priest shall make an atonement for him concerning his ignorance wherein he erred and knew *it* not, and it shall be forgiven him. valuation

19 It *is* a trespass offering: he has certainly trespassed against the LORD.

CHAPTER 6

AND the LORD spoke to Mo'ses, saying,

2 If a soul sin, and commit a trespass against the LORD, and lie to his neighbor in that which was delivered him to keep, or in fellowship, or in a thing taken away by violence, or has deceived his neighbor;

person - bargaining - robbery

3 Or have found that which was lost, and lies concerning it, and swears falsely; in any of all these that a man does, sinning therein:

4 Then it shall be, because he has sinned, and is guilty, that he shall restore that which he took violently away, or the thing which he has deceitfully gotten, or that which was delivered him to keep, or the lost thing which he found, responsible

5 Or all that about which he has <u>sworn</u> <u>falsely</u>; he shall even restore it in the principal, and shall add the fifth part more thereto, *and* give it to him to whom it <u>appertains</u>, in the day of his trespass offering. lied about - belongs

6 And he shall bring his trespass offering to the LORD, a ram without blemish out of the flock, with your estimation, for a trespass offering, to the priest:

7 And the priest shall make an atonement for him before the LORD: and it shall be forgiven him for any thing of all that he has done in trespassing therein.

8 And the LORD spoke to Mo'ses, saying,

9 Command Aar'on and his sons, saying, This *is* the law of the burned offering: It *is* the burned offering, because of the burning upon the altar all night to the morning, and the fire of the altar shall be burning in it.

10 And the priest shall put on his linen garment, and his linen breeches shall he put upon his flesh, and take up the ashes which the fire has consumed with the burned offering on the altar, and he shall put them beside the altar.

11 And he shall put off his garments, and put on other garments, and carry forth the ashes outside the camp to a clean place.

12 And the fire upon the altar shall be burning in it; it shall not be put out: and the priest shall burn wood on it every morning, and lay the burned offering in order upon it; and he shall burn thereon the fat of the peace offerings.

13 The fire shall ever be burning upon the altar; it shall never go out.

14 And this *is* the <u>law</u> of the <u>meat</u> offering: the sons of Aar'on shall offer it before the LORD, before the altar. rule - grain

15 And he shall take of it his handful, of the flour of the <u>meat</u> offering, and of the oil thereof, and all the frankincense which *is* upon the <u>meat</u> offering, and shall burn *it* upon the altar *for* a sweet savor, *even* the <u>memorial</u> of it, to the LORD. token part

16 And the remainder thereof shall Aar'on and his sons eat: with <u>unleavened</u> bread shall it be eaten in the holy place; in the court of the tabernacle of the congregation they shall eat it. without yeast

17 It shall not be baked with <u>leaven</u>. I have given it *to them for* their <u>portion</u> of My offerings made by fire; it *is* most holy, as *is* the sin offering, and as the trespass offering. yeast - share

18 All the males among the children of Aar'on shall eat of it. *It shall be* a <u>statute</u> for ever in your generations concerning the offerings of the LORD made by fire: every one that touches them shall be <u>holy</u>. ordinance - set apart

19 And the LORD spoke to Mo'ses, saying,

20 This *is* the offering of Aar'on and of his sons, which they shall offer to the LORD in the day when he is anointed; the tenth part of an ephah of fine flour for a meat offering perpetual, half of it in the morning, and half thereof at night.

21 In a pan it shall be made with oil; *and when it is* <u>baked,</u> you shall bring it in: *and* the <u>baked</u> pieces of the meat offering shall you offer *for* a <u>sweet savor</u> to the LORD. soaked - soothing aroma

22 And the priest of his sons that is anointed in his stead shall offer it: *it is* a <u>statute</u> for ever to the LORD; it shall be <u>wholly burned.</u>ordinance - entirely offered to the Lord

23 For every meat offering for the priest shall be wholly burned: it shall not be eaten.

24 And the LORD spoke to Mo'ses, saying,

25 Speak to Aar'on and to his sons, saying, This *is* the law of the sin offering: In the place where the burned offering is killed shall the sin offering be killed before the LORD: it *is* most holy.

26 The priest that offer it for sin shall eat it: in the holy place shall it be eaten, in the court of the tabernacle of the congregation.

27 Whatsoever shall touch the flesh thereof shall be holy: and when there is sprinkled of the blood thereof upon any garment, you shall wash that whereon it was sprinkled in the <u>holy place</u>. set apart

28 But the earthen vessel wherein it is <u>sodden</u> shall be broken: and if it be <u>sodden</u> in a brazen pot, it shall be both scoured, and rinsed in water. boiled

29 All the males among the priests shall eat thereof: it is most holy.

30 And no sin offering, whereof *any* of the blood is brought into the tabernacle of the congregation to reconcile *with* in the holy *place*, shall be eaten: it shall be burned in the fire.

CHAPTER 7

LIKEWISE this *is* the law of the <u>trespass</u> offering: it *is* most holy. guilt

2 In the place where they kill the burned offering shall they kill the <u>trespass</u> offering: and the blood thereof shall he sprinkle round about upon the altar.

3 And he shall offer of it all the fat thereof; the rump, and the fat that covers the inwards,

4 And the two kidneys, and the fat that *is* on them, which *is* by the flanks, and the <u>caul</u> *that is* above the liver, with the kidneys, it shall he take away: lobe

5 And the priest shall burn them upon the altar *for* an offering made by fire to the LORD: it *is* a <u>trespass</u> offering. guilt

6 Every male among the priests shall eat thereof: it shall be eaten in the holy place: it *is* most holy.

7 As the sin offering *is*, so *is* the <u>trespass</u> offering: *there is* one <u>law</u> for them: the priest that makes atonement therewith shall have *it*. procedure

8 And the priest that offers any man's burned offering, *even* the priest shall have <u>to</u> himself the skin of the burned offering which he has offered. for

9 And all the <u>meat</u> offering that is baked in the oven, and all that is dressed in the fryingpan, and in the pan, shall be the priest's that offer it. grain

10 And every <u>meat</u> offering, mingled with oil, and dry, shall all the sons of Aar'on have, one *as much* as another.

11 And this *is* the <u>law</u> of the sacrifice

of peace offerings, which he shall offer to the LORD.   procedure

12 If he offer it for a thanksgiving, then he shall offer with the sacrifice of thanksgiving <u>unleavened</u> cakes mingled with oil, and <u>unleavened</u> wafers anointed with oil, and cakes mingled with oil, of fine flour, fried.

HEB. 13:15 without yeast

13 Besides the cakes, he shall offer *for* his offering <u>leavened</u> bread with the sacrifice of thanksgiving of his peace offerings.   with yeast

14 And of it he shall offer one out of the whole <u>oblation</u> *for* an heave offering to the LORD, *and* it shall be the priest's that sprinkles the blood of the peace offerings.   offering

15 And the flesh of the sacrifice of his peace offerings for thanksgiving shall be eaten the same day that it is offered; he shall not leave any of it until the morning.

16 But if the sacrifice of his offering *be* a <u>vow</u>, or a voluntary offering, it shall be eaten the same day that he offers his sacrifice: and on the morrow also the remainder of it shall be eaten: promise

17 But the remainder of the flesh of the sacrifice on the third day shall be burned with fire.

18 And if *any* of the flesh of the sacrifice of his peace offerings be eaten at all on the third day, it shall not be accepted, neither shall it be imputed to him that offers it: it shall be an <u>abomination</u>, and the <u>soul</u> that eats of it shall bear his iniquity.

offensive thing - person

19 And the flesh that touches any unclean *thing* shall not be eaten; it shall be burned with fire: and as for the flesh, all that be clean shall eat thereof.

20 But the <u>soul</u> that eats *of* the flesh of the sacrifice of peace offerings, that *pertain* to the LORD, having his uncleanness upon him, even that <u>soul</u> shall be cut off from his people. person

21 Moreover the <u>soul</u> that shall touch any unclean *thing*, as the uncleanness of man, or *any* unclean beast, or any abominable unclean *thing*, and eat of the flesh of the sacrifice of peace offerings, which *pertain* to the LORD, *even* that <u>soul</u> shall be cut off from his people.

22 And the LORD spoke to Mo'ses, saying,

23 Speak to the children of Is'ra-el, saying, You shall eat no manner of fat, of ox, or of sheep, or of goat.

24 And the fat of the beast that dies of itself, and the fat of that which is torn with beasts, may be used in any other use: but you shall in no wise eat of it.

25 For whosoever eats the fat of the beast, of which men offer an offering made by fire to the LORD, even the <u>soul</u> that eats *it* shall be cut off from his people.

26 Moreover you shall eat no manner of blood, *whether it be* of fowl or of beast, in any of your dwellings.

27 Whatsoever <u>soul</u> *it be* that eats any manner of blood, even that <u>soul</u> shall be cut off from his people.   person

28 And the LORD spoke to Mo'ses, saying,

29 Speak to the children of Is'ra-el,

saying, He that offers the sacrifice of his peace offerings to the LORD shall bring his <u>oblation</u> to the LORD of the sacrifice of his peace offerings. _{offering}

30 His own hands shall bring the offerings of the LORD made by fire, the fat with the breast, it shall he bring, that the breast may be waved *for* a wave offering before the LORD.

31 And the priest shall burn the fat upon the altar: but the breast shall be Aar'on's and his sons'.

32 And the right shoulder shall you give to the priest *for* an heave offering of the sacrifices of your peace offerings.

33 He among the sons of Aar'on, that offers the blood of the peace offerings, and the fat, shall have the right shoulder for *his* part.

34 For the wave breast and the heave shoulder have I taken of the children of Is'ra-el from off the sacrifices of their peace offerings, and have given them to Aar'on the priest and to his sons <u>by a statute</u> for ever from among the children of Is'ra-el.   as their due

35 This *is the portion* of the anointing of Aar'on, and of the anointing of his sons, out of the offerings of the LORD made by fire, in the day *when* he presented them to minister to the LORD in the priest's office;

36 Which the LORD commanded to be given them of the children of Is'ra-el, in the day that He anointed them, *by* a statute for ever throughout their generations.

37 This *is* the <u>law</u> of the burned offering, of the <u>meat</u> offering, and of the sin offering, and of the trespass offering, and of the consecrations, and of the sacrifice of the peace offerings; _{procedure - grain}

38 Which the LORD commanded Mo'ses in mount Si'nai, in the day that He commanded the children of Is'ra-el to offer their <u>oblations</u> to the LORD, in the wilderness of Si'nai.   offerings

CHAPTER 8

AND the LORD spoke to Mo'ses, saying,

2 Take Aar'on and his sons with him, and the garments, and the anointing oil, and a bullock for the sin offering, and two rams, and a basket of <u>unleavened</u> bread; _{without yeast}

3 And gather you all the congregation together to <u>the door</u> of the tabernacle of the congregation.   in front of

4 And Mo'ses did as the LORD commanded him; and the assembly was gathered together to the door of the tabernacle of the congregation.

5 And Mo'ses said to the congregation, This *is* the thing which the LORD commanded to be done.

6 And Mo'ses brought Aar'on and his sons, and washed them with water.

7 And he put upon him the coat, and girded him with the girdle, and clothed him with the robe, and put the <u>ephod</u> upon him, and he girded him with the <u>curious girdle</u> of the ephod, and bound *it* to him therewith.   priestly robe - artistic band

8 And he put the breastplate upon him: also he put in the breastplate the <u>U'rim and the Thum'mim</u>.   Light and Perfection

9 And he put the <u>mitre</u> upon his head; also upon the <u>mitre</u>, *even* upon his forefront, did he put the golden plate, the holy crown; as the Lord commanded Mo'ses. turban

10 And Mo'ses took the anointing oil, and anointed the tabernacle and all that *was* therein, and sanctified them.

11 And he sprinkled thereof upon the altar seven times, and anointed the altar and all its vessels, both the laver and its foot, to sanctify them.

12 And he poured of the anointing oil upon Aar'on's head, and anointed him, to sanctify him.

13 And Mo'ses brought Aar'on's sons, and put coats upon them, and girded them with girdles, and put bonnets upon them; as the Lord commanded Mo'ses. headpieces

14 And he brought the bullock for the sin offering: and Aar'on and his sons laid their hands upon the head of the bullock for the sin offering.

15 And he slew *it*; and Mo'ses took the blood, and put *it* upon the horns of the altar round about with his finger, and purified the altar, and poured the blood at the bottom of the altar, and sanctified it, to make <u>reconciliation</u> upon it. atonement

16 And he took all the fat that *was* upon the inwards, and the <u>caul</u> *above* the liver, and the two kidneys, and their fat, and Mo'ses burned *it* upon the altar. lobe

17 But the bullock, and its hide, its flesh, and its dung, he burned with fire outside the camp; as the Lord commanded Mo'ses.

18 And he brought the ram for the burned offering: and Aar'on and his sons laid their hands upon the head of the ram.

19 And he killed *it*; and Mo'ses sprinkled the blood upon the altar round about.

20 And he cut the ram into pieces; and Mo'ses burned the head, and the pieces, and the fat.

21 And he washed the inwards and the legs in water; and Mo'ses burned the whole ram upon the altar: it *was* a burned sacrifice for a <u>sweet savor</u>, *and* an offering made by fire to the Lord; as the Lord commanded Mo'ses. soothing aroma

22 And he brought the other ram, the ram of <u>consecration</u>: and Aar'on and his sons laid their hands upon the head of the ram. ordination

23 And he slew *it*; and Mo'ses took of the blood of it, and put *it* upon the tip of Aar'on's right ear, and upon the thumb of his right hand, and upon the <u>great</u> toe of his right foot. big

24 And he brought Aar'on's sons, and Mo'ses put of the blood upon the tip of their right ear, and upon the thumbs of their right hands, and upon the great toes of their right feet: and Mo'ses sprinkled the blood upon the altar round about.

25 And he took the fat, and the rump, and all the fat that *was* upon the inwards, and the <u>caul</u> *above* the liver, and the two kidneys, and their fat, and the right shoulder: lobe

26 And out of the basket of <u>unleavened</u> bread, that *was* before the Lord,

he took one <u>unleavened</u> cake, and a cake of oiled bread, and one wafer, and put *them* on the fat, and upon the right shoulder: without yeast

27 And he put all upon Aar'on's hands, and upon his sons' hands, and waved them *for* a wave offering before the LORD.

28 And Mo'ses took them from off their hands, and burned *them* on the altar upon the burned offering: they *were* consecrations for a sweet savor: it *is* an offering made by fire to the LORD.

29 And Mo'ses took the breast, and waved it *for* a wave offering before the LORD: *for* of the ram of consecration it was Mo'ses' part; as the LORD commanded Mo'ses.

30 And Mo'ses took of the anointing oil, and of the blood which *was* upon the altar, and sprinkled *it* upon Aar'on, *and* upon his garments, and upon his sons, and upon his sons' garments with him; and sanctified Aar'on, *and* his garments, and his sons, and his sons' garments with him.

31 And Mo'ses said to Aar'on and to his sons, Boil the flesh *at* the door of the tabernacle of the congregation: and there eat it with the bread that *is* in the basket of consecrations, as I commanded, saying, Aar'on and his sons shall eat it.

32 And that which remains of the flesh and of the bread shall you burn with fire.

33 And you shall not go out of the door of the tabernacle of the congregation *in* seven days, until the days of your <u>con-</u> secration be at an end: for seven days shall he <u>consecrate</u> you.   ordination - ordain

34 As he has done this day, *so* the LORD has commanded to do, to make an <u>atonement</u> for you.   a reconciliation

35 Therefore shall you abide *at* the door of the tabernacle of the congregation day and night seven days, and <u>keep the charge</u> of the LORD, that you die not: for so I am commanded.   obey the ordinances

36 So Aar'on and his sons did all things which the LORD commanded by the hand of Mo'ses.

CHAPTER 9

AND it came to pass on the eighth day, *that* Mo'ses called Aar'on and his sons, and the elders of Is'ra-el;

2 And he said to Aar'on, Take you a young calf for a sin offering, and a ram for a burned offering, without blemish, and offer *them* before the LORD.

3 And to the children of Is'ra-el you shall speak, saying, Take you a kid of the goats for a sin offering; and a calf and a lamb, *both* of the first year, without blemish, for a burned offering;

4 Also a bullock and a ram for peace offerings, to sacrifice before the LORD; and a <u>meat</u> offering mingled with oil: for to day the LORD will appear to you.   grain

5 And they brought *that* which Mo'ses commanded before the tabernacle of the congregation: and all the congregation drew near and stood before the LORD.

6 And Mo'ses said, This *is* the thing which the LORD commanded that you

should do: and the glory of the LORD shall appear to you.

7 And Mo'ses said to Aar'on, Go to the altar, and offer your sin offering, and your burned offering, and make an atonement for yourself, and for the people: and offer the offering of the people, and make an atonement for them; as the LORD commanded.

8 Aar'on therefore went to the altar, and slew the calf of the sin offering, which *was* for <u>himself</u>. his own sins

9 And the sons of Aar'on brought the blood to him: and he dipped his finger in the blood, and put *it* upon the horns of the altar, and poured out the blood at the bottom of the altar:

10 But the fat, and the kidneys, and the <u>caul</u> above the liver of the sin offering, he burned upon the altar; as the LORD commanded Mo'ses. lobe

11 And the flesh and the hide he burned with fire outside the camp.

12 And he slew the burned offering; and Aar'on's sons presented to him the blood, which he sprinkled round about upon the altar.

13 And they presented the burned offering to him, with the pieces thereof, and the head: and he burned *them* upon the altar.

14 And he did wash the inwards and the legs, and burned *them* upon the burned offering on the altar.

15 And he brought the people's offering, and took the goat, which *was* the sin offering for the people, and slew it, and offered it for sin, as the first.

16 And he brought the burned offering, and offered it according to the manner.

17 And he brought the <u>meat</u> offering, and took an handful thereof, and burned *it* upon the altar, beside the burned <u>sacrifice</u> of the morning. grain - offering

18 He slew also the bullock and the ram *for a* sacrifice of peace offerings, which *was* for the people: and Aar'on's sons presented to him the blood, which he sprinkled upon the altar round about,

19 And the fat of the bullock and of the ram, the rump, and that which covers *the inwards*, and the kidneys, and the <u>caul</u> *above* the liver: lobe

20 And they put the fat upon the breasts, and he burned the fat upon the altar:

21 And the breasts and the right shoulder Aar'on waved *for* a wave offering before the LORD; as Mo'ses commanded.

22 And Aar'on lifted up his hand toward the people, and blessed them, and came down from offering of the sin offering, and the burned offering, and peace offerings.

23 And Mo'ses and Aar'on went into the tabernacle of the congregation, and came out, and blessed the people: and the glory of the LORD appeared to all the people.

24 And there came a fire out from before the LORD, and consumed upon the altar the burned offering and the fat: *which* when all the people saw, they shouted, and fell on their faces.

CHAPTER 10

AND Na'dab and A-bi'hu, the sons of Aar'on, took either of them his censer, and put fire therein, and put incense thereon, and offered strange fire before the LORD, which He commanded them not. _{unlawful}

2 And there went out fire from the LORD, and devoured them, and they died before the LORD.

3 Then Mo'ses said to Aar'on, This *is it* that the LORD spoke, saying, I will be sanctified in them that come near Me, and before all the people I will be glorified. And Aar'on held his peace. _{honored}

4 And Mo'ses called Mish'a-el and El'za-phan, the sons of Uz'zi-el the uncle of Aar'on, and said to them, Come near, carry your brethren from before the sanctuary out of the camp. _{in front}

5 So they went near, and carried them in their coats out of the camp; as Mo'ses had said.

6 And Mo'ses said to Aar'on, and to E-le-a'zar and to Ith'a-mar, his sons, Uncover not your heads, neither rend your clothes; less you die, and less wrath come upon all the people: but let your brethren, the whole house of Is'ra-el, bewail the burning which the LORD has kindled.

7 And you shall not go out from the door of the tabernacle of the congregation, less you die: for the anointing oil of the LORD *is* upon you. And they did according to the word of Mo'ses.

8 And the LORD spoke to Aar'on, saying,

9 Do not drink wine nor strong drink, you, nor your sons with you, when you go into the tabernacle of the congregation, less you die: *it shall be* a statute for ever throughout your generations: _{ordinance}

10 And that you may put difference between holy and unholy, and between unclean and clean; _{profane}

11 And that you may teach the children of Is'ra-el all the statutes which the LORD has spoken to them by the hand of Mo'ses. _{show}

12 And Mo'ses spoke to Aar'on, and to E-le-a'zar and to Ith'a-mar, his sons that were left, Take the meat offering that remains of the offerings of the LORD made by fire, and eat it without leaven beside the altar: for it *is* most holy: _{grain - yeast - use only for this}

13 And you shall eat it in the holy place, because it *is* your due, and your sons' due, of the sacrifices of the LORD made by fire: for so I am commanded. _{share}

14 And the wave breast and heave shoulder shall you eat in a clean place; you, and your sons, and your daughters with you: for *they be* your due, and your sons' due, *which* are given out of the sacrifices of peace offerings of the children of Is'ra-el.

15 The heave shoulder and the wave breast shall they bring with the offerings made by fire of the fat, to wave *it* for a wave offering before the LORD; and it shall be yours, and your sons' with

you, by a statute for ever; as the Lord has commanded.

16 And Mo'ses diligently sought the goat of the sin offering, and, behold, it was burned: and he was angry with E-le-a'zar and Ith'a-mar, the sons of Aar'on *which were* left *alive,* saying,

17 Wherefore have you not eaten the sin offering in the holy place, seeing it *is* most holy, and *God* has given it you to bear the iniquity of the congregation, to make atonement for them before the Lord?

18 Behold, the blood of it was not brought in within the holy *place*: you should indeed have eaten it in the holy *place*, as I commanded.

19 And Aar'on said to Mo'ses, Behold, this day have they offered their sin offering and their burned offering before the Lord; and such things have <u>befallen</u> me: and *if* I had eaten the sin offering to day, should it have been accepted in the sight of the Lord?   <small>happened to</small>

20 And when Mo'ses heard *that,* he was content.

CHAPTER 11

AND the Lord spoke to Mo'ses and to Aar'on, saying to them,

2 Speak to the children of Is'ra-el, saying, These *are* the beasts which you shall eat among all the beasts that *are* on the earth.

3 Whatsoever parts the hoof, and is <u>clovenfooted</u>, *and* chews the cud, among the beasts, that shall you eat.   <small>split hoof</small>

4 Nevertheless these shall you not eat of them that chew the cud, or of them that divide the hoof: *as* the camel, because it chews the cud, but divides not the hoof; it *is* <u>unclean</u> to you.   <small>ACTS 10:14 unfit</small>

5 And the coney, because it chews the cud, but divides not the hoof; it *is* <u>unclean</u> to you.

6 And the hare, because it chews the cud, but divides not the hoof; it *is* <u>unclean</u> to you.

7 And the swine, though it divide the hoof, and be <u>clovenfooted</u>, yet it chews not the cud; it *is* <u>unclean</u> to you.

8 Of their flesh shall you not eat, and their carcase shall you not touch; they *are* <u>unclean</u> to you.

9 These shall you eat of all that *are* in the waters: whatsoever has fins and scales in the waters, in the seas, and in the rivers, them shall you eat.

10 And all that have not fins and scales in the seas, and in the rivers, of all that move in the waters, and of any living thing which *is* in the waters, they *shall be* an <u>abomination</u> to you: <small>detestable things</small>

11 They shall be even an <u>abomination</u> to you; you shall not eat of their flesh, but you shall have their carcases in <u>abomination</u>.

12 Whatsoever has no fins nor scales in the waters, that *shall* be an <u>abomination</u> to you.

13 And these *are they which* you shall have in <u>abomination</u> among the fowls; they shall not be eaten, they *are* an <u>abomination</u>: the eagle, and the <u>ossifrage</u>, and the ospray,   <small>vulture</small>

14 And the vulture, and the <u>kite</u> after its kind;   <small>hawk</small>

15 Every raven after its kind;

16 And the owl, and the night hawk, and the cuckow, and the hawk after its kind,

17 And the little owl, and the cormorant, and the great owl,

18 And the swan, and the pelican, and the <u>gier eagle</u>,   carrion vulture

19 And the stork, the heron after its kind, and the lapwing, and the bat.

20 All fowls that creep, going upon *all* four, *shall be* an <u>abomination</u> to you.   detestable

21 Yet these may you eat of every flying creeping thing that goes upon *all* four, which have legs above their feet, to leap with upon the earth;

22 *Even* these of them you may eat; the locust after its kind, and the bald locust after its kind, and the beetle after its kind, and the grasshopper after its kind.

23 But all *other* flying creeping things, which have four feet, *shall be* an <u>abomination</u> to you.

24 And for these you shall be <u>unclean:</u> whosoever touches the carcase of them shall be <u>unclean</u> until the even.   unfit

25 And whosoever <u>bears anything</u> of the carcase of them shall wash his clothes, and be unclean until the even.   carries any

26 *The carcases* of every beast which divides the hoof, and *is* not <u>clovenfooted</u>, nor chews the cud, *are* <u>unclean</u> to you: every one that touches them shall be <u>unclean</u>.   split hoof

27 And whatsoever goes upon its paws, among all manner of beasts that go on *all* four, those *are* <u>unclean</u> to you: whoso touches their carcase shall be <u>unclean</u> until the <u>even</u>.   unfit - evening

28 And he that bears the carcase of them shall wash his clothes, and be <u>unclean</u> until the even: they *are* <u>unclean</u> to you.   unfit

29 These also *shall be* <u>unclean</u> to you among the creeping things that creep upon the earth; the weasel, and the mouse, and the <u>tortoise</u> after its kind,   thorn tailed lizard

30 And the ferret, and the chameleon, and the lizard, and the snail, and the mole.

31 These *are* <u>unclean</u> to you among all that creep: whosoever does touch them, when they be dead, shall be <u>unclean</u> until the <u>even</u>.   evening

32 And upon whatsoever *any* of them, when they are dead, does fall, it shall be <u>unclean</u>; whether *it be* any vessel of wood, or <u>raiment</u>, or skin, or sack, whatsoever vessel *it be*, wherein *any* work is done, it must be put into water, and it shall be <u>unclean</u> until the even; so it shall be cleansed.   clothing

33 And every earthen vessel, whereinto *any* of them falls, whatsoever *is* in it shall be <u>unclean</u>; and you shall break it.   unfit

34 Of all meat which may be eaten, *that* on which *such* water comes shall be unclean: and all drink that may be drunk in every *such* vessel shall be <u>unclean</u>.

35 And every *thing* whereupon *any* *part* of their carcase falls shall be unclean; *whether it be* oven, or <u>ranges</u> for pots, they shall be broken down: *for* they *are* <u>unclean</u>, and shall be <u>unclean</u> to you.   hearth

36 Nevertheless a <u>fountain</u> or <u>pit</u>, *wherein there is* plenty of water, shall be clean: but that which touches their carcase shall be <u>unclean</u>.   spring - cistern - unfit

37 And *if any part* of their carcase fall upon any sowing seed which is to be sown, it *shall be* clean.

38 But if *any* water be put upon the seed, and *any part* of their carcase fall thereon, it *shall be* <u>unclean to you</u>.   i.e., for food

39 And if any beast, of which you may eat, die; he that touches the carcase thereof shall be <u>unclean</u> until the even.

40 And he that eats of the carcase of it shall wash his clothes, and be <u>unclean</u> until the <u>even</u>: he also that <u>bears</u> the carcase of it shall wash his clothes, and be <u>unclean</u> until the <u>even</u>.   unfit - evening - carries

41 And every creeping thing that creeps upon the earth *shall be* an <u>abomination</u>; it shall not be eaten.

42 Whatsoever goes upon the belly, and whatsoever goes upon *all* four, or whatsoever has more feet among all creeping things that creep upon the earth, them you shall not eat; for they *are* an <u>abomination</u>.   detestable

43 You shall not make yourselves <u>abominable</u> with any creeping thing that creeps, neither shall you make yourselves <u>unclean</u> with them, that you should be defiled thereby.   unfit

44 For I *am* the LORD your <u>God</u>: you shall therefore <u>sanctify</u> yourselves, and you shall be holy; for I *am* holy: neither shall you defile yourselves with any manner of creeping thing that creeps upon the earth.   1 PET, 1:16 Elohim^{p.f.} - consecrate

45 For I *am* the LORD that brings you up out of the land of E'gypt, to be your <u>God</u>: you shall therefore be <u>holy</u>, for I *am* <u>holy</u>.   Elohim^{p.f.} - separate

46 This *is* the <u>law</u> of the beasts, and of the fowl, and of every living creature that moves in the waters, and of every creature that creeps upon the earth: regulation

47 To make a difference between the <u>unclean</u> and the clean, and between the beast that may be eaten and the beast that may not be eaten.   unfit

CHAPTER 12

AND the LORD spoke to Mo'ses, saying,

2 Speak to the children of Is'ra-el, saying, If a woman have conceived seed, and born a man child: then she shall be <u>unclean</u> seven days; according to the days of the separation for her infirmity shall she be <u>unclean</u>.

3 And in the eighth day the flesh of his foreskin shall be circumcised.

4 And she shall then continue in the blood of her purifying three and thirty days; she shall touch no hallowed thing, nor come into the sanctuary, until the days of her purifying be fulfilled.

5 But if she bear a maid child, then she shall be <u>unclean</u> two weeks, as in her separation: and she shall continue in the blood of her purifying <u>threescore *and* six</u> days.   66 days

6 And when the days of her purifying are fulfilled, for a son, or for a daughter, she shall bring a lamb of the first year for a burned offering, and a young pigeon, or a turtledove, for a sin offer-

ing, to the door of the tabernacle of the congregation, to the priest:

7 Who shall offer it before the LORD, and make an <u>atonement</u> for her; and she shall be cleansed from the issue of her blood. This *is* the law for her that has born a male or a female.   a reconcilation

8 And if she be not able to bring a lamb, then she shall bring two <u>turtles</u>, or two young pigeons; the one for the burned offering, and the other for a sin offering: and the priest shall make an atonement for her, and she shall be <u>clean</u>.   LUKE 2:24 turtle-doves - fit

CHAPTER 13

AND the LORD spoke to Mo'ses and Aar'on, saying,

2 When a man shall have in the skin of his flesh a <u>rising</u>, a scab, or bright spot, and it be in the skin of his flesh *like* the <u>plague</u> of leprosy; then he shall be brought to Aar'on the priest, or to one of his sons the priests: swelling - infection

3 And the priest shall look on the plague in the skin of the flesh: and *when* the hair in the <u>plague</u> is turned white, and the <u>plague</u> in sight *be* deeper than the skin of his flesh, it *is* a plague of leprosy: and the priest shall look on him, and pronounce him <u>unclean</u>.   unfit

4 If the bright spot *be* white in the skin of his flesh, and in sight *be* not deeper than the skin, and the hair thereof be not turned white; then the priest shall <u>shut up</u> *him that has* the plague seven days: isolate

5 And the priest shall look on him the seventh day: and, behold, *if* the <u>plague</u> in his sight <u>be at a stay</u>, *and* the <u>plague</u> spread not in the skin; then the priest shall shut him up seven days more: infection - has not changed

6 And the priest shall look on him again the seventh day: and, behold, *if* the <u>plague</u> *be* somewhat <u>dark</u>, *and* the <u>plague</u> spread not in the skin, the priest shall pronounce him clean: it *is but* a scab: and he shall wash his clothes, and be clean.   faded

7 But if the scab spread much abroad in the skin, after that he has been seen of the priest for his cleansing, he shall be seen of the priest again:

8 And *if* the priest see that, behold, the scab spreads in the skin, then the priest shall pronounce him <u>unclean</u>: it *is* a leprosy.   unfit

9 When the <u>plague</u> of leprosy is in a man, then he shall be brought to the priest;

10 And the priest shall see *him*: and, behold, *if* the rising *be* white in the skin, and it have turned the hair white, and *there be* <u>quick raw</u> flesh in the rising;   sensitive

11 It *is* an <u>old</u> leprosy in the skin of his flesh, and the priest shall pronounce him <u>unclean</u>, and shall not <u>shut</u> him up: for he *is* <u>unclean</u>.   chronic - isolate

12 And if a leprosy break out abroad in the skin, and the leprosy cover all the skin of *him that has* the <u>plague</u> from his head even to his foot, wheresoever the priest looks;   infection

13 Then the priest shall consider: and, behold, *if* the leprosy have covered all his flesh, he shall pronounce *him* clean

that has the <u>plague</u>: it is all turned white: he *is* clean. <small>infection</small>

14 But when raw flesh appears in him, he shall be <u>unclean</u>. <small>unfit</small>

15 And the priest shall see the raw flesh, and pronounce him to be <u>unclean</u>: *for* the raw flesh *is* <u>unclean</u>: it *is* a leprosy.

16 Or if the raw flesh turn again, and be changed to white, he shall come to the priest;

17 And the priest shall see him: and, behold, *if* the <u>plague</u> be turned into white; then the priest shall pronounce *him* clean *that has* the <u>plague</u>: he is clean.

18 The flesh also, in which, *even* in the skin thereof, was a boil, and is healed,

19 And in the place of the boil there be a <u>white rising</u>, or a bright spot, white, and somewhat reddish, and it be showed to the priest; <small>swelling</small>

20 And if, when the priest sees it, behold, it *be* in sight lower than the skin, and the hair thereof be turned white; the priest shall pronounce him <u>unclean</u>: it *is* a <u>plague</u> of leprosy broken out of the boil. <small>infection</small>

21 But if the priest look on it, and, behold, *there be* no white hairs therein, and *if* it *be* not lower than the skin, but be somewhat dark; then the priest shall <u>shut him up</u> seven days: <small>isolate</small>

22 And if it spread much abroad in the skin, then the priest shall pronounce him <u>unclean</u>: it *is* a <u>plague</u>. <small>unfit - infection</small>

23 But if the bright spot <u>stay in its</u> place, *and* spread not, it *is* a burning boil; and the priest shall pronounce him clean. <small>remain in</small>

24 Or if there be *any* flesh, in the skin whereof *there is* a hot burning, and the quick *flesh* that burns have a white bright spot, somewhat reddish, or white;

25 Then the priest shall look upon it: and, behold, *if* the hair in the bright spot be turned white, and it *be in* sight deeper than the skin; it *is* a leprosy broken out of the burning: wherefore the priest shall pronounce him <u>unclean</u>: it *is* the <u>plague</u> of leprosy. <small>unfit - infection</small>

26 But if the priest look on it, and, behold, *there be* no white hair in the bright spot, and it *be* no <u>lower</u> than the *other* skin, but *be* somewhat dark; then the priest shall <u>shut him up</u> seven days: <small>deeper - isolate</small>

27 And the priest shall look upon him the seventh day: *and* if it be spread much abroad in the skin, then the priest shall pronounce him <u>unclean</u>: it *is* the <u>plague</u> of leprosy.

28 And if the bright spot stay in its place, *and* spread not in the skin, but it *be* somewhat dark; it *is* a rising of the burning, and the priest shall pronounce him clean: for it *is* an inflammation of the burning.

29 If a man or woman have a <u>plague</u> upon the head or the beard;

30 Then the priest shall see the <u>plague</u>: and, behold, if it *be* in sight deeper than the skin; *and there be* in it a yellow thin hair; then the priest shall pronounce him <u>unclean</u>: it *is* a dry <u>scall</u>, *even* a leprosy upon the head or beard. <small>infection - scale</small>

31 And if the priest look on the plague of the <u>scall</u>, and, behold, it *be* not in sight deeper than the skin, and *that there* is no black hair in it; then the priest shall shut up *him that has* the <u>plague</u> of the <u>scall</u> seven days: infection - scale

32 And in the seventh day the priest shall look on the <u>plague:</u> and, behold, if the <u>scall</u> spread not, and there be in it no yellow hair, and the <u>scall</u> *be* not in sight deeper than the skin;

33 He shall be shaven, but the <u>scall</u> shall he not shave; and the priest shall shut up *him that has* the <u>scall</u> seven days more:

34 And in the seventh day the priest shall look on the <u>scall</u>: and, behold, *if* the <u>scall</u> be not spread in the skin, nor *be* in sight deeper than the skin; then the priest shall <u>pronounce</u> him clean: and he shall wash his clothes, and be clean. declare

35 But if the <u>scall</u> spread much in the skin after his cleansing; scale

36 Then the priest shall look on him: and, behold, if the <u>scall</u> be spread in the skin, the priest shall not seek for yellow hair; he *is* <u>unclean</u>. unfit

37 But if the <u>scall</u> be in his sight at a stay, and *that* there is black hair grown up therein; the scall is healed, he *is* clean: and the priest shall pronounce him clean.

38 If a man also or a woman have in the skin of their flesh bright spots, *even* white <u>bright spots</u>; pimples

39 Then the priest shall look: and, behold, *if* the bright spots in the skin of their flesh *be* darkish white; it *is* a <u>freck-</u> led spot *that* grows in the skin; he *is* clean. eczema

40 And the man whose hair is fallen off his head, he *is* bald; *yet is* he clean.

41 And he that has his hair fallen off from the part of his head toward his face, he *is* forehead bald: *yet is* he clean.

42 And if there be in the bald head, or bald forehead, a white reddish sore; it *is* a leprosy sprung up in his bald head, or his bald forehead.

43 Then the priest shall look upon it: and, behold, *if* the <u>rising</u> of the sore *be* white reddish in his bald head, or in his bald forehead, as the leprosy appears in the skin of the flesh; swelling

44 He is a leprous man, he *is* <u>unclean</u>: the priest shall pronounce him utterly <u>unclean</u>; his <u>plague</u> *is* in his head. unfit - infection

45 And the leper in whom the <u>plague</u> *is*, his clothes shall be rent, and his head bare, and he shall put a covering upon his upper lip, and shall cry, <u>Unclean</u>, <u>unclean</u>. infection

46 All the days wherein the <u>plague</u> *shall be* in him he shall be defiled; he *is* <u>unclean</u>: he shall <u>dwell</u> alone; outside the camp *shall* his habitation be. live

47 The garment also that the <u>plague</u> of leprosy is in, *whether it be* a woollen garment, or a linen garment; mark of the

48 Whether *it be* in the <u>warp, or woof</u>; of linen, or of woollen; whether in a skin, or in any thing made of skin; weaving or texture

49 And if the <u>plague</u> be greenish or reddish in the garment, or in the skin, either in the <u>warp, or in the woof</u>, or in

any thing of skin; it *is* a <u>plague</u> of leprosy, and shall be showed to the priest: <small>MARK 1:44 LUKE 5:14 mark</small>

50 And the priest shall look upon the <u>plague</u>, and <u>shut up</u> *it that has* the <u>plague</u> seven days: <small>infection - quarantine</small>

51 And he shall look on the <u>plague</u> on the seventh day: if the <u>plague</u> be spread in the garment, either in the <u>warp, or in the woof,</u> or in a skin, *or* in any work that is made of skin ; the plague *is* a <u>fretting</u> leprosy; it *is* <u>unclean</u>.   <small>mark - unfit</small>

52 He shall therefore burn that garment, whether <u>warp or woof</u>, in woollen or in linen, or any thing of skin, wherein the <u>plague</u> is: for it *is* a <u>fretting</u> leprosy; it shall be burned in the fire.   <small>weaving or in texture - spreading</small>

53 And if the priest shall look, and, behold, the <u>plague</u> be not spread in the garment, either in the <u>warp, or in the woof</u>, or in any thing of skin; <small>mark</small>

54 Then the priest shall command that they wash *the thing* wherein the <u>plague</u> *is*, and he shall shut it up seven days more: <small>infection</small>

55 And the pricst shall look on the <u>plague</u>, after that it is washed: and, behold, *if* the plague have not changed its color, and the <u>plague</u> be not spread; it *is* <u>unclean</u>; you shall burn it in the fire; it *is* <u>fret inward</u>, *whether* it *be* bare inside or outside.   <small>i.e., eaten away within</small>

56 And if the priest look, and, behold, the <u>plague</u> *be* somewhat <u>dark</u> after the washing of it; then he shall <u>rend</u> it out of the garment, or out of the skin, or out of the <u>warp, or out of the woof</u>:   <small>faded - cut</small>

57 And if it appear still in the garment, either in the <u>warp, or in the woof</u>, or in any thing of skin; it *is* a spreading *<u>plague</u>*: you shall burn that wherein the <u>plague</u> *is* with fire.   <small>mark</small>

58 And the garment, either <u>warp, or woof</u>, or whatsoever thing of skin *it be*, which you shall wash, if the <u>plague</u> be departed from them, then it shall be washed the second time, and shall be clean. <small>weaving or in texture - infection</small>

59 This *is* the law of the <u>plague</u> of leprosy in a garment of woollen or linen, either in the <u>warp, or woof</u>, or any thing of skins, to pronounce it clean, or to pronounce it <u>unclean</u>. <small>unfit</small>

CHAPTER 14

AND the LᴏRD spoke to Mo'ses, saying,

2 This shall be the law of the leper in the day of his cleansing: He shall be brought to the priest:

3 And the priest shall go forth out of the camp; and the priest shall look, and, behold, *if* the <u>plague</u> of leprosy be healed in the leper;   <small>infection</small>

4 Then shall the priest command to take for him that is to be cleansed two birds alive *and* clean, and cedar wood, and scarlet, and hyssop:

5 And the priest shall command that one of the birds be killed in an earthen vessel over running water:

6 As for the living bird, he shall take it, and the cedar wood, and the scarlet, and the hyssop, and shall dip them and the living bird in the blood of the bird *that was* killed over the running water:

7 And he shall sprinkle upon him that is to be cleansed from the leprosy seven times, and shall <u>pronounce</u> him clean, and shall let the living bird loose into the open field.   declare

8 And he that is to be cleansed shall wash his clothes, and shave off all his hair, and wash himself in water, that he may be clean: and after that he shall come into the camp, and shall <u>tarry abroad</u> out of his tent seven days.   delay outside

9 But it shall be on the seventh day, that he shall shave all his hair off his head and his beard and his eyebrows, even all his hair he shall shave off: and he shall wash his clothes, also he shall wash his flesh in water, and he shall be clean.

10 And on the eighth day he shall take two he lambs without blemish, and one ewe lamb of the first year without blemish, and three tenth deals of fine flour *for* a meat offering, mingled with oil, and one <u>log</u> of oil.   pint

11 And the priest that makes *him* clean shall present the man that is to be made clean, and those things, before the LORD, *at* the door of the tabernacle of the congregation:

12 And the priest shall take one he lamb, and offer him for a <u>trespass</u> offering, and the <u>log</u> of oil, and wave them *for* a wave offering before the LORD: guilt

13 And he shall slay the lamb in the place where he shall kill the sin offering and the burned offering, in the holy place: for as the sin offering *is* the priest's, *so is* the trespass offering: it *is* most holy:

14 And the priest shall take *some* of the blood of the <u>trespass</u> offering, and the priest shall put *it* upon the tip of the right ear of him that is to be cleansed, and upon the thumb of his right hand, and upon the <u>great</u> toe of his right foot: guilt - big

15 And the priest shall take *some* of the <u>log</u> of oil, and pour *it* into the palm of his own left hand: pint

16 And the priest shall dip his right finger in the oil that *is* in his left hand, and shall sprinkle of the oil with his finger seven times before the LORD:

17 And of the rest of the oil that *is* in his hand shall the priest put upon the tip of the right ear of him that is to be cleansed, and upon the thumb of his right hand, and upon the <u>great</u> toe of his right foot, upon the blood of the <u>trespass</u> offering:

18 And the remnant of the oil that is in the priest's hand he shall pour upon the head of him that is to be cleansed: and the priest shall make an <u>atonement</u> for him before the LORD.   reconciliation

19 And the priest shall offer the sin offering, and make an <u>atonement</u> for him that is to be cleansed from his uncleanness; and afterward he shall kill the burned offering:

20 And the priest shall offer the burned offering and the <u>meat</u> offering upon the altar: and the priest shall make an atonement for him, and he shall be clean.   grain

21 And if he *be* poor, and cannot get so much; then he shall take one lamb *for* a <u>trespass</u> offering to be waved, to make an atonement for him, and one

tenth deal of fine flour mingled with oil for a <u>meat</u> offering, and a <u>log</u> of oil;
22 And two turtledoves, or two young pigeons, such as he is able to get; and the one shall be a sin offering, and the other a burned offering. guilt - grain - pint
23 And he shall bring them on the eighth day for his cleansing to the priest, <u>to</u> the door of the tabernacle of the congregation, before the LORD. in front
24 And the priest shall take the lamb of the trespass offering, and the <u>log</u> of oil, and the priest shall wave them *for* a wave offering before the LORD:
25 And he shall kill the lamb of the trespass offering, and the priest shall take *some* of the blood of the trespass offering, and put *it* upon the tip of the right ear of him that is to be cleansed, and upon the thumb of his right hand, and upon the <u>great</u> toe of his right foot:
26 And the priest shall pour of the oil into the palm of his own left hand:
27 And the priest shall sprinkle with his right finger *some* of the oil that *is* in his left hand seven times before the LORD:
28 And the priest shall put of the oil that *is* in his hand upon the tip of the right ear of him that is to be cleansed, and upon the thumb of his right hand, and upon the <u>great</u> toe of his right foot, upon the place of the blood of the trespass offering: big
29 And the rest of the oil that *is* in the priest's hand he shall put upon the head of him that is to be cleansed, to make an atonement for him before the LORD.

30 And he shall offer the one of the turtledoves, or of the young pigeons, such as he can get;
31 *Even* such as he is able to get, the one *for* a sin offering, and the other *for* a burned offering, with the meat offering: and the priest shall make an atonement for him that is to be cleansed before the LORD.
32 This *is* the <u>law</u> *of him* in whom *is* the <u>plague</u> of leprosy, <u>whose hand is not able to get</u> *that which pertains* to his cleansing. procedure - infection - who cannot afford
33 And the LORD spoke to Mo'ses and to Aar'on, saying,
34 When you be come into the land of Ca'naan, which I give to you for a possession, and I put the plague of leprosy in a house of the land of your possession;
35 And he that owns the house shall come and tell the priest, saying, It seems to me *there is* as it were a <u>plague</u> in the house: mark of leprosy
36 Then the priest shall command that they empty the house, before the priest go *into it* to see the <u>plague</u>, that all that *is* in the house be not made <u>unclean</u>: and afterward the priest shall go in to see the house: unfit
37 And he shall look on the <u>plague</u>, and, behold, *if* the <u>plague</u> *be* in the walls of the house with hollow <u>strakes</u>, greenish or reddish, which in sight *are* lower than the <u>wall</u>; streaks - surface
38 Then the priest shall go out of the house to the door of the house, and <u>shut up</u> the house seven days: quarantine
39 And the priest shall come again the seventh day, and shall look: and,

behold, *if* the plague be spread in the walls of the house; _{infection}

40 Then the priest shall command that they take away the stones in which the plague *is*, and they shall cast them into an unclean place outside the city:

41 And he shall cause the house to be scraped within round about, and they shall pour out the dust that they scrape off outside the city into an unclean place: _{all around inside - unfit}

42 And they shall take other stones, and put *them* in the place of those stones; and he shall take other mortar, and shall plaster the house.

43 And if the plague come again, and break out in the house, after that he has taken away the stones, and after he has scraped the house, and after it is plastered; _{infection}

44 Then the priest shall come and look, and, behold, *if* the plague be spread in the house, it *is* a fretting leprosy in the house: it *is* unclean. _{spreading}

45 And he shall break down the house, the stones of it, and the timber thereof, and all the mortar of the house; and he shall carry *them* forth out of the city into an unclean place. _{unfit}

46 Moreover he that goes into the house all the while that it is shut up shall be unclean until the even.

47 And he that lies in the house shall wash his clothes; and he that eats in the house shall wash his clothes.

48 And if the priest shall come in, and look *upon it*, and, behold, the plague has not spread in the house, after the house was plastered: then the priest shall pronounce the house clean, because the plague is healed. _{mark - infection}

49 And he shall take to cleanse the house two birds, and cedar wood, and scarlet, and hyssop:

50 And he shall kill the one of the birds in an earthen vessel over running water:

51 And he shall take the cedar wood, and the hyssop, and the scarlet, and the living bird, and dip them in the blood of the slain bird, and in the running water, and sprinkle the house seven times:

52 And he shall cleanse the house with the blood of the bird, and with the running water, and with the living bird, and with the cedar wood, and with the hyssop, and with the scarlet: _{in a ceremonial way}

53 But he shall let go the living bird out of the city into the open fields, and make an atonement for the house: and it shall be clean.

54 This *is* the law for all manner of plague of leprosy, and scall, _{procedure - mark - scale}

55 And for the leprosy of a garment, and of a house,

56 And for a rising, and for a scab, and for a bright spot:

57 To teach when *it is* unclean, and when *it is* clean: this *is* the law of leprosy. _{unfit - fit}

CHAPTER 15

AND the LORD spoke to Mo'ses and to Aar'on, saying,

2 Speak to the children of Is'ra-el, and say to them, When any man has a running issue out of his flesh, *because of* his issue he *is* unclean. _{discharge}

3 And this shall be his uncleanness in his issue: whether his flesh run with its <u>issue</u>, or his flesh be stopped from its issue, it *is* his uncleanness. _{discharge}

4 Every bed, whereon he lies that has the <u>issue</u>, is unclean: and every thing, whereon he sits, shall be unclean.

5 And whosoever touches his bed shall wash his clothes, and bathe *himself* in water, and be unclean until the even.

6 And he that sits on *any* thing whereon he sat that has the <u>issue</u> shall wash his clothes, and bathe *himself* in water, and be <u>unclean</u> until the even. _{discharge - unfit}

7 And he that touches the flesh of him that has the <u>issue</u> shall wash his clothes, and bathe *himself* in water, and be <u>unclean</u> until the even.

8 And if he that has the <u>issue</u> spit upon him that is clean; then he shall wash his clothes, and bathe *himself* in water, and be unclean until the even.

9 And what saddle soever he rides upon that has the issue shall be unclean.

10 And whosoever touches any thing that was under him shall be unclean until the even: and he that bears *any of* those things shall wash his clothes, and bathe *himself* in water, and be unclean until the even.

11 And whomsoever he touches that has the <u>issue</u>, and has not rinsed his hands in water, he shall wash his clothes, and bathe *himself* in water, and be unclean until the even. _{discharge}

12 And the vessel of earth, that he touches which hath the <u>issue</u>, shall be <u>broken</u>: and every vessel of wood shall be rinsed in water. _{discharge - destroyed}

13 And when he that has an <u>issue</u> is cleansed of his issue; then he shall number to himself seven days for his cleansing, and wash his clothes, and bathe his flesh in running water, and shall be clean.

14 And on the eighth day he shall take to him two turtledoves, or two young pigeons, and come before the LORD to the door of the tabernacle of the congregation, and give them to the priest:

15 And the priest shall offer them, the one *for* a sin offering, and the other *for* a burned offering; and the priest shall make an <u>atonement</u> for him before the LORD for his issue. _{reconciliation}

16 And if any man's <u>seed of copulation</u> go out from him, then he shall wash all his flesh in water, and be unclean until the even. _{seminal emission - unfit}

17 And every garment, and every skin, whereon is the <u>seed of copulation</u>, shall be washed with water, and be <u>unclean</u> until the even.

18 The woman also with whom man shall lie *with* <u>seed of copulation</u>, they shall *both* bathe *themselves* in water, and be <u>unclean</u> until the even.

19 And if a woman have an <u>issue</u>, *and* her <u>issue</u> in her flesh be blood, she shall be <u>put apart</u> seven days: and whosoever touches her shall be <u>unclean</u> until the even. _{discharge - kept separate}

20 And every thing that she lies upon in her separation shall be <u>un-</u>

<u>clean</u>: every thing also that she sits upon shall be <u>unclean</u>.   _{unfit}

21 And whosoever touches her bed shall wash his clothes, and bathe *himself* in water, and be <u>unclean</u> until the even.

22 And whosoever touches any thing that she sat upon shall wash his clothes, and bathe *himself* in water, and be <u>unclean</u> until the even.

23 And if it *be* on *her* bed, or on any thing whereon she sits, when he touches it, he shall be <u>unclean</u> until the even.

24 And if any man lie with her at all, and her <u>flowers</u> be upon him, he shall be <u>unclean</u> seven days; and all the bed whereon he lies shall be <u>unclean</u>.   _{menstrual impurity}

25 And if a woman have an <u>issue</u> of her blood many days out of the time of her separation, or if it run beyond the time of her separation; all the days of the <u>issue</u> of her uncleanness shall be as the days of her separation: she *shall be* <u>unclean</u>.   _{MATT. 9:20 discharge}

26 Every bed whereon she lies all the days of her <u>issue</u> shall be to her as the bed of her separation: and whatsoever she sits upon shall be <u>unclean</u>, as the uncleanness of her separation.

27 And whosoever touches those things shall be <u>unclean</u>, and shall wash his clothes, and bathe *himself* in water, and be <u>unclean</u> until the even.   _{unfit}

28 But if she be cleansed of her issue, then she shall number to herself seven days, and after that she shall be clean.

29 And on the eighth day she shall take to her two <u>turtles</u>, or two young pigeons, and bring them to the priest, to the door of the tabernacle of the congregation.   _{turtledoves}

30 And the priest shall offer the one *for* a sin offering, and the other *for* a burned offering; and the priest shall make an atonement for her before the LORD for the <u>issue</u> of her uncleanness.   _{discharge}

31 Thus shall you separate the children of Is'ra-el from their uncleanness; that they die not in their uncleanness, when they defile My tabernacle that *is* among them.

32 This *is* the <u>law</u> of him that has an issue, and *of him* whose seed goes from him, and is defiled therewith;   _{regulation}

33 And of her that is sick of her <u>flowers</u>, and of him that has an <u>issue</u>, of the man, and of the woman, and of him that lies with her that is unclean.   _{menstrual impurity - discharge - unfit}

CHAPTER 16

A ND the LORD spoke to Mo'ses after the death of the two sons of Aar'on, when they offered before the LORD, and died;

2 And the LORD said to Mo'ses, Speak to Aar'on your brother, that he come not at all times into the holy *place* within the veil before the mercy seat, which *is* upon the ark; that he die not: for I will appear in the cloud upon the mercy seat.   _{HEB. 6:19}

3 Thus shall Aar'on come into the holy *place*: with a young bullock for a sin offering, and a ram for a burned offering.

4 He shall put on the holy linen coat, and he shall have the linen breeches

upon his flesh, and shall be girded with a linen girdle, and with the linen <u>mitre</u> shall he be attired: these *are* holy garments; therefore shall he wash his flesh in water, and *so* put them on. turban

5 And he shall take of the congregation of the children of Is'ra-el two <u>kids</u> of the goats for a sin offering, and one ram for a burnt offering. male goats

6 And Aar'on shall offer his bullock of the sin offering, which *is* for himself, and make an <u>atonement</u> for himself, and for his house. offering

7 And he shall take the two goats, and present them before the LORD *at* the door of the tabernacle of the congregation.

8 And Aar'on shall cast lots upon the two goats; one lot for the LORD, and the other lot for the scapegoat.

9 And Aar'on shall bring the goat upon which the LORD's lot fell, and offer him *for* a sin offering.

10 But the goat, on which the lot fell to be the scapegoat, shall be presented alive before the LORD, to make an atonement with him, *and* to let him go for a scapegoat into the wilderness. 1 JOHN 2:2

11 And Aar'on shall bring the bullock of the sin offering, which *is* for himself, and shall make an atonement for himself, and for his house, and shall kill the bullock of the sin offering which *is* for himself:

12 And he shall take a censer full of burning coals of fire from off the altar before the LORD, and his hands full of sweet incense beaten small, and bring *it* within the veil:

13 And he shall put the incense upon the fire before the LORD, that the cloud of the incense may cover the mercy seat that *is* upon the testimony, that he die not:

14 And he shall take of the blood of the bullock, and sprinkle *it* with his finger upon the mercy seat eastward; and before the mercy seat shall he sprinkle of the blood with his finger seven times.

15 Then shall he kill the goat of the sin offering, that *is* for the people, and bring its blood within the veil, and do with that blood as he did with the blood of the bullock, and sprinkle it upon the mercy seat, and before the mercy seat:

16 And he shall make an atonement for the holy *place*, because of the <u>uncleanness</u> of the children of Is'ra-el, and because of their transgressions in all their sins: and so shall he do for the tabernacle of the congregation, that remains among them in the midst of their <u>uncleanness</u>. unfitness

17 And there shall be no man in the tabernacle of the congregation when he goes in to make an atonement in the holy *place*, until he come out, and have made an atonement for himself, and for his household, and for all the congregation of Is'ra-el.

18 And he shall go out to the altar that *is* before the LORD, and make an atonement for it; and shall take of the blood of the bullock, and of the blood of the goat, and put *it* upon the horns of the altar round about.

19 And he shall sprinkle of the blood upon it with his finger seven times, and

cleanse it, and <u>hallow</u> it from the <u>un-cleanness</u> of the children of Is'ra-el.

           consecrate - unfitness

20 And when he has made an end of <u>reconciling</u> the holy *place*, and the tabernacle of the congregation, and the altar, he shall bring the live goat: atoning for

21 And Aar'on shall lay both his hands upon the head of the live goat, and confess over him all the <u>iniquities</u> of the children of Is'ra-el, and all their transgressions in all their sins, putting them upon the head of the goat, and shall send *him* away by the hand of a fit man into the wilderness: sins

22 And the goat shall <u>bear</u> upon him all their iniquities to a <u>land not inhab-ited</u>: and he shall let go the goat in the wilderness.   carry - a solitary land

23 And Aar'on shall come into the tabernacle of the congregation, and shall put off the linen garments, which he put on when he went into the holy *place*, and shall leave them there:

24 And he shall wash his flesh with water in the holy place, and put on his garments, and come forth, and offer his burned offering, and the burned offering of the people, and make an atonement for himself, and for the people.

25 And the fat of the sin offering shall he burn upon the altar.

26 And he that let go the goat for the <u>scapegoat</u> shall wash his clothes, and bathe his flesh in water, and afterward come into the camp.   Lit. goat of departure

27 And the bullock *for* the sin offering, and the goat *for* the sin offering, whose blood was brought in to make atonement in the holy *place*, shall *one* carry forth outside the camp; and they shall burn in the fire their skins, and their flesh, and their dung.   HEB. 13:11

28 And he that burns them shall wash his clothes, and bathe his flesh in water, and afterward he shall come into the camp.

29 And *this* shall be a <u>statute</u> for ever to you: *that* in the seventh month, on the tenth *day* of the month, you shall <u>afflict your souls</u>, and do no work at all, *whether it be* one of your own country, or a <u>stranger</u> that <u>sojourns</u> among you: law - humble yourselves - alien - lives

30 For on that day shall *the priest* make an <u>atonement</u> for you, to cleanse you, *that* you may be clean from all your sins before the LORD.

           ceremony of reconciliation

31 It *shall be* a <u>sabbath</u> of rest to you, and you shall <u>afflict your souls</u>, by a <u>statute</u> for ever.   day

32 And the priest, whom he shall anoint, and whom he shall consecrate to minister in the priest's office in his father's stead, shall make the <u>atonement</u>, and shall put on the linen clothes, *even* the holy garments:

33 And he shall make an <u>atonement</u> for the holy sanctuary, and he shall make an <u>atonement</u> for the tabernacle of the congregation, and for the altar, and he shall make an <u>atonement</u> for the priests, and for all the people of the congregation.

34 And this shall be an everlasting <u>statute</u> to you, to make an <u>atonement</u> for the children of Is'ra-el for all their sins once a year. And he did as the LORD commanded Mo'ses.   law

CHAPTER 17

A ND the Lord spoke to Mo'ses, saying,

2 Speak to Aar'on, and to his sons, and to all the children of Is'ra-el, and say to them; This *is* the thing which the Lord has commanded, saying,

3 What man soever *there be* of the house of Is'ra-el, that kills an ox, or lamb, or goat, in the camp, or that kill *it* <u>out of</u> the camp,   outside

4 And brings it not to the door of the tabernacle of the congregation, to offer an offering to the Lord before the tabernacle of the Lord; blood shall be <u>imputed</u> to that man; he has shed blood; and that man shall be <u>cut off</u> from among his people: reckoned - destroyed

5 To the end that the children of Is'ra-el may bring their sacrifices, which they offer in the open field, even that they may bring them to the Lord, to the door of the tabernacle of the congregation, to the priest, and offer them *for* peace offerings to the Lord.

6 And the priest shall sprinkle the blood upon the altar of the Lord *at* the door of the tabernacle of the congregation, and burn the fat for a sweet savor to the Lord.

7 And they shall no more offer their sacrifices to <u>devils</u>, after whom they have gone a whoring. This shall be a <u>statute</u> for ever to them throughout their generations.   demons - law

8 And you shalt say to them, Whatsoever man *there be* of the house of Is'ra-el, or of the strangers which <u>so-</u>journ among you, that offers a burned offering or sacrifice,   stay

9 And brings it not to the door of the tabernacle of the congregation, to offer it to the Lord; even that man shall be <u>cut off</u> from among his people.   destroyed

10 And whatsoever man *there be* of the house of Is'ra-el, or of the strangers that <u>sojourn</u> among you, that eats any manner of blood; I will even set My face against that <u>soul</u> that eats blood, and will <u>cut him off</u> from among his people.   stay - man

11 For the life of the flesh *is* in the blood: and I have given it to you upon the altar to make an atonement for your <u>souls</u>: for it *is* the <u>blood *that* makes an atonement</u> for the soul.

the death of the sacrifice

12 Therefore I said to the children of Is'ra-el, No <u>soul</u> of you shall eat blood, neither shall any stranger that <u>sojourns</u> among you eat blood.   person

13 And whatsoever man *there be* of the children of Is'ra-el, or of the strangers that <u>sojourn</u> among you, which hunts and catches any beast or fowl that may be eaten; he shall even pour out the blood thereof, and cover it with dust.   stay

14 For *it is* the life of all flesh; the blood of it *is* for the life thereof: therefore I said to the children of Is'ra-el, You shall eat the blood of no manner of flesh: for the life of all flesh *is* the blood thereof: whosoever eats it shall be cut off.

15 And every <u>soul</u> that eats that which died *of itself*, or that which was

M16 G4R

332 304

torn *with beasts*, *whether it be* one of your own country, or a stranger, he shall both wash his clothes, and bathe *himself* in water, and be <u>unclean</u> until the even: then shall he be clean. <small>one - unfit</small>

16 But if he wash *them* not, nor bathe his flesh; then he shall bear his <u>iniquity</u>. <small>guilt</small>

CHAPTER 18

AND the L**ORD** spoke to Mo'ses, saying,

2 Speak to the children of Is'ra-el, and say to them, I am the L**ORD** your <u>God</u>. <small>Elohim^{p.f.}</small>

3 After the doings of the land of E'gypt, wherein you dwelt, shall you not do: and after the doings of the land of Ca'naan, where I bring you, shall you not do: neither shall you walk in their <u>ordinances</u>. <small>to which - ways</small>

4 You shall do My <u>judgments</u>, and keep My <u>ordinances</u>, to walk therein: I *am* the L**ORD** your <u>God</u>. <small>laws</small>

5 You shall therefore keep My <u>stat-utes</u>, and My <u>judgments</u>: which if a man <u>do</u>, he shall live in them: I *am* the L**ORD**. <small>ROM. 10:5 GAL. 3:12 rules - practices</small>

6 None of you shall approach to any that is near of kin to him, to uncover *their* nakedness: I *am* the L**ORD**.

7 The nakedness of your father, or the nakedness of your mother, shall you not uncover: she *is* your mother; you shall not uncover her nakedness.

8 The nakedness of your father's wife shall you not uncover: it *is* your father's nakedness.

9 The nakedness of your sister, the daughter of your father, or daughter of your mother, *whether she be* born at home, or born abroad, *even* their nakedness you shall not uncover.

10 The nakedness of your son's daugh-ter, or of your daughter's daughter, *even* their nakedness you shall not uncover: for theirs *is* your own nakedness.

11 The nakedness of your father's wife's daughter, begotten of your fa-ther, she *is* your sister, you shall not uncover her nakedness.

12 You shall not uncover the naked-ness of your father's sister: she *is* your father's near kinswoman.

13 You shall not uncover the naked-ness of your mother's sister: for she *is* your mother's near kinswoman.

14 You shall not uncover the naked-ness of your father's brother, you shall not approach to his wife: she *is* your aunt.

15 You shall not uncover the naked-ness of your daughter in law: she *is* your son's wife; you shall not un-cover her nakedness.

16 You shall not uncover the naked-ness of your brother's wife: it *is* your brother's nakedness.

17 You shall not uncover the naked-ness of a woman and her daughter, nei-ther shall you take her son's daughter, or her daughter's daughter, to uncover her nakedness; *for* they *are* her near kinswomen: it *is* <u>wickedness</u>. <small>sinful</small>

18 Neither shall you take a wife to her sister, to <u>vex</u> *her*, to uncover her nakedness, beside the other in her life *time*. <small>irritate</small>

19 Also you shall not approach to a woman to uncover her nakedness, as

long as she is put apart for her un-cleanness.

20 Moreover you shall not <u>lie car-nally</u> with your neighbor's wife, to defile yourself with her. have intercourse

21 And you shall not let any of your <u>seed</u> pass through *the fire* to Mo'lech, neither shall you profane the name of your God: I *am* the LORD. offspring

22 You shall not lie with mankind, as with womankind: it *is* <u>abomination</u>. sin

23 Neither shall you lie with any beast to defile yourself therewith: neither shall any woman stand be-fore a beast to lie down thereto: it *is* <u>confusion</u>. perversion

24 Defile not you yourselves in any of these things: for in all these the nations are defiled which I cast out before you:

25 And the land is defiled: therefore I do visit the iniquity thereof upon it, and the land itself vomits out her inhabitants.

26 You shall therefore <u>keep</u> My <u>stat-utes</u> and My judgments, and shall not commit *any* of these <u>abominations:</u> *neither* any of your own nation, nor any <u>stranger</u> that <u>sojourns</u> among you: obey - laws - alien - lives

27 (For all these <u>abominations</u> have the men of the land done, which *were* before you, and the land is defiled;)

28 That the land spew not you out also, when you defile it, as it spewed out the nations that *were* before you.

29 For whosoever shall commit any of these <u>abominations</u>, even the <u>souls</u> that commit *them* shall be <u>cut off</u> from among their people. sins - persons - destroyed

30 Therefore shall you keep My ordi-nance, that *you* commit not *any one* of these <u>abominable</u> customs, which were committed before you, and that you defile not yourselves therein: I *am* the LORD your <u>God</u>. detestable

CHAPTER 19

AND the LORD spoke to Mo'ses, saying,

2 Speak to all the congregation of the children of Is'ra-el, and say to them, You shall be holy: for I the LORD your <u>God</u> *am* <u>holy</u>. Elohim^{p-f} - set apart

3 You shall <u>fear</u> every man his mother, and his father, and keep My <u>sabbaths</u>: I *am* the LORD your <u>God</u>. revere - rest days

4 Turn you not to idols, nor make to yourselves <u>molten gods</u>: I *am* the LORD your <u>God</u>. images

5 And if you offer a sacrifice of peace offerings to the LORD, you shall offer it at your own will.

6 It shall be eaten the same day you offer it, and on the morrow: and if any remain until the third day, it shall be burned in the fire. any

7 And if it be eaten at all on the third day, it *is* <u>abominable</u>; it shall not be accepted. an offense

8 Therefore *every one* that eats it shall bear his iniquity, because he has profaned the hallowed thing of the LORD: and that <u>soul</u> shall be cut off from among his people. person

9 And when you reap the harvest of your land, you shall not wholly reap the corners of your field, neither shall

you gather the gleanings of your harvest.
10 And you shall not glean your vineyard, neither shall you gather *every
grape* of your vineyard; you shall leave
them for the poor and stranger: I *am*
the LORD your <u>God</u>.   the fallen fruit - Elohim[p.f.]
11 You shall not steal, neither deal
falsely, neither lie one to another.
12 And you shall not swear by My
name falsely, neither shall you profane the name of thy <u>God</u>: I *am* the
LORD.   MATT. 5:34
13 You shall not defraud your neighbor, neither rob *him*: the wages of
him that is hired shall not abide with
you all night until the morning. MATT.20:8
14 You shall not curse the deaf, nor
put a stumblingblock before the
blind, but shall <u>fear</u> your <u>God</u>: I *am*
the LORD.   revere - Elohim[p.f.]
15 You shall do no unrighteousness in
judgment: you shall not respect the
person of the poor, nor honor the person of the mighty: *but* in righteousness shall you judge your neighbor.
16 You shall not go up and down *as* a
talebearer among your people: neither
shall you <u>stand against the blood</u> of
your neighbor: I *am* the LORD. act against the life
17 You shall not <u>hate</u> your brother
in your heart: you shall in any wise
rebuke your neighbor, and not <u>suf-
fer sin upon him</u>. dislike - incur sin because of him
18 You shall not <u>avenge</u>, nor bear
any grudge against the children of
your people, but you shall love your
neighbor as yourself: I *am* the
LORD. MATT 5:43 MATT. 19:19 MARK 12:31 MATT 22:39
JAMES 2:8 GAL. 5:14 LUKE 10:27 ROM 13:9 retaliate
19 You shall <u>keep</u> My <u>statutes</u>. You

shall not let your cattle <u>gender</u> with a
diverse kind: you shall not sow your
field with mingled seed: neither shall
a garment mingled of linen and
woollen come upon you. obey - laws - breed
20 And whosoever lies carnally with a
woman, that *is* a bondmaid, betrothed
to an husband, and not at all redeemed,
nor freedom given her; she shall be
scourged; they shall not be put to
death, because she was not free.
21 And he shall bring his <u>trespass</u> offering to the LORD, to the door of the
tabernacle of the congregation, *even* a
ram for a trespass offering.   guilt
22 And the priest shall make an
atonement for him with the ram of
the trespass offering before the
LORD for his sin which he has done:
and the sin which he has done shall
be forgiven him.
23 And when you shall come into the
land, and shall have planted all
manner of trees for food, then you
shall count the fruit thereof as
<u>uncircumcised</u>: three years shall it be
as <u>uncircumcised</u> to you: it shall not
be eaten of.   forbidden
24 But in the fourth year all the fruit
thereof shall be <u>holy</u> to praise the
LORD *with*.   set apart
25 And in the fifth year shall you eat
of the fruit thereof, that it may yield
to you the increase thereof: I *am* the
LORD your <u>God</u>.   Elohim[p.f.]
26 You shall not eat *any thing* with
the blood: neither shall you use <u>en-
chantment</u>, nor <u>observe times</u>.
     divination - soothsaying
27 You shall not round the <u>corners</u> of

your heads, neither shall you mar the <u>corners</u> of your beard.   side growth

28 You shall not make any cuttings in your flesh for the dead, nor <u>print</u> any marks upon you: I *am* the Lord.   tattoo

29 Do not prostitute your daughter, to cause her to be a whore; less the land fall to whoredom, and the land become full of wickedness.

30 Ye shall keep My <u>sabbaths</u>, and reverence My sanctuary: I *am* the Lord.   rest days

31 Regard not them that have <u>familiar spirits</u>, neither seek after <u>wizards</u>, to be defiled by them: I *am* the Lord your <u>God</u>.   mediums - diviners

32 You shall rise up before the <u>hoary head</u>, and honor the face of the old man, and <u>fear</u> your <u>God</u>: I *am* the Lord.   aged - revere - Elohim[p.f.]

33 And if a stranger <u>sojourn</u> with you in your land, you shall not <u>vex</u> him.   resides - trouble

34 *But* the <u>stranger</u> that dwells with you shall be to you as <u>one born</u> among you, and you shall love him as yourself; for you were <u>strangers</u> in the land of E'gypt: I *am* the Lord your <u>God</u>.   foreigner - the native - aliens

35 You shall do no <u>unrighteousness</u> in judgment, in <u>meteyard</u>, in weight, or in <u>measure</u>.   wrong - measurements - capacity

36 <u>Just</u> balances, <u>just</u> weights, a <u>just</u> ephah, and a <u>just</u> hin, shall you have: I *am* the Lord your <u>God</u>, which brought you out of the land of E'gypt.   fair - Elohim[p.f.]

37 Therefore shall you observe all My <u>statutes</u>, and all My judgments, and do them: I *am* the Lord.   laws

CHAPTER 20

AND the Lord spoke to Mo'ses, saying,

2 Again, you shall say to the children of Is'ra-el, Whosoever *he be* of the children of Is'ra-el, or of the <u>strangers</u> that <u>sojourn</u> in Is'ra-el, that gives *any* of his <u>seed</u> to Mo'lech; he shall surely be put to death: the people of the land shall stone him with stones.   foreigners - temporarily resides - offspring

3 And I will set My face against that man, and will <u>cut him off</u> from among his people; because he has given of his <u>seed</u> to Mo'lech, to defile My sanctuary, and to profane My holy name.   destroy him

4 And if the people of the land do any ways hide their eyes from the man, when he gives of his <u>seed</u> to Mo'lech, and kill him not:

5 Then I will set My face against that man, and against his family, and will cut him off, and all that go a whoring after him, to commit whoredom with Mo'lech, from among their people.

6 And the <u>soul</u> that turns after such as have <u>familiar spirits</u>, and after <u>wizards</u>, to go a whoring after them, I will even set My face against that <u>soul</u>, and will <u>cut him off</u> from among his people.   mediums - person - diviners

7 Sanctify yourselves therefore, and be you holy: for I *am* the Lord your <u>God</u>.   Elohim[p.f.]

8 And you shall <u>keep</u> My <u>statutes</u>, and do them: I *am* the Lord which <u>sanctify you</u>.   obey - laws - sets you apart

9 For every one that curses his fa-

ther or his mother shall be surely put to death: he has cursed his father or his mother; his blood *shall be* upon him.

10 And the man that commits adultery with *another* man's wife, *even he* that commits adultery with his neighbor's wife, the adulterer and the adulteress shall surely be put to death.

11 And the man that lies with his father's wife has uncovered his father's nakedness: both of them shall surely be put to death; their blood *shall be* upon them.

12 And if a man lie with his daughter in law, both of them shall surely be put to death: they have <u>wrought</u> confusion; their blood *shall be* upon them. _{worked}

13 If a man also lie with mankind, as he lies with a woman, both of them have committed an <u>abomination</u>: they shall surely be put to death; their blood *shall be* upon them. _{a detestable act}

14 And if a man take a wife and her mother, it *is* wickedness: they shall be burned with fire, both he and they; that there be no wickedness among you.

15 And if a man lie with a beast, he shall surely be put to death: and you shall slay the beast.

16 And if a woman approach to any beast, and lie down thereto, you shall kill the woman, and the beast: they shall surely be put to death; their blood *shall be* upon them.

17 And if a man shall take his sister, his father's daughter, or his mother's daughter, and see her nakedness, and she see his nakedness; it *is* a wicked thing; and they shall be <u>cut off</u> in the sight of their people: he has uncovered his sister's nakedness; he shall bear his iniquity.

18 And if a man shall lie with a woman having her sickness, and shall uncover her nakedness; he has discovered her fountain, and she has uncovered the fountain of her blood: and both of them shall be <u>cut off</u> from among their people. _{destroyed}

19 And you shall not uncover the nakedness of your mother's sister, nor of your father's sister: for he uncovers his near kin: they shall bear their iniquity.

20 And if a man shall lie with his uncle's wife, he has uncovered his uncle's nakedness: they shall bear their sin; they shall die childless.

21 And if a man shall take his brother's wife, it *is* an <u>unclean thing</u>: he has uncovered his brother's nakedness; they shall be childless. _{an impure deed}

22 You shall therefore keep all My <u>statutes</u>, and all My judgments, and do them: that the land, where I bring you to dwell therein, spew you not out. _{laws}

23 And you shall not walk in the manners of the nation, which I cast out before you: for they committed all these things, and therefore I abhorred them.

24 But I have said to you, You shall inherit their land, and I will give it to you to possess it, a land that flows with milk and honey: I *am* the LORD your God, which have <u>separated</u> you from *other* people. _{divided}

25 You shall therefore put difference between clean beasts and <u>unclean</u>, and between <u>unclean</u> fowls and clean: and

you shall not make <u>your souls abomi-</u><u>nable</u> by beast, or by fowl, or by any manner of living thing that creeps on the ground, which I have separated from you as unclean. <small>unfit - yourselves detestable</small>

26 And you shall be holy to Me: for I the LORD *am* holy, and have severed you from *other* people, that you should be Mine.

27 A man also or woman that has a <u>familiar spirit</u>, or that is a <u>wizard</u>, shall surely be put to death: they shall stone them with stones: their blood *shall be* upon them. <small>mediums - diviners</small>

CHAPTER 21

AND the LORD said to Mo'ses, Speak to the priests the sons of Aar'on, and say to them, There shall none be defiled for the dead among his people:

2 <u>But</u> for his kin, that is near to him, *that is*, for his mother, and for his father, and for his son, and for his daughter, and for his brother, <small>Except</small>

3 And for his sister a virgin, that is near to him, which has had no husband; for her may he be defiled.

4 <u>But</u> he shall not defile himself, *being* a chief man among his people, to profane himself.

5 They shall not make baldness upon their head, neither shall they shave off the <u>corner</u> of their beard, nor make any cuttings in their flesh. <small>side growth</small>

6 They shall be holy to their God, and not profane the name of their God: for the offerings of the LORD made by

fire, *and* the bread of their God, they do offer: therefore they shall be holy.

7 <u>They</u> shall not take a wife *that* is a whore, or profane; neither shall they take a woman put away from her husband: for he *is* holy to his <u>God</u>. <small>Priests - Elohim^{p.f.}</small>

8 You shall <u>sanctify</u> him therefore; for he offers the bread of your <u>God</u>: he shall be holy to you: for I the LORD, which sanctify you, *am* holy. <small>set apart</small>

9 And the daughter of any priest, if she <u>profane</u> herself by playing the whore, she <u>profanes</u> her father: she shall be burned with fire. <small>defile - disgraces</small>

10 And *he that is* the high priest among his brethren, upon whose head the anointing oil was poured, and that is consecrated to put on the garments, shall not uncover his head, nor rend his clothes;

11 Neither shall he go in to any dead body, nor defile himself for his father, or for his mother;

12 Neither shall he go out of the sanctuary, nor <u>profane</u> the sanctuary of his <u>God</u>; for the crown of the anointing oil of his <u>God</u> *is* upon him: I am the LORD. <small>desecrate - Elohim^{p.f.}</small>

13 And he shall take a wife in her virginity.

14 A widow, or a divorced woman, or <u>profane</u>, *or* an <u>harlot</u>, these shall he not take: but he shall take a virgin of his own people to wife. <small>prostitute</small>

15 Neither shall he <u>profane</u> his <u>seed</u> among his people: for I the LORD do sanctify him. <small>defile - offspring</small>

16 And the LORD spoke to Mo'ses, saying,

17 Speak to Aar'on, saying, Whosoever *he be* of your <u>seed</u> in their generations that has *any* <u>blemish,</u> let him not approach to <u>offer</u> the bread of his God.   offspring - defect - serve as priest

18 For whatsoever man *he be* that has a <u>blemish</u>, he shall not approach: a blind man, or a lame, or he that has a flat nose, or any thing superfluous,

19 Or a man that is brokenfooted, or brokenhanded,

20 Or crookback, or a dwarf, or that has a blemish in his eye, or be scurvy, or <u>scabbed</u>, or has his <u>stones</u> broken;   skin disease - testicles

21 No man that has a <u>blemish</u> of the <u>seed</u> of Aar'on the priest shall come near to offer the offerings of the LORD made by fire: he has a <u>blemish;</u> he shall not come near to offer the bread of his <u>God</u>.   defect - offspring - Elohim^{p.f.}

22 He shall eat the bread of his <u>God</u>, *both* of the most holy, and of the holy.

23 Only he shall not go in to the veil, nor come near to the altar, because he has a blemish; that he <u>profane</u> not My sanctuaries: for I the LORD do sanctify them.   serve as priest - defile

24 And Mo'ses told *it* to Aar'on, and to his sons, and to all the children of Is'ra-el.

CHAPTER 22

AND the LORD spoke to Mo'ses, saying,

2 Speak to Aar'on and to his sons, that they separate themselves from the holy things of the children of Is'ra-el, and that they <u>profane</u> not My holy name *in those things* which they hallow to Me: I *am* the LORD.   defile

3 Say to them, Whosoever *he be* of all your <u>seed</u> among your generations, that goes to the <u>holy things</u>, which the children of Is'ra-el hallow to the LORD, having his <u>uncleanness</u> upon him, that <u>soul</u> shall be cut off from My presence: I *am* the LORD.   descendants - serve as priest - ceremonially unfit - person

4 What man soever of the <u>seed</u> of Aar'on *is* a leper, or has a <u>running issue</u>; he shall not eat of the holy things, until he be clean. And whoso touches any thing *that is* <u>unclean</u> by the dead, or a man whose seed goes from him;   bodily discharge - defiled

5 Or whosoever touches any creeping thing, whereby he may be made <u>unclean</u>, or a man of whom he may take <u>uncleanness</u>, whatsoever <u>uncleanness</u> he has;   unfit - unfitness

6 The <u>soul</u> which has touched any such shall be <u>unclean</u> until even, and <u>shall not eat</u> of the holy things, unless he wash his flesh with water.   person - i.e., as priest

7 And when the sun is down, he shall be clean, and shall afterward eat of the holy things; because it *is* his food.

8 That which dies of itself, or is torn *with beasts*, he shall not eat to defile himself therewith: I am the LORD.

9 They shall therefore <u>keep</u> My <u>ordinance</u>, less they bear sin for it, and die therefore, if they profane it: I the LORD do sanctify them.   obey - requirements

10 There shall no stranger eat *of* the <u>holy thing</u>: a <u>sojourner</u> of the priest, or

an hired servant, shall not eat *of* the holy thing.   sacred offering - guest

11 But if the priest buy *any* <u>soul</u> with his money, he shall eat of it, and he that is born in his house: they shall eat of his <u>meat</u>.   slave - food

12 If the priest's daughter also be *married* to a <u>stranger</u>, she may not eat of an offering of the holy things.

13 But if the priest's daughter be a widow, or divorced, and have no child, and is returned to her father's house, as in her youth, she shall eat of her father's <u>meat</u>: but there shall no <u>stranger</u> eat thereof.   alien

14 And if a man eat *of* the holy thing unwittingly, then he shall put the fifth *part* thereof to it, and shall give *it* to the priest with the holy thing.

15 And they shall not <u>profane</u> the holy things of the children of Is'ra-el, which they offer to the LORD;   desecrate

16 Or allow them to bear the iniquity of trespass, when they eat their holy things: for I the LORD do sanctify them.

17 And the LORD spoke to Mo'ses, saying,

18 Speak to Aar'on, and to his sons, and to all the children of Is'ra-el, and say to them, Whatsoever *he be* of the house of Is'ra-el, or of the strangers in Is'ra-el, that will offer his <u>oblation</u> for all his vows, and for all his freewill offerings, which they will offer to the LORD for a burned offering;   offering

19 *You shall offer* at your own will a male without <u>blemish</u>, of the <u>beeves</u>, of the sheep, or of the goats   .defect - beef cattle

20 But whatsoever has a <u>blemish</u>, *that* shall you not offer: for it shall not be acceptable for you.   defect

21 And whosoever offers a sacrifice of peace offerings to the LORD to accomplish *his* vow, or a freewill offering in <u>beeves</u> or sheep, it shall be perfect to be accepted; there shall be no <u>blemish</u> therein.   beef cattle

22 Blind, or broken, or maimed, or having a <u>wen</u>, or scurvy, or <u>scabbed</u>, you shall not offer these to the LORD, nor make an offering by fire of them upon the altar to the LORD.   a running sore - skin disease

23 Either a bullock or a lamb that has any thing <u>superfluous</u> or lacking in his parts, that may you offer *for* a freewill offering; but <u>for</u> a vow it shall not be accepted.   deformed - required offering

24 You shall not offer to the LORD that which is bruised, or crushed, or broken, or cut; neither shall you make *any offering thereof* in your land.

25 Neither from a stranger's hand shall you offer the bread of your <u>God</u> of any of these; because their corruption *is* in them, *and* <u>blemishes</u> *be* in them: they shall not be accepted for you.   Elohim^p.f.

26 And the LORD spoke to Mo'ses, saying,

27 When a bullock, or a sheep, or a goat, is brought forth, then it shall be seven days under the <u>dam</u>; and from the eighth day and thereafter it shall be accepted for an offering made by fire to the LORD.   mother

28 And *whether it* be cow or ewe, you shall not kill it and her young both in one day.

29 And when you will offer a sacrifice of thanksgiving to the LORD, offer *it* at your own will. free giving

30 On the same day it shall be eaten up; you shall leave none of it until the morrow: I *am* the LORD.

31 Therefore shall you keep My commandments, and do them: I *am* the LORD.

32 Neither shall you profane My holy name; but I will be hallowed among the children of Is'ra-el: I *am* the LORD which hallow you, defile - sanctified

33 That brought you out of the land of E'gypt, to be your God: I *am* the LORD. Elohim^p.f.

CHAPTER 23

AND the LORD spoke to Mo'ses, saying,

2 Speak to the children of Is'ra-el, and say to them, *Concerning* the feasts of the LORD, which you shall proclaim *to be* holy convocations, *even* these *are* My feasts. assemblies

3 Six days shall work be done: but the seventh day *is* the sabbath of rest, an holy convocation; you shall do no work *therein*: it *is* the sabbath of the LORD in all your dwellings. LUKE 13:14 rest day - homes

4 These *are* the feasts of the LORD, *even* holy convocations, which you shall proclaim in their seasons.

5 In the fourteenth *day* of the first month at even *is* the LORD's passover.

6 And on the fifteenth day of the same month *is* the feast of unleavened bread to the LORD: seven days you must eat unleavened bread. without yeast

7 In the first day you shall have an holy convocation: you shall do no servile work therein. assembly - regular

8 But you shall offer an offering made by fire to the LORD seven days: in the seventh day *is* an holy convocation: you shall do no servile work *therein*.

9 And the LORD spoke to Mo'ses, saying,

10 Speak to the children of Is'ra-el, and say to them, When you be come into the land which I give to you, and shall reap the harvest thereof, then you shall bring a sheaf of the firstfruits of your harvest to the priest: handful

11 And he shall wave the sheaf before the LORD, to be accepted for you: on the morrow after the sabbath the priest shall wave it. present - rest day

12 And you shall offer that day when you wave the sheaf an he lamb without blemish of the first year for a burned offering to the LORD. defect

13 And the meat offering thereof *shall be* two tenth deals of fine flour mingled with oil, an offering made by fire to the LORD *for* a sweet savor: and the drink offering thereof *shall* be of wine, the fourth *part* of an hin. grain - soothing aroma

14 And you shall eat neither bread, nor parched corn, nor green ears, until the selfsame day that you have brought an offering to your God: *it shall be* a statute for ever throughout your generations in all your dwellings. grain - Elohim^p.f. - law

15 And you shall count to you from the morrow after the sabbath, from the day that you brought the sheaf of the wave offering; seven sabbaths shall be complete: rest day

16 Even to the morrow after the seventh <u>sabbath</u> shall you number <u>fifty days</u>; and you shall offer a new <u>meat</u> offering to the LORD.   rest day - Pentecost - grain
17 You shall bring out of your habitations two wave loaves of two tenth deals: they shall be of fine flour; they shall be baked with <u>leaven</u>; *they are* the firstfruits to the LORD.   yeast
18 And you shall offer with the bread seven lambs without <u>blemish</u> of the first year, and one young bullock, and two rams: they shall be *for* a burned offering to thc LORD, with their <u>meat</u> offering, and their drink offerings, *even* an offering made by fire, of sweet savor to the LORD.   defect - grain
19 Then you shall sacrifice one kid of the goats for a sin offering, and two lambs of the first year for a sacrifice of peace offerings.
20 And the priest shall wave them with the bread of the firstfruits *for* a wave offering before the LORD, with the two lambs: they shall be holy to the LORD for the priest.
21 And you shall proclaim on the selfsame day, *that* it may be an holy <u>convocation</u> to you: you shall do no <u>servile</u> work *therein*: *it shall be* a <u>statute</u> for ever in all your dwellings throughout your generations.
                    assembly - regular - ordinance
22 And when you reap the harvest of your land, you shall not make clean riddance of the corners of your field when you reap, neither shall you gather any gleaning of your harvest: you shall leave them to the poor, and to the stranger: I *am* the LORD your <u>God</u>.   Elohim^p.f.

23 And the LORD spoke to Mo'ses, saying,
24 Speak to the children of Is'ra-el, saying, In the seventh month, in the first *day* of the month, shall you have a <u>sabbath</u>, a memorial of blowing of trumpets, an holy <u>convocation</u>.   rest day
25 You shall do no <u>servile</u> work *therein*: but you shall offer an offering made by fire to the LORD.   regular
26 And the LORD spoke to Mo'ses, saying,
27 Also on the tenth *day* of this seventh month *there shall be* a day of atonement: it shall be an holy <u>convocation</u> to you; and you shall <u>afflict</u> your <u>souls</u>, and offer an offering made by fire to the LORD.   asscmbly - humble - persons
28 And you shall do no work in that same day: for it *is* a day of atonemcnt, to make an atonement for you before the LORD your God.
29 For whatsoever <u>soul</u> *it be* that shall not be afflicted in that same day, he shall be cut off from among his people.
30 And whatsoever <u>soul</u> *it be* that does any work in that same day, the same <u>soul</u> will I destroy from among his people.   person
31 You shall do no manner of work: *it shall be* a <u>statute</u> for ever throughout your generations in all your dwellings.   ordinance
32 *It shall be* to you a <u>sabbath</u> of rest, and you shall <u>afflict</u> your <u>souls</u>: in the ninth *day* of the month at even, from even to even, shall you celebrate your <u>sabbath</u>.   rest day - humble - selves
33 And the LORD spoke to Mo'ses, saying,

34 Speak to the children of Is'ra-el, saying, The fifteenth day of this seventh month *shall* be the feast of tabernacles *for* seven days to the LORD.

35 On the first day *shall be* an holy convocation: you shall do no servile work *therein*.   assembly - regular

36 Seven days you shall offer an offering made by fire to the LORD: on the eighth day shall be an holy convocation to you; and you shall offer an offering made by fire to the LORD: it *is* a solemn assembly; *and* you shall do no servile work *therein*.

37 These *are* the feasts of the LORD, which you shall proclaim *to be* holy convocations, to offer an offering made by fire to the LORD, a burnt offering, and a meat offering, a sacrifice, and drink offerings, every thing upon its day:

38 Beside the sabbaths of the LORD, and beside your gifts, and beside all your vows, and beside all your freewill offerings, which you give to the LORD.   rest days

39 Also in the fifteenth day of the seventh month, when you have gathered in the fruit of the land, you shall keep a feast to the LORD seven days: on the first day *shall be* a sabbath, and on the eighth day *shall be* a sabbath.

40 And you shall take you on the first day the boughs of goodly trees, branches of palm trees, and the boughs of thick trees, and willows of the brook; and you shall rejoice before the LORD your God seven days.   REV 7:9 Elohim^{p.f.}

41 And you shall keep it a feast to the LORD seven days in the year. *It* shall be a statute for ever in your generations: you shall celebrate it in the seventh month.   ordinance

42 You shall dwell in booths seven days; all that are Is'ra-el-ites born shall dwell in booths: tents

43 That your generations may know that I made the children of Is'ra-el to dwell in booths, when I brought them out of the land of E'gypt: I *am* the LORD your God.

44 And Mo'ses declared to the children of Is'ra-el the feasts of the LORD.   festivals

CHAPTER 24

AND the LORD spoke to Mo'ses, saying,

2 Command the children of Is'ra-el, that they bring to you pure oil olive beaten for the light, to cause the lamps to burn continually.

3 Outside the veil of the testimony, in the tabernacle of the congregation, shall Aar'on order it from the evening to the morning before the LORD continually: *it shall be* a statute for ever in your generations.   ark with the law - ordinance

4 He shall order the lamps upon the pure candlestick before the LORD continually.   keep

5 And you shall take fine flour, and bake twelve cakes thereof: two tenth deals shall be in one cake.

6 And you shall set them in two rows, six on a row, upon the pure table before the LORD.   pure gold

7 And you shall put pure frankincense upon *each* row, that it may be on

the bread for a <u>memorial</u>, *even* an offering made by fire to the LORD. remembrance

8 Every <u>sabbath</u> he shall set it in order before the LORD continually, *being taken* from the children of Is'ra-el by an everlasting <u>covenant</u>. rest day - agreement

9 And it shall be Aar'on's and his sons'; and they shall eat it in the holy place: for it *is* most holy to him of the offerings of the LORD made by fire by a perpetual statute.

10 And the son of an Is'ra-el-it-ish woman, whose father *was* an E-gyp'tian, went out among the children of Is'ra-el: and this son of the Is'ra-el-it-ish *woman* and a man of Is'ra-el <u>strove</u> together in the camp; struggled

11 And the Is'ra-el-it-ish woman's son blasphemed the name *of the* LORD, and cursed. And they brought him to Mo'ses: (and his mother's name *was* Shel'o-mith, the daughter of Dib'ri, of the tribe of Dan:)

12 And they put him in <u>ward</u>, that the mind of the LORD might be showed them. custody

13 And the LORD spoke to Mo'ses, saying,

14 Bring forth him that has cursed outside the camp; and let all that heard *him* lay their hands upon his head, and let all the congregation stone him.

15 And you shall speak to the children of Is'ra-el, saying, Whosoever curses his <u>God</u> shall <u>bear his sin</u>.
Elohim^p.f. - to be held responsible

16 And he that <u>blasphemes</u> the name of the LORD, he shall surely be put to death, *and* all the congregation shall certainly stone him: as well the <u>stranger</u>, as he that is born in the land, when he <u>blasphemes</u> the name *of the LORD*, shall be put to death. MATT. 26:65 MARK 14:64 JOHN 10:33 JOHN 19:7 curses - alien

17 And he that kills any man shall surely be put to death.

18 And he that kills a beast shall make it good; beast for beast

19 And if a man cause a <u>blemish</u> in his neighbor; as he has done, so shall it be done to him; an injury

20 Breach for breach, eye for eye, tooth for tooth: as he has caused a <u>blemish</u> in a man, so shall it be done to him *again*.

21 And he that kills a beast, he shall restore it: and he that kills a man, he shall be put to death.

22 You shall have one manner of law, as well for the stranger, as for one of your own country: for I *am* the LORD your <u>God</u>. Elohim^p.f.

23 And Mo'ses spoke to the children of Is'ra-el, that they should bring forth him that had cursed out of the camp, and stone him with stones. And the children of Is'ra-el did as the LORD commanded Mo'ses.

CHAPTER 25

AND the LORD spoke to Mo'ses in mount Si'nai, saying,

2 Speak to the children of Is'ra-el, and say to them, When you come into the land which I give you, then shall the land keep a <u>sabbath</u> to the LORD. rest day

3 Six years you shall sow your field, and six years you shall prune your vineyard, and gather in the fruit thereof;

4 But in the seventh year shall be a <u>sab-bath of rest</u> to the land, a <u>sabbath</u> for the LORD: you shall neither sow your field, nor prune your vineyard.   rest year

5 That which grows of its own ac-cord of your harvest you shall not reap, neither gather the grapes of your vine undressed: *for* it is a year of rest to the land.

6 And the <u>sabbath</u> of the land shall be <u>meat</u> for you; for you, and for your servant, and for your maid, and for your hired servant, and for your stranger that <u>sojourns</u> with you,   (products) - food - resides

7 And for your cattle, and for the beast that *are* in your land, shall all the increase thereof be <u>meat</u>.   food

8 And you shall number seven <u>sabbaths</u> of years to you, seven times seven years; and the space of the seven <u>sabbaths</u> of years shall be to you forty and nine years.   rests

9 Then shall you cause the trumpet of the jubilee to sound on the tenth *day* of the seventh month, in the day of atonement shall you make the trumpet sound throughout all your land.

10 And you shall hallow the fiftieth year, and proclaim liberty through-out *all* the land to all the inhabitants thereof: it shall be a jubilee to you; and you shall return every man to his possession, and you shall return every man to his family.

11 A jubilee shall that fiftieth year be to you: you shall not sow, neither reap that which grows of itself in it, nor gather *the grapes* in it of your vine undressed.

12 For it *is* the jubilee; it shall be <u>holy</u> to you: you shall eat the increase thereof out of the field.   for you alone

13 In the year of this jubilee you shall return every man to his possession.

14 And if you sell *anything* to your neighbor, or <u>buy</u> anything of your neighbor's hand, you shall not op-press one another:

15 According to the number of years after the jubilee you shall buy of your neighbor, *and* according to the number of years of the fruits he shall sell to you:

16 According to the multitude of years you shall increase the price thereof, and according to the fewness of years you shall diminish the price of it: for *according* to the number *of the years* of the fruits dos he sell to you.

17 You shall not therefore <u>oppress</u> one another; but you shall <u>fear</u> your God: for I *am* the LORD your <u>God</u>.

take advantage - reverence - Elohim[p.f.]

18 Wherefore you shall do My <u>stat-utes</u>, and keep My <u>judgments</u>, and do them; and you shall dwell in the land in safety.   ordinances - i.e., rules

19 And the land shall yield her fruit, and you shall eat your fill, and dwell therein in safety.

20 And if you shall say, What shall we eat the seventh year? behold, we shall not sow, nor gather in our increase:

21 Then I will command my blessing upon you in the sixth year, and it shall bring forth fruit for three years.

22 And you shall sow the eighth year, and eat *yet* of old fruit until the ninth

year; until her fruits come in you shall eat *of* the old *store*.

23 The land shall not be sold for ever: for the land *is* Mine; for you *are* strangers and sojourners with Me. _{permanently - aliens - tenants}

24 And in all the land of your possession you shall grant a redemption for the land.

25 If your brother be waxen poor, and has sold away *some* of his possession, and if any of his kin come to redeem it, then shall he redeem that which his brother sold. _{has become}

26 And if the man have none to redeem it, and himself be able to redeem it;

27 Then let him count the years of the sale thereof, and restore the overplus to the man to whom he sold it; that he may return to his possession.

28 But if he be not able to restore *it* to him, then that which is sold shall remain in the hand of him that has bought it until the year of jubilee: and in the jubilee it shall go out, and he shall return to his possession.

29 And if a man sell a dwelling house in a walled city, then he may redeem it within a whole year after it is sold; *within* a full year may he redeem it.

30 And if it be not redeemed within the space of a full year, then the house that *is* in the walled city shall be established for ever to him that bought it throughout his generations: it shall not go out in the jubilee.

31 But the houses of the villages which have no wall round about them shall be counted as the fields of the country: they may be redeemed, and they shall go out in the jubilee.

32 Notwithstanding the cities of the Le'vites, *and* the houses of the cities of their possession, may the Le'vites redeem at any time.

33 And if a man purchase of the Le'vites, then the house that was sold, and the city of his possession, shall go out in *the year of* jubilee: for the houses of the cities of the Le'vites *are* their possession among the children of Is'ra-el.

34 But the field of the suburbs of their cities may not be sold; for it *is* their perpetual possession. _{pasture land}

35 And if your brother be waxen poor, and fallen in decay with you; then you shall relieve him: *yea, though he be* a stranger, or a sojourner; that he may live with you. _{has become - alien - temporary resident}

36 Take you no usury of him, or increase: but fear your God; that your brother may live with you. _{interest revere - Elohim[p.f.]}

37 You shalt not give him your money upon usury, nor lend him your victuals for increase.

38 I *am* the LORD your God, which brought you forth out of the land of E'gypt, to give you the land of Ca'naan, *and* to be your God. _{Elohim[p.f.]}

39 And if your brother *that dwells* by you be waxen poor, and be sold to you; you shall not compel him to serve as a bondservant: _{has become - sells himself}

40 *But* as an hired servant, *and* as a sojourner, he shall be with you, *and* shall serve you to the year of jubilee: _{temporary resident}

41 And *then* shall he depart from

you, *both* he and his children with him, and shall return to his own family, and to the possession of his fathers shall he return.

42 For they *are* My servants, which I brought forth out of the land of E'gypt: they shall not be sold as bondmen.   ROM. 6:22

43 You shall not rule over him with rigor; but shall fear your God.

COL. 4:1   severity - revere - Elohim^{p.f.}

44 Both your bondmen, and your bondmaids, which you shall have, *shall be* of the heathen that are round about you; of them shall you buy bondmen and bondmaids.   nations

45 Moreover of the children of the strangers that do sojourn among you, of them shall you buy, and of their families that *are* with you, which they fathered in your land: and they shall be your possession.   reside

46 And you shall take them as an inheritance for your children after you, to inherit *them for* a possession; they shall be your bondmen for ever: but over your brethren the children of Is'ra-el, you shall not rule one over another with rigor.   severity

47 And if a sojourner or stranger wax rich by you, and your brother *that* dwells by him wax poor, and sell himself to the stranger *or* sojourner by you, or to the stock of the stranger's family: resident - alien - grow

48 After that he is sold he may be redeemed again; one of his brethren may redeem him:

49 Either his uncle, or his uncle's son, may redeem him, or *any* that is near of kin to him of his family may redeem him; or if he be able, he may redeem himself.

50 And he shall reckon with him that bought him from the year that he was sold to him to the year of jubilee: and the price of his sale shall be according to the number of years, according to the time of an hired servant shall it be with him.

51 If *there be* yet many years *behind*, according to them he shall give again the price of his redemption out of the money that he was bought for.

52 And if there remain but few years to the year of jubilee, then he shall count with him, *and* according to his years shall he give him again the price of his redemption.

53 *And* as a yearly hired servant shall he be with him: *and the other* shall not rule with rigor over him in your sight.   severity

54 And if he be not redeemed in these *years*, then he shall go out in the year of jubilee, *both* he, and his children with him.

55 For to Me the children of Is'ra-el *are* servants; they *are* My servants whom I brought forth out of the land of E'gypt: I *am* the LORD your God.

CHAPTER 26

YOU shall make you no idols nor graven image, neither rear you up a standing image, neither shall you set up *any* image of stone in your land, to bow down to it: for I *am* the LORD your God.   pillar - Elohim^{p.f.}

2 You shall keep My sabbaths, and

reverence My sanctuary: I *am* the LORD.

observe - rest days

3 If you walk in My <u>statutes</u>, and <u>keep</u> My commandments, and <u>do</u> them;

decrees - obey

4 Then I will give you rain in due season, and the land shall yield her increase, and the trees of the field shall yield their fruit.

5 And your threshing shall reach to the vintage, and the vintage shall reach to the sowing time: and you shall eat your bread to the full, and dwell in your land safely.

6 And I will give peace in the land, and you shall lie down, and none shall make *you* afraid: and I will rid evil beasts out of the land, <u>neither shall the sword go</u> through your land.

there will be no war

7 And you shall chase your enemies, and they shall fall before you by the sword.

8 And five of you shall chase an hundred, and an hundred of you shall put ten thousand to flight: and your enemies shall fall before you by the sword.

9 For I will have respect to you, and make you fruitful, and multiply you, and establish My <u>covenant</u> with you.

agreement

10 And you shall eat old <u>store</u>, and bring forth the old because of the new.

supply

11 And I will set My tabernacle among you: and My soul shall not abhor you.

12 And I will walk among you, and will be your <u>God</u>, and you shall be My people. 2 COR. 6:12 2 COR. 6:16 Elohim[p.f.]

13 I *am* the LORD your <u>God</u>, which brought you forth out of the land of E'gypt, that you should not be their <u>bondmen</u>; and I have broken the bands of your yoke, and made you go <u>upright</u>.

slaves - free

14 But if you will not <u>hearken</u> to Me, and will not do all these commandments;

listen

15 And if you shall despise My <u>statutes</u>, or if your <u>soul abhor</u> My judgments, so that you will not do all My commandments, *but* that you break My <u>covenant</u>:

decrees - heart reject - agreement

16 I also will do this to you; I will even appoint over you terror, <u>consumption</u>, and the <u>burning ague</u>, that shall consume the eyes, and cause sorrow of heart: and you shall sow your seed <u>in vain</u>, for your enemies shall eat it.

wasting diseases - -fever - foolishly

17 And I will set My face against you, and you shall be slain before your enemies: they that <u>hate</u> you shall reign over you; and you shall flee when none pursue you.

abhor

18 And if you will not yet for all this <u>hearken</u> to Me, then I will punish you seven times more for your sins.

listen

19 And I will break the pride of your power; and I will make your heaven as iron, and your earth as brass:

20 And your strength shall be spent in vain: for your land shall not yield her increase, neither shall the trees of the land yield their fruits.

21 And if you walk contrary to Me, and will not hearken to Me; I will bring seven times more underline{plagues} upon you according to your sins.

REV. 15:1 afflictions

22 I will also send wild beasts among you, which shall rob you of your children, and destroy your cattle, and make you few in number; and your *high* ways shall be desolate.

23 And if you will not be reformed by Me by these things, but will walk contrary to Me;

24 Then will I also walk contrary to you, and will punish you yet seven times for your sins.

25 And I will bring a sword upon you, that shall avenge the quarrel of *My* underline{covenant}: and when you are gathered together inside your cities, I will send the pestilence among you; and you shall be delivered into the hand of the enemy.

agreement

26 *And* when I have broken the staff of your bread, ten women shall bake your bread in one oven, and they shall deliver *you* your bread again by weight: and you shall eat, and not be satisfied.

27 And if you will not for all this underline{hearken} to Me, but walk contrary to Me;

listen

28 Then I will walk contrary to you also in fury; and I, even I, will chastise you seven times for your sins.

29 And you shall eat the flesh of your sons, and the flesh of your daughters shall you eat.

30 And I will destroy your high places, and cut down your images, and cast your carcases upon the carcases of your idols, and My underline{soul} shall abhor you.

being

31 And I will make your cities waste, and bring your sanctuaries to desolation, and I will not smell the savor of your sweet odors.

32 And I will bring the land into desolation: and your enemies which dwell therein shall be astonished at it.

33 And I will scatter you among the heathen, and will draw out a sword after you: and your land shall be desolate, and your cities waste.

34 Then shall the land enjoy her underline{sabbaths}, as long as it lies desolate, and you *be* in your enemies' land; *even* then shall the land rest, and enjoy her underline{sabbaths}.

rests

35 As long as it lies desolate it shall rest; because it did not rest in your underline{sabbaths}, when you dwelt upon it.

36 And upon them that are left *alive* of you I will send a underline{faintness} into their hearts in the lands of their enemies; and the sound of a shaken leaf shall chase them; and they shall flee, as fleeing from a sword; and they shall fall when none pursues.

uneasiness

37 And they shall fall one upon another, as it were before a sword, when none pursues: and you shall have no power to stand before your enemies.

38 And you shall perish among the heathen, and the land of your enemies shall eat you up.

39 And they that are left of you shall underline{pine} away in their iniquity in your enemies' lands; and also in the iniquities of their fathers shall they underline{pine} away with them.

waste

40 If they shall confess their iniquity, and the iniquity of their fathers, with their trespass which they trespassed against Me, and that also they have walked contrary to Me;   2 CHRON. 7:14

41 And *that* I also have walked contrary to them, and have brought them into the land of their enemies; if then their uncircumcised hearts be humbled, and they then accept of the punishment of their iniquity:

42 Then will I remember My <u>covenant</u> with Ja'cob, and also My <u>covenant</u> with I'saac, and also My <u>covenant</u> with A'bra-ham will I remember; and I will remember the land.   agreement

43 The land also shall be left of them, and shall enjoy her <u>sabbaths</u>, while she lies desolate without them: and they shall accept of the punishment of their iniquity: because, even because they despised My judgments, and because their soul abhorred My <u>statutes</u>. rests - decrees

44 And yet for all that, when they be in the land of their enemies, I will not <u>cast</u> them away, neither will I abhor them, to destroy them utterly, and to break My <u>covenant</u> with them: for I *am* the LORD their <u>God</u>. reject - agreement -Elohim p.f.

45 But I will for their sakes remember the <u>covenant</u> of their ancestors, whom I brought forth out of the land of E'gypt in the sight of the heathen, that I might be their God: I *am* the LORD.

46 These *are* the statutes and judgments and laws, which the LORD made between Him and the children of Is'ra-el in mount Si'nai by the hand of Mo'ses.

CHAPTER 27

AND the LORD spoke to Mo'ses, saying,

2 Speak to the children of Is'ra-el, and say to them, When a man shall make a <u>singular</u> vow, the persons *shall be* for the LORD by your <u>estimation</u>.   special - evaluation

3 And your <u>estimation</u> shall be of the male from twenty years old even to sixty years old, even your <u>estimation</u> shall be fifty shekels of silver, after the shekel of the sanctuary.

4 And if it *be* a female, then your <u>estimation</u> shall be thirty shekels.

5 And if *it be* from five years old even to twenty years <u>old</u>, then your <u>estimation</u> shall be of the male twenty shekels, and for the female ten shekels.

6 And if *it be* from a month old even to five years old, then your <u>estimation</u> shall be of the male five shekels of silver, and for the female your <u>estimation</u> *shall be* three shekels of silver.   evaluation

7 And if *it be* from sixty years old and above; if *it be* a male, then your <u>estimation</u> shall be fifteen shekels, and for the female ten shekels.

8 But if he be poorer than your <u>estimation</u>, then he shall present himself before the priest, and the priest shall value him; according to his ability that vowed shall the priest value him.

9 And if *it be* a beast, whereof men bring an offering to the LORD, all that *any man* gives of such to the LORD shall be <u>holy</u>.   only for this use

10 He shall not alter it, nor change it, a good for a bad, or a bad for a good:

and if he shall at all change beast for beast, then it and the exchange thereof shall be <u>holy</u>.   only for this use

11 And if *it be* any <u>unclean</u> beast, of which they do not offer a sacrifice to the LORD, then he shall present the beast before the priest: unfit

12 And the priest shall value it, whether it be good or bad: as you value it, *who are* the priest, so shall it be.

13 But if he will at all redeem it, then he shall add a fifth *part* thereof to your <u>estimation</u>.   valuation

14 And when a man shall <u>sanctify</u> his house *to be* <u>holy</u> to the LORD, then the priest shall <u>estimate</u> it, whether it be good or bad: as the priest shall <u>estimate</u> it, so shall it stand.   consecrate - value

15 And if he that <u>sanctified</u> it will <u>redeem</u> his house, then he shall add the fifth *part* of the money of your <u>estimation</u> to it, and it shall be his.   buy back

16 And if a man shall <u>sanctify</u> to the LORD *some part* of a field of his possession, then your <u>estimation</u> shall be according to the seed thereof: an homer of barley seed *shall be valued* at fifty shekels of silver.

17 If he <u>sanctify</u> his field from the year of jubilee, according to your <u>estimation</u> it shall stand.   consecrate - valuation

18 But if he <u>sanctify</u> his field after the jubilee, then the priest shall reckon to him the money according to the years that remain, even to the year of the jubilee, and it shall be abated from your <u>estimation</u>.   value

19 And if he that <u>sanctified</u> the field will in any wise redeem it, then he shall add the fifth *part* of the money of your <u>estimation</u> to it, and it shall be assured to him.   consecrated - valuation

20 And if he will not redeem the field, or if he have sold the field to another man, it shall not be redeemed any more.

21 But the field, when it goes out in the jubilee, shall be holy to the LORD, as a field devoted; the possession thereof shall be the priest's.

22 And if *a man* <u>sanctify</u> to the LORD a field which he has bought, which *is* not of the fields of his possession;

23 Then the priest shall reckon to him the worth of your <u>estimation</u>, *even* to the year of the jubilee: and he shall give your <u>estimation</u> in that day, *as* a holy thing to the LORD.   valuation

24 In the year of the jubilee the field shall return to him of whom it was bought, *even* to him to whom the possession of the land *did belong*.

25 And all your estimations shall be according to the shekel of the sanctuary: twenty gerahs shall be the shekel.

26 Only the <u>firstling</u> of the beasts, which should be the LORD's firstling, no man shall sanctify it; whether *it be* ox, or sheep: it *is* the LORD's.   first born

27 And if *it be* of an <u>unclean</u> beast, then he shall redeem *it* according to your <u>estimation</u>, and shall add a fifth *part* of it thereto: or if it be not redeemed, then it shall be sold according to your <u>estimation</u>.   unfit

28 <u>Notwithstanding</u> no <u>devoted thing</u>, that a man shall devote to the Lord of all that he has, *both* of man and beast, and of the field of his possession, shall be sold or redeemed: every <u>devoted thing</u> *is* most holy to the Lord.   <small>Nevertheless - dedicated to God</small>

29 None devoted, which shall be devoted of men, shall be redeemed; *but* shall surely be put to death.

30 And all the tithe of the land, *whether* of the seed of the land, *or* of the fruit of the tree, *is* the Lord's: *it is* <u>holy</u> to the Lord.   <small>set apart</small>

31 And if a man will at all redeem *any* of his tithes, he shall add thereto the fifth *part* thereof.

32 And concerning the tithe of the herd, or of the flock, *even* of whatsoever passes under the rod, the tenth shall be holy to the Lord.

33 He shall not search whether it be good or bad, neither shall he change it: and if he change it at all, then both it and the change thereof shall be holy; it shall not be redeemed.

34 These *are* the commandments, which the Lord commanded Mo'ses for the children of Is'ra-el in mount Si'nai.

NUMBERS

OUTLINE

SURVEY

The Book of Numbers takes its name in our English versions, as it did in the Latin and Greek also, from the two censuses reported in the narrative. Actually the book is a division of the larger unit, the Pentateuch. Among the Jewish scribes it was known mainly as "In the Wilderness," which in Hebrew is one word, *Bemidbar*, a title taken from the first verse. This is appropriate, since the theme of the book is the vicissitudes and victories of the people of Israel from the time they left the area of Sinai until they reached the borders of the Promised Land.

Numbers seems at times to be a rather loosely-knit collection of data, narrative and ritual or civil law. Yet these data are always pertinent to the history, while the legal enactments often arise out of the exigencies of the situation in life, such as the allowance for a special Passover (9.1-14) in circumstances which precluded observance of the regular Passover; or the claim of the daughters of Zelophehad (27.1-11) which called forth the Lord's provision for the inheritance by daughters where there is no surviving son.

Historically, Numbers begins where Exodus ends, with necessary allowance, of course, for the scattered narrative sections of Leviticus. It covers a period of approximately forty years in the story of Israel's advance upon Palestine. While these are usually described as years of wandering, it is fairly clear that the people lived south of Canaan proper, partly in the area known as the Negev, not far from Kadesh Barnea, for about thirty-seven years. During this time the tabernacle was the focal point of civil as well as religious life, since it was here that Moses carried out his administrative duties. It may be assumed that the people followed the domestic pursuits of nomads, living in tents, pasturing flocks in the semi-arid steppes. These circumstances required special divine provision of food and water.

God is presented in Numbers as a sovereign Who demands absolute obedience to His holy will, but Who also shows mercy to the penitent and believing. As a father nurtures and chastens his children, so God directs Israel His beloved. He chooses to deal with men through mediators. Of these Moses is unique, though others may be endowed with prophetic gifts and even a heathen, Balaam, may be used, since God is the God of the spirits of all flesh.

Several references to Numbers are found in the New Testament, where the deliverance from Egypt is regarded as an earthly pattern of eternal redemption. The wilderness experiences are said to be recorded for our admonition (1 Co 10.11). Our Lord Jesus Christ used the incident of the brazen serpent in illustration of the way He Himself was to be lifted up so that those who believe in Him might not perish but have everlasting life.

AUTHOR

Both Jews and Christians traditionally have regarded Moses as the author of Numbers. Since the Mosaic period is at least thirteen hundred years before Christ, the book in its present form has passed through many hands, and even in the Hebrew itself has been transliterated from one type of script to another. Undoubtedly there are scribal or editorial additions here and there. Extremes of literary criticism have tried to deny that Moses could have written any of the book and have attempted to partition it into documents dating from several periods of Israel's history. Archaeologi-

cal discoveries, however, have shown the antiquity of laws, institutions and living conditions described in Numbers. The view that Numbers comes from Moses and the period in which he lived is supported also by the great veneration which the Jews had for Moses and the sacred writings attributed to him.

D.W.K.

THE FORTH BOOK OF MOSES COMMONLY CALLED

NUMBERS

Arranging the People
for the Wilderness
March

CHAPTER 1

AND the LORD spoke to Mo'ses in the wilderness of Si'nai, in the tabernacle of the congregation, on the first *day* of the second month, in the second year after they were come out of the land of E'gypt, saying,

2 Take you the sum of all the congregation of the children of Is'ra-el, after their families, by the house of their fathers, with the number of *their* names, every male by their polls; _{Take a census}

3 From twenty years old and upward, all that are able to go forth to war in Is'ra-el: you and Aar'on shall number them by their armies. _{count}

4 And with you there shall be a man of every tribe; every one head of the house of his fathers.

5 And these *are* the names of the men that shall stand with you: of *the* tribe of Reu'ben; E-li'zur the son of Shed'e-ur.

6 Of Sim'e-on; She-lu'mi-el the son of Zu-ri-shad'da-i.

7 Of Ju'dah; Nah'shon the son of Am-min'a-dab.

8 Of Is'sa-char; Ne-than'e-el the son of Zu'ar.

9 Of Zeb'u-lun; E-li'ab the son of He'lon.

10 Of the children of Jo'seph: of E'phra-im; E-lish'a-ma the son of Am-mi'hud: of Ma-nas'seh; Ga-ma'li-el the son of Pe-dah'zur.

11 Of Ben'ja-min; Ab'i-dan the son of Gid-e-o'ni.

12 Of Dan; A-hi-e'zer the son of Am-mi-shad'da-i.

13 Of Ash'er; Pa'gi-el the son of Oc'ran.

14 Of Gad; E-li'a-saph the son of Deu'el.

15 Of Naph'ta-li; A-hi'ra the son of E'nan.

16 These *were* the renowned of the congregation, princes of the tribes of their fathers, heads of thousands in Is'ra-el.

17 And Mo'ses and Aar'on took these men which are expressed by *their* names:

18 And they assembled all the congregation together on the first *day* of the second month, and they declared their pedigrees after their families, by the house of their fathers, according to the number of the names, from twenty years old and upward, by their polls. _{ancestry}

19 As the LORD commanded Mo'ses, so he numbered them in the wilderness of Si'nai.

20 And the children of Reu'ben, Is'ra-el's eldest son, by their generations, after their families, by the house of their fathers, according to the number of the

names, by their polls, every male from twenty years old and upward, all that were <u>able</u> to go forth to war;

physically fit

21 Those that were numbered of them, *even* of the tribe of Reu'ben, *were* forty and six thousand and five hundred.

22 Of the children of Sim'e-on, by their generations, after their families, by the house of their fathers, those that were numbered of them, according to the number of the names, by their polls, every male from twenty years old and upward, all that were able to go forth to war;

23 Those that were numbered of them, *even* of the tribe of Sim'e-on, *were* fifty and nine thousand and three hundred.

24 Of the children of Gad, by their generations, after their families, by the house of their fathers, according to the number of the names, from twenty years old and upward, all that were able to go forth to war;

25 Those that were numbered of them, *even* of the tribe of Gad, *were* forty and five thousand six hundred and fifty.

26 Of the children of Ju'dah, by their generations, after their families, by the house of their fathers, according to the number of the names, from twenty years old and upward, all that were able to go forth to war;

27 Those that were numbered of them, *even* of the tribe of Ju'dah, *were* threescore and fourteen thousand and six hundred.

28 Of the children of Is'sa-char, by their generations, after their families, by the house of their fathers, according to the number of the names, from twenty years old and upward, all that were able to go forth to war;

29 Those that were numbered of them, *even* of the tribe of Is'sa-char, *were* fifty and four thousand and four hundred.

30 Of the children of Zeb'u-lun, by their generations, after their families, by the house of their fathers, according to the number of the names, from twenty years old and upward, all that were able to go forth to war;

31 Those that were numbered of them, *even* of the tribe of Zeb'u-lun, *were* fifty and seven thousand and four hundred.

32 Of the children of Jo'seph, *namely*, of the children of E'phra-im, by their generations, after their families, by the house of their fathers, according to the number of the names, from twenty years old and upward, all that were able to go forth to war;

33 Those that were numbered of them, *even* of the tribe of E'phra-im, *were* forty thousand and five hundred.

34 Of the children of Ma-nas'seh, by their generations, after their families, by the house of their fathers, according to the number of the names, from twenty years old and upward, all that were able to go forth to war;

35 Those that were numbered of them, *even* of the tribe of Ma-nas'seh, *were* thirty and two thousand and two hundred.

36 Of the children of Ben'ja-min,

by their generations, after their families, by the house of their fathers, according to the number of the names, from twenty years old and upward, all that were able to go forth to war;

37 Those that were numbered of them, *even* of the tribe of Ben'ja-min, *were* thirty and five thousand and four hundred.

38 Of the children of Dan, by their generations, after their families, by the house of their fathers, according to the number of the names, from twenty years old and upward, all that were able to go forth to war;

39 Those that were numbered of them, *even* of the tribe of Dan, *were* threescore and two thousand and seven hundred.

40 Of the children of Ash'er, by their generations, after their families, by the house of their fathers, according to the number of the names, from twenty years old and upward, all that were able to go forth to war;

41 Those that were numbered of them, *even* of the tribe of Ash'er, *were* forty and one thousand and five hundred.

42 Of the children of Naph'ta-li, throughout their generations, after their families, by the house of their fathers, according to the number of the names, from twenty years old and upward, all that were able to go forth to war;

43 Those that were numbered of them, *even* of the tribe of Naph'ta-li, *were* fifty and three thousand and four hundred.

44 These *are* those that were num-bered, which Mo'ses and Aar'on numbered, and the princes of Is'ra-el, *being* twelve men: each one was for the house of his fathers.　leaders

45 So were all those that were num-bered of the children of Is'ra-el, by the house of their fathers, from twenty years old and upward, all that were able to go forth to war in Is'ra-el;

46 Even all they that were numbered were six hundred thousand and three thousand and five hundred and fifty.

47 But the Le'vites after the tribe of their fathers were not numbered among them.

48 For the Lord had spoken to Mo'ses, saying,

49 Only you shall not number the tribe of Le'vi, neither take the sum of them among the children of Is'ra-el:

50 But you shall appoint the Le'vites over the tabernacle of testimony, and over all the vessels thereof, and over all things that *belong* to it: they shall bear the tabernacle, and all the ves-sels thereof; and they shall minister to it, and shall encamp round about the tabernacle.

51 And when the tabernacle sets for-ward, the Le'vites shall take it down: and when the tabernacle is to be pitched, the Le'vites shall set it up: and the stranger that comes near shall be put to death.　is to move - set up

52 And the children of Is'ra-el shall pitch their tents, every man by his own camp, and every man by his own stan-dard, throughout their hosts.　flag

53 But the Le'vites shall pitch round about the tabernacle of testimony, that

there be no <u>wrath</u> upon the congregation of the children of Is'ra-el: and the Le'vites shall keep the <u>charge</u> of the tabernacle of testimony.   <small>judgment - responsibility</small>

54 And the children of Is'ra-el did according to all that the Lord commanded Mo'ses, so did they.

CHAPTER 2

AND the Lord spoke to Mo'ses and to Aar'on, saying,

2 Every man of the children of Is'ra-el shall <u>pitch</u> by his own <u>standard</u>, with the <u>ensign</u> of their father's house: <u>far off about</u> the tabernacle of the congregation shall they <u>pitch</u>.   <small>set up - flag - banner - around</small>

3 And on the east side toward the rising of the sun shall they of the <u>standard</u> of the camp of Ju'dah <u>pitch</u> throughout their <u>armies</u>: and Nah'shon the son of Am-min'a-dab *shall be* captain of the children of Ju'dah.   <small>divisions</small>

4 And his host, and those that were numbered of them, *were* threescore and fourteen thousand and six hundred.

5 And those that do <u>pitch</u> next to him *shall be* the tribe of Is'sa-char: and Ne-than'e-el the son of Zu'ar *shall be* captain of the children of Is'sa-char.

6 And his host, and those that were numbered thereof, *were* fifty and four thousand and four hundred.

7 *Then* the tribe of Zeb'u-lun: and E-li'ab the son of He'lon *shall be* captain of the children of Zeb'u-lun.

8 And his host, and those that were numbered thereof, *were* fifty and seven thousand and four hundred.

9 All that were numbered in the camp of Ju'dah *were* an hundred thousand and fourscore thousand and six thousand and four hundred, throughout their armies. These shall first <u>set forth</u>.   <small>go</small>

10 On the south side *shall be* the <u>standard</u> of the camp of Reu'ben according to their armies: and the captain of the children of Reu'ben *shall be* E-li'zur the son of Shed'e-ur.   <small>flag</small>

11 And his host, and those that were numbered thereof, *were* forty and six thousand and five hundred.

12 And those which <u>pitch</u> by him *shall be* the tribe of Sim'e-on: and the captain of the children of Sim'e-on *shall be* She-lu'mi-el the son of Zu-ri-shad'da-i.   <small>setup</small>

13 And his host, and those that were numbered of them, *were* fifty and nine thousand and three hundred.

14 Then the tribe of Gad: and the captain of the sons of Gad *shall be* E-li'a-saph the son of Reu'el.

15 And his host, and those that were numbered of them, *were* forty and five thousand and six hundred and fifty.

16 All that were numbered in the camp of Reu'ben *were* an hundred thousand and fifty and one thousand and four hundred and fifty, throughout their armies. And they shall set forth in the second rank.

17 Then the tabernacle of the congregation shall set forward with the camp of the Le'vites in the midst of the camp: as they encamp, so shall they set forward, every man in his place by their <u>standards</u>.   <small>flags</small>

18 On the west side *shall be* the <u>standard</u> of the camp of E'phra-im ac-

cording to their armies: and the captain of the sons of E'phra-im *shall be* E-lish'a-ma the son of Am-mi'hud. flag

19 And his host, and those that were numbered of them, *were* forty thousand and five hundred.

20 And by him *shall be* the tribe of Ma-nas'seh: and the captain of the children of Ma-nas'seh *shall be* Ga-ma'li-el the son of Pe-dah'zur.

21 And his host, and those that were numbered of them, *were* thirty and two thousand and two hundred.

22 Then the tribe of Ben'ja-min: and the captain of the sons of Ben'ja-min *shall be* Ab'i-dan the son of Gid-c-o'ni.

23 And his host, and those that were numbered of them, *were* thirty and five thousand and four hundred.

24 All that were numbered of the camp of E'phra-im *were* an hundred thousand and eight thousand and an hundred, throughout their armies. And they shall go forward in the third <u>rank</u>. group

25 The <u>standard</u> of the camp of Dan *shall be* on the north side by their armies: and the captain of the children of Dan *shall be* A-hi-e'zer the son of Am-mi-shad'da-i. flag

26 And his host, and those that were numbered of them, *were* threescore and two thousand and seven hundred.

27 And those that encamp by him *shall be* the tribe of Ash'er: and the captain of the children of Ash'er *shall be* Pa'gi-el the son of Oc'ran.

28 And his host, and those that were numbered of them, *were* forty and one thousand and five hundred.

29 Then the tribe of Naph'ta-li: and the captain of the children of Naph'ta-li *shall be* A-hi'ra the son of E'nan.

30 And his host, and those that were numbered of them, *were* fifty and three thousand and four hundred.

31 All they that were numbered in the camp of Dan *were* an hundred thousand and fifty and seven thousand and six hundred. They shall go <u>hindmost</u> with their <u>standards</u>. last - flag

32 These *are* those which were numbered of the children of Is'ra-el by the house of their fathers: all those that were numbered of the camps throughout their hosts *were* six hundred thousand and three thousand and five hundred and fifty.

33 But the Le'vites were not numbered among the children of Is'ra-el; as the Lord commanded Mo'ses.

34 And the children of Is'ra-el did according to all that the LORD commanded Mo'ses: so they <u>pitched</u> by their <u>standards</u>, and so thcy set forward, every one after their families, according to the house of their fathers. camped - banners

CHAPTER 3

THESE also *are* the generations of Aar'on and Mo'ses in the day *that* the Lord spoke with Mo'ses in mount Si'nai.

2 And these *are* the names of the sons of Aar'on; Na'dab the firstborn, and A-bi'hu, E-le-a'zar, and Ith'a-mar.

3 These *are* the names of the sons of Aar'on, the priests which were

anointed, whom he <u>consecrated</u> to minister in the priest's office. ordained

M10 4 And Na'dab and A-bi'hu died before the LORD, when they offered strange fire before the LORD, in the wilderness of Si'nai, and they had no children: and E-le-a'zar and Ith'a-mar <u>ministered</u> in the priest's office in the sight of Aar'on their father. served

237

5 And the LORD spoke to Mo'ses, saying,

6 Bring the tribe of Le'vi near, and present them before Aar'on the priest, that they may <u>minister</u> to him.

7 And they shall keep his charge, and the charge of the whole congregation before the tabernacle of the congregation, to do the service of the tabernacle.

8 And they shall keep all the <u>instruments</u> of the tabernacle of the congregation, and the charge of the children of Is'ra-el, to do the service of the tabernacle. furnishings

9 And you shall give the Le'vites to Aar'on and to his sons: they *are* wholly given to him out of the children of Is'ra-el.

10 And you shall appoint Aar'on and his sons, and they shall <u>wait</u> on their priest's office: and the stranger that comes near shall be put to death. care for

11 And the LORD spoke to Mo'ses, saying,

12 And I, behold, I have taken the Le'vites from among the children of Is'ra-el instead of all the firstborn that opens the <u>matrix</u> among the children of Is'ra-el: therefore the Le'vites shall be Mine; womb

13 Because all the firstborn *are* Mine; *for* on the day that I smote all the firstborn in the land of E'gypt I hallowed to Me all the firstborn in Is'ra-el, both man and beast: Mine shall they be: I *am* the LORD.

14 And the LORD spoke to Mo'ses in the wilderness of Si'nai, saying,

15 Number the children of Le'vi after the house of their fathers, by their families: every male from a month old and upward shall you <u>number</u> them. count

16 And Mo'ses numbered them according to the word of the LORD, as he was commanded.

17 And these were the sons of Le'vi by their names; Ger'shon, and Ko'hath, and Me-ra'ri.

18 And these *are* the names of the sons of Ger'shon by their families; Lib'ni, and Shim'e-i.

19 And the sons of Ko'hath by their families; Am'ram, and Iz'e-har, He'bron, and Uz'zi-el.

20 And the sons of Me-ra'ri by their families; Mah'li, and Mu'shi. These *are* the families of the Le'vites according to the house of their fathers.

21 Of Ger'shon *was* the family of the Lib'nites, and the family of the Shim'ites: these *are* the families of the Ger'shon-ites.

22 Those that were numbered of them, according to the number of all the males, from a month old and upward, *even* those that were numbered of them *were* seven thousand and five hundred.

23 The families of the Ger'shon-ites

shall <u>pitch</u> behind the tabernacle westward. <small>camp</small>

24 And the <u>chief</u> of the house of the father of the Ger'shon-ites *shall be* E-li'a-saph the son of La'el. <small>leader</small>

25 And the <u>charge</u> of the sons of Ger'shon in the tabernacle of the congregation *shall be* the tabernacle, and the tent, the covering thereof, and the hanging for the door of the tabernacle of the congregation, <small>duties</small>

26 And the hangings of the court, and the curtain for the door of the court, which *is* by the tabernacle, and by the altar round about, and the cords of it for all the service thereof.

27 And of Ko'hath *was* the family of the Am'ram-ites, and the family of the Iz'e-har-ites, and the family of the He'bron-ites, and the family of the Uz'zi-el-ites: these *are* the families of the Ko'hath-ites.

28 In the number of all the males, from a month old and upward, *were* eight thousand and six hundred, keeping the charge of the sanctuary.

29 The families of the sons of Ko'hath shall <u>pitch</u> on the side of the tabernacle southward. <small>camp</small>

30 And the <u>chief</u> of the house of the father of the families of the Ko'hath-ites *shall be* E-liz'a-phan the son of Uz'zi-el. <small>leader</small>

31 And their <u>charge</u> *shall be* the ark, and the table, and the candlestick, and the altars, and the vessels of the sanctuary wherewith they minister, and the hanging, and all the service thereof. <small>duties</small>

32 And E-le-a'zar the son of Aar'on the priest *shall be* chief over the chief of the Le'vites, *and have* the oversight of them that keep the <u>charge</u> of the sanctuary. <small>duties</small>

33 Of Me-ra'ri *was* the family of the Mah'lites, and the family of the Mu'shites: these *are* the families of Me-ra'ri.

34 And those that were numbered of them, according to the number of all the males, from a month old and upward, *were* six thousand and two hundred.

35 And the <u>chief</u> of the house of the father of the families of Me-ra'ri *was* Zu'ri-el the son of Ab-i-ha'il: *these* shall <u>pitch</u> on the side of the tabernacle northward. <small>leader - camp</small>

36 And *under* the <u>custody and charge</u> of the sons of Me-ra'ri *shall be* the boards of the tabernacle, and the bars thereof, and the pillars thereof, and the sockets thereof, and all the vessels thereof, and all that serves thereto, <small>appointed duties</small>

37 And the pillars of the court round about, and their sockets, and their pins, and their cords.

38 But those that <u>encamp</u> before the tabernacle toward the east, *even* before the tabernacle of the congregation eastward, *shall be* Mo'ses, and Aar'on and his sons, keeping the <u>charge</u> of the sanctuary for the charge of the children of Is'ra-el; and the stranger that comes near shall be put to death. <small>camp - responsibility</small>

39 All that were numbered of the Le'vites, which Mo'ses and Aar'on numbered at the commandment of the LORD, throughout their families, all the

males from a month old and upward, *were* twenty and two thousand.

40 And the LORD said to Mo'ses, <u>Number</u> all the firstborn of the males of the children of Is'ra-el from a month old and upward, and take the number of their names.   _{count}

41 And you shall take the Le'vites for Me (I *am* the LORD) instead of all the firstborn among the children of Is'ra-el; and the cattle of the Le'vites instead of all the firstlings among the cattle of the children of Is'ra-el.

42 And Mo'ses numbered, as the LORD commanded him, all the firstborn among the children of Is'ra-el.

43 And all the firstborn males by the number of names, from a month old and upward, of those that were numbered of them, were twenty and two thousand two hundred and threescore and thirteen.

44 And the LORD spoke to Mo'ses, saying,

45 Take the Le'vites instead of all the firstborn among the children of Is'ra-el, and the cattle of the Le'vites instead of their cattle; and the Le'vites shall be Mine: I *am* the LORD.

46 And for those that are to be redeemed of the two hundred and threescore and thirteen of the firstborn of the children of Is'ra-el, which are more than the Le'vites;

47 You shall even take five shekels apiece by the poll, after the shekel of the sanctuary shall you take *them*: (the shekel *is* twenty gerahs:)

48 And you shall give the money, wherewith the odd number of them is to be redeemed, to Aar'on and to his sons.

49 And Mo'ses took the redemption money of them that were over and above them that were redeemed by the Le'vites:

50 Of the firstborn of the children of Is'ra-el took he the money; a thousand three hundred and threescore and five *shekels*, after the shekel of the sanctuary:

51 And Mo'ses gave the money of them that were redeemed to Aar'on and to his sons, according to the word of the LORD, as the LORD commanded Mo'ses.

CHAPTER 4

AND the LORD spoke to Mo'ses and to Aar'on, saying,

2 Take the sum of the sons of Ko'hath from among the sons of Le'vi, after their families, by the house of their fathers,

3 From thirty years old and upward even until fifty years old, all that enter into the host, to do the work in the tabernacle of the congregation.

4 This *shall be* the service of the sons of Ko'hath in the tabernacle of the congregation, *about* the most holy things:

5 And when the camp sets forward, Aar'on shall come, and his sons, and they shall take down the covering veil, and cover the ark of testimony with it:

6 And shall put thereon the covering of badgers' skins, and shall spread over

it a cloth wholly of blue, and shall put in the staves thereof.   poles

7 And upon the table of showbread they shall spread a cloth of blue, and put thereon the dishes, and the spoons, and the bowls, and covers to cover with: and the continual bread shall be thereon: consecrated bread

8 And they shall spread upon them a cloth of scarlet, and cover the same with a covering of badgers' skins, and shall put in the staves thereof.

9 And they shall take a cloth of blue, and cover the candlestick of the light, and its lamps, and its tongs, and its snuffdishes, and all the oil vessels thereof, wherewith they minister to it:

10 And they shall put it and all the vessels thereof within a covering of badgers' skins, and shall put *it* upon a bar.

11 And upon the golden altar they shall spread a cloth of blue, and cover it with a covering of badgers' skins, and shall put to the staves thereof:

12 And they shall take all the instruments of ministry, wherewith they minister in the sanctuary, and put *them* in a cloth of blue, and cover them with a covering of badgers' skins, and shall put *them* on a bar: articles - serve

13 And they shall take away the ashes from the altar, and spread a purple cloth thereon:

14 And they shall put upon it all the vessels thereof, wherewith they minister about it, *even* the censers, the fleshhooks, and the shovels, and the basins, all the vessels of the altar; and they shall spread upon it a covering of badgers' skins, and put to the staves of it.   firepans - bowls - poles

15 And when Aar'on and his sons have made an end of covering the sanctuary, and all the vessels of the sanctuary, as the camp is to set forward; after that, the sons of Ko'hath shall come to bear *it*: but they shall not touch *any* holy thing, less they die. These *things are* the burden of the sons of Ko'hath in the tabernacle of the congregation.   sacred

16 And to the office of E-le-a'zar the son of Aar'on the priest *pertains* the oil for the light, and the sweet incense, and the daily meat offering, and the anointing oil, *and* the oversight of all the tabernacle, and of all that therein is, in the sanctuary, and in the vessels thereof.

17 And the LORD spoke to Mo'ses and to Aar'on, saying,

18 Cut you not off the tribe of the families of the Ko'hath-ites from among the Le'vites:

19 But thus do to them, that they may live, and not die, when they approach to the most holy things: Aar'on and his sons shall go in, and appoint them every one to his service and to his burden: assign

20 But they shall not go in to see when the holy things are covered, less they die.

21 And the LORD spoke to Mo'ses, saying,

22 Take also the sum of the sons of Ger'shon, throughout the houses of their fathers, by their families;

23 From thirty years old and upward

until fifty years old shall you number them; all that enter in to perform the service, to do the work in the tabernacle of the congregation.

24 This *is* the service of the families of the Ger'shon-ites, to serve, and for burdens: _{carrying}

25 And they shall bear the curtains of the tabernacle, and the tabernacle of the congregation, its covering, and the covering of the badgers' skins that *is* above upon it, and the hanging for the door of the tabernacle of the congregation,

26 And the hangings of the court, and the hanging for the door of the gate of the court, which *is* by the tabernacle and by the altar round about, and their cords, and all the instruments of their service, and all that is made for them: so shall they serve.

27 At the appointment of Aar'on and his sons shall be all the service of the sons of the Ger'shon-ites, in all their burdens, and in all their service: and you shall appoint to them in charge all their burdens. _{assign}

28 This *is* the service of the families of the sons of Ger'shon in the tabernacle of the congregation: and their charge *shall be* under the hand of Ith'a-mar the son of Aar'on the priest. _{direction}

29 As for the sons of Me-ra'ri, you shall number them after their families, by the house of their fathers;

30 From thirty years old and upward even to fifty years old shall you number them, every one that enters into the service, to do the work of the tabernacle of the congregation.

31 And this *is* the charge of their burden, according to all their service in the tabernacle of the congregation; the boards of the tabernacle, and the bars thereof, and the pillars thereof, and sockets thereof, _{duty - loads}

32 And the pillars of the court round about, and their sockets, and their pins, and their cords, with all their instruments, and with all their service: and by name you shall reckon the instruments of the charge of their burden. _{equipment - articles}

33 This *is* the service of the families of the sons of Me-ra'ri, according to all their service, in the tabernacle of the congregation, under the hand of Ith'a-mar the son of Aar'on the priest.

34 And Mo'ses and Aar'on and the chief of the congregation numbered the sons of the Ko'hath-ites after their families, and after the house of their fathers,

35 From thirty years old and upward even to fifty years old, every one that enters into the service, for the work in the tabernacle of the congregation:

36 And those that were numbered of them by their families were two thousand seven hundred and fifty.

37 These *were* they that were numbered of the families of the Ko'hath-ites, all that might do service in the tabernacle of the congregation, which Mo'ses and Aar'on did number according to the commandment of the LORD by the hand of Mo'ses.

38 And those that were numbered of the sons of Ger'shon, throughout their

families, and by the house of their fathers,

39 From thirty years old and upward even to fifty years old, every one that enters into the service, for the work in the tabernacle of the congregation,

40 Even those that were numbered of them, throughout their families, by the house of their fathers, were two thousand and six hundred and thirty.

41 These *are* they that were numbered of the families of the sons of Ger'shon, of all that might do service in the tabernacle of the congregation, whom Mo'ses and Aar'on did number according to the commandment of the LORD.

42 And those that were numbered of the families of the sons of Me-ra'ri, throughout their families, by the house of their fathers,

43 From thirty years old and upward even to fifty years old, every one that enters into the service, for the work in the tabernacle of the congregation,

44 Even those that were numbered of them after their families, were three thousand and two hundred.

45 These *be* those that were numbered of the families of the sons of Me-ra'ri, whom Mo'ses and Aar'on numbered according to the word of the LORD by the hand of Mo'ses.

46 All those that were numbered of the Le'vites, whom Mo'ses and Aar'on and the chief of Is'ra-el numbered, after their families, and after the house of their fathers,

47 From thirty years old and upward even to fifty years old, every one that came to do the service of the ministry, and the service of the burden in the tabernacle of the congregation,

48 Even those that were numbered of them, were eight thousand and five hundred and <u>fourscore</u>. ₈₀ 80

49 According to the commandment of the LORD they were numbered by the hand of Mo'ses, every one according to his service, and according to his <u>burden</u>: thus were they numbered of him, as the LORD commanded Mo'ses.   carrying

CHAPTER 5

AND the LORD spoke to Mo'ses, saying,

2 Command the children of Is'ra-el, that they put out of the camp every leper, and every one that has <u>an issue</u>, and whosoever is defiled by the dead: a discharge

3 Both male and female shall you put out, outside the camp shall you put them; that they <u>defile</u> not their camps, in the midst whereof I dwell.   contaminate

4 And the children of Is'ra-el did so, and put them out outside the camp: as the LORD spoke to Mo'ses, so did the children of Is'ra-el.

5 And the LORD spoke to Mo'ses, saying,

6 Speak to the children of Is'ra-el, When a man or woman shall commit any sin that men commit, to do a trespass against the LORD, and that person be guilty;

7 Then they shall confess their sin which they have done: and he shall <u>recompense</u> his trespass with the principal

thereof, and add to it the fifth *part* thereof, and give *it* to *him* against whom he has trespassed. _{pay}

8 But if the man have no <u>kinsman</u> to <u>recompense</u> the trespass to, let the trespass be <u>recompensed</u> to the LORD, *even* to the priest; beside the ram of the atonement, whereby an atonement shall be made for him. _{relative - pay}

9 And every offering of all the holy things of the children of Is'ra-el, which they bring to the priest, shall be his.

10 And every man's <u>hallowed</u> things shall be his: whatsoever any man gives the priest, it shall be his. _{sacred}

11 And the LORD spoke to Mo'ses, saying,

12 Speak to the children of Is'ra-el, and say to them, If any man's wife go aside, and <u>commit a trespass</u> against him, _{is unfaithful}

13 And a man lie with her carnally, and it be hid from the eyes of her husband, and be kept close, and she be defiled, and *there be* no witness against her, neither she be <u>taken with the manner</u>; _{caught in the act}

14 And the spirit of jealousy come upon him, and he be jealous of his wife, and she be defiled: or if the spirit of jealousy come upon him, and he be jealous of his wife, and she be not defiled:

15 Then shall the man bring his wife to the priest, and he shall bring her offering for her, the tenth *part* of an ephah of barley meal; he shall pour no oil upon it, nor put frankincense thereon; for it *is* an offering of jealousy,

an offering of memorial, bringing iniquity to remembrance.

16 And the priest shall bring her near, and set her before the LORD:

17 And the priest shall take holy water in an earthen vessel; and of the dust that is in the floor of the tabernacle the priest shall take, and put *it* into the water:

18 And the priest shall set the woman before the LORD, and uncover the woman's head, and put the offering of memorial in her hands, which *is* the jealousy offering: and the priest shall have in his hand the bitter water that causes the curse:

19 And the priest shall charge her by an oath, and say to the woman, If no man have lain with you, and if you have not gone aside to uncleanness *with another* instead of your husband, be you free from this bitter water that causes the curse:

20 But if you have gone aside *to another* instead of your husband, and if you be defiled, and some man have lain with you beside your husband:

21 Then the priest shall charge the woman with an oath of cursing, and the priest shall say to the woman, The LORD make you a curse and an oath among your people, when the LORD does make your thigh to rot, and your belly to swell;

22 And this water that causes the curse shall go into your <u>bowels,</u> to make *your* belly to swell, and *your* thigh to rot: And the woman shall say, Amen, amen. _{inward parts}

23 And the priest shall write these

curses in a book, and he shall blot *them* out with the bitter water:

24 And he shall cause the woman to drink the bitter water that causes the curse: and the water that causes the curse shall enter into her, *and become* bitter.

25 Then the priest shall take the jealousy offering out of the woman's hand, and shall wave the offering before the LORD, and offer it upon the altar:

26 And the priest shall take an handful of the offering, *even* the memorial thereof, and burn *it* upon the altar, and afterward shall cause the woman to drink the water.

27 And when he has made her to drink the water, then it shall come to pass, *that*, if she be defiled, and have done trespass against her husband, that the water that causes the curse shall enter into her, *and become* bitter, and her belly shall swell, and her thigh shall rot: and the woman shall be <u>a curse</u> among her people.   an outcast

28 And if the woman be not defiled, but be clean; then she shall be free, and shall conceive seed.

29 This *is* the law of jealousies, when a wife goes aside *to another* instead of her husband, and is defiled;

30 Or when the spirit of jealousy comes upon him, and he be jealous over his wife, and shall set the woman before the LORD, and the priest shall execute upon her all this law.

31 Then shall the man be guiltless from iniquity, and this woman shall bear her <u>iniquity</u>.   guilt

CHAPTER 6

AND the LORD spoke to Mo'ses, saying,

2 Speak to the children of Is'rael, and say to them, When either man or woman shall <u>separate</u> *themselves* to <u>vow a vow</u> of a Naz'arite, to <u>separate</u> *themselves* to the LORD: dedicate - pledge a pledge

3 He shall separate *himself* from wine and strong drink, and shall drink no vinegar of wine, or vinegar of strong drink, neither shall he drink any liquor of grapes, nor eat moist grapes, or dried.   LUKE 1:15

4 All the days of his separation shall he eat nothing that is made of the <u>vine tree</u>, from the kernels even to the husk.   grape vine

5 All the days of the vow of his separation there shall no razor come upon his head: until the days be fulfilled, in the which he separates *himself* to the LORD, he shall be <u>holy</u>, and shall let the locks of the hair of his head grow.   separated

6 All the days that he separates *himself* to the LORD he shall <u>come at</u> no dead body.   touch

7 He shall not make himself unclean for his father, or for his mother, for his brother, or for his sister, when they die: because the consecration of his <u>God</u> *is* upon his head.   Elohim^{p.f}

8 All the days of his separation he *is* <u>holy</u> to the LORD.   consecrated

9 And if any man die very suddenly by him, and he has defiled the head of his consecration; then he shall shave his

head in the day of his cleansing, on the seventh day shall he shave it.

10 And on the eighth day he shall bring two <u>turtles</u>, or two young pigeons, to the priest, to the door of the tabernacle of the congregation: doves

11 And the priest shall offer the one for a sin offering, and the other for a burned offering, and make an atonement for him, for that he sinned by the dead, and shall hallow his head that same day.

12 And he shall consecrate to the LORD the days of his separation, and shall bring a lamb of the first year for a trespass offering: but the days that were before shall be lost, because his separation was defiled.

13 And this *is* the law of the Naz'a-rite, when the days of his separation are fulfilled: he shall be brought to the door of the tabernacle of the congregation:

14 And he shall offer his offering to the LORD, one he lamb of the first year without <u>blemish</u> for a burned offering, and one ewe lamb of the first year without <u>blemish</u> for a sin offering, and one ram without <u>blemish</u> for peace offerings,   defect

15 And a basket of <u>unleavened</u> bread, cakes of fine flour mingled with oil, and wafers of <u>unleavened</u> bread anointed with oil, and their <u>meat</u> offering, and their drink offerings.   i.e., without yeast - grain

16 And the priest shall bring *them* before the LORD, and shall offer his sin offering, and his burned offering:

17 And he shall offer the ram *for* a sacrifice of peace offerings to the LORD, with the basket of <u>unleavened</u> bread: the priest shall offer also his <u>mea</u>t offering, and his drink offering.   i.e., without yeast - grain

18 And the Naz'a-rite shall shave the head of his separation *at* the door of the tabernacle of the congregation, and shall take the hair of the head of his separation, and put *it* in the fire which *is* under the sacrifice of the peace offerings.

19 And the priest shall take the <u>sodden</u> shoulder of the ram, and one <u>unleavened</u> cake out of the basket, and one <u>unleavened</u> wafer, and shall put *them* upon the hands of the Naz'a-rite, after *the hair of* his separation is shaven: boiled

20 And the priest shall <u>wave</u> them *for* a wave offering before the LORD: this *is* holy for the priest, with the wave breast and heave shoulder: and after that the Naz'a-rite may drink wine.   present

21 This *is* the law of the Naz'a-rite who has <u>vowed</u>, *and of* his offering to the LORD for his separation, beside *that* that his hand shall get: according to the <u>vow</u> which he <u>vowed</u>, so he must do after the law of his separation.   pledged

22 And the LORD spoke to Mo'ses, saying,

23 Speak to Aar'on and to his sons, saying, On this wise you shall bless the children of Is'ra-el, saying to them,

24 The LORD bless you, and keep you.

25 The LORD make His face shine upon you, and be gracious to you:

M27

26 The LORD lift up His countenance upon you, and give you peace.

27 And they shall <u>put</u> My name upon the children of Is'ra-el; and I will bless them. _{invoke}

CHAPTER 7

AND it came to pass on the day that Mo'ses had fully set up the tabernacle, and had anointed it, and sanctified it, and all the instruments thereof, both the altar and all the vessels thereof, and had anointed them, and sanctified them;

2 That the princes of Is'ra-el, heads of the house of their fathers, who *were* the princes of the tribes, <u>and</u> were over them that were numbered, offered: _{who}

3 And they brought their offering before the LORD, six covered wagons, and twelve oxen; a wagon for two of the princes, and for each one an ox: and they brought them before the tabernacle.

4 And the LORD spoke to Mo'ses, saying,

5 Take *it* of them, that they may be <u>to do the service</u> of the tabernacle of the congregation; and you shall give them to the Le'vites, to every man according to his service. _{used in the work}

6 And Mo'ses took the wagons and the oxen, and gave them to the Le'vites.

7 Two wagons and four oxen he gave to the sons of Ger'shon, according to their service:

8 And four wagons and eight oxen he gave to the sons of Me-ra'ri, according to their service, under the hand of Ith'a-mar the son of Aar'on the priest.

9 But to the sons of Ko'hath he gave none: because the service of the sanctuary belonging to them *was that* they should bear upon their shoulders.

10 And the princes offered for dedicating of the altar in the day that it was anointed, even the princes offered their offering before the altar.

11 And the LORD said to Mo'ses, They shall offer their offering, each prince on his day, for the dedicating of the altar.

12 And he that offered his offering the first day was Nah'shon the son of Am-min'a-dab, of the tribe of Ju'dah:

13 And his offering *was* one silver <u>charger</u>, the weight thereof *was* an hundred and thirty *shekels*, one silver bowl of seventy shekels, after the shekel of the sanctuary; both of them *were* full of fine flour mingled with oil for a meat offering: _{plate}

14 One spoon of ten *shekels* of gold, full of incense:

15 One young bullock, one ram, one lamb of the first year, for a burned offering:

16 One kid of the goats for a sin offering:

17 And for a sacrifice of peace offerings, two oxen, five rams, five he goats, five lambs of the first year: this *was* the offering of Nah'shon the son of Am-min'a-dab.

18 On the second day Ne-than'e-el the son of Zu'ar, prince of Is'sa-char, did offer:

19 He offered *for* his offering one silver <u>charger</u>, the weight whereof *was* an hundred and thirty *shekels*, one silver bowl of seventy shekels, after the shekel of the sanctuary; both of them full of fine flour mingled with oil for a meat offering: _{plate}

20 One spoon of gold of ten *shekels*, full of incense:

21 One young bullock, one ram, one lamb of the first year, for a burned offering:

22 One kid of the goats for a sin offering:

23 And for a sacrifice of peace offerings, two oxen, five rams, five he goats, five lambs of the first year: this *was* the offering of Ne-than'e-el the son of Zu'ar.

24 On the third day E-li'ab the son of He'lon, prince of the children of Zeb'u-lun, *did offer*:

25 His offering *was* one silver <u>charger</u>, the weight whereof *was* an hundred and thirty *shekels*, one silver bowl of seventy shekels, after the shekel of the sanctuary; both of them full of fine flour <u>mingled</u> with oil for a <u>meat</u> offering: _{mixed - grain}

26 One golden spoon of ten *shekels*, full of incense:

27 One young bullock, one ram, one lamb of the first year, for a burned offering:

28 One kid of the goats for a sin offering:

29 And for a sacrifice of peace offerings, two oxen, five rams, five he goats, five lambs of the first year: this *was* the offering of E-li'ab the son of He'lon.

30 On the fourth day E-li'zur the son of Shed'e-ur, prince of the children of Reu'ben, *did offer*:

31 His offering *was* one silver <u>charger</u> of the weight of an hundred and thirty *shekels*, one silver bowl of seventy shekels, after the shekel of the sanctuary; both of them full of fine flour mingled with oil for a <u>meat</u> offering: _{plate - grain}

32 One golden spoon of ten *shekels*, full of incense:

33 One young bullock, one ram, one lamb of the first year, for a burned offering:

34 One kid of the goats for a sin offering:

35 And for a sacrifice of peace offerings, two oxen, five rams, five he goats, five lambs of the first year: this *was* the offering of E-li'zur the son of Shed'e-ur.

36 On the fifth day She-lu'mi-el the son of Zu-ri-shad'da-i, prince of the children of Sim'e-on, *did offer*:

37 His offering *was* one silver <u>charger</u>, the weight whereof *was* an hundred and thirty *shekels*, one silver bowl of seventy shekels, after the shekel of the sanctuary; both of them full of fine flour mingled with oil for a <u>meat</u> offering: _{plate - grain}

38 One golden spoon of ten *shekels*, full of incense:

39 One young bullock, one ram, one lamb of the first year, for a burned offering:

40 One kid of the goats for a sin offering:

41 And for a sacrifice of peace offerings, two oxen, five rams, five he goats, five lambs of the first year: this *was* the

offering of She-lu'mi-el the son of Zu-ri-shad'da-i.

42 On the sixth day E-li'a-saph the son of Deu'el, prince of the children of Gad, *offered*:

43 His offering *was* one silver <u>charger</u> of the weight of an hundred and thirty *shekels*, a silver bowl of seventy shekels, after the shekel of the sanctuary; both of them full of fine flour mingled with oil for a meat offering: ᵖˡᵃᵗᵉ

44 One golden spoon of ten *shekels*, full of incense:

45 One young bullock, one ram, one lamb of the first year, for a burned offering:

46 One kid of the goats for a sin offering:

47 And for a sacrifice of peace offerings, two oxen, five rams, five he goats, five lambs of the first year: this *was* the offering of E-li'a-saph the son of Deu'el.

48 On the seventh day E-lish'a-ma the son of Am-mi'hud, prince of the children of E'phra-im, *offered*:

49 His offering *was* one silver <u>charger</u>, the weight whereof *was* an hundred and thirty *shekels*, one silver bowl of seventy shekels, after the shekel of the sanctuary; both of them full of fine flour mingled with oil for a <u>meat</u> offering: ᵖˡᵃᵗᵉ ⁻ ᵍʳᵃⁱⁿ

50 One golden spoon of ten *shekels*, full of incense:

51 One young bullock, one ram, one lamb of the first year, for a burned offering:

52 One kid of the goats for a sin offering:

53 And for a sacrifice of peace offerings, two oxen, five rams, five he goats, five lambs of the first year: this *was* the offering of E-lish'a-ma the son of Am-mi'hud.

54 On the eighth day *offered* Ga-ma'li-el the son of Pe-dah'zur, prince of the children of Ma-nas'seh:

55 His offering *was* one silver <u>charger</u> of the weight of an hundred and thirty *shekels*, one silver bowl of seventy shekels, after the shekel of the sanctuary; both of them full of fine flour mingled with oil for a <u>meat</u> offering: ᵖˡᵃᵗᵉ ⁻ ᵍʳᵃⁱⁿ

56 One golden spoon of ten *shekels*, full of incense:

57 One young bullock, one ram, one lamb of the first year, for a burned offering:

58 One kid of the goats for a sin offering:

59 And for a sacrifice of peace offerings, two oxen, five rams, five he goats, five lambs of the first year: this *was* the offering of Ga-ma'li-el the son of Pe-dah'zur.

60 On the ninth day Ab'i-dan the son of Gid-e-o'ni, prince of the children of Ben'ja-min, *offered*:

61 His offering *was* one silver <u>charger</u>, the weight whereof *was* an hundred and thirty *shekels*, one silver bowl of seventy shekels, after the shekel of the sanctuary; both of them full of fine flour mingled with oil for a <u>meat</u> offering: ᵖˡᵃᵗᵉ ⁻ ᵍʳᵃⁱⁿ

62 One golden spoon of ten *shekels*, full of incense:

63 One young bullock, one ram, one

lamb of the first year, for a burned offering:

64 One kid of the goats for a sin offering:

65 And for a sacrifice of peace offerings, two oxen, five rams, five he goats, five lambs of the first year: this *was* the offering of Ab'i-dan the son of Gid-e-o'ni.

66 On the tenth day A-hi-e'zer the son of Am-mi-shad'da-i, prince of the children of Dan, *offered*:

67 His offering *was* one silver <u>charger</u>, the weight whereof *was* an hundred and thirty *shekels*, one silver bowl of seventy shekels, after the shekel of the sanctuary; both of them full of fine flour mingled with oil for a <u>meat</u> offering:

plate - grain

68 One golden spoon of ten *shekels*, full of incense:

69 One young bullock, one ram, one lamb of the first year, for a burned offering:

70 One kid of the goats for a sin offering:

71 And for a sacrifice of peace offerings, two oxen, five rams, five he goats, five lambs of the first year: this *was* the offering of A-hi-e'zer the son of Am-mi-shad'da-i.

72 On the eleventh day Pa'gi-el the son of Oc'ran, prince of the children of Ash'er, *offered*:

73 His offering *was* one silver <u>charger</u>, the weight whereof *was* an hundred and thirty *shekels*, one silver bowl of seventy shekels, after the shekel of the sanctuary; both of them full of fine

flour <u>mingled</u> with oil for a <u>meat</u> offering:

plate - mixed - grain

74 One golden spoon of ten *shekels*, full of incense:

75 One young bullock, one ram, one lamb of the first year, for a burned offering:

76 One kid of the goats for a sin offering:

77 And for a sacrifice of peace offerings, two oxen, five rams, five he goats, five lambs of the first year: this *was* the offering of Pa'gi-el the son of Oc'ran.

78 On the twelfth day A-hi'ra the son of E'nan, prince of the children of Naph'ta-li, *offered*:

79 His offering *was* one silver <u>charger</u>, the weight whereof *was* an hundred and thirty *shekels*, one silver bowl of seventy shekels, after the shekel of the sanctuary; both of them full of fine flour <u>mingled</u> with oil for a <u>meat</u> offering:

80 One golden spoon of ten *shekels*, full of incense:

81 One young bullock, one ram, one lamb of the first year, for a burned offering:

82 One kid of the goats for a sin offering:

83 And for a sacrifice of peace offerings, two oxen, five rams, five he goats, five lambs of the first year: this *was* the offering of A-hi'ra the son of E'nan.

84 This *was* the dedication of the altar, in the day when it was anointed, by the princes of Is'ra-el: twelve <u>charg</u>ers of silver, twelve silver bowls, twelve spoons of gold: plates

85 Each <u>charger</u> of silver *weighing* an

hundred and thirty *shekels*, each bowl seventy: all the silver vessels *weighed* two thousand and four hundred *shekels*, after the shekel of the sanctuary: plate
86 The golden spoons *were* twelve, full of incense, *weighing* ten *shekels* apiece, after the shekel of the sanctuary: all the gold of the spoons *was* an hundred and twenty *shekels*.
87 All the oxen for the burned offering *were* twelve bullocks, the rams twelve, the lambs of the first year twelve, with their <u>meat</u> offering: and the kids of the goats for sin offering twelve. grain
88 And all the oxen for the sacrifice of the peace offerings *were* twenty and four bullocks, the rams sixty, the he goats sixty, the lambs of the first year sixty. This *was* the dedication of the altar, after that it was anointed.
89 And when Mo'ses was gone into the tabernacle of the congregation to speak with Him, then he heard the voice of One speaking to him from off the mercy seat that *was* upon the ark of testimony, from between the two cherubims: and He spoke to him.

CHAPTER 8

AND the LORD spoke to Mo'ses, saying,
2 Speak to Aar'on, and say to him, When you <u>light</u> the lamps, the seven lamps shall give light over against the candlestick. set up
3 And Aar'on did so; he lighted the lamps thereof over against the candlestick, as the LORD commanded Mo'ses.
4 And this work of the candlestick *was of* <u>beaten</u> gold, to the shaft thereof, to the flowers thereof, *was* <u>beaten</u> work: according to the pattern which the LORD had showed Mo'ses, so he made the candlestick. hammered
5 And the LORD spoke to Mo'ses, saying,
6 Take the Le'vites from among the children of Is'ra-el, and cleanse them.
7 And thus shall you do to them, to cleanse them: Sprinkle water of purifying upon them, and let them shave all their flesh, and let them wash their clothes, and *so* make themselves clean.
8 Then let them take a young bullock with his <u>meat</u> offering, *even* fine flour mingled with oil, and another young bullock shall you take for a sin offering. grain
9 And you shall bring the Le'vites before the tabernacle of the congregation: and you shall gather the whole assembly of the children of Is'ra-el together:
10 And you shall bring the Le'vites before the LORD: and the children of Is'ra-el shall put their hands upon the Le'vites:
11 And Aar'on shall offer the Le'vites before the LORD *for* an offering of the children of Is'ra-el, that they may <u>execute</u> the service of the LORD. do
12 And the Le'vites shall lay their hands upon the heads of the bullocks: and you shall offer the one *for* a sin offering, and the other *for* a burned offering, to the LORD, to make an atonement for the Le'vites.
13 And you shall set the Le'vites before Aar'on, and before his sons, and

offer them *for* an offering to the LORD.

14 Thus shall you separate the Le'vites from among the children of Is'ra-el: and the Le'vites shall be Mine.

15 And after that shall the Le'vites go in to do the service of the tabernacle of the congregation: and you shall cleanse them, and offer them *for* an offering.

16 For they *are* wholly given to Me from among the children of Is'ra-el; instead of such as open every womb, *even instead of* the firstborn of all the children of Is'ra-el, have I taken them to Me.

17 For all the firstborn of the children of Is'ra-el *are* Mine, *both* man and beast: on the day that I smote every firstborn in the land of E'gypt I <u>sanctified them</u> for Myself.   set them apart

18 And I have taken the Le'vites for all the firstborn of the children of Is'ra-el.

19 And I have given the Le'vites *as* a gift to Aar'on and to his sons from among the children of Is'ra-el, to do the service of the children of Is'ra-el in the tabernacle of the congregation, and to make an atonement for the children of Is'ra-el: that there be no <u>plague</u> among the children of Is'ra-el, when the children of Is'ra-el come near to the sanctuary.   punishment

20 And Mo'ses, and Aar'on, and all the congregation of the children of Is'ra-el, did to the Le'vites according to all that the LORD commanded Mo'ses concerning the Le'vites, so did the children of Is'ra-el to them.

21 And the Le'vites were <u>purified</u>, and they washed their clothes; and Aar'on offered them *as* an offering before the LORD; and Aar'on made an atonement for them to cleanse them.   cleansed

22 And after that went the Le'vites in to do their service in the tabernacle of the congregation before Aar'on, and before his sons: as the LORD had commanded Mo'ses concerning the Le'vites, so did they to them.

23 And the LORD spoke to Mo'ses, saying,

24 This *is it* that *belongs* to the Le'vites: from twenty and five years old and upward they shall go in to wait upon the service of the tabernacle of the congregation:

25 And from the age of fifty years they shall cease waiting upon the service *thereof*, and shall serve no more:

26 But shall minister with their brethren in the tabernacle of the congregation, to keep the <u>charge</u>, and shall do no service. Thus shall you do to the Le'vites <u>touching their charge</u>.   duties - concerning their responsibilities

CHAPTER 9

AND the LORD spoke to Mo'ses in the wilderness of Si'nai, in the first month of the second year after they were come out of the land of E'gypt, saying,

2 Let the children of Is'ra-el also keep the passover at its appointed season.

3 In the fourteenth day of this month, at even, you shall keep it in its appointed season: according to all the rites of it,

and according to all the ceremonies thereof, shall you keep it.

4 And Mo'ses spoke to the children of Is'ra-el, that they should keep the passover.

5 And they kept the passover on the fourteenth day of the first month at even in the wilderness of Si'nai: according to all that the LORD commanded Mo'ses, so did the children of Is'ra-el.

6 And there were certain men, who were defiled by the dead body of a man, that they could not keep the passover on that day: and they came before Mo'ses and before Aar'on on that day: unclean

7 And those men said to him, We *are* defiled by the dead body of a man: wherefore are we kept back, that we may not offer an offering of the LORD in its appointed season among the children of Is'ra-el? restrained from sharing

8 And Mo'ses said to them, Stand still, and I will hear what the LORD will command concerning you. wait

9 And the LORD spoke to Mo'ses, saying,

10 Speak to the children of Is'ra-el, saying, If any man of you or of your posterity shall be unclean by reason of a dead body, or *be* in a journey afar off, yet he shall keep the passover to the LORD. descendants - unfit

11 The fourteenth day of the second month at even they shall keep it, *and* eat it with unleavened bread and bitter *herbs*. without yeast

12 They shall leave none of it to the morning, nor break any bone of it: according to all the ordinances of the passover they shall keep it. regulations

13 But the man that *is* clean, and is not in a journey, and forbears to keep the passover, even the same soul shall be cut off from among his people: because he brought not the offering of the LORD in its appointed season, that man shall bear his sin.

person - destroyed - at the appointed time

14 And if a stranger shall sojourn among you, and will keep the passover to the LORD; according to the ordinance of the passover, and according to the manner thereof, so shall he do: you shall have one ordinance, both for the stranger, and for him that was born in the land. stay

15 And on the day that the tabernacle was reared up the cloud covered the tabernacle, *namely*, the tent of the testimony: and at even there was upon the tabernacle as it were the appearance of fire, until the morning.

16 So it was alway: the cloud covered it *by day*, and the appearance of fire by night.

17 And when the cloud was taken up from the tabernacle, then after that the children of Is'ra-el journeyed: and in the place where the cloud abode, there the children of Is'ra-el pitched their tents. lifted

18 At the commandment of the LORD the children of Is'ra-el journeyed, and at the commandment of the LORD they pitched: as long as the cloud abode upon the tabernacle they rested in their tents. camped

19 And when the cloud tarried long upon the tabernacle many days, then

the children of Is'ra-el kept the <u>charge</u> of the LORD, and journeyed not.   _{order}

20 And *so* it was, when the cloud was a few days upon the tabernacle; according to the commandment of the LORD they abode in their tents, and according to the commandment of the LORD they journeyed.

21 And *so* it was, when the cloud abode from <u>even</u> to the morning, and *that* the cloud was taken up in the morning, then they journeyed: whether *it was* by day or by night that the cloud was taken up, they journeyed.   _{evening}

22 Or *whether it were* two days, or a month, or a year, that the cloud tarried upon the tabernacle, remaining thereon, the children of Is'ra-el <u>abode</u> in their tents, and journeyed not: but when it was taken up, they journeyed.   _{remained}

23 At the commandment of the LORD they rested in the tents, and at the commandment of the LORD they journeyed: they kept the <u>charge</u> of the LORD, at the commandment of the LORD by the hand of Mo'ses.   _{order}

CHAPTER 10

AND the LORD spoke to Mo'ses, saying,

2 Make you two trumpets of silver; of a whole piece shall you make them: that you may use them for the calling of the assembly, and for the journeying of the camps.

3 And when they shall blow with them, all the assembly shall assemble themselves to you at the door of the tabernacle of the congregation.

4 And if they blow *but* with one *trumpet*, then the princes, *which are* heads of the thousands of Is'ra-el, shall gather themselves to you.

5 When you blow an alarm, then the camps that lie on the east parts shall go forward.

6 When you blow an alarm the second time, then the camps that lie on the south side shall <u>take their journey</u>: they shall blow an alarm for their journeys.   _{set out}

7 But when the congregation is to be gathered together, you shall blow, but you shall not sound an alarm.

8 And the sons of Aar'on, the priests, shall blow with the trumpets; and they shall be to you for <u>an ordinance</u> for ever throughout your generations. _{a rule}

9 And if you go to war in your land against the enemy that oppresses you, then you shall blow an alarm with the trumpets; and you shall be remembered before the LORD your <u>God</u>, and you shall be saved from your enemies.   _{Elohim^{p.fi}}

10 Also in the day of your gladness, and in your <u>solemn</u> days, and in the beginnings of your months, you shall blow with the trumpets over your burned offerings, and over the sacrifices of your peace offerings; that they may be to you for a memorial before your <u>God</u>: I *am* the LORD your <u>God</u>.   _{appointed}

11 And it came to pass on the twentieth *day* of the second month, in the second year, that the cloud was taken up from off the tabernacle of the testimony.

12 And the children of Is'ra-el took their journeys out of the wilderness of

Si'nai; and the cloud rested in the wilderness of Pa'ran.

13 And they first took their journey according to the commandment of the LORD by the hand of Mo'ses.

14 In the first *place* went the <u>standard</u> of the camp of the children of Ju'dah according to their armies: and over his host *was* Nah'shon the son of Am-min'a-dab.   flag

15 And over the host of the tribe of the children of Is'sa-char *was* Ne-than'e-el the son of Zu'ar.

16 And over the host of the tribe of the children of Zeb'u-lun *was* E-li'ab the son of He'lon.

17 And the tabernacle was taken down; and the sons of Ger'shon and the sons of Me-ra'ri set forward, <u>bearing</u> the tabernacle.   carrying

18 And the <u>standard</u> of the camp of Reu'ben set forward according to their <u>armies</u>: and over his host *was* E-li'zur the son of Shed'e-ur.   tribes

19 And over the host of the tribe of the children of Sim'e-on *was* She-lu'mi-el the son of Zu-ri-shad'da-i.

20 And over the host of the tribe of the children of Gad *was* E-li'a-saph the son of Deu'el.

21 And the Ko'hath-ites set forward, bearing the sanctuary: and *the other* did set up the tabernacle against they came.

22 And the <u>standard</u> of the camp of the children of E'phra-im set forward according to their <u>armies</u>: and over his host *was* E-lish'a-ma the son of Am-mi'hud.   flag - tribes

23 And over the host of the tribe of the children of Ma-nas'seh *was* Ga-ma'li-el the son of Pe-dah'zur.

24 And over the host of the tribe of the children of Ben'ja-min *was* Ab'i-dan the son of Gid-e-o'ni.

25 And the <u>standard</u> of the camp of the children of Dan set forward, *which was* the <u>rearward</u> of all the camps throughout their hosts: and over his host *was* A-hi-e'zer the son of Am-mi-shad'da-i.   flag - rear guard

26 And over the host of the tribe of the children of Ash'er *was* Pa'gi-el the son of Oc'ran.

27 And over the host of the tribe of the children of Naph'ta-li *was* A-hi'ra the son of E'nan.

28 Thus *were* the <u>journeyings</u> of the children of Is'ra-el according to their armies, when they set forward.   travels

29 And Mo'ses said to Ho-bab, the son of Ra-gu'el the Mid'i-an-ite, Mo'ses' father in law, We are journeying to the place of which the LORD said, I will give it you: come you with us, and we will do you good: for the LORD has <u>spoken</u> good concerning Is'ra-el.   promised

30 And he said to him, I will not go; but I will depart to my own land, and to my kindred.

31 And he said, Leave us not, I pray you; forasmuch as you know how we are to encamp in the wilderness, and you may be to us instead of eyes.

32 And it shall be, if you go with us, yea, it shall be, that <u>what goodness</u> the LORD shall do to us, the same will we do to you.   whatever good

33 And they departed from the

mount of the LORD three days' journey: and the ark of the <u>covenant</u> of the LORD went before them in the three days' journey, to search out a resting place for them.　　agreement

34 And the cloud of the LORD *was* upon them by day, when they went out of the camp.

35 And it came to pass, when the ark set forward, that Mo'ses said, Rise up, LORD, and let Your enemies be scattered; and let them that <u>hate</u> You flee before You.　　abhor

36 And when it rested, he said, Return, O LORD, to the many thousands of Is'ra-el.

CHAPTER 11

M27
GI
|
|
|
|
232
|
|
237

AND *when* the people complained, it displeased the LORD: and the LORD heard *it*; and His anger was kindled; and the fire of the LORD burned among them, and consumed *them that were* in the uttermost parts of the camp.

2 And the people cried to Mo'ses; and when Mo'ses prayed to the LORD, the fire was <u>quenched</u>.　　put out

3 And he called the name of the place <u>Tab'e-rah</u>: because the fire of the LORD burned among them.　　i.e., a burning

4 And the mixed multitude that *was* among them <u>fell a lusting</u>: and the children of Is'ra-el also wept again, and said, Who shall give us flesh to eat?　　1 COR. 10:6　had greedy desires

5 We remember the fish, which we did eat in E'gypt <u>freely</u>; the cucumbers, and the melons, and the leeks, and the onions, and the garlic: at no cost

6 But now our <u>soul</u> *is* dried <u>away</u>:

there is nothing at all, beside this manna, *before* our eyes.　　body - up

7 And the manna *was* as coriander seed, and the color thereof as the color of <u>bdellium</u>.　　resin

8 *And* the people went about, and gathered *it*, and ground *it* in mills, or beat *it* in a mortar, and baked *it* in pans, and made cakes of it: and the taste of it was as the taste of fresh oil.

9 And when the dew fell upon the camp in the night, the manna fell upon it.

10 Then Mo'ses heard the people weep throughout their families, every man in the door of his tent: and the anger of the LORD was <u>kindled greatly</u>; Mo'ses also was displeased.　　exceedingly angry

GI
234

11 And Mo'ses said to the LORD, Wherefore have You afflicted Your servant? and wherefore have I not found favor in Your sight, that You lay the <u>burden</u> of all this people upon me?　　responsibility

12 Have I conceived all this people? have I begotten them, that You should say to me, Carry them in your bosom, as a nursing father bears the sucking child, to the land which You <u>swear</u> to their fathers?　　promised

13 From where should I have <u>flesh</u> to give to all this people? for they weep to me, saying, Give us <u>flesh</u>, that we may eat.　　meat

14 I am not able to <u>bear</u> all this people alone, because *it is* too heavy for me.　　carry

15 And if You <u>deal thus with me</u>, kill me, I pray You, <u>out of hand</u>, if I have

found favor in Your sight; and let me not see my wretchedness.

treat me this way - at once

16 And the LORD said to Mo'ses, Gather to Me seventy men of the elders of Is'ra-el, whom you know to be the elders of the people, and officers over them; and bring them to the tabernacle of the congregation, that they may stand there with you.

17 And I will come down and talk with you there: and I will take of the Spirit which *is* upon you, and will put *it* upon them; and they shall bear the burden of the people with you, that you bear *it* not yourself alone.

carry the responsibility

18 And say you to the people, Sanctify yourselves against to morrow, and you shall eat flesh: for you have wept in the ears of the LORD, saying, Who shall give us flesh to eat? for *it was* well with us in E'gypt: therefore the LORD will give you flesh, and you shall eat.

Consecrate - meat

19 You shall not eat one day, nor two days, nor five days, neither ten days, nor twenty days;

20 *But* even a whole month, until it come out at your nostrils, and it be loathsome to you: because that you have despised the LORD which *is* among you, and have wept before Him, saying, Why came we forth out of E'gypt?

disgusting - rejected

21 And Mo'ses said, The people, among whom I *am, are* six hundred thousand footmen; and You have said, I will give them flesh, that they may eat a whole month.

food

22 Shall the flocks and the herds be slain for them, to suffice them? or shall all the fish of the sea be gathered together for them, to suffice them?

be enough for

23 And the LORD said to Mo'ses, Is the LORD's hand waxed short? you shall see now whether My word shall come to pass to you or not.

limited

24 And Mo'ses went out, and told the people the words of the LORD, and gathered the seventy men of the elders of the people, and set them round about the tabernacle.

25 And the LORD came down in a cloud, and spoke to him, and took of the Spirit that *was* upon him, and gave *It* to the seventy elders: and it came to pass, *that*, when the Spirit rested upon them, they prophesied, and did not cease.

26 But there remained two *of the* men in the camp, the name of the one *was* El'dad, and the name of the other Me'dad: and the Spirit rested upon them; and they *were* of them that were written, but went not out to the tabernacle: and they prophesied in the camp.

27 And there ran a young man, and told Mo'ses, and said, El'dad and Me'dad do prophesy in the camp.

28 And Josh'u-a the son of Nun, the servant of Mo'ses, *one* of his young men, answered and said, My lord Mo'ses, forbid them.

29 And Mo'ses said to him, Envy you for my sake? would God that all the LORD's people were prophets, *and* that the LORD would put His Spirit upon them!

MARK 9:39

30 And Mo'ses got him into the camp, he and the elders of Is'ra-el.

31 And there went forth a wind from the LORD, and brought quails from the sea, and let *them* fall by the camp, as it were a day's journey on this side, and as it were a day's journey on the other side, round about the camp, and as it were two cubits *high* upon the face of the earth.

32 And the people stood up all that day, and all *that* night, and all the next day, and they gathered the quails: he that gathered least gathered ten homers: and they spread *them* all abroad for themselves round about the camp.

33 And while the <u>flesh</u> *was* yet between their teeth, before it was chewed, the wrath of the LORD was kindled against the people, and the LORD <u>smote</u> the people with a very great plague._{meat - struck}

34 And he called the name of that place Kib'roth-hat-ta'a-vah: because there they buried the people that lusted.

35 *And* the people journeyed from Kib'roth-hat-ta'a-vah to Ha-ze'roth; and abode at Ha-ze'roth.

CHAPTER 12

AND Mir'i-am and Aar'on spoke against Mo'ses because of the E-thi-o'pi-an woman whom he had married: for he had married an E-thi-o'pi-an woman.

2 And they said, Has the LORD indeed spoken only by Mo'ses? has He not spoken also by us? And the LORD heard *it*.

3 (Now the man Mo'ses *was* very <u>meek</u>, above all the men which *were* upon the face of the earth.) _{humble}

4 And the LORD spoke suddenly to Mo'ses, and to Aar'on, and to Mir'i-am, Come out you three to the tabernacle of the congregation. And they three came out.

5 And the LORD came down in the pillar of the cloud, and stood *in* the door of the tabernacle, and called Aar'on and Mir'i-am: and they both came forth.

6 And He said, Hear now My words: If there be a prophet among you, *I* the LORD will make Myself known to him in a vision, *and* will speak to him in a dream.

7 My servant Mo'ses *is* not so, who *is* faithful in all My house.   HEB. 3:2

8 With him will I speak mouth to mouth, even <u>apparently</u>, and not <u>in</u> <u>dark speeches</u>; and the <u>similitude</u> of the LORD shall he behold: wherefore then were you not afraid to speak against My servant Mo'ses?

_{openly - in riddles - form}

9 And the anger of the LORD was kindled against them; and He departed.

10 And the cloud departed from off the tabernacle; and, behold, Mir'i-am *became* leprous, *white* as snow: and Aar'on looked upon Mir'i-am, and, behold, *she was* leprous.

11 And Aar'on said to Mo'ses, Alas, my lord, I beseech you, lay not the sin upon us, wherein we have done foolishly, and wherein we have sinned.

12 Let her not be as one dead, of whom the flesh is half consumed when he comes out of his mother's womb.

13 And Mo'ses cried to the LORD,

saying, Heal her now, O God, I beseech You.   _{pray}

14 And the LORD said to Mo'ses, If
her father had but spit in her face,
should she not be ashamed seven
days? let her be shut out from the
camp seven days, and after that let
her be received in *again*.   _{confined}

15 And Mir'i-am was shut out from
the camp seven days: and the people
journeyed not till Mir'i-am was
brought in *again*.

16 And afterward the people removed
from Ha-ze'roth, and pitched in the
wilderness of Pa'ran.   _{camped}

CHAPTER 13

AND the LORD spoke to Mo'ses,
saying,

2 Send you men, that they may search
the land of Ca'naan, which I give to
the children of Is'ra-el: of every tribe
of their fathers shall you send a man,
every one a ruler among them.   _{spy out}

3 And Mo'ses by the commandment
of the LORD sent them from the wilderness of Pa'ran: all those men *were*
heads of the children of Is'ra-el.

4 And these *were* their names: of the
tribe of Reu'ben, Sham-mu'a the son
of Zac'cur.

5 Of the tribe of Sim'e-on, Sha'phat
the son of Ho'ri.

6 Of the tribe of Ju'dah, Ca'leb the son
of Je-phun'neh.

7 Of the tribe of Is'sa-char, I'gal the
son of Jo'seph.

8 Of the tribe of E'phra-im, O-she'a
the son of Nun.

9 Of the tribe of Ben'ja-min, Pal'ti the
son of Ra'phu.

10 Of the tribe of Zeb'u-lun, Gad'di-el
the son of So'di.

11 Of the tribe of Jo'seph, *namely*, of
the tribe of Ma-nas'seh, Gad'di the
son of Su'si.

12 Of the tribe of Dan, Am'mi-el the
son of Ge-mal'li.

13 Of the tribe of Ash'er, Se'thur the
son of Mi'chael.

14 Of the tribe of Naph'ta-li, Nah'bi the
son of Voph'si.

15 Of the tribe of Gad, Ge-u'el the son
of Ma'chi.

16 These *are* the names of the men
which Mo'ses sent to spy out the land.
And Mo'ses called O-she'a the son
of Nun Je-hosh'u-a.

17 And Mo'ses sent them to spy out
the land of Ca'naan, and said to them,
Get you up this *way* southward, and
go up into the mountain:

18 And see the land, what it *is*; and
the people that dwell therein, whether
they *be* strong or weak, few or many;
      _{assess}

19 And what the land *is* that they
dwell in, whether it *be* good or bad;
and what cities *they be* that they
dwell in, whether in tents, or in
strong holds;   _{open camps}

20 And what the land *is*, whether it
be fat or lean, whether there be wood
therein, or not. And be you of good
courage, and bring of the fruit of the
land. Now the time *was* the time of
the firstripe grapes.

21 So they went up, and searched
the land from the wilderness of Zin

to Re'hob, as men come to Ha'math. 22 And they ascended by the <u>south</u>, and came to He'bron; where A-hi'man, She'shai, and Tal'mai, the children of A'nak, *were*. (Now He'bron was built seven years before Zo'an in E'gypt.) i.e., Negev
23 And they came to the <u>brook</u> of Esh'col, and cut down from there a branch with one cluster of grapes, and they bare it between two upon a staff; and *they brought* of the pomegran-ates, and of the figs. valley
24 The place was called the <u>brook</u> Esh'col, because of the cluster of grapes which the children of Is'ra-el cut down from there.
25 And they returned from searching of the land after forty days.
26 And they went and came to Mo'ses, and to Aar'on, and to all the congregation of the children of Is'ra-el, to the wilderness of Pa'ran, to Ka'desh; and brought back word to them, and to all the congregation, and showed them the fruit of the land.
27 And they told him, and said, We came to the land where you sent us, and surely it flows with milk and honey; and this *is* the fruit of it.
28 Nevertheless the people *be* strong that dwell in the land, and the cities *are* walled, *and* very great: and moreover we saw the children of A'nak there.
29 The Am'a-lek-ites dwell in the land of the south: and the Hit'tites, and the Jeb'u-sites, and the Am'or-ites, dwell in the mountains: and the Ca'naan-ites dwell by the sea, and by the coast of Jor'dan.

30 And Ca'leb stilled the people be-fore Mo'ses, and said, Let us go up at once, and <u>possess</u> it; for we are well able to overcome it. occupy
31 But the men that went up with him said, We be not able to go up against the people; for they *are* stronger than we.
32 And they brought up an evil report of the land which they had searched to the children of Is'ra-el, saying, The land, through which we have gone to search it, *is* a land that <u>eats up</u> the inhabitants thereof; and all the people that we saw in it *are* men of a great stature. devours
33 And there we saw the giants, the sons of A'nak, *which come* of the giants: and we were in our own sight as grasshop-pers, and so we were in their sight.

CHAPTER 14

AND all the congregation <u>lifted up their voice</u>, and cried; and the people wept that night.
HEB. 3:16-19 made loud lament
2 And all the children of Is'ra-el <u>mur-mured</u> against Mo'ses and against Aar'on: and the whole congregation said to them, Would God that we had died in the land of E'gypt! or would God we had died in this wilderness! grumbled
3 And wherefore has the LORD brought us to this land, to fall by <u>the sword</u>, that our wives and our children should be a prey? were it not better for us to return into E'gypt? wars
4 And they said one to another, Let us make a captain, and let us return into E'gypt. ACTS 7:39

5 Then Mo'ses and Aar'on fell on their faces before all the assembly of the congregation of the children of Is'ra-el.

6 And Josh'u-a the son of Nun, and Ca'leb the son of Je-phun'neh, *which were* of them that searched the land, rent their clothes: tore

7 And they spoke to all the company of the children of Is'ra-el, saying, The land, which we passed through to search it, *is* an exceeding good land.

8 If the LORD delight in us, then He will bring us into this land, and give it us; a land which flows with milk and honey.

9 Only rebel not you against the LORD, neither fear you the people of the land; for they *are* bread for us: their defence is departed from them, and the LORD *is* with us: fear them not.   protection

10 But all the congregation bade stone them with stones. And the glory of the LORD appeared in the tabernacle of the congregation before all the children of Is'ra-el.   said

11 And the LORD said to Mo'ses, How long will this people provoke Me? and how long will it before they believe Me, for all the signs which I have showed among them? spurn - miracles

12 I will smite them with the pestilence, and disinherit them, and will make of you a greater nation and mightier than they.

13 And Mo'ses said to the LORD, Then the E-gyptians shall hear *it*, (for You brought up this people in Your might from among them;)

14 And they will tell *it* to the inhabitants of this land: *for* they have heard that You LORD *are* among this people, that You LORD are seen face to face, and *that* Your cloud stands over them, and *that* You go before them, by day time in a pillar of a cloud, and in a pillar of fire by night.

15 Now *if* You shall kill *all* this people as one man, then the nations which have heard the fame of You will speak, saying,

16 Because the LORD was not able to bring this people into the land which He swear to them, therefore He has slain them in the wilderness.

17 And now, I beseech You, let the power of my Lord be great, according as You have spoken, saying,   pray - displayed

18 The LORD *is* long suffering, and of great mercy, forgiving iniquity and transgression, and by no means clearing *the guilty*, visiting the iniquity of the fathers upon the children to the third and fourth *generation*. slow to anger

19 Pardon, I beseech You, the iniquity of this people according to the greatness of Your mercy, and as You have forgiven this people, from E'gypt even until now.

20 And the LORD said, I have pardoned according to your word:

21 But *as* truly *as* I live, all the earth shall be filled with the glory of the LORD.

22 Because all those men which have seen My glory, and My miracles, which I did in E'gypt and in the wilderness, and have tempted Me now these ten times, and have not hearkened to My voice;

23 Surely they shall not see the land which I swear to their fathers, neither shall any of them that provoked Me see it:

24 But My servant Ca'leb, because he had another spirit with him, and has followed Me fully, him will I bring into the land whereto he went; and his seed shall possess it.   descendants

25 (Now the Am'a-lek-ites and the Ca'naan-ites dwelt in the valley.) To morrow turn you, and get you into the wilderness by the way of the Red sea.

26 And the LORD spoke to Mo'ses and to Aar'on, saying,

27 How long *shall I bear with* this evil congregation, which murmur against Me? I have heard the murmurings of the children of Is'ra-el, which they murmur against Me.   wicked - grumble

28 Say to them, *As truly as* I live, says the LORD, as you have spoken in My ears, so will I do to you:

29 Your carcases shall fall in this wilderness; and all that were numbered of you, according to your whole number, from twenty years old and upward, which have murmured against Me,   1 COR. 10:5 corpses

30 Doubtless you shall not come into the land, *concerning* which I swear to make you dwell therein, save Ca'leb the son of Je-phun'neh, and Josh'u-a the son of Nun.

31 But your little ones, which you said should be a prey, them will I bring in, and they shall know the land which you have despised. enjoy - rejected

32 But *as for* you, your carcases, they shall fall in this wilderness.

33 And your children shall wander in the wilderness forty years, and bear your whoredoms, until your carcases be wasted in the wilderness.

be shepherds - i.e., faithlessness - corpses

34 After the number of the days in which you searched the land, *even* forty days, each day for a year, shall you bear your iniquities, *even* forty years, and you shall know My breach of promise.   opposition

35 I the LORD have said, I will surely do it to all this evil congregation, that are gathered together against Me: in this wilderness they shall be consumed, and there they shall die. wicked

36 And the men, which Mo'ses sent to search the land, who returned, and made all the congregation to murmur against him, by bringing up a slander upon the land, spy out - grumble - bad report

37 Even those men that did bring up the evil report upon the land, died by the plague before the LORD.   affliction

38 But Josh'u-a the son of Nun, and Ca'leb the son of Je-phun'neh, *which were* of the men that went to search the land, lived *still*.

39 And Mo'ses told these sayings to all the children of Is'ra-el: and the people mourned greatly.

40 And they rose up early in the morning, and got them up into the top of the mountain, saying, Lo, we *be here*, and will go up to the place which the LORD has promised: for we have sinned.

41 And Mo'ses said, Wherefore now do you transgress the commandment of the LORD? but it shall not prosper. succeed

42 Go not up, for the LORD *is* not

among you; that you be not <u>smitten</u>
before your enemies.   defeated
43 For the Am'a-lek-ites and the
Ca'naan-ites *are* there before you, and
you shall fall by the sword: because
you are turned away from the LORD,
therefore the LORD will not be with you.
44 But they <u>presumed to go</u> up to the
hill top: nevertheless the ark of the
<u>covenant</u> of the LORD, and Mo'ses, de-
parted not out of the camp.

heedlessly went - agreement

45 Then the Am'a-lek-ites came down,
and the Ca'naan-ites which dwelt in
that hill, and smote them, and <u>discom-
fited</u> them, *even* to Hor'mah.   beat

CHAPTER 15

A ND the LORD spoke to Mo'ses,
saying,
2 Speak to the children of Is'ra-el,
and say to them, When you be come
into the land <u>of your habitations</u>,
which I give to you,   where you are to live
3 And will make an offering by fire
to the LORD, a burned offering, or a
sacrifice in performing a vow, or in a
freewill offering, or in your <u>solemn</u>
feasts, to make a <u>sweet savor</u> to the
LORD, of the herd, or of the flock:

appointed - soothing aroma

4 Then shall he that offers his offering to the LORD bring a meat offering
of a tenth deal of flour mingled with
the fourth *part* of an hin of oil.
5 And the fourth *part* of an hin of
wine for a drink offering shall you
prepare with the burned offering or
sacrifice, for one lamb.

6 Or for a ram, you shall prepare *for*
a meat offering two tenth deals of
flour mingled with the third *part* of
an hin of oil.
7 And for a drink offering you shall
offer the third *part* of an hin of
wine, *for* a <u>sweet savor</u> to the LORD.

soothing aroma

8 And when you prepare a bullock
for a burned offering, or *for* a sacrifice in <u>performing a vow</u>, or peace
offerings to the LORD: fulfilling a promise
9 Then shall he bring with a bullock a
meat offering of three tenth deals of
flour mingled with half an hin of oil.
10 And you shall bring for a drink
offering half an hin of wine, *for* an
offering made by fire, of a sweet savor to the LORD.
11 Thus shall it be done for one bullock, or for one ram, or for a lamb, or a
kid.
12 According to the number that you
shall prepare, so shall you do to every one according to their number.
13 All that are <u>born</u> of the country shall
do these things after this manner, in
offering an offering made by fire, of a
sweet savor to the LORD.   native born
14 And if a <u>stranger sojourn</u> with you,
or whosoever *be* among you in your
generations, and will offer an offering
made by fire, of a sweet savor to the
LORD; as you do, so he shall do. alien stays
15 <u>One ordinance</u> *shall be both* for
you of the congregation, and also for
the <u>stranger</u> that <u>sojourns</u> *with you*,
an <u>ordinance</u> for ever in your generations: as you *are*, so shall the
<u>stranger</u> be before the LORD. The same rule
16 One law and one <u>manner</u> shall be

for you, and for the stranger that sojourns with you. regulation - stays

17 And the LORD spoke to Mo'ses, saying,

18 Speak to the children of Is'ra-el, and say to them, When you come into the land where I bring you,

19 Then it shall be, that, when you eat of the bread of the land, you shall offer up an heave offering to the LORD.

20 You shall offer up a cake of the first of your dough *for* an heave offering: as *you do* the heave offering of the threshingfloor, so shall you heave it.

21 Of the first of your dough you shall give to the LORD an heave offering in your generations.

22 And if you have erred, and not observed all these commandments, which the LORD has spoken to Mo'ses, failed

23 *Even* all that the LORD has commanded you by the hand of Mo'ses, from the day that the LORD commanded Mo'ses, and hereafter among your generations;

24 Then it shall be, if *it* be committed by ignorance without the knowledge of the congregation, that all the congregation shall offer one young bullock for a burned offering, for a sweet savor to the LORD, with his meat offering, and his drink offering, according to the manner, and one kid of the goats for a sin offering. error - regulation

25 And the priest shall make an atonement for all the congregation of the children of Is'ra-el, and it shall be forgiven them; for it *is* ignorance: and they shall bring their offering, a sacrifice made by fire to the LORD, and their sin offering before the LORD, for their ignorance: error

26 And it shall be forgiven all the congregation of the children of Is'ra-el, and the stranger that sojourns among them; seeing all the people *were* in ignorance. alien - lives

27 And if any soul sin through ignorance, then he shall bring a she goat of the first year for a sin offering.person

28 And the priest shall make an atonement for the soul that sins ignorantly, when he sins by ignorance before the LORD, to make an atonement for him; and it shall be forgiven him.

29 You shall have one law for him that sins through ignorance, *both for* him that is born among the children of Is'ra-el, and for the stranger that sojourns among them. alien - lives

30 But the soul that does *anything* presumptuously, *whether he be* born in the land, or a stranger, the same reproaches the LORD; and that soul shall be cut off from among his people. anything with a high hand - destroyed

31 Because he has despised the word of the LORD, and has broken His commandment, that soul shall utterly be cut off; his iniquity *shall be* upon him. person

32 And while the children of Is'ra-el were in the wilderness, they found a man that gathered sticks upon the sabbath day.

33 And they that found him gathering sticks brought him to Mo'ses and Aar'on, and to all the congregation.

34 And they put him in ward, because

it was not <u>declared</u> what should be done to him. custody - revealed

35 And the LORD said to Mo'ses, The man shall be surely put to death: all the congregation shall stone him with stones outside the camp.

36 And all the congregation brought him outside the camp, and stoned him with stones, and he died; as the LORD commanded Mo'ses.

37 And the LORD spoke to Mo'ses, saying,

38 Speak to the children of Is'ra-el, and bid them that they make them fringes in the borders of their garments throughout their generations, and that they put upon the fringe of the borders a ribbon of blue:

39 And it shall be to you for a fringe, that you may look upon it, and remember all the commandments of the LORD, and do them; and that you seek not after your own heart and your own eyes, after which you use to go a <u>whoring</u>: i.e., away from God

40 That you may remember, and do all My commandments, and be holy to your God.

41 I *am* the LORD your <u>God</u>, which brought you out of the land of E'gypt, to be your <u>God</u>: I *am* the LORD your <u>God</u>. Elohim^{p.f.}

CHAPTER 16

NOW Ko'rah, the son of Iz'har, the son of Ko'hath, the son of Le'vi, and Da'than and A-bi'ram, the sons of E-li'ab, and On, the son of Pe'leth, sons of Reu'ben, took *men*:

2 And they rose up before Mo'ses, with certain of the children of Is'ra-el, two hundred and fifty princes of the assembly, famous in the congregation, men of renown:

3 And they gathered themselves together against Mo'ses and against Aar'on, and said to them, *You take* too much upon you, seeing all the congregation *are* holy, every one of them, and the LORD *is* among them: wherefore then lift you up yourselves above the congregation of the LORD? assume

4 And when Mo'ses heard *it*, he fell upon his face:

5 And he spoke to Ko'rah and to all his company, saying, Even to morrow the LORD will show who *are* His, and *who is* holy; and will cause *him* to come near to Him: even *him* whom He has chosen will He cause to come near to Him. 2 Tim 2:19

6 This do; Take you <u>censers</u>, Ko'rah, and all his company; firepots

7 And put fire therein, and put incense in them before the LORD to morrow: and it shall be *that* the man whom the LORD does choose, he *shall be* <u>holy</u>: *you take* too much upon you, you sons of Le'vi. set apart

8 And Mo'ses said to Ko'rah, Hear, I pray you, you sons of Le'vi:

9 *Seems it but* a small thing to you, that the God of Is'ra-el has separated you from the congregation of Is'ra-el, to bring you near to Himself to do the service of the tabernacle of the LORD, and to stand before the congregation to minister to them?

10 And He has brought you near *to*

Him, and all your brethren the sons of Le'vi with you: and seek you the priesthood also?

11 For which cause *both* you and all your company *are* gathered together against the LORD: and what *is* Aar'on, that you murmur against him?   grumble

12 And Mo'ses sent to call Da'than and A-bi'ram, the sons of E-li'ab: which said, We will not come up:

13 *Is it* a small thing that you have brought us up out of a land that flows with milk and honey, to kill us in the wilderness, except you make yourself altogether a prince over us?

14 Moreover you have not brought us into a land that flows with milk and honey, or given us inheritance of fields and vineyards: will you put out the eyes of these men? we will not come up.

15 And Mo'ses was very angry, and said to the LORD, Respect not You their offering: I have not taken one ass from them, neither have I hurt one of them.

16 And Mo'ses said to Ko'rah, Be you and all your company before the LORD, you, and they, and Aar'on, to morrow:

17 And take every man his censer, and put incense in them, and bring you before the LORD every man his censer, two hundred and fifty censers; you also, and Aar'on, each *of you* his censer.   firepot

18 And they took every man his censer, and put fire in them, and laid incense thereon, and stood in the door of the tabernacle of the congregation with Mo'ses and Aar'on.

19 And Ko'rah gathered all the congregation against them to the door of the tabernacle of the congregation: and the glory of the LORD appeared to all the congregation.

20 And the LORD spoke to Mo'ses and to Aar'on, saying,

21 Separate yourselves from among this congregation, that I may consume them in a moment.   destroy

22 And they fell upon their faces, and said, O God, the God of the spirits of all flesh, shall one man sin, and will You be angry with all the congregation?   El$^{s.f.}$ - Elohim$^{p.f.}$

23 And the LORD spoke to Mo'-ses, saying,

24 Speak to the congregation, saying, Get you up from about the tabernacle of Ko'rah, Da'than, and A-bi'ram.

25 And Mo'ses rose up and went to Da'than and A-bi'ram; and the elders of Is'ra-el followed him.

26 And he spoke to the congregation, saying, Depart, I pray you, from the tents of these wicked men, and touch nothing of theirs, less you be consumed in all their sins.

27 So they got up from the tabernacle of Ko'rah, Da'than, and A-bi'ram, on every side: and Da'than and A-bi'ram came out, and stood in the door of their tents, and their wives, and their sons, and their little children.

28 And Mo'ses said, Hereby you shall know that the LORD has sent me to do all these works; for *I have* not *done them* of my own mind.   JOHN 5:30

29 If these men die the common death

of all men, or if they be visited after the visitation of all men; *then* the LORD has not sent me.   REV. 11:5

30 But if the LORD make a new thing, and the earth open her mouth, and swallow them up, with all that *appertain* to them, and they go down <u>quick</u> into the pit; then you shall understand that these men have <u>provoked</u> the LORD.

living (alive) - spurned

31 And it came to pass, as he had made an end of speaking all these words, that the ground <u>clave asunder</u> that *was* under them: *split apart*

32 And the earth opened its mouth, and swallowed them up, and their houses, and all the men that *appertained* to Ko'rah, and all *their* goods.

33 They, and all that *appertained* to them, went down alive into the pit, and the earth closed upon them: and they perished from among the congregation.

34 And all Is'ra-el that *were* round about them fled at the cry of them: for they said, Less the earth swallow us up *also*.

35 And there came out a fire from the LORD, and <u>consumed</u> the two hundred and fifty men that offered incense.   *destroyed*

36 And the LORD spoke to Mo'ses, saying,

37 Speak to E-le-a'zar the son of Aar'on the priest, that he take up the <u>censers</u> out of the burning, and scatter you the fire yonder; for they are hallowed.   *firepans*

38 The <u>censers</u> of these sinners against their own souls, let them make them broad plates *for* a covering of the altar: for they offered them before the LORD, therefore they are hallowed: and they shall be a sign to the children of Is'ra-el.   *firepans*

39 And E-le-a'zar the priest took the brazen <u>censers</u>, wherewith they that were burned had offered; and they were made broad *plates for* a covering of the altar:

40 *To be* a <u>memorial</u> to the children of Is'ra-el, that no stranger, which *is* not of the <u>seed</u> of Aar'on, come near to offer incense before the LORD; that he be not as Ko'rah, and as his company: as the LORD said to him by the hand of Mo'ses.   *reminder - descendants*

41 But on the morrow all the congregation of the children of Is'ra-el <u>murmured</u> against Mo'ses and against Aar'on, saying, You have killed the people of the LORD.   1 COR. 10:10 - *grumbled*

42 And it came to pass, when the congregation was gathered against Mo'ses and against Aar'on, that they looked toward the tabernacle of the congregation: and, behold, the cloud covered it, and the glory of the LORD appeared.

43 And Mo'ses and Aar'on came before the tabernacle of the congregation.

44 And the LORD spoke to Mo'ses, saying,

45 Get you up from among this congregation, that I may consume them as in a moment. And they fell upon their faces.

46 And Mo'ses said to Aar'on, Take a <u>censer</u>, and put fire therein from off the altar, and put on incense, and go quickly to the congregation, and make an atonement for them: for there

is wrath gone out from the LORD; the <u>plague</u> is begun. firepans - sickness

47 And Aar'on took as Mo'ses commanded, and ran into the midst of the congregation; and, behold, the <u>plague</u> was begun among the people: and he put on incense, and made an atonement for the people.

48 And he stood between the dead and the living; and the <u>plague</u> was <u>stayed</u>. stopped

49 Now they that died in the plague were fourteen thousand and seven hundred, beside them that died about the matter of Ko'rah.

50 And Aar'on returned to Mo'ses to the door of the tabernacle of the congregation: and the plague was stayed.

CHAPTER 17

AND the LORD spoke to Mo'ses, saying,

2 Speak to the children of Is'ra-el, and take of every one of them a rod according to the house of *their* fathers, of all their princes according to the house of their fathers twelve rods: write you every man's name upon his rod.

3 And you shall write Aar'on's name upon the rod of Le'vi: for one rod *shall be* for the head of the house of their fathers.

4 And you shall lay them up in the tabernacle of the congregation before the testimony, where I will meet with you.

5 And it shall come to pass, *that* the man's rod, whom I shall choose, shall blossom: and I will make to cease from Me the <u>murmurings</u> of the children of Is'ra-el, whereby they <u>murmur</u> against you. grumblings

6 And Mo'ses spoke to the children of Is'ra-el, and every one of their princes gave him a rod <u>apiece</u>, for each prince one, according to their fathers' houses, *even* twelve rods: and the rod of Aar'on *was* among their rods. each

7 And Mo'ses laid up the rods before the LORD in the tabernacle of witness.

8 And it came to pass, that on the morrow Mo'ses went into the tabernacle of witness; and, behold, the rod of Aar'on for the house of Le'vi was budded, and brought forth buds, and bloomed blossoms, and <u>yielded</u> almonds. HEB. 9:4 produced

9 And Mo'ses brought out all the rods from before the LORD to all the children of Is'ra-el: and they looked, and took every man his rod.

10 And the LORD said to Mo'ses, Bring Aar'on's rod again before the testimony, to be kept for a token against the rebels; and you shall quite take away their <u>murmurings</u> from Me, that they die not. grumblings

11 And Mo'ses did *so*: as the LORD commanded him, so did he.

12 And the children of Is'ra-el spoke to Mo'ses, saying, Behold, we die, we perish, we all perish.

13 Whosoever comes any thing near to the tabernacle of the LORD shall die: shall we be <u>consumed with dying</u>? perish completely

CHAPTER 18

AND the LORD said to Aar'on, You and your sons and your father's house with you shall <u>bear the iniquity</u> of the sanctuary: and you and your sons with you shall bear the iniquity of your priesthood.

be responsible for offenses against

2 And your brethren also of the tribe of Le'vi, the tribe of your father, bring you with you, that they may be joined to you, and minister to you: but you and your sons with you *shall minister* before the tabernacle of <u>witness</u>. testimony

3 And they shall <u>keep your charge</u>, and the <u>charge</u> of all the tabernacle: only they shall not come near the vessels of the sanctuary and the altar, that neither they, nor you also, die.   i.e., be responsible

4 And they shall be joined to you, and <u>keep the charge</u> of the tabernacle of the congregation, for all the service of the tabernacle: and a stranger shall not come near to you.

5 And you shall keep the <u>charge</u> of the sanctuary, and the <u>charge</u> of the altar: that there be no <u>wrath any more</u> upon the children of Is'ra-el.

responsibility - further judgment

6 And I, behold, I have taken your brethren the Le'vites from among the children of Is'ra-el: to you *they are* given *as* a gift for the LORD, to do the service of the tabernacle of the congregation.

7 Therefore you and your sons with you shall keep your priest's office for every thing of the altar, and within the veil; and you shall serve: I have given your priest's office *to you as* a service

of <u>gift</u>: and the stranger that comes near shall be put to death.   i.e., free will

8 And the LORD spoke to Aar'on, Behold, I also have given you the <u>charge</u> of my heave offerings of all the hallowed things of the children of Is'ra-el; to you have I given them by reason of the anointing, and to your sons, by an ordinance for ever.   responsibility

9 This shall be yours of the most holy things, *reserved* from the fire: every <u>oblation</u> of theirs, every <u>meat</u> offering of theirs, and every sin offering of theirs, and every trespass offering of theirs, which they shall render to Me, *shall be* most holy for you and for your sons.   gift - grain

10 In the most <u>holy</u> *place* shall you eat it; every male shall eat it: it shall be <u>holy</u> to you.   separated

11 And this *is* yours; the heave offering of their gift, with all the wave offerings of the children of Is'ra-el: I have given them to you, and to your sons and to your daughters with you, by a <u>statute</u> for ever: every one that is <u>clean</u> in your house shall eat of it.

allotment - cleansed from sin

12 All the best of the oil, and all the best of the wine, and of the wheat, the firstfruits of them which they shall offer to the LORD, them have I given you.

13 *And* whatsoever is first ripe in the land, which they shall bring to the LORD, shall be yours; every one that is clean in your house shall eat *of* it.

14 Every thing devoted in Is'ra-el shall be yours.

15 Every thing that opens the <u>matrix</u> in all flesh, which they bring to

the LORD, *whether it be* of men or beasts, shall be yours: nevertheless the firstborn of man shall you surely redeem, and the firstling of <u>unclean</u> beasts shall you redeem. _{womb - unfit}

16 And those that are to be redeemed from a month old shall you redeem, according to your estimation, for the money of five shekels, after the shekel of the sanctuary, which *is* twenty gerahs.

17 But the firstling of a cow, or the firstling of a sheep, or the firstling of a goat, you shall not redeem; they *are* holy: you shall sprinkle their blood upon the altar, and shall burn their fat *for* an offering made by fire, for a sweet savor to the LORD.

18 And the flesh of them shall be yours, as the wave breast and as the right shoulder are yours.

19 All the heave offerings of the holy things, which the children of Is'ra-el offer to the LORD, have I given you, and your sons and your daughters with you, by a statute for ever: it *is* a <u>covenant of salt</u> for ever before the LORD to you and to your seed with you.   *i.e., an unbreakable promise*

20 And the LORD spoke to Aar'on, You shall have no inheritance in their land, neither shall you have any part among them: I *am* your part and your inheritance among the children of Is'ra-el.

21 And, behold, I have given the children of Le'vi all the tenth in Is'ra-el for <u>an inheritance,</u> for their service which they serve, *even* the service of the tabernacle of the congregation.   *their share*

22 Neither must the children of Is'ra-el hereafter come near the tabernacle of the congregation, less they bear sin, and die.

23 But the Le'vites shall <u>do</u> the service of the tabernacle of the congregation, and they shall bear their iniquity: *it shall be* a <u>statute</u> for ever throughout your generations, that among the children of Is'ra-el they have no inheritance.   *perform - ordinance*

24 But the tithes of the children of Is'ra-el, which they offer *as* an heave offering to the LORD, I have given to the Le'vites to inherit: therefore I have said to them, Among the children of Is'ra-el they shall have no <u>inheritance</u>.   *share*

25 And the LORD spoke to Mo'ses, saying,

26 Thus speak to the Le'vites, and say to them, When you take of the children of Is'ra-el the tithes which I have given you from them for your inheritance, then you shall offer up an heave offering of it for the LORD, *even* a tenth *part* of the tithe.

27 And *this* your heave offering shall be reckoned to you, as though *it were* the <u>corn</u> of the threshingfloor, and as the fulness of the winepress.   *grain*

28 Thus you also shall offer an heave offering to the LORD of all your tithes, which you receive of the children of Is'ra-el; and you shall give thereof the LORD's heave offering to Aar'on the priest.

29 Out of all your gifts you shall offer every heave offering of the LORD, of all

the best thereof, *even* the hallowed part thereof out of it.

30 Therefore you shall say to them, When you have heaved the best thereof from it, then it shall be counted to the Le'vites as the increase of the threshingfloor, and as the increase of the winepress.

31 And you shall eat it in every place, you and your households: for it *is* your <u>reward</u> for your service in the tabernacle of the congregation. _{wages}

32 And you shall bear no sin by reason of it, when you have heaved from it the best of it: neither shall you pollute the holy things of the children of Is'ra-el, less you die.

CHAPTER 19

AND the Lᴏʀᴅ spoke to Mo'ses and to Aar'on, saying,

2 This *is* the ordinance of the law which the Lᴏʀᴅ has commanded, saying, Speak to the children of Is'ra-el, that they bring you a red heifer without <u>spot</u>, wherein *is* no <u>blemis</u>h, *and* upon which never came yoke;   _{defect - defect}

3 And you shall give it to E-le-a'zar the priest, that he may bring it forth outside the camp, and *one* shall slay it before his face:

4 And E-le-a'zar the priest shall take of its blood with his finger, and sprinkle of its blood directly before the tabernacle of the congregation seven times:

5 And *one* shall burn the heifer in its sight; its skin, and its flesh, and its blood, with its dung, shall he burn:

6 And the priest shall take cedar wood, and hyssop, and scarlet, and cast *it* into the midst of the burning of the heifer.

7 Then the priest shall wash his clothes, and he shall bathe his flesh in water, and afterward he shall come into the camp, and the priest shall be <u>unclean</u> until <u>the even</u>.   _{unfit - evening}

8 And he that burns it shall wash his clothes in water, and bathe his flesh in water, and shall be unclean until the even.

9 And a man *that is* clean shall gather up the ashes of the heifer, and lay *them* up outside the camp in a clean place, and it shall be kept for the congregation of the children of Is'ra-el for a water of separation: it *is* a <u>purification</u> for sin.   _{offering}

10 And he that gathers the ashes of the heifer shall wash his clothes, and be <u>unclean</u> until <u>the even</u>: and it shall be to the children of Is'ra-el, and to the <u>stranger</u> that <u>sojourns</u> among them, for a <u>statute</u> for ever.

_{unfit - alien - lives - ordinance}

11 He that touches the dead body of any man shall be <u>unclean</u> seven days.

12 He shall purify himself with it on the third day, and on the seventh day he shall be clean: but if he purify not himself the third day, then the seventh day he shall not be clean.

13 Whosoever touches the dead body of any man that is dead, and purifies not himself, defiles the tabernacle of the Lᴏʀᴅ; and that <u>soul</u> shall be cut off from Is'ra-el: because the water of separation was not sprinkled upon him,

he shall be unclean; his <u>uncleanness</u> *is* yet upon him.   person - unfitness

14 This *is* the law, when a man dies in a tent: all that come into the tent, and all that *is* in the tent, shall be <u>unclean</u> seven days.   unfit

15 And every open vessel, which has no covering bound upon it, *is* <u>unclean</u>.

16 And whosoever touches one that is slain with a sword in the open fields, or a dead body, or a bone of a man, or a grave, shall be <u>unclean</u> seven days.

17 And for an <u>unclean</u> *person* they shall take of the ashes of the burned heifer of purification for sin, and running water shall be put thereto in a vessel:

18 And a clean person shall take hyssop, and dip *it* in the water, and sprinkle *it* upon the tent, and upon all the vessels, and upon the persons that were there, and upon him that touched a bone, or one slain, or one dead, or a grave:

19 And the clean *person* shall sprinkle upon the unclean on the third day, and on the seventh day: and on the seventh day he shall purify himself, and wash his clothes, and bathe himself in water, and shall be clean at <u>even</u>.   evening

20 But the man that shall be <u>unclean</u>, and shall not purify himself, that <u>soul</u> shall be cut off from among the congregation, because he has defiled the sanctuary of the LORD: the water of separation has not been sprinkled upon him; he *is* <u>unclean</u>.   unfit - person

21 And it shall be a perpetual <u>statute</u> to them, that he that sprinkles the water of separation shall wash his clothes; and he that touches the water of separation shall be <u>unclean</u> until <u>even</u>.   ordinance - unfit - evening

22 And whatsoever the <u>unclean</u> *person* touches shall be <u>unclean</u>; and the <u>soul</u> that touches *it* shall be <u>unclean</u> until <u>even</u>.

CHAPTER 20

THEN came the children of Is'ra-el, *even* the whole congregation, into the desert of Zin in the first month: and the people abode in Ka'desh; and Mir'i-am died there, and was buried there.

2 And there was no water for the congregation: and they gathered themselves together against Mo'ses and against Aar'on.

3 And the people <u>chode with</u> Mo'ses, and spoke, saying, Would God that we had died when our brethren died before the LORD!   rebuked

4 And why have you brought up the congregation of the LORD into this wilderness, that we and our cattle should die there?

5 And wherefore have you made us to come up out of E'gypt, to bring us in to this evil place? it *is* no place of seed, or of figs, or of vines, or of pomegranates; neither *is* there any water to drink.

6 And Mo'ses and Aar'on went from the presence of the assembly to the door of the tabernacle of the congregation, and they fell upon their faces: and the glory of the LORD appeared to them.

7 And the LORD spoke to Mo'ses, saying,

8 Take the rod, and gather you the assembly together, you, and Aar'on your brother, and speak you to the rock before their eyes; and it shall give forth its water, and you shall bring forth to them water out of the rock: so you shall give the congregation and their beasts drink.

9 And Mo'ses took the rod from before the LORD, as He commanded him.

10 And Mo'ses and Aar'on gathered the congregation together before the rock, and he said to them, Hear now, you rebels; must we bring you water out of this rock?

11 And Mo'ses lifted up his hand, and with his rod he <u>smote</u> the rock twice: and the water came out abundantly, and the congregation drank, and their beasts *also*.   struck

12 And the LORD spoke to Mo'ses and Aar'on, Because you believed Me not, to <u>sanctify Me</u> in the eyes of the children of Is'ra-el, therefore you shall not bring this congregation into the land which I have given them.   i.e., make My Holiness apparent

13 This *is* the water of Mer'i-bah; because the children of Is'ra-el strove with the LORD, and He was sanctified in them.

14 And Mo'ses sent messengers from Ka'desh to the king of E'dom, Thus says your brother Is'ra-el, You know all the <u>travail</u> that has befallen us: hardships

15 How our fathers went down into E'gypt, and we have dwelt in E'gypt a long time; and the E-gyptians <u>vexed</u> us, and our fathers: mistreated

16 And when we cried to the LORD, He heard our voice, and sent an <u>angel</u>, and has brought us forth out of E'gypt: and, behold, we *are* in Ka'desh, a city in the uttermost of your border: messenger

17 Let us pass, I pray you, through your country: we will not pass through the fields, or through the vineyards, neither will we drink *of* the water of the wells: we will go by the king's *high* way, we will not turn to the right hand nor to the left, until we have passed your borders.

18 And E'dom said to him, You shall not pass by me, less I come out against you with the sword.

19 And the children of Is'ra-el said to him, We will go by the high way: and if I and my cattle drink of your water, then I will pay for it: I will only, without *doing* any thing *else*, go through on my feet.

20 And he said, you shall not go through. And E'dom came out against him with much people, and with a strong hand.

21 Thus E'dom refused to give Is'ra-el passage through his border: wherefore Is'ra-el turned away from him.

22 And the children of Is'ra-el, *even* the whole congregation, journeyed from Ka'desh, and came to mount Hor.

23 And the LORD spoke to Mo'ses and Aar'on in mount Hor, by the coast of the land of E'dom, saying,

24 Aar'on shall be <u>gathered to his</u>

people: for he shall not enter into the land which I have given to the children of Is'ra-el, because you rebelled against My word at the water of Mer'i-bah.   buried

25 Take Aar'on and E-le-a'zar his son, and bring them up to mount Hor:

26 And strip Aar'on of his garments, and put them upon E-le-a'zar his son: and Aar'on shall be gathered *to his people*, and shall die there.

27 And Mo'ses did as the LORD commanded: and they went up into mount Hor in the sight of all the congregation.

28 And Mo'ses stripped Aar'on of his garments, and put them upon E-le-a'zar his son; and Aar'on died there in the top of the mount: and Mo'ses and E-le-a'zar came down from the mount.

29 And when all the congregation saw that Aar'on was dead, they mourned for Aar'on thirty days, *even* all the house of Is'ra-el.

CHAPTER 21

AND *when* king A'rad the Ca'naan-ite, which dwelt in the south, heard tell that Is'ra-el came by the way of the spies; then he fought against Is'ra-el, and took *some* of them prisoners.

2 And Is'ra-el vowed a vow to the LORD, and said, If You will indeed deliver this people into my hand, then I will utterly destroy their cities.   make a pledge

3 And the LORD hearkened to the voice of Is'ra-el, and delivered up the Ca'naan-ites; and they utterly destroyed them and their cities: and he called the name of the place Hor'mah.

4 And they journeyed from mount Hor by the way of the Red sea, to compass the land of E'dom: and the soul of the people was much discouraged because of the way.   go around

5 And the people spoke against God, and against Mo'ses, Wherefore have you brought us up out of E'gypt to die in the wilderness? for *there is* no bread, neither *is there any* water; and our soul loathes this light bread.   1 COR. 10:5 people detests   M10 | | 262

6 And the LORD sent fiery serpents among the people, and they bit the people; and much people of Is'ra-el died.

7 Therefore the people came to Mo'ses, and said, We have sinned, for we have spoken against the LORD, and against you; pray to the LORD, that He take away the serpents from us. And Mo'ses prayed for the people.   LUKE 13:3 objected to   M27 | | |

8 And the LORD said to Mo'ses, Make you a fiery serpent, and set it upon a pole: and it shall come to pass, that every one that is bitten, when he looks upon it, shall live.   G4H — | | 290

9 And Mo'ses made a serpent of brass, and put it upon a pole, and it came to pass, that if a serpent had bitten any man, when he beheld the serpent of brass, he lived.   JOHN 3:14   288

10 And the children of Is'ra-el set forward, and pitched in O'both.   camped

11 And they journeyed from O'both, and pitched at Ij'e-ab'a-rim, in the wilderness which *is* before Mo'ab, toward the sunrising.   i.e., Heaps of Ab'r-im

12 From there they removed, and pitched in the valley of Za'red.   camped

13 From there they removed, and <u>pitched</u> on the other side of Ar'non, which *is* in the wilderness that comes out of the coasts of the Am'or-ites: for Ar'non *is* the border of Mo'ab, between Mo'ab and the Am'or-ites. camped

14 Wherefore it is said in the book of the wars of the LORD, What He did in the Red sea, and in the brooks of Ar'non,

15 And at the stream of the brooks that goes down to the dwelling of Ar, and lies upon the border of Mo'ab.

16 And from there *they went* to Be'er: that *is* the well whereof the LORD spoke to Mo'ses, Gather the people together, and I will give them water.

17 Then Is'ra-el sang this song, <u>Spring up, O well</u>; <u>sing</u> you to it: Ascend - answer

18 The princes dug the well, the nobles of the people dug it, by *the direction of* the lawgiver, with their staves. And from the wilderness *they went* to Mat'ta-nah:

19 And from Mat'ta-nah to Na-ha'li-el: and from Na-ha'li-el to Ba'moth:

20 And from Ba'moth *in* the valley, that *is* in the <u>country</u> of Mo'ab, to the top of Pis'gah, which looks toward Jesh'i-mon. land

21 And Is'ra-el sent messengers to Si'hon king of the Am'or-ites, saying,

22 Let me pass through your land: we will not turn into the fields, or into the vineyards; we will not drink *of* the waters of the well: *but* we will go along by the king's *high* way, until we be past your borders.

23 And Si'hon would not allow Is'ra-el to pass through his border: but Si'hon gathered all his people together, and <u>went out against</u> Is'ra-el into the wilderness: and he came to Ja'haz, and fought against Is'ra-el. attacked

24 And Is'ra-el smote him with the edge of the sword, and <u>possessed</u> his land from Ar'non to Jab'bok, even to the children of Am'mon: for the border of the children of Am'mon *was* strong. took over

25 And Is'ra-el took all these cities: and Is'ra-el dwelt in all the cities of the Am'or-ites, in Hesh'bon, and in all the villages thereof.

26 For Hesh'bon *was* the city of Si'hon the king of the Am'or-ites, who had fought against the former king of Mo'ab, and taken all his land out of his hand, even to Ar'non.

27 Wherefore <u>they</u> that speak in proverbs say, Come into Hesh'bon, let the city of Si'hon be built and prepared: the poets

28 For there is a fire gone out of Hesh'bon, a flame from the city of Si'hon: it has consumed Ar of Mo'ab, *and* the lords of the high places of Ar'non.

29 Woe to you, Mo'ab! you are undone, O people of Che'mosh: he has given his sons that escaped, and his daughters, into captivity to Si'hon king of the Am'or-ites.

30 We have shot at them; Hesh'bon is perished even to Di'bon, and we have <u>laid them waste</u> even to No'phah, which *reache*s to Med'e-ba. demolished them

31 Thus Is'ra-el dwelt in the land of the Am'or-ites.

32 And Mo'ses sent to spy out Ja-a'zer, and they took the villages thereof, and drove out the Am'or-ites that *were* there.

33 And they turned and went up by the way of Ba'shan: and Og the king of Ba'shan went out against them, he, and all his people, to the battle at Ed're-i.

34 And the LORD said to Mo'ses, Fear him not: for I have delivered him into your hand, and all his people, and his land; and you shall do to him as you did to Si'hon king of the Am'or-ites, which dwelt at Hesh'bon.

35 So they <u>smote</u> him, and his sons, and all his people, until there was none left him alive: and they possessed his land.   killed

CHAPTER 22

AND the children of Is'ra-el set forward, and <u>pitched</u> in the plains of Mo'ab on this side Jor'dan *by* Jer'i-cho.   camped

2 And Ba'lak the son of Zip'por saw all that Is'ra-el had done to the Am'or-ites.

3 And Mo'ab was <u>sore</u> afraid of the people, because they *were* many: and Mo'ab was distressed because of the children of Is'ra-el.   very

4 And Mo'ab said to the elders of Mid'i-an, Now shall this company <u>lick up all</u> *that are* round about us, as the ox licks up the grass of the field. And Ba'lak the son of Zip'por *was* king of the Mo'ab-ites at that time.   defeat in battle

5 He sent messengers therefore to Ba'laam the son of Be'or to Pe'thor, which *is* by the river of the land of the children of his people, to call him, saying, Behold, there is a people come out from E'gypt: behold, they cover the face of the earth, and they abide opposite me: 2 PET. 2:15

6 Come now therefore, I pray you, <u>curse me this people</u>; for they *are* too mighty for me: perhaps I shall prevail, *that* we may smite them, and *that* I may drive them out of the land: for I know that he whom you bless is blessed, and he whom you curse *is* cursed.   smite them

7 And the elders of Mo'ab and the elders of Mid'i-an departed with the <u>rewards of divination</u> in their hand; and they came to Ba'laam, and spoke to him the words of Ba'lak.   fees for fortune telling

8 And he said to them, Lodge here this night, and I will bring you word again, as the LORD shall speak to me: and the princes of Mo'ab abode with Ba'laam.

9 And God came to Ba'laam, and said, What men *are* these with you?

10 And Ba'laam said to God, Ba'lak the son of Zip'por, king of Mo'ab, has sent to me, *saying*,

11 Behold, *there is* a people come out of E'gypt, which covers the face of the earth: come now, curse me them; perhaps I shall be able to overcome them, and drive them out.

12 And God said to Ba'laam, You shall not go with them; you shall not curse the people: for they *are* blessed.

13 And Ba'laam rose up in the morning, and said to the princes of Ba'lak, Get you into your land: for the LORD refuses to give me <u>leave</u> to go with you. _{permission}

permission

14 And the princes of Mo'ab rose up, and they went to Ba'lak, and said, Ba'laam refuses to come with us.

15 And Ba'lak sent yet again princes, more, and more honorable than they.

16 And they came to Ba'laam, and said to him, Thus says Ba'lak the son of Zip'por, Let nothing, I pray you, hinder you from coming to me:

17 For I will promote you to very great honor, and I will do whatsoever you say to me: come therefore, I pray you, curse me this people.

18 And Ba'laam answered and said to the servants of Ba'lak, If Ba'lak would give me his house full of silver and gold, I cannot go beyond the word of the LORD my <u>God</u>, to do less or more.

Elohim^{p.f.}

19 Now therefore, I pray you, tarry you also here this night, that I may know what the LORD will say to me more.

20 And <u>God</u> came to Ba'laam at night, and said to him, If the men come to call you, rise up, *and* go with them; but yet the word which I shall say to you, that shall you do.

21 And Ba'laam rose up in the morning, and saddled his ass, and went with the princes of Mo'ab.

22 And <u>God's</u> anger was kindled because he went: and the <u>angel</u> of the LORD stood in the way for an adversary against him. Now he was riding upon his ass, and his two servants *were* with him.

messenger

23 And the ass saw the <u>angel</u> of the LORD standing in the way, and his sword drawn in his hand: and the ass turned aside out of the way, and went into the field: and Ba'laam smote the ass, to turn her into the way. 2 PET. 2:16

24 But the <u>angel</u> of the LORD stood in a path of the vineyards, a wall *being* on this side, and a wall on that side.

25 And when the ass saw the <u>angel</u> of the LORD, she <u>thrust</u> herself to the wall, and <u>crushed</u> Ba'laam's foot against the wall: and he smote her again.　　　JUDE 11 pushed - pressed

26 And the <u>angel</u> of the LORD went further, and stood in a <u>narrow</u> place, where *was* no way to turn either to the right hand or to the left.

27 And when the ass saw the <u>angel</u> of the LORD, she fell down under Ba'laam: and Ba'laam's anger was kindled, and he smote the ass with a staff.　　　　messenger stick

28 And the LORD opened the mouth of the ass, and she said to Ba'laam, What have I done to you, that you have smitten me these three times?

29 And Ba'laam said to the ass, Because you have <u>mocked</u> me: I would there were a sword in my hand, for now would I kill you.

ridiculed

30 And the ass said to Ba'laam, *Am* not I your ass, upon which you have ridden ever since *I was* yours to this day? was I ever <u>wont</u> to do so to you? And he said, Nay.　　　in a habit

31 Then the LORD opened the eyes of Ba'laam, and he saw the <u>angel</u> of the

LORD standing in the way, and his sword drawn in his hand: and he bowed down his head, and fell flat on his face. _{messenger}

32 And the <u>angel</u> of the LORD said to him, Wherefore have you smitten your ass these three times? behold, I went out to <u>withstand</u> you, because *your* way is <u>perverse</u> before me:

messenger - oppose - contrary

33 And the ass saw me, and turned from me these three times: unless she had turned from me, surely now also I had slain you, and saved her alive.

34 And Ba'laam said to the <u>angel</u> of the LORD, I have sinned; for I knew not that you stood in the way against me: now therefore, if it displease you, I will get me back again.

35 And the <u>angel</u> of the LORD said to Ba'laam, Go with the men: but only the word that I shall speak to you, that you shall speak. So Ba'laam went with the princes of Ba'lak.

36 And when Ba'lak heard that Ba'laam was come, he went out to meet him to a city of Mo'ab, which *is* in the border of Ar'non, which *is* in the utmost coast.

37 And Ba'lak said to Ba'laam, Did I not earnestly send to you to call you? wherefore came you not to me? am I not able indeed to promote you to honor?

38 And Ba'laam said to Ba'lak, Lo, I am come to you: have I now any power at all to say any thing? the word that God puts in my mouth, that shall I speak.

39 And Ba'laam went with Ba'lak, and they came to Kir'jath-hu'zoth.

40 And Ba'lak offered oxen and sheep, and sent to Ba'laam, and to the princes that *were* with him.

41 And it came to pass on the morrow, that Ba'lak took Ba'laam, and brought him up into the high places of Ba'al, that from there he might see the <u>utmost</u> *part* of the people. _{farthest}

CHAPTER 23

AND Ba'laam said to Ba'lak, Build me here seven altars, and prepare me here seven oxen and seven rams.

2 And Ba'lak did as Ba'laam had spoken; and Ba'lak and Ba'laam offered on *every* altar a bullock and a ram.

3 And Ba'laam said to Ba'lak, Stand by your burned offering, and I will go: perhaps the LORD will come to meet me: and whatsoever He shows me I will tell you. And he went to an high place.

4 And <u>God</u> met Ba'laam: and he said to Him, I have prepared seven altars, and I have offered upon *every* altar a bullock and a ram. _{Elohim^{p.f.}}

5 And the LORD put a word in Ba'laam's mouth, and said, Return to Ba'lak, and thus you shall speak.

6 And he returned to him, and, lo, he stood by his burned sacrifice, he, and all the princes of Mo'ab.

7 And he <u>took up his parable</u>, and said, Ba'lak the king of Mo'ab has brought me from A'ram, out of the mountains of the east, *saying*, Come, curse me Ja'cob, and come, defy Is'ra-el. _{began his discourse}

8 How shall I curse, whom <u>God</u> has not cursed? or how shall I defy, *whom* the LORD has not defied? El.s.f.
9 For from the top of the rocks I see him, and from the hills I behold him: lo, the people shall dwell alone, and shall not be reckoned among the nations.
10 Who can count the dust of Ja'cob, and the number of the fourth *part* of Is'ra-el? Let me die the death of the righteous, and let my last end be like his!
11 And Ba'lak said to Ba'laam, What have you done to me? I took you to curse my enemies, and, behold, you have blessed *them* altogether.
12 And he answered and said, Must I not take heed to speak that which the LORD has put in my mouth?
13 And Ba'lak said to him, Come, I pray you, with me to another place, from where you may see them: you shall see but the utmost part of them, and shall not see them all: and curse me them from there.
14 And he brought him into the field of Zo'phim, to the top of Pis'gah, and built seven altars, and offered a bullock and a ram on *every* altar.
15 And he said to Ba'lak, Stand here by your burned offering, while I meet *the LORD* yonder.
16 And the LORD met Ba'laam, and put a word in his mouth, and said, Go again to Ba'lak, and say thus.
17 And when he came to him, behold, he stood by his burned offering, and the princes of Mo'ab with him. And Ba'lak said to him, What has the LORD spoken?
18 And he took up his parable, and said, Rise up, Ba'lak, and hear; hearken to me, you son of Zip'por:
19 <u>God</u> *is* not a man, that He should lie; neither the son of man, that He should repent: has He said, and shall He not do *it*? or has He spoken, and shall He not make it good? El.s.f.
20 Behold, I have received *commandment* to bless: and He has blessed; and I cannot reverse it.
21 He has not beheld iniquity in Ja'cob, neither has He seen <u>perverseness</u> in Is'ra-el: the LORD his <u>God</u> *is* with him, and the shout of a king *is* among them. trouble - Elohim p.f.
22 <u>God</u> brought them out of E'gypt; He has as it were the strength of an <u>unicorn</u>. El.s.f. - wild ox
23 Surely *there is* no <u>enchantment</u> against Ja'cob, neither *is there* any <u>divination</u> against Is'ra-el: according to this time it shall be said of Ja'cob and of Is'ra-el, What has God wrought! sorcery - fortune telling
24 Behold, the people shall rise up as a great lion, and lift up himself as a young lion: he shall not lie down until he eat *of* the prey, and drink the blood of the slain.
25 And Ba'lak said to Ba'laam, Neither curse them at all, nor bless them at all.
26 But Ba'laam answered and said to Ba'lak, Told not I you, saying, All that the LORD speaks, that I must do?
27 And Ba'lak said to Ba'laam, Come, I pray you, I will bring you

to another place; perhaps it will please God that you may curse me them from there.   Elohim^{p.f}

28 And Ba'lak brought Ba'laam to the top of Pe'or, that looks toward Jesh'i-mon.

29 And Ba'laam said to Ba'lak, Build me here seven altars, and prepare me here seven bullocks and seven rams.

30 And Ba'lak did as Ba'laam had said, and offered a bullock and a ram on *every* altar.

CHAPTER 24

AND when Ba'laam saw that it pleased the LORD to bless Is'ra-el, he went not, as at other times, to seek for enchantments, but he set his face toward the wilderness.   omens

2 And Ba'laam lifted up his eyes, and he saw Is'ra-el abiding *in his tents* according to their tribes; and the Spirit of God came upon him.

3 And he took up his parable, and said, Ba'laam the son of Be'or has said, and the man whose eyes are open has said:

4 He has said, which heard the words of God, which saw the vision of the Almighty, falling *into a trance*, but having his eyes open: El^{s.f.} - Shaddai

5 How goodly are your tents, O Ja'cob, *and* your tabernacles, O Is'ra-el!

6 As the valleys are they spread forth, as gardens by the river's side, as the trees of lign aloes which the LORD has planted, *and* as cedar trees beside the waters.

7 He shall pour the water out of his buckets, and his seed *shall be* in many waters, and his king shall be higher than A'gag, and his kingdom shall be exalted.

8 God brought him forth out of E'gypt; he has as it were the strength of an unicorn: he shall eat up the nations his enemies, and shall break their bones, and pierce *them* through with his arrows.   El^{s.f.} - wild ox

9 He couched, he lay down as a lion, and as a great lion: who shall stir him up? Blessed *is* he that blesses you, and cursed *is* he that curses you.

10 And Ba'lak's anger was kindled against Ba'laam, and he smote his hands together: and Ba'lak said to Ba'laam, I called you to curse my enemies, and, behold, you have altogether blessed *them* these three times.

11 Therefore now flee you to your place: I thought to promote you to great honor; but, lo, the LORD has kept you from honor.

12 And Ba'laam said to Ba'lak, Spoke I not also to your messengers which you sent to me, saying,

13 If Ba'lak would give me his house full of silver and gold, I cannot go beyond the commandment of the LORD, to do *either* good or bad of my own mind; *but* what the LORD says, that will I speak?

14 And now, behold, I go to my people: come *therefore, and* I will advertise you what this people shall do to your people in the latter days.   counsel

15 And he took up his parable, and said, Ba'laam the son of Be'or has

said, and the man whose eyes are open has said:

16 He has said, which heard the words of <u>God</u>, and knew the knowledge of the Most High, *which* saw the vision of the Almighty, falling *into a trance*, but having his eyes open: El s.f.

17 I shall see Him, but not now: I shall behold Him, but not near: there shall come a Star out of Ja'cob, and a Sceptre shall rise out of Is'ra-el, and shall smite the corners of Mo'ab, and destroy all the children of Sheth. MATT. 2:2

18 And E'dom shall be a possession, Se'ir also shall be a possession for his enemies; and Is'ra-el shall do <u>valiantly</u>. grow strong

19 Out of Ja'cob shall come He that <u>shall have dominion</u>, and shall destroy him that remains of the city. shall rule

20 And when he looked on Am'a-lek, he took up his parable, and said, Am'a-lek *was* the first of the nations; but his latter end *shall be* that he perish for ever.

21 And he looked on the Ken'ites, and took up his parable, and said, Strong is your dwellingplace, and you put your nest in a rock.

22 Nevertheless the Ken'ite shall be wasted, until As'shur shall carry you away captive.

23 And he took up his parable, and said, Alas, who shall live when <u>God</u> does this! El s.f.

24 And ships *shall come* from the coast of Chit'tim, and shall afflict As'shur, and shall afflict E'ber, and he also shall perish for ever.

25 And Ba'laam rose up, and went and returned to his place: and Ba'lak also went his way.

CHAPTER 25

AND Is'ra-el abode in Shit'tim, and the people began to <u>commit whoredom</u> with the daughters of Mo'ab. have illicit relations

2 And they called the people to the sacrifices of their gods: and the people did eat, and bowed down to their gods.

3 And Is'ra-el joined himself to Ba'al-pe'or: and the anger of the LORD was <u>kindled</u> against Is'ra-el. aroused

4 And the LORD said to Mo'ses, Take all the heads of the people, and hang them up before the LORD against the sun, that the fierce anger of the LORD may be turned away from Is'ra-el.

5 And Mo'ses said to the judges of Is'ra-el, Slay you every one his men that were joined to Ba'al-pe'or.

6 And, behold, one of the children of Is'ra-el came and brought to his brethren a Mid'i-an-it-ish woman in the sight of Mo'ses, and in the sight of all the congregation of the children of Is'ra-el, who *were* weeping *before* the door of the tabernacle of the congregation.

7 And when Phin'e-has, the son of E-le-a'zar, the son of Aar'on the priest, saw *it*, he rose up from among the congregation, and took a javelin in his hand;

8 And he went after the man of Is'ra-el into the tent, and thrust both of them through, the man of Is'ra-el, and the woman through her belly. So the

plague was stayed from the children of Is'ra-el.

9 And those that died in the plague were twenty and four thousand.

10 And the LORD spoke to Mo'ses, saying,

11 Phin'e-has, the son of E-le-a'zar, the son of Aar'on the priest, has turned My <u>wrath</u> away from the children of Is'ra-el, while he was zealous for My sake among them, that I <u>consumed</u> not the children of Is'ra-el in My jealousy.   anger - destroyed

12 Wherefore say, Behold, I give to him My <u>covenant</u> of peace: agreement

13 And he shall have it, and his <u>seed</u> after him, *even* the <u>covenant</u> of an everlasting priesthood; because he was zealous for his <u>God</u>, and <u>made an atonement</u> for the children of Is'ra-el.   descendants - effected reconciliation

14 Now the name of the Is'ra-el-ite that was slain, *even* that was slain with the Mid'i-an-it-ish woman, *was* Zim'ri, the son of Sa'lu, a prince of a chief house among the Sim'e-on-ites.

15 And the name of the Mid'i-an-it-ish woman that *was* slain was Coz'bi, the daughter of Zur; he *was* head over a people, *and* of a chief house in Mid'i-an.

16 And the LORD spoke to Mo'ses, saying,

17 <u>Vex</u> the Mid'i-an-ites, and <u>smite</u> them: fight - strike

18 For they <u>vex</u> you with their <u>wiles</u>, wherewith they have <u>beguiled</u> you in the matter of Pe'or, and in the matter of Coz'bi, the daughter of a prince of

Mid'i-an, their sister, which was slain in the day of the <u>plague</u> for Pe'or's sake.   fight - tricks - deceived - sickness

CHAPTER 26

AND it came to pass after the plague, that the LORD spoke to Mo'ses and to E-le-a'zar the son of Aar'on the priest, saying,

2 <u>Take the sum</u> of all the congregation of the children of Is'ra-el, from twenty years old and upward, throughout their fathers' house, all that are able to go to war in Is'ra-el.   Take a census

3 And Mo'ses and E-le-a'zar the priest spoke with them in the plains of Mo'ab by Jor'dan *near* Jer'i-cho, saying,

4 *Take the sum of the people*, from twenty years old and upward; as the LORD commanded Mo'ses and the children of Is'ra-el, which went forth out of the land of E'gypt.

5 Reu'ben, the eldest son of Is'ra-el: the children of Reu'ben; Ha'noch, *of whom comes* the family of the Ha'noch-ites: of Pal'lu, the family of the Pal'lu-ites:

6 Of Hez'ron, the family of the Hez'ron-ites: of Car'mi, the family of the Car'mites.

7 These *are* the families of the Reu'ben-ites: and they that were numbered of them were forty and three thousand and seven hundred and thirty.

8 And the sons of Pal'lu; E-li'ab.

9 And the sons of E-li'ab; Ne-mu'el, and Da'than, and A-bi'ram. This *is that* Da'than and A-bi'ram, *which were* famous in the congregation, who <u>strove</u>

against Mo'ses and against Aar'on in the company of Ko'rah, when they strove against the LORD: _{rebelled}

10 And the earth opened its mouth, and swallowed them up together with Ko'rah, when that company died, what time the fire devoured two hundred and fifty men: and they became a sign.

11 Notwithstanding the children of Ko'rah died not.

12 The sons of Sim'e-on after their families: of Ne-mu'el, the family of the Ne-mu'el-ites: of Ja'min, the family of the Ja'min-ites: of Ja'chin, the family of the Ja'chin-ites:

13 Of Ze'rah, the family of the Zar'hites: of Sha'ul, the family of the Sha'ul-ites.

14 These *are* the families of the Sim'e-on-ites, twenty and two thousand and two hundred.

15 The children of Gad after their families: of Ze'phon, the family of the Ze'phon-ites: of Hag'gi, the family of the Hag'gites: of Shu'ni, the family of the Shu-nites:

16 Of Oz'ni, the family of the Oz'nites: of E'ri, the family of the E'rites:

17 Of A'rod, the family of the A'rod-ites: of A-re'li, the family of the A-re'lites.

18 These *are* the families of the children of Gad according to those that were numbered of them, forty thousand and five hundred.

19 The sons of Ju'dah *were* Er and O'nan: and Er and O'nan died in the land of Ca'naan.

20 And the sons of Ju'dah after their families were; of She'lah, the family of the She'lan-ites: of Pha'rez, the family of the Phar'zites: of Ze'rah, the family of the Zar'hites.

21 And the sons of Pha'rez were; of Hez'ron, the family of the Hez'ron-ites: of Ha'mul, the family of the Ha'mul-ites.

22 These *are* the families of Ju'dah according to those that were numbered of them, threescore and sixteen thousand and five hundred.

23 *Of* the sons of Is'sa-char after their families: *of* To'la, the family of the To'la-ites: of Pu'a, the family of the Pu'nites:

24 Of Jash'ub, the family of the Jash'ub-ites: of Shim'ron, the family of the Shim'ron-ites.

25 These *are* the families of Is'sa-char according to those that were numbered of them, threescore and four thousand and three hundred.

26 *Of* the sons of Zeb'u-lun after their families: of Se'red, the family of the Sar'dites: of E'lon, the family of the E'lon-ites: of Jah'le-el, the family of the Jah'le-el-ites.

27 These *are* the families of the Zeb'u-lun-ites according to those that were numbered of them, threescore thousand and five hundred.

28 The sons of Jo'seph after their families *were* Ma-nas'seh and E'phra-im.

29 Of the sons of Ma-nas'seh: of Ma'chir, the family of the Ma'chir-ites: and Ma'chir fathered Gil'e-ad: of Gil'e-ad *come* the family of the Gil'e-ad-ites.

30 These *are* the sons of Gil'e-ad: *of*

Je-e'zer, the family of the Je-e'zer-ites: of He'lek, the family of the He'lek-ites: 31 And *of* As'ri-el, the family of the As'ri-el-ites: and *of* Shechem, the family of the She'chem-ites:

32 And *of* She-mi'da, the family of the She-mi'da-ites: and *of* He'pher, the family of the He'pher-ites.

33 And Ze-lo'phe-had the son of He'pher had no sons, but daughters: and the names of the daughters of Ze-lo'phe-had *were* Mah'lah, and No'ah, Hog'lah, Mil'cah, and Tir'zah.

34 These *are* the families of Ma-nas'seh, and those that were numbered of them, fifty and two thousand and seven hundred.

35 These *are* the sons of E'phra-im after their families: of Shu'the-lah, the family of the Shu'thal-hites: of Be'cher, the family of the Bach'rites: of Ta'han, the family of the Ta'han-ites.

36 And these *are* the sons of Shu'the-lah: of E'ran, the family of the E'ran-ites.

37 These *are* the families of the sons of E'phra-im according to those that were numbered of them, thirty and two thousand and five hundred. These *are* the sons of Jo'seph after their families.

38 The sons of Ben'ja-min after their families: of Be'la, the family of the Be'la-ites: of Ash'bel, the family of the Ash'bel-ites: of A-hi'ram, the family of the A-hi'ram-ites:

39 Of Shu'pham, the family of the Shu'pham-ites: of Hu'pham, the family of the Hu'pham-ites.

40 And the sons of Be'la were Ard and Na'a-man: *of Ard*, the family of the Ard'ites: and of Na'a-man, the family of the Na'a-mites.

41 These *are* the sons of Ben'ja-min after their families: and they that were numbered of them *were* forty and five thousand and six hundred.

42 These *are* the sons of Dan after their families: of Shu'ham, the family of the Shu'ham-ites. These *are* the families of Dan after their families.

43 All the families of the Shu'ham-ites, according to those that were numbered of them, *were* threescore and four thousand and four hundred.

44 *Of* the children of Ash'er after their families: of Jim'na, the family of the Jim'nites: of Jes'u-i, the family of the Jes'u-ites: of Be-ri'ah, the family of the Be-ri'tes.

45 Of the sons of Be-ri'ah: of He'ber, the family of the He'ber-ites: of Mal'chi-el, the family of the Mal'chi-el-ites.

46 And the name of the daughter of Ash'er *was* Sa'rah.

47 These *are* the families of the sons of Ash'er according to those that were numbered of them; *who were* fifty and three thousand and four hundred.

48 *Of* the sons of Naph'ta-li after their families: of Jah'ze-el, the family of the Jah'ze-el-ites: of Gu'ni, the family of the Gu'nites:

49 Of Je'zer, the family of the Je'zer-ites: of Shil'lem, the family of the Shil'lem-ites.

50 These *are* the families of Naph'ta-li according to their families: and they that were numbered of them *were* forty and five thousand and four hundred.

51 These *were* the numbered of the children of Is'ra-el, six hundred thousand and a thousand seven hundred and thirty.

52 And the LORD spoke to Mo'ses, saying,

53 To these the land shall be divided for an inheritance according to the number of names.

54 To many you shall give the more inheritance, and to few you shall give the less inheritance: to every one shall his inheritance be given according to those that were numbered of him.

55 Notwithstanding the land shall be divided by lot: according to the names of the tribes of their fathers they shall inherit.

56 According to the lot shall the possession thereof be divided between many and few.

57 And these *are* they that were numbered of the Le'vites after their families: of Ger'shon, the family of the Ger'shon-ites: of Ko'hath, the family of the Ko'hath-ites: of Me-ra'ri, the family of the Me-ra'rites.

58 These *are* the families of the Le'vites: the family of the Lib'nites, the family of the He'bron-ites, the family of the Mah'lites, the family of the Mu'shites, the family of the Ko'rath-ites. And Ko'hath begat Am'ram.

59 And the name of Am'ram's wife was Joch'e-bed, the daughter of Le'vi, whom *her mother* bare to Le'vi in E'gypt: and she bare to Am'ram Aar'on and Mo'ses, and Mir'i-am their sister. ^{bore}

60 And to Aar'on was born Na'-dab, and A-bi'hu, E-le-a'zar, and Ith'a-mar.

61 And Na'dab and A-bi'hu died, when they offered strange fire before the LORD. ^{unauthorized}

62 And those that were numbered of them were twenty and three thousand, all males from a month old and upward: for they were not numbered among the children of Is'ra-el, because there was no inheritance given them among the children of Is'ra-el.

63 These *are* they that were numbered by Mo'ses and E-le-a'zar the priest, who numbered the children of Is'ra-el in the plains of Mo'ab by Jor'dan *near* Jer'i-cho.

64 But among these there was not a man of them whom Mo'ses and Aar'on the priest numbered, when they numbered the children of Is'ra-el in the wilderness of Si'nai.

65 For the LORD had said of them, They shall surely die in the wilderness. And there was not left a man of them, save Ca'leb the son of Je-phun'neh, and Josh'u-a the son of Nun.

CHAPTER 27

THEN came the daughters of Ze-lo'phe-had, the son of He'pher, the son of Gil'e-ad, the son of Ma'chir, the son of Ma-nas'seh, of the families of Ma-nas'seh the son of Jo'seph: and these *are* the names of his daughters; Mah'lah, No'ah, and Hog'lah, and Mil'cah, and Tir'zah.

2 And they stood before Mo'ses, and before E-le-a'zar the priest, and before

the princes and all the congregation, *by* the door of the tabernacle of the congregation, saying,

3 Our father died in the wilderness, and he was not in the company of them that gathered themselves together against the LORD in the company of Ko'rah; but died in his own sin, and had no sons.

4 Why should the name of our father be <u>done away</u> from among his family, because he has no son? Give to us *therefore* a <u>possession</u> among the brethren of our father.   withdrawn - property

5 And Mo'ses brought their cause before the LORD.

6 And the LORD spoke to Mo'ses, saying,

7 The daughters of Ze-lo'phe-had speak right: you shall surely give them a possession of an inheritance among their father's brethren; and you shall cause the inheritance of their father to pass to them.

8 And you shall speak to the children of Is'ra-el, saying, If a man die, and have no son, then you shall cause his inheritance to pass to his daughter.

9 And if he have no daughter, then you shall give his inheritance to his brethren.

10 And if he have no brethren, then you shall give his inheritance to his father's brethren.

11 And if his father have no brethren, then you shall give his inheritance to his kinsman that is next to him of his family, and he shall possess it: and it shall be to the children of Is'ra-el a statute of judgment, as the LORD commanded Mo'ses.

12 And the LORD said to Mo'ses, Get you up into this mount Ab'a-rim, and see the land which I have given to the children of Is'ra-el.

13 And when you have seen it, <u>you also shall be gathered to your people,</u> as Aar'on your brother was gathered.

you will die

14 For you rebelled against My commandment in the desert of Zin, in the strife of the congregation, to <u>sanctify Me</u> at the water before their eyes: that is the water of Mer'i-bah in Ka'desh in the wilderness of Zin.

M10 — | — | — | — | 351

i.e., make My holiness apparent

15 And Mo'ses spoke to the LORD, saying,

16 Let the LORD, the <u>God</u> of the spirits of all flesh, set a man over the congregation,   Elohim[p.f.]

17 Which may go out before them, and which may go in before them, and which may lead them out, and which may bring them in; that the congregation of the LORD be not as sheep which have no shepherd.

18 And the LORD said to Mo'ses, Take you Josh'u-a the son of Nun, a man in whom *is* the Spirit, and lay <u>your hand</u> upon him;   transfer authority

G5 — | — | 390

19 And set him before E-le-a'zar the priest, and before all the congregation; and give him a <u>charge</u> in their sight.   commission

20 And you shall put *some* of your honor upon him, that all the congregation of the children of Is'ra-el may be obedient.

21 And he shall stand before E-le-a'zar the priest, who shall ask *counsel* for him after the judgment of U'rim before the LORD: at his word shall they go out, and at his word they shall come in, *both* he, and all the children of Is'ra-el with him, even all the congregation. i.e.,Light

22 And Mo'ses did as the LORD commanded him: and he took Josh'u-a, and set him before E-le-a'zar the priest, and before all the congregation:

23 And he laid his hands upon him, and gave him a charge, as the LORD commanded by the hand of Mo'ses.

CHAPTER 28

AND the LORD spoke to Mo'ses, saying,

2 Command the children of Is'ra-el, and say to them, My offering, *and* My bread for My sacrifices made by fire, *for* a sweet savor to Me, shall you observe to offer to Me in their due season. soothing aroma

3 And you shall say to them, This *is* the offering made by fire which you shall offer to the LORD; two lambs of the first year without spot day by day, *for* a continual burned offering. defect

4 The one lamb shall you offer in the morning, and the other lamb shall you offer at even;

5 And a tenth *part* of an ephah of flour for a meat offering, mingled with the fourth *part* of an hin of beaten oil.

6 *It is* a continual burned offering, which was ordained in mount Si'nai for a sweet savor, a sacrifice made by fire to the LORD. instituted

7 And the drink offering thereof *shall be* the fourth *part* of an hin for the one lamb: in the holy *place* shall you cause the strong wine to be poured to the LORD *for* a drink offering.

8 And the other lamb shall you offer at even: as the meat offering of the morning, and as the drink offering thereof, you shall offer *it*, a sacrifice made by fire, of a sweet savor to the LORD. grain - soothing aroma

9 And on the sabbath day two lambs of the first year without spot, and two tenth deals of flour *for* a meat offering, mingled with oil, and the drink offering thereof:

10 *This is* the burned offering of every sabbath, beside the continual burned offering, and his drink offering. rest day

11 And in the beginnings of your months you shall offer a burned offering to the LORD; two young bullocks, and one ram, seven lambs of the first year without spot;

12 And three tenth deals of flour *for* a meat offering, mingled with oil, for one bullock; and two tenth deals of flour *for* a meat offering, mingled with oil, for one ram; grain

13 And a several tenth deal of flour mingled with oil *for* a meat offering to one lamb; for a burned offering of a sweet savor, a sacrifice made by fire to the LORD. soothing aroma

14 And their drink offerings shall be half an hin of wine to a bullock, and the third *part* of an hin to a ram, and a fourth *part* of an hin to a lamb: this *is* the burned offering of every month throughout the months of the year.

15 And one kid of the goats for a sin offering to the LORD shall be offered, beside the continual burned offering, and his drink offering.

16 And in the fourteenth day of the first month *is* the passover of the LORD.

17 And in the fifteenth day of this month *is* the feast: seven days shall unleavened bread be eaten. i.e., without yeast

18 In the first day *shall be* an holy convocation; you shall do no manner of servile work *therein*: sacred assembly - regular

19 But you shall offer a sacrifice made by fire *for* a burned offering to the LORD; two young bullocks, and one ram, and seven lambs of the first year: they shall be to you without blemish: defect

20 And their meat offering *shall be of* flour mingled with oil: three tenth deals shall you offer for a bullock, and two tenth deals for a ram;

21 A several tenth deal shall you offer for every lamb, throughout the seven lambs:

22 And one goat *for* a sin offering, to make an atonement for you. a reconciliation

23 You shall offer these beside the burned offering in the morning, which *is* for a continual burned offering.

24 After this manner you shall offer daily, throughout the seven days, the meat of the sacrifice made by fire, of a sweet savor to the LORD: it shall be offered beside the continual burned offering, and his drink offering.

25 And on the seventh day you shall have an holy convocation; you shall do no servile work. sacred assembly - regular

26 Also in the day of the firstfruits, when you bring a new meat offering to the LORD, after your weeks *be out*, you shall have an holy convocation; you shall do no servile work: sacred assembly - regular

27 But you shall offer the burned offering for a sweet savor to the LORD; two young bullocks, one ram, seven lambs of the first year;

28 And their meat offering of flour mingled with oil, three tenth deals to one bullock, two tenth deals to one ram, grain

29 A several tenth deal to one lamb, throughout the seven lambs;

30 *And* one kid of the goats, to make an atonement for you. a reconciliation

31 You shall offer *them* beside the continual burned offering, and his meat offering, (they shall be to you without blemish) and their drink offerings. defect

CHAPTER 29

AND in the seventh month, on the first *day* of the month, you shall have an holy convocation; you shall do no servile work: it is a day of blowing the trumpets to you. sacred assembly - regular

2 And you shall offer a burned offering for a sweet savor to the LORD; one young bullock, one ram, *and* seven lambs of the first year without blemish: defect

3 And their meat offering *shall be of* flour mingled with oil, three tenth deals for a bullock, *and* two tenth deals for a ram,

4 And one tenth deal for one lamb, throughout the seven lambs:

5 And one kid of the goats *for* a sin offering, to make an atonement for you:

6 Beside the burned offering of the month, and his meat offering, and the daily burned offering, and his <u>meat</u> offering, and their drink offerings, according to their manner, for a sweet savor, a sacrifice made by fire to the LORD. _{grain}

7 And you shall have on the tenth *day* of this seventh month an <u>holy convocation</u>; and you shall afflict your souls: you shall not do any work *therein*: _{sacred assembly}

8 But you shall offer a burned offering to the LORD *for* a sweet savor; one young bullock, one ram, *and* seven lambs of the first year; they shall be to you without <u>blemish</u>: _{defect}

9 And their meat offering *shall be of* flour mingled with oil, three tenth deals to a bullock, *and* two tenth deals to one ram,

10 A several tenth deal for one lamb, throughout the seven lambs:

11 One kid of the goats *for* a sin offering; beside the sin offering of atonement, and the continual burned offering, and the meat offering of it, and their drink offerings.

12 And on the fifteenth day of the seventh month you shall have an <u>holy convocation</u>; you shall do no <u>servile</u> work, and you shall keep a feast to the LORD seven days: _{sacred assembly - regular}

13 And you shall offer a burned offering, a sacrifice made by fire, of a sweet savor to the LORD; thirteen young bullocks, two rams, *and* fourteen lambs of the first year; they shall be without <u>blemish</u>:

14 And their meat offering *shall be of* flour mingled with oil, three tenth deals to every bullock of the thirteen bullocks, two tenth deals to each ram of the two rams,

15 And a several tenth deal to each lamb of the fourteen lambs:

16 And one kid of the goats *for* a sin offering; beside the continual burned offering, his meat offering, and his drink offering.

17 And on the second day *you shall offer* twelve young bullocks, two rams, fourteen lambs of the first year without spot:

18 And their <u>meat</u> offering and their drink offerings for the bullocks, for the rams, and for the lambs, *shall be* according to their number, after the manner: _{grain}

19 And one kid of the goats *for* a sin offering; beside the continual burned offering, and the meat offering thereof, and their drink offerings.

20 And on the third day eleven bullocks, two rams, fourteen lambs of the first year without <u>blemish</u>; _{defect}

21 And their meat offering and their drink offerings for the bullocks, for the rams, and for the lambs, *shall be* according to their number, after the manner:

22 And one goat *for* a sin offering; beside the continual burned offering, and his meat offering, and his drink offering.

23 And on the fourth day ten bullocks, two rams, *and* fourteen lambs of the first year without <u>blemish</u>:

24 Their meat offering and their drink offerings for the bullocks, for the rams,

and for the lambs, *shall be* according to their number, after the <u>manner</u>:
  _{ordinance}
25 And one kid of the goats *for* a sin offering; beside the continual burned offering, his meat offering, and his drink offering.
26 And on the fifth day nine bullocks, two rams, *and* fourteen lambs of the first year without spot:
27 And their meat offering and their drink offerings for the bullocks, for the rams, and for the lambs, *shall be* according to their number, after the <u>manner</u>:
28 And one goat *for* a sin offering; beside the continual burned offering, and his meat offering, and his drink offering.
29 And on the sixth day eight bullocks, two rams, *and* fourteen lambs of the first year without <u>blemish</u>: _{defect}
30 And their meat offering and their drink offerings for the bullocks, for the rams, and for the lambs, *shall be* according to their number, after the manner:
31 And one goat *for* a sin offering; beside the continual burned offering, his meat offering, and his drink offering.
32 And on the seventh day seven bullocks, two rams, *and* fourteen lambs of the first year without blemish:
33 And their meat offering and their drink offerings for the bullocks, for the rams, and for the lambs, *shall be* according to their number, after the manner:
34 And one goat *for* a sin offering; beside the continual burned offering, his meat offering, and his drink offering.

35 On the eighth day you shall have a <u>solemn assembly</u>: you shall do no <u>servile</u> work *therein*: _{sacred assembly - regular}
36 But you shall offer a burned offering, a sacrifice made by fire, of a sweet savor to the LORD: one bullock, one ram, seven lambs of the first year without <u>blemish</u>: _{defect}
37 Their meat offering and their drink offerings for the bullock, for the ram, and for the lambs, *shall be* according to their number, after the <u>manner</u>: _{ordinance}
38 And one goat *for* a sin offering; beside the continual burned offering, and his meat offering, and his drink offering.
39 These *things* you shall <u>do</u> to the LORD in your <u>set feasts</u>, beside your vows, and your freewill offerings, for your burned offerings, and for your <u>meat</u> offerings, and for your drink offerings, and for your peace offerings. _{present - appointed times - grain}
40 And Mo'ses told the children of Is'ra-el according to all that the LORD commanded Mo'ses.

CHAPTER 30

AND Mo'ses spoke to the heads of the tribes concerning the children of Is'ra-el, saying, This *is* the thing which the LORD has commanded.
2 If a man <u>vow a vow</u> to the LORD, or swear an oath to <u>bind his soul</u> with a bond; he shall not break his word, he shall do according to all that proceeds out of his mouth. _{make a pledge - obligate himself}
3 If a woman also <u>vow a vow</u> to the

LORD, and bind *herself* by a bond, *being* in her father's house in her youth;

4 And her father hear her vow, and her bond wherewith she has bound her soul, and her father shall hold his peace at her: then all her vows shall stand, and every bond wherewith she has bound her soul shall stand.   pledge - herself - says nothing to her

5 But if her father disallow her in the day that he hears; not any of her vows, or of her bonds wherewith she has bound her soul, shall stand: and the LORD shall forgive her, because her father disallowed her.   forbid - pledges - herself

6 And if she had at all an husband, when she vowed, or uttered anything out of her lips, wherewith she bound her soul;

7 And her husband heard *it*, and held his peace at her in the day that he heard *it*: then her vows shall stand, and her bonds wherewith she bound her soul shall stand.

8 But if her husband disallowed her on the day that he heard *it*; then he shall make her vow which she vowed, and that which she uttered with her lips, wherewith she bound her soul, of none effect: and the LORD shall forgive her.   herself

9 But every vow of a widow, and of her that is divorced, wherewith they have bound their souls, shall stand against her.   pledge

10 And if she vowed in her husband's house, or bound her soul by a bond with an oath;

11 And her husband heard *it*, and held his peace at her, *and* disallowed her not: then all her vows shall stand, and every bond wherewith she bound her soul shall stand.

12 But if her husband has utterly made them void on the day he heard *them*; *then* whatsoever proceeded out of her lips concerning her vows, or concerning the bond of her soul, shall not stand: her husband has made them void; and the LORD shall forgive her.   pledges - herself - invalid

13 Every vow, and every binding oath to afflict the soul, her husband may establish it, or her husband may make it void.

14 But if her husband altogether hold his peace at her from day to day; then he establishes all her vows, or all her bonds, which *are* upon her: he confirms them, because he held his peace at her in the day that he heard *them*.

15 But if he shall any ways make them void after that he has heard *them*; then he shall bear her iniquity.

16 These *are* the statutes, which the LORD commanded Mo'ses, between a man and his wife, between the father and his daughter, *being yet* in her youth in her father's house.   regulations

CHAPTER 31

AND the LORD spoke to Mo'ses, saying,

2 Avenge the children of Is'ra-el of the Mid'i-an-ites: afterward shall you be gathered to your people.   on

3 And Mo'ses spoke to the people, saying, Arm some of yourselves to the war, and let them go against the

Mid'i-an-ites, and avenge the LORD of Mid'i-an.

4 Of every tribe a thousand, throughout all the tribes of Is'ra-el, shall you send to the war.

5 So there were delivered out of the thousands of Is'ra-el, a thousand of *every* tribe, twelve thousand armed for war.

6 And Mo'ses sent them to the war, a thousand of *every* tribe, them and Phin'e-has the son of E-le-a'zar the priest, to the war, with the holy instruments, and the trumpets to blow in his hand.

7 And they warred against the Mid'i-an-ites, as the LORD commanded Mo'ses; and they slew all the males.

8 And they slew the kings of Mid'i-an, beside the rest of them that were slain; *namely*, E'vi, and Re'kem, and Zur, and Hur, and Re'ba, five kings of Mid'i-an: Ba'laam also the son of Be'or they slew with the sword.

9 And the children of Is'ra-el took *all* the women of Mid'i-an captives, and their little ones, and took the spoil of all their cattle, and all their flocks, and all their goods.

10 And they burned all their cities wherein they dwelled, and all their goodly castles, with fire.

11 And they took all the spoil, and all the prey, *both* of men and of beasts.

12 And they brought the captives, and the prey, and the spoil, to Mo'ses, and E-le-a'zar the priest, and to the congregation of the children of Is'ra-el, to the camp at the plains of Mo'ab, which *are* by Jor'dan *near* Jer'i-cho.

13 And Mo'ses, and E-le-a'zar the priest, and all the princes of the congregation, went forth to meet them outside the camp.

14 And Mo'ses was angry with the officers of the host, *with* the captains over thousands, and captains over hundreds, which came from the battle.

15 And Mo'ses said to them, Have you saved all the women alive?

16 Behold, these caused the children of Is'ra-el, through the counsel of Ba'laam, to commit trespass against the LORD in the matter of Pe'or, and there was a <u>plague</u> among the congregation of the LORD.   REV. 2:14 sickness

17 Now therefore kill every male among the little ones, and kill every woman that has known man by lying with him.

18 But all the women children, that have not known a man by lying with him, keep alive for yourselves.

19 And do you abide outside the camp seven days: whosoever has killed any person, and whosoever has touched any slain, purify *both* yourselves and your captives on the third day, and on the seventh day.

20 And purify all *your* <u>raiment</u>, and all that is made of skins, and all work of goats' *hair*, and all things made of wood.   garment

21 And E-le-a'zar the priest said to the men of war which went to the battle, This *is* the <u>ordinance</u> of the law which the LORD commanded Mo'ses; requirement

22 Only the gold, and the silver, the brass, the iron, the tin, and the lead,
23 Every thing that may abide the fire, you shall make *it* go through the fire, and it shall be clean: nevertheless it shall be <u>purified</u> with the water of separation: and all that abides not the fire you shall make go through the water. ceremonially purified
24 And you shall wash your clothes on the seventh day, and you shall be clean, and afterward you shall come into the camp.
25 And the Lord spoke to Mo'ses, saying,
26 Take the sum of the <u>prey</u> that was taken, *both* of man and of beast, you, and E-le-a'zar the priest, and the chief fathers of the congregation: booty
27 And divide the prey into two parts; between them that took the war upon them, who went out to battle, and between all the congregation:
28 And levy a <u>tribute</u> to the Lord of the men of war which went out to battle: one <u>soul</u> of five hundred, *both* of the persons, and of the <u>beeves</u>, and of the asses, and of the sheep: tax - person - cattle
29 Take *it* of their half, and give *it* to E-le-a'zar the priest, *for* an heave offering of the Lord.
30 And of the children of Is'ra-el's half, you shall take one portion of fifty, of the persons, of the <u>beeves</u>, of the asses, and of the flocks, of all manner of beasts, and give them to the Le'vites, which keep the charge of the tabernacle of the Lord.
31 And Mo'ses and E-le-a'zar the priest did as the Lord commanded Mo'ses.
32 And the booty, *being* the rest of the prey which the men of war had caught, was six hundred thousand and seventy thousand and five thousand sheep,
33 And <u>threescore and twelve thousand beeves</u>, 72,000 cattle
34 And <u>threescore and one thousand asses</u>, 61,000 donkeys
35 And thirty and two thousand persons in all, of women that had not known man by lying with him.
36 And the half, *which was* the portion of them that went out to war, was in number three hundred thousand and seven and thirty thousand and five hundred sheep:
37 And the Lord's <u>tribute</u> of the sheep was <u>six hundred and threescore and fifteen</u>. tax - 675
38 And the beeves *were* thirty and six thousand; of which the Lord's tribute *was* <u>threescore and twelve</u>. 72
39 And the asses *were* thirty thousand and five hundred; of which the Lord's tribute *was* <u>threescore and one</u>. 61
40 And the persons *were* sixteen thousand; of which the Lord's <u>tribute</u> *was* thirty and two persons.
41 And Mo'ses gave the <u>tribute</u>, *which was* the Lord's heave offering, to E-le-a'zar the priest, as the Lord commanded Mo'ses. tax
42 And of the children of Is'ra-el's half, which Mo'ses divided from the men that warred,
43 (Now the *half that pertained to* the congregation was three hundred

thousand and thirty thousand *and* seven thousand and five hundred sheep,

44 And thirty and six thousand <u>beeves</u>,　_{cattle}

45 And thirty thousand asses and five hundred,

46 And sixteen thousand persons;)

47 Even of the children of Is'ra-el's half, Mo'ses took one portion of fifty, *both* of man and of beast, and gave them to the Le'vites, which kept the <u>charge</u> of the tabernacle of the LORD; as the LORD commanded Mo'ses.　_{responsibility}

48 And the officers which *were* over thousands of the host, the captains of thousands, and captains of hundreds, came near to Mo'ses:

49 And they said to Mo'ses, Your servants have taken the sum of the men of war which *are* under our <u>charge</u>, and there lacks not one man of us.　_{command}

50 We have therefore brought an <u>oblation</u> for the LORD, what every man has gotten, of jewels of gold, chains, and bracelets, rings, earrings, and <u>tablets</u>, to make an atonement for <u>our souls</u> before the LORD.　_{offering - necklaces - ourselves}

51 And Mo'ses and E-le-a'zar the priest took the gold of them, *even* all <u>wrought</u> jewels.　_{artful}

52 And all the gold of the offering that they offered up to the LORD, of the captains of thousands, and of the captains of hundreds, was sixteen thousand seven hundred and fifty shekels.

53 (*For* the men of war had taken spoil, every man for himself.)

54 And Mo'ses and E-le-a'zar the priest took the gold of the captains of thousands and of hundreds, and brought it into the tabernacle of the congregation, *for* a <u>memorial</u> for the children of Is'ra-el before the LORD.　_{remembrance}

CHAPTER 32

NOW the children of Reu'ben and the children of Gad had a very great multitude of cattle: and when they saw the land of Ja'zer, and the land of Gil'e-ad, that, behold, the place *was* a place for cattle;

2 The children of Gad and the children of Reu'ben came and spoke to Mo'ses, and to E-le-a'zar the priest, and to the princes of the congregation, saying,

3 At'a-roth, and Di'bon, and Ja'zer, and Nim'rah, and Hesh'bon, and E-le-a'leh, and She'bam, and Ne'bo, and Be'on,

4 *Even* the country which the LORD <u>smote</u> before the congregation of Is'ra-el, *is* a land for cattle, and your servants have cattle:　_{conquered}

5 Wherefore, said they, if we have found grace in your sight, let this land be given to your servants for a possession, *and* bring us not over Jor'dan.

6 And Mo'ses said to the children of Gad and to the children of Reu'ben, Shall your brethren go to war, and shall you sit here?

7 And wherefore <u>discourage</u> you the heart of the children of Is'ra-el from going over into the land which the LORD has given them?　_{restrain}

8 Thus did your fathers, when I sent

them from Ka'desh-bar'ne-a to see the land.

9 For when they went up to the valley of Esh'col, and saw the land, they discouraged the heart of the children of Is'ra-el, that they should not go into the land which the LORD had given them.

10 And the LORD's anger <u>was kindled</u> the same time, and He swear, saying, _{burned}

11 Surely none of the men that came up out of E'gypt, from twenty years old and upward, shall see the land which I swear to A'bra-ham, to I'saac, and to Ja'cob; because they have not wholly <u>followed</u> Me: _{obeyed}

12 Save Ca'leb the son of Je-phun'neh the Kenez-ite, and Josh'u-a the son of Nun: for they have wholly followed the LORD.

13 And the LORD's anger <u>was kindled</u> against Is'ra-el, and He made them wander in the wilderness forty years, until all the generation, that had done <u>evil</u> in the sight of the LORD, was consumed. _{Wrong}

14 And, behold, you are risen up in your fathers' stead, <u>an increase</u> of sinful men, to augment yet the fierce anger of the LORD toward Is'ra-el. _{a brood}

15 For if you turn away from after Him, He will yet again leave them in the wilderness; and you shall destroy all this people.

16 And they came near to him, and said, We will build sheepfolds here for our cattle, and cities for our little ones:

17 But we ourselves will go ready armed before the children of Is'ra-el, until we have brought them to their place: and our little ones shall dwell in the fenced cities because of the inhabitants of the land.

18 We will not return to our houses, until the children of Is'ra-el have <u>in-herited</u> every man his inheritance. _{received}

19 For we will not inherit with them on yonder side Jor'dan, or <u>forward</u>; because our inheritance is fallen to us on this side Jor'dan eastward. _{beyond}

20 And Mo'ses said to them, If you will do this thing, if you will go armed before the LORD to war,

21 And will go all of you armed over Jor'dan before the LORD, until He has driven out His enemies from before Him,

22 And the land be subdued before the LORD: then afterward you shall return, and be <u>guiltless</u> before the LORD, and before Is'ra-el; and this land shall be your possession before the LORD. _{free of obligation}

23 But if you will not do so, behold, you have sinned against the LORD: and be sure your sin will find you out.

24 Build you cities for your little ones, and folds for your sheep; and do that which has proceeded out of your mouth.

25 And the children of Gad and the children of Reu'ben spoke to Mo'ses, saying, Your servants will do as my lord commands.

26 Our little ones, our wives, our flocks, and all our cattle, shall be there in the cities of Gil'e-ad:

27 But your servants will pass over, every man armed for war, before the LORD to battle, as my lord says.

28 So concerning them Mo'ses commanded E-le-a'zar the priest, and Josh'u-a the son of Nun, and the chief fathers of the tribes of the children of Is'ra-el:

29 And Mo'ses said to them, If the children of Gad and the children of Reu'ben will pass with you over Jor'dan, every man armed to battle, before the LORD, and the land shall be subdued before you; then you shall give them the land of Gil'e-ad for a possession:

30 But if they will not pass over with you armed, they shall have possessions among you in the land of Ca'naan.

31 And the children of Gad and the children of Reu'ben answered, saying, As the LORD has said to your servants, so will we do.

32 We will pass over armed before the LORD into the land of Ca'naan, that the possession of our inheritance on this side Jor'dan *may be* ours.

33 And Mo'ses gave to them, *even* to the children of Gad, and to the children of Reu'ben, and to half the tribe of Ma-nas'seh the son of Jo'seph, the kingdom of Si'hon king of the Am'or-ites, and the kingdom of Og king of Ba'shan, the land, with the cities thereof in the coasts, *even* the cities of the country round about.

34 And the children of Gad built Di'bon, and At'a-roth, and Ar'o-er,

35 And At'roth, Sho'phan, and Ja-a'zer, and Jog'-be-hah,

36 And Beth-nim'rah, and Beth-ha'ran, fenced cities: and folds for sheep.

37 And the children of Reu'ben built Hesh'bon, and E-le-a'leh, and Kir-jath-a'im,

38 And Ne'bo, and Ba'al-me'on, (their names being changed,) and Shib'mah: and gave other names to the cities which they builded.

39 And the children of Ma'chir the son of Ma-nas'seh went to Gil'e-ad, and took it, and <u>dispossessed</u> the Am'or-ite which *was* in it.   _{drove out}

40 And Mo'ses gave Gil'e-ad to Ma'chir the son of Ma-nas'seh; and he dwelled therein.

41 And Ja'ir the son of Ma-nas'seh went and took the small towns thereof, and called them Ha'voth-ja'ir.

42 And No'bah went and took Ke'nath, and the villages thereof, and called it No'bah, after his own name.

CHAPTER 33

THESE *are* the journeys of the children of Is'ra-el, which went forth out of the land of E'gypt with their armies under the hand of Mo'ses and Aar'on.

2 And Mo'ses wrote their goings out according to their journeys by the commandment of the LORD: and these *are* their journeys according to their goings out.

3 And they departed from Ra-me'ses in the first month, on the fifteenth day of the first month; on the morrow after the passover the children of Is'ra-el went out with an high hand in the sight of all the Egyptians.

PISA

4 For the E-gyptians buried all *their* firstborn, which the LORD had smitten among them: upon their gods also the LORD executed judgments.

5 And the children of Is'ra-el removed from Ra-me'ses, and pitched in Suc'coth.

6 And they departed from Suc'coth, and <u>pitched</u> in E'tham, which *is* in the edge of the wilderness. camped

7 And they removed from E'tham, and turned again to Pi-ha-hi'roth, which *is* before Ba'al-ze'phon: and they <u>pitched</u> before Mig'dol.

8 And they departed from before Pi-ha-hi'roth, and passed through the midst of the sea into the wilderness, and went three days' journey in the wilderness of E'tham, and <u>pitched</u> in Ma'rah.

9 And they removed from Ma'rah, and came to E'lim: and in E'lim *were* twelve fountains of water, and threescore and ten palm trees; and they <u>pitched</u> there.

10 And they removed from E'lim, and <u>encamped</u> by the Red sea. camped

11 And they removed from the Red sea, and <u>encamped</u> in the wilderness of Sin.

12 And they took their journey out of the wilderness of Sin, and <u>encamped</u> in Doph'kah.

13 And they departed from Doph'kah, and <u>encamped</u> in A'lush.

14 And they removed from A'lush, and encamped at Reph'i-dim, where was no water for the people to drink.

15 And they departed from Reph'i-dim, and <u>pitched</u> in the wilderness of Si'nai.

16 And they <u>removed</u> from the desert of Si'nai, and <u>pitched</u> at Kib'roth-hat-ta'a-vah. left - camped

17 And they departed from Kib'roth-hat-ta'a-vah, and <u>encamped</u> at Ha-ze'roth.

18 And they departed from Ha-ze'roth, and <u>pitched</u> in Rith'mah.

19 And they departed from Rith'mah, and <u>pitched</u> at Rim'mon-pa'rez.

20 And they departed from Rim'mon-pa'rez, and <u>pitched</u> in Lib'nah.

21 And they removed from Lib'nah, and <u>pitched</u> at Ris'sah.

22 And they journeyed from Ris'sah, and <u>pitched</u> in Ke-hel'a-thah. camped

23 And they went from Ke-hel'a-thah, and <u>pitched</u> in mount Sha'pher.

24 And they removed from mount Sha'pher, and <u>encamped</u> in Har'a-dah.

25 And they removed from Har'a-dah, and <u>pitched</u> in Mak-he'loth.

26 And they removed from Mak-he'loth, and <u>encamped</u> at Ta'hath.

27 And they departed from Ta'hath, and <u>pitched</u> at Ta'rah.

28 And they removed from Ta'rah, and <u>pitched</u> in Mith'cah.

29 And they went from Mith'cah, and <u>pitched</u> in Hash-mo'nah.

30 And they departed from Hash-mo'nah, and <u>encamped</u> at Mo-se'roth. camped

31 And they departed from Mo-se'roth, and <u>pitched</u> in Ben-e-ja'a-kan.

32 And they removed from Ben-e-ja'a-kan, and <u>encamped</u> at Hor-ha-gid'-gad.

33 And they went from Hor-ha-gid'gad, and <u>pitched</u> in Jot'ba-thah.

34 And they removed from Jot'ba-thah, and <u>encamped</u> at E-bro'nah.   camped

35 And they departed from E-bro'nah, and <u>encamped</u> at E'zi-on-ga'ber.

36 And they removed from E'zi-on-ga'ber, and <u>pitched</u> in the wilderness of Zin, which *is* Ka'desh.

37 And they removed from Ka'desh, and <u>pitched</u> in mount Hor, in the edge of the land of E'dom.   camped

38 And Aar'on the priest went up into mount Hor at the commandment of the LORD, and died there, in the fortieth year after the children of Is'ra-el were come out of the land of E'gypt, in the first *day* of the fifth month.

39 And Aar'on *was* an hundred and twenty and three years old when he died in mount Hor.

40 And king A'rad the Ca'naan-ite, which dwelt in the south in the land of Ca'naan, heard of the coming of the children of Is'ra-el.

41 And they departed from mount Hor, and <u>pitched</u> in Zal-mo'nah.   camped

42 And they departed from Zal-mo'nah, and <u>pitched</u> in Pu'non.

43 And they departed from Pu'non, and <u>pitched</u> in O'both.

44 And they departed from O'both, and <u>pitched</u> in Ij'e-ab'a-rim, in the border of Mo'ab.

45 And they departed from I'im, and <u>pitched</u> in Di'bon-gad.

46 And they removed from Di'bon-gad, and <u>encamped</u> in Al'mon-dib-la-tha'im.   camped

47 And they removed from Al'mon-dib-la-tha'im, and <u>pitched</u> in the mountains of Ab'a-rim, before Ne'bo.

48 And they departed from the mountains of Ab'a-rim, and <u>pitched</u> in the plains of Mo'ab by Jor'dan *near* Jer'i-cho.   camped

49 And they <u>pitched</u> by Jor'dan, from Beth-jes'i-moth *even* to A'bel-shit'-tim in the plains of Mo'ab.

50 And the LORD spoke to Mo'ses in the plains of Mo'ab by Jor'dan *near* Jer'i-cho, saying,

51 Speak to the children of Is'ra-el, and say to them, When you are passed over Jor'dan into the land of Ca'naan;

52 Then you shall drive out all the inhabitants of the land from before you, and destroy all their <u>pictures</u>, and destroy all their molten images, and <u>quite pluck down</u> all their high places: carved figures - destroy

53 And you shall dispossess *the inhabitants* of the land, and dwell therein: for I have given you the land to possess it.

54 And you shall divide the land by lot for an inheritance among your families: *and* to <u>the more</u> you shall give <u>the more</u> inheritance, and to the fewer you shall give the less inheritance: every man's *inheritance* shall be in the place where his lot falls; according to the tribes of your fathers you shall inherit.   a larger

55 But if you will not drive out the inhabitants of the land from before you; then it shall come to pass, that those which you let remain of them *shall be* pricks in your eyes, and thorns in your sides, and shall <u>vex</u> you in the land wherein you dwell.   trouble

56 Moreover it shall come to pass, *that* I shall do to you, as I thought to do to them.

CHAPTER 34

A ND the LORD spoke to Mo'ses, saying,

2 Command the children of Is'ra-el, and say to them, When you come into the land of Ca'naan; (this *is* the land that shall fall to you for an inheritance, *even* the land of Ca'naan with the coasts thereof:)

3 Then your south quarter shall be from the wilderness of Zin along by the coast of E'dom, and your south border shall be the outmost coast of the <u>Salt</u> Sea eastward: i.e., Dead

4 And your border shall turn from the south to the ascent of A-krab'bim, and pass on to Zin: and the going forth thereof shall be from the south to Ka'desh-bar'ne-a, and shall go on to Ha'zar-ad'dar, and pass on to Az'mon:

5 And the border shall <u>bring a compass</u> from Az'mon to the river of E'gypt, and the goings out of it shall be at the sea.   take a turn

6 And *as for* the western border, you shall even have the <u>Great</u> Sea for a border: this shall be your west border.   i.e., Mediterranean

7 And this shall be your north border: from the <u>Great</u> Sea you shall point out for you mount Hor:

8 From mount Hor you shall point out *your border* to the entrance of Ha'math; and the goings forth of the border shall be to Zedad:

9 And the border shall go on to Ziph'ron, and the goings out of it shall be at Ha'zar-e'nan: this shall be your north border.

10 And you shall point out your east border from Ha'zar-e'nan to She'pham:

11 And the coast shall go down from She'pham to Rib'lah, on the east side of A'in; and the border shall descend, and shall reach to the side of the Sea of <u>Chin'ne-reth</u> eastward: i.e., Galilee

12 And the border shall go down to Jor'dan, and the goings out of it shall be at the <u>Salt</u> Sea: this shall be your land with the coasts thereof round about.   i.e., Dead

13 And Mo'ses commanded the children of Is'ra-el, saying, This *is* the land which you shall inherit by lot, which the LORD commanded to give to the nine tribes, and to the half tribe:

14 For the tribe of the children of Reu'ben according to the house of their fathers, and the tribe of the children of Gad according to the house of their fathers, have received *their inheritance*; and half the tribe of Ma-nas'seh have received their inheritance:

15 The two tribes and the half tribe have received their inheritance on this side Jor'dan *near* Jer'i-cho eastward, toward the sunrising.

16 And the LORD spoke to Mo'ses, saying,

17 These *are* the names of the men which shall divide the land to you: E-le-a'zar the priest, and Josh'u-a the son of Nun.

18 And you shall take one prince of every tribe, to divide the land by inheritance.

19 And the names of the men *are*

these: Of the tribe of Ju'dah, Ca'leb the son of Je-phun'neh.

20 And of the tribe of the children of Sim'e-on, She-mu'el the son of Am-mi'hud.

21 Of the tribe of Ben'ja-min, E-li'dad the son of Chis'lon.

22 And the prince of the tribe of the children of Dan, Buk'ki the son of Jog'li.

23 The prince of the children of Jo'seph, for the tribe of the children of Ma-nas'seh, Han'ni'el the son of E'phod.

24 And the prince of the tribe of the children of E'phra-im, Ke-mu'el the son of Shiph'tan.

25 And the prince of the tribe of the children of Zeb'u-lun, E-liz'a-phan the son of Par'nach.

26 And the prince of the tribe of the children of Is'sa-char, Pal'ti-el the son of Az'zan.

27 And the prince of the tribe of the children of Ash'er, A'hi'hud the son of Shel'o-mi.

28 And the prince of the tribe of the children of Naph'ta-li, Ped'a-hel the son of Am-mi'hud.

29 These *are they* whom the LORD commanded to divide the inheritance to the children of Is'ra-el in the land of Ca'naan.

CHAPTER 35

AND the LORD spoke to Mo'ses in the plains of Mo'ab by Jor'dan *near* Jer'i-cho, saying,

2 Command the children of Is'ra-el, that they give to the Le'vites of the inheritance of their possession cities to dwell in; and you shall give *also* to the Le'vites suburbs for the cities round about them.   open land

3 And the cities shall they have to dwell in; and the suburbs of them shall be for their cattle, and for their goods, and for all their beasts.

4 And the suburbs of the cities, which you shall give to the Le'vites, *shall reach* from the wall of the city and outward a thousand cubits round about.

5 And you shall measure from without the city on the east side two thousand cubits, and on the south side two thousand cubits, and on the west side two thousand cubits, and on the north side two thousand cubits; and the city shall be in the midst: this *shall be* to them the suburbs of the cities.

6 And among the cities which you shall give to the Le'vites *there shall be* six cities for refuge, which you shall appoint for the manslayer, that he may flee there: and to them you shall add forty and two cities. in addition

7 *So* all the cities which you shall give to the Le'vites *shall be* forty and eight cities: them *shall you give* with their suburbs.   open land

8 And the cities which you shall give *shall be* of the possession of the children of Is'ra-el: from *them that have* many you shall give many; but from *them that have* few you shall give few: every one shall give of his cities to the Le'vites according to his inheritance which he inherits.   they

9 And the Lord spoke to Mo'ses, saying,

10 Speak to the children of Is'ra-el, and say to them, When you be come over Jor'dan into the land of Ca'naan;

11 Then you shall appoint you cities to be cities of <u>refuge</u> for you; that the slayer may flee there, which kills any person at <u>unawares</u>.

safety - unintentionally

12 And they shall be to you cities for refuge from the avenger; that the manslayer die not, until he stand before the congregation in judgment.

13 And of these cities which you shall give six cities shall you have for refuge.

14 You shall give three cities on this side Jor'dan, and three cities shall you give in the land of Ca'naan, *which* shall be cities of refuge.

15 These six cities shall be a refuge, *both* for the children of Is'ra-el, and for the <u>stranger</u>, and for the <u>sojourner</u> among them: that every one that kills any person <u>unawares</u> may flee there.

alien - temporary resident - unintentionally

16 And if he <u>smite</u> him with an instrument of iron, so that he die, he *is* a murderer: the murderer shall surely be put to death.

strike

17 And if he <u>smite</u> him with throwing a stone, wherewith he may die, and he die, he *is* a murderer: the murderer shall surely be put to death.

18 Or *if* he <u>smite</u> him with an <u>hand</u> <u>weapon</u> of wood, wherewith he may die, and he die, he *is* a murderer: the murderer shall surely be put to death.

club

19 The revenger of blood himself shall slay the murderer: when he meets him, he shall slay him.

20 But if he <u>thrust</u> him of hatred, or hurl at him by laying of wait, that he die;

pushed

21 Or in enmity <u>smite</u> him with his hand, that he die: he that smote *him* shall surely be put to death; *for* he *is* a murderer: the revenger of blood shall slay the murderer, when he meets him.

strike

22 But if he <u>thrust</u> him suddenly without enmity, or have cast upon him any thing without laying of wait,

23 Or with any stone, wherewith a man may die, seeing *him* not, and cast *it* upon him, that he die, and *was* not his enemy, neither sought his harm:

24 Then the congregation shall judge between the slayer and the revenger of blood according to these judgments:

25 And the congregation shall deliver the slayer out of the hand of the revenger of blood, and the congregation shall restore him to the city of his refuge, <u>where</u> he was fled: and he shall abide in it to the death of the high priest, which was anointed with the holy oil.

to which

26 But if the slayer shall at any time <u>come outside</u> the border of the city of his refuge, where he was fled;

go beyond

27 And the revenger of blood find him without the borders of the city of his refuge, and the revenger of blood kill the slayer; he shall not be guilty of blood:

28 Because he should have remained in the city of his refuge until the death

of the high priest: but after the death of the high priest the slayer shall return into the land of his possession.

29 So these *things* shall be for a statute of judgment to you throughout your generations in all your dwellings.   law

30 Whoso kills any person, the murderer shall be put to death by the mouth of witnesses: but one witness shall not testify against any person *to cause him* to die.   accuser

31 Moreover you shall take no satisfaction for the life of a murderer, which *is* guilty of death: but he shall be surely put to death.   ransom

32 And you shall take no satisfaction for him that is fled to the city of his refuge, that he should come again to dwell in the land, until the death of the priest.

33 So you shall not pollute the land wherein you *are*: for blood it defiles the land: and the land cannot be cleansed of the blood that is shed therein, but by the blood of him that shed it.

34 Defile not therefore the land which you shall inhabit, wherein I dwell: for I the LORD dwell among the children of Is'ra-el.

CHAPTER 36

AND the chief fathers of the families of the children of Gil'e-ad, the son of Ma'chir, the son of Ma-nas'seh, of the families of the sons of Jo'seph, came near, and spoke before Mo'ses, and before the princes, the chief fathers of the children of Is'ra-el: heads

2 And they said, The LORD commanded my lord to give the land for an inheritance by lot to the children of Is'ra-el: and my lord was commanded by the LORD to give the inheritance of Ze-lo'phe-had our brother to his daughters.

3 And if they be married to any of the sons of the *other* tribes of the children of Is'ra-el, then shall their inheritance be taken from the inheritance of our fathers, and shall be put to the inheritance of the tribe whereto they are received: so shall it be taken from the lot of our inheritance.

4 And when the jubilee of the children of Is'ra-el shall be, then shall their inheritance be put to the inheritance of the tribe whereto they are received: so shall their inheritance be taken away from the inheritance of the tribe of our fathers.

5 And Mo'ses commanded the children of Is'ra-el according to the word of the LORD, saying, The tribe of the sons of Jo'seph has said well.

6 This *is* the thing which the LORD does command concerning the daughters of Ze-lo'phe-had, saying, Let them marry to whom they think best; only to the family of the tribe of their father shall they marry.

7 So shall not the inheritance of the children of Is'ra-el remove from tribe to tribe: for every one of the children of Is'ra-el shall keep himself to the inheritance of the tribe of his fathers.

8 And every daughter, that possesses an inheritance in any tribe of the chil-

dren of Is'ra-el, shall be wife to one of the family of the tribe of her father, that the children of Is'ra-el may enjoy every man the inheritance of his fathers.

9 Neither shall the inheritance remove from *one* tribe to another tribe; but every one of the tribes of the children of Is'ra-el shall keep himself to his own inheritance.

10 Even as the LORD commanded Mo'ses, so did the daughters of Ze-lo'phe-had:

11 For Mah'lah, Tir'zah, and Hog'-lah, and Mil'cah, and No'ah, the daughters of Ze-lo'phe-had, were married to their <u>father's brothers' sons</u>: first cousins

12 *And* they were married into the families of the sons of Ma-nas'seh the son of Jo'seph, and their inheritance remained in the tribe of the family of their father.

13 These *are* the commandments and the judgments, which the LORD commanded by the hand of Mo'ses to the children of Is'ra-el in the plains of Mo'ab by Jor'dan *near* Jer'i-cho.

DEUTERONOMY

OUTLINE

SURVEY

The name of the Book of Deuteronomy, or "Second Law," suggests its nature and purpose. Standing, as it properly does in our Bibles, as the last of the Five Books of Moses, it summarizes and brings to focus the message embodied in the four preceding books. This does not mean that it is a mere repetition of what has been said previously. Deuteronomy is, it is true, set in the historical events which have been given previously, particularly in Exodus and Numbers. However, it goes beyond those records in that it both interprets and adapts them.

Throughout this book, events are charged with meaning. Moses gives a good deal of history; but in nearly every case he relates events to the spiritual lesson which they underscore. He takes the legislation which the Lord had given to Israel nearly forty years before and adapts it to conditions of settled life in the land to which Israel was soon to go.

The nation of Israel was, when this book was written, in the land of Moab, to the east of the Jordan River and the Dead Sea. Once before, Israel had failed, through lack of faith, to enter Palestine. Now thirty-eight years later, Moses gathers the company together, and seeks to infuse faith which will enable the chosen people to move ahead in obedience. Before them lies their inheritance. Dangers, seen and unseen, lie ahead. With them is their God, Whom they have come to know better during their experiences in the peninsula of Sinai, with its ruggedness and bleakness.

Moses sees, correctly, that their major perils will be in the area of their spiritual life; so the major thrust of his message is spiritual. The Lord their God is *One*; it is He Who has delivered them from bondage. He has given them the law. He has entered into covenant relation with them. They are His people. He demands exclusive devotion and worship. His ways are known to them. By long experience, Israel has learned that the Lord honors obedience and punishes transgression. Now, in a new sense, Israel is on her own, under the Lord and in her new home.

The book covers the entire range of questions which arise out of this new phase in Israel's life. Her attitude toward the Lord is, of course, the major problem. Moses, with all of the earnestness which he can summon, calls Israel to trust the Lord with the whole heart, and to make His law the continual monitor of her life. This law, if observed, will infuse her entire life, and make her a people distinctive among nations. Blessings will follow and the nations will recognize that her God is the Lord. But if Israel shall go the way of the nations about her, and forget her God, then afflictions will seize her, and ultimately she will be scattered among the nations.

Throughout the book, the emphasis is upon faith-plus-obedience. In a real sense, this is its keynote.

AUTHOR

Throughout the Book of Deuteronomy, Moses is declared to be the author of the addresses which make up the major part of the work. It is obvious that the account of his death, given at the end, is the work of another writer, quite probably Joshua. It is thus entirely proper to refer to Deuteronomy as the Fifth Book of Moses.

H.B.K.

THE FIFTH BOOK OF MOSES COMMONLY CALLED

DEUTERONOMY

> "Second Law"
> Moses' Final Words

CHAPTER 1

THESE *be* the words which Mo'ses spoke to all Is'ra-el on this side Jor'dan in the wilderness, in the plain opposite the Red *sea*, between Pa'ran, and To'phel, and La'ban, and Ha-ze'roth, and Diz'a-hab.

2 (*There are* eleven days' *journey* from Ho'reb by the way of mount Se'ir to Ka'desh-bar'ne-a.)

3 And it came to pass in the fortieth year, in the eleventh month, on the first *day* of the month, *that* Mo'ses spoke to the children of Is'ra-el, according to all that the LORD had given him in commandment to them;

4 After he had slain Si'hon the king of the Am'or-ites, which dwelt in Hesh'bon, and Og the king of Ba'shan, which dwelled at As'ta-roth in Ed're-i:

5 On this side Jor'dan, in the land of Mo'ab, began Mo'ses to declare this law, saying,

6 The LORD our God spoke to us in Ho'reb, saying, You have dwelled long enough in this mount: Elohim p.f.

7 Turn you, and take your journey, and go to the mount of the Am'or-ites, and to all *the places* near there to, in the plain, in the hills, and in the vale, and in the south, and by the sea side, to the land of the Ca'naan-ites, and to Leb'a-non, to the great river, the river Eu-phra'tes. valley

8 Behold, I have set the land before you: go in and possess the land which the LORD swear to your fathers, A'bra-ham, I'saac, and Ja'cob, to give to them and to their seed after them. promised - descendants

9 And I spoke to you at that time, saying, I am not able to bear you myself alone: cannot carry all the responsibility

10 The LORD your God has multiplied you, and, behold, you *are* this day as the stars of heaven for multitude.

11 (The LORD God of your fathers make you a thousand times so many more as you *are*, and bless you, as He has promised you!) Jehovah s.f. Elohim p.f.

12 How can I myself alone bear your cumbrance, and your burden, and your strife? endure - problems

13 Take you wise men, and understanding, and known among your tribes, and I will make them rulers over you. chiefs

14 And you answered me, and said, The thing which you have spoken is good *for us* to do. purpose

15 So I took the chief of your tribes, wise men, and known, and made them heads over you, captains over thousands, and captains over hundreds, and captains over fifties, and captains over tens, and officers among your tribes. appointed

16 And I <u>charged</u> your judges at that time, saying, Hear *the* <u>causes</u> between your brethren, and judge righteously between *every* man and his brother, and the stranger *that is* with him. instructed - problems

17 You shall not respect persons in judgment; *but* you shall hear the small as well as the great; you shall not be afraid of the face of man; for the judgment *is* <u>God's</u>: and the <u>cause</u> that is too hard for you, bring *it* to me, and I will hear it. Elohim^{p.f.} - case

18 And I commanded you at that time all the things which you should do.

19 And when we departed from Ho'reb, we went through all that great and terrible wilderness, which you saw by the way of the mountain of the Am'or-ites, as the LORD our God commanded us; and we came to Ka'desh-bar'ne-a.

20 And I said to you, You are come to the mountain of the Am'or-ites, which the LORD our <u>God</u> does give to us.

21 Behold, the LORD your <u>God</u> has set the land before you: go up *and* possess *it*, as the <u>LORD God</u> of your fathers has said to you; fear not, neither be discouraged. Jehovah^{s.f.} Elohim^{p.f.}

22 And you came near to me every one of you, and said, We will send men before us, and they shall <u>search</u> us out the land, and bring us word again by what way we must go up, and into what cities we shall come. spy

23 And the saying pleased me well: and I took twelve men of you, one of a tribe:

24 And they turned and went up into the mountain, and came to the valley of Esh'col, and searched it out.

25 And they took of the fruit of the land in their hands, and brought *it* down to us, and brought us word again, and said, *It is* a good land which the LORD our <u>God</u> does give us. Elohim^{p.f.}

26 Notwithstanding you would not go up, but rebelled against the commandment of the LORD your <u>God</u>:

27 And you <u>murmured</u> in your tents, and said, Because the LORD <u>hated</u> us, He has brought us forth out of the land of E'gypt, to deliver us into the hand of the Am'or-ites, to destroy us. grumbled - abhored

28 Where shall we go up? our brethren have discouraged our heart, saying, The people *is* greater and taller than we; the cities *are* great and walled up to heaven; and moreover we have seen the sons of the An'akims there.

29 Then I said to you, Dread not, neither be afraid of them.

30 The LORD your <u>God</u> which goes before you, He shall fight for you, according to all that He did for you in E'gypt before your eyes;

31 And in the wilderness, where you have seen how that the LORD your <u>God</u> bare you, as a man does bear his son, in all the way that you went, until you came into this place.

32 Yet in this <u>thing</u> you did not believe the LORD your <u>God</u>, matter - Elohim^{p.f.}

33 Who went in the way before you, to search you out a place to pitch your tents *in*, in fire by night, to show you by

what way you should go, and in a cloud by day.

34 And the LORD heard the voice of your words, and was angry, and swear, saying,   *i.e., sound - promised*

35 Surely there shall not one of these men of this evil generation see that good land, which I swear to give to your fathers,

36 Save Ca'leb the son of Je-phun'neh; he shall see it, and to him will I give the land that he has trodden upon, and to his children, because he has wholly followed the LORD.   *set foot - fully obeyed*

37 Also the LORD was angry with me for your sakes, saying, You also shall not go in there.

38 *But* Josh'u-a the son of Nun, which stands before you, he shall go in there: encourage him: for he shall cause Is'ra-el to inherit it.

39 Moreover your little ones, which you said should be a prey, and your children, which in that day had no knowledge between good and evil, they shall go in there, and to them will I give it, and they shall possess it.   *would be taken captive*

40 But *as for* you, turn you, and take your journey into the wilderness by the way of the Red Sea.

41 Then you answered and said to me, We have sinned against the LORD, we will go up and fight, according to all that the LORD our God commanded us. And when you had girded on every man his weapons of war, you were ready to go up into the hill.   *Elohim*p.f.

42 And the LORD said to me, Say to them, Go not up, neither fight; for I *am* not among you; less you be smitten before your enemies.   *defeated*

43 So I spoke to you; and you would not hear, but rebelled against the commandment of the LORD, and went presumptuously up into the hill.   *arrogantly*

44 And the Am'or-ites, which dwelled in that mountain, came out against you, and chased you, as bees do, and destroyed you in Se'ir, *even* to Hor'mah.

45 And you returned and wept before the LORD; but the LORD would not hearken to your voice, nor give ear to you.

46 So you abode in Ka'desh many days, according to the days that you abode *there*.

CHAPTER 2

THEN we turned, and took our journey into the wilderness by the way of the Red sea, as the LORD spoke to me: and we compassed mount Se'ir many days.   *went around*

2 And the LORD spoke to me, saying,

3 You have compassed this mountain long enough: turn you northward.   *gone arouond*

4 And command you the people, saying, You *are* to pass through the coast of your brethren the children of E'sau, which dwell in Se'ir; and they shall be afraid of you: take you good heed to yourselves therefore: *be cautious*

5 Meddle not with them; for I will not give you of their land, no, not so much as a foot breadth; because I have given

mount Se'ir to E'sau *for* a possession.   provoke
6 You shall buy <u>meat</u> of them for
money, that you may eat; and you
shall also buy water of them for
money, that you may drink.   food
7 For the LORD your <u>God</u> has blessed
you in all the works of your hand:
He knows your walking through this
great wilderness: these forty years
the LORD your <u>God</u> *has been* with
you; you have lacked nothing. Elohim P.f.
8 And when we passed by from our
brethren the children of E'sau, which
dwelt in Se'ir, through the way of
the plain from E'lath, and from E'zi-
on-ga'ber, we turned and passed by
the way of the wilderness of Mo'ab.
9 And the LORD said to me, <u>Distress</u>
not the Mo'ab-ites, neither contend
with them in battle: for I will not give
you of their land *for* a possession; because I have given Ar to the children
of Lot *for* a possession.   Harass
10 The E'mims dwelled therein in
times past, a people great, and
many, and tall, as the An'a-kims;
11 Which also were accounted giants, as the An'a-kims; but the
Mo'ab-ites call them E'mims.
12 The Ho'rims also dwelled in Se'ir
beforetime; but the children of E'sau
succeeded them, when they had destroyed them from before them, and
dwelled in their stead; as Is'ra-el did
to the land of his possession, which
the LORD gave to them.
13 Now rise up, said I, and get you
over the <u>brook</u> Ze'red. And we went
over the <u>brook</u> Ze'red.   valley

14 And the space in which we came
from Ka'desh-bar'ne-a, until we were
come over the <u>brook</u> Ze'red, *was*
thirty and eight years; until all the generation of the men of war were <u>wasted
out</u> from among the <u>host</u>, as the LORD
swear to them.   valley - perished - camp
15 For indeed the hand of the LORD
was against them, to destroy them
from among the host, until they were
consumed.
16 So it came to pass, when all the
men of war were consumed and dead
from among the people,
17 That the LORD spoke to me, saying,
18 You are to pass over through Ar,
the <u>coast</u> of Mo'ab, this day: border
19 And *when* you come near oppo-
site the children of Am'mon, distress
them not, nor meddle with them: for
I will not give you of the land of the
children of Am'mon *any* possession;
because I have given it to the children of Lot *for* a possession.
20 (That also was accounted a land
of giants: giants dwelled therein in
<u>old time</u>; and the Am'mon-ites call
them Zam-zum'mims;   formerly
21 A people great, and many, and
tall, as the An'a-kims; but the LORD
destroyed them before them; and
they succeeded them, and dwelled
in their stead:
22 As He did to the children of E'sau,
which dwelled in Se'ir, when He destroyed the Ho'rims from before
them; and they succeeded them, and
dwelled in their stead even to this day:
23 And the A'vims which dwelled in

Ha-ze'rim, *even* to Az'zah, the Caph'to-rims, which came forth out of Caph'tor, destroyed them, and dwelled in their stead.)   Gaza

24 Rise you up, take your journey, and pass over the river Ar'non: behold, I have given into your hand Si'hon the Am'or-ite, king of Hesh'bon, and his land: begin to possess *it*, and contend with him in battle.

25 This day will I begin to put the dread of you and the fear of you upon the nations *that are* under the whole heaven, who shall hear report of you, and shall tremble, and be in anguish because of you.

26 And I sent messengers out of the wilderness of Ked'e-moth to Si'hon king of Hesh'bon with words of peace, saying,

27 Let me pass through your land: I will go along by the high way, I will neither turn to the right hand nor to the left.

28 You shall sell me meat for money, that I may eat; and give me water for money, that I may drink: only I will pass through on my feet;

29 (As the children of E'sau which dwell in Se'ir, and the Mo'ab-ites which dwell in Ar, did to me;) until I shall pass over Jor'dan into the land which the LORD our God gives us.

30 But Si'hon king of Hesh'bon would not let us pass by him: for the LORD your God hardened his spirit, and made his heart obstinate, that He might deliver him into your hand, as *appears* this day.   Elohim^p.f.

31 And the LORD said to me, Be-hold, I have begun to give Si'hon and his land before you: begin to possess, that you may inherit his land.

32 Then Si'hon came out against us, he and all his people, to fight at Ja'haz.

33 And the LORD our God deliv-ered him before us; and we smote him, and his sons, and all his people.   Elohim^p.f. - gave us victory over - struck

34 And we took all his cities at that time, and utterly destroyed the men, and the women, and the little ones, of every city, we left none to remain:

35 Only the cattle we took for a prey to ourselves, and the spoil of the cities which we took.   as booty

36 From Ar'o-er, which *is* by the brink of the river of Ar'non, and *from* the city that *is* by the river, even to Gil'e-ad, there was not one city too strong for us: the LORD our God de-livered all to us:

37 Only to the land of the children of Am'mon you came not, *nor* to any place of the river Jab'bok, nor to the cities in the mountains, nor to whatsoever the LORD our God for-bad us.   Elohim^p.f.

CHAPTER 3

THEN turned, and went up the way to Ba'shan: and Og the king of Ba'shan came out against us, he and all his people, to battle at Ed're-i.

2 And the LORD said to me, Fear him not: for I will deliver him, and all his people, and his land, into your hand; and you shall do to him as you

did to Si'hon king of the Am'or-ites, which dwelled at Hesh'bon.

3 So the LORD our <u>God</u> delivered into our hands Og also, the king of Ba'shan, and all his people: and we <u>smote</u> him until none was left to him remaining. Elohim^{p.f.} - destroyed

4 And we took all his cities at that time, there was not a city which we took not from them, threescore cities, all the region of Ar'gob, the kingdom of Og in Ba'shan.

5 All these cities *were* <u>fenced</u> with high walls, gates, and bars; beside <u>unwalled</u> towns a great many. fortified - rural

6 And we utterly destroyed them, as we did to Si'hon king of Hesh'bon, utterly destroying the men, women, and children, of every city.

7 But all the cattle, and the spoil of the cities, we took for a prey to ourselves.

8 And we took at that time out of the hand of the two kings of the Am'or-ites the land that *was* on this side Jor'dan, from the river of Ar'non unto mount Her'mon;

9 (*Which* Her'mon the Si-do'ni-ans call Sir'i-on; and the Am'or-ites call it She'nir;)

10 All the cities of the plain, and all Gil'e-ad, and all Ba'shan, to Sal'chah and Ed're-i, cities of the kingdom of Og in Ba'shan.

11 For only Og king of Ba'shan remained of the remnant of giants; behold, his bedstead *was* a bedstead of iron; *is* it not in Rab'bath of the children of Am'mon? nine cubits *was* the length thereof, and four cubits the breadth of it, after the cubit of a man.

12 And this land, *which* we possessed at that time, from Ar'o-er, which *is* by the river Ar'non, and half mount Gil'e-ad, and the cities thereof, gave I to the Reu'ben-ites and to the Gad'ites.

13 And the rest of Gil'e-ad, and all Ba'shan, *being* the kingdom of Og, gave I to the half tribe of Ma-nas'seh; all the region of Ar'gob, with all Ba'shan, which was called the land of giants.

14 Ja'ir the son of Ma-nas'seh took all the country of Ar'gob to the coasts of Gesh'u-ri and Ma-ach'a-thi; and called them after his own name, Ba'shan-ha'voth-ja'ir, to this day.

15 And I gave Gil'e-ad to Ma'chir.

16 And to the Reu'ben-ites and to the Gad'ites I gave from Gil'e-ad even to the river Ar'non half the valley, and the border even to the river Jab'bok, *which is* the border of the children of Am'mon;

17 The plain also, and Jor'dan, and the coast *thereof*, from Chin'ne-reth even to the sea of the plain, *even* the <u>Salt</u> sea, under Ash'doth-pis'gah eastward. Dead

18 And I commanded you at that time, saying, The LORD your <u>God</u> has given you this land to possess it: you shall pass over armed before your brethren the children of Is'ra-el, all *that are* <u>meet</u> for the war. Elohim^{p.f.} - able-bodied

19 But your wives, and your little ones, and your cattle, (*for* I know that you have much cattle,) shall abide in your cities which I have given you;

20 Until the LORD have given rest to your brethren, as well as to you,

and *until* they also possess the land which the LORD your God has given them beyond Jor'dan: and *then* shall you return every man to his possession, which I have given you. Elohim[p.f.]

21 And I commanded Josh'u-a at that time, saying, Your eyes have seen all that the LORD your God has done to these two kings: so shall the LORD do to all the kingdoms where you pass.

22 You shall not fear them: for the LORD your God He shall fight for you.

23 And I besought the LORD at that time, saying,

24 O Lord GOD, You have begun to show Your servant Your greatness, and Your mighty hand: for what God *is there* in heaven or in earth, that can do according to Your works, and according to Your might? Adonay[p.f.] Jevovah[s.f.]

25 I pray You, let me go over, and see the good land that *is* beyond Jor'dan, that goodly mountain, and Leb'a-non.

26 But the LORD was angry with me for your sakes, and would not hear me: and the LORD said to me, Let it suffice you; speak no more to Me of this matter.

27 Get you up into the top of Pis'gah, and lift up your eyes westward, and northward, and southward, and eastward, and behold *it* with your eyes: for you shall not go over this Jor'dan.

28 But charge Josh'u-a, and encourage him, and strengthen him: for he shall go over before this people, and he shall cause them to inherit the land which you shall see. commission

29 So we abode in the valley over against Beth-pe'or.

CHAPTER 4

NOW therefore hearken, O Is'ra-el, to the statutes and to the judgments, which I teach you, for to do *them*, that you may live, and go in and possess the land which the LORD God of your fathers gives you. decrees - live in - Jehovah[s.f.] Elohim[p.f.]

2 You shall not add to the word which I command you, neither shall you diminish *anything* from it, that you may keep the commandments of the LORD your God which I command you. take away - obey - Elohim[p.f.]

3 Your eyes have seen what the LORD did because of Ba-al-pe'or: for all the men that followed Ba-al-pe'or, the LORD your God has destroyed them from among you.

4 But you that did cling to the LORD your God *are* alive every one of you this day. held fast

5 Behold, I have taught you statutes and judgments, even as the LORD my God commanded me, that you should do so in the land where you go to possess it. laws - Elohim[p.f.]

6 Keep therefore and do *them*; for this *is* your wisdom and your understanding in the sight of the nations, which shall hear all these statutes, and say, Surely this great nation *is* a wise and understanding people.

7 For what nation *is there so* great, who *has* God *so* near to them, as the LORD our God *is* in all *things that* we call upon him for? Elohim[p.f.]

8 And what nation *is there so* great, that has <u>statutes</u> and <u>judgments</u> *so* righteous as all this law, which I set before you this day?   decrees - laws

9 Only <u>take heed</u> to yourself, and <u>keep your soul</u> diligently, less you forget the things which your eyes have seen, and less they depart from your heart all the days of your life: but teach them your sons, and your sons' sons;   be careful - watch yourselves

M03 10 *Specially* the day that you stood before the LORD your God in Ho'reb, when the LORD said to me, Gather Me the people together, and I will make them hear My words, that they may learn to <u>fear</u> Me all the days that they shall live upon the earth, and *that* they 290 may teach their children.   reverence

11 And you came near and stood under the mountain; and the mountain burned with fire to the midst of heaven, with darkness, clouds, and thick darkness.

12 And the LORD spoke to you out of the midst of the fire: you heard the voice of the words, but saw no <u>similitude</u>; only *you heard* a voice.   form

13 And He declared to you His <u>covenant</u>, which He commanded you to perform, *even* ten commandments; and He wrote them upon two tables of stone.   agreement

P03 14 And the LORD commanded me at that time to teach you <u>statutes</u> and <u>judgments</u>, that you might <u>do</u> them in the land where you go over 295 to <u>possess</u> it.   perform - live in

15 Take you therefore good heed to yourselves; for you saw no manner of si-militude on the day *that* the LORD spoke to you in Ho'reb out of the midst of the fire: form

16 Less you corrupt *yourselves*, and make you a graven image, the <u>similitude</u> of any figure, the likeness of male or female,

17 The likeness of any beast that *is* on the earth, the likeness of any winged fowl that flys in the air,

18 The likeness of any thing that creeps on the ground, the likeness of any fish that *is* in the waters beneath the earth:

19 And less you lift up your eyes to heaven, and when you see the sun, and the moon, and the stars, *even* all the host of heaven, should be driven to worship them, and serve them, which the LORD your <u>God</u> has <u>divided</u> to all nations under the whole heaven.   Elohim^p.f. - allotted

20 But the LORD has taken you, and brought you forth out of the iron furnace, *even* out of E'gypt, to be to Him a people of inheritance, as *you are* this day.

21 Furthermore the LORD was angry GI with me for your sakes, and swear that I should not go over Jor'dan, and that I should not go in to that good land, which the LORD your <u>God</u> gives you *for* an inheritance: 290

22 But I must die in this land, I must not go over Jor'dan: but you shall go over, and <u>possess</u> that good land.   live in

23 Take heed to yourselves, less you P02 forget the <u>covenant</u> of the LORD your God, which He made with you, and

make you a graven image, *or* the likeness of any *thing*, which the LORD your God has forbidden you. agreement

24 For the LORD your God *is* a consuming fire, *even* a jealous God. HEB. 12:29 Jehovah$^{s.f.}$ - Elohim$^{p.f.}$ - destroying - El$^{s.f.}$

25 When you shall father children, and children's children, and you shall have remained long in the land, and shall corrupt *yourselves*, and make a graven image, *or* the likeness of any *thing*, and shall do evil in the sight of the LORD your God, to provoke Him to anger: Elohim$^{p.f.}$

26 I call heaven and earth to witness against you this day, that you shall soon utterly perish from off the land whereto you go over Jor'dan to possess it; you shall not prolong *your* days upon it, but shall utterly be destroyed. extend

27 And the LORD shall scatter you among the nations, and you shall be left few in number among the heathen, where the LORD shall lead you. people

28 And there you shall serve gods, the work of men's hands, wood and stone, which neither see, nor hear, nor eat, nor smell.

29 But if from there you shall seek the LORD your God, you shall find *Him*, if you seek Him with all your heart and with all your soul.

30 When you are in tribulation, and all these things are come upon you, *even* in the latter days, if you turn to the LORD your God, and shall be obedient to His voice; distress - future - Elohim$^{p.f.}$

31 (For the LORD your God *is* a merciful God;) He will not forsake you, neither destroy you, nor forget the covenant of your fathers which He sware to them. Jehovah$^{s.f.}$ - Elohim$^{p.f.}$ - El$^{s.f.}$ - agreement

32 For ask now of the days that are past, which were before you, since the day that God created man upon the earth, and *ask* from the one side of heaven to the other, whether there has been *any such thing* as this great thing is, or has been heard like it?

33 Did *ever* people hear the voice of God speaking out of the midst of the fire, as you have heard, and live?

34 Or has God assayed to go *and* take Him a nation from the midst of *another* nation, by temptations, by signs, and by wonders, and by war, and by a mighty hand, and by a stretched out arm, and by great terrors, according to all that the LORD your God did for you in E'gypt before your eyes? ever tried - trials - awesome deeds

35 To you it was showed, that you might know that the LORD He *is* God; *there is* none else beside Him.

36 Out of heaven He made you to hear His voice, that He might instruct you: and upon earth He showed you His great fire; and you heard His words out of the midst of the fire.

37 And because He loved your fathers, therefore He chose their seed after them, and brought you out in His sight with His mighty power out of E'gypt; descendants - by His presence

38 To drive out nations from before you greater and mightier than you *are*, to bring you in, to give you their land *for* an inheritance, *as it is* this day.

39 Know therefore this day, and con-

sider *it* in your heart, that the Lord He *is* God in heaven above, and upon the earth beneath: *there is* none else. Elohim^{p.f.}

40 You shall keep therefore His statutes, and His commandments, which I command you this day, that it may go well with you, and with your children after you, and that you may <u>prolong *your* days</u> upon the earth, which the Lord your God gives you, for ever. live long

41 Then Mo'ses severed three cities on this side Jor'dan toward the sunrising;

42 That the <u>slayer</u> might flee there, which should kill his neighbor <u>unawares</u>, and <u>hated him not</u> in times past; and that fleeing to one of these cities he might live:

manslayer - accidentally - without malice

43 *Namely*, Be'zer in the wilderness, in the plain country, of the Reu'benites; and Ra'moth in Gil'e-ad, of the Gad'ites; and Go'lan in Ba'shan, of the Ma-nas'sites.

44 And this *is* the law which Mo'ses set before the children of Is'ra-el:

45 These *are* the testimonies, and the <u>statutes</u>, and the <u>judgments</u>, which Mo'ses spoke to the children of Is'ra-el, after they came forth out of E'gypt, decrees - laws

46 On this side Jor'dan, in the valley over against Beth-pe'or, in the land of Si'hon king of the Am'orites, who dwelled at Hesh'bon, whom Mo'ses and the children of Is'ra-el <u>smote</u>, after they were come forth out of E'gypt: defeated

47 And they possessed his land, and the land of Og king of Ba'shan, two kings of the Am'or-ites, which *were* on this side Jor'dan toward the <u>sunrising</u>; east

48 From Ar'o-er, which *is* by the bank of the river Ar'non, even to mount Zi'on, which *is* Her'mon,

49 And all the plain on this side Jor'dan eastward, even to the sea of the plain, under the springs of Pis'gah.

CHAPTER 5

AND Mo'ses called all Is'ra-el, and said to them, Hear, O Is'ra-el, the <u>statutes</u> and <u>judgments</u> which I speak in your ears this day, that you may learn them, and <u>keep</u>, and do them. decrees - laws - follow

2 The Lord our God made a <u>covenant</u> with us in Ho'reb. Elohim^{p.f.} - agreement

3 The Lord made not this <u>covenant</u> with our fathers, but with us, *even* us, who *are* all of us here alive this day.

4 The Lord talked with you face to face in the mount out of the midst of the fire,

5 (I stood between the Lord and you at that time, to <u>show</u> you the word of the Lord: for you were afraid by reason of the fire, and went not up into the mount;) saying, declare to

6 I *am* the Lord your God, which brought you out of the land of E'gypt, from the house of <u>bondage</u>. slavery

7 You shall have none other gods before Me.

8 You shall not make you *any* graven image, *or* any likeness *of any thing* that *is* in heaven above, or that *is* in the earth beneath, or that is in the waters beneath the earth:

9 You shall not <u>bow down</u> yourself to them, nor serve them: for I the LORD your <u>God</u> *am* a jealous <u>God</u>, visiting the iniquity of the fathers upon the children to the third and fourth <u>generation</u> of them that <u>hate</u> Me,   worship - Jehovah^s.f. - Elohim^p.f. - El^s.f. - abhor
10 And showing mercy to thousands of them that love Me and <u>keep</u> My commandments.   obey
11 You shall not take the name of the LORD your <u>God</u> in vain: for the LORD will not hold *him* <u>guiltless</u> that takes His name in vain.   innocent
12 Keep the <u>sabbath</u> day to <u>sanctify it</u>, as the LORD your <u>God</u> has commanded you.   rest day - set it apart
13 Six days you shall labor, and do all your work:
14 But the seventh day *is* the <u>sabbath</u> of the LORD your <u>God</u>: *in it* you shall not do any work, you, nor your son, nor your daughter, nor your manservant, nor your maidservant, nor your ox, nor your ass, nor any of your cattle, nor your stranger that *is* inside your gates; that your manservant and your maidservant may rest as well as you.   rest day
15 And remember that you were a servant in the land of E'gypt, and *that* the LORD your <u>God</u> brought you out from there through a <u>mighty</u> hand and by a stretched out arm: therefore the LORD your <u>God</u> commanded you to <u>keep</u> the <u>sabbath</u> day.   Elohim^p.f. - powerful - rest
16 Honor your father and your mother, as the LORD your <u>God</u> has commanded you; that your days may be prolonged, and that it may go well with you, in the land which the LORD your <u>God</u> gives you.

        MARK 10:19 EPH. 6:3 Elohim^p.f.
17 You shall not kill.   MATT. 5:21
18 Neither shall you commit adultery.   MATT 5:27
19 Neither shall you steal.
20 Neither shall you bear false witness against your neighbor.
21 Neither shall you desire your neighbor's wife, neither shall you <u>covet</u> your neighbor's house, his field, or his manservant, or his maidservant, his ox, or his ass, or any *thing* that *is* your neighbor's.   ROM. 7:7 desire
22 These words the LORD spoke to all your assembly in the mount out of the midst of the fire, of the cloud, and of the thick darkness, with a great voice: and He added no more. And He wrote them in two tables of stone, and delivered them to me.
23 And it came to pass, when you heard the voice out of the midst of the darkness, (for the mountain did burn with fire,) that you came near to me, even all the heads of your tribes, and your elders;
24 And you said, Behold, the LORD our <u>God</u> has showed us His glory and His greatness, and we have heard His voice out of the midst of the fire: we have seen this day that God does talk with man, and He lives.   Elohim^p.f.
25 Now therefore why should we die? for this great fire will <u>consume</u> us: if we hear the voice of the LORD our <u>God</u> any more, then we shall die.   destroy
26 For who *is there of* all flesh, that has heard the voice of the living <u>God</u>

speaking out of the midst of the fire, as we *have*, and lived?

27 Go you near, and hear all that the LORD our God shall say: and speak you to us all that the LORD our God shall speak to you; and we will hear *it*, and do *it*.   Elohim^{p.f.}

28 And the LORD heard the voice of your words, when you spoke to me; and the LORD said to me, I have heard the voice of the words of this people, which they have spoken to you: they have well said all that they have spoken.

29 O that there were such an heart in them, that they would fear Me, and keep all My commandments always, that it might be well with them, and with their children for ever!   reverence - obey

30 Go say to them, Get you into your tents again.

31 But as for you, stand you here by Me, and I will speak to you all the commandments, and the statutes, and the judgments, which you shall teach them, that they may do *them* in the land which I give them to possess it.

32 You shall observe to do therefore as the LORD your God has commanded you: you shall not turn aside to the right hand or to the left.   Elohim^{p.f.}

33 You shall walk in all the ways which the LORD your God has commanded you, that you may live, and *that it may be* well with you, and *that you* may prolong *your* days in the land which you shall possess.

CHAPTER 6

NOW these *are* the commandments, the statutes, and the judgments, which the LORD your God commanded to teach you, that you might do *them* in the land where you go to possess it: decrees - Elohim^{p.f.}

2 That you might fear the LORD your God, to keep all His statutes and His commandments, which I command you, you, and your son, and your son's son, all the days of your life; and that your days may be prolonged. honor - Elohim^{p.f.}

3 Hear therefore, O Is'ra-el, and observe to do *it*; that it may be well with you, and that you may increase mightily, as the LORD God of your fathers has promised you, in the land that flows with milk and honey.   be careful - multiply greatly

4 Hear, O Is'ra-el: The LORD our God *is* one LORD:

   MARK 12:29 1 COR. 8:4 Jehovah - Elohim^{p.f.} - Jehovah

5 And you shall love the LORD your God with all your heart, and with all your soul, and with all your might.   MATT. 22:37 LUKE 10:25

6 And these words, which I command you this day, shall be in your heart:

7 And you shall teach them diligently to your children, and shall talk of them when you sit in your house, and when you walk by the way, and when you lay down, and when you rise up.   impress on

8 And you shall bind them for a sign upon your hand, and they shall be as frontlets between your eyes.

9 And you shall write them upon the posts of your house, and on your gates.

10 And it shall be, when the LORD your

God shall have brought you into the land which He swear to your fathers, to A'bra-ham, to I'saac, and to Ja'cob, to give you great and goodly cities, which you builded not, Elohim^{p.f.} - promised

11 And houses full of all good *things*, which you filled not, and wells dug, which you dug not, vineyards and olive trees, which you planted not; when you shall have eaten and be full;

12 *Then* beware less you forget the LORD, which brought you forth out of the land of E'gypt, from the house of bondage.

13 You shall fear the LORD your God, and serve Him, and shall swear by His name. MATT. 4:10 LUKE 4:8 reverence

14 You shall not go after other gods, of the gods of the people which *are* round about you; 2 COR. 6:14

15 (For the LORD your God *is* a jealous God among you) less the anger of the LORD your God be kindled against you, and destroy you from off the face of the earth. Jehovah - Elohim^{p.f.} - El^{s.f.}

16 You shall not tempt the LORD your God, as you tempted *Him* in Mas'sah. MATT. 4:7 LUKE 4:12 test

17 You shall diligently keep the commandments of the LORD your God, and His testimonies, and His statutes, which He has commanded you. obey

18 And you shall do *that which is* right and good in the sight of the LORD: that it may be well with you, and that you may go in and possess the good land which the LORD swear to your fathers,

19 To cast out all your enemies from before you, as the LORD has spoken.

20 *And* when your son asks you in time to come, saying, What *mean* the testimonies, and the statutes, and the judgments, which the LORD our God has commanded you? decrees

21 Then you shall say to your son, We were Pha'raoh's bondmen in E'-gypt; and the LORD brought us out of E'gypt with a mighty hand: slaves - powerful

22 And the LORD showed signs and wonders, great and sore, upon E'gypt, upon Pha'raoh, and upon all his household, before our eyes: terrible

23 And He brought us out from there, that He might bring us in, to give us the land which He swear to our fathers.

24 And the LORD commanded us to do all these statutes, to fear the LORD our God, for our good always, that He might preserve us alive, as *it is* at this day. decrees - reverence - Elohim^{p.f.}

25 And it shall be our righteousness, if we observe to do all these commandments before the LORD our God, as He has commanded us. are careful to obey

CHAPTER 7

WHEN the LORD your God shall bring you into the land where you go to possess it, and has cast out many nations before you, the Hit'-tites, and the Gir'ga-shites, and the Am'or-ites, and the Ca'naan-ites, and the Per'iz-zites, and the Hi'vites, and the Jeb'u-sites, seven nations greater and mightier than you; Elohim^{p.f.}

2 And when the LORD your God shall

deliver them before you; you shall smite them, *and* utterly destroy them; you shall make no <u>covenant</u> with them, nor show mercy to them: Elohim[p.f.] - agreement

3 Neither shall you make marriages with them; your daughter you shall not give to his son, nor his daughter shall you take to your son.   2 COR. 6:14

4 For they will turn away your son from following Me, that they may serve other gods: so will the anger of the LORD be kindled against you, and destroy you suddenly.   1 COR. 10:6

5 But thus shall you deal with them; you shall destroy their altars, and break down their images, and cut down their groves, and burn their graven images with fire.

6 For you *are* an holy people to the LORD your <u>God</u>: the LORD your <u>God</u> has chosen you to be a <u>special people</u> to Himself, <u>above</u> all people that *are* upon the face of the earth.   special treasure - out of

7 The LORD did not set His love upon you, nor choose you, because you were more in number than any people; for you *were* the fewest of all people:

8 But because the LORD loved you, and because He would keep the <u>oath</u> which He had sworn to your fathers, has the LORD brought you out with a mighty hand, and re-deemed you out of the house of <u>bondmen</u>, from the hand of Pha'-raoh king of E'gypt.   promise - slavery

9 Know therefore that the <u>LORD</u> your <u>God</u>, He *is* <u>God</u>, the faithful <u>God</u>, which keeps <u>covenant</u> and mercy with them that love Him and keep His commandments to a thousand gen-erations;   Jehovah - Elohim[p.f.] - Elohim[p.f.] - agreement

10 And repays them that <u>hate</u> Him to their face, to destroy them: He will not be <u>slack</u> to him that <u>hates</u> Him, He will repay him to his face.   abhor - slow

11 You shall therefore keep the com-mandments, and the <u>statutes</u>, and the judgments, which I command you this day, to do them.   decrees

12 Wherefore it shall come to pass, if you hearken to these judgments, and keep, and do them, that the LORD your <u>God</u> shall keep to you the <u>cov-enant</u> and the mercy which He swear to your fathers: Elohim[p.f.] - agreement

13 And He will love you, and bless you, and multiply you: He will also bless the <u>fruit</u> of your womb, and the <u>fruit</u> of your land, your <u>corn</u>, and your wine, and your oil, the increase of your <u>kine</u>, and the flocks of your sheep, in the land which He <u>swear</u> to your fathers to give you.   children - crops - grain - cattle - promised

14 You shall be blessed above all people: there shall not be male or female barren among you, or among your cattle.

15 And the LORD will take away from you all sickness, and will put none of the <u>evil</u> diseases of E'gypt, which you know, upon you; but will lay them upon all *them* that <u>hate</u> you.   horrible - dislike

16 And you shall <u>consume</u> all the people which the LORD your <u>God</u> shall deliver you; your eye shall have no pity upon them: neither shall you serve their gods; for that *will be* a <u>snare</u> to you.   destroy - lure

17 If you shall say in your heart,

These nations *are* <u>more</u> than I; how can I <u>dispossess them</u>?_{stronger - drive them out}

18 You shall not be afraid of them: *but* shall well remember what the Lord your <u>God</u> did to Pha'roah, and to all E'gypt; _{Elohim^{p.f.}}

19 The great <u>temptations</u> which your eyes saw, and the signs, and the wonders, and <u>the mighty hand,</u> <u>and the stretched out arm</u>, whereby the Lord your <u>God</u> brought you out: so shall the Lord your <u>God</u> do to all the people of whom you are afraid. _{testing - power}

20 Moreover the Lord your <u>God</u> will <u>send the hornet among them</u>, until they that are left, and hide themselves from you, be destroyed._{cause to be put to flight}

21 You shall not be affrighted at them: for the Lord your <u>God</u> *is* among you, a mighty <u>God</u> and <u>terrible</u>. _{Elohim^{p.f.} - El^{s.f.} - awe inspiring}

22 And the Lord your <u>God</u> will put out those nations before you by little and little: you may not <u>consume</u> them at once, less the beasts of the field increase upon you. _{eliminate}

23 But the Lord your <u>God</u> shall deliver them to you, and shall destroy them with a mighty destruction, until they be destroyed. _{Elohim^{p.f.}}

24 And He shall deliver their kings into your hand, and you shall destroy their name from under heaven: there shall no man be able to stand before you, until you have destroyed them.

25 The <u>graven images</u> of their gods shall you burn with fire: you shall not <u>desire</u> the silver or gold *that is* on them, nor take *it* to you, less you be <u>snared</u> therein: for it *is* an <u>abomination</u> to the Lord your <u>God</u>.

_{idols - covet - trapped - detestable - Elohim^{p.f.}}

26 Neither shall you bring an <u>abomination</u> into your house, less you be <u>a cursed thing</u> like it: *but* you shall utterly detest it, and you shall utterly abhor it; for it *is* a <u>cursed thing</u>.

_{evil - set apart for destruction}

CHAPTER 8

ALL the commandments which I command you this day shall you <u>observe</u> to do, that you may live, and multiply, and go in and possess the land which the Lord <u>swear</u> to your fathers. _{be careful - promised}

2 And you shall remember all the way which the Lord your <u>God</u> led you these forty years in the wilderness, to humble you, *and* to <u>prove</u> you, to <u>know</u> what *was* in your heart, whether you would keep His commandments, or no. _{Elohim^{p.f.} - test - learn}

3 And He humbled you, and allowed you to hunger, and fed you with manna, which you knew not, neither did your fathers know; that He might make you know that man does not live by bread only, but by every *word* that proceeds out of the mouth of the Lord does man live. _{MATT. 4:4 LUKE 4:3}

4 Your <u>raiment</u> waxed not old upon you, neither did your foot swell, these forty years. _{garment}

5 You shall also <u>consider</u> in your heart, that, as a man chastens his son, *so* the Lord your <u>God</u> chastens you. _{remember - Elohim^{p.f.}}

6 Therefore you shall keep the com-

mandments of the Lord your <u>God</u>, to walk in His ways, and to <u>fear</u> Him.   Elohim^{p.f.} - reverence

7 For the Lord your <u>God</u> brings you into a good land, a land of brooks of water, of fountains and depths that spring out of valleys and hills;

8 A land of wheat, and barley, and vines, and fig trees, and pomegranates; a land of oil olive, and honey;

9 A land wherein you shall eat bread without scarceness, you shall not lack any *thing* in it; a land whose stones *are* iron, and out of whose hills you may dig <u>brass</u>.   copper

10 When you have eaten and are full, then you shall bless the Lord your God for the good land which He has given you.   Elohim^{p.f.}

11 Beware that you forget not the Lord your <u>God</u>, in not keeping His commandments, and His judgments, and His statutes, which I command you this day:

12 Less *when* you have eaten and are <u>full</u>, and have built goodly houses, and dwelled *therein*;   satisfied

13 And *when* your herds and your flocks multiply, and your silver and your gold is <u>multiplied</u>, and all that you have is <u>multiplied</u>;   increased

14 Then <u>your heart be lifted up</u>, and you forget the Lord your <u>God</u>, which brought you forth out of the land of E'gypt, from the house of bondage;   you become proud

15 Who led you through that great and terrible wilderness, *wherein were* fiery serpents, and scorpions, and drought, where *there was* no water;

Who brought you forth water out of the rock of flint;

16 Who fed you in the wilderness with manna, which your fathers knew not, that He might humble you, and that He might <u>prove</u> you, to do you good at your latter end;   test

17 And you say in <u>your heart</u>, My power and the might of *my* hand has gotten me this wealth.   to yourself

18 But you shall remember the Lord your <u>God</u>: for *it is* He that gives you power to get wealth, that He may <u>establish His covenant</u> which He swear to your fathers, as *it is* this day.   confirm His agreement

19 And it shall be, if you do at all forget the Lord your <u>God</u>, and walk after other gods, and serve them, and worship them, I testify against you this day that you shall surely perish.   Elohim^{p.f.}

20 As the nations which the Lord destroys before your face, so shall you perish; because you would not be obedient to the voice of the Lord your <u>God</u>.

CHAPTER 9

HEAR, O Is'ra-el: You *are* to pass over Jor'dan this day, to go in to possess nations greater and mightier than yourself, cities great and <u>fenced</u> up to heaven,   defended

2 A people great and tall, the children of the An'a-kims, whom you know, and *of whom* you have heard *say*, Who can stand before the children of A'nak!

3 Understand therefore this day, that the Lord your <u>God</u> *is* He which goes over before you; *as* a consuming fire

He shall destroy them, and He shall bring them down before your face: so shall you drive them out, and destroy them quickly, as the LORD has said to you. Elohim^p.f. - you

M03

4 Speak not you in your heart, after that the LORD your God has cast them out from before you, saying, For my righteousness the LORD has brought me in to possess this land: but for the wickedness of these nations the LORD does drive them out from before you. evil

5 Not for your righteousness, or for the uprightness of your heart, do you go to possess their land: but for the wickedness of these nations the LORD your God does drive them out from before you, and that He may perform the word which the LORD swear to your fathers, A'bra-ham, I'saac, and Ja'cob. accomplish His promise

6 Understand therefore, that the LORD your God gives you not this good land to possess it for your righteousness; for you *are* a stiffnecked people. stubborn

300 GI

7 Remember, *and* forget not, how you provoked the LORD your God to wrath in the wilderness: from the day that you did depart out of the land of E'gypt, until you came to this place, you have been rebellious against the LORD. irritated - disobedient

8 Also in Ho'reb you provoked the LORD to wrath, so that the LORD was angry with you to have destroyed you. anger

299

9 When I was gone up into the mount to receive the tables of stone, *even* the tables of the covenant which the LORD made with you, then I abode in the mount forty days and forty nights, I neither did eat bread nor drink water: LUKE 4:2 agreement - stayed

10 And the LORD delivered to me two tables of stone written with the finger of God; and on them *was written* according to all the words, which the LORD spoke with you in the mount out of the midst of the fire in the day of the assembly. Elohim^p.f.

11 And it came to pass at the end of forty days and forty nights, *that* the LORD gave me the two tables of stone, *even* the tables of the covenant. agreement

12 And the LORD said to me, Arise, get you down quickly from here; for your people which you have brought forth out of E'gypt have corrupted *themselves*; they are quickly turned aside out of the way which I commanded them; they have made them a molten image. done wrong

13 Furthermore the LORD spoke to me, saying, I have seen this people, and, behold, it *is* a stiffnecked people: stubborn

14 Let Me alone, that I may destroy them, and blot out their name from under heaven: and I will make of you a nation mightier and greater than they.

15 So I turned and came down from the mount, and the mount burned with fire: and the two tables of the covenant *were* in my two hands. agreement

16 And I looked, and, behold, you had sinned against the LORD your God, *and* had made you a molten calf: you had turned aside quickly out of the way which the LORD had commanded you. Elohim^p.f.

17 And I took the two tables, and cast them out of my two hands, and broke them before your eyes.

18 And I fell down before the LORD, as at the first, forty days and forty nights: I did neither eat bread, nor drink water, because of all your sins which you sinned, in doing wickedly in the sight of the LORD, to provoke Him to anger.   fasted

19 For I was afraid of the anger and hot displeasure, wherewith the LORD was angry against you to destroy you. But the LORD hearkened to me at that time also.   HEB. 12:21

20 And the LORD was very angry with Aar'on to have destroyed him: and I prayed for Aar'on also the same time.

21 And I took your sin, the calf which you had made, and burned it with fire, and stamped it, *and* ground *it* very small, *even* until it was as small as dust: and I cast the dust thereof into the brook that descended out of the mount.

22 And at Tab'e-rah, and at Mas'sah, and at Kib'roth-hat-ta'a-vah, you provoked the LORD to wrath.   irritated - anger

23 Likewise when the LORD sent you from Ka'desh-bar'ne-a, saying, Go up and possess the land which I have given you; then you rebelled against the commandment of the LORD your God, and you believed Him not, nor hearkened to His voice.   Elohim^p.f. - obeyed

24 You have been rebellious against the LORD from the day that I knew you.

25 Thus I fell down before the LORD forty days and forty nights, as I fell down *at the first*; because the LORD had said He would destroy you.

26 I prayed therefore to the LORD, and said, O Lord GOD, destroy not Your people and Your inheritance, which You have redeemed through Your greatness, which You have brought forth out of E'gypt with a mighty hand.

Adonay^p.f. Jehovah - What belongs to you - power - strength

27 Remember Your servants, A'braham, I'saac, and Ja'cob; look not to the stubbornness of this people, nor to their wickedness, nor to their sin:

28 Less the land where You brought us out say, Because the LORD was not able to bring them into the land which He promised them, and because He hated them, He has brought them out to slay them in the wilderness.   people

29 Yet they *are* Your people and Your inheritance, which You brought out by Your mighty power and by Your stretched out arm.

CHAPTER 10

AT that time the LORD said to me, Hew you two tables of stone like to the first, and come up to Me into the mount, and make you an ark of wood.   cut

2 And I will write on the tables the words that were in the first tables which you broke, and you shall put them in the ark.

3 And I made an ark *of* shittim wood, and hewed two tables of stone like to the first, and went up into the mount, having the two tables in my hand.

4 And He wrote on the tables, according to the first writing, the ten commandments, which the LORD spoke to

you in the mount out of the midst of the fire in the day of the assembly: and the LORD gave them to me. words

5 And I turned myself and came down from the mount, and put the tables in the ark which I had made; and there they be, as the LORD commanded me.

6 And the children of Is'ra-el took their journey from Be-e'roth of the children of Ja'a-kan to Mo-se'ra: there Aar'on died, and there he was buried; and E-le-a'zar his son ministered in the priest's office in his stead. place

7 From there they journeyed to Gud'go-dah; and from Gud'go-dah to Jot'bath, a land of rivers of waters.

8 At that time the LORD separated the tribe of Le'vi, to bear the ark of the covenant of the LORD, to stand before the LORD to minister to Him, and to bless in His name, to this day. set apart - agreement

9 Wherefore Le'vi has no part nor inheritance with his brethren; the LORD is his inheritance, according as the LORD your God promised him. Elohim^p.f.

10 And I stayed in the mount, according to the first time, forty days and forty nights; and the LORD hearkened to me at that time also, *and* the LORD would not destroy you.

11 And the LORD said to me, Arise, take *your* journey before the people, that they may go in and possess the land, which I swear to their fathers to give to them. proceed on

12 And now, Is'ra-el, what does the LORD your God require of you, but to fear the LORD your God, to walk in all His ways, and to love Him, and to serve the LORD your God with all your heart and with all your soul, Elohim^p.f. - reverence

13 To keep the commandments of the LORD, and His statutes, which I command you this day for your good? benefit

14 Behold, the heaven and the heaven of heavens *is* the LORD's your God, the earth *also*, with all that therein *is*.

15 Only the LORD had a delight in your fathers to love them, and He chose their seed after them, *even* you above all people, as *it is* this day. 1 PET. 2:9 set His affection on - descendants

16 Circumcise therefore the foreskin of your heart, and be no more stiffnecked. stubborn

17 For the LORD your God *is* God of gods, and Lord of lords, a great God, a mighty, and a terrible, which regards not persons, nor takes reward: ROM. 2:11 REV. 19:16 -

Jehovah - Elohim^p.f. - Elohim^p.f. - Adonay - El^s.f. - awe-inspiring

18 He does execute the judgment of the fatherless and widow, and loves the stranger, in giving him food and raiment. garment

19 Love you therefore the stranger: for you were strangers in the land of E'gypt.

20 You shall fear the LORD your God; him shall you serve, and to Him shall you cling, and swear by His name. revere - Elohim^p.f.

21 He *is* your praise, and He *is* your God, that has done for you these great and terrible things, which your eyes have seen.

22 Your fathers went down into E'gypt with threescore and ten persons; and now the LORD your God has made you as the stars of heaven for multitude. ACTS 7:14

CHAPTER 11

THEREFORE you shall love the LORD your <u>God</u>, and <u>keep His charge</u>, and His <u>statutes</u>, and His <u>judgments</u>, and his commandments, alway. obey His requirements - decrees

2 And know you this day: for *I speak* not with your children which have not known, and which have not seen the chastisement of the LORD your God, His greatness, His mighty hand, and His stretched out arm,

3 And His miracles, and His acts, which He did in the midst of E'gypt to Pha'raoh the king of E'gypt, and to all His land;

4 And what He did to the army of E'gypt, to their horses, and to their chariots; how He made the water of the Red sea to overflow them as they pursued after you, and *how* the LORD has destroyed them to this day;

5 And what He did to you in the wilderness, until you came into this place;

6 And what He did to Da'than and A-bi'rim, the sons of E-li'ab, the son of Reu'ben: how the earth <u>opened her mouth</u>, and swallowed them up, and their households, and their tents, and all the substance that *was* in their possession, in the midst of all Is'ra-el: split like a chasm

7 But your eyes have seen all the great acts of the LORD which He did.

8 Therefore shall you keep all the commandments which I command you this day, that you may be strong, and go in and possess the land, when you go to possess it;

9 And that you may prolong *your* days in the land, which the LORD sware to your fathers to give to them and to their seed, a land that flows with milk and honey.

10 For the land, where you go in to possess it, *is* not as the land of E'gypt, from where you came out, where you sowed your seed, and <u>watered *it* with your foot</u>, as a garden of herbs: i.e., treadmill

11 But the land, where you go to possess it, *is* a land of hills and valleys, *and* drinks water of the rain of heaven: received

12 A land which the LORD your <u>God cares</u> for: the eyes of the LORD your <u>God</u> *are* always upon it, from the beginning of the year even to the end of the year. provides - Elohim[p.f.]

13 And it shall come to pass, if you shall hearken diligently to my commandments which I command you this day, to love the LORD your <u>God</u>, and to serve Him with all your heart and with all your soul,

14 That I will give *you* the rain of your land in its due season, the first rain and the latter rain, that you may gather in your <u>corn</u>, and your wine, and your oil. grain

15 And I will send grass in your fields for your cattle, that you may eat and be <u>full</u>. satisfied

16 Take heed to yourselves, that your heart be not deceived, and you turn aside, and serve other gods, and worship them;

17 And *then* the LORD's <u>wrath be kindled</u> against you, and He <u>shut up</u> the

heaven, that there be no rain, and that the land yield not her fruit; and *less* you perish quickly from off the good land which the LORD gives you.   anger will burn - close - die

18 Therefore shall you lay up these my words in your heart and in your soul, and bind them for a sign upon your hand, that they may be as frontlets between your eyes.

19 And you shall teach them your children, speaking of them when you sit in your house, and when you walk by the way, when you lay down, and when you rise up.

20 And you shall write them upon the door posts of your house, and upon your gates: i.e., city gates

21 That your days may be multiplied, and the days of your children, in the land which the LORD swear to your fathers to give them, as the days of heaven upon the earth.   forever

22 For if you shall diligently keep all these commandments which I command you, to do them, to love the LORD your God, to walk in all His ways, and to cleave to Him;

Elohim^{p.f.} - hold fast

23 Then will the LORD drive out all these nations from before you, and you shall possess greater nations and mightier than yourselves.

24 Every place whereon the soles of your feet shall tread shall be yours: from the wilderness and Leb'a-non, from the river, the river Eu-phra'tes, even to the uttermost sea shall your coast be.   Mediterranean

25 There shall no man be able to stand before you: *for* the LORD your God shall lay the fear of you and the dread of you upon all the land that you shall tread upon, as He has said to you.   resist - Elohim^{p.f.}

26 Behold, I set before you this day a blessing and a curse;

27 A blessing, if you obey the commandments of the LORD your God, which I command you this day:

28 And a curse, if you will not obey the commandments of the LORD your God, but turn aside out of the way which I command you this day, to go after other gods, which you have not known.

29 And it shall come to pass, when the LORD your God has brought you in to the land where you go to possess it, that you shall put the blessing upon mount Ger'i-zim, and the curse upon mount E'bal.   where you are entering

30 *Are* they not on the other side Jor'-dan, by the way where the sun goes down, in the land of the Ca'naan-ites, which dwell in the champaign over against Gil'gal, beside the plains of Mo'reh?   Arabah - oaks

31 For you shall pass over Jor'dan to go in to possess the land which the LORD your God gives you, and you shall possess it, and dwell therein.

32 And you shall observe to do all the statutes and judgments which I set before you this day.   decrees - laws

CHAPTER 12

THESE *are* the statutes and judgments, which you shall observe to do

in the land, which the Lord God of your fathers gives you to possess it, all the days that you live upon the earth. decrees - laws - Jehovah[s.f.] - Elohim[p.f.]

2 You shall utterly destroy all the places, wherein the nations which you shall <u>possess</u> served their gods, upon the high mountains, and upon the hills, and under every green tree: conquer

3 And you shall overthrow their altars, and break their pillars, and burn their groves with fire; and you shall hew down the graven images of their gods, and destroy the names of them out of that place.

4 You shall not do so to the Lord your <u>God</u>. Elohim[p.f.]

5 But to the place which the Lord your <u>God</u> shall choose out of all your tribes to put His name there, *even* to His <u>habitation</u> shall you seek, and there you shall come: dwelling

6 And there you shall bring your burned offerings, and your sacrifices, and your tithes, and heave offerings of your hand, and your vows, and your freewill offerings, and the firstlings of your herds and of your flocks:

7 And there you shall eat before the Lord your <u>God</u>, and you shall rejoice in all that you put your hand to, you and your households, wherein the Lord your <u>God</u> has blessed you. Elohim[p.f.]

8 You shall not do after all *the things* that we do here this day, every man whatsoever is right in his own eyes.

9 For you are not as yet come to <u>the rest</u> and to the <u>inheritance</u>, which the Lord your <u>God</u> gives you. resting place - possessions

10 But *when* you go over Jor'dan, and dwell in the land which the Lord your <u>God</u> gives you to inherit, and *when* He gives you rest from all your enemies round about, so that you dwell in safety;

11 Then there shall be a place which the Lord your <u>God</u> shall choose to cause His name to dwell there; there shall you bring all that I command you; your burned offerings, and your sacrifices, your tithes, and the heave offering of your hand, and all your <u>choice vows</u> which you <u>vow</u> to the Lord: Elohim[p.f.] - special pledges - pledge

12 And you shall rejoice before the Lord your <u>God</u>, you, and your sons, and your daughters, and your menservants, and your maidservants, and the Le'vite that *is* inside your gates; forasmuch as he has no part nor inheritance with you.

13 Take heed to yourself that you offer not your burned offerings in every place that you see:

14 But in the place which the Lord shall choose in one of your tribes, there you shall offer your burned offerings, and there you shall do all that I command you.

15 Notwithstanding you may kill and eat flesh in all your <u>gates</u>, whatsoever your soul <u>lusts</u> after, according to the blessing of the Lord your <u>God</u> which He has given you: the unclean and the clean may eat thereof, as of the <u>roebuck</u>, and as of the <u>hart</u>. i.e., city gates - desire - gazelle - stag

16 Only you shall not eat the blood; you shall pour it upon the earth as water.

17 You may not eat inside your <u>gates</u> the tithe of your corn, or of your wine, or of your oil, or the firstlings of your herds or of your flock, nor any of your vows which you vow, nor your freewill offerings, or heave offering of your hand: i.e., city gates

18 But you must eat them before the Lord your <u>God</u> in the place which the Lord your <u>God</u> shall choose, you, and your son, and your daughter, and your manservant, and your maidservant, and the Le'vite that *is* inside your gates: and you shall rejoice before the Lord your <u>God</u> in all that you put your hands to.   Elohim^{p.f.}

19 <u>Take heed</u> to yourself that you forsake not the Le'vite as long as you live upon the earth.   Be - careful

20 When the Lord your <u>God</u> shall enlarge your border, as He has promised you, and you shall say, I will eat <u>flesh</u>, because your <u>soul</u> longs to eat <u>flesh</u>; you may eat <u>flesh</u>, whatsoever <u>your soul</u> <u>lusts after</u>.   meat - you - desire

21 If the place which the Lord your <u>God</u> has chosen to put His name there be too far from you, then you shall kill of your herd and of your flock, which the Lord has given you, as I have commanded you, and you shall eat in your <u>gates</u> whatsoever your soul <u>lusts after</u>.   i.e., city gates

22 Even as the <u>roebuck</u> and the <u>hart</u> is eaten, so you shall eat them: the unclean and the clean shall eat *of* them alike.   gazelle - stag

23 Only be sure that you eat not the blood: for the blood *is* the life; and you may not eat the life with the <u>flesh</u>.   meat

24 You shall not eat it; you shall pour it upon the earth as water.

25 You shall not eat it; that it may go well with you, and with you or children after you, when you shall do *that which is* right in the sight of the Lord.

26 Only your <u>holy</u> things which you have, and your <u>vows</u>, you shall take, and go to the place which the Lord shall choose: consecrated - pledges

27 And you shall offer your burned offerings, the <u>flesh</u> and the blood, upon the altar of the Lord your <u>God</u>: and the blood of your sacrifices shall be poured out upon the altar of the Lord your <u>God</u>, and you shall eat the <u>flesh</u>.

28 Observe and hear all these words which I command you, that it may go well with you, and with your children after you for ever, when you do *that which is* good and right in the sight of the Lord your <u>God</u>.   Elohim^{p.f.}

29 When the Lord your <u>God</u> shall <u>cut off</u> the nations from before you, where you go to possess them, and you succeed them, and dwell in their land;   Elohim^{p.f.} - destroy

30 Take heed to yourself that you be not <u>snared</u> by following them, after that they be destroyed from before you; and that you <u>enquire not</u> after their gods, saying, How did these nations serve their gods? even so will I do likewise.   trapped - take no interest

31 You shall not do so to the Lord your <u>God</u>: for every <u>abomination</u> to the Lord, which He <u>hates</u> have they done to their gods; for even

their sons and their daughters they have burned in the fire to their gods.   Elohim[p.f.] - detestable - abhored

32 What thing soever I command you, <u>observe</u> to do it: you shall not add thereto, nor <u>diminish</u> from it.

REV. 22:18 be careful - take away

CHAPTER 13

IF there arise among you a prophet, or a dreamer of dreams, and give you a sign or a wonder,   MATT. 24:24

2 And the sign or the wonder come to pass, whereof he spoke to you, saying, Let us go after other gods, which you have not known, and let us serve them;

3 You shall not hearken to the words of that prophet, or that dreamer of dreams: for the LORD your <u>God</u> prove you, to know whether you love the LORD your <u>God</u> with all your heart and with all your soul.   Elohim[p.f.]

4 You shall <u>walk after</u> the LORD your <u>God</u>, and <u>fear</u> Him, and keep His commandments, and obey His voice, and you shall serve Him, and cling to Him.   follow - revere

5 And that prophet, or that dreamer of dreams, shall be put to death; because he has spoken to turn *you* away from the LORD your <u>God</u>, which brought you out of the land of E'gypt, and redeemed you out of the house of bondage, to <u>thrust</u> you out of the way which the LORD your God commanded you to walk in. So shall you put the evil away from the midst of you.   i.e., - lead astray

6 If your brother, the son of your mother, or your son, or your daughter, or the wife of your bosom, or your friend, which *is* as your own soul, entice you secretly, saying, Let us go and serve other gods, which you have not known, you, nor your fathers;

7 *Namely*, of the gods of the people which *are* round about you, near to you, or far off from you, from the *one* end of the earth even to the *other* end of the earth;

8 You shall not <u>consent</u> to him, nor hearken to him; neither shall your eye pity him, neither shall you spare, neither shall you conceal him: yield

9 But you shall surely kill him; your hand shall be first upon him to put him to death, and afterwards the hand of all the people.

10 And you shall stone him with stones, that he die; because he has sought to thrust you away from the LORD your <u>God</u>, which brought you out of the land of E'gypt, from the house of bondage.   Elohim[p.f.]

11 And all Is'ra-el shall hear, and fear, and shall do no more any such wickedness as this is among you.

12 If you shall hear *say* in one of your cities, which the LORD your <u>God</u> has given you to dwell there, saying,

13 *Certain* men, the children of <u>Be'li-al</u>, are gone out from among you, and have withdrawn the inhabitants of their city, saying, Let us go and serve other gods, which you have not known;   Satan

14 Then shall you enquire, and make search, and ask diligently; and, behold, *if it be* truth, and the thing certain, *that*

such abomination is wrought among you;

15 You shall surely <u>smite</u> the inhabitants of that city with the edge of the sword, destroying it utterly, and all that *is* therein, and the cattle thereof, with the edge of the sword. _{strike}

16 And you shall gather all the <u>spoil of it</u> into the midst of the street thereof, and shall burn with fire the city, and all the spoil thereof every <u>whit</u>, for the LORD your <u>God</u>: and it shall be an heap for ever; it shall not be built again. _{booty - piece - Elohim^{p.f.}}

17 And there shall cling nothing of the cursed thing to your hand: that the LORD may turn from the fierceness of His anger, and show you mercy, and have compassion upon you, and <u>multiply you</u>, as He has sworn to your fathers; _{increase your numbers}

18 When you shall <u>hearken</u> to the voice of the LORD your God, to keep all His commandments which I command you this day, to do *that which is* right in the <u>eyes</u> of the LORD your <u>God</u>. _{listen - sight}

CHAPTER 14

YOU *are* the children of the LORD your <u>God</u>: you shall not <u>cut</u> yourselves, nor <u>make</u> any baldness between your eyes for the dead.

_{Elohim^{p.f.} - disfigure - shave}

2 For you *are* an holy people to the LORD your <u>God</u>, and the LORD has chosen you to be a <u>peculiar people</u> to Himself, above all the nations that *are* upon the earth. _{treasured possession}

3 You shall not eat any <u>abominable</u> thing. _{detestable}

4 These *are* the beasts which you shall eat: the ox, the sheep, and the goat,

5 The <u>hart</u>, and the <u>roebuck</u>, and the fallow deer, and the wild goat, and the <u>pygarg</u>, and the wild ox, and the <u>chamois</u>. _{stag - gazelle - antelope - mountain sheep}

6 And every beast that parts the hoof, and <u>cleaves</u> the cleft into two claws, *and* chews the cud among the beasts, that you shall eat. _{splits}

7 Nevertheless these you shall not eat of them that chew the cud, or of them that divide the <u>cloven</u> hoof; *as* the camel, and the hare, and the coney: for they chew the cud, but divide not the hoof; *therefore* they *are* <u>unclean</u> to you. _{split - unfit}

8 And the swine, because it divides the hoof, yet chews not the cud, it *is* unclean to you: you shall not eat of their flesh, nor touch their dead carcase.

9 These you shall eat of all that *are* in the waters: all that have fins and scales shall you eat:

10 And whatsoever has not fins and scales you may not eat; it *is* unclean to you.

11 *Of* all <u>clean</u> birds you shall eat. _{fit}

12 But these *are they* of which you shall not eat: the eagle, and the <u>ossifrage</u>, and the ospray, _{vulture}

13 And the <u>glede</u>, and the <u>kite</u>, and the vulture after its kind, _{buzzard - falcon}

14 And every raven after its kind,

15 And the owl, and the night hawk, and the <u>cuckow</u>, and the hawk after its kind, _{gull}

16 The little owl, and the great owl, and the swan,

17 And the pelican, and the gier eagle, and the cormorant, _{carrion vulture}
18 And the stork, and the heron after its kind, and the lapwing, and the bat.
19 And every creeping thing that flies *is* unclean to you: they shall not be eaten. _{teeming life}
20 *But of* all clean fowls you may eat. _{birds}
21 You shall not eat *of* any thing that dies of itself: you shall give it to the stranger that *is* in your gates, that he may eat it; or you may sell it to an alien: for you *are* an holy people to the LORD your God. You shall not seethe a kid in its mother's milk. _{boil}
22 You shall truly tithe all the increase of your seed, that the field brings forth year by year. _{produce from what you sow}
23 And you shall eat before the LORD your God, in the place which He shall choose to place His name there, the tithe of your corn, of your wine, and of your oil, and the firstlings of your herds and of your flocks; that you may learn to fear the LORD your God always. _{revere}
24 And if the way be too long for you, so that you are not able to carry it; *or* if the place be too far from you, which the LORD your God shall choose to set His name there, when the LORD your God has blessed you:
25 Then shall you turn *it* into money, and bind up the money in your hand, and shall go to the place which the LORD your God shall choose:
26 And you shall bestow that money for whatsoever your soul lusts after, _{exchange - Elohim^{p.f.}} for oxen, or for sheep, or for wine, or for strong drink, or for whatsoever your soul desires: and you shall eat there before the LORD your God, and you shall rejoice, you, and your household, _{spend - heart - Elohim^{p.f.} - do it with gladness}
27 And the Le'vite that *is* inside your gates; you shall not forsake him; for he has no part nor inheritance with you.
28 At the end of three years you shall bring forth all the tithe of your increase the same year, and shall lay *it* up inside your gates: _{deposit - i.e., city gates}
29 And the Le'vite, (because he has no part nor inheritance with you,) and the stranger, and the fatherless, and the widow, which *are* inside your gates, shall come, and shall eat and be satisfied; that the LORD your God may bless you in all the work of your hand which you do.

CHAPTER 15

AT the end of *every* seven years you shall make a release. _{remission of debts}
2 And this *is* the manner of the release: Every creditor that lends *any-thing* to his neighbor shall release *it*; he shall not exact *it* of his neighbor, or of his brother; because it is called the LORD's release.
3 Of a foreigner you may exact *it* *again*: but *that* which is your with your brother your hand shall release;
4 Save when there shall be no poor among you; for the LORD shall greatly bless you in the land which the LORD your God gives you *for* an inheritance to possess it: _{Elohim^{p.f.}}

5 Only if you carefully <u>hearken</u> to the voice of the LORD your <u>God</u>, to observe to do all these commandments which I command you this day.   listen - Elohim^p.f.

6 For the LORD your <u>God</u> blesses you, as He promised you: and you shall lend to many nations, but you shalt not borrow; and you shall reign over many nations, but they shall not reign over you.

7 If there be among you a poor man of one of your brethren inside any of your <u>gates</u> in your land which the LORD your <u>God</u> gives you, you shall not harden your heart, nor <u>shut</u> your hand from your poor brother: i.e., city gates - close

8 But you shall open your hand wide to him, and shall surely lend him sufficient for his need, *in that* which he wants.   MATT. 5:42

9 Beware that there be not a thought in your wicked heart, saying, The seventh year, the year of release, is at hand; and your eye <u>be evil</u> against your poor brother, and you give him nothing; and he <u>cry</u> to the LORD against you, and it be sin to you.   is hostile - appeal

10 You shall surely give him, and your heart shall not be <u>grieved</u> when you give to him: because that for this thing the LORD your <u>God</u> shall bless you in all your works, and in all that you put your hand to.   grudging

11 For the poor shall never cease out of the land: therefore I command you, saying, You shall <u>open your hand wide to</u> your brother, to your poor, and to your needy, in your land.   MATT. 26:11 MARK 14:7 give freely

12 *And if* your brother, an He'brew man, or an He'brew woman, <u>be sold to you</u>, and serve you six years; then in the seventh year you shall let him go free from you.   obligated economically

13 And when you send him out free from you, you shall not let him go away <u>empty</u>:   empty handed

14 You shall furnish him liberally out of your flock, and out of your <u>floor</u>, and out of your winepress: *of that* wherewith the LORD your <u>God</u> has blessed you you shall give to him.   threshing floor

15 And you shall remember that you were a <u>bondman</u> in the land of E'gypt, and the LORD your <u>God</u> redeemed you: therefore I command you this thing today.   slave - Elohim^p.f.

16 And it shall be, if he say to you, I will not go away from you; because he loves you and your house, because he is <u>well with you</u>;   well off

17 Then you shall take an awl, and thrust *it* through his ear to the door, and he shall be your servant for ever. And also to you or maidservant you shall do likewise.

18 It shall not seem <u>hard</u> to you, when you send him away free from you; for he has been worth a double hired servant *to you,* in serving you six years: and the LORD your God shall bless you in all that you do.   a hardship

19 All the firstling males that come of your herd and of your flock you shall <u>sanctify</u> to the LORD your <u>God</u>: you shall do no work with the firstling of your bullock, nor shear the firstling of your sheep.   consecrate - Elohim^p.f.

20 You shall eat *it* before the LORD

your <u>God</u> year by year in the place which the LORD shall choose, you and your household. Elohim^{p.f.}

21 And if there be *any* blemish therein, *as if it be* lame, or blind, *or have* any ill blemish, you shall not <u>sacrifice</u> it to the LORD your God. offer

22 You shall eat it inside your <u>gates</u>: the unclean and the clean *person shall eat it* alike, as the <u>roebuck</u>, and as the <u>hart</u>. i.e., city gates - gazelle - stag

23 Only you shall not eat the blood thereof; you shall pour it upon the ground as water.

CHAPTER 16

OBSERVE the month of A'bib, and keep the passover to the LORD your <u>God</u>: for in the month of A'bib the LORD your <u>God</u> brought you forth out of E'gypt by night. Elohim^{p.f.}

2 You shall therefore <u>sacrifice</u> the passover to the LORD your God, of the flock and the herd, in the place which the LORD shall choose to place His name there. offer

3 You shall eat no <u>leavened</u> bread with it; seven days shall you eat <u>unleavened</u> bread therewith, *even* the bread of <u>affliction</u>; for you came forth out of the land of E'gypt in haste: that you may remember the day when you came forth out of the land of E'gypt all the days of your life. with yeast - without yeast - distress

4 And there shall be no <u>leavened</u> bread seen with you in all your coast seven days; neither shall there *any thing* of the flesh, which you sacrificed the first day at even, remain all night until the morning. with yeast

5 You may not <u>sacrifice</u> the passover inside any of your <u>gates</u>, which the LORD your <u>God</u> gives you: offer - i.e., city gates

6 But at the place which the LORD your <u>God</u> shall choose to place His name in, there you shall <u>sacrifice</u> the passover at even, at the going down of the sun, at the season that you came forth out of E'gypt. offer

7 And you shall roast and eat *it* in the place which the LORD your God shall choose: and you shall <u>turn</u> in the morning, and go to your tents. return

8 Six days you shall eat <u>unleavened</u> bread: and on the seventh day *shall be* a solemn assembly to the LORD your <u>God</u>: you shall do no work *therein*. Elohim^{p.f.}

9 Seven weeks shall you number to you: begin to number the seven weeks from *such time as* you <u>begin</u> *to put* the sickle to the corn. start to reap

10 And you shall keep the feast of weeks to the LORD your <u>God</u> with a <u>tribute</u> of a freewill offering of your hand, which you shall give *to the LORD your God*, according as the LORD your <u>God</u> has blessed you: Jehovah^{s.f.} - Elohim^{p.f.} - offering

11 And you shall rejoice before the LORD your <u>God</u>, you, and your son, and your daughter, and your manservant, and your maidservant, and the Le'vite that *is* inside your gates, and the stranger, and the fatherless, and the widow, that *are* among you, in the place which the LORD your God has chosen to place His name there.

12 And you shall remember that you were a <u>bondman</u> in E'gypt: and you shall <u>observe</u> and do these <u>statutes</u>.

slave - follow carefully - decrees

13 You shall observe the feast of tabernacles seven days, after that you have gathered in your <u>corn</u> and your wine:

grain

14 And you shall rejoice in your feast, you, and your son, and your daughter, and your manservant, and your maidservant, and the Le'vite, the stranger, and the fatherless, and the widow, that *are* inside your gates.

15 Seven days shall you keep a solemn feast to the LORD your <u>God</u> in the place which the LORD shall choose: because the LORD your <u>God</u> shall bless you in all your increase, and in all the works of your hands, therefore you shall surely rejoice.

Elohim^{p.f.}

16 Three times in a year shall all your males appear before the LORD your <u>God</u> in the place which He shall choose; in the feast of <u>unleavened</u> bread, and in the feast of weeks, and in the feast of tabernacles: and they shall not appear before the LORD <u>empty</u>:

without yeast - empty-handed

17 Every man *shall give* as he is able, according to the blessing of the LORD your God which He has given you.

18 Judges and officers shall you make you in all your <u>gates</u>, which the LORD your God gives you, throughout your tribes: and they shall judge the people with just judgment.

i.e. city gates

19 You shall not twist judgment; you shall not respect persons, neither take a <u>gift</u>: for a <u>gift</u> does blind the eyes of the wise, and <u>pervert</u> the words of the righteous.

bribe - twist

20 That which is altogether <u>just</u> shall you follow, that you may live, and inherit the land which the LORD your God gives you.

right

21 You shall not plant you a grove of any trees near to the altar of the LORD your <u>God</u>, which you shall make you.

Elohim^{p.f.}

22 Neither shall you set you up *any* image; which the LORD your <u>God</u> <u>hates</u>.

abhors

CHAPTER 17

YOU shall not sacrifice to the LORD your <u>God</u> *any* bullock, or sheep, wherein is blemish, *or* any evil-favoredness: for that *is* an <u>abomination</u> to the LORD your <u>God</u>.

Elohim^{p.f.} - detestable

2 If there be found among you, inside any of your <u>gates</u> which the LORD your <u>God</u> gives you, man or woman, that has wrought wickedness in the sight of the LORD your <u>God</u>, in <u>transgressing His covenant</u>,

i.e., city gates - violation of His agreement

3 And has gone and served other gods, and worshiped them, either the sun, or moon, or any of the host of heaven, which I have not commanded;

4 And it be told you, and you have heard *of it*, and enquired diligently, and, behold, *it be* true, *and* the thing certain, *that* such <u>abomination is wrought</u> in Is'ra-el:

detestable thing is done

5 Then shall you bring forth that man or that woman, which have committed that wicked thing, to your

gates, *even* that man or that woman, and shall <u>stone</u> them with stones, till they die. i.e., city gates - execute

6 At the mouth of two witnesses, or three witnesses, shall he that is worthy of death be put to death; *but* at the mouth of one witness he shall not be put to death. JOHN 7:51 HEB. 10:28

7 The hands of the witnesses shall be first upon him to put him to death, and afterward the hands of all the people. So you shall put the evil away from among you. 1 COR. 5:13

8 If there arise a matter too hard for you in judgment, between blood and blood, between plea and plea, and between stroke and stroke, *be-ing* matters of <u>controversy</u> inside your gates: then shall you arise, and get you up into the place which the LORD your <u>God</u> shall choose; dispute

9 And you shall come to the priests the Le'vites, and to the judge that shall be in those days, and enquire; and they shall show you the sentence of judgment:

10 And you shall do according to the sentence, which they of that place which the LORD shall choose shall show you; and you shall observe to do according to all that they <u>inform you</u>: will declare

11 According to the sentence of the law which they shall teach you, and according to the judgment which they shall tell you, you shall do: you shall not decline from the <u>sentence</u> which they shall show you, *to* the right hand, nor *to* the left. terms

12 And the man that will do pre-sumptuously, and will not <u>hearken</u> to the priest that stands to minister there before the LORD your <u>God</u>, or to the judge, even that man shall die: and you shall put away the evil from Is'ra-el. arrogantly - listen - Elohim^{p.f.}

13 And all the people shall hear, and fear, and do no more <u>presumptuously</u>.

14 When you are come to the land which the LORD your <u>God</u> gives you, and shall possess it, and shall dwell therein, and shall say, I will set a king over me, like as all the nations that *are* about me;

15 You shall in any wise <u>set</u> *him* king over you, whom the LORD your <u>God</u> shall choose: *one* from among your brethren shall you set king over you: you may not set a <u>stranger</u> over you, which *is* not your brother. make - foreigner

16 But he shall not multiply horses to himself, nor cause the people to return to E'gypt, to the end that he should multiply horses: forasmuch as the LORD has said to you, You shall hereafter return no more that way.

17 Neither shall he <u>multiply</u> wives to himself, that his heart turn not away: neither shall he greatly <u>multiply</u> to himself silver and gold. take many

18 And it shall be, when he sits upon the throne of his kingdom, that he shall write him a copy of this law in a book out of *that which is* before the priests the Le'vites:

19 And it shall be with him, and he shall read therein all the days of his life: that he may learn to <u>fear</u> the LORD his

God, to keep all the words of this law and these <u>statutes</u>, to do them:

revere - decrees

20 That his heart be not lifted up above his brethren, and that he turn not aside from the commandment, *to* the right hand, or *to* the left: to the end that he may prolong *his* days in his kingdom, he, and his children, in the midst of Is'ra-el.

CHAPTER 18

THE priests the Le'vites, *and* all the tribe of Le'vi, shall have no part nor inheritance with Is'ra-el: they shall eat the offerings of the LORD made by fire, and His inheritance.   1 COR. 9:13

2 Therefore shall they have no inheritance among their brethren: the LORD *is* their inheritance, as He has said to them.

3 And this shall be the priest's <u>due</u> from the people, from them that offer a sacrifice, whether *it be* ox or sheep; and they shall give to the priest the shoulder, and the two cheeks, and the <u>maw</u>.

right - inner parts

4 The firstfruit *also* of your <u>corn</u>, of your wine, and of your oil, and the first of the fleece of your sheep, shall you give him.

grain

5 For the LORD your <u>God</u> has chosen him out of all your tribes, to stand to minister in the name of the LORD, him and his sons for ever.   Elohim^{p.f.}

6 And if a Le'vite come from any of your <u>gates</u> out of all Is'ra-el, where he <u>sojourned</u>, and come with all the desire of his mind to the place which the LORD shall choose;   i.e., city gates - resides

7 Then he shall minister in the name of the LORD his <u>God</u>, as all his brethren the Le'vites *do*, which stand there before the LORD.   Elohim^{p.f.}

8 They shall have <u>like</u> portions to eat, beside that which comes of the sale of his <u>patrimony</u>.   equal - fathers' estates

9 When you are come into the land which the LORD your <u>God</u> gives you, you shall not learn to do after the <u>abominations</u> of those nations.   detestable things

10 There shall not be found among you *any one* that makes his son or his daughter to <u>pass through the fire</u>, *or* that uses <u>divination</u>, *or* an observer of times, or an <u>enchanter</u>, or a witch,   pagan rite - fortune telling - magician

11 Or a charmer, or a consulter with <u>familiar spirits</u>, or a <u>wizard</u>, or a <u>necromancer</u>.   spells - medium - consults the dead

12 For all that do these things *are* <u>an abomination</u> to the LORD: and because of these <u>abominations</u> the LORD your <u>God</u> does drive them out from before you.   detestable

13 You shall be <u>perfect</u> with the LORD your <u>God</u>.   blameless

14 For these nations, which you shall possess, <u>hearkened</u> to observers of times, and to <u>diviners</u>: but as for you, the LORD your <u>God</u> has not permitted you so *to do*.   fortune tellers - Elohim^{p.f.}

15 The LORD your <u>God</u> will raise up to you a Prophet from the midst of you, of your brethren, like to me; to Him you shall hearken;   ACTS 7:37

JOHN 1:45 ACTS 2:22 ACTS 3:22 ACTS 7:37 JOHN 1:21

16 According to all that you desired of the LORD your <u>God</u> in Ho'reb in the day of the assembly, saying, Let

me not hear again the voice of the LORD my God, neither let me see this great fire any more, that I die not.   Elohim^{p.f.}

17 And the LORD said to me, They have well *spoken that* which they have spoken.

18 I will raise them up a Prophet from among their brethren, like to you, and will put My words in his mouth; and he shall speak to them all that I shall command him.

JOHN 1:21 JOHN 6:14 JOHN 4:25

19 And it shall come to pass, *that* whosoever will not hearken to My words which he shall speak in My name, I will require *it* of him.

20 But the prophet, which shall presume to speak a word in My name, which I have not commanded him to speak, or that shall speak in the name of other gods, even that prophet shall die.

21 And if you say in your heart, How shall we know the word which the LORD has not spoken?

22 When a prophet speaks in the name of the LORD, if the thing follow not, nor come to pass, that *is* the thing which the LORD has not spoken, *but* the prophet has spoken it presumptuously: you shall not be afraid of him.   arrogance

CHAPTER 19

WHEN the LORD your God has cut off the nations, whose land the LORD your God gives you, and you succeed them, and dwell in their cities, and in their houses;   Elohim^{p.f.} destroyed

2 You shall separate three cities for you in the midst of your land, which the LORD your God gives you to possess it.   Elohim^{p.f.}

3 You shall prepare you a way, and divide the coasts of your land, which the LORD your God gives you to inherit, into three parts, that every slayer may flee there.   build - borders

4 And this *is* the case of the slayer, which shall flee there, that he may live: Whoso kills his neighbor ignorantly, whom he hated not in time past;   unintentionally - had no malice

5 As when a man goes into the wood with his neighbor to hew wood, and his hand brought a stroke with the ax to cut down the tree, and the head slips from the helve, and light upon his neighbor, that he die; he shall flee to one of those cities, and live:

cut - iron - handle - strikes

6 Less the avenger of the blood pursue the slayer, while his heart is hot, and overtake him, because the way is long, and slay him; whereas he *was* not worthy of death, inasmuch as he hated him not in time past.

too great - had no malice

7 Wherefore I command you, saying, You shall separate three cities for you.

8 And if the LORD your God enlarge your coast, as he has sworn to your fathers, and give you all the land which He promised to give to your fathers;   Elohim^{p.f.}

9 If you shall keep all these commandments to do them, which I command you this day, to love the LORD your God, and to walk ever in His ways;

then shall you add three cities more for you, beside these three:

10 That innocent blood be not shed in your land, which the LORD your <u>God</u> gives you *for* an inheritance, and *so* blood be upon you.   Elohim^{p.f.}

11 But if any man <u>hate</u> his neighbor, and <u>lie in wait for</u> him, and rise up against him, and smite him mortally that he die, and flees into one of these cities: abhors - plot to kill

12 Then the elders of his city shall send and bring him from there, and deliver him into the hand of the avenger of blood, that he may die.

13 Your eye shall not pity him, but you shall put away *the guilt of* innocent blood from Is'ra-el, that it may go well with you.

14 You shall not remove your neighbor's landmark, which they of old time have set in your inheritance, which you shall inherit in the land that the LORD your <u>God</u> gives you to possess it.   Elohim^{p.f.}

15 One witness shall not rise up against a man for any iniquity, or for any sin, in any sin that he sins: at the mouth of two witnesses, or at the mouth of three witnesses, shall the matter be established. JOHN 8:17 2 COR. 13:1

16 If a false witness rise up against any man to testify against him *that which* is wrong;

17 Then both the men, between whom the controversy *is*, shall stand before the LORD, before the priests and the judges, which shall be in those days;

18 And the judges shall make diligent <u>inquisition</u>: and, behold, *if* the witness *be* a false witness, and has testified falsely against his brother;   investigate throughly

19 Then shall you do to him, as he had thought to have done to his brother: so shall you put the evil away from among you.

20 And those which remain shall hear, and fear, and shall from now on commit no more any such evil among you.

21 And your eye shall not pity; *but* life *shall go* for life, eye for eye, tooth for tooth, hand for hand, foot for foot.   MATT. 5:38

CHAPTER 20

WHEN you go out to battle against your enemies, and see horses, and chariots, *and* a people more than you, be not afraid of them: for the LORD your <u>God</u> *is* with you, which brought you up out of the land of E'gypt.   Elohim^{p.f.}

2 And it shall be, when you are come near to the battle, that the priest shall approach and speak to the people,

3 And shall say to them, Hear, O Is'ra-el, you approach this day to battle against your enemies: let not your hearts faint, fear not, and do not tremble, neither be you terrified because of them;

4 For the LORD your <u>God</u> *is* He that goes with you, to fight for you against your enemies, to save you.   Elohim^{p.f.}

5 And the officers shall speak to the people, saying, What man *is there* that has built a new house, and has

not dedicated it? let him go and return to his house, less he die in the battle, and another man dedicate it.

6 And what man *is he* that has planted a vineyard, and has not *yet* eaten of it? let him *also* go and return to his house, less he die in the battle, and another man eat of it.

7 And what man *is there* that has betrothed a wife, and has not taken her? let him go and return to his house, less he die in the battle, and another man take her.

8 And the officers shall speak further to the people, and they shall say, What man *is there that is* fearful and fainthearted? let him go and return to his house, less his brethren's heart faint as well as his heart.

9 And it shall be, when the officers have made an end of speaking to the people, that they shall make captains of the armies to lead the people.

10 When you come near to a city to fight against it, then proclaim peace to it.

11 And it shall be, if it make you answer of peace, and open to you, then it shall be, *that* all the people *that is* found therein shall be <u>tributaries</u> to you, and they shall serve you.   _{forced labor}

12 And if it will make no peace with you, but will make war against you, then you shall besiege it:

13 And when the Lord your <u>God</u> has delivered it into your hands, you shall smite every male thereof with the edge of the sword: Elohim^{p.f.}

14 But the women, and the little ones, and the cattle, and all that is in the city,

even all the <u>spoil</u> thereof, shall you take to yourself; and you shall eat the <u>spoil</u> of your enemies, which the Lord your God has given you.   _{booty}

15 Thus shall you do to all the cities *which are* very far off from you, which *are* not of the cities of these nations.

16 But of the cities of these people, which the Lord your <u>God</u> does give you *for* an inheritance, you shall save alive nothing that breathes: Elohim^{p.f.}

17 But you shall utterly destroy them; *namely*, the Hit'tites, and the Am'or-ites, the Ca'naan-ites, and the Per'iz-zites, the Hi'vites, and the Jeb'u-sites; as the Lord your <u>God</u> has commanded you:

18 That they teach you not to do after all their <u>abominations</u>, which they have done to their gods; so should you sin against the Lord your God.   _{detestable ways}

19 When you shall besiege a city a long time, in making war against it to take it, you shall not destroy the trees thereof by forcing an ax against them: for you may eat of them, and you shall not cut them down (for the tree of the field *is* man's *life*) to employ *them* in the siege:

20 Only the trees which you know that they *be* not trees for <u>meat</u>, you shall destroy and cut them down; and you shall build bulwarks against the city that makes war with you, until it be subdued.   _{food}

CHAPTER 21

IF *one* be found slain in the land which the Lord your <u>God</u> gives you to

possess it, lying in the field, *and* it be not known who has slain him:

2 Then your elders and your judges shall come forth, and they shall <u>measure</u> to the cities which *are* round about him that is slain: the distance

Elohim^{p.f.}

3 And it shall be, *that* the city *which is* next to the slain man, even the elders of that city shall take an heifer, which <u>has not been wrought with</u>, *and* which has not drawn in the yoke;   has not been worked

4 And the elders of that city shall bring down the heifer to a rough valley, which is neither <u>eared</u> nor sown, and shall strike off the heifer's neck there in the valley: ploughed

5 And the priests the sons of Le'vi shall come near; for them the Lord your <u>God</u> has chosen to minister to him, and to bless in the name of the Lord; and by their word shall every <u>controversy</u> and every <u>stroke</u> be *tried*:   Elohim^{p.f.} - dispute - assault

6 And all the elders of that city, *that are* next to the slain *man*, shall wash their hands over the heifer that is beheaded in the valley:

7 And they shall answer and say, Our hands have not shed this blood, neither have our eyes seen *it*.

8 Be merciful, O Lord, to Your people Is'ra-el, whom You have redeemed, and lay not innocent blood to Your people of Is'ra-el's charge. And the blood shall be forgiven them.

9 So shall you put away the *guilt of* innocent blood from among you, when you shall do *that which is* right in the sight of the Lord.

10 When you go forth to war against your enemies, and the Lord your <u>God</u> has delivered them into your hands, and you have taken them captive,

Elohim^{p.f.}

11 And see among the captives a beautiful woman, and has a desire to her, that you would have her to your wife;

12 Then you shall bring her home to your house; and she shall shave her head, and <u>pare</u> her nails;   trim

13 And she shall put the <u>raiment</u> of her captivity from off her, and shall remain in your house, and <u>bewail</u> her father and her mother a full month: and after that you shall go in to her, and be her husband, and she shall be your wife.   clothes - mourn

14 And it shall be, if you have no delight in her, then you shall let her go where she will; but you shall not sell her at all for money, you shall not make merchandise of her, because you have humbled her.

15 If a man have two wives, one beloved, and another <u>hated</u>, and they have born him children, *both* the beloved and the <u>hated</u>; and *if* the firstborn son be hers that was <u>hated</u>: unloved

16 Then it shall be, when he makes his sons to inherit *that* which he has, *that* he may not make the son of the beloved firstborn before the son of the <u>hated</u>, *which is indeed* the firstborn:

17 But he shall acknowledge the son of the <u>hated</u> *for* the firstborn, by giving him a double portion of all that he has: for he *is* the beginning of his

M22

318

strength; the right of the firstborn *is* his. unloved

18 If a man have a stubborn and rebellious son, which will not obey the voice of his father, or the voice of his mother, and *that*, when they have chastened him, will not hearken to them:

19 Then shall his father and his mother lay hold on him, and bring him out to the elders of his city, and to the gate of his place;

20 And they shall say to the elders of his city, This our son *is* stubborn and rebellious, he will not obey our voice; *he is* a glutton, and a drunkard.

21 And all the men of his city shall stone him with stones, that he die: so shall you put evil away from among you; and all Is'ra-el shall hear, and fear. execute

22 And if a man have committed a sin worthy of death, and he be to be put to death, and you hang him on a tree: ACTS 5:30

23 His body shall not remain all night upon the tree, but you shall in any wise bury him that day; (for he that is hanged *is* accursed of God;) that your land be not defiled, which the LORD your God gives you *for* an inheritance.

MARK 15:42 JOHN 19:31 GAL. 3:13 Elohim^{p.f.}

CHAPTER 22

YOU shall not see your brother's ox or his sheep go astray, and hide yourself from them: you shall in any case bring them again to your brother. 2 And if your brother *be* not near to you, or if you know him not, then you shall bring it to your own house, and it shall be with you until your brother seek after it, and you shall restore it to him again.

3 In like manner shall you do with his ass; and so shall you do with his raiment; and with all lost thing of your brother's, which he has lost, and you have found, shall you do likewise: you may not hide yourself.

garment - avoid responsibility

4 You shall not see your brother's ass or his ox fall down by the way, and hide yourself from them: you shall surely help him to lift *them* up again. road

5 The woman shall not wear that which pertains to a man, neither shall a man put on a woman's garment: for all that do so *are* abomination to the LORD your God. detestable - Elohim^{p.f.}

6 If a bird's nest chance to be before you in the way in any tree, or on the ground, *whether they be* young ones, or eggs, and the dam sitting upon the young, or upon the eggs, you shall not take the dam with the young: mother

7 *But* you shall in any wise let the dam go, and take the young to you; that it may be well with you, and *that* you may prolong *your* days.

8 When you build a new house, then you shall make a battlement for your roof, that you bring not blood upon your house, if any man fall from there.

parapet

9 You shall not sow your vineyard with divers seeds: less the fruit of your seed which you have sown, and the fruit of your vineyard, be defiled. various

10 You shall not plow with an ox and an ass together. 2 COR. 6:14

11 You shall not wear a garment

of <u>divers sorts</u>, *as* of woollen and linen together. various fabrics

12 You shall make you fringes upon the four <u>quarters</u> of your <u>vesture</u>, wherewith you cover *yourself*. corners - cloak

13 If any man take a wife, and go in to her, and <u>hate</u> her, turns against

14 And give occasions of speech against her, and bring up an evil name upon her, and say, I took this woman, and when I came to her, I found her not a <u>maid</u>: virgin

15 Then shall the father of the <u>damsel</u>, and her mother, take and bring forth *the tokens of* the damsel's virginity to the elders of the city in the gate: young girl

16 And the damsel's father shall say to the elders, I gave my daughter to this man <u>to wife</u>, and he <u>hates</u> her; in marriage - dislikes

17 And, lo, he has given occasions of speech *against her*, saying, I found not your daughter a <u>maid</u>; and yet these *are the tokens of* my daughter's virginity. And they shall spread the cloth before the elders of the city. virgin

18 And the elders of that city shall take that man and chastise him;

19 And they shall <u>amerce</u> him in an hundred <u>shekels</u> of silver, and give *them* to the father of the <u>damsel</u>, because he has brought up an evil name upon a virgin of Is'ra-el: and she shall be his wife; he may not put her away all his days. fine

20 But if this thing be true, *and the tokens of* virginity be not found for the <u>damsel</u>: young girl

21 Then they shall bring out the <u>damsel</u> to the door of her father's house, and the men of her city shall stone her with stones that she die: because she has wrought folly in Is'ra-el, to play the whore in her father's house: so shall you put <u>evil</u> away from among you. young girl - wrong

22 If a man be found lying with a woman married to an husband, then they shall both of them die, *both* the man that lay with the woman, and the woman: so shall you put away evil from Is'ra-el.

23 If a <u>damsel</u> *that is* a virgin be betrothed to an husband, and a man find her in the city, and lie with her;

24 Then you shall bring them both out to the gate of that city, and you shall stone them with stones that they die; the <u>damsel</u>, because she cried not, *being* in the city; and the man, because he has humbled his neighbor's wife: so you shall put away evil from among you.

25 But if a man find a betrothed <u>damsel</u> in the field, and the man <u>force</u> her, and lie with her: then the man only that lay with her shall die: rape

26 But to the <u>damsel</u> you shall do nothing; *there is* in the <u>damsel</u> no sin *worthy* of death: for as when a man rise against his neighbor, and slays him, even so *is* this matter: young girl

27 For he found her in the field, *and* the betrothed <u>damsel</u> cried, and *there was* none to save her.

28 If a man find a <u>damsel</u> *that is* a virgin, which is not betrothed, and lay

hold on her, and lie with her, and they be found; _{young girl}

29 Then the man that lay with her shall give to the <u>damsel's</u> father fifty *shekels* of silver, and she shall be his wife; because he has humbled her, he may not put her away all his days.

30 A man shall not take his father's wife, nor <u>discover</u> his father's skirt. 1 COR. 5:1 uncover

CHAPTER 23

HE that is wounded in the <u>stones</u>, or has his privy member cut off, shall not enter into the congregation of the LORD. testicles

2 A <u>bastard</u> shall not enter into the <u>congregation</u> of the LORD; even to his tenth generation shall he not enter into the <u>congregation</u> of the LORD. ie born of a harlot - assemblies

3 An Am'mon-ite or Mo'ab-ite shall not enter into the congregation of the LORD; even to their tenth generation shall they not enter into the congregation of the LORD for ever:

4 Because they met you not with bread and with water in the way, when you came forth out of E'gypt; and because they hired against you Ba'laam the son of Be'or of Pe'thor of Mes-o-po-ta'mi-a, to curse you.

5 Nevertheless the LORD your <u>God</u> would not <u>hearken</u> to Ba'laam; but the LORD your <u>God</u> turned the curse into a blessing to you, because the LORD your <u>God</u> loved you. Elohim^{p.f.} - listen

6 You shall not seek their peace nor their prosperity all your days for ever.

7 You shall not abhor an E'dom-ite; for he *is* your brother: you shall not abhor an E-gyp'tian; because you were a stranger in his land.

8 The children that are begotten of them shall enter into the congregation of the LORD in their third generation.

9 When the host goes forth against your enemies, then keep you from every wicked thing.

10 If there be among you any man, that is not clean by reason of uncleanness that chances him by night, then shall he go abroad out of the camp, he shall not come inside the camp:

11 But it shall be, when evening comes on, he shall wash *himself* with water: and when the sun is down, he shall come into the camp *again*.

12 You shall have a place also outside the camp, where you shall go forth abroad:

13 And you shall have a <u>paddle</u> upon your weapon; and it shall be, when you will ease yourself abroad, you shall dig therewith, and shall turn back and cover that which comes from you: spade

14 For the LORD your <u>God</u> walks in the midst of your camp, to deliver you, and to give up your enemies before you; therefore shall your camp be holy: that He see no unclean thing in you, and turn away from you. Elohim^{p.f.}

15 You shall not <u>deliver</u> to his master the servant which is escaped from his master to you: hand over

16 He shall dwell with you, *even* among you, in that place which he shall choose in one of your gates, where it <u>likes</u> him best: you shall not oppress him. pleases

17 There shall be no whore of the daughters of Is'ra-el, nor a sodomite of the sons of Is'ra-el.

18 You shall not bring the hire of a whore, or the <u>price</u> of a dog, into the house of the Lord your <u>God</u> for any vow: for even both these *are* <u>abomination</u> to the Lord your God.

MATT. 27:6   MARK 2:23   wages - detestable

19 You shall not lend upon <u>usury</u> to your brother; <u>usury</u> of money, <u>usury</u> of victuals, <u>usury</u> of any thing that is lent upon <u>usury</u>:   interest

20 To a stranger you may lend upon <u>usury</u>; but to your brother you shall not lend upon <u>usury</u>: that the Lord your <u>God</u> may bless you in all that you set your hand to in the land where you go to possess it.

21 When you shall <u>vow a vow</u> to the Lord your God, you shall not <u>slack</u> to pay it: for the Lord your God will surely require it of you; and it would be sin in you.   make a pledge - slow

22 But if you shall <u>forbear to vow</u>, it shall be no sin in you.   refrain from pledging

23 That which is gone out of your lips you shall keep and perform; *even* a freewill offering, according as you have <u>vowed</u> to the Lord your God, which you have promised with your mouth.   pledged - Elohim[p.f.]

24 When you come into your neighbor's vineyard, then you may eat grapes your fill at your own pleasure; but you shall not put *any* in your vessel.

25 When you come into the standing <u>corn</u> of your neighbor, then you may pluck the ears with your hand; but you shall not move a <u>sickle</u> to your neighbor's standing <u>corn</u>.

LUKE 6:1   MARK 2:23   wield - grain

CHAPTER 24

WHEN a man has taken a wife, and married her, and it come to pass that she find no <u>favor</u> in his eyes, because he has found some uncleanness in her: then let him write her a bill of divorcement, and give *it* in her hand, and send her out of his house MARK 10:4 desire

2 And when she is departed out of his house, she may go and be another man's *wife*.

3 And *if* the latter husband <u>hate</u> her, and write her a bill of divorcement, and gives *it* in her hand, and sends her out of his house; or if the latter husband die, which took her *to be* his wife;   turns against

4 Her former husband, which sent her away, may not take her again to be his wife, after that she is defiled; for that *is* <u>abomination</u> before the Lord: and you shall not cause the land to sin, which the Lord your <u>God</u> gives you *for* an inheritance.   detestable - Elohim[p.f.]

5 When a man has taken a new wife, he shall not go out to war, neither shall he be charged with any business: *but* he shall be free at home one year, and shall cheer up his wife which he has taken.   LUKE 14:20

6 No man shall take the <u>nether</u> or the upper millstone to pledge: for he takes *a man's* life to pledge.   lower

7 If a man be found stealing any of his brethren of the children of Is'ra-el, and makes merchandise of him, or sells him; then that thief shall die;

M46
M22

754

437

and you shall put evil away from among you.

8 Take heed in the <u>plague</u> of leprosy, that you <u>observe diligently</u>, and do according to all that the priests the Le'vites shall teach you: as I commanded them, *so* you shall observe to do.　　infection - be cautious

9 Remember what the LORD your <u>God</u> did to Mir'i-am by the way, after that you were come forth out of E'gypt.

10 When you do lend your brother any thing, you shall not go into his house to bring his pledge.

11 You shall stand abroad, and the man to whom you do lend shall bring out the <u>pledge</u> abroad to you.　collateral

12 And if the man *be* poor, you shall <u>not sleep with his pledge</u>:　not keep it overnight

13 In any case you shall deliver him the <u>pledge</u> again when the sun goes down, that he may sleep in his own <u>raiment</u>, and bless you: and it shall be righteousness to you before the LORD your <u>God</u>.　collateral - cloak - Elohim^{p.f.}

14 You shall not oppress an hired servant *that is* poor and needy, *whether he be* of your brethren, or of your strangers that *are* in your land inside your gates:

15 At his day you shall give *him* his <u>hire</u>, neither shall the sun go down upon it; for he *is* poor, and sets his heart upon it: less he cry against you to the LORD, and it be sin to you.　wages

16 The fathers shall not be put to death for the children, neither shall the children be put to death for the fathers: every man shall be put to death for his own sin.

17 You shall not pervert the judgment of the stranger, *nor* of the fatherless; nor take a widow's <u>raiment</u> to <u>pledge</u>:　clothes

18 But you shall remember that you were a <u>bondman</u> in E'gypt, and the LORD your <u>God</u> redeemed you from there: therefore I command you to do this thing.　slave - Elohim^{p.f.}

19 When you cut down your harvest in your field, and have forgot a sheaf in the field, you shall not go again to bring it: it shall be for the stranger, for the fatherless, and for the widow: that the LORD your <u>God</u> may bless you in all the work of your hands.

20 When you beat your olive tree, you shall not go over the boughs again: it shall be for the stranger, for the fatherless, and for the widow.

21 When you gather the grapes of your vineyard, you shall not glean *it* afterward: it shall be for the stranger, for the fatherless, and for the widow.

22 And you shall remember that you were a <u>bondman</u> in the land of E'gypt: therefore I command you to do this thing.　slave

CHAPTER 25

IF there be a <u>controversy</u> between men, and they come <u>to judgment</u>, that *the judges* may judge them; then they shall justify the righteous, and condemn the wicked.　dispute - to court

2 And it shall be, if the wicked man *be* worthy to be beaten, that the judge shall cause him to lie down, and to be

beaten before his face, according to his fault, by a certain number.

3 Forty stripes he may give him, *and* not exceed: less, *if* he should exceed, and beat him above these with many stripes, then your brother should seem vile to you. LUKE 12:48 2 COR. 11:24

4 You shall not muzzle the ox when he treads out *the* corn.

1 COR. 9:9 1 TIM 5:18 treading - grain

5 If brethren dwell together, and one of them die, and have no child, the wife of the dead shall not marry without to a stranger: her husband's brother shall go in to her, and take her to him to wife, and perform the duty of an husband's brother to her.

MARK 22:24 MARK 12:19 outside the family

6 And it shall be, *that* the firstborn which she bears shall succeed in the name of his brother *which* is dead, that his name be not put out of Is'ra-el.

7 And if the man like not to take his brother's wife, then let his brother's wife go up to the gate to the elders, and say, My husband's brother refuses to raise up to his brother a name in Is'ra-el, he will not perform the duty of my husband's brother.

8 Then the elders of his city shall call him, and speak to him: and *if* he stand *to it*, and say, I like not to take her;

9 Then shall his brother's wife come to him in the presence of the elders, and loose his shoe from off his foot, and spit in his face, and shall answer and say, So shall it be done to that man that will not build up his brother's house.   take off

10 And his name shall be called in Is'-ra-el, The house of him that has his shoe loosed.

11 When men strive together one with another, and the wife of the one draws near for to deliver her husband out of the hand of him that smite him, and puts forth her hand, and takes him by the secrets: genitals

12 Then you shall cut off her hand, your eye shall not pity *her*.

13 You shall not have in your bag divers weights, a great and a small.   different

14 You shall not have in your house divers measures, a great and a small.

15 *But* you shall have a perfect and just weight, a perfect and just measure shall you have: that your days may be lengthened in the land which the LORD your God gives you. Elohim^p.f.

16 For all that do such things, *and* all that do unrighteously, *are* an abomination to the LORD your God.   detestable

17 Remember what Am'a-lek did to you by the way, when you were come forth out of E'gypt;

18 How he met you by the way, and smote the hindmost of you, *even* all *that were* feeble behind you, when you *were* faint and weary; and he feared not God.   reverenced

19 Therefore it shall be, when the LORD your God has given you rest from all your enemies round about, in the land which the LORD your God gives you *for* an inheritance to possess it, *that* you shall blot out the remembrance of Am'a-lek from under heaven; you shall not forget *it*.   Elohim^p.f.

CHAPTER 26

AND it shall be, when you *are* come in to the land which the LORD your <u>God</u> gives you *for* an inheritance, and possess it, and dwell therein;

2 That you shall take of the first of all the fruit of the earth, which you shall bring of your land that the LORD your <u>God</u> gives you, and shall put *it* in a basket, and shall go to the place which the LORD your <u>God</u> shall choose to <u>place</u> His name there.

Elohim^{p.f.} - establish

3 And you shall go to the priest that shall be in those days, and say to him, I profess this day to the LORD your <u>God</u>, that I am come to the country which the LORD swear to our fathers for to give us.

4 And the priest shall take the basket out of your hand, and set it down before the altar of the LORD your <u>God</u>.

5 And you shall speak and say before the LORD your <u>God</u>, A <u>Syr'i-an</u> ready to perish *was* my father, and he went down into E'gypt, and <u>sojourned</u> there with a few, and became there a nation, great, mighty, and populous:

Aramean - lived as an alien

6 And the E-gyptians <u>evil entreated us</u>, and afflicted us, and laid upon us hard <u>bondage</u>:

mistreated us - slavery

7 And when we cried to the LORD God of our fathers, the LORD heard our voice, and looked on our affliction, and our labor, and our oppression:

8 And the LORD brought us forth out of E'gypt with a mighty hand, and with an outstretched arm, and with great terribleness, and with signs, and with wonders:

9 And He has brought us into this place, and has given us this land, *even* a land that flows with milk and honey.

10 And now, behold, I have brought the firstfruits of the land, which You, O LORD, have given me. And you shall <u>set</u> it before the LORD your God, and worship before the LORD your God:

offer

11 And you shall rejoice in every good *thing* which the LORD your <u>God</u> has given to you, and to your house, you, and the Le'vite, and the stranger that *is* among you.

Elohim^{p.f.}

12 When you have made an end of tithing all the tithes of your increase the third year, *which is* the year of tithing, and have given *it* to the Le'vite, the stranger, the fatherless, and the widow, that they may eat inside your gates, and be filled;

13 Then you shall say before the LORD your <u>God</u>, I have brought away the hallowed things out of *my* house, and also have given them to the Le'vite, and to the stranger, to the fatherless, and to the widow, according to all Your commandments which You have commanded me: I have not transgressed Your commandments, neither have I forgotten *them*:

Elohim^{p.f.}

14 I have not eaten thereof in my <u>mourning</u>, neither have I taken away *aught* thereof for *any* <u>unclean</u> *use*, nor given *aught* thereof for the dead: *but* I have hearkened to the voice of the

LORD my God, *and* have done according to all that You have commanded me.   distress - any - unfit - Elohim[p.f.]

15 Look down from Your holy habitation, from heaven, and bless Your people Is'ra-el, and the land which You have given us, as You swear to our fathers, a land that flows with milk and honey.

16 This day the LORD your God has commanded you to do these statutes and judgments: you shall therefore keep and do them with all your heart, and with all your soul.   decrees - laws

17 You have avouched the LORD this day to be your God, and to walk in His ways, and to keep His statutes, and His commandments, and His judgments, and to hearken to His voice: declared

18 And the LORD has avouched you this day to be His peculiar people, as He has promised you, and that *you* should keep all His commandments;   treasured possession

19 And to make you high above all nations which He has made, in praise, and in name, and in honor; and that you may be an holy people to the LORD your God, as He has spoken.   set you up - consecrated

CHAPTER 27

AND Mo'ses with the elders of Is'ra-el commanded the people, saying, Keep all the commandments which I command you this day.   obey

2 And it shall be on the day when you shall pass over Jor'dan to the land which the LORD your God gives you,

that you shall set you up great stones, and plaster them with plaster: Elohim[p.f.]

3 And you shall write upon them all the words of this law, when you are passed over, that you may go in to the land which the LORD your God gives you, a land that flows with milk and honey; as the LORD God of your fathers has promised you.

4 Therefore it shall be when you be gone over Jor'dan, *that* you shall set up these stones, which I command you this day, in mount E'bal, and you shall plaster them with plaster.

5 And there shall you build an altar to the LORD your God, an altar of stones: you shall not lift up *any* iron *tool* upon them.

6 You shall build the altar of the LORD your God of whole stones: and you shall offer burned offerings thereon to the LORD your God: field

7 And you shall offer peace offerings, and shall eat there, and rejoice before the LORD your God.   Elohim[p.f.]

8 And you shall write upon the stones all the words of this law very plainly.

9 And Mo'ses and the priests the Le'vites spoke to all Is'ra-el, saying, Take heed, and hearken, O Is'ra-el; this day you are become the people of the LORD your God.

10 You shall therefore obey the voice of the LORD your God, and do His commandments and His statutes, which I command you this day.   Elohim[p.f.]

11 And Mo'ses charged the people the same day, saying,

12 These shall stand upon mount

Ger'i-zim to bless the people, when you are come over Jor'dan; Sim'e-on, and Le'vi, and Ju'dah, and Is-sa-char, and Jo'seph, and Ben'ja-min:

13 And these shall stand upon mount E'bal to curse; Reu'ben, Gad, and Ash'er, and Zeb'u-lun, Dan, and Naph'ta-li.

14 And the Le'vites shall speak, and say to all the men of Is'ra-el with a loud voice,

15 Cursed *be* the man that makes *any* graven or molten image, an <u>abomination</u> to the LORD, the work of the hands of the craftsman, and puts *it* in *a secret place*. And all the people shall answer and say, Amen.

a detestable thing - hidden

16 Cursed *be* he that sets light by his father or his mother. And all the people shall say, Amen.

17 Cursed *be* he that removes his neighbor's <u>landmark</u>. And all the people shall say, Amen.   boundary mark

18 Cursed *be* he that <u>makes</u> the blind to wander out of the way. And all the people shall say, Amen.   misleads

19 Cursed *be* he that <u>perverts</u> the judgment of the stranger, father-less, and widow. And all the people shall say, Amen.   distorts

20 Cursed *be* he that lies with his father's wife; because he uncovers his father's skirt. And all the people shall say, Amen.

21 Cursed *be* he that lies with any manner of beast. And all the people shall say, Amen.

22 Cursed *be* he that lies with his sister, the daughter of his father, or the daughter of his mother. And all the people shall say, Amen.

23 Cursed *be* he that lies with his mother in law. And all the people shall say, Amen.

24 Cursed *be* he that <u>smites</u> his neighbor secretly. And all the people shall say, Amen.   strikes

25 Cursed *be* he that <u>takes reward</u> to slay an innocent person. And all the people shall say, Amen.   accepts a bribe

26 Cursed *be* he that <u>confirms</u> not all the words of this law to do them. And all the people shall say, Amen.   GAL. 3:10 uphold

CHAPTER 28

AND it shall come to pass, if you shall hearken diligently to the voice of the LORD your <u>God</u>, to observe *and* to do all His commandments which I command you this day, that the LORD your <u>God</u> will set you on high above all nations of the earth: Elohim[p.f.]

2 And all these blessings shall come on you, and overtake you if you shall <u>hearken</u> to the voice of the LORD your <u>God</u>.   obey

3 Blessed *shall* you *be* in the city, and blessed *shall* you *be* in the field.

4 Blessed *shall be* the <u>fruit</u> of your body, and the <u>fruit</u> of your ground, and the <u>fruit</u> of your cattle, the increase of your <u>kine</u>, and the flocks of your sheep.   offspring - produce - offspring - cows

5 Blessed *shall be* your basket and your store.

6 Blessed *shall* you *be* when you come in, and blessed *shall* you be when you go out.

7 The LORD shall cause your enemies that rise up against you to be <u>smitten</u> before your face: they shall come out against you one way, and flee before you seven ways. *defeated*

8 The LORD shall command the blessing upon you in your storehouses, and in all that you set your hand to; and He shall bless you in the land which the LORD your <u>God</u> gives you.

9 The LORD shall establish you an holy people to Himself, as He has sworn to you, if you shall keep the commandments of the LORD your <u>God</u>, and walk in His ways. *Elohim*^{p.f.}

10 And all people of the earth shall see that you are called by the name of the LORD; and they shall be afraid of you.

11 And the LORD shall make you <u>plenteous</u> in goods, in the fruit of your body, and in the fruit of your cattle, and in the fruit of your ground, in the land which the LORD swear to your fathers to give you. *abound*

12 The LORD shall open to you His <u>good treasure</u>, the heaven to give the rain to your land in its season, and to bless all the work of your hand: and you shall lend to many nations, and you shall not borrow. *storehouse*

13 And the LORD shall make you <u>the head</u>, and not the tail; and you shall be above only, and you shall not be beneath; if that you <u>hearken</u> to the commandments of the LORD your <u>God</u>, which I command you this day, to <u>observe</u> and to do *them*: *more important - listen - take note*

14 And you shall not <u>go aside</u> from any of the words which I command you this day, *to* the right hand, or *to* the left, to go after other gods to serve them. *turn aside*

15 But it shall come to pass, if you will not <u>hearken</u> to the voice of the LORD your <u>God</u>, to observe to do all His commandments and His statutes which I command you this day; that all these curses shall come upon you, and overtake you: *listen - Elohim*^{p.f.}

16 Cursed *shall* you *be* in the city, and cursed *shall* you *be* in the field.

17 Cursed *shall be* your basket and your store.

18 Cursed *shall be* the <u>fruit</u> of your body, and the <u>fruit</u> of your land, the increase of your <u>kine</u>, and the flocks of your sheep. *offspring - produce - cattle*

19 Cursed *shall* you *be* when you come in, and cursed *shall* you *be* when you go out.

20 The LORD shall send upon you cursing, <u>vexation</u>, and rebuke, in all that you set your hand to for to do, until you be destroyed, and until you perish quickly; because of the wickedness of your doings, whereby you have forsaken Me. *confusion*

21 The LORD shall make the <u>pestilence</u> cling to you, until He have <u>consumed</u> you from off the land, where you got to possess it. *disease - destroyed*

22 The LORD shall smite you with a consumption, and with a fever, and with an inflammation, and with an extreme burning, and with the sword, and

with <u>blasting</u>, and with mildew; and they shall pursue you until you perish.

blight

23 And your heaven that *is* over your head shall be <u>brass</u>, and the earth that *is* under you *shall be* <u>iron</u>.

i.e., solid, not emitting rain - unproductive

24 The Lord shall make the rain of your land powder and dust: from heaven shall it come down upon you, until you be destroyed.

25 The Lord shall cause you to be <u>smitten</u> before your enemies: you shall go out one way against them, and flee seven ways before them: and shall be removed into all the kingdoms of the earth.

defeated

26 And your carcase shall be meat to all fowls of the air, and to the beasts of the earth, and no man shall <u>fray</u> *them* away.

frighten

27 The Lord will smite you with the <u>botch</u> of E'gypt, and with the <u>emerods</u>, and with the scab, and with the itch, whereof you can not be healed.

boils - tumors

28 The Lord shall smite you with <u>madness</u>, and blindness, and <u>astonishment of heart:</u>

mental disorder - bewilderment

29 And you shall grope at noonday, as the blind grope in darkness, and you shall not prosper in your ways: and you shall be only oppressed and <u>spoiled</u> evermore, and no man shall save *you*.

robbed

30 You shall betroth a wife, and another man shall lie with her: you shall build an house, and you shall not dwell therein: you shall plant a vineyard, and shall not gather the grapes thereof.

31 Your ox *shall be* slain before your eyes, and you shall not eat thereof: your ass *shall be* violently taken away from before your face, and shall not be restored to you: your sheep *shall be* given to your enemies, and you shall have none to rescue *them*.

32 Your sons and your daughters *shall be* given to another people, and your eyes shall look, and <u>fail</u> *with longing* for them all the day long: and *there shall be* no might in your hand.

yearn

33 The fruit of your land, and all your labors, shall a nation which you know not <u>eat up</u>; and you shall be only oppressed and crushed alway:

take away

34 So that you shall be mad for the sight of your eyes which you shall see.

35 The Lord shall smite you in the knees, and in the legs, with a sore <u>botch</u> that cannot be healed, from the sole of your foot to the top of your head.

boil

36 The Lord shall bring you, and your king which you shall set over you, to a nation which neither you nor your fathers have known; and there shall you serve other gods, wood and stone.

37 And you shall become an astonishment, a proverb, and a byword, among all nations where the Lord shall lead you.

38 You shall carry much seed out into the field, and shall gather *but* little in; for the locust shall <u>consume</u> it.

devour

39 You shall plant vineyards, and dress *them*, but shall neither drink *of* the wine, nor gather *the grapes*; for the worms shall eat them.

40 You shall have olive trees through-out all your <u>coasts</u>, but you shall not anoint *yourself* with the oil; for your olive shall <u>cast</u> *its fruit*. _{country - lose}

41 You shall father sons and daughters, but you shall not enjoy them; for they shall <u>go into captivity</u>. _{taken as slaves}

42 All your trees and fruit of your land shall the locust <u>consume</u>. _{devour}

43 The stranger that *is* inside you shall get up above you very high; and you shall come down very low.

44 He shall lend to you, and you shall not lend to him: he shall be the <u>head</u>, and you shall be the tail. _{important one}

45 Moreover all these curses shall come upon you, and shall pursue you, and overtake you, till you be destroyed; because you hearkened not to the voice of the LORD your <u>God</u>, to keep His commandments and His statutes which He commanded you: _{Elohim^{p.f.}}

46 And they shall be upon you for a sign and for a <u>wonder</u>, and upon your <u>seed</u> for ever. _{miracle - descendants}

47 Because you served not the LORD your <u>God</u> with joyfulness, and with gladness of heart, for the abundance of all *things*;

48 Therefore shall you serve your enemies which the LORD shall send against you, in hunger, and in thirst, and in nakedness, and in want of all *things*: and he shall put a <u>yoke of iron</u> upon your neck, until He have destroyed you. _{oppression}

49 The LORD shall bring a nation against you from far, from the end of the earth, *as swift* as the eagle flies; a nation whose <u>tongue</u> you shall not understand; _{language}

50 A nation of fierce countenance, which shall not <u>regard</u> the person of the old, nor show favor to the young: _{respect}

51 And he shall eat the fruit of your cattle, and the fruit of your land, until you be destroyed: which *also* shall not leave you *either* corn, wine, or oil, *or* the increase of your <u>kine</u>, or flocks of your sheep, until he have destroyed you. _{cattle}

52 And he shall besiege you in all your gates, until your high and <u>fenced</u> walls come down, wherein you trusted, throughout all your land: and he shall besiege you in all your gates throughout all your land, which the LORD your <u>God</u> has given you. _{fortified - Elohim^{p.f.}}

53 And you shall eat the <u>fruit</u> of your own body, the flesh of your sons and of your daughters, which the LORD your <u>God</u> has given you, in the siege, and in the <u>straitness</u>, wherewith your enemies shall distress you: _{children - hardship}

54 So *that* the man *that* is tender among you, and very delicate, his eye shall be evil toward his brother, and toward the wife of his bosom, and toward the remnant of his children which he shall leave:

55 So that he will not give to any of them of the flesh of his children whom he shall eat: because he has nothing left him in the siege, and in the <u>straitness</u>, wherewith your enemies shall <u>distress</u> you in all your gates. _{oppress}

56 The <u>tender</u> and <u>delicate</u> woman among you, which would not adventure to set the sole of her foot upon the

ground for delicateness and tenderness, her eye shall be <u>evil</u> toward the husband of her bosom, and toward her son, and toward her daughter,

young - weak - hostile

57 And toward her young one that comes out from between her feet, and toward her children which she shall bear: for she shall eat them for want of all *things* secretly in the siege and <u>straitness</u>, wherewith your enemy shall distress you in your gates. hardship

58 If you will not observe to do all the words of this law that are written in this book, that you may <u>fear</u> this glorious and <u>fearful</u> name, THE LORD YOUR <u>GOD</u>;

reverence - awesome - Elohim^{p.f.}

59 Then the LORD will make your <u>plagues</u> wonderful, and the <u>plagues</u> of your <u>seed</u>, *even* great <u>plagues</u>, and of long continuance, and sore sicknesses, and of long continuance. sickness - offspring

60 Moreover He will bring upon you all the diseases of E'gypt, which you were afraid of; and they shall cling to you.

61 Also every sickness, and every <u>plague</u>, which *is* not written in the book of this law, them will the LORD bring upon you, until you be destroyed. disaster

62 And you shall be left few in number, whereas you were as the stars of heaven for multitude; because you would not obey the voice of the LORD your <u>God</u>. Elohim^{p.f.}

63 And it shall come to pass, *that* as the LORD rejoiced over you to do you good, and to multiply you; so the LORD will rejoice over you to destroy you, and to bring you to nothing; and you shall be plucked from off the land where you go to possess it.

64 And the LORD shall scatter you among all people, from the one end of the earth even to the other; and there you shall serve other gods, which neither you nor your fathers have known, *even* wood and stone.

65 And among these nations shall you find no ease, neither shall the sole of your foot have rest: but the LORD shall give you there a trembling heart, and failing of eyes, and <u>sorrow of mind</u>: despairing heart

66 And your life shall hang in doubt before you; and you shall <u>fear</u> day and night, and shall have none assurance of your life: he in dread

67 In the morning you shall say, Would God it were <u>even</u>! and at <u>even</u> you shall say, Would God it were morning! for the <u>fear</u> of your heart wherewith you shall <u>fear</u>, and for the sight of your eyes which you shall see. night - dread

68 And the LORD shall bring you into E'gypt again with ships, by the way whereof I spoke to you, You shall see it no more again: and there you shall be sold to your enemies for <u>bondmen</u> and <u>bondwomen</u>, and no man shall buy *you*. slaves

CHAPTER 29

THESE *are* the words of the <u>covenant</u>, which the LORD commanded Mo'ses to make with the children of Is'ra-el in the land of Mo'ab, beside the <u>covenant</u> which He made with them in Ho'reb. agreement

2 And Mo'ses called to all Is'ra-el, and said to them, You have seen all that the LORD did before your eyes in the land of E'gypt to Pha'raoh, and to all his servants, and to all his land;

3 The great temptations which your eyes have seen, the signs, and those great miracles: trials

4 Yet the LORD has not given you an heart to perceive, and eyes to see, and ears to hear, to this day. ROM. 11:8 know

5 And I have led you forty years in the wilderness: your clothes are not waxen old upon you, and your shoe is not waxen old upon your foot. grown

6 You have not eaten bread, neither have you drunk wine or strong drink: that you might know that I *am* the LORD your God. Elohim p.f.

7 And when you came to this place, Si'hon the king of Hesh'bon, and Og the king of Ba'shan, came out against us to battle, and we smote them:

8 And we took their land, and gave it for an inheritance to the Reu'ben-ites, and to the Gad'ites, and to the half tribe of Ma-nas'seh.

9 Keep therefore the words of this covenant, and do them, that you may prosper in all that you do. agreement

10 You stand this day all of you before the LORD your God; your captains of your tribes, your elders, and your officers, *with* all the men of Is'ra-el, Elohim p.f.

11 Your little ones, your wives, and your stranger that *is* in your camp, from the hewer of your wood to the drawer of your water:

12 That you should enter into covenant with the LORD your God, and into His oath, which the LORD your God makes with you this day: agreement - Elohim p.f.

13 That He may establish you to day for a people to Himself, and *that* He may be to you a God, as He has said to you, and as He has sworn to your fathers, to A'bra-ham, to I'saac, and to Ja'cob.

14 Neither with you only do I make this covenant and this oath;

15 But with *him* that stands here with us this day before the LORD our God, and also with *him* that *is* not here with us this day:

16 (For you know how we have dwelled in the land of E'gypt; and how we came through the nations which you passed by;

17 And you have seen their abominations, and their idols, wood and stone, silver and gold, which *were* among them:) detestable images

18 Less there should be among you man, or woman, or family, or tribe, whose heart turns away this day from the LORD our God, to go *and* serve the gods of these nations; less there should be among you a root that bears gall and wormwood; HEB. 12:15 Elohim p.f.

19 And it come to pass, when he hears the words of this curse, that he bless himself in his heart, saying, I shall have peace, though I walk in the imagination of my heart, to add drunkenness to thirst:

20 The LORD will not spare him, but then the anger of the LORD and His jealousy shall smoke against that man,

and all the curses that are written in this book shall lie upon him, and the LORD shall blot out his name from under heaven. _{burn}

21 And the LORD shall separate him to evil out of all the tribes of Is'ra-el, according to all the curses of the <u>covenant</u> that are written in this book of the law: _{agreement}

22 So that the generation to come of your children that shall rise up after you, and the <u>stranger</u> that shall come from a far land, shall say, when they see the <u>plagues</u> of that land, and the sicknesses which the LORD has laid upon it; _{foreigner - desolations}

23 *And that* the whole land thereof *is* brimstone, and salt, *and* burning, *that* it is not sown, nor bears, nor any grass grows therein, like the overthrow of Sod'om, and Go-mor'rah, Ad'-mah, and Ze-bo'im, which the LORD overthrew in His anger, and in His wrath:

24 Even all nations shall say, Wherefore has the LORD done thus to this land? what *means* the heat of this great anger?

25 Then men shall say, Because they have <u>forsaken the covenant</u> of the <u>LORD God</u> of their fathers, which He made with them when He brought them forth out of the land of E'gypt: _{broken the agreement - Jehovah^{s.f.} Elohim^{p.f.}}

26 For they went and served other gods, and worshiped them, gods whom they knew not, and *whom* He had not given to them:

27 And the anger of the LORD was kindled against this land, to bring upon it all the curses that are written in this book:

28 And the LORD <u>rooted</u> them out of their land in anger, and in wrath, and in great indignation, and cast them into another land, as *it is* this day. _{uprooted}

29 The <u>secret *things* belong</u> to the LORD our <u>God</u>: but those *things which are* revealed *belong* to us and to our children for ever, that we may do all the words of this law. _{hidden realities - Elohim^{p.f.}}

CHAPTER 30

AND it shall come to pass, when all these things are come upon you, the blessing and the curse, which I have set before you, and you shall <u>call *them* to mind</u> among all the nations, where the LORD your God has driven you, _{remember}

2 And shall <u>return</u> to the LORD your God, and shall obey His voice according to all that I command you this day, you and your children, with all your heart, and with all your soul; _{turn again}

3 That then the LORD your <u>God will turn your captivity</u>, and have compassion upon you, and will return and gather you from all the nations, where the LORD your God has scattered you. _{restore you from captivity}

4 If *any* of yours be driven out to the <u>outmost *parts*</u> of heaven, from there will the LORD your <u>God</u> gather you, and from there will He bring you: _{to the ends of the earth - Elohim^{p.f.}}

5 And the LORD your <u>God</u> will bring you into the land which your fathers possessed, and you shall possess it;

and He will do you good, and multiply you above your fathers.

6 And the LORD your God will circumcise your heart, and the heart of your seed, to love the LORD your God with all your heart, and with all your soul, that you may live.   Elohim^{p.f.}

7 And the LORD your God will put all these curses upon your enemies, and on them that hate you, which persecuted you.

8 And you shall return and obey the voice of the LORD, and do all His commandments which I command you this day.

9 And the LORD your God will make you plenteous in every work of your hand, in the fruit of your body, and in the fruit of your cattle, and in the fruit of your land, for good: for the LORD will again rejoice over you for good, as He rejoiced over your fathers: prosperous - offspring

10 If you shall hearken to the voice of the LORD your God, to keep His commandments and His statutes which are written in this book of the law, *and* if you turn to the LORD your God with all your heart, and with all your soul.   listen - Elohim^{p.f.} - decrees

11 For this commandment which I command you this day, it *is* not hidden from you, neither is it far off.   too difficult for

12 It *is* not in heaven, that you should say, Who shall go up for us to heaven, and bring it to us, that we may hear it, and do it?   ROM. 10:6

13 Neither *is* it beyond the sea, that you should say, Who shall go over the sea for us, and bring it to us, that we may hear it, and do it?

14 But the word *is* very near to you, in your mouth, and in your heart, that you may do it.   ROM. 10:8

15 See, I have set before you this day life and good, and death and evil;

16 In that I command you this day to love the LORD your God, to walk in His ways, and to keep His commandments and His statutes and His judgments, that you may live and multiply: and the LORD your God shall bless you in the land where you go to possess it.   Elohim^{p.f.}

17 But if your heart turn away, so that you will not hear, but shall be drawn away, and worship other gods, and serve them;

18 I denounce to you this day, that you shall surely perish, *and that* you shall not prolong *your* days upon the land, where you pass over Jor'dan to go to possess it.

19 I call heaven and earth to record this day against you, *that* I have set before you life and death, blessing and cursing: therefore choose life, that both you and your seed may live: to witness - descendants

20 That you may love the LORD your God, *and* that you may obey His voice, and that you may cling to Him: for He *is* your life, and the length of your days: that you may dwell in the land which the LORD swear to your fathers, to A'bra-ham, to I'saac, and to Ja'cob, to give them.

CHAPTER 31

AND Mo'ses went and spoke these words to all Is'ra-el.

2 And he said to them, I *am* an hundred and twenty years old this day; I can no more go out and come in: also the LORD has said to me, You shall not go over this Jor'dan.

3 The LORD your <u>God</u>, He will go over before you, *and* He will destroy these nations from before you, and you shall <u>possess</u> them: *and* Josh'u-a, he shall go over before you, as the LORD has said. Elohim^{p.f.} - take possession of

4 And the LORD shall do to them as He did to Si'hon and to Og, kings of the Am'or-ites, and to the land of them, whom He destroyed.

5 And the LORD shall give them up before your face, that you may do to them according to all the commandments which I have commanded you.

6 Be strong and of a good courage, fear not, nor be afraid of them: for the LORD your <u>God</u>, He *it is* that does go with you; He will not fail you, nor forsake you.   HEB. 13:5

7 And Mo'ses called to Josh'u-a, and said to him in the sight of all Is'ra-el, Be strong and of a good courage: for you must go with this people to the land which the LORD has sworn to their fathers to give them; and you shall cause them to inherit it.

8 And the LORD, He *it is* that does go before you; He will be with you, He will not fail you, neither forsake you: fear not, neither be dismayed. HEB. 13:5

9 And Mo'ses wrote this law, and delivered it to the priests the sons of Le'vi, which bare the ark of the <u>covenant</u> of the LORD, and to all the elders of Is'ra-el.   agreement

10 And Mo'ses commanded them, saying, At the end of *every* seven years, in the <u>solemnity</u> of the year of release, in the feast of tabernacles, time

11 When all Is'ra-el is come to appear before the LORD your <u>God</u> in the place which He shall choose, you shall read this law before all Is'ra-el in their hearing.   Elohim^{p.f.}

12 Gather the people together, men, and women, and children, and your <u>stranger</u> that *is* inside your gates, that they may hear, and that they may learn, and <u>fear</u> the LORD your God, and observe to do all the words of this law: alien - reverence

13 And *that* their children, which have not known *any thing*, may hear, and learn to <u>fear</u> the LORD your <u>God</u>, <u>as long as you live in the land where you go over Jor'dan to possess</u> it. revere - take

14 And the LORD said to Mo'ses, Behold, your days approach that you must die: call Josh'u-a, and present yourselves in the tabernacle of the congregation, that I may give him a <u>charge</u>. And Mo'ses and Josh'u-a went, and presented themselves in the tabernacle of the congregation.   commission

15 And the LORD appeared in the tabernacle in a pillar of a cloud: and the pillar of the cloud stood over the door of the tabernacle.

16 And the LORD said to Mo'ses, Behold, you shall sleep with your fathers; and this people will rise up, and <u>go a whoring</u> after the gods of the strangers of the land, where they go *to be* among them, and will forsake Me,

and break My covenant which I have made with them.

be unfaithful to God - agreement

17 Then My anger shall be kindled against them in that day, and I will forsake them, and I will hide My face from them, and they shall be devoured, and many evils and troubles shall befall them; so that they will say in that day, Are not these evils come upon us, because our God is not among us?   destroyed

18 And I will surely hide My face in that day for all the evils which they shall have wrought, in that they are turned to other gods.   done

19 Now therefore write you this song for you, and teach it the children of Is'ra-el: put it in their mouths, that this song may be a witness for Me against the children of Is'ra-el.

20 For when I shall have brought them into the land which I swear to their fathers, that flows with milk and honey; and they shall have eaten and filled themselves, and waxen fat; then will they turn to other gods, and serve them, and provoke Me, and break My covenant.   become - agreement

21 And it shall come to pass, when many evils and troubles are befallen them, that this song shall testify against them as a witness; for it shall not be forgotten out of the mouths of their seed: for I know their imagination which they go about, even now, before I have brought them into the land which I swear.   descendants

22 Mo'ses therefore wrote this song the same day, and taught it the children of Is'ra-el.

23 And he gave Josh'u-a the son of Nun a charge, and said, Be strong and of a good courage: for you shall bring the children of Is'ra-el into the land which I swear to them: and I will be with you.   commission

24 And it came to pass, when Mo'ses had made an end of writing the words of this law in a book, until they were finished,

25 That Mo'ses commanded the Le'vites, which bare the ark of the covenant of the LORD, saying,   agreement

26 Take this book of the law, and put it in the side of the ark of the covenant of the LORD your God, that it may be there for a witness against you.   Elohim

27 For I know your rebellion, and your stiff neck: behold, while I am yet alive with you this day, you have been rebellious against the LORD; and how much more after my death?   disobedience - stubbornness

28 Gather to me all the elders of your tribes, and your officers, that I may speak these words in their ears, and call heaven and earth to record against them.   hearing

29 For I know that after my death you will utterly corrupt *yourselves*, and turn aside from the way which I have commanded you; and evil will befall you in the latter days; because you will do evil in the sight of the LORD, to provoke Him to anger through the work of your hands.

30 And Mo'ses spoke in the ears of all the congregation of Is'ra-el the words of this song, until they were ended.

CHAPTER 32

GIVE ear, O you heavens, and I will speak; and hear, O earth, the words of my mouth.

2 My <u>doctrine</u> shall drop as the rain, my speech shall distil as the dew, as the small rain upon the tender herb, and as the showers upon the grass: _{teaching}

3 Because I will <u>publish</u> the name of the LORD: ascribe you greatness to our <u>God</u>. proclaim - Elohim^{p.f.}

4 *He is* the Rock, His work *is* perfect: for all His ways *are* judgment: a God of truth and without iniquity, just and right *is* He.

5 They have corrupted themselves, their spot *is* not *the spot* of His children: *they are* a perverse and <u>crooked</u> generation. crafty

6 Do you thus <u>requite</u> the LORD, O foolish people and unwise? *is* not He your father *that* has bought you? has He not made you, and established you? JOHN 8:41 repay

7 Remember the days of old, consider the years of many generations: ask your father, and he will show you; your elders, and they will tell you.

8 When the <u>Most High</u> divided to the nations their inheritance, when He separated the sons of Ad'am, He set the bounds of the people according to the number of the children of Is'ra-el. El Elyon^{s.f.}

9 For the LORD's portion *is* His people; Ja'cob *is* the lot of His inheritance.

10 He found him in a desert land, and in the waste howling wilderness; He led him about, He instructed him, He kept him as the apple of His eye.

11 As an eagle stirs up her nest, flutters over her young, spreads abroad her wings, takes them, bears them on her wings:

12 *So* the LORD alone did lead him, and *there was* no strange god with him.

13 He made him ride on the high places of the earth, that he might eat the increase of the fields; and He made him to suck honey out of the rock, and oil out of the flinty rock;

14 Butter of <u>kine</u>, and milk of sheep, with fat of lambs, and rams of the breed of Ba'shan, and goats, with the fat of kidneys of wheat; and you did drink the pure blood of the grape. cows

15 But Jeshu-run <u>waxed</u> fat, and kicked: you are <u>waxen</u> fat, you are grown thick, you are covered *with fatness*; then he forsook <u>God</u> *which* made him, and <u>lightly esteemed</u> the Rock of his <u>salvation</u>. grew - Eloah^{s.f.} - scorned - i.e., Heb. Jeshua

16 They provoked Him to jealousy with strange *gods*, with <u>abominations</u> provoked they Him to anger. detestable idols

17 They sacrificed to devils, not to <u>God</u>; to gods whom they knew not, to new *gods that* came newly up, whom your fathers <u>feared</u> not. 1 COR. 10:20 Eloah^{s.f.} - dreaded

18 Of the Rock *that* fathered you you are unmindful, and have forgotten God that formed you.

19 And when the LORD *saw it*, He <u>abhorred</u> *them*, because of the provoking of His sons, and of His daughters. spurned

20 And He said, I will hide My face from them, I will see what their end *shall be*: for they *are* a very <u>froward</u>

generation, children in whom *is* no faith.

^{perverse}

21 They have moved Me to jealousy with *that which is* not <u>God</u>; they have provoked Me to anger with their <u>vanities</u>: and I will move them to jealousy with *those which are* not a people; I will provoke them to anger with a foolish nation.   ROM. 10:19 - 1 COR. 10:22 - El^{s.f.} - worthless idols

22 For a fire is kindled in My anger, and shall burn to the lowest hell, and shall consume the earth with her increase, and set on fire the foundations of the mountains.

23 I will heap mischiefs upon them; I will spend Mine arrows upon them.

24 *They shall be* burned with hunger, and devoured with burning heat, and with bitter destruction: I will also send the teeth of beasts upon them, with the poison of serpents of the dust.

25 The sword outside, and terror inside, shall destroy both the young man and the virgin, the suckling *also* with the man of gray hairs.

26 I said, I would scatter them into corners, I would make the remembrance of them to cease from among men:

27 Were it not that I <u>feared</u> the <u>wrath</u> of the enemy, less their adversaries should behave themselves strangely, *and* less they should say, Our hand *is* high, and the LORD has not done all this.   ^{dreaded - anger}

28 For they *are* a nation void of counsel, neither *is there any* understanding in them.

29 O that they were wise, *that* they understood this, *that* they would consider their latter end!

30 How should one chase a thousand, and two put ten thousand to flight, except their Rock had sold them, and the LORD had shut them up?

31 For their rock *is* not as our Rock, even our enemies themselves *being* judges.

32 For their vine *is* of the vine of Sod'om, and of the fields of Gomor'rah: their grapes *are* grapes of gall, their clusters *are* bitter:

33 Their wine *is* the poison of dragons, and the cruel venom of asps.

34 *Is* not this laid up in store with Me, *and* sealed up among My treasures?

35 To Me *belongs* vengeance, and recompence; their foot shall slide in *due* time: for the day of their calamity *is* at hand, and the things that shall come upon them <u>make haste</u>.

ROM. 12:19 HEB. 10:30 are coming soon

36 For the LORD shall judge His people, and repent Himself for His servants, when He see that *their* power is gone, and *there is* none shut up, or left.

37 And He shall say, Where *are* their gods, *their* rock in whom they trusted,

38 Which did eat the fat of their sacrifices, *and* drank the wine of their drink offerings? let them rise up and help you, and be your protection.

39 See now that I, *even I, am* He, and *there is* no god with Me: I kill, and I make alive; I wound, and I heal: neither *is there any* that can deliver out of My hand.

40 For I lift up My hand to heaven, and say, I live for ever.

41 If I whet My glittering sword, and

My hand take hold on judgment; I will render vengeance to My enemies, and will reward them that <u>hate</u> Me. abhor

42 I will make My arrows drunk with blood, and My sword shall devour flesh; *and that* with the blood of the slain and of the captives, from the beginning of revenges upon the enemy.

43 Rejoice, O you nations, *with* His people: for He will avenge the blood of His servants, and will render vengeance to His adversaries, and will be merciful to His land, *and* to His people. ROM. 15:10 REV. 19:2

44 And Mo'ses came and spoke all the words of this song in the ears of the people, he, and <u>Ho-she'a</u> the son of Nun. Joshua

45 And Mo'ses made an end of speaking all these words to all Is'ra-el:

46 And he said to them, Set your hearts to all the words which I testify among you this day, which you shall command your children to observe to do, all the words of this law.

47 For it *is* not a vain thing for you; because it *is* your life: and through this thing you shall prolong *your* days in the land, where you go over Jor'dan to possess it.

48 And the LORD spoke to Mo'ses that selfsame day, saying,

49 Get you up into this mountain Ab'a-rim, *to* mount Ne'bo, which *is* in the land of Mo'ab, that *is* opposite Jer'i-cho; and behold the land of Ca'naan, which I give to the children of Is'ra-el for a possession:

50 And die in the mount where you go up, and be gathered to your people; as Aar'on your brother died in mount Hor, and was gathered to his people:

51 Because you trespassed against Me among the children of Is'ra-el at the waters of Mer'i-bah-Ka'desh, in the wilderness of Zin; because you sanctified Me not in the midst of the children of Is'ra-el.

52 Yet you shall see the land before *you*; but you shall not go there to the land which I give the children of Is'ra-el.

CHAPTER 33

AND this *is* the blessing, wherewith Mo'ses the man of God blessed the children of Is'ra-el before his death.

2 And he said, The LORD came from Si'nai, and rose up from Se'ir to them; He shined forth from mount Pa'ran, and He came with ten thousands of saints: from His right hand *went* a fiery law for them.

3 Yea, He loved the people; all His saints *are* in Your hand: and they sat down at Your feet; *every one* shall receive of Your words.

4 Mo'ses commanded us a law, *even* the inheritance of the congregation of Ja'cob.

5 And he was king in Jeshu-run, when the heads of the people *and* the tribes of Is'ra-el were gathered together.

6 Let Reu'ben live, and not die; and let *not* his men be few.

7 And this *is the blessing* of Ju'dah: and he said, Hear, LORD, the voice of Ju'dah, and bring him to his people: let his hands be sufficient for him; and

be You an help *to him* from his enemies.

8 And of Le'vi he said, *Let* Your Thum'mim and Your U'rim *be* with Your holy one, whom You did prove at Mas'sah, *and with* whom You did strive at the waters of Mer'i-bah;

lights and perfecrion

9 Who said to his father and to his mother, I have not seen him; neither did he acknowledge his brethren, nor knew his own children: for they have observed Your word, and kept Your covenant.

watched - agreement

10 They shall teach Ja'cob Your judgments, and Is'ra-el Your law: they shall put incense before You, and whole burned sacrifice upon Your altar.

11 Bless, LORD, his substance, and accept the work of his hands: smite through the loins of them that rise against him, and of them that hate him, that they rise not again.

12 *And* of Ben'ja-min he said, The beloved of the LORD shall dwell in safety by Him; *and the* LORD shall cover him all the day long, and he shall dwell between His shoulders.

13 And of Jo'seph he said, Blessed of the LORD *be* his land, for the precious things of heaven, for the dew, and for the deep that couches beneath,

14 And for the precious fruits *brought forth* by the sun, and for the precious things put forth by the moon,

15 And for the chief things of the ancient mountains, and for the precious things of the lasting hills,

everlasting

16 And for the precious things of the earth and fulness thereof, and *for* the good will of him that dwelled in the bush: let *the blessing* come upon the head of Jo'seph, and upon the top of the head of him *that was* separated from his brethren.

17 His glory *is like* the firstling of his bullock, and his horns *are like* the horns of unicorns: with them he shall push the people together to the ends of the earth: and they *are* the ten thousands of E'phra-im, and they are the thousands of Ma-nas'seh.

18 And of Zeb'u-lun he said, Rejoice, Zeb'u-lun, in your going out; and, Is'sa-char, in your tents.

19 They shall call the people to the mountain; there they shall offer sacrifices of righteousness: for they shall suck *of* the abundance of the seas, and *of* treasures hid in the sand.

20 And of Gad he said, Blessed be he that enlarged Gad: he dwells as a lion, and tears the arm with the crown of the head.

21 And he provided the first part for himself, because there, *in* a portion of the lawgiver, *was he* seated; and he came with the heads of the people, he executed the justice of the LORD, and His judgments with Is'ra-el.

22 And of Dan he said, Dan *is* a lion's whelp: he shall leap from Ba'shan.

23 And of Naph'ta-li he said, O Naph'ta-li, satisfied with favor, and full with the blessing of the LORD: possess you the west and the south.

24 And of Ash'er he said, *Let* Ash'er *be* blessed with children; let him be

acceptable to his brethren, and let him dip his foot in oil.

25 Your shoes *shall be* iron and brass; and as your days, *so shall* your strength *be*.

26 *There is* none like to the God of Jeshu-run, *Who* rides upon the heaven in Your help, and in His excellency on the sky.

27 The eternal <u>God</u> *is your* refuge, and underneath *are* the everlasting arms: and He shall thrust out the enemy from before you; and shall say, Destroy *them*.   Elohim^{p.f.}

28 Is'ra-el then shall dwell in safety alone: the fountain of Ja'cob *shall be* upon a land of <u>corn</u> and wine; also His heavens shall drop down dew. grain

29 Happy *are* you, O Is'ra-el: who *is* like to you, O people saved by the LORD, the shield of your help, and who *is* the sword of your excellency! and your enemies shall be found liars to you; and you shall <u>tread upon</u> their high places.   trample down

CHAPTER 34

AND Mo'ses went up from the plains of Mo'ab to the mountain of Ne'bo, to the top of Pis'gah, that *is* opposite Jer'i-cho. And the LORD showed him all the land of Gil'e-ad, to Dan,

2 And all Naph'ta-li, and the land of E'phra-im, and Ma-nas'seh, and all the land of Ju'dah, to the <u>utmost sea</u>,   Mediterranean

3 And the <u>south</u>, and the plain of the valley of Jer'i-cho, the city of palm trees, to Zo'ar.   i.e., Negev

4 And the LORD said to him, This *is* the land which I swear to A'bra-ham, to I'saac, and to Ja'cob, saying, I will give it to your <u>seed</u>: I have caused you to see *it* with your eyes, but you shall not go over there.   offspring

5 So Mo'ses the servant of the LORD died there in the land of Mo'ab, according to the word of the LORD.

6 And He buried him in a valley in the land of Mo'ab, opposite Bethpe'or: but no man knows of his <u>sepulcher</u> to this day.   grave

7 And Mo'ses *was* an hundred and twenty years old when he died: his eye was not dim, nor his natural force <u>abated</u>.   lessened

8 And the children of Is'ra-el wept for Mo'ses in the plains of Mo'ab thirty days: so the days of weeping *and* mourning for Mo'ses were ended.

9 And Josh'u-a the son of Nun was full of the spirit of wisdom; for Mo'ses had laid his hands upon him: and the children of Is'ra-el hearkened to him, and did as the LORD commanded Mo'ses.

10 And there arose not a prophet since in Is'ra-el like to Mo'ses, whom the LORD knew face to face,

11 In all the signs and the wonders, which the LORD sent him to do in the land of E'gypt to Pha'raoh, and to all His servants, and to all His land,

12 And in all that mighty hand, and in all the <u>great terror</u> which Mo'ses showed in the sight of all Is'ra-el.   awesome deeds

JOSHUA

OUTLINE

SURVEY

The Book of Joshua is a sequel to the Pentateuch. Moses died in the land of Moab, within sight of the promised land. To Joshua, his successor, was left the mission of leading Israel across the Jordan into Canaan.

The greater part of the book describes the conquest of Canaan and the division of the land among the tribes of Israel. After the fall of Jericho and Ai, and the capitulation of Gibeon, in central Canaan, Joshua was confronted by two successive coalitions of Canaanite states, one in the south with the king of Jerusalem at its head, and the other in the north under Jabin of Hazor. Through divine assistance Joshua was able to conquer both south and north, and to apportion the land among the tribes. Pockets of resistance continued, however, and it was the responsibility of each tribe to occupy the land assigned to it. The Book of Joshua records the history of Israel from Joshua's appointment as Moses' successor to his death at the age of 110.

AUTHOR

The title of the book implies that Joshua is its principle character. The book itself is anonymous, although there is strong internal evidence that it was written by an eyewitness to many of the events which it describes.

In its present form, however, the book is later than Joshua, whose death it records. The conquest of Debir by Othniel and of Laish (Leshem) by the Danites took place after the death of Joshua.

The book may be the work of one of the "elders that outlived Joshua" who made use of material written by Joshua himself (24.26; cf. 24.1-25).

C.F.P.

THE BOOK OF
JOSHUA

"Jehovah Saves"
Bringing Down Walls

CHAPTER 1

NOW after the death of Mo'ses the servant of the LORD it came to pass, that the LORD spoke to Josh'u-a the son of Nun, Mo'ses' minister, saying,

2 Mo'ses My servant is dead; now therefore arise, go over this Jor'dan, you, and all this people, to the land which I do give to them, *even* to the children of Is'ra-el.

3 Every place that the sole of your foot shall tread upon, that have I given to you, as I said to Mo'ses.

4 From the wilderness and this Leb'a-non even to the great river, the river Eu-phra'tes, all the land of the Hit'tites, and to the Great sea toward the going down of the sun, shall be your coast.   Mediterranean - territory

5 There shall not any man be able to stand before you all the days of your life: as I was with Mo'ses, *so* I will be with you: I will not fail you, nor forsake you.   HEB. 13:5

6 Be strong and of a good courage: for to this people shall you divide for an inheritance the land, which I swear to their fathers to give them.

7 Only be you strong and very courageous, that you may observe to do according to all the law, which Mo'ses My servant commanded you: turn not from it *to* the right hand or *to* the left,

that you may prosper wherever you go.

8 This book of the law shall not depart out of your mouth; but you shall meditate therein day and night, that you may observe to do according to all that is written therein: for then you shall make your way prosperous, and then you shall have good success.   i.e., never forgotten

9 Have not I commanded you? Be strong and of a good courage; be not afraid, neither be you dismayed: for the LORD your God *is* with you wherever you go.

10 Then Josh'u-a commanded the officers of the people, saying,

11 Pass through the host, and command the people, saying, Prepare you victuals; for within three days you shall pass over this Jor'dan, to go in to possess the land, which the LORD your God gives you to possess it.   provisions

12 And to the Reu'ben-ites, and to the Gad'ites, and to half the tribe of Ma-nas'seh, spoke Josh'u-a, saying,

13 Remember the word which Mo'ses the servant of the LORD commanded you, saying, The LORD your God has given you rest, and has given you this land.   Elohim[p.f.]

14 Your wives, your little ones, and your cattle, shall remain in the land which Mo'ses gave you on this side

Jor'dan; but you shall pass before your brethren armed, all the mighty men of valor, and help them;

15 Until the LORD have given your brethren <u>rest</u>, as *He has given* you, and they also have possessed the land which the LORD your <u>God</u> gives them: then you shall return to the land of your possession, and enjoy it, which Mo'ses the LORD's servant gave you on this side Jor'dan toward the <u>sunrising</u>.   peace - Elohim[p.f] east

16 And they answered Josh'u-a, saying, All that you command us we will do, and wherever you send us, we will go.

17 According as we <u>hearkened</u> to Mo'ses in all things, so will we <u>hearken</u> to you: only the LORD your <u>God</u> be with you, as He was with Mo'ses.   listen

18 Whosoever *he be* that does rebel against your commandment, and will not hearken to your words in all that you command him, he shall be put to death: only be strong and of a good courage.

CHAPTER 2

AND Josh'u-a the son of Nun sent out of Shit'tim two men to spy secretly, saying, Go view the land, even Jer'i-cho. And they went, and came into an harlot's house, named Ra'hab, and lodged there.

2 And it was told the king of Jer'i-cho, saying, Behold, there came men in here to night of the children of Is'ra-el to search out the country.

3 And the king of Jer'i-cho sent to Ra'hab, saying, Bring forth the men that are come to you, which are entered into your house: for they be come to search out all the country.

4 And the woman took the two men, and hid them, and said thus, There came men to me, but I knew not where they *were*:

5 And it came to pass *about the time* of shutting of the gate, when it was dark, that the men went out: where the men went I know not: pursue after them quickly; for you shall overtake them.

6 But she had brought them up to the roof of the house, and hid them with the stalks of flax, which she had <u>laid</u> in order upon the roof.   arranged

7 And the men pursued after them the way to Jor'dan to the fords: and as soon as they which pursued after them were gone out, they shut the gate.

8 And before they were laid down, she came up to them upon the roof;

9 And she said to the men, I know that the LORD has given you the land, and that your terror is fallen upon us, and that all the inhabitants of the land faint because of you.

10 For we have heard how the LORD dried up the water of the Red sea for you, when you came out of E'gypt; and what you did to the two kings of the Am'or-ites, that *were* on the other side Jor'dan, Si'hon and Og, whom you utterly destroyed.

11 And as soon as we had heard *these things*, our hearts did melt, neither did there remain any more courage in any man, because of you: for the LORD

your God, He *is* God in heaven above, and in earth beneath.   Elohim [p.f.]

12 Now therefore, I pray you, swear to me by the LORD, since I have showed you kindness, that you will also show kindness to my father's house, and give me a true token: promise

13 And *that* you will save alive my father, and my mother, and my brethren, and my sisters, and all that they have, and deliver our lives from death.

14 And the men answered her, Our life for yours, if you utter not this our business. And it shall be, when the LORD has given us the land, that we will deal kindly and truly with you.

15 Then she let them down by a cord through the window: for her house *was* upon the town wall, and she dwells upon the wall. JAMES 2:25 i.e., built into

16 And she said to them, Get you to the mountain, less the pursuers meet you; and hide yourselves there three days, until the pursuers be returned: and afterward may you go your way.

17 And the men said to her, We *will be* blameless of this your oath which you have made us swear.   free

18 Behold, *when* we come into the land, you shall bind this line of scarlet thread in the window which you did let us down by: and you shall bring your father, and your mother, and your brethren, and all your father's household, home to you.

19 And it shall be, *that* whosoever shall go out of the doors of your house into the street, his blood *shall be* upon his head, and we *will be* guiltless: and whosoever shall be with you in the house, his blood *shall be* on our head, if *any* hand be upon him.

MATT. 27:25   free - our responsibility

20 And if you utter this our business, then we will be quit of your oath which you have made us to swear.   HEB. 11:31 - free

21 And she said, According to your words, so *be* it. And she sent them away, and they departed: and she bound the scarlet line in the window.

22 And they went, and came to the mountain, and abode there three days, until the pursuers were returned: and the pursuers sought *them* throughout all the way, but found *them* not.

23 So the two men returned, and descended from the mountain, and passed over, and came to Josh'u-a the son of Nun, and told him all *things* that befell them:

24 And they said to Josh'u-a, Truly the LORD has delivered into our hands all the land; for even all the inhabitants of the country do faint because of us.

CHAPTER 3

AND Josh'u-a rose early in the morning; and they removed from Shit'tim, and came to Jor'dan, he and all the children of Is'ra-el, and lodged there before they passed over.

2 And it came to pass after three days, that the officers went through the host;

3 And they commanded the people, saying, When you see the ark of the covenant of the LORD your God, and the priests the Le'vites bearing it, then you

shall remove from your place, and go after it.   agreement - Elohimᵖᶠ - carrying

4 Yet there shall be a space between you and it, about two thousand cubits by measure: come not near to it, that you may know the way by which you must go: for you have not passed *this* way heretofore.

5 And Josh'u-a said to the people, Sanctify yourselves: for to morrow the LORD will do wonders among you.

6 And Josh'u-a spoke to the priests, saying, Take up the ark of the <u>covenant</u>, and pass over before the people. And they took up the ark of the <u>covenant</u>, and went before the people.

7 And the LORD said to Josh'u-a, This day will I begin to magnify you in the sight of all Is'ra-el, that they may know that, as I was with Mo'ses, *so* I will be with you.

8 And you shall command the priests that bear the ark of the <u>covenant</u>, saying, When you are come to the brink of the water of Jor'dan, you shall stand still in Jor'dan.   agreement

9 And Josh'u-a said to the children of Is'ra-el, Come here, and hear the words of the LORD your <u>God</u>.   Elohim

10 And Josh'u-a said, Hereby you shall <u>know</u> that the living <u>God</u> *is* among you, and *that* He will without fail drive out from before you the Ca'naan-ites, and the Hit'tites, and the Hi'vites, and the Per'iz-zites, and the Gir'ga-shites, and the Am'or-ites, and the Jeb'u-sites.   understand - Elˢᶠ

11 Behold, the ark of the <u>covenant</u> of the Lord of all the earth passes over before you into Jor'dan.   agreement - Adonˢᶠ

12 Now therefore take you twelve men out of the tribes of Is'ra-el, out of every tribe a man.

13 And it shall come to pass, as soon as the soles of the feet of the priests that bear the ark of the LORD, the Lord of all the earth, shall rest in the waters of Jor'dan, *that* the waters of Jor'dan shall be cut off *from* the waters that come down from above; and they shall stand upon an heap.

14 And it came to pass, when the people removed from their tents, to pass over Jor'dan, and the priests bearing the ark of the <u>covenant</u> before the people;   ACTS 7:44 agreement

15 And as they that bare the ark were come to Jor'dan, and the feet of the priests that bare the ark were dipped in the brim of the water, (for Jor'dan overflows all its banks all the time of harvest,)

16 That the waters which came down from above stood *and* rose up upon an heap very far from the city Ad'am, that *is* beside Zar'e-tan: and those that came down toward the sea of the plain, *even* the <u>Salt</u> sea, failed, *and* were cut off: and the people passed over right against Jer'i-cho.   i.e., Dead

17 And the priests that bare the ark of the <u>covenant</u> of the LORD stood firm on dry ground in the midst of Jor'dan, and all the Is'ra-el-ites passed over on dry ground, until all the people <u>were passed clean over</u> Jor'dan.   had finished crossing the

CHAPTER 4

AND it came to pass, when all the people <u>were clean passed over</u> Jor'dan, that the LORD spoke to Josh'u-a, saying, finished crossing

2 Take you twelve men out of the people, out of every tribe a man,

3 And command you them, saying, Take you here out of the midst of Jor'dan, out of the place where the priests' feet stood firm, twelve stones, and you shall carry them over with you, and leave them in the lodging place, where you shall lodge this night.

4 Then Josh'u-a called the twelve men, whom he had prepared of the children of Is'ra-el, out of every tribe a man:

5 And Josh'u-a said to them, <u>Pass over</u> before the ark of the LORD your <u>God</u> into the midst of Jor'dan, and take you up every man of you a stone upon his shoulder, according to the number of the tribes of the children of Is'ra-el: cross - Elohim^{p.f.}

6 That this may be a <u>sign</u> among you, *that* when your children ask *their fathers* in time to come, saying, What <u>*mean*</u> <u>you</u> by these stones? memorial - is signified

7 Then you shall answer them, That the waters of Jor'dan were <u>cut off</u> before the ark of the <u>Covenant</u> of the LORD; when it passed over Jor'dan, the waters of Jor'dan were cut off: and these stones shall be for a memorial to the children of Is'ra-el for ever. held back - agreement

8 And the children of Is'ra-el did so as Josh'u-a commanded, and took up twelve stones out of the midst of Jor'dan, as the LORD spoke to Josh'u-a, according to the number of the tribes of the children of Is'ra-el, and carried them over with them to the place where they lodged, and laid them down there.

9 And Josh'u-a set up twelve stones in the midst of Jor'dan, in the place where the feet of the priests which bare the ark of the <u>covenant</u> stood: and they are there to this day. agreement

10 For the priests which bare the ark stood in the midst of Jor'dan, until everything was finished that the LORD commanded Josh'u-a to speak to the people, according to all that Mo'ses commanded Josh'u-a: and the people <u>hasted</u> and passed over. JOHN 19:30　hurried

11 And it came to pass, when all the people were <u>clean passed</u> over, that the ark of the LORD passed over, and the priests, in the presence of the people. finished crossing

12 And the children of Reu'ben, and the children of Gad, and half the tribe of Ma-nas'seh, passed over armed before the children of Is'ra-el, as Mo'ses spoke to them:

13 About forty thousand <u>prepared</u> for war passed over before the LORD to battle, to the plains of Jer'i-cho. equipped

14 On that day the LORD <u>magnified</u> Josh'u-a in the sight of all Is'ra-el; and they <u>feared</u> him, as they <u>feared</u> Mo'ses, all the days of his life. exalted - revered

15 And the LORD spoke to Josh'u-a, saying,

16 Command the priests that bear the ark of the testimony, that they come up out of Jor'dan.

PISA - - - - - 381

17 Josh'u-a therefore commanded the priests, saying, Come you up out of Jor'dan.

18 And it came to pass, when the priests that bare the ark of the <u>covenant</u> of the LORD were come up out of the midst of Jor'dan, *and* the soles of the priests' feet were lifted up to the dry land, that the waters of Jor'dan returned to their place, and flowed over all its banks, as *they did* before. agreement

19 And the people came up out of Jor'dan on the tenth *day* of the first month, and encamped in Gil'gal, in the east border of Jer'i-cho.

20 And those twelve stones, which they took out of Jor'dan, did Josh'u-a <u>pitch</u> in Gil'gal. set up

21 And he spoke to the children of Is'ra-el, saying, When your children shall ask their fathers in time to come, saying, What *mean* these stones?

22 Then you shall let your children know, saying, Is'ra-el came over this Jor'dan on dry land.

23 For the LORD your <u>God</u> dried up the waters of Jor'dan from before you, until you were passed over, as the LORD your <u>God</u> did to the Red sea, which He dried up from before us, until we were gone over: Elohim^{p-f}

24 That all the people of the earth might know the hand of the LORD, that it *is* mighty: that you might <u>fear</u> the LORD your God for ever. reverence

CHAPTER 5

AND it came to pass, when all the kings of the Am'or-ites, which *were* on the side of Jor'dan westward, and all the kings of the Ca'naan-ites, which *were* by the sea, heard that the LORD had dried up the waters of Jor'dan from before the children of Is'ra-el, until we were passed over, that <u>their heart melted</u>, neither was there spirit in them any more, because of the children of Is'ra-el. they lost their courage

2 At that time the LORD said to Josh'u-a, Make you sharp knives, and circumcise again the children of Is'ra-el the second time.

3 And Josh'u-a made him sharp knives, and circumcised the children of Is'ra-el at the hill of the foreskins.

4 And this *is* the cause why Josh'u-a did circumcise: All the people that came out of E'gypt, *that were* males, *even* all the men of war, died in the wilderness by the way, after they came out of E'gypt.

5 Now all the people that came out were circumcised: but all the people *that were* born in the wilderness by the way as they came forth out of E'gypt, *them* they had not circumcised.

6 For the children of Is'ra-el walked forty years in the wilderness, till all the people *that were* men of war, which came out of E'gypt, were consumed, because they obeyed not the voice of the LORD: to whom the LORD swear that He would not show them the land, which the LORD swear to their fathers that He would give us, a land that flows with milk and honey.

7 And their children, *whom* He raised

up in their stead, them Josh'u-a circumcised: for they were uncircumcised, because they had not circumcised them by the way.

8 And it came to pass, when they had done circumcising all the people, that they abode in their places in the camp, till they were <u>whole</u>.   healed

9 And the LORD said to Josh'u-a, This day have I rolled away the reproach of E'gypt from off you. Wherefore the name of the place is called Gil'gal to this day.

10 And the children of Is'ra-el encamped in Gil'gal, and kept the passover on the fourteenth day of the month at <u>even</u> in the plains of Jer'i-cho.   evening

11 And they did eat of the <u>old corn</u> of the land on the <u>morrow</u> after the passover, <u>unleavened</u> cakes, and <u>parched</u> *corn* in the selfsame day.   produce - next day - without yeast - roasted grain

12 And the manna ceased on the morrow after they had eaten of the old <u>corn</u> of the land; neither had the children of Is'ra-el manna any more; but they did eat of the fruit of the land of Ca'naan that year.

13 And it came to pass, when Josh'u-a was by Jer'i-cho, that he lifted up his eyes and looked, and, behold, there stood a man opposite him with his sword drawn in his hand: and Josh'u-a went to him, and said to him, *Are* you for us, or for our adversaries?

14 And he said, Nay; but *as* captain of the host of the LORD am I now come. And Josh'u-a fell on his face to the earth, and did worship, and said to

him, What says my lord to his servant?

15 And the captain of the LORD's host said to Josh'u-a, Loose your shoe from off your foot; for the place whereon you stand *is* holy. And Josh'u-a did so.

CHAPTER 6

NOW Jer'i-cho was <u>straitly</u> shut up because of the children of Is'ra-el: none went out, and none came in.   tightly

2 And the LORD said to Josh'u-a, See, I have given into your hand Jer'i-cho, and the king thereof, *and* the mighty men of valor.

3 And you shall <u>compass</u> the city, all *you* men of war, *and* go round about the city once. Thus shall you do six days.   go around

4 And seven priests shall bear before the ark seven trumpets of rams' horns: and the seventh day you shall <u>compass</u> the city seven times, and the priests shall blow with the trumpets.

5 And it shall come to pass, that when they make a long *blast* with the ram's horn, *and* when you hear the sound of the trumpet, all the people shall shout with a great shout; and the wall of the city shall fall down flat, and the people shall <u>ascend</u> up every man straight before him.   go i.e., to battle

6 And Josh'u-a the son of Nun called the priests, and said to them, Take up the ark of the <u>covenant</u>, and let seven priests bear seven trumpets of rams' horns before the ark of the LORD.   agreement

7 And he said to the people, Pass

on, and <u>compass</u> the city, and let him that is armed pass on before the ark of the LORD. HEB. 11:30 go around 8 And it came to pass, when Josh'u-a had spoken to the people, that the seven priests bearing the seven trumpets of rams' horns passed on before the LORD, and blew with the trumpets: and the ark of the <u>covenant</u> of the LORD followed them. agreement

9 And the armed men went before the priests that blew with the trumpets, and the <u>rearward</u> came after the ark, *the priests* going on, and blowing with the trumpets. rear guard

10 And Josh'u-a had commanded the people, saying, You shall not shout, nor make any noise with your voice, neither shall *any* word proceed out of your mouth, until the day I bid you shout; then shall you shout.

11 So the ark of the LORD <u>com-passed</u> the city, going about *it* once: and they came into the camp, and lodged in the camp. circled

12 And Josh'u-a rose early in the morning, and the priests took up the ark of the LORD.

13 And seven priests bearing seven trumpets of rams' horns before the ark of the LORD went on continually, and blew with the trumpets: and the armed men went before them; but the <u>rearward</u> came after the ark of the LORD, *the priests* going on, and blowing with the trumpets.

14 And the second day they <u>com-passed</u> the city once, and returned into the camp: so they did six days. circled

15 And it came to pass on the seventh day, that they rose early about the dawning of the day, and <u>compassed</u> the city after the same manner seven times: only on that day they <u>com-passed</u> the city seven times. circled

16 And it came to pass at the seventh time, when the priests blew with the trumpets, Josh'u-a said to the people, Shout; for the LORD has given you the city.

17 And the city shall be accursed, *even* it, and all that *are* therein, to the LORD: only Ra'hab the harlot shall live, she and all that *are* with her in the house, because she hid the messengers that we sent.

18 And you, in any wise keep *your-selves* from the accursed thing, less you make *yourselves* accursed, when you take of the accursed thing, and make the camp of Is'ra-el a curse, and trouble it.

19 But all the silver, and gold, and vessels of brass and iron, *are* <u>conse-crated</u> to the LORD: they shall <u>come</u> into the treasury of the LORD. holy - go

20 So the people shouted when *the priests* blew with the trumpets: and it came to pass, when the people heard the sound of the trumpet, and the people shouted with a great shout, that the wall fell down flat, so that the people went up into the city, every man straight before him, and they took the city.

21 And they utterly destroyed all that was in the city, both man and woman, young and old, and ox, and sheep, and ass, with the edge of the sword.

22 But Josh'u-a had said to the two

men that had spied out the country, Go into the harlot's house, and bring out from there the woman, and all that she has, as you swear to her.

23 And the young men that were spies went in, and brought out Ra'hab, and her father, and her mother, and her brethren, and all that she had; and they brought out all her <u>kindred</u>, and left them out-side the camp of Is'ra-el.   relatives

24 And they burned the city with fire, and all that *was* therein: only the sil-ver, and the gold, and the vessels of brass and of iron, they put into the treasury of the house of the LORD.

25 And Josh'u-a saved Ra'hab the har-lot alive, and her father's household, and all that she had; and she dwelled in Is'ra-el *even* to this day; because she hid the messengers, which Josh'u-a sent to spy out Jer'i-cho.

26 And Josh'u-a <u>adjured</u> *them* at that time, saying, Cursed *be* the man before the LORD, that rises up and builds this city Jer'i-cho: he shall lay the foundation thereof in his firstborn, and in his youngest *son* shall he set up the gates of it.   i.e., required oath of them

27 So the LORD was with Josh'u-a; and his fame was *noised* through-out all the country.   spread

CHAPTER 7

BUT the children of Is'ra-el com mitted a trespass in the <u>accursed thing</u>: for A'chan, the son of Car'mi, the son of Zab'di, the son of Ze'rah, of the tribe of Ju'dah, took of the <u>accursed thing</u>: and the anger of the LORD <u>was kindled</u> against the children of Is'ra-el.   things under the ban - burned

2 And Josh'u-a sent men from Jer'i-cho to A'i, which *is* beside Beth-a'ven, on the east side of Beth'-el, and spoke to them, saying, Go up and <u>view</u> the country. And the men went up and <u>viewed</u> A'i.   spy out

3 And they returned to Josh'u-a, and said to him, Let not all the people go up; but let about two or three thou-sand men go up and smite A'i; *and* make not all the people to labor there; for they *are but* few.

4 So there went up there of the people about three thousand men: and they fled before the men of A'i.

5 And the men of A'i smote of them about thirty and six men: for they chased them *from* before the gate *even* to Sheb'a-rim, and smote them <u>in the going down</u>: wherefore the hearts of the people melted, and became as water.   on the descent

6 And Josh'u-a <u>rent</u> his clothes, and fell to the earth upon his face before the ark of the LORD until the eventide, he and the elders of Is'ra-el, and <u>put dust upon their heads</u>.   tore - mourned

7 And Josh'u-a said, Alas, O <u>Lord GOD</u>, wherefore have You at all brought this people over Jor'dan, to deliver us into the hand of the Am'or-ites, to destroy us? <u>would to God</u> we had been content, and dwelled on the other side Jor'dan!   Adonay^p.f. Jehovah - if only

8 O Lord, what shall I say, when Is'ra-el turns their backs before their enemies!

9 For the Ca'naan-ites and all the inhabitants of the land shall hear *of it*, and shall <u>environ</u> us round, and cut off our name from the earth: and what will you do to Your great name? surround

10 And the LORD said to Josh'u-a, <u>Get you up</u>; why you thus upon your face? stand up

11 Is'ra-el has sinned, and they have also transgressed My <u>covenant</u> which I commanded them: for they have even taken of the <u>accursed</u> thing, and have also stolen, and <u>dissembled</u> also, and they have put *it* even among their own stuff. agreement - banned - deceived

12 Therefore the children of Is'ra-el could not stand before their enemies, *but* turned *their* backs before their enemies, because they were <u>accursed</u>: neither will I be with you any more, except you destroy the <u>accursed</u> from among you.

13 Up, <u>sanctify</u> the people, and say, Sanctify yourselves against to morrow: for thus says the LORD God of Is'ra-el, *There is* an <u>accursed</u> thing in the midst of you, O Is'ra-el: you can not stand before your enemies, until you take away the <u>accursed</u> thing from among you. consecrate

14 In the morning therefore you shall be brought according to your tribes: and it shall be, *that* the tribe which the LORD takes shall come according to the families *thereof*; and the family which the LORD shall take shall come by households; and the household which the LORD shall take shall come man by man.

15 And it shall be, *that* he that is taken with the <u>accursed</u> thing shall be <u>burned</u> with fire, he and all that he has: because he has <u>transgressed</u> the <u>covenant</u> of the LORD, and because he has wrought folly in Is'ra-el. banned - destroyed - violated the agreement

16 So Josh'u-a rose up early in the morning, and brought Is'ra-el by their tribes; and the tribe of Ju'dah was <u>taken</u>: pointed out

17 And he brought the family of Ju'dah; and he took the family of the Zar'hites: and he brought the family of the Zar'hites man by man; and Zab'di was taken:

18 And he brought his household man by man; and A'chan, the son of Car'mi, the son of Zab'di, the son of Ze'rah, of the tribe of Ju'dah, was taken.

19 And Josh'u-a said to A'chan, My son, give, I pray you, glory to the <u>LORD God</u> of Is'ra-el, and make confession to Him; and tell me now what you have done; hide *it* not from me. Jehovah[s.f.] Elohim[p.f.]

20 And A'chan answered Josh'u-a, and said, Indeed I have sinned against the <u>LORD God</u> of Is'ra-el, and <u>thus and thus have I done</u>: this is what I did

21 When I saw among the spoils a goodly Bab'y-lo-nish <u>garment</u>, and two hundred shekels of silver, and a wedge of gold of fifty shekels weight, then I <u>coveted</u> them, and took them; and, behold, they *are* hid in the earth in the midst of my tent, and the silver under it. mantle - wanted

22 So Josh'u-a sent messengers, and they ran to the tent; and, behold,

it was hid in his tent, and the silver under it.

23 And they took them out of the midst of the tent, and brought them to Josh'u-a, and to all the children of Is'ra-el, and laid them out before the LORD.

24 And Josh'u-a, and all Is'ra-el with him, took A'chan the son of Ze'rah, and the silver, and the garment, and the wedge of gold, and his sons, and his daughters, and his oxen, and his asses, and his sheep, and his tent, and all that he had: and they brought them to the valley of A'chor.

25 And Josh'u-a said, Why have you troubled us? the LORD shall trouble you this day. And all Is'ra-el stoned him with stones, and burned them with fire, after they had stoned them with stones.

26 And they raised over him a great heap of stones to this day. So the LORD turned from the fierceness of His anger. Wherefore the name of that place was called, The valley of A'chor, to this day.

monument - Trouble

CHAPTER 8

AND the LORD said to Josh'u-a, Fear not, neither be you dismayed: take all the people of war with you, and arise, go up to A'i: see, I have given into your hand the king of A'i, and his people, and his city, and his land:

2 And you shall do to A'i and her king as you did to Jer'i-cho and her king: only the spoil thereof, and the cattle thereof, shall you take for a prey to yourselves: lay you an ambush for the city behind it.

3 So Josh'u-a arose, and all the people of war, to go up against A'i: and Josh'u-a chose out thirty thousand mighty men of valor, and sent them away by night.

4 And he commanded them, saying, Behold, you shall lie in wait against the city, *even* behind the city: go not very far from the city, but be you all ready:

5 And I, and all the people that *are* with me, will approach to the city: and it shall come to pass, when they come out against us, as at the first, that we will flee before them,

6 (For they will come out after us) till we have drawn them from the city; for they will say, They flee before us, as at the first: therefore we will flee before them.

7 Then you shall rise up from the ambush, and seize upon the city: for the LORD your God will deliver it into your hand.

8 And it shall be, when you have taken the city, *that* you shall set the city on fire: according to the commandment of the LORD shall you do. See, I have commanded you.

9 Josh'u-a therefore sent them forth: and they went to lie in ambush, and abode between Beth'-el and A'i, on the west side of A'i: but Josh'u-a lodged that night among the people.

10 And Josh'u-a rose up early in the morning, and numbered the people, and went up, he and the elders of Is'ra-el, before the people to A'i.

marched

11 And all the people, *even the people* of war that *were* with him, went up, and drew near, and came before the city, and underline{pitched} on the north side of A'i: now *there was* a valley between them and A'i.   camped

12 And he took about five thousand men, and set them to lie in ambush between Beth'-el and A'i, on the west side of the city.

13 And when they had set the people, *even* all the host that *was* on the north of the city, and their liers in wait on the west of the city, Josh'u-a went that night into the midst of the valley.   ambushers

14 And it came to pass, when the king of A'i saw *it*, that they hasted and rose up early, and the men of the city went out against Is'ra-el to battle, he and all his people, at a time appointed, before the plain; but he knew not that *there were* liers in ambush against him behind the city.

15 And Josh'u-a and all Is'ra-el made as if they were beaten before them, and fled by the way of the wilderness.

16 And all the people that were in A'i *were* called together to pursue after them: and they pursued after Josh'u-a, and were drawn away from the city.

17 And there was not a man left in A'i or Beth'-el, that went not after Is'ra-el: and they left the city open, and pursued after Is'ra-el.

18 And the LORD said to Josh'u-a, Stretch out the spear that *is* in your hand toward A'i; for I will give it into your hand. And Josh'u-a stretched out the spear that *he had* in his hand toward the city.

19 And the ambush arose quickly out of their place, and they ran as soon as he had stretched out his hand: and they entered into the city, and took it, and hasted and set the city on fire.   hurried

20 And when the men of A'i looked behind them, they saw, and, behold, the smoke of the city ascended up to heaven, and they had no power to flee this way or that way: and the people that fled to the wilderness turned back upon the pursuers.

21 And when Josh'u-a and all Is'ra-el saw that the ambush had taken the city, and that the smoke of the city ascended, then they turned again, and slew the men of A'i.

22 And the other issued out of the city against them; so they were in the midst of Is'ra-el, some on this side, and some on that side: and they smote them, so that they let none of them remain or escape.   destroyed

23 And the king of A'i they took alive, and brought him to Josh'u-a.

24 And it came to pass, when Is'ra-el had made an end of slaying all the inhabitants of A'i in the field, in the wilderness wherein they chased them, and when they were all fallen on the edge of the sword, until they were consumed, that all the Is'ra-el-ites returned to A'i, and smote it with the edge of the sword.   finished - killed by - destroyed

25 And *so* it was, *that* all that fell that day, both of men and women, *were* twelve thousand, *even* all the men of A'i.

26 For Josh'u-a drew not his hand

back, wherewith he stretched out the spear, until he had utterly destroyed all the inhabitants of A'i. did not call a halt

27 Only the cattle and the spoil of that city Is'ra-el took for a prey to themselves, according to the word of the LORD which He commanded Josh'u-a.

28 And Josh'u-a burned A'i, and made it an heap for ever, *even* a desolation to this day. ruin

29 And the king of A'i he hanged on a tree until eventide: and as soon as the sun was down, Josh'u-a commanded that they should take his carcase down from the tree, and cast it at the entering of the gate of the city, and raise thereon a great heap of stones, *that remains* to this day. body

30 Then Josh'u-a built an altar to the LORD God of Is'ra-el in mount E'bal, Jehovah^s.f. Elohim^p.f.

31 As Mo'ses the servant of the LORD commanded the children of Is'ra-el, as it is written in the book of the law of Mo'ses, an altar of whole stones, over which no man has lift up *any* iron: and they offered thereon burned offerings to the LORD, and sacrificed peace offerings.

32 And he wrote there upon the stones a copy of the law of Mo'ses, which he wrote in the presence of the children of Is'ra-el.

33 And all Is'ra-el, and their elders, and officers, and their judges, stood on this side the ark and on that side before the priests the Le'vites, which bare the ark of the covenant of the LORD, as well the stranger, as he that was born among them; half of them opposite mount Ger'i-zim, and half of them opposite mount E'bal; as Mo'ses the servant of the LORD had commanded before, that they should bless the people of Is'ra-el.

both sides of the ark - agreement - aliens

34 And afterward he read all the words of the law, the blessings and cursings, according to all that is written in the book of the law.

35 There was not a word of all that Mo'ses commanded, which Josh'u-a read not before all the congregation of Is'ra-el, with the women, and the little ones, and the strangers that were conversant among them.

CHAPTER 9

AND it came to pass, when all the kings which *were* on this side Jor'dan, in the hills, and in the valleys, and in all the coasts of the great sea over against Leb'a-non, the Hit'-tite, and the Am'or-ite, the Ca'naan-ite, the Per'iz-zite, the Hi'vite, and the Jeb'u-site, heard *thereof*;

2 That they gathered themselves together, to fight with Josh'u-a and with Is'ra-el, with one accord. purpose

3 And when the inhabitants of Gib'e-on heard what Josh'u-a had done to Jer'i-cho and to A'i,

4 They did work wilily, and went and made as if they had been ambassadors, and took old sacks upon their asses, and wine bottles, old, and rent, and bound up; craftily - skins

5 And old shoes and clouted upon their feet, and old garments upon them;

and all the bread of their provision was dry *and* mouldy. _{patched sandals}

6 And they went to Josh'u-a to the camp at Gil'gal, and said to him, and to the men of Is'ra-el, We be come from a far country: now therefore make you a <u>league</u> with us. _{treaty}

7 And the men of Is'ra-el said to the Hi'vites, Perhaps you dwell among us; and how shall we make a <u>league</u> with you?

8 And they said to Josh'u-a, We *are* your servants. And Josh'u-a said to them, Who *are* you? and from where come you?

9 And they said to him, From a very far country your servants are come because of the <u>name</u> of the LORD your God: for we have heard the fame of him, and all that He did in E'gypt, _{fame}

10 And all that He did to the two kings of the Am'or-ites, that *were* beyond Jor'dan, to Si'hon king of Hesh'bon, and to Og king of Ba'shan, which *was* at Ash'ta-roth.

11 Wherefore our elders and all the inhabitants of our country spoke to us, saying, Take victuals with you for the journey, and go to meet them, and say to them, We *are* your servants: therefore now make you a <u>league</u> with us. _{treaty}

12 This our bread we took hot *for* our provision out of our houses on the day we came forth to go to you; but now, behold, it is dry, and it is mouldy:

13 And these <u>bottles</u> of wine, which we filled, *were* new; and, behold, they be <u>rent</u>: and these our garments and our shoes are become old by reason of the very long journey. _{wineskins - torn}

14 And the men took of their <u>victuals</u>, and asked not *counsel* at the mouth of the LORD. _{provisions}

15 And Josh'u-a made peace with them, and made a league with them, to let them live: and the princes of the congregation swear to them.

16 And it came to pass at the end of three days after they had made a league with them, that they heard that they *were* their neighbors, and *that* they dwelled among them.

17 And the children of Is'ra-el journeyed, and came to their cities on the third day. Now their cities *were* Gib'e-on, and Che-phi'rah, and Be-e'roth, and Kir'jath-je'a-rim.

18 And the children of Is'ra-el <u>smote</u> them not, because the princes of the congregation had sworn to them by the LORD God of Is'ra-el. And all the congregation <u>murmured</u> against the princes. _{attacked - grumbled}

19 But all the princes said to all the congregation, We have <u>sworn</u> to them by the <u>LORD God</u> of Is'ra-el: now therefore we may not touch them. _{promised - Jehovah^{s.f.} Elohim^{p.f.}}

20 This we will do to them; we will even let them live, less <u>wrath</u> be upon us, because of the oath which we swear to them. _{judgment}

21 And the princes said to them, Let them live; but let them be <u>hewers of wood</u> and drawers of water to all the congregation; as the princes had promised them. _{woodcutters}

22 And Josh'u-a called for them,

and he spoke to them, saying, Wherefore have you <u>beguiled</u> us, saying, We *are* very far from you; when you dwell among us? <small>deceived</small>
23 Now therefore you *are* cursed, and there shall none of you be freed from being bondmen, and <u>hewers of wood</u> and drawers of water for the house of my <u>God</u>. <small>woodcutters - Elohim p.f.</small>
24 And they answered Josh'u-a, and said, Because it was <u>certainly</u> told your servants, how that the LORD your <u>God</u> commanded His servant Mo'ses to give you all the land, and to destroy all the inhabitants of the land from before you, therefore we were <u>sore</u> afraid of our lives because of you, and have done this thing. <small>clearly - very</small>
25 And now, behold, we *are* in your hand: as it seems good and right to you to do to us, do.
26 And so did he to them, and delivered them out of the hand of the children of Is'ra-el, that they slew them not.
27 And Josh'u-a made them that day <u>hewers of wood</u> and drawers of water for the congregation, and for the altar of the LORD, even to this day, in the place which he should choose.

CHAPTER 10

NOW it came to pass, when A-don'i-ze'dec king of Je-ru'sa-lem had heard how Josh'u-a had taken it, and had utterly destroyed it; as he had done to Jer'i-cho and her king, so he had done to A'i and her king; and how the inhabitants of Gib'e-on had made peace with Is'ra-el, and were among them;
2 That they feared greatly, because Gib'e-on *was* a great city, as one of the royal cities, and because it *was* greater than A'i, and all the men thereof *were* mighty.
3 Wherefore A-don'i-ze'dec king of Je-ru'sa-lem sent to Ho'ham king of He'bron, and to Pi'ram king of Jar'muth, and to Ja-phi'a king of La'chish, and to De'bir king of Eg'lon, saying,
4 Come up to me, and help me, that we may <u>smite</u> Gib'e-on: for it has made peace with Josh'u-a and with the children of Is'ra-el. <small>attack</small>
5 Therefore the five kings of the Am'or-ites, the king of Je-ru'sa-lem, the king of He'bron, the king of Jar'muth, the king of La'chish, the king of Eg'lon, gathered themselves together, and went up, they and all their hosts, and encamped before Gib'e-on, and made war against it.
6 And the men of Gib'e-on sent to Josh'u-a to the camp to Gil'gal, saying, <u>Slack</u> not your hand from your servants; come up to us quickly, and save us, and help us: for all the kings of the Am'or-ites that dwell in the mountains are gathered together against us. <small>abandon</small>
7 So Josh'u-a ascended from Gil'gal, he, and all the people of war with him, and all the <u>mighty</u> men of valor. <small>brave</small>
8 And the LORD said to Josh'u-a, Fear them not: for I have delivered

them into your hand; <u>there shall not</u> <u>a man of them stand before you</u>.

<small>i.e., killed all</small>

9 Josh'u-a therefore came to them suddenly, *and* went up from Gil'gal all night.

10 And the Lord <u>discomfited</u> them before Is'ra-el, and slew them with a great slaughter at Gib'e-on, and chased them along the way that goes up to Beth-ho'ron, and smote them to A-ze'kah, and to Mak-ke'dah.

<small>confounded</small>

11 And it came to pass, as they fled from before Is'ra-el, *and* were in the going down to Beth-ho'ron, that the Lord cast down great stones from heaven upon them to A-ze'kah, and they died: *they were* more which died with hailstones than *they* whom the children of Is'ra-el slew with the sword.

12 Then spoke Josh'u-a to the Lord in the day when the Lord delivered up the Am'or-ites before the children of Is'ra-el, and he said in the sight of Is'ra-el, Sun, stand you still upon Gib'e-on; and you, Moon, in the valley of Aj'a-lon.

13 And the sun stood still, and the moon stayed, until the people had avenged themselves upon their enemies. *Is* not this written in the book of Ja'sher? So the sun stood still in the midst of heaven, and <u>hasted not</u> to go down about a whole day. <small>delayed</small>

14 And there was no day like that before it or after it, that the Lord <u>hearkened</u> to the voice of a man: for the Lord fought for Is'ra-el. <small>listened</small>

15 And Josh'u-a returned, and all Is'ra-el with him, to the camp to Gil'gal.

16 But these five kings fled, and hid themselves in a cave at Mak-ke'dah.

17 And it was told Josh'u-a, saying, The five kings are found hid in a cave at Mak-ke'dah.

18 And Josh'u-a said, Roll great stones upon the mouth of the cave, and <u>set</u> men by it for to <u>keep</u> them: <small>assign - guard</small>

19 And stay you not, *but* pursue after your enemies, and smite the hindmost of them; allow them not to enter into their cities: for the Lord your God has delivered them into your hand.

20 And it came to pass, when Josh'u-a and the children of Is'ra-el had made an end of slaying them with a very great slaughter, till they were <u>consumed</u>, that the rest *which* remained of them entered into <u>fenced</u> cities. <small>destroyed - fortified</small>

21 And all the people returned to the camp to Josh'u-a at Mak-ke'dah in peace: none <u>moved his tongue</u> against any of the children of Is'ra-el. <small>uttered a word</small>

22 Then said Josh'u-a, Open the mouth of the cave, and bring out those five kings to me out of the cave.

23 And they did so, and brought forth those five kings to him out of the cave, the king of Je-ru'sa-lem, the king of He'bron, the king of Jar'muth, the king of La'chish, *and* the king of Eg'lon.

24 And it came to pass, when they brought out those kings to Josh'u-a, that Josh'u-a called for all the men of Is'ra-el, and said to the captains of the men of war which went with him, Come near, <u>put your feet upon the</u>

necks of these kings. And they came near, and put their feet upon the necks of them.   i.e., symbol of mastery

25 And Josh'u-a said to them, Fear not, nor be dismayed, be strong and of good courage: for thus shall the LORD do to all your enemies against whom you fight.

26 And afterward Josh'u-a smote them, and slew them, and hanged them on five trees: and they were hanging upon the trees until the evening.   struck

27 And it came to pass at the time of the going down of the sun, *that* Josh'u-a commanded, and they took them down off the trees, and cast them into the cave wherein they had been hid, and laid great stones in the cave's mouth, *which remain* until this very day.

28 And that day Josh'u-a took Mak-ke'dah, and smote it with the edge of the sword, and the king thereof he utterly destroyed, them, and all the souls that *were* therein; he let none remain: and he did to the king of Mak-ke'dah as he did to the king of Jer'i-cho.   people

29 Then Josh'u-a passed from Mak-ke'dah, and all Is'ra-el with him, to Lib'nah, and fought against Lib'nah:

30 And the LORD delivered it also, and the king thereof, into the hand of Is'ra-el; and he smote it with the edge of the sword, and all the souls that *were* therein; he let none remain in it; but did to the king thereof as he did to the king of Jer'i-cho.

31 And Josh'u-a passed from Lib'-nah, and all Is'ra-el with him, to La'-chish, and encamped against it, and fought against it:

32 And the LORD delivered La'chish into the hand of Is'ra-el, which took it on the second day, and smote it with the edge of the sword, and all the souls that *were* therein, according to all that he had done to Lib'nah.   people

33 Then Ho'ram king of Ge'zer came up to help La'chish; and Josh'u-a smote him and his people, until he had left him none remaining.

34 And from La'chish Josh'u-a passed to Eg'lon, and all Is'ra-el with him; and they encamped against it, and fought against it:

35 And they took it on that day, and smote it with the edge of the sword, and all the souls that *were* therein he utterly destroyed that day, according to all that he had done to La'chish.   people

36 And Josh'u-a went up from Eg'lon, and all Is'ra-el with him, to He'bron; and they fought against it:

37 And they took it, and smote it with the edge of the sword, and the king thereof, and all the cities thereof, and all the souls that *were* therein; he left none remaining, according to all that he had done to Eg'lon; but destroyed it utterly, and all the souls that *were* therein.

38 And Josh'u-a returned, and all Is'ra-el with him, to De'bir; and fought against it:

39 And he took it, and the king thereof, and all the cities thereof; and they smote them with the edge of the sword, and utterly destroyed all the souls that *were* therein; he left none re-maining: as he had done to He'bron, so

he did to De'bir, and to the king thereof; as he had done also to Lib'nah, and to her king. *people*

40 So Josh'u-a <u>smote</u> all the country of the hills, and of the south, and of the <u>vale</u>, and of the <u>springs</u>, and all their kings: he left none remaining, but utterly destroyed all that breathed, as the LORD God of Is'ra-el commanded.

*struck - foothills - mountain slopes - Jehovah*s.f. *Elohim*p.f.

41 And Josh'u-a smote them from Ka'desh-bar'ne-a even to Ga'za, and all the country of Go'shen, even to Gib'e-on.

42 And all these kings and their land did Josh'u-a take at one time, because the LORD God of Is'ra-el fought for Is'ra-el.

43 And Josh'u-a returned, and all Is'ra-el with him, to the camp to Gil'gal.

CHAPTER 11

AND it came to pass, when Ja'bin king of Ha'zor had heard *those things*, that he sent to Jo'bab king of Ma'don, and to the king of Shim'ron, and to the king of Ach'shaph,

2 And to the kings that *were* on the north of the mountains, and of the plains south of Chin'ne-roth, and in the valley, and in the borders of Dor on the west,

3 *And to* the Ca'naan-ite on the east and on the west, and *to* the Am'or-ite, and the Hit'tite, and the Per'iz-zite, and the Jeb'u-site in the mountains, and to the Hi'vite under Her'mon in the land of Miz-peh.

4 And they went out, they and all their hosts with them, much people, even as the sand that is upon the sea shore in multitude, with horses and chariots very many.

5 And when all these kings were <u>met together</u>, they came and <u>pitched</u> together at the waters of Me'rom, to fight against Is'ra-el. *agreed to meet - camped*

6 And the LORD said to Josh'u-a, Be not afraid because of them: for to morrow about this time will I deliver them up all slain before Is'ra-el: you shall <u>hough</u> their horses, and burn their chariots with fire. *hamstring*

7 So Josh'u-a came, and all the people of war with him, against them by the waters of Me'rom suddenly; and they fell upon them.

8 And the LORD delivered them into the hand of Is'ra-el, who smote them, and chased them to great Zi'don, and to Mis're-photh-ma'im, and to the valley of Miz-peh eastward; and they smote them, until they left them none remaining.

9 And Josh'u-a did to them as the LORD bade him: he <u>houghed</u> their horses, and burned their chariots with fire. *hamstrung*

10 And Josh'u-a at that time turned back, and took Ha'zor, and smote the king thereof with the sword: for Ha'zor beforetime was the head of all those kingdoms.

11 And they <u>smote</u> all the <u>souls</u> that *were* therein with the edge of the sword, utterly destroying *them*: there was not any left to breathe: and he burned Ha'zor with fire. *struck - people*

12 And all the cities of those kings, and all the kings of them, did Josh'u-a take, and smote them with the edge of the sword, *and* he utterly destroyed them, as Mo'ses the servant of the LORD commanded.

13 But *as for* the cities that stood still in their strength, Is'ra-el burned none of them, save Ha'zor only; *that* did Josh'u-a burn.

14 And all the spoil of these cities, and the cattle, the children of Is'ra-el took for a prey to themselves; but every man they smote with the edge of the sword, until they had destroyed them, neither left they any to breathe.

M03

381

15 As the LORD commanded Mo'ses his servant, so did Mo'ses command Josh'u-a, and so did Josh'u-a; he left nothing undone of all that the LORD commanded Mo'ses.

16 So Josh'u-a took all that land, the hills, and all the south country, and all the land of Go'shen, and the valley, and the plain, and the mountain of Is'ra-el, and the valley of the same;

17 *Even* from the mount Ha'lak, that goes up to Se'ir, even to Ba'al-gad in the valley of Leb'a-non under mount Her'mon: and all their kings he took, and smote them, and slew them.

18 Josh'u-a made war a long time with all those kings.

19 There was not a city that made peace with the children of Is'ra-el, save the Hi'vites the inhabitants of Gib'e-on: all *other* they took in battle.

20 For it was of the LORD to harden their hearts, that they should come against Is'ra-el in battle, that he might destroy them utterly, *and* that they might have no favor, but that he might destroy them, as the LORD commanded Mo'ses.

mercy

21 And at that time came Josh'u-a, and cut off the An'a-kims from the mountains, from He'bron, from De'bir, from A'nab, and from all the mountains of Ju'dah, and from all the mountains of Is'ra-el: Josh'u-a destroyed them utterly with their cities.

22 There was none of the An'a-kims left in the land of the children of Is'ra-el: only in Ga'za, in Gath, and in Ash'dod, there remained.

23 So Josh'u-a took the whole land, according to all that the LORD said to Mo'ses; and Josh'u-a gave it for an inheritance to Is'ra-el according to their divisions by their tribes. And the land rested from war.

CHAPTER 12

NOW these *are* the kings of the land, which the children of Is'ra-el smote, and possessed their land on the other side Jor'dan toward the rising of the sun, from the river Ar'non to mount Her'mon, and all the plain on the east: defeated

2 Si'hon king of the Am'or-ites, who dwelled in Hesh'bon, *and* ruled from Ar'o-er, which *is* upon the bank of the river Ar'non, and from the middle of the river, and from half Gil'e-ad, even to the river Jab'bok, *which is* the border of the children of Am'mon;

3 And from the plain to the sea of Chin'ne-roth on the east, and to the

sea of the plain, *even* the Salt sea on the east, the way to Beth-jesh'i-moth; and from the south, under Ash'doth-pis'gah: *i.e., Galilee - i.e., Dead*

4 And the coast of Og king of Ba'shan, *which was* of the remnant of the giants, that dwelled at Ash'ta-roth and at Ed're-i,

5 And reigned in mount Her'mon, and in Sal'cah, and in all Ba'shan, to the border of the Gesh'u-rites and the Ma-ach'a-thites, and half Gil'e-ad, the border of Si'hon king of Hesh'bon.

6 Them did Mo'ses the servant of the LORD and the children of Is'ra-el smite: and Mo'ses the servant of the LORD gave it *for* a possession to the Reu'ben-ites, and the Gad'ites, and the half tribe of Ma-nas'seh.

7 And these *are* the kings of the country which Josh'u-a and the children of Is'ra-el smote on this side Jor'dan on the west, from Ba'al-gad in the valley of Leb'a-non even to the mount Ha'lak, that goes up to Se'ir; which Josh'u-a gave to the tribes of Is'ra-el *for* a possession according to their divisions; *their own*

8 In the mountains, and in the valleys, and in the plains, and in the springs, and in the wilderness, and in the south country; the Hit'tites, the Am'or-ites, and the Ca'naan-ites, the Per'iz-zites, the Hi'vites, and the Jeb'u-sites:

9 The king of Jer'i-cho, one; the king of A'i, which *is* beside Beth'-el, one;

10 The king of Je-ru'sa-lem, one; the king of He'bron, one;

11 The king of Jar'muth, one; the king of La'chish, one;

12 The king of Eg'lon, one; the king of Ge'zer, one;

13 The king of De'bir, one; the king of Geder, one;

14 The king of Hor'mah, one; the king of A'rad, one;

15 The king of Lib'nah, one; the king of A-dul'lam, one;

16 The king of Mak-ke'dah, one; the king of Beth'-el, one;

17 The king of Tap'pu-ah, one; the king of He'pher, one;

18 The king of A'phek, one; the king of La-shar'on, one;

19 The king of Ma'don, one; the king of Ha'zor, one;

20 The king of Shim'ron-me'ron, one; the king of Ach'shaph, one;

21 The king of Ta'a-nach, one; the king of Me-gid'do, one;

22 The king of Ke'desh, one; the king of Jok'ne-am of Car'mel, one;

23 The king of Dor in the coast of Dor, one; the king of the nations of Gil'gal, one; *height*

24 The king of Tir'zah, one: all the kings thirty and one.

CHAPTER 13

NOW Josh'u-a was old and stricken in years; *and* the LORD said to him, You are old *and* stricken in years, and there remains yet very much land to be possessed. *taken over*

2 This *is* the land that yet remains: all the borders of the Phi-lis'tines, and all Gesh'u-ri,

3 From Si'hor, which *is* before E'gypt, even to the borders of Ek'ron northward, *which* is counted to the Ca'naanite: five lords of the Phi-lis'tines; the Ga'zath-ites, and the Ash'doth-ites, the Esh'ka-lon-ites, the Git-tites, and the Ek'ron-ites; also the A'vites:

4 From the south, all the land of the Ca'naan-ites, and Me-a'rah that *is* beside the Si-do'ni-ans, to A'phek, to the borders of the Am'or-ites:

5 And the land of the Gib'lites, and all Leb'a-non, toward the sunrising, from Ba'al-gad under mount Her'mon to the entering into Ha'math.

6 All the inhabitants of the hill country from Leb'a-non to Mis're-photh-ma'im, *and* all the Si-do'ni-ans, them will I drive out from before the children of Is'ra-el: only <u>divide</u> you it by lot to the Is'ra-el-ites for an inheritance, as I have commanded you.   allot

7 Now therefore divide this land for an inheritance to the nine tribes, and the half tribe of Ma-nas'seh,

8 With whom the Reu'ben-ites and the Gad'ites have received their inheritance, which Mo'ses gave them, beyond Jor'dan eastward, *even* as Mo'ses the servant of the LORD gave them;

9 From Ar'o-er, that *is* upon the bank of the river Ar'non, and the city that *is* in the midst of the river, and all the plain of Med'e-ba to Di'bon;

10 And all the cities of Si'hon king of the Am'or-ites, which reigned in Hesh'bon, to the border of the children of Am'mon;

11 And Gil'e-ad, and the border of the Gesh'u-rites and Ma-ach'a-thites, and all mount Her'mon, and all Ba'shan to Sal'cah;

12 All the kingdom of Og in Ba'shan, which reigned in Ash'ta-roth and in Ed're-i, who remained of the remnant of the giants: for these did Mo'ses <u>smite</u>, and <u>cast them out</u>.   defeat - took their land

13 Nevertheless the children of Is'ra-el expelled not the Gesh'u-rites, nor the Ma-ach'a-thites: but the Gesh'u-rites and the Ma-ach'a-thites dwell among the Is'ra-el-ites until this day.

14 Only to the tribe of Le'vi he gave none inheritance; the <u>sacrifices</u> of the Lord God of Is'ra-el made by fire *are* their inheritance, as He said to them.   offerings - Jehovahs.f. Elohim[p.f.]

15 And Mo'ses gave to the tribe of the children of Reu'ben *inheritance* <u>according</u> to their families.   divided

16 And their coast was from Ar'o-er, that *is* on the bank of the river Ar'non, and the city that *is* in the midst of the river, and all the plain by Med'e-ba;

17 Hesh'bon, and all her cities that *are* in the plain; Di'bon, and Ba'moth-ba'al, and Beth-ba'al-me'on,

18 And Ja-ha'za, and Ked'e-moth, and Meph'a-ath,

19 And Kir-jath-a'im, and Sib'mah, and Za'reth-sha'har in the mount of the valley,

20 And Beth-pe'or, and Ash'doth-pis'gah, and Beth-jesh'i-moth,

21 And all the cities of the plain, and all the kingdom of Si'hon king of the Am'or-ites, which reigned in Hesh'bon, whom Mo'ses smote with the princes of Mid'i-an, E'vi, and Re'kem, and Zur,

M11 | | | 387

and Hur, and Re'ba, *which were* chiefs of Si'hon, dwelling in the country.

22 Ba'laam also the son of Be'or, the soothsayer, did the children of Is'ra-el slay with the sword among them that were slain by them.   fortune teller

23 And the border of the children of Reu'ben was Jor'dan, and the border *thereof*. This *was* the inheritance of the children of Reu'ben after their families, the cities and the villages thereof.

24 And Mo'ses gave *inheritance* to the tribe of Gad, *even* to the children of Gad according to their families.

25 And their coast was Ja'zer, and all the cities of Gil'e-ad, and half the land of the children of Am'mon, to Ar'o-er that *is* before Rab'bah;   territory

26 And from Hesh'bon to Ra'math-miz'peh, and Bet'o-nim; and from Ma-ha-na'im to the border of De'bir;

27 And in the valley, Beth-a'ram, and Beth-nim'rah, and Suc'coth, and Za'phon, the rest of the kingdom of Si'hon king of Hesh'bon, Jor'dan and *his* border, *even* to the edge of the sea of Chin'ne-reth on the other side Jor'dan eastward.

28 This *is* the inheritance of the children of Gad after their families, the cities, and their villages.

29 And Mo'ses gave *inheritance* to the half tribe of Ma-nas'seh: and *this* was *the possession* of the half tribe of the children of Ma-nas'seh by their families.

30 And their coast was from Ma-ha-na'im, all Ba'shan, all the kingdom of Og king of Ba'shan, and all the towns of Ja'ir, which are in Ba'shan, threescore cities: 60

31 And half Gil'e-ad, and Ash'ta-roth, and Ed're-i, cities of the kingdom of Og in Ba'shan, *were pertaining to* the children of Ma'chir the son of Ma-nas'seh, *even* to the one half of the children of Ma'chir by their families.   were for

32 These *are the countries* which Mo'ses did distribute for inheritance in the plains of Mo'ab, on the other side Jor'dan, by Jer'i-cho, eastward.   apportion

33 But to the tribe of Le'vi Mo'ses gave not *any* inheritance: the LORD God of Is'ra-el *was* their inheritance, as he said to them.

CHAPTER 14

AND these *are the countries* which the children of Is'ra-el inherited in the land of Ca'naan, which E-le-a'zar the priest, and Josh'u-a the son of Nun, and the heads of the fathers of the tribes of the children of Is'ra-el, distributed for inheritance to them.

2 By lot *was* their inheritance, as the LORD commanded by the hand of Mo'ses, for the nine tribes, and *for* the half tribe.

3 For Mo'ses had given the inheritance of two tribes and an half tribe on the other side Jor'dan: but to the Le'vites he gave none inheritance among them.

4 For the children of Jo'seph were two tribes, Ma-nas'seh and E'phra-im: therefore they gave no part to the Le'vites in the land, save cities to dwell

in, with their suburbs for their cattle and for their substance.

share - except - pasture lands

5 As the LORD commanded Mo'ses, so the children of Is'ra-el did, and they divided the land.

6 Then the children of Ju'dah came to Josh'u-a in Gil'gal: and Ca'leb the son of Je-phun'neh the Ken'ez-ite said to him, You know the thing that the LORD said to Mo'ses the man of God concerning me and you in Ka'desh-bar'ne-a.

7 Forty years old *was* I when Mo'ses the servant of the LORD sent me from Ka'desh-bar'ne-a to espy out the land; and I brought him word again *as it was* in my heart.

spy

8 Nevertheless my brethren that went up with me made the heart of the people melt: but I wholly followed the LORD my God.

obeyed wholeheartedly

9 And Mo'ses swear on that day, saying, Surely the land whereon your feet have trodden shall be your inheritance, and your children's for ever, because you have wholly followed the LORD my God.

promised - Elohim[p.f.]

10 And now, behold, the LORD has kept me alive, as He said, these forty and five years, even since the LORD spoke this word to Mo'ses, while *the children of* Is'ra-el wandered in the wilderness: and now, lo, I *am* this day fourscore and five years old.

11 As yet I *am as* strong this day as *I was* in the day that Mo'ses sent me: as my strength *was* then, even so *is* my strength now, for war, both to go out, and to come in.

12 Now therefore give me this mountain, whereof the LORD spoke in that day; for you heard in that day how the An'a-kims *were* there, and *that* the cities *were* great *and* fenced: if so be the LORD *will be* with me, then I shall be able to drive them out, as the LORD said.

fortified

13 And Josh'u-a blessed him, and gave to Ca'leb the son of Je-phun'neh He'bron for an inheritance.

14 He'bron therefore became the inheritance of Ca'leb the son of Je-phun'neh the Ken'ez-ite to this day, because that he wholly followed the LORD God of Is'ra-el.

15 And the name of He'bron before *was* Kir'jath-ar'ba; *which Ar'ba was* a great man among the An'a-kims. And the land had rest from war.

peace

CHAPTER 15

THIS then was the lot of the tribe of the children of Ju'dah by their families; even to the border of E'dom the wilderness of Zin southward *was* the uttermost part of the south coast.

allotment - boundary

2 And their south border was from the shore of the Salt sea, from the bay that looks southward:

Dead

3 And it went out to the south side to Ma-al'eh-a-crab'bim, and passed along to Zin, and ascended up on the south side to Ka'desh-bar'ne-a, and passed along to Hez'ron, and went up to A'dar, and brought a compass to Kar'ka-a:

circled around

4 *From there* it passed toward Az'-mon, and went out to the river of E'-

gypt; and the <u>goings out</u> of that <u>coast</u> were at the sea: this shall be your south <u>coast</u>.   <small>end - boundary</small>

5 And the east border *was* the <u>Salt</u> sea, *even* to the end of Jor'dan. And *their* border in the north quarter *was* from the bay of the sea at the uttermost part of Jor'dan: <small>Dead</small>

6 And the border went up to Beth-hog'la, and passed along by the north of Beth-ar'a-bah; and the border went up to the <u>stone</u> of Bo'han the son of Reu'ben: <small>marker</small>

7 And the border went up toward De'bir from the valley of A'chor, and so northward, looking toward Gil'gal, that *is* before the going up to A-dum'mim, which *is* on the south side of the river: and the border passed toward the waters of En-she'mesh, and the goings out thereof were at En'ro'gel:

8 And the border went up by the valley of the son of Hin'nom to the south side of the Jeb'u-site; the same *is* Je-ru'sa-lem: and the border went up to the top of the mountain that *lies* before the valley of Hin'nom westward, which is at the end of the valley of the giants northward:

9 And the border was drawn from the top of the hill to the fountain of the water of Neph'to-ah, and went out to the cities of mount E'phron; and the border was drawn to Ba'al-ah, which *is* Kir'jath-je'a-rim:

10 And the border <u>compassed</u> from Ba'al-ah westward to mount Se'ir, and passed along to the side of mount Je'a-rim, which *is* Ches'a-lon, on

the north side, and went down to Beth-she'mesh, and passed on to Tim'nah: <small>curved</small>

11 And the border went out to the side of Ek'ron northward: and the border was drawn to Shi'cron, and passed along to mount Ba'al-ah, and went out to Jab'ne-el; and the goings out of the border were at the sea.

12 And the west border *was* to the <u>Great</u> sea, and the coast *thereof*. This *is* the coast of the children of Ju'dah round about according to their families.   <small>i.e., Mediterranean</small>

13 And to Ca'leb the son of Je-phun'neh he gave a part among the children of Ju'dah, according to the commandment of the LORD to Josh'u-a, even the city of Ar'ba the father of A'nak, which *city is* He'bron.

14 And Ca'leb drove from there the three sons of A'nak, She'shai, and A-hi'man, and Tal'mai, the children of A'nak.

15 And he went up from there to the inhabitants of De'bir: and the name of De'bir before *was* Kir'jath-se'pher.

16 And Ca'leb said, He that smite Kir'jath-se'pher, and takes it, to him will I give Ach'sah my daughter to wife.

17 And Oth'ni-el the son of Ke'naz, the brother of Ca'leb, took it: and he gave him Ach'sah his daughter to wife.

18 And it came to pass, as she came *to him*, that she moved him to ask of her father a field: and she lighted *off* the ass; and Ca'leb said to her, What would you?

19 Who answered, Give me a blessing; for you have given me a south land; give me also springs of water. And he gave her the upper springs, and the <u>nether</u> springs. _{lower}

20 This *is* the inheritance of the tribe of the children of Ju'dah according to their families.

21 And the uttermost cities of the tribe of the children of Ju'dah toward the coast of E'dom southward were Kab'ze-el, and E'der, and Ja'gur,

22 And Ki'nah, and Di-mo'nah, and Ad'a-dah,

23 And Ke'desh, and Ha'zor, and Ith'nan,

24 Ziph, and Te'lem, and Be'a-loth,

25 And Ha'zor, Ha-dat'tah, and Ke'ri-oth, *and* Hez'ron, which *is* Ha'zor,

26 A'mam, and She'ma, and Mol'a-dah,

27 And Ha'zar-gad'dah, and Hesh'mon, and Beth-pa'let,

28 And Ha'zar-shu'al, and Be'er-she'ba, and Biz-joth'jah,

29 Ba'al-ah, and I'im, and A'zem,

30 And El'to-lad, and Che'sil, and Hor'mah,

31 And Zik'lag, and Mad-man'nah, and San-san'nah,

32 And Leb'a-oth, and Shil'him, and A'in, and Rim'mon: all the cities *are* twenty and nine, with their villages:

33 *And* in the valley, Esh'ta-ol, and Zo're-ah, and Ash'nah,

34 And Za-no'ah, and En-gan'nim, Tap'pu-ah, and E'nam,

35 Jar'muth, and A-dul'lam, So'coh, and A-ze'kah,

36 And Shar-a'im, and Ad-i-tha'im, and Ge-de'rah, and Ged-e-roth-a'im; fourteen cities with their villages:

37 Ze'nan, and Had'a-shah, and Mig'dal-gad,

38 And Dil'e-an, and Miz-peh, and Jok'the-el,

39 La'chish, and Boz'kath, and Eg'lon,

40 And Cab'bon, and Lah'mam, and Kith'lish,

41 And Ge-de'roth, Beth-da'gon, and Na'a-mah, and Mak-ke'dah; sixteen cities with their villages:

42 Lib'nah, and E'ther, and A'shan,

43 And Jiph'tah, and Ash'nah, and Ne'zib,

44 And Kei'lah, and Ach'zib, and Ma-re'shah; nine cities with their villages:

45 Ek'ron, with her towns and her villages:

46 From Ek'ron even to the sea, all that *lay* near Ash'dod, with their villages:

47 Ash'dod with her towns and her villages, Ga'za with her towns and her villages, to the river of E'gypt, and the <u>Great</u> sea, and the border *thereof*: _{i.e., Mediterranean}

48 And in the mountains, Sha'mir, and Jat'tir, and So'coh,

49 And Dan'nah, and Kir'jath-san'nah, which *is* De'bir,

50 And A'nab, and Esh'te-moh, and A'nim,

51 And Go'shen, and Ho'lon, and Gi'loh; eleven cities with their villages:

52 A'rab, and Du'mah, and E'she-an,

53 And Ja'num, and Beth-tap'pu-ah, and A-phe'kah,

54 And Hum'tah, and Kir'jath-ar'ba, which *is* He'bron, and Zi'or; nine cities with their villages:

55 Ma'on, Car'mel, and Ziph, and Jut'tah,

56 And Jez're-el, and Jok'de-am, and Za-no'ah,

57 Cain, Gib'e-ah, and Tim'nah; ten cities with their villages:

58 Hal'hul, Beth'-zur, and Ge'dor,

59 And Ma'a-rath, and Beth-a'noth, and El'te-kon; six cities with their villages:

60 Kir'jath-ba'al, which *is* Kir'jath-je'a-rim, and Rab'bah; two cities with their villages:

61 In the wilderness, Beth-ar'a-bah, Mid'din, and Sec'a-cah,

62 And Nib'shan, and the city of Salt, and En-ge'di; six cities with their villages.

63 As for the Jeb'u-sites the inhabitants of Je-ru'sa-lem, the children of Ju'dah could not drive them out: but the Jeb'u-sites dwell with the children of Ju'dah at Je-ru'sa-lem to this day.

CHAPTER 16

AND the lot of the children of Jo'seph <u>fell</u> from Jor'dan by Jer'i-cho, to the water of Jer'i-cho on the east, to the wilderness that goes up from Jer'i-cho throughout mount Beth'-el, _{went}

2 And goes out from Beth'-el to Luz, and passes along to the borders of Ar'chi to At'a-roth,

3 And goes down westward to the coast of Japh-le'ti, to the coast of Beth-ho'ron the <u>nether</u>, and to Ge'zer: and the <u>goings out thereof are</u> at the sea. _{lower - i.e., end}

4 So the children of Jo'seph, Ma-nas'seh and E'phra-im, took their inheritance.

5 And the border of the children of E'phra-im according to their families was *thus*: even the border of their inheritance on the east side was At'a-roth-ad'dar, to Beth-ho'ron the upper;

6 And the border went <u>out toward the sea</u> to Mich'me-thah on the north side; and the border went about eastward to Ta'a-nath-shi'loh, and passed by it on the east to Ja-no'hah; _{westward at}

7 And it went down from Ja-no'hah to At'a-roth, and to Na'a-rath, and came to Jer'i-cho, and went out at Jor'dan.

8 The border went out from Tap'pu-ah westward to the river Ka'nah; and the <u>goings out thereof were</u> at the sea. This *is* the inheritance of the tribe of the children of E'phra-im by their families. _{i.e., end}

9 And the separate cities for the children of E'phra-im *were* among the inheritance of the children of Ma-nas'seh, all the cities with their villages.

10 And they drove not out the Ca'naan-ites that dwelled in Ge'zer: but the Ca'naan-ites dwell among the E'phra-im-ites to this day, and serve <u>under tribute</u>. _{i.e. forced laborers}

CHAPTER 17

THERE was also a lot for the tribe of Ma-nas'seh; for he *was* the firstborn

of Jo'seph; *that is*, for Ma'chir the firstborn of Ma-nas'seh, the father of Gil'e-ad: because he was a <u>man of war</u>, therefore he had Gil'e-ad and Ba'shan.   great soldier

2 There was also *a lot* for the rest of the children of Ma-nas'seh by their families; for the children of A-bi-e'zer, and for the children of He'lek, and for the children of As'ri-el, and for the children of She'chem, and for the children of He'pher, and for the children of She-mi'da: these *were* the male children of Ma-nas'seh the son of Jo'seph by their families.

3 But Ze-lo'phe-had, the son of He'pher, the son of Gil'e-ad, the son of Ma'chir, the son of Ma-nas'seh, had no sons, but daughters: and these *are* the names of his daughters, Mah'lah, and No'ah, Hog'lah, Mil'cah, and Tir'zah.

4 And they came near before E-le-a'zar the priest, and before Josh'u-a the son of Nun, and before the princes, saying, The LORD commanded Mo'ses to give us <u>an inheritance</u> among our brethren. Therefore according to the commandment of the LORD he gave them an inheritance among the brethren of their father.   a share

5 And there fell ten portions to Ma-nas'seh, beside the land of Gil'e-ad and Ba'shan, which *were* on the other side Jor'dan;

6 Because the daughters of Ma-nas'seh had an inheritance among his sons: and the rest of Ma-nas'seh's sons had the land of Gil'e-ad.

7 And the <u>coast</u> of Ma-nas'seh was from Ash'er to Mich'me-thah, that <u>lies</u> before She'chem; and the border went along on the right hand to the inhabitants of En-tap'pu-ah.   territory - was

8 *Now* Ma-nas'seh had the land of Tap'pu-ah: but Tap'pu-ah on the border of Ma-nas'seh *belonged* to the children of E'phra-im;

9 And the coast descended to the river Ka'nah, southward of the river: these cities of E'phra-im *are* among the cities of Ma-nas'seh: the coast of Ma-nas'seh also *was* on the north side of the river, and the outgoings of it were at the sea:

10 Southward *it was* E'phra-im's, and northward *it was* Ma-nas'seh's, and the sea is his <u>border</u>; and they met together in Ash'er on the north, and in Is'sa-char on the east.   boundary

11 And Ma-nas'seh had in Is'sa-char and in Ash'er Beth-she'an and her towns, and Ib'le-am and her towns, and the inhabitants of Dor and her towns, and the inhabitants of En'-dor and her towns, and the inhabitants of Ta'a-nach and her towns, and the inhabitants of Me-gid'do and her towns, *even* three countries.

12 Yet the children of Ma-nas'seh could not drive out *the inhabitants of* those cities; but the Ca'naan-ites would dwell in that land.

13 Yet it came to pass, when the children of Is'ra-el <u>were waxen</u> strong, that they put the Ca'naan-ites to <u>tribute</u>; but did not utterly drive them out.   grew - forced labor

14 And the children of Jo'seph spoke to Josh'u-a, saying, Why have you

given me *but* one lot and one portion to inherit, seeing I *am* a great people, forasmuch as the LORD has blessed me until now? allotment

15 And Josh'u-a answered them, If you *be* a great people, *then* get you up to the wood *country*, and cut down for yourself there in the land of the Per'iz-zites and of the giants, if mount E'phra-im be too narrow for you. small

16 And the children of Jo'seph said, The hill is not enough for us: and all the Ca'naan-ites that dwell in the land of the valley have chariots of iron, *both they* who *are* of Beth-she'an and her towns, and *they* who *are* of the valley of Jez're-el.

17 And Josh'u-a spoke to the house of Jo'seph, *even* to E'phra-im and to Ma-nas'seh, saying, You *are* a great people, and have great power: you shall not have one lot *only*: allotment

18 But the mountain shall be yours; for it *is* a wood, and you shall cut it down: and the outgoings of it shall be yours: for you shall drive out the Ca'naan-ites, though they have iron chariots, *and* though they *be* strong. forest - territory

CHAPTER 18

AND the whole congregation of the children of Is'ra-el assembled together at Shi'loh, and set up the tabernacle of the congregation there. And the land was subdued before them.

2 And there remained among the children of Is'ra-el seven tribes, which had not yet received their inheritance.

3 And Josh'u-a said to the children of Is'ra-el, How long *are* you slack to go to possess the land, which the LORD God of your fathers has given you?

4 Give out from among you three men for *each* tribe: and I will send them, and they shall rise, and go through the land, and describe it according to the inheritance of them; and they shall come *again* to me.

5 And they shall divide it into seven parts: Ju'dah shall abide in their coast on the south, and the house of Jo'seph shall abide in their coasts on the north. its territory

6 You shall therefore describe the land *into* seven parts, and bring *the description* here to me, that I may cast lots for you here before the LORD our God. diagram - Elohim^{p.f.}

7 But the Le'vites have no part among you; for the priesthood of the LORD *is* their inheritance: and Gad, and Reu'ben, and half the tribe of Ma-nas'seh, have received their inheritance beyond Jor'dan on the east, which Mo'ses the servant of the LORD gave them.

8 And the men arose, and went away: and Josh'u-a charged them that went to describe the land, saying, Go and walk through the land, and describe it, and come again to me, that I may here cast lots for you before the LORD in Shi'loh. commanded

9 And the men went and passed through the land, and described it by cities into seven parts in a book, and came *again* to Josh'u-a to the host at Shi'loh. divisions - scroll

10 And Josh'u-a cast lots for them

in Shi'loh before the LORD: and there Josh'u-a divided the land to the children of Is'ra-el according to their underlineddivisions. ^(family groups)

11 And the lot of the tribe of the children of Ben'ja-min came up according to their families: and the coast of their lot came forth between the children of Ju'dah and the children of Jo'seph. ^(territory)

12 And their border on the north side was from Jor'dan; and the border went up to the side of Jer'i-cho on the north side, and went up through the mountains westward; and the goings out thereof were at the wilderness of Beth-a'ven. ^(i.e., end)

13 And the border went over from there toward Luz, to the side of Luz, which *is* Beth'-el, southward; and the border descended to At'a-roth-a'dar, near the hill that *lies* on the south side of the nether Beth-ho'ron. ^(lower)

14 And the border was drawn from there, and compassed the corner of the sea southward, from the hill that *lies* before Beth-ho'ron southward; and the goings out thereof were at Kir'jath-ba'al, which *is* Kir'jath-je'a-rim, a city of the children of Ju'dah: this *was* the west quarter. ^(turned around - side)

15 And the south quarter *was* from the end of Kir'jath-je'a-rim, and the border went out on the west, and went out to the well of waters of Neph'to-ah:

16 And the border came down to the end of the mountain that *lies* before the valley of the son of Hin'nom, *and* which *is* in the valley of the giants on the north, and descended to the valley of Hin'nom, to the side of Je-bu'si on the south, and descended to En-ro'gel,

17 And was drawn from the north, and went forth to En-she'mesh, and went forth toward Gel'i-loth, which *is* opposite the going up of A-dum'mim, and descended to the stone of Bo'han the son of Reu'ben, ^(curved - the ascent - marker)

18 And passed along toward the side over against Ar'a-bah northward, and went down to Ar'a-bah:

19 And the border passed along to the side of Beth-hog'lah northward: and the outgoings of the border were at the north bay of the Salt sea at the south end of Jor'dan: this *was* the south coast. ^(end - Dead)

20 And Jor'dan was the border of it on the east side. This *was* the inheritance of the children of Ben'ja-min, by the coasts thereof round about, according to their families. ^(boundaries)

21 Now the cities of the tribe of the children of Ben'ja-min according to their families were Jer'i-cho, and Beth-hog'lah, and the valley of Ke'ziz,

22 And Beth-ar'a-bah, and Zem-a-ra'im, and Beth'-el,

23 And A'vim, and Pa'rah, and Oph'rah,

24 And Che'phar-ha-am'mo-nai, and Oph'ni, and Ga'ba; twelve cities with their villages:

25 Gib'e-on, and Ra'mah, and Be-e'roth,

26 And Miz-peh, and Che-phi'rah, and Mo'zah,

27 And Re'kem, and Ir'pe-el, and Tar'a-lah,

28 And Ze'lah, E'leph, and Je-bu'si, which *is* Je-ru'sa-lem, Gib'e-ath, *and* Kir'jath; fourteen cities with their villages. This *is* the inheritance of the children of Ben'ja-min according to their families.

CHAPTER 19

AND the second lot came forth to Sim'e-on, *even* for the tribe of the children of Sim'e-on according to their families: and their inheritance was within the inheritance of the children of Ju'dah.

2 And they had in their inheritance Be'er-she'ba, or She'ba, and Mol'a-dah,

3 And Ha'zar-shu'al, and Ba'lah, and A'zem,

4 And El'to-lad, and Be'thul, and Hor'mah,

5 And Zik'lag, and Beth-mar'ca-both, and Ha'zar-su'sah,

6 And Beth-leb'a-oth, and Sha-ru'hen; thirteen cities and their villages:

7 A'in, Rem'mon, and E'ther, and A'shan; four cities and their villages:

8 And all the villages that *were* round about these cities to Ba'al-ath-be'er, Ra'math of the south. This *is* the inheritance of the tribe of the children of Sim'e-on according to their families.

9 Out of the portion of the children of Ju'dah *was* the inheritance of the children of Sim'e-on: for the part of the children of Ju'dah was too much for them: therefore the children of Sim'e-on had their inheritance within the inheritance of them.

10 And the third lot came up for the children of Zeb'u-lun according to their families: and the <u>border</u> of their <u>inheritance</u> was to Sa'rid: territory - land

11 And their border went up toward the sea, and Mar'a-lah, and reached to Dab'ba-sheth, and reached to the river that is before Jok'ne-am;

12 And turned from Sa'rid eastward toward the sunrising to the border of Chis'loth-ta'bor, and then goes out to Dab'e-rath, and goes up to Ja-phi'a,

13 And from there passes on along on the east to Git'tah-he'pher, to It'tah-ka'zin, and goes out to Rem'mon-meth'o-ar to Ne-ah;

14 And the border <u>compasses</u> it on the north side to Han'na-thon: and the <u>outgoings</u> thereof are in the valley of Jiph'thah-el: goes around - i.e., end

15 And Kat'tath, and Na-hal'lal, and Shim'ron, and I-da'lah, and Beth'-le-hem: twelve cities with their villages.

16 This *is* the <u>inheritance</u> of the children of Zeb'u-lun according to their families, these cities with their villages.   land

17 *And* the fourth lot came out to Is'sa-char, for the children of Is'sa-char according to their families.

18 And their border was toward Jez're-el, and Che-sul'loth, and Shu'nem,

19 And Haph-ra'im, and Shi'hon, and An-a-ha'rath,

20 And Rab'bith, and Kish'i-on, and A'bez,

21 And Re'meth, and En-gan'nim, and En-had'dah, and Beth-paz'zez;

22 And the <u>coast</u> reacheth to Ta'bor,

and Sha-haz'i-mah, and Beth-she'mesh; and the <u>outgoings</u> of their border were at Jor'dan: sixteen cities with their villages. boundary - i.e., extreme limits

23 This *is* the inheritance of the tribe of the children of Is'sa-char according to their families, the cities and their villages.

24 And the fifth lot came out for the tribe of the children of Ash'er according to their families.

25 And their border was Hel'kath, and Ha'li, and Be'ten, and Ach'shaph,

26 And A-lam'me-lech, and A'mad, and Mi'she-al; and reaches to Car'mel westward, and to Shi'hor-lib'nath;

27 And turns toward the sunrising to Beth-da'gon, and reaches to Zeb'u-lun, and to the valley of Jiph'thah-el toward the north side of Beth-e'mek, and Ne'i-el, and goes out to Ca'bul on the left hand,

28 And He'bron, and Re'hob, and Ham'mon, and Ka'nah, *even* to great Zi'don;

29 And *then* the <u>coast</u> turns to Ra'mah, and to the strong city Tyre; and the coast turns to Ho'sah; and the outgoings thereof are at the sea <u>from the coast to</u> Ach'zib: boundary - in the region of

30 Um'mah also, and A'phek, and Re'hob: twenty and two cities with their villages.

31 This *is* the inheritance of the tribe of the children of Ash'er according to their families, these cities with their villages.

32 The sixth lot came out to the children of Naph'ta-li, *even* for the children of Naph'ta-li according to their families.

33 And their coast was from He'leph, from Al'lon to Za-a-nan'nim, and Ad'a-mi, Ne'keb, and Jab'ne-el, to La'kum; and the outgoings thereof were at Jor'dan:

34 And *then* the <u>coast</u> turns westward to Az'noth-ta'bor, and goes out from there to Huk'kok, and reaches to Zeb'u-lun on the south side, and reaches to Ash'er on the west side, and to Ju'dah upon Jor'dan toward the <u>sunrising</u>. boundary - east

35 And the <u>fenced</u> cities *are* Zid'dim, Zer, and Ham'math, Rak'kath, and Chin'ne-reth, fortified

36 And Ad'a-mah, and Ra'mah, and Ha'zor,

37 And Ke'desh, and Ed're-i, and En-ha'zor,

38 And I'ron, and Mig'dal-el, Ho'rem, and Beth-a'nath, and Beth-she'mesh; nineteen cities with their villages.

39 This *is* the inheritance of the tribe of the children of Naph'ta-li according to their families, the cities and their villages.

40 *And* the seventh lot came out for the tribe of the children of Dan according to their families.

41 And the coast of their inheritance was Zo'rah, and Esh'ta-ol, and Ir-she'mesh,

42 And Sha-al-ab'bin, and Aj'a-lon, and Jeth'lah,

43 And E'lon, and Thim'na-thah, and Ek'ron,

44 And El'te-keh, and Gib'be-thon, and Ba'al-ath,

45 And Je'hud, and Ben'e-be'rak, and Gath-rim'mon,

46 And Me-jar'kon, and Rak'kon, with the border before Ja'pho. Joppa

47 And the coast of the children of Dan went out *too little* for them: therefore the children of Dan went up to fight against Le'shem, and took it, and smote it with the edge of the sword, and possessed it, and dwelled therein, and called Le'shem, Dan, after the name of Dan their father.

48 This is the inheritance of the tribe of the children of Dan according to their families, these cities with their villages.

49 When they had made an end of dividing the land for inheritance by their coasts, the children of Is'ra-el gave an inheritance to Josh'u-a the son of Nun among them:

finished apportioning - by its borders

50 According to the word of the LORD they gave him the city which he asked, *even* Tim'nath-se'rah in mount E'phra-im: and he built the city, and dwelled therein.

51 These *are* the inheritances, which E-le-a'zar the priest, and Josh'u-a the son of Nun, and the heads of the fathers of the tribes of the children of Is'ra-el, divided for an inheritance by lot in Shi'loh before the LORD, at the door of the tabernacle of the congregation. So they made an end of dividing the country.

CHAPTER 20

THE LORD also spoke to Josh'u-a, saying,

2 Speak to the children of Is'ra-el, saying, Appoint out for you cities of refuge, whereof I spoke to you by the hand of Mo'ses: Designate the

3 That the slayer that kills *any* person unawares *and* unwittingly may flee there: and they shall be your refuge from the avenger of blood.

unintentionally - without premeditation

4 And when he that does flee to one of those cities shall stand at the entering of the gate of the city, and shall declare his cause in the ears of the elders of that city, they shall take him into the city to them, and give him a place, that he may dwell among them. state his case

5 And if the avenger of blood pursue after him, then they shall not deliver the slayer up into his hand; because he smote his neighbor unwittingly, and hated him not beforetime. without premeditation - without malice

6 And he shall dwell in that city, until he stand before the congregation for judgment, *and* until the death of the high priest that shall be in those days: then shall the slayer return, and come to his own city, and to his own house, to the city from where he fled.

stand trial

7 And they appointed Ke'desh in Gal'i-lee in mount Naph'ta-li, and She'chem in mount E'phra-im, and Kir'jath-ar'ba, which *is* He'bron, in the mountain of Ju'dah.

8 And on the other side Jor'dan by Jer'i-cho eastward, they assigned Be'zer in the wilderness upon the plain out of the tribe of Reu'ben, and Ra'moth in

Gil'e-ad out of the tribe of Gad, and Go'lan in Ba'shan out of the tribe of Ma-nas'seh.

9 These were the cities appointed for all the children of Is'ra-el, and for the <u>stranger</u> that <u>sojourns</u> among them, that whosoever kills *any* person <u>at unawares</u> might flee there, and not die by the hand of the avenger of blood, until he stood before the congregation.   <small>alien - lives temporarily - by accident</small>

CHAPTER 21

THEN came near <u>heads</u> of the fathers of the Le'vites to E-le-a'zar the priest, and to Josh'u-a the son of Nun, and to the heads of the fathers of the tribes of the children of Is'ra-el;<small>leaders</small>

2 And they spoke to them at Shi'loh in the land of Ca'naan, saying, The LORD commanded by the hand of Mo'ses to give us cities to dwell in, with the <u>suburbs</u> thereof for our cattle.   <small>pasture lands</small>

3 And the children of Is'ra-el gave to the Le'vites out of their inheritance, at the commandment of the LORD, these cities and their <u>suburbs</u>.

4 And the <u>lot</u> came out for the families of the Ko'hath-ites: and the children of Aar'on the priest, *which were* of the Le'vites, had by lot out of the tribe of Ju'dah, and out of the tribe of Sim'e-on, and out of the tribe of Ben'ja-min, thirteen cities.   <small>share</small>

5 And the rest of the children of Ko'hath *had* by lot out of the families of the tribe of E'phra-im, and out of the tribe of Dan, and out of the half tribe of Ma-nas'seh, ten cities.

6 And the children of Ger'shon *had* by lot out of the families of the tribe of Is'sa-char, and out of the tribe of Ash'er, and out of the tribe of Naph-ta'li, and out of the half tribe of Ma-nas'seh in Ba'shan, thirteen cities.

7 The children of Me-ra'ri by their families *had* out of the tribe of Reu'ben, and out of the tribe of Gad, and out of the tribe of Zeb'u-lun, twelve cities.

8 And the children of Is'ra-el gave by lot to the Le'vites these cities with their <u>suburbs</u>, as the LORD commanded by the hand of Mo'ses.   <small>pasture lands</small>

9 And they gave out of the tribe of the children of Ju'dah, and out of the tribe of the children of Sim'e-on, these cities which are *here* <u>mentioned</u> by name,   <small>called</small>

10 Which the children of Aar'on, *being* of the families of the Ko'hath-ites, *who were* of the children of Le'vi, had: for theirs was the first lot.

11 And they gave them the city of Ar'ba the father of A'nak, which *city is* He'bron, in the hill *country* of Ju'dah, with the <u>suburbs</u> thereof round about it.

12 But the fields of the city, and the villages thereof, gave they to Ca'leb the son of Je-phun'neh for his possession.

13 Thus they gave to the children of Aar'on the priest He'bron with her <u>suburbs</u>, *to be* a city of refuge for the slayer; and Lib'nah with her <u>suburbs</u>,

14 And Jat'tir with her <u>suburbs</u>, and Esh-te-mo'a with her <u>suburbs</u>,

15 And Ho'lon with her <u>suburbs</u>, and De'bir with her <u>suburbs</u>,   <small>pasture lands</small>

16 And A'in with her <u>suburbs</u>, and

Jut'tah with her suburbs, *and* Beth-she'mesh with her suburbs; nine cities out of those two tribes. pasture lands
17 And out of the tribe of Ben'ja-min, Gib'e-on with her suburbs, Ge'ba with her suburbs,
18 An'a-thoth with her suburbs, and Al'mon with her suburbs; four cities.
19 All the cities of the children of Aar'on, the priests, were thirteen cities with their suburbs.
20 And the families of the children of Ko'hath, the Le'vites which remained of the children of Ko'hath, even they had the cities of their lot out of the tribe of E'phra-im. share
21 For they gave them She'chem with her suburbs in mount E'phra-im, *to be* a city of refuge for the slayer; and Ge'zer with her suburbs, protection
22 And Kib'za-im with her suburbs, and Beth-ho'ron with her suburbs; four cities. pasture lands
23 And out of the tribe of Dan, El'te-keh with her suburbs, Gib'be-thon with her suburbs,
24 Aij'a-lon with her suburbs, Gath-rim'mon with her suburbs; four cities.
25 And out of the half tribe of Ma-nas'seh, Ta'nach with her suburbs, and Gath-rim'mon with her suburbs; two cities.
26 All the cities were ten with their suburbs for the families of the children of Ko'hath that remained.
27 And to the children of Ger'shon, of the families of the Le'vites, out of the *other* half tribe of Ma-nas'seh *they* gave Go'lan in Ba'shan with her suburbs, *to be* a city of refuge for the slayer; and Be-esh'-te-rah with her suburbs; two cities. pasture lands
28 And out of the tribe of Is'sa-char, Ki'shon with her suburbs, Dab'a-reh with her suburbs,
29 Jar'muth with her suburbs, En-gan'nim with her suburbs; four cities.
30 And out of the tribe of Ash'er, Mi'shal with her suburbs, Ab'don with her suburbs,
31 Hel'kath with her suburbs, and Re'hob with her suburbs; four cities.
32 And out of the tribe of Naph'ta-li, Ke'desh in Gal'i-lee with her suburbs, *to be* a city of refuge for the slayer; and Ham'moth-dor with her suburbs, and Kar'tan with her suburbs; three cities.
33 All the cities of the Ger'shon-ites according to their families *were* thirteen cities with their suburbs.
34 And to the families of the children of Me-ra'ri, the rest of the Le'vites, out of the tribe of Zeb'u-lun, Jok'ne-am with her suburbs, and Kar'tah with her suburbs, pasture lands
35 Dim'nah with her suburbs, Na'ha-lal with her suburbs; four cities.
36 And out of the tribe of Reu'ben, Be'zer with her suburbs, and Ja-ha'zah with her suburbs,
37 Ked'e-moth with her suburbs, and Meph'a-ath with her suburbs; four cities.
38 And out of the tribe of Gad, Ra'moth in Gil'e-ad with her suburbs, *to be* a city of refuge for the slayer; and Ma-ha-na'im with her suburbs, protection
39 Hesh'bon with her suburbs, Ja'zer with her suburbs; four cities in all. pasture lands

40 So all the cities for the children of Me-ra'ri by their families, which were remaining of the families of the Le'-vites, were *by* their lot twelve cities.

41 All the cities of the Le'vites within the possession of the children of Is'ra-el *were* forty and eight cities with their <u>suburbs</u>.   pasture lands

42 These cities were every one with their <u>suburbs</u> round about them: thus *were* all these cities.

43 And the LORD gave to Is'ra-el all the land which He swear to give to their fathers; and they possessed it, and dwelled therein.

44 And the LORD gave them rest round about, according to all that He swear to their fathers: and there stood not a man of all their enemies before them; the LORD delivered all their enemies into their hand.

45 There failed nothing of any good thing which the LORD had spoken to the house of Is'ra-el; all came to pass.

CHAPTER 22

THEN Josh'u-a called the Reu'ben-ites, and the Gad'ites, and the half tribe of Ma-nas'seh,

2 And said to them, You have <u>kept</u> all that Mo'ses the servant of the LORD commanded you, and have obeyed my voice in all that I commanded you: done

3 You have not left your brethren these many days to this day, but have <u>kept the charge</u> of the commandment of the LORD your God.   carried out the mission

4 And now the LORD your God has given rest to your brethren, as he promised them: therefore now return you, and get you to your tents, *and* to the land of your possession, which Mo'ses the servant of the LORD gave you on the other side Jor'dan.

5 But take diligent heed to do the commandment and the law, which Mo'ses the servant of the LORD charged you, to love the LORD your God, and to walk in all His ways, and to keep His commandments, and to cling to Him, and to serve Him with all your heart and with all your <u>soul</u>.   Elohim^{p.f.} - being

6 So Josh'u-a blessed them, and sent them away: and they went to their tents.

7 Now to the *one* half of the tribe of Ma-nas'seh Mo'ses had given <u>*possession*</u> in Ba'shan: but to the *other* half thereof gave Josh'u-a among their brethren on this side Jor'dan westward. And when Josh'u-a sent them away also to their tents, then he blessed them,   land

8 And he spoke to them, saying, Return with much riches to your tents, and with very much cattle, with silver, and with gold, and with brass, and with iron, and with very much <u>raiment</u>: divide the spoil of your enemies with your brethren.   clothing

9 And the children of Reu'ben and the children of Gad and the half tribe of Ma-nas'seh returned, and departed from the children of Is'ra-el out of Shi'loh, which *is* in the land of Ca'naan, to go to the country of Gil'e-ad, to the land of their possession, whereof they

<u>were possessed</u>, according to the word of the Lord by the hand of Mo'ses. <small>had acquired</small>
10 And when they came to the borders of Jor'dan, that *are* in the land of Ca'naan, the children of Reu'ben and the children of Gad and the half tribe of Ma-nas'seh built there an altar by Jor'dan, a great altar <u>to see to</u>. <small>in appearance</small>
11 And the children of Is'ra-el <u>heard say</u>, Behold, the children of Reu'ben and the children of Gad and the half tribe of Ma-nas'seh have built an altar opposite the land of Ca'naan, in the borders of Jor'dan, at the passage of the children of Is'ra-el. <small>heard it said</small>
12 And when the children of Is'ra-el heard *of it*, the whole congregation of the children of Is'ra-el <u>gathered</u> themselves together at Shi'loh, to go up to war against them. <small>assembled</small>
13 And the children of Is'ra-el sent to the children of Reu'ben, and to the children of Gad, and to the half tribe of Ma-nas'seh, into the land of Gil'e-ad, Phin'e-has the son of E-le-a'zar the priest,
14 And with him ten princes, of each chief house a prince throughout all the tribes of Is'ra-el; and each one *was* an head of the house of their fathers among the thousands of Is'ra-el.
15 And they came to the children of Reu'ben, and to the children of Gad, and to the half tribe of Ma-nas'seh, to the land of Gil'e-ad, and they spoke with them, saying,
16 Thus says the whole congregation of the Lord, What <u>trespass</u> *is* this that you have committed against the <u>God</u> of Is'ra-el, to turn away this day from following the Lord, in that you have built you an altar, that you might rebel this day against the Lord? <small>wrong doing - Elohim^{p.f.}</small>
17 *Is* the iniquity of Pe'or too little for us, from which we are not cleansed until this day, although there was a <u>plague</u> in the congregation of the Lord, <small>sickness</small>
18 But that you must turn away this day from following the Lord? and it will be, *seeing* you rebel to day against the Lord, that to morrow He will be angry with the whole congregation of Is'ra-el.
19 <u>Notwithstanding</u>, if the land of your possession *be* <u>unclean</u>, *then* pass you over to the land of the possession of the Lord, wherein the Lord's tabernacle dwells, and take possession among us: but rebel not against the Lord, nor rebel against us, in building you an altar <u>beside</u> the altar of the Lord our God. <small>However - unfit - in addition to</small>
20 Did not A'chan the son of Ze'rah commit a <u>trespass</u> in the <u>accursed thing</u>, and wrath fell on all the congregation of Is'ra-el? and that man perished not alone in his iniquity. <small>things under the ban</small>
21 Then the children of Reu'ben and the children of Gad and the half tribe of Ma-nas'seh answered, and said to the heads of the thousands of Is'ra-el,
22 The <u>Lord God</u> of gods, the <u>Lord</u> God of gods, He knows, and Is'ra-el He shall know; if *it be* in rebellion, or if

in transgression against the LORD, (save us not this day,)   JehovahEl[s.f.] - spare
23 That we have built us an altar to turn from following the LORD, or if to offer thereon burned offering or meat offering, or if to offer peace offerings thereon, let the LORD himself require *it*;   grain - call us to account
24 And if we have not *rather* done it for fear of *this* thing, saying, In time to come your children might speak to our children, saying, What have you to do with the LORD God of Is'ra-el?   concern - Jehovah[s.f.] Elohim[p.f.]
25 For the LORD has made Jor'dan a border between us and you, you children of Reu'ben and children of Gad; you have no part in the LORD: so shall your children make our children cease from fearing the LORD.   respecting
26 Therefore we said, Let us now prepare to build us an altar, not for burned offering, nor for sacrifice:
27 But *that* it *may be* a witness between us, and you, and our generations after us, that we might do the service of the LORD before Him with our burned offerings, and with our sacrifices, and with our peace offerings; that your children may not say to our children in time to come, You have no part in the LORD.   share
28 Therefore said we, that it shall be, when they should *so* say to us or to our generations in time to come, that we may say *again*, Behold the pattern of the altar of the LORD, which our fathers made, not for burned offerings, nor for sacrifices; but it *is* a witness between us and you.

29 God forbid that we should rebel against the LORD, and turn this day from following the LORD, to build an altar for burned offerings, for meat offerings, or for sacrifices, beside the altar of the LORD our God that *is* before His tabernacle.   grain - Elohim[p.f.]
30 And when Phin'e-has the priest, and the princes of the congregation and heads of the thousands of Is'ra-el which *were* with him, heard the words that the children of Reu'ben and the children of Gad and the children of Ma-nas'seh spoke, it pleased them.   i.e., pleasing in their eyes
31 And Phin'e-has the son of E-le-a'zar the priest said to the children of Reu'ben, and to the children of Gad, and to the children of Ma-nas'seh, This day we perceive that the LORD *is* among us, because you have not committed this trespass against the LORD: now you have delivered the children of Is'ra-el out of the hand of the LORD.
32 And Phin'e-has the son of E-le-a'zar the priest, and the princes, returned from the children of Reu'ben, and from the children of Gad, out of the land of Gil'e-ad, to the land of Ca'naan, to the children of Is'ra-el, and brought them word again.
33 And the thing pleased the children of Is'ra-el; and the children of Is'ra-el blessed God, and did not intend to go up against them in battle, to destroy the land wherein the children of Reu'ben and Gad dwelled.
34 And the children of Reu'ben and the children of Gad called the altar *Witness:* for it *shall be* a witness between us that the LORD *is* God.

CHAPTER 23

AND it came to pass a long time after that the LORD had given rest to Is'ra-el from all their enemies round about, that Josh'u-a <u>waxed</u> old *and* stricken in age. grew

2 And Josh'u-a called for all Is'ra-el, *and* for their elders, and for their heads, and for their judges, and for their officers, and said to them, I am old *and* stricken in age:

3 And you have seen all that the LORD your <u>God</u> has done to all these nations because of you; for the LORD your <u>God</u> *is* He that has fought for you. Elohim^{p.f.}

4 Behold, I have divided to you by lot these nations that remain, to be an inheritance for your tribes, from Jor'dan, with all the nations that I have <u>cut off</u>, even to the <u>Great</u> Sea westward. destroyed - i.e., Mediterranean

5 And the LORD your <u>God</u>, He shall expel them from before you, and drive them from out of your sight; and you shall possess their land, as the LORD your <u>God</u> has promised to you.

6 Be you therefore very courageous to keep and to do all that is written in the book of the law of Mo'ses, that you turn not aside therefrom *to* the right hand or *to* the left;

7 That you come not among these nations, these that remain among you; neither make mention of the name of their gods, nor cause to swear *by them*, neither serve them, nor bow yourselves to them:

8 But cling to the LORD your <u>God</u>, as you have done to this day. Elohim^{p.f.}

9 For the LORD has driven out from before you great nations and strong: but *as for* you, no man has been able to <u>stand before</u> you to this day. withstand

10 One man of you shall chase a thousand: for the LORD your <u>God</u>, He *it is* that fights for you, as He has promised you.

11 Take good heed therefore to yourselves, that you love the LORD your <u>God</u>. Elohim^{p.f.}

12 Else if you do in any wise go back, and cling to the remnant of these nations, *even* these that remain among you, and shall make marriages with them, and <u>go in to</u> them, and they to you: associated with

13 Know for a certainty that the LORD your <u>God</u> will no more drive out *any of* these nations from before you; but they shall be <u>snares</u> and traps to you, and <u>scourges in</u> your sides, and thorns in your eyes, until you perish from off this good land which the LORD your <u>God</u> has given you. lures - a whip on

14 And, behold, this day I *am* <u>going the way of all the earth</u>: and you know in all your hearts and in all your souls, that not one thing has failed of all the good things which the LORD your <u>God</u> spoke concerning you; all are come to pass to you, *and* not one thing has failed thereof. will die

15 Therefore it shall come to pass, *that* as all good things are come upon you, which the LORD your <u>God</u> promised you; so shall the LORD bring upon

you all evil things, until He have destroyed you from off this good land which the LORD your God has given you.   Elohim[p.f.]

16 <u>When</u> you have transgressed the <u>covenant</u> of the LORD your God, which He commanded you, and have gone and served other gods, and bowed yourselves to them; then shall the anger of the LORD be kindled against you, and you shall perish quickly from off the good land which He has given to you.   If - agreement

CHAPTER 24

AND Josh'u-a gathered all the tribes of Is'ra-el to She'chem, and called for the elders of Is'ra-el, and for their heads, and for their judges, and for their officers; and they presented themselves before God.

2 And Josh'u-a said to all the people, Thus says the LORD God of Is'ra-el, Your fathers dwelled on the other side of the <u>flood</u> in old time, *even* Te'rah, the father of A'bra-ham, and the father of Na'chor: and they served other gods.   river i.e., Euphrates

3 And I took your father A'bra-ham from the other side of the flood, and led him throughout all the land of Ca'naan, and multiplied his <u>seed</u>, and gave him I'saac.   descendants

4 And I gave to I'saac Ja'cob and E'sau: and I gave to E'sau mount Se'ir, to possess it; but Ja'cob and his children went down into E'gypt.

5 I sent Mo'ses also and Aar'on, and I <u>plagued</u> E'gypt, according to that which I did among them: and afterward I brought you out.   afflicted

6 And I brought your fathers out of E'gypt: and you came to the sea; and the E-gyp'tians pursued after your fathers with chariots and horsemen to the Red sea.

7 And when they cried to the LORD, he put darkness between you and the E-gyp'tians, and brought the sea upon them, and <u>covered</u> them; and your eyes have seen what I have done in E'gypt: and you dwelled in the wilderness a long season.   drowned

8 And I brought you into the land of the Am'or-ites, which dwelled on the other side Jor'dan; and they fought with you: and I gave them into your hand, that you might possess their land; and I destroyed them from before you.

9 Then Ba'lak the son of Zip'por, king of Mo'ab, arose and warred against Is'ra-el, and sent and called Ba'laam the son of Be'or to curse you:

10 But I would not hearken to Ba'laam; therefore he blessed you still: so I delivered you out of his hand.

11 And you went over Jor'dan, and came to Jer'i-cho: and the men of Jer'i-cho fought against you, the Am'or-ites, and the Per'iz-zites, and the Ca'naan-ites, and the Hit'tites, and the Gir'ga-shites, the Hi'vites, and the Jeb'u-sites; and I delivered them into your hand.

12 And I sent the hornet before you, which drove them out from before you, *even* the two kings of the Am'or-ites; but not with your sword, nor with your bow.

13 And I have given you a land for which you did not labor, and cities which you built not, and you dwell in them; of the vineyards and oliveyards which you planted not do you eat.

14 Now therefore <u>fear</u> the LORD, and serve Him in sincerity and in truth: and put away the gods which your fathers served on the other side of the <u>flood</u>, and in E'gypt; and serve you the LORD.   reverence - river i.e., Euphrates

15 And if it seem evil to you to serve the LORD, choose you this day whom you will serve; whether the gods which your fathers served that *were* on the other side of the flood, or the gods of the Am'or-ites, in whose land you dwell: but as for me and my house, we will serve the LORD.

16 And the people answered and said, God forbid that we should forsake the LORD, to serve other gods;

17 For the LORD our <u>God</u>, He *it is* that brought us up and our fathers out of the land of E'gypt, from the house of bondage, and which did those great signs in our sight, and preserved us in all the way <u>wherein</u> we went, and among all the people through whom we passed: Elohim^p.f. - in which

18 And the LORD drove out from before us all the people, even the Am'or-ites which dwelled in the land: *therefore* will we also serve the LORD; for He *is* our <u>God</u>.

19 And Josh'u-a said to the people, You cannot serve the <u>LORD</u>: for He *is* an holy <u>God</u>; He *is* a jealous <u>God</u>; He will not forgive your transgressions nor your sins. Jehovah^s.f. - Elohim^p.f. - El^s.f.

20 If you forsake the LORD, and serve <u>strange</u> gods, then He will turn and <u>do you hurt</u>, and <u>consume</u> you, after that He has done you good.   ACTS 7:43 foreign - bring disaster - destroy

21 And the people said to Josh'u-a, Nay; but we will serve the LORD.

22 And Josh'u-a said to the people, You *are* witnesses against yourselves that you have chosen you the LORD, to serve Him. And they said, *We are* witnesses.

23 Now therefore put away, *said he*, the <u>strange</u> gods which *are* among you, and <u>incline</u> your heart to the LORD God of Is'ra-el.   yield

24 And the people said to Josh'u-a, The LORD our God will we serve, and His voice will we obey.

25 So Josh'u-a made a <u>covenant</u> with the people that day, and set them a <u>statute</u> and an ordinance in She'chem.   agreement - decree

26 And Josh'u-a wrote these words in the book of the law of God, and took a great stone, and set it up there under an oak, that *was* by the sanctuary of the LORD.

27 And Josh'u-a said to all the people, Behold, this stone shall be a witness to us; for it has heard all the words of the LORD which He spoke to us: it shall be therefore a witness to you, less you deny your <u>God</u>.   Elohim^p.f.

28 So Josh'u-a let the people depart, every man to his inheritance.

29 And it came to pass after these things, that Josh'u-a the son of Nun, the servant of the LORD, died, *being* an hundred and ten years old.

30 And they buried him in the border

of his inheritance in Tim'nath-se'rah, which *is* in mount E'phra-im, on the north side of the hill of Ga'ash.

31 And Is'ra-el served the LORD all the days of Josh'u-a, and all the days of the elders that <u>overlived</u> Josh'u-a, and which had known all the works of the LORD, that He had done for Is'ra-el.   ^{survived}

32 And the bones of Jo'seph, which the children of Is'ra-el brought up out of E'gypt, buried they in She'chem, in a parcel of ground which Ja'cob bought of the sons of Ha'mor the father of She'chem for an hundred pieces of silver: and it became the inheritance of the children of Jo'seph.   ACTS 7:16

33 And E-le-a'zar the son of Aar'on died; and they buried him in a hill *that* <u>pertained</u> to Phin'e-has his son, which was given him in mount E'phra-im.   ^{belonged}

JUDGES

OUTLINE

SURVEY

The title of the Book of Judges was probably suggested by verse 16 of chapter 2: "Nevertheless the LORD raised up judges, which delivered them out of the hand of those that spoiled them." These judges were Spirit-filled persons who, in times of national emergencies, led the people in war and, having delivered them from the bondage of foreign oppression, continued to lead the people in peace. They functioned both as military and as civil magistrates.

By inviting two or more tribes for concerted action, several of the judges paved the way for the union of the twelve tribes in the future monarchy.

In the threefold divisions of the Hebrew Bible—the Law, the Prophets, and the Writings—the Book of Judges is found among the Prophets.

The Book of Judges contains the account of the thirteen judges who ruled Israel from the death of Joshua until the time of Eli and Samuel. It is possible that some of the judges ruled simultaneously in different parts of the land. The period of time covered in the Book of Judges is approximately four hundred years.

Judges is valuable for the historical evidence it presents of the development of the religion of Israel during the early years of the conquest. The book covers the period of transition from unsettled and disintegrated tribal life to the organization of a federation that eventually led to the forming of a monarchy. The struggles of the various tribes, with their individual problems, amid an alien population are seen more clearly in Judges than in the Pentateuch or in Joshua.

Although the later prophets make a greater appeal to men's consciences, the Book of Judges presents a philosophy of history that commands the attention of the modern Christian. The neglect of the Lord's ordinances and the worship of false gods lead to punishment, while sincere repentance brings about divine favor. The fact that God deals with nations in view of their attitude toward His moral laws merits our present day consideration.

AUTHOR

In the absence of precise data, several suggestions have been made concerning authorship of the Book of Judges. The most probable opinion is that Samuel, in addition to his office of prophet or seer, compiled the book. The time of writing may have been during his retirement from public life. The internal evidence implies that the book was in existence before the conquest of Jerusalem by David. Undoubtedly the writer made use of written records left by previous judges, relative to the times and events of their respective governments.

F.E.Y.

THE BOOK OF

JUDGES

CHAPTER 1

God Raises Up
Deliverers

NOW after the death of Josh'u-a it came to pass, that the children of Is'ra-el asked the LORD, saying, Who shall go up for us against the Ca'naan-ites first, to fight against them?

2 And the LORD said, Ju'dah shall go up: behold, I have delivered the land into his hand.

3 And Ju'dah said to Sim'e-on his brother, Come up with me into my lot, that we may fight against the Ca'naan-ites; and I likewise will go with you into your lot. So Sim'e-on went with him. territory

4 And Ju'dah went up; and the LORD delivered the Ca'naan-ites and the Per'iz-zites into their hand: and they slew of them in Be'zek ten thousand men.

5 And they found A-don'i-be'zek in Be'zek: and they fought against him, and they slew the Ca'naan-ites and the Per'iz-zites.

6 But A-don'i-be'zek fled; and they pursued after him, and caught him, and cut off his thumbs and his great toes. big

7 And A-don'i-be'zek said, Three-score and ten kings, having their thumbs and their great toes cut off, gathered their meat under my table: as I have done, so God has requited me. And they brought him to Je-ru'sa-lem, and there he died. scraps - Elohim p.f.

8 Now the children of Ju'dah had fought against Je-ru'sa-lem, and had taken it, and smitten it with the edge of the sword, and set the city on fire.

9 And afterward the children of Ju'dah went down to fight against the Ca'naan-ites, that dwelled in the mountain, and in the south, and in the valley.

10 And Ju'dah went against the Ca'naan-ites that dwelled in He'bron: (now the name of He'bron before was Kir'jath-ar'ba:) and they slew She'shai, and A-hi'man, and Tal'mai. advanced

11 And from there he went against the inhabitants of De'bir: and the name of De'bir before was Kir'jath-se'pher:

12 And Ca'leb said, He that smites Kir'jath-se'pher, and takes it, to him will I give Ach'sah my daughter to wife.

13 And Oth'ni-el the son of Ke'naz, Ca'leb's younger brother, took it: and he gave him Ach'sah his daughter to wife.

14 And it came to pass, when she came to him, that she moved him to ask of her father a field: and she lighted from off the ass; and Ca'leb said to her, What will you?

15 And she said to him, Give me a blessing: for you have given me a south land; give me also springs of water. And Ca'leb gave her the upper springs and the nether springs. lower

16 And the children of the Ken'ite,

Mo'ses' father in law, went up out of the city of palm trees with the children of Ju'dah into the wilderness of Ju'dah, which *lies* in the south of A'rad; and they went and dwelled among the people.

17 And Ju'dah went with Sim'e-on his brother, and they slew the Ca'naan-ites that inhabited Ze'phath, and utterly destroyed it. And the name of the city was called Hor'mah.

18 Also Ju'dah took Ga'za with the coast thereof, and As'ke-lon with the coast thereof, and Ek'ron with the coast thereof.

19 And the LORD was with Ju'dah; and he drove out *the inhabitants of* the mountain; but could not drive out the inhabitants of the valley, because they had chariots of iron.

20 And they gave He'bron to Ca'leb, as Mo'ses said: and he <u>expelled from there</u> the three sons of A'nak.   drove from it

21 And the children of Ben'ja-min did not drive out the Jeb'u-sites that inhabited Je-ru'sa-lem; but the Jeb'u-sites dwell with the children of Ben'ja-min in Je-ru'sa-lem to this day.

22 And the <u>house</u> of Jo'seph, they also went up against Beth'-el: and the LORD *was* with them.   family

23 And the <u>house</u> of Jo'seph sent to <u>descry</u> Beth'-el. (Now the name of the city before *was* Luz.)   spy out

24 And the spies saw a man come forth out of the city, and they said to him, Show us, we pray you, the entrance into the city, and we will show you mercy.

25 And when he showed them the entrance into the city, they smote the city with the edge of the sword; but they let go the man and all his family.

26 And the man went into the land of the Hit'tites, and built a city, and called the name thereof Luz: which *is* the name thereof to this day.

27 Neither did Ma-nas'seh drive out *the inhabitants of* Beth-she'an and her towns, nor Ta'a-nach and her towns, nor the inhabitants of Dor and her towns, nor the inhabitants of Ib'le-am and her towns, nor the inhabitants of Me-gid'do and her towns: but the Ca'naan-ites <u>would dwell</u> in that land.   persisted in living

28 And it came to pass, when Is'ra-el was strong, that they put the Ca'naan-ites to <u>tribute</u>, and did not utterly drive them out.   forced labor

29 Neither did E'phra-im drive out the Ca'naan-ites that dwelled in Ge'zer; but the Ca'naan-ites dwelled in Ge'zer among them.

30 Neither did Zeb'u-lun drive out the inhabitants of Kit'ron, nor the inhabitants of Na'ha-lol; but the Ca'naan-ites dwelled among them, and became <u>tributaries</u>.

31 Neither did Ash'er drive out the inhabitants of Ac'cho, nor the inhabitants of Zi'don, nor of Ah'lab, nor of Ach'zib, nor of Hel'bah, nor of A'phik, nor of Re'hob:

32 But the Ash'er-ites dwelled among the Ca'naan-ites, the inhabitants of the land: for they did not drive them out.

33 Neither did Naph'ta-li drive out the inhabitants of Beth-she'mesh, nor the inhabitants of Beth-a'nath; but he

dwelled among the Ca'naan-ites, the inhabitants of the land: nevertheless the inhabitants of Beth-she'mesh and of Beth-a'nath became <u>tribu-taries</u> to them.   forced labor

34 And the Am'or-ites forced the children of Dan into the mountain: for they would not permit them to come down to the valley:

35 But the Am'or-ites would dwell in mount He'res in Aij'a-lon, and in Sha-al'bim: yet the hand of the house of Jo'seph prevailed, so that they became <u>tributaries</u>.

36 And the coast of the Am'or-ites *was* from the going up to A-krab'bim, from the rock, and upward.

CHAPTER 2

AND an angel of the LORD came up from Gil'gal to Bo'chim, and said, I made you to go up out of E'gypt, and have brought you to the land which I swear to your fathers; and I said, I will never break My <u>covenant</u> with you.   agreement

2 And you shall make no league with the inhabitants of this land; you shall <u>throw</u> down their altars: but you have not obeyed My voice: why have you done this?   tear

3 Wherefore I also said, I will not drive them out from before you; but they shall be *as thorns* in your sides, and their gods shall be a <u>snare</u> to you.   lure

4 And it came to pass, when the angel of the LORD spoke these words to all the children of Is'ra-el, that the people <u>lifted up their voice</u>, and wept.   cried out

5 And they called the name of that place <u>Bo'chim</u>: and they sacrificed there to the LORD.   i.e., Weepers

6 And when Josh'u-a had let the people go, the children of Is'ra-el went every man to his inheritance to possess the land.

7 And the people served the LORD all the days of Josh'u-a, and all the days of the elders that outlived Josh'u-a, who had seen all the great works of the LORD, that He did for Is'ra-el.

8 And Josh'u-a the son of Nun, the servant of the LORD, died, *being* an hundred and ten years old.

9 And they buried him in the border of his inheritance in Tim'nath-he'res, in the mount of E'phra-im, on the north side of the hill Ga'ash.

10 And also all that generation <u>were gathered to their fathers</u>: and there arose another generation after them, which knew not the LORD, nor yet the works which He had done for Is'ra-el.   died

11 And the children of Is'ra-el did evil in the sight of the LORD, and served Ba'al-im:

12 And they forsook the <u>LORD God</u> of their fathers, which brought them out of the land of E'gypt, and fol-lowed other gods, of the gods of the people that *were* round about them, and <u>bowed themselves to</u> them, and provoked the LORD to an-ger.   Jehovah^s.c. Elohim^p.f. - worshipped

13 And they forsook the LORD, and served Ba'al and Ash'ta-roth.

14 And the anger of the LORD was

hot against Is'ra-el, and He delivered them into the hands of spoilers that spoiled them, and He sold them into the hands of their enemies round about, so that they could not any longer stand before their enemies.

15 Wherever they went out, the hand of the LORD <u>was against</u> them for evil, as the LORD had said, and as the LORD had sworn to them: and they were greatly distressed. defeated

16 Nevertheless the LORD raised up judges, which delivered them out of the hand of those that <u>spoiled</u> them. plundered

17 And yet they would not hearken to their judges, but they <u>went a</u> <u>whoring</u> after other gods, and bowed themselves to them: they turned quickly out of the way which their fathers walked in, obeying the commandments of the LORD; *but* they did not so. prostituted themselves

18 And when the LORD raised them up judges, then the LORD was with the judge, and delivered them out of the hand of their enemies all the days of the judge: for it <u>repented</u> the LORD because of their groanings by reason of them that oppressed them and <u>vexed</u> them. grieved - afflicted

19 And it came to pass, when the judge was dead, *that* they returned, and <u>cor-</u><u>rupted</u> *themselves* more than their fathers, in following other gods to serve them, and to bow down to them; they ceased not from their own doings, nor from their stubborn way. practiced evil

20 And the anger of the LORD was hot against Is'ra-el; and He said, Because that this people has transgressed My <u>covenant</u> which I commanded their fathers, and have not hearkened to My voice; agreement

21 I also will not hereafter drive out any from before them of the nations which Josh'u-a left when he died:

22 That through them I may <u>prove</u> Is'ra-el, whether they will keep the way of the LORD to walk therein, as their fathers did keep *it*, or not. test

23 Therefore the LORD left those nations, without driving them out hastily; neither delivered He them into the hand of Josh'u-a.

CHAPTER 3

NOW these *are* the nations which the LORD left, to <u>prove</u> Is'ra-el by them, *even* as many *of Is'ra-el* as had not <u>known</u> all the wars of Ca'naan; test - experienced

2 Only that the generations of the children of Is'ra-el might <u>know</u>, to teach them war, at the least such as before knew nothing thereof; understand

3 *Namely*, five lords of the Phi-lis'tines, and all the Ca'naan-ites, and the Si-do'ni-ans, and the Hi'vites that dwelled in mount Leb'a-non, from mount Ba'al-her'mon to the entering in of Ha'math.

4 And they were to <u>prove</u> Is'ra-el by them, to <u>know</u> whether they would hearken to the commandments of the LORD, which He commanded their fathers by the hand of Mo'ses. find out

5 And the children of Is'ra-el dwelled among the Ca'naan-ites, Hit'tites, and

Am'or-ites, and Per'iz-zites, and Hi'vites, and Jeb'u-sites:

6 And they took their daughters to be their wives, and gave their daughters to their sons, and served their gods.

7 And the children of Is'ra-el did evil in the sight of the LORD, and forgat the LORD their God, and served Ba'al-im and the <u>groves</u>. idols

8 Therefore the anger of the LORD was hot against Is'ra-el, and He sold them into the hand of Chu'shan-rish-a-tha'im king of Mes-o-po-ta'mi-a: and the children of Is'ra-el served Chu'shan-rish-a-tha'im eight years.

9 And when the children of Is'ra-el cried to the LORD, the LORD raised up a <u>deliverer</u> to the children of Is'ra-el, who delivered them, *even* Oth'ni-el the son of Ke'naz, Ca'leb's younger brother. savior

10 And the Spirit of the LORD came upon him, and he judged Is'ra-el, and went out to war: and the LORD delivered Chu'shan-rish-a-tha'im king of Mes-o-po-ta'mi-a into his hand; and his hand prevailed against Chu'shan-rish-a-tha'im .

11 And the land had rest forty years. And Oth'ni-el the son of Ke'naz died.

12 And the children of Is'ra-el did evil again in the sight of the LORD: and the LORD strengthened Eg'lon the king of Mo'ab against Is'ra-el, because they had done evil in the sight of the LORD.

13 And he <u>gathered to</u> him the children of Am'mon and Am'a-lek, and went and <u>smote</u> Is'ra-el, and possessed the city of palm trees. recruited to - defeated

14 So the children of Is'ra-el served Eg'lon the king of Mo'ab eighteen years.

15 But when the children of Is'ra-el cried to the LORD, the LORD raised them up a deliverer, E'hud the son of Ge'ra, a Ben'ja-mite, a man lefthanded: and by him the children of Is'ra-el sent <u>a present</u> to Eg'lon the king of Mo'ab. tribute

16 But E'hud made him a <u>dagger</u> which had two edges, of a cubit length; and he did <u>gird</u> it under his <u>raiment</u> upon his right thigh. sword - fasten - cloak

17 And he brought the <u>present</u> to Eg'lon king of Mo'ab: and Eg'lon *was* a very fat man.

18 And when he had <u>made an end to offer the present</u>, he sent away the people that <u>bare</u> the present. finished presenting the tribute - carried

19 But he himself turned again from the quarries that *were* <u>by</u> Gil'gal, and said, I have a secret errand to you, O king: who said, <u>Keep silence</u>. And all that stood by him went out from him. at - leave us alone

20 And E'hud came to him; and he was sitting in a summer parlor, which he had for himself alone. And E'hud said, I have a message from God to you. And he arose out of *his* seat.

21 And E'hud put forth his left hand, and took the dagger from his right thigh, and thrust it into his belly:

22 And the <u>haft</u> also went in after the blade; and the fat closed upon the blade, so that he could not draw the dagger out of his belly; and the <u>dirt</u> came out. hilt - refuse

23 Then E'hud went forth through

the porch, and shut the doors of the parlor upon him, and lockcd them.

24 When he was gone out, his servants came; and when they saw that, behold, the doors of the parlor *were* locked, they said, Surely he <u>covers his feet</u> in his summer chamber. is relieving himself

25 And they tarried till they were ashamed: and, behold, he opened not the doors of the parlor; therefore they took a key, and opened *them*: and, behold, their lord *was* fallen down dead on the earth.

26 And E'hud escaped while they tarried, and passed beyond the <u>quarries</u>, and escaped to Se'i-rath. idols

27 And it came to pass, when he was come, that he blew a trumpet in the mountain of E'phra-im, and the children of Is'ra-el went down with him from the mount, and he <u>before</u> them. led

28 And he said to them, Follow after me: for the LORD has delivered your enemies the Mo'ab-ites into your hand. And they went down after him, and took the fords of Jor'dan toward Mo'ab, and allowed not a man to pass over.

29 And they slew of Mo'ab at that time about ten thousand men, all <u>lusty</u>, and all men of valor; and there escaped not a man. robust

30 So Mo'ab was <u>subdued</u> that day under the hand of Is'ra-el. And the land had rest <u>fourscore</u> years. defeated - 80

31 And after him was Sham'gar the son of A'nath, which slew of the Phi-lis'tines six hundred men with an ox <u>goad</u>: and he also delivered Is'ra-el. stick

CHAPTER 4

AND the children of Is'ra-el again did evil in the sight of the LORD, when E'hud was dead.

2 And the LORD <u>sold them into the hand</u> of Ja'bin king of Ca'naan, that reigned in Ha'zor; the captain of whose host *was* Sis'e-ra, which dwelled in Ha-ro'sheth of the Gen'tiles. i.e., they became slaves

3 And the children of Is'ra-el cried to the LORD: for he had nine hundred chariots of iron; and twenty years he mightily oppressed the children of Is'ra-el.

4 And Deb'o-rah, a prophetess, the wife of Lap'i-doth, she judged Is'ra-el at that time.

5 And she dwelled under the palm tree of Deb'o-rah between Ra'mah and Beth'-el in mount E'phra-im: and the children of Is'ra-el came up to her for judgment.

6 And she sent and called Ba'rak the son of A-bin'o-am out of Ke'desh-naph'ta-li, and said to him, Has not the LORD God of Is'ra-el commanded, *saying*, Go and draw toward mount Ta'bor, and take with you ten thousand men of the children of Naph'ta-li and of the children of Zeb'u-lun?

7 And I will <u>draw to</u> you to the river Ki'shon Sis'e-ra, the captain of Ja'bin's army, with his chariots and his multitude; and I will <u>deliver</u> him into your hand. lure - give

8 And Ba'rak said to her, If you will go with me, then I will go: but if you will not go with me, *then* I will not go.

9 And she said, I will surely go with you: notwithstanding the journey that you take shall not be for your honor; for the LORD shall sell Sis'e-ra into the hand of a woman. And Deb'o-rah arose, and went with Ba'rak to Ke'desh.

10 And Ba'rak called Zeb'u-lun and Naph'ta-li to Ke'desh; and he went up with ten thousand men at his feet: and Deb'o-rah went up with him.

11 Now He'ber the Ken'ite, *which was* of the children of Ho'bab the father in law of Mo'ses, had severed himself from the Ken-ites, and <u>pitched his tent</u> to the plain of Za-a-na'im, which *is* by Ke'desh. _{camped}

12 And they showed Sis'e-ra that Ba'rak the son of A-bin'o-am <u>was</u> gone up to mount Ta'bor. _{had}

13 And Sis'e-ra gathered together all his chariots, *even* nine hundred chariots of iron, and all the people that *were* with him, from Ha-ro'sheth of the <u>Gen'tiles</u> to the river of Ki'shon. _{nations}

14 And Deb'o-rah said to Ba'rak, Up; for this *is* the day in which the LORD has delivered Sis'e-ra into your hand: is not the LORD <u>gone out</u> before you? So Ba'rak went down from mount Ta'bor, and ten thousand men after him. _{gone ahead}

15 And the LORD <u>discomfited</u> Sis'e-ra, and all *his* chariots, and all *his* host, with the edge of the sword before Ba'rak; so that Sis'e-ra lighted down off *his* chariot, and fled away on his feet. _{routed}

16 But Ba'rak pursued after the chariots, and after the <u>host</u>, to Ha-ro'sheth of the Gen'tiles: and all the <u>host</u> of Sis'e-ra <u>fell upon the edge of the sword</u>; *and* there was not a man left. _{army - were killed}

17 However Sis'e-ra fled away on his feet to the tent of Ja'el the wife of He'ber the Ken'ite: for *there was* peace between Ja'bin the king of Ha'zor and the house of He'ber the Ken'ite.

18 And Ja'el went out to meet Sis'e-ra, and said to him, <u>Turn in</u>, my lord, <u>turn</u> in to me; fear not. And when he had turned in to her into the tent, she <u>covered</u> him with a <u>mantle</u>. _{Come - hid - rug}

19 And he said to her, Give me, I pray you, a little water to drink; for I am thirsty. And she opened a bottle of milk, and gave him drink, and <u>covered</u> him.

20 Again he said to her, Stand in the door of the tent, and it shall be, when any man does come and enquire of you, and say, Is there any man here? that you shall say, No.

21 Then Ja'el He'ber's wife took a <u>nail</u> of the tent, and took an hammer in her hand, and went softly to him, and <u>smote</u> the <u>nail</u> into his temples, and fastened it into the ground: for he was fast asleep and weary. So he died. _{tent peg - drove}

22 And, behold, as Ba'rak pursued Sis'e-ra, Ja'el came out to meet him, and said to him, Come, and I will show you the man whom you seek. And when he came into her *tent*, behold, Sis'e-ra lay dead, and the nail was in his temples.

23 So God <u>subdued</u> on that day Ja'-

bin the king of Ca'naan before the children of Is'ra-el.   defeated

24 And the hand of the children of Is'ra-el prospered, and prevailed against Ja'bin the king of Ca'naan, until they had destroyed Ja'bin king of Ca'naan.

CHAPTER 5

THEN sang Deb'o-rah and Ba'rak the son of A-bin'o-am on that day, saying,

2 Praise you the LORD for <u>the avenging of</u> Is'ra-el, when the people willingly offered themselves. bringing victory to

3 Hear, O you kings; give ear, O you princes; I, *even* I, will sing to the LORD; I will sing *praise* to the LORD God of Is'ra-el.

4 LORD, when You went out of Se'ir, when You marched out of the field of E'dom, the earth trembled, and the heavens dropped, the clouds also dropped water.

5 The mountains <u>melted</u> from before the LORD, *even* that Si'nai from before the <u>LORD God</u> of Is'ra-el.   quaked - Jehovah s.f. Elohim p.f.

6 In the days of Sham'gar the son of A'nath, in the days of Ja'el, the highways were unoccupied, and the travellers walked through byways.

7 The *inhabitants of* the villages ceased, they ceased in Is'ra-el, until that I Deb'o-rah arose, that I arose a <u>mother</u> in Is'ra-el.   woman leader

8 They chose new gods; then *was* war in the gates: was there a shield or spear seen among forty thousand in Is'ra-el?

9 My heart *is* toward the governors of Is'ra-el, that offered themselves willingly among the people. Bless you the LORD.

10 Speak, you that <u>ride on white asses</u>, you that sit in judgment, and walk by the way.   hold public office

11 *They that are delivered* from the noise of archers in the places of drawing water, there shall they rehearse the righteous acts of the LORD, *even* the righteous acts *toward the inhabitants* of His villages in Is'ra-el: then shall the people of the LORD <u>go down to the gates</u>.   defend themselves

12 Awake, awake, Deb'o-rah: awake, awake, utter a song: arise, Ba'rak, and lead your captivity captive, you son of A-bin'o-am.

13 Then he made him that remains have dominion over the nobles among the people: the LORD made me have dominion over the mighty.

14 Out of E'phra-im *was there* a <u>root</u> of them against Am'a-lek; after you, Ben'ja-min, among your people; out of Ma'chir came down governors, and out of Zeb'u-lun they that handle the pen of the writer.   few

15 And the <u>princes</u> of Is'sa-char *were* with Deb'o-rah; even Is'sa-char, and also Ba'rak: he was sent on foot into the valley. For the divisions of Reu'ben *there were* great thoughts of heart.   rulers

16 Why abode you among the sheepfolds, to hear the bleatings of the flocks? <u>For</u> the divisions of Reu'ben *there were* great searchings of heart. In

17 Gil'e-ad abode beyond Jor'dan: and why did Dan remain in ships?

Ash'er continued on the sea shore, and abode in his breaches.

18 Zeb'u-lun and Naph'ta-li *were* a people *that* jeoparded their lives to the death in the high places of the field. _{risked}

19 The kings came *and* fought, then fought the kings of Ca'naan in Ta'a-nach by the waters of Me-gid'do; they took no gain of money.

20 They fought from heaven; the stars in their courses fought against Sis'e-ra.

21 The river of Ki'shon swept them away, that ancient river, the river Ki'shon. O my soul, you have trodden down strength.

22 Then were the horsehoofs broken by the means of the prancings, the prancings of their mighty ones.

23 Curse you Me'roz, said the angel of the LORD, curse you bitterly the inhabitants thereof; because they came not to the help of the LORD, to the help of the LORD against the mighty. _{messenger}

24 Blessed above women shall Ja'el the wife of He'ber the Ken'ite be, blessed shall she be above women in the tent.

25 He asked water, *and* she gave *him* milk; she brought forth butter in a lordly dish.

26 She put her hand to the nail, and her right hand to the workmen's hammer; and with the hammer she smote Sis'e-ra, she smote off his head, when she had pierced and stricken through his temples.

27 At her feet he bowed, he fell, he lay down: at her feet he bowed, he fell: where he bowed, there he fell down dead.

28 The mother of Sis'e-ra looked out at a window, and cried through the lattice, Why is his chariot *so* long in coming? why tarry the wheels of his chariots?

29 Her wise ladies answered her, yea, she returned answer to herself,

30 Have they not sped? have they *not* divided the prey; to every man a damsel *or* two; to Sis'e-ra a prey of divers colors, a prey of divers colors of needlework, of divers colors of needlework on both sides, *meet* for the necks of *them that take* the spoil? _{found - young woman - various}

31 So let all your enemies perish, O LORD: but *let* them that love Him *be as* the sun when it goes forth in his might. And the land had rest forty years.

CHAPTER 6

AND the children of Is'ra-el did evil in the sight of the LORD: and the LORD delivered them into the hand of Mid'i-an seven years. _{sinned - under the control}

2 And the hand of Mid'i-an prevailed against Is'ra-el: *and* because of the Mid'i-an-ites the children of Is'ra-el made them the dens which *are* in the mountains, and caves, and strong holds.

3 And *so* it was, when Is'ra-el had sown, that the Mid'i-an-ites came up, and the Am'a-lek-ites, and the children of the east, even they came up against them; _{invaded the country}

4 And they encamped against them, and destroyed the increase of the earth,

till you come to Ga'za, and left no sustenance for Is'ra-el, neither sheep, nor ox, nor ass.   produce - living thing

5 For they came up with their cattle and their tents, and they came as grasshoppers for multitude; *for* both they and their camels were without number: and they entered into the land to destroy it.

6 And Is'ra-el was greatly impoverished because of the Mid'i-an-ites; and the children of Is'ra-el cried to the LORD.

7 And it came to pass, when the children of Is'ra-el cried to the LORD because of the Mid'i-an-ites,

8 That the LORD sent a prophet to the children of Is'ra-el, which said to them, Thus says the LORD God of Is'ra-el, I brought you up from E'gypt, and brought you forth out of the house of bondage;

Jehovah$^{s.f.}$ - Adonay Elohim$^{p.f.}$

9 And I delivered you out of the hand of the E-gyp'tians, and out of the hand of all that oppressed you, and drove them out from before you, and gave you their land;

10 And I said to you, I *am* the LORD your God; fear not the gods of the Am'or-ites, in whose land you dwell: but you have not obeyed My voice.   Elohim$^{p.f.}$ - heed

11 And there came an angel of the LORD, and sat under an oak which *was* in Oph'rah, that *pertained* to Jo'ash the A'bi-ez'rite: and his son Gid'e-on threshed wheat by the winepress, to hide *it* from the Mid'i-an-ites.   messenger - save

12 And the angel of the LORD appeared to him, and said to him,

The LORD *is* with you, you mighty man of valor.   messenger

13 And Gid'e-on said to him, Oh my Lord, if the LORD be with us, why then is all this befallen us? and where *be* all His miracles which our fathers told us of, saying, Did not the LORD bring us up from E'gypt? but now the LORD has forsaken us, and delivered us into the hands of the Mid'i-an-ites.   Adon$^{s.f.}$ - Jehovah$^{s.f.}$ - happened to - wonders

14 And the LORD looked upon him, and said, Go in this your might, and you shall save Is'ra-el from the hand of the Mid'i-an-ites: have not I sent you?

15 And he said to Him, Oh my Lord, wherewith shall I save Is'ra-el? behold, my family *is* poor in Ma-nas'seh, and I *am* the least in my father's house.

16 And the LORD said to him, Surely I will be with you, and you shall smite the Mid'i-an-ites as one man.   strike down

17 And he said to Him, If now I have found grace in Your sight, then show me a sign that You talk with me.

18 Depart not from here, I pray You, until I come to You, and bring forth my present, and set *it* before You. And He said, I will tarry until you come again.

19 And Gid'e-on went in, and made ready a kid, and unleavened cakes of an ephah of flour: the flesh he put in a basket, and he put the broth in a pot, and brought *it* out to him under the oak, and presented *it*.   i.e., without yeast

20 And the angel of God said to

him, Take the <u>flesh</u> and the <u>unleavened</u> cakes, and lay *them* upon this rock, and pour out the broth. And he did so. messenger - meat - without yeast

21 Then the <u>angel</u> of the LORD put forth the end of the staff that *was* in his hand, and touched the <u>flesh</u> and the <u>unleavened</u> cakes; and there rose up fire out of the rock, and consumed the <u>flesh</u> and the <u>unleavened</u> cakes. Then the angel of the LORD departed out of his sight.

22 And when Gid'e-on <u>perceived</u> that he *was* an <u>angel</u> of the LORD, Gid'e-on said, Alas, O <u>Lord GOD</u>! for because I have seen an <u>angel</u> of the LORD face to face. saw - Adonay^{p.f.} Jehovah

23 And the LORD said to him, Peace *be* to you; fear not: you shall not die.

24 Then Gid'e-on built an altar there to the LORD, and called it <u>Jeho'vah-sha'lom</u>: to this day it *is* yet in Oph'rah of the A'bi-ez'rites.

The LORD is peace

25 And it came to pass the same night, that the LORD said to him, Take your father's young bullock, even the second bullock of seven years old, and throw down the altar of Ba'al that your father has, and cut down the grove that is by it:

26 And build an altar to the LORD your <u>God</u> upon the top of this rock, in the ordered place, and take the second bullock, and offer a burned sacrifice with the wood of the grove which you shall cut down. Elohim^{p.f.}

27 Then Gid'e-on took ten men of his servants, and did as the LORD had said to him: and *so* it was, because he feared his father's household, and the men of the city, that he could not do *it* by day, that he did *it* by night.

28 And when the men of the city arose early in the morning, behold, the altar of Ba'al was cast down, and the <u>grove</u> was cut down that *was* by it, and the second bullock was offered upon the altar *that was* built. idols

29 And they said one to another, Who has done this thing? And when they enquired and asked, they said, Gid'e-on the son of Jo'ash has done this thing.

30 Then the men of the city said to Jo'ash, Bring out your son, that he may die: because he has <u>cast</u> down the altar of Ba'al, and because he has cut down the <u>grove</u> that *was* by it.broken

31 And Jo'ash said to all that stood against him, Will you plead for Ba'al? will you save him? he that will plead for him, let him be put to death while *it is yet* morning: if he *be* a god, let him plead for himself, because *one* has cast down his altar.

32 Therefore on that day he called him Je-rub'ba-al, saying, Let Ba'al <u>plead</u> against him, because he has thrown down his altar. contend

33 Then all the Mid'i-an-ites and the Am'a-lek-ites and the children of the east were gathered together, and went over, and <u>pitched</u> in the valley of Jez're-el. camped

34 But the Spirit of the LORD came upon Gid'e-on, and he blew a trumpet; and A'bi-e'zer was gathered after him.

35 And he sent messengers throughout all Ma-nas'seh; who also was <u>gath-</u>

ered after him: and he sent messengers to Ash'er, and to Zeb'u-lun, and to Naph'ta-li; and they came up to meet them. called together to follow

36 And Gid'e-on said to God, If You will save Is'ra-el <u>by mine hand</u>, as You have said, through me

37 Behold, I will put a fleece of wool in the floor; *and* if the dew be on the fleece only, and *it be* dry upon all the earth *beside*, then shall I know that You will save Is'ra-el by my hand, as You have said.

38 And it was so: for he rose up early on the <u>morrow</u>, and thrust the fleece together, and wringed the dew out of the fleece, a bowl full of water. next day

39 And Gid'e-on said to God, Let not Your anger be hot against me, and I will speak but this once: let me prove, I pray You, but this once with the fleece; let it now be dry only upon the fleece, and upon all the ground let there be dew.

40 And <u>God</u> did so that night: for it was dry upon the fleece only, and there was dew on all the ground. Elohim^{p.f.}

CHAPTER 7

THEN Je-rub'ba-al, who *is* Gid'e-on, and all the people that *were* with him, rose up early, and <u>pitched</u> beside the well of Ha'rod: so that the host of the Mid'i-an-ites were on the north side of them, by the hill of Mo'reh, in the valley. camped

2 And the LORD said to Gid'e-on, The people that *are* with you *are* too many for Me to give the Mid'i-an-ites into their hands, less Is'ra-el vaunt themselves against Me, saying, My own hand has saved me.

3 Now therefore go to, proclaim in the <u>ears</u> of the people, saying, Whosoever *is* <u>fearful</u> and afraid, let him <u>return</u> and depart early from mount Gil'e-ad. And there returned of the people twenty and two thousand; and there remained ten thousand. hearing - trembling - turn back

4 And the LORD said to Gid'e-on, The people *are* yet *too* many; bring them down to the water, and I will <u>try</u> them for you there: and it shall be, *that* of whom I say to you, This shall go with you, the same shall go with you; and of whomsoever I say to you, This shall not go with you, the same shall not go. test

5 So he brought down the people to the water: and the LORD said to Gid'e-on, Every one that laps of the water with his tongue, as a dog laps, him shall you set by himself; likewise every one that bows down upon his knees to drink.

6 And the number of them that lapped, *putting* their hand to their mouth, were three hundred men: but all the rest of the people bowed down upon their knees to drink water.

7 And the LORD said to Gid'e-on, By the three hundred men that lapped will I save you, and deliver the Mid'i-an-ites into your hand: and let all the *other* people go every man <u>to his place</u>. to his home

8 So the people took victuals in their hand, and their trumpets: and he sent

all *the rest of* Is'ra-el every man to his tent, and retained those three hundred men: and the <u>host</u> of Mid'i-an was beneath him in the valley.   army

9 And it came to pass the same night, that the LORD said to him, Arise, get you down to the host; for I have delivered it into your hand.

10 But if you fear to go down, go you with Phu'rah your servant down to the host:

11 And you shall hear what they say; and afterward shall your hands be strengthened to go down to the host. Then went he down with Phu'rah his servant to the outside of the armed men that *were* in the <u>host</u>.

12 And the Mid'i-an-ites and the Am'a-lek-ites and all the children of the east lay along in the valley like grasshoppers for multitude; and their camels *were* without number, as the sand by the sea side for multitude.

13 And when Gid'e-on was come, behold, *there was* a man that told a dream to his fellow, and said, Behold, I dreamed a dream, and, lo, a cake of barley bread tumbled into the host of Mid'i-an, and came to a tent, and smote it that it fell, and overturned it, that the tent lay <u>along</u>.   flat

14 And his fellow answered and said, This is nothing else <u>save</u> the sword of Gid'e-on the son of Jo'ash, a man of Is'ra-el: *for* into his hand has God delivered Mid'i-an, and all the <u>host</u>.   less than - army

15 And it was so, when Gid'e-on heard the telling of the dream, and the interpretation thereof, that he worshiped, and returned into the <u>host</u> of Is'ra-el, and said, Arise; for the LORD has delivered into your hand the host of Mid'i-an.   army

16 And he divided the three hundred men into three companies, and he put a trumpet in every man's hand, with empty pitchers, and <u>lamps</u> within the pitchers.   torches

17 And he said to them, Look on me, and do <u>likewise</u>: and, behold, when I come to the outside of the camp, it shall be that, as I do, so shall you do.   the same

18 When I blow with a trumpet, I and all that *are* with me, then blow you the trumpets also on every side of all the camp, and say, *The sword of the LORD, and of Gid'e-on.*

19 So Gid'e-on, and the hundred men that *were* with him, came to the outside of the camp in the beginning of the middle watch; and they had but newly set the watch: and they blew the trumpets, and broke the pitchers that were in their hands.

20 And the three companies blew the trumpets, and broke the pitchers, and held the <u>lamps</u> in their left hands, and the trumpets in their right hands to blow *with*: and they cried, The sword of the LORD, and of Gid'e-on.   Jehovah

21 And they stood every man in his place round about the camp: and all the <u>host</u> ran, and cried, and fled.   army

22 And the three hundred blew the trumpets, and the LORD set every man's sword against <u>his fellow</u>, even throughout all the <u>host</u>: and the <u>host</u> fled to Beth-shit'tah in Zer'e-rath, *and* to the

border of A'bel-me-ho'lah, to Tab'bath. <small>each other - army</small>

23 And the men of Is'ra-el <u>gathered themselves</u> together out of Naph'ta-li, and out of Ash'er, and out of all Ma-nas'seh, and pursued after the Mid'i-an-ites. <small>were summoned</small>

24 And Gid'e-on sent messengers throughout all mount E'phra-im, saying, Come down against the Mid'i-an-ites, and take before them the waters to Beth-ba'rah and Jor'dan. Then all the men of E'phra-im gathered themselves together, and took the waters to Beth-ba'rah and Jor'dan.

25 And they took two princes of the Mid'i-an-ites, O'reb and Ze'eb; and they slew O'reb upon the rock O'reb, and Ze'eb they slew at the winepress of Ze'eb, and pursued Mid'i-an, and brought the heads of O'reb and Ze'eb to Gid'e-on on the other side Jor'dan.

CHAPTER 8

AND the men of E'phra-im said to him, Why have you served us thus, that you called us not, when you went to fight with the Mid'i-an-ites? And they did <u>chide</u> with him sharply. <small>contend</small>

2 And he said to them, What have I done now in comparison of you? *Is* not the gleaning of the grapes of E'phra-im better than the vintage of A'bi-e'zer?

3 <u>God</u> has delivered into your hands the princes of Mid'i-an, O'reb and Ze'eb: and what was I able to do in comparison of you? Then their anger <u>was</u>

abated toward him, when he had said that. <small>Elohim^{p-f} - subsided</small>

4 And Gid'e-on came to Jor'dan, *and* passed over, he, and the three hundred men that were with him, faint, yet pursuing *them*.

5 And he said to the men of Suc'coth, Give, I pray you, loaves of bread to the people that follow me; for they *be* faint, and I am pursuing after Ze'bah and Zal-mun'na, kings of Mid'i-an.

6 And the princes of Suc'coth said, *Are* the hands of Ze'bah and Zal-mun'na now in your hand, that we should give bread to your army?

7 And Gid'e-on said, Therefore when the LORD has delivered Ze'bah and Zal-mun'na into my hand, then I will <u>tear your flesh</u> with the thorns of the wilderness and with briers. <small>thrash your bodies</small>

8 And he went up from there to Pe-nu'el, and spoke to them likewise: and the men of Pe-nu'el answered him as the men of Suc'coth had answered *him*.

9 And he spoke also to the men of Pe-nu'el, saying, When I come again in <u>peace</u>, I will break down this tower. <small>triumph</small>

10 Now Ze'bah and Zal-mun'na *were* in Kar'kor, and their hosts with them, about fifteen thousand *men*, all that were left of all the <u>hosts</u> of the children of the east: for there fell an hundred and twenty thousand men that drew sword. <small>army</small>

11 And Gid'e-on went up by the way of them that dwelled in tents on the east of No'bah and Jog'be-hah, and <u>smote</u> the host: for the host was secure. <small>attacked</small>

12 And when Ze'bah and Zal-mun'na fled, he pursued after them, and took the two kings of Mid'i-an, Ze'bah and Zal-mun'na, and discomfited all the host.

13 And Gid'e-on the son of Jo'ash returned from battle before the sun *was up,*

14 And caught a young man of the men of Suc'coth, and inquired of him: and he described to him the princes of Suc'coth, and the elders thereof, *even* threescore and seventeen men.

15 And he came to the men of Suc'coth, and said, Behold Ze'bah and Zal-mun'na, with whom you did upbraid me, saying, *Are* the hands of Ze'bah and Zal-mun'na now in your hand, that we should give bread to your men *that are* weary?

16 And he took the elders of the city, and thorns of the wilderness and briers, and with them he taught the men of Suc'coth.

17 And he beat down the tower of Pe-nu'el, and slew the men of the city.

18 Then said he to Ze'bah and Zal-mun'na, What manner of men *were they* whom you slew at Ta'bor? And they answered, As you *are*, so *were* they; each one resembled the children of a king.

19 And he said, They *were* my brethren, *even* the sons of my mother: as the LORD lives, if you had saved them alive, I would not slay you.

20 And he said to Je'ther his firstborn, Up, *and* slay them. But the youth drew not his sword: for he feared, because he *was* yet a youth.

21 Then Ze'bah and Zal-mun'na said, Rise you, and fall upon us: for as the man *is, so is* his strength. And Gid'e-on arose, and slew Ze'bah and Zal-mun'na, and took away the <u>ornaments</u> that *were* on their camels' necks. crescents

22 Then the men of Is'ra-el said to Gid'e-on, Rule you over us, both you, and your son, and your son's son also: for you have delivered us from the hand of Mid'i-an.

23 And Gid'e-on said to them, I will not rule over you, neither shall my son rule over you: the LORD shall rule over you.   G4A 407

24 And Gid'e-on said to them, I would desire a request of you, that you would give me every man the earrings of his <u>prey</u>. (For they had golden earrings, because they *were* Ish'ma-el-ites.)   spoil

25 And they answered, We will willingly give *them*. And they spread a garment, and did cast therein every man the earrings of his <u>prey</u>.

26 And the weight of the golden earrings that he requested was a thousand and seven hundred *shekels* of gold; beside ornaments, and <u>collars</u>, and purple <u>raiment</u> that *was* on the kings of Mid'i-an, and beside the chains that *were* about their camels' necks.   pendants - clothing

27 And Gid'e-on made an <u>ephod</u> thereof, and put it in his city, *even* in Oph'rah: and all Is'ra-el went there <u>a whoring</u> after it: which thing became a <u>snare</u> to Gid'e-on, and to his house.   M10 409

priestly garment - i.e., worshipping - lure

28 Thus was Mid'i-an subdued before the children of Is'ra-el, so that they

lifted up their heads no more. And the country was in quietness forty years in the days of Gid'e-on.   *were a force*

29 And Je-rub'ba-al the son of Jo'ash went and dwelled in his own house.

30 And Gid'e-on had threescore and ten sons of his body begotten: for he had many wives.   *70*

31 And his concubine that *was* in She'chem, she also bare him a son, whose name he called A-bim'e-lech.

32 And Gid'e-on the son of Jo'ash died in a good old age, and was buried in the sepulcher of Jo'ash his father, in Oph'rah of the A'bi-ez'rites.   *tomb*

33 And it came to pass, as soon as Gid'e-on was dead, that the children of Is'ra-el turned again, and went a whoring after Ba'al-im, and made Ba'al-be'rith their god.   *i.e., worshipping*

34 And the children of Is'ra-el remembered not the LORD their God, who had delivered them out of the hands of all their enemies on every side:

35 Neither showed they kindness to the house of Je-rub'ba-al, *namely*, Gid'e-on, according to all the goodness which he had showed to Is'ra-el.

CHAPTER 9

AND A-bim'e-lech the son of Je-rub'ba-al went to She'chem to his mother's brethren, and communed with them, and with all the family of the house of his mother's father, saying,   *spoke*

2 Speak, I pray you, in the ears of all the men of She'chem, Whether *is* better for you, either that all the sons of Je-rub'ba-al, *which are* threescore and ten persons, reign over you, or that one reign over you? remember also that I *am* your bone and your flesh.   *70 - your relative*

3 And his mother's brethren spoke of him in the ears of all the men of She'chem all these words: and their hearts inclined to follow A-bim'e-lech; for they said, He is our brother.

4 And they gave him threescore and ten *pieces* of silver out of the house of Ba'al-be'rith, wherewith A-bim'e-lech hired vain and light persons, which followed him.   *worthless and reckless*

5 And he went to his father's house at Oph'rah, and slew his brethren the sons of Je-rub'ba-al, *being* threescore and ten persons, upon one stone: notwithstanding yet Jo'tham the youngest son of Je-rub'ba-al was left; for he hid himself.   *spot*

6 And all the men of She'chem gathered together, and all the house of Mil'lo, and went, and made A-bim'e-lech king, by the plain of the pillar that *was* in She'chem.

7 And when they told *it* to Jo'tham, he went and stood in the top of mount Ger'i-zim, and lifted up his voice, and cried, and said to them, Hearken to me, you men of She'chem, that God may hearken to you.   *listen*

8 The trees went forth *on a time* to anoint a king over them; and they said to the olive tree, Reign you over us.

9 But the olive tree said to them, Should I leave my fatness, wherewith by me they honor God and man, and go to be promoted over the trees?   *waving*

10 And the trees said to the fig tree, Come you, *and* reign over us.

11 But the fig tree said to them, Should I forsake my sweetness, and my good fruit, and go to be promoted over the trees?

12 Then said the trees to the vine, Come you, *and* reign over us.

13 And the vine said to them, Should I leave my wine, which cheers God and man, and go to be promoted over the trees?

14 Then said all the trees to the bramble, Come you, *and* reign over us.   thornbush

15 And the bramble said to the trees, If in truth you anoint me king over you, *then* come *and* put your trust in my shadow: and if not, let fire come out of the bramble, and devour the cedars of Leb'a-non.

16 Now therefore, if you have done truly and sincerely, in that you have made A-bim'e-lech king, and if you have dealt well with Je-rub'ba-al and his house, and have done to him according to the deserving of his hands;   deeds

17 (For my father fought for you, and adventured his life far, and delivered you out of the hand of Mid'i-an: risked

18 And you are risen up against my father's house this day, and have slain his sons, threescore and ten persons, upon one stone, and have made A-bim'e-lech, the son of his maidservant, king over the men of She'chem, because he *is* your brother;)   70 - spot

19 If you then have dealt truly and sincerely with Je-rub'ba-al and with his house this day, *then* rejoice you in A-bim'e-lech, and let him also rejoice in you:

20 But if not, let fire come out from A-bim'e-lech, and devour the men of She'chem, and the house of Mil'lo; and let fire come out from the men of She'chem, and from the house of Mil'lo, and devour A-bim'e-lech.   destruction

21 And Jo'tham ran away, and fled, and went to Be'er, and dwelled there, for fear of A-bim'e-lech his brother.

22 When A-bim'e-lech had reigned three years over Is'ra-el,

23 Then God sent an evil spirit between A-bim'e-lech and the men of She'chem; and the men of She'chem dealt treacherously with A-bim'e-lech: Elohim^p.f

24 That the cruelty *done* to the three-score and ten sons of Je-rub'ba-al might come, and their blood be laid upon A-bim'e-lech their brother, which slew them; and upon the men of She'chem, which aided him in the killing of his brethren.   70

25 And the men of She'chem set liers in wait for him in the top of the mountains, and they robbed all that came along that way by them: and it was told A-bim'e-lech.   men in ambush

26 And Ga'al the son of E'bed came with his brethren, and went over to She'chem: and the men of She'chem put their confidence in him.

27 And they went out into the fields, and gathered their vineyards, and trampled *the grapes*, and made merry, and went into the house of their god, and did eat and drink, and cursed A-bim'e-lech.   celebrated

28 And Ga'al the son of E'bed said, Who *is* A-bim'e-lech, and who *is* She'-

chem, that we should serve him? *is* not *he* the son of Je-rub'ba-al? and Ze'bul his officer? serve the men of Ha'mor the father of She'chem: for why should we serve him?

29 And would to God this people were under my hand! then would I remove A-bim'e-lech. And he said to A-bim'e-lech, Increase your army, and come out.

30 And when Ze'bul the ruler of the city heard the words of Ga'al the son of E'bed, his anger <u>was kindled</u>. burned

31 And he sent messengers to A-bim'e-lech <u>privily</u>, saying, Behold, Ga'al the son of E'bed and his brethren be come to She'chem; and, behold, they fortify the city against you. deceitfully

32 Now therefore <u>up</u> by night, you and the people that *is* with you, and lie in wait in the field: arise

33 And it shall be, *that* in the morning, as soon as the sun is up, you shall rise early, and set upon the city: and, behold, *when* he and the people that *is* with him come out against you, then may you do to them as you shall find occasion.

34 And A-bim'e-lech rose up, and all the people that *were* with him, by night, and they laid wait against She'chem in four companies.

35 And Ga'al the son of E'bed went out, and stood in the <u>entering</u> of the gate of the city: and A-bim'e-lech rose up, and the people that *were* with him, from lying in <u>wait</u>. entrance - ambush

36 And when Ga'al saw the people, he said to Ze'bul, Behold, there come

people down from the top of the mountains. And Ze'bul said to him, You see the shadow of the mountains as *if they were* men.

37 And Ga'al spoke again and said, See there come people down by the middle of the land, and another company come along by the <u>plain</u> of Me-on'e-nim. oak

38 Then said Ze'bul to him, Where *is* now your <u>mouth</u>, wherewith you said, Who *is* A-bim'e-lech, that we should serve him? *is* not this the people that you have despised? go out, I pray now, and fight with them. boasting

39 And Ga'al went out before the men of She'chem, and fought with A-bim'e-lech.

40 And A-bim'e-lech chased him, and he fled before him, and many were overthrown *and* wounded, *even* to the <u>entering</u> of the gate. entrance

41 And A-bim'e-lech dwelled at A-ru'mah: and Ze'bul <u>thrust</u> out Ga'al and his brethren, that they should not dwell in She'chem. drove

42 And it came to pass on the <u>morrow</u>, that the people went out into the field; and they told A-bim'e-lech. next day

43 And he took the people, and divided them into three companies, and laid wait in the field, and looked, and, behold, the people *were* come forth out of the city; and he rose up against them, and smote them.

44 And A-bim'e-lech, and the company that *was* with him, rushed forward, and <u>stood</u> in the <u>entering</u> of the

gate of the city: and the two *other* companies ran upon all *the people* that *were* in the fields, and slew them.   _{occupied - entrance}

45 And A-bim'e-lech fought against the city all that day; and he took the city, and slew the people that *was* therein, and beat down the city, and <u>sowed</u> it with salt.   _{scattered}

46 And when all the men of the tower of She'chem heard *that*, they entered into an hold of the house of the god Be'rith.

47 And it was told A-bim'e-lech, that all the men of the tower of She'chem were gathered together.

48 And A-bim'e-lech got him up to mount Zal'mon, he and all the people that *were* with him; and A-bim'e-lech took an ax in his hand, and cut down a bough from the trees, and took it, and laid *it* on his shoulder, and said to the people that *were* with him, What you have seen me do, make haste, *and* do *as* I *have done.*

49 And all the people likewise cut down every man his bough, and followed A-bim'e-lech, and put *them* to the <u>hold</u>, and set the <u>hold</u> on fire upon them; so that all the men of the tower of She'chem died also, about a thousand men and women.   _{chamber}

50 Then went A-bim'e-lech to The'bez, and <u>encamped</u> against The'bez, and took it.   _{besieged}

51 But there was a strong tower within the city, and there fled all the men and women, and all they of the city, and shut *it* to them, and got them up to the top of the tower.

52 And A-bim'e-lech came to the tower, and fought against it, and <u>went hard to</u> the door of the tower to burn it with fire.   _{approached}

53 And a certain woman cast a piece of a millstone upon A-bim'e-lech's head, and all to break his skull.

54 Then he called hastily to the young man his armorbearer, and said to him, Draw your sword, and slay me, that men say not of me, A woman slew him. And his young man thrust him through, and he died.

55 And when the men of Is'ra-el saw that A-bim'e-lech was dead, they departed every man to his <u>place</u>.   _{home}

56 Thus God rendered the wickedness of A-bim'e-lech, which he did to his father, in slaying his seventy brethren:

57 And all the evil of the men of She'chem did <u>God render</u> upon their heads: and upon them came the curse of Jo'tham the son of Je-rub'ba-al.   _{Elohim^{p.f.} -return}

CHAPTER 10

AND after A-bim'e-lech there arose to defend Is'ra-el To'la the son of Pu'ah, the son of Do'do, a man of Is'sa-char; and he dwelled in Sha'mir in mount E'phra-im.

2 And he judged Is'ra-el twenty and three years, and died, and was buried in Sha'mir.

3 And after him arose Ja'ir, a Gil'e-ad-ite, and judged Is'ra-el twenty and two years.

4 And he had thirty sons that rode on thirty ass colts, and they had thirty cities, which are called Ha'voth-ja'ir

to this day, which *are* in the land of Gil'e-ad.

5 And Ja'ir died, and was buried in Ca'mon.

6 And the children of Is'ra-el did evil again in the sight of the LORD, and served Ba'al-im, and Ash'ta-roth, and the gods of Syr'i-a, and the gods of Zi'don, and the gods of Mo'ab, and the gods of the children of Am'mon, and the gods of the Phi-lis'tines, and forsook the LORD, and served not Him.

7 And the anger of the LORD was hot against Is'ra-el, and He sold them into the hands of the Phi-lis'tines, and into the hands of the children of Am'mon.

8 And that year they <u>vexed</u> and oppressed the children of Is'ra-el: eighteen years, all the children of Is'ra-el that *were* on the other side Jor'dan in the land of the Am'or-ites, which is in Gil'e-ad. _{afflicted}

9 Moreover the children of Am'mon passed over Jor'dan to fight also against Ju'dah, and against Ben'ja-min, and against the house of E'phra-im; so that Is'ra-el was <u>sore</u> distressed. _{greatly}

10 And the children of Is'ra-el cried to the LORD, saying, We have sinned against you, both because we have forsaken our <u>God</u>, and also served Ba'al-im. _{Elohim}^{p.f.}

11 And the LORD said to the children of Is'ra-el, *Did* not *I deliver you* from the E-gyp'tians, and from the Am'or-ites, from the children of Am'mon, and from the Phi-lis'tines?

12 The Zi-do'ni-ans also, and the Am'a-lek-ites, and the Ma'on-ites, did oppress you; and you cried to Me, and I delivered you out of their hand.

13 Yet you have forsaken Me, and served other gods: wherefore I will deliver you no more.

14 Go and <u>cry</u> to the gods which you have chosen; let them deliver you in the time of your <u>tribulation</u>. _{call - distress}

15 And the children of Is'ra-el said to the LORD, We have sinned: do You to us whatsoever seems good to You; deliver us only, we pray You, this day.

16 And they put away the <u>strange</u> gods from among them, and served the LORD: and His soul was grieved for the misery of Is'ra-el. _{foreign}

17 Then the children of Am'mon were <u>gathered</u> together, and encamped in Gil'e-ad. And the children of Is'ra-el assembled themselves together, and encamped in Miz'peh. _{summoned}

18 And the people *and* princes of Gil'e-ad said one to another, What man *is he* that will begin to fight against the children of Am'mon? he shall be <u>head over</u> all the inhabitants of Gil'e-ad. _{leader of}

CHAPTER 11

NOW Jeph'thah the Gil'e-ad-ite *was* a mighty man of valor, and he *was* the son of an harlot: and Gil'e-ad fathered Jeph'thah.

2 And Gil'e-ad's wife bare him sons; and his wife's sons grew up, and they thrust out Jeph'thah, and said to him, You shall not inherit in our father's house; for you are the son of <u>a strange</u> woman. _{another}

3 Then Jeph'thah fled from his brethren, and dwelled in the land of Tob: and there were gathered vain men to Jeph'thah, and went out with him. worthless

4 And it came to pass in process of time, that the children of Am'mon made war against Is'ra-el. after a while

5 And it was so, that when the children of Am'mon made war against Is'ra-el, the elders of Gil'e-ad went to bring Jeph'thah out of the land of Tob:

6 And they said to Jeph'thah, Come, and be our captain, that we may fight with the children of Am'mon.

7 And Jeph'thah said to the elders of Gil'e-ad, Did not you hate me, and expel me out of my father's house? and why are you come to me now when you are in distress? dislike - trouble

8 And the elders of Gil'e-ad said to Jeph'thah, Therefore we turn again to you now, that you may go with us, and fight against the children of Am'mon, and be our head over all the inhabitants of Gil'e-ad. return - leader

9 And Jeph'thah said to the elders of Gil'e-ad, If you bring me home again to fight against the children of Am'mon, and the LORD deliver them before me, shall I be your head?

10 And the elders of Gil'e-ad said to Jeph'thah, The LORD be witness between us, if we do not so according to your words.

11 Then Jeph'thah went with the elders of Gil'e-ad, and the people made him head and captain over them: and Jeph'thah uttered all his words before the LORD in Miz'peh.

12 And Jeph'thah sent messengers to the king of the children of Am'mon, saying, What have you to do with me, that you are come against me to fight in my land?

13 And the king of the children of Am'mon answered to the messengers of Jeph'thah, Because Is'ra-el took away my land, when they came up out of E'gypt, from Ar'non even to Jab'bok, and to Jor'dan: now therefore restore those *lands* again peaceably.

14 And Jeph'thah sent messengers again to the king of the children of Am'mon:

15 And said to him, Thus says Jeph'thah, Is'ra-el took not away the land of Mo'ab, nor the land of the children of Am'mon:

16 But when Is'ra-el came up from E'gypt, and walked through the wilderness to the Red sea, and came to Ka'desh;

17 Then Is'ra-el sent messengers to the king of E'dom, saying, Let me, I pray you, pass through your land: but the king of E'dom would not hearken *thereto*. And in like manner they sent to the king of Mo'ab: but he would not *consent*: and Is'ra-el abode in Ka'desh. listen

18 Then they went along through the wilderness, and compassed the land of E'dom, and the land of Mo'ab, and came by the east side of the land of Mo'ab, and pitched on the other side of Ar'non, but came not inside the border of Mo'ab: for Ar'non *was* the border of Mo'ab. around

19 And Is'ra-el sent messengers to Si'hon king of the Am'or-ites, the king of Hesh'bon; and Is'ra-el said to him, Let us pass, we pray you, through your land into my place.

20 But Si'hon trusted not Is'ra-el to pass through his <u>coast</u>: but Si'hon gathered all his people together, and <u>pitched</u> in Ja'haz, and fought against Is'ra-el. territory - camped

21 And the LORD God of Is'ra-el delivered Si'hon and all his people into the hand of Is'ra-el, and they smote them: so Is'ra-el <u>possessed</u> all the land of the Am'or-ites, the inhabitants of that country. took over

22 And they possessed all the <u>coasts</u> of the Am'or-ites, from Ar'non even to Jab'bok, and from the wilderness even to Jor'dan.

23 So now the LORD God of Is'ra-el has <u>dispossessed</u> the Am'or-ites from before His people Is'ra-el, and should you possess it? driven out

24 Will not you possess that which Che'mosh your god gives you to possess? So whomsoever the LORD our God shall drive out from before us, them will we possess.

25 And now *are* you any thing better than Ba'lak the son of Zip'por, king of Mo'ab? did he ever strive against Is'ra-el, or did he ever fight against them,

26 While Is'ra-el dwelled in Hesh'bon and her towns, and in Ar'o-er and her towns, and in all the cities that *be* along by the coasts of Ar'non, three hundred years? why therefore did you not <u>recover</u> *them* within that time? retake

27 Wherefore I have not sinned against you, but you do me wrong to war against me: the LORD the Judge be judge this day between the children of Is'ra-el and the children of Am'mon.

28 However the king of the children of Am'mon hearkened not to the words of Jeph'thah which he sent him.

29 Then the Spirit of the LORD came upon Jeph'thah, and he passed over Gil'e-ad, and Ma-nas'seh, and passed over Miz'peh of Gil'e-ad, and from Miz'peh of Gil'e-ad he passed over *to* the children of Am'mon.

30 And Jeph'thah <u>vowed a vow</u> to the LORD, and said, If You shall without fail deliver the children of Am'mon into my hands, make a pledge

31 Then it shall be, that whatsoever comes forth of the doors of my house to meet me, when I return in <u>peace</u> from the children of Am'mon, shall surely be the LORD's, and I will offer it up for a burned offering. triumph

32 So Jeph'thah passed over to the children of Am'mon to fight against them; and the LORD delivered them into his hands.

33 And he <u>smote</u> them from Ar'o-er, *even* till you come to Min'nith, even twenty cities, and to the plain of the vineyards, with a very great slaughter. Thus the children of Am'mon were subdued before the children of Is'ra-el. devastated

34 And Jeph'thah came to Miz'peh to his house, and, behold, his daughter came out to meet him with timbrels and with dances: and she *was his* only child; beside her he had neither son nor daughter.

35 And it came to pass, when he saw her, that he <u>rent</u> his clothes, and said, Alas, my daughter! you have brought me very low, and you are one of them that trouble me: for I have opened my mouth to the LORD, and I cannot go back. ^{tore}

36 And she said to him, My father, *if* you have opened your mouth to the LORD, do to me according to that which has proceeded out of your mouth; forasmuch as the LORD has taken vengeance for you of your enemies, *even* of the children of Am'mon.

37 And she said to her father, Let this thing be done for me: let me alone two months, that I may go up and down upon the mountains, and <u>bewail</u> my virginity, I and my <u>fellows</u>. ^{lament - companions}

38 And he said, Go. And he sent her away *for* two months: and she went with her companions, and bewailed her virginity upon the mountains.

39 And it came to pass at the end of two months, that she returned to her father, who did with her *according* to his vow which he had vowed: and she knew no man. And it was a custom in Is'ra-el,

40 *That* the daughters of Is'ra-el went yearly to lament the daughter of Jeph'thah the Gil'e-ad-ite four days in a year.

CHAPTER 12

AND the men of E'phra-im <u>gathered themselves</u> together, and went northward, and said to Jeph'thah, Wherefore passed you over to fight against the children of Am'mon, and did not call us to go with you? we will burn your house upon you with fire. ^{were summoned}

2 And Jeph'thah said to them, I and my people were at great strife with the children of Am'mon; and when I called you, you delivered me not out of their hands.

3 And when I saw that you delivered *me* not, I put my life in my hands, and <u>passed</u> over against the children of Am'mon, and the LORD delivered them into my hand: wherefore then are you come up to me this day, to fight against me? ^{crossed}

4 Then Jeph'thah gathered together all the men of Gil'e-ad, and fought with E'phra-im: and the men of Gil'e-ad smote E'phra-im, because they said, You Gil'e-ad-ites *are* fugitives of E'phra-im among the E'phra-im-ites, *and* among the Ma-nas'sites.

5 And the Gil'e-ad-ites took the passages of Jor'dan before the E'phra-im-ites: and it was *so*, that when those E'phra-im-ites which were escaped said, Let me go over; that the men of Gil'e-ad said to him, *Are* you an E'phra-im-ite? If he said, Nay;

6 Then said they to him, Say now Shib'bo-leth: and he said Sib'bo-leth: for he could not <u>frame to pronounce</u> *it* right. Then they took him, and slew him at the passages of Jor'dan: and there fell at that time of the E'phra-im-ites forty and two thousand. ^{enunciate}

7 And Jeph'thah judged Is'ra-el six years. Then died Jeph'thah the Gil'e-

ad-ite, and was buried in *one of* the cities of Gil'e-ad.

8 And after him Ib'zan of Beth'-le-hem judged Is'ra-el.

9 And he had thirty sons, and thirty daughters, *whom* he sent abroad, and took in thirty daughters from abroad for his sons. And he judged Is'ra-el seven years.

10 Then died Ib'zan, and was buried at Beth'-le-hem.

11 And after him E'lon, a Zeb'u-lon-ite, judged Is'ra-el; and he judged Is'ra-el ten years.

12 And E'lon the Zeb'u-lon-ite died, and was buried in Aij'a-lon in the country of Zeb'u-lun.

13 And after him Ab'don the son of Hil'lel, a Pir'a-thon-ite, judged Is'ra-el.

14 And he had forty sons and thirty nephews, that rode on threescore and ten ass colts: and he judged Is'ra-el eight years.

15 And Ab'don the son of Hil'lel the Pir'a-thon-ite died, and was buried in Pir'a-thon in the land of E'phra-im, in the mount of the Am'a-lek-ites.

CHAPTER 13

M10

AND the children of Is'ra-el did evil again in the sight of the LORD; and the LORD delivered them into the hand of the Phi-lis'tines forty years. sinned

413

2 And there was a certain man of Zo'rah, of the family of the Dan'ites, whose name *was* Ma-no'ah; and his wife was barren, and bare not.

3 And the angel of the LORD appeared to the woman, and said to her, Behold now, you *are* barren, and bear not: but you shall conceive, and bear a son. messenger

4 Now therefore beware, I pray you, and drink not wine nor strong drink, and eat not any unclean *thing*: be careful - unfit

5 For, lo, you shall conceive, and bear a son; and no razor shall come on his head: for the child shall be a Naz'a-rite to God from the womb: and he shall begin to deliver Is'ra-el out of the hand of the Phi-lis'tines. rescue

6 Then the woman came and told her husband, saying, A man of God came to me, and his countenance was like the countenance of an angel of God, very terrible: but I asked him not from where he was, neither told he me his name: awesome

7 But he said to me, Behold, you shall conceive, and bear a son; and now drink no wine nor strong drink, neither eat any unclean *thing*: for the child shall be a Naz'a-rite to God from the womb to the day of his death. birth

8 Then Ma-no'ah entreated the LORD, and said, O my Lord, let the man of God which You did send come again to us, and teach us what we shall do to the child that shall be born. Elohim p.f.

9 And God hearkened to the voice of Ma-no'ah; and the angel of God came again to the woman as she sat in the field: but Ma-no'ah her husband *was* not with her. listened - messenger

GIG
G
410
855

10 And the woman made haste, and ran, and showed her husband, and said

to him, Behold, the man has appeared to me, that came to me the *other* day. _{told}

11 And Ma-no'ah arose, and went after his wife, and came to the man, and said to him, *Are* you the man that spoke to the woman? And he said, I *am*.

12 And Ma-no'ah said, Now let your words come to pass. How shall we order the child, and *how* shall we do to him?

13 And the angel of the LORD said to Ma-no'ah, Of all that I said to the woman let her beware. _{messenger}

14 She may not eat of any *thing* that comes of the vine, neither let her drink wine or strong drink, nor eat any unclean *thing*: all that I commanded her let her observe.

15 And Ma-no'ah said to the angel of the LORD, I pray you, let us detain you, until we shall have made ready a kid for you. _{keep}

16 And the angel of the LORD said to Ma-no'ah, Though you detain me, I will not eat of your bread: and if you will offer a burned offering, you must offer it to the LORD. For Ma-no'ah knew not that he *was* an angel of the LORD. _{food}

17 And Ma-no'ah said to the angel of the LORD, What *is* your name, that when your sayings come to pass we may do you honor? _{messenger - praise you}

18 And the angel of the LORD said to him, Why ask you thus after my name, seeing it *is* secret? _{beyond understanding}

19 So Ma-no'ah took a kid with a meat offering, and offered *it* upon a rock to the LORD: and *the angel* did wonderously; and Ma-no'ah and his wife looked on. _{messenger - grain}

20 For it came to pass, when the flame went up toward heaven from off the altar, that the angel of the LORD ascended in the flame of the altar. And Ma-no'ah and his wife looked on *it*, and fell on their faces to the ground. _{went up}

21 But the angel of the LORD did no more appear to Ma-no'ah and to his wife. Then Ma-no'ah knew that he was an angel of the LORD. _{realized}

22 And Ma-no'ah said to his wife, We shall surely die, because we have seen God. _{Elohim^{p.f.}}

23 But his wife said to him, If the LORD were pleased to kill us, He would not have received a burned offering and a meat offering at our hands, neither would He have showed us all these *things*, nor would as at this time have told us *such things* as these.

24 And the woman bare a son, and called his name Sam'son: and the child grew, and the LORD blessed him.

25 And the Spirit of the LORD began to move him at times in the camp of Dan between Zo'rah and Esh'ta-ol. _{stir}

CHAPTER 14

AND Sam'son went down to Tim'nath, and saw a woman in Tim'nath of the daughters of the Phi-lis'tines.

2 And he came up, and told his father and his mother, and said, I have seen a woman in Tim'nath of the daughters of

the Phi-lis'tines: now therefore get her for me to wife.

3 Then his father and his mother said to him, *Is there* never a woman among the daughters of your brethren, or among all my people, that you go to take a wife of the uncircumcised Phi-lis'tines? And Sam'son said to his father, Get her for me; for she pleases me well.

4 But his father and his mother knew not that it *was* of the LORD, that He sought an <u>occasion against</u> the Phi-lis'tines: for at that time the Phi-lis'tines had dominion over Is'ra-el.   opportunity to confront

5 Then went Sam'son down, and his father and his mother, to Tim'nath, and came to the vine-yards of Tim'nath: and, behold, a young lion roared against him.

6 And the Spirit of the LORD came mightily upon him, and he <u>rent</u> him as he would have <u>rent</u> a kid, and *he had* nothing in his hand: but he told not his father or his mother what he had done.   tore

7 And he went down, and talked with the woman; and she pleased Sam'son well.

8 And after a time he returned to take her, and he turned aside to see the carcase of the lion: and, behold, *there* was a swarm of bees and honey in the carcase of the lion.

9 And he took thereof in his hands, and went on eating, and came to his father and mother, and he gave them, and they did eat: but he told not them that he had taken the honey out of the carcase of the lion.

10 So his father went down to the woman: and Sam'son made there a feast; for so used the young men to do.

11 And it came to pass, when they saw him, that they brought thirty companions to be with him.

12 And Sam'son said to them, I will now put forth a riddle to you: if you can certainly declare it me within the seven days of the feast, and find *it* out, then I will give you thirty <u>sheets</u> and thirty change of gar-ments: linen wrappers

13 But if you cannot <u>declare</u> *it* me, then shall you give mc thirty <u>sheets</u> and thirty change of <u>garments</u>. And they said to him, Put forth your riddle, that we may hear it.   tell - clothing

14 And he said to them, Out of the eater came forth <u>meat</u>, and out of the strong came forth sweetness. And they could not in three days ex-pound the riddle.   something to eat

15 And it came to pass on the seventh day, that they said to Sam'son's wife, Entice your husband, that he may declare to us the riddle, less we burn you and your father's house with fire: have you called us to take that we have? *is it* not *so*?

16 And Sam'son's wife wept before him, and said, You do but <u>hate</u> me, and love me not: you have put forth a riddle to the children of my people, and have not told *it* me. And he said to her, Behold, I have not told it my father nor my mother, and shall I tell *it* you?   dislike

17 And she wept before him the seven days, while their feast lasted: and it came to pass on the seventh day, that he told her, because she <u>lay sore upon</u> him: and she told the riddle to the children of her people.   pressed

18 And the men of the city said to him on the seventh day before the sun went down, What *is* sweeter than honey? and what *is* stronger than a lion? And he said to them, If you had not plowed with my heifer, you had not found out my riddle.

19 And the Spirit of the LORD came upon him, and he went down to Ash'ke-lon, and slew thirty men of them, and took their spoil, and gave change of garments to them which <u>expounded</u> the riddle. And his anger was kindled, and he went up to his father's house.   told

20 But Sam'son's wife was *given* to his companion, whom he had used as his friend.

CHAPTER 15

BUT it came to pass within a while after, in the time of wheat harvest, that Sam'son visited his wife with a kid; and he said, I will go in to my wife into the chamber. But her father <u>would not allow</u> him to go in.   did not let

2 And her father said, I <u>verily</u> thought that you had utterly <u>hated</u> her; therefore I gave her to your companion: *is* not her younger sister fairer than she? take her, I pray you, instead of her.   truly - abhorred

3 And Sam'son said concerning them, Now shall I be more blameless than the Phi-lis'tines, though I do them a <u>displeasure</u>.   harm

4 And Sam'son went and caught three hundred foxes, and took <u>firebrands</u>, and turned tail to tail, and put a firebrand in the midst between two tails.   torches

5 And when he had set the <u>brands</u> on fire, he let *them* go into the standing <u>corn</u> of the Phi-lis'tines, and burned up both the shocks, and also the standing <u>corn</u>, with the vineyards *and* olives.   torches - grain

6 Then the Phi-lis'tines said, Who has done this? And they answered, Sam'son, the son in law of the Tim'nite, because he had taken his wife, and given her to his companion. And the Phi-lis'tines came up, and burned her and her father with fire.

7 And Sam'son said to them, Though you have done this, yet will I be avenged of you, and after that I will cease.

8 And he smote them hip and thigh with a great slaughter: and he went down and dwelled in the <u>top</u> of the rock E'tam.   cleft

9 Then the Phi-lis'tines went up, and <u>pitched</u> in Ju'dah, and spread themselves in Le'hi.   camped

10 And the men of Ju'dah said, Why are you come up against us? And they answered, To <u>bind</u> Sam'son are we come up, to do to him as he has done to us.   capture

11 Then three thousand men of Ju'dah went to the <u>top</u> of the rock E'tam, and said to Sam'son, Know you not that the Phi-lis'tines *are* rulers over us? what *is* this *that* you have done to

us? And he said to them, As they did to me, so have I done to them.

12 And they said to him, We are come down to bind you, that we may deliver you into the hand of the Phi-lis'tines. And Sam'son said to them, Swear to me, that you will not fall upon me yourselves.

13 And they spoke to him, saying, No; but we will bind you fast, and deliver you into their hand: but surely we will not kill you. And they bound him with two new cords, and brought him up from the rock.

14 *And* when he came to Le'hi, the Phi-lis'tines shouted against him: and the Spirit of the Lord came mightily upon him, and the cords that were upon his arms became as flax that was burned with fire, and his bands loosed from off his hands.

15 And he found a <u>new</u> jawbone of an ass, and put forth his hand, and took it, and slew a thousand men therewith. fresh

16 And Sam'son said, With the jawbone of an ass, heaps upon heaps, with the jaw of an ass have I slain a thousand men.

17 And it came to pass, when he had made an end of speaking, that he cast away the jawbone out of his hand, and called that place <u>Ra'math-le'hi</u>.   i.e., The high place of the jawbone

18 And he was sore athirst, and called on the Lord, and said, You have given this great deliverance into the hand of Your servant: and now shall I die for thirst, and fall into the hand of the uncircumcised?

19 But God clave an hollow place that *was* in the jaw, and there came water thereout; and when he had drunk, his spirit came again, and he revived: wherefore he called the name thereof En-hak'ko-re, which *is* in Le'hi to this day.

20 And he judged Is'ra-el in the days of the Phi-lis'tines twenty years.

CHAPTER 16

THEN went Sam'son to Ga'za, and saw there an harlot, and went in to her.

2 *And it was told* the Ga'zites, saying, Sam'son is come here. And they compassed *him* in, and laid wait for him all night in the gate of the city, and were quiet all the night, saying, In the morning, when it is day, we shall kill him.

3 And Sam'son lay till midnight, and arose at midnight, and took the doors of the gate of the city, and the two posts, and went away with them, bar and all, and put them upon his shoulders, and carried *them* up to the top of an hill that is before He'bron.

4 And it came to pass afterward, that he loved a woman in the valley of So'rek, whose name *was* De-li'lah.

5 And the lords of the Phi-lis'tines came up to her, and said to her, Entice him, and see wherein his great strength *lies*, and by what *means* we may prevail against him, that we may bind him to <u>afflict</u> him: and we will give you every one of us eleven hundred *pieces* of silver.   subdue

6 And De-li'lah said to Sam'son, Tell me, I pray you, wherein your great

strength *lies*, and wherewith you might be bound to afflict you.

7 And Sam'son said to her, If they bind me with seven green withes that were never dried, then shall I be weak, and be as another man. fresh cords

8 Then the lords of the Phi-lis'tines brought up to her seven green withes which had not been dried, and she bound him with them.

9 *Now there* were men lying in wait, abiding with her in the chamber. And she said to him, The Phi-lis'tines *be* upon you, Sam'son. And he broke the withes, as a thread of tow is broken when it touches the fire. So his strength was not known. straw

10 And De-li'lah said to Sam'son, Behold, you have mocked me, and told me lies: now tell me, I pray you, wherewith you might be bound.

11 And he said to her, If they bind me fast with new ropes that never were occupied, then shall I be weak, and be as another man. tightly - used

12 De-li'lah therefore took new ropes, and bound him therewith, and said to him, The Phi-lis'tines *be* upon you, Sam'son. And *there were* liers in wait abiding in the chamber. And he broke them from off his arms like a thread. ambushers

13 And De-li'lah said to Sam'son, Previously you have mocked me, and told me lies: tell me wherewith you might be bound. And he said to her, If you weave the seven locks of my head with the web.

14 And she fastened *it* with the pin, and said to him, The Phi-lis'tines *be* upon you, Sam'son. And he awaked out of his sleep, and went away with the pin of the beam, and with the web.

15 And she said to him, How can you say, I love you, when your heart *is* not with me? you have mocked me these three times, and have not told me wherein your great strength *lies*.

16 And it came to pass, when she pressed him daily with her words, and urged him, *so* that his soul was vexed to death; annoyed

17 That he told her all his heart, and said to her, There has not come a razor upon my head; for I *have been a* Naz'a-rite to God from my mother's womb: if I be shaven, then my strength will go from me, and I shall become weak, and be like any *other* man.

18 And when De-li'lah saw that he had told her all his heart, she sent and called for the lords of the Phi-lis'tines, saying, Come up this once, for he has showed me all his heart. Then the lords of the Phi-lis'tines came up to her, and brought money in their hand.

19 And she made him sleep upon her knees; and she called for a man, and she caused him to shave off the seven locks of his head; and she began to afflict him, and his strength went from him.

20 And she said, The Phi-lis'tines *be* upon you, Sam'son. And he awoke out of his sleep, and said, I will go out as at other times before, and shake myself. And he knew not that the LORD was departed from him.

21 But the Phi-lis'tines took him, and put out his eyes, and brought him

down to Ga'za, and bound him with <u>fetters</u> of brass; and he did grind in the prison house. chains

22 However the hair of his head began to grow again after he was shaven.

23 Then the lords of the Phi-lis'tines gathered them together for to offer a great sacrifice to Da'gon their god, and to rejoice: for they said, Our god has delivered Sam'son our enemy into our hand.

24 And when the people saw him, they praised their god: for they said, Our god has delivered into our hands our enemy, and the destroyer of our country, which slew many of us.

25 And it came to pass, when their hearts were merry, that they said, Call for Sam'son, that he may <u>make us sport</u>. And they called for Sam'son out of the prison house; and he made them sport: and they set him between the pillars, amuse us

26 And Sam'son said to the lad that held him by the hand, Allow me that I may feel the pillars whereupon the house stands, that I may lean upon them.

7 Now the house was full of men and women; and all the lords of the Phi-lis'tines *were* there; and *there were* upon the roof about three thousand men and women, that beheld while Sam'son made sport.

28 And Sam'son called to the LORD, and said, O <u>Lord GOD</u>, remember me, I pray You, and strengthen me, I pray You, only this once, O God,

that I may be <u>at once</u> avenged of the Phi-lis'tines for my two eyes. Adonay^p.f. Jehovah - at one blow

29 And Sam'son took hold of the two middle pillars upon which the house stood, and on which it was borne up, of the one with his right hand, and of the other with his left.

30 And Sam'son said, Let me die with the Phi-lis'tines. And he bowed himself with *all his* might; and the house fell upon the lords, and upon all the people that *were* therein. So the dead which he slew at his death were more than *they* which he slew in his life.

31 Then his brethren and all the house of his father came down, and took him, and brought *him* up, and buried him between Zo'rah and Esh'ta-ol in the burying place of Ma-no'ah his father. And he judged Is'ra-el twenty years.

CHAPTER 17

AND there was a man of mount E'phra-im, whose name *was* Mi'cah.

2 And he said to his mother, The eleven hundred *shekels* of silver that were taken from you, about which you cursed, and spoke of also in my ears, behold, the silver *is* with me; I took it. And his mother said, Blessed *be you* of the LORD, my son.

3 And when he had restored the eleven hundred *shekels* of silver to his mother, his mother said, I had wholly dedicated the silver to the LORD from my hand for my son, to make a

graven image and a molten image: now therefore I will restore it to you.   carved - cast

4 Yet he restored the money to his mother; and his mother took two hundred *shekels* of silver, and gave them to the founder, who made thereof a graven image and a molten image: and they were in the house of Mi'cah.   silversmith

5 And the man Mi'cah had an house of gods, and made an ephod, and teraphim, and consecrated one of his sons, who became his priest.   priestly garment - household idols

6 In those days *there was* no king in Is'ra-el, *but* every man did *that which was* right in his own eyes.

7 And there was a young man out of Beth'-le-hem-ju'dah of the family of Ju'dah, who *was* a Le'vite, and he sojourned there.   lived

8 And the man departed out of the city from Beth'-le-hem-ju'dah to sojourn where he could find *a place*: and he came to mount E'phra-im to the house of Mi'cah, as he journeyed.   stay

9 And Mi'cah said to him, from where come you? And he said to him, I *am* a Le'vite of Beth'-le-hem-ju'dah, and I go to sojourn where I may find *a place*.

10 And Mi'cah said to him, Dwell with me, and be to me a father and a priest, and I will give you ten *shekels* of silver by the year, and a suit of apparel, and your victuals. So the Le'vite went in.

11 And the Le'vite was content to dwell with the man; and the young man was to him as one of his sons.

12 And Mi'cah consecrated the Le'vite; and the young man became his priest, and was in the house of Mi'cah.

13 Then said Mi'cah, Now know I that the LORD will do me good, seeing I have a Le'vite to *my* priest.

CHAPTER 18

IN those days *there was* no king in Is'ra-el: and in those days the tribe of the Dan'ites sought them an inheritance to dwell in; for to that day *all their* inheritance had not fallen to them among the tribes of Is'ra-el.

2 And the children of Dan sent of their family five men from their coasts, men of valor, from Zo'rah, and from Esh'ta-ol, to spy out the land, and to search it; and they said to them, Go, search the land: who when they came to mount E'phra-im, to the house of Mi'cah, they lodged there.   clan

3 When they *were* by the house of Mi'cah, they knew the voice of the young man the Le'vite: and they turned in there, and said to him, Who brought you here? and what make you in this *place*? and what have you here?

4 And he said to them, Thus and thus deals Mi'cah with me, and has hired me, and I am his priest.

5 And they said to him, Ask counsel, we pray you, of God, that we may know whether our way which we go shall be prosperous.   Inquire - Elohim[p.f.]

6 And the priest said to them, Go in peace: before the LORD is your way wherein you go.

7 Then the five men departed, and

came to La'ish, and saw the people that *were* therein, how they dwelled careless, after the manner of the Zi-do'ni-ans, quiet and secure; and *there was* no magistrate in the land, that might put *them* to shame in *any* thing; and they *were* far from the Zi-do'ni-ans, and had no business with *any* man.

8 And they came to their brethren to Zo'rah and Esh'ta-ol: and their brethren said to them, What *say* you?

9 And they said, Arise, that we may go up against them: for we have seen the land, and, behold, it *is* very good: and *are* you still? be not slothful to go, *and* to enter to possess the land.   sitting still

10 When you go, you shall come to a people secure, and to a large land: for God has given it into your hands; a place where *there is* no want of any thing that *is* in the earth.   Elohim ᵖ·ᶠ·

11 And there went from there of the family of the Dan'ites, out of Zo'rah and out of Esh'ta-ol, six hundred men appointed with weapons of war.

12 And they went up, and pitched in Kir'jath-je'a-rim, in Ju'dah: wherefore they called that place Ma'ha-neh-dan to this day: behold, *it is* behind Kir'jath-je'a-rim.   camped

13 And they passed from there to mount E'phra-im, and came to the house of Mi'cah.

14 Then answered the five men that went to spy out the country of La'ish, and said to their brethren, Do you know that there is in these houses an ephod, and teraphim, and a graven image, and a molten image? now therefore consider what you have to do.   priestly garment - household idols - carved - cast idol

15 And they turned aside there, and came to the house of the young man the Le'vite, *even* to the house of Mi'cah, and saluted him.   greeted

16 And the six hundred men appointed with their weapons of war, which *were* of the children of Dan, stood by the entering of the gate.

17 And the five men that went to spy out the land went up, *and* came in there, *and* took the graven image, and the ephod, and the teraphim, and the molten image: and the priest stood in the entering of the gate with the six hundred men *that were* appointed with weapons of war.   armed

18 And these went into Mi'cah's house, and brought the carved image, the ephod, and the teraphim, and the molten image. Then said the priest to them, What do you?

19 And they said to him, Hold your peace, lay your hand upon your mouth, and go with us, and be to us a father and a priest: *is it* better for you to be a priest to the house of one man, or that you be a priest to a tribe and a family in Is'ra-el?

20 And the priest's heart was glad, and he took the ephod, and the teraphim, and the graven image, and went in the midst of the people.   priestly garment - household idols - carved idol

21 So they turned and departed, and put the little ones and the cattle and the carriage before them.   riches

22 *And* when they were a good way

from the house of Mi'cah, the men that *were* in the houses near to Mi'cah's house were gathered together, and overtook the children of Dan.

23 And they cried to the children of Dan. And they turned their faces, and said to Mi'cah, What ails you, that you come with such a company?

24 And he said, You have taken away my <u>gods</u> which I made, and the priest, and you are gone away: and what have I more? and what *is* this *that* you say to me, What ails you?   idols

25 And the children of Dan said to him, Let not your voice be heard among us, less angry fellows run upon you, and you lose your life, with the lives of your household.

26 And the children of Dan went their way: and when Mi'cah saw that they *were* too strong for him, he turned and went back to his house.

27 And they took *the things* which Mi'cah had made, and the priest which he had, and came to La'ish, to a people *that were* <u>at quiet</u> and secure: and they <u>smote</u> them with the edge of the sword, and burned the city with fire.   peaceful - attacked

28 And *there was* no deliverer, because it *was* far from Zi'don, and they had no business with *any* man; and it was in the valley that *lies* by Beth-re'hob. And they built a city, and dwelled therein.

29 And they called the name of the city Dan, after the name of Dan their father, who was born to Is'ra-el: however the name of the city *was* La'ish at the first.

30 And the children of Dan set up the graven image: and Jon'a-than, the son of Ger'shom, the son of Manas'seh, he and his sons were priests to the tribe of Dan until the day of the captivity of the land.

31 And they set them up Mi'cah's graven image, which he made, all the time that the house of God was in Shi'loh.

CHAPTER 19

AND it came to pass in those days, when *there was* no king in Is'ra-el, that there was a certain Le'vite sojourning on the side of mount E'phra-im, who took to him a concubine out of Beth'-le-hem-ju'dah.

2 And his concubine played the whore against him, and went away from him to her father's house to Beth'-le-hem-ju'dah, and was there four whole months.

3 And her husband arose, and went after her, to speak friendly to her, *and* to bring her again, having his servant with him, and a couple of asses: and she brought him into her father's house: and when the father of the <u>damsel</u> saw him, he rejoiced to meet him.   young woman

4 And his father in law, the <u>damsel's</u> father, <u>retained</u> him; and he abode with him three days: so they did eat and drink, and lodged there.   detained

5 And it came to pass on the fourth day, when they arose early in the morning, that he rose up to depart: and the <u>damsel's</u> father said to his son in law,

Comfort your heart with a morsel of bread, and afterward go your way.

6 And they sat down, and did eat and drink both of them together: for the <u>damsel's</u> father had said to the man, Be content, I pray you, and tarry all night, and <u>let your heart be merry</u>. young woman - enjoy yourself

7 And when the man rose up to depart, his father in law urged him: therefore he lodged there again.

8 And he arose early in the morning on the fifth day to depart: and the <u>damsel's</u> father said, Comfort your heart, I pray you. And they tarried until afternoon, and they did eat both of them.

9 And when the man rose up to depart, he, and his concubine, and his servant, his father in law, the <u>damsel's</u> father, said to him, Behold, now the day draws toward evening, I pray you tarry all night: behold, the day grows to an end, lodge here, that your heart may be merry; and to morrow get you early on your way, that you may go <u>home</u>. to your tent

10 But the man would not tarry that night, but he rose up and departed, and came opposite Je'bus, which *is* Je-ru'sa-lem; and *there were* with him two asses saddled, his concubine also *was* with him.

11 *And* when they *were* by <u>Je'bus</u>, the day was far spent; and the servant said to his master, Come, I pray you, and let us turn in into this city of the Jeb'usites, and lodge in it. i.e., Jerusalem

12 And his master said to him, We will not turn aside here into the city of a stranger, that is not of the children of Is'ra-el; we will pass over to Gib'e-ah.

13 And he said to his servant, Come, and let us draw near to one of these places to lodge all night, in Gib'e-ah, or in Ra'mah.

14 And they passed on and went their way; and the sun went down upon them *when they were* by Gib'e-ah, which *belongs* to Ben'ja-min.

15 And they turned aside there, to go in *and* to lodge in Gib'e-ah: and when he went in, he sat him down in a street of the city: for *there was* no man that took them into his house to lodging.

16 And, behold, there came an old man from his work out of the field at even, which *was* also of mount E'phra-im; and he sojourned in Gib'e-ah: but the men of the place *were* Ben'ja-mites.

17 And when he had lifted up his eyes, he saw a <u>wayfaring</u> man in the street of the city: and the old man said, Where go you? and where come you? traveling

18 And he said to him, We *are* passing from Beth'-le-hem-ju'dah toward the side of mount E'phra-im; from there *am* I: and I went to Beth'-le-hem-ju'dah, but I *am now* going to the house of the LORD; and there *is* no man that receives me to house.

19 Yet there is both straw and <u>provender</u> for our asses; and there is bread and wine also for me, and for your handmaid, and for the young man *which is* with your servants: *there is* no want of any thing. fodder

20 And the old man said, Peace *be* with you; howsoever *let* all your wants *lie* upon me; only lodge not in the street.

21 So he brought him into his house, and gave <u>provender</u> to the asses: and they <u>washed their feet</u>, and did eat and drink. fodder - bathed

22 *Now* as they were making their hearts merry, behold, the men of the city, certain sons of Be'li-al, beset the house round about, *and* beat at the door, and spoke to the master of the house, the old man, saying, Bring forth the man that came into your house, that we may know him.

23 And the man, the master of the house, went out to them, and said to them, Nay, my brethren, *nay*, I pray you, do not *so* wickedly; seeing that this man is come into my house, do not this folly.

24 Behold, *here is* my daughter a maiden, and his concubine; them I will bring out now, and humble you them, and do with them what seems good to you: but to this man do not so vile a thing.

25 But the men would not hearken to him: so the man took his concubine, and brought her forth to them; and they knew her, and abused her all the night until the morning: and when the day began to <u>spring</u>, they let her go. dawn

26 Then came the woman in the dawning of the day, and fell down at the door of the man's house where her lord *was*, till it was light.

27 And her lord rose up in the morning, and opened the doors of the house, and went out to go his way: and, behold, the woman his concubine was fallen down *at* the door of the house, and her hands *were* upon the threshold.

28 And he said to her, Up, and let us be going. But none answered. Then the man took her *up* upon an ass, and the man rose up, and got him to his place.

29 And when he was come into his house, he took a knife, and laid hold on his concubine, and <u>divided</u> her, *together* with her bones, into twelve pieces, and sent her into all the coasts of Is'ra-el. cut

30 And it was so, that all that saw it said, There was no such deed done nor seen from the day that the children of Is'ra-el came up out of the land of E'gypt to this day: consider of it, take <u>advice</u>, and speak *your minds*. counsel - up

CHAPTER 20

THEN all the children of Is'ra-el went out, and the congregation was gathered together as one man, from Dan even to Be'er-she'ba, with the land of Gil'e-ad, to the LORD in Miz'peh.

2 And the chief of all the people, *even* of all the tribes of Is'ra-el, presented themselves in the assembly of the people of <u>God</u>, four hundred thousand footmen that drew sword. Elohim p.f.

3 (Now the children of Ben'ja-min heard that the children of Is'ra-el were gone up to Miz'peh.) Then said the children of Is'ra-el, Tell *us*, how was this wickedness?

4 And the Le'vite, the husband of the woman that was slain, answered and

said, I came into Gib'e-ah that *be-longs* to Ben'ja-min, I and my concubine, to lodge.

5 And the men of Gib'e-ah rose against me, and beset the house round about upon me by night, *and* thought to have slain me: and my concubine have they <u>forced</u>, that she is dead. ravished

6 And I took my concubine, and cut her in pieces, and sent her throughout all the country of the inheritance of Is'ra-el: for they have committed <u>lewdness and folly</u> in Is'ra-el. disgraceful conduct

7 Behold, you *are* all children of Is'ra-el; give here your advice and counsel.

8 And all the people arose as one man, saying, We will not any *of us* go to his tent, neither will we any *of us* turn into his house.

9 But now this *shall be* the thing which we will do to Gib'e-ah; *we will go up* by lot against it;

10 And we will take ten men of an hundred throughout all the tribes of Is'ra-el, and an hundred of a thousand, and a thousand out of ten thousand, to bring victual for the people, that they may do, when they come to Gib'e-ah of Ben'ja-min, according to all the <u>folly</u> that they have wrought in Is'ra-el.

11 So all the men of Is'ra-el were gathered against the city, knit together as one man.

12 And the tribes of Is'ra-el sent men through all the tribe of Ben'ja-min, saying, What wickedness *is* this that is done among you?

13 Now therefore deliver *us* the men, the children of <u>Be'li-al</u>, which *are* in Gib'e-ah, that we may put them to death, and put away evil from Is'ra-el. But the children of Ben'ja-min would not hearken to the voice of their brethren the children of Is'ra-el: i.e., Satan

14 But the children of Ben'ja-min gathered themselves together out of the cities to Gib'e-ah, to go out to battle against the children of Is'ra-el.

15 And the children of Ben'ja-min were numbered at that time out of the cities twenty and six thousand men that drew sword, beside the inhabitants of Gib'e-ah, which were numbered seven hundred chosen men.

16 Among all this people *there were* seven hundred chosen men left-handed; every one could sling stones at an hair *breadth*, and not miss.

17 And the men of Is'ra-el, beside Ben'ja-min, were numbered four hundred thousand men that drew sword: all these *were* men of war.

18 And the children of Is'ra-el arose, and went up to the house of <u>God</u>, and asked counsel of <u>God</u>, and said, Which of us shall go up first to the battle against the children of Ben'ja-min? And the LORD said, Ju'dah *shall go up* first. El s.f. - Elohim p.f.

19 And the children of Is'ra-el rose up in the morning, and encamped against Gib'e-ah.

20 And the men of Is'ra-el went out to battle against Ben'ja-min; and the men of Is'ra-el put themselves in array to fight against them at Gib'e-ah.

21 And the children of Ben'ja-min came forth out of Gib'e-ah, and de-

stroyed down to the ground of the Israelites that day twenty and two thousand men.

22 And the people the men of Is'ra-el encouraged themselves, and set their battle again in array in the place where they put themselves in array the first day.

23 (And the children of Is'ra-el went up and wept before the LORD until even, and asked counsel of the LORD, saying, Shall I go up again to battle against the children of Ben'ja-min my brother? And the LORD said, Go up against him.)

24 And the children of Is'ra-el came near against the children of Ben'ja-min the second day.

25 And Ben'ja-min went forth against them out of Gib'e-ah the second day, and destroyed down to the ground of the children of Is'ra-el again eighteen thousand men; all these drew the sword.

26 Then all the children of Is'ra-el, and all the people, went up, and came to the house of God, and wept, and sat there before the LORD, and fasted that day until even, and offered burned offerings and peace offerings before the LORD.

27 And the children of Is'ra-el enquired of the LORD, (for the ark of the covenant of God *was* there in those days,   agreement

28 And Phin'e-has, the son of E-le-a'zar, the son of Aar'on, stood before it in those days,) saying, Shall I yet again go out to battle against the children of Ben'ja-min my brother, or shall I cease?

And the LORD said, Go up; for tomorrow I will deliver them into your hand.

29 And Is'ra-el set liers in wait round about Gib'e-ah.   set an ambush

30 And the children of Is'ra-el went up against the children of Ben'ja-min on the third day, and put themselves in array against Gib'e-ah, as at other times.

31 And the children of Ben'ja-min went out against the people, *and* were drawn away from the city; and they began to smite of the people, *and* kill, as at other times, in the highways, of which one goes up to the house of God, and the other to Gib'e-ah in the field, about thirty men of Is'ra-el.

32 And the children of Ben'ja-min said, They *are* smitten down before us, as at the first. But the children of Is'ra-el said, Let us flee, and draw them from the city to the highways.   retreat

33 And all the men of Is'ra-el rose up out of their place, and put themselves in array at Ba'al-ta'mar: and the liers in wait of Is'ra-el came forth out of their places, *even* out of the meadows of Gib'e-ah.

34 And there came against Gib'e-ah ten thousand chosen men out of all Is'ra-el, and the battle was sore: but they knew not that evil *was* near them. heavy

35 And the LORD smote Ben'ja-min before Is'ra-el: and the children of Is'ra-el destroyed of the Ben'ja-mites that day twenty and five thousand and an hundred men: all these drew the sword.   experienced soldiers

36 So the children of Ben'ja-min saw that they were smitten: for the men of

Is'ra-el gave place to the Ben'ja-mites, because they trusted to the <u>liers in wait</u> which they had set beside Gib'e-ah. men in ambush

37 And the <u>liers in wait</u> hasted, and rushed upon Gib'e-ah; and the <u>liers in wait</u> drew *themselves* along, and smote all the city with the edge of the sword.

38 Now there was an appointed <u>sign</u> between the men of Is'ra-el and the <u>liers in wait</u>, that they should make a great flame with smoke rise up out of the city. signal

39 And when the men of Is'ra-el retired in the battle, Ben'ja-min began to smite *and* kill of the men of Is'ra-el about thirty persons: for they said, Surely they are smitten down before us, as *in* the first battle.

40 But when the flame began to arise up out of the city with a pillar of smoke, the Benj'a-mites looked behind them, and, behold, the <u>flame</u> of the city <u>ascended up to heaven</u>. whole - i.e., went up in smoke

41 And when the men of Is'ra-el turned again, the men of Ben'ja-min were <u>amazed</u>: for they saw that <u>evil</u> was come upon them. terrified - disaster

42 Therefore they <u>turned *their* backs</u> before the men of Is'ra-el to the way of the wilderness; but the battle overtook them; and them which *came* out of the cities they destroyed in the midst of them. fled

43 *Thus* they inclosed the Ben'ja-mites round about, *and* chased them, *and* <u>trode them down</u> with ease opposite Gib'e-ah toward the <u>sunrising</u>. overran them - east

44 And there fell of Ben'ja-min eighteen thousand men; all these *were* men of valor.

45 And they turned and fled toward the wilderness to the rock of Rim'mon: and they <u>gleaned</u> of them in the highways five thousand men; and pursued hard after them to Gi'dom, and slew two thousand men of them. caught

46 So that all which <u>fell</u> that day of Ben'ja-min were twenty and five thousand men that drew the sword; all these *were* <u>men of valor</u>. died - valiant warriors

47 But six hundred men turned and fled to the wilderness to the rock Rim'mon, and abode in the rock Rim'mon four months.

48 And the men of Is'ra-el turned again upon the children of Ben'ja-min, and smote them with the edge of the sword, as well the men of *every* city, as the beast, and all that came to hand: also they set on fire all the cities that they came to.

CHAPTER 21

NOW the men of Is'ra-el had sworn in Miz'peh, saying, There shall not any of us give his daughter to Ben'ja-min to wife.

2 And the people came to the house of <u>God</u>, and abode there till even before <u>God</u>, and lifted up their voices, and wept sore; El^{s.f.} - Elohim^{p.f.}

3 And said, O LORD God of Is'ra-el, why is this come to pass in Is'ra-el, that there should be to day one tribe lacking in Is'ra-el? Jehovah^{s.f.} Elohim^{p.f.}

4 And it came to pass on the <u>morrow</u>, that the people rose early, and built there an altar, and offered burned offerings and peace offering. _{next day}

5 And the children of Is'ra-el said, Who *is there* among all the tribes of Is'ra-el that came not up with the <u>congregation</u> to the LORD? For they had made a great oath concerning him that came not up to the LORD to Miz'peh, saying, He shall surely be put to death. _{assembly}

6 And the children of Is'ra-el <u>repented them</u> for Ben'ja-min their brother, and said, There is one tribe cut off from Is'ra-el this day. _{were sorry}

7 How shall we do for wives for them that remain, seeing we have sworn by the LORD that we will not give them of our daughters <u>to wives</u>? _{in marriage}

8 And they said, What one *is there* of the tribes of Is'ra-el that came not up to Miz'peh to the LORD? And, behold, there came none to the camp from Ja'besh-gil'e-ad to the assembly.

9 For the <u>people were numbered</u>, and, behold, *there were* none of the inhabitants of Ja'besh-gil'e-ad there. _{census was taken}

10 And the congregation sent there twelve thousand men of the <u>valiantest</u>, and commanded them, saying, Go and smite the inhabitants of Ja'besh-gil'e-ad with the edge of the sword, with the women and the children. _{valiant warriors}

11 And this *is* the thing that you shall do, You shall utterly destroy every male, and every woman that has lain by man.

12 And they found among the inhabitants of Ja'besh-gil'e-ad four hundred young virgins, that had known no man by lying with any male: and they brought them to the camp to Shi'loh, which is in the land of Ca'naan.

13 And the whole congregation sent *some* to speak to the children of Ben'ja-min that *were* in the rock Rim'mon, and to <u>call peaceably</u> to them. _{proclaim peace}

14 And Ben'ja-min came again at that time; and they gave them wives which they had saved alive of the women of Ja'besh-gil'e-ad : and yet so they sufficed them not.

15 And the people <u>repented them</u> for Ben'ja-min, because that the LORD had made a breach in the tribes of Is'ra-el. _{were sorry}

16 Then the elders of the congregation said, How shall we do for wives for them that remain, seeing the women are destroyed out of Ben'ja-min?

17 And they said, *There must be* an inheritance for them that be escaped of Ben'ja-min, that a tribe be not destroyed out of Is'ra-el.

18 However we may not give them wives of our daughters: for the children of Is'ra-el have sworn, saying, Cursed *be* he that gives a wife to Ben'ja-min.

19 Then they said, Behold, *there is* a feast of the LORD in Shi'loh yearly *in a place* which *is* on the north side of Beth'-el, on the east side of the highway that goes up from Beth'-el to She'chem, and on the south of Le'bo-nah.

20 Therefore they commanded the children of Ben'ja-min, saying, Go and lie in wait in the vineyards; _{hide}

21 And see, and, behold, if the daughters of Shi'loh come out to dance in dances, then come you out of the vineyards, and catch you every man his wife of the daughters of Shi'loh, and go to the land of Ben'ja-min.

22 And it shall be, when their fathers or their brethren come to us to complain, that we will say to them, Be favorable to them for our sakes: because we reserved not to each man his wife in the war: for you did not give to them at this time, *that* you should be guilty. _{Be kind}

23 And the children of Ben'ja-min did so, and took *them* wives, according to their number, of them that danced, whom they caught: and they went and returned to their inheritance, and repaired the cities, and dwelled in them. _{rebuilt}

24 And the children of Is'ra-el departed from there at that time, every man to his tribe and to his family, and they went out from there every man to his inheritance.

25 In those days *there was* no king in Is'ra-el: every man did *that which was* right in his own eyes.

RUTH

OUTLINE

GRIEVOUS VISITATIONS 1.1–5
FAR-REACHING DECISIONS 1.6–22
A SURPRISING ENCOUNTER 2.1–23
WHOLEHEARTED DEDICATION 3.1–18
COMPLETE REDEMPTION 4.1–17
SIGNIFICANT GENEALOGY 4.18–22

SURVEY

The Book of Ruth describes the providential guidance of God in the life and adventures of an Israelite family. Through the death of the father and his two sons in a foreign country, the name and inheritance of this family are endangered. Man's extremity, however, is God's opportunity. Owing to the action of a kinsman with a noble view of his obligations, the hereditary line remains unbroken. The union of Boaz the Hebrew and Ruth the Moabitess becomes the avenue of God's fulfilment of His gracious purpose. In relation to the whole message of the Scriptures, the book supplies a perspective of the history of Christmas and the event of Pentecost. The genealogy culminates in the theocratic king David to whose line the promise of the advent of the Messiah is given. This occurs with the inclusion of a Moabite ancestress, whereby the pentecostal perspective of the universal meaning of the Messiah is opened: He is not only Savior of Israel but of the human race.

AUTHOR

In the Greek and later translations, the Book of Ruth follows that of the Judges, since it was in their time that the history related in this book took place. In the Hebrew Bible, it forms a part of the so-called Holy Writings (Hagiographa), a subdivision of the five scrolls read in public on the great feast days of Israel. As the climax of the history of Ruth falls in harvest time, this narrative was customarily read at the Weeks or Wheat Harvest Feast—later called the Feast of Pentecost. The author is unknown. The announcement in 1.1 that the story took place in "the days when the judges ruled" indicates that the era of the judges belonged to the past. The way in which the author writes about David in 4.17 and the genealogy of 4.18–22 show that the author knew of the splendor of the reign of David. This consideration favors a time of writing before the kingship lost its glory, thus possibly in the latter time of David or immediately thereafter.

P.A.V.

THE BOOK OF
RUTH

CHAPTER 1

NOW it came to pass in the days when the judges <u>ruled</u>, that there was a famine in the land. And a certain man of Beth`-le-hem-ju'dah went to <u>sojourn</u> in the country of Mo'ab, he, and his wife, and his two sons. *governed - temporarily live*

2 And the name of the man *was* E-lim'e-lech, and the name of his wife Na-o'mi, and the name of his two sons Mah'lon and Chil'i-on, Eph'rath-ites of Beth'-le-hem-ju'dah. And they came into the country of Mo'ab, and <u>continued</u> there. *lived*

3 And E-lim'e-lech Na-o`mi's husband died; and she was left, and her two sons.

4 And they took them wives of the women of Mo'ab; the name of the one *was* Or'pah, and the name of the other Ruth: and they dwelled there about ten years.

5 And Mah'lon and Chil'i-on died also both of them; and the woman was left of her two sons and her husband.

6 Then she arose with her daughters in law, that she might return from the country of Mo'ab: for she had heard in the country of Mo'ab how that the Lord had visited His people in giving them bread.

7 Wherefore she went forth out of the place where she was, and her two daughters in law with her; and they went on the way to return to the land of Ju'dah.

8 And Na-o`mi said to her two daughters in law, Go, return each to her mother's house: the Lord deal kindly with you, as you have dealt with the <u>dead</u>, and with me. *their dead husbands*

9 The Lord grant you that you may find rest, each *of you* in the house of her husband. Then she kissed them; and they lifted up their voice, and wept.

10 And they said to her, Surely we will return with you to your people.

11 And Na-o`mi said, Turn again, my daughters: why will you go with me? *are* there yet *any more* sons in my womb, that they may be your husbands?

12 Turn again, my daughters, go *your way*; for I am too old to have an husband. If I should say, I have hope, *if* I should have an husband also to night, and should also bear sons;

13 Would you tarry for them till they were grown? would you stay for them from having husbands? nay, my daughters; for it grieves me much for your sakes that the hand of the Lord is gone out against me.

14 And they lifted up their voice, and wept again: and Or'pah kissed her mother in law; but Ruth clung to her.

15 And she said, Behold, your sister in

law is gone back to her people, and to her gods: return you after your sister in law.

16 And Ruth said, Entreat me not to leave you, *or* to <u>return</u> from following after you: for where you go, I will go; and where you <u>lodge</u>, I will <u>lodge</u>: your people *shall be* my people, and your <u>God</u> my <u>God</u>: turn back - stay - Elohim^{p.f.}

17 Where you die, will I die, and there will I be buried: the LORD do so to me, and more also, *if anything* but death part you and me.

18 When she saw that she was <u>stedfastly minded</u> to go with her, then she <u>left speaking</u> her.

determined - said no more

19 So they two went until they came to Beth'-le-hem. And it came to pass, when they were come to Beth'-le-hem, that all the city was moved about them, and <u>they</u> said, *Is* this Na-o`mi?

the women

20 And she said to them, Call me not Na-o`mi, call me Ma'ra: for the Almighty has dealt very bitterly with me.

21 I went out full, and the LORD has brought me home again empty: why *then* call you me Na-o`mi, seeing the LORD has <u>testified</u> against me, and the Almighty has afflicted me?

witnessed

22 So Na-o`mi returned, and Ruth the Mo'ab-it-ess, her daughter in law, with her, which returned out of the country of Mo'ab: and they came to Beth'-le-hem in the beginning of barley harvest.

CHAPTER 2

AND Na-o`mi had a kinsman of her husband's, a mighty man of wealth, of the family of E-lim'e-lech; and his name *was* Bo'az.

2 And Ruth the Mo'ab-it-ess said to Na-o`mi, Let me now go to the field, and <u>glean</u> ears of <u>corn</u> after *him* in whose sight I shall find grace. And she said to her, Go, my daughter.

gather (leftover) - grain

3 And she went, and came, and <u>gleaned</u> in the field after the reapers: and <u>her hap was</u> to light on a part of the field *belonging* to Bo'az, who *was* of the kindred of E-lim'e-lech.

she happened

4 And behold, Bo'az came from Beth'-le-hem, and said to the reapers, The LORD *be* with you. And they answered him, The LORD bless you.

5 Then said Bo'az to his servant that was set over the reapers, Whose <u>damsel</u> *is* this?

young woman

6 And the servant that was set over the reapers answered and said, It *is* the Mo'ab-it-ish <u>damsel</u> that came back with Na-o`mi out of the country of Mo'ab:

7 And she said, I pray you, let me glean and gather after the reapers among the sheaves: so she came, and has continued even from the morning until now, that she tarried a little in the house.

8 Then said Bo'az to Ruth, Hear you not, my daughter? Go not to <u>glean</u> in another field, neither go from here, but abide here <u>fast</u> by my maidens:

gather - near

9 *Let* your eyes *be* on the field that they do reap, and go you after them: have I not <u>charged</u> the young men that they shall not <u>touch</u> you? and when

you are athirst, go to the vessels, and drink of *that* which the young men have drawn. _{commanded - molest}

10 Then she fell on her face, and bowed herself to the ground, and said to him, Why have I found grace in your eyes, that you should take <u>knowledge</u> of me, seeing I *am* a stranger? _{notice}

11 And Bo'az answered and said to her, It has fully been showed me, all that you have done to your mother in law since the death of your husband: and *how* you have left your father and your mother, and the land of your nativity, and are come to a people which you knew not heretofore.

12 The Lord <u>recompense</u> your work, and a full reward be given you of the Lord God of Is'ra-el, under whose wings you are come to trust. _{reward - Jehovah Elohim}

13 Then she said, Let me find favor in your sight, my lord; for that you have comforted me, and for that you have spoken friendly to your handmaid, though I be not like to one of your handmaidens.

14 And Bo'az said to her, At mealtime come you here, and eat of the bread, and dip your morsel in the vinegar. And she sat beside the reapers: and he reached her parched *corn*, and she did eat, and was sufficed, and left.

15 And when she was risen up to <u>glean</u>, Bo'az commanded his young men, saying, Let her glean even among the sheaves, and <u>reproach</u> her not: _{gather - insult}

16 And let fall also *some* of the handfuls of purpose for her, and leave *them*, that she may <u>glean</u> *them*, and rebuke her not. _{gather}

17 So she <u>gleaned</u> in the field until even, and beat out that she had <u>gleaned</u>: and it was about an ephah of barley.

18 And she took *it* up, and went into the city: and her mother in law saw what she had <u>gleaned</u>: and she brought forth, and gave to her that she had reserved after she was sufficed.

19 And her mother in law said to her, Where have you <u>gleaned</u> to day? and where <u>wroughtest</u> you? blessed be he that did take knowledge of you. And she showed her mother in law with whom she had <u>wrought</u>, and said, The man's name with whom I wrought to day *is* Bo'az. _{did you work}

20 And Na-o'mi said to her daughter in law, Blessed *be* he of the Lord, who has not left off His kindness to the living and to the dead. And Na-o'mi said to her, The man *is* near of kin to us, one of our next kinsmen.

21 And Ruth the Mo'ab-it-ess said, he said to me also, you shall <u>keep fast</u> by my young men, until they have ended all my harvest. _{stay near}

22 And Na-o'mi said to Ruth her daughter in law, *It is* good, my daughter, that you go out with his maidens, that they meet you not in any other field.

23 So she kept fast by the maidens of Bo'az to <u>glean</u> to the end of barley harvest and of wheat harvest; and dwelled with her mother in law. _{gather}

CHAPTER 3

THEN Na-o`mi her mother in law said to her, My daughter, shall I not seek <u>rest</u> for you, that it may be well with you? security

2 And now *is* not Bo'az of our kindred, with whose maidens you were? Behold, he winnow barley to night in the threshingfloor.

3 Wash yourself therefore, and anoint you, and put your <u>raiment</u> upon you, and get you down to the floor: *but* make not yourself known to the man, until he shall have done eating and drinking. clothing

4 And it shall be, when he lies down, that you shall <u>mark</u> the place where he shall lie, and you shall go in, and uncover his feet, and lay you down; and he will tell you what you shall do. notice

5 And she said to her, All that you say to me I will do.

6 And she went down to the floor, and did according to all that her mother in law bade her.

7 And when Bo'az had eaten and drunk, and his heart was <u>merry</u>, he went to lie down at the end of the heap of corn: and she came softly, and uncovered his feet, and laid her down. cheerful

8 And it came to pass at midnight, that the man was <u>afraid</u>, and turned himself: and, behold, a woman lay at his feet. startled

9 And he said, Who *are* you? And she answered, I *am* Ruth your handmaid: spread therefore your skirt over your handmaid; for you *are* a near kinsman.

10 And he said, Blessed *be* you of the Lord, my daughter: *for* you have showed more kindness in the latter end than at the beginning, inasmuch as you followed not young men, whether poor or rich.

11 And now, my daughter, fear not; I will do to you all that you require: for all the city of my people does know that you *are* a virtuous woman.

12 And now it is true that I *am your* near kinsman: however there is a kinsman nearer than I.

13 Tarry this night, and it shall be in the morning, *that* if he will perform to you the part of a kinsman, well; let him do the kinsman's part: but if he will not do the part of a kinsman to you, then will I do the part of a kinsman to you, *as* the Lord lives: lie down until the morning.

14 And she lay at his feet until the morning: and she rose up before one could know another. And he said, Let it not be known that a woman came into the floor.

15 Also he said, Bring the <u>veil</u> that *you have* upon you, and hold it. And when she held it, he measured six *measures* of barley, and laid *it* on her: and she went into the city. cloak

16 And when she came to her mother in law, she said, <u>Who are you</u>, my daughter? And she told her all that the man had done to her. How did it go

17 And she said, These six *measures* of barley gave he me; for he said to me, Go not empty to your mother in law.

18 Then said she, Sit still, my daughter, until you know how the matter will fall: for the man will not be in rest, until he have finished the thing this day.

CHAPTER 4

THEN went Bo'az up to the gate, and sat him down there: and, behold, the kinsman of whom Bo'az spoke came by; to whom he said, Ho, such a one! turn aside, sit down here. And he turned aside, and sat down.

2 And he took ten men of the elders of the city, and said, Sit you down here. And they sat down.

3 And he said to the kinsman, Na-o`mi, that is come again out of the country of Mo'ab, sells a <u>parcel</u> of land, which *was* our brother E-lim`e-lech's: piece

4 And I thought to <u>advertise</u> you, saying, Buy *it* before the inhabitants, and before the elders of my people. If you will redeem *it*, redeem *it*: but if you will not redeem *it*, *then* tell me, that I may know: for *there is* none to redeem *it* beside you; and I *am* after you. And he said, I will redeem *it*.   inform

5 Then said Bo'az, What day you buy the field of the hand <u>of</u> Na-o`mi, you must buy *it* also of Ruth the Mo'ab-it-ess, the wife of the dead, to raise up the name of the dead upon his inheritance.   from

6 And the kinsman said, I cannot redeem *it* for myself, less I <u>mar</u> my own inheritance: redeem you my <u>right</u> to yourself; for I cannot redeem *it*.   endanger

7 Now this *was the manner* in former time in Is'ra-el concerning redeeming and concerning <u>changing</u>, for to confirm all things; a man plucked off his shoe, and gave *it* to his neighbor: and this *was* a testimony in Is'ra-el.   the exchange of land

8 Therefore the kinsman said to Bo'az, Buy *it* for you. So he drew off his shoe.

9 And Bo'az said to the elders, and *to* all the people, You *are* witnesses this day, that I have bought all that *was* E-lim`e-lech's, and all that *was* Chil`i-on's and Mah`lon's, of the hand of Na-o`mi.

10 Moreover Ruth the Mo'ab-it-ess, the wife of Mah'lon, have I purchased to be my wife, to raise up the name of the dead upon his inheritance, that the name of the dead be not cut off from among his brethren, and from the gate of his place: you *are* witnesses this day.

11 And all the people that *were* in the gate, and the elders, said, *We are* witnesses. The LORD make the woman that is come into your house like Ra'chel and like Le'ah, which two did build the house of Is'ra-el: and do you worthily in Eph'ra-tah, and be famous in Beth'-le-hem:

12 And let your house be like the house of Pha'rez, whom Ta'mar <u>bare</u> to Ju'dah, of the <u>seed</u> which the LORD shall give you of this young woman.

bore - offspring

13 So Bo'az took Ruth, and she was his wife: and when he went in to her, the LORD gave her conception, and she bare a son.

14 And the women said to Na-o`mi, Blessed *be* the LORD, which has not left you this day without a <u>kinsman</u>, that his name may be famous in Is'ra-el.

<small>redeemer</small>

15 And he shall be to you a <u>restorer</u> of *your* life, and a <u>nourisher</u> of your old age: for your daughter in law, which loves you, which is better to you than seven sons, has born him.

<small>renewer - sustainer</small>

16 And Na-o`mi took the child, and laid it in her bosom, and became nurse to it.

17 And the women her neighbors gave it a name, saying, There is a son born to Na-o`mi; and they called his name O'bed: he *is* the father of Jes'se, the father of Da'vid.

18 Now these *are* the generations of Pha'rez: Pha'rez fathered Hez'ron,

19 And Hez'ron fathered Ram, and Ram fathered Am-min'a-dab,

20 And Am-min'a-dab fathered Nah'-shon, and Nah'shon fathered Sal'mon,

21 And Sal'mon fathered Bo'az, and Bo'az fathered O'bed,

22 And O'bed fathered Jes'se, and Jes'se fathered Da'vid.

1 AND 2 SAMUEL

OUTLINE

OVERTHROW OF ABSALOM AND RETURN OF DAVID 18.6—24.25

Defeat of Israel and Death of Absalom 18.6—19.8

Gain and Loss 18.6–18

David's Reception of the News 18.19-33

Joab Rebukes Mourning David 19.1-8

David's Return to Jerusalem 19.9-43

Sheba's Rebellion 20.1-26

Famine on Account of Saul's Crime 21.1-14

Finale of the Goliath Feud 21.15-22

David's Song of Deliverance 22.1-51

Last Words of David 23.1-7

List of Chief of David's Mighty Men 23.8-39

Taking of the Census and God's Chastisement 24.1-15

God's Intervention and David's Intercession 24.16-25

SURVEY

The Books of Samuel record the transition from a theocracy to a monarchy, and the establishment of the monarchy. The story begins in the closing days of the Judges and leaves us with the aged David securely enthroned as king over Israel and Judah. The other two great figures are Samuel and Saul.

Samuel was the last of the judges and the first of the prophets. He was a man of great piety and spiritual discernment and wholly dedicated to the realization of God's purposes for Israel. Although not of Aaronic descent, he succeeded Eli in the priestly office. He seems to have been the first to have established an institution for the training of young men for the prophetic calling. He was called upon to guide Israel in some of the greatest crises of her history, and he falls little short of the stature of Moses. Without any desire on his part, he found himself in the role of "kingmaker," commissioned to anoint Saul, the first king, and David, Israel's greatest king.

Saul, the king, is an enigmatic character. A man of great physical courage, he lacked, nevertheless, that constancy of purpose essential to greatness. His fickleness of temperament impaired all his personal relationships, and a morbid fear of potential rivals preyed on his mind and affected his reason. From a humble background he was called to the highest station in the land. In the end, with no achievement to entitle him to a royal tomb, his bones were returned to his native place.

David is one of the great figures of Biblical history. Like Saul, he came from a humble background, but his gifts were of the highest order. He was a born leader of men, able to win and retain their allegiance. Some of his most faithful servants came from outside Judah and Israel. Ittai, for instance, was from Gath. David was a wise administrator and a good judge of human nature. His ability to make quick decisions is well illustrated by his solution of the delicate problem that arose over Mephibosheth (2 S 19.24 ff.). He was a highly gifted poet, whose songs of praise enriched the worship, first of the temple, and then of the Christian Church. To rise so high and at so great a cost would have made him strong, one would have thought, to withstand temptation. Alas, his powers of resistance were no greater than those of other men. Even when we make full allowance for the age in which he lived, he was no stalwart when faced with temptation. Despite his frailty, he saw clearly the purposes of God for His people, and foresaw the coming of the messianic King, Whom he in his life so imperfectly portrayed.

The Books of Samuel provide an indispensable chapter in the record of God's dealings with the people of Israel, and their preservation and preparation for their twofold purpose: to be the recipients of the oracles of God, and to bring forth in due time "great David's greater Son."

AUTHOR

We are nowhere told who wrote these books. The statement in 1 Chronicles 29.29 strongly suggests that Samuel was joint author with Nathan and Gad.

W.J.M.

THE FIRST BOOK OF
SAMUEL

CHAPTER 1

NOW there was a certain man of Ramath-a'im-zo'phim, of mount E'phra-im, and his name *was* El'ka-nah, the son of Jer'o-ham, the son of E-li'hu, the son of To'hu, the son of Zuph, an Eph'rath-ite:

2 And he had two wives; the name of the one *was* Han'nah, and the name of the other Pe-nin'nah: and Pe-nin'nah had children, but Han'nah had no children.

3 And this man went up out of his city yearly to worship and to sacrifice to the LORD of hosts in Shi'loh. And the two sons of E'li, Hoph'ni and Phin'e-has, the priests of the LORD, *were* there.   Jehovah^s.f. Tsebaoth

4 And when the time was that El'ka-nah offered, he gave to Pe-nin'nah his wife, and to all her sons and her daughters, portions: sacrificed

5 But to Han'nah he gave a worthy portion; for he loved Han'nah: but the LORD had shut up her womb.   double

6 And her adversary also provoked her sore, for to make her fret, because the LORD had shut up her womb.   bitterly - irritable

7 And *as* he did so year by year, when she went up to the house of the LORD, so she provoked her; therefore she wept, and did not eat.

8 Then said El'ka-nah her husband to her, Han'nah, why weep you? and why eat you not? and why is your heart grieved? *am* not I better to you than ten sons?   sad

9 So Han'nah rose up after they had eaten in Shi'loh, and after they had drunk. Now E'li the priest sat upon a seat by a post of the temple of the LORD.

10 And she *was* in bitterness of soul, and prayed to the LORD, and wept sore.   bitterly

11 And she vowed a vow, and said, O LORD of hosts, if You will indeed look on the affliction of Your handmaid, and remember me, and not forget Your handmaid, but will give to Your handmaid a man child, then I will give him to the LORD all the days of his life, and there shall no razor come upon his head.   made a pledge - Jehovah^s.f. Tsebaoth

12 And it came to pass, as she continued praying before the LORD, that E'li marked her mouth.   noticed

13 Now Han'nah, she spoke in her heart; only her lips moved, but her voice was not heard: therefore E'li thought she had been drunken.

14 And E'li said to her, How long will you be drunken? put away your wine from you.

15 And Han'nah answered and said, No, my lord, I *am* a woman of a sorrowful spirit: I have drunk neither wine

nor strong drink, but have <u>poured</u> out my soul before the LORD.   prayed earnestly

16 Count not your handmaid for a <u>daughter</u> of Be'li-al: for out of the abundance of my <u>complaint</u> and <u>grief</u> have I spoken <u>hereto</u>.   worthless woman - provocation - concern - up to now

17 Then E'li answered and said, Go in peace: and the <u>God</u> of Is'ra-el grant *you* your petition that you have asked of Him.   Elohim^{p.f.}

18 And she said, Let your handmaid find grace in your sight. So the woman went her way, and did eat, and her countenance was no more *sad*.

19 And they rose up in the morning early, and worshiped before the LORD, and returned, and came to their house to Ra'mah: and El'ka-nah knew Han'nah his wife; and the LORD remembered her.

20 Wherefore it came to pass, when the time was come about after Han'nah had conceived, that she bare a son, and called his name <u>Sam'u-el</u>, *saying*, Because I have asked him of the LORD.   asked of God

21 And the man El'ka-nah, and all his house, went up to offer to the LORD the yearly sacrifice, and his <u>vow</u>.   pledge

22 But Han'nah went not up; for she said to her husband, *I will not go up* until the child be weaned, and *then* I will bring him, that he may appear before the LORD, and there abide for ever.

23 And El'ka-nah her husband said to her, Do what seems you good; tarry until you have weaned him; only the LORD <u>establish</u> His word. So the woman abode, and gave her son suck until she weaned him.   confirm

24 And when she had weaned him, she took him up with her, with three bullocks, and one ephah of flour, and a bottle of wine, and brought him to the house of the LORD in Shi'loh: and the child *was* young.

25 And they slew a bullock, and brought the child to E'li.

26 And she said, Oh my lord, *as* your soul lives, my lord, I *am* the woman that stood by you here, praying to the LORD.

27 For this child I prayed; and the LORD has given me my petition which I asked of Him:

28 Therefore also I have <u>lent</u> him to the LORD; as long as he lives he shall be <u>lent</u> to the LORD. And he worshiped the LORD there.   dedicated

CHAPTER 2

AND Han'nah prayed, and said, My heart rejoices in the LORD, my <u>horn</u> is exalted in the LORD: my mouth is enlarged over my enemies; because I rejoice in Your <u>salvation</u>.   i.e., strength - Jeshua

2 *There is* none holy as the LORD: for *there is* none beside You: neither *is there* any rock like our <u>God</u>.   Elohim^{p.f.}

3 Talk no more so exceeding proudly; let *not* arrogancy come out of your mouth: for the LORD *is* a God of knowledge, and by Him actions are <u>weighed</u>.   i.e., judged

4 The bows of the mighty men *are* broken, and they that stumbled are girded with strength.

5 *They that were* full have hired out themselves for bread; and *they that were* hungry ceased: so that the barren has born seven; and she that has many children is <u>waxed</u> feeble.   grows

6 The LORD kills, and makes alive: He brings down to the <u>grave</u>, and brings up.   Sheol

7 The LORD makes poor, and makes rich: He brings low, and lifts up.

8 He raises up the poor out of the dust, *and* lifts up the beggar from the dunghill, to set *them* among princes, and to make them inherit the throne of glory: for the pillars of the earth *are* the LORD's, and He has set the world upon them.

9 He will keep the feet of His saints, and the wicked shall be silent in darkness; for by strength shall no man prevail.

10 The adversaries of the LORD shall be broken to pieces; out of heaven shall He thunder upon them: the LORD shall judge the ends of the earth; and He shall give strength to His king, and exalt the horn of His anointed.

11 And El'ka-nah went to Ra'mah to his house. And the child did <u>minister</u> to the LORD before E'li the priest.   serve

12 Now the sons of E'li *were* sons of <u>Be'li-al</u>; they knew not the LORD. i.e., Satan

13 And the priests' custom with the people *was*, *that*, when any man offered sacrifice, the priest's servant came, while the flesh was in <u>seething</u>, with a <u>fleshhook</u> of three teeth in his hand;   boiling - fork

14 And he struck *it* into the pan, or kettle, or caldron, or pot; all that the <u>fleshhook</u> brought up the priest took for himself. So they did in Shi'loh to all the Is'ra-el-ites that came there.

15 Also before they burned the fat, the priest's servant came, and said to the man that sacrificed, Give flesh to roast for the priest; for he will not have <u>sodden flesh</u> of you, but raw.   boiled meat

16 And *if* any man said to him, Let them not fail to burn the fat <u>presently</u>, and *then* take *as much* as <u>your soul</u> desires; then he would answer him, *Nay*; but you shall give *it me* now: and if not, I will take *it* by force.   first - you

17 Wherefore the sin of the young men was very great before the LORD: for men abhorred the offering of the LORD.

18 But Sam'u-el ministered before the LORD, *being* a child, girded with a linen <u>ephod</u>.   priestly garment

19 Moreover his mother made him a little coat, and brought *it* to him from year to year, when she came up with her husband to offer the yearly sacrifice.

20 And E'li blessed El'ka-nah and his wife, and said, The LORD give you <u>seed of</u> this woman for the loan which is lent to the LORD. And they went to their own home.   children from

21 And the LORD <u>visited</u> Han'nah, so that she conceived, and bare three sons and two daughters. And the child Sam'u-el grew before the LORD.   was gracious to

22 Now E'li was very old, and heard all that his sons did to all Is'ra-el; and how they lay with the women

that assembled *at* the door of the tabernacle of the congregation.

23 And he said to them, Why do you such things? for I hear of your evil dealings by all this people.   wicked deeds

24 Nay, my sons; for *it is* no good report that I hear: you make the LORD's people to transgress.   lead

25 If one man sin against another, the judge shall judge him: but if a man sin against the LORD, who shall entreat for him? Notwithstanding they hearkened not to the voice of their father, because the LORD would slay them.

26 And the child Sam'u-el grew on, and was in favor both with the LORD, and also with men.

27 And there came a man of God to E'li, and said to him, Thus says the LORD, Did I plainly appear to the house of your father, when they were in E'gypt in Pha'raoh's house?   Elohim^p.f.

28 And did I choose him out of all the tribes of Is'ra-el *to be* My priest, to offer upon My altar, to burn incense, to wear an ephod before Me? and did I give to the house of your father all the offerings made by fire of the children of Is'ra-el?   priestly garment

29 Wherefore kick you at My sacrifice and at My offering, which I have commanded *in My* habitation; and honor your sons above Me, to make yourselves fat with the chiefest of all the offerings of Is'ra-el My people?   scorn - first

30 Wherefore the LORD God of Is'ra-el says, I said indeed *that* your house, and the house of your father, should walk before Me for ever: but now the LORD says, Be it far from Me; for them that honor Me I will honor, and they that despise Me shall be lightly esteemed.   Jehovah^s.f. - Elohim^p.f.

31 Behold, the days come, that I will cut off your arm, and the arm of your father's house, that there shall not be an old man in your house.   break your strength - strength

32 And you shall see an enemy *in My* habitation, in all *the wealth* which *God* shall give Is'ra-el: and there shall not be an old man in your house for ever.

33 And the man of yours, *whom* I shall not cut off from My altar, *shall be* to consume your eyes, and to grieve your heart: and all the increase of your house shall die in the flower of their age.   blind - prime

34 And this *shall be* a sign to you, that shall come upon your two sons, on Hoph'ni and Phin'e-has; in one day they shall die both of them.

35 And I will raise Me up a faithful priest, *that* shall do according to *that* which *is* in My heart and in My mind: and I will build him a sure house; and he shall walk before My anointed for ever.

36 And it shall come to pass, *that* every one that is left in your house shall come *and* crouch to him for a piece of silver and a morsel of bread, and shall say, Put me, I pray you, into one of the priests' offices, that I may eat a piece of bread.   loaf - Assign

CHAPTER 3

AND the child Sam'u-el minis-tered to the LORD before E'li. And the word of the LORD was pre-cious in those days; *there was* no open vision. ^{rare}

2 And it came to pass at that time, when E'li *was* laid down in his place, and his eyes began to wax dim, *that* he could not see; ^{grow}

3 And before the lamp of God went out in the temple of the LORD, where the ark of God *was*, and Sam'u-el was laid down to *sleep*; ^{Elohim p.f.}

4 That the LORD called Sam'u-el: and he answered, Here *am* I.

5 And he ran to E'li, and said, Here *am* I; for you called me. And he said, I called not; lie down again. And he went and lay down.

6 And the LORD called yet again, Sam'u-el. And Sam'u-el arose and went to E'li, and said, Here *am* I; for you did call me. And he answered, I called not, my son; lie down again.

7 Now Sam'u-el did not yet know the LORD, neither was the word of the LORD yet revealed to him.

8 And the LORD called Sam'u-el again the third time. And he arose and went to E'li, and said, Here *am* I; for you did call me. And E'li perceived that the LORD had called the child.

9 Therefore E'li said to Sam'u-el, Go, lie down: and it shall be, if He call you, that you shall say, Speak, LORD; for Your servant hears. So Sam'u-el went and lay down in his place.

10 And the LORD came, and stood, and called as at other times, Sam'u-el, Sam'u-el. Then Sam'u-el answered, Speak; for Your servant hears.

11 And the LORD said to Sam'u-el, Behold, I will do a thing in Is'ra-el, at which both the ears of every one that hears it shall tingle. ^{ring (in amazement)}

12 In that day I will perform against E'li *all things* which I have spoken concerning his house: when I be-gin, I will also make an end.

13 For I have told him that I will judge his house for ever for the in-iquity which he know; because his sons made themselves vile, and he restrained them not.

14 And therefore I have sworn to the house of E'li, that the iniquity of E'li's house shall not be purged with sacrifice nor offering for ever. ^{not be atoned}

15 And Sam'u-el lay until the morn-ing, and opened the doors of the house of the LORD. And Sam'u-el feared to show E'li the vision.

16 Then E'li called Sam'u-el, and said, Sam'u-el, my son. And he answered, Here *am* I.

17 And he said, What *is* the thing that *the LORD* has said to you? I pray you hide *it* not from me: God do so to you, and more also, if you hide *any* thing from me of all the things that He said to you. ^{Elohim p.f.}

18 And Sam'u-el told him every whit, and hid nothing from him. And he said, It *is* the LORD: let Him do what seems Him good. ^{thing}

19 And Sam'u-el grew, and the

LORD was with him, and <u>did let none of his words fall to the ground</u>. heard him when he prayed

20 And all Is'ra-el from Dan even to Be'er-she'ba knew that Sam'u-el *was* <u>established</u> *to be* a prophet of the LORD. confirmed

21 And the LORD appeared again in Shi'loh: for the LORD revealed Himself to Sam'u-el in Shi'loh by the word of the LORD.

CHAPTER 4

AND the word of Sam'u-el came to all Is'ra-el. Now Is'ra-el went out against the Phi-lis'tines to battle, and <u>pitched</u> beside Eb'en-e'zer: and the Phi-lis'tines <u>pitched</u> in A'phek. camped

2 And the Phi-lis'tines put themselves in array against Is'ra-el: and when they joined battle, Is'ra-el was <u>smitten</u> before the Phi-lis'tines: and they slew of the army in the field about four thousand men. defeated

3 And when the people were come into the camp, the elders of Is'ra-el said, Wherefore has the LORD <u>smitten</u> us to day before the Phi-lis'tines? Let us bring the ark of the <u>covenant</u> of the LORD out of Shi'loh to us, that, when it comes among us, it may save us out of the hand of our enemies. agreement

4 So the people sent to Shi'loh, that they might bring from there the ark of the <u>covenant</u> of the <u>LORD of hosts</u>, which dwells *between* the cherubims: and the two sons of E'li, Hoph'ni and Phin'e-has, *were* there with the ark of the <u>covenant</u> of <u>God</u>. Jehovah^{s.f.} Elohe Tsebaoth

5 And when the ark of the <u>covenant</u> of the LORD came into the camp, all Is'ra-el shouted with a great shout, so that the earth rang again. agreement

6 And when the Phi-lis'tines heard the noise of the shout, they said, What *means* the noise of this great shout in the camp of the He'brews? And they understood that the ark of the LORD was come into the camp.

7 And the Phi-lis'tines were afraid, for they said, <u>God</u> is come into the camp. And they said, Woe to us! for there has not been such a thing heretofore. Elohim^{p.f.}

8 Woe to us! who shall deliver us out of the hand of these mighty <u>Gods</u>? these *are* the <u>Gods</u> that <u>smote</u> the E-gyp'tians with all the plagues in the wilderness. struck

9 Be strong, and <u>quit</u> yourselves like men, O you Phi-lis'tines, that you be not servants to the He'brews, as they have been to you: <u>quit</u> yourselves like men, and fight. act

10 And the Phi-lis'tines fought, and Is'ra-el was <u>smitten</u>, and they fled every man into his tent: and there was a very great slaughter; for there fell of Is'ra-el thirty thousand footmen. defeated

11 And the ark of <u>God</u> was taken; and the two sons of E'li, Hoph'ni and Phin'e-has, were slain.

12 And there ran a man of Ben'ja-min out of the army, and came to Shi'loh the same day with his clothes <u>rent</u>, and with <u>earth upon his head</u>. torn - i.e., as a sign of grief

13 And when he came, lo, E'li sat upon a seat by the wayside watching:

for his <u>heart trembled</u> for the ark of <u>God</u>. And when the man came into the city, and told *it*, all the city cried out. _{i.e., was concerned - Elohim^{p.f.}}

14 And when E'li heard the noise of the crying, he said, What *means* the noise of this tumult? And the man came in hastily, and told E'li.

15 Now E'li was ninety and eight years old; and his eyes were <u>dim</u>, that he could not see. _{weak}

16 And the man said to E'li, I *am* he that came out of the army, and I fled to day out of the army. And he said, What is there done, my son?

17 And the messenger answered and said, Is'ra-el is fled before the Phi-lis'tines, and there has been also a great slaughter among the people, and your two sons also, Hoph'ni and Phin'e-has, are dead, and the ark of <u>God</u> is taken.

18 And it came to pass, when he made mention of the ark of <u>God</u>, that he fell from off the seat backward by the side of the gate, and his neck broke, and he died: for he was an old man, and heavy. And he had judged Is'ra-el forty years. _{Elohim^{p.f.}}

19 And his daughter in law, Phin'e-has' wife, was with child, *near* to be delivered: and when she heard the tidings that the ark of <u>God</u> was taken, and that her father in law and her husband were dead, she bowed herself and <u>travailed</u>; for her pains came upon her. _{gave birth}

20 And about the time of her death the women that stood by her said to her, Fear not; for you have born a son. But she answered not, neither did she regard *it*.

21 And she named the child I'-cha-bod, saying, The glory is departed from Is'ra-el: because the ark of <u>God</u> was taken, and because of her father in law and her husband. _{Elohim^{p.f.}}

22 And she said, The glory is departed from Is'ra-el: for the ark of <u>God</u> is taken.

CHAPTER 5

AND the Phi-lis'tines took the ark of <u>God</u>, and brought it from Eb'en-e'zer to Ash'dod.

2 When the Phi-lis'tines took the ark of <u>God</u>, they brought it into the house of Da'gon, and set it by Da'gon. _{Elohim^{p.f.}}

3 And when they of Ash'dod arose early on the morrow, behold, Da'gon *was* fallen upon his face to the earth before the ark of the LORD. And they took Da'gon, and set him in his place again.

4 And when they arose early on the morrow morning, behold, Da'gon *was* fallen upon his face to the ground before the ark of the LORD; and the head of Da'gon and both the palms of his hands *were* cut off upon the threshold; only *the stump of* Da'gon was left to him.

5 Therefore neither the priests of Da'gon, nor any that come into Da'gon's house, tread on the threshold of Da'gon in Ash'dod to this day.

6 But the hand of the LORD was heavy upon them of Ash'dod, and He destroyed them, and smote them with <u>emerods</u>, *even* Ash'dod and the coasts thereof. _{tumors}

7 And when the men of Ash'dod saw that *it was* so, they said, The ark of the <u>God</u> of Is'ra-el shall not abide with us: for His hand is <u>sore</u> upon us, and upon Da'gon our god. Elohim^p.f. - severe

8 They sent therefore and gathered all the lords of the Phi-lis'tines to them, and said, What shall we do with the ark of the <u>God</u> of Is'ra-el? And they answered, Let the ark of the <u>God</u> of Is'ra-el be carried about to Gath. And they carried the ark of the <u>God</u> of Is'ra-el about *there*.

9 And it was *so*, that, after they had carried it about, the hand of the LORD was against the city with a very great destruction: and He smote the men of the city, both small and great, and they had <u>emerods</u> in their secret parts. tumors

10 Therefore they sent the ark of <u>God</u> to Ek'ron. And it came to pass, as the ark of <u>God</u> came to Ek'ron, that the Ek'ron-ites cried out, saying, They have brought about the ark of the <u>God</u> of Is'ra-el to us, to <u>slay</u> us and our people. kill

11 So they sent and gathered together all the lords of the Phi-lis'tines, and said, Send away the ark of the <u>God</u> of Is'ra-el, and let it go again to its own place, that it slay us not, and our people: for there was a deadly destruction throughout all the city; the hand of <u>God</u> was very heavy there. Elohim^p.f.

12 And the men that died not were <u>smitten</u> with the emerods: and the cry of the city went up to heaven. afflicted

CHAPTER 6

AND the ark of the LORD was in the country of the Phi-lis'tines seven months.

2 And the Phi-lis'tines called for the priests and the <u>diviners</u>, saying, What shall we do to the ark of the LORD? tell us wherewith we shall send it to its place. soothsayers

3 And they said, If you send away the ark of the God of Is'ra-el, send it not <u>empty</u>; but in any wise return Him a trespass offering: then you shall be healed, and it shall be known to you why His hand is not removed from you. without a gift

4 Then said they, What *shall be* the trespass offering which we shall return to Him? They answered, Five golden <u>emerods</u>, and five golden mice, *according to* the number of the lords of the Phi-lis'tines: for one plague *was* on you all, and on your lords. tumors

5 Wherefore you shall make <u>images</u> of your emerods, and <u>images</u> of your mice that mar the land; and you shall give glory to the <u>God</u> of Is'ra-el: perhaps He will <u>lighten</u> His hand from off you, and from off your gods, and from off your land. Elohim^p.f. - likenesses - ease

6 Wherefore then do you harden your hearts, as the E-gyp'tians and Pha'raoh hardened their hearts? when He had wrought wonderfully among them, did they not let the people go, and they departed?

7 Now therefore make a new cart, and take two milch <u>kine</u>, on which

there has come no yoke, and tie the <u>kine</u> to the cart, and bring their calves home from them: _{cows}

8 And take the ark of the LORD, and lay it upon the cart; and put the jewels of gold, which you return Him *for* a trespass offering, in a <u>coffer</u> by the side thereof; and send it away, that it may go. _{chest}

9 And see, if it goes up by the way of his own <u>coast</u> to Beth-she'mesh, *then* He has done us this great evil: but if not, then we shall know that *it is* not His hand *that* smote us; it *was* a chance *that* happened to us. _{territory}

10 And the men did so; and took two milch <u>kine</u>, and tied them to the cart, and shut up their calves at home:

11 And they laid the ark of the LORD upon the cart, and the <u>coffer</u> with the mice of gold and the images of their emerods.

12 And the <u>kine</u> took the straight way to the way of Beth-she'mesh, *and* went along the highway, <u>lowing</u> as they went, and turned not aside *to* the right hand or *to* the left; and the lords of the Phi-lis'tines went after them to the border of Beth-she'mesh. _{cows bellowing}

13 And *they of* Beth-she'mesh *were* reaping their wheat harvest in the valley: and they lifted up their eyes, and saw the ark, and rejoiced to see *it*.

14 And the cart came into the field of Josh'u-a, a Beth-she'mite, and stood there, where *there was* a great stone: and they <u>clave</u> the wood of the cart, and offered the <u>kine</u> a burned offering to the LORD. _{split}

15 And the Le'vites took down the ark of the LORD, and the <u>coffer</u> that *was* with it, wherein the jewels of gold *were*, and put *them* on the great stone: and the men of Beth-she'mesh offered burned offerings and sacrificed sacrifices the same day to the LORD. _{chest}

16 And when the five lords of the Phi-lis'tines had seen *it*, they returned to Ek'ron the same day.

17 And these *are* the golden <u>emerods</u> which the Phi-lis'tines returned *for* a trespass offering to the LORD; for Ash'dod one, for Ga'za one, for As'ke-lon one, for Gath one, for Ek'ron one; _{tumors}

18 And the golden mice, *according to* the number of all the cities of the Phi-lis'tines *belonging* to the five lords, *both* of <u>fenced</u> cities, and of country villages, even to the great *stone of* A'bel, whereon they set down the ark of the LORD: *which stone remains* to this day in the field of Josh'u-a, the Beth-she'mite. _{fortified}

19 And He <u>smote</u> the men of Beth-she'mesh, because they had looked into the ark of the LORD, even He smote of the people fifty thousand and threescore and ten men: and the people lamented, because the LORD had smitten *many* of the people with a great slaughter. _{struck down}

20 And the men of Beth-she'mesh said, Who is able to stand before this holy <u>LORD God</u>? and to whom shall He go up from us? _{Jehovah^{s.f.} Elohim^{p.f.}}

21 And they sent messengers to the inhabitants of Kir'jath-je'a-rim, saying, The Phi-lis'tines have brought again the

ark of the LORD; come you down, *and* bring it up to you.

CHAPTER 7

AND the men of Kir'jath-je'a-rim came, and brought up the ark of the LORD, and brought it into the house of A-bin'a-dab in the hill, and <u>sanctified</u> E-le'a-zar his son to keep the ark of the LORD.   _{consecrated}
2 And it came to pass, while the ark abode in Kir'jath-je'a-rim, that the time was long; for it was twenty years: and all the house of Is'ra-el lamented after the LORD.
3 And Sam'u-el spoke to all the house of Is'ra-el, saying, If you do return to the LORD with all your hearts, *then* put away the <u>strange</u> gods and Ash'ta-roth from among you, and prepare your hearts to the LORD, and serve Him only: and He will <u>deliver</u> you out of the hand of the Phi-lis'tines.   _{foreign - save}
4 Then the children of Is'ra-el did put away Ba'al-im and Ash'ta-roth, and served the LORD only.
5 And Sam'u-el said, Gather all Is'ra-el to Miz'peh, and I will pray for you to the LORD.
6 And they gathered together to Miz'peh, and drew water, and poured it out before the LORD, and fasted on that day, and said there, We have sinned against the LORD. And Sam'u-el judged the children of Is'ra-el in Miz'peh.
7 And when the Phi-lis'tines heard that the children of Is'ra-el were gathered together to Miz'peh, the lords of the Phi-lis'tines went up against Is'ra-el. And when the children of Is'ra-el heard *it*, they were afraid of the Phi-lis'tines.
8 And the children of Is'ra-el said to Sam'u-el, Cease not to cry to the LORD our <u>God</u> for us, that He will save us out of the hand of the Phi-lis'tines.   _{Elohim^{p.f.}}
9 And Sam'u-el took a sucking lamb, and offered *it for* a burned offering wholly to the LORD: and Sam'u-el cried to the LORD for Is'ra-el; and the LORD heard him.
10 And as Sam'u-el was offering up the burned offering, the Phi-lis'tines drew near to battle against Is'ra-el: but the LORD thundered with a great thunder on that day upon the Phi-lis'tines, and <u>discom-fited</u> them; and they were smitten before Is'ra-el.   _{overwhelmed}
11 And the men of Is'ra-el went out of Miz'peh, and pursued the Phi-lis'tines, and <u>smote</u> them, until *they came* under Beth'-car.   _{destroyed}
12 Then Sam'u-el took a stone, and set *it* between Miz'peh and Shen, and called the name of it <u>Eb'en-e'zer</u>, saying, Thus far has the LORD helped us.   _{The stone of help}
13 So the Phi-lis'tines were subdued, and they came no more into the coast of Is'ra-el: and the <u>hand</u> of the LORD was against the Phi-lis'tines all the days of Sam'u-el.   _{providence}
14 And the cities which the Phi-lis'tines had taken from Is'ra-el were restored to Is'ra-el, from Ek-ron even to Gath; and the <u>coasts</u> thereof did Is'ra-el deliver <u>out of the hands</u> of the

Phi-lis'tines. And there was peace between Is'ra-el and the Am'or-ites. Territory - from the power

15 And Sam'u-el judged Is'ra-el all the days of his life.

16 And he went from year to year in circuit to Beth'-el, and Gil'gal, and Miz'peh, and judged Is'ra-el in all those places.

17 And his return *was* to Ra'mah; for there *was* his house; and there he judged Is'ra-el; and there he built an altar to the LORD.

CHAPTER 8

AND it came to pass, when Sam'u-el was old, that he made his sons judges over Is'ra-el.

2 Now the name of his firstborn was Jo'el; and the name of his second, A-bi'ah: *they were* judges in Be'er-she'ba.

3 And his sons walked not in his ways, but turned aside after lucre, and took bribes, and perverted judgment. money

4 Then all the elders of Is'ra-el gathered themselves together, and came to Sam'u-el to Ra'mah,

5 And said to him, Behold, you are old, and your sons walk not in your ways: now make us a king to judge us like all the nations.

6 But the thing displeased Sam'u-el, when they said, Give us a king to judge us. And Sam'u-el prayed to the LORD.

7 And the LORD said to Sam'u-el, Hearken to the voice of the people in all that they say to you: for they have not rejected you, but they have rejected Me, that I should not reign over them. Listen

8 According to all the works which they have done since the day that I brought them up out of E'gypt even to this day, wherewith they have forsaken Me, and served other gods, so do they also to you.

9 Now therefore hearken to their voice: however yet protest solemnly to them, and show them the manner of the king that shall reign over them. listen

10 And Sam'u-el told all the words of the LORD to the people that asked of him a king.

11 And he said, This will be the manner of the king that shall reign over you: He will take your sons, and appoint *them* for himself, for his chariots, and *to be* his horsemen; and *some* shall run before his chariots.

12 And he will appoint him captains over thousands, and captains over fifties; and *will set them* to ear his ground, and to reap his harvest, and to make his instruments of war, and instruments of his chariots. plow

13 And he will take your daughters *to be* confectionaries, and *to be* cooks, and *to be* bakers. perfumers

14 And he will take your fields, and your vineyards, and your oliveyards, *even* the best *of them*, and give *them* to his servants.

15 And he will take the tenth of your seed, and of your vineyards, and give to his officers, and to his servants.

16 And he will take your menservants, and your maidservants, and your

goodliest young men, and your asses, and put *them* to his work. best

17 He will take the tenth of your sheep: and you shall be his servants.   flocks - slaves

18 And you shall cry out in that day because of your king which you shall have chosen you; and the LORD will not hear you in that day.

19 Nevertheless the people refused to obey the voice of Sam'u-el; and they said, Nay; but we will have a king over us;

20 That we also may be like all the nations; and that our king may judge us, and go out before us, and fight our battles.   lead

21 And Sam'u-el heard all the words of the people, and he rehearsed them in the ears of the LORD.   repeated

22 And the LORD said to Sam'u-el, Hearken to their voice, and make them a king. And Sam'u-el said to the men of Is'ra-el, Go you every man to his city.   Listen

CHAPTER 9

NOW there was a man of Ben'ja-min, whose name *was* Kish, the son of A-bi'el, the son of Ze'ror, the son of Be-cho'rath, the son of A-phi'ah, a Ben'ja-mite, a mighty man of power.   valor

2 And he had a son, whose name *was* Saul, a choice young man, and a goodly: and *there was* not among the children of Is'ra-el a goodlier person than he: from his shoulders and upward *he was* higher than any of the people.   handsome - taller

3 And the asses of Kish Saul's father were lost. And Kish said to Saul his son, Take now one of the servants with you, and arise, go seek the asses.

4 And he passed through mount E'phra-im, and passed through the land of Shal'i-sha, but they found *them* not: then they passed through the land of Sha'lim, and *there they were* not: and he passed through the land of the Ben'ja-mites, but they found *them* not.

5 *And* when they were come to the land of Zuph, Saul said to his servant that was with him, Come, and let us return; less my father leave *caring* for the asses, and take thought for us.   cease

6 And he said to him, Behold now, *there is* in this city a man of God, and *he is* an honorable man; all that he says comes surely to pass: now let us go there; perhaps he can show us our way that we should go.

7 Then said Saul to his servant, But, behold, *if* we go, what shall we bring the man? for the bread is spent in our vessels, and *there is* not a present to bring to the man of God: what have we?   gone - Elohim[p.f.]

8 And the servant answered Saul again, and said, Behold, I have here at hand the fourth part of a shekel of silver: *that* will I give to the man of God, to tell us our way.

9 (Beforetime in Is'ra-el, when a man went to enquire of God, thus he spoke, Come, and let us go to the seer: for *he that is* now *called* a Prophet was beforetime called a Seer.)

10 Then said Saul to his servant, Well

said; come, let us go. So they went to the city where the man of God was. _{Elohim}^{p.f.}

11 *And* as they went up the hill to the city, they found young maidens going out to draw water, and said to them, Is the seer here?

12 And they answered them, and said, He is; behold, *he is* before you: make haste now, for he came to day to the city; for *there is* a sacrifice of the people to day in the high place:

13 As soon as you be come into the city, you shall immediately find him, before he go up to the high place to eat: for the people will not eat until he come, because he does bless the sacrifice; *and* afterwards they eat that be bidden. Now therefore get you up; for about this time you shall find him. _{at once}

14 And they went up into the city: *and* when they were come into the city, behold, Sam'u-el came out against them, for to go up to the high place. _{toward}

15 Now the Lord had told Sam'u-el in his ear a day before Saul came, saying,

16 To morrow about this time I will send you a man out of the land of Ben'ja-min, and you shall anoint him *to be* captain over My people Is'ra-el, that he may save My people out of the hand of the Phi-lis'tines: for I have looked upon My people, because their cry is come to Me. _{prayer}

17 And when Sam'u-el saw Saul, the Lord said to him, Behold the man whom I spoke to you of! this same shall reign over My people.

18 Then Saul drew near to Sam'u-el in the gate, and said, Tell me, I pray you, where the seer's house *is*.

19 And Sam'u-el answered Saul, and said, I *am* the seer: go up before me to the high place; for you shall eat with me to day, and to morrow I will let you go, and will tell you all that *is* in your heart.

20 And as for your asses that were lost three days ago, set not your mind on them; for they are found. And on whom *is* all the desire of Is'ra-el? *Is it* not on you, and on all your father's house?

21 And Saul answered and said, *Am* not I a Ben'ja-mite, of the smallest of the tribes of Is'ra-el? and my family the least of all the families of the tribe of Ben'ja-min? wherefore then speak you so to me?

22 And Sam'u-el took Saul and his servant, and brought them into the parlor, and made them sit in the chief place among them that were bidden, which *were* about thirty persons. _{hall}

23 And Sam'u-el said to the cook, Bring the portion which I gave you, of which I said to you, Set it by you.

24 And the cook took up the shoulder, and *that* which *was* upon it, and set *it* before Saul. And *Sam'u-el* said, Behold that which is left! set *it* before you, *and* eat: for to this time has it been kept for you since I said, I have invited the people. So Saul did eat with Sam'u-el that day. _{leg}

25 And when they were come down from the high place into the city, *Sam'u-el* communed with Saul upon the top of the house. _{spoke}

26 And they arose early: and it came to pass about the <u>spring</u> of the day, that Sam'u-el called Saul to the top of the house, saying, Up, that I may send you away. And Saul arose, and they went out both of them, he and Sam'u-el, abroad.   _{daybreak}

27 *And* as they were going down to the end of the city, Sam'u-el said to Saul, Bid the servant pass on before us, (and he passed on,) but stand you still a while, that I may show you the word of <u>God</u>.   Elohim^{p.f.}

CHAPTER 10

THEN Sam'u-el took a <u>vial</u> of oil, and poured *it* upon his head, and kissed him, and said, *Is it* not because the LORD has anointed you *to be* captain over His inheritance?   _{flask}

2 When you are departed from me to day, then you shall find two men by Ra'chel's <u>sepulcher</u> in the border of Ben'ja-min at Zel'zah; and they will say to you, The asses which you went to seek are found: and, lo, your father has left the care of the asses, and sorrow for you, saying, What shall I do for my son?   _{tomb}

3 Then shall you go on forward from there, and you shall come to the <u>plain</u> of Ta'bor, and there shall meet you three men going up to <u>God</u> to Beth'-el, one carrying three kids, and another carrying three loaves of bread, and another carrying a bottle of wine: oak - Elohim^{p.f.}

4 And they will <u>salute</u> you, and give you two *loaves* of bread; which you shall receive of their hands.   _{greet}

5 After that you shall come to the hill of <u>God</u>, where *is* the garrison of the Phi-lis'tines: and it shall come to pass, when you are come there to the city, that you shall meet a company of prophets coming down from the high place with a <u>psaltery</u>, and a tabret, and a pipe, and a harp, before them; and they shall prophesy: Elohim^{p.f.} - lyres

6 And the Spirit of the LORD will come upon you, and you shall prophesy with them, and shall be turned into another man.

7 And let it be, when these signs are come to you, *that* you do as occasion serve you; for <u>God</u> *is* with you.

8 And you shall go down before me to Gil'gal; and, behold, I will come down to you, to offer burned offerings, *and* to sacrifice sacrifices of peace offerings: seven days shall you tarry, till I come to you, and show you what you shall do.

9 And it was *so*, that when he had turned his back to go from Sam'u-el, <u>God</u> gave him <u>another</u> heart: and all those signs came to pass that day.   Elohim^{p.f.} - a changed

10 And when they came there to the hill, behold, a company of prophets met him; and the Spirit of <u>God</u> came upon him, and he prophesied among them.

11 And it came to pass, when all that knew him beforetime saw that, behold, he prophesied among the prophets, then the people said one to another, What *is* this *that* is come to the son of Kish? *Is* Saul also among the prophets?   MATT. 13:57

12 And one of the same place answered and said, But who *is* their father? Therefore it became a proverb, *Is* Saul also among the prophets?

13 And when he had made an end of prophesying, he came to the high place.

14 And Saul's uncle said to him and to his servant, Where went you? And he said, To seek the asses: and when we saw that *they were* no where, we came to Sam'u-el.

15 And Saul's uncle said, Tell me, I pray you, what Sam'u-el said to you.

16 And Saul said to his uncle, He told us plainly that the asses were found. But of the matter of the kingdom, whereof Sam'u-el spoke, he told him not.

17 And Sam'u-el called the people together to the LORD to Miz'peh;

18 And said to the children of Is'ra-el, Thus says the LORD God of Is'ra-el, I brought up Is'ra-el out of E'gypt, and delivered you out of the hand of the E-gyp'tians, and out of the hand of all kingdoms, *and* of them that oppressed you: ^{Jehovah^{s.f.} Elohim^{p.f.}}

19 And you have this day rejected your <u>God</u>, who Himself saved you out of all your adversities and your tribulations; and you have said to Him, *Nay*, but set a king over us. Now therefore <u>present</u> yourselves before the LORD by your tribes, and by your thousands.   Elohim^{p.f.} - come

20 And when Sam'u-el had caused all the tribes of Is'ra-el to come near, the tribe of Ben'ja-min was taken.

21 When he had caused the tribe of Ben'ja-min to come near by their families, the family of Ma'tri was taken, and Saul the son of Kish was taken: and when they sought him, he could not be found.

22 Therefore they <u>enquired</u> of the LORD further, if the man should yet come *there*. And the LORD answered, Behold, he has hid himself among the stuff.   asked

23 And they ran and brought him from there: and when he stood among the people, he was <u>higher</u> than any of the people from his shoulders and upward.   taller

24 And Sam'u-el said to all the people, See you him whom the LORD has chosen, that *there is* none like him among all the people? And all the people shouted, and said, <u>God save the king</u>.   Long live the king

25 Then Sam'u-el told the people the manner of the kingdom, and wrote *it* in a book, and laid *it* up before the LORD. And Sam'u-el sent all the people away, every man to his house.

26 And Saul also went home to Gib'e-ah; and there went with him a band of men, whose hearts God had touched.

27 But the children of <u>Be'li-al</u> said, How shall this man save us? And they despised him, and brought him no presents. But he held his peace.   i.e., Satan

CHAPTER 11

THEN Na'hash the Am'mon-ite came up, and <u>encamped against</u> Ja'besh-gil'e-ad: and all the men of Ja'besh said to Na'hash, Make a <u>covenant</u> with us, and we will serve you.   besieged - agreement

2 And Na'hash the Am'mon-ite answered them, On this *condition* will I make *a* <u>covenant</u> with you, that I may thrust out all your right eyes, and lay it *for* a reproach upon all Is'ra-el. agreement

3 And the elders of Ja'besh said to him, Give us seven days' respite, that we may send messengers to all the <u>coasts</u> of Is'ra-el: and then, if *there be* no man to <u>save</u> us, we will come out to you.   territory - deliver

4 Then came the messengers to Gib'e-ah of Saul, and told the tidings in the ears of the people: and all the people lifted up their voices, and wept.

5 And, behold, Saul came after the herd out of the field; and Saul said, What *ails* the people that they weep? And they told him the tidings of the men of Ja'besh.

6 And the Spirit of God came upon Saul when he heard those tidings, and his anger was kindled greatly.

7 And he took a yoke of oxen, and hewed them in pieces, and sent *them* throughout all the <u>coasts</u> of Is'ra-el by the hands of messengers, saying, Whosoever comes not forth after Saul and after Sam'u-el, so shall it be done to his oxen. And the <u>fear</u> of the LORD fell on the people, and they came out <u>with one consent</u>.   territory - dread - as one man

8 And when he numbered them in Be'zek, the children of Is'ra-el were three hundred thousand, and the men of Ju'dah thirty thousand.

9 And they said to the messengers that came, Thus shall you say to the men of Ja'besh-gil'e-ad, To morrow, by *that time* the sun be hot, you shall have

help. And the messengers came and showed *it* to the men of Ja'besh; and they were glad. deliverance

10 Therefore the men of Ja'besh said, To morrow we will come out to you, and you shall do with us all that seems good to you.

11 And it was *so* on the morrow, that Saul put the people in three companies; and they came into the midst of the <u>host in the morning watch</u>, and slew the Am'mon-ites until the heat of the day: and it came to pass, that they which remained were scattered, so that two of them were not left together. camp - in the forenoon

12 And the people said to Sam'u-el, Who *is* he that said, Shall Saul reign over us? bring the men, that we may put them to death.

13 And Saul said, There shall not a man be put to death this day: for to day the LORD has wrought salvation in Is'ra-el.

14 Then said Sam'u-el to the people, Come, and let us go to Gil'gal, and renew the kingdom there.

15 And all the people went to Gil'gal; and there they made Saul king before the LORD in Gil'gal; and there they sacrificed sacrifices of peace offerings before the LORD; and there Saul and all the men of Is'ra-el rejoiced greatly.

CHAPTER 12

AND Sam'u-el said to all Is'ra-el, Behold, I have <u>hearkened</u> to your voice in all that you said to me, and have made a king over you.   listened

2 And now, behold, the king walks before you: and I am old and grayheaded; and, behold, my sons *are* with you: and I have walked before you from my childhood to this day.

3 Behold, here I *am*: witness against me before the LORD, and before His anointed: whose ox have I taken? or whose ass have I taken? or whom have I defrauded? whom have I oppressed? or of whose hand have I received *any* bribe to blind my eyes therewith? and I will restore it you.

4 And they said, You have not defrauded us, nor oppressed us, neither have you taken anything of any man's hand.

5 And he said to them, The LORD *is* witness against you, and His anointed *is* witness this day, that you have not found anything in my hand. And they answered, *He is* witness.

6 And Sam'u-el said to the people, *It is* the LORD that <u>advanced</u> Mo'ses and Aar'on, and that brought your fathers up out of the land of E'gypt.

appointed

7 Now therefore <u>stand still</u>, that I may reason with you before the LORD of all the righteous acts of the LORD, which He did to you and to your fathers. take your stand

8 When Ja'cob was come into E'gypt, and your fathers cried to the LORD, then the LORD sent Mo'ses and Aar'on, which brought forth your fathers out of E'gypt, and made them dwell in this place.

9 And when they forgot the LORD their <u>God</u>, He <u>sold</u> them into the hand of Sis'e-ra, captain of the host of Ha'zor, and into the hand of the Phi-lis'tines, and into the hand of the king of Mo'ab, and they fought against them. Elohim^{p.f.} - i.e., gave them to be slaves

10 And they cried to the LORD, and said, We have sinned, because we have forsaken the LORD, and have served Ba'al-im and Ash'ta-roth: but now deliver us out of the hand of our enemies, and we will serve You.

11 And the LORD sent Je-rub'ba-al, and Be'dan, and Jeph'thah, and Sam'u-el, and delivered you out of the hand of your enemies on every side, and you dwelled safe.

12 And when you saw that Na'hash the king of the children of Am'mon came against you, you said to me, Nay; but a king shall reign over us: when the LORD your <u>God</u> *was* your king. Elohim^{p.f.}

13 Now therefore behold the king whom you have chosen, *and* whom you have desired! and, behold, the LORD has set a king over you.

14 If you will <u>fear</u> the LORD, and serve Him, and obey His voice, and not rebel against the commandment of the LORD, then shall both you and also the king that reigns over you continue <u>following</u> the LORD your God: reverence - obeying

15 But if you will not obey the voice of the LORD, but rebel against the commandment of the LORD, then shall the hand of the LORD be against you, as *it was* against your fathers.

16 Now therefore stand and see this great thing, which the LORD will do before your eyes.

17 *Is it* not wheat harvest to day? I

will call to the Lord, and He shall send thunder and rain; that you may perceive and see that your wickedness *is* great, which you have done in the sight of the Lord, in asking you a king.

18 So Sam'u-el called to the Lord; and the Lord sent thunder and rain that day: and all the people greatly feared the Lord and Sam'u-el.

stood in awe of

19 And all the people said to Sam'u-el, Pray for your servants to the Lord your God, that we die not: for we have added to all our sins *this* evil, to ask us a king.

Elohim p.f.

20 And Sam'u-el said to the people, Fear not: you have done all this wickedness: yet turn not aside from following the Lord, but serve the Lord with all your heart;

21 And turn you not aside: for *then should you go* after vain *things*, which cannot profit nor deliver; for they *are* vain.

22 For the Lord will not forsake His people for His great name's sake: because it has pleased the Lord to make you His people.

ROM. 11:1

23 Moreover as for me, God forbid that I should sin against the Lord in ceasing to pray for you: but I will teach you the good and the right way:

24 Only fear the Lord and serve Him in truth with all your heart: for consider how great *things* He has done for you.

reverence

25 But if you shall still do wickedly, you shall be consumed, both you and your king.

CHAPTER 13

SAUL reigned one year; and when he had reigned two years over Is'ra-el,

2 Saul chose him three thousand *men* of Is'ra-el; *whereof* two thousand were with Saul in Mich'mash and in mount Beth'-el, and a thousand were with Jon'a-than in Gib'e-ah of Ben'ja-min: and the rest of the people he sent every man to his tent.

3 And Jon'a-than smote the garrison of the Phi-lis'tines that *was* in Ge'ba, and the Phi-lis'tines heard *of it*. And Saul blew the trumpet throughout all the land, saying, Let the He'brews hear.

attacked

4 And all Is'ra-el heard say *that* Saul had smitten a garrison of the Phi-lis'tines, and *that* Is'ra-el also was had in abomination with the Phi-lis'tines. And the people were called together after Saul to Gil'gal.

had become odious to

5 And the Phi-lis'tines gathered themselves together to fight with Is'ra-el, thirty thousand chariots, and six thousand horsemen, and people as the sand which *is* on the sea shore in multitude: and they came up, and pitched in Mich'mash, eastward from Beth-a'ven.

camped

6 When the men of Is'ra-el saw that they were in a strait, (for the people were distressed,) then the people did hide themselves in caves, and in thickets, and in rocks, and in high places, and in pits.

critical situation

7 And *some of* the He'brews went over Jor'dan to the land of Gad and Gil'e-ad. As for Saul, he *was* yet in Gil'-

gal, and all the people followed him trembling.

8 And he tarried seven days, according to the set time that Sam'u-el *had appointed*: but Sam'u-el came not to Gil'gal; and the people were scattered from him.

9 And Saul said, Bring here a burned offering to me, and peace offerings. And he offered the burned offering.

10 And it came to pass, that as soon as he had made an end of offering the burned offering, behold, Sam'u-el came; and Saul went out to meet him, that he might <u>salute</u> him.　greet

11 And Sam'u-el said, What have you done? And Saul said, Because I saw that the people were scattered from me, and *that* you came not within the days appointed, and *that* the Phi-lis'tines gathered themselves together at Mich'mash;

12 Therefore said I, The Phi-lis'tines will come down now upon me to Gil'gal, and I have not <u>made</u> <u>supplication</u> to the LORD: I forced myself therefore, and offered a burned offering.　asked the favor

13 And Sam'u-el said to Saul, You have done foolishly: you have not <u>kept</u> the commandment of the LORD your <u>God</u>, which He commanded you: for now would the LORD have established your kingdom upon Is'ra-el for ever.　obeyed - Elohim

14 But now your kingdom shall not continue: the LORD has sought Him a man after His own heart, and the LORD has commanded Him *to be* captain over His people, because you have not kept *that* which the LORD commanded you.　ACTS 13:22 obeyed

15 And Sam'u-el arose, and got him up from Gil'gal to Gib'e-ah of Ben'ja-min. And Saul numbered the people *that were* present with him, about six hundred men.

16 And Saul, and Jon'a-than his son, and the people *that were* present with them, abode in Gib'e-ah of Ben'ja-min: but the Phi-lis'tines encamped in Mich'mash.

17 And the <u>spoilers</u> came out of the camp of the Phi-lis'tines in three companies: one company turned to the way *that leads* to Oph'rah, to the land of Shu'al:　raiders

18 And another company turned the way *to* Beth-ho'ron: and another company turned *to* the way of the border that looks to the valley of Ze-bo'im toward the wilderness.

19 Now there was no smith found throughout all the land of Is'ra-el: for the Phi-lis'tines said, Less the He'brews make *them* swords or spears:

20 But all the Is'ra-el-ites went down to the Phi-lis'tines, to sharpen every man his <u>share</u>, and his <u>coulter</u>, and his ax, and his <u>mattock</u>.　sickle - farm tool - hoe

21 Yet they had a file for the <u>mattocks</u>, and for the <u>coulters</u>, and for the forks, and for the axes, and to sharpen the goads.

22 So it came to pass in the day of battle, that there was neither sword nor spear found in the hand of any of the people that *were* with Saul and Jon'a-than: but with Saul and with Jon'a-than his son was there found.

23 And the garrison of the Phi-lis'tines went out to the passage of Mich'mash.

CHAPTER 14

NOW it came to pass upon a day, that Jon'a-than the son of Saul said to the young man that <u>bare</u> his armor, Come, and let us go over to the Phi-lis'tines' garrison, that *is* on the other side. But he told not his father. carried

2 And Saul tarried in the <u>uttermost part</u> of Gib'e-ah under a pomegranate tree which *is* in Mig'ron: and the people that *were* with him *were* about six hundred men; outskirts

3 And A-hi'ah, the son of A-hi'tub, I-cha-bod's brother, the son of Phin'e-has, the son of E'li, the LORD's priest in Shi'loh, wearing an <u>ephod</u>. And the people knew not that Jon'a-than was gone. priestly garment

4 And between the passages, by which Jon'a-than sought to go over to the Phi-lis'tines' garrison, *there was* a sharp rock on the one side, and a sharp rock on the other side: and the name of the one *was* Bo'zez, and the name of the other Se'neh.

5 The forefront of the one *was* situate northward over against Mich'mash, and the other southward opposite Gib'e-ah.

6 And Jon'a-than said to the young man that bare his armor, Come, and let us go over to the garrison of these uncircumcised: it may be that the LORD will work for us: for *there is* no <u>restraint</u> to the LORD to save by many or by few. limitation

7 And his armorbearer said to him, Do all that *is* in your heart: turn you; behold, I *am* with you according to your heart.

8 Then said Jon'a-than, Behold, we will pass over to *these* men, and we will <u>discover</u> ourselves to them. reveal

9 If they say thus to us, Tarry until we come to you; then we will stand still in our place, and will not go up to them.

10 But if they say thus, Come up to us; then we will go up: for the LORD has delivered them into our hand: and this *shall be* a sign to us.

11 And both of them <u>discovered</u> themselves to the garrison of the Phi-lis'tines: and the Phi-lis'tines said, Behold, the He'brews come forth out of the holes where they had hid themselves. revealed

12 And the men of the garrison answered Jon'a-than and his armorbearer, and said, Come up to us, and we will show you a thing. And Jon'a-than said to his armorbearer, Come up after me: for the LORD has delivered them into the hand of Is'ra-el.

13 And Jon'a-than climbed up upon his hands and upon his feet, and his armorbearer after him: and they fell before Jon'a-than; and his armorbearer slew after him.

14 And that first slaughter, which Jon'a-than and his armorbearer made, was about twenty men, within as it were an half acre of land, *which* a yoke *of oxen might plow*.

15 And there was trembling in the host, in the field, and among all the

people: the garrison, and the <u>spoil-ers</u>, they also trembled, and the earth quaked: so it was a very great trembling. raiders

16 And the watchmen of Saul in Gib'e-ah of Ben'ja-min looked; and, behold, the multitude melted away, and they went on beating down *one another*.

17 Then said Saul to the people that *were* with him, Number now, and see who is gone from us. And when they had numbered, behold, Jon'a-than and his armorbearer *were* not *there*.

18 And Saul said to A-hi'ah, Bring here the ark of <u>God</u>. For the ark of God was at that time with the chil-dren of Is'ra-el. Elohim^{p.f.}

19 And it came to pass, while Saul talked to the priest, that the <u>noise</u> that *was* in the host of the Phi-lis'tines went on and increased: and Saul said to the priest, Withdraw your hand. commotion

20 And Saul and all the people that *were* with him assembled themselves, and they came to the battle: and, be-hold, every man's sword was against his fellow, *and there was* a very great discomfiture.

21 Moreover the He'brews *that* were with the Phi-lis'tines before that time, which went up with them into the camp *from the country* round about, even they also *turned* to be with the Is'ra-el-ites that *were* with Saul and Jon'a-than.

22 Likewise all the men of Is'ra-el which had hid themselves in mount E'phra-im, *when* they heard that the Phi-lis'tines fled, even they also fol-lowed hard after them in the battle.

23 So the Lord saved Is'ra-el that day: and the battle passed over to Beth-a'ven.

24 And the men of Is'ra-el were dis-tressed that day: for Saul had <u>ad-jured</u> the people, saying, Cursed *be* the man that eats *any* food until evening, that I may be avenged on my enemies. So none of the people tasted *any* food. bound under oath

25 And all *they of* the land came to a wood; and there was honey upon the ground.

26 And when the people were come into the <u>wood</u>, behold, the honey dropped; but no man put his hand to his mouth: for the people feared the oath. forest

27 But Jon'a-than heard not when his father <u>charged</u> the people with the oath: wherefore he put forth the end of the rod that *was* in his hand, and dipped it in an honeycomb, and put his hand to his mouth; and his eyes were <u>enlightened</u>. bound - brightened

28 Then answered one of the people, and said, Your father <u>straitly charged</u> the people with an oath, saying, Cursed *be* the man that eats *any* food this day. And the people were faint. strickly bound

29 Then said Jon'a-than, My father has troubled the land: see, I pray you, how mine eyes have <u>been en-lightened</u>, because I tasted a little of this honey. brightened

30 How much more, if <u>haply</u> the people had eaten freely to day of the <u>spoil</u> of their enemies which they found? for

had there not been now a much greater slaughter among the Phi-lis'tines?   only - booty

31 And they <u>smote</u> the Phi-lis'tines that day from Mich'mash to Aij'a-lon: and the people were very faint.   struck down

32 And the people flew upon the spoil, and took sheep, and oxen, and calves, and slew *them* on the ground: and the people did eat *them* with the blood.

33 Then they told Saul, saying, Be-hold, the people sin against the LORD, in that they eat with the blood. And he said, You have <u>transgressed</u>: roll a great stone to me this day.   broken faith

34 And Saul said, Disperse your-selves among the people, and say to them, Bring me here every man his ox, and every man his sheep, and slay *them* here, and eat; and sin not against the LORD in eating with the blood. And all the people brought every man his ox <u>with him</u> that night, and slew *them* there.   in his hand

35 And Saul built an altar to the LORD: the same was the first altar that he built to the LORD.

36 And Saul said, Let us go down after the Phi-lis'tines by night, and spoil them until the morning light, and let us not leave a man of them. And they said, Do whatsoever seems good to you. Then said the priest, Let us draw near here to <u>God</u>.   Elohim^p.f.

37 And Saul asked <u>counsel of God</u>, Shall I go down after the Phi-lis'tines? will You deliver them into the hand of Is'ra-el? But He an-swered him not that day.   inquired

38 And Saul said, Draw you near here, all the chief of the people: and know and see wherein this sin has been this day.

39 For, *as* the LORD lives, which saves Is'ra-el, though it be in Jon'a-than my son, he shall surely die. But *there was* not a man among all the people *that* answered him.

40 Then said he to all Is'ra-el, Be you on one side, and I and Jon'a-than my son will be on the other side. And the people said to Saul, Do what seems good to you.

41 Therefore Saul said to the LORD God of Is'ra-el, <u>Give a perfect *lot*</u>. And Saul and Jon'a-than were taken: but the people escaped.
                    Give me the right answer

42 And Saul said, Cast *lots* between me and Jon'a-than my son. And Jon'a-than was taken.

43 Then Saul said to Jon'a-than, Tell me what you have done. And Jon'a-than told him, and said, I did but taste a little honey with the end of the rod that *was* in my hand, *and*, lo, I must die.

44 And Saul answered, <u>God</u> do so and more also: for you shall surely die, Jon'a-than.   Elohim^p.f.

45 And the people said to Saul, Shall Jon'a-than die, who has <u>wrought</u> this great <u>salvation</u> in Is'ra-el? God for-bid: *as* the LORD lives, there shall not one hair of his head fall to the ground; for he has <u>wrought</u> with <u>God</u> this day. So the people rescued Jon'a-than, that he died not.

LUKE 21:18 brought about - i.e., Heb. Jeshua - worked

46 Then Saul <u>went up from following</u>

the Phi-lis'tines: and the Phi-lis'tines went to their own place.　stopped pursuing

47 So Saul took the kingdom over Is'ra-el, and fought against all his enemies on every side, against Mo'ab, and against the children of Am'mon, and against E'dom, and against the kings of Zo'bah, and against the Phi-lis'tines: and wherever he turned himself, he vexed *them*.　harassed

48 And he gathered an host, and smote the Am'a-lek-ites, and delivered Is'ra-el out of the hands of them that spoiled them.

49 Now the sons of Saul were Jon'a-than, and Ish'u-i, and Mel'chi-shu'a: and the names of his two daughters *were these*; the name of the firstborn Me'rab, and the name of the younger Mi'chal:

50 And the name of Saul's wife *was* A-hin'o-am, the daughter of A-him'a-az: and the name of the captain of his host *was* Ab'ner, the son of Ner, Saul's uncle.

51 And Kish *was* the father of Saul; and Ner the father of Ab'ner *was* the son of A-bi'el.

52 And there was sore war against the Phi-lis'tines all the days of Saul: and when Saul saw any strong man, or any valiant man, he took him to him.　a severe

CHAPTER 15

SAM'U-EL also said to Saul, The LORD sent me to anoint you *to be* king over His people, over Is'ra-el: now therefore hearken you to the voice of the words of the LORD.

2 Thus says the LORD of hosts, I remember *that* which Am'a-lek did to Is'ra-el, how he laid *wait* for him in the way, when he came up from E'gypt.　Jehovah's Tsebaoth

3 Now go and smite Am'a-lek, and utterly destroy all that they have, and spare them not; but slay both man and woman, infant and suckling, ox and sheep, camel and ass.　attack

4 And Saul gathered the people together, and numbered them in Tel'a-im, two hundred thousand footmen, and ten thousand men of Ju'dah.

5 And Saul came to a city of Am'a-lek, and laid wait in the valley.

6 And Saul said to the Ken'ites, Go, depart, get you down from among the Am'a-lek-ites, less I destroy you with them: for you showed kindness to all the children of Is'ra-el, when they came up out of E'gypt. So the Ken'ites departed from among the Am'a-lek-ites.

7 And Saul smote the Am'a-lek-ites from Hav'i-lah *until* you come to Shur, that *is* opposite E'gypt.

8 And he took A'gag the king of the Am'a-lek-ites alive, and utterly destroyed all the people with the edge of the sword.

9 But Saul and the people spared A'gag, and the best of the sheep, and of the oxen, and of the fatlings, and the lambs, and all *that was* good, and would not utterly destroy them: but every thing *that was* vile and refuse, that they destroyed utterly.

10 Then came the word of the LORD to Sam'u-el, saying,

11 It <u>repents</u> Me that I have set up Saul *to be* king: for he is turned back from following Me, and has not <u>per-formed</u> My commandments. And it grieved Sam'u-el; and he cried to the LORD all night.   grieved - carried out

12 And when Sam'u-el rose early to meet Saul in the morning, it was told Sam'u-el, saying, Saul came to Car'mel, and, behold, he set him up a place, and is gone about, and passed on, and gone down to Gil'gal.

13 And Sam'u-el came to Saul: and Saul said to him, Blessed *be* you of the LORD: I have <u>performed</u> the commandment of the LORD.

14 And Sam'u-el said, What *means* then this bleating of the sheep in my ears, and the lowing of the oxen which I hear?

15 And Saul said, They have brought them from the Am'a-lek-ites: for the people spared the best of the sheep and of the oxen, to sacrifice to the LORD your <u>God</u>; and the rest we have utterly destroyed.   Elohim^p.f.

16 Then Sam'u-el said to Saul, Stay, and I will tell you what the LORD has said to me this night. And he said to him, Say on.

17 And Sam'u-el said, When you *were* little in your own sight, *were* you not *made* the head of the tribes of Is'ra-el, and the LORD anointed you king over Is'ra-el?

18 And the LORD sent you on a journey, and said, Go and utterly destroy the sinners the Am'a-lek-ites, and fight against them until they be <u>consumed</u>.   destroyed

19 Why then did you not obey the voice of the LORD, but did <u>fly upon</u> the spoil, and did evil in the sight of the LORD?   rush upon the booty

20 And Saul said to Sam'u-el, Yea, I have obeyed the voice of the LORD, and have gone the way which the LORD sent me, and have brought A'gag the king of Am'a-lek, and have utterly destroyed the Am'a-lek-ites.

21 But the people took of the <u>spoil</u>, sheep and oxen, the chief of the things which should have been utterly destroyed, to sacrifice to the LORD your God in Gil'gal.   booty

22 And Sam'u-el said, Has the LORD *as great* delight in burned offerings and sacrifices, as in obeying the voice of the LORD? Behold, to obey *is* better than sacrifice, *and* to hearken than the fat of rams.   MARK 12:33

23 For rebellion *is as* the sin of <u>witchcraft</u>, and stubbornness *is as* iniquity and idolatry. Because you have rejected the word of the LORD, He has also rejected you from *being* king.   fortune telling

24 And Saul said to Sam'u-el, I have sinned: for I have transgressed the commandment of the LORD, and your words: because I feared the people, and obeyed their voice.

25 Now therefore, I pray you, pardon my sin, and turn again with me, that I may worship the LORD.

26 And Sam'u-el said to Saul, I will not return with you: for you have rejected the word of the LORD, and the LORD has rejected you from being king over Is'ra-el.

27 And as Sam'u-el turned about to go away, he laid hold upon the skirt of his mantle, and it <u>rent</u>.   tore

28 And Sam'u-el said to him, The LORD has <u>rent</u> the kingdom of Is'ra-el from you this day, and has given it to a neighbor of yours, *that is* better than you.

29 And also the Strength of Is'ra-el will not lie nor <u>repent</u>: for He is not a man, that He should <u>repent</u>.   change His mind

30 Then he said, I have sinned: *yet* <u>honor</u> me now, I pray you, before the elders of my people, and before Is'ra-el, and turn again with me, that I may worship the LORD your God.   treat me with honor - Elohim^{p.f.}

31 So Sam'u-el turned again after Saul; and Saul worshiped the LORD.

32 Then said Sam'u-el, Bring you here to me A'gag the king of the Am'a-lek-ites. And A'gag came to him <u>delicately</u>. And A'gag said, Surely the bitterness of death is past.   in chains

33 And Sam'u-el said, As your sword has made women childless, so shall your mother be childless among women. And Sam'u-el hewed A'gag in pieces before the LORD in Gil'gal.

34 Then Sam'u-el went to Ra'mah; and Saul went up to his house to Gib'e-ah of Saul.

35 And Sam'u-el came no more to see Saul until the day of his death: nevertheless Sam'u-el mourned for Saul: and the LORD <u>repented</u> that He had made Saul king over Is'ra-el.   regretted

CHAPTER 16

AND the LORD said to Sam'u-el, How long will you <u>mourn</u> for Saul, seeing I have rejected him from <u>reigning</u> over Is'ra-el? fill your horn with oil, and go, I will send you to Jes'se the Beth'-le-hem-ite: for I have <u>provided</u> Me a king among his sons.   grieve - being king - selected

2 And Sam'u-el said, How can I go? if Saul hear *it*, he will kill me. And the LORD said, Take an heifer with you, and say, I am come to sacrifice to the LORD.

3 And call Jes'se to the sacrifice, and I will show you what you shall do: and you shall anoint to Me *him* whom I <u>name to you</u>.   designate

4 And Sam'u-el did that which the LORD spoke, and came to Beth'-le-hem. And the elders of the town trembled at his coming, and said, Come you peaceably?

5 And he said, Peaceably: I am come to sacrifice to the LORD: <u>sanctify</u> yourselves, and come with me to the sacrifice. And he sanctified Jes'se and his sons, and called them to the sacrifice.   consecrate

6 And it came to pass, when they were come, that he looked on E-li'ab, and said, Surely the LORD's anointed *is* before Him.

7 But the LORD said to Sam'u-el, Look not on his countenance, or on the height of his stature; because I have <u>refused</u> him: for *the LORD sees* not as man sees; for man looks on the outward appearance, but the LORD looks on the heart.   LUKE 16:15 rejected

8 Then Jes'se called A-bin'a-dab, and made him pass before Sam'u-el. And he

said, Neither has the LORD chosen this.

9 Then Jes'se made Sham'mah to pass by. And he said, Neither has the LORD chosen this.

10 Again, Jes'se made seven of his sons to pass before Sam'u-el. And Sam'u-el said to Jes'se, The LORD has not chosen these.

11 And Sam'u-el said to Jes'se, Are here all *your* children? And he said, There remains yet the youngest, and, behold, he keeps the sheep. And Sam'u-el said to Jes'se, Send and bring him: for we will not sit down till he come here.

12 And he sent, and brought him in. Now he *was* ruddy, *and* with of a beautiful countenance, and goodly to look to. And the LORD said, Arise, anoint him: for this *is* he.   handsome

13 Then Sam'u-el took the horn of oil, and anointed him in the midst of his brethren: and the Spirit of the LORD came upon Da'vid from that day forward. So Sam'u-el rose up, and went to Ra'mah.

14 But the Spirit of the LORD departed from Saul, and an evil spirit from the LORD troubled him.   terrorized

15 And Saul's servants said to him, Behold now, an evil spirit from God troubles you.

16 Let our lord now command your servants, *which are* before you, to seek out a man, *who is* a cunning player on an harp: and it shall come to pass, when the evil spirit from God is upon you, that he shall play with his hand, and you shall be well.   Elohim^{p.f.}

17 And Saul said to his servants, Provide me now a man that can play well, and bring *him* to me.

18 Then answered one of the servants, and said, Behold, I have seen a son of Jes'se the Beth'-le-hem-ite, *that is* cunning in playing, and a mighty valiant man, and a man of war, and prudent in matters, and a comely person, and the LORD *is* with him.

19 Wherefore Saul sent messengers to Jes'se, and said, Send me Da'vid your son, which *is* with the sheep.

20 And Jes'se took an ass *laden* with bread, and a bottle of wine, and a kid, and sent *them* by Da'vid his son to Saul.

21 And Da'vid came to Saul, and stood before him: and he loved him greatly; and he became his armorbearer.   attended

22 And Saul sent to Jes'se, saying, Let Da'vid, I pray you, stand before me; for he has found favor in my sight.

23 And it came to pass, when the *evil* spirit from God was upon Saul, that Da'vid took an harp, and played with his hand: so Saul was refreshed, and was well, and the evil spirit departed from him.   Elohim^{p.f.}

CHAPTER 17

NOW the Phi-lis'tines gathered together their armies to battle, and were gathered together at Sho'choh, which *belongs* to Ju'dah, and pitched

between Sho'choh and A-ze'kah, in E'phes-dam'mim.

2 And Saul and the men of Is'ra-el were gathered together, and pitched by the valley of E'lah, and <u>set the battle in array</u> against the Phi-lis'tines. <small>arranged their battle lines</small>

3 And the Phi-lis'tines stood on a mountain on the one side, and Is'ra-el stood on a mountain on the other side: and *there was* a valley between them.

4 And there went out a champion out of the camp of the Phi-lis'tines, named Go-li'ath, of Gath, whose height *was* <u>six cubits and a span</u>. <small>9 feet 9 inches</small>

5 And *he had* an helmet of brass upon his head, and he *was* <u>armed</u> with a coat of <u>mail</u>; and the weight of the coat *was* five thousand shek-els of brass. <small>clothed - armor</small>

6 And *he had* <u>greaves</u> of brass upon his legs, and a <u>target</u> of brass be-tween his shoulders. <small>leg guards - covering</small>

7 And the staff of his spear *was* like a weaver's beam; and his spear's head *weighed* <u>six hundred shekels</u> of iron: and one bearing a shield went before him. <small>20 pounds</small>

8 And he stood and cried to the armies of Is'ra-el, and said to them, Why are you come out <u>to set *your* battle in array</u>? *am* not I a Phi-lis'tine, and you servants to Saul? choose you a man for you, and let him come down to me. <small>and line up for battle</small>

9 If he be able to fight with me, and to kill me, then will we be your ser-vants: but if I prevail against him, and kill him, then shall you be our servants, and serve us.

10 And the Phi-lis'tine said, I <u>defy</u> the armies of Is'ra-el this day; give me a man, that we may fight together. <small>challenge</small>

11 When Saul and all Is'ra-el heard those words of the Phi-lis'tine, they were dismayed, and greatly afraid.

12 Now Da'vid *was* the son of that Eph'rath-ite of Beth'-le-hem-ju'dah, whose name *was* Jes'se; and he had eight sons: and the man <u>went</u> among men *for* an old man in the days of Saul. <small>passed</small>

13 And the three eldest sons of Jes'se went *and* followed Saul to the battle: and the names of his three sons that went to the battle *were* E-li'ab the firstborn, and next to him A-bin'a-dab, and the third Sham'mah.

14 And Da'vid *was* the youngest: and the three eldest followed Saul.

15 But Da'vid went and returned from Saul to feed his father's sheep at Beth'-le-hem.

16 And the Phi-lis'tine drew near morning and evening, and presented himself forty days.

17 And Jes'se said to Da'vid his son, Take now for your brethren an ephah of this parched *corn*, and these ten loaves, and run to the camp to your brethren; <small>grain</small>

18 And carry these ten cheeses to the captain of *their* thousand, and look how your brethren fare, and take their <u>pledge</u>. <small>token of receipt</small>

19 Now Saul, and they, and all the men of Is'ra-el, *were* in the valley of E'lah, fighting with the Phi-lis'tines.

20 And Da'vid rose up early in the morning, and left the sheep with a keeper, and took, and went, as Jes'se

had commanded him; and he came to the <u>trench</u>, as the host was going forth to the fight, and shouted for the battle.   <small>circle of the camp</small>

21 For Is'ra-el and the Phi-lis'tines had put the battle in array, army against army.   <small>army</small>

22 And Da'vid left his <u>carriage</u> in the hand of the keeper of the <u>carriage</u>, and ran into the army, and came and <u>saluted</u> his brethren.   <small>baggage - greeted</small>

23 And as he talked with them, behold, there came up the champion, the Phi-lis'tine of Gath, Go-li'ath by name, out of the armies of the Phi-lis'tines, and spoke according to the same words: and Da'vid heard *them*.

24 And all the men of Is'ra-el, when they saw the man, fled from him, and were <u>sore</u> afraid.   <small>greatly</small>

25 And the men of Is'ra-el said, Have you seen this man that is come up? surely to defy Is'ra-el is he come up: and it shall be, *that* the man who kills him, the king will enrich him with great riches, and will give him his daughter, and make his father's house free in Is'ra-el.

26 And Da'vid spoke to the men that stood by him, saying, What shall be done to the man that kills this Phi-lis'tine, and takes away the <u>reproach</u> from Is'ra-el? for who *is* this uncircumcised Phi-lis'tine, that he should <u>defy</u> the armies of the living <u>God</u>?   <small>disgrace - challenge - Elohim^{p.f.}</small>

27 And the people answered him after this manner, saying, So shall it be done to the man that kills him.

28 And E-li'ab his eldest brother heard when he spoke to the men; and E-li'ab's anger was kindled against Da'vid, and he said, Why came you down here? and with whom have you left those few sheep in the wilderness? I know your pride, and the <u>naughtiness</u> of your heart; for you are come down that you might see the battle.   <small>wickedness</small>

29 And Da'vid said, What have I now done? *Is there* not a cause?

30 And he turned from him toward another, and spoke <u>after the same manner</u>: and the people answered him again after the former manner.   <small>as before</small>

31 And when the words were heard which Da'vid spoke, they <u>rehearsed</u> *them* before Saul: and he sent for him.   <small>told</small>

32 And Da'vid said to Saul, Let no man's heart fail because of him; your servant will go and fight with this Phi-lis'tine.

33 And Saul said to Da'vid, You are not able to go against this Phi-lis'tine to fight with him: for you *are but* a youth, and he a man of war from his youth.

34 And Da'vid said to Saul, Your servant kept his father's sheep, and there came a lion, and a bear, and took a lamb out of the flock:

35 And I went out after him, and smote it, and delivered *it* out of its mouth: and when it arose against me, I caught *it* by its beard, and smote it, and slew it.

36 Your servant slew both the lion and the bear: and this uncircumcised Phi-lis'tine shall be as one of them, seeing he has defied the armies of the living <u>God</u>.   <small>Elohim^{p.f.}</small>

37 Da'vid said moreover, The LORD that delivered me out of the paw of the lion, and out of the paw of the bear, He will deliver me out of the hand of this Phi-lis'tine. And Saul said to Da'vid, Go, and the LORD be with you.

38 And Saul <u>armed</u> Da'vid with his armor, and he put an helmet of brass upon his head; also he <u>armed</u> him with a coat of mail.   clothed

39 And Da'vid girded his sword upon his armor, and he <u>assayed</u> to go; for he had not proved *it*. And Da'vid said to Saul, I cannot go with these; for I have not <u>proved</u> *them*. And Da'vid put them off him.   wanted - tried it out

40 And he took his staff in his hand, and chose him five smooth stones out of the <u>brook</u>, and put them in a shepherd's bag which he had, even in a <u>scrip</u>; and his sling *was* in his hand: and he drew near to the Phi-lis'tine.   valley - pouch

41 And the Phi-lis'tine came on and drew near to Da'vid; and the man that bare the shield *went* before him.

42 And when the Phi-lis'tine looked about, and saw Da'vid, he <u>disdained</u> him: for he was *but* a youth, and ruddy, and of a fair countenance.   despised

43 And the Phi-lis'tine said to Da'vid, *Am* I a dog, that you come to me with <u>staves</u>? And the Phi-lis'tine cursed Da'vid by his gods.   sticks

44 And the Phi-lis'tine said to Da'vid, Come to me, and I will give your flesh to the fowls of the air, and to the beasts of the field.

45 Then said Da'vid to the Phi-lis'-tine, You come to me with a sword, and with a spear, and with a shield: but I come to you in the name of the <u>LORD of hosts</u>, the <u>God</u> of the armies of Is'ra-el, whom you have defied.   Jehovah[s.f.] Tsebaoth

46 This day will the LORD deliver you into my hand; and I will <u>smite you</u>, and take your head from you; and I will give the carcases of the host of the Phi-lis'tines this day to the fowls of the air, and to the wild beasts of the earth; that all the earth may know that there is a God in Is'ra-el.   strike you down

47 And all this assembly shall know that the LORD saves not with sword and spear: for the battle *is* the LORD's, and He will give you into our hands.

48 And it came to pass, when the Phi-lis'tine arose, and came and drew near to meet Da'vid, that Da'vid <u>hasted</u>, and ran toward the army to meet the Phi-lis'tine.   hurried

49 And Da'vid put his hand in his bag, and took from it a stone, and slang *it*, and smote the Phi-lis'tine in his forehead, that the stone sunk into his forehead; and he fell upon his face to the earth.

50 So Da'vid prevailed over the Phi-lis'tine with a sling and with a stone, and smote the Phi-lis'tine, and slew him; but *there was* no sword in the hand of Da'vid.

51 Therefore Da'vid ran, and stood upon the Phi-lis'tine, and took his sword, and drew it out of the sheath thereof, and slew him, and cut off his head therewith. And when the Phi-lis'tines saw their champion was dead, they fled.

52 And the men of Is'ra-el and of Ju'dah arose, and shouted, and pursued the Phi-lis'tines, <u>until you come</u> to the valley, and to the gates of Ek'ron. And the wounded of the Phi-lis'tines fell down by the way to Sha-a-ra'im, even to Gath, and to Ek'ron. _{as far as}

53 And the children of Is'ra-el returned from chasing after the Phi-lis'tines, and they <u>spoiled their tents</u>. _{plundered their camp}

54 And Da'vid took the head of the Phi-lis'tine, and brought it to Je-ru'sa-lem; but he put his armor in his tent.

55 And when Saul saw Da'vid go forth against the Phi-lis'tine, he said to Ab'ner, the captain of the host, Ab'ner, whose son is this youth? And Ab'ner said, *As* <u>your soul lives</u>, O king, I cannot tell. _{By your life}

56 And the king said, Enquire you whose son the <u>stripling</u> *is*. _{youth}

57 And as Da'vid returned from the slaughter of the Phi-lis'tine, Ab'ner took him, and brought him before Saul with the head of the Phi-lis'tine in his hand.

58 And Saul said to him, Whose son *are* you, *you* young man? And Da'vid answered, *I am* the son of your servant Jes'se the Beth'-le-hem-ite.

CHAPTER 18

AND it came to pass, when he had <u>made an end of</u> speaking to Saul, that the soul of Jon'a-than <u>was knit</u> with the soul of Da'vid, and Jon'a-than loved him as his own soul. _{finished - i.e., became fast friends}

2 And Saul took him that day, and would let him go no more home to his father's house.

3 Then Jon'a-than and Da'vid made a <u>covenant</u>, because he loved him as his own soul. _{agreement} ^{P02 470}

4 And Jon'a-than stripped himself of the robe that *was* upon him, and gave it to Da'vid, and his garments, even to his sword, and to his bow, and to his girdle.

5 And Da'vid went out wherever Saul sent him, *and* behaved himself wisely: and Saul set him over the men of war, and he was accepted in the sight of all the people, and also in the sight of Saul's servants.

6 And it came to pass as they came, when Da'vid was returned from the slaughter of the Phi-lis'tine, that the women came out of all cities of Is'ra-el, singing and dancing, to meet king Saul, with tabrets, with joy, and with instruments of music.

7 And the women <u>answered *one another*</u> as they played, and said, Saul has slain his thousands, and Da'vid his ten thousands. _{sang}

8 And Saul was very angry, and the saying displeased him; and he said, They have ascribed to Da'vid ten thousands, and to me they have ascribed *but* thousands: and *what* can he have more but the kingdom? ^{M20 535}

9 And Saul <u>eyed</u> Da'vid from that day and forward. _{looked at David with suspicion}

10 And it came to pass on the <u>morrow</u>, that the evil spirit from <u>God</u> came upon Saul, and he prophesied in the midst of the house: and Da'vid played with his hand, as at other times: and *there was* a javelin in Saul's hand. _{next day - Elohim^{p.c.}}

11 And Saul cast the javelin; for he said, I will smite Da'vid even to the wall *with it*. And Da'vid <u>avoided</u> out of his presence twice. _{escaped}

12 And Saul was afraid of Da'vid, because the LORD was with him, and was departed from Saul.

13 Therefore Saul <u>removed</u> him from him, and made him his captain over a thousand; and he went out and came in before the people. _{sent}

14 And Da'vid behaved himself wisely in all his ways; and the LORD *was* with him.

15 Wherefore when Saul saw that he behaved himself very wisely, he <u>was afraid of</u> him. _{dreaded}

16 But all Is'ra-el and Ju'dah loved Da'vid, because he went out and came in before them.

17 And Saul said to Da'vid, Behold my elder daughter Me'rab, her will I give you to wife: only be you valiant for me, and fight the LORD's battles. For Saul said, Let not my hand be upon him, but let the hand of the Phi-lis'tines be upon him.

18 And Da'vid said to Saul, Who *am* I? and what *is* my life, *or* my father's family in Is'ra-el, that I should be son in law to the king?

19 But it came to pass at the time when Me'rab Saul's daughter should have been given to Da'vid, that she was given to A'dri-el the Me-hol'ath-ite to wife.

20 And Mi'chal Saul's daughter loved Da'vid: and they told Saul, and the thing pleased him.

21 And Saul said, I will give him her, that she may be a <u>snare</u> to him, and that the hand of the Phi-lis'tines may be against him. Wherefore Saul said to Da'vid, You shall this day be my son in law <u>in *the one* of the two</u>. _{lure - a second time}

22 And Saul commanded his servants, *saying*, <u>Commune</u> with Da'vid secretly, and say, Behold, the king has delight in you, and all his servants love you: now therefore be the king's son in law. _{Speak}

23 And Saul's servants spoke those words in the ears of Da'vid. And Da'vid said, Seem it to you *a* light *thing* to be a king's son in law, seeing that *I am* a poor man, and lightly esteemed?

24 And the servants of Saul told him, saying, On this manner spoke Da'vid.

25 And Saul said, Thus shall you say to Da'vid, The king desires not any dowry, but an hundred foreskins of the Phi-lis'tines, to be avenged of the king's enemies. But Saul thought to make Da'vid <u>fall</u> by the hand of the Phi-lis'tines. _{killed}

26 And when his servants told Da'vid these words, it pleased Da'vid well to be the king's son in law: and the days were not expired.

27 Wherefore Da'vid arose and went, he and his men, and slew of the Phi-lis'tines two hundred men; and Da'vid brought their foreskins, and they gave them in full <u>tale</u> to the king, that he might be the king's son in law. And Saul gave him Mi'chal his daughter to wife. _{number}

28 And Saul saw and knew that the

LORD *was* with Da'vid, and *that* Mi'chal Saul's daughter loved him. 29 And Saul was yet the more afraid of Da'vid; and Saul became Da'vid's enemy <u>continually</u>. the rest of his days

30 Then the princes of the Phi-lis'tines went forth: and it came to pass, after they went forth, *that* Da'vid behaved himself more wisely than all the servants of Saul; so that his name was much set by.

CHAPTER 19

AND Saul spoke to Jon'a-than his son, and to all his servants, that they should kill Da'vid. 2 But Jon'a-than Saul's son de-lighted much in Da'vid: and Jon'a-than told Da'vid, saying, Saul my father seeks to kill you: now there-fore, I pray you, take heed to your-self until the morning, and abide in a secret *place*, and hide yourself: 3 And I will go out and stand be-side my father in the field where you *are*, and I will <u>commune</u> with my father of you; and what I see, that I will tell you. speak

4 And Jon'a-than spoke good of Da'vid to Saul his father, and said to him, Let not the king sin against his servant, against Da'vid; be-cause he has not sinned against you, and because his works *have been* <u>to you-ward very good</u>:

very beneficial to you

5 For he did put his life in his hand, and slew the Phi-lis'tine, and the LORD wrought a great salvation for all Is'ra-el: you saw *it*, and did rejoice:

why then will you sin against inno-cent blood, to slay Da'vid without a cause? 6 And Saul hearkened to the voice of Jon'a-than: and Saul swear, *As* the LORD lives, he shall not be slain. 7 And Jon'a-than called Da'vid, and Jon'a-than showed him all those things. And Jon'a-than brought Da'vid to Saul, and he was in his presence, as in times past. 8 And there was war again: and Da'vid went out, and fought with the Phi-lis'tines, and slew them with a great slaughter; and they fled from him. 9 And the evil spirit from the LORD was upon Saul, as he sat in his house with his javelin in his hand: and Da'vid played <u>with *his* hand</u>. harp

10 And Saul sought to <u>smite</u> Da'vid even to the wall with the javelin; but he slipped away out of Saul's pres-ence, and he smote the javelin into the wall: and Da'vid fled, and es-caped that night. pin

11 Saul also sent messengers to Da'vid's house, to watch him, and to slay him in the morning: and Mi'chal Da'vid's wife told him, say-ing, If you save not your life to night, to morrow you shall be slain. 12 So Mi'chal let Da'vid down through a window: and he went, and fled, and escaped. 13 And Mi'chal took an image, and laid *it* in the bed, and put a pillow of goats' *hair* for his <u>bolster</u>, and covered *it* with a cloth. head

14 And when Saul sent messengers to take Da'vid, she said, he is sick.

15 And Saul sent the messengers *again* to see Da'vid, saying, Bring him up to me in the bed, that I may slay him.

16 And when the messengers were come in, behold, *there was* an image in the bed, with a pillow of goats' *hair* for his <u>bolster</u>. head

17 And Saul said to Mi'chal, Why have you deceived me so, and sent away my enemy, that he is escaped? And Mi'chal answered Saul, He said to me, Let me go; why should I kill you?

18 So Da'vid fled, and escaped, and came to Sam'u-el to Ra'mah, and told him all that Saul had done to him. And he and Sam'u-el went and dwelled in Na'ioth.

19 And it was told Saul, saying, Behold, Da'vid *is* at Na'ioth in Ra'mah.

20 And Saul sent messengers to take Da'vid: and when they saw the company of the prophets prophesying, and Sam'u-el standing *as* appointed over them, the Spirit of <u>God</u> was upon the messengers of Saul, and they also prophesied. Elohim^{p.f.}

21 And when it was told Saul, he sent other messengers, and they prophesied likewise. And Saul sent messengers again the third time, and they prophesied also.

22 Then went he also to Ra'mah, and came to a great well that *is* in Se'chu: and he asked and said, Where *are* Sam'u-el and Da'vid? And *one* said, Behold, *they be* at Na'ioth in Ra'mah.

23 And he went there to Na'ioth in Ra'mah: and the Spirit of <u>God</u> was upon him also, and he went on, and prophesied, until he came to Na'ioth in Ra'mah. Elohim^{p.f.}

24 And he stripped off his clothes also, and prophesied before Sam'u-el in like manner, and lay down naked all that day and all that night. Wherefore they say, *Is* Saul also among the prophets?

CHAPTER 20

AND Da'vid fled from Na'ioth in Ra'mah, and came and said before Jon'a-than, What have I done? what *is* my iniquity? and what *is* my sin before your father, that he seeks my life?

2 And he said to him, God forbid; you shall not die: behold, my father will do nothing either great or small, but that he will show it me: and why should my father hide this thing from me? it *is* not *so*.

3 And Da'vid swear moreover, and said, Your father certainly knows that I have found grace in your eyes; and he says, Let not Jon'a-than know this, less he be grieved: but truly *as* the LORD lives, and *as* <u>your soul</u> lives, *there is* but a step between me and death. you

4 Then said Jon'a-than to Da'vid, Whatsoever <u>your soul desires</u>, I will even do *it* for you. you say

5 And Da'vid said to Jon'a-than, Behold, to morrow *is* the new moon, and I should not fail to sit with the king <u>at meat</u>: but let me go, that I may hide myself in the field to the third *day* at even. to eat

6 If your father at all miss me, then say,

Da'vid earnestly asked *leave* of me that he might run to Beth'-le-hem his city: for *there is* a yearly sacrifice there for all the family.

7 If he say thus, *It is* well; your servant shall have peace: but if he be very angry, *then* be sure that evil is determined by him.

8 Therefore you shall deal kindly with your servant; for you have brought your servant into a <u>covenant</u> of the LORD with you: notwithstanding, if there be in me iniquity, slay me yourself; for why should you bring me to your father?   agreement

9 And Jon'a-than said, Far be it from you: for if I knew certainly that evil were determined by my father to come upon you, then would not I tell it you?

10 Then said Da'vid to Jon'a-than, Who shall tell me? or what *if* your father answer you roughly?

11 And Jon'a-than said to Da'vid, Come, and let us go out into the field. And they went out both of them into the field.

12 And Jon'a-than said to Da'vid, O <u>LORD God</u> of Is'ra-el, when I have sounded my father about to morrow any time, *or* the third *day*, and, behold, *if there be* good toward Da'vid, and I then send not to you, and show it you;   Jehovah$^{s.f.}$ Elohim$^{p.f.}$

13 The LORD do so and much more to Jon'a-than: but if it please my father *to do* you evil, then I will show it you, and send you away, that you may go in peace: and the LORD be with you, as He has been with my father.

14 And you shall not only while yet I live show me the kindness of the LORD, that I die not:

15 But *also* you shall not cut off your kindness from my house for ever: no, not when the LORD has cut off the enemies of Da'vid every one from the face of the earth.

16 So Jon'a-than made *a* <u>covenant</u> with the <u>house</u> of Da'vid, *saying*, Let the LORD even require *it* at the hand of Da'vid's enemies.   agreement - family

17 And Jon'a-than caused Da'vid to <u>swear</u> again, because he loved him: for he loved him as he loved his own <u>soul</u>.   promise - life

18 Then Jon'a-than said to Da'vid, To morrow *is* the new moon: and you shall be missed, because your seat will be empty.

19 And *when* you have stayed three days, *then* you shall go down quickly, and come to the place where you did hide yourself when the business was *in hand*, and shall remain by the <u>stone E'zel</u>.   stone heap

20 And I will shoot three arrows on the side *thereof*, as though I shot at a mark.

21 And, behold, I will send a lad, *saying*, Go, find out the arrows. If I expressly say to the lad, Behold, the arrows *are* on this side of you, take them; then come you: for *there is* peace to you, and no hurt; *as* the LORD lives.

22 But if I say thus to the young man, Behold, the arrows *are* beyond you; go your way: for the LORD has sent you away.

23 And *as touching* the matter which you and I have spoken of, behold, the

LORD *be* between you and me for ever. 24 So Da'vid hid himself in the field: and when the new moon was come, the king sat him down to eat meat. 25 And the king sat upon his seat, as at other times, *even* upon a seat by the wall: and Jon'a-than arose, and Ab'ner sat by Saul's side, and Da'vid's place was empty. 26 Nevertheless Saul spoke not any thing that day: for he thought, Something has befallen him, he *is* not clean; surely he *is* not clean. _{unfit} 27 And it came to pass on the morrow, *which was* the second *day* of the month, that Da'vid's place was empty: and Saul said to Jon'a-than his son, Wherefore come not the son of Jes'se to meat, neither yesterday, nor to day? _{the meal} 28 And Jon'a-than answered Saul, Da'vid earnestly asked *leave* of me *to go* to Beth'-le-hem: 29 And he said, Let me go, I pray you; for our family has a sacrifice in the city; and my brother, he has commanded me *to be there*: and now, if I have found favor in your eyes, let me get away, I pray you, and see my brethren. Therefore he comes not to the king's table. 30 Then Saul's anger was kindled against Jon'a-than, and he said to him, You son of the perverse rebellious *woman*, do not I know that you have chosen the son of Jes'se to your own confusion, and to the confusion of your mother's nakedness? 31 For as long as the son of Jes'se lives upon the ground, you shall not be established, nor your kingdom. Wherefore now send and bring him to me, for he shall surely die. 32 And Jon'a-than answered Saul his father, and said to him, Wherefore shall he be slain? what has he done? 33 And Saul cast a javelin at him to smite him: whereby Jon'a-than knew that it was determined of his father to slay Da'vid. _{spear - strike him down} 34 So Jon'a-than arose from the table in fierce anger, and did eat no meat the second day of the month: for he was grieved for Da'vid, because his father had done him shame. _{food - sorry} 35 And it came to pass in the morning, that Jon'a-than went out into the field at the time appointed with Da'vid, and a little lad with him. 36 And he said to his lad, Run, find out now the arrows which I shoot. *And* as the lad ran, he shot an arrow beyond him. 37 And when the lad was come to the place of the arrow which Jon'a-than had shot, Jon'a-than cried after the lad, and said, *Is* not the arrow beyond you? 38 And Jon'a-than cried after the lad, Make speed, haste, stay not. And Jon'a-than's lad gathered up the arrows, and came to his master. _{do not stop} 39 But the lad knew not any thing: only Jon'a-than and Da'vid knew the matter. 40 And Jon'a-than gave his artillery to his lad, and said to him, Go, carry *them* to the city. _{weapons} 41 *And* as soon as the lad was gone, Da'vid arose out of *a place* toward the

south, and fell on his face to the ground, and bowed himself three times: and they kissed one another, and wept one with another, until Da'vid exceeded. but David more

42 And Jon'a-than said to Da'vid, Go in peace, forasmuch as we have sworn both of us in the name of the LORD, saying, The LORD be between me and you, and between my seed and your seed for ever. And he arose and departed: and Jon'a-than went into the city. descendants

CHAPTER 21

THEN came Da'vid to Nob to A-him'e-lech the priest: and A-him'e-lech was afraid at the meeting of Da'vid, and said to him, Why are you alone, and no man with you?

2 And Da'vid said to A-him'e-lech the priest, The king has commanded me a business, and has said to me, Let no man know any thing of the business whereabout I send you, and what I have commanded you: and I have appointed my servants to such and such a place.

3 Now therefore what is under your hand? give me five loaves of bread in my hand, or what there is present.

4 And the priest answered Da'vid, and said, There is no common bread under my hand, but there is hallowed bread; if the young men have kept themselves at least from women. consecrated

5 And Da'vid answered the priest, and said to him, Of a truth women have been kept from us about these three days, since I came out, and the vessels of the young men are holy, and the bread is in a manner common, yea, though it were sanctified this day in the vessel. made holy

6 So the priest gave him hallowed bread: for there was no bread there but the showbread, that was taken from before the LORD, to put hot bread in the day when it was taken away. fresh

7 Now a certain man of the servants of Saul was there that day, detained before the LORD; and his name was Do'eg, an E'dom-ite, the chiefest of the herdmen that belonged to Saul. taking time to worship

8 And Da'vid said to A-him'e-lech, And is there not here under your hand spear or sword? for I have neither brought my sword nor my weapons with me, because the king's business required haste. was urgent

9 And the priest said, The sword of Go-li'ath the Phi-lis'tine, whom you slew in the valley of E'lah, behold, it is here wrapped in a cloth behind the ephod: if you will take that, take it: for there is no other save that here. And Da'vid said, There is none like that; give it me.

10 And Da'vid arose, and fled that day for fear of Saul, and went to A'chish the king of Gath.

11 And the servants of A'chish said to him, Is not this Da'vid the king of the land? did they not sing one to another of him in dances, saying, Saul has slain his thousands, and Da'vid his ten thousands?

12 And Da'vid laid up these words in

his heart, and was sore afraid of A'chish the king of Gath. <small>made special note of</small>
13 And he changed his behavior before them, and <u>feigned</u> himself mad in their hands, and <u>scrabbled</u> on the doors of the gate, and let his spittle fall down upon his beard. <small>preferred to be demented - scribbled</small>
14 Then said A'chish to his servants, Lo, you see the man is <u>mad</u>: why *then* have you brought him to me? <small>demented</small>
15 Have I need of mad men, that you have brought this *fellow* to play the <u>mad</u> man in my presence? shall this *fellow* come into my house?

CHAPTER 22

DA'VID therefore departed *from there*, and escaped to the cave A-dul'lam: and when his brethren and all his father's house heard *it*, they went down there to him.
2 And every one *that was* in distress, and every one that *was* in debt, and every one *that was* <u>discontented</u>, gathered themselves to him; and he became a captain over them: and there were with him about four hundred men. <small>bitter of soul</small>
3 And Da'vid went there to Miz'peh of Mo'ab: and he said to the king of Mo'ab, Let my father and my mother, I pray you, <u>come forth</u>, *and be* with you, till I know what <u>God</u> will do for me. <small>come and stay - Elohim^{p.f.}</small>
4 And he brought them before the king of Mo'ab: and they dwelled with him all the while that Da'vid was in the <u>hold</u>. <small>stronghold</small>
5 And the prophet Gad said to Da'vid, Abide not in the <u>hold</u>; depart, and get you into the land of Ju'dah. Then Da'vid departed, and came into the forest of Ha'reth. <small>stronghold</small>
6 When Saul heard that Da'vid was discovered, and the men that *were* with him, (now Saul abode in Gib'e-ah under a tree in Ra'mah, having his spear in his hand, and all his servants *were* standing about him;)
7 Then Saul said to his servants that stood about him, Hear now, you Ben'ja-mites; will the son of Jes'se give every one of you fields and vineyards, *and* make you all captains of thousands, and captains of hundreds;
8 That all of you have conspired against me, and *there is* none that show me that my son has made a league with the son of Jes'se, and *there is* none of you that is sorry for me, or show to me that my son has stirred up my servant against me, to lie in wait, as at this day?
9 Then answered Do'eg the E'dom-ite, which was set over the servants of Saul, and said, I saw the son of Jes'se coming to Nob, to A-him'e-lech the son of A-hi'tub.
10 And he enquired of the LORD for him, and gave him <u>victuals</u>, and gave him the sword of Go-li'ath the Phi-lis'tine. <small>provisions</small>
11 Then the king sent to call A-him'e-lech the priest, the son of A-hi'tub, and all his father's house, the priests that *were* in Nob: and they came all of them to the king.
12 And Saul said, Hear now, you son

of A-hi'tub. And he answered, Here I *am*, my lord.

13 And Saul said to him, Why have you conspired against me, you and the son of Jes'se, in that you have given him bread, and a sword, and <u>have enquired of God</u> for him, that he should rise against me, to lie in wait, as at this day? _{prayed to - Elohim}^{pf.}

14 Then A-him'e-lech answered the king, and said, And who *is so* faithful among all your servants as Da'vid, which is the king's son in law, and goes at your bidding, and is <u>honorable</u> in your house? _{respected}

15 Did I then begin to enquire of <u>God</u> for him? be it far from me: let not the king impute *any* thing to his servant, *nor* to all the house of my father: for your servant knew nothing of all this, less or more.

16 And the king said, You shall surely die, A-him'e-lech, you, and all your father's house.

17 And the king said to the <u>footmen</u> that stood about him, Turn, and slay the priests of the LORD; because their hand also *is* with Da'vid, and because they knew when he fled, and did not show it to me. But the servants of the king would not put forth their hand to fall upon the priests of the LORD. _{guards}

18 And the king said to Do'eg, Turn you, and <u>fall upon</u> the priests. And Do'eg the E'dom-ite turned, and he fell upon the priests, and slew on that day <u>fourscore and five</u> persons that did wear a linen <u>ephod</u>.

_{attacked - 85 - priestly garments}

19 And Nob, the city of the priests, <u>smote he</u> with the edge of the sword, both men and women, children and sucklings, and oxen, and asses, and sheep, with the edge of the sword. _{he attacked}

20 And one of the sons of A-him'e-lech the son of A-hi'tub, named A-bi'a-thar, escaped, and fled after Da'vid.

21 And A-bi'a-thar showed Da'vid that Saul had slain the LORD's priests.

22 And Da'vid said to A-bi'a-thar, I knew *it* that day, when Do'eg the E'dom-ite *was* there, that he would surely tell Saul: I have occasioned *the death* of all the persons of your father's <u>house</u>. _{household}

23 Abide you with me, fear not: for he that seeks my life seeks your life: but with me you *shall be* in <u>safeguard</u>. _{safe}

CHAPTER 23

THEN they told Da'vid, saying, Behold, the Phi-lis'tines fight against Kei'lah, and they rob the threshingfloors.

2 Therefore Da'vid enquired of the LORD, saying, Shall I go and <u>smite</u> these Phi-lis'tines? And the LORD said to Da'vid, Go, and <u>smite</u> the Phi-lis'tines, and save Kei'lah. _{attack}

3 And Da'vid's men said to him, Behold, we be afraid here in Ju'dah: how much more then if we come to Kei'lah against the armies of the Phi-lis'tines?

4 Then Da'vid enquired of the LORD yet again. And the LORD answered him and said, Arise, go down to Kei'lah; for I will deliver the Phi-lis'tines into your hand.

5 So Da'vid and his men went to Kei'lah, and fought with the Phi-lis'tines, and brought away their cattle, and smote them with a great slaughter. So Da'vid saved the inhabitants of Kei'lah.

6 And it came to pass, when A-bi'a-thar the son of A-him'e-lech fled to Da'vid to Kei'lah, *that* he came down *with* an ephod in his hand. priestly garment

7 And it was told Saul that Da'vid was come to Kei'lah. And Saul said, God has delivered him into my hand; for he is shut in, by entering into a town that has gates and bars. Elohim^p.f. - surrounded

8 And Saul called all the people together to war, to go down to Kei'lah, to besiege Da'vid and his men.

9 And Da'vid knew that Saul secretly practised mischief against him; and he said to A-bi'a-thar the priest, Bring here the ephod. plotted evil - priestly garment

10 Then said Da'vid, O Lord God of Is'ra-el, your servant has certainly heard that Saul seeks to come to Kei'lah, to destroy the city for my sake. Jehovah^s.f. Elohim^p.f.

11 Will the men of Kei'lah deliver me up into his hand? will Saul come down, as your servant has heard? O Lord God of Is'ra-el, I beseech you, tell Your servant. And the Lord said, He will come down. pray

12 Then said Da'vid, Will the men of Kei'lah deliver me and my men into the hand of Saul? And the Lord said, They will deliver *you* up. surrender

13 Then Da'vid and his men, *which were* about six hundred, arose and departed out of Kei'lah, and went wherever they could go. And it was told Saul that Da'vid was escaped from Kei'lah; and he forbare to go forth. ceased

14 And Da'vid abode in the wilderness in strong holds, and remained in a mountain in the wilderness of Ziph. And Saul sought him every day, but God delivered him not into his hand. lived - Elohim^p.f.

15 And Da'vid saw that Saul was come out to seek his life: and Da'vid *was* in the wilderness of Ziph in a wood. forest

16 And Jon'a-than Saul's son arose, and went to Da'vid into the wood, and strengthened his hand in God. encouraged him

17 And he said to him, Fear not: for the hand of Saul my father shall not find you; and you shall be king over Is'ra-el, and I shall be next to you; and that also Saul my father know.

18 And they two made a covenant before the Lord: and Da'vid abode in the wood, and Jon'a-than went to his house. agreement - forest

19 Then came up the Ziph'ites to Saul to Gib'e-ah, saying, Does not Da'vid hide himself with us in strong holds in the wood, in the hill of Hach'i-lah, which *is* on the south of Jesh'i-mon?

20 Now therefore, O king, come down according to all the desire of your soul to come down; and our part *shall be* to deliver him into the king's hand.

21 And Saul said, Blessed *be you* of the Lord; for you have compassion on me.

22 Go, I pray you, prepare yet, and

know and see his place where his <u>haunt</u> is, *and* who has seen him there: for it is told me *that* he deals very <u>subtilly</u>.   foot - cunning

23 See therefore, and take knowledge of all the lurking places where he hides himself, and come you again to me with the certainty, and I will go with you: and it shall come to pass, if he be in the land, that I will search him out throughout all the thousands of Ju'dah.

24 And they arose, and went to Ziph before Saul: but Da'vid and his men *were* in the wilderness of Ma'on, in the plain on the south of Jesh'i-mon.

25 Saul also and his men went to seek *him*. And they told Da'vid: wherefore he came down <u>into a rock</u>, and abode in the wilderness of Ma'on. And when Saul heard *that*, he pursued after Da'vid in the wilderness of Ma'on.   to the rock

26 And Saul went on this side of the mountain, and Da'vid and his men on that side of the mountain: and Da'vid made haste to get away for fear of Saul; for Saul and his men <u>compassed</u> Da'vid and his men round about to take them.   surrounded

27 But there came a messenger to Saul, saying, Haste you, and come; for the Phi-lis'tines have invaded the land.

28 Wherefore Saul returned from pursuing after Da'vid, and went against the Phi-lis'tines: therefore they called that place Se'la-ham-mah-le'koth.

29 And Da'vid went up from there, and dwelled in strong holds at En-ge'di.

CHAPTER 24

AND it came to pass, when Saul was returned from following the Phi-lis'tines, that it was told him, saying, Behold, Da'vid *is* in the wilderness of En-ge'di.

2 Then Saul took three thousand chosen men out of all Is'ra-el, and went to seek Da'vid and his men upon the rocks of the wild goats.

3 And he came to the <u>sheepcotes</u> by the way, where *was* a cave; and Saul went in <u>to cover his feet</u>: and Da'vid and his men remained in the <u>sides</u> of the cave. sheepfolds - relieve himself - back

4 And the men of Da'vid said to him, Behold the day of which the Lord said to you, Behold, I will deliver your enemy into your hand, that you may do to him as it shall seem good to you. Then Da'vid arose, and cut off the skirt of Saul's robe <u>privily</u>. secretly

5 And it came to pass afterward, that Da'vid's heart smote him, because he had cut off Saul's skirt.

6 And he said to his men, The Lord forbid that I should do this thing to my master, the Lord's anointed, to stretch forth mine hand against him, seeing he *is* the anointed of the Lord.

7 So Da'vid <u>stayed</u> his servants with these words, and allowed them not to rise against Saul. But Saul rose up out of the cave, and went on *his* way.   persuaded

8 Da'vid also arose afterward, and went out of the cave, and cried after Saul, saying, My lord the king. And when Saul looked behind him, Da'vid

stooped with his face to the earth, and bowed himself.

9 And Da'vid said to Saul, Wherefore hear you men's words, saying, Behold, Da'vid seeks your hurt?

10 Behold, this day your eyes have seen how that the LORD had delivered you to day into my hand in the cave: and *some* bade *me* kill you: but *my eye* spared you; and I said, I will not put forth my hand against my lord; for he *is* the LORD's anointed.

11 Moreover, my father, see, yea, see the skirt of your robe in my hand: for in that I cut off the skirt of your robe, and killed you not, know you and see that *there is* neither evil nor transgression in my hand, and I have not sinned against you; yet you hunt my soul to take it.

12 The LORD judge between me and you, and the LORD avenge me of you: but my hand shall not be upon you.

13 As says the proverb of the ancients, Wickedness proceeds from the wicked: but my hand shall not be upon you.

14 After whom is the king of Is'ra-el come out? after whom do you pursue? after a dead dog, after a flea.

15 The LORD therefore be judge, and judge between me and you, and see, and plead my cause, and deliver me out of your hand.

16 And it came to pass, when Da'vid had made an end of speaking these words to Saul, that Saul said, *Is* this your voice, my son Da'vid? And Saul lifted up his voice, and wept.

17 And he said to Da'vid, You *are* more righteous than I: for you have rewarded me good, whereas I have rewarded you evil.

18 And you have showed this day how that you have dealt well with me: forasmuch as when the LORD had delivered me into your hand, you killed me not.

19 For if a man find his enemy, will he let him go well away? wherefore the LORD reward you good for that you have done to me this day.   away safely

20 And now, behold, I know well that you shall surely be king, and that the kingdom of Is'ra-el shall be established in your hand.

21 Swear now therefore to me by the LORD, that you will not cut off my seed after me, and that you will not destroy my name out of my father's house.   Promised - descendants

22 And Da'vid swear to Saul. And Saul went home; but Da'vid and his men got them up to the hold.   stronghold

CHAPTER 25

AND Sam'u-el died; and all the Is'ra-el-ites were gathered together, and lamented him, and buried him in his house at Ra'mah. And Da'vid arose, and went down to the wilderness of Pa'ran.

2 And *there was* a man in Ma'on, whose possessions *were* in Car'mel; and the man *was* very great, and he had three thousand sheep, and a thousand goats: and he was shearing his sheep in Car'mel.   business was

3 Now the name of the man *was* Na'bal; and the name of his wife Ab'i-gail: and *she was* a woman of good understanding, and of a beautiful countenance: but the man *was* churlish and evil in his doings; and he *was* of the house of Ca'leb.   harsh
4 And Da'vid heard in the wilderness that Na'bal did shear his sheep.
5 And Da'vid sent out ten young men, and Da'vid said to the young men, Get you up to Car'mel, and go to Na'bal, and greet him in my name:
6 And thus shall you say to him that lives *in prosperity*, Peace *be* both to you, and peace *be* to your house, and peace *be* to all that you have.   LUKE 10:5
7 And now I have heard that you have shearers: now your shepherds which were with us, we hurt them not, neither was there anything missing to them, all the while they were in Car'mel.
8 Ask your young men, and they will show you. Wherefore let the young men find favor in your eyes: for we come in a good day: give, I pray you, whatsoever comes to your hand to your servants, and to your son Da'vid.
9 And when Da'vid's young men came, they spoke to Na'bal according to all those words in the name of Da'vid, and ceased.
10 And Na'bal answered Da'vid's servants, and said, Who *is* Da'vid? and who *is* the son of Jes'se? there be many servants now a days that break away every man from his master.
11 Shall I then take my bread, and my water, and my flesh that I have killed for my shearers, and give *it* to men, whom I know not where they *be*?   butchered meat
12 So Da'vid's young men turned their way, and went again, and came and told him all those sayings.
13 And Da'vid said to his men, Gird you on every man his sword. And they girded on every man his sword; and Da'vid also girded on his sword: and there went up after Da'vid about four hundred men; and two hundred abode by the stuff.   stayed with the baggage
14 But one of the young men told Ab'i-gail, Na'bal's wife, saying, Behold, Da'vid sent messengers out of the wilderness to salute our master; and he railed on them.
15 But the men *were* very good to us, and we were not hurt, neither missed we any thing, as long as we were conversant with them, when we were in the fields:
16 They were a wall to us both by night and day, all the while we were with them keeping the sheep.   protection
17 Now therefore know and consider what you will do; for evil is determined against our master, and against all his household: for he *is* such a son of Be'li-al, that *a man* cannot speak to him.   worthless man
18 Then Ab'i-gail made haste, and took two hundred loaves, and two bottles of wine, and five sheep ready dressed, and five measures of parched *corn*, and an hundred clusters of raisins, and two hundred cakes of figs, and laid *them* on asses.

19 And she said to her servants, Go on before me; behold, I come after you. But she told not her husband Na'bal.
20 And it was *so*, *as* she rode on the ass, that she came down by the covert of the hill, and, behold, Da'vid and his men came down against her; and she met them.
21 Now Da'vid had said, Surely in vain have I kept all that this *fellow* has in the wilderness, so that nothing was missed of all that *pertained* to him: and he has requited me evil for good. <small>returned</small>
22 So and more also do God to the enemies of Da'vid, if I leave of all that *pertain* to him by the morning light any that urinates against the wall.
23 And when Ab'i-gail saw Da'vid, she hasted, and lighted off the ass, and fell before Da'vid on her face, and bowed herself to the ground,
24 And fell at his feet, and said, Upon me, my lord, *upon* me *let this* iniquity *be*: and let your handmaid, I pray you, speak in your audience, and hear the words of your handmaid.
25 Let not my lord, I pray you, regard this man of Be'li-al, *even* Na'bal: for as his name *is*, so *is* he; Na'bal *is* his name, and folly *is* with him: but I your handmaid saw not the young men of my lord, whom you did send.
26 Now therefore, my lord, *as* the LORD lives, and *as* your soul lives, seeing the LORD has withheld you from coming to *shed* blood, and from avenging yourself with your own hand, now let your enemies, and they that seek evil to my lord, be as Na'bal.

27 And now this blessing which your handmaid has brought to my lord, let it even be given to the young men that follow my lord.
28 I pray you, forgive the trespass of your handmaid: for the LORD will certainly make my lord a <u>sure</u> house; because my lord fights the battles of the LORD, and evil has not been found in you *all* your days. <small>faithful</small>
29 Yet a man is risen to pursue you, and to seek your <u>soul</u>: but the <u>soul</u> of my lord shall be <u>bound</u> in the bundle of life with the LORD your God; and the <u>souls</u> of your enemies, them shall He sling out, *as out* of the middle of a sling. <small>person - body - secure</small>
30 And it shall come to pass, when the LORD shall have done to my lord according to all the good that He has spoken concerning you, and shall have appointed you ruler over Is'ra-el;
31 That this shall be no grief to you, nor offence of heart to my lord, either that you have shed blood causeless, or that my lord has avenged himself: but when the LORD shall have dealt well with my lord, then remember your handmaid.
32 And Da'vid said to Ab'i-gail, Blessed *be* the <u>LORD God</u> of Is'ra-el, which sent you this day to meet me: <small>LUKE 1:68</small>
33 And blessed *be* your advice, and blessed *be* you, which have kept me this day from coming to *shed* blood, and from avenging myself with my own hand. <small>Jehovah^s.f. Elohim^p.f.</small>
34 For in very deed, as the <u>LORD God</u> of Is'ra-el lives, which has kept me back from hurting you, except you

<small>G4H</small>
<small>553</small>

had hasted and come to meet me, surely there had not been left to Na'bal by the morning light any that urinates against the wall. Jehovah^{s-f.} Elohim^{p-f.}

35 So Da'vid received of her hand *that* which she had brought him, and said to her, Go up in peace to your house; see, I have hearkened to your voice, and have accepted your person. <small>listened - request</small>

36 And Ab'i-gail came to Na'bal; and, behold, he held a feast in his house, like the feast of a king; and Na'bal's heart *was* merry within him, for he *was* very drunken: wherefore she told him nothing, less or more, until the morning light.

37 But it came to pass in the morning, when the wine was gone out of Na'bal, and his wife had told him these things, that his heart died within him, and he became *as* a stone. <small>he lost all confidence</small>

38 And it came to pass about ten days *after*, that the LORD smote Na'bal, that he died.

39 And when Da'vid heard that Na'bal was dead, he said, Blessed *be* the LORD, that has pleaded the cause of my reproach from the hand of Na'bal, and has kept His servant from evil: for the LORD has returned the wickedness of Na'bal upon his own head. And Da'vid sent and communed with Ab'i-gail, to take her to him to wife. <small>contempt - talked</small>

40 And when the servants of Da'vid were come to Ab'i-gail to Car'mel, they spoke to her, saying, Da'vid sent us to you, to take you to him to wife.

41 And she arose, and bowed herself on *her* face to the earth, and said, Behold, *let* your handmaid *be* a servant to wash the feet of the servants of my lord. <small>LUKE 7:38</small>

42 And Ab'i-gail hasted, and arose, and rode upon an ass, with five damsels of hers that went after her; and she went after the messengers of Da'vid, and became his wife. <small>young women - attended</small>

43 Da'vid also took A-hin'o-am of Jez're-el; and they were also both of them his wives.

44 But Saul had given Mi'chal his daughter, Da'vid's wife, to Phal'ti the son of La'ish, which *was* of Gal'lim.

CHAPTER 26

AND the Ziph'ites came to Saul to Gib'e-ah, saying, Does not Da'vid hide himself in the hill of Hach'i-lah, *which is* before Jesh'i-mon?

2 Then Saul arose, and went down to the wilderness of Ziph, having three thousand chosen men of Is'ra-el with him, to seek Da'vid in the wilderness of Ziph.

3 And Saul pitched in the hill of Hach'i-lah, which *is* before Jesh'i-mon, by the way. But Da'vid abode in the wilderness, and he saw that Saul came after him into the wilderness. <small>camped</small>

4 Da'vid therefore sent out spies, and understood that Saul was come in very deed.

5 And Da'vid arose, and came to the place where Saul had pitched: and Da'vid beheld the place where Saul lay, and Ab'ner the son of Ner, the captain of his host: and Saul lay in the trench,

and the people <u>pitched</u> round about him.   circle of the camp - camped

6 Then answered Da'vid and said to A-him'e-lech the Hit'tite, and to A-bish'a-i the son of Zer-u-i'ah, brother to Jo'ab, saying, Who will go down with me to Saul to the camp? And A-bish'a-i said, I will go down with you.

7 So Da'vid and A-bish'a-i came to the people by night: and, behold, Saul lay sleeping within the trench, and his spear stuck in the ground at his <u>bolster</u>: but Ab'ner and the people lay round about him.   head

8 Then said A-bish'a-i to Da'vid, God has delivered your enemy into your hand this day: now therefore let me <u>smite</u> him, I pray you, with the spear even to the earth <u>at once</u>, and I will not *smite* him the second time.

strike - with one stroke

9 And Da'vid said to A-bish'a-i, Destroy him not: for who can <u>stretch forth</u> his hand against the LORD's anointed, and be guiltless?   lay

10 Da'vid said furthermore, *As* the LORD lives, the LORD shall <u>smite</u> him; or his day shall come to die; or he shall descend into battle, and perish.   strike

11 The LORD forbid that I should stretch forth my hand against the LORD's anointed: but, I pray you, take you now the spear that *is* at his <u>bolster</u>, and the <u>cruse</u> of water, and let us go.   head - jug

12 So Da'vid took the spear and the cruse of water from Saul's bolster; and they got them away, and no man saw *it*, nor knew *it*, neither awaked: for they *were* all asleep; because a deep sleep from the LORD was fallen upon them.

13 Then Da'vid went over to the other side, and stood on the top of an hill afar off; a great space *being* between them:

14 And Da'vid cried to the people, and to Ab'ner the son of Ner, saying, Answer you not, Ab'ner? Then Ab'ner answered and said, Who *are* you *that* cries to the king?

15 And Da'vid said to Ab'ner, *Are* not you a *valiant* man? and who *is* like to you in Is'ra-el? wherefore then have you not kept your lord the king? for there came one of the people in to destroy the king your lord.

16 This thing *is* not good that you have done. *As* the LORD lives, you *are* worthy to die, because you have not <u>kept</u> your master, the LORD's anointed. And now see where the king's spear *is*, and the <u>cruse</u> of water that *was* at his <u>bolster</u>.   guarded - jug - head

17 And Saul knew Da'vid's voice, and said, *Is* this your voice, my son Da'vid? And Da'vid said, *It is* my voice, my lord, O king.

18 And he said, Wherefore does my lord thus pursue after his servant? for what have I done? or what evil *is* in my hand?

19 Now therefore, I pray you, let my lord the king hear the words of his servant. If the LORD have stirred you up against me, let Him accept an offering: but if *they be* the children of men, cursed *be* they before the LORD; for they have driven me out this day from abiding in the inheritance of the LORD, saying, Go, serve other gods.

20 Now therefore, let not my blood fall to the earth <u>before the face</u> of the LORD: for the king of Is'ra-el is come out to seek a flea, as when one does hunt a partridge in the mountains. <small>away from the presence</small>

21 Then said Saul, I have sinned: return, my son Da'vid: for I will no more do you harm, because my <u>soul</u> was precious in your eyes this day: behold, I have played the fool, and have erred exceedingly. <small>life</small>

22 And Da'vid answered and said, Behold the king's spear! and let one of the young men come over and bring it.

23 The LORD render to every man His righteousness and His faithfulness: for the LORD delivered you into *my* hand to day, but I would not stretch forth my hand against the LORD's anointed.

24 And, behold, as your life was much set by this day in my eyes, so let my life be much set by in the eyes of the LORD, and let Him deliver me out of all tribulation.

25 Then Saul said to Da'vid, Blessed *be* you, my son Da'vid: you shall both do great *things*, and also shall still prevail. So Da'vid went on his way, and Saul returned to his place.

CHAPTER 27

AND Da'vid said in his heart, I shall now perish one day by the hand of Saul: *there is* nothing better for me than that I should speedily escape into the land of the Phi-lis'tines; and Saul shall despair of me, to seek me any more in any coast of Is'ra-el: so shall I escape out of his hand.

2 And Da'vid arose, and he passed over with the six hundred men that *were* with him to A'chish, the son of Ma'och, king of Gath.

3 And Da'vid dwelled with A'chish at Gath, he and his men, every man with his household, *even* Da'vid with his two wives, A-hin'o-am the Jez're-el-it-ess, and Ab'i-gail the Car'mel-it-ess, Na'bal's wife.

4 And it was told Saul that Da'vid was fled to Gath: and he sought no more again for him.

5 And Da'vid said to A'chish, If I have now found grace in your eyes, let them give me a place in some town in the country, that I may dwell there: for why should your servant dwell in the royal city with you?

6 Then A'chish gave him Zik'lag that day: wherefore Zik'lag pertain to the kings of Ju'dah to this day.

7 And the time that Da'vid dwelled in the country of the Phi-lis'tines was a full year and four months.

8 And Da'vid and his men went up, and invaded the Gesh'u-rites, and the Gez'rites, and the Am'a-lek-ites: for those *nations were* <u>of old</u> the inhabitants of the land, as you go to Shur, even to the land of E'gypt. <small>from ancient times</small>

9 And Da'vid <u>smote</u> the land, and left neither man nor woman alive, and took away the sheep, and the oxen, and the asses, and the camels, and the apparel, and returned, and came to A'chish. <small>attacked</small>

10 And A'chish said, Where have you made a <u>road</u> to day? And Da'vid said, Against the south of Ju'dah, and against the south of the Je-rah'me-el-ites, and against the south of the Ken'ites. ^{raid}

11 And Da'vid saved neither man nor woman alive, to bring *tidings* to Gath, saying, Less they should tell on us, saying, So did Da'vid, and so <u>*will be* his manner</u> all the while he dwells in the country of the Phi-lis'tines. ^{was his practice}

12 And A'chish believed Da'vid, saying, He has made his people Is'ra-el utterly to abhor him; therefore he shall be my servant for ever.

CHAPTER 28

AND it came to pass in those days, that the Phi-lis'tines gathered their armies together for warfare, to fight with Is'ra-el. And A'chish said to Da'vid, Know you assuredly, that you shall go out with me to battle, you and your men.

2 And Da'vid said to A'chish, Surely you shall know what your servant can do. And A'chish said to Da'vid, Therefore will I make you keeper of my head for ever.

3 Now Sam'u-el was dead, and all Is'ra-el had lamented him, and buried him in Ra'mah, even in his own city. And Saul had put away <u>those</u> that had familiar spirits, and the wizards, out of the land. ^{mediums}

4 And the Phi-lis'tines gathered themselves together, and came and <u>pitched</u> in Shu'nem: and Saul gathered all Is'ra-el together, and they pitched in Gil-bo'a. ^{camped}

5 And when Saul saw the host of the Phi-lis'tines, he was afraid, and his heart greatly trembled.

6 And when Saul enquired of the LORD, the LORD answered him not, neither by dreams, nor by U'rim, nor by prophets.

7 Then said Saul to his servants, Seek me a woman that <u>has a familiar spirit</u>, that I may go to her, and enquire of her. And his servants said to him, Behold, *there is* a woman that has a familiar spirit at En'-dor. ^{is a medium}

8 And Saul disguised himself, and put on other <u>raiment</u>, and he went, and two men with him, and they came to the woman by night: and he said, I pray you, divine to me by the <u>familiar spirit</u>, and bring me *him* up, whom I shall name to you. ^{clothes}

9 And the woman said to him, Behold, you know what Saul has done, how he has cut off those that have <u>familiar spirits</u>, and the <u>wizards</u>, out of the land: wherefore then lay you a <u>snare</u> for my life, to cause me to die? ^{mediums - spiritists - trap}

10 And Saul swear to her by the LORD, saying, *As* the LORD lives, there shall no punishment happen to you for this thing.

11 Then said the woman, Whom shall I bring up to you? And he said, Bring me up Sam'u-el.

12 And when the woman saw Sam'u-el, she cried with a loud voice: and the woman spoke to Saul, saying, Why have you deceived me? for you *are* Saul.

13 And the king said to her, Be not afraid: for what saw you? And the woman said to Saul, I saw <u>gods</u> ascending out of the earth. _{spirits}

14 And he said to her, What form *is* he of? And she said, An old man comes up; and he *is* covered with a mantle. And Saul perceived that it *was* Sam'u-el, and he stooped with *his* face to the ground, and bowed himself.

15 And Sam'u-el said to Saul, Why have you <u>disquieted</u> me, to bring me up? And Saul answered, I am sore distressed; for the Phi-lis'tines make war against me, and <u>God</u> is departed from me, and answers me no more, neither by prophets, nor by dreams: therefore I have called you, that you may make known to me what I shall do.

disturbed - Elohim^{p.f.}

16 Then said Sam'u-el, Why then do you ask of me, seeing the Lord is departed from you, and is become your enemy?

17 And the Lord has done to him, as He spoke by me: for the Lord has rent the kingdom out of your hand, and given it to your neighbor, *even* to Da'vid:

18 Because you obeyed not the voice of the Lord, nor executed His fierce wrath upon Am'a-lek, therefore has the Lord done this thing to you this day.

19 Moreover the Lord will also <u>deliver</u> Is'ra-el with you into the hand of the Phi-lis'tines: and to morrow *shall* you and your sons *be* with me: the Lord also shall deliver the host of Is'ra-el into the hand of the Phi-lis'tines. _{give over}

20 Then Saul fell immediately <u>all along</u> on the earth, and was <u>sore</u> afraid, because of the words of Sam'u-el: and there was no strength in him; for he had eaten no bread all the day, nor all the night. _{full length - very}

21 And the woman came to Saul, and saw that he was sore troubled, and said to him, Behold, your handmaid has obeyed your voice, and I have put my life in my hand, and have <u>hearkened</u> to your words which you spoke to me. _{listened}

22 Now therefore, I pray you, hearken you also to the voice of your handmaid, and let me set a <u>morsel</u> of bread before you; and eat, that you may have strength, when you go on your way. _{piece}

23 But he refused, and said, I will not eat. But his servants, together with the woman, <u>compelled</u> him; and he hearkened to their voice. So he arose from the earth, and sat upon the bed. _{urged}

24 And the woman had a fat calf in the house; and she <u>hasted</u>, and killed it, and took flour, and kneaded *it*, and did bake <u>unleavened</u> bread thereof:

hurried - without yeast

25 And she brought *it* before Saul, and before his servants; and they did eat. Then they rose up, and went away that night.

CHAPTER 29

NOW the Phi-lis'tines gathered together all their armies to A'phek:

and the Is'ra-el-ites <u>pitched</u> by a fountain which *is* in Jez're-el. _{camped}

2 And the lords of the Phi-lis'tines passed on by hundreds, and by thousands: but Da'vid and his men passed on <u>in the rearward</u> with A'chish. _{behind him}

3 Then said the princes of the Phi-lis'tines, What *do* these He'brews *here*? And A'chish said to the princes of the Phi-lis'tines, *Is* not this Da'vid, the servant of Saul the king of Is'ra-el, which has been with me these days, or these years, and I have found no fault in him since he <u>fell *to me*</u> to this day? _{deserted to me}

4 And the princes of the Phi-lis'tines were angry with him; and the princes of the Phi-lis'tines said to him, Make this fellow return, that he may go again to his place which you have appointed him, and let him not go down with us to battle, less in the battle he be an adversary to us: for wherewith should he reconcile himself to his master? *should it* not *be* with the heads of these men?

5 *Is* not this Da'vid, of whom they sang one to another in dances, saying, Saul slew his thousands, and Da'vid his ten thousands?

6 Then A'chish called Da'vid, and said to him, Surely, *as* the LORD lives, you have been upright, and your <u>going out and your coming in</u> with me in the host *is* good in my sight: for I have not found evil in you since the day of your coming to me to this day: nevertheless the lords <u>favor you not</u>. _{daily walk - do not approve}

7 Wherefore now return, and go in peace, that you displease not the lords of the Phi-lis'tines.

8 And Da'vid said to A'chish, But what have I done? and what have you found in your servant so long as I have been with you to this day, that I may not go fight against the enemies of my lord the king?

9 And A'chish answered and said to Da'vid, I know that you *are* good in my sight, as an <u>angel</u> of <u>God</u>: notwithstanding the princes of the Phi-lis'tines have said, He shall not go up with us to the battle. _{messenger - Elohim^{p.f.}}

10 Wherefore now rise up early in the morning with your master's servants that are come with you: and as soon as you be up early in the morning, and have light, depart.

11 So Da'vid and his men rose up early to depart in the morning, to return into the land of the Phi-lis'tines. And the Phi-lis'tines went up to Jez're-el.

CHAPTER 30

AND it came to pass, when Da'vid and his men were come to Zik'lag on the third day, that the Am'a-lek-ites had invaded the south, and Zik'lag, and smitten Zik'lag, and burned it with fire;

2 And had taken the women captives, that *were* therein: they slew not any, either great or small, but carried *them* away, and went on their way.

3 So Da'vid and his men came to the city, and, behold, *it was* burned with fire; and their wives, and their sons, and their daughters, were taken captives.

4 Then Da'vid and the people that *were* with him lifted up their voice and wept, until they had no more power to weep.
5 And Da'vid's two wives were taken captives, A-hin'o-am the Jez're-el-it-ess, and Ab'i-gail the wife of Na'bal the Car-mel'ite.
6 And Da'vid was greatly distressed; for the people spoke of stoning him, because the soul of all the people was grieved, every man for his sons and for his daughters: but Da'vid <u>encouraged</u> himself in the LORD his <u>God</u>. <small>strengthened</small>
7 And Da'vid said to A-bi'a-thar the priest, A-him'e-lech's son, I pray you, bring me here the ephod. And A-bi'a-thar brought from there the ephod to Da'vid.
8 And Da'vid enquired at the LORD, saying, Shall I pursue after this troop? shall I overtake them? And He answered him, Pursue: for you shall surely overtake *them*, and without fail recover *all*.
9 So Da'vid went, he and the six hundred men that *were* with him, and came to the brook Be'sor, where those that were left behind stayed.
10 But Da'vid pursued, he and four hundred men: for two hundred abode behind, which were so <u>faint</u> that they could not go over the brook Be'sor. <small>weak</small>
11 And they found an E-gyp'tian in the field, and brought him to Da'vid, and gave him bread, and he did eat; and they made him drink water;
12 And they gave him a piece of a cake of figs, and two clusters of raisins: and when he had eaten, his spirit <u>came</u>

again to him: for he had eaten no bread, nor drunk *any* water, three days and three nights. <small>revived</small>
13 And Da'vid said to him, To whom *belong* you? and where *are* you from? And he said, I *am* a young man of E'gypt, servant to an Am'a-lek-ite; and my master left me, because three days <u>agone</u> I fell sick. <small>ago</small>
14 We made an invasion *upon* the south of the Cher'eth-ites, and upon *the coast* which *belongs* to Ju'dah, and upon the south of Ca'leb; and we burned Zik'lag with fire.
15 And Da'vid said to him, Can you bring me down to this company? And he said, <u>Swear</u> to me by <u>God</u>, that you will neither kill me, nor deliver me into the hands of my master, and I will bring you down to this company. <small>Promise - Elohim^{p.f.}</small>
16 And when he had brought him down, behold, *they were* spread abroad upon all the earth, eating and drinking, and dancing, because of all the great <u>spoil</u> that they had taken out of the land of the Phi-lis'tines, and out of the land of Ju'dah. <small>booty</small>
17 And Da'vid <u>smote</u> them from the twilight even to the evening of the next day: and there escaped not a man of them, save four hundred young men, which rode upon camels, and fled. <small>fought</small>
18 And Da'vid recovered all that the Am'a-lek-ites had carried away: and Da'vid rescued his two wives.
19 And there was nothing lacking to them, neither small nor great, neither sons nor daughters, neither spoil, nor

any *thing* that they had taken to them: Da'vid recovered all.

20 And Da'vid took all the flocks and the herds, *which* they drove before those *other* cattle, and said, This *is* Da'vid's spoil.

21 And Da'vid came to the two hundred men, which were so faint that they could not follow Da'vid, whom they had made also to abide at the brook Be'sor: and they went forth to meet Da'vid, and to meet the people that *were* with him: and when Da'vid came near to the people, he <u>saluted</u> them.   greeted

22 Then answered all the wicked men and <u>*men* of Be'li-al</u>, of those that went with Da'vid, and said, Because they went not with us, we will not give them *anything* of the spoil that we have recovered, save to every man his wife and his children, that they may lead *them* away, and depart.   worthless men

23 Then said Da'vid, You shall not do so, my brethren, with that which the LORD has given us, who has preserved us, and delivered the company that came against us into our hand.

24 For who will hearken to you in this matter? but as his part *is* that goes down to the battle, so *shall* his part *be* that tarries by the stuff: they shall part alike.

25 And it was *so* from that day forward, that he made it a <u>statute</u> and an ordinance for Is'ra-el to this day.   decree

26 And when Da'vid came to Zik'lag, he sent of the <u>spoil</u> to the elders of Ju'dah, *even* to his friends, saying,

Behold a present for you of the spoil of the enemies of the LORD;   booty

27 To *them* which *were* in Beth'-el, and to *them* which *were* in south Ra'moth, and to *them* which *were* in Jat'tir,

28 And to *them* which *were* in Ar'o-er, and to *them* which *were* in Siph'moth, and to *them* which *were* in Esh-te-mo'a,

29 And to *them* which *were* in Ra'chal, and to *them* which *were* in the cities of the Je-rah'me-el-ites, and to *them* which *were* in the cities of the Ken'ites,

30 And to *them* which *were* in Hor'mah, and to *them* which *were* in Chor-a'shan, and to *them* which *were* in A'thach,

31 And to *them* which *were* in He'bron, and to all the places where Da'vid himself and his men were wont to haunt.

CHAPTER 31

NOW the Phi-lis'tines fought against Is'ra-el: and the men of Is'ra-el fled from before the Phi-lis'tines, and fell down slain in mount Gil-bo'a.

2 And the Phi-lis'tines followed hard upon Saul and upon his sons; and the Phi-lis'tines slew Jon'a-than, and A-bin'a-dab, and Mel'chi-shu'a, Saul's sons.

3 And the battle went <u>sore</u> against Saul, and the archers hit him; and he was sore wounded of the archers.   severely

4 Then said Saul to his armorbearer, Draw your sword, and thrust me through therewith; less these uncircum-

cised come and thrust me through, and abuse me. But his armorbearer would not; for he was sore afraid. Therefore Saul took a sword, and fell upon it. *make sport of me - greatly*

5 And when his armorbearer saw that Saul was dead, he fell likewise upon his sword, and died with him.

6 So Saul died, and his three sons, and his armorbearer, and all his men, that same day together.

7 And when the men of Is'ra-el that *were* on the other side of the valley, and *they* that *were* on the other side Jor'dan, saw that the men of Is'ra-el fled, and that Saul and his sons were dead, they forsook the cities, and fled; and the Phi-lis'tines came and dwelled in them.

8 And it came to pass on the morrow, when the Phi-lis'tines came to strip the slain, that they found Saul and his three sons fallen in mount Gil-bo'a.

next day

9 And they cut off his head, and stripped off his armor, and sent into the land of the Phi-lis'tines round about, to publish *it in* the house of their idols, and among the people.

10 And they put his armor in the house of Ash'ta-roth: and they fastened his body to the wall of Beth'-shan.

11 And when the inhabitants of Ja'besh-gil'e-ad heard of that which the Phi-lis'tines had done to Saul;

12 All the valiant men arose, and went all night, and took the body of Saul and the bodies of his sons from the wall of Beth'-shan, and came to Ja'besh, and burned them there.

13 And they took their bones, and buried *them* under a tree at Ja'besh, and fasted seven days.

THE SECOND BOOK OF
SAMUEL

The Reign of David
the Beloved

CHAPTER 1

NOW it came to pass after the death of Saul, when Da'vid was returned from the slaughter of the Am'a-lek-ites, and Da'vid had abode two days in Zik'lag;

2 It came even to pass on the third day, that, behold, a man came out of the camp from Saul with his clothes rent, and earth upon his head: and *so* it was, when he came to Da'vid, that he fell to the earth, and did obei-sance.

torn - i.e., an act of obedience

3 And Da'vid said to him, From where come you? And he said to him, Out of the camp of Is'ra-el am I escaped.

4 And Da'vid said to him, How went the matter? I pray you, tell me. And he answered, That the people are fled from the battle, and many of the people also are fallen and dead; and Saul and Jon'a-than his son are dead also.

5 And Da'vid said to the young man that told him, How know you that Saul and Jon'a-than his son be dead?

6 And the young man that told him said, As I happened by chance upon mount Gil-bo'a, behold, Saul leaned upon his spear; and, lo, the chariots and horsemen followed hard after him.

accidentally was

7 And when he looked behind him, he saw me, and called to me. And I answered, Here *am* I.

8 And he said to me, Who *are* you? And I answered him, I *am* an Am'a-lek-ite.

9 He said to me again, Stand, I pray you, upon me, and slay me: for anguish is come upon me, because my life *is* yet whole in me.

by - still lingers in me

10 So I stood upon him, and slew him, because I was sure that he could not live after that he was fallen: and I took the crown that *was* upon his head, and the bracelet that *was* on his arm, and have brought them here to my lord.

11 Then Da'vid took hold on his clothes, and rent them; and likewise all the men that *were* with him:

tore

12 And they mourned, and wept, and fasted until even, for Saul, and for Jon'a-than his son, and for the people of the LORD, and for the house of Is'ra-el; because they were fallen by the sword.

13 And Da'vid said to the young man that told him, Where *are* you from? And he answered, I *am* the son of a stranger, an Am'a-lek-ite.

14 And Da'vid said to him, How were you not afraid to stretch forth your hand to destroy the LORD's anointed?

15 And Da'vid called one of the

young men, and said, Go near, *and* <u>fall upon him</u>. And he <u>smote</u> him that he died.   cut him down - struck

16 And Da'vid said to him, Your blood *be* upon your head; for <u>your mouth has testified against you</u>, saying, I have slain the LORD's anointed.   you said yourself

17 And Da'vid lamented with this lamentation over Saul and over Jon'a-than his son:

18 (Also he bade them teach the children of Judah *the use of* the bow: behold, *it is* written in the book of Ja'sher.)

19 The beauty of Is'ra-el is slain upon your high places: how are the mighty fallen!

20 Tell *it* not in Gath, publish *it* not in the streets of As'ke-lon; less the daughters of the Phi-lis'tines rejoice, less the daughters of the uncircumcised triumph.

21 You mountains of Gil-bo'a, *let there be* no dew, neither *let there be* rain, upon you, nor fields of offerings: for there the shield of the mighty is vilely cast away, the shield of Saul, *as though he had* not *been* anointed with oil.

22 From the blood of the slain, from the fat of the mighty, the bow of Jon'a-than turned not back, and the sword of Saul returned not empty.

23 Saul and Jon'a-than *were* lovely and pleasant in their lives, and in their death they were not divided: they were swifter than eagles, they were stronger than lions.

24 You daughters of Is'ra-el, weep over Saul, who clothed you in scarlet, with *other* delights, who put on ornaments of gold upon your apparel.

25 How are the mighty fallen in the midst of the battle! O Jon'a-than, *you were* slain in your high places.

26 I am distressed for you, my brother Jon'a-than: very pleasant have you been to me: your love to me was wonderful, passing the love of women.

27 How are the mighty fallen, and the weapons of war perished!

CHAPTER 2

AND it came to pass after this, that Da'vid inquired of the LORD, saying, Shall I go up into any of the cities of Ju'dah? And the LORD said to him, Go up. And Da'vid said, Where shall I go up? And He said, To He'bron.

2 So Da'vid went up there, and his two wives also, A-hin'o-am the Jez'reel-it-ess, and Ab'i-gail Na'bal's wife the Car'mel-ite.

3 And his men that *were* with him did Da'vid bring up, every man with his household: and they dwelled in the cities of He'bron.

4 And the men of Ju'dah came, and there they anointed Da'vid king over the house of Ju'dah. And they told Da'vid, saying, *That* the men of Ja'besh-gil'e-ad *were they* that buried Saul.

5 And Da'vid sent messengers to the men of Ja'besh-gil'e-ad, and said to them, Blessed *be* you of the LORD, that you have showed this kindness to your lord, *even* to Saul, and have buried him.

6 And now the LORD <u>show</u> kindness and truth to you: and I also will <u>requite</u> you this kindness, because you have done this thing. _{do - return}

7 Therefore now let your hands be strengthened, and be you valiant: for your master Saul is dead, and also the house of Ju'dah have anointed me king over them.

8 But Ab'ner the son of Ner, captain of Saul's host, took Ish-bo'sheth the son of Saul, and brought him over to Ma-ha-na'im;

9 And made him king over Gil'e-ad, and over the Ash'ur-ites, and over Jez're-el, and over E'phra-im, and over Ben'ja-min, and over all Is'ra-el.

10 Ish-bo'sheth Saul's son *was* forty years old when he began to reign over Is'ra-el, and reigned two years. But the house of Ju'dah followed Da'vid.

11 And the time that Da'vid was king in He'bron over the house of Ju'dah was seven years and six months.

12 And Ab'ner the son of Ner, and the servants of Ish-bo'sheth the son of Saul, went out from Ma-ha-na'im to Gib'e-on.

13 And Jo'ab the son of Zer-u-i'ah, and the servants of Da'vid, went out, and met together by the pool of Gib'e-on: and they sat down, the one on the one side of the pool, and the other on the other side of the pool.

14 And Ab'ner said to Jo'ab, Let the young men now arise, and <u>play</u> before us. And Jo'ab said, Let them arise. _{hold a contest}

15 Then there arose and went over by number twelve <u>of</u> Ben'ja-min, which *pertained* to Ish-bo'sheth the son of Saul, and twelve of the servants of Da'vid. _{for}

16 And they caught every one his fellow by the head, and *thrust* his sword in his fellow's side; so they fell down together: wherefore that place was called Hel'kath-haz'zu-rim, which *is* in Gib'e-on.

17 And there was a very <u>sore</u> battle that day; and Ab'ner was beaten, and the men of Is'ra-el, before the servants of Da'vid. _{severe}

18 And there were three sons of Zer-u-i'ah there, Jo'ab, and A-bish'a-i, and A'sa-hel: and A'sa-hel *was as* light of foot as a wild <u>roe</u>. _{gazelle}

19 And A'sa-hel pursued after Ab'ner; and in going he turned not to the right hand nor to the left from following Ab'ner.

20 Then Ab'ner looked behind him, and said, *Are* you A'sa-hel? And he answered, I *am*.

21 And Ab'ner said to him, Turn you aside to your right hand or to your left, and lay you hold on one of the young men, and take you his armor. But A'sa-hel would not turn aside from following of him.

22 And Ab'ner said again to A'sa-hel, Turn you aside from following me: <u>wherefore</u> should I <u>smite</u> you to the ground? how then should I hold up my face to Jo'ab your brother? _{why - strike}

23 However he refused to turn aside: wherefore Ab'ner with the <u>hinder</u> end of the spear smote him under the fifth *rib*, that the spear came out behind him; and he fell down there, and died

in the same place: and it came to pass, *that* as many as came to the place where A'sa-hel fell down and died stood still. _{blunt}

24 Jo'ab also and A'bish'a-i pursued after Ab'ner: and the sun went down when they were come to the hill of Am'mah, that *lies* before Gi'ah by the way of the wilderness of Gib'e-on.

25 And the children of Ben'ja-min gathered themselves together after Ab'ner, and became one troop, and stood on the top of an hill. rallied - unified

26 Then Ab'ner called to Jo'ab, and said, Shall the sword devour for ever? know you not that it will be bitterness in the latter end? how long shall it be then, before you bid the people return from following their brethren?

27 And Jo'ab said, *As* God lives, unless you had spoken, surely then in the morning the people had gone up every one from following his brother. Elohim^{p.f.} - ceased pursuing

28 So Jo'ab blew a trumpet, and all the people stood still, and pursued after Is'ra-el no more, neither fought they any more.

29 And Ab'ner and his men walked all that night through the plain, and passed over Jor'dan, and went through all Bith'ron, and they came to Ma-ha-na'im.

30 And Jo'ab returned from following Ab'ner: and when he had gathered all the people together, there lacked of Da'vid's servants nineteen men and A'sa-hel.

31 But the servants of Da'vid had smitten of Ben'ja-min, and of Ab'ner's men, *so that* three hundred and threescore men died. struck down - 360

32 And they took up A'sa-hel, and buried him in the sepulcher of his father, which *was in* Beth'-le'hem. And Jo'ab and his men went all night, and they came to He'bron at break of day. tomb

CHAPTER 3

NOW there was long war between the house of Saul and the house of Da'vid: but Da'vid waxed stronger and stronger, and the house of Saul waxed weaker and weaker. grew

2 And to Da'vid were sons born in He'bron: and his firstborn was Am'non, of A-hin'o-am the Jez're-el-it-ess;

3 And his second, Chil'e-ab, of Ab'i-gail the wife of Na'bal the Car'mel-ite; and the third, Ab'sa-lom the son of Ma'a-cah the daughter of Tal'mai king of Ge'shur;

4 And the fourth, Ad-o-ni'jah the son of Hag'gith; and the fifth, Sheph-a-ti'ah the son of Ab'i-tal;

5 And the sixth, Ith're-am, by Eg'lah Da'vid's wife. These were born to Da'vid in He'bron.

6 And it came to pass, while there was war between the house of Saul and the house of Da'vid, that Ab'ner made himself strong for the house of Saul.

7 And Saul had a concubine, whose name *was* Riz'pah, the daughter of A-i'ah: and *Ish-bo'sheth* said to Ab'ner, Why have you gone in to my father's concubine?

8 Then was Ab'ner very angry for the

words of Ish-bo'sheth, and said, *Am* I a dog's head, which against Ju'dah do show kindness this day to the house of Saul your father, to his brethren, and to his friends, and have not delivered you into the hand of Da'vid, that you charge me to day with a fault concerning this woman? 9 So do <u>God</u> to Ab'ner, and more also, except, as the Lord has <u>sworn</u> to Da'vid, even so I do to him;

Elohim^{p.f.} - promised

Elohim^{p.f.} - promised

10 To <u>translate</u> the kingdom from the house of Saul, and to set up the throne of Da'vid over Is'ra-el and over Ju'dah, from Dan even to Be'er-she'ba.   transfer

11 And he could not answer Ab'ner a word again, because he feared him.

12 And Ab'ner sent messengers to Da'vid on his behalf, saying, Whose *is* the land? saying *also*, Make your <u>league</u> with me, and, behold, my hand *shall be* with you, to bring about all Israel to you.   agreement

13 And he said, Well; I will make a league with you: but one thing I require of you, that is, You shall not see my face, except you first bring Mi'chal Saul's daughter, when you come to see my face.

14 And Da'vid sent messengers to Ish-bo'sheth Saul's son, saying, Deliver *me* my wife Mi'chal, which I <u>espoused</u> to me for an hundred foreskins of the Phi-lis'tines.   engaged

15 And Ish-bo'sheth sent, and took her from *her* husband, *even* from Phal'ti-el the son of La'ish.

16 And her husband went with her along weeping behind her to Ba-hu'rim. Then said Ab'ner to him, Go, return. And he returned.   weeping as he went

17 And Ab'ner had communication with the elders of Israel, saying, You sought for Da'vid in times past *to be* king over you:

18 Now then *do it*: for the Lord has spoken of Da'vid, saying, By the hand of My servant Da'vid I will save My people Is'ra-el out of the hand of the Phi-lis'tines, and out of the hand of all their enemies.

19 And Ab'ner also spoke in the ears of Ben'ja-min: and Ab'ner went also to speak in the ears of Da'vid in He'bron all that seemed good to Is'ra-el, and that seemed good to the whole house of Ben'ja-min.

20 So Ab'ner came to Da'vid to He'bron, and twenty men with him. And Da'vid made Ab'ner and the men that *were* with him a feast.

21 And Ab'ner said to Da'vid, I will arise and go, and will gather all Is'ra-el to my lord the king, that they may make a <u>league</u> with you, and that you may reign over all that your heart desires And Da'vid sent Ab'ner away; and he went in peace.   agreement

22 And, Behold, the servants of Da'vid and Jo'ab came from *pursuing* a troop, and brought in a great <u>spoil</u> with them: but Ab'ner *was* not with Da'vid in He'bron; for he had sent him away, and he was gone in peace.   booty

23 When Jo'ab and all the host that *was* with him were come, they told Jo'ab, saying, Ab'ner the son of Ner came

to the king, and he has sent him away, and he is gone in peace.

24 Then Jo'ab came to the king, and said, What have you done? behold, Ab'ner came to you; why *is* it *that* you have sent him away, and he is quite gone?

25 You know Ab'ner the son of Ner, that he came to deceive you, and to know your going out and your coming in, and to know all that you do.

26 And when Jo'ab was come out from Da'vid, he sent messengers after Ab'ner, which brought him again from the well of Si'rah: but Da'vid knew *it* not.

27 And when Ab'ner was returned to He'bron, Jo'ab took him aside in the gate to speak with him <u>quietly</u>, and <u>smote</u> him there under the fifth *rib*, that he died, for the blood of A'sa-hel his brother.   privately - struck

28 And afterward when Da'vid heard *it*, he said, I and my kingdom *are* <u>guiltless</u> before the LORD for ever from the blood of Ab'ner the son of Ner: innocent

29 Let it rest on the head of Jo'ab, and on all his father's <u>house</u>; and let there not fail from the house of Jo'ab one that has an issue, or that is a leper, or that leans on a staff, or that falls on the sword, or that lacks bread.   family

30 So Jo'ab and A-bish'a-i his brother slew Ab-ner, because he had slain their brother A'sa-hel at Gib'e-on in the battle.

31 And Da'vid said to Jo'ab, and to all the people that *were* with him, <u>Rend</u> your clothes, and gird you with sackcloth, and mourn before Ab'ner. And king Da'vid *himself* followed the <u>bier</u>.   Tear - casket

32 And they buried Ab'ner in He'bron: and the king lifted up his voice, and wept at the grave of Ab'ner; and all the people wept.

33 And the king lamented over Ab'ner, and said, Died Ab'ner as a fool dies?

34 Your hands *were* not bound, nor your feet put into fetters: as a man falls before wicked men, *so* fell you. And all the people wept again over him.

35 And when all the people came to cause Da'vid to eat meat while it was yet day, Da'vid swear, saying, So do God to me, and more also, if I taste bread, or anything else, till the sun be down.   Elohim[p.f.]

36 And all the people took notice *of* it, and it pleased them: as whatsoever the king did pleased all the people.

37 For all the people and all Is'ra-el understood that day that it was not of the king to slay Ab'ner the son of Ner.

38 And the king said to his servants, Know you not that there is a prince and a great man fallen this day in Is'ra-el?

39 And I *am* this day weak, though anointed king; and these men the sons of Zer-u-i'ah *be* too <u>hard</u> for me: the LORD shall reward the doer of evil according to his wickedness.   difficult

CHAPTER 4

AND when Saul's son heard that Ab'ner was dead in He'bron, his hands

were feeble, and all the Is'ra-el-ites were troubled.

2 And Saul's son had two men *that were* captains of <u>bands</u>: the name of the one *was* Ba'a-nah, and the name of the other Re'chab, the sons of Rim'mon a Be-e'roth-ite, of the children of Ben'ja-min: (for Be-e'roth also was <u>reckoned</u> to Ben'ja-min: i.e., military units - considered part of

3 And the Be-e'roth-ites fled to Git'ta-im, and were <u>sojourners</u> there until this day.)   resident non-citizens

4 And Jon'a-than, Saul's son, had a son *that was* lame of *his* feet. He was five years old when the tidings came of Saul and Jon'a-than out of Jez're-el, and his nurse took him up, and fled: and it came to pass, as she made haste to flee, that he fell, and became lame. And his name *was* Me-phib'o-sheth.

5 And the sons of Rim-mon the Be-e'roth-ite, Re'chab and Ba'a-nah, went, and came about the heat of the day to the house of Ish-bo'sheth, who lay on a bed at noon.

6 And they came there into the midst of the house, *as though* <u>they would have brought wheat</u>; and they <u>smote</u> him under the fifth *rib*: and Re'chab and Ba'a-nah his brother escaped.

      if to get wheat - struck

7 For when they came into the house, he lay on his bed in his bedchamber, and they smote him, and slew him, and beheaded him, and took his head, and got them away through the plain all night.

8 And they brought the head of Ish-bo'sheth to Da'vid to He'bron, and said to the king, Behold the head of Ish-bo'sheth the son of Saul your enemy, which sought your life; and the LORD has avenged my lord the king this day of Saul, and of his <u>seed</u>.   offspring

9 And Da'vid answered Re'chab and Ba'a-nah his brother, the sons of Rim'mon the Be-e'roth-ite, and said to them, *As* the LORD lives, who has redeemed my soul out of all adversity,

10 When one told me, saying, Behold, Saul is dead, thinking to have brought good tidings, I took hold of him, and slew him in Zik'lag, who *thought* that I would have given him a reward for his tidings:

11 How much more, when wicked men have slain a righteous person in his own house upon his bed? shall I not therefore now require his blood of your hand, and take you away from the earth?

12 And Da'vid commanded his young men, and they slew them, and cut off their hands and their feet, and hanged *them* up over the pool in He'bron. But they took the head of Ish-bo'sheth, and buried *it* in the <u>sepulcher</u> of Ab'ner in He'bron.   tomb

CHAPTER 5

THEN came all the tribes of Is'ra-el to Da'vid to He'bron, and spoke, saying, Behold, we *are* your bone and your flesh.

2 Also in time past, when Saul was king over us, you were he that led out and brought in Is'ra-el: and the LORD said to you, You shall feed My

people Is'ra-el, and you shall be a captain over Is'ra-el.

3 So all the elders of Is'ra-el came to the king to He'bron; and king Da'vid made a <u>league</u> with them in He'bron before the LORD: and they anointed Da'vid king over Is'ra-el.   agreement

4 Da'vid *was* thirty years old when he began to reign, *and* he reigned forty years.

5 In He'bron he reigned over Ju'dah seven years and six months: and in Je-ru'sa-lem he reigned thirty and three years over all Is'ra-el and Ju'dah.

6 And the king and his men went to Je-ru'sa-lem to the Jeb'u-sites, the inhabitants of the land: which spoke <u>to</u> Da'vid, saying, Except you take away the blind and the lame, you shall not come in here: thinking, Da'vid cannot come in here.   against

7 Nevertheless Da'vid took the strong hold of Zi'on: the same *is* the city of Da'vid.

8 And Da'vid said on that day, Whosoever <u>gets up to the gutter</u>, and smites the Jeb'u-sites, and the lame and the blind, *that are* hated of Da'vid's soul, *he shall be chief and captain*. Wherefore they said, The blind and the lame shall not come into the house.   goes through the water tunnel

9 So Da'vid dwelled in the fort, and called it the <u>city of Da'vid</u>. And Da'vid built round about from Mil'lo and inward.   i.e., Citadel

10 And Da'vid went on, and grew great, and the <u>LORD God of hosts</u> *was* with him.   Jehovah^{s-f} Elohe Tsebaoth

11 And Hi'ram king of Tyre sent messengers to Da'vid, and cedar trees, and carpenters, and masons: and they built Da'vid an house.

12 And Da'vid <u>perceived</u> that the LORD had established him king over Is'ra-el, and that He had exalted his kingdom for His people Is'ra-el's sake.   realized

13 And Da'vid took *him* more concubines and wives out of Je-ru'sa-lem, after he was come from He'bron: and there were yet sons and daughters born to Da'vid.

14 And these *be* the names of those that were born to him in Je-ru'sa-lem; Sham-mu'ah, and Sho'bab, and Na'than, and Sol'o-mon,

15 Ib'har also, and El-i-shu'a, and Ne'pheg, and Ja-phi'a,

16 And E-lish'a-ma, and E-li'a-da, and E-liph'a-let.

17 But when the Phi-lis'tines heard that they had anointed Da'vid king over Is'ra-el, all the Phi'lis'tines came up to <u>seek</u> Da'vid; and Da'vid heard *of it*, and went down to the <u>hold</u>.   search for - stronghold

18 The Phi-lis'tines also came and spread themselves in the valley of Reph'a-im.

19 And Da'vid enquired of the LORD, saying, Shall I go up to the Phi-lis'tines? will You deliver them into my hand? And the LORD said to Da'vid, Go up: for I will doubtless deliver the Phi-lis'tines into your hand.

20 And Da'vid came to Ba'al-per'a-zim, and Da'vid smote them there, and said, The LORD has broken forth upon my enemies before me, as the breach

of waters. Therefore he called the name of that place Ba'al-per'a-zim.

21 And there they left their <u>images</u>, and Da'vid and his men <u>burned them</u>. idols - carried them away

22 And the Phi-lis'tines came up yet again, and spread themselves in the valley of Reph'a-im.

23 And when Da'vid enquired of the LORD, He said, You shall not go up; *but* <u>bring a compass</u> behind them, and come upon them opposite the mulberry trees. circle around

24 And let it be, when you hear the sound of a <u>going</u> in the tops of the <u>mulberry</u> trees, that then you shall bestir yourself: for then shall the LORD go out before you, to smite the host of the Phi-lis'tines. marching - balsam

25 And Da'vid did so, as the LORD had commanded him; and <u>smote</u> the Phi-lis'tines from Ge'ba until you come to Ga'zer. struck down

CHAPTER 6

AGAIN, Da'vid gathered together all *the* chosen *men* of Is'ra-el, thirty thousand.

2 And Da'vid arose, and went with all the people that *were* with him from Ba'a-le of Ju'dah, to bring up from there the ark of <u>God</u>, whose name is called by the name of the LORD of hosts that dwells *between* the cherubims.

Jehovah^{s.f.} Tsebaoth - who is enthroned above

3 And they set the ark of <u>God</u> upon a new cart, and brought it out of the house of A-bin'a-dab that *was* in Gib'e-ah: and Uz'zah and A-hi'o, the sons of A-bin'a-dab, drove the new cart. on the hill

4 And they brought it out of the house of A-bin'a-dab which *was* at Gib'e-ah, <u>accompanying</u> the ark of <u>God</u>: and A-hi'o went before the ark. Elohim^{p.f.} - with

5 And Da'vid and all the house of Is'ra-el played before the LORD on all manner of *instruments made of* fir wood, even on harps, and on <u>psalteries</u>, and on timbrels, and on cornets, and on cymbals. lyres

6 And when they came to Na'chon's threshingfloor, Uz'zah put forth *his hand* to the ark of <u>God</u>, and took hold of it; for the oxen <u>shook</u> *it*. nearly upset it

7 And the anger of the LORD <u>was kindled</u> against Uz'zah; and <u>God</u> smote him there for *his* <u>error</u>; and there he died by the ark of <u>God</u>. burned - irreverence

8 And Da'vid was displeased, because the LORD had made a <u>breach</u> upon Uz'zah: and he called the name of the place Pe'rez-uz'zah to this day. violent work

9 And Da'vid was afraid of the LORD that day, and said, How shall the ark of the LORD come to me?

10 So Da'vid would not <u>remove</u> the ark of the LORD to him into the <u>city of Da'vid</u>: but Da'vid carried it aside into the house of O'bed-e'dom the Git'tite. take i.e., Citadel

11 And the ark of the LORD continued in the house of O'bed-e'dom the Git'tite three months: and the LORD blessed O'bed-e'dom, and all his household.

12 And it was told king Da'vid, saying, The LORD has blessed the house of O'bed-e'dom, and all that *per-*

tains to him, because of the ark of God. So Da'vid went and brought up the ark of God from the house of O'bed-e'dom into the city of Da'vid with gladness. Elohim^p.f.

13 And it was *so*, that when they that bare the ark of the LORD had gone six paces, he sacrificed oxen and fatlings.

14 And Da'vid danced before the LORD with all *his* might; and Da'vid *was* girded with a linen ephod. priestly garment

15 So Da'vid and all the house of Is'ra-el brought up the ark of the LORD with shouting, and with the sound of the trumpet.

16 And as the ark of the LORD came into the city of Da'vid, Mi'chal Saul's daughter looked through a window, and saw king Da'vid leaping and dancing before the LORD; and she despised him in her heart.

17 And they brought in the ark of the LORD, and set it in his place, in the midst of the tabernacle that Da'vid had pitched for it: and Da'vid offered burned offerings and peace offerings before the LORD.

18 And as soon as Da'vid had made an end of offering burned offerings and peace offerings, he blessed the people in the name of the LORD of hosts. Jehovah^s.f. Tsebaoth

19 And he dealt among all the people, *even* among the whole multitude of Is'ra-el, as well to the women as men, to every one a cake of bread, and a good piece *of flesh*, and a flagon *of wine*. So all the people departed every one to his house.

20 Then Da'vid returned to bless his household. And Mi'chal the daughter of Saul came out to meet Da'vid, and said, How glorious was the king of Is'ra-el to day, who uncovered himself to day in the eyes of the handmaids of his servants, as one of the vain fellows shamelessly uncovers himself! vulgar

21 And Da'vid said to Mi'chal, *It was* before the LORD, which chose me before your father, and before all his house, to appoint me ruler over the people of the LORD, over Is'ra-el: therefore will I play before the LORD. celebrate

22 And I will yet be more vile than thus, and will be base in my own sight: and of the maidservants which you have spoken of, of them shall I be had in honor.

23 Therefore Mi'chal the daughter of Saul had no child to the day of her death.

CHAPTER 7

AND it came to pass, when the king sat in his house, and the LORD had given him rest round about from all his enemies;

2 That the king said to Na'than the prophet, See now, I dwell in an house of cedar, but the ark of God dwells within curtains. Elohim^p.f. - within tent

3 And Na'than said to the king, Go, do all that *is* in your heart; for the LORD *is* with you.

4 And it came to pass that night, that the word of the LORD came to Na'than, saying,

5 Go and tell My servant Da'vid,

Thus says the LORD, Shall you build Me an house for Me to dwell in?

6 Whereas I have not dwelled in *any* house since the time that I brought up the children of Is'ra-el out of E'gypt, even to this day, but have <u>walked</u> in a tent and in a tabernacle.   traveled

7 In all *the places* wherein I have <u>walked</u> with all the children of Is'ra-el spoke I a word with any of the tribes of Is'ra-el, whom I commanded to feed My people Is'ra-el, saying, Why build you not Me an house of cedar?

8 Now therefore so shall you say to My servant Da'vid, Thus says the <u>LORD of hosts</u>, I took you from the <u>sheepcote</u>, from following the sheep, to be ruler over My people, over Is'ra-el: Jehovah^{s.f.} - Tsebaoth - pasture

9 And I was with you wherever you went, and have <u>cut off</u> all your enemies out of your sight, and have made you a great name, like to the name of the great *men* that *are* in the earth.   destroyed

10 Moreover I will appoint a place for My people Is'ra-el, and will <u>plant</u> them, that they may dwell in a place of their own, and move no more; neither shall the children of wickedness afflict them any more, as <u>beforetime</u>,   provide a place for - previously

11 And as since the time that I commanded judges *to be* over My people Is'-ra-el, and have caused you to rest from all your enemies. Also the LORD tell you that He will make you an <u>house</u>.   i.e., family lineage

12 And when your days be fulfilled, and you shall sleep with your fathers, I will set up your <u>seed</u> after you, which shall proceed out of your bowels, and I will establish his kingdom.   descendants

13 He shall build an house for My name, and I will stablish the throne of his kingdom for ever.

14 I will be his father, and he shall be My son. If he commit iniquity, I will chasten him with the rod of men, and with the stripes of the children of men: HEB. 1:5

15 But My mercy shall not depart away from him, as I took *it* from Saul, whom I put away before you.

16 And your house and your kingdom shall be established for ever before you: your throne shall be established for ever.   LUKE 1:33

17 According to all these words, and according to all this vision, so did Na'than speak to Da'vid.

18 Then went king Da'vid in, and sat before the LORD, and he said, Who *am* I, O Lord GOD? and what *is* my <u>house</u>, that You have brought me this far?   Adonay^{p.f.} Jehovah - i.e., family lineage

19 And this was yet a small thing in Your sight, O Lord GOD; but You have spoken also of your servant's house for a great while to come. And *is* this the <u>manner</u> of man, O Lord GOD?   custom

20 And what can Da'vid say more to You? for You, Lord GOD, know Your servant.

21 For Your word's sake, and according to Your own heart, have You done all these great things, to make Your servant know *them*.

22 Wherefore You are great, O LORD God: for *there is* none like You, neither *is there any* <u>God</u> beside You, according

to all that we have heard with our ears.

23 And what one nation in the earth *is* like Your people, *even* like Is-ra-el, whom <u>God</u> went to redeem for a people to Himself, and to make Him a <u>name</u>, and to do for you great things and <u>terrible</u>, for Your land, before Your people, which You redeemed to You from E'gypt, *from* the nations and their gods? Elohim^(p.f.) - reputation - amazing

24 For You have <u>confirmed</u> to Yourself Your people Is'ra-el *to be* a people to You for ever: and You, LORD, are become their <u>God</u>. established

25 And now, O LORD God, the word that You have spoken concerning Your servant, and concerning his house, establish *it* for ever, and do as You have said. MATT. 19:28 Jehovah^(s.f.) Elohim^(p.f.)

26 And let Your name be magnified for ever, saying, The LORD of hosts *is* the God over Is'ra-el: and let the house of Your servant Da'vid be established before You.

27 For you, O LORD of hosts, God of Is'ra-el, have revealed to Your servant, saying, I will build You an house: therefore has Your servant found in his heart to pray this prayer to You. Jehovah^(s.f.) Tsebaoth

28 And now, O Lord GOD, You *are* that <u>God</u>, and Your words be true, and You have promised this goodness to Your servant: Adonay^(p.f.) Jehovah

29 Therefore now let it please you to bless the house of Your servant, that it may continue for ever before You: for You, O Lord GOD, have spoken *it*: and with Your blessing let the house of Your servant be blessed for ever.

CHAPTER 8

AND after this it came to pass, that Da'vid <u>smote</u> the Phi-lis'tines, and subdued them: and Da'vid took Me'theg-am'mah out of the hand of the Phi-lis'tines. defeated

2 And he <u>smote</u> Mo'ab, and measured them with a line, <u>casting them down to</u> the ground; even with two lines measured he to put to death, and with one full line to keep alive. And *so* the Mo'ab-ites became Da'vid's servants, *and* brought gifts. making them lie down on

3 Da'vid <u>smote</u> also Had-ad-e'zer, the son of Re'hob, king of Zo'bah, as he went to recover his <u>border</u> at the river Eu-phra'tes. rule

4 And Da'vid took from him a thousand *chariots*, and seven hundred horsemen, and twenty thousand footmen: and Da'vid <u>houghed</u> all the chariot *horses*, but reserved of them *for* an hundred chariots. hamstrung

5 And when the Syr'i-ans of Da-mas'cus came to <u>succour</u> Had-ad-e'zer king of Zo'bah, Da'vid slew of the Syr'i-ans two and twenty thousand men. help

6 Then Da'vid put garrisons in Syr'i-a of Da-mas'cus: and the Syr'i-ans became servants to Da'vid, *and* brought <u>gifts</u>. And the LORD <u>preserved</u> Da'vid wherever he went. tribute - helped

7 And Da'vid took the shields of gold that were on the servants of Had-ad-e'zer, and brought them to Je-ru'sa-lem.

8 And from Be'tah, and from Ber'o-thai, cities of Had-ad-e'zer, king Da'vid took <u>exceeding</u> much <u>brass</u>. very - bronze

9 When To'i king of Ha'math heard that Da'vid had smitten all the host of Had-ad-e'zer,

10 Then To'i sent Jo'ram his son to king Da'vid, to <u>salute</u> him, and to bless him, because he had fought against Had-ad-e'zer, and smitten him: for Had-ad-e'zer had wars with To'i. And *Jo'ram* brought with him vessels of silver, and vessels of gold, and vessels of brass: greet

11 Which also king Da'vid did dedicate to the LORD, with the silver and gold that he had dedicated of all nations which he subdued;

12 Of Syr'i-a, and of Mo'ab, and of the children of Am'mon, and of the Phi-lis'tines, and of Am'a-lek, and of the spoil of Had-ad-e'zer, son of Re'hob, king of Zo'bah.

13 And Da'vid got *him* a name when he returned from <u>smiting</u> of the <u>Syr'i-ans</u> in the valley of salt, *being* eighteen thousand *men*.   killing - Edomites

14 And he put garrisons in E'dom; throughout all E'dom put he garrisons, and all they of E'dom became Da'vid's servants. And the LORD <u>preserved</u> Da'vid wherever he went.   helped

15 And Da'vid reigned over all Is'rael; and Da'vid <u>executed</u> judgment and justice to all his people.   administered

16 And Jo'ab the son of Zer-u-i'ah *was* over the host; and Je-hosh'a-phat the son of A-hi'lud *was* recorder;

17 And Za'dok the son of A-hi'tub, and A-him'e-lech the son of A-bi'a-thar, *were* the priests; and Ser-a-i'ah was the scribe;

18 And Be-na'iah the son of Je-hoi'a-da *was over* both the Cher'eth-ites and the Pe'leth-ites; and Da'vid's sons were chief <u>rulers</u>.   ministers

CHAPTER 9

AND Da'vid said, Is there yet any that is left of the house of Saul, that I may show him kindness for Jon'a-than's sake?

2 And *there was* of the house of Saul a servant whose name *was* Zi'ba. And when they had called him to Da'vid, the king said to him, *Are* you Zi'ba? And he said, Your servant *is he*.

3 And the king said, *Is* there not yet any of the house of Saul, that I may show the kindness of <u>God</u> to him? And Zi'ba said to the king, Jon'a-than has yet a son, *which is* lame on *his* feet.   Elohim^{p.f.}

4 And the king said to him, Where *is* he? And Zi'ba said to the king, Behold, he *is* in the house of Ma'chir, the son of Am'mi-el, in Lo-de'bar.

5 Then king Da'vid sent, and brought him out of the house of Ma'chir, the son of Am'mi-el, from Lo-de'bar.

6 Now when Me-phib'o-sheth, the son of Jon'a-than, the son of Saul, was come to Da'vid, he fell on his face, and did reverence. And Da'vid said, Me-phib'o-sheth. And he answered, Behold your servant!

7 And Da'vid said to him, Fear not: for I will surely show you kindness for Jon'a-than your father's sake, and will restore you all the land of Saul your

father; and you shall eat bread at my table continually.

8 And he bowed himself, and said, What *is* your servant, that you should look upon such a <u>dead dog</u> as I *am*? worthless person

9 Then the king called to Zi'ba, Saul's servant, and said to him, I have given to your master's son all that pertained to Saul and to all his house.

10 You therefore, and your sons, and your servants, shall <u>till</u> the land for him, and you shall bring in *the fruits*, that your master's son may have food to eat: but Me-phib'o-sheth your master's son shall eat bread always at my table. Now Zi'ba had fifteen sons and twenty servants. cultivate

11 Then said Zi'ba to the king, According to all that my lord the king has commanded his servant, so shall your servant do. As for Me-phib'o-sheth, *said the king*, he shall eat at my table, as one of the king's sons.

12 And Me-phib'o-sheth had a young son, whose name *was* Mi'cha. And all that dwelled in the house of Zi'ba *were* servants to Me-phib'o-sheth.

13 So Me-phib'o-sheth dwelled in Je-ru'sa-lem: for he did eat continually at the king's table; and was lame on both his feet.

CHAPTER 10

AND it came to pass after this, that the king of the children of Am'mon died, and Ha'nun his son reigned in his stead.

2 Then said Da'vid, I will show kindness to Ha'nun the son of Na'hash, as his father showed kindness to me. And Da'vid sent to comfort him by the hand of his servants for his father. And Da'vid's servants came into the land of the children of Am'mon.

3 And the princes of the children of Am'mon said to Ha'nun their lord, Think you that Da'vid does honor your father, that he has sent comforters to you? has not Da'vid *rather* sent his servants to you, to search the city, and to spy it out, and to overthrow it?

4 Wherefore Ha'nun took Da'vid's servants, and shaved off the one half of their beards, and cut off their garments in the middle, *even* to their buttocks, and sent them away.

5 When they told *it* to Da'vid, he sent to meet them, because the men were greatly <u>ashamed</u>: and the king said, <u>Tarry</u> at Jer'i-cho until your beards be grown, and *then* return. humiliated - Wait

6 And when the children of Am'mon saw that they <u>stank</u> before Da'vid, the children of Am'mon sent and hired the Syr'i-ans of Beth-re'hob, and the Syr'i-ans of Zo'ba, twenty thousand footmen, and of king Ma'a-cah a thousand men, and of <u>Ish'-tob</u> twelve thousand men. had become odious - the men of Tob

7 And when Da'vid heard of *it*, he sent Jo'ab, and all the host of the mighty men.

8 And the children of Am'mon came out, and put the battle in array at the entering in of the gate: and the Syr'i-

ans of Zo'ba, and of Re'hob, and Ish'-tob, and Ma'a-cah, *were* by themselves in the field.

9 When Jo'ab saw that the front of the battle was against him before and behind, he chose of all the choice *men* of Is'ra-el, and put *them* in array against the Syr'i-ans:

10 And the rest of the people he delivered into the hand of A-bish'a-i his brother, that he might put *them* in array against the children of Am'mon.

11 And he said, If the Syr'i-ans be too strong for me, then you shall help me: but if the children of Am'mon be too strong for you, then I will come and help you.

12 Be of good courage, and let us play the men for our people, and for the cities of our <u>God</u>: and the Lord do that which seems Him good. Elohim^{p.f}

13 And Jo'ab drew near, and the people that *were* with him, to the battle against the Syr'i-ans: and they fled before him.

14 And when the children of Am'mon saw that the Syr'i-ans were fled, then fled they also before A-bish'a-i, and entered into the city. So Jo'ab returned from the children of Am'mon, and came to Je-ru'sa-lem.

15 And when the Syr'i-ans saw that they were smitten before Is'ra-el, they gathered themselves together.

16 And Had-ar-e'zer sent, and brought out the Syr'i-ans that *were* beyond the <u>river</u>: and they came to He'lam; and Sho'bach the captain of the host of Had-ar-e'zer *went* before them. i.e., Euphrates

17 And when it was told Da'vid, he gathered all Is'ra-el together, and passed over Jor'dan, and came to He'lam. And the Syr'i-ans set themselves in array against Da'vid, and fought with him.

18 And the Syr'i-ans fled before Is'ra-el; and Da'vid slew *the men of* seven hundred chariots of the Syr'i-ans, and forty thousand horsemen, and <u>smote</u> Sho'bach the captain of their host, who died there. struck

19 And when all the kings *that were* servants to Had-ar-e'zer saw that they were <u>smitten</u> before Is'ra-el, they made peace with Is'ra-el, and <u>served</u> them. So the Syr'i-ans <u>feared</u> to help the children of Am'mon any more. destroyed - were subject to - were afraid

CHAPTER 11

AND it came to pass, <u>after the year was expired</u>, at the time when kings go forth *to battle*, that Da'vid sent Jo'ab, and his servants with him, and all Is'ra-el; and they destroyed the children of Am'mon, and besieged Rab'bah. But Da'vid tarried still at Je-ru'sa-lem. i.e., in the spring

2 And it came to pass in an eveningtide, that Da'vid arose from off his bed, and walked upon the roof of the king's house: and from the roof he saw a woman washing herself; and the woman *was* very beautiful to look upon.

3 And Da'vid sent and enquired after the woman. And *one* said, *Is* not this Bath'-she-ba, the daughter of E-li'am, the wife of U-ri'ah the Hit'tite?

4 And Da'vid sent messengers, and took her; and she came in to him, and he lay with her; for she was purified from her uncleanness: and she returned to her house.

5 And the woman conceived, and sent and told Da'vid, and said, I *am* with child.

6 And Da'vid sent to Jo'ab, *saying,* Send me U-ri'ah the Hit'tite. And Jo'ab sent U-ri'ah to Da'vid.

7 And when U-ri'ah was come to him, Da'vid <u>demanded</u> *of him* how Jo'ab did, and how the people did, and how the war prospered.   asked

8 And Da'vid said to U-ri'ah, Go down to your house, and <u>wash your feet</u>. And U-ri'ah departed out of the king's house, and there followed him a <u>mess</u> *of meat* from the king.   refresh yourself - present

9 But U-ri'ah slept at the door of the king's house with all the servants of his lord, and went not down to his house.

10 And when they had told Da'vid, saying, U-ri'ah went not down to his house, Da'vid said to U-ri'ah, Came you not from *your* journey? why *then* did you not go down to your house?

11 And U-ri'ah said to Da'vid, The ark, and Is'ra-el, and Ju'dah, abide in tents; and my lord Jo'ab, and the servants of my lord, are encamped in the open fields; shall I then go into mine house, to eat and to drink, and to lie with my wife? *as* you live, and *as* your soul lives I will not do this thing.

12 And Da'vid said to U-ri'ah, Tarry here to day also, and to morrow I will let you depart. So U-ri'ah abode in Je-ru'sa-lem that day, and the morrow.

13 And when Da'vid had called him, he did eat and drink before him; and he made him drunk: and at even he went out to lie on his bed with the servants of his lord, but went not down to his house.

14 And it came to pass in the morning, that Da'vid wrote a letter to Jo'ab, and sent *it* by the hand of U-ri'ah.

15 And he wrote in the letter, saying, Set you U-ri'ah in the forefront of the hottest battle, and <u>retire</u> you from him, that he may be smitten, and die.   withdraw

16 And it came to pass, when Jo'ab observed the city, that he assigned U-ri'ah to a place where he knew that <u>valiant men</u> *were*.   the strongest defenders

17 And the men of the city went out, and fought with Jo'ab: and there fell *some* of the people of the servants of Da'-vid; and U-ri'ah the Hit'tite died also.

18 Then Jo'ab sent and told Da'vid all the things concerning the war;

19 And charged the messenger, saying, When you have made an end of telling the matters of the war to the king,

20 And if so be that the king's wrath arise, and he say to you, Wherefore approached you so near to the city when you did fight? knew you not that they would shoot from the wall?

21 Who smote A-bim'e-lech the son of Je-rub'be-sheth? did not a woman cast a piece of a millstone upon him from the wall, that he died in The'bez? why went you near the wall? then say

you, Your servant U-ri'ah the Hit'tite is dead also.

22 So the messenger went, and came and showed Da'vid all that Jo'ab had sent him for.

23 And the messenger said to Da'vid, Surely the men prevailed against us, and came out to us into the field, and we were upon them even to the entering of the gate.

24 And the shooters shot from off the wall upon your servants; and *some* of the king's servants be dead, and your servant U-ri'ah the Hit'tite is dead also.

25 Then Da'vid said to the messenger, Thus shall you say to Jo'ab, Let not this thing displease you, for the sword devour one as well as another: make your battle more strong against the city, and overthrow it: and encourage you him.

26 And when the wife of U-ri'ah heard that U-ri'ah her husband was dead, she mourned for her husband.

27 And when the mourning was past, Da'vid sent and brought her to his house, and she became his wife, and bare him a son. But the thing that Da'vid had done displeased the LORD.

CHAPTER 12

A ND the LORD sent Na'than to Da'vid. And he came to him, and said to him, There were two men in one city; the one rich, and the other poor.

2 The rich *man* had exceeding many flocks and herds:

3 But the poor *man* had nothing, save one little ewe lamb, which he had bought and nourished up: and it grew up together with him, and with his children; it did eat of his own <u>meat</u>, and drank of his own cup, and lay in his bosom, and was to him as a daughter.   food

4 And there came a traveler to the rich man, and he <u>spared</u> to take of his own flock and of his own herd, to dress for the wayfaring man that was come to him; but took the poor man's lamb, and <u>dressed</u> it for the man that was come to him.   was unwilling - prepared

5 And Da'vid's anger was greatly kindled against the man; and he said to Na'than, *As* the LORD lives, the man that has done this *thing* <u>shall</u> <u>surely die</u>:   ought to die

6 And he shall restore the lamb fourfold, because he did this thing, and because he had no pity.

7 And Na'than said to Da'vid, you *are* the man. Thus says the <u>LORD</u> <u>God</u> of Is'ra-el, I anointed you king over Is'ra-el, and I <u>delivered</u> you out of the hand of Saul;   Jehovah[s.f.] Elohim[p.f.] - rescued

8 And I gave you your master's house, and your master's wives into your bosom, and gave you the house of Is'ra-el and of Ju'dah; and if *that had been* too little, I would moreover have given to you <u>such and such</u> things.   more

9 Wherefore have you despised the commandment of the LORD, to do evil in His sight? you have killed U-ri'ah the Hit'tite with the sword, and have taken his wife *to be* your wife, and have slain him with the sword of the children of Am'mon.

M28
M23

553

P15B
M11

535

10 Now therefore the sword shall never depart from your house; because you have despised Me, and have taken the wife of U-ri'ah the Hit'tite to be your wife.

11 Thus says the Lord, Behold, I will raise up evil against you out of your own house, and I will take your wives before your eyes, and give *them* to your neighbor, and he shall lie with your wives <u>in the sight</u> of this sun.   i.e., publicly

12 For you did *it* secretly: but I will do this thing before all Is'ra-el, and <u>before the sun</u>.   i.e., publicly

13 And Da'vid said to Na'than, I have sinned against the Lord. And Na'than said to Da'vid, The Lord also has put away your sin; you shall not die.

14 However, because by this deed you have given great occasion to the enemies of the Lord to <u>blaspheme</u>, the child also *that is* born to you shall surely die.   show utter contempt

15 And Na'than departed to his house. And the Lord struck the child that U-ri'ah's wife bare to Da'vid, and it was very sick.

16 Da'vid therefore <u>besought God</u> for the child; and Da'vid fasted, and went in, and lay all night upon the earth.   appealed to

17 And the elders of his house arose, *and went* to him, to raise him up from the earth: but he would not, neither did he eat bread with them.

18 And it came to pass on the seventh day, that the child died. And the servants of Da'vid <u>feared</u> to tell him that the child was dead: for they said, Behold, while the child was yet alive, we spoke to him, and he would not hearken to our voice: how will he then <u>vex</u> himself, if we tell him that the child is dead?   were afraid - harm

19 But when Da'vid saw that his servants whispered, Da'vid perceived that the child was dead: therefore Da'vid said to his servants, Is the child dead? And they said, he is dead.

20 Then Da'vid arose from the earth, and washed, and anointed *himself*, and changed his apparel, and came into the house of the Lord, and worshiped: then he came to his own house; and when he <u>required</u>, they set bread before him, and he did eat.   asked

21 Then said his servants to him, What thing *is* this that you have done? you did fast and weep for the child, *while it was* alive; but when the child was dead, you did rise and eat bread.

22 And he said, While the child was yet alive, I fasted and wept: for I said, Who can tell *whether* God will be gracious to me, that the child may live?

23 But now he is dead, why should I fast? can I bring him back again? I shall go to him, but he shall not return to me.

24 And Da'vid comforted Bath'-she-ba his wife, and went in to her, and lay with her: and she bare a son, and he called his name Sol'o-mon: and the Lord loved him.

25 And he sent by the hand of Na'than the prophet; and he called his name Jed-i-di'ah, because of the Lord.

26 And Jo'ab fought against Rab'-

bah of the children of Am'mon, and took the royal city.

27 And Jo'ab sent messengers to Da'vid, and said, I have fought against Rab'bah, and have taken the city of waters.

28 Now therefore gather the rest of the people together, and encamp against the city, and take it: less I take the city, and it be called after my name.

29 And Da'vid gathered all the people together, and went to Rab'bah, and fought against it, and took it.

30 And he took their king's crown from off his head, the weight whereof *was* a talent of gold with the precious stones: and it was *set* on Da'vid's head. And he brought forth the spoil of the city in great abundance.   about 100 pounds

31 And he brought forth the people that *were* therein, and put *them* under saws, and under harrows of iron, and under axes of iron, and made them pass through the brickkiln: and thus did he to all the cities of the children of Am'mon. So Da'vid and all the people returned to Je-ru'salem.   made them work with - work at

CHAPTER 13

AND it came to pass after this, that Ab'sa-lom the son of Da'vid had a fair sister, whose name *was* Ta'mar; and Am'non the son of Da'vid loved her.   desired

2 And Am'non was so vexed, that he fell sick for his sister Ta'mar; for she *was* a virgin; and Am'non thought it hard for him to do any thing to her.   miserable - impossible

3 But Am'non had a friend, whose name *was* Jon'a-dab, the son of Shim'e-ah Da'vid's brother: and Jon'a-dab *was* a very subtle man.

4 And he said to him, Why *are* you, *being* the king's son, lean from day to day? will you not tell me? And Am'non said to him, I love Ta'mar, my brother Ab'sa-lom's sister.   depressed

5 And Jon'a-dab said to him, Lay you down on your bed, and make yourself sick: and when your father comes to see you, say to him, I pray you, Let my sister Ta'mar come, and give me meat, and dress the meat in my sight, that I may see *it*, and eat *it* at her hand.   pretend - food - prepare the food

6 So Am'non lay down, and made himself sick: and when the king was come to see him, Am'non said to the king, I pray you, let Ta'mar my sister come, and make me a couple of cakes in my sight, that I may eat at her hand.

7 Then Da'vid sent home to Ta'mar, saying, Go now to your brother Am'non's house, and dress him meat.

8 So Ta'mar went to her brother Am'non's house; and he was laid down. And she took flour, and kneaded *it*, and made cakes in his sight, and did bake the cakes.

9 And she took a pan, and poured *them* out before him; but he refused to eat. And Am'non said, Have out all men from me. And they went out every man from him.

10 And Am'non said to Ta'mar, Bring the meat into the chamber, that I may eat of your hand. And Ta'mar took the cakes which she had made,

and brought *them* into the chamber to Am'non her brother.

11 And when she had brought *them* to him to eat, he took hold of her, and said to her, Come lie with me, my sister.

12 And she answered him, Nay, my brother, do not <u>force</u> me; for no such thing ought to be done in Is'ra-el: do not you this <u>folly</u>. degrade me - disgusting thing

13 And I, where shall I cause my shame to go? and as for you, you shall be as one of the fools in Is'ra-el. Now therefore, I pray you, speak to the king; for he will not withhold me from you.

14 However he would not hearken to her voice: but, being stronger than she, forced her, and lay with her.

15 Then Am'non <u>hated</u> her <u>exceedingly</u>; so that the hatred wherewith he hated her *was* greater than the love wherewith he had loved her. And Am'non said to her, Arise, be gone. disliked - intensely

16 And she said to him, *There is* no cause: this evil in sending me away *is* greater than the other that you did to me. But he would not hearken to her.

17 Then he called his servant that ministered to him, and said, Put now this *woman* out from me, and bolt the door after her.

18 And *she had* a <u>garment</u> of <u>divers</u> colors upon her: for with such robes were the king's daughters *that were* virgins appareled. Then his servant brought her out, and bolted the door after her. full length robe - various

19 And Ta'mar put ashes on her head, and <u>rent</u> her garment of divers colors that *was* on her, and laid her hand on her head, and went on crying. tore

20 And Ab'sa-lom her brother said to her, Has Am'non your brother been with you? but hold now your peace, my sister: he *is* your brother; regard not this thing. So Ta'mar remained desolate in her brother Ab'sa-lom's house.

21 But when king Da'vid heard of all these things, he was very angry.

22 And Ab'sa-lom spoke to his brother Am'non neither good nor bad: for Ab'sa-lom hated Am'non, because he had <u>forced</u> his sister Ta'mar. degraded

23 And it came to pass after two full years, that Ab'sa-lom had sheepshearers in Ba'al-ha'zor, which *is* beside E'phra-im: and Ab'sa-lom invited all the king's sons.

24 And Ab'sa-lom came to the king, and said, Behold now, your servant has sheepshearers; let the king, I beseech you, and his servants go with your servant.

25 And the king said to Ab'sa-lom, Nay, my son, let us not all now go, less we be <u>chargeable</u> to you. And he <u>pressed</u> him: however he would not go, but blessed him. burdensome - urged

26 Then said Ab'sa-lom, If not, I pray you, let my brother Am'non go with us. And the king said to him, Why should he go with you?

27 But Ab'sa-lom <u>pressed</u> him, that he let Am'non and all the king's sons go with him. urged

M23 | | | 558

28 Now Ab'sa-lom had commanded his servants, saying, Mark you now when Am'non's heart is merry with wine, and when I say to you, <u>Smite</u> Am'non; then kill him, fear not: have not I commanded you? be coura-geous, and be valiant. Strike
29 And the servants of Ab'sa-lom did to Am'non as Ab'sa-lom had commanded. Then all the king's sons arose, and every man got him up upon his mule, and fled.
30 And it came to pass, while they were in the way, that tidings came to Da'vid, saying, Ab'sa-lom has slain all the king's sons, and there is not one of them left.
31 Then the king arose, and tare his garments, and lay on the earth; and all his servants stood by with their clothes <u>rent</u>. torn
32 And Jon'a-dab, the son of Shim'e-ah Da'vid's brother, an-swered and said, Let not my lord sup-pose *that* they have slain all the young men the king's sons; for Am'non only is dead: for by the <u>appointment</u> of Ab'sa-lom this has been determined from the day that he <u>forced</u> his sister Ta'mar. intent - degraded
33 Now therefore let not my lord the king take the thing to his heart, to think that all the king's sons are dead: for Am'non only is dead.
34 But Ab'sa-lom fled. And the young man that kept the watch lifted up his eyes, and looked, and, be-hold, there came <u>much</u> people by the way of the hill side behind him. many
35 And Jon'a-dab said to the king, Behold, the king's sons come: as your servant said, so it is.
36 And it came to pass, as soon as he had <u>made an end</u> of speaking, that, behold, the king's sons came, and lifted up their voice and wept: and the king also and all his servants wept very <u>sore</u>. finished - bitterly
37 But Ab'sa-lom fled, and went to Tal'mai, the son of Am-mi'hud, king of Ge'shur. And *Da'vid* mourned for his son every day.
38 So Ab'sa-lom fled, and went to Ge'shur, and was there three years.
39 And *the soul of* king Da'vid longed to go forth to Ab'sa-lom: for he was <u>comforted</u> concerning Am'non, see-ing he was dead. heart - consoled

CHAPTER 14

NOW Jo'ab the son of Zer-u-i'ah perceived that the king's heart *was* <u>toward</u> Ab'sa-lom. inclined toward
2 And Jo'ab sent to Te-ko'ah, and brought from there a wise woman, and said to her, I pray you, <u>feign</u> your-self to be a mourner, and put on now mourning apparel, and anoint not yourself with oil, but be as a woman that had a long time mourned for the dead: pretend
3 And come to the king, and speak <u>on this manner</u> to him. So Jo'ab put the words in her mouth. in this way
4 And when the woman of Te-ko'ah spoke to the king, she fell on her face to the ground, and <u>did obei-sance</u>, and said, Help, O king. prostrated herself
5 And the king said to her, What

ails you? And she answered, I *am* indeed a widow woman, and my husband is dead.

6 And your handmaid had two sons, and they two <u>strove</u> together in the field, and *there was* none to part them, but the one <u>smote</u> the other, and slew him.   fought - struck

7 And, behold, the whole family is risen against your handmaid, and they said, Deliver him that smote his brother, that we may kill him, for the life of his brother whom he slew; and we will destroy the heir also: and so they shall <u>quench my coal</u> which is left, and shall not leave to my husband *neither* name nor remainder upon the earth.   i.e., destroy the last of my family

8 And the king said to the woman, Go to your house, and I will give <u>charge</u> concerning you.   instruction

9 And the woman of Te-ko'ah said to the king, My lord, O king, the iniquity *be* on me, and on my father's house: and the king and his throne *be* guiltless.

10 And the king said, Whosoever says *anything* to you, bring him to me, and he shall not touch you any more.

11 Then said she, I pray you, let the king remember the LORD your <u>God</u>, that you would not allow the <u>revengers</u> of blood to destroy any more, less they destroy my son. And he said, *As* the LORD lives, there shall not one hair of your son fall to the earth.   avengers

12 Then the woman said, Let your handmaid, I pray you, speak *one* word to my lord the king. And he said, Say on.

13 And the woman said, Wherefore then have you thought such a thing against the people of <u>God</u>? for the king does speak this thing as one which is <u>faulty</u>, in that the king does not bring home again his banished.   Elohim^(p.f.) - guilty

14 For we must needs die, and *are* as water spilt on the ground, which cannot be gathered up again; neither does <u>God</u> respect *any* person: yet does He devise means, that His banished be not <u>expelled</u> from Him.   cast out

15 Now therefore that I am come to speak of this thing to my lord the king, *it is* because the people have made me afraid: and your handmaid said, I will now speak to the king; it may be that the king will perform the request of his handmaid.

16 For the king will hear, to deliver his handmaid out of the hand of the man *that would* destroy me and my son together out of the inheritance of <u>God</u>.

17 Then your handmaid said, The word of my lord the king shall now be comfortable: for as an <u>angel</u> of God, so *is* my lord the king to discern good and bad: therefore the LORD your <u>God</u> will be with you.   messenger - Elohim^(p.f.)

18 Then the king answered and said to the woman, Hide not from me, I pray you, the thing that I shall ask you. And the woman said, Let my lord the king now speak.

19 And the king said, *Is not* the hand of Jo'ab with you in all this? And the woman answered and said, *As* your soul

M05 —
|
|
|
681

lives, my lord the king, none can turn to the right hand or to the left from anything that my lord the king has spoken: for your servant Jo'ab, he <u>bade</u> me, and he put all these words in the mouth of your handmaid: *instructed*

20 To bring about this form of speech has your servant Jo'ab done this thing: and my lord *is* wise, according to the wisdom of an angel of <u>God</u>, to know all *things* that *are* in the earth. *Elohim* p.f.

21 And the king said to Jo'ab, Behold now, I have done this thing: go therefore, bring the young man Ab'sa-lom again.

22 And Jo'ab fell to the ground on his face, and bowed himself, and thanked the king: and Jo'ab said, To day your servant knows that I have found grace in your sight, my lord, O king, in that the king has fulfilled the <u>request</u> of his servant. *word*

23 So Jo'ab arose and went to Ge'shur, and brought Ab'sa-lom to Je-ru'sa-lem.

24 And the king said, Let him turn to his own house, and let him not <u>see</u> my face. So Ab'sa-lom returned to his own house, and saw not the king's face. *come to see*

25 But in all Is'ra-el there was none to be so much praised as Ab'sa-lom for his beauty: from the sole of his foot even to the crown of his head there was no <u>blemish</u> in him. *defect*

26 And when he <u>polled</u> his head, (for it was at every year's end that he polled *it*: because *the hair* was heavy on him, therefore he polled it:) he weighed the hair of his head at two hundred shekels after the king's weight. *cut*

27 And to Ab'sa-lom there were born three sons, and one daughter, whose name *was* Ta'mar: she was a woman of a <u>fair countenance</u>. *beautiful appearance*

28 So Ab'sa-lom dwelled two full years in Je-ru'sa-lem, and saw not the king's face.

29 Therefore Ab'sa-lom sent for Jo'ab, to have sent him to the king; but he would not come to him: and when he sent again the second time, he would not come.

30 Therefore he said to his servants, See, Jo'ab's field is near mine, and he has barley there; go and set it on fire. And Ab'sa-lom's servants set the field on fire.

31 Then Jo'ab arose, and came to Ab'sa-lom to *his* house, and said to him, Why have your servants set my field on fire?

32 And Ab'sa-lom answered Jo'ab, Behold, I sent to you, saying, Come here, that I may send you to the king, to say, Wherefore am I come from Ge'shur? *it had been* good for me *to have been* there still: now therefore let me <u>see the king's face</u>; and if there be *any* iniquity in me, let him kill me. *meet with the king*

33 So Jo'ab came to the king, and told him: and when he had called for Ab'sa-lom, he came to the king, and bowed himself on his face to the ground before the king: and the king kissed Ab'sa-lom.

CHAPTER 15

AND it came to pass after this, that Ab'sa-lom prepared him chariots and horses, and fifty men to run before him.

2 And Ab'sa-lom rose up early, and stood beside the way of the gate: and it was *so*, that when any man that had a controversy came to the king for judgment, then Ab'sa-lom called to him, and said, Of what city *are* you? And he said, Your servant *is* of one of the tribes of Is'ra-el.

3 And Ab'sa-lom said to him, See, your matters *are* good and right; but *there is* no man <u>deputed</u> of the king to hear you.   representing

4 Ab'sa-lom said moreover, Oh that I were made judge in the land, that every man which has any suit or cause might come to me, and I would do him justice!

5 And it was *so*, that when any man came near *to him* to <u>do him obei-sance</u>, he put forth his hand, and took him, and kissed him.

          prostrate himself

6 And on this manner did Ab'sa-lom to all Is'ra-el that came to the king for judgment: so Ab'sa-lom stole the hearts of the men of Is'ra-el.

7 And it came to pass after forty years, that Ab'sa-lom said to the king, I pray you, let me go and <u>pay</u> my <u>vow</u>, which I have vowed to the LORD, in He'bron.   fulfill - pledge

8 For your servant <u>vowed a vow</u> while I abode at Ge'shur in Syr'i-a, saying, If the LORD shall bring me again indeed to Je-ru'sa-lem, then I will serve the LORD.   made a pledge

9 And the king said to him, Go in peace. So he arose, and went to He'bron.

10 But Ab'sa-lom sent <u>spies</u> throughout all the tribes of Is'ra-el, saying, As soon as you hear the sound of the trumpet, then you shall say, Ab'sa-lom reigns in He'bron.   secret messengers

11 And with Ab'sa-lom went two hundred men out of Je-ru'sa-lem, *that were* called; and they went in their <u>simplicity</u>, and they knew not any thing.   innocence

12 And Ab'sa-lom sent for A-hith'o-phel the Gi'lo-nite, Da'vid's counselor, from his city, *even* from Gi'loh, while he offered sacrifices. And the conspiracy was strong; for the people <u>increased</u> continually with Ab'sa-lom.   were increasing in numbers

13 And there came a messenger to Da'vid, saying, The hearts of the men of Is'ra-el are <u>after</u> Ab'sa-lom.   with

14 And Da'vid said to all his servants that were with him at Je-ru'sa-lem, Arise, and let us flee; for we shall not *else* escape from Ab'sa-lom: make speed to depart, less he overtake us suddenly, and bring evil upon us, and <u>smite</u> the city with the edge of the sword.

          otherwise - strike

15 And the king's servants said to the king, Behold, your servants *are ready to do* whatsoever my lord the king shall <u>appoint</u>.   decide

16 And the king went forth, and all his household after him. And the king

left ten women, *which were* concubines, to keep the house.

17 And the king went forth, and all
the people after him, and tarried in a
place that was far off. stayed

18 And all his servants passed on
beside him; and all the Cher'eth-ites,
and all the Pe'leth-ites, and all the
Git'tites, six hundred men which
came after him from Gath, passed
on before the king. traveled

19 Then said the king to It'ta-i the
Git'tite, Why go you also with us?
return to your place, and abide with
the king: for you *are* a stranger, and
also an exile.

20 Whereas you came *but* yesterday,
should I this day make you go up
and down with us? seeing I go where
I may, return you, and take back
your brethren: mercy and truth *be*
with you.

21 And It'ta-i answered the king, and
said, *As* the LORD lives, and *as* my
lord the king lives, surely in what
place my lord the king shall be,
whether in death or life, even there
also will thy servant be.

22 And Da-vid said to It'ta-i, Go and
pass over. And It'ta-i the Git'tite
passed over, and all his men, and all
the little ones that *were* with him.

23 And all the country wept with a
loud voice, and all the people
passed over: the king also himself
passed over the brook Kid'ron, and
all the people passed over, toward
the way of the wilderness. traveled

24 And lo Za'dok also, and all the
Le'vites *were* with him, bearing the ark

of the covenant of God: and they
set down the ark of God; and A-
bi'a-thar went up, until all the
people had done passing out of the
city. agreement - Elohim^p.f. - finished traveling

25 And the king said to Za'dok, Carry
back the ark of God into the city: if I
shall find favor in the eyes of the LORD,
He will bring me again, and show me
both it, and His habitation:

26 But if He thus say, I have no delight in you; behold, *here am I*, let Him
do to me as seems good to Him.

27 The king said also to Za'dok the
priest, *Are not* you a seer? return into
the city in peace, and your two sons
with you, A-him'a-az your son, and
Jon'a-than the son of A-bi'a-thar. prophet

28 See, I will tarry in the plain of the
wilderness, until there come word
from you to certify me. inform

29 Za'dok therefore and A-bi'a-thar
carried the ark of God again to Je-
ru'sa-lem: and they tarried there. Elohim^p.f.

30 And Da'vid went up by the ascent of *mount* Ol'i-vet, and wept as
he went up, and had his head covered, and he went barefoot: and all
the people that *was* with him covered every man his head, and they
went up, weeping as they went up.

31 And *one* told Da'vid, saying, A-
hith'o-phel *is* among the conspirators
with Ab'sa-lom. And Da'vid said, O
LORD, I pray you, turn the counsel of
A-hith'o-phel into foolishness.

32 And it came to pass, that *when*
Da'vid was come to the top *of the
mount*, where he worshiped God, behold, Hu'shai the Ar'chite came to meet

him with his coat <u>rent</u>, and earth
upon his head: Elohim^{p.f.} - torn
33 To whom Da'vid said, If you <u>pass</u>
on with me, then you shall be a burden to me: travel
34 But if you return to the city, and
say to Ab'sa-lom, I will be your servant, O king; *as* I *have been* your
father's servant formerly, so *will* I
now also *be* your servant: then may
you for me <u>defeat</u> the counsel of A-
hith'o-phel. frustrate
35 And *have you* not there with you
Za'dok and A-bi'a-thar the priests?
therefore it shall be, *that* what thing
soever you shall hear <u>out of</u> the
king's house, you shall tell *it* to
Za'dok and A-bi'a-thar the priests.
from
36 Behold, *they have* there with them
their two sons, A-him'a-az Za'dok's
son, and Jon'a-than A-bi'a-thar's
son; and by them you shall send to
me every thing that you can hear.
37 So Hu'shai Da'vid's friend came
into the city, and Ab'sa-lom came
into Je-ru'sa-lem.

CHAPTER 16

AND when Da'vid was a little past
the top *of the hill*, behold, Zi'ba
the servant of Me-phib'o-sheth met
him, with a couple of asses saddled,
and upon them two hundred *loaves*
of bread, and an hundred bunches
of raisins, and an hundred of summer fruits, and a bottle of wine.
2 And the king said to Zi'ba, What
mean you by these? And Zi'ba said,
The asses *be* for the king's household
to ride on; and the bread and summer fruit for the young men to eat;
and the wine, that such as be faint
in the wilderness may drink.
3 And the king said, And where *is*
your master's son? And Zi'ba said
to the king, Behold, he abides at Je-
ru'sa-lem: for he said, To day shall
the house of Is'ra-el restore me the
kingdom of my father.
4 Then said the king to Zi'ba, Behold, you *are* all that *pertained* to
Me-phib'o-sheth. And Zi'ba said,
I humbly <u>beseech</u> you *that* I may
find <u>grace</u> in your sight, my lord, O
king. belonged - beg - favor
5 And when king Da'vid came to Ba-
hu'rim, behold, there came out a man
of the family of the house of Saul,
whose name *was* Shim'e-i, the son
of Ge'ra: he came forth, and cursed
still as he came.
6 And he cast stones at Da'vid, and
at all the servants of king Da'vid: and
all the people and all the mighty men
were on his right hand and on his left.
7 And thus said Shim'e-i when he
cursed, <u>Come</u> out, come out, you
bloody man, and you <u>man of Be'li-
al</u>: Get - a worthless fellow
8 The LORD has returned upon you
all the blood of the house of Saul,
in whose stead you have reigned; and
the LORD has delivered the kingdom
into the hand of Ab'sa-lom your son:
and, behold, you *are taken* in your
mischief, because you *are* a <u>bloody
man</u>. man of bloodshed
9 Then said A-bish'a-i the son of Zer-
u-i'ah to the king, Why should this
dead dog curse my lord the king?

let me go over, I pray you, and take off his head.   cut

10 And the king said, What have I to do with you, you sons of Zer-u-i'ah? so let him curse, because the LORD has said to him, Curse Da'vid. Who shall then say, Wherefore have you done so?

11 And Da'vid said to A-bish'a-i, and to all his servants, Behold, my son, which came forth of my bowels, seeks my life: how much more now *may this* Ben'ja-mite *do it*? let him alone, and let him curse; for the LORD has bidden him.   insides

12 It may be that the LORD will look on my affliction, and that the LORD will requite me good for his cursing this day.

13 And as Da'vid and his men went by the way, Shim'e-i went along on the hill's side opposite him, and cursed as he went, and threw stones at him, and cast dust.

14 And the king, and all the people that *were* with him, came weary, and refreshed themselves there.

15 And Ab'sa-lom, and all the people the men of Is'ra-el, came to Je-ru'sa-lem, and A-hith'o-phel with him.

16 And it came to pass, when Hu'shai the Ar'chite, Da'vid's friend, was come to Ab'sa-lom, that Hu'shai said to Ab'sa-lom, God save the king, God save the king.   long live

17 And Ab'sa-lom said to Hu'shai, *Is* this your kindness to your friend? why went you not with your friend?

18 And Hu'shai said to Ab'sa-lom, Nay; but whom the LORD, and this people, and all the men of Is'ra-el,

choose, his will I be, and with him will I abide.   remain

19 And again, whom should I serve? *should I* not *serve* in the presence of his son? as I have served in your father's presence, so will I be in your presence.

20 Then said Ab'sa-lom to A-hith'o-phel, Give counsel among you what we shall do.

21 And A-hith'o-phel said to Ab'sa-lom, Go in to your father's concubines, which he has left to keep the house; and all Israel shall hear that you are abhorred of your father: then shall the hands of all that *are* with you be strong.

22 So they spread Ab'sa-lom a tent upon the top of the house; and Ab'sa-lom went in to his father's concubines in the sight of all Is'ra-el.

23 And the counsel of A-hith'o-phel, which he counselled in those days, *was* as if a man had enquired at the oracle of God: so *was* all the counsel of A-hith'o-phel both with Da'vid and with Ab'sa-lom.   advice - Elohim^p.f.

CHAPTER 17

MOREOVER A-hith'o-phel said to Ab'sa-lom, Let me now choose out twelve thousand men, and I will arise and pursue after Da'vid this night:

2 And I will come upon him while he *is* weary and weak handed, and will make him afraid: and all the people that *are* with him shall flee; and I will smite the king only:

                        exhausted - terrify him - strike down

3 And I will bring back all the people

to you: the man whom you seek *is* as if all returned: *so* all the people shall be in peace.

4 And the saying pleased Ab'sa-lom well, and all the elders of Is'ra-el.

5 Then said Ab'sa-lom, Call now Hu'shai the Ar'chite also, and let us hear likewise what he says.

6 And when Hu'shai was come to Ab'sa-lom, Ab'sa-lom spoke to him, saying, A-hith'o-phel has spoken after this manner: shall we do *after* his saying? if not; speak you.

7 And Hu'shai said to Ab'sa-lom, The counsel that A-hith'o-phel has given *is* not good at this time.   advice

8 For, said Hu'shai, you know your father and his men, that they *be* mighty men, and they *be* chafed in their minds, as a bear robbed of her whelps in the field: and your father *is* a man of war, and will not lodge with the people.   fierce - cubs - spend the night

9 Behold, he is hid now in some pit, or in some *other* place: and it will come to pass, when some of them be overthrown at the first, that whosoever hears it will say, There is a slaughter among the people that follow Ab'sa-lom.   fallen

10 And he also *that is* valiant, whose heart *is* as the heart of a lion, shall utterly melt: for all Is'ra-el knows that your father *is* a mighty man, and *they* which *be* with him *are* valiant men.   brave

11 Therefore I counsel that all Is'ra-el be generally gathered to you, from Dan even to Be'er-she'ba, as the sand that *is* by the sea for multitude; and that you go to battle in your own person.

12 So shall we come upon him in some place where he shall be found, and we will light upon him as the dew falls on the ground: and of him and of all the men that *are* with him there shall not be left so much as one.

13 Moreover, if he be gotten into a city, then shall all Is'ra-el bring ropes to that city, and we will draw it into the river, until there be not one small stone found there.

14 And Ab'sa-lom and all the men of Is'ra-el said, The counsel of Hu'shai the Ar'chite is better than the counsel of A-hith'o-phel. For the LORD had appointed to defeat the good counsel of A-hith'o-phel, to the intent that the LORD might bring evil upon A'bsa-lom.   ordained

15 Then said Hu'shai to Za'dok and to A-bi'a-thar the priests, Thus and thus did A-hith'o-phel counsel Ab'sa-lom and the elders of Is'ra-el; and thus and thus have I counseled.

16 Now therefore send quickly, and tell Da'vid, saying, Lodge not this night in the plains of the wilderness, but speedily pass over; less the king be swallowed up, and all the people that *are* with him.   Do not spend

17 Now Jon'a-than and A-him'a-az stayed by En-ro'gel; for they might not be seen to come into the city: and a wench went and told them; and they went and told king Da'vid.   maidservant

18 Nevertheless a lad saw them, and told Ab'sa-lom: but they went both of them away quickly, and came to a

man's house in Ba-hu'rim, which had a well in his court; into which they went down.

19 And the woman took and spread a covering over the well's mouth, and spread ground <u>corn</u> thereon; and the thing was not known. grain

20 And when Ab'sa-lom's servants came to the woman to the house, they said, Where *is* A-him'a-az and Jon'a-than? And the woman said to them, They be gone over the brook of water. And when they had sought and could not find *them*, they returned to Je-ru'sa-lem.

21 And it came to pass, after they were departed, that they came up out of the well, and went and told king Da'vid, and said to Da'vid, Arise, and <u>pass quickly</u> over the water: for thus has A-hith'o-phel counselled against you. travel

22 Then Da'vid arose, and all the people that *were* with him, and they <u>passed</u> over Jor'dan: by the <u>morning light</u> there lacked not one of them that was not gone over Jor'dan. traveled - dawn

23 And when A-hith'o-phel saw that his counsel was not followed, he saddled *his* ass, and arose, and got him home to his house, to his city, and put his household in order, and hanged himself, and died, and was buried in the <u>sepulcher</u> of his father. tomb

24 Then Da'vid came to Ma-ha-na'im. And Ab'sa-lom <u>passed</u> over Jor'dan, he and all the men of Is'ra-el with him.

25 And Ab'sa-lom made Am'a-sa captain of the host instead of Jo'ab: which Am'a-sa *was* a man's son, whose name was Ith'ra an Is'ra-el-ite, that went in to Ab'i-gail the daughter of Na'hash, sister to Zer-u-i'ah Jo'ab's mother.

26 So Is'ra-el and Ab'sa-lom <u>pitched</u> in the land of Gil'e-ad. camped

27 And it came to pass, when Da'vid was come to Ma-ha-na'im, that Sho'bi the son of Na'hash of Rab'bah of the children of Am'mon, and Ma'chir the son of Am'mi-el of Lo-de'bar, and Bar-zil'la-i the Gil'e-ad-ite of Ro-ge'lim,

28 Brought beds, and <u>basins</u>, and earthen vessels, and wheat, and barley, and flour, and parched *corn*, and beans, and lentils, and parched *pulse*, bowls - seeds

29 And honey, and butter, and sheep, and cheese of <u>kine</u>, for Da'vid, and for the people that *were* with him, to eat: for they said, The people *is* hungry, and weary, and thirsty, in the wilderness. the herd - are

CHAPTER 18

AND Da'vid numbered the people that *were* with him, and set captains of thousands and captains of hundreds over them.

2 And Da'vid sent forth a third part of the people under the hand of Jo'ab, and a third part under the hand of A-bish'a-i the son of Zer-u-i'ah, Jo'ab's brother, and a third part under the hand of It'ta-i the Git'tite. And the king said to the people, I will surely go forth with you myself also.

3 But the people answered, You shall not go forth: for if we flee away, they will not care for us; neither if half of us die, will they care for us: but now *you are* worth ten thousand of us: therefore now *it is* better that you <u>succour</u> us out of the city. _{provide help for}
4 And the king said to them, What seems you best I will do. And the king stood by the gate side, and all the people came out by hundreds and by thousands.
5 And the king commanded Jo'ab and A-bish'a-i and It'ta-i, saying, *Deal* gently for my sake with the young man, *even* with Ab'sa-lom. And all the people heard when the king gave all the captains <u>charge</u> concerning Ab'sa-lom._{orders}
6 So the people went out into the field against Is'ra-el: and the battle *was* in the <u>wood</u> of E'phra-im; _{forest}
7 Where the people of Is'ra-el were slain before the servants of Da'vid, and there was there a great slaughter that day of twenty thousand *men*.
8 For the battle was there scattered over the face of all the country: and the <u>wood</u> <u>devoured more people</u> that day than the sword devoured. _{claimed more lives}
9 And Ab'sa-lom met the servants of Da'vid. And Ab'sa-lom rode upon a mule, and the mule went under the thick boughs of a great oak, and his head caught hold of the oak, and he was <u>taken</u> up between the heaven and the earth; and the mule that *was* under him went away. _{left hanging}
10 And a certain man saw *it*, and told Jo'ab, and said, Behold, I saw Ab'sa-lom hanged in an oak.

11 And Jo'ab said to the man that told him, And, behold, you saw *him*, and why did you not smite him there to the ground? and I would have given you ten *shekels* of silver, and a girdle.
12 And the man said to Jo'ab, Though I should receive a thousand *shekels* of silver in my hand, *yet* would I not put forth my hand against the king's son: for in our hearing the king <u>charged</u> you and A-bish'a-i and It'ta-i, saying, Beware that none *touch* the young man Ab'sa-lom. _{ordered}
13 Otherwise I should have wrought falsehood against my own life: for there is no matter hid from the king, and you yourself would have set yourself against *me*.
14 Then said Jo'ab, I may not <u>tarry thus</u> with you. And he took three <u>darts</u> in his hand, and thrust them through the heart of Ab'sa-lom, while he *was* yet alive in the midst of the oak. _{waste time - arrows}
15 And ten young men that bare Jo'ab's armor <u>compassed about</u> and <u>smote</u> Ab'sa-lom, and slew him. _{gathered around - struck}
16 And Jo'ab blew the trumpet, and the people returned from pursuing after Is'ra-el: for Jo'ab held back the people.
17 And they took Ab'sa-lom, and cast him into a great pit in the wood, and laid a very great heap of stones upon him: and all Is'ra-el fled every one to his tent.
18 Now Ab'sa-lom in his lifetime had taken and reared up for himself a <u>pillar</u>, which *is* in the king's <u>dale</u>: for he said, I have no son to keep my name in

remembrance: and he called the pillar after his own name: and it is called to this day, Ab'sa-lom's place. _{monument - valley}

19 Then said A-him'a-az the son of Za'dok, Let me now run, and bear the king tidings, how that the LORD has avenged him of his enemies.

20 And Jo'ab said to him, You shall not bear tidings this day, but you shall bear tidings another day: but this day you shall bear no tidings, because the king's son is dead.

21 Then said Jo'ab to Cu'shi, Go tell the king what you have seen. And Cu'shi bowed himself to Jo'ab, and ran.

22 Then said A-him'a-az the son of Za'dok yet again to Jo'ab, But <u>howsoever</u>, let me, I pray you, also run after Cu'shi. And Jo'ab said, Wherefore will you run, my son, seeing that you <u>have no tidings ready</u>?

whatever happened - will not be paid for the news

23 But <u>howsoever</u>, *said he*, let me run. And he said to him, Run. Then A-him'a-az ran by the way of the plain, and <u>overran</u> Cu'shi. _{passed by}

24 And Da'vid sat between the two gates: and the watchman went up to the roof over the gate to the wall, and lifted up his eyes, and looked, and behold a man running alone.

25 And the watchman cried, and told the king. And the king said, If he *be* alone, <u>*there is* tidings in his mouth</u>. And he came <u>apace, and drew near</u>. _{he is bringing news - nearer and nearer}

26 And the watchman saw another man running: and the watchman called to the <u>porter</u>, and said, Behold *an-* other man running alone. And the king said, He also brings tidings. _{gatekeeper}

27 And the watchman said, Me thinks the running of the foremost is like the running of A-him'a-az the son of Za'dok. And the king said, He *is* a good man, and comes with good tidings.

28 And A-him'a-az called, and said to the king, All is well. And he fell down to the earth upon his face before the king, and said, Blessed *be* the LORD your <u>God</u>, which has delivered up the men that lifted up their hand against my lord the king. _{Elohim p.f.}

29 And the king said, Is the young man Ab'sa-lom safe? And A-him'a-az answered, When Jo'ab sent the king's servant, and *me* your servant, I saw a great tumult, but I knew not what *it was*.

30 And the king said *to him*, Turn aside, *and* stand here. And he turned aside, and stood still.

31 And, behold, Cu'shi came; and Cu'shi said, Tidings, my lord the king: for the LORD has <u>avenged</u> you this day of all them that rose up against you. _{freed}

32 And the king said to Cu'shi, *Is* the young man Ab'sa-lom safe? And Cu'shi answered, The enemies of my lord the king, and all that rise against you to do *you* hurt, be as *that* young man *is*.

33 And the king was much moved, and went up to the chamber over the gate, and wept: and as he went, thus he said, O my son Ab'sa-lom, my son, my son Ab'sa-lom! would God I had died for you, O Ab'sa-lom, my son, my son!

CHAPTER 19

AND it was told Jo'ab, Behold, the king weeps and mourns for Ab'sa-lom.

2 And the victory that day was *turned* into mourning to all the people: for the people heard say that day how the king was grieved for his son.

3 And the people got them <u>by stealth</u> that day into the city, as people being ashamed steal away when they flee in battle. _{secretly}

4 But the king covered his face, and the king cried with a loud voice, O my son Ab'sa-lom, O Ab'sa-lom, my son, my son!

5 And Jo'ab came into the house to the king, and said, You have shamed this day the faces of all your servants, which this day have saved your life, and the lives of your sons and of your daughters, and the lives of your wives, and the lives of your concubines;

6 In that you love your enemies, and hate your friends. For you have declared this day, that you <u>regard</u> neither princes nor servants: for this day I perceive, that if Ab'sa-lom had lived, and all we had died this day, then it had pleased you well. _{respect}

7 Now therefore arise, go forth, and speak <u>comfortably</u> to your servants: for I swear by the LORD, if you go not forth, there <u>will not tarry one</u> with you this night: and that will be worse to you than all the evil that befell you from your youth until now.

_{kindly - not one will remain}

8 Then the king arose, and sat in the gate. And they told to all the people, saying, Behold, the king does sit in the gate. And all the people came before the king: for Is'ra-el had fled every man to his tent.

9 And all the people were at strife throughout all the tribes of Is'ra-el, saying, The king saved us out of the hand of our enemies, and he delivered us out of the hand of the Phi-lis'tines; and now he is fled out of the land for Ab'sa-lom.

10 And Ab'sa-lom, whom we anointed over us, is dead in battle. Now therefore why speak you not a word of bringing the king back?

11 And king Da'vid sent to Za'dok and to A-bi'a-thar the priests, saying, Speak to the elders of Ju'dah, saying, Why are you the last to bring the king back to his house? seeing the speech of all Is'ra-el is come to the king, <u>even to his house</u>. _{at his quarters}

12 You *are* my brethren, you *are* my bones and my flesh: wherefore then are you the last to bring back the king?

13 And say you to Am'a-sa, *Are* you not of my bone, and of my flesh? <u>God</u> do so to me, and more also, if you be not captain of the host before me continually in the <u>room</u> of Jo'ab.

_{Elohim^{p.f.} - place}

14 And he bowed the heart of all the men of Ju'dah, even as *the heart of* one man; so that they sent *this word* to the king, Return you, and all your servants.

15 So the king returned, and came to Jor'dan. And Ju'dah came to Gil'gal, to

go to meet the king, to conduct the king over Jor'dan.

16 And Shim'e-i the son of Ge'ra, a Ben'ja-mite, which *was* of Ba-hu'rim, hasted and came down with the men of Ju'dah to meet king Da'vid.

17 And *there were* a thousand men of Ben'ja-min with him, and Zi'ba the servant of the house of Saul, and his fifteen sons and his twenty servants with him; and they went over Jor'dan before the king.

18 And there went over a ferry boat to carry over the king's household, and to do what he thought good. And Shim'e-i the son of Ge'ra fell down before the king, as he was come over Jor'dan;

19 And said to the king, Let not my lord <u>impute iniquity to me</u>, neither do you remember that which your servant did perversely the day that my lord the king went out of Je-ru'sa-lem, that the king should take it to his heart.   consider me guilty

20 For your servant does know that I have sinned: therefore, behold, I am come the first this day of all the house of Jo'seph to go down to meet my lord the king.

21 But A-bish'a-i the son of Zer-u-i'ah answered and said, Shall not Shim'e-i be put to death for this, because he cursed the LORD's anointed?

22 And Da'vid said, What have I to do with you, you sons of Zer-u-i'ah, that you should this day be adversaries to me? shall there any man be put to death this day in Is'ra-el? for do not I know that I *am* this day king over Is'ra-el?

23 Therefore the king said to Shim'e-i, You shall not die. And the king <u>swear to him</u>.   promised

24 And Me-phib'o-sheth the son of Saul came down to meet the king, and had neither <u>dressed</u> his feet, nor trimmed his beard, nor washed his clothes, from the day the king departed until the day he came *again* in peace.   cared for

25 And it came to pass, when he was come to Je-ru'sa-lem to meet the king, that the king said to him, Why went not you with me, Me-phib'o-sheth?

26 And he answered, My lord, O king, my servant deceived me: for your servant said, I will saddle me an ass, that I may ride thereon, and go <u>to</u> the king; because your servant *is* lame.   with

27 And he has slandered your servant to my lord the king; but my lord the king *is* as <u>an angel</u> of <u>God</u>: do therefore *what is* good in your eyes.

a messenger - Elohim[p.f.]

28 For all *of* my father's house were but dead men before my lord the king: yet did you set your servant among them that did eat at your own table. What right therefore have I yet to <u>cry</u> any more to the king?   complain

29 And the king said to him, Why speak you any more of your matters? I have said, You and Zi'ba divide the land.

30 And Me-phib'o-sheth said to the king, Yea, let him take all, forasmuch

as my lord the king is come again in peace to his own house.

31 And Bar-zil'la-i the Gil'e-ad-ite came down from Ro-ge'lim, and went over Jor'dan with the king, to conduct him over Jor'dan.

32 Now Bar-zil'la-i was a very aged man, *even* <u>fourscore</u> years old: and he had provided the king of sustenance while he lay at Ma-ha-na'im; for he *was* a very great man. ₈₀

33 And the king said to Bar-zil'la-i, Come you over with me, and I will feed you with me in Je-ru'sa-lem.

34 And Bar-zil'la-i said to the king, How long have I to live, that I should go up with the king to Je-ru'sa-lem?

35 I *am* this day <u>fourscore</u> years old: *and* can I discern between good and evil? can your servant taste what I eat or what I drink? can I hear any more the voice of singing men and singing women? why then should your servant be yet a burden to my lord the king?

36 Your servant will go a little way over Jor'dan with the king: and why should the king <u>recompense</u> it me with such a reward? compensate

37 Let your servant, I pray you, turn back again, that I may die in my own city, *and be buried* by the grave of my father and of my mother. But behold your servant Chim'ham; let him go over with my lord the king; and do to him what shall seem good to you.

38 And the king answered, Chim'ham shall go over with me, and I will do to him that which shall seem good to you: and whatsoever you shall <u>require</u> of me, *that* will I do for you. choose

39 And all the people went over Jor'dan. And when the king was come over, the king kissed Bar-zil'la-i, and blessed him; and he returned to his own place.

40 Then the king went on to Gil'gal, and Chim'ham went on with him: and all the people of Ju'dah <u>conducted</u> the king, and also half the people of Is'ra-el. accompanied

41 And, behold, all the men of Is'ra-el came to the king, and said to the king, Why have our brethren the men of Ju'dah stolen you away, and have brought the king, and his household, and all Da'vid's men with him, over Jor'dan?

42 And all the men of Ju'dah answered the men of Is'ra-el, Because the king is near of kin to us: why then be you angry for this matter? have we eaten at all of the king's *cost*? or has he given us any gift?

43 And the men of Is'ra-el answered the men of Ju'dah, and said, We have ten parts in the king, and we have also more *right* in Da'vid than you: why then did you despise us, that our advice should not be first had in bringing back our king? And the words of the men of Ju'dah were <u>fiercer</u> than the words of the men of Is'ra-el. harsher

CHAPTER 20

AND there happened to be there a man of Be'li-al, whose name *was* She'ba, the son of Bich'ri, a Ben'ja-

mite: and he blew a trumpet, and said, We have no part in Da'vid, neither have we inheritance in the son of Jes'se: every man to his tents, O Is'ra-el. _{worthless man}

2 So every man of Is'ra-el went up from after Da'vid, *and* followed She'ba the son of Bich'ri: but the men of Ju'dah clung to their king, from Jor'dan even to Je-ru'sa-lem.

3 And Da'vid came to his house at Je-ru'sa-lem; and the king took the ten women *his* concubines, whom he had left to keep the house, and put them in <u>ward</u>, and fed them, but went not in to them. So they were shut up to the day of their death, living in widowhood. _{confinement}

4 Then said the king to Am'a-sa, <u>Assemble me</u> the men of Ju'dah within three days, and be you here present. _{Call out}

5 So Am'a-sa went to assemble *the men* of Ju'dah: but he <u>tarried</u> longer than the set time which he had appointed him. _{delayed}

6 And Da'vid said to A-bish'a-i, Now shall She'ba the son of Bich'ri do us more harm than *did* Ab'sa-lom: take you your lord's servants, and pursue after him, less he get him <u>fenced</u> cities, and escape us. _{fortified}

7 And there went out after him Jo'ab's men, and the Cher'eth-ites, and the Pe'leth-ites, and all the mighty men: and they went out of Je-ru'sa-lem, to pursue after She'ba the son of Bich'ri.

8 When they *were* at the great stone which *is* in Gib'e-on, Am'a-sa <u>went before</u> them. And Jo'ab's garment that he had put on was girded to him, and upon it a <u>girdle</u> *with* a sword fastened upon his loins in the sheath thereof; and as he went forth it fell out. _{came to - waistband}

9 And Jo'ab said to Am'a-sa, *Are* you in health, my brother? And Jo'ab took Am'a-sa by the beard with the right hand to kiss him.

10 But Am'a-sa took no heed to the sword that *was* in Jo'ab's hand: so he smote him therewith in the fifth *rib*, and shed out his <u>bowels</u> to the ground, and struck him not again; and he died. So Jo'ab and A-bish'a-i his brother pursued after She'ba the son of Bich'ri. _{intestines}

11 And one of Jo'ab's men stood by him, and said, He that favors Jo'ab, and he that *is* for Da'vid, *let him go* after Jo'ab.

12 And Am'a-sa wallowed in blood in the midst of the highway. And when the man saw that all the people stood still, he removed Am'a-sa out of the highway into the field, and cast a cloth upon him, when he saw that every one that came by him stood still.

13 When he was removed out of the highway, all the people went on after Jo'ab, to pursue after She'ba the son of Bich'ri.

14 And he went through all the tribes of Is'ra-el to A'bel, and to Beth-ma'a-chah, and all the Be'rites: and they were gathered together, and went also after him.

15 And they came and besieged him in A'bel of Beth-ma'a-chah, and they cast up a <u>bank</u> against the city, and *it*

stood in the trench: and all the people that *were* with Jo'ab battered the wall, to throw it down. mound - it stood by the rampart
16 Then cried a wise woman out of the city, Hear, hear; say, I pray you, to Jo'ab, Come near here, that I may speak with you.
17 And when he was come near to her, the woman said, *Are* you Jo'ab? And he answered, I *am he*. Then she said to him, Hear the words of your handmaid. And he answered, I do hear.
18 Then she spoke, saying, They were wont to speak in old time, saying, They shall surely ask *counsel* at A'bel: and so they ended *the matter*. accustomed
19 *I am one of them that are* peaceable *and* faithful in Is'ra-el: you seek to destroy a city and a mother in Is'ra-el: why will you swallow up the inheritance of the LORD?
20 And Jo'ab answered and said, Far be it, far be it from me, that I should swallow up or destroy.
21 The matter *is* not so: but a man of mount E'phra-im, She'ba the son of Bich'ri by name, has lifted up his hand against the king, *even* against Da'vid: deliver him only, and I will depart from the city. And the woman said to Jo'ab, Behold, his head shall be thrown to you over the wall.
22 Then the woman went to all the people in her wisdom. And they cut off the head of She'ba the son of Bich'ri, and cast *it* out to Jo'ab. And he blew a trumpet, and they retired from the city, every man to his tent. And Jo'ab returned to Je-ru'sa-lem to the king. disbursed

23 Now Jo'ab was over all the host of Is'ra-el: and Be-na'iah the son of Je-hoi'a-da *was* over the Cher'eth-ites and over the Pe'leth-ites:
24 And A-do'ram *was* over the tribute: and Je-hosh'a-phat the son of A-hi'lud *was* recorder:
25 And She'va *was* scribe: and Za'dok and A-bi'a-thar *were* the priests:
26 And I'ra also the Ja'ir-ite was a chief ruler about Da'vid. priest

CHAPTER 21

THEN there was a famine in the days of Da'vid three years, year after year; and Da'vid enquired of the LORD. And the LORD answered, *It is* for Saul, and for *his* bloody house, because he slew the Gib'e-on-ites.
2 And the king called the Gib'e-on-ites, and said to them; (now the Gib'e-on-ites *were* not of the children of Is'ra-el, but of the remnant of the Am'or-ites; and the children of Is'ra-el had sworn to them: and Saul sought to slay them in his zeal to the children of Is'ra-el and Ju'dah.)
3 Therefore Da'vid said to the Gib'e-on-ites, What shall I do for you? and wherewith shall I make the atonement, that you may bless the inheritance of the LORD?
4 And the Gib'e-on-ites said to him, We will have no silver nor gold of Saul, nor of his house; neither for us shall you kill any man in Is-rael. And he said, What you shall say, *that* will I do for you.
5 And they answered the king, The

man that <u>consumed</u> us, and that <u>devised</u> against us *that* we should be destroyed from remaining in any of the coasts of Israel, destroyed - plotted
6 Let seven men of his sons be delivered to us, and we will hang them up to the LORD in Gib'e-ah of Saul, *whom* the LORD did choose. And the king said, I will give *them*.
7 But the king spared Me-phib'o-sheth, the son of Jon'a-than the son of Saul, because of the LORD's oath that *was* between them, between Da'vid and Jon'a-than the son of Saul.
8 But the king took the two sons of Riz'pah the daughter of A-i'ah, whom she bare to Saul, Ar-mo'ni and Me-phib'o-sheth; and the five sons of Mi'chal the daughter of Saul, whom she brought up for A'dri-el the son of Bar-zil'la-i the Me-hol'ath-ite:
9 And he delivered them into the hands of the Gib'e-on-ites, and they hanged them in the hill before the LORD: and they fell *all* seven together, and were put to death in the *days* of harvest, in the first days, in the beginning of barley harvest.
10 And Riz'pah the daughter of A-i'ah took sackcloth, and spread it for her upon the rock, from the beginning of harvest until water dropped upon them out of heaven, and allowed neither the birds of the air to rest on them by day, nor the beasts of the field by night.
11 And it was told Da'vid what Riz'pah the daughter of A-i'ah, the concubine of Saul, had done.
12 And Da'vid went and took the bones of Saul and the bones of Jon'a-than his son from the men of Ja'besh-gil'e-ad, which had stolen them from the street of Beth'-shan, where the Phi-lis'tines had hanged them, when the Phi-lis'tines had slain Saul in Gil-bo'a:
13 And he brought up from there the bones of Saul and the bones of Jon'a-than his son; and they gathered the bones of them that were hanged.
14 And the bones of Saul and Jon'a-than his son buried they in the country of Ben'ja-min in Ze'lah, in the <u>sepulcher</u> of Kish his father: and they performed all that the king commanded. And after that <u>God was entreated</u> for the land. tomb - Elohim^{p.f.} - heard the prayer
15 Moreover the Phi-lis'tines had yet war again with Is'ra-el; and Da'vid went down, and his servants with him, and fought against the Phi-lis'tines: and Da'vid <u>waxed</u> faint. became
16 And Ish'bi-be'nob, which *was* of the sons of the giant, the weight of whose spear *weighed* three hundred *shekels* of brass in weight, he being girded with a new *sword*, thought to have slain Da'vid.
17 But A-bish'a-i the son of Zer-u-i'ah <u>succoured</u> him, and <u>smote</u> the Phi-lis'tine, and killed him. Then the men of Da'vid swear to him, saying, You shall go no more out with us to battle, that you quench not the light of Is'ra-el. helped - struck
18 And it came to pass after this, that there was again a battle with the Phi-lis'tines at Gob: then Sib'be-chai the Hu'shath-ite slew Saph, which *was* of the sons of the giant.

19 And there was again a battle in Gob with the Phi-lis'tines, where El-ha'nan the son of Ja-ar'e-or'e-gim, a Beth'-le-hem-ite, slew *the brother of* Go-li'ath the Git'tite, the staff of whose spear *was* like a weaver's beam.

20 And there was yet a battle in Gath, where was a man of *great* stature, that had on every hand six fingers, and on every foot six toes, four and twenty in number; and he also was born to the giant.

21 And when he <u>defied</u> Is'ra-el, Jon'a-than the son of Shim'e-ah the brother of Da'vid slew him.   taunted

22 These four were born to the giant in Gath, and fell by the hand of Da'-vid, and by the hand of his servants.

CHAPTER 22

AND Da'vid spoke to the LORD the words of this song in the day *that* the LORD had delivered him out of the hand of all his enemies, and out of the hand of Saul:

2 And he said, The LORD *is* my rock, and my fortress, and my deliverer;

3 The <u>God</u> of my rock; in Him will I trust: *He is* my shield, and the horn of my salvation, my high tower, and my refuge, my savior; You save me from violence.   Elohim^{p.f.}

4 I will call on the LORD, *who is* worthy to be praised: so shall I be saved from my enemies.

5 When the waves of death compassed me, the floods of ungodly men made me afraid;

6 The sorrows of hell compassed me about; the snares of death <u>prevented</u> me;   confronted

7 In my distress I called upon the LORD, and cried to my <u>God</u>: and He did hear my voice out of His temple, and my cry *did enter* into His ears.   Elohim^{p.f.}

8 Then the earth shook and trembled; the foundations of heaven moved and shook, because He was angry.

9 There went up a smoke out of His nostrils, and fire out of His mouth devoured: coals were kindled by it.

10 He bowed the heavens also, and came down; and darkness *was* under his feet.

11 And He rode upon a cherub, and did fly: and He was seen upon the wings of the wind.

12 And he made darkness pavilions round about Him, dark waters, *and* thick clouds of the skies.

13 Through the brightness before Him were coals of fire kindled.

14 The LORD thundered from heaven, and the Most High uttered His voice.

15 And He sent out arrows, and scattered them; lightning, and discomfited them.

16 And the channels of the sea appeared, the foundations of the world were <u>discovered</u>, at the rebuking of the LORD, at the blast of the breath of His nostrils.   laid bare

17 He sent from above, He took me; He drew me out of many waters;

18 He delivered me from my strong enemy, *and* from them that hated me: for they were too strong for me.

19 They <u>prevented</u> me in the day of

my calamity: but the LORD was my <u>stay</u>.   confronted - support

20 He brought me forth also into a large place: He delivered me, because He delighted in me.

21 The LORD rewarded me according to my righteousness: according to the cleanness of my hands has He recompensed me.

22 For I have kept the ways of the LORD, and have not wickedly departed from my <u>God</u>.   Elohim$^{p.f.}$

23 For all His judgments *were* before me: and as *for* His statutes, I did not depart from them.

24 I was also upright before Him, and have kept myself from my iniquity.

25 Therefore the LORD has <u>recompensed</u> me according to my righteousness; according to my cleanness in His eye sight.   rewarded

26 With the merciful You will show Yourself merciful, *and* with the upright man You will show Yourself upright.   MATT. 5:7

27 With the pure You will show Yourself pure; and with the <u>froward</u> You will show Yourself <u>unsavory</u>.   perverted - shrewed

28 And the afflicted people You will save: but Your eyes *are* upon the haughty, *that* You may bring *them* down.

29 For you *are* my lamp, O LORD: and the LORD will lighten my darkness.

30 For by You I have run through a troop: by my <u>God</u> have I leaped over a wall.   Elohim$^{p.f.}$

31 *As for* God, His way *is* perfect; the word of the LORD *is* tried: He *is* a <u>buckler</u> to all them that trust in Him.   shield

32 For who *is* God, save the LORD? and who *is* a rock, save our <u>God</u>?
El$^{s.f.}$ - Jehovah - Elohim$^{p.f.}$

33 God *is* my strength *and* power: and He makes my way perfect.

34 He makes my feet like <u>hinds'</u> *feet*: and sets me upon my high places.   deer's

35 He teaches my hands <u>to war</u>; so that a bow of steel is broken by my arms.   for war

36 You have also given me the shield of Your salvation: and Your gentleness has made me great.

37 You have enlarged my steps under me; so that my feet did not slip.

38 I have pursued my enemies, and destroyed them; and turned not again until I had consumed them.

39 And I have consumed them, and wounded them, that they could not arise: yea, they are fallen under my feet.

40 For You have girded me with strength to battle: them that rose up against me have You subdued under me.

41 You have also given me the necks of my enemies, that I might destroy them that <u>hate</u> me.   disrespect

42 They looked, but *there was* none to save; *even* to the LORD, but He answered them not.

43 Then did I beat them as small as the dust of the earth, I did stamp them as the mire of the street, *and* did spread them abroad.

44 You also have delivered me from

the strivings of my people, you have kept me *to be* head of the heathen: a people *which* I knew not shall serve me. nations

45 Strangers shall submit themselves to me: as soon as they hear, they shall be obedient to me.

46 Strangers shall fade away, and they shall be afraid out of their close places. come trembling out of their fortresses

47 The LORD lives; and blessed *be* my rock; and exalted be the God of the rock of my salvation. Elohim^{p.f.}

48 It *is* God that avenges me, and that brings down the people under me,

49 And that brings me forth from my enemies: You also have lifted me up on high above them that rose up against me: You have delivered me from the violent man.

50 Therefore I will give thanks to You, O LORD, among the heathen, and I will sing praises to Your name. nations

51 *He is* the tower of salvation for his king: and shows mercy to his anointed, to Da'vid, and to his seed for evermore. descendants

CHAPTER 23

NOW these *be* the last words of Da'vid. Da'vid the son of Jes'se said, and the man *who was* raised up on high, the anointed of the God of Ja'cob, and the sweet psalmist of Is'ra-el, said, singer

2 The Spirit of the LORD spoke by me, and His word *was* in my tongue.

3 The God of Is'ra-el said, the Rock of Is'ra-el spoke to me, He that rules over men *must be* just, ruling in the fear of God. Elohim^{p.f.} - respect

4 And *he shall be* as the light of the morning, *when* the sun rises, *even* a morning without clouds; *as* the tender grass *springing* out of the earth by clear shining after rain.

5 Although my house *be* not so with God; yet He has made with me an everlasting covenant, ordered in all *things*, and sure: for *this is* all my salvation, and all *my* desire, although He make *it* not to grow.

6 But the *sons* of Be'li-al *shall be* all of them as thorns thrust away, because they cannot be taken with hands: worthless men

7 But the man *that* shall touch them must be fenced with iron and the staff of a spear; and they shall be utterly burned with fire in the *same* place. armed

8 These *be* the names of the mighty men whom Da'vid had: The Tach'mo-nite that sat in the seat, chief among the captains; the same *was* Ad'i-no the Ez'nite: *he lift up his spear* against eight hundred, whom he slew at one time.

9 And after him *was* E-le-a'zar the son of Do'do the A-ho'hite, *one* of the three mighty men with Da'vid, when they defied the Phi-lis'tines *that* were there gathered together to battle, and the men of Is'ra-el were gone away:

10 He arose, and smote the Phi-lis'tines until his hand was weary, and his hand clung to the sword: and the LORD wrought a great victory that day; and the people returned after him only to spoil. take plunder

11 And after him *was* Sham'mah the

son of Ag'e-e the Ha'ra-rite. And the Phi-lis'tines were gathered together into a troop, where was a piece of ground full of lentils: and the people fled from the Phi-lis'tines.

12 But he stood in the midst of the ground, and defended it, and slew the Phi-lis'tines: and the LORD wrought a great victory.

13 And three of the thirty chief went down, and came to Da'vid in the harvest time to the cave of A-dul'lam: and the troop of the Phi-lis'tines <u>pitched</u> in the valley of Reph'a-im.   were encamped

14 And Da'vid *was* then in <u>an hold</u>, and the garrison of the Phi-lis'tines *was* then *in* Beth'-le-hem.   the stronghold

15 And Da'vid longed, and said, Oh that one would give me drink of the water of the well of Beth'-le-hem, which *is* by the gate!

16 And the three mighty men broke through the host of the Phi-lis'tines, and drew water out of the well of Beth'-le-hem, that *was* by the gate, and took *it*, and brought *it* to Da'vid: nevertheless he would not drink thereof, but poured it out to the LORD.

17 And he said, Be it far from me, O LORD, that I should do this: *is not this* the blood of the men that went in jeopardy of their lives? therefore he would not drink it. These things did these three mighty men.

18 And A-bish'a-i, the brother of Jo'ab, the son of Zer-u-i'ah, was chief among three. And he lifted up his spear against three hundred, *and* slew *them*, and had the <u>name</u> among three.   reputation

19 Was he not most honorable of three? therefore he was their captain: however he attained not to the *first* three.

20 And Be-na'iah the son of Je-hoi'ada, the son of a valiant man, of Kab'ze-el, who had done many acts, he slew two lionlike men of Mo'ab: he went down also and slew a lion in the midst of a pit in time of snow:

21 And he slew an E-gyp'tian, <u>a goodly</u> man: and the E-gyp'tian had a spear in his hand; but he went down to him with a staff, and plucked the spear out of the E-gyp'tian's hand, and slew him with his own spear.   an impressive

22 These *things* did Be-na'iah the son of Je-hoi'a-da, and had the name among three mighty men.

23 He was more honorable than the thirty, but he attained not to the *first* three. And Da'vid set him over his guard.

24 A'sa-hel the brother of Jo'ab *was* one of the thirty; El-ha'nan the son of Do'do of Beth'-le-hem,

25 Sham'mah the Ha'rod-ite, El'i-ka the Ha'rod-ite,

26 He'lez the Pal'tite, I'ra the son of Ik'kesh the Te-ko'ite,

27 A-bi-e'zer the An'e-thoth-ite, Me-bun'nai the Hu'shath-ite,

28 Zal'mon the A-ho'hite, Ma-har'a-i the Ne-toph'a-thite,

29 He'leb the son of Ba'a-nah, a Ne-toph'a-thite, It'ta-i the son of Ri'bai out of Gib'e-ah of the children of Ben'ja-min,

30 Be-na'iah the Pir'a-thon-ite, Hid'da-i of the <u>brooks</u> of Ga'ash,   streambeds

31 A'bi-al'bon the Ar'bath-ite, Az'ma-veth the Bar-hu'mite,

32 E-li'ah-ba the Sha-al'bo-nite, of the sons of Ja'shen, Jon'a-than,

33 Sham'mah the Ha'ra-rite, A-hi'am the son of Sha'rar the Ha'ra-rite,

34 E-liph'e-let the son of A-has'ba-i, the son of the Ma-ach'a-thite, E-li'am the son of A-hith'o-phel the Gi'lo-nite,

35 Hez'ra-i the Car'mel-ite, Pa'a-rai the Ar'bite,

36 I'gal the son of Na'than of Zo'bah, Ba'ni the Gad'ite,

37 Ze'lek the Am'mon-ite, Na'ha-ri the Be-e'roth-ite, armorbearer to Jo'ab the son of Zer-u-i'ah,

38 I'ra an Ith'rite, Ga'reb an Ith'rite,

39 U-ri'ah the Hit'tite: thirty and seven in all.

CHAPTER 24

A ND again the anger of the LORD <u>was kindled</u> against Is'ra-el, and He moved Da'vid against them to say, Go, number Is'ra-el and Ju'dah.   burned

2 For the king said to Jo'ab the captain of the host, which *was* with him, Go now through all the tribes of Is'ra-el, from Dan even to Be'er-she'ba, and number you the people, that I may know the number of the people.

3 And Jo'ab said to the king, Now the LORD your <u>God</u> add to the people, how many soever they be, an hundredfold, and that the eyes of my lord the king may see *it*: but why does my lord the king <u>delight</u> in this thing?   Elohim^p.f. - desire

4 <u>Notwithstanding</u> the king's word prevailed against Jo'ab, and against the captains of the host. And Jo'ab and the captains of the host went out from the presence of the king, to number the people of Is'ra-el.   Nevertheless

5 And they passed over Jor'dan, and <u>pitched</u> in Ar'o-er, on the right side of the city that *lies* in the midst of the <u>river</u> of Gad, and toward Ja'zer: camped - valley

6 Then they came to Gil'e-ad, and to the land of Tah'tim-hod'shi; and they came to Dan-ja'an, and about to Zi'don,

7 And came to the strong hold of Tyre, and to all the cities of the Hi'vites, and of the Ca'naan-ites: and they went out to the south of Ju'dah, *even* to Be'er-she'ba.

8 So when they had gone through all the land, they came to Je-ru'sa-lem at the end of nine months and twenty days.

9 And Jo'ab gave up the sum of the number of the people to the king: and there were in Is'ra-el eight hundred thousand <u>valiant</u> men that drew the sword; and the men of Ju'dah *were* five hundred thousand men.   strong

10 And Da'vid's heart smote him after that he had numbered the people. And Da'vid said to the LORD, I have sinned greatly in that I have done: and now, I <u>beseech</u> You, O LORD, take away the iniquity of Your servant; for I have done very foolishly.   pray

11 For when Da'vid was up in the morning, the word of the LORD came

to the prophet Gad, Da'vid's <u>seer</u>, saying,   prophet

12 Go and say to Da'vid, Thus says the LORD, I offer you three *things*; choose you one of them, that I may *do it* to you.

13 So Gad came to Da'vid, and told him, and said to him, Shall seven years of famine come to you in your land? or will you flee three months before your enemies, while they pursue you? or that there be three days' pestilence in your land? now <u>advise</u>, and see what answer I shall return to Him that sent me.   consider

14 And Da'vid said to Gad, I am in a great <u>strait</u>: let us fall now into the hand of the LORD; for His mercies *are* great: and let me not fall into the hand of man.   distress

15 So the LORD sent a pestilence upon Is'ra-el from the morning even to the time appointed: and there died of the people from Dan even to Be'er-she'ba seventy thousand men.

16 And when the <u>angel</u> stretched out his hand upon Je-ru'sa-lem to destroy it, the LORD <u>repented</u> Him of the evil, and said to the angel that destroyed the people, It is enough: <u>stay</u> now your hand. And the angel of the LORD was by the threshingplace of A-rau'nah the Jeb'u-site.   messenger - regretted - held back

17 And Da'vid spoke to the LORD when he saw the angel that smote the people, and said, Lo, I have sinned, and I have done wickedly: but these sheep, what have they done? let Your hand, I pray You, be against me, and against my father's house.

18 And Gad came that day to Da'vid, and said to him, Go up, rear an altar to the LORD in the threshingfloor of A-rau'nah the Jeb'u-site.

19 And Da'vid, according to the saying of Gad, went up as the LORD commanded.

20 And A-rau'nah looked, and saw the king and his servants coming on toward him: and A-rau'nah went out, and bowed himself before the king on his face upon the ground.

21 And A-rau'nah said, Why is my lord the king come to his servant? And Da'vid said, To buy the threshingfloor of you, to build an altar to the LORD, that the plague may be stayed from the people.

22 And A-rau'nah said to Da'vid, Let my lord the king take and offer up what *seems* good to him: behold, *here be* oxen for burned sacrifice, and threshing instruments and *other* <u>instruments</u> of the oxen for wood.   the yokes

23 All these *things* did A-rau'nah, *as* a king, give to the king. And A-rau'nah said to the king, The LORD your <u>God</u> accept you.   Elohim[p.f.]

24 And the king said to A-rau'nah, Nay; but I will surely buy *it* of you at a price: neither will I offer burned offerings to the LORD my <u>God</u> of that which does cost me nothing. So Da'vid bought the threshingfloor and the oxen for fifty shekels of silver.

25 And Da'vid built there an altar to the LORD, and offered burned offerings and peace offerings. So the LORD was entreated for the land, and the plague was <u>stayed</u> from Is'ra-el.

held back

1 AND 2 KINGS

OUTLINE

SURVEY

The aim of these books is nowhere clearly stated. But even a casual reading will make clear that the writer set out to demonstrate that although Israel stood in covenant relationship with God, most of her kings had rejected and outraged the covenant obligations.

The kings of both Judah and Israel are passed in review and, as far as possible, treated contemporaneously. The worth of each king is determined by comparison with two kings of former years, King David who held closely to the covenant, and King Jeroboam of Israel who forsook the covenant.

Comparison in this way shows whether a given king "walked in the ways of David his father" or "in the ways of Jeroboam the son of Nebat."

It is evident that the writer of Kings found that on this basis very few of the kings of Israel or Judah kept the covenant with God. Notable exceptions were Asa (1 K 15), Jehoshaphat (1 K 22), Hezekiah (2 K 18—20) and Josiah (2 K 22—23), and even these had some defects.

David realized the ideal more closely than any. His parting advice to his son Solomon was that he should keep God's commandments (1 K 2.3). In that course lay the only hope of prosperity and peace. To depart from that way was to risk divine judgment.

Loyalty to God's covenant was an ancient requirement in Israel. It stemmed from Abraham, but found national expression at the time of the Exodus when Israel, recently delivered from Egypt, stood at Mount Sinai and entered into a solemn covenant with God (Ex 19.5; 24.3-8). Thereafter Israel was to be God's own people, set apart from the nations, obedient to His commandments and loyal to Him. The Israelites were forbidden to enter into covenants with other nations or other gods. Adherence to the covenant with God would result in blessing; departure from it would result in cursing and judgment. These principles are clearly worked out in 2 K 17-23.

The writer traces the story of Israel's kings from Solomon to the last king of Judah. In a frank, honest fashion he records the sad story of the rejection of the covenant by most of the rulers. The final collapse of Israel before Assyria (2 K 17) and of Judah before Babylon (2 K 25) was a demonstration of the truth of the principle underlying the book and came as no surprise to men of spiritual discernment.

In later days the two Books of Kings remained as a warning to the remnant of God's people, and thus provided a practical lesson in the truth that rejection of God's covenant, being a sinful and rebellious act, can only result in divine judgment.

AUTHOR

The author of Kings is unknown. He had access to written records such as the "Book of the acts of Solomon" (1 K 11.41), the "Book of the chronicles of the kings of Israel" (1 K 14.19, and elsewhere), and the "Book of the chronicles of the kings of Judah" (1 Kings 14.29, and elsewhere), which were probably official annals. He may also have used earlier compilations made possibly by some of the prophets.

The final compiler must have lived beyond the downfall of Judah in 586 B.C., for he recorded the release of Jehoiachin in about 560 B.C. (2 K 25.27–30).

We may speculate from his interest in the covenant that he was a prophet roughly contemporary with Jeremiah, and that he wrote in the first half of the sixth century B.C.

J.A.T.

THE FIRST BOOK OF
KINGS

CHAPTER 1

NOW king Da'vid was old *and* stricken in years; and they covered him with clothes, but he got no heat.

2 Wherefore his servants said to him, Let there be sought for my lord the king a young virgin: and let her stand before the king, and let her cherish him, and let her lie in your bosom, that my lord the king may get heat. attend

3 So they sought for a fair damsel throughout all the coasts of Is'ra-el, and found Ab'i-shag a Shu'nam-mite, and brought her to the king. young woman

4 And the damsel *was* very fair, and cherished the king, and ministered to him: but the king knew her not. nursed

5 Then Ad-o-ni'jah the son of Hag'gith exalted himself, saying, I will be king: and he prepared him chariots and horsemen, and fifty men to run before him.

6 And his father had not displeased him at any time in saying, Why have you done so? and he also *was a* very goodly *man*; and *his mother* bare him after Ab'sa-lom. handsome - gave birth to

7 And he conferred with Jo'ab the son of Zer-u-i'ah, and with A-bi'a-thar the priest: and they following Ad-o-ni'jah helped *him*.

8 But Za'dok the priest, and Be-na'iah the son of Je-hoi'a-da, and Na'than the prophet, and Shim'e-i, and Re'i, and the mighty men which *belonged* to Da'vid, were not with Ad-o-ni'jah.

9 And Ad-o-ni'jah slew sheep and oxen and fat cattle by the stone of Zo'he-leth, which *is* by En-ro'gel, and called all his brethren the king's sons, and all the men of Ju'dah the king's servants: the well Rogel - invited

10 But Na'than the prophet, and Be-na'iah, and the mighty men, and Sol'o-mon his brother, he called not.

11 Wherefore Na'than spoke to Bath'-she-ba the mother of Sol'o-mon, saying, Have you not heard that Ad-o-ni'jah the son of Hag'gith does reign, and Da'vid our lord knows *it* not?

12 Now therefore come, let me, I pray you, give you counsel, that you may save your own life, and the life of your son Sol'o-mon. advice

13 Go and get you in to king Da'vid, and say to him, Did not you, my lord, O king, swear to your handmaid, saying, Assuredly Sol'o-mon your son shall reign after me, and he shall sit upon my throne? why then does Ad-o-ni'jah reign?

14 Behold, while you yet talk there with the king, I also will come in after you, and confirm your words.

15 And Bath'-she-ba went in to the king into the chamber: and the king was very old; and Ab'i-shag the Shu'-nam-mite ministered to the king.

16 And Bath'-she-ba bowed, and did obeisance to the king. And the king said, What <u>would you</u>?   _{do you wish}

17 And she said to him, My lord, you swear by the LORD your <u>God</u> to your handmaid, *saying*, Assuredly Sol'o-mon your son shall reign after me, and he shall sit upon my throne.   _{Elohim^{p.f.}}

18 And now, behold, Ad-o-ni'jah reigns; and now, my lord the king, you know *it* not:

19 And he has slain oxen and fat cattle and sheep in abundance, and has <u>called</u> all the sons of the king, and A-bi'a-thar the priest, and Jo'ab the captain of the host: but Sol'o-mon your servant has he not <u>called</u>.   _{invited}

20 And you, my lord, O king, the eyes of all Is'ra-el *are* upon you, that you should tell them who shall sit on the throne of my lord the king after him.

21 Otherwise it shall come to pass, when my lord the king shall sleep with his fathers, that I and my son Sol'o-mon shall be counted offenders.

22 And, lo, while she yet talked with the king, Na'than the prophet also came in.

23 And they told the king, saying, Behold Na'than the prophet. And when he was come in before the king, he bowed himself before the king with his face to the ground.

24 And Na'than said, My lord, O king, have you said, Ad-o-ni'jah shall reign after me, and he shall sit upon my throne?

25 For he is gone down this day, and has slain oxen and fat cattle and sheep in abundance, and has called all the king's sons, and the captains of the host, and A-bi'a-thar the priest; and, behold, they eat and drink before him, and say, <u>God save</u> king Ad-o-ni'jah.   _{Long live}

26 But me, *even* me your servant, and Za'dok the priest, and Be-na'iah the son of Je-hoi'a-da, and your servant Sol'o-mon, has he not called.

27 Is this thing done by my lord the king, and you have not showed *it* to your servant, who should sit on the throne of my lord the king after him?

28 Then king Da'vid answered and said, Call me Bath'-she-ba. And she came into the king's presence, and stood before the king.

29 And the king swear, and said, *As* the LORD lives, that has redeemed my soul out of all distress,

30 Even as I swear to you by the LORD God of Is'ra-el, saying, Assuredly Sol'o-mon your son shall reign after me, and he shall sit upon my throne in my stead; even so will I certainly do this day.   _{Jehovah^{s.f.} Elohim^{p.f.}}

31 Then Bath'-she-ba bowed with *her* face to the earth, and did reverence to the king, and said, Let my lord king Da'vid live for ever.

32 And king Da'vid said, Call me Za'dok the priest, and Na'than the prophet, and Be-na'iah the son of Je-hoi'a-da. And they came before the king.

33 The king also said to them, Take with you the servants of your lord, and cause Sol'o-mon my son to

ride upon my own mule, and bring him down to Gi'hon:

34 And let Za'dok the priest and Na'than the prophet anoint him there king over Is'ra-el: and blow you with the trumpet, and say, <u>God save</u> king Sol'o-mon.   Long live

35 Then you shall come up after him, that he may come and sit upon my throne; for he shall be king in my stead: and I have appointed him to be ruler over Is'ra-el and over Ju'dah.

36 And Be-na'iah the son of Je-hoi'a-da answered the king, and said, Amen: the Lord God of my lord the king say so *too*. Jehovah^{s.f.} Elohim^{p.f.}

37 As the Lord has been with my lord the king, even so be he with Sol'o-mon, and make his throne greater than the throne of my lord king Da'vid.

38 So Za'dok the priest, and Na'than the prophet, and Be-na'iah the son of Je-hoi'a-da, and the Cher'eth-ites, and the Pe'leth-ites, went down, and caused Sol'o-mon to ride upon king Da'vid's mule, and brought him to Gi'hon.

39 And Za'dok the priest took an horn of oil out of the tabernacle, and anointed Sol'o-mon. And they blew the trumpet; and all the people said, <u>God save</u> king Sol'o-mon.   Long live

40 And all the people came up after him, and the people piped with <u>pipes</u>, and rejoiced with great joy, so that the earth <u>rent</u> with the sound of them.   flutes - shook

41 And Ad-o-ni'jah and all the guests that *were* with him heard *it* as they had <u>made an end</u> of eating. And when Jo'ab heard the sound of the trumpet, he said, Why *is this* noise of the city being in an uproar?   finished

42 And while he yet spoke, behold, Jon'a-than the son of A-bi'a-thar the priest came: and Ad-o-ni'jah said to him, Come in; for you *are* a <u>valiant</u> man, and bring good tidings.   good soldier

43 And Jon'a-than answered and said to Ad-o-ni'jah, <u>Verily</u> our lord king Da'vid has made Sol'o-mon king.   truly

44 And the king has sent with him Za'dok the priest, and Na'than the prophet, and Be-na'iah the son of Je-hoi'a-da, and the Cher'eth-itcs, and thc Pe'leth-ites, and they have caused him to ride upon the king's mule:

45 And Za'dok the priest and Na'than the prophet have anointed him king in Gi'hon: and they are come up from there rejoicing, so that the city rang again. This *is* the noise that you havc heard.

46 And also Sol'o-mon sits on the throne of the kingdom.

47 And moreover the king's servants came to bless our lord king Da'vid, saying, <u>God</u> make the name of Sol'o-mon better than your name, and make his throne greater than your throne. And the king bowed himself upon the bed.

48 And also thus said the king, Blessed *be* the Lord God of Is'ra-el, which has given *one* to sit on my throne this day, my eyes even see-ing *it*.   Jehovah^{s.f.} Elohim^{p.f.}

49 And all the guests that *were* with Ad-o-ni'jah were afraid, and rose up, and went every man his way.

50 And Ad-o-ni'jah <u>feared</u> because

of Sol'o-mon, and arose, and went, and <u>caught</u> hold on the horns of the altar. was afraid - took

51 And it was told Sol'o-mon, saying, Behold, Ad-o-ni'jah <u>fears</u> king Sol'o-mon: for, lo, he has caught hold on the horns of the altar, saying, Let king Sol'o-mon swear to me to day that he will not slay his servant with the sword.

52 And Sol'o-mon said, If he will show himself a worthy man, there shall not an hair of him fall to the earth: but if wickedness shall be found in him, he shall die.

53 So king Sol'o-mon sent, and they brought him down from the altar. And he came and bowed himself to king Sol'o-mon: and Sol'o-mon said to him, Go to your house.

CHAPTER 2

NOW the days of Da'vid drew near that he should die; and he <u>charged</u> Sol'o-mon his son, saying, commanded

2 I go the way of all the earth: be you strong therefore, and show yourself a man;

3 And keep the <u>charge</u> of the LORD your <u>God</u>, to walk in His ways, to keep His statutes, and His commandments, and His judgments, and His testimonies, as it is written in the law of Mo'ses, that you may prosper in all that you do, and wherever you turn yourself: requirements - Elohim^{p.f.}

4 That the LORD may <u>continue</u> His word which He spoke concerning me, saying, If your children take heed to their way, to walk before Me in truth

with all their heart and with all their soul, there shall not fail you (said He) a man on the throne of Is'ra-el. carry out

5 Moreover you know also what Jo'ab the son of Zer-u-i'ah did to me, *and* what he did to the two captains of the hosts of Is'ra-el, to Ab'ner the son of Ner, and to Am'a-sa the son of Je'ther, whom he slew, and shed the blood of war in peace, and put the blood of war upon his <u>girdle</u> that *was* about his loins, and in his shoes that *were* on his feet. waistband

6 Do therefore according to your wisdom, and let not his <u>hoar</u> head go down to <u>the grave</u> in peace. gray - Sheol

7 But show kindness to the sons of Bar-zil'la-i the Gil'e-ad-ite, and let them be of those that eat at your table: for so they came to me when I fled <u>because of</u> Ab'sa-lom your brother. from

8 And, behold, *you have* with you Shim'e-i the son of Ge'ra, a Ben'jamite of Ba-hu'rim, which cursed me with a grievous curse in the day when I went to Ma-ha-na'im: but he came down to meet me at Jor'dan, and I <u>swear</u> to him by the LORD, saying, I will not put you to death with the sword. promised

9 Now therefore hold him not guiltless: for you *are* a wise man, and know what you ought to do to him; but his <u>hoar</u> head bring you down to the grave with blood. gray

10 So Da'vid slept with his fathers, and was buried in the city of Da'vid.

11 And the days that Da'vid reigned over Is'ra-el *were* forty years: seven years reigned he in He'bron, and thirty

and three years reigned he in Je-ru'sa-lem.

12 Then sat Sol'o-mon upon the throne of Da'vid his father; and his kingdom was established <u>greatly</u>. firmly

13 And Ad-o-ni'jah the son of Hag'gith came to Bath'-she-ba the mother of Sol'o-mon. And she said, Come you peaceably? And he said, Peaceably.

14 He said moreover, I have <u>some-what</u> to say to you. And she said, Say on. something

15 And he said, You know that the kingdom was mine, and *that* all Is'ra-el set their faces on me, that I should reign: however the kingdom is turned about, and is become my brother's: for it was his from the LORD.

16 And now I ask one petition of you, deny me not. And she said to him, Say on.

17 And he said, Speak, I pray you, to Sol'o-mon the king, (for he will not say you nay,) that he give me Ab'i-shag the Shu'nam-mite to wife.

18 And Bath'-she-ba said, Well; I will speak for you to the king.

19 Bath'-she-ba therefore went to king Sol'o-mon, to speak to him for Ad-o-ni'jah. And the king rose up to meet her, and bowed himself to her, and sat down on his throne, and caused a <u>seat</u> to be set for the king's mother; and she sat on his right hand. throne

20 Then she said, I desire one small petition of you; *I pray you*, say me not nay. And the king said to her, Ask on, my mother: for I will not say you nay.

21 And she said, Let Ab'i-shag the Shu'nam-mite be given to Ad-o-ni'jah your brother to wife.

22 And king Sol'o-mon answered and said to his mother, And why do you ask Ab'i-shag the Shu'nam-mite for Ad-o-ni'jah? ask for him the kingdom also; for he *is* my elder brother; even for him, and for A-bi'a-thar the priest, and for Jo'ab the son of Zer-u-i'ah.

23 Then king Sol'o-mon swear by the LORD, saying, <u>God</u> do so to me, and more also, if Ad-o-ni'jah have not spoken this word against his own life.

24 Now therefore, *as* the LORD lives, which has established me, and set me on the throne of Da'vid my father, and who has made me an house, as he promised, Ad-o-ni'jah shall be put to death this day.

25 And king Sol'o-mon sent by the hand of Be-na'iah the son of Je-hoi'a-da; and he <u>fell</u> upon him that he died. attacked

26 And to A-bi'a-thar the priest said the king, Get you to An'a-thoth, to your own fields; for you *are* worthy of death: but I will not at this time put you to death, because you bare the ark of the <u>Lord GOD</u> before Da'vid my father, and because you have been afflicted in all wherein my father was afflicted. Adonay^p.f. Jehovah^s.f.

27 So Sol'o-mon thrust out A-bi'a-thar from being priest to the LORD; that he might fulfill the word of the LORD, which He spoke concerning the house of E'li in Shi'loh.

28 Then tidings came to Jo'ab: for

Jo'ab had turned after Ad-o-ni'jah, though he turned not after Ab'sa-lom. And Jo'ab fled to the tabernacle of the LORD, and caught hold on the horns of the altar.

29 And it was told king Sol'o-mon that Jo'ab was fled to the tabernacle of the LORD; and, behold, *he is* by the altar. Then Sol'o-mon sent Be-na'iah the son of Je-hoi'a-da, saying, Go, <u>fall</u> upon him. _{attack}

30 And Be-na'iah came to the tabernacle of the LORD, and said to him, Thus says the king, Come forth. And he said, Nay; but I will die here. And Be-na'iah brought the king word again, saying, Thus said Jo'ab, and thus he answered me.

31 And the king said to him, Do as he has said, and fall upon him, and bury him; that you may take away the innocent blood, which Jo'ab shed, from me, and from the house of my father.

32 And the LORD shall return his blood upon his own head, who fell upon two men more righteous and better than he, and slew them with the sword, my father Da'vid not knowing *thereof*, <u>to wit</u>, Ab'ner the son of Ner, captain of the host of Is'ra-el, and Am'a-sa the son of Je'ther, captain of the host of Ju'dah. _{i.e., that is}

33 Their blood shall therefore return upon the head of Jo'ab, and upon the head of his <u>seed</u> for ever: but upon Da'vid, and upon his <u>seed</u>, and upon his house, and upon his throne, shall there be peace for ever from the LORD. _{descendants}

34 So Be-na'iah the son of Je-hoi'a-da went up, and <u>fell upon</u> him, and slew him: and he was buried in his own house in the wilderness. _{attacked}

35 And the king put Be-na'iah the son of Je-hoi'a-da in his <u>room</u> over the <u>host</u>: and Za'dok the priest did the king put in the <u>room</u> of A-bi'a-thar. _{place - army}

36 And the king sent and called for Shim'e-i, and said to him, Build you an house in Je-ru'sa-lem, and dwell there, and go not forth from there any where.

37 For it shall be, *that* on the day you go out, and pass over the brook Kid'ron, you shall know for certain that you shall surely die: your blood shall be upon your own head.

38 And Shim'e-i said to the king, The saying *is* good: as my lord the king has said, so will your servant do. And Shim'e-i dwelled in Je-ru'sa-lem many days.

39 And it came to pass at the end of three years, that two of the servants of Shim'e-i ran away to A'chish son of Ma'a-chah king of Gath. And they told Shim'e-i, saying, Behold, your servants *be* in Gath.

40 And Shim'e-i arose, and saddled his ass, and went to Gath to A'chish to seek his servants: and Shim'e-i went, and brought his servants from Gath.

41 And it was told Sol'o-mon that Shim'e-i had gone from Je-ru'sa-lem to Gath, and was come again.

42 And the king sent and called for Shim'e-i, and said to him, Did I not make you to swear by the LORD, and <u>protested</u> to you, saying, Know for a

certain, on the day you go out, and walk abroad anywere, that you shall surely die? and you said to me, The word *that* I have heard *is* good.

solemnly warn

43 Why then have you not kept the oath of the LORD, and the commandment that I have <u>charged</u> you with? commanded

44 The king said moreover to Shim'e-i, You know all the wickedness which your heart <u>is privy to</u>, that you did to Da'vid my father: therefore the LORD shall return your wickedness upon your own head; acknowledge

45 And king Sol'o-mon *shall be* blessed, and the throne of Da'vid shall be established before the LORD for ever.

46 So the king commanded Be-na'iah the son of Je-hoi'a-da; which went out, and <u>fell</u> upon him, that he died. And the kingdom was established in the hand of Sol'o-mon. attacked

CHAPTER 3

AND Sol'o-mon made <u>affinity</u> with Pha'raoh king of E'gypt, and took Pha'raoh's daughter, and brought her into the city of Da'vid, until he had made an end of building his own house, and the house of the LORD, and the wall of Je-ru'sa-lem round about. an alliance

2 Only the people sacrificed in high places, because there was no house built to the name of the LORD, until those days.

3 And Sol'o-mon loved the LORD, walking in the statutes of Da'vid his father: only he sacrificed and burned incense in high places.

4 And the king went to Gib'e-on to sacrifice there; for that *was* the great high place: a thousand burned offerings did Sol'o-mon offer upon that altar.

5 In Gib'e-on the LORD appeared to Sol'o-mon in a dream by night: and God said, Ask what I shall give you.

6 And Sol'o-mon said, You have showed to Your servant Da'vid my father great mercy, according as he walked before You in truth, and in righteousness, and in uprightness of heart with You; and You have kept for him this great kindness, that You have given him a son to sit on his throne, as *it is* this day.

7 And now, O LORD my <u>God</u>, You have made Your servant king instead of Da'vid my father: and I *am but* a little child: I know not *how* to go out or come in. Elohim^{p.f.}

8 And Your servant *is* in the midst of Your people which You have chosen, a great people, that cannot be numbered nor counted for multitude.

9 Give therefore Your servant an understanding heart to judge Your people, that I may discern between good and bad: for who is able to judge this Your so great a people? HEB. 5:14

10 And the speech pleased the Lord, that Sol'o-mon had asked this thing.

11 And <u>God</u> said to him, Because you have asked this thing, and have not asked for yourself long life; neither have asked riches for yourself, nor have asked the life of your enemies; but have asked for yourself understanding to discern judgment;

12 Behold, I have done according to your words: lo, I have given you a wise and an understanding heart; so that there was none like you before you, neither after you shall any arise like to you.

13 And I have also given you that which you have not asked, both riches, and honor: so that there shall not be any among the kings like to you all your days.

14 And if you will walk in My ways, to keep My statutes and My commandments, as your father Da'vid did walk, then I will lengthen your days. obey - prolong

15 And Sol'o-mon awoke; and, behold, *it was* a dream. And he came to Je-ru'sa-lem, and stood before the ark of the covenant of the LORD, and offered up burned offerings, and offered peace offerings, and made a feast to all his servants. agreement

16 Then came there two women, *that were* harlots, to the king, and stood before him.

17 And the one woman said, O my lord, I and this woman dwell in one house; and I was delivered of a child with her in the house.

18 And it came to pass the third day after that I was delivered, that this woman was delivered also: and we *were* together; *there was* no stranger with us in the house, save we two in the house. no one - except

19 And this woman's child died in the night; because she overlaid it. lay on it

20 And she arose at midnight, and took my son from beside me, while your handmaid slept, and laid it in her bosom, and laid her dead child in my bosom.

21 And when I rose in the morning to give my child suck, behold, it was dead: but when I had considered it in the morning, behold, it was not my son, which I did bear.

nurse my child - looked

22 And the other woman said, Nay; but the living *is* my son, and the dead *is* your son. And this said, No; but the dead *is* your son, and the living *is* my son. Thus they spoke before the king.

23 Then said the king, The one says, This *is* my son that lives, and your son *is* the dead: and the other says, Nay; but your son *is* the dead, and my son *is* the living.

24 And the king said, Bring me a sword. And they brought a sword before the king.

25 And the king said, Divide the living child in two, and give half to the one, and half to the other.

26 Then spoke the woman whose the living child *was* to the king, for her bowels yearned upon her son, and she said, O my lord, give her the living child, and in no wise slay it. But the other said, Let it be neither mine nor yours, *but* divide *it*. heart

27 Then the king answered and said, Give her the living child, and in no wise slay it: she *is* the mother thereof.

28 And all Is'ra-el heard of the judgment which the king had judged; and they feared the king: for they saw that the wisdom of God *was* in him, to do judgment. Elohim[n.f.]

CHAPTER 4

So king Sol'o-mon was king over all Is'ra-el.

2 And these *were* the princes which he had; Az-a-ri'ah the son of Za'dok the priest,

3 El-i-ho'reph and A-hi'ah, the sons of Shi'sha, scribes; Je-hosh'a-phat the son of A-hi'lud, the recorder.

4 And Be-na'iah the son of Je-hoi'a-da *was* over the host: and Za'dok and A-bi'a-thar *were* the priests: army

5 And Az-a-ri'ah the son of Na'than *was* over the officers: and Za'bud the son of Na'than *was* principal officer, *and* the king's friend:

6 And A-hi'shar *was* over the household: and Ad-o-ni'ram the son of Ab'da *was* over the tribute.   forced labor

7 And Sol'o-mon had twelve officers over all Is'ra-el, which provided victuals for the king and his household: each man his month in a year made provision.   provisions

8 And these *are* their names: The son of Hur, in mount E'phra-im:

9 The son of De'kar, in Ma'kaz, and in Sha-al'bim, and Beth-she'mesh, and E'lon-beth-ha'nan:

10 The son of He'sed, in Ar'u-both; to him *pertained* So'choh, and all the land of He'pher:

11 The son of A-bin'a-dab, in all the region of Dor; which had Ta'phath the daughter of Sol'o-mon to wife:

12 Ba'a-na the son of A-hi'lud; *to him pertained* Ta'a-nach and Me-gid'do, and all Beth-she'an, which *is* by Zar'ta-nah beneath Jez're-el, from Beth-she'-an to A'bel-me-ho'lah, *even* to *the place that is* beyond Jok'ne-am:

13 The son of Ge'ber, in Ra'moth-gil'e-ad; to him *pertained* the towns of Ja'ir the son of Ma-nas'seh, which *are* in Gil'e-ad; to him *also pertained* the region of Ar'gob, which is in Ba'shan, threescore great cities with walls and brasen bars: belonged - 60

14 A-hin'a-dab the son of Id'do *had* Ma-ha-na'im:

15 A-him'a-az *was* in Naph'ta-li; he also took Bas'math the daughter of Sol'o-mon to wife: as his

16 Ba'a-nah the son of Hu'shai *was* in Ash'er and in A'loth:

17 Je-hosh'a-phat the son of Par'u-ah, in Is'sa-char:

18 Shim'e-i the son of E'lah, in Ben'ja-min:

19 Ge'ber the son of U'ri *was* in the country of Gil'e-ad, *in* the country of Si'hon king of the Am'or-ites, and of Og king of Ba'shan; and *he was* the only officer which *was* in the land.

20 Ju'dah and Is'ra-el *were* many, as the sand which *is* by the sea in multitude, eating and drinking, and making merry.

21 And Sol'o-mon reigned over all kingdoms from the river to the land of the Phi-lis'tines, and to the border of E'gypt: they brought presents, and served Sol'o-mon all the days of his life.   Euphrates - tribute

22 And Sol'o-mon's provision for one day was thirty measures of fine flour, and threescore measures of meal,

23 Ten fat oxen, and twenty oxen out of the pastures, and an hundred sheep,

beside harts, and <u>roebucks</u>, and fallowdeer, and fatted fowl. _{gazelles}

24 For he had dominion over all *the region* on this side the river, from Tiph'sah even to <u>Az'zah</u>, over all the kings on this side the river: and he had peace on all sides round about him. _{Gaza}

25 And Ju'dah and Is'ra-el dwelled safely, every man under his vine and <u>under his fig tree</u>, from Dan even to Be'er-she'ba, all the days of Sol'o-mon. _{with his own}

26 And Sol'o-mon had forty thousand stalls of horses for his chariots, and twelve thousand horsemen.

27 And those officers provided <u>victual</u> for king Sol'o-mon, and for all that came to king Sol'o-mon's table, every man in his month: they lacked nothing. _{provisions}

28 Barley also and straw for the horses and <u>dromedaries</u> brought they to the place where *the officers* were, every man according to his <u>charge</u>. _{riding horses - responsibility}

29 And <u>God</u> gave Sol'o-mon wisdom and understanding exceeding much, and <u>largeness</u> of heart, even as the sand that *is* on the sea shore. _{Elohim^{p.f.} - discernment}

30 And Sol'o-mon's wisdom excelled the wisdom of all the children of the east country, and all the wisdom of E'gypt.

31 For he was wiser than all men; than E'than the Ez'ra-hite, and He'man, and Chal'col, and Dar'da, the sons of Ma'hol: and his fame was in all nations round about.

32 And he spoke three thousand prov-

erbs: and his songs were a thousand and five.

33 And he spoke of trees, from the cedar tree that *is* in Leb'a-non even to the hyssop that springs out of the wall: he spoke also of beasts, and of fowl, and of creeping things, and of fishes.

34 And there came of all people to hear the wisdom of Sol'o-mon, from all kings of the earth, which had heard of his wisdom.

CHAPTER 5

AND Hi'ram king of Tyre sent his servants to Sol'o-mon; for he had heard that they had <u>anointed</u> him king in the room of his father: for Hi'ram was ever a lover of Da'vid. _{installed}

2 And Sol'o-mon sent to Hi'ram, saying,

3 You know how that Da'vid my father could not build an house to the name of the LORD his <u>God</u> for the wars which were about him on every side, until the LORD put them under <u>the soles of his feet</u>. _{Elohim^{p.f.} - his control}

4 But now the LORD my <u>God</u> has given me rest on every side, *so that there is* neither adversary nor <u>evil occurrent</u>. _{disaster}

5 And, behold, I purpose to build an house to the name of the LORD my <u>God</u>, as the LORD spoke to Da'vid my father, saying, your son, whom I will set upon your throne in your room, he shall build an house to My name.

6 Now therefore command you that they <u>hew</u> me cedar trees out of Leb'a-non; and my servants shall be with your

servants: and to you will I give hire for your servants according to all that you shall <u>appoint</u>: for you know that *there is* not among us any that <u>can skill</u> to <u>hew</u> timber like to the Si-do'ni-ans. cut - say - knows how

7 And it came to pass, when Hi'ram heard the words of Sol'o-mon, that he rejoiced greatly, and said, Blessed *be* the LORD this day, which has given to Da'vid a wise son over this great people.

8 And Hi'ram sent to Sol'o-mon, saying, I have considered the things which you sent to me for: *and* I will do all your desire concerning timber of cedar, and concerning timber of fir.

9 My servants shall bring *them* down from Leb'a-non to the sea: and I will convey them by sea in <u>floats</u> to the place that you shall <u>appoint</u> me, and will cause them to be discharged there, and you shall receive *them*: and you shall accomplish my desire, in giving food for my household. rafts - direct

10 So Hi'ram gave Sol'o-mon cedar trees and fir trees *according to* all his desire.

11 And Sol'o-mon gave Hi'ram twenty thousand measures of wheat *for* food to his household, and twenty measures of pure oil: thus gave Sol'o-mon to Hi'ram year by year.

12 And the LORD gave Sol'o-mon wisdom, as He promised him: and there was peace between Hi'ram and Sol'o-mon; and they two made a <u>league</u> together. agreement

13 And king Sol'o-mon raised a <u>levy</u> out of all Is'ra-el; and the <u>levy</u> was thirty thousand men. muster

14 And he sent them to Leb'a-non, ten thousand a month <u>by courses</u>: a month they were in Leb'a-non, *and* two months at home: and Ad-o-ni'ram *was* over the <u>levy</u>. in relays - forced laborers

15 And Sol'o-mon had <u>threescore and ten</u> thousand that bare burdens, and fourscore thousand hewers in the mountains; 70

16 Beside the chief of Sol'o-mon's officers which *were* over the work, three thousand and three hundred, which ruled over the people that wrought in the work.

17 And the king commanded, and they brought great stones, costly stones, *and* <u>hewed</u> stones, to lay the foundation of the house. cut

18 And Sol'o-mon's builders and Hi'ram's builders did hew *them*, and the stonesquarers: so they prepared timber and stones to build the house.

CHAPTER 6

AND it came to pass in the four hundred and eightieth year after the children of Is'ra-el were come out of the land of E'gypt, in the fourth year of Sol'o-mon's reign over Is'ra-el, in the month Zif, which *is* the second month, that he began to build the house of the LORD.

2 And the house which king Sol'o-mon built for the LORD, the length thereof *was* <u>threescore</u> cubits, and the breadth thereof twenty *cubits*, and the height thereof thirty cubits. 60

3 And the porch before the temple of

the house, twenty cubits *was* the length thereof, according to the breadth of the house; *and* ten cubits *was* the breadth thereof before the house.

4 And for the house he made windows of <u>narrow lights</u>.   with artistic frames

5 And against the wall of the house he built <u>chambers</u> round about, *against* the walls of the house round about, *both* of the <u>temple</u> and of the <u>oracle</u>: and he made <u>chambers</u> round about: a structure - nave - inner sanctuary

6 The <u>nethermost chamber</u> *was* five cubits broad, and the middle *was* six cubits broad, and the third *was* seven cubits broad: for without *in the wall* of the house he made <u>narrowed rests</u> round about, that *the beams* should not be fastened in the walls of the house.   lowest floor - offsets

7 And the house, when it was in building, was built of stone made ready before it was brought there: so that there was neither hammer nor axe *nor* any tool of iron heard in the house, while it was in building.

8 The door for the <u>middle</u> chamber *was* in the right side of the house: and they went up with winding stairs into the middle *chamber*, and out of the middle into the third.   lowest side

9 So he built the house, and finished it; and covered the house with beams and boards of cedar.

10 And *then* he built <u>chambers</u> against all the house, five cubits high: and they rested on the house with timber of cedar.   stories

11 And the word of the LORD came to Sol'o-mon, saying,

12 *Concerning* this house which you are in building, if you will walk in My statutes, and execute My judgments, and keep all My commandments to walk in them; then will I perform My word with you, which I spoke to Da'vid your father:

13 And I will dwell among the children of Is'ra-el, and will not forsake My people Is'ra-el.

14 So Sol'o-mon built the house, and finished it.

15 And he built the walls of the house within with boards of cedar, <u>both</u> the floor of the house, <u>and</u> the walls of the ceiling: *and* he covered *them* on the inside with wood, and covered the floor of the house with planks of fir.   from - to

16 And he built twenty cubits on the sides of the house, both the floor and the walls with boards of cedar: he even built *them* for it within, *even* for the <u>oracle</u>, *even* for the most holy *place*.   inner sanctuary

17 And the house, that *is*, the <u>temple</u> before it, was forty cubits *long*.   nave

18 And the cedar of the house within *was* carved with <u>knops</u> and open flowers: all *was* cedar; there was no stone seen.   gourds

19 And the <u>oracle</u> he prepared in the house within, to set there the ark of the <u>covenant</u> of the LORD.   agreement

20 And the oracle in the forepart *was* twenty cubits in length, and twenty cubits in breadth, and twenty cubits in the height thereof: and he overlaid it with pure gold; and *so* covered the altar *which was of* cedar.

21 So Sol'o-mon overlaid the house inside with pure gold: and he made a partition by the chains of gold before the <u>oracle</u>; and he overlaid it with gold. inside - inner sanctuary
22 And the whole house he overlaid with gold, until he had finished all the house: also the whole altar that *was* by the <u>oracle</u> he overlaid with gold.
23 And within the <u>oracle</u> he made two cherubims *of* olive tree, *each* ten cubits high.
24 And five cubits *was* the one wing of the cherub, and five cubits the other wing of the cherub: from the uttermost part of the one wing to the <u>uttermost part of</u> the other *were* ten cubits. end
25 And the other cherub *was* ten cubits: both the cherubims *were* of one measure and one size.
26 The height of the one cherub *was* ten cubits, and so *was it* of the other cherub.
27 And he set the cherubims inside the inner house: and they stretched forth the wings of the cherubims, so that the wing of the one touched the *one* wall, and the wing of the other cherub touched the other wall; and their wings touched one another in the midst of the house.
28 And he overlaid the cherubims with gold.
29 And he carved all the walls of the house round about with carved figures of cherubims and palm trees and open flowers, inside and outside.
30 And the floor of the house he overlaid with gold, inside and outside.

31 And for the <u>entering</u> of the <u>oracle</u> he made doors *of* olive <u>tree</u>: the lintel *and* side posts *were* <u>a fifth part</u> <u>*of the wall*</u>. entrance - wood - five-sided
32 The two doors also *were of* olive <u>tree</u>; and he carved upon them carvings of cherubims and palm trees and open flowers, and overlaid *them* with gold, and spread gold upon the cherubims, and upon the palm trees. wood
33 So also made he for the door of the temple posts *of* olive <u>tree</u>, a <u>fourth part</u> *of the wall*. four-sided
34 And the two doors *were of* fir <u>tree</u>: the two <u>leaves</u> of the one door *were* <u>folding</u>, and the two <u>leaves</u> of the other door *were* <u>folding</u>. panels - pivoting
35 And he carved *thereon* cherubims and palm trees and open flowers: and covered *them* with gold fitted upon the carved work.
36 And he built the inner court with three rows of hewed stone, and a row of cedar beams.
37 In the fourth year was the foundation of the house of the LORD laid, in the month Zif:
38 And in the eleventh year, in the month Bul, which *is* the eighth month, was the house finished throughout all the parts thereof, and according to all the fashion of it. So was he seven years in building it.

CHAPTER 7

BUT Sol'o-mon was building his own house thirteen years, and he finished all his house.

2 He built also the house of the forest of Leb'a-non; the length thereof *was* an hundred cubits, and the breadth thereof fifty cubits, and the height thereof thirty cubits, upon four rows of cedar pillars, with cedar beams upon the pillars.

3 And *it was* covered with cedar above upon the beams, that *lay* on forty five pillars, fifteen *in* a row.

4 And *there were* <u>windows</u> *in* three rows, and <u>light</u> *was* against <u>light</u> *in* three ranks.

window frames - window

5 And all the doors and posts *were* square, with the windows: and <u>light</u> *was* <u>against</u> <u>light</u> *in* three <u>ranks</u>.

opposite - sets

6 And he made a <u>porch</u> of pillars; the length thereof *was* fifty cubits, and the breadth thereof thirty cubits: and the porch *was* before them: and the *other* pillars and the thick beam *were* before them.

hall

7 Then he made a <u>porch</u> for the throne where he might judge, *even* the <u>porch</u> of judgment: and *it was* covered with cedar from one side of the floor to the other.

8 And his house where he dwelled *had* another court inside the <u>porch</u>, *which* was of the like work. Sol'o-mon made also an house for Pha'raoh's daughter, whom he had taken *to wife*, <u>like to</u> this <u>porch</u>.

similar to

9 All these *were of* costly stones, according to the measures of <u>hewed</u> stones, sawed with saws, inside and outside, even from the foundation to the <u>coping</u>, and *so* on the outside toward the great court.

cut - eaves

10 And the foundation *was of* costly stones, even great stones, stones of ten cubits, and stones of eight cubits.

11 And above *were* costly stones, after the measures of <u>hewed</u> stones, and cedars.

12 And the great court round about *was* with three rows of <u>hewed</u> stones, and a row of cedar beams, both for the inner court of the house of the LORD, and for the <u>porch</u> of the house.

cut - hall

13 And king Sol'o-mon sent and brought Hi'ram out of Tyre.

14 He *was* a widow's son of the tribe of Naph'ta-li, and his father *was* a man of Tyre, a worker in brass: and he was filled with wisdom, and understanding, and <u>cunning</u> to work all works in brass. And he came to king Sol'o-mon, and wrought all his work.

skill

15 For he cast two pillars of brass, of eighteen cubits high apiece: and a line of twelve cubits <u>did compass</u> either of them about.

went around

16 And he made two <u>chapiters</u> *of* molten <u>brass</u>, to set upon the tops of the pillars: the height of the one chapiter *was* five cubits, and the height of the other chapiter *was* five cubits:

capitals - bronze

17 *And* nets of checker work, and wreaths of chain work, for the chapiters which *were* upon the top of the pillars; seven for the one <u>chapiter</u>, and seven for the other <u>chapiter</u>.

18 And he made the pillars, and two rows round about upon the one network, to cover the <u>chapiters</u> that *were*

upon the top, with pomegranates: and so did he for the other <u>chapter</u>.capitals
19 And the <u>chapiters</u> that *were* upon the top of the pillars *were* of lily work in the porch, four cubits.
20 And the <u>chapiters</u> upon the two pillars *had pomegranates* also above, over against the <u>belly</u> which *was* by the network: and the pomegranates *were* two hundred in rows round about upon the other chapiter.   projection
21 And he set up the pillars in the porch of the <u>temple</u>: and he set up the right pillar, and called the name thereof Ja'chin: and he set up the left pillar, and called the name thereof Bo'az. nave
22 And upon the top of the pillars *was* lily work: so was the work of the pillars finished.
23 And he made a <u>molten</u> sea, ten cubits from the one brim to the other: *it was* round all about, and his height *was* five cubits: and a line of thirty cubits did compass it round about.   cast metal
24 And under the brim of it round about *there were* <u>knops</u> <u>compassing</u> it, ten in a cubit, <u>compassing</u> the sea round about: the knops *were* cast in two rows, when it was cast.gourds - encircling
25 It stood upon twelve oxen, three looking toward the north, and three looking toward the west, and three looking toward the south, and three looking toward the east: and the sea was *set* above upon them, and all their hinder parts *were* inward.
26 And it *was* an hand breadth thick, and the brim thereof was wrought like the brim of a cup, with flowers of lilies: it contained two thousand baths.

27 And he made ten <u>bases</u> of <u>brass</u>; four cubits *was* the length of one base, and four cubits the breadth thereof, and three cubits the height of it.   stands - bronze.
28 And the work of the <u>bases was</u> on this *manner*: they had borders, and the borders *were* between the <u>ledges</u>:   stands - uprights
29 And on the borders that *were* between the <u>ledges</u> *were* lions, oxen, and cherubims: and upon the <u>ledges</u> *there was* a base above: and beneath the lions and oxen *were* certain additions made of thin work.
30 And every base had four <u>brazen</u> wheels, and <u>plates</u> of <u>brass</u>: and the four <u>corners</u> thereof had <u>undersetters</u>: under the laver *were* <u>undersetters</u> molten, at the side of every addition.

bronze - axles - bronze - feet - supports

31 And the mouth of it inside the <u>chapiter</u> and above *was* a cubit: but the mouth thereof *was* round *after* the work of the base, a cubit and an half: and also upon the mouth of it *were* gravings with their borders, foursquare, not round.   capitals
32 And under the borders *were* four wheels; and the <u>axletrees</u> of the wheels *were joined* to the base: and the height of a wheel *was* a cubit and half a cubit.   axles
33 And the work of the wheels *was* like the work of a chariot wheel: their <u>axletrees</u>, and their <u>naves</u>, and their <u>felloes</u>, and their spokes, *were* all <u>molten</u>.   hubs - rims - cast
34 And *there were* four <u>undersetters</u> to the four corners of one base: *and* the undersetters *were* of the very base itself.

35 And in the top of the base *was there* a round <u>compass</u> of half a cubit high: and on the top of the base the ledges thereof and the borders thereof *were* of the same.   band
36 For on the plates of the <u>ledges</u> thereof, and on the <u>borders</u> thereof, he <u>graved</u> cherubims, lions, and palm trees, according to the <u>proportion</u> of every one, and additions round about.   uprights - surfaces - engraved - size
37 After this *manner* he made the ten bases: all of them had <u>one</u> casting, <u>one</u> measure, *and* <u>one</u> size.the same
38 Then made he ten lavers of brass: one laver contained forty baths: *and* every laver was four cubits: *and* upon every one of the ten bases one laver.
39 And he put five bases on the right side of the house, and five on the left side of the house: and he set the sea on the right side of the house eastward over against the south.
40 And Hi'ram made the lavers, and the shovels, and the basins. So Hi'ram <u>made an end</u> of doing all the work that he made king Sol'o-mon for the house of the LORD: finished
41 The two pillars, and the *two* bowls of the <u>chapiters</u> that *were* on the top of the two pillars; and the two networks, to cover the two bowls of the <u>chapiters</u> which *were* upon the top of the pillars;   capitals
42 And four hundred pomegranates for the two networks, *even* two rows of pomegranates for one network, to cover the two bowls of the <u>chapiters</u> that *were* <u>upon</u> the pillars;   on top of

43 And the ten bases, and ten lavers on the bases;
44 And one sea, and twelve oxen under the sea;
45 And the pots, and the shovels, and the basins: and all these vessels, which Hi'ram made to king Sol'o-mon for the house of the LORD, *were of* bright brass.
46 In the plain of Jor'dan did the king cast them, in the clay ground between Suc'coth and Zar'than.
47 And Sol'o-mon left all the vessels *unweighed*, because they were exceeding many: neither was the weight of the brass found out.
48 And Sol'o-mon made all the vessels that *pertained* to the house of the LORD: the altar of gold, and the table of gold, whereupon the showbread *was*,
49 And the candlesticks of pure gold, five on the right *side*, and five on the left, before the <u>oracle</u>, with the flowers, and the lamps, and the tongs *of* gold,   inner sanctuary
50 And the bowls, and the snuffers, and the basins, and the spoons, and the <u>censers</u> *of* pure gold; and the hinges *of* gold, *both* for the doors of the inner house, the most holy *place*, *and* for the doors of the house, *to* <u>wit</u>, of the temple.   firepans - that is
51 So was ended all the work that king Sol'o-mon made for the house of the LORD. And Sol'o-mon brought in the things which Da'vid his father had dedicated; *even* the silver, and the gold, and the vessels, did he put among the treasures of the house of the LORD.

CHAPTER 8

THEN Sol'o-mon assembled the elders of Is'ra-el, and all the heads of the tribes, the <u>chief</u> of the fathers of the children of Is'ra-el, to king Sol'o-mon in Je-ru'sa-lem, that they might bring up the ark of the <u>cov-enant</u> of the LORD out of the city of Da'vid, which *is* Zi'on. heads - agreement

2 And all the men of Is'ra-el assembled themselves to king Sol'o-mon at the feast in the month Eth'a-nim, which is the seventh month.

3 And all the elders of Is'ra-el came, and the priests took up the ark.

4 And they brought up the ark of the LORD, and the tabernacle of the congregation, and all the holy vessels that *were* in the tabernacle, even those did the priests and the Le'vites bring up.

5 And king Sol'o-mon, and all the congregation of Is'ra-el, that were assembled to him, *were* with him before the ark, sacrificing sheep and oxen, that could not be told nor numbered for multitude.

6 And the priests brought in the ark of the <u>covenant</u> of the LORD to his place, into the <u>oracle</u> of the house, to the most holy *place*, *even* under the wings of the cherubims. agreement - inner sanctuary

7 For the cherubims spread forth *their* two wings over the place of the ark, and the cherubims covered the ark and the <u>staves</u> thereof above. poles

8 And they drew out the <u>staves</u>, that the ends of the staves were seen out in the holy *place* before the <u>oracle</u>, and they were not seen outside: and there they are to this day. inner sanctuary

9 *There was* nothing in the ark save the two tables of stone, which Mo'ses put there at Ho'reb, when the LORD made *a* <u>covenant</u> with the children of Is'ra-el, when they came out of the land of E'gypt. agreement

10 And it came to pass, when the priests were come out of the holy *place*, that the cloud filled the house of the LORD, REV. 15:8

11 So that the priests could not stand to minister because of the cloud: for the glory of the LORD had filled the house of the LORD.

12 Then spoke Sol'o-mon, The LORD said that He would dwell in the thick darkness.

13 I have surely built You an house to dwell in, a <u>settled</u> place for You to abide in for ever. princely

14 And the king turned his face about, and blessed all the congregation of Is'ra-el: (and all the congregation of Is'ra-el stood;)

15 And he said, Blessed *be* the <u>LORD</u> <u>God</u> of Is'ra-el, which spoke with His mouth to Da'vid my father, and has with His hand fulfilled *it*, saying, Jehovah^{s-f} Elohim^{p-f}

16 Since the day that I brought forth My people Is'ra-el out of E'gypt, I chose no city out of all the tribes of Is'ra-el to build an house, that My name might be therein; but I chose Da'vid to be over My people Is'ra-el.

17 And it was <u>in the heart</u> of Da'vid

my father to build an house for the name of the Lord God of Is'ra-el.

the intention

18 And the Lord said to Da'vid my father, Whereas it was in your heart to build an house to My name, you did well that it was in your heart.

19 Nevertheless you shall not build the house; but your son that shall come forth out of your loins, he shall build the house to My name.

20 And the Lord has performed His word that He spoke, and I am risen up in the <u>room</u> of Da'vid my father, and sit on the throne of Is'ra-el, as the Lord <u>promised</u>, and have built an house for the name of the Lord God of Is'ra-el.   place - spoke - Jehovah^{s.f.} - Elohim^{p.f.}

21 And I have set there a place for the ark, wherein *is* the <u>covenant</u> of the Lord, which He made with our fathers, when He brought them out of the land of E'gypt.   agreement

22 And Sol'o-mon stood before the altar of the Lord in the presence of all the congregation of Is'ra-el, and spread forth his hands toward heaven:

23 And he said, Lord God of Is'ra-el, *there is* no <u>God</u> like You, in heaven above, or on earth beneath, who keeps <u>covenant</u> and mercy with Your servants that walk before You with all their heart:

24 Who have kept with Your servant Da'vid my father that You promised him: You spoke also with Your mouth, and have fulfilled *it* with Your hand, as *it is* this day.

25 Therefore now, Lord God of Is'ra-el, keep with Your servant Da'vid my father that You promised him, saying, There shall not fail you a man in My sight to sit on the throne of Is'ra-el; so that your children take heed to their way, that they walk before Me as you have walked before Me.   Jehovah^{s.f.}   Elohim^{p.f.}

26 And now, O <u>God</u> of Is'ra-el, let Your word, I pray You, be verified, which You spoke to Your servant Da'vid my father.

27 But will <u>God</u> indeed dwell on the earth? behold, the heaven and heaven of heavens cannot contain You; how much less this house that I have builded?   Elohim^{p.f.}

28 Yet have <u>You respect</u> to the prayer of Your servant, and to his supplication, O Lord my <u>God</u>, to hearken to the cry and to the prayer, which Your servant prays before You to day: regard

29 That Your eyes may be open toward this house night and day, *even* toward the place of which You have said, My name shall be there: that You may hearken to the prayer which Your servant shall make toward this place.

30 And hearken You to the supplication of Your servant, and of Your people Is'ra-el, when they shall pray toward this place: and hear You in heaven Your dwelling place: and when You hear, forgive.

31 If any man trespass against his neighbor, and an <u>oath</u> be laid upon him to cause him to swear, and the <u>oath</u> come before your altar in this house: pledge

32 Then hear You in heaven, and do, and judge Your servants, condemning the wicked, to bring his way upon his head; and justifying the righteous, to give him according to his righteousness.

33 When Your people Is'ra-el be smitten down before the enemy, because they have sinned against You, and shall turn again to You, and confess Your name, and pray, and make supplication to You in this house:

34 Then hear You in heaven, and forgive the sin of Your people Is'ra-el, and bring them again to the land which You gave to their fathers.

35 When heaven is shut up, and there is no rain, because they have sinned against You; if they pray to-ward this place, and confess Your name, and turn from their sin, when You afflict them:

36 Then hear You in heaven, and forgive the sin of Your servants, and of Your people Is'ra-el, that You teach them the good way wherein they should walk, and give rain upon Your land, which You have given to Your people for an inheritance.

37 If there be in the land famine, if there be pestilence, blasting, mildew, locust, *or* if there be caterpillar; if their enemy besiege them in the land of their cities; whatsoever plague, whatsoever sickness *there be*;

38 What prayer and supplication soever be *made* by any man, *or* by all Your people Is'ra-el, which shall know every man the plague of his own heart, and spread forth his hands toward this house:

39 Then hear You in heaven Your dwelling place, and forgive, and do, and give to every man according to his ways, whose heart You know; (for You, *even* You only, know the hearts of all the children of men;)

40 That they may fear You all the days that they live in the land which You gave to our fathers.

41 Moreover concerning a stranger, that *is* not of Your people Is'ra-el, but come out of a far country for Your name's sake;

42 (For they shall hear of Your great name, and of Your strong hand, and of Your stretched out arm;) when he shall come and pray toward this house;

43 Hear You in heaven Your dwelling place, and do according to all that the stranger calls to You for: that all people of the earth may know Your name, to fear You, as *do* Your people Is'ra-el; and that they may know that this house, which I have builded, is called by Your name.

44 If Your people go out to battle against their enemy, wherever You shall send them, and shall pray to the LORD toward the city which You have chosen, and *toward* the house that I have built for Your name:

45 Then hear You in heaven their prayer and their supplication, and maintain their cause.

46 If they sin against You, (for *there is* no man that sins not,) and You be angry with them, and deliver them to the enemy, so that they carry them

M27
G4H-555
M28-691

away captives to the land of the enemy, far or near;

47 *Yet* if they shall <u>bethink</u> themselves in the land where they were carried captives, and repent, and make <u>supplication</u> to You in the land of them that carried them captives, saying, We have sinned, and have done <u>perversely</u>, we have committed wickedness;

change their minds - iniquity

48 And *so* return to You with all their heart, and with all their soul, in the land of their enemies, which led them away captive, and pray to You toward their land, which You gave to their fathers, the city which You have chosen, and the house which I have built for Your name:

49 Then hear You their prayer and their <u>supplication</u> in heaven Your dwelling place, and maintain their <u>cause</u>,

appeal - justice

50 And forgive Your people that have sinned against You, and all their transgressions wherein they have transgressed against You, and give them compassion before them who carried them captive, that they may have compassion on them:

51 For they *be* Your people, and Your inheritance, which You brought forth out of E'gypt, from the midst of the furnace of iron:

52 That Your eyes may be open to the <u>supplication</u> of Your servant, and to the supplication of Your people Is'ra-el, to hearken to them in all that they call for to You.

53 For You did separate them from among all the people of the earth, to be Your inheritance, as You spoke by the hand of Moses Your servant, when You brought our fathers out of E'gypt, O Lord GOD.

Jehovah^{s.f.} Elohim^{p.f.}

54 And it was *so*, that when Sol'o-mon had made an end of praying all this prayer and supplication to the LORD, he arose from before the altar of the LORD, from kneeling on his knees with his hands spread up to heaven.

55 And he stood, and blessed all the congregation of Is'ra-el with a loud voice, saying,

56 Blessed *be* the LORD, that has given rest to His people Is'ra-el, according to all that He promised: there has not failed one word of all His good promise, which He promised by the hand of Mo'ses His servant.

57 The LORD our <u>God</u> be with us, as He was with our fathers: let Him not leave us, nor forsake us:

Elohim^{p.f.}

58 That He may <u>incline</u> our hearts to Him, to walk in all His ways, and to keep His commandments, and His statutes, and His judgments, which He commanded our fathers.

turn

59 And let these my words, wherewith I have made <u>supplication</u> before the LORD, be near to the LORD our <u>God</u> day and night, that He maintain the cause of His servant, and the cause of His people Is'ra-el <u>at all times</u>, as the matter shall require:

appeal - each day

60 That all the people of the earth may <u>know</u> that the LORD *is* God, *and that there is* none else.

understand - Elohim^{p.f.}

61 Let your heart therefore be <u>perfect</u> <u>with</u> the LORD our <u>God</u>, to walk in His

statutes, and to keep His commandments, as at this day.

wholly devoted to - Elohim[p.f.]

62 And the king, and all Is'ra-el with him, offered sacrifice before the LORD.
63 And Sol'o-mon offered a sacrifice of peace offerings, which he offered to the LORD, two and twenty thousand oxen, and an hundred and twenty thousand sheep. So the king and all the children of Is'ra-el dedicated the house of the LORD.
64 The same day did the king <u>hallow</u> the middle of the court that *was* before the house of the LORD: for there he offered burned offerings, and meat offerings, and the fat of the peace offerings: because the brazen altar that *was* before the LORD *was* too little to receive the burned offerings, and meat offerings, and the fat of the peace offerings.[consecrate]
65 And at that time Sol'o-mon held a feast, and all Is'ra-el with him, a great congregation, from the entering in of Ha'math to the river of E'gypt, before the LORD our <u>God</u>, seven days and seven days, *even* fourteen days.
66 On the eighth day he sent the people away: and they <u>blessed</u> the king, and went to their tents joyful and glad of heart for all the goodness that the LORD had done for Da'vid His servant, and for Is'ra-el His people.[thanked]

CHAPTER 9

A ND it came to pass, when Sol'o-mon had finished the building of the house of the LORD, and the king's house, and all Sol'o-mon's <u>desire</u> which he was pleased to do,[wishes]
2 That the LORD appeared to Sol'o-mon the second time, as He had appeared to him at Gib'e-on.
3 And the LORD said to him, I have heard your prayer and your <u>supplication</u>, that you have made before Me: I have <u>hallowed</u> this house, which you have built, to put My name there for ever; and My eyes and My heart shall be there perpetually.[appeal - consecrated]

G4H
593

4 And if you will walk before Me, as Da'vid your father walked, in integrity of heart, and in uprightness, to do according to all that I have commanded you, *and* will keep My statutes and My judgments:
5 Then I will establish the throne of your kingdom upon Is'ra-el for ever, as I promised to Da'vid your father, saying, There shall not fail you a man upon the throne of Is'ra-el.
6 *But* if you shall at all turn from following Me, you or your children, and will not keep My commandments *and* My statutes which I have set before you, but go and serve other gods, and worship them:

M11
559 P04

7 Then will I <u>cut off</u> Is'ra-el out of the land which I have given them; and this house, which I have hallowed for My name, will I cast out of My sight; and Is'ra-el shall be a proverb and a byword among all people:[destroy]

854

8 And at this house, *which* is high, every one that passes by it shall be astonished, and shall <u>hiss;</u> and they shall say, Why has the LORD done thus to this land, and to this house?[scoff]

9 And they shall answer, Because they forsook the Lord their <u>God</u>, who brought forth their fathers out of the land of E'gypt, and have taken hold upon other gods, and have worshiped them, and served them: therefore has the Lord brought upon them all this evil.   Elohim^{p.f.}

10 And it came to pass at the end of twenty years, when Sol'o-mon had built the two houses, the house of the Lord, and the king's house,

11 (*Now* Hi'ram the king of Tyre had furnished Sol'o-mon with cedar trees and fir trees, and with gold, according to all his desire,) that then king Sol'o-mon gave Hi'ram twenty cities in the land of Gal'i-lee.

12 And Hi'ram came out from Tyre to see the cities which Sol'o-mon had given him; and they pleased him not.

13 And he said, What cities *are* these which you have given me, my brother? And he called them the land of <u>Ca'bul</u> to this day.   Displeasing

14 And Hi'ram sent to the king sixscore talents of gold.

15 And this *is* the reason of the levy which king Sol'o-mon raised; for to build the house of the Lord, and his own house, and Mil'lo, and the wall of Je-ru'sa-lem, and Ha'zor, and Me-gid'do, and Ge'zer.

16 *For* Pha'raoh king of E'gypt had gone up, and taken Ge'zer, and burned it with fire, and slain the Ca'naan-ites that dwelled in the city, and given it *for* a present to his daughter, Sol'o-mon's wife.

17 And Sol'o-mon built Ge'zer, and Beth-ho'ron the <u>nether,</u>   lower

18 And Ba'al-ath, and Tad'mor in the wilderness, in the land,

19 And all the cities of store that Sol'o-mon had, and cities for his chariots, and cities for his horsemen, and that which Sol'o-mon desired to build in Je-ru'sa-lem, and in Leb'a-non, and in all the land of his dominion.

20 *And* all the people *that were* left of the Am'or-ites, Hit'tites, Per'iz-zites, Hi'vites, and Jeb'u-sites, which *were* not of the children of Is'ra-el,

21 Their children that were left after them in the land, whom the children of Is'ra-el also were not able utterly to destroy, upon those did Sol'o-mon levy a tribute of bondservice to this day.

22 But of the children of Is'ra-el did Sol'o-mon make no <u>bondmen</u>: but they *were* men of war, and his servants, and his princes, and his captains, and rulers of his chariots, and his horsemen.   slaves

23 These *were* the chief of the officers that *were* over Sol'o-mon's work, five hundred and fifty, which bare rule over the people that <u>wrought in</u> the work.   were doing

24 But Pha'raoh's daughter came up out of the city of Da'vid to her house which *Sol'o-mon* had built for her: then did he build Mil'lo.

25 And three times in a year did Sol'o-mon offer burned offerings and peace offerings upon the altar which he built to the Lord, and he burned incense upon the altar that *was* before the Lord. So he finished the house.

26 And king Sol'o-mon made a

navy of ships in E'zi-on-ge'ber, which is beside E'loth, on the shore of the Red sea, in the land of E'dom.

27 And Hi'ram sent in the navy his servants, shipmen that had knowledge of the sea, with the servants of Sol'o-mon.

28 And they came to O'phir, and brought from there gold, four hundred and twenty talents, and brought *it* to king Sol'o-mon.

CHAPTER 10

AND when the queen of She'ba heard of the <u>fame</u> of Sol'o-mon concerning the name of the LORD, she came to prove him with hard questions. MATT. 12:42 reputation

2 And she came to Je-ru'sa-lem with a very great <u>train</u>, with camels that bare spices, and very much gold, and precious stones: and when she was come to Sol'o-mon, she communed with him of all that was <u>in her heart</u>. retinue - on her mind

3 And Sol'o-mon <u>told</u> her all her questions: there was not *any* thing hid from the king, which he told her not. answered

4 And when the queen of She'ba had seen all Sol'o-mon's wisdom, and the house that he had built,

5 And the <u>meat</u> of his table, and the sitting of his servants, and the attendance of his ministers, and their apparel, and his cupbearers, and his ascent by which he went up to the house of the LORD; there was no more spirit in her. food

6 And she said to the king, It was a true report that I heard in my own land of your acts and of your wisdom.

7 However I believed not the words, until I came, and my eyes had seen *it*: and, behold, the half was not told me: your wisdom and prosperity exceeds the fame which I heard.

8 Happy *are* your men, happy *are* these your servants, which stand continually before you, *and* that hear your wisdom.

9 Blessed be the LORD your <u>God</u>, which delighted in you, to set you on the throne of Is'ra-el: because the LORD loved Is'ra-el for ever, therefore made He you king, to do judgment and justice. Elohim P.f.

10 And she gave the king an hundred and twenty talents of gold, and of spices very great store, and precious stones: there came no more such abundance of spices as these which the queen of She'ba gave to king Sol'o-mon.

11 And the navy also of Hi'ram, that brought gold from O'phir, brought in from O'phir <u>great plenty of</u> almug trees, and precious stones. very many

12 And the king made of the almug trees pillars for the house of the LORD, and for the king's house, harps also and <u>psalteries</u> for singers: there came no such almug trees, nor were seen to this day. lyres

13 And king Sol'o-mon gave to the queen of She'ba all <u>her desire</u>, whatsoever she asked, beside *that* which Sol'o-mon gave her of his royal bounty. So she turned and went to her own country, she and her servants. she wanted

14 Now the weight of gold that

came to Sol'o-mon in one year was six hundred threescore and six talents of gold,

15 Beside *that he had* of the merchantmen, and of the traffic of the spice merchants, and of all the kings of A-ra'bi-a, and of the governors of the country.

16 And king Sol'o-mon made two hundred <u>targets</u> *of* beaten gold: six hundred *shekels* of gold went to one target.   _{large shields}

17 And *he made* three hundred shields *of* beaten gold; three pound of gold went to one shield: and the king put them in the house of the forest of Leb'a-non.

18 Moreover the king made a great throne of ivory, and overlaid it with the best gold.

19 The throne had six steps, and the top of the throne *was* round behind: and *there were* stays on either side on the place of the seat, and two lions stood beside the <u>stays</u>.   _{arms}

20 And twelve lions stood there on the one side and on the other upon the six steps: there was not the <u>like made</u> in any kingdom.   _{equal}

21 And all king Sol'o-mon's drinking vessels *were of* gold, and all the vessels of the house of the forest of Leb'a-non *were of* pure gold; none *were of* silver: it was <u>nothing accounted</u> of in the days of Sol'o-mon.   _{not valuable}

22 For the king had at sea a navy of Thar'shish with the navy of Hi'ram: once in three years came the navy of Thar'shish, bringing gold, and silver, ivory, and apes, and peacocks.

23 So king Sol'o-mon exceeded all the kings of the earth for riches and for wisdom.

24 And all the earth <u>sought</u> to Sol'o-mon, to hear his wisdom, which <u>God</u> had put in his heart.   _{consulted - Elohim^{p.f.}}

25 And they brought every man his present, vessels of silver, and vessels of gold, and garments, and armor, and spices, horses, and mules, a rate year by year.

26 And Sol'o-mon gathered together chariots and horsemen: and he had a thousand and four hundred chariots, and twelve thousand horsemen, whom he <u>bestowed</u> in the cities for chariots, and with the king at Je-ru'sa-lem.   _{stationed}

27 And the king made silver *to be* in Je-ru'sa-lem as stones, and cedars made he *to be* as the sycamore trees that *are* in the <u>vale</u>, for abundance.   _{lowland}

28 And Sol'o-mon had horses brought out of E'gypt, and linen yarn: the king's merchants received the linen yarn at a price.

29 And a chariot came up and went out of E'gypt for six hundred *shekels* of silver, and an horse for an hundred and fifty: and so for all the kings of the Hit'tites, and for the kings of Syr'i-a, did they bring *them* out by their <u>means</u>.   _{expense}

CHAPTER 11

BUT king Sol'o-mon loved many <u>strange</u> women, together with the daughter of Pha'raoh, women of the Mo'ab-ites, Am'mon-ites, E'dom-ites, Zi-do'ni-ans, *and* Hit'tites;   _{foreign}

2 Of the nations *concerning* which the LORD said to the children of Is'ra-el, You shall not go in to them, neither shall they come in to you: *for* surely they will turn away your heart after their gods: Sol'o-mon clung to these in love.

3 And he had seven hundred wives, princesses, and three hundred concubines: and his wives turned away his heart.

4 For it came to pass, when Sol'o-mon was old, *that* his wives turned away his heart <u>after</u> other gods: and his heart was not <u>perfect</u> with the LORD his <u>God</u>, as *was* the heart of Da'vid his father.

to follow - wholly devoted - Elohim

5 For Sol'o-mon <u>went</u> after Ash'to-reth the goddess of the Zi-do'ni-ans, and after Mil'com the <u>abomination</u> of the Am'mon-ites. followed - detestable idol

6 And Sol'o-mon did evil in the sight of the LORD, and <u>went</u> not fully after the LORD, *as did* Da'vid his father.

7 Then did Sol'o-mon build an <u>high place</u> for Che'mosh, the <u>abomination</u> of Mo'ab, in the hill that *is* before Je-ru'sa-lem, and for Mo'lech, the <u>abomination</u> of the children of Am'mon. shrine

8 And likewise did he for all his <u>strange</u> wives, which burned incense and sacrificed to their gods. foreign

9 And the LORD was angry with Sol'o-mon, because his heart was turned from the LORD God of Is'ra-el, which had appeared to him twice,

10 And had <u>commanded</u> him concerning this thing, that he should not go after other gods: but he <u>kept not</u> that which the LORD commanded.

forbidden - did not observe

11 Wherefore the LORD said to Sol'o-mon, Forasmuch as this is done of you, and you have not kept My <u>covenant</u> and My <u>statutes</u>, which I have commanded you, I will surely <u>rend</u> the kingdom from you, and will give it to your servant.

agreement - decrees - tear

12 Notwithstanding in your days I will not do it for Da'vid your father's sake: *but* I will rend it out of the hand of your son.

13 However I will not <u>rend</u> away all the kingdom; *but* will give one tribe to your son for Da'vid My servant's sake, and for Je-ru'sa-lem's sake which I have chosen.

14 And the LORD <u>stirred</u> up an adversary to Sol'o-mon, Ha'dad the E'dom-ite: he *was* of the king's <u>seed</u> in E'dom. raised - offspring

15 For it came to pass, when Da'vid was in E'dom, and Jo'ab the captain of the host was gone up to bury the slain, after he had smitten every male in E'dom;

16 (For six months did Jo'ab remain there with all Is'ra-el, until he had cut off every male in E'dom:)

17 That Ha'dad fled, he and certain E'dom-ites of his father's servants with him, to go into E'gypt; Ha'dad *being* yet a little child.

18 And they arose out of Mid'i-an, and came to Pa'ran: and they took men with them out of Pa'ran, and they came

to E'gypt, to Pha'raoh king of E'gypt; which gave him an house, and <u>appointed</u> him <u>victuals</u>, and gave him land. assigned - food

19 And Ha'dad found great favor in the sight of Pha'raoh, so that he gave him <u>to wife</u> the sister of his own wife, the sister of Tah'pen-es the queen. in marriage

20 And the sister of Tah'pen-es bare him Ge-nu'bath his son, whom Tah'-pen-es weaned in Pha'raoh's house: and Ge-nu'bath was in Pha'raoh's household among the sons of Pha'raoh.

21 And when Ha'dad heard in E'gypt that Da'vid slept with his fathers, and that Jo'ab the captain of the host was dead, Ha'dad said to Pha'raoh, Let me depart, that I may go to my own country.

22 Then Pha'raoh said to him, But what have you lacked with me, that, behold, you seek to go to your own country? And he answered, Nothing: however let me go in any <u>wise</u>. case

23 And <u>God</u> <u>stirred</u> him up *another* adversary, Re'zon the son of E-li'a-dah, which fled from his lord Hadad-e'zer king of Zo'bah: Elohim^{p.f.} - raised

24 And he gathered men to him, and became captain over a band, when Da'vid slew them *of Zo'bah*: and they went to Da-mas'cus, and dwelled therein, and reigned in Da-mas'cus.

25 And he was an adversary to Is'ra-el all the days of Sol'o-mon, beside the <u>mischief</u> that Ha'dad *did*: and he <u>abhorred</u> Is'ra-el, and reigned over Syr'i-a. trouble - was hostile to

26 And Jer-o-bo'am the son of Ne'-bat, an Eph'rath-ite of Zer'e-da, Sol'o-mon's servant, whose mother's name *was* Ze-ru'ah, a widow woman, even he <u>lifted up</u> *his* <u>hand</u> against the king. rebelled

27 And this *was* the cause that he lifted up *his* hand against the king: Sol'o-mon built Mil'lo, *and* <u>repaired</u> the breaches of the city of Da'vid his father. closed up

28 And the man Jer-o-bo'am *was* a mighty man of valor: and Sol'o-mon seeing the young man that he was industrious, he made him ruler over all the <u>charge</u> of the house of Jo'seph. labor force

29 And it came to pass at that time when Jer-o-bo'am went out of Je-ru'sa-lem, that the prophet A-hi'jah the Shi'lo-nite found him in the way; and he had <u>clad</u> himself with a new garment; and they two *were* alone in the field: dressed

30 And A-hi'jah caught the new garment that *was* on him, and <u>rent</u> it *in* twelve pieces: tore

31 And he said to Jer-o-bo'am, Take you ten pieces: for thus says the Lord, the <u>God</u> of Is'ra-el, Behold, I will <u>rend</u> the kingdom out of the hand of Sol'o-mon, and will give ten tribes to you: tear

32 (But he shall have one tribe for My servant Da'vid's sake, and for Je-ru'sa-lem's sake, the city which I have chosen out of all the tribes of Is'ra-el:)

33 Because that they have forsaken Me, and have worshiped Ash'to-reth the goddess of the Zi-do'ni-ans, Che'mosh the god of the Mo'ab-ites, and Mil'com the god of the children of Am'mon, and have not walked in My

ways, to do *that which is* right in My eyes, and *to keep* My statutes and My judgments, as *did* Da'vid his father.

34 However I will not take the whole kingdom out of his hand: but I will make him prince all the days of his life for Da'vid My servant's sake, whom I chose, because he kept My commandments and My statutes:

35 But I will take the kingdom out of his son's hand, and will give it to you, *even* ten tribes.

36 And to his son will I give one tribe, that Da'vid My servant may have a <u>light</u> always before Me in Je-ru'sa-lem, the city which I have chosen Me to put My name there.   lamp

37 And I will take you, and you shall reign according to all that your soul desires, and shall be king over Is'ra-el.

38 And it shall be, if you will hearken to all that I command you, and will walk in My ways, and do *that is* right in My sight, to keep My statutes and My commandments, as Da'vid My servant did; that I will be with you, and build you a <u>sure</u> house, as I built for Da'vid, and will give Is'ra-el to you.   an enduring

39 And I will for this <u>afflict</u> the <u>seed</u> of Da'vid, but not for ever.   humble descendants

40 Sol'o-mon sought therefore to kill Jer-o-bo'am. And Jer-o-bo'am arose, and fled into E'gypt, to Shi'shak king of E'gypt, and was in E'gypt until the death of Sol'o-mon.

41 And the rest of the <u>acts</u> of Sol'o-mon, and all that he did, and his wisdom, *are* they not written in the book of the acts of Sol'o-mon?   events

42 And the time that Sol'o-mon reigned in Je-ru'sa-lem over all Is'ra-el *was* forty years.

43 And Sol'o-mon slept with his fathers, and was buried in the city of Da'vid his father: and Re-ho-bo'am his son reigned in his stead.

CHAPTER 12

AND Re-ho-bo'am went to She'chem: for all Is'ra-el were come to She'chem to make him king.

2 And it came to pass, when Jer-o-bo'am the son of Ne'bat, who was yet in E'gypt, heard *of it*, (for he was fled from the presence of king Sol'o-mon, and Jer-o-bo'am dwelled in E'gypt;)

3 That they sent and called him. And Jer-o-bo'am and all the congregation of Is'ra-el came, and spoke to Re-ho-bo'am, saying,

4 Your father made our yoke <u>grievous</u>: now therefore make you the <u>grievous</u> service of your father, and his heavy yoke which he put upon us, lighter, and we will serve you.   hard

5 And he said to them, Depart yet *for* three days, then come again to me. And the people departed.

6 And king Re-ho-bo'am consulted with the old men, that stood before Sol'o-mon his father while he yet lived, and said, How do you advise that I may answer this people?

7 And they spoke to him, saying, If you will be a servant to this people

this day, and will serve them, and answer them, and speak good words to them, then they will be your servants for ever.

8 But he forsook the counsel of the old men, which they had given him, and consulted with the young men that were grown up with him, *and* which <u>stood before</u> him: served

9 And he said to them, What <u>counsel</u> give you that we may answer this people, who have spoken to me, saying, Make the yoke which your father did put upon us lighter?   advice

10 And the young men that were grown up with him spoke to him, saying, Thus shall you speak to this people that spoke to you, saying, Your father made our yoke heavy, but make you *it* lighter to us; thus shall you say to them, My little *finger* shall be thicker than my father's loins.

11 And now whereas my father did <u>lade</u> you with a heavy yoke, I will add to your yoke: my father has <u>chastised</u> you with whips, but I will <u>chastise</u> you with <u>scorpions</u>.   load - disciplined - i.e., whip with tips

12 So Jer-o-bo'am and all the people came to Re-ho-bo'am the third day, as the king had appointed, saying, Come to me again the third day.

13 And the king answered the people <u>roughly</u>, and <u>forsook</u> the old men's <u>counsel</u> that they gave him;   harshly - rejected

14 And spoke to them after the <u>counsel</u> of the young men, saying, My father made your yoke heavy, and I will add to your yoke: my father *also* <u>chastised</u> you with whips, but I will chastise you with scorpions.

15 Wherefore the king hearkened not to the people; for the cause was from the LORD, that He might perform His saying, which the LORD spoke by A-hi'jah the Shi'lo-nite to Jer-o-bo'am the son of Ne'bat.

16 So when all Is'ra-el saw that the king <u>hearkened not</u> to them, the people answered the king, saying, What portion have we in Da'vid? neither *have we* inheritance in the son of Jes'se: to your tents, O Is'ra-el: now see to your own house, Da'vid. So Is'ra-el departed to their tents.   did not listen

17 But *as for* the children of Is'ra-el which dwelled in the cities of Ju'dah, Re-ho-bo'am reigned over them.

18 Then king Re-ho-bo'am sent A-do'ram, who *was* over the <u>tribute</u>; and all Is'ra-el stoned him with stones, that he died. Therefore king Re-ho-bo'am made speed to get him up to his chariot, to flee to Je-ru'sa-lem.   forced labor

19 So Is'ra-el rebelled against the <u>house</u> of Da'vid to this day.   family

20 And it came to pass, when all Is'ra-el heard that Jer-o-bo'am was come again, that they sent and called him to the congregation, and made him king over all Is'ra-el: there was none that followed the house of Da'vid, but the tribe of Ju'dah only.

21 And when Re-ho-bo'am was come to Je-ru'sa-lem, he assembled all the house of Ju'dah, with the tribe of Ben'ja-min, an <u>hundred and fourscore</u> thousand chosen men, which were warriors, to fight against the house of Is'ra-el, to bring the kingdom again to Re-ho-bo'am the son of Sol'o-mon.   180

22 But the word of <u>God</u> came to Shem-a-i'ah the man of <u>God</u>, saying,   Elohim^{p.f.}

23 Speak to Re-ho-bo'am, the son of Sol'o-mon, king of Ju'dah, and to all the house of Ju'dah and Ben'ja-min, and to the remnant of the people, saying,

24 Thus says the LORD, You shall not go up, nor fight against your brethren the children of Is'ra-el: return every man to his house; for this thing is from Me. They <u>hearkened</u> therefore to the word of the LORD, and returned to depart, according to the word of the LORD.   listened

25 Then Jer-o-bo'am built She'chem in mount E'phra-im, and dwelled therein; and went out from there, and built Pe-nu'el.

26 And Jer-o-bo'am said in his heart, Now shall the kingdom return to the house of Da'vid:

27 If this people go up to do sacrifice in the house of the LORD at Je-ru'sa-lem, then shall the heart of this people turn again to their lord, *even* to Re-ho-bo'am king of Ju'dah, and they shall kill me, and go again to Re-ho-bo'am king of Ju'dah.

28 Whereupon the king took counsel, and made two calves *of* gold, and said to them, It is too much for you to go up to Je-ru'sa-lem: behold your gods, O Is'ra-el, which brought you up out of the land of E'gypt.

29 And he set the one in Beth'-el, and the other put he in Dan.

30 And this thing became a sin: for the people went *to worship* before the one, *even* to Dan.

31 And he made an <u>house of</u> high places, and made priests <u>of the lowest</u> of the people, which were not of the sons of Le'vi.   temple shine on - from all sorts

32 And Jer-o-bo'am <u>ordained</u> a feast in the eighth month, on the fifteenth day of the month, like to the feast that *is* in Ju'dah, and he offered upon the altar. So did he in Beth'-el, sacrificing to the calves that he had made: and he placed in Beth'-el the priests of the <u>high places</u> which he had made.   instituted - shrines

33 So he offered upon the altar which he had made in Beth'-el the fifteenth day of the eighth month, *even* in the month which he had devised of his own heart; and <u>ordained</u> a feast to the children of Is'ra-el: and he offered upon the altar, and burned incense.

CHAPTER 13

AND, behold, there came a man of <u>God</u> out of Ju'dah <u>by the word</u> of the LORD to Beth'-el: and Jer-o-bo'am stood by the altar to burn incense.   Elohim^{p.f.} - directed

2 And he cried against the altar <u>in the word</u> of the LORD, and said, O altar, altar, thus says the LORD; Behold, a child shall be born to the house of Da'vid, Jo-si'ah by name; and upon you shall he <u>offer</u> the priests of the high places that burn incense upon you, and men's bones shall be burned upon you.   by the direction - sacrifice

3 And he gave a sign the same day, saying, This *is* the sign which the LORD

has spoken; Behold, the altar shall be <u>rent</u>, and the ashes that *are* upon it shall be poured out.   split apart

4 And it came to pass, when king Jer-o-bo'am heard the saying of the man of <u>God</u>, which had cried against the altar in Beth'-el, that he put forth his hand from the altar, saying, Lay hold on him. And his hand, which he put forth against him, dried up, so that he could not pull it in again to him.   Elohim^{p.f.}

5 The altar also was rent, and the ashes poured out from the altar, according to the sign which the man of <u>God</u> had given by the word of the L<small>ORD</small>.

6 And the king answered and said to the man of <u>God</u>, <u>Entreat now the face</u> <u>of</u> the L<small>ORD</small> your <u>God</u>, and pray for me, that my hand may be restored me again. And the man of <u>God</u> besought the L<small>ORD</small>, and the king's hand was restored him again, and became as *it was* before.   Elohim^{p.f.} - intercede with

7 And the king said to the man of <u>God</u>, Come home with me, and refresh yourself, and I will give you a <u>reward</u>.   gift

8 And the man of <u>God</u> said to the king, If you will give me half your house, I will not go in with you, neither will I eat bread nor drink water in this place:

9 For so was it <u>charged</u> me by the word of the L<small>ORD</small>, saying, Eat no bread, nor drink water, nor turn again by the same way that you came.   commanded

10 So he went another way, and returned not by the way that he came to Beth'-el.

11 Now there dwelled an old prophet in Beth'-el; and his sons came and told him all the works that the man of <u>God</u> had done that day in Beth'-el: the words which he had spoken to the king, them they told also to their father.   Elohim^{p.f.}

12 And their father said to them, What way went he? For his sons had seen what way the man of <u>God</u> went, which came from Ju'dah.

13 And he said to his sons, Saddle me the ass. So they saddled him the ass: and he rode thereon,

14 And went after the man of <u>God</u>, and found him sitting under an oak: and he said to him, *Are* you the man of <u>God</u> that came from Ju'dah? And he said, I *am*.

15 Then he said to him, Come home with me, and eat <u>bread</u>.   some food

16 And he said, I may not return with you, nor go in with you: neither will I eat bread nor drink water with you in this place:

17 For it was <u>said</u> to me by the word of the L<small>ORD</small>, You shall eat no <u>bread</u> nor drink water there, nor turn again to go by the way that you came.   told - food

18 He said to him, I *am* a prophet also as you *are*; and an <u>angel</u> spoke to me by the word of the L<small>ORD</small>, saying, Bring him back with you into your house, that he may eat bread and drink water. *But* he lied to him.   messenger

19 So he went back with him, and did eat bread in his house, and drank water.

20 And it came to pass, as they sat at the table, that the word of the LORD came to the prophet that brought him back:

21 And he cried to the man of <u>God</u> that came from Ju'dah, saying, Thus says the LORD, Forasmuch as you have disobeyed the mouth of the LORD, and have not kept the commandment which the LORD your <u>God</u> commanded you,   Elohim^{p.f.}

22 But came back, and have eaten <u>bread</u> and drunk water in the place, of the which *the Lord* did say to you, Eat no <u>bread</u>, and drink no water; your carcase shall not come to the <u>sepulcher</u> of your fathers.   food - grave

23 And it came to pass, after he had eaten bread, and after he had drunk, that he saddled for him the ass, *to wit*, for the prophet whom he had brought back.   that is

24 And when he was gone, a lion met him by the way, and slew him: and his carcase was cast in the way, and the ass stood by it, the lion also stood by the carcase.

25 And, behold, men passed by, and saw the carcase cast in the way, and the lion standing by the carcase: and they came and told *it* in the city where the old prophet dwelled.

26 And when the prophet that brought him back from the way heard *thereof*, he said, It *is* the man of <u>God</u>, who was disobedient to the <u>word</u> of the LORD: therefore the LORD has delivered him to the lion, which has <u>torn</u> him, and slain him, according to the word of the LORD, which He spoke to him.   command - mauled

27 And he spoke to his sons, saying, Saddle me the ass. And they saddled *him*.

28 And he went and found his carcase cast in the way, and the ass and the lion standing by the carcase: the lion had not eaten the carcase, nor <u>torn</u> the ass.

29 And the prophet took up the carcase of the man of <u>God</u>, and laid it upon the ass, and brought it back: and the old prophet came to the city, to mourn and to bury him.   Elohim^{p.f.}

30 And he laid his carcase in his own grave; and they mourned over him, *saying*, Alas, my brother!

31 And it came to pass, after he had buried him, that he spoke to his sons, saying, When I am dead, then bury me in the <u>sepulcher</u> wherein the man of <u>God</u> *is* buried; lay my bones beside his bones: grave

32 For the saying which he cried by the word of the LORD against the altar in Beth'-el, and against all the houses of the high places which *are* in the cities of Sa-ma'ri-a, shall surely come to pass.   declared

33 After this thing Jer-o-bo'am returned not from his evil way, but made again <u>of the lowest</u> of the people priests of the high places: whosoever would, he consecrated him, and he became *one* of the priests of the high places.   from all sorts

34 And this thing became sin to the house of Jer-o-bo'am, even to cut *it* off, and to destroy *it* from off the face of the earth.

CHAPTER 14

AT that time A-bi'jah the son of Jer-o-bo'am fell sick.

2 And Jer-o-bo'am said to his wife, Arise, I pray you, and disguise yourself, that you be not known to be the wife of Jer-o-bo'am; and get you to Shi'loh: behold, there *is* A-hi'jah the prophet, which told me that *I should be* king over this people.

3 And take with you ten loaves, and <u>cracknels</u>, and a <u>cruse</u> of honey, and go to him: he shall tell you what shall become of the child.   cakes - jar

4 And Jer-o-bo'am's wife did so, and arose, and went to Shi'loh, and came to the house of A-hi'jah. But A-hi'jah could not see; for his eyes were <u>set</u> by reason of his age.   dim

5 And the LORD said to A-hi'jah, Behold, the wife of Jer-o-bo'am come to ask a thing of you for her son; for he *is* sick: thus and thus shall you say to her: for it shall be, when she come in, that she shall feign herself *to be* another *woman*.

6 And it was *so*, when A-hi'jah heard the sound of her feet, as she came in at the door, that he said, Come in, you wife of Jer-o-bo'am; why <u>feignest</u> you yourself *to be* another? for I *am* sent to you *with* <u>heavy</u> tidings.   pretend - harsh

7 Go, tell Jer-o-bo'am, Thus says the <u>LORD God</u> of Is'ra-el, Forasmuch as I exalted you from among the people, and made you prince over My people Is'ra-el, Jehovah^{s.f.} Elohim^{p.f.}

8 And <u>rent</u> the kingdom away from the house of Da'vid, and gave it you: and *yet* you have not been as My servant Da'vid, who kept My commandments, and who followed Me with all his heart, to do *that* only *which was* right in My eyes;   tore

9 But have done evil above all that were before you: for you have gone and made you other gods, and molten images, to provoke Me to anger, and have <u>cast</u> Me behind your back: thrust

10 Therefore, behold, I will bring evil upon the house of Jer-o-bo'am, and will cut off from Jer-o-bo'am him that urinates against the wall, *and* him that is shut up and left in Is'ra-el, and will take away the remnant of the house of Jer-o-bo'am, as a man takes away dung, till it be all gone.

11 Him that dies of Jer-o-bo'am in the city shall the dogs eat; and him that dies in the field shall the fowls of the air eat: for the LORD has spoken *it*.

12 Arise you therefore, get you to your own house: *and* when your feet enter into the city, the child shall die.

13 And all Is'ra-el shall mourn for him, and bury him: for he only of Jer-o-bo'am shall come to the grave, because in him there is found *some* good thing toward the LORD God of Is'ra-el in the house of Jer-o-bo'am.   Jehovah^{s.f.} Elohim^{p.f.}

14 Moreover the LORD shall raise Him up a king over Is'ra-el, who shall cut off the house of Jer-o-bo'am that day: but what? even now.

15 For the LORD shall <u>smite</u> Is'ra-el, as a reed is shaken in the water, and He shall root up Is'ra-el out of this good land, which He gave to their fathers,

and shall scatter them beyond the river, because they have made their groves, provoking the LORD to anger. <small>strike - shrines to the goddess Asherah</small>

16 And He shall give Is'ra-el up because of the sins of Jer-o-bo'am, who did sin, and who made Is'ra-el to sin.

17 And Jer-o-bo'am's wife arose, and departed, and came to Tir'zah: *and* when she came to the threshold of the door, the child died;

18 And they buried him; and all Is'ra-el mourned for him, according to the word of the LORD, which He spoke by the hand of His servant A-hi'jah the prophet.

19 And the rest of the acts of Jer-o-bo'am, how he warred, and how he reigned, behold, they *are* written in the book of the chronicles of the kings of Is'ra-el.

20 And the days which Jer-o-bo'am reigned *were* two and twenty years: and he slept with his fathers, and Na'dab his son reigned in his stead.

21 And Re-ho-bo'am the son of Sol'o-mon reigned in Ju'dah. Re-ho-bo'am *was* forty and one years old when he began to reign, and he reigned seventeen years in Je-ru'sa-lem, the city which the LORD did choose out of all the tribes of Is'ra-el, to put His name there. And his mother's name *was* Na'a-mah an Am'mon-it-ess.

22 And Ju'dah did evil in the sight of the LORD, and they provoked Him to jealousy with their sins which they had committed, above all that their fathers had done.

23 For they also built them <u>high</u> places, and <u>images</u>, and groves, on every high hill, and under every green tree. <small>shrines - sacred pillars</small>

24 And there were also <u>sodomites</u> in the land: *and* they did according to all the <u>abominations</u> of the nations which the LORD cast out before the children of Is'ra-el. <small>male cult prostitutes - detestable practices</small>

25 And it came to pass in the fifth year of king Re-ho-bo'am, *that* Shi'shak king of E'gypt came up against Je-ru'sa-lem:

26 And he took away the treasures of the house of the LORD, and the treasures of the king's house; he even took away all: and he took away all the shields of gold which Sol'o-mon had made.

27 And king Re-ho-bo'am made in their stead brazen shields, and committed *them* to the hands of the chief of the guard, which kept the door of the king's house.

28 And it was *so*, when the king went into the house of the LORD, that the guard <u>bare</u> them, and brought them back into the guard <u>chamber</u>. <small>carried - room</small>

29 Now the rest of the acts of Re-ho-bo'am, and all that he did, *are* they not written in the book of the chronicles of the kings of Ju'dah?

30 And there was war between Re-ho-bo'am and Jer-o-bo'am all *their* days.

31 And Re-ho-bo'am slept with his fathers, and was buried with his fathers in the city of Da'vid. And his mother's name *was* Na'a-mah an Am'mon-it-ess. And A-bi'jam his son reigned in his stead.

CHAPTER 15

NOW in the eighteenth year of king Jer-o-bo'am the son of Ne'bat reigned A-bi'jam over Ju'dah.

2 Three years reigned he in Je-ru'sa-lem. And his mother's name *was* Ma'a-chah, the daughter of A-bish'a-lom.

3 And he walked in all the sins of his father, which he had done before him: and his heart was not perfect with the LORD his <u>God</u>, as the heart of Da'vid his father.   Elohim[p.f.]

4 Nevertheless for Da'vid's sake did the LORD his <u>God</u> give him a <u>lamp</u> in Je-ru'sa-lem, to set up his son after him, and to establish Je-ru'sa-lem:

                                    i.e., rule

5 Because Da'vid did *that which was* right in the eyes of the LORD, and turned not aside from any *thing* that he commanded him all the days of his life, save only in the matter of U-ri'ah the Hit'tite.

6 And there was war between Re-ho-bo'am and Jer-o-bo'am all the days of his life.

7 Now the rest of the acts of A-bi'jam, and all that he did, *are* they not written in the book of the chronicles of the kings of Ju'dah? And there was war between A-bi'jam and Jer-o-bo'am.

8 And A-bi'jam slept with his fathers; and they buried him in the city of Da'vid: and A'sa his son reigned in his stead.

9 And in the twentieth year of Jer-o-bo'am king of Is'ra-el reigned A'sa over Ju'dah.

10 And forty and one years reigned he in Je-ru'sa-lem. And his mother's name *was* Ma'a-chah, the daughter of A-bish'a-lom.

11 And A'sa did *that which was* right in the eyes of the LORD, as *did* Da'vid his father.

12 And he took away the <u>sodomites</u> out of the land, and removed all the idols that his fathers had made.

                          male cult prostitutes

13 And also Ma'a-chah his mother, even her he removed from *being* queen, because she had made an idol in a <u>grove</u>; and A'sa destroyed her idol, and burned *it* by the brook Kid'ron.   shrine for the goddess Asherah

14 But the high places were not removed: nevertheless A'sa's heart was perfect with the LORD all his days.

15 And he brought in the things which his father had dedicated, and the things which himself had dedicated, into the house of the LORD, silver, and gold, and vessels.

16 And there was war between A'sa and Ba'a-sha king of Is'ra-el all their days.

17 And Ba'a-sha king of Is'ra-el went up against Ju'dah, and built Ra'mah, that he might <u>not suffer</u> any to go out or come in to A'sa king of Ju'dah.

                                    prevent

18 Then A'sa took all the silver and the gold *that were* left in the treasures of the house of the LORD, and the treasures of the king's house, and delivered them into the hand of his servants: and king A'sa sent them to Ben-ha'dad, the son of Tab'ri-mon, the son of He'zi-on, king of Syr'i-a, that dwelled at Da-mas'cus, saying,

19 *There is* a <u>league</u> between me and you, *and* between my father and your father: behold, I have sent to you a present of silver and gold; come and break your league with Ba'a-sha king of Is'ra-el, that he may depart from me. _{treaty}

20 So Ben-ha'dad hearkened to king A'sa, and sent the captains of the hosts which he had against the cities of Is'ra-el, and smote I'jon, and Dan, and A'bel-beth-ma'a-chah, and all Cin'ne-roth, with all the land of Naph'ta-li.

21 And it came to pass, when Ba'a-sha heard *thereof*, that he left off building of Ra'mah, and dwelled in Tir'zah.

22 Then king A'sa made a proclamation throughout all Ju'dah; none *was* <u>exempted</u>: and they took away the stones of Ra'mah, and the timber thereof, wherewith Ba'a-sha had builded; and king A'sa built with them Ge-ba of Ben'ja-min, and Miz'pah._{left out}

23 The rest of all the acts of A'sa, and all his might, and all that he did, and the cities which he built, *are* they not written in the book of the chronicles of the kings of Ju'dah? Nevertheless in the time of his old age he was diseased in his feet.

24 And A'sa <u>slept</u> with his fathers, and was buried with his fathers in the city of Da'vid his father: and Je-hosh'a-phat his son reigned in his stead. _{died}

25 And Na'dab the son of Jer-o-bo'am began to reign over Is'ra-el in the second year of A'sa king of Ju'dah, and reigned over Is'ra-el two years.

26 And he did evil in the sight of the LORD, and walked in the way of his father, and in his sin wherewith he made Is'ra-el to sin.

27 And Ba'a-sha the son of A-hi'jah, of the house of Is'sa-char, conspired against him; and Ba'a-sha <u>smote him</u> at Gib'be-thon, which *belonged* to the Phi-lis'tines; for Na'dab and all Is'ra-el laid siege to Gib'be-thon.

_{struck him down}

28 Even in the third year of A'sa king of Ju'dah did Ba'a-sha slay him, and reigned in his stead.

29 And it came to pass, when he reigned, *that* he smote all the house of Jer-o-bo'am; he left not to Jer-o-bo'am any that breathed, until he had destroyed him, according to the saying of the LORD, which He spoke by His servant A-hi'jah the Shi'lo-nite:

30 Because of the sins of Jer-o-bo'am which he sinned, and which he made Is'ra-el sin, by his provocation wherewith he provoked the <u>LORD God</u> of Is'ra-el to anger.

_{Jehovah^{s.f.} Elohim^{p.f.}}

31 Now the rest of the acts of Na'dab, and all that he did, *are* they not written in the book of the chronicles of the kings of Is'ra-el?

32 And there was war between A'sa and Ba'a-sha king of Is'ra-el all their days.

33 In the third year of A'sa king of Ju'dah began Ba'a-sha the son of A-hi'jah to reign over all Is'ra-el in Tir'zah, twenty and four years.

34 And he did evil in the sight of the LORD, and walked in the way of Jer-o-bo'am, and in his sin wherewith he made Is'ra-el to sin.

CHAPTER 16

THEN the word of the LORD came to Je'hu the son of Ha-na'ni against Ba'a-sha, saying,

2 Forasmuch as I exalted you out of the dust, and made you prince over My people Is'ra-el; and you have walked in the way of Jer-o-bo'am, and have made My people Is'ra-el to sin, to provoke Me to anger with their sins; _{Because - lifted}

3 Behold, I will take away the posterity of Ba'a-sha, and the posterity of his house; and will make your house like the house of Jer-o-bo'am the son of Ne'bat.

4 Him that dies of Ba'a-sha in the city shall the dogs eat; and him that dies of his in the fields shall the fowls of the air eat.

5 Now the rest of the acts of Ba'a-sha, and what he did, and his might, *are* they not written in the book of the chronicles of the kings of Is'ra-el?

6 So Ba'a-sha slept with his fathers, and was buried in Tir'zah: and E'lah his son reigned in his stead. _{died}

7 And also by the hand of the prophet Je'hu the son of Ha-na'ni came the word of the LORD against Ba'a-sha, and against his house, even for all the evil that he did in the sight of the LORD, in provoking Him to anger with the work of his hands, in being like the house of Jer-o-bo'am; and because he killed him.

8 In the twenty and sixth year of A'sa king of Ju'dah began E'lah the son of Ba'a-sha to reign over Is'ra-el in Tir'zah, two years.

9 And his servant Zim-ri, captain of half *his* chariots, conspired against him, as he was in Tir'zah, drinking himself drunk in the house of Ar'za steward of *his* house in Tir'zah.

10 And Zim-ri went in and smote him, and killed him, in the twenty and seventh year of A'sa king of Ju'dah, and reigned in his stead. _{struck}

11 And it came to pass, when he began to reign, as soon as he sat on his throne, *that* he slew all the house of Ba'a-sha: he left him not one that urinates against a wall, neither of his kinsfolks, nor of his friends.

12 Thus did Zim-ri destroy all the house of Ba'a-sha, according to the word of the LORD, which He spoke against Ba'a-sha by Je'hu the prophet,

13 For all the sins of Ba'a-sha, and the sins of E'lah his son, by which they sinned, and by which they made Is'ra-el to sin, in provoking the LORD God of Is'ra-el to anger with their vanities. _{Jehovah Elohim - worthless idols}

14 Now the rest of the acts of E'lah, and all that he did, *are* they not written in the book of the chronicles of the kings of Is'ra-el?

15 In the twenty and seventh year of A'sa king of Ju'dah did Zim-ri reign seven days in Tir'zah. And the people were encamped against Gib'be-thon, which *belonged* to the Phi-lis'tines.

16 And the people *that were* encamped heard say, Zim-ri has conspired, and has also slain the king: wherefore all Is'ra-el made Om'ri, the captain of the host, king over Is'ra-el that day in the camp.

17 And Om'ri went up from Gib'be-

thon, and all Is'ra-el with him, and they besieged Tir'zah.

18 And it came to pass, when Zim-ri saw that the city was taken, that he went into the palace of the king's house, and burned the king's house over him with fire, and died,

19 For his sins which he sinned in doing evil in the sight of the LORD, in walking in the way of Jer-o-bo'am, and in his sin which he did, to make Is'ra-el to sin.

20 Now the rest of the acts of Zim-ri, and his treason that he wrought, *are* they not written in the book of the chronicles of the kings of Is'ra-el?

21 Then were the people of Is'ra-el divided into two parts: half of the people followed Tib'ni the son of Gi'nath, to make him king; and half followed Om'ri.

22 But the people that followed Om'ri prevailed against the people that followed Tib'ni the son of Gi'nath: so Tib'ni died, and Om'ri reigned.

23 In the thirty and first year of A'sa king of Ju'dah began Om'ri to reign over Is'ra-el, twelve years: six years reigned he in Tir'zah.

24 And he bought the hill Sa-ma'ri-a of She'mer for two talents of silver, and built on the hill, and called the name of the city which he built, after the name of She'mer, owner of the hill, Sa-ma'ri-a.

25 But Om'ri wrought evil in the eyes of the LORD, and did worse than all that *were* before him.

26 For he walked in all the way of Jer-o-bo'am the son of Ne'bat, and in his sin wherewith he made Is'ra-el to sin, to provoke the LORD God of Is'ra-el to anger with their vanities.   Jehovah^s.f. Elohim^p.f.

27 Now the rest of the acts of Om'ri which he did, and his might that he showed, *are* they not written in the book of the chronicles of the kings of Is'ra-el?

28 So Om'ri slept with his fathers, and was buried in Sa-ma'ri-a: and A'hab his son reigned in his stead.

29 And in the thirty and eighth year of A'sa king of Ju'dah began A'hab the son of Om'ri to reign over Is'ra-el: and A'hab the son of Om'ri reigned over Is'ra-el in Sa-ma'ri-a twenty and two years.

30 And A'hab the son of Om'ri did evil in the sight of the LORD above all that *were* before him.   more than

31 And it came to pass, as if it had been a light thing for him to walk in the sins of Jer-o-bo'am the son of Ne'bat, that he took to wife Jez'e-bel the daughter of Eth'ba-al king of the Zi-do'ni-ans, and went and served Ba'al, and worshiped him.

32 And he reared up an altar for Ba'al in the house of Ba'al, which he had built in Sa-ma'ri-a.   erected

33 And A'hab made a grove; and A'hab did more to provoke the LORD God of Is'ra-el to anger than all the kings of Is'ra-el that were before him.   shrine of goddess Asherah

34 In his days did Hi'el the Beth'-el-ite build Jer'i-cho: he laid the foundation thereof in A-bi'ram his firstborn,

and set up the gates thereof in his youngest *son* Se'gub, according to the word of the LORD, which He spoke by Josh'u-a the son of Nun.

CHAPTER 17

AND E-li'jah the Tish'bite, *who was* of the inhabitants of Gil'e-ad, said to A'hab, *As* the LORD God of Is'ra-el lives, before whom I stand, there shall not be dew nor rain these years, but according to my word.   LUKE 4:25 JAMES 5:17 whom I serve

2 And the word of the LORD came to him, saying,

3 Get you from here, and turn you eastward, and hide yourself by the brook Che'rith, that *is* before Jor'dan.

4 And it shall be, *that* you shall drink of the brook; and I have commanded the ravens to feed you there.

5 So he went and did according to the word of the LORD: for he went and dwelled by the brook Che'rith, that *is* before Jor'dan.   stayed

6 And the ravens brought him bread and flesh in the morning, and bread and flesh in the evening; and he drank of the brook.

7 And it came to pass after a while, that the brook dried up, because there had been no rain in the land.

8 And the word of the LORD came to him, saying,

9 Arise, get you to Zar'e-phath, which *belongs* to Zi'don, and dwell there: behold, I have commanded a widow woman there to sustain you.   provide for

10 So he arose and went to Zar'e-phath. And when he came to the gate of the city, behold, the widow woman *was* there gathering of sticks: and he called to her, and said, Bring me, I pray you, a little water in a vessel, that I may drink.

11 And as she was going to bring *it*, he called to her, and said, Bring me, I pray you, a morsel of bread in your hand.

12 And she said, *As* the LORD your God lives, I have not a cake, but an handful of meal in a barrel, and a little oil in a cruse: and, behold, I *am* gathering two sticks, that I may go in and dress it for me and my son, that we may eat it, and die.   Elohim^{p.f.} - jar - prepare

13 And E-li'jah said to her, Fear not; go *and* do as you have said: but make me thereof a little cake first, and bring *it* to me, and after make for you and for your son.

14 For thus says the LORD God of Is'ra-el, The barrel of meal shall not waste, neither shall the cruse of oil fail, until the day *that* the LORD sends rain upon the earth.   Jehovah^{s.f.} Elohim^{p.f.}

15 And she went and did according to the saying of E-li'jah: and she, and he, and her house, did eat *many* days.   a full year

16 *And* the barrel of meal wasted not, neither did the cruse of oil fail, according to the word of the LORD, which He spoke by E-li'jah.   was not exhausted - jar

17 And it came to pass after these things, *that* the son of the woman, the mistress of the house, fell sick; and his sickness was so sore, that there was no breath left in him.   bad

18 And she said to E-li'jah, What have I to do with you, O you man of <u>God</u>? are you come to me to call my sin to remembrance, and to slay my son? Elohim^{p.f.}

19 And he said to her, Give me your son. And he took him out of her bosom, and carried him up into a loft, where he <u>abode</u>, and laid him upon his own bed. lived

20 And he cried to the LORD, and said, O LORD my <u>God</u>, have You also brought evil upon the widow with whom I <u>sojourn</u>, by slaying her son? am staying

21 And he stretched himself upon the child three times, and cried to the LORD, and said, O LORD my <u>God</u>, I pray You, let this child's soul come into him again.

22 And the LORD heard the voice of E-li'jah; and the soul of the child came into him again, and he revived.

23 And E-li'jah took the child, and brought him down out of the <u>chamber</u> into the house, and <u>delivered</u> him to his mother: and E-li'jah said, See, your son lives. room - gave

24 And the woman said to E-li'jah, Now by this I know that you *are* a man of <u>God</u>, *and* that the word of the LORD in your mouth *is* truth. JOHN 3:2 prophet - Elohim^{p.f.}

CHAPTER 18

AND it came to pass *after* many days, that the word of the LORD came to E-li'jah in the third year, saying, Go, show yourself to A'hab; and I will send rain upon the earth.

2 And E-li'jah went to show himself to A'hab. And *there was* a <u>sore</u> famine in Sa-ma'ri-a. severe

3 And A'hab called O-ba-di'ah, which *was* the governor of *his* house. (Now O-ba-di'ah <u>feared</u> the LORD greatly: revered

4 For it *was so*, when Jez'e-bel <u>cut off</u> the prophets of the LORD, that O-ba-di'ah took an hundred prophets, and hid them by fifty in a cave, and fed them with bread and water.) came about - destroyed

5 And A'hab said to O-ba-di'ah, Go into the land, to all fountains of water, and to all brooks: perhaps you may find grass to save the horses and mules alive, that we lose not all the beasts.

6 So they divided the land between them to pass throughout it: A'hab went one way by himself, and O-ba-di'ah went another way by himself.

7 And as O-ba-di'ah was in the way, behold, E-li'jah met him: and he knew him, and <u>fell on his face</u>, and said, *Are* you that my lord E-li'jah? i.e., bowed - Is it

8 And he answered him, I *am*: go, tell your lord, Behold, E-li'jah *is here*.

9 And he said, What have I sinned, that you would deliver your servant into the hand of A'hab, to slay me?

10 *As* the LORD your <u>God</u> lives, there is no nation or kingdom, where my lord has not sent to seek you: and when they said, *he is* not *there*; he <u>took an oath of the kingdom and nation</u>, that they found you not.

Elohim^{p.f.} - made kingdom and nation swear

11 And now you say, Go, tell your lord, Behold, E-li'jah *is here*.

12 And it shall come to pass, *as soon as* I am gone from you, that the Spirit of the LORD shall carry you where I know not; and *so* when I come and tell A'hab, and he cannot find you he shall slay me: but I your servant <u>fear</u> the LORD from my youth.   revered

13 Was it not told my lord what I did when Jez'e-bel <u>slew</u> the prophets of the LORD, how I hid an hundred men of the LORD's prophets by fifty in a cave, and fed them with bread and water?   killed

14 And now you say, Go, tell your lord, Behold, E-li'jah *is here*: and he shall slay me.

15 And E-li'jah said, *As* the <u>LORD of hosts</u> lives, before whom I stand, I will surely <u>show</u> myself to him to day.   Jehovah Tsebaoth - present

16 So O-ba-di'ah went to meet A'hab, and told him: and A'hab went to meet E-li'jah.

17 And it came to pass, when A'hab saw E-li'jah, that A'hab said to him, *Are* you he that troubles Is'ra-el?

18 And he answered, I have not troubled Is'ra-el; but you, and your father's house, in that you have forsaken the commandments of the LORD, and you have followed Ba'al-im.

19 Now therefore send, *and* gather to me all Is'ra-el to mount Car'mel, and the prophets of Ba'al four hundred and fifty, and the prophets of the groves four hundred, which eat at Jez'e-bel's table.

20 So A'hab sent to all the children of Is'ra-el, and gathered the prophets together to mount Car'mel.

21 And E-li'jah came to all the people, and said, How long <u>halt you</u> between two opinions? if the LORD *be* <u>God</u>, follow Him: but if Ba'al, *then* follow him. And the people answered him not a word. will you hesitate - Elohim^p.f.

22 Then said E-li'jah to the people, I, *even* I only, remain a prophet of the LORD; but Ba'al's prophets *are* four hundred and fifty men.

23 Let them therefore give us two bullocks; and let them choose one bullock for themselves, and cut it in pieces, and lay *it* on wood, and put no fire *under*: and I will <u>dress</u> the other bullock, and lay *it* on wood, and put no fire *under*:   prepare

24 And <u>call</u> you on the name of your gods, and I will call on the name of the LORD: and the <u>God</u> that answers by fire, let Him be <u>God</u>. And all the people answered and said, It is well spoken. pray

25 And E-li'jah said to the prophets of Ba'al, Choose you one bullock for yourselves, and <u>dress</u> *it* first; for *you are* many; and call on the name of your gods, but put no fire *under*.

26 And they took the bullock which was given them, and they <u>dressed</u> *it*, and called on the name of Ba'al from morning even until noon, saying, O Ba'al, <u>hear</u> us. But *there was* no voice, nor any that answered. And they <u>leaped</u> upon the altar which was made.   answer - limped around i.e., in a ritual dance

27 And it came to pass at noon, that E-li'jah mocked them, and said, Cry aloud: for he *is* a god; either he is talking, or he is pursuing, or he is in a journey, *or* perhaps he sleeps, and must be awaked.

28 And they cried aloud, and cut themselves after their manner with knives and lancets, till the blood gushed out upon them.

29 And it came to pass, when midday was past, and they prophesied until the *time* of the offering of the *evening* sacrifice, that *there was* neither voice, nor any to answer, nor any that <u>regarded</u>.   paid attention

30 And E-li'jah said to all the people, Come near to me. And all the people came near to him. And he repaired the altar of the LORD *that was* broken down.

31 And E-li'jah took twelve stones, according to the number of the tribes of the sons of Ja'cob, to whom the word of the LORD came, saying, Is'ra-el shall be your name:

32 And with the stones he built an altar in the name of the LORD: and he made a trench about the altar, as great as would contain two measures of seed.

33 And he put the wood in order, and cut the bullock in pieces, and laid *it* on the wood, and said, Fill four barrels with water, and pour *it* on the burnt sacrifice, and on the wood.

34 And he said, Do *it* the second time. And they did it the second time. And he said, Do *it* the third time. And they did *it* the third time.

35 And the water ran round about the altar; and he filled the trench also with water.

36 And it came to pass at *the time of* the offering of the *evening* sacrifice, that E-li'jah the prophet came near, and said, <u>LORD</u> God of A'bra-ham, I'saac, and of Is'ra-el, let it be known this day that You *are* <u>God</u> in Is'ra-el, and *that* I *am* Your servant, and *that* I have done all these things at Your word.   Elohim^p.f.

37 Hear me, O LORD, hear me, that this people may know that You *are* the <u>LORD God</u>, and *that* You have turned their heart back again.   Jehovah^s.f. Elohim^p.f.

38 Then the fire of the LORD fell, and consumed the burned sacrifice, and the wood, and the stones, and the dust, and licked up the water that *was* in the trench.

39 And when all the people saw *it*, they fell on their faces: and they said, The LORD, He *is* the <u>God</u>; <u>the LORD,</u> He *is* the <u>God</u>.   Elohim^p.f. Jehovah^s.f. - Elohim^p.f.

40 And E-li'jah said to them, Take the prophets of Ba'al; let not one of them escape. And they took them: and E-li'jah brought them down to the brook Ki'shon, and slew them there.

41 And E-li'jah said to A'hab, Get you up, eat and drink; for *there is* a sound of abundance of rain.

42 So A'hab went up to eat and to drink. And E-li'jah went up to the top of Car'mel; and he cast himself down upon the earth, and put his face between his knees,

43 And said to his servant, Go up now, look toward the sea. And he went up, and looked, and said, *There is* nothing. And he said, Go again seven times.

44 And it came to pass at the seventh time, that he said, Behold, there arises a little cloud out of the sea, like a man's hand. And he said, Go up, say to A'hab, Prepare *your chariot*, and get you down, that the rain stop you not.

45 And it came to pass in the mean while, that the heaven was black with clouds and wind, and there was a great rain. And A'hab rode, and went to Jez're-el.   JAMES 5:18

46 And the hand of the LORD was on E-li'jah; and he girded up his loins, and <u>ran before</u> A'hab to the entrance of Jez're-el.   outran

CHAPTER 19

AND A'hab told Jez'e-bel all that E-li'jah had done, and <u>withal</u> how he had slain all the prophets with the sword.   all about

2 Then Jez'e-bel sent a messenger to E-li'jah, saying, So let the gods do *to me*, and more also, if I make not your life as the life of one of them by to morrow about this time.

3 And when he saw *that*, he arose, and <u>went</u> for his life, and came to Be'er-she'ba, which *belongs* to Ju'dah, and left his servant there.   ran

4 But he himself went a day's journey into the wilderness, and came and sat down under a juniper tree: and he requested for himself that he might die; and said, It is enough; now, O LORD, take away my life; for I *am* not better than my fathers.

5 And as he lay and slept under a juniper tree, behold, then an <u>angel</u> touched him, and said to him, Arise *and* eat.   messenger

6 And he looked, and, behold, *there was* a <u>cake</u> baked on the coals, and a <u>cruse</u> of water at his head. And he did eat and drink, and laid him down again.   bread cake - jar

7 And the <u>angel</u> of the LORD came again the second time, and touched him, and said, Arise *and* eat; because the journey *is* too great for you.

8 And he arose, and did eat and drink, and went in the strength of that <u>meat</u> forty days and forty nights to Ho'reb the mount of <u>God</u>.   MATT. 4:2 food - Elohim p.f.

9 And he came there to a cave, and lodged there; and, behold, the word of the LORD *came* to him, and He said to him, What do you here, E-li'jah?

10 And he said, I have been very <u>jealous</u> for the <u>LORD God</u> of hosts: for the children of Is'ra-el have forsaken Your <u>covenant</u>, thrown down Your altars, and slain Your prophets with the sword; and I, *even* I only, am left; and they seek my life, to take it away.

    ROM. 11:2-3 zealous - Jehovah s.f. Elohe Tsebaoth - agreement

11 And He said, Go forth, and stand upon the mount before the LORD. And, behold, the LORD passed by, and a great and strong wind <u>rent</u> the mountains, and broke in pieces the rocks before the LORD; *but* the LORD *was* not in the wind: and after the wind an earthquake; *but* the LORD *was* not in the earthquake: was tearing

12 And after the earthquake a fire; *but* the LORD *was* not in the fire: and after the fire a still small voice.

13 And it was *so*, when E-li'jah heard *it*, that he <u>wrapped</u> his face in his mantle, and went out, and stood in the entering in of the cave. And, behold, *there*

came a voice to him, and said, What do you here, E-li'jah? covered
14 And he said, I have been very <u>jealous</u> for the Lord God of hosts: because the children of Is'ra-el have forsaken Your <u>covenant</u>, thrown down Your altars, and slain Your prophets with the sword; and I, *even* I only, am left; and they seek my life, to take it away. zealous - Jehovah^{s.f.} Elohe Tsebaoth - agreement
15 And the Lord said to him, Go, return on your way to the wilderness of Da-mas'cus: and when you come, anoint Haz'a-el *to be* king over Syr'i-a:
16 And Je'hu the son of Nim'shi shall you anoint to be king over Is'ra-el: and E-li'sha the son of Sha'phat of A'bel-me-ho'lah shall you anoint *to be* prophet in your <u>room</u>. place
17 And it shall come to pass, *that* him that escapes the sword of Haz'a-el shall Je'hu slay: and him that escapes from the sword of Je'hu shall E-li'sha slay.
18 Yet I <u>have left</u> Me seven thousand in Is'ra-el, all the knees which have not bowed to Ba'al, and every mouth which has not kissed him. ROM. 11:4 will leave
19 So he departed from there, and found E-li'sha the son of Sha'phat, who *was* plowing *with* twelve yoke *of oxen* before him, and he with the twelfth: and E-li'jah passed by him, and cast his mantle upon him.
20 And he left the oxen, and ran after E-li'jah, and said, Let me, I pray you, kiss my father and my mother, and *then* I will follow you. And he said to him, Go back again: for what have I done to you? MATT. 8:21 LUKE 9:61

21 And he returned back from him, and took a yoke of oxen, and slew them, and boiled their flesh with the <u>instruments</u> of the oxen, and gave to the people, and they did eat. Then he arose, and went after E-li'jah, and ministered to him. implements

CHAPTER 20

AND Ben-ha'dad the king of Syr'i-a gathered all his <u>host</u> together: and *there were* thirty and two kings with him, and horses, and chariots: and he went up and besieged Sa-ma'ri-a, and warred against it. army
2 And he sent messengers to A'hab king of Is'ra-el into the city, and said to him, Thus says Ben-ha'dad,
3 Your silver and your gold *is* mine; your wives also and your children, *even* the <u>goodliest</u>, *are* mine. most beautiful
4 And the king of Is'ra-el answered and said, My lord, O king, according to your saying, I *am* yours, and all that I have.
5 And the messengers came again, and said, Thus speaks Ben-ha'dad, saying, Although I have sent to you, saying, You shall deliver me your silver, and your gold, and your wives, and your children;
6 Yet I will send my servants to you to morrow about this time, and they shall search your house, and the houses of your servants; and it shall be, *that* whatsoever is <u>pleasant</u> in your eyes, they shall put it in their hand, and take *it* away. desirable
7 Then the king of Is'ra-el called all

the elders of the land, and said, <u>Mark</u>, I pray you, and see how this *man* <u>seeks</u> <u>mischief</u>: for he sent to me for my wives, and for my children, and for my silver, and for my gold; and I denied him not.   notice - is looking for trouble

8 And all the elders and all the people said to him, Hearken not *to him*, nor consent.

9 Wherefore he said to the messengers of Ben-ha'dad, Tell my lord the king, All that you did send for to your servant at the first I will do: but this thing I may not do. And the messengers departed, and brought him word again.

10 And Ben-ha'dad sent to him, and said, The gods do so to me, and more also, if the dust of Sa-ma'ri-a shall suffice for handfuls for all the people that follow me.

11 And the king of Is'ra-el answered and said, Tell *him*, Let not him that gird on *his* <u>harness</u> boast himself as he that puts it off.   armor

12 And it came to pass, when *Ben-ha'dad* heard this message, as he *was* drinking, he and the kings in the pavilions, that he said to his servants, <u>Set</u> *yourselves in array*. And they <u>set</u> *themselves in array* against the city.   Station

13 And, behold, there came a prophet to A'hab king of Is'ra-el, saying, Thus says the LORD, Have you seen all this great multitude? behold, I will deliver it into your hand this day; and you shall know that I *am* the LORD.

14 And A'hab said, By whom? And he said, Thus says the LORD, *Even* by the young men of the princes of the provinces. Then he said, Who shall order the battle? And he answered, You.

15 Then he numbered the young men of the princes of the provinces, and they were two hundred and thirty two: and after them he numbered all the people, *even* all the children of Is'ra-el, *being* seven thousand.

16 And they went out at noon. But Ben-ha'dad *was* drinking himself drunk in the pavilions, he and the kings, the thirty and two kings that helped him.

17 And the young men of the princes of the provinces went out first; and Ben-ha'dad sent out, and they told him, saying, There are men come out of Sa-ma'ri-a.

18 And he said, Whether they be come out for peace, take them alive; or whether they be come out for war, take them alive.

19 So these young men of the princes of the provinces came out of the city, and the army which followed them.

20 And they slew every one his man: and the Syr'i-ans fled; and Is'ra-el pursued them: and Ben-ha'dad the king of Syr'i-a escaped on an horse with the horsemen.

21 And the king of Is'ra-el went out, and <u>smote</u> the horses and chariots, and slew the Syr'i-ans with a great slaughter.   struck

22 And the prophet came to the king of Is'ra-el, and said to him, Go, strengthen yourself, and <u>mark</u>, and see what you do: for at the return of the year the king of Syr'i-a will come up against you.   notice

23 And the servants of the king of

Syr'i-a said to him, Their gods *are* gods of the hills; therefore they were stronger than we; but let us fight against them in the plain, and surely we shall be stronger than they.

24 And do this thing, Take the kings away, every man out of his place, and put captains in their <u>rooms</u>: _{places}

25 And <u>number</u> you an army, like the army that you have lost, horse for horse, and chariot for chariot: and we will fight against them in the plain, *and* surely we shall be stronger than they. And he hearkened to their voice, and did so. _{assemble}

26 And it came to pass at the return of the year, that Ben-ha'dad numbered the Syr'i-ans, and went up to A'phek, to fight against Is'ra-el.

27 And the children of Is'ra-el were numbered, and were all present, and went against them: and the children of Is'ra-el <u>pitched</u> before them like two little flocks of kids; but the Syr'i-ans filled the country. _{camped}

28 And there came a man of <u>God</u>, and spoke to the king of Is'ra-el, and said, Thus says the LORD, Because the Syr'i-ans have said, The LORD *is* <u>God</u> of the hills, but He *is* not <u>God</u> of the valleys, therefore will I deliver all this great multitude into your hand, and you shall <u>know</u> that I *am* the LORD. _{Elohim^{p.f.} - understand}

29 And they <u>pitched</u> one over against the other seven days. And *so* it was, that in the seventh day the battle was joined: and the children of Is'ra-el slew of the Syr'i-ans an hundred thousand footmen in one day.

30 But the rest fled to A'phek, into the city; and *there* a wall fell upon twenty and seven thousand of the men *that were* left. And Ben-ha'dad fled, and came into the city, into an inner <u>chamber</u>. _{room}

31 And his servants said to him, Behold now, we have heard that the kings of the house of Is'ra-el *are* merciful kings: let us, I pray you, put sackcloth on our loins, and ropes upon our heads, and go out to the king of Is'ra-el: perhaps he will save your life. _{perhaps}

32 So they girded sackcloth on their loins, and *put* ropes on their heads, and came to the king of Is'ra-el, and said, Your servant Ben-ha'dad says, I pray you, let me live. And he said, *Is* he yet alive? he *is* my brother.

33 Now the men did diligently observe whether *any thing would come* from him, and did hastily catch *it*: and they said, Your brother Ben-ha'dad. Then he said, Go you, bring him. Then Ben-ha'dad came forth to him; and he caused him to come up into the chariot.

34 And *Ben-ha'dad* said to him, The cities, which my father took from your father, I will restore; and you shall make streets for you in Da-mas'cus, as my father made in Sa-ma'ri-a. Then *said A'hab*, I will send you away with this <u>covenant</u>. So he made a <u>covenant</u> with him, and sent him away. _{agreement}

35 And a certain man of the sons of the prophets said to his neighbor in the word of the LORD, Smite me, I pray you. And the man refused to <u>smite</u> him. _{Strike}

36 Then said he to him, Because you have not obeyed the voice of the LORD, behold, as soon as you are departed from me, a lion shall slay you. And as soon as he was departed from him, a lion found him, and slew him.
37 Then he found another man, and said, <u>Smite</u> me, I pray you. And the man smote him, so that in smiting he wounded *him*. Strike
38 So the prophet departed, and waited for the king by the way, and disguised himself with <u>ashes</u> upon his face. headband
39 And as the king passed by, he cried to the king: and he said, Your servant went out into the midst of the battle; and, behold, a man turned aside, and brought a man to me, and said, <u>Keep</u> this man: if by any means he be missing, then shall your life be for his life, or else you shall pay a talent of silver. Guard
40 And as your servant was busy here and there, he was gone. And the king of Is'ra-el said to him, So *shall* your judgment *be*; yourself have decided *it*.
41 And he hasted, and took the ashes away from his face; and the king of Is'ra-el <u>discerned</u> him that he *was* of the prophets. recognized
42 And he said to him, Thus says the LORD, Because you have let go out of *your* hand a man whom I appointed to utter destruction, therefore your life shall go for his life, and your people for his people.
43 And the king of Is'ra-el went to his house <u>heavy</u> and <u>displeased</u>, and came to Sa-ma'ri-a. sullen - angry

CHAPTER 21

AND it came to pass after these things, *that* Na'both the Jez're-el-ite had a vineyard, which was in Jez're-el, <u>hard</u> by the palace of A'hab king of Sa-ma'ri-a. close to
2 And A'hab spoke to Na'both, saying, Give me your vineyard, that I may have it for a garden of herbs, because it *is* near to my house: and I will give you for it a better vineyard than it; *or*, if it seem good to you, I will give you the worth of it in money.
3 And Na'both said to A'hab, The LORD forbid it me, that I should give the inheritance of my fathers to you.
4 And A'hab came into his house <u>heavy</u> and displeased because of the word which Na'both the Jez're-el-ite had spoken to him: for he had said, I will not give you the inheritance of my fathers. And he laid him down upon his bed, and turned away his face, and would eat no <u>bread</u>. unhappy - food
5 But Jez'e-bel his wife came to him, and said to him, Why is your spirit so sad, that you eat no <u>bread</u>?
6 And he said to her, Because I spoke to Na'both the Jez're-el-ite, and said to him, Give me your vineyard for money; or else, if it please you, I will give you *another* vineyard for it: and he answered, I will not give you my vineyard.
7 And Jez'e-bel his wife said to him, Do you now govern the kingdom of Is'ra-el? arise, and *eat* bread, and let your heart be merry: I will give

you the vineyard of Na'both the Jez're-el-ite.

8 So she wrote letters in A'hab's name, and sealed *them* with his seal, and sent the letters to the elders and to the nobles that *were* in his city, dwelling with Na'both.

9 And she wrote in the letters, saying, Proclaim a fast, and set Na'both on high among the people:

10 And set two men, <u>sons of Be'li-al</u>, before him, to bear witness against him, saying, You did blaspheme <u>God</u> and the king. And *then* carry him out, and stone him, that he may die. worthless men

11 And the men of his city, *even* the elders and the nobles who were the inhabitants in his city, did as Jez'e-bel had sent to them, *and* as it *was* written in the letters which she had sent to them.

12 They proclaimed a fast, and set Na'both on high among the people.

13 And there came in two men, children of Be'li-al, and sat before him: and the men of Be'li-al witnessed against him, *even* against Na'both, in the presence of the people, saying, Na'both did <u>blaspheme God</u> and the king. Then they carried him forth out of the city, and stoned him with stones, that he died. cursed - Elohim^{p.f.}

14 Then they sent to Jez'e-bel, saying, Na'both is stoned, and is dead.

15 And it came to pass, when Jez'e-bel heard that Na'both was stoned, and was dead, that Jez'e-bel said to A'hab, Arise, take possession of the vineyard of Na'both the Jez're-el-ite, which he refused to give you for money: for Na'both is not alive, but dead.

16 And it came to pass, when A'hab heard that Na'both was dead, that A'hab rose up to go down to the vineyard of Na'both the Jez're-el-ite, to take possession of it.

17 And the word of the LORD came to E-li'jah the Tish'bite, saying,

18 Arise, go down to meet A'hab king of Is'ra-el, which *is* in Sa-ma'ri-a: behold, *he is* in the vineyard of Na'both, where he is gone down to possess it.

19 And you shall speak to him, saying, Thus says the LORD, Have you killed, and also taken possession? And you shall speak to him, saying, Thus says the LORD, In the place where dogs licked the blood of Na'both shall dogs lick your blood, even yours.

20 And A'hab said to E-li'jah, Have you found me, O my enemy? And he answered, I have found *you*: because you have sold yourself to work evil in the sight of the LORD.

21 Behold, I will bring evil upon you, and will take away your posterity, and will cut off from A'hab him that urinates against the wall, and him that is shut up and left in Is'ra-el,

22 And will make your house like the house of Jer-o-bo'am the son of Ne'bat, and like the house of Ba'a-sha the son of A-hi'jah, for the provocation wherewith you have provoked *Me* to anger, and made Is'ra-el to sin.

23 And of Jez'e-bel also spoke the LORD, saying, The dogs shall eat Jez'e-bel by the <u>wall</u> of Jez're-el. ditch

24 Him that dies of A'hab in the city the dogs shall eat; and him that dies in the field shall the fowls of the air eat.

25 But there was none like to A'hab, which did sell himself to <u>work</u> wickedness in the sight of the LORD, whom Jez'e-bel his wife <u>stirred up</u>. _{do - incited}

26 And he <u>did very abominably</u> in following idols, according to all *things* as did the Am'or-ites, whom the LORD cast out before the children of Is'ra-el. _{behaved vilely}

27 And it came to pass, when A'hab heard those words, that he <u>rent</u> his clothes, and put sackcloth upon his flesh, and fasted, and lay in sackcloth, and went <u>softly</u>. _{tore - dejectedly}

28 And the word of the LORD came to E-li'jah the Tish'bite, saying,

29 See you how A'hab humbles himself before Me? because he humbles himself before Me, I will not bring the evil in his days: *but* in his son's days will I bring the evil upon his house.

CHAPTER 22

A ND they continued three years without war between Syr'i-a and Is'ra-el.

2 And it came to pass in the third year, that Je-hosh'a-phat the king of Ju'dah came down to the king of Is'ra-el.

3 And the king of Is'ra-el said to his servants, Know you that Ra'moth in Gil'e-ad *is* ours, and we *be* still, *and* take it not out of the hand of the king of Syr'i-a?

4 And he said to Je-hosh'a-phat, Will you go with me to battle to Ra'moth-gil'e-ad? And Je-hosh'a-phat said to the king of Is'ra-el, I *am* as you *are*, my people as your people, my horses as your horses.

5 And Je-hosh'a-phat said to the king of Is'ra-el, Enquire, I pray you, <u>at</u> the word of the LORD to day. _{for}

6 Then the king of Is'ra-el gathered the prophets together, about four hundred men, and said to them, Shall I go against Ra'moth-gil'e-ad to battle, or shall I <u>forbear</u>? And they said, Go up; for the Lord shall deliver *it* into the hand of the king. _{refrain}

7 And Je-hosh'a-phat said, *Is there* not here a prophet of the LORD besides, that we might enquire of him?

8 And the king of Is'ra-el said to Je-hosh'a-phat, *There is* yet one man, Mi-ca'iah the son of Im'lah, by whom we may enquire of the LORD: but I hate him; for he does not prophesy good concerning me, but evil. And Je-hosh'-a-phat said, Let not the king say so.

9 Then the king of Is'ra-el called an officer, and said, Hasten here Mi-ca'iah the son of Im'lah.

10 And the king of Is'ra-el and Je-hosh'a-phat the king of Ju'dah sat each on his throne, having put on their robes, in a <u>void</u> place in the entrance of the gate of Sa-ma'ri-a; and all the prophets prophesied before them. _{an open}

11 And Zed-e-ki'ah the son of Che-na'a-nah made him horns of iron: and he said, Thus says the LORD, With these shall you push the Syr'i-ans, until you have consumed them.

12 And all the prophets prophesied so, saying, Go up to Ra'moth-gil'e-ad, and prosper: for the LORD shall deliver *it* into the king's hand. Attack
13 And the messenger that was gone to call Mi-ca'iah spoke to him, saying, Behold now, the words of the prophets *declare* good to the king with one mouth: let your word, I pray you, be like the word of one of them, and speak *that which is* good.
14 And Mi-ca'iah said, *As* the LORD lives, what the LORD says to me, that will I speak.
15 So he came to the king. And the king said to him, Mi-ca'iah, shall we go against Ra'moth-gil'e-ad to battle, or shall we forbear? And he answered him, Go, and prosper: for the LORD shall deliver *it* into the hand of the king. refrain
16 And the king said to him, How many times shall I adjure you that you tell me nothing but *that which is* true in the name of the LORD?
17 And he said, I saw all Is'ra-el scattered upon the hills, as sheep that have not a shepherd: and the LORD said, These have no master: let them return every man to his house in peace. MATT. 9:36
18 And the king of Is'ra-el said to Je-hosh'a-phat, Did I not tell you that he would prophesy no good concerning me, but evil?
19 And he said, Hear you therefore the word of the LORD: I saw the LORD sitting on His throne, and all the host of heaven standing by Him on His right hand and on His left.

20 And the LORD said, Who shall persuade A'hab, that he may go up and fall at Ra'moth-gil'e-ad? And one said on this manner, and another said on that manner.
21 And there came forth a spirit, and stood before the LORD, and said, I will persuade him.
22 And the LORD said to him, Wherewith? And he said, I will go forth, and I will be a lying spirit in the mouth of all his prophets. And He said, You shall persuade *him*, and prevail also: go forth, and do so.
23 Now therefore, behold, the LORD has put a lying spirit in the mouth of all these your prophets, and the LORD has spoken evil concerning you.
24 But Zed-e-ki'ah the son of Che-na'a-nah went near, and smote Mi-ca'iah on the cheek, and said, Which way went the Spirit of the LORD from me to speak to you? struck
25 And Mi-ca'iah said, Behold, you shall see in that day, when you shall go into an inner chamber to hide yourself. room
26 And the king of Is'ra-el said, Take Mi-ca'iah, and carry him back to A'mon the governor of the city, and to Jo'ash the king's son;
27 And say, Thus says the king, Put this *fellow* in the prison, and feed him with bread of affliction and with water of affliction, until I come in peace.
28 And Mi-ca'iah said, If you return at all in peace, the LORD has not spoken by me. And he said, Hearken, O people, every one of you. Listen

29 So the king of Is'ra-el and Je-hosh'a-phat the king of Ju'dah went up to Ra'moth-gil'e-ad.

30 And the king of Is'ra-el said to Je-hosh'a-phat, I will disguise myself, and enter into the battle; but put you on your robes. And the king of Is'ra-el disguised himself, and went into the battle.

31 But the king of Syr'i-a commanded his thirty and two captains that had rule over his chariots, saying, Fight neither with small nor great, save only with the king of Is'ra-el. except

32 And it came to pass, when the captains of the chariots saw Je-hosh'a-phat, that they said, Surely it *is* the king of Is'ra-el. And they turned aside to fight against him: and Je-hosh'a-phat cried out.

33 And it came to pass, when the captains of the chariots perceived that it *was* not the king of Is'ra-el, that they turned back from pursuing him.

34 And a *certain* man drew a bow at a venture, and smote the king of Is'ra-el between the joints of the harness: wherefore he said to the driver of his chariot, Turn your hand, and carry me out of the host; for I am wounded. random - armor - army

35 And the battle increased that day: and the king was stayed up in his chariot against the Syr'i-ans, and died at even: and the blood ran out of the wound into the midst of the chariot. propped - evening - bottom

36 And there went a proclamation throughout the host about the going down of the sun, saying, Every man to his city, and every man to his own country. army

37 So the king died, and was brought to Sa-ma'ri-a; and they buried the king in Sa-ma'ri-a.

38 And *one* washed the chariot in the pool of Sa-ma'ri-a; and the dogs licked up his blood; and they washed his armor; according to the word of the LORD which He spoke.

39 Now the rest of the acts of A'hab, and all that he did, and the ivory house which he made, and all the cities that he built, *are* they not written in the book of the chronicles of the kings of Is'ra-el?

40 So A'hab slept with his fathers; and A-ha-zi'ah his son reigned in his stead. died

41 And Je-hosh'a-phat the son of A'sa began to reign over Ju'dah in the fourth year of A'hab king of Is'ra-el.

42 Je-hosh'a-phat *was* thirty and five years old when he began to reign; and he reigned twenty and five years in Je-ru'sa-lem. And his mother's name *was* A-zu'bah the daughter of Shil'hi.

43 And he walked in all the ways of A'sa his father; he turned not aside from it, doing *that which was* right in the eyes of the LORD: nevertheless the high places were not taken away; *for* the people offered and burned incense yet in the high places. shrines

44 And Je-hosh'a-phat made peace with the king of Is'ra-el.

45 Now the rest of the acts of Je-hosh'-a-phat, and his might that he showed, and how he warred, *are* they

not written in the book of the chronicles of the kings of Ju'dah?

M23 | 46 And the remnant of the sodomites, which remained in the days of his father A'sa, he took out of the land. 905

male cult prostitutes

47 *There was* then no king in E'dom: a deputy *was* king.

48 Je-hosh'a-phat made ships of Thar'shish to go to O'phir for gold: but they went not; for the ships were broken at E'zi-on-ge'ber.

49 Then said A-ha-zi'ah the son of A'hab to Je-hosh'a-phat, Let my servants go with your servants in the ships. But Je-hosh'a-phat would not.

50 And Je-hosh'a-phat slept with his fathers, and was buried with his fathers in the city of Da'vid his father: and Je-ho'ram his son reigned in his stead.

died

51 A-ha-zi'ah the son of A'hab began to reign over Is'ra-el in Sama'ri-a the seventeenth year of Jehosh'a-phat king of Ju'dah, and reigned two years over Is'ra-el.

52 And he did evil in the sight of the LORD, and walked in the way of his father, and in the way of his mother, and in the way of Jer-obo'am the son of Ne'bat, who made Is'ra-el to sin:

53 For he served Ba'al, and worshiped him, and provoked to anger the LORD God of Is'ra-el, according to all that his father had done.

Jehovah s.f. Elohim p.f. - just as   808

G1 609

THE BOOK OF SECOND
KINGS

CHAPTER 1

THEN Mo'ab rebelled against Is'ra-el after the death of A'hab.

2 And A-ha-zi'ah fell down through a lattice in his upper chamber that *was* in Sa-ma'ri-a, and was sick: and he sent messengers, and said to them, Go, enquire of Ba'al-ze'bub the god of Ek'ron whether I shall recover of this disease.   MATT. 10:25

3 But the <u>angel</u> of the LORD said to E-li'jah the Tish'bite, Arise, go up to meet the messengers of the king of Sa-ma'ri-a, and say to them, *Is it* not because *there is* not a God in Is'ra-el, *that* you go to enquire of Ba'al-ze'bub the god of Ek'ron?   messenger

4 Now therefore thus says the LORD, You shall not come down from that bed on which you are gone up, but shall surely die. And E-li'jah departed.

5 And when the messengers turned back to him, he said to them, Why are you now <u>turned back</u>?   returned

6 And they said to him, There came a man up to meet us, and said to us, Go, <u>turn again</u> to the king that sent you, and say to him, Thus says the LORD, *Is it* not because *there is* not a God in Is'ra-el, *that* you send to enquire of Ba'al-ze'bub the god of Ek'ron? therefore you shall not come down from that bed on which you are gone up, but shall surely die. return

7 And he said to them, What <u>manner</u> of man *was he* which came up to meet you, and told you these words?   kind

8 And they answered him, *he was* an hairy man, and <u>girt</u> with a girdle of leather about his loins. And he said, It *is* E-li'jah the Tish'bite.   bound

9 Then the king sent to him a captain of fifty with his fifty. And he went up to him: and, behold, he sat on the top of an hill. And he spoke to him, You man of God, the king has said, Come down.

10 And E-li'jah answered and said to the captain of fifty, If I *be* a man of God, then let fire come down from heaven, and <u>consume</u> you and your fifty. And there came down fire from heaven, and <u>consumed</u> him and his fifty.   destroy

11 Again also he sent to him another captain of fifty with his fifty. And he answered and said to him, O man of God, thus has the king said, Come down quickly.   REV. 20:9

12 And E-li'jah answered and said to them, If I *be* a man of God, let fire come down from heaven, and <u>consume</u> you and your fifty. And the fire of God came down from heaven, and <u>consumed</u> him and his fifty.

13 And he sent again a captain of the third fifty with his fifty. And the third captain of fifty went up, and came and <u>fell</u> on his knees before E-li'jah,

and <u>besought</u> him, and said to him, O man of God, I pray you, let my life, and the life of these fifty your servants, be precious in your sight. _{bowed - begged}
14 Behold, there came fire down from heaven, and burned up the two captains of the former fifties with their fifties: therefore let my life now be precious in your sight.
15 And the <u>angel</u> of the LORD said to E-li'jah, Go down with him: be not afraid of him. And he arose, and went down with him to the king.   _{messenger}
16 And he said to him, Thus says the LORD, Forasmuch as you have sent messengers to enquire of Ba'al-ze'bub the god of Ek'ron, *is it* not because *there is* no God in Is'ra-el to enquire of His word? therefore you shall not come down off that bed on which you are gone up, but shall surely die.
17 So he died according to the word of the LORD which E-li'jah had spoken. And Je-ho'ram reigned in his stead in the second year of Je-ho'ram the son of Je-hosh'a-phat king of Ju'dah; because he had no son.
18 Now the rest of the acts of A-ha-zi'ah which he did, *are* they not written in the book of the chronicles of the kings of Is'ra-el?

CHAPTER 2

AND it came to pass, when the LORD would take up E-li'jah into heaven by a whirlwind, that E-li'jah went with E-li'sha from Gil'gal.
2 And E-li'jah said to E-li'sha, Tarry here, I pray you; for the LORD has sent me to Beth'-el. And E-li'sha said *to him, As* the LORD lives, and *as* your soul lives, I will not leave you. So they went down to Beth'-el.
3 And the sons of the prophets that *were* at Beth'-el came forth to E-li'sha, and said to him, Know you that the LORD will take away your master from <u>your head</u> today? And he said, Yea, I know *it*; hold you your peace.   _{being your leader}
4 And E-li'jah said to him, E-li'sha, tarry here, I pray you; for the LORD has sent me to Jer'i-cho. And he said, *As* the LORD lives, and *as* your soul lives, I will not leave you. So they came to Jer'i-cho.
5 And the sons of the prophets that *were* at Jer'i-cho came to E-li'sha, and said to him, Know you that the LORD will take away your master from <u>your head</u> today? And he answered, Yea, I know *it*; <u>hold you your peace</u>.   _{be still}
6 And E-li'jah said to him, Tarry, I pray you, here; for the LORD has sent me to Jor'dan. And he said, *As* the LORD lives, and *as* your soul lives, I will not leave you. And they two went on.
7 And fifty men of the sons of the prophets went, and stood <u>to view afar off</u>: and they two stood by Jor'dan.   _{opposite them}
8 And E-li'jah took his mantle, and wrapped *it* together, and smote the waters, and they were divided here and there, so that they two went over on dry ground.
9 And it came to pass, when they were gone over, that E-li'jah said to

E-li'sha, Ask what I shall do for you, before I be taken away from you. And E-li'sha said, I pray you, let a double portion of your spirit be upon me.

10 And he said, You have asked a hard thing: *nevertheless*, if you see me *when I am* taken from you, it shall be so to you; but if not, it shall not be *so*.

11 And it came to pass, as they still went on, and talked, that, behold, *there appeared* a chariot of fire, and horses of fire, and parted them both asunder; and E-li'jah went up by a whirlwind into heaven.   REV. 11:12

12 And E-li'sha saw *it*, and he cried, My father, my father, the chariot of Is'ra-el, and the horsemen thereof. And he saw him no more: and he took hold of his own clothes, and <u>rent</u> them in two pieces.   tore

13 He took up also the mantle of E-li'jah that fell from him, and went back, and stood by the bank of Jor'dan;

14 And he took the mantle of E-li'jah that fell from him, and <u>smote</u> the waters, and said, Where *is* the <u>LORD</u> <u>God</u> of E-li'jah? and when he also had <u>smitten</u> the waters, they parted here and there: and E-li'sha went over.   Jehovah[s.f.] Elohim[p.f.] - struck

15 And when the sons of the prophets which *were* to view at Jer'i-cho saw him, they said, The spirit of E-li'jah does rest on E-li'sha. And they came to meet him, and bowed themselves to the ground before him.

16 And they said to him, Behold now, there be with your servants fifty strong men; let them go, we pray you, and seek your master: less perhaps the Spirit of the LORD has taken him up, and cast him upon some mountain, or into some valley. And he said, You shall not send.

17 And when they urged him till he was ashamed, he said, Send. They sent therefore fifty men; and they <u>sought</u> three days, but found him not.   searched

18 And when they came again to him, (for he tarried at Jer'i-cho,) he said to them, Did I not say to you, Go not?

19 And the men of the city said to E-li'sha, Behold, I pray you, the <u>situation</u> of this city *is* pleasant, as my lord sees: but the water *is* nothing, and the ground <u>barren</u>.   location - unfruitful

20 And he said, Bring me a new <u>cruse</u>, and put salt therein. And they brought *it* to him.   jar

21 And he went forth to the spring of the waters, and cast the salt in there, and said, Thus says the LORD, I have healed these waters; there shall not be from there any more death or barren *land*.

22 So the waters were healed to this day, according to the saying of E-li'sha which he spoke.

23 And he went up from there to Beth'-el: and as he was going up by the way, there came forth <u>little children</u> out of the city, and mocked him, and said to him, Go up, you bald head; go up, you bald head.   young lads

24 And he turned back, and looked on them, and cursed them in the name of the LORD. And there came forth two she bears out of the wood, and tare forty and two children of them.

25 And he went from there to mount Car'mel, and from there he returned to Sa-ma'ri-a.

CHAPTER 3

NOW Je-ho'ram the son of A'hab began to reign over Is'ra-el in Sa-ma'ri-a the eighteenth year of Je-hosh'a-phat king of Ju'dah, and reigned twelve years. 2 And he <u>wrought</u> evil in the sight of the LORD; but not like his father, and like his mother: for he put away the <u>image</u> of Ba'al that his father had made.   did - sacred pillar 3 Nevertheless he clung to the sins of Jer-o-bo'am the son of Ne'bat, which made Is'ra-el to sin; he departed not therefrom. 4 And Me'sha king of Mo'ab was a sheepmaster, and rendered to the king of Is'ra-el an hundred thousand lambs, and an hundred thousand rams, with the wool. 5 But it came to pass, when A'hab was dead, that the king of Mo'ab rebelled against the king of Is'ra-el. 6 And king Je-ho'ram went out of Sa-ma'ri-a the same time, and <u>numbered</u> all Is'ra-el.   mobilized 7 And he went and sent to Je-hosh'a-phat the king of Ju'dah, saying, The king of Mo'ab has rebelled against me: will you go with me against Mo'ab to battle? And he said, I will go up: I *am* as you *are*, my people as your people, *and* my horses as your horses. 8 And he said, Which way shall we go up? And he answered, The way through the wilderness of E'dom. 9 So the king of Is'ra-el went, and the king of Ju'dah, and the king of E'dom: and they <u>brought a compass</u> of seven days' journey: and there was no water for the host, and for the cattle that followed them.   made a circuit 10 And the king of Is'ra-el said, Alas! that the LORD has called these three kings together, to deliver them into the hand of Mo'ab! 11 But Je-hosh'a-phat said, *Is there* not here a prophet of the LORD, that we may enquire of the LORD by him? And one of the king of Is'ra-el's servants answered and said, Here *is* E-li'sha the son of Sha'phat, <u>which poured water on the hands</u> of E-li'jah.   i.e., was the personal servant 12 And Je-hosh'a-phat said, The word of the LORD is with him. So the king of Is'ra-el and Je-hosh'a-phat and the king of E'dom went down to him. 13 And E-li'sha said to the king of Is'ra-el, What have I to do with you? get you to the prophets of your father, and to the prophets of your mother. And the king of Is'ra-el said to him, Nay: for the LORD has called these three kings together, to deliver them into the hand of Mo'ab. 14 And E-li'sha said, *As* the <u>LORD of hosts</u> lives, before whom I stand, surely, were it not that I regard the presence of Je-hosh'a-phat the king of Ju'dah, I would not look toward you, nor see you.   Jehovahs Tsebaoth s.f. 15 But now bring me a minstrel. And it came to pass, when the minstrel

played, that the hand of the LORD came upon him.

16 And he said, Thus says the LORD, Make this valley full of ditches.

17 For thus says the LORD, You shall not see wind, neither shall you see rain; yet that valley shall be filled with water, that you may drink, both you, and your cattle, and your beasts.

18 And this is *but* a light thing in the sight of the LORD: He will deliver the Mo'ab-ites also into your hand.   an easy

19 And you shall smite every fenced city, and every choice city, and shall fell every good tree, and stop all wells of water, and mar every good piece of land with stones.   strike - fortified

20 And it came to pass in the morning, when the meat offering was offered, that, behold, there came water by the way of E'dom, and the country was filled with water.   sacrificed

21 And when all the Mo'ab-ites heard that the kings were come up to fight against them, they gathered all that were able to put on armor, and upward, and stood in the border.   assembled - older

22 And they rose up early in the morning, and the sun shone upon the water, and the Mo'ab-ites saw the water on the other side *as* red as blood:

23 And they said, This *is* blood: the kings are surely slain, and they have smitten one another: now therefore, Mo'ab, to the spoil.   slaughtered - struck

24 And when they came to the camp of Is'ra-el, the Is'ra-el-ites rose up and smote the Mo'ab-ites, so that they fled before them: but they went forward smiting the Mo'ab-ites, even in *their* country.   attacking

25 And they beat down the cities, and on every good piece of land cast every man his stone, and filled it; and they stopped all the wells of water, and felled all the good trees: only in Kir-har'a-seth left they the stones thereof; however the slingers went about *it*, and smote it.   destroyed - struck

26 And when the king of Mo'ab saw that the battle was too sore for him, he took with him seven hundred men that drew swords, to break through *even* to the king of E'dom: but they could not.   fierce

27 Then he took his eldest son that should have reigned in his stead, and offered him *for* a burned offering upon the wall. And there was great indignation against Is'ra-el: and they departed from him, and returned to *their own* land.

CHAPTER 4

NOW there cried a certain woman of the wives of the sons of the prophets to E-li'sha, saying, Your servant my husband is dead; and you know that your servant did fear the LORD: and the creditor is come to take to him my two sons to be bondmen.   revered - slaves

2 And E-li'sha said to her, What shall I do for you? tell me, what have you in the house? And she said, your handmaid has not any thing in the house, save a pot of oil.

3 Then he said, Go, borrow you ves-

sels abroad of all your neighbors, *even* empty vessels; borrow <u>not a few</u>. many

4 And when you are come in, you shall shut the door upon you and upon your sons, and shall pour out into all those vessels, and you shall set aside that which is full.

5 So she went from him, and shut the door upon her and upon her sons, who brought *the vessels* to her; and she poured out.

6 And it came to pass, when the vessels were full, that she said to her son, Bring me yet a vessel. And he said to her, *There is* not a vessel more. And the oil <u>stayed</u>.   stopped flowing

7 Then she came and told the man of God. And he said, Go, sell the oil, and pay your debt, and live you and your children of the rest.

8 And <u>it fell on</u> a day, that E-li'sha passed to Shu'nem, where *was* a great woman; and she constrained him to eat <u>bread</u>. And *so* it was, *that* as oft as he passed by, he turned in there to eat <u>bread</u>.   there came - food

9 And she said to her husband, Behold now, I perceive that this *is* an holy man of God, which passes by us continually.

10 Let us make a little chamber, I pray you, on the wall; and let us set for him there a bed, and a table, and a stool, and a candlestick: and it shall be, when he comes to us, that he shall turn in there.

11 And it fell on a day, that he came there, and he turned into the chamber, and lay there.

12 And he said to Ge-ha'zi his ser-

vant, Call this Shu'nam-mite. And when he had called her, she stood before him.

13 And he said to him, Say now to her, Behold, you have <u>been careful</u> for us with all this care; what *is* to be done for you? would you be spoken for to the king, or to the captain of the host? And she answered, I dwell among my own people.   showed care

14 And he said, What then *is* to be done for her? And Ge-ha'zi answered, <u>Verily</u> she has no child, and her husband is old.   Truly

15 And he said, Call her. And when he had called her, she stood in the door.

16 And he said, About this season, <u>according to the time of life</u>, you shall embrace a son. And she said, Nay, my lord, *you* man of God, do not lie to your handmaid.   next year

17 And the woman conceived, and bare a son at that season that E-li'sha had said to her, according to the time of life.

18 And when the child was grown, it fell on a day, that he went out to his father to the reapers.

19 And he said to his father, My head, my head. And he said to <u>a lad</u>, Carry him to his mother.   his servant

20 And when he had taken him, and brought him to his mother, he sat on her knees till noon, and *then* died.

21 And she went up, and laid him on the bed of the man of God, and shut *the door* upon him, and went out.

22 And she called to her husband, and said, Send me, I pray you, one of

the young men, and one of the asses, that I may run to the man of <u>God</u>, and come again.   Elohim^{p.f.}

23 And he said, Wherefore will you go to him to day? *it is* neither new moon, nor sabbath. And she said, *It shall be* well.

24 Then she saddled an ass, and said to her servant, Drive, and go forward; slack not *your* riding for me, except I bid you.

25 So she went and came to the man of God to mount Car'mel. And it came to pass, when the man of God saw her afar off, that he said to Ge-ha'zi his servant, Behold, *yonder is* that Shu'nam-mite:

26 Run now, I pray you, to meet her, and say to her, *Is it* well with you? *is it* well with your husband? *is it* well with the child? And she answered, *It is* well.

27 And when she came to the man of God to the hill, she caught him by the feet: but Ge-ha'zi came near to thrust her away. And the man of God said, Let her alone; for her soul *is* <u>vexed</u> within her: and the LORD has hid *it* from me, and has not told me.   troubled

28 Then she said, Did I desire a son of my lord? did I not say, Do not deceive me?

29 Then he said to Ge-ha'zi, Gird up your loins, and take my staff in your hand, and go your way: if you meet any man, <u>salute</u> him not; and if any <u>salute</u> you, answer him not again: and lay my staff upon the face of the child.   greet

30 And the mother of the child said, *As* the LORD lives, and *as* your soul lives,

I will not leave you. And he arose, and followed her.

31 And Ge-ha'zi passed on before them, and laid the staff upon the face of the child; but *there was* neither voice, nor <u>hearing</u>. Wherefore he went again to meet him, and told him, saying, The child is not awaked.   response

32 And when E-li'sha was come into the house, behold, the child was dead, *and* laid upon his bed.

33 He went in therefore, and shut the door upon them two, and prayed to the LORD.

34 And he went up, and lay upon the child, and put his mouth upon his mouth, and his eyes upon his eyes, and his hands upon his hands: and he stretched himself upon the child; and the flesh of the child <u>waxed</u> warm.   became

35 Then he returned, and walked in the house to and fro; and went up, and stretched himself upon him: and the child sneezed seven times, and the child opened his eyes.

36 And he called Ge-ha'zi, and said, Call this Shu'nam-mite. So he called her. And when she was come in to him, he said, Take up your son.

37 Then she went in, and fell at his feet, and bowed herself to the ground, and took up her son, and went out.

38 And E-li'sha came again to Gil'gal: and *there was* a <u>dearth</u> in the land; and the sons of the prophets *were* sitting before him: and he said to his servant, Set on the great pot, and <u>see pottage</u> for the sons of the prophets.   famine - cook stew

39 And one went out into the field to

gather herbs, and found a wild vine, and gathered thereof wild gourds his lap full, and came and shred *them* into the pot of pottage: for they knew *them* not.

40 So they poured out for the men to eat. And it came to pass, as they were eating of the pottage, that they cried out, and said, O *you* man of <u>God</u>, *there is* death in the pot. And they could not eat *thereof*. Elohim^{p.f.}

41 But he said, Then bring meal. And he cast *it* into the pot; and he said, Pour out for the people, that they may eat. And there was no <u>harm</u> in the pot. evil thing

42 And there came a man from Ba'al-shal'i-sha, and brought the man of God bread of the firstfruits, twenty loaves of barley, and full ears of <u>corn</u> in the <u>husk</u> thereof. And he said, Give to the people, that they may eat. MARK 6:37 LUKE 9:13 grain - sack

43 And his <u>servitor</u> said, What, should I set this before an hundred men? he said again, Give the people, that they may eat: for thus says the LORD, They shall eat, and shall leave *thereof*. LUKE 9:17 attendant

44 So he set *it* before them, and they did eat, and left *thereof*, according to the word of the LORD. some

CHAPTER 5

NOW Na'a-man, captain of the host of the king of Syr'i-a, was a great man with his master, and <u>honorable</u>, because by him the LORD had given de-liverance to Syr'i-a: he was also a mighty man in valor, *but he was* a leper. highly regarded

2 And the Syr'i-ans had gone out by companies, and had brought away captive out of the land of Is'ra-el a little <u>maid</u>; and she <u>waited</u> on Na'a-man's wife. girl - served

3 And she said to her mistress, Would God my lord *were* with the prophet that *is* in Sa-ma'ri-a! for he would <u>re-cover</u> him of his leprosy. cure

4 And *one* went in, and told his lord, saying, Thus and thus said the maid that *is* of the land of Is'ra-el.

5 And the king of Syr'i-a said, Go <u>to</u>, go, and I will send a letter to the king of Is'ra-el. And he departed, and took with him ten talents of silver, and six thousand *pieces* of gold, and ten changes of <u>raiment</u>. there - clothes

6 And he brought the letter to the king of Is'ra-el, saying, Now when this letter is come to you, behold, I have *therewith* sent Na'a-man my servant to you, that you may <u>recover</u> him of his leprosy. cure

7 And it came to pass, when the king of Is'ra-el had read the letter, that he <u>rent</u> his clothes, and said, *Am* I God, to kill and to make alive, that this man does send to me to <u>recover</u> a man of his leprosy? wherefore consider, I pray you, and see how he seeks a quarrel against me. tore

8 And it was *so*, when E-li'sha the man of God had heard that the king of Is'ra-el had <u>rent</u> his clothes, that he sent to the king, saying, Why have you <u>rent</u> your clothes? let him come now to

me, and he shall <u>know</u> that there is a prophet in Is'ra-el. _{understand}

9 So Na'a-man came with his horses and with his chariot, and <u>stood</u> at the door of the house of E-li'sha. _{stopped}

10 And E-li'sha sent a messenger to him, saying, Go and wash in Jor'dan seven times, and your flesh shall come again to you, and you shall be <u>clean</u>. _{made well}

11 But Na'a-man was angry, and went away, and said, Behold, I thought, he will surely come out to me, and stand, and call on the name of the LORD his God, and <u>strike</u> his hand over the place, and recover the leper. _{wave}

12 *Are* not Ab'a-na and Phar'par, rivers of Da-mas'cus, better than all the waters of Is'ra-el? may I not wash in them, and be clean? So he turned and went away in a rage.

13 And his servants came near, and spoke to him, and said, My father, *if* the prophet had bid you *do some* great thing, would you not have done *it*? how much rather then, when he says to you, Wash, and be clean?

14 Then went he down, and dipped himself seven times in Jor'dan, according to the saying of the man of God: and his flesh came again like to the flesh of a little child, and he was <u>clean</u>. _{LUKE 4:27 - Elohim^{n.f.} - made well}

15 And he returned to the man of God, he and all his company, and came, and stood before him: and he said, Behold, now I know that *there is* no God in all the earth, but in Is'ra-el: now therefore, I pray you, take a <u>blessing</u> of your servant. _{present}

16 But he said, *As* the LORD lives, before whom I stand, I will receive none. And he urged him to take *it*; but he refused.

17 And Na'a-man said, Shall there not then, I pray you, be given to your servant two mules' burden of earth? for your servant will hereafter offer neither burned offering nor sacrifice to other gods, but to the LORD.

18 In this thing the LORD pardon your servant, *that* when my master goes into the house of Rim'mon to worship there, and he leans on my hand, and I bow myself in the house of Rim'mon: when I bow down myself in the house of Rim'mon, the LORD pardon your servant in this thing.

19 And he said to him, Go in peace. So he departed from him a little way.

20 But Ge-ha'zi, the servant of E-li'sha the man of God, said, Behold, my master has spared Na'a-man this Syr'i-an, in not receiving at his hands that which he brought: but, *as* the LORD lives, I will run after him, and take <u>somewhat</u> of him. _{something}

21 So Ge-ha'zi followed after Na'a-man. And when Na'a-man saw *him* running after him, he <u>lighted</u> down from the chariot to meet him, and said, *Is* all well? _{came}

22 And he said, All *is* well. My master has sent me, saying, Behold, even now there be come to me from mount E'phra-im two young men of the sons of the prophets: give them, I pray you, a talent of silver, and two changes of garments.

23 And Na'a-man said, Be content, take two talents. And he urged him, and bound two talents of silver in two bags, with two changes of garments, and laid *them* upon two of his servants; and they bare *them* before him.
24 And when he came to the <u>tower</u>, he took *them* from their hand, and <u>bestowed</u> *them* in the house: and he let the men go, and they departed.   <small>hill - put</small>
25 But he went in, and stood before his master. And E-li'sha said to him, Where *come you*, Ge-ha'zi? And he said, Your servant went no where.
26 And he said to him, <u>Went not my heart</u> *with you,* when the man turned again from his chariot to meet you? *Is it* a time to receive money, and to receive garments, and oliveyards, and vineyards, and sheep, and oxen, and menservants, and maidservants?   <small>Was not my spirit</small>
27 The leprosy therefore of Na'a-man shall cling to you, and to your <u>seed</u> for ever. And he went out from his presence a leper *as white* as snow.   <small>descendants</small>

CHAPTER 6

AND the sons of the prophets said to E-li'sha, Behold now, the place where we dwell with you is too <u>strait</u> for us.   <small>small</small>
2 Let us go, we pray you, to Jor'dan, and take from there every man a beam, and let us make us a place there, where we may dwell. And he answered, Go you.
3 And one said, Be content, I pray you, and go with your servants. And he answered, I will go.
4 So he went with them. And when they came to Jor'dan, they cut down wood.
5 But as one was felling a beam, the ax head fell into the water: and he cried, and said, Alas, master! for it was borrowed.
6 And the man of God said, Where fell it? And he showed him the place. And he cut down a stick, and cast *it* in there; and the iron did <u>swim</u>.   <small>float</small>
7 Therefore said he, Take *it* up to you. And he put out his hand, and took it.
8 Then the king of Syr'i-a warred against Is'ra-el, and took counsel with his servants, saying, In such and such a place *shall be* my camp.
9 And the man of God sent to the king of Is'ra-el, saying, Beware that you pass not such a place; for there the Syr'i-ans are come down.
10 And the king of Is'ra-el sent to the place which the man of God told him and warned him of, and <u>saved</u> himself there, <u>not once nor twice</u>.   <small>guarded - several times</small>
11 Therefore the heart of the king of Syr'i-a was <u>sore troubled</u> for this thing; and he called his servants, and said to them, Will you not show me which of us *is* for the king of Is'ra-el?   <small>enraged</small>
12 And one of his servants said, <u>None</u>, my lord, O king: but E-li'sha, the prophet that *is* in Is'ra-el, tells the king of Is'ra-el the words that you speak in <u>your bedchamber</u>.   <small>No - privacy</small>
13 And he said, Go and spy where

he *is*, that I may send and bring him. And it was told him, saying, Behold, *he is* in Do'than.

14 Therefore sent he there horses, and chariots, and a great host: and they came by night, and com-passed the city about. surrounded

15 And when the servant of the man of God was risen early, and gone forth, behold, an host com-passed the city both with horses and chariots. And his servant said to him, Alas, my master! how shall we do?

16 And he answered, Fear not: for they that *be* with us *are* more than they that *be* with them. ROM. 8:31

17 And E-li'sha prayed, and said, LORD, I pray you, open his eyes, that he may see. And the LORD opened the eyes of the young man; and he saw: and, behold, the mountain *was* full of horses and chari-ots of fire round about E-li'sha.

18 And when they came down to him, E-li'sha prayed to the LORD, and said, Smite this people, I pray You, with blindness. And He smote them with blindness according to the word of E-li'sha. Strike

19 And E-li'sha said to them, This *is* not the way, neither *is* this the city: follow me, and I will bring you to the man whom you seek. But he led them to Sa-ma'ri-a.

20 And it came to pass, when they were come into Sa-ma'ri-a, that E-li'-sha said, LORD, open the eyes of these *men*, that they may see. And the LORD opened their eyes, and they saw; and, behold, *they were* in the midst of Sa-ma'ri-a.

21 And the king of Is'ra-el said to E-li'sha, when he saw them, my father, shall I smite *them*? shall I smite *them*? kill

22 And he answered, You shall not smite *them*: would you smite those whom you have taken captive with your sword and with your bow? set bread and water before them, that they may eat and drink, and go to their master. ROM. 12:20

23 And he prepared great provision for them: and when they had eaten and drunk, he sent them away, and they went to their master. So the bands of Syr'i-a came no more into the land of Is'ra-el. a great feast

24 And it came to pass after this, that Ben-ha'dad king of Syr'i-a gathered all his host, and went up, and besieged Sa-ma'ri-a.

25 And there was a great famine in Sa-ma'ri-a: and, behold, they besieged it, until an ass's head was *sold* for fourscore *pieces* of silver, and the fourth part of a cab of dove's dung for five *pieces* of silver.

26 And as the king of Is'ra-el was passing by upon the wall, there cried a woman to him, saying, Help, my lord, O king.

27 And he said, If the LORD do not help you, where shall I help you? out of the barnfloor, or out of the winepress?

28 And the king said to her, What ails you? And she answered, This woman said to me, Give your son, that we may eat him to day, and we will eat my son to morrow. is the matter with

29 So we boiled my son, and did eat him: and I said to her on the next day, Give your son, that we may eat him: and she has hid her son.

30 And it came to pass, when the king heard the words of the woman, that he <u>rent</u> his clothes; and he passed by upon the wall, and the people looked, and, behold, *he had* sackcloth <u>within</u> upon his flesh. _{tore - beneath}

31 Then he said, God do so and more also to me, if the head of E-li'sha the son of Sha'phat shall stand on him this day.

32 But E-li'sha sat in his house, and the elders sat with him; and *the king* sent a man from before him: but before the messenger came to him, he said to the elders, See you how this son of a murderer has sent to take away my head? look, when the messenger come, shut the door, and hold him fast at the door: *is* not the sound of his master's feet behind him?

33 And while he yet talked with them, behold, the messenger came down to him: and he said, Behold, this evil *is* of the LORD; <u>what</u> should I wait for the LORD any longer? why

CHAPTER 7

_{P15C}

THEN E-li'sha said, Hear you the word of the LORD; Thus says the LORD, Tomorrow about this time *shall* a measure of fine flour *be sold* for a shekel, and two measures of barley for a shekel, in the gate of Sa-ma'ri-a.

₁₀₀₆

2 Then a lord on whose hand the king leaned answered the man of <u>God</u>, and said, Behold, *if* the LORD would make windows in heaven, might this thing be? And he said, Behold, you shall see *it* with your eyes, but shall not eat thereof. Elohim^{p.f.}

3 And there were four leprous men at the entering in of the gate: and they said one to another, Why sit we here until we die?

4 If we say, We will enter into the city, then the famine *is* in the city, and we shall die there: and if we sit still here, we die also. Now therefore come, and let us <u>fall</u> to the host of the Syr'i-ans: if they save us alive, we shall live; and if they kill us, we shall but die. go over

5 And they rose up in the twilight, to go to the camp of the Syr'i-ans: and when they were come to the <u>uttermost part</u> of the camp of Syr'i-a, behold, *there was* no man there. outskirts

6 For the Lord had made the host of the Syr'i-ans to hear a noise of chariots, and a noise of horses, *even* the noise of a great host: and they said one to another, Lo, the king of Is'ra-el has hired against us the kings of the Hit'tites, and the kings of the E-gyp'tians, to come upon us.

7 Wherefore they arose and fled in the twilight, and left their tents, and their horses, and their asses, even the camp as it *was*, and fled for their life.

8 And when these lepers came to the <u>uttermost part</u> of the camp, they went into one tent, and did eat and drink, and carried from there silver, and gold, and <u>raiment</u>, and went and hid *it*; and came again, and entered into another tent,

and carried from there *also*, and went and hid *it*.   _{outskirts - clothes}
9 Then they said one to another, We do not well: this day *is* a day of good tidings, and we hold our peace: if we tarry till the morning light, some mischief will come upon us: now therefore come, that we may go and tell the king's household.
10 So they came and called to the porter of the city: and they told them, saying, We came to the camp of the Syr'i-ans, and, behold, *there was* no man there, neither voice of man, but horses tied, and asses tied, and the tents as they *were*.   _{gatekeeper}
11 And he called the porters; and they told *it* to the king's house within.
12 And the king arose in the night, and said to his servants, I will now show you what the Syr'i-ans have done to us. They know that we *be* hungry; therefore are they gone out of the camp to hide themselves in the field, saying, When they come out of the city, we shall catch them alive, and get into the city.   _{i.e., set up an ambush}
13 And one of his servants answered and said, Let *some* take, I pray you, five of the horses that remain, which are left in the city, (behold, they *are* as all the multitude of Is'ra-el that are left in it: behold, *I say*, they *are* even as all the multitude of the Is'ra-el-ites that are consumed:) and let us send and see.   _{doomed}
14 They took therefore two chariot horses; and the king sent after the host of the Syr'i-ans, saying, Go and see.   _{chariots with}

15 And they went after them to Jor'dan: and, lo, all the way *was* full of garments and vessels, which the Syr'i-ans had cast away in their haste. And the messengers returned, and told the king.
16 And the people went out, and spoiled the tents of the Syr'i-ans. So a measure of fine flour was *sold* for a shekel, and two measures of barley for a shekel, according to the word of the LORD.   _{plundered}
17 And the king appointed the lord on whose hand he leaned to have the charge of the gate: and the people trode upon him in the gate, and he died, as the man of God had said, who spoke when the king came down to him.   _{trampled - i.e., prophet}
18 And it came to pass as the man of God had spoken to the king, saying, Two measures of barley for a shekel, and a measure of fine flour for a shekel, shall be to morrow about this time in the gate of Sa-ma'ri-a:
19 And that lord answered the man of God, and said, Now, behold, *if* the LORD should make windows in heaven, might such a thing be? And he said, Behold, you shall see it with your eyes, but shall not eat thereof.
20 And so it fell out to him: for the people trode upon him in the gate, and he died.   _{happened}

CHAPTER 8

THEN spoke E-li'sha to the woman, whose son he had restored to life, saying, Arise, and go you and your household, and sojourn whereso-

ever you can <u>sojourn</u>: for the LORD has called for a famine; and it shall also come upon the land seven years. temporarily live
2 And the woman arose, and did after the saying of the man of God: and she went with her household, and sojourned in the land of the Phi-lis'tines seven years.
3 And it came to pass at the seven years' end, that the woman returned out of the land of the Phi-lis'tines: and she went forth to <u>cry</u> to the king for her house and for her land. beg
4 And the king talked with Ge-ha'zi the servant of the man of God, saying, Tell me, I pray you, all the great things that E-li'sha has done.
5 And it came to pass, as he was telling the king how he had restored a dead body to life, that, behold, the woman, whose son he had restored to life, <u>cried</u> to the king for her house and for her land. And Ge-ha'zi said, My lord, O king, this *is* the woman, and this *is* her son, whom E-li'sha restored to life.
6 And when the king asked the woman, she told him. So the king appointed to her a certain officer, saying, Restore all that *was* hers, and all the fruits of the field since the day that she left the land, even until now.
7 And E-li'sha came to Da-mas'cus; and Ben-ha'dad the king of Syr'i-a was sick; and it was told him, saying, The man of God is come here.
8 And the king said to Haz'a-el, Take a present in your hand, and go, meet the <u>man of God</u>, and enquire of

the LORD by him, saying, Shall I recover of this disease? i.e., prophet
9 So Haz'a-el went to meet him, and took a present with him, even of every good thing of Da-mas'cus, forty camels' burden, and came and stood before him, and said, Your son Ben-ha'dad king of Syr'i-a has sent me to you, saying, Shall I recover of this disease?
10 And E-li'sha said to him, Go, say to him, You may certainly recover: however the LORD has showed me that he shall surely die.
11 And he <u>settled his countenance</u> stedfastly, until he was ashamed: and the man of God wept. stared at him
12 And Haz'a-el said, Why weeps my lord? And he answered, Because I know the evil that you will do to the children of Is'ra-el: their strong holds will you set on fire, and their young men will you slay with the sword, and will dash their children, and rip up their women with child.
13 And Haz'a-el said, But what, *is* your servant a dog, that he should do this great thing? And E-li'sha answered, The LORD has showed me that you *shall be* king over Syr'i-a.
14 So he departed from E-li'sha, and came to his master; who said to him, What said E-li'sha to you? And he answered, He told me *that* you should surely <u>recover</u>. get well
15 And it came to pass on the morrow, that he took a thick cloth, and dipped *it* in water, and spread *it* on his face, so that he died: and Haz'a-el reigned in his stead.
16 And in the fifth year of Jo'ram

the son of A'hab king of Is'ra-el, Je-hosh'a-phat *being* then king of Ju'dah, Je-ho'ram the son of Je-hosh'a-phat king of Ju'dah <u>began to reign</u>. _{became king}

17 Thirty and two years old was he when he began to reign; and he reigned eight years in Je-ru'sa-lem.

18 And he walked in the way of the kings of Is'ra-el, as did the house of A'hab: for the daughter of A'hab was his wife: and he did evil in the sight of the LORD.

19 Yet the LORD would not destroy Ju'dah for Da'vid His servant's sake, as He promised him to give him alway a <u>light</u>, *and* to his children. _{i.e., rule}

20 In his days E'dom revolted from under the hand of Ju'dah, and made a king over themselves.

21 So Jo'ram went over to Za'ir, and all the chariots with him: and he rose by night, and smote the E'dom-ites which <u>compassed</u> him about, and the captains of the chariots: and the people fled into their tents. _{surrounded}

22 Yet E'dom revolted from under the hand of Ju'dah to this day. Then Lib'nah revolted at the same time.

23 And the rest of the acts of Jo'ram, and all that he did, *are* they not written in the book of the chronicles of the kings of Ju'dah?

24 And Jo'ram slept with his fathers, and was buried with his fathers in the city of Da'vid: and A-ha-zi'ah his son reigned in his stead.

25 In the twelfth year of Jo'ram the son of A'hab king of Is'ra-el did A-ha-zi'ah the son of Je-ho'ram king of Ju'dah begin to reign.

26 Two and twenty years old *was* A-ha-zi'ah when he began to reign; and he reigned one year in Je-ru'sa-lem. And his mother's name *was* Ath-a-li'ah, the daughter of Om'ri king of Is'ra-el.

27 And he walked in the way of the house of A'hab, and did evil in the sight of the LORD, as *did* the house of A'hab: for he *was* the son in law of the house of A'hab.

28 And he went with Jo'ram the son of A'hab to the war against Haz'a-el king of Syr'i-a in Ra'moth-gil'e-ad; and the Syr'i-ans wounded Jo'ram.

29 And king Jo'ram went back to be healed in Jez're-el of the wounds which the Syr'i-ans had given him at Ra'mah, when he fought against Haz'a-el king of Syr'i-a. And A-ha-zi'ah the son of Je-ho'ram king of Ju'dah went down to see Jo'ram the son of A'hab in Jez're-el, because he was <u>sick</u>, _{wounded}

CHAPTER 9

AND E-li'sha the prophet called one of the children of the prophets, and said to him, <u>Gird</u> up your <u>loins</u>, and take this box of oil in your hand, and go to Ra'moth-gil'e-ad: _{Bind - waist}

2 And when you come there, <u>look</u> out there Je'hu the son of Je-hosh'a-phat the son of Nim'shi, and go in, and make him arise up from among his brethren, and carry him to an inner <u>chamber</u>; _{search - room}

3 Then take the <u>box</u> of oil, and pour *it* on his head, and say, Thus says the LORD, I have anointed you king over

Is'ra-el. Then open the door, and flee, and tarry not. _{flask}

4 So the young man, *even* the young man the prophet, went to Ra'moth-gil'e-ad.

5 And when he came, behold, the captains of the <u>host</u> *were* sitting; and he said, I have an <u>errand</u> to you, O captain. And Je'hu said, To which of all us? And he said, To you, O captain. _{army - message}

6 And he arose, and went into the house; and he poured the oil on his head, and said to him, Thus says the Lord God of Is'ra-el, I have anointed you king over the people of the Lord, *even* over Is'ra-el. _{Jehovah^{s-f.} Elohim^{p-f.}}

7 And you shall <u>smite</u> the house of A'hab your master, that I may avenge the blood of My servants the prophets, and the blood of all the servants of the Lord, at the hand of Jez'e-bel. _{strike}

8 For the whole house of A'hab shall perish: and I will cut off from A'hab <u>him that</u> <u>urinates</u> <u>against the wall</u>, and him that is shut up and left in Is'ra-el: _{every male}

9 And I will make the house of A'hab like the house of Jer-o-bo'am the son of Ne'bat, and like the house of Ba'a-sha the son of A-hi'jah:

10 And the dogs shall eat Jez'e-bel in the portion of Jez're-el, and *there shall be* none to bury *her*. And he opened the door, and fled.

11 Then Je'hu came forth to the servants of his lord: and *one* said to him, *Is* all well? why came this mad *fellow* to you? And he said to them, You know the man, and his <u>communication</u>. _{talk}

12 And they said, *It is* <u>false</u>; tell us now. And he said, Thus and thus spoke he to me, saying, Thus says the Lord, I have anointed you king over Is'ra-el. _{a lie}

13 Then they hasted, and took every man his garment, and put *it* under him on the top of the stairs, and blew with trumpets, saying, Je'hu is king.

14 So Je'hu the son of Je-hosh'a-phat the son of Nim'shi <u>conspired</u> against Jo'ram. (Now Jo'ram had kept Ra'moth-gil'e-ad, he and all Is'ra-el, because of Haz'a-el king of Syr'i-a. _{plotted}

15 But king Jo'ram was returned to be healed in Jez're-el of the wounds which the Syr'i-ans had given him, when he fought with Haz'a-el king of Syr'i-a.) And Je'hu said, If it be your minds, *then* let none go forth *nor* escape out of the city to go to tell *it* in Jez're-el.

16 So Je'hu rode in a chariot, and went to Jez're-el; for Jo'ram lay there. And A-ha-zi'ah king of Ju'dah was come down to see Jo'ram.

17 And there stood a watchman on the tower in Jez're-el, and he spied the company of Je'hu as he came, and said, I see a company. And Jo'ram said, Take an horseman, and send to meet them, and let him say, *Is it* <u>peace</u>? _{Do you come in peace}

18 So there went one on horseback to meet him, and said, Thus says the king, *Is it* peace? And Je'hu said, What have you to do with peace? <u>turn you</u> behind me. And the watchman told, saying,

The messenger came to them, but he comes not again. _{fall in}
19 Then he sent out a second on horseback, which came to them, and said, Thus says the king, *Is it* peace? And Je'hu answered, What have you to do with peace? turn you behind me.
20 And the watchman told, saying, He came even to them, and come not again: and the driving *is* like the driving of Je'hu the son of Nim'shi; for he drives furiously.
21 And Jo'ram said, Make ready. And his chariot was made ready. And Jo'ram king of Is'ra-el and A-ha-zi'ah king of Ju'dah went out, each in his chariot, and they went out against Je'hu, and met him in the portion of Na'both the Jez're-el-ite. _{found}
22 And it came to pass, when Jo'ram saw Je'hu, that he said, *Is it* peace, Je'hu? And he answered, What peace, so long as the whoredoms of your mother Jez'e-bel and her witch-crafts *are so* many? _{Do you come in peace}
23 And Jo'ram turned his hands, and fled, and said to A-ha-zi'ah, *There is* treachery, O A-ha-zi'ah. _{treason}
24 And Je'hu drew a bow with his full strength, and smote Je-ho'ram between his arms, and the arrow went out at his heart, and he sunk down in his chariot.
25 Then said Je'hu to Bid'kar his captain, Take up, *and* cast him in the portion of the field of Na'both the Jez're-el-ite: for remember how that, when I and you rode together after A'hab his father, the LORD laid this burden upon him _{made this prophecy about}
26 Surely I have seen yesterday the blood of Na'both, and the blood of his sons, says the LORD; and I will requite you in this plat, says the LORD. Now therefore take *and* cast him into the plat *of ground*, according to the word of the LORD.
27 But when A-ha-zi'ah the king of Ju'dah saw *this*, he fled by the way of the garden house. And Je'hu followed after him, and said, Smite him also in the chariot. *And they did so* at the going up to Gur, which *is* by Ib'le-am. And he fled to Me-gid'do, and died there. _{strike}
28 And his servants carried him in a chariot to Je-ru'sa-lem, and buried him in his sepulcher with his fathers in the city of Da'vid. _{grave}
29 And in the eleventh year of Jo'ram the son of A'hab began A-ha-zi'ah to reign over Ju'dah.
30 And when Je'hu was come to Jez're-el, Jez'e-bel heard *of it*; and she painted her face, and tired her head, and looked out at a window. _{eyes - adorned}
31 And as Je'hu entered in at the gate, she said, *Had* Zim'ri peace, who slew his master?
32 And he lifted up his face to the window, and said, Who *is* on my side? who? And there looked out to him two *or* three eunuchs. _{officials}
33 And he said, Throw her down. So they threw her down: and *some* of her blood was sprinkled on the wall, and on the horses: and he trode her under foot.
34 And when he was come in, he did eat and drink, and said, Go, see now this cursed *woman*, and bury her: for she *is* a king's daughter.

35 And they went to bury her: but they found no more of her than the skull, and the feet, and the palms of *her* hands.
36 Wherefore they came again, and told him. And he said, This *is* the word of the LORD, which He spoke by His servant E-li'jah the Tish'bite, saying, In the <u>portion</u> of Jez're-el shall dogs eat the flesh of Jez'e-bel: territory
37 And the carcase of Jez'e-bel shall be as dung upon the face of the field in the portion of Jez're-el; *so* that they shall not say, This *is* Jez'e-bel.

CHAPTER 10

A ND A'hab had seventy sons in Sa-ma'ri-a. And Je'hu wrote letters, and sent to Sa-ma'ri-a, to the rulers of Jez're-el, to the elders, and to them that brought up A'hab's *children*, saying,
2 Now as soon as this letter come to you, seeing your master's sons *are* with you, and *there are* with you chariots and horses, a <u>fenced</u> city also, and armor; fortified
3 Look <u>even out</u> the best and <u>meetest</u> of your master's sons, and set *him* on his father's throne, and fight for your master's house. choose - most worthy
4 But they were exceedingly afraid, and said, Behold, two kings <u>stood not before</u> him: how then shall we stand? could not resist
5 And he that *was* over the house, and he that *was* over the city, the elders also, and the bringers up *of the children*, sent to Je'hu, saying, We *are* your ser-vants, and will do all that you shall bid us; we will not make any king: do you *that which is* good in your eyes.
6 Then he wrote a letter the second time to them, saying, If you *be* <u>mine</u>, and *if* you will hearken to my voice, take you the heads of the men your master's sons, and come to me to Jez're-el by to morrow this time. Now the king's sons, *being* seventy per-sons, *were* with the great men of the city, which brought them up. on my side
7 And it came to pass, when the let-ter came to them, that they took the king's sons, and slew seventy per-sons, and put their heads in baskets, and sent him *them* to Jez're-el.
8 And there came a messenger, and told him, saying, They have brought the heads of the king's sons. And he said, Lay you them in two heaps at the <u>entering</u> in of the gate until the morning. entrance
9 And it came to pass in the morning, that he went out, and stood, and said to all the people, You *be* <u>righteous</u>: behold, I conspired against my master, and slew him: but who slew all these? just
10 Know now that there shall fall to the earth nothing of the word of the LORD, which the LORD spoke con-cerning the house of A'hab: for the LORD has done *that* which He spoke by His servant E-li'jah.
11 So Je'hu slew all that remained of the house of A'hab in Jez're-el, and all his great men, and his <u>kinsfolks</u>, and his priests, until he left him none remaining. close friends
12 And he arose and departed, and

came to Sa-ma'ri-a. *And* as he *was* at the shearing house in the way,

13 Je'hu met with the brethren of A-ha-zi'ah king of Ju'dah, and said, Who *are* you? And they answered, We *are* the brethren of A-ha-zi'ah; and we go down to <u>salute</u> the children of the king and the children of the queen.   greet

14 And he said, Take them alive. And they took them alive, and slew them at the pit of the shearing house, *even* two and forty men; neither left he any of them.

15 And when he was departed from there, he lighted on Je-hon'a-dab the son of Re'chab *coming* to meet him: and he <u>saluted</u> him, and said to him, Is your heart right, as my heart *is* with your heart? And Je-hon'a-dab answered, It is. If it be, give *me* your hand. And he gave *him* his hand; and he took him up to him into the chariot.

16 And he said, Come with me, and see my zeal for the LORD. So they made him ride in his chariot.

17 And when he came to Sa-ma'ri-a, he slew all that remained to A'hab in Sa-ma'ri-a, till he had destroyed him, according to the saying of the LORD, which He spoke to E-li'jah.

18 And Je'hu gathered all the people together, and said to them, A'hab served Ba'al a little; *but* Je'hu shall serve him much.

19 Now therefore call to me all the prophets of Ba'al, all his servants, and all his priests; let none be <u>wanting</u>: for I have a great sacrifice *to do* to Ba'al; whosoever shall be wanting, he shall not live. But Je'hu did *it* in subtilty, to the intent that he might destroy the worshippers of Ba'al.   missing

20 And Je'hu said, Proclaim a solemn assembly for Ba'al. And they proclaimed *it*.

21 And Je'hu sent through all Is'ra-el: and all the worshippers of Ba'al came, so that there was not a man left that came not. And they came into the house of Ba'al; and the house of Ba'al was full from one end to another.

22 And he said to him that *was* over the <u>vestry</u>, Bring forth vestments for all the worshippers of Ba'al. And he brought them forth vestments.   wardrobe

23 And Je'hu went, and Je-hon'a-dab the son of Re'chab, into the house of Ba'al, and said to the worshippers of Ba'al, Search, and <u>look</u> that there be here with you none of the servants of the LORD, but the worshippers of Ba'al only.   see

24 And when they went in to offer sacrifices and burned offerings, Je'hu appointed <u>fourscore</u> men outside, and said, *If* any of the men whom I have brought into your hands escape, *he that lets him go*, his life *shall be* for the life of him.₈₀

25 And it came to pass, as soon as he had made an end of offering the burned offering, that Je'hu said to the guard and to the captains, Go in, *and* slay them; let none come forth. And they <u>smote</u> them with the edge of the sword; and the guard and the captains cast *them* out, and went to the city of the house of Ba'al.   struck

26 And they brought forth the <u>images</u>

out of the house of Ba'al, and burned them. sacred pillars

27 And they broke down the <u>image</u> of Ba'al, and broke down the house of Ba'al, and made it a <u>draught house</u> to this day. latrine

28 Thus Je'hu destroyed Ba'al out of Is'ra-el.

29 However *from* the sins of Jer-o-bo'am the son of Ne'bat, who made Is'ra-el to sin, Je'hu departed not from after them, *to wit*, the golden calves that *were* in Beth'-el, and that *were* in Dan. that is

30 And the LORD said to Je'hu, Because you have done well in executing *that which is* right in My eyes, *and* have done to the house of A'hab according to all that *was* in My heart, your children of the fourth *generation* shall sit on the throne of Is'ra-el.

31 But Je'hu took no heed to walk in the law of the LORD God of Is'ra-el with all his heart: for he departed not from the sins of Jer-o-bo'am, which made Is'ra-el to sin.

32 In those days the LORD began to <u>cut Is'ra-el short</u>: and Haz'a-el <u>smote</u> them in all the <u>coasts</u> of Is'ra-el; reduce the size of Israel - struck - borders

33 From Jor'dan eastward, all the land of Gil'e-ad, the Gad'ites, and the Reu'ben-ites, and the Ma-nas'sites, from Ar'o-er, which *is* by the <u>river</u> Ar'non, even Gil'e-ad and Ba'shan. valley of the

34 Now the rest of the acts of Je'hu, and all that he did, and all his might, *are* they not written in the book of the chronicles of the kings of Is'ra-el?

35 And Je'hu slept with his fathers: and they buried him in Sa-ma'ri-a. And Je-ho'a-haz his son reigned in his stead.

36 And the time that Je'hu reigned over Is'ra-el in Sa-ma'ri-a *was* twenty and eight years.

CHAPTER 11

AND when Ath-a-li'ah the mother of A-ha-zi'ah saw that her son was dead, she arose and destroyed all the <u>seed royal</u>. royal offsprings

2 But Je-hosh'e-ba, the daughter of king Jo'ram, sister of A-ha-zi'ah, took Jo'ash the son of A-ha-zi'ah, and <u>stole</u> him from among the king's sons *which were* slain; and they hid him, *even* him and his nurse, in the bedchamber from Ath-a-li'ah, so that he was not slain. took

3 And he was with her hid in the house of the LORD six years. And Ath-a-li'ah did reign over the land.

4 And the seventh year Je-hoi'a-da sent and brought the rulers over hundreds, with the captains and the guard, and brought them to him into the house of the LORD, and made a <u>covenant</u> with them, and took an oath of them in the house of the LORD, and showed them the king's son. agreement

5 And he commanded them, saying, This *is* the thing that you shall do; A third part of you that <u>enter</u> in on the <u>sabbath</u> shall even be <u>keepers of the watch</u> of the king's house; come - rest day - guards

6 And a third part *shall be* at the gate of Sur; and a third part at the gate behind the guard: so shall you keep the watch of the house, that it be not broken down.

7 And two <u>parts</u> of all you that go forth on the <u>sabbath</u>, even they shall keep the watch of the house of the LORD about the king. companies - rest day

8 And you shall <u>compass</u> the king round about, every man with his weapons in his hand: and he that come within the <u>ranges</u>, let him be slain: and be you with the king as he goes out and as he comes in. surround - rank

9 And the captains over the hundreds did according to all *things* that Je-hoi'a-da the priest commanded: and they took every man his men that were to come in on the <u>sabbath</u>, with them that should go out on the <u>sabbath</u>, and came to Je-hoi'a-da the priest.

10 And to the captains over hundreds did the priest give king Da'vid's spears and shields, that *were* in the temple of the LORD.

11 And the guard stood, every man with his weapons in his hand, round about the king, from the right corner of the temple to the left corner of the temple, *along* by the altar and the temple.

12 And he brought forth the king's son, and put the crown upon him, and *gave him* the testimony; and they made him king, and anointed him; and they clapped their hands, and said, <u>God save</u> the king. Long live

13 And when Ath-a-li'ah heard the noise of the guard *and* of the people, she came to the people into the temple of the LORD.

14 And when she looked, behold, the king stood by a pillar, as the manner *was,* and the princes and the trumpeters by the king, and all the people of the land rejoiced, and blew with trumpets: and Ath-a-li'ah <u>rent</u> her clothes, and cried, Treason, Treason. tore

15 But Je-hoi'a-da the priest commanded the captains of the hundreds, the officers of the host, and said to them, <u>Have her forth outside the ranges</u>: and him that follows her kill with the sword. For the priest had said, Let her not be slain in the house of the LORD. Bring her outside the ranks

16 And they laid hands on her; and she went by the <u>way</u> by the which the horses came into the king's house: and there was she slain. gate

17 And Je-hoi'a-da made a <u>covenant</u> between the LORD and the king and the people, that they should be the LORD's people; between the king also and the people. agreement

18 And all the people of the land went into the house of Ba'al, and broke it down; its altars and its <u>images</u> broke they in pieces thoroughly, and slew Mat'tan the priest of Ba'al before the altars. And the priest appointed officers over the house of the LORD. idols

19 And he took the rulers over hundreds, and the captains, and the guard, and all the people of the land; and they brought down the king from the house of the LORD, and came by the way of the gate of the guard to the king's house. And he sat on the throne of the kings.

20 And all the people of the land rejoiced, and the city was in quiet: and they slew Ath-a-li'ah with the sword *beside* the king's house.

21 Seven years old *was* Je-ho'ash when he began to reign.

CHAPTER 12

IN the seventh year of Je'hu Je-ho'ash began to reign; and forty years reigned he in Je-ru'sa-lem. And his mother's name *was* Zib'i-ah of Be'er-she'ba.

2 And Je-ho'ash did *that which was* right in the sight of the LORD all his days wherein Je-hoi'a-da the priest instructed him.

3 But the high places were not taken away: the people still sacrificed and burned incense in the high places.

4 And Je-ho'ash said to the priests, All the money of the dedicated things that is brought into the house of the LORD, *even* the money of every one that passes *the account*, the money that every man is set at, *and* all the money that comes into any man's heart to bring into the house of the LORD,   sacred - assessed - i.e., given willingly

5 Let the priests take *it* to them, every man of his acquaintance: and let them repair the breaches of the house, wheresoever any breach shall be found. damages

6 But it was *so, that* in the three and twentieth year of king Je-ho'ash the priests had not repaired the breaches of the house.

7 Then king Je-ho'ash called for Je-hoi'a-da the priest, and the *other* priests, and said to them, Why repair you not the breaches of the house? now therefore receive no *more* money of your acquaintance, but deliver it for the breaches of the house.

8 And the priests consented to receive no *more* money of the people, neither to repair the breaches of the house. damages

9 But Je-hoi'a-da the priest took a chest, and bored a hole in the lid of it, and set it beside the altar, on the right side as one comes into the house of the LORD: and the priests that kept the door put therein all the money *that was* brought into the house of the LORD.

10 And it was *so,* when they saw that *there was* much money in the chest, that the king's scribe and the high priest came up, and they put up in bags, and told the money that was found in the house of the LORD.   secretary - tied it - counted

11 And they gave the money, being told, into the hands of them that did the work, that had the oversight of the house of the LORD: and they laid it out to the carpenters and builders, that wrought upon the house of the LORD,   paid - worked

12 And to masons, and hewers of stone, and to buy timber and hewed stone to repair the breaches of the house of the LORD, and for all that was laid out for the house to repair *it*.   stonecutters

13 However there were not made for the house of the LORD bowls of silver, snuffers, basins, trumpets, any vessels of gold, or vessels of silver, of the money *that was* brought into the house of the LORD:

14 But they gave that to the workmen, and repaired therewith the house of the LORD.

15 Moreover they reckoned not with

the men, into whose hand they delivered the money to be bestowed on workmen: for they dealt faithfully. did not require an accounting from
16 The trespass money and sin money was not brought into the house of the LORD: it was the priests'.
17 Then Haz'a-el king of Syr'i-a went up, and fought against Gath, and took it: and Haz'a-el set his face <u>to go</u> up to Je-ru'sa-lem.   i.e., to fight
18 And Je-ho'ash king of Ju'dah took all the hallowed things that Je-hosh'a-phat, and Je-ho'ram, and A-ha-zi'ah, his fathers, kings of Ju'dah, had dedicated, and his own hallowed things, and all the gold *that was* found in the treasures of the house of the LORD, and in the king's house, and sent *it* to Haz'a-el king of Syr'i-a: and he <u>went away</u> from Je-ru'sa-lem.   withdrew
19 And the rest of the acts of Jo'ash, and all that he did, *are* they not written in the book of the chronicles of the kings of Ju'dah?
20 And his servants arose, and made a conspiracy, and slew Jo'ash in the house of Mil'lo, which goes down to Sil'la.
21 For Joz'a-char the son of Shim'e-ath, and Je-hoz'a-bad the son of Sho'mer, his servants, <u>smote</u> him, and he died; and they buried him with his fathers in the city of Da'vid: and Am-a-zi'ah his son reigned in his stead. struck

CHAPTER 13

IN the three and twentieth year of Jo'ash the son of A-ha-zi'ah king of Ju'-dah Je-ho'a-haz the son of Je'hu began to reign over Is'ra-el in Sa-ma'ri-a, *and reigned* seventeen years.
2 And he did *that which was* evil in the sight of the LORD, and followed the sins of Jer-o-bo'am the son of Ne'bat, which made Is'ra-el to sin; he departed not from there.
3 And the anger of the LORD was kindled against Is'ra-el, and He <u>delivered</u> them into the hand of Haz'a-el king of Syr'i-a, and into the hand of Ben-ha'dad the son of Haz'a-el, all *their* days.   gave
4 And Je-ho'a-haz besought the LORD, and the LORD hearkened to him: for He saw the oppression of Is'ra-el, because the king of Syr'i-a oppressed them.
5 (And the LORD gave Is'ra-el a savior, so that they went out from under the hand of the Syr'i-ans: and the children of Is'ra-el dwelled in their tents, as beforetime.
6 Nevertheless they departed not from the sins of the house of Jer-o-bo'am, who made Is'ra-el sin, *but* walked therein: and there remained the <u>grove</u> also in Sa-ma'ri-a.)   Asherah shrine
7 Neither did he leave of the people to Je-ho'a-haz but fifty horsemen, and ten chariots, and ten thousand footmen; for the king of Syr'i-a had destroyed them, and had made them like the dust by threshing.
8 Now the rest of the acts of Je-ho'a-haz, and all that he did, and his might, *are* they not written in the book of the chronicles of the kings of Is'ra-el?

9 And Je-ho'a-haz <u>slept</u> with his fathers; and they buried him in Sa-ma'ri-a: and Jo'ash his son reigned in his stead. _{died}

10 In the thirty and seventh year of Jo'ash king of Ju'dah began Je-ho'ash the son of Je-ho'a-haz to reign over Is'ra-el in Sa-ma'ri-a, *and reigned* sixteen years.

11 And he did *that which was* evil in the sight of the LORD; he departed not from all the sins of Jer-o-bo'am the son of Ne'bat, who made Is'ra-el sin: *but* he walked <u>therein</u>. _{in them}

12 And the rest of the acts of Jo'ash, and all that he did, and his might wherewith he fought against Am-a-zi'ah king of Ju'dah, *are* they not written in the book of the chronicles of the kings of Is'ra-el?

13 And Jo'ash <u>slept</u> with his fathers; and Jer-o-bo'am sat upon his throne: and Jo'ash was buried in Sa-ma'ri-a with the kings of Is'ra-el.

14 Now E-li'sha was fallen sick of his sickness whereof he died. And Jo'ash the king of Is'ra-el came down to him, and wept over <u>his face</u>, and said, O my father, my father, the chariot of Is'ra-el, and the horsemen thereof. _{him}

15 And E-li'sha said to him, Take bow and arrows. And he took to him bow and arrows.

16 And he said to the king of Is'ra-el, Put your hand upon the bow. And he put his hand *upon it*: and E-li'sha put his hands upon the king's hands.

17 And he said, Open the window eastward. And he opened *it*. Then E-li'sha said, Shoot. And he shot. And he said, The arrow of the LORD's deliverance, and the arrow of deliverance from Syr'i-a: for you shall <u>smite</u> the Syr'i-ans in A'phek, till you have consumed *them*. _{defeat}

18 And he said, Take the arrows. And he took *them*. And he said to the king of Is'ra-el, <u>Smite</u> upon the ground. And he smote thrice, and <u>stayed</u>. _{Strike - stopped}

19 And the man of God was angry with him, and said, You should have <u>smitten</u> five or six times; then had you <u>smitten</u> Syr'i-a till you had <u>consumed</u> *it*: whereas now you shall <u>smite</u> Syr'i-a *but* thrice. _{destroyed}

20 And E-li'sha died, and they buried him. And the bands of the Mo'ab-ites invaded the land at the coming in of the year.

21 And it came to pass, as they were burying a man, that, behold, they spied a band *of men*; and they cast the man into the <u>sepulcher</u> of E-li'sha: and when the man was let down, and touched the bones of E-li'sha, he revived, and stood up on his feet. _{tomb}

22 But Haz'a-el king of Syr'i-a oppressed Is'ra-el all the days of Je-ho'a-haz.

23 And the LORD was gracious to them, and had compassion on them, and <u>had respect</u> to them, because of His <u>covenant</u> with A'bra-ham, I'saac, and Ja'cob, and would not destroy them, neither cast He them from His presence as yet. _{paid attention - agreement}

24 So Haz'a-el king of Syr'i-a died; and Ben-ha'dad his son reigned in his stead.

25 And Je-ho'ash the son of Je-ho'a-haz took again out of the hand of Ben-ha'dad the son of Haz'a-el the cities, which he had taken out of the hand of Je-ho'a-haz his father by war. Three times did Jo'ash beat him, and recovered the cities of Is'ra-el.

CHAPTER 14

IN the second year of Jo'ash son of Je-ho'a-haz king of Is'ra-el reigned Am-a-zi'ah the son of Jo'ash king of Ju'dah.

2 He was twenty and five years old when he began to reign, and reigned twenty and nine years in Je-ru'sa-lem. And his mother's name *was* Je-ho-ad'dan of Je-ru'sa-lem.

3 And he did *that which was* right in the sight of the LORD, yet not like Da'vid his father: he did according to all things as Jo'ash his father did.

4 However the high places were not taken away: as yet the people did sacrifice and burned incense on the high places.

5 And it came to pass, as soon as the kingdom was underline{confirmed} in his hand, that he underline{slew} his servants which had slain the king his father. firmly - killed

6 But the children of the murderers he slew not: according to that which is written in the book of the law of Mo'ses, wherein the LORD commanded, saying, The fathers shall not be put to death for the children, nor the children be put to death for the fathers; but every man shall be put to death for his own sin.

7 He slew of E'dom in the valley of salt ten thousand, and took Se'lah by war, and called the name of it Jok'the-el to this day.

8 Then Am-a-zi'ah sent messengers to Je-ho'ash, the son of Je-ho'a-haz son of Je'hu, king of Is'ra-el, saying, Come, let us look one another in the face.

9 And Je-ho'ash the king of Is'ra-el sent to Am-a-zi'ah king of Ju'dah, saying, The thistle that *was* in Leb'a-non sent to the cedar that *was* in Leb'a-non, saying, Give your daughter to my son to wife: and there passed by a wild beast that *was* in Leb'a-non, and trode down the thistle.

10 You have indeed smitten E'dom, and your heart has lifted you up: glory *of this*, and tarry at home: for why should you meddle to *your* hurt, that you should fall, *even* you, and Ju'dah with you?

11 But Am-a-zi'ah would not hear. Therefore Je-ho'ash king of Is'ra-el went up; and he and Am-a-zi'ah king of Ju'dah looked one another in the face at Beth-she'mesh, which *belongs* to Ju'dah.

12 And Ju'dah was underline{put to the worse} before Is'ra-el; and they fled every man to their tents. routed

13 And Je-ho'ash king of Is'ra-el took Am-a-zi'ah king of Ju'dah, the son of Je-ho'ash the son of A-ha-zi'ah, at Beth-she'mesh, and came to Je-ru'sa-lem, and broke down the wall of Je-ru'sa-lem from the gate of E'phra-im to the corner gate, four hundred cubits.

14 And he took all the gold and silver, and all the vessels that were found in the house of the LORD, and in the trea-

sures of the king's house, and hostages, and returned to Sa-ma'ri-a.
15 Now the rest of the acts of Je-ho'ash which he did, and his <u>might</u>, and how he fought with Am-a-zi'ah king of Ju'dah, *are* they not written in the book of the chronicles of the kings of Is'ra-el? _{achievements}
16 And Je-ho'ash <u>slept</u> with his fathers, and was buried in Sa-ma'ri-a with the kings of Is'ra-el; and Jer-o-bo'am his son reigned in his stead. _{died}
17 And Am-a-zi'ah the son of Jo'ash king of Ju'dah lived after the death of Je-ho'ash son of Je-ho'a-haz king of Is'ra-el fifteen years.
18 And the rest of the acts of Am-a-zi'ah, *are* they not written in the book of the chronicles of the kings of Ju'dah?
19 Now they made a conspiracy against him in Je-ru'sa-lem: and he fled to La'chish; but they sent after him to La'chish, and slew him there.
20 And they brought him on horses: and he was buried at Je-ru'sa-lem with his fathers in the city of Da'vid.
21 And all the people of Ju'dah took Az-a-ri'ah, which *was* sixteen years old, and made him king instead of his father Am-a-zi'ah.
22 He built E'lath, and restored it to Ju'dah, after that the king <u>slept</u> with his fathers.
23 In the fifteenth year of Am-a-zi'ah the son of Jo'ash king of Ju'dah Jer-o-bo'am the son of Jo'ash king of Is'ra-el began to reign in Sa-ma'ri-a, *and reigned* forty and one years.
24 And he did *that which was* evil in the sight of the LORD: he departed not

from all the sins of Jer-o-bo'am the son of Ne'bat, who made Is'ra-el to sin.
25 He restored the <u>coast</u> of Is'ra-el from the entering of Ha'math to the sea of the plain, according to the word of the LORD God of Is'ra-el, which He spoke by the hand of His servant Jo'nah, the son of A-mit'ta-i, the prophet, which *was* of Gath-he'pher. _{boundaries}
26 For the LORD saw the <u>affliction</u> of Is'ra-el, *that it was* very bitter: for *there was* not any <u>shut up, nor any left</u>, nor any helper for Is'ra-el. _{suffering - slave nor free}
27 And the LORD said not that He would blot out the name of Is'ra-el from under heaven: but He saved them by the hand of Jer-o-bo'am the son of Jo'ash.
28 Now the rest of the acts of Jer-o-bo'am, and all that he did, and his might, how he warred, and how he recovered Da-mas'cus, and Ha'math, *which belonged* to Ju'dah, for Is'ra-el, *are* they not written in the book of the chronicles of the kings of Is'ra-el?
29 And Jer-o-bo'am slept with his fathers, *even* with the kings of Is'ra-el; and Zach-a-ri'ah his son reigned in his stead.

CHAPTER 15

IN the twenty and seventh year of Jer-o-bo'am king of Is'ra-el began Az-a-ri'ah son of Am-a-zi'ah king of Ju'dah to reign.
2 Sixteen years old was he when he began to reign, and he reigned two and fifty years in Je-ru'sa-lem. And his

mother's name *was* Jech-o-li'ah of Je-ru'sa-lem.

3 And he did *that which was* right in the sight of the Lord, according to all that his father Am-a-zi'ah had done;

4 <u>Save that</u> the high places were not removed: the people sacrificed and burned incense still on the high places. _{Only}

5 And the Lord <u>smote</u> the king, so that he was a leper to the day of his death, and dwelled in a <u>several</u> house. And Jo'tham the king's son *was* over the house, judging the people of the land. _{struck - separate}

6 And the rest of the acts of Az-a-ri'ah, and all that he did, *are* they not written in the book of the <u>chronicles</u> of the kings of Ju'dah? _{annals}

7 So Az-a-ri'ah <u>slept</u> with his fathers; and they buried him with his fathers in the city of Da'vid: and Jo'tham his son reigned in his stead. _{died}

8 In the thirty and eighth year of Az-a-ri'ah king of Ju'dah did Zach-a-ri'ah the son of Jer-o-bo'am reign over Is'ra-el in Sa-ma'ri-a six months.

9 And he did *that which was* evil in the sight of the Lord, as his fathers had done: he departed not from the sins of Jer-o-bo'am the son of Ne'bat, who made Is'ra-el to sin.

10 And Shal'lum the son of Ja'besh conspired against him, and smote him <u>before the people</u>, and slew him, and reigned in his stead. _{publicly}

11 And the rest of the acts of Zach-a-ri'ah, behold, they *are* written in the book of the <u>chronicles</u> of the kings of Is'ra-el. _{annals}

12 This *was* the word of the Lord which he spoke to Je'hu, saying, your sons shall sit on the throne of Is'ra-el to the fourth *generation*. And so it came to pass.

13 Shal'lum the son of Ja'besh began to reign in the nine and thirtieth year of Uz-zi'ah king of Ju'dah; and he reigned a full month in Sa-ma'ri-a.

14 For Men'a-hem the son of Ga'di went up from Tir'zah, and came to Sa-ma'ri-a, and <u>smote</u> Shal'lum the son of Ja'besh in Sa-ma'ri-a, and slew him, and reigned in his stead. _{struck}

15 And the rest of the acts of Shal'lum, and his conspiracy which he made, behold, they *are* written in the book of the chronicles of the kings of Is'ra-el.

16 Then Men'a-hem smote Tiph'sah, and all that *were* therein, and the coasts thereof from Tir'zah: because they opened not *to him*, therefore he <u>smote</u> *it*; *and* all the women therein that were with child he ripped up. _{sacked}

17 In the nine and thirtieth year of Az-a-ri'ah king of Ju'dah began Men'a-hem the son of Ga'di to reign over Is'ra-el, *and reigned* ten years in Sa-ma'ri-a.

18 And he did *that which was* evil in the sight of the Lord: he departed not all his days from the sins of Jer-o-bo'am the son of Ne'bat, who made Is'ra-el to sin.

19 *And* Pul the king of As-syr'i-a came against the land: and Men'a-hem gave Pul a thousand talents of silver, that his hand might be with him to <u>confirm</u> the kingdom in his hand. _{strengthen}

20 And Men'a-hem <u>exacted</u> the

money of Is'ra-el, *even* of all the mighty men of wealth, of each man fifty shekels of silver, to give to the king of As-syr'i-a. So the king of As-syr'i-a turned back, and stayed not there in the land. _{took}

21 And the rest of the acts of Men'a-hem, and all that he did, *are* they not written in the book of the chronicles of the kings of Is'ra-el?

22 And Men'a-hem slept with his fathers; and Pek-a-hi'ah his son reigned in his stead.

23 In the fiftieth year of Az-a-ri'ah king of Ju'dah Pek-a-hi'ah the son of Men'a-hem began to reign over Is'ra-el in Sa-ma'ri-a, *and reigned* two years.

24 And he did *that which was* evil in the sight of the LORD: he departed not from the sins of Jer-o-bo'am the son of Ne'bat, who made Is'ra-el to sin.

25 But Pe'kah the son of Rem-a-li'ah, a captain of his, conspired against him, and smote him in Sa-ma'ri-a, in the palace of the king's house, with Ar'gob and A-ri'eh, and with him fifty men of the Gil'e-ad-ites: and he killed him, and reigned in his room.   _{struck - ruled - place}

26 And the rest of the acts of Pek-a-hi'ah, and all that he did, behold, they *are* written in the book of the chronicles of the kings of Is'ra-el.

27 In the two and fiftieth year of Az-a-ri'ah king of Ju'dah Pe'kah the son of Rem-a-li'ah began to reign over Is'ra-el in Sa-ma'ri-a, *and reigned* twenty years.

28 And he did *that which was* evil in the sight of the LORD: he departed not from the sins of Jer-o-bo'am the son of Ne'bat, who made Is'ra-el to sin.

29 In the days of Pe'kah king of Is'ra-el came Tig'lath-pi-le'ser king of As-syr'i-a, and took I'jon, and A'bel-beth-ma'a-chah, and Ja-no'ah, and Ke'desh, and Ha'zor, and Gil'e-ad, and Gal'i-lee, all the land of Naph'ta-li, and carried them captive to As-syr'i-a.

30 And Ho-she'a the son of E'lah made a conspiracy against Pe'kah the son of Rem-a-li'ah, and smote him, and slew him, and reigned in his stead, in the twentieth year of Jo'tham the son of Uz-zi'ah.

31 And the rest of the acts of Pe'kah, and all that he did, behold, they *are* written in the book of thc chronicles of the kings of Is'ra-el.

32 In the second year of Pe'kah the son of Rem-a-li'ah king of Is'ra-el began Jo'tham the son of Uz-zi'ah king of Ju'dah to reign.   _{rule}

33 Five and twenty years old was he when he began to reign, and he reigned sixteen years in Je-ru'sa-lem. And his mother's name *was* Je-ru'sha, the daughter of Za'dok.

34 And he did *that which was* right in the sight of the LORD: he did according to all that his father Uz-zi'ah had done.

35 However the high places were not removed: the people sacrificed and burned incense still in the high places. He built the higher gate of the house of the LORD.

36 Now the rest of the acts of Jo'tham, and all that he did, *are* they not written in the book of the chronicles of the kings of Ju'dah?   _{annals}

37 In those days the LORD began to send against Ju'dah Re'zin the king of

Syr'i-a, and Pe'kah the son of Rem-a-li'ah.

38 And Jo'tham <u>slept</u> with his fathers, and was buried with his fathers in the city of Da'vid his father: and A'haz his son <u>reigned</u> in his stead.   died - ruled

CHAPTER 16

IN the seventeenth year of Pe'kah the son of Rem-a-li'ah A'haz the son of Jo'tham king of Ju'dah began to reign.

2 Twenty years old *was* A'haz when he began to reign, and reigned sixteen years in Je-ru'sa-lem, and did not *that which was* right in the sight of the LORD his God, like Da'vid his father.

3 But he walked in the way of the kings of Is'ra-el, yea, and made his son to pass through the fire, according to the <u>abominations</u> of the heathen, whom the LORD cast out from before the children of Is'ra-el.   detestable ways

4 And he sacrificed and burned incense in the high places, and on the hills, and under every green tree.

5 Then Re'zin king of Syr'i-a and Pe'kah son of Rem-a-li'ah king of Is'ra-el came up to Je-ru'sa-lem to war: and they besieged A'haz, but could not <u>overcome</u> *him*.   overpower

6 At that time Re'zin king of Syr'i-a recovered E'lath to Syr'i-a, and drove the Jews from E'lath: and the Syr'i-ans came to E'lath, and dwelled there to this day.

7 So A'haz sent messengers to Tig'lath-pi-le'ser king of As-syr'i-a, saying, I *am* your servant and your son: come up, and <u>save</u> me out of the hand of the king

of Syr'i-a, and out of the hand of the king of Is'ra-el, which rise up against me.   deliver

8 And A'haz took the silver and gold that was found in the house of the LORD, and in the <u>treasures</u> of the king's house, and sent *it for* a present to the king of As-syr'i-a.   treasuries

9 And the king of As-syr'i-a hearkened to him: for the king of As-syr'i-a went up against Da-mas'cus, and <u>took</u> it, and carried *the people of* it captive to Kir, and slew Re'zin. captured

10 And king A'haz went to Da-mas'cus to meet Tig'lath-pi-le'ser king of As-syr'i-a, and saw an altar that *was* at Da-mas'cus: and king A'haz sent to U-ri'jah the priest the <u>fashion</u> of the altar, and the pattern of it, according to all the workmanship thereof.   model

11 And U-ri'jah the priest built an altar according to all that king A'haz had sent from Da-mas'cus: so U-ri'jah the priest made *it* <u>against</u> king A'haz came from Da-mas'cus.   before

12 And when the king was come from Da-mas'cus, the king saw the altar: and the king approached to the altar, and offered thereon.

13 And he burned his burned offering and his <u>meat</u> offering, and poured his drink offering, and sprinkled the blood of his peace offerings, upon the altar. grain

14 And he brought also the brazen altar, which *was* <u>before</u> the LORD, from the forefront of the house, from between the altar and the house of the LORD, and put it on the north side of the altar.   dedicated to

15 And king A'haz commanded U-ri'jah the priest, saying, Upon the great altar burn the morning burned offering, and the evening <u>meat</u> offering, and the king's burned sacrifice, and his <u>meat</u> offering, with the burned offering of all the people of the land, and their meat offering, and their drink offerings; and sprinkle upon it all the blood of the burned offering, and all the blood of the sacrifice: and the brazen altar shall be for me to <u>enquire *by*</u>. seek guidance

16 Thus did U-ri'jah the priest, according to all that king A'haz commanded.

17 And king A'haz cut off the borders of the bases, and removed the laver from off them; and took down the sea from off the brazen oxen that *were* under it, and put it upon a pavement of stones.

18 And the <u>covert</u> for the <u>sabbath</u> that they had built in the house, and the king's entry without, <u>turned</u> he from the house of the LORD for the king of As-syr'i-a.

covered corridor - rest day - removed

19 Now the rest of the acts of A'haz which he did, *are* they not written in the book of the chronicles of the kings of Ju'dah?

20 And A'haz <u>slept</u> with his fathers, and was buried with his fathers in the city of Da'vid: and Hez-e-ki'ah his son <u>reigned</u> in his <u>stead</u>. died - ruled - place

CHAPTER 17

IN the twelfth year of A'haz king of Ju'dah began Ho-she'a the son of E'-lah to reign in Sa-ma'ri-a over Is'ra-el nine years.

2 And he did *that which was* evil in the sight of the LORD, but not as the kings of Is'ra-el that were before him.

3 Against him came up Shal-man-e'ser king of As-syr'i-a; and Ho-she'a became his servant, and gave him <u>presents</u>. tribute

4 And the king of As-syr'i-a found conspiracy in Ho-she'a: for he had sent messengers to So king of E'gypt, and brought no <u>present</u> to the king of As-syr'i-a, as *he had done* year by year: therefore the king of As-syr'i-a shut him up, and bound him in prison.

5 Then the king of As-syr'i-a came up throughout all the land, and went up to Sa-ma'ri-a, and besieged it three years.

6 In the ninth year of Ho-she'a the king of As-syr'i-a took Sa-ma'ri-a, and carried Is'ra-el away into As-syr'i-a, and placed them in Ha'lah and in Ha'bor *by* the river of Go'zan, and in the cities of the Medes.

7 For *so* it was, that the children of Is'ra-el had sinned against the LORD their God, which had brought them up out of the land of E'gypt, from under the hand of Pha'raoh king of E'gypt, and had <u>feared</u> other gods, revered

8 And walked in the statutes of the heathen, whom the LORD cast out from before the children of Is'ra-el, and of the kings of Is'ra-el, which they had made.

9 And the children of Is'ra-el did secretly *those* things that *were* not right against the LORD their <u>God</u>, and they

built them high places in all their cities, from the tower of the watchmen to the <u>fenced</u> city.   <small>fortified - Elohim^{p.f.}</small>

10 And they set them up <u>images</u> and <u>groves</u> in every high hill, and under every green tree: <small>sacred pillars - Asherah idols</small>

11 And there they burned incense in all the high places, as *did* the <u>heathen</u> whom the Lord carried away before them; and <u>wrought</u> wicked things to provoke the Lord to anger: <small>nations - did</small>

12 For they served idols, whereof the Lord had said to them, You shall not do this thing.

13 Yet the Lord testified against Is'ra-el, and against Ju'dah, by all the prophets, *and by* all the seers, saying, Turn you from your evil ways, and keep My commandments *and* My statutes, according to all the law which I commanded your fathers, and which I sent to you by My servants the prophets.

14 <u>Notwithstanding</u> they would not hear, but <u>hardened</u> their necks, like to the neck of their fathers, that did not believe in the Lord their God.   <small>ACTS 7:51 However - became stubborn</small>

15 And they rejected His <u>statutes</u>, and His <u>covenant</u> that He made with their fathers, and His testimonies which He testified against them; and they followed vanity, and became vain, and went after the heathen that *were* round about them, *concerning* whom the Lord had charged them, that they should not do like them.   <small>decrees - agreement</small>

16 And they left all the commandments of the Lord their God, and made them molten images, *even* two calves, and made a grove, and worshiped <u>all the host of heaven</u>, and served Ba'al.   <small>i.e., sun, moon, and stars</small>

17 And they caused their sons and their daughters to pass through the fire, and used <u>divination</u> and <u>enchantments</u>, and sold themselves to do evil in the sight of the Lord, to provoke Him to anger.   <small>fortune telling - sorcery</small>

18 Therefore the Lord was very angry with Is'ra-el, and removed them out of His sight: there was none left but the tribe of Ju'dah only.

19 Also Ju'dah kept not the commandments of the Lord their God, but walked in the <u>statutes</u> of Is'ra-el which they <u>made</u>.   <small>customs - introduced</small>

20 And the Lord rejected all the <u>seed</u> of Is'ra-el, and afflicted them, and delivered them into the hand of spoilers, until He had cast them out of His sight.   <small>descendants</small>

21 For He <u>rent</u> Is'ra-el from the house of Da'vid; and they made Jer-o-bo'am the son of Ne'bat king: and Jer-o-bo'am drove Is'ra-el from following the Lord, and made them sin a great sin.   <small>tore</small>

22 For the children of Is'ra-el walked in all the sins of Jer-o-bo'am which he did; they departed not from them;

23 Until the Lord removed Is'ra-el out of His sight, as He had said by all His servants the prophets. So was Is'ra-el carried away out of their own land to As-syr'i-a to this day.

24 And the king of As-syr'i-a brought *men* from Bab'y-lon, and from Cu'thah, and from A'va, and from Ha'math, and from Seph-ar-va'im, and placed *them* in the cities of Sa-ma'ri-a

instead of the children of Is'ra-el and they possessed Sa-ma'ri-a, and dwelt in the cities thereof.

25 And *so* it was at the beginning of their dwelling there, *that* they <u>feared</u> not the LORD: therefore the LORD sent lions among them, which slew *some* of them.   worshipped

26 Wherefore they spoke to the king of As-syr'i-a, saying, The nations which you have removed, and placed in the cities of Sa-ma'ri-a, know not the <u>manner</u> of the God of the land: therefore He has sent lions among them, and, behold, they slay them, because they know not the <u>manner</u> of the God of the land.   custom

27 Then the king of As-syr'i-a commanded, saying, Carry there one of the priests whom you brought from there; and let them go and dwell there, and let him teach them the <u>man-ner</u> of the God of the land.

28 Then one of the priests whom they had carried away from Sa-ma'ri-a came and dwelled in Beth'-el, and taught them how they should <u>fear</u> the LORD.   revere

29 However every nation made gods of their own, and put *them* in the houses of the high places which the Sa-mar'i-tans had made, every nation in their cities wherein they dwelled.   But

30 And the men of Bab'y-lon made Suc'coth-be'noth, and the men of Cuth made Ner'gal, and the men of Ha'math made Ash'i-ma,

31 And the A'vites made Nib'haz and Tar'tak, and the Seph'ar-vites burned their children in fire to A-dram'me-lech and A-nam'me-lech, the gods of Seph-ar-va'im.

32 So they <u>feared</u> the LORD, and made to themselves <u>of the lowest of them</u> priests of the high places, which sacrificed for them in the houses of the high places.   revered - from the common people

33 They <u>feared</u> the LORD, and served their own gods, after the <u>manner</u> of the nations whom they carried away from there.   custom

34 To this day they do after the former <u>manners</u>: they <u>fear</u> not the LORD, neither do they after their <u>statutes</u>, or after their ordinances, or after the law and commandment which the LORD commanded the children of Ja'cob, whom He named Is'ra-el;   decrees

35 With whom the LORD had made a <u>covenant</u>, and charged them, saying, You shall not fear other gods, nor bow yourselves to them, nor serve them, nor sacrifice to them: agreement

36 But the LORD, who brought you up out of the land of E'gypt with great power and a stretched out arm, Him shall you <u>fear</u>, and Him shall you worship, and to Him shall you do sacrifice.   reverence

37 And the statutes, and the ordinances, and the law, and the commandment, which He wrote for you, you shall observe to do for evermore; and you shall not <u>fear</u> other gods.   respect

38 And the <u>covenant</u> that I have made with you you shall not forget; neither shall you fear other gods.

39 But the LORD your God you shall fear; and He shall deliver you out of the hand of all your enemies.

40 However they did not <u>hearken</u>, but they did after their former manner. _{listen}
41 So these nations feared the LORD, and served their graven images, both their children, and their children's children: as did their fathers, so do they to this day.

CHAPTER 18

NOW it came to pass in the third year of Ho-she'a son of E'lah king of Is'ra-el, *that* Hez-e-ki'ah the son of A'haz king of Ju'dah began to reign.
2 Twenty and five years old was he when he began to reign; and he reigned twenty and nine years in Je-ru'sa-lem. His mother's name also *was* A'bi, the daughter of Zach-a-ri'ah.
3 And he did *that which was* right in the sight of the LORD, according to all that Da'vid his father did.
4 He removed the high places, and broke the <u>images</u>, and cut down the <u>groves</u>, and broke in pieces the brazen serpent that Mo'ses had made: for to those days the children of Is'ra-el did burn incense to it: and he called it <u>Ne-hush'tan</u>.

sacred pillars - Asherah idols - i.e., a piece of bronze

5 He trusted in the <u>LORD God</u> of Is'ra-el; so that after him was none like him among all the kings of Ju'dah, nor *any* that were before him. Jehovah^{s.f.} Elohim^{p.f.}
6 For he clung to the LORD, *and* departed not from following Him, but kept His commandments, which the LORD commanded Mo'ses. _{obeyed}
7 And the LORD was with him; *and* he prospered wherever he went forth:

and he rebelled against the king of As-syr'i-a, and served him not.
8 He smote the Phi-lis'tines, *even* to Ga'za, and the borders thereof, from the tower of the watchmen to the <u>fenced</u> city. _{fortified}
9 And it came to pass in the fourth year of king Hez-e-ki'ah, which *was* the seventh year of Ho-she'a son of E'lah king of Is'ra-el, *that* Shal-man-e'ser king of As-syr'i-a came up against Sa-ma'ri-a, and besieged it.
10 And at the end of three years they took it: *even* in the sixth year of Hez-e-ki'ah, that *is* the ninth year of Ho-she'a king of Is'ra-el, Sa-ma'ri-a was taken.
11 And the king of As-syr'i-a did carry away Is'ra-el to As-syr'i-a, and put them in Ha'lah and in Ha'bor *by* the river of Go'zan, and in the cities of the Medes:
12 Because they obeyed not the voice of the LORD their God, but transgressed His <u>covenant</u>, *and* all that Mo'ses the servant of the LORD commanded, and would not hear *them*, nor do *them*. _{agreement}
13 Now in the fourteenth year of king Hez-e-ki'ah did Sen-nach'e-rib king of As-syr'i-a come up against all the <u>fenced</u> cities of Ju'dah, and took them. _{fortified}
14 And Hez-e-ki'ah king of Ju'dah sent to the king of As-syr'i-a to La'chish, saying, I have <u>offended</u>; return from me: that which you put on me will I bear. And the king of As-syr'i-a appointed to Hez-e-ki'ah king of Ju'dah three hundred talents of silver and thirty talents of gold. _{done wrong}

15 And Hez-e-ki'ah gave *him* all the silver that was found in the house of the LORD, and in the <u>treasures</u> of the king's house.   treasuries

16 At that time did Hez-e-ki'ah <u>cut off</u> *the gold from* the doors of the temple of the LORD, and *from* the pillars which Hez-e-ki'ah king of Ju'dah had overlaid, and gave it to the king of As-syr'i-a.   strip

17 And the king of As-syr'i-a sent Tar'tan and Rab'sa-ris and Rab'-sha-keh from La'chish to king Hez-e-ki'ah with a great host against Je-ru'sa-lem. And they went up and came to Je-ru'sa-lem. And when they were come up, they came and stood by the conduit of the upper pool, which *is* in the highway of the fuller's field.

18 And when they had called to the king, there came out to them E-li'a-kim the son of Hil-ki'ah, which *was* over the household, and Sheb'na the <u>scribe</u>, and Jo'ah the son of A'saph the recorder.   secretary

19 And Rab'-sha-keh said to them, Speak you now to Hez-e-ki'ah, Thus says the great king, the king of As-syr'i-a, What confidence *is* this wherein you trust?

20 You say, (but *they are but* <u>vain</u> words,) *I have* counsel and strength for the war. Now on whom do you trust, that you rebell against me?   empty

21 Now, behold, you trust upon the staff of this bruised reed, *even* upon E'gypt, on which if a man lean, it will go into his hand, and pierce it: so *is* Pha'raoh king of E'gypt to all that trust on <u>him</u>.

22 But if you say to me, We trust in the LORD our <u>God</u>: *is* not that He, whose <u>high places</u> and whose altars Hez-e-ki'ah has taken away, and has said to Ju'dah and Je-ru'sa-lem, You shall worship before this altar in Je-ru'sa-lem?   Elohim$^{p.f.}$ - shrines

23 Now therefore, I pray you, <u>give pledges to</u> my lord the king of As-syr'i-a, and I will deliver you two thousand horses, if you be able on your part to set riders upon them.   make a bargain with

24 How then will you turn away the face of one captain of the least of my master's servants, and put your trust on E'gypt for chariots and for horsemen?

25 Am I now come up without the LORD against this place to destroy it? The LORD said to me, Go up against this land, and destroy it.

26 Then said E-li'a-kim the son of Hil-ki'ah, and Sheb'na, and Jo'ah, to Rab'-sha-keh, Speak, I pray you, to your servants in the Syr'i-an language; for we understand *it*: and talk not with us in the Jews' language in the <u>ears</u> of the people that *are* on the wall.   hearing

27 But Rab'-sha-keh said to them, Has my master sent me to your master, and to you, to speak these words? *has he* not *sent me* to the men which sit on the wall, that they may eat their own dung, and drink their own urine with you?

28 Then Rab'-sha-keh stood and cried with a loud voice in the Jews' language, and spoke, saying, Hear the word of the great king, the king of As-syr'i-a:

29 Thus says the king, Let not Hez-e-ki'ah <u>deceive</u> you: for he shall not be able to deliver you out of his hand: mislead

30 Neither let Hez-e-ki'ah make you trust in the LORD, saying, The LORD will surely deliver us, and this city shall not be delivered into the hand of the king of As-syr'i-a.

31 Hearken not to Hez-e-ki'ah: for thus says the king of As-syr'i-a, Make <u>*an agreement*</u> with me by a present, and come out to me, and *then* eat you every man of his own vine, and every one of his fig tree, and drink you every one the waters of his cistern: your peace

32 Until I come and take you away to a land like your own land, a land of <u>corn</u> and wine, a land of bread and vineyards, a land of oil olive and of honey, that you may live, and not die: and hearken not to Hez-e-ki'ah, when he <u>persuades</u> you, saying, The LORD will deliver us. grain - misleads

33 Has any of the gods of the nations delivered at all his land out of the hand of the king of As-syr'i-a?

34 Where *are* the gods of Ha'math, and of Ar'pad? where *are* the gods of Sephar-va'im, He'na, and I'vah? have they delivered Sa-ma'ri-a out of my hand?

35 Who *are* they among all the gods of the countries, that have delivered their country out of my hand, that the LORD should deliver Je-ru'salem out of my hand?

36 But the people held their peace, and answered him not a word: for the king's commandment was, saying, Answer him not.

37 Then came E-li'a-kim the son of Hil-ki'ah, which *was* over the household, and Sheb'na the scribe, and Jo'ah the son of A'saph the recorder, to Hez-e-ki'ah with *their* clothes <u>rent</u>, and told him the words of Rab'-sha-keh. torn

CHAPTER 19

AND it came to pass, when king Hez-e-ki'ah heard *it*, that he <u>rent</u> his clothes, and covered himself with sackcloth, and went into the house of the LORD.

2 And he sent E-li'a-kim, which *was* over the household, and Sheb'na the scribe, and the elders of the priests, covered with sackcloth, to I-sa'iah the prophet the son of A'moz.

3 And they said to him, Thus says Hez-e-ki'ah, This day *is* a day of trouble, and of rebuke, and <u>blasphemy</u>: for the children are come to the birth, and *there is* not strength to bring forth. disgrace

4 It may be the LORD your God will hear all the words of Rab'-sha-keh, whom the king of As-syr'i-a his master has sent to reproach the living God; and will <u>reprove</u> the words which the LORD your <u>God</u> has heard: wherefore lift up *your* prayer for the remnant that are left. ROM. 11:5 Elohim^{p.f.} - criticize

5 So the servants of king Hez-e-ki'ah came to I-sa'iah.

6 And I-sa'iah said to them, Thus shall you say to your master, Thus says the LORD, Be not afraid of the words which you have heard, with which the servants of the king of As-syr'i-a have <u>blasphemed</u> Me. reviled

7 Behold, I will send a <u>blast upon</u> him, and he shall hear a rumor, and shall return to his own land; and I will cause him to fall by the sword in his own land. spirit in

8 So Rab'-sha-keh returned, and found the king of As-syr'i-a warring against Lib'nah: for he had heard that he was departed from La'chish.

9 And when he heard say of Tir'ha-kah king of E-thi-o'pi-a, Behold, he is come out to fight against you: he sent messengers again to Hez-e-ki'ah, saying,

10 Thus shall you speak to Hez-e-ki'ah king of Ju'dah, saying, Let not your God in whom you trust deceive you, saying, Je-ru'sa-lem shall not be delivered into the hand of the king of As-syr'i-a.

11 Behold, you have heard what the kings of As-syr'i-a have done to all lands, by destroying them <u>utterly</u>: and shall you be <u>delivered</u>? completely - spared

12 Have the gods of the nations delivered them which my fathers have destroyed; *as* Go'zan, and Ha'ran, and Re'zeph, and the children of E'den which *were* in The-la'sar?

13 Where *is* the king of Ha'math, and the king of Ar'pad, and the king of the city of Seph-ar-va'im, of He'na, and I'vah?

14 And Hez-e-ki'ah received the letter of the hand of the messengers, and read it: and Hez-e-ki'ah went up into the house of the LORD, and spread it before the LORD.

15 And Hez-e-ki'ah prayed before the LORD, and said, O LORD God of Is'ra-el, which dwell *between* the cherubims, You are the God, *even* You alone, of all the kingdoms of the earth; You have made heaven and earth.

16 LORD, bow down Your ear, and hear: open, LORD, Your eyes, and see: and hear the words of Sen-nach'e-rib, which has sent him to <u>reproach</u> the living God. insult

17 Of a truth, LORD, the kings of As-syr'i-a have destroyed the nations and their lands,

18 And have cast their gods into the fire: for they *were* no gods, but the work of men's hands, wood and stone: therefore they have destroyed them.

19 Now therefore, O LORD our God, I beseech You, save You us out of his hand, that all the kingdoms of the earth may know that You *are* the LORD God, *even* You only. Jehovah^{s.f.} Elohim^{p.f.}

20 Then I-sa'iah the son of A'moz sent to Hez-e-ki'ah, saying, Thus says the <u>LORD God</u> of Is'ra-el, *That* which you have prayed to Me against Sen-nach'e-rib king of As-syr'i-a I have heard. Jehovah^{s.f.} Elohim^{p.f.}

21 This *is* the word that the LORD has spoken concerning him; The virgin the daughter of Zi'on has despised you, *and* laughed you to scorn; the daughter of Je-ru'sa-lem has shaken her head at you.

22 Whom have you <u>reproached</u> and <u>blasphemed?</u> and against whom have you exalted *your* voice, and lifted up your eyes on high? *even* against the Holy *One* of Is'ra-el. insulted - reviled

23 By your messengers you have <u>reproached</u> the Lord, and have said,

With the multitude of my chariots I am come up to the height of the mountains, to the sides of Leb'a-non, and will cut down the tall ce-dar trees thereof, *and* the choice fir trees thereof: and I will enter into the lodgings of its borders, *and into* the forest of his Car'mel.

24 I have digged and drunk strange wa-ters, and with the sole of my feet have I dried up all the rivers of besieged places.

25 Have you not heard long ago *how* I have done it, *and* of ancient times that I have formed it? now have I brought it to pass, that you should be to lay waste <u>fenced</u> cities *into* ruinous heaps.   fortified

26 Therefore their inhabitants were of small <u>power</u>, they were dis-mayed and confounded; they were *as* the grass of the field, and *as* the green herb, *as* the grass on the housetops, and *as corn* blasted before it be grown up.   strength - grain

27 But I know your abode, and your going out, and your coming in, and your rage against Me.

28 Because your rage against Me and your tumult is come up into My ears, therefore I will put My hook in your nose, and My bridle in your lips, and I will turn you back by the way by which you came.

29 And this *shall be* a sign to you, You shall eat this year such things as grow of themselves, and in the second year that which springs of the same; and in the third year sow you, and reap, and plant vineyards, and eat the fruits thereof.

30 And the remnant that is escaped of the house of Ju'dah shall yet again take root downward, and bear fruit upward.

31 For out of Je-ru'sa-lem shall go forth a remnant, and they that es-cape out of mount Zi'on: the zeal of the LORD *of hosts* shall do this.

32 Therefore thus says the LORD concerning the king of As-syr'i-a, He shall not come into this city, nor shoot an arrow there, nor come before it with shield, nor cast a <u>bank</u> against it.   siege mound

33 By the way that he came, by the same shall he return, and shall not come into this city, says the LORD.

34 For I will defend this city, to save it, for My own sake, and for My servant Da'vid's sake.

35 And it came to pass that night, that the <u>angel</u> of the LORD went out, and <u>smote</u> in the camp of the As-syr'i-ans an <u>hundred fourscore and five</u> thousand: and when they arose early in the morning, behold, they *were* all dead corpses. messenger - struck - 185

36 So Sen-nach'e-rib king of As-syr'i-a departed, and went and re-turned, and dwelled at Nin'e-veh.

37 And it came to pass, as he was worshipping in the house of Nis'roch his god, that A-dram'me-lech and Sha-re'zer his sons smote him with the sword: and they escaped into the land of Ar-me'ni-a. And E'sar-had'don his son reigned in his stead.

CHAPTER 20

IN those days was Hez-e-ki'ah sick to death. And the prophet I-sa'iah the son of A'moz came to him, and said

to him, Thus says the LORD, Set your house in order; for you shall die, and not live.

2 Then he turned his face to the wall, and prayed to the LORD, saying,

3 I beseech You, O LORD, remember now how I have walked before You in truth and with a perfect heart, and have done *that which is* good in Your sight. And Hez-e-ki'ah wept sore. beg - bitterly

4 And it came to pass, afore I-sa'iah was gone out into the middle court, that the word of the LORD came to him, saying,

5 Turn again, and tell Hez-e-ki'ah the captain of My people, Thus says the LORD, the God of Da'vid your father, I have heard your prayer, I have seen your tears: behold, I will heal you: on the third day you shall go up to the house of the LORD.

6 And I will add to your days fifteen years; and I will deliver you and this city out of the hand of the king of As-syr'i-a; and I will defend this city for My own sake, and for My servant Da'vid's sake.

7 And I-sa'iah said, Take a lump of figs. And they took and laid *it* on the boil, and he recovered.

8 And Hez-e-ki'ah said to I-sa'iah, What *shall be* the sign that the LORD will heal me, and that I shall go up into the house of the LORD the third day?

9 And I-sa'iah said, This sign shall you have of the LORD, that the LORD will do the thing that He has spoken: shall the shadow go forward ten degrees, or go back ten degrees? steps

10 And Hez-e-ki'ah answered, It is a light thing for the shadow to go down ten degrees: nay, but let the shadow return backward ten degrees. easy

11 And I-sa'iah the prophet cried to the LORD: and He brought the shadow ten degrees backward, by which it had gone down in the dial of A'haz.

12 At that time Be-ro'dach-bal'a-dan, the son of Bal'a-dan, king of Bab'y-lon, sent letters and a present to Hez-e-ki'ah: for he had heard that Hez-e-ki'ah had been sick.

13 And Hez-e-ki'ah hearkened to them, and showed them all the house of his precious things, the silver, and the gold, and the spices, and the precious ointment, and *all* the house of his armor, and all that was found in his treasures: there was nothing in his house, nor in all his dominion, that Hez-e-ki'ah showed them not. listened

14 Then came I-sa'iah the prophet to king Hez-e-ki'ah, and said to him, What said these men? and from where came they to you? And Hez-e-ki'ah said, They are come from a far country, *even* from Bab'y-lon.

15 And he said, What have they seen in your house? And Hez-e-ki'ah answered, All *the things* that *are* in my house have they seen: there is nothing among my treasures that I have not showed them.

16 And I-sa'iah said to Hez-e-ki'ah, Hear the word of the LORD.

17 Behold, the days come, that all that *is* in your house, and that which your fathers have laid up in store to

this day, shall be carried into Bab'y-lon: nothing shall be left, says the LORD.
18 And of your sons that shall issue from you, which you shall father, shall they take away; and they shall be eunuchs in the palace of the king of Bab'y-lon.
19 Then said Hez-e-ki'ah to I-sa'-iah, Good *is* the word of the LORD which you have spoken. And he said, *Is it* not *good*, if peace and truth be in my days?
20 And the rest of the acts of Hez-e-ki'ah, and all his might, and how he made a pool, and a conduit, and brought water into the city, *are* they not written in the book of the chronicles of the kings of Ju'dah?
21 And Hez-e-ki'ah <u>slept</u> with his fathers: and Ma-nas'seh his son reigned in his stead.   died

CHAPTER 21

MA-NAS'SEH *was* twelve years old when he began to <u>reign</u>, and <u>reigned</u> fifty and five years in Je-ru'sa-lem. And his mother's name *was* Heph'zi-bah. rule
2 And he did *that which was* evil in the sight of the LORD, after the <u>abominations</u> of the heathen, whom the LORD cast out before the children of Is'ra-el.   detestable practices
3 For he built up again the high places which Hez-e-ki'ah his father had destroyed; and he reared up altars for Ba'al, and made a grove, as did A'hab king of Is'ra-el; and worshiped all the host of heaven, and served them.

4 And he built altars in the house of the LORD, of which the LORD said, In Je-ru'sa-lem will I put My name.
5 And he built altars for all the host of heaven in the two courts of the house of the LORD.
6 And he made his son <u>pass through the fire</u>, and observed <u>times</u>, and used enchantments, and dealt with <u>familiar spirits</u> and <u>wizards</u>: he <u>wrought</u> much wickedness in the sight of the LORD, to provoke *Him* to anger.

i.e., pagan ritual - witchcraft - mediums - spiritists - did

7 And he set a graven image of the grove that he had made in the house, of which the LORD said to Da'vid, and to Sol'o-mon his son, In this house, and in Je-ru'sa-lem, which I have chosen out of all tribes of Is'ra-el, will I put My name for ever:
8 Neither will I make the feet of Is'ra-el move any more out of the land which I gave their fathers; only if they will observe to do according to all that I have commanded them, and according to all the law that My servant Mo'ses commanded them.
9 But they hearkened not: and Ma-nas'seh seduced them to do more evil than did the nations whom the LORD destroyed before the children of Is'ra-el.
10 And the LORD spoke by His servants the prophets, saying,
11 Because Ma-nas'seh king of Ju'dah hath done these <u>abominations</u>, *and* has done wickedly above all that the Am'or-ites did, which *were* before him, and has made Ju'dah also to sin with his idols: detestable sins
12 Therefore thus says the LORD

God of Is'ra-el, Behold, I *am* bringing *such* evil upon Je-ru'sa-lem and Ju'dah, that whosoever hears of it, <u>both his ears shall tingle</u>. i.e., he will be utterly astonished

13 And I will stretch over Je-ru'sa-lem the line of Sa-ma'ri-a, and the plummet of the house of A'hab: and I will wipe Je-ru'sa-lem as *a man* wipes a dish, wiping *it*, and turning *it* upside down.

14 And I will forsake the remnant of My <u>inheritance</u>, and deliver them into the hand of their enemies; and they shall become a prey and <u>a spoil to</u> all their enemies; i.e., people who belong to me - plundered by

15 Because they have done *that which was* evil in My sight, and have provoked Me to anger, since the day their fathers came forth out of E'gypt, even to this day.

16 Moreover Ma-nas'seh shed innocent blood very much, till he had filled Je-ru'sa-lem from one end to another; beside his sin wherewith he made Ju'dah to sin, in doing *that which was* evil in the sight of the LORD.

17 Now the rest of the acts of Ma-nas'seh, and all that he did, and his sin that he sinned, *are* they not written in the book of the chronicles of the kings of Ju'dah?

18 And Ma-nas'seh <u>slept</u> with his fathers, and was buried in the garden of his own house, in the garden of Uz'za: and A'mon his son reigned in his stead. died

19 A'mon *was* twenty and two years old when he began to <u>reign</u>, and he <u>reigned</u> two years in Je-ru'sa-lem. And his mother's name *was* Me-shul'le-meth, the daughter of Ha'ruz of Jot'bah. rule

20 And he did *that which was* evil in the sight of the LORD, as his father Ma-nas'seh did.

21 And he walked in all the way that his father walked in, and served the idols that his father served, and worshiped them:

22 And he forsook the LORD God of his fathers, and walked not in the way of the LORD.

23 And the servants of A'mon conspired against him, and slew the king in his own house.

24 And the people of the land slew all them that had conspired against king A'mon; and the people of the land made Jo-si'ah his son king in his stead.

25 Now the rest of the acts of A'mon which he did, *are* they not written in the book of the chronicles of the kings of Ju'dah?

26 And he was buried in his <u>sepulcher</u> in the garden of Uz'za: and Jo-si'ah his son reigned in his stead. tomb

CHAPTER 22

JO-SI'AH *was* eight years old when he began to <u>reign</u>, and he <u>reigned</u> thirty and one years in Je-ru'sa-lem. And his mother's name *was* Je-di'dah, the daughter of Ad-a-i'ah of Bos'cath. rule

2 And he did *that which was* right in the sight of the LORD, and walked in all the way of Da'vid his father, and turned not aside to the right hand or to the left.

3 And it came to pass in the eighteenth year of king Jo-si'ah, *that* the king sent Sha'phan the son of Az-a-li'ah, the son of Me-shul'lam, the scribe, to the house of the LORD, saying,

4 Go up to Hil-ki'ah the high priest, that he may <u>sum</u> the silver which is brought into the house of the LORD, which the keepers of the door have gathered of the people: count

5 And let them deliver it into the hand of the doers of the work, that have the oversight of the house of the LORD: and let them give it to the doers of the work which *is* in the house of the LORD, to repair the <u>breaches</u> of the house,   damage

6 To carpenters, and builders, and masons, and to buy timber and <u>hewn</u> stone to repair the house. dressed

7 However there was no reckoning made with them of the money that was delivered into their hand, because they dealt faithfully.

8 And Hil-ki'ah the high priest said to Sha'phan the <u>scribe</u>, I have found the book of the law in the house of the LORD. And Hil-ki'ah gave the book to Sha'phan, and he read it.   secretary

9 And Sha'phan the scribe came to the king, and brought the king word again, and said, Your servants have <u>gathered</u> the money that was found in the house, and have delivered it into the hand of them that do the work, that have the oversight of the house of the LORD.   emptied out

10 And Sha'phan the scribe showed the king, saying, Hil-ki'ah the priest has delivered me a book. And Sha'phan read it before the king.

11 And it came to pass, when the king had heard the words of the book of the law, that he <u>rent</u> his clothes.   tore

12 And the king commanded Hil-ki'ah the priest, and A-hi'kam the son of Sha'phan, and Ach'bor the son of Mi-cha'iah, and Sha'phan the scribe, and A-sa-hi'ah a servant of the king's, saying,

13 Go you, <u>enquire</u> of the LORD for me, and for the people, and for all Ju'dah, concerning the words of this book that is found: for great *is* the wrath of the LORD that is kindled against us, because our fathers have not hearkened to the words of this book, to do according to all that which is written concerning us.   seek

14 So Hil-ki'ah the priest, and A-hi'kam, and Ach'bor, and Sha'phan, and A-sa-hi'ah, went to Hul'dah the prophetess, the wife of Shal'lum the son of Tik'vah, the son of Har'has, keeper of the wardrobe; (now she dwelled in Je-ru'sa-lem in the <u>college</u>;) and they <u>communed</u> with her.   second quarter - spoke

15 And she said to them, Thus says the <u>LORD God</u> of Is'ra-el, Tell the man that sent you to me, Jehovah[s.f.] Elohim[p.f.]

16 Thus says the LORD, Behold, I will bring evil upon this place, and upon the inhabitants thereof, *even* all the words of the book which the king of Ju'dah has read:

17 Because they have forsaken Me, and have burned incense to other gods, that they might provoke Me to anger with all the works of their hands;

therefore My wrath shall be kindled against this place, and shall not be quenched.

18 But to the king of Ju'dah which sent you to enquire of the LORD, thus shall you say to him, Thus says the LORD God of Is'ra-el, *As touching* the words which you have heard;

19 Because your heart was <u>tender</u>, and you have humbled yourself before the LORD, when you heard what I spoke against this place, and against the inhabitants thereof, that they should become a desolation and a curse, and have rent your clothes, and wept before Me; I also have heard *you*, says the LORD. responsive

20 Behold therefore, I will <u>gather</u> you to your fathers, and you shall be <u>gathered</u> into your grave in peace; and your eyes shall not see all the evil which I will bring upon this place. And they brought the king word again. take

CHAPTER 23

AND the king sent, and they gathered to him all the elders of Ju'dah and of Je-ru'sa-lem.

2 And the king went up into the house of the LORD, and all the men of Ju'dah and all the inhabitants of Je-ru'sa-lem with him, and the priests, and the prophets, and all the people, both small and great: and he read in their ears all the words of the book of the <u>covenant</u> which was found in the house of the LORD. agreement

3 And the king stood by a pillar, and made a <u>covenant</u> before the LORD, to walk after the LORD, and to keep His commandments and His testimonies and His statutes with all *their* heart and all *their* soul, to perform the words of this covenant that were written in this book. And all the people stood to the <u>covenant</u>. agreement

4 And the king commanded Hil-ki'ah the high priest, and the priests of the second order, and the keepers of the door, to bring forth out of the temple of the LORD all the vessels that were made for Ba'al, and for the grove, and for all the host of heaven: and he burned them outside Je-ru'sa-lem in the fields of Kid'ron, and carried the ashes of them to Beth'-el.

5 And he <u>put down</u> the idolatrous priests, whom the kings of Ju'dah had ordained to burn incense in the <u>high places</u> in the cities of Ju'dah, and in the places round about Je-ru'sa-lem; them also that burned incense to Ba'al, to the sun, and to the moon, and to the planets, and to all the host of heaven. dismissed - shrines

6 And he brought out the <u>grove</u> from the house of the LORD, outside Je-ru'sa-lem, to the brook Kid'ron, and burned it at the brook Kid'ron, and stamped *it* small to powder, and cast the powder thereof upon the graves of the children of the people. Asherah idol

7 And he broke down the houses of the <u>sodomites</u>, that *were* by the house of the LORD, where the women wove hangings for the <u>grove</u>. male cult prostitutes

8 And he brought all the priests out of the cities of Ju'dah, and <u>defiled the high</u>

places where the priests had burned incense, from Ge'ba to Be'er-she'ba, and broke down the high places of the gates that *were* in the entering in of the gate of Josh'u-a the governor of the city, which *were* on a man's left hand at the gate of the city.   broke down the shrines

9 Nevertheless the priests of the high places came not up to the altar of the LORD in Je-ru'sa-lem, but they did eat of the unleavened bread among their brethren.   without yeast

10 And he defiled To'pheth, which *is* in the valley of the children of Hin'nom, that no man might make his son or his daughter to pass through the fire to Mo'lech.   desecrated

11 And he took away the horses that the kings of Ju'dah had given to the sun, at the entering in of the house of the LORD, by the chamber of Na'than-me'lech the chamberlain, which *was* in the suburbs, and burned the chariots of the sun with fire.   entrance - official

12 And the altars that *were* on the top of the upper chamber of A'haz, which the kings of Ju'dah had made, and the altars which Ma-nas'seh had made in the two courts of the house of the LORD, did the king beat down, and broke *them* down from there, and cast the dust of them into the brook Kid'ron.   break

13 And the high places that *were* before Je-ru'sa-lem, which *were* on the right hand of the mount of corruption, which Sol'o-mon the king of Is'ra-el had builded for Ash'to-reth the abomination of the Zi-do'ni-ans, and for Che'mosh the abomination of the Mo'-ab-ites, and for Mil'com the abomination of the children of Am'mon, did the king defile.   shrines - detestable god - desecrate

14 And he broke in pieces the images, and cut down the groves, and filled their places with the bones of men.   Asherah idols

15 Moreover the altar that *was* at Beth'-el, *and* the high place which Jer-o-bo'am the son of Ne'bat, who made Is'ra-el to sin, had made, both that altar and the high place he broke down, and burned the high place, *and* stamped *it* small to powder, and burned the grove.

16 And as Jo-si'ah turned himself, he spied the sepulchres that *were* there in the mount, and sent, and took the bones out of the sepulchres, and burned *them* upon the altar, and polluted it, according to the word of the LORD which the man of God proclaimed, who proclaimed these words.   tombs

17 Then he said, What title *is* that that I see? And the men of the city told him, *It is* the sepulcher of the man of God, which came from Ju'dah, and proclaimed these things that you have done against the altar of Beth'-el.   tombstone

18 And he said, Let him alone; let no man move his bones. So they let his bones alone, with the bones of the prophet that came out of Sa-ma'ri-a.

19 And all the houses also of the high places that *were* in the cities of Sa-ma'ri-a, which the kings of Is'ra-el had made to provoke *the* LORD to anger, Jo-si'ah took away, and did to them according to all the acts that he had done in Beth'-el.   temples

20 And he slew all the priests of the <u>high places</u> that *were* there upon the altars, and burned men's bones upon them, and returned to Je-ru'sa-lem. _{shrines}

21 And the king commanded all the people, saying, Keep the passover to the LORD your God, as *it is* written in the book of this <u>covenant</u>. _{agreement}

22 Surely there was not holden such a passover from the days of the judges that judged Is'ra-el, nor in all the days of the kings of Is'ra-el, nor of the kings of Ju'dah;

23 But in the eighteenth year of king Jo-si'ah, *wherein* this passover was holden to the LORD in Je-ru'sa-lem.

24 Moreover the *workers with* <u>familiar spirits</u>, and the <u>wizards</u>, and the <u>images</u>, and the idols, and all the <u>abominations</u> that were spied in the land of Ju'dah and in Je-ru'sa-lem, did Jo-si'ah put away, that he might perform the words of the law which were written in the book that Hil-ki'ah the priest found in the house of the LORD.

_{mediums - spiritists - household goods - detestable things}

25 And like to him was there no king before him, that turned to the LORD with all his heart, and with all his soul, and with all his might, according to all the law of Mo'ses; neither after him arose there *any* like him.

26 Notwithstanding the LORD turned not from the fierceness of His great wrath, wherewith His anger was kindled against Ju'dah, because of all the provocations that Ma-nas'seh had provoked Him with.

27 And the LORD said, I will remove Ju'dah also out of My sight, as I have removed Is'ra-el, and will cast off this city Je-ru'sa-lem which I have chosen, and the house of which I said, My name shall be there.

28 Now the rest of the acts of Jo-si'ah, and all that he did, *are* they not written in the book of the chronicles of the kings of Ju'dah?

29 In his days Pha'raoh-ne'choh king of E'gypt went up against the king of As-syr'i-a to the river Eu-phra'tes: and king Jo-si'ah went against him; and he slew him at Me-gid'do, when he had seen him.

30 And his servants carried him in a chariot dead from Me-gid'do, and brought him to Je-ru'sa-lem, and buried him in his own <u>sepulcher</u>. And the people of the land took Je-ho'a-haz the son of Jo-si'ah, and anointed him, and made him king in his father's stead. _{tomb}

31 Je-ho'a-haz *was* twenty and three years old when he began to reign; and he reigned three months in Je-ru'sa-lem. And his mother's name *was* Ha-mu'tal, the daughter of Jer-e-mi'ah of Lib'nah.

32 And he did *that which was* evil in the sight of the LORD, according to all that his fathers had done.

33 And Pha'raoh-ne'choh put him in bands at Rib'lah in the land of Ha'math, that he might not reign in Je-ru'sa-lem; and put the land to a tribute of an hundred talents of silver, and a talent of gold.

34 And Pha'raoh-ne'choh made E-li'a-kim the son of Jo-si'ah king in the <u>room</u> of Jo-si'ah his father, and <u>turned</u>

his name to Je-hoi'a-kim, and took Je-ho'a-haz away: and he came to E'gypt, and died there.   place - changed

35 And Je-hoi'a-kim gave the silver and the gold to Pha'raoh; but he taxed the land to give the money according to the commandment of Pha'raoh: he exacted the silver and the gold of the people of the land, of every one according to his taxation, to give *it* to Pha'raoh-ne'choh.

36 Je-hoi'a-kim *was* twenty and five years old when he began to reign; and he reigned eleven years in Je-ru'sa-lem. And his mother's name *was* Ze-bu'dah, the daughter of Pe-da'iah of Ru'mah.

37 And he did *that which was* evil in the sight of the LORD, according to all that his fathers had done.

CHAPTER 24

IN his days Neb-u-chad-nez'zar king of Bab'y-lon came up, and Je-hoi'a-kim became his servant three years: then he turned and rebelled against him.

2 And the LORD sent against him <u>bands</u> of the Chal'dees, and <u>bands</u> of the Syr'i-ans, and <u>bands</u> of the Mo'ab-ites, and <u>bands</u> of the children of Am'mon, and sent them against Ju'dah to destroy it, according to the word of the LORD, which He spoke by His servants the prophets.   raiders

3 Surely at the commandment of the LORD came *this* upon Ju'dah, to remove *them* out of His sight, for the sins of Ma-nas'seh, according to all that he did;

4 And also for the innocent blood that he shed: for he filled Je-ru'sa-lem with innocent blood; which the LORD would not pardon.

5 Now the rest of the acts of Je-hoi'a-kim, and all that he did, *are* they not written in the book of the chronicles of the kings of Ju'dah?

6 So Je-hoi'a-kim slept with his fathers: and Je-hoi'a-chin his son reigned in his stead.

7 And the king of E'gypt came not again any more out of his land: for the king of Bab'y-lon had taken from the river of E'gypt to the river Eu-phra'tes all that pertained to the king of E'gypt.

8 Je-hoi'a-chin *was* eighteen years old when he began to reign, and he reigned in Je-ru'sa-lem three months. And his mother's name *was* Ne-hush'ta, the daughter of El'na-than of Je-ru'sa-lem.

9 And he did *that which was* evil in the sight of the LORD, according to all that his father had done.

10 At that time the servants of Neb-u-chad-nez'zar king of Bab'y-lon came up against Je-ru'sa-lem, and the city was besieged.

11 And Neb-u-chad-nez'zar king of Bab'y-lon came against the city, and his servants did besiege it.

12 And Je-hoi'a-chin the king of Ju'dah went out to the king of Bab'y-lon, he, and his mother, and his servants, and his princes, and his officers: and the king of Bab'y-lon took him in the eighth year of his reign.

13 And he carried out from there all the treasures of the house of the LORD, and the treasures of the king's house, and cut in pieces all the vessels of gold which Sol'o-mon king of Is'ra-el had made in the temple of the LORD, as the LORD had said.

14 And he carried away all Je-ru'sa-lem, and all the princes, and all the mighty men of valor, *even* ten thousand captives, and all the craftsmen and smiths: none remained, save the poorest sort of the people of the land. led

15 And he carried away Je-hoi'a-chin to Bab'y-lon, and the king's mother, and the king's wives, and his officers, and the mighty of the land, *those* carried he into captivity from Je-ru'sa-lem to Bab'y-lon.

16 And all the men of might, *even* seven thousand, and craftsmen and smiths a thousand, all *that were* strong *and* apt for war, even them the king of Bab'y-lon brought captive to Bab'y-lon. fit

17 And the king of Bab'y-lon made Mat-ta-ni'ah his father's brother king in his stead, and changed his name to Zed-e-ki'ah.

18 Zed-e-ki'ah *was* twenty and one years old when he began to reign, and he reigned eleven years in Je-ru'sa-lem. And his mother's name *was* Ha-mu'tal, the daughter of Jer-e-mi'ah of Lib'nah.

19 And he did *that which was* evil in the sight of the LORD, according to all that Je-hoi'a-kim had done.

20 For through the anger of the LORD it came to pass in Je-ru'sa-lem and Ju'-dah, until He had cast them out from his presence, that Zed-e-ki'ah rebelled against the king of Bab'y-lon.

CHAPTER 25

AND it came to pass in the ninth year of his reign, in the tenth month, in the tenth *day* of the month, *that* Neb-u-chad-nez'zar king of Bab'y-lon came, he, and all his host, against Je-ru'sa-lem, and pitched against it; and they built forts against it round about. rule - camped

2 And the city was besieged to the eleventh year of king Zed-e-ki'ah.

3 And on the ninth *day* of the *fourth* month the famine prevailed in the city, and there was no bread for the people of the land.

4 And the city was broken up, and all the men of war *fled* by night by the way of the gate between two walls, which *is* by the king's garden: (now the Chal'dees *were* against the city round about:) and *the king* went the way toward the plain.

5 And the army of the Chal'dees pursued after the king, and overtook him in the plains of Jer'i-cho: and all his army were scattered from him.

6 So they took the king, and brought him up to the king of Bab'y-lon to Rib'lah; and they gave judgment upon him.

7 And they slew the sons of Zed-e-ki'ah before his eyes, and put out the eyes of Zed-e-ki'ah, and bound him with fetters of brass, and carried him to Bab'y-lon. bronze

8 And in the fifth month, on the

seventh *day* of the month, which *is* the nineteenth year of king Neb-u-chad-nez'zar king of Bab'y-lon, came Neb'u-zar-a'dan, captain of the guard, a servant of the king of Bab'y-lon, unto Je-ru'sa-lem:

9 And he burned the house of the LORD, and the king's house, and all the houses of Je-ru'sa-lem, and every great *man's* house burned he with fire.

10 And all the army of the Chal'dees, that *were with* the captain of the guard, broke down the walls of Je-ru'sa-lem round about.

11 Now the rest of the people *that were* left in the city, and the fugitives that fell away to the king of Bab'y-lon, with the remnant of the multitude, did Neb'u-zar-a'dan the captain of the guard carry away.

12 But the captain of the guard left of the poor of the land *to be* vinedressers and husbandmen. farmers

13 And the pillars of brass that *were* in the house of the LORD, and the bases, and the brazen sea that *was* in the house of the LORD, did the Chal'dees break in pieces, and carried the brass of them to Bab'y-lon.   bronze

14 And the pots, and the shovels, and the snuffers, and the spoons, and all the vessels of brass wherewith they ministered, took they away.

15 And the firepans, and the bowls, *and* such things as *were* of gold, *in* gold, and of silver, *in* silver, the captain of the guard took away.

16 The two pillars, one sea, and the bases which Sol'o-mon had made for the house of the LORD; the brass of all these vessels was without weight.

17 The height of the one pillar *was* eighteen cubits, and the chapiter upon it *was* brass: and the height of the chapiter three cubits; and the wreathen work, and pomegranates upon the chapiter round about, all of brass: and like to these had the second pillar with wreathen work.   capital - decorated

18 And the captain of the guard took Ser-a-i'ah the chief priest, and Zeph-a-ni'ah the second priest, and the three keepers of the door:

19 And out of the city he took an officer that was set over the men of war, and five men of them that were in the king's presence, which were found in the city, and the principal scribe of the host, which mustered the people of the land, and threescore men of the people of the land *that were* found in the city:

20 And Neb'u-zar-a'dan captain of the guard took these, and brought them to the king of Bab'y-lon to Rib'lah:

21 And the king of Bab'y-lon smote them, and slew them at Rib'lah in the land of Ha'math. So Ju'dah was carried away out of their land. attacked

22 And *as for* the people that remained in the land of Ju'dah, whom Neb-u-chad-nez'zar king of Bab'y-lon had left, even over them he made Ged-a-li'ah the son of A-hi'kam, the son of Sha'phan, ruler.

23 And when all the captains of the armies, they and their men, heard that the king of Bab'y-lon had made Ged-a-li'ah governor, there came to Ged-a-li'ah to Miz'pah, even Ish'ma-el the son

of Neth-a-ni'ah, and Jo-ha'nan the son of Ca-re'ah, and Ser-a-i'ah the son of Tan'hu-meth the Ne-toph'a-thite, and Ja-az-a-ni'ah the son of a Ma-ach'a-thite, they and their men.

24 And Ged-a-li'ah swear to them, and to their men, and said to them, Fear not to be the servants of the Chal'dees: dwell in the land, and serve the king of Bab'y-lon; and it shall be well with you.

25 But it came to pass in the seventh month, that Ish'ma-el the son of Neth-a-ni'ah, the son of E-lish'a-ma, of the <u>seed royal</u>, came, and ten men with him, and <u>smote</u> Ged-a-li'ah, that he died, and the Jews and the Chal'dees that were with him at Miz'pah. _{royal family - struck}

royal family - struck

26 And all the people, both small and great, and the captains of the armies, arose, and came to E'gypt: for they were afraid of the Chal'dees.

27 And it came to pass in the seven and thirtieth year of the captivity of Je-hoi'a-chin king of Ju'dah, in the twelfth month, on the seven and twentieth *day* of the month, *that* E'vil-me-ro'dach king of Bab'y-lon in the year that he began to reign did <u>lift up the head of</u> Je-hoi'a-chin king of Ju'dah out of prison;   release

28 And he spoke kindly to him, and set his throne above the throne of the kings that *were* with him in Bab'y-lon;

29 And changed his prison garments: and he <u>did eat bread continually before</u> him all the days of his life.   had his meals with

30 And his allowance *was* a continual allowance given him of the king, a daily rate for every day, all the days of his life.

1 AND 2 CHRONICLES

OUTLINE

SURVEY

In the Hebrew Scriptures, our two Books of Chronicles were originally one. The translators of the Greek Septuagint (about 200 B.C.) were the first to make the division. Jerome (d. A.D. 420) adopted this division in the Latin Vulgate. The Hebrew title was "Dibrey hay-yamim," that is, "Acts of the Days," or record of daily happenings. The Septuagint calls Chronicles "Paraleipomena," meaning "things omitted" in the Books of Samuel and Kings. Chronicles, however, often deals with the same facts as these books, but presents them with a different aim and in a different manner. The title *Chronicles* was adopted from Jerome's term *Chronicon*. It is not an unsuitable name.

It seems clear that when the chronicler set himself to cover the same ground as Samuel and Kings, he desired to present from his own point of view the history of God's people from the days of Samuel to the Captivity. His nation needed rebuilding on a solid spiritual foundation, for their long captivity had caused a serious break in their relationship to the ideals and traditions of their own people. Formerly, they had belonged to a theocracy where the civil and religious rulers were equally expected to honor God's truth and law.

Now, under the Persian monarchy, the king was a foreigner and a pagan who knew not the God of Israel. Only through a vigorous and strict ecclesiastical organization could the religious unity of the nation be maintained. The Jews felt increasingly that the promised perpetual Davidic sovereignty was concerned with a spiritual rather than a secular kingdom. Hence the writing of the Book of Chronicles. It was not a case of a crafty priestly caste imposing their ideas as against the prophets, as liberal critics used to declare. Those who had returned from the Captivity must be made to see their proper connection with the Lord's people.

After recounting the history of man before David's time, the chronicler shows the higher meaning of the promises made to David's line, especially in regard to the coming Messiah. The past attitude of kings to religious matters is emphasized rather than their civil undertakings. The immense importance of the temple, the priesthood, the religious rites, and the moral law is stressed. It is shown that when the kings dishonor God's law, signal punishment fell upon them, while those who honor God's ordinances prospered. The Book of Chronicles is markedly didactic and dwells upon the blessings which follow on a genuine religious life. It must have had an uplifting effect on the national religion. Only such parts of their history as illustrated the ecclesiastical (which was now the only sacred sphere) were dwelt upon; the story of the ten apostate tribes, for example, is dropped as not being conducive to spiritual uplift.

AUTHOR

The Books of Chronicles, Ezra, and Nehemiah are closely connected, and breathe the same spirit. Chronicles is the antecedent of the other two, which deal with the events after the Captivity. The Talmud, and most Jewish writers, as well as the Fathers of the Christian Church, ascribed Chronicles to Ezra. The Books of Chronicles and Ezra are similar in diction and outlook. It has been objected that Chronicles contains accounts of events later than Ezra's time. We may well accept Ezra as the main author (or compiler), even if some additions were made later, although many conservative scholars see no need to acknowledge such additions.

The Book of Chronicles was compiled from a wealth of historical data in earlier registers and records, besides Samuel and Kings. A careful study of the book has led many trustworthy scholars to place its date between 430 and 400 B.C. There is no need to postulate a later date.

A.M.R.

THE FIRST BOOK OF
CHRONICLES

Genealogies and
the Reign of David

CHAPTER 1

A D'AM, Sheth, E'nosh,
2 Ke'nan, Ma-ha'la-le-el, Je'red,
3 He'noch, Me-thu'se-lah, La'mech,
4 No'ah, Shem, Ham, and Ja'pheth.
5 The sons of Ja'pheth; Go'mer, and
Ma'gog, and Mad'a-i, and Ja'van, and
Tu'bal, and Me'shech, and Ti'ras.
6 And the sons of Go'mer; Ash'che-
naz, and Ri'phath, and To-gar'mah.
7 And the sons of Ja'van; E-li'shah, and
Tar'shish, Kit'tim, and Dod'a-nim.
8 The sons of Ham; Cush, and Miz'ra-
im, Put, and Ca'naan.
9 And the sons of Cush; Se'ba, and
Hav'i-lah, and Sab'ta, and Ra'a-mah,
and Sab'te-cha. And the sons of Ra'a-
mah; She'ba, and De'dan.
10 And Cush fathered Nim'rod: he
began to be mighty upon the earth.
11 And Miz'ra-im fathered Lu'dim,
and An'a-mim, and Le'ha-bim, and
Naph'tu-him,
12 And Path-ru'sim, and Cas'lu-him, (of
whom came the Phi-lis'tines,) and
Caph'tho-rim.
13 And Ca'naan fathered Zi'don his
firstborn, and Heth,
14 The Jeb'u-site also, and the Am'or-
ite, and the Gir'ga-shite,
15 And the Hi'vite, and the Ark'ite, and
the Sin'ite,
16 And the Ar'vad-ite, and the Zem'a-
rite, and the Ha'math-ite.

17 The sons of Shem; E'lam, and
Assh'ur, and Ar-phax'ad, and Lud, and
A'ram, and Uz, and Hul, and Ge'ther,
and Me'shech.
18 And Ar-phax'ad fathered She'lah,
and She'lah begat E'ber.
19 And to E'ber were born two sons:
the name of the one *was* Pe'leg; because in his days the earth was divided: and his brother's name *was*
Jok'tan.
20 And Jok'tan fathered Al-mo'dad,
and She'leph, and Ha'zar-ma'veth,
and Je'rah,
21 Ha-do'ram also, and U'zal, and
Dik'lah,
22 And E'bal, and A-bim'a-el, and
She'ba,
23 And O'phir, and Hav'i-lah, and
Jo'bab. All these *were* the sons of
Jok'tan.
24 Shem, Ar-phax'ad, She'lah,
25 E'ber, Pe'leg, Re'u,
26 Se'rug, Na'hor, Te'rah,
27 A'bram; the same *is* A'bra-ham.
28 The sons of A'bra-ham; I'saac, and
Ish'ma-el.
29 These *are* their generations: The
firstborn of Ish'ma-el, Ne-ba'ioth; then
Ke'dar, and Ad'be-el, and Mib'sam,
30 Mish'ma, and Du'mah, Mas'sa,
Ha'dad, and Te'ma,
31 Je'tur, Na'phish, and Ked'e-mah.
These are the sons of Ish'ma-el.

32 Now the sons of Ke-tu'rah, A'bra-ham's concubine: she bare Zim'ran, and Jok'shan, and Me'dan, and Mid'i-an, and Ish'bak, and Shu'ah. And the sons of Jok'shan; She'ba, and De'dan.

33 And the sons of Mid'i-an; E'phah, and E'pher, and He'noch, and A-bi'da, and El'da-ah. All these *are* the sons of Ke-tu'rah.

34 And A'bra-ham fathered I'saac. The sons of I'saac; E'sau and Is'ra-el.

35 The sons of E'sau; El'i-phaz, Reu'el, and Je'ush, and Ja-a'lam, and Ko'rah.

36 The sons of El'i-phaz; Te'man, and O'mar, Ze'phi, and Ga'tam, Ke'naz, and Tim'na, and Am'a-lek.

37 The sons of Reu'el; Na'hath, Ze'rah, Sham'mah, and Miz'zah.

38 And the sons of Se'ir; Lo'tan, and Sho'bal, and Zib'e-on, and A'nah, and Di'shon, and E'zer, and Di'shan.

39 And the sons of Lo'tan; Ho'ri, and Ho'mam: and Tim'na *was* Lo'tan's sister.

40 The sons of Sho'bal; A-li'an, and Man'a-hath, and E'bal, She'phi, and O'nam. And the sons of Zib'e-on; A-i'ah, and A'nah.

41 The sons of A'nah; Di'shon. And the sons of Di'shon; Am'ram, and Esh'ban, and Ith'ran, and Che'ran.

42 The sons of E'zer; Bil'han, and Za'van, *and* Ja'kan. The sons of Di'shan; Uz, and A'ran.

43 Now these *are* the kings that reigned in the land of E'dom before *any* king reigned over the children of Is'ra-el; Be'la the son of Be'or: and the name of his city *was* Din'ha-bah.

44 And when Be'la was dead, Jo'bab the son of Ze'rah of Boz'rah reigned in his stead.

45 And when Jo'bab was dead, Hu'sham of the land of the Te'man-ites reigned in his stead. _{place}

46 And when Hu'sham was dead, Ha'dad the son of Be'dad, which smote Mid'i-an in the field of Mo'ab, reigned in his stead: and the name of his city *was* A'vith. _{defeated}

47 And when Ha'dad was dead, Sam'lah of Mas're-kah reigned in his stead.

48 And when Sam'lah was dead, Sha'ul of Re-ho'both by the river reigned in his stead.

49 And when Sha'ul was dead, Ba'al-ha'nan the son of Ach'bor reigned in his stead.

50 And when Ba'al-ha'nan was dead, Ha'dad reigned in his stead: and the name of his city *was* Pa'i; and his wife's name *was* Me-het'a-bel, the daughter of Ma'tred, the daughter of Mez'a-hab.

51 Ha'dad died also. And the chiefs of E'dom were; chief Tim'nah, chief A-li'ah, chief Je'theth,

52 Chief A-ho-lib'a-mah, chief E'lah, chief Pi'non,

53 Chief Ke'naz, chief Te'man, chief Mib'zar,

54 Chief Mag'di-el, chief I'ram. These *are* the chiefs of E'dom.

CHAPTER 2

THESE *are* the sons of Is'ra-el; Reu'ben, Sim'e-on, Le'vi, and Ju'dah, Is'sa-char, and Zeb'u-lun, _{Jacob}

2 Dan, Jo'seph, and Ben'ja-min, Naph'ta-li, Gad, and Ash'er.

3 The sons of Ju'dah; Er, and O'nan, and She'lah: *which* three were born to him of the daughter of Shu'a the Ca'naan-it-ess. And Er, the firstborn of Ju'dah, was evil in the sight of the LORD; and he slew him.

4 And Ta'mar his daughter in law bare him Pha'rez and Ze'rah. All the sons of Ju'dah *were* five.

5 The sons of Pha'rez; Hez'ron, and Ha'mul.

6 And the sons of Ze'rah; Zim'ri, and E'than, and He'man, and Cal'col, and Da'ra: five of them in all.

7 And the sons of Car'mi; A'char, the troubler of Is'ra-el, who transgressed in the thing accursed.

8 And the sons of E'than; Az-a-ri'ah.

9 The sons also of Hez'ron, that were born to him; Je-rah'me-el, and Ram, and Che-lu'bai.

10 And Ram fathered Am-min'a-dab; and Am-min'a-dab fathered Nah'shon, prince of the children of Ju'dah;

11 And Nah'shon fathered Sal'ma, and Sal'ma fathered Bo'az,

12 And Bo'az fathered O'bed, and O'bed fathered Jes'se,

13 And Jes'se fathered his firstborn E-li'ab, and A-bin'a-dab the second, and Shim'ma the third,

14 Ne-than'e-el the fourth, Rad'da-i the fifth,

15 O'zem the sixth, Da'vid the seventh:

16 Whose sisters *were* Zer-u-i'ah, and Ab'i-gail. And the sons of Zer-u-i'ah; A-bish'a-i, and Jo'ab, and A'sa-hel, three.

17 And Ab'i-gail bare Am'a-sa: and the father of Am'a-sa *was* Je'ther the Ish'me-el-ite.

18 And Ca'leb the son of Hez'ron fathered *children* of A-zu'bah *his* wife, and of Je'ri-oth: her sons *are* these; Je'sher, and Sho'bab, and Ar'don.

19 And when A-zu'bah was dead, Ca'leb took to him Eph'rath, which bare him Hur.   married

20 And Hur fathered U'ri, and U'ri fathered Be-zal'e-el.

21 And afterward Hez'ron went in to the daughter of Ma'chir the father of Gil'e-ad, whom he married when he *was* threescore years old; and she bare him Se'gub.   60

22 And Se'gub fathered Ja'ir, who had three and twenty cities in the land of Gil'e-ad.

23 And he took Ge'shur, and A'ram, with the towns of Ja'ir, from them, with Ke'nath, and the towns thereof, *even* threescore cities. All these *belonged to* the sons of Ma'chir the father of Gil'e-ad.

24 And after that Hez'ron was dead in Ca'leb-eph'ra-tah, then A-bi'ah Hez'ron's wife bare him Ash'ur the father of Te-ko'a.

25 And the sons of Je-rah'me-el the firstborn of Hez'ron were, Ram the firstborn, and Bu'nah, and O'ren, and O'zem, *and* A-hi'jah.

26 Je-rah'me-el had also another wife, whose name *was* At'a-rah; she *was* the mother of O'nam.

27 And the sons of Ram the firstborn

of Je-rah'me-el were, Ma'az, and Ja'min, and E'ker.

28 And the sons of O'nam were, Sham'ma-i, and Ja'da. And the sons of Sham'ma-i; Na'dab, and Ab'i-shur.

29 And the name of the wife of Ab'i-shur *was* Ab-i-ha'il, and she bare him Ah'ban, and Mo'lid.

30 And the sons of Na'dab; Se'led, and Ap'pa-im: but Se'led died without children. ^sons^

31 And the sons of Ap'pa-im; Ish'i. And the sons of Ish'i; She'shan. And the children of She'shan; Ah'lai.

32 And the sons of Ja'da the brother of Sham'ma-i; Je'ther, and Jon'a-than: and Je'ther died without children.

33 And the sons of Jon'a-than; Pe'leth, and Za'za. These were the sons of Je-rah'me-el.

34 Now She'shan had no sons, but daughters. And She'shan had a servant, an E-gyp'tian, whose name *was* Jar'ha.

35 And She'shan gave his daughter to Jar'ha his servant to wife; and she bare him At'tai. ^in marriage^

36 And At'tai fathered Na'than, and Na'than fathered Za'bad,

37 And Za'bad fathered Eph'lal, and Eph'lal fathered O'bed,

38 And O'bed fathered Je'hu, and Je'hu fathered Az-a-ri'ah,

39 And Az-a-ri'ah fathered He'lez, and He'lez fathered E-le'a-sah,

40 And E-le'a-sah fathered Si'sam'a-i, and Si'sam'a-i fathered Shal'lum,

41 And Shal'lum fathered Jek-a-mi'ah, and Jek-a-mi'ah fathered E-lish'a-ma.

42 Now the sons of Ca'leb the brother of Je-rah'me-el *were*, Me'sha his firstborn, which *was* the father of Ziph; and the sons of Ma-re'shah the father of He'bron.

43 And the sons of He'bron; Ko'rah, and Tap'pu-ah, and Re'kem, and She'ma.

44 And She'ma fathered Ra'ham, the father of Jor'ko-am: and Re'kem fathered Sham'ma-i.

45 And the son of Sham'ma-i *was* Ma'on: and Ma'on *was* the father of Beth'-zur.

46 And E'phah, Ca'leb's concubine, bare Ha'ran, and Mo'za, and Ga'zez: and Ha'ran fathered Ga'zez.

47 And the sons of Jah'da-i; Re'gem, and Jo'tham, and Ge'sham, and Pe'let, and E'phah, and Sha'aph.

48 Ma'a-chah, Ca'leb's concubine, bare She'ber, and Tir'ha-nah.

49 She bare also Sha'aph the father of Mad-man'nah, She'va the father of Mach'be-nah, and the father of Gib'e-a: and the daughter of Ca'leb *was* Ach'sa.

50 These were the sons of Ca'leb the son of Hur, the firstborn of Eph'ra-tah; Sho'bal the father of Kir'jath-je'a-rim,

51 Sal'ma the father of Beth'-le-hem, Ha'reph the father of Beth-ga'der.

52 And Sho'bal the father of Kir'jath-je'a-rim had sons; Har'o-eh, *and* half of the Ma-na'heth-ites.

53 And the families of Kir'jath-je'a-rim; the Ithrites, and the Pu'hites, and the Shu'math-ites, and the Mish'ra-ites; of them came the Za're-ath-ites, and the Esh'ta-ul-ites.

54 The sons of Sal'ma; Beth'-le-hem, and the Ne-toph'a-thites, At'a-roth, the house of Jo'ab, and half of the Ma-na'heth-ites, the Zo'rites.

55 And the families of the scribes which dwelled at Ja'bez; the Ti'rath-ites, the Shim'e-ath-ites, *and* Su'chath-ites. These *are* the Ken-ites that came of He'math, the father of the house of Re'chab.

CHAPTER 3

NOW these were the sons of Da'vid, which were born to him in He'bron; the firstborn Am'non, of A-hin'o-am the Jez're-el-it-ess; the second Dan'iel, of Ab'i-gail the Car'mel-it-ess:

2 The third, Ab'sa-lom the son of Ma'a-chah the daughter of Tal'mai king of Ge'shur: the fourth, Ad-o-ni'jah the son of Hag'gith:

3 The fifth, Sheph-a-ti'ah of Ab'i-tal: the sixth, Ith're-am by Eg'lah his wife.

4 *These* six were born to him in He'bron; and there he reigned seven years and six months: and in Je-ru'sa-lem he reigned thirty and three years.

5 And these were born to him in Je-ru'sa-lem; Shim'e-a, and Sho'bab, and Na'than, and Sol'o-mon, four, of Bath'-shu-a the daughter of Am'mi-el:

6 Ib'har also, and E-lish'a-ma, and E-liph'e-let,

7 And No'gah, and Ne'pheg, and Ja-phi'a,

8 And E-lish'a-ma, and E-li'a-da, and E-liph'e-let, nine.

9 *These were* all the sons of Da'vid, beside the sons of the concubines, and Ta'mar their sister.

10 And Sol'o-mon's son *was* Re-ho-bo'am, A-bi'a his son, A'sa his son, Je-hosh'a-phat his son,

11 Jo'ram his son, A-ha-zi'ah his son, Jo'ash his son,

12 Am-a-zi'ah his son, Az-a-ri'ah his son, Jo'tham his son,

13 A'haz his son, Hez-e-ki'ah his son, Ma-nas'seh his son,

14 A'mon his son, Jo-si'ah his son.

15 And the sons of Jo-si'ah *were*, the firstborn Jo-ha'nan, the second Je-hoi'a-kim, the third Zed-e-ki'ah, the fourth Shal'lum.

16 And the sons of Je-hoi'a-kim: Jec-o-ni'ah his son, Zed-e-ki'ah his son.

17 And the sons of Jec-o-ni'ah; As'sir, Sa-la'-thi-el his son,

18 Mal-chi'ram also, and Pe-da'iah, and She-na'zar, Jec-a-mi'ah, Hosh'a-ma, and Ned-a-bi'ah.

19 And the sons of Pe-da'iah *were*, Ze-rub'ba-bel, and Shim'e-i: and the sons of Ze-rub'ba-bel; Me-shul'lam, and Han-a-ni'ah, and Shel'o-mith their sister:

20 And Ha-shu'bah, and O'hel, and Ber-e-chi'ah, and Has-a-di'ah, Ju'shab-he'sed, five.

21 And the sons of Han-a-ni'ah; Pel-a-ti'ah, and Je'sa'iah: the sons of Reph-a-i'ah, the sons of Ar'nan, the sons of O-ba-di'ah, the sons of Shech-a'ni'ah.

22 And the sons of Shech-a'ni'ah; Shem-a-i'ah; and the sons of Shem-a-i'ah; Hat'tush, and Ig'e-al, and Ba-ri'ah, and Ne-a-ri'ah, and Sha'phat, six.

23 And the sons of Ne-a-ri'ah; El-i-o-

e'na-i, and Hez-e-ki'ah, and Az'ri-kam, three.

24 And the sons of El-i-o-e'na-i *were*, Hod-a-i'ah, and E-li'a-shib, and Pel-a-i'ah, and Ak'kub, and Jo-ha'nan, and Dal-a-i'ah, and An-a'ni, seven.

CHAPTER 4

THE sons of Ju'dah; Pha'rez, Hez'ron, and Car'mi, and Hur, and Sho'bal.

2 And Re-a-i'ah the son of Sho'bal fathered Ja'hath; and Ja'hath fathered A-hu'ma-i and La'had. These *are* the families of the Zo'rath-ites.

3 And these *were of* the father of E'tam; Jez're-el, and Ish'ma, and Id'bash: and the name of their sister *was* Haz-e-lel-po'ni:

4 And Pe-nu'el the father of Ge'dor, and E'zer the father of Hu'shah. These *are* the sons of Hur, the firstborn of Eph'ra-tah, the father of Beth'-le-hem.

5 And Ash'ur the father of Te-ko'a had two wives, He'lah and Na'a-rah.

6 And Na'a-rah bare him A-hu'zam, and He'pher, and Tem'e-ni, and Ha-a-hash'ta-ri. These *were* the sons of Na'a-rah.

7 And the sons of He'lah *were*, Ze'reth, and Jez'o-ar, and Eth-nan.

8 And Coz fathered A'nub, and Zo-be'bah, and the families of A-har'-hel the son of Ha'rum.

9 And Ja'bez was more <u>honorable</u> than his brethren: and his mother called his name Ja'bez, saying, Because I bare him with sorrow.   famous

10 And Ja'bez called on the God of Is'ra-el, saying, Oh that You would bless me indeed, and enlarge my <u>coast</u>, and that Your hand might be with me, and that You would keep *me* from evil, that it may not grieve me! And God granted him that which he requested.   territory

11 And Che'lub the brother of Shu'ah fathered Me'hir, which *was* the father of Esh'ton.

12 And Esh'ton fathered Beth-ra'pha, and Pa-se'ah, and Te-hin'nah the father of Ir-na'hash. These *are* the men of Re'chah.

13 And the sons of Ke'naz; Oth'ni-el, and Ser-a-i'ah: and the sons of Oth'ni-el; Ha'thath.

14 And Me-on'o-thai fathered Oph'rah: and Ser-a-i'ah fathered Jo'ab, the father of the <u>valley</u> of Char'a-shim; for they were craftsmen.   inhabitants

15 And the sons of Ca'leb the son of Je-phun'neh; I'ru, E'lah, and Na'am: and the sons of E'lah, even Ke'naz.

16 And the sons of Je-ha-le'le-el; Ziph, and Zi'phah, Tir'i-a, and A-sa're-el.

17 And the sons of Ez'ra *were*, Je'ther, and Me'red, and E'pher, and Ja'lon: and she bare Mir'i-am, and Sham'ma-i, and Ish'bah the father of Esh-te-mo'a.

18 And his wife Je-hi-di-jah bare Je'red the father of Ge'dor, and He'ber the father of So'cho, and Je-ku'thi-el the father of Za-no'ah. And these *are* the sons of Bith'i-ah the daughter of Pha'raoh, which Me'red took.

19 And the sons of *his* wife Ho-di'ah

the sister of Na'ham, the father of Kei'lah the Gar'mite, and Esh-te-mo'a the Ma-ach'a-thite.

20 And the sons of Shi'mon *were*, Am'non, and Rin'nah, Ben-ha'nan, and Ti'lon. And the sons of Ish'i *were*, Zo'heth, and Ben-zo'heth.

21 The sons of She'lah the son of Ju'dah *were*, Er the father of Le'cah, and La'a-dah the father of Ma-re'shah, and the families of the house of them that wrought fine linen, of the house of Ash-be'a,

22 And Jo'kim, and the men of Cho'ze-ba, and Jo'ash, and Sa'raph, who had the dominion in Mo'ab, and Jash'u-bi-le'hem. And *these are* ancient things.   records

23 These *were* the potters, and those that dwelled among plants and hedges: there they dwelled with the king for his work.

24 The sons of Sim'e-on *were*, Ne-mu'el, and Ja'min, Ja'rib, Ze'rah, *and* Sha'ul:

25 Shal'lum his son, Mib'sam his son, Mish'ma his son.

26 And the sons of Mish'ma; Ha-mu'el his son, Zac'chur his son, Shim'e-i his son.

27 And Shim'e-i had sixteen sons and six daughters; but his brethren had not many children, neither did all their family multiply, like to the children of Ju'dah.

28 And they dwelled at Be'er-she'ba, and Mol'a-dah, and Ha'zar-shu'al,

29 And at Bil'hah, and at E'zem, and at To'lad,

30 And at Beth-u'el, and at Hor'mah, and at Zik'lag,

31 And at Beth-mar'ca-both, and Ha'zar-su'sim, and at Beth-bir'e-i, and at Sha-a-ra'im. These *were* their cities to the reign of Da'vid.

32 And their villages *were*, E'tam, and A'in, Rim'mon, and To'chen, and A'shan, five cities:

33 And all their villages that *were* round about the same cities, to Ba'al. These *were* their habitations, and their genealogy.   _{settlements}

34 And Me-sho'bab, and Jam'lech, and Jo'shah the son of Am-a-zi'ah,

35 And Jo'el, and Je'hu the son of Jos-i-bi'ah, the son of Ser-a-i'ah, the son of A'si-el,

36 And El-i-o-e'na-i, and Ja-ak'o-bah, and Jesh-o-ha-i'ah, and A-sa-i'ah, and A-di'el, and Je-sim'i-el, and Be-na'iah,

37 And Zi'za the son of Shi'phi, the son of Al'lon, the son of Je-da'iah, the son of Shim'ri, the son of Shem-a-i'ah;

38 These mentioned by *their* names *were* princes in their families: and the house of their fathers increased greatly.   _{leaders}

39 And they went to the entrance of Ge'dor, *even* to the east side of the valley, to seek pasture for their flocks.

40 And they found fat pasture and good, and the land *was* wide, and quiet, and peaceable; for *they* of Ham had dwelled there of old.   _{rich}

41 And these written by name came in the days of Hez-e-ki'ah king of Ju'dah, and smote their tents, and the habitations that were found there, and destroyed them utterly to this day,

and dwelled in their <u>rooms</u>: because *there was* pasture there for their flocks. attacked - places

42 And *some* of them, *even* of the sons of Sim'e-on, five hundred men, went to mount Se'ir, having for their captains Pel-a-ti'ah, and Ne-a-ri'ah, and Reph-a-i'ah, and Uz'zi-el, the sons of Ish'i.

43 And they <u>smote</u> the rest of the Am'a-lek-ites that were escaped, and dwelled there to this day. destroyed

CHAPTER 5

NOW the sons of Reu'ben the firstborn of Is'ra-el, (for he *was* the firstborn; but, forasmuch as he <u>defiled</u> his father's bed, his birth-right was given to the sons of Jo'seph the son of Is'ra-el: and the genealogy is not to be reckoned af-ter the birthright. did evil on

2 For Ju'dah prevailed above his breth-ren, and of him *came* the chief ruler; but the <u>birthright</u> *was* Jo'seph's:) blessing

3 The sons, *I say*, of Reu'ben the first-born of Is'ra-el *were*, Ha'noch, and Pal'lu, Hez'ron, and Car'mi.

4 The sons of Jo'el; Shem-a-i'ah his son, Gog his son, Shim'e-i his son,

5 Mi'cah his son, Re-a-i'a his son, Ba'al his son,

6 Be-e'rah his son, whom Til'gath-pil-ne'ser king of As-syr'i-a carried away *captive*: he *was* prince of the Reu'ben-ites.

7 And his brethren by their families, when the genealogy of their genera-tions was reckoned, *were* the chief, Je-i'el, and Zech-a-ri'ah,

8 And Be'la the son of A'zaz, the son of She'ma, the son of Jo'el, who dwelled in Ar'o-er, even to Ne'bo and Ba'al-me-on:

9 And eastward he inhabited to the entering in of the wilderness from the river Eu-phra'tes: because their cattle were <u>multiplied</u> in the land of Gil'e-ad. increased

10 And in the days of Saul they made war with the Ha'gar-ites, who fell by their hand: and they dwelled in their tents throughout all the east *land* of Gil'e-ad.

11 And the children of Gad dwelled opposite them, in the land of Ba'shan to Sal'cah:

12 Jo'el the chief, and Sha'pham the next, and Ja-a'nai, and Sha'phat in Ba'shan.

13 And their brethren of the house of their fathers *were*, Mi'chael, and Me-shul'lam, and She'ba, and Jo'ra-i, and Ja'chan, and Zi'a, and He'ber, seven.

14 These *are* the children of Ab-i-ha'il the son of Hu'ri, the son of Ja-ro'ah, the son of Gil'e-ad, the son of Mi'chael, the son of Je-shish'a-i, the son of Jah'do, the son of Buz;

15 A'hi the son of Ab'di-el, the son of Gu'ni, chief of the house of their fa-thers.

16 And they dwelled in Gil'e-ad in Ba'shan, and in her towns, and in all the suburbs of Shar'on, upon their borders.

17 All these were reckoned by genealo-gies in the days of Jo'tham king of Ju'dah, and in the days of Jer-o-bo'am king of Is'ra-el.

18 The sons of Reu'ben, and the Gad'ites, and half the tribe of Ma-nas'seh, of <u>valiant</u> men, men able to bear

buckler and sword, and to shoot with bow, and skilful in war, *were* four and forty thousand seven hundred and three-score, that went out to the war. brave - shield

19 And they made war with the Ha'gar-ites, with Je'tur, and Ne'phish, and No'dab.

20 And they were helped against them, and the Ha'gar-ites were de-livered into their hand, and all that *were* with them: for they cried to God in the battle, and He was entreated of them; because they put their trust in Him.   Elohim^p.f. - answered

21 And they took away their cattle; of their camels fifty thousand, and of sheep two hundred and fifty thou-sand, and of asses two thousand, and of men an hundred thousand.

22 For there fell down many slain, because the war *was* of God. And they dwelled in their steads until the captivity.   places

23 And the children of the half tribe of Ma-nas'seh dwelled in the land: they increased from Ba'shan to Ba'al-her'mon and Se'nir, and to mount Her'mon.

24 And these *were* the heads of the house of their fathers, even E'pher, and Ish'i, and E-li'el, and Az'ri-el, and Jer-e-mi'ah, and Hod-a-vi'ah, and Jah'di-el, mighty men of valor, famous men, *and* heads of the house of their fathers.

25 And they transgressed against the God of their fathers, and went a whor-ing after the gods of the people of the land, whom God destroyed be-fore them.   Elohim^p.f. - played the harlot

26 And the God of Is'ra-el stirred up the spirit of Pul king of As-syr'i-a, and the spirit of Til'gath-pil-ne'ser king of As-syr'i-a, and he carried them away, even the Reu'ben-ites, and the Gad-ites, and the half tribe of Ma-nas'seh, and brought them to Ha'lah, and Ha'bor, and Ha'ra, and to the river Go'zan, to this day.   Elohim^p.f.

CHAPTER 6

THE sons of Le'vi; Ger'shon, Ko'hath, and Me-ra'ri.

2 And the sons of Ko'hath; Am'ram, Iz'har, and He'bron, and Uz'zi-el.

3 And the children of Am'ram; Aar'on, and Mo'ses, and Mir'i-am. The sons also of Aar'on; Na'dab, and A-bi'hu, E-le-a'zar, and Ith'a-mar.

4 E-le-a'zar fathered Phin'e-has, Phin'e-has fathered A-bish'u-a,

5 And A-bish'u-a fathered Buk'ki, and Buk'ki fathered Uz'zi,

6 And Uz'zi fathered Zer-a-hi'ah, and Zer-a-hi'ah fathered Me-ra'ioth,

7 Me-ra'ioth fathered Am-a-ri'ah, and Am-a-ri'ah fathered A-hi'tub,

8 And A-hi'tub fathered Za'dok, and Za'dok fathered A-him'a-az,

9 And A-him'a-az fathered Az-a-ri'ah, and Az-a-ri'ah fathered Jo-ha'nan,

10 And Jo-ha'nan fathered Az-a-ri'ah, (he *it is* that executed the priest's office in the temple that Sol'o-mon built in Je-ru'sa-lem:)   served

11 And Az-a-ri'ah fathered Am-a-ri'ah, and Am-a-ri'ah fathered A-hi'tub,

12 And A-hi'tub fathered Za'dok, and Za'dok fathered Shal'lum,

13 And Shal'lum fathered Hil-ki'ah, and Hil-ki'ah fathered Az-a-ri'ah,

14 And Az-a-ri'ah fathered Ser-a-i'ah, and Ser-a-i'ah fathered Je-hoz'a-dak,

15 And Je-hoz'a-dak went *into captivity*, when the LORD carried away Ju'dah and Je-ru'sa-lem by the hand of Neb-u-chad-nez'zar.

16 The sons of Le'vi; Ger'shom, Ko'hath, and Me-ra'ri.

17 And these *be* the names of the sons of Ger'shom; Lib'ni, and Shim'e-i.

18 And the sons of Ko'hath *were*, Am'ram, and Iz'har, and He'bron, and Uz'zi-el.

19 The sons of Me-ra'ri; Mah'li, and Mu'shi. And these *are* the families of the Le'vites according to their fathers.

20 Of Ger'shom; Lib'ni his son, Ja'hath his son, Zim'mah his son,

21 Jo'ah his son, Id'do his son, Ze'rah his son, Je-at'e-rai his son.

22 The sons of Ko'hath; Am-min'a-dab his son, Ko'rah his son, As'sir his son,

23 El'ka-nah his son, and E-bi'a-saph his son, and As'sir his son,

24 Ta'hath his son, U'ri-el his son, Uz-zi'ah his son, and Sha'ul his son.

25 And the sons of El'ka-nah; A-mas'a-i, and A-hi'moth.

26 *As for* El'ka-nah: the sons of El'ka-nah; Zo'phai his son, and Na'hath his son,

27 E-li'ab his son, Jer'o-ham his son, El'ka-nah his son.

28 And the sons of Sam'u-el; the firstborn Vash'ni, and A-bi'ah.

29 The sons of Me-ra'ri; Mah'li, Lib'-ni his son, Shim'e-i his son, Uz'za his son,

30 Shim'e-a his son, Hag-gi'ah his son, A-sa-i'ah his son.

31 And these *are they* whom Da'vid set over the service of song in the house of the LORD, after that the ark had rest.

32 And they ministered before the dwelling place of the tabernacle of the congregation with singing, until Sol'o-mon had built the house of the LORD in Je-ru'sa-lem: and *then* they waited on their office according to their order.   performed - regulation

33 And these *are* they that waited with their children. Of the sons of the Ko'hath-ites: He'man a singer, the son of Jo'el, the son of She-mu'el,   served

34 The son of El'ka-nah, the son of Jer'o-ham, the son of E-li'el, the son of To'ah,

35 The son of Zuph, the son of El'ka-nah, the son of Ma'hath, the son of A-mas'a-i,

36 The son of El'ka-nah, the son of Jo'el, the son of Az-a-ri'ah, the son of Zeph-a-ni'ah,

37 The son of Ta'hath, the son of As'sir, the son of E-bi'a-saph, the son of Ko'rah,

38 The son of Iz'har, the son of Ko'hath, the son of Le'vi, the son of Is'ra-el.

39 And his brother A'saph, who stood on his right hand, *even* A'saph the son of Ber-a-chi'ah, the son of Shim'e-a,

40 The son of Mi'chael, the son of Ba-a-se'iah, the son of Mal-chi'ah,

41 The son of Eth'ni, the son of Ze'rah, the son of Ad-a-i'ah,

42 The son of E'than, the son of Zim'mah, the son of Shim'e-i,

43 The son of Ja'hath, the son of Ger'shom, the son of Le'vi.

44 And their brethren the sons of Me-ra'ri *stood* on the left hand: E'than the son of Kish'i, the son of Ab'di, the son of Mal'luch,

45 The son of Hash-a-bi'ah, the son of Am-a-zi'ah, the son of Hil-ki'ah,

46 The son of Am'zi, the son of Ba'ni, the son of Sha'mer,

47 The son of Mah'li, the son of Mu'shi, the son of Me-ra'ri, the son of Le'vi.

48 Their brethren also the Le'vites *were* appointed to all manner of service of the tabernacle of the house of God.

49 But Aar'on and his sons offered upon the altar of the burned offering, and on the altar of incense, *and were appointed* for all the work of the *place* most holy, and to make an atonement for Is'ra-el, according to all that Mo'ses the servant of God had commanded.

50 And these *are* the sons of Aar'on; E-le-a'zar his son, Phin'e-has his son, A-bish'u-a his son,

51 Buk'ki his son, Uz'zi his son, Zer-a-hi'ah his son,

52 Me-ra'ioth his son, Am-a-ri'ah his son, A-hi'tub his son,

53 Za'dok his son, A-him'a-az his son.

54 Now these *are* their dwelling places throughout their <u>castles</u> in their <u>coasts</u>, of the sons of Aar'on, of the families of the Ko'hath-ites: for theirs was the lot. <small>camps - borders</small>

55 And they gave them He'bron in the land of Ju'dah, and the <u>suburbs</u> thereof round about it. <small>pasture land</small>

56 But the fields of the city, and the villages thereof, they gave to Ca'leb the son of Je-phun'neh.

57 And to the sons of Aar'on they gave the cities of Ju'dah, *namely*, He'bron, *the city* of refuge, and Lib'nah with her <u>suburbs</u>, and Jat'tir, and Esh-te-mo'a, with their <u>suburbs</u>,

58 And Hi'len with her <u>suburbs</u>, De'bir with her <u>suburbs</u>,

59 And A'shan with her <u>suburbs</u>, and Beth-she'mesh with her <u>suburbs</u>:

60 And out of the tribe of Ben'ja-min; Ge'ba with her <u>suburbs</u>, and Al'e-meth with her <u>suburbs</u>, and An'a-thoth with her <u>suburbs</u>. All their cities throughout their families *were* thirteen cities. <small>pasture lands</small>

61 And to the sons of Ko'hath, *which were* left of the family of that tribe, *were cities given* out of the half tribe, *namely, out of* the half *tribe* of Ma-nas'seh, by lot, ten cities.

62 And to the sons of Ger'shom throughout their families out of the tribe of Is'sa-char, and out of the tribe of Ash'er, and out of the tribe of Ma-nas'seh in Ba'shan, thirteen cities.

63 To the sons of Me-ra'ri *were given* by lot, throughout their families, out of the tribe of Reu'ben, and out of the tribe of Gad, and out of the tribe of Zeb'u-lun, twelve cities.

64 And the children of Is'ra-el gave to the Le'vites *these* cities with their <u>suburbs</u>.

65 And they <u>gave by lot</u> out of the tribe of the children of Ju'dah, and out

of the tribe of the children of Sim'e-on, and out of the tribe of the children of Ben'ja-min, these cities, which are called by *their* names. allotted

66 And *the residue* of the families of the sons of Ko'hath had cities of their <u>coasts</u> out of the tribe of E'phra-im. balance - territory

67 And they gave to them, *of* the cities of refuge, Shechem in mount E'phra-im with her <u>suburbs</u>; *they gave* also Ge'zer with her <u>suburbs</u>, pasture lands

68 And Jok'me-am with her <u>suburbs</u>, and Beth-ho'ron with her <u>suburbs</u>,

69 And Aij'a-lon with her <u>suburbs</u>, and Gath-rim'mon with her <u>suburbs</u>:

70 And out of the half tribe of Ma-nas'seh; A'ner with her <u>suburbs</u>, and Bil'e-am with her <u>suburbs</u>, for the family of the remnant of the sons of Ko'hath.

71 To the sons of Ger'shom *were given* out of the family of the half tribe of Ma-nas'seh, Go'lan in Ba'shan with her <u>suburbs</u>, and Ash'ta-roth with her <u>suburbs</u>:

72 And out of the tribe of Is'sa-char; Ke'desh with her <u>suburbs</u>, Dab'e-rath with her <u>suburbs</u>, pasture lands

73 And Ra'moth with her <u>suburbs</u>, and A'nem with her <u>suburbs</u>:

74 And out of the tribe of Ash'er; Ma'shal with her <u>suburbs</u>, and Ab'don with her <u>suburbs</u>, pasture lands

75 And Hu'kok with her <u>suburbs</u>, and Re'hob with her <u>suburbs</u>:

76 And out of the tribe of Naph'ta-li; Ke'desh in Gal'i-lee with her <u>suburbs</u>, and Ham'mon with her <u>suburbs</u>, and Kir-jath-a'im with her <u>suburbs</u>.

77 To the rest of the children of Me-ra'ri *were given* out of the tribe of Zeb'u-lun, Rim'mon with her <u>suburbs</u>, Ta'bor with her <u>suburbs</u>: pasture lands

78 And on the other side Jor'dan by Jer'i-cho, on the east side of Jor'dan, *were given them* out of the tribe of Reu'ben, Be'zer in the wilderness with her <u>suburbs</u>, and Jah'zah with her <u>suburbs</u>,

79 Ked'e-moth also with her <u>suburbs</u>, and Meph'a-ath with her <u>suburbs</u>:

80 And out of the tribe of Gad; Ra'moth in Gil'e-ad with her <u>suburbs</u>, and Ma-ha-na'im with her <u>suburbs</u>,

81 And Hesh'bon with her <u>suburbs</u>, and Ja'zer with her <u>suburbs</u>.

CHAPTER 7

NOW the sons of Is'sa-char *were*, To'la, and Pu'ah, Jash'ub, and Shim'rom, four.

2 And the sons of To'la; Uz'zi, and Reph-a-i'ah, and Je'ri-el, and Jah'ma-i, and Jib'sam, and She-mu'el, heads of their father's house, *to that is*, of To'la: *they were* valiant men of might in their generations; whose number *was* in the days of Da'vid two and twenty thousand and six hundred.

3 And the sons of Uz'zi; Iz-ra-hi'ah: and the sons of Iz-ra-hi'ah; Mi'chael, and O-ba-di'ah, and Jo'el, Ish-i'ah, five: all of them chief men.

4 And with them, by their generations, after the house of their fathers, *were* bands of soldiers for war, six and thirty thousand *men*: for they had many wives and sons.

5 And their brethren among all the

families of Is'sa-char *were* <u>valiant</u> men of might, reckoned in all by their genealogies fourscore and seven thousand.   strong

6 *The sons* of Ben'ja-min; Be'la, and Be'cher, and Je-di'a-el, three.

7 And the sons of Be'la; Ez'bon, and Uz'zi, and Uz'zi-el, and Jer'i-moth, and I'ri, five; heads of the house of *their* fathers, mighty men of valor; and were reckoned by their genealogies twenty and two thousand and thirty and four.

8 And the sons of Be'cher; Ze'mi-ra, and Jo'ash, and E-li-e'zer, and El-i-o-e'na-i, and Om'ri, and Jer'i-moth, and A-bi'ah, and An'a-thoth, and Al'a-meth. All these *are* the sons of Be'cher.

9 And the number of them, after their genealogy by their <u>generations</u>, heads of the house of their fathers, mighty men of valor, *was* twenty thousand and two hundred.   families

10 The sons also of Je-di'a-el; Bil'han: and the sons of Bil'han; Je'ush, and Ben'ja-min, and E'hud, and Che-na'a-nah, and Ze'than, and Thar'shish, and A-hish'a-har.

11 All these the sons of Je-di'a-el, by the heads of their fathers, mighty men of valor, *were* seventeen thousand and two hundred *soldiers*, fit to go out for war *and* battle.

12 Shup'pim also, and Hup'pim, the children of Ir, *and* Hu'shim, the sons of A'her.

13 The sons of Naph'ta-li; Jah'zi-el, and Gu'ni, and Je'zer, and Shal'lum, the sons of Bil'hah.

14 The sons of Ma-nas'seh; Ash'ri-el, whom she bare: (*but* his concubine the A'ram-it-ess bare Ma'chir the father of Gil'e-ad:

15 And Ma'chir took to wife *the sister* of Hup'pim and Shup'pim, whose sister's name *was* Ma'a-chah;) and the name of the second *was* Ze-lo'phe-had: and Ze-lo'phe-had had daughters.

16 And Ma'a-chah the wife of Ma'chir bare a son, and she called his name Pe'resh; and the name of his brother *was* She'resh; and his sons *were* U'lam and Ra'kem.

17 And the sons of U'lam; Be'dan. These *were* the sons of Gil'e-ad, the son of Ma'chir, the son of Ma-nas'seh.

18 And his sister Ham-mol'e-keth bare I'shod, and A-bi-e'zer, and Ma-ha'lah.

19 And the sons of She-mi'dah were, A-hi'an, and She'chem, and Lik'hi, and A'ni-am.

20 And the sons of E'phra-im; Shu'the-lah, and Be'red his son, and Ta'hath his son, and El'a-dah his son, and Ta'hath his son,

21 And Za'bad his son, and Shu'the-lah his son, and E'zer, and E'le-ad, whom the men of Gath *that were* born in *that* land slew, because they came down to <u>take away</u> their cattle.   steal

22 And E'phra-im their father mourned many days, and his brethren came to comfort him.

23 And when he went in to his wife, she conceived, and bare a son, and he called his name Be-ri'ah, because it went evil with his house.

24 (And his daughter *was* She'rah, who built Beth-ho'ron the <u>nether</u>, and the upper, and Uz'-zen-she'rah.)   lower

25 And Re'phah *was* his son, also Re'sheph, and Te'lah his son, and Ta'han his son,

26 La'a-dan his son, Am-mi'hud his son, E-lish'a-ma his son,

27 Non his son, Je-hosh'u-ah his son.

28 And their possessions and habitations *were*, Beth'-el and the towns thereof, and eastward Na'a-ran, and westward Ge'zer, with the towns thereof; She'chem also and the towns thereof, to Ga'za and the towns thereof:

29 And by the borders of the children of Ma-nas'seh, Beth-she'an and her towns, Ta'a-nach and her towns, Me-gid'do and her towns, Dor and her towns. In these dwelled the children of Jo'seph the son of Is'ra-el.

30 The sons of Ash'er; Im'nah, and Is'u-ah, and Ish'u-ai, and Be-ri'ah, and Se'rah their sister.

31 And the sons of Be-ri'ah; He'ber, and Mal'chi-el, who *is* the father of Bir'za-vith.

32 And He'ber fathered Japh'let, and Sho'mer, and Ho'tham, and Shu'a their sister.

33 And the sons of Japh'let; Pa'sach, and Bim'hal, and Ash'vath. These *are* the children of Japh'let.

34 And the sons of Sha'mer; A'hi, and Roh'gah, Je-hub'bah, and A'ram.

35 And the sons of his brother He'lem; Zo'phah, and Im'na, and She'lesh, and A'mal.

36 The sons of Zo'phah; Su'ah, and Har'ne-pher, and Shu'al, and Be'ri, and Im'rah,

37 Be'zer, and Hod, and Sham'ma, and Shil'shah, and Ith'ran, and Be-e'ra.

38 And the sons of Je'ther; Je-phun'neh, and Pis'pah, and A'ra.

39 And the sons of Ul'la; A'rah, and Han'i-el, and Re-zi'a.

40 All these *were* the children of Ash'er, heads of *their* father's house, choice *and* mighty men of valor, chief of the princes. And the number throughout the genealogy of them that were apt to the war *and* to battle *was* twenty and six thousand men.

CHAPTER 8

NOW Ben'ja-min fathered Be'la his firstborn, Ash'bel the second, and A-har'ah the third,

2 No'hah the fourth, and Ra'pha the fifth.

3 And the sons of Be'la were, Ad'dar, and Ge'ra, and A-bi'hud,

4 And A-bish'u-a, and Na'a-man, and A-ho'ah,

5 And Ge'ra, and She-phu'phan, and Hu'ram.

6 And these *are* the sons of E'hud: these are the heads of the fathers of the inhabitants of Ge'ba, and they re-moved them to Man'a-hath: _{exiled}

7 And Na'a-man, and A-hi'ah, and Ge'ra, he removed them, and fathered Uz'za, and A-hi'hud.

8 And Sha-ha-ra'im fathered *children* in the country of Mo'ab, after he had sent them away; Hu'shim and Ba'a-ra *were* his wives.

9 And he fathered of Ho'desh his wife, Jo'bab, and Zib'i-a, and Me'sha, and Mal'cham,

10 And Je'uz, and Shach-i'a, and Mir'ma. These *were* his sons, heads of the fathers.

11 And of Hu'shim he fathered Ab'i-tub, and El'pa-al.

12 The sons of El'pa-al; E'ber, and Mi'sham, and Sha'med, who built O'no, and Lod, with the towns thereof:

13 Be-ri'ah also, and She'ma, who *were* heads of the fathers of the inhabitants of Aij'a-lon, who drove away the inhabitants of Gath:

14 And A-hi'o, Sha'shak, and Jer'e-moth,

15 And Zeb-a-di'ah, and A'rad, and A'der,

16 And Mi'chael, and Is'pah, and Jo'ha, the sons of Be-ri'ah;

17 And Zeb-a-di'ah, and Me-shul'lam, and Hez'e-ki, and He'ber,

18 Ish'me-rai also, and Jez-li'ah, and Jo'bab, the sons of El'pa-al;

19 And Ja'kim, and Zich'ri, and Zab'di,

20 And E-li-e'na-i, and Zil'thai, and E-li'el,

21 And Ad-a-i'ah, and Ber-a-i'ah, and Shim'rath, the sons of Shim'hi;

22 And Ish'pan, and He'ber, and E-li'el,

23 And Ab'don, and Zich'ri, and Ha'nan,

24 And Han-a-ni'ah, and E'lam, and An-to-thi'jah,

25 And Iph-e-de'iah, and Pe-nu'el, the sons of Sha'shak;

26 And Sham-she-ra'i, and She-ha-ri'ah, and Ath-a-li'ah,

27 And Jar'e-si'ah, and E-li'ah, and Zich'ri, the sons of Jer'o-ham.

28 These *were* heads of the fathers, by their generations, chief *men*. These dwelled in Je-ru'sa-lem.

29 And at Gib'e-on dwelled the father of Gib'e-on; whose wife's name *was* Ma'a-chah:

30 And his firstborn son Ab'don, and Zur, and Kish, and Ba'al, and Na'dab,

31 And Ge'dor, and A-hi'o, and Za'cher.

32 And Mik'loth fathered Shim'e-ah. And these also dwelled with their brethren in Je-ru'sa-lem, opposite them.

33 And Ner fathered Kish, and Kish fathered Saul, and Saul fathered Jon'a-than, and Mal-chi-shu'a, and A-bin'a-dab, and Esh-ba'al.

34 And the son of Jon'a-than *was* Mer'ib-ba'al; and Mer'ib-ba'al fathered Mi'cah.

35 And the sons of Mi'cah *were*, Pi'thon, and Me'lech, and Ta're-a, and A'haz.

36 And A'haz fathered Je-ho'a-dah; and Je-ho'a-dah fathered Al'e-meth, and Az'ma-veth, and Zim'ri; and Zim'ri fathered Mo'za,

37 And Mo'za fathered Bin'e-a: Ra'pha *was* his son, E-le'a-sah his son, A'zel his son:

38 And A'zel had six sons, whose names *are* these, Az'ri-kam, Boch'e-ru, and Ish'ma-el, and She-a-ri'ah, and O-ba-di'ah, and Ha'nan. All these *were* the sons of A'zel.

39 And the sons of E'shek his brother *were*, U'lam his firstborn, Je'nush the second, and E-liph'e-let the third.

40 And the sons of U'lam were

mighty men of valor, archers, and had many sons, and sons' sons, an hundred and fifty. All these *are* of the sons of Ben'ja-min.

CHAPTER 9

SO all Is'ra-el were <u>reckoned</u> by genealogies; and, behold, they *were* written in the book of the kings of Is'ra-el and Ju'dah, *who* were carried away to Bab'y-lon for their <u>transgression</u>. enrolled - unfaithfulness

2 Now the first inhabitants that *dwelled* in their possessions in their cities *were*, the Is'ra-el-ites, the priests, Le'vites, and the <u>Neth'i-nims</u>. temple servants

3 And in Je-ru'sa-lem dwelled of the children of Ju'dah, and of the children of Ben'ja-min, and of the children of E'phra-im, and Ma-nas'seh;

4 U'tha-i the son of Am-mi'hud, the son of Om'ri, the son of Im'ri, the son of Ba'ni, of the children of Pha'rez the son of Ju'dah.

5 And of the Shi'lo-nites; A-sa-i'ah the firstborn, and his sons.

6 And of the sons of Ze'rah; Je-u'el, and their brethren, six hundred and ninety.

7 And of the sons of Ben'ja-min; Sal'lu the son of Me-shul'lam, the son of Hod-a-vi'ah, the son of Has-e-nu'ah,

8 And Ib-ne'iah the son of Jer'o-ham, and E'lah the son of Uz'zi, the son of Mich'ri, and Me-shul'lam the son of Sheph-a-thi'ah, the son of Re-u'el, the son of Ib-ni'jah;

9 And their brethren, according to their <u>generations</u>, nine hundred and fif-

ty and six. All these men *were* chief of the fathers in the house of their fathers. families

10 And of the priests; Je-da'iah, and Je-hoi'a-rib, and Ja'chin,

11 And Az-a-ri'ah the son of Hil-ki'ah, the son of Me-shul'lam, the son of Za'dok, the son of Me-ra'ioth, the son of A-hi'tub, the ruler of the house of <u>God</u>; Elohim^{p.f.}

12 And Ad-a-i'ah the son of Jer'o-ham, the son of Pash'ur, the son of Mal-chi'jah, and Ma-as'i-ai the son of A-di'el, the son of Jah'ze-rah, the son of Me-shul'lam, the son of Me-shil'le-mith, the son of Im'mer;

13 And their brethren, heads of the house of their fathers, a thousand and seven hundred and threescore; very able men for the work of the service of the house of <u>God</u>.

14 And of the Le'vites; Shem-a-i'ah the son of Has'shub, the son of Az'ri-kam, the son of Hash-a-bi'ah, of the sons of Me-ra'ri;

15 And Bak-bak'kar, He'resh, and Ga'lal, and Mat-ta-ni'ah the son of Mi'cah, the son of Zich'ri, the son of A'saph;

16 And O-ba-di'ah the son of Shem-a-i'ah, the son of Ga'lal, the son of Jed'u-thun, and Ber-e-chi'ah the son of A'sa, the son of El'ka-nah, that dwelled in the villages of the Ne-toph'a-thites.

17 And the <u>porters</u> *were*, Shal'lum, and Ak'kub, and Tal'mon, and A-hi'man, and their brethren: Shal'lum *was* the chief; gatekeepers

18 Who previously *waited* in the king's

gate eastward: they *were* <u>porters</u> in the companies of the children of Le'vi. gatekeepers

19 And Shal'lum the son of Ko're, the son of E-bi'a-saph, the son of Ko'rah, and his brethren, of the house of his father, the Ko'rah-ites, *were* <u>over</u> the work of the service, keepers of the <u>gates</u> of the tabernacle: and their fathers, *being* over the host of the LORD, *were* keepers of the <u>entry</u>. in charge of - thresholds - entrance

20 And Phin'e-has the son of E-le-a'zar was the ruler over them in time past, *and* the LORD *was* with him.

21 *And* Zech-a-ri'ah the son of Me-shel-e-mi'ah *was* <u>porter</u> of the door of the tabernacle of the congregation.

22 All these *which were* chosen to be <u>porters</u> in the <u>gates</u> *were* two hundred and twelve. These were reckoned by their genealogy in their villages, whom Da'vid and Sam'u-el the seer <u>did ordain</u> in their <u>set office</u>. appointed - office of trust

23 So they and their children *had* the oversight of the <u>gates</u> of the house of the LORD, *namely*, the house of the tabernacle, <u>by wards</u>. entrance - as guards

24 In four quarters were the <u>porters</u>, toward the east, west, north, and south. gatekeepers

25 And their brethren, *which were* in their villages, *were* to come after seven days from time to time with them.

26 For these Le'vites, the four chief <u>porters</u>, were in *their* <u>set office</u>, and were over the <u>chambers</u> and treasuries of the house of <u>God</u>. rooms - Elohim^{p.f.}

27 And they lodged round about the house of <u>God</u>, because the <u>charge</u> *was* upon them, and the opening thereof every morning *pertained* to them. Elohim^{p.f.} - responsibility

28 And *certain* of them had the <u>charge</u> of the ministering vessels, that they should bring them in and out by <u>tale</u>. count

29 *Some* of them also *were* appointed to oversee the vessels, and all the <u>instruments</u> of the sanctuary, and the fine flour, and the wine, and the oil, and the frankincense, and the spices. utensils

30 And *some* of the sons of the priests made the ointment of the spices.

31 And Mat-ti-thi'ah, *one* of the Le'vites, who *was* the firstborn of Shal'lum the Ko'rah-ite, had the <u>set office</u> over the things that were made in the pans. office of trust

32 And *other* of their brethren, of the sons of the Ko'hath-ites, *were* over the showbread, to prepare *it* every sabbath. rest day

33 And these *are* the singers, chief of the fathers of the Le'vites, *who* remaining in the chambers *were* free: for they were employed in *that* work day and night.

34 These chief fathers of the Le'vites *were* chief throughout their generations; these dwelt at Je-ru'sa-lem.

35 And in Gib'e-on dwelled the father of Gib'e-on, Je-hi'el, whose wife's name *was* Ma'a-chah:

36 And his firstborn son Ab'don, then Zur, and Kish, and Ba'al, and Ner, and Na'dab,

37 And Ge'dor, and A-hi'o, and Zech-a-ri'ah, and Mik'loth.

38 And Mik'loth fathered Shim'e-am.

And they also dwelled with their brethren at Je-ru'sa-lem, opposite their brethren.

39 And Ner fathered Kish; and Kish fathered Saul; and Saul fathered Jon'a-than, and Mal-chi-shu'a, and A-bin'a-dab, and Esh-ba'al.

40 And the son of Jon'a-than *was* Mer'ib-ba'al: and Mer'ib-ba'al fathered Mi'cah.

41 And the sons of Mi'cah *were*, Pi'thon, and Me'lech, and Tah-re'a, *and A'haz*.

42 And A'haz fathered Ja'rah; and Ja'rah fathered Al'e-meth, and Az'ma-veth, and Zim'ri; and Zim'ri fathered Mo'za;

43 And Mo'za fathered Bin'e-a; and Reph-a-i'ah his son, E-le'a-sah his son, A'zel his son.

44 And A'zel had six sons, whose names *are* these, Az'ri-kam, Boch'e-ru, and Ish'ma-el, and She-a-ri'ah, and O-ba-di'ah, and Ha'nan: these *were* the sons of A'zel.

CHAPTER 10

NOW the Phi-lis'tines fought against Is'ra-el; and the men of Is'ra-el fled from before the Phi-lis'tines, and <u>fell down slain</u> in mount Gil-bo'a.   were killed

2 And the Phi-lis'tines followed hard after Saul, and after his sons; and the Phi-lis'tines slew Jon'a-than, and A-bin'a-dab, and Mal-chi-shu'a, the sons of Saul.

3 And the battle <u>went sore</u> against Saul, and the archers hit him, and he was wounded of the archers.   was fierce

4 Then said Saul to his armorbearer, Draw your sword, and thrust me through therewith; less these uncircumcised come and <u>abuse</u> me. But his armorbearer would not; for he was <u>sore</u> afraid. So Saul took a sword, and fell upon it.   torture - greatly

5 And when his armorbearer saw that Saul was dead, he fell likewise on the sword, and died.

6 So Saul died, and his three sons, and all his house died together.

7 And when all the men of Is'ra-el that *were* in the valley saw that they fled, and that Saul and his sons were dead, then they forsook their cities, and fled: and the Phi-lis'tines came and dwelled in them.

8 And it came to pass on the morrow, when the Phi-lis'tines came to <u>strip</u> the slain, that they found Saul and his sons fallen in mount Gil-bo'a.   rob

9 And when they had <u>stripped</u> him, they took his head, and his armor, and sent into the land of the Phi-lis'tines round about, to carry tidings to their idols, and to the people.

10 And they put his armor in the house of their gods, and fastened his head in the temple of Da'gon.

11 And when all Ja'besh-gil'e-ad heard all that the Phi-lis'tines had done to Saul,

12 They arose, all the valiant men, and took away the body of Saul, and the bodies of his sons, and brought them to Ja'besh, and buried their bones under the oak in Ja'besh, and fasted seven days.

13 So Saul died for his transgression which he committed against the

LORD, *even* against the word of the LORD, which he kept not, and also for asking *counsel* of *one that had* a familiar spirit, to enquire *of it*;   i.e., fortune teller

14 And enquired not of the LORD: therefore He slew him, and turned the kingdom to Da'vid the son of Jes'se.

CHAPTER 11

THEN all Is'ra-el gathered themselves to Da'vid to He'bron, saying, Behold, we *are* your bone and your flesh.

2 And moreover in time past, even when Saul was king, you *were* he that led out and brought in Is'ra-el: and the LORD your God said to you, You shall feed My people Is'ra-el, and you shall be ruler over My people Is'ra-el. Elohim p.f.

3 Therefore came all the elders of Is'ra-el to the king to He'bron; and Da'vid made a covenant with them in He'bron before the LORD; and they anointed Da'vid king over Is'ra-el, according to the word of the LORD by Sam'u-el.   agreement - consecrated

4 And Da'vid and all Is'ra-el went to Je-ru'sa-lem, which *is* Je'bus; where the Jeb'u-sites *were*, the inhabitants of the land.

5 And the inhabitants of Je'bus said to Da'vid, You shall not come here. Nevertheless Da'vid took the castle of Zi'on, which *is* the city of Da'vid.   stronghold - i.e., Jerusalem

6 And Da'vid said, Whosoever smite the Jeb'u-sites first shall be chief and captain. So Jo'ab the son of Zer-u-i'ah went first up, and was chief.   strikes down

7 And Da'vid dwelled in the castle; therefore they called it the city of Da'vid.   i.e., Jerusalem

8 And he built the city round about, even from Mil'lo round about: and Jo'ab repaired the rest of the city.

9 So Da'vid waxed greater and greater: for the LORD of hosts *was* with him.   became - Jehovah Tsebaoth

10 These also *are* the chief of the mighty men whom Da'vid had, who strengthened themselves with him in his kingdom, *and* with all Is'ra-el, to make him king, according to the word of the LORD concerning Is'ra-el.

11 And this *is* the number of the mighty men whom Da'vid had; Ja-sho'be-am, an Hach'mo-nite, the chief of the captains: he lifted up his spear against three hundred slain *by him* at one time.

12 And after him *was* E-le-a'zar the son of Do'do, the A-ho'hite, who *was* one of the three mighties.

13 He was with Da'vid at Pas-dam'mim, and there the Phi-lis'tines were gathered together to battle, where was a parcel of ground full of barley; and the people fled from before the Phi-lis'tines.

14 And they set themselves in the midst of *that* parcel, and delivered it, and slew the Phi-lis'tines; and the LORD saved *them* by a great deliverance.

15 Now three of the thirty captains went down to the rock to Da'vid, into the cave of A-dul'lam; and the host of the Phi-lis'tines encamped in the valley of Reph'a-im.

16 And Da'vid *was* then in the hold, and the Phi-lis'tines' garrison *was* then at Beth'-le-hem.   stronghold

17 And Da'vid longed, and said, Oh that one would give me drink of the water of the well of Beth'-le-hem, that *is* at the gate!

18 And the three broke through the host of the Phi-lis'tines, and drew water out of the well of Beth'-le-hem, that *was* by the gate, and took *it*, and brought *it* to Da'vid: but Da'vid would not drink *of* it, but poured it out to the LORD,

19 And said, My God forbid it me, that I should do this thing: shall I drink the blood of these men that have put their lives in jeopardy? for with *the jeopardy of* their lives they brought it. Therefore he would not drink it. These things did these three mightiest. — Elohim^p.f.

20 And A-bish'a-i the brother of Jo'ab, he was chief of the three: for lifting up his spear against three hundred, he slew *them*, and had a name among the three. — reputation

21 Of the three, he was more honorable than the two; for he was their captain: however he attained not to the *first* three.

22 Be-na'iah the son of Je-hoi'a-da, the son of a valiant man of Kab'zeel, who had done many acts; he slew two lionlike men of Mo'ab: also he went down and slew a lion in a pit in a snowy day. — strong

23 And he slew an E-gyp'tian, a man of *great* stature, five cubits high; and in the E-gyp'tian's hand *was* a spear like a weaver's beam; and he went down to him with a staff, and plucked the spear out of the E-gyp'tian's hand, and slew him with his own spear.

24 These *things* did Be-na'iah the son of Je-hoi'a-da, and had the name among the three mighties.

25 Behold, he was honorable among the thirty, but attained not to the *first* three: and Da'vid set him over his guard.

26 Also the valiant men of the armies *were*, A'sa-hel the brother of Jo'ab, El-ha'nan the son of Do'do of Beth'-le-hem,

27 Sham'moth the Ha'ro-rite, He'lez the Pel'o-nite,

28 I'ra the son of Ik'kesh the Te-ko'ite, A-bi-e'zer the An'toth-ite,

29 Sib'be-cai the Hu'shath-ite, I'lai the A-ho'hite,

30 Ma-har'a-i the Ne-toph'a-thite, He'led the son of Ba'a-nah the Ne-toph'a-thite,

31 Ith'a-i the son of Ri'bai of Gib'e-ah, *that pertained* to the children of Ben'ja-min, Be-na'iah the Pir'a-thon-ite,

32 Hu'rai of the brooks of Ga'ash, A-bi'el the Ar'bath-ite,

33 Az'ma-veth the Ba-ha'rum-ite, E-li'ah-ba the Sha-al'bo-nite,

34 The sons of Ha'shem the Gi'zo-nite, Jon'a-than the son of Sha'ge the Ha'ra-rite,

35 A-hi'am the son of Sa'car the Ha'ra-rite, El'i-phal the son of Ur,

36 He'pher the Mech'e-rath-ite, A-hi'jah the Pel'o-nite,

37 Hez'ro the Car'mel-ite, Na'a-rai the son of Ez'ba-i,

38 Jo'el the brother of Na'than, Mib'har the son of Hag-ge'ri,

39 Ze'lek the Am'mon-ite, Na-har'a-i

the Be'roth-ite, the armorbearer of Jo'ab the son of Zer-u-i'ah,

40 I'ra the Ith'rite, Ga'reb the Ith'rite,

41 U-ri'ah the Hit'tite, Za'bad the son of Ah'lai,

42 Ad'i-na the son of Shi'za the Reu'ben-ite, a captain of the Reu'ben-ites, and thirty with him,

43 Ha'nan the son of Ma'a-chah, and Josh'a-phat the Mith'nite,

44 Uz-zi'a the Ash'te-rath-ite, Sha'ma and Je-hi'el the sons of Ho'than the Ar'o-er-ite,

45 Je-di'a-el the son of Shim'ri, and Jo'ha his brother, the Ti'zite,

46 E-li'el the Ma'ha-vite, and Jer'i-bai, and Josh-a-vi'ah, the sons of El'na-am, and Ith'mah the Mo'ab-ite,

47 E-li'el, and O'bed, and Ja'si-el the Mes'o-ba-ite.

CHAPTER 12

NOW these *are* they that came to Da'vid to Zik'lag, while he yet kept himself <u>close</u> because of Saul the son of Kish: and they *were* among the mighty men, helpers of the war. banished

2 *They were* armed with bows, and could use both the right hand and the left in *hurling* stones and *shooting* arrows out of a bow, *even* of Saul's brethren of Ben'ja-min.

3 The chief *was* A-hi-e'zer, then Jo'ash, the sons of She-ma'ah the Gib'e-ath-ite; and Je'zi-el, and Pe'let, the sons of Az'ma-veth; and Ber'a-chah, and Je'hu the An'toth-ite,

4 And Is-ma-i'ah the Gib'e-on-ite, a mighty man among the thirty, and over the thirty; and Jer-e-mi'ah, and Ja-ha'zi-el, and Jo-ha'nan, and Jos'a-bad the Ged'e-rath-ite,

5 E-lu'za-i, and Jer'i-moth, and Be-a-li'ah, and Shem-a-ri'ah, and Sheph-a-ti'ah the Har'u-phite,

6 El'ka-nah, and Je-si'ah, and A-zar'e-el, and Jo-e'zer, and Ja-sho'be-am, the Kor'hites,

7 And Jo-e'lah, and Zeb-a-di'ah, the sons of Jer'o-ham of Ge'dor.

8 And of the Gad'ites there <u>separated themselves</u> to Da'vid into the <u>hold</u> to the wilderness men of might, *and* men of war *fit* for the battle, that could handle shield and <u>buckler</u>, whose faces *were like* the faces of lions, and *were* as swift as the <u>roes</u> upon the mountains;   came over - stronghold - spear - gazelles

9 E'zer the first, O-ba-di'ah the second, E-li'ab the third,

10 Mish-man'nah the fourth, Jer-e-mi'ah the fifth,

11 At'tai the sixth, E-li'el the seventh,

12 Jo-ha'nan the eighth, El'za-bad the ninth,

13 Jer-e-mi'ah the tenth, Mach'ba-nai the eleventh.

14 These *were* of the sons of Gad, captains of the host: one of the least *was* <u>over</u> an hundred, and the greatest <u>over</u> a thousand.   equal to

15 These *are* they that went over Jor'dan in the first month, when it had overflown all its banks; and they put to flight all *them* of the valleys, *both* toward the east, and toward the west.

16 And there came of the children of Ben'ja-min and Ju'dah to the <u>hold</u> to Da'vid.   stronghold

17 And Da'vid went out to meet them, and answered and said to them, If you be come peaceably to me to help me, my heart shall be <u>knit</u> to you: but if *you be come* to betray me to my enemies, seeing *there is* no <u>wrong</u> in my hands, the <u>God</u> of our fathers look *thereon*, and rebuke *it*.   united - violence - Elohim^{p.f.}

18 Then the spirit came upon A-mas'a-i, *who was* chief of the captains, *and he said*, Yours *are we*, Da'vid, and on your side, you son of Jes'se: peace, peace *be* to you, and peace *be* to your helpers; for your <u>God</u> helps you. Then Da'vid received them, and made them captains of the band.

19 And there <u>fell</u> *some* of Ma-nas'seh to Da'vid, when he came with the Phi-lis'tines against Saul to battle: but they helped them not: for the lords of the Phi-lis'tines upon <u>ad-viscment</u> sent him away, saying, he will <u>fall</u> to his master Saul to *the jeopardy of* our heads.   deserted - consultation

20 As he went to Zik'lag, there <u>fell</u> to him of Ma-nas'seh, Ad'nah, and Joz'a-bad, and Je-di'a-el, and Mi'chael, and Joz'a-bad, and E-li'hu, and Zil'thai, captains of the thousands that *were* of Ma-nas'seh.

21 And they helped Da'vid against the band *of the <u>rovers</u>*: for they *were* all mighty men of valor, and were captains in the host.   raiders

22 For at *that* time day by day there came to Da'vid to help him, until *it* was a great host, like the <u>host</u> of God.   army - Elohim^{p.f.}

23 And these *are* the numbers of the <u>bands</u> *that were* ready armed to the war, *and* came to Da'vid to He'bron, to turn the kingdom of Saul to him, according to the word of the LORD.   divisions

24 The children of Ju'dah that bare shield and spear *were* six thousand and eight hundred, ready armed to the war.

25 Of the children of Sim'e-on, mighty men of valor for the war, seven thousand and one hundred.

26 Of the children of Le'vi four thousand and six hundred.

27 And Je-hoi'a-da *was* the leader of the Aar'on-ites, and with him *were* three thousand and seven hundred;

28 And Za'dok, a young man mighty of valor, and of his father's house twenty and two captains.

29 And of the children of Ben'ja-min, the kindred of Saul, three thousand: for previously the greatest part of them had kept <u>the ward of</u> the house of Saul.   allegiance to

30 And of the children of E'phra-im twenty thousand and eight hundred, mighty men of valor, famous throughout the house of their fathers.

31 And of the half tribe of Ma-nas'seh eighteen thousand, which were <u>expressed</u> by name, to come and make Da'vid king.   designated

32 And of the children of Is'sa-char, *which were men* that had understanding of the times, to know what Is'ra-el ought to do; the heads of them *were* two hundred; and all their brethren *were* at their commandment.

33 Of Zeb'u-lun, such as went forth to

battle, expert in war, with all <u>instru-</u><u>ments</u> of war, fifty thousand, which could keep rank: *they were* not of double heart.   weapons

34 And of Naph'ta-li a thousand captains, and with them with shield and spear thirty and seven thousand.

35 And of the Dan'ites expert in war twenty and eight thousand and six hundred.

36 And of Ash'er, such as went forth to battle, expert in war, forty thousand.

37 And on the other side of Jor'dan, of the Reu'ben-ites, and the Gad'ites, and of the half tribe of Ma-nas'seh, with all manner of <u>instruments</u> of war for the battle, an hundred and twenty thousand.

38 All these men of war, that could keep rank, came with a <u>perfect</u> heart to He'bron, to make Da'vid king over all Is'ra-el: and all the rest also of Is'ra-el *were* of one heart to make Da'vid king.   sincere

39 And there they were with Da'vid three days, eating and drinking: for their brethren had prepared for them.

40 Moreover they that were near them, *even* to Is'sa-char and Zeb'u-lun and Naph'ta-li, brought bread on asses, and on camels, and on mules, and on oxen, *and* meat, meal, cakes of figs, and bunches of raisins, and wine, and oil, and oxen, and sheep abundantly: for *there was* joy in Is'ra-el.

CHAPTER 13

AND Da'vid consulted with the captains of thousands and hundreds, *and* with every leader.

2 And Da'vid said to all the congregation of Is'ra-el, If *it seem* good to you, and *that it be* of the LORD our <u>God</u>, let us send abroad to our brethren every where, *that <u>are</u> left* in all the land of Is'ra-el, and with them *also* to the priests and Le'vites *which are* in their cities *and* suburbs, that they may gather themselves to us: Elohim^p.f. - remain

3 And let us bring again the ark of our God to us: for we enquired not at it in the days of Saul.

4 And all the congregation said that they would do so: for the thing was right in the eyes of all the people.

5 So Da'vid gathered all Is'ra-el together, from Shi'hor of E'gypt even to the entering of He'math, to bring the ark of <u>God</u> from Kir'jath-je'a-rim.   Elohim^p.f.

6 And Da'vid went up, and all Is'ra-el, to Ba'al-ah, *that is,* to Kir'jath-je'a-rim, which *belonged* to Ju'dah, to bring up from there the ark of <u>God</u> the LORD, that dwells *between* the cherubims, whose name is called *on it.*

7 And they carried the ark of <u>God</u> in a new cart out of the house of A-bin'a-dab: and Uz'za and A-hi'o drove the cart.

8 And Da'vid and all Is'ra-el <u>played</u> before <u>God</u> with all *their* might, and with singing, and with harps, and with <u>psalteries</u>, and with timbrels, and with cymbals, and with trumpets.   celebrated - lyres

9 And when they came to the threshingfloor of Chi'don, Uz'za put forth his hand to hold the ark; for the oxen <u>stumbled</u>.   nearly upset it

10 And the anger of the LORD was

kindled against Uz'za, and He <u>smote</u> him, because he put his hand to the ark: and there he died before <u>God</u>. struck
11 And Da'vid was displeased, because the LORD had made a breach upon Uz'za: wherefore that place is called <u>Pe'rez-uz'za</u> to this day.

i.e., the break through of Uzza

12 And Da'vid was afraid of <u>God</u> that day, saying, How shall I bring the ark of <u>God</u> *home* to me? Elohim^{p.f.}
13 So Da'vid brought not the ark *home* to himself to the <u>city of Da'vid</u>, but carried it aside into the house of O'bed-e'dom the Git'tite. *i.e., Jerusalem*
14 And the ark of <u>God</u> remained with the family of O'bed-e'dom in his house three months. And the LORD blessed the house of O'bed-e'dom, and all that he had.

CHAPTER 14

NOW Hi'ram king of Tyre sent messengers to Da'vid, and timber of cedars, with masons and carpenters, to build him an house.
2 And Da'vid perceived that the LORD had confirmed him king over Is'ra-el, for his kingdom was <u>lifted up on high</u>, because of his people Is'ra-el.

highly exalted

3 And Da'vid took more wives at Je-ru'sa-lem: and Da'vid fathered more sons and daughters.
4 Now these *are* the names of *his* children which he had in Je-ru'sa-lem; Sham-mu'a, and Sho'bab, Na'than, and Sol'o-mon,
5 And Ib'har, and El-i-shu'a, and El'pa-let,
6 And No'gah, and Ne'pheg, and Ja-phi'a,
7 And E-lish'a-ma, and Be-el-i'a-da, and E-liph'a-let.
8 And when the Phi-lis'tines heard that Da'vid was <u>anointed</u> king over all Is'ra-el, all the Phi-lis'tines went up to seek Da'vid. And Da'vid heard *of it*, and went out against them.

consecrated

9 And the Phi-lis'tines came and <u>spread</u> themselves in the valley of Reph'a-im. made a raid
10 And Da'vid enquired of <u>God</u>, saying, Shall I go up against the Phi-lis'tines? And will You deliver them into my hand? And the LORD said to him, Go up; for I will deliver them into your hand. Elohim^{p.f.}
11 So they came up to Ba'al-per'a-zim; and Da'vid smote them there. Then Da'vid said, <u>God</u> has broken in upon my enemies by my hand like <u>the breaking forth</u> of waters: therefore they called the name of that place Ba'al-per'a-zim. a flood
12 And when they had left their <u>gods</u> there, Da'vid gave a commandment, and they were burned with fire.

i.e., idols

13 And the Phi-lis'tines yet again spread themselves abroad in the valley.
14 Therefore Da'vid <u>enquired</u> again of <u>God</u>; and <u>God</u> said to him, Go not up after them; turn away from them, and come upon them opposite the mulberry trees. prayed
15 And it shall be, when you shall hear a sound of going in the tops of the mulberry trees, *that* then you shall go

out to battle: for God is gone forth before you to smite the host of the Phi-lis'tines.

16 Da'vid therefore did as <u>God</u> commanded him: and they <u>smote</u> the <u>host</u> of the Phi-lis'tines from Gib'e-on even to Ga'zer.   Elohim^(p.f.) - struck - army

17 And the fame of Da'vid went out into all lands; and the LORD brought the <u>fear</u> of him upon all nations. respect

CHAPTER 15

A ND *Da'vid* made him houses in the <u>city of Da'vid</u>, and prepared a place for the ark of <u>God</u>, and <u>pitched</u> for it a tent.   i.e., Jerusalem - made

2 Then Da'vid said, None ought to carry the ark of <u>God</u> but the Le'vites: for them has the LORD chosen to carry the ark of <u>God</u>, and to minister to Him for ever.

3 And Da'vid gathered all Is'ra-el together to Je-ru'sa-lem, to bring up the ark of the LORD to its place, which he had prepared for it.

4 And Da'vid assembled the children of Aar'on, and the Le'vites:

5 Of the sons of Ko'hath; U'ri-el the chief, and his <u>brethren</u> an hundred and twenty: relatives

6 Of the sons of Me-ra'ri; A-sa-i'ah the chief, and his brethren two hundred and twenty:

7 Of the sons of Ger'shom; Jo'el the chief, and his brethren an hundred and thirty:

8 Of the sons of E-liz'a-phan; Shem-a-i'ah the chief, and his brethren two hundred:

9 Of the sons of He'bron; E-li'el the chief, and his brethren fourscore:

10 Of the sons of Uz'zi-el; Am-min'a-dab the chief, and his brethren an hundred and twelve.

11 And Da'vid called for Za'dok and A-bi'a-thar the priests, and for the Le'vites, for U'ri-el, A-sa-i'ah, and Jo'el, Shem-a-i'ah, and E-li'el, and Am-min'a-dab,

12 And said to them, You *are* the chief of the fathers of the Le'vites: <u>sanctify</u> yourselves, *both* you and your brethren, that you may bring up the ark of the LORD God of Is'ra-el to *the place that* I have prepared for it.   consecrate

13 For because you *did it* not at the first, the LORD our God made a breach upon us, for that we sought Him not <u>after the due order</u>.   according to the ordinance

14 So the priests and the Le'vites <u>sanctified</u> themselves to bring up the ark of the LORD God of Is'ra-el.

consecrated

15 And the children of the Le'vites bare the ark of <u>God</u> upon their shoulders with the <u>staves</u> thereon, as Mo'ses commanded according to the word of the LORD.   Elohim^(p.f.) - poles

16 And Da'vid spoke to the chief of the Le'vites to appoint their brethren *to be* the singers with instruments of music, <u>psalteries</u> and harps and cymbals, sounding, by <u>lifting up the voice</u> with joy.   lyres - singing

17 So the Le'vites appointed He'man the son of Jo'el; and of his brethren, A'saph the son of Ber-e-chi'ah; and of the sons of Me-ra'ri their brethren, E'than the son of Kush-a'iah;

18 And with them their brethren of the second *degree*, Zech-a-ri'ah, Bcn, and Ja-a'zi-el, and She-mir'a-moth, and Je-hi'el, and Un'ni, E-li'ab, and Be-na'iah, and Ma-a-se'iah, and Mat-ti-thi'ah, and E-liph'e-leh, and Mik-ne'iah, and O'bed-e'dom, and Je-i'el, the <u>porters</u>. gatekeepers

19 So the singers, He'man, A'saph, and E'than, *were appointed* to sound with cymbals of brass;

20 And Zech-a-ri'ah, and A'zi-el, and She-mir'a-moth, and Je-hi'el, and Un'ni, and E-li'ab, and Ma-a-se'iah, and Be-na'iah, with <u>psalteries</u> on Al'a-moth; lyres

21 And Mat-ti-thi'ah, and E-liph'e-leh, and Mik-ne'iah, and O'bed-e'dom, and Je-i'el, and Az-a-zi'ah, with harps on the Shem'i-nith to excel.

22 And Chen-a-ni'ah, chief of the Le'vites, *was* for song: he instructed about thc song, because he *was* <u>skillful</u>. trained

23 And Ber-e-chi'ah and El'ka-nah *were* doorkeepers for the ark.

24 And Sheb-a-ni'ah, and Je-hosh'a-phat, and Ne-than'e-el, and A-mas'a-i, and Zech-a-ri'ah, and Be-na'iah, and E-li-e'zer, the priests, did blow with the trumpets before the ark of <u>God</u>: and O'bed-e'dom and Je-hi'ah *were* doorkeepers for the ark. Elohim^{p.f.}

25 So Da'vid, and the elders of Is'ra-el, and the captains over thousands, went to bring up the ark of the <u>covenant</u> of the LORD out of the house of O'bed-e'dom with joy. agreement

26 And it came to pass, when <u>God</u> helped the Le'vites that bare the ark of the <u>covenant</u> of the LORD, that they offered seven bullocks and seven rams. Elohim^{p.f.} - agreement

27 And Da'vid *was* clothed with a robe of fine linen, and all the Le'vites that bare the ark, and the singers, and Chen-a-ni'ah the master of the song with the singers: Da'vid also *had* upon him an <u>ephod</u> of linen. priestly garment

28 Thus all Is'ra-el brought up the ark of the <u>covenant</u> of the LORD with shouting, and with sound of the cornet, and with trumpets, and with cymbals, making a noise with <u>psalteries</u> and harps. lyres

29 And it came to pass, *as* the ark of the <u>covenant</u> of the LORD came to the city of Da'vid, that Mi'chal the daughter of Saul looking out at a window saw king Da'vid dancing and playing: and she despised him in her heart.

CHAPTER 16

SO they brought the ark of <u>God</u>, and set it in the midst of the tent that Da'vid had <u>pitched</u> for it: and they offered burned sacrifices and peace offerings before <u>God</u>. Elohim^{p.f.} - set up

2 And when Da'vid had <u>made an end of</u> offering the burned offerings and the peace offerings, he blessed the people in the name of the LORD. finished

3 And he <u>dealt</u> to every one of Is'ra-el, both man and woman, to every one a loaf of bread, and a good piece of flesh, and a flagon *of wine*. distributed

4 And he appointed *certain* of the Le'vites to minister before the ark of

the LORD, and to <u>record</u>, and to thank and praise the LORD God of Is'ra-el: Jehovah^{s.f.} Elohim^{p.f.} - celebrate

5 A'saph the chief, and next to him Zech-a-ri'ah, Je-i'el, and She-mir'a-moth, and Je-hi'el, and Mat-ti-thi'ah, and E-li'ab, and Be-na'iah, and O'bed-e'dom: and Je-i'el with <u>psalteries</u> and with harps; but A'saph made a sound with cymbals;   lyres

6 Be-na'iah also and Ja-ha'zi-el the priests with trumpets continually before the ark of the <u>covenant</u> of <u>God</u>.   agreement

7 Then on that day Da'vid delivered first *this psalm* to thank the LORD into the hand of A'saph and his brethren.

8 Give thanks to the LORD, call upon His name, make known His deeds among the people.

9 Sing to Him, sing psalms to Him, talk you of all His wondrous works.

10 Glory you in His holy name: let the heart of them rejoice that seek the LORD.

11 Seek the LORD and His strength, seek His face continually.   MATT. 6:33

12 Remember His marvellous works that He has done, His wonders, and the <u>judgments</u> of His mouth;   wisdom

13 O <u>you seed</u> of Is'ra-el His servant, you children of Ja'cob, His chosen ones.   descendants

14 He *is* the LORD our <u>God</u>; His judgments *are* in all the earth.   Elohim^{p.f.}

15 Be you mindful always of His <u>covenant</u>; the word *which* He commanded to a thousand generations;   agreement

16 *Even of the <u>covenant</u>* which He made with A'bra-ham, 'and of His oath to I'saac;   agreement

17 And has confirmed the same to Ja'cob for a law, *and* to Is'ra-el *for* an everlasting <u>covenant</u>,

18 Saying, To you will I give the land of Ca'naan, the <u>lot</u> of your inheritance;   portion

19 When you were but few, even a few, and strangers in it.

20 And *when* they went from nation to nation, and from *one* kingdom to another people;

21 He allowed no man to do them wrong: yea, He reproved kings for their sakes,

22 *Saying*, Touch not My anointed, and do My prophets no harm.

23 Sing to the LORD, all the earth; show forth from day to day His <u>salvation</u>.   i.e., Heb. Jeshua

24 Declare His glory among the heathen; His marvellous works among all nations.

25 For great *is* the LORD, and greatly to be praised: He also *is* to be <u>feared</u> above all gods.   revered

26 For all the gods of the people *are* idols: but the LORD made the heavens.

27 Glory and honor *are* in His presence; strength and gladness *are* in His place.

28 Give to the LORD, you kindreds of the people, give to the LORD glory and strength.

29 Give to the LORD the glory *due* to His name: bring an offering, and come before Him: worship the LORD in the beauty of holiness.

30 <u>Fear</u> before Him, all the earth: the world also shall be stable, that it be not moved.   Tremble

31 Let the heavens be glad, and let the earth rejoice: and let *men* say among the nations, The LORD reigns.

32 Let the sea roar, and the fulness thereof: let the fields rejoice, and all that *is* therein.

33 Then shall the trees of the wood sing out at the presence of the LORD, because He comes to judge the earth.

34 O give thanks to the LORD; for *He is* good; for His mercy *endures* for ever.

35 And say you, Save us, O <u>God</u> of our salvation, and gather us together, and deliver us from the heathen, that we may give thanks to Your holy name, *and* glory in Your praise. Elohim^p.f.

36 Blessed *be* the <u>LORD God</u> of Is'ra-el for ever and ever. And all the people said, Amen, and praised the LORD.   Jehovah^s.f. Elohim^p.f.

37 So he left there before the ark of the <u>covenant</u> of the LORD A'saph and his brethren, to <u>minister</u> before the ark continually, as every day's work required: agreement - serve

38 And O'bed-e'dom with their brethren, <u>threescore and eight</u>; O'bed-e'dom also the son of Jed'u-thun and Ho'sah *to be* <u>porters</u>:   68 - doorkeepers

39 And Za'dok the priest, and his brethren the priests, before the tabernacle of the LORD in the <u>high place</u> that *was* at Gib'e-on,   shrine

40 To offer burned offerings to the LORD upon the altar of the burned offering continually morning and evening,

and *to do* according to all that is written in the law of the LORD, which He commanded Is'ra-el;

41 And with them He'man and Jed'u-thun, and the rest that were chosen, who were <u>expressed</u> by name, to give thanks to the LORD, because His mercy *endures* for ever;   designated

42 And with them He'man and Jed'u-thun with trumpets and cymbals for those that should make a sound, and with musical instruments of <u>God</u>. And the sons of Jed'u-thun *were* <u>porters</u>.   Elohim^p.f. - doorkeepers

43 And all the people departed every man to his house: and Da'vid returned to bless his house.

CHAPTER 17

NOW it came to pass, as Da'vid sat in his house, that Da'vid said to Na'than the prophet, Lo, I dwell in an house of cedars, but the ark of the <u>covenant</u> of the LORD *remains* under <u>curtains</u>.   agreement - a tent

2 Then Na'than said to Da'vid, Do all that *is* in your heart; for <u>God</u> *is* with you.

3 And it came to pass the same night, that the word of <u>God</u> came to Na'than, saying,   Elohim^p.f.

4 Go and tell Da'vid My servant, Thus says the LORD, You shall not build Me an house to dwell in:

5 For I have not dwelled in an house since the day that I brought up Is'ra-el to this day; but have <u>gone</u> from tent to tent, and from *one* tabernacle *to another*.   i.e., moved

6 Wheresoever I have walked with all Is'ra-el, <u>spoke</u> I a word to any of the judges of Is'ra-el, whom I commanded to feed My people, saying, Why have you not built Me an house of cedars? did I ever say

7 Now therefore thus shall you say to My servant Da'vid, Thus says the Lord <u>of hosts</u>, I took you from the <u>sheepcote</u>, *even* from following the sheep, that you should be ruler over My people Is'ra-el: Jehovah Tsebaoth - pasture

8 And I have been with you wherever you have walked, and have <u>cut off</u> all your enemies from before you, and have made you a <u>name</u> like the <u>name</u> of the great men that *are* in the earth. destroyed - reputation

9 Also I will <u>ordain</u> a place for My people Is'ra-el, and will <u>plant</u> them, and they shall dwell in their place, and shall be moved no more; neither shall the children of wickedness <u>waste</u> them any more, as at the beginning, appoint - establish - oppress

10 And since the time that I commanded judges *to be* over My people Is'ra-el. Moreover I will subdue all your enemies. Furthermore I tell you that the Lord will build you an house.

11 And it shall come to pass, when your days be <u>expired</u> that you must go *to be* <u>with your fathers,</u> that I will raise up your <u>seed</u> after you, which shall be of your sons; and I will establish his kingdom. fulfilled - die - descendants

12 He shall build Me an house, and I will stablish his throne for ever.

13 I will be his father, and he shall be My son: and I will not take My mercy away from him, as I took *it* from *him* that was before you:

14 But I will settle him in My house and in My kingdom for ever: and his throne shall be established for evermore. ACTS 2:30

15 According to all these words, and according to all this vision, so did Na'than speak to Da'vid.

16 And Da'vid the king came and sat before the Lord, and said, Who *am* I, O Lord <u>God</u>, and what *is* my house, that You have brought me presently? Jehovah^{s.f.} Elohim^{p.f.}

17 And *yet* this was a small thing in Your eyes, O <u>God</u>; for You have *also* spoken of Your servant's house for a great while to come, and have regarded me according to the <u>estate</u> of a man of high degree, O Lord <u>God</u>. Elohim^{p.f.} - standard - Jehovah^{s.f.} Elohim^{p.f.}

18 What can Da'vid *speak* more to You for the honor of Your servant? for You know Your servant.

19 O Lord, for Your servant's sake, and according to Your own heart, have You done all this greatness, in making known all *these* great things.

20 O Lord, *there is* none like You, neither *is there any* <u>God</u> beside You, according to all that we have heard with our ears.

21 And what one nation in the earth *is* like Your people Is'ra-el, whom God went to redeem *to be* His own people, to make You a name of greatness and terribleness, by driving out nations from before Your people, whom You have redeemed out of E'gypt?

22 For Your people Is'ra-el did You

make Your own people for ever; and You, Lord, became their <u>God</u>.   Elohim^{p.f.}
23 Therefore now, Lord, let the thing that You have spoken concerning Your servant and concerning his house be established for ever, and do as You have said.

24 Let it even be established, that Your name may be magnified for ever, saying, The Lord of hosts *is* the God of Is'ra-el, *even* a God to Is'ra-el: and *let* the house of Da'vid Your servant *be* established before You.   Jehovah^{s.f.} Tsebaoth
25 For You, O my God, have told Your servant that You will build him an house: therefore Your servant has found *in his heart* to pray before You.
26 And now, Lord, You are <u>God</u>, and have promised this goodness to Your servant: Elohim^{p.f.}
27 Now therefore let it please You to bless the house of Your servant, that it may be before You for ever: for You bless, O Lord, and *it shall be* blessed for ever.

CHAPTER 18

NOW after this it came to pass, that Da'vid <u>smote</u> the Phi-lis'tines, and subdued them, and took Gath and her towns out of the hand of the Phi-lis'tines.   defeated
2 And he <u>smote</u> Mo'ab; and the Mo'ab-ites became Da'vid's servants, *and* brought gifts.
3 And Da'vid <u>smote</u> Had-ar-e'zer king of Zo'bah to Ha'math, as he went to stablish his dominion by the river Eu-phra'tes.

4 And Da'vid took from him a thousand chariots, and seven thousand horsemen, and twenty thousand footmen: Da'vid also <u>houghed</u> all the chariot *horses*, but reserved of them an hundred chariots.   hamstrung
5 And when the Syr'i-ans of Da-mas'cus came to help Had-ar-e'zer king of Zo'bah, Da'vid slew of the Syr'i-ans two and twenty thousand men.
6 Then Da'vid put *garrisons* in Syr'i-a-da-mas'cus; and the Syr'i-ans became Da'vid's servants, *and* brought gifts. Thus the Lord preserved Da'vid wherever he went.   tribute
7 And Da'vid took the shields of gold that were on the servants of Had-ar-e'zer, and brought them to Je-ru'sa-lem.
8 Likewise from Tib'hath, and from Chun, cities of Had-ar-e'zer, brought Da'vid very much brass, wherewith Sol'o-mon made the brazen sea, and the pillars, and the vessels of brass.
9 Now when To'u king of Ha'math heard how Da'vid had smitten all the host of Had-ar-e'zer king of Zo'bah;
10 He sent Ha-do'ram his son to king Da'vid, to enquire of his welfare, and to congratulate him, because he had fought against Had-ar-e'zer, and <u>smitten</u> him; (for Had-ar-e'zer had war with To'u;) and *with him* all manner of vessels of gold and silver and brass.   defeated
11 Them also king Da'vid dedicated to the Lord, with the silver and the gold that he brought from all *these* nations; from E'dom, and from Mo'ab, and from the children of Am'mon, and from the Phi-lis'tines, and from Am'a-lek.

12 Moreover A-bish'a-i the son of Zer-u-i'ah slew of the E'dom-ites in the valley of salt eighteen thousand.

13 And he put garrisons in E'dom; and all the E'dom-ites became Da'vid's servants. Thus the LORD preserved Da'vid wherever he went.

14 So Da'vid reigned over all Is'ra-el, and <u>executed</u> judgment and justice among all his people.   administered

15 And Jo'ab the son of Zer-u-i'ah *was* over the host; and Je-hosh'a-phat the son of A-hi'lud, recorder.

16 And Za'dok the son of A-hi'tub, and A-bim'e-lech the son of A-bi'a-thar, *were* the priests; and Shav'sha was scribe;

17 And Be-na'iah the son of Je-hoi'a-da *was* over the Cher'eth-ites and the Pe'leth-ites; and the sons of Da'vid *were* chief <u>about the king</u>.   at the king's side

CHAPTER 19

NOW it came to pass after this, that Na'hash the king of the children of Am'mon died, and his son reigned in his stead.

2 And Da'vid said, I will show kindness to Ha'nun the son of Na'hash, because his father showed kindness to me. And Da'vid sent messengers to comfort him concerning his father. So the servants of Da'vid came into the land of the children of Am'mon to Ha'nun, to comfort him.

3 But the princes of the children of Am'mon said to Ha'nun, Think you that Da'vid does honor your father, that he has sent comforters to you? are not his servants come to you for to search, and to overthrow, and to spy out the land?

4 Wherefore Ha'nun took Da'vid's servants, and shaved them, and cut off their garments in the midst <u>hard</u> by their buttocks, and sent them away.   close

5 Then there went *certain*, and told Da'vid how the men were <u>served</u>. And he sent to meet them: for the men were greatly ashamed. And the king said, Tarry at Jer'i-cho until your beards be grown, and *then* return.   treated

6 And when the children of Am'mon saw that they had made themselves <u>odious</u> to Da'vid, Ha'nun and the children of Am'mon sent a thousand talents of silver to hire them chariots and horsemen out of Mes-o-po-ta'mi-a, and out of Syr'i-a-ma'a-chah, and out of Zo'bah.   a stench

7 So they hired thirty and two thousand chariots, and the king of Ma'a-chah and his people; who came and <u>pitched</u> before Med'e-ba. And the children of Am'mon gathered themselves together from their cities, and came to battle.   camped

8 And when Da'vid heard *of it*, he sent Jo'ab, and all the host of the mighty men.

9 And the children of Am'mon came out, and put the battle in array before the gate of the city: and the kings that were come *were* by themselves in the field.

10 Now when Jo'ab saw that the battle was set against him before and behind, he chose out of all the choice of

Is'ra-el, and put *them* in array against the Syr'i-ans.

11 And the rest of the people he delivered to the hand of A-bish'a-i his brother, and they set *themselves* in array against the children of Am'mon.

12 And he said, If the Syr'i-ans be too strong for me, then you shall help me: but if the children of Am'mon be too strong for you, then I will help you.

13 Be of good courage, and let us behave ourselves <u>valiantly</u> for our people, and for the cities of our God: and let the LORD do *that which is* good in His sight.   courageously

14 So Jo'ab and the people that *were* with him drew near before the Syr'i-ans to the battle; and they fled before him.

15 And when the children of Am'mon saw that the Syr'i-ans were fled, they likewise fled before A-bish'a-i his brother, and entered into the city. Then Jo'ab came to Je-ru'sa-lem.

16 And when the Syr'i-ans saw that they were <u>put to the worse</u> before Is'ra-el, they sent messengers, and drew forth the Syr'i-ans that *were* beyond the river: and Sho'phach the captain of the host of Had-ar-e'zer *went* before them.   being defeated

17 And it was told Da'vid; and he gathered all Is'ra-el, and passed over Jor'dan, and came upon them, and set *the battle* in array against them. So when Da'vid had <u>put the battle in array</u> against the Syr'i-ans, they fought with him.   formed his battle lines

18 But the Syr'i-ans fled before Is'ra-el; and Da'vid slew of the Syr'i-ans seven thousand *men which fought in* chariots, and forty thousand footmen, and killed Sho'phach the captain of the host.

19 And when the servants of Had-ar-e'zer saw that they were <u>put to the worse</u> before Is'ra-el, they made peace with Da'vid, and became his servants: neither would the Syr'i-ans help the children of Am'mon any more.   being defeated

CHAPTER 20

AND it came to pass, that after the year was expired, at the time that kings go out *to battle*, Jo'ab led forth the power of the army, and <u>wasted</u> the country of the children of Am'mon, and came and besieged Rab'bah. But Da'vid <u>tarried</u> at Je-ru'sa-lem. And Jo'ab smote Rab'bah, and destroyed it.   destroyed - stayed

2 And Da'vid took the crown of their king from off his head, and found it to weigh a talent of gold, and *there were* precious stones in it; and it was set upon Da'vid's head: and he brought also exceeding much <u>spoil</u> out of the city.   plunder

3 And he brought out the people that *were* in it, and cut *them* with saws, and with harrows of iron, and with axes. Even so dealt Da'vid with all the cities of the children of Am'mon. And Da'vid and all the people returned to Je-ru'sa-lem.

4 And it came to pass after this, that there arose war at Ge'zer with the Phi-lis'tines; at which time Sib'be-chai the Hu'shath-ite slew Sip'pai, *that was*

of the children of the giant: and they were subdued.

5 And there was war again with the Phi-lis'tines; and El-ha'nan the son of Ja'ir slew Lah'mi the brother of Go-li'ath the Git'tite, whose spear staff *was* like a weaver's beam.

6 And yet again there was war at Gath, where was a man of *great* stature, whose fingers and toes *were* four and twenty, six *on each hand*, and six *on each foot*: and he also was the son of the giant.

7 But when he <u>defied</u> Is'ra-el, Jon'a-than the son of Shim'e-a Da'vid's brother slew him.   taunted

8 These were born to the giant in Gath; and they fell by the hand of Da'vid, and by the hand of his servants.

CHAPTER 21

AND Sa'tan <u>stood</u> up against Is'ra-el, and <u>provoked</u> Da'vid to <u>number</u> Is'ra-el. rose - incited - take a census in

2 And Da'vid said to Jo'ab and to the rulers of the people, Go, number Is'ra-el from Be'er-she'ba even to Dan; and bring the number of them to me, that I may know *it*.

3 And Jo'ab answered, The LORD make His people an hundred times so many more as they *be*: but, my lord the king, *are* they not all my lord's servants? why then does my lord require this thing? why will he be a cause of <u>trespass</u> to Is'ra-el?   guilt

4 Nevertheless the king's word prevailed against Jo'ab. Wherefore Jo'ab departed, and went throughout all Is'ra-el, and came to Je-ru'sa-lem.

5 And Jo'ab gave the sum of the number of the people to Da'vid. And all *they of* Is'ra-el were a thousand thousand and an hundred thousand men that drew sword: and Ju'dah *was* <u>four hundred threescore and ten thousand</u> men that drew sword.   470,000

6 But Le'vi and Ben'ja-min counted he not among them: for the king's word was abominable to Jo'ab.

7 And <u>God</u> was displeased with this thing; therefore He <u>smote</u> Is'ra-el.

Elohim^{p.f.} - struck

8 And Da'vid said to <u>God</u>, I have sinned greatly, because I have done this thing: but now, I <u>beseech</u> You, <u>do</u> away the iniquity of Your servant; for I have done very foolishly.   beg - take

9 And the LORD spoke to Gad, Da'vid's seer, saying,

10 Go and tell Da'vid, saying, Thus says the LORD, I offer you three *things*: choose you one of them, that I may do *it* to you.

11 So Gad came to Da'vid, and said to him, Thus says the LORD, Choose you.

12 Either three years' famine; or three months to be destroyed before your foes, while that the sword of your enemies overtakes *you*; or else three days the sword of the LORD, even the pestilence, in the land, and the <u>angel</u> of the LORD destroying throughout all the <u>coasts</u> of Is'ra-el. Now therefore advise yourself what word I shall bring again to Him that sent me. messenger - territory

13 And Da'vid said to Gad, I am in

<u>a great strait</u>: let me fall now into the hand of the LORD; for very great *are* His mercies: but let me not fall into the hand of man.   deep distress

14 So the LORD sent pestilence upon Is'ra-el: and there fell of Is'ra-el seventy thousand men.

15 And <u>God</u> sent an <u>angel</u> to Je-ru'salem to destroy it: and as he was destroying, the LORD beheld, and He <u>repented</u> Him of the evil, and said to the <u>angel</u> that destroyed, It is enough, stay now your hand. And the <u>angel</u> of the LORD stood by the threshingfloor of Or'nan the Jeb'usite.   Elohim^{p.f.} - messenger - regretted

16 And Da'vid lifted up his eyes, and saw the <u>angel</u> of the LORD stand between the earth and the heaven, having a drawn sword in his hand stretched out over Je-ru'sa-lem. Then Da'vid and the elders *of Is'ra-el, who were* clothed in sackcloth, fell upon their faces.

17 And Da'vid said to <u>God</u>, *Is it* not I *that* commanded the people to be numbered? even I it is that have sinned and done evil indeed; but *as for* these sheep, what have they done? let Your hand, I pray You, O LORD my <u>God</u>, be on me, and on my father's house; but not on Your people, that they should be plagued.   Elohim^{p.f.}

18 Then the <u>angel</u> of the LORD commanded Gad to say to Da'vid, that Da'vid should go up, and set up an altar to the LORD in the threshingfloor of Or'nan the Jeb'u-site.

19 And Da'vid went up at the saying of Gad, which he spoke in the name of the LORD.

20 And Or'nan turned back, and saw the <u>angel</u>; and his four sons with him hid themselves. Now Or'nan was threshing wheat.   messenger

21 And as Da'vid came to Or'nan, Or'nan looked and saw Da'vid, and went out of the threshingfloor, and bowed himself to Da'vid with *his* face to the ground.

22 Then Da'vid said to Or'nan, Grant me the place of *this* threshingfloor, that I may build an altar therein to the LORD: you shall grant it me for the full price: that the <u>plague</u> may be stayed from the people.   Give - epidemic

23 And Or'nan said to Da'vid, Take *it* to you, and let my lord the king do *that which is* good in his eyes: lo, I give *you* the oxen *also* for burned offerings, and the threshing instruments for wood, and the wheat for the meat offering; I give it all.

24 And king Da'vid said to Or'nan, Nay; but I will <u>verily</u> buy it for the full price: for I will not take *that* which *is* yours for the LORD, nor offer burned offerings without cost.   surely

25 So Da'vid gave to Or'nan for the place six hundred shekels of gold by weight.

26 And Da'vid built there an altar to the LORD, and offered burned offerings and peace offerings, and called upon the LORD; and He answered him from heaven by fire upon the altar of burned offering.

27 And the LORD commanded the <u>angel</u>; and he put up his sword again into <u>the</u> sheath thereof.   messenger - its

28 At that time when Da'vid saw

that the LORD had answered him in the threshingfloor of Or'nan the Jeb'usite, then he sacrificed there. worshipped 29 For the tabernacle of the LORD, which Mo'ses made in the wilderness, and the altar of the burned offering, *were* at that season in the high place at Gib'e-on.

30 But Da'vid could not go before it to enquire of God: for he was afraid because of the sword of the angel of the LORD. Elohim^p.f. - messenger

CHAPTER 22

THEN Da'vid said, This *is* the house of the LORD God, and this *is* the altar of the burned offering for Is'ra-el. Jehovah^s.f. Elohim^p.f.
2 And Da'vid commanded to gather together the strangers that *were* in the land of Is'ra-el; and he set masons to hew wrought stones to build the house of God. prepare dressed
3 And Da'vid prepared iron in abundance for the nails for the doors of the gates, and for the joinings; and brass in abundance without weight; beyond measure
4 Also cedar trees in abundance: for the Zi-do'ni-ans and they of Tyre brought much cedar wood to Da'vid.
5 And Da'vid said, Sol'o-mon my son *is* young and tender, and the house *that is* to be built for the LORD *must be* exceeding magnifical, of fame and of glory throughout all countries: I will *therefore* now make preparation for it. So Da'vid prepared abundantly before his death.
6 Then he called for Sol'o-mon his son, and charged him to build an house for the LORD God of Is'ra-el. commanded
7 And Da'vid said to Sol'o-mon, My son, as for me, it was in my mind to build an house to the name of the LORD my God: Elohim^p.f.
8 But the word of the LORD came to me, saying, You have shed blood abundantly, and have made great wars: you shall not build an house to My name, because you have shed much blood upon the earth in My sight.
9 Behold, a son shall be born to you, who shall be a man of rest; and I will give him rest from all his enemies round about: for his name shall be Sol'o-mon, and I will give peace and quietness to Is'ra-el in his days. peace - i.e., Peaceful
10 He shall build an house for My name; and he shall be My son, and I *will be* his father; and I will establish the throne of his kingdom over Is'ra-el for ever.
11 Now, my son, the LORD be with you; and prosper you, and build the house of the LORD your God, as He has said of you.
12 Only the LORD give you wisdom and understanding, and give you charge concerning Is'ra-el, that you may keep the law of the LORD your God. obey - Jehovah^s.f. - Elohim^p.f.
13 Then shall you prosper, if you take heed to fulfill the statutes and judgments which the LORD charged Mo'ses with concerning Is'ra-el: be strong, and of good courage; dread not, nor be dismayed.
14 Now, behold, in my trouble I have prepared for the house of the LORD an

hundred thousand talents of gold, and a thousand thousand talents of silver; and of brass and iron without weight; for it is in abundance: timber also and stone have I prepared; and you may add thereto.

15 Moreover *there are* workmen with you in abundance, hewers and workers of stone and timber, and all manner of <u>cunning</u> men for every manner of work. skillful

16 Of the gold, the silver, and the brass, and the iron, *there is* no number. Arise *therefore*, and be doing, and the LORD be with you.

17 Da'vid also commanded all the princes of Is'ra-el to help Sol'o-mon his son, *saying,*

18 *Is* not the LORD your <u>God</u> with you? and has He *not* given you <u>rest</u> on every side? for He has given the inhabitants of the land <u>into my hand</u>; and the land is <u>subdued</u> before the LORD, and before His people.

Elohim^p.f. - peace - over to me - conquered

19 Now set your heart and your soul to seek the LORD your <u>God</u>; arise therefore, and build you the sanctuary of the <u>LORD God</u>, to bring the ark of the <u>covenant</u> of the LORD, and the holy vessels of <u>God</u>, into the house that is to be built to the name of the LORD. Jehovah^s.f. Elohim^p.f. - agreement

CHAPTER 23

SO when Da'vid was old and full of days, he made Sol'o-mon his son king over Is'ra-el.

2 And he gathered together all the princes of Is'ra-el, with the priests and the Le'vites.

3 Now the Le'vites were numbered from the age of thirty years and upward: and their number by their polls, man by man, was thirty and eight thousand.

4 Of which, twenty and four thousand *were* <u>to set forward</u> the work of the house of the LORD; and six thousand *were* officers and judges: to supervise

5 Moreover four thousand *were* <u>porters</u>; and four thousand praised the LORD with the instruments which I made, *said Da'vid*, to praise *therewith*. gatekeepers

6 And Da'vid divided them into <u>courses</u> among the sons of Le'vi, *namely*, Ger'shon, Ko'hath, and Me-ra'ri. divisions

7 Of the Ger'shon-ites were, La'a-dan, and Shim'e-i.

8 The sons of La'a-dan; the chief *was* Je-hi'el, and Ze'tham, and Jo'el, three.

9 The sons of Shim'e-i; Shel'o-mith, and Ha'zi-el, and Ha'ran, three. These *were* the chief of the fathers of La'a-dan.

10 And the sons of Shim'e-i *were*, Ja'hath, Zi'na, and Je'ush, and Be-ri'ah. These four *were* the sons of Shim'e-i.

11 And Ja'hath was the chief, and Zi'zah the second: but Je'ush and Be-ri'ah had not many sons; therefore they were in one <u>reckoning</u>, according to *their* father's house. family

12 The sons of Ko'hath; Am'ram, Iz'har, He'bron, and Uz'zi-el, four.

13 The sons of Am'ram; Aar'on and Mo'ses: and Aar'on was separated, that

he should sanctify the most holy things, he and his sons for ever, to burn incense before the LORD, to minister to Him, and to bless in His name for ever.

14 Now *concerning* Mo'ses the man of <u>God</u>, his sons were named of the tribe of Le'vi.   Elohim^p.f.

15 The sons of Mo'ses *were*, Ger'shom, and E-li-e'zer.

16 Of the sons of Ger'shom, Sheb'u-el *was* the chief.

17 And the sons of E-li-e'zer *were*, Re-ha-bi'ah <u>the chief</u>. And E-li-e'zer had none other sons; but the sons of Re-ha-bi'ah were very many.   was the first

18 Of the sons of Iz'har; Shel'o-mith the chief.

19 Of the sons of He'bron; Je-ri'ah the first, Am-a-ri'ah the second, Ja-ha'zi-el the third, and Jek-a-me'am the fourth.

20 Of the sons of Uz'zi-el; Mi'cah the first, and Je-si'ah the second.

21 The sons of Me-ra'ri; Mah'li, and Mu'shi. The sons of Mah'li; E-le-a'zar, and Kish.

22 And E-le-a'zar died, and had no sons, but daughters: and their <u>brethren</u> the sons of Kish took them.   kinsmen

23 The sons of Mu'shi; Mah'li, and E'der, and Jer'e-moth, three.

24 These *were* the sons of Le'vi after the house of their fathers; *even* the chief of the fathers, as they were counted by number of names by their <u>polls</u>, that did the work for the service of the house of the LORD, from the age of twenty years and upward.   census

25 For Da'vid said, The <u>LORD God</u> of Is'ra-el has given rest to His people,

that they may dwell in Je-ru'sa-lem for ever: Jehovah^s.f. Elohim^p.f.

26 And also to the Le'vites; they shall no *more* carry the tabernacle, nor any vessels of it for the service thereof.

27 For by the last words of Da'vid the Le'vites *were* numbered from twenty years old and above:

28 Because their <u>office</u> *was* to wait on the sons of Aar'on for the service of the house of the LORD, in the courts, and in the <u>chambers</u>, and in the purifying of all holy things, and the work of the service of the house of God;   responsibility - side rooms

29 Both for the showbread, and for the fine flour for meat offering, and for the unleavened cakes, and for *that which is baked in* the pan, and for that which is fried, and for all manner of measure and size;

30 And to stand every morning to thank and praise the LORD, and likewise at even;

31 And to offer all burned sacrifices to the LORD in the <u>sabbaths</u>, in the new moons, and on the set feasts, by number, according to the order commanded to them, continually before the LORD: rest days

32 And that they should <u>keep the charge</u> of the tabernacle of the congregation, and the <u>charge</u> of the holy *place*, and the <u>charge</u> of the sons of Aar'on their brethren, in the service of the house of the LORD. be responsible for

CHAPTER 24

N OW *these are* the divisions of the sons of Aar'on. The sons of Aar'-

on; Na'dab, and A-bi'hu, E-le-a'zar, and Ith'a-mar.

2 But Na'dab and A-bi'hu died before their father, and had no children: therefore E-le-a'zar and Ith'a-mar <u>executed</u> the priest's office. ^{served}

3 And Da'vid distributed them, both Za'dok of the sons of E-le-a'zar, and A-him'e-lech of the sons of Ith'a-mar, according to their offices in their service.

4 And there were more chief men found of the sons of E-le-a'zar than of the sons of Ith'a-mar; and *thus* were they divided. Among the sons of E-le-a'zar *there were* sixteen chief men of the house of *their* fathers, and eight among the sons of Ith'a-mar according to the house of their fathers.

5 Thus were they divided by lot, one sort with another; for the governors of the sanctuary, and governors *of the house* of God, were of the sons of E-le-a'zar, and of the sons of Ith'a-mar.

6 And Shem-a-i'ah the son of Ne-than'e-el the scribe, *one* of the Le'vites, wrote them before the king, and the princes, and Za'dok the priest, and A-him'e-lech the son of A-bi'a-thar, and *before* the chief of the fathers of the priests and Le'vites: one principal household being taken for E-le-a'zar, and *one* taken for Ith'a-mar.

7 Now the first lot came forth to Je-hoi'a-rib, the second to Je-da'iah,

8 The third to Ha'rim, the fourth to Se-o'rim,

9 The fifth to Mal-chi'jah, the sixth to Mij'a-min,

10 The seventh to Hak'koz, the eighth to A-bi'jah,

11 The ninth to Jesh'u-ah, the tenth to Shech-a'ni'ah,

12 The eleventh to E-li'a-shib, the twelfth to Ja'kim,

13 The thirteenth to Hup'pah, the fourteenth to Je'sheb'e-ab,

14 The fifteenth to Bil'gah, the sixteenth to Im'mer,

15 The seventeenth to He'zir, the eighteenth to Aph'ses,

16 The nineteenth to Peth-a-hi'ah, the twentieth to Je-hez'e-kel,

17 The one and twentieth to Ja'chin, the two and twentieth to Ga'mul,

18 The three and twentieth to Del-a-i'ah, the four and twentieth to Ma'a-zi'ah.

19 These *were* the <u>orderings</u> of them in their service to come into the house of the LORD, according to their manner, under Aar'on their father, as the LORD God of Is'ra-el had commanded him.

^{appointed order - Jehovah}^{s.f.} ^{Elohim}^{p.f.}

20 And the rest of the sons of Le'vi *were these*: Of the sons of Am'ram; Shu'ba-el: of the sons of Shu'ba-el; Jeh-de'iah.

21 Concerning Re-ha-bi'ah: of the sons of Re-ha-bi'ah, the first *was* Issh-i'ah.

22 Of the Iz'har-ites; Shel'o-moth: of the sons of Shel'o-moth; Ja'hath.

23 And the sons of *He'bron*; Je-ri'ah *the first*, Am-a-ri'ah the second, Ja-ha'zi-el the third, Jek-a-me'am the fourth.

24 *Of* the sons of Uz'zi-el; Mi'chah: of the sons of Mi'chah; Sha'mir.

25 The brother of Mi'chah *was* Issh-i'ah: of the sons of Issh-i'ah; Zech-a-ri'ah.

26 The sons of Me-ra'ri *were* Mah'li and Mu'shi: the sons of Ja-a-zi'ah; Be'no.

27 The sons of Me-ra'ri by Ja-a-zi'ah; Be'no, and Sho'ham, and Zac'cur, and Ib'ri.

28 Of Mah'li *came* E-le-a'zar, who had no sons.

29 Concerning Kish: the son of Kish *was* Je-rah'me-el.

30 The sons also of Mu'shi; Mah'li, and E'der, and Jer'i-moth. These *were* the sons of the Le'vites after the house of their fathers.

31 These likewise cast lots opposite their brethren the sons of Aar'on in the presence of Da'vid the king, and Za'dok, and A-him'e-lech, and the chief of the fathers of the priests and Le'vites, even the principal fathers opposite their younger brethren.

CHAPTER 25

MOREOVER Da'vid and the captains of the host separated to the service of the sons of A'saph, and of He'man, and of Jed'u-thun, who should prophesy with harps, with psalteries, and with cymbals: and the number of the workmen according to their service was: set apart - lyres

2 Of the sons of A'saph; Zac'cur, and Jo'seph, and Neth-a-ni'ah, and As-a-re'lah, the sons of A'saph under the hands of A'saph, which prophesied according to the order of the king.   spoke

3 Of Jed'u-thun: the sons of Jed'u-thun; Ged-a-li'ah, and Ze'ri, and Je-sha'iah, Hash-a-bi'ah, and Mat-ti-thi'-ah, six, under the hands of their father Jed'u-thun, who prophesied with a harp, to give thanks and to praise the LORD.

4 Of He'man: the sons of He'man; Buk-ki'ah, Mat-ta-ni'ah, Uz'zi-el, Sheb'u-el, and Jer'i-moth, Han-a-ni'ah, Ha-na'ni, E-li'a-thah, Gid-dal'ti, and Ro-mam'ti-e'zer, Josh-bek'a-shah, Mal'lo-thi, Ho'thir, *and* Ma-ha'zi-oth:

5 All these *were* the sons of He'man the king's seer in the words of God, to lift up the horn. And God gave to He'man fourteen sons and three daughters.   Elohim^{p.f.}

6 All these *were* under the hands of their father for song *in* the house of the LORD, with cymbals, psalteries, and harps, for the service of the house of God, according to the king's order to A'saph, Jed'u-thun, and He'man.   lyres

7 So the number of them, with their brethren that were instructed in the songs of the LORD, *even* all that were cunning, was two hundred fourscore and eight.   skillful - 288

8 And they cast lots, ward against *ward*, as well the small as the great, the teacher as the scholar.   for their duties

9 Now the first lot came forth for A'saph to Jo'seph: the second to Ged-a-li'ah, who with his brethren and sons *were* twelve:

10 The third to Zac'cur, *he*, his sons, and his brethren, *were* twelve:

11 The fourth to Iz'ri, *he*, his sons, and his brethren, *were* twelve:

12 The fifth to Neth-a-ni'ah, *he*, his sons, and his brethren, *were* twelve:

13 The sixth to Buk-ki'ah, *he*, his sons, and his brethren, *were* twelve:
14 The seventh to Je-shar'e-lah, *he*, his sons, and his brethren, *were* twelve:
15 The eighth to Je-sha'iah, *he*, his sons, and his brethren, *were* twelve:
16 The ninth to Mat-ta-ni'ah, *he*, his sons, and his brethren, *were* twelve:
17 The tenth to Shim'e-i, *he*, his sons, and his brethren, *were* twelve:
18 The eleventh to A-zar'e-el, *he*, his sons, and his brethren, *were* twelve:
19 The twelfth to Hash-a-bi'ah, *he*, his sons, and his brethren, *were* twelve:
20 The thirteenth to Shu'ba-el, *he*, his sons, and his brethren, *were* twelve:
21 The fourteenth to Mat-ti-thi'ah, *he*, his sons, and his brethren, *were* twelve:
22 The fifteenth to Jer'e-moth, *he*, his sons, and his brethren, *were* twelve:
23 The sixteenth to Han-a-ni'ah, *he*, his sons, and his brethren, *were* twelve:
24 The seventeenth to Josh-bek'a-shah, *he*, his sons, and his brethren, *were* twelve:
25 The eighteenth to Ha-na'ni, *he*, his sons, and his brethren, *were* twelve:
26 The nineteenth to Mal'lo-thi, *he*, his sons, and his brethren, *were* twelve:
27 The twentieth to E-li'a-thah, *he*, his sons, and his brethren, *were* twelve:
28 The one and twentieth to Ho'thir, *he*, his sons, and his brethren, *were* twelve:
29 The two and twentieth to Gid-dal'ti, *he*, his sons, and his brethren, *were* twelve:
30 The three and twentieth to Ma-ha'zi-oth, *he*, his sons, and his brethren, *were* twelve:
31 The four and twentieth to Ro-mam'ti-e'zer, *he*, his sons, and his brethren, *were* twelve.

CHAPTER 26

CONCERNING the divisions of the <u>porters</u>: Of the Kor'hites *was* Me-shel-e-mi'ah the son of Ko're, of the sons of A'saph. gatekeepers
2 And the sons of Me-shel-e-mi'ah *were*, Zech-a-ri'ah the firstborn, Je-di'a-el the second, Zeb-a-di'ah the third, Jath'ni-el the fourth,
3 E'lam the fifth, Je-ho-ha'nan the sixth, El-i-o-e'na-i the seventh.
4 Moreover the sons of O'bed-e'dom *were*, Shem-a-i'ah the firstborn, Je-hoz'a-bad the second, Jo'ah the third, and Sa'car the fourth, and Ne-than'e-el the fifth,
5 Am'mi-el the sixth, Is'sa-char the seventh, Pe-ul'thai the eighth: for God blessed <u>him</u>. i.e., Obed-edom
6 Also to Shem-a-i'ah his son were sons born, that ruled throughout the house of their father: for they *were* mighty men of valor.
7 The sons of Shem-a-i'ah; Oth'ni, and Re'pha-el, and O'bed, El'za-bad, whose brethren *were* strong men, E-li'hu, and Sem-a-chi'ah.
8 All these of the sons of O'bed-e'dom: they and their sons and their brethren, able men for strength for the service, *were* <u>threescore and two</u> of O'bed-e'dom. 62
9 And Me-shel-e-mi'ah had sons and brethren, strong men, eighteen.
10 Also Ho'sah, of the children of

Me-ra'ri, had sons; Sim'ri the chief, (for *though* he was not the firstborn, yet his father made him the chief;)

11 Hil-ki'ah the second, Teb-a-li'ah the third, Zech-a-ri'ah the fourth: all the sons and brethren of Ho'sah *were* thirteen.

12 Among these *were* the divisions of the <u>porters</u>, *even* among the chief men, *having* <u>wards</u> one against another, to minister in the house of the LORD. gatekeepers - guards

13 And they cast lots, as well the small as the great, according to the house of their fathers, for every gate.

14 And the lot eastward fell to Shel-e-mi'ah. Then for Zech-a-ri'ah his son, a wise counselor, they cast lots; and his lot came out northward.

15 To O'bed-e'dom southward; and to his sons the house of A-sup'pim.

16 To Shup'pim and Ho'sah *the lot came forth* westward, with the gate Shal'le-cheth, by the <u>causeway</u> of the going up, <u>ward</u> against <u>ward</u>. ramp - guard

17 Eastward *were* six Le'vites, northward four a day, southward four a day, and toward <u>A-sup'pim</u> two *and* two. the storehouse

18 At Par'bar westward, four at the <u>causeway</u>, *and* two at Par'bar. ramp

19 These *are* the divisions of the <u>porters</u> among the sons of Ko're, and among the sons of Me-ra'ri. gatekeepers

20 And of the Le'vites, A-hi'jah *was* over the treasures of the house of <u>God</u>, and over the treasures of the <u>dedicated</u> things. Elohim^{p.f.} - holy

21 *As concerning* the sons of La'a-dan; the sons of the Ger'shon-ite La'a-dan, chief fathers, *even* of La'a-dan the Ger'shon-ite, *were* Je-hi'e-li.

22 The sons of Je-hi'e-li; Ze'tham, and Jo'el his brother, *which were* over the treasures of the house of the LORD.

23 Of the Am'ram-ites, *and* the Iz'har-ites, the He'bron-ites, *and* the Uz'zi-el-ites:

24 And Sheb'u-el the son of Ger'shom, the son of Mo'ses, *was* ruler of the treasures.

25 And his brethren by E-li-e'zer; Re-ha-bi'ah his son, and Je-sha'iah his son, and Jo'ram his son, and Zich'ri his son, and Shel'o-mith his son.

26 Which Shel'o-mith and his brethren *were* over all the treasures of the dedicated things, which Da'vid the king, and the chief fathers, the captains over thousands and hundreds, and the captains of the host, had dedicated.

27 Out of the <u>spoils</u> won in battles did they dedicate to <u>maintain</u> the house of the LORD. plunder - repair

28 And all that Sam'u-el the seer, and Saul the son of Kish, and Ab'ner the son of Ner, and Jo'ab the son of Zer-u-i'ah, had dedicated; *and* whosoever had dedicated *any thing*, *it was* under the hand of Shel'o-mith, and of his brethren.

29 Of the Iz'har-ites, Chen-a-ni'ah and his sons *were* for the outward business over Is'ra-el, for officers and judges.

30 *And* of the He'bron-ites, Hash-a-bi'ah and his brethren, men of valor, a thousand and seven hundred, *were* officers among them of Is'ra-el on this side Jor'dan westward in all the business of

the LORD, and in the service of the king. 31 Among the He'bron-ites *was* Je-ri'jah the chief, *even* among the He'bron'ites, according to the generations of his fathers. In the fortieth year of the reign of Da'vid they were sought for, and there were found among them mighty men of valor at Ja'zer of Gil'e-ad.

32 And his brethren, men of valor, *were* two thousand and seven hundred chief fathers, whom king Da'vid made rulers over the Reu'ben-ites, the Gad'ites, and the half tribe of Ma-nas'seh, for every matter pertaining to God, and affairs of the king. Elohim^p.f.

CHAPTER 27

NOW the children of Is'ra-el after their number, *to that is*, the chief fathers and captains of thousands and hundreds, and their officers that served the king in any matter of the courses, which came in and went out month by month throughout all the months of the year, of every course *were* twenty and four thousand. divisions

2 Over the first course for the first month *was* Ja-sho'be-am the son of Zab'di-el: and in his course *were* twenty and four thousand.

3 Of the children of Pe'rez *was* the chief of all the captains of the host for the first month.

4 And over the course of the second month *was* Dod'a-i an A-ho'hite, and of his course *was* Mik'loth also the ruler: in his course likewise *were* twenty and four thousand.

5 The third captain of the host for the third month *was* Be-na'iah the son of Je-hoi'a-da, a chief priest: and in his course *were* twenty and four thousand.

6 This *is that* Be-na'iah, *who was* mighty *among* the thirty, and above the thirty: and in his course *was* Am-miz'a-bad his son. division

7 The fourth *captain* for the fourth month *was* A'sa-hel the brother of Jo'ab, and Zeb-a-di'ah his son after him: and in his course *were* twenty and four thousand.

8 The fifth captain for the fifth month *was* Sham'huth the Iz'ra-hite: and in his course *were* twenty and four thousand.

9 The sixth *captain* for the sixth month *was* I'ra the son of Ik'kesh the Te-ko'ite: and in his course *were* twenty and four thousand. division

10 The seventh *captain* for the seventh month *was* He'lez the Pel'o-nite, of the children of E'phra-im: and in his course *were* twenty and four thousand.

11 The eighth *captain* for the eighth month *was* Sib'be-cai the Hu'shath-ite, of the Zar'hites: and in his course *were* twenty and four thousand.

12 The ninth *captain* for the ninth month *was* A-bi-e'zer the An'e-toth-ite, of the Ben'ja-mites: and in his course *were* twenty and four thousand.

13 The tenth *captain* for the tenth month *was* Ma-har'a-i the Ne-toph'a-thite, of the Zar'hites: and in his course *were* twenty and four thousand.

14 The eleventh *captain* for the eleventh month *was* Be-na'iah the Pir'a-thon-ite, of the children of E'phra-im:

and in his <u>course</u> *were* twenty and four thousand.

15 The twelfth *captain* for the twelfth month *was* Hel'da-i the Ne-toph'a-thite, of Oth'ni-el: and in his <u>course</u> *were* twenty and four thousand._{division}

16 Furthermore over the tribes of Is'ra-el: the ruler of the Reu'ben-ites *was* E-li-e'zer the son of Zich'ri: of the Sim'e-on-ites, Sheph-a-ti'ah the son of Ma'a-chah:

17 Of the Le'vites, Hash-a-bi'ah the son of Ke-mu'el: of the Aar'on-ites, Za'dok:

18 Of Ju'dah, E-li'hu, *one* of the brethren of Da'vid: of Is'sa-char, Om'ri the son of Mi'chael:

19 Of Zeb'u-lun, Ish-ma-i'ah the son of O-ba-di'ah: of Naph'ta-li, Jer'i-moth the son of Az'ri-el:

20 Of the children of E'phra-im, Ho-she'a the son of Az-a-zi'ah: of the half tribe of Ma-nas'seh, Jo'el the son of Pe-da'iah:

21 Of the half *tribe* of Ma-nas'seh in Gil'e-ad, Id'do the son of Zech-a-ri'ah: of Ben'ja-min, Ja-a'si-el the son of Ab'ner:

22 Of Dan, A-zar'e-el the son of Jer'o-ham. These *were* the princes of the tribes of Is'ra-el.

23 But Da'vid took not the number of them from twenty years old and under: because the LORD had said He would increase Is'ra-el like to the stars of the heavens.

24 Jo'ab the son of Zer-u-i'ah began to number, but he finished not, because there fell wrath for it against Is'ra-el;

neither was the number <u>put</u> in the account of the chronicles of king Da'vid. _{included}

25 And over the king's treasures *was* Az'ma-veth the son of A-di'el: and over the storehouses in the fields, in the cities, and in the villages, and in the castles, *was* Je-hon'a-than the son of Uz-zi'ah:

26 And over them that did the work of the field for tillage of the ground *was* Ez'ri the son of Che'lub:

27 And over the vineyards *was* Shim'e-i the Ra'math-ite: over the increase of the vineyards for the wine cellars *was* Zab'di the Shiph'mite:

28 And over the olive trees and the sycamore trees that *were* in the low plains *was* Ba'al-ha'nan the Ged'e-rite: and over the cellars of oil *was* Jo'ash:

29 And over the herds that fed in Shar'on *was* Shit'ra-i the Shar'on-ite: and over the herds *that were* in the valleys *was* Sha'phat the son of Ad'la-i:

30 Over the camels also *was* O'bil the Ish'ma-el-ite: and over the asses *was* Jeh-de'iah the Me-ron'o-thite:

31 And over the flocks *was* Ja'ziz the Ha'ger-ite. All these *were* the rulers of the <u>substance</u> which *was* king Da'vid's. _{property}

32 Also Jon'a-than Da'vid's uncle was a counselor, a wise man, and a <u>scribe</u>: and Je-hi'el the son of Hach'mo-ni *was* with the king's sons: _{secretary}

33 And A-hith'o-phel *was* the king's counselor: and Hu'shai the Ar'chite *was* the king's companion:

34 And after A-hith'o-phel *was* Je-hoi'a-da the son of Be-na'iah, and A-

bi'a-thar: and the general of the king's army *was* Jo'ab.

CHAPTER 28

AND Da'vid assembled all the princes of Is'ra-el, the princes of the tribes, and the captains of the companies that ministered to the king by <u>course</u>, and the captains over the thousands, and captains over the hundreds, and the stewards over all the <u>substance</u> and possession of the king, and of his sons, with the <u>officers</u>, and with the mighty men, and with all the valiant men, to Je-ru'sa-lem.

divisions - property - officials

2 Then Da'vid the king stood up upon his feet, and said, Hear me, my brethren, and my people: *As for me*, I *had* in my heart to build an house of rest for the ark of the <u>covenant</u> of the LORD, and for the footstool of our <u>God</u>, and had made ready for the building: agreement

3 But <u>God</u> said to me, You shall not build an house for My name, because you *have been* a man of war, and have shed blood.   Elohim^p.f.

4 However the <u>LORD God</u> of Is'ra-el chose me before all the house of my father to be king over Is'ra-el for ever: for He has chosen Ju'dah *to be* the ruler; and of the house of Ju'dah, the house of my father; and among the sons of my father He liked me to make *me* king over all Is'ra-el: Jehovah^s.f. Elohim^p.f.

5 And of all my sons, (for the LORD has given me many sons,) He has chosen Sol'o-mon my son to sit upon the throne of the kingdom of the LORD over Is'ra-el.

6 And He said to me, Sol'o-mon your son, he shall build My house and My courts: for I have chosen him *to be* My son, and I will be his father.

7 Moreover I will establish his kingdom for ever, if he be <u>constant</u> to do My commandments and My judgments, as at this day.   faithful

8 Now therefore in the sight of all Is'ra-el the congregation of the LORD, and in the audience of our <u>God</u>, keep and seek for all the commandments of the LORD your <u>God</u>: that you may possess this good land, and leave *it* for an inheritance for your children after you for ever.   Elohim^p.f.

9 And you, Sol'o-mon my son, know you the <u>God</u> of your father, and serve Him with a perfect heart and with a willing mind: for the LORD searches all hearts, and understands all the imaginations of the thoughts: if you seek Him, He will be found of you; but if you forsake Him, He will cast you off for ever.

10 Take heed now; for the LORD has chosen you to build an house for the sanctuary: be strong, and do *it*.

11 Then Da'vid gave to Sol'o-mon his son the <u>pattern</u> of the porch, and of the houses thereof, and of the treasuries thereof, and of the upper chambers thereof, and of the inner <u>parlors</u> thereof, and of the place of the mercy seat,   plan - halls

12 And the pattern of all that he had by the spirit, of the courts of the house of the LORD, and of all the chambers round about, of the treasuries of the

house of <u>God</u>, and of the treasuries of the dedicated things: Elohim^{p.f.}

13 Also for the <u>courses</u> of the priests and the Le'vites, and for all the work of the service of the house of the Lord, and for all the vessels of service in the house of the Lord.   divisions

14 *He gave* of gold by weight for *things* of gold, for all <u>instruments</u> of all manner of service; *silver also* for all <u>instruments</u> of silver by weight, for all <u>instruments</u> of every kind of service: utensils

15 Even the weight for the candlesticks of gold, and for their lamps of gold, by weight for every candlestick, and for the lamps thereof: and for the candlesticks of silver by weight, *both* for the candlestick, and *also* for the lamps thereof, according to the use of every candlestick.

16 And by weight *he gave* gold for the tables of showbread, for every table; and *likewise* silver for the tables of silver:

17 Also pure gold for the <u>flesh-hooks</u>, and the bowls, and the <u>cups</u>: and for the golden basins *he gave gold* by weight for every basin; and *likewise silver* by weight for every basin of silver: forks - pitchers

18 And for the altar of incense refined gold by weight; and gold for the pattern of the chariot of the cherubims, that spread out *their wings*, and covered the ark of the <u>covenant</u> of the Lord.   agreement

19 All *this*, *said Da'vid*, the Lord made me understand in writing by *His* hand upon me, *even* all the works of this pattern.

20 And Da'vid said to Sol'o-mon his son, Be strong and of good courage, and do *it*: fear not, nor be dismayed: for the Lord God, *even* my <u>God</u>, *will be* with you; He will not fail you, nor forsake you, until you have finished all the work for the service of the house of the Lord.   Jehovah^{s.f.} Elohim^{p.f.}

21 And, behold, the <u>courses</u> of the priests and the Le'vites, *even they shall be with you* for all the service of the house of God: and *there shall be* with you for all manner of workmanship every willing skilful man, for any manner of service: also the princes and all the people *will be* wholly at your commandment.   divisions

CHAPTER 29

FURTHERMORE Da'vid the king said to all the congregation, Sol'o-mon my son, whom alone God has chosen, *is yet* young and <u>tender</u>, and the work *is* great: for the <u>palace</u> *is* not for man, but for the Lord God.   inexperienced - i.e., temple - Jehovah Elohim

2 Now I have prepared with all my might for the house of my God the gold for *things to be made* of gold, and the silver for *things* of silver, and the brass for *things* of brass, the iron for *things* of iron, and wood for *things* of wood; onyx stones, and *stones* to be set, <u>glistering</u> stones, and of <u>divers</u> colors, and all manner of precious stones, and marble stones in abundance. antimony - various

3 Moreover, because I have set my affection to the house of my God, I have of my own <u>proper good</u>, of gold and

silver, *which* I have given to the house of my God, over and above all that I have prepared for the holy house, personal treasure

4 *Even* three thousand talents of gold, of the gold of O'phir, and seven thousand talents of refined silver, to overlay the walls of the houses *with*:

5 The gold for *things* of gold, and the silver for *things* of silver, and for all manner of work *to be made* by the hands of artificers. And who *then* is willing to consecrate his service this day to the LORD? craftsmen

6 Then the chief of the fathers and princes of the tribes of Is'ra-el, and the captains of thousands and of hundreds, with the rulers of the king's work, offered willingly, gave

7 And gave for the service of the house of God of gold five thousand talents and ten thousand drams, and of silver ten thousand talents, and of brass eighteen thousand talents, and one hundred thousand talents of iron.

8 And they with whom *precious* stones were found gave *them* to the treasure of the house of the LORD, by the hand of Je-hi'el the Ger'shon-ite.

9 Then the people rejoiced, for that they offered willingly, because with perfect heart they offered willingly to the LORD: and Da'vid the king also rejoiced with great joy. a whole

10 Wherefore Da'vid blessed the LORD before all the congregation: and Da'vid said, Blessed *be* You, LORD God of Is'ra-el our father, for ever and ever.

11 Yours, O LORD, *is* the greatness, and the power, and the glory, and the victory, and the majesty: for all *that is* in the heaven and in the earth *is Yours*; Yours *is* the kingdom, O LORD, and You are exalted as head above all.

12 Both riches and honor *come* of You, and You reign over all; and in Your hand *is* power and might; and in Your hand *it is* to make great, and to give strength to all. ROM. 11:36

13 Now therefore, our God, we thank You, and praise Your glorious name.

14 But who *am* I, and what *is* my people, that we should be able to offer so willingly after this sort? for all things *come* of You, and of Your own have we given You.

15 For we *are* strangers before you, and sojourners, as *were* all our fathers: our days on the earth *are* as a shadow, and *there is* none abiding. resident aliens - no hope

16 O LORD our God, all this store that we have prepared to build You an house for Your holy name *come* of Your hand, and is all Your own. abundance

17 I know also, my God, that You try the heart, and have pleasure in uprightness. As for me, in the uprightness of my heart I have willingly offered all these things: and now have I seen with joy Your people, which are present here, to offer willingly to You. test - given

18 O LORD God of A'bra-ham, I'saac, and of Is'ra-el, our fathers, keep this for ever in the imagination of the thoughts of the heart of Your people, and prepare their heart to You: direct

19 And give to Sol'o-mon my son a perfect heart, to keep Your commandments, Your testimonies, and Your statutes, and to do all *these things*, and to build the palace, *for* the which I have made provision.   i.e., temple

20 And Da'vid said to all the congregation, Now bless the Lord your God. And all the congregation blessed the Lord God of their fathers, and bowed down their heads, and worshiped the Lord, and the king.

         Jehovah^{s.f.} Elohim^{p.f.}

21 And they sacrificed sacrifices to the Lord, and offered burned offerings to the Lord, on the morrow after that day, *even* a thousand bullocks, a thousand rams, *and* a thousand lambs, with their drink offerings, and sacrifices in abundance for all Is'ra-el: day

22 And did eat and drink before the Lord on that day with great gladness. And they made Sol'o-mon the son of Da'vid king the second time, and anointed *him* to the Lord *to be* the chief governor, and Za'dok *to be* priest.   ruler

23 Then Sol'o-mon sat on the throne of the Lord as king instead of Da'vid his father, and prospered; and all Is'ra-el obeyed him.

24 And all the princes, and the mighty men, and all the sons likewise of king Da'vid, submitted themselves to Sol'o-mon the king.

25 And the Lord magnified Sol'o-mon exceedingly in the sight of all Is'ra-el, and bestowed upon him *such* royal majesty as had not been on any king before him in Is'ra-el.

26 Thus Da'vid the son of Jes'se reigned over all Is'ra-el.

27 And the time that he reigned over Is'ra-el *was* forty years; seven years reigned he in He'bron, and thirty and three *years* reigned he in Je-ru'salem.

28 And he died in a good old age, full of days, riches, and honor: and Sol'o-mon his son reigned in his stead.   place

29 Now the acts of Da'vid the king, first and last, behold, they *are* written in the book of Sam'u-el the seer, and in the book of Na'than the prophet, and in the book of Gad the seer,

30 With all his reign and his might, and the times that went over him, and over Is'ra-el, and over all the kingdoms of the countries.

THE SECOND BOOK OF THE
CHRONICLES

Solomon and
the Kings of Judah

CHAPTER 1

AND Sol'o-mon the son of Da'vid was strengthened in his kingdom, and the LORD his <u>God</u> *was* with him, and magnified him exceedingly. Elohim^{p.f.}

2 Then Sol'o-mon spoke to all Is'ra-el, to the captains of thousands and of hundreds, and to the judges, and to every governor in all Is'ra-el, the chief of the fathers.

3 So Sol'o-mon, and all the congregation with him, went to the <u>high place</u> that *was* at Gib'e-on; for there was the tabernacle of the congregation of <u>God</u>, which Mo'-ses the servant of the LORD had made in the wilderness. shrine - Elohim^{p.f.}

4 But the ark of <u>God</u> had Da'vid brought up from Kir'jath-je'a-rim to *the place which* Da'vid had prepared for it: for he had <u>pitched</u> a tent for it at Je-ru'sa-lem. set up

5 Moreover the brazen altar, that Be-zal'e-el the son of U'ri, the son of Hur, had made, he put before the tabernacle of the LORD: and Sol'o-mon and the congregation sought to it.

6 And Sol'o-mon went up there to the brazen altar before the LORD, which *was* at the tabernacle of the congregation, and offered a thousand burned offerings upon it.

7 In that night did <u>God</u> appear to Sol'o-mon, and said to him, Ask what I shall give you.

8 And Sol'o-mon said to <u>God</u>, You have showed great mercy to Da'vid my father, and have made me to reign in his <u>stead</u>. Elohim^{p.f.} - place

9 Now, O <u>LORD God</u>, let Your promise to Da'vid my father be <u>established</u>: for You have made me king over a people like the dust of the earth in multitude. Jehovah^{s.f.} Elohim^{p.f.} - fulfilled

10 Give me now wisdom and knowledge, that I may go out and come in before this people: for who can <u>judge</u> this Your people, *that is so* great? rule

11 And <u>God</u> said to Sol'o-mon, Because this was in your heart, and you have not asked riches, wealth, or honor, nor the life of your enemies, neither yet have asked long life; but have asked wisdom and knowledge for yourself, that you may <u>judge</u> My people, over whom I have made you king:

12 Wisdom and knowledge *is* granted to you; and I will give you riches, and wealth, and honor, such as none of the kings have had that *have been* before you, neither shall there any after you have the like.

13 Then Sol'o-mon came *from his journey* to the <u>high place</u> that *was* at Gib'e-on to Je-ru'sa-lem, from before the tabernacle of the congregation, and reigned over Is'ra-el. shrine

14 And Sol'o-mon gathered chariots and horsemen: and he had a thousand

and four hundred chariots, and twelve thousand horsemen, which he placed in the chariot cities, and with the king at Je-ru'sa-lem.

15 And the king made silver and gold at Je-ru'sa-lem *as plenteous* as stones, and cedar trees made he as the sycamore trees that *are* in the vale for abundance.   lowlands

16 And Sol'o-mon had horses brought out of E'gypt, and linen yarn: the king's merchants received the linen yarn at a price.

17 And they brought up, and brought forth out of E'gypt a chariot for six hundred *shekels* of silver, and an horse for an hundred and fifty: and so brought they out *horses* for all the kings of the Hit'tites, and for the kings of Syr'i-a, by their means.   the same

CHAPTER 2

AND Sol'o-mon determined to build an house for the name of the LORD, and an house for his kingdom.

2 And Sol'o-mon told out three-score and ten thousand men to bear burdens, and fourscore thousand to hew in the mountain, and three thousand and six hundred to oversee them.   assigned - 70,000 - 80,000 - cut

3 And Sol'o-mon sent to Hu'ram the king of Tyre, saying, As you did deal with Da'vid my father, and did send him cedars to build him an house to dwell therein, *even so deal with me.*

4 Behold, I build an house to the name of the LORD my God, to dedicate *it* to Him, *and* to burn before Him sweet incense, and for the continual showbread, and for the burned offerings morning and evening, on the sabbaths, and on the new moons, and on the solemn feasts of the LORD our God. This *is an ordinance* for ever to Is'ra-el.   rest days

5 And the house which I build *is* great: for great *is* our God above all gods.   Elohim[p.f.]

6 But who is able to build Him an house, seeing the heaven and heaven of heavens cannot contain Him? who *am* I then, that I should build Him an house, save only to burn sacrifice before Him?

7 Send me now therefore a man cunning to work in gold, and in silver, and in brass, and in iron, and in purple, and crimson, and blue, and that can skill to grave with the cunning men that *are* with me in Ju'dah and in Je-ru'sa-lem, whom Da'vid my father did provide.   skillful - know how to engrave

8 Send me also cedar trees, fir trees, and algum trees, out of Leb'a-non: for I know that your servants can skill to cut timber in Leb'a-non; and, behold, my servants *shall be* with your servants,

9 Even to prepare me timber in abundance: for the house which I am about to build *shall be* wonderful great.

10 And, behold, I will give to your servants, the hewers that cut timber, twenty thousand measures of beaten wheat, and twenty thousand measures of barley, and twenty thousand baths of wine, and twenty thousand baths of oil.   woodsmen - crushed

11 Then Hu'ram the king of Tyre answered in writing, which he sent to Sol'o-mon, Because the LORD has

loved His people, He has made you king over them.

12 Hu'ram said moreover, Blessed *be* the LORD God of Is'ra-el, that made heaven and earth, who has given to Da'vid the king a wise son, underlined with prudence and understanding, that might build an house for the LORD, and an house for his kingdom. Jehovah[s.f.] Elohim[p.f.] - endowed

13 And now I have sent a cunning man, endued with understanding, of Hu'ram my father's, skillful

14 The son of a woman of the daughters of Dan, and his father *was* a man of Tyre, skillful to work in gold, and in silver, in brass, in iron, in stone, and in timber, in purple, in blue, and in fine linen, and in crimson; also to grave any manner of graving, and to find out every device which shall be put to him, with your cunning men, and with the cunning men of my LORD Da'vid your father. execute any design

15 Now therefore the wheat, and the barley, the oil, and the wine, which my LORD has spoken of, let him send to his servants:

16 And we will cut wood out of Leb'a-non, as much as you shall need: and we will bring it to you in floats by sea to Jop'pa; and you shall carry it up to Je-ru'sa-lem. rafts

17 And Sol'o-mon numbered all the strangers that *were* in the land of Is'ra-el, after the numbering wherewith Da'vid his father had numbered them; and they were found an hundred and fifty thousand and three thousand and six hundred.

18 And he set threescore and ten thousand of them *to be* bearers of burdens, and fourscore thousand *to be* hewers in the mountain, and three thousand and six hundred overseers to set the people a work. 70,000 - 80,000 - stonecutters

CHAPTER 3

THEN Sol'o-mon began to build the house of the LORD at Je-ru'sa-lem in mount Mo-ri'ah, where *the* LORD appeared to Da'vid his father, in the place that Da'vid had prepared in the threshingfloor of Or'nan the Jeb'u-site.

2 And he began to build in the second *day* of the second month, in the fourth year of his reign.

3 Now these *are the things wherein* Sol'o-mon was instructed for the building of the house of God. The length by cubits after the first measure *was* threescore cubits, and the breadth twenty cubits. Elohim[p.f.] - 60

4 And the porch that *was* in the front *of the house*, the length *of it was* according to the breadth of the house, twenty cubits, and the height *was* an hundred and twenty: and he overlaid it within with pure gold.

5 And the greater house he ceiled with fir tree, which he overlaid with fine gold, and set thereon palm trees and chains.

6 And he garnished the house with precious stones for beauty: and the gold *was* gold of Par-va'im. adorned

7 He overlaid also the house, the beams, the posts, and the walls thereof,

and the doors thereof, with gold; and <u>graved</u> cherubims on the walls. _{carved}

8 And he made the most holy house, the length whereof *was* according to the breadth of the house, twenty cubits, and the breadth thereof twenty cubits: and he overlaid it with fine gold, *amounting* to six hundred talents.

9 And the weight of the nails *was* fifty shekels of gold. And he overlaid the upper chambers with gold.

10 And in the most holy house he made two cherubims of <u>image</u> work, and overlaid them with gold. _{sculptured}

11 And the wings of the cherubims *were* twenty cubits long: one wing *of the one cherub was* five cubits, reaching to the wall of the house: and the other wing *was likewise* five cubits, reaching to the wing of the other cherub.

12 And *one* wing of the other cherub *was* five cubits, reaching to the wall of the house: and the other wing *was* five cubits *also*, joining to the wing of the other cherub.

13 The wings of these cherubims spread themselves forth twenty cubits: and they stood on their feet, and their faces *were* inward.

14 And he made the veil *of* blue, and purple, and crimson, and fine linen, and wrought cherubims thereon.

15 Also he made before the house two pillars of thirty and five cubits high, and the <u>chapiter</u> that *was* on the top of each of them *was* five cubits. _{capital}

16 And he made chains, *as* in the <u>oracle</u>, and put *them* on the heads of the pillars; and made an hundred pomegranates, and put *them* on the chains. _{inner sanctuary}

17 And he <u>reared up</u> the pillars before the temple, one on the right hand, and the other on the left; and called the name of that on the right hand Ja'chin, and the name of that on the left Bo'az. _{erected}

CHAPTER 4

MOREOVER he made an altar of brass, twenty cubits the length thereof, and twenty cubits the breadth thereof, and ten cubits the height thereof.

2 Also he made a molten sea of ten cubits from brim to brim, round in compass, and five cubits the height thereof; and a line of thirty cubits <u>did compass it round about</u>. _{i.e., its circumference}

3 And under it *was* the <u>similitude</u> of oxen, which <u>did compass it round about</u>: ten in a cubit, compassing the sea round about. Two rows of oxen *were* cast, when it was cast. _{likeness - encircled it}

4 It stood upon twelve oxen, three looking toward the north, and three looking toward the west, and three looking toward the south, and three looking toward the east: and the <u>sea</u> *was set* above upon them, and all their <u>hinder parts</u> *were* inward. _{large basin - hindquarters}

5 And the thickness of it *was* an <u>handbreadth</u>, and the brim of it like the work of the brim of a cup, with flowers of lilies; *and* it received and held three thousand baths. _{3 inches}

6 He made also ten <u>lavers</u>, and put

five on the right hand, and five on the left, to wash in them: such things as they offered for the burned offering they washed in them; but the sea *was* for the priests to wash in. washbasins

7 And he made ten underline{candlesticks} of gold according to their form, and set *them* in the temple, five on the right hand, and five on the left. lampstands

8 He made also ten tables, and placed *them* in the temple, five on the right side, and five on the left. And he made an hundred basins of gold. bowls

9 Furthermore he made the court of the priests, and the great court, and doors for the court, and overlaid the doors of them with brass.

10 And he set the sea on the right side of the east end, over against the south.

11 And Hu'ram made the pots, and the shovels, and the basins. And Hu'ram finished the work that he was to make for king Sol'o-mon for the house of God; Elohim^{p.f.}

12 *That is*, the two pillars, and the pommels, and the chapiters *which were* on the top of the two pillars, and the two wreaths to cover the two pommels of the chapiters which *were* on the top of the pillars; bowls - capitals

13 And four hundred pomegranates on the two wreaths; two rows of pomegranates on each wreath, to cover the two pommels of the chapiters which *were* upon the pillars.

14 He made also bases, and lavers made he upon the bases; basins

15 One sea, and twelve oxen under it.

16 The pots also, and the shovels, and the fleshhooks, and all their instruments, did Hu'ram his father make to king Sol'o-mon for the house of the LORD of bright brass. forks - utensils

17 In the plain of Jor'dan did the king cast them, in the clay ground between Suc'coth and Ze-red'a-thah.

18 Thus Sol'o-mon made all these vessels in great abundance: for the weight of the brass could not be found out.

19 And Sol'o-mon made all the vessels that *were for* the house of God, the golden altar also, and the tables whereon the showbread *was set*; Elohim^{p.f.}

20 Moreover the candlesticks with their lamps, that they should burn after the manner before the oracle, of pure gold; inner sanctuary

21 And the flowers, and the lamps, and the tongs, *made he of* gold, *and* that perfect gold;

22 And the snuffers, and the basins, and the spoons, and the censers, *of* pure gold: and the entry of the house, the inner doors thereof for the most holy *place*, and the doors of the house of the temple, *were of* gold. bowls - firepans

CHAPTER 5

THUS all the work that Sol'o-mon made for the house of the LORD was finished: and Sol'o-mon brought in *all* the things that Da'vid his father had dedicated; and the silver, and the gold, and all the instruments, put he among the treasures of the house of God. utensils - Elohim^{p.f.}

2 Then Sol'o-mon assembled the elders of Is'ra-el, and all the heads of the

tribes, the chief of the fathers of the children of Is'ra-el, to Je-ru'sa-lem, to bring up the ark of the <u>covenant</u> of the LORD out of the city of Da'vid, which *is* Zi'on.   _{agreement}

3 Wherefore all the men of Is'ra-el assembled themselves to the king in the feast which *was* in the seventh month.

4 And all the elders of Is'ra-el came; and the Le'vites took up the ark.

5 And they brought up the ark, and the tabernacle of the congregation, and all the holy vessels that *were* in the tabernacle, these did the priests *and* the Le'vites bring up.

6 Also king Sol'o-mon, and all the congregation of Is'ra-el that were assembled to him before the ark, sacrificed sheep and oxen, which could not be <u>told</u> nor numbered for multitude.   _{counted}

7 And the priests brought in the ark of the <u>covenant</u> of the LORD to its place, to the <u>oracle</u> of the house, into the most holy *place,* *even* under the wings of the cherubims: _{agreement - inner sanctuary}

8 For the cherubims spread forth *their* wings over the place of the ark, and the cherubims covered the ark and the <u>staves</u> thereof above.   _{poles}

9 And they drew out the <u>staves</u> *of the ark,* that the ends of the <u>staves</u> were seen from the ark before the <u>oracle</u>; but they were not seen without. And there it is to this day.

10 *There was* nothing in the ark <u>save</u> the two tables which Mo'ses put *therein* at Ho'reb, when the LORD made *a cov-*

enant with the children of Is'ra-el, when they came out of E'gypt.   _{except - agreement}

11 And it came to pass, when the priests were come out of the holy *place*: (for all the priests *that were* present were sanctified, *and* did not *then* wait by <u>course</u>:   _{division}

12 Also the Le'vites *which were* the singers, all of them of A'saph, of He'man, of Jed'u-thun, with their sons and their brethren, *being* arrayed in white linen, having cymbals and <u>psalteries</u> and harps, stood at the east end of the altar, and with them an hundred and twenty priests sounding with trumpets:)   _{lyres}

13 It came even to pass, as the trumpeters and singers *were* <u>as one</u>, to make one sound to be heard in praising and thanking the LORD; and when they lifted up *their* voice with the trumpets and cymbals and instruments of music, and praised the LORD, *saying*, For *He is* good; for His mercy *endure* for ever: that *then* the house was filled with a cloud, *even* the house of the LORD;   _{in unison}

14 So that the priests could not <u>stand to minister</u> by reason of the cloud: for the glory of the LORD had filled the house of God.   _{perform the service}

CHAPTER 6

THEN said Sol'o-mon, The LORD has said that He would dwell in the thick darkness.

2 But I have built an house of habitation for You, and a place for Your dwelling for ever.

3 And the king turned his face, and

blessed the whole congregation of Is'ra-el: and all the congregation of Is'ra-el stood.

4 And he said, Blessed *be* the L̲o̲r̲d̲ G̲o̲d̲ of Is'ra-el, who has with His hands fulfilled *that* which He spoke with His mouth to my father Da'vid, saying, Jehovah^{s.f.} Elohim^{p.f.}

5 Since the day that I brought forth My people out of the land of E'gypt I chose no city among all the tribes of Is'ra-el to build an house in, that My name might be there; neither chose I any man to be a ruler over My people Is'ra-el:

6 But I have chosen Je-ru'sa-lem, that My name might be there; and have chosen Da'vid to be over My people Is'ra-el.

7 Now it was in the heart of Da'vid my father to build an house for the name of the L̲o̲r̲d̲ G̲o̲d̲ of Is'ra-el. Jehovah^{s.f.} Elohim^{p.f.}

8 But the L̲o̲r̲d̲ said to Da'vid my father, Forasmuch as it was in your heart to build an house for My name, you did well in that it was in your heart:

9 Notwithstanding you shall not build the house; but your son which shall come forth out of your loins, he shall build the house for My name.

10 The L̲o̲r̲d̲ therefore has performed His word that He has spoken: for I am risen up in the room of Da'vid my father, and am set on the throne of Is'ra-el, as the L̲o̲r̲d̲ promised, and have built the house for the name of the L̲o̲r̲d̲ G̲o̲d̲ of Is'ra-el.

11 And in it have I put the ark, wherein *is* the c̲o̲v̲e̲n̲a̲n̲t̲ of the L̲o̲r̲d̲, that He made with the children of Is'ra-el. agreement

12 And he stood before the altar of the L̲o̲r̲d̲ in the presence of all the congregation of Is'ra-el, and spread forth his hands:

13 For Sol'o-mon had made a brazen scaffold, of five cubits long, and five cubits broad, and three cubits high, and had set it in the midst of the court: and upon it he stood, and kneeled down upon his knees before all the congregation of Is'ra-el, and spread forth his hands toward heaven,

14 And said, O L̲o̲r̲d̲ G̲o̲d̲ of Is'ra-el, *there is* no G̲o̲d̲ like You in the heaven, nor in the earth; which keeps c̲o̲v̲e̲n̲a̲n̲t̲, and *shows* mercy to Your servants, that walk before You with all their hearts: Jehovah^{s.f.} Elohim^{p.f.}

15 You which have kept with Your servant Da'vid my father that which You have promised him; and spoke with Your mouth, and have fulfilled *it* with Your hand, as *it is* this day.

16 Now therefore, O L̲o̲r̲d̲ G̲o̲d̲ of Is'ra-el, k̲e̲e̲p̲ with Your servant Da'vid my father that which You have promised him, saying, There shall not fail you a man in My sight to sit upon the throne of Is'ra-el; yet so that your children take heed to their way to walk in My law, as you have walked before Me. continue

17 Now then, O L̲o̲r̲d̲ G̲o̲d̲ of Is'ra-el, let Your word be verified, which You have spoken to Your servant Da'vid.

18 But will God i̲n̲ ̲v̲e̲r̲y̲ ̲d̲e̲e̲d̲ dwell with men on the earth? behold, heaven

and the heaven of heavens cannot contain You; how much less this house which I have built! indeed

19 Have respect therefore to the prayer of Your servant, and to his supplication, O LORD my God, to hearken to the cry and the prayer which Your servant prays before You: appeal

20 That Your eyes may be open upon this house day and night, upon the place whereof You have said that You would put Your name there; to hearken to the prayer which Your servant prays toward this place. in

21 Hearken therefore to the supplications of Your servant, and of Your people Is'ra-el, which they shall make toward this place: hear You from Your dwelling place, *even* from heaven; and when You hear, forgive. pray

22 If a man sin against his neighbor, and an oath be laid upon him to make him swear, and the oath come before Your altar in this house; promise

23 Then hear You from heaven, and do, and judge Your servants, by requiting the wicked, by recompensing his way upon his own head; and by justifying the righteous, by giving him according to his righteousness. punishing - bringing

M29 24 And if Your people Is'ra-el be put to the worse before the enemy, because they have sinned against You; and shall return and confess Your name, and pray and make supplication before You in this house; appeal

25 Then hear You from the heavens, and forgive the sin of Your people Is'ra-el, and bring them again to the land which You gave to them and to their fathers. M29

26 When the heaven is shut up, and there is no rain, because they have sinned against You; *yet* if they pray toward this place, and confess Your name, and turn from their sin, when You do afflict them;

27 Then hear You from heaven, and forgive the sin of Your servants, and of Your people Is'ra-el, when You have taught them the good way, wherein they should walk; and send rain upon Your land, which You have given to Your people for an inheritance.

28 If there be dearth in the land, if there be pestilence, if there be blasting, or mildew, locusts, or caterpillers; if their enemies besiege them in the cities of their land; whatsoever sore or whatsoever sickness *there be*: famine - plague - blight

29 *Then* what prayer *or* what supplication soever shall be made of any man, or of all Your people Is'ra-el, when every one shall know his own sore and his own grief, and shall spread forth his hands in this house: appeal

30 Then hear You from heaven Your dwelling place, and forgive, and render to every man according to all his ways, whose heart You know; (for You only know the hearts of the children of men:)

31 That they may fear You, to walk in Your ways, so long as they live in the land which You gave to our fathers. reverence

32 Moreover concerning the stranger, which is not of Your people Is'ra-el, but is come from a far country for Your

great name's sake, and Your mighty hand, and Your stretched out arm; if they come and pray in this house; foreigner 33 Then hear You from the heavens, *even* from Your dwelling place, and do according to all that the stranger calls to You for; that all people of the earth may know Your name, and <u>fear</u> You, as *do* Your people Is'ra-el, and may know that this house which I have built is called by Your name. reverence - temple 34 If your people go out to war against their enemies by the way that You shall send them, and they pray to You toward this city which You have chosen, and the house which I have built for Your name; 35 Then hear You from the heavens their prayer and their <u>supplication</u>, and <u>maintain</u> their cause. appeal - uphold 36 If they sin against You, (for *there is* no man which sins not,) and You be angry with them, and deliver them over before *their* enemies, and they carry them away captives to a land far off or near; 37 Yet *if* they <u>bethink</u> themselves in the land where they are carried captive, and turn and pray to You in the land of their captivity, saying, We have sinned, we have done <u>amiss</u>, and have dealt wickedly; take thought - wrong 38 If they return to You with all their heart and with all their soul in the land of their captivity, where they have carried them captives, and pray toward their land, which You gave to their fathers, and *toward* the city which You have chosen, and toward the house which I have built for Your name:

39 Then hear You from the heavens, *even* from your dwelling place, their prayer and their <u>supplications</u>, and <u>maintain</u> their cause, and forgive Your people which have sinned against You. appeals - uphold 40 Now, my <u>God</u>, let, I <u>beseech</u> You, Your eyes be open, and *let* Your ears *be* <u>attent</u> to the prayer *that is made* in this place . Elohim[p.f.] - beg - attentive 41 Now therefore arise, O L<small>ORD</small> God, into Your resting place, You, and the ark of Your strength: let Your priests, O L<small>ORD</small> God, be clothed with salvation, and let Your saints rejoice in goodness. Jehovah[e.f.] Elohim[n.f.] 42 O L<small>ORD</small> God, <u>turn not away</u> the face of Your anointed: remember the mercies of Da'vid Your servant. do not reject

CHAPTER 7

NOW when Sol'o-mon had made an end of praying, the fire came down from heaven, and consumed the burned offering and the sacrifices; and the glory of the L<small>ORD</small> filled the house. 2 And the priests could not enter into the house of the L<small>ORD</small>, because the glory of the L<small>ORD</small> had filled the L<small>ORD</small>'s house. 3 And when all the children of Is'ra-el saw how the fire came down, and the glory of the L<small>ORD</small> upon the house, they bowed themselves with their faces to the ground upon the pavement, and worshiped, and praised the L<small>ORD</small>, *saying*, For *He is* good; for His mercy *endures* for ever. 4 Then the king and all the people offered sacrifices before the L<small>ORD</small>.

5 And king Sol'o-mon offered a sacrifice of twenty and two thousand oxen, and an hundred and twenty thousand sheep: so the king and all the people dedicated the house of God.

6 And the priests waited on their offices: the Le'vites also with instruments of music of the LORD, which Da'vid the king had made to praise the LORD, because His mercy *endures* for ever, when Da'vid praised by their ministry; and the priests sounded trumpets before them, and all Is'ra-el stood.

7 Moreover Sol'o-mon hallowed the middle of the court that *was* before the house of the LORD: for there he offered burned offerings, and the fat of the peace offerings, because the brazen altar which Sol'o-mon had made was not able to receive the burned offerings, and the meat offerings, and the fat.

8 Also at the same time Sol'o-mon kept the feast seven days, and all Is'ra-el with him, a very great congregation, from the entering in of Ha'math to the river of E'gypt.   entrance

9 And in the eighth day they made a solemn assembly: for they kept the dedication of the altar seven days, and the feast seven days.

10 And on the three and twentieth day of the seventh month he sent the people away into their tents, glad and merry in heart for the goodness that the LORD had showed to Da'vid, and to Sol'o-mon, and to Is'ra-el His people.

11 Thus Sol'o-mon finished the house of the LORD, and the king's house: and all that came into Sol'o-mon's heart to make in the house of the LORD, and in his own house, he prosperously effected.

12 And the LORD appeared to Sol'o-mon by night, and said to him, I have heard your prayer, and have chosen this place to Myself for an house of sacrifice.

13 If I shut up heaven that there be no rain, or if I command the locusts to devour the land, or if I send pestilence among My people;

14 If My people, which are called by My name, shall humble themselves, and pray, and seek My face, and turn from their wicked ways; then will I hear from heaven, and will forgive their sin, and will heal their land.

15 Now My eyes shall be open, and My ears attent to the prayer *that is made* in this place.   attentive

16 For now have I chosen and sanctified this house, that My name may be there for ever: and My eyes and My heart shall be there perpetually.

17 And as for you, if you will walk before Me, as Da'vid your father walked, and do according to all that I have commanded you, and shall observe My statutes and My judgments;   decrees - laws

18 Then will I stablish the throne of your kingdom, according as I have covenanted with Da'vid your father, saying, There shall not fail you a man *to be* ruler in Is'ra-el.   agreed

19 But if you turn away, and forsake My statutes and My commandments, which I have set before you, and shall go and serve other gods, and worship them;

20 Then will I pluck them up by the

roots out of My land which I have given them; and this house, which I have *sanctified* for My name, will I cast out of My sight, and will make it *to be* a proverb and a byword among all nations.   i.e., Israel - consecrated

21 And this house, which is high, shall be an astonishment to every one that passes by it; so that he shall say, Why has the LORD done thus to this land, and to this house?   i.e., temple - exalted

22 And it shall be answered, Because they forsook the LORD God of their fathers, which brought them forth out of the land of E'gypt, and laid hold on other gods, and worshiped them, and served them: therefore has He brought all this evil upon them. adopted

CHAPTER 8

A ND it came to pass at the end of twenty years, wherein Sol'o-mon had built the house of the LORD, and his own house,

2 That the cities which Hu'ram had restored to Sol'o-mon, Sol'o-mon built them, and caused the children of Is'ra-el to dwell there.   given

3 And Sol'o-mon went to Ha'math-zo'bah, and prevailed against it.

4 And he built Tad'mor in the wilderness, and all the store cities, which he built in Ha'math.   storage

5 Also he built Beth-ho'ron the upper, and Beth-ho'ron the nether, fenced cities, with walls, gates, and bars;   lower - fortified

6 And Ba'al-ath, and all the store cities that Sol'o-mon had, and all the chariot cities, and the cities of the horsemen, and all that Sol'o-mon desired to build in Je-ru'sa-lem, and in Leb'a-non, and throughout all the land of his dominion.   storage

7 *As for* all the people *that were* left of the Hit'tites, and the Am'or-ites, and the Per'iz-zites, and the Hi'vites, and the Jeb'u-sites, which *were* not of Is'ra-el,

8 *But* of their children, who were left after them in the land, whom the children of Is'ra-el consumed not, them did Sol'o-mon make to pay tribute until this day.   serve as laborers

9 But of the children of Is'ra-el did Sol'o-mon make no servants for his work; but they *were* men of war, and chief of his captains, and captains of his chariots and horsemen.   slaves - commanders

10 And these *were* the chief of king Sol'o-mon's officers, *even* two hundred and fifty, that bare rule over the people.

11 And Sol'o-mon brought up the daughter of Pha'raoh out of the city of Da'vid to the house that he had built for her: for he said, my wife shall not dwell in the house of Da'vid king of Is'ra-el, because *the places are* holy, whereto the ark of the LORD has come.

12 Then Sol'o-mon offered burned offerings to the LORD on the altar of the LORD, which he had built before the porch,

13 Even after a certain rate every day, offering according to the commandment of Mo'ses, on the sabbaths, and on the new moons, and on the solemn feasts, three times in the year, *even* in the feast of unleavened bread, and in

the feast of weeks, and in the feast of tabernacles.   rest days - without yeast

14 And he appointed, according to the order of Da'vid his father, the courses of the priests to their service, and the Le'vites to their charges, to praise and minister before the priests, as the duty of every day required: the porters also by their courses at every gate: for so had Da'vid the man of God commanded.   duties - gatekeepers - divisions

15 And they departed not from the commandment of the king to the priests and Le'vites concerning any matter, or concerning the treasures.   deviated

16 Now all the work of Sol'o-mon was prepared to the day of the foundation of the house of the LORD, and until it was finished. *So* the house of the LORD was perfected.   from - finished

17 Then went Sol'o-mon to E'zi-on-ge'ber, and to E'loth, at the sea side in the land of E'dom.

18 And Hu'ram sent him by the hands of his servants ships, and servants that had knowledge of the sea; and they went with the servants of Sol'o-mon to O'phir, and took from there four hundred and fifty talents of gold, and brought *them* to king Sol'o-mon.

CHAPTER 9

A ND when the queen of She'ba heard of the fame of Sol'o-mon, she came to prove Sol'o-mon with hard questions at Je-ru'sa-lem, with a very great company, and camels that bare spices, and gold in abundance, and precious stones: and when she was come to Sol'o-mon, she communed with him of all that was in her heart. MATT. 12:42 test - carried - spoke

2 And Sol'o-mon told her all her questions: and there was nothing hid from Sol'o-mon which he told her not. answered

3 And when the queen of She'ba had seen the wisdom of Sol'o-mon, and the house that he had built,

4 And the meat of his table, and the sitting of his servants, and the attendance of his ministers, and their apparel; his cupbearers also, and their apparel; and his ascent by which he went up into the house of the LORD; there was no more spirit in her.   food - seating - butlers - stairway

5 And she said to the king, *It was* a true report which I heard in my own land of your acts, and of your wisdom: your words

6 However I believed not their words, until I came, and my eyes had seen *it*: and, behold, the one half of the greatness of your wisdom was not told me: *for* you exceed the fame that I heard.

7 Happy *are* your men, and happy *are* these your servants, which stand continually before you, and hear your wisdom.

8 Blessed be the LORD your God, which delighted in you to set you on His throne, *to be* king for the LORD your God: because your God loved Is'ra-el, to establish them for ever, therefore made He you king over them, to do judgment and justice.   Elohim p.f.

9 And she gave the king an hundred and twenty talents of gold, and of spices great abundance, and precious

stones: neither was there any such spice as the queen of She'ba gave king Sol'o-mon.

10 And the servants also of Hu'ram, and the servants of Sol'o-mon, which brought gold from O'phir, brought algum trees and precious stones.

11 And the king made *of* the algum trees <u>terraces</u> to the house of the LORD, and to the king's palace, and <u>harps</u> and <u>psalteries</u> for singers: and there were none such seen before in the land of Ju'dah. <small>steps - lyres</small>

12 And king Sol'o-mon gave to the queen of She'ba all her desire, whatsoever she asked, beside *that* which she had brought to the king. So she turned, and went away to her own land, she and her servants.

13 Now the weight of gold that came to Sol'o-mon in one year was six hundred and threescore and six talents of gold;

14 Beside *that which* <u>chapmen</u> and merchants brought. And all the kings of A-ra'bi-a and governors of the country brought gold and silver to Sol'o-mon. <small>traders</small>

15 And king Sol'o-mon made two hundred <u>targets</u> *of* beaten gold: six hundred *shekels* of beaten gold went to one <u>target</u>. <small>large shields</small>

16 And three hundred shields *made he of* beaten gold: three hundred *shekels* of gold went to one shield. And the king put them in the house of the forest of Leb'a-non.

17 Moreover the king made a great throne of ivory, and overlaid it with pure gold.

18 And *there were* six steps to the throne, with a footstool of gold, *which were* fastened to the throne, and <u>stays</u> on each side of the sitting place, and two lions standing by the <u>stays</u>: <small>arms</small>

19 And twelve lions stood there on the one side and on the other upon the six steps. There was not the like made in any kingdom.

20 And all the drinking vessels of king Sol'o-mon *were of* gold, and all the vessels of the house of the forest of Leb'a-non *were of* pure gold: none *were of* silver; it was *not* <u>any thing accounted of</u> in the days of Sol'o-mon. <small>considered valuable</small>

21 For the king's ships went to Tar'shish with the servants of Hu'ram: every three years once came the ships of Tar'shish bringing gold, and silver, ivory, and apes, and peacocks.

22 And king Sol'o-mon passed all the kings of the earth in riches and wisdom.

23 And all the kings of the earth sought the presence of Sol'o-mon, to hear his wisdom, that <u>God</u> had put in his heart. <small>Elohim^{p.f.}</small>

24 And they brought every man his present, vessels of silver, and vessels of gold, and <u>raiment</u>, <u>harness</u>, and spices, horses, and mules, a rate year by year. <small>garments - weaponry</small>

25 And Sol'o-mon had four thousand stalls for horses and chariots, and twelve thousand horsemen; whom he bestowed in the chariot cities, and with the king at Je-ru'sa-lem.

26 And he reigned over all the kings from the river even to the land of the Phi-lis'tines, and to the border of E'gypt.

27 And the king made silver in Je-ru'sa-lem *as* stones, and cedar trees made he as the sycamore trees that *are* in the low plains in abundance. _{as common as}
28 And they brought to Sol'o-mon horses out of E'gypt, and out of all lands.
29 Now the rest of the acts of Sol'o-mon, first and last, *are* they not written in the book of Na'than the prophet, and in the prophecy of A-hi'jah the Shi'lo-nite, and in the visions of Id'do the seer against Jer-o-bo'am the son of Ne'bat? _{concerning}
30 And Sol'o-mon reigned in Je-ru'sa-lem over all Is'ra-el forty years.
31 And Sol'o-mon slept with his fathers, and he was buried in the city of Da'vid his father: and Re-ho-bo'am his son reigned in his stead.

CHAPTER 10

AND Re-ho-bo'am went to She'chem: for to She'chem were all Is'ra-el come to make him king.
2 And it came to pass, when Jer-o-bo'am the son of Ne'bat, who *was* in E'gypt, where he had fled from the presence of Sol'o-mon the king, heard *it*, that Jer-o-bo'am returned out of E'gypt.
3 And they sent and called him. So Jer-o-bo'am and all Is'ra-el came and spoke to Re-ho-bo'am, saying,
4 Your father made our yoke grievous: now therefore ease you somewhat the grievous servitude of your father, and his heavy yoke that he put upon us, and we will serve you.

5 And he said to them, Come again to me after three days. And the people departed.
6 And king Re-ho-bo'am took counsel with the old men that had stood before Sol'o-mon his father while he yet lived, saying, What counsel give you *me* to return answer to this people? _{consulted - served}
7 And they spoke to him, saying, If you be kind to this people, and please them, and speak good words to them, they will be your servants for ever.
8 But he forsook the counsel which the old men gave him, and took counsel with the young men that were brought up with him, that stood before him.
9 And he said to them, What advice give you that we may return answer to this people, which have spoken to me, saying, Ease somewhat the yoke that your father did put upon us?
10 And the young men that were brought up with him spoke to him, saying, Thus shall you answer the people that spoke to you, saying, Your father made our yoke heavy, but make you *it* somewhat lighter for us; thus shall you say to them, My little *finger* shall be thicker than my father's loins. _{waist}
11 For whereas my father put a heavy yoke upon you, I will put more to your yoke: my father chastised you with whips, but I *will chastise you* with scorpions. _{i.e., whips with tips}
12 So Jer-o-bo'am and all the people came to Re-ho-bo'am on the third day, as the king bade, saying, Come again to me on the third day. _{directed}

13 And the king answered them roughly; and king Re-ho-bo'am forsook the counsel of the old men,   harshly - advice
14 And answered them after the advice of the young men, saying, My father made your yoke heavy, but I will add thereto: my father chastised you with whips, but I *will chastise you* with scorpions.   i.e., whips with metal tip
15 So the king hearkened not to the people: for the cause was of God, that the LORD might perform His word, which He spoke by the hand of A-hi'jah the Shi'lo-nite to Jer-o-bo'am the son of Ne'bat.   turn of events - Elohim^p.f.
16 And when all Is'ra-el *saw* that the king would not hearken to them, the people answered the king, saying, What portion have we in Da'vid? and *we have* none inheritance in the son of Jes'se: every man to your tents, O Is'ra-el: *and* now, Da'vid, see to your own house. So all Is'ra-el went to their tents.   return home - homes
17 But *as for* the children of Is'ra-el that dwelled in the cities of Ju'dah, Re-ho-bo'am reigned over them.
18 Then king Re-ho-bo'am sent Ha-do'ram that *was* over the tribute; and the children of Is'ra-el stoned him with stones, that he died. But king Re-ho-bo'am made speed to get him up to *his* chariot, to flee to Je-ru'sa-lem.   forced labor - hurried
19 And Is'ra-el rebelled against the house of Da'vid to this day.

CHAPTER 11

AND when Re-ho-bo'am was come to Je-ru'sa-lem, he gathered of the house of Ju'dah and Ben'ja-min an hundred and fourscore thousand chosen *men*, which were warriors, to fight against Is'ra-el, that he might bring the kingdom again to Re-ho-bo'am.   assembled
2 But the word of the LORD came to Shem-a-i'ah the man of God, saying,
3 Speak to Re-ho-bo'am the son of Sol'o-mon, king of Ju'dah, and to all Is'ra-el in Ju'dah and Ben'ja-min, saying,
4 Thus says the LORD, You shall not go up, nor fight against your brethren: return every man to his house: for this thing is done of Me. And they obeyed the words of the LORD, and returned from going against Jer-o-bo'am.   from
5 And Re-ho-bo'am dwelled in Je-ru'sa-lem, and built cities for defence in Ju'dah.
6 He built even Beth'-le-hem, and E'tam, and Te-ko'a,
7 And Beth'-zur, and Sho'co, and A-dul'lam,
8 And Gath, and Ma-re'shah, and Ziph,
9 And Ad-o-ra'im, and La'chish, and A-ze'kah,
10 And Zo'rah, and Aij'a-lon, and He'bron, which *are* in Ju'dah and in Ben'ja-min fenced cities.   fortified
11 And he fortified the strong holds, and put captains in them, and store of victual, and of oil and wine.   food
12 And in every several city *he put* shields and spears, and made them exceeding strong, having Ju'dah and Ben'ja-min on his side.
13 And the priests and the Le'vites

that *were* in all Is'ra-el <u>resorted to</u> him out of all their <u>coasts</u>. stood with - districts

14 For the Le'vites left their <u>sub-urbs</u> and their possession, and came to Ju'dah and Je-ru'sa-lem: for Jer-o-bo'am and his sons had cast them off from <u>executing</u> the priest's office to the LORD: pasture lands - serving

15 And he ordained him priests for the high places, and for the <u>devils</u>, and for the calves which he had made. goats

16 And <u>after them</u> out of all the tribes of Is'ra-el such as set their hearts to seek the LORD God of Is'ra-el came to Je-ru'sa-lem, to sacrifice to the LORD God of their fathers. there followed them

17 So they strengthened the kingdom of Ju'dah, and made Re-ho-bo'am the son of Sol'o-mon strong, three years: for three years they walked in the way of Da'vid and Sol'o-mon.

18 And Re-ho-bo'am took him Ma'ha-lath the daughter of Jer'i-moth the son of Da'vid to wife, *and* Ab-i-ha'il the daughter of E-li'ab the son of Jes'se;

19 Which bare him children; Je'ush, and Sham-a-ri'ah, and Za'ham.

20 And after her he took Ma'a-chah the daughter of Ab'sa-lom; which bare him A-bi'jah, and At'tai, and Zi'za, and Shel'o-mith.

21 And Re-ho-bo'am loved Ma'a-chah the daughter of Ab'sa-lom above all his wives and his concubines: (for he took eighteen wives, and threescore concubines; and fathered twenty and eight sons, and threescore daughters.)

22 And Re-ho-bo'am made A-bi'jah the son of Ma'a-chah the chief, *to be* ruler among his brethren: for *he* thought to make him king.

23 And he dealt wisely, and dispersed of all his children throughout all the countries of Ju'dah and Ben'ja-min, to every <u>fenced</u> city: and he gave them victual in abundance. And he <u>desired</u> many wives. fortified - sought for them

CHAPTER 12

AND it came to pass, when Re-ho-bo'am had established the kingdom, and had strengthened himself, he forsook the law of the LORD, and all Is'ra-el with him.

2 And it came to pass, *that* in the fifth year of king Re-ho-bo'am Shi'shak king of E'gypt came up against Je-ru'sa-lem, because they had <u>transgressed</u> against the LORD, been unfaithful to

3 With twelve hundred chariots, and threescore thousand horsemen: and the people *were* without number that came with him out of E'gypt; the Lu'bims, the Suk'ki-ims, and the E-thi-o'pi-ans.

4 And he took the <u>fenced</u> cities which *pertained* to Ju'dah, and came to Je-ru'sa-lem. fortified

5 Then came Shem-a-i'ah the prophet to Re-ho-bo'am, and *to* the princes of Ju'dah, that were gathered together to Je-ru'sa-lem because of Shi'shak, and said to them, Thus says the LORD, You have forsaken Me, and therefore have I also left you in the hand of Shi'shak.

6 Whereupon the princes of Is'ra-el and the king humbled themselves; and they said, The LORD *is* righteous.

7 And when the Lord saw that they humbled themselves, the word of the Lord came to Shem-a-i'ah, saying, They have humbled themselves; *therefore* I will not destroy them, but I will grant them <u>some</u> deliverance; and My wrath shall not be poured out upon Je-ru'sa-lem by the hand of Shi'shak. some measure of

8 Nevertheless they shall be his servants; that they may <u>know</u> My service, and the service of the kingdoms of the countries. respect

9 So Shi'shak king of E'gypt came up against Je-ru'sa-lem, and took away the treasures of the house of the Lord, and the treasures of the king's house; he took all: he carried away also the shields of gold which Sol'o-mon had made.

10 Instead of which king Re-ho-bo'am made shields of brass, and committed *them* to the hands of the <u>chief</u> of the guard, that kept the entrance of the king's house. captain

11 And when the king entered into the house of the Lord, the guard came and brought them, and brought them again into the guard chamber.

12 And when he humbled himself, the wrath of the Lord turned from him, that He would not destroy *him* altogether: and also in Ju'dah things went well.

13 So king Re-ho-bo'am strengthened himself in Je-ru'sa-lem, and reigned: for Re-ho-bo'am *was* one and forty years old when he began to reign, and he reigned seventeen years in Je-ru'-sa-lem, the city which the Lord had chosen out of all the tribes of Is'ra-el, to put His name there. And his mother's name *was* Na'a-mah an Am'mon-it-ess.

14 And he did evil, because he prepared not his heart to seek the Lord.

15 Now the acts of Re-ho-bo'am, first and last, *are* they not written in the book of Shem-a-i'ah the prophet, and of Id'do the seer concerning genealogies? And *there were* wars between Re-ho-bo'am and Jer-o-bo'am continually.

16 And Re-ho-bo'am slept with his fathers, and was buried in the city of Da'vid: and A-bi'jah his son reigned in his stead.

CHAPTER 13

NOW in the eighteenth year of king Jer-o-bo'am began A-bi'jah to reign over Ju'dah.

2 He reigned three years in Je-ru'sa-lem. His mother's name also *was* Mi-cha'iah the daughter of U'ri-el of Gib'e-ah. And there was war between A-bi'jah and Jer-o-bo'am.

3 And A-bi'jah set the battle in array with an army of valiant men of war, *even* four hundred thousand chosen men: Jer-o-bo'am also set the battle in array against him with eight hundred thousand chosen men, *being* mighty men of valor.

4 And A-bi'jah stood up upon <u>mount</u> Zem-a-ra'im, which *is* in mount E'phra-im, and said, Hear me, you Jer-o-bo'am, and all Is'ra-el; the hill country of

5 Ought you not to know that the Lord God of Is'ra-el gave the kingdom

over Is'ra-el to Da'vid for ever, *even* to him and to his sons by a <u>cov-enant of salt</u>?   i.e., agreement of preservation

6 Yet Jer-o-bo'am the son of Ne'bat, the servant of Sol'o-mon the son of Da'vid, <u>is risen up</u>, and has rebelled against his LORD. become a leader

7 And there are gathered to him <u>vain men</u>, <u>the children of Be'li-al</u>, and have strengthened themselves against Re-ho-bo'am the son of Sol'o-mon, when Re-ho-bo'am was young and tenderhearted, and could not withstand them.   scoundrels - i.e., Satan

8 And now you think to withstand the kingdom of the LORD in the hand of the sons of Da'vid; and you *be* a great multitude, and *there are* with you golden calves, which Jer-o-bo'am made you for gods.

9 Have you not cast out the priests of the LORD, the sons of Aar'on, and the Le'vites, and have made you priests after the manner of the nations of *other* lands? so that whosoever comes to consecrate himself with a young bul-lock and seven rams, *the same* may be a priest of *them that are* no gods.

10 But as for us, the LORD *is* our <u>God</u>, and we have not forsaken Him; and the priests, which minis-ter to the LORD, *are* the sons of Aar'on, and the Le'vites *wait* upon *their* business: Elohim^{p.f.} - attend to their work

11 And they burn to the LORD every morning and every evening burned sac-rifices and sweet incense: the showbread also *set they in order* upon the <u>pure</u> table; and the candlestick of gold with the lamps thereof, to burn every

evening: for we <u>keep the charge</u> of the LORD our <u>God</u>; but you have for-saken Him.   clean - observe the requirements - Elohim^{p.f.}

12 And, behold, <u>God</u> Himself *is* with us for *our* captain, and His priests with sounding trumpets to cry alarm against you. O children of Is'ra-el, fight you not against the LORD God of your fa-thers; for you shall not prosper.

13 But Jer-o-bo'am <u>caused</u> an ambushment to come about behind them: so they were before Ju'dah, and the ambushment *was* behind them. set up

14 And when Ju'dah looked back, be-hold, the battle *was* before and behind: and they cried to the LORD, and the priests sounded with the trumpets.

15 Then the men of Ju'dah gave a shout: and as the men of Ju'dah shouted, it came to pass, that <u>God smote</u> Jer-o-bo'am and all Is'ra-el be-fore A-bi'jah and Ju'dah. Elohim^{p.f.} - defeated

16 And the children of Is'ra-el fled before Ju'dah: and <u>God</u> delivered them into their hand.

17 And A-bi'jah and his people slew them with a great slaughter: so there fell down slain of Is'ra-el five hun-dred thousand chosen men.

18 Thus the children of Is'ra-el were <u>brought under</u> at that time, and the children of Ju'dah prevailed, be-cause they relied upon the <u>LORD God</u> of their fathers.   subdued - Jehovah^{s.f.} Elohim^{p.f.}

19 And A-bi'jah pursued after Jer-o-bo'am, and took cities from him, Beth'el with the towns thereof, and Jesh'a-nah with the towns thereof, and E'phra-in with the towns thereof.

20 Neither did Jer-o-bo'am recover

strength again in the days of A-bi'jah: and the LORD struck him, and he died.
21 But A-bi'jah <u>waxed mighty</u>, and married fourteen wives, and fathered twenty and two sons, and sixteen daughters.   grew in strength
22 And the rest of the acts of A-bi'jah, and his ways, and his sayings, *are* written in the story of the prophet Id'do.

CHAPTER 14

S O A-bi'jah slept with his fathers, and they buried him in the city of Da'vid: and A'sa his son reigned in his stead. In his days the land was quiet ten years.
2 And A'sa did *that which was* good and right in the eyes of the LORD his <u>God</u>:   Elohim^p.f.
3 For he took away the <u>altars</u> of the strange *gods*, and the <u>high places</u>, and broke down the images, and cut down the groves: foreign alters - shrines - pillars - Asherah idols
4 And commanded Ju'dah to seek the <u>LORD God</u> of their fathers, and to do the law and the commandment.   Jehovah^s.f. Elohim^p.f.
5 Also he took away out of all the cities of Ju'dah the <u>high places</u> and the images: and the kingdom was quiet before him.   shrines
6 And he built <u>fenced</u> cities in Ju'dah: for the land had <u>rest</u>, and he had no war in those years; because the LORD had given him <u>rest</u>.   fortified - peace
7 Therefore he said to Ju'dah, Let us build these cities, and make about *them* walls, and towers, gates, and bars,

while the land *is* yet before us; because we have sought the LORD our God, we have sought *Him*, and He has given us rest on every side. So they built and prospered.   Elohim^p.f.
8 And A'sa had an army *of men* that bare <u>targets</u> and spears, out of Ju'dah three hundred thousand; and out of Ben'ja-min, that bare shields and drew bows, two hundred and fourscore thousand: all these *were* mighty men of valor.   shields
9 And there came out against them Ze'rah the E-thi-o'pi-an with an host of a thousand thousand, and three hundred chariots; and came to Ma-re'shah.
10 Then A'sa went out against him, and they set the battle in array in the valley of Zeph'a-thah at Ma-re'shah.
11 And A'sa cried to the LORD his God, and said, LORD, *it is* nothing with You to help, whether with many, or with them that have no <u>power</u>: help us, O LORD our <u>God</u>; for we rest on You, and in Your name we go against this multitude. O LORD, You *are* our <u>God</u>; let not man prevail against You.   Elohim^p.f. strength - win
12 So the LORD <u>smote</u> the E-thi-o'pi-ans before A'sa, and before Ju'dah; and the E-thi-o'pi-ans fled.   routed
13 And A'sa and the people that *were* with him pursued them to Ge'rar: and the E-thi-o'pi-ans were overthrown, that they could not recover themselves; for they were destroyed before the LORD, and before His host; and they carried away very much <u>spoil</u>.   plunder

14 And they <u>smote</u> all the cities round about Ge'rar; for the <u>fear</u> of the LORD came upon them: and they <u>spoiled</u> all the cities; for there was exceeding much <u>spoil</u> in them. destroyed - dread - plundered
15 They <u>smote</u> also the <u>tents</u> of <u>cattle</u>, and carried away sheep and camels in abundance, and returned to Je-ru'sa-lem. struck - camps - herdsmen

CHAPTER 15

AND the Spirit of <u>God</u> came upon Az-a-ri'ah the son of O'ded: Elohim^p.f.
2 And he went out to meet A'sa, and said to him, Hear you me, A'sa, and all Ju'dah and Ben'ja-min; The LORD *is* with you, while you be with Him; and if you seek Him, He will be found of you; but if you forsake Him, He will forsake you.   JAMES 4:8
3 Now for a long season Is'ra-el *has been* without the true <u>God</u>, and without a teaching priest, and without law.
4 But when they in their trouble did turn to the <u>LORD God</u> of Is'ra-el, and sought Him, He was found of them.   Jehovah^s.f. Elohim^p.f.
5 And in those times *there was* no peace to him that went out, nor to him that came in, but great <u>vexations</u> *were* upon all the inhabitants of the countries. disturbances
6 And nation was <u>destroyed</u> of nation, and city of city: for <u>God</u> did <u>vex</u> them with all adversity.   LUKE 21:10 crushed - Elohim^p.f. - trouble
7 Be you strong therefore, and <u>let not your hands be weak</u>: for your work shall be rewarded. do not lose courage
8 And when A'sa heard these words, and the prophecy of O'ded the prophet, he took courage, and put away the <u>abominable</u> idols out of all the land of Ju'dah and Ben'ja-min, and out of the cities which he had taken from <u>mount</u> E'phra-im, and <u>renewed</u> the altar of the LORD, that *was* before the porch of the LORD.   detestable - the hill country - restored
9 And he gathered all Ju'dah and Ben'ja-min, and the strangers with them out of E'phra-im and Ma-nas'seh, and out of Sim'e-on: for they <u>fell</u> to him out of Is'ra-el in abundance, when they saw that the LORD his God *was* with him.   defected
10 So they gathered themselves together at Je-ru'sa-lem in the third month, in the fifteenth year of the reign of A'sa.
11 And they offered to the LORD <u>the same time</u>, of the <u>spoil</u> *which* they had brought, seven hundred oxen and seven thousand sheep.   that day - plunder
12 And they entered into a <u>covenant</u> to seek the <u>LORD God</u> of their fathers with all their heart and with all their soul;   agreement - Jehovah^s.f. Elohim^p.f.
13 That whosoever would not seek the <u>LORD God</u> of Is'ra-el should be put to death, whether small or great, whether man or woman.   Jehovah^s.f. Elohim^p.f.
14 And they swear to the LORD with a loud voice, and with shouting, and with trumpets, and with cornets.
15 And all Ju'dah rejoiced at the oath: for they had sworn with all their heart, and sought Him with their whole desire; and He was found of them: and the LORD gave them <u>rest</u> round about.   peace
16 And also *concerning* Ma'a-chah

the <u>mother</u> of A'sa the king, he removed her from *being* queen, because she had made an idol <u>in a grove</u>: and A'sa cut down her idol, and <u>stamped</u> *it*, and burned *it* at the brook Kid'ron. grandmother - for Asherah - crushed

17 But the high places were not taken away out of Is'ra-el: nevertheless the heart of A'sa was perfect all his days.

18 And he brought into the house of God the things that his father had dedicated, and that he himself had dedicated, silver, and gold, and vessels.

19 And there was no *more* war to the five and thirtieth year of the reign of A'sa.

CHAPTER 16

IN the six and thirtieth year of the reign of A'sa Ba'a-sha king of Is'ra-el came up against Ju'dah, and built Ra'mah, to the intent that he might let none go out or come in to A'sa king of Ju'dah.

2 Then A'sa brought out silver and gold out of the treasures of the house of the LORD and of the king's house, and sent to Ben-ha'dad king of Syr'i-a, that dwelled at Da-mas'cus, saying,

3 *There is* a <u>league</u> between me and you, as *there was* between my father and your father: behold, I have sent you silver and gold; go, break your league with Ba'a-sha king of Is'ra-el, that he may <u>depart</u> from me. treaty - withdraw

4 And Ben-ha'dad hearkened to king A'sa, and sent the captains of his armies against the cities of Is'ra-el; and they smote I'jon, and Dan, and A'bel-ma'im, and all the store cities of Naph'ta-li.

5 And it came to pass, when Ba'a-sha heard *it*, that he left off building of Ra'mah, and let his work cease.

6 Then A'sa the king took all Ju'dah; and they carried away the stones of Ra'mah, and the timber thereof, <u>wherewith</u> Ba'a-sha <u>was</u> building; and he built therewith Ge'ba and Miz'pah. with which - had been

7 And at that time Ha-na'ni the seer came to A'sa king of Ju'dah, and said to him, Because you have relied on the king of Syr'i-a, and not relied on the LORD your <u>God</u>, therefore is the host of the king of Syr'i-a escaped out of your hand. Elohim^{p.f.}

8 Were not the E-thi-o'pi-ans and the <u>Lu'bims</u> a huge host, with very many chariots and horsemen? yet, because you did rely on the LORD, He delivered them into your hand. Libyans

9 For the eyes of the LORD run to and fro throughout the whole earth, to show Himself strong in the behalf of *them* whose heart *is* perfect toward Him. <u>Herein</u> you have done foolishly: therefore from hereafter you shall have wars. In this

10 Then A'sa was angry with the seer, and put him in a prison house; for *he was* in a rage with him because of this *thing*. And A'sa <u>oppressed</u> *some* of the people the same time. crushed

11 And, behold, the acts of A'sa, first and last, lo, they *are* written in the book of the kings of Ju'dah and Is'ra-el.

12 And A'sa in the thirty and ninth year of his reign was diseased in his

feet, until his disease *was* exceeding *great*: yet in his disease he <u>sought not to</u> the Lord, but to the physicians.   did not seek

13 And A'sa slept with his fathers, and died in the one and fortieth year of his reign.

14 And they buried him in his own <u>sepulchers</u>, which he had <u>made</u> for himself in the city of Da'vid, and laid him in the bed which was filled with sweet odors and divers kinds *of spices* prepared by the apothecaries' art: and they made a very great burning for him.   tomb - cut out

CHAPTER 17

AND Je-hosh'a-phat his son reigned in his stead, and strengthened himself against Is'ra-el.

2 And he placed <u>forces</u> in all the <u>fenced</u> cities of Ju'dah, and set garrisons in the land of Ju'dah, and in the cities of E'phra-im, which A'sa his father had taken.   troops - fortified

3 And the Lord was with Je-hosh'a-phat, because he walked in the <u>first ways</u> of his father Da'vid, and sought not <u>to</u> Ba'al-im;   example - help from

4 But sought to the *Lord* <u>God</u> of his father, and walked in His commandments, and not after the doings of Is'ra-el.   Jehovah^{s.f.} Elohim^{p.f.}

5 Therefore the Lord stablished the kingdom in his hand; and all Ju'dah brought to Je-hosh'a-phat <u>presents</u>; and he had riches and honor in abundance.   tribute

6 And his heart was lifted up in the ways of the Lord: moreover he took away the <u>high places</u> and <u>groves</u> out of Ju'dah.   shrines - Asherah idols

7 Also in the third year of his reign he sent to his princes, *even* to Ben-ha'il, and to O-ba-di'ah, and to Zech-a-ri'ah, and to Ne-than'e-el, and to Mi-cha'-iah, to teach in the cities of Ju'dah.

8 And with them *he sent* Le'vites, *even* Shem-a-i'ah, and Neth-a-ni'ah, and Zeb-a-di'ah, and A'sa-hel, and She-mir'a-moth, and Je-hon'a-than, and Ad-o-ni'jah, and To-bi'jah, and Tob-ad-o-ni'jah, Le'vites; and with them E-lish'a-ma and Je-ho'ram, priests.

9 And they taught in Ju'dah, and *had* the book of the law of the Lord with them, and went about throughout all the cities of Ju'dah, and taught the people.

10 And the <u>fear</u> of the Lord fell upon all the kingdoms of the lands that *were* round about Ju'dah, so that they made no war against Je-hosh'a-phat.   dread

11 Also *some* of the Phi-lis'tines brought Je-hosh'a-phat presents, and tribute silver; and the A-ra'bi-ans brought him flocks, seven thousand and seven hundred rams, and seven thousand and seven hundred he goats.

12 And Je-hosh'a-phat <u>waxed</u> great exceedingly; and he built in Ju'dah <u>castles</u>, and cities of store.   grew - fortresses

13 And he had much business in the cities of Ju'dah: and the men of war, mighty men of valor, *were* in Je-ru'sa-lem.

14 And these *are* the numbers of them according to the house of their fathers: Of Ju'dah, the captains of thousands;

Ad'nah the chief, and with him mighty men of valor three hundred thousand.

15 And next to him *was* Je-ho-ha'nan the captain, and with him <u>two hundred and fourscore</u> thousand. ₂₈₀

16 And <u>next</u> him *was* Am-a-si'ah the son of Zich'ri, who willingly offered himself to the LORD; and with him two hundred thousand mighty men of valor. _{next to}

17 And of Ben'ja-min; E-li'a-da a mighty man of valor, and with him armed men with bow and shield two hundred thousand.

18 And <u>next</u> him *was* Je-hoz'a-bad, and with him an <u>hundred and fourscore</u> thousand ready prepared for the war. ₁₈₀

19 These <u>waited</u> on the king, beside *those* whom the king put in the <u>fenced</u> cities throughout all Ju'dah. _{served - fortified}

CHAPTER 18

NOW Je-hosh'a-phat had riches and honor in abundance, and <u>joined affinity</u> with A'hab. _{allied himself by marriage}

2 And after *certain* years he went down to A'hab to Sa-ma'ri-a. And A'hab killed sheep and oxen for him in abundance, and for the people that *he had* with him, and persuaded him to go up <u>*with him*</u> to Ra'moth-gil'e-ad. _{against}

3 And A'hab king of Is'ra-el said to Je-hosh'a-phat king of Ju'dah, Will you go with me to Ra'moth-gil'e-ad? And he answered him, I *am* as you *are*, and my people as your people; and *we will be* with you in the war.

4 And Je-hosh'a-phat said to the king of Is'ra-el, Enquire, I pray you, <u>at</u> the word of the LORD to day. _{for}

5 Therefore the king of Is'ra-el gathered together of prophets four hundred men, and said to them, Shall we go to Ra'moth-gil'e-ad to battle, or shall I forbear? And they said, Go up; for <u>God</u> will deliver *it* into the king's hand. _{Elohim^{p.f.}}

6 But Je-hosh'a-phat said, *Is there* not here a prophet of the LORD <u>besides</u>, that we might enquire of him? _{more}

7 And the king of Is'ra-el said to Je-hosh'a-phat, *There is* yet one man, by whom we may enquire of the LORD: but I hate him; for he never prophesied good to me, but always evil: the same *is* Mi-ca'iah the son of Im'la. And Je-hosh'a-phat said, Let not the king say so.

8 And the king of Is'ra-el called for one *of his* <u>officers</u>, and said, Bring quickly Mi-ca'iah the son of Im'la. _{officials}

9 And the king of Is'ra-el and Je-hosh'a-phat king of Ju'dah sat <u>either</u> of them on his throne, clothed in *their* robes, and they sat in <u>a void</u> place at the entering in of the gate of Sa-ma'ri-a; and all the prophets prophesied before them. _{each - an open}

10 And Zed-e-ki'ah the son of Che-na'a-nah had made him horns of iron, and said, Thus says the LORD, With these you shall push Syr'i-a until they be consumed.

11 And all the prophets prophesied so, saying, Go up to Ra'moth-gil'e-ad, and prosper: for the LORD shall deliver *it* into the hand of the king.

12 And the messenger that went to

call Mi-ca'iah spoke to him, saying, Behold, the words of the prophets *declare* good to the king with one <u>assent</u>; let your word therefore, I pray you, be like one of theirs, and speak you good. ₍voice₎

13 And Mi-ca'iah said, *As* the LORD lives, even what my <u>God</u> says, that will I speak. ₍Elohimᵖᶠ₎

14 And when he was come to the king, the king said to him, Mi-ca'iah, shall we go to Ra'moth-gil'e-ad to battle, or shall I <u>forbear</u>? And he said, Go you up, and prosper, and they shall be delivered into your hand. ₍refrain₎

15 And the king said to him, How many times shall I <u>adjure</u> you that you say nothing but the truth to me in the name of the LORD? ₍command₎

16 Then he said, I did see all Is'ra-el scattered upon the mountains, as sheep that have no shepherd: and the LORD said, These have no master; let them return *therefore* every man to his house in peace.

17 And the king of Is'ra-el said to Je-hosh'a-phat, Did I not tell you *that* he would not prophesy good to me, but evil?

18 Again he said, Therefore hear the word of the LORD; I saw the LORD sitting upon His throne, and all the host of heaven standing on His right hand and *on* His left.

19 And the LORD said, Who shall entice A'hab king of Is'ra-el, that he may go up and <u>fall</u> at Ra'moth-gil'e-ad? And one spoke saying after this manner, and another saying after that manner. ₍be killed₎

20 Then there came out a spirit, and stood before the LORD, and said, I will entice him. And the LORD said to him, <u>Wherewith</u>? ₍How₎

21 And he said, I will go out, and be a lying spirit in the mouth of all his prophets. And *the* LORD said, You shall entice *him*, and you shall also prevail: go out, and do *even* so.

22 Now therefore, behold, the LORD has put a lying spirit in the mouth of these your prophets, and the LORD has spoken evil against you.

23 Then Zed-e-ki'ah the son of Che-na'a-nah came near, and <u>smote</u> Mi-ca'iah upon the cheek, and said, Which way went the Spirit of the LORD from me to speak to you? ₍struck₎

24 And Mi-ca'iah said, Behold, you shall see on that day when you shall go into an inner chamber to hide yourself.

25 Then the king of Is'ra-el said, Take you Mi-ca'iah, and carry him back to A'mon the governor of the city, and to Jo'ash the king's son;

26 And say, Thus says the king, Put this *fellow* in the prison, and feed him with bread of affliction and with water <u>of affliction</u>, until I return in peace. ₍sparingly₎

27 And Mi-ca'iah said, If you certainly return in peace, *then* has not the LORD spoken by me. And he said, <u>Hearken</u>, all you people. ₍Listen₎

28 So the king of Is'ra-el and Je-hosh'a-phat the king of Ju'dah went up to Ra'moth-gil'e-ad.

29 And the king of Is'ra-el said to Je-hosh'a-phat, I will disguise myself, and will go to the battle; but put you

on your robes. So the king of Is'ra-el disguised himself; and they went to the battle.

30 Now the king of Syr'i-a had commanded the captains of the chariots that *were* with him, saying, Fight you not with small or great, <u>save</u> only with the king of Is'ra-el. except

31 And it came to pass, when the captains of the chariots saw Je-hosh'a-phat, that they said, It *is* the king of Is'ra-el. Therefore they <u>compassed about</u> him to fight: but Je-hosh'a-phat cried out, and the LORD helped him; and <u>God</u> moved them *to depart* from him. surrounded - Elohim[p.f.]

32 For it came to pass, that, when the captains of the chariots <u>perceived</u> that it was not the king of Is'ra-el, they turned back again from pursuing him. saw

33 And a *certain* man drew a bow at <u>a venture</u>, and smote the king of Is'ra-el between the joints of the <u>harness</u>: therefore he said to his chariot man, Turn your hand, that you may carry me out of the host; for I am wounded. random - armor

34 And the battle increased that day: however the king of Is'ra-el stayed *himself* up in *his* chariot against the Syr'i-ans until the <u>even</u>: and about the time of the sun going down he died. evening

CHAPTER 19

AND Je-hosh'a-phat the king of Ju'dah returned to his house in peace to Je-ru'sa-lem.

2 And Je'hu the son of Ha-na'ni the seer went out to meet him, and said to king Je-hosh'a-phat, Should you help the ungodly, and love them that <u>hate</u> the LORD? therefore is wrath upon you from before the LORD. despise

3 Nevertheless there are good things found in you, in that you have taken away the <u>groves</u> out of the land, and have prepared your heart to seek <u>God</u>. Asherah idols - Elohim[p.f.]

4 And Je-hosh'a-phat dwelled at Je-ru'sa-lem: and he went out again <u>through</u> the people from Be'er-she'ba to <u>mount</u> E'phra-im, and brought them back to the LORD <u>God of</u> their fathers.

Among - the hill country of - Jehovah[s.f.] Elohim[p.f.]

5 And he set judges in the land throughout all the <u>fenced</u> cities of Ju'dah, city by city, fortified

6 And said to the judges, Take heed what you do: for you judge not for man, but for the LORD, who *is* with you <u>in the</u> judgment. when you render

7 Wherefore now let the <u>fear</u> of the LORD be upon you; take heed and do *it*: for *there is* no iniquity with the LORD our <u>God</u>, nor respect of persons, nor taking of gifts. reverence - Elohim[p.f.]

8 Moreover in Je-ru'sa-lem did Je-hosh'a-phat set of the Le'vites, and *of* the priests, and of the <u>chief</u> of the fathers of Is'ra-el, for the judgment of the LORD, and for controversies, when they returned to Je-ru'sa-lem. heads

9 And he <u>charged</u> them, saying, Thus shall you do in the fear of the LORD, faithfully, and <u>with a perfect heart</u>. commanded - wholeheartedly

10 And what cause soever shall come to you of your brethren that dwell in their cities, between blood and blood,

between law and commandment, statutes and judgments, you shall even warn them that they trespass not against the LORD, and *so* wrath come upon you, and upon your brethren: this do, and you shall not trespass.

11 And, behold, Am-a-ri-ah the chief priest *is* over you in all matters of the LORD; and Zeb-a-di'ah the son of Ish'ma-el, the ruler of the house of Ju'dah, for all the king's matters: also the Le'vites *shall be* officers before you. Deal courageously, and the LORD shall be with the good. Act

CHAPTER 20

IT came to pass after this also, *that* the children of Mo'ab, and the children of Am'mon, and with them *other* beside the Am'mon-ites, came against Je-hosh'a-phat to battle.

2 Then there came some that told Je-hosh'a-phat, saying, There come a great multitude against you from beyond the sea on this side Syr'i-a; and, behold, they *be* in Haz'a-zon-ta'mar, which *is* En-ge'di.

3 And Je-hosh'a-phat feared, and set himself to seek the LORD, and proclaimed a fast throughout all Ju'dah.   was afraid -turned

4 And Ju'dah gathered themselves together, to ask *help* of the LORD: even out of all the cities of Ju'dah they came to seek the LORD.

5 And Je-hosh'a-phat stood in the congregation of Ju'dah and Je-ru'sa-lem, in the house of the LORD, before the new court,

6 And said, O LORD God of our fathers, *are* not You God in heaven? and rule *not* You over all the kingdoms of the heathen? and in Your hand *is there not* power and might, so that none is able to withstand You?   Jehovah[s.f.] Elohim[p.f.]

7 *Are* not You our God, *who* did drive out the inhabitants of this land before Your people Is'ra-el, and gave it to the seed of A'bra-ham Your friend for ever?   Elohim[p.f.] - descendants

8 And they dwelled therein, and have built You a sanctuary therein for Your name, saying,

9 If, *when* evil comes upon us, *as* the sword, judgment, or pestilence, or famine, we stand before this house, and in Your presence, (for Your name *is* in this house,) and cry to You in our affliction, then You will hear and help.

10 And now, behold, the children of Am'mon and Mo'ab and mount Se'ir, whom You would not let Is'ra-el invade, when they came out of the land of E'gypt, but they turned from them, and destroyed them not;

11 Behold, *I say, how* they reward us, to come to cast us out of Your possession, which You have given us to inherit.

12 O our God, will You not judge them? for we have no might against this great company that comes against us; neither know we what to do: but our eyes *are* upon You.   Elohim[p.f.]

13 And all Ju'dah stood before the LORD, with their little ones, their wives, and their children.

14 Then upon Ja-ha'zi-el the son of Zech-a-ri'ah, the son of Be-na'iah, the

son of Je-i'el, the son of Mat-ta-ni'ah, a Le'vite of the sons of A'saph, came the Spirit of the LORD in the midst of the congregation; presence

15 And he said, Hearken you, all Ju'dah, and you inhabitants of Je-ru'sa-lem, and you king Je-hosh'a-phat, Thus says the LORD to you, Be not afraid nor dismayed by reason of this great multitude; for the battle *is* not yours, but God's.

Listen - Elohim[P.F.]

16 To morrow go you down against them: behold, they come up by the cliff of Ziz; and you shall find them at the end of the brook, before the wilderness of Jer'u-el. ascent

17 You shall not *need* to fight in this *battle*: set yourselves, stand you *still*, and see the salvation of the LORD with you, O Ju'dah and Je-ru'sa-lem: fear not, nor be dismayed; to morrow go out against them: for the LORD *will be* with you.

18 And Je-hosh'a-phat bowed his head with *his* face to the ground: and all Ju'dah and the inhabitants of Je-ru'sa-lem fell before the LORD, worshipping the LORD.

19 And the Le'vites, of the children of the Ko'hath-ites, and of the children of the Kor'hites, stood up to praise the LORD God of Is'ra-el with a loud voice on high. Jehovah[s.f.] Elohim[p.f.]

20 And they rose early in the morning, and went forth into the wilderness of Te-ko'a: and as they went forth, Je-hosh'a-phat stood and said, Hear me, O Ju'dah, and you inhabitants of Je-ru'sa-lem; Believe in the LORD your God, so shall you be established; believe His prophets, so shall you prosper. safely kept

21 And when he had consulted with the people, he appointed singers to the LORD, and that should praise the beauty of holiness, as they went out before the army, and to say, Praise the LORD; for His mercy *endures* for ever.

22 And when they began to sing and to praise, the LORD set ambushments against the children of Am'mon, Mo'ab, and mount Se'ir, which were come against Ju'dah; and they were smitten. routed

23 For the children of Am'mon and Mo'ab stood up against the inhabitants of mount Se'ir, utterly to slay and destroy *them*: and when they had made an end of the inhabitants of Se'ir, every one helped to destroy another. finished with

24 And when Ju'dah came toward the watch tower in the wilderness, they looked to the multitude, and, behold, they *were* dead bodies fallen to the earth, and none escaped.

25 And when Je-hosh'a-phat and his people came to take away the spoil of them, they found among them in abundance both riches with the dead bodies, and precious jewels, which they stripped off for themselves, more than they could carry away: and they were three days in gathering of the spoil, it was so much.

26 And on the fourth day they assembled themselves in the valley of Ber'a-chah; for there they blessed the LORD: therefore the name of the same place was called, The valley of Ber'a-chah, to this day.

27 Then they returned, every man of Ju'dah and Je-ru'sa-lem, and Je-hosh'a-phat in the forefront of them, to go again to Je-ru'sa-lem with joy; for the LORD had made them to rejoice over their enemies.

28 And they came to Je-ru'sa-lem with underline psalteries and harps and trumpets to the house of the LORD.   lyres

29 And the fear of God was on all the kingdoms of *those* countries, when they had heard that the LORD fought against the enemies of Is'ra-el.   dread - Elohim^p.f.

30 So the realm of Je-hosh'a-phat was quiet: for his God gave him rest round about.

31 And Je-hosh'a-phat reigned over Ju'dah: *he was* thirty and five years old when he began to reign, and he reigned twenty and five years in Je-ru'sa-lem. And his mother's name *was* A-zu'bah the daughter of Shil'hi.

32 And he walked in the way of A'sa his father, and departed not from it, doing *that which was* right in the sight of the LORD.

33 However the high places were not taken away: for as yet the people had not prepared their hearts to the God of their fathers.   shrines - Elohim^p.f.

34 Now the rest of the acts of Je-hosh'a-phat, first and last, behold, they *are* written in the book of Je'hu the son of Ha-na'ni, who *is* mentioned in the book of the kings of Is'ra-el.

35 And after this did Je-hosh'a-phat king of Ju'dah join himself with A-ha-zi'ah king of Is'ra-el, who did very wickedly:

36 And he joined himself with him to make ships to go to Tar'shish: and they made the ships in E'zi-on-ga'ber.

37 Then E-li-e'zer the son of Dod'a-vah of Ma-re'shah prophesied against Je-hosh'a-phat, saying, Because you have joined yourself with A-ha-zi'ah, the LORD have broken your works. And the ships were broken, that they were not able to go to Tar'shish.

CHAPTER 21

NOW Je-hosh'a-phat slept with his fathers, and was buried with his fathers in the city of Da'vid. And Je-ho'ram his son reigned in his stead.

2 And he had brethren the sons of Je-hosh'a-phat, Az-a-ri'ah, and Je-hi'el, and Zech-a-ri'ah, and Az-a-ri'ah, and Mi'chael, and Sheph-a-ti'ah: all these *were* the sons of Je-hosh'a-phat king of Is'ra-el.

3 And their father gave them great gifts of silver, and of gold, and of precious things, with fenced cities in Ju'dah: but the kingdom gave he to Je-ho'ram; because he *was* the firstborn.   fortified

4 Now when Je-ho'ram was risen up to the kingdom of his father, he strengthened himself, and slew all his brethren with the sword, and *divers* also of the princes of Is'ra-el.   took over - secured - some

5 Je-ho'ram *was* thirty and two years old when he began to reign, and he reigned eight years in Je-ru'sa-lem.

6 And he walked in the way of the kings of Is'ra-el, like as did the house of A'hab: for he had the daughter of A'hab to wife: and he wrought *that which* was evil in the eyes of the LORD.   did

7 However the LORD would not destroy the house of Da'vid, because of the <u>covenant</u> that He had made with Da'vid, and as He promised to give a <u>light</u> to him and to his sons for ever.   Yet - agreement - yoke, i.e., rule

8 In his days the E'dom-ites revolted from under the <u>dominion</u> of Ju'dah, and made themselves a king.   rule

9 Then Je-ho'ram went forth with his princes, and all his chariots with him: and he rose up by night, and smote the E'dom-ites which <u>compassed</u> him in, and the captains of the chariots. surrounded

10 So the E'dom-ites revolted from under the hand of Ju'dah to this day. The same time *also* did Lib'nah revolt from under his hand; because he had forsaken the <u>LORD God</u> of his fathers.   Jehovah^s.f. Elohim^p.f.

11 Moreover he made <u>high places</u> in the mountains of Ju'dah, and caused the inhabitants of Je-ru'sa-lem to commit fornication, and <u>compelled</u> Ju'dah *thereto*.   shrines - led

12 And there came a writing to him from E-li'jah the prophet, saying, Thus says the <u>LORD God</u> of Da'vid your father, Because you have not walked in the ways of Je-hosh'a-phat your father, nor in the ways of A'sa king of Ju'dah,

13 But have walked in the way of the kings of Is'ra-el, and have made Ju'dah and the inhabitants of Je-ru'sa-lem to go a whoring, like to the whoredoms of the house of A'hab, and also have slain your brethren of your father's house, *which were* better than yourself:

14 Behold, with a great plague will the LORD smite your people, and your children, and your wives, and all your goods:

15 And you *shall have* great sickness by disease of your bowels, until your bowels fall out by reason of the sickness day by day.

16 Moreover the LORD stirred up against Je-ho'ram the spirit of the Phi-lis'tines, and of the A-ra'bi-ans, that *were* near the E-thi-o'pi-ans:

17 And they came up into Ju'dah, and broke into it, and carried away all the <u>substance</u> that was found in the king's house, and his sons also, and his wives; so that there was <u>never</u> a son left him, save Je-ho'a-haz, the youngest of his sons.   possessions - no

18 And after all this the LORD smote him in his bowels with an incurable disease.

19 And it came to pass, that in process of time, after the end of two years, his bowels fell out by reason of his sickness: so he died <u>of sore diseases</u>. And his people made <u>no burning for him</u>, like the burning of his fathers.   in great pain - no fire in his honor

20 Thirty and two years old was he when he began to reign, and he reigned in Je-ru'sa-lem eight years, and departed without <u>being desired</u>. However they buried him in the city of Da'vid, but not in the <u>sepulchers</u> of the kings.   anyone's regret - tombs

CHAPTER 22

AND the inhabitants of Je-ru'sa-lem made A-ha-zi'ah his youngest son king in his stead: for the band of men that came with the A-ra'bi-ans to the

camp had slain all the eldest. So A-ha-zi'ah the son of Je-ho'ram king of Ju'dah reigned.

2 Forty and two years old *was* A-ha-zi'ah when he began to reign, and he reigned one year in Je-ru'sa-lem. His mother's name also *was* Ath-a-li'ah the daughter of Om'ri.

3 He also walked in the ways of the house of A'hab: for his mother was his <u>counselor</u> to do wickedly.   advisor

4 Wherefore he did evil in the sight of the LORD like the house of A'hab: for they were his counselors after the death of his father to his destruction.

5 He walked also after their counsel, and went with Je-ho'ram the son of A'hab king of Is'ra-el to war against Haz'a-el king of Syr'i-a at Ra'moth-gil'e-ad: and the Syr'i-ans smote Jo'ram.

6 And he returned to be healed in Jez're-el because of the wounds which were given him at Ra'mah, when he fought with Haz'a-el king of Syr'i-a. And Az-a-ri'ah the son of Je-ho'ram king of Ju'dah went down to see Je-ho'ram the son of A'hab at Jez're-el, because he was sick.

7 And the destruction of A-ha-zi'ah was of <u>God</u> <u>by coming</u> to Jo'ram: for when he <u>was</u> come, he went out with Je-ho'ram against Je'hu the son of Nim'shi, whom the LORD had anointed to <u>cut off</u> the house of A'hab.   Elohim^{p.f.} - because he went - had - destroy

8 And it came to pass, that, when Je'hu was executing judgment upon the house of A'hab, and found the princes of Ju'dah, and the sons of the brethren of A-ha-zi'ah, that ministered to A-ha-zi'ah, he slew them.

9 And he sought A-ha-zi'ah: and they caught him, (for he was hid in Sa-ma'ri-a,) and brought him to Je'hu: and when they had slain him, they buried him: Because, said they, he *is* the son of Je-hosh'a-phat, who sought the LORD with all his heart. So the house of A-ha-zi'ah had no power to <u>keep still</u> the kingdom.   retain control of

10 But when Ath-a-li'ah the mother of A-ha-zi'ah saw that her son was dead, she arose and destroyed all the <u>seed royal</u> of the house of Ju'dah.   royal offspring

11 But Je-ho-shab'e-ath, the daughter of the king, took Jo'ash the son of A-ha-zi'ah, and stole him from among the king's sons that were slain, and put him and his nurse in a bedchamber. So Je-ho-shab'e-ath, the daughter of king Je-ho'ram, the wife of Je-hoi'a-da the priest, (for she was the sister of A-ha-zi'ah,) hid him from Ath-a-li'ah, so that she slew him not.

12 And he was with them hid in the house of <u>God</u> six years: and Ath-a-li'ah reigned over the land.   Elohim^{p.f.}

CHAPTER 23

AND in the seventh year Je-hoi'a-da strengthened himself, and took the captains of hundreds, Az-a-ri'ah the son of Jer'o-ham, and Ish'ma-el the son of Je-ho-ha'nan, and Az-a-ri'ah the son of O'bed, and Ma-a-se'iah the son of Ad-a-i'ah, and E-lish'a-phat the son of Zich'ri, into <u>covenant</u> with him.   agreement

2 And they went about in Ju'dah, and

gathered the Le'vites out of all the cities of Ju'dah, and the chief of the fathers of Is'ra-el, and they came to Je-ru'sa-lem.

3 And all the congregation made a <u>covenant</u> with the king in the house of <u>God</u>. And he said to them, Behold, the king's son shall reign, as the LORD has said of the sons of Da'vid. agreement - Elohim p.f.

4 This *is* the thing that you shall do; A third part of you entering on the <u>sabbath</u>, of the priests and of the Le'vites, *shall be* <u>porters of the doors</u>; rest day - gatekeepers

5 And a third part *shall be* at the king's house; and a third part at the gate of the foundation: and all the people *shall be* in the courts of the house of the LORD.

6 But let none come into the house of the LORD, save the priests, and they that minister of the Le'vites; they shall go in, for they *are* holy: but all the people shall keep the <u>watch</u> of the LORD. command

7 And the Le'vites shall <u>compass</u> the king round about, every man with his weapons in his hand; and whosoever *else* comes into the house, he shall be put to death: but be you with the king when he comes in, and when he goes out. surround

8 So the Le'vites and all Ju'dah did according to all things that Je-hoi'a-da the priest had commanded, and took every man his men that were to come in on the sabbath, with them that were to go *out* on the sabbath: for Je-hoi'a-da the priest dismissed not the <u>courses</u>. divisions

9 Moreover Je-hoi'a-da the priest delivered to the captains of hundreds spears, and <u>bucklers</u>, and shields, that *had been* king Da'vid's, which *were* in the house of God. large shields

10 And he set all the people, every man having his weapon in his hand, from the right side of the temple to the left side of the temple, along by the altar and the temple, by the king round about.

11 Then they brought out the king's son, and put upon him the crown, and *gave him* the testimony, and made him king. And Je-hoi'a-da and his sons anointed him, and said, <u>God save</u> the king. Long live

12 Now when Ath-a-li'ah heard the noise of the people running and praising the king, she came to the people into the house of the LORD:

13 And she looked, and, behold, the king stood at his pillar at the <u>entering</u> in, and the princes and the trumpets by the king: and all the people of the land rejoiced, and sounded with trumpets, also the singers with instruments of music, and such as taught to sing praise. Then Ath-a-li'ah <u>rent</u> her clothes, and said, Treason, Treason. entrance - tore

14 Then Je-hoi'a-da the priest brought out the captains of hundreds that were set over the host, and said to them, <u>Have</u> her forth <u>of the ranges</u>: and whoso follows her, let him be slain with the sword. For the priest said, Slay her not in the house of the LORD. Bring - from - ranks

15 So they laid hands on her; and when she was come to the entering of

the horse gate by the king's house, they slew her there.

16 And Je-hoi'a-da made a <u>covenant</u> between him, and between all the people, and between the king, that they should be the LORD's people.   agreement

17 Then all the people went to the house of Ba'al, and broke it down, and broke his altars and his images in pieces, and slew Mat'tan the priest of Ba'al before the altars.

18 Also Je-hoi'a-da <u>appointed</u> the offices of the house of the LORD by the hand of the priests the Le'vites, whom Da'vid had <u>distributed</u> in the house of the LORD, to offer the burned offerings of the LORD, as *it is* written in the law of Mo'ses, with rejoicing and with singing, *as it was ordained* by Da'vid.   assigned - placed

19 And he set the <u>porters</u> at the gates of the house of the LORD, that none *which was* unclean in any <u>thing</u> should enter in.   gatekeepers - way

20 And he took the captains of hundreds, and the nobles, and the governors of the people, and all the people of the land, and brought down the king from the house of the LORD: and they came through the <u>high</u> gate into the king's house, and set the king upon the throne of the kingdom.   upper

21 And all the people of the land rejoiced: and the city was quiet, after that they had slain Ath-a-li'ah with the sword.

CHAPTER 24

J O'ASH *was* seven years old when he began to reign, and he reigned forty years in Je-ru'sa-lem. His mother's name also *was* Zib'i-ah of Be'er-she'ba.

2 And Jo'ash did *that which was* right in the sight of the LORD all the days of Je-hoi'a-da the priest.

3 And Je-hoi'a-da took for him two wives; and he fathered sons and daughters.

4 And it came to pass after this, *that* Jo'ash was minded to repair the house of the LORD.

5 And he gathered together the priests and the Le'vites, and said to them, Go out to the cities of Ju'dah, and gather of all Is'ra-el money to repair the house of your <u>God</u> from year to year, and see that you <u>hasten</u> the matter. However the Le'vites hastened *it* not.   Elohim^{p.f} - quickly do

6 And the king called for Je-hoi'a-da the chief, and said to him, Why have you not required of the Le'vites to bring in out of Ju'dah and out of Je-ru'sa-lem the <u>collection</u>, *according to the commandment* of Mo'ses the servant of the LORD, and of the congregation of Is'ra-el, for the tabernacle of witness?   levy

7 For the sons of Ath-a-li'ah, that wicked woman, had <u>broken up</u> the house of <u>God</u>; and also all the dedicated things of the house of the LORD did they <u>bestow</u> upon Ba'al-im.   damaged - Elohim^{p.f} - use - the Baals

8 And at the king's commandment they made a chest, and set it outside at the gate of the house of the LORD.

9 And they made a proclamation through Ju'dah and Je-ru'sa-lem, to bring in to the LORD the collection *that*

Mo'ses the servant of <u>God</u> *laid* upon Is'ra-el in the wilderness.   Elohim^{p.f.}

10 And all the princes and all the people rejoiced, and brought in, and cast into the chest, until they had made an end.

11 Now it came to pass, that at what time the chest was brought to the king's office by the hand of the Le'vites, and when they saw that *there was* much money, the king's scribe and the high priest's officer came and emptied the chest, and took it, and carried it to his place again. Thus they did day by day, and gathered money in abundance.

12 And the king and Je-hoi'a-da gave it to such as did the work of the service of the house of the LORD, and hired masons and carpenters to repair the house of the LORD, and also such as <u>wrought</u> iron and <u>brass</u> to mend the house of the LORD.   worked with - bronze

13 So the workmen <u>wrought</u>, and the work <u>was perfected</u> by them, and they set the house of God <u>in its state</u>, and strengthened it.

labored - progressed - according to its specifications

14 And when they had finished *it*, they brought the rest of the money before the king and Je-hoi'a-da, whereof were made <u>vessels</u> for the house of the LORD, *even* <u>vessels</u> to minister, and to offer *with*, and <u>spoons</u>, and <u>vessels</u> of gold and silver. And they offered burned offerings in the house of the LORD continually all the days of Je-hoi'a-da.   utensils - pans

15 But Je-hoi'a-da <u>waxed</u> old, and was full of days when he died; an hun-dred and thirty years old *was he* when he died.   grew

16 And they buried him in the city of Da'vid among the kings, because he had done good in Is'ra-el, both toward <u>God</u>, and toward his house.   Elohim^{p.f.}

17 Now after the death of Je-hoi'a-da came the princes of Ju'dah, and <u>made obeisance</u> to the king. Then the king <u>hearkened</u> to them.   bowed down - listened

18 And they left the house of the LORD God of their fathers, and served groves and idols: and wrath came upon Ju'dah and Je-ru'sa-lem for this their trespass.

19 Yet He sent prophets to them, to bring them again to the LORD; and they testified against them: but they would not give ear.

20 And the Spirit of <u>God</u> <u>came</u> upon Zech-a-ri'ah the son of Je-hoi'a-da the priest, which stood above the people, and said to them, Thus says God, Why transgress you the commandments of the LORD, that you cannot prosper? because you have forsaken the LORD, He has also forsaken you.   Elohim^{p.f.} - clothed

21 And they conspired against him, and stoned him with stones at the commandment of the king in the court of the house of the LORD.

22 Thus Jo'ash the king remembered not the kindness which Je-hoi'a-da his father had done to him, but slew his son. And when he died, he said, The LORD look upon *it*, and require *it*.

23 And it came to pass at the end of the year, *that* the host of Syr'i-a came up against him: and they came to Ju'dah and Je-ru'sa-lem, and destroyed all

the princes of the people from among the people, and sent all the spoil of them to the king of Da-mas'cus. plunder

24 For the army of the Syr'i-ans came with a small company of men, and the LORD delivered a very great host into their hand, because they had forsaken the LORD God of their fathers. So they executed judgment against Jo'ash.

25 And when they were departed from him, (for they left him in great diseases,) his own servants conspired against him for the blood of the sons of Je-hoi'a-da the priest, and slew him on his bed, and he died: and they buried him in the city of Da'vid, but they buried him not in the sepulchers of the kings. very sick - tombs

26 And these are they that conspired against him; Za'bad the son of Shim'e-ath an Am'mon-it-ess, and Je-hoz'a-bad the son of Shim'rith a Mo'ab-it-ess.

27 Now *concerning* his sons, and the greatness of the burdens *laid* upon him, and the repairing of the house of God, behold, they *are* written in the story of the book of the kings. And Am-a'zi'ah his son reigned in his stead. Elohim^p.f. - treatise

CHAPTER 25

A M-A-ZI'AH *was* twenty and five years old *when* he began to reign, and he reigned twenty and nine years in Je-ru'sa-lem. And his mother's name *was* Je-ho-ad'dan of Je-ru'sa-lem.

2 And he did *that which was* right in the sight of the LORD, but not with a perfect heart. whole

3 Now it came to pass, when the kingdom was established to him, that he slew his servants that had killed the king his father. firmly in his grasp

4 But he slew not their children, but *did* as *it is* written in the law in the book of Mo'ses, where the LORD commanded, saying, The fathers shall not die for the children, neither shall the children die for the fathers, but every man shall die for his own sin.

5 Moreover Am-a-zi'ah gathered Ju'dah together, and made them captains over thousands, and captains over hundreds, according to the houses of *their* fathers, throughout all Ju'dah and Ben'ja-min: and he numbered them from twenty years old and above, and found them three hundred thousand choice *men, able* to go forth to war, that could handle spear and shield.

6 He hired also an hundred thousand mighty men of valor out of Is'ra-el for an hundred talents of silver.

7 But there came a man of God to him, saying, O king, let not the army of Is'ra-el go with you; for the LORD *is* not with Is'ra-el, *that is, with* all the children of E'phra-im. Elohim^p.f.

8 But if you will go, do *it*, be strong for the battle: God shall make you fall before the enemy: for God has power to help, and to cast down.

9 And Am-a-zi'ah said to the man of God, But what shall we do for the hundred talents which I have given to the army of Is'ra-el? And the man of God answered, The LORD is able to give you much more than this. troops

10 Then Am-a-zi'ah separated them, *that is,* the army that was come to him

out of E'phra-im, to go home again: wherefore their anger was greatly kindled against Ju'dah, and they returned home in great anger.

11 And Am-a-zi'ah <u>strengthened</u> himself, and led forth his people, and went to the <u>valley of salt</u>, and <u>smote</u> of the children of Se'ir ten thousand.   took courage - i.e., Dead Sea area - struck

12 And *other* ten thousand *left* alive did the children of Ju'dah carry away captive, and brought them to the top of the rock, and cast them down from the top of the rock, that they all were broken in pieces.

13 But the soldiers of the army which Am-a-zi'ah sent back, that they should not go with him to battle, fell upon the cities of Ju'dah, from Sa-ma'ri-a even to Beth-ho'ron, and smote three thousand of them, and took much <u>spoil</u>. plunder

14 Now it came to pass, after that Am-a-zi'ah was come from the slaughter of the E'dom-ites, that he brought the gods of the children of Se'ir, and set them up *to be* his gods, and bowed down himself before them, and burned incense to them.

15 Wherefore the anger of the LORD was kindled against Am-a-zi'ah, and He sent to him a prophet, which said to him, Why have you sought after the gods of the people, which could not deliver their own people out of your hand?

16 And it came to pass, as he talked with him, that *the king* said to him, Are you made of the king's counsel? <u>forbear</u>; why should you be smitten? Then the prophet forbare, and said, I know that <u>God</u> has <u>determined</u> to destroy you, because you have done this, and have not hearkened to my <u>counsel</u>.   refrain - Elohim^{p.f.} - planned - advice

17 Then Am-a-zi'ah king of Ju'dah took advice, and sent to Jo'ash, the son of Je-ho'a-haz, the son of Je'hu, king of Is'ra-el, saying, Come, <u>let us see one another in the face</u>.   "meet me face to face"

18 And Jo'ash king of Is'ra-el sent to Am-a-zi'ah king of Ju'dah, saying, The thistle that *was* in Leb'a-non sent to the cedar that *was* in Leb'a-non, saying, Give your daughter to my son to wife: and there passed by a wild beast that *was* in Leb'a-non, and trampled down the thistle.

19 You say, Lo, you have smitten the E'dom-ites; and your heart <u>lifts you up to boast</u>: abide now at home; why should you <u>meddle</u> to *your* hurt, that you should fall, *even* you, and Ju'dah with you?   has become proud in boasting - ask for trouble

20 But Am-a-zi'ah would not hear; for it *came* of <u>God</u>, that He might deliver them into the hand *of their enemies*, because they sought after the gods of E'dom.   Elohim^{p.f.}

21 So Jo'ash the king of Is'ra-el went up; and they saw one another in the face, *both* he and Am-a-zi'ah king of Ju'dah, at Beth-she'mesh, which *belongs* to Ju'dah.

22 And Ju'dah was <u>put to the worse</u> before Is'ra-el, and they fled every man to his tent.   defeated

23 And Jo'ash the king of Is'ra-el took Am-a-zi'ah king of Ju'dah, the son

of Jo'ash, the son of Je-ho'a-haz, at Beth-she'mesh, and brought him to Je-ru'sa-lem, and broke down the wall of Je-ru'sa-lem from the gate of E'phra-im to the corner gate, four hundred cubits.

24 And *he took* all the gold and the silver, and all the vessels that were found in the house of God with O'bed-e'dom, and the treasures of the king's house, the hostages also, and returned to Sa-ma'ri-a.

25 And Am-a-zi'ah the son of Jo'ash king of Ju'dah lived after the death of Jo'ash son of Je-ho'a-haz king of Is'ra-el fifteen years.

26 Now the rest of the acts of Am-a-zi'ah, first and last, behold, *are* they not written in the book of the kings of Ju'dah and Is'ra-el?

27 Now after the time that Am-a-zi'ah did turn away from following the LORD they made a conspiracy against him in Je-ru'sa-lem; and he fled to La'chish: but they sent to La'chish after him, and slew him there.

28 And they brought him upon horses, and buried him with his fathers in the city of Ju'dah.

CHAPTER 26

THEN all the people of Ju'dah took Uz-zi'ah, who *was* sixteen years old, and made him king in the room of his father Am-a-zi'ah.   place

2 He built E'loth, and restored it to Ju'dah, after that the king slept with his fathers.

3 Sixteen years old *was* Uz-zi'ah when he began to reign, and he reigned fifty and two years in Je-ru'sa-lem. His mother's name also *was* Jec-o-li'ah of Je-ru'sa-lem.

4 And he did *that which was* right in the sight of the LORD, according to all that his father Am-a-zi'ah did.

5 And he sought God in the days of Zech-a-ri'ah, who had understanding in the visions of God: and as long as he sought the LORD, God made him to prosper. Elohim^{p.f.}

6 And he went forth and warred against the Phi-lis'tines, and broke down the wall of Gath, and the wall of Jab'neh, and the wall of Ash'dod, and built cities about Ash'dod, and among the Phi-lis'tines.

7 And God helped him against the Phi-lis'tines, and against the A-ra'bi-ans that dwelled in Gur-ba'al, and the Me-hu'nims.

8 And the Am'mon-ites gave gifts to Uz-zi'ah: and his name spread abroad *even* to the entering in of E'gypt; for he strengthened *himself* exceedingly.

9 Moreover Uz-zi'ah built towers in Je-ru'sa-lem at the corner gate, and at the valley gate, and at the turning *of the wall*, and fortified them.

10 Also he built towers in the desert, and dug many wells: for he had much cattle, both in the low country, and in the plains: husbandmen *also*, and vine dressers in the mountains, and in Car'mel: for he loved husbandry. cisterns - plowmen - the soil

11 Moreover Uz-zi'ah had an host of fighting men, that went out to war by bands, according to the number of their account by the hand of Je-i'el the scribe

and Ma-a-se'iah the ruler, under the hand of Han-a-ni'ah, *one* of the king's captains.

12 The whole number of the chief of the fathers of the mighty men of valor *were* two thousand and six hundred.

13 And under their hand *was* an army, three hundred thousand and seven thousand and five hundred, that made war with mighty power, to help the king against the enemy.

14 And Uz-zi'ah prepared for them throughout all the host shields, and spears, and helmets, and <u>habergeons</u>, and bows, and slings *to cast* stones. body armor

15 And he made in Je-ru'sa-lem engines, invented by <u>cunning</u> men, to be on the towers and upon the bulwarks, to shoot arrows and great stones with. And his name spread far abroad; for he was marvellously helped, till he was strong. skillful

16 But when he was strong, his heart was lifted up to *his* destruction: for he transgressed against the LORD his <u>God</u>, and went into the temple of the LORD to burn incense upon the altar of incense. Elohim^{p.f.}

17 And Az-a-ri'ah the priest went in after him, and with him <u>fourscore</u> priests of the LORD, *that* were <u>valiant</u> men: 80 - courageous

18 And they withstood Uz-zi'ah the king, and said to him, *It* <u>appertains</u> not to you, Uz-zi'ah, to burn incense to the LORD, but to the priests the sons of Aar'on, that are consecrated to burn incense: go out of the sanctuary; for you have trespassed; neither *shall it be* for your honor from the <u>LORD</u> God. is not proper for you - Jehovah^{s.f.} Elohim^{p.f.}

19 Then Uz-zi'ah was angry, and *had* a censer in his hand to burn incense: and while he was angry with the priests, the leprosy even rose up in his forehead before the priests in the house of the LORD, from beside the incense altar.

20 And Az-a-ri'ah the chief priest, and all the priests, looked upon him, and, behold, he *was* leprous in his forehead, and they thrust him out from there; yea, himself <u>hasted</u> also to go out, because the LORD had <u>smitten</u> him. hurried - afflicted

21 And Uz-zi'ah the king was a leper to the day of his death, and dwelled in a <u>several</u> house, *being* a leper; for he was cut off from the house of the LORD: and Jo'tham his son *was* over the king's house, judging the people of the land. separate

22 Now the rest of the acts of Uz-zi'ah, first and last, did I-sa'iah the prophet, the son of A'moz, write.

23 So Uz-zi'ah slept with his fathers, and they buried him with his fathers in the field of the burial which *belonged* to the kings; for they said, He *is* a leper: and Jo'tham his son reigned in his stead.

CHAPTER 27

JO'THAM *was* twenty and five years old when he began to reign, and he reigned sixteen years in Je-ru'sa-lem. His mother's name also *was* Je-ru'-shah, the daughter of Za'dok.

2 And he did *that which was* right in the sight of the LORD, according to all that his father Uz-zi'ah did: however he entered not into the temple of the LORD. And the people did yet corruptly.   continued to act

3 He built the high gate of the house of the LORD, and on the wall of O'phel he built much.

4 Moreover he built cities in the mountains of Ju'dah, and in the forests he built castles and towers.   hill country - fortresses

5 He fought also with the king of the Am'mon-ites, and prevailed against them. And the children of Am'mon gave him the same year an hundred talents of silver, and ten thousand measures of wheat, and ten thousand of barley. So much did the children of Am'mon pay to him, both the second year, and the third.   Elohim$^{p.f.}$ - defeated

6 So Jo'tham became mighty, because he prepared his ways before the LORD his God.   walked steadfastly - Elohim$^{p.f.}$

7 Now the rest of the acts of Jo'tham, and all his wars, and his ways, lo, they *are* written in the book of the kings of Is'ra-el and Ju'dah.

8 He was five and twenty years old when he began to reign, and reigned sixteen years in Je-ru'sa-lem.

9 And Jo'tham slept with his fathers, and they buried him in the city of Da'vid: and A'haz his son reigned in his stead.

CHAPTER 28

A'HAZ *was* twenty years old when he began to reign, and he reigned six-teen years in Je-ru'sa-lem: but he did not *that which was* right in the sight of the LORD, like Da'vid his father:

2 For he walked in the ways of the kings of Is'ra-el, and made also molten images for Ba'al-im.   cast idols - the Baals

3 Moreover he burned incense in the valley of the son of Hin'nom, and burned his children in the fire, after the abominations of the heathen whom the LORD had cast out before the children of Is'ra-el.

4 He sacrificed also and burned incense in the high places, and on the hills, and under every green tree.   shrines

5 Wherefore the LORD his God delivered him into the hand of the king of Syr'i-a; and they smote him, and carried away a great multitude of them captives, and brought *them* to Da-mas'cus. And he was also delivered into the hand of the king of Is'ra-el, who smote him with a great slaughter.   defeated

6 For Pe'kah the son of Rem-a-li'ah slew in Ju'dah an hundred and twenty thousand in one day, *which were* all valiant men; because they had forsaken the LORD God of their fathers.   courageous - Jehovah$^{s.f.}$ Elohim$^{p.f.}$

7 And Zich'ri, a mighty man of E'phra-im, slew Ma-a-se'iah the king's son, and Az'ri-kam the governor of the house, and El'ka-nah *that was* next to the king.   second in command

8 And the children of Is'ra-el carried away captive of their brethren two hundred thousand, women, sons, and daughters, and took also away much spoil from them, and brought the spoil to Sa-ma'ri-a.   plunder

9 But a prophet of the LORD was there, whose name *was* O'ded: and he went out before the host that came to Sa-ma'ri-a, and said to them, Behold, because the LORD God of your fathers was angry with Ju'dah, He has delivered them into your hand, and you have slain them in a rage *that* reaches up to heaven. Jehovah^s.f. Elohim^p.f.

10 And now you purpose to keep under the children of Ju'dah and Je-ru'sa-lem for bondmen and bondwomen to you: *but are there* not with you, even with you, sins against the LORD your God? subdue - slaves - Elohim^p.f.

11 Now hear me therefore, and deliver the captives again, which you have taken captive of your brethren: for the fierce wrath of the LORD *is* upon you.

12 Then certain of the heads of the children of E'phra-im, Az-a-ri'ah the son of Jo-ha'nan, Ber-e-chi'ah the son of Me-shil'le-moth, and Je-hiz-ki'ah the son of Shal'lum, and Am'a-sa the son of Had'la-i, stood up against them that came from the war,

13 And said to them, You shall not bring in the captives here: for whereas we have offended against the LORD *already*, you intend to add *more* to our sins and to our trespass: for our trespass is great, and *there is* fierce wrath against Is'ra-el.

14 So the armed men left the captives and the spoil before the princes and all the congregation. plunder

15 And the men which were expressed by name rose up, and took the captives, and with the spoil clothed all that were naked among them, and arrayed them, and shod them, and gave them to eat and to drink, and anointed them, and carried all the feeble of them upon asses, and brought them to Jer'i-cho, the city of palm trees, to their brethren: then they returned to Sa-ma'ri-a. designated - plunder

16 At that time did king A'haz send to the kings of As-syr'i-a to help him.

17 For again the E'dom-ites had come and smitten Ju'dah, and carried away captives. attacked

18 The Phi-lis'tines also had invaded the cities of the low country, and of the south of Ju'dah, and had taken Beth-she'mesh, and Aj'a-lon, and Ge-de'roth, and Sho'cho with the villages thereof, and Tim'nah with the villages thereof, Gim'zo also and the villages thereof: and they dwelled there.

19 For the LORD brought Ju'dah low because of A'haz king of Is'ra-el; for he made Ju'dah naked, and transgressed sore against the LORD. much

20 And Til'gath-pil-ne'ser king of As-syr'i-a came to him, and distressed him, but strengthened him not. afflicted - would not help him

21 For A'haz took away a portion *out* of the house of the LORD, and *out* of the house of the king, and of the princes, and gave *it* to the king of As-syr'i-a: but he helped him not.

22 And in the time of his distress did he trespass yet more against the LORD: this *is that* king A'haz.

23 For he sacrificed to the gods of Da-mas'cus, which smote him: and he said, Because the gods of the kings of

Syr'i-a help them, *therefore* will I sacrifice to them, that they may help me. But they were the ruin of him, and of all Is'ra-el. _{defeated}

24 And A'haz gathered together the vessels of the house of <u>God</u>, and cut in pieces the <u>vessels</u> of the house of <u>God</u>, and shut up the doors of the house of the LORD, and he made him altars in every corner of Je-ru'sa-lem. _{Elohim^{p.f.} - utensils}

25 And in <u>every several</u> city of Ju'dah he made <u>high places</u> to burn incense to other gods, and provoked to anger the LORD God of his fathers. _{every - shrines - Jehovah^{s.f.} Elohim^{p.f.}}

26 Now the rest of his acts and of all his ways, first and last, behold, they *are* written in the book of the kings of Ju'dah and Is'ra-el.

27 And A'haz slept with his fathers, and they buried him in the city, *even* in Je-ru'sa-lem: but they brought him not into the <u>sepulchers</u> of the kings of Is'ra-el: and Hez-e-ki'ah his son reigned in his <u>stead</u>. _{tombs - place}

CHAPTER 29

HEZ-E-KI'AH began to reign *when he was* five and twenty years old, and he reigned nine and twenty years in Je-ru'sa-lem. And his mother's name *was* A-bi'jah, the daughter of Zech-a-ri'ah.

2 And he did *that which was* right in the sight of the LORD, according to all that Da'vid his father had done.

3 He in the first year of his reign, in the first month, opened the doors of the house of the LORD, and repaired them.

4 And he brought in the priests and the Le'vites, and gathered them together into the east <u>street</u>, _{square}

5 And said to them, Hear me, you Le'vites, <u>sanctify</u> now yourselves, and <u>sanctify</u> the house of the LORD God of your fathers, and carry forth the <u>filthiness</u> out of the holy *place*. _{consecrate - defilement}

6 For our fathers have <u>trespassed</u>, and done *that which was* evil in the eyes of the LORD our <u>God</u>, and have forsaken Him, and have turned away their faces from the <u>habitation</u> of the LORD, and turned *their* backs. _{been unfaithful - dwelling place}

7 Also they have shut up the doors of the porch, and put out the lamps, and have not burned incense nor offered burned offerings in the holy *place* to the <u>God</u> of Is'ra-el. _{Elohim^{p.f.}}

8 Wherefore the wrath of the LORD was upon Ju'dah and Je-ru'sa-lem, and He has delivered them to trouble, to astonishment, and to hissing, as you see with your eyes.

9 For, lo, our fathers have fallen by the sword, and our sons and our daughters and our wives *are* in captivity for this.

10 Now *it is* in my heart to make a <u>covenant</u> with the LORD God of Is'ra-el, that His fierce wrath may turn away from us. _{agreement - Jehovah^{s.f.} Elohim^{p.f.}}

11 My sons, be not now negligent: for the LORD has chosen you to stand before Him, to serve Him, and that you should minister to Him, and burn incense.

12 Then the Le'vites arose, Ma'-

hath the son of A-mas'a-i, and Jo'el the son of Az-a-ri'ah, of the sons of the Ko'hath-ites: and of the sons of Me-ra'ri, Kish the son of Ab'di, and Az-a-ri'ah the son of Je-hal'e-lel: and of the Ger'shon-ites; Jo'ah the son of Zim'mah, and E'den the son of Jo'ah :

13 And of the sons of El'za-phan; Shim'ri, and Je-i'el: and of the sons of A'saph; Zech-a-ri'ah, and Mat-ta-ni'ah:

14 And of the sons of He'man; Je-hi'el, and Shim'e-i: and of the sons of Jed'u-thun; Shem-a-i'ah, and Uz'zi-el.

15 And they gathered their brethren, and <u>sanctified</u> themselves, and came, according to the commandment of the king, by the words of the LORD, to cleanse the house of the LORD. consecrated

16 And the priests went into the inner part of the house of the LORD, to cleanse *it*, and brought out all the <u>uncleanness</u> that they found in the temple of the LORD into the court of the house of the LORD. And the Le'vites took *it*, to carry *it* out abroad into the brook Kid'ron. defilement

17 Now they began on the first *day* of the first month to sanctify, and on the eighth day of the month came they to the porch of the LORD: so they sanctified the house of the LORD in eight days; and in the sixteenth day of the first month they made an end.

18 Then they went in to Hez-e-ki'ah the king, and said, We have cleansed all the house of the LORD, and the altar of burned offering, with all the <u>vessels</u> thereof, and the showbread table, with all the <u>vessels</u> thereof. utensils

19 Moreover all the vessels, which king A'haz in his reign <u>did cast away</u> in his transgression, have we prepared and sanctified, and, behold, they *are* before the altar of the LORD. discarded

20 Then Hez-e-ki'ah the king rose early, and gathered the rulers of the city, and went up to the house of the LORD.

21 And they brought seven bullocks, and seven rams, and seven lambs, and seven he goats, for a sin offering for the kingdom, and for the sanctuary, and for Ju'dah. And he commanded the priests the sons of Aar'on to offer *them* on the altar of the LORD.

22 So they killed the bullocks, and the priests received the blood, and sprinkled *it* on the altar: likewise, when they had killed the rams, they sprinkled the blood upon the altar: they killed also the lambs, and they sprinkled the blood upon the altar.

23 And they brought <u>forth</u> the he goats *for* the sin offering before the king and the congregation; and they laid their hands upon them: near

24 And the priests killed them, and they made <u>reconciliation</u> with their blood upon the altar, to make an atonement for all Is'ra-el: for the king commanded *that* the burned offering and the sin offering *should be made* for all Is'ra-el. i.e., sin offering

25 And he set the Le'vites in the house of the LORD with cymbals, with <u>psalteries</u>, and with harps, according to the commandment of Da'vid, and of Gad the king's seer, and Na'than the

prophet: for *so was* the commandment of the LORD by His prophets. lyres
26 And the Le'vites stood with the
instruments of Da'vid, and the
priests with the trumpets.
27 And Hez-e-ki'ah commanded to
offer the burned offering upon the altar. And when the burned offering began, the song of the LORD began *also*
with the trumpets, and with the instruments *ordained* by Da'vid king
of Is'ra-el.
28 And all the congregation worshiped, and the singers sang, and
the trumpeters sounded: *and* all *this
continued* until the burned offering
was finished.
29 And when they had made an end
of offering, the king and all that
were present with him bowed themselves, and worshiped.
30 Moreover Hez-e-ki'ah the king
and the princes commanded the
Le'vites to sing praise to the LORD
with the words of Da'vid, and of
A'saph the seer. And they sang
praises with gladness, and they
bowed their heads and worshiped.
31 Then Hez-e-ki'ah answered and
said, Now you have consecrated
yourselves to the LORD, come near
and bring sacrifices and thank offerings into the house of the LORD. And
the congregation brought in sacrifices
and thank offerings; and as many as
were of a free heart burned offerings.
32 And the number of the burned offerings, which the congregation brought,
was threescore and ten bullocks, an hundred rams, *and* two hundred lambs:

all these *were* for a burned offering
to the LORD.
33 And the consecrated things *were* six
hundred oxen and three thousand sheep.
34 But the priests were too few, so
that they could not <u>flay</u> all the
burned offerings: wherefore their
brethren the Le'vites did help them,
till the work was ended, and until the
other priests had <u>sanctified</u> themselves: for the Le'vites *were* more
upright in heart to <u>sanctify</u> themselves than the priests. skin - consecrated
35 And also the burned offerings *were*
in abundance, with the fat of the peace
offerings, and the drink offerings for *every* burned offering. So the service of
the house of the LORD was set in order.
36 And Hez-e-ki'ah rejoiced, and all the
people, that God had prepared the
people: for the thing was *done* suddenly.

CHAPTER 30

AND Hez-e-ki'ah sent to all
Is'ra-el and Ju'dah, and wrote
letters also to E'phra-im and Ma-
nas'seh, that they should come to
the house of the LORD at Je-ru'sa-
lem, to keep the passover to the
<u>LORD God</u> of Is'ra-el. Jehovah's.f. Elohimᵖ.f.
2 For the king had taken counsel,
and his princes, and all the congregation in Je-ru'sa-lem, to keep the
passover in the second month.
3 For they could not keep it at that time,
because the priests had not <u>sanctified</u>
themselves <u>sufficiently</u>, neither had the
people gathered themselves together
to Je-ru'sa-lem. consecrated - in sufficient numbers

4 And the thing pleased the king and all the congregation.

5 So they established a decree to make proclamation throughout all Is'ra-el, from Be'er-she'ba even to Dan, that they should come to keep the passover to the LORD God of Is'ra-el at Je-ru'sa-lem: for they had not done *it* of a long *time in such sort* as it was written.

6 So the posts went with the letters from the king and his princes throughout all Is'ra-el and Ju'dah, and according to the commandment of the king, saying, You children of Is'ra-el, turn again to the LORD God of A'braham, I'saac, and Is'ra-el, and He will return to the remnant of you, that are escaped out of the hand of the kings of As-syr'i-a. Jehovah^s.f. Elohim^p.f.

7 And be not you like your fathers, and like your brethren, which trespassed against the LORD God of their fathers, *who* therefore gave them up to desolation, as you see. were unfaithful

8 Now be you not stiffnecked, as your fathers *were, but* yield yourselves to the LORD, and enter into His sanctuary, which He has sanctified for ever: and serve the LORD your God, that the fierceness of His wrath may turn away from you. stubborn - consecrated - Elohim^p.f.

9 For if you turn again to the LORD, your brethren and your children *shall find* compassion before them that lead them captive, so that they shall come again into this land: for the LORD your God *is* gracious and merciful, and will not turn away *His* face from you, if you return to Him.

10 So the posts passed from city to city through the country of E'phra-im and Ma-nas'seh even to Zeb'u-lun: but they laughed them to scorn, and mocked them. couriers

11 Nevertheless divers of Ash'er and Ma-nas'seh and of Zeb'u-lun humbled themselves, and came to Je-ru'sa-lem. some people

12 Also in Ju'dah the hand of God was to give them one heart to do the commandment of the king and of the princes, by the word of the LORD. Elohim^p.f. - unity

13 And there assembled at Je-ru'sa-lem much people to keep the feast of unleavened bread in the second month, a very great congregation.

14 And they arose and took away the altars that *were* in Je-ru'sa-lem, and all the altars for incense took they away, and cast *them* into the brook Kid'ron.

15 Then they killed the passover on the fourteenth *day* of the second month: and the priests and the Le'vites were ashamed, and sanctified themselves, and brought in the burned offerings into the house of the LORD. humbled themselves - consecrated

16 And they stood in their place after their manner, according to the law of Mo'ses the man of God: the priests sprinkled the blood, *which they received* of the hand of the Le'vites. custom - Elohim^p.f.

17 For *there were* many in the congregation that were not sanctified: therefore the Le'vites had the charge of the killing of the passovers for every one *that was* not clean, to sanctify *them* to the LORD. consecrated

18 For a multitude of the people, *even*

many of E'phra-im, and Ma-nas'seh, Is'sa-char, and Zeb'u-lun, had not cleansed themselves, yet did they eat the passover otherwise than it was written. But Hez-e-ki'ah prayed for them, saying, The good Lord pardon every one

19 *That* prepare his heart to seek God, the Lord God of his fathers, though *he be* not *cleansed* according to the purification of the sanctuary.   Jehovah[s.f.] Elohim[p.f.]

20 And the Lord hearkened to Hez-e-ki'ah, and healed the people.   listened

21 And the children of Is'ra-el that were present at Je-ru'sa-lem kept the feast of unleavened bread seven days with great gladness: and the Le'vites and the priests praised the Lord day by day, *singing* with loud instruments to the Lord.   without yeast

22 And Hez-e-ki'ah spoke comfortably to all the Le'vites that taught the good knowledge of the Lord: and they did eat throughout the feast seven days, offering peace offerings, and making confession to the Lord God of their fathers.   encouragingly - Jehovah[s.f.] Elohim[p.f.]

23 And the whole assembly took counsel to keep other seven days: and they kept *other* seven days with gladness.

24 For Hez-e-ki'ah king of Ju'dah did give to the congregation a thousand bullocks and seven thousand sheep; and the princes gave to the congregation a thousand bullocks and ten thousand sheep: and a great number of priests sanctified themselves.

25 And all the congregation of Ju'-dah, with the priests and the Le'vites, and all the congregation that came out of Is'ra-el, and the strangers that came out of the land of Is'ra-el, and that dwelled in Ju'dah, rejoiced.

26 So there was great joy in Je-ru'sa-lem: for since the time of Sol'o-mon the son of Da'vid king of Is'ra-el *there was* not the like in Je-ru'sa-lem.

27 Then the priests the Le'vites arose and blessed the people: and their voice was heard, and their prayer came *up* to His holy dwelling place, *even* to heaven.

CHAPTER 31

NOW when all this was finished, all Is'ra-el that were present went out to the cities of Ju'dah, and broke the images in pieces, and cut down the groves, and threw down the high places and the altars out of all Ju'dah and Ben'ja-min, in E'phra-im also and Manas'seh, until they had utterly destroyed them all. Then all the children of Is'ra-el returned, every man to his possession, into their own cities.   Asherah idols - shrines

2 And Hez-e-ki'ah appointed the courses of the priests and the Le'vites after their courses, every man according to his service, the priests and Le'vites for burned offerings and for peace offerings, to minister, and to give thanks, and to praise in the gates of the tents of the Lord.   camp

3 *He appointed* also the king's portion of his substance for the burned offerings, *that is*, for the morning and evening burned offerings, and the burned offerings for the sabbaths, and for the new

moons, and for the set feasts, as *it is* written in the law of the LORD. share - goods
4 Moreover he commanded the people that dwelled in Je-ru'sa-lem to give the <u>portion of</u> the priests and the Le'vites, that they might be encouraged in the law of the LORD. share due to
5 And as soon as the commandment came abroad, the children of Is'ra-el brought in abundance the firstfruits of <u>corn</u>, wine, and oil, and honey, and of all the increase of the fields; and the tithe of all *things* brought they in abundantly. grain
6 And *concerning* the children of Is'ra-el and Ju'dah, that dwelled in the cities of Ju'dah, they also brought in the tithe of oxen and sheep, and the tithe of holy things which were consecrated to the LORD their <u>God</u>, and laid *them* by heaps. Elohim^p.f.
7 In the third month they began to lay the foundation of the heaps, and finished *them* in the seventh month.
8 And when Hez-e-ki'ah and the princes came and saw the heaps, they blessed the LORD, and His people Is'ra-el.
9 Then Hez-e-ki'ah questioned with the priests and the Le'vites concerning the heaps.
10 And Az-a-ri'ah the chief priest of the house of Za'dok answered him, and said, Since *the people* began to bring the offerings into the house of the LORD, we have had enough to eat, and have left plenty: for the LORD has blessed His people; and that which is left *is* this great store.
11 Then Hez-e-ki'ah commanded to prepare <u>chambers</u> in the house of the LORD; and they prepared *them*, rooms
12 And brought in the offerings and the tithes and the dedicated *things* faithfully: over which Con-o-ni'ah the Le'vite *was* ruler, and Shim'e-i his brother *was* the next.
13 And Je-hi'el, and Az-a-zi'ah, and Na'hath, and A'sa-hel, and Jer'i-moth, and Joz'a-bad, and E-li'el, and Is-ma-chi'ah, and Ma'hath, and Be-na'iah, *were* overseers under the hand of Con-o-ni'ah and Shim'e-i his brother, at the commandment of Hez-e-ki'ah the king, and Az-a-ri'ah the ruler of the house of God.
14 And Ko're the son of Im'nah the Le'vite, the <u>porter toward the east</u>, *was* over the freewill offerings of <u>God</u>, to distribute the <u>oblations</u> of the LORD, and the most holy things. keeper of the east gate - Elohim^p.f. - offerings
15 And next him *were* E'den, and Mi-ni'a-min, and Jesh'u-a, and Shem-a-i'ah, Am-a-ri'ah, and Shec-a-ni'ah, in the cities of the priests, in *their* <u>set</u> office, to give to their brethren by <u>courses</u>, as well to the great as to the small: assigned - divisions
16 Beside their genealogy of males, from three years old and upward, *even* to every one that enters into the house of the LORD, his daily <u>portion</u> for their service in their charges according to their <u>courses</u>; obligations
17 Both to the genealogy of the priests by the house of their fathers, and the Le'vites from twenty years old and upward, in their charges by their courses;

18 And to the genealogy of all their little ones, their wives, and their sons, and their daughters, through all the congregation: for in their set office they sanctified themselves in <u>holiness</u>: solemn service

19 Also of the sons of Aar'on the priests, *which were* in the fields of the <u>suburbs</u> of their cities, in every several city, the men that were expressed by name, to give portions to all the males among the priests, and to all that were reckoned by genealogies among the Le'vites. pasture lands

20 And thus did Hez-e-ki'ah throughout all Ju'dah, and <u>wrought</u> *that which was* good and right and <u>truth</u> before the Lord his <u>God</u>. did - true - Elohim^{p.f.}

21 And in every work that he began in the service of the house of <u>God</u>, and in the law, and in the commandments, to seek his <u>God</u>, he did *it* <u>with all his heart</u>, and prospered. wholehearted

CHAPTER 32

AFTER these things, and the establishment thereof, Sennach'e-rib king of As-syr'i-a came, and entered into Ju'dah, and encamped against the <u>fenced</u> cities, and thought to win them for himself. fortified

2 And when Hez-e-ki'ah saw that Sen-nach'e-rib was come, and that he <u>was purposed</u> to fight against Je-ru'sa-lem, intended

3 He took counsel with his princes and his mighty men to stop the waters of the <u>fountains</u> which *were* outside the city: and they did help him. springs

4 So there was gathered much people together, who stopped all the fountains, and the brook that ran through the midst of the land, saying, Why should the kings of As-syr'i-a come, and find much water?

5 Also he strengthened himself, and built up all the wall that was broken, and raised *it* up to the towers, and another wall outside, and repaired Mil'lo *in* the <u>city of Da'vid</u>, and made <u>darts</u> and shields in abundance. i.e., Jerusalem - weapons

6 And he set captains of war over the people, and gathered them together to him in the <u>street</u> of the gate of the city, and spoke <u>comfortably</u> to them, saying, square - encouragingly

7 Be strong and courageous, be not afraid nor dismayed for the king of As-syr'i-a, nor for all the multitude that *is* with him: for *there be* more with us than with him:

8 With him *is* an arm of flesh; but with us *is* the Lord our <u>God</u> to help us, and to fight our battles. And the people <u>rested themselves</u> upon the words of Hez-e-ki'ah king of Ju'dah. Elohim^{p.f.} - relied

9 After this did Sen-nach'e-rib king of As-syr'i-a send his servants to Je-ru'sa-lem, (but he *himself laid siege* against La'chish, and all his power with him,) to Hez-e-ki'ah king of Ju'dah, and to all Ju'dah that *were* at Je-ru'sa-lem, saying,

10 Thus says Sen-nach'e-rib king of As-syr'i-a, Whereon do you trust, that you abide in the siege in Je-ru'sa-lem?

11 Do not Hez-e-ki'ah persuade you to give over yourselves to die by

famine and by thirst, saying, The LORD our <u>God</u> shall deliver us out of the hand of the king of As-syr'i-a? Elohim^{p.f.} 12 Has not the same Hez-e-ki'ah taken away his <u>high places</u> and his altars, and commanded Ju'dah and Je-ru'sa-lem, saying, You shall worship before one altar, and burn incense upon it? shrines
13 Know you not what I and my fathers have done to all the people of *other* lands? were the gods of the nations of those lands any ways able to deliver their lands out of my hand?
14 Who *was there* among all the gods of those nations that my fathers utterly destroyed, that could deliver his people out of my hand, that your God should be able to deliver you out of my hand?
15 Now therefore let not Hez-e-ki'ah deceive you, nor persuade you on this manner, neither yet believe him: for no god of any nation or kingdom was able to deliver his people out of my hand, and out of the hand of my fathers: how much less shall your <u>God</u> deliver you out of my hand?
16 And his servants spoke yet *more* against the <u>LORD God</u>, and against His servant Hez-e-ki'ah. Jehovah^{s.f.} Elohim^{p.f.}
17 He wrote also letters to <u>rail on</u> the <u>LORD God</u> of Is'ra-el, and to speak against Him, saying, As the gods of the nations of *other* lands have not delivered their people out of my hand, so shall not the <u>God</u> of Hez-e-ki'ah deliver his people out of my hand. insult - Jehovah^{s.f.} Elohim^{p.f.}
18 Then they cried with a loud voice in the Jews' speech to the people of Je-ru'sa-lem that *were* on the wall, to <u>affright</u> them, and to <u>trouble</u> them; that they might take the city. frighten - terrify
19 And they spoke against the <u>God</u> of Je-ru'sa-lem, as against the gods of the people of the earth, *which were* the work of the hands of man. Elohim^{p.f.}
20 And for this *cause* Hez-e-ki'ah the king, and the prophet I-sa'iah the son of A'moz, prayed and cried to heaven.
21 And the LORD sent an <u>angel</u>, which cut off all the mighty men of valor, and the leaders and captains in the camp of the king of As-syr'i-a. So he returned with shame of face to his own land. And when he was come into the house of his god, they that came forth of his own <u>bowels</u> slew him there with the sword. messenger - insides
22 Thus the LORD saved Hez-e-ki'ah and the inhabitants of Je-ru'sa-lem from the hand of Sen-nach'e-rib the king of As-syr'i-a, and from the hand of all *other*, and guided them on every side. others
23 And many brought gifts to the LORD to Je-ru'sa-lem, and <u>presents</u> to Hez-e-ki'ah king of Ju'dah: so that he was magnified in the sight of all nations from therefore. choice things
24 In those days Hez-e-ki'ah was <u>sick to the death</u>, and prayed to the LORD: and He spoke to him, and He gave him a <u>sign</u>. mortally ill - miraculous sign
25 But Hez-e-ki'ah rendered not again according to the benefit *done* to him; for his heart was <u>lifted up</u>: therefore there was wrath upon him, and upon Ju'dah and Je-ru'sa-lem. proud

26 Notwithstanding Hez-e-ki'ah humbled himself for the pride of his heart, *both* he and the inhabitants of Je-ru'sa-lem, so that the wrath of the LORD came not upon them in the days of Hez-e-ki'ah.

27 And Hez-e-ki'ah had exceeding much riches and honor: and he made himself treasuries for silver, and for gold, and for precious stones, and for spices, and for shields, and for all manner of <u>pleasant jewels</u>;   valuable articles

28 Storehouses also for the increase of <u>corn</u>, and wine, and oil; and stalls for all manner of beasts, and <u>cotes</u> for flocks.   grain - sheepfolds

29 Moreover he provided him cities, and possessions of flocks and herds in abundance: for <u>God</u> had given him <u>substance very much</u>.   Elohim^{p.f.} - great wealth

30 This same Hez-e-ki'ah also stopped the upper watercourse of Gi'hon, and brought it straight down to the west side of the city of Da'vid. And Hez-e-ki'ah prospered in all his works.

31 However in *the business of* the ambassadors of the princes of Bab'y-lon, who sent to him to enquire of the wonder that was *done* in the land, <u>God</u> left him, to <u>try</u> him, that He might know all *that was* in his heart.   And even - test

32 Now the rest of the acts of Hez-e-ki'ah, and his goodness, behold, they *are* written in the vision of I-sa'iah the prophet, the son of A'moz, *and* in the book of the kings of Ju'dah and Is'ra-el.

33 And Hez-e-ki'ah slept with his fathers, and they buried him in the chiefest of the <u>sepulchers</u> of the sons of Da'vid: and all Ju'dah and the inhabitants of Je-ru'sa-lem did him honor at his death. And Ma-nas'seh his son reigned in his stead.   tombs

CHAPTER 33

MA-NAS'SEH *was* twelve years old when he began to reign, and he reigned fifty and five years in Je-ru'sa-lem:

2 But did *that which was* evil in the sight of the LORD, like to the <u>abominations</u> of the heathen, whom the LORD had cast out before the children of Is'ra-el.   detestable practices

3 For he built again the high places which Hez-e-ki'ah his father had broken down, and he <u>reared up</u> altars for Ba'al-im, and made groves, and worshiped all the host of heaven, and served them.   erected

4 Also he built altars in the house of the LORD, whereof the LORD had said, In Je-ru'sa-lem shall My name be for ever.

5 And he built altars for all the host of heaven in the two courts of the house of the LORD.

6 And he caused his children to pass through the fire in the valley of the son of Hin'nom: also he <u>observed times</u>, and used enchantments, and used <u>witchcraft</u>, and dealt with a <u>familiar spirit</u>, and with <u>wizards</u>: he <u>wrought</u> much evil in the sight of the LORD, to provoke Him to anger.   practiced witchcraft - sorcery - medium - spiritists - did

7 And he set a carved image, the idol which he had made, in the <u>house</u> of God, of which God had said to Da'vid

and to Sol'o-mon his son, In this house, and in Je-ru'sa-lcm, which I have chosen before all the tribes of Is'ra-el, will I put My name for ever: temple - Elohim^p.f.
8 Neither will I any more remove the foot of Is'ra-el from out of the land which I have appointed for your fathers; so that they will take heed to do all that I have commanded them, according to the whole law and the statutes and the ordinances by the hand of Mo'ses.
9 So Ma-nas'seh made Ju'dah and the inhabitants of Je-ru'sa-lem to err, *and* to do worse than the heathen, whom the LORD had destroyed before the children of Is'ra-el.
10 And the LORD spoke to Ma-nas'seh, and to his people: but they would not <u>hearken</u>. listen
11 Wherefore the LORD brought upon them the captains of the host of the king of As-syr'i-a, which took Ma-nas'seh <u>among the thorns</u>, and bound him with fetters, and carried him to Bab'y-lon. with hooks
12 And when he was in <u>affliction</u>, he besought the LORD his <u>God</u>, and humbled himself greatly before the <u>God</u> of his fathers, distressed - Elohim^p.f.
13 And prayed to Him: and He was <u>entreated of him</u>, and heard his <u>supplication</u>, and brought him again to Je-ru'sa-lem into his kingdom. Then Ma-nas'seh knew that the LORD He *was* God. moved by his plea - appeal - Elohim^p.f.
14 Now after this he built a wall outside the <u>city of Da'vid</u>, on the west side of Gi'hon, in the valley, even to the entering in at the fish gate, and <u>compassed</u>

about O'phel, and raised it up a very great height, and put captains of war in all the <u>fenced</u> cities of Ju'dah. i.e., Jerusalem - encircled - fortified
15 And he took away the strange gods, and the idol out of the house of the LORD, and all the altars that he had built in the mount of the house of the LORD, and in Je-ru'sa-lem, and cast *them* out of the city.
16 And he repaired the altar of the LORD, and sacrificed thereon peace offerings and thank offerings, and commanded Ju'dah to serve the <u>LORD God</u> of Is'ra-el. Jehovah^s.f. Elohim^p.f.
17 Nevertheless the people did sacrifice still in the <u>high places</u>, *yet* to the LORD their <u>God</u> only. shrines - Elohim^p.f.
18 Now the rest of the acts of Ma-nas'seh, and his prayer to his God, and the words of the seers that spoke to him in the name of the LORD God of Is'ra-el, behold, they *are written* in the book of the kings of Is'ra-el.
19 His prayer also, and *how God* was entreated of him, and all his sin, and his trespass, and the places wherein he built high places, and set up <u>groves</u> and graven images, before he was humbled: behold, they *are* written among the <u>sayings</u> of the seers. Asherah idols - history
20 So Ma-nas'seh slept with his fathers, and they buried him in his own house: and A'mon his son reigned in his stead.
21 A'mon *was* two and twenty years old when he began to reign, and reigned two years in Je-ru'sa-lem.
22 But he did *that which was* evil in

the sight of the LORD, as did Ma-nas'seh his father: for A'mon sacrificed to all the <u>carved images</u> which Ma-nas'seh his father had made, and served them;   idols

23 And humbled not himself before the LORD, as Ma-nas'seh his father had humbled himself; but A'mon <u>trespassed more and more</u>.   increased his guilt

24 And his servants conspired against him, and slew him in his own house.

25 But the people of the land slew all them that had conspired against king A'mon; and the people of the land made Jo-si'ah his son king in his stead.

CHAPTER 34

JO-SI'AH *was* eight years old when he began to reign, and he reigned in Je-ru'sa-lem one and thirty years.

2 And he did *that which was* right in the sight of the LORD, and walked in the ways of Da'vid his father, and <u>declined</u> *neither* to the right hand, nor to the left.   turned aside

3 For in the eighth year of his reign, while he was yet young, he began to seek after the <u>God</u> of Da'vid his father: and in the twelfth year he began to <u>purge</u> Ju'dah and Je-ru'sa-lem from the <u>high places</u>, and the <u>groves</u>, and the carved images, and the molten <u>images</u>.   Elohim^{p.f.} cleanse - shrines - Asherah idols - idols

4 And they broke down the altars of Ba'al-im in his presence; and the images, that *were* on high above them, he cut down; and the <u>groves</u>, and the carved images, and the molten <u>images</u>, he broke in pieces, and made dust *of*

them, and scattered *it* upon the graves of them that had sacrificed to them.

5 And he burned the bones of the priests upon their altars, and cleansed Ju'dah and Je-ru'sa-lem.

6 And *so did he* in the cities of Ma-nas'seh, and E'phra-im, and Sim'e-on, even to Naph'ta-li, with their <u>mattocks</u> round about.   ruins

7 And when he had broken down the altars and the <u>groves</u>, and had beaten the graven <u>images</u> into powder, and cut down all the idols throughout all the land of Is'ra-el, he returned to Je-ru'sa-lem.   Asherah idols - idols

8 Now in the eighteenth year of his reign, when he had <u>purged</u> the land, and the house, he sent Sha'phan the son of Az-a-li'ah, and Ma-a-se'iah the governor of the city, and Jo'ah the son of Jo'a-haz the recorder, to repair the house of the LORD his <u>God</u>.   cleanse - Elohim^{p.f.}

9 And when they came to Hil-ki'ah the high priest, they delivered the money that was brought into the house of <u>God</u>, which the Le'vites that kept the doors had gathered of the hand of Ma-nas'seh and E'phra-im, and of all the remnant of Is'ra-el, and of all Ju'dah and Ben'ja-min; and they returned to Je-ru'sa-lem.

10 And they put *it* in the hand of the workmen that had the oversight of the house of the LORD, and they gave it to the workmen that <u>wrought</u> in the house of the LORD, to repair and <u>amend</u> the house: worked - restore

11 Even to the <u>artificers</u> and builders gave they *it*, to buy <u>hewn</u> stone, and

timber for couplings, and to floor the houses which the kings of Ju'dah had destroyed. carpenters - quarried

12 And the men did the work faithfully: and the overseers of them *were* Ja'hath and O-ba-di'ah, the Le'vites, of the sons of Me-ra'ri; and Zech-a-ri'ah and Me-shul'lam, of the sons of the Ko'hath-ites, to set *it* forward; and *other of* the Le'vites, all that could skill of instruments of music. were skillful with

13 Also *they were* over the bearers of burdens, and *were* overseers of all that wrought the work in any manner of service: and of the Le'vites *there were* scribes, and officers, and porters. gatekeepers

14 And when they brought out the money that was brought into the house of the LORD, Hil-ki'ah the priest found a book of the law of the LORD *given* by Mo'ses. the

15 And Hil-ki'ah answered and said to Sha'phan the scribe, I have found the book of the law in the house of the LORD. And Hil-ki'ah delivered the book to Sha'phan.

16 And Sha'phan carried the book to the king, and brought the king word back again, saying, All that was committed to your servants, they do *it*.

17 And they have gathered together the money that was found in the house of the LORD, and have delivered it into the hand of the overseers, and to the hand of the workmen. emptied out

18 Then Sha'phan the scribe told the king, saying, Hil-ki'ah the priest has given me a book. And Sha'phan read it before the king.

19 And it came to pass, when the king had heard the words of the law, that he rent his clothes. tore

20 And the king commanded Hil-ki'ah, and A-hi'kam the son of Sha'phan, and Ab'don the son of Mi'cah, and Sha'phan the scribe, and A-sa-i'ah a servant of the king's, saying,

21 Go, enquire of the LORD for me, and for them that are left in Is'ra-el and in Ju'dah, concerning the words of the book that is found: for great *is* the wrath of the LORD that is poured out upon us, because our fathers have not kept the word of the LORD, to do after all that is written in this book.

22 And Hil-ki'ah, and *they* that the king *had appointed*, went to Hul'dah the prophetess, the wife of Shal'lum the son of Tik'vath, the son of Has'rah, keeper of the wardrobe; (now she dwelled in Je-ru'sa-lem in the college:) and they spoke to her to that *effect*. second quarter

23 And she answered them, Thus says the LORD God of Is'ra-el, Tell you the man that sent you to me, Jehovah^{s.f.} Elohim^{p.f.}

24 Thus says the LORD, Behold, I will bring evil upon this place, and upon the inhabitants thereof, *even* all the curses that are written in the book which they have read before the king of Ju'dah:

25 Because they have forsaken Me, and have burned incense to other gods, that they might provoke Me to anger with all the works of their hands; therefore My wrath shall be poured out upon this place, and shall not be quenched.

26 And as for the king of Ju'dah, who

sent you to enquire of the LORD, so shall you say to him, Thus says the LORD God of Is'ra-el *concerning* the words which you have heard;

Jehovah^s.f. Elohim^p.f.

27 Because your heart was tender, and you did humble yourself before God, when you heard His words against this place, and against the inhabitants thereof, and humbled yourself before Me, and did rend your clothes, and weep before Me; I have even heard *you* also, says the LORD.　　Elohim^p.f. - tear

28 Behold, I will gather you to your fathers, and you shall be gathered to your grave in peace, neither shall your eyes see all the evil that I will bring upon this place, and upon the inhabitants of the same. So they brought the king word again.

29 Then the king sent and gathered together all the elders of Ju'dah and Je-ru'sa-lem.

30 And the king went up into the house of the LORD, and all the men of Ju'dah, and the inhabitants of Je-ru'sa-lem, and the priests, and the Le'vites, and all the people, great and small: and he read in their ears all the words of the book of the covenant that was found in the house of the LORD.

31 And the king stood in his place, and made a covenant before the LORD, to walk after the LORD, and to keep His commandments, and His testimonies, and His statutes, with all his heart, and with all his soul, to perform the words of the covenant which are written in this book.　　agreement - earnestly

32 And he caused all that were present in Je-ru'sa-lem and Ben'ja-min to stand *to it*. And the inhabitants of Je-ru'sa-lem did according to the covenant of God, the God of their fathers.　　pledge - agreement - Elohim^p.f.

33 And Jo-si'ah took away all the abominations out of all the countries that *pertained* to the children of Is'ra-el, and made all that were present in Is'ra-el to serve, *even* to serve the LORD their God. *And* all his days they departed not from following the LORD, the God of their fathers.　　detestable idols

CHAPTER 35

MOREOVER Jo-si'ah kept a passover to the LORD in Je-ru'sa-lem: and they killed the passover on the fourteenth *day* of the first month.

2 And he set the priests in their charges, and encouraged them to the service of the house of the LORD, offices

3 And said to the Le'vites that taught all Is'ra-el, which were holy to the LORD, Put the holy ark in the house which Sol'o-mon the son of Da'vid king of Is'ra-el did build; *it shall* not *be* a burden upon *your* shoulders: serve now the LORD your God, and His people Is'ra-el,　　carried

4 And prepare *yourselves* by the houses of your fathers, after your courses, according to the writing of Da'vid king of Is'ra-el, and according to the writing of Sol'o-mon his son.　　families - divisions

5 And stand in the holy *place* according to the divisions of the families of the fathers of your brethren the people, and

after the division of the families of the Le'vites.

6 So kill the passover, and <u>sanctify</u> yourselves, and prepare your brethren, that *they* may do according to the word of the LORD by the hand of Mo'ses.   consecrate

7 And Jo-si'ah gave to the people, of the flock, lambs and kids, all for the passover offerings, for all that were present, to the number of thirty thousand, and three thousand bullocks: these *were* of the king's <u>substance</u>. possessions

8 And his princes gave willingly to the pcople, to the priests, and to the Le'vites: Hil-ki'ah and Zech-a-ri'ah and Je-hi'el, rulers of the house of <u>God</u>, gave to the priests for the passover offerings two thousand and six hundred *small cattle*, and three hundred oxen.   Elohim

9 Con-a-ni'ah also, and Shem-a-i'ah and Ne-than'e-el, his brethren, and Hash-a-bi'ah and Je-i'el and Joz'a-bad, chief of the Le'vites, gave to the Le'vites for passover offerings five thousand *small cattle*, and five hundred oxen.

10 So the service was prepared, and the priests stood in their place, and the Le'vites in their <u>courses</u>, according to the king's commandment.   divisions

11 And they killed the passover, and the priests sprinkled *the blood* from their hands, and the Le'vites <u>flayed</u> *them*.   skinned

12 And they removed the burned offerings, that they might give according to the divisions of the families of the people, to offer to the LORD, as *it is* written in the book of Mo'ses. And so *did they* with the oxen.

13 And they roasted the passover with fire according <u>to the ordinance</u>: but the *other* holy *offerings* <u>sod</u> they in pots, and in caldrons, and in pans, and divided *them* speedily among all the people.   as prescribed - boiled

14 And afterward they made ready for themselves, and for the priests: because the priests the sons of Aar'on *were busied* in offering of burned offerings and the fat until night; therefore the Le'vites prepared for themselves, and for the priests the sons of Aar'on.

15 And the singers the sons of A'saph *were* in their <u>place</u>, according to the commandment of Da'vid, and A'saph, and He'man, and Jed'u-thun the king's seer; and the <u>porters</u> *waited* at every gate; they might not depart from their service; for their brethren the Le'vites prepared for them.   station - gatekeepers

16 So all the service of the LORD was prepared the same day, to keep the passover, and to offer burned offerings upon the altar of the LORD, according to the commandment of king Jo-si'ah.

17 And the children of Is'ra-el that were present kept the passover at that time, and the feast of <u>unleavened</u> bread seven days.   without yeast

18 And there was no passover like to that kept in Is'ra-el from the days of Sam'u-el the prophet; neither did all the kings of Is'ra-el keep such a passover as Jo-si'ah kept, and the priests, and the Le'vites, and all Ju'dah and Is'ra-el that were present, and the inhabitants of Je-ru'sa-lem.

19 In the eighteenth year of the reign of Jo-si'ah was this passover kept.

20 After all this, when Jo-si'ah had prepared the temple, Ne'cho king of E'gypt came up to fight against Char'che-mish by Eu-phra'tes: and Jo-si'ah went out against him.

21 But he sent ambassadors to him, saying, What have I to do with you, you king of Ju'dah? *I come* not against you this day, but against the house wherewith I have war: for God commanded me to make haste: forbear you from *meddling with* God, who *is* with me, that He destroy you not.   _{government - Elohim}^{p.f.} - refrain

22 Nevertheless Jo-si'ah would not turn his face from him, but disguised himself, that he might fight with him, and hearkened not to the words of Ne'cho from the mouth of God, and came to fight in the valley of Me-gid'do.

23 And the archers shot at king Jo-si'ah; and the king said to his servants, Have me away; for I am sore wounded.   Take - badly

24 His servants therefore took him out of that chariot, and put him in the second chariot that he had; and they brought him to Je-ru'sa-lem, and he died, and was buried in *one of* the sepulchers of his fathers. And all Ju'dah and Je-ru'sa-lem mourned for Jo-si'ah.

25 And Jer-e-mi'ah lamented for Jo-si'ah: and all the singing men and the singing women spoke of Jo-si'ah in their lamentations to this day, and made them an ordinance in Is'ra-el: and, behold, they *are* written in the lamentations.

26 Now the rest of the acts of Jo-si'ah, and his goodness, according to *that which was* written in the law of the LORD,

27 And his deeds, first and last, behold, they *are* written in the book of the kings of Is'ra-el and Ju'dah.

CHAPTER 36

THEN the people of the land took Je-ho'a-haz the son of Jo-si'ah, and made him king in his father's stead in Je-ru'sa-lem.   place

2 Je-ho'a-haz *was* twenty and three years old when he began to reign, and he reigned three months in Je-ru'sa-lem.

3 And the king of E'gypt put him down at Je-ru'sa-lem, and condemned the land in an hundred talents of silver and a talent of gold.   deposed him - assessed

4 And the king of E'gypt made E-li'a-kim his brother king over Ju'dah and Je-ru'sa-lem, and turned his name to Je-hoi'a-kim. And Ne'cho took Je-ho'a-haz his brother, and carried him to E'gypt.   changed

5 Je-hoi'a-kim *was* twenty and five years old when he began to reign, and he reigned eleven years in Je-ru'sa-lem: and he did *that which was* evil in the sight of the LORD his God.   Elohim^{p.f.}

6 Against him came up Neb-u-chad-nez'zar king of Bab'y-lon, and bound him in fetters, to carry him to Bab'y-lon.   chains

7 Neb-u-chad-nez'zar also carried of

the vessels of the house of the Lord to Bab'y-lon, and put them in his temple at Bab'y-lon.

8 Now the rest of the acts of Je-hoi'a-kim, and his abominations which he did, and that which was found in him, behold, they *are* written in the book of the kings of Is'ra-el and Ju'dah: and Je-hoi'a-chin his son reigned in his stead.

9 Je-hoi'a-chin *was* eight years old when he began to reign, and he reigned three months and ten days in Je-ru'sa-lem: and he did *that which was* evil in the sight of the Lord.

10 And when the year was expired, king Neb-u-chad-nez'zar sent, and brought him to Bab'y-lon, with the goodly vessels of the house of the Lord, and made Zed-e-ki'ah his brother king over Ju'dah and Je-ru'sa-lem.

11 Zed-e-ki'ah *was* one and twenty years old when he began to reign, and reigned eleven years in Je-ru'sa-lem.

M010 12 And he did *that which was* evil in the sight of the Lord his God, *and* humbled not himself before Jer-e-mi'ah the prophet *speaking* from 780 the mouth of the Lord.   Elohim^p.f.

13 And he also rebelled against king Neb-u-chad-nez'zar, who had made him swear by God: but he stiffened his neck, and hardened his heart from turning to the Lord God of Is'ra-el.   Jehovah^s.f. Elohim^p.f.

14 Moreover all the chief of the priests, and the people, transgressed very much after all the abominations of the heathen; and polluted the house of the Lord which He had hallowed in Je-ru'sa-lem.   detestable practices - made holy

15 And the Lord God of their fathers sent to them by His messengers, rising up betimes, and sending; because He had compassion on His people, and on His dwelling place: again and again

16 But they mocked the messengers of God, and despised His words, and misused His prophets, until the wrath of the Lord arose against His people, till *there was* no remedy.   MATT. 5:12 MATT. 23:34 scoffed at

17 Therefore He brought upon them the king of the Chal'dees, who slew their young men with the sword in the house of their sanctuary, and had no compassion upon young man or maiden, old man, or him that stooped for age: He gave *them* all into his hand.

18 And all the vessels of the house of God, great and small, and the treasures of the house of the Lord, and the treasures of the king, and of his princes; all *these* he brought to Bab'y-lon.   articles - Elohim^p.f.

19 And they burned the house of God, and broke down the wall of Je-ru'sa-lem, and burned all the palaces thereof with fire, and destroyed all the goodly vessels thereof.   valuables

20 And them that had escaped from the sword carried he away to Bab'y-lon; where they were servants to him and his sons until the reign of the kingdom of Per'sia:

21 To fulfill the word of the Lord by the mouth of Jer-e-mi'ah, until the land had enjoyed her sabbaths: *for* as long as she lay desolate she kept sabbath, to fulfill threescore and ten years.   rest days - 70

22 Now in the first year of Cy'rus king of Per'sia, that the word of the LORD *spoken* by the mouth of Jer-e-mi'ah might be accomplished, the LORD stirred up the spirit of Cy'rus king of Per'sia, that he made a proclamation throughout all his kingdom, and *put it* also in writing, saying,

moved the heart

23 Thus says Cy'rus king of Per'sia, All the kingdoms of the earth has the LORD God of heaven given me; and He has charged me to build Him an house in Je-ru'sa-lem, which *is* in Ju'dah. Who *is there* among you of all His people? The LORD his God *be* with him, and let him go up.

Jehovah^{s.f.} Elohim^{p.f.}

EZRA

OUTLINE

SURVEY

This book contains almost all that is known of the history of the Jews between 538 B.C., when Cyrus the Persian conquered Babylon, and 457 B.C., when Ezra came to Jerusalem. Note the connection of 1.1-3 with the ending of Chronicles.

The hand of God is seen in causing King Cyrus to allow the Jews to return from exile in Babylon and to rebuild the ruined temple (1.1-11). Yet many Jews preferred the comforts of civilized Babylon rather than the hardships of poverty-stricken Judea (2.1-70). Those who returned began by putting God first (3.1-13), yet allowed their enemies to stop the building of the temple and city (4.1-24). After sixteen years revival came through the preaching of Haggai and Zechariah, and the temple was completed by 516 B.C. despite further opposition (5.1—6.22).

A gap of nearly sixty years is followed in 457 B.C. by the coming of Ezra (7.1-10), commissioned by the Persian king to teach and enforce the Jewish law (7.11-28). Ezra gathered a new generation of exiles to come back with him and made the dangerous journey without escort (8.1-36). Almost at once he was faced with the problem of mixed marriages between Jews and heathen, and, after prayer and confession, he was able to carry most of the people with him in a thorough examination of this scandal, and in causing them to make a new covenant with the Lord (9.1—10.44).

The book demonstrates God's use of heathen rulers to fulfil His purposes, and gives encouragement and warning to the people of God. They may be frightened by opposition when God means them to go forward; they may be content with the standards of the pagan world; or they may have the faith of Ezra and the prophets.

AUTHOR

The author, or compiler, is unknown, but may have been Ezra himself. He made use of existing documents for events not witnessed personally. Two sections of the book are in Aramaic (4.8—6.18 and 7.12-26). This Semitic language was in common use throughout the Near East at this time.

J.S.W.

THE BOOK OF

EZRA

CHAPTER 1

NOW in the first year of Cy'rus king of Per'sia, that the word of the LORD by the mouth of Jer-e-mi'ah might be fulfilled, the LORD <u>stirred up the spirit</u> of Cy'rus king of Per'sia, that he made a proclamation throughout all his kingdom, and *put it* also in writing, saying, _{moved the heart}

G4 2 Thus says Cy'rus king of Per'sia, The <u>LORD God</u> of heaven has given me all the kingdoms of the earth; and He has <u>charged</u> me to build Him an house at Je-ru'sa-lem, which *is* in Ju'dah. _{Jehovah^{s.f.} - Elohim^{p.f.} - appointed}

3 Who *is there* among you of all His people? his <u>God</u> be with him, and let him go up to Je-ru'sa-lem, which *is* in Ju'dah, and build the house of the <u>LORD God</u> of Is'ra-el, (He *is* the 758 God,) which *is* in Je-ru'sa-lem.

4 And whosoever remains in any place where he <u>sojourns</u>, let the men of <u>his</u> place help him with silver, and with gold, and with goods, and with beasts, beside the freewill offering for the house of <u>God</u> that *is* in Je-ru'sa-lem. _{lives temporarily - that - Elohim^{p.f.}}

5 Then rose up the chief of the fathers of Ju'dah and Ben'ja-min, and the priests, and the Le'vites, with all *them* whose spirit <u>God</u> had raised, to go up to build the house of the LORD which *is* in Je-ru'sa-lem. _{Elohim^{p.f.}}

6 And all they that *were* about them <u>strengthened</u> their hands with <u>vessels</u> of silver, with gold, with goods, and with beasts, and with precious things, beside all *that* was willingly offered. _{encouraged - articles}

7 Also Cy'rus the king brought forth the vessels of the house of the LORD, which Neb-u-chad-nez'zar had brought forth out of Je-ru'sa-lem, and had put them in the <u>house</u> of his gods; _{temple}

8 Even those did Cy'rus king of Per'sia bring forth by the hand of Mith're-dath the treasurer, and <u>numbered</u> them to Shesh-baz'zar, the prince of Ju'dah. _{counted}

9 And this *is* the number of them: thirty <u>chargers</u> of gold, a thousand <u>chargers</u> of silver, nine and twenty knives, _{dishes}

10 Thirty basins of gold, silver basins of a second *sort* four hundred and ten, *and* other <u>vessels</u> a thousand. _{articles}

11 All the <u>vessels</u> of gold and of silver *were* five thousand and four hundred. All *these* did Shesh-baz'zar bring up with *them of* the captivity that were brought up from Bab'y-lon to Je-ru'sa-lem.

CHAPTER 2

NOW these *are* the children of the province that went up out of the

captivity, of those which had been carried away, whom Neb-u-chad-nez'zar the king of Bab'y-lon had carried away to Bab'y-lon, and came again to Je-ru'sa-lem and Ju'dah, every one to his city;

2 Which came with Ze-rub'ba-bel: Jesh'u-a, Ne-he-mi'ah, Ser-a-i'ah, Re-el-a'iah, Mor'de-cai, Bil'shan, Miz'par, Big'va-i, Re'hum, Ba'a-nah. The number of the men of the people of Is'ra-el:

3 The children of Pa'rosh, two thousand an hundred seventy and two.

4 The children of Sheph-a-ti'ah, three hundred seventy and two.

5 The children of A'rah, seven hundred seventy and five.

6 The children of Pa'hath-mo'ab, of the children of Jesh'u-a *and* Jo'ab, two thousand eight hundred and twelve.

7 The children of E'lam, a thousand two hundred fifty and four.

8 The children of Zat'tu, nine hundred forty and five.

9 The children of Zac'ca-i, seven hundred and <u>threescore</u>. 60

10 The children of Ba'ni, six hundred forty and two.

11 The children of Beb'a-i, six hundred twenty and three.

12 The children of Az'gad, a thousand two hundred twenty and two.

13 The children of A-don'i-kam, six hundred sixty and six.

14 The children of Big'va-i, two thousand fifty and six.

15 The children of A'din, four hundred fifty and four.

16 The children of A'ter of Hez-e-ki'ah, ninety and eight.

17 The children of Be'zai, three hundred twenty and three.

18 The children of Jo'rah, an hundred and twelve.

19 The children of Ha'shum, two hundred twenty and three.

20 The children of Gib'bar, ninety and five.

21 The children of Beth'-le-hem, an hundred twenty and three.

22 The men of Ne-to'phah, fifty and six.

23 The men of An'a-thoth, an hundred twenty and eight.

24 The children of Az'ma-veth, forty and two.

25 The children of Kir'jath-a'rim, Che-phi'rah, and Be-e'roth, seven hundred and forty and three.

26 The children of Ra'mah and Ga'ba, six hundred twenty and one.

27 The men of Mich'mas, an hundred twenty and two.

28 The men of Beth'-el and A'i, two hundred twenty and three.

29 The children of Ne'bo, fifty and two.

30 The children of Mag'bish, an hundred fifty and six.

31 The children of the other E'lam, a thousand two hundred fifty and four.

32 The children of Ha'rim, three hundred and twenty.

33 The children of Lod, Ha'did, and O'no, seven hundred twenty and five.

34 The children of Jer'i-cho, three hundred forty and five.

35 The children of Se-na'ah, three thousand and six hundred and thirty.

36 The priests: the children of Je-da'iah, of the house of Jesh'u-a, nine hundred seventy and three.

37 The children of Im'mer, a thousand fifty and two.

38 The children of Pash'ur, a thousand two hundred forty and seven.

39 The children of Ha'rim, a thousand and seventeen.

40 The Le'vites: the children of Jesh'u-a and Kad'mi-el, of the children of Hod-a-vi'ah, seventy and four.

41 The singers: the children of A'saph, an hundred twenty and eight.

42 The children of the porters: the children of Shal'lum, the children of A'ter, the children of Tal'mon, the children of Ak'kub, the children of Hat'i-ta, the children of Sho'ba-i, *in* all an hundred thirty and nine. ᵍᵃᵗᵉᵏᵉᵉᵖᵉʳˢ

43 The Neth'i-nims: the children of Zi'ha, the children of Ha-su'pha, the children of Tab'ba-oth,

44 The children of Ke'ros, the children of Si'a-ha, the children of Pa'don,

45 The children of Leb'a-nah, the children of Hag'a-bah, the children of Ak'kub,

46 The children of Ha'gab, the children of Shal'ma-i, the children of Ha'nan,

47 The children of Gid'del, the children of Ga'har, the children of Re-a-i'ah,

48 The children of Re'zin, the children of Ne-ko'da, the children of Gaz'zam,

49 The children of Uz'za, the children of Pa-se'ah, the children of Be'sai,

50 The children of As'nah, the chil-dren of Me-hu'nim, the children of Ne-phu'sim,

51 The children of Bak'buk, the children of Ha-ku'pha, the children of Har'hur,

52 The children of Baz'luth, the children of Me-hi'da, the children of Har'sha,

53 The children of Bar'kos, the children of Sis'e-ra, the children of Tha'mah,

54 The children of Ne-zi'ah, the children of Hat'i-pha.

55 The children of Sol'o-mon's servants: the children of So'ta-i, the children of Soph'e-reth, the children of Pe-ru'da,

56 The children of Ja-a'lah, the children of Dar'kon, the children of Gid'del,

57 The children of Sheph-a-ti'ah, the children of Hat'til, the children of Poch'e-reth of Ze-ba'im, the children of A'mi.

58 All the Neth'i-nims, and the children of Sol'o-mon's servants, *were* three hundred ninety and two.

59 And these *were* they which went up from Tel-me'lah, Tel-har'sa, Che'rub, Ad'dan, *and* Im'mer: but they could not show their father's house, and their seed, whether they *were* of Is'ra-el: ᵈᵉˢᶜᵉⁿᵈᵃⁿᵗˢ

60 The children of Del-a-i'ah, the children of To-bi'ah, the children of Ne-ko'da, six hundred fifty and two.

61 And of the children of the priests: the children of Ha-ba'iah, the children of Koz, the children of Bar-zil'la-i; which took a wife of the daugh-

ters of Bar-zil'la-i the Gil'e-ad-ite, and was called after their name:

62 These sought their register *among* those that were reckoned by genealogy, but they were not found: therefore were they, as <u>polluted</u>, <u>put</u> from the priesthood. unclean - excluded

63 And the <u>Tir'sha-tha</u> said to them, that they should not eat of the most holy things, till there stood up a priest with <u>U'rim and with Thum'mim</u>.

governor - The Blacks and Whites i.e., dice used for divination

64 The whole congregation together *was* forty and two thousand three hundred *and* threescore,

65 Beside their servants and their maids, of whom *there were* seven thousand three hundred thirty and seven: and *there were* among them two hundred singing men and singing women.

66 Their horses *were* seven hundred thirty and six; their mules, two hundred forty and five;

67 Their camels, four hundred thirty and five; *their* asses, six thousand seven hundred and twenty.

68 And *some* of the chief of the fathers, when they came to the house of the LORD which *is* at Je-ru'sa-lem, offered freely for the house of <u>God</u> to set it up in its place: Elohim^{p.f.}

69 They gave after their ability to the treasure of the work threescore and one thousand drams of gold, and five thousand pound of silver, and one hundred priests' garments.

70 So the priests, and the Le'vites, and *some* of the people, and the singers, and the <u>porters</u>, and the Neth'i-nims, dwelled in their cities, and all Is'ra-el in their cities. gatekeepers

CHAPTER 3

A**ND** when the seventh month was come, and the children of Is'ra-el *were* in the cities, the people gathered themselves together <u>as one man</u> to Je-ru'sa'lem. in unity

2 Then stood up Jesh'u-a the son of Joz'a-dak, and his brethren the priests, and Ze-rub'ba-bel the son of She-al'ti-el, and his brethren, and builded the altar of the <u>God</u> of Is'ra-el, to offer burned offerings thereon, as *it is* written in the law of Mo'ses the man of <u>God</u>. Elohim^{p.f.}

3 And they set the altar upon <u>its bases</u>; for <u>fear *was* upon them</u> because of the people of those countries: and they offered burned offerings thereon to the LORD, *even* burned offerings morning and evening. its foundation - they were terrified

4 They kept also the feast of tabernacles, as *it is* written, and *offered* the daily burned offerings <u>by number</u>, according to the custom, as the duty of every day required; with the required

5 And afterward *offered* the continual burned offering, both of the new moons, and of all the set feasts of the LORD that were consecrated, and of every one that willingly offered a freewill offering to the LORD.

6 From the first day of the seventh month began they to offer burned offerings to the LORD. But the foundation of the temple of the LORD was not *yet* laid.

7 They gave money also to the masons, and to the carpenters; and <u>meat</u>, and drink, and oil, to them of Zi'don, and to them of Tyre, to bring cedar trees from Leb'a-non to the sea of Jop'pa, according to the grant that they had of Cy'rus king of Per'sia. _{food}

8 Now in the second year of their coming to the house of <u>God</u> at Je-ru'sa-lem, in the second month, began Ze-rub'ba-bel the son of She-al'ti-el, and Jesh'u-a the son of Joz'a-dak, and the remnant of their brethren the priests and the Le'vites, and all they that were come out of the captivity to Je-ru'sa-lem; and appointed the Le'vites, from twenty years old and upward, to <u>set forward</u> the work of the house of the Lord. _{Elohim^p.f. - oversee}

9 Then stood Jesh'u-a *with* his sons and his brethren, Kad'mi-el and his sons, the sons of Ju'dah, <u>together</u>, to <u>set forward</u> the workmen in the house of <u>God</u>: the sons of Hen'a-dad, *with* their sons and their brethren the Le'vites. _{united}

10 And when the builders laid the foundation of the temple of the Lord, they <u>set</u> the priests in their apparel with trumpets, and the Le'vites the sons of A'saph with cymbals, to praise the Lord, after the ordinance of Da'vid king of Is'ra-el. _{placed/assigned}

11 And they sang together by course in praising and giving thanks to the Lord; because *He is* good, for His mercy *endures* for ever toward Is'ra-el. And all the people shouted with a great shout, when they praised the Lord, because the foundation of the house of the Lord was laid.

12 But many of the priests and Le'vites and chief of the fathers, *who were* <u>ancient</u> men, that had seen the first house, when the foundation of this house was laid before their eyes, wept with a loud voice; and many shouted aloud for joy: _{old}

13 So that the people could not discern the noise of the shout of joy from the noise of the weeping of the people: for the people shouted with a loud shout, and the noise was heard afar off.

CHAPTER 4

NOW when the <u>adversaries</u> of Ju'dah and Ben'ja-min heard that the children of the captivity builded the temple to the <u>Lord God</u> of Is'ra-el; _{enemies - Jehovah^s.f. Elohim^p.f.}

2 Then they came to Ze-rub'ba-bel, and to the chief of the fathers, and said to them, Let us build with you: for we seek your <u>God</u>, as you *do*; and we do sacrifice to Him since the days of E'sar-had'don king of As'sur, which brought us up here. _{Elohim^p.f.}

3 But Ze-rub'ba-bel, and Jesh'u-a, and the rest of the chief of the fathers of Is'ra-el, said to them, You have nothing to do with us to build an house to our <u>God</u>; but we ourselves together will build to the <u>Lord God</u> of Is'ra-el, as king Cy'rus the king of Per'sia has commanded us. _{Elohim^p.f. - Jehovah^s.f. Elohim^p.f.}

4 Then the people of the land <u>weakened the hands of</u> the people of Ju'dah, and troubled them in building, _{discouraged}

5 And hired counselors against them, to frustrate their purpose, all the days

of Cy'rus king of Per'sia, even until the reign of Da-ri'us king of Per'sia.
6 And in the reign of A-has-u-e'rus, in the beginning of his reign, wrote they *to him* an accusation against the inhabitants of Ju'dah and Je-ru'sa-lem.
7 And in the days of Ar-tax-erx'es wrote Bish'lam, Mith're-dath, Ta'bel, and the rest of their companions, to Ar-tax-erx'es king of Per'sia; and the writing of the letter *was* written in the Syr'i-an tongue, and interpreted in the Syr'i-an tongue.
8 Re'hum the chancellor and Shim'shai the <u>scribe</u> wrote a letter against Je-ru'sa-lem to Ar-tax-erx'es the king in this sort: secretary
9 Then *wrote* Re'hum the chancellor, and Shim'shai the <u>scribe</u>, and the rest of their companions; the Di'na-ites, the A-phar'sath-chites, the Tar'pel-ites, the A-phar'sites, the Ar'che-vites, the Bab-y-lo'ni-ans, the Su'san-chites, the De-ha'vites, *and* the E'lam-ites,
10 And the rest of the nations whom the great and noble As-nap'par brought over, and <u>set</u> in the cities of Sa-ma'ri-a, and the rest *that are* on this side the river, and at such a time.   settled
11 This *is* the copy of the letter that they sent to him, *even* to Ar-tax-erx'es the king; your servants the men on this side the river, and at such a time.
12 Be it known to the king, that the Jews which came up from you to us are come to Je-ru'sa-lem, building the rebellious and the bad city, and have set up the walls *thereof*, and joined the foundations.

13 Be it known now to the king, that, if this city be builded, and the walls set up *again*, *then* will they not pay toll, tribute, and custom, and *so* you shall <u>endamage</u> the revenue of the kings.   damage
14 Now because we <u>have maintenance from *the king's*</u> palace, and it was not <u>meet</u> for us to see the king's dishonor, therefore have we sent and certified the king;   are in the service of the - fitting
15 That search may be made in the book of the records of your fathers: so shall you find in the book of the records, and know that this city *is* a rebellious city, and hurtful to kings and provinces, and that they have <u>moved</u> sedition inside the same of old time: for which cause was this city destroyed.   incited
16 We certify the king that, if this city be builded *again*, and the walls thereof set up, by this means you shall have no <u>portion</u> on this side the river.   possession
17 *Then* sent the king an answer to Re'hum the chancellor, and *to* Shim'shai the scribe, and *to* the rest of their companions that dwell in Sa-ma'ri-a, and *to* the rest beyond the river, Peace, and at such a time.
18 The letter which you sent to us has been plainly read before me.
19 And I <u>commanded</u>, and search has been made, and it is found that this city of old time has made insurrection against kings, and *that* rebellion and sedition have been made therein.   issued an order
20 There have been mighty kings also over Je-ru'sa-lem, which have ruled

over all *countries* beyond the river; and toll, tribute, and custom, was paid to them.

21 <u>Give you now commandment</u> to cause these men to cease, and that this city be not builded, un- til *another* commandment shall be given from me.   Now issue an order

22 Take heed now that you fail not to do this: why should damage grow to the hurt of the kings?

23 Now when the copy of king Ar- tax-erx'es' letter *was* read before Re'hum, and Shim'shai the <u>scribe</u>, and their companions, they went up in haste to Je-ru'sa-lem to the Jews, and made them to cease by force and power.   secretary

24 Then ceased the work of the house of God which *is* at Je-ru'sa-lem. So it ceased to the second year of the reign of Da-ri'us king of Per'sia.

CHAPTER 5

THEN the prophets, Hag'ga-i the prophet, and Zech-a-ri'ah the son of Id'do, prophesied to the Jews that *were* in Ju'dah and Je- ru'sa-lem in the name of the God of Is'ra-el, <u>even to</u> them.   who was over

2 Then rose up Ze-rub'ba-bel the son of She-al'ti-el, and Jesh'u-a the son of Joz'a-dak, and began to build the house of God which *is* at Je- ru'sa-lem: and with them *were* the prophets of God helping them.

3 At the same time came to them Tatnai, governor on this side the river, and She'thar-boz'na-i, and their com- panions, and said thus to them, Who

has commanded you to build this house, and to make up this wall?

4 Then said we to them after this manner, What are the names of the men that make this building?

5 But the eye of their God was upon the elders of the Jews, that they could not cause them to cease, till the matter came to Da-ri'us: and then they returned answer by letter concerning this *matter*.

6 The copy of the letter that Tat'na-i, governor on this side the river, and She'thar-boz'na-i, and his companions the A-phar'sach- ites, which *were* on this side the river, sent to Da-ri'us the king:

7 They sent a letter to him, wherein was written thus; To Da-ri'us the king, all peace.

8 Be it known to the king, that we went into the province of Ju-de'a, to the <u>house</u> of the great God, which is built with <u>great</u> stones, and timber is laid in the walls, and this work goes fast on, and prospers in their hands.   temple - huge

9 Then asked we those elders, *and* said to them thus, Who com- manded you to build this house, and to make up these walls?

10 We asked their names also, to <u>certify</u> you, that we might write the names of the men that *were* the chief of them.   inform

11 And thus they returned us answer, saying, We are the servants of the God of heaven and earth, and build the <u>house</u> that was built these many

years ago, which a great king of Is-ra'el builded and set up. _{temple}

12 But after that our fathers had pro-voked the God of heaven to wrath, He gave them into the hand of Neb-u-chad-nez'zar the king of Bab'y-lon, the Chal-de'an, who destroyed this house, and carried the people away into Bab'y-lon.

13 But in the first year of Cy'rus the king of Bab'y-lon *the same* king Cy'rus made a decree to build this <u>house</u> of God.

14 And the vessels also of gold and silver of the <u>house</u> of God, which Neb-u-chad-nez'zar took out of the temple that *was* in Je-ru'sa-lem, and brought them into the temple of Bab'y-lon, those did Cy'rus the king take out of the temple of Bab'y-lon, and they were delivered to *one,* whose name *was* Shesh-baz'zar, whom he had made governor;

15 And said to him, Take these vessels, go, carry them into the temple that *is* in Je-ru'sa-lem, and let the <u>house</u> of God be built in its place. _{temple}

16 Then came the same Shesh-baz'zar, *and* laid the foundation of the <u>house</u> of God which *is* in Je-ru'sa-lem: and since that time even until now has it been in building, and *yet* it is not finished. _{temple}

17 Now therefore, if *it seem* good to the king, let there be search made in the king's treasure house, which *is* there at Bab'y-lon, whether it be *so,* that a de-cree was made of Cy'rus the king to build this house of God at Je-ru'sa-lem,

and let the king send his pleasure to us concerning this matter.

CHAPTER 6

THEN Da-ri'us the king made a decree, and search was made in the house of the <u>rolls</u>, where the trea-sures were laid up in Bab'y-lon. _{archives}

2 And there was found at Ach'me-tha, in the palace that *is* in the prov-ince of the Medes, a roll, and therein *was* a record thus written:

3 In the first year of Cy'rus the king *the same* Cy'rus the king made a de-cree *concerning* the house of God at Je-ru'sa-lem, Let the house be built, the place where they offered sacri-fices, and let the foundations thereof be strongly laid; the height thereof <u>threescore</u> cubits, *and* the breadth thereof <u>threescore</u> cubits; ₆₀

4 *With* three rows of great stones, and a row of new timber: and let the expenses be given out of the <u>king's house</u>: _{royal treasury}

5 And also let the golden and silver vessels of the house of God, which Neb-u-chad-nez'zar took forth out of the temple which *is* at Je-ru'sa-lem, and brought to Bab'y-lon, be re-stored, and <u>brought again</u> to the temple which *is* at Je-ru'sa-lem, *ev-ery one* to its place, and place *them* in the <u>house</u> of God. _{returned - temple}

6 Now *therefore,* Tat'na-i, governor beyond the river, She'thar-boz'na-i, and your companions the A-phar'sach-ites, which *are* beyond the river, be you far from there:

7 Let the work of this house of God

alone; let the governor of the Jews and the elders of the Jews build this <u>house</u> of God in its place. _{temple}

8 Moreover I make a decree what you shall do to the elders of these Jews for the building of this <u>house</u> of God: that of the king's goods, *even* of the tribute beyond the river, forthwith expenses be given to these men, that they be not hindered.

9 And that which they have need of, both young bullocks, and rams, and lambs, for the burned offerings of the God of heaven, wheat, salt, wine, and oil, according to the appointment of the priests which *are* at Je-ru'sa-lem, let it be given them day by day without fail:

10 That they may offer sacrifices of sweet savors to the God of heaven, and pray for the life of the king, and of his sons.

11 Also I have made a decree, that whosoever shall alter this word, let timber be pulled down from his house, and being set up, let him be <u>hanged</u> thereon; and let his house be made a <u>dunghill</u> for this. _{impaled - refuse heap}

12 And the God that has caused His name to dwell there destroy all kings and people, that shall put to their hand to alter *and* to destroy this <u>house</u> of God which *is* at Je-ru'sa-lem. I Da-ri'us have made a decree; let it be done with speed. _{temple}

13 Then Tat'na-i, governor on this side the river, She'thar-boz'na-i, and their companions, according to that which Da-ri'us the king had sent, so they did speedily.

14 And the elders of the Jews built, and they prospered through the prophesying of Hag'ga-i the prophet and Zech-a-ri'ah the son of Id'do. And they built, and finished *it*, according to the commandment of the God of Is'ra-el, and according to the commandment of Cy'rus, and Da-ri'us, and Ar-tax-erx'es king of Per'sia.

15 And this <u>house</u> was finished on the third day of the month A'dar, which was in the sixth year of the reign of Da-ri'us the king.

16 And the children of Is'ra-el, the priests, and the Le'vites, and the rest of the children of the captivity, kept the dedication of this <u>house</u> of God with joy, _{temple}

17 And offered at the dedication of this <u>house</u> of God an hundred bullocks, two hundred rams, four hundred lambs; and for a sin offering for all Is'ra-el, twelve he goats, according to the number of the tribes of Is'ra-el.

18 And they set the priests in their divisions, and the Le'vites in their <u>courses</u>, for the service of God, which *is* at Je-ru'sa-lem; as it is written in the book of Mo'ses. _{orders}

19 And the children of the captivity kept the passover upon the fourteenth *day* of the first month.

20 For the priests and the Le'vites were purified together, all of them *were* pure, and killed the passover for all the children of the captivity, and for their brethren the priests, and for themselves.

21 And the children of Is'ra-el, which were come again out of captivity, and all such as had separated themselves

to them from the <u>filthiness</u> of the heathen of the land, to seek the LORD
God of Is'ra-el, did eat, evil practices
22 And kept the feast of <u>unleav-
ened</u> bread seven days with joy:
for the LORD had made them joyful, and turned the heart of the
king of As-syr'i-a to them, to
strengthen their hands in the work
of the <u>house</u> of <u>God</u>, the <u>God</u> of
Is'ra-el. i.e., without yeast - temple - Elohim^{p.f.}

CHAPTER 7

NOW after these things, in the reign
of Ar-tax-erx'es king of Per'sia,
Ez'ra the son of Ser-a-i'ah, the son
of Az-a-ri'ah, the son of Hil-ki'ah,
2 The son of Shal'lum, the son of
Za'dok, the son of A-hi'tub,
3 The son of Am-a-ri'ah, the son of
Az-a-ri'ah, the son of Me-ra'ioth,
4 The son of Zer-a-hi'ah, the son of
Uz'zi, the son of Buk'ki,
5 The son of A-bish'u-a, the son of
Phin'e-has, the son of E-le-a'zar, the
son of Aar'on the chief priest:
6 This Ez'ra went up from Bab'y-
lon; and he *was* a <u>ready</u> scribe in
the law of Mo'ses, which the <u>LORD</u>
<u>God</u> of Is'ra-el had given: and the
king granted him all his request, according to the hand of the LORD his
God upon him. skilled - Jehovah^{s.f.} Elohim^{p.f.}
7 And there went up *some* of the chil-
dren of Is'ra-el, and of the priests,
and the Le'vites, and the singers, and
the porters, and the Neth'i-nims, to
Je-ru'sa-lem, in the seventh year of
Ar-tax-erx'es the king.
8 And he came to Je-ru'sa-lem in the
fifth month, which *was* in the seventh year of the king.
9 For upon the first *day* of the first
month began he to go up from
Bab'y-lon, and on the first *day* of
the fifth month came he to Je-ru'sa-
lem, according to the good hand of
his <u>God</u> upon him. Elohim^{p.f.}
10 For Ez'ra had prepared his heart
to <u>seek</u> the law of the LORD, and to
do *it*, and to teach in Is'ra-el <u>stat-
utes</u> and judgments. study - decrees
11 Now this *is* the copy of the letter that
the king Ar-tax-erx'es gave to Ez'ra the
priest, the scribe, *even* a scribe of the
words of the commandments of the
LORD, and of his statutes to Is'ra-el.
12 Ar-tax-erx'es, king of kings, to
Ez'ra the priest, a scribe of the law
of the God of heaven, perfect *peace*,
and at such a time.
13 I make a decree, that all they of the
people of Is'ra-el, and *of* his priests
and Le'vites, in my realm, which are
minded of their own freewill to go up
to Je-ru'sa-lem, go with you.
14 Forasmuch as you are sent of the
king, and of his seven counselors, to
enquire concerning Ju'dah and Je-
ru'sa-lem, according to the law of
your God which *is* in your hand;
15 And to carry the silver and gold,
which the king and his counselors
have freely offered to the God of
Is'ra-el, whose habitation *is* in Je-
ru'sa-lem,
16 And all the silver and gold that you
can find in all the province of Bab'y-
lon, with the freewill offering of the
people, and of the priests, offering

willingly for the <u>house</u> of their God which *is* in Je-ru'sa-lem: temple

17 That you may buy speedily with this money bullocks, rams, lambs, with their <u>meat</u> offerings and their drink offerings, and offer them upon the altar of the house of your God which *is* in Je-ru'sa-lem. grain

18 And whatsoever shall seem good to you, and to your brethren, to do with the rest of the silver and the gold, that do after the will of your God.

19 The <u>vessels</u> also that are given you for the service of the <u>house</u> of your God, *those* deliver you before the God of Je-ru'sa-lem. utensils

20 And whatsoever more shall be needful for the <u>house</u> of your God, which you shall have occasion to bestow, bestow *it* out of the king's treasure house.

21 And I, *even* I Ar-tax-erx'es the king, do make a decree to all the treasurers which *are* beyond the <u>river</u>, that whatsoever Ez'ra the priest, the scribe of the law of the God of heaven, shall require of you, it be done speedily, i.e., Euphrates

22 To an hundred talents of silver, and to an hundred measures of wheat, and to an hundred baths of wine, and to an hundred baths of oil, and salt without prescribing *how much.*

23 Whatsoever is commanded by the God of heaven, let it be <u>diligently</u> done for the <u>house</u> of the God of heaven: for why should there be wrath against the realm of the king and his sons? zealously - temple

24 Also we certify you, that touching any of the priests and Le'vites, singers, porters, Neth'i-nims, or ministers of this house of God, it shall not be lawful to impose toll, tribute, or custom, upon them. gatekeepers

25 And you, Ez'ra, after the wisdom of your God, that *is* in your hand, set magistrates and judges, which may judge all the people that *are* beyond the <u>river</u>, all such as know the laws of your God; and teach you them that know *them* not.

26 And whosoever will not do the law of your God, and the law of the king, let judgment be executed speedily upon him, whether *it be* to death, or <u>to banishment,</u> or to confiscation of goods, or to imprisonment. for rooting out

27 Blessed *be* the Lord <u>God</u> of our fathers, which has put *such a thing* as this in the king's heart, to beautify the house of the Lord which *is* in Je-ru'sa-lem: Jehovah^{s.f.} Elohim^{p.f.}

28 And have extended mercy to me before the king, and his counselors, and before all the king's mighty princes. And I was strengthened as the hand of the Lord my <u>God</u> *was* upon me, and I gathered together out of Is'rael chief men to go up with me. Elohim^{p.f.}

CHAPTER 8

THESE *are* now the chief of their fathers, and *this is* the genealogy of them that went up with me from Bab'y-lon, in the reign of Ar-tax-erx'es the king.

2 Of the sons of Phin'e-has; Ger'shom: of the sons of Ith'a-mar; Dan'iel: of the sons of Da'vid; Hat'tush.

3 Of the sons of Shech-a'ni'ah, of the sons of Pha'rosh; Zech-a-ri'ah: and with him were reckoned by genealogy of the males an hundred and fifty.

4 Of the sons of Pa'hath-mo'ab; El-i-ho-e'na-i the son of Zer-a-hi'ah, and with him two hundred males.

5 Of the sons of Shech-a'ni'ah; the son of Ja-ha'zi-el, and with him three hundred males.

6 Of the sons also of A'din; E'bed the son of Jon'a-than, and with him fifty males.

7 And of the sons of E'lam; Je-sha'iah the son of Ath-a-li'ah, and with him seventy males.

8 And of the sons of Sheph-a-ti'ah; Zeb-a-di'ah the son of Mi'chael, and with him fourscore males.

9 Of the sons of Jo'ab; O-ba-di'ah the son of Je-hi'el, and with him two hundred and eighteen males.

10 And of the sons of Shel'o-mith; the son of Jos-i-phi'ah, and with him an <u>hundred and threescore</u> males. 160

11 And of the sons of Beb'a-i; Zech-a-ri'ah the son of Beb'a-i, and with him twenty and eight males.

12 And of the sons of Az'gad; Jo-ha'nan <u>the son</u> of Hak'ka-tan, and with him an hundred and ten males. the youngest son

13 And of the last sons of A-don'i-kam, whose names *are* these, E-liph'e-let, Je-i'el, and Shem-a-i'ah, and with them threescore males.

14 Of the sons also of Big'va-i; U'tha-i, and Zab'bud, and with them seventy males.

15 And I gathered them together to the river that runs to A-ha'va; and there abode we in tents three days: and I viewed the people, and the priests, and found there none of the sons of Le'vi.

16 Then sent I for E-li-e'zer, for A'ri-el, for Shem-a-i'ah, and for El'na-than, and for Ja'rib, and for El'na-than, and for Na'than, and for Zech-a-ri'ah, and for Me-shul'lam, chief men; also for Joi'a-rib, and for El'na-than, men of understanding.

17 And I sent them with command-ment to Id'do the chief at the place Ca-siph'i-a, and I told them what they should say to Id'do, *and* to his brethren the Neth-i'nims, at the place Ca'siph'i-a, that they should bring to us ministers for the house of our <u>God</u>.

18 And by the good hand of our <u>God</u> upon us they brought us a man of understanding, of the sons of Mah'li, the son of Le'vi, the son of Is'ra-el; and Sher-e-bi'ah, with his sons and his brethren, eighteen; Elohim^{p.f.}

19 And Hash-a-bi'ah, and with him Je-sha'iah of the sons of Me-ra'ri, his brethren and their sons, twenty;

20 Also of the Neth'i-nims, whom Da'vid and the princes had appointed for the service of the Le'vites, two hun-dred and twenty Neth'i-nims: all of them were <u>expressed</u> by name. designated

21 Then I proclaimed a fast there, at the river of A-ha'va, that we might <u>afflict</u> ourselves before our <u>God</u>, to seek of Him a right way for us, and for our little ones, and for all our substance. humble

22 For I was ashamed to require of the king a band of soldiers and horsemen to help us against the enemy in the way: because we had spoken to the king, saying, The hand of our God *is* upon all them for good that seek Him; but His power and His wrath *is* against all them that forsake Him.

23 So we fasted and besought our God for this: and He was entreated of us.   Elohim^{p.f.}

24 Then I separated twelve of the chief of the priests, Sher-e-bi'ah, Hash-a-bi'ah, and ten of their brethren with them,

25 And weighed to them the silver, and the gold, and the vessels, *even* the offering of the house of our God, which the king, and his counselors, and his lords, and all Is'ra-el *there* present, had offered:

26 I even weighed to their hand six hundred and fifty talents of silver, and silver vessels an hundred talents, *and* of gold an hundred talents;

27 Also twenty basins of gold, of a thousand drams; and two vessels of fine copper, precious as gold. bowls-bronze

28 And I said to them, You *are* holy to the LORD; the vessels *are* holy also; and the silver and the gold *are* a freewill offering to the LORD God of your fathers.   Jehovah^{s.f.} Elohim^{p.f.}

29 Watch you, and keep *them*, until you weigh *them* before the chief of the priests and the Le'vites, and chief of the fathers of Is'ra-el, at Je-ru'sa-lem, in the chambers of the house of the LORD. storerooms-temple

30 So took the priests and the Le'vites

the weight of the silver, and the gold, and the vessels, to bring *them* to Je-ru'sa-lem to the house of our God.   Elohim^{p.f.}

31 Then we departed from the river of A-ha'va on the twelfth *day* of the first month, to go to Je-ru'sa-lem: and the hand of our God was upon us, and He delivered us from the hand of the enemy, and of such as lay in wait by the way.

32 And we came to Je-ru'sa-lem, and abode there three days.

33 Now on the fourth day was the silver and the gold and the vessels weighed in the house of our God by the hand of Mer'e-moth the son of U-ri'ah the priest; and with him was E-le-a'zar the son of Phin'e-has; and with them *was* Joz'a-bad the son of Jesh'u-a, and No-a-di'ah the son of Bin'nu-i, Le'vites;

34 By number *and* by weight of every one: and all the weight was written at that time.

35 *Also* the children of those that had been carried away, which were come out of the captivity, offered burned offerings to the God of Is'ra-el, twelve bullocks for all Is'ra-el, ninety and six rams, seventy and seven lambs, twelve he goats *for* a sin offering: all *this was* a burned offering to the LORD.

36 And they delivered the king's commissions to the king's lieutenants, and to the governors on this side the river: and they furthered the people, and the house of God.

edicts - beyond - i.e., Euphrates - supported - temple

CHAPTER 9

NOW when these things were done, the princes came to me, saying, The people of Is'ra-el, and the priests, and the Le'vites, have not separated themselves from the people of the lands, *doing* according to their abominations, *even* of the Ca'-naan-ites, the Hit'tites, the Per'iz-zites, the Jeb'u-sites, the Am'mon-ites, the Mo'ab-ites, the E-gyptians, and the Am'or-ites. detestable practices

2 For they have taken of their daughters for themselves, and for their sons: so that the holy seed have mingled themselves with the people of *those* lands: yea, the hand of the princes and rulers has been chief in this trespass. unfaithfulness

3 And when I heard this thing, I rent my garment and my mantle, and plucked off the hair of my head and of my beard, and sat down astonished tore - robe - appalled

4 Then were assembled to me every one that trembled at the words of the God of Is'ra-el, because of the transgression of those that had been carried away; and I sat astonished until the evening sacrifice. Elohim^{p.f.}

5 And at the evening sacrifice I arose up from my heaviness; and having rent my garment and my mantle, I fell upon my knees, and spread out my hands to the LORD my God,

6 And said, O my God, I am ashamed and blush to lift up my face to You, my God: for our iniquities are in-creased over *our* head, and our trespass is grown up to the heav-ens. Elohim^{p.f.}

7 Since the days of our fathers *have* we *been* in a great trespass to this day; and for our iniquities have we, our kings, *and* our priests, been de-livered into the hand of the kings of the lands, to the sword, to captivity, and to a spoil, and to confusion of face, as *it is* this day. plunder - open shame

8 And now for a little space grace has been *showed* from the LORD our God, to leave us a remnant to escape, and to give us a nail in His holy place, that our God may lighten our eyes, and give us a little reviving in our bondage. i.e., a place in the promised land

9 For we *were* bondmen; yet our God has not forsaken us in our bondage, but has extended mercy to us in the sight of the kings of Per'sia, to give us a reviving, to set up the house of our God, and to repair the desolations thereof, and to give us a wall in Ju'dah and in Je-ru'sa-lem. slaves - temple - ruins

10 And now, O our God, what shall we say after this? for we have for-saken Your commandments, Elohim^{p.f.}

11 Which You have commanded by Your servants the prophets, saying, The land, to which you go to pos-sess it, is an unclean land with the filthiness of the people of the lands, with their abominations, which have filled it from one end to another with their uncleanness. detestable practices

12 Now therefore give not your daugh-ters to their sons, neither take their daughters to your sons, nor seek their peace or their wealth for ever: that

you may be strong, and eat the good of the land, and leave *it* for an inheritance to your children for ever.

13 And after all that is come upon us for our evil deeds, and for our great trespass, seeing that You our God have punished us less than our iniquities *deserve*, and have given us *such* deliverance as this;

14 <u>Should</u> we again break Your commandments, and <u>join in affinity</u> with the people of these <u>abominations</u>? would not You be angry with us till You had <u>consumed</u> *us*, so that *there should be* no remnant nor escaping?

Shall - intermarry - detestable practices - destroyed

15 O LORD God of Is'ra-el, You *are* righteous: for we remain yet escaped, as *it is* this day: behold, we *are* before You in our trespasses: for we cannot stand before You because of this.

Jehovah^{s.f.} Elohim^{p.f.}

CHAPTER 10

NOW <u>when</u> Ez'ra had prayed, and when he had confessed, weeping and casting himself down before the house of <u>God</u>, there assembled to him out of Is'ra-el a very great congregation of men and women and children: for the people wept <u>very sore</u>.

while - Elohim^{p.f.} - bitterly

2 And Shech-a'ni'ah the son of Je-hi'el, *one* of the sons of E'lam, answered and said to Ez'ra, We have <u>trespassed against</u> our <u>God</u>, and have <u>taken strange</u> wives of the people of the land: yet now there is hope in Is'ra-el concerning this thing.

been unfaithful to - married foreign

3 Now therefore let us make a <u>cov-enant</u> with our <u>God</u> to put away all the wives, and such as are born of them, according to the <u>counsel</u> of my lord, and of those that <u>tremble</u> at the commandment of our <u>God</u>; and let it be done according to the law. agreement - Elohim^{p.f.} - advice - are distressed

4 Arise; for *this* matter *belongs* to you: we also *will be* with you: be of good courage, and do *it*.

5 Then arose Ez'ra, and made the chief priests, the Le'vites, and all Is'ra-el, to <u>swear</u> that they should do according to this word. And they swear. promise

6 Then Ez'ra rose up from before the house of <u>God</u>, and went into the chamber of Jo-ha'nan the son of E-li'a-shib: and *when* he came there, he did eat no bread, nor drink water: for he mourned because of the <u>transgression</u> of them that had been carried away. unfaithfulness

7 And they made <u>proclamation</u> throughout Ju'dah and Je-ru'sa-lem to all the children of the captivity, that they should gather themselves together to Je-ru'sa-lem; public notice

8 And that whosoever would not come within three days, according to the counsel of the princes and the elders, all his substance should be <u>forfeited</u>, and himself separated from the congregation of those that had been carried away. confiscated

9 Then all the men of Ju'dah and Ben'ja-min gathered themselves together to Je-ru'sa-lem within three days. It *was* the ninth month, on the twentieth *day* of the month; and all the

people sat in the street of the house of <u>God</u>, <u>trembling</u> because of *this* matter, and for the great rain.   temple - greatly distressed

10 And Ez'ra the priest stood up, and said to them, You have transgressed, and have <u>taken strange</u> wives, to increase the <u>trespass</u> of Is'ra-el.   married foreign - guilt

11 Now therefore make confession to the <u>Lord God</u> of your fathers, and do His <u>pleasure</u>: and separate yourselves from the people of the land, and from the <u>strange</u> wives.   will - foreign

12 Then all the congregation answered and said with a loud voice, As you have said, so must we do.

13 But the people *are* many, and *it is* a time of much rain, and we are not able to stand outside, neither *is this* a work of one day or two: for we are many that have <u>transgressed</u> in this thing.   sinned

14 Let now our <u>rulers</u> of all the congregation stand, and let all them which have taken <u>strange</u> wives in our cities come at appointed times, and with them the elders of every city, and the judges thereof, until the fierce wrath of our <u>God</u> for this matter be turned from us.   leaders - Elohim^{p.f.}

15 Only Jon'a-than the son of A'sahel and Ja-ha-zi'ah the son of Tik'vah were <u>employed about</u> this *matter*: and Me-shul'lam and Shab-beth'a-i the Le'vite helped them.   opposed to

16 And the children of the captivity did so. And Ez'ra the priest, *with* certain <u>chief</u> of the fathers, after the house of their fathers, and all of them by *their*

names, were separated, and sat down in the first day of the tenth month to examine the matter.   heads

17 And they <u>made an end</u> with all the men that had <u>taken strange</u> wives by the first day of the first month.   finished investigating - foreign

18 And among the sons of the priests there were found that had taken strange wives: *namely*, of the sons of Jesh'u-a the son of Joz'a-dak, and his brethren; Ma-a-se'iah, and E-li-e'zer, and Ja'rib, and Ged-a-li'ah.

19 And they <u>gave their hands</u> that they would put away their wives; and *being* guilty, *they offered* a ram of the flock for their <u>trespass</u>.   pledged - guilt

20 And of the sons of Im'mer; Hana'ni, and Zeb-a-di'ah.

21 And of the sons of Ha'rim; Ma-a-se'iah, and E-li'jah, and Shem-a-i'ah, and Je-hi'el, and Uz-zi'ah.

22 And of the sons of Pash'ur; El-i-o-e'na-i, Ma-a-se'iah, Ish'ma-el, Nethan'e-el, Joz'a-bad, and El'a-sah.

23 Also of the Le'vites; Joz'a-bad, and Shim'e-i, and Ke-la'iah, (the same *is* Kel'i-ta,) Peth-a-hi'ah, Ju'dah, and E-li-e'zer.

24 Of the singers also; E-li'a-shib: and of the <u>porters</u>; Shal'lum, and Te'lem, and U'ri.   gatekeepers

25 Moreover of Is'ra-el: of the sons of Pa'rosh; Ra-mi'ah, and Je-zi'ah, and Mal-chi'ah, and Mi'a-min, and E-le-a'zar, and Mal-chi'jah, and Be-na'iah.

26 And of the sons of E'lam; Mat-ta-ni'ah, Zech-a-ri'ah, and Je-hi'el, and Ab'di, and Jer'e-moth, and E-li'ah.

27 And of the sons of Zat'tu; El-i-o-e'na-i, E-li'a-shib, Mat-ta-ni'ah, and Jer'e-moth, and Za'bad, and A-zi'za.

28 Of the sons of Beb'a-i; Je-ho-ha'nan, Han-a-ni'ah, Zab'bai, *and* Ath'lai.

29 And of the sons of Ba'ni; Me-shul'lam, Mal'luch, and Ad-a-i'ah, Jash'ub, and She'al, and Ra'moth.

30 And of the sons of Pa'hath-mo'ab; Ad'na, and Che'lal, Be-na'iah, Ma-a-se'iah, Mat-ta-ni'ah, Be-zal'e-el, and Bin'nu-i, and Ma-nas'seh.

31 And *of* the sons of Ha'rim; E-li-e'zer, Ish-i'jah, Mal-chi'ah, Shem-a-i'ah, Shim'e-on,

32 Ben'ja-min, Mal'luch, *and* Shem-a-ri'ah.

33 Of the sons of Ha'shum; Mat-te-na'i, Mat'ta-thah, Za'bad, E-liph'e-let, Jer'e-mai, Ma-nas'seh, *and* Shim'e-i.

34 Of the sons of Ba'ni; Ma-ad'ai, Am'ram, and U'el,

35 Be-na'iah, Be-de'iah, Chel'luh,

36 Va-ni'ah, Mer-e-moth, E-li'a-shib,

37 Mat-ta-ni'ah, Mat-te-na'i, and Ja'a-sau,

38 And Ba'ni, and Bin'nu-i, Shim'e-i,

39 And Shel-e-mi'ah, and Na'than, and Ad-a-i'ah,

40 Mach-na-de'bai, Shash'a-i, Shar'a-i,

41 A-zar'e-el, and Shel-e-mi'ah, Shem-a-ri'ah,

42 Shal'lum, Am-a-ri'ah, *and* Jo'seph.

43 Of the sons of Ne'bo; Je-i'el, Mat-ti-thi'ah, Za'bad, Ze-bi'na, Ja-da'u, and Jo'el, Be-na'iah.

44 All these had taken strange wives: and *some* of them had wives by whom they had children.

foreign

M46 ------ 1089

NEHEMIAH

OUTLINE

SURVEY

This book is a lesson in prayer, sacrifice, and tenacity. Nehemiah, the chief figure, gave up a responsible and wealthy position with the king of Persia in 445 B.C. in order to rebuild the walls of Jerusalem, and rally the Jews as a nation (1.1—3.32). His work brought intense opposition from powerful men round about, but Nehemiah overcame threatened attacks by taking wise defense measures (4.1-23), disunity within by squarely facing the problem and by personal example (5.1-19), and false accusations by insight and courage (6.1-14).

When the wall was completed, he took steps to have the city fully inhabited (6.15—7.73), but above all, he arranged for Ezra to read the law so that the people could mold their lives by it (8.1-18). He and the nation confessed the national sins, sought God's forgiveness, and set their seal to a renewed covenant with God (9.1—10.39). People were brought into the city, arrangements made for the worship, and the walls were dedicated (11.1—12.47). But as the years went by, the people kept declining from God's ideal, and Nehemiah had to bring about fresh reforms even in the teeth of opposition (13.1-31).

The book shows the need for prayer and firmness in the work of God. Nehemiah's prayers make an excellent study.

AUTHOR

It is usually thought that Ezra and Nehemiah were originally one book. The compiler here made use of personal memoirs of Nehemiah, as well as other material.

J.S.W.

THE BOOK OF
NEHEMIAH

"Comforted of Jehovah"
Rebuilding Fallen Walls

CHAPTER 1

THE words of Ne-he-mi'ah the son of Hach-a-li'ah. And it came to pass in the month Chis'leu, in the twentieth year, as I was in Shu'shan the palace,

2 That Ha-na'ni, one of my brethren, came, he and *certain* men of Ju'dah; and I asked them concerning the Jews that had escaped, which were left of the captivity, and concerning Je-ru'sa-lem.

3 And they said to me, The remnant that are left of the captivity there in the province *are* in great affliction and reproach: the wall of Je-ru'sa-lem also *is* broken down, and the gates thereof are burned with fire. distress

4 And it came to pass, when I heard these words, that I sat down and wept, and mourned *certain* days, and fasted, and prayed before the God of heaven, Elohim^p.f.

5 And said, I beseech You, O LORD God of heaven, the great and terrible God, that keeps covenant and mercy for them that love Him and observe His commandments:

beg - Jehovah^s.f. Elohim^p.f. - awesome - El^s.f. - agreement - keep

6 Let Your ear now be attentive, and Your eyes open, that You may hear the prayer of your servant, which I pray before You now, day and night, for the children of Is'ra-el Your servants,

and confess the sins of the children of Is'ra-el, which we have sinned against You: both I and my father's house have sinned.

7 We have dealt very corruptly against You, and have not kept the commandments, nor the statutes, nor the judgments, which You commanded Your servant Mo'ses.

8 Remember, I beseech You the word that You commanded Your servant Mo'ses, saying, *If* you transgress, I will scatter you abroad among the nations: beg

9 But *if* you turn to Me, and keep My commandments, and do them; though there were of you cast out to the uttermost part of the heaven, *yet* will I gather them from there, and will bring them to the place that I have chosen to set My name there.

10 Now these *are* Your servants and Your people, whom You have redeemed by Your great power, and by Your strong hand.

11 O Lord, I beseech You, let now Your ear be attentive to the prayer of Your servant, and to the prayer of Your servants, who desire to fear Your name: and prosper, I pray You, Your servant this day, and grant him mercy in the sight of this man. For I was the king's cupbearer. beg - revere

CHAPTER 2

AND it came to pass in the month Ni'san, in the twentieth year of Ar-tax-erx'es the king, *that* wine *was* before him: and I took up the wine, and gave *it* to the king. Now I had not been *beforetime* sad in his presence.

2 Wherefore the king said to me, Why *is* your countenance sad, seeing you *are* not sick? this *is* nothing *else* but sorrow of heart. Then I was very <u>sore</u> afraid,   much

3 And said to the king, Let the king live for ever: why should not my countenance be sad, when the city, the place of my fathers' <u>sepulchers</u>, *lies* waste, and the gates thereof are consumed with fire?   tombs

4 Then the king said to me, For what do you makc rcqucst? So I prayed to the <u>God</u> of heaven.   Elohim[p.f.]

5 And I said to the king, If it please the king, and if your servant have found favor in your sight, that you would send me to Ju'dah, to the city of my fathers' <u>sepulchers</u>, that I may build it.

6 And the king said to me, (the <u>queen</u> also sitting by him,) For how long shall your journey be? and when will you return? So it pleased the king to send me; and I set him a time.   wife

7 Moreover I said to the king, If it please the king, let letters be given me to the governors beyond the <u>river</u>, that they may <u>convey me over</u> till I come into Ju'dah;   i.e. Euphrates - allow me to pass

8 And a letter to A'saph the keeper of the king's forest, that he may give me timber to make beams for the gates of the palace which *appertained* to the house, and for the wall of the city, and for the house that I shall enter into. And the king granted me, according to the good hand of my <u>God</u> upon me.

9 Then I came to the governors beyond the river, and gave them the king's letters. Now the king had sent captains of the army and horsemen with me.

10 When San-bal'lat the Hor'o-nite, and To-bi'ah the servant, the Am'monite, heard *of it*, it grieved them exceedingly that there was come a man to seek the welfare of the children of Is'ra-el.

11 So I came to Je-ru'sa-lem, and was there three days.

12 And I arose in the night, I and some few men with me; neither told I *any* man what my <u>God</u> had put in my heart to do at Je-ru'sa-lem: neither *was there any* beast with me, save the beast that I rode upon.   Elohim[p.f.]

13 And I went out by night by the gate of the valley, even before the dragon well, and to the <u>dung port</u>, and <u>viewed</u> the walls of Je-ru'sa-lem, which were broken down, and the gates thereof were <u>consumed</u> with fire.   rubbish gate - inspected - destroyed

14 Then I went on to the gate of the fountain, and to the king's pool: but *there was* no place for the beast *that was* under me to pass.

15 Then went I up in the night by the brook, and <u>viewed</u> the wall, and turned back, and entered by the gate of the valley, and *so* returned. inspected

16 And the rulers knew not where I went, or what I did; neither had I as yet told *it* to the Jews, nor to the priests, nor to the nobles, nor to the rulers, nor to the rest that did the work.

17 Then said I to them, You see the distress that we *are* in, how Je-ru'sa-lem *lies* <u>waste</u>, and the gates thereof are <u>burned</u> with fire: come, and let us build up the wall of Je-ru'sa-lem, that we be no more a <u>reproach</u>. desolate - destroyed - disgrace

18 Then I told them of the hand of my <u>God</u> which was good upon me; as also the king's words that he had spoken to me. And they said, Let us rise up and build. So they <u>strengthened their hands for</u> *this* good *work*. Elohim^p.f. - began

19 But when San-bal'lat the Hor'o-nite, and To-bi'ah the servant, the Am'mon-ite, and Ge'shem the A-ra'bi-an, heard *it*, they laughed us to scorn, and despised us, and said, What *is* this thing that you do? will you rebel against the king?

20 Then answered I them, and said to them, The <u>God</u> of heaven, He will prosper us; therefore we His servants will arise and build: but you have no portion, nor right, nor memorial, in Je-ru'sa-lem. Elohim^p.f.

CHAPTER 3

THEN E-li'a-shib the high priest rose up with his brethren the priests, and they built the sheep gate; they sanctified it, and set up the doors of it; even to the tower of Me'ah they sanctified it, to the tower of Ha-nan'e-el.

2 And next to him built the men of Jer-i'cho. And next to them built Zac'cur the son of Im'ri.

3 But the fish gate did the sons of Has-se-na'ah build, who *also* laid the beams thereof, and set up the doors thereof, the locks thereof, and the bars thereof.

4 And next to them repaired Mer'e-moth the son of U-ri'jah, the son of Koz. And next to them repaired Me-shul'lam the son of Ber-e-chi'ah, the son of Me-shez'a-be-el. And next to them repaired Za'dok the son of Ba'a-na.

5 And next to them the Te-ko'ites repaired; but their nobles put not their necks to the work of their <u>lord</u>. supervisor

6 Moreover the old gate repaired Je-hoi'a-da the son of Pa-se'ah, and Me-shul'lam the son of Bes-o-de'iah; they laid the beams thereof, and set up the doors <u>thereof</u>, and the locks thereof, and the bars thereof. of it

7 And next to them repaired Mel-a-ti'ah the Gib'e-on-ite, and Ja'don the Me-ron'o-thite, the men of Gib'e-on, and of Miz'pah, to the throne of the governor on this side the river.

8 Next to him repaired Uz'zi-el the son of Har-ha-i'ah, of the goldsmiths. Next to him also repaired Han-a-ni'ah the son of *one of* the apothecaries, and they fortified Je-ru'sa-lem to the broad wall.

9 And next to them repaired Reph-a-i'ah the son of Hur, the ruler of the half part of Je-ru'sa-lem.

10 And next to them repaired Je-da'iah the son of Ha-ru'maph, even

opposite his house. And next to him repaired Hat'tush the son of Hash-ab-ni'ah.

11 Mal-chi'jah the son of Ha'rim, and Ha'shub the son of Pa-hath-mo'ab, repaired the other piece, and the tower of the furnaces.   section

12 And next to him repaired Shal'lum the son of Ha-lo'hesh, the ruler of the half part of Je-ru'sa-lem, he and his daughters.

13 The valley gate repaired Ha'nun, and the inhabitants of Za-no'ah; they built it, and set up the doors thereof, the locks thereof, and the bars thereof, and a thousand cubits on the wall to the dung gate.

14 But the dung gate repaired Mal-chi'ah the son of Re'chab, the ruler of part of Beth-hac'ce-rem; he built it, and set up the doors thereof, the locks thereof, and the bars thereof.   of it - bolts

15 But the gate of the fountain repaired Shal'lun the son of Col-ho'zeh, the ruler of part of Miz'pah; he built it, and covered it, and set up the doors thereof, the locks thereof, and the bars thereof, and the wall of the pool of Si-lo'ah by the king's garden, and to the stairs that go down from the city of Da'vid.

16 After him repaired Ne-he-mi'ah the son of Az'buk, the ruler of the half part of Beth'-zur, to *the place* opposite the sepulchers of Da'vid, and to the pool that was made, and to the house of the mighty.   tombs

17 After him repaired the Le'vites, Re'hum the son of Ba'ni. Next to him repaired Hash-a-bi'ah, the ruler of the half part of Kei'lah, in his part.

18 After him repaired their brethren, Bav'a-i the son of Hen'a-dad, the ruler of the half part of Kei'lah.

19 And next to him repaired E'zer the son of Jesh'u-a, the ruler of Miz'pah, another piece opposite the going up to the armory at the turning *of the wall*.   section

20 After him Ba'ruch the son of Zab'bai earnestly repaired the other piece, from the turning *of the wall* to the door of the house of E-li'a-shib the high priest.

21 After him repaired Mer'e-moth the son of U-ri'jah the son of Koz another piece, from the door of the house of E-li'a-shib even to the end of the house of E-li'a-shib.

22 And after him repaired the priests, the men of the plain.   valley

23 After him repaired Ben'ja-min and Ha'shub opposite their house. After him repaired Az-a-ri'ah the son of Ma-a-se'iah the son of An-a-ni'ah by his house.

24 After him repaired Bin'nu-i the son of Hen'a-dad another piece, from the house of Az-a-ri'ah to the turning *of the wall*, even to the corner.   section

25 Pa'lal the son of U'za-i, opposite the turning *of the wall*, and the tower which lies out from the king's high house, that *was* by the court of the prison. After him Pe-da'iah the son of Pa'rosh.

26 Moreover the Neth'i-nims dwelled in O'phel, to *the place* opposite the

water gate toward the east, and the tower that lies out.

<small>temple servants - made repairs as far as - projects</small>

27 After them the Te-ko'ites repaired another piece, opposite the great tower that lies out, even to the wall of O'phel.   <small>section</small>

28 From above the horse gate repaired the priests, every one opposite his house.

29 After them repaired Za'dok the son of Im'mer opposite his house. After him repaired also Shem-a-i'ah the son of Shech-a-ni'ah, the keeper of the east gate.

30 After him repaired Han-a-ni'ah the son of Shel-e-mi'ah, and Ha'nun the sixth son of Za'laph, another piece. After him repaired Me-shul'lam the son of Ber-e-chi'ah opposite his chamber.   <small>grain - cell</small>

31 After him repaired Mal-chi'ah the goldsmith's son to the place of the Neth'i-nims, and of the merchants, opposite the gate Miph'kad, and to the going up of the corner.

32 And between the going up of the corner to the sheep gate repaired the goldsmiths and the merchants.

CHAPTER 4

BUT it came to pass, that when San-bal'lat heard that we built the wall, he was angry, and took great indignation, and mocked the Jews.

2 And he spoke before his brethren and the army of Sa-ma'ri-a, and said, What do these feeble Jews? will they fortify themselves? will they sacrifice? will they make an end in a day? will they revive the stones out of the heaps of the rubbish which are burned?   <small>finish - bring to life</small>

3 Now To-bi'ah the Am'mon-ite *was* by him, and he said, Even that which they build, if a fox go up, he shall even break down their stone wall. <small>jackal</small>

4 Hear, O our God; for we are despised: and turn their reproach upon their own head, and give them for a prey in the land of captivity: <small>Elohim^{p.f.}</small>

5 And cover not their iniquity, and let not their sin be blotted out from before You: for they have provoked *You* to anger before the builders.

6 So built we the wall; and all the wall was joined together to the half thereof: for the people had a mind to work.

7 But it came to pass, *that* when San-bal'lat, and To-bi'ah, and the A-ra'bi-ans, and the Am'mon-ites, and the Ash'dod-ites, heard that the walls of Je-ru'sa-lem were made up, *and* that the breaches began to be stopped, then they were very angry,   <small>being repaired - gaps</small>

8 And conspired all of them together to come *and* to fight against Je-ru'sa-lem, and to hinder it.

9 Nevertheless we made our prayer to our God, and set a watch against them day and night, because of them.

10 And Ju'dah said, The strength of the bearers of burdens is decayed, and *there is* much rubbish; so that we are not able to build the wall.   <small>failing - debris</small>

11 And our adversaries said, They shall not know, neither see, till we come in the midst among them, and slay them, and cause the work to cease.

12 And it came to pass, that when the Jews which dwelled by them came, they said to us ten times, From all places where you shall return to us *they will be upon you.*

13 Therefore set I in the lower places behind the wall, *and* on the <u>higher</u> places, I even set the people <u>after</u> their families with their swords, their spears, and their bows.   bare - according to

14 And I looked, and rose up, and said to the nobles, and to the rulers, and to the rest of the people, Be not you afraid of them: remember the Lord, *which is* great and <u>terrible</u>, and fight for your brethren, your sons, and your daughters, your wives, and your houses.   awesome

15 And it came to pass, when our enemies heard that it was known to us, and <u>God</u> had <u>brought their counsel to nought</u>, that we returned all of us to the wall, every one to his work.   Elohim^{p.f.} - frustrated their plans

16 And it came to pass from that time forth, *that* the half of my servants <u>wrought in</u> the work, and the other half of them held both the spears, the shields, and the bows, and the <u>habergeons</u>; and the rulers *were* behind all the house of Ju'dah. carried on - breastplates

17 They which builded on the wall, and they that bare burdens, with those that <u>laded</u>, *every one* with one of his hands <u>wrought in</u> the work, and with the other *hand* held a weapon.   loaded

18 For the builders, every one had his sword girded by his side, and *so* builded. And he that sounded the trumpet *was* by me.

19 And I said to the nobles, and to the rulers, and to the rest of the people, The work *is* great and large, and we are separated upon the wall, one far from another.

20 In what place *therefore* you hear the sound of the trumpet, <u>resort</u> <u>you there to us</u>: our <u>God</u> shall fight for us.   rally to us there - Elohim^{p.f.}

21 So we labored in the work: and half of them held the spears from the rising of the morning till the stars appeared.

22 Likewise at the same time said I to the people, Let every one with his servant lodge within Je-ru'sa-lem, that in the night they may be a guard to us, and labor on the day.

23 So neither I, nor my brethren, nor my servants, nor the men of the guard which followed me, none of us put off our clothes, *saving* that every one <u>put them off for washing.</u>   but - took his weapon to the water

CHAPTER 5

AND there was a great cry of the people and of their wives against their brethren the Jews.

2 For there were that said, We, our sons, and our daughters, *are* many: therefore we take up <u>corn</u> *for them*, that we may eat, and live.   grain

3 *Some* also there were that said, We have mortgaged our lands, vineyards, and houses, that we might buy <u>corn</u>, because of the <u>dearth</u>. grain - famine

4 There were also that said, We have borrowed money for the king's tribute, *and that upon* our lands and vineyards.

5 Yet now our flesh *is* as the flesh of our brethren, our children as their children: and, lo, we bring into <u>bondage</u> our sons and our daughters to be servants, and *some* of our daughters are brought to <u>bondage</u> *already*: neither *is it* in our power *to redeem them*; for other men have our lands and vineyards.   _{slavery}

6 And I was very angry when I heard their cry and these words.

7 Then I consulted with myself, and I rebuked the nobles, and the rulers, and said to them, You exact usury, every one of his brother. And I <u>set</u> a great <u>assembly</u> against them.   _{held - meeting}

8 And I said to them, We after our ability have redeemed our brethren the Jews, which were sold to the heathen; and will you even sell your brethren? or shall they be sold to us? Then held they their peace, and found nothing *to answer*.

9 Also I said, It *is* not good that you do: ought you not to walk in the <u>fear</u> of our <u>God</u> because of the <u>reproach</u> of the heathen our enemies?   _{reverence - criticism}

10 I likewise, *and* my brethren, and my servants, <u>might exact of</u> them money and <u>corn</u>: I pray you, let us leave off this <u>usury</u>.   _{are lending - interest}

11 Restore, I pray you, to them, even this day, their lands, their vineyards, their oliveyards, and their houses, also the hundredth *part* of the money, and of the <u>corn</u>, the wine, and the oil, that you exact of them.   _{grain}

12 Then said they, We will restore *them*, and will require nothing of them; so will we do as you say. Then I called the priests, and took an oath of them, that they should do according to this promise.

13 Also I shook my lap, and said, So <u>God</u> shake out every man from his house, and from his labor, that performs not this promise, even thus be he shaken out, and emptied. And all the congregation said, Amen, and praised the LORD. And the people did according to this promise.   _{Elohim^{p.f.}}

14 Moreover from the time that I was appointed to be their governor in the land of Ju'dah, from the twentieth year even to the two and thirtieth year of Ar-tax-erx'es the king, *that is*, twelve years, I and my brethren have not eaten the <u>bread</u> of the governor.   _{food allowance}

15 But the former governors that *had been* before me were chargeable to the people, and had taken of them bread and wine, beside forty shekels of silver; yea, even their servants bare rule over the people: but so did not I, because of the <u>fear</u> of <u>God</u>.   _{reverence - Elohim^{p.f.}}

16 Yea, also I continued in the work of this wall, neither bought we any land: and all my servants *were* gathered there to the work.

17 Moreover *there were* at my table an hundred and fifty of the Jews and rulers, beside those that came to us from among the heathen that *are* about us.

18 Now *that* which was prepared *for me* daily *was* one ox *and* six choice sheep; also fowls were prepared for me, and once in ten days store of all sorts of wine: yet for all this required not I the

bread of the governor, because the <u>bondage</u> was heavy upon this people. _{servitude}

19 Think upon me, my <u>God</u>, for good, *according* to all that I have done for this people. _{Elohim^{p.f.}}

CHAPTER 6

NOW it came to pass, when San-bal'lat, and To-bi'ah, and Ge'shem the A-ra'bi-an, and the rest of our enemies, heard that I had built the wall, and *that* there was no <u>breach</u> left therein; (though at that time I had not set up the doors upon the gates;) _{gap}

2 That San-bal'lat and Ge'shem sent to me, saying, Come, let us meet together in *some one of* the villages in the plain of O'no. But they thought to do me <u>mischief</u>. _{harm}

3 And I sent messengers to them, saying, I *am* doing a great work, so that I cannot come down: why should the work cease, while I leave it, and come down to you?

4 Yet they sent to me four times after this sort; and I answered them after the same manner.

5 Then sent San-bal'lat his servant to me in like manner the fifth time with an open letter in his hand;

6 Wherein *was* written, It is reported among the <u>heathen</u>, and Gash'mu says *it, that* you and the Jews think to rebel: for which cause you built the wall, that you may be their king, according to these words. _{nations}

7 And you have also appointed prophets to preach of you at Je-ru'sa-lem, saying, *There is* a king in Ju'dah:

and now shall it be reported to the king according to these words. Come now therefore, and let us take counsel together.

8 Then I sent to him, saying, There are no such things done as you say, but you <u>feign</u> them out of your own heart. _{are inventing}

9 For they all made us afraid, saying, Their hands shall be weakened from the work, that it be not done. Now therefore, *O God*, strengthen my hands.

10 Afterward I came to the house of Shem-a-i'ah the son of Del-a-i'ah the son of Me-het'a-beel, who *was* <u>shut up</u>; and he said, Let us meet together in the house of <u>God</u>, inside the temple, and let us shut the doors of the temple: for they will come to slay you; yea, in the night will they come to slay you. _{confined}

11 And I said, Should such a man as I flee? and who is *there*, that, *being* as I *am*, would go into the temple to save his life? I will not go in.

12 And, lo, I perceived that <u>God</u> had not sent him; but that he pronounced this prophecy against me: for To-bi'ah and San-bal'lat had hired him. _{Elohim^{p.f.}}

13 Therefore *was* he hired, that I should be afraid, and do so, and sin, and *that* they might have *matter* for an evil report, that they might <u>reproach</u> me. _{discredit}

14 My <u>God</u>, think You upon To-bi'ah and San-bal'lat according to these their works, and on the prophetess No-a-di'ah, and the rest of the prophets, that would have <u>put me in fear</u>. _{frightened me}

15 So the wall was finished in the

twenty and fifth *day* of *the month* E'lul, in fifty and two days.

16 And it came to pass, that when all our enemies heard *thereof*, and all the heathen that *were* about us saw *these things*, they were much cast down in their own eyes: for they perceived that this work was <u>wrought</u> of our <u>God</u>. accomplished - Elohim^{p.f.}

17 Moreover in those days the nobles of Ju'dah sent many letters to To-bi'ah, and *the letters* of To-bi'ah came to them.

18 For *there were* many in Ju'dah <u>sworn</u> to him, because he *was* the son in law of Shech-a-ni'ah the son of A'rah; and his son Jo-ha'nan had taken the daughter of Me-shul'lam the son of Ber-e-chi'ah. bound by oath

19 Also they reported his good deeds before me, and uttered my words to him. *And* To-bi'ah sent letters to put me in fear.

CHAPTER 7

NOW it came to pass, when the wall was built, and I had set up the doors, and the <u>porters</u> and the singers and the Le'vites were appointed, gatekeepers

2 That I gave my brother Ha-na'ni, and Han-a-ni'ah the ruler of the palace, <u>charge</u> over Je-ru'sa-lem: for he *was* a faithful man, and <u>feared</u> <u>God</u> above many. command - revered - Elohim^{p.f.}

3 And I said to them, Let not the gates of Je-ru'sa-lem be opened until the sun be hot; and while they stand <u>by</u>, let them shut the doors, and bar *them*: and appoint <u>watches</u> of the inhabitants of Je-ru'sa-lem, every one in his <u>watch</u>, and every one *to be* opposite his house. on guard - guards - post

4 Now the city *was* large and <u>great</u>: but the people *were* few therein, and the houses *were* not builded. spacious

5 And my <u>God</u> put into my heart to gather together the nobles, and the rulers, and the people, that they might be reckoned by genealogy. And I found a register of the genealogy of them which came up at the first, and found written therein, Elohim^{p.f.}

6 These *are* the children of the province, that went up out of the captivity, of those that had been carried away, whom Neb-u-chad-nez'zar the king of Bab'y-lon had carried away, and came again to Je-ru'sa-lem and to Ju'dah, every one to his city;

7 Who came with Ze-rub'ba-bel, Jesh'u-a, Ne-he-mi'ah, Az-a-ri'ah, Ra-a-mi'ah, Na-ham'a-ni, Mor'de-cai, Bil'shan, Mis'pe-reth, Big'va-i, Ne'hum, Ba'a-nah. The number, *I say*, of the men of the people of Is'ra-el *was this*;

8 The children of Pa'rosh, two thousand an hundred seventy and two.

9 The children of Sheph-a-ti'ah, three hundred seventy and two.

10 The children of A'rah, six hundred fifty and two.

11 The children of Pa'hath-mo'ab, of the children of Jesh'u-a and Jo'ab, two thousand and eight hundred *and* eighteen.

12 The children of E'lam, a thousand two hundred fifty and four.

13 The children of Zat'tu, eight hundred forty and five.

14 The children of Zac'ca-i, seven hundred and threescore.

15 The children of Bin'nu-i, six hundred forty and eight.

16 The children of Beb'a-i, six hundred twenty and eight.

17 The children of Az'gad, two thousand three hundred twenty and two.

18 The children of A-don'i-kam, six hundred threescore and seven.

19 The children of Big'va-i, two thousand threescore and seven.

20 The children of A'din, six hundred fifty and five.

21 The children of A'ter of Hez-e-ki'ah, ninety and eight.

22 The children of Ha'shum, three hundred twenty and eight.

23 The children of Be'zai, three hundred twenty and four.

24 The children of Ha'riph, an hundred and twelve.

25 The children of Gib'e-on, ninety and five.

26 The men of Beth'-le-hem and Ne-to-phah, an hundred fourscore and eight.

27 The men of An'a-thoth, an hundred twenty and eight.

28 The men of Beth-az'ma-veth, forty and two.

29 The men of Kir'jath-je'a-rim, Che-phi'rah, and Be-e'roth, seven hundred forty and three.

30 The men of Ra'mah and Ga'ba, six hundred twenty and one.

31 The men of Mich'mas, an hundred and twenty and two.

32 The men of Beth'-el and A'i, an hundred twenty and three.

33 The men of the other Ne'bo, fifty and two.

34 The children of the other E'lam, a thousand two hundred fifty and four.

35 The children of Ha'rim, three hundred and twenty.

36 The children of Jer'i-cho, three hundred forty and five.

37 The children of Lod, Ha'did, and O'no, seven hundred twenty and one.

38 The children of Se-na'ah, three thousand nine hundred and thirty.

39 The priests: the children of Je-da'iah, of the house of Jesh'u-a, nine hundred seventy and three.

40 The children of Im'mer, a thousand fifty and two.

41 The children of Pash'ur, a thousand two hundred forty and seven.

42 The children of Ha'rim, a thousand and seventeen.

43 The Le'vites: the children of Jesh'u-a, of Kad'mi-el, *and* of the children of Ho-de'vah, seventy and four.

44 The singers: the children of A'saph, an hundred forty and eight.

45 The porters: the children of Shal'lum, the children of A'ter, the children of Tal'mon, the children of Ak'kub, the children of Hat'i-ta, the children of Sho'ba-i, an hundred thirty and eight. gatekeepers

46 The Neth'i-nims: the children of Zi'ha, the children of Ha-su'pha, the children of Tab'ba-oth,

47 The children of Ke'ros, the children of Si'a, the children of Pa'don,

48 The children of Leb'a-na, the children of Hag'a-ba, the children of Shal'ma-i,

49 The children of Ha'nan, the children of Gid'del, the children of Ga'har,
50 The children of Re-a-i'ah, the children of Re'zin, the children of Ne-ko'da,
51 The children of Gaz'zam, the children of Uz'za, the children of Pha-se'ah,
52 The children of Be'sai, the children of Me-u'nim, the children of Ne-phish'e-sim,
53 The children of Bak'buk, the children of Ha-ku'pha, the children of Har'hur,
54 The children of Baz'lith, the children of Me-hi'da, the children of Har'sha,
55 The children of Bar'kos, the children of Sis'e-ra, the children of Ta'mah,
56 The children of Ne-zi'ah, the children of Hat'i-pha.
57 The children of Sol'o-mon's servants: the children of So'ta-i, the children of Soph'e-reth, the children of Pe-ri'da,
58 The children of Ja-a'la, the children of Dar'kon, the children of Gid'del,
59 The children of Sheph-a-ti'ah, the children of Hat'til, the children of Poch'e-reth of Ze-ba'im, the children of A'mon.
60 All the Neth'i-nims, and the children of Sol-o'mon's servants, *were* three hundred ninety and two.
61 And these *were* they which went up *also* from Tel-me'lah, Tel-ha-re'sha, Che'rub, Ad'don, and Im'mer: but they could not show their father's <u>house</u>, nor

their <u>seed</u>, whether they *were* of Is'ra-el.   temple - descendants
62 The children of Del-a-i'ah, the children of To-bi'ah, the children of Ne-ko'da, six hundred forty and two.
63 And of the priests: the children of Ha-ba'iah, the children of Koz, the children of Bar-zil'la-i, which took *one* of the daughters of Bar-zil'la-i the Gil'e-ad-ite to wife, and was called after their name.
64 These sought their register *among* those that were reckoned by genealogy, but it was not found: therefore were they, as polluted, put from the priesthood.
65 And the Tir'sha-tha said to them, that they should not eat of the most holy things, till there stood *up* a priest with <u>U'rim and Thum'mim</u>.   Light and Perfection
66 The whole congregation together *was* forty and two thousand three hundred and threescore,
67 Beside their manservants and their maidservants, of whom *there were* seven thousand three hundred thirty and seven: and they had two hundred forty and five singing men and singing women.
68 Their horses, seven hundred thirty and six: their mules, two hundred forty and five:
69 *Their* camels, four hundred thirty and five: six thousand seven hundred and twenty asses.
70 And some of the <u>chief</u> of the fathers gave to the work. The Tir'sha-tha gave to the treasure a thousand

drams of gold, fifty basins, five hundred and thirty priests' garments. heads
71 And *some* of the chief of the fathers gave to the treasure of the work twenty thousand drams of gold, and two thousand and two hundred pound of silver.
72 And *that* which the rest of the people gave *was* twenty thousand drams of gold, and two thousand pound of silver, and threescore and seven priests' garments.
73 So the priests, and the Le'vites, and the <u>porters</u>, and the singers, and *some* of the people, and the Neth'i-nims, and all Is'ra-el, dwelled in their cities; and when the seventh month came, the children of Is'ra-el *were* in their cities.   gatekeepers

CHAPTER 8

AND all the people gathered themselves together as one man into the <u>street</u> that *was* before the water gate; and they spoke to Ez'ra the scribe to bring the book of the law of Mo'ses, which the LORD had commanded to Is'ra-el.   square
2 And Ez'ra the priest brought the law before the congregation both of men and women, and all that could hear with understanding, upon the first day of the seventh month.
3 And he read <u>therein</u> before the street that *was* before the water gate from the morning until midday, before the men and the women, and those that could understand; and the ears of all the people *were attentive* to the book of the law.   from it

4 And Ez'ra the scribe stood upon a <u>pulpit of wood</u>, which they had made for the purpose; and beside him stood Mat-ti-thi'ah, and She'ma, and An-a-i'ah, and U-ri'jah, and Hil-ki'ah, and Ma-a-se'iah, on his right hand; and on his left hand, Pe-da'iah, and Mish'a-el, and Mal-chi'ah, and Ha'shum, and Hash-bad'a-na, Zech-a-ri'ah, *and* Me-shul'lam.   platform
5 And Ez'ra opened the book in the <u>sight</u> of all the people; (for he was above all the people;) and when he opened it, all the people stood up: eyes
6 And Ez'ra blessed the LORD, the great <u>God</u>. And all the people answered, Amen, Amen, with lifting up their hands: and they bowed their heads, and worshiped the LORD with *their* faces to the ground.   Elohim p.f.
7 Also Jesh'u-a, and Ba'ni, and Sher-e-bi'ah, Ja'min, Ak'kub, Shab-beth'a-i, Ho-di'jah, Ma-a-se'iah, Kel'i-ta, Az-a-ri'ah, Joz'a-bad, Ha'nan, Pel-a-i'ah, and the Le'vites, caused the people to understand the law: and the people *stood* in their place.
8 So they read in the book in the law of <u>God</u> distinctly, and gave the sense, and caused *them* to understand the reading.
9 And Ne-he-mi'ah, which *is* the Tir'sha-tha, and Ez'ra the priest the scribe, and the Le'vites that taught the people, said to all the people, This day *is* holy to the LORD your <u>God</u>; mourn not, nor weep. For all the people wept, when they heard the words of the law.

10 Then he said to them, Go your way, eat the fat, and drink the sweet, and send portions to them for whom nothing is prepared: for *this* day *is* holy to our Lord: neither be you sorry; for the joy of the Lord is your strength.   Adonay^{p.f.}

11 So the Le'vites stilled all the people, saying, Hold your peace, for the day *is* holy; neither be you grieved.   depressed

12 And all the people went their way to eat, and to drink, and to send portions, and to make great mirth, because they had understood the words that were declared to them.

13 And on the second day were gathered together the chief of the fathers of all the people, the priests, and the Le'vites, to Ez'ra the scribe, even to understand the words of the law.

14 And they found written in the law which the Lord had commanded by Mo'ses, that the children of Is'ra-el should dwell in booths in the feast of the seventh month: huts

15 And that they should publish and proclaim in all their cities, and in Je-ru'salem, saying, Go forth to the mount, and bring olive branches, and pine branches, and myrtle branches, and palm branches, and branches of thick trees, to make booths, as *it is* written.

16 So the people went forth, and brought *them*, and made themselves booths, every one upon the roof of his house, and in their courts, and in the courts of the house of God, and in the street of the water gate, and in the street of the gate of E'phra-im.   Elohim^{p.f.}

17 And all the congregation of them that were come again out of the captivity made booths, and sat under the booths: for since the days of Jesh'u-a the son of Nun to that day had not the children of Is'ra-el done so. And there was very great gladness.   lived in - shelters

18 Also day by day, from the first day to the last day, he read in the book of the law of God. And they kept the feast seven days; and on the eighth day *was* a solemn assembly, according to the manner.   Elohim^{p.f.}

CHAPTER 9

NOW in the twenty and fourth day of this month the children of Is'ra-el were assembled with fasting, and with sackclothes, and earth upon them.

2 And the seed of Is'ra-el separated themselves from all strangers, and stood and confessed their sins, and the iniquities of their fathers.   descendants

3 And they stood up in their place, and read in the book of the law of the Lord their God *one* fourth part of the day; and *another* fourth part they confessed, and worshiped the Lord their God.   Elohim^{p.f.}

4 Then stood up upon the stairs, of the Le'vites, Jesh'u-a, and Ba'ni, Kad'mi-el, Sheb-a-ni'ah, Bun'ni, Sher-e-bi'ah, Ba'ni, *and* Chen'a-ni, and cried with a loud voice to the Lord their God.   platform

5 Then the Le'vites, Jesh'u-a, and Kad'mi-el, Ba'ni, Hash-ab-ni'ah, Sher-e-bi'ah, Ho-di'jah, Sheb-a-ni'ah, *and* Peth-a-hi'ah, said, Stand up *and* bless

the Lord your God for ever and ever: and blessed be Your glorious name, which is exalted above all blessing and praise.   Elohim^p.f.

6 You, *even* You, *are* Lord alone; You have made heaven, the heaven of heavens, with all their host, the earth, and all *things* that *are* therein, the seas, and all that *is* therein, and You preserve them all; and the host of heaven worships You.   sustain

7 You *are* the Lord the God, who did choose A'bram, and brought him forth out of Ur of the Chal'dees, and gave him the name of A'bra-ham;   Elohim^p.f.

8 And found his heart faithful before You, and made a covenant with him to give the land of the Ca'naan-ites, the Hit'tites, the Am'or-ites, and the Per'iz-zites, and the Jeb'u-sites, and the Gir'ga-shites, to give *it, I say*, to his seed, and have performed Your words; for You *are* righteous: agreement

9 And did see the affliction of our fathers in E'gypt, and heard their cry by the Red sea;   suffering

10 And showed signs and wonders upon Pha'raoh, and on all his servants, and on all the people of his land: for you knew that they dealt proudly against them. So did You get You a name, as *it is* this day.   acted arrogantly

11 And You did divide the sea before them, so that they went through the midst of the sea on the dry land; and their persecutors You threw into the deeps, as a stone into the mighty waters.

12 Moreover You led them in the day by a cloudy pillar; and in the night by a pillar of fire, to give them light in the way wherein they should go.

13 You came down also upon mount Si'nai, and spoke with them from heaven, and gave them right judgments, and true laws, good statutes and commandments:

14 And made known to them Your holy sabbath, and commanded them precepts, statutes, and laws, by the hand of Mo'ses Your servant: rest day - decrees

15 And gave them bread from heaven for their hunger, and brought forth water for them out of the rock for their thirst, and promised them that they should go in to possess the land which You had sworn to give them.

16 But they and our fathers dealt proudly, and hardened their necks, and hearkened not to Your commandments,   acted arrogantly

17 And refused to obey, neither were mindful of Your wonders that You did among them; but hardened their necks, and in their rebellion appointed a captain to return to their bondage: but You *are* a God ready to pardon, gracious and merciful, slow to anger, and of great kindness, and forsook them not.   Eloahs^s.f.

18 Yea, when they had made them a molten calf, and said, This *is* your God that brought you up out of E'gypt, and had wrought great provocations;   Elohim^p.f. - committed

19 Yet You in Your manifold mercies forsook them not in the wilderness: the pillar of the cloud departed not from them by day, to lead them in the

way; neither the pillar of fire by night, to show them light, and the way wherein they should go.   great

20 You gave also Your good Spirit to instruct them, and withheld not Your manna from their mouth, and gave them water for their thirst.

21 Yea, forty years did You sustain them in the wilderness, *so that* they lacked nothing; their clothes waxed not old, and their feet swelled not.   grew

22 Moreover You gave them kingdoms and nations, and did divide them into corners: so they possessed the land of Si'hon, and the land of the king of Hesh'bon, and the land of Og king of Ba'shan.   allot - boundaries

23 Their children also multiplied You as the stars of heaven, and brought them into the land, concerning which You had promised to their fathers, that they should go in to possess *it*.

24 So the children went in and possessed the land, and You subdued before them the inhabitants of the land, the Ca'naan-ites, and gave them into their hands, with their kings, and the people of the land, that they might do with them as they would.   desired

25 And they took strong cities, and a fat land, and possessed houses full of all goods, wells dug, vineyards, and oliveyards, and fruit trees in abundance: so they did eat, and were filled, and became fat, and delighted themselves in Your great goodness.   cisterns - rich

26 Nevertheless they were disobedient, and rebelled against You, and cast Your law behind their backs, and slew

Your prophets which testified against them to turn them to You, and they wrought great provocations.   put - admonished - committed

27 Therefore You delivered them into the hand of their enemies, who vexed them: and in the time of their trouble, when they cried to You, You heard *them* from heaven; and according to Your manifold mercies You gave them saviors, who saved them out of the hand of their enemies.   oppressed - great

28 But after they had rest, they did evil again before You: therefore left You them in the hand of their enemies, so that they had the dominion over them: yet when they returned, and cried to You, You heard *them* from heaven; and many times did You deliver them according to Your mercies;

29 And testified against them, that You might bring them again to Your law: yet they dealt proudly, and hearkened not to Your commandments, but sinned against Your judgments, (which if a man do, he shall live in them;) and withdrew the shoulder, and hardened their neck, and would not hear.   acted arrogantly - turned away - were stubborn

30 Yet many years did You forbear them, and testified against them by Your Spirit in Your prophets: yet would they not give ear: therefore gave You them into the hand of the people of the lands.

31 Nevertheless for Your great mercies' sake You did not utterly con-

sume them, nor forsake them; for You *are* a gracious and merciful God.

G4 32 Now therefore, our <u>God</u>, the great, the mighty, and the <u>terrible</u> God, who keeps <u>covenant</u> and mercy, let not all the trouble seem little before You, that has come upon us, on our kings, on our princes, and on our priests, and on our prophets, and on our fathers, and on all Your people, since the time of the kings of As-syr'i-a to this day.

798

Elohim^{p.f.} - awesome - El^{s.f.} - agreement

33 However You *are* just in all that is brought upon us; for You have done right, but we have done wickedly:

34 Neither have our kings, our princes, our priests, nor our fathers, kept Your law, nor hearkened to Your commandments and Your testimonies, wherewith You did <u>testify against</u> them.   admonish

35 For they have not served You in their kingdom, and in Your great goodness that You gave them, and in the large and <u>fat</u> land which You gave before them, neither turned they from their wicked works.   rich

36 Behold, we *are* servants this day, and *for* the land that You gave to our fathers to eat the fruit thereof and the good thereof, behold, we *are* servants in it:

37 And it yields much <u>increase</u> to the kings whom You have set over us because of our sins: also they have dominion over our bodies, and over our cattle, at their pleasure, and we *are* in great distress.   harvest

38 And because of all this we make a sure <u>*covenant*</u>, and write *it*; and our princes, Le'vites, *and* priests, seal *to it*.   agreement

CHAPTER 10

NOW those that sealed *were*, Ne-he-mi'ah, the Tir'sha-tha, the son of Hach-a-li'ah, and Zid-ki'jah,

2 Ser-a-i'ah, Az-a-ri'ah, Jer-e-mi'ah,

3 Pash'ur, Am-a-ri'ah, Mal-chi'jah,

4 Hat'tush, Sheb-a-ni'ah, Mal'luch,

5 Ha'rim, Mer'e-moth, O-ba-di'ah,

6 Dan'iel, Gin'ne-thon, Ba'ruch,

7 Me-shul'lam, A-bi'jah, Mij'a-min,

8 Ma-a-zi'ah, Bil'ga-i, Shem-a-i'ah: these *were* the priests.

9 And the Le'vites: both Jesh'u-a the son of Az-a-ni'ah, Bin'nu-i of the sons of Hen'a-dad, Kad'mi-el;

10 And their brethren, Sheb-a-ni'ah, Ho-di'jah, Kel'i-ta, Pel-a-i'ah, Ha'nan,

11 Mi'cha, Re'hob, Hash-a-bi'ah,

12 Zac'cur, Sher-e-bi'ah, Sheb-a-ni'ah,

13 Ho-di'jah, Ba'ni, Ben'i-nu.

14 The chief of the people; Pa'rosh, Pa'hath-mo'ab, E'lam, Zat'thu, Ba'ni,

15 Bun'ni, Az'gad, Beb'a-i,

16 Ad-o-ni'jah, Big'va-i, A'din,

17 A'ter, Hiz-ki'jah, Az'zur,

18 Ho-di'jah, Ha'shum, Be'zai,

19 Ha'riph, An'a-thoth, Neb'a-i,

20 Mag'pi-ash, Me-shul'lam, He'zir,

21 Me-shez'a-be-el, Za'dok, Jad-du'a,

22 Pel-a-ti'ah, Ha'nan, An-a-i'ah,

23 Ho-she'a, Han-a-ni'ah, Ha'shub,

24 Hal-lo'hesh, Pil'e-ha, Sho'bek,

25 Re'hum, Ha-shab'nah, Ma-a-se'iah,

26 And A-hi'jah, Ha'nan, A'nan,
27 Mal'luch, Ha'rim, Ba-a-nah.
28 And the rest of the people, the priests, the Le'vites, the <u>porters</u>, the singers, the Neth'i-nims, and all they that had separated themselves from the people of the lands to the law of <u>God</u>, their wives, their sons, and their daughters, every one having knowledge, and having understanding; _{gatekeepers - Elohim^{p.f.}}
29 They cling to their brethren, their nobles, and entered into a curse, and into an oath, to walk in <u>God's</u> law, which was given by Mo'ses the servant of <u>God</u>, and to observe and do all the commandments of the <u>LORD</u> our <u>Lord</u>, and His judgments and His statutes; _{Jehovah^{s.f.} - Adonay^{p.f.}}
30 And that we would not give our daughters to the people of the land, nor take their daughters for our sons:
31 And *if* the people of the land bring <u>ware</u> or any <u>victuals</u> on the <u>sabbath</u> day to sell, *that* we would not buy it of them on the <u>sabbath</u>, or on the holy day: and *that* we would <u>leave</u> the seventh year, and the <u>exaction</u> of every debt. _{merchandise - food - rest day - forego - interest}
32 Also we made <u>ordinances</u> for us, to charge ourselves yearly with the third part of a shekel for the service of the <u>house</u> of our God; _{laws - temple}
33 For the showbread, and for the continual meat offering, and for the continual burned offering, of the <u>sabbaths</u>, of the new moons, for the set feasts, and for the holy *things*, and for the sin offerings to make an atonement for Is'ra-el, and *for* all the work of the <u>house</u> of our God. _{rest days - temple}
34 And we cast the lots among the priests, the Le'vites, and the people, for the wood offering, to bring *it* into the <u>house</u> of our <u>God</u>, after the houses of our fathers, at times appointed year by year, to burn upon the altar of the LORD our <u>God</u>, as *it is* written in the law: _{Elohim^{p.f.}}
35 And to bring the firstfruits of our ground, and the firstfruits of all fruit of all trees, year by year, to the <u>house</u> of the LORD:
36 Also the firstborn of our sons, and of our cattle, as *it is* written in the law, and the firstlings of our herds and of our flocks, to bring to the <u>house</u> of our <u>God</u>, to the priests that minister in the <u>house</u> of our <u>God</u>: _{temple}
37 And *that* we should bring the firstfruits of our dough, and our offerings, and the fruit of all manner of trees, of wine and of oil, to the priests, to the <u>chambers</u> of the <u>house</u> of our <u>God</u>; and the tithes of our ground to the Le'vites, that the same Le'vites might have the tithes in all the <u>cities</u> of our tillage. _{storerooms - temple - Elohim^{p.f.} - rural towns}
38 And the priest the son of Aar'on shall be with the Le'vites, when the Le'vites take tithes: and the Le'vites shall bring up the tithe of the tithes to the <u>house</u> of our <u>God</u>, to the <u>chambers</u>, into the treasure house. _{Elohim^{p.f.}}
39 For the children of Is'ra-el and the children of Le'vi shall bring the offering of the <u>corn</u>, of the new wine, and the oil, to the chambers, where *are* the vessels of the sanctuary, and the priests

that minister, and the <u>porters</u>, and the singers: and we will not forsake the house of our <u>God</u>. grain - gatekeepers - Elohim^{p.f.}

CHAPTER 11

AND the rulers of the people dwelled at Je-ru'sa-lem: the rest of the people also cast lots, to bring one of ten to dwell in Je-ru'sa-lem the holy city, and nine parts *to dwell* in *other* cities.

2 And the people blessed all the men, that willingly offered themselves to dwell at Je-ru'sa-lem.

3 Now these *are* the chief of the province that dwelled in Je-ru'sa-lem: but in the cities of Ju'dah dwelled every one in his possession in their cities, *that is*, Is'ra-el, the priests, and the Le'vites, and the Neth'i-nims, and the children of Sol'o-mon's servants.

4 And at Je-ru'sa-lem dwelled *certain* of the children of Ju'dah, and of the children of Ben'ja-min. Of the children of Ju'dah; Ath-a-i'ah the son of Uz-zi'ah, the son of Zech-a-ri'ah, the son of Am-a-ri'ah, the son of Sheph-a-ti'ah, the son of Ma-ha'la-le-el, of the children of Pe'rez;

5 And Ma-a-se'iah the son of Ba'ruch, the son of Col-ho'zeh, the son of Ha-za'iah, the son of Ad-a-i'ah, the son of Joi'a-rib, the son of Zech-a-ri'ah, the son of Shi-lo'ni.

6 All the sons of Pe'rez that dwelled at Je-ru'sa-lem *were* <u>four hundred three-score and eight</u> <u>valiant</u> men. 468 - brave

7 And these *are* the sons of Ben'ja-min; Sal'lu the son of Me-shul'lam, the son of Jo'ed, the son of Pe-da'iah, the son of Kol-a-i'ah, the son of Ma-a-se'iah, the son of Ith'i-el, the son of Je'sa'iah.

8 And after him Gab'ba-i, Sal'la-i, nine hundred twenty and eight.

9 And Jo'el the son of Zich'ri *was* their overseer: and Ju'dah the son of Se-nu'ah *was* second over the city.

10 Of the priests: Je-da'iah the son of Joi'a-rib, Ja'chin.

11 Ser-a-i'ah the son of Hil-ki'ah, the son of Me-shul'lam, the son of Za'dok, the son of Me-ra'ioth, the son of A-hi'tub, *was* the ruler of the <u>house</u> of <u>God</u>. temple - Elohim^{p.f.}

12 And their brethren that did the work of the house *were* eight hundred twenty and two: and Ad-a-i'ah the son of Jer'o-ham, the son of Pel-a-li'ah, the son of Am'zi, the son of Zech-a-ri'ah, the son of Pash'ur, the son of Mal-chi'ah,

13 And his brethren, chief of the fathers, two hundred forty and two: and A-mash'a-i the son of A-zar'e-el, the son of A-has'a-i, the son of Me-shil'le-moth, the son of Im'mer,

14 And their brethren, mighty men of valor, an hundred twenty and eight: and their overseer *was* Zab'di-el, the son of *one of* the great men.

15 Also of the Le'vites: Shem-a-i'ah the son of Ha'shub, the son of Az'ri-kam, the son of Hash-a-bi'ah, the son of Bun'ni;

16 And Shab-beth'a-i and Joz'a-bad, of the <u>chief</u> of the Le'-vites, *had* <u>the oversight</u> of the <u>outward</u> business of the <u>house</u> of <u>God</u>. leaders - were in charge - outside - temple

17 And Mat-ta-ni'ah the son of Mi'cha, the son of Zab'di, the son of A'saph, *was* the <u>principal</u> to begin the thanksgiving in prayer: and Bak-buk-i'ah the second among his brethren, and Ab'da the son of Sham-mu'a, the son of Ga'lal, the son of Jed'u-thun.   leader

18 All the Le'vites in the holy city *were* two hundred fourscore and four.

19 Moreover the <u>porters</u>, Ak'kub, Tal'mon, and their brethren that kept the gates, *were* an hundred seventy and two.   gatekeepers

20 And the residue of Is'ra-el, of the priests, *and* the Le'vites, *were* in all the cities of Ju'dah, every one in his inheritance.

21 But the Neth'i-nims dwelled in O'phel: and Zi'ha and Gis'pa *were* over the Neth'i-nims.

22 The overseer also of the Le'vites at Je-ru'sa-lem *was* Uz'zi the son of Ba'ni, the son of Hash-a-bi'ah, the son of Mat-ta-ni'ah, the son of Mi'cha. Of the sons of A'saph, the singers *were* over the <u>business</u> of the <u>house</u> of <u>God</u>.   service - temple - Elohim^{P.f.}

23 For *it was* the king's commandment concerning them, that a certain portion should be for the singers, due for every day.

24 And Peth-a-hi'ah the son of Me-shez'a-be-el, of the children of Ze'rah the son of Ju'dah, <u>*was* at the king's hand</u> in all matters concerning the people.   represented the king

25 And for the villages, with their fields, *some* of the children of Ju'dah dwelled at Kir'jath-ar'ba, and *in* the villages thereof, and at Di'bon, and *in* the villages thereof, and at Je-kab'ze-el, and *in* the villages thereof,

26 And at Jesh'u-a, and at Mol'a-dah, and at Beth-phe'let,

27 And at Ha'zar-shu'al, and at Be'er-she'ba, and *in* the villages thereof,

28 And at Zik'lag, and at Mek'o-nah, and in the villages thereof,

29 And at En-rim'mon, and at Za're-ah, and at Jar'muth,

30 Za-no'ah, A-dul'lam, and *in* their villages, at La'chish, and the fields thereof, at A-ze'kah, and *in* the villages thereof. And they dwelled from Be'er-she'ba to the valley of Hin'nom.

31 The children also of Ben'ja-min from Ge'ba *dwelled* at Mich'mash, and A-i'ja, and Beth'-el, and *in* their villages,

32 *And* at An'a-thoth, Nob, An-a-ni'ah,

33 Ha'zor, Ra'mah, Git'ta-im,

34 Ha'did, Ze-bo'im, Ne-bal'lat,

35 Lod, and O'no, the valley of craftsmen.

36 And of the Le'vites *were* divisions *in* Ju'dah, *and* in Ben'ja-min.

CHAPTER 12

NOW these *are* the priests and the Le'vites that went up with Ze-rub'ba-bel the son of She-al'ti-el, and Jesh'u-a: Ser-a-i'ah, Jer-e-mi'ah, Ez'ra,

2 Am-a-ri'ah, Mal'luch, Hat'tush,

3 Shech-a-ni'ah, Re'hum, Mer'e-moth,

4 Id'do, Gin'ne-tho, A-bi'jah,

5 Mi'a-min, Ma-a-di'ah, Bil'gah,

6 Shem-a-i'ah, and Joi'a-rib, Je-da'iah,

7 Sal'lu, A'mok, Hil-ki'ah, Je-da'iah. These *were* the chief of the priests and of their brethren in the days of Jesh'u-a.

8 Moreover the Le'vites: Jesh'u-a, Bin'nu-i, Kad'mi-el, Sher-e-bi'ah, Ju'dah, *and* Mat-ta-ni'ah, *which was* over the thanksgiving, he and his brethren.

9 Also Bak-buk-i'ah and Un'ni, their brethren, *were* opposite them in the <u>watches</u>.   service divisions

10 And Jesh'u-a fathered Joi'a-kim, Joi'a-kim also fathered E-li'a-shib, and E-li'a-shib fathered Joi'a-da,

11 And Joi'a-da fathered Jon'a-than, and Jon'a-than fathered Jad-du'a.

12 And in the days of Joi'a-kim were priests, the chief of the fathers: of Ser-a-i'ah, Mer-a-i'ah; of Jer-e-mi'ah, Han-a-ni'ah;

13 Of Ez'ra, Me-shul'lam; of Am-a-ri'ah, Je-ho-ha'nan;

14 Of Mel'i-cu, Jon'a-than; of Sheb-a-ni'ah, Jo'seph;

15 Of Ha'rim, Ad'na; of Me-ra'ioth, Hel'ka-i;

16 Of Id'do, Zech-a-ri'ah; of Gin'ne-thon, Me-shul'lam;

17 Of A-bi'jah, Zich'ri; of Mi-ni'a-min, of Mo-a-di'ah, Pil'tai;

18 Of Bil'gah, Sham-mu'a; of Shem-a-i'ah, Je-hon'a-than;

19 And of Joi'a-rib, Mat-te-na'i; of Je-da'iah, Uz'zi;

20 Of Sal'la-i, Kal'la-i; of A'mok, E'ber;

21 Of Hil-ki'ah, Hash-a-bi'ah; of Je-da'iah, Ne-than'e-el.

22 The Le'vites in the days of E-li'a-shib, Joi'a-da, and Jo-ha'nan, and Jad-du'a, *were* recorded chief of the fathers: also the priests, <u>to</u> the reign of Da-ri'us the Per'sian.   in

23 The sons of Le'vi, the chief of the fathers, *were* written in the book of the chronicles, even until the days of Jo-ha'nan the son of E-li'a-shib.

24 And the chief of the Le'vites: Hash-a-bi'ah, Sher-e-bi'ah, and Jesh'u-a the son of Kad'mi-el, with their brethren opposite them, to praise *and* to give thanks, according to the commandment of Da'vid the man of <u>God</u>, <u>ward opposite ward</u>.   Elohim^{p.f.} - division to division

25 Mat-ta-ni'ah, and Bak-buk-i'ah, O-ba-di'ah, Me-shul'lam, Tal'mon, Ak'kub, *were* <u>porters</u> keeping the <u>ward</u> at the <u>thresholds</u> of the gates.   gatekeepers - watch - storehouses

26 These *were* in the days of Joi'a-kim the son of Jesh'u-a, the son of Joz'a-dak, and in the days of Ne-he-mi'ah the governor, and of Ez'ra the priest, the scribe.

27 And at the dedication of the wall of Je-ru'sa-lem they sought the Le'vites out of all their places, to bring them to Je-ru'sa-lem, to <u>keep</u> the dedication with gladness, both with thanksgivings, and with singing, *with* cymbals, <u>psalteries</u>, and with harps.   observe - lyres

28 And the sons of the singers gathered themselves together, both out of the plain country round about Je-ru'sa-lem, and from the villages of Ne-toph'a-thi;

29 Also from the house of Gil'gal, and

out of the fields of Ge'ba and Az'ma-veth: for the singers had built them villages round about Je-ru'sa-lem.

30 And the priests and the Le'vites purified themselves, and purified the people, and the gates, and the wall.

31 Then I brought up the princes of Ju'dah upon the wall, and appointed two great *companies of them that gave* thanks, *whereof one* went on the right hand upon the wall toward the <u>dung</u> gate: _{rubbish}

32 And after them went Hosh-a-i'ah, and half of the princes of Ju'dah,

33 And Az-a-ri'ah, Ez'ra, and Me-shul'lam,

34 Ju'dah, and Ben'ja-min, and Shem-a-i'ah, and Jer-e-mi'ah,

35 And *certain* of the priests' sons with trumpets; *namely*, Zech-a-ri'ah the son of Jon'a-than, the son of Shem-a-i'ah, the son of Mat-ta-ni'ah, the son of Mi-cha'iah, the son of Zac'cur, the son of A'saph:

36 And his brethren, Shem-a-i'ah, and A-zar'a-el, Mil-a-la'i, Gil'a-lai, Ma-a'i, Ne-than'e-el, and Ju'dah, Ha-na'ni, with the musical instruments of Da'vid the man of <u>God</u>, and Ez'ra the scribe before them.   _{Elohim^{p.f.}}

37 And at the fountain gate, which was opposite them, they went up by the stairs of the city of Da'vid, at the going up of the wall, above the house of Da'vid, even to the water gate eastward.

38 And the other *company of them that gave* thanks went opposite *them*, and I after them, and the half of the people upon the wall, from beyond the tower of the furnaces even to the broad wall;

39 And from above the gate of E'phra-im, and above the old gate, and above the fish gate, and the tower of Ha-nan'e-el, and the tower of Me'ah, even to the sheep gate: and they stood still in the prison gate.

40 So stood the two *companies of them that gave* thanks in the <u>house</u> of <u>God</u>, and I, and the half of the rulers with me: _{temple - Elohim^{p.f.}}

41 And the priests; E-li'a-kim, Ma-a-se'iah, Mi-ni'a-min, Mi-cha'iah, El-i-o-e'na-i, Zech-a-ri'ah, *and* Han-a-ni'ah, with trumpets;

42 And Ma-a-se'iah, and Shem-a-i'ah, and E-le-a'zar, and Uz'zi, and Je-ho-ha'nan, and Mal-chi'jah, and E'lam, and E'zer. And the singers sang loud, with Jez-ra-hi'ah *their* overseer.

43 Also that day they offered great sacrifices, and rejoiced: for <u>God</u> had made them rejoice with great joy: the wives also and the children rejoiced: so that the joy of Je-ru'sa-lem was heard even afar off.   _{Elohim^{p.f.}}

44 And at that time were some appointed over the <u>chambers</u> for the treasures, for the offerings, for the firstfruits, and for the tithes, to gather into them out of the fields of the cities the portions of the law for the priests and Le'vites: for Ju'dah rejoiced for the priests and for the Le'vites <u>that waited</u>.   _{storerooms - who served}

45 And both the singers and the <u>porters</u> kept the <u>ward</u> of their God, and the <u>ward</u> of the purification, according to

the commandment of Da'vid, *and* of Sol'o-mon his son. gatekeepers - service
46 For in the days of Da'vid and A'saph of old *there were* chief of the singers, and songs of praise and thanksgiving to God. Elohim^p.f.
47 And all Is'ra-el in the days of Ze-rub'ba-bel, and in the days of Ne-he-mi'ah, gave the portions of the singers and the porters, every day his portion: and they sanctified *holy things* to the Le'vites; and the Le'vites sanctified *them* to the children of Aar'on. gatekeepers - consecrated

CHAPTER 13

O N that day they read in the book of Mo'ses in the audience of the people; and therein was found written, that the Am'mon-ite and the Mo'ab-ite should not come into the congregation of God for ever;
2 Because they met not the children of Is'ra-el with bread and with water, but hired Ba'laam against them, that he should curse them: however our God turned the curse into a blessing.
3 Now it came to pass, when they had heard the law, that they separated from Is'ra-el all the mixed multitude.
4 And before this, E-li'a-shib the priest, having the oversight of the chamber of the house of our God, *was* allied to To-bi'ah: temple - Elohim^p.f.
5 And he had prepared for him a great chamber, where aforetime they laid the meat offerings, the frankincense, and the vessels, and the tithes of the corn, the new wine, and the oil, which was commanded *to be given* to the Le'vites, and the singers, and the porters; and the offerings of the priests. large room - grain - gatekeepers
6 But in all this *time* was not I at Je-ru'sa-lem: for in the two and thirtieth year of Ar-tax-erx'es king of Bab'y-lon came I to the king, and after certain days obtained I leave of the king: asked
7 And I came to Je-ru'sa-lem, and understood of the evil that E-li'a-shib did for To-bi'ah, in preparing him a chamber in the courts of the house of God. room - temple - Elohim^p.f.
8 And it grieved me sore: therefore I cast forth all the household stuff of To-bi'ah out of the chamber. much
9 Then I commanded, and they cleansed the chambers: and there brought I again the vessels of the house of God, with the meat offering and the frankincense. utensils
10 And I perceived that the portions of the Le'vites had not been given *them*: for the Le'vites and the singers, that did the work, were fled every one to his field.
11 Then contended I with the rulers, and said, Why is the house of God forsaken? And I gathered them together, and set them in their place. temple - Elohim^p.f.
12 Then brought all Ju'dah the tithe of the corn and the new wine and the oil to the treasuries. grain - storehouses
13 And I made treasurers over the treasuries, Shel-e-mi'ah the priest, and Za'dok the scribe, and of the Le'vites, Pe-da'iah: and next to them *was* Ha'nan the son of Zac'cur, the son of Mat-ta-ni'ah: for they were counted faithful,

and their <u>office</u> *was* to distribute to their brethren.   job

14 Remember me, O my <u>God</u>, concerning this, and wipe not out my good deeds that I have done for the <u>house</u> of my God, and for the <u>offices</u> thereof.   Elohim^{p.f.} - temple

15 In those days saw I in Ju'dah *some* treading wine presses on the <u>sabbath</u>, and bringing in sheaves, and lading asses; as also wine, grapes, and figs, and all *manner of* burdens, which they brought into Je-ru'sa-lem on the <u>sabbath</u> day: and I testified *against them* in the day wherein they sold victuals.   rest day

16 There dwelled men of Tyre also therein, which brought fish, and all manner of <u>ware</u>, and sold on the <u>sabbath</u> to the children of Ju'dah, and in Je-ru'sa-lem.   merchandise

17 Then I <u>contended</u> with the nobles of Ju'dah, and said to them, What evil thing *is* this that you do, and profane the <u>sabbath</u> day?   rebuked - rest day

18 Did not your fathers thus, and did not our <u>God</u> bring all this evil upon us, and upon this city? yet you bring more wrath upon Is'ra-el by profaning the <u>sabbath</u>.   Elohim^{p.f.}

19 And it came to pass, that when the gates of Je-ru'sa-lem began to be dark before the sabbath, I commanded that the gates should be shut, and charged that they should not be opened till after the <u>sabbath</u>: and *some* of my servants set I at the gates, *that* there should no burden be brought in on the <u>sabbath</u> day.   rest

20 So the merchants and sellers of all kind of <u>ware</u> lodged outside Je-ru'sa-lem once or twice.   merchandise

21 Then I <u>testified against</u> them, and said to them, Why lodge you about the wall? if you do *so* again, I will lay hands on you. From that time forth came they no *more* on the <u>sabbath</u>.   warned

22 And I commanded the Le'vites that they should cleanse themselves, and *that* they should come *and* keep the gates, to <u>sanctify</u> the <u>sabbath</u> day. Remember me, O my <u>God</u>, *concerning* this also, and spare me according to the greatness of Your mercy.   consecrate - rest - Elohim^{p.f.}

23 In those days also saw I Jews *that* had married wives of Ash'dod, of Am'mon, and of Mo'ab:

24 And their children spoke half in the speech of Ash'dod, and could not speak in the Jews' language, but according to the language of each people.

25 And I contended with them, and <u>cursed</u> them, and <u>smote</u> certain of them, and plucked off their hair, and made them swear by God, *saying*, You shall not give your daughters to their sons, nor take their daughters to your sons, or for yourselves.   reviled - struck

26 Did not Sol'o-mon king of Is'ra-el sin by these things? yet among many nations was there no king like him, who was beloved of his <u>God</u>, and <u>God</u> made him king over all Is'ra-el: nevertheless even him did <u>outlandish</u> women cause to sin.   Elohim^{p.f.} - foreign

27 Shall we then <u>hearken</u> to you to

M10

806

do all this great evil, to transgress against our God in marrying strange wives? listen - Elohim^p.f. - foreign

28 And *one* of the sons of Joi'a-da, the son of E-li'a-shib the high priest, *was* son in law to San-bal'lat the Hor'o-nite: therefore I chased him from me.

29 Remember them, O my God, because they have defiled the priesthood, and the covenant of the priesthood, and of the Le'vites. Elohim^p.f. - agreement

30 Thus cleansed I them from all strangers, and appointed the wards of the priests and the Le'vites, every one in his business; foreigners - duties for - own task

31 And for the wood offering, at times appointed, and for the firstfruits. Remember me, O my God, for good.

ESTHER

OUTLINE

SURVEY

The Book of Esther graphically depicts the victorious struggles of the dispersed Jews during the time of the Persian king Ahasuerus against the nefarious plottings of a certain prime minister named Haman. Although God's name is not once mentioned in this book, His hand is continually manifested in all the circumstantial details of the story. Esther, by her beauty, supplants Vashti as queen; Mordecai, by his skill, supplants Haman as prime minister. All the characters from the king down to the obsequious slaves play their parts at just the right time. Haman is the incarnation of evil; Mordecai, the essence of goodness; Ahasuerus, though weak and pliable, has strong points also. Esther, cousin and ward of Mordecai, becomes the heroine of the story by her willingness to risk her life and position, at the behest of Mordecai, for her own people in their time of dire need.

AUTHOR

No certain evidence is obtainable regarding the author of the Book of Esther. It has been attributed to various persons (Ezra, Joiakim, Mordecai, men of the Great Synagogue). There is nothing intrinsically improbable in ascribing the book to Mordecai, a principal character and a custodian of all the relevant facts involved.

Unlike works of fiction and romance, the Book of Esther is thoroughly entrenched in history and documented by specific dates. This book, like Haggai's prophecy (1.1, 15; 2.1, 10, 20), is dated according to the reign of Ahasuerus, who is commonly equated with Xerxes I (485—465 B.C.) of ancient times. Modern excavations at Shushan (that is, Susa) have confirmed substantially the accuracy of the author, who must have had a personal knowledge of the people and events of the story.

Perhaps no other book of the Bible has been attacked as bitterly and vehemently as the Book of Esther. Because of its spirit of nationalism and vindictiveness, critics have declared it unworthy of a place in the sacred Canon. If, however, one will approach this story reverently, humbly relying upon the Spirit of God to teach him, he will find truths that will satisfy the mind and edify the soul. The more one studies this matchless story, the more he will conclude that its deeper truths must be dug out like gold nuggets.

W.B.

THE BOOK OF

ESTHER

"A Star"
A Woman Risks Her
Life for Her People

CHAPTER 1

NOW it came to pass in the days of A-has-u-e'rus, (this *is* A-has-u-e'rus which reigned, from Ind'ia even to E-thi-o'pi-a, *over* an hundred and seven and twenty provinces:)

2 *That* in those days, when the king A-has-u-e'rus sat on the throne of his kingdom, which *was* in Shu'shan the palace,

3 In the third year of his reign, he made a feast to all his princes and his servants; the power of Per'sia and Me'di-a, the nobles and princes of the provinces, *being* before him:

4 When he showed the riches of his glorious kingdom and the honor of his excellent majesty many days, *even* an hundred and fourscore days. 180

5 And when these days were expired, the king made a feast to all the people that were present in Shu'shan the palace, both to great and small, seven days, in the court of the garden of the king's palace;

6 *Where were* white, green, and blue, *hangings*, fastened with cords of fine linen and purple to silver rings and pillars of marble: the beds *were of* gold and silver, upon a pavement of red, and blue, and white, and black, marble. mosaic pavement

7 And they gave *them* drink in vessels of gold, (the vessels being diverse one from another,) and royal wine in abundance, according to the state of the king. various - liberality

8 And the drinking *was* according to the law; none did compel: for so the king had appointed to all the officers of his house, that they should do according to every man's pleasure. no compulsion

9 Also Vash'ti the queen made a feast for the women *in* the royal house which *belonged* to king A-has-u-e'rus.

10 On the seventh day, when the heart of the king was merry with wine, he commanded Me-hu'man, Biz'tha, Har-bo'na, Big'tha, and A-bag'tha, Ze'thar, and Car'cas, the seven chamberlains that served in the presence of A-has-u-e'rus the king, officials

11 To bring Vash'ti the queen before the king with the crown royal, to show the people and the princes her beauty: for she *was* fair to look on.

12 But the queen Vash'ti refused to come at the king's commandment by *his* chamberlains: therefore was the king very angry, and his anger burned in him.

13 Then the king said to the wise men, which knew the times, (for so *was* the king's manner toward all that knew law and judgment:

14 And the next to him *was* Car-she'na, She'thar, Ad'ma-tha, Tar'shish, Me'res, Mar'se-na, *and* Me-mu'can,

the seven princes of Per'sia and Me'di-a, which saw the king's face, *and* which sat the first in the kingdom;)

15 What shall we do to the queen Vash'ti according to law, because she has not performed the commandment of the king A-has-u-e'rus by the chamberlains?

16 And Me-mu'can answered before the king and the princes, Vash'ti the queen has not done wrong to the king only, but also to all the princes, and to all the people that *are* in all the provinces of the king A-has-u-e'rus.

17 For *this* deed of the queen shall come abroad to all women, so that they shall despise their husbands in their eyes, when it shall be reported, The king A-has-u-e'rus commanded Vash'ti the queen to be brought in before him, but she came not.

18 *Likewise* shall the <u>ladies</u> of Per'sia and Me'di-a say this day to all the king's princes, which have heard of the deed of the queen. Thus *shall there arise* too much contempt and wrath.   women of nobility

19 If it please the king, let there go a royal commandment from him, and let it be written among the laws of the Per'sians and the Medes, that it be not <u>altered</u>, That Vash'ti come no more before king A-has-u-e'rus; and let the king give her <u>royal</u> estate to another that is better than she.   repealed - position

20 And when the king's decree which he shall make shall be published throughout all his empire, (for it is great,) all the wives shall give to their husbands honor, both to great and small.

21 And the saying pleased the king and the princes; and the king did according to the word of Me-mu'can:

22 For he sent letters into all the king's provinces, into every province according to the writing thereof, and to every people after their language, that every man should bear rule in his own house, and that *it* should be published according to the language of every people.

CHAPTER 2

AFTER these things, when the wrath of king A-has-u-e'rus was appeased, he remembered Vash'ti, and what she had done, and what was decreed against her.   M28 | 786

2 Then said the king's servants that ministered to him, Let there be fair young virgins sought for the king:

3 And let the king appoint officers in all the provinces of his kingdom, that they may gather together all the fair young virgins to Shu'shan the palace, to the house of the women, to the custody of He'ge the king's <u>chamberlain</u>, keeper of the women; and let their things for purification be given *them*:   official

4 And let the maiden which pleases the king be queen instead of Vash'ti. And the thing pleased the king; and he did so.

5 *Now* in Shu'shan the palace there was a certain Jew, whose name *was* Mor'de-cai, the son of Ja'ir, the son of

Shim'e-i, the son of Kish, a Ben'ja-mite;

6 Who had been carried away from Je-ru'sa-lem with the captivity which had been carried away with Jec-o-ni'ah king of Ju'dah, whom Neb-u-chad-nez'zar the king of Bab'y-lon had carried away.

7 And he <u>brought up</u> Ha-das'sah, that *is*, Es'ther, his uncle's daughter: for she had neither father nor mother, and the maid *was* fair and beautiful; whom Mor'de-cai, when her father and mother were dead, took for his own daughter. reared

8 So it came to pass, when the king's commandment and his decree was heard, and when many maidens were gathered together to Shu'shan the palace, to the custody of Heg'a-i, that Es'ther was brought also to the king's house, to the custody of Heg'a-i, keeper of the women.

9 And the maiden pleased him, and she obtained kindness of him; and he speedily gave her her things for purification, with such things as belonged to her, and seven maidens, *which were* <u>meet</u> to be given her, out of the king's house: and he preferred her and her maids to the best *place* of the house of the women. fit

10 Es'ther had not <u>showed</u> her people nor her kindred: for Mor'de-cai had charged her that she should not show *it*. revealed

11 And Mor'de-cai walked every day before the court of the women's house, to know how Es'ther did, and what should become of her.

12 Now when every maid's turn was come to go in to king A-has-u-e'rus, after that she had been twelve months, according to the manner of the women, (for so were the days of their purifications accomplished, *that is*, six months with oil of myrrh, and six months with sweet odors, and with *other* things for the purifying of the women;)

13 Then thus came *every* maiden to the king; whatsoever she desired was given her to go with her out of the house of the women to the king's house.

14 In the evening she went, and on the morrow she returned into the second house of the women, to the custody of Sha-ash'gaz, the king's <u>chamberlain</u>, which kept the concubines: she came in to the king no more, except the king delighted in her, and that she were called by name. official

15 Now when the turn of Es'ther, the daughter of Ab-i-ha'il the uncle of Mor'de-cai, who had taken her for his daughter, was come to go in to the king, she required nothing but what Heg'a-i the king's chamberlain, the keeper of the women, <u>appointed</u>. And Es'ther obtained favor in the sight of all them that looked upon her. advised

16 So Es'ther was taken to king A-has-u-e'rus into his house royal in the tenth month, which *is* the month Te'beth, in the seventh year of his reign.

17 And the king loved Es'ther above all the women, and she obtained grace and <u>favor</u> in his sight more than all the

virgins; so that he set the royal crown upon her head, and made her queen instead of Vash'ti. kindness

18 Then the king made a great feast to all his princes and his servants, *even* Es'ther's feast; and he made a release to the provinces, and gave gifts, according to the state of the king. holiday for

19 And when the virgins were gathered together the second time, then Mor'de-cai sat in the king's gate.

20 Es'ther had not *yet* showed her kindred nor her people; as Mor'de-cai had charged her: for Es'ther did the commandment of Mor'de-cai, like as when she was brought up with him. revealed - commanded - as instructed

21 In those days, while Mor'de-cai sat in the king's gate, two of the king's chamberlains, Big'than and Te'resh, of those which kept the door, were angry, and sought to lay hand on the king A-has-u-e'rus. officials - guarded

22 And the thing was known to Mor'de-cai, who told *it* to Es'ther the queen; and Es'ther certified the king *thereof* in Mor'de-cai's name. plot

23 And when inquisition was made of the matter, it was found out; therefore they were both hanged on a tree: and it was written in the book of the chronicles before the king. investigation

CHAPTER 3

AFTER these things did king A-has-u-e'rus promote Ha'man the son of Ham'med'a-tha the A'gag-ite, and ad-vanced him, and set his seat above all the princes that *were* with him. established his authority

2 And all the king's servants, that *were* in the king's gate, bowed, and reverenced Ha'man: for the king had so commanded concerning him. But Mor'de-cai bowed not, nor did *him* reverence.

3 Then the king's servants, which *were* in the king's gate, said to Mor'de-cai, Why transgresses you the king's commandment?

4 Now it came to pass, when they spoke daily to him, and he hearkened not to them, that they told Ha'man, to see whether Mor'de-cai's matters would stand: for he had told them that he *was* a Jew. reason

5 And when Ha'man saw that Mor'de-cai bowed not, nor did him reverence, then was Ha'man full of wrath.

6 And he thought scorn to lay hands on Mor'de-cai alone; for they had showed him the people of Mor'de-cai: wherefore Ha'man sought to destroy all the Jews that *were* throughout the whole kingdom of A-has-u-e'rus, *even* the people of Mor'de-cai. disdained

7 In the first month, that *is*, the month Ni'san, in the twelfth year of king A-has-u-e'rus, they cast Pur, that *is*, the lot, before Ha'man from day to day, and from month to month, *to* the twelfth *month*, that *is*, the month A'dar.

8 And Ha'man said to king A-has-u-e'rus, There is a certain people scattered abroad and dispersed among the people in all the provinces of your

kingdom; and their laws *are* di-verse from all people; neither keep they the king's laws: there-fore it *is* not for the king's profit to allow them. _{different}

9 If it please the king, let it be writ-ten that they may be destroyed: and I will pay ten thousand talents of sil-ver to the hands of those that have the charge of the business, to bring *it* into the king's treasuries. _{carry out this}

10 And the king took his ring from his hand, and gave it to Ha'man the son of Ham'med'a-tha the A'gag-ite, the Jews' enemy.

11 And the king said to Ha'man, The silver *is* given to you, the people also, to do with them as it seems good to you.

12 Then were the king's scribes called on the thirteenth day of the first month, and there was written according to all that Ha'man had commanded to the king's lieutenants, and to the gover-nors that *were* over every province, and to the rulers of every people of every province according to the writ-ing thereof, and *to* every people after their language; in the name of king A-has-u-e'rus was it written, and sealed with the king's ring. _{secretaries}

13 And the letters were sent by posts into all the king's provinces, to de-stroy, to kill, and to cause to per-ish, all Jews, both young and old, little children and women, in one day, *even* upon the thirteenth *day* of the twelfth month, which *is* the month A'dar, and *to take* the spoil of them for a prey. _{couriers - possessions - plunder}

14 The copy of the writing for a commandment to be given in ev-ery province was published to all people, that they should be ready against that day. _{an edict}

15 The posts went out, being has-tened by the king's commandment, and the decree was given in Shu'shan the palace. And the king and Ha'man sat down to drink; but the city Shu'shan was perplexed. _{couriers - in confusion}

CHAPTER 4

WHEN Mor'de-cai perceived all that was done, Mor'de-cai rent his clothes, and put on sackcloth with ashes, and went out into the midst of the city, and cried with a loud and a bitter cry;

2 And came even before the king's gate: for none *might* enter into the king's gate clothed with sackcloth. _{as far as}

3 And in every province, wherever the king's commandment and his decree came, *there was* great mourning among the Jews, and fasting, and weeping, and wailing; and many lay in sackcloth and ashes.

4 So Es'ther's maids and her chamberlains came and told *it* her. Then was the queen exceedingly grieved; and she sent raiment to clothe Mor'de-cai, and to take away his sackcloth from him: but he received *it* not. _{officials - garments}

5 Then called Es'ther for Ha'tach, *one* of the king's chamberlains, whom he had appointed to attend upon her, and gave him a com-mandment to Mor'de-cai, to know what it *was*, and why it *was*.

6 So Ha'tach went forth to Mor'de-cai to the <u>street</u> of the city, which *was* before the king's gate. open square

7 And Mor'de-cai told him of all that had happened to him, and of the sum of the money that Ha'man had promised to pay to the king's treasuries for the Jews, to destroy them.

8 Also he gave him the copy of the writing of the decree that was given at Shu'shan to destroy them, to show *it* to Es'ther, and to declare *it* to her, and to <u>charge</u> her that she should go in to the king, to make supplication to him, and to make request before him for her people. order

9 And Ha'tach came and told Es'ther the words of Mor'de-cai.

10 Again Es'ther spoke to Ha'tach, and gave him <u>commandment</u> to Mor'de-cai; a reply

11 All the king's servants, and the people of the king's provinces, do know, that whosoever, whether man or woman, shall come to the king into the inner court, who is not called, *there is* one law of his to put *him* to death, except such to whom the king shall hold out the golden scepter, that he may live: but I have not been called to come in to the king these thirty days.

12 And they told to Mor'de-cai Es'ther's words.

13 Then Mor'de-cai commanded to answer Es'ther, Think not with yourself that you shall escape in the king's house, more than all the Jews.

14 For if you altogether hold your peace at this time, *then* shall there en-largement and deliverance arise to the Jews from another place; but you and your father's house shall be destroyed: and who know whether you are come to the kingdom for *such* a time as this? relief

15 Then Es'ther bade *them* return Mor'de-cai *this answer*,

16 Go, gather together all the Jews that are present in Shu'shan, and fast you for me, and neither eat nor drink three days, night or day: I also and my maidens will fast likewise; and so will I go in to the king, which *is* not according to the law: and if I perish, I perish.

17 So Mor'de-cai went his way, and did according to all that Es'ther had commanded him.

CHAPTER 5

NOW it came to pass on the third day, that Es'ther put on *her* royal *apparel*, and stood in the inner court of the king's house, opposite the king's house: and the king sat upon his royal throne in the royal house, opposite the gate of the house.

2 And it was so, when the king saw Es'ther the queen standing in the court, *that* she obtained favor in his sight: and the king held out to Es'ther the golden scepter that *was* in his hand. So Es'ther drew near, and touched the top of the scepter.

3 Then said the king to her, What will you, queen Es'ther? and what *is* your request? it shall be even given you to the half of the kingdom. MARK 6:23

4 And Es'ther answered, If *it seem*

good to the king, let the king and Ha'man come this day to the banquet that I have prepared for him.

5 Then the king said, Cause Ha'man to make haste, that he may do as Es'ther has said. So the king and Ha'man came to the banquet that Es'ther had prepared.

6 And the king said to Es'ther at the banquet of wine, What *is* your petition? and it shall be granted you: and what *is* your request? even to the half of the kingdom it shall be performed.

7 Then answered Es'ther, and said, My petition and my request *is*;

8 If I have found favor in the sight of the king, and if it please the king to grant my petition, and to perform my request, let the king and Ha'man come to the banquet that I shall prepare for them, and I will do to morrow as the king has said.

9 Then went Ha'man forth that day joyful and with a glad heart: but when Ha'man saw Mor'de-cai in the king's gate, that he stood not up, nor moved for him, he was full of indignation against Mor'de-cai.

10 Nevertheless Ha'man refrained himself: and when he came home, he sent and called for his friends, and Ze'resh his wife.

11 And Ha'man told them of the glory of his riches, and the multitude of his children, and all *the things* wherein the king had promoted him, and how he had advanced him above the princes and servants of the king.

12 Ha'man said moreover, Yea, Es'ther the queen did let no man come in with the king to the banquet that she had prepared but myself; and to morrow am I invited to her also with the king.

13 Yet all this avails me nothing, so long as I see Mor'de-cai the Jew sitting at the king's gate.

14 Then said Ze'resh his wife and all his friends to him, Let a gallows be made of fifty cubits high, and to morrow speak you to the king that Mor'de-cai may be hanged thereon: then go you in merrily with the king to the banquet. And the thing pleased Ha'man; and he caused the gallows to be made.

CHAPTER 6

ON that night could not the king sleep, and he commanded to bring the book of records of the chronicles; and they were read before the king.

2 And it was found written, that Mor'de-cai had told of Big'tha-na and Te'resh, two of the king's <u>chamberlains</u>, the keepers of the door, who sought to lay hand on the king A-has-u-e'rus. _{officials}

3 And the king said, What honor and dignity has been done to Mor'de-cai for this? Then said the king's servants that ministered to him, There is nothing done for him.

4 And the king said, Who *is* in the court? Now Ha'man was come into the outward court of the king's house, to speak to the king to hang Mor'de-cai

on the gallows that he had prepared for him.

5 And the king's servants said to him, Behold, Ha'man stands in the court. And the king said, Let him come in.

6 So Ha'man came in. And the king said to him, What shall be done to the man whom the king delights to honor? Now Ha'man thought in his heart, To whom would the king delight to do honor more than to myself?

7 And Ha'man answered the king, For the man whom the king <u>delights</u> to honor,

desires

8 Let the royal apparel be brought which the king *uses* to wear, and the horse that the king rides upon, and the crown royal which is set upon his head:

9 And let this apparel and horse be delivered to the hand of one of the king's most noble princes, that they may array the man *with* whom the king delights to honor, and <u>bring</u> him on horseback through the street of the city, and proclaim before him, Thus shall it be done to the man whom the king delights to honor.

lead

10 Then the king said to Ha'man, Make haste, *and* take the <u>apparel</u> and the horse, as you have said, and do even so to Mor'de-cai the Jew, that sits at the king's gate: let nothing fail of all that you have spoken.

robes

11 Then took Ha'man the apparel and the horse, and arrayed Mor'de-cai, and brought him on horseback through the street of the city, and proclaimed before him, Thus shall it be done to the man whom the king delights to honor.

12 And Mor'de-cai came again to the king's gate. But Ha'man hasted to his house mourning, and having his head covered.

13 And Ha'man told Ze'resh his wife and all his friends every *thing* that had befallen him. Then said his wise men and Ze'resh his wife to him, If Mor'de-cai <u>be of the seed of the Jews</u>, before whom you have begun to fall, you shall not prevail against him, but shall surely fall before him.

is of Jewish origin

14 And while they *were* yet talking with him, came the king's <u>chamberlains</u>, and hasted to bring Ha'man to the banquet that Es'ther had prepared.

officials

CHAPTER 7

SO the king and Ha'man came to banquet with Es'ther the queen.

2 And the king said again to Es'ther on the second day at the banquet of wine, What *is* your petition, queen Es'ther? and it shall be granted you: and what *is* your request? and it shall be performed, *even* to the half of the kingdom.

3 Then Es'ther the queen answered and said, If I have found favor in your sight, O king, and if it please the king, let my life be given me at my petition, and my people at my request:

4 For we are sold, I and my people, to be destroyed, to be slain, and to perish. But if we had been sold for <u>bondmen and bondwomen</u>, I had held my

tongue, although the enemy could not <u>counterveil</u> the king's damage. slaves - justify

5 Then the king A-has-u-e′rus answered and said to Es′ther the queen, Who is he, and where is he, that dare presume in his heart to do so?

6 And Es′ther said, The <u>adversary</u> and enemy *is* this wicked Ha′man. Then Ha′man was afraid before the king and the queen. foe

7 And the king arising from the banquet of wine in his wrath *went* into the palace garden: and Ha′man stood up to make request for his life to Es′ther the queen; for he saw that there was evil determined against him by the king.

8 Then the king returned out of the palace garden into the place of the banquet of wine; and Ha′man was fallen upon the bed whereon Es′ther *was*. Then said the king, Will he force the queen also <u>before</u> me in the house? As the word went out of the king's mouth, they covered Ha′man's face. with

9 And Har-bo′nah, one of the <u>chamberlains</u>, said before the king, Behold also, the gallows fifty cubits high, which Ha′man had made for Mor′de-cai, who had spoken good for the king, stands in the house of Ha′man. Then the king said, Hang him thereon. officials

10 So they hanged Ha′man on the gallows that he had prepared for Mor′de-cai. Then was the king's wrath pacified.

CHAPTER 8

ON that day did the king A-has-u-e′rus give the house of Ha′man the Jews' enemy to Es′ther the queen. And Mor′de-cai came before the king; for Es′ther had told what he *was* to her.

2 And the king took off his ring, which he had taken from Ha′man, and gave it to Mor′de-cai. And Es′ther set Mor′de-cai over the house of Ha′man.

3 And Es′ther spoke yet again before the king, and fell down at his feet, and <u>besought</u> him with tears to put away the mischief of Ha′man the A′gag-ite, and his device that he had devised against the Jews. implored

4 Then the king held out the golden scepter toward Es′ther. So Es′ther arose, and stood before the king,

5 And said, If it please the king, and if I have found favor in his sight, and the thing *seem* right before the king, and I *be* pleasing in his eyes, let it be written to reverse the letters devised by Ha′man the son of Hammed′a-tha the A′gag-ite, which he wrote to destroy the Jews which *are* in all the king's provinces:

6 For how can I endure to see the evil that shall come to my people? or how can I endure to see the destruction of my kindred?

7 Then the king A-has-u-e′rus said to Es′ther the queen and to Mor′de-cai the Jew, Behold, I have given Es′ther the house of Ha′man, and him they have hanged upon the gallows, because he laid his hand upon the Jews.

8 Write you also for the Jews, <u>as it likes you</u>, in the king's name, and seal *it* with the king's ring: for the writing

which is written in the king's name, and sealed with the king's ring, may no man reverse. as you see fit

9 Then were the king's scribes called at that time in the third month, that *is*, the month Si'van, on the three and twentieth *day* thereof; and it was written according to all that Mor'de-cai commanded to the Jews, and to the lieutenants, and the deputies and rulers of the provinces which *are* from Ind'ia to E-thi-o'pi-a, an hundred twenty and seven provinces, to every province according to the writing thereof, and to every people after their language, and to the Jews according to their writing, and according to their language.

10 And he wrote in the king A-has-u-e'rus' name, and sealed *it* with the king's ring, and sent letters by posts on horseback, *and* riders on mules, camels, *and* young dromedaries: couriers

11 Wherein the king granted the Jews which *were* in every city to gather themselves together, and to stand for their life, to destroy, to slay, and to cause to perish, all the power of the people and province that would assault them, *both* little ones and women, and *to take* the spoil of them for a prey, possessions - plunder

12 Upon one day in all the provinces of king A-has-u-e'rus, *namely*, upon the thirteenth *day* of the twelfth month, which *is* the month A'dar.

13 The copy of the writing for a commandment to be given in every province *was* published to all people, and that the Jews should be ready against that day to avenge themselves on their enemies.

14 *So* the posts that rode upon mules *and* camels went out, being hastened and pressed on by the king's commandment. And the decree was given at Shu'shan the palace. impelled

15 And Mor'de-cai went out from the presence of the king in royal apparel of blue and white, and with a great crown of gold, and with a garment of fine linen and purple: and the city of Shu'shan rejoiced and was glad.

16 The Jews had light, and gladness, and joy, and honor.

17 And in every province, and in every city, wherever the king's commandment and his decree came, the Jews had joy and gladness, a feast and a good day. And many of the people of the land became Jews; for the fear of the Jews fell upon them. dread

CHAPTER 9

NOW in the twelfth month, that *is*, the month A'dar, on the thirteenth day of the same, when the king's commandment and his decree drew near to be put in execution, in the day that the enemies of the Jews hoped to have power over them, (though it was turned to the contrary, that the Jews had rule over them that hated them;)

2 The Jews gathered themselves together in their cities throughout all the provinces of the king A-has-u-e'rus, to lay hand on such as sought their hurt: and no man could withstand them; for the fear of them fell upon all people. dread

3 And all the rulers of the provinces, and the lieutenants, and the deputies, and officers of the king, helped the Jews; because the <u>fear</u> of Mor'de-cai fell upon them.   dread
4 For Mor'de-cai *was* great in the king's house, and his fame went out throughout all the provinces: for this man Mor'de-cai <u>waxed</u> greater and greater.   became
5 Thus the Jews <u>smote</u> all their enemies with the stroke of the sword, and slaughter, and destruction, and did what they would to those that <u>hated</u> them.   struck - despised
6 And in Shu'shan the palace the Jews slew and destroyed five hundred men.
7 And Par-shan'da-tha, and Dal'phon, and As'pa-tha,
8 And Por'a-tha, and Ad-a-li'a, and A-rid'a-tha,
9 And Par-mash'ta, and A-ris'a-i, and A-rid'a-i, and Va-jez'a-tha,
10 The ten sons of Ha'man the son of Ham-med'a-tha, the enemy of the Jews, slew they; but on the <u>spoil</u> laid they not their hand.   possessions
11 On that day the number of those that were slain in Shu'shan the palace was <u>brought before</u> the king.   reported to
12 And the king said to Es'ther the queen, The Jews have slain and destroyed five hundred men in Shu'shan the palace, and the ten sons of Ha'man; what have they done in the rest of the king's provinces? now what *is* your petition? and it shall be granted you: or what *is* your request further? and it shall be done.
13 Then said Es'ther, If it please the king, let it be granted to the Jews which *are* in Shu'shan to do to morrow also according to this day's decree, and let Ha'man's ten sons be hanged upon the gallows.
14 And the king commanded it so to be done: and the decree was given at Shu'shan; and they hanged Ha'man's ten sons.
15 For the Jews that *were* in Shu'shan gathered themselves together on the fourteenth day also of the month A'dar, and slew three hundred men at Shu'shan; but on the <u>prey</u> they laid not their hand.   plunder
16 But the other Jews that *were* in the king's provinces gathered themselves together, and stood for their lives, and had rest from their enemies, and slew of their foes seventy and five thousand, but they laid not their hands on the <u>prey</u>,
17 On the thirteenth day of the month A'dar; and on the fourteenth day of the same rested they, and made it a day of feasting and gladness.
18 But the Jews that *were* at Shu'shan assembled together on the thirteenth *day* thereof; and on the fourteenth thereof; and on the fifteenth *day* of the same they rested, and made it a day of feasting and gladness.
19 Therefore the Jews of the villages, that dwelled in the unwalled towns, made the fourteenth day of the month A'dar *a day of* gladness and feasting, and a

good day, and of sending <u>por-tions</u> one to another. presents

20 And Mor'de-cai wrote these things, and sent letters to all the Jews that *were* in all the provinces of the king A-has-u-e'rus, *both* near and far,

21 To stablish *this* among them, that they should keep the fourteenth day of the month A'dar, and the fifteenth day of the same, yearly,

22 As the days wherein the Jews rested from their enemies, and the month which was turned to them from sorrow to joy, and from mourning into a good day: that they should make them days of feasting and joy, and of sending <u>portions</u> one to another, and gifts to the poor.

23 And the Jews undertook to do as they had begun, and as Mor'de-cai had written to them;

24 Because Ha'man the son of Ham-med'a-tha, the A'gag-ite, the enemy of all the Jews, had <u>devised</u> against the Jews to destroy them, and had cast Pur, that *is*, the lot, to <u>consume</u> them, and to destroy them; plotted - disturb

25 But when *Es'ther* came before the king, he commanded by letters that his wicked <u>device</u>, which he de-vised against the Jews, should re-turn upon his own head, and that he and his sons should be hanged on the gallows. i.e., the plot - scheme

26 Wherefore they called these days Pu'rim after the name of <u>Pur</u>. Therefore for all the words of this letter, and *of that* which they had seen concerning this matter, and which had come to them, Lot

27 The Jews <u>ordained</u>, and took upon them, and upon their <u>seed</u>, and upon all such as joined themselves to them, so as it should not fail, that they would keep these two days ac-cording to their writing, and accord-ing to their *appointed* time every year; established - descendants

28 And *that* these days *should be* re-membered and kept throughout every generation, every family, every prov-ince, and every city; and *that* these days of Pu'rim should not fail from among the Jews, nor the <u>memorial</u> of them perish from their <u>seed</u>. memory

29 Then Es'ther the queen, the daugh-ter of Ab-i-ha'il, and Mor'de-cai the Jew, wrote with all authority, to con-firm this second letter of Pu'rim.

30 And he sent the letters to all the Jews, to the hundred twenty and seven prov-inces of the kingdom of A-has-u-e'rus, *with* words of peace and truth,

31 To confirm these days of Pu'rim in their times *appointed*, according as Mor'de-cai the Jew and Es'ther the queen had enjoined them, and as they had decreed for themselves and for their <u>seed</u>, the matters of the fastings and their <u>cry</u>. lamentations

32 And the decree of Es'ther con-firmed these matters of Pu'rim; and it was written in the book.

CHAPTER 10

AND the king A-has-u-e'rus laid a tribute upon the land, and *upon* the isles of the sea.

2 And all the acts of his power and of his might, and the declaration of the

greatness of Mor'de-cai, whereto the king <u>advanced</u> him, *are* they not written in the book of the chronicles of the kings of Me'di-a and Per'sia?

3 For Mor'de-cai the Jew *was* next to king A-has-u-e'rus, and great among the Jews, and accepted of the multitude of his brethren, seeking the <u>wealth</u> of his people, and speaking peace to all his <u>seed</u>.

raised

good - descendants

JOB

OUTLINE

SURVEY

The book's clearly developed pattern—prologue, speeches, and epilogue, plus the cycles within the speeches themselves—shows that this is a theological interpretation of certain events in the life of a man named Job. From beginning to end the author is intent on answering one basic question: What is the meaning of faith?

A tribal chieftain of outstanding piety and integrity, Job is blessed by God with such wordly prosperity that he is "the greatest of all the men of the East." (1.3). Suddenly Job suffers a complete reversal of fortune. The victim of a series of great calamities, he is deprived of all his possessions and his children (1.13-19). His body is covered by a repulsive disease (2.7). Three friends, ostensibly coming to comfort Job, insist that his suffering is a punishment for sin, and that therefore his only recourse is to repent. But Job vehemently rejects this solution, affirming his uprightness and his consequent inability to understand his plight. Another friend, Elihu, suggests that Job is undergoing a discipline of love sent by God to deter him from further sin. This interpretation also is rejected by Job. Finally God answers Job's repeated request for a direct explanation of his sufferings, not by a justification of His actions, nor by an immediate solution, but by His presentation of Himself in wisdom and power. This is enough for Job; he sees that, God being what He is, there must be a solution, and in this he rests his faith.

Although the theme of suffering and its cause is dominant throughout the book, this serves a wider purpose in the mind of the author: to show that the certainty of faith lies not in outward circumstances, nor in speculative explanations, but in the encounter of faith in an omniscient and omnipotent God.

AUTHOR

The book does not give any certain indication of its authorship or time of composition. Although many today claim Exilic or post-Exilic authorship (sixth to third century B.C.), traditionally the date has been placed in patriarchal times (sixteenth century B.C.), or in Solomonic days (tenth century B.C.).

R.B.L.

THE BOOK OF

JOB

CHAPTER 1

THERE was a man in the land of Uz, whose name *was* Job; and that man was <u>perfect</u> and upright, and one that <u>feared</u> <u>God</u>, and <u>eschewed</u> evil.

blameless - revered - Elohim^{p.f.} - shunned

2 And there were born to him seven sons and three daughters.
3 His <u>substance</u> also was seven thousand sheep, and three thousand camels, and five hundred yoke of oxen, and five hundred she asses, and a very great household; so that this man was the greatest of all the men of the east.   possessions
4 And his sons went and feasted *in their* houses, every one his day; and sent and called for their three sisters to eat and to drink with them.
5 And it was so, when the days of *their* feasting were gone about, that Job sent and <u>sanctified</u> them, and rose up early in the morning, and offered burned offerings *according* to the number of them all: for Job said, It may be that my sons have sinned, and cursed <u>God</u> in their hearts. Thus did Job continually.   consecrated - Elohim^{p.f.}
6 Now there was a day when the sons of God came to present themselves before the LORD, and Sa'tan came also among them.
7 And the LORD said to Sa'tan, Where come you? Then Sa'tan an-swered the LORD, and said, From going to and fro in the earth, and from walking up and down in it.
8 And the LORD said to Sa'tan, Have you considered My servant Job, that *there is* none like him in the earth, a <u>perfect</u> and an upright man, one that <u>fears</u> God, and <u>eschewed</u> evil?   blameless - reveres - shuns
9 Then Sa'tan answered the LORD, and said, Does Job <u>fear</u> <u>God</u> for nothing?   revere - Elohim^{p.f}
10 Have not You made an <u>hedge</u> about him, and about his house, and about all that he has on every side? You have blessed the work of his hands, and his <u>substance</u> is increased in the land.   barrier - possessions
11 But put forth Your hand now, and touch all that he has, and he will curse You to Your face.
12 And the LORD said to Sa'tan, Behold, all that he has *is* in your power; only upon himself put not forth your hand. So Sa'tan went forth from the presence of the LORD.
13 And there was a day when his sons and his daughters *were* eating and drinking wine in their eldest brother's house:
14 And there came a messenger to Job, and said, The oxen were plowing, and the asses feeding beside them:
15 And the Sa-be'ans fell *upon them*,

and took them away; yea, they have slain the servants with the edge of the sword; and I only am escaped alone to tell you.

16 While he *was* yet speaking, there came also another, and said, The fire of God is fallen from heaven, and has burned up the sheep, and the servants, and consumed them; and I only am escaped alone to tell you. burned them up

17 While he *was* yet speaking, there came also another, and said, The Chal-de'ans made out three bands, and fell upon the camels, and have carried them away, yea, and slain the servants with the edge of the sword; and I only am escaped alone to tell you. made a raid

18 While he *was* yet speaking, there came also another, and said, Your sons and your daughters *were* eating and drinking wine in their eldest brother's house:

19 And, behold, there came a great wind from the wilderness, and smote the four corners of the house, and it fell upon the young men, and they are dead; and I only am escaped alone to tell you. struck - collapsed

20 Then Job arose, and rent his mantle, and shaved his head, and fell down upon the ground, and worshiped, tore - robe

21 And said, Naked came I out of my mother's womb, and naked shall I return there: the LORD gave, and the LORD has taken away; blessed be the name of the LORD.

22 In all this Job sinned not, nor charged God foolishly. JAMES 5:11 blamed

CHAPTER 2

AGAIN there was a day when the sons of God came to present themselves before the LORD, and Sa'tan came also among them to present himself before the LORD. Elohim p.f.

2 And the LORD said to Sa'tan, From where come you? And Sa'tan answered the LORD, and said, From going to and fro in the earth, and from walking up and down in it.

3 And the LORD said to Sa'tan, Have you considered My servant Job, that *there is* none like him in the earth, a perfect and an upright man, one that fears God, and eschews evil? and still he holds fast his integrity, although you moved Me against him, to destroy him without cause. blameless - reveres - shuns

4 And Sa'tan answered the LORD, and said, Skin for skin, yea, all that a man has will he give for his life.

5 But put forth Your hand now, and touch his bone and his flesh, and he will curse you to Your face.

6 And the LORD said to Sa'tan, Behold, he *is* in your hand; but save his life. 2 COR. 12:7

7 So went Sa'tan forth from the presence of the LORD, and smote Job with sore boils from the sole of his foot to his crown. HEB. 5:5

8 And he took him a potsherd to scrape himself with; and he sat down among the ashes. piece of broken pottery

9 Then said his wife to him, Do you still retain your integrity? curse God, and die. renounce

10 But he said to her, You speak as one of the foolish women speak. What? shall we receive good at the hand of God, and shall we not receive evil? In all this did not Job sin with his lips.

11 Now when Job's three friends heard of all this evil that was come upon him, they came every one from his own place; El'i-phaz the Te'man-ite, and Bil'dad the Shu'hite, and Zo'phar the Na'a-math-ite: for they had made an appointment together to come to mourn with him and to comfort him.

12 And when they lifted up their eyes afar off, and <u>knew</u> him not, they lifted up their voice, and wept; and they <u>rent</u> every one his mantle, and sprinkled dust upon their heads toward heaven.   recognized - tore

13 So they sat down with him upon the ground seven days and seven nights, and none spoke a word to him: for they saw that *his* grief was very great.

CHAPTER 3

A FTER this opened Job his mouth, and cursed his day.

2 And Job spoke, and said,

3 Let the day perish wherein I was born, and the night *in which* it was said, There is a man child conceived.

4 Let that day be darkness; let not <u>God</u> regard it from above, neither let the light shine upon it.   Eloah s.f.

5 Let darkness and the shadow of death stain it; let a cloud dwell upon it; let the blackness of the day terrify it.

6 *As for* that night, let darkness seize upon it; let it not be joined to the days of the year, let it not come into the number of the months.

7 Lo, let that night be <u>solitary</u>, let no joyful voice come therein.   barren

8 Let them curse it that curse the day, who are ready to raise up their mourning.

9 Let the stars of the twilight thereof be dark; let it look for light, but *have* none; neither let it see the dawning of the day:

10 Because it shut not up the doors of my *mother's* womb, nor hid sorrow from my eyes.

11 Why died I not from the womb? *why* did I *not* <u>give up the ghost</u> when I came out of the belly?   expire

12 Why did the knees prevent me? or why the breasts that I should suck?

13 For now should I have lain still and been quiet, I should have slept: then had I been at rest,

14 With kings and counselors of the earth, which built desolate places for themselves;

15 Or with princes that had gold, who filled their houses with silver:

16 Or as an hidden <u>untimely birth</u> I had not been; as infants *which* never saw light.   stillborn

17 There the wicked cease *from* troubling; and there the weary be at rest.

18 *There* the prisoners rest together; they hear not the voice of the oppressor.

19 The small and great are there; and the servant *is* free from his master.

20 Wherefore is light given to him

that is in misery, and life to the bitter *in* soul;

21 Which long for death, but it *come* not; and dig for it more than for <u>hid</u> treasures; hidden

22 Which rejoice exceedingly, *and* are glad, when they can find the grave?

23 *Why is light given* to a man whose way is hid, and whom <u>God</u> has hedged in? Eloah^{s.f.}

24 For my sighing comes before I eat, and my <u>roarings</u> are poured out like the waters. groans

25 For the thing which I greatly feared is come upon me, and that which I was afraid of is come to me.

26 I was not in safety, neither had I rest, neither was I quiet; yet trouble came.

CHAPTER 4

THEN El'i-phaz the Te'man-ite answered and said,

2 *If* we <u>assay</u> to <u>commune</u> with you, will you be grieved? but who can withhold himself from speaking? venture - talk

3 Behold, you have instructed many, and you have strengthened the weak hands.

4 Your words have <u>upholden</u> him that was falling, and you have strengthened the feeble knees. helped

5 But now it is come upon you, and you faint; it touches you, and you are troubled.

6 *Is* not *this* your <u>fear</u>, your confidence, your hope, and the uprightness of your ways? reverence

7 Remember, I pray you, who *ever* perished, being innocent? or where were thc righteous cut off?

8 Even as I have seen, they that plow iniquity, and sow wickedness, reap the same.

9 By the blast of God they perish, and by the <u>breath of His nostrils</u> are they consumed. blast of His anger

10 The roaring of the lion, and the voice of the fierce lion, and the teeth of the young lions, are broken.

11 The old lion perishes for lack of prey, and the stout lion's whelps are scattered abroad.

12 Now a thing was secretly brought to me, and my ear received a little thereof.

13 In thoughts from the visions of the night, when deep sleep falls on men,

14 <u>Fear</u> came upon me, and trembling, which made all my bones to shake. dread

15 Then a spirit passed before my face; the hair of my flesh stood up:

16 It stood still, but I could not discern the form thereof: an image *was* before my eyes, *there was* silence, and I heard a <u>voice</u>, *saying*, hushed voice

17 Shall mortal man be more just than God? shall a man be more pure than his maker?

18 Behold, He put no trust in His servants; and His <u>angels</u> He charged with folly: messengers

19 How much less *in* them that dwell in houses of clay, whose foundation *is* in the dust, *which* are crushed before the moth?

20 They are destroyed from morning

to evening: they perish for ever without any regarding *it*.

21 Does not their excellency *which is* in them go away? they die, even without wisdom.

CHAPTER 5

CALL now, if there be any that will answer you; and to which of the saints will you turn?

2 For wrath kills the foolish man, and envy slays the silly one.

3 I have seen the foolish taking root: but suddenly I cursed his habitation.

4 His children are far from safety, and they are crushed in the gate, neither *is there* any to deliver *them*.

5 Whose harvest the hungry eats up, and takes it even out of the thorns, and the robber swallows up their underline{substance}.   wealth

6 Although affliction comes not forth of the dust, neither does trouble spring out of the ground;

7 Yet man is born to trouble, as the sparks fly upward.

8 I would seek to God, and to God would I commit my cause: El^{s.f.} - Elohim^{p.f.}

9 Which does great things and unsearchable; marvellous things without number:

10 Who gives rain upon the earth, and sends waters upon the fields:

11 To set up on high those that be low; that those which mourn may be exalted to safety.

12 He disappoints the underline{devices} of the crafty, so that their hands cannot perform *their* underline{enterprise}.   plotting - intentions

13 He takes the wise in their own craftiness: and the counsel of the underline{froward} is underline{carried headlong}.   1 COR. 3:19 cunning - quickly thwarted

14 They meet with darkness in the daytime, and grope in the noonday as in the night.

15 But He saves the poor from the sword, from their mouth, and from the hand of the mighty.

16 So the poor has hope, and iniquity stops her mouth.

17 Behold, happy *is* the man whom God corrects: therefore despise not you the chastening of the underline{Almighty}:   Eloah^{s.f.} - Shaddai

18 For He underline{makes sore}, and binds up: He wounds, and His hands make whole.   inflicts pain

19 He shall deliver you in six troubles: yea, in seven there shall no evil touch you.

20 In famine He shall redeem you from death: and in war from the power of the sword.

21 You shall be hid from the scourge of the tongue: neither shall you be afraid of destruction when it comes.

22 At destruction and famine you shall laugh: neither shall you be afraid of the beasts of the earth.

23 For you shall be in league with the stones of the field: and the beasts of the field shall be at peace with you.

24 And you shall know that your tabernacle *shall be* in peace; and you shall visit your habitation, and shall not sin.

25 You shall know also that your underline{seed}

shall be great, and your offspring as the grass of the earth. _{descendants}

26 You shall come to *your* grave in a full age, like as a <u>shock of corn</u> comes in in his season. _{stack of grain}

27 Lo this, we have searched it, so it *is*; hear it, and know you *it* for your good.

CHAPTER 6

BUT Job answered and said,
2 Oh that my grief were <u>throughly</u> weighed, and my calamity laid in the balances together! _{actually}

3 For now it would be heavier than the sand of the sea: therefore my words are <u>swallowed up</u>. _{rash}

4 For the arrows of the <u>Almighty</u> *are* within me, the poison whereof drinks up my spirit: the terrors of <u>God</u> do set themselves in array against me. _{Shaddai - Eloah s.f.}

5 Does the wild ass bray when he has grass? or lows the ox over his fodder?

6 Can that which is <u>unsavory</u> be eaten without salt? or is there *any* taste in the white of an egg? _{tasteless}

7 The things *that* my soul refused to touch *are* as my sorrowful meat.

8 Oh that I might have my request; and that <u>God</u> would grant *me* the thing that I long for! _{Eloah s.f.}

9 Even that it would please <u>God</u> to destroy me; that He would let loose His hand, and cut me off!

10 Then should I yet have comfort; yea, I would harden myself in sorrow: let Him not spare; for I have not concealed the words of the Holy One.

11 What *is* my strength, that I should hope? and what *is* my end, that I should prolong my life?

12 *Is* my strength the strength of stones? or *is* my flesh of <u>brass</u>? _{bronze}

13 *Is* not my help in me? and is wisdom driven quite from me?

14 To him that is afflicted pity *should be showed* from his friend; but he forsakes the <u>fear</u> of the Almighty. _{reverence}

15 My brethren have dealt deceitfully as a brook, *and* as the stream of brooks they pass away;

16 Which are blackish by reason of the ice, *and* wherein the snow is hid:

17 What time they <u>wax</u> warm, they vanish: when it is hot, they are consumed out of their place. _{grow}

18 The paths of their way are turned aside; they go to nothing, and perish.

19 The troops of Te'ma looked, the companies of She'ba waited for them.

20 They were <u>confounded</u> because they had hoped; they came there, and were ashamed. _{distressed}

21 For now you are nothing; you see *my* casting down, and are afraid.

22 Did I say, Bring to me? or, Give a reward for me of your substance?

23 Or, Deliver me from the enemy's hand? or, Redeem me from the hand of the mighty?

24 Teach me, and I will hold my tongue: and cause me to understand wherein I have erred.

25 How forcible are right words! but what does your arguing <u>reprove</u>? _{prove}

26 Do you imagine to <u>reprove</u> words,

and the speeches of one that is desperate, *which are* as wind?   correct my

27 Yea, you overwhelm the fatherless, and you dig *a pit* for your friend.

28 Now therefore be content, look upon me; for *it is* evident to you if I lie.

29 <u>Return</u>, I pray you, let it not be <u>iniquity</u>; yea, return again, my righteousness *is* in it.   Relent - unjust

30 Is there iniquity in my tongue? cannot my taste discern perverse things?

CHAPTER 7

M — | 826 | **I**S *there* not an appointed time to man upon earth? *are not* his days also like the days of an <u>hireling</u>?   temporary worker

2 As a servant <u>earnestly desires the shadow</u>, and as an <u>hireling</u> looks for *the reward* of his work: longs for shade - worker

3 So am I made to possess months of vanity, and wearisome nights are appointed to me.

4 When I lie down, I say, When shall I arise, and the night be gone? and I am full of tossings to and fro to the dawning of the day.

5 My flesh is clothed with worms and clods of dust; my skin is broken, and become loathsome.

6 My days are swifter than a weaver's shuttle, and are spent without hope.

7 O remember that my life *is* wind: my eye shall no more see good.

8 The eye of him that has seen me shall see me no *more*: your eyes *are* upon me, and I *am* <u>not</u>.   no more

9 *As* the cloud is consumed and vanishes away: so he that goes down to the grave shall come up no *more*.

10 He shall return no more to his house, neither shall his place know him any more.

11 Therefore I will not refrain my mouth; I will speak in the anguish of my spirit; I will complain in the bitterness of my soul.

12 *Am* I a sea, or a <u>whale</u>, that You set a <u>watch</u> over me?   sea monster - guard

13 When I say, My bed shall comfort me, my couch shall ease my complaint;

14 Then You scare me with dreams, and terrifiy me through visions:

15 So that <u>my soul</u> chooses strangling, *and* death rather than my life.   M06 - 830

16 I loathe *it*; I would not live always: let me alone; for my days *are* vanity.

17 What *is* man, that You should magnify him? and that You should set Your heart upon him?   M05 -- 808

18 And *that* You should <u>visit</u> him every morning, *and* <u>try</u> him every moment?   examine - test

19 How long will You not depart from me, nor let me alone till I swallow down my spittle?

20 I have sinned; what shall I do to You, O You preserver of men? why have You set me as a mark against You, so that I am a burden to myself?

21 And why do You not pardon my transgression, and take away my iniquity? for now shall I <u>sleep in the dust</u>; and You shall seek me in the morning, but I *shall* not *be*.   be dead in the grave

CHAPTER 8

THEN answered Bil'dad the Shu'hite, and said,

2 How long will you speak these *things*? and *how long shall* the words of your mouth *be like* a strong wind?

3 Does <u>God</u> pervert judgment? or does the <u>Almighty</u> <u>pervert</u> justice?

El^{s.f.} - Shaddai - twist

4 If your children have sinned against Him, and He have cast them away for their transgression;

5 If you would seek to God betimes, and make your supplication to the Almighty;

6 If you *were* pure and upright; surely now He would <u>awake</u> for you, and make the habitation of your righteousness prosperous. rouse Himself

7 Though your beginning was small, yet your latter end should greatly increase.

8 For <u>inquire</u>, I pray you, of the former age, and prepare yourself to the search of their fathers: ask

9 (For we *are but of* yesterday, and know nothing, because our days upon earth *are* a shadow:)

10 Shall not they teach you, *and* tell you, and utter words out of their heart?

11 Can the <u>rush</u> grow up without mire? can the <u>flag</u> grow without water? papyrus - rushes

12 While it *is* yet in his greenness, *and* not cut down, it withers before any *other* herb.

13 So *are* the paths of all that forget God; and the hypocrite's hope shall perish:

14 Whose hope shall be cut off, and whose trust *shall be* a spider's web.

15 He shall lean upon his house, but it shall not stand: he shall hold it fast, but it shall not endure.

16 He *is* green before the sun, and his branch shoots forth in his garden.

17 His roots are wrapped about the heap, *and* sees the place of stones.

18 If he destroy him from his place, then *it* shall deny him, *saying*, I have not seen you.

19 Behold, this *is* the joy of His way, and out of the earth shall others grow.

20 Behold, God will not <u>cast away</u> a <u>perfect</u> *man*, neither will He help the evil doers: reject - blameless

21 Till He fill your mouth with laughing, and your lips with rejoicing.

22 They that <u>hate</u> you shall be clothed with shame; and the dwelling place of the wicked shall <u>come to nothing</u>. despise - not be

CHAPTER 9

THEN Job answered and said,

2 I know *it is* so of a truth: but how should man be just with God?

3 If he will <u>contend</u> with Him, he cannot answer Him one of a thousand. dispute

4 *He is* wise in heart, and mighty in strength: who has hardened *himself* against Him, and has prospered?

5 Which removes the mountains, and they know not: which overturns them in His anger.

6 Which shakes the earth out of her place, and the pillars thereof tremble.

7 Which commands the sun, and it rises not; and seals up the stars.

8 Which alone spreads out the heavens, and treads upon the waves of the sea.

9 Which makes Arc-tu'rus, O-ri'on, and Ple'ia-des, and the underline(chambers) of the south.   constellations

10 Which does great things past finding out; yea, and wonders without number.

11 Lo, He goes by me, and I see *Him* not: He passes on also, but I perceive Him not.

12 Behold, He takes away, who can hinder Him? who will say to Him, What do You?

13 *If* God will not withdraw His anger, the proud helpers do stoop under Him.   Eloah^s.f.

14 How much less shall I answer Him, *and* choose out my words *to reason* with Him?

15 Whom, though I were righteous, *yet* would I not answer, *but* I would make supplication to my judge.

16 If I had called, and He had answered me; *yet* would I not believe that He had hearkened to my voice.

17 For He breaks me with a tempest, and multiplies my wounds without cause.

18 He will not allow me to take my breath, but fills me with bitterness.

19 If *I speak* of strength, lo, *He is* strong: and if of underline(judgment), who shall set me a time *to plead*?   justice

20 If I justify myself, my own mouth shall condemn me: *if I say,* I *am* perfect, it shall also prove me underline(perverse).   guilty

21 *Though* I *were* perfect, *yet* would I not know my soul: I would despise my life.

22 This *is* one *thing*, therefore I said *it*, He destroys the perfect and the wicked.

23 If the scourge slay suddenly, He will laugh at the trial of the innocent.

24 The earth is given into the hand of the wicked: He covers the faces of the judges thereof; if not, where, *and* who *is* He?

25 Now my days are swifter than a underline(post): they flee away, they see no good.   runner

26 They are passed away as the swift ships: as the eagle *that* hurried to the prey.

27 If I say, I will forget my complaint, I will leave off my underline(heaviness), and comfort *myself*:   sad countenance

28 I am afraid of all my sorrows, I know that You will not hold me innocent.

29 *If* I be wicked, why then labor I in vain?

30 If I wash myself with snow water, and make my hands never so clean;

31 Yet shall You plunge me in the ditch, and my own clothes shall abhor me.

32 For *He is* not a man, as I *am, that* I should answer Him, *and* we should come together in underline(judgment).   court

33 Neither is there any underline(daysman) between us, *that* might lay his hand upon us both.   arbitrator

34 Let Him take His <u>rod</u> away from me, and let not His fear terrify me: _{chastisement}
35 *Then* would I speak, and not <u>fear</u> Him; but *it is* not so with me.   _{reverence}

CHAPTER 10

MY soul is weary of my life; I will leave my complaint upon myself; I will speak in the bitterness of my soul.
2 I will say to <u>God</u>, Do not condemn me; show me wherefore You contend with me.   _{Eloah s.f.}
3 *Is it* good to You that You should oppress, that You should despise the work of Your hands, and shine upon the counsel of the wicked?
4 Have You eyes of flesh? or see You as man sees?
5 *Are* Your days as the days of man? *are* Your years as man's days,
6 That You enquire after my iniquity, and search after my sin?
7 You know that I am not wicked; and *there is* none that can deliver out of Your hand.
8 Your hands <u>have made</u> me and fashioned me together round about; yet You do destroy me.   _{shaped}
9 Remember, I <u>beseech</u> You, that You have made me as the clay; and will You bring me into dust again?   _{beg}
10 Have You not poured me out as milk, and curdled me like cheese?
11 You have clothed me with skin and flesh, and have <u>fenced</u> me with bones and sinews.   _{knit}
12 You have granted me life and favor, and Your visitation has preserved my spirit.

13 And these *things* have You hid in Your heart: I know that this *is* with You.
14 If I sin, then You mark me, and You will not acquit me from my iniquity.
15 If I be wicked, woe to me; and *if* I be righteous, *yet* will I not lift up my head. *I am* full of confusion; therefore see You my affliction;
16 For it increases. You hunt me as a fierce lion: and again You show Yourself marvellous upon me.
17 You renew Your witnesses against me, and increase Your indignation upon me; changes and war *are* against me.
18 Wherefore then have you brought me forth out of the womb? Oh that I had given up the ghost, and no eye had seen me!
19 I should have been as though I had not been; I should have been carried from the womb to the grave.
20 *Are* not my days few? cease *then, and* let me alone, that I may take comfort a little,
21 Before I go *where* I shall not return, *even* to the land of darkness and the shadow of death;
22 A land of darkness, as darkness *itself; and* of the shadow of death, without any order, and *where* the light *is* as darkness.

CHAPTER 11

THEN answered Zo'phar the Na'a-math-ite, and said,
2 Should not the multitude of words

be answered? and should a man full of talk be justified?

3 Should your lies make men <u>hold their peace</u>? and when you mock, shall no man make you ashamed? _{silent}

4 For you have said, my <u>doctrine</u> *is* pure, and I am clean in your eyes. _{teaching}

5 But oh that <u>God</u> would speak, and open His lips against you; _{Eloah^{s.f.}}

6 And that He would show you the secrets of wisdom, that *they are* double to that which is! Know therefore that God <u>exacts</u> of you *less* than your iniquity *deserves*. _{demands}

7 Can you by searching find out <u>God</u>? can you find out the <u>Almighty</u> to perfection? _{Eloah^{s.f.} - Shaddai}

8 *It is* as high as heaven; what can you do? deeper than hell; what can you know?

9 The measure thereof *is* longer than the earth, and broader than the sea.

10 If He cut off, and shut up, or gather together, then who can hinder Him?

11 For He knows vain men: He sees wickedness also; will He not then consider *it*?

12 For vain man would be wise, though man be born *like* a wild ass's colt.

13 If you prepare your heart, and stretch out your hands toward Him;

14 If iniquity *be* in your hand, put it far away, and let not wickedness dwell in your <u>tabernacles</u>. _{tents}

15 For then shall you lift up your face without spot; yea, you shall be steadfast, and shall not <u>fear</u>: _{be afraid}

16 Because you shall forget *your* misery, *and* remember *it* as waters *that* pass away:

17 And *your* <u>age</u> shall be clearer than the noonday; you shall shine forth, you shall be as the morning. _{life}

18 And you shall be secure, because there is hope; yea, you shall dig *about you, and* you shall take your rest in safety.

19 Also you shall lie down, and none shall make *you* afraid; yea, many shall <u>make suit to you</u>. _{seek you out}

20 But the eyes of the wicked shall fail, and they shall not escape, and their hope *shall be as* the giving up of the ghost.

CHAPTER 12

AND Job answered and said,
2 No doubt but you *are* the people, and wisdom shall die with you.

3 But I have understanding as well as you; I *am* not inferior to you: yea, who knows not such things as these?

4 I am *as* one mocked of his neighbor, who calls upon God, and He answers him: the just upright *man is* laughed to scorn.

5 He that is ready to slip with *his* feet *is as* a lamp despised in the thought of him that is at ease.

6 The <u>tabernacles</u> of robbers prosper, and they that provoke <u>God</u> are secure; into whose hand <u>God</u> brings *abundantly*. _{tents - El^{s.f.} - Eloah^{s.f.}}

7 But ask now the beasts, and they shall teach you; and the fowls of the air, and they shall tell you:

8 Or speak to the earth, and it shall teach you: and the fishes of the sea shall declare to you.
9 Who knows not in all these that the hand of the LORD has wrought this?
10 In whose hand *is* the soul of every living thing, and the breath of all mankind.
11 Does not the ear <u>try</u> words? and the mouth taste His meat? _{test}
12 With the ancient *is* wisdom; and in <u>length of days</u> understanding._{long life}
13 With Him *is* wisdom and strength, He has counsel and understanding.
14 Behold, He breaks down, and it cannot be built again: He shuts up a man, and there can be no opening.
15 Behold, He withholds the waters, and they dry up: also He sends them out, and they overturn the earth.
16 With Him *is* strength and wisdom: the deceived and the deceiver *are* His.
17 He leads counselors away <u>spoiled</u>, and makes the judges fools. _{stripped}
18 He loosens the bond of kings, and girds their loins with a girdle.
19 He leads princes away <u>spoiled</u>, and overthrows the mighty.
20 He removes away the speech of the trusty, and takes away the understanding of the aged.
21 He pours contempt upon princes, and weakens the strength of the mighty.
22 He discovers deep things out of darkness, and brings out to light the shadow of death.
23 He increases the nations, and destroys them: He enlarges the nations, and straitens them *again*.
24 He takes away the heart of the chief of the people of the earth, and causes them to wander in a wilderness *where there is* no way.
25 They grope in the dark without light, and He makes them to stagger like *a* drunken *man*.

CHAPTER 13

L O, my eye has seen all *this*, my ear has heard and understood it.
2 What you know, *the same* do I know also: I *am* not inferior to you.
3 Surely I would speak to the <u>Almighty</u>, and I desire to reason with <u>God</u>. _{Shaddai - El^{s.f.}}
4 But you *are* forgers of lies, you *are* all physicians of no value.
5 O that you would altogether hold your peace! and it should be your wisdom.
6 Hear now my reasoning, and hearken to the pleadings of my lips.
7 Will you speak <u>wickedly</u> for God? and talk deceitfully for Him? _{unjustly}
8 Will you accept His person? will you contend for God?
9 Is it good that He should search you out? or as one man mocks another, do you *so* mock Him?
10 He will surely <u>reprove</u> you, if you do secretly accept persons. _{rebuke}
11 Shall not His excellency make you afraid? and His dread fall upon you?
12 Your remembrances *are* like to ashes, your bodies to bodies of clay.

13 Hold your peace, let me alone, that I may speak, and let come on me what *will*.

14 Wherefore do I take my flesh in my teeth, and put my life in my hand?

15 Though He slay me, yet will I trust in Him: but I will maintain my own ways before Him.

16 He also *shall be* my <u>salvation</u>: for an hypocrite shall not come before Him.   i.e., Heb. Jeshua

17 Hear diligently my speech, and my declaration with your ears.

18 Behold now, I have ordered *my* cause; I know that I shall be justified.

19 Who *is* he *that* will plead with me? for now, if I hold my tongue, I shall give up the ghost.

20 Only do not two *things* to me: then will I not hide myself from You.

21 Withdraw Your hand far from me: and let not Your dread make me afraid.

22 Then call You, and I will answer: or let me speak, and answer You me.

23 How many *are* my iniquities and sins? make me to know my transgression and my sin.

24 Wherefore hide You Your face, and hold me for Your enemy?

25 Will You break a leaf driven to and fro? and will You pursue the dry stubble?

26 For You write bitter things against me, and make me to possess the iniquities of my youth.

27 You put my feet also in the stocks, and look <u>narrowly</u> to all my paths; You set a print upon the heels of my feet.   closely

28 And he, as a rotten thing, consumes, as a garment that is moth eaten.

CHAPTER 14

MAN *that is* born of a woman is of <u>few days</u>, and full of trouble.   short lived

2 He comes forth like a flower, and is cut down: he flees also as a shadow, and continues not.

3 And do You open your eyes upon such an one, and bring me into judgment with You?

4 Who can bring a clean *thing* out of an unclean? not one.

5 Seeing his days *are* <u>determined</u>, the number of his months *are* with You, You have appointed his bounds that he cannot pass;   decreed

6 Turn from him, that he may <u>rest</u>, till he shall accomplish, as an <u>hireling</u>, his day.   have peace - temporary worker

7 For there is hope of a tree, if it be cut down, that it will sprout again, and that the tender branch thereof will not cease.

8 Though the root thereof <u>wax</u> old in the earth, and the stock thereof die in the ground;   grow

9 *Yet* through the scent of water it will bud, and bring forth boughs like a plant.

10 But man dies, and wastes away: yea, man <u>gives up the ghost</u>, and where *is* he?   expires

11 *As* the waters fail from the sea, and the flood decays and dries up:

12 So man lies down, and rises not: till the heavens *be* no more, they shall

not awake, nor be raised out of their sleep.

13 O that You would hide me in the grave, that You would <u>keep me se-cret</u>, until your wrath be past, that You would appoint me a set time, and remember me!

conceal me

14 If a man die, shall he live *again*? all the days of my appointed time will I wait, till my change come.

15 You shall call, and I will answer You: You will have a desire to the work of Your hands.

16 For now You number my steps: do You not watch over my sin?

17 My transgression *is* sealed up in a bag, and You sew up my iniquity.

18 And surely the mountain <u>falling come to nothing</u>, and the rock is removed out of its place.

erodes and crumbles

19 The waters wear the stones: You wash away the things which grow *out* of the dust of the earth; and You destroy the hope of man.

20 You prevail for ever against him, and he passes: you change his countenance, and send him away.

21 His sons come to honor, and he knows *it* not; and they are brought low, but he perceives *it* not of them.

22 But his flesh upon him shall have pain, and his soul within him shall mourn.

CHAPTER 15

THEN answered El'i-phaz the Te'man-ite, and said,

2 Should a wise man utter vain knowledge, and fill his belly with the east wind?

3 Should he reason with unprofitable talk? or with speeches wherewith he can do no good?

4 Yea, you cast off <u>fear</u>, and <u>restrain</u> prayer before God.

reverence - hinder

5 For your mouth utters your iniquity, and you choose the tongue of the crafty.

6 Your own mouth condemns you, and not I: yea, your own lips testify against you.

LUKE 19:22

7 *Are* you the first man *that* was born? or were you made before the hills?

8 Have you heard the secret of <u>God</u>? and do you <u>restrain</u> wisdom to yourself?

*Eloah*ˢ·ᶠ *- limit*

9 What know you, that we know not? *what* understand you, which *is* not in us?

10 With us *are* both the grayheaded and very aged men, much elder than your father.

11 *Are* the consolations of God small with you? is there any secret thing with you?

12 Why does your heart carry you away? and what do your eyes wink at,

13 That you turn your spirit against God, and lets *such* words go out of your mouth?

14 What *is* man, that he should be clean? and *he which is* born of a woman, that he should be righteous?

15 Behold, He puts no trust in His saints; yea, the heavens are not clean in His sight.

16 How much more <u>abominable</u> and filthy *is* man, which drinks iniquity like water? detestable

17 I will show you, hear me; and that *which* I have seen I will declare;

18 Which wise men have told from their fathers, and have not hid *it*:

19 To whom alone the earth was given, and no stranger passed among them.

20 The wicked man <u>travails</u> with pain all *his* days, and the number of years is hidden to the oppressor. writhes

21 A dreadful sound *is* in his ears: in prosperity the <u>destroyer</u> shall come upon him. i.e., Satan

22 He believes not that he shall return out of darkness, and he is <u>waited</u> for of the sword. destined

23 He wanders abroad for bread, *saying*, Where *is it*? he knows that the day of darkness is ready at his hand.

24 Trouble and anguish shall make him afraid; they shall prevail against him, as a king ready to the battle.

25 For he stretches out his hand against <u>God</u>, and <u>strengthens</u> himself against the <u>Almighty</u>.
El^{s.f.} - vaunts - Shaddai

26 He runs upon Him, *even* on *his* neck, upon the thick <u>bosses of his bucklers</u>: masses of his shields

27 Because he covers his face with his fatness, and makes <u>collops</u> of fat on *his* flanks. bulges

28 And he dwells in desolate cities, *and* in houses which no man inhabits, which are ready to become heaps.

29 He shall not be rich, neither shall his <u>substance</u> continue, neither shall he prolong <u>the perfection</u> thereof upon the earth. wealth - its prosperity

30 He shall not depart out of darkness; the flame shall dry up his branches, and by the breath of his mouth shall he go away.

31 Let not him that is deceived trust in vanity: for vanity shall be his <u>recompence</u>. reward

32 It shall be accomplished before his time, and his branch shall not be green.

33 He shall shake off his unripe grape as the vine, and shall cast off his flower as the olive.

34 For the congregation of <u>hypocrites</u> *shall be* desolate, and fire shall consume the tabernacles of <u>bribery</u>. godless - the corrupt

35 They conceive mischief, and bring forth vanity, and their belly prepares deceit.

CHAPTER 16

THEN Job answered and said,

2 I have heard many such things: miserable comforters *are* you all.

3 Shall <u>vain</u> words have an end? or what emboldens you that you answer? empty

4 I also could speak as you *do*: if your soul were in my soul's stead, I could heap up words against you, and shake my head at you.

5 *But* I would <u>strengthen</u> you with my mouth, and the moving of my lips should <u>assuage</u> *your grief*. encourage - lessen

6 Though I speak, my grief is not <u>assuaged</u>: and *though* I forbear, what am I eased? lessened

7 But now He has made me weary:

You have made desolate all my company.

8 And You have filled me with wrinkles, *which is* a witness *against me*: and my leanness rising up in me bears witness to my face.

9 He tears *me* in His wrath, who hates me: He gnashes upon me with His teeth; my enemy sharpens his eyes upon me.

10 They have <u>gaped</u> upon me with their mouth; they have smitten me upon the cheek reproachfully; they have gathered themselves together against me.   jeered at

11 God has delivered me to the ungodly, and turned me over into the hands of the wicked.

12 I was at ease, but He has <u>broken me asunder</u>: He has also taken *me* by my neck, and shaken me to pieces, and set me up for His <u>mark</u>.   shattered me - target

13 His archers <u>compass</u> me round about, He clasps my reins asunder, and does not spare; He pours out my gall upon the ground.   surround

14 He breaks me with breach upon breach, He runs upon me like a giant.

15 I have sewed sackcloth upon my skin, and defiled my horn in the dust.

16 My face is foul with weeping, and on my eyelids *is* the shadow of death;

17 Not for *any* injustice in my hands: also my prayer *is* pure.

18 O earth, cover not you my blood, and let my cry have no place.

19 Also now, behold, my witness *is* in heaven, and my record *is* on high.

20 My friends scorn me: *but* my eye pours out *tears* to <u>God</u>.   Eloahs.f.

21 O that one might plead for a man with God, as a man *pleads* for his <u>neighbor</u>!   friend

22 When a few years are come, then I shall go the way *where* I shall not return.

CHAPTER 17

MY <u>breath</u> is corrupt, my days are extinct, the graves *are ready* for me.   spirit

2 *Are there* not mockers with me? and does not my eye <u>continue</u> in their provocation?   gaze on

3 Lay down now, put me in a surety with you; who *is* he *that* will strike hands with me?

4 For You have hid their heart from understanding: therefore shall You not exalt *them*.

5 He that speaks flattery to *his* friends, even the eyes of his children shall fail.

6 He has made me also a byword of the people; and <u>aforetime</u> I was as a <u>tabret</u>.   before - one at whom people spit

7 My eye also is dim by reason of sorrow, and all my members *are* as a shadow.

8 Upright *men* shall be astonished at this, and the innocent shall stir up himself against the <u>hypocrite</u>.   godless

9 The righteous also shall hold on his way, and he that has clean hands shall be stronger and stronger.

10 But as for you all, do you return,

and come now: for I cannot find *one* wise *man* among you.

11 My days are past, my purposes are broken off, *even* the thoughts of my heart.

12 They change the night into day: the light *is* short because of darkness.

13 If I wait, the grave *is* my house: I have made my bed in the darkness.

14 I have said to <u>corruption</u>, you *are* my father: to the worm, *you are* my mother, and my sister.   decay

15 And where *is* now my hope? as for my hope, who shall see it?

16 They shall go down to the bars of the pit, when *our* <u>rest</u> together *is* in the dust.   burial

CHAPTER 18

THEN answered Bil'dad the Shu'hite, and said,

2 How long *will it be before* you make an end of words? mark, and afterwards we will speak.

3 Wherefore are we counted as beasts, *and* reputed vile in your sight?

4 He tears himself in his anger: shall the earth be forsaken for you? and shall the rock be removed out of his place?

5 Yea, the light of the wicked shall be put out, and the spark of his fire shall not shine.

6 The light shall be dark in his <u>tab</u>ernacle, and his <u>candle</u> shall be put out with him.   tent - lamp

7 The steps of his strength shall be straitened, and his own counsel shall cast him down.

8 For he is cast into a net by his own feet, and he walks <u>upon a snare</u>.   into its mesh

9 The <u>gin</u> shall take *him* by the heel, *and* the <u>robber</u> shall prevail against him.   snare - trap

10 The snare *is* laid for him in the ground, and a trap for him in the way.

11 Terrors shall make him afraid on every side, and shall drive him to his feet.

12 His strength shall be hungerbitten, and destruction *shall be* ready at his side.

13 It shall devour the strength of his skin: *even* the firstborn of death shall devour his strength.

14 His confidence shall be rooted out of his <u>tabernacle</u>, and it shall bring him to the king of terrors.   tent

15 It shall dwell in his <u>tabernacle</u>, because *it is* none of his: brimstone shall be scattered upon his habitation.

16 His roots shall be dried up beneath, and above shall his branch be cut off.

17 His remembrance shall perish from the earth, and he shall have no name in the street.

18 He shall be driven from light into darkness, and chased out of the world.

19 He shall neither have son nor nephew among his people, nor any remaining in his dwellings.

20 They that come after *him* shall be astonished at his <u>day</u>, as they that went before were <u>affrighted</u>.   fate - seized with fright

21 Surely such *are* the dwellings of the wicked, and this *is* the place *of him that* knows not God.

CHAPTER 19

THEN Job answered and said, 2 How long will you <u>vex my soul</u>, and break me in pieces with words? torment me

3 These ten times have you <u>reproached</u> me: you are not ashamed *that* you make yourselves <u>strange</u> to me. insulted - foreign

4 And be it indeed *that* I have erred, my error remains with myself.

5 If indeed you will magnify *yourselves* against me, and plead against me my <u>reproach</u>: humiliation

6 Know now that <u>God</u> has overthrown me, and has <u>compassed</u> me with His net. Eloah^{s.f.} - encircled

7 Behold, I cry out of <u>wrong</u>, but I am not heard: I cry aloud, but *there is* no <u>judgment</u>. violence - justice

8 He has <u>fenced</u> up my way that I cannot pass, and He has set darkness in my paths. walled

9 He has stripped me of my glory, and taken the crown *from* my head.

10 He has destroyed me on every side, and I am gone: and my hope has He removed like a tree.

11 He has also kindled His wrath against me, and He counts me to Him as *one of* His enemies.

12 His troops come together, and raise up their way against me, and encamp round about my <u>tabernacle</u>. tent

13 He has put my brethren far from me, and my acquaintance are verily estranged from me.

14 My kinsfolk have failed, and my <u>familiar</u> friends have forgotten me. intimate

15 They that dwell in my house, and my maids, count me for a stranger: I am an alien in their sight.

16 I called my servant, and he gave *me* no answer; I entreated him with my mouth.

17 My breath is <u>strange</u> to my wife, though I entreated for the children's *sake* of my own body. offensive

18 Yea, young children despised me; I arose, and they spoke against me.

19 All my <u>inward friends</u> abhorred me: and they whom I loved arc turned against me. associates

20 My bone clings to my skin and to my flesh, and I am escaped with the skin of my teeth.

21 Have pity upon me, have pity upon me, O you my friends; for the hand of <u>God</u> has touched me. Eloah^{s.f.}

22 Why do you persecute me as God, and are not satisfied with my flesh?

23 Oh that my words were now written! oh that they were printed in a book!

24 That they were <u>graven</u> with an iron pen and lead in the rock for ever! engraved

25 For I know *that* my redeemer lives, and *that* He shall stand at the latter *day* upon the earth:

26 And *though* after my skin *worms* destroy this *body*, yet in my flesh shall I see God:

27 Whom I shall see for myself, and

my eyes shall behold, and not another; *though* my <u>reins</u> be consumed within me. heart

28 But you should say, Why persecute we him, seeing the root of the matter is found in me?

29 Be you afraid of the sword: for wrath *brings* the punishments of the sword, that you may know *there is* a judgment.

CHAPTER 20

THEN answered Zo'phar the Na'a-math-ite, and said,

2 Therefore do my thoughts cause me to answer, and for *this* I make haste.

3 I have heard the <u>check of my reproach</u>, and the spirit of my understanding causes me to answer. correction of my criticism

4 Know you *not* this of old, since man was placed upon earth,

5 That the triumphing of the wicked *is* short, and the joy of the <u>hypocrite</u> *but* for a moment? godless

6 Though his excellency mount up to the heavens, and his head reach to the clouds;

7 *Yet* he shall perish for ever like his own dung: they which have seen him shall say, Where *is* he?

8 He shall fly away as a dream, and shall not be found: yea, he shall be chased away as a vision of the night.

9 The eye also *which* saw him shall *see him* no more; neither shall his place any more behold him.

10 His children shall seek to <u>please</u> the poor, and his hands shall restore their goods. favor

11 His bones are full *of the sin* of his youth, which shall lie down with him in the dust.

12 Though wickedness be sweet in his mouth, *though* he hide it under his tongue;

13 *Though* he spare it, and forsake it not; but keep it still within his mouth:

14 *Yet* his <u>meat</u> in his bowels is <u>turned</u>, *it is* the <u>gall</u> of asps within him. food - changed - venom

15 He has swallowed down riches, and he shall vomit them up again: <u>God</u> shall cast them out of his belly. Els.f.

16 He shall suck the poison of asps: the viper's tongue shall slay him.

17 He shall not see the rivers, the floods, the brooks of honey and butter.

18 That which he labored for shall he restore, and shall not <u>swallow *it* down</u>: according to *his* substance *shall* the restitution *be*, and he shall not rejoice *therein*. be able to keep it

19 Because he has oppressed *and* has forsaken the poor; *because* he has violently taken away an house which he built <u>not</u>; was not his

20 Surely he shall not feel quietness in his belly, he shall not save of that which he desired.

21 There shall none of his <u>meat</u> be left; therefore shall no man look for his goods. food

22 In the fulness of his sufficiency he shall be in <u>straits</u>: every hand of the wicked shall come upon him. distress

23 *When* he is about to fill his belly, God shall cast the fury of His wrath

upon him, and shall rain *it* upon him while he is eating.

24 He shall flee from the iron weapon, *and* the bow of steel shall strike him through.

25 It is drawn, and comes out of the body; yea, the glittering sword comes out of his gall: terrors *are* upon him.

26 All darkness *shall be* hid in his secret places: a fire not blown shall consume him; it shall go ill with him that is left in his <u>tabernacle</u>.   tent

27 The heaven shall reveal his iniquity; and the earth shall rise up against him.

28 The increase of his house shall depart, *and his goods* shall flow away in the day of his wrath.

29 This *is* the portion of a wicked man from <u>God</u>, and the heritage <u>appointed</u> to him by <u>God</u>.

Elohim^{p.f.} - decreed - El^{s.f.}

CHAPTER 21

BUT Job answered and said,
2 Hear diligently my speech, and let this be your <u>consolations</u>.   comfort

3 <u>Suffer</u> me that I may speak; and after that I have spoken, mock on.   Bear with

4 As for me, *is* my complaint to man? and if *it were so*, why should not my spirit be troubled?

5 <u>Mark</u> me, and be astonished, and lay *your* hand upon *your* mouth.   Look at

6 Even when I remember I am afraid, and trembling takes hold on my flesh.

7 Wherefore do the wicked live, become old, yea, are mighty in power?

8 Their seed is established in their sight with them, and their offspring before their eyes.

9 Their houses *are* safe from <u>fear</u>, neither *is* the rod of God upon them.   dread

10 Their bull <u>genders</u>, and fails not; their cow calves, and <u>casts not</u> her calf.   mates - does not abort

11 They send forth their little ones like a flock, and their children dance.

12 They take the timbrel and harp, and rejoice at the sound of the organ.

13 They spend their days in wealth, and in a moment go down to the grave.

14 Therefore they say to <u>God</u>, Depart from us; for we desire not the knowledge of Your ways.   El^{s.f.}

15 What *is* the Almighty, that we should serve Him? and what profit should we have, if we pray to Him?

16 Lo, their good *is* not in their hand: the counsel of the wicked is far from me.

17 How oft is the candle of the wicked put out! and *how oft* comes their destruction upon them! *God* distributes sorrows in His anger.

18 They are as stubble before the wind, and as chaff that the storm carries away.

19 God lays up his iniquity for his children: He rewards him, and he shall know *it*.

20 His eyes shall see his destruction, and he shall drink of the wrath of the Almighty.

21 For what pleasure *has* he in his house after him, when the number of his months is cut off in the midst?

22 Shall *any* teach God knowledge?

seeing He judges those that are high.

23 One dies in his full strength, being wholly at ease and quiet.

24 His breasts are full of milk, and his bones are moistened with marrow.

25 And another dies in the bitterness of his soul, and never eats with pleasure.

26 They shall lie down alike in the dust, and the worms shall cover them.

27 Behold, I know your thoughts, and the underline{devices} *which you* wrongfully imagine against me.   plans

28 For you say, Where *is* the house of the prince? and where *are* the dwelling places of the wicked?

29 Have you not asked them that go by the way? and do you not know their underline{tokens},   indications

30 That the wicked is reserved to the day of destruction? they shall be brought forth to the day of wrath.

31 Who shall declare his way to his face? and who shall repay him *what* he has done?

32 Yet shall he be brought to the grave, and shall remain in the tomb.

33 The clods of the valley shall be sweet to him, and every man shall draw after him, as *there are* innumerable before him.

34 How then comfort you me in vain, seeing in your answers there remains falsehood?

CHAPTER 22

THEN El'i-phaz the Te'man-ite answered and said,

2 Can a man be profitable to underline{God}, as he that is wise may be profitable to himself?   El^{s.f.}

3 *Is it* any pleasure to the underline{Almighty}, that you are righteous? or *is it* gain *to Him*, that you make your ways perfect?   Shaddai

4 Will He reprove you for underline{fear} of you? will He enter with you into judgment?   reverence

5 *Is* not your wickedness great? and your iniquities underline{infinite}?   without end

6 For you have taken a pledge from your brother underline{for nothing}, and stripped the naked of their clothing.   without cause

7 You have not given water to the weary to drink, and you have withheld bread from the hungry.

8 But *as for* the mighty man, he had the earth; and the honorable man dwelled in it.

9 You have sent widows away empty, and the arms of the fatherless have been broken.

10 Therefore underline{snares} *are* round about you, and sudden fear troubles you;   lures

11 Or darkness, *that* you can not see; and abundance of waters cover you.

12 *Is* not underline{God} in the height of heaven? and behold the height of the stars, how high they are!   Eloah^{s.f.}

13 And you say, How does underline{God} know? can He judge through the dark cloud?   El^{s.f.}

14 Thick clouds *are* a covering to Him, that He sees not; and He walks in the circuit of heaven.

15 Have you marked the old way which wicked men have trodden?

16 Which were cut down out of time, whose foundation was <u>overflown</u> with a flood: washed away

17 Which said to <u>God</u>, Depart from us: and what can the <u>Almighty</u> do for them?   El⁵·ᶠ - Shaddai

18 Yet He filled their houses with good *things*: but the <u>counsel</u> of the wicked is far from me.   advice

19 The righteous see *it*, and are glad: and the innocent laugh them to scorn.

20 Whereas our <u>substance</u> is not cut down, but the remnant of them the fire <u>consumes</u>.   possessions - destroys

21 Acquaint now yourself with Him, and be at peace: thereby good shall come to you.

22 Receive, I pray you, the law from His mouth, and lay up His words in your heart.

23 If you return to the Almighty, you shall be <u>built up</u>, you shall put away iniquity far from your tabernacles.   restored

24 Then shall you lay up gold as dust, and the *gold* of O'phir as the stones of the brooks.

25 Yea, the Almighty shall be your defence, and you shall have plenty of silver.

26 For then shall you have your delight in the <u>Almighty</u>, and shall lift up your face to <u>God</u>.   Shaddai - Eloah⁵·ᶠ·

27 You shall make your prayer to Him, and He shall hear you, and you shall pay your vows.

28 You shall also decree a thing, and it shall be established to you: and the light shall shine upon your ways.

29 When *men* are cast down, then you shall say, *There is* lifting up; and He shall save the humble person.

30 He shall deliver the island of the innocent: and *it* is delivered by the pureness of your hands.

CHAPTER 23

THEN Job answered and said,
2 Even to day *is* my complaint bitter: <u>my stroke is heavier than</u> my groaning.   His hand is heavy despite

3 Oh that I knew where I might find Him! *that* I might come *even* to His seat!

4 I would order *my* cause before Him, and fill my mouth with arguments.

5 I would know the words *which* He would answer me, and understand what He would say to me.

6 Will He plead against me with *His* great power? No; but He would put *strength* in me.

7 There the righteous might dispute with Him; so should I be delivered for ever from my judge.

8 Behold, I go forward, but He *is* not *there*; and backward, but I cannot perceive Him:

9 On the left hand, where He does work, but I cannot behold *Him*: He hides Himself on the right hand, that I cannot see *Him*:

10 But He knows the way that I take: *when* He has tried me, I shall come forth as gold.

11 My foot has held His steps, His way have I kept, and not declined.

12 Neither have I gone back from the commandment of His lips; I have esteemed the words of His mouth more than my necessary *food*.

13 But He *is* in one *mind*, and who can turn Him? and *what* His soul desires, even *that* He does. unique

14 For He performs *the thing that is* appointed for me: and many such *things are* with Him.

15 Therefore am I troubled at His presence: when I consider, I am afraid of Him.

16 For God makes my heart soft, and the Almighty troubles me: El^s.f.

17 Because I was not cut off before the darkness, *neither* has He covered the darkness from my face.

CHAPTER 24

WHY, seeing times are not hidden from the Almighty, do they that know Him not see His days? Shaddai

2 *Some* remove the landmarks; they violently take away flocks, and feed *thereof*.

3 They drive away the ass of the fatherless, they take the widow's ox for a pledge.

4 They turn the needy out of the way: the poor of the earth hide themselves together.

5 Behold, *as* wild asses in the desert, go they forth to their work; rising betimes for a prey: the wilderness *yields* food for them *and* for *their* children. in time

6 They reap *every one* his corn in the field: and they gather the vintage of the wicked. grain

7 They cause the naked to lodge without clothing, that *they have* no covering in the cold.

8 They are wet with the showers of the mountains, and embrace the rock for want of a shelter.

9 They pluck the fatherless from the breast, and take a pledge of the poor. against

10 They cause *him* to go naked without clothing, and they take away the sheaf *from* the hungry; sheaves/i.e., wheat

11 *Which* make oil inside their walls, *and* tread *their* winepresses, and suffer thirst.

12 Men groan from out of the city, and the soul of the wounded cries out: yet God lays not folly *to them*. Eloah^s.f.

13 They are of those that rebel against the light; they know not the ways thereof, nor abide in the paths thereof.

14 The murderer rising with the light kills the poor and needy, and in the night is as a thief.

15 The eye also of the adulterer waits for the twilight, saying, No eye shall see me: and disguises *his* face.

16 In the dark they dig through houses, *which* they had marked for themselves in the daytime: they know not the light.

17 For the morning *is* to them even as the shadow of death: if *one* know them, *they are in* the terrors of the shadow of death. deep darkness

18 He *is* swift as the waters; their portion is cursed in the earth: he beholds not the way of the vineyards.

19 Drought and heat consume the snow waters: *so does* the grave *those which* have sinned.

20 The womb shall forget him; the worm shall feed sweetly on him; he shall be no more remembered; and wickedness shall be broken as a tree.

21 He <u>evil entreats</u> the barren *that* bears not: and does not good to the widow. _{wrongs}

22 He draws also the mighty with His power: He rises up, and no *man* is sure of life.

23 *Though* it be given him *to be* in safety, whereon he rests; yet His eyes *are* upon their ways.

24 They are <u>exalted</u> for a little while, but are gone and brought low; they are taken out of the way as all *other*, and cut off as the tops of the ears of corn. _{prosperous - grain}

25 And if *it be* not *so* now, who will make me a liar, and make my speech nothing worth?

CHAPTER 25

THEN answered Bil'dad the Shu'hite, and said,

2 Dominion and <u>fear</u> *are* with Him, He makes peace in His high places. _{awe}

3 Is there any number of His armies? and upon whom does not His light arise?

4 How then can man be justified with <u>God</u>? or how can he be clean *that is* born of a woman? _{El^{s.f.}}

5 Behold even to the moon, and it shiness not; yea, the stars are not pure in his sight.

6 How much less man, *that is* a worm? and the son of man, *which is* a worm?

CHAPTER 26

BUT Job answered and said,

2 How have you helped *him that is* without power? *how* save you the arm *that has* no strength?

3 How have you counselled *him that has* no wisdom? and *how* have you plentifully declared the thing as it is?

4 To whom have you uttered words? and whose spirit came from you?

5 Dead *things* are formed from under the waters, and the inhabitants thereof.

6 Hell *is* naked before Him, and destruction has no covering.

7 He stretches out the north over the empty place, *and* hangs the earth upon nothing.

8 He binds up the waters in His thick clouds; and the cloud is not <u>rent</u> under them. _{torn}

9 He holds back the face of His throne, *and* spreads His cloud upon it.

10 He has <u>compassed</u> the waters with bounds, until the day and night come to an end. _{marked}

11 The pillars of heaven tremble and are <u>astonished</u> at His reproof. _{aghast}

12 He divides the sea with His power, and by His understanding He smites through the proud.

13 By His spirit He has garnished

M05 - - 848

P25 - 849
GIP - 846

the heavens; His hand has formed the crooked serpent.   gliding

14 Lo, these *are* parts of His ways: but how little a portion is heard of Him? but the thunder of His power who can understand?

CHAPTER 27

MOREOVER Job continued his parable, and said,

2 *As* God lives, *who* has taken away my judgment; and the Almighty, *who* has vexed my soul;   El ˢ·ᶠ· - Shaddai - troubled

3 All the while my breath *is* in me, and the Spirit of God *is* in my nostrils;

4 My lips shall not speak wickedness, nor my tongue utter deceit.

5 God forbid that I should justify you: till I die I will not remove my integrity from me.   put away

6 My righteousness I hold fast, and will not let it go: my heart shall not reproach *me* so long as I live.

7 Let my enemy be as the wicked, and he that rises up against me as the unrighteous.

8 For what *is* the hope of the hypocrite, though he has gained, when God takes away his soul?   MATT. 16:26 godless

9 Will God hear his cry when trouble comes upon him?

10 Will he delight himself in the Almighty? will he always call upon God?   Shaddai - Eloah ˢ·ᶠ·

11 I will teach you by the hand of God: *that* which *is* with the Almighty will I not conceal.   El ˢ·ᶠ·

12 Behold, all you yourselves have seen *it*; why then are you thus altogether vain?

13 This *is* the portion of a wicked man with God, and the heritage of oppressors, *which* they shall receive of the Almighty.   El ˢ·ᶠ·

14 If his children be multiplied, *it is* for the sword: and his offspring shall not be satisfied with bread.

15 Those that remain of him shall be buried in death: and his widows shall not weep.

16 Though he heap up silver as the dust, and prepare raiment as the clay;   garments

17 He may prepare it, but the just shall put *it* on, and the innocent shall divide the silver.

18 He builds his house as a moth, and as a booth *that* the keeper makes.

19 The rich man shall lie down, but he shall not be gathered: he opens his eyes, and he *is* not.

20 Terrors take hold on him as waters, a tempest steals him away in the night.

21 The east wind carries him away, and he departs: and as a storm hurls him out of his place.

22 For God shall cast upon him, and not spare: he would fain flee out of His hand.   surely try to

23 *Men* shall clap their hands at him, and shall hiss him out of his place.

CHAPTER 28

SURELY there is a vein for the silver, and a place for gold *where* they fine *it*.   mine

2 Iron is taken out of the earth, and brass *is* molten *out of* the stone.

3 He sets an end to darkness, and searches out all perfection: the stones of darkness, and the shadow of death.

4 The flood breaks out from the inhabitant; *even the waters* forgotten of the foot: they are dried up, they are gone away from men.

5 *As for* the earth, out of it comes bread: and under it is turned up as it were fire.

6 The stones of it *are* the place of sapphires: and it has dust of gold.

7 *There is* a path which no fowl knows, and which the <u>vulture's</u> eye has not seen: falcon's

8 The lion's whelps have not trodden it, nor the fierce lion passed by it.

9 He puts forth His hand upon the rock; He overturns the mountains by the roots.

10 He cuts out rivers among the rocks; and His eye sees every precious thing.

11 He binds the floods from overflowing; and *the thing that is* hid brings He forth to light.

12 But where shall wisdom be found? and where *is* the place of understanding?

13 Man knows not the price thereof; neither is it found in the land of the living.

14 The depth says, It *is* not in me: and the sea says, *It is* not with me.

15 It cannot be gotten for gold, neither shall silver be weighed *for* the price thereof.

16 It cannot be valued with the gold of O'phir, with the precious onyx, or the sapphire.

17 The gold and the crystal cannot equal it: and the exchange of it *shall not be for* jewels of fine gold.

18 No mention shall be made of coral, or of pearls: for the price of wisdom *is* above rubies.

19 The topaz of E-thi-o'pi-a shall not equal it, neither shall it be valued with pure gold.

20 Where then comes wisdom? and where *is* the place of understanding?

21 Seeing it is hid from the eyes of all living, and kept close from the fowls of the air.

22 Destruction and death say, We have heard the fame thereof with our ears.

23 <u>God</u> understands the way thereof, and He knows the place thereof.   Elohim[p.f.]

24 For He looks to the ends of the earth, *and* sees under the whole heaven;

25 To make the weight for the winds; and He weighs the waters by measure.

26 When He made a decree for the rain, and a way for the lightning of the thunder:

27 Then did He see it, and declare it; He prepared it, yea, and searched it out.

28 And to man He said, Behold, the <u>fear</u> of the Lord, that *is* wisdom; and to depart from evil *is* understanding.   reverence

CHAPTER 29

MOREOVER Job continued his parable, and said,

2 Oh that I were as *in* months past, as *in* the days *when* God preserved me;

3 When His candle shined upon my head, *and when* by His light I walked *through* darkness;

4 As I was in the days of my youth, when the secret of God *was* upon my tabernacle;   Eloah^{s.f.} - tent

5 When the Almighty *was* yet with me, *when* my children *were* about me;

6 When I washed my steps with butter, and the rock poured me out rivers of oil;

7 When I went out to the gate through the city, *when* I prepared my seat in the street!

8 The young men saw me, and hid themselves: and the aged arose, *and* stood up.

9 The princes refrained talking, and laid *their* hand on their mouth.

10 The nobles held their peace, and their tongue clung to the roof of their mouth.

11 When the ear heard *me*, then it blessed me; and when the eye saw *me*, it gave witness to me:

12 Because I delivered the poor that cried, and the fatherless, and *him that had* none to help him.

13 The blessing of him that was ready to perish came upon me: and I caused the widow's heart to sing for joy.

14 I put on righteousness, and it clothed me: my judgment *was* as a robe and a diadem.   turban

15 I was eyes to the blind, and feet *was* I to the lame.

16 I *was* a father to the poor: and the cause *which* I knew not I searched out.

17 And I broke the jaws of the wicked, and plucked the spoil out of his teeth.

18 Then I said, I shall die in my nest, and I shall multiply *my* days as the sand.   i.e., own house

19 My root *was* spread out by the waters, and the dew lay all night upon my branch.

20 My glory *was* fresh in me, and my bow was renewed in my hand.   new

21 To me *men* gave ear, and waited, and kept silence at my counsel.

22 After my words they spoke not again; and my speech dropped upon them.

23 And they waited for me as for the rain; and they opened their mouth wide *as* for the latter rain.

24 *If* I laughed on them, they believed *it* not; and the light of my countenance they cast not down.

was precious to them

25 I chose out their way, and sat chief, and dwelled as a king in the army, as one *that* comforts the mourners.

CHAPTER 30

BUT now *they that are* younger than I have me in derision, whose fathers I would have disdained to have set with the dogs of my flock.   refused

2 Yea, whereto *might* the strength of their hands *profit* me, in whom old age was perished?   how

3 For want and famine *they were* <u>solitary</u>; fleeing into the wilderness in former time desolate and waste. gaunt

4 Who cut up mallows by the bushes, and juniper roots *for* their <u>meat</u>. food

5 They were driven forth from among *men*, (they cried after them as *after* a thief;)

6 To dwell in the cliffs of the valleys, *in* caves of the earth, and *in* the rocks.

7 Among the bushes they <u>brayed</u>; under the nettles they were gathered together. cried out

8 *They were* children of fools, yea, children of <u>base</u> men: they were viler than the earth. nameless

9 And now am I their song, yea, I am their byword.

10 They abhor me, they flee far from me, and <u>spare</u> not to spit in my face. refrain

11 Because He has loosed my <u>cord</u>, and afflicted me, they have also let loose the <u>bridle</u> before me. bowstring - restraint

12 Upon *my* right *hand* rise the youth; they push away my feet, and they raise up against me the ways of their destruction.

13 They mar my path, they set forward my calamity, they have no helper.

14 They came *upon me* as a wide <u>breaking in</u> *of waters*: in the desolation they rolled themselves *upon me*. flood

15 Terrors are turned upon me: they pursue my soul as the wind: and my welfare passes away as a cloud.

16 And now my soul is poured out upon me; the days of affliction have taken hold upon me.

17 My bones are pierced in me in the night season: and my sinews take no rest.

18 By the great force *of my disease* is my garment <u>changed</u>: it binds me about as the collar of my coat. distorted

19 He has cast me into the mire, and I am become like dust and ashes.

20 I cry to You, and You do not hear me: I stand up, and You regard me *not*.

21 You are become cruel to me: with Your strong hand You <u>oppose</u> Yourself against me. attack

22 You lift me up to the wind; You cause me to ride *upon it*, and <u>dissolve my substance</u>. destroys property

23 For I know *that* You will bring me *to* death, and *to* the house appointed for all living.

24 However he will not stretch out *his* hand to the grave, though they cry in his destruction.

25 Did not I weep for him that was in trouble? was *not* my soul grieved for the poor?

26 When I looked for good, then evil came *to me*: and when I waited for light, there came darkness.

27 My <u>bowels boiled</u>, and rested not: the days of affliction <u>prevented</u> me. insides churned - confronted

28 I went mourning without the sun: I stood up, *and* I cried in the congregation.

29 I am a brother to <u>dragons</u>, and a companion to <u>owls</u>. jackals - ostriches

30 My skin is black upon me, and my bones are burned with heat.

31 My harp also is *turned* to mourning, and my organ into the voice of them that weep.

CHAPTER 31

I MADE a <u>covenant</u> with my eyes; why then should I think upon a <u>maid</u>?   agreement - virgin

2 For what portion of <u>God</u> *is there* from above? and *what* inheritance of the <u>Almighty</u> from on high?   Eloah^s.f. - Shaddai

3 *Is* not destruction to the wicked? and a strange *punishment* to the workers of iniquity?

4 Does not He see my ways, and count all my steps?

5 If I have walked with vanity, or if my foot has hasted to deceit;

6 Let me be weighed in an even balance, that <u>God</u> may know my integrity.

7 If my step has turned out of the way, and my heart walked after my eyes, and if any blot has clung to my hands;

8 *Then* let me sow, and let another eat; yea, let my offspring be rooted out.

9 If my heart have been <u>deceived</u> by a woman, or *if* I have laid wait at my neighbor's door;   enticed

10 *Then* let my wife <u>grind to</u> another, and let others bow down upon her.   serve

11 For this *is* an heinous crime; yea, it *is* an iniquity *to be punished by* the judges.

12 For it *is* a fire *that* consumes to destruction, and would root out all my increase.

13 If I did despise the cause of my manservant or of my maidservant, when they contended with me;

14 What then shall I do when God rises up? and when He visits, what shall I answer Him?

15 Did not He that made me in the womb make him? and did not one fashion us in the womb?

16 If I have withheld the poor from *their* desire, or have caused the eyes of the widow to fail;

17 Or have eaten my morsel myself alone, and the fatherless has not eaten thereof;

18 (For from my youth he was brought up with me, as *with* a father, and I have guided her from my mother's womb;)

19 If I have seen any perish for want of clothing, or any poor without covering;

20 If his loins have not blessed me, and *if* he were *not* warmed with the fleece of my sheep;

21 If I have lifted up my hand against the fatherless, when I saw my help in the gate:

22 *Then* let my arm fall from my shoulder blade, and my arm be broken from the bone.

23 For destruction *from* <u>God</u> *was* a terror to me, and by reason of His <u>highness</u> I could not endure.   El^s.f. - splendor

24 If I have made gold my hope, or have said to the fine gold, *You are* my confidence;

25 If I rejoiced because my wealth

was great, and because my hand had gotten much;

26 If I beheld the sun when it shined, or the moon walking *in* brightness;

27 And my heart has been secretly enticed, or my mouth has kissed my hand:

28 This also *were* an iniquity *to be punished by* the judge: for I should have denied the God *that is* above.

29 If I rejoiced at the destruction of him that <u>hated</u> me, or lifted up myself when evil found him: despised

30 Neither have I allowed my mouth to sin by wishing a curse to his soul.

31 If the men of my <u>tabernacle</u> said not, Oh that we had of his flesh! we cannot be satisfied.   tent

32 The stranger did not lodge in the street: *but* I opened my doors to the traveler.

33 If I covered my transgressions as Ad'am, by hiding my iniquity in my bosom:

34 Did I <u>fear</u> a great multitude, or did the contempt of families terrify me, that I kept silence, *and* went not out of the door?   dread

35 Oh that one would hear me! behold, my desire *is, that* the Almighty would answer me, and *that* my <u>adversary</u> had written a book.   prosecutor

36 Surely I would take it upon my shoulder, *and* bind it *as* a crown to me.

37 I would declare to him the number of my steps; as a prince would I go near to him.

38 If my land cry against me, or that the furrows likewise thereof complain;

39 If I have eaten the fruits thereof without money, or have caused the owners thereof to lose their life:

40 Let thistles grow instead of wheat, and <u>cockle</u> instead of barley. The words of Job are ended.   weeds

CHAPTER 32

SO these three men ceased to answer Job, because *he* was righteous in his own eyes.

2 Then was kindled the wrath of E-li'hu the son of Bar'a-chel the Bu'zite, of the kindred of Ram: against Job was his wrath kindled, because he justified himself rather than <u>God</u>.   Elohim P.f.

3 Also against his three friends was his wrath kindled, because they had found no answer, and *yet* had condemned Job.

4 Now E-li'hu had waited till Job had spoken, because they *were* elder than he.

5 When E-li'hu saw that *there was* no answer in the mouth of *these* three men, then his wrath was kindled.

6 And E-li'hu the son of Bar'a-chel the Bu'zite answered and said, I *am* young, and you *are* very old; wherefore I was afraid, and dare not show you my opinion.

7 I said, Days should speak, and multitude of years should teach wisdom.

8 But *there is* a spirit in man: and the inspiration of the <u>Almighty</u> gives them understanding.   Shaddai

9 Great men are not *always* wise: neither do the aged understand judgment.

10 Therefore I said, Hearken to me; I also will show my opinion.

11 Behold, I waited for your words; I gave ear to your reasons, while you <u>searched out</u> what to say. pondered

12 Yea, I attended to you, and, behold, *there was* none of you that convinced Job, *or* that answered his words:

13 Less you should say, We have found out wisdom: <u>God</u> thrusts him down, not man. El^s.f.

14 Now he has not directed *his* words against me: neither will I answer him with your speeches.

15 They were amazed, they answered no more: they left off speaking.

16 When I had waited, (for they spoke not, but stood still, *and* answered no more;)

17 *I said*, I will answer also my part, I also will show my opinion.

18 For I am full of matter, the spirit within me constrains me.

19 Behold, my <u>belly</u> *is* as wine *which* has no vent; it is ready to burst like new <u>bottles</u>. heart - wineskins

20 I will speak, that I may be refreshed: I will open my lips and answer.

21 Let me not, I pray you, <u>accept</u> any man's person, neither let me give flattering titles to man. be partial to

22 For I know not to give flattering titles; *in so doing* my maker would soon take me away.

CHAPTER 33

WHEREFORE, Job, I pray you, hear my <u>speeches</u>, and <u>hearken</u> to all my words. arguments - listen

2 Behold, now I have opened my mouth, my tongue has spoken in my mouth.

3 My words *shall be of* the uprightness of my heart: and my lips shall utter knowledge clearly.

4 The Spirit of <u>God</u> has made me, and the breath of the <u>Almighty</u> has given me life. El^s.f. - Shaddai

5 If you can answer me, set *your* words in order before me, stand up.

6 Behold, I *am* according to your wish in God's stead: I also am formed out of the clay.

7 Behold, my terror shall not make you afraid, neither shall my hand be heavy upon you.

8 Surely you have spoken in <u>my hearing</u>, and I have heard the voice of *your* words, *saying*, my ears

9 I am clean without transgression, I *am* innocent; neither *is there* iniquity in me.

10 Behold, He finds occasions against me, He counts me for His enemy,

11 He puts my feet in the stocks, He marks all my paths.

12 Behold, *in* this you are not <u>just</u>: I will answer you, that God is greater than man. right

13 Why do you <u>strive against</u> Him? for He gives not account of any of His matters. complain to

14 For <u>God</u> speaks once, yea twice, *yet man* perceives it not. El^s.f.

15 In a dream, in a vision of the night, when deep sleep falls upon men, in slumberings upon the bed;

16 Then He opens the ears of men, and seals their instruction,

17 That He may withdraw man *from his* purpose, and hide pride from man.   ^{wrongdoing}

18 He keeps back his soul from the pit, and his life from perishing by the sword.

19 He is chastened also with pain upon his bed, and the multitude of his bones with strong *pain*:

20 So that his life abhors bread, and his soul dainty meat.

21 His flesh is consumed away, that it cannot be seen; and his bones *that* were not seen stick out.

22 Yea, his soul draw near to the grave, and his life to the destroyers.

23 If there be a messenger with him, an interpreter, one among a thousand, to show to man his uprightness:

24 Then He is gracious to him, and says, Deliver him from going down to the pit: I have found a ransom.   ^{i.e., atonement}

25 His flesh shall be fresher than a child's: he shall return to the days of his youth:

26 He shall pray to God, and He will be favorable to Him: and he shall see His face with joy: for He will render to man His righteousness.   ^{Eloah s.f.}

27 He looks upon men, and *if any* say, I have sinned, and perverted *that which was* right, and it profited me not;   ^{LUKE 15:21}

28 He will deliver his soul from going into the pit, and his life shall see the light.

29 Lo, all these *things* works God oftentimes with man,   ^{El s.f.}

30 To bring back his soul from the pit, to be enlightened with the light of the living.

31 Mark well, O Job, hearken to me: hold your peace, and I will speak.

32 If you have any thing to say, answer me: speak, for I desire to justify you.

33 If not, hearken to me: hold your peace, and I shall teach you wisdom.

CHAPTER 34

FURTHERMORE E-li'hu answered and said,

2 Hear my words, O you wise *men*; and give ear to me, you that have knowledge.

3 For the ear tries words, as the mouth tastes meat.   ^{hears}

4 Let us choose to us judgment: let us know among ourselves what *is* good.

5 For Job has said, I am righteous: and God has taken away my judgment.   ^{El s.f.}

6 Should I lie against my right? my wound *is* incurable without transgression.   ^{faults of my own}

7 What man *is* like Job, *who* drinks up scorning like water?   ^{derision}

8 Which goes in company with the workers of iniquity, and walks with wicked men.

9 For he has said, It profits a man nothing that he should delight himself with God.

10 Therefore hearken to me, you men of understanding: far be it from God, *that He should do* wickedness; and

from the Almighty, *that He should commit* iniquity.

11 For the work of a man shall He render to him, and cause every man to find according to *his* ways.

12 Yea, surely God will not do wickedly, neither will the Almighty pervert judgment.   El^s.f. - justice

13 Who has given Him a charge over the earth? or who has disposed the whole world?

14 If He set His heart upon man, *if* He gather to Himself His spirit and His breath;

15 All flesh shall perish together, and man shall turn again to dust.

16 If now *you have* understanding, hear this: hearken to the voice of my words.

17 Shall even he that hates right govern? and will you condemn him that is most just?   despises

18 *Is it fit* to say to a king, *You are* wicked? *and* to princes, *You are* ungodly?

19 *How much less to him* that accepts not the persons of princes, nor regards the rich more than the poor? for they all *are* the work of his hands.

20 In a moment shall they die, and the people shall be troubled at midnight, and pass away: and the mighty shall be taken away without hand.

21 For His eyes *are* upon the ways of man, and He sees all his goings.

22 *There is* no darkness, nor shadow of death, where the workers of iniquity may hide themselves.

23 For He will not lay upon man more *than right*; that he should enter into judgment with God.   argument - El^s.f.

24 He shall break in pieces mighty men without number, and set others in their stead.   inquiry - place

25 Therefore He knows their works, and He overturns *them* in the night, so that they are destroyed.

26 He strikes them as wicked men in the open sight of others;

27 Because they turned back from Him, and would not consider any of His ways:

28 So that they cause the cry of the poor to come to Him, and He hear the cry of the afflicted.   needy

29 When He gives quietness, who then can make trouble? and when He hides *His* face, who then can behold Him? whether *it be done* against a nation, or against a man only:

30 That the hypocrite reign not, less the people be ensnared.   godless - trapped

31 Surely it is meet to be said to God, I have borne *chastisement*, I will not offend *any more*:   fitting - El^s.f.

32 *That which* I see not teach You me: if I have done iniquity, I will do no more.

33 *Should it be* according to your mind? He will recompense it, whether you refuse, or whether you choose; and not I: therefore speak what you know.

34 Let men of understanding tell me, and let a wise man hearken to me.

35 Job has spoken without knowledge, and his words *were* without wisdom.

36 My desire *is that* Job may be tried to the end because of *his* answers <u>for</u> wicked men. ^{like}

37 For he adds rebellion to his sin, he claps *his hands* among us, and multiplies his words against God.

CHAPTER 35

E-LI'HU spoke moreover, and said, 2 Think you this to be <u>right</u>, *that* you said, My righteousness *is* more than God's? ^{according to justice}

3 For you said, What advantage will it be to you? *and,* What profit shall I have, *if I be cleansed* from my sin?

4 I will answer you, and your companions with you.

5 Look to the heavens, and see; and behold the clouds *which* are higher than you.

6 If you sin, what do you against Him? or *if* your transgressions be multiplied, what do you to Him?

7 If you be righteous, what gives you Him? or what receives He of your hand? ^{ROM. 11:35}

8 Your wickedness *may hurt* a man as you *are*; and your righteousness *may profit* the son of man.

9 By reason of the multitude of oppressions they make *the oppressed* to cry: they cry out by reason of the arm of the mighty.

10 But none says, Where *is* God my maker, who gives songs in the night;

11 Who teaches us more than the beasts of the earth, and makes us wiser than the fowls of heaven?

12 There they cry, but none gives answer, because of the pride of evil men.

13 Surely <u>God</u> will not hear vanity, neither will the <u>Almighty</u> regard it. ^{El^{s.f.} - Shaddai}

14 Although you say you shall not see Him, *yet* judgment *is* before Him; therefore trust you in Him.

15 But now, because *it is* not *so,* He has visited in His anger; yet He know *it* not in great extremity:

16 Therefore does Job open his mouth in vain; he multiplies words without knowledge.

CHAPTER 36

E-LI'HU also proceeded, and said, 2 Allow me a little, and I will show you that *I have* yet to speak on God's behalf. ^{there is yet more to be said in}

3 I will bring my knowledge from afar, and will ascribe righteousness to my Maker.

4 For truly my words *shall* not *be* false: He that is perfect in knowledge *is* with you.

5 Behold, <u>God</u> *is* mighty, and despises not *any*: He *is* mighty in strength *and* wisdom. ^{El^{s.f.}}

6 He preserves not the life of the wicked: but gives right to the poor.

7 He withdraws not His eyes from the righteous: but with kings *are they* on the throne; yea, He does establish them for ever, and they are exalted.

8 And if *they be* bound in fetters, *and* be <u>holden</u> in <u>cords</u> of affliction; ^{caught - bonds}

9 Then He shows them their work,

and their transgressions that they have exceeded.

10 He opens also their ear to discipline, and commands that they return from iniquity.

11 If they obey and serve *Him*, they shall spend their days in prosperity, and their years in pleasures.

12 But if they obey not, they shall perish by the sword, and they shall die without knowledge.

13 But the hypocrites in heart heap up wrath: they cry not when He binds them.   godless

14 They die in youth, and their life *is* among the unclean.

15 He delivers the poor in his affliction, and opens their ears in oppression.

16 Even so would He have removed you out of the strait *into* a broad place, where *there is* no straitness; and that which should be set on your table *should be* full of fatness.   mouth of distress - constraint

17 But you have fulfilled the judgment of the wicked: judgment and justice take hold *on you.*

18 Because *there is* wrath, *beware* less He take you away with *His* stroke: then a great ransom cannot deliver you.

19 Will He esteem your riches? *no,* not gold, nor all the forces of strength.

20 Desire not the night, when people are cut off in their place.

21 Take heed, regard not iniquity: for this have you chosen rather than affliction.

22 Behold, God exalts by His power: who teaches like Him?   El^s.t.

23 Who has enjoined Him His way? or who can say, You have wrought iniquity?   appointed - done wrong

24 Remember that you magnify His work, which men behold.

25 Every man may see it; man may behold *it* afar off.

26 Behold, God *is* great, and we know *Him* not, neither can the number of His years be searched out.   understand

27 For He makes small the drops of water: they pour down rain according to the vapor thereof:

28 Which the clouds do drop *and* distil upon man abundantly.

29 Also can *any* understand the spreadings of the clouds, *or* the noise of His tabernacle?

30 Behold, He spreads His light upon it, and covers the bottom of the sea.

31 For by them judges He the people; He gives meat in abundance.

32 With clouds He covers the light; and commands it *not to shine* by *the cloud* that comes between.

33 The noise thereof shows concerning it, the cattle also concerning the vapor.

CHAPTER 37

AT this also my heart trembles, and is moved out of its place.

2 Hear attentively the noise of His voice, and the sound *that* goes out of His mouth.

3 He directs it under the whole

heaven, and His lightning to the ends of the earth.

4 After it a voice roars: He thunders with the voice of His excellency; and He will not <u>stay</u> them when His voice is heard. stop - 1COR2

5 <u>God</u> thunders marvellously with His voice; great things does He, which we cannot comprehend. El^{s.f.}

6 For He says to the snow, Be you *on* the earth; likewise to the small rain, and to the great rain of His strength.

7 He seals up the hand of every man; that all men may know His work.

8 Then the beasts go into dens, and remain in their places.

9 Out of the south comes the whirlwind: and cold out of the north.

10 By the breath of <u>God</u> frost is given: and the breadth of the waters is <u>straitened</u>. frozen

11 Also by watering He wearies the thick cloud: He scatters His bright cloud:

12 And it is turned round about by His counsels: that they may do whatsoever He commands them upon the face of the world in the earth.

13 He causes it to come, whether for correction, or for His land, or for mercy.

14 Hearken to this, O Job: stand still, and consider the wondrous works of God.

15 Do you know when <u>God</u> disposed them, and caused the light of His cloud to shine? Eloah^{s.f.}

16 Do you know the balancings of the clouds, the wondrous works of Him which is perfect in knowledge?

17 How your garments *are* warm, when He quiets the earth by the south *wind*?

18 Have you with Him spread out the sky, *which is* strong, *and* as a <u>molten looking glass</u>? mirror

19 Teach us what we shall say to Him; *for* we cannot order *our speech* by reason of <u>darkness</u>. i.e. lack of understanding

20 Shall it be told Him that I speak? if a man speak, surely he shall be swallowed up.

21 And now *men* see not the bright light which *is* in the clouds: but the wind passes, and cleanses them.

22 Fair weather comes out of the north: with <u>God</u> *is* <u>terrible</u> majesty. Eloath^{s.f.} - awesome

23 *Touching* the <u>Almighty</u>, we cannot find Him out: *He is* excellent in power, and in judgment, and in plenty of justice: He will not afflict. Shaddai

24 Men do therefore <u>fear</u> Him: He respects not any *that are* wise of heart. revere

CHAPTER 38

THEN the Lord answered Job out of the whirlwind, and said,

2 Who *is* this that darkens counsel by words without knowledge?

3 Gird up now your loins like a man; for I will demand of you, and answer you Me.

4 Where were you when I laid the foundations of the earth? declare, if you have understanding.

5 Who has laid the measures thereof, if you know? or who has stretched the line upon it?

6 Whereupon are the foundations thereof fastened? or who laid the corner stone thereof;

7 When the morning stars sang together, and all the sons of <u>God</u> shouted for joy? Elohim^{p.6}

Elohim^{p.6}

8 Or *who* shut up the sea with doors, when it broke forth, *as if* it had issued out of the womb?

9 When I made the cloud the garment thereof, and thick darkness a <u>swaddling</u> band for it, i.e., wrapping

10 And broke up for it My decreed *place*, and set bars and doors,

11 And said, Presently shall you come, but no further: and here shall your proud waves be stayed?

12 Have you commanded the morning since your days; *and* caused the <u>dayspring</u> to know its place; dawn

13 That it might take hold of the ends of the earth, that the wicked might be shaken out of it?

14 It is turned as clay *to* the seal; and they stand as a garment.

15 And from the wicked their light is witholden, and the high arm shall be broken.

16 Have you entered into the springs of the sea? or have you walked in the search of the depth?

17 Have the gates of death been opened to you? or have you seen the doors of the shadow of death?

18 Have you perceived the breadth of the earth? declare if you know it all.

19 Where *is* the way *where* light dwells? and *as for* darkness, where *is* the place thereof,

20 That you should take it to the bound thereof, and that you should know the paths *to* the house thereof?

21 Know you *it*, because you were then born? or *because* the number of your days *is* great?

22 Have you entered into the treasures of the snow? or have you seen the <u>treasures</u> of the hail, storehouses

23 Which I have reserved against the time of trouble, against the day of battle and war?

24 By what way is the light parted, *which* scatters the east wind upon the earth?

25 Who has divided a watercourse for the overflowing of waters, or a way for the lightning of thunder;

26 To cause it to rain on the earth, *where* no man *is; on* the wilderness, wherein *there is* no man;

27 To satisfy the desolate and waste *ground*; and to cause the bud of the tender herb to spring forth?

28 Has the rain a father? or who has fathered the drops of dew?

29 Out of whose womb came the ice? and the <u>hoary</u> frost of heaven, who has <u>gendered it</u>? white - given it birth

30 The waters are hid as *with* a stone, and the face of the deep is frozen.

31 Can you bind the <u>sweet influences</u> of Ple'ia-des, or loose the bands of O-ri'on? chains

32 Can you bring forth <u>Maz'za-roth</u> in his season? or can you guide Arc-tu'rus with his sons? the constellations

33 Know you the <u>ordinances</u> of

heaven? can you set the dominion thereof in the earth?   laws

34 Can you lift up your voice to the clouds, that abundance of waters may cover you?

35 Can you send lightnings, that they may go, and say to you Here we *are*?

36 Who has put wisdom in the inward parts? or who has given understanding to the heart?

37 Who can number the clouds in wisdom? or who can <u>stay</u> the <u>bottles</u> of heaven,   tip - water jars

38 When the dust grows into hardness, and the clods cling fast together?

39 Will you hunt the prey for the lion? or fill the appetite of the young lions,

40 When they crouch in *their* dens, *and* abide in the covert to lie in wait?

41 Who provides for the raven its food? when its young ones cry to God, they wander for lack of mcat.

CHAPTER 39

KNOW you the time when the wild goats of the rock bring forth? *or* can you mark when the <u>hinds</u> do calve?   deer

2 Can you number the months *that* they fulfill? or know you the time when they bring forth?

3 They bow themselves, they bring forth their young ones, they cast out their <u>sorrows</u>.   labor pains

4 Their young ones are in good liking, they grow up <u>with corn</u>; they go forth, and return not to them.   in the field

5 Who has sent out the wild ass free? or who has loosed the bands of the wild ass?

6 Whose house I have made the wilderness, and the barren land his dwellings.

7 He scorns the multitude of the city, neither regards he the crying of the driver.

8 The range of the mountains *is* his pasture, and he searches after every green thing.

9 Will the <u>unicorn</u> be willing to serve you, or abide by your <u>crib</u>?   wild ox - food crib

10 Can you bind the <u>unicorn</u> with his band in the furrow? or will he harrow the valleys after you?

11 Will you trust him, because his strength *is* great? or will you leave your labor to him?

12 Will you believe him, that he will bring home your <u>seed</u>, and gather *it into* your barn?   grain

13 *Gave you* the goodly wings to the peacocks? or wings and feathers to the ostrich?

14 Which leaves her eggs in the earth, and warms them in dust,

15 And forgets that the foot may crush them, or that the wild beast may break them.

16 She is hardened against her young ones, as though *they were* not hers: her labor is in vain without <u>fear</u>;   care

17 Because <u>God</u> has deprived her of wisdom, neither has He imparted to her understanding.   Eloath^{s.f.}

18 What time she lifts up herself on high, she <u>scorns</u> the horse and its rider.   laughs at

19 Have you given the horse strength? have you clothed its neck with thunder?

20 Can you make him afraid as a grasshopper? the glory of its nostrils *is* terrible.

21 He paws in the valley, and rejoices in *his* strength: he goes on to meet the armed men.

22 He mocks at fear, and is not <u>affrighted</u>; neither turns he back from the sword.   afraid

23 The quiver rattles against him, the glittering spear and the shield.

24 He swallows the ground with fierceness and rage: neither believes he that *it is* the sound of the trumpet.

25 He says among the trumpets, Ha, ha; and he smells the battle afar off, the thunder of the captains, and the shouting.

26 Does the hawk fly by your wisdom, *and* stretch her wings toward the south?

27 Does the eagle mount up at your command, and make her nest on high?

28 She dwells and abides on the rock, upon the crag of the rock, and the strong place.

29 From there she <u>seeks the prey,</u> *and* her eyes behold afar off.   spies out food

30 Her young ones also suck up blood: and where the slain *are*, there *is* she.

CHAPTER 40

MOREOVER the LORD answered Job, and said,

2 Shall he that contends with the Almighty instruct *Him*? he that reproves <u>God,</u> let him answer it.   Shaddai - Eloah^{s.f.}

3 Then Job answered the LORD, and said,

4 Behold, I am vile; what shall I answer You? I will lay my hand upon my mouth.

5 Once have I spoken; but I will not answer: yea, twice; but I will proceed no further.

6 Then answered the LORD to Job out of the whirlwind, and said,

7 Gird up your loins now like a man: I will demand of you, and declare you to Me.

8 Will you also disannul My judgment? will you condemn Me, that you may be righteous?

9 Have you an arm like God? or can you thunder with a voice like Him?

10 Deck yourself now *with* majesty and excellency; and array yourself with glory and beauty.

11 Cast abroad the rage of your wrath: and behold every one *that is* proud, and <u>abase him</u>.   bring him low

12 Look on every one *that is* proud, *and* bring him low; and tread down the wicked in their place.

13 Hide them in the dust together; *and* bind their faces in secret.

14 Then will I also confess to you that your own right hand can save you.

15 Behold now <u>behemoth</u>, which I made with you; he eats grass as an ox.   elephant

16 Lo now, his strength *is* in his loins, and his force *is* in the navel of his belly.

17 He moves his tail like a cedar: the sinews of his <u>stones</u> are wrapped together. *thighs*

18 His bones *are as* strong pieces of brass; his bones *are* like bars of iron.

19 He *is* the chief of the ways of God: He that made him can make his sword to approach *to him*.

20 Surely the mountains bring him forth food, where all the beasts of the field play.

21 He lies under the shady trees, in the covert of the reed, and <u>fens</u>. *marsh*

22 The shady trees cover him *with* their shadow; thc willows of the brook <u>compass</u> him about. *surround*

23 Behold, he drinks up a river, *and* hurries not: he <u>trusts</u> that he can draw up Jor'dan into his mouth. *is confident*

24 He takes it with his eyes: *his* nose pierces through <u>snares</u>. *barbs*

CHAPTER 41

CAN you draw out <u>levia-than</u> with an hook? or his tongue with a cord *which* you let down? *i.e. crocodile*

2 Can you put an hook into his nose? or bore his jaw through with a thorn?

3 Will he make many supplications to you? will he speak soft *words* to you?

4 Will he make a <u>covenant</u> with you? will you take him for a servant for ever? *agreement*

5 Will you play with him as *with* a bird? or will you bind him for your maidens?

6 Shall the companions make a banquet of him? shall they part him among the merchants?

7 Can you fill his skin with barbed irons? or his head with fish spears?

8 Lay your hand upon him, remember the battle, do no more.

9 Behold, the hope of him is <u>in vain</u>: shall not *one* be cast down even at the sight of him? *false*

10 None *is so* fierce that dare stir him up: who then is able to stand before Me?

11 Who has <u>prevented</u> Me, that I should repay *him? whatsoever is* under the whole heaven is Mine.

ROM. 11:35 Lit. anticipated

12 I will not conceal his parts, nor his power, nor his comely proportion.

13 Who can <u>discover the face</u> of his garment? *or* who can come *to him* with his double bridle? *strip off the outside*

14 Who can open the doors of his face? his teeth *are* terrible round about.

15 *His* scales *are his* pride, shut up together *as with* a close seal.

16 One is so near to another, that no air can come between them.

17 They are joined one to another, they stick together, that they cannot be <u>sundered</u>. *separated*

18 By his sneezings a light does shine, and his eyes *are* like the eyelids of the morning.

19 Out of his mouth go burning lamps, *and* sparks of fire leap out.

20 Out of his nostrils goes smoke, as *out* of a <u>seething</u> pot or caldron. *boiling*

21 His breath kindles coals, and a flame goes out of his mouth.

22 In his neck remains strength,

and sorrow is turned into joy before him.

23 The <u>flakes</u> of his flesh are joined together: they are firm in themselves; they cannot be moved. folds

24 His heart is as firm as a stone; yea, as hard as a piece of the <u>nether</u> *millstone*. lower

25 When he raises up himself, the mighty are afraid: by reason of <u>breakings</u> they purify themselves.

consternation

26 The sword of him that lays at him cannot hold: the spear, the dart, nor the <u>habergeon</u>. javelin

27 He esteems iron as straw, *and* brass as rotten wood.

28 The arrow cannot make him flee: slingstones are turned with him into stubble.

29 Darts are counted as stubble: he laughs at the shaking of a spear.

30 Sharp stones *are* under him: he spreads sharp pointed things upon the mire.

31 He makes the deep to boil like a pot: he makes the sea like a pot of ointment.

32 He makes a path to shine after him; *one* would think the deep *to be* <u>hoary</u>. grey-haired

33 Upon earth there is not his like, who is made without fear.

34 He beholds all high *things*: he *is* a king over all the children of pride.

CHAPTER 42

THEN Job answered the LORD, and said,

2 I know that You can do every *thing*, and *that* no thought can be withheld from You.

3 Who *is* he that hides counsel without knowledge? therefore have I uttered that I understood not; things too wonderful for me, which I knew not.

4 Hear, I <u>beseech</u> You, and I will speak: I will demand of You, and declare You to me. beg

5 I have heard of You by the hearing of the ear: but now my eye sees You.

6 Wherefore I <u>abhor</u> *myself*, and repent in dust and ashes. despise

7 And it was *so*, that after the LORD had spoken these words to Job, the LORD said to El'i-phaz the Te'man-ite, My wrath is kindled against you, and against your two friends: for you have not spoken of Me *the thing that is* right, as My servant Job *has*.

8 Therefore take to you now seven bullocks and seven rams, and go to My servant Job, and offer up for yourselves a burned offering; and My servant Job shall pray for you: for him will I accept: less I deal with you *after your* folly, in that you have not spoken of Me *the thing which is* right, like My servant Job.

9 So El'i-phaz the Te'man-ite and Bil'dad the Shu'hite *and* Zo'phar the Na'a-math-ite went, and did according as the LORD commanded them: the LORD also accepted Job.

10 And the LORD <u>turned the captivity</u>

of Job, when he prayed for his friends: also the LORD gave Job twice as much as he had before.

restored the fortunes

11 Then came there to him all his brethren, and all his sisters, and all they that had been of his acquaintance before, and did eat bread with him in his house: and they <u>bemoaned</u> him, and comforted him over all the evil that the LORD had brought upon him: every man also gave him a piece of money, and every one an earring of gold.   *consoled*

12 So the LORD blessed the latter end of Job more than his beginning: for he had fourteen thousand sheep, and six thousand camels, and a thousand yoke of oxen, and a thousand she asses.

13 He had also seven sons and three daughters.

14 And he called the name of the first, Je-mi'-ma; and the name of the second, Ke-zi'a; and the name of the third, Ker'en-hap'puch.

15 And in all the land were no women found *so* fair as the daughters of Job: and their father gave them inheritance among their brethren.

16 After this lived Job an hundred and forty years, and saw his sons, and his sons' sons, *even* four generations.

17 So Job died, *being* old and full of days.

PSALMS

An outline of the Psalter must be general, since the individual psalms were apparently not collected with particular regard to subject or author. Possibly musical considerations partly determined the present arrangement. The Psalter is divided into five books, each marked at the end by a doxology. Of more significance than a general outline in the study of the Psalms is their classification according to subject matter.

OUTLINE

BOOK I, THE GENESIS BOOK CHIEFLY PRAYERS OF FAITH IN ADVERSITY 1—41
   (Exceptions: Praise Psalms, 8, 24, 29, 33; Royal, 2, 21; Psalms of Righteousness, 1, 15;
      Penitential, 32; Revelation, 19)

BOOK II, THE EXODUS BOOK CHIEFLY PRAYERS OF FAITH IN ADVERSITY 42—72
   (Exceptions: Praise Psalms, 47, 48, 50, 65—68; Royal, 45, 72; Penitential, 51; Imprecation, 58,
      59)

BOOK III, THE LEVITICUS BOOK PSALMS OF TRUST, ESPECIALLY IN NATIONAL DISTRESS 73—89
   (Exceptions: Praise Psalms, 75, 76; Historical, 78, 81; Love for Zion or for Temple, 84, 87;
      Rebuke to Wicked, 82)

BOOK IV, THE NUMBERS BOOK PSALMS OF PRAISE 90—106
   (Exceptions: Faith in Adversity, 90, 91, 94, 102; Historical, 105, 106; Psalm of Righteousness,
      101)

BOOK V, THE DEUTERONOMY BOOK MINGLED PSALMS, CHIEFLY PRAISE AND TRUST IN TROUBLE
      107—150
   (Exceptions: Royal Psalms, 110, 132; National Distress, 129, 137; Psalms of Righteousness, 112,
      116; Revelation, 119; Love for Zion, 122)
   (Special Categories in Book V: Songs of Degrees, 120—134; Hallel Psalms of Praise, 113—118,
      136, and 146—150)

SURVEY

The Psalms, half of which are ascribed by title to David, the sweet singer of Israel, by and large come from Israel's golden age, about 1000 B.C. Some were doubtless written later, even in the Captivity (for example, Ps 137). They express great truths in poetic style, calculated to reach the deep springs of the heart. They should teach us that head knowledge is not enough; the heart must be touched by God's redeeming grace.

Hebrew poetry does not consist in rhyme, but principally in repetition of the thought in a parallel clause, thus: "He hath not dealt with us after our sins, nor rewarded us according to our inquities" (Ps 103.10). Attention to this parallelism will occasionally help to interpret obscure words by the clearer parallel. Another device frequently found in poetry is dramatization. David does not write just for himself; he writes for others. Using the same poetic device, Shelley wrote "The Cloud," recounting the experiences of a cloud in the first person. The psalmists wrote for all of us, and we may take their prayers and praises as our own. When interpreting the Messianic Psalms, we must remember that here too David sometimes would write in the first person, yet give in vivid detail the experiences of the Messiah.

About half of the Psalms may be classified as prayers of faith in time of trouble. Such precious psalms as 23, 91, 121, and many others, sustain us in time of deepest need. We do well to memorize and recall these psalms often, so as to be fortified with the Word when testing comes. About forty

more psalms are devoted to the subject of praise. The note of praise to God should be a part of a Christian's very breath, and such psalms as 100 and 103 should have large place in our devotions.

Detailed classification of the Psalms is difficult because they are highly poetic and one psalm may touch on different themes. But we suggest several categories: Psalms of the Righteous Man are represented by 1, 15, 101, 112, and 133. Six may be called Royal Psalms, 2, 21, 45, 72, 110, and 132. Psalms 32 and 51 are usually called Penitential, along with parts of 38, 130, and 143. The Imprecatory Psalms ask vengeance on God's enemies: 69, 101, 137, and parts of 35, 55, and 58. There are at least four Historical Psalms: 78, 81, 105, and 106. Two emphasize Revelation, 19 and 119.

The Messianic Psalms applied to Christ in the New Testament are: 2, 8, 16, 22, 40, 41, 45, 68, 69, 89, 102, 109, 110, and 118. Some of these are typically messianic, that is, written of our general experiences, but applied to Christ. Others are directly predictive. Psalms 2, 45, and 110 predict the messianic King. In Psalm 45.6, the Messiah is God; in 110, He is the priest-king and David's Lord; in 2, He is God's Son to be worshiped. Other psalms speak of His suffering (22), His sacrifice (40), His resurrection (16.10, 11). In Psalm 89, He is the One Who brings to completion the Davidic Covenant in fulfilment of Israel's hopes.

AUTHOR

According to the titles, David was the author of seventy-three psalms, Asaph of twelve, the Sons of Korah, eleven, Solomon, two, and Moses and Ethan each one. No author is mentioned in the case of fifty psalms. The Greek Septuagint adds Haggai and Zechariah as authors of five.

The value of the titles has been disputed, but they were obviously much older than 200 B.C., for the Septuagint, translated at about that time, misunderstood several of the musical notations of the titles. Poetic compositions embedded in the pre-Exilic historic books show a similar use of titles (Hk 3.1; Is 38.9; 2 S 1.17; 23.1). Psalm 18, attributed to David by its title, is also said in 2 Samuel 22.1 to have been written by him. This reputation of David as a musician is mentioned repeatedly (2 S 23.1; 1 S 16.18; Am 6.5). Chronicles is quite explicit that David gathered temple choirs and composed psalms for them (1 Ch 16.4, 5; 25.1-5). The enigmatic musical terms of the titles are often associated by Chronicles with this work of David (1 Ch 15.20, 21; 16.4; compare the titles of Pss 46, 12, 38; and 105.1, 148.1; and others). Finally, Christ based an important argument on the validity of the title of Psalm 110 (Mk 12.36). There seems to be no positive evidence against the traditional view that most of the psalms were written around 1000 B.C., as the titles say. New evidence from the Dead Sea Scrolls forbids placing any of them as late as the Second Century B.C., as some scholars had once held.

R.L.H.

THE PSALMS

PSALM 1

Songs of Adoration
Thanksgiving to God;
Prophecy

BLESSED *is* the man that walks not in the counsel of the ungodly, nor stands in the way of sinners, nor sits in the seat of the scornful. Fortunate

2 But his delight *is* in the law of the LORD; and in His law does he meditate day and night. ROM.7:22

3 And he shall be like a tree planted by the rivers of water, that brings forth its fruit in its season; its leaf also shall not wither; and whatsoever he does shall prosper. whatever

4 The ungodly *are* not so: but *are* like the chaff which the wind drives away.

5 Therefore the ungodly shall not stand in the judgment, nor sinners in the congregation of the righteous. rise - assembly

6 For the LORD knows the way of the righteous: but the way of the ungodly shall perish.

PSALM 2

WHY do the heathen rage, and the people imagine a vain thing? nations

2 The kings of the earth set themselves, and the rulers take counsel together, against the LORD, and against His Anointed, *saying,* ACTS 4:25,27 i.e., Messiah-Christ

3 Let us break their bands asunder, and cast away their cords from us.

4 He that sits in the heavens shall laugh: the Lord shall have them in derision.

5 Then shall He speak to them in His anger, and vex them in His sore displeasure. terrify - fury

6 Yet have I set My king upon My holy hill of Zi'on. REV. 14:1 installed

7 I will declare the decree: the LORD has said to me, You *are* My Son; this day have I begotten You. HEB. 5:5 MATT. 3:17 MATT. 17:5 ACTS 13:33 HEB. 1:5 tell of

8 Ask of Me, and I shall give *You* the heathen *for* Your inheritance, and the uttermost parts of the earth *for* your possession. nations

9 You shall break them with a rod of iron; You shall dash them in pieces like a potter's vessel. REV. 2:27

10 Be wise now therefore, O you kings: be instructed, you judges of the earth.

11 Serve the LORD with fear, and rejoice with trembling. reverence

12 Kiss the Son, less He be angry, and you perish *from* the way, when His wrath is kindled but a little. Blessed *are* all they that put their trust in Him. Fortunate

PSALM 3

A Psalm of David, when he fled from Absalom his son

LORD, how are they increased that trouble me! many *are* they that rise up against me.

2 Many *there be* which say of my soul, *There is* no help for him in God. Se'lah. Elohim p.f. me

3 But You, O LORD, *are* a shield for me; my glory, and the lifter up of my head.

4 I cried to the LORD with my

voice, and He heard me out of His holy <u>hill</u>. Se'lah.   mountain

5 I laid me down and slept; I awaked; for the LORD sustained me.

6 I will not be afraid of ten thousands of people, that have set *themselves* against me round about.

7 Arise, O LORD; save me, O my God: for You have smitten all my enemies *upon* the cheek bone; You have broken the teeth of the ungodly.

8 Salvation *belongs* to the LORD: Your blessing *is* upon Your people. Se'lah.

P15A–843

PSALM 4

To the chief Musician on Neginoth. A Psalm of David

HEAR me when I call, O God of my righteousness: You have <u>en</u>larged me *when I was* in distress; have mercy upon me, and hear my prayer. relieved

2 O you sons of men, how long *will you turn* my glory into shame? *how long* will you love vanity, *and* seek after <u>leasing</u>? Se'lah.   falsehood

3 But know that the LORD has set apart him that is godly for Himself: the LORD will hear when I call to Him.

4 Stand in awe, and sin not: commune with your own heart upon your bed, and be still. Se'lah.

5 Offer the sacrifices of righteousness, and put your trust in the LORD.

6 *There be* many that say, Who will show us *any* good? LORD, lift You up the light of Your countenance upon us.

7 You have put gladness in my heart,

P15A–1042

more than in the time *that* their <u>corn</u> and their wine increased.   grain

8 I will both lay me down in peace, and sleep: for You, LORD, only make me dwell in safety.

PSALM 5

To the chief Musician upon Nehiloth, A Psalm of David

GIVE ear to my words, O LORD, consider my <u>meditation</u>.   sighing

2 Hearken to the voice of my cry, my King, and my God: for to You will I pray.   Elohim p.f.

3 My voice shall You hear in the morning, O LORD; in the morning will I direct *my prayer* to You, and will look up.

4 For You *are* not a God that has pleasure in wickedness: neither shall evil dwell with You.

5 The foolish shall not stand in Your sight: You <u>hate</u> all workers of iniquity.   despise

6 You shall destroy them that speak <u>leasing</u>: the LORD will abhor the bloody and deceitful man.   falsehood

7 But as for me, I will come *into* Your house in the multitude of Your mercy: *and* in Your <u>fear</u> will I worship toward Your holy temple. reverence

8 Lead me, O LORD, in Your righteousness because of my enemies; make Your way straight before my face.

9 For *there is* no faithfulness in their mouth; their inward part *is* very wickedness; their throat *is* an open <u>sepulcher</u>; they flatter with their tongue.   ROM. 3:10,13 tomb

10 Destroy You them, O God; let

MJ3–895

them fall by their own counsels; cast them out in the multitude of their transgressions; for they have rebelled against You.

11 But let all those that put their trust in You rejoice: let them ever shout for joy, because You defend them: let them also that love Your name be joyful in You.

12 For You, Lord, will bless the righteous; with favor will You <u>compass</u> him as *with* a shield.   surround

PSALM 6

To the chief Musician on Neginoth upon Sheminith, A Psalm of David

O LORD, rebuke me not in Your anger, neither chasten me in Your hot displeasure.

2 Have mercy upon me, O Lord; for I *am* weak: O Lord, heal me; for my bones are <u>vexed</u>.   dismayed

3 My soul is also <u>sore vexed</u>: but You, O Lord, how long?   greatly dismayed

4 Return, O Lord, deliver my soul: oh save me for Your mercies' sake.

5 For in death *there is* no remembrance of You: in the grave who shall give You thanks?

6 I am weary with my groaning; <u>all the night</u> make I my bed to swim; I water my couch with my tears.   every

7 My eye is <u>consumed</u> because of grief; it <u>waxes</u> old because of all my enemies.   wasted away - has become

8 Depart from me, all you workers of iniquity; for the Lord has heard the voice of my weeping.   MATT. 25:41

9 The Lord has heard my supplication; the Lord will receive my prayer.

10 Let all my enemies be ashamed and <u>sore vexed</u>: let them return *and* be ashamed suddenly.   greatly dismayed

PSALM 7

Shiggaion of David, which he sang to the LORD, concerning the words of Cush the Benjamite

O LORD my God, in You do I put my trust: save me from all them that persecute me, and deliver me:

2 Less he tear my soul like a lion, <u>rending</u> *it* in pieces, while *there is* none to deliver.   tearing

3 O Lord my <u>God</u>, if I have done this; if there be iniquity in my hands;

4 If I have rewarded evil to him that was at peace with me; (yea, I have delivered him that without cause is mine enemy:)   Elohim[p.f.]

5 Let the enemy persecute my soul, and take *it*; yea, let him tread down my life upon the earth, and lay my honor in the dust. Se'lah.

6 Arise, O Lord, in Your anger, lift up Yourself because of the rage of my enemies: and awake for me *to* the judgment *that* You have commanded.

7 So shall the congregation of the people <u>compass</u> You about: for their sakes therefore return You on high.   surround

8 The Lord shall judge the people: judge me, O Lord, according to my righteousness, and according to my integrity *that is* in me.

9 Oh let the wickedness of the wicked

come to an end; but establish the just: for the righteous God tries the hearts and reins.   secure - emotions

10 My defense *is* of God, which saves the upright in heart.

G1 11 God judges the righteous, and God is angry *with the wicked* every day.   Elohim^p.f. - El^s.f.

853

12 If he turn not, He will whet His sword; He has bent His bow, and made it ready.   sharpen

13 He has also prepared for him the instruments of death; He ordains His arrows against the persecutors.

14 Behold, he travails with iniquity, and has conceived mischief, and brought forth falsehood.

15 He made a pit, and dug it, and is fallen into the ditch *which* he made.

16 His mischief shall return upon his own head, and his violent dealing shall come down upon his own pate.   head

17 I will praise the Lord according to His righteousness: and will sing praise to the name of the Lord Most High.   Jehovah^s.f. - Elyon

PSALM 8

To the chief Musician Gittith, A Psalm of David

G4 **O** LORD our Lord, how excellent *is* Your name in all the earth! who have set Your glory above the heavens.

2 Out of the mouth of babes and sucklings have You ordained strength because of Your enemies, that You might still the enemy and the avenger.   MATT. 21:16 nursing babies

3 When I consider Your heavens, the work of Your fingers, the moon and the stars, which You have ordained;

4 What is man, that You are mindful of him? and the son of man, that You visit him?   HEB. 2:6 pay attention to

5 For You have made him a little lower than the angels, and have crowned him with glory and honor.   HEB. 2:7

6 You made him to have dominion over the works of Your hands; You have put all *things* under his feet: 1 COR. 15:27 EPH. 1:22 HEB. 2:8

7 All sheep and oxen, yea, and the beasts of the field;

8 The fowl of the air, and the fish of the sea, *and whatsoever* passes through the paths of the seas.

9 O Lord our Lord, how excellent *is* Your name in all the earth!   majestic

854

PSALM 9

To the chief Musician upon Muthlabben, A Psalm of David

I WILL praise *You*, O Lord, with my whole heart; I will show forth all Your marvellous works.   tell

2 I will be glad and rejoice in You: I will sing praise to Your name, O You Most High.

3 When my enemies are turned back, they shall fall and perish at Your presence.

4 For You have maintained my right and my cause; You sat in the throne judging right.   t

5 You have rebuked the heathen, You have destroyed the wicked, You have put out their name for ever and ever.   nations

6 O you enemy, destructions are

come to a perpetual end: and You have destroyed cities; their memorial is perished with them.

7 But the LORD shall endure for ever: He has prepared His throne for judgment.

8 And He shall judge the world in righteousness, He shall minister judgment to the people in uprightness.   ACTS 17:31

9 The LORD also will be a refuge for the oppressed, a refuge in times of trouble.

10 And they that know Your name will put their trust in You: for You, LORD, have not forsaken them that seek you.

11 Sing praises to the LORD, which dwells in Zi'on: declare among the people His doings.

12 When He makes inquisition for blood, He remembers them: He forgets not the cry of the humble.

13 Have mercy upon me, O LORD; consider my trouble *which I suffer* of them that hate me, You that lifts me up from the gates of death: persecute

14 That I may show forth all Your praise in the gates of the daughter of Zi'on: I will rejoice in Your salvation.   i.e., publicly

15 The heathen are sunk down in the pit *that* they made: in the net which they hid is their own foot taken. nations

16 The LORD is known *by* the judgment *which* He executes: the wicked is snared in the work of his own hands. Hig-ga'ion. Se'lah.   trapped

17 The wicked shall be turned into hell, *and* all the nations that forget God.

18 For the needy shall not always be forgotten: the expectation of the poor shall *not* perish for ever.

19 Arise, O LORD; let not man prevail: let the heathen be judged in Your sight.

20 Put them in fear, O LORD: *that* the nations may know themselves *to be but* men. Se'lah.   dread

PSALM 10

WHY stand You afar off, O LORD? *why* hide You *Yourself* in times of trouble?

2 The wicked in *his* pride does persecute the poor: let them be taken in the devices that they have imagined.

3 For the wicked boasts of his heart's desire, and blesses the covetous, *whom* the LORD abhors.

4 The wicked, through the pride of his countenance, will not seek *after God*: God *is* not in all his thoughts. Elohim[p.f.]

5 His ways are always grievous; Your judgments *are* far above out of his sight: *as for* all his enemies, he puffs at them.   snorts

6 He has said in his heart, I shall not be moved: for *I shall* never *be* in adversity.   trouble

7 His mouth is full of cursing and deceit and fraud: under his tongue *is* mischief and vanity.   ROM. 3:14

8 He sits in the lurking places of the villages: in the secret places does he murder the innocent: his eyes are privily set against the poor.   hidden - secretly

9 He lies in wait secretly as a lion in his den: he lies in wait to catch the poor: he does catch the poor, when he draws him into his net.

10 He crouches, *and* humbles himself, that the poor may fall by his strong ones.

11 He has said in his heart, God has forgotten: He hides His face; He will never see *it*.

12 Arise, O LORD; O God, lift up Your hand: forget not the humble.

13 Wherefore does the wicked contemn God? he has said in his heart, You will not require *it*.

revile - call me to account

14 You have seen *it*; for You behold mischief and spite, to requite *it* with Your hand: the poor commits himself to You; You are the helper of the fatherless.

repay

15 Break You the arm of the wicked and the evil *man*: seek out his wickedness *till* You find none.

16 The LORD *is* King for ever and ever: the heathen are perished out of His land.

nations

17 LORD, You have heard the desire of the humble: You will prepare their heart, You will cause Your ear to hear:

petition

18 To judge the fatherless and the oppressed, that the man of the earth may no more oppress.

PSALM 11

To the chief Musician, A Psalm of David

IN the LORD put I my trust: how say you to my soul, Flee *as* a bird to your mountain?

take refuge

2 For, lo, the wicked bend *their* bow, they make ready their arrow upon the string, that they may privily shoot at the upright in heart.

i.e., in the shadows

3 If the foundations be destroyed, what can the righteous do?

truth

4 The LORD *is* in His holy temple, the LORD's throne *is* in heaven: His eyes behold, His eyelids try, the children of men.

5 The LORD tries the righteous: but the wicked and him that loves violence His soul hates.

tests

6 Upon the wicked He shall rain snares, fire and brimstone, and an horrible tempest: *this shall be* the portion of their cup.

7 For the righteous LORD loves righteousness; His countenance does behold the upright.

PSALM 12

To the chief Musician upon Sheminith, A Psalm of David

HELP, LORD; for the godly man ceases; for the faithful fail from among the children of men.

2 They speak vanity every one with his neighbor: *with* flattering lips *and* with a double heart do they speak.

falsehood - deception

3 The LORD shall cut off all flattering lips, *and* the tongue that speaks proud things:

4 Who have said, With our tongue will we prevail; our lips *are* our own: who *is* lord over us?

5 For the oppression of the poor, for the sighing of the needy, now will I arise, says the LORD; I will set *him* in safety *from him* that puffs at him.

groaning - malign

6 The words of the L<small>ORD</small> *are* pure words: *as* silver <u>tried</u> in a furnace of earth, purified seven times. refined

7 You shall keep <u>them</u>, O L<small>ORD</small>, You shall preserve <u>them</u> from this generation for ever. i.e., the godly

8 The wicked walk on every side, when the vilest men are exalted.

PSALM 13

To the chief Musician, A Psalm of David

HOW long will You forget me, O L<small>ORD</small>? for ever? how long will You hide Your face from me?

2 How long <u>shall I take counsel in my soul</u>, *having* sorrow in my heart daily? how long shall my enemy be exalted over me? i.e., must I wrestle with my thoughts

3 Consider *and* hear me, O L<small>ORD</small> my God: lighten my eyes, less I sleep the *sleep of* death;

4 Less my enemy say, I have prevailed against him; *and* those that trouble me rejoice when I am moved.

5 But I have trusted in Your mercy; my heart shall rejoice in Your salvation.

6 I will sing to the L<small>ORD</small>, because He has dealt bountifully with me.

PSALM 14

To the chief Musician, A Psalm of David

THE fool has said in his heart, *There is* no God. They are corrupt, they have done <u>abominable</u> works, *there is* none that does good. detestable

2 The L<small>ORD</small> looked down from heaven upon the children of men, to see if there were any that did understand, *and* seek God.

3 They are all gone aside, they are *all* together become <u>filthy</u>: *there is* none that does good, no, not one. ROM.3:12 corrupt

4 Have all the workers of iniquity no knowledge? who eat up my people *as* they eat bread, and call not upon the L<small>ORD</small>.

5 There were they in great <u>fear</u>: for God *is* in the generation of the righteous. dread

6 You have shamed the counsel of the poor, because the L<small>ORD</small> *is* his refuge.

7 Oh that the <u>salvation</u> of Is'ra-el *were come* out of Zi'on! when the L<small>ORD</small> brings back the captivity of His people, Ja'cob shall rejoice, *and* Is'ra-el shall be glad. i.e., Heb. Jeshua

PSALM 15

A Psalm of David

LORD, who shall <u>abide</u> in Your <u>tabernacle</u>? who shall dwell in Your holy hill? dwell - tent

2 He that walks uprightly, and works righteousness, and speaks the truth in his heart.

3 *He that* backbites not with his tongue, nor does evil to his neighbor, <u>nor takes up a reproach</u> against his neighbor. casts no slur

4 In whose eyes a vile person is <u>contemned</u>; but he honors them that fear the L<small>ORD</small>. *He that* swears to *his own* hurt, and changes not. despised

5 *He that* puts not out his money <u>to usury</u>, nor takes reward against the

innocent. He that does these *things* shall never be moved.   for interest

PSALM 16

Michtam of David

PRESERVE me, O God: for in You do I put my trust.   Elsf

2 *O my soul,* you have said to the LORD, You *are* my Lord: my goodness *extends* not to You;   Adonahy.p.f.

3 *But* to the saints that *are* in the earth, and *to* the excellent, in whom *is* all my delight.   holy ones

4 Their sorrows shall be multiplied *that* hasten *after* another *god*: their drink offerings of blood will I not offer, nor take up their names into my lips.

5 The LORD *is* the portion of my inheritance and of my cup: You maintain my lot.

6 The lines are fallen to me in pleasant *places*; yea, I have a goodly heritage.

7 I will bless the LORD, who has given me counsel: my reins also instruct me in the night seasons.   guidance - mind

8 I have set the LORD always before me: because *He is* at my right hand, I shall not be moved.   ACTS 2:25

9 Therefore my heart is glad, and my glory rejoices: my flesh also shall rest in hope.

10 For You will not leave my soul in hell; neither will You allow Your Holy One to see corruption. ACTS 2:31 ACTS 13:35

11 You will show me the path of life: in Your presence *is* fulness of joy; at Your right hand *there are* pleasures for evermore.

PSALM 17

A Prayer of David

HEAR the right, O LORD, attend to my cry, give ear to my prayer, *that goes* not out of feigned lips.   deceitful

2 Let my sentence come forth from Your presence; let Your eyes behold the things that are equal.   judgment

3 You have proved my heart; You have visited *me* in the night; You have tried me, *and* shall find nothing; I am purposed *that* my mouth shall not transgress.   tried - examined - no evil in me

4 Concerning the works of men, by the word of Your lips I have kept *me from* the paths of the destroyer.   violent

5 Hold up my goings in Your paths, *that* my footsteps slip not.

6 I have called upon You, for You will hear me, O God: incline Your ear to me, *and hear* my speech.

7 Show your marvellous lovingkindness, O You that saves by Your right hand them which put their trust *in You* from those that rise up *against them*.

8 Keep me as the apple of the eye, hide me under the shadow of Your wings,

9 From the wicked that oppress me, *from* my deadly enemies, *who* compass me about.   surround

10 They are inclosed in their own fat: with their mouth they speak proudly.

11 They have now compassed us in our steps: they have set their eyes bowing down to the earth;

12 Like as a lion *that* is greedy of his

M09
GIP— 877
P03 —1052
P25 — 859
850
M16
853

prey, and as it were a young lion lurking in secret places.

13 Arise, O LORD, <u>disappoint</u> him, cast him down: deliver my soul from the wicked, *which is* Your sword: confront

14 From men *which are* Your hand, O LORD, from men of the world, *which have* their portion in *this* life, and whose belly You fill with Your hid *treasure*: they are full of children, and leave the rest of their *substance* to their babes.

15 As for me, I will behold Your face in righteousness: I shall be satisfied, when I awake, with Your likeness.

G4A — 855
G4H — 856
M09 — 873

PSALM 18

To the chief Musician, A Psalm of David, the servant of the LORD, who spoke to the LORD the words of *this song in the day *that* the LORD delivered him from the hand of all his enemies, and from the hand of Saul: And he said

I WILL love You, O LORD, my strength.

2 The LORD *is* my rock, and my fortress, and my deliverer; my <u>God</u>, my strength, in whom I will trust; my <u>buckler</u>, and the <u>horn</u> of my salvation, *and* my high tower.   Elˢ·ᶠ· - shield - i.e., strength

3 I will call upon the LORD, *who is worthy* to be praised: so shall I be saved from my enemies.

M42
G4C - 861

860

4 The sorrows of death <u>compassed</u> me, and the floods of ungodly men made me afraid.   surrounded

5 The sorrows of hell compassed me about: the <u>snares</u> of death prevented me.   traps

6 In my distress I called upon the LORD, and cried to my God: He heard my voice out of His temple, and my cry came before Him, *even* into His ears.

7 Then the earth shook and trembled; the foundations also of the hills moved and were shaken, because He was angry.

8 There went up a smoke out of His nostrils, and fire out of His mouth devoured: coals were kindled by it.

9 He bowed the heavens also, and came down: and darkness *was* under His feet.

10 And He rode upon a cherub, and did fly: yea, He did fly upon the wings of the wind.

11 He made darkness His secret place; His <u>pavilion</u> round about Him *were* dark waters *and* thick clouds of the skies.   canopy

12 At the brightness *that was* before Him His thick clouds passed, hail *stones* and coals of fire.

13 The LORD also thundered in the heavens, and the Highest gave His voice; hail *stones* and coals of fire.

14 Yea, He sent out His arrows, and scattered them; and He shot out lightnings, and <u>discomfited</u> them.   overwhelmed

15 Then the channels of waters were seen, and the foundations of the world were discovered at Your rebuke, O LORD, at the blast of the breath of Your nostrils.

16 He sent from above, He took me, He drew me out of many waters.

17 He delivered me from my strong

enemy, and from them which <u>hated</u>
me: for they were too strong for
me.   despised

M36-860
18 They <u>prevented</u> me in the
day of my calamity: but the
LORD was my <u>stay</u>.   confronted - support
19 He brought me forth also into a
<u>large</u> place; He delivered me, be-
cause He delighted in me.   broad
20 The LORD rewarded me according to my righteousness; according to the cleanness of my hands
has He recompensed me.
21 For I have kept the ways of the
LORD, and have not wickedly de-
parted from my <u>God</u>.   Elohim ᴾ·ᶠ·
22 For all His <u>judgments</u> were before me, and I did not put away His
<u>statutes</u> from me.   ordinances - decrees
23 I was also upright before Him, and
I kept myself from my iniquity.
24 Therefore has the LORD recompensed me according to my righteousness, according to the cleanness of my hands in His eyesight.
25 With the merciful You will show
Yourself merciful; with an upright
man You will show Yourself upright;
26 With the pure You will show Yourself pure; and with the <u>froward</u> You will
show Yourself <u>froward</u>.   crooked - astute
27 For You will save the afflicted
people; but will bring down high
looks.
28 For You will light my candle:
the LORD my God will enlighten
my darkness.
29 For by You I have run through
a troop; and by my God have I
leaped over a wall.

30 As for God, His way is perfect: the
word of the LORD is tried: He is a <u>buck-</u>
<u>ler</u> to all those that trust in Him.   shield
31 For who is God save the LORD?
or who is a rock save our God?
32 It is God that girds me with
strength, and makes my way perfect.
33 He makes my feet like <u>hinds'</u>
feet, and sets me upon my high
places.   deer
34 He teaches my hands to war,
so that a bow of <u>steel</u> is broken
by my arms.   bronze
35 You have also given me the shield
of Your salvation: and Your right
hand has held me up, and Your
gentleness has made me great.
36 You have <u>enlarged my steps un-</u>
<u>der</u> me, that my feet did not slip.
                                    supported
37 I have pursued my enemies, and
overtaken them: neither did I turn
again till they were consumed.
38 I have wounded them that they
were not able to rise: they are fallen
under my feet.
39 For You have <u>girded</u> me with
strength to the battle: You have
subdued under me those that
rose up against me.   armed
40 You have also given me the necks
of my enemies; that I might destroy
them that <u>hate</u> me.   despise
41 They cried, but there was none
to save them: even to the LORD, but
He answered them not.
42 Then did I beat them small as
the dust before the wind: I did cast
them out as the dirt in the streets.
43 You have delivered me from the

M03-856

strivings of the people; *and* You have made me the head of the <u>hea-then</u>: a people *whom* I have not known shall serve me.   nations

44 As soon as they hear of me, they shall obey me: the strangers shall <u>submit</u> themselves to me.   yield

45 The strangers shall fade away, and be afraid out of their <u>close places</u>.   strongholds

46 The Lord live; and blessed *be* my rock; and let the <u>God</u> of my salvation be exalted.   Elohim^{p.f.}

47 *It is* <u>God</u> that avenges me, and subdues the people under me.   El^{s.f.}

48 He delivers me from my enemies: yea, You lift me up above those that rise up against me: You have delivered me from the violent man.

49 Therefore will I give <u>thanks</u> to you, O Lord, among the heathen, and sing praises to Your name.   ROM. 15:9 praise

50 Great deliverance gives He to His king; and shows mercy to His anointed, to David, and to his <u>seed</u> for evermore.   descendants

PSALM 19

To the chief Musician, A Psalm of David

THE heavens <u>declare</u> the glory of God; and the <u>firmament</u> shows His handywork.   are telling of - expanse

2 Day to day utters speech, and night to night shows knowledge.

3 *There is* no <u>speech</u> nor language, *where* their voice is not heard.   word

4 Their line is gone out through all the earth, and their words to the end of the world. In them has He set a <u>tabernacle</u> for the sun,   ROM. 10:18 tent

5 Which *is* as a bridegroom coming out of his chamber, *and* rejoices as a strong man to run a race.

6 <u>His</u> going forth *is* from the end of the heaven, and <u>his</u> circuit to the ends of it: and there is nothing hid from the heat thereof.   i.e., the sun

7 The law of the Lord *is* perfect, converting the soul: the testimony of the Lord *is* sure, making wise the simple.

8 The <u>statutes</u> of the Lord *are* right, rejoicing the heart: the commandment of the Lord *is* pure, enlightening the eyes.   precepts

9 The <u>fear</u> of the Lord *is* clean, enduring for ever: the judgments of the Lord *are* true *and* righteous altogether.   reverence

10 More to be desired *are they* than gold, yea, than much fine gold: sweeter also than honey and the honeycomb.

11 Moreover by them is Your servant warned: *and* in keeping of them *there is* great reward.

12 Who can understand *his* errors? cleanse You me from secret *faults*.

13 Keep back Your servant also from presumptuous *sins*; let them not have dominion over me: then shall I be upright, and I shall be innocent from the great transgression.

14 Let the words of my mouth, and the meditation of my heart, be acceptable in your sight, O Lord, my <u>strength</u>, and my redeemer.   rock

PSALM 20

To the chief Musician, A Psalm of David

THE LORD hear you in the day of trouble; the name of the God of Ja'cob defend you; answer
2 Send you help from the sanctuary, and strengthen you out of Zi'on;
3 Remember all your offerings, and accept your burned sacrifice; Se'lah.
4 Grant you according to your own heart, and fulfill all your counsel. purpose
5 We will rejoice in your salvation, and in the name of our God we will set up *our* banners: the LORD fulfill all your petitions. i.e., Heb. Jeshua
6 Now know I that the LORD saves His anointed; He will hear him from His holy heaven with the saving strength of His right hand.
7 Some *trust* in chariots, and some in horses: but we will remember the name of the LORD our God. boast
8 They are brought down and fallen: but we are risen, and stand upright.
9 Save, LORD: let the king hear us when we call.

PSALM 21

To the chief Musician, A Psalm of David

THE king shall joy in Your strength, O LORD; and in Your salvation how greatly shall he rejoice! i.e., Heb. Jeshua
2 You have given him his heart's desire, and have not withheld the request of his lips. Se'lah.
3 For You prevents him with the blessings of goodness: You set a crown of pure gold on his head. welcome
4 He asked life of You, *and* You gave *it* him, *even* length of days for ever and ever.
5 His glory *is* great in Your salvation: honor and majesty have You laid upon him.
6 For You have made him most blessed for ever: You have made him exceeding glad with Your countenance. presence
7 For the king trusts in the LORD, and through the mercy of the Most High he shall not be moved. shaken
8 Your hand shall find out all Your enemies: Your right hand shall find out those that hate You. despise
9 You shall make them as a fiery oven in the time of Your anger: the LORD shall swallow them up in His anger, and the fire shall devour them.
10 Their fruit shall You destroy from the earth, and their seed from among the children of men. offspring - descendants
11 For they intended evil against You: they imagined a mischievous device, *which* they are not able *to perform*.
12 Therefore shall You make them turn their back, *when* You shall make ready *Your arrows* upon Your strings against the face of them.
13 Be You exalted, LORD, in Your own strength: *so* will we sing and praise Your power.

PSALM 22

To the chief Musician upon Aijeleth Shahar, A Psalm of David

MY God, my God, why have You forsaken me? *why are You so* far from helping me, *and from* the words of my roaring? Matt. 27:46 Mark 15:34 Elᵉᶠ. - groaning

2 O my God, I cry in the daytime, but You hear not; and in the night season, and am not silent. Elohimᵖ·ᶠ·

3 But You *are* holy, *O You* that inhabites the praises of Is'ra-el.

4 Our fathers trusted in You: they trusted, and You did deliver them.

5 They cried to You, and were delivered: they trusted in You, and were not confounded. disappointed

6 But I *am* a worm, and no man; a reproach of men, and despised of the people.

7 All they that see me laugh me to scorn: they shoot out the lip, they shake the head, *saying,* hurl insults

8 He trusted on the LORD *that* He would deliver him: let Him deliver him, seeing he delighted in Him. MATT. 27:43 MARK 15:31 relied on

9 But You *are* He that took me out of the womb: You did make me hope *when I was* upon my mother's breasts.

10 I was cast upon You from the womb: You *are* my God from my mother's belly. Elᵉᶠ.

11 Be not far from me; for trouble *is* near; for *there is* none to help. MATT. 27:46

12 Many bulls have compassed me: strong *bulls* of Ba'shan have beset me round. surrounded - encircled me

13 They gaped upon me *with* their mouths, *as* a ravening and a roaring lion.

14 I am poured out like water, and all my bones are out of joint: my heart is like wax; it is melted in the midst of my bowels. within me

15 My strength is dried up like a potsherd; and my tongue clings to my jaws; and You have brought me into the dust of death. i.e., piece of broken pottery

16 For dogs have compassed me: the assembly of the wicked have inclosed me: they pierced my hands and my feet.

17 I may tell all my bones: they look *and* stare upon me. count

18 They part my garments among them, and cast lots upon my vesture. MATT. 27:35 MARK 15:24 JOHN 19:24 for my clothing

19 But be not You far from me, O LORD: O my strength, haste You to help me.

20 Deliver my soul from the sword; my darling from the power of the dog. precious life

21 Save me from the lion's mouth: for You have heard me from the horns of the unicorns. 2 TIM. 4:17 wild oxen

22 I will declare Your name to my brethren: in the midst of the congregation will I praise You. HEB. 2:12

23 You that fear the LORD, praise Him; all you the seed of Ja'cob, glorify Him; and fear Him, all you the seed of Is'ra-el. reverence - descendants

24 For He has not despised nor abhorred the affliction of the afflicted; neither has He hid His face from him; but when he cried to Him, He heard.

25 My praise *shall be* of You in the

great congregation: I will pay my vows before them that <u>fear</u> Him. *honor*

26 The <u>meek</u> shall eat and be satisfied: they shall praise the LORD that seek Him: your heart shall live for ever. *afflicted*

27 All the ends of the world shall remember and turn to the LORD: and all the kindreds of the nations shall worship before You.

28 For the kingdom *is* the LORD's: and He *is* the governor among the nations.

29 All *they that be* <u>fat</u> upon earth shall eat and worship: all they that go down to the dust shall bow before Him: and none can keep alive his own soul. *prosperous*

30 <u>A seed</u> shall serve Him; it shall be accounted to the Lord for a generation. *Posterity*

31 They shall come, and shall declare His righteousness to a people that shall be born, that He has done *this*.

PSALM 23

A Psalm of David

THE LORD *is* my shepherd; I shall <u>not want</u>. *lack nothing*

2 He makes me to lie down in green pastures: He leads me beside the still waters.

3 He restores my soul: He leads me in the paths of righteousness for His name's sake.

4 Yea, though I walk through the valley of the shadow of death, I will fear no evil: for You *are* with me; Your rod and Your staff they comfort me.

5 You prepare a table before me in the presence of my enemies: You anoint my head with oil; my cup runs over.

6 Surely goodness and mercy shall follow me all the days of my life: and I will dwell in the house of the LORD for ever.

PSALM 24

A Psalm of David

THE earth *is* the LORD's, and the <u>fulness thereof</u>; the world, and they that dwell therein. *1 COR. 10:26 all it contains*

2 For He has founded it upon the seas, and established it upon the floods. *rivers*

3 Who shall ascend into the hill of the LORD? or who shall stand in His holy place?

4 He that has clean hands, and a pure heart; who has not lifted up his soul to <u>vanity</u>, nor sworn deceitfully. *i.e. wickedly*

5 He shall receive the blessing from the LORD, and righteousness from the <u>God</u> of his salvation. *Elohim*ᵖ.ᶠ

6 This *is* the generation of them that seek Him, that seek Your face, O Ja'cob. Se'lah.

7 Lift up your heads, O you gates; and be you lifted up, you everlasting doors; and the King of glory shall come in.

8 Who *is* this King of glory? The LORD strong and mighty, the LORD mighty in battle.

9 Lift up your heads, O you gates; even lift *them* up, you everlasting doors; and the King of glory shall come in.

10 Who is this King of glory? The

LORD of hosts, He *is* the King of glory. Se'lah.   Jehovah Tsebaoth

PSALM 25

A Psalm of David

TO you, O LORD, do I lift up my soul.

2 O my God, I trust in You: let me not be ashamed, let not my enemies triumph over me.

3 Yea, let none that wait on You be ashamed: let them be ashamed which transgress without cause.

4 Show me Your ways, O LORD; teach me Your paths.

5 Lead me in Your truth, and teach me: for You *are* the God of my salvation; on You do I wait all the day.

6 Remember, O LORD, Your tender mercies and Your lovingkindnesss; for they *have been* ever of old.

7 Remember not the sins of my youth, nor my transgressions: according to Your mercy remember You me for Your goodness' sake, O LORD.

8 Good and upright *is* the LORD: therefore will He teach sinners in the way.

9 The meek will He guide in judgment: and the meek will He teach His way.   humble

10 All the paths of the LORD *are* mercy and truth to such as keep His covenant and His testimonies.   obey - agreement

11 For Your name's sake, O LORD, pardon my iniquity; for it *is* great.

12 What man *is* he that fears the LORD? him shall He teach in the way *that* he shall choose.   reveres

13 His soul shall dwell at ease; and his seed shall inherit the earth.   descendants

14 The secret of the LORD *is* with them that fear Him; and He will show them His covenant.   reverence - agreement

15 My eyes *are* ever toward the LORD; for He shall pluck my feet out of the net.

16 Turn You to me, and have mercy upon me; for I *am* desolate and afflicted.

17 The troubles of my heart are enlarged: *O* bring You me out of my distresses.

18 Look upon my affliction and my pain; and forgive all my sins.

19 Consider my enemies; for they are many; and they hate me with cruel hatred.

20 O keep my soul, and deliver me: let me not be ashamed; for I put my trust in You.

21 Let integrity and uprightness preserve me; for I wait on You.   trust

22 Redeem Is'ra-el, O God, out of all his troubles.   Elohim[p.f.]

PSALM 26

A Psalm of David

JUDGE me, O LORD; for I have walked in my integrity: I have trusted also in the LORD; *therefore* I shall not slide.   waver

2 Examine me, O LORD, and prove me; try my reins and my heart.   emotions

3 For Your lovingkindness *is* before my eyes: and I have walked in Your truth.

4 I have not sat with vain persons, neither will I go in with <u>dissemblers</u>.   pretenders

5 I have <u>hated</u> the congregation of evildoers; and will not sit with the wicked.   abhorred

6 I will wash my hands in innocency: so will I <u>compass</u> Your altar, O LORD: MATT. 27:24 go about

7 That I may <u>publish</u> with the voice of thanksgiving, and tell of all Your wondrous works.   proclaim

8 LORD, I have loved the habitation of Your house, and the place where Your honor dwells.

9 Gather not my soul with sinners, nor my life with bloody men:

10 In whose hands *is* mischief, and their right hand is full of bribes.

11 But as for me, I will walk in my integrity: redeem me, and be merciful to me.

12 My foot stands in an even place: in the congregations will I bless the LORD.

PSALM 27

A Psalm of David

THE LORD *is* my light and my salvation; whom shall I fear? the LORD *is* the strength of my life; of whom shall I be afraid?

2 When the wicked, *even* my enemies and my foes, came upon me to eat up my flesh, they stumbled and fell.

3 Though an host should encamp against me, my heart shall not fear: though war should rise against me, <u>in this</u> *will* I *be* confident.   in spite of this

4 One *thing* have I desired of the LORD, that will I seek after; that I may dwell in the house of the LORD all the days of my life, to behold the beauty of the LORD, and to enquire in His temple.

5 For in the time of trouble He shall hide me in His pavilion: in the secret of His tabernacle shall He hide me; He shall set me up upon a rock.

6 And now shall my head be <u>lifted up</u> above my enemies round about me: therefore will I offer in His tabernacle sacrifices of joy; I will sing, yea, I will sing praises to the LORD.   exalted

7 Hear, O LORD, *when* I cry with my voice: <u>have mercy also upon me</u>, and answer me.   be gracious to

8 *When You said*, Seek you My face; my heart said to You, Your face, LORD, will I seek.

9 Hide not Your face *far* from me; put not Your servant away in anger: You have been my help; leave me not, neither forsake me, O God of my salvation.

10 When my father and my mother forsake me, then the LORD will take me up.

11 Teach me Your way, O LORD, and lead me in a plain path, because of my enemies.

12 Deliver me not over to the will of my enemies: for false witnesses are risen up against me, and such as breathe out cruelty.   MATT. 26:60

13 *I had fainted*, unless I had believed to see the goodness of the LORD in the land of the living.

14 <u>Wait</u> on the LORD: be of good courage, and He shall strengthen your heart: wait, I say, on the LORD.   Trust

PSALM 28

A Psalm of David

TO You will I cry, O LORD my rock; be not silent to me: less, *if* You be silent to me, I become like them that go down into the pit.

2 Hear the voice of my supplications, when I cry to You, when I lift up my hands toward Your <u>holy oracle</u>.   inner sanctuary

3 Draw me not away with the wicked, and with the workers of iniquity, which speak peace to their neighbor, but <u>mischief</u> *is* in their hearts.   evil

4 Give them according to their deeds, and according to the wickedness of their endeavours: give them after the work of their hands; render to them their desert.

5 Because they <u>regard not</u> the works of the LORD, nor the operation of His hands, He shall destroy them, and not build them up.   paid no attention to

6 Blessed *be* the LORD, because He has heard the voice of my supplications.

7 The LORD *is* my strength and my shield; my heart trusted in Him, and I am helped: therefore my heart greatly rejoices; and with my song will I praise Him.

8 The LORD *is* their strength, and He *is* the saving strength of His anointed.

9 Save Your people, and bless Your inheritance: feed them also, and lift them up for ever.

PSALM 29

A Psalm of David

GIVE to the LORD, O you mighty, give to the LORD glory and strength.

2 Give to the LORD the glory due to His name; worship the LORD in <u>the beauty of holiness</u>.   holy array

3 The voice of the LORD *is* upon the waters: the <u>God</u> of glory thunders: the LORD *is* upon many waters.   El^{s.f.}

4 The voice of the LORD *is* powerful; the voice of the LORD *is* full of majesty.

5 The voice of the LORD <u>breaks</u> the cedars; yea, the LORD <u>breaks</u> the cedars of Leb'a-non.   i.e., is in command

6 He makes them also to <u>skip like a calf</u>; Leb'a-non and Sir'i-on like a young unicorn.   i.e., obey

7 The voice of the LORD divides the flames of fire.

8 The voice of the LORD shakes the wilderness; the LORD shakes the wilderness of Ka'desh.

9 The voice of the LORD makes the <u>hinds</u> to calve, and discovers the forests: and in His temple does every one speak of *His* glory.   deer

10 The LORD sits upon the flood; yea, the LORD sits King for ever.

11 The LORD will give strength to His people; the LORD will bless His people with peace.

PSALM 30

A Psalm and Song *at* the dedication of the house of David

I WILL <u>extol</u> You, O LORD; for You have lifted me up, and have not made my foes to rejoice over me. *exalt*

2 O LORD my <u>God</u>, I cried to You, and You have healed me. *Elohim*ᵖˑ

3 O LORD, You have brought up my soul from the grave: You have kept me alive, that I should not go down to the pit.

4 Sing to the LORD, O you saints of His, and give thanks at the remembrance of His holiness.

5 For His anger *endures but* a moment; in His favor *is* life: weeping may endure for a night, but joy *comes* in the morning.

6 And in my prosperity I said, I shall never be moved.

7 LORD, by Your favor You have made my mountain to stand strong: you did hide Your face, *and* I was troubled.

8 I cried to You, O LORD; and to the LORD I made supplication.

9 What profit *is there* in my blood, when I go down to the pit? Shall the dust praise You? shall it declare Your truth?

10 Hear, O LORD, and have mercy upon me: LORD, be You my helper.

11 You have turned for me my mourning into dancing: You have put off my sackcloth, and girded me with gladness;

12 To the end that *my* <u>glory</u> may sing praise to You, and not be silent. O

LORD my God, I will give thanks to You for ever. *heart*

PSALM 31

To the chief Musician, A Psalm of David

IN You, O LORD, do I put my trust; let me never be ashamed: deliver me in Your righteousness.

2 Bow down Your ear to me; deliver me speedily: be You my strong rock, for an house of defence to save me.

3 For You *are* my rock and my fortress; therefore for Your name's sake lead me, and guide me.

4 <u>Pull</u> me out of the net that they have laid <u>privily</u> for me: for You *are* my strength. *Free - secretly*

5 Into Your hand I commit my spirit: You have redeemed me, O LORD God of truth. *LUKE 23:46*

6 I have <u>hated</u> them that regard <u>lying vanities</u>: but I trust in the LORD. *despised - vain idols*

7 I will be glad and rejoice in Your mercy: for You have considered my trouble; You have known my soul in adversities;

8 And have not <u>shut me up</u> into the hand of the enemy: You have set my feet in a large room. *given me over*

9 Have mercy upon me, O LORD, for I am in trouble: my eye is consumed with grief, *yea*, my soul and my <u>belly</u>. *body*

10 For my life is spent with grief, and my years with sighing: my strength fails because of my iniquity, and my bones are consumed.

11 I was a reproach among all my enemies, but especially among my neighbors, and a <u>fear</u> to my acquaintance: they that did see me without fled from me. dread

12 I am forgotten as a dead man out of mind: I am like a broken vessel.

13 For I have heard the slander of many: <u>fear</u> *was* on every side: while they took counsel together against me, they devised to take away my life. MATT. 27:1 terror

14 But I trusted in You, O LORD: I said, You *are* my <u>God</u>. Elohim p.f.

15 My times *are* in Your hand: deliver me from the hands of my enemies, and from them that persecute me.

16 Make Your face to shine upon Your servant: save me for Your mercies' sake.

17 Let me not be ashamed, O LORD; for I have called upon You: let the wicked be ashamed, *and* let them be silent in the <u>grave</u>. Sheol

18 Let the lying lips be put to silence; which speak <u>grievous</u> things proudly and contemptuously against the righteous. arrogantly

19 *Oh* how great *is* Your goodness, which You have laid up for them that <u>fear</u> You; *which* You have wrought for them that trust in You before the sons of men! reverence

20 You shall hide them in the secret of Your presence from the pride of man: You shall keep them secretly in a <u>pavilion</u> from the strife of tongues. shelter

21 Blessed *be* the LORD: for He has showed me His marvellous kindness in a <u>strong</u> city. besieged

22 For I said in my haste, I am cut off from before Your eyes: nevertheless You heard the voice of my <u>supplications</u> when I cried to You. appeals

23 O love the LORD, all you His saints: *for* the LORD preserves the faithful, and plentifully rewards the proud doer.

24 Be of good courage, and He shall strengthen your heart, all you that hope in the LORD. 1 COR. 16:13

PSALM 32

A Psalm of David, Maschil

BLESSED *is he whose* transgression *is* forgiven, *whose* sin *is* covered. ROM. 4:7 Fortunate

2 <u>Blessed</u> *is* the man to whom the LORD <u>imputes</u> not <u>iniquity</u>, and in whose spirit *there is* no <u>guile</u>. counts - sin - deceit

3 When I kept silence, my bones <u>waxed</u> old through my <u>roaring</u> all the day long. grew - groaning

4 For day and night Your hand was heavy upon me: my moisture is turned into the drought of summer. Se'lah.

5 I acknowledged my sin to You, and my <u>iniquity</u> have I not hid. I said, I will confess my transgresions to the LORD; and You forgave the iniquity of my sin. Se'lah. guilt

6 For this shall every one that is godly pray to You in a time when You may be found: surely in the floods of great waters they shall not come near to him.

7 You *are* my hiding place; You shall preserve me from trouble; You shall

compass me about with songs of deliverance. Se'lah. *surround*

8 I will instruct you and teach you in the way which you shall go: I will guide you with My eye. *counsel*

9 Be you not as the horse, *or* as the mule, *which* have no understanding: whose mouth must be held in with bit and bridle, less they come near to you.

10 Many sorrows *shall be* to the wicked: but he that trusts in the LORD, mercy shall compass him about.

11 Be glad in the LORD, and rejoice, you righteous: and shout for joy, all *you that are* upright in heart.

PSALM 33

REJOICE in the LORD, O you righteous: *for* praise is comely for the upright.

2 Praise the LORD with harp: sing to Him with the psaltery *and* an instrument of ten strings. *lyre*

3 Sing to Him a new song; play skilfully with a loud noise.

4 For the word of the LORD *is* right; and all His works *are done* in truth.

5 He loves righteousness and judgment: the earth is full of the goodness of the LORD.

justice - unfailing love

6 By the word of the LORD were the heavens made; and all the host of them by the breath of His mouth.

7 He gathers the waters of the sea together as an heap: He lays up the depth in storehouses.

8 Let all the earth fear the LORD: let all the inhabitants of the world stand in awe of Him. *reverence*

9 For He spoke, and it was *done*; He commanded, and it stood fast.

10 The LORD brings the counsel of the heathen to nothing: he makes the devices of the people of none effect. *nations - plans*

11 The counsel of the LORD stands for ever, the thoughts of His heart to all generations.

12 Blessed *is* the nation whose God *is* the LORD; *and* the people *whom* He has chosen for His own inheritance. *Fortunate - Elohim*[p.f.]

13 The LORD looks from heaven; He beholds all the sons of men.

14 From the place of His habitation He looks upon all the inhabitants of the earth.

15 He fashions their hearts alike; He considers all their works.

16 There is no king saved by the multitude of an host: a mighty man is not delivered by much strength.

17 An horse *is* a vain thing for safety: neither shall he deliver *any* by his great strength. *false hope*

18 Behold, the eye of the LORD *is* upon them that fear Him, upon them that hope in His mercy; *revere*

19 To deliver their soul from death, and to keep them alive in famine.

20 Our soul waits for the LORD: He *is* our help and our shield.

21 For our heart shall rejoice in Him, because we have trusted in His holy name.

22 Let Your mercy, O LORD, be upon us, according as we hope in You.

PSALM 34

A Psalm of David, when he changed his behavior before Abimelech, who drove him away, and he departed

I WILL bless the LORD at all times: His praise *shall* continually *be* in my mouth.   EPH. 5:20

2 My soul shall make her boast in the LORD: the humble shall hear *thereof*, and be glad.

3 O magnify the LORD with me, and let us exalt His name together.

4 I sought the LORD, and He heard me, and delivered me from all my fears.

5 They looked to Him, and were lightened: and their faces were not ashamed.

6 This poor man cried, and the LORD heard *him*, and saved him out of all his troubles.

7 The angel of the LORD encamps round about them that fear Him, and delivers them.   messenger

8 O taste and see that the LORD *is* good: blessed *is* the man *that* trusts in Him.   1 PET. 2:3 fortunate

9 O fear the LORD, you His saints: for *there is* no want to them that fear Him.   reverence

10 The young lions do lack, and suffer hunger: but they that seek the LORD shall not want any good *thing*.

11 Come, you children, hearken to me: I will teach you the fear of the LORD.   reverence

12 What man *is he that* desires life, *and* loves *many* days, that he may see good?

13 Keep your tongue from evil, and your lips from speaking guile.   deceit

14 Depart from evil, and do good; seek peace, and pursue it.

15 The eyes of the LORD *are* upon the righteous, and His ears *are open* to their cry.   1 PET. 3:12

16 The face of the LORD *is* against them that do evil, to cut off the remembrance of them from the earth.

17 The *righteous* cry, and the LORD hears, and delivers them out of all their troubles.   rescues

18 The LORD *is* near to them that are of a broken heart; and saves such as be of a contrite spirit.

19 Many *are* the afflictions of the righteous: but the LORD delivers him out of them all.

20 He keeps all his bones: not one of them is broken.   JOHN 19:36

21 Evil shall slay the wicked: and they that hate the righteous shall be desolate.

22 The LORD redeems the soul of His servants: and none of them that trust in Him shall be desolate.

PSALM 35

A Psalm of David

PLEAD *my cause*, O LORD, with them that strive with me: fight against them that fight against me.

2 Take hold of shield and buckler, and stand up for mine help.   large shield and small shield

3 Draw out also the spear, and stop

the way against them that persecute me: say to my soul, I *am* your
<u>salvation</u>.   the battle ax - i.e., Heb. Jeshua
4 Let them be <u>confounded</u> and put
to shame that seek after my soul: let
them be turned back and brought to
confusion that devise my hurt. ashamed
5 Let them be as chaff before the
wind: and let the <u>angel</u> of the
LORD chase *them*.   messenger
6 Let their way be dark and slip-
pery: and let the <u>angel</u> of the LORD
persecute them.
7 For without cause have they hid for
me their net *in* a pit, *which* without
cause they have dug for my soul.
8 Let destruction come upon him at
unawares; and let his net that he has
hid catch himself: into that very destruction let him fall.
9 And my soul shall be joyful in the
LORD: it shall rejoice in His salvation.
10 All my bones shall say, LORD, who
is like to You, which delivers the poor
from him that is too strong for him,
yea, the poor and the needy from
him that spoils him?
11 False witnesses did rise up; they
laid to my charge *things* that I
knew not.
12 They rewarded me evil for good
to the <u>spoiling</u> of my soul.   bereavement
13 But as for me, when they were sick,
my clothing *was* sackcloth: I humbled
my soul with fasting; and my prayer
returned into my own bosom.
14 I behaved myself as though *he*
had been my friend *or* brother: I
bowed down heavily, as one that
mourns *for his* mother.

15 But in my <u>adversity</u> they rejoiced, and gathered themselves together: *yea*, the <u>abjects</u> gathered
themselves together against me,
and I knew *it* not; they did tear *me*,
and ceased not   stumbling - smiters
16 With hypocritical mockers in feasts,
they gnashed upon me with their teeth.
17 Lord, how long will You look
on? rescue my soul from their
destructions, my <u>darling</u> from
the lions.   precious life
18 I will give You thanks in the great
congregation: I will praise You
among much people.
19 Let not them that are my enemies
wrongfully rejoice over me: *neither*
let them wink with the eye that <u>hate</u>
me without a cause.   abhor
20 For they speak not peace: but
they devise deceitful matters against
them that are quiet in the land.
21 Yea, they opened their mouth
wide against me, *and* said, Aha, aha,
our eye has seen *it*.
22 *This* You have seen, O LORD:
keep not silence: O <u>Lord</u>, be not
far from me.   Adonahy[p.f.]
23 Stir up Yourself, and awake to my
judgment, *even* to my cause, my
God and my <u>Lord</u>.   Elohim[p.f.] - Adonahy[p.f.]
24 Judge me, O LORD my God, ac-
cording to Your righteousness; and
let them not rejoice over me.
25 Let them not say in their hearts,
Ah, so would we have it: let them not
say, We have swallowed him up.
26 Let them be ashamed and brought
to <u>confusion</u> together that rejoice at
my hurt: let them be clothed with

shame and dishonor that magnify *themselves* against me.   humiliation

27 Let them shout for joy, and be glad, that favor my righteous cause: yea, let them say continually, Let the LORD be magnified, which has pleasure in the prosperity of His servant.

28 And my tongue shall speak of Your righteousness *and* of Your praise all the day long.

PSALM 36

To the chief Musician, A Psalm of David the servant of the LORD

THE transgression of the wicked says within my heart, *that there is* no <u>fear</u> of God before his eyes.   ROM. 3:18 reverence

2 For he flatters himself in his own eyes, until his iniquity be found to be <u>hateful</u>.   despiseful

3 The words of his mouth *are* iniquity and deceit: he has left off to be wise, *and* to do good.

4 He devises mischief upon his bed; he sets himself in a way *that is* not good; he abhors not evil.

5 Your mercy, O LORD, *is* in the heavens; *and* Your faithfulness *reaches* to the clouds.

6 Your righteousness *is* like the great mountains; Your judgments *are* a great deep: O LORD, You preserve man and beast.

7 How <u>excellent</u> *is* Your lovingkindness, O God! therefore the children of men <u>put their trust under</u> the shadow of Your wings. priceless - take refuge in

8 They shall be abundantly satisfied with the <u>fatness</u> of Your house; and

You shall make them drink of the river of Your pleasures.   riches

9 For with You *is* the fountain of life: in Your light shall we see light.

10 O continue Your lovingkindness to them that know You; and Your righteousness to the upright in heart.

11 Let not the foot of pride come against me, and let not the hand of the wicked <u>remove me</u>.   drive me away

12 There are the workers of iniquity fallen: they are cast down, and shall not be able to rise.

PSALM 37

A Psalm of David

FRET not Yourself because of evildoers, neither be you envious against the workers of iniquity.

2 For they shall soon be cut down like the grass, and wither as the green herb.

3 Trust in the LORD, and do good; *so* shall you dwell in the land, and verily you shall be fed.

4 Delight yourself also in the LORD; and He shall give you the desires of your heart.

5 Commit your way to the LORD; trust also in Him; and He shall bring *it* to pass.

6 And He shall bring forth your righteousness as the light, and your judgment as the noonday.

7 Rest in the LORD, and wait patiently for him: <u>fret</u> not yourself because of him who prospers in his way, because of the man who brings wicked devices to pass.   worry

8 Cease from anger, and forsake wrath: fret not yourself in any wise to do evil.

9 For evildoers shall be <u>cut off</u>: but those that wait upon the Lord, they shall inherit the earth.   destroyed

10 For yet a little while, and the wicked *shall* not *be*: yea, you shall diligently consider his place, and it *shall* not *be*.

11 But the <u>meek</u> shall inherit the earth; and shall delight themselves in the abundance of peace.   MATT. 5:5 humble

12 The wicked plots against the just, and gnashes upon him with his teeth.

13 The Lord shall laugh at him: for He sees that his day is coming.

14 The wicked have drawn out the sword, and have bent their bow, to cast down the poor and needy, *and* to slay such as be of upright conversation.

15 Their sword shall enter into their own heart, and their bows shall be broken.

16 A little that a righteous man has *is* better than the riches of many wicked.

17 For the arms of the wicked shall be broken: but the Lord upholds the righteous.

18 The Lord knows the days of the upright: and their inheritance shall be for ever.

19 They shall not be ashamed in the evil time: and in the days of famine they shall be satisfied.

20 But the wicked shall perish, and the enemies of the Lord *shall be* as the fat of lambs: they shall consume; into smoke shall they consume away.

21 The wicked borrows, and pays not again: but the righteous <u>shows</u> <u>mercy</u>, and gives.   is gracious

22 For *such as be* blessed of Him shall inherit the earth; and *they that be* cursed of Him shall be cut off.

23 The steps of a *good* man are ordered by the Lord: and He delights in his way.

24 Though he fall, he shall not be utterly cast down: for the Lord upholds *him with* His hand.

25 I have been young, and *now* am old; yet have I not seen the righteous forsaken, nor his seed begging bread.

26 *He is* ever merciful, and lends; and His <u>seed</u> *is* blessed.   descendants

27 Depart from evil, and do good; and dwell for evermore.

28 For the Lord loves <u>judgment</u>, and forsakes not His saints; they are preserved for ever: but the <u>seed</u> of the wicked shall be cut off.   justice

29 The righteous shall inherit the land, and dwell therein for ever.

30 The mouth of the righteous speaks wisdom, and his tongue talks of judgment.

31 The law of his <u>God</u> *is* in his heart; none of his steps shall <u>slide</u>.   Elohim^p.f. - slip

32 The wicked watches the righteous, and seeks to slay him.

33 The Lord will not leave him in his hand, nor condemn him when he is judged.

34 Wait on the Lord, and keep His way, and He shall exalt you to inherit

the land: when the wicked are cut off, you shall see *it*.

35 I have seen the wicked in great power, and spreading himself like a <u>green bay</u> tree.   luxuriant

36 Yet he passed away, and, lo, he *was* not: yea, I sought him, but he could not be found.

37 Mark the perfect *man*, and behold the upright: for the end of *that* man *is* <u>peace</u>.   posterity

38 But the transgressors shall be destroyed together: the end of the wicked shall be cut off.

39 But the salvation of the righteous *is* of the LORD: *He is* their strength in the time of trouble.

40 And the LORD shall help them, and deliver them: He shall deliver them from the wicked, and save them, because they trust in Him.

PSALM 38

A Psalm of David, to bring to remembrance

O LORD, rebuke me not in Your wrath: neither chasten me in Your hot displeasure.

2 For Your arrows <u>stick fast in</u> me, and Your hand presses me <u>sore</u>.   pierce - down

3 *There is* no soundness in my flesh because of Your anger; neither *is there any* rest in my bones because of my sin.

4 For my iniquities are gone over my head: as an heavy burden they are too heavy for me.

5 My <u>wounds</u> stink *and* are corrupt because of my foolishness.   stripes

6 I am troubled; I am bowed down greatly; I go mourning all the day long.

7 For my loins are filled with a <u>loathsome *disease*</u>: and *there is* no soundness in my flesh.   searing pain

8 I am feeble and <u>sore broken</u>: I <u>have roared</u> by reason of the disquietness of my heart.   badly crushed - groan

9 Lord, all my desire *is* before You; and my groaning is not hid from You.

10 My heart pants, my strength fails me: as for the light of my eyes, it also is gone from me.

11 My lovers and my friends stand aloof from my <u>sore</u>; and my kinsmen stand afar off.   plague

12 They also that seek after my life lay <u>snares</u> *for me*: and they that seek my hurt speak mischievous things, and imagine deceits all the day long.   traps

13 But I, as a deaf *man*, heard not; and *I was* as a dumb man *that* opens not his mouth.

14 Thus I was as a man that hears not, and in whose mouth *are* no <u>reproofs</u>.   arguments

15 For in You, O LORD, do I hope: You will hear, O Lord my <u>God</u>.

Adonahy[p.f.] - Elohim[p.f.]

16 For I said, *Hear me*, less *otherwise* they should rejoice over me: when my foot slips, they magnify *themselves* against me.

17 For I *am* ready to <u>halt</u>, and my sorrow *is* continually before me.   fall

18 For I will declare my iniquity; I will be sorry for my sin.

19 But my enemies *are* <u>lively</u>, *and* they are strong: and they that <u>hate</u> me wrongfully are multiplied.   vigorous - abhor

20 They also that render evil for good are my adversaries; because I follow *the thing that* good *is*.
21 Forsake me not, O Lᴏʀᴅ: O my God, be not far from me.
22 Make haste to help me, O Lord my salvation.

PSALM 39

To the chief Musician, even To Jeduthun, A Psalm of David

I SAID, I will take heed to my ways, that I sin not with my tongue: I will keep my mouth with a bridle, while the wicked is before me.
2 I was dumb with silence, I held my peace, *even* from good; and my sorrow <u>was stirred</u>.   increased
3 My heart was hot within me, while I was musing the fire burned: *then* spoke I with my tongue,
4 Lᴏʀᴅ, make me to know my end, and the measure of my days, what it *is; that* I may know how frail I *am*.
5 Behold, You have made my days *as* an handbreadth; and my age *is* as nothing before You: <u>verily</u> every man at his best state *is* <u>altogether vanity</u>. Se'lah.   surely - as nothing
6 Surely every man walks in a vain show: surely they are disquieted in vain: he heaps up *riches*, and knows not who shall gather them.
7 And now, Lord, what wait I for? my hope *is* in You.
8 Deliver me from all my transgressions: make me not the reproach of the foolish.

9 I was dumb, I opened not my mouth; because You did *it*.
10 Remove Your <u>stroke</u> away from me: I am consumed by the blow of Your hand.   plague
11 When You with rebukes do correct man for iniquity, You make his beauty to consume away like a moth: surely every man *is* <u>vanity</u>. Se'lah.   as nothing
12 Hear my prayer, O Lᴏʀᴅ, and give ear to my cry; hold not Your peace at my tears: for I *am* a stranger with You, *and* a <u>sojourner</u>, as all my fathers *were*.   HEB. 11:13 temporary resident
13 O spare me, that I may recover strength, before I go from here, and be no more.

PSALM 40

To the chief Musician, A Psalm of David

I WAITED patiently for the Lᴏʀᴅ; and He inclined to me, and heard my cry.
2 He brought me up also out of an horrible pit, out of the miry clay, and set my feet upon a rock, *and* established my goings.
3 And He has put a new song in my mouth, *even* praise to our <u>God</u>: many shall see *it*, and fear, and shall trust in the Lᴏʀᴅ.   Elohim ᴾ·ᶠ·
4 <u>Blessed</u> *is* that man that makes the Lᴏʀᴅ his trust, and respects not the proud, nor such as turn aside to lies.   Fortunate
5 Many, O Lᴏʀᴅ my God, *are* Your wonderful works *which* You have done, and Your thoughts *which are* to us-ward:

they cannot be reckoned up in order to You: *if* I would declare and speak *of them*, they are more than can be numbered.

6 Sacrifice and offering You did not desire; my ears have You opened: burned offering and sin offering have You not required.   HEB. 10:5-7

7 Then said I, Lo, I come: in the volume of the book *it is* written of me,

8 I delight to do Your will, O my God: yea, Your law *is* within my heart.   HEB. 10:7

9 I have preached righteousness in the great congregation: lo, I have not <u>refrained</u> my lips, O LORD, You know.   held back

10 I have not hid Your righteousness within my heart; I have declared Your faithfulness and Your salvation: I have not concealed Your lovingkindness and Your truth from the great congregation.   ACTS 20:20

11 Withhold not You Your tender mercies from me, O LORD: let Your lovingkindness and Your truth continually preserve me.

12 For innumerable evils have <u>compassed</u> me about: my iniquities have taken hold upon me, so that I am not able to look up; they are more than the hairs of my head: therefore my heart fails me.   surrounded

13 Be pleased, O LORD, to deliver me: O LORD, make haste to help me.

14 Let them be ashamed and confounded together that seek after my soul to destroy it; let them be driven backward and put to shame that wish me evil.

15 Let them be desolate for a reward of their shame that say to me, Aha, aha.

16 Let all those that seek You rejoice and be glad in You: let such as love Your salvation say continually, The LORD be magnified.

17 But I *am* poor and needy; *yet* the Lord thinks upon me: You *are* my help and my deliverer; make no tarrying, O my God.

PSALM 41

To the chief Musician, A Psalm of David

BLESSED *is* he that considers the poor: the LORD will deliver him in time of trouble.   Fortunate

2 The LORD will <u>preserve</u> him, and keep him alive; *and* he shall be <u>blessed</u> upon the earth: and You will not deliver him to the will of his enemies.   protect

3 The LORD will strengthen him upon the bed of <u>languishing</u>: You will <u>make all his bed in his sickness</u>.   sickness - restore him to health

4 I said, LORD, be merciful to me: heal my soul; for I have sinned against You.

5 My enemies speak evil of me, When shall he die, and his name perish?

6 And if he come to see *me*, he speaks <u>vanity</u>: his heart gathers iniquity to itself; *when* he goes abroad, he tells *it*.   i.e. wickedly

7 All that <u>hate</u> me whisper together against me: against me do they devise my hurt.   despise

8 An evil disease, *say they*, <u>cleaves fast</u> to him: and *now* that he lies he shall rise up no more. is poured out
9 Yea, my own familiar friend, in whom I trusted, which did eat of my bread, has lifted up *his* heel against me. MARK 14:18 JOHN 13:18-21 JOHN 17:12
10 But You, O LORD, be merciful to me, and raise me up, that I may requite them.
11 By this I know that You favor me, because my enemy does not triumph over me.
12 And as for me, You uphold me in my integrity, and sets me before Your face for ever.
13 <u>Blessed</u> *be* the <u>LORD God</u> of Is'ra-el from everlasting, and to everlasting. Amen, and Amen. Praise - Jehovah^{s.f.} Elohim^{p.f.}

PSALM 42

To the chief Musician, Maschil, for the sons of Korah

AS the <u>hart</u> pants after the water brooks, so pants my soul after You, O God. deer
2 My soul thirsts for God, for the living <u>God</u>: when shall I come and appear before God? El^{s.f.}
3 My tears have been my <u>meat</u> day and night, while they continually say to me, Where *is* your God? food
4 When I remember these *things*, I pour out my soul in me: for I had gone with the multitude, I went with them to the house of God, with the voice of joy and praise, with a multitude that kept <u>holyday</u>. the festival

5 Why are you cast down, O my soul? and *why* arc you disquieted in me? hope you in God: for I shall yet praise Him *for* the help of His <u>countenance</u>. presence
6 O my God, my soul is cast down within me: therefore will I remember You from the land of Jor'dan, and of the Her'mon-ites, from the hill Mi'zar.
7 Deep calls to deep at the noise of Your <u>waterspouts</u>: all Your waves and Your billows are gone over me. waterfalls
8 *Yet* the LORD will command His lovingkindness in the daytime, and in the night His song *shall be* with me, *and* my prayer to the God of my life.
9 I will say to God my rock, Why have You forgotten me? why go I mourning because of the oppression of the enemy?
10 *As* with a sword in my bones, my enemies reproach me; while they say daily to me, Where *is* your God?
11 Why are you cast down, O my soul? and why are you disquieted within me? hope you in God: for I shall yet praise Him, *who is* the <u>health</u> of my countenance, and my God. help

PSALM 43

JUDGE me, O God, and plead my cause against an ungodly nation: O deliver me from the deceitful and unjust man.
2 For You *are* the God of my <u>strength</u>: why do You cast me off? why go I mourning because of the oppression of the enemy? stronghold
3 O send out Your light and Your truth:

let them lead me; let them bring me to Your holy hill, and to Your tabernacles.

4 Then will I go to the altar of God, to God my exceeding joy: yea, upon the harp will I praise You, O God my God. Els.f.

5 Why are you cast down, O my soul? and why are you <u>disquieted</u> within me? hope in God: for I shall yet praise Him, *who is* the <u>health</u> of my countenance, and my God.

troubled - help

PSALM 44

To the chief Musician for the sons of Korah, Maschil

WE have heard with our ears, O <u>God</u>, our fathers have told us, *what* work You did in their days, in the times of old. Elohim p.f.

2 *How* You did drive out the <u>heathen</u> with Your hand, and planted them; *how* You did afflict the people, and cast them out. nations

3 For they got not the land in possession by their own sword, neither did their own arm save them: but Your right hand, and Your arm, and the light of Your countenance, because You had a favor to them.

4 You are my King, O God: command deliverances for Ja'cob.

5 Through You will we push down our enemies: through Your name will we tread them under that rise up against us.

6 For I will not trust in my bow, neither shall my sword save me.

7 But You have saved us from our enemies, and have put them to shame that <u>hated</u> us. despised

8 In God we boast all the day long, and praise Your name for ever. Se'lah.

9 But You have cast off, and put us to shame; and go not forth with our armies.

10 You make us to turn back from the enemy: and they which hate us spoil for themselves.

11 You have given us like sheep *appointed* for meat; and have scattered us among the <u>heathen</u>. to be eaten - nations

12 You sell Your people for <u>nought</u>, and do not increase *Your wealth* by their price. little profit

13 You make us a reproach to our neighbor, a scorn and a derision to them that are round about us.

14 You make us a byword among the <u>heathen</u>, a shaking of the head among the people.

15 My confusion *is* continually before me, and the shame of my face has covered me,

16 For the voice of him that reproaches and blasphemes; by reason of the enemy and avenger.

17 All this is come upon us; yet have we not forgotten You, neither have we dealt falsely in Your <u>covenant</u>. agreement

18 Our heart is not turned back, neither have our steps <u>declined</u> from Your way; deviated

19 Though You have <u>sore broken</u> us in the place of <u>dragons</u>, and covered us with the shadow of death. crushed - jackals

20 If we have forgotten the name of

our <u>God</u>, or <u>stretched out</u> our hands to a strange god; Els.f. - extended

GID - 886

21 Shall not God search this out? for He knows the secrets of the heart.

22 Yea, for Your sake are we killed all the day long; we are counted as sheep for the slaughter. ROM. 8:36

23 Awake, why sleep You, O Lord? arise, cast *us* not off for ever.

24 Wherefore hide You Your face, *and* forget our affliction and our oppression?

25 For our soul is bowed down to the dust: our belly clings to the earth.

26 Arise for our help, and redeem us for Your mercies' sake.

PSALM 45

To the chief Musician upon Shoshannim, for the sons of Korah, *Maschil, A Song of loves

MY heart <u>is inditing</u> a good matter: I speak of the things which I have made <u>touching</u> the king: my tongue *is* the pen of a ready writer. overflows with - for

GIL 875

2 You are fairer than the children of men: grace is poured into Your lips: therefore <u>God</u> has blessed You for ever. Elohim p.f.

3 <u>Gird</u> <u>Your sword upon</u> *Your* <u>thigh</u>, O *most* mighty, with Your glory and Your majesty. Prepare for war

4 And in Your majesty ride prosperously because of truth and meekness *and* righteousness; and Your right hand shall teach You <u>terrible</u> things. awesome

5 Your arrows *are* sharp in the heart of the king's enemies; *whereby* the people fall under You.

6 Your throne, O God, *is* for ever and ever: the scepter of Your kingdom *is* a <u>right</u> scepter. HEB. 1:8 true

7 You love righteousness, and <u>hate</u> wickedness: therefore God, Your God, has anointed You with the oil of gladness above Your fellows. HEB. 1:9 despise

8 All Your garments *smell* of myrrh, and aloes, *and* cassia, out of the ivory palaces, <u>whereby they</u> have made You glad. i.e., stringed instruments

9 Kings' daughters *were* among Your honorable women: upon Your right hand did stand the queen in gold of O'phir.

10 Hearken, O daughter, and consider, and <u>incline</u> <u>your ear</u>; forget also your own people, and your father's house; listen

11 So shall the king greatly desire your beauty: for He *is* your <u>Lord</u>; and worship you Him. Adon s.f.

12 And the daughter of Tyre *shall be there* with a gift; even the rich among the people shall intreat Your favor.

13 The king's daughter *is* all glorious within: her clothing *is* <u>of wrought</u> gold. interwoven with

14 She shall be brought to the king in <u>raiment of needlework</u>: the virgins her companions that follow her shall be brought to you. embroidered clothing

15 With gladness and rejoicing shall they be brought: they shall enter into the king's palace.

16 Instead of your fathers shall be your children, whom you may make princes in all the earth.

17 I will make Your name to be remembered in all generations: therefore shall the people praise You for ever and ever.

PSALM 46

To the chief Musician for the sons of Korah, A Song upon Alamoth

GOD *is* our refuge and strength, a very present help in trouble.
2 Therefore will not we fear, though the earth be removed, and though the mountains be carried into the midst of the sea;
3 *Though* the waters thereof roar *and* be troubled, *though* the mountains shake with the swelling thereof. Se'lah.
4 *There is* a river, the streams whereof shall make glad the city of God, the holy *place* of the tabernacles of the Most High.
5 God *is* in the midst of her; she shall not be moved: God shall help her, *and that* right early.　Elohim[p.f.]
6 The heathen raged, the kingdoms were moved: He uttered His voice, the earth melted.　nations
7 The LORD of hosts *is* with us; the God of Ja'cob *is* our refuge. Se'lah.　Jehovah Tsebaoth
8 Come, behold the works of the LORD, what desolations He has made in the earth.　see
9 He makes wars to cease to the end of the earth; He breaks the bow, and cuts the spear in sunder; He burns the chariot in the fire.　two
10 Be still, and know that I *am* God: I will be exalted among the heathen, I will be exalted in the earth.
11 The LORD of hosts *is* with us; the God of Ja'cob *is* our refuge. Se'lah.

PSALM 47

To the chief Musician, A Psalm for the sons of Korah

O CLAP your hands, all you people; shout to God with the voice of triumph.
2 For the LORD Most High *is* terrible; *He is* a great King over all the earth.　Jehovah[s.f.] Eleyon - awesome
3 He shall subdue the people under us, and the nations under our feet.
4 He shall choose our inheritance for us, the excellency of Ja'cob whom He loved. Se'lah.
5 God is gone up with a shout, the LORD with the sound of a trumpet.
6 Sing praises to God, sing praises: sing praises to our King, sing praises.
7 For God *is* the King of all the earth: sing you praises with understanding.
8 God reigns over the heathen: God sits upon the throne of His holiness.　REV. 4:9　nations
9 The princes of the people are gathered together, *even* the people of the God of A'bra-ham: for the shields of the earth *belong* to God: He is greatly exalted.　Elohim[p.f.] - powerful

PSALM 48

A Song and Psalm for the sons of Korah

GREAT *is* the LORD, and greatly to be praised in the city of our God, *in* the mountain of His holiness.

2 Beautiful for situation, the joy of the whole earth, is mount Zi'on, *on* the sides of the north, the city of the great King.

3 <u>God is known</u> in her palaces for a refuge.   Elohim^p.f. - has made Himself known

4 For, lo, the kings were assembled, they passed by together.

5 They saw *it, and* so they marveled; they were troubled, *and* hasted away.

6 <u>Fear</u> took hold upon them there, *and* pain, as of a woman in <u>travail</u>.   Trembling - labor

7 You break the ships of Tar'shish with an east wind.

8 As we have heard, so have we seen in the city of the <u>LORD of hosts</u>, in the city of our God: God will establish it for ever. Se'lah.   Jehovah Tsebaoth

9 We have thought of Your lovingkindness, O God, in the midst of Your temple.

10 According to Your name, O God, so *is* Your praise to the ends of the earth: Your right hand is full of righteousness.

11 Let mount Zi'on rejoice, let the <u>daughters</u> of Ju'dah be glad, because of Your judgments.   villages

12 Walk about Zi'on, and go round about her: <u>tell</u> the towers thereof.   count

13 <u>Mark</u> you well her <u>bulwarks</u>, consider her palaces; that you may tell *it* to the generation following.   Notice - ramparts

14 For this God *is* our God for ever and ever: He will be our guide *even* to death.

PSALM 49

To the chief Musician, A Psalm for the sons of Korah

HEAR this, all *you* people; give ear, all *you* inhabitants of the world:

2 Both low and high, rich and poor, together.

3 My mouth shall speak of wisdom; and the meditation of my heart *shall be* of understanding.

4 I will incline my ear to a parable: I will open my dark saying upon the harp.

5 Wherefore should I fear in the days of evil, *when* the iniquity of my heels shall <u>compass</u> me about?   surround

6 They that trust in their wealth, and boast themselves in the multitude of their riches;

7 <u>None</u> *of them* can by any means redeem his brother, nor give to God a ransom for him: no man

8 (For the redemption of their soul *is* <u>precious</u>, and it ceases for ever:)   costly

9 That he should still live for ever, *and* not see <u>corruption</u>.   decay

10 For he sees *that* wise men die, likewise the fool and the <u>brutish</u> person perish, and leave their wealth to others.   senseless

11 Their inward thought *is, that* their houses *shall continue* for ever, *and* their dwelling places to all generations; they call *their* lands after their own names.

12 Nevertheless man *being* in honor <u>abides not</u>: he is like the beasts *that* perish.   will not endure

13 This their way *is* their folly: yet

their posterity approve their sayings. Se'lah.

14 Like sheep they are laid in the grave; death shall feed on them; and the upright shall have dominion over them in the morning; and their beauty shall consume in the grave from their dwelling.

15 But God will redeem my soul from the power of the grave: for He shall receive me. Se'lah.   ACTS 2:31

16 Be not you afraid when one is made rich, when the glory of his house is increased;

17 For when he dies he shall carry nothing away: his glory shall not descend after him.

18 Though while he lived he blessed his soul: and *men* will praise you, when you do well to yourself.   For - congratulated himself

19 He shall go to the generation of his fathers; they shall never see light.

20 Man *that is* in honor, and understands not, is like the beasts *that* perish.

PSALM 50

A Psalm of Asaph

THE mighty God, *even* the LORD, has spoken, and called the earth from the rising of the sun to the going down thereof.   throughout the whole day

2 Out of Zi'on, the perfection of beauty, God has shined.   Elohim^p.f.

3 Our God shall come, and shall not keep silence: a fire shall devour before Him, and it shall be very tempestuous round about Him.   destroy

4 He shall call to the heavens from above, and to the earth, that He may judge His people.

5 Gather My saints together to Me; those that have made a covenant with Me by sacrifice.   godly ones - agreement

6 And the heavens shall declare His righteousness: for God *is* judge Himself. Se'lah.

7 Hear, O My people, and I will speak; O Is'ra-el, and I will testify against you: I *am* God, *even* your God.

8 I will not reprove you for your sacrifices or your burned offerings, *to have been* continually before Me.   rebuke

9 I will take no bullock out of your house, *nor* he goats out of your folds.

10 For every beast of the forest *is* Mine, *and* the cattle upon a thousand hills.

11 I know all the fowls of the mountains: and the wild beasts of the field *are* Mine.

12 If I were hungry, I would not tell you: for the world *is* Mine, and the fulness thereof.

13 Will I eat the flesh of bulls, or drink the blood of goats?

14 Offer to God thanksgiving; and pay your vows to the Most High:

15 And call upon Me in the day of trouble: I will deliver you, and you shall glorify Me.

16 But to the wicked God says, What have you to do to declare My statutes, or *that* you should take My covenant in your mouth?   What right - tell of My decrees

17 Seeing you hate instruction, and cast My words behind you.   despise

18 When you saw a thief, then you consented with him, and have been partaker with adulterers.

19 You give your mouth to evil, and your tongue <u>frame</u>s deceit. *speaks*

20 You sit *and* speak against your brother; you slander your own mother's son.

21 These *things* have you done, and I kept silence; you thought that I was altogether *such as one* as yourself: *but* I will <u>reprove</u> you, and set *them* in <u>order</u> before your eyes. *rebuke - detail*

22 Now consider this, you that forget God, less I tear *you* in pieces, and *there be* none to deliver.

23 Whoso offers praise glorifies Me: and to him that orders *his* <u>conversation</u> *aright* will I show the salvation of God. *way*

PSALM 51

To the chief Musician, A Psalm of David, when Nathan the prophet came to him, after he had gone in to Bathsheba

HAVE mercy upon me, O God, according to Your lovingkindness: according to the multitude of Your tender mercies blot out my transgressions.

2 Wash me throughly from my iniquity, and cleanse me from my sin.

3 For I acknowledge my transgressions: and my sin *is* ever before me.

4 Against You, You only, have I sinned, and done *this* evil in Your sight: that You might be justified when You speak, *and* be <u>clear</u> when You judge. *ROM. 3:4 blameless*

5 Behold, I was shapen in iniquity; and in sin did my mother conceive me.

6 Behold, You desire truth in the inward parts: and in the hidden *part* You shall make me to know wisdom.

7 Purge me with hyssop, and I shall be clean: wash me, and I shall be whiter than snow.

8 Make me to hear joy and gladness; *that* the bones *which* You have broken may rejoice.

9 Hide Your face from my sins, and blot out all my iniquities.

10 Create in me a clean heart, O God; and renew a right spirit within me.

11 Cast me not away from Your presence; and take not Your Holy Spirit from me.

12 Restore to me the joy of Your salvation; and uphold me *with* Your <u>free</u> spirit. *willing*

13 *Then* will I teach transgressors Your ways; and sinners shall be converted to You.

14 Deliver me from <u>bloodguiltiness</u>, O God, You God of my salvation: *and* my tongue shall sing aloud of Your righteousness. *sins that deserve death*

15 Lord, open You my lips; and my mouth shall show forth Your praise.

16 For You desire not sacrifice; else would I give *it*: You delight not in burned offering.

17 The sacrifices of <u>God</u> *are* a broken spirit: a broken and a contrite heart, O God, You will not despise. *Elohim^p.f*

18 Do good in Your good pleasure to Zi'on: build You the walls of Je-ru'sa-lem.

19 Then shall You be pleased with the sacrifices of righteousness, with burned offering and whole burned offering: then shall they offer bullocks upon Your altar.

PSALM 52

To the chief Musician, Maschil, A Psalm of David when Doeg the Edomite came and told Saul, and said to him, David is come to the house of Ahimelech

WHY boast you yourself in mischief, O mighty man? the goodness of God *endures* continually.
2 Your tongue <u>devises</u> mischiefs; like a sharp razor, working deceitfully.   plots
3 You love evil more than good; *and* lying rather than to speak righteousness. Se'lah.
4 You love all devouring words, O *you* deceitful tongue.
5 God shall likewise destroy you for ever, He shall take you away, and pluck you out of *your* dwelling place, and root you out of the land of the living. Se'lah.
6 The righteous also shall see, and fear, and shall laugh at him:
7 Lo, *this is* the man *that* made not God his strength; but trusted in the abundance of his riches, *and* strengthened himself in his wickedness.
8 But I *am* like a green olive tree in the house of God: I trust in the mercy of God for ever and ever.
9 I will praise You for ever, because You have done *it*: and I will wait on Your name; for *it is* good before Your <u>saints</u>.   godly ones

PSALM 53

To the chief Musician upon Mahalath, Maschil, A Psalm of David

THE fool has said in his heart, *There is* no God. Corrupt are they, and have done abominable iniquity: *there is* none that does good.
2 <u>God</u> looked down from heaven upon the children of men, to see if there were *any* that did understand, that did seek God.   Elohim^p.f.
3 Every one of them is gone back: they are altogether become <u>filthy</u>; *there is* none that does good, no, not one.   corrupt
4 Have the workers of iniquity no knowledge? who eat up my people *as* they eat bread: they have not called upon God.
5 There were they in great fear, *where* no fear was: for God has scattered the bones of him that encamps *against* you: you have put *them* to shame, because God has despised them.
6 Oh that the <u>salvation</u> of Is'ra-el *were come* out of Zi'on! When God brings back the captivity of His people, Ja'cob shall rejoice, *and* Is'ra-el shall be glad.   i.e., Heb. Jeshua

PSALM 54

To the chief Musician on Neginoth, Maschil, A Psalm of David, when the Ziphims came and said to Saul, Does not David hide himself with us

SAVE me, O God, by Your name, and judge me by Your strength. Elohim^p.f.

2 Hear my prayer, O God; give ear to the words of my mouth.

3 For strangers are risen up against me, and oppressors seek after my soul: they have not set God before them. Se'lah.

4 Behold, God *is* my helper: the Lord *is* with them that uphold my soul.

5 He shall reward evil to my enemies: <u>cut them off</u> in Your truth.

destroy them

6 I will freely sacrifice to You: I will praise Your name, O LORD; for *it is* good.

7 For He has delivered me out of all trouble: and my eye has <u>seen</u> <u>*His desire*</u> upon my enemies.

looked with satisfaction

PSALM 55

To the chief Musician on Neginoth, Maschil, A Psalm of David

GIVE ear to my prayer, O God; and hide not Yourself from my <u>supplication</u>.

appeal

2 Attend to me, and hear me: I mourn in my complaint, and make a noise;

3 Because of the voice of the enemy, because of the oppression of the wicked: for they cast iniquity upon me, and in wrath they hate me.

4 My heart is <u>sore pained</u> within me: and the terrors of death are fallen upon me.

in anguish

5 Fearfulness and trembling are come upon me, and horror has overwhelmed me.

6 And I said, Oh that I had wings like a dove! *for then* would I fly away, and be at rest.

7 Lo, *then* would I wander far off, *and* remain in the wilderness. Se'lah.

8 I would hasten my escape from the windy storm *and* tempest.

9 Destroy, O Lord, *and* <u>divide their</u> <u>tongues</u>: for I have seen violence and strife in the city.

bring confusion

10 Day and night they go about it upon the walls thereof: <u>mischief</u> also and sorrow *are* in the midst of it.

malice

11 Wickedness *is* in the midst thereof: deceit and <u>guile</u> depart not from her streets.

oppression

12 For *it was* not an enemy *that* reproached me; then I could have borne *it*: neither *was it* he that <u>hated</u> me *that* did magnify *himself* against me; then I would have hid myself from him.

despised

13 But *it was* you, a man my equal, my guide, and my acquaintance.

14 We took sweet counsel together, *and* walked to the <u>house</u> of God in <u>company</u>.

i.e., temple - the throng

15 Let death seize upon them, *and* let them go down <u>quick</u> into <u>hell</u>: for wickedness *is* in their dwellings, *and* among them.

alive - i.e., Sheol

16 As for me, I will call upon <u>God</u>; and the LORD shall save me.

Elohim[p.f.] - Jehovah[s.f.]

17 Evening, and morning, and at noon, will I pray, and cry aloud: and He shall hear my voice.

18 He has delivered my soul in peace from the battle *that was* against me: for there were many with me.

19 <u>God</u> shall hear, and afflict them,

even he that abides of old. Se'lah. Because they have no changes, therefore they <u>fear</u> not <u>God</u>. El^s.f. - honor - Elohim^p.f.

20 He has put forth his hands against such as be at peace with him: he has broken his <u>covenant</u>. agreement

21 *The words* of his mouth were smoother than butter, but war *was* in his heart: his words were softer than oil, yet *were* they <u>drawn swords</u>. ready to wound

22 Cast your burden upon the LORD, and He shall sustain you: He shall never allow the righteous to be moved. 1 PET. 5:7

23 But You, O God, shall bring them down into the pit of destruction: bloody and deceitful men shall not live out half their days; but I will trust in You.

PSALM 56

To the chief Musician upon Jonath-elem-rechokim, Michtam of David, when the Philistines took him in Gath

BE merciful to me, O God: for <u>man would swallow me up</u>; he fighting daily oppresses me.

2 My enemies would daily swallow *me* up: for *they be* many that fight against me, O You most High.

3 <u>What time I am afraid, I will trust in You</u> When

4 <u>In God I will praise His word, in</u> God I have put my trust; I will not <u>fear what flesh can do to me</u>.

5 Every day they twist my words: all their thoughts *are* against me for evil.

6 They gather themselves together,

they hide themselves, they <u>mark</u> my steps, when they wait for my soul. watch

7 Shall they escape by iniquity? in *Your* anger cast down the people, O <u>God</u>. Elohim^p.f.

8 You <u>tell</u> my wanderings: put You my tears into Your bottle: *are they* not in Your book? has taken account

9 When I cry *to You*, then shall my enemies turn back: this I know; for God *is* for me.

10 In God will I praise *His* word: in the LORD will I praise *His* word.

11 In God have I put my trust: I will not be afraid what man can do to me.

12 Your <u>vows</u> *are* upon me, O God: I will render praises to You. promises

13 For You have delivered my soul from death: *will* not *You deliver* my feet from falling, that I may walk before God in the light of the living?

PSALM 57

To the chief Musician, Al-taschith, Michtam of David, when he fled from Saul in the cave

BE merciful to me, O God, be merciful to me: for my soul trusts in You: yea, in <u>the shadow of Your wings</u> will I make my refuge, until *these* calamities be overpast. your care

2 I will cry to God Most High; to God that performs *all things* for me.

3 He shall send from heaven, and save me *from* the reproach of him that would <u>swallow me up</u>. Se'lah. God shall send forth His mercy and His truth. trample upon me

4 My soul *is* among lions: *and* I lie *even among* them that are set on fire, *even* the sons of men, whose teeth *are* spears and arrows, and their tongue a sharp sword.

5 Be You exalted, O God, above the heavens; *let* Your glory *be* above all the earth.

6 They have prepared a net for my steps; my soul is bowed down: they have dug a pit before me, into the midst whereof they are fallen *themselves*. Se'lah.

7 My heart is fixed, O God, my heart is fixed: I will sing and give praise.

8 Awake up, my glory; awake, psaltery and harp: I *myself* will awake early.   lyre

9 I will praise You, O Lord, among the people: I will sing to You among the nations.

10 For Your mercy *is* great to the heavens, and Your truth to the clouds.

11 Be You exalted, O God, above the heavens: *let* Your glory *be* above all the earth.

4 Their poison *is* like the poison of a serpent: *they are* like the deaf adder *that* stops her ear;

5 Which will not hearken to the voice of charmers, charming never so wisely.

6 Break their teeth, O God, in their mouth: break out the great teeth of the young lions, O LORD.   shatter

7 Let them melt away as waters *which* run continually: *when* He bends *His bow to shoot* His arrows, let them be as cut in pieces.   flow

8 As a snail *which* melts, let *every one of them* pass away: *like* the untimely birth of a woman, *that* they may not see the sun.   i.e., secretes slime

9 Before your pots can feel the thorns, He shall take them away as with a whirlwind, both living, and in *His* wrath.

10 The righteous shall rejoice when he sees the vengeance: He shall wash his feet in the blood of the wicked.

11 So that a man shall say, Verily *there is* a reward for the righteous: verily He is a God that judges in the earth.   Surely

PSALM 58

To the chief Musician, Al-taschith, Michtam of David

DO you indeed speak righteousness, O congregation? do you judge uprightly, O you sons of men? 2 Yea, in heart you work wickedness; you weigh the violence of your hands in the earth.   do - mete out

3 The wicked are estranged from the womb: they go astray as soon as they be born, speaking lies.   birth

PSALM 59

To the chief Musician, Al-taschith, Michtam of David, when Saul sent, and they watched the house to kill him

DELIVER me from my enemies, O my God: defend me from them that rise up against me. 2 Deliver me from the workers of iniquity, and save me from bloody men. 3 For, lo, they lie in wait for my soul: the mighty are gathered against me; not

M27

for my transgression, nor *for* my sin, O LORD.

4 They run and prepare themselves without *my* fault: awake to help me, and behold.

5 You therefore, O LORD God of hosts, the God of Is'ra-el, awake to visit all the heathen: be not merciful to any wicked transgressors. Se'lah.   Jehovah[s-f.] Elohim[p-f.] of Tsebaoth - nations

6 They return at evening: they make a noise like a dog, and go round about the city.   howl

7 Behold, they belch out with their mouth: swords *are* in their lips: for who, *say they*, does hear?

8 But You, O LORD, shall laugh at them; You shall have all the heathen in derision.

9 *Because* of his strength will I wait upon You: for God *is* my defence.

10 The God of my mercy shall prevent me: God shall let me see *my desire* upon my enemies.   meet

11 Slay them not, less my people forget: scatter them by Your power; and bring them down, O Lord our shield.

12 *For* the sin of their mouth *and* the words of their lips let them even be taken in their pride: and for cursing and lying *which* they speak.

13 Consume *them* in wrath, consume *them*, that they *may* not *be*: and let them know that God rules in Ja'cob to the ends of the earth. Se'lah.

14 And at evening let them return; *and* let them make a noise like a dog, and go round about the city.

15 Let them wander up and down for meat, and grudge if they be not satisfied.   growl

16 But I will sing of Your power; yea, I will sing aloud of Your mercy in the morning: for You have been my defence and refuge in the day of my trouble.

17 To You, O my strength, will I sing: for God *is* my defence, *and* the God of my mercy.

M27

900

PSALM 60

To the chief Musician upon Shushaneduth, Michtam of David, to teach; when he strove with Aram-naharaim, and with Aram-zobah, when Joab returned, and smote of Edom in the Valley of Salt twelve thousand

O GOD, You have cast us off, You have scattered us, You have been displeased; O turn Yourself to us again.

2 You have made the earth to tremble; You have broken it: heal the breaches thereof; for it shakes.

3 You have showed Your people hard things: You have made us to drink the wine of astonishment.

4 You have given a banner to them that fear You, that it may be displayed because of the truth. Se'lah.   reverence

5 That Your beloved may be delivered; save *with* Your right hand, and hear me.

6 God has spoken in His holiness; I will rejoice, I will divide She'chem, and mete out the valley of Suc'coth.   Elohim[p-f.]

7 Gil'e-ad *is* Mine, and Ma-nas'seh *is* Mine; E'phra-im also *is* the strength of Mine head; Ju'dah *is* My lawgiver;

8 Mo'ab *is* My washpot; over E'dom will I cast out My shoe: Phi-lis'tia, triumph you because of Me.

9 Who will bring me *into* the strong city? who will lead me into E'dom?

10 *Will* not You, O God, *which* had cast us off? and *You*, O God, *which* did not go out with our armies?

11 Give us help from trouble: for vain *is* the help of man.   worthless

12 Through God we shall do val-iantly: for He *it is that* shall tread down our enemies.   gain the victory

PSALM 61

To the chief Musician upon Neginah, A Psalm of David

HEAR my cry, O God; attend to my prayer.   listen

2 From the end of the earth will I cry to You, when my heart is over-whelmed: lead me to the rock *that* is higher than I.

3 For You have been a shelter for me, *and* a strong tower from the enemy.

4 I will abide in Your tabernacle for ever: I will trust in the covert of Your wings. Se'lah.   shelter

5 For You, O God, have heard my vows: You have given *me* the heritage of those that fear Your name.   reverence

6 You will prolong the king's life: *and* his years as many generations.

7 He shall abide before God for ever: O prepare mercy and truth, *which* may preserve him.   sit enthroned - protect

8 So will I sing praise to Your name for ever, that I may daily perform my vows.   promises

PSALM 62

To the chief Musician, to Jeduthun, A Psalm of David

TRULY my soul waits upon God: from Him *comes* my salvation.

2 He only *is* my rock and my salva-tion; *He is* my defence; I shall not be greatly moved.   stronghold

3 How long will you imagine mis-chief against a man? you shall be slain all of you: as a bowing wall *shall you be, and as* a tottering fence.   leaning

4 They only consult to cast *him* down from his excellency: they delight in lies: they bless with their mouth, but they curse inwardly. Se'lah.

5 My soul, wait you only upon God; for my expectation *is* from Him.

6 He only *is* my rock and my salvation: *He is* my defence; I shall not be moved.

7 In God *is* my salvation and my glory: the rock of my strength, *and* my refuge, *is* in God.   Elohim[p.f.]

8 Trust in Him at all times; you people, pour out your heart before Him: God *is* a refuge for us. Se'lah.

9 Surely men of low degree *are* van-ity, *and* men of high degree *are* a lie: to be laid in the balance, they *are* al-together *lighter* than vanity. nothing - a breath

10 Trust not in oppression, and be-come not vain in robbery: if riches increase, set not your heart *upon them*.   LUKE 12:15

11 God has spoken once; twice have

M07 -- 923

M48 --- 954

I heard this; that power *belongs* to God.

12 Also to You, O Lord, *belongs* mercy: for You <u>render</u> to every man according to his work.   ROM. 2:6 REV. 2:23 reward

PSALM 63

A Psalm of David, when he was in the wilderness of Judah

O GOD, You *are* my God; early will I seek You: my soul thirsts for You, my flesh longs for You in a dry and thirsty land, where no water is;

2 To see Your power and Your glory, so *as* I have seen You in the sanctuary.

3 Because Your lovingkindness *is* better than life, my lips shall praise you.

4 Thus will I <u>bless</u> You while I live: I will lift up my hands in Your name.   praise

5 My soul shall be satisfied as *with* <u>marrow and fatness</u>; and my mouth shall praise *You* with joyful lips: the richest of foods

6 When I remember You upon my bed, *and* meditate on You in the *night* watches.

7 Because You have been my help, therefore in the <u>shadow</u> of Your <u>wings</u> will I rejoice.   protection - presence

8 My soul <u>follows hard after</u> You: Your right hand upholds me.   clings to

9 But those *that* seek my soul, to destroy *it*, shall go into the lower parts of the earth.

10 They shall fall by the sword: they shall be a <u>portion</u> for foxes.   prey

11 But the king shall rejoice in God; every one that swears by Him shall glory: but the mouth of them that speak lies shall be stopped.

PSALM 64

To the chief Musician, A Psalm of David

HEAR my voice, O <u>God</u>, in my prayer: preserve my life from <u>fear</u> of the enemy.   Elohim[p.f.] - the dread

2 Hide me from the <u>secret counsel</u> of the wicked; from the <u>insurrection</u> of the workers of iniquity: conspiracy - tumult

3 Who <u>whet</u> their tongue like a sword, *and* bend *their bows to shoot* their arrows, *even* bitter words: sharpen

4 That they may shoot in secret at the perfect: suddenly do they shoot at him, and fear not.

5 They encourage themselves *in* an evil matter: they <u>commune</u> of laying <u>snares privily</u>; they say, Who shall see them?   talk - traps secretly

6 They <u>search out iniquities</u>; they accomplish a diligent search: both the inward *thought* of every one *of them*, and the heart, *is* deep.   devise injustices

7 But God shall shoot at them *with* an arrow; suddenly shall they be wounded.

8 So they shall make <u>their own tongue</u> to fall upon themselves: all that see them shall flee away. the blame

9 And all men shall <u>fear</u>, and shall declare the work of God; for they shall wisely consider of His doing.   reverence

10 The righteous shall be glad in the LORD, and shall trust in Him; and all the upright in heart shall glory.

PSALM 65

To the chief Musician, A Psalm and
Song of David

PRAISE waits for You, O God, in Zi'on: and to You shall the vow be performed.

2 O You that hears prayer, to You shall all flesh come.

3 Iniquities prevail against me: *as for* our transgressions, You shall purge them away.

4 <u>Blessed</u> *is the man whom* You choose, and cause to approach *to You, that* he may dwell in Your courts: we shall be satisfied with the goodness of Your house, *even* of Your holy temple.   Fortunate

5 *By* <u>terrible things</u> in righteousness will You answer us, O God of our salvation; *who are* the confidence of all the ends of the earth, and of them that are afar off *upon* the sea: awesome deeds

6 Which by His strength sets fast the mountains; *being* girded with power:

7 Which <u>stills</u> the noise of the seas, the noise of their waves, and the tumult of the people.   quiets

8 They also that dwell in the uttermost parts are afraid at Your <u>tokens</u>: You make the outgoings of the morning and evening to rejoice.   signs

9 You <u>visit</u> the earth, and water it: You greatly enriched it with the river of God, *which* is full of water: You prepare them <u>corn</u>, when You have so provided for it.   cares for - grain

10 You water the ridges thereof abundantly: You settle the furrows thereof:

You make it soft with showers: You bless the springing thereof.

11 You crown the year with Your goodness; and Your paths drop fatness.

12 They drop *upon* the pastures of the wilderness: and the little hills rejoice on every side.

13 The pastures are clothed with flocks; the valleys also are covered over with <u>corn</u>; they shout for joy, they also sing.   grain

PSALM 66

To the chief Musician, A Song or Psalm

MAKE a joyful noise to God, all you <u>lands</u>: Elohim$^{p.f}$ - i.e., people

2 Sing forth the honor of His name: make His praise glorious.

3 Say to God, How <u>terrible</u> *are You in* Your works! through the greatness of Your power shall Your enemies submit themselves to You.   awesome

4 All the earth shall worship You, and shall sing to You; they shall sing *to* Your name. Se'lah.

5 Come and see the works of God: *He is* <u>terrible</u> *in His* doing toward the children of men.

6 He turned the sea into dry *land*: they went through the <u>flood</u> on foot: there did we rejoice in Him.   river

7 He rules by His power for ever; His eyes behold the nations: let not the rebellious exalt themselves. Se'lah.

8 O bless our God, you people, and make the voice of His praise to be heard:

9 Which holds <u>our soul</u> in life, and allows not our feet to be moved. us

10 For You, O God, have <u>proved</u> us: You have tried us, as silver is tried. tested
11 You brought us into the net; You laid <u>affliction</u> upon our loins.

a crushing burden

12 You have caused men to ride over our heads; we went through fire and through water: but You brought us out into <u>a wealthy</u> *place.* an abundant
13 I will go into Your house with burned offerings: I will pay You my vows,
14 Which my lips have uttered, and my mouth has spoken, when I was in trouble.
15 I will offer to You burned sacrifices of fatlings, with the incense of rams; I will offer bullocks with goats. Se'lah.
16 Come *and* hear, all you that <u>fear</u> God, and I will declare what He has done for my soul. revere
17 I cried to Him with my mouth, and He was <u>extolled</u> with my tongue. praised
18 If I regard <u>iniquity</u> in my heart, the Lord will not hear *me:* wickedness
19 *But* <u>verily</u> God has heard *me*; He has attended to the voice of my prayer. surely
20 Blessed *be* God, which has not turned away my prayer, nor His mercy from me.

PSALM 67

To the chief Musician on Neginoth, A Psalm or Song

GOD be merciful to us, and bless us; *and* cause His face to shine upon us; Se'lah.

2 That Your way may be known upon earth, Your <u>saving health</u> among all nations. salvation
3 Let the people praise You, O God; let all the people praise You.
4 O let the nations be glad and sing for joy: for You shall judge the people righteously, and govern the nations upon earth. Se'lah.
5 Let the people praise You, O God; let all the people praise You.
6 *Then* shall the earth yield her increase; *and* God, *even* our own God, shall bless us.
7 God shall bless us; and all the ends of the earth shall <u>fear</u> Him. reverence

PSALM 68

To the chief Musician, A Psalm or Song of David

LET God arise, let His enemies be scattered: let them also that <u>hate</u> Him flee before Him. despise
2 As smoke is driven away, *so* drive *them* away: as wax melts before the fire, *so* let the wicked perish at the presence of God.
3 But let the righteous be glad; let them rejoice before God: yea, let them exceedingly rejoice.
4 Sing to God, sing praises to His name: <u>extol</u> Him that <u>rides upon</u> the heavens by His name <u>JAH</u>, and rejoice before Him.

praise - rules - i.e., the LORD

5 A father of the fatherless, and a judge of the widows, *is* God in His holy habitation.
6 God sets the <u>solitary</u> in families:

M42 - 1087

G4B

886

He brings out those which are bound with chains: but the rebellious dwell in a dry *land*.   lonely

7 O God, when You went forth before Your people, when You did march through the wilderness; Se'lah:

8 The earth shook, the heavens also <u>dropped</u> at the presence of God: *even* Si'nai itself *was moved* at the presence of God, the God of Is'ra-el.   dropped rain

9 You, O God, did send a plentiful rain, whereby You did confirm Your inheritance, when it was weary.

10 Your congregation has dwelled therein: You, O God, have prepared of Your goodness for the poor.

11 The Lord gave the word: great *was* the company of those that published *it*.

12 Kings of armies did flee <u>apace</u>: and she that tarried at home divided the spoil.   indeed

13 Though you <u>have lain</u> among the pots, *yet shall you be as* the wings of a dove covered with silver, and her feathers with yellow gold.   lie

14 When the Almighty scattered kings in it, it was *white* as snow in Sal'mon.

15 The hill of God *is as* the hill of Ba'shan; an high hill *as* the hill of Ba'shan.

16 Why leap you, you high hills? *this is* the hill *which* God desires to dwell in; yea, the LORD will dwell *in it* for ever.

17 The chariots of <u>God</u> *are* twenty thousand, *even* thousands of <u>angels</u>: the <u>Lord</u> *is* among them, *as in* Si'nai, in the holy *place*.   Elohim^p.f. - messengers - Adonahy^p.f.

18 You have ascended on high, You

have led captivity captive: You have received gifts for men; yea, *for* the rebellious also, that the LORD God might dwell *among them*.   EPH.4:8 Jah Elohim^p.f.

19 Blessed *be* the Lord, *who* daily loads us *with benefits, even* the God of our <u>salvation</u>. Se'lah.

El^s.f. - i.e., Heb. Jeshua

20 *He that is* our God *is* the God of salvation; and to <u>GOD the Lord</u> *belong* the issues from death.   Jehovah^s.f. Adonay^p.f.

21 But God shall wound the head of His enemies, *and* the hairy scalp of such an one as goes on still in his trespasses.

22 The Lord said, I will bring again from Ba'shan, I will bring *My people* again from the depths of the sea:

23 That your foot may be dipped in the blood of *your* enemies, *and* the tongue of your dogs in the same.

24 They have seen Your <u>goings</u>, O God; *even* the <u>goings</u> of my God, my King, in the sanctuary.   procession

25 The singers went before, the players on instruments *followed* after; <u>among them were</u> the <u>damsels</u> playing with <u>timbrels</u>.   in the midst of - maidens - tambourines

26 Bless you God in the congregations, *even* the Lord, from the fountain of Is'ra-el.

27 There *is* little Ben'ja-min *with* their ruler, the princes of Ju'dah *and* their council, the princes of Zeb'u-lun, *and* the princes of Naph'ta-li.

28 Your God has commanded your strength: strengthen, O God, that which You have wrought for us.

29 Because of Your temple at Je-ru'salem shall kings bring presents to You.

30 Rebuke the company of spearmen,

the multitude of the bulls, with the calves of the people, *till every one* submit himself with pieces of silver: scatter You the people *that* delight in war.

31 Princes shall come out of E'gypt; E-thi-o'pi-a shall soon stretch out her hands to God.

32 Sing to God, you kingdoms of the earth; O sing praises to the Lord; Se'lah: Elohim^{p.f.} - Adonahy^{p.f.}

33 To Him that rides upon the heavens of heavens, *which were* of old; lo, He does send out His voice, *and that* a mighty voice.

34 Ascribe you strength to God: His excellency *is* over Is'ra-el, and His strength *is* in the clouds.   skies

35 O God, *You are* terrible out of Your holy places: the God of Is'ra-el *is* He that gives strength and power to *His* people. Blessed *be* God.   awesome - El^{s.f.} - Elohim^{p.f.}

PSALM 69

To the chief Musician upon Shoshannim, A Psalm of David

SAVE me, O God; for the waters are come in to *my* soul.

2 I sink in deep mire, where *there is* no standing: I am come into deep waters, where the floods overflow me.

3 I am weary of my crying: my throat is dried: my eyes fail while I wait for my God.

4 They that hate me without a cause are more than the hairs of my head: they that would destroy me, *being* my enemies wrongfully, are mighty: then I restored *that* which I took not away.   JOHN 15:25 think less of

5 O God, You know my foolishness; and my sins are not hid from You.

6 Let not them that wait on You, O Lord GOD of hosts, be ashamed for my sake: let not those that seek You be confounded for my sake, O God of Is'ra-el.   Adonay^{p.f.} Jehovah^{s.f.} Tsebaoth

7 Because for Your sake I have borne reproach; shame has covered my face.

8 I am become a stranger to my brethren, and an alien to my mother's children.

9 For the zeal of Your house has eaten me up; and the reproaches of them that reproached You are fallen upon me.   JOHN 2:17 ROM. 15:3

10 When I wept, *and chastened* my soul with fasting, that was to my reproach.

11 I made sackcloth also my garment; and I became a proverb to them.

12 They that sit in the gate speak against me; and I *was* the song of the drunkards.

13 But as for me, my prayer *is* to You, O LORD, *in* an acceptable time: O God, in the multitude of Your mercy hear me, in the truth of Your salvation.

14 Deliver me out of the mire, and let me not sink: let me be delivered from them that hate me, and out of the deep waters.   despise

15 Let not the waterflood overflow me, neither let the deep swallow me up, and let not the pit shut her mouth upon me.

16 Hear me, O LORD; for your lovingkindness *is* good: turn to me accord-

ing to the multitude of Your tender mercies.

17 And hide not Your face from Your servant; for I am in trouble: hear me speedily.

18 Draw near to my soul, *and* redeem it: deliver me because of my enemies.

19 You have known my reproach, and my shame, and my dishonor: my adversaries *are* all before You.

20 Reproach has broken my heart; and I am full of heaviness: and I looked *for some* to take pity, but *there was* none; and for comforters, but I found none.

21 They gave me also gall for my <u>meat</u>; and in my thirst they gave me vinegar to drink. MATT. 27:48 JOHN 19:28 food

22 Let their table become a <u>snare</u> before them: and *that which should have been* for *their* welfare, *let it become* a trap. ROM. 11:9 lure

23 Let their eyes be darkened, that they see not; and make their loins continually to shake.

24 Pour out Your indignation upon them, and let Your wrathful anger take hold of them. REV. 16:1

25 Let their habitation be desolate; *and* let none dwell in their tents. ACTS 1:20 MATT. 23:38

26 For they persecute *him* whom You have smitten; and they talk to the grief of those whom You have wounded.

27 <u>Add iniquity to their iniquity</u>: and let them not come into Your righteousness. Charge them with sin upon sin

28 Let them be blotted out of the book of the living, and not be written with the righteous.

29 But I *am* poor and sorrowful: let Your <u>salvation</u>, O God, set me up on high. i.e., Heb. Jeshua

30 I will praise the name of <u>God</u> with a song, and will magnify Him with thanksgiving. Elohim[p.f.]

31 *This* also shall please the LORD better than an ox *or* bullock that has horns and <u>hoofs</u>. divided hoofs

32 The humble shall see *this*, and <u>be glad</u>: and your heart shall live that seek God. rejoice

33 For the LORD hears the poor, and despises not His prisoners.

34 Let the heaven and earth praise Him, the seas, and everything that moves therein.

35 For God will save Zi'on, and will build the cities of Ju'dah: that they may dwell there, and have it in possession.

36 The <u>seed</u> also of His servants shall inherit it: and they that love His name shall dwell therein. descendants

PSALM 70

To the chief Musician, A Psalm of David, to bring to remembrance

MAKE *haste*, O God, to deliver me; make haste to help me, O LORD.

2 Let them be ashamed and confounded that seek after <u>my soul</u>: let them be turned backward, and put to confusion, that desire my hurt. me

3 Let them be turned back for a reward of their shame that say, Aha, aha.

4 Let all those that seek You rejoice and be glad in You: and let such as

love Your salvation say continually,
Let God be magnified.

5 But I *am* <u>poor</u> and needy: make
haste to me, O God: You *are* my
help and my deliverer; O LORD,
<u>make no tarrying</u>.   afflicted - do not delay

PSALM 71

IN you, O LORD, do I put my trust:
let me never be put to confusion.

2 Deliver me in Your righteousness,
and cause me to escape: incline Your
ear to me, and save me.

3 Be You my strong habitation,
whereto I may continually resort:
You have given commandment to
save me; for You *are* my rock and
my fortress.

4 Deliver me, O my God, out of the
hand of the wicked, out of the hand
of the unrighteous and cruel man.

5 For You *are* my hope, O <u>Lord</u>
<u>GOD</u>: *You are* my trust from my
youth.   Adonay^p.f. Jehovah^s.f.

6 By You have I been <u>holden up</u>
from the womb: You are He that
took me out of my mother's <u>bow-</u>
<u>els</u>: my praise *shall be* continu-
ally of You.   sustained - insides

7 I am as a <u>wonder</u> to many; but You
are my strong refuge.   marvel

8 Let my mouth be filled *with* Your
praise *and with* Your honor all the day.

9 Cast me not off in the time of
old age; forsake me not when my
strength fails.

10 For my enemies speak against me;
and they that <u>lay wait</u> for my <u>soul</u>
<u>take counsel</u> together,   watch - conspire

11 Saying, God has forsaken him:
persecute and take him; for *there*
is none to deliver *him*.

12 O God, be not far from me: O
my God, make haste for my help.

13 Let them be confounded *and* consumed that are adversaries to my soul;
let them be covered *with* reproach
and dishonor that seek my hurt.

14 But I will hope continually, and
will yet praise You more and more.

15 My mouth shall show forth Your
righteousness *and* Your salvation
all the day; for I know not the numbers *thereof*.

16 I will go in the strength of
the <u>Lord GOD</u>: I will make mention of Your righteousness, *even*
of You only.   Adonay^p.f. Jehovah^s.f.

17 O God, You have taught me from
my youth: and presently have I declared Your wondrous works.

18 Now also when I am old and
grayheaded, O <u>God</u>, forsake me not;
until I have showed Your strength to
this generation, *and* Your power to
every one *that* is to come.   Elohim^p.f.

19 Your righteousness also, O God,
is very high, who have done great
things: O God, who *is* like to You!

20 *You*, which have showed me great
and <u>sore</u> troubles, shall quicken me
again, and shall bring me up again
from the depths of the earth.   many

21 You shall increase my greatness,
and comfort me on every side.

22 I will also praise You with the
<u>psaltery</u>, *even* Your truth, O my God:
to You will I sing with the harp, O
You Holy One of Is'ra-el.   lyre

23 My lips shall greatly rejoice when I sing to You; and my soul, which You have redeemed.

24 My tongue also shall talk of Your righteousness all the day long: for they are <u>confounded</u>, for they are brought to shame, that seek my hurt.   confused

PSALM 72

A Psalm for Solomon

GIVE the king Your judgments, O <u>God</u>, and Your righteousness to the king's son.   Elohim^p.f.

2 He shall judge Your people with righteousness, and Your poor with judgment.

3 The mountains shall bring peace to the people, and the little hills, by righteousness.

4 He shall judge the poor of the people, he shall save the children of the needy, and shall break in pieces the oppressor.

5 They shall <u>fear</u> You as long as the sun and moon endure, throughout all generations.   dread

6 He shall come down like rain upon the mown grass: as showers *that* water the earth.

7 In his days shall the righteous flourish; and abundance of peace so long as the moon endures.

8 He shall have dominion also from sea to sea, and from the river to the ends of the earth.

9 They that dwell in the wilderness shall bow before him; and his enemies shall lick the dust.

10 The kings of Tar'shish and of the isles shall bring presents: the kings of She'ba and Se'ba shall offer gifts.

11 Yea, all kings shall fall down before him: all nations shall serve him.

12 For he shall deliver the needy when he cries; the poor also, and *him* that has no helper.

13 He shall spare the poor and needy, and shall save the souls of the needy.

14 He shall redeem their soul from deceit and violence: and precious shall their blood be in his sight.

15 And he shall live, and to him shall be given of the gold of She'ba: prayer also shall be made for him continually; *and* daily shall he be praised.

16 There shall be an <u>handful</u> of <u>corn</u> in the earth upon the top of the mountains; the fruit thereof shall shake like Leb'a-non: and *they* of the city shall flourish like grass of the earth.   abundance - grain

17 His name shall endure for ever: His name shall be continued as long as the sun: and *men* shall be blessed in Him: all nations shall call Him blessed.

18 Blessed *be* the Lord <u>God</u>, the God of Is'ra-el, who only does wondrous things.   Jehovah^s.f. Elohim^p.f.

19 And blessed *be* His glorious name for ever: and let the whole earth be filled *with* His glory; Amen, and Amen.

20 The prayers of Da'vid the son of Jes'se are ended.

PSALM 73

A Psalm of Asaph

TRULY God *is* good to Is'ra-el, *even* to such as are of a clean heart.

2 But as for me, my feet were al-most gone; my steps had well near slipped.

3 For I was envious at the foolish, *when* I saw the prosperity of the wicked.

4 For *there are* no bands in their death: but their strength *is* firm.   at

5 They *are* not in trouble *as other* men; neither are they plagued like *other* men.

6 Therefore pride compasses them about as a chain; violence covers them *as* a garment.   surrounds

7 Their eyes stand out with fatness: they have more than heart could wish.

8 They are corrupt, and speak wickedly *concerning* oppression: they speak loftily.

9 They set their mouth against the heavens, and their tongue walks through the earth.

10 Therefore his people return here: and waters of a full *cup* are wrung out to them.   abundance

11 And they say, How does God know? and is there knowledge in the Most High?

12 Behold, these *are* the ungodly, who prosper in the world; they increase *in* riches.

13 Verily I have cleansed my heart *in* vain, and washed my hands in innocency.   Surely

14 For all the day long have I been plagued, and chastened every morning.   stricken - punished

15 If I say, I will speak thus; behold, I should offend *against* the generation of Your children.

16 When I thought to know this, it *was* too painful for me;   oppressive

17 Until I went into the sanctuary of God; *then* understood I their end.   final destiny

18 Surely You did set them in slippery places: You casted them down into destruction.

19 How are they *brought* into desolation, as in a moment! they are utterly consumed with terrors.

20 As a dream when *one* awakes *so,* O Lord, when You awake, You shall despise their image.

21 Thus my heart was grieved, and I was pricked in my reins.   pierced within

22 So foolish *was* I, and ignorant: I was *as* a beast before You.

23 Nevertheless I *am* continually with You: You have held *me* by my right hand.

24 You shall guide me with Your counsel, and afterward receive me *to* glory.

25 Whom have I in heaven *but You?* and *there is* none upon earth *that* I desire beside You.

26 My flesh and my heart fails: *but* God *is* the strength of my heart, and my portion for ever.   Elohim p.f.

27 For, lo, they that are far from You shall perish: You have destroyed all them that go a whoring from You.   are unfaithful to

28 But *it is* good for me to draw near to God: I have put my trust in the Lord GOD, that I may declare all Your works.

HEB. 10:22 Adonay p.f. Jehovah s.f.

PSALM 74

Maschil of Asaph

O GOD, why have You cast *us* off for ever? *why* does Your anger smoke against the sheep of Your pasture?

2 Remember Your congregation, *which* You have purchased of old; the <u>rod</u> of Your inheritance, *which* You have redeemed; this mount Zi'on, wherein You have dwelled. tribe

3 Lift up Your feet to the perpetual desolations; *even* all *that* the enemy has done wickedly in the sanctuary.

4 Your enemies <u>roar</u> in the midst of Your congregations; they set up their <u>ensigns</u> *for* signs. threaten - standards

5 *A man* was famous according as he had lifted up axes upon the thick trees.

6 But now they break down the carved work thereof at once with axes and hammers.

7 They have cast fire into Your <u>sanctuary</u>, they have defiled *by casting down* the dwelling place of Your name to the ground. i.e., temple

8 They said in their hearts, Let us destroy them together: they have burned up all the synagogues of God in the land.

9 We see not our signs: *there is* no more any prophet: neither *is there* among us any that knows how long.

10 O <u>God</u>, how long shall the adversary <u>reproach</u>? shall the enemy blaspheme Your name for ever? Elohim p.f. - revile

11 Why withdraw You Your hand, even Your right hand? pluck *it* out of Your bosom.

12 For God *is* my King of old, working salvation in the midst of the earth.

13 You did divide the sea by Your strength: You broke the heads of the <u>dragons</u> in the waters. sea monsters

14 You broke the heads of <u>leviathan</u> in pieces, *and* gave him *to be* meat to the people inhabiting the wilderness. crocodile

15 You did cling the fountain and the flood: You dried up mighty rivers.

16 The day *is* Yours, the night also *is* Yours: You have prepared the light and the sun.

17 You have set all the borders of the earth: You have made summer and winter.

18 Remember this, *that* the enemy has <u>reproached</u>, O LORD, and *that* the foolish people have <u>blasphemed</u> Your name. mocked - spurned

19 O deliver not the soul of Your <u>turtledove</u> to the multitude *of the wicked*: forget not the congregation of Your poor for ever. i.e., beloved

20 Have respect to the <u>covenant</u>: for the dark places of the earth are full of the habitations of cruelty. agreement

21 O let not the oppressed return ashamed: let the poor and needy praise Your name.

22 Arise, O God, plead Your own cause: remember how the foolish man <u>reproachs</u> You daily. mock

23 Forget not the voice of Your enemies: the tumult of those that rise up against You increases continually.

PSALM 75

To the chief Musician, Al-taschith, A Psalm or Song of Asaph

TO you, O God, do we give thanks, *to You* do we give thanks: for *that* Your name is near Your wondrous works declare.

Elohim[p.f.]

2 When I shall receive the congregation I will judge uprightly.
3 The earth and all the inhabitants thereof are dissolved: I bear up the pillars of it. Se'lah.
4 I said to the fools, Deal not foolishly: and to the wicked, Lift not up the horn:
5 Lift not up your horn on high: speak *not with* a stiff neck.   i.e., strength - insolent pride
6 For promotion *comes* neither from the east, nor from the west, nor from the south.
7 But God *is* the judge: He puts down one, and sets up another.
8 For in the hand of the LORD *there is* a cup, and the wine is red; it is full of mixture; and He pours out of the same: but the dregs thereof, all the wicked of the earth shall wring *them* out, *and* drink *them*.
9 But I will declare for ever; I will sing praises to the God of Ja'cob.
10 All the horns of the wicked also will I cut off; *but* the horns of the righteous shall be exalted.

PSALM 76

To the chief Musician on Neginoth, A Psalm or Song of Asaph

IN Ju'dah *is* God known: His name *is* great in Is'ra-el.
2 In Sa'lem also is His tabernacle, and His dwelling place in Zi'on.
3 There broke He the arrows of the bow, the shield, and the sword, and the battle. Se'lah.
4 You *are* more glorious *and* excellent than the mountains of prey.
5 The stouthearted are spoiled, they have slept their sleep: and none of the men of might have found their hands.
6 At your rebuke, O God of Ja'cob, both the chariot and horse are cast into a dead sleep.   Elohim[p.f.]
7 You, *even* You, *are* to be feared: and who may stand in Your sight when once You are angry?

REV. 6:17   revered   894

8 You did cause judgment to be heard from heaven; the earth feared, and was still,
9 When God arose to judgment, to save all the meek of the earth. Se'lah.
10 Surely the wrath of man shall praise You: the remainder of wrath shall You restrain.
11 Vow, and pay to the LORD your God: let all that be round about Him bring presents to Him that ought to be feared.
12 He shall cut off the spirit of princes: *He is* terrible to the kings of the earth.   awesome

PSALM 77

To the chief Musician, to Jeduthun, A Psalm of Asaph

I CRIED to God with my voice, *even* to God with my voice; and He gave ear to me.   *listened*

2 In the day of my trouble I sought the Lord: my sore ran in the night, and ceased not: my soul refused to be comforted.   *heart ached*

3 I remembered God, and was troubled: I complained, and my spirit was overwhelmed. Se'lah.   *Elohim*ᵖᶠ

4 You hold my eyes waking: I am so troubled that I cannot speak.

5 I have considered the days of old, the years of ancient times.

6 I call to remembrance my song in the night: I commune with my own heart: and my spirit made diligent search.

7 Will the Lord cast off for ever? and will He be favorable no more?

8 Is His mercy clean gone for ever? does *His* promise fail for evermore?

9 Has God forgotten to be gracious? has He in anger shut up His tender mercies? Se'lah.

10 And I said, This *is* my infirmity: *but I will remember* the years of the right hand of the Most High.   *grief*

11 I will remember the works of the LORD: surely I will remember Your wonders of old.

12 I will meditate also of all Your work, and talk of Your doings.

13 Your way, O God, *is* in the sanctuary: who *is so* great a God as *our* God?

14 You *are* the God that does wonders: You have declared Your strength among the people.

15 You have with *Your* arm redeemed Your people, the sons of Ja'cob and Jo'seph. Se'lah.

16 The waters saw You, O God, the waters saw You; they were afraid: the depths also were troubled.   *convulsed*

17 The clouds poured out water: the skies sent out a sound: Your arrows also went abroad.

18 The voice of Your thunder *was* in the heaven: the lightnings lightened the world: the earth trembled and shook.

19 Your way *is* in the sea, and Your path in the great waters, and Your footsteps are not known.

20 You led Your people like a flock by the hand of Mo'ses and Aar'on.

PSALM 78

Maschil of Asaph

G IVE ear, O my people, *to* my law: incline your ears to the words of my mouth.   *listen*

2 I will open my mouth in a parable: I will utter dark sayings of old: MATT. 13:35

3 Which we have heard and known, and our fathers have told us.   *understood*

4 We will not hide *them* from their children, showing to the generation to come the praises of the LORD, and His strength, and His wonderful works that He has done.

5 For He established a testimony in Ja'cob, and appointed a law in Is'ra-el, which He commanded our fathers, that

they should make them known to their children:

6 That the generation to come might know *them, even* the children *which* should be born; *who* should arise and declare *them* to their children:

7 That they might set their hope in God, and not forget the works of God, but keep His commandments: El^s.f.

8 And might not be as their fathers, a stubborn and rebellious generation; a generation *that* set not their heart aright, and whose spirit was not steadfast with God. did not prepare

9 The children of E'phra-im, *being* armed, *and* carrying bows, turned back in the day of battle.

10 They kept not the covenant of God, and refused to walk in His law; agreement

11 And forgot His works, and His wonders that He had showed them.

12 Marvellous things did He in the sight of their fathers, in the land of E'gypt, *in* the field of Zo'an.

13 He divided the sea, and caused them to pass through; and He made the waters to stand as an heap.

14 In the daytime also He led them with a cloud, and all the night with a light of fire.

15 He clave the rocks in the wilderness, and gave *them* drink as *out of* the great depths. split

16 He brought streams also out of the rock, and caused waters to run down like rivers.

17 And they sinned yet more against Him by provoking the Most High in the wilderness.

18 And they tempted God in their heart by asking meat for their lust. food

19 Yea, they spoke against God; they said, Can God furnish a table in the wilderness? Elohim^p.f. - El^s.f. - prepare

20 Behold, He smote the rock, that the waters gushed out, and the streams overflowed; can He give bread also? can He provide flesh for His people? struck

21 Therefore the LORD heard *this*, and was angry: so a fire was kindled against Ja'cob, and anger also came up against Is'ra-el;

22 Because they believed not in God, and trusted not in His salvation: i.e., Jeshua

23 Though He had commanded the clouds from above, and opened the doors of heaven,

24 And had rained down manna upon them to eat, and had given them of the corn of heaven.

25 Man did eat angels' food: He sent them meat to the full. food

26 He caused an east wind to blow in the heaven: and by His power He brought in the south wind.

27 He rained flesh also upon them as dust, and feathered fowls like as the sand of the sea: meat

28 And He let *it* fall in the midst of their camp, round about their habitations.

29 So they did eat, and were well filled: for He gave them their own desire;

30 They were not estranged from their lust. But while their meat *was* yet in their mouths, separated - desire

31 The anger of God came upon

them, and slew the fattest of them, and smote down the chosen *men* of Is'ra-el.

32 For all this they sinned still, and believed not for His wondrous works.

33 Therefore their days did He consume in vanity, and their years in trouble.

34 When He slew them, then they sought Him: and they returned and enquired early after <u>God</u>.   El s.f.

35 And they remembered that God *was* their rock, and <u>the high God</u> their redeemer.   El Elyon

36 Nevertheless they did flatter Him with their mouth, and they lied to Him with their tongues.

37 For their heart was not right with Him, neither were they <u>steadfast</u> in His <u>covenant</u>.   ACTS 8:21 faithful - agreement

38 But He, *being* full of compassion, forgave *their* iniquity, and destroyed *them* not: yea, many a time turned He His anger away, and did not stir up all His wrath.

39 For He remembered that they *were but* flesh; a wind that passes away, and comes not again.

40 How oft did they <u>provoke</u> Him in the wilderness, *and* grieve Him in the desert!   rebel against

41 Yea, they turned back and tempted God, and limited the Holy One of Is'ra-el.

42 They remembered not His hand, *nor* the day when He delivered them from the enemy.

43 How He had <u>wrought</u> His signs in E'gypt, and His wonders in the field of Zo'an: performed

44 And had turned their rivers into blood; and their <u>floods</u>, that they could not drink.   streams

45 He sent <u>divers</u> sorts of flies among them, which devoured them; and frogs, which destroyed them.   various

46 He gave also their <u>increase</u> to the caterpiller, and their labor to the locust.   crops

47 He destroyed their vines with hail, and their sycamore trees with frost.

48 He gave up their cattle also to the hail, and their flocks to hot thunderbolts.

49 He cast upon them the fierceness of His anger, wrath, and indignation, and trouble, by sending evil <u>angels</u> *among them*.   messengers

50 He made a way to His anger; He spared not their soul from death, but gave their life over to the pestilence;

51 And smote all the firstborn in E'gypt; the chief of *their* strength in the tabernacles of Ham:

52 But made His own people to go forth like sheep, and guided them in the wilderness like a flock.

53 And He led them on safely, so that they feared not: but the sea overwhelmed their enemies.

54 And He brought them to the border of His sanctuary, *even to* this mountain, *which* His right hand had purchased.

55 He cast out the <u>heathen</u> also before them, and divided them an inheritance by line, and made the tribes of Is'ra-el to dwell in their tents.   nations

56 Yet they <u>tempted</u> and provoked

the <u>Most High God</u>, and kept not His testimonies: tested - Elohim^{p.f.} Eleyon

57 But turned back, and dealt unfaithfully like their fathers: they were turned aside like a deceitful bow.

58 For they provoked Him to anger with their <u>high places</u>, and moved Him to jealousy with their graven <u>images</u>.   shrines - idols

59 When God heard *this*, He was angry, and greatly abhorred Is'ra-el:

60 So that He forsook the tabernacle of Shi'loh, the tent *which* He placed among men;

61 And delivered His strength into captivity, and His glory into the enemy's hand.

62 He gave His people over also to the sword; and was angry with His inheritance.

63 The fire consumed their young men; and their maidens were not given to marriage.

64 Their priests fell by the sword; and their widows made no lamentation.

65 Then the Lord awaked as one out of sleep, *and* like a mighty man that shouts by reason of wine.

66 And He <u>smote</u> His enemies <u>in the hinder parts</u>: He put them to a perpetual reproach.   drove - backwards

67 Moreover He refused the <u>tabernacle</u> of Jo'seph, and chose not the tribe of E'phra-im: tent

68 But chose the tribe of Ju'dah, the mount Zi'on which He loved.

69 And He built His sanctuary like high *palaces*, like the earth which He has established for ever.

70 He chose Da'vid also His servant, and took him from the sheepfolds:

71 From following the ewes great with young He brought him to feed Ja'cob His people, and Is'ra-el His inheritance.

72 So He fed them according to the integrity of His heart; and guided them by the skilfulness of His hands.

PSALM 79

A Psalm of Asaph

O GOD, the <u>heathen</u> are come into Your inheritance; Your holy temple have they defiled; they have laid Je-ru'sa-lem <u>on heaps</u>.
Elohim^{p.f.} - nations - in ruins

2 The dead bodies of Your servants have they given *to be* <u>meat</u> to the fowls of the heaven, the flesh of Your saints to the beasts of the earth.   food

3 Their blood have they shed like water round about Je-ru'sa-lem; and *there was* none to bury *them*.

4 We are become a reproach to our neighbor, a scorn and derision on to them that are round about us.

5 How long, LORD? Will You be angry for ever? shall Your jealousy burn like fire?

6 Pour out Your anger upon the <u>heathen</u> that have not known You, and upon the kingdoms that have not called upon Your name.   nations

7 For they have <u>devoured</u> Ja'cob, and laid waste His dwelling place.   destroyed

8 O remember not against us former iniquities: let Your tender mercies speedily <u>prevent</u> us: for we are brought very low.   come before

9 Help us, O God of our salvation, for the glory of Your name: and deliver us, and purge away our sins, for Your name's sake.

10 Why should the heathen say, Where *is* their God? let him be known among the heathen in our sight *by* the revenging of the blood of Your servants *which is* shed.   nations - time

11 Let the sighing of the prisoner come before You; according to the greatness of Your power preserve You those that are appointed to die;

Lit. arm save

12 And render to our neighbors sevenfold into their bosom their reproach, wherewith they have reproached You, O Lord.   return

13 So we Your people and sheep of Your pasture will give You thanks for ever: we will show forth Your praise to all generations.

PSALM 80

To the chief Musician upon Shoshannim-eduth, A Psalm of Asaph

GIVE ear, O Shepherd of Is'rael, You that leads Jo'seph like a flock; You that dwell *between* the cherubims, shine forth.

2 Before E'phra-im and Ben'ja-min and Ma-nas'seh stir up Your strength, and come *and* save us.

3 Turn us again, O God, and cause Your face to shine; and we shall be saved.

4 O LORD God of hosts, how long will You be angry against the prayer of Your people?   Jehovah^{s.f.} Elohim^{p.f.} Tsebaoth

5 You feed them with the bread of tears; and give them tears to drink in great measure.   i.e., in sorrow

6 You make us a strife to our neighbors: and our enemies laugh among themselves.

7 Turn us again, O God of hosts, and cause Your face to shine; and we shall be saved.   Restore

8 You have brought a vine out of E'gypt: You have cast out the heathen, and planted it.   i.e., Israel - nations

9 You prepared *room* before it, and did cause it to take deep root, and it filled the land.

10 The hills were covered with the shadow of it, and the boughs thereof *were like* the goodly cedars.   mighty

11 She sent out her boughs to the sea, and her branches to the river.

12 Why have You *then* broken down her hedges, so that all they which pass by the way do pluck her?

13 The boar out of the wood does waste it, and the wild beast of the field does devour it.   forest - ravage

14 Return, we beseech You, O God of hosts: look down from heaven, and behold, and visit this vine;   beg

15 And the vineyard which Your right hand has planted, and the branch *that* You made strong for Yourself.

16 *It is* burned with fire, *it is* cut down: they perish at the rebuke of Your countenance.   presence

17 Let Your hand be upon the man of Your right hand, upon the son of man *whom* You made strong for Yourself.

18 So will not we go back from You:

quicken us, and we will call upon Your name.   revive

19 <u>Turn</u> us again, O LORD God of hosts, cause Your face to shine; and we shall be saved.   Restore

PSALM 81

To the chief Musician upon Gittith, A Psalm of Asaph

SING aloud to <u>God</u> our strength: make a joyful noise to the <u>God</u> of Ja'cob.   Elohim^{p.f.}

2 Take a psalm, and bring here the timbrel, the pleasant harp with the <u>psaltery</u>.   lyre

3 Blow up the trumpet in the new moon, in the time appointed, on our solemn feast day.

4 For this *was* a <u>statute</u> for Is'ra-el, *and* a law of the God of Ja'cob. decree

5 This He ordained in Jo'seph *for* a testimony, when He went out through the land of E'gypt: *where* I heard a language *that* I understood not.

6 I removed his shoulder from the burden: his hands were delivered from the <u>pots</u>.   baskets

7 You called in trouble, and I delivered you; I answered you in the secret place of thunder: I <u>proved</u> you at the waters of Meribah. Se'lah.   tested

8 Hear, O My people, and I will testify to you: O Is'ra-el, if you will hearken to Me;

9 There shall no strange god be in you; neither shall you worship any strange god.

10 I *am* the LORD your God, which brought you out of the land of E'gypt: open your mouth wide, and I will fill it.

11 But My people would not hearken to My voice; and Is'ra-el would none of Me.

12 So I gave them up to their own hearts' lust: *and* they walked in their own counsels.

13 Oh that My people had hearkened to Me, *and* Is'ra-el had walked in My ways!

14 I should soon have subdued their enemies, and turned My hand against their adversaries.

15 The haters of the LORD should have submitted themselves to Him: but their time should have endured for ever.

16 He should have fed them also with the finest of the wheat: and with honey out of the rock should I have satisfied you.

PSALM 82

A Psalm of Asaph

GOD stands in the congregation of the mighty; He judges among the gods.

2 How long will you judge unjustly, and accept the persons of the wicked? Se'lah.

3 Defend the poor and fatherless: do justice to the afflicted and needy.

4 Deliver the poor and needy: <u>rid</u> *them* out of the hand of the wicked.   deliver

5 They know not, neither will they understand; they walk on in darkness: all the foundations of the earth <u>are</u> out of course.   are shaken

6 I have said, You *are* gods; and all of you *are* children of the most High. JOHN 10:33

7 But you shall die like men, and fall like one of the princes.

8 Arise, O God, judge the earth: for You shall inherit all nations.

PSALM 83

A Song or Psalm of Asaph

KEEP not Your silence, O God: hold not Your peace, and be not still, O God. Elohim^{p.f.} - El^{s.f.}

2 For, lo, Your enemies make a tumult: and they that hate You have lifted up the head.   are astir - abhor - exalted themselves

3 They have taken crafty counsel against Your people, and consulted against Your hidden ones.

4 They have said, Come, and let us cut them off from *being* a nation; that the name of Is'ra-el may be no more in remembrance.

5 For they have consulted together with one consent: they are confederate against You: mind - united

6 The tabernacles of E'dom, and the Ish'ma-el-ites; of Mo'ab, and the Ha'gar-enes;   tents

7 Ge'bal, and Am'mon, and Am'a-lek; the Phi-lis'tines with the inhabitants of Tyre;

8 As'sur also is joined with them: they have helped the children of Lot. Se'lah.

9 Do to them as *to* the Mid'i-an-ites; as *to* Sis'e-ra, as *to* Ja'bin, at the brook of Ki'son:

10 *Which* perished at En'-dor: they became *as* dung for the earth.   refuse

11 Make their nobles like O'reb, and like Ze'eb: yea, all their princes as Ze'bah, and as Zal-mun'na:

12 Who said, Let us take to ourselves the houses of God in possession.

13 O my God, make them like a wheel; as the stubble before the wind.

14 As the fire burns a wood, and as the flame sets the mountains on fire;

15 So persecute them with Your tempest, and make them afraid with Your storm.

16 Fill their faces with shame; that they may seek Your name, O Lord.

17 Let them be confounded and troubled for ever; yea, let them be put to shame, and perish:

18 That *men* may know that You, whose name alone *is* **JE-HO'VAH**, *are* the Most High over all the earth.   the LORD

PSALM 84

To the chief Musician upon Gittith, A Psalm for the sons of Korah

HOW amiable *are* Your tabernacles, O Lord of hosts!   lovely - Jehovah Tsebaoth

2 My soul longs, yea, even faints for the courts of the Lord: my heart and my flesh cries out for the living God.   El^{s.f.}

3 Yea, the sparrow has found an house, and the swallow a nest for herself, where she may lay her young, *even* Your altars, O Lord of hosts, my King, and my God.

4 Blessed *are* they that dwell in Your house: they will be still praising You. Se'lah.

5 Blessed *is* the man whose strength *is*

in You; in whose heart *are* the ways *of them*.

6 *Who* passing through the valley of Ba'ca make it a well; the rain also fills the pools.

7 They go from <u>strength to strength</u>, *every one of them* in Zi'on appears before God.   company to company

8 O LORD God of hosts, hear my prayer: give ear, O God of Ja'cob. Se'lah.

9 Behold, O God our shield, and look upon the face of Your anointed.

10 For a day in Your courts *is* better than a thousand. I had rather be a doorkeeper in the house of my God, than to dwell in the tents of wickedness.

11 For the <u>LORD God</u> *is* a sun and shield: the LORD will give grace and glory: no good *thing* will He withhold from them that walk uprightly.   Jehovah[s.f.] Elohim[p.f.]

12 O <u>LORD of hosts</u>, blessed *is* the man that trusts in you.   Jehovah Tsebaoth

PSALM 85

To the chief Musician, A Psalm for the sons of Korah

LORD, You have been favorable to Your land: You have brought back the captivity of Ja'cob.

2 You have forgiven the iniquity of Your people, You have covered all their sin. Se'lah.

3 You have taken away all Your wrath: You have turned *Yourself* from the fierceness of Your anger.

4 Turn us, O <u>God</u> of our salvation, and cause Your anger toward us to cease.   Elohim[p.f.]

5 Will You be angry with us for ever? will You <u>draw out</u> Your anger to all generations?   extend

6 Will You not revive us again: that Your people may rejoice in You?

7 Show us Your mercy, O LORD, and grant us Your salvation.

8 I will hear what God the LORD will speak: for He will speak peace to His people, and to His <u>saints</u>: but let them not turn again to <u>folly</u>.   godly ones - sin

9 Surely His salvation *is* near them that <u>fear</u> Him; that glory may dwell in our land.   reverence

10 Mercy and truth are met together; righteousness and peace have kissed *each other*.

11 Truth shall spring out of the earth; and righteousness shall look down from heaven.

12 Yea, the LORD shall give *that which is* good; and our land shall yield her <u>increase</u>.   harvest

13 Righteousness shall go before Him; and shall set us in the way of His steps.

PSALM 86

A Prayer of David

BOW down Your ear, O LORD, hear me: for I *am* poor and needy.

2 <u>Preserve</u> my <u>soul</u>; for I *am* <u>holy</u>: O You my God, save Your servant that trusts in You.   Guard - life - a godly man

3 Be merciful to me, O Lord: for I cry to You daily.

4 Rejoice the soul of Your servant: for to You, O Lord, do I lift up my soul.
5 For You, Lord, *are* good, and ready to forgive; and plenteous in mercy to all them that call upon You.
6 Give ear, O LORD, to my prayer; and attend to the voice of my sup-plications.   appeal
7 In the day of my trouble I will call upon You: for You will answer me.
8 Among the gods *there is* none like to You, O Lord; neither *are there any works* like to Your works.
9 All nations whom You have made shall come and worship before You, O Lord; and shall glorify Your name.
10 For You *are* great, and do won-drous things: You *are* God alone.
11 Teach me Your way, O LORD; I will walk in Your truth: unite my heart to fear Your name.   revere
12 I will praise You, O Lord my God, with all my heart: and I will glorify Your name for evermore.

Adonahy[p.l.] - Elohim[p.f.]

13 For great *is* Your mercy toward me: and You have delivered my soul from the lowest hell.   i.e., Sheol
14 O God, the proud are risen against me, and the assemblies of violent *men* have sought after my soul; and have not set You before them.
15 But You, O Lord, *are* a God full of compassion, and gracious, long-suffering, and plenteous in mercy and truth.   Adonahy[p.f.] - El[s.f.] - patient
16 O turn to me, and have mercy upon me; give Your strength to Your servant, and save the son of Your handmaid.   be gracious to

17 Show me a token for good; that they which hate me may see *it*, and be ashamed: because You, LORD, have helped me, and com-forted me.   sign - despise

PSALM 87

A Psalm or Song for the sons of Korah

HIS foundation *is* in the holy mountains.
2 The LORD loves the gates of Zi'on more than all the dwellings of Ja'cob.
3 Glorious things are spoken of You, O city of God. Se'lah.   Elohim[p.f.]
4 I will make mention of Ra'hab and Bab'y-lon to them that know Me: behold Phi-lis'tia, and Tyre, with E-thi-o'pi-a; this *man* was born there.
5 And of Zi'on it shall be said, This and that man was born in her: and the Highest Himself shall es-tablish her.
6 The LORD shall count, when He writes up the people, *that* this *man* was born there. Se'lah.   record
7 As well the singers as the players on instruments *shall be there*: all My springs *are* in you.

PSALM 88

A Song or Psalm for the sons of Korah, to the chief Musician upon Mahalath Leannoth, Maschil of Heman the Ezrahite

O LORD God of my salvation, I have cried day *and* night before You:
2 Let my prayer come before You: incline Your ear to my cry;   listen

3 For my soul is full of troubles: and my life draws near to the grave.   i.e., Sheol

4 I am counted with them that go down into the pit: I am as a man *that has* no strength: i.e., are dying

5 <u>Free</u> among the dead, like the slain that lie in the grave, whom You remember no more: and they are cut off from Your hand.   Forsaken

6 You have laid me in the lowest pit, in darkness, in the deeps.

7 Your anger lies <u>hard</u> upon me, and You have afflicted *me* with all Your waves. Se'lah.   heavy

8 You have put away my acquaintance far from me; You have made me <u>an abomination</u> to them: *I am* shut up, and I cannot come forth.   repulsive

9 My eye mourns by reason of affliction: Lord, I have called daily upon You, I have stretched out my hands to You.

10 Will You show wonders to the dead? shall the dead arise *and* praise You? Se'lah.

11 Shall Your lovingkindness be declared in the grave? *or* Your faithfulness in destruction?

12 Shall Your wonders be known in the dark? and Your righteousness in the land of forgetfulness?

13 But to You have I cried, O Lord; and in the morning shall my prayer <u>prevent</u> You.   come before

14 Lord, why cast You off my soul? *why* hide You Your face from me?

15 I *am* afflicted and ready to die from *my* youth up: *while* I suffer Your terrors I am distracted.

16 Your fierce anger goes over me; Your terrors have cut me off.

17 They came round about me daily like <u>water</u>; they <u>compassed</u> me <u>about together</u>.   a flood - engulfed - completely

18 Lover and friend have You put far from me, *and* my acquaintance into darkness.

PSALM 89

Maschil of Ethan the Ezrahite

I WILL sing of the mercies of the Lord for ever: with my mouth will I make known Your faithfulness to all generations.

2 For I have said, Mercy shall be built up for ever: Your faithfulness shall You establish in the very heavens.

3 I have made a <u>covenant</u> with My chosen, I have sworn to Da'vid My servant,   agreement

4 Your <u>seed</u> will I establish for ever, and build up your throne to all generations. Se'lah.   line

5 And the heavens shall praise Your wonders, O Lord: Your faithfulness also in the congregation of the saints.

6 For who in the heaven can be compared to the Lord? *who* among the sons of the mighty can be likened to the Lord?

7 <u>God</u> is greatly to be <u>feared</u> in the assembly of the saints, and to be had in reverence of all *them that are* about Him.   El^s.f. - revered

8 O <u>Lord God of hosts</u>, who *is* a

strong Lord like to You? or to Your faithfulness round about You?

Jehovah[s.f.] Elohim[p.f.] Tsebaoth

9 You rule the raging of the sea: when the waves thereof arise, You still them.
10 You have broken Ra'hab in pieces, as one that is slain; You have scattered Your enemies with Your strong arm.   i.e., Egypt
11 The heavens *are* Yours, the earth also *is* Yours: *as for* the world and the fulness thereof, You have founded them.
12 The north and the south You have created them: Ta'bor and Her'mon shall rejoice in Your name.
13 You have a mighty arm: strong is Your hand, *and* high is Your right hand.
14 Justice and judgment *are* the habitation of Your throne: mercy and truth shall go before Your face.   foundation
15 Blessed *is* the people that know the joyful sound: they shall walk, O Lord, in the light of Your countenance.   presence
16 In your name shall they rejoice all the day: and in Your righteousness shall they be exalted.
17 For You *are* the glory of their strength: and in Your favor our horn shall be exalted.   i.e., strength
18 For the Lord *is* our defence; and the Holy One of Is'ra-el *is* our king.
19 Then You spoke in vision to Your holy one, and said, I have laid help upon *one that is* mighty; I have exalted *one* chosen out of the people.
20 I have found Da'vid My servant; with My holy oil have I anointed him:

21 With whom My hand shall be established: My arm also shall strengthen him.
22 The enemy shall not exact upon him; nor the son of wickedness afflict him.
23 And I will beat down his foes before his face, and plague them that hate him.   despise
24 But My faithfulness and My mercy *shall be* with him: and in My name shall his horn be exalted.   authority
25 I will set his hand also in the sea, and his right hand in the rivers.
26 He shall cry to Me, You *are* my father, my God, and the rock of my salvation.   i.e., strength
27 Also I will make him *My* firstborn, higher than the kings of the earth. REV. 1:5
28 My mercy will I keep for him for evermore, and My covenant shall stand fast with him.   REV. 21:7 agreement
29 His seed also will I make *to endure* for ever, and his throne as the days of heaven.   line
30 If his children forsake My law, and walk not in My judgments;
31 If they break My statutes, and keep not My commandments;   decrees - obey
32 Then will I visit their transgression with the rod, and their iniquity with stripes.   punish - sin
33 Nevertheless My lovingkindness will I not utterly take from him, nor allow My faithfulness to fail.   completely
34 My covenant will I not break, nor alter the thing that is gone out of My lips.   agreement - violate - change - word
35 Once have I sworn by My holiness that I will not lie to Da'vid.

36 His <u>seed</u> shall endure for ever, and his throne as the sun before Me.　line

37 It shall be established for ever as the moon, and *as* a faithful witness in heaven. Se'lah.

38 But You have cast off and abhorred, You have been angry with Your <u>anointed</u>.　own

39 You have made void the <u>covenant</u> of Your servant: You have profaned his crown *by casting it* to the ground.

40 You have broken down all his <u>hedges</u>; You have brought his strong holds to ruin.　walls

41 All that pass by the way <u>spoil</u> him: he is a reproach to his neighbor.　plunder

42 You have set up the right hand of his adversaries; You have made all his enemies to rejoice.

43 You have also turned the edge of his sword, and have not <u>made</u> him to stand in the battle.　supported

44 You have made his glory to cease, and cast his throne down to the ground.

45 The days of his youth have You shortened: You have covered him with shame. Se'lah.

46 How long, LORD? will You hide yourself for ever? shall Your anger burn like fire?

47 Remember how short my time is: wherefore have You made all men in vain?

48 What man *is he that* lives, and shall not see death? shall he deliver his soul from the hand of the grave? Se'lah.

49 Lord, where *are* Your former lovingkindness, *which* You swear to Da'vid in Your truth?

50 Remember, Lord, the reproach of Your servants; *how* I do bear in my bosom *the reproach of* all the mighty people;

51 Wherewith Your enemies have reproached, O LORD; wherewith they have reproached the footsteps of Your anointed.

52 Blessed *be* the LORD for evermore. Amen, and Amen.

PSALM 90

A Prayer of Moses the man of God

LORD, You have been our dwelling place in all generations.

2 Before the mountains were brought forth, or ever You had formed the earth and the world, even from everlasting to everlasting, You *are* God.

3 You turn man to destruction; and say, Return, you children of men.

4 For a thousand years in Your sight *are but* as yesterday when it is past, and *as* a watch in the night.　2 PET. 3:8

5 You carried them away as with a flood; they are *as* a sleep: in the morning *they are* like grass *which* grows up.

6 In the morning it flourishs, and grows up; in the evening it is cut down, and withers.

7 For we are <u>consumed</u> by Your anger, and by Your wrath are we troubled.　destroyed

8 You have set our iniquities before You, our secret *sins* in the light of Your <u>countenance</u>.　presence

9 For all our days are passed away in Your wrath: we spend our years as a tale *that is told*.

10 The days of our years *are* <u>three-score years and ten</u>; and if by reason of strength *they be* <u>fourscore years</u>, yet *is* their <u>strength</u> labor and sorrow; for it is soon cut off, and we fly away.　　70 - 80 - span

11 Who knows the power of Your anger? even according to Your <u>fear</u>, *so is* Your anger.　　honor

12 So teach *us* to number our days, that we may apply *our* hearts to wisdom.

13 Return, O Lord, how long? and let it <u>repent</u> You concerning Your servants.　　grieve

14 O satisfy us early with Your mercy; that we may rejoice and be glad all our days.

15 Make us glad according to the days *wherein* You have afflicted us, *and* the years *wherein* we have seen evil.

16 Let Your work appear to Your servants, and Your glory to their children.

17 And let the beauty of the Lord our God be upon us: and establish You the work of our hands upon us; yea, the work of our hands establish You it.

PSALM 91

HE that dwells in the secret place of the Most High shall abide under the shadow of the <u>Almighty</u>. Shaddai

2 I will say of the Lord, *He is* my refuge and my fortress: my <u>God</u>; in Him will I trust.　　Elohim ᵖ·ᶠ·

3 Surely He shall deliver you from the <u>snare</u> of the fowler, *and* from the <u>noisome</u> pestilence.　　lure - deadly

4 He shall cover you with His feathers, and under His wings shall you trust: His truth *shall be* your shield and <u>buckler</u>.　　bulwark

5 You shall not be afraid for the terror by night; *nor* for the arrow *that* flies by day;

6 *Nor* for the <u>pestilence</u> *that* walks in darkness; *nor* for the destruction *that* <u>wastes</u> at noonday.　　sickness - destroys

7 A thousand shall fall at your side, and ten thousand at your right hand; *but* it shall not come near you.

8 Only with your eyes shall you behold and see the reward of the wicked.

9 Because you have made the Lord, *which is* my refuge, *even* the Most High, your habitation;

10 There shall no evil befall you, neither shall any plague come near your <u>dwelling</u>.　　tent

11 For He shall give His <u>angels</u> charge over you, to keep you in all your ways.　　MATT. 4:6　LUKE 4:10　messengers

12 They shall <u>bear</u> you up in *their* hands, less you dash your foot against a stone.　　lift

13 You shall tread upon the lion and adder: the young lion and the dragon shall you trample under feet.

14 Because he has set his love upon Me, therefore will I deliver him: I will <u>set him on high</u>, because he has known My name.　　exalt him

15 He shall call upon Me, and I will answer him: I *will be* with him in trouble; I will deliver him, and honor him.

16 With long life will I satisfy him, and show him My salvation.

PSALM 92

A Psalm or Song for the sabbath day

IT *is a* good *thing* to give thanks to the LORD, and to sing praises to Your name, O Most High:

2 To <u>show forth</u> Your lovingkindness in the morning, and Your faithfulness <u>every</u> night,   declare - by

3 Upon an instrument of ten strings, and upon the <u>psaltery</u>; upon the harp with a <u>solemn sound</u>.   lyre - deep tone

4 For You, LORD, have made me glad through Your work: I will triumph in the works of Your hands.

5 O LORD, how great are Your works! *and* Your thoughts are very deep.

6 A <u>brutish</u> man knows not; neither does a fool understand this.   senseless

7 When the wicked spring as the grass, and when all the workers of iniquity do flourish; *it is* that they shall be destroyed for ever:

8 But You, LORD, *are* <u>*most*</u> high for evermore.   exalted

9 For, lo, Your enemies, O LORD, for, lo, Your enemies shall perish; all the workers of iniquity shall be scattered.

10 But my <u>horn</u> shall You exalt like *the horn of* an <u>unicorn</u>: I shall be anointed with fresh oil.   i.e., strength - wild ox

11 My eye also shall see *my desire* on my enemies, *and* my ears shall hear *my desire* of the wicked that rise up against me.

12 The righteous shall <u>flourish</u> like the palm tree: he shall grow like a cedar in Leb'a-non.   prosper

13 Those that be planted in the house of the LORD shall flourish in the courts of our God.

14 They shall still bring forth fruit in old age; they shall be fat and flourishing;

15 To <u>show</u> that the LORD *is* upright: *He is* my rock, and *there is* no unrighteousness in Him.   declare

PSALM 93

THE LORD reigns, He is clothed with majesty; the LORD is clothed with strength, *wherewith* He has girded Himself: the world also is stablished, that it cannot be <u>moved</u>.   shaken

2 Your throne *is* established of old: You *are* from everlasting.

3 The floods have lifted up, O LORD, the floods have lifted up their voice; the floods lift up their waves.

4 The LORD on high *is* mightier than the noise of many waters, *yea, than* the mighty waves of the sea.

5 Your testimonies are <u>very sure</u>: holiness <u>become</u> Your house, O LORD, for ever.   fully confirmed - adorns

PSALM 94

O LORD <u>God</u>, to whom vengeance belongs; O <u>God</u>, to whom vengeance belongs, show Yourself.   El s.f.

2 Lift up Yourself, You judge of the earth: render a reward to the proud.

3 LORD, how long shall the wicked, how long shall the wicked triumph?

4 *How long* shall they utter *and* speak <u>hard things</u>? *and* all the workers of iniquity boast themselves?   arrogantly

5 They break in pieces Your people, O Lord, and afflict Your heritage.
6 They slay the widow and the stranger, and murder the fatherless.
7 Yet they say, The Lord shall not see, neither shall the God of Ja'cob regard *it*.
8 Understand, you brutish among the people: and *you* fools, when will you be wise? senseless
9 He that planted the ear, shall He not hear? He that formed the eye, shall He not see?
10 He that chastises the heathen, shall not He correct? He that teaches man knowledge, *shall not He know*? punishes - nations
11 The Lord knows the thoughts of man, that they *are* vanity. 1 COR. 3:20 futile
12 Blessed *is* the man whom You chasten, O Lord, and teaches him out of Your law; disciplines
13 That You may give him rest from the days of adversity, until the pit be dug for the wicked. relief
14 For the Lord will not cast off His people, neither will He forsake His inheritance. ROM. 11:2
15 But judgment shall return to righteousness: and all the upright in heart shall follow it.
16 Who will rise up for me against the evildoers? *or* who will stand up for me against the workers of iniquity?
17 Unless the Lord *had been* my help, my soul had almost dwelled in silence.
18 When I said, my foot slips; Your mercy, O Lord, held me up.
19 In the multitude of my thoughts within me Your comforts delight my soul.
20 Shall the throne of iniquity have fellowship with You, which frames mischief by a law? be allied
21 They gather themselves together against the soul of the righteous, and condemn the innocent blood.
22 But the Lord is my defence; and my God *is* the rock of my refuge.
23 And He shall bring upon them their own iniquity, and shall cut them off in their own wickedness; *yea*, the Lord our God shall cut them off.

PSALM 95

O COME, let us sing to the Lord: let us make a joyful noise to the rock of our salvation.
2 Let us come before His presence with thanksgiving, and make a joyful noise to Him with psalms.
3 For the Lord *is* a great God, and a great King above all gods. El[s.f.] - rulers
4 In His hand *are* the deep places of the earth: the strength of the hills *is* His also.
5 The sea *is* His, and He made it: and His hands formed the dry *land*.
6 O come, let us worship and bow down: let us kneel before the Lord our maker. PHIL. 2:10
7 For He *is* our God; and we *are* the people of His pasture, and the sheep of His hand. To day if you will hear His voice, HEB. 4:8 Elohim[p.f.]
8 Harden not your heart, as in the provocation, *and* as *in* the day of temptation in the wilderness:

9 When your fathers <u>tempted</u> Me, <u>proved</u> Me, and saw My work.   tested - tried

10 Forty years long was I grieved with *this* generation, and said, It *is* a people that do err in their heart, and they have not known My ways:

11 To whom I swear in My anger that they should not enter into My rest.   HEB. 3:11 HEB. 4:3,5

PSALM 96

O SING to the LORD a new song: sing to the LORD, all the earth.

2 Sing to the LORD, bless His name; show forth His salvation from day to day.

3 Declare His glory among the <u>heathen</u>, His wonders among all people.   nations

4 For the LORD *is* great, and greatly to be praised: He *is* to be <u>feared</u> above all <u>gods</u>.   revered - rulers

5 For all the gods of the nations *are* idols: but the LORD made the heavens.

6 Honor and majesty *are* before Him: strength and beauty *are* in His sanctuary.

7 Give to the LORD, O you kindreds of the people, give to the LORD glory and strength.

8 Give to the LORD the glory *due to* His name: bring an offering, and come into His courts.

9 O worship the LORD in the beauty of holiness: <u>fear</u> before Him, all the earth.   tremble

10 Say among the <u>heathen</u> *that* the LORD reigns: the world also shall be established that it shall not be <u>moved</u>: He shall judge the people righteously.   nations - shaken

11 Let the heavens rejoice, and let the earth be glad; let the sea roar, and the fulness thereof.

12 Let the field be joyful, and all that *is* therein: then shall all the trees of the <u>wood</u> rejoice   forest

13 Before the LORD: for He comes, for He comes to judge the earth: He shall judge the world with righteousness, and the people with His truth.   REV. 19:11

PSALM 97

THE LORD reigns; let the earth rejoice; let the multitude of <u>isles</u> be glad *thereof*.   distant lands

2 Clouds and darkness *are* round about Him: righteousness and judgment *are* the <u>habitation</u> of His throne.   foundation

3 A fire goes before Him, and burned up His enemies round about.

4 His lightnings enlightened the world: the earth saw, and trembled.

5 The hills melted like wax at the presence of the <u>LORD</u>, at the presence of the <u>Lord</u> of the whole earth.   Jehovah[s.f.] - Adon[s.f.]

6 The heavens declare His righteousness, and all the people see His glory.

7 Confounded be all they that serve graven <u>images</u>, that boast themselves of idols: worship Him, all *you* gods.   idols

8 Zi'on heard, and was glad; and the daughters of Ju'dah rejoiced because of Your judgments, O LORD.

9 For You, LORD, *are* high above all the earth: You are exalted far above all gods.

10 You that love the LORD, <u>hate</u> evil: He <u>preserve</u> the souls of His <u>saints</u>; He delivers them out of the hand of the wicked. abhor - guards - faithful ones
11 Light is sown for the righteous, and gladness for the upright in heart.
12 Rejoice in the LORD, your righteous; and give thanks at the remembrance of His holiness.

PSALM 98

A Psalm

O SING to the LORD a new song; for He has done marvellous things: His right hand, and His holy arm, has gotten Him the victory.
2 The LORD has made known His <u>salvation</u>: His righteousness has He openly showed in the sight of the <u>heathen</u>. i.e., Heb. Jeshua - nations
3 He has remembered His mercy and His truth toward the house of Is'ra-el: all the ends of the earth have seen the <u>salvation</u> of our God. LUKE 3:6 i.e., Heb. Jeshua
4 Make a joyful noise to the LORD, all the earth: make a loud noise, and rejoice, and sing praise.
5 Sing to the LORD with the harp; with the harp, and the voice of a psalm.
6 With trumpets and sound of cornet make a joyful noise before the LORD, the King.
7 Let the sea roar, and the fulness thereof; the world, and they that dwell therein.
8 Let the floods clap *their* hands: let the hills be joyful together
9 Before the LORD; for He comes to judge the earth: with righteousness shall He judge the world, and the people with <u>equity</u>. fairness

PSALM 99

THE LORD reigns; let the people <u>tremble</u>: He sits *between* the cherubims; let the earth be moved. be impressed
2 The LORD *is* great in Zi'on; and He *is* high above all the people.
3 Let them praise Your great and <u>terrible</u> name; *for* it *is* holy. awesome
4 The king's strength also loves <u>judgment</u>; You do <u>establish equity</u>, You execute judg<u>ment</u> and righteousness in Ja'cob. justice - make fairness the rule
5 Exalt you the LORD our God, and worship at His footstool; *for* He *is* holy.
6 Mo'ses and Aar'on among His priests, and Sam'u-el among them that call upon His name; they called upon the LORD, and He answered them.
7 He spoke to them in the cloudy pillar: they kept His testimonies, and the <u>ordinance</u> *that* He gave them. statute
8 You answered them, O LORD our God: You were a God that forgave them, though You took vengeance of their <u>inventions</u>. deeds
9 Exalt the LORD our <u>God</u>, and worship at His holy <u>hill</u>; for the LORD our <u>God</u> *is* holy. Elohim^{p.f.} - presence

PSALM 100

A Psalm of praise

MAKE a joyful noise to the LORD, all <u>you lands</u>.the earth, i.e., nations
2 Serve the LORD with gladness: come before His presence with singing.

3 Know you that the LORD He *is* God: *it is* He *that* has made us, and not we ourselves; *we are* His people, and the sheep of His pasture.　EPH. 2:10

4 Enter into His gates with thanksgiving, *and* into His courts with praise: be thankful to Him, *and* bless His name.

5 For the LORD *is* good; His mercy *is* everlasting; and His truth *endures* to all generations.

PSALM 101

A Psalm of David

I WILL sing of mercy and judgment: to You, O LORD, will I sing.

2 I will behave myself wisely in a perfect way. O when will You come to me? I will walk within my house with a perfect heart.

3 I will set no wicked thing before my eyes: I <u>hate</u> the work of them that turn aside; *it* shall not cling to me.　despise

4 A <u>froward</u> heart shall depart from Me: I will not <u>know</u> a wicked *person*.　perverse - esteem

5 Whoso <u>privily</u> slanders his neighbor, him will I cut off: him that has an high look and a proud heart will not I allow.　secretly

6 My eyes *shall be* upon the faithful of the land, that they may dwell with Me: he that walks in a <u>perfect</u> way, he shall serve Me.　blameless

7 He that works deceit shall not dwell within My house: he that tells lies shall not <u>tarry</u> in My sight.　dwell

8 I will early destroy all the wicked of the land; that I may cut off all wicked doers from the city of the LORD.

PSALM 102

A Prayer of the afflicted, when he is overwhelmed, and pours out his complaint before the LORD

HEAR my prayer, O LORD, and let my cry come to You.

2 Hide not Your face from me in the day *when* I am in trouble; incline Your ear to me: in the day *when* I call answer me speedily.

3 For my days are consumed like smoke, and my bones are burned as an hearth.

4 My heart is smitten, and withered like grass; so that I forget to eat my bread.

5 By reason of the voice of my groaning my bones cling to my skin.

6 I am like a pelican of the wilderness: I am like an owl of the desert.

7 I watch, and am as a sparrow alone upon the house top.

8 My enemies reproach me all the day; *and* they that are mad against me are sworn against me.

9 For I have eaten ashes like bread, and mingled my drink with weeping,

10 Because of Your indignation and Your wrath: for You have lifted me up, and cast me down.

11 My days *are* like a shadow that declines; and I am withered like grass.

12 But You, O LORD, shall endure for ever; and Your remembrance to all generations.

13 You shall arise, *and* have mercy upon Zi'on: for the time to favor her, yea, the set time, is come.

14 For Your servants take pleasure in her stones, and favor the dust thereof.

15 So the heathen shall fear the name of the Lord, and all the kings of the earth Your glory.   nations

16 When the Lord shall build up Zi'on, He shall appear in His glory.

17 He will regard the prayer of the destitute, and not despise their prayer.

18 This shall be written for the generation to come: and the people which shall be created shall praise the Lord.

19 For He has looked down from the height of His sanctuary; from heaven did the Lord behold the earth;

20 To hear the groaning of the prisoner; to loose those that are appointed to death;

21 To declare the name of the Lord in Zi'on, and His praise in Je-ru'sa-lem;

22 When the people are gathered together, and the kingdoms, to serve the Lord.

23 He weakened my strength in the way; He shortened my days.

24 I said, O my God, take me not away in the midst of my days: Your years are throughout all generations.

25 Of old have You laid the foundation of the earth: and the heavens are the work of Your hands.   HEB. 1:10

26 They shall perish, but You shall endure: yea, all of them shall wax old like a garment; as a vesture shall You change them, and they shall be changed: HEB. 1:11 wear out - clothing

27 But You are the same, and Your years shall have no end.   HEB. 1:12

28 The children of Your servants shall continue, and their seed shall be established before You.   descendants

PSALM 103

A Psalm of David

BLESS the Lord, O my soul: and all that is within me, *bless* His holy name.

2 Bless the Lord, O my soul, and forget not all His benefits: none of

3 Who forgives all your iniquities; who heal all your diseases;

4 Who redeems your life from destruction; who crowns you with lovingkindness and tender mercies;

5 Who satisfies your mouth with good *things; so that* your youth is renewed like the eagle's.

6 The Lord executes righteousness and judgment for all that are oppressed.

7 He made known His ways to Mo'ses, His acts to the children of Is'ra-el.

8 The Lord *is* merciful and gracious, slow to anger, and plenteous in mercy.

9 He will not always chide: neither will He keep *His anger* for ever.   contend

10 He has not dealt with us after our sins; nor rewarded us according to our iniquities.

11 For as the heaven is high above the earth, *so* great is His mercy toward them that fear Him.   revere

12 As far as the east is from the west, *so* far has He removed our transgressions from us.

13 Like as a father pities *his* children, *so* the Lord pities them that fear Him.   revere

14 For He knows our frame; He remembers that we *are* dust.

15 *As for* man, his days *are* as grass: as a flower of the field, so he flourishes.

16 For the wind passes over it, and it is gone; and the place thereof shall <u>know</u> it no more.   ^{remember}

17 But the mercy of the LORD *is* from everlasting to everlasting upon them that <u>fear</u> Him, and His righteousness to children's children;   ^{revere}

18 To such as keep His <u>covenant</u>, and to those that remember His commandments to do them.   ^{agreement}

19 The LORD has prepared His throne in the heavens; and His kingdom rules over all.

20 Bless the LORD, you His <u>angels</u>, that excel in strength, that do His commandments, hearkening to the voice of His word.   ^{messengers}

21 Bless you the LORD, all *you* His hosts; *you* ministers of His, that do His pleasure.

22 Bless the LORD, all His works in all places of His dominion: bless the LORD, O my soul.

PSALM 104

BLESS the LORD, O my soul. O LORD my God, You are very great; You are clothed with honor and majesty.

2 Who covers *Yourself* with light as *with* a garment: who stretches out the heavens like a curtain:

3 Who lays the beams of His chambers in the waters: who makes the clouds His chariot: who walks upon the wings of the wind:

4 Who makes His <u>angels</u> spirits; His <u>ministers</u> a flaming fire: ^{HEB. 1:7 messengers - servants}

5 *Who* laid the foundations of the earth, *that* it should not be removed for ever.

6 You covered it with the <u>deep</u> as *with* a garment: the waters stood above the mountains.   ^{ocean}

7 At Your rebuke they fled; at the voice of Your thunder they hasted away.

8 They go up by the mountains; they go down by the valleys to the place which You have founded for them.

9 You have set a bound that they may not pass over; that they turn not again to cover the earth.

10 He sends the springs into the valleys, *which* run among the hills.

11 They give drink to every beast of the field: the wild asses quench their thirst.

12 By them shall the fowls of the heaven have their habitation, *which* sing among the branches.

13 He waters the hills from His <u>chambers</u>: the earth is satisfied with the fruit of Your works.   ^{dwelling place}

14 He causes the grass to grow for the cattle, and herb for the <u>service</u> of man: that he may bring forth food out of the earth;   ^{labor}

15 And wine *that* makes glad the heart of man, *and* oil to make *his* face to shine, and bread *which* strengthens man's heart.

16 The trees of the LORD are full *of* *sap*; the cedars of Leb'a-non, which He has planted;

17 Where the birds make their nests: *as for* the stork, the fir trees *are* her house.

18 The high hills *are* a refuge for the wild goats; *and* the rocks for the conies.

19 He appointed the moon for seasons: the sun knows its going down.

20 You make darkness, and it is night: wherein all the beasts of the forest do creep *forth*.

21 The young lions roar after their prey, and seek their meat from God.

22 The sun arises, they gather themselves together, and lay them down in their dens.

23 Man goes forth to his work and to his labor until the evening.

24 O LORD, how <u>manifold</u> are Your works! in wisdom have You made them all: the earth is full of Your riches.   many

25 *So is* this great and wide sea, wherein *are* things creeping innumerable, both small and great beasts.

26 There go the ships: *there is* that <u>leviathan</u>, *whom* You have <u>made</u> to play therein.   i.e., crocodile - formed

27 These wait all upon You; that You may give *them* their <u>meat</u> in due season.   food

28 *That* You give them they gather: You open Your hand, they are filled with good.

29 You hide Your face, they are troubled: You take away their breath, they die, and return to their dust.

30 You send forth Your Spirit, they are created: and You renew the face of the earth.

31 The glory of the LORD shall <u>endure</u> for ever: the LORD shall rejoice in His works.   be

32 He looks on the earth, and it <u>trembles</u>: He touches the hills, and they smoke.   is shaken

33 I will sing to the LORD as long as I live: I will sing praise to my <u>God</u> while I have my being.   Elohim[p.f.]

34 My meditation of Him shall be sweet: I will be glad in the LORD.

35 Let the sinners <u>be consumed</u> out of the earth, and let the wicked be no more. Bless you the LORD, O my soul. Praise you the LORD.   vanish

PSALM 105

O GIVE thanks to the LORD; call upon His name: make known His deeds among the people.

2 Sing to Him, sing psalms to Him: talk you of all His wondrous works.

3 Glory you in His holy name: let the heart of them rejoice that seek the LORD.

4 Seek the LORD, and His strength: seek His face <u>evermore</u>.   continually

5 Remember His marvellous works that He has done; His wonders, and the judgments of His mouth;

6 O you seed of A'bra-ham His servant, you children of Ja'cob His chosen.

7 He *is* the LORD our God: His judgments *are* in all the earth.

8 He has remembered His <u>covenant</u> for ever, the word *which* He commanded to a thousand generations.   agreement

9 Which *covenant* He made with A'bra-ham, and His oath to I'saac; _{agreement}

10 And confirmed the same to Ja'cob for a law, *and* to Is'ra-el *for* an everlasting covenant: _{agreement}

11 Saying, To you will I give the land of Ca'naan, the lot of your inheritance:

12 When they were *but* a few men in number; yea, very few, and strangers in it. _{temporary residents}

13 When they went from one nation to another, from *one* kingdom to another people;

14 He allowed no man to do them wrong: yea, He reproved kings for their sakes; _{rebuked}

15 *Saying*, Touch not My anointed, and do My prophets no harm.

16 Moreover He called for a famine upon the land: He broke the whole staff of bread.

17 He sent a man before them, *even* Jo'seph, *who* was sold for a servant:

18 Whose feet they hurt with fetters: he was laid in iron:

19 Until the time that his word came: the word of the LORD tried him.

20 The king sent and loosed him; *even* the ruler of the people, and let him go free.

21 He made him lord of his house, and ruler of all his substance: _{possessions}

22 To bind his princes at his pleasure; and teach his senators wisdom. _{elders}

23 Is'ra-el also came into E'gypt; and Ja'cob sojourned in the land of Ham. _{lived}

24 And He increased His people greatly; and made them stronger than their enemies.

25 He turned their heart to hate His people, to deal subtilly with His servants. _{despise}

26 He sent Mo'ses His servant; *and* Aar'on whom He had chosen.

27 They showed His signs among them, and wonders in the land of Ham. _{miracles}

28 He sent darkness, and made it dark; and they rebelled not against His word.

29 He turned their waters into blood, and slew their fish.

30 Their land brought forth frogs in abundance, in the chambers of their kings. _{rooms}

31 He spoke, and there came divers sorts of flies, *and* lice in all their coasts.

32 He gave them hail for rain, *and* flaming fire in their land.

33 He smote their vines also and their fig trees; and broke the trees of their coasts. _{territory}

34 He spoke, and the locusts came, and caterpillers, and that without number,

35 And did eat up all the herbs in their land, and devoured the fruit of their ground.

36 He smote also all the firstborn in their land, the chief of all their strength.

37 He brought them forth also with silver and gold: and *there was* not one feeble *person* among their tribes.

38 E'gypt was glad when they departed: for the fear of them fell upon them.

39 He spread a cloud for a covering; and fire to give light in the night.

40 *The people* asked, and He brought quails, and satisfied them with the bread of heaven.

41 He opened the rock, and the waters gushed out; they ran in the dry places *like* a river.

42 For He remembered His holy promise, *and* A'bra-ham His servant.

43 And He brought forth His people with joy, *and* His chosen with gladness:

44 And gave them the lands of the heathen: and they inherited the labor of the people;

45 That they might observe His statutes, and keep His laws. Praise you the LORD.

PSALM 106

PRAISE you the LORD. O give thanks to the LORD; for *He is* good: for His mercy *endures* for ever.

2 Who can utter the mighty acts of the LORD? *who* can show forth all His praise?

3 Blessed *are* they that keep judgment, *and* he that does righteousness at all times.

4 Remember me, O LORD, with the favor *that You bear to* Your people: O visit me with Your salvation;

come to

5 That I may see the good of Your chosen, that I may rejoice in the gladness of Your nation, that I may glory with Your inheritance.

6 We have sinned with our fathers, we have committed iniquity, we have done wickedly.

7 Our fathers understood not Your wonders in E'gypt; they remembered not the multitude of Your mercies; but provoked *Him* at the sea, *even* at the Red sea.

8 Nevertheless He saved them for His name's sake, that He might make His mighty power to be known.

9 He rebuked the Red sea also, and it was dried up: so He led them through the depths, as through the wilderness.

10 And He saved them from the hand of him that hated *them*, and redeemed them from the hand of the enemy.

11 And the waters covered their enemies: there was not one of them left.

12 Then believed they His words; they sang His praise.

13 They soon forgot His works; they waited not for His counsel:

14 But lusted exceedingly in the wilderness, and tempted God in the desert.

15 And He gave them their request; but sent leanness into their soul.

16 They envied Mo'ses also in the camp, *and* Aar'on the saint of the LORD.

holy one

17 The earth opened and swallowed up Da'than, and covered the company of A-bi'ram.

18 And a fire was kindled in their company; the flame burned up the wicked.

19 They made a calf in Ho'reb, and worshiped the molten image.

20 Thus they changed their glory into the similitude of an ox that eats grass.

ROM. 1:23

21 They forgot God their Savior, which had done great things in E'gypt; Elohim[p.f]

22 Wondrous works in the land of Ham, *and* terrible things by the Red sea.   El^s-f.

23 Therefore He said that He would destroy them, had not Mo'ses His chosen stood before Him in the breach, to turn away His wrath, less He should destroy *them*.

24 Yea, they despised the pleasant land, they believed not His word:

25 But murmured in their tents, *and* hearkened not to the voice of the LORD.

26 Therefore He lifted up His hand against them, to overthrow them in the wilderness:

27 To overthrow their <u>seed</u> also among the nations, and to scatter them in the lands.   descendants

28 They joined themselves also to Ba'al-pe'or, and ate the sacrifices of the dead.

29 Thus they provoked *Him* to anger with their <u>inventions</u>: and the plague broke in upon them.   deeds

30 Then stood up Phin'e-has, and executed judgment: and *so* the plague was <u>stayed</u>.   checked

31 And that was counted to him for righteousness to all generations for evermore.

32 They angered *Him* also at the waters of strife, so that it went ill with Mo'ses for their sakes:

33 Because they provoked His Spirit, so that he spoke <u>unadvisedly</u> with his lips.   foolishly

34 They did not destroy the nations, concerning whom the LORD commanded them:

35 But were mingled among the heathen, and learned their works.

36 And they served their idols: which were a <u>snare</u> to them.   trap

37 Yea, they sacrificed their sons and their daughters to <u>devils</u>,   evil spirits

38 And shed innocent blood, *even* the blood of their sons and of their daughters, whom they sacrificed to the idols of Ca'naan: and the land was polluted with blood.

39 Thus were they <u>defiled</u> with their own works, and went a whoring with their own <u>inventions</u>.   unclean - deeds

40 Therefore was the anger of the LORD kindled against His people, insomuch that He abhorred His own inheritance.

41 And He gave them into the hand of the <u>heathen</u>; and they that <u>hated</u> them ruled over them.   nations - despised

42 Their enemies also oppressed them, and they were brought into subjection under their hand.

43 Many times did He deliver them; but they provoked *Him* with their counsel, and were brought low for their iniquity.

44 Nevertheless He <u>regarded</u> their affliction, when He heard their cry: noticed

45 And He remembered for them His <u>covenant</u>, and <u>repented</u> according to the multitude of His mercies.   agreement - regretted

46 He made them also to be pitied of all those that carried them captives.

47 Save us, O LORD our God, and gather us from among the <u>heathen</u>, to give thanks to Your holy name, *and* to triumph in Your praise.   nations

48 Blessed *be* the LORD God of Is'ra-el from everlasting to everlasting: and let all the people say, Amen. Praise you the LORD.

PSALM 107

O GIVE thanks to the LORD, for *He is* good: for His mercy *endures* for ever.

2 Let the redeemed of the LORD say *so*, whom He has redeemed from the hand of the enemy;

3 And gathered them out of the lands, from the east, and from the west, from the north, and from the south.

4 They wandered in the wilderness in a solitary way; they found no city to dwell in.

5 Hungry and thirsty, their soul fainted in them.

6 Then they cried to the LORD in their trouble, *and* He delivered them out of their distresses.

7 And He led them forth by the right way, that they might go to a city of habitation.

8 Oh that *men* would praise the LORD *for* His goodness, and *for* His wonderful works to the children of men!

9 For He satisfies the longing soul, and fills the hungry soul with goodness.

10 Such as sit in darkness and in the shadow of death, *being* bound in affliction and iron;   prisoners

11 Because they rebelled against the words of God, and contemned the counsel of the Most High:

El⁻ᶠ. - spurned

12 Therefore He brought down their heart with labor; they fell down, and *there was* none to help.

13 Then they cried to the LORD in their trouble, *and* He saved them out of their distresses.

14 He brought them out of darkness and the shadow of death, and broke their bands in sunder.   two

15 Oh that *men* would praise the LORD *for* His goodness, and *for* His wonderful works to the children of men!

16 For He has broken the gates of brass, and cut the bars of iron in sunder.

17 Fools because of their transgression, and because of their iniquities, are afflicted.

18 Their soul abhors all manner of meat; and they draw near to the gates of death.

19 Then they cry to the LORD in their trouble, *and* He saves them out of their distresses.

20 He sent His word, and healed them, and delivered *them* from their destructions.

21 Oh that *men* would praise the LORD *for* His goodness, and *for* His wonderful works to the children of men!

22 And let them sacrifice the sacrifices of thanksgiving, and declare His works with rejoicing.   joyful singing

23 They that go down to the sea in ships, that do business in great waters;

24 These see the works of the LORD, and His wonders in the deep.   ocean

25 For He commands, and raises

the stormy wind, which lifts up the waves thereof.

26 They mount up to the heaven, they go down again to the depths: their soul is melted because of trouble.

27 They reel to and fro, and stagger like a drunken man, and are at their wit's end.

28 Then they cry to the LORD in their trouble, and He brings them out of their distresses.

29 He makes the storm a calm, so that the waves thereof are still.

30 Then are they glad because they be quiet; so He brings them to their desired haven.

31 Oh that *men* would praise the LORD *for* His goodness, and *for* His wonderful works to the children of men!

32 Let them exalt Him also in the congregation of the people, and praise Him in the assembly of the elders.

33 He turns rivers into a wilderness, and the watersprings into dry ground;

34 A fruitful land into barrenness, for the wickedness of them that dwell therein.

35 He turns the wilderness into a standing water, and dry ground into watersprings.

36 And there He makes the hungry to dwell, that they may prepare a city for habitation;

37 And sow the fields, and plant vineyards, which may yield fruits of increase.

38 He blesses them also, so that they are multiplied greatly; and allows not their cattle to decrease.

39 Again, they are <u>minished</u> and brought low through oppression, affliction, and sorrow. diminished

40 He pours contempt upon princes, and causes them to wander in <u>the wilderness</u>, *where there is* no way. a pathless waste

41 Yet sets He the poor on high from affliction, and makes *him* families like a flock.

42 The righteous shall see *it*, and rejoice: and all iniquity shall stop her mouth.

43 Whoso *is* wise, and will observe these *things*, even they shall understand the lovingkindness of the LORD.

PSALM 108

A Song or Psalm of David

O GOD, my heart is fixed; I will sing and give praise, even with my glory.

2 Awake, <u>psaltery</u> and harp: I *myself* will awake early. lyre

3 I will praise You, O LORD, among the people: and I will sing praises to You among the nations.

4 For Your mercy *is* great above the heavens: and Your truth *reaches* to the clouds.

5 Be You exalted, O <u>God</u>, above the heavens: and Your glory above all the earth; Elohim p.f.

6 That Your beloved may be delivered: save *with* Your right hand, and answer me.

7 God has spoken in His holiness; I will rejoice, I will divide She'chem, and <u>mete</u> out the valley of Suc'coth. measure

8 Gil'e-ad *is* Mine; Ma-nas'seh *is* Mine; E'phra-im also *is* the strength of Mine head; Ju'dah *is* My lawgiver; 9 Mo'ab *is* My washpot; over E'dom will I cast out My shoe; over Phi-lis'tia will I triumph.

10 Who will bring me into the strong city? who will lead me into E'dom?

11 *Will* not *You*, O God, *who* has cast us off? and will not You, O God, go forth with our hosts?

12 Give us help from trouble: for vain *is* the help of man.

13 Through God we shall <u>do valiantly</u>: for He *it is that* shall tread down our enemies. gain victory

PSALM 109

To the chief Musician, A Psalm of David

HOLD not Your peace, O <u>God</u> of my praise; Elohim[p.f.]

2 For the mouth of the wicked and the mouth of the <u>deceitful</u> are opened against me: they have spoken against me with a lying tongue. lawless

3 They <u>compassed</u> me about also with words of <u>hatred</u>; and fought against me without a cause. surrounded - disrespect

4 For my love they are my adversaries: but I *give myself to* prayer.

5 And they have rewarded me evil for good, and <u>hatred</u> for my love.

6 Set You a wicked man over him: and let Sa'tan stand at his right hand.

7 When he shall be judged, let him be condemned: and let his prayer become sin.

8 Let his days be few; *and* let another take his <u>office</u>. ACTS 1:20 leadership

9 Let his children be fatherless, and his wife a widow.

10 Let his children be continually <u>vagabonds</u>, and beg: let them seek *their bread* also out of their desolate places. wanderers

11 Let the <u>extortioner catch</u> all that he has; and let the strangers spoil his labor. creditor seize

12 Let there be none to extend mercy to him: neither let there be any to favor his fatherless children.

13 Let his <u>posterity</u> be cut off; *and* in the generation following let their name be blotted out. descendants

14 Let the iniquity of his fathers be remembered with the L ORD; and let not the sin of his mother be blotted out.

15 Let them be before the L ORD continually, that he may cut off the memory of them from the earth.

16 Because that he remembered not to show mercy, but persecuted the poor and needy man, that he might even slay the <u>broken</u> in heart. despondent

17 As he loved cursing, so let it come to him: as he delighted not in blessing, so let it be far from him.

18 As he clothed himself with cursing like as with his garment, so let it come into his <u>bowels</u> like water, and like oil into his bones. body

19 Let it be to him as the garment *which* covers him, and for a girdle wherewith he is girded continually.

20 *Let* this *be* the reward of my adversaries from the L ORD, and of them that <u>speak evil</u> against my soul. think harm

21 But do You for me, O GOD the Lord, for Your name's sake: because Your mercy *is* good, deliver You me. Jehovah^{s-f.} Adonay^{p-f.}

22 For I *am* poor and needy, and my heart is wounded within me.

23 I am gone like the shadow when it declines: I am tossed up and down as the locust.

24 My knees are weak through fasting; and my flesh fails of fatness.

25 I became also a reproach to them: *when* they looked upon me they shaked their heads. MATT. 27:39 object of scorn

26 Help me, O LORD my God: O save me according to Your mercy:

27 That they may know that this *is* Your hand; *that* You, LORD, have done it.

28 Let them curse, but bless You: when they arise, let them be ashamed; but let Your servant rejoice. defeated

29 Let my adversaries be clothed with shame, and let them cover themselves with their own confusion, as with a mantle. robe

30 I will greatly praise the LORD with my mouth; yea, I will praise Him among the multitude.

31 For He shall stand at the right hand of the poor, to save *him* from those that condemn his soul. judge

PSALM 110

A Psalm of David

THE LORD said to my Lord, Sit You at My right hand, until I make Your enemies Your footstool. MATT. 22:44
MARK 12:35 HEB. 1:3 LUKE 20:43 ACTS 2:34 HEB.
10:13 1 COR. 15:25 EPH. 1:20 HEB. 1:13 Jehovah^{s-f.} - Adon^{p-f.}

2 The LORD shall send the rod of Your strength out of Zi'on: rule You in the midst of Your enemies.

3 Your people *shall* be willing in the day of Your power, in the beauties of holiness from the womb of the morning: You have the dew of Your youth. volunteer freely

4 The LORD has sworn, and will not repent, You *are* a priest for ever after the order of Melchiz'e-dek. HEB. 5:6 HEB. 6:20 HEB. 7:21

5 The Lord at Your right hand shall strike through kings in the day of His wrath. shatter

6 He shall judge among the heathen, He shall fill *the places* with the dead bodies; He shall wound the heads over many countries.

nations - shatter the leaders

7 He shall drink of the brook in the way: therefore shall He lift up the head.

PSALM 111

PRAISE you the LORD. I will praise the LORD with *my* whole heart, in the assembly of the upright, and *in* the congregation. MATT. 22:44

2 The works of the LORD *are* great, sought out of all them that have pleasure therein.

3 His work *is* honorable and glorious: and His righteousness endures for ever.

4 He has made His wonderful works to be remembered: the LORD *is* gracious and full of compassion.

5 He has given meat to them that fear Him: He will ever be mindful of His covenant. food - revere - agreement

6 He has showed His people the

power of His works, that He may give them the <u>heritage</u> of the <u>heathen</u>.

lands - nations

7 The works of His hands *are* <u>verity</u> and <u>judgment</u>; all His commandments *are* sure.

truth - justice

8 They stand fast for ever and ever, *and are* done in truth and uprightness.

9 He sent redemption to His people: He has commanded His covenant for ever: holy and reverend *is* His name.

10 The <u>fear</u> of the Lord *is* the beginning of wisdom: a good understanding have all they that do *His commandments*: His praise endures for ever.

reverence

PSALM 112

PRAISE you the Lord. Blessed *is* the man *that* <u>fears</u> the Lord, *that* delights greatly in His commandments.

2 His <u>seed</u> shall be mighty upon earth: the generation of the upright shall be blessed.

descendants

3 Wealth and riches *shall be* in His house: and His righteousness endures for ever.

4 To the upright there arises light in the darkness: *He is* gracious, and full of compassion, and righteous.

5 A good man shows favor, and lends: he will guide his affairs with discretion.

6 Surely he shall not be <u>moved</u> for ever: the righteous shall be in everlasting remembrance.

shaken

7 He shall not be afraid of evil tidings: his heart is fixed, trusting in the Lord.

8 His heart *is* established, he shall not be afraid, until he see *his desire* upon his enemies.

9 He has dispersed, He has given to the poor; His righteousness endures for ever; His <u>horn</u> shall be exalted with honor.

2 COR. 9:9 i.e., strength

10 The wicked shall see *it*, and be grieved; He shall gnash with his teeth, and melt away: the desire of the wicked shall perish.

PSALM 113

PRAISE you the Lord. Praise, O you servants of the Lord, praise the name of the Lord.

2 Blessed be the name of the Lord from this time forth and for evermore.

3 From the rising of the sun to the going down of the same the Lord's name *is* to be praised.

4 The Lord *is* high above all nations, *and* His glory above the heavens.

5 Who *is* like to the Lord our <u>God</u>, who dwells on high,

Elohim^p.f.

6 Who humbles *Himself* to behold *the things that are* in heaven, and in the earth!

7 He raises up the poor out of the dust, *and* lifts the needy out of the <u>dunghill</u>;

rubbish heap

8 That He may set *him* with princes, *even* with the princes of His people.

9 He makes the barren woman to keep house, *and to be* a joyful mother of children. Praise you the Lord.

PSALM 114

WHEN Is'ra-el went out of E'gypt, the house of Ja'cob from a people of <u>strange</u> language;

foreign

2 Ju'dah was His sanctuary, *and* Is'ra-el His dominion.

3 The sea saw *it*, and fled: Jor'dan was driven back.

4 The mountains skipped like rams, *and* the little hills like lambs.

5 What *ails* you, O you sea, that you fled? you Jor'dan, *that* you were driven back?

6 You mountains, *that* you skipped like rams; *and* you little hills, like lambs?

7 Tremble, you earth, at the presence of the <u>Lord</u>, at the presence of the <u>God</u> of Ja'cob;   Adon^s.f. - Eloah^s.f.

8 Which <u>turned</u> the rock *into* a <u>standing</u> water, the flint into a fountain of waters.   changed - pool of

PSALM 115

NOT to us, O Lord, not to us, but to Your name give glory, for Your mercy, *and* for Your truth's sake.

2 Wherefore should the heathen say, Where *is* now their God?

3 But our God *is* in the heavens: He has done whatsoever He has pleased.

4 Their idols *are* silver and gold, the work of men's hands.

5 They have mouths, but they speak not: eyes have they, but they see not:

6 They have ears, but they hear not: noses have they, but they smell not:

7 They have hands, but they handle not: feet have they, but they walk not: neither speak they through their throat.

8 They that make them are like to them; *so is* every one that trusts in them.

9 O Is'ra-el, trust you in the Lord: He *is* their help and their shield.

10 O house of Aar'on, trust in the Lord: He *is* their help and their shield.

11 You that <u>fear</u> the Lord, trust in the Lord: He *is* their help and their shield.   revere

12 The Lord has been mindful of us: He will bless *us*; He will bless the house of Is'ra-el; He will bless the house of Aar'on.

13 He will bless them that <u>fear</u> the Lord, *both* small and great.   REV. 19:5

14 The Lord shall increase you more and more, you and your children.

15 You *are* blessed of the Lord which made heaven and earth.

16 The heaven, *even* the heavens, *are* the Lord's: but the earth has He given to the children of men.

17 The dead praise not the Lord, neither any that go down into silence.

18 But we will bless the Lord from this time forth and for evermore. Praise the Lord.

PSALM 116

I LOVE the Lord, because He has heard my voice *and* my supplications.

2 Because He has <u>inclined</u> His ear to me, therefore will I call upon *Him* as long as I live.   turned

3 The sorrows of death <u>compassed</u> me, and the pains of <u>hell</u> got hold upon me: I found trouble and sorrow.   entangled - i.e. sheol

4 Then called I upon the name of the Lord; O Lord, I <u>beseech</u> You, deliver my soul.   beg

5 Gracious *is* the Lord, and righteous; yea, our <u>God</u> *is* merciful.   Elohim^p.f.

6 The LORD preserves the simple: I was brought low, and He helped me.

7 Return to your rest, O my soul; for the LORD has dealt bountifully with you.

8 For You have delivered my soul from death, my eyes from tears, *and* my feet from falling.

9 I will walk before the LORD in the land of the living.

10 I believed, therefore have I spoken: I was greatly afflicted: 2 COR. 4:13

11 I said in my haste, All men *are* liars. ROM. 3:4

12 What shall I render to the LORD *for* all His benefits toward me?

13 I will take the cup of salvation, and call upon the name of the LORD.

14 I will pay my vows to the LORD now in the presence of all His people.

15 Precious in the sight of the LORD *is* the death of His saints.

16 O LORD, truly I *am* Your servant; I *am* Your servant, *and* the son of Your handmaid: You have loosed my bonds.

17 I will offer to You the sacrifice of thanksgiving, and will call upon the name of the LORD.

18 I will pay my vows to the LORD now in the presence of all His people,

19 In the courts of the LORD's house, in the midst of you, O Je-ru'sa-lem. Praise you the LORD.

PSALM 117

O PRAISE the LORD, all you nations: praise him, all you people. ROM. 15:9,11

2 For His merciful kindness is great toward us: and the truth of the LORD *endures* for ever. Praise you the LORD.

PSALM 118

O GIVE thanks to the LORD; for *He is* good: because His mercy *endures* for ever.

2 Let Is'ra-el now say, that His mercy *endures* for ever.

3 Let the house of Aar'on now say, that His mercy *endures* for ever.

4 Let them now that <u>fear</u> the LORD say, that His mercy *endures* for ever. revere

5 I called upon the LORD in distress: the LORD answered me, *and set me* in a large place.

6 The LORD *is* on my side; I will not fear: what can man do to me?

ROM. 8:31 HEB. 13:6

7 The LORD takes my part with them that help me: therefore shall I see *my desire* upon them that hate me.

8 *It is* better to trust in the LORD than to put confidence in man.

9 *It is* better to trust in the LORD than to put confidence in princes.

10 All nations <u>compassed</u> me about: but in the name of the LORD will I destroy them. surround

11 They <u>compassed</u> me about; yea, they <u>compassed</u> me about: but in the name of the LORD I will destroy them.

12 They <u>compassed</u> me about like bees; they are quenched as the fire of thorns: for in the name of the LORD I will destroy them.

13 You have thrust sore at me that I might fall: but the LORD helped me.

14 The LORD *is* my strength and song, and is become my <u>salvation</u>. i.e., Jeshua

15 The voice of rejoicing and salvation *is* in the <u>tabernacles</u> of the righteous: the right hand of the Lord does valiantly. tents

16 The right hand of the Lord is exalted: the right hand of the Lord does valiantly.

17 I shall not die, but live, and declare the works of the Lord.

18 The Lord has chastened me <u>sore</u>: but He has not given me over to death. much

19 Open to me the gates of righteousness: I will go into them, *and* I will praise the Lord:

20 This gate of the Lord, into which the righteous shall enter.

21 I will praise You: for You have heard me, and are become my <u>salvation</u>. i.e., Heb. Jeshua

22 The <u>stone</u> *which* the builders refused is become the head *stone* of the corner. LUKE 20:17 MATT. 21:42 ACTS 4:11 1 PET. 2:6 i.e., referring to Christ

23 This is the Lord's doing; it *is* marvellous in our eyes. MARK 12:11

24 This *is* the day *which* the Lord has made; we will rejoice and be glad in it. REV. 19:7

25 Save now, I <u>beseech</u> You, O Lord: O Lord, I <u>beseech</u> You, send now prosperity. beg

26 <u>Blessed</u> *be* he that comes in the name of the Lord: we have blessed you out of the house of the Lord. MATT 21:9 MATT. 23:39 MARK 11:9 LUKE 13:35 JOHN 12:13 LUKE 19:38 Fortunate

27 God *is* the Lord, which has showed us light: bind the sacrifice with cords, *even* to the horns of the altar.

28 You *are* my <u>God</u>, and I will praise You: *You are* my <u>God</u>, I will exalt You. El^s.f. - Elohim^p.f.

29 O give thanks to the Lord; for *He is* good: for His mercy *endures* for ever.

PSALM 119

ALEPH

BLESSED *are* the <u>undefiled</u> in the way, who walk in the law of the Lord. Happy - blameless

2 <u>Blessed</u> *are* they that <u>keep</u> His testimonies, *and that* seek Him with the whole heart. obey

3 They also do no <u>iniquity</u>: they walk in His ways. unrighteousness

4 You have commanded *us* to keep Your <u>precepts</u> diligently. ordinances

5 O that my ways were directed to keep Your <u>statutes</u>! decrees

6 Then shall I not be <u>ashamed</u>, when I have respect to all Your commandments. embarrassed

7 I will praise You with <u>uprightness of heart</u>, when I shall have learned Your righteous judgments. whole heart

8 I will keep Your <u>statutes</u>: O forsake me not utterly. decrees

BETH

9 Wherewithal shall a young man cleanse his way? by taking heed *thereto* according to Your word.

10 With my whole heart have I sought you: O let me not wander from Your commandments.

11 Your word have I hid in my heart, that I might not sin against you.

12 Blessed *are* You, O Lord: teach me Your <u>statutes</u>. decrees

13 With my lips have I declared all the judgments of Your mouth. ordinances
14 I have rejoiced in the way of Your testimonies, as *much as* in all riches.
15 I will meditate in Your precepts, and have respect to Your ways.

regard

16 I will delight myself in Your statutes: I will not forget Your word. decrees

GIMEL

17 Deal bountifully with Your servant, *that* I may live, and keep Your word.

obey

18 Open You my eyes, that I may behold wondrous things out of Your law.
19 I *am* a stranger in the earth: hide not Your commandments from me.
20 My soul breaks for the longing *that it has* to Your judgments at all times.
21 You have rebuked the proud *that are* cursed, which do err from Your commandments.
22 Remove from me reproach and contempt; for I have kept Your testimonies.
23 Princes also did sit *and* speak against me: *but* Your servant did meditate in Your statutes.

decrees

24 Your testimonies also *are* my delight *and* my counselors.

DALETH

25 My soul clings to the dust: quicken You me according to Your word.

enliven

26 I have declared my ways, and You heard me: teach me Your statutes.

decrees

27 Make me to understand the way of Your precepts: so shall I talk of Your wondrous works.

ordinances - meditate on

28 My soul melts for heaviness: strengthen You me according to Your word.

weeps - sorrow

29 Remove from me the way of lying: and grant me Your law graciously.
30 I have chosen the way of truth: Your judgments have I laid *before me*.
31 I have stuck to Your testimonies: O LORD, put me not to shame.

cling

32 I will run the way of Your commandments, when You shall enlarge my heart.

HE

33 Teach me, O LORD, the way of Your statutes; and I shall keep it *to* the end.

decrees

34 Give me understanding, and I shall keep your law; yea, I shall observe it with *my* whole heart.
35 Make me to go in the path of Your commandments; for therein do I delight.
36 Incline my heart to Your testimonies, and not to covetousness.
37 Turn away my eyes from beholding vanity; *and* quicken You me in Your way.

renew

38 Stablish Your word to Your servant, who *is* devoted to Your fear.

reverence

39 Turn away my reproach which I fear: for Your judgments *are* good.
40 Behold, I have longed after Your precepts: quicken me in Your righteousness.

M13 - 956

VAU

41 Let Your mercies come also to me, O Lord, *even* Your <u>salvation</u>, according to Your word.   i.e., Heb. Jeshua

42 So shall I have <u>wherewith</u> to answer him that reproaches me: for I trust in Your word.   a word

43 And take not the word of truth utterly out of my mouth; for I have hoped in Your <u>judgments</u>.   ordinances

44 So shall I keep Your law continually for ever and ever.

45 And I will walk at liberty: for I seek Your <u>precepts</u>.   ordinances

46 I will speak of Your testimonies also before kings, and will not be ashamed.   MATT. 10:18

47 And I will delight myself in Your commandments, which I have loved.

48 My hands also will I lift up to Your commandments, which I have loved; and I will meditate in Your <u>statutes</u>.   decrees

ZAIN

49 Remember the word to Your servant, upon which You have caused me to hope.

50 This *is* my comfort in my affliction: for Your word has <u>quickened</u> me.   renewed

51 The <u>proud</u> have had me greatly in derision: *yet* have I not declined from Your law.   arrogant

52 I remembered Your judgments of old, O Lord; and have comforted myself.

53 Horror has taken hold upon me because of the wicked that forsake Your law.

54 Your <u>statutes</u> have been my songs in the house of my pilgrimage.   decrees

55 I have remembered Your name, O Lord, in the night, and have kept Your law.

56 This I had, because I kept Your <u>precepts</u>.   ordinances

CHETH

57 *You are* my portion, O Lord: I have said that I would keep Your words.

58 I entreated Your favor with *my* whole heart: be merciful to me according to Your word.

59 I thought on my ways, and turned my feet to Your testimonies.

60 I made haste, and delayed not to <u>keep</u> Your commandments.   obey

61 The <u>bands</u> of the wicked have robbed me: *but* I have not forgotten Your law.   cords

62 At midnight I will rise to give thanks to You because of Your righteous judgments.

63 I *am* a companion of all *them* that <u>fear</u> You, and of them that keep Your <u>precepts</u>.   revere

64 The earth, O Lord, is full of Your <u>mercy</u>: teach me Your <u>statutes</u>.   kindness - decrees

TETH

65 You have dealt well with Your servant, O Lord, according to Your word.

66 Teach me good judgment and knowledge: for I have believed Your commandments.

67 Before I was afflicted I went astray: but now have I kept Your word.

68 You *are* good, and do good; teach me Your <u>statutes</u>. decrees

69 The proud have <u>forged</u> a lie against me: *but* I will keep Your <u>precepts</u> with *my* whole heart. prepared - ordinances

70 Their heart is as fat as grease; *but* I delight in Your law.

71 *It is* good for me that I have been afflicted; that I might learn Your <u>statutes</u>. decrees

72 The law of Your mouth is better to me than thousands of gold and silver.

JOD

73 Your hands have made me and fashioned me: give me understanding, that I may learn Your commandments.

74 They that <u>fear</u> You will be glad when they see me; because I have hoped in Your word. revere

75 I know, O Lord, that Your judgments *are* right, and *that* You in faithfulness have afflicted me.

76 Let, I pray You, Your merciful kindness be for my comfort, according to Your word to Your servant.

77 Let Your <u>tender mercies</u> come to me, that I may live: for Your law *is* my delight. compassion

78 Let the proud be ashamed; for they dealt perversely with me without a cause: *but* I will meditate in Your <u>precepts</u>. ordinances

79 Let those that <u>fear</u> You turn to me, and those that have known Your testimonies. reverence

80 Let my heart be <u>sound</u> in Your <u>statutes</u>; that I be not ashamed. blameless - decrees

CAPH

81 My soul faints for Your salvation: *but* I hope in Your word.

82 My eyes fail for Your word, saying, When will You comfort me?

83 For I am become like a <u>bottle</u> in the smoke; *yet* do I not forget Your <u>statutes</u>. wineskins - decrees

84 How many *are* the days of Your servant? when will You execute judgment on them that persecute me?

85 The proud have digged pits for me, which *are* not after Your law.

86 All Your commandments *are* faithful: they persecute me wrongfully; help You me.

87 They had almost consumed me upon earth; but I forsook not Your <u>precepts</u>. ordinances

88 <u>Quicken</u> me after Your lovingkindness; so shall I keep the testimony of Your mouth. Renew

LAMED

89 For ever, O Lord, Your word is settled in heaven.

90 Your faithfulness *is* to all generations: You have established the earth, and it <u>abide</u>. endures

91 They <u>continue</u> this day according to Your <u>ordinances</u>: for all *are* Your servants. stand - laws

92 Unless Your law *had been* my delights, I should then have perished in my affliction.

93 I will never forget Your <u>precepts</u>: for with them You have <u>quickened</u> me. ordinances - renewed

94 I *am* Yours, save me; for I have sought Your <u>precepts</u>.

95 The wicked have waited for me to destroy me: *but* I will consider Your testimonies.

96 I have seen an end of all perfection: *but* Your commandment *is* exceeding broad.

MEM

97 O how love I Your law! it *is* my meditation all the day.

98 You through Your commandments have made me wiser than my enemies: for they *are* ever with me.

99 I have more understanding than all my teachers: for Your testimonies *are* my meditation.

100 I understand more than the ancients, because I keep Your precepts.   ordinances

101 I have refrained my feet from every evil way, that I might keep Your word.

102 I have not departed from Your judgments: for You have taught me.

103 How sweet are Your words to my taste! *yea, sweeter* than honey to my mouth!

104 Through Your precepts I get understanding: therefore I hate every false way.   despise

NUN

105 Your word *is* a lamp to my feet, and a light to my path.

106 I have sworn, and I will perform *it*, that I will keep Your righteous judgments.

107 I am afflicted very much: quicken me, O LORD, according to Your word.   renew

108 Accept, I beseech You, the freewill offerings of my mouth, O LORD, and teach me Your judgments.   beg

109 My soul *is* continually in my hand: yet do I not forget Your law.

110 The wicked have laid a snare for me: yet I erred not from Your precepts.   trap - ordinances

111 Your testimonies have I taken as an heritage for ever: for they *are* the rejoicing of my heart.

112 I have inclined my heart to perform Your statutes always, *even to* the end.   keep - decrees

SAMECH

113 I hate *vain* thoughts: but Your law do I love.   abhor

114 You *are* my hiding place and my shield: I hope in Your word.

115 Depart from me, you evildoers: for I will keep the commandments of my God.

116 Uphold me according to Your word, that I may live: and let me not be ashamed of my hope.   ROM. 5:5

117 Hold You me up, and I shall be safe: and I will have respect to Your statutes continually.   regard

118 You have trodden down all them that err from Your statutes: for their deceit *is* falsehood.   rejected - decrees

119 You put away all the wicked of the earth *like* dross: therefore I love Your testimonies.   refuse

120 My flesh trembles for fear of You; and I am afraid of Your judgments.

AIN

121 I have done judgment and justice: leave me not to my oppressors.

122 Be surety for Your servant for good: let not the proud oppress me.

123 My eyes fail for Your salvation, and for the word of Your righteousness.

124 Deal with Your servant according to Your mercy, and teach me Your statutes. decrees

125 I *am* Your servant; give me understanding, that I may know Your testimonies.

126 *It is* time for *You*, LORD, to work: *for* they have made void Your law.

127 Therefore I love Your commandments above gold; yea, above fine gold.

128 Therefore I esteem all *Your* precepts *concerning* all *things to be* right; *and* I hate every false way. ordinances - despise

PE

129 Your testimonies *are* wonderful: therefore does my soul keep them. obey

130 The entrance of Your words gives light; it gives understanding to the simple.

131 I opened my mouth, and panted: for I longed for Your commandments.

132 Look You upon me, and be merciful to me, as You use to do to those that love Your name.

133 Order my steps in Your word: and let not any iniquity have dominion over me. ROM. 6:12 Establish

134 Deliver me from the oppression of man: so will I keep Your precepts.

135 Make Your face to shine upon Your servant; and teach me Your statutes. decrees

136 Rivers of waters run down my eyes, because they keep not Your law.

TZADDI

137 Righteous *are* You, O LORD, and upright *are* Your judgments. REV. 16:7

138 Your testimonies *that* You have commanded *are* righteous and very faithful. rules

139 My zeal has consumed me, because my enemies have forgotten Your words. wears me out

140 Your word *is* very pure: therefore Your servant loves it.

141 I *am* small and despised: *yet* do not I forget Your precepts. ordinances

142 Your righteousness *is* an everlasting righteousness, and Your law *is* the truth. JOHN 17:17

143 Trouble and anguish have taken hold on me: *yet* Your commandments *are* my delights.

144 The righteousness of Your testimonies *is* everlasting: give me understanding, and I shall live.

KOPH

145 I cried with *my* whole heart; hear me, O LORD: I will keep Your statutes. decrees

146 I cried to You; save me, and I shall keep Your testimonies.

147 I prevented the dawning of the morning, and cried: I hoped in Your word.

148 My eyes prevent the *night*

watches, that I might meditate in Your word. _{anticipate}

149 Hear my voice according to Your lovingkindness: O LORD, <u>quicken</u> me according to Your judgment. _{renew}

150 They draw near that follow after mischief: they are far from Your law.

151 You *are* near, O LORD; and all Your commandments *are* truth.

152 Concerning Your testimonies, I have known of old that You have founded them for ever.

RESH

153 Consider my affliction, and deliver me: for I do not forget Your law.

154 Plead my cause, and deliver me: <u>quicken</u> me according to Your word.

155 Salvation *is* far from the wicked: for they seek not Your <u>statutes</u>. _{decrees}

156 Great *are* Your tender mercies, O LORD: <u>quicken</u> me according to Your judgments. _{renew}

157 Many *are* my persecutors and my enemies; *yet* do I not <u>decline</u> from Your testimonies. _{turn aside}

158 I beheld the transgressors, and was grieved; because they kept not Your word.

159 Consider how I love Your <u>precepts</u>: <u>quicken</u> me, O LORD, according to Your lovingkindness. _{ordinances - renew}

160 Your word *is* true *from* the beginning: and every one of Your righteous judgments *endures* for ever.

SCHIN

161 <u>Princes</u> have persecuted me without a cause: but my heart stands in awe of Your word. _{Rulers}

162 I rejoice at Your word, as one that finds great spoil.

163 I <u>hate</u> and abhor <u>lying</u>: *but* Your law do I love. _{despise - falsehood}

164 Seven times a day do I praise You because of Your righteous judgments.

165 Great peace have they which love Your law: and nothing shall offend them.

166 LORD, I have hoped for Your salvation, and done Your commandments.

167 My soul has kept Your testimonies; and I love them exceedingly.

168 I have kept Your <u>precepts</u> and Your testimonies: for all my ways *are* before You. _{ordinances}

TAU

169 Let my cry come near before You, O LORD: give me understanding according to Your word.

170 Let my supplication come before You: deliver me according to Your word.

171 My lips shall utter praise, when You have taught me Your <u>statutes</u>. _{decrees}

172 My tongue shall speak of Your word: for all Your commandments *are* righteousness.

173 Let Your hand help me; for I have chosen Your <u>precepts</u>.

174 I have longed for Your salvation, O LORD; and Your law *is* my delight.

175 Let my soul live, and it shall praise You; and let Your judgments help me.

176 I have gone astray like a lost sheep; seek Your servant; for I do not forget Your commandments.

PSALM 120

A Song of degrees

IN my distress I cried to the LORD, and He heard me.

2 Deliver my soul, O LORD, from lying lips, *and* from a deceitful tongue.

3 What shall be given to you? or what shall be done to you, you <u>false tongue</u>?   deceiver

4 Sharp arrows of the mighty, with coals of juniper.

5 Woe is me, that I sojourn in Me'sech, *that* I dwell in the tents of Ke'dar!

6 My soul has long dwelled with him that <u>hates</u> peace.   opposed

7 I *am for* peace: but when I speak, they *are* for war.

PSALM 121

A Song of degrees

I WILL lift up my eyes to the hills from where comes my help.

2 My help *comes* from the LORD, which made heaven and earth.

3 He will not allow your foot to <u>be moved</u>: He that keeps you will not slumber.   slip

4 Behold, He that keeps Is'ra-el shall neither slumber nor sleep.

5 The LORD *is* your keeper: the LORD *is* your shade upon your right hand.

6 The sun shall not smite you by day, nor the moon by night.   REV. 7:16

7 The LORD shall preserve you from all evil: He shall preserve your soul.

8 The LORD shall preserve your going out and your coming in from this time forth, and even for evermore.

PSALM 122

A Song of degrees of David

I WAS glad when they said to me, Let us go into the house of the LORD.

2 Our feet shall stand within your gates, O Je-ru'sa-lem.

3 Je-ru'sa-lem is builded as a city that is compact together:

4 Where the tribes go up, the tribes of the LORD, to the testimony of Is'ra-el, to give thanks to the name of the LORD.

5 For there are set thrones of judgment, the thrones of the house of David.

6 Pray for the peace of Je-ru'sa-lem: they shall prosper that love you.

7 Peace be inside your walls, *and* prosperity inside your palaces.

8 For my brethren and companions' sakes, I will now say, Peace *be* within you.

9 Because of the house of the LORD our God I will seek your good.

PSALM 123

A Song of degrees

TO You lift I up my eyes, O You that dwells in the heavens.

2 Behold, as the eyes of servants *look* to the hand of their masters, *and* as the eyes of a maiden to the hand of her mistress; so our eyes *wait* <u>upon</u> the LORD our <u>God</u>, until that He have mercy upon us.   look to - Elohim^{p.f.}

3 Have mercy upon us, O LORD, have mercy upon us: for we are exceedingly filled with contempt.

4 Our soul is exceedingly filled with the scorning of those that are at ease, *and* with the contempt of the proud.

PSALM 124

A Song of degrees of David

IF *it had not been* the LORD who was on our side, now may Is'ra-el say;
2 If *it had not been* the LORD who was on our side, when men rose up against us:
3 Then they had swallowed us up alive, when their anger was kindled against us:
4 Then the waters had overwhelmed us, the stream had gone over our soul:
5 Then the <u>proud</u> waters <u>had gone</u> over our soul.　　　raging - would have swept
6 Blessed *be* the LORD, who has not given us *as* a prey to their teeth.
7 Our soul is escaped as a bird out of the <u>snare</u> of the <u>fowlers</u>: the <u>snare</u> is broken, and we are escaped.
　　　　　　　　　　　　trap - trappers
8 Our help *is* in the name of the LORD, who made heaven and earth.

GIA - 963
M09 - 938

PSALM 125

A Song of degrees

THEY that trust in the LORD *shall* be as mount Zi'on, *which* cannot be removed, *but* abides for ever.
2 *As* the mountains *are* round about Je-ru'sa-lem, so the LORD *is* round about His people from <u>here after</u> even for ever.　　　now on
3 For the rod of the wicked shall not rest upon the lot of the righteous; less

the righteous put forth their hands to iniquity.
4 Do good, O LORD, to *those that be* good, and to *them that are* upright in their hearts.
5 As for such as turn aside to their crooked ways, the LORD shall lead them forth with the workers of iniquity: *but* peace *shall be* upon Is'ra-el.　　GAL. 6:16

PSALM 126

A Song of degrees

WHEN the LORD <u>turned again</u> the captivity of Zi'on, we were like them that dream. brought back
2 Then was our mouth filled with laughter, and our tongue with singing: then said they among the <u>hea-then</u>, The LORD has done great things for them.　　　nations
3 The LORD has done great things for us; *whereof* we are glad.
4 <u>Turn again</u> our captivity, O LORD, as the streams in the south.　Restore
5 They that sow in tears shall reap in joy.
6 He that goes forth and weeps, bearing precious seed, shall doubtless come again with rejoicing, bringing his sheaves *with him*.

PSALM 127

A Song of degrees for Solomon

EXCEPT the LORD build the house, they labor in vain that build it: except the LORD keep the city, the watchman wakes *but* in vain.
2 *It is* vain for you to rise up early, to

M22 — | |
M16 — | |
P12 — | |
933
949
1051

sit up late, to eat the bread of sorrows: *for* so He gives His beloved sleep.

3 Lo, children *are* an heritage of the Lord: *and* the fruit of the womb *is His* reward.　　　　　　EPH. 6:4

4 As arrows *are* in the hand of a mighty man; so *are* children of the youth.

5 Happy *is* the man that has his quiver full of them: they shall not be ashamed, but they shall speak with the enemies in the gate.　　meet

PSALM 128

A Song of degrees

BLESSED *is* every one that fears the Lord; that walks in His ways.　　　　　　　　reveres

2 For you shall eat the labor of your hands: happy *shall* you *be*, and it *shall be* well with you.

3 Your wife *shall be* as a fruitful vine by the sides of your house: your children like olive plants round about your table.

4 Behold, that thus shall the man be blessed that fears the Lord.

5 The Lord shall bless you out of Zi'on: and you shall see the good of Je-ru'sa-lem all the days of your life.

6 Yea, you shall see your children's children, *and* peace upon Is'ra-el.

PSALM 129

A Song of degrees

MANY a time have they afflicted me from my youth, may Is'ra-el now say:

2 Many a time have they afflicted me from my youth: yet they have not prevailed against me.　　　　oppressed

3 The plowers plowed upon my back: they made long their furrows.

4 The Lord *is* righteous: He has cut asunder the cords of the wicked.

5 Let them all be confounded and turned back that hate Zi'on.　　despise

6 Let them be as the grass *upon* the house tops, which withers afore it grows up:

7 Wherewith the mower fills not his hand; nor he that binds sheaves his bosom.

8 Neither do they which go by say, The blessing of the Lord *be* upon you: we bless you in the name of the Lord.

PSALM 130

A Song of degrees

OUT of the depths have I cried to You O Lord.

2 Lord, hear my voice: let Your ears be attentive to the voice of my supplications.

3 If You, Lord, should mark iniquities, O Lord, who shall stand?

Jah[s.f.] - Adonahy[s.f.]

4 But *there is* forgiveness with You, that You may be feared.　　revered

5 I wait for the Lord, my soul does wait, and in His word do I hope.

6 My soul *waits* for the Lord more than they that watch for the morning: *I say, more than* they that watch for the morning.

7 Let Is'ra-el hope in the Lord: for with the Lord *there is* mercy, and with Him *is* plenteous redemption.　　loving-kindness

8 And He shall redeem Is'ra-el from all its iniquities.   TIT. 2:14

PSALM 131

A Song of degrees of David

LORD, my heart is not <u>haughty</u>, nor my eyes lofty: neither do I <u>exercise</u> myself in great matters, or in things too <u>high</u> for me.<small>proud - involve - difficult</small>
2 Surely I have behaved and quieted myself, as a child that is weaned of his mother: my soul *is* even as a weaned child.
3 Let Is'ra-el hope in the LORD from hereafter and for ever.

PSALM 132

A Song of degrees

LORD, remember David, *and* all his afflictions:
2 How he swear to the LORD, *and* vowed to the mighty *God* of Ja'cob;
3 Surely I will not come into the <u>tabernacle</u> of my house, nor go up into my bed;   <small>tent</small>
4 I will not give sleep to my eyes, *or* slumber to my eyelids,
5 Until I find out a place for the LORD, an habitation for the mighty *God* of Ja'cob.   ACTS 7:46
6 Lo, we heard of it at Eph'ra-tah: we found it in the fields of the wood.
7 We will go into His tabernacles: we will worship at His footstool.
8 Arise, O LORD, into Your rest; You, and the ark of Your strength.
9 Let Your priests be clothed with righteousness; and let Your saints shout for joy.

10 For Your servant Da'vid's sake turn not away the face of Your anointed.
11 The LORD has sworn *in* truth to Da'vid; He will not turn from it; Of the fruit of your body will I set upon your throne.   ACTS 2:30
12 If your children will keep My <u>covenant</u> and My testimony that I shall teach them, their children shall also sit upon your throne for evermore. <small>agreement</small>
13 For the LORD has chosen Zi'on; He has desired *it* for His <u>habitation</u>.   <small>dwelling</small>
14 This *is* My rest for ever: here will I dwell; for I have desired it.
15 I will abundantly bless her provision: I will satisfy her poor with bread.
16 I will also clothe her priests with salvation: and her <u>saints</u> shall shout aloud for joy.   <small>godly ones</small>
17 There will I make the <u>horn</u> of Da'vid to bud: I have ordained a lamp for My anointed.   <small>i.e., authority</small>
18 His enemies will I clothe with shame: but upon himself shall his crown flourish.

PSALM 133

A Song of degrees of David

BEHOLD, how good and how pleasant *it is* for brethren to dwell together in unity!
2 *It is* like the precious ointment upon the head, that ran down upon the beard, *even* Aar'on's beard: that went down to the skirts of his garments;
3 As the dew of Her'mon, *and as the dew* that descended upon the mountains of Zi'on: for there the LORD com-

-manded the blessing, *even* life for evermore.

PSALM 134

A Song of degrees

BEHOLD, bless you the LORD, all *you* servants of the LORD, which by night stand in the house of the LORD.
2 Lift up your hands *in* the sanctuary, and bless the LORD.
3 The LORD that made heaven and earth bless you out of Zi'on.

PSALM 135

PRAISE you the LORD. Praise you the name of the LORD; praise *Him*, O you servants of the LORD.
2 You that stand in the house of the LORD, in the courts of the house of our God,
3 Praise the LORD; for the LORD *is* good: sing praises to His name; for *it is* pleasant.
4 For the LORD has chosen Ja'cob to Himself, *and* Is'ra-el for His peculiar treasure.   own possession
5 For I know that the LORD *is* great, and *that* our Lord *is* above all gods.   Adon.s.f.
6 Whatsoever the LORD pleased, *that* did he in heaven, and in earth, in the seas, and all deep places.
7 He causes the vapors to ascend from the ends of the earth; He makes lightnings for the rain; He brings the wind out of His treasuries.
8 Who smote the firstborn of E'gypt, both of man and beast.

9 *Who* sent tokens and wonders into the midst of you, O E'gypt, upon Pha'raoh, and upon all his servants.
10 Who smote great nations, and slew mighty kings;
11 Si'hon king of the Am'or-ites, and Og king of Ba'shan, and all the kingdoms of Ca'naan:
12 And gave their land *for* an heritage, an heritage to Is'ra-el His people.
13 Your name, O LORD, *endures* for ever; *and* Your memorial, O LORD, throughout all generations.
14 For the LORD will judge His people, and He will repent Himself concerning His servants.

HEB. 10:30 have compassion on

15 The idols of the heathen *are* silver and gold, the work of men's hands.nations
16 They have mouths, but they speak not; eyes have they, but they see not;
17 They have ears, but they hear not; neither is there *any* breath in their mouths.
18 They that make them *are* like to them: *so is* every one that trusts in them.   will be
19 Bless the LORD, O house of Is'ra-el: bless the LORD, O house of Aar'on:
20 Bless the LORD, O house of Le'vi: you that fear the LORD, bless the LORD.   revere
21 Blessed be the LORD out of Zi'on, which dwells at Je-ru'sa-lem. Praise you the LORD.

PSALM 136

O GIVE thanks to the LORD; for *He is* good: for His mercy *endures* for ever.

2 O give thanks to the God of gods: for His mercy *endures* for ever.

Elohim^{p.f.}

3 O give thanks to the Lord of lords: for His mercy *endures* for ever.

4 To Him who alone does great wonders: for His mercy *endures* for ever.

5 To Him that by wisdom made the heavens: for His mercy *endures* for ever.

6 To Him that stretched out the earth above the waters: for His mercy *endures* for ever.

7 To Him that made great lights: for His mercy *endures* for ever:

8 The sun to rule by day: for His mercy *endures* for ever:

9 The moon and stars to rule by night: for His mercy *endures* for ever.

10 To Him that smote E'gypt in their firstborn: for His mercy *endures* for ever:

11 And brought out Is'ra-el from among them: for His mercy *endures* for ever:

12 With a strong hand, and with a stretched out arm: for His mercy *endures* for ever.

13 To Him which divided the Red sea into parts: for His mercy *endures* for ever:

14 And made Is'ra-el to pass through the midst of it: for His mercy *endures* for ever:

15 But overthrew Pha'raoh and his host in the Red sea: for His mercy *endures* for ever.

16 To Him which led his people through the wilderness: for His mercy *endures* for ever.

17 To Him which smote great kings: for His mercy *endures* for ever:

18 And slew famous kings: for His mercy *endures* for ever:

19 Si'hon king of the Am'or-ites: for His mercy *endures* for ever:

20 And Og the king of Ba'shan: for His mercy *endures* for ever:

21 And gave their land for an heritage: for His mercy *endures* for ever:

22 *Even* an heritage to Is'ra-el His servant: for His mercy *endures* for ever.

23 Who remembered us in our low estate: for His mercy *endures* for ever:

24 And has redeemed us from our enemies: for His mercy *endures* for ever.

25 Who gives food to all flesh: for His mercy *endures* for ever.

26 O give thanks to the God of heaven: for His mercy *endures* for ever.

El^{s.f.}

PSALM 137

BY the rivers of Bab'y-lon, there we sat down, yea, we wept, when we remembered Zi'on.

2 We hanged our harps upon the willows in the midst thereof.

3 For there they that carried us away captive required of us a song; and they that wasted us *required of us* mirth, *saying*, Sing us *one* of the songs of Zi'on.

4 How shall we sing the LORD's song in a strange land?

5 If I forget you, O Je-ru'sa-lem, let my right hand forget *her cunning*.

6 If I do not remember you, let my

GID - 937

tongue cling to the roof of my mouth; if I <u>prefer</u> not Je-ru'sa-lem above my chief joy.   *exalt*

7 Remember, O LORD, the children of E'dom in the day of Je-ru'sa-lem; who said, <u>Rase</u> *it*, <u>rase</u> *it*, *even* to the foundation thereof.   *Raze*

8 O daughter of Bab'y-lon, who are to be destroyed; happy *shall he be*, that rewards you as you have served us.

9 Happy *shall he be*, that takes and dashes your little ones against the stones.

PSALM 138

A Psalm of David

I WILL praise You with my whole heart: before the gods will I sing praise to You.

2 I will worship <u>toward</u> Your holy temple, and praise Your name for Your lovingkindness and for Your truth: for You have magnified Your word above all Your name.   *facing*

3 In the day when I cried You answered me, *and* strengthened me *with* strength in my soul.

4 All the kings of the earth shall praise You, O LORD, when they hear the words of Your mouth.

5 Yea, they shall sing in the ways of the LORD: for great *is* the glory of the LORD.

6 Though the LORD *be* high, yet has He <u>respect</u> to the lowly: but the proud He knows afar off.   *regard*

7 Though I walk in the midst of trouble, You will revive me: You shall stretch forth Your hand against the wrath of my enemies, and Your right hand shall save me.

8 The LORD will <u>perfect</u> *that which* concerns me: Your mercy, O LORD, *endures* for ever: forsake not the works of Your own hands.   *accomplish*

PSALM 139

To the chief Musician, A Psalm of David

O LORD, You have searched me, and known *me*.

2 You know my downsitting and my uprising, You understand my thought afar off.   ROM. 8:27

3 You <u>compass</u> my path and my lying down, and are acquainted *with* all my ways.   *discerns*

4 For *there is* not a word in my tongue, *but*, lo, O LORD, You know it altogether.

5 You have beset me behind and before, and laid Your hand upon me.

6 *Such* knowledge *is* too wonderful for me; it is high, I cannot *attain* to it.

7 Where shall I go from Your Spirit? or where shall I flee from Your presence?

8 If I ascend up into heaven, You *are* there: if I make my bed in hell, behold, You *are there*.

9 *If* I take the wings of the morning, *and* dwell in the uttermost parts of the sea;

10 Even there shall your hand lead me, and Your right hand shall hold me.

11 If I say, Surely the darkness

shall cover me; even the night shall be light about me.

12 Yea, the darkness hides not from You; but the night shines as the day: the darkness and the light *are* both alike *to You*.

13 For You have possessed my <u>reins</u>: You have covered me in my mother's womb.   inward parts

14 I will praise You; for I am fearfully *and* wonderfully made: marvellous *are* Your works; and *that* my soul knows right well.

15 My substance was not hid from You, when I was made in secret, *and* curiously wrought in the lowest parts of the earth.

16 Your eyes did see my substance, yet being unperfect; and in Your book all *my members* were written, *which* in continuance were fashioned, when *as yet there was* none of them.

17 How precious also are Your thoughts to me, O <u>God</u>! how great is the sum of them!   El^s.f.

18 *If* I should count them, they are more in number than the sand: when I awake, I am still with You.

19 Surely You will slay the wicked, O God: depart from me therefore, you bloody men.

20 For they speak against You <u>wickedly</u>, *and* Your enemies take *Your name* in vain.   rebelliously

21 Do not I <u>hate</u> them, O LORD, that <u>hate</u> You? and am not I grieved with those that rise up against You?   despise

22 I <u>hate</u> them with <u>perfect</u> hatred: I count them my enemies.   utmost

23 Search me, O God, and know my heart: try me, and know my thoughts:

24 And see if *there be any* wicked way in me, and lead me in the way everlasting.

PSALM 140

To the chief Musician, A Psalm of David

DELIVER me, O LORD, from the evil man: preserve me from the violent man;

2 <u>Which imagine</u> mischiefs in their *heart*; continually are they gathered together *for* war.   Who devise

3 They have sharpened their tongues like a serpent; adders' poison *is* under their lips. Se'lah.   ROM. 3:13

4 Keep me, O LORD, from the hands of the <u>wicked</u>; preserve me from the violent man; who have purposed to overthrow my goings.   lawless

5 The proud have hid a <u>snare</u> for me, and cords; they have spread a net by the wayside; they have set <u>gins</u> for me. Se'lah.   trap - lures

6 I said to the LORD, You *are* my <u>God</u>: hear the voice of my supplications, O LORD.   El^s.f.

7 O <u>GOD the Lord</u>, the strength of my <u>salvation</u>, You have covered my head in the day of battle.

Jehovah^s.f. Adonay^p.f. - Jeshua

8 Grant not, O LORD, the desires of the wicked: further not his wicked device; *less* they exalt themselves. Se'lah.

9 *As for* the head of those that <u>compass</u> me about, let the mischief of their own lips cover them.   surround

10 Let burning coals fall upon them: let them be cast into the fire; into deep pits, that they rise not up again.
11 Let not an evil speaker be established in the earth: evil shall hunt the violent man to overthrow *him*.
12 I know that the LORD will maintain the cause of the afflicted, *and* the right of the poor.
13 Surely the righteous shall give thanks to Your name: the upright shall dwell in Your presence.

PSALM 141

A Psalm of David

LORD, I cry to You: make haste to me; give ear to my voice, when I cry to You.
2 Let my prayer be set forth before You *as* incense; *and* the lifting up of my hands as the evening sacrifice.
3 Set a watch, O LORD, before my mouth; keep the door of my lips.
4 Incline not my heart to *any* evil thing, to practise wicked works with men that work iniquity: and let me not eat of their underlined dainties. delicacies
5 Let the righteous smite me; *it shall be* a kindness: and let him reprove me; *it shall be* an excellent oil, *which* shall not break my head: for yet my prayer also *shall be* in their calamities.
6 When their judges are overthrown in stony places, they shall hear my words; for they are sweet. rulers
7 Our bones are scattered at the grave's mouth, as when one cuts and clings *wood* upon the earth.

8 But my eyes *are* to you, O GOD the Lord: in You is my trust; leave not my soul destitute. Jehovah s.f. Adonahy p.f.
9 Keep me from the snares *which* they have laid for me, and the gins of the workers of iniquity. traps - lures
10 Let the wicked fall into their own nets, until that I with escape.

PSALM 142

Maschil of David; A Prayer when he was in the cave

I CRIED to the LORD with my voice; with my voice to the LORD did I make my supplication.
2 I poured out my complaint before Him; I showed before Him my trouble.
3 When my spirit was overwhelmed within me, then You knew my path. In the way wherein I walked have they privily laid a snare for me. secretly - trap
4 I looked on *my* right hand, and beheld, but *there was* no man that would know me: refuge failed me; no man cared for my soul.
5 I cried to You, O LORD: I said, You *are* my refuge *and* my portion in the land of the living.
6 Attend to my cry; for I am brought very low: deliver me from my persecutors; for they are stronger than I. Listen
7 Bring my soul out of prison, that I may praise Your name: the righteous shall compass me about; for You shall deal bountifully with me. surround

PSALM 143

A Psalm of David

HEAR my prayer, O LORD, give ear to my supplications: in Your faithfulness answer me, *and* in Your righteousness.
2 And enter not into judgment with Your servant: for in Your sight shall no man living be justified.

GAL. 2:16

3 For the enemy has persecuted my soul; he has <u>smitten</u> my life down to the ground; he has made me to dwell in darkness, as those that have been long dead.　struck
4 Therefore is my spirit overwhelmed within me; my heart within me is desolate.
5 I remember the days of old; I meditate on all Your works; I <u>muse on</u> the work of Your hands.　consider
6 I stretch forth my hands to You: my soul *thirsts* after You, as a thirsty land. Se'lah.
7 Hear me speedily, O LORD: my spirit fails: hide not Your face from me, less I be like to them that go down into the pit.
8 Cause me to hear Your lovingkindness in the morning; for in You do I trust: cause me to know the way wherein I should walk; for I lift up my soul to You.
9 Deliver me, O LORD, from my enemies: I flee to You to hide me.
10 Teach me to do Your will; for You *are* my <u>God</u>: Your Spirit *is* good; lead me into the land of uprightness.　Elohim[p.f.]

11 <u>Quicken</u> me, O LORD, for Your name's sake: for Your righteousness' sake bring my soul out of trouble. Revive
12 And of Your mercy cut off my enemies, and destroy all them that afflict my soul: for I *am* Your servant.

PSALM 144

A Psalm of David

BLESSED *be* the LORD my strength, which teaches my hands to war, *and* my fingers to fight:
2 My <u>goodness</u>, and my fortress; my high tower, and my <u>deliverer</u>; my shield, and *He* in whom I trust; who subdues my people under me.

lovingkindness - liberator

3 LORD, what *is* man, that You take knowledge of him! *or* the son of man, that You make account of him!
4 Man is like to vanity: his days *are* as a shadow that passes away.
5 Bow Your heavens, O LORD, and come down: touch the mountains, and they shall smoke.
6 Cast forth lightning, and scatter them: shoot out Your arrows, and destroy them.
7 Send Your hand from above; rid me, and deliver me out of great waters, from the hand of <u>strange children</u>;　foreigners
8 Whose mouth speaks <u>vanity</u>, and their right hand *is* a right hand of falsehood.　i.e. wickedly
9 I will sing a new song to You, O God: upon a <u>psaltery</u> *and* an instrument of ten strings will I sing praises to You.　lyre

10 *It is He* that gives <u>salvation</u> to kings: who delivers Da'vid His servant from the hurtful sword. _{victory}

11 Rid me, and deliver me from the hand of strange children, whose mouth speaks <u>vanity</u>, and their right hand *is* a right hand of falsehood: _{i.e. wickedly}

12 That our sons *may be* as plants grown up in their youth; *that* our daughters *may be* as corner stones, polished *after* the similitude of a palace:

13 *That* our garners *may be* full, affording all manner of store: *that* our sheep may bring forth thousands and ten thousands in our streets:

14 *That* our oxen *may be* strong to labor; *that there be* no breaking in, nor going out; that *there be* no complaining in our streets.

15 Happy *is that* people, that is in such a case: *yea*, happy *is that* people, whose God *is* the LORD.

PSALM 145

David's Psalm of praise

I WILL extol You, my <u>God</u>, O king; and I will bless Your name for ever and ever. _{Elohim p.f.}

2 Every day will I bless You; and I will praise Your name for ever and ever.

3 Great *is* the LORD, and greatly to be praised; and His greatness *is* unsearchable.

4 One generation shall praise Your works to another, and shall declare Your mighty acts.

5 I will speak of the glorious honor of Your majesty, and of Your wondrous works.

6 And *men* shall speak of the might of Your <u>terrible</u> acts: and I will declare Your greatness. _{awesome}

7 They shall <u>abundantly</u> utter the memory of Your great goodness, and shall sing of Your righteousness. _{eagerly}

8 The LORD *is* gracious, and full of compassion; slow to anger, and of great mercy.

9 The LORD *is* good to all: and His tender mercies *are* over all His works.

10 All Your works shall praise You, O LORD; and Your saints shall bless You.

11 They shall speak of the glory of Your kingdom, and talk of Your power;

12 To make known to the sons of men His mighty acts, and the glorious majesty of His kingdom.

13 Your kingdom *is* an everlasting kingdom, and Your dominion *endures* throughout all generations.

14 The LORD upholds all that fall, and raises up all *those that be* bowed down.

15 The eyes of all <u>wait upon</u> You; and You give them their meat in due season. _{look to}

16 You open Your hand, and satisfy the desire of every living thing.

17 The LORD *is* righteous in all His ways, and <u>holy</u> in all His works. _{merciful}

18 The LORD *is* near to all them that call upon Him, to all that call upon Him in truth.

19 He will fulfill the desire of them that <u>fear</u> Him: He also will hear their cry, and will save them. _{revere}

20 The LORD preserves all them that

love Him: but all the wicked will
He destroy.

21 My mouth shall speak the praise
of the LORD: and let all flesh bless
His holy name for ever and ever.

PSALM 146

PRAISE you the LORD. Praise the
LORD, O my soul.

2 While I live will I praise the LORD:
I will sing praises to my God while
I have any being.

M07 - 943

3 Put not your trust in princes,
nor in the son of man, in whom
there is no help.

4 His breath goes forth, he returns
to his earth; in that very day his
thoughts perish.

G4

5 Happy *is he* that *has* the <u>God</u> of
Ja'cob for his help, whose hope *is*
in the LORD his <u>God</u>:   El^s.f. - Elohim^p.f.

6 Which made heaven, and earth, the
sea, and all that therein *is*: which
keeps truth for ever: REV. 14:7 ACTS 4:24

7 Which executes judgment for the oppressed: which gives food to the hungry. The LORD loosens the prisoners:

8 The LORD opens *the eyes of* the
blind: the LORD raises them that are
bowed down: the LORD loves the
righteous: MATT. 9:30

9 The LORD <u>preserves</u> the strangers; He relieves the fatherless
and widow: but the way of the
wicked He turns upside down.

watches over

10 The LORD shall reign for ever, *even*
your God, O Zi'on, to all generations. Praise you the LORD.

943

PSALM 147

PRAISE you the LORD: for *it is*
good to sing praises to our
God; for *it is* pleasant; *and* praise
is <u>comely</u>.   fitting

2 The LORD does build up Je-ru'sa-
lem: He gathers together the outcasts
of Is'ra-el.

3 He heals the broken in heart, and
binds up their wounds.

4 He <u>tells</u> the number of the stars;
He calls them all by *their* names.
counts

5 Great *is* our Lord, and of great
power: His understanding *is* infinite.

6 The LORD lifts up the <u>meek</u>: He
casts the wicked down to the
ground.   humble

M35 - 963

7 Sing to the LORD with thanksgiving; sing praise upon the harp to
our <u>God</u>:   Elohim^p.f.

8 Who covers the heaven with
clouds, who prepares rain for the
earth, who makes grass to grow upon
the mountains.

9 He gives to the beast His food,
and to the young ravens which cry.

10 He delights not in the strength
of the horse: He takes not pleasure
in the legs of a man.

11 The LORD takes pleasure in
them that <u>fear</u> Him, in those that
hope in His mercy.   revere

12 Praise the LORD, O Je-ru'sa-lem;
praise your <u>God</u>, O Zi'on.   Elohim^p.f.

13 For He has strengthened the
bars of your gates; He has blessed
your children within you.

14 He makes peace *in* your borders,
and fills you with the finest of the wheat.

15 He sends forth His commandment *upon* earth: His word runs
very swiftly.
16 He gives snow like wool: He scatters the hoarfrost like ashes.
17 He casts forth His ice like morsels:
who can stand before His cold?
18 He sends out His word, and melts
them: He causes His wind to blow,
and the waters flow.
19 He shows His word to Ja'cob,
His statutes and His judgments to
Is'ra-el.   ROM. 3:2
20 He has not dealt so with any nation: and *as for His* judgments, they
have not known them. Praise you the
LORD.

PSALM 148

PRAISE you the LORD. Praise
you the LORD from the heavens: praise Him in the heights.
2 Praise you Him, all His angels:
praise you Him, all His hosts.messengers
3 Praise you Him, sun and moon:
praise Him, all you stars of light.
4 Praise Him, you heavens of heavens, and you waters that *be* above
the heavens.
5 Let them praise the name of the
LORD: for He commanded, and they
were created.
6 He has also stablished them for
ever and ever: He has made a decree
which shall not pass.
7 Praise the LORD from the earth, you
dragons, and all deeps:
8 Fire, and hail; snow, and vapor;
stormy wind fulfilling His word:

9 Mountains, and all hills; fruitful
trees, and all cedars:
10 Beasts, and all cattle; creeping
things, and flying fowl:
11 Kings of the earth, and all people;
princes, and all judges of the earth:
12 Both young men, and maidens;
old men, and children:
13 Let them praise the name of the
LORD: for His name alone is excellent;
His glory *is* above the earth and heaven.
14 He also exalts the horn of His
people, the praise of all His
saints; *even* of the children of
Is'ra-el, a people near to Him.
Praise you the LORD.   i.e., king

PSALM 149

PRAISE you the LORD. Sing to
the LORD a new song, *and* His
praise in the congregation of saints.
2 Let Is'ra-el rejoice in Him that
made him: let the children of Zi'on
be joyful in their King.
3 Let them praise His name in the
dance: let them sing praises to Him
with the timbrel and harp.
4 For the LORD takes pleasure in
His people: He will beautify the
meek with salvation.   humble
5 Let the saints be joyful in glory:
let them sing aloud upon their beds.
6 *Let* the high *praises* of God *be* in
their mouth, and a twoedged sword
in their hand;   El s.f.
7 To execute vengeance upon the
heathen, *and* punishments upon the
people;   nations
8 To bind their kings with chains,
and their nobles with fetters of iron;

9 To execute upon them the judgment written: this honor have all His
saints. Praise you the LORD.

PSALM 150

PRAISE you the LORD. Praise God
in His sanctuary: praise Him in
the firmament of His power.   Jah - El^{s.f.}
2 Praise Him for His mighty acts:
praise Him according to His excellent greatness.

3 Praise Him with the sound of the
trumpet: praise Him with the psaltery and harp.   lyre
4 Praise Him with the timbrel and
dance: praise Him with stringed instruments and organs.
5 Praise Him upon the loud cymbals: praise Him upon the high
sounding cymbals.
6 Let every thing that has breath
praise the LORD. Praise you the LORD.

M03 - 950

PROVERBS

OUTLINE

SURVEY

In Proverbs, wisdom begins with God; His centrality is assumed throughout. The wise, upright, righteous, and godly are equated. They are those who trust and know their God, and mirror this by their just and loving conduct toward their fellows in accordance with divinely-approved principles. Good and bad are linked with reward and penalty, because God embodies in Himself both love and justice and so must promote good and obviate evil.

The positive and negative standards in Proverbs afford a valuable test of personal conduct. Christ enjoins His disciples to be "wise as serpents . . ." (Mt. 10.16). The wisdom of Proverbs is the Old Testament pendant to the many practical exhortations in the New Testament letters, a fact true of both the great fourteenfold discourse and the vast series of pithy instructions and observations of which most of this book consists, bearing on many aspects of daily life.

AUTHOR

Proverbs 1.1 and 2 name Solomon as main author; 10.1—22.16 are directly his. The first group of "words of the wise" in 22.17—24.22 he has incorporated ("my knowledge," 22.17); and 24.23-34 were perhaps added by him, or by Hezekiah's men along with Solomon's second big series, chapters 25 through 29. The discourses, chapters 1 through 9, are undated, but there was good ancient Oriental precedent for Solomon's possibly prefixing them as an introduction to the main proverbs. Agur, Lemuel and the Good Wife poem are of unknown date, but could have been added at the earliest in Hezekiah's time, though perhaps later. Thus the earliest date for the present book of Proverbs would be in Hezekiah's reign just after 700 B.C., but it may be some time later.

External considerations support the tenth to seventh century B.C. date implied by the rubrics. Written proverbial literature was then already ancient in the Near East; and recent studies (not all published) of linguistic contacts and literary background from North-Canaanitic (Ugaritic), Egyptian, Mesopotamian and Hittite sources would also indicate a date for Proverbs in the first half of the first millennium B.C.

K.A.K.

THE PROVERBS

Practical Guidance
For Everyday Life

CHAPTER 1

THE proverbs of Sol'o-mon the son of Da'vid, king of Is'ra-el;

2 To know wisdom and instruction; to perceive the words of understanding;

3 To receive the instruction of wisdom, justice, and judgment, and equity;

4 To give <u>subtilty</u> to the simple, to the young man knowledge and discretion. _prudence_

5 A wise _man_ will hear, and will increase learning; and a man of understanding shall attain to wise counsels:

6 To understand a proverb, and the <u>interpretation</u>; the words of the wise, and their dark sayings. _meaning_

7 The <u>fear</u> of the LORD _is_ the beginning of knowledge: _but_ fools despise wisdom and instruction. _reverence_

8 My son, hear the instruction of your father, and forsake not the law of your mother:

9 For they _shall be_ an ornament of grace to your head, and chains about your neck.

10 My son, if sinners entice you, consent you not.

11 If they say, Come with us, let us lay wait for blood, let us <u>lurk privily for</u> the innocent without cause: _ambush_

12 Let us swallow them up alive as the grave; <u>and</u> whole, as those that go down into the <u>pit</u>: _even - abyss_

13 We shall find all precious substance, we shall fill our houses with spoil:

14 Cast in your lot among us; let us all have one purse:

15 My son, walk not you in the way with them; refrain your foot from their path:

16 For their feet run to evil, and make haste to shed blood.

17 Surely in vain the net is spread in the sight of any bird.

18 And they lay wait for their _own_ blood; they lurk <u>privily</u> for their _own_ lives. _secretly_

19 So _are_ the ways of every one that is greedy of gain; _which_ takes away the life of the owners thereof.

20 Wisdom cries without; she utters her voice in the streets:

21 She cries in the chief place of <u>concourse</u>, in the openings of the gates: in the city she utters her words, _saying_, _streets_

22 How long, you <u>simple</u> ones, will you love simplicity? and the scorners delight in their scorning, and fools hate knowledge? _naive_

23 Turn you at my <u>reproof</u>: behold, I will pour out my spirit to you, I will make known my words to you. _correction_

24 Because I have called, and you refused; I have stretched out my hand, and no man regarded;

25 But you have set at nought all my counsel, and <u>would</u> none of my reproof: _wanted_

26 I also will laugh at your calamity; I will mock when your <u>fear</u> comes; _dread_

27 When your <u>fear</u> comes as desolation, and your destruction comes
as a whirlwind; when distress and
anguish comes upon you.   dread

28 Then shall they call upon me, but
I will not answer; they shall seek me
early, but they shall not find me:

29 For that they <u>hated</u> knowledge,
and did not choose the <u>fear</u> of the
LORD: despised - reverence

30 They would none of my counsel:
they despised all my reproof.

31 Therefore shall they eat of the fruit
of their own way, and be filled with
their own devices.

32 For the <u>turning away</u> of the
simple shall slay them, and the
<u>prosperity</u> of fools shall destroy
them.   waywardness - complacency

33 But whoso hearkens to me shall
dwell safely, and shall be quiet from
fear of evil.

CHAPTER 2

M Y son, if you will receive my
words, and <u>hide</u> my commandments with you;   treasure

2 So that you incline your ear to
wisdom, *and* apply your heart to
understanding;

3 Yea, if you seek after knowledge,
and lift up your voice for understanding;

4 If you seek her as silver, and
search for her as *for* hid treasures;

5 Then shall you understand the <u>fear</u>
of the LORD, and find the knowledge
of <u>God</u>.   reverence - Jehovah^{s.f.} - Elohim^{p.f.}

6 For the LORD gives wisdom: out of

His mouth *comes* knowledge and understanding.

7 He lays up sound wisdom for the
righteous: *He is* a <u>buckler</u> to them
that walk uprightly.   shield

8 He keeps the paths of judgment, and
preserves the way of His saints.

9 Then shall you understand righteousness, and judgment, and equity; *yea*, every good path.

10 When wisdom enters into your
heart, and knowledge is pleasant to
your soul;

11 <u>Discretion</u> shall preserve you, understanding shall keep you:

12 To deliver you from the way of
the evil *man*, from the man that speak
<u>froward</u> things;   perverse

13 Who leave the paths of uprightness, to walk in the ways of darkness;

14 Who rejoice to do evil, *and* delight in the <u>frowardness</u> of the wicked;

15 Whose ways *are* crooked, and
they <u>froward</u> in their paths:

16 To deliver you from the strange
woman, *even* from the stranger
which flatters with her words;

17 Which forsakes the guide of her
youth, and forgets the <u>covenant</u> of
her <u>God</u>.   agreement - Elohim^{p.f.}

18 For her house <u>inclines</u> to death,
and her paths to the dead.   sinks down

19 None that go to her return again,
neither take they hold of the paths
of life.

20 That you may walk in the way
of good *men*, and keep the paths
of the righteous.

21 For the upright shall dwell in the

land, and the perfect shall remain in it.
22 But the wicked shall be cut off from the earth, and the transgressors shall be rooted out of it.

CHAPTER 3

MY son, forget not my law; but let your heart keep my commandments:

2 For length of days, and long life, and peace, shall they add to you.

3 Let not mercy and truth forsake you: bind them about your neck; write them upon the table of your heart:

4 So shall you find favor and good <u>understanding</u> in the sight of <u>God</u> and man.   repute - Elohim^p.f.

5 Trust in the LORD with all your heart; and lean not to your own understanding.

6 In all your ways acknowledge Him, and He shall direct your paths.

7 Be not wise in your own eyes: fear the LORD, and depart from evil.

8 It shall be <u>health</u> to your <u>navel</u>, and <u>marrow</u> to your bones.   healing - body - refreshment

9 Honor the LORD with your substance, and with the firstfruits of all your increase:

10 So shall your barns be filled with plenty, and your <u>presses</u> shall burst out with new wine.   vats

11 My son, despise not the chastening of the LORD; neither be weary of His correction: HEB. 12:5

12 For whom the LORD loves He corrects; even as a father the son *in whom* he delights.   REV. 3:19

13 Happy *is* the man *that* finds wisdom, and the man *that* gets understanding.

14 For the merchandise of it *is* better than the merchandise of silver, and the gain thereof than fine gold.

15 <u>She</u> *is* more precious than rubies: and all the things you can desire are not to be compared to her.   wisdom

16 Length of days *is* in her right hand; *and* in her left hand riches and honor.

17 Her ways *are* ways of pleasantness, and all her paths *are* peace.

18 <u>She</u> *is* a tree of life to them that lay hold upon her: and happy *is every one* that retains her.   wisdom

19 The LORD by wisdom has founded the earth; by understanding has He established the heavens.

20 By His knowledge the depths are broken up, and the clouds drop down the dew.

21 My son, let not them depart from your eyes: keep sound wisdom and discretion:

22 So shall they be life to your soul, and grace to your neck.

23 Then shall you walk in your way safely, and your foot shall not stumble.

24 When you lie down, you shall not be afraid: yea, you shall lie down, and your sleep shall be sweet.

25 Be not afraid of sudden <u>fear</u>, neither of the desolation of the wicked, when it comes.   disaster

26 For the LORD shall be your confidence, and shall keep your foot from being taken.

27 Withhold not good from them to

whom it is due, when it is in the power of your hand to do *it*.

28 Say not to your neighbor, Go, and come again, and to morrow I will give; when you have it by you.

29 Devise not evil against your neighbor, seeing he dwells securely by you.

30 Strive not with a man without cause, if he have done you no harm.

31 Envy you not the oppressor, and choose none of his ways.

32 For the <u>froward</u> *is* <u>abomination</u> to the LORD: but His secret *is* with the righteous.   perverse man - detestable

33 The curse of the LORD *is* in the house of the wicked: but He blesses the habitation of the just.

34 Surely He scorns the scorners: but He gives grace to the lowly.

         1 PET 5:5   JAMES 4:6

35 The wise shall inherit glory: but shame shall be the promotion of fools.

CHAPTER 4

HEAR, you children, the instruction of a father, and attend to know understanding.

2 For I give you good <u>doctrine</u>, forsake you not my law.   teaching

3 For I was my father's son, tender and only *beloved* in the sight of my mother.

4 He taught me also, and said to me, Let your heart retain my words: keep my commandments, and live.

5 Get wisdom, get understanding: forget *it* not; neither <u>decline</u> from the words of my mouth.   turn away

6 Forsake her not, and she shall pre-serve you: love her, and she shall keep you.

7 Wisdom *is* the principal thing; *therefore* get wisdom: and with all your getting get understanding.

8 Exalt her, and she shall promote you: she shall bring you to honor, when you do embrace her.

9 She shall give to your head an ornament of grace: a crown of glory shall she deliver to you.

10 Hear, O my son, and receive my sayings; and the years of your life shall be many.

11 I have taught you in the way of wisdom; I have led you in right paths.

12 When you go, your steps shall not be <u>straitened</u>; and when you run you shall not stumble.   hampered

13 Take fast hold of instruction; let *her* not go: keep her; for she *is* your life.

14 Enter not into the path of the wicked, and go not in the way of evil *men*.

15 Avoid it, pass not by it, turn from it, and pass away.

16 For they sleep not, except they have done mischief; and their sleep is taken away, unless they cause *some* to fall.

17 For they eat the bread of wickedness, and drink the wine of violence.

18 But the path of the just *is* as the shining light, that shines more and more to the perfect day.

19 The way of the wicked *is* as darkness: they know not at what they stumble.

20 My son, attend to my words; incline your ear to my sayings.

21 Let them not depart from your eyes; keep them in the midst of your heart.
22 For they *are* life to those that find them, and health to all their flesh.
23 Keep your heart with all diligence; for out of it *are* the issues of life.
24 Put away from you a froward mouth, and perverse lips put far from you.   deceitful - devious
25 Let your eyes look right on, and let your eyelids look straight before you.
26 Ponder the path of your feet, and let all your ways be established.
27 Turn not to the right hand nor to the left: remove your foot from evil.

CHAPTER 5

MY son, attend to my wisdom, *and* bow your ear to my understanding:
2 That you may regard discretion, and *that* your lips may keep knowledge.
3 For the lips of a strange woman drop *as* an honeycomb, and her mouth *is* smoother than oil:
4 But her end is bitter as wormwood, sharp as a twoedged sword.
5 Her feet go down to death; her steps take hold on hell.   Sheol
6 Less you should ponder the path of life, her ways are moveable, *that* you can not know *them*.

    reflect - crooked

7 Hear me now therefore, O you children, and depart not from the words of my mouth.
8 Remove your way far from her, and come not near the door of her house:

9 Less you give your honor to others, and your years to the cruel:
10 Less strangers be filled with your wealth; and your labors *be* in the house of a stranger;   alien
11 And you mourn at the last, when your flesh and your body are consumed,
12 And say, How have I hated instruction, and my heart despised reproof;   despised
13 And have not obeyed the voice of my teachers, nor inclined my ear to them that instructed me!
14 I was almost in all evil in the midst of the congregation and assembly.
15 Drink waters out of your own cistern, and running waters out of your own well.
16 Let your fountains be dispersed abroad, *and* rivers of waters in the streets.
17 Let them be only your own, and not strangers' with you.
18 Let your fountain be blessed: and rejoice with the wife of your youth.
19 *Let her be as* the loving hind and pleasant roe; let her breasts satisfy you at all times; and be you ravished always with her love.   deer
20 And why will you, my son, be ravished with a strange woman, and embrace the bosom of a stranger?

    captivated

21 For the ways of man *are* before the eyes of the LORD, and He ponders all his goings.
22 His own iniquities shall take the wicked himself, and he shall be holden with the cords of his sins.   held
23 He shall die without instruction;

and in the greatness of his folly he shall go astray.

CHAPTER 6

MY son, if you be <u>surety</u> for your friend, *if* you have <u>stricken your hand</u> with a stranger, <small>guarantee - i.e., made a pledge</small>

2 You are snared with the words of your mouth, you are taken with the words of your mouth.

3 Do this now, my son, and deliver yourself, when you are come into the hand of your <u>friend</u>; go, humble yourself, and make sure your <u>friend</u>. <small>neighbor</small>

4 Give not sleep to your eyes, nor slumber to your eyelids.

5 Deliver yourself as a roe from the hand *of the hunter*, and as a bird from the hand of the fowler.

6 Go to the ant, you sluggard; consider its ways, and be wise:

7 Which having no guide, overseer, or ruler,

8 Provides her meat in the summer, *and* gathers her food in the harvest.

9 How long will you sleep, O sluggard? when will you arise out of your sleep?

10 *Yet* a little sleep, a little slumber, a little folding of the hands to sleep:

11 So shall your poverty come as one that travels, and your want as an armed man.

12 A naughty person, a wicked man, walks with a <u>froward</u> mouth. <small>corrupt</small>

13 He winks with his eyes, he speaks with his feet, he <u>teaches</u> with his fingers; <small>points</small>

14 <u>Frowardness</u> *is* in his heart, he de-vises mischief continually; he sows discord. <small>deceit</small>

15 Therefore shall his calamity come suddenly; suddenly shall he be broken without remedy.

16 These six *things* does the LORD <u>hate</u>: yea, seven *are* <u>an abomination</u> to Him: <small>detest - detestable</small>

17 A proud look, a lying tongue, and hands that shed innocent blood,

18 An heart that devises wicked <u>imaginations</u>, feet that be swift in running to mischief, <small>plans</small>

19 A false witness *that* speaks lies, and he that sows discord among brethren.

20 My son, keep your father's commandment, and forsake not the law of your mother: <small>EPH. 6:1</small>

21 Bind them continually upon your heart, *and* tie them about your neck.

22 When you go, it shall lead you; when you sleep, it shall keep you; and *when* you awake, it shall talk with you.

23 For the commandment *is* a lamp; and the law *is* light; and <u>reproofs</u> of instruction *are* the way of life: <small>corrections</small>

24 To keep you from the evil woman, from the flattery of the tongue of a <u>strange</u> woman. <small>foreign</small>

25 Lust not after her beauty in your heart; neither let her take you with her eyelids. <small>MATT. 5:28</small>

26 For by means of a <u>whorish woman</u> *a man is brought* to a piece of bread: and the adulteress will hunt for the precious life. <small>prostitute</small>

27 Can a man take fire in his bosom, and his clothes not be burned?

28 Can one go upon hot coals, and his feet not be burned?

29 So he that goes in to his neighbor's wife; whosoever touches her shall not be innocent.

30 *Men* do not despise a thief, if he steal to satisfy his soul when he is hungry;

31 But *if* he be found, he shall restore sevenfold; he shall give all the substance of his house.

32 *But* whoso commits adultery with a woman lacks understanding: he *that* does it destroys his own soul.

33 A wound and dishonor shall he get; and his reproach shall not be wiped away.

34 For jealousy *is* the rage of a man: therefore he will not spare in the day of vengeance.

35 He will not <u>regard</u> any ransom; neither will he rest content, though you give many gifts. accept

CHAPTER 7

MY son, keep my words, and lay up my commandments with you.

2 Keep my commandments, and live; and my law as the apple of your eye.

3 Bind them upon your fingers, write them upon the table of your heart.

4 Say to wisdom, You *are* my sister; and call understanding *your* kinswoman:

5 That they may keep you from the <u>strange woman</u>, from the <u>stranger</u> *which* flatters with her words. adulteress - foreigner

6 For at the window of my house I looked through my casement,

7 And beheld among the simple ones, I discerned among the youths, a young man void of understanding,

8 Passing through the street near her corner; and he went the way to her house,

9 In the twilight, in the evening, in the black and dark night:

10 And, behold, there met him a woman *with* the attire of an harlot, and subtil of heart.

11 (She *is* loud and stubborn; her feet abide not in her house:

12 Now *is she* without, now in the streets, and lies in wait at every corner.)

13 So she caught him, and kissed him, *and* with an <u>impudent</u> face said to him, brazen

14 *I have* peace offerings with me; this day have I paid my vows.

15 Therefore came I forth to meet you, diligently to seek your face, and I have found you.

16 I have decked my bed with coverings of tapestry, with carved *works*, with fine linen of E'gypt.

17 I have perfumed my bed with myrrh, aloes, and cinnamon.

18 Come, let us take our fill of love until the morning: let us <u>solace</u> ourselves with <u>loves</u>. enjoy - caresses

19 For the <u>goodman</u> *is* not at home, he is gone a long journey: husband

20 He has taken a bag of money with him, *and* will come home at the day appointed.

21 With her much fair speech she caused him to yield, with the flattering of her lips she forced him.

22 He goes after her immediately, as an ox goes to the slaughter, or as a fool to the correction of the stocks;

23 Till a dart strike through his liver; as a bird hastens to the snare, and knows not that it *is* for his life.

24 <u>Hearken</u> to me now therefore, O you children, and attend to the words of my mouth. _{Listen}

25 Let not your heart decline to her ways, go not astray in her paths.

26 For she has cast down many wounded: yea, many strong *men* have been slain by her.

27 Her house *is* the way to <u>hell</u>, going down to the chambers of death. _{Sheol}

CHAPTER 8

DOES not wisdom cry? and understanding put forth her voice?

2 She stands in the top of high places, by the way in the places of the paths.

3 She cries at the gates, at the entry of the city, at the coming in at the doors,

4 To you, O men, I call; and my voice *is* to the sons of man.

5 O you <u>simple</u>, understand wisdom: and, you fools, be you of an understanding heart. _{naive}

6 Hear; for I will speak of excellent things; and the opening of my lips *shall be* right things.

7 For my mouth shall speak truth; and wickedness *is* an <u>abomination</u> to my lips. _{detestable}

8 All the words of my mouth *are* in righteousness; *there is* nothing <u>fro-ward</u> or perverse in them. _{crooked}

9 They *are* all plain to him that understands, and right to them that find knowledge.

10 Receive my instruction, and not silver; and knowledge rather than choice gold.

11 For wisdom *is* better than rubies; and all the things that may be desired are not to be compared to it.

12 I wisdom dwell with prudence, and find out knowledge of witty inventions.

13 The <u>fear</u> of the LORD *is* to <u>hate</u> evil: pride, and arrogancy, and the evil way, and the <u>froward</u> mouth, do I <u>hate</u>. _{reverence - despise - perverted}

14 Counsel *is* mine, and sound wisdom: I *am* understanding; I have strength.

15 By me kings reign, and princes decree justice. _{ROM. 13:1}

16 By me princes rule, and nobles, *even* all the judges of the earth.

17 I love them that love me; and those that seek me early shall find me. _{MATT. 14:21}

18 Riches and honor *are* with me; *yea*, durable riches and righteousness.

19 My fruit *is* better than gold, yea, than fine gold; and my revenue than choice silver.

20 I lead in the way of righteousness, in the midst of the paths of judgment:

21 That I may cause those that love me to inherit <u>substance</u>; and I will fill their treasures. _{wealth}

22 The LORD possessed me in the beginning of His way, before His works of old. _{COL. 1:17}

23 I was set up from everlasting, from the beginning, or ever the earth was.

24 When *there were* no depths, I was brought forth; when *there were* no fountains abounding with water.

25 Before the mountains were settled, before the hills was I brought forth:

26 While as yet He had not made the earth, nor the fields, nor the highest part of the dust of the world.

27 When He prepared the heavens, I *was* there: when He <u>set a compass</u> upon the face of the depth: _{inscribed a circle}

28 When He established the clouds above: when He strengthened the fountains of the deep:

29 When He gave to the sea His decree, that the waters should not pass His commandment: when He appointed the foundations of the earth:

30 Then I was by Him, *as* one brought up *with Him*: and I was daily *His* delight, rejoicing always before Him;

31 Rejoicing in the habitable part of His earth; and my delights *were* with the sons of men.

32 Now therefore hearken to me, O you children: for <u>blessed</u> *are they that* keep my ways. LUKE 11:28 fortunate

33 Hear instruction, and be wise, and refuse it not.

34 <u>Blessed</u> *is* the man that hears me, watching daily at my gates, waiting at the posts of my doors.

35 For whoso finds me finds life, and shall obtain favor of the LORD.

36 But he that sins against me wrongs his own soul: all they that <u>hate</u> me love death. despise

CHAPTER 9

WISDOM has built her house, she has hewn out her seven pillars:

2 She has killed her beasts; she has mingled her wine; she has also furnished her table.

3 She has sent forth her maidens: she cries upon the highest places of the city,

4 Whoso *is* simple, let him turn in here: *as for* him that <u>want</u> understanding, she says to him, lacks

5 Come, eat of my bread, and drink of the wine *which* I have mingled.

6 Forsake the foolish, and live; and go in the way of understanding.

7 He that <u>reprove</u> a <u>scorner</u> gets to himself shame: and he that rebukes a wicked *man gets* himself a blot. corrects - mocker

8 Reprove not a <u>scorner</u>, less he <u>hate</u> you: rebuke a wise man, and he will love you. despise

9 Give *instruction* to a wise *man*, and he will be yet wiser: teach a just *man*, and he will increase in learning.

10 The <u>fear</u> of the LORD *is* the beginning of wisdom: and the knowledge of the holy *is* understanding. reverence

11 For by me your days shall be multiplied, and the years of your life shall be increased.

12 If you be wise, you shall be wise for yourself: but *if* you scorn, you alone shall bear *it*.

13 A foolish woman *is* clamorous: *she is* simple, and knows nothing.

14 For she sits at the door of her house, on a seat in the high places of the city,

15 To call <u>passengers</u> who go right on their ways: those passing

16 Whoso *is* <u>simple</u>, let him turn in here: and *as for* him that wants understanding, she says to him, naïve

17 Stolen waters are sweet, and bread *eaten* in secret is pleasant.

18 But he knows not that the dead *are* there; *and that* her guests *are* in the depths of <u>hell</u>. Sheol

CHAPTER 10

THE proverbs of Sol'o-mon. A wise son makes a glad father: but a foolish son *is* the heaviness of his mother.

2 Treasures of wickedness profit nothing: but righteousness delivers from death.

3 The LORD will not allow the soul of the righteous to famish: but He casts away the substance of the wicked.

4 He becomes poor that deals *with* a <u>slack</u> hand: but the hand of the diligent makes rich. negligent

5 He that gathers in summer *is* a wise son: *but* he that sleeps in harvest *is* a son that causes shame.

6 Blessings *are* upon the head of the just: but violence covers the mouth of the wicked.

7 The memory of the just *is* <u>blessed</u>: but the name of the wicked shall rot. a blessing

8 The wise in heart will receive commandments: but a <u>prating</u> fool shall fall. babbling

9 He that walks uprightly walks <u>surely</u>: but he that perverts his ways shall be known. securely

10 He that winks with the eye causes sorrow: but a prating fool shall fall.

11 The mouth of a righteous *man is* a well of life: but violence covers the mouth of the wicked.

12 <u>Hatred</u> stirs up strifes: but love covers all sins. 1 PET. 4:8 Disliking

13 In the lips of him that has understanding wisdom is found: but a rod *is* for the back of him that is void of understanding.

14 Wise *men* lay up knowledge: but the mouth of the foolish *is* near destruction.

15 The rich man's wealth *is* his strong city: the destruction of the poor *is* their poverty.

16 The labor of the righteous *tends* to life: the fruit of the wicked to sin.

17 He *is in* the way of life <u>that keeps</u> instruction: but he that refuses reproof errs. who heeds

18 He that hides <u>hatred</u> *with* lying lips, and he that utters a slander, *is* a fool. dislikes

19 In the multitude of words there wants not sin: but he that refrains his lips *is* wise.

20 The tongue of the just *is as* choice silver: the heart of the wicked *is* little worth.

21 The lips of the righteous feed many: but fools die for want of wisdom.

22 The blessing of the LORD, it make rich, and He adds no sorrow with it.

23 *It is* as sport to a fool to do mischief: but a man of understanding has wisdom.

24 The <u>fear</u> of the wicked, it shall come upon him: but the desire of the righteous shall be granted.   dread

25 As the whirlwind passes, so *is* the wicked no *more*: but the righteous *is* an everlasting foundation.

26 As vinegar to the teeth, and as smoke to the eyes, so *is* the sluggard to them that send him.

27 The <u>fear</u> of the LORD <u>prolongs</u> days: but the years of the wicked shall be shortened.   reverence - adds

28 The hope of the righteous *shall be* gladness: but the expectation of the wicked shall perish.

29 The way of the LORD *is* strength to the upright: but destruction *shall be* to the workers of iniquity.

30 The righteous shall never be removed: but the wicked shall not inhabit the earth.

31 The mouth of the just brings forth wisdom: but the <u>froward</u> tongue shall be cut out.   perverted

32 The lips of the righteous know what is acceptable: but the mouth of the wicked *speaks* <u>frowardness</u>.   perversion

CHAPTER 11

A FALSE balance *is* <u>abomination</u> to the LORD: but a just weight *is* His delight.   detestable

2 *When* pride comes, then comes shame: but with the lowly *is* wisdom.

3 The integrity of the upright shall guide them: but the perverseness of transgressors shall destroy them.

4 Riches profit not in the day of wrath: but righteousness delivers from death.

5 The righteousness of the perfect shall direct his way: but the wicked shall fall by his own wickedness.

6 The righteousness of the upright shall deliver them: but transgressors shall be taken in *their own* naughtiness.

7 When a wicked man dies, *his* expectation shall perish: and the hope of unjust *men* perishes.

8 The righteous is delivered out of trouble, and the wicked comes in his <u>stead</u>.   place

9 An hypocrite with *his* mouth destroys his neighbor: but through knowledge shall the just be delivered.

10 When it goes well with the righteous, the city rejoices: and when the wicked perish, *there is* shouting.

11 By the blessing of the upright the city is exalted: but it is overthrown by the mouth of the wicked.

12 He that <u>is void</u> of wisdom despises his neighbor: but a man of understanding holds his peace.   lacks

13 A <u>talebearer</u> reveals secrets: but he that is of a faithful spirit conceals the matter.   gossip

14 Where no <u>counsel</u> *is*, the people fall: but in the multitude of counselors *there is* safety.   guidance

15 He that is <u>surety</u> for a stranger shall <u>smart</u> *for it*: and he that <u>hates</u> suretyship is <u>sure</u>.   guarantee - suffer - despises - safe

16 A gracious woman retains honor: and strong *men* retain riches.

17 The merciful man does good to

his own soul: but *he that is* cruel troubles his own flesh.

18 The wicked works a deceitful work: but to him that sows righteousness *shall be* a sure reward.

19 As righteousness *tends* to life: so he that pursues evil *pursues it* to his own death.

20 They that are of a <u>froward</u> heart *are* <u>abomination</u> to the Lord: but *such as are* upright in *their* way *are* His delight.   perverse - detestable

21 *Though* hand *join* in hand, the wicked shall not be unpunished: but the seed of the righteous shall be delivered.

22 *As a* jewel of gold in a swine's snout, *so is* a fair woman which is without discretion.

23 The desire of the righteous *is* only good: *but* the expectation of the wicked *is* wrath.

24 There is that scatters, and yet increases; and *there is* that withholds more than is <u>meet</u>, but *it tends* to poverty.   justly due

25 The liberal soul shall be made fat: and he that waters shall be watered also himself.

26 He that withholds <u>corn</u>, the people shall curse him: but blessing *shall be* upon the head of him that sells *it*.   grain

27 He that diligently seeks good procures favor: but he that seeks mischief, it shall come to him.

28 He that trusts in his riches shall fall: but the righteous shall flourish as a branch.

29 He that troubles his own house

shall inherit the wind: and the fool *shall be* servant to the wise of heart.

30 The fruit of the righteous *is* a tree of life; and he that wins souls *is* wise.

31 Behold, the righteous shall be <u>recompensed</u> in the earth: much more the wicked and the sinner.

                  1 PET. 4:18   rewarded

CHAPTER 12

WHOSO loves instruction loves knowledge: but he that <u>hates</u> reproof *is* <u>brutish</u>.   despises - stupid

2 A good *man* obtains favor of the Lord: but a man of wicked <u>devices</u> will He condemn.   plans

3 A man shall not be established by wickedness: but the root of the righteous shall not be moved.

4 A virtuous woman *is* a crown to her husband: but she that makes ashamed *is* as rottenness in his bones.

5 The thoughts of the righteous *are* right: *but* the <u>counsels</u> of the wicked *are* deceit.   advice

6 The words of the wicked *are* to lie in wait for blood: but the mouth of the upright shall deliver them.

7 The wicked are overthrown, and *are* not: but the house of the righteous shall stand.

8 A man shall be commended according to his wisdom: but he that is of a perverse <u>heart</u> shall be despised.   mind

9 *He that is* despised, and has a servant, *is* better than he that honors himself, and lacks bread.

10 A righteous *man* regards the life

of his beast: but the tender mercies of the wicked *are* cruel.

11 He that tills his land shall be satisfied with bread: but he that follows vain *persons is* void of understanding.

12 The wicked desires the <u>net</u> of evil *men*: but the root of the righteous yields *fruit*.   plunder

13 The wicked is <u>snared</u> by the transgression of *his* lips: but the just shall come out of trouble.   trapped

14 A man shall be satisfied with good by the fruit of *his* mouth: and the recompence of a man's hands shall be rendered to him.

15 The way of a fool *is* right in his own eyes: but he that hearkens to counsel *is* wise.

16 A fool's wrath is presently known: but a prudent *man* covers shame.

17 *He that* speaks truth shows forth righteousness: but a false witness deceit.

18 There is that speaks like the piercings of a sword: but the tongue of the wise *is* health.

19 The lip of truth shall be established for ever: but a lying tongue *is* but for a moment.

20 Deceit *is* in the heart of them that imagine evil: but to the counselors of peace *is* joy.

21 There shall no evil happen to the just: but the wicked shall be filled with <u>mischief</u>.   trouble

22 Lying lips *are* <u>abomination</u> to the LORD: but they that deal truly *are* His delight.   detestable

23 A prudent man conceals knowledge: but the heart of fools proclaims foolishness.

24 The hand of the diligent shall bear rule: but the slothful shall be under tribute.

25 Heaviness in the heart of man makes it stoop: but a good word makes it glad.

26 The righteous *is* more excellent than his neighbor: but the way of the wicked seduces them.

27 The slothful *man* roasts not that which he took in hunting: but the <u>substance</u> of a diligent man *is* precious.   possessions

28 In the way of righteousness *is* life; and *in* the pathway *thereof there is* no death.

CHAPTER 13

A WISE son *hears* his father's instruction: but a scorner hears not rebuke.

2 A man shall eat good by the fruit of *his* mouth: but the soul of the transgressors *shall eat* violence.

3 He that keeps his mouth keeps his life: *but* he that opens wide his lips shall have destruction.

4 The soul of the sluggard desires, and *has* nothing: but the soul of the diligent shall be made fat.

5 A righteous *man* <u>hates</u> lying: but a wicked *man* is <u>loathsome</u>, and comes to shame.   despises - disgusting

6 Righteousness keeps *him that is* upright in the way: but wickedness overthrows the sinner.

7 There is that makes himself rich,

yet *has* nothing: *there is* that makes himself poor, yet *has* great riches.

8 The ransom of a man's life *are* his riches: but the poor hears not rebuke.

9 The light of the righteous rejoices: but the lamp of the wicked shall be put out.

10 Only by pride comes contention: but with the well advised *is* wisdom.

11 Wealth *gotten* by <u>vanity</u> shall be diminished: but he that gathers by labor shall increase. <small>fraud</small>

12 Hope deferred makes the heart sick: but *when* the desire comes, *it is* a tree of life.

13 Whoso despises the word shall be destroyed: but he that <u>fears</u> the commandment shall be rewarded. <small>respects</small>

14 The law of the wise *is* a fountain of life, to depart from the <u>snares</u> of death. <small>lures</small>

15 Good understanding gives favor: but the way of transgressors *is* hard.

16 Every prudent *man* deals with knowledge: but a fool <u>lays open</u> *his* folly. <small>exposes</small>

17 A wicked messenger falls into mischief: but a faithful ambassador *is* health.

18 Poverty and shame *shall be to* him that refuses instruction: but he that regards <u>reproof</u> shall be honored. <small>correction</small>

19 The desire accomplished is sweet to the soul: but *it is* <u>abomination</u> to fools to depart from evil. <small>detestable</small>

20 He that walks with wise *men* shall be wise: but a companion of fools shall be destroyed.

21 Evil pursues sinners: but to the righteous good shall be repaid.

22 A good *man* leaves an inheritance to his children's children: and the wealth of the sinner *is* laid up for the just.

23 Much food *is in* the <u>tillage</u> of the poor: but there is *that is* destroyed for want of judgment. <small>fallow ground</small>

24 He that spares his rod <u>hates</u> his son: but he that loves him chastens him <u>betimes</u>. <small>despises - diligently</small>

25 The righteous eats to the satisfying of his soul: but the belly of the wicked shall want.

CHAPTER 14

EVERY wise woman builds her house: but the foolish <u>plucks</u> it down with her hands. <small>tears</small>

2 He that walks in his uprightness <u>fears</u> the LORD: but *he that is* perverse in his ways despises Him. <small>reveres</small>

3 In the mouth of the foolish *is* a rod of pride: but the lips of the wise shall preserve them.

4 Where no oxen *are*, the crib *is* clean: but much increase *is* by the strength of the ox.

5 A faithful witness will not lie: but a false witness will utter lies.

6 A scorner seeks wisdom, and *find it* not: but knowledge *is* easy to him that understands.

7 Go from the presence of a foolish man, when you perceive not *in him* the <u>lips</u> of knowledge. <small>words</small>

8 The wisdom of the prudent is to understand his way: but the folly of fools *is* deceit.

9 Fools make a mock at sin: but among the righteous *there is* favor.

10 The heart knows its own bitterness; and a stranger does not <u>intermeddle with</u> its joy. _{share}

11 The house of the wicked shall be overthrown: but the tabernacle of the upright shall flourish.

12 There is a way which seems right to a man, but the end thereof *are* the ways of death.

13 Even in laughter the heart is sorrowful; and the end of that mirth *is* heaviness.

14 The backslider in heart shall be filled with its own ways: and a good man *shall be satisfied* from himself.

15 The simple believes every word: but the prudent *man* <u>looks well</u> to his going. _{gives thought}

16 A wise *man* <u>fears</u>, and departs from evil: but the fool rages, and is confident. _{is cautious}

17 *He that is* soon angry deals foolishly: and a man of wicked devices is hated.

18 The simple inherit folly: but the prudent are crowned with knowledge.

19 The evil bow before the good; and the wicked at the gates of the righteous.

20 The poor is <u>hated</u> even of his own neighbor: but the rich *has* many friends. _{despised}

21 He that despises his neighbor sins but he that has mercy on the poor, happy *is* he.

22 Do they not err that devise evil? but mercy and truth *shall be* to them that devise good.

23 In all labor there is profit: but the talk of the lips *tends* only to penury.

24 The crown of the wise *is* their riches: *but* the foolishness of fools *is* folly.

25 A true witness delivers souls: but a deceitful *witness* speaks lies.

26 In the <u>fear</u> of the LORD *is* strong confidence: and his children shall have a place of refuge. _{reverence}

27 The <u>fear</u> of the LORD *is* a fountain of life, to depart from the snares of death.

28 In the multitude of people *is* the king's honor: but in the want of people *is* the destruction of the prince.

29 *He that is* slow to anger *is* of great understanding: but *he that is* hasty of spirit exalts folly. _{JAMES 1:19}

30 A sound heart *is* the life of the flesh: but envy the rottenness of the bones.

31 He that oppresses the poor reproaches his Maker: but he that honors Him has mercy on the poor.

32 The wicked is driven away in his wickedness: but the righteous has hope in his death.

33 Wisdom rests in the heart of him that has understanding: but *that which is* in the midst of fools is made known.

34 Righteousness exalts a nation: but sin *is* a reproach to any people.

35 The king's favor *is* toward a wise servant: but his anger *is against* him that causes shame.

CHAPTER 15

A SOFT answer turns away anger: but grievous words stir up anger.

2 The tongue of the wise uses knowledge aright: but the mouth of fools pours out foolishness.

3 The eyes of the LORD *are* in every place, beholding the evil and the good.

4 A <u>wholesome</u> tongue *is a* tree of life: but <u>perverseness</u> therein *is* a breach in the spirit.   soothing - deceitfulness

5 A fool <u>despises</u> his father's instruction: but he that regards <u>reproof</u> is prudent.   spurns - correction

6 In the house of the righteous *is* much treasure: but in the revenues of the wicked is trouble.

7 The lips of the wise disperse knowledge: but the heart of the foolish *does* not so.

8 The sacrifice of the wicked *is* <u>an abomination</u> to the LORD: but the prayer of the upright *is* His delight.   detestable

9 The way of the wicked *is* <u>an abomination</u> to the LORD: but He loves him that follow after righteousness.

10 <u>Correction</u> *is* grievous to him that forsakes the way: *and* he that hates <u>reproof</u> shall die.   Stern discipline

11 Hell and destruction *are* before the LORD: how much more then the hearts of the children of men?

12 A scorner loves not one that reproves him: neither will he go to the wise.

13 A merry heart makes a cheerful countenance: but by sorrow of the heart the spirit is broken.

14 The heart of him that has understanding seeks knowledge: but the mouth of fools feeds on foolishness.

15 All the days of the afflicted *are* evil: but he that is of a merry heart *has* a continual feast.

16 Better *is* little with the <u>fear</u> of the LORD than great treasure and trouble therewith.   reverence

17 Better *is* a dinner of herbs where love is, than a <u>stalled</u> ox and <u>hatred</u> therewith.   fattened - emnity

18 A <u>wrathful</u> man stirs up strife: but *he that is* slow to anger appeases strife.   hot-tempered

19 The way of the <u>slothful</u> *man is* as an hedge of thorns: but the way of the righteous *is* made plain.   sluggard

20 A wise son makes a glad father: but a foolish man despises his mother.

21 Folly *is* joy to *him that is* destitute of wisdom: but a man of understanding walks uprightly.   EPH. 5:15

22 Without counsel purposes are disappointed: but in the multitude of counselors they are established.

23 A man has joy by the answer of his mouth: and a word *spoken* in due season, how good *is it!*

24 The way of life *is* above to the wise, that he may depart from hell beneath.

25 The LORD will destroy the house of the proud: but He will establish the border of the widow.

26 The thoughts of the wicked *are* <u>an abomination</u> to the LORD: but *the words* of the pure *are* pleasant words.   detestable

27 He that is greedy of gain troubles his own house; but he that <u>hates gifts</u> shall live.   despises - bribes

28 The heart of the righteous studies

to answer: but the mouth of the wicked pours out evil things.

29 The Lord *is* far from the wicked: but He hears the prayer of the righteous.

30 The light of the eyes rejoices the heart: *and* a good report makes the bones fat.

31 The ear that hears the reproof of life abides among the wise. correction

32 He that refuses instruction despises his own soul: but he that hears reproof gets understanding. heeds

33 The fear of the Lord *is* the instruction of wisdom; and before honor *is* humility. reverence

CHAPTER 16

THE preparations of the heart in man, and the answer of the tongue, *is* from the Lord. inclinations

2 All the ways of a man *are* clean in his own eyes; but the Lord weighs the spirits. motives

3 Commit your works to the Lord, and your thoughts shall be established.

4 The Lord has made all *things* for Himself: yea, even the wicked for the day of evil. ROM. 9:22

5 Every one *that is* proud in heart *is* an abomination to the Lord: *though* hand *join* in hand, he shall not be unpunished. detestable

6 By mercy and truth iniquity is purged: and by the fear of the Lord *men* depart from evil. atoned for - reverence

7 When a man's ways please the Lord, He makes even his enemies to be at peace with him.

8 Better *is* a little with righteousness than great revenues without right.

9 A man's heart devises his way: but the Lord directs his steps. plans

10 A divine sentence *is* in the lips of the king: His mouth transgresses not in judgment. decision

11 A just weight and balance *are* the Lord's: all the weights of the bag *are* His work. concern

12 *It is* an abomination to kings to commit wickedness: for the throne is established by righteousness. detestable

13 Righteous lips *are* the delight of kings; and they love him that speaks right.

14 The anger of a king *is as* messengers of death: but a wise man will pacify it.

15 In the light of the king's countenance *is* life; and his favor *is* as a cloud of the latter rain.

16 How much better *is it* to get wisdom than gold! and to get understanding rather to be chosen than silver!

17 The highway of the upright *is* to depart from evil: he that keeps his way preserves his soul.

18 Pride *goes* before destruction, and an haughty spirit before a fall.

19 Better *it is to be* of an humble spirit with the lowly, than to divide the spoil with the proud.

20 He that handles a matter wisely shall find good: and whoso trusts in the Lord, happy *is* he.

21 The wise in heart shall be called prudent: and the sweetness of the lips increases learning.

22 Understanding *is* a wellspring of

life to him that has it: but the instruction of fools *is* folly.

23 The heart of the wise teaches his mouth, and adds learning to his lips.

24 Pleasant words *are as* an honeycomb, sweet to the soul, and health to the bones.

25 There is a way that seems right to a man, but the end thereof *are* the ways of death.

26 He that labors for himself; for his mouth craves it of him.

27 An ungodly man digs up evil: and in his lips *there is* as a burning fire.

28 A underline:froward man sows strife: and a whisperer separates chief friends.   perverse

29 A violent man entices his neighbor, and leads him into the way *that is* not good.

30 He shuts his eyes to devise froward things: moving his lips he brings evil to pass.

31 The hoary head *is* a crown of glory, *if* it be found in the way of righteousness.   A gray

32 *He that is* slow to anger *is* better than the mighty; and he that rules his spirit than he that takes a city.

33 The lot is cast into the lap; but the whole disposing thereof *is* of the LORD.

CHAPTER 17

BETTER *is* a dry morsel, and quietness therewith, than an house full of sacrifices *with* strife.

2 A wise servant shall have rule over a son that causes shame, and shall have part of the inheritance among the brethren.

3 The fining pot *is* for silver, and the furnace for gold: but the LORD tries the hearts.   refining - tests

4 A wicked doer gives heed to false lips; *and* a liar gives ear to a naughty tongue.

5 Whoso mocks the poor reproaches his Maker: *and* he that is glad at calamities shall not be unpunished.

6 Children's children *are* the crown of old men; and the glory of children *are* their fathers.

7 Excellent speech becomes not a fool: much less do lying lips a prince.

8 A gift *is as* a precious stone in the eyes of him that has it: where it turns, it prospers.

9 He that covers a transgression seeks love; but he that repeats a matter separates *very* friends.

10 A reproof enters more into a wise man than an hundred stripes into a fool.   correction

11 An evil *man* seeks only rebellion: therefore a cruel messenger shall be sent against him.

12 Let a bear robbed of her whelps meet a man, rather than a fool in his folly.

13 Whoso rewards evil for good, evil shall not depart from his house.

14 The beginning of strife *is as* when one lets out water: therefore leave off contention, before it be meddled with.

15 He that justifies the wicked, and he that condemns the just, even they both *are* abomination to the LORD.   detestable

16 Why *is there* a price in the

hand of a fool to get wisdom, seeing *he has* no heart *to it?*

17 A friend loves at all times, and a brother is born for adversity.

18 A man <u>void</u> of understanding <u>strikes hands,</u> *and* becomes <u>surety</u> in the presence of his friend.

empty - pledges - security

19 He loves transgression that loves strife: *and* he that exalts his gate seeks destruction.

20 He that has a <u>froward</u> heart finds no good: and he that has a <u>perverse</u> tongue falls into mischief.

crooked - deceitful

21 He that fathers a fool *does it* to his sorrow: and the father of a fool has no joy.

22 A merry heart does good *like* a medicine: but a broken spirit dries the bones.

23 A wicked *man* takes a gift out of the bosom to pervert the ways of judgment.

24 Wisdom *is* before him that has understanding; but the eyes of a fool *are* in the ends of the earth.

25 A foolish son *is* a grief to his father, and bitterness to her that bare him.

26 Also to punish the just *is* not good, *nor* to strike princes for equity.

27 He that has knowledge spares his words: *and* a man of understanding is of an excellent spirit.

28 Even a fool, when he holds his peace, is counted wise: *and* he that shuts his lips *is esteemed* a man of understanding.

CHAPTER 18

THROUGH desire a man, having separated himself, seeks *and* <u>meddles</u> with all wisdom. quarrels

2 A fool has no delight in understanding, but that his heart may discover itself.

3 When the wicked comes, *then* comes also contempt, and with ignominy reproach.

4 The words of a man's mouth *are as* deep waters, *and* the wellspring of wisdom *as* a flowing brook.

5 *It is* not good to accept the person of the wicked, to overthrow the righteous in judgment.

6 A fool's lips enter into contention, and his mouth calls for <u>strokes.</u>

blows

7 A fool's mouth *is* his destruction, and his lips *are* the snare of his soul.

8 The words of a talebearer *are* as wounds, and they go down into the innermost parts of the belly.

9 He also that is slothful in his work is brother to him that is a great waster.

10 The name of the LORD *is* a strong tower: the righteous runs into it, and is safe.

11 The rich man's wealth *is* his strong city, and as an high wall in his own conceit.

12 Before destruction the heart of man is haughty, and before honor *is* humility.

13 He that answer a matter before he hears *it*, it *is* folly and shame to him.

14 The spirit of a man will <u>sustain</u> his

infirmity; but a wounded spirit who can bear? _{endure}

15 The heart of the prudent gets knowledge; and the ear of the wise seeks knowledge.

16 A man's gift makes room for him, and brings him before great men.

17 *He that is* first in his own cause *seems* just; but his neighbor comes and <u>searches</u> him. _{questions}

18 The lot causes contentions to cease, and parts between the mighty.

19 A brother offended *is harder to be won* than a strong city: and *their* contentions *are* like the bars of a castle.

20 A man's belly shall be satisfied with the fruit of his mouth; *and* with the increase of his lips shall he be filled.

21 Death and life *are* in the power of the tongue: and they that love it shall eat the fruit thereof.

22 *Whoso* finds a wife finds a good *thing*, and obtains favor of the LORD.

23 The poor uses entreaties; but the rich answers roughly.

24 A man *that has* friends must show himself friendly: and there is a friend *that* sticks closer than a brother.

CHAPTER 19

BETTER *is* the poor that walks in his integrity, than *he that is* <u>perverse</u> in his <u>lips</u>, and is a fool. _{deceitful - speech}

2 Also, *that* the soul *be* without knowledge, *it is* not good; and he that hastens with *his* feet sins.

3 The foolishness of man <u>perverts</u> his way: and his heart <u>frets</u> against the LORD. _{ruins - rages}

4 Wealth makes many friends; but the poor is separated from his neighbor.

5 A false witness shall not be unpunished, and *he that* speaks lies shall not escape.

6 Many will entreat the favor of the prince: and every man *is* a friend to him that gives gifts.

7 All the brethren of the poor do <u>hate</u> him: how much more do his friends go far from him? he pursues *them with* words, *yet* they *are* wanting *to him*. _{despise}

8 He that gets wisdom loves his own soul: he that keeps understanding shall find good.

9 A false witness shall not be unpunished, and *he that* speaks lies shall perish.

10 Delight is not <u>seemly</u> for a fool; much less for a servant to have rule over princes. _{fitting}

11 The <u>discretion</u> of a man defers his anger; and *it is* his glory to pass over a transgression. _{wisdom}

12 The king's anger *is* as the roaring of a lion; but his favor *is* as dew upon the grass.

13 A foolish son *is* the calamity of his father: and the contentions of a wife *are* a continual dropping.

14 House and riches *are* the inheritance of fathers: and a prudent wife *is* from the LORD.

15 <u>Slothfulness</u> casts into a deep sleep; and an idle soul shall suffer hunger. _{Laziness}

16 He that keeps the commandment keeps his own soul; *but* he that despises his ways shall die.

17 He that has pity upon the poor

lends to the LORD; and that which he has given will He pay him again.

MATT. 25:40

18 Chasten your son while there is hope, and let not your soul spare for his crying.

19 A man of great anger shall suffer punishment: for if you deliver *him*, yet you must do it again.

20 Hear counsel, and receive instruction, that you may be wise in your latter end.

21 *There are* many devices in a man's heart; nevertheless the counsel of the LORD, that shall stand. plans - purpose

22 The desire of a man *is* his kindness: and a poor man *is* better than a liar.

23 The fear of the LORD *tends* to life: and *he that has it* shall abide satisfied; he shall not be visited with evil.

reverence

24 A slothful *man* hides his hand in *his* bosom, and will not so much as bring it to his mouth again. lazy

25 Smite a scorner, and the simple will beware: and reprove one that has understanding, *and* he will understand knowledge. learn

26 He that wastes *his* father, *and* chases away *his* mother, *is* a son that causes shame, and brings reproach.

27 Cease, my son, to hear the instruction *that causes* to err from the words of knowledge.

28 An ungodly witness scorns judgment: and the mouth of the wicked devours iniquity.

29 Judgments are prepared for scorners, and stripes for the back of fools.

CHAPTER 20

WINE *is* a mocker, strong drink *is* raging: and whosoever is deceived thereby is not wise.

2 The fear of a king *is* as the roaring of a lion: *whoso* provokes him to anger sins *against* his own soul. terror

3 *It is* an honor for a man to cease from strife: but every fool will be meddling.

4 The sluggard will not plow by reason of the cold; *therefore* shall he beg in harvest, and *have* nothing.

5 Counsel in the heart of man *is like* deep water; but a man of understanding will draw it out.

6 Most men will proclaim every one his own goodness: but a faithful man who can find?

7 The just *man* walks in his integrity: his children *are* blessed after him.

8 A king that sits in the throne of judgment scatters away all evil with his eyes. disperses

9 Who can say, I have made my heart clean, I am pure from my sin?

10 Divers weights, *and* divers measures, both of them *are* alike abomination to the LORD. Differing - detestable

11 Even a child is known by his doings, whether his work *be* pure, and whether *it be* right.

12 The hearing ear, and the seeing eye, the LORD has made even both of them.

13 Love not sleep, less you come to poverty; open your eyes, *and* you shall be satisfied with bread.

14 *It is* <u>naught</u>, *it is* <u>naught</u>, says the buyer: but when he is gone his way, then he boasts.   no good

15 There is gold, and a multitude of rubies: but the <u>lips</u> of knowledge *are* a precious jewel.   thoughts

16 Take his garment that is surety *for* a stranger: and take a pledge of him for a strange woman.

17 Bread of deceit *is* sweet to a man; but afterwards his mouth shall be filled with gravel.

18 *Every* purpose is established by counsel: and with good advice make war.

19 He that goes about *as* a tale-bearer reveals secrets: therefore meddle not with him that flatters with his lips.

20 Whoso curses his father or his mother, his lamp shall be put out in obscure darkness.

21 An inheritance *may be* gotten hastily at the beginning; but the end thereof shall not be blessed.

22 Say not you, I will recompense evil; *but* wait on the LORD, and He shall save you.   ROM. 12:17

23 <u>Divers</u> weights *are* <u>an abomination</u> to the LORD; and a false balance *is* not good.   Differing - detestable

24 Man's goings *are* of the LORD; how can a man then understand his own way?

25 *It is* a <u>snare</u> to the man *who* devours *that which is* holy, and after vows to make enquiry.   trap

26 A wise king scatters the wicked, and brings the wheel over them.

27 The spirit of man is the candle of the LORD, searching all the inward parts of the belly.

28 Mercy and truth preserve the king: and his throne is upholden by mercy.

29 The glory of young men *is* their strength: and the beauty of old men *is* the gray head.

30 The blueness of a wound cleans away evil: so *do* stripes the inward parts of the belly.

CHAPTER 21

THE king's heart *is* in the hand of the LORD, *as* the rivers of water: He turns it wherever He will.

2 Every way of a man *is* right in his own eyes: but the LORD ponders the hearts.

3 To do justice and judgment *is* more acceptable to the LORD than sacrifice.

4 An high look, and a proud heart, *and* the plowing of the wicked, *is* sin.

5 The thoughts of the diligent *tend* only to plenteousness; but of every one *that is* hasty only to want.

6 The getting of treasures by a lying tongue *is* a vanity tossed to and fro of them that seek death.

7 The robbery of the wicked shall destroy them; because they refuse to do judgment.

8 The way of man *is* <u>froward</u> and strange: but *as for* the pure, his work *is* right.   perverse

9 *It is* better to dwell in a corner of the housetop, than with a brawling woman in a wide house.

10 The soul of the wicked desires

evil: his neighbor finds no favor in his eyes.

11 When the scorner is punished, the simple is made wise: and when the wise is instructed, he receives knowledge.

12 The righteous *man* wisely considers the house of the wicked: *but God* overthrows the wicked for *their* wickedness.

13 Whoso stops his ears at the cry of the poor, he also shall cry himself, but shall not be heard.

14 A gift in secret pacifies anger: and a reward in the bosom strong wrath.

15 *It is* joy to the just to do judgment: but destruction *shall be* to the workers of iniquity.

16 The man that wanders out of the way of understanding shall remain in the congregation of the dead.

17 He that loves pleasure *shall be* a poor man: he that loves wine and oil shall not be rich.

18 The wicked *shall be* a ransom for the righteous, and the transgressor for the upright.

19 *It is* better to dwell in the wilderness, than with a contentious and an angry woman.

20 *There is* treasure to be desired and oil in the dwelling of the wise; but a foolish man spends it up.

21 He that follows after righteousness and mercy finds life, righteousness, and honor.

22 A wise *man* scales the city of the mighty, and casts down the strength of the confidence thereof.

23 Whoso keeps his mouth and his tongue keeps his soul from troubles.

24 Proud *and* haughty scorner *is* his name, who deals in proud anger.

25 The desire of the slothful kills him; for his hands refuse to labor.

26 He covets greedily all the day long: but the righteous gives and spares not.

27 The sacrifice of the wicked *is* abomination: how much more, *when* he brings it with a wicked mind? detestable

28 A false witness shall perish: but the man that hears speaks constantly.

29 A wicked man hardens his face: but *as for* the upright, he directs his way.

30 *There is* no wisdom nor understanding nor counsel against the LORD.

31 The horse *is* prepared against the day of battle: but safety *is* of the LORD.

CHAPTER 22

A GOOD name *is* rather to be chosen than great riches, *and* loving favor rather than silver and gold.

2 The rich and poor meet together: the LORD *is* the maker of them all.

3 A prudent *man* foresees the evil, and hides himself: but the simple pass on, and are punished.

4 By humility *and* the fear of the LORD *are* riches, and honor, and life. The reward of - reverence

5 Thorns *and* snares *are* in the way of the froward: he that does keep his soul shall be far from them. traps - perverse

6 Train up a child in the way he

should go: and when he is old, he will not depart from it. EPH. 6:4

7 The rich rules over the poor, and the borrower *is* servant to the lender.

8 He that sows iniquity shall reap vanity: and the rod of his anger shall fail.

9 He that has a bountiful eye shall be blessed; for he gives of his bread to the poor.

10 Cast out the scorner, and contention shall go out; yea, strife and reproach shall cease.

11 He that loves pureness of heart, *for* the grace of his lips the king *shall be* his friend. good will

12 The eyes of the LORD preserve knowledge, and He overthrows the words of the transgressor.

13 The slothful *man* says, *There is* a lion without, I shall be slain in the streets. lazy

14 The mouth of strange women *is* a deep pit: he that is abhorred of the LORD shall fall therein.

15 Foolishness *is* bound in the heart of a child; *but* the rod of correction shall drive it far from him.

16 He that oppresses the poor to increase his *riches, and* he that gives to the rich, *shall* surely *come* to want.

17 Bow down your ear, and hear the words of the wise, and apply your heart to my knowledge.

18 For *it is* a pleasant thing if you keep them within you; they shall with be fitted in your lips.

19 That your trust may be in the LORD, I have made known to you this day, even to you. especially

20 Have not I written to you excellent things in counsels and knowledge,

21 That I might make you know the certainty of the words of truth; that you might answer the words of truth to them that send to you?

22 Rob not the poor, because he *is* poor: neither oppress the afflicted in the gate:

23 For the LORD will plead their cause, and spoil the soul of those that spoiled them.

24 Make no friendship with an angry man; and with a furious man you shall not go: hot-tempered

25 Less you learn his ways, and get a snare to your soul. trap - yourself

26 Be not you *one* of them that strike hands, *or* of them that are sureties for debts. give pledges - guarantees

27 If you have nothing to pay, why should he take away your bed from under you?

28 Remove not the ancient landmark, which your fathers have set.

29 See you a man diligent in his business? he shall stand before kings; he shall not stand before mean *men*. obscure

CHAPTER 23

WHEN you sit to eat with a ruler, consider diligently what *is* before you:

2 And put a knife to your throat, if you *be* a man given to appetite.

3 Be not desirous of his dainties: for they *are* deceitful meat. delicacies

4 Labor not to be rich: cease from your own wisdom.

5 Will you set your eyes upon that which is not? for *riches* certainly make themselves wings; they fly away as an eagle toward heaven.

6 Eat you not the bread of *him that has* an evil eye, neither desire you his dainty meats: delicacies

7 For as he thinks in his heart, so *is* he: Eat and drink, says he to you; but his heart *is* not with you.

8 The morsel *which* you have eaten shall you vomit up, and lose your sweet words.

9 Speak not in the ears of a fool: for he will despise the wisdom of your words.

10 Remove not the old landmark; and enter not into the fields of the fatherless:

11 For their redeemer *is* mighty; He shall plead their cause with you.

12 Apply your heart to instruction, and your ears to the words of knowledge.

13 Withhold not correction from the child: for *if* you beat him with the rod, he shall not die.

14 You shall beat him with the rod, and shall deliver his soul from hell.

15 My son, if your heart be wise, my heart shall rejoice, even mine.

16 Yea, my reins shall rejoice, when your lips speak right things. inmost being

17 Let not your heart envy sinners: but *be you* in the fear of the LORD all the day long. reverence

18 For surely there is an end; and your expectation shall not be cut off.

19 Hear you, my son, and be wise, and guide your heart in the way.

20 Be not among winebibbers; among riotous eaters of flesh:

21 For the drunkard and the glutton shall come to poverty: and drowsiness shall clothe *a man* with rags.

22 Hearken to your father that fathered you, and despise not your mother when she is old. Listen

23 Buy the truth, and sell *it* not; *also* wisdom, and instruction, and understanding.

24 The fathers of the righteous shall greatly rejoice: and he that fathers a wise *child* shall have joy of him.

25 Your father and your mother shall be glad, and she that bare you shall rejoice.

26 My son, give me your heart, and let your eyes observe my ways.

27 For a whore *is* a deep ditch; and a strange woman *is* a narrow pit. prostitute - adulterous

28 She also lies in wait as *for* a prey, and increases the transgressors among men.

29 Who has woe? who has sorrow? who has contentions? who has babbling? who has wounds without cause? who has redness of eyes?

30 They that tarry long at the wine; they that go to seek mixed wine.

31 Look not you upon the wine when it is red, when it gives its color in the cup, *when* it moves itself aright.

32 At the last it bites like a serpent, and stings like an adder.

33 Your eyes shall behold strange women, and your heart shall utter perverse things. adulterous - mind

34 Yea, you shall be as he that lies

down in the midst of the sea, or as
he that lies upon the top of a mast.
35 They have stricken me, *shall you
say, and* I was not sick; they have
beaten me, *and* I felt *it* not: when shall
I awake? I will seek it yet again.

CHAPTER 24

BE not you envious against evil
men, neither desire to be with them.
2 For their heart studies destruction, and their lips talk of mischief.   thoughts
3 Through wisdom is an house
builded; and by understanding it
is established:
4 And by knowledge shall the
chambers be filled with all precious
and pleasant riches.
5 A wise man *is* strong; yea, a man
of knowledge increases strength.
6 For by wise counsel you shall
make your war: and in multitude of
counselors *there is* safety.
7 Wisdom *is* too high for a fool: he
opens not his mouth in the gate.
8 He that devises to do evil shall be
called a mischievous person.
9 The thought of foolishness *is*
sin: and the scorner *is* an abomination to men.   detestable
10 *If* you faint in the day of adversity, your strength *is* small.   are lazy
11 If you forbear to deliver *them
that are* drawn to death, and *those
that are* ready to be slain;
12 If you say, Behold, we knew it not;
does not he that ponders the heart consider *it*? and he that keeps your
soul, does *not* he know *it*? and shall

not he render to *every* man according to his works?
13 My son, eat you honey, because
it is good; and the honeycomb,
which is sweet to your taste:
14 So *shall* the knowledge of wisdom
be to your soul: when you have found
it, then there shall be a reward, and
your expectation shall not be cut off.
15 Lay not wait, O wicked *man*,
against the dwelling of the righteous;
spoil not his resting place: destroy
16 For a just *man* falls seven times,
and rises up again: but the wicked
shall fall into mischief.
17 Rejoice not when your enemy falls,
and let not your heart be glad when
he stumbles:
18 Less the LORD *see it*, and it displease Him, and He turn away His
wrath from him.
19 Fret not yourself because of evil
men, neither be you envious at the
wicked;
20 For there shall be no reward to
the evil *man*; the candle of the
wicked shall be put out.
21 My son, fear you the LORD and
the king: *and* meddle not with them
that are given to change: reverence
22 For their calamity shall rise suddenly; and who knows the ruin of
them both?
23 These *things* also *belong* to the
wise. *It is* not good to have respect
of persons in judgment.
24 He that says to the wicked, you
are righteous; him shall the people
curse, nations shall abhor him:
25 But to them that rebuke *him* shall

be delight, and a good blessing shall come upon them.

26 *Every man* shall <u>kiss</u> *his* lips that gives a right answer. praise

27 Prepare your work without, and make it fit for yourself in the field; and afterwards build your house.

28 Be not a witness against your neighbor without cause; and deceive *not* with your lips.

29 Say not, I will do so to him as he has done to me: I will render to the man according to his work.

M29 - - 974

30 I went by the field of the slothful, and by the vineyard of the man <u>void</u> of understanding; lacking

31 And, lo, it was all grown over with thorns, *and* nettles had covered the face thereof, and the stone wall thereof was broken down.

32 Then I saw, *and* considered *it* well: I looked upon *it, and* received instruction.

33 *Yet* a little sleep, a little slumber, a little folding of the hands to sleep:

34 So shall your poverty come *as* <u>one that travels</u>; and your want as an armed man. a vagabond

CHAPTER 25

THESE *are* also proverbs of Sol'o-mon, which the men of Hez-e-ki'ah king of Ju'dah copied out.

2 *It is* the glory of <u>God</u> to conceal a thing: but the honor of kings *is* to search out a matter. Elohim p-f

3 The heaven for height, and the earth for depth, and the heart of kings *is* unsearchable.

4 Take away the dross from the silver, and there shall come forth a vessel for the <u>finer</u>. refiner

5 Take away the wicked *from* before the king, and his throne shall be established in righteousness.

6 <u>Put not forth</u> yourself in the presence of the king, and stand not in the place of great *men*: Do not exalt

7 For better *it is* that it be said to you, Come up here; than that you should be put lower in the presence of the prince whom your eyes have seen. LUKE 14:8

8 Go not forth hastily to strive, less *you know not* what to do in the end thereof, when your neighbor has put you to shame.

M37 - 975

9 Debate your cause with your neighbor *himself*; and <u>discover</u> not a secret to another: betray

10 Less he that hears *it* put you to shame, and your infamy turn not away.

11 A word fitly spoken *is like* apples of gold in pictures of silver.

12 *As* an earring of gold, and an ornament of fine gold, *so is* a wise reprover upon an obedient ear.

13 As the cold of snow in the time of harvest, *so is* a faithful messenger to them that send him: for he refreshes the soul of his masters.

14 Whoso boasts himself of a false gift *is like* clouds and wind without rain.

15 By <u>long forbearing</u> is a prince persuaded, and a soft tongue breaks the bone. patience

16 Have you found honey? eat so

much as is sufficient for you, less you be filled therewith, and vomit it.

17 Withdraw your foot from your neighbor's house; less he be weary of you, and *so* hate you. despise

18 A man that bears false witness against his neighbor *is* a maul, and a sword, and a sharp arrow. club

19 Confidence in an unfaithful man in time of trouble *is like* a broken tooth, and a foot out of joint.

20 *As* he that takes away a garment in cold weather, *and as* vinegar upon nitre, so *is* he that sings songs to an heavy heart. soda

21 If your enemy be hungry, give him bread to eat; and if he be thirsty, give him water to drink:

22 For you shall heap coals of fire upon his head, and the LORD shall reward you. ROM. 12:20

23 The north wind drives away rain: so *does* an angry countenance a backbiting tongue.

24 *It is* better to dwell in the corner of the housetop, than with a brawling woman and in a wide house.

25 *As* cold waters to a thirsty soul, so *is* good news from a far country.

26 A righteous man falling down before the wicked *is as* a troubled fountain, and a corrupt spring.

27 *It is* not good to eat much honey: so *for men* to search their own glory *is not* glory.

28 He that *has* no rule over his own spirit *is like* a city *that is* broken down, *and* without walls.

CHAPTER 26

AS snow in summer, and as rain in harvest, so honor is not seemly for a fool. fitting

2 As the bird by wandering, as the swallow by flying, so the curse causeless shall not come.

3 A whip for the horse, a bridle for the ass, and a rod for the fool's back.

4 Answer not a fool according to his folly, less you also be like to him.

5 Answer a fool according to his folly, less he be wise in his own conceit.

6 He that sends a message by the hand of a fool cuts off the feet, *and* drinks damage.

7 The legs of the lame are not equal: so *is* a parable in the mouth of fools.

8 As he that binds a stone in a sling, so *is* he that gives honor to a fool.

9 *As* a thorn goes up into the hand of a drunkard, so *is* a parable in the mouth of fools.

10 The great *God* that formed all *things* both rewards the fool, and rewards transgressors.

11 As a dog returns to its vomit, *so* a fool returns to his folly.
2 PET. 2:22

12 See you a man wise in his own conceit? *there is* more hope of a fool than of him.

13 The slothful *man* says, *There is* a lion in the way; a lion *is* in the streets. lazy

14 *As* the door turns upon its hinges, so *does* the slothful upon his bed.

15 The slothful hides his hand in *his*

bosom; it grieves him to bring it again to his mouth. _{lazy}

16 The <u>sluggard</u> *is* wiser in his own conceit than seven men that can render a reason. _{lazy}

17 He that passes by, *and* meddles with strife *belonging* not to him, *is like* one that takes a dog by the ears.

18 As a mad *man* who casts firebrands, arrows, and death,

19 So *is* the man *that* deceives his neighbor, and says, Am not I <u>in sport</u>? _{joking}

20 Where no wood is, *there* the fire goes out: so where *there is* no <u>talebearer</u>, the strife ceases. _{gossip}

21 *As* coals *are* to burning coals, and wood to fire; so *is* a contentious man to kindle strife.

22 The words of a talebearer *are* as wounds, and they go down into the innermost parts of the belly.

23 Burning lips and a wicked heart *are like* a <u>potsherd</u> covered with silver dross. _{earthen vessel}

24 He that <u>hates dissembles</u> with his lips, and lays up deceit within him; _{despises - disguises it}

25 When he speaks fair, believe him not: for *there are* seven <u>abominations</u> in his heart. _{detestable things}

26 *Whose* <u>hatred</u> is covered by deceit, his wickedness shall be showed before the *whole* congregation. _{malice}

27 Whoso digs a pit shall fall therein: and he that rolls a stone, it will return upon him.

28 A lying tongue <u>hates</u> *those that are* afflicted by it; and a flattering mouth works ruin.

CHAPTER 27

BOAST not yourself of to morrow; for you know not what a day may bring forth.

2 Let another man praise you, and not your own mouth; a stranger, and not your own lips.

3 A stone *is* heavy, and the sand weighty; but a fool's anger *is* heavier than them both.

4 Anger *is* cruel, and <u>anger</u> *is* outrageous; but who *is* able to stand before envy? _{fury}

5 Open rebuke *is* better than secret love.

6 Faithful *are* the wounds of a friend; but the kisses of an enemy *are* deceitful.

7 The full soul loaths an honeycomb; but to the hungry soul every bitter thing is sweet.

8 As a bird that wanders from her nest, so *is* a man that wanders from his place.

9 Ointment and perfume rejoice the heart: so *does* the sweetness of a man's friend by hearty counsel.

10 Your own friend, and your father's friend, forsake not; neither go into your brother's house in the day of your calamity: *for* better *is* a neighbor *that is* near than a brother far off.

11 My son, be wise, and make my heart glad, that I may answer him that reproaches me.

12 A prudent *man* foresees the evil, *and* hides himself; *but* the <u>simple</u> pass on, *and* are punished. _{naive}

13 Take his garment that is <u>surety</u> for

a stranger, and take a pledge of him for a <u>strange</u> woman.   guarantee - adulteress

14 He that blesses his friend with a loud voice, rising early in the morning, it shall be counted a curse to him.

15 A continual dropping in a very rainy day and a contentious woman are alike.

16 Whosoever <u>hides</u> her <u>hides</u> the wind, and the ointment of his right hand, *which* <u>bewrays</u> *itself.*   restrain - betrays

17 Iron sharpens iron; so a man sharpens the countenance of his friend.

18 Whoso <u>keeps</u> the fig tree shall eat the fruit thereof: so he that waits on his master shall be honored.   tends

19 As in water face *answers* to face, so the heart of man to man.   reflects

20 Hell and destruction are never full; so the eyes of man are never satisfied.

21 *As* the fining pot for silver, and the furnace for gold; so *is* a man to his praise.

22 Though you should <u>bray</u> a fool in a mortar among <u>wheat</u> with a pestle, *yet* will not his foolishness depart from him.   grind - grain

23 Be you diligent to know the state of your flocks, *and* look well to your herds.

24 For riches *are* not for ever: and does the crown *endure* to every generation?

25 The hay appears, and the tender grass shows itself, and herbs of the mountains are gathered.

26 The lambs *are* for your clothing, and the goats *are* the price of the field.

27 And *you shall have* goats' milk enough for your food, for the food of your household, and *for* the <u>maintenance</u> for your maidens.   nourishment

CHAPTER 28

THE wicked flee when no man pursues: but the righteous are bold as a lion.

2 For the transgression of a land many *are* the princes thereof: but by a man of understanding *and* knowledge the state *thereof* shall be prolonged.

3 A poor man that oppresses the poor *is like* a sweeping rain which leaves no food.

4 They that forsake the law praise the wicked: but such as keep the law contend with them.

5 Evil men understand not judgment: but they that seek the LORD understand all *things.*

6 Better *is* the poor that walks in his uprightness, than *he that is* perverse *in his* ways, though he *be* rich.

7 Whoso keeps the law *is* a wise son: but he that is a companion of <u>riotous *men*</u> shames his father.   gluttons

8 He that by usury and unjust gain increases his substance, he shall gather it for him that will pity the poor.

9 He that turns away his ear from hearing the law, even his prayer *shall be* abomination.

10 Whoso causes the righteous to go astray in an evil way, he shall fall himself into his own pit: but the upright shall have good *things* in possession.

11 The rich man *is* wise in his own conceit; but the poor that has understanding searches him out.

12 When righteous *men* do rejoice, there is great glory: but when the wicked rise, a man is hidden.

13 He that covers his sins shall not prosper: but whoso confesses and forsakes *them* shall have mercy.

14 Happy *is* the man that <u>fears</u> always: but he that hardens his heart shall fall into mischief.　is respectful

15 *As* a roaring lion, and a ranging bear; *so is* a wicked ruler over the poor people.

16 The prince that <u>wants</u> understanding *is* also a great oppressor: *but* he that <u>hates</u> covetousness shall prolong *his* days.　lacks - abhors

17 A man that does violence to the blood of *any* person shall flee <u>to the pit</u>; let no man <u>stay</u> him.　until death - support

18 Whoso walks uprightly shall be saved: but *he that is* <u>perverse</u> *in his* ways shall fall at once.　crooked

19 He that tills his land shall have plenty of bread: but he that follows after vain *persons* shall have poverty enough.　works

20 A faithful man shall abound with blessings: but he that makes haste to be rich shall not be innocent.

21 To have respect of persons *is* not good: for for a piece of bread *that* man will transgress.

22 He that hastens to be rich *has* an evil eye, and considers not that poverty shall come upon him.

23 He that rebukes a man afterwards shall find more favor than he that flatters with the tongue.

24 Whoso robs his father or his mother, and says, *It is* no transgression; the same *is* the companion of a destroyer.

25 He that is of a proud heart stirs up strife: but he that puts his trust in the LORD shall be made fat.

26 He that trusts in his own heart is a fool: but whoso walks wisely, he shall be delivered.

27 He that gives to the poor shall not lack: but he that hides his eyes shall have many a curse.

28 When the wicked rise, men hide themselves: but when they perish, the righteous increase.

CHAPTER 29

HE, that being often <u>reproved</u> hardens *his* neck, shall suddenly be destroyed, and that without remedy.　corrected

2 When the righteous are in authority, the people rejoice: but when the wicked bears rule, the people mourn.

3 Whoso loves wisdom rejoices his father: but he that keeps company with harlots spends *his* substance.

4 The king by judgment establishes the land: but he that receives gifts overthrows it.

5 A man that flatters his neighbor spreads a net for his feet.

6 In the transgression of an evil man *there is* a <u>snare</u>: but the righteous does sing and rejoice.　trap

7 The righteous considers the cause of the poor: *but* the wicked regards not to know *it*.

8 Scornful men bring a city into a <u>snare</u>: but wise *men* turn away anger.

9 *If* a wise man contends with a foolish man, whether he rage or laugh, *there is* no rest.

10 The bloodthirsty <u>hate</u> the upright: but the just seek his <u>soul</u>.   despise - life

11 A fool utters all his mind: but a wise *man* keeps it in till afterwards.

12 If a ruler hearken to lies, all his servants *are* wicked.

13 The poor and the deceitful man meet together: the LORD lightens both their eyes.

14 The king that faithfully judges the poor, his throne shall be established for ever.

15 The rod and <u>reproof</u> give wisdom: but a child left *to himself* brings his mother to shame.   correction

16 When the wicked are multiplied, transgression increases: but the righteous shall see their fall.

17 Correct your son, and he shall give you rest; yea, he shall give delight to your soul.

18 Where *there is* no vision, the people perish: but he that keeps the law, happy *is* he.

19 A servant will not be corrected by words: for though he understand he will not answer.

20 See you a man *that is* hasty in his words? *there is* more hope of a fool than of him.

21 He that <u>delicately brings up</u> his servant from a child shall have him become *his* son at the length.   pampers

22 An angry man stirs up strife, and a furious man abounds in transgression.

23 A man's pride shall bring him low:

but honor shall uphold the humble in spirit.

24 Whoso is partner with a thief <u>hates</u> his own soul: he hears cursing, and <u>bewrays</u> *it* not.   despises - tells

25 The <u>fear</u> of man brings a <u>snare</u>: but whoso puts his trust in the LORD shall be safe.   1 TIM. 6:16   dread - trap

26 Many seek the ruler's favor; but every man's judgment *comes* from the LORD.

27 An unjust man *is* <u>an abomination</u> to the just: and *he that is* upright in the way *is* <u>abomination</u> to the wicked.   detestable

CHAPTER 30

THE words of A'gur the son of Ja'keh, *even* the prophecy: the man spoke to Ith'i-el, even to Ith'i-el and U'cal,

2 Surely I *am* more <u>brutish</u> than *any* man, and have not the understanding of a man.   ignorant

3 I neither learned wisdom, nor have the knowledge of the holy.

4 Who has ascended up into heaven, or descended? who has gathered the wind in His fists? who has bound the waters in a garment? who has established all the ends of the earth? what *is* His name, and what *is* His son's name, if you can tell?   JOHN 3:13

5 Every word of God *is* pure: He *is* a shield to them that put their trust in Him.

6 Add you not to His words, less He reprove you, and you be found a liar.

7 Two *things* have I required of You; deny me *them* not before I die:

8 Remove far from me vanity and lies: give me neither poverty nor riches; feed me with food convenient for me:

9 Less I be full, and deny *You*, and say, Who *is* the L<small>ORD</small>? or less I be poor, and steal, and take the name of my God *in vain.*   Jehovah^{s.f.} - Elohim^{p.f.}

10 Accuse not a servant to his master, less he curse you, and you be found guilty.   slander

11 *There is* a generation *that* curses their father, and does not bless their mother.

12 *There is* a generation *that are* pure in their own eyes, and *yet* is not washed from their filthiness.

13 *There is* a generation, O how lofty are their eyes! and their eyelids are lifted up.

14 *There is* a generation, whose teeth *are as* swords, and their jaw teeth *as* knives, to devour the poor from off the earth, and the needy from *among* men.

15 The horseleach has two daughters, *crying*, Give, give. There are three *things that* are never satisfied, *yea*, four *things* say not, *It is* enough:

16 The grave; and the barren womb; the earth *that* is not filled with water; and the fire *that* says not, *It is* enough.

17 The eye *that* mocks at *his* father, and despises to obey *his* mother, the ravens of the valley shall pick it out, and the young eagles shall eat it.

18 There be three *things which* are too wonderful for me, yea, four which I know not:

19 The way of an eagle in the air; the way of a serpent upon a rock; the way of a ship in the midst of the sea; and the way of a man with a maid.

20 Such *is* the way of an adulterous woman; she eats, and wipes her mouth, and says, I have done no wickedness.

21 For three *things* the earth is disquieted, and for four *which* it cannot bear:

22 For a servant when he reigns; and a fool when he is filled with meat;

23 For an odious *woman* when she is married; and an handmaid that is heir to her mistress.   unloved

24 There be four *things which are* little upon the earth, but they *are* exceeding wise:

25 The ants *are* a people not strong, yet they prepare their meat in the summer;

26 The conies *are but* a feeble folk, yet make they their houses in the rocks;

27 The locusts have no king, yet go they forth all of them by bands;

28 The spider takes hold with its hands, and is in kings' palaces.

29 There be three *things* which go well, yea, four are comely in going: stately

30 A lion *which is* strongest among beasts, and turns not away for any;

31 A greyhound; an he goat also; and a king, against whom *there is* no rising up.   fighting cock

32 If you have done foolishly in lifting up yourself, or if you have thought evil, *lay* your hand upon your mouth.

33 Surely the churning of milk brings forth butter, and the wringing of the

nose brings forth blood: so the forcing of wrath brings forth strife.

CHAPTER 31

THE words of king Lem'u-el, the prophecy that his mother taught him.

2 What, my son? and what, the son of my womb? and what, the son of my vows?

3 Give not your strength to women, nor your ways to that which destroys kings.

4 *It is* not for kings, O Lem'u-el, *it is* not for kings to drink wine; nor for princes strong drink:

5 Less they drink, and forget the law, and <u>pervert</u> the judgment of any of the <u>afflicted</u>.　　deprived - oppressed

6 Give strong drink to him that is ready to perish, and wine to those that be of <u>heavy</u> hearts.　　anguished

7 Let him drink, and forget his poverty, and remember his misery no more.

8 Open your mouth for the dumb in the cause of all such as are appointed to destruction.

9 Open your mouth, judge righteously, and plead the cause of the poor and needy.

10 Who can find a virtuous woman? for her price *is* far above rubies.

11 The heart of her husband does safely trust in her, so that he shall have no need of spoil.

12 She will do him good and not evil all the days of her life.

13 She seeks wool, and flax, and works willingly with her hands.

14 She is like the merchants' ships; she brings her food from afar.

15 She rises also while it is yet night, and <u>gives meat</u> to her household, and a portion to her maidens.　　provides food

16 She considers a field, and buys it: with the fruit of her hands she plants a vineyard.

17 She girds her loins with strength, and strengthens her arms.

18 She perceives that her merchandise *is* good: her candle goes not out by night.

19 She lays her hands to the spindle, and her hands hold the distaff.

20 She stretches out her hand to the poor; yea, she reaches forth her hands to the needy.

21 She is not afraid of the snow for her household: for all her household *are* clothed with <u>scarlet</u>.　　i.e., the best

22 She makes herself coverings of tapestry; her clothing *is* silk and purple.

23 Her husband is known in the gates, when he sits among the elders of the land.

24 She makes fine linen, and sells *it*; and delivers <u>girdles</u> to the merchant.　　waistbands

25 Strength and honor *are* her clothing; and she shall rejoice in time to come.

26 She opens her mouth with wisdom; and in her tongue *is* the law of kindness.

27 She looks well to the ways of her household, and eats not the bread of idleness.

28 Her children arise up, and call her

blessed; her husband *also*, and he praises her.

29 Many daughters have done vir-tuously, but you excel them all.

nobly

30 Favor *is* deceitful, and beauty *is* vain: *but* a woman *that* fear the LORD, she shall be praised.

reverences

31 Give her of the fruit of her hands; and let her own works praise her in the gates.

ECCLESIASTES

OUTLINE

Old Age 11.8—12.7
    Age and Youth 11.8–10
    Remember God before Age Comes 12.1–7
The Text and the Preacher 12.8–12
Practical Piety in View of Judgment 12.13,14

SURVEY AND AUTHOR

Who is Ecclesiastes? The term means "assembly-man," that is, either the man who calls a religious assembly (Nu 10.7) or one who is its spokesman, its preacher. Our spokesman was not a priest with law, nor a prophet with the word, but a wise man with counsel (Jr 18.18), much of whose work resembles the Book of Proverbs.

From 1.1 it is popularly inferred that he is Solomon, first of Israel's wise men (12.9, 11; cf. 1 K 3.12; 4.29–34); at least, part of the book was thought to reflect that sage's experiences.

Yet it may be asked whether Solomon, third king of Israel, would at any time in his history have used the past tense to say, "I was king over Israel in Jerusalem" (1.12)? Could he have confessed that the attempt to be wise "was far from" him (7.23)? Under his efficient government would he have described oppressors as men with power against whom there was no redress (4.1; 5.8; 8.9; 10.5–7; cf. 1 K 4.20, 25)?

When did this Qoheleth (the only name he has in the Hebrew, "assemblyman," really the title of his office) write? Evidently when Israel groaned under foreign oppressors (possibly Persian, between 444 and 331 B.C., though some would say Greek). The apocryphal Ecclesiasticus by Jesus ben Sirach, about 160 B.C., seems to quote the earlier work of Ecclesiastes.

Where? Near the house of God (5.1) where men come and go from the place of the holy (8.10). Knowledge of the outside world shown in the book could have been acquired right there in Jerusalem.

Whose book, then, was it intended to be? Though it is in the Hebrew language, its distinctive marks of Israel are few. God's covenant name is never used; Israel is mentioned once. Our proverb-monger speaks to the children of men (1.13, and so forth), to mankind. Pointing out man's natural folly and darkness, he prepares the way for the wisdom and light of the Gospel.

Why such a book in the canon? The rabbis disputed the consistency of the writer, but the book to them was already part of their Bible. Here is no blind optimism: more than a score of life's pressing problems are too clearly seen for that. Here is no cynical pessimism, for the author is a believer in a God of righteousness (8.12, 13, and elsewhere). Here is clear-eyed realism that faces the fun and fury, the triumphs and defeats, the pattern of light and shade, only to conclude that the whole thing is a puff of wind (1.2; 12.8; and so forth), yet paradoxically, the whole of man's life must be reverence and obedience to God, for to Him at last one must give full account (12.13, 14).

                                                        W.G.B.

ECCLESIASTES
OR, THE PREACHER

CHAPTER 1

King Solomon's
Final Advice

THE words of the <u>Preacher</u>, the son of Da'vid, king in Je-ru'sa-lem.

i.e., Solomon

2 Vanity of vanities, says the <u>Preacher</u>, vanity of vanities; all *is* vanity.

ROM. 8:20

3 What profit has a man of all his labor which he <u>takes</u> under the sun? does

4 *One* generation passes away, and *another* generation comes: but the earth abides for ever.

5 The sun also arises, and the sun goes down, and hastes to its place where it arose.

6 The wind goes toward the south, and turns about to the north; it whirls about continually, and the wind returns again according to its circuits.

JOHN 3:8

7 All the rivers run into the sea; yet the sea *is* not full; to the place from where the rivers come, there they return again.

8 All things *are* <u>full of labor</u>; man cannot utter *it*: the eye is not satisfied with seeing, nor the ear filled with hearing. wearisome

9 The thing that has been, it *is that* which shall be; and that which is done *is* that which shall be done: and *there is* no new *thing* under the sun.

10 Is there *any* thing whereof it may be said, See, this *is* new? it has been already of old time, which was before us.

11 *There is* no remembrance of former *things*; neither shall there be *any* remembrance of *things* that are to come with *those* that shall come after.

12 I the <u>Preacher</u> was king over Is'ra-el in Je-ru-sa-lem. *i.e., Solomon*

13 And I gave my heart to seek and search out by wisdom concerning all *things* that are done under heaven: this <u>sore travail</u> has <u>God</u> given to the sons of man to be <u>exercised</u> therewith.

heavy task - Elohim ᵖ·ᶠ· - afflicted

14 I have seen all the works that are done under the sun; and, behold, all *is* vanity and <u>vexation of spirit</u>.

chasing after the wind

15 *That which is* crooked cannot be made straight: and that which is <u>wanting</u> cannot be numbered. lacking

16 I communed with my own heart, saying, Lo, I am come to great estate, and have gotten more wisdom than all *they* that have been before me in Je-ru'sa-lem: yea, my heart had great experience of wisdom and knowledge.

17 And I gave my heart to know wisdom, and to know madness and folly: I perceived that this also is <u>vexation of spirit</u>.

18 For in much wisdom *is* much grief: and he that increases knowledge increases sorrow.

CHAPTER 2

I SAID in my heart, Go to now, I will prove you with mirth, therefore

enjoy pleasure: and, behold, this also *is* vanity.

2 I said of laughter, *It is* mad: and of mirth, What does it?

3 I sought in my heart to give myself to wine, yet acquainting my heart with wisdom; and to lay hold on folly, till I might see what *was* that good for the sons of men, which they should do under the heaven all the days of their life.

4 I made me great works; I built me houses; I planted me vineyards:

5 I made me gardens and orchards, and I planted trees in them of all *kind of* fruits:

6 I made me pools of water, to <u>water</u> therewith the wood that brings forth trees: i.e., irrigate

7 I got *me* servants and maidens, and had servants born in my house; also I had great possessions of great and small cattle above all that were in Je-ru'sa-lem before me:

8 I gathered me also silver and gold, and the peculiar treasure of kings and of the provinces: I got me men singers and women singers, and the delights of the sons of men, *as* musical instruments, and that of all sorts.

9 So I was great, and increased more than all that were before me in Je-ru'sa-lem: also my wisdom remained with me.

10 And whatsoever my eyes desired I kept not from them, I withheld not my heart from any joy; for my heart rejoiced in all my labor: and this was my portion of all my labor.

11 Then I looked on all the works that my hands had wrought, and on the labor that I had labored to do: and, behold, all *was* vanity and <u>vexation of spirit</u>, and *there was* no profit under the sun.   chasing after the wind

12 And I turned myself to behold wisdom, and madness, and folly: for what *can* the man *do* that comes after the king? *even* that which has been already done.

13 Then I saw that wisdom excels folly, as far as light excels darkness.

14 The wise man's eyes *are* in his head; but the fool walks in darkness: and I myself perceived also that one event happens to them all.

15 Then said I in my heart, As it happens to the fool, so it happens even to me; and why was I then more wise? Then I said in my heart, that this also *is* vanity.

16 For *there is* no remembrance of the wise more than of the fool for ever; seeing that which now *is* in the days to come shall all be forgotten. And how dies the wise *man*? as the fool.

17 Therefore I <u>hated</u> life; because the work that is wrought under the sun *is* grievous to me: for all *is* vanity and <u>vexation of spirit</u>.   abhorred - chasing after the wind

18 Yea, I <u>hated</u> all my labor which I had taken under the sun: because I should leave it to the man that shall be after me.

19 And who knows whether he shall be a wise *man* or a fool? yet shall he have rule over all my labor wherein I have labored, and wherein I have showed myself wise under the sun. This *is* also vanity.

20 Therefore I went about to cause my heart to despair of all the labor which I took under the sun.

21 For there is a man whose labor *is* in wisdom, and in knowledge, and in equity; yet to a man that has not labored therein shall he leave it *for* his portion. This also *is* vanity and a great evil.   skill - inheritance

22 For what has man of all his labor, and of the vexation of his heart, wherein he has labored under the sun?   anxious striving

23 For all his days *are* sorrows, and his travail grief; yea, his heart takes not rest in the night. This is also vanity. labor is

24 *There is* nothing better for a man, *than* that he should eat and drink, and *that* he should make his soul enjoy good in his labor. This also I saw, that it *was* from the hand of God.   himself - Elohim^p.f.

25 For who can eat, or who else can hasten *hereto*, more than I?

26 For God gives to a man that *is* good in His sight wisdom, and knowledge, and joy: but to the sinner He gives travail, to gather and to heap up, that He may give to *him that is* good before God. This also *is* vanity and vexation of spirit.   what - chasing after the wind

CHAPTER 3

TO every *thing there is* a season, and a time to every purpose under the heaven:

2 A time to be born, and a time to die; a time to plant, and a time to pluck up *that which is* planted;   HEB. 9:27

3 A time to kill, and a time to heal; a time to break down, and a time to build up;

4 A time to weep, and a time to laugh; a time to mourn, and a time to dance;

5 A time to cast away stones, and a time to gather stones together; a time to embrace, and a time to refrain from embracing;   shun

6 A time to get, and a time to lose; a time to keep, and a time to cast away;

7 A time to rend, and a time to sew; a time to keep silence, and a time to speak;

8 A time to love, and a time to hate; a time of war, and a time of peace.

9 What profit has he that works in that wherein he labors?

10 I have seen the travail, which God has given to the sons of men to be exercised in it.   task - Elohim^p.f. - occupied

11 He has made every *thing* beautiful in its time: also He has set the world in their heart, so that no man can find out the work that God makes from the beginning to the end.

12 I know that *there is* no good in them, but for *a man* to rejoice, and to do good in his life.

13 And also that every man should eat and drink, and enjoy the good of all his labor, it *is* the gift of God.   Elohim^p.f.

14 I know that, whatsoever God does, it shall be for ever: nothing can be put to it, nor any thing taken from it: and God does *it*, that *men* should fear before Him.

15 That which has been is now; and

that which is to be has already been; and <u>God</u> <u>requires</u> that which is past. Elohim^{p.f.} - seeks

16 And moreover I saw under the sun the place of judgment, *that* wickedness *was* there; and the place of righteousness, *that* iniquity *was* there.

17 I said in my heart, <u>God</u> shall judge the righteous and the wicked: for *there is* a time there for every purpose and for every work.

18 I said in my heart concerning the estate of the sons of men, that <u>God</u> might <u>manifest</u> them, and that they might see that they themselves are beasts. lest

19 For that which befalls the sons of men befalls beasts; even one thing befalls them: as the one dies, so dies the other; yea, they have all one breath; so that a man has no preeminence above a beast: for all *is* vanity.

20 All go to one place; all are of the dust, and all turn to dust again.

21 Who knows the spirit of man that goes upward, and the spirit of the beast that goes downward to the earth?

22 Wherefore I perceive that *there is* nothing better, than that a man should rejoice in his own works; for that *is* his <u>portion</u>: for who shall bring him to see what shall be after him? lot

CHAPTER 4

SO I returned, and considered all the oppressions that are done under the sun: and behold the tears of *such as were* oppressed, and they had no comforter; and on the side of their oppressors *there was* power; but they had no comforter.

2 Wherefore I praised the dead which are already dead more than the living which are yet alive.

3 Yea, better *is he* than both they, which has not yet been, who has not seen the evil work that is done under the sun.

4 Again, I considered all <u>travail</u>, and every <u>right work</u>, that for this a man is envied of his neighbor. This *is* also vanity and <u>vexation of spirit</u>. labor - skill - chasing after the wind

5 The fool folds his hands together, and eats his own flesh.

6 Better *is* an handful *with* quietness, than both the hands full *with* <u>travail</u> and <u>vexation of spirit</u>. labor

7 Then I returned, and I saw vanity under the sun.

8 There is one *alone*, and *there is* not a second; yea, he has neither child nor brother: yet *is there* no end of all his labor; neither is his eye satisfied with riches; neither *says he,* For whom do I labor, and bereave my soul of good? This *is* also vanity, yea, it *is* a <u>sore travail</u>. great task

9 Two *are* better than one; because they have a good reward for their labor.

10 For if they fall, the one will lift up his fellow: but woe to him *that is* alone when he falls; for *he has* not another to help him up.

11 Again, if two lie together, then they have heat: but how can one be warm *alone*?

12 And if one prevail against him,

two shall withstand him; and a three-fold cord is not quickly broken.

13 Better *is* a poor and a wise child than an old and foolish king, who will no more be admonished.

14 For out of prison he comes to reign; whereas also *he that is* born in his kingdom becomes poor.

15 I considered all the living which walk under the sun, with the second child that shall stand up in his stead.

16 *There is* no end of all the people, *even* of all that have been before them: they also that come after shall not rejoice in him. Surely this also *is* vanity and vexation of spirit.   chasing after the wind

CHAPTER 5

KEEP your foot when you go to the house of God, and be more ready to hear, than to give the sacrifice of fools: for they consider not that they do evil.   Elohim[p.f.]

2 Be not rash with your mouth, and let not your heart be hasty to utter *any* thing before God: for God *is* in heaven, and you upon earth: therefore let your words be few.

3 For a dream comes through the multitude of business; and a fool's voice *is known* by multitude of words.

4 When you vow a vow to God, defer not to pay it; for *He has* no pleasure in fools: pay that which you have vowed.   swear a promise

5 Better *is it* that you should not vow, than that you should vow and not pay.   ACTS 5:4 promise

6 Allow not your mouth to cause your flesh to sin; neither say you before the angel, that it *was* an error: wherefore should God be angry at your voice, and destroy the work of your hands?

7 For in the multitude of dreams and many words *there are* also *divers* vanities: but fear you God.   is emptiness - revere - Elohim[p.f.]

8 If you see the oppression of the poor, and violent perverting of judgment and justice in a province, marvel not at the matter: for *he that is* higher than the highest regards; and *there be* higher than they.   denial

9 Moreover the profit of the earth is for all: the king *himself* is served by the field.

10 He that loves silver shall not be satisfied with silver; nor he that loves abundance with increase: this *is* also vanity.

11 When goods increase, they are increased that eat them: and what good *is there* to the owners thereof, saving the beholding *of them* with their eyes?

12 The sleep of a laboring man *is* sweet, whether he eat little or much: but the abundance of the rich will not allow him to sleep.

13 There is a sore evil *which* I have seen under the sun, *namely*, riches kept for the owners thereof to their hurt.   great

14 But those riches perish by evil travail: and he fathered a son, and *there is* nothing in his hand.   effort

15 As he came forth of his mother's womb, naked shall he return to go as he came, and shall take nothing of his labor, which he may carry away in his hand.

M48 — 989

16 And this also *is* a <u>sore</u> evil, *that* in all points as he came, so shall he go: and what profit has he that has labored for the wind?   <small>great</small>

17 All his days also he eats in darkness, and *he has* much sorrow and wrath with his sickness.

18 Behold *that* which I have seen: *it is* good and <u>comely</u> *for one* to eat and to drink, and to enjoy the good of all his labor that he takes under the sun all the days of his life, which <u>God</u> gives him: for it *is* his portion.   <small>proper - Elohim^{p.f.}</small>

19 Every man also to whom <u>God</u> has given riches and wealth, and has given him power to eat thereof, and to take his portion, and to rejoice in his labor; this *is* the gift of <u>God</u>.

20 For he shall not much remember the days of his life; because <u>God</u> answers *him* in the joy of his heart.

CHAPTER 6

THERE is an evil which I have seen under the sun, and it *is* common among men:

2 A man to whom <u>God</u> has given riches, wealth, and honor, so that he wants nothing for his soul of all that he desires yet <u>God</u> gives him not power to eat thereof, but a stranger eats it: this *is* <u>vanity</u>, and it *is* an evil disease.   <small>Elohim^{p.f.} - futility</small>

3 If a man fathers an hundred *children*, and live many years, so that the days of his years be many, and his soul be not filled with good, and also *that* he have no burial; I say, *that* an untimely birth *is* better than he.

4 For he comes in with vanity, and departs in darkness, and his name shall be covered with darkness.

5 Moreover he has not seen the sun, nor known *any thing*: this has more rest than the other.

6 Yea, though he live a thousand years twice *told*, yet has he seen no good: do not all go to one place?

7 All the labor of man *is* for his mouth, and yet the appetite is not filled.

8 For what has the wise more than the fool? what has the poor, that knows to walk before the living?

9 Better *is* the sight of the eyes than the wandering of the desire: this *is* also vanity and <u>vexation of spirit</u>.   <small>chasing after the wind</small>

10 That which has been is named already, and it is known that it *is* man: neither may he contend with him that is mightier than he.

11 Seeing there be many things that increase vanity, what *is* man the better?

12 For who knows what *is* good for man in *this* life, all the days of his vain life which he spends as a shadow? for who can tell a man what shall be after him under the sun?

CHAPTER 7

A GOOD name *is* better than precious ointment; and the day of death than the day of one's birth.

2 *It is* better to go to the house of mourning, than to go to the house of feasting: for that *is* the end of all men; and the living will lay *it* to his heart.

3 Sorrow *is* better than laughter: for

by the sadness of the countenance the heart is made better.   2 COR. 7:10

4 The heart of the wise *is* in the house of mourning; but the heart of fools *is* in the house of mirth.

5 *It is* better to hear the rebuke of the wise, than for a man to hear the song of fools.

6 For as the crackling of thorns under a pot, so *is* the laughter of the fool: this also *is* vanity.

7 Surely oppression makes a wise man mad; and a gift destroys the heart.

8 Better *is* the end of a thing than the beginning thereof: *and* the patient in spirit *is* better than the proud in spirit.

9 Be not hasty in your spirit to be angry: for anger rests in the bosom of fools.

10 Say not you, What is *the cause* that the former days were better than these? for you do not enquire wisely concerning this.

11 Wisdom *is* good with an inheritance: and *by it there is* profit to them that see the sun.

12 For wisdom *is* a <u>defence</u>, *and* money *is* a <u>defence</u>: but the <u>excellency</u> of knowledge *is, that* wisdom gives life to them that have it.   protection - advantage

13 Consider the work of <u>God</u>: for who can make *that* straight, which He has made crooked?   Elohim[p.f.]

14 In the day of prosperity be joyful, but in the day of adversity consider: <u>God</u> also has set the one over against the other, to the end that man should find nothing after him.

15 All *things* have I seen in the days of my vanity: there is a just *man* that perishes in his righteousness, and there is a wicked *man* that prolongs *his life* in his wickedness.

16 Be not righteous over much; neither make yourself over wise: why should you destroy youself?   ROM. 12:3

17 Be not over much wicked, neither be you foolish: why should you die before your time?

18 *It is* good that you should take hold of this; yea, also from this withdraw not your hand: for he that <u>fears</u> <u>God</u> shall come forth of them all.   reveres - Elohim[p.f.]

19 Wisdom strengthens the wise more than ten mighty *men* which are in the city.

20 For *there is* not a just man upon earth, that does good, and sins not.   1 JOHN 1:8

21 Also take no <u>heed</u> to all words that are spoken; less you hear your servant curse you: attention

22 For oftentimes also your own heart knows that you yourself likewise have cursed others.

23 All this have I proved by wisdom: I said, I will be wise; but it *was* far from me.

24 That which is far off, and exceeding deep, who can find it out?

25 I <u>applied my heart</u> to know, and to search, and to seek out wisdom, and the reason *of things*, and to know the wickedness of folly, even of foolishness *and* madness: directed my mind

26 And I find more bitter than death the woman, whose heart *is* <u>snares</u> and <u>nets</u>, *and* her hands *as* <u>bands</u>: whoso

pleases <u>God</u> shall escape from her; but the sinner shall be taken by her.

<small>i.e., luring - i.e., enticing - chains - Elohim^{p.f.}</small>

27 Behold, this have I found, says the preacher, *counting* one by one, to find out the account:

28 Which yet my soul seeks, but I find not: one man among a thousand have I found; but a woman among all those have I not found.

29 Lo, this only have I found, that <u>God</u> has made man upright; but they have sought out many <u>inventions</u>. <small>Elohim^{p.f.} - schemes</small>

CHAPTER 8

WHO *is* as the wise *man*? and who knows the interpretation of a thing? a man's wisdom makes his face to shine, and the boldness of his face shall be changed.

2 I *counsel you* to keep the king's commandment, and *that* in regard of the oath of <u>God</u>.

3 Be not hasty to go out of his sight: <u>stand</u> not in an evil thing; for he does whatsoever pleases him. <small>join</small>

4 Where the word of a king *is, there is* power: and who may say to him, What do you?

5 Whoso keeps the commandment shall feel no evil thing: and a wise man's heart discerns both time and judgment.

6 Because to every purpose there is time and judgment, therefore the misery of man *is* great upon him.

7 For he knows not that which shall be: for who can tell him when it shall be?

8 *There is* no man that has power over the spirit to retain the spirit; neither *has he* power in the day of death: and *there is* no discharge in *that* war; neither shall wickedness deliver those that are given to it.

9 All this have I seen, and applied my heart to every work that is done under the sun: *there is* a time wherein one man rules over another to his own hurt.

10 And so I saw the wicked buried, who had come and gone from the place of the holy, and they were forgotten in the city where they had so done: this *is* also vanity.

11 Because sentence against an evil work is not executed speedily, therefore the heart of the sons of men is fully set in them to do evil.

12 Though a sinner do evil an hundred times, and his *days* be prolonged, yet surely I know that it shall be well with them that <u>fear</u> God, which <u>fear</u> before Him: <small>reverence - Elohim^{p.f.}</small>

13 But it shall not be well with the wicked, neither shall he prolong *his* days, *which are* as a shadow; because he <u>fears not</u> before <u>God</u>. <small>is not revered</small>

14 There is a vanity which is done upon the earth; that there be just *men*, to whom it happens according to the work of the wicked; again, there be wicked *men*, to whom it happens according to the work of the righteous: I said that this also *is* vanity.

15 Then I commended mirth, because a man has no better thing under the sun, than to eat, and to drink, and to be merry: for that shall abide with him of

his labor the days of his life, which God gives him under the sun.   Elohim^p.f.

16 When I applied my heart to know wisdom, and to see the business that is done upon the earth: (for also *there is that* neither day nor night sees sleep with his eyes:)

17 Then I beheld all the work of God, that a man cannot find out the work that is done under the sun: because though a man labor to seek *it* out, yet he shall not find *it*; yea farther; though a wise *man* think to know *it*, yet shall he not be able to find *it*.

CHAPTER 9

FOR all this I considered in my heart even to declare all this, that the righteous, and the wise, and their works, *are* in the hand of God: no man knows either love or hatred *by* all *that is* before them.   Elohim^p.f.

2 All *things come* alike to all: *there is* one event to the righteous, and to the wicked; to the good and to the clean, and to the unclean; to him that sacrifices and to him that sacrifices not: as *is* the good, so *is* the sinner; *and* he that swears, as *he* that fears an oath.

3 This *is* an evil among all *things* that are done under the sun, that *there is* one event to all: yea, also the heart of the sons of men is full of evil, and madness *is* in their heart while they live, and after that *they go* to the dead.

4 For to him that is joined to all the living there is hope: for a living dog is better than a dead lion.

5 For the living know that they shall die: but the dead know not any thing, neither have they any more a reward; for the memory of them is forgotten.

6 Also their love, and their hatred, and their envy, is now perished; neither have they any more a portion for ever in any *thing* that is done under the sun.

7 Go your way, eat your bread with joy, and drink your wine with a merry heart; for God now accepts your works.   Elohim^p.f.

8 Let your garments be always white; and let your head lack no ointment.

9 Live joyfully with the wife whom you love all the days of the life of your vanity, which he has given you under the sun, all the days of your vanity: for that *is* your portion in *this* life, and in your labor which you take under the sun.

10 Whatsoever your hand finds to do, do *it* with your might; for *there is* no work, nor device, nor knowledge, nor wisdom, in the grave, where you go.   planning

11 I returned, and saw under the sun, that the race *is* not to the swift, nor the battle to the strong, neither yet bread to the wise, nor yet riches to men of understanding, nor yet favor to men of skill; but time and chance happens to them all.

12 For man also know not his time: as the fishes that are taken in an evil net, and as the birds that are caught in the snare; so *are* the sons of men snared in an evil time, when it falls suddenly upon them.   trap - trapped

13 This wisdom have I seen also

under the sun, and it *seemed* great to me:

14 *There was* a little city, and few men inside it; and there came a great king against it, and besieged it, and built great bulwarks against it:

15 Now there was found in it a poor wise man, and he by his wisdom delivered the city; yet no man remembered that same poor man.

16 Then said I, Wisdom *is* better than strength: nevertheless the poor man's wisdom *is* despised, and his words are not heard.

17 The words of wise *men are* heard in quiet more than the cry of him that rules among fools.　shouting

18 Wisdom *is* better than weapons of war: but one sinner destroys much good.

CHAPTER 10

DEAD flies cause the ointment of the apothecary to send forth a stinking savor: *so does* a little folly him that is in reputation for wisdom *and* honor.　odor

2 A wise man's heart *is* at his right hand; but a fool's heart at his left.

3 Yea also, when he that is a fool walks by the way, his wisdom fails *him*, and he says to every one *that* he *is* a fool.

4 If the spirit of the ruler rise up against you, leave not your place; for yielding pacifies great offences.

5 There is an evil *which* I have seen under the sun, as an error *which* proceeds from the ruler:　goes forth

6 Folly is set in great dignity, and the rich sit in low place.　exalted places

7 I have seen servants upon horses, and princes walking as servants upon the earth.

8 He that digs a pit shall fall into it; and whoso breaks an hedge, a serpent shall bite him.

9 Whoso removes stones shall be hurt therewith; *and* he that cleaves wood shall be endangered thereby.　splits

10 If the iron be blunt, **and he do** not whet the edge, then must he put to more strength: but wisdom *is* profitable to direct.　sharpen - success

11 Surely the serpent will bite without enchantment; and a babbler is no better.

12 The words of a wise man's mouth *are* gracious; but the lips of a fool will swallow up himself.

13 The beginning of the words of his mouth *is* foolishness: and the end of his talk *is* mischievous madness.

14 A fool also is full of words: a man cannot tell what shall be; and what shall be after him, who can tell him?

15 The labor of the foolish wearies every one of them, because he knows not how to go to the city.

16 Woe to you, O land, when your king *is* a child, and your princes eat in the morning!　i.e., feast

17 Blessed *are* you, O land, when your king *is* the son of nobles, and your princes eat in due season, for strength, and not for drunkenness!　Fortunate

18 By much slothfulness the building decays; and through idleness of the hands the house drops through.　laziness

19 A feast is made for laughter, and wine makes merry: but money answers all *things*.

20 Curse not the king, no not in your thought; and curse not the rich in your bedchamber: for a bird of the air shall carry the voice, and that which has wings shall tell the matter.   ACTS 23:5

CHAPTER 11

CAST your bread upon the waters: for you shall find it after many days.

2 Give a portion to seven, and also to eight; for you know not what evil shall <u>be</u> upon the earth.   come

3 If the clouds be full of rain, they empty *themselves* upon the earth: and if the tree fall toward the south, or toward the north, in the place where the tree falls, there it <u>shall be</u>.   lies

4 He that observes the wind shall not sow; and he that <u>regards</u> the clouds shall not reap.   watches

5 As you know not what *is* the way of the <u>spirit</u>, *nor* how the bones *do grow* in the womb of her that is with child: even so you know not the works of <u>God</u> who makes all.   wind - Elohim[p.f.]

6 In the morning sow your seed, and in the evening withhold not your hand: for you know not whether shall prosper, either this or that, or which they both *shall be* alike good.

7 Truly the light *is* sweet, and a pleasant *thing it is* for the eyes to behold the sun:

8 But if a man live many years, *and* rejoice in them all; yet let him remember the days of darkness; for they shall be many. All that comes *is* vanity.

9 Rejoice, O young man, in your youth; and let your heart cheer you in the days of your youth, and walk in the ways of your heart, and in the sight of your eyes: but know you, that for all these *things* <u>God</u> will bring you into judgment. Elohim[p.f.]

10 Therefore remove sorrow from your heart, and put away evil from your flesh: for childhood and youth *are* vanity.

CHAPTER 12

REMEMBER now your Creator in the days of your youth, while the evil days come not, nor the years draw near, when you shall say, I have no pleasure in them;

2 While the sun, or the light, or the moon, or the stars, be not darkened, nor the clouds return after the rain:

3 In the day when the <u>keepers</u> of the <u>house</u> shall tremble, and the <u>strong men</u> shall bow themselves, and the <u>grinders</u> cease because they are few, and those that look out of the <u>windows</u> be darkened, i.e., lips - i.e., mouth - i.e., legs - i.e., teeth - i.e., eyes

4 And the <u>doors</u> shall be shut in the streets, when the sound of the <u>grinding is low</u>, and he shall <u>rise up</u> at the voice of the bird, and all the daughters of music shall be <u>brought low</u>; i.e., ears - no teeth - awaken - not heard

5 Also *when* they shall be afraid of *that which is* <u>high</u>, and <u>fears *shall be* in the way</u>, and the <u>almond tree</u> shall flourish, and the <u>grasshopper</u> shall be a burden, and <u>desire</u> shall fail: because

man goes to his <u>long home</u>, and the mourners go about the streets: i.e., thoughts of

God in heaven - i.e., fear now of death - i.e., gray hair - i.e.,

slightest weight - i.e., sexual desire - i.e., death eternal

6 Or ever the <u>silver cord</u> be loosed, or the <u>golden bowl</u> be broken, or the <u>pitcher</u> be broken at the fountain, or the <u>wheel broken at the cistern</u>.   i.e., spinal cord?

throat? - i.e., cranium? stomach? - i.e., heart - i.e., heart as a pump

7 Then shall the <u>dust</u> return to the earth as it was: and the spirit shall return to <u>God</u> who gave it.

i.e., body - Elohim^{p.f.}

8 Vanity of vanities, says the preacher; all *is* vanity.

9 And moreover, because the preacher was wise, he still taught the people knowledge; yea, he gave good heed, and sought out, *and* set in order many proverbs.

10 The preacher sought to find out acceptable words: and *that which was* written *was* upright, *even* words of truth.

11 The words of the wise *are* as <u>goads</u>, and as nails fastened *by* the masters of assemblies, *which* are given from one shepherd. i.e., challenges

12 And further, <u>by these</u>, my son, be admonished: of making many books *there is* no end; and much study *is* a weariness of the flesh.   i.e., words of truth

13 Let us hear the conclusion of the whole matter: <u>Fear God</u>, and keep His commandments: for this *is* the whole *duty* of man.   Reverence - Elohim^{p.f.}

14 For <u>God</u> shall bring every work into judgment, with every secret thing, whether *it be* good, or whether *it be* evil.   ROM. 2:16

THE SONG OF SOLOMON

OUTLINE

SURVEY

This book describes the love and marriage of Solomon (called "the beloved") and a country maiden (called "the Shulamite"). It consists entirely of speeches, chiefly by the Shulamite and Solomon. Because it is ancient oriental poetry, it differs widely from the way a devout present-day writer might present the same basic ideas. It depicts the beauty of a pure love between man and woman, which ripens into an undying mutual devotion. The basic message is the purity and sacredness of love and marriage—a message much needed in our day of broken marriage vows and easy divorces.

At the same time the Song reminds us that back of all pure human love is the greatest, deepest love of all—the love of God Who gave His Son to redeem sinners, and the love of the Son of God Who suffered and died for His Bride, the Church. The Song is not an allegory nor a type, but a parable of the divine love which is the background and source of all true human love.

AUTHOR

The title (1.1) indicates Solomon is the author. This accords well with the contents of the book, especially the descriptions of nature. No convincing case has been presented against Solomon's authorship. He was king of Israel about 973-933 B.C.

J.G.V.

THE SONG OF SOLOMON

True Love is Pure;
Christ's Love for
His Church

CHAPTER 1

THE song of songs, which *is* Sol'o-mon's.

2 Let him kiss me with the kisses of his mouth: for your love *is* better than wine.

3 Because of the savor of your good ointments your name *is as* ointment poured forth, therefore do the virgins love you. fragrance - perfumes - maidens

4 Draw me, we will run after you: the king has brought me into his chambers: we will be glad and rejoice in you, we will remember your love more than wine: the upright love you.

5 I *am* black, but comely, O you daughters of Je-ru'sa-lem, as the tents of Ke'dar, as the curtains of Sol'o-mon.

6 Look not upon me, because I *am* black, because the sun has looked upon me: my mother's children were angry with me; they made me the keeper of the vineyards; *but* my own vineyard have I not kept.

7 Tell me, O you whom my soul loves, where you feed, where you make *your flock* to rest at noon: for why should I be as one that turns aside by the flocks of your companions?

8 If you know not, O you fairest among women, go your way forth by the footsteps of the flock, and feed your kids beside the shepherds' tents.

9 I have compared you, O my love, to a company of horses in Pha'raoh's chariots.

10 Your cheeks are comely with rows *of jewels*, your neck with chains *of gold*.

11 We will make you borders of gold with studs of silver. ornaments - beads

12 While the king *sits* at his table, my spikenard sends forth the smell thereof. perfume

13 A bundle of myrrh *is* my wellbeloved to me; he shall lie all night between my breasts. fragrant resin

14 My beloved *is* to me *as* a cluster of camphire in the vineyards of En-ge'di.

15 Behold, you *are* fair, my love; behold, you *are* fair; you *have* doves' eyes.

16 Behold, you *are* fair, my beloved, yea, pleasant: also our bed *is* green. couch - luxuriant

17 The beams of our house *are* cedar, *and* our rafters of fir.

CHAPTER 2

I *AM* the rose of Shar'on, *and* the lily of the valleys.

2 As the lily among thorns, so *is* my love among the daughters.

3 As the apple tree among the trees of the wood, so *is* my beloved among the sons. I sat down under his shadow with great delight, and his fruit *was* sweet to my taste.

4 He brought me to the banqueting house, and his banner over me *was* love.

5 Stay me with flagons, comfort me with apples: for I *am* sick of love. raisin cakes - lovesick

6 His left hand *is* under my head, and his right hand does embrace me.

7 I <u>charge</u> you, O you daughters of Je-ru'sa-lem, by the <u>roes</u>, and by the <u>hinds</u> of the field, that you stir not up, nor awake *my* love, till he please.   adjure - gazelles - does

8 The voice of my beloved! behold, he comes leaping upon the mountains, skipping upon the hills.

9 My beloved is like a roe or a young hart: behold, he stands behind our wall, he looks forth at the windows, showing himself through the lattice.

10 My beloved spoke, and said to me, Rise up, my love, my fair one, and come away.

11 For, lo, the winter is past, the rain is over *and* gone;

12 The flowers appear on the earth; the time of the singing *of birds* is come, and the voice of the <u>turtle</u> is heard in our land;   turtle dove

13 The fig tree puts forth her green figs, and the vines *with* the tender grape give a *good* smell. Arise, my love, my fair one, and come away.

14 O my dove, *that are* in the clefts of the rock, in the secret *places* of the stairs, let me see your <u>countenance</u>, let me hear your voice; for sweet *is* your voice, and your <u>countenance</u> *is* comely.   lovely face

15 Take us the foxes, the little foxes, that spoil the vines: for our vines *have* tender grapes.

16 My beloved *is* mine, and I *am* his: he feeds among the lilies.

17 Until the day break, and the shadows flee away, turn, my beloved, and be you like a <u>roe</u> or a young <u>hart</u> upon the mountains of Be'ther.   gazell - stag

CHAPTER 3

BY night on my bed I sought him whom my soul loves: I sought him, but I found him not.

2 I will rise now, and go about the city in the streets, and in the broad ways I will seek him whom my soul loves: I sought him, but I found him not.

3 The watchmen that go about the city found me: *to whom I said*, Saw you him whom my soul loves?

4 *It was* but a little that I passed from them, but I found him whom my soul loves: I held him, and would not let him go, until I had brought him into my mother's house, and into the <u>chamber</u> of her that conceived me.   room

5 I charge you, O you daughters of Je-ru'sa-lem, by the <u>roes</u>, and by the <u>hinds</u> of the field, that you stir not up, nor awake *my* love, till he please.   gazelles - does

6 Who *is* this that comes out of the wilderness like pillars of smoke, perfumed with <u>myrrh</u> and <u>frankincense</u>, with all <u>powders</u> of the merchant?   fragrant resin - spices

7 Behold his <u>bed</u>, which *is* Sol'o-mon's; <u>threescore</u> valiant men *are* about it, of the valiant of Is'ra-el.   traveling couch - 60

8 They all hold swords, *being* expert in war: every man *has* his sword upon his thigh because of <u>fear</u> in the night.   terrors

9 King Sol'o-mon made himself a chariot of the wood of Leb'a-non.

10 He made the pillars thereof *of* sil-

ver, the bottom thereof *of* gold, the covering of it *of* purple, the midst thcreof being paved *with* love, for the daughters of Je-ru'sa-lem.

11 Go forth, O you daughters of Zi'on, and behold king Sol'o-mon with the crown wherewith his mother crowned him in the day of his espousals, and in the day of the gladness of his heart.

CHAPTER 4

BEHOLD, you *are* fair, my love; behold, you *are* fair; you *have* doves' eyes within your locks: your hair *is* as a flock of goats, that appear from mount Gil'e-ad.

2 Your teeth *are* like a flock *of sheep that are even* shorn, which came up from the washing; whereof every one bear twins, and none *is* barren among them.

3 Your lips *are* like a thread of scarlet, and your speech *is* comely: your temples *are* like a piece of a pomegranate within your locks.

4 Your neck *is* like the tower of Da'vid builded for an armory, whereon there hang a thousand <u>bucklers</u>, all shields of mighty men. shields

5 Your two breasts *are* like two young roes that are twins, which feed among the lilies.

6 Until the day break, and the shadows flee away, I will get me to the mountain of <u>myrrh</u>, and to the hill of <u>frankincense</u>. fragrant resin

7 You *are* all fair, my love; *there is* no <u>spot</u> in you. EPH. 5:27 blemish

8 Come with me from Leb'a-non, *my* spouse, with me from Leb'a-non: look from the top of Am'a-na, from the top of She'nir and Her'mon, from the lions' dens, from the mountains of the leopards.

9 You have ravished my heart, my sister, *my* spouse; you have ravished my heart with one of your eyes, with one chain of your neck.

10 How fair is your love, my sister, *my* spouse! how much better is your love than wine! and the <u>smell</u> of your <u>ointments</u> than all spices! fragrance - perfumes

11 Your lips, O *my* spouse, drop *as* the honeycomb: honey and milk *are* under your tongue; and the smell of your garments *is* like the smell of Leb'a-non.

12 A garden inclosed *is* my sister, *my* spouse; a spring shut up, a fountain sealed.

13 Your plants *are* an orchard of pomegranates, with pleasant fruits; camphire, with spikenard,

14 Spikenard and saffron; calamus and cinnamon, with all trees of <u>frankincense</u>; <u>myrrh</u> and aloes, with all the chief spices: fragrant resin

15 A fountain of gardens, a well of living waters, and streams from Leb'a-non.

16 Awake, O north wind; and come, you south; blow upon my garden, *that* the spices thereof may flow out. Let my beloved come into his garden, and eat his pleasant fruits.

CHAPTER 5

I AM come into my garden, my sister, *my* spouse: I have gathered my

myrrh with my spice; I have eaten my honeycomb with my honey; I have drunk my wine with my milk: eat, O friends; drink, yea, drink abundantly, O beloved.

2 I sleep, but my heart wakes: *it is* the voice of my beloved that knocks, *saying*, Open to me, my sister, my love, my dove, my undefiled: for my head is filled with dew, *and* my locks with the drops of the night.

3 I have put off my coat; how shall I put it on? I have washed my feet; how shall I defile them?

4 My beloved put in his hand by the hole *of the door*, and my bowels were moved for him.

5 I rose up to open to my beloved; and my hands dropped *with* <u>myrrh</u>, and my fingers *with* sweet smelling <u>myrrh</u>, upon the handles of the lock.   _{fragrant resin}

6 I opened to my beloved; but my beloved had withdrawn himself, *and* was gone: my soul failed when he spoke: I sought him, but I could not find him; I called him, but he gave me no answer.

7 The watchmen that went about the city found me, they smote me, they wounded me; the keepers of the walls took away my veil from me.

8 I <u>charge</u> you, O daughters of Je-ru'sa-lem, if you find my beloved, that you tell him, that I *am* <u>sick of love</u>.   _{adjure - lovesick}

9 What *is* your beloved more than *another* beloved, O you fairest among women? what *is* your beloved more than *another* beloved, that you do so charge us?

10 My beloved *is* white and ruddy, the <u>chiefest</u> among ten thousand.   _{outstanding}

11 His head *is as* the most fine gold, his locks *are* bushy, *and* black as a raven.

12 His eyes *are* as *the eyes* of doves by the rivers of waters, washed with milk, *and* <u>fitly set</u>.   _{mounted like jewels}

13 His cheeks *are* as a bed of spices, *as* sweet flowers: his lips *like* lilies, dropping <u>sweet</u> smelling <u>myrrh</u>.   _{fragrant - fragrant resin}

14 His hands *are as* gold rings set with the beryl: his belly *is as* bright ivory overlaid *with* sapphires.

15 His legs *are as* pillars of marble, set upon sockets of fine gold: his countenance *is* as Leb'a-non, excellent as the cedars.

16 His mouth *is* most sweet: yea, he *is* altogether lovely. This *is* my beloved, and this *is* my friend, O daughters of Je-ru'sa-lem.

CHAPTER 6

WHERE is your beloved gone, O you fairest among women? where is your beloved turned aside? that we may seek him with you.

2 My beloved is gone down into his garden, to the beds of spices, to feed in the gardens, and to gather lilies.

3 I *am* my beloved's, and my beloved *is* mine: he feeds among the lilies.

4 You *are* beautiful, O my love, as Tir'zah, comely as Je-ru'sa-lem, <u>terrible</u> as *an army* with banners.   _{awesome}

5 Turn away your eyes from me, for they have overcome me: your hair *is* as a

flock of goats that appear from Gil'e-ad.

6 Your teeth *are* as a flock of sheep which go up from the washing, whereof every one bears twins, and *there is* not one <u>barren</u> among them. _{lost}

7 As a piece of a pomegranate *are* your temples within your <u>locks</u>. _{veil}

8 There are <u>threescore</u> queens, and <u>fourscore</u> concubines, and <u>virgins</u> without number. _{60 - 80 - maidens}

9 My dove, my <u>undefiled</u> is *but* one; she *is* the *only* one of her mother, she *is* the choice *one* of her that bare her. The daughters saw her, and blessed her; *yea*, the queens and the concubines, and they praised her. _{perfect one}

10 Who *is* she *that* looks forth as the morning, fair as the moon, clear as the sun, *and* <u>terrible</u> as *an army* with banners? _{awesome}

11 I went down into the garden of nuts to see the fruits of the valley, *and* to see whether the vine flourished, *and* the pomegranates budded.

12 Or ever I was aware, my soul made me *like* the chariots of Am-mi'-na-dib.

13 Return, return, O Shu'lam-ite; return, return, that we may look upon you. What will you see in the Shu'lam-ite? As it were the company of two armies.

CHAPTER 7

HOW beautiful are your feet with shoes, O prince's daughter! the joints of your thighs *are* like jewels, the work of the hands of a cunning workman.

2 Your navel *is like* a round goblet, *which* wants not liquor: your belly *is like* an heap of wheat set about with lilies.

3 Your two breasts *are* like two young <u>roes</u> *that are* twins. _{gazelles}

4 Your neck *is* as a tower of ivory; your eyes *like* the fishpools in Hesh'bon, by the gate of Bath-rab'bim: your nose *is* as the tower of Leb'a-non which looks toward Damas'cus.

5 Your head upon you *is* like Car'mel, and the hair of your head like purple; the king *is* <u>held</u> in the galleries. _{captive}

6 How fair and how pleasant are you, O love, for delights!

7 This your stature is like to a palm tree, and your breasts to clusters *of grapes*.

8 I said, I will go up to the palm tree, I will take hold of the boughs thereof: now also your breasts shall be as clusters of the vine, and the smell of your nose like apples;

9 And the roof of your mouth like the best wine for my beloved, that goes *down* sweetly, causing the lips of those that are asleep to speak.

10 I *am* my beloved's, and his desire *is* toward me.

11 Come, my beloved, let us go forth into the field; let us lodge in the villages.

12 Let us get up early to the vineyards; let us see if the vine flourish, *whether* the tender grape <u>appear</u>, *and* the pomegranates bud forth: there will I give you my loves. _{open}

13 The mandrakes give a smell, and at our gates *are* all manner of pleasant *fruits*, new and old, *which* I have laid up for you, O my beloved.

CHAPTER 8

O THAT you *were* as my brother, that sucked the breasts of my mother! *when* I should find you without, I would kiss you; yea, I should not be despised.

2 I would lead you, *and* bring you into my mother's house, *who* would instruct me: I would cause you to drink of spiced wine of the juice of my pomegranate.

3 His left hand *should be* under my head, and his right hand should embrace me.

4 I charge you, O daughters of Je-ru'sa-lem, that you stir not up, nor awake *my* love, until he please.

5 Who *is* this that comes up from the wilderness, leaning upon her beloved? I raised you up under the apple tree: there your mother brought you forth: there she brought you forth *that* bare you.

6 Set me as a seal upon your heart, as a seal upon your arm: for love *is* strong as death; jealousy *is* cruel as the grave: the coals thereof *are* coals of fire, *which has* a most vehement flame.

severe - flashes

7 Many waters cannot quench love, neither can the floods drown it: if a man would give all the substance of his house for love, it would utterly be contemned.

8 We have a little sister, and she has no breasts: what shall we do for our sister in the day when she shall be spoken for?

9 If she *be* a wall, we will build upon her a palace of silver: and if she *be* a door, we will inclose her with boards of cedar.

10 I *am* a wall, and my breasts like towers: then was I in his eyes as one that found favor.

peace

11 Sol'o-mon had a vineyard at Ba'al-ha'mon; he let out the vineyard to keepers; every one for the fruit thereof was to bring a thousand *pieces* of silver.

12 My vineyard, which *is* mine, *is* before me: you, O Sol'o-mon, *must have* a thousand, and those that keep the fruit thereof two hundred.

13 You that dwell in the gardens, the companions hearken to your voice: cause me to hear *it*.

14 Make haste, my beloved, and be you like to a roe or to a young hart upon the mountains of spices.

gazell - stag

ISAIAH

OUTLINE

SURVEY

Isaiah is deservedly known as the Evangelical Prophet, because he gives the fullest and clearest exposition of the Gospel of Jesus Christ to be found anywhere in the Old Testament. Somewhat like the Epistle to the Romans in the New Testament, Isaiah serves as a compendium of the great doctrines of the pre-Christian age, and treats of almost every cardinal theme in the gamut of theology. Special emphasis is given to the doctrine of God, in His omnipotence, His omniscience, and His redemptive love. As over against the imaginary gods of the idol-worshipping heathen, He reveals Himself as the one true God, the sovereign Creator of the universe, Who ordains all the events of history according to His own master plan. In demonstration of the authority and inspiration of His word, He marvelously fulfills the predictions uttered by His prophets long before. He is the upholder of the moral law, Who brings into judgment all of the ungodly nations of the heathen, even the wealthiest and most powerful of them, and consigns them to the ash heap of eternity, while His chosen people live on to glorify His name.

It is above all as the Holy One of Israel that Isaiah presents the Lord Who moved him to prophesy. As the Holy One, He requires above and beyond the formalities of sacrificial worship the living sacrifice of a godly life. To this end He brings the most powerful suasions to bear upon the consciences of His people, both in the form of prophetic warning and appeal, and in the pressures of

chastisement designed to lead them to repentance. But as the Holy One *of Israel* He shows Himself forth to be unalterably committed to His convenant people, and the faithful guarantor of His gracious promises to forgive them when repentant and to deliver them from the power of their enemies. He shows Himself ready to rescue them from the assaults of their arrogant Gentile oppressors, or to bring them back from enslavement and exile to the Land of Promise.

Yet in the final analysis, even the Israelite believers, nurtured upon the Old Testament and enjoying unpurchasable privileges of access to God, are shown to be inherently sinful and unable to save themselves from evil. Their ultimate deliverance can only come through a Savior, the divine-human Messiah. This virgin-born Immanuel, who is the mighty God Himself, will establish His throne as King over all the earth and enforce the demands of God's holy law, as He establishes universal peace, goodness and truth all over the world. And yet this kingly Messiah is to achieve His triumph only as the Servant of Jehovah, rejected and despised by His own people, and presenting His sacred body as an atonement for their sins. Through this suffering and death He shall bring deliverance of soul not only to the true believers of national Israel but also to those Gentiles of distant lands who open their hearts to receive His truth. Both Jew and Gentile shall be gathered into the fold of faith and constitute the rejoicing subjects of His Millennial Kingdom, which is destined to establish God's rule and settle God's peace upon the whole earth.

AUTHOR

Isaiah, the son of Amoz, seems to have come from a well-to-do and respected Jerusalemite family, for not only is his father's name recorded, but he also enjoyed intimate relations with the royal family and the highest officials of the government. Although he may have begun his prophetic ministry in the latter end of Uzziah's reign, he records the year of Uzziah's death (probably 740 B.C.) as the time when he received a special anointing and commission from God in the temple (ch. 6). He was bidden to preach boldly and uncompromisingly a message of warning and denunciation against his people for their ungodliness of life and idolatry of worship, and to summon the nation to thoroughgoing repentance and reformation. He was hated and opposed by idolatrous King Ahaz, favored and respected by King Hezekiah (716-698 B.C.)—who nevertheless disregarded his warnings against alliance with Egypt—and he was probably martyred by Hezekiah's depraved and brutal son, King Manasseh, somewhere around 680 B.C.

G.L.A. Jr.

THE BOOK OF

ISAIAH

CHAPTER 1

"Salvation of Jehovah"
As Enemies Attack the Promise of
the Messiah's Coming Comforts

THE vision of I-sa'iah the son of A'moz, which he saw concerning Ju'dah and Je-ru'sa-lem in the days of Uz-zi'ah, Jo'tham, A'haz, *and* Hez-e-ki'ah, kings of Ju'dah.

2 Hear, O heavens, and give ear, O earth: for the LORD has spoken, I have nourished and brought up children, and they have rebelled against Me.

3 The ox know its owner, and the ass its master's crib: *but* Is'ra-el does not know, My people do not consider.   manger

4 Ah sinful nation, a people laden with iniquity, a seed of evildoers, children that are corrupters: they have forsaken the LORD, they have provoked the Holy One of Is'ra-el to anger, they are gone away backward.   guilt - turned from Him

5 Why should you be stricken any more? you will revolt more and more: the whole head is sick, and the whole heart faint.

6 From the sole of the foot even to the head *there is* no soundness in it; *but* wounds, and bruises, and putrifying sores: they have not been closed, neither bound up, neither mollified with ointment.   cleansed

7 Your country *is* desolate, your cities *are* burned with fire: your land, strangers devour it in your presence, and *it is* desolate, as overthrown by strangers.   strip

8 And the daughter of Zi'on is left as a cottage in a vineyard, as a lodge in a garden of cucumbers, as a besieged city.   shelter

9 Except the LORD of hosts had left to us a very small remnant, we should have been as Sod'om, *and we* should have been like to Go-mor'rah.   ROM. 9:29   Jehovah[s.f.] Tsebaoth

10 Hear the word of the LORD, you rulers of Sod'om; give ear to the law of our God, you people of Go-mor'rah.   Jehovah[s.f.] - Elohim[p.f.]

11 To what purpose *is* the multitude of your sacrifices to Me? says the LORD: I am full of the burned offerings of rams, and the fat of fed beasts; and I delight not in the blood of bullocks, or of lambs, or of he goats.

12 When you come to appear before Me, who has required this at your hand, to tread My courts?   trample

13 Bring no more vain oblations; incense is an abomination to Me; the new moons and sabbaths, the calling of assemblies, I cannot away with; *it is* iniquity, even the solemn meeting.

worthless - offerings - detestable - rest days - evil

14 Your new moons and your appointed feasts My soul hates: they are a trouble to Me; I am weary to bear *them*.   abhors

15 And when you spread forth your hands, I will hide My eyes from you:

yea, when you make many prayers, I will not hear: your hands are full of <u>blood</u>. evil deeds

16 Wash you, make you clean; put away the evil of your doings from before My eyes; cease to do evil; ROM. 12:9

17 Learn to do well; seek judgment, <u>relieve</u> the oppressed, judge the fatherless, plead for the widow. encourage

18 Come now, and let us reason together, says the LORD: though your sins be as scarlet, they shall be as white as snow; though they be red like crimson, they shall be as wool.

19 If you be willing and obedient, you shall eat the good of the land:

20 But if you refuse and rebel, you shall be <u>devoured</u> with the sword: for the mouth of the LORD has spoken *it*. destroyed

21 How is the faithful city become an harlot! it was full of judgment; righteousness lodged in it; but now murderers.

22 Your silver is become dross, your wine mixed with water:

23 Your princes *are* rebellious, and companions of thieves: every one loves <u>gifts</u>, and follows after rewards: they judge not the fatherless, neither does the cause of the widow come to them. bribes

24 Therefore says the <u>Lord</u>, the <u>LORD of hosts</u>, the mighty One of Is'ra-el, Ah, I will <u>ease Me</u> of My adversaries, and avenge Me of My enemies: Adon^{s.f.} - Jehovah^{s.f.} Tsebaoth - be relieved

25 And I will turn My hand upon you, and <u>purely purge</u> away your dross, and take away all your tin: smelt

26 And I will restore your judges as at the first, and your counselors as at the beginning: afterward you shall be called, The city of righteousness, the faithful city.

27 Zi'on shall be redeemed with judgment, and her converts with righteousness.

28 And the destruction of the transgressors and of the sinners *shall be* together, and they that forsake the LORD shall <u>be consumed</u>. 2 THESS. 1:8 perish

29 For they shall be ashamed of the <u>oaks</u> which you have desired, and you shall be <u>confounded</u> for the gardens that you have chosen. i.e., pagan shrines - disgraced

30 For you shall be as an oak whose leaf fades, and as a garden that has no water.

31 And the strong shall be as <u>tow</u>, and <u>the maker of it</u> as a spark, and they shall both burn together, and none shall quench *them*. straw - his work

CHAPTER 2

THE word that I-sa'iah the son of A'moz saw concerning Ju'dah and Je-ru'sa-lem.

2 And it shall come to pass in the last days, *that* the mountain of the LORD's house shall be established in the top of the mountains, and shall be exalted above the hills; and all nations shall flow to it.

3 And many people shall go and say, Come you, and let us go up to the mountain <u>of the</u> LORD, to the house of the <u>God</u> of Ja'cob; and He will teach us of His ways, and we will walk in His

paths: for out of Zi'on shall go forth the law, and the word of the LORD from Je-ru'sa-lem.   Jehovah[s.f.] - Elohim[p.f.]

4 And He shall judge among the nations, and shall rebuke many people: and they shall beat their swords into plowshares, and their spears into pruninghooks: nation shall not lift up sword against nation, neither shall they learn war any more.

5 O house of Ja'cob, come you, and let us walk in the light of the LORD.EPH. 5:8

6 Therefore You have forsaken Your people the house of Ja'cob, because they be replenished from the east, and *are* soothsayers like the Phi-lis'tines, and they please themselves in the children of strangers.

7 Their land also is full of silver and gold, neither *is there any* end of their treasures; their land is also full of horses, neither *is there any* end of their chariots:

8 Their land also is full of idols; they worship the work of their own hands, that which their own fingers have made:

9 And the <u>mean</u> man <u>bows down</u> and the great man humbles himself therefore: forgive them not.

common - is humbled

10 Enter into the <u>rock</u>, and hide you in the dust, for <u>fear</u> of the LORD, and for the glory of His majesty. caves - dread

11 The <u>lofty</u> looks of man shall be humbled, and the haughtiness of men shall be <u>bowed down</u>, and the LORD alone shall be exalted in that day. prowl

12 For the day of the LORD of hosts *shall be* upon every *one that is* proud and lofty, and upon every *one that is* lifted up; and he shall be brought low: Jehovah[s.f.] Tsebaoth

13 And upon all the cedars of Leb'a-non, *that are* high and lifted up, and upon all the oaks of Ba'shan,

14 And upon all the high mountains, and upon all the hills *that are* lifted up,

15 And upon every high tower, and upon every <u>fenced</u> wall,   fortified

16 And upon all the ships of Tar'-shish, and upon all pleasant pictures.

17 And the <u>loftiness</u> of man shall be <u>bowed down</u>, and the haughtiness of men shall be made low: and the LORD alone shall be exalted in that day. arrogance

18 And the idols He shall utterly abolish.

19 And they shall go into the holes of the rocks, and into the caves of the earth, for <u>fear</u> of the LORD, and for the glory of His majesty, when He arises to shake terribly the earth. dread

20 In that day a man shall <u>cast</u> his idols of silver, and his idols of gold, which they made *each one* for himself to worship, to the moles and to the bats;   throw away

21 To go into the clefts of the rocks, and into the tops of the ragged rocks, for <u>fear</u> of the LORD, and for the glory of His majesty, when He arises to shake terribly the earth.

22 Cease you from man, whose breath *is* in his nostrils: for wherein is he to be accounted of?

CHAPTER 3

FOR, behold, the <u>Lord</u>, the LORD of <u>hosts</u>, does take away from Je-ru'sa-

lem and from Ju'dah the <u>stay</u> and the <u>staff</u>, the whole <u>stay</u> of bread, and the whole <u>stay</u> of water,

Adon^{s.f.} - Jehovah^{s.f.} Tsebaoth - supply - i.e., support

2 The mighty man, and the man of war, the judge, and the prophet, and the <u>prudent</u>, and the <u>ancient</u>,   diviner - elder

3 The captain of fifty, and the honorable man, and the counselor, and the cunning <u>artificer</u>, and the eloquent orator.   magician

4 And I will give children *to be* their princes, and babes shall rule over them.

5 And the people shall be oppressed, every one by another, and every one by his neighbor: the child shall behave himself proudly against the <u>ancient</u>, and the <u>base</u> against the honorable.   elder - inferior

6 When a man shall take hold of his brother of the house of his father, *saying*, You have clothing, be you our ruler, and *let* this ruin *be* under your hand:

7 In that day shall he <u>swear</u>, saying, I will not be an <u>healer</u>; for in my house *is* neither bread nor clothing: make me not a ruler of the people.   protest - helper

8 For Je-ru'sa-lem is ruined, and Ju'dah is fallen: because their tongue and their doings *are* against the LORD, to provoke the eyes of His glory.

9 The show of their countenance does witness against them; and they <u>declare</u> their sin as Sod'om, they hide *it* not. Woe to their soul! for they have rewarded evil to themselves.   display

10 Say you to the righteous, that *it shall be* well *with him*: for they shall eat the fruit of their doings.

11 Woe to the wicked! *it shall be* ill *with him*: for the reward of his hands shall be given him.

12 *As for* My people, children *are* their oppressors, and women rule over them. O My people, they which lead you cause *you* to err, and destroy the way of your paths.

13 The LORD stands up to plead, and stands to judge the people.

14 The LORD will enter into judgment with the <u>ancients</u> of His people, and the princes thereof: for you have <u>eaten up</u> the vineyard; the spoil of the poor *is* in your houses.   elders - ruined

15 What mean you *that* you beat My people to pieces, and grind the faces of the poor? says the <u>Lord GOD of hosts</u>.   Adonay^{p.f.} Jehovah^{s.f.} Tsebaoth

16 Moreover the LORD says, Because the daughters of Zi'on are haughty, and walk with stretched forth necks and <u>wanton</u> eyes, walking and <u>mincing</u> *as* they go, and making a tinkling with their feet: seductive - skipping

17 Therefore the LORD will smite with a scab the crown of the head of the daughters of Zi'on, and the LORD will <u>discover</u> their secret parts.   bare

18 In that day the Lord will take away the <u>bravery</u> of *their* <u>tinkling ornaments</u> *about their feet*, and *their* <u>cauls</u>, and *their* round <u>tires</u> like the moon,   beauty - anklets - headbands - tiaras

19 The <u>chains</u>, and the bracelets, and the <u>mufflers</u>,   earrings - veils

20 The bonnets, and the ornaments of the legs, and the <u>headbands</u>, and the <u>tablets</u>, and the earrings,   sashes - perfume boxes

21 The rings, and <u>nose jewels</u>,

22 The changeable suits of apparel, and the mantles, and the <u>wimples</u>, and the <u>crisping pins</u>, <small>cloaks - money purses</small>
23 The <u>glasses</u>, and the fine linen, and the <u>hoods</u>, and the veils. <small>hand mirrors - turbans</small>
24 And it shall come to pass, *that* instead of sweet smell there shall be stink; and instead of a girdle a <u>rent</u>; and instead of well set hair baldness; and instead of <u>a stomacher</u> a girding of sackcloth; *and* burning instead of beauty. <small>rope - fine clothes</small>
25 Your men shall fall by the sword, and your mighty in the war.
26 And her gates shall lament and mourn; and she *being* <u>desolate</u> shall sit upon the ground. <small>deserted</small>

CHAPTER 4

AND in that day seven women shall take hold of one man, saying, We will eat our own bread, and wear our own apparel: only let us be called by your name, to take away our reproach.<small>LUKE 1:25</small>
2 In that day shall the Branch of the LORD be beautiful and glorious, and the fruit of the earth *shall be* excellent and comely for them that are escaped of Is'ra-el.
3 And it shall come to pass, *that he that is* left in Zi'on, and *he that* remains in Je-ru'sa-lem, shall be called holy, *even* every one that is written among the living in Je-ru'sa-lem:
4 When the Lord shall have washed away the filth of the daughters of Zi'on, and shall have purged the blood of Je-ru'sa-lem from the midst thereof by the spirit of judgment, and by the spirit of burning.

5 And the LORD will create <u>upon</u> every dwelling place of mount Zi'on, and upon her assemblies, a cloud and smoke by day, and the shining of a flaming fire by night: for upon all the glory *shall be* a <u>defence</u>. <small>over - canopy</small>
6 And there shall be a tabernacle for a shadow in the daytime from the heat, and for a place of refuge, and for <u>a covert</u> from storm and from rain.<small>the protection</small>

CHAPTER 5

NOW will I sing to My wellbeloved a song of My beloved touching His vineyard. My wellbeloved has a vineyard in a very <u>fruitful</u> hill: <small>fertile</small>
2 And He <u>fenced it</u>, and gathered out the stones thereof, and planted it with the choicest vine, and built a tower in the midst of it, and also <u>made</u> a winepress therein: and He <u>looked</u> that it should bring forth grapes, and it brought forth wild grapes. <small>dug it up - cut out - expected</small>
3 And now, O inhabitants of Je-ru'sa-lem, and men of Ju'dah, judge, I pray you, between Me and My vineyard.
4 What could have been done more to My vineyard, that I have not done in it? wherefore, when I looked that it should bring forth grapes, brought it forth wild grapes? <small>LUKE 20:9</small>
5 And now <u>go to</u>; I will tell you what I will do to My vineyard: I will take away the hedge thereof, and it shall be eaten up; *and* break down the wall thereof, and it shall be trodden down: <small>JOHN 15:1 listen</small>
6 And I will lay it waste: it shall not be pruned, nor dug; but there shall

come up briers and thorns: I will also command the clouds that they rain no rain upon it.

7 For the vineyard of the LORD of hosts *is* the house of Is'ra-el, and the men of Ju'dah His pleasant plant: and He looked for judgment, but behold oppression; for righteousness, but behold a cry. Jehovah^{s.f.} Tsebaoth

8 Woe to them that join house to house, *that* lay field to field, till *there be* no place, that they may be placed alone in the midst of the earth!

9 In my ears *said* the LORD of hosts, Of a truth many houses shall be desolate, *even* great and fair, without inhabitant.

10 Yea, ten acres of vineyard shall yield one bath, and the seed of an homer shall yield an ephah.

11 Woe to them that rise up early in the morning, *that* they may follow strong drink; that continue until night, *till* wine inflame them! pursue

12 And the harp, and the viol, the tabret, and pipe, and wine, are in their feasts: but they regard not the work of the LORD, neither consider the operation of His hands.

13 Therefore my people are gone into captivity, because *they have* no knowledge: and their honorable men *are* famished, and their multitude dried up with thirst.

14 Therefore hell has enlarged herself, and opened her mouth without measure: and their glory, and their multitude, and their pomp, and he that rejoices, shall descend into it. Sheol (Heb.)

15 And the mean man shall be brought down, and the mighty man shall be humbled, and the eyes of the lofty shall be humbled:

16 But the LORD of hosts shall be exalted in judgment, and God that is holy shall be sanctified in righteousness. Jehovah^{s.f.} Tsebaoth - holy

17 Then shall the lambs feed after their manner, and the waste places of the fat ones shall strangers eat.

18 Woe to them that draw iniquity with cords of vanity, and sin as it were with a cart rope: drag - falsehood

19 That say, Let Him make speed, *and* hasten His work, that we may see *it*: and let the counsel of the Holy One of Is'ra-el draw near and come, that we may know *it*!

20 Woe to them that call evil good, and good evil; that put darkness for light, and light for darkness; that put bitter for sweet, and sweet for bitter!

21 Woe to *them that are* wise in their own eyes, and prudent in their own sight! ROM. 1:22

22 Woe to *them that are* mighty to drink wine, and men of strength to mingle strong drink:

23 Which justify the wicked for reward, and take away the righteousness of the righteous from him! acquit - bribes

24 Therefore as the fire devours the stubble, and the flame consumes the chaff, *so* their root shall be as rottenness, and their blossom shall go up as dust: because they have cast away the law of the LORD of hosts, and despised the word of the Holy One of Is'ra-el. Jehovah^{s.f.} Tsebaoth

25 Therefore is the anger of the LORD kindled against His people, and He has stretched <u>forth</u> His hand against them, and has smitten them: and the hills did tremble, and their carcases *were* torn in the midst of the streets. For all this His anger is not turned away, but His hand *is* stretched out still.   out

26 And He will lift up an <u>ensign</u> to the nations from far, and will <u>hiss</u> to them from the end of the earth: and, behold, they shall come with speed swiftly: banner - call

27 None shall be weary nor stumble among them; none shall slumber nor sleep; neither shall the girdle of their loins be loosed, nor the <u>latchet</u> of their shoes be broken: thong

28 Whose arrows *are* sharp, and all their bows bent, their horses' hoofs shall be counted like flint, and their wheels like a whirlwind:

29 Their roaring *shall be* like a lion, they shall roar like young lions: yea, they shall roar, and lay hold of the prey, and shall carry *it* away safe, and none shall deliver *it*.

30 And in that day they shall roar against them like the roaring of the sea: and if *one* look to the land, behold darkness *and* sorrow, and the light is darkened in the heavens thereof.

CHAPTER 6

IN the year that king Uz-zi'ah died I saw also the Lord sitting upon a throne, high and lifted up, and His <u>train</u> filled the temple.   JOHN 12:41 train of His robe

2 Above it stood the seraphims: each one had six wings; with two he covered his face, and with two he covered his feet, and with two he did fly.

3 And one cried to another, and said, Holy, holy, holy, *is* the <u>LORD</u> of hosts: the whole earth *is* full of His glory.   REV. 4:8 Jehovah[s.f.] Tsebaoth

4 And the posts of the door moved at the voice of him that cried, and the house was filled with smoke.

5 Then said I, Woe *is* me! for I am undone; because I *am* a man of unclean lips, and I dwell in the midst of a people of unclean lips: for my eyes have seen the King, the <u>LORD</u> of hosts.   Jehovah[s.f.] Tsebaoth

6 Then flew one of the seraphims to me, having a live coal in his hand, *which* he had taken with the tongs from off the altar:

7 And he laid *it* upon my mouth, and said, Lo, this has touched your lips; and your <u>iniquity</u> is taken away, and your sin <u>purged</u>.   guilt - forgiven

8 Also I heard the voice of the Lord, saying, Whom shall I send, and who will go for Us? Then said I, Here *am* I; send me.

9 And He said, Go, and tell this people, Hear you indeed, but understand not; and see you indeed, but perceive not.   LUKE 8:10 ACTS 28:26

10 Make the heart of this people fat, and make their ears heavy, and shut their eyes; less they see with their eyes, and hear with their ears, and understand with their heart, and convert, and be healed.

MATT. 13:14 MARK 4:12 JOHN 12:40 ACTS 28:26

11 Then said I, Lord, how long? And

He answered, Until the cities be wasted without inhabitant, and the houses without man, and the land be utterly desolate,

12 And the LORD have removed men far away, and *there be* a great forsaking in the midst of the land.

13 But yet in it *shall be* a tenth, and *it* shall return, and shall be eaten: as a teil tree, and as an oak, whose substance *is* in them, when they cast *their leaves*: *so* the holy seed *shall be* the substance thereof.   elm

CHAPTER 7

AND it came to pass in the days of A'haz the son of Jo'tham, the son of Uz-zi'ah, king of Ju'dah, *that* Re'zin the king of Syr'i-a, and Pe'kah the son of Rem-a-li'ah, king of Is'ra-el, went up toward Je-ru'sa-lem to war against it, but could not prevail against it.

2 And it was told the house of Da'vid, saying, Syr'i-a is confederate with E'phra-im. And his heart was moved, and the heart of his people, as the trees of the wood are moved with the wind.   allied

3 Then said the LORD to I-sa'iah, Go forth now to meet A'haz, you, and She'ar-ja'shub your son, at the end of the conduit of the upper pool in the highway of the fuller's field;

4 And say to him, Take heed, and be quiet; fear not, neither be fainthearted for the two tails of these smoking firebrands, for the fierce anger of Re'zin with Syr'i-a, and of the son of Rem-a-li'ah.   care

5 Because Syr'i-a, E'phra-im, and the son of Rem-a-li'ah, have taken evil counsel against you, saying,   planned evil

6 Let us go up against Ju'dah, and vex it, and let us make a breach therein for us, and set a king in the midst of it, *even* the son of Ta'be-al: terrorize - force an entrance

7 Thus says the Lord GOD, It shall not stand, neither shall it come to pass.   Adonay p.f. Jehovah

8 For the head of Syr'i-a *is* Damas'cus, and the head of Damas'cus *is* Re'zin; and within threescore and five years shall E'phra-im be broken, that it be not a people. 65

9 And the head of E'phra-im *is* Sama'ri-a, and the head of Sa-ma'ri-a *is* Rem-a-li'ah's son. If you will not believe, surely you shall not be established.   stand at all

10 Moreover the LORD spoke again to A'haz, saying,

11 Ask you a sign of the LORD your God; ask it either in the depth, or in the height above.   Jehovah s.f. - Elohim p.f. - of Sheol (Heb.) - of heaven

12 But A'haz said, I will not ask, neither will I tempt the LORD.   test

13 And he said, Hear you now, O house of Da'vid; *Is it* a small thing for you to weary men, but will you weary my God also?

14 Therefore the Lord Himself shall give you a sign; Behold, a virgin shall conceive, and bear a son, and shall call His name Im-man'u-el.

MATT. 1:23 Adonay p.f. - God with us

15 Butter and honey shall He eat, that He may know to refuse the evil, and choose the good.

16 For before the child shall know to refuse the evil, and choose the good, the

land that you <u>abhor</u> shall be forsaken of both her kings.   despise

17 The L ORD shall bring upon you, and upon your people, and upon your father's house, days that have not come, from the day that E'phra-im departed from Ju'dah; *even* the king of As-syr'i-a.

18 And it shall come to pass in that day, *that* the L ORD shall <u>hiss</u> for the fly that *is* in the <u>uttermost</u> part of the rivers of E'gypt, and for the bee that *is* in the land of As-syr'i-a.   call - remotest

19 And they shall come, and shall rest all of them in the desolate valleys, and in the holes of the rocks, and upon all thorns, and upon all bushes.

20 In the same day shall the Lord shave with a razor that is hired, *namely*, by them beyond the river, by the king of As-syr'i-a, the head, and the hair of the feet: and it shall also <u>consume</u> the beard.   remove

21 And it shall come to pass in that day, *that* a man shall <u>nourish</u> a young cow, and two sheep;   keep alive

22 And it shall come to pass, for the abundance of milk *that* they shall give he shall eat butter: for butter and honey shall every one eat that is left in the land.

23 And it shall come to pass in that day, *that* every place shall be, where there were a thousand vines at a thousand silverlings, it shall *even* be for briers and thorns.

24 With arrows and with bows shall *men* come there; because all the land shall become briers and thorns.

25 And *on* all hills that shall be dug with the mattock, there shall not come there the fear of briers and thorns: but it shall be for the sending forth of oxen, and for the treading of <u>lesser cattle</u>.   sheep

CHAPTER 8

MOREOVER the L ORD said to me, Take you a great roll, and write in it with a man's pen concerning Ma'her-shal'al-hash'-baz.

2 And I took to me faithful witnesses to record, U-ri'ah the priest, and Zech-a-ri'ah the son of Je-ber-e-chi'ah.

3 And I <u>went to</u> the prophetess; and she conceived, and bare a son. Then said the L ORD to me, Call his name Ma'her-shal'al-hash'-baz.   married

4 For before the child <u>shall have knowledge</u> to cry, My father, and my mother, the riches of Da-mas'cus and the spoil of Sa-ma'ri-a shall be taken away <u>before</u> the king of As-syr'i-a.   knows how - by

5 The L ORD spoke also to me again, saying,

6 Forasmuch as this people refuse the waters of Shi-lo'ah that go softly, and rejoice in Re'zin and Rem-a-li'ah's son;

7 Now therefore, behold, the Lord brings up upon them the waters of the <u>river</u>, strong and many, *even* the king of As-syr'i-a, and all his glory: and it shall <u>come</u> up over all its channels, and go over all its banks: i.e. Euphrates - rise

8 And it shall pass through Ju'dah; it shall overflow and go over, He shall reach *even* to the neck; and the stretch-

P15C—— 1014

P15C-1054

ing out of its wings shall fill the breadth of Your land, O Im-man'u-el.

9 Associate yourselves, O you people, and you shall be broken in pieces; and give ear, all you of far countries: gird yourselves, and you shall be broken in pieces; gird yourselves, and you shall be broken in pieces.

10 Take counsel together, and it shall come to nothing; speak the word, and it shall not stand: for God *is* with us.

11 For the LORD spoke thus to me with a <u>strong hand</u>, and instructed me that I should not walk in the way of this people, saying, mighty power

12 Say you not, A <u>confederacy</u>, to all *them to* whom this people shall say, A <u>confederacy</u>; neither fear you their fear, nor be afraid. conspiracy

13 <u>Sanctify</u> the LORD of hosts Himself; and *let* Him *be* your <u>fear</u>, and *let* Him *be* your dread.

1 PET. 3:15 Holy is - Jehovah^{s.f.} Tsebaoth - respected One

14 And He shall be for a <u>sanctuary</u>; but for a stone of stumbling and for a rock of <u>offence</u> to both the houses of Is'ra-el, for a <u>gin</u> and for a <u>snare</u> to the inhabitants of Je-ru'sa-lem.

LUKE 20:18 refuge - confusion - trap - lure

15 And many among them shall stumble, and fall, and be broken, and be <u>snared</u>, and be taken.

16 <u>Bind up</u> the <u>testimony</u>, seal the law among My disciples. Protect - records

17 And I will <u>wait</u> upon the LORD, that hides His face from the house of Ja'cob, and I will look for Him. call

18 Behold, I and the children whom the LORD has given me *are* for signs and for wonders in Is'ra-el from the LORD of hosts, which dwells in mount Zi'on. HEB. 2:13 Jehovah^{s.f.} Tsebaoth

19 And when they shall say to you, Seek to them that have <u>familiar spirits</u>, and to <u>wizards</u> that <u>peep</u>, and that mutter: should not a people seek to their <u>God</u>? for the living to the dead?

mediums - spiritists - whisper - Elohim^{p.f.}

20 To the law and to the testimony: if they speak not according to this word, *it is* because *there is* no light in them.

21 And they shall pass through it, <u>hardly bestead</u> and hungry: and it shall come to pass, that when they shall be hungry, they shall fret themselves, and curse their king and their <u>God</u>, and look upward. hard pressed

22 And they shall look to the earth; and behold trouble and darkness, dimness of anguish; and *they shall be* driven to darkness.

CHAPTER 9

NEVERTHELESS the dimness *shall* not *be* such as *was* in her <u>vexation</u>, when at the first He lightly afflicted the land of Zeb'u-lun and the land of Naph'ta-li, and afterward did more grievously afflict *her by* the way of the sea, beyond Jor'dan, in Gal'i-lee of the nations. anguish

2 The people that walked in darkness have seen a great light: they that dwell in the land of the shadow of death, upon them has the light shined. LUKE 1:79

3 You have multiplied the nation, *and* not increased the joy: they joy before You according to the joy in harvest, *and* as *men* rejoice when they divide the spoil.

4 For You have <u>broken</u> the yoke of his burden, and the staff of his shoulder, the rod of his oppressor, as in the day of Mid'i-an.   shattered

5 <u>For</u> every battle of the warrior *is* with confused noise, and garments rolled in blood; but *this* shall be with burning *and* fuel <u>of</u> fire.   Usually - for the

6 For to us a <u>Child</u> is born, to us a Son is given: and the government shall be upon His shoulder: and His name shall be called Wonderful, Counselor, <u>The Mighty God</u>, The Everlasting Father, The Prince of Peace.   LUKE 2:11 i.e., Jesus Christ - El^{s.f.} Gibbor

7 Of the increase of *His* government and peace *there shall be* no end, upon the throne of Da'vid, and upon his kingdom, to order it, and to establish it with judgment and with justice from henceforth even for ever. The <u>zeal</u> of the Lord <u>of hosts</u> will <u>perform</u> this.

    burning desire - Jehovahs.f. Tsebaoth - accomplish

8 The Lord sent a word into Ja'cob, and it has <u>lighted</u> upon Is'ra-el.   fallen

9 And all the people shall know, *even* E'phra-im and the inhabitant of Sa-ma'ri-a, that say in the pride and <u>stoutness</u> of heart,   arrogance

10 The bricks are fallen down, but we will build with <u>hewn</u> stones: the sycamores are cut down, but we will <u>change</u> *them into* cedars.

    smooth - replace - with

11 Therefore the Lord shall <u>set</u> up the adversaries of Re'zin against him, and join his enemies together;   raise

12 The Syr'i-ans before, and the Phi-lis'tines behind; and they shall devour Is'ra-el with open mouth. For all this

His anger is not turned away, but His hand *is* stretched out still.

13 For the people turn not to Him that <u>smite</u> them, neither do they seek the Lord of hosts.

    struck - Jehovah^{s.f.} Tsebaoth

14 Therefore the Lord will cut off from Is'ra-el head and tail, branch and <u>rush</u>, in one day.   bulrush

15 The <u>ancient</u> and honorable, he *is* the head; and the prophet that teaches lies, he *is* the tail.   elder

16 For the leaders of this people cause *them* to err; and *they that are* led of them *are* destroyed.

17 Therefore the Lord shall have no joy in their young men, neither shall have mercy on their fatherless and widows: for every one *is* an hypocrite and an evildoer, and every mouth speaks folly. For all this His anger is not turned away, but His hand *is* stretched out still.

18 For wickedness burns as the fire: it shall devour the briers and thorns, and shall kindle in the thickets of the forest, and they shall mount up *like* the lifting up of smoke.

19 Through the anger of the Lord <u>of hosts</u> is the land darkened, and the people shall be as the fuel of the fire: no man shall spare his brother.   Jehovah^{s.f.} Tsebaoth

20 And he shall <u>snatch</u> on the right hand, and be hungry; and he shall eat on the left hand, and they shall not be satisfied: they shall eat every man the flesh of his own arm:

    slice off what is

21 Ma-nas'seh, E'phra-im; and E'-

phra-im, Ma-nas'seh: *and* they to-gether *shall be* against Ju'dah. For all this His anger is not turned away, but His hand *is* stretched out still.

CHAPTER 10

WOE to them that decree un-righteous decrees, and that write grievousness *which* they have pre-scribed;

2 To turn aside the needy from judg-ment, and to take away the right from the poor of My people, that widows may be their prey, and *that* they may rob the fatherless!

3 And what will you do in the day of visitation, and in the desolation *which* shall come from far? to whom will you flee for help? and where will you leave your glory?

4 Without Me they shall <u>bow down under</u> the prisoners, and they shall fall under the slain. For all this His anger is not turned away, but His hand *is* stretched out still.   _{cringe among}

5 O As-syr'i-an, the rod of My an-ger, and the staff in their hand is My indignation.

6 I will send him against an <u>hypo-critical</u> nation, and against the people of My wrath will I give him a charge, to take the spoil, and to take the prey, and to tread them down like the mire of the streets.   _{godless}

7 However he means not so, neither does his heart think so; but *it is* in his heart to destroy and cut off na-tions not a few.

8 For he says, *Are* not my princes <u>al-together</u> kings?   _{all}

9 *Is* not Cal'no <u>as</u> Car'che-mish? *is* not Ha'math <u>as</u> Ar'pad? *is* not Sa-ma'ri-a <u>as</u> Da-mas'cus?   _{as good as}

10 As my hand has found the king-doms of the idols, and whose graven images did excel them of Je-ru'sa-lem and of Sa-ma'ri-a;

11 Shall I not, as I have done to Sa-ma'ri-a and her <u>idols</u>, so do to Je-ru'sa-lem and her <u>idols</u>?   _{images}

12 Wherefore it shall come to pass, *that* when the Lord has <u>performed</u> His whole work upon mount Zi'on and on Je-ru'sa-lem, I will punish the fruit of the stout heart of the king of As-syr'i-a, and the glory of his <u>high looks</u>.   _{finished - haughtiness}

13 For he says, By the strength of my hand I have done *it*, and by my wisdom; for I am prudent: and I have removed the bounds of the people, and have robbed their treasures, and I have put down the inhabitants like a <u>val-iant</u> *man*:   _{mighty}

14 And my hand has found as a nest the riches of the people: and as one gathers eggs *that are* left, have I gathered all the earth; and there was none that moved the wing, or opened the mouth, or peeped.

15 Shall the ax boast itself against him that <u>hews</u> therewith? *or* shall the saw magnify itself against him that shakes it? as if the rod should shake *itself* against them that lift it up, *or* as if the staff should lift up *itself, as if it were* no wood.   _{chops}

16 Therefore shall the Lord, the Lord

of hosts, send among his fat ones leanness; and under his glory he shall kindle a burning like the burning of a fire. Adon^{s.f.} - Adonay^{p.f.} Tsebaoth

17 And the light of Is'ra-el shall be for a fire, and his Holy One for a flame: and it shall burn and devour his thorns and his briers in one day;

18 And shall consume the glory of his forest, and of his fruitful field, both soul and body: and they shall be as when a standardbearer faints.

19 And the rest of the trees of his forest shall be few, that a child may write them.

20 And it shall come to pass in that day, *that* the remnant of Is'ra-el, and such as are escaped of the house of Ja'cob, shall no more again stay upon him that smote them; but shall stay upon the LORD, the Holy One of Is'ra-el, in truth. rely - struck

21 The remnant shall return, *even* the remnant of Ja'cob, to the Mighty God.

El^{s.f.} Gibbor

22 For though your people Is'ra-el be as the sand of the sea, *yet* a remnant of them shall return: the consumption decreed shall overflow with righteousness. ROM. 9:27 destruction

23 For the Lord GOD of hosts shall make a consumption, even determined, in the midst of all the land.

Adonay^{p.f.} - Jehovah^{s.f.} Tsebaoth

24 Therefore thus says the Lord GOD of hosts, O My people that dwell in Zi'on, be not afraid of the As-syr'i-an: he shall smite you with a rod, and shall lift up his staff against you, after the manner of E'gypt.

25 For yet a very little while, and the indignation shall cease, and My anger in their destruction.

26 And the LORD of hosts shall stir up a scourge for him according to the slaughter of Mid'i-an at the rock of O'reb: and *as* his rod *was* upon the sea, so shall he lift it up after the manner of E'gypt. Jehovah^{s.f.} Tsebaoth - enemy

27 And it shall come to pass in that day, *that* his burden shall be taken away from off your shoulder, and his yoke from off your neck, and the yoke shall be destroyed because of the anointing. i.e., control

28 He is come to A-i'ath, he is passed to Mig'ron; at Mich'mash he has laid up his carriages: baggage

29 They are gone over the passage: they have taken up their lodging at Ge'ba; Ra'mah is afraid; Gib'e-ah of Saul is fled.

30 Lift up your voice, O daughter of Gal'lim: cause it to be heard to La'ish, O poor An'a-thoth.

31 Mad-me'nah is removed; the inhabitants of Ge'bim gather themselves to flee.

32 As yet shall he remain at Nob that day: he shall shake his hand *against* the mount of the daughter of Zi'on, the hill of Je-ru'sa-lem.

33 Behold, the Lord, the LORD of hosts, shall lop the bough with terror: and the high ones of stature *shall be* hewn down, and the haughty shall be humbled. Adon^{s.f.} - Adonay^{p.f.} Tsebaoth - cut off - tall

34 And He shall cut down the thickets of the forest with iron, and Leb'a-non shall fall by a mighty one. an iron ax

CHAPTER 11

AND there shall come forth a rod out of the stem of Jes'se, and a Branch shall grow out of his roots:

REV. 22:16 i.e., The Christ

2 And the Spirit of the LORD shall rest upon Him, the spirit of wisdom and understanding, the spirit of counsel and might, the spirit of knowledge and of the fear of the LORD;   REV. 1:4 reverence

3 And shall make Him of quick understanding in the fear of the LORD: and He shall not judge after the sight of His eyes, neither reprove after the hearing of His ears: delight - honor - by

4 But with righteousness shall He judge the poor, and reprove with equity for the meek of the earth: and He shall smite the earth with the rod of His mouth, and with the breath of His lips shall He slay the wicked.   2 THESS. 2:8 decide

5 And righteousness shall be the girdle of His loins, and faithfulness the girdle of His reins.

EPH. 6:14 sash - i.e., strength - waist i.e., emotions

6 The wolf also shall dwell with the lamb, and the leopard shall lie down with the kid; and the calf and the young lion and the fatling together; and a little child shall lead them.

7 And the cow and the bear shall feed; their young ones shall lie down together: and the lion shall eat straw like the ox.

8 And the sucking child shall play on the hole of the asp, and the weaned child shall put his hand on the cockatrice' den.   viper's

9 They shall not hurt nor destroy in all My holy mountain: for the earth shall be full of the knowledge of the LORD, as the waters cover the sea.

10 And in that day there shall be a root of Jes'se, which shall stand for an ensign of the people; to it shall the Gen'tiles seek: and His rest shall be glorious.   ROM. 15:12 signal

11 And it shall come to pass in that day, *that* the Lord shall set His hand again the second time to recover the remnant of His people, which shall be left, from As-syr'i-a, and from E'gypt, and from Path'ros, and from Cush, and from E'lam, and from Shi'nar, and from Ha'math, and from the islands of the sea.

12 And He shall set up an ensign for the nations, and shall assemble the outcasts of Is'ra-el, and gather together the dispersed of Ju'dah from the four corners of the earth.   1 PET. 4:14

13 The envy also of E'phra-im shall depart, and the adversaries of Ju'dah shall be cut off: E'phra-im shall not envy Ju'dah, and Ju'dah shall not vex E'phra-im.   trouble

14 But they shall fly upon the shoulders of the Phi-lis'tines toward the west; they shall spoil them of the east together: they shall lay their hand upon E'dom and Mo'ab; and the children of Am'mon shall obey them.   plunder

15 And the LORD shall utterly destroy the tongue of the E-gyp'tian sea; and with His mighty wind shall He shake His hand over the river, and shall smite it in the seven streams, and make *men* go over dryshod.

16 And there shall be an highway for the remnant of His people, which shall

be left, from As-syr'i-a; like as it was to Is'ra-el in the day that he came up out of the land of E'gypt.

CHAPTER 12

AND in that day you shall say, O LORD, I will praise You: though You were angry with me, Your anger is turned away, and You comforted me.

2 Behold, God *is* my salvation; I will trust, and not be afraid: for the LORD JE-HO'VAH *is* my strength and *my* song; He also is become my salvation.

3 Therefore with joy shall you draw water out of the wells of salvation.

4 And in that day shall you say, Praise the LORD, call upon His name, declare His doings among the people, make mention that His name is exalted.

5 Sing to the LORD; for He has done excellent things: this *is* known in all the earth.

6 Cry out and shout, you inhabitant of Zi'on: for great *is* the Holy One of Is'ra-el in the midst of you.

CHAPTER 13

THE burden of Bab'y-lon, which I-sa'iah the son of A'moz did see.

2 Lift you up a banner upon the high mountain, exalt the voice to them, shake the hand, that they may go into the gates of the nobles.   raise up

3 I have commanded My sanctified ones, I have also called My mighty ones for My anger, *even* them that re-joice in My highness.   consecrated - triumph

4 The noise of a multitude in the mountains, like as of a great people; a tumultuous noise of the kingdoms of nations gathered together: the LORD of hosts musters the host of the battle.   Jehovah's f. Tsebaoth - assembles

5 They come from a far country, from the end of heaven, *even* the LORD, and the weapons of His indignation, to de-stroy the whole land.   instruments

6 Howl you; for the day of the LORD *is* at hand; it shall come as a destruc-tion from the Almighty.   Wail

7 Therefore shall all hands be faint, and every man's heart shall melt: weak

8 And they shall be afraid: pangs and sorrows shall take hold of them; they shall be in pain as a woman that travails: they shall be amazed one at another; their faces *shall be as* flames.   JOHN 16:23 JOHN 16:20-21

9 Behold, the day of the LORD come, cruel both with wrath and fierce anger, to lay the land desolate: and He shall destroy the sinners thereof out of it.

10 For the stars of heaven and the con-stellations thereof shall not give their light: the sun shall be darkened in its going forth, and the moon shall not cause her light to shine. MATT. 24:29 LUKE 21:25

11 And I will punish the world for *their* evil, and the wicked for their iniquity; and I will cause the arrogancy of the proud to cease, and will lay low the haughtiness of the terrible.   tyrants

12 I will make a man more precious than fine gold; even a man than the golden wedge of O'phir.   scarcer

13 Therefore I will shake the heavens, and the earth shall remove out of her place, in the wrath of the LORD of

hosts, and in the day of His fierce anger. *Jehovah*[s.f.] *Tsebaoth*

14 And it shall be as the chased <u>roe</u>, and as a sheep that no man takes up: they shall every man turn to his own people, and flee every one into his own land. *gazell*

15 Every one that is found shall be thrust through; and every one that is joined *to them* shall fall by the sword.

16 Their children also shall be dashed to pieces before their eyes; their houses shall be spoiled, and their wives ravished.

17 Behold, I will stir up the Medes against them, which shall not regard silver; and *as for* gold, they shall not delight in it.

18 *Their* bows also shall dash the young men to pieces; and they shall have no pity on the fruit of the womb; their eye shall not spare children.

19 And Bab'y-lon, the glory of kingdoms, the beauty of the Chal'dees' excellency, shall be as when <u>God</u> overthrew Sod'om and Go-mor'rah. *Elohim*[p.f.]

20 It shall never be inhabited, neither shall it be dwelled in from generation to generation: neither shall the A-ra'bi-an pitch tent there; neither shall the shepherds make their fold there.

21 But wild beasts of the desert shall lie there; and their houses shall be full of <u>doleful</u> creatures; and owls shall dwell there, and satyrs shall dance there. *howling*

22 And the wild beasts of the <u>islands</u> shall cry in their <u>desolate</u> houses, and <u>dragons</u> in *their* pleasant palaces: and

her time *is* near to come, and her days shall not be prolonged. *borders - empty - jackals*

CHAPTER 14

FOR the LORD will have mercy on Ja'cob, and will yet choose Is'ra-el, and set them in their own land: and the strangers shall be joined with them, and they shall <u>cling</u> to the house of Ja'cob.

2 And the people shall take them, and bring them to their place: and the house of Is'ra-el shall possess them in the land of the LORD for servants and handmaids: and they shall take them captives, whose captives they were; and they shall rule over their oppressors.

3 And it shall come to pass in the day that the LORD shall give you rest from your sorrow, and from your <u>fear</u>, and from the <u>hard bondage</u> wherein you were made to serve, *turmoil - harsh slavery*

4 That you shall take up this <u>proverb</u> against the king of Bab'y-lon, and say, How has the oppressor ceased! the golden city ceased! *saying*

5 The LORD has broken the staff of the wicked, *and* the scepter of the rulers.

6 He who smote the people in anger with a continual stroke, he that ruled the nations in anger, is persecuted, *and* none hinders.

7 The whole earth is at rest, *and* is quiet: they break forth into singing.

8 Yea, the fir trees rejoice at you, *and* the cedars of Leb'a-non, *saying*, Since you are laid down, no <u>feller</u> is come up against us. *tree cutter*

9 Hell from beneath is moved for you

to meet *you* at your coming: it stir up the dead for you, *even* all the <u>chief ones</u> of the earth; it has raised up from their thrones all the kings of the nations. leaders
10 All they shall speak and say to you, Are you also become weak as we? are you become like to us?
11 Your pomp is brought down to the grave, *and* the noise of your <u>viols</u>: the worm is spread under you, and the worms cover you.   lutes
12 How are you fallen from heaven, O <u>Lu'ci·fer</u>, son of the morning! *how* are you cut down to the ground, which did weaken the nations!   (Satan), morning star
13 For you have said in your heart, I will ascend into heaven, I will exalt my throne above the stars of God: I will sit also <u>upon</u> the mount of the congregation, in the sides of the north: i.e., in control
14 I will ascend above the heights of the clouds; I will be like the Most High.
15 Yet you shall be brought down to hell, to the sides of the pit.
16 They that see you shall narrowly look upon you, *and* consider you, *saying, Is* this the man that made the earth to tremble, that did shake kingdoms;
17 *That* made the world as a wilderness, and destroyed the cities thereof; *that* opened not the house of his prisoners?
18 All the kings of the nations, *even* all of them, lie in glory, every one in his own <u>house</u>.   tomb
19 But you are cast out of your grave like an <u>abominable</u> branch, *and as* the <u>raiment</u> of those that are slain, thrust through with a sword, that go down to the stones of the pit; as a carcase trodden under feet.   detestable - clothing
20 You shall not be joined with them in burial, because you have destroyed your land, *and* slain your people: the <u>seed</u> of evildoers shall never be <u>renowned</u>.   offspring - honored
21 Prepare slaughter for his children for <u>the iniquity</u> of their fathers; that they do not rise, nor possess the land, nor fill the face of the world with cities. sins
22 For I will rise up against them, **says the Lord of hosts**, and cut off from Bab'y·lon the name, and remnant, and son, and nephew, **says the** Lord.   Jehovah^s.f. Tsebaoth
23 I will also make it a possession for the <u>bittern,</u> and pools of water: and I will sweep it with the <u>besom</u> of destruction, **says the Lord of hosts**.   hedgehog - broom
24 The <u>Lord of hosts</u> has sworn, saying, Surely as I have thought, so shall it come to pass; and as I have purposed, *so* shall it stand:
25 That I will break the As·syr'i·an in My land, and upon My mountains tread him under foot: then shall his yoke <u>depart</u> from off them, and his burden depart from off their shoulders.   be removed
26 This *is* the purpose that is purposed upon the whole earth: and this *is* the hand that is stretched out upon all the nations.
27 For the <u>Lord of hosts</u> has purposed, and who shall disannul *it*? and His hand *is* stretched out, and who shall turn it back?   Jehovah^s.f. Tsebaoth
28 In the year that king A'haz died <u>was this burden</u>.   this oracle came

29 Rejoice not you, whole Pal-es-ti'na, because the rod of Him that smote you is broken: for out of the serpent's root shall come forth a <u>cockatrice</u>, and its fruit *shall be* a fiery flying serpent. viper

30 And the firstborn of the <u>poor</u> shall feed, and the needy shall lie down in safety: and I will kill your root with famine, and he shall slay your remnant. helpless

31 Howl, O gate; cry, O city; you, whole Pal-es-ti'na, *are* dissolved: for there shall come from the north a smoke, and none *shall be* alone in its appointed times.

32 What shall *one* then answer the messengers of the nation? That the LORD has founded Zi'on, and the <u>poor</u> of His people shall <u>trust</u> in it. afflicted - find refuge

CHAPTER 15

THE burden of Mo'ab. Because in the night Ar of Mo'ab is laid waste, *and* <u>brought to silence</u>; because in the night Kir of Mo'ab is laid waste, *and* <u>brought to silence</u>; ruined

2 He is gone up to Ba'jith, and to Di'bon, the high places, to weep: Mo'ab shall howl over Ne'bo, and over Med'e-ba: on all their heads *shall be* baldness, *and* every beard cut off.

3 In their streets they shall gird themselves with sackcloth: on the tops of their houses, and in their streets, every one shall howl, weeping abundantly.

4 And Hesh'bon shall cry, and E-le-a'leh: their voice shall be heard *even* to Ja'haz: therefore the armed sol-diers of Mo'ab shall cry out; his life shall be <u>grievous</u> to him. a misery

5 My heart shall cry out for Mo'ab; his fugitives *shall flee* to Zo'ar, an heifer of three years old: for by the mounting up of Lu'hith with weeping shall they go it up; for in the way of Hor-o-na'im they shall raise up a cry of destruction.

6 For the waters of Nim'rim shall be desolate: for the hay is withered away, the grass fails, there is no green thing.

7 Therefore the abundance they have gotten, and that which they have laid up, shall they carry away to the brook of the willows.

8 For the cry <u>is</u> gone round about the borders of Mo'ab; the <u>howling</u> thereof to Eg'la-im, and the <u>howling</u> thereof to Be'er-e'lim. of distress has - wailing

9 For the waters of Di'mon shall be full of blood: for I will bring more upon Di'mon, lions upon him that escapes of Mo'ab, and upon the remnant of the land.

CHAPTER 16

SEND you the lamb to the ruler of the land from Se'la to the wilderness, to the mount of the daughter of Zi'on.

2 For it shall be, *that*, as a wandering bird cast out of the nest, *so* the daughters of Mo'ab shall be at the fords of Ar'non.

3 Take counsel, execute judgment; make your shadow as the night in the midst of the noonday; hide the outcasts; <u>bewray</u> not him that wanders. betray

4 Let My outcasts dwell with you, Mo'ab; be you a <u>covert</u> to them from the face of the spoiler: for the extortioner is at an end, the spoiler ceases, the oppressors are consumed out of the land. _{shelter}

5 And in mercy shall the throne be established: and he shall sit upon it in truth in the tabernacle of Da'vid, judging, and seeking judgment, and <u>hasting</u> righteousness. _{prompt}

6 We have heard of the pride of Mo'ab; *he is* very proud: *even* of his haughtiness, and his pride, and his wrath: *but* his lies *shall* not *be* so.

7 Therefore shall Mo'ab howl for Mo'ab, every one shall howl: for the foundations of Kir-har'e-seth shall you mourn; surely *they are* stricken.

8 For the fields of Hesh'bon languish, *and* the vine of Sib'mah: the lords of the <u>heathen</u> have broken down the principal plants thereof, they are come *even* to Ja'zer, they wandered *through* the wilderness: her branches are stretched out, they are gone over the sea. _{nations}

9 Therefore I will bewail with the weeping of Ja'zer the vine of Sib'mah: I will water you with My tears, O Hesh'bon, and E-le-a'leh: for the shouting for your summer fruits and for your harvest is fallen.

10 And gladness is taken away, and joy out of the plentiful field; and in the vineyards there shall be no singing, neither shall there be shouting: the treaders shall tread out no wine in *their* presses; I have made *their* vintage shouting to cease.

11 Wherefore My <u>bowels</u> shall sound like an harp for Mo'ab, and My inward parts for Kir-ha'resh. _{heart}

12 And it shall come to pass, when it is seen that Mo'ab is weary on the high place, that he shall come to his sanctuary to pray; but he shall not <u>prevail</u>. _{have power}

13 This *is* the word that the LORD has spoken concerning Mo'ab since that time.

14 But now the LORD has spoken, saying, Within three years, as the years of an hireling, and the glory of Mo'ab shall be <u>contemned,</u> with all that great multitude; and the remnant *shall be* very small *and* feeble. _{degraded}

CHAPTER 17

THE burden of Da-mas'cus. Behold, Da-mas'cus is taken away from *being* a city, and it shall be a ruinous heap.

2 The cities of Ar'o-er *are* forsaken: they shall be for flocks, which shall lie down, and none shall make *them* afraid.

3 The fortress also shall cease from E'phra-im, and the kingdom from Da-mas'cus, and the remnant of Syr'i-a: they shall be as the glory of the children of Is'ra-el, says the LORD of hosts. _{Jehovah^{s.f.} Tsebaoth}

4 And in that day it shall come to pass, *that* the glory of Ja'cob shall be made thin, and the fatness of his flesh shall <u>wax</u> lean. _{become}

5 And it shall be as when the harvestman gathers the corn, and reaps the ears with his arm; and it shall be as

he that gathers ears in the valley of Reph'a-im.

6 Yet gleaning grapes shall be left in it, as the shaking of an olive tree, two *or* three berries in the top of the uppermost bough, four *or* five in the outmost fruitful branches thereof, says the L<small>ORD</small> God of Is'ra-el. <small>Jehovah^{s.f.} Elohim^{p.f.}</small>

7 At that day shall a man look to his Maker, and his eyes shall have respect to the Holy One of Is'ra-el.

8 And he shall not look to the altars, the work of his hands, neither shall respect *that* which his fingers have made, either the groves, or the images.   <small>idols</small>

9 In that day shall his strong cities be as a forsaken bough, and an uppermost branch, which they left because of the children of Is'ra-el: and there shall be desolation.

10 Because you have forgotten the God of your salvation, and have not been mindful of the rock of your strength, therefore shall you plant pleasant plants, and shall set it with strange slips:

<small>Elohim^{p.f.} - i.e., God-Christ - imported vines</small>

11 In the day shall you make your plant to grow, and in the morning shall you make your seed to flourish: *but* the harvest *shall be* a heap in the day of grief and of desperate sorrow. <small>as nothing</small>

12 Woe to the multitude of many people, *which* make a noise like the noise of the seas; and to the rushing of nations, *that* make a rushing like the rushing of mighty waters!

13 The nations shall rush like the rushing of many waters: but *God* shall rebuke them, and they shall flee far off, and shall be chased as the chaff of the mountains before the wind, and like a rolling thing before the whirlwind.

14 And behold at eveningtide trouble; *and* before the morning he *is* not. This *is* the portion of them that spoil us, and the lot of them that rob us. <small>no more</small>

CHAPTER 18

WOE to the land shadowing with wings, which *is* beyond the rivers of E-thi-o'pi-a: <small>?Ethopia - of whirring wings</small>

2 That sends ambassadors by the sea, even in vessels of bulrushes upon the waters, *saying*, Go, you swift messengers, to a nation scattered and peeled, to a people terrible from their beginning presently; a nation meted out and trodden down, whose land the rivers have spoiled! <small>smooth - now - parcelled - treading down - divided</small>

3 All you inhabitants of the world, and dwellers on the earth, see you, when He lifts up an ensign on the mountains; and when He blows a trumpet, hear you.   <small>banner</small>

4 For so the L<small>ORD</small> said to me, I will take My rest, and I will consider in My dwelling place like a clear heat upon herbs, *and* like a cloud of dew in the heat of harvest.   <small>be silent - look from</small>

5 For afore the harvest, when the bud is perfect, and the sour grape is ripening in the flower, He shall both cut off the sprigs with pruning hooks, and take away *and* cut down the branches.

6 They shall be left together to the fowls of the mountains, and to the beasts of the earth: and the fowls shall summer upon them, and all the beasts of the earth shall winter upon them.

7 In that time shall the present be brought to the L ORD of hosts of a people scattered and peeled, and from a people terrible from their beginning presently; a nation meted out and trodden under foot, whose land the rivers have spoiled, to the place of the name of the L ORD of hosts, the mount Zi'on.

Jehovah^{s.f.} Tsebaoth - smooth - now - parcelled - divided

CHAPTER 19

THE burden of E'gypt. Behold, the L ORD rides upon a swift cloud, and shall come into E'gypt: and the idols of E'gypt shall be moved at His presence, and the heart of E'gypt shall melt in the midst of it.
2 And I will set the E-gyp'tians against the E-gyp'tians: and they shall fight every one against his brother, and every one against his neighbor; city against city, *and* kingdom against kingdom.
3 And the spirit of E'gypt shall fail in the midst thereof; and I will destroy the counsel thereof: and they shall seek to the idols, and to the charmers, and to them that have familiar spirits, and to the wizards.

confound - mediums - spiritists

4 And the E-gyp'tians will I give over into the hand of a cruel lord; and a fierce king shall rule over them, says the Lord, the L ORD of hosts.   Adon^{s.f.} - Adonay^{p.f.} Tsebaoth
5 And the waters shall fail from the sea, and the river shall be wasted and dried up.
6 And they shall turn the rivers far away; *and* the brooks of defence shall be emptied and dried up: the reeds and flags shall wither.
7 The paper reeds by the brooks, by the mouth of the brooks, and every thing sown by the brooks, shall wither, be driven away, and be no *more*.   bulrushes - i.e., Nile - edge
8 The fishers also shall mourn, and all they that cast angle into the brooks shall lament, and they that spread nets upon the waters shall languish.   hooks
9 Moreover they that work in fine flax, and they that weave networks, shall be confounded.   linen cloths - dejected
10 And they shall be broken in the purposes thereof, all that make sluices *and* ponds for fish.   defeated - dams
11 Surely the princes of Zo'an *are* fools, the counsel of the wise counselors of Pha'raoh is become brutish: how say you to Pha'raoh, I *am* the son of the wise, the son of ancient kings?   stupid
12 Where *are* they? where *are* your wise *men*? and let them tell you now, and let them know what the L ORD of hosts has purposed upon E'gypt.   Jehovah^{s.f.} Tsebaoth - planned against
13 The princes of Zo'an are become fools, the princes of Noph are deceived; they have also seduced E'gypt, *even they that are* the stay of the tribes thereof.
14 The L ORD has mingled a perverse spirit in the midst thereof: and they have caused E'gypt to err in every work thereof, as a drunken *man* staggers in his vomit.   distorted
15 Neither shall there be *any* work for E'gypt, which the head or tail, branch or rush, may do.

16 In that day shall E'gypt be like to women: and it shall be afraid and fear because of the shaking of the hand of the Lord of hosts, which He shakes over it. _{Jehovah^{s.f.} Tsebaoth}

17 And the land of Ju'dah shall be a terror to E'gypt, every one that makes mention thereof shall be afraid in himself, because of the counsel of the Lord of hosts, which He has determined against it.

18 In that day shall five cities in the land of E'gypt speak the language of Ca'naan, and swear to the Lord of hosts; one shall be called, The city of destruction.

19 In that day shall there be an altar to the Lord in the midst of the land of E'gypt, and a pillar at the border thereof to the Lord.

20 And it shall be for a sign and for a witness to the Lord of hosts in the land of E'gypt: for they shall cry to the Lord because of the oppressors, and He shall send them a Savior, and a Great One, and He shall deliver them. _{Jehovah^{s.f.} Tsebaoth}

21 And the Lord shall be known to E'gypt, and the E-gyp'tians shall know the Lord in that day, and shall do sacrifice and oblation; yea, they shall vow a vow to the Lord, and perform *it*. _{make Himself - make a pledge}

22 And the Lord shall smite E'gypt: He shall smite and heal *it*: and they shall return *even* to the Lord, and He shall be entreated of them, and shall heal them.

23 In that day shall there be a highway out of E'gypt to As-syr'i-a, and the As-syr'i-an shall come into E'gypt, and the E-gyp'tian into As-syr'i-a, and the E-gyp'tians shall serve with the As-syr'i-ans.

24 In that day shall Is'ra-el be the third with E'gypt and with As-syr'i-a, *even* a blessing in the midst of the land: _{third party}

25 Whom the Lord of hosts shall bless, saying, Blessed *be* E'gypt My people, and As-syr'i-a the work of My hands, and Is'ra-el My inheritance. _{Jehovah^{s.f.} Tsebaoth}

CHAPTER 20

IN the year that Tar'tan came to Ash'dod, (when Sar'gon the king of As-syr'i-a sent him,) and fought against Ash"dod, and took it;

2 At the same time spoke the Lord by I-sa'iah the son of A'moz, saying, Go and loose the sackcloth from off your loins, and put off your shoe from your foot. And he did so, walking naked and barefoot.

3 And the Lord said, Like as My servant I-sa'iah has walked naked and barefoot three years *for* a sign and wonder upon E'gypt and upon E-thi-o'pi-a;

4 So shall the king of As-syr'i-a lead away the E-gyp'tians prisoners, and the E-thi-o'pi-ans captives, young and old, naked and barefoot, even with *their* buttocks uncovered, to the shame of E'gypt.

5 And they shall be afraid and ashamed of E-thi-o'pi-a their expectation, and of E'gypt their glory.

6 And the inhabitant of this isle shall

say in that day, Behold, such *is* our expectation, where we flee for help to be delivered from the king of As-syr'i-a: and how shall we escape?　　coast

CHAPTER 21

THE <u>burden</u> of the desert of the sea. As whirlwinds in the south pass through; *so* it comes from the desert, from a terrible land.　　message
2 A grievous vision is declared to me; the treacherous dealer deals treacherously, and the <u>spoiler spoils</u>. Go up, O E'lam: besiege, O Me'di-a; all the sighing thereof have I made to cease.　　destroyer still destroys
3 Therefore are my loins filled with pain: pangs have taken hold upon me, as the pangs of a woman that travail: I was bowed down at the hearing *of it*; I was dismayed at the seeing *of it*.
4 My heart panted, fearfulness affrighted me: the night of my pleasure has he turned into <u>fear</u> to me.　　trembling
5 Prepare the table, watch in the watchtower, eat, drink: arise, you princes, *and* anoint the shield.
6 For thus has the Lord said to me, Go, set a watchman, let him declare what he sees.
7 And he saw a chariot *with* a couple of horsemen, a chariot of asses, *and* a chariot of camels; and he hearkened diligently with much heed:
8 And he <u>cried</u>, A lion: My lord, I stand continually upon the watchtower in the daytime, and I am set in my <u>ward</u> whole nights:　　called like - guard

9 And, behold, here comes a chariot of men, *with* a couple of horsemen. And he answered and said, Bab'y-lon is fallen, is fallen; and all the <u>graven images</u> of her gods he has broken to the ground.

REV. 14:8 REV. 18:2　carved idols

10 O my threshing, and the corn of my floor: that which I have heard of the L<small>ORD</small> <u>of hosts</u>, the <u>God</u> of Is'ra-el, have I declared to you.

Jehovah^{s.f.} Tsebaoth - Elohim^{p.f.}

11 The burden of Du'mah. He calls to me out of Se'ir, Watchman, what of the night? Watchman, what of the night?
12 The watchman said, The morning comes, and also the night: if you will enquire, enquire you: return, come.
13 The burden upon A-ra'bi-a. In the forest in A-ra'bi-a shall you lodge, O you travelling companies of Ded'a-nim.
14 The inhabitants of the land of Tema brought water to him that was thirsty, they <u>prevented</u> with their bread him that fled.　　met
15 For they fled from the swords, from the drawn sword, and from the bent bow, and from the grievousness of war.
16 For thus has the Lord said to me, Within a year, according to the years of an hireling, and all the glory of Ke'dar shall fail:
17 And the <u>residue</u> of the number of archers, the mighty men of the children of Ke'dar, shall be diminished: for the L<small>ORD</small> <u>God</u> of Is'ra-el has spoken *it*.　　remainder - Jehovah^{s.f.} Elohim^{p.f.}

CHAPTER 22

THE burden of the valley of vision. What ails you now, that you are wholly gone up to the housetops?

2 You that are full of <u>stirs</u>, a tumultuous city, a joyous city: your slain *men are* not slain with the sword, nor dead in battle.   noises

3 All your rulers are fled together, they are bound by the archers: all that are found in you are bound together, *which* have fled from far.

4 Therefore said I, <u>Look</u> away from me; I will weep bitterly, labor not to comfort me, because of the <u>spoiling</u> of the daughter of my people.

Turn - destruction

5 For *it is* a day of trouble, and of treading down, and of <u>perplexity</u> by the <u>Lord G</u>OD <u>of hosts</u> in the valley of vision, breaking down the walls, and of crying to the mountains.

confusion - Adonay[p.f.] Jehovah[s.f.] Tsebaoth

6 And E'lam bare the quiver with chariots of men *and* horsemen, and Kir uncovered the shield.

7 And it shall come to pass, *that* your choicest valleys shall be full of chariots, and the horsemen shall set themselves in array at the <u>gate</u>.entrance

8 And he discovered the covering of Ju'dah, and you did look in that day to the armor of the house of the forest.

9 You have seen also the breaches of the city of Da'vid, that they are many: and you gathered together the waters of the lower pool.

10 And you have numbered the houses of Je-ru'sa-lem, and the houses have you broken down to fortify the wall.

11 You made also a <u>ditch</u> between the two walls for the water of the old pool: but you have not looked to the Maker thereof, neither had respect to Him that fashioned it long ago.   reservoir

12 And in that day did the <u>Lord G</u>OD <u>of hosts</u> call to weeping, and to mourning, and to baldness, and to girding with sackcloth:

Adonay[p.f.] Jehovah[s.f.] Tsebaoth

13 And behold joy and gladness, slaying oxen, and killing sheep, eating flesh, and drinking wine: let us eat and drink; for to morrow we shall die.   1 COR. 15:32

14 And it was revealed in my ears by the L ORD of hosts, Surely this iniquity shall not be purged from you till you die, says the Lord <u>G</u>OD <u>of hosts</u>.

Adonay[p.f.] Jehovah[s.f.] Tsebaoth

15 Thus says the Lord <u>G</u>OD <u>of hosts,</u> Go, get you to this treasurer, *even* to Sheb'na, which *is* over the house, *and say,*

16 What have you here? and whom have you here, that you have hewed you out a <u>sepulcher</u> here, *as* he that hews him out a <u>sepulcher</u> on high, *and* that grave an habitation for himself in a rock?   tomb

17 Behold, the L ORD will carry you away with a mighty captivity, and will surely <u>cover</u> you.   grasp

18 He will surely violently turn and toss you *like* a ball into a large country: there shall you die, and there the chariots of your glory *shall be* the shame of your lord's house.

19 And I will drive you from your station, and from your state shall he pull you down.

20 And it shall come to pass in that day, that I will call My servant E-li′a-kim the son of Hil-ki′ah:

21 And I will clothe him with your robe, and strengthen him with your girdle, and I will commit your government into his hand: and he shall be a father to the inhabitants of Je-ru′sa-lem, and to the house of Ju′dah.

22 And the key of the house of Da′vid will I lay upon his shoulder; so he shall open, and none shall shut; and he shall shut, and none shall open.   REV. 3:7

23 And I will fasten him as a nail in a sure place; and he shall be for a glorious throne to his father's house.

24 And they shall hang upon him all the glory of his father's house, the offspring and the issue, all vessels of small quantity, from the vessels of cups, even to all the vessels of flagons.   bowls - jars

25 In that day, says the LORD of hosts, shall the nail that is fastened in the sure place be removed, and be cut down, and fall; and the burden that *was* upon it shall be cut off: for the LORD has spoken *it*.   Jehovah[s.f.] Tsebaoth

CHAPTER 23

THE burden of Tyre. Howl, you ships of Tar′shish; for it is laid waste, so that there is no house, no entering in: from the land of Chit′tim it is revealed to them.

2 Be still, you inhabitants of the isle; you whom the merchants of Zi′don, that pass over the sea, have replenished.   enriched

3 And by great waters the seed of Si′hor, the harvest of the river, *is* her revenue; and she is a mart of nations.   market

4 Be you ashamed, O Zi′don: for the sea has spoken, *even* the strength of the sea, saying, I travail not, nor bring forth children, neither do I nourish up young men, *nor* bring up virgins.

5 As at the report concerning E′gypt, *so* shall they be sorely pained at the report of Tyre.

6 Pass you over to Tar′shish; howl, you inhabitants of the isle.   coast

7 *Is* this your joyous *city*, whose antiquity *is* of ancient days? her own feet shall carry her afar off to sojourn.   live

8 Who has taken this counsel against Tyre, the crowning *city*, whose merchants *are* princes, whose trafficers *are* the honorable of the earth?   traders

9 The LORD of hosts has purposed it, to stain the pride of all glory, *and* to bring into contempt all the honorable of the earth.   Jehovah[s.f.] Tsebaoth

10 Pass through your land as a river, O daughter of Tar′shish: *there is* no more strength.   Overflow - restraint

11 He stretched out His hand over the sea, He shook the kingdoms: the LORD has given a commandment against the merchant *city*, to destroy the strong holds thereof.   i.e., Canaan

12 And He said, You shall no more rejoice, O you oppressed virgin, daughter of Zi′don: arise, pass over to Chit′tim; there also shall you have no rest.

13 Behold the land of the Chal-de′ans; this people was not, *till* the As-syr′-

i-an founded it for them that dwell in the wilderness: they set up the towers thereof, they <u>raised up</u> the palaces thereof; *and* He brought it to ruin. stripped

14 Howl, you ships of Tar'shish: for your strength is <u>laid waste</u>.REV. 18:17 destroyed

15 And it shall come to pass in that day, that Tyre shall be forgotten seventy years, according to the days of one king: after the end of seventy years shall Tyre sing as an harlot.

16 Take an harp, go about the city, you harlot that have been forgotten; make sweet melody, sing many songs, that you may be remembered.

17 And it shall come to pass after the end of seventy years, that the LORD will visit Tyre, and she shall turn to her <u>hire</u>, and shall commit fornication with all the kingdoms of the world upon the face of the earth. REV. 17:2 employment

18 And her merchandise and her <u>hire</u> shall be holiness to the LORD: it shall not be treasured nor laid up; for her merchandise shall be for them that dwell before the LORD, to eat sufficiently, and for durable clothing.

CHAPTER 24

BEHOLD, the LORD makes the earth empty, and makes it waste, and turns it upside down, and scatters abroad the inhabitants thereof.

2 And it shall be, as with the people, so with the priest; as with the servant, so with his master; as with the maid, so with her mistress; as with the buyer, so with the seller; as with the lender, so with the borrower; as with the taker of usury, so with the giver of usury to him.

3 The land shall be utterly emptied, and utterly <u>spoiled</u>: for the LORD has spoken this word. plundered

4 The earth mourns *and* fades away, the world languishes *and* fades away, the haughty people of the earth do languish.

5 The earth also is defiled under the inhabitants thereof; because they have transgressed the laws, changed the ordinance, broken the everlasting <u>covenant</u>. agreement

6 Therefore has the curse devoured the earth, and they that dwell therein are <u>desolate</u>: therefore the inhabitants of the earth are burned, and few men left. guilty

7 The new wine mourns, the vine languishes, all the merryhearted do sigh.

8 The mirth of <u>tabrets</u> ceases, the noise of them that rejoice ends, the joy of the harp ceases. tambourines

9 They shall not drink wine with a song; strong drink shall be bitter to them that drink it.

10 The city of confusion is broken down: every house is shut up, that no man may come in.

11 There is a crying for wine in the streets; all joy is darkened, the mirth of the land is gone.

12 In the city is left desolation, and the gate is smitten with destruction.

13 When thus it shall be in the midst of the land among the people, *there shall be* as the shaking of an olive

tree, *and* as the gleaning grapes when the vintage is done.

14 They shall lift up their voice, they shall sing for the majesty of the Lord, they shall cry aloud from the sea.

15 Wherefore glorify you the Lord in the <u>fires</u>, *even* the name of the <u>Lord God</u> of Is'ra-el in the <u>isles</u> of the sea.   light - Jehovah^{s.f.} Elohim^{p.f.} - furthermost

16 From the <u>uttermost part</u> of the earth have we heard songs, *even* glory to the righteous. But I said, <u>My leanness, my leanness</u>, woe to me! the treacherous dealers have dealt treacherously; yea, the treacherous dealers have dealt very treacherously. ends - I waste away

17 <u>Fear</u>, and the <u>pit</u>, and the <u>snare</u>, *are* upon you, O inhabitant of the earth.   Terror - abyss - lure

18 And it shall come to pass, *that* he who flees from the <u>noise of the fear</u> shall fall into the <u>pit</u>; and he that comes up out of the midst of the pit shall be taken in the <u>snare</u>: for the windows from on high are open, and the foundations of the earth do shake.   report of disaster - trap

19 The earth is utterly broken down, the earth is clean dissolved, the earth is moved exceedingly.

20 The earth shall <u>reel</u> to and fro like a drunkard, and shall be removed like a cottage; and the transgression thereof shall be heavy upon it; and it shall fall, and not rise again.   stagger

21 And it shall come to pass in that day, *that* the Lord shall <u>punish</u> the host of the high ones *that are* on high, and the kings of the earth upon the earth.   judge

22 And they shall be gathered together, *as* prisoners are gathered in the <u>pit</u>, and shall be shut up in the prison, and after many days shall they be <u>visited</u>.   abyss - punished

23 Then the moon shall be confounded, and the sun ashamed, when the <u>Lord of hosts</u> shall reign in mount Zi'on, and in Je-ru'sa-lem, and before His <u>ancients</u> gloriously.   REV. 21:23 Jehovah^{s.f.} Tsebaoth - elders

CHAPTER 25

O LORD, You *are* my <u>God</u>; I will exalt You, I will praise Your name; for You have done wonderful *things*; *Your* counsels of old *are* faithfulness *and* truth.   Elohim^{p.f.}

2 For You have made of a city an heap; *of* a <u>defenced</u> city a ruin: a palace of strangers to be no city; it shall never be built.   fortified

3 Therefore shall the strong people glorify You, the city of <u>the terrible</u> nations shall fear You.   ruthless

4 For You have been a strength to the poor, a strength to the needy in his distress, a refuge from the storm, a shadow from the heat, when the blast of the terrible ones *is* as a storm *against* the wall.

5 You shall bring down the noise of strangers, as the heat in a dry place; *even* the heat with the shadow of a cloud: the <u>branch</u> of the <u>terrible ones</u> shall be <u>brought low</u>.   song - ruthless - stilled

6 And in this mountain shall the <u>Lord of hosts</u> make to all people a feast of fat things, a feast of wines on

the <u>lees</u>, of fat things full of marrow, of wines on the <u>lees</u> well refined.

<small>Jehovah^{s.f.} Tsebaoth - dregs(stronger wine)</small>

7 And He will destroy in this mountain the face of the covering cast over all people, and the veil that is spread over all nations.

8 He will swallow up death in victory; and the <u>Lord G</u>OD will wipe away tears from off all faces; and the rebuke of His people shall He take away from off all the earth: for the L ORD has spoken *it*. <small>REV. 21:4 1 COR. 15:54 Adonay^{p.f.} Jehovah</small>

9 And it shall be said in that day, Lo, this *is* our <u>God</u>; we have waited for Him, and He will save us: this *is* the L ORD; we have waited for Him, we will be glad and rejoice in His salvation. <small>Elohim^{p.f.}</small>

10 For in this mountain shall the hand of the L ORD rest, and Mo'ab shall be <u>trodden down</u> under Him, even as straw is <u>trodden down</u> for the dunghill. <small>on - trampled</small>

11 And He shall spread forth His hands in the midst of them, as he that swims spreads forth *his hands* to swim: and He shall bring down their pride together with the <u>spoils</u> of their hands. <small>work</small>

12 And the fortress of the high fort of your walls shall He bring down, lay low, *and* bring to the ground, *even* to the dust.

CHAPTER 26

IN that day shall this song be sung in the land of Ju'dah; We have a strong city; <u>salvation</u> will *God* appoint *for* walls and bulwarks. <small>i.e., Heb. Jeshua</small>

2 Open you the gates, that the righteous nation which <u>keeps the truth</u> may enter in. <small>remains faithful</small>

3 You will keep *him* in perfect peace, *whose* mind *is* stayed *on You*: because he trusts in You.

4 Trust you in the L ORD for ever: for in the LORD JE-HO'VAH *is* everlasting strength: <small>Jah</small>

5 For He <u>brings down</u> them that dwell on high; the lofty city, He lays it low; He lays it low, *even* to the ground; He brings it *even* to the dust. <small>humbles</small>

6 The foot shall <u>tread it down</u>, *even* the feet of the poor, *and* the steps of the needy. <small>trample it</small>

7 The way of the just *is* uprightness: You, most upright, do <u>weigh</u> the path of the just. <small>prepare</small>

8 Yea, in the way of Your judgments, O L ORD, have we waited for You; the desire of *our* soul *is* to Your name, and to the remembrance of You.

9 With my soul have I desired You in the night; yea, with my spirit within me will I seek You early: for when Your judgments *are* in the earth, the inhabitants of the world will learn righteousness.

10 Let favor be showed to the wicked, *yet* will he not learn righteousness: in the land of uprightness will he deal unjustly, and will not <u>behold</u> the majesty of the L ORD. <small>perceive</small>

11 L ORD, *when* Your hand is lifted up, they will not see: *but* they shall see, and be ashamed for *their* envy <u>at the people</u>; yea, the fire of Your enemies shall devour them. <small>HEB. 10:27 i.e., against God's people</small>

12 LORD, You will <u>ordain</u> peace for us: for You also have wrought all our works in us.   establish - for

13 O LORD our <u>God</u>, *other* lords beside You have had dominion over us: *but* by You only will we make mention of Your name.   Elohim^p.f.

14 *They are* dead, they shall not live; *they are* deceased, they shall not rise: therefore have You <u>visited</u> and destroyed them, and made all their memory to perish.   i.e., with judgment

15 You have increased the nation, O LORD, You have increased the nation: You are glorified: You had removed *it* far *to* all the ends of the earth.

16 LORD, in trouble have they visited You, they poured out a prayer *when* Your chastening *was* upon them.

17 Like as a woman with child, *that* draws near the time of her delivery, is in pain, *and* cries out in her pangs; so have we been in Your sight, O LORD.

18 We have been with child, we have been in pain, we have as it were brought forth wind; we have not <u>wrought</u> any deliverance in the earth; neither have the inhabitants of the world fallen.   worked

19 Your dead *men* shall live, *together with* my dead body shall they arise. Awake and sing, you that dwell in dust: for your dew *is as* the dew of herbs, and the earth shall cast out the dead.

20 Come, my people, enter you into your chambers, and shut your doors about you: hide yourself as it were for a little moment, until the indignation be overpast.   HEB. 10:37

21 For, behold, the LORD comes out of His place to punish the inhabitants of the earth for their iniquity: the earth also shall disclose her blood, and shall no more cover her slain.

CHAPTER 27

IN that day the LORD with His <u>sore</u> and great and strong sword shall punish <u>leviathan</u> the piercing serpent, even <u>leviathan</u> that crooked serpent; and He shall slay the <u>dragon</u> that *is* in the sea.   REV. 20:2 fierce - crocodile - monster

2 In that day sing you to her, A vineyard of red wine.

3 I the LORD do <u>keep</u> it; I will water it every moment: less *any* hurt it, I will keep it night and day.   watch over

4 Fury *is* not in Me: who would set the briers *and* thorns against Me in battle? I would <u>go through</u> them, I would burn them together.   march against

5 Or let him <u>take hold</u> of My strength, *that* he may make peace with Me; *and* he shall make peace with Me.   i.e., grasp

6 He shall cause them that come of Ja'cob to take root: Is'ra-el shall blossom and bud, and fill the face of the world with fruit.

7 Has He smitten him, as He smote those that smote Him? *or is* He slain according to the slaughter of them that are slain by Him?

8 In measure, when it shoots forth, You will debate with it: He stays His rough wind in the day of the east wind.

9 By this therefore shall the iniquity of Ja'cob be purged; and this *is* all the fruit to take away his sin; when he makes all the stones of the altar as

chalkstones that are beaten in sunder, the groves and <u>images</u> shall not stand up. idols

10 Yet the <u>defenced</u> city *shall be* desolate, *and* the habitation forsaken, and left like a wilderness: there shall the calf feed, and there shall he lie down, and consume the branches thereof. unfortified

11 When the boughs thereof are withered, they shall be broken off: the women come, *and* set them on fire: for it *is* a people of no understanding: therefore He that made them will not have mercy on them, and He that formed them will show them no favor.

12 And it shall come to pass in that day, *that* the LORD shall <u>beat off</u> from the channel of the river to the stream of E'gypt, and you shall be gathered one by one, O you children of Is'ra-el. thresh

13 And it shall come to pass in that day, *that* the great trumpet shall be blown, and they shall come which were ready to perish in the land of As-syr'i-a, and the outcasts in the land of E'gypt, and shall worship the LORD in the holy mount at Je-ru'sa-lem.

CHAPTER 28

WOE to the crown of pride, to the drunkards of E'phra-im, whose glorious beauty *is* a fading flower, which *are* on the head of the <u>fat</u> valleys of them that are overcome with wine! fertile

2 Behold, the Lord has a mighty and strong one, *which* as a tempest of hail *and* a destroying storm, as a flood of mighty waters overflowing, shall cast down to the earth with the hand.

3 The crown of pride, the drunkards of E'phra-im, shall be trodden under feet:

4 And the glorious beauty, which *is* on the head of the fat valley, shall be a fading flower, *and* as the <u>hasty fruit</u> before the summer; which *when* he that looks upon it sees, while it is yet in his hand he eats it up. first ripe fig

5 In that day shall the Lord of hosts be for a crown of glory, and for a diadem of beauty, to the residue of His people, Jehovah^{s.f.} Tsebaoth

6 And for a spirit of judgment to him that sits in judgment, and for strength to them that turn the battle to the gate.

7 But they also <u>have erred</u> through wine, and through strong drink are <u>out of the way</u>; the priest and the prophet have erred through strong drink, they are swallowed up of wine, they are out of the way through strong drink; they <u>err</u> in vision, they stumble *in* judgment. sinned - staggering

8 For all tables are full of vomit *and* filthiness, *so that there is* no place *clean*.

9 Whom shall He teach knowledge? and whom shall He make to understand <u>doctrine</u>? *them that are* weaned from the milk, *and* drawn from the breasts. the message

10 For <u>precept</u> *must be* upon <u>precept</u>, <u>precept</u> upon <u>precept</u>; line upon line, line upon line; here a little, *and* there a little: rule

11 For with <u>stammering</u> lips and another tongue will He speak to this people. 1 COR. 14:21 foreign

12 To whom He said, This *is* the rest

wherewith you may cause the weary to rest; and this *is* the refreshing: yet they would not hear.

13 But the word of the LORD was to them precept upon precept, precept upon precept; line upon line, line upon line; here a little, *and* there a little; that they might go, and fall backward, and be broken, and snared, and taken.   rule - trapped

14 Wherefore hear the word of the LORD, you scornful men, that rule this people which *is* in Je-ru'sa-lem.

15 Because you have said, We have made a covenant with death, and with hell are we at agreement; when the overflowing scourge shall pass through, it shall not come to us: for we have made lies our refuge, and under falsehood have we hid ourselves: agreement

16 Therefore thus says the Lord GOD, Behold, I lay in Zi'on for a foundation a stone, a tried stone, a precious corner *stone*, a sure foundation: he that believes shall not make haste.

MATT. 21:42 ROM. 9:33 1 PET. 2:6 Adonay^p.f. Jehovah

17 Judgment also will I lay to the line, and righteousness to the plummet: and the hail shall sweep away the refuge of lies, and the waters shall overflow the hiding place.   Justice

18 And your covenant with death shall be disannulled, and your agreement with hell shall not stand; when the overflowing scourge shall pass through, then you shall be trodden down by it.   agreement - beaten

19 From the time that it goes forth it shall take you: for morning by morning shall it pass over, by day and by night: and it shall be a vexation only *to* understand the report.   sheer terror - what it means

20 For the bed is shorter than that *a man* can stretch himself *on it*: and the covering narrower than that he can wrap himself *in it*.   too small

21 For the LORD shall rise up as *in* mount Per'a-zim, He shall be angry as *in* the valley of Gib'e-on, that He may do His work, His strange work; and bring to pass His act, His strange act.   extraordinary

22 Now therefore be you not mockers, less your bands be made strong: for I have heard from the Lord GOD of hosts a consumption, even determined upon the whole earth.

scoffers - fetters - Adonay^p.f. Jehovah^s.f. Tsebaoth - destruction

23 Give you ear, and hear my voice; hearken, and hear my speech.   listen

24 Does the plowman plow all day to sow? does he open and break the clods of his ground?   farmer

25 When he has made plain the face thereof, does he not cast abroad the fitches, and scatter the cummin, and cast in the principal wheat and the appointed barley and the rye in their place?   sow - dill

26 For his God does instruct him to discretion, *and* does teach him. Elohim^p.f.

27 For the fitches are not threshed with a threshing instrument, neither is a cart wheel turned about upon the cummin; but the fitches are beaten out with a staff, and the cummin with a rod.   dill

28 Bread *corn* is bruised; because he will not ever be threshing it, nor break *it with* the wheel of his cart, nor bruise it *with* his horsemen.   grain - ground

29 This also comes forth from the Lord of hosts, *which* is wonderful in counsel, *and* excellent in working. Jehovah^{s.f.} Tsebaoth

CHAPTER 29

WOE to A'ri-el, to A'ri-el, the city *where* Da'vid dwells! add you year to year; let them kill sacrifices. i.e. Jerusalem
2 Yet I will distress A'ri-el, and there shall be heaviness and sorrow: and it shall be to me as A'ri-el.
3 And I will camp against you round about, and will lay siege against you with a mount, and I will raise forts against you. siegeworks
4 And you shall be brought down, *and* shall speak out of the ground, and your speech shall be low out of the dust, and your voice shall be, as of one that has a familiar spirit, out of the ground, and your speech shall whisper out of the dust.
5 Moreover the multitude of your strangers shall be like small dust, and the multitude of the terrible ones *shall be* as chaff that passes away: yea, it shall be at an instant suddenly. enemies - ruthless
6 You shall be visited of the Lord of hosts with thunder, and with earthquake, and great noise, with storm and tempest, and the flame of devouring fire. Jehovah^{s.f.} Tsebaoth
7 And the multitude of all the nations that fight against A'ri-el, even all that fight against her and her munition, and that distress her, shall be as a dream of a night vision. i.e., Jerusalem - fortress
8 It shall even be as when an hungry man dreams, and, behold, he eats; but he awakes, and his soul is empty: or as when a thirsty man dreams, and, behold, he drinks; but he awakes, and, behold, *he is* faint, and his soul has appetite: so shall the multitude of all the nations be, that fight against mount Zi'on.
9 Stay yourselves, and wonder; cry you out, and cry: they are drunken, but not with wine; they stagger, but not with strong drink. be amazed
10 For the Lord has poured out upon you the spirit of deep sleep, and has closed your eyes: the prophets and your rulers, the seers has He covered. ROM. 11:8
11 And the vision of all is become to you as the words of a book that is sealed, which *men* deliver to one that is learned, saying, Read this, I pray you: and he says, I cannot; for it *is* sealed:
12 And the book is delivered to him that is not learned, saying, Read this, I pray you: and he says, I am not learned.
13 Wherefore the Lord said, Forasmuch as this people draw near *Me* with their mouth, and with their lips do honor Me, but have removed their heart far from Me, and their fear toward Me is taught by the precept of men: MATT. 15:8 reverence - rule
14 Therefore, behold, I will proceed to do a marvellous work among this people, *even* a marvellous work and a wonder: for the wisdom of their wise *men* shall perish, and the understanding of their prudent *men* shall be hid. 1 COR. 1:19
15 Woe to them that seek deep to hide their counsel from the Lord, and their works are in the dark, and they

say, Who sees us? and who know us?

plans

16 Surely your turning of things upside down shall be esteemed as the potter's clay: for shall the work say of him that made it, He made me not? or shall the thing framed say of him that framed it, He had no understanding?

17 *Is* it not yet a very little while, and Leb'a-non shall be turned into a fruitful field, and the fruitful field shall be esteemed as a forest?

18 And in that day shall the deaf hear the words of the book, and the eyes of the blind shall see out of obscurity, and out of darkness. LUKE 7:22

19 The meek also shall increase *their* joy in the LORD, and the poor among men shall rejoice in the Holy One of Is'ra-el.

humble

20 For the terrible one is brought to nothing, and the scorner is consumed, and all that watch for iniquity are cut off:

ruthless - evil

21 That make a man an offender for a word, and lay a snare for him that reproves in the gate, and turn aside the just for a thing of nothing.

trap

22 Therefore thus says the LORD, who redeemed A'bra-ham, concerning the house of Ja'cob, Ja'cob shall not now be ashamed, neither shall his face now wax pale.

grow

23 But when he sees his children, the work of My hands, in the midst of him, they shall sanctify My name, and sanctify the Holy One of Ja'cob, and shall fear the God of Is'ra-el.

stand in awe of

24 They also that erred in spirit shall come to understanding, and they that murmured shall learn doctrine.

complained - accept instruction

CHAPTER 30

WOE to the rebellious children, says the LORD, that take counsel, but not of Me; and that cover with a covering, but not of My Spirit, that they may add sin to sin: *execute a plan - make an alliance*

2 That walk to go down into E'gypt, and have not asked at My mouth; to strengthen themselves in the strength of Pha'raoh, and to trust in the shadow of E'gypt!

consulted me

3 Therefore shall the strength of Pha'raoh be your shame, and the trust in the shadow of E'gypt *your* confusion.

4 For his princes were at Zo'an, and his ambassadors came to Ha'nes.

5 They were all ashamed of a people *that* could not profit them, nor be an help nor profit, but a shame, and also a reproach.

6 The burden of the beasts of the south: into the land of trouble and anguish, from where *come* the young and old lion, the viper and fiery flying serpent, they will carry their riches upon the shoulders of young asses, and their treasures upon the bunches of camels, to a people *that* shall not profit *them*.

humps

7 For the E-gyp'tians shall help in vain, and to no purpose: therefore have I cried concerning this, Their strength *is* to sit still.

8 Now go, write it before them in a table, and note it in a book, that it may

be for the time to come for ever and ever:　　_{tablet}

9 That this *is* a rebellious people, lying children, children *that* will not hear the law of the LORD:　　listen to

10 Which say to the seers, See not; and to the prophets, Prophesy not to us right things, speak to us smooth things, prophesy deceits:

11 Get you out of the way, turn aside out of the path, cause the Holy One of Is'ra-el to cease from before us.

12 Wherefore thus says the Holy One of Is'ra-el, Because you despise this word, and trust in oppression and perverseness, and stay thereon:　　extortion - trust

13 Therefore this iniquity shall be to you as a breach ready to fall, swelling out in a near wall, whose breaking comes suddenly at an instant.

14 And He shall break it as the breaking of the potters' vessel that is broken in pieces; He shall not spare: so that there shall not be found in the bursting of it a sherd to take fire from the hearth, or to take water *with* out of the pit.　　fragment

15 For thus says the Lord GOD, the Holy One of Is'ra-el; In returning and rest shall you be saved; in quietness and in confidence shall be your strength: and you would not.

Adonay[p.f.] Jehovah

16 But you said, No; for we will flee upon horses; therefore shall you flee: and, We will ride upon the swift; therefore shall they that pursue you be swift.

17 One thousand *shall flee* at the rebuke of one; at the rebuke of five shall you flee: till you be left as a beacon upon the top of a mountain, and as an ensign on an hill.　　a flag

18 And therefore will the LORD wait, that He may be gracious to you, and therefore will He be exalted, that He may have mercy upon you: for the LORD *is* a God of judgment: blessed *are* all they that wait for Him.　　Jehovah[s.f.] - Elohim[p.f.]

19 For the people shall dwell in Zi'on at Je-ru'sa-lem: you shall weep no more: He will be very gracious to you at the voice of your cry; when He shall hear it, He will answer you.

20 And *though* the Lord give you the bread of adversity, and the water of affliction, yet shall not your teachers be removed into a corner any more, but your eyes shall see your teachers:

21 And your ears shall hear a word behind you, saying, This *is* the way, walk you in it, when you turn to the right hand, and when you turn to the left.

22 You shall defile also the covering of your graven images of silver, and the ornament of your molten images of gold: you shall cast them away as a menstruous cloth; you shall say to it, Get you from here.　　carved idols

23 Then shall He give the rain of your seed, that you shall sow the ground with; and bread of the increase of the earth, and it shall be fat and plenteous: in that day shall your cattle feed in large pastures.

24 The oxen likewise and the young asses that ear the ground shall eat clean provender, which has been winnowed with the shovel and with the fan.　　work - good fodder

25 And there shall be upon every high mountain, and upon every high hill, rivers *and* streams of waters in the day of the great slaughter, when the towers fall.

26 Moreover the light of the moon shall be as the light of the sun, and the light of the sun shall be sevenfold, as the light of seven days, in the day that the LORD binds up the breach of His people, and heals the stroke of their wound.

27 Behold, the name of the LORD comes from far, burning *with* His anger, and the burden *thereof is* heavy: His lips are full of indignation, and His tongue as a devouring fire:

28 And His breath, as an overflowing stream, shall reach to the midst of the neck, to sift the nations with the sieve of vanity: and *there shall be* a bridle in the jaws of the people, causing *them* to err.   which leads to ruin - i.e. falsehood

29 You shall have a song, as in the night *when* a holy solemnity is kept; and gladness of heart, as when one goes with a pipe to come into the mountain of the LORD, to the Mighty One of Is'ra-el.

30 And the LORD shall cause His glorious voice to be heard, and shall show the lighting down of His arm, with the indignation of *His* anger, and *with* the flame of a devouring fire, *with* scattering, and tempest, and hailstones.   majestic

31 For through the voice of the LORD shall the As-syr'i-an be beaten down, *which* smote with a rod.   shattered - struck

32 And *in* every place where the grounded staff shall pass, which the LORD shall lay upon him, *it* shall be with tabrets and harps: and in battles of shaking will He fight with it.   them

33 For To'phet *is* ordained of old; yea, for the king it is prepared; he has made *it* deep *and* large: the pile thereof *is* fire and much wood; the breath of the LORD, like a stream of brimstone, does kindle it.

CHAPTER 31

WOE to them that go down to E'gypt for help; and stay on horses, and trust in chariots, because *they are* many; and in horsemen, because they are very strong; but they look not to the Holy One of Is'ra-el, neither seek the LORD!   rely

2 Yet He also *is* wise, and will bring evil, and will not call back His words: but will arise against the house of the evildoers, and against the help of them that work iniquity.   support

3 Now the E-gyp'tians *are* men, and not God; and their horses flesh, and not spirit. When the LORD shall stretch out His hand, both he that helps shall fall, and he that is helped shall fall down, and they all shall fail together.

4 For thus has the LORD spoken to me, Like as the lion and the young lion roaring on its prey, when a multitude of shepherds is called forth against him, *he* will not be afraid of their voice, nor abase himself for the noise of them: so shall the LORD of hosts come down to fight for mount Zi'on, and for the hill thereof.

                Jehovah^{s.f.} Tsebaoth

5 As birds flying, so will the LORD of

hosts defend Je-ru'sa-lem; defending also He will deliver *it*; *and* passing over He will preserve *it*. Jehovah^{s-f} Tsebaoth
6 Turn you to *Him from* whom the children of Is'ra-el have deeply revolted.
7 For in that day every man shall cast away his idols of silver, and his idols of gold, which your own hands have made to you *for* a sin.
8 Then shall the As-syr'i-an fall with the sword, not of a mighty man; and the sword, not of a mean man, shall devour him: but he shall flee from the sword, and his young men shall be <u>discomfited</u>. for forced labor
9 And he shall pass over to his strong hold for <u>fear</u>, and his princes shall be afraid of the <u>ensign</u>, says the LORD, whose fire *is* in Zi'on, and His furnace in Je-ru'sa-lem.

terror - battle standard

CHAPTER 32

BEHOLD, a king shall reign in righteousness, and princes shall rule in judgment.
2 And a man shall be as an hiding place from the wind, and a <u>covert</u> from the tempest; as rivers of water in a dry place, as the shadow of a great rock in a weary land. shelter
3 And the eyes of them that see shall not be <u>dim</u>, and the ears of them that hear shall <u>hearken</u>. blind - listen
4 The heart also of the <u>rash</u> shall understand knowledge, and the tongue of the stammerers shall be ready to speak plainly. hasty

5 The <u>vile</u> person shall be no more called <u>liberal</u>, nor the <u>churl</u> said *to be* bountiful. foolish - noble - peasant
6 For the <u>vile</u> person will speak <u>villany</u>, and his heart will work iniquity, to practise <u>hypocrisy</u>, and to utter error against the LORD, to make empty the soul of the hungry, and he will cause the drink of the thirsty to fail. folly - ungodliness
7 The instruments also of the <u>churl</u> *are* evil: he devises wicked devices to destroy the poor with lying words, even when the needy speaks right. scoundrel
8 But the <u>liberal</u> devises <u>liberal</u> things; and by <u>liberal</u> things shall he stand. noble
9 Rise up, you women that are at ease; hear my voice, you careless daughters; give ear to my speech.
10 Many days and years shall you be troubled, you careless women: for the vintage shall fail, the gathering shall not come.
11 Tremble, you women that are at ease; be troubled, you careless ones: strip you, and make you bare, and gird *sackcloth* upon *your* loins.
12 They shall lament for the teats, for the pleasant fields, for the fruitful vine.
13 Upon the land of my people shall come up thorns *and* briers; yea, upon all the houses of joy *in* the joyous city:
14 Because the palaces shall be forsaken; the multitude of the city shall be left; the forts and towers shall be for dens for ever, a joy of wild asses, a pasture of flocks;

15 Until the Spirit be poured upon us from on high, and the wilderness be a fruitful field, and the fruitful field be counted for a forest.

16 Then judgment shall dwell in the wilderness, and righteousness remain in the fruitful field.

17 And the work of righteousness shall be peace; and the effect of righteousness quietness and assurance for ever.   JAMES 3:18

18 And my people shall dwell in a peaceable habitation, and in <u>sure</u> dwellings, and in quiet resting places;   secure

19 When it shall hail, coming down on the forest; and the city shall be <u>low in a low place</u>.   leveled completely

20 Blessed *are* you that sow beside all waters, that send forth *there* the feet of the ox and the ass.

CHAPTER 33

WOE to you that <u>spoils</u>, and you *were* not <u>spoiled</u>; and deals treacherously, and they dealt not treacherously with you! when you shall cease to <u>spoil</u>, you shall be <u>spoiled</u>; *and* when you shall make an end to deal treacherously, they shall deal treacherously with you.   destroys - destroyed

2 O LORD, be gracious to us; we have waited for You: be You their arm every morning, our <u>salvation</u> also in the time of trouble.   i.e., Heb. Jeshua

3 At the noise of the tumult the people fled; at the lifting up of Yourself the nations were scattered.

4 And your <u>spoil</u> shall be gathered *like* the gathering of the caterpiller: as the running to and fro of locusts shall he run upon them.   plunder

5 The LORD is exalted; for He dwells on high: He has filled Zi'on with judgment and righteousness.

6 And wisdom and knowledge shall be the stability of Your times, *and* strength of salvation: the <u>fear</u> of the LORD *is* his treasure.   reverence

7 Behold, their <u>valiant</u> ones shall cry without: the ambassadors of peace shall weep bitterly.   brave

8 The highways lie waste, the wayfaring man ceases: he has broken the <u>covenant</u>, he has despised the cities, he regards no man.   agreement

9 The earth mourns *and* languishes: Leb'a-non is ashamed *and* <u>hewn</u> down: Shar'on is like a wilderness; and Ba'shan and Car'mel shake off *their fruits*.   cut

10 Now will I rise, says the LORD; now will I be exalted; now will I lift up Myself.

11 You shall conceive chaff, you shall bring forth stubble: your breath, *as* fire, shall devour you.

12 And the people shall be *as* the burnings of lime: *as* thorns cut up shall they be burned in the fire.

13 Hear, you *that are* far off, what I have done; and, you *that are* near, acknowledge My might.

14 The sinners in Zi'on are afraid; <u>fearfulness</u> has <u>surprised</u> the <u>hypocrites</u>. Who among us shall dwell with the devouring fire? who among us shall dwell with everlasting burnings?   trembling - seized - godless ones

15 He that walks righteously, and speaks uprightly; he that despises the gain of oppressions, that shakes his hands from holding of bribes, that stops his ears from hearing of blood, and shuts his eyes from seeing evil; _{unjust gains - violence}

16 He shall dwell on high: his place of defence *shall be* the munitions of rocks: bread shall be given him; his waters *shall be* sure.

17 Your eyes shall see the king in His beauty: they shall behold the land that is very far off.

18 Your heart shall meditate terror. Where *is* the scribe? where *is* the receiver? where *is* he that counted the towers? _{1 COR. 1:20 think about former}

19 You shall not see a fierce people, a people of a deeper speech than you can perceive; of a stammering tongue, *that you can* not understand.

_{i.e., foreign}

20 Look upon Zi'on, the city of our solemnities: your eyes shall see Je-ru'sa-lem a quiet habitation, a tabernacle *that* shall not be taken down; not one of the stakes thereof shall ever be removed, neither shall any of the cords thereof be broken. _{tent}

21 But there the glorious LORD *will be* to us a place of broad rivers *and* streams; wherein shall go no galley with oars, neither shall gallant ship pass thereby. _{boat}

22 For the LORD *is* our Judge, the LORD *is* our Lawgiver, the LORD *is* our King; He will save us.

23 Your tacklings are loosed; they could not well strengthen their mast, they could not spread the sail: then is the prey of a great spoil divided; the lame take the prey. _{loot}

24 And the inhabitant shall not say, I am sick: the people that dwell therein *shall be* forgiven *their* iniquity.

CHAPTER 34

COME near, you nations, to hear; and hearken, you people: let the earth hear, and all that is therein; the world, and all things that come forth of it.

2 For the indignation of the LORD *is* upon all nations, and *His* fury upon all their armies: He has utterly destroyed them, He has delivered them to the slaughter.

3 Their slain also shall be cast out, and their stink shall come up out of their carcases, and the mountains shall be melted with their blood.

4 And all the host of heaven shall be dissolved, and the heavens shall be rolled together as a scroll: and all their host shall fall down, as the leaf falls off from the vine, and as a falling *fig* from the fig tree. _{2 PET. 3:12 REV. 6:13}

5 For My sword shall be bathed in heaven: behold, it shall come down upon I-du-me'a, and upon the people of My curse, to judgment.

6 The sword of the LORD is filled with blood, it is made fat with fatness, *and* with the blood of lambs and goats, with the fat of the kidneys of rams: for the LORD has a sacrifice in Boz'rah, and a great slaughter in the land of I-du-me'a.

7 And the unicorns shall come down with them, and the bullocks with the

bulls; and their land shall be soaked with blood, and their dust made fat with fatness.   wild oxen

8 For *it is* the day of the LORD's ven-geance, *and* the year of recompences for the controversy of Zi'on.

9 And the streams thereof shall be turned into pitch, and the dust thereof into brimstone, and the land thereof shall become burning pitch.   tar

10 It shall not be quenched night nor day; the smoke thereof shall go up for ever: from generation to genera-tion it shall lie waste; none shall pass through it for ever and ever.   live

11 But the cormorant and the bittern shall possess it; the owl also and the raven shall dwell in it: and He shall stretch out upon it the line of confu-sion, and the stones of emptiness.

pelican - hedgehog

12 They shall call the nobles thereof to the kingdom, but none *shall be* there, and all its princes shall be nothing.

13 And thorns shall come up in its palaces, nettles and brambles in the fortresses thereof: and it shall be an habitation of dragons, *and* a court for owls.   jackals - ostriches

14 The wild beasts of the desert shall also meet with the wild beasts of the island, and the satyr shall cry to its fellow; the screech owl also shall rest there, and find for herself a place of rest.   hyenas - shaggy goat

15 There shall the great owl make its nest, and lay, and hatch, and gather under its shadow: there shall the vultures also be gathered, every one with its mate.

16 Seek you out of the book of the LORD, and read: no one of these shall fail, none shall want its mate: for My mouth it has commanded, and His Spirit it has gathered them.

17 And He has cast the lot for them, and His hand has divided it to them by line: they shall possess it for ever, from generation to generation shall they dwell therein.

CHAPTER 35

THE wilderness and the solitary place shall be glad for them; and the desert shall rejoice, and blossom as the rose.

2 It shall blossom abundantly, and rejoice even with joy and singing: the glory of Leb'a-non shall be given to it, the excellency of Car'mel and Shar'on, they shall see the glory of the LORD, *and* the excellency of our God.   Elohim[p.f.]

3 Strengthen you the weak hands, and confirm the feeble knees.

4 Say to them *that are* of a fearful heart, Be strong, fear not: behold, your God will come *with* vengeance, *even* God *with* a recompence; He will come and save you.   1 THESS. 5:4 anxious

5 Then the eyes of the blind shall be opened, and the ears of the deaf shall be unstopped.   MATT. 11:5

6 Then shall the lame *man* leap as an hart, and the tongue of the dumb sing: for in the wilderness shall waters break out, and streams in the desert.   deer

7 And the parched ground shall be-come a pool, and the thirsty land springs of water: in the habitation of

<u>dragons</u>, where each lay, *shall be* grass with reeds and rushes. crocodiles

8 And an highway shall be there, and a way, and it shall be called the way of holiness; the unclean shall not pass over it; but it *shall be* for those: the wayfaring men, though fools, shall not err *therein*.

9 No lion shall be there, nor *any* ravenous beast shall go up thereon, it shall not be found there; but the redeemed shall walk *there*:

10 And the ransomed of the LORD shall return, and come to Zi'on with songs and everlasting joy upon their heads: they shall obtain joy and gladness, and sorrow and sighing shall flee away.

CHAPTER 36

N OW it came to pass in the fourteenth year of king Hez-e-ki'ah, *that* Sen-nach'e-rib king of As-syr'i-a came up against all the <u>defenced</u> cities of Ju'dah, and took them. unfortified

2 And the king of As-syr'i-a sent Rab'sha-keh from La'chish to Je-ru'sa-lem to king Hez-e-ki'ah with a great army. And he stood by the conduit of the upper pool in the highway of the fuller's field.

3 Then came forth to him E-li'a-kim, Hil-ki'ah's son, which was over the house, and Sheb'na the scribe, and Jo'ah, A'saph's son, the recorder.

4 And Rab'sha-keh said to them, Say you now to Hez-e-ki'ah, Thus says the great king, the king of As-syr'i-a, What confidence *is* this wherein you trusts?

5 I say, *say you*, (but *they are but* <u>vain</u> words) *I have* counsel and strength for war: now on whom do you trust, that you rebel against me? empty

6 Lo, you trust in the staff of this broken reed, on E'gypt; whereon if a man lean, it will go into his hand, and pierce it: so *is* Pha'raoh king of E'gypt to all that trust in him.

7 But if you say to me, We trust in the LORD our <u>God</u>: *is it* not He, whose high places and whose altars Hez-e-ki'ah has taken away, and said to Ju'dah and to Je-ru'sa-lem, You shall worship before this altar? Elohim^p.f.

8 Now therefore <u>give pledges</u>, I pray you, <u>to</u> my master the king of As-syr'i-a, and I will give you two thousand horses, if you be able on your part to set riders upon them. make an agreement - with

9 How then will you turn away the face of one captain of the least of my master's servants, and put your trust on E'gypt for chariots and for horsemen?

10 And am I now come up without the LORD against this land to destroy it? the LORD said to me, Go up against this land, and destroy it.

11 Then said E-li'a-kim and Sheb'na and Jo'ah to Rab'sha-keh, Speak, I pray you, to your servants in the Syr'i-an language; for we understand *it*: and speak not to us in the Jews' language, in the <u>ears</u> of the people that *are* on the wall. hearing

12 But Rab'sha-keh said, Has my master sent me to your master and to

M07 — 1072

you to speak these words? *has he not sent me* to the men that sit upon the wall, that they may eat their own dung, and drink their own urine with you? _{refuse} *refuse*

13 Then Rab'sha-keh stood, and cried with a loud voice in the Jews' language, and said, Hear you the words of the great king, the king of As-syr'i-a.

14 Thus says the king, Let not Hez-e-ki'ah deceive you: for he shall not be able to deliver you.

15 Neither let Hez-e-ki'ah make you trust in the LORD, saying, The LORD will surely deliver us: this city shall not be delivered into the hand of the king of As-syr'i-a.

16 Hearken not to Hez-e-ki'ah: for thus says the king of As-syr'i-a, Make *an agreement* with me *by* a present, and come out to me: and eat you every one of his vine, and every one of his fig tree, and drink you every one the waters of his own cistern;

17 Until I come and take you away to a land like your own land, a land of corn and wine, a land of bread and vineyards. *grain*

18 *Beware* less Hez-e-ki'ah persuade you, saying, The LORD will deliver us. Has any of the gods of the nations delivered his land out of the hand of the king of As-syr'i-a?

19 Where *are* the gods of Ha'math and Ar'phad? where *are* the gods of Seph-ar-va'im? and have they delivered Sa-ma'ri-a out of my hand?

20 Who *are they* among all the gods of these lands, that have delivered their land out of my hand, that the LORD should deliver Je-ru'sa-lem out of my hand?

21 But they held their peace, and answered him not a word: for the king's commandment was, saying, Answer him not. *were silent*

22 Then came E-li'a-kim, the son of Hil-ki'ah, that *was* over the household, and Sheb'na the scribe, and Jo'ah, the son of A'saph, the recorder, to Hez-e-ki'ah with *their* clothes rent, and told him the words of Rab'sha-keh.

CHAPTER 37

AND it came to pass, when king Hez-e-ki'ah heard *it*, that he rent his clothes, and covered himself with sackcloth, and went into the house of the LORD.

2 And he sent E-li'a-kim, who *was* over the household, and Sheb'na the scribe, and the elders of the priests covered with sackcloth, to I-sa'iah the prophet the son of A'moz.

3 And they said to him, Thus says Hez-e-ki'ah, This day *is* a day of trouble, and of rebuke, and of blasphemy: for the children are come to the birth, and *there is* not strength to bring forth. *rejection*

4 It may be the LORD your God will hear the words of Rab'sha-keh, whom the king of As-syr'i-a his master has sent to reproach the living God, and will reprove the words which the LORD your God has heard: wherefore lift up *your* prayer for the remnant that is left. Jehovah^{s.f.} - Elohim^{p.f.} - rebuke

5 So the servants of king Hez-e-ki'ah came to I-sa'iah.

6 And I-sa'iah said to them, Thus shall you say to your master, Thus says the LORD, Be not afraid of the words that you have heard, wherewith the servants of the king of As-syr'i-a have blasphemed Me.

7 Behold, I will send a blast upon him, and he shall hear a rumor, and return to his own land; and I will cause him to <u>fall</u> by the sword in his own land. _{be killed}

8 So Rab'sha-keh returned, and found the king of As-syr'i-a warring against Lib'nah: for he had heard that he was departed from La'chish.

9 And he heard <u>say</u> concerning Tir'ha-kah king of E-thi-o'pi-a, He is come forth to make war with you. And when he heard *it*, he sent messengers to Hez-e-ki'ah, saying, _{a report}

10 Thus shall you speak to Hez-e-ki'ah king of Ju'dah, saying, Let not your God, in whom you trust, deceive you, saying, Je-ru'sa-lem shall not be given into the hand of the king of As-syr'i-a.

11 Behold, you have heard what the kings of As-syr'i-a have done to all lands by destroying them utterly; and shall you be delivered?

12 Have the gods of the nations delivered them which my fathers have destroyed, *as* Go'zan, and Ha'ran, and Re'zeph, and the children of E'den which *were* in Te-las'sar?

13 Where *is* the king of Ha'math, and the king of Ar'phad, and the king of the city of Seph-ar-va'im, He'na, and I'vah?

14 And Hez-e-ki'ah received the letter from the hand of the messengers, and read it: and Hez-e-ki'ah went up to the house of the LORD, and spread it before the LORD.

15 And Hez-e-ki'ah prayed to the LORD, saying,

16 O <u>LORD of hosts</u>, <u>God</u> of Is'ra-el, that dwells *between* the cherubims, You *are* the <u>God</u>, *even* You alone, of all the kingdoms of the earth: You have made heaven and earth. _{Jehovah^{s.f.} Tsebaoth - Elohim^{p.f.}}

17 Incline Your ear, O LORD, and hear; open Your eyes, O LORD, and see: and hear all the words of Sen-nach'e-rib, which has sent to reproach the living God.

18 Of a truth, LORD, the kings of As-syr'i-a have laid waste all the nations, and their <u>countries</u>, _{lands}

19 And have cast their gods into the fire: for they *were* no gods, but the work of men's hands, wood and stone: therefore <u>they</u> have destroyed them.

20 Now therefore, O LORD our <u>God</u>, save us from his hand, that all the kingdoms of the earth may know that You *are* the LORD, *even* You only.

21 Then I-sa'iah the son of A'moz sent to Hez-e-ki'ah, saying, Thus says the <u>LORD God</u> of Is'ra-el, <u>Whereas</u> you have prayed to Me against Sen-nach'e-rib king of As-syr'i-a: _{Jehovah^{s.f.} Elohim^{p.f.} - Because}

22 This *is* the word which the LORD has spoken concerning him; The virgin, the daughter of Zi'on, has despised you, *and* laughed you to scorn; the daughter of Je-ru'sa-lem has shaken her head at you.

23 Whom have you reproached and blasphemed? and against whom have you underline(exalted) *your* voice, and lifted up your eyes on high? *even* against the Holy One of Is'ra-el.

raised

24 By your servants have you reproached the Lord, and have said, By the multitude of my chariots am I come up to the height of the mountains, to the sides of Leb'a-non; and I will cut down the tall cedars thereof, *and* the choice fir trees thereof: and I will enter into the height of its border, *and* the forest of its Car'mel.

25 I have dug, and drunk water; and with the sole of my feet have I dried up all the rivers of the besieged places.

26 Have you not heard long ago, *how* I have done it; *and* of ancient times, that I have formed it? now have I brought it to pass, that you should be to lay waste defenced cities *into* ruinous heaps.

destroy -unfortified

27 Therefore their inhabitants *were* of small power, they were dismayed and confounded: they were *as* the grass of the field, and *as* the green herb, *as* the grass on the house tops, and *as* corn blasted before it be grown up.

weak - grain - scorched

28 But I know your abode, and your going out, and your coming in, and your rage against Me.

dwelling place

29 Because your rage against Me, and your tumult, is come up into My ears, therefore will I put My hook in your nose, and My bridle in your lips, and I will turn you back by the way by which you came.

30 And this *shall be* a sign to you, You shall eat *this* year such as grows of itself; and the second year that which springs of the same: and in the third year sow you, and reap, and plant vineyards, and eat the fruit thereof.

31 And the remnant that is escaped of the house of Ju'dah shall again take root downward, and bear fruit upward:

32 For out of Je-ru'sa-lem shall go forth a remnant, and they that escape out of mount Zi'on: the zeal of the LORD of hosts shall do this.

Jehovah^{s.f.} Tsebaoth

33 Therefore thus says the LORD concerning the king of As-syr'i-a, He shall not come into this city, nor shoot an arrow there, nor come before it with shields, nor cast a bank against it.

build a seige ramp

34 By the way that he came, by the same shall he return, and shall not come into this city, says the LORD.

35 For I will defend this city to save it for My own sake, and for My servant Da'vid's sake.

36 Then the angel of the LORD went forth, and smote in the camp of the As-syr'i-ans a hundred and fourscore and five thousand: and when they arose early in the morning, behold, they *were* all dead corpses.

messenger - 185,000

37 So Sen-nach'e-rib king of As-syr'i-a departed, and went and returned, and dwelled at Nin'e-veh.

38 And it came to pass, as he was worshipping in the house of Nis'roch his god, that A-dram'me-lech and Sha-

re'zer his sons smote him with the sword; and they escaped into the land of Ar-me'ni-a: and E'sar-had'don his son reigned in his stead.

CHAPTER 38

IN those days was Hez-e-ki'ah sick to death. And I-sa'iah the prophet the son of A'moz came to him, and said to him, Thus says the LORD, Set your house in order: for you shall die, and not live.

2 Then Hez-e-ki'ah turned his face toward the wall, and prayed to the LORD,

3 And said, Remember now, O LORD, I <u>beseech</u> You, how I have walked before You in truth and with a perfect heart, and have done *that which is* good in Your sight. And Hez-e-ki'ah wept <u>sore</u>.　　beg - bitterly

4 Then came the word of the LORD to I-sa'iah, saying,

5 Go, and say to Hez-e-ki'ah, Thus says the LORD, the <u>God</u> of Da'vid your father, I have heard your prayer, I have seen your tears: behold, I will add to your days fifteen years.　　Elohim^p.f.

6 And I will deliver you and this city out of the hand of the king of As-syr'i-a: and I will defend this city.

7 And this *shall be* a sign to you from the LORD, that the LORD will do this thing that He has spoken;

8 Behold, I will bring again the shadow of the degrees, which is gone down in the sun dial of A'haz, ten degrees backward. So the sun returned ten degrees, by which degrees it was gone down.

9 The writing of Hez-e-ki'ah king of Ju'dah, when he had been sick, and was recovered of his sickness:

10 I said in the cutting off of my days, I shall go to the gates of the grave: I am deprived of the residue of my years.

11 I said, I shall not see the LORD, *even* the LORD, in the land of the living: I shall behold man no more with the inhabitants of the world.

12 My age is departed, and is removed from me as a shepherd's tent: I have cut off like a weaver my life: He will cut me off with pining sickness: from day *even* to night will You make an end of me.

13 I <u>reckoned</u> till morning, *that*, as a lion, so will He break all my bones: from day *even* to night will You make an end of me.　　waited patiently

14 Like a crane *or* a swallow, so did I chatter: I did mourn as a dove: my eyes fail *with looking* upward: O LORD, I am oppressed; undertake for me.

15 What shall I say? He has both spoken to me, and Himself has done *it*: I shall go softly all my years in the bitterness of my soul.

16 O Lord, by these *things men* live, and in all these *things is* the life of my spirit: so will You <u>recover</u> me, and make me to live.　　restore

17 Behold, for peace I had great bitterness: but You have in love to my soul *delivered it* from the pit of corruption: for You have cast all my sins behind Your back.

18 For the grave cannot praise You, death can *not* celebrate You: they that go down into the pit cannot hope for Your <u>truth</u>.   faithfulness
19 The living, the living, he shall praise You, as I *do* this day: the father to the children shall make known Your truth.
20 The LORD *was ready* to save me: therefore we will sing my songs to the stringed instruments all the days of our life in the house of the LORD.
21 For I-sa'iah had said, Let them take a lump of figs, and lay *it* for a plaster upon the boil, and he shall recover.
22 Hez-e-ki'ah also had said, What *is* the sign that I shall go up to the house of the LORD?

CHAPTER 39

AT that time Me-ro'dach-bal'a-dan, the son of Bal'a-dan, king of Bab'y-lon, sent letters and a present to Hez-e-ki'ah: for he had heard that he had been sick, and was recovered.
2 And Hez-e-ki'ah was glad of them, and showed them the house of his precious <u>things</u>, the silver, and the gold, and the spices, and the precious ointment, and all the house of his armor, and all that was found in his treasures: there was nothing in his house, nor in all his dominion, that Hez-e-ki'ah showed them not.   treasures
3 Then came I-sa'iah the prophet to king Hez-e-ki'ah, and said to him, What said these men? and from where came they to you? And Hez-e-ki'ah said, They are come from a far country to me, *even* from Bab'y-lon.
4 Then said he, What have they seen in your house? And Hez-e-ki'ah answered, All that *is* in my house have they seen: there is nothing among my treasures that I have not showed them.
5 Then said I-sa'iah to Hez-e-ki'ah, Hear the word of the <u>LORD</u> of hosts: Jehovah^{s.f.} Tsebaoth
6 Behold, the days come, that all that *is* in your house, and *that* which your fathers have laid up in store until this day, shall be carried to Bab'y-lon: nothing shall be left, says the LORD.
7 And of your sons that shall <u>issue from</u> you, which you shall father, shall they take away; and they shall be eunuchs in the palace of the king of Bab'y-lon.   be born to
8 Then said Hez-e-ki'ah to I-sa'iah, Good *is* the word of the LORD which you have spoken. He said moreover, For there shall be peace and truth in my days.

CHAPTER 40

COMFORT you, comfort you G.4 My people, says your <u>God</u>.   Elohim^{p.f.}
2 Speak you <u>comfortably</u> to Je-ru'sa-lem, and cry to her, that her <u>warfare</u> is accomplished, that her iniquity is pardoned: for she has received of the LORD's hand double for all her sins.   kindly - hard service
3 The voice of him that cries in the wilderness, Prepare you the way of the LORD, make straight in the desert a highway for our <u>God</u>.
MATT. 3:3 MATT 11:10 MARK 1:3 LUKE 3:4 JOHN 1:23

4 Every valley shall be exalted, and every mountain and hill shall be made low: and the crooked shall be made straight, and the rough places plain:

5 And the glory of the LORD shall be revealed, and all flesh shall see *it* together: for the mouth of the LORD has spoken *it*.

6 The voice said, Cry. And he said, What shall I cry? All flesh *is* grass, and all the goodliness thereof *is* as the flower of the field: 1 PET. 1:24

7 The grass withers, the flower fades: because the Spirit of the LORD blows upon it: surely the people *is* grass.   JAMES 1:6

8 The grass withers, the flower fades: but the word of our God shall stand for ever.   Elohim^p.f.

9 O Zi'on, that brings good tidings, get you up into the high mountain; O Je-ru'sa-lem, that brings good tidings, lift up your voice with strength; lift *it* up, be not afraid; say to the cities of Ju'dah, Behold your God!

10 Behold, the Lord GOD will come with strong *hand*, and His arm shall rule for Him: behold, His reward *is* with Him, and His work before Him.   REV. 22:12 Adonay^p.f. Jehovah - might

11 He shall feed His flock like a shepherd: He shall gather the lambs with His arm, and carry *them* in His bosom, *and* shall gently lead those that are with young.   JOHN 10:11

12 Who has measured the waters in the hollow of His hand, and meted out heaven with the span, and comprehended the dust of the earth in a measure, and weighed the mountains in scales, and the hills in a balance? marked off

13 Who has directed the Spirit of the LORD, or *being* His counselor has taught Him?   ROM.11:34 1 COR 2:16

14 With whom took He counsel, and *who* instructed Him, and taught Him in the path of judgment, and taught Him knowledge, and showed to Him the way of understanding?   ROM. 11:34 justice

15 Behold, the nations *are* as a drop of a bucket, and are counted as the small dust of the balance: behold, He takes up the isles as a very little thing.   lifts - distant lands

16 And Leb'a-non *is* not sufficient to burn, nor the beasts thereof sufficient for a burned offering.

17 All nations before Him *are* as nothing; and they are counted to Him less than nothing, and vanity.

18 To whom then will you liken God? or what likeness will you compare to Him?

19 The workman melts a graven image, and the goldsmith spreads it over with gold, and casts silver chains.

20 He that *is* so impoverished that he has no oblation chooses a tree *that* will not rot; he seeks to him a cunning workman to prepare a graven image, *that* shall not be moved.   offering - skillful

21 Have you not known? have you not heard? has it not been told you from the beginning? have you not understood from the foundations of the earth?

22 *It is* He that sits upon the circle of the earth, and the inhabitants thereof

are as grasshoppers; that stretches out the heavens as a curtain, and spreads them out as a tent to dwell in:

23 That brings the princes to nothing; He makes the judges of the earth as vanity.

24 Yea, they shall not be planted; yea, they shall not be sown: yea, their stock shall not take root in the earth: and He shall also blow upon them, and they shall wither, and the whirlwind shall take them away as stubble.

25 To whom then will you liken Me, or shall I be equal? says the Holy One.

26 Lift up your eyes on high, and behold who has created these *things*, that brings out their host by number: He calls them all by names by the greatness of His might, for that *He is* strong in power; not one fails.

27 Why say you, O Ja'cob, and speak, O Is'ra-el, My way is hid from the LORD, and my judgment is passed over from my God?

justice - by - Elohim^(p.f.)

28 Have you not known? have you not heard, *that* the everlasting God, the LORD, the Creator of the ends of the earth, faints not, neither is weary? *there is* no searching of His understanding.

29 He gives power to the faint; and to *them that have* no might He increases strength.

30 Even the youths shall faint and be weary, and the young men shall utterly fall:

31 But they that wait upon the LORD shall renew *their* strength; they shall mount up with wings as eagles; they shall run, and not be weary; *and* they shall walk, and not faint.   hope in

CHAPTER 41

KEEP silence before Me, O islands; and let the people renew *their* strength: let them come near; then let them speak: let us come near together to judgment.

2 Who raised up the righteous *man* from the east, called him to His foot, gave the nations before him, and made *him* rule over kings? He gave *them* as the dust to his sword, *and* as driven stubble to his bow.

3 He pursued them, *and* passed safely; *even* by the way *that* he had not gone with his feet.

4 Who has wrought and done *it*, calling the generations from the beginning? I the LORD, the First, and with the Last; I *am* He.

5 The isles saw *it*, and feared; the ends of the earth were afraid, drew near, and came.   distant lands

6 They helped every one his neighbor; and *every one* said to his brother, Be of good courage.   brave

7 So the carpenter encouraged the goldsmith, *and* he that smooths *with* the hammer him that smote the anvil, saying, It *is* ready for the soldering: and he fastened it with nails, *that* it should not be moved.   smelter

8 But you, Is'ra-el, *are* My servant, Ja'cob whom I have chosen, the seed of A'bra-ham My friend.

HEB. 2:16 descendants

9 *You* whom I have taken from the ends of the earth, and called you from

the chief men thereof, and said to you, you *are* My servant; I have chosen you, and not cast you away.

10 Fear you not; for I *am* with you: be not dismayed; for I *am* your <u>God</u>: I will strengthen you; yea, I will help you; yea, I will uphold you with the right hand of My righteousness. Elohim^{p.f.}

11 Behold, all they that were incensed against you shall be ashamed and confounded: they shall be as nothing; and they that strive with you shall perish.

12 You shall seek them, and shall not find them, *even* them that contended with you: they that war against you shall be as nothing, and as a thing of <u>nought</u>. non-existent

13 For I the Lᴏʀᴅ your <u>God</u> will hold your right hand, saying to you, Fear not; I will help you.

14 Fear not, you worm Ja'cob, *and* you men of Is'ra-el; I will help you, says the Lᴏʀᴅ, and your redeemer, the Holy One of Is'ra-el.

15 Behold, I will make you a new sharp threshing instrument having teeth: you shall thresh the mountains, and beat *them* small, and shall make the hills as chaff.

16 You shall fan them, and the wind shall carry them away, and the whirlwind shall scatter them: and you shall rejoice in the Lᴏʀᴅ, *and* shall glory in the Holy One of Is'ra-el.

17 *When* the poor and needy seek water, and *there is* none, *and* their tongue fails for thirst, I the Lᴏʀᴅ will hear them, *I* the <u>God</u> of Is'ra-el will not forsake them. ROM. 11:2 Elohim^{p.f.}

18 I will open rivers in high places, and fountains in the midst of the valleys: I will make the wilderness a pool of water, and the dry land springs of water.

19 I will plant in the wilderness the cedar, the shittah tree, and the myrtle, and the oil tree; I will set in the desert the fir tree, *and* the pine, and the box tree together:

20 That they may see, and know, and consider, and understand together, that the hand of the Lᴏʀᴅ has done this, and the Holy One of Is'ra-el has created it.

21 Produce <u>your cause</u>, says the Lᴏʀᴅ; bring forth your strong *reasons*, says the King of Ja'cob.

your argument

22 Let them bring *them* forth, and show us what shall happen: let them show the former things, what they *be*, that we may consider them, and know the latter end of them; or declare us things for to come.

23 Show the things that are to come hereafter, that we may know that you *are* gods: yea, do good, or do evil, that we may be dismayed, and behold *it* together.

24 Behold, you *are* of <u>nothing</u>, and your work of <u>nothing</u>: an <u>abomination</u> *is he that* chooses you.

no account - amounts to nothing - detestable

25 I have raised up *one* from the north, and he shall come: from the <u>rising of the sun</u> shall he call upon My name: and he shall come upon princes as *upon* mortar, and as the potter treads clay. i.e., east

26 Who has declared from the beginning, that we may know? and beforetime, that we may say, *He is* righteous? yea, *there is* none that shows, yea, *there is* none that declares, yea, *there is* none that hears your words.

27 The first *shall say* to Zi'on, Behold, behold them: and I will give to Je-ru'salem one that brings good tidings.

28 For I beheld, and *there was* no man; even among them, and *there was* no counselor, that, when I asked of them, could <u>answer a word</u>. give an answer

29 Behold, they *are* all <u>vanity</u>; their works *are* <u>nothing</u>: their molten images *are* wind and confusion. empty - worthless

CHAPTER 42

BEHOLD My Servant, whom I uphold; My elect, *in whom* My soul delights; I have put My Spirit upon Him: He shall bring forth judgment to the Gen'tiles.

MATT. 3:17 MATT. 12:17 MARK 1:11 JOHN 17:4

2 He shall not cry, nor lift up, nor cause His voice to be heard in the street.

3 A bruised reed shall He not break, and the smoking flax shall He not quench: He shall bring forth judgment <u>to truth</u>. faithfully

4 He shall not fail nor be discouraged, till He have set judgment in the earth: and the isles shall wait for His law.

5 Thus says God the LORD, He that created the heavens, and stretched them out; He that spread forth the earth, and that which comes out of it; He that gives breath to the people upon it, and spirit to them that walk therein: ACTS 17:25

6 I the LORD have called you in righteousness, and will hold your hand, and will keep you, and give you for a <u>covenant</u> of the people, for a light of the Gen'tiles; LUKE 2:32 agreement

7 To open the blind eyes, to bring out the prisoners from the prison, *and* them that sit in darkness out of the prison house. ACTS 26:18

8 I *am* the LORD: that *is* My name: and My glory will I not give to another, neither My praise to <u>graven images</u>. idols

9 Behold, the former things are come to pass, and new things do I declare: before they spring forth I tell you of them.

10 Sing to the LORD a new song, *and* His praise from the end of the earth, you that go down to the sea, and all that is therein; the <u>isles</u>, and the inhabitants thereof. distant lands

11 Let the wilderness and the cities thereof lift up *their voice*, the villages *that* Ke'dar does inhabit: let the inhabitants of the rock sing, let them shout from the top of the mountains.

12 Let them give glory to the LORD, and declare His praise in the islands.

13 The LORD shall go forth as a mighty man, He shall <u>stir up jealousy</u> like a man of war: He shall cry, yea, roar; He shall prevail against His enemies. arouse His zeal

14 I have long time <u>holden</u> My peace; I have been still, *and* refrained Myself: *now* will I cry like a travailing woman; I will destroy and <u>devour</u> at once. kept - consume

15 I will make waste mountains and

hills, and dry up all their herbs; and I will make the rivers <u>islands</u>, and I will dry up the pools.   coastlands

16 And I will bring the blind by a way *that* they knew not; I will lead them in paths *that* they have not known: I will make darkness light before them, and crooked things straight. These things will I do to them, and not forsake them.

17 They shall be turned back, they shall be greatly ashamed, that trust in graven <u>images</u>, that say to the molten <u>images</u>, You *are* our gods.   idols

18 Hear, you deaf; and look, you blind, that you may see.

19 Who *is* blind, but My servant? or deaf, as My messenger *that* I sent? who *is* blind as *he that is* perfect, and blind as the LORD's servant?

20 Seeing many things, but you observe not; opening the ears, but he hears not.

21 The LORD is well pleased for His righteousness' sake; He will magnify the law, and make *it* honorable.

22 But this *is* a people robbed and <u>spoiled</u>; *they are* all of them <u>snared</u> in holes, and they are hid in prison houses: they are for a prey, and none delivers; for <u>a spoil</u>, and none says, Restore.   stripped - trapped - plundered

23 Who among you will give ear to this? *who* will <u>hearken</u> and hear for the time to come?   listen

24 Who gave Ja'cob for <u>a spoil</u>, and Is'ra-el to the robbers? did not the LORD, He against whom we have sinned? for they would not walk in His ways, neither were they obedient to His law.   plunder

25 Therefore He has poured upon him the fury of His anger, and the strength of battle: and it has set him on fire round about, yet he knew not; and it burned him, yet he laid *it* not to heart.

CHAPTER 43

BUT now thus says the LORD that created you, O Ja'cob, and He that formed you, O Is'ra-el, Fear not: for I have redeemed you, I have called *you* by your name; you *are* Mine.

2 When you pass through the waters, I *will be* with you; and through the rivers, they shall not overflow you: when you walk through the fire, you shall not be burned; neither shall the flame kindle upon you.

3 For I *am* the LORD your <u>God</u>, the Holy One of Is'ra-el, your Savior: I gave E'gypt *for* your ransom, E-thi-o'pi-a and Se'ba for you.   Elohim[p.f.]

4 Since you were precious in My sight, you have been honorable, and I have loved you: therefore will I give men for you, and people for your life.

5 Fear not: for I *am* with you: I will bring your <u>seed</u> from the east, and gather you from the west;   ACTS 18:10 offspring

6 I will say to the north, Give up; and to the south, Keep not back: bring My sons from far, and My daughters from the ends of the earth;

7 *Even* every one that is called by My name: for I have created him for My glory, I have formed him; yea, I have made him.

8 Bring forth the blind people that have eyes, and the deaf that have ears. 9 Let all the nations be gathered together, and let the people be assembled: who among them can declare this, and show us former things? let them bring forth their witnesses, that they may be justified: or let them hear, and say, *It is* truth.

10 You *are* My witnesses, says the LORD, and My servant whom I have chosen: that you may <u>know</u> and believe Me, and understand that I *am* He: before Me there was <u>no God</u> <u>formed</u>, neither shall there be after Me.

respect - nothing formed of God

11 I, *even* I, *am* the LORD; and beside Me *there is* no savior. 12 I have declared, and have saved, and I have showed, when *there was* no strange *god* among you: therefore you *are* My witnesses, says the LORD, that I *am* God. 13 Yea, before the day *was* I *am* He; and *there is* none that can deliver out of My hand: I will work, and who shall <u>let</u> it?

reverse

14 Thus says the LORD, your redeemer, the Holy One of Is'ra-el; For your sake I have sent to Bab'y-lon, and have brought down all their nobles, and the Chal-de'ans, whose cry *is* in the ships. 15 I *am* the LORD, your Holy One, the creator of Is'ra-el, your King. 16 Thus says the LORD, which makes a way in the sea, and a path in the mighty waters; 17 Which brings forth the chariot and horse, the army and the power;

they shall lie down together, they shall not rise: they are extinct, they are quenched as <u>tow</u>.

i.e., wick

18 Remember you not the former things, neither consider the things of old. 19 Behold, I will do a new thing; now it shall spring forth; shall you not know it? I will even make a way in the wilderness, *and* rivers in the desert.

REV. 21:5

20 The beast of the field shall honor Me, the <u>dragons</u> and the <u>owls</u>: because I give waters in the wilderness, *and* rivers in the desert, to give drink to My people, My chosen.

jackels - ostriches

21 This people have I formed for Myself; they shall show forth My praise. 22 But you have not called upon Me, O Ja'cob; but you have been weary of Me, O Is'ra-el. 23 You have not brought Me the <u>small cattle</u> of your burned offerings; neither have you honored Me with your sacrifices. I have not caused you to serve with an offering, nor <u>wearied</u> you with incense.

sheep - troubled

24 You have bought Me no sweet cane with money, neither have you filled Me with the fat of your sacrifices: but you have made Me to <u>serve</u> with your sins, you have wearied Me with your <u>iniquities</u>.

labor - offenses

25 I, *even* I, *am* He that blots out your transgressions for My own sake, and will not remember your sins. 26 Put Me in remembrance: let us plead together: <u>declare you</u>, that you may be justified.

state your cause

27 Your first father has sinned, and

your teachers have transgressed against Me.

28 Therefore I have profaned the princes of the sanctuary, and have given Ja'cob to the curse, and Is'ra-el to reproaches.

CHAPTER 44

YET now hear, O Ja'cob My servant; and Is'ra-el, whom I have chosen:

2 Thus says the LORD that made you, and formed you from the womb, *which* will help you; Fear not, O Ja'cob, My servant; and you, Jes'u-run, whom I have chosen. REV. 1:17

3 For I will pour water upon him that is thirsty, and floods upon the dry ground: I will pour My Spirit upon your <u>seed</u>, and My blessing upon your offspring: JOHN 7:38 descendants

4 And they shall spring up *as* among the grass, as willows by the water courses.

5 One shall say, I *am* the LORD's; and another shall call *himself* by the name of Ja'cob; and another shall <u>subscribe *with* h</u>is hand to the LORD, and surname *himself* by the name of Is'ra-el. write on

6 Thus says the LORD the King of Is'ra-el, and his redeemer the LORD of hosts; I *am* the First, and I *am* the Last; and beside Me *there* is no God.

REV. 2:8 REV. 22:13 Jehovah[s.f.] - Jehovah[s.f.] Tsebaoth - Elohim[p.f.]

7 And who, as I, shall call, and shall declare it, and set it in order for Me, since I appointed the ancient people? and the things that are coming, and shall come, let them show to them.

8 Fear you not, neither be afraid: have not I told you from that time, and have declared *it*? you *are* even My witnesses. Is there a God beside Me? yea, *there is* no God; I know not *any*. Eloah[s.f.] Rock (Heb. Tsur) - Rock

9 They that make a graven <u>image</u> *are* all of them vanity; and their <u>delectable</u> things shall not profit; and they *are* their own witnesses; they see not, nor know; that they may be ashamed. idol - desirable

10 Who has formed a god, or molten a graven <u>image</u> *that* is <u>profitable</u> for nothing? good

11 Behold, all his fellows shall be ashamed: and the workmen, they *are* of men: let them all be gathered together, let them stand up; *yet* they shall fear, *and* they shall be ashamed together.

12 The smith with <u>the tongs</u> both works in the coals, and fashions it with hammers, and works it with the strength of his arms: yea, he is hungry, and his strength fails: he drinks no water, and is faint. an axe

13 The carpenter stretches out *his* <u>rule</u>; he marks it out with a <u>line</u>; he fits it with planes, and he marks it out with the compass, and makes it after the figure of a man, according to the beauty of a man; that it may remain in the house. line - marker

14 He <u>hews</u> him down cedars, and takes the cypress and the oak, which he <u>strengthens</u> for himself among the trees of the forest: he plants an ash, and the rain does nourish *it*.

cuts - secures

15 Then shall it be for a man to burn: for he will take thereof, and warm himself; yea, he kindles *it*, and bakes

bread; yea, he makes a god, and worships *it*; he makes it a graven <u>image</u>, and falls down thereto.   idol

16 He burns part thereof in the fire; with part thereof he eats flesh; he roasts roast, and is satisfied: yea, he warms *himself*, and says, Aha, I am warm, I have seen the fire:

17 And the residue thereof he makes a god, *even* his graven <u>image</u>: he falls down to it, and worships *it*, and prays to it, and says, Deliver me; for you *are* my god.

18 They have not known nor understood: for He has shut their eyes, that they cannot see; *and* their hearts, that they cannot understand.

19 And none<u> considers in his heart</u>, neither *is there* knowledge nor understanding to say, I have burned part of it in the fire; yea, also I have baked bread upon the coals thereof; I have roasted flesh, and eaten *it*: and shall I make the residue thereof <u>an abomination</u>? shall I fall down to the stock of a tree?   stops to think - detestable

20 He feeds on ashes: a deceived heart has turned him aside, that he cannot <u>deliver</u> his soul, nor say, *Is there* not a lie in my right hand?   rescue

21 Remember these, O Ja'cob and Is'ra-el; for you *are* My servant: I have formed you; you *are* My servant: O Is'ra-el, you shall not be forgotten of Me.

22 I have blotted out, as a thick cloud, your transgressions, and, as a cloud, your sins: return to Me; for I have redeemed you.   1 COR. 6:20

23 Sing, O you heavens; for the LORD has done *it*: shout, you lower parts of the earth: break forth into singing, you mountains, O forest, and every tree therein: for the LORD has redeemed Ja'cob, and glorified Himself in Is'ra-el.   REV. 18:20

24 Thus says the LORD, your redeemer, and He that formed you from the womb, I *am* the LORD that makes all *things*; that stretches forth the heavens alone; that spreads abroad the earth by Myself;

25 That frustrates the tokens of the liars, and makes <u>diviners</u> mad; that turns wise *men* backward, and makes their knowledge foolish;   astrologers

26 That confirms the word of His servant, and performs the counsel of His messengers; that says to Je-ru'sa-lem, You shall be inhabited; and to the cities of Ju'dah, You shall be built, and I will raise up the <u>decayed places</u> thereof: ruins

27 That says to the deep, Be dry, and I will dry up your rivers:

28 That says of Cy'rus, *he is* My shepherd, and shall perform all My pleasure: even saying to Je-ru'sa-lem, You shall be built; and to the temple, Your foundation shall be laid.

CHAPTER 45

THUS says the LORD to His anointed, to Cy'rus, whose right hand I have <u>holden</u>, to subdue nations before him; and I will loose the loins of kings, to open before him the two <u>leaved</u> gates; and the gates shall not be shut;   supported - paneled

2 I will go before you, and make the crooked places straight: I will break in

pieces the gates of brass, and cut in sunder the bars of iron:

3 And I will give you the treasures of darkness, and hidden riches of secret places, that you may know that I, the LORD, which call *you* by your name, *am* the God of Is'ra-el. COL. 2:3 Elohim[p.f.]

4 For Ja'cob My servant's sake, and Is'ra-el My elect, I have even called you by your name: I have surnamed you, though you have not known Me.

5 I *am* the LORD, and *there is* none else, *there is* no God beside Me: I girded you, though you have not known Me:

6 That they may know from the rising of the sun, and from the west, that *there is* none beside Me. I *am* the LORD, and *there is* none else.

7 I form the light, and create darkness: I make peace, and create evil: I the LORD do all these *things*.

8 Drop down, you heavens, from above, and let the skies pour down righteousness: let the earth open, and let them bring forth salvation, and let righteousness spring up together; I the LORD have created it.

9 Woe to him that strives with his Maker! *Let* the potsherd *strive* with the potsherds of the earth. Shall the clay say to him that fashions it, What make you? or your work, He has no hands? ROM. 9:20 earthenware vessel

10 Woe to him that says to *his* father, What fathered you? or to the woman, What have you brought forth?

11 Thus says the LORD, the Holy One of Is'ra-el, and his Maker, Ask Me of things to come concerning My sons,

and concerning the work of My hands command you Me.

12 I have made the earth, and created man upon it: I, *even* My hands, have stretched out the heavens, and all their host have I commanded.

13 I have raised him up in righteousness, and I will direct all his ways: he shall build My city, and he shall let go My captives, not for price nor reward, says the LORD of hosts. guide - payment - Jehovah[s.f.] Tsebaoth

14 Thus says the LORD, The labor of E'gypt, and merchandise of E-thi-o'pi-a and of the Sa-be'ans, men of stature, shall come over to you, and they shall be yours: they shall come after you; in chains they shall come over, and they shall fall down to you, they shall make supplication to you, *saying*, Surely God *is* in you; and *there is* none else, *there is* no God. 1 COR. 14:25 El[s.f.] - Elohim[p.f.]

15 Verily you *are* a God that hides Yourself, O God of Is'ra-el, the Savior.

16 They shall be ashamed, and also confounded, all of them: they shall go to confusion together *that are* makers of idols.

17 *But* Is'ra-el shall be saved in the LORD with an everlasting salvation: you shall not be ashamed nor confounded world without end.

18 For thus says the LORD that created the heavens; God Himself that formed the earth and made it; He has established it, He created it not in vain, He formed it to be inhabited: I *am* the LORD; and *there is* none else. purposeless

19 I have not spoken in secret, in a dark place of the earth: I said not to

the <u>seed</u> of Ja'cob, Seek you Me <u>in vain</u>: I the LORD speak righteousness, I declare things that are right. offspring - purposeless

20 Assemble yourselves and come; draw near together, you *that are* escaped of the nations: they have no knowledge that set up the wood of their graven <u>image</u>, and pray to a god *that* cannot save. idols

21 Tell you, and bring *them* near; yea, let them take counsel together: who has declared this from ancient time? *who* has told it from that time? *have* not I the LORD? and *there is* no <u>God</u> else beside Me; a just <u>God</u> and a Savior; *there is* none beside Me. Elohim^{p.f.} - El^{s.f.}

22 Look to Me, and be you saved, all the ends of the earth: for I *am* God, and *there is* none else.

23 I have sworn by Myself, the word is gone out of My mouth *in* righteousness, and shall not return, That to Me every knee shall bow, every tongue shall swear. ROM. 14:11

24 Surely, shall *one* say, in the LORD have I righteousness and strength: *even* to Him shall *men* come; and all that are incensed against Him shall be ashamed.

25 In the LORD shall all the <u>seed</u> of Is'ra-el be justified, and shall glory. descendants

CHAPTER 46

BEL bows down, Ne'bo stoops, their idols were upon the beasts, and upon the cattle: your carriages *were* heavy loaden; *they are* a burden to the weary *beast*.

2 They stoop, they bow down together; they could not deliver the bur-den, but themselves are gone into captivity.

3 Hearken to Me, O house of Ja'cob, and all the remnant of the house of Is'ra-el, which are borne *by Me* from the belly, which are carried from the womb:

4 And *even* to *your* old age I *am* He; and *even* to <u>hoar</u> hairs will I carry *you*: I have made, and I will bear; even I will carry, and will deliver *you*. gray

5 To whom will you liken Me, and make *Me* equal, and compare Me, that we may be like?

6 They lavish gold out of the bag, and weigh silver in the balance, *and* hire a goldsmith; and he makes it a god: they <u>fall</u> down, yea, they worship. bow

7 They bear it upon the shoulder, they carry it, and set it in its place, and it stands; from its place shall it not <u>remove</u>: yea, *one* shall cry to it, yet can it not answer, nor save him out of his trouble. move

8 Remember this, and <u>show yourselves men</u>: bring *it* again to mind, O you transgressors. i.e., act like men

9 Remember the former things of old: for I *am* <u>God</u>, and *there is* none else; *I am* <u>God</u>, and *there is* none like Me, El^{s.f.} - Elohim^{p.f.}

10 Declaring the end from the beginning, and from ancient times *the things* that are not *yet* done, saying, My counsel shall stand, and I will do all My pleasure:

11 Calling a ravenous bird from the east, the man that <u>executes</u> My counsel from a far country: yea, I have spoken *it*, I will also bring it to pass; I have purposed *it*, I will also do it. performs

12 <u>Hearken</u> to Me, you stouthearted, that *are* far from righteousness:

Listen

13 I bring near My righteousness; it shall not be far off, and My salvation shall not <u>tarry</u>: and I will place salvation in Zi'on for Is'ra-el My glory.

be delayed

CHAPTER 47

COME down, and sit in the dust, O virgin daughter of Bab'y-lon, sit on the ground: *there is* no throne, O daughter of the Chal-de'ans: for you shall no more be called tender and delicate.

2 Take the millstones, and grind meal: uncover your locks, make bare the leg, uncover the thigh, pass over the rivers.

3 Your nakedness shall be uncovered, yea, your shame shall be seen: I will take vengeance, and I will not meet *you as* a man.

4 *As for* our redeemer, the Lord of <u>hosts</u> *is* His name, the Holy One of Is'ra-el.

Jehovah^{s.f.} Tsebaoth

5 Sit you silent, and get you into darkness, O daughter of the Chal-de'ans: for you shall no more be called, The lady of kingdoms.

6 I was angry with My people, I have polluted My inheritance, and given them into your hand: you did show them no mercy; upon the <u>ancient</u> have you very heavily laid your yoke.

aged

7 And you said, I shall be a lady for ever: *so* that you did not lay these things to your heart, neither did remember the latter end of it.

8 Therefore hear now this, *you that are* given to pleasures, that dwell carelessly, that say in your heart, I *am*, and none else beside me; I shall not sit *as* a widow, neither shall I know the loss of children:

REV. 18:7

9 But these two *things* shall come to you in a moment in one day, the loss of children, and widowhood: they shall come upon you in their perfection for the multitude of your sorceries, *and* for the great abundance of your enchantments.

10 For you have trusted in your wickedness: you have said, None sees me. Your wisdom and your knowledge, it has perverted you; and you have said in your heart, I *am*, and none else beside me.

11 Therefore shall evil come upon you; you shall not know from where it rises: and mischief shall fall upon you; you shall not be able to put it off: and desolation shall come upon you suddenly, *which* you shall not know.

12 Stand now with your enchantments, and with the multitude of your sorceries, wherein you have labored from your youth; if so be you shall be able to profit, if so be you may prevail.

13 You are wearied in the multitude of your <u>counsels</u>. Let now the astrologers, the stargazers, the monthly prognosticators, stand up, and save you from *these things* that shall come upon you.

advice

14 Behold, they shall be as stubble; the fire shall burn them; they shall not deliver themselves from the power of the flame: *there shall* not *be* a coal to warm at, *nor* fire to sit before it.

15 Thus shall they be to you with whom you have labored, *even* your merchants, from your youth: they shall wander every one to his quarter; none shall save you.   own way

CHAPTER 48

HEAR you this, O house of Ja'cob,which are called by the name of Is'ra-el, and are come forth out of the waters of Ju'dah, which swear by the name of the LORD, and make mention of the God of Is'ra-el, *but* not in truth, nor in righteousness.   Elohim^{p.f.}

2 For they call themselves of the holy city, and stay themselves upon the God of Is'ra-el; The LORD of hosts *is* His name.   Jehovah^{s.f.} Tsebaoth

3 I have declared the former things from the beginning; and they went forth out of My mouth, and I showed them; I did *them* suddenly, and they came to pass.

4 Because I knew that you *are* obstinate, and your neck *is* an iron sinew, and your brow brass;   stubborn - muscle

5 I have even from the beginning declared *it* to you; before it came to pass I showed *it* you: less you should say, My idol has done them, and my graven image, and my molten image, has commanded them.   idol

6 You have heard, see all this; and will not you declare *it*? I have showed you new things from this time, even hidden things, and you did not know them.

7 They are created now, and not from the beginning; even before the day when you heard them not; less you should say, Behold, I knew them.

8 Yea, you heard not; yea, you knew not; yea, from that time *that* your ear was not opened: for I knew that you would deal very treacherously, and was called a transgressor from the womb.

9 For My name's sake will I defer My anger, and for My praise will I refrain for you, that I cut you not off.   delay

10 Behold, I have refined you, but not with silver; I have chosen you in the furnace of affliction.   as

11 For My own sake, *even* for My own sake, will I do *it*: for how should *My name* be polluted? and I will not give My glory to another.   profaned

12 Hearken to Me, O Ja'cob and Is'ra-el, My called; I *am* He; I *am* the First, I also *am* the Last. REV. 22:13

13 My hand also has laid the foundation of the earth, and My right hand has spanned the heavens: *when* I call to them, they stand up together.   spread

14 All you, assemble yourselves, and hear; which among them has declared these *things*? The LORD has loved him: He will do His pleasure on Bab'y-lon, and His arm *shall be on* the Chal-de'ans.

15 I, *even* I, have spoken; yea, I have called him: I have brought him, and He shall make his way prosperous.

16 Come you near to me, hear you this; I have not spoken in secret from the beginning; from the time that it was, there *am* I: and now the Lord God, and His Spirit, has sent me.

Adonay[p.f.] Jehovah

17 Thus says the LORD, your redeemer, the Holy One of Is'ra-el; I *am* the LORD your God which teaches you to profit, which leads you by the way *that* you should go.

Elohim[p.f.]

18 O that you had hearkened to My commandments! then had your peace been as a river, and your righteousness as the waves of the sea:

paid attention

19 Your seed also had been as the sand, and the offspring of your bowels like the gravel thereof; his name should not have been cut off nor destroyed from before Me.

descendants - your offspring

20 Go you forth of Bab'y-lon, flee you from the Chal-de'ans, with a voice of singing declare you, tell this, utter it *even* to the end of the earth; say you, The LORD has redeemed His servant Ja'cob.

21 And they thirsted not *when* He led them through the deserts: He caused the waters to flow out of the rock for them: He clave the rock also, and the waters gushed out.

split

22 *There is* no peace, says the LORD, to the wicked.

CHAPTER 49

LISTEN, O isles, to Me; and hearken, you people, from far; The LORD has called Me from the womb; from the bowels of My mother has he made mention of My name.

distant lands   body

2 And He has made My mouth like a sharp sword; in the shadow of His hand has He hid Me, and made Me a polished shaft; in His quiver has He hid Me;

3 And said to Me, You *are* My servant, O Is'ra-el, in whom I will be glorified.

4 Then I said, I have labored in vain, I have spent My strength for nothing, and in vain: *yet* surely My judgment *is* with the LORD, and My work with My God.

nothing - Elohim[p.f.]

5 And now, says the LORD that formed me from the womb *to be* His servant, to bring Ja'cob again to Him, Though Is'ra-el be not gathered, yet shall I be glorious in the eyes of the LORD, and My God shall be My strength.

6 And He said, It is a light thing that you should be My servant to raise up the tribes of Ja'cob, and to restore the preserved of Is'ra-el: I will also give You for a light to the Gen'tiles, that You may be My salvation to the end of the earth.

ACTS 13:47 i.e., Heb. Jeshua

7 Thus says the LORD, the Redeemer of Is'ra-el, *and* his Holy One, to Him whom man despises, to Him whom the nation abhors, to a servant of rulers, Kings shall see and arise, princes also shall worship, because of the LORD that is faithful, *and* the Holy One of Is'ra-el, and He shall choose you.

8 Thus says the LORD, In an acceptable time have I heard you, and in a day of salvation have I helped you:

and I will preserve you, and give you for a <u>covenant</u> of the people, to establish the earth, to cause to inherit the desolate heritages;   2 COR. 6:2   agreement

9 That you may say to the prisoners, Go forth; to them that *are* in darkness, Show yourselves. They shall feed in the ways, and their pastures *shall be* in all high places.

10 They shall not hunger nor thirst; neither shall the heat nor sun smite them: for He that has mercy on them shall lead them, even by the springs of water shall He guide them.   REV. 7:16

11 And I will make all My mountains a way, and My highways shall be exalted.

12 Behold, these shall come from far: and, lo, these from the north and from the west; and these from the land of Si'nim.

13 Sing, O heavens; and be joyful, O earth; and break forth into singing, O mountains: for the LORD has comforted His people, and will have mercy upon His <u>afflicted</u>.   oppressed ones

14 But Zi'on said, The LORD has forsaken me, and my Lord has forgotten me.

15 Can a woman forget her sucking child, that she should not have compassion on the son of her womb? yea, they may forget, yet will I not forget you.

16 Behold, I have graven you upon the palms of *My* hands; your walls *are* continually before Me.

17 Your children shall make haste; your destroyers and they that made you waste shall go forth of you.

18 Lift up your eyes round about, and behold: all these gather themselves together, *and* come to you. *As* I live, says the LORD, you shall surely clothe you with them all, as with an ornament, and bind them *on you*, as a bride *does*.

19 For your <u>waste</u> and your <u>desolate</u> places, and the land of your destruction, shall even now be too narrow by reason of the inhabitants, and they that swallowed you up shall be far away.   empty - ruined

20 The children which you shall have, after you have lost the other, shall say again in your ears, The place *is* too strait for me: give place to me that I may dwell.

21 Then shall you say in your heart, Who has fathered me these, seeing I have lost my children, and am desolate, a captive, and <u>removing to and fro</u>? and who has brought up these? Behold, I was left alone; these, where *had* they *been*?   a wanderer

22 Thus says the Lord GOD, Behold, I will lift up My hand to the <u>Gen'tiles</u>, and set up My standard to the people: and they shall bring your sons in *their* arms, and your daughters shall be carried upon *their* shoulders.   Adonay^p.f. Jehovah^s.f. - Nations

23 And kings shall be your nursing fathers, and their queens your nursing mothers: they shall bow down to you *with* their face toward the earth, and lick up the dust of your feet; and you shall know that I *am* the LORD: for they shall not be ashamed that wait for Me.   ROM. 10:11

24 Shall the prey be taken from the mighty, or the lawful captive delivered?

25 But thus says the LORD, Even the captives of the mighty shall be taken away, and the prey of the terrible shall be delivered: for I will contend with him that contends with you, and I will save your children.

26 And I will feed them that oppress you with their own flesh; and they shall be drunken with their own blood, as with sweet wine: and all flesh shall know that I the LORD *am* your Savior and your Redeemer, the Mighty One of Ja'cob. new

CHAPTER 50

THUS says the LORD, Where *is* the bill of your mother's divorcement, whom I have put away? or which of My creditors *is it* to whom I have sold you? Behold, for your iniquities have you sold yourselves, and for your transgressions is your mother put away. sins - wrongdoings

2 Why, when I came, *was there* no man? when I called, *was there* none to answer? Is My hand shortened at all, that it cannot redeem? or have I no power to deliver? behold, at My rebuke I dry up the sea, I make the rivers a wilderness: their fish stink, because *there is* no water, and die for thirst.

3 I clothe the heavens with blackness, and I make sackcloth their covering.

4 The Lord GOD has given me the tongue of the learned, that I should know how to speak a word in season to *him that is* weary: He wakens morning by morning, He wakens my ear to hear as the learned. Adonay^{p.f.} Jehovah - opens

5 The Lord GOD has opened my ear, and I was not rebellious, neither turned away back. Adonay^{p.f.} Jehovah

6 I gave my back to the smiters, and my cheeks to them that plucked off the hair: I hid not my face from shame and spitting. MATT. 27:26

7 For the Lord GOD will help me; therefore shall I not be confounded: therefore have I set my face like a flint, and I know that I shall not be ashamed. disappointed

8 *He is* near that justifies me; who will contend with me? let us stand together: who *is* my adversary? let him come near to me. vindicates

9 Behold, the Lord GOD will help me; who *is* he *that* shall condemn me? lo, they all shall wax old as a garment; the moth shall eat them up. Adonay^{p.f.} Jehovah - wear out

10 Who *is* among you that fears the LORD, that obeys the voice of His servant, that walks *in* darkness, and has no light? let him trust in the name of the LORD, and stay upon his God. revere - rely - Elohim^{p.f.}

11 Behold, all you that kindle a fire, that compass *yourselves* about with sparks: walk in the light of your fire, and in the sparks *that* you have kindled. This shall you have of my hand; you shall lie down in sorrow. encircle

CHAPTER 51

HEARKEN to Me, you that follow after righteousness, you that seek the LORD: look to the rock *where* you are hewn, and to the hole of the pit *from where* you are dug. Listen - pursue - cut

2 Look to A'bra-ham your father, and to Sarah *that* bare you: for I called him alone, and blessed him, and increased him.

3 For the LORD shall comfort Zi'on: He will comfort all her waste places; and He will make her wilderness like E'den, and her desert like the garden of the LORD; joy and gladness shall be found therein, thanksgiving, and the voice of melody.

4 Hearken to Me, My people; and give ear to Me, O My nation: for a law shall proceed from Me, and I will make My judgment to rest for a light of the people.   Listen

5 My righteousness *is* near; My salvation is gone forth, and My arms shall judge the people; the isles shall wait upon Me, and on My arm shall they trust.   distant lands

6 Lift up your eyes to the heavens, and look upon the earth beneath: for the heavens shall vanish away like smoke, and the earth shall wax old like a garment, and they that dwell therein shall die in like manner: but My salvation shall be for ever, and My righteousness shall not be abolished.   wear out - i.e., Heb. Jeshua - fail

7 Hearken to Me, you that know righteousness, the people in whose heart *is* My law; fear you not the reproach of men, neither be you afraid of their revilings.

8 For the moth shall eat them up like a garment, and the worm shall eat them like wool: but My righteousness shall be for ever, and My salvation from generation to generation.   i.e., Heb. Jeshua

9 Awake, awake, put on strength, O arm of the LORD; awake, as in the ancient days, in the generations of old. *Are* You not it that has cut Ra'hab, *and* wounded the dragon?   days of old - i.e., Egypt - monster

10 *Are* You not it which has dried the sea, the waters of the great deep; that has made the depths of the sea a way for the ransomed to pass over?   Was it not you

11 Therefore the redeemed of the LORD shall return, and come with singing to Zi'on; and everlasting joy *shall be* upon their head: they shall obtain gladness and joy; *and* sorrow and mourning shall flee away.

12 I, *even* I, *am* He that comforts you: who *are* you, that you should be afraid of a man *that* shall die, and of the son of man *which* shall be made *as* grass;

13 And forgets the LORD your maker, that has stretched forth the heavens, and laid the foundations of the earth; and have feared continually every day because of the fury of the oppressor, as if he were ready to destroy? and where *is* the fury of the oppressor?

14 The captive exile hastens that he may be loosed, and that he should not die in the pit, nor that his bread should fail.

15 But I *am* the LORD your God, that divided the sea, whose waves roared: The LORD of hosts *is* His name.   Jehovah[s.f.] - Elohim[p.f.] - Jehovah[s.f.] Tsebaoth

16 And I have put My words in your mouth, and I have covered you in the

shadow of My hand, that I may plant the heavens, and lay the foundations of the earth, and say to Zi'on, You *are* My people.   establish

17 Awake, awake, stand up, O Je-ru'sa-lem, which have drunk at the hand of the LORD the cup of His fury; you have drunken the dregs of the cup of trembling, *and* wrung *them* out.

18 *There is* none to guide her among all the sons *whom* she has brought forth; neither *is there any* that takes her by the hand of all the sons *that* she has brought up.

19 These two *things* are come to you; who shall be sorry for you? desolation, and destruction, and the famine, and the sword: by whom shall I comfort you?

20 Your sons have fainted, they lie at the head of all the streets, as a wild bull in a net: they are full of the fury of the LORD, the rebuke of your God.   wrath - Elohim^{p.f.}

21 Therefore hear now this, you afflicted, and drunken, but not with wine:

22 Thus says your Lord the LORD, and your God *that* pleads the cause of His people, Behold, I have taken out of your hand the cup of trembling, *even* the dregs of the cup of My fury; you shall no more drink it again: Adonay^{p.f.} - Jehovah^{s.f.}

23 But I will put it into the hand of them that afflict you; which have said to your soul, Bow down, that we may go over: and you have laid your body as the ground, and as the street, to them that went over.

CHAPTER 52

AWAKE, awake; put on your strength, O Zi'on; put on your beautiful garments, O Je-ru'sa-lem, the holy city: for hereafter there shall no more come into you the uncircumcised and the unclean.   REV. 21:27   unbelieving

2 Shake yourself from the dust; arise, *and* sit down, O Je-ru'sa-lem: loose yourself from the bands of your neck, O captive daughter of Zi'on.

3 For thus says the LORD, You have sold yourselves for nothing; and you shall be redeemed without money.

4 For thus says the Lord GOD, My people went down aforetime into E'gypt to sojourn there; and the As-syr'i-an oppressed them without cause.   Adonay^{p.f.} Jehovah - live

5 Now therefore, what have I here, says the LORD, that My people is taken away for nothing? they that rule over them make them to howl, says the LORD; and My name continually every day *is* blasphemed.   ROM. 2:24

6 Therefore My people shall know My name: therefore *they shall know* in that day that I *am* He that does speak: behold, *it is* I.

7 How beautiful upon the mountains are the feet of him that brings good tidings, that publishes peace; that brings good tidings of good, that publishes salvation; that says to Zi'on, Your God reigns!   ROM. 10:15   Elohim^{p.f.}

8 Your watchmen shall lift up the voice; with the voice together shall they sing: for they shall see eye to eye, when the LORD shall bring again Zi'on.   restore

9 Break forth into joy, sing together, you waste places of Je-ru'sa-lem: for the LORD has comforted His people, He has redeemed Je-ru'sa-lem.

10 The LORD has <u>made bare</u> His holy arm in the eyes of all the nations; and all the ends of the earth shall see the salvation of our <u>God</u>.

LUKE 3:6   LUKE 2:30   revealed - Elohim^{p.f.}

11 Depart you, depart you, go you out from there, touch no unclean *thing*; go you out of the midst of her; be you clean, that bear the vessels of the LORD.   2 COR. 6:17

12 For you shall not go out with haste, nor go by flight: for the LORD will go before you; and the <u>God</u> of Is'ra-el *will be* your <u>rearward</u>. rear guard

P.04 13 Behold, My servant shall deal prudently, He shall be exalted and extolled, and be very high.

14 As many were astonished at you; His visage was so marred more than any man, and His form more than the sons of men:

15 So shall He <u>sprinkle</u> many nations; the kings shall shut their mouths at Him: for *that* which had not been told them shall they see; and *that* which they had not heard shall they consider.   ROM. 15:21 startle

CHAPTER 53

P.04 **W**HO has believed our <u>report</u>? and to whom is the arm of the LORD <u>revealed</u>? JOHN 12:38 ROM. 10:16 message

2 For He shall grow up before Him as a tender plant, and as a root out of a dry ground: He has no form nor comeliness; and when we shall see Him,

there *is* no beauty that we should desire Him.

3 He is despised and rejected of men; a man of sorrows, and acquainted with grief: and we hid as it were *our* faces from Him; He was despised, and we <u>esteemed Him not</u>.   did not respect Him

4 Surely He has borne our <u>griefs</u>, and carried our <u>sorrows</u>: yet we did <u>esteem</u> Him stricken, smitten of <u>God</u>, and afflicted. MATT. 8:17 sickness - pains - Elohim^{p.f.}

5 But He *was* wounded for our transgressions, *He was* bruised for our iniquities: the chastisement of our peace *was* upon Him; and with His <u>stripes</u> we are healed.   ROM. 4:25 wounds

6 All we like sheep have gone astray; we have turned every one to his own way; and the LORD has laid on Him the <u>iniquity</u> of us all.   1 PET. 2:25 sin

7 He was oppressed, and He was afflicted, yet He opened not His mouth: He is brought as a lamb to the slaughter, and as a sheep before her shearers is dumb, so He opens not His mouth.   MATT. 27:12 ACTS 8:32

8 He was taken from prison and from judgment: and who shall declare His generation? for He was cut off out of the land of the living: for the transgression of my people was He stricken.

9 And He <u>made</u> His grave with the wicked, and with the rich in His death; because He had done no violence, neither *was any* deceit in His mouth.

1 PET. 2:22 MATT. 27:57 1 COR. 15:3 was assigned

10 Yet it pleased the LORD to bruise Him; He has put *Him* to grief: when you shall make His soul an offering for sin, He shall see *His* <u>seed</u>, He

shall prolong *His* days, and the pleasure of the LORD shall prosper in His hand. adopted children - disciples

11 He shall see of the <u>travail</u> of His soul, *and* shall be satisfied: by His knowledge shall My righteous servant justify many; for He shall bear their iniquities. LUKE 23:34 suffering

12 Therefore will I divide Him *a portion* with the great, and He shall divide the spoil with the strong; because He has poured out His soul to death: and He was numbered with the transgressors; and He bare the sin of many, and made intercession for the transgressors.

MARK 15:28 LUKE 22:37 1 COR. 15:3 1 PET. 2:24

CHAPTER 54

SING, O <u>barren</u>, you *that* did not bear; break forth into singing, and cry aloud, you *that* did not <u>travail</u> with child: for more *are* the children of the desolate than the children of the married wife, **says the** LORD. GAL. 4:27 i.e., Jerusalem - suffer

2 Enlarge the place of your tent, and let them stretch forth the curtains of your habitations: spare not, lengthen your cords, and strengthen your stakes;

3 For you shall break forth on the right hand and on the left; and your <u>seed</u> shall <u>inherit</u> the <u>Gen'tiles</u>, and make the desolate cities to be inhabited. descendants - possess - Nations

4 Fear not; for you shall not be ashamed: neither be you <u>confounded</u>; for you shall not be put to shame: for you shall forget the shame of your youth, and shall not remember the reproach of your widowhood any more. humiliated

5 For your Maker *is* your husband; the <u>LORD of hosts</u> *is* His name; and your Redeemer the Holy One of Is'ra-el; The <u>God</u> of the whole earth shall He be called. Jehovah[s.f.] Tsebaoth - Elohim[p.f.]

6 For the LORD has called you as a woman forsaken and grieved in spirit, and a wife of youth, when you were <u>refused,</u> **says your** <u>God</u>. rejected

7 For a small moment have I forsaken you; but with great mercies will I gather you.

8 In a little anger I hid My face from you for a moment; but with everlasting kindness will I have mercy on you, **says the** LORD **your Redeemer.**

9 For this *is as* the waters of No'ah to Me: for *as* I have sworn that the waters of No'ah should no more go over the earth; so have I sworn that I would not be angry with you, nor rebuke you.

10 For the mountains shall depart, and the hills be removed; but My kindness shall not depart from you, neither shall the <u>covenant</u> of My peace be removed, **says the** LORD **that has mercy on you.** agreement

11 O you afflicted, tossed with tempest, *and* not comforted, behold, I will lay your stones with fair colors, and lay your foundations with sapphires.

12 And I will make your <u>windows</u> of agates, and your gates of carbuncles, and all your borders of pleasant stones. battlements

13 And <u>all</u> your children *shall be* taught

of the LORD; and great *shall be* the peace of your children. JOHN 6:45

14 In righteousness shall you be established: you shall be far from oppression; for you shall not <u>fear</u>: and from terror; for it shall not come near you. be afraid

15 Behold, they shall surely gather together, *but* not by Me: whosoever shall gather together against you shall fall for your sake.

16 Behold, I have created the smith that blows the coals in the fire, and that brings forth an instrument for his work; and I have created the <u>waster</u> to destroy. i.e., Satan-destroyer

17 No weapon that is formed against you shall prosper; and every tongue *that* shall rise against you in judgment you shall condemn. This *is* the heritage of the servants of the LORD, and their righteousness *is* of Me, says the LORD.

CHAPTER 55

Ho, every one that thirsts, come you to the <u>waters</u>, and he that has no money; come you, buy, and eat; yea, come, buy <u>wine</u> and <u>milk</u> without money and without price. REV. 22:17 spirit - joy - nourishment

2 Wherefore do you spend money for *that which is* not bread? and your labor for *that which* satisfies not? hearken diligently to Me, and eat *you that which is* good, and let your soul delight itself in fatness. MATT. 5:6 JOHN 6:27

3 Incline your ear, and come to Me: hear, and your soul shall live; and I will make an everlasting <u>covenant</u> with you, *even* the <u>sure</u> mercies of Da'vid. ACTS 13:34 agreement - confirmed

4 Behold, I have given him *for* a witness to the people, a leader and commander to the people.

5 Behold, you shall call a nation *that* you know not, and nations *that* knew not you shall run to you because of the LORD your <u>God</u>, and for the Holy One of Is'ra-el; for He has glorified you.

6 Seek you the LORD while He may be found, call you upon Him while He is near:

7 Let the wicked forsake his way, and the unrighteous man his thoughts: and let him return to the LORD, and He will have mercy upon him; and to our <u>God</u>, for He will <u>abundantly</u> pardon. Elohim[p.f.] - freely

8 For My thoughts *are* not your thoughts, neither *are* your ways My ways, says the LORD.

9 For *as* the heavens are higher than the earth, so are My ways higher than your ways, and My thoughts than your thoughts.

10 For as the rain comes down, and the snow from heaven, and returns not there, but waters the earth, and makes it bring forth and bud, that it may give seed to the sower, and bread to the eater: 2 COR. 9:10

11 So shall My word be that goes forth out of My mouth: it shall not return to Me <u>void</u>, but it shall accomplish that which I please, and it shall prosper *in the thing* whereto I sent it. i.e., without result

12 For you shall go out with joy, and

be led forth with peace: the mountains and the hills shall break forth before you into singing, and all the trees of the field shall clap *their* hands.

13 Instead of the thorn shall come up the fir tree, and instead of the brier shall come up the myrtle tree: and it shall be to the LORD for a name, for an everlasting sign *that* shall not be cut off.

CHAPTER 56

THUS says the LORD, Keep you judgment, and do justice: for My salvation *is* near to come, and My righteousness to be revealed.   *i.e., Heb. Jeshua*

2 Blessed *is* the man *that* does this, and the son of man *that* lays hold on it; that keeps the sabbath from polluting it, and keeps his hand from doing any evil.   *rest day*

3 Neither let the son of the stranger, that has joined himself to the LORD, speak, saying, The LORD has utterly separated me from His people: neither let the eunuch say, Behold, I *am* a dry tree.

4 For thus says the LORD to the eunuchs that keep My sabbaths, and choose *the things* that please Me, and take hold of My covenant;

hold fast by - agreement

5 Even to them will I give in My house and inside My walls a place and a name better than of sons and of daughters: I will give them an everlasting name, that shall not be cut off.

6 Also the sons of the stranger, that join themselves to the LORD, to serve Him, and to love the name of the LORD, to be His servants, every one that keeps the sabbath from polluting it, and takes hold of My covenant;

rest day - profaning

7 Even them will I bring to My holy mountain, and make them joyful in My house of prayer: their burned offerings and their sacrifices *shall be* accepted upon My altar; for My house shall be called an house of prayer for all people. MATT. 21:13 MARK 11:17

8 The Lord GOD which gathers the outcasts of Is'ra-el says, Yet will I gather *others* to him, beside those that are gathered to him.   JOHN 10:16 *Adonay*[p.f.] *Jehovah*

9 All you beasts of the field, come to devour, *yea*, all you beasts in the forest.   *eat*

10 His watchmen *are* blind: they are all ignorant, they *are* all dumb dogs, they cannot bark; sleeping, lying down, loving to slumber.   *voiceless men*

11 Yea, *they are* greedy dogs *which* can never have enough, and they *are* shepherds *that* cannot understand: they all look to their own way, every one for his gain, from his quarter.

symbolic of man - every

12 Come you, *say they*, I will bring wine, and we will fill ourselves with strong drink; and to morrow shall be as this day, *and* much more abundant.

CHAPTER 57

THE righteous perish, and no man lays *it* to heart: and merciful men *are* taken away, none considering that the righteous is taken away from the evil *to come*.   *devout*

2 He shall enter into peace: they shall

rest in their beds, *each one* walking *in* his uprightness.   go in

3 But draw near here, you sons of the sorceress, the <u>seed</u> of the adulterer and the <u>whore</u>.   offspring - prostitute

4 Against whom do you sport yourselves? against whom make you a wide mouth, *and* <u>draw</u> out the tongue? *are* you not children of transgression, a seed of falsehood,_{stick}

5 Enflaming yourselves with idols under every green tree, slaying the children in the valleys under the clifts of the rocks?

6 Among the smooth *stones* of the stream *is* your portion; they, they *are* your lot: even to them have you poured a drink offering, you have offered a <u>meat</u> offering. Should I receive comfort in these?   grain

7 Upon a lofty and high mountain have you set your bed: even there went you up to offer sacrifice.

8 Behind the doors also and the posts have you set up your remembrance: for you have <u>discovered</u> *yourself to another* than Me, and are gone up; you have enlarged your bed, and made you *a* <u>covenant</u> with them; you loved their bed where you saw *it*.

uncovered - agreement

9 And you went to the king with ointment, and did increase your perfumes, and did send your messengers far off, and did debase *yourself even* to hell.

10 You are wearied in the greatness of your way; *yet* said you not, There is no hope: you have found the life of your hand; therefore you were not grieved.

11 And of whom have you been afraid or feared, that you have lied, and have not remembered Me, nor laid *it* to your heart? have not I <u>held My peace</u> even of old, and you <u>fear</u> Me not?   i.e., remained silent - honored

12 I will declare your righteousness, and your works; for they shall not profit you.

13 When you cry, let your <u>companies</u> deliver you; but the wind shall carry them all away; <u>vanity</u> shall take *them*: but he that puts his trust in Me shall possess the land, and shall inherit My holy mountain;   collection of idols - deceit

14 And shall say, Cast you up, cast you up, prepare the way, take up the stumblingblock out of the way of My people.

15 For thus says the high and lofty One that inhabits eternity, whose name *is* Holy; I dwell in the high and holy *place*, with him also *that is* of a contrite and humble spirit, to revive the spirit of the humble, and to revive the heart of the contrite ones.

16 For I will not contend for ever, neither will I be always angry: for the spirit should fail before Me, and the souls *which* I have made.

17 For the <u>iniquity</u> of his covetousness was I angry, and <u>smote</u> him: I hid Me, and was angry, and he went on <u>frowardly</u> in the way of his heart.   sin - struck - rebelliously

18 I have seen his ways, and will heal him: I will lead him also, and restore comforts to him and to his mourners.

19 I create the <u>fruit</u> of the lips; Peace, peace to *him that is* far off, and to *him*

M07
|
|
|
|
1111

M35
|
|
|
|
1337

P02
|
|
1075

that is near, says the LORD; and I will heal him. ACTS 2:39 EPH. 2:19 praise

20 But the wicked *are* like the troubled sea, when it cannot rest, whose waters cast up mire and dirt.

21 *There is* no peace, says my God, to the wicked. Elohim[p.f.]

M10-1074

CHAPTER 58

CRY aloud, spare not, lift up your voice like a trumpet, and show My people their transgression, and the house of Ja'cob their sins. do not hold back

2 Yet they seek Me daily, and delight to know My ways, as a nation that did righteousness, and forsook not the ordinance of their God: they ask of Me the ordinances of justice; they take delight in approaching to God. Elohim[p.f.]

3 Why have we fasted, *say they*, and you see not? *why* have we afflicted our soul, and you take no knowledge? Behold, in the day of your fast you find pleasure, and exact all your labors.

4 Behold, you fast for strife and debate, and to smite with the fist of wickedness: you shall not fast as *you do this* day, to make your voice to be heard on high.

5 Is it such a fast that I have chosen? a day for a man to afflict his soul? *is it* to bow down his head as a bulrush, and to spread sackcloth and ashes *under him*? will you call this a fast, and an acceptable day to the LORD? humble himself

6 *Is* not this the fast that I have chosen? to loose the bands of wickedness, to do the heavy burdens, and to let the oppressed go free, and that you break every yoke?

7 *Is it* not to deal your bread to the hungry, and that you bring the poor that are cast out to your house? when you see the naked, that you cover him; and that you hide not yourself from your own flesh? divide - wandering

8 Then shall your light break forth as the morning, and your health shall spring forth speedily: and your righteousness shall go before you; the glory of the LORD shall be your rearward. rear guard

9 Then shall you call, and the LORD shall answer; you shall cry, and He shall say, Here I *am*. If you take away from the midst of you the yoke, the putting forth of the finger, and speaking vanity; i.e. wickedly

10 And *if* you draw out your soul to the hungry, and satisfy the afflicted soul; then shall your light rise in obscurity, and your darkness *be* as the noon day: oppressed

11 And the LORD shall guide you continually, and satisfy your soul in drought, and make fat your bones: and you shall be like a watered garden, and like a spring of water, whose waters fail not. give strength to

G4H 1078

12 And *they that shall be* of you shall build the old waste places: you shall raise up the foundations of many generations; and you shall be called, The repairer of the breach, The restorer of paths to dwell in. ancient ruins

13 If you turn away your foot from the sabbath, *from* doing your pleasure on My holy day; and call the sabbath a delight, the holy of the LORD, honorable; and shall honor Him, not doing

your own ways, nor finding your own pleasure, nor speaking *your own* words: rest day

14 Then shall you delight yourself in the LORD; and I will cause you to ride upon the high places of the earth, and feed you with the heritage of Ja'cob your father: for the mouth of the LORD has spoken *it.*

CHAPTER 59

BEHOLD, the LORD's hand is not shortened, that it cannot save; neither His ear heavy, that it cannot hear:

2 But your <u>iniquities</u> have separated between you and your God, and your sins have hid *His* face from you, that He will not hear. sins

3 For your hands are defiled with <u>blood</u>, and your fingers with iniquity; your lips have spoken lies, your tongue has muttered <u>perverseness</u>.

wrongdoing - wickedness

4 None call for <u>justice</u>, nor *any* plead <u>for</u> truth: they trust in vanity, and speak lies; they conceive mischief, and bring forth iniquity.

righteousness - in

5 They hatch <u>cockatrice'</u> eggs, and weave the spider's web: he that eats of their eggs dies, and that which is crushed breaks out into a viper. adders'

6 Their webs shall not become garments, neither shall they <u>cover</u> themselves with their works: their works *are* works of iniquity, and the act of violence *is* in their hands. clothe

7 Their feet run to evil, and they make haste to shed innocent blood: their thoughts *are* thoughts of <u>iniquity</u>;

wasting and destruction *are* in their paths. ROM. 3:15-16 evil

8 The way of peace they know not; and *there is* no judgment in their goings: they have made them crooked paths: whosoever goes therein shall not know peace. ROM. 3:10

9 Therefore is judgment far from us, neither does justice overtake us: we wait for light, but behold obscurity; for brightness, *but* we walk in darkness.

10 We grope for the wall like the blind, and we grope as if *we had* no eyes: we stumble at noon day as in the night; *we are* in desolate places as dead *men*.

11 We roar all like bears, and mourn sore like doves: we look for judgment, but *there is* none; for salvation, *but* it is far off from us.

12 For our transgressions are multiplied before You, and our sins testify against us: for our transgressions *are* with us; and *as for* our <u>iniquities</u>, we know them; sins

13 In transgressing and <u>lying</u> against the LORD, and departing away from our <u>God</u>, speaking oppression and revolt, conceiving and uttering from the heart words of falsehood.

acting deceptively - Elohim^{p.f}

14 And judgment is turned away backward, and justice stands afar off: for truth is fallen in the street, and equity cannot enter.

15 Yea, truth fails; and he *that* departs from evil makes himself a <u>prey</u>: and the LORD saw *it*, and it displeased Him that *there was* no <u>judgment</u>. victim - justice

16 And He saw that *there was* no

man, and wondered that *there was* no intercessor: therefore His arm brought salvation to Him; and His righteousness, it sustained Him.

17 For He put on righteousness as a breastplate, and an helmet of salvation upon His head; and He put on the garments of vengeance *for* clothing, and was clad with zeal as a cloak.

18 According to *their* deeds, accordingly He will repay, fury to His adversaries, recompence to His enemies; to the <u>islands</u> He will repay recompence. coastlands

19 So shall they <u>fear</u> the name of the LORD from the west, and His glory from the rising of the sun. When the enemy shall come in like a flood, the Spirit of the LORD shall lift up a standard against him. revere

20 And the <u>Redeemer</u> shall come to Zi'on, and to them that turn from transgression in Ja'cob, says the LORD. ROM. 11:26 i.e., Christ

21 As for Me, this *is* My <u>covenant</u> with them, says the LORD; My Spirit that *is* upon you, and My words which I have put in your mouth, shall not depart out of your mouth, nor out of the mouth of your <u>seed</u>, nor out of the mouth of your <u>seed's seed</u>, says the LORD, from hereafter and for ever. agreement - offspring - descendants

CHAPTER 60

ARISE, shine; for your light is come, and the glory of the LORD is risen upon you.

2 For, behold, the darkness shall cover the earth, and gross darkness the people: but the LORD shall arise upon you, and His glory shall be seen upon you.

3 And the <u>Gen'tiles</u> shall come to your light, and kings to the brightness of your rising. Nations

4 Lift up your eyes round about, and see: all they gather themselves together, they come to you: your sons shall come from far, and your daughters shall be nursed at *your* side.

5 Then you shall see, and flow together, and your heart shall fear, and be enlarged; because the abundance of the sea shall be converted to you, the forces of the Gen'tiles shall come to you.

6 The multitude of camels shall cover you, the <u>dromedaries</u> of Mid'i-an and E'phah; all they from She'ba shall come: they shall bring gold and incense; and they shall show forth the praises of the LORD. camels

7 All the flocks of Ke'dar shall be gathered together to you, the rams of Ne-ba'ioth shall minister to you: they shall come up with acceptance on My altar, and I will glorify the house of My glory.

8 Who *are* these *that* fly as a cloud, and as the doves to their windows?

9 Surely the <u>isles</u> shall wait for Me, and the ships of Tar'shish first, to bring your sons from far, their silver and their gold with them, to the name of the LORD your God, and to the Holy One of Is'ra-el, because He has glorified you. distant lands

10 And the sons of strangers shall build up your walls, and their kings shall

minister to you: for in My wrath I smote you, but in My favor have I had mercy on you.

11 Therefore your gates shall be open continually; they shall not be shut day nor night; that *men* may bring to you the <u>forces</u> of the Gen'tiles, and *that* their kings *may be* brought.

REV. 21:25 wealth - Nations

12 For the nation and kingdom that will not serve you shall perish; yea, *those* nations shall be utterly <u>wasted</u>.   ruined

13 The glory of Leb'a-non shall come to you, the fir tree, the pine tree, and the box together, to beautify the place of My sanctuary; and I will make the place of My feet glorious.

14 The sons also of them that afflicted you shall come bending to you; and all they that despised you shall bow themselves down at the soles of your feet; and they shall call you, The city of the LORD, The Zi'on of the Holy One of Is'ra-el. REV. 3:9

15 Whereas you have been forsaken and <u>hated</u>, so that no man went through *you*, I will make you an eternal excellency, a joy of many generations. despised

16 You shall also suck the milk of the Gen'tiles, and shall suck the breast of kings: and you shall know that I the LORD *am* your Savior and your Redeemer, the Mighty One of Ja'cob.

17 For brass I will bring gold, and for iron I will bring silver, and for wood brass, and for stones iron: I will also make your officers peace, and your <u>exactors</u> righteousness. overseers

18 Violence shall no more be heard in your land, wasting nor destruction inside your borders; but you shall call your walls <u>Salvation</u>, and your gates Praise. i.e., Heb. Jeshua

19 The sun shall be no more your light by day; neither for brightness shall the moon give light to you: but the LORD shall be to you an everlasting light, and your <u>God</u> your glory. Elohim^{p.f.}

20 Your sun shall no more go down; neither shall your moon withdraw itself: for the LORD shall be your everlasting light, and the days of your mourning shall be ended.

21 Your people also *shall be* all righteous: they shall inherit the land for ever, the branch of My planting, the work of My hands, that I may be glorified. MATT. 15:13

22 A little one shall become a thousand, and a small one a strong nation: I the LORD will hasten it in his time.

CHAPTER 61

THE Spirit of the Lord GOD *is* upon me; because the LORD has anointed me to preach good tidings to the meek; he has sent me to bind up the brokenhearted, to proclaim liberty to the captives, and the opening of the prison to *them that are* bound; 2 COR. 3:17

2 To proclaim the acceptable year of the LORD, and the day of vengeance of our <u>God</u>; to comfort all that mourn; MATT. 5:4 LUKE 4:19-21 Elohim^{p.f.}

3 To <u>appoint</u> to them that mourn in Zi'on, to give to them beauty for ashes, the oil of joy for mourning, the garment of praise for the spirit of heaviness; that they might be called trees of

righteousness, the planting of the LORD, that He might be glorified. 1 COR. 3:9 proclaim

4 And they shall build the old wastes, they shall raise up the former desolations, and they shall repair the waste cities, the desolations of many generations.

5 And strangers shall stand and feed your flocks, and the sons of the alien *shall be* your plowmen and your vinedressers.

6 But you shall be named the Priests of the LORD: *men* shall call you the Ministers of our God: you shall eat the riches of the Gen'tiles, and in their glory shall you boast yourselves.

REV. 1:6　Elohim[p.f.] - Nations - wealth

7 For your shame *you shall have* double; and *for* confusion they shall rejoice in their portion: therefore in their land they shall possess the double: everlasting joy shall be to them.

8 For I the LORD love judgment, I hate robbery for burned offering; and I will direct their work in truth, and I will make an everlasting covenant with them.　　　despise - agreement

9 And their seed shall be known among the Gen'tiles, and their offspring among the people: all that see them shall acknowledge them, that they *are* the seed *which* the LORD has blessed.　　offspring - descendants

10 I will greatly rejoice in the LORD, my soul shall be joyful in my God; for He has clothed me with the garments of salvation, he has covered me with the robe of righteousness, as a bridegroom decks *himself* with ornaments, and as a bride adorns *herself* with her jewels.　　Elohim[p.f.]

11 For as the earth brings forth her bud, and as the garden causes the things that are sown in it to spring forth; so the Lord GOD will cause righteousness and praise to spring forth before all the nations.　　Adonay[p.f.] Jehovah

CHAPTER 62

FOR Zi'on's sake will I not hold My peace, and for Je-ru'salem's sake I will not rest, until the righteousness thereof go forth as brightness, and the salvation thereof as a lamp *that* burns.　　keep - i.e. Heb. Jeshua

2 And the Gen'tiles shall see your righteousness, and all kings your glory: and you shall be called by a new name, which the mouth of the LORD shall name.　　REV. 2:17 REV. 3:12 Nations

3 You shall also be a crown of glory in the hand of the LORD, and a royal diadem in the hand of your God.

Lit. turban

4 You shall no more be termed Forsaken; neither shall your land any more be termed Desolate: but you shall be called Heph'zi-bah, and your land Beu'lah: for the LORD delights in you, and your land shall be married.

5 For *as* a young man marries a virgin, *so* shall your sons marry you: and *as* the bridegroom rejoices over the bride, *so* shall your God rejoice over you.　　Elohim[p.f.]

6 I have set watchmen upon your walls, O Je-ru'sa-lem, *which* shall never hold their peace day nor night: you that make mention of the LORD, keep not silence,　　keep

7 And give Him no rest, till He establish, and till He make Je-ru'sa-lem a praise in the earth.

8 The LORD has sworn by His right hand, and by the arm of His strength, Surely I will no more give your <u>corn</u> *to be* <u>meat</u> for your enemies; and the sons of the stranger shall not drink your wine, for the which you have labored. _{grain - food}

9 But they that have gathered it shall eat it, and praise the LORD; and they that have brought it together shall drink it in the courts of My <u>holiness</u>. _{sanctuary}

10 Go through, go through the gates; prepare you the way of the people; cast up, cast up the highway; gather out the stones; lift up a <u>standard</u> for the people. _{banner (Heb.)}

11 Behold, the LORD has proclaimed to the end of the <u>world</u>, Say you to the daughter of Zi'on, Behold, your salvation comes; behold, His reward *is* with him, and His <u>work</u> before Him. _{MATT. 21:5 earth - recompense}

12 And they shall call them, The holy people, The redeemed of the LORD: and you shall be called, Sought out, A city not forsaken.

CHAPTER 63

WHO *is* this that comes from E'dom, with dyed garments from Boz'rah? this *that is* glorious in His apparel, travelling in the greatness of His strength? I that speak in righteousness, mighty to save.

2 Why *are You* red in Your apparel, and Your garments like him that treads in the winefat?

3 I have trodden the winepress alone; and of the people *there was* none with Me: for I will tread them in My anger, and trample them in My fury; and their blood shall be sprinkled upon My garments, and I will stain all My <u>raiment</u>. _{garments}

4 For the day of vengeance *is* in My heart, and the year of My redeemed is come.

5 And I looked, and *there was* none to help; and I wondered that *there was* none to uphold: therefore My own arm brought salvation to Me; and My fury, it upheld Me.

6 And I will tread down the people in My anger, and make them drunk in My <u>fury</u>, and I will bring down their strength to the earth. _{wrath}

7 I will mention the lovingkindnesss of the LORD, *and* the praises of the LORD, according to all that the LORD has bestowed on us, and the great goodness toward the house of Is'ra-el, which He has bestowed on them according to His mercies, and according to the multitude of His lovingkindnesss.

8 For He said, Surely they *are* My people, children *that* will not <u>lie</u>: so He was their Savior. _{deal falsely}

9 In all their affliction He was afflicted, and the <u>angel</u> of His presence saved them: in His love and in His pity He redeemed them; and He bare them, and carried them all the days of old. _{messenger}

10 But they rebelled, and <u>vexed</u> His Holy Spirit: therefore He was turned to be their enemy, *and* He fought against them. _{grieved}

11 Then He remembered the days of old, Mo's, *and* His people, *say-ing*, Where *is* He that brought them up out of the sea with the shepherd of His flock? where *is* He that put His Holy Spirit within him? HEB. 13:20

12 That led *them* by the right hand of Mo's with His glorious arm, divid-ing the water before them, to make Himself an everlasting name? mighty

13 That led them through the deep, as an horse in the wilderness, *that* they should not stumble?

14 As a beast goes down into the valley, the Spirit of the Lord caused him to rest: so did You lead Your people, to make Yourself a glorious name. the cattle

15 Look down from heaven, and behold from the habitation of Your holiness and of Your glory: where *is* Your zeal and Your strength, the sounding of Your bowels and of Your mercies toward me? are they restrained? i.e., the murmur of your compassion

16 Doubtless You *are* our father, though A'bra-ham be ignorant of us, and Is'ra-el acknowledge us not: You, O Lord, *are* our father, our redeemer; Your name *is* from everlasting.

17 O Lord, why have You made us to err from Your ways, *and* hardened our heart from Your fear? Return for Your servants' sake, the tribes of Your inheritance. stray - honor

18 The people of Your holiness have possessed *it* but a little while: our adversaries have trodden down Your sanctuary. LUKE 21:24

19 We are *Yours*: You never bare rule over them; they were not called by Your name.

CHAPTER 64

OH that You would rend the heavens, that You would come down, that the mountains might flow down at Your presence, open

2 As *when* the melting fire burns, the fire causes the waters to boil, to make Your name known to Your ad-versaries, *that* the nations may tremble at Your presence!

3 When You did terrible things *which* we looked not for, You came down, the mountains flowed down at Your presence.

4 For since the beginning of the world *men* have not heard, nor per-ceived by the ear, neither has the eye seen, O God, beside You, *what* He has prepared for him that waits for Him. 1 COR. 2:9 Elohim p.f.

5 You meet him that rejoices and works righteousness, *those that* re-member You in Your ways: behold, You are angry; for we have sinned: in those is continuance, and we shall be saved.

6 But we are all as an unclean *thing*, and all our righteousnesses *are* as filthy rags; and we all do fade as a leaf; and our iniquities, like the wind, have taken us away.

7 And *there is* none that calls upon Your name, that stirs up himself to take hold of You: for You have hid Your face from us, and have consumed us, because of our iniquities. destroyed

8 But now, O LORD, you *are* our father; we *are* the clay, and You our potter; and we all *are* the work of Your hand.
9 Be not angry <u>very sore</u>, O LORD, neither remember <u>iniquity</u> for ever: behold, see, we <u>beseech</u> You, we *are* all Your people.   beyond measure - our sins - beg
10 Your holy cities are a wilderness, Zi'on is a wilderness, Je-ru'sa-lem a desolation.
11 Our holy and our beautiful house, where our fathers praised You, is burned up with fire: and all our pleasant things are <u>laid waste</u>.   in ruins
12 Will You refrain Yourself for these *things*, O LORD? will You <u>hold</u> Your peace, and <u>afflict</u> us <u>very sore</u>?   keep - punish - beyond measure

CHAPTER 65

I AM sought of *them that* asked not *for Me*; I am found of *them that* sought Me not: I said, Behold Me, behold Me, to a nation *that* was not called by My name.   ROM. 10:20
2 I have spread out My hands all the day to a rebellious people, which walks in a way *that was* not good, after their own thoughts;   ROM. 10:21
3 A people that provokes Me to anger continually to My face; that sacrifices in <u>gardens</u>, and burns incense upon <u>altars of brick</u>;   pagan shrines - pagan altars
4 Which remain among the graves, and lodge in the monuments, which eat swine's flesh, and broth of <u>abominable</u> *things is in* their vessels;   detestable
5 Which say, Stand by yourself, come not near to me; for I am holier than you. These *are* a smoke in My nose, a fire that burns all the day.
6 Behold, *it is* written before Me: I will not keep silence, but will recompense, even recompense into their bosom,
7 Your iniquities, and the iniquities of your fathers together, says the LORD, which have burned incense upon the mountains, and blasphemed Me upon the hills: therefore will I <u>measure</u> their former work into their bosom.   pay back
8 Thus says the LORD, As the new wine is found in the cluster, and *one* says, Destroy it not; for a blessing *is* in it: so will I do for My servants' sakes, that I may not destroy them all.
9 And I will bring forth a <u>seed</u> out of Ja'cob, and out of Ju'dah an inheritor of My mountains: and My elect shall inherit it, and My servants shall dwell there.   descendants
10 And Shar'on shall be a fold of flocks, and the valley of A'chor a place for the herds to lie down in, for My people that have sought Me.
11 But you *are* they that forsake the LORD, that forget My holy mountain, that prepare a table for that troop, and that furnish the drink offering to that number.
12 Therefore will I number you to the sword, and you shall all bow down to the slaughter: because when I called, you did not answer; when I spoke, you did not hear; but did evil before My eyes, and did choose *that* wherein I delighted not.
13 Therefore thus says the Lord GOD, Behold, My servants shall eat, but you shall be hungry: behold, My ser-

vants shall drink, but you shall be thirsty: behold, My servants shall rejoice, but you shall be ashamed:

14 Behold, My servants shall sing for joy of heart, but you shall cry for sorrow of heart, and shall <u>howl</u> <u>for vexation of spirit</u>._{cry out with a heavy heart}

15 And you shall leave your name for a curse to My chosen: for the <u>Lord G</u>OD shall slay you, and call His servants by another name:

Adonay^{p.f.} Jehovah

16 That he who blesses himself in the earth shall bless himself in the <u>God</u> of truth; and he that swears in the earth shall swear by the <u>God</u> of truth; because the former troubles are forgotten, and because they are hid from My eyes. Elohim^{p.f.}

17 For, behold, I create new heavens and a new earth: and the former shall not be remembered, nor come into mind. 2 PET. 3:13

18 But be you glad and rejoice for ever *in that* which I create: for, behold, I create Je-ru'sa-lem a rejoicing, and her people a joy.

19 And I will rejoice in Je-ru'sa-lem, and joy in My people: and the voice of weeping shall be no more heard in her, nor the voice of crying.

20 There shall be no more there an infant of days, nor an old man that has not filled his days: for the child shall die an hundred years old; but the sinner *being* an hundred years old shall be accursed.

21 And they shall build houses, and inhabit *them*; and they shall plant vineyards, and eat the fruit of them.

22 They shall not build, and another inhabit; they shall not plant, and another eat: for as the days of a tree *are* the days of My people, and My elect shall long enjoy the work of their hands.

23 They shall not labor in vain, nor bring forth for trouble; for they *are* the <u>seed</u> of the blessed of the LORD, and their offspring with them. _{descendants}

24 And it shall come to pass, that before they call, I will answer; and while they are yet speaking, I will hear.

25 The wolf and the lamb shall feed together, and the lion shall eat straw like the bullock: and dust *shall be* the serpent's <u>meat</u>. They shall not hurt nor destroy in all My holy mountain, says the LORD. _{food}

CHAPTER 66

THUS says the LORD, The heaven *is* My throne, and the earth *is* My footstool: where *is* the house that you build to Me? and where *is* the place of My rest? MATT. 5:35 ACTS 7:49

2 For all those *things* has My hand made, and all those *things* have been, says the LORD: but to this *man* will I look, *even* to *him that is* poor and of a contrite spirit, and trembles at My word.

3 He that kills an ox *is as if* he slew a man; he that sacrifices a lamb, *as if* he cut off a dog's neck; he that offers an oblation, *as if he offered* swine's blood; he that burns incense, *as if* he blessed an idol. Yea, they have chosen their own ways, and their soul delights in their <u>abominations</u>. _{detestable ways}

4 I also will choose their <u>delusions</u>, and will bring their <u>fears</u> upon them; because when I called, none did answer; when I spoke, they did not hear: but they did evil before My eyes, and chose *that* in which I delighted not.   <small>punishment - dread</small>

5 Hear the word of the LORD, you that tremble at His word; Your brethren that <u>hated</u> you, that cast you out for My name's sake, said, Let the LORD be glorified: but He shall appear to your joy, and they shall be ashamed. <small>despised</small>

6 A voice of noise from the city, a voice from the temple, a voice of the LORD that renders recompence to His enemies.   <small>REV. 16:17</small>

7 Before she <u>travailed</u>, she brought forth; before her pain came, she was delivered of a man child. <small>REV. 12:5 suffered</small>

8 Who has heard such a thing? who has seen such things? Shall the earth be made to bring forth in one day? *or* shall a nation be born at once? for as soon as Zi'on travailed, she brought forth her children.

9 Shall I bring to the birth, and not cause to bring forth? says the LORD: shall I <u>cause to bring forth</u>, and shut *the womb*? says your <u>God</u>. <small>give delivery - Elohim^{p.f.}</small>

10 Rejoice you with Je-ru'sa-lem, and be glad with her, all you that love her: rejoice for joy with her, all you that mourn for her:

11 That you may suck, and be satisfied with the breasts of her <u>consolations</u>; that you may milk out, and be delighted with the abundance of her glory.   <small>comforts</small>

12 For thus says the LORD, Behold, I will extend peace to her like a river, and the glory of the Gen'tiles like a flowing stream: then shall you suck, you shall be borne upon *her* sides, and be dandled upon *her* knees.

13 As one whom his mother comforts, so will I comfort you; and you shall be comforted in Je-ru'sa-lem.

14 And when you see *this*, your heart shall rejoice, and your bones shall flourish like an herb: and the hand of the LORD shall be known toward His servants, and *His* indignation toward His enemies.

15 For, behold, the LORD will come with fire, and with His chariots like a whirlwind, to render His anger with fury, and His rebuke with flames of fire.

16 For by fire and by His sword will the LORD plead with all flesh: and the slain of the LORD shall be many.

17 They that <u>sanctify</u> themselves, and purify themselves in the gardens behind one *tree* in the midst, eating swine's flesh, and the <u>abomination</u>, and the mouse, shall be consumed together, says the LORD.

<small>consecrate - detestable things</small>

18 For I *know* their works and their thoughts: it shall come, that I will gather all nations and tongues; and they shall come, and see My glory.

19 And I will set a sign among them, and I will send those that escape of them to the nations, *to* Tar'shish, Pul, and Lud, that draw the bow, *to* Tu'bal, and Ja'van, *to* the <u>isles</u> afar off, that have not heard My fame, neither have seen My glory; and they shall declare My glory among the Gen'tiles.   <small>distant lands</small>

20 And they shall bring all your brethren *for* an offering to the LORD out of all nations upon horses, and in chariots, and in litters, and upon mules, and upon swift beasts, to My holy mountain Je-ru'sa-lem, says the LORD, as the children of Is'ra-el bring an offering in a clean vessel into the house of the LORD.

21 And I will also take of them for priests *and* for Le'vites, says the LORD.

22 For as the new heavens and the new earth, which I will make, shall remain before Me, says the LORD, so shall your seed and your name remain.

REV. 21 descendants

23 And it shall come to pass, *that* from one new moon to another, and from one sabbath to another, shall all flesh come to worship before Me, says the LORD.

rest day

24 And they shall go forth, and look upon the carcases of the men that have transgressed against Me: for their worm shall not die, neither shall their fire be quenched; and they shall be an abhorring to all flesh.

MARK 9:46 loathsome

JEREMIAH

Outline

JEREMIAH, GOD'S WITNESS TO THE NATION: THE LORD OMNIPOTENT REIGNETH 46.1—52.34
  "The Prophet Concerning the Nations" 46.1; Egypt 46.2-28; Philistia 47.1-7; Moab 48.1-47;
      Ammon 49.1-6; Edom 49.7-22; Damascus 49.23-27; Kedar 49.28, 29; Hazor 49.30-33;
      Elam 49.34-39; Babylon 50.1—51.64; Judah 52.1-34.

SURVEY

Jeremiah's long ministry of over forty years stretched from 625 B.C. until a few years after Judah ceased to be a state in 586 B.C. Over fifty years of religious apostasy under Manasseh were eventually followed by religious reform under Josiah (621-607 B.C.). Jeremiah supported the reform with enthusiasm until he realized that it was not changing the people's hearts. Two years after Josiah's death, the battle of Carchemish (605 B.C.) established Babylonian control over western Asia. From that time Jeremiah advocated submission to Babylon, but without success. Under the last four kings of Judah, twenty-one years of religious apostasy and political weakness made the fall of Jerusalem in 586 B.C., and exile, inevitable.

The distressing circumstances in which Jeremiah worked, and the extraordinary extent to which idolatry had replaced revealed religion in Judah, are clearly mirrored in Jeremiah's prophecies. So also is Jeremiah's spiritual anguish occasioned by this apostasy. Yet he was no pessimist. He was essentially God's warrior, but a warrior who was also watchman and witness. Chapter 1 describes Jeremiah's call to prophethood. Chapters 2 through 13 enable us to reconstruct the conditions in which he prophesied, while chapters 14 through 33 mirror his awareness of, and his fellowship with, God (cf. also 1.1-19). The warrior then emerges as God's watchman (34.1—45.5) and God's witness (46.1—52.34).

In Jeremiah's oracles, God, the moral governor of the world, is Israel's covenant God. Through Israel He sought to achieve moral purposes. Alas, the northern kingdom's adulteries with the Baalim compelled God to divorce (that is, exile) her. Judah, the southern kingdom, failed to learn from Israel's experience. She outdid Israel in sexual impurities, yet Judah repudiated the charges of religious infidelity. Therefore God must judge her.

Repentance might have stayed divorce proceedings (exile), her adulteries notwithstanding, so great is the Lord's grace. But so established was Judah in lewdness that she was incapable of moral amendment. Gradually social virtues disappeared. Sacrifices and ritual failed as substitutes for repentance and righteousness. Judah's appalling sinfulness meant that sin must be congenital, hence her moral inability. It sprang from a sinful nature. Judgment was inescapable, and exile. But exile was not the final word.

A remnant would return to live under Messiah's rule in religious and social security. Messiah's righteous rule over a righteous people helps explain Jeremiah's doctrine of the New Covenant. People would be righteous because their hearts would be renewed. They would obey God's laws from the heart spontaneously. The New Covenant, insuring forgiveness and inward moral dynamic, would transcend the legalism of the Old Covenant. Eventually through Christ's sacrificial death, and the inward, regenerative activity of the Holy Spirit, the New Covenant became a reality.

AUTHOR

No principle is discernible in the arrangement of Jeremiah's prophecies. Oracles under Judah's last five kings do not follow chronological sequence. The chapter sequence in Hebrew differs from the order in the Septuagint, and the latter shows considerable though unimportant omissions. This suggests a different editorial revision. Jeremiah dictated his prophecies and Baruch wrote them down (36.1-8, 32). The disorderly arrangement might be evidence of primitiveness. The New Testament contains numerous references to Jeremiah.

                                                                              J.G.S.S.T.

THE BOOK OF
JEREMIAH

CHAPTER 1

"Appointed by Jehovah" to Announce that the Babylonians Are Coming

THE words of Jer-e-mi'ah the son of Hil-ki'ah, of the priests that *were* in An'a-thoth in the land of Ben'ja-min:

2 To whom the word of the LORD came in the days of Jo-si'ah the son of A'mon king of Ju'dah, in the thirteenth year of his reign.

3 It came also in the days of Je-hoi'a-kim the son of Jo-si'ah king of Ju'dah, to the end of the eleventh year of Zed-e-ki'ah the son of Jo-si'ah king of Ju'dah, to the carrying away of Je-ru'sa-lem captive in the fifth month.

4 Then the word of the LORD came to me, saying,

5 Before I formed you in the belly I knew you; and before you came forth out of the womb I <u>sanctified</u> you, *and* I ordained you a prophet to the nations.   GAL. 1:15 consecrated

6 Then said I, Ah, <u>Lord GOD</u>! behold, I cannot speak: for I *am* a child.   Adonay[p.f.] Jehovah

7 But the LORD said to me, Say not, I *am* a child: for you shall go to all that I shall send you, and whatsoever I command you you shall speak.

8 Be not afraid of their faces: for I *am* with you to deliver you, says the LORD.

9 Then the LORD put forth His hand, and touched my mouth. And the LORD said to me, Behold, I have put My words in your mouth.

10 See, I have this day set you over the nations and over the kingdoms, to root out, and to pull down, and to destroy, and to throw down, to build, and to plant.

11 Moreover the word of the LORD came to me, saying, Jer-e-mi'ah, what see you? And I said, I see a rod of an almond tree.

12 Then said the LORD to me, You have well seen: for I will <u>hasten</u> My word to perform it.   watch over

13 And the word of the LORD came to me the second time, saying, What see you? And I said, I see a seething pot; and the face thereof *is* toward the north.

14 Then the LORD said to me, Out of the north an evil shall break forth upon all the inhabitants of the land.

15 For, lo, I will call all the families of the kingdoms of the north, **says** the LORD; and they shall come, and they shall set every one his throne at the entering of the gates of Je-ru'sa-lem, and against all the walls thereof round about, and against all the cities of Ju'dah.

16 And I will utter My judgments against them <u>touching</u> all their wickedness, who have forsaken Me, and have burned incense to other gods, and worshiped the works of their own hands.   concerning

17 You therefore gird up your loins, and arise, and speak to them all that

I command you: be not dismayed at their faces, less I <u>confound</u> you before them. _{dismay}

18 For, behold, I have made you this day a <u>defenced</u> city, and an iron pillar, and brazen walls against the whole land, against the kings of Ju'dah, against the princes thereof, against the priests thereof, and against the people of the land. _{unfortified}

19 And they shall fight against you; but they shall not prevail against you; for I *am* with you, says the LORD, to deliver you.

CHAPTER 2

MOREOVER the word of the LORD came to me, saying,

2 Go and cry in the ears of Je-ru'salem, saying, Thus says the LORD; I remember you, the kindness of your youth, the love of your <u>espousals</u>, when you <u>went</u> after Me in the wilderness, in a land *that* was not sown. _{betrothals - followed}

3 Is'ra-el *was* holiness to the LORD, and the firstfruits of His increase: all that devour him shall <u>offend;</u> evil shall come upon them, says the LORD. _{be guilty}

4 Hear you the word of the LORD, O house of Ja'cob, and all the families of the house of Is'ra-el:

5 Thus says the LORD, What iniquity have your fathers found in Me, that they are gone far from Me, and have walked after vanity, and are become vain?

6 Neither said they, Where *is* the LORD that brought us up out of the land of E'gypt, that led us through the wilderness, through a land of deserts and of pits, through a land of drought, and of the shadow of death, through a land that no man passed through, and where no man dwelled?

7 And I brought you into a plentiful country, to eat the fruit thereof and the goodness thereof; but when you entered, you defiled My land, and made My heritage an <u>abomination</u>. _{detestable}

8 The priests said not, Where *is* the LORD? and they that handle the law knew Me not: the pastors also transgressed against Me, and the prophets prophesied by Ba'al, and walked after *things that* do not profit.

9 Wherefore I will yet plead with you, says the LORD, and with your children's children will I plead.

10 For <u>pass over</u> the <u>isles</u> of Chit'tim, and see; and send to Ke'dar, and consider diligently, and see if there be such a thing.

_{cross over to - distant lands}

11 Has a nation changed *their* gods, which *are* yet no gods? but My people have changed their glory for *that which* does not profit.

12 Be astonished, O you heavens, at this, and be horribly afraid, be you <u>very desolate</u>, says the LORD. _{in despair}

13 For My people have committed two evils; they have forsaken Me the fountain of living waters, *and* <u>hewed</u> them out cisterns, broken cisterns, that can hold no water. _{cut}

14 *Is* Is'ra-el a servant? *is* he a homeborn *slave*? why is he <u>spoiled</u>? _{plundered}

15 The young lions roared upon him, *and* yelled, and they made his land

waste: his cities are burned without inhabitant.   a ruin

16 Also the children of Noph and Ta'hap'a-nes have broken the crown of your head.

17 Have you not procured this to yourself, in that you have forsaken the LORD your God, when he led you by the way?   Elohim^p.f.

18 And now what have you to do in the way of E'gypt, to drink the waters of Si'hor? or what have you to do in the way of As-syr'i-a, to drink the waters of the river?

19 Your own wickedness shall correct you, and your backslidings shall reprove you: know therefore and see that *it is* an evil *thing* and bitter, that you have forsaken the LORD your God, and that My fear *is* not in you, says the Lord GOD of hosts.

Jehovah^s.f. - Elohim^p.f. - dread - Adonay^p.f. Jehovah^s.f. Tsebaoth

20 For of old time I have broken your yoke, *and* burst your bands; and you said, I will not transgress; when upon every high hill and under every green tree you wander, playing the harlot.

21 Yet I had planted you a noble vine, wholly a right seed: how then are you turned into the degenerate plant of a strange vine to Me?

22 For though you wash you with nitre, and take you much soap, *yet* your iniquity is marked before Me, says the Lord GOD.

                    i.e., lye soap - sin - Adonay^p.f. Jehovah

23 How can you say, I am not polluted, I have not gone after Ba'al-im? see your way in the valley, know what you have done: *you are* a swift dromedary traversing her ways; unclean - camel

24 A wild ass used to the wilderness, *that* snuffs up the wind at her pleasure; in her occasion who can turn her away? all they that seek her will not weary themselves; in her month they shall find her.

25 Withhold your foot from being unshod, and your throat from thirst: but you said, There is no hope: no; for I have loved strangers, and after them will I go.

26 As the thief is ashamed when he is found, so is the house of Is'ra-el ashamed; they, their kings, their princes, and their priests, and their prophets,

27 Saying to a stock, You *are* my father; and to a stone, You have brought me forth: for they have turned *their* back to Me, and not *their* face: but in the time of their trouble they will say, Arise, and save us.   i.e., wooden idol

28 But where *are* your gods that you have made you? let them arise, if they can save you in the time of your trouble: for *according to* the number of your cities are your gods, O Ju'dah.   evil

29 Why will you plead with Me? you all have transgressed against Me, says the LORD.

30 In vain have I smitten your children; they received no correction: your own sword has devoured your prophets, like a destroying lion.

31 O generation, see you the word of the LORD. Have I been a wilderness to Is'ra-el? a land of darkness?

why say My people, We are lords; we will come no more to You?

32 Can a maid forget her ornaments, *or* a bride her attire? yet My people have forgotten Me days without number.

33 Why trim you your way to seek love? therefore have you also taught the wicked ones your ways. prepare - i.e., women

34 Also in your skirts is found the blood of the souls of the poor innocents: I have not found it by secret search, but upon all these.

35 Yet you say, Because I am innocent, surely His anger shall turn from me. Behold, I will plead with you, because you say, I have not sinned.

36 Why gad you about so much to change your way? you also shall be ashamed of E'gypt, as you were ashamed of As-syr'i-a.

37 Yea, you shall go forth from him, and your hands upon your head: for the Lord has rejected your confidences, and you shall not prosper in them.

CHAPTER 3

THEY say, If a man put away his wife, and she go from him, and become another man's, shall he return to her again? shall not that land be greatly polluted? but you have played the harlot with many lovers; yet return again to Me, says the Lord. completely unclean

2 Lift up your eyes to the high places, and see where you have not been lain with. In the ways have you sat for them, as the A-ra'bi-an in the wilderness; and you have polluted the land with your whoredoms and with your wickedness. made unclean

3 Therefore the showers have been withholden, and there has been no latter rain; and you had a whore's forehead, you refused to be ashamed.

4 Will you not from this time cry to Me, My father, You *are* the guide of my youth?

5 Will He reserve *His anger* for ever? will He keep *it* to the end? Behold, you have spoken and done evil things as you could.

6 The Lord said also to me in the days of Jo-si'ah the king, Have you seen *that* which backsliding Is'ra-el has done? she is gone up upon every high mountain and under every green tree, and there has played the harlot.

7 And I said after she had done all these *things*, Turn you to Me. But she returned not. And her treacherous sister Ju'dah saw *it*.

8 And I saw, when for all the causes whereby backsliding Is'ra-el committed adultery I had put her away, and given her a bill of divorce; yet her treacherous sister Ju'dah feared not, but went and played the harlot also. unfaithfulness

9 And it came to pass through the lightness of her whoredom, that she defiled the land, and committed adultery with stones and with stocks. frivolity - harlotry - unfaithfulness

10 And yet for all this her treacherous sister Ju'dah has not turned to me with her whole heart, but feignedly, says the Lord. in deception

11 And the Lord said to me, The

backsliding Is'ra-el has justified herself more than treacherous Ju'dah.

12 Go and proclaim these words toward the north, and say, Return, you backsliding Is'ra-el, says the LORD; *and* I will not cause My anger to fall upon you: for I *am* merciful, says the LORD, *and* I will not keep *anger* for ever.

13 Only acknowledge your iniquity, that you have transgressed against the LORD your <u>God</u>, and have scattered your ways to the strangers under every green tree, and you have not obeyed My voice, says the LORD.   Elohim^{p.f.}

14 Turn, O backsliding children, says the LORD; for I am married to you: and I will take you one of a city, and two of a family, and I will bring you to Zi'on:

15 And I will give you pastors according to My heart, which shall feed you with knowledge and understanding.

16 And it shall come to pass, when you be multiplied and increased in the land, in those days, says the LORD, they shall say no more, The ark of the <u>covenant</u> of the LORD: neither shall it come to mind: neither shall they remember it; neither shall they visit *it*; neither shall *that* be <u>done any more</u>.   agreement - it be made again

17 At that time they shall call Je-ru'sa-lem the throne of the LORD; and all the nations shall be gathered to it, to the name of the LORD, to Je-ru'sa-lem: neither shall they walk any more after the <u>imagination</u> of their evil heart.   stubborness

18 In those days the house of Ju'dah shall walk with the house of Is'ra-el, and they shall come together out of the land of the north to the land that I have given for an inheritance to your fathers.

19 But I said, How shall I put you among the children, and give you a pleasant land, a goodly heritage of the hosts of nations? and I said, You shall call Me, My father; and shall not turn away from Me.

20 Surely *as* a wife treacherously departs from her husband, so have you dealt treacherously with Me, O house of Is'ra-el, says the LORD.

21 A voice was heard upon the high places, weeping *and* supplications of the children of Is'ra-el: for they have perverted their way, *and* they have forgotten the LORD their <u>God</u>.   Elohim^{p.f.}

22 Return, you backsliding children, *and* I will heal your backslidings. Behold, we come to You; for You *are* the LORD our God.

23 Truly in vain *is salvation hoped for* from the hills, *and from* the multitude of mountains: truly in the LORD our <u>God</u> *is* the salvation of Is'ra-el.

24 For shame has devoured the labor of our fathers from our youth; their flocks and their herds, their sons and their daughters.

25 We lie down in our shame, and our confusion covers us: for we have sinned against the LORD our <u>God</u>, we and our fathers, from our youth even to this day, and have not obeyed the voice of the LORD our <u>God</u>.   Elohim^{p.f.}

CHAPTER 4

IF you will return, O Is'ra-el, says the LORD, return to Me: and if you will put away your abominations out of My sight, then shall you not remove.   detestable things
2 And you shall swear, The LORD lives, in truth, in judgment, and in righteousness; and the nations shall bless themselves in Him, and in Him shall they glory.
3 For thus says the LORD to the men of Ju'dah and Je-ru'sa-lem, Break up your fallow ground, and sow not among thorns.
4 Circumcise yourselves to the LORD, and take away the foreskins of your heart, you men of Ju'dah and inhabitants of Je-ru'sa-lem: less My fury come forth like fire, and burn that none can quench *it*, because of the evil of your doings.
5 Declare you in Ju'dah, and publish in Je-ru'sa-lem; and say, Blow you the trumpet in the land: cry, gather together, and say, Assemble yourselves, and let us go into the defenced cities.   unfortified
6 Set up the standard toward Zi'on: retire, stay not: for I will bring evil from the north, and a great destruction.   banner
7 The lion is come up from his thicket, and the destroyer of the Gen'tiles is on his way; he is gone forth from his place to make your land desolate; *and* your cities shall be laid waste, without an inhabitant.
8 For this gird you with sackcloth, la-ment and howl: for the fierce anger of the LORD is not turned back from us.
9 And it shall come to pass at that day, says the LORD, *that* the heart of the king shall perish, and the heart of the princes; and the priests shall be astonished, and the prophets shall wonder.
10 Then said I, Ah, Lord GOD! surely You have greatly deceived this people and Je-ru'sa-lem, saying, You shall have peace; whereas the sword reaches to the soul.   Adonay^p.f. Jehovah
11 At that time shall it be said to this people and to Je-ru'sa-lem, A dry wind of the high places in the wilderness toward the daughter of My people, not to fan, nor to cleanse,
12 *Even* a full wind from those *places* shall come to Me: now also will I give sentence against them.   pronounce judgment
13 Behold, he shall come up as clouds, and his chariots *shall be* as a whirlwind: his horses are swifter than eagles. Woe to us! for we are spoiled.   robbed
14 O Je-ru'sa-lem, wash your heart from wickedness, that you may be saved. How long shall your vain thoughts lodge within you?   wicked
15 For a voice declares from Dan, and publishes affliction from mount E'phra-im.   proclaims
16 Make you mention to the nations; behold, publish against Je-ru'sa-lem, *that* watchers come from a far country, and give out their voice against the cities of Ju'dah.
17 As keepers of a field, are they against her round about; because she has

been rebellious against Me, says the LORD.

18 Your way and your doings have procured these *things* to you; this *is* your wickedness, because it is bitter, because it reaches to your heart.

19 My <u>bowels</u>, my <u>bowels</u>! I am pained at my very heart; my heart makes a noise in me; I cannot hold my peace, because you have heard, O my soul, the sound of the trumpet, the alarm of war.   i.e., the emotions

20 Destruction upon destruction is cried; for the whole land is <u>spoiled</u>: suddenly are my tents spoiled, *and* my curtains in a moment.   robbed

21 How long shall I see the <u>standard</u>, *and* hear the sound of the trumpet?   banner

22 For My people *are* foolish, they have not known Me; they *are* <u>sottish</u> children, and they have <u>none</u> understanding: they *are* wise to do evil, but to do good they have no knowledge.   stupid - no

23 I beheld the earth, and, lo, *it was* without form, and void; and the heavens, and they *had* no light.

24 I beheld the mountains, and, lo, they trembled, and all the hills moved lightly.

25 I beheld, and, lo, *there was* no man, and all the birds of the heavens were fled.

26 I beheld, and, lo, the fruitful place *was* a wilderness, and all the cities thereof were broken down at the presence of the LORD, *and* by His fierce anger.

27 For thus has the LORD said, The whole land shall be <u>desolate</u>; yet will I not make a full end.   a waste

28 For this shall the earth mourn, and the heavens above be black: because I have spoken *it*, I have purposed *it*, and will not repent, neither will I turn back from it.

29 The whole city shall flee for the noise of the horsemen and bowmen; they shall go into thickets, and climb up upon the rocks: every city *shall be* forsaken, and not a man dwell therein.

30 And *when* you *are* <u>spoiled</u>, what will you do? Though you cloth yourself with crimson, though you deck you with ornaments of gold, though you <u>rent</u> your face with painting, in vain shall you make yourself fair; *your* lovers will despise you, they will seek your life.   robbed - cover

31 For I have heard a voice as of a woman in travail, *and* the anguish as of her that brings forth her first child, the voice of the daughter of Zi'on, *that* bewails herself, *that* spreads her hands, *saying*, Woe *is* me now! for my soul is <u>wearied</u> because of murderers.   faint

CHAPTER 5

RUN you to and fro through the streets of Je-ru'sa-lem, and see now, and know, and seek in the broad places thereof, if you can find a man, if there be *any* that <u>executes</u> <u>judgment</u>, that seeks the truth; and I will pardon <u>it</u>.   does justice - i.e., Jerusalem

2 And though they say, The LORD lives; surely they swear falsely.

3 O LORD, *are* not Your eyes upon

the truth? You have <u>stricken</u> them, but they have not grieved; You have <u>consumed</u> them, *but* they have refused to receive correction: they have made their faces harder than a rock; they have refused to return. smitten - crushed

4 Therefore I said, Surely these *are* poor; they are foolish: for they know not the way of the LORD, *nor* the <u>judgment</u> of their <u>God</u>. justice - Elohim^{p.f.}

5 I will get me to the great men, and will speak to them; for they have known the way of the LORD, *and* the judgment of their <u>God</u>: but these have altogether broken the yoke, *and* burst the bonds.

6 Wherefore a lion out of the forest shall slay them, *and* a wolf of the evenings shall <u>spoil</u> them, a leopard shall watch over their cities: every one that goes out from there shall be torn in pieces: because their transgressions are many, *and* their backslidings are increased. destroy

7 How shall I pardon you for this? your children have forsaken Me, and sworn by *them that are* no gods: when I had fed them to the full, they then committed adultery, and assembled themselves <u>by troops in</u> the harlots' houses. and thronged to

8 They were *as* fed horses in the morning: every one neighed after his neighbor's wife.

9 Shall I not <u>visit</u> for these *things*? says the LORD: and shall not My soul be avenged on such a nation as this? i.e., punish

10 Go you up upon her walls, and destroy; but make not a full end: take away her battlements; for they *are* not the LORD's.

11 For the house of Is'ra-el and the house of Ju'dah have dealt very treacherously against Me, says the LORD.

12 They have belied the LORD, and said, *It is* not He; neither shall evil come upon us; neither shall we see sword nor famine:

13 And the prophets shall become wind, and the word *is* not in them: thus shall it be done to them.

14 Wherefore thus says the <u>LORD</u> <u>God of hosts</u>, Because you speak this word, behold, I will make My words in your mouth fire, and this people wood, and it shall devour them. Jehovah^{s.f.} Elohe Tsebaoth

15 Lo, I will bring a nation upon you from far, O house of Is'ra-el, says the LORD: it *is* a mighty nation, it *is* an ancient nation, a nation whose language you know not, neither understand what they say.

16 Their quiver *is* as an open <u>sepulcher</u>, they *are* all mighty men. tomb

17 And they shall eat up your harvest, and your bread, *which* your sons and your daughters should eat: they shall eat up your flocks and your herds: they shall eat up your vines and your fig trees: they shall impoverish your <u>fenced</u> cities, wherein you trusted, with the sword. fortified

18 Nevertheless in those days, says the LORD, I will not make a full end with you.

19 And it shall come to pass, when you shall say, Why does the LORD our <u>God</u> all these *things* to us? then

shall you answer them, Like as you have forsaken Me, and served <u>strange</u> gods in your land, so shall you serve strangers in a land *that is* not yours. Elohim[p.f.] - foreign

20 Declare this in the house of Ja'cob, and publish it in Ju'dah, saying,

21 Hear now this, O foolish people, and without understanding; which have eyes, and see not; which have ears, and hear not: LUKE 8:10

22 Fear you not me? says the LORD: will you not tremble at My presence, which have placed the sand *for* the bound of the sea by a perpetual decree, that it cannot pass it: and though the waves thereof toss themselves, yet can they not prevail; though they roar, yet can they not pass over it?

23 But this people has a revolting and a rebellious heart; they are revolted and gone.

24 Neither say they in their heart, Let us now <u>fear</u> the LORD our <u>God</u>, that gives rain, both the former and the latter, in His season: He reserves to us the appointed weeks of the harvest.   revere - Elohim[p.f.]

25 Your iniquities have turned away these *things*, and your sins have <u>withholden</u> good *things* from you.   withheld

26 For among My people are found wicked *men*: they lay wait, as he that sets <u>snares</u>; they set a trap, they catch men.   lures

27 As a cage is full of birds, so *are* their houses full of deceit: therefore they are become great, and <u>waxen</u> rich.

28 They are <u>waxen</u> fat, they shine: yea, they <u>overpass</u> the deeds of the wicked: they judge not the cause, the cause of the fatherless, yet they prosper; and the right of the needy do they not judge.   become - excel in

29 Shall I not <u>visit</u> for these *things*? says the LORD: shall not My soul be avenged on such a nation as this?   i.e., punish

30 <u>A wonderful</u> and horrible thing is committed in the land;   An appalling

31 The prophets prophesy falsely, and the priests bear rule by their means; and My people love *to have it* so: and what will you do in the end thereof?

CHAPTER 6

O YOU children of Ben'ja-min, gather yourselves to flee out of the midst of Je-ru'sa-lem, and blow the trumpet in Te-ko'a, and set up a sign of fire in Beth-hac'ce-rem: for evil appears out of the north, and great destruction.

2 I have likened the daughter of Zi'on to a comely and delicate *woman*.

3 The shepherds with their flocks shall come to her; they shall <u>pitch</u> *their* tents against her round about; they shall feed every one in his place.   set up

4 Prepare you war against her; arise, and let us go up at noon. Woe to us! for the day goes away, for the shadows of the evening are stretched out.

5 Arise, and let us go by night, and let us destroy her palaces.

6 For thus has the LORD <u>of hosts</u> said, <u>Hew</u> you down trees, and <u>cast a mount</u> against Je-ru'sa-lem: this *is* the city to be visited; she *is* wholly oppression in the midst of her.   Jehovah[s.f.] Tsebaoth - Cut - i.e., build fortifications

7 As a fountain casts out her waters, so she casts out her wickedness: violence and spoil is heard in her; before Me continually *is* <u>grief</u> and wounds.   _{suffering}

8 Be you instructed, O Je-ru'salem, less My soul depart from you; less I make you desolate, a land not inhabited.

9 Thus said the <u>LORD of hosts,</u> They shall <u>throughly glean</u> the remnant of Is'ra-el as a vine: turn back your hand as a grapegatherer into the baskets.

Jehovah^{s.f.} Tsebaoth - i.e., pick clean

10 To whom shall I speak, and give warning, that they may hear? behold, their ear *is* uncircumcised, and they cannot hearken: behold, the word of the LORD is to them a reproach; they have no delight in it.

11 Therefore I am full of the fury of the LORD; I am weary with holding in: I will pour it out upon the children abroad, and upon the assembly of young men together: for even the husband with the wife shall be taken, the aged with *him that is* full of days.

12 And their houses shall be turned to others, *with their* fields and wives together: for I will stretch out My hand upon the inhabitants of the land, says the LORD.

13 For from the least of them even to the greatest of them every one *is* given to covetousness; and from the prophet even to the priest every one deals falsely.

14 They have healed also the hurt *of the daughter* of My people <u>slightly</u>, say-ing, Peace, peace; when *there is* no peace.   _{i.e., superficially}

15 Were they ashamed when they had committed <u>abomination</u>? nay, they were not at all ashamed, neither could they blush: therefore they shall fall among them that fall: at the time *that* I visit them they shall be cast down, says the LORD.   _{detestable acts}

16 Thus says the LORD, Stand you in the ways, and see, and ask for the old paths, where *is* the good way, and walk therein, and you shall find rest for your souls. But they said, We will not walk *therein*.

17 Also I set watchmen over you, *saying*, Hearken to the sound of the trumpet. But they said, We will not hearken.

18 Therefore hear, you nations, and <u>know</u>, O congregation, what *is* among them.   _{realize}

19 Hear, O earth: behold, I will bring evil upon this people, *even* the fruit of their thoughts, because they have not hearkened to My words, nor to My law, but rejected it.

20 To what purpose comes there to Me incense from She'ba, and the sweet cane from a far country? your burned offerings *are* not acceptable, nor your sacrifices sweet to Me.

21 Therefore thus says the LORD, Behold, I will lay stumblingblocks before this people, and the fathers and the sons together shall fall upon them; the neighbor and his friend shall perish.

22 Thus says the LORD, Behold, a people comes from the north country, and a great nation shall be raised from the <u>sides</u> of the earth.   _{i.e., uttermost parts}

23 They shall lay hold on bow and spear; they *are* cruel, and have no mercy; their voice roars like the sea; and they ride upon horses, set in array as men for war against you, O daughter of Zi'on.

24 We have heard the fame thereof: our hands <u>wax</u> feeble: anguish has taken hold of us, *and* pain, as of a woman in travail. _{grow}

25 Go not forth into the field, nor walk by the way; for the sword of the enemy *and* fear *is* on every side.

26 O daughter of My people, gird *you* with sackcloth, and wallow yourself in ashes: make you mourning, *as for* an only son, most bitter lamentation: for the <u>spoiler</u> shall suddenly come upon us.   _{destroyer}

27 I have set you *for* a tower *and* a fortress among My people, that you may know and <u>try</u> their way.   _{test}

28 They *are* all grievous revolters, walking with slanders: *they are* brass and iron; they *are* all corrupters.

29 The bellows <u>are burned</u>, the lead is consumed of the fire; the <u>founder</u> melts in vain: for the wicked are not plucked away.   _{blow - metal worker}

30 <u>Reprobate</u> silver shall *men* call them, because the LORD has rejected them.   _{Rejected}

CHAPTER 7

T HE word that came to Jer-e-mi'ah from the LORD, saying,

2 Stand in the gate of the LORD's house, and proclaim there this word, and say, Hear the word of the LORD, all

you of Ju'dah, that enter in at these gates to worship the LORD.

3 Thus says the <u>LORD of hosts</u>, the <u>God</u> of Is'ra-el, Amend your ways and your doings, and I will cause you to dwell in this place.

_{Jehovah^{s.f.} Tsebaoth - Elohim^{p.f.}}

4 Trust you not in lying words, saying, The temple of the LORD, The temple of the LORD, The temple of the LORD, *are* these.

5 For if you throughly amend your ways and your doings; if you throughly execute <u>judgment</u> between a man and his neighbor;   _{justice}

6 *If* you oppress not the stranger, the fatherless, and the widow, and shed not innocent blood in this place, neither walk after other gods to your hurt:

7 Then will I cause you to dwell in this place, in the land that I gave to your fathers, for ever and ever.

8 Behold, you trust in lying words, that cannot profit.

9 Will you steal, murder, and commit adultery, and swear falsely, and burn incense to Ba'al, and walk after other gods whom you know not;

10 And come and stand before Me in this house, which is called by My name, and say, We are delivered to do all these <u>abominations</u>? _{detestable things}

11 Is this house, which is called by My name, become a den of robbers in your eyes? Behold, even I have seen *it*, says the LORD.   MATT. 21:13 MARK 11:17

12 But go you now to My place which *was* in Shi'loh, where I set My name at the first, and see what I did to it for the wickedness of My people Is'ra-el.

13 And now, because you have done all these works, says the LORD, and I spoke to you, rising up early and speaking, but you heard not; and I called you, but you answered not;

14 Therefore will I do to *this* house, which is called by My name, wherein you trust, and to the place which I gave to you and to your fathers, as I have done to Shi'loh.

15 And I will cast you out of My sight, as I have cast out all your brethren, *even* the whole seed of E'phra-im. people

16 Therefore pray not you for this people, neither lift up cry nor prayer for them, neither make intercession to Me: for I will not hear you.

17 See you not what they do in the cities of Ju'dah and in the streets of Je-ru'sa-lem?

18 The children gather wood, and the fathers kindle the fire, and the women knead *their* dough, to make cakes to the queen of heaven, and to pour out drink offerings to other gods, that they may provoke Me to anger.

probably Astarte, the moon-godess

19 Do they provoke Me to anger? says the LORD: *do they* not *provoke* themselves to the confusion of their own faces?

20 Therefore thus says the Lord GOD; Behold, My anger and My fury shall be poured out upon this place, upon man, and upon beast, and upon the trees of the field, and upon the fruit of the ground; and it shall burn, and shall not be quenched. Adonay^p.f. Jehovah

21 Thus says the LORD of hosts, the God of Is'ra-el; Put your burned offerings to your sacrifices, and eat flesh. Jehovah^s.f. Tsebaoth - Elohim^p.f.

22 For I spoke not to your fathers, nor commanded them in the day that I brought them out of the land of E'gypt, concerning burned offerings or sacrifices:

23 But this thing commanded I them, saying, Obey My voice, and I will be your God, and you shall be My people: and walk you in all the ways that I have commanded you, that it may be well to you.

24 But they hearkened not, nor inclined their ear, but walked in the counsels *and* in the imagination of their evil heart, and went backward, and not forward.

25 Since the day that your fathers came forth out of the land of E'gypt to this day I have even sent to you all My servants the prophets, daily rising up early and sending *them*:

26 Yet they hearkened not to Me, nor inclined their ear, but hardened their neck: they did worse than their fathers.

27 Therefore you shall speak all these words to them; but they will not hearken to you: you shall also call to them; but they will not answer you.

28 But you shall say to them, This *is* a nation that obeys not the voice of the LORD their God, nor receives correction: truth is perished, and is cut off from their mouth. Elohim^p.f.

29 Cut off your hair, *O* Je-ru'sa-lem, and cast *it* away, and take up a

lamentation on high places; for the LORD has rejected and forsaken the generation of His wrath.

30 For the children of Ju'dah have done evil in My sight, says the LORD: they have set their <u>abominations</u> in the house which is called by My name, to pollute it. detestable things

31 And they have built the high places of To'phet, which *is* in the valley of the son of Hin'nom, to burn their sons and their daughters in the fire; which I commanded *them* not, neither came it into My heart.

32 Therefore, behold, the days come, says the LORD, that it shall no more be called To'phet, nor the valley of the son of Hin'nom, but the valley of slaughter: for they shall bury in To'phet, till there be no place.

33 And the <u>carcases</u> of this people shall be meat for the fowls of the heaven, and for the beasts of the earth; and none shall <u>fray</u> *them* away. corpses - frighten

34 Then will I cause to cease from the cities of Ju'dah, and from the streets of Je-ru'sa-lem, the voice of mirth, and the voice of gladness, the voice of the bridegroom, and the voice of the bride: for the land shall be desolate.

CHAPTER 8

AT that time, says the LORD, they shall bring out the bones of the kings of Ju'dah, and the bones of his princes, and the bones of the priests, and the bones of the prophets, and the bones of the inhabitants of Je-ru'sa-lem, out of their graves:

2 And they shall spread them before the sun, and the moon, and all the host of heaven, whom they have loved, and whom they have served, and after whom they have walked, and whom they have sought, and whom they have worshiped: they shall not be gathered, nor be buried; they shall be for dung upon the face of the earth.

3 And death shall be chosen rather than life by all the <u>residue of them</u> that remain of this evil family, which remain in all the places where I have driven them, says the LORD of hosts.

remnant - Jehovah^{s.f.} Tsebaoth

4 Moreover you shall say to them, Thus says the LORD; Shall they fall, and not arise? shall he turn away, and not return?

5 Why *then* is this people of Je-ru'sa-lem slidden back by a perpetual backsliding? they hold fast deceit, they refuse to return.

6 I hearkened and heard, *but* they spoke not aright: no man repented him of his wickedness, saying, What have I done? every one turned to his course, as the horse rushes into the battle.

7 Yea, the stork in the heaven knows her appointed times; and the <u>turtle</u> and the crane and the swallow observe the time of their coming; but My people know not the <u>judgment</u> of the LORD. turtledove - justice

8 How do you say, We *are* wise, and the law of the LORD *is* with us? Lo, certainly in vain made He *it*; the pen of the scribes *is* <u>in vain</u>. deceitful

9 The wise *men* are ashamed, they are dismayed and taken: lo, they have re-

jected the word of the LORD; and what wisdom *is* in them?

10 Therefore will I give their wives to others, *and* their fields to them that shall inherit *them*: for every one from the least even to the greatest is given to covetousness, from the prophet even to the priest every one deals falsely.

11 For they have healed the hurt of the daughter of My people slightly, saying, Peace, peace; when *there is* no peace.

12 Were they ashamed when they had committed <u>abomination</u>? nay, they were not at all ashamed, neither could they blush: therefore shall they fall among them that fall: in the time of their visitation they shall be cast down, says the LORD.   detestable acts

13 I will surely consume them, says the LORD: *there shall be* no grapes on the vine, nor figs on the fig tree, and the leaf shall fade; and *the things that* I have given them shall pass away from them.   MATT. 21:19

14 Why do we sit still? assemble yourselves, and let us enter <u>into the</u> <u>defenced</u> cities, and let us be silent there: for the LORD our <u>God</u> has put us to silence, and given us <u>water of gall</u> to drink, because we have sinned against the LORD.

not fortified - Elohim^{p.f.} - poisoned water

15 We looked for peace, but no good *came; and* for a time of health, and behold trouble!

16 The snorting of his horses was heard from Dan: the whole land trembled at the sound of the neighing of his strong ones; for they are come, and

have devoured the land, and all that is in it; the city, and those that dwell therein.

17 For, behold, I will send serpents, <u>cockatrices</u>, among you, which *will* not *be* charmed, and they shall bite you, says the LORD.   adders

18 *When* I would comfort myself against sorrow, my heart *is* faint in me.

19 Behold the voice of the cry of the daughter of my people because of them that dwell in a far country: *Is* not the LORD in Zi'on? *is* not her king in her? Why have they provoked Me to anger with their <u>graven images</u>, *and* with strange vanities?   i.e. carved idols

20 The harvest is past, the summer is ended, and we are not saved.

21 For the hurt of the daughter of my people am I hurt; I am black; astonishment has taken hold on me.

22 *Is there* no balm in Gil'e-ad; *is there* no physician there? why then is not the health of the daughter of my people <u>recovered</u>?   restored

CHAPTER 9

OH that my head were waters, and my eyes a fountain of tears, that I might weep day and night for the slain of the daughter of my people!

2 Oh that I had in the wilderness a lodging place of wayfaring men; that I might leave my people, and go from them! for they *be* all adulterers, an assembly of <u>treacherous</u> men.   deceitful

3 And they bend their tongues *like* their bow *for* lies: but they are not valiant for the truth upon the earth; for

they proceed from evil to evil, and they know not Me, says the LORD.   respect

4 Take you heed every one of his neighbor, and trust you not in any brother: for every brother will utterly supplant, and every neighbor will walk with slanders.   craftily

5 And they will deceive every one his neighbor, and will not speak the truth: they have taught their tongue to speak lies, *and* weary themselves to commit iniquity.   sinning

6 Your habitation *is* in the midst of deceit; through deceit they refuse to know Me, says the LORD.

7 Therefore thus says the LORD of hosts, Behold, I will melt them, and try them; for how shall I do for the daughter of My people?

Jehovah^{s.f.} Tsebaoth - refine(by fire) - test

8 Their tongue *is as* an arrow shot out; it speaks deceit: *one* speaks peaceably to his neighbor with his mouth, but in heart he lays his wait.

9 Shall I not visit them for these *things*? says the LORD: shall not My soul be avenged on such a nation as this?

10 For the mountains will I take up a weeping and wailing, and for the habitations of the wilderness a lamentation, because they are burned up, so that none can pass through *them*; neither can *men* hear the voice of the cattle; both the fowl of the heavens and the beast are fled, they are gone.   pastures - desolate

11 And I will make Je-ru'sa-lem heaps, *and* a den of dragons; and I will make the cities of Ju'dah desolate, without an inhabitant.   ruins - jackals

12 Who *is* the wise man, that may understand this? and *who is he* to whom the mouth of the LORD has spoken, that he may declare it, for what the land perish *and* is burned up like a wilderness, that none passes through?

13 And the LORD says, Because they have forsaken My law which I set before them, and have not obeyed My voice, neither walked therein;

14 But have walked after the imagination of their own heart, and after Ba'al-im, which their fathers taught them: stubborness

15 Therefore thus says the LORD of hosts, the God of Is'ra-el; Behold, I will feed them, *even* this people, with wormwood, and give them water of gall to drink.

REV. 8:11   Jehovah^{s.f.} Tsebaoth - Elohim^{p.f.} - poison

16 I will scatter them also among the heathen, whom neither they nor their fathers have known: and I will send a sword after them, till I have consumed them.

17 Thus says the LORD of hosts, Consider you, and call for the mourning women, that they may come; and send for cunning *women*, that they may come: i.e., skilled (at mourning)

18 And let them make haste, and take up a wailing for us, that our eyes may run down with tears, and our eyelids gush out with waters.

19 For a voice of wailing is heard out of Zi'on, How are we spoiled! we are greatly confounded, because we have forsaken the land, because our dwellings have cast *us* out.

20 Yet hear the word of the LORD, O you women, and let your ear receive the

word of His mouth, and teach your daughters wailing, and every one her neighbor lamentation.

21 For death is come up into our windows, *and* is entered into our palaces, to cut off the children from without, *and* the young men from the streets.

22 Speak, Thus says the LORD, Even the carcases of men shall fall as dung upon the open field, and as the handful after the harvestman, and none shall gather *them*.

23 Thus says the LORD, Let not the wise *man* glory in his wisdom, neither let the mighty *man* glory in his might, let not the rich *man* glory in his riches:

24 But let him that glories glory in this, that he understands and knows Me, that I *am* the LORD which exercise lovingkindness, judgment, and righteousness, in the earth: for in these *things* I delight, says the LORD.

1 COR. 1:31 2 COR. 10:17 justice

25 Behold, the days come, says the LORD, that I will punish all *them which are* circumcised with the uncircumcised; ROM. 2:25

26 E'gypt, and Ju'dah, and E'dom, and the children of Am'mon, and Mo'ab, and all *that are* in the utmost corners, that dwell in the wilderness: for all *these* nations *are* uncircumcised, and all the house of Is'ra-el *are* uncircumcised in the heart.

CHAPTER 10

HEAR you the word which the LORD speaks to you, O house of Is'ra-el:

2 Thus says the LORD, Learn not the way of the heathen, and be not dismayed at the signs of heaven; for the heathen are dismayed at them.

3 For the customs of the people *are* vain: for *one* cuts a tree out of the forest, the work of the hands of the workman, with the ax. a delusion

4 They deck it with silver and with gold; they fasten it with nails and with hammers, that it move not.

5 They *are* upright as the palm tree, but speak not: they must needs be borne, because they cannot go. Be not afraid of them; for they cannot do evil, neither also *is it* in them to do good. carried - i.e., own power

6 Forasmuch as *there is* none like to You, O LORD; You *are* great, and Your name *is* great in might.

7 Who would not fear You, O King of nations? for to You does it appertain: forasmuch as among all the wise *men* of the nations, and in all their kingdoms, *there is* none like to You. REV. 15:4 revere

8 But they are altogether brutish and foolish: the stock *is* a doctrine of vanities. i.e., stupid

9 Silver spread into plates is brought from Tar'shish, and gold from U'phaz, the work of the workman, and of the hands of the founder: blue and purple *is* their clothing: they *are* all the work of cunning *men*. goldsmith - skillful

10 But the LORD *is* the true God, He *is* the living God, and an everlasting king: at His anger the earth shall tremble, and the nations shall not be able to abide His indignation. Elohim[p-f] eternal

11 Thus shall you say to them, The gods that have not made the heavens

and the earth, *even* they shall perish from the earth, and from under these heavens.

12 He has made the earth by His power, He has established the world by His wisdom, and has stretched out the heavens by His discretion.

13 When He utters His voice, *there is* a multitude of waters in the heavens, and He causes the vapors to ascend from the ends of the earth; He makes lightnings with rain, and brings forth the wind out of His treasures.

14 Every man is <u>brutish</u> in *his* knowledge: every <u>founder</u> is confounded by the <u>graven image</u>: for his molten image *is* falsehood, and *there is* no breath in them.   i.e., stupid - goldsmith - idol

15 They *are* vanity, *and* the work of <u>errors</u>: in the time of their visitation they shall perish.   mockery

16 The portion of Ja'cob *is* not like them: for He *is* the former of all *things*; and Is'ra-el *is* the <u>rod</u> of His inheritance: The <u>Lord of hosts</u> *is* His name.   tribe - Jehovah^{s.f.} Tsebaoth

17 Gather up your wares out of the land, O inhabitant of the fortress.

18 For thus says the Lord, Behold, I will sling out the inhabitants of the land at this once, and will distress them, that they may find *it so.*

19 Woe is me for my hurt! my wound is grievous: but I said, Truly this *is* a grief, and I must bear it.

20 My tabernacle is spoiled, and all my cords are broken: my children are gone forth of me, and they *are* not: *there is* none to stretch forth my tent any more, and to set up my curtains.

21 For the <u>pastors</u> are become <u>brutish</u>, and have not sought the Lord: therefore they shall not prosper, and all their flocks shall be scattered.   shepherds - i.e., stupid

22 Behold, the <u>noise</u> of <u>the bruit</u> is come, and a great commotion out of the north country, to make the cities of Ju'dah desolate, *and* a den of <u>dragons</u>.   sound - a report - jackals

23 O Lord, I know that the way of man *is* not in himself: *it is* not in man that walks to direct his steps.

24 O Lord, correct me, but with judgment; not in Your anger, less You bring me to nothing.

25 Pour out Your fury upon the heathen that know You not, and upon the families that call not on Your name: for they have eaten up Ja'cob, and devoured him, and consumed him, and have made his habitation desolate.

CHAPTER 11

THE word that came to Jer-e-mi'ah from the Lord, saying,

2 Hear you the words of this <u>covenant</u>, and speak to the men of Ju'dah, and to the inhabitants of Je-ru'sa-lem;   agreement

3 And say you to them, Thus says the <u>Lord God</u> of Is'ra-el; Cursed *be* the man that obeys not the words of this <u>covenant</u>,   Jehovah^{s.f.} Elohim^{p.f.}

4 Which I commanded your fathers in the day *that* I brought them forth out of the land of E'gypt, from the iron furnace, saying, Obey My voice, and do them, according to all which I com-

mand you: so shall you be My people, and I will be your God: Elohim^{p.f.} *Elohim*

5 That I may <u>perform</u> the oath which I have sworn to your fathers, to give them a land flowing with milk and honey, as *it is* this day. Then answered I, and said, So be it, O LORD. fulfill

6 Then the LORD said to me, Proclaim all these words in the cities of Ju'dah, and in the streets of Je-ru'sa-lem, saying, Hear you the words of this <u>covenant</u>, and do them. agreement

7 For I earnestly protested to your fathers in the day *that* I brought them up out of the land of E'gypt, *even* to this day, rising early and protesting, saying, Obey My voice.

8 Yet they obeyed not, nor inclined their ear, but walked every one in the <u>imagination</u> of their evil heart: therefore I will bring upon them all the words of this <u>covenant</u>, which I commanded *them* to do; but they did *them* not. stubborness - agreement

9 And the LORD said to me, A conspiracy is found among the men of Ju'dah, and among the inhabitants of Je-ru'sa-lem.

10 They are turned back to the <u>iniquities</u> of their forefathers, which refused to hear My words; and they went after other gods to serve them: the house of Is'ra-el and the house of Ju'dah have broken My <u>covenant</u> which I made with their fathers. sins

11 Therefore thus says the LORD, Behold, I will bring evil upon them, which they shall not be able to escape; and though they shall cry to Me, I will not hearken to them.

12 Then shall the cities of Ju'dah and inhabitants of Je-ru'sa-lem go, and cry to the gods to whom they offer incense: but they shall not save them at all in the time of their trouble.

13 For *according to* the number of your cities were your gods, O Ju'dah; and *according to* the number of the streets of Je-ru'sa-lem have you set up altars to *that* shameful thing, *even* altars to burn incense to Ba'al.

14 Therefore pray not you for this people, neither lift up a cry or prayer for them: for I will not hear *them* in the time that they cry to Me for their trouble.

15 What has My beloved to do in My house, *seeing* she has <u>wrought lewdness</u> with many, and the holy flesh is passed from you? when you do evil, then you rejoice. done evil things

16 The LORD called your name, A green olive tree, fair, *and* of goodly fruit: with the noise of a great tumult He has kindled fire upon it, and the branches of it are broken.

17 For the LORD of hosts, that planted you, has pronounced evil against you, for the evil of the house of Is'ra-el and of the house of Ju'dah, which they have done against themselves to provoke Me to anger in offering incense to Ba'al. Jehovah^{s.f.} Tsebaoth

18 And the LORD has given me knowledge *of it*, and I know *it*: then You shows me their doings.

19 But I *was* like a lamb *or* an ox *that* is brought to the slaughter; and I knew not that they had devised devices against me, *saying*, Let us destroy the

tree with the fruit thereof, and let us cut him off from the land of the living, that his name may be no more remembered.

20 But, O Lord of hosts, that judges righteously, that tries the reins and the heart, let me see Your vengeance on them: for to You have I revealed my cause.   Jehovah^{s.f.} Tsebaoth

21 Therefore thus says the Lord of the men of An'a-thoth, that seek your life, saying, Prophesy not in the name of the Lord, that you die not by our hand:

22 Therefore thus says the Lord of hosts, Behold, I will punish them: the young men shall die by the sword; their sons and their daughters shall die by famine:

23 And there shall be no remnant of them: for I will bring evil upon the men of An'a-thoth, *even* the year of their visitation.   i.e., judgment

CHAPTER 12

RIGHTEOUS *are* You, O Lord, when I plead with You: yet let me talk with You of *Your* judgments: Why does the way of the wicked prosper? *why* are all they happy that deal very treacherously?

2 You have planted them, yea, they have taken root: they grow, yea, they bring forth fruit: You *are* near in their mouth, and far from their reins.   MATT. 15:8 i.e., heart

3 But You, O Lord, know me: You have seen me, and tried my heart toward You: pull them out like sheep for the slaughter, and prepare them for the day of slaughter.   tested

4 How long shall the land mourn, and the herbs of every field wither, for the wickedness of them that dwell therein? the beasts are consumed, and the birds; because they said, He shall not see our last end.

5 If you have run with the footmen, and they have wearied you, then how can you contend with horses? and *if* in the land of peace, *wherein* you trusted, *they wearied you*, then how will you do in the swelling of Jordan?

6 For even your brethren, and the house of your father, even they have dealt treacherously with you; yea, they have called a multitude after you: believe them not, though they speak fair words to you.

7 I have forsaken My house, I have left My heritage; I have given the dearly beloved of My soul into the hand of her enemies.

8 My heritage is to Me as a lion in the forest; it cries out against Me: therefore have I hated it.   despised

9 My heritage *is* to Me *as* a speckled bird, the birds round about *are* against her; come you, assemble all the beasts of the field, come to devour.

10 Many pastors have destroyed My vineyard, they have trodden My portion under foot, they have made My pleasant portion a desolate wilderness.

11 They have made it desolate, *and being* desolate it mourns to Me; the whole land is made desolate, because no man lays *it* to heart.

12 The spoilers are come upon all high places through the wilderness: for the sword of the Lord shall devour

from the *one* end of the land even to the *other* end of the land: no flesh shall have peace. destroyers

13 They have sown wheat, but shall reap thorns: they have put themselves to pain, *but* shall not profit: and they shall be ashamed of your <u>revenues</u> because of the fierce anger of the LORD. harvest

14 Thus says the LORD against all My evil neighbors, that touch the inheritance which I have caused My people Is'ra-el to inherit; Behold, I will pluck them out of their land, and pluck out the house of Ju'dah from among them.

15 And it shall come to pass, after that I have plucked them out I will return, and have compassion on them, and will bring them again, every man to his heritage, and every man to his land.

16 And it shall come to pass, if they will diligently learn the ways of My people, to swear by My name, The LORD lives; as they taught My people to swear by Ba'al; then shall they be built in the midst of My people.

17 But if they will not obey, I will utterly pluck up and destroy that nation, says the LORD.

CHAPTER 13

THUS says the LORD to me, Go and get you a linen <u>girdle</u>, and put it upon your loins, and put it not in water. waistband

2 So I got a <u>girdle</u> according to the word of the LORD, and put *it* on my loins.

3 And the word of the LORD came to me the second time, saying,

4 Take the <u>girdle</u> that you have <u>got</u>, which *is* upon your loins, and arise, go to Eu-phra'tes, and hide it there in a hole of the rock. waistband - bought

5 So I went, and hid it by Eu-phra'tes, as the LORD commanded me.

6 And it came to pass after many days, that the LORD said to me, Arise, go to Eu-phra'tes, and take the <u>girdle</u> from there, which I commanded you to hide there.

7 Then I went to Eu-phra'tes, and digged, and took the <u>girdle</u> from the place where I had hid it: and, behold, the <u>girdle</u> was marred, it was profitable for nothing.

8 Then the word of the LORD came to me, saying,

9 Thus says the LORD, After this manner will I <u>mar</u> the pride of Ju'dah, and the great pride of Je-ru'sa-lem. destroy

10 This evil people, which refuse to hear My words, which walk in the <u>imagination</u> of their heart, and walk after other gods, to serve them, and to worship them, shall even be as this <u>girdle</u>, which is good for nothing. stubbornness - waistband

11 For as the <u>girdle</u> clings to the loins of a man, so have I caused to cling to me the whole house of Is'ra-el and the whole house of Ju'dah, says the LORD; that they might be to Me for a people, and for a name, and for a praise, and for a glory: but they would not hear.

12 Therefore you shall speak to them this word; Thus says the <u>LORD</u>

God of Is'ra-el, Every bottle shall be filled with wine: and they shall say to you, Do we not certainly know that every bottle shall be filled with wine?   Jehovah^s.f. Elohim^p.f.

13 Then shall you say to them, Thus says the LORD, Behold, I will fill all the inhabitants of this land, even the kings that sit upon Da'vid's throne, and the priests, and the prophets, and all the inhabitants of Je-ru'sa-lem, with drunkenness.

14 And I will dash them one against another, even the fathers and the sons together, says the LORD: I will not pity, nor spare, nor have mercy, but destroy them.

15 Hear you, and give ear; be not proud: for the LORD has spoken.

16 Give glory to the LORD your God, before He cause darkness, and before your feet stumble upon the dark mountains, and, while you look for light, He turn it into the shadow of death, *and* make *it* gross darkness. Elohim^p.f.

17 But if you will not hear it, my soul shall weep in secret places for *your* pride; and my eye shall weep sore, and run down with tears, because the LORD's flock is carried away captive.   indeed

18 Say to the king and to the queen, Humble yourselves, sit down: for your principalities shall come down, *even* the crown of your glory. chief places

19 The cities of the south shall be shut up, and none shall open *them*: Ju'dah shall be carried away captive all of it, it shall be wholly carried away captive.

20 Lift up your eyes, and behold them that come from the north: where *is* the flock *that* was given you, your beautiful flock?

21 What will you say when He shall punish you? for you have taught them *to be* captains, *and* as chief over you: shall not sorrows take you, as a woman in travail?

22 And if you say in your heart, Why come these things upon me? For the greatness of your iniquity are your skirts discovered, *and* your heels made bare.   uncovered

23 Can the E-thi-o'pi-an change his skin, or the leopard its spots? *then* may you also do good, that are accustomed to do evil.

24 Therefore will I scatter them as the stubble that passes away by the wind of the wilderness.

25 This *is* your lot, the portion of your measures from Me, says the LORD; because you have forgotten Me, and trusted in falsehood.

26 Therefore will I discover your skirts upon your face, that your shame may appear.

27 I have seen your adulteries, and your neighings, the lewdness of your whoredom, *and* your abominations on the hills in the fields. Woe to you, O Je-ru'sa-lem! will you not be made clean? when *shall it* once *be*?   detestable acts

CHAPTER 14

THE word of the LORD that came to Jer-e-mi'ah concerning the dearth.   drought

2 Ju'dah mourns, and the gates thereof languish; they are black to

the ground; and the cry of Je-ru'sa-lem is gone up.

3 And their nobles have sent their little ones to the waters: they came to the pits, *and* found no water; they returned with their vessels empty; they were ashamed and confounded, and covered their heads.

4 Because the ground is <u>chapt</u>, for there was no rain in the earth, the plowmen were ashamed, they covered their heads. _{cracked}

5 Yea, the <u>hind</u> also calved in the field, and forsook *it*, because there was no grass. _{doe}

6 And the wild asses did stand in the high places, they snuffed up the wind like <u>dragons</u>; their eyes <u>did fail</u>, because *there was* no grass. _{jackals - became weak}

7 O LORD, though our iniquities testify against us, do You *it* for Your name's sake: for our backslidings are many; we have sinned against You.

8 O the Hope of Is'ra-el, the Savior thereof in time of trouble, why should You be as a <u>stranger</u> in the land, and as a wayfaring man *that* turns aside to tarry for a night? _{temporary resident}

9 Why should You be as a man astonished, as a mighty man *that* cannot save? yet You, O LORD, *are* in the midst of us, and we <u>are called by</u> Your name; leave us not. _{bear}

10 Thus says the LORD to this people, Thus have they loved to wander, they have not <u>refrained</u> their feet, therefore the LORD does not accept them; He will now remember their iniquity, and visit their sins. _{restrained}

11 Then said the LORD to me, Pray not for this people for *their* good.

12 When they fast, I will not hear their cry; and when they offer burned offering and an oblation, I will not accept them: but I will consume them by the sword, and by the famine, and by the pestilence.

13 Then said I, Ah, <u>Lord GOD</u>! behold, the prophets say to them, You shall not see the sword, neither shall you have famine; but I will give you <u>assured</u> peace in this place. _{Adonay^{b.f.} Jehovah - true}

14 Then the LORD said to me, The prophets prophesy lies in My name: I sent them not, neither have I commanded them, neither spoke to them: they prophesy to you a false vision and <u>divination</u>, and a thing of nothing, and the deceit of their heart. _{insights}

15 Therefore thus says the LORD concerning the prophets that prophesy in My name, and I sent them not, yet they say, Sword and famine shall not be in this land; By sword and famine shall those prophets be consumed.

16 And the people to whom they prophesy shall be cast out in the streets of Je-ru'sa-lem because of the famine and the sword; and they shall have none to bury them, them, their wives, nor their sons, nor their daughters: for I will <u>pour</u> their wickedness upon them. _{bring}

17 Therefore you shall say this word to them; Let my eyes run down with tears night and day, and let them not cease: for the virgin daughter

of My people is broken with a great breach, with a very grievous blow.
18 If I go forth into the field, then behold the slain with the sword! and if I enter into the city, then behold them that are sick with famine! yea, both the prophet and the priest go about into a land that they know not.
19 Have You utterly rejected Ju'dah? has Your soul <u>loathed</u> Zi'on? why have You smitten us, and *there is* no healing for us? we looked for peace, and *there is* no good; and for the time of healing, and behold trouble!   despised

20 We acknowledge, O LORD, our wickedness, *and* the iniquity of our fathers: for we have sinned against You.

21 Do not abhor *us*, for Your name's sake, do not disgrace the throne of Your glory: remember, break not Your <u>covenant</u> with us.   agreement

22 Are there *any* among the vanities of the Gen'tiles that can cause rain? or can the heavens give showers? *are* not You He, O LORD our <u>God</u>? therefore we will wait upon You: for You have made all these *things*.   Elohim^p.f.

CHAPTER 15

THEN said the LORD to me, Though Mo'ses and Sam'u-el stood before Me, *yet* My mind *could* not *be* <u>toward</u> this people: cast *them* out of My sight, and let them go forth.   with
2 And it shall come to pass, if they say to you, Where shall we go forth? then you shall tell them, Thus says the LORD; Such as *are* for death, to death; and such as *are* for the sword, to the sword; and such as *are* for the famine, to the famine; and such as *are* for the captivity, to the captivity.
3 And I will appoint over them four <u>kinds</u>, says the LORD: the sword to slay, and the dogs to tear, and the fowls of the heaven, and the beasts of the earth, to devour and destroy.   i.e., kinds of doom
4 And I will cause them to be removed into all kingdoms of the earth, because of Ma-nas'seh the son of Hez-e-ki'ah king of Ju'dah, for *that* which he did in Je-ru'sa-lem.
5 For who shall have pity upon you, O Je-ru'sa-lem? or who shall bemoan you? or who shall go aside to ask how you do?
6 You have forsaken Me, says the LORD, you are gone backward: therefore will I stretch out My hand against you, and destroy you; I am weary with <u>repenting</u>.   grieving
7 And I will fan them with a fan in the gates of the land; I will bereave *them* of children, I will destroy My people, *since* they return not from their ways.
8 Their widows are increased to Me above the sand of the seas: I have brought upon them against the mother of the young men a spoiler at noonday: I have caused *him* to fall upon it suddenly, and terrors upon the city.
9 She that has borne seven languishs: she has given up the ghost; her sun is gone down while *it was* yet day: she has been ashamed and confounded: and the residue of them will I

deliver to the sword before their enemies, says the LORD.

10 Woe is me, my mother, that you have borne me a man of strife and a man of contention to the whole earth! I have neither lent on usury, nor men have lent to me on usury; *yet* every one of them does curse me.   land - interest

11 The LORD said, Verily it shall be well with your remnant; verily I will cause the enemy to entreat you *well* in the time of evil and in the time of affliction.   Truly

12 Shall iron break the northern iron and the steel?   bronze

13 Your substance and your treasures will I give to the spoil without price, and *that* for all your sins, even in all your borders.   plunderer

14 And I will make *you* to pass with your enemies into a land *which* you know not: for a fire is kindled in My anger, *which* shall burn upon you.   be enslaved

15 O LORD, You know: remember me, and visit me, and revenge me of my persecutors; take me not away in Your longsuffering: know that for Your sake I have suffered rebuke.   take notice of

16 Your words were found, and I did eat them; and Your word was to me the joy and rejoicing of my heart: for I am called by Your name, O LORD God of hosts.   Jehovah\ s.f. Elohe Tsebaoth

17 I sat not in the assembly of the mockers, nor rejoiced; I sat alone because of your hand: for You have filled me with indignation.   jokers

18 Why is my pain perpetual, and my wound incurable, *which* refuses to be healed? will You be altogether to me as a liar, *and as* waters *that* fail?

19 Therefore thus says the LORD, If you return, then will I bring you again, *and* you shall stand before Me: and if you take forth the precious from the vile, you shall be as My mouth: let them return to you; but return not you to them.   i.e., separate

20 And I will make you to this people a fenced brazen wall: and they shall fight against you, but they shall not prevail against you: for I *am* with you to save you and to deliver you, says the LORD.   fortified

21 And I will deliver you out of the hand of the wicked, and I will redeem you out of the hand of the terrible.

CHAPTER 16

THE word of the LORD came also to me, saying,

2 You shall not take you a wife, neither shall you have sons or daughters in this place.

3 For thus says the LORD concerning the sons and concerning the daughters that are born in this place, and concerning their mothers that bare them, and concerning their fathers that fathered them in this land;

4 They shall die of grievous deaths; they shall not be lamented; neither shall they be buried; *but* they shall be as dung upon the face of the earth: and they shall be consumed by the sword, and by famine; and their carcases shall be meat for the fowls of heaven, and for the beasts of the earth.

5 For thus says the LORD, Enter not into the house of mourning, neither go to lament nor bemoan them: for I have taken away My peace from this people, says the LORD, *even* lovingkindness and mercies.

6 Both the great and the small shall die in this land: they shall not be buried, neither shall *men* lament for them, nor cut themselves, nor make themselves bald for them:

7 Neither shall *men* <u>tear *themselves*</u> for them in mourning, to comfort them for the dead; neither shall *men* give them the cup of consolation to drink for their father or for their mother. <small>break bread</small>

8 You shall not also go into the house of feasting, to sit with them to eat and to drink.

9 For thus says the <u>LORD of hosts</u>, the God of Is'ra-el; Behold, I will cause to cease out of this place in your eyes, and in your days, the voice of <u>mirth</u>, and the voice of gladness, the voice of the bridegroom, and the voice of the bride. <small>Jehovah^{s.f.} Tsebaoth - rejoicing</small>

10 And it shall come to pass, when you shall show this people all these words, and they shall say to you, Why has the LORD pronounced all this great evil against us? or what *is* our <u>iniquity</u>? or what *is* our sin that we have committed against the LORD our <u>God</u>? <small>wrong - Elohim^{p.f.}</small>

11 Then shall you say to them, Because your fathers have forsaken Me, says the LORD, and have walked after other gods, and have served them, and have worshiped them, and have forsaken Me, and have not kept My law;

12 And you have done worse than your fathers; for, behold, you walk every one after the imagination of his evil heart, that they may not hearken to Me:

13 Therefore will I cast you out of this land into a land that you know not, *neither* you nor your fathers; and there shall you serve other gods day and night; where I will not show you favor.

14 Therefore, behold, the days come, says the LORD, that it shall no more be said, The LORD lives, that brought up the children of Is'ra-el out of the land of E'gypt;

15 But, The LORD lives, that brought up the children of Is'ra-el from the land of the north, and from all the lands where he had driven them: and I will bring them again into their land that I gave unto their fathers.

16 Behold, I will send for many <u>fishers</u>, says the LORD, and they shall fish them; and after will I send for many hunters, and they shall hunt them from every mountain, and from every hill, and out of the <u>holes</u> of the rocks. <small>fishermen - crevices</small>

17 For My eyes *are* upon all their ways: they are not hid from My face, neither is their <u>iniquity</u> hid from My eyes. <small>sin</small>

18 And first I will recompense their <u>iniquity</u> and their sin double; because they have defiled My land, they have filled My inheritance with the carcases of their detestable and abominable things. <small>wickedness</small>

19 O LORD, my strength, and my fortress, and my refuge in the day of affliction, the Gen'tiles shall come to You

G4T — 1371

from the ends of the earth, and shall say, Surely our fathers have inherited lies, vanity, and *things* wherein *there is* no profit.

20 Shall a man make gods to himself, and they *are* no gods?

21 Therefore, behold, I will this once cause them to know, I will cause them to know My hand and My might; and they shall know that My name *is* The LORD.

CHAPTER 17

THE sin of Ju'dah *is* written with a pen of iron, *and* with the point of a diamond: *it is* graven upon the table of their heart, and upon the horns of your altars;

2 Until their children remember their altars and their groves by the green trees upon the high hills.   shrines

3 O My mountain in the field, I will give you substance *and* all your treasures to the spoil, *and* your high places for sin, throughout all your borders.   i.e., own places - be plundered

4 And you, even yourself, shall discontinue from your heritage that I gave you; and I will cause you to serve your enemies in the land which you know not: for you have kindled a fire in My anger, *which* shall burn for ever.   loose

5 Thus says the LORD; Cursed *be* the man that trusts in man, and makes flesh his arm, and whose heart departs from the LORD.

6 For he shall be like the heath in the desert, and shall not see when good comes; but shall inhabit the parched places in the wilderness, *in* a salt land and not inhabited.   bush

7 Blessed *is* the man that trusts in the LORD, and whose hope the LORD is.

8 For he shall be as a tree planted by the waters, and *that* spreads out her roots by the river, and shall not see when heat comes, but her leaf shall be green; and shall not be careful in the year of drought, neither shall cease from yielding fruit.   dread

9 The heart *is* deceitful above all *things*, and desperately wicked: who can know it?

10 I the LORD search the heart, *I* try the reins, even to give every man according to his ways, *and* according to the fruit of his doings. ROM. 2:6   REV. 2:23   test the emotions - i.e., repay

11 *As* the partridge sits *on eggs*, and hatches *them* not; *so* he that gets riches, and not by right, shall leave them in the midst of his days, and at his end shall be a fool.

12 A glorious high throne from the beginning *is* the place of Our sanctuary.

13 O LORD, the hope of Is'ra-el, all that forsake You shall be ashamed, *and* they that depart from me shall be written in the earth, because they have forsaken the LORD, the fountain of living waters.

14 Heal me, O LORD, and I shall be healed; save me, and I shall be saved: for You *are* my praise.

15 Behold, they say to me, Where *is* the word of the LORD? let it come now.

16 As for me, I have not hastened from *being* a pastor to follow You: neither have I desired the woeful day;

You know: that which came out of my lips was *right* before You.   shepherd

17 Be not a terror to me: You *are* my hope in the day of evil.   refuge

18 Let them be confounded that persecute me, but let not me be confounded: let them be dismayed, but let not me be dismayed: bring upon them the day of evil, and destroy them with double destruction.   twofold

19 Thus said the LORD to me; Go and stand in the gate of the children of the people, whereby the kings of Ju'dah come in, and by the which they go out, and in all the gates of Je-ru'sa-lem;

20 And say to them, Hear you the word of the LORD, you kings of Ju'dah, and all Ju'dah, and all the inhabitants of Je-ru'sa-lem, that enter in by these gates:

21 Thus says the LORD; Take heed to yourselves, and bear no burden on the sabbath day, nor bring *it* in by the gates of Je-ru'sa-lem;   JOHN 5:10 rest

22 Neither carry forth a burden out of your houses on the sabbath day, neither do you any work, but hallow you the sabbath day, as I commanded your fathers.

23 But they obeyed not, neither inclined their ear, but made their neck stiff, that they might not hear, nor receive instruction.   i.e., listened - i.e., were rebellious

24 And it shall come to pass, if you diligently hearken to Me, says the LORD, to bring in no burden through the gates of this city on the sabbath day, but hallow the sabbath day, to do no work therein;   rest

25 Then shall there enter into the gates of this city kings and princes sitting upon the throne of Da'vid, riding in chariots and on horses, they, and their princes, the men of Ju'dah, and the inhabitants of Je-ru'sa-lem: and this city shall remain for ever.

26 And they shall come from the cities of Ju'dah, and from the places about Je-ru'sa-lem, and from the land of Ben'ja-min, and from the plain, and from the mountains, and from the south, bringing burned offerings, and sacrifices, and meat offerings, and incense, and bringing sacrifices of praise, to the house of the LORD.

27 But if you will not hearken to Me to hallow the sabbath day, and not to bear a burden, even entering in at the gates of Je-ru'sa-lem on the sabbath day; then will I kindle a fire in the gates thereof, and it shall devour the palaces of Je-ru'sa-lem, and it shall not be quenched.   make holy - rest

CHAPTER 18

THE word which came to Jer-e-mi'ah from the LORD, saying,

2 Arise, and go down to the potter's house, and there I will cause you to hear My words.

3 Then I went down to the potter's house, and, behold, he wrought a work on the wheels.   was making

4 And the vessel that he made of clay was marred in the hand of the potter: so he made it again another vessel, as seemed good to the potter to make *it*.

5 Then the word of the LORD came to me, saying,

6 O house of Is'ra-el, cannot I do with

you as this potter? says the LORD. Behold, as the clay *is* in the potter's hand, so *are* you in My hand, O house of Is'ra-el.

7 At *what* instant I shall speak concerning a nation, and concerning a kingdom, to pluck up, and to pull down, and to destroy *it*;

8 If that nation, against whom I have pronounced, turn from their evil, I will <u>repent</u> of the evil that I thought to do to them.   grieve

9 And *at what* instant I shall speak concerning a nation, and concerning a kingdom, to build and to plant *it*;

10 If it do evil in My sight, that it obey not My voice, then I will <u>repent</u> of the good, wherewith I said I would benefit them.

11 Now therefore go to, speak to the men of Ju'dah, and to the inhabitants of Je-ru'sa-lem, saying, Thus says the LORD; Behold, I <u>frame</u> evil against you, and devise a device against you: return you now every one from his evil way, and make your ways and your doings good.   fashion

12 And they said, There is no hope: but we will walk after our own <u>devices</u>, and we will every one do the <u>imagination</u> of his evil heart.

plans - stubbornness

13 Therefore thus says the LORD; Ask you now among the <u>heathen</u>, who has heard such things: the virgin of Is'ra-el has done a very horrible thing.   nations

14 Will *a man* leave the snow of Leb'a-non *which comes* from the rock of the field? *or* shall the cold flowing waters that come from another place be forsaken?

15 Because My people have forgotten Me, they have <u>burned incense</u> to vanity, and they have caused them to stumble in their ways *from* the ancient paths, to walk in paths, *in* a way not cast up;   worshiped

16 To make their land desolate, *and* a perpetual hissing; every one that passes thereby shall be astonished, and wag his head.

17 I will scatter them as with an east wind before <u>the</u> enemy; I will show them the back, and not the face, in the day of their calamity.   i.e., My

18 Then said they, Come, and let us devise devices against Jer-e-mi'ah; for <u>the</u> law shall not perish from the priest, nor counsel from the wise, nor <u>the</u> word from the prophet. Come, and let us smite him with the tongue, and let us not give heed to any of his words.

19 Give heed to me, O LORD, and hearken to the voice of them that contend with me.

20 Shall evil be recompensed for good? for they have dug a pit for my soul. Remember that I stood before You to speak good for them, *and* to turn away Your wrath from them.

21 Therefore deliver up their children to the famine, and <u>pour out their</u> *blood* by the force of the sword; and let their wives be bereaved of their children, and *be* widows; and let their men be put to death; *let* their young men *be* slain by the sword in battle.   bring death

22 Let a cry be heard from their houses, when You shall bring a troop

suddenly upon them: for they have dug a pit to take me, and hid <u>snares</u> for my feet.   traps

^{G4H} 23 Yet, LORD, You know all their coun-
G1 sel against me to slay me: forgive not
their iniquity, neither blot out their sin
from Your sight, but let them be over-
thrown before You; deal *thus* with
¹³⁵⁵
¹¹¹⁶ them in the time of Your anger.

CHAPTER 19

THUS says the LORD, Go and <u>get a</u> potter's <u>earthen</u> <u>bottle</u>, and *take* of the <u>ancients</u> of the people, and of the <u>ancients</u> of the priests;   buy - clay jar - elders

2 And go forth to the valley of the son of Hin'nom, which *is* by the en-try of the east gate, and proclaim there the words that I shall tell you,

3 And say, Hear you the word of the LORD, O kings of Ju'dah, and inhabitants of Je-ru'sa-lem; Thus says the LORD of hosts, the <u>God</u> of Is'ra-el; Behold, I will bring evil upon this place, the which who-soever hears, his ears shall tingle.

Jehovah^{s.f.} - Jehovah^{s.f.} Tsebaoth - Elohim^{p.f.}

4 Because they have forsaken Me, and have estranged this place, and have burned incense in it to other gods, whom neither they nor their fathers have known, nor the kings of Ju'dah, and have filled this place with the blood of innocents;

5 They have built also the high places of Ba'al, to burn their sons with fire *for* burned offerings to Ba'al, which I commanded not, nor spoke *it*, nei-ther came *it* into My mind:

6 Therefore, behold, the days come,

says the LORD, that this place shall no more be called To'phet, nor the val-ley of the son of Hin'nom, but the valley of slaughter.

7 And I will make void the counsel of Ju'dah and Je-ru'sa-lem in this place; and I will cause them to fall by the sword before their enemies, and by the hands of them that seek their lives: and their carcases will I give to be meat for the fowls of the heaven, and for the beasts of the earth.

8 And I will make this city deso-late, and an <u>hissing</u>; every one that passes thereby shall be astonished and <u>hiss</u> because of all the plagues thereof.   i.e., object of scorn - i.e., scoff

9 And I will cause them to eat the flesh of their sons and the flesh of their daughters, and they shall eat every one the flesh of his friend in the siege and <u>straitness</u>, wherewith their enemies, and they that seek their lives, shall <u>straiten</u> them.   hardship - oppress

10 Then shall you break the bottle in the sight of the men that go with you,

11 And shall say to them, Thus says the LORD of hosts; Even so will I break this people and this city, as *one* breaks a potter's vessel, that cannot be made whole again: and they shall bury *them* in To'phet, till *there be* no place to bury.   Jehovah^{s.f.} Tsebaoth

12 Thus will I do to this place, says the LORD, and to the inhabitants thereof, and *even* make this city as To'phet:

13 And the houses of Je-ru'sa-lem, and the houses of the kings of Ju'dah, shall be defiled as the place of To'phet,

because of all the houses upon whose roofs they have <u>burned incense</u> to all the host of heaven, and have poured out drink offerings to other gods.   worshiped

14 Then came Jer-e-mi'ah from To'phet, where the LORD had sent him to prophesy; and he stood in the court of the LORD's house; and said to all the people,

15 Thus says the <u>LORD of hosts</u>, the <u>God</u> of Is'ra-el; Behold, I will bring upon this city and upon all her towns all the evil that I have pronounced against it, because they have hardened their necks, that they might not hear My words.   Jehovah[a.f.] Tsebaoth - Elohim[p.f.]

CHAPTER 20

NOW Pash'ur the son of Im'mer the priest, who *was* also chief governor in the house of the LORD, heard that Jer-e-mi'ah prophesied these things.

2 Then Pash'ur <u>smote</u> Jer-e-mi'ah the prophet, and put him in <u>the stocks</u> that *were* in the high gate of Ben'ja-min, which *was* by the house of the LORD.   beat - prison

3 And it came to pass on the morrow, that Pash'ur brought forth Jer-e-mi'ah out of <u>the stocks</u>. Then said Jer-e-mi'ah to him, The LORD has not called your name Pash'ur, but <u>Ma'gor-mis'sa-bib</u>.

      prison - i.e., terror on every side

4 For thus says the LORD, Behold, I will make you a terror to yourself, and to all your friends: and they shall fall by the sword of their enemies, and your eyes shall behold *it*: and I will give all Ju'dah into the hand of the king of Bab'y-lon, and he shall carry them captive into Bab'y-lon, and shall slay them with the sword.

5 Moreover I will deliver all the strength of this city, and all the labors thereof, and all the precious things thereof, and all the treasures of the kings of Ju'dah will I give into the hand of their enemies, which shall <u>spoil</u> them, and take them, and carry them to Bab'y-lon.   plunder

6 And you, Pash'ur, and all that dwell in your house shall go into captivity: and you shall come to Bab'y-lon, and there you shall die, and shall be buried there, you, and all your friends, to whom you have prophesied lies.   ACTS 7:43

7 O LORD, You have <u>deceived</u> me, and I was <u>deceived</u>: You are stronger than I, and have prevailed: I am in derision daily, every one mocks me.   persuaded

8 For since I spoke, I cried out, I cried violence and spoil; because the word of the LORD was made a reproach to me, and a derision, daily.

9 Then I said, I will not make mention of Him, nor speak any more in His name. But *His word* was in my heart as a burning fire shut up in my bones, and I was weary with forbearing, and I could not *stay*.

10 For I heard the defaming of many, fear on every side. Report, *say they*, and we will report it. All my <u>familiars</u> watched for my <u>halting</u>, *saying*,

Perhaps he will be enticed, and we shall prevail against him, and we shall take our revenge on him. trusted friend - stumbling

11 But the LORD *is* with me as a mighty <u>terrible one</u>: therefore my persecutors shall stumble, and they shall not prevail: they shall be greatly ashamed; for they shall not prosper: *their* everlasting confusion shall never be forgotten. master

12 But, O LORD <u>of hosts</u>, that tries the righteous, *and* sees the <u>reins</u> and the heart, let me see Your vengeance on them: for to You have I opened my cause.

Jehovah^{s.f.} Tsebaoth - i.e., emotions

13 Sing to the LORD, praise you the LORD: for He has delivered the <u>soul</u> of the poor from the hand of evildoers. i.e., life

14 Cursed *be* the day wherein I was born: let not the day wherein my mother bare me be blessed.

15 Cursed *be* the man who brought tidings to my father, saying, A man child is born to you; making him very glad.

16 And let that man be as the cities which the LORD overthrew, and <u>repented</u> not: and let him hear the cry in the morning, and the shouting at noontide; regretted

17 Because he slew me not from the womb; or that my mother might have been my grave, and her womb *to be* always great *with me.*

18 Why came I forth out of the womb to see labor and sorrow, that my days should be consumed with shame?

CHAPTER 21

THE word which came to Jer-e-mi'ah from the LORD, when king Zed-e-ki'ah sent to him Pash'ur the son of Mel-chi'ah, and Zeph-a-ni'ah the son of Ma-a-se'iah the priest, saying,

2 Enquire, I pray you, of the LORD for us; for Neb-u-chad-rez'zar king of Bab'y-lon makes war against us; if so be that the LORD will deal with us according to all His wondrous works, that he may go up from us.

3 Then said Jer-e-mi'ah to them, Thus shall you say to Zed-e-ki'ah:

4 Thus says the LORD God of Is'ra-el; Behold, I will turn <u>back</u> the weapons of war that *are* in your hands, wherewith you fight against the king of Bab'y-lon, and *against* the Chal-de'ans, which besiege you outside the walls, and I will assemble them into the midst of this city. Jehovah^{s.f.} Elohim^{p.f.} - against you

5 And I Myself will fight against you with an outstretched hand and with a strong arm, even in anger, and in fury, and in great <u>wrath</u>. indignation

6 And I will smite the inhabitants of this city, both man and beast: they shall die of a great pestilence.

7 And afterward, says the LORD, I will deliver Zed-e-ki'ah king of Ju'dah, and his servants, and the people, and such as are left in this city from the pestilence, from the sword, and from the famine, into the hand of Neb-u-chad-rez'zar king of Bab'y-lon, and into the hand of their enemies, and into the hand of those that seek their life: and

he shall smite them with the edge of the sword; he shall not spare them, neither have pity, nor have mercy.

8 And to this people you shall say, Thus says the LORD; Behold, I set before you the way of life, and the way of death.

9 He that abides in this city shall die by the sword, and by the famine, and by the pestilence: but he that goes out, and <u>falls</u> to the Chalde'ans that besiege you, he shall live, and his life shall be to him for a <u>prey</u>. surrenders - booty

10 For I have set My face against this city for evil, and not for good, says the LORD: it shall be given into the hand of the king of Bab'y-lon, and he shall burn it with fire.

11 And touching the house of the king of Ju'dah, *say*, Hear you the word of the LORD;

12 O house of Da'vid, thus says the LORD; Execute judgment in the morning, and deliver *him that is* <u>spoiled</u> out of the hand of the oppressor, less My fury go out like fire, and burn that none can quench *it*, because of the evil of your doings. robbed

13 Behold, I *am* against you, O inhabitant of the valley, *and* rock of the plain, says the LORD; which say, Who shall come down against us? or who shall enter into our habitations?

14 But I will punish you according to the fruit of your doings, says the LORD: and I will kindle a fire in the forest thereof, and it shall devour all things round about it.

CHAPTER 22

THUS says the LORD; Go down to the house of the king of Ju'dah, and speak there this word,

2 And say, Hear the word of the LORD, O king of Ju'dah, that sits upon the throne of Da'vid, you, and your servants, and your people that enter in by these gates:

3 Thus says the LORD; <u>Execute you judgment</u> and righteousness, and deliver the <u>spoiled</u> out of the hand of the oppressor: and do no wrong, do no violence to the stranger, the fatherless, nor the widow, neither shed innocent blood in this place. Do justice - robbed

4 For if you do this thing indeed, then shall there enter in by the gates of this house kings sitting upon the throne of Da'vid, riding in chariots and on horses, he, and his servants, and his people.

5 But if you will not <u>hear</u> these words, I swear by Myself, says the LORD, that this house shall become a <u>desolation</u>. MATT. 23:38 obey - ruin

6 For thus says the LORD to the king's house of Ju'dah; You *are* Gil'e-ad to me, *and* the head of Leb'a-non: *yet* surely I will make you a wilderness, *and* cities *which* are not inhabited.

7 And I will prepare destroyers against you, every one with his weapons: and they shall cut down your choice cedars, and cast *them* into the fire.

8 And many nations shall pass by this city, and they shall say every man to his neighbor, Why has the LORD done thus to this great city?

9 Then they shall answer, Because they have forsaken the <u>covenant</u> of the LORD their <u>God</u>, and worshiped other gods, and served them. agreement - Elohim^{p.f.}

10 Weep you not for the dead, neither bemoan him: *but* weep <u>sore</u> for him that goes away: for he shall return no more, nor see his native country. bitterly

11 For thus says the LORD touching Shal'lum the son of Jo-si'ah king of Ju'dah, which reigned instead of Jo-si'ah his father, which went forth out of this place; He shall not return there any more:

12 But he shall die in the place where they have led him captive, and shall see this land no more.

13 Woe to him that builds his house by unrighteousness, and his chambers by wrong; *that* uses his neighbor's service without wages, and gives him not for his work;

14 That says, I will build me a wide house and large chambers, and cuts him out windows; and *it is* ceiled with cedar, and painted with vermilion.

15 Shall you reign, because you <u>closest *yourself* in cedar</u>? did not your father eat and drink, and do judgment and justice, *and* then *it was* well with him? try to excell (Heb.)

16 He judged the cause of the poor and needy; then *it was* well *with him: was* not this to <u>know</u> Me? says the LORD. honor

17 But your eyes and your heart *are* not but for your covetousness, and for to shed innocent blood, and for oppression, and for <u>violence</u>, to do *it*.extortion (Heb.)

18 Therefore thus says the LORD concerning Je-hoi'a-kim the son of Jo-si'ah king of Ju'dah; They shall not lament for him, *saying*, Ah my brother! or, Ah sister! they shall not lament for him, *saying*, Ah lord! or, Ah his glory!

19 He shall be buried with the burial of an ass, drawn and cast forth beyond the gates of Je-ru'sa-lem.

20 Go up to Leb'a-non, and cry; and lift up your voice in Ba'shan, and cry from the passages: for all your lovers are destroyed.

21 I spoke to you in your prosperity; *but* you said, I will not hear. This *has been* your manner from your youth, that you obey not My voice.

22 The wind shall eat up all your pastors, and your lovers shall go into captivity: surely then shall you be ashamed and confounded for all your wickedness.

23 O inhabitant of Leb'a-non, that makes your nest in the cedars, how gracious shall you be when pangs come upon you, the pain as of a woman in travail!

24 *As* I live, says the LORD, though Co-ni'ah the son of Je-hoi'a-kim king of Ju'dah were the <u>signet</u> upon My right hand, yet would I pluck you from there; ring

25 And I will give you into the hand of them that seek your life, and into the hand *of them* whose face you <u>fearest</u>, even into the hand of Neb-u-chad-rez'zar king of Bab'y-lon, and into the hand of the Chal-de'ans. dread

26 And I will cast you out, and your mother that bare you, into another country, where you were not born; and there shall you die.

27 But to the land whereto they desire to return, there shall they not return.

28 *Is* this man Co-ni'ah a despised broken idol? *is he* a vessel wherein *is* no pleasure? wherefore are they cast out, he and his <u>seed</u>, and are cast into a land which they know not? descendants

29 O earth, earth, earth, hear the word of the LORD.

30 Thus says the LORD, Write you this man childless, a man *that* shall not prosper in his days: for no man of his seed shall prosper, sitting upon the throne of Da'vid, and ruling any more in Ju'dah.

CHAPTER 23

WOE be to the <u>pastors</u> that destroy and scatter the sheep of My pasture! says the LORD. JOHN 10:8 shepherds

2 Therefore thus says the <u>LORD God</u> of Is'ra-el against the pastors that feed My people; You have scattered My flock, and driven them away, and have not visited them: behold, I will <u>visit</u> upon you the evil of your doings, says the LORD. Jehovah^s.f. Elohim^p.f. - allow

3 And I will gather the remnant of My flock out of all countries where I have driven them, and will bring them again to their folds; and they shall be fruitful and increase.

4 And I will set up shepherds over them which shall feed them: and they shall fear no more, nor be dismayed, neither shall they be lacking, says the LORD.

5 Behold, the days come, says the LORD, that I will raise to Da'vid a righteous Branch, and a King shall reign and prosper, and shall execute judgment and justice in the earth. MATT. 2:2

6 In His days Ju'dah shall be saved, and Is'ra-el shall dwell safely: and this *is* His name whereby He shall be called, THE LORD OUR RIGHTEOUSNESS.

7 Therefore, behold, the days come, says the LORD, that they shall no more say, The LORD lives, which brought up the children of Is'ra-el out of the land of E'gypt;

8 But, The LORD lives, which brought up and which led the <u>seed</u> of the house of Is'ra-el out of the north country, and from all countries where I had driven them; and they shall dwell in their own land. descendants

9 My heart within me is broken because of the prophets; all my bones shake; I am like a drunken man, and like a man whom wine has overcome, because of the LORD, and because of the words of His holiness.

10 For the land is full of adulterers; for because of <u>swearing</u> the land mourns; the pleasant places of the wilderness are dried up, and their course is evil, and their force *is* not right. a curse (Heb.)

11 For both prophet and priest are profane; yea, in My house have I found their wickedness, says the LORD.

12 Wherefore their way shall be to

them as slippery *ways* in the darkness: they shall be driven on, and fall therein: for I will bring evil upon them, *even* the year of their visitation, says the LORD.

13 And I have seen folly <u>in</u> the prophets of Sa-ma'ri-a; they prophesied in Ba'al, and caused My people Is'ra-el to err.   by

14 I have seen also in the prophets of Je-ru'sa-lem an horrible thing: they commit adultery, and walk in lies: they strengthen also the hands of evildoers, that none does return from his wickedness: they are all of them to Me as Sod'om, and the inhabitants thereof as Go-mor'rah.

15 Therefore thus says the <u>LORD of hosts</u> concerning the prophets; Behold, I will feed them with <u>wormwood</u>, and make them drink the water of <u>gall</u>: for from the prophets of Je-ru'sa-lem is <u>profaneness</u> gone forth into all the land.   Jehovah[s.f.] Tsebaoth - i.e., bitterness - godlessness

16 Thus says the <u>LORD of hosts,</u> Hearken not to the words of the prophets that prophesy to you: they make you vain: they speak a vision of their own heart, *and* not out of the mouth of the LORD.

17 They say still to them that despise Me, The LORD has said, You shall have peace; and they say to every one that walks after the imagination of his own heart, No evil shall come upon you.

18 For who has stood in the <u>counsel</u> of the LORD, and has perceived and heard His word? who has <u>marked</u> His word, and heard *it*?   private thoughts - heeded

19 Behold, a whirlwind of the LORD is gone forth in fury, even a grievous whirlwind: it shall fall grievously upon the head of the wicked.

20 The anger of the LORD shall not return, until He have executed, and till He have performed the thoughts of His heart: in the latter days you shall <u>consider</u> it perfectly.   understand

21 I have not sent these prophets, yet they ran: I have not spoken to them, yet they prophesied.

22 But if they had <u>stood in My counsel</u>, and had caused My people to hear My words, then they should have turned them from their evil way, and from the evil of their doings.   i.e., understood My mind

23 *Am* I a <u>God</u> at hand, says the LORD, and not a <u>God</u> afar off?   Elohim[p.f.]

24 Can any hide himself in secret places that I shall not see him? says the LORD. Do not I fill heaven and earth? says the LORD.

25 I have heard what the prophets said, that prophesy lies in My name, saying, I have dreamed, I have dreamed.

26 How long shall *this* be in the heart of the prophets that prophesy lies? yea, *they are* prophets of the deceit of their own heart;

27 Which think to <u>cause</u> My people to forget My name by their dreams which they tell every man to his neighbor, as their fathers have forgotten My name for Ba'al.   make

28 The prophet that has a dream, let him tell a dream; and he that has My word, let him speak My word faithfully.

What *is* the chaff to the wheat? says the LORD.

29 *Is* not My word like as a fire? says the LORD; and like a hammer *that* breaks the rock in pieces?

30 Therefore, behold, I *am* against the prophets, says the LORD, that steal My words every one from his neighbor.

31 Behold, I *am* against the prophets, says the LORD, that use their tongues, and say, He says.

32 Behold, I *am* against them that prophesy false dreams, says the LORD, and do tell them, and cause My people to err by their lies, and by their lightness; yet I sent them not, nor commanded them: therefore they shall not profit this people at all, says the LORD.   boasting

33 And when this people, or the prophet, or a priest, shall ask you, saying, What *is* the burden of the LORD? you shall then say to them, What burden? I will even forsake you, says the LORD.   message

34 And *as for* the prophet, and the priest, and the people, that shall say, The burden of the LORD, I will even punish that man and his house.

35 Thus shall you say every one to his neighbor, and every one to his brother, What has the LORD answered? and, What has the LORD spoken?

36 And the burden of the LORD shall you mention no more: for every man's word shall be his burden; for you have perverted the words of the living God, of the LORD of hosts our God.

Jehovah[s.f.] - message - Elohim[p.f.] - Jehovah[s.f.] Tsebaoth - Elohim[p.f.]

37 Thus shall you say to the prophet, What has the LORD answered you? and, What has the LORD spoken?

38 But since you say, The burden of the LORD; therefore thus says the LORD; Because you say this word, The burden of the LORD, and I have sent to you, saying, You shall not say, The burden of the LORD;   message

39 Therefore, behold, I, even I, will utterly forget you, and I will forsake you, and the city that I gave you and your fathers, *and cast you* out of My presence:

40 And I will bring an everlasting reproach upon you, and a perpetual shame, which shall not be forgotten.

CHAPTER 24

THE LORD showed me, and, behold, two baskets of figs *were* set before the temple of the LORD, after that Neb-u-chad-rez'zar king of Bab'y-lon had carried away captive Jec-o-ni'ah the son of Je-hoi'a-kim king of Ju'dah, and the princes of Ju'dah, with the carpenters and smiths, from Je-ru'sa-lem, and had brought them to Bab'y-lon.

2 One basket *had* very good figs, *even* like the figs *that are* first ripe: and the other basket *had* very naughty figs, which could not be eaten, they were so bad.   bad

3 Then said the LORD to me, What see you, Jer-e-mi'ah? And I said, Figs; the good figs, very good; and the evil, very evil, that cannot be eaten, they are so evil.

4 Again the word of the LORD came to me, saying,

5 Thus says the Lord, the <u>God</u> of Is'ra-el; Like these good figs, so will I <u>acknowledge</u> them that are carried away captive of Ju'dah, whom I have sent out of this place into the land of the Chal-de'ans for *their* good.   Elohim^{n.f.} - regard

6 For I will set My eyes upon them for good, and I will bring them again to this land: and I will build them, and not pull *them* down; and I will plant them, and not pluck *them* up.

7 And I will give them an heart to know Me, that I *am* the Lord: and they shall be My people, and I will be their <u>God</u>: for they shall return to Me with their whole heart.

8 And as the <u>evil</u> figs, which cannot be eaten, they are so <u>evil</u>; surely thus says the Lord, So will I give Zed-e-ki'ah the king of Ju'dah, and his princes, and the residue of Je-ru'sa-lem, that remain in this land, and them that dwell in the land of E'gypt: bad

9 And I will deliver them to be removed into all the kingdoms of the earth for *their* hurt, *to be* a reproach and a proverb, a taunt and a curse, in all places where I shall drive them.

10 And I will send the sword, the famine, and the pestilence, among them, till they be <u>consumed</u> from off the land that I gave to them and to their fathers.   destroyed

CHAPTER 25

THE word that came to Jer-e-mi'ah concerning all the people of Ju'dah in the fourth year of Je-hoi'a-kim the son of Jo-si'ah king of Ju'dah, that *was* the first year of Neb-u-chad-rez'zar king of Bab'y-lon;

2 The which Jer-e-mi'ah the prophet spoke to all the people of Ju'dah, and to all the inhabitants of Je-ru'sa-lem, saying,

3 From the thirteenth year of Jo-si'ah the son of A'mon king of Ju'dah, even to this day, that *is* the three and twentieth year, the word of the Lord has come to me, and I have spoken to you, rising early and speaking; but you have not <u>hearkened</u>.   listened

4 And the Lord has sent to you all His servants the prophets, rising early and sending *them*; but you have not <u>hearkened</u>, nor inclined your ear to hear.

5 They said, Turn you again now every one from his evil way, and from the evil of your doings, and dwell in the land that the Lord has given to you and to your fathers for ever and ever:

6 And go not after other gods to serve them, and to worship them, and provoke Me not to anger with the works of your hands; and I will do you no <u>hurt</u>.   harm

7 Yet you have not <u>hearkened</u> to Me, says the Lord; that you might provoke Me to anger with the works of your hands to your own hurt.   Listened

8 Therefore thus says the <u>Lord of hosts</u>; Because you have not heard My words,   Jehovah^{s.f.} Tsebaoth

9 Behold, I will send and take all the families of the north, says the Lord, and Neb-u-chad-rez'zar the king of Bab'y-lon, My servant, and will bring

them against this land, and against the inhabitants thereof, and against all these nations round about, and will utterly destroy them, and make them an astonishment, and an <u>hissing</u>, and perpetual desolations. *i.e., object of scorn*

10 Moreover I will take from them the voice of mirth, and the voice of gladness, the voice of the bridegroom, and the voice of the bride, the sound of the millstones, and the light of the candle.

11 And this whole land shall be a desolation, *and* an <u>astonishment</u>; and these nations shall serve the king of Bab'y-lon seventy years. *a horror*

12 And it shall come to pass, when seventy years are accomplished, *that* I will punish the king of Bab'y-lon, and that nation, says the LORD, for their iniquity, and the land of the Chal-de'ans, and will make it perpetual desolations.

13 And I will bring upon that land all My words which I have pronounced against it, *even* all that is written in this book, which Jer-e-mi'ah has prophesied against all the nations.

14 For many nations and great kings shall serve themselves of them also: and I will recompense them according to their deeds, and according to the works of their own hands.

15 For thus says the <u>LORD God</u> of Is'ra-el to me; Take the wine cup of this <u>fury</u> at My hand, and cause all the nations, to whom I send you, to drink it. *Jehovah Elohim - violent anger*

16 And they shall drink, and <u>be</u> <u>moved</u>, and be mad, because of the sword that I will send among them. *stagger*

17 Then took I the cup at the LORD's hand, and made all the nations to drink, to whom the LORD had sent me:

18 *That is*, Je-ru'sa-lem, and the cities of Ju'dah, and the kings thereof, and the princes thereof, to make them a desolation, an astonishment, an <u>hissing</u>, and a curse; as *it is* this day; *i.e., scorn*

19 Pha'raoh king of E'gypt, and his servants, and his princes, and all his people;

20 And all the mingled people, and all the kings of the land of Uz, and all the kings of the land of the Phi-lis'tines, and Ash'ke-lon, and Az'zah, and Ek'ron, and the remnant of Ash'dod,

21 E'dom, and Mo'ab, and the children of Am'mon,

22 And all the kings of Ty'rus, and all the kings of Zi'don, and the kings of the isles which *are* beyond the sea,

23 De'dan, and Te'ma, and Buz, and all *that are* in the utmost corners,

24 And all the kings of A-ra'bi-a, and all the kings of the mingled people that dwell in the desert,

25 And all the kings of Zim'ri, and all the kings of E'lam, and all the kings of the Medes,

26 And all the kings of the north, far and near, one with another, and all the kingdoms of the world, which *are* upon the face of the earth: and the king of She'shach shall drink after them.

27 Therefore you shall say to them, Thus says the <u>LORD of hosts</u>, the <u>God</u> of Is'ra-el; Drink you, and be

drunken, and spew, and fall, and rise no more, because of the sword which I will send among you.   REV. 18:3 Jehovah[s.f.] Tsebaoth - Elohim[p.f.]

28 And it shall be, if they refuse to take the cup at your hand to drink, then shall you say to them, Thus says the LORD of hosts; You shall certainly drink.

29 For, lo, I begin to bring <u>evil</u> on the city which is called by My name, and should you be utterly unpunished? You shall not be unpunished: for I will call for a sword upon all the inhabitants of the earth, says the LORD of hosts.   calamity - Jehovah[s.f.] Tsebaoth

30 Therefore prophesy you against them all these words, and say to them, The LORD shall roar from on high, and utter His voice from His holy habitation; He shall mightily roar upon His habitation; He shall give a shout, as they that tread *the grapes*, against all the inhabitants of the earth.

31 A noise shall come *even* to the ends of the earth; for the LORD has a controversy with the nations, He will plead with all flesh; He will give them *that are* wicked to the sword, says the LORD.

32 Thus says the LORD of hosts, Behold, evil shall go forth from nation to nation, and a great whirlwind shall be raised up from the coasts of the earth.

33 And the slain of the LORD shall be at that day from *one* end of the earth even to the *other* end of the earth: they shall not be lamented, neither gathered, nor buried; they shall be dung upon the ground.

34 Howl, you shepherds, and cry; and wallow yourselves *in the ashes*, you principal of the flock: for the days of your slaughter and of your dispersions <u>are accomplished</u>; and you shall fall like a <u>pleasant</u> vessel.   have come - choice

35 And the shepherds shall have no way to flee, nor the <u>principal</u> of the flock to escape.   master

36 A voice of the cry of the shepherds, and an <u>howling</u> of the principal of the flock, *shall be heard*: for the LORD has <u>spoiled</u> their pasture.   wailing - destroyed

37 And the peaceable habitations are cut down because of the fierce anger of the LORD.

38 He has forsaken His <u>covert</u>, as the lion: for their land is desolate because of the fierceness of the <u>oppressor</u>, and because of His fierce anger.   hiding place - oppressing sword

CHAPTER 26

IN the beginning of the reign of Je-hoi'a-kim the son of Jo-si'ah king of Ju'dah came this word from the LORD, saying,

2 Thus says the LORD; Stand in the court of the LORD's house, and speak to all the cities of Ju'dah, which come to worship in the LORD's house, all the words that I command you to speak to them; <u>diminish</u> not a word: MATT. 28:20 omit

3 If so be they will hearken, and turn every man from his evil way, that I may <u>repent</u> Me of the evil, which I purpose to do to them because of the evil of their doings.   grieve

4 And you shall say to them, Thus says the LORD; If you will not <u>hearken</u>

to Me, to walk in My law, which I have set before you, _{listen}

5 To <u>hearken</u> to the words of My servants the prophets, whom I sent to you, both rising up early, and sending *them*, but you have not <u>hearkened</u>;

6 Then will I make this house like Shi'loh, and will make this city a curse to all the nations of the earth.

7 So the priests and the prophets and all the people heard Jer-e-mi'ah speaking these words in the house of the LORD.

8 Now it came to pass, when Jer-e-mi'ah had made an end of speaking all that the LORD had commanded *him* to speak to all the people, that the priests and the prophets and all the people took him, saying, you shall surely die.

9 Why have you prophesied in the name of the LORD, saying, This house shall be like Shi'loh, and this city shall be desolate without an inhabitant? And all the people were gathered against Jer-e-mi'ah in the house of the LORD.

10 When the princes of Ju'dah heard these things, then they came up from the king's house to the house of the LORD, and sat down in the entry of the new gate of the LORD's *house*.

11 Then spoke the priests and the prophets to the princes and to all the people, saying, This man *is* worthy to die; for he has prophesied against this city, as you have heard with your ears.

12 Then spoke Jer-e-mi'ah to all the princes and to all the people, saying, The LORD sent me to prophesy against this house and against this city all the words that you have heard.

13 Therefore now amend your ways and your doings, and obey the voice of the LORD your <u>God</u>; and the LORD will <u>repent</u> Him of the evil that He has pronounced against you. _{Elohim^{p.f.} - relent}

14 As for me, behold, I *am* in your hand: do with me as seems good and <u>meet</u> to you. _{proper}

15 But know you for certain, that if you put me to death, you shall surely bring innocent blood upon yourselves, and upon this city, and upon the inhabitants thereof: for of a truth the LORD has sent me to you to speak all these words in your ears.

16 Then said the princes and all the people to the priests and to the prophets; This man *is* not worthy to die: for he has spoken to us in the name of the LORD our <u>God</u>. _{Elohim^{p.f.}}

17 Then rose up certain of the elders of the land, and spoke to all the assembly of the people, saying,

18 Mi'cah the Mo'ras-thite prophesied in the days of Hez-e-ki'ah king of Ju'dah, and spoke to all the people of Ju'dah, saying, Thus says the <u>LORD of hosts</u>; Zi'on shall be plowed *like* a field, and Je-ru'sa-lem shall become heaps, and the mountain of the house as the high places of a forest. _{Jehovah^{s.f.} Tsebaoth}

19 Did Hez-e-ki'ah king of Ju'dah and all Ju'dah put him at all to death? did he not <u>fear</u> the LORD, and besought the LORD, and the LORD <u>repented</u> Him of the evil which He had pronounced against them? Thus might we procure great evil against our souls. _{revere - regretted}

M03 — | — | 1210

20 And there was also a man that prophesied in the name of the LORD, U-ri'jah the son of Shem-a-i'ah of Kir'jath-je'a-rim, who prophesied against this city and against this land according to all the words of Jer-e-mi'ah:

21 And when Je-hoi'a-kim the king, with all his mighty men, and all the princes, heard his words, the king sought to put him to death: but when U-ri'jah heard it, he was afraid, and fled, and went into E'gypt;

22 And Je-hoi'a-kim the king sent men into E'gypt, *namely*, El'na-than the son of Ach'bor, and *certain* men with him into E'gypt.

23 And they brought forth U-ri'jah out of E'gypt, and brought him to Je-hoi'a-kim the king; who slew him with the sword, and cast his dead body into the graves of the common people.

24 Nevertheless the hand of A-hi'kam the son of Sha'phan was with Jer-e-mi'ah, that they should not give him into the hand of the people to put him to death.

CHAPTER 27

IN the beginning of the reign of Je-hoi'a-kim the son of Jo-si'ah king of Ju'dah came this word to Jer-e-mi'ah from the LORD, saying,

2 Thus says the LORD to me; Make you bonds and yokes, and put them upon your neck,

3 And send them to the king of E'dom, and to the king of Mo'ab, and to the king of the Am'mon-ites, and to the king of Ty'rus, and to the king of Zi'-don, by the hand of the messengers which come to Je-ru'sa-lem to Zed-e-ki'ah king of Ju'dah;

4 And command them to say to their masters, Thus says the LORD of hosts, the God of Is'ra-el; Thus shall you say to your masters;

*Jehovah*s.f. *Tsebaoth - Elohim*p.f.

5 I have made the earth, the man and the beast that *are* upon the ground, by My great power and by My outstretched arm, and have given it to whom it seemed meet to Me.   *right*

6 And now have I given all these lands into the hand of Neb-u-chad-nez'zar the king of Bab'y-lon, My servant; and the beasts of the field have I given him also to serve him.

7 And all nations shall serve him, and his son, and his son's son, until the very time of his land come: and then many nations and great kings shall serve themselves of him.

8 And it shall come to pass, *that* the nation and kingdom which will not serve the same Neb-u-chad-nez'zar the king of Bab'y-lon, and that will not put their neck under the yoke of the king of Bab'y-lon, that nation will I punish, says the LORD, with the sword, and with the famine, and with the pestilence, until I have consumed them by his hand.

9 Therefore hearken not you to your prophets, nor to your diviners, nor to your dreamers, nor to your enchanters, nor to your sorcerers, which speak to you, saying, You shall not serve the king of Bab'y-lon: soothsayers - magicians - wizards

10 For they prophesy a lie to you,

to remove you far from your land; and that I should drive you out, and you should perish.

11 But the nations that <u>bring</u> their neck under the yoke of the king of Bab'y-lon, and serve him, those will I let remain still in their own land, says the LORD; and they shall till it, and dwell therein. _{bow}

12 I spoke also to Zed-e-ki'ah king of Ju'dah according to all these words, saying, <u>Bring</u> your necks under the yoke of the king of Bab'y-lon, and serve him and his people, and live.

13 Why will you die, you and your people, by the sword, by the famine, and by the pestilence, as the LORD has spoken against the nation that will not serve the king of Bab'y-lon?

14 Therefore <u>hearken</u> not to the words of the prophets that speak to you, saying, You shall not serve the king of Bab'y-lon: for they prophesy a lie to you. _{listen}

15 For I have not sent them, says the LORD, yet they prophesy a lie in My name; that I might drive you out, and that you might perish, you, and the prophets that prophesy to you.

16 Also I spoke to the priests and to all this people, saying, Thus says the LORD; <u>Hearken</u> not to the words of your prophets that prophesy to you, saying, Behold, the vessels of the LORD's house shall now shortly be brought again from Bab'y-lon: for they prophesy a lie to you. _{listen}

17 <u>Hearken</u> not to them; serve the king of Bab'y-lon, and live: why should this city be laid waste?

18 But if they *be* prophets, and if the word of the LORD be with them, let them now make intercession to the LORD of hosts, that the vessels which are left in the house of the LORD, and *in* the house of the king of Ju'dah, and at Je-ru'sa-lem, go not to Bab'y-lon. Jehovah^{s.f.} - Tsebaoth

19 For thus says the LORD of hosts concerning the pillars, and concerning the sea, and concerning the bases, and concerning the residue of the vessels that remain in this city,

20 Which Neb-u-chad-nez'zar king of Bab'y-lon took not, when he carried away captive Jec-o-ni'ah the son of Je-hoi'a-kim king of Ju'dah from Je-ru'sa-lem to Bab'y-lon, and all the nobles of Ju'dah and Je-ru'sa-lem;

21 Yea, thus says the LORD of hosts, the God of Is'ra-el, concerning the vessels that remain *in* the house of the LORD, and in the house of the king of Ju'dah and of Je-ru'sa-lem;

Jehovah^{s.f.} Tsebaoth - Elohim^{p.f.} - Jehovah^{s.f.}

22 They shall be carried to Bab'y-lon, and there shall they be until the day that I visit them, says the LORD; then will I bring them up, and restore them to this place.

CHAPTER 28

AND it came to pass the same year, in the beginning of the reign of Zed-e-ki'ah king of Ju'dah, in the fourth year, *and* in the fifth month, *that* Han-a-ni'ah the son of A'zur the prophet, which *was* of Gib'e-on, spoke to me in the house

of the LORD, in the presence of the priests and of all the people, saying,

2 Thus speaks the LORD of hosts, the God of Is'ra-el, saying, I have broken the yoke of the king of Bab'y-lon.   Jehovah^s.f. Tsebaoth - Elohim^p.f. - destroyed the power

3 Within two full years will I bring again into this place all the vessels of the LORD's house, that Neb-u-chad-nez'zar king of Bab'y-lon took away from this place, and carried them to Bab'y-lon:

4 And I will bring again to this place Jec-o-ni'ah the son of Je-hoi'a-kim king of Ju'dah, with all the captives of Ju'dah, that went into Bab'y-lon, says the LORD: for I will break the yoke of the king of Bab'y-lon.

5 Then the prophet Jer-e-mi'ah said to the prophet Han-a-ni'ah in the presence of the priests, and in the presence of all the people that stood in the house of the LORD,

6 Even the prophet Jer-e-mi'ah said, Amen: the LORD do so: the LORD perform your words which you have prophesied, to bring again the vessels of the LORD's house, and all that is carried away captive, from Bab'y-lon into this place.

7 Nevertheless hear you now this word that I speak in your ears, and in the ears of all the people;

8 The prophets that have been before me and before you of old prophesied both against many countries, and against great kingdoms, of war, and of evil, and of pestilence.

9 The prophet which prophesies of peace, when the word of the prophet shall come to pass, *then* shall the prophet be known, that the LORD has truly sent him.

10 Then Han-a-ni'ah the prophet took the yoke from off the prophet Jer-e-mi'ah's neck, and broke it.

11 And Han-a-ni'ah spoke in the presence of all the people, saying, Thus says the LORD; Even so will I break the yoke of Neb-u-chad-nez'zar king of Bab'y-lon from the neck of all nations within the space of two full years. And the prophet Jer-e-mi'ah went his way.

12 Then the word of the LORD came to Jer-e-mi'ah *the prophet*, after that Han-a-ni'ah the prophet had broken the yoke from off the neck of the prophet Jer-e-mi'ah, saying,

13 Go and tell Han-a-ni'ah, saying, Thus says the LORD; You have broken the yokes of wood; but you shall make for them yokes of iron.

14 For thus says the LORD of hosts, the God of Is'ra-el; I have put a yoke of iron upon the neck of all these nations, that they may serve Neb-u-chad-nez'zar king of Bab'y-lon; and they shall serve him: and I have given him the beasts of the field also.   Jehovah^s.f. Tsebaoth - Elohim^p.f.

15 Then said the prophet Jer-e-mi'ah to Han-a-ni'ah the prophet, Hear now, Han-a-ni'ah; The LORD has not sent you; but you make this people to trust in a lie.

16 Therefore thus says the LORD; Behold, I will cast you from off the face of the earth: this year you shall die, because you have taught rebellion against the LORD.

17 So Han-a-ni'ah the prophet died the same year in the seventh month.

CHAPTER 29

NOW these *are* the words of the letter that Jer-e-mi'ah the prophet sent from Je-ru'sa-lem to the residue of the elders which were carried away captives, and to the priests, and to the prophets, and to all the people whom Neb-u-chad-nez'zar had carried away captive from Je-ru'sa-lem to Bab'y-lon; rest
2 (After that Jec-o-ni'ah the king, and the queen, and the eunuchs, the princes of Ju'dah and Je-ru'sa-lem, and the carpenters, and the smiths, were departed from Je-ru'sa-lem;) court officials
3 By the hand of El'-a-sah the son of Sha'phan, and Gem-a-ri'ah the son of Hil-ki'ah, (whom Zed-e-ki'ah king of Ju'dah sent to Bab'y-lon to Neb-u-chad-nez'zar king of Bab'y-lon) saying,
4 Thus says the LORD of hosts, the God of Is'ra-el, to all that are carried away captives, whom I have caused to be carried away from Je-ru'sa-lem to Bab'y-lon; Jehovah[s.f.] Tsebaoth - Elohim[p.f.]
5 Build you houses, and dwell *in them*; and plant gardens, and eat the fruit of them;
6 Take you wives, and father sons and daughters; and take wives for your sons, and give your daughters to husbands, that they may bear sons and daughters; that you may be increased there, and not diminished.
7 And seek the peace of the city where I have caused you to be carried away captives, and pray to the LORD

for it: for in the peace thereof shall you have peace.
8 For thus says the LORD of hosts, the God of Is'ra-el; Let not your prophets and your diviners, that *be* in the midst of you, deceive you, neither hearken to your dreams which you cause to be dreamed. Jehovah[s.f.] Tsebaoth - Elohim[p.f.] soothsayers
9 For they prophesy falsely to you in My name: I have not sent them, says the LORD.
10 For thus says the LORD, That after seventy years be accomplished at Bab'y-lon I will visit you, and perform My good word toward you, in causing you to return to this place.
11 For I know the thoughts that I think toward you, says the LORD, thoughts of peace, and not of evil, to give you an expected end. hopeful
12 Then shall you call upon Me, and you shall go and pray to Me, and I will hearken to you. listen
13 And you shall seek Me, and find *Me*, when you shall search for Me with all your heart.
14 And I will be found of you, says the LORD: and I will turn away your captivity, and I will gather you from all the nations, and from all the places where I have driven you, says the LORD; and I will bring you again into the place where I caused you to be carried away captive.
15 Because you have said, The LORD has raised us up prophets in Bab'y-lon;
16 *Know* that thus says the LORD of

P04 | 1134 GID | 12

M16 --- 1281

the king that sits upon the throne of Da'vid, and of all the people that dwell in this city, *and* of your brethren that are not gone forth with you into captivity;

17 Thus says the LORD of hosts; Behold, I will send upon them the sword, the famine, and the pestilence, and will make them like vile figs, that cannot be eaten, they are so evil.   Jehovah^{s.f.} Tsebaoth - spoiled - bad

18 And I will persecute them with the sword, with the famine, and with the pestilence, and will deliver them to be removed to all the kingdoms of the earth, to be a curse, and an astonishment, and an hissing, and a reproach, among all the nations where I have driven them: horror - whistling

19 Because they have not hearkened to My words, says the LORD, which I sent to them by My servants the prophets, rising up early and sending *them*; but you would not hear, says the LORD.   listened

20 Hear you therefore the word of the LORD, all you of the captivity, whom I have sent from Je-ru'sa-lem to Bab'y-lon:

21 Thus says the LORD of hosts, the God of Is'ra-el, of A'hab the son of Kol-a-i'ah, and of Zed-e-ki'ah the son of Ma-a-se'iah, which prophesy a lie to you in My name; Behold, I will deliver them into the hand of Neb-u-chad-rez'zar king of Bab'y-lon; and he shall slay them before your eyes;   Jehovah^{s.f.} Tsebaoth - Elohim^{p.f.}

22 And of them shall be taken up a curse by all the captivity of Ju'dah which *are* in Bab'y-lon, saying, The LORD make you like Zed-e-ki'ah and like A'hab, whom the king of Bab'y-lon roasted in the fire;

23 Because they have committed villany in Is'ra-el, and have committed adultery with their neighbors' wives, and have spoken lying words in my name, which I have not commanded them; even I know, and *am* a witness, says the LORD.

24 *Thus* shall you also speak to Shem-a-i'ah the Ne-hel'a-mite, saying,

25 Thus speaks the LORD of hosts, the God of Is'ra-el, saying, Because you have sent letters in your name to all the people that *are* at Je-ru'sa-lem, and to Zeph-a-ni'ah the son of Ma-a-se'iah the priest, and to all the priests, saying,   Jehovah^{s.f.} Tsebaoth - Elohim^{p.f.}

26 The LORD has made you priest in the stead of Je-hoi'a-da the priest, that you should be officers in the house of the LORD, for every man *that is* mad, and makes himself a prophet, that you should put him in prison, and in the stocks.

27 Now therefore why have you not reproved Jer-e-mi'ah of An'a-thoth, which makes himself a prophet to you?

28 For therefore he sent to us *in* Bab'y-lon, saying, This *captivity is* long: build you houses, and dwell *in them*; and plant gardens, and eat the fruit of them.

29 And Zeph-a-ni'ah the priest read this letter in the ears of Jer-e-mi'ah the prophet.

30 Then came the word of the LORD to Jer-e-mi'ah, saying,

31 Send to all them of the captivity,

saying, Thus says the LORD concerning Shem-a-i'ah the Ne-hel'a-mite; Because that Shem-a-i'ah has prophesied to you, and I sent him not, and he caused you to trust in a lie:

32 Therefore thus says the LORD; Behold, I will punish Shem-a-i'ah the Ne-hel'a-mite, and his <u>seed</u>: he shall not have a man to dwell among this people; neither shall he behold the good that I will do for My people, says the LORD; because he has taught rebellion against the LORD. *descendants*

CHAPTER 30

THE word that came to Jer-e-mi'ah from the LORD, saying,

2 Thus speaks the <u>LORD God</u> of Is'ra-el, saying, Write you all the words that I have spoken to you in a book. *Jehovah^s.f. Elohim^p.f.*

3 For, lo, the days come, says the LORD, that I will bring again the captivity of My people Is'ra-el and Ju'dah, says the LORD: and I will cause them to return to the land that I gave to their fathers, and they shall possess it.

4 And these *are* the words that the LORD spoke concerning Is'ra-el and concerning Ju'dah.

5 For thus says the LORD; We have heard a voice of trembling, of <u>fear</u>, and not of peace. *dread*

6 Ask you now, and see whether a man <u>does travail with child</u>? why do I see every man with his hands on his loins, as a woman in <u>travail</u>, and all faces are turned into paleness? *can give birth - childbirth*

7 Alas! for that day *is* great, so that none *is* like it: it *is* even the time of Ja'cob's trouble; but he shall be saved out of it.

8 For it shall come to pass in that day, says the <u>LORD of hosts</u>, *that* I will break his <u>yoke from off your neck</u>, and will burst your bonds, and strangers shall no more serve themselves of him: *Jehovah^s.f. Tsebaoth - power over you*

9 But they shall serve the LORD their <u>God</u>, and Da'vid their king, whom I will raise up to them. *Elohim^p.f.*

10 Therefore fear you not, O My servant Ja'cob, says the LORD; neither be dismayed, O Is'ra-el: for, lo, I will save you from afar, and your <u>seed</u> from the land of their captivity; and Ja'cob shall return, and shall be in rest, and be quiet, and none shall make *him* afraid. *i.e., offspring*

11 For I *am* with you, says the LORD, to save you: though I make a full end of all nations where I have scattered you, yet will I not make a full end of you: but I will correct you in measure, and will not leave you altogether unpunished.

12 For thus says the LORD, Your bruise *is* incurable, *and* your wound *is* grievous.

13 *There is* none to plead your cause, that you may be bound up: you have no healing medicines.

14 All your lovers have forgotten you; they seek you not; for I have wounded you with the wound of an enemy, with the chastisement of a cruel one, for the multitude of your iniquity; *because* your sins were increased.

15 Why cry you for your affliction? your sorrow *is* incurable for the multitude of your iniquity: *because* your sins were increased, I have done these things to you.

16 Therefore all they that devour you shall be devoured; and all your adversaries, every one of them, shall go into captivity; and they that <u>spoil</u> you shall be a <u>spoil</u>, and all that prey upon you will I give for a prey. plunder

17 For I will restore health to you, and I will heal you of your wounds, says the Lord; because they called you an outcast, *saying*, This *is* Zi'on, whom no man seeks after.

18 Thus says the Lord; Behold, I will bring again the captivity of Ja'cob's tents, and have mercy on his dwellingplaces; and the city shall be built upon her own <u>heap</u>, and the palace shall remain after the manner thereof. ruin

19 And out of them shall proceed thanksgiving and the voice of them that make merry: and I will multiply them, and they shall not be few; I will also glorify them, and they shall not be small.

20 Their children also shall be as <u>aforetime</u>, and their congregation shall be established before Me, and I will punish all that oppress them. formerly

21 And their nobles shall be of themselves, and their governor shall proceed from the midst of them; and I will cause him to draw near, and he shall approach to Me: for who *is* this that engaged his heart to approach to Me? says the Lord.

22 And you shall be My people, and I will be your <u>God</u>. Elohim^{p.f.}

23 Behold, the <u>whirlwind</u> of the Lord goes forth with <u>fury</u>, a continuing <u>whirlwind</u>: it shall fall with pain upon the head of the wicked. tempest - violent anger

24 The fierce anger of the Lord shall not return, until He have done *it*, and until He have performed the intents of His heart: in the latter days you shall consider it.

CHAPTER 31

AT the same time, says the Lord, will I be the <u>God</u> of all the families of Is'ra-el, and they shall be My people.

2 Thus says the Lord, The people *which were* left of the sword found grace in the wilderness; *even* Is'ra-el, when I went to cause him to rest.

3 The Lord has appeared of old to me, *saying*, Yea, I have loved you with an everlasting love: therefore with lovingkindness have I drawn you. JOHN 6:44

4 Again I will build you, and you shall be built, O virgin of Is'ra-el: you shall again be adorned with your <u>tabrets</u>, and shall go forth in the dances of them that make merry. tambourines

5 You shall yet plant vines upon the mountains of Sa-ma'ri-a: the planters shall plant, and shall eat *them* as common things.

6 For there shall be a day, *that* the watchmen upon the mount E'phra-im shall cry, Arise you, and let us go up to Zi'on to the Lord our <u>God</u>. Elohim^{p.f.}

7 For thus says the Lord; Sing with

gladness for Ja'cob, and shout among the chief of the nations: publish you, praise you, and say, O LORD, save your people, the remnant of Is'ra-el.

8 Behold, I will bring them from the north country, and gather them from the <u>coasts</u> of the earth, *and* with them the blind and the lame, the woman with child and her that travails with child together: a great company shall return there.   i.e., distant lands

9 They shall come with weeping, and with supplications will I lead them: I will cause them to walk by the rivers of waters in a straight way, wherein they shall not stumble: for I am a father to Is'ra-el, and E'phra-im *is* My firstborn.

10 Hear the word of the LORD, O you nations, and declare *it* in the <u>isles</u> afar off, and say, He that scattered Is'ra-el will gather him, and keep him, as a shepherd *does* his flock.   coastlands

11 For the LORD has redeemed Ja'cob, and ransomed him from the hand of *him that was* stronger than he.

12 Therefore they shall come and sing in the height of Zi'on, and shall flow together to the goodness of the LORD, for wheat, and for wine, and for oil, and for the young of the flock and of the herd: and their soul shall be as a watered garden; and they shall not sorrow any more at all.

13 Then shall the virgin rejoice in the dance, both young men and old together: for I will turn their mourning into joy, and will comfort them, and make them rejoice from their sorrow.

14 And I will <u>satiate</u> the soul of the priests with <u>fatness</u>, and My people shall be satisfied with My goodness, says the LORD.   satisfy - abundance

15 Thus says the LORD; A voice was heard in Ra'mah, lamentation, *and* bitter weeping; Ra'hel weeping for her children refused to be comforted for her children, because they *were* not.   MATT. 2:18

16 Thus says the LORD; Refrain your voice from weeping, and your eyes from tears: for your work shall be rewarded, says the LORD; and they shall come again from the land of the enemy.

17 And there is hope in your end, says the LORD, that your children shall come again to their own border.

18 I have surely heard E'phra-im bemoaning himself *thus*; You have chastised me, and I was chastised, as a bullock unaccustomed *to the yoke*: turn You me, and I shall be turned; for You *are* the LORD my <u>God</u>.   Elohim^{p.f.}

19 Surely after that I was turned, I <u>repented</u>; and after that I was instructed, I <u>smote upon</u> *my* thigh: I was ashamed, yea, even confounded, because I did bear the reproach of my youth.   struck - regretted

20 *Is* E'phra-im My dear son? *is he* a pleasant child? for since I spoke against him, I do earnestly remember him still: therefore My <u>bowels</u> are troubled for him; I will surely have mercy upon him, says the LORD.   feelings

21 Set you up <u>waymarks</u>, make you <u>high heaps</u>: set your heart toward the highway, *even* the way *which* you went: turn again, O virgin of Is'ra-el, turn again to these your cities.   roadmarks - guideposts

22 How long will you go about, O you backsliding daughter? for the

L<small>ORD</small> has created a new thing in the earth, A woman shall <u>compass</u> a man.   encircle

23 Thus says the L<small>ORD</small> of hosts, the <u>God</u> of Is'ra-el; As yet they shall use this speech in the land of Ju'dah and in the cities thereof, when I shall bring again their captivity; The L<small>ORD</small> bless you, O habitation of justice, *and* mountain of holiness.   Jehovah^{s.f.} Tsebaoth - Elohim^{p.f.}

24 And there shall dwell in Ju'dah itself, and in all the cities thereof together, husbandmen, and they *that* go forth with flocks.

25 For I have <u>satiated</u> the weary soul, and I have replenished every sorrowful soul.   satisfied

26 Upon this I awaked, and beheld; and my sleep was sweet to me.

27 Behold, the days come, says the L<small>ORD</small>, that I will sow the house of Is'ra-el and the house of Ju'dah with the <u>seed</u> of man, and with the <u>seed</u> of beast.   offspring

28 And it shall come to pass, *that* like as I have watched over them, to pluck up, and to break down, and to throw down, and to destroy, and to afflict; so will I watch over them, to build, and to plant, says the L<small>ORD</small>.

29 In those days they shall say no more, The fathers have eaten a sour grape, and the children's teeth are set on edge.

30 But every one shall die for his own iniquity: every man that eats the sour grape, his teeth shall be set on edge.

31 Behold, the days come, says the L<small>ORD</small>, that I will make a new <u>covenant</u> with the house of Is'ra-el, and with the house of Ju'dah: 2 COR. 3:6   HEB. 8:6   agreement

32 Not according to the <u>covenant</u> that I made with their fathers in the day *that* I took them by the hand to bring them out of the land of E'gypt; which My <u>covenant</u> they broke, although I was an husband to them, says the L<small>ORD</small>:

33 But this *shall be* the <u>covenant</u> that I will make with the house of Is'ra-el; After those days, says the L<small>ORD</small>, I will put My law in their inward parts, and write it in their hearts; and will be their <u>God</u>, and they shall be My people.   ROM. 11:27   HEB. 8:10   HEB. 10:16   Elohim^{p.f.}

34 And they shall teach no more every man his neighbor, and every man his brother, saying, Know the L<small>ORD</small>: for they shall all know Me, from the least of them to the greatest of them, says the L<small>ORD</small>: for I will forgive their iniquity, and I will remember their sin no more.

35 Thus says the L<small>ORD</small>, which gives the sun for a light by day, *and* the ordinances of the moon and of the stars for a light by night, which divides the sea when the waves thereof roar; The L<small>ORD</small> of hosts *is* His name: Jehovah^{s.f.} Tsebaoth

36 If those ordinances depart from before Me, says the L<small>ORD</small>, *then* the <u>seed</u> of Is'ra-el also shall cease from being a nation before Me for ever.   offspring

37 Thus says the L<small>ORD</small>; If heaven above can be measured, and the foundations of the earth searched out beneath, I will also cast off all the <u>seed</u> of Is'ra-el for all that they have done, says the L<small>ORD</small>.   descendants

38 Behold, the days come, says the

LORD, that the city shall be built to the LORD from the tower of Ha-nan'e-el to the gate of the corner.

39 And the measuring line shall yet go forth over against it upon the hill Ga'reb, and shall compass about to Go'ath. *then turn*

40 And the whole valley of the dead bodies, and of the ashes, and all the fields to the brook of Kid'ron, to the corner of the horse gate toward the east, *shall be* holy to the LORD; it shall not be plucked up, nor thrown down any more for ever.

CHAPTER 32

THE word that came to Jer-e-mi'ah from the LORD in the tenth year of Zed-e-ki'ah king of Ju'dah, which *was* the eighteenth year of Neb-u-chad-rez'zar.

2 For then the king of Bab'y-lon's army besieged Je-ru'sa-lem: and Jer-e-mi'ah the prophet was shut up in the court of the prison, which *was* in the king of Ju'dah's house.

3 For Zed-e-ki'ah king of Ju'dah had shut him up, saying, Why do you prophesy, and say, Thus says the LORD, Behold, I will give this city into the hand of the king of Bab'y-lon, and he shall take it;

4 And Zed-e-ki'ah king of Ju'dah shall not escape out of the hand of the Chal-de'ans, but shall surely be delivered into the hand of the king of Bab'y-lon, and shall speak with him mouth to mouth, and his eyes shall behold his eyes;

5 And he shall lead Zed-e-ki'ah to Bab'y-lon, and there shall he be until I visit him, says the LORD: though you fight with the Chal-de'ans, you shall not prosper.

6 And Jer-e-mi'ah said, The word of the LORD came to me, saying,

7 Behold, Ha-nam'e-el the son of Shal'lum your uncle shall come to you, saying, Buy you my field that *is* in An'a-thoth: for the right of redemption *is* your to buy *it*.

8 So Ha-nam'e-el my uncle's son came to me in the court of the prison according to the word of the LORD, and said to me, Buy my field, I pray you, that *is* in An'a-thoth, which *is* in the country of Ben'ja-min: for the right of inheritance *is* yours, and the redemption *is* yours; buy *it* for yourself. Then I knew that this *was* the word of the LORD.

9 And I bought the field of Ha-nam'e-el my uncle's son, that *was* in An'a-thoth, and weighed him the money, *even* seventeen shekels of silver.

10 And I subscribed the underline{evidence}, and sealed *it*, and took witnesses, and weighed *him* the money in the balances. *deed*

11 So I took the evidence of the purchase, *both* that which was sealed *according* to the law and custom, and that which was open:

12 And I gave the evidence of the purchase to Ba'ruch the son of Ne-ri'ah, the son of Ma-a-se'iah, in the sight of Ha-nam'e-el my uncle's *son*, and in the presence of the witnesses

that subscribed the book of the purchase, before all the Jews that sat in the court of the prison.

13 And I charged Ba'ruch before them, saying,

14 Thus says the LORD of hosts, the God of Is'ra-el; Take these evidences, this evidence of the purchase, both which is sealed, and this evidence which is open; and put them in an earthen vessel, that they may continue many days.

Jehovah^{s.f.} Tsebaoth - Elohim^{p.f.} - deed

15 For thus says the LORD of hosts, the God of Is'ra-el; Houses and fields and vineyards shall be possessed again in this land.

16 Now when I had delivered the evidence of the purchase to Ba'ruch the son of Ne-ri'ah, I prayed to the LORD, saying,

17 Ah Lord GOD! behold, You have made the heaven and the earth by Your great power and stretched out arm, *and* there is nothing too hard for You:

LUKE 18:27 Adonay^{p.f.} Jehovah

18 You show lovingkindness to thousands, and recompense the iniquity of the fathers into the bosom of their children after them: the Great, the Mighty God, the LORD of hosts, *is* His name,

El^{s.f.} - Jehovah^{s.f.} Tsebaoth

19 Great in counsel, and mighty in work: for Your eyes *are* open upon all the ways of the sons of men: to give every one according to his ways, and according to the fruit of his doings: deed

20 Which have set signs and wonders in the land of E'gypt, *even* to this day, and in Is'ra-el, and among *other*

men; and have made You a name, as at this day;

21 And have brought forth Your people Is'ra-el out of the land of E'gypt with signs, and with wonders, and with a strong hand, and with a stretched out arm, and with great terror;

22 And have given them this land, which You did swear to their fathers to give them, a land flowing with milk and honey;

23 And they came in, and possessed it; but they obeyed not Your voice, neither walked in Your law; they have done nothing of all that You commanded them to do: therefore You have caused all this evil to come upon them:

24 Behold the mounts, they are come to the city to take it; and the city is given into the hand of the Chal-de'ans, that fight against it, because of the sword, and of the famine, and of the pestilence: and what You have spoken is come to pass; and, behold, You see *it*.

25 And You have said to me, O Lord GOD, Buy you the field for money, and take witnesses; for the city is given into the hand of the Chal-de'ans.

Adonay^{p.f.} Jehovah^{s.f.}

26 Then came the word of the LORD to Jer-e-mi'ah, saying,

27 Behold, I *am* the LORD, the God of all flesh: is there any thing too hard for Me?

Elohim^{p.f.}

28 Therefore thus says the LORD; Behold, I will give this city into the hand of the Chal-de'ans, and into the hand of Neb-u-chad-rez'zar king of Bab'y-lon, and he shall take it:

29 And the Chal-de'ans, that fight against this city, shall come and set fire on this city, and burn it with the houses, upon whose roofs they have <u>offered incense</u> to Ba'al, and poured out drink offerings to other gods, to provoke Me to anger.   _{worshiped}

30 For the children of Is'ra-el and the children of Ju'dah have only done evil before Me from their youth: for the children of Is'ra-el have only provoked Me to anger with the work of their hands, says the LORD.

31 For this city has been to Me *as a* <u>provocation</u> of My anger and of My fury from the day that they built it even to this day; that I should remove it from before My face,   _{irritation}

32 Because of all the evil of the children of Is'ra-el and of the children of Ju'dah, which they have done to provoke Me to anger, they, their kings, their princes, their priests, and their prophets, and the men of Ju'dah, and the inhabitants of Je-ru'sa-lem.

33 And they have turned to Me the back, and not the face: though I taught them, rising up early and teaching *them*, yet they have not hearkened to receive instruction.

34 But they set their <u>abominations</u> in the <u>house</u>, which is called by My name, to defile it.   _{detestable things - temple}

35 And they built the high places of Ba'al, which *are* in the valley of the son of Hin'nom, to cause their sons and their daughters to pass through *the fire* to Mo'lech; which I commanded them not, neither came it into My mind, that they should do this <u>abomination</u>, to cause Ju'dah to sin._{detestable thing}

36 And now therefore thus says the LORD, the <u>God</u> of Is'ra-el, concerning this city, whereof you say, It shall be delivered into the hand of the king of Bab'y-lon by the sword, and by the famine, and by the pestilence;   Elohim^{p.f.}

37 Behold, I will gather them out of all countries, where I have driven them in My anger, and in My fury, and in great anger; and I will bring them again to this place, and I will cause them to dwell safely:

38 And they shall be My people, and I will be their <u>God</u>:   Elohim^{p.f.}

39 And I will give them one heart, and one way, that they may <u>fear</u> Me for ever, for the good of them, and of their children after them: _{revere}

40 And I will make an everlasting <u>covenant</u> with them, that I will not turn away from them, to do them good; but I will put My <u>fear</u> in their hearts, that they shall not depart from Me.   _{agreement - respect}

41 Yea, I will rejoice over them to do them good, and I will plant them in this land <u>assuredly</u> with My whole heart and with My whole soul.   _{in truth}

42 For thus says the LORD; Like as I have brought all this great evil upon this people, so will I bring upon them all the good that I have promised them.

43 And fields shall be bought in this land, whereof you say, *It is* desolate without man or beast; it is given into the hand of the Chal-de'ans.

44 Men shall buy fields for money, and <u>subscribe evidences</u>, and seal *them*,

and take witnesses in the land of Ben'ja-min, and in the places about Je-ru'sa-lem, and in the cities of Ju'dah, and in the cities of the mountains, and in the cities of the valley, and in the cities of the south: for I will cause their captivity to return, says the LORD. sign deeds

CHAPTER 33

MOREOVER the word of the LORD came to Jer-e-mi'ah the second time, while he was yet shut up in the court of the prison, saying,

2 Thus says the LORD the maker thereof, the LORD that formed it, to establish it; the LORD *is* His name;

3 Call to Me, and I will answer you, and show you great and mighty things, which you know not. unsearchable

4 For thus says the LORD, the God of Is'ra-el, concerning the houses of this city, and concerning the houses of the kings of Ju'dah, which are thrown down by the mounts, and by the sword; Elohim^p.f. - siege ramps

5 They come to fight with the Chal-de'ans, but *it is* to fill them with the dead bodies of men, whom I have slain in My anger and in My fury, and for all whose wickedness I have hid My face from this city.

6 Behold, I will bring it health and cure, and I will cure them, and will reveal to them the abundance of peace and truth.

7 And I will cause the captivity of Ju'dah and the captivity of Is'ra-el to return, and will build them, as at the first.

8 And I will cleanse them from all their iniquity, whereby they have sinned against Me; and I will pardon all their iniquities, whereby they have sinned, and whereby they have transgressed against Me. sins

9 And it shall be to Me a name of joy, a praise and an honor before all the nations of the earth, which shall hear all the good that I do to them: and they shall fear and tremble for all the goodness and for all the prosperity that I procure to it. be in awe

10 Thus says the LORD; Again there shall be heard in this place, which you say *shall be* desolate without man and without beast, *even* in the cities of Ju'dah, and in the streets of Je-ru'sa-lem, that are desolate, without man, and without inhabitant, and without beast, deserted - a waste

11 The voice of joy, and the voice of gladness, the voice of the bridegroom, and the voice of the bride, the voice of them that shall say, Praise the LORD of hosts: for the LORD *is* good; for His mercy *endures* for ever: *and* of them that shall bring the sacrifice of praise into the house of the LORD. For I will cause to return the captivity of the land, as at the first, says the LORD. Jehovah^s.f. Tsebaoth - Jehovah^s.f.

12 Thus says the LORD of hosts; Again in this place, which is desolate without man and without beast, and in all the cities thereof, shall be an habitation of shepherds causing *their* flocks to lie down.

13 In the cities of the mountains, in the cities of the vale, and in the cities of

the south, and in the land of Ben'ja-min, and in the places about Je-ru'sa-lem, and in the cities of Ju'dah, shall the flocks pass again under the hands of him that <u>telleth</u> *them*, says the LORD.   numbers

14 Behold, the days come, says the LORD, that I will perform that good thing which I have promised to the house of Is'ra-el and to the house of Ju'dah.

15 In those days, and at that time, will I cause the <u>Branch</u> of righteousness to grow up to Da'vid; and He shall execute judgment and righteousness in the land. i.e., Jesus Christ

16 In those days shall Ju'dah be saved, and Je-ru'sa-lem shall dwell safely: and this *is the name* wherewith she shall be called, The LORD our righteousness.

17 For thus says the LORD; Da'vid shall never <u>want</u> a man to sit upon the throne of the house of Is'ra-el;
     lack

18 Neither shall the priests the Le'vites <u>want</u> a man before Me to offer burned offerings, and to <u>kindle meat</u> offerings, and to do sacrifice continually.   burn again

19 And the word of the LORD came to Jer-e-mi'ah, saying,

20 Thus says the LORD; If you can break My <u>covenant</u> of the day, and My <u>covenant</u> of the night, and that there should not be day and night in their season;   agreement

21 *Then* may also My <u>covenant</u> be broken with Da'vid My servant, that he should not have a son to reign upon his throne; and with the Le'vites the priests, My ministers.

22 As the host of heaven cannot be numbered, neither the sand of the sea measured: so will I multiply the <u>seed</u> of Da'vid My servant, and the Le'-vites that minister to Me.   descendants

23 Moreover the word of the LORD came to Jer-e-mi'ah, saying,

24 Consider you not what this people have spoken, saying, The two families which the LORD has chosen, He has even cast them off? thus they have despised My people, that they should be no more a nation before them.

25 Thus says the LORD; If My <u>covenant</u> *be* not with day and night, *and if* I have not appointed the ordinances of heaven and earth;   agreement

26 Then will I cast away the <u>seed</u> of Ja'cob, and Da'vid My servant, *so* that I will not take *any* of his <u>seed</u> *to be* rulers over the <u>seed</u> of A'bra-ham, I'saac, and Ja'cob: for I will cause their captivity to return, and have mercy on them.   descendants

CHAPTER 34

THE word which came to Jer-e-mi'ah from the LORD, when Neb-u-chad-nez'zar king of Bab'y-lon, and all his army, and all the kingdoms of the earth of his dominion, and all the people, fought against Je-ru'sa-lem, and against all the cities thereof, saying,

2 Thus says the LORD, the <u>God</u> of Is'ra-el; Go and speak to Zed-e-ki'ah king of Ju'dah, and tell him, Thus says the LORD; Behold, I will give this city into

the hand of the king of Bab'y-lon, and he shall burn it with fire: Elohim^{p.f.}

3 And you shall not escape out of his hand, but shall surely be taken, and delivered into his hand; and your eyes shall behold the eyes of the king of Bab'y-lon, and he shall speak with you mouth to mouth, and you shall go to Bab'y-lon.   face to face

4 Yet hear the word of the LORD, O Zed-e-ki'ah king of Ju'dah; Thus says the LORD of you, You shall not die by the sword:

5 *But* you shall die in peace: and with the burnings of your fathers, the former kings which were before you, so shall they burn *odors* for you; and they will lament you, *saying*, Ah lord! for I have pronounced the word, says the LORD.

6 Then Jer-e-mi'ah the prophet spoke all these words to Zed-e-ki'ah king of Ju'dah in Je-ru'sa-lem,

7 When the king of Bab'y-lon's army fought against Je-ru'sa-lem, and against all the cities of Ju'dah that were left, against La'chish, and against A-ze'kah: for these defenced cities remained of the cities of Ju'dah.

8 *This is* the word that came to Jer-e-mi'ah from the LORD, after that the king Zed-e-ki'ah had made a covenant with all the people which *were* at Je-ru'sa-lem, to proclaim liberty to them;   agreement

9 That every man should let his manservant, and every man his maidservant, *being* an He'brew or an He'brew-ess, go free; that none should serve

himself of them, *that is*, of a Jew his brother.

10 Now when all the princes, and all the people, which had entered into the covenant, heard that every one should let his manservant, and every one his maidservant, go free, that none should serve themselves of them any more, then they obeyed, and let *them* go.   agreement

11 But afterward they turned, and caused the servants and the handmaids, whom they had let go free, to return, and brought them into subjection for servants and for handmaids.

12 Therefore the word of the LORD came to Jer-e-mi'ah from the LORD, saying,

13 Thus says the LORD, the God of Is'ra-el; I made a covenant with your fathers in the day that I brought them forth out of the land of E'gypt, out of the house of bondmen, saying,   Elohim^{p.f.} - agreement

14 At the end of seven years let you go every man his brother an He'brew, which has been sold to you; and when he has served you six years, you shall let him go free from you: but your fathers hearkened not to Me, neither inclined their ear.   sold himself

15 And you were now turned, and had done right in My sight, in proclaiming liberty every man to his neighbor; and you had made a covenant before Me in the house which is called by My name:

16 But you turned and polluted My name, and caused every man his servant, and every man his handmaid, whom you had set at liberty at their plea-

P15A

1242

sure, to return, and brought them into subjection, to be to you for servants and for handmaids.

17 Therefore thus says the LORD; You have not hearkened to Me, in proclaiming liberty, every one to his brother, and every man to his neighbor: behold, I proclaim a liberty for you, says the LORD, to the sword, to the pestilence, and to the famine; and I will make you to be removed into all the kingdoms of the earth.

18 And I will give the men that have <u>transgressed</u> My <u>covenant</u>, which have not performed the words of the <u>covenant</u> which they had made before Me, when they cut the calf in two, and passed between the parts thereof, violated - agreement

19 The princes of Ju'dah, and the princes of Je-ru'sa-lem, the eunuchs, and the priests, and all the people of the land, which passed between the parts of the calf;

20 I will even give them into the hand of their enemies, and into the hand of them that seek their life: and their dead bodies shall be for meat to the fowls of the heaven, and to the beasts of the earth.

21 And Zed-e-ki'ah king of Ju'dah and his princes will I give into the hand of their enemies, and into the hand of them that seek their life, and into the hand of the king of Bab'y-lon's army, which are gone up from you.

22 Behold, I will command, says the LORD, and cause them to return to this city; and they shall fight against it, and take it, and burn it with fire: and I will make the cities of Ju'dah a <u>desolation</u> without an inhabitant. waste

CHAPTER 35

THE word which came to Jer-e-mi'ah from the LORD in the days of Je-hoi'a-kim the son of Jo-si'ah king of Ju'dah, saying,

2 Go to the house of the Re'chab-ites, and speak to them, and bring them into the house of the LORD, into one of the chambers, and give them wine to drink.

3 Then I took Ja-az-a-ni'ah the son of Jer-e-mi'ah, the son of Hab-a-zi-ni'ah, and his brethren, and all his sons, and the whole house of the Re'chab-ites;

4 And I brought them into the house of the LORD, into the <u>chamber</u> of the sons of Ha'nan, the son of Ig-da-li'ah, a man of <u>God</u>, which *was* by the <u>chamber</u> of the princes, which *was* above the <u>chamber</u> of Ma-a-se'iah the son of Shal'lum, the <u>keeper of the door</u>: room - Elohim^(p.f.) - doorkeeper

5 And I set before the sons of the house of the Re'chab-ites pots full of wine, and cups, and I said to them, Drink you wine.

6 But they said, We will drink no wine: for Jon'a-dab the son of Re'chab our father commanded us, saying, You shall drink no wine, *neither you*, nor your sons for ever:

7 Neither shall you build house, nor sow seed, nor plant vineyard, nor have *any*: but all your days you shall dwell in tents; that you may live many days in the land where you *be* strangers.

8 Thus have we obeyed the voice of

Jon'a-dab the son of Re'chab our father in all that he has charged us, to drink no wine all our days, we, our wives, our sons, nor our daughters;

9 Nor to build houses for us to dwell in: neither have we vineyard, nor field, nor seed:

10 But we have dwelled in tents, and have obeyed, and done according to all that Jon'a-dab our father commanded us.

11 But it came to pass, when Neb-u-chad-rez'zar king of Bab'y-lon came up into the land, that we said, Come, and let us go to Je-ru'sa-lem for <u>fear</u> of the army of the Chal-de'ans, and for <u>fear</u> of the army of the Syr'i-ans: so we dwell at Je-ru'sa-lem.   dread

12 Then came the word of the LORD to Jer-e-mi'ah, saying,

13 Thus says the <u>LORD of hosts</u>, the <u>God</u> of Is'ra-el; Go and tell the men of Ju'dah and the inhabitants of Je-ru'sa-lem, Will you not receive instruction to <u>hearken</u> to My words? says the <u>LORD</u>.

Jehovah[s.f.] Tsebaoth - Elohim[p.f.] - Listen - Jehovah[s.f.]

14 The words of Jon'a-dab the son of Re'chab, that he commanded his sons not to drink wine, are performed; for to this day they drink none, but obey their father's commandment: notwithstanding I have spoken to you, rising early and speaking; but you hearkened not to Me.

15 I have sent also to you all My servants the prophets, rising up early and sending *them*, saying, Return you now every man from his evil way, and amend your doings, and go not after other gods to serve them, and you shall dwell in the land which I have given to you and to your fathers: but you have not inclined your ear, nor hearkened to Me.

16 Because the sons of Jon'a-dab the son of Re'chab have performed the commandment of their father, which he commanded them; but this people have not hearkened to Me:

17 Therefore thus says the <u>LORD</u> <u>God of hosts</u>, the <u>God</u> of Is'ra-el; Behold, I will bring upon Ju'dah and upon all the inhabitants of Je-ru'sa-lem all the evil that I have pronounced against them: because I have spoken to them, but they have not heard; and I have called to them, but they have not answered.

Jehovah[s.f.] Elohe Tsebaoth - Elohim[p.f.]

18 And Jer-e-mi'ah said to the house of the Re'chab-ites, Thus says the <u>LORD of hosts</u>, the <u>God</u> of Is'ra-el; Because you have obeyed the commandment of Jon'a-dab your father, and kept all his <u>precepts</u>, and done according to all that he has commanded you: instructions

19 Therefore thus says the <u>LORD of hosts</u>, the <u>God</u> of Is'ra-el; Jon'a-dab the son of Re'chab shall not <u>want</u> a man to stand before Me for ever.   lack

CHAPTER 36

AND it came to pass in the fourth year of Je-hoi'a-kim the son of Jo-si'ah king of Ju'dah, *that* this word came to Jer-e-mi'ah from the LORD, saying,

2 Take you a roll of a book, and write therein all the words that I have spoken

to you against Is'ra-el, and against Ju'dah, and against all the nations, from the day I spoke to you, from the days of Jo-si'ah, even to this day.

3 It may be that the house of Ju'dah will hear all the evil which I purpose to do to them; that they may return every man from his evil way; that I may forgive their iniquity and their sin.

4 Then Jer-e-mi'ah called Ba'ruch the son of Ne-ri'ah: and Ba'ruch wrote from the mouth of Jer-e-mi'ah all the words of the LORD, which He had spoken to him, upon a roll of a book.

5 And Jer-e-mi'ah commanded Ba'ruch, saying, *I am* shut up; I cannot go into the house of the LORD: restricted

6 Therefore go you, and read in the roll, which you have written from my mouth, the words of the LORD in the ears of the people in the LORD's house upon the fasting day: and also you shall read them in the ears of all Ju'dah that come out of their cities.

7 It may be they will present their supplication before the LORD, and will return every one from his evil way: for great *is* the anger and the fury that the LORD has pronounced against this people.

8 And Ba'ruch the son of Ne-ri'ah did according to all that Jer-e-mi'ah the prophet commanded him, reading in the book the words of the LORD in the LORD's house.

9 And it came to pass in the fifth year of Je-hoi'a-kim the son of Jo-si'ah king of Ju'dah, in the ninth month, *that* they proclaimed a fast before the LORD to all the people in Je-ru'sa-lem, and to all the people that came from the cities of Ju'dah to Je-ru'sa-lem.

10 Then read Ba'ruch in the book the words of Jer-e-mi'ah in the house of the LORD, in the chamber of Gem-a-ri'ah the son of Sha'phan the scribe, in the higher court, at the entry of the new gate of the LORD's house, in the ears of all the people.   room

11 When Mi-cha'iah the son of Gem-a-ri'ah, the son of Sha'phan, had heard out of the book all the words of the LORD,

12 Then he went down into the king's house, into the scribe's chamber: and, lo, all the princes sat there, *even* E-lish'a-ma the scribe, and Del-a-i'ah the son of Shem-a-i'ah, and El'na-than the son of Ach'bor, and Gem-a-ri'ah the son of Sha'phan, and Zed-e-ki'ah the son of Han-a-ni'ah, and all the princes.

13 Then Mi-cha'iah declared to them all the words that he had heard, when Ba'ruch read the book in the ears of the people.

14 Therefore all the princes sent Je-hu'di the son of Neth-a-ni'ah, the son of Shel-e-mi'ah, the son of Cu'shi, to Ba'ruch, saying, Take in your hand the roll wherein you have read in the ears of the people, and come. So Ba'ruch the son of Ne-ri'ah took the roll in his hand, and came to them.

15 And they said to him, Sit down now, and read it in our ears. So Ba'ruch read *it* in their ears.

16 Now it came to pass, when they had heard all the words, they were afraid both one and other, and said

to Ba'ruch, We will surely tell the king of all these words.

17 And they asked Ba'ruch, saying, Tell us now, How did you write all these words at his mouth?

18 Then Ba'ruch answered them, He pronounced all these words to me with his mouth, and I wrote *them* with ink in the book.

19 Then said the princes to Ba'ruch, Go, hide you, you and Jer-e-mi'ah; and let no man know where you be.

20 And they went in to the king into the court, but they laid up the roll in the <u>chamber</u> of E-lish'a-ma the scribe, and told all the words in the ears of the king.　　room

21 So the king sent Je-hu'di to bring the roll: and he took it out of E-lish'a-ma the scribe's <u>chamber</u>. And Je-hu'di read it in the ears of the king, and in the ears of all the princes which stood beside the king.

22 Now the king sat in the winterhouse in the ninth month: and *there was a fire* on the hearth burning before him.

23 And it came to pass, *that* when Je-hu'di had read three or four leaves, he cut it with the penknife, and cast *it* into the fire that *was* on the hearth, until all the roll was consumed in the fire that *was* on the hearth.

24 Yet they were not afraid, nor rent their garments, *neither* the king, nor any of his servants that heard all these words.

25 Nevertheless El'na-than and Del-a-i'ah and Gem-a-ri'ah had made intercession to the king that he would not burn the roll: but he would not hear them.

26 But the king commanded Je-rah'me-el the son of Ham'me-lech, and Ser-a-i'ah the son of Az'ri-el, and Shel-e-mi'ah the son of Ab'de-el, to take Ba'ruch the scribe and Jer-e-mi'ah the prophet: but the LORD hid them.

27 Then the word of the LORD came to Jer-e-mi'ah, after that the king had burned the roll, and the words which Ba'ruch wrote at the mouth of Jer-e-mi'ah, saying,

28 Take you again another roll, and write in it all the former words that were in the first roll, which Je-hoi'a-kim the king of Ju'dah has burned.

29 And you shall say to Je-hoi'a-kim king of Ju'dah, Thus says the LORD; You have burned this roll, saying, Why have you written therein, saying, The king of Bab'y-lon shall certainly come and destroy this land, and shall cause to cease from there man and beast?

30 Therefore thus says the LORD of Je-hoi'a-kim king of Ju'dah; He shall have none to sit upon the throne of Da'vid: and his dead body shall be cast out in the day to the heat, and in the night to the frost.

31 And I will punish him and his <u>seed</u> and his servants for their <u>iniquity</u>; and I will bring upon them, and upon the inhabitants of Je-ru'sa-lem, and upon the men of Ju'dah, all the evil that I have pronounced against them; but they hearkened not.　　descendants - wickedness

32 Then took Jer-e-mi'ah another roll, and gave it to Ba'ruch the scribe, the son of Ne-ri'ah; who wrote therein

from the mouth of Jer-e-mi'ah all the words of the book which Je-hoi'a-kim king of Ju'dah had burned in the fire: and there were added besides to them many like words.

CHAPTER 37

AND king Zed-e-ki'ah the son of Jo-si'ah reigned instead of Co-ni'ah the son of Je-hoi'a-kim, whom Neb-u-chad-rez'zar king of Bab'y-lon made king in the land of Ju'dah.

2 But neither he, nor his servants, nor the people of the land, did <u>hearken</u> to the words of the LORD, which He spoke by the prophet Jer-e-mi'ah._{listen}

3 And Zed-e-ki'ah the king sent Je'hu-cal the son of Shel-e-mi'ah and Zeph-a-ni'ah the son of Ma-a-se'iah the priest to the prophet Jer-e-mi'ah, saying, Pray now to the LORD our <u>God</u> for us. Elohim^{p.f.}

4 Now Jer-e-mi'ah came in and went out among the people: for they had not put him into prison.

5 Then Pha'raoh's army was come forth out of E'gypt: and when the Chal-de'ans that besieged Je-ru'sa-lem heard tidings of them, they departed from Je-ru'sa-lem.

6 Then came the word of the LORD to the prophet Jer-e-mi'ah, saying,

7 Thus says the LORD, the <u>God</u> of Is'ra-el; Thus shall you say to the king of Ju'dah, that sent you to Me to enquire of Me; Behold, Pha'raoh's army, which is come forth to help you, shall return to E'gypt into their own land. Elohim^{p.f.}

8 And the Chal-de'ans shall come again, and fight against this city, and take it, and burn it with fire.

9 Thus says the LORD; Deceive not yourselves, saying, The Chal-de'ans shall surely depart from us: for they shall not depart.

10 For though you had smitten the whole army of the Chal-de'ans that fight against you, and there remained *but* wounded men among them, *yet* should they rise up every man in his tent, and burn this city with fire.

11 And it came to pass, that when the army of the Chal-de'ans was broken up from Je-ru'sa-lem for <u>fear</u> of Pha'raoh's army, dread

12 Then Jer-e-mi'ah went forth out of Je-ru'sa-lem to go into the land of Ben'ja-min, to <u>separate himself there</u> in the midst of the people. receive a portion there

13 And when he was in the gate of Ben'ja-min, a captain of the ward *was* there, whose name *was* I-ri'jah, the son of Shel-e-mi'ah, the son of Han-a-ni'ah; and he took Jer-e-mi'ah the prophet, saying, You <u>fall away</u> to the Chal-de'ans. are deserting

14 Then said Jer-e-mi'ah, *It is* false; I fall not away to the Chal-de'ans. But he hearkened not to him: so I-ri'jah took Jer-e-mi'ah, and brought him to the princes.

15 Why the princes were angry with Jer-e-mi'ah, and smote him, and put him in prison in the house of Jon'a-than the scribe: for they had made that the prison.

16 When Jer-e-mi'ah was entered into the dungeon, and into the <u>cabins</u>,

and Jer-e-mi'ah had remained there many days;   vaulted cell

17 Then Zed-e-ki'ah the king sent, and took him out: and the king asked him secretly in his house, and said, Is there *any* word from the LORD? And Jer-e-mi'ah said, There is: for, said He, you shall be delivered into the hand of the king of Bab'y-lon.

18 Moreover Jer-e-mi'ah said to king Zed-e-ki'ah, What have I offended against you, or against your servants, or against this people, that you have put me in prison?

19 Where *are* now your prophets which prophesied to you, saying, The king of Bab'y-lon shall not come against you, nor against this land?

20 Therefore hear now, I pray you, O my lord the king: let my supplication, I pray you, be accepted before you; that you cause me not to return to the house of Jon'a-than the scribe, less I die there.

21 Then Zed-e-ki'ah the king commanded that they should commit Jer-e-mi'ah into the court of the prison, and that they should give him daily a piece of bread out of the bakers' street, until all the bread in the city were spent. Thus Jer-e-mi'ah remained in the court of the prison.

CHAPTER 38

THEN Sheph-a-ti'ah the son of Mat'tan, and Ged-a-li'ah the son of Pash'ur, and Ju'cal the son of Shel-e-mi'ah, and Pash'ur the son of Mal-chi'ah, heard the words that Jer-e-mi'ah had spoken to all the people, saying,

2 Thus says the LORD, He that remains in this city shall die by the sword, by the famine, and by the pestilence: but he that goes forth to the Chal-de'ans shall live; for he shall have his life for a prey, and shall live.   goes over

3 Thus says the LORD, This city shall surely be given into the hand of the king of Bab'y-lon's army, which shall take it.

4 Therefore the princes said to the king, We beseech you, let this man be put to death: for thus he weakens the hands of the men of war that remain in this city, and the hands of all the people, in speaking such words to them: for this man seeks not the welfare of this people, but the hurt.   beg - soldiers - good

5 Then Zed-e-ki'ah the king said, Behold, he *is* in your hand: for the king *is* not *he that* can do *any* thing against you.

6 Then took they Jer-e-mi'ah, and cast him into the dungeon of Mal-chi'ah the son of Ham'me-lech, that *was* in the court of the prison: and they let down Jer-e-mi'ah with cords. And in the dungeon *there was* no water, but mire: so Jer-e-mi'ah sunk in the mire.

7 Now when E'bed-me'lech the E-thi-o'pi-an, one of the eunuchs which was in the king's house, heard that they had put Jer-e-mi'ah in the dungeon; the king then sitting in the gate of Ben'ja-min;

8 E'bed-me'lech went forth out of the king's house, and spoke to the king, saying,

9 My lord the king, these men have done evil in all that they have done to

Jer-e-mi'ah the prophet, whom they have cast into the dungeon; and he is <u>like</u> to die for hunger in the place where he is: for *there is* no more bread in the city. _{likely}

10 Then the king commanded E'bed-me'lech the E-thi-o'pi-an, saying, Take from here thirty men with you, and take up Jer-e-mi'ah the prophet out of the dungeon, before he die.

11 So E'bed-me'lech took the men with him, and went into the house of the king under the treasury, and took from there old <u>cast clouts</u> and old <u>rotten rags</u>, and let them down by cords into the dungeon to Jer-e-mi'ah. _{clothes - worn out}

12 And E'bed-me'lech the E-thi-o'pi-an said to Jer-e-mi'ah, Put now *these* old <u>cast clouts</u> and <u>rotten</u> rags under your armholes under the cords. And Jer-e-mi'ah did so.

13 So they drew up Jer-e-mi'ah with cords, and took him up out of the dungeon: and Jer-e-mi'ah remained in the court of the prison.

14 Then Zed-e-ki'ah the king sent, and took Jer-e-mi'ah the prophet to him into the third entry that *is* in the house of the LORD: and the king said to Jer-e-mi'ah, I will ask you a thing; hide nothing from me.

15 Then Jer-e-mi'ah said to Zed-e-ki'ah, If I declare *it* to you, will you not surely put me to death? and if I give you counsel, will you not hearken to me?

16 So Zed-e-ki'ah the king swear secretly to Jer-e-mi'ah, saying, *As* the LORD lives, that made us this soul, I will not put you to death, neither will I give you into the hand of these men that seek your life.

17 Then said Jer-e-mi'ah to Zed-e-ki'ah, Thus says the LORD, <u>the God of hosts</u>, the <u>God</u> of Is'ra-el; If you will assuredly <u>go forth</u> to the king of Bab'y-lon's princes, then your soul shall live, and this city shall not be burned with fire; and you shall live, and your house:

_{Jehovah^{s.f.} Elohe Tsebaoth - Elohim^{p.f.} - surrender}

18 But if you will not <u>go forth</u> to the king of Bab'y-lon's princes, then shall this city be given into the hand of the Chal-de'ans, and they shall burn it with fire, and you shall not escape out of their hand.

19 And Zed-e-ki'ah the king said to Jer-e-mi'ah, I am afraid of the Jews that are fallen to the Chal-de'ans, less they deliver me into their hand, and they <u>mock</u> me. _{abuse}

20 But Jer-e-mi'ah said, They shall not deliver *you*. Obey, I <u>beseech</u> you, the voice of the LORD, which I speak to you: so it shall be well to you, and your soul shall live. _{beg}

21 But if you refuse to <u>go forth</u>, this *is* the word that the LORD has showed me:

22 And, behold, all the women that are left in the king of Ju'dah's house *shall be* brought forth to the king of Bab'y-lon's princes, and those *women* shall say, Your friends have set you on, and have prevailed against you: your feet are sunk in the mire, *and* they are turned away back.

23 So they shall bring out all your

wives and your children to the Chal-de'ans: and you shall not escape out of their hand, but shall be taken by the hand of the king of Bab'y-lon: and you shall cause this city to be burned with fire.

24 Then said Zed-e-ki'ah to Jer-e-mi'ah, Let no man know of these words, and you shall not die.

25 But if the princes hear that I have talked with you, and they come to you, and say to you, Declare to us now what you have said to the king, hide it not from us, and we will not put you to death; also what the king said to you:

26 Then you shall say to them, I presented my supplication before the king, that he would not cause me to return to Jon'a-than's house, to die there.

27 Then came all the princes to Jer-e-mi'ah, and asked him: and he told them according to all these words that the king had commanded. So they left off speaking with him; for the matter was not perceived.   ceased - overheard

28 So Jer-e-mi'ah abode in the court of the prison until the day that Je-ru'sa-lem was taken: and he was *there* when Je-ru'sa-lem was taken.

CHAPTER 39

IN the ninth year of Zed-e-ki'ah king of Ju'dah, in the tenth month, came Neb-u-chad-rez'zar king of Bab'y-lon and all his army against Je-ru'sa-lem, and they besieged it.

2 *And* in the eleventh year of Zed-e-ki'ah, in the fourth month, the ninth *day* of the month, the city was broken up.

3 And all the princes of the king of Bab'y-lon came in, and sat in the middle gate, *even* Ner'gal-sha-re'zer, Sam'gar-ne'bo, Sar-se'chim, Rab'-sa-ris, Ner'gal-sha-re'zer, Rab'-mag, with all the residue of the princes of the king of Bab'y-lon.   rest

4 And it came to pass, *that* when Zed-e-ki'ah the king of Ju'dah saw them, and all the men of war, then they fled, and went forth out of the city by night, by the way of the king's garden, by the gate between the two walls: and he went out the way of the plain.   soldiers

5 But the Chal-de'ans' army pursued after them, and overtook Zed-e-ki'ah in the plains of Jer'i-cho: and when they had taken him, they brought him up to Neb-u-chad-nez'zar king of Bab'y-lon to Rib'lah in the land of Ha'math, where he gave judgment upon him.   passed sentence

6 Then the king of Bab'y-lon slew the sons of Zed-e-ki'ah in Rib'lah before his eyes: also the king of Bab'y-lon slew all the nobles of Ju'dah.

7 Moreover he put out Zed-e-ki'ah's eyes, and bound him with chains, to carry him to Bab'y-lon.

8 And the Chal-de'ans burned the king's house, and the houses of the people, with fire, and broke down the walls of Je-ru'sa-lem.

9 Then Neb'u-zar-a'dan the captain of the guard carried away captive into Bab'y-lon the remnant of the people that remained in the city, and those

that <u>fell away</u>, that fell to him, with the rest of the people that remained.   commander - deserted

10 But Neb'u-zar-a'dan the captain of the guard left of the poor of the people, which had nothing, in the land of Ju'dah, and gave them vineyards and fields at <u>the same</u> time. that

11 Now Neb-u-chad-rez'zar king of Bab'y-lon gave charge concerning Jer-e-mi'ah to Neb'u-zar-a'dan the captain of the guard, saying,

12 Take him, and look <u>well to</u> him, and do him no harm; but do to him even as he shall say to. after

13 So Neb'u-zar-a'dan the captain of the guard sent, and Neb-u-shas'ban, Rab'-sa-ris, and Ner'gal-sha-re'zer, Rab'-mag, and all the king of Bab'y-lon's princes;

14 Even they sent, and took Jer-e-mi'ah out of the court of the prison, and committed him to Ged-a-li'ah the son of A-hi'kam the son of Sha'phan, that he should carry him home: so he dwelled among the people.

15 Now the word of the LORD came to Jer-e-mi'ah, while he was shut up in the court of the prison, saying,

16 Go and speak to E'bed-me'lech the E-thi-o'pi-an, saying, Thus says the Lord of hosts, the <u>God</u> of Is'ra-el; Behold, I will bring My words upon this city for evil, and not for good; and they shall be *accomplished* in that day before you. Jehovah^{s.f.} Tsebaoth - Elohim^{p.f.}

17 But I will deliver you in that day, says the LORD: and you shall not be given into the hand of the men of whom you *are* afraid.

18 For I will surely deliver you, and you shall not fall by the sword, but your life shall be for a prey to you: because you have put your trust in Me, says the LORD.

CHAPTER 40

THE word that came to Jer-e-mi'ah from the LORD, after that Neb'u-zar-a'dan the captain of the guard had let him go from Ra'mah, when he had taken him being bound in chains among all that were carried away captive of Je-ru'sa-lem and Ju'dah, which were carried away captive unto Bab'y-lon.

2 And the captain of the guard took Jer-e-mi'ah, and said to him, The LORD your <u>God</u> has pronounced this evil upon this place. Elohim^{p.f.}

3 Now the LORD has brought *it*, and done according as He has said: because you have sinned against the LORD, and have not obeyed His voice, therefore this thing is come upon you.

4 And now, behold, I loose you this day from the chains which *were* upon your hand. If it seem good to you to come with me into Bab'y-lon, come; and I will look well to you: but if it seem ill to you to come with me into Bab'y-lon, <u>forbear</u>: behold, all the land *is* before you: where it seems good and convenient for you to go, there go. never mind

5 Now while he was not yet gone back, *he said*, Go back also to Ged-a-li'ah the son of A-hi'kam the son of

Sha'phan, whom the king of Bab'y-lon has made governor over the cities of Ju'dah, and dwell with him among the people: or go wheresoever it seems convenient to you to go. So the captain of the guard gave him victuals and a <u>reward</u>, and let him go. ^{gift}

6 Then went Jer-e-mi'ah to Ged-a-li'ah the son of A-hi'kam to Miz'pah; and dwelled with him among the people that were left in the land.

7 Now when all the captains of the forces which *were* in the fields, *even* they and their men, heard that the king of Bab'y-lon had made Ged-a-li'ah the son of A-hi'kam governor in the land, and had committed to him men, and women, and children, and of the poor of the land, of them that were not carried away captive to Bab'y-lon;

8 Then they came to Ged-a-li'ah to Miz'pah, even Ish'ma-el the son of Neth-a-ni'ah, and Jo-ha'nan and Jon'a-than the sons of Ka-re'ah, and Ser-a-i'ah the son of Tan'hu-meth, and the sons of E'phai the Ne-toph'a-thite, and Jez-a-ni'ah the son of a Ma-ach'a-thite, they and their men.

9 And Ged-a-li'ah the son of A-hi'kam the son of Sha'phan swear to them and to their men, saying, Fear not to serve the Chal-de'ans: dwell in the land, and serve the king of Bab'y-lon, and it shall be well with you.

10 As for me, behold, I will dwell at Miz'pah to serve the Chal-de'ans, which will come to us: but you, gather you wine, and summer fruits, and oil,

and put *them* in your vessels, and dwell in your cities that you have taken.

11 Likewise when all the Jews that *were* in Mo'ab, and among the Am'mon-ites, and in E'dom, and that *were* in all the countries, heard that the king of Bab'y-lon had left a remnant of Ju'dah, and that he had set over them Ged-a-li'ah the son of A-hi'kam the son of Sha'phan;

12 Even all the Jews returned out of all places where they were driven, and came to the land of Ju'dah, to Ged-a-li'ah, to Miz'pah, and gathered wine and summer fruits very much.

13 Moreover Jo-ha'nan the son of Ka-re'ah, and all the captains of the forces that *were* in the fields, came to Ged-a-li'ah to Miz'pah,

14 And said to him, Do you certainly know that Ba'a-lis the king of the Am'mon-ites has sent Ish'ma-el the son of Neth-a-ni'ah to slay you? But Ged-a-li'ah the son of A-hi'kam believed them not.

15 Then Jo-ha'nan the son of Ka-re'ah spoke to Ged-a-li'ah in Miz'pah secretly, saying, Let me go, I pray you, and I will slay Ish'ma-el the son of Neth-a-ni'ah, and no man shall know *it*: why should he slay you, that all the Jews which are gathered to you should be scattered, and the remnant in Ju'dah perish?

16 But Ged-a-li'ah the son of A-hi'kam said to Jo-ha'nan the son of Ka-re'ah, You shall not do this thing: for you speak falsely of Ish'ma-el.

CHAPTER 41

NOW it came to pass in the seventh month, *that* Ish'ma-el the son of Neth-a-ni'ah the son of E-lish'a-ma, of the <u>seed royal</u>, and the princes of the king, even ten men with him, came to Ged-a-li'ah the son of A-hi'kam to Miz'pah; and there they did eat bread together in Miz'pah.   royal family
2 Then arose Ish'ma-el the son of Neth-a-ni'ah, and the ten men that were with him, and smote Ged-a-li'ah the son of A-hi'kam the son of Sha'phan with the sword, and slew him, whom the king of Bab'y-lon had made governor over the land.
3 Ish'ma-el also slew all the Jews that were with him, *even* with Ged-a-li'ah, at Miz'pah, and the Chal-de'ans that were found there, *and* the <u>men</u> of war.   soldiers
4 And it came to pass the second day after he had slain Ged-a-li'ah, and no man knew *it*,
5 That there came certain from She'chem, from Shi'loh, and from Sa-ma'ri-a, *even* <u>fourscore</u> men, having their beards shaven, and their clothes rent, and having cut themselves, with offerings and incense in their hand, to bring *them* to the house of the LORD. 80
6 And Ish'ma-el the son of Neth-a-ni'ah went forth from Miz'pah to meet them, weeping all along as he went: and it came to pass, as he met them, he said to them, Come to Ged-a-li'ah the son of A-hi'kam.
7 And it was *so*, when they came into the midst of the city, that Ish'ma-el the son of Neth-a-ni'ah slew them, *and cast* *them* into the midst of the pit, he, and the men that *were* with him.
8 But ten men were found among them that said to Ish'ma-el, Slay us not: for we have treasures in the field, of wheat, and of barley, and of oil, and of honey. So he forbare, and slew them not among their brethren.
9 Now the <u>pit</u> wherein Ish'ma-el had cast all the dead bodies of the men, whom he had slain because of Ged-a-li'ah, *was* it which A'sa the king had made <u>for fear</u> of Ba'a-sha king of Is'ra-el: *and* Ish'ma-el the son of Neth-a-ni'ah filled it with *them that were* slain.   cistern - on account
10 Then Ish'ma-el carried away captive all the <u>residue</u> of the people that *were* in Miz'pah, *even* the king's daughters, and all the people that remained in Miz'pah, whom Neb'u-zar-a'dan the captain of the guard had committed to Ged-a-li'ah the son of A-hi'kam: and Ish'ma-el the son of Neth-a-ni'ah carried them away captive, and departed to go over to the Am'mon-ites.   rest
11 But when Jo-ha'nan the son of Ka-re'ah, and all the captains of the forces that *were* with him, heard of all the evil that Ish'ma-el the son of Neth-a-ni'ah had done,
12 Then they took all the men, and went to fight with Ish'ma-el the son of Neth-a-ni'ah, and found him by the great waters that *are* in Gib'e-on.
13 Now it came to pass, *that* when all the people which *were* with Ish'ma-el saw Jo-ha'nan the son of Ka-re'ah, and all the captains of the forces that *were* with him, then they were glad.

14 So all the people that Ish'ma-el had carried away captive from Miz'pah <u>cast about</u> and returned, and went to Jo-ha'nan the son of Ka-re'ah.   turned around

15 But Ish'ma-el the son of Neth-a-ni'ah escaped from Jo-ha'nan with eight men, and went to the Am'mon-ites.

16 Then took Jo-ha'nan the son of Ka-re'ah, and all the captains of the forces that *were* with him, all the remnant of the people whom he had recovered from Ish'ma-el the son of Neth-a-ni'ah, from Miz'pah, after *that* he had slain Ged-a-li'ah the son of A-hi'kam, *even* mighty men of war, and the women, and the children, and the eunuchs, whom he had brought again from Gib'e-on:

17 And they departed, and dwelled in the habitation of Chim'ham, which is by Beth'-le-hem, to go to enter into E'gypt,

18 Because of the Chal-de'ans: for they were afraid of them, because Ish'ma-el the son of Neth-a-ni'ah had slain Ged-a-li'ah the son of A-hi'kam, whom the king of Bab'y-lon made governor in the land.

CHAPTER 42

THEN all the captains of the forces, and Jo-ha'nan the son of Ka-re'ah, and Jez-a-ni'ah the son of Hosh-a-i'ah, and all the people from the least even to the greatest, came near,

2 And said to Jer-e-mi'ah the prophet, <u>Let</u>, we <u>beseech</u> you, our supplication be accepted before you, and pray for us to the LORD your <u>God</u>, even for all this remnant; (for we are left *but* a few of many, as your eyes do behold us:)   Please - beg - Elohim^p.f.

3 That the LORD your <u>God</u> may show us the way wherein we may walk, and the thing that we may do.

4 Then Jer-e-mi'ah the prophet said to them, I have heard *you*; behold, I will pray to the LORD your <u>God</u> according to your words; and it shall come to pass, *that* whatsoever thing the LORD shall answer you, I will declare *it* to you; I will keep nothing back from you.

5 Then they said to Jer-e-mi'ah, The LORD be a true and faithful witness between us, if we do not even according to all things for the which the LORD your <u>God</u> shall send you to us.   Elohim^p.f.

6 Whether *it be* good, or whether *it be* evil, we will obey the voice of the LORD our <u>God</u>, to whom we send you; that it may be well with us, when we obey the voice of the LORD our <u>God</u>.

7 And it came to pass after ten days, that the word of the LORD came to Jer-e-mi'ah.

8 Then called he Jo-ha'nan the son of Ka-re'ah, and all the captains of the forces which *were* with him, and all the people from the least even to the greatest,

9 And said to them, Thus says the LORD, the <u>God</u> of Is'ra-el, to whom you sent me to present your supplication before him;

10 If you will still abide in this land, then will I build you, and not pull *you* down, and I will plant you, and not

pluck *you* up: for I <u>repent</u> Me of the evil that I have done to you. _{grieve}

11 Be not afraid of the king of Bab'y-lon, of whom you are afraid; be not afraid of him, says the LORD: for I *am* with you to save you, and to deliver you from his hand.

12 And I will show mercies to you, that he may have mercy upon you, and cause you to return to your own land.

13 But if you say, We will not dwell in this land, neither obey the voice of the LORD your <u>God</u>, _{Elohim^{p.f.}}

14 Saying, No; but we will go into the land of E'gypt, where we shall sce no war, nor hear the sound of the trumpet, nor have hunger of bread; and there will we dwell:

15 And now therefore hear the word of the LORD, you remnant of Ju'dah; Thus says the <u>LORD of hosts</u>, the <u>God</u> of Is'ra-el; If you wholly set your faces to enter into E'gypt, and go to <u>sojourn</u> there; _{Jehovah^{s.f.} Tsebaoth - reside}

16 Then it shall come to pass, *that* the sword, which you feared, shall overtake you there in the land of E'gypt, and the famine, whereof you were afraid, shall follow close after you there in E'gypt; and there you shall die.

17 So shall it be with all the men that <u>set their faces</u> to go into E'gypt to <u>sojourn</u> there; they shall die by the sword, by the famine, and by the pestilence: and none of them shall remain or escape from the evil that I will bring upon them. _{are determined - reside}

18 For thus says the <u>LORD of hosts</u>, the <u>God</u> of Is'ra-el; As My anger and My fury has been poured forth upon the inhabitants of Je-ru'sa-lem; so shall My fury be poured forth upon you, when you shall enter into E'gypt: and you shall be an <u>execration</u>, and an astonishment, and a curse, and a reproach; and you shall see this place no more. _{Jehovah^{s.f.} Tsebaoth - Elohim^{p.f.} - curse}

19 The LORD has said concerning you, O you remnant of Ju'dah; Go you not into E'gypt: know certainly that I have <u>admonished</u> you this day. _{warned}

20 For you <u>dissembled</u> in your hearts, when you sent me to the LORD your <u>God</u>, saying, Pray for us to the LORD our <u>God</u>; and according to all that the LORD our God shall say, so declare to us, and we will do *it*. _{are deceived - Elohim^{p.f.}}

21 And *now* I have this day declared *it* to you; but you have not obeyed the voice of the LORD your <u>God</u>, nor any *thing* for the which He has sent me to you.

22 Now therefore know certainly that you shall die by the sword, by the famine, and by the pestilence, in the place where you desire to go *and* to <u>sojourn</u>. _{reside}

CHAPTER 43

AND it came to pass, *that* when Jer-e-mi'ah had made an end of speaking to all the people all the words of the LORD their <u>God</u>, for which the LORD their <u>God</u> had sent him to them, *even* all these words, _{Elohim^{p.f.}}

2 Then spoke Az-a-ri'ah the son of Hosh-a-i'ah, and Jo-ha'nan the son of Ka-re'ah, and all the proud men, saying to Jer-e-mi'ah, You speak falsely:

the LORD our God has not sent you to say, Go not into E'gypt to so-journ there: Elohim^{p.f.} - reside

3 But Ba'ruch the son of Ne-ri'ah sets you on against us, for to deliver us into the hand of the Chal-de'ans, that they might put us to death, and carry us away captives into Bab'y-lon.   is inciting you

4 So Jo-ha'nan the son of Ka-re'ah, and all the captains of the forces, and all the people, obeyed not the voice of the LORD, to dwell in the land of Ju'dah.

5 But Jo-ha'nan the son of Ka-re'ah, and all the captains of the forces, took all the remnant of Ju'dah, that were returned from all nations, where they had been driven, to dwell in the land of Ju'dah;

6 *Even* men, and women, and chil-dren, and the king's daughters, and every person that Neb'u-zar-a'dan the captain of the guard had left with Ged-a-li'ah the son of A-hi'kam the son of Sha'phan, and Jer-e-mi'ah the prophet, and Ba'ruch the son of Ne-ri'ah.

7 So they came into the land of E'gypt: for they obeyed not the voice of the LORD: thus came they *even* to Tah'pan-hes.

8 Then came the word of the LORD to Jer-e-mi'ah in Tah'pan-hes, saying,

9 Take great stones in your hand, and hide them in the clay in the brickkiln, which *is* at the entry of Pha'raoh's house in Tah'pan-hes, in the sight of the men of Ju'dah;   bury

10 And say to them, Thus says the LORD of hosts, the God of Is'ra-el; Behold,

I will send and take Neb-u-chad-rez'zar the king of Bab'y-lon, My servant, and will set his throne upon these stones that I have hid; and he shall spread his royal pavil-ion over them.   Jehovah^{s.f.} Tsebaoth - Elohim^{p.f.}

11 And when he comes, he shall smite the land of E'gypt, *and deliver* such *as are* for death to death; and such *as are* for captivity to captivity; and such *as are* for the sword to the sword.

12 And I will kindle a fire in the houses of the gods of E'gypt; and he shall burn them, and carry them away cap-tives: and he shall array himself with the land of E'gypt, as a shepherd puts on his garment; and he shall go forth from there in peace.

13 He shall break also the images of Beth-she'mesh, that *is* in the land of E'gypt; and the houses of the gods of the E-gyp'tians shall he burn with fire.

CHAPTER 44

THE word that came to Jer-e-mi'ah concerning all the Jews which dwell in the land of E'gypt, which dwell at Mig'dol, and at Tah'pan-hes, and at Noph, and in the country of Path'ros, saying,

2 Thus says the LORD of hosts, the God of Is'ra-el; You have seen all the evil that I have brought upon Je-ru'sa-lem, and upon all the cities of Ju'dah; and, behold, this day they *are* a desolation, and no man dwells therein,   Jehovah^{s.f.} Tsebaoth - Elohim^{p.f.} - in ruins

3 Because of their wickedness which they have committed to provoke Me to anger, in that they went to burn in-

cense, *and* to serve other gods, whom they knew not, *neither* they, you, nor your fathers. worship
4 However I sent to you all My servants the prophets, rising early and sending *them*, saying, Oh, do not this abominable thing that I hate. detestable thing - despise
5 But they hearkened not, nor inclined their ear to turn from their wickedness, to burn no incense to other gods. listened
6 Wherefore My fury and My anger was poured forth, and was kindled in the cities of Ju'dah and in the streets of Je-ru'sa-lem; and they are wasted *and* desolate, as at this day. ruined
7 Therefore now thus says the LORD, the God of hosts, the God of Is'ra-el; Wherefore commit you *this* great evil against your souls, to cut off from you man and woman, child and suckling, out of Ju'dah, to leave you none to remain; Jehovahˢ·ᶠ Elohe Tsebaoth - Elohimᵖ·ᶠ
8 In that you provoke Me to anger with the works of your hands, burning incense to other gods in the land of E'gypt, where you be gone to dwell, that you might cut yourselves off, and that you might be a curse and a reproach among all the nations of the earth? worshiping
9 Have you forgotten the wickedness of your fathers, and the wickedness of the kings of Ju'dah, and the wickedness of their wives, and your own wickedness, and the wickedness of your wives, which they have committed in the land of Ju'dah, and in the streets of Je-ru'sa-lem?

10 They are not humbled *even* to this day, neither have they feared, nor walked in My law, nor in My statutes, that I set before you and before your fathers. revered - decrees
11 Therefore thus says the LORD of hosts, the God of Is'ra-el; Behold, I will set My face against you for evil, and to cut off all Ju'dah. Jehovahˢ·ᶠ Tsebaoth - Elohimᵖ·ᶠ - bring disaster
12 And I will take the remnant of Ju'dah, that have set their faces to go into the land of E'gypt to sojourn there, and they shall all be consumed, *and* fall in the land of E'gypt; they shall *even* be consumed by the sword *and* by the famine: they shall die, from the least even to the greatest, by the sword and by the famine: and they shall be an execration, *and* an astonishment, and a curse, and a reproach. reside - curse
13 For I will punish them that dwell in the land of E'gypt, as I have punished Je-ru'sa-lem, by the sword, by the famine, and by the pestilence:
14 So that none of the remnant of Ju'dah, which are gone into the land of E'gypt to sojourn there, shall escape or remain, that they should return into the land of Ju'dah, to the which they have a desire to return to dwell there: for none shall return but such as shall escape. live
15 Then all the men which knew that their wives had burned incense to other gods, and all the women that stood by, a great multitude, even all the people that dwelled in the land of E'gypt, in Path'ros, answered Jer-e-mi'ah, saying, worshiped

16 *As for* the word that you have spoken to us in the name of the LORD, we will not hearken to you.

17 But we will certainly do whatsoever thing goes forth out of our own mouth, to burn incense to the <u>queen of heaven</u>, and to pour out drink offerings to her, as we have done, we, and our fathers, our kings, and our princes, in the cities of Ju'dah, and in the streets of Je-ru'sa-lem: for *then* had we plenty of victuals, and were well, and saw no evil.

worshiped - female deity idol

18 But since we left off to <u>burn incense</u> to the <u>queen of heaven</u>, and to pour out drink offerings to her, we have <u>wanted</u> all *things*, and have been consumed by the sword and by the famine.   lacked

19 And when we burned incense to the <u>queen of heaven</u>, and poured out drink offerings to her, did we make her cakes to worship her, and pour out drink offerings to her, without our men?

20 Then Jer-e-mi'ah said to all the people, to the men, and to the women, and to all the people which had given him *that* answer, saying,

21 The incense that you burned in the cities of Ju'dah, and in the streets of Je-ru'sa-lem, you, and your fathers, your kings, and your princes, and the people of the land, did not the LORD remember them, and came it *not* into His mind?

22 So that the LORD could no longer bear, because of the evil of your doings, *and* because of the <u>abominations</u> which you have committed; therefore is your land a desolation, and an astonishment, and a curse, without an inhabitant, as at this day.   detestable things

23 Because you have burned incense, and because you have sinned against the LORD, and have not obeyed the voice of the LORD, nor walked in His law, nor in His statutes, nor in His testimonies; therefore this evil is happened to you, as at this day.

24 Moreover Jer-e-mi'ah said to all the people, and to all the women, Hear the word of the LORD, all Ju'dah that *are* in the land of E'gypt:

25 Thus says the <u>LORD of hosts</u>, the God of Is'ra-el, saying; You and your wives have both spoken with your mouths, and fulfilled with your hand, saying, We will surely perform our <u>vows</u> that we have <u>vowed</u>, to burn incense to the <u>queen of heaven</u>, and to pour out drink offerings to her: you will surely accomplish your vows, and surely perform your vows.

Jehovah^s.f. Tsebaoth - Elohim^p.f. - promises - female deity idol

26 Therefore hear you the word of the LORD, all Ju'dah that dwell in the land of E'gypt; Behold, I have sworn by My great name, says the LORD, that My name shall no more be named in the mouth of any man of Ju'dah in all the land of E'gypt, saying, The <u>Lord GOD</u> lives.   HEB. 6:13 Adonay^p.f. Jehovah

27 Behold, I will watch over them for evil, and not for good: and all the men of Ju'dah that *are* in the land of E'gypt shall be consumed by the sword and by the famine, until there be an end of them.

28 Yet a small number that escape the sword shall return out of the land of

E'gypt into the land of Ju'dah, and all the remnant of Ju'dah, that are gone into the land of E'gypt to <u>so-journ</u> there, shall know whose words shall stand, Mine, or theirs. _{reside}

29 And this *shall be* a sign to you, says the LORD, that I will punish you in this place, that you may know that My words shall surely stand against you for evil:

30 Thus says the LORD; Behold, I will give Pha'raoh-hoph'ra king of E'gypt into the hand of his enemies, and into the hand of them that seek his life; as I gave Zed-e-ki'ah king of Ju'dah into the hand of Neb-u-chad-rez'zar king of Bab'y-lon, his enemy, and that sought his life.

CHAPTER 45

THE word that Jer-e-mi'ah the prophet spoke to Ba'ruch the son of Ne-ri'ah, when he had written these words in a book at the mouth of Jer-e-mi'ah, in the fourth year of Je-hoi'a-kim the son of Jo-si'ah king of Ju'dah, saying,

2 Thus said the LORD, the <u>God</u> of Is'ra-el, to you, O Ba'ruch; _{Elohim p.f.}

3 You did say, Woe is me now! for the LORD has added grief to my sorrow; I fainted in my sighing, and I find no rest.

4 Thus shall; you say to him, The LORD says thus; Behold, *that* which I have built will I break down, and that which I have planted I will pluck up, even this whole land.

5 And seek you great things for yourself? seek *them* not: for, behold, I will bring evil upon all flesh, says the LORD: but your life will I give to you for a <u>prey</u> in all places where you go. _{booty}

CHAPTER 46

THE word of the LORD which came to Jer-e-mi'ah the prophet <u>against</u> the <u>Gen'tiles</u>; _{concerning - Nations}

2 Against E'gypt, against the army of Pha'raoh-ne'cho king of E'gypt, which was by the river Eu-phra'tes in Car'che-mish, which Neb-u-chad-rez'zar king of Bab'y-lon smote in the fourth year of Je-hoi'a-kim the son of Jo-si'ah king of Ju'dah.

3 <u>Order</u> you the <u>buckler</u> and shield, and draw near to battle.
_{Prepare - i.e., small shield}

4 Harness the horses; and get up, you horsemen, and stand forth with *your* helmets; <u>furbish</u> the spears, *and* put on the <u>brigandines</u>._{polish - armor}

5 Why have I seen them dismayed *and* turned away back? and their mighty ones are <u>beaten down</u>, and are fled apace, and look not back: *for* <u>fear</u> *was* round about, says the LORD. _{defeated - terror}

6 Let not the swift flee away, nor the mighty man escape; they shall stumble, and fall toward the north by the river Eu-phra'tes.

7 Who *is* this *that* comes up as a flood, whose waters are moved as the rivers?

8 E'gypt rises up like a flood, and *its* waters are moved like the rivers; and he

said, I will go up, *and* will cover the earth; I will destroy the city and the inhabitants thereof.

9 Come up, you horses; and rage, you chariots; and let the mighty men come forth; the E-thi-o'pi-ans and the Lib'y-ans, that handle the shield; and the Lyd'i-ans, that handle *and* bend the bow.

10 For this *is* the day of the Lord GOD of hosts, a day of vengeance, that He may avenge Him of His adversaries: and the sword shall devour, and it shall be satiate and made drunk with their blood: for the Lord GOD of hosts has a sacrifice in the north country by the river Eu-phra'tes.   Adonay^{p.f.} Jehovah Tsebaoth - satisfied

11 Go up into Gil'e-ad, and take balm, O virgin, the daughter of E'gypt: in vain shall you use many medicines; *for* you shall not be cured.

12 The nations have heard of your shame, and your cry has filled the land: for the mighty man has stumbled against the mighty, *and* they are fallen both together.

13 The word that the LORD spoke to Jer-e-mi'ah the prophet, how Neb-u-chad-rez'zar king of Bab'y-lon should come *and* smite the land of E'gypt.

14 Declare you in E'gypt, and publish in Mig'dol, and publish in Noph and in Tah'pan-hes: say you, Stand fast, and prepare you; for the sword shall devour round about you.

15 Why are your valiant *men* swept away? they stood not, because the LORD did drive them.

16 He made many to fall, yea, one fell upon another: and they said, Arise, and let us go again to our own people, and to the land of our nativity, from the oppressing sword.

17 They did cry there, Pha'raoh king of E'gypt *is but* a noise; he has passed the time appointed.

18 *As* I live, says the King, whose name *is* the LORD of hosts, Surely as Ta'bor *is* among the mountains, and as Car'mel by the sea, *so* shall he come.   Jehovah^{s.f.} Tsebaoth

19 O you daughter dwelling in E'gypt, furnish yourself to go into captivity: for Noph shall be waste and desolate without an inhabitant.   prepare

20 E'gypt *is like* a very fair heifer, *but* destruction comes; it comes out of the north.

21 Also her hired men *are* in the midst of her like fatted bullocks; for they also are turned back, *and* are fled away together: they did not stand, because the day of their calamity was come upon them, *and* the time of their visitation.

22 The voice thereof shall go like a serpent; for they shall march with an army, and come against her with axes, as hewers of wood.

23 They shall cut down her forest, says the LORD, though it cannot be searched; because they are more than the grasshoppers, and *are* innumerable.

24 The daughter of E'gypt shall be confounded; she shall be delivered into the hand of the people of the north.

25 The LORD of hosts, the God of Is'ra-el, says; Behold, I will punish the multitude of No, and Pha'raoh, and E'-

gypt, with their gods, and their kings; even Pha'raoh, and *all* them that trust in him: Jehovah^{s.f.} Tsebaoth - Elohim^{p.f.}
26 And I will deliver them into the hand of those that seek their lives, and into the hand of Neb-u-chad-rez'zar king of Bab'y-lon, and into the hand of his servants: and afterward it shall be inhabited, as in the days of old, says the LORD.
27 But fear not you, O My servant Ja'cob, and be not dismayed, O Is'ra-el: for, behold, I will save you from afar off, and your seed from the land of their captivity; and Ja'cob shall return, and be in rest and at ease, and none shall make *him* afraid. descendants
28 Fear you not, O Ja'cob My servant, says the LORD: for I *am* with you; for I will make a full end of all the nations where I have driven you: but I will not make a full end of you, but correct you in measure; yet will I not leave you wholly unpunished.

CHAPTER 47

THE word of the LORD that came to Jer-e-mi'ah the prophet against the Phi-lis'tines, before that Pha'raoh smote Ga'za.
2 Thus says the LORD; Behold, waters rise up out of the north, and shall be an overflowing flood, and shall overflow the land, and all that is therein; the city, and them that dwell therein: then the men shall cry, and all the inhabitants of the land shall howl. cry out
3 At the noise of the stamping of the hoofs of his strong *horses*, at the rushing of his chariots, *and at* the rumbling of his wheels, the fathers shall not look back to *their* children for feebleness of hands;
4 Because of the day that comes to spoil all the Phi-lis'tines, *and* to cut off from Ty'rus and Zi'don every helper that remains: for the LORD will spoil the Phi-lis'tines, the remnant of the country of Caph'tor. destroy - i.e., Crete
5 Baldness is come upon Ga'za; Ash'ke-lon is cut off *with* the remnant of their valley: how long will you cut yourself?
6 O you sword of the LORD, how long *will it be* before you be quiet? put up yourself into your scabbard, rest, and be still.
7 How can it be quiet, seeing the LORD has given it a charge against Ash'ke-lon, and against the sea shore? there has He appointed it. you

CHAPTER 48

AGAINST Mo'ab thus says the LORD of hosts, the God of Is'ra-el; Woe to Ne'bo! for it is spoiled: Kir-i-a-tha'im is confounded *and* taken: Mis'gab is confounded and dismayed. Jehovah^{s.f.} Tsebaoth - Elohim^{p.f.}
2 *There shall be* no more praise of Mo'ab: in Hesh'bon they have devised evil against it; come, and let us cut it off from *being* a nation. Also you shall be cut down, O Madmen; the sword shall pursue you. silenced
3 A voice of crying *shall be* from Hor-o-na'im, spoiling and great destruction.
4 Mo'ab is destroyed; her little ones have caused a cry to be heard.

5 For in the going up of Lu'hith continual weeping shall go up; for in the going down of Hor-o-na'im the enemies have heard a cry of destruction.

6 Flee, save your lives, and be like the <u>heath</u> in the wilderness.   bush

7 For because you have trusted in your works and in your treasures, you shall also be taken: and Che'mosh shall go forth into captivity *with* his priests and his princes together.

8 And the <u>spoiler</u> shall come upon every city, and no city shall escape: the valley also shall perish, and the plain shall be destroyed, as the LORD has spoken.   destroyer

9 Give wings to Mo'ab, that it may flee and get away: for the cities thereof shall be desolate, without any to dwell therein.

10 Cursed *be* he that does the work of the LORD deceitfully, and cursed *be* he that keeps back his sword from blood.

11 Mo'ab has been at ease from his youth, and he has settled on his <u>lees</u>, and has not been emptied from vessel to vessel, neither has he gone into captivity: therefore his taste remained in him, and his scent is not changed.   dregs-strong wine

12 Therefore, behold, the days come, says the LORD, that I will send to him wanderers, that shall cause him to wander, and shall empty his vessels, and break their bottles.

13 And Mo'ab shall be ashamed of Che'mosh, as the house of Is'ra-el was ashamed of Beth'-el their confidence.

14 How say you, We *are* mighty and strong men for the war?

15 Mo'ab is spoiled, and gone up *out of* her cities, and his chosen young men are gone down to the slaughter, says the King, whose name *is* the LORD of hosts.

   Jehovah[s.f.] Tsebaoth

16 The calamity of Mo'ab *is* near to come, and his affliction hastens fast.

17 All you that are about him, bemoan him; and all you that know his name, say, How is the strong staff broken, *and* the beautiful rod!

18 You daughter that does inhabit Di'bon, come down from *your* glory, and sit in thirst; for the <u>spoiler</u> of Mo'ab shall come upon you, *and* he shall destroy your strong holds.   destroyer

19 O inhabitant of Ar'o-er, stand by the way, and <u>espy</u>; ask him that flees, and her that escapes, *and* say, What is done?   watch

20 Mo'ab is confounded; for it is broken down: howl and cry; tell you it in Ar'non, that Mo'ab is spoiled,

21 And judgment is come upon the plain country; upon Ho'lon, and upon Ja-ha'zah, and upon Meph'a-ath,

22 And upon Di'bon, and upon Ne'bo, and upon Beth-dib-la-tha'im,

23 And upon Kir-i-a-tha'im, and upon Beth-ga'mul, and upon Beth-me'on,

24 And upon Ke'ri-oth, and upon Boz'rah, and upon all the cities of the land of Mo'ab, far or near.

25 The <u>horn</u> of Mo'ab is cut off, and his arm is broken, says the LORD. i.e., strength

26 Make you him drunken: for he

magnified *himself* against the Lord: Mo'ab also shall wallow in his vomit, and he also shall be in derision.

27 For was not Is'ra-el a derision to you? was he found among thieves? for <u>since</u> you spoke of him, you <u>skipped</u> for joy.

each time - you jump

28 O you that dwell in Mo'ab, leave the cities, and dwell in the rock, and be like the dove *that* makes her nest in the sides of the hole's mouth.

29 We have heard the pride of Mo'ab, (he is exceeding proud) his loftiness, and his arrogancy, and his pride, and the haughtiness of his heart.

30 I know his anger, says the Lord; but *it shall* not *be* so; his lies shall not so effect *it*.

31 Therefore will I howl for Mo'ab, and I will cry out for all Mo'ab; *My heart* shall mourn for the men of Kir-he'res.

32 O vine of Sib'mah, I will weep for you with the weeping of Ja'zer: your plants are gone over the sea, they reach *even* to the sea of Ja'zer: the <u>spoiler</u> is fallen upon your summer fruits and upon your vintage.

destroyer

33 And joy and gladness is taken from the plentiful field, and from the land of Mo'ab; and I have caused wine to fail from the winepresses: none shall tread with shouting; *their* shouting *shall be* no shouting.

34 From the cry of Hesh'bon *even* to E-le-a'leh, *and even* to Ja'haz, have they uttered their voice, from Zo'ar *even* to Hor-o-na'im, *as* an heifer of three years old: for the waters also of Nim'rim shall be desolate.

35 Moreover I will cause to cease in Mo'ab, says the Lord, him that offers in the <u>high places</u>, and him that <u>burns incense</u> to his gods.

shrines - worships

36 Therefore My heart shall sound for Mo'ab like pipes, and My heart shall sound like pipes for the men of Kir-he'res: because the riches *that* he has gotten are perished.

37 For every head *shall be* bald, and every beard clipped: upon all the hands *shall be* cuttings, and upon the loins sackcloth.

38 *There shall be* <u>lamentation</u> generally upon all the housetops of Mo'ab, and in the streets thereof: for I have broken Mo'ab like a vessel wherein *is* no pleasure, says the Lord.

mourning

39 They shall howl, *saying*, How is it broken down! how has Mo'ab turned the back with shame! so shall Mo'ab be a derision and a dismaying to all them about him.

40 For thus says the Lord; Behold, he shall fly as an eagle, and shall spread his wings over Mo'ab.

41 <u>Ke'ri-oth is</u> taken, and the strong holds are surprised, and the mighty men's hearts in Mo'ab at that day shall be as the heart of a woman in her pangs.

The cities are

42 And Mo'ab shall be destroyed from *being* a people, because he has magnified *himself* against the Lord.

43 <u>Fear</u>, and the <u>pit</u>, and the <u>snare</u>, *shall be* upon you, O inhabitant of Mo'ab, says the Lord.

Terror - abyss - lure

44 He that flees from the <u>fear</u> shall fall into the <u>pit</u>; and he that gets up out of the <u>pit</u> shall be taken in the

snare: for I will bring upon it, *even* upon Mo'ab, the year of their visitation, says the LORD.   terror - abyss - trap

45 They that fled stood under the shadow of Hesh'bon because of the force: but a fire shall come forth out of Hesh'bon, and a flame from the midst of Si'hon, and shall devour the corner of Mo'ab, and the crown of the head of the tumultuous ones.

46 Woe be to you, O Mo'ab! the people of Che'mosh perishes: for your sons are taken captives, and your daughters captives.

47 Yet will I bring again the captivity of Mo'ab in the latter days, says the LORD. Thus far *is* the judgment of Mo'ab.

CHAPTER 49

CONCERNING the Am'monites, thus says the LORD; Has Is'ra-el no sons? has he no heir? why *then* does their king inherit Gad, and his people dwell in his cities?   take possession of

2 Therefore, behold, the days come, says the LORD, that I will cause an alarm of war to be heard in Rab'bah of the Am'mon-ites; and it shall be a desolate heap, and her daughters shall be burned with fire: then shall Is'ra-el be heir to them that were his heirs, says the LORD.   mound of ruins

3 Howl, O Hesh'bon, for A'i is spoiled: cry, you daughters of Rab'bah, gird you with sackcloth; lament, and run to and fro by the hedges; for their king shall go into captivity, *and* his priests and his princes together.

4 Why glory you in the valleys, your flowing valley, O backsliding daughter? that trusted in her treasures, *saying*, Who shall come to me?

5 Behold, I will bring a fear upon you, says the Lord GOD of hosts, from all those that be about you; and you shall be driven out every man right forth; and none shall gather up him that wanders.   terror - Adonay[p.f.] Jehovah Tsebaoth

6 And afterward I will bring again the captivity of the children of Am'mon, says the LORD.

7 Concerning E'dom, thus says the LORD of hosts; *Is* wisdom no more in Te'man? is counsel perished from the prudent? is their wisdom vanished?   Jehovah[s.f.] Tsebaoth

8 Flee you, turn back, dwell deep, O inhabitants of De'dan; for I will bring the calamity of E'sau upon him, the time *that* I will visit him.

9 If grapegatherers come to you, would they not leave *some* gleaning grapes? if thieves by night, they will destroy till they have enough.   until

10 But I have made E'sau bare, I have uncovered his secret places, and he shall not be able to hide himself: his seed is spoiled, and his brethren, and his neighbors, and he *is* not.   offspring - destroyed

11 Leave your fatherless children, I will preserve *them* alive; and let your widows trust in me.

12 For thus says the LORD; Behold, they whose judgment *was* not to drink of the cup have assuredly drunken; and *are* you he *that* shall altogether go un-

punished? you shall not go unpunished, but you shall surely drink *of it.*

13 For I have sworn by Myself, says the LORD, that Boz'rah shall become a desolation, a reproach, a waste, and a curse; and all the cities thereof shall be perpetual wastes.

14 I have heard a rumor from the LORD, and an ambassador is sent to the heathen, *saying*, Gather you together, and come against her, and rise up to the battle.

15 For, lo, I will make you small among the heathen, *and* despised among men.

16 Your terribleness has deceived you, *and* the pride of your heart, O you that dwells in the clefts of the rock, that holds the height of the hill: though you should make your nest as high as the eagle, I will bring you down from there, says the LORD.

terror

17 Also E'dom shall be a desolation: every one that goes by it shall be astonished, and shall hiss at all the plagues thereof.

i.e., scoff

18 As in the overthrow of Sod'om and Go-mor'rah and the neighbor *cities* thereof, says the LORD, no man shall abide there, neither shall a son of man dwell in it.

19 Behold, he shall come up like a lion from the swelling of Jor'dan against the habitation of the strong: but I will suddenly make him run away from her: and who *is* a chosen *man, that* I may appoint over her? for who is like Me? and who will appoint Me the time? and who *is* that shepherd that will stand before Me?

20 Therefore hear the counsel of the LORD, that He has taken against E'dom; and His purposes, that He has purposed against the inhabitants of Te'man: Surely the least of the flock shall draw them out: surely He shall make their habitations desolate with them.

21 The earth is moved at the noise of their fall, at the cry the noise thereof was heard in the Red sea.

22 Behold, He shall come up and fly as the eagle, and spread His wings over Boz'rah: and at that day shall the heart of the mighty men of E'dom be as the heart of a woman in her pangs.

23 Concerning Da-mas'cus. Ha'math is confounded, and Ar'pad: for they have heard evil tidings: they are fainthearted; *there is* sorrow on the sea; it cannot be quiet.

disheartened - anxiety

24 Da-mas'cus is waxed feeble, *and* turns herself to flee, and fear has seized on *her*: anguish and sorrows have taken her, as a woman in travail.

grown - panic - childbirth

25 How is the city of praise not left, the city of My joy!

26 Therefore her young men shall fall in her streets, and all the men of war shall be cut off in that day, says the LORD of hosts.

Jehovah[s.f.] Tsebaoth

27 And I will kindle a fire in the wall of Da-mas'cus, and it shall consume the palaces of Ben-ha'dad.

28 Concerning Ke'dar, and concerning the kingdoms of Ha'zor, which Neb-u-chad-rez'zar king of Bab'ylon shall smite, thus says the LORD; Arise you, go up to Ke'dar, and spoil the men of the east.

rob

29 Their tents and their flocks shall they take away: they shall take to themselves their curtains, and all their vessels, and their camels; and they shall cry to them, <u>Fear</u> *is* on every side.   Terror

30 Flee, get you far off, dwell deep, O you inhabitants of Ha'zor, says the LORD; for Neb-u-chad-rez'zar king of Bab'y-lon has <u>taken counsel</u> against you, and has conceived a purpose against you.   devised a plan

31 Arise, get you up to the wealthy nation, that dwells without care, says the LORD, which have neither gates nor bars, *which* dwell alone.

32 And their camels shall be a booty, and the multitude of their cattle a <u>spoil</u>: and I will scatter into all winds them *that are* in the utmost corners; and I will bring their calamity from all sides thereof, says the LORD.   booty

33 And Ha'zor shall be a dwelling for dragons, *and* a desolation for ever: there shall no man abide there, nor *any* son of man dwell in it.

34 The word of the LORD that came to Jer-e-mi'ah the prophet against E'lam in the beginning of the reign of Zed-e-ki'ah king of Ju'dah, saying,

35 Thus says the <u>LORD of hosts</u>: Behold, I will break the <u>bow</u> of E'lam, the chief of their might.

Jehovah^s.f. Tsebaoth - i.e., power

36 And upon E'lam will I bring the four winds from the four quarters of heaven, and will scatter them toward all those winds; and there shall be no nation where the outcasts of E'lam shall not come.   REV. 7:1

37 For I will cause E'lam to be <u>dismayed</u> before their enemies, and before them that seek their life: and I will bring evil upon them, *even* My fierce anger, says the LORD; and I will send the sword after them, till I have consumed them: shattered

38 And I will <u>set</u> My throne in E'lam, and will destroy from there the king and the princes, says the LORD.   lift

39 But it shall come to pass in the latter days, *that* I will bring again the captivity of E'lam, says the LORD.

CHAPTER 50

THE word that the LORD spoke against Bab'y-lon *and* against the land of the Chal-de'ans by Jer-e-mi'ah the prophet.

2 Declare you among the nations, and publish, and <u>set</u> up a standard; publish, *and* conceal not: say, Bab'y-lon is taken, Bel is confounded, Me-ro'dach is broken in pieces; her idols are confounded, her images are broken in pieces.   lift

3 For out of the north there comes up a nation against her, which shall make her land desolate, and none shall dwell therein: they shall remove, they shall depart, both man and beast.

4 In those days, and in that time, says the LORD, the children of Is'ra-el shall come, they and the children of Ju'dah together, going and weeping: they shall go, and seek the LORD their God.

5 They shall ask the way to Zi'on with their faces aside there, *saying*, Come, and let us join ourselves to the LORD in

a perpetual <u>covenant</u> *that* shall not be forgotten. agreement

6 My people has been lost sheep: their shepherds have caused them to go astray, they have turned them away *on* the mountains: they have gone from mountain to hill, they have forgotten their <u>restingplace</u>. refuge

7 All that found them have devoured them: and their adversaries said, We offend not, because they have sinned against the LORD, the habitation of justice, even the LORD, the hope of their fathers.

8 Remove out of the midst of Bab'y-lon, and go forth out of the land of the Chal-de'ans, and be as the <u>he goats</u> before the flocks. i.e., leader

9 For, lo, I will raise and cause to come up against Bab'y-lon an assembly of great nations from the north country: and they shall set themselves in array against her; from there she shall be taken: their arrows *shall be* as of a mighty expert man; none shall return in vain.

10 And Chal-de'a shall be a <u>spoil</u>: all that <u>spoil</u> her shall be satisfied, says the LORD. plunder

11 Because you were glad, because you rejoiced, O you destroyers of My heritage, because you are grown fat as the heifer at grass, and bellow as bulls;

12 Your mother shall be <u>sore</u> confounded; she that bare you shall be ashamed: behold, the <u>hindermost</u> of the nations *shall be* a wilderness, a dry land, and a desert. greatly - least

13 Because of the anger of the LORD it shall not be inhabited, but it shall be wholly desolate: every one that goes by Bab'y-lon shall be astonished, and <u>hiss</u> at all her plagues. anger - i.e., scoff

14 Put yourselves in array against Bab'y-lon round about: all you that bend the bow, shoot at her, spare no arrows: for she has sinned against the LORD.

15 Shout against her round about: she has given her hand: her foundations are fallen, her walls are thrown down: for it *is* the vengeance of the LORD: take vengeance upon her; as she has done, do to her.

16 Cut off the sower from Bab'y-lon, and him that handles the sickle in the time of harvest: <u>for fear</u> of the oppressing sword they shall turn every one to his people, and they shall flee every one to his own land. because

17 Is'ra-el *is* a scattered sheep; the lions have driven *him* away: first the king of As-syr'i-a has devoured him; and last this Neb-u-chad-rez'zar king of Bab'y-lon has broken his bones.

18 Therefore thus says the <u>LORD of hosts</u>, the <u>God</u> of Is'ra-el; Behold, I will punish the king of Bab'y-lon and his land, as I have punished the king of As-syr'i-a. Jehovah^s.f. Tsebaoth - Elohim^p.f.

19 And I will bring Is'ra-el again to his habitation, and he shall feed on Car'mel and Ba'shan, and his soul shall be satisfied upon mount E'phra-im and Gil'e-ad.

20 In those days, and in that time, says the LORD, the iniquity of Is'ra-el shall be sought for, and *there shall be* none; and the sins of Ju'dah, and they shall not be found: for I will pardon them whom I <u>reserve</u>. save

21 Go up against the land of Mer-a-tha'im, *even* against it, and against the inhabitants of Pe'kod: <u>waste</u> and utterly destroy after them, says the LORD, and do according to all that I have commanded you. _{slay}

22 A sound of battle *is* in the land, and of great destruction.

23 How is the hammer of the whole earth cut asunder and broken! how is Bab'y-lon become a desolation among the nations!

24 I have laid a <u>snare</u> for you, and you are also taken, O Bab'y-lon, and you were not aware: you are found, and also caught, because you have striven against the LORD. _{trap}

25 The LORD has opened His armory, and has brought forth the weapons of His indignation: for this *is* the work of the <u>Lord GOD of hosts</u> in the land of the Chal-de'ans. _{Adonay^{p.f.} Jehovah Tsebaoth}

26 Come against her from the <u>utmost</u> border, open her storehouses: cast her up as heaps, and destroy her utterly: let nothing of her be left. _{farthest}

27 Slay all her bullocks; let them go down to the slaughter: woe to them! for their day is come, the time of their visitation.

28 The voice of them that flee and escape out of the land of Bab'y-lon, to declare in Zi'on the vengeance of the LORD our <u>God</u>, the vengeance of His temple. _{Elohim^{p.f.}}

29 Call together the archers against Bab'y-lon: all you that bend the bow, camp against it round about; let none thereof escape: recompense her according to her work; according to all that she has done, do to her: for she has been proud against the LORD, against the Holy One of Is'ra-el.

30 Therefore shall her young men fall in the streets, and all her men of war shall be cut off in that day, says the LORD.

31 Behold, I *am* against you, *O you* most proud, says the <u>Lord GOD of hosts</u>: for your day is come, the time *that* I will visit you. _{Adonay^{p.f.} Jehovah Tsebaoth}

32 And the most proud shall stumble and fall, and none shall raise him up: and I will kindle a fire in his cities, and it shall devour all round about him.

33 Thus says the <u>LORD of hosts</u>; The children of Is'ra-el and the children of Ju'dah *were* oppressed together: and all that took them captives held them fast; they refused to let them go. _{Jehovah^{s.f.} Tsebaoth}

34 Their Redeemer *is* strong; the <u>LORD of hosts</u> *is* His name: He shall throughly plead their cause, that He may give rest to the land, and disquiet the inhabitants of Bab'y-lon.

35 A sword *is* upon the Chal-de'ans, says the LORD, and upon the inhabitants of Bab'y-lon, and upon her princes, and upon her wise *men*.

36 A sword *is* upon the liars; and they shall <u>dote</u>: a sword *is* upon her mighty men; and they shall be dismayed. _{become fools}

37 A sword *is* upon their horses, and upon their chariots, and upon all the mingled people that *are* in the midst of her; and they shall become as women: a sword *is* upon her treasures; and they shall be robbed.

38 A drought *is* upon her waters; and they shall be dried up: for it *is* the land of graven images, and they are mad upon *their* idols. idols - over

39 Therefore the wild beasts of the desert with the wild beasts of the islands shall dwell *there*, and the owls shall dwell therein: and it shall be no more inhabited for ever; neither shall it be dwelled in from generation to generation. REV. 18:2

40 As God overthrew Sod'om and Go-mor'rah and the neighbor *cities* thereof, says the LORD; *so* shall no man abide there, neither shall any son of man dwell therein. Elohim[p.f.]

41 Behold, a people shall come from the north, and a great nation, and many kings shall be raised up from the coasts of the earth.

42 They shall hold the bow and the lance: they *are* cruel, and will not show mercy: their voice shall roar like the sea, and they shall ride upon horses, *every one* put in array, like a man to the battle, against you, O daughter of Bab'y-lon.

43 The king of Bab'y-lon has heard the report of them, and his hands waxed feeble: anguish took hold of him, *and* pangs as of a woman in travail. grew

44 Behold, he shall come up like a lion from the swelling of Jor'dan to the habitation of the strong: but I will make them suddenly run away from her: and who *is* a chosen *man, that* I may appoint over her? for who *is* like Me? and who will appoint Me the time?

and who *is* that shepherd that will stand before Me? flooding - decide

45 Therefore hear you the counsel of the LORD, that He has taken against Bab'y-lon; and His purposes, that He has purposed against the land of the Chal-de'ans: Surely the least of the flock shall draw them out: surely He shall make *their* habitation desolate with them. plan

46 At the noise of the taking of Bab'y-lon the earth is moved, and the cry is heard among the nations.

CHAPTER 51

THUS says the LORD; Behold, I will raise up against Bab'y-lon, and against them that dwell in the midst of them that rise up against Me, a destroying wind;

2 And will send to Bab'y-lon fanners, that shall fan her, and shall empty her land: for in the day of trouble they shall be against her round about. strangers - window

3 Against *him that* bends let the archer bend his bow, and against *him that* lifts himself up in his brigandine: and spare you not her young men; destroy you utterly all her host. armor

4 Thus the slain shall fall in the land of the Chal-de'ans, and *they that are* thrust through in her streets.

5 For Is'ra-el *has* not *been* forsaken, nor Ju'dah of his God, of the LORD of hosts; though their land was filled with sin against the Holy One of Is'ra-el. Elohim[p.f.] - Jehovah[s.f.] Tsebaoth

6 Flee out of the midst of Bab'y-lon, and deliver every man his soul: be not

cut off in her <u>iniquity</u>; for this *is* the time of the LORD's vengeance; He will render to her a recompence.   punishment - life

7 Bab'y-lon *has been* a golden cup in the LORD's hand, that made all the earth drunken: the nations have drunken of her wine; therefore the nations are mad.   REV. 14:8 REV. 14:10-11 REV. 17:4

8 Bab'y-lon is suddenly fallen and destroyed: <u>howl</u> for her; take balm for her pain, if so be she may be healed.   lament

9 We would have healed Bab'y-lon, but she is not healed: forsake her, and let us go every one into his own country: for her judgment reaches to heaven, and is lifted up *even* to the skies.   REV. 18:5

10 The LORD has brought forth our righteousness: come, and let us declare in Zi'on the work of the LORD our God.

11 Make <u>bright</u> the arrows; gather the shields: the LORD has raised up the spirit of the kings of the Medes: for His <u>device</u> *is* against Bab'y-lon, to destroy it; because it *is* the vengeance of the LORD, the vengeance of His temple.   sharp - purpose

12 Set up the <u>standard</u> upon the walls of Bab'y-lon, make the watch strong, set up the watchmen, prepare the <u>ambushes</u>: for the LORD has both devised and done that which He spoke against the inhabitants of Bab'y-lon.   banner - defenses

13 O you that dwell upon many waters, abundant in treasures, your end is come, *and* the measure of your <u>covetousness</u>.   lifespan

14 The <u>LORD of hosts</u> has sworn by Himself, *saying*, Surely I will fill you with men, as with <u>caterpillers</u>; and they shall lift up a shout against you.   Jehovah^s.f. Tsebaoth - locust

15 He has made the earth by His power, He has established the world by His wisdom, and has stretched out the heaven by His understanding.

16 When He utters *His* voice, *there is* a <u>multitude</u> of waters in the heavens; and He causes the vapors to ascend from the ends of the earth: He makes lightnings with rain, and brings forth the wind out of His treasures.   tumult

17 Every man is <u>brutish</u> by *his* knowledge; every founder is confounded by the graven <u>image</u>: for his molten <u>image</u> *is* falsehood, and *there is* no breath in them.   stupid - idols

18 They *are* vanity, the work of <u>errors</u>: in the time of their <u>visitation</u> they shall perish.   mockery - judgment

19 The portion of Ja'cob *is* not like them; for He *is* the former of all things: and Is'ra-el *is* the <u>rod</u> of His inheritance: the <u>LORD of hosts</u> *is* His name.   tribe - Jehovah^s.f. - Tsebaoth

20 You *are* My battle ax *and* weapons of war: for with you will I break in pieces the nations, and with you will I destroy kingdoms;

21 And with you will I break in pieces the horse and its rider; and with you will I break in pieces the chariot and its rider;

22 With you also will I break in pieces man and woman; and with you will I break in pieces old and young; and with you will I break in pieces the young man and the maid;

23 I will also break in pieces with you

the shepherd and his flock; and with you will I break in pieces the husbandman and his yoke of oxen; and with you will I break in pieces captains and rulers.

24 And I will render to Bab'y-lon and to all the inhabitants of Chal-de'a all their evil that they have done in Zi'on in your sight, says the LORD.

25 Behold, I *am* against you, O destroying <u>mountain</u>, says the LORD, which destroys all the earth: and I will stretch out My hand upon you, and roll you down from the rocks, and will make you a <u>burnt mountain</u>.

i.e., power - i.c., ruined

26 And they shall not take of you a stone for a corner, nor a stone for foundations; but you shall be <u>desolate</u> for ever, says the LORD.   ruined

27 Set you up a <u>standard</u> in the land, blow the trumpet among the nations, prepare the nations against her, call together against her the kingdoms of Ar'a-rat, Min'ni, and Ash'che-naz; appoint a captain against her; cause the horses to come up as the rough <u>caterpillers</u>.   banner - locust

28 Prepare against her the nations with the kings of the Medes, the captains thereof, and all the rulers thereof, and all the land of his dominion.

29 And the land shall tremble and sorrow: for every purpose of the LORD shall be performed against Bab'y-lon, to make the land of Bab'y-lon a <u>desolation</u> without an inhabitant.   waste place

30 The mighty men of Bab'y-lon have forborn to fight, they have remained in *their* <u>holds</u>: their might has failed;

they became as women: they have burned her dwellingplaces; her bars are broken.   strongholds

31 One post shall run to meet another, and one messenger to meet another, to show the king of Bab'y-lon that his city is taken <u>at *one* end</u>, from end to end

32 And that the passages are <u>stopped</u>, and the reeds they have burned with fire, and the men of war are affrighted.   seized

33 For thus says the <u>LORD of hosts</u>, the <u>God</u> of Is'ra-el; The daughter of Bab'y-lon *is* like a threshingfloor, *it is* time to thresh her: yet a little while, and the time of her harvest shall come.   Jehovah^{s.f.} Tsebaoth - Elohim^{p.f.}

34 Neb-u-chad-rez'zar the king of Bab'y-lon has devoured me, he has crushed me, he has made me an empty vessel, he has swallowed me up like a dragon, he has filled his belly with my delicates, he has cast me out.

35 The violence done to me and to my flesh *be* upon Bab'y-lon, shall the inhabitant of Zi'on say; and my blood upon the inhabitants of Chal-de'a, shall Je-ru'sa-lem say.

36 Therefore thus says the LORD; Behold, I will plead your cause, and take vengeance for you; and I will dry up her sea, and make her springs dry.

37 And Bab'y-lon shall become <u>heaps</u>, a dwellingplace for <u>dragons</u>, an <u>astonishment</u>, and an <u>hissing</u>, without an inhabitant.   ruins - jackals - object of horror - i.e., scorn

38 They shall roar together like lions: they shall yell as lions' whelps.

39 In their heat I will make their

feasts, and I will make them drunken, that they may rejoice, and sleep a perpetual sleep, and not wake, **says the** LORD.

40 I will bring them down like lambs to the slaughter, like rams with he goats.

41 How is She'shach taken! and how is the praise of the whole earth surprised! how is Bab'y-lon become an astonishment among the nations!

42 The <u>sea</u> is come up upon Bab'y-lon: she is covered with the multitude of the waves thereof.   i.e., flooded Euphrates

43 Her cities are a desolation, a dry land, and a wilderness, a land wherein no man dwells, neither does *any* son of man pass thereby.

44 And I will punish Bel in Bab'y-lon, and I will bring forth out of his mouth that which he has swallowed up: and the nations shall not flow together any more to him: yea, the wall of Bab'y-lon shall fall.

45 My people, go you out of the midst of her, and deliver you every man his soul from the fierce anger of the LORD.

46 And <u>less</u> your heart faint, and you <u>fear</u> for the rumor that shall be heard in the land; a rumor shall both come *one* year, and after that in *another* year *shall come* a rumor, and violence in the land, ruler against ruler.   let not - be afraid

47 Therefore, behold, the days come, that I will <u>do</u> judgment upon the <u>graven images</u> of Bab'y-lon: and her whole land shall be confounded, and all her slain shall fall in the midst of her.   pass - carved idols

48 Then the heaven and the earth, and all that *is* therein, shall sing for Bab'y-lon: for the <u>spoilers</u> shall come to her from the north, **says the** LORD.   destroyers

49 As Bab'y-lon *has caused* the slain of Is'ra-el to fall, so at Bab'y-lon shall fall the slain of all the <u>earth</u>.   REV. 18:24 land

50 You that have escaped the sword, go away, stand not still: remember the LORD afar off, and let Je-ru'sa-lem come into your mind.

51 We are confounded, because we have heard reproach: shame has covered our faces: for strangers are come into the <u>sanctuaries</u> of the LORD's house.   holy places

52 Wherefore, behold, the days come, **says the** LORD, that I will <u>do</u> judgment upon her <u>graven images</u>: and through all her land the wounded shall groan.   pass - carved idols

53 Though Bab'y-lon should mount up to heaven, and though she should fortify the height of her strength, *yet* from Me shall <u>spoilers</u> come to her, **says the** LORD.   destroyers

54 A sound of a cry *come* from Bab'y-lon, and great destruction from the land of the Chal-de'ans:

55 Because the LORD has spoiled Bab'y-lon, and destroyed out of her the great voice; when her waves do roar like great waters, a noise of their voice is uttered:

56 Because the <u>spoiler</u> is come upon her, *even* upon Bab'y-lon, and her mighty men are taken, every one of their bows is broken: for the LORD God of recompences shall surely <u>requite</u>.   pay back

57 And I will make drunk her princes, and her wise *men*, her captains, and her rulers, and her mighty men: and they shall sleep a perpetual sleep, and not wake, says the King, whose name *is* the LORD of hosts. Jehovah^s.f. Tsebaoth

58 Thus says the LORD of hosts; The broad walls of Bab'y-lon shall be utterly broken, and her high gates shall be burned with fire; and the people shall labor in vain, and the folk in the fire, and they shall be weary. nations for

59 The word which Jer-e-mi'ah the prophet commanded Ser-a-i'ah the son of Ne-ri'ah, the son of Ma-a-se'iah, when he went with Zed-e-ki'ah the king of Ju'dah into Bab'y-lon in the fourth year of his reign. And *this* Ser-a-i'ah *was* a quiet prince.

60 So Jer-e-mi'ah wrote in a book all the evil that should come upon Bab'y-lon, *even* all these words that are written against Bab'y-lon.

61 And Jer-e-mi'ah said to Ser-a-i'ah, When you come to Bab'y-lon, and shall see, and shall read all these words;

62 Then shall you say, O LORD, you have spoken against this place, to cut it off, that none shall remain in it, neither man nor beast, but that it shall be desolate for ever. uninhabited

63 And it shall be, when you have made an end of reading this book, *that* you shall bind a stone to it, and cast it into the midst of Eu-phra'tes: REV. 18:21

64 And you shall say, Thus shall Bab'y-lon sink, and shall not rise from the evil that I will bring upon her: and

they shall be weary. Thus far *are* the words of Jer-e-mi'ah.

CHAPTER 52

ZED-E-KI'AH *was* one and twenty years old when he began to reign, and he reigned eleven years in Je-ru'sa-lem. And his mother's name *was* Ha-mu'tal the daughter of Jer-e-mi'ah of Lib'nah.

2 And he did *that which was* evil in the eyes of the LORD, according to all that Je-hoi'a-kim had done.

3 For through the anger of the LORD it came to pass in Je-ru'sa-lem and Ju'dah, till He had cast them out from His presence, that Zed-e-ki'ah rebelled against the king of Bab'y-lon.

4 And it came to pass in the ninth year of his reign, in the tenth month, in the tenth *day* of the month, *that* Neb-u-chad-rez'zar king of Bab'y-lon came, he and all his army, against Je-ru'sa-lem, and pitched against it, and built forts against it round about. camped

5 So the city was besieged to the eleventh year of king Zed-e-ki'ah.

6 And in the fourth month, in the ninth *day* of the month, the famine was sore in the city, so that there was no bread for the people of the land. severe

7 Then the city was broken up, and all the men of war fled, and went forth out of the city by night by the way of the gate between the two walls, which *was* by the king's garden; (now the Chal-de'ans *were* by the city round about:) and they went by the way of the plain. into

8 But the army of the Chal-de'ans pursued after the king, and overtook Zed-e-ki'ah in the plains of Jer'i-cho; and all his army was scattered from him.

9 Then they took the king, and carried him up to the king of Bab'y-lon to Rib'lah in the land of Ha'math; where he gave judgment upon him.

10 And the king of Bab'y-lon slew the sons of Zed-e-ki'ah before his eyes: he slew also all the princes of Ju'dah in Rib'lah.

11 Then he put out the eyes of Zed-e-ki'ah; and the king of Bab'y-lon bound him in chains, and carried him to Bab'y-lon, and put him in prison till the day of his death.

12 Now in the fifth month, in the tenth *day* of the month, which *was* the nineteenth year of Neb-u-chad-rez'zar king of Bab'y-lon, came Neb'u-zar-a'dan, captain of the guard, *which* served the king of Bab'y-lon, into Je-ru'sa-lem,

13 And burned the house of the LORD, and the king's house; and all the houses of Je-ru'sa-lem, and all the houses of the great *men*, burned he with fire:

14 And all the army of the Chal-de'ans, that *were* with the captain of the guard, broke down all the walls of Je-ru'sa-lem round about.

15 Then Neb'u-zar-a'dan the captain of the guard carried away captive *certain* of the poor of the people, and the residue of the people that remained in the city, and those that fell away, that fell to the king of Bab'y-lon, and the rest of the multitude.　　rest - deserted

16 But Neb'u-zar-a'dan the captain of the guard left *certain* of the poor of the land for vinedressers and for husbandmen.

17 Also the pillars of brass that *were* in the house of the LORD, and the bases, and the brazen sea that *was* in the house of the LORD, the Chal-de'ans broke, and carried all the brass of them to Bab'y-lon. broke in pieces

18 The caldrons also, and the shovels, and the snuffers, and the bowls, and the spoons, and all the vessels of brass wherewith they ministered, took they away.　　basins

19 And the basins, and the firepans, and the bowls, and the caldrons, and the candlesticks, and the spoons, and the cups; *that* which *was* of gold *in* gold, and *that* which *was* of silver *in* silver, took the captain of the guard away.　　censers

20 The two pillars, one sea, and twelve brazen bulls that *were* under the bases, which king Sol'o-mon had made in the house of the LORD: the brass of all these vessels was without weight.　　beyond

21 And *concerning* the pillars, the height of one pillar *was* eighteen cubits; and a fillet of twelve cubits did compass it; and the thickness thereof *was* four fingers: *it was* hollow.　　in circumference - 3 in.

22 And a chapiter of brass *was* upon it; and the height of one chapiter *was* five cubits, with network and pomegranates upon the chapiters round about, all *of* brass. The second pillar also and the pomegranates *were* like to these.　　capital

23 And there were ninety and six pomegranates on a side; *and* all the pomegranates upon the network *were* an hundred round about.

24 And the captain of the guard took Ser-a-i'ah the chief priest, and Zeph-a-ni'ah the second priest, and the three keepers of the door:

25 He took also out of the city an eunuch, which had the charge of the men of war; and seven men of them that were near the king's person, which were found in the city; and the principal scribe of the host, who mustered the people of the land; and threescore men of the people of the land, that were found in the midst of the city.

₆₀

26 So Neb'u-zar-a'dan the captain of the guard took them, and brought them to the king of Bab'y-lon to Rib'lah.

27 And the king of Bab'y-lon smote them, and put them to death in Rib'lah in the land of Ha'math. Thus Ju'dah was carried away captive out of his own land.

struck

28 This *is* the people whom Neb-u-chad-rez'zar carried away captive: in the seventh year three thousand Jews and three and twenty:

29 In the eighteenth year of Neb-u-chad-rez'zar he carried away captive from Je-ru'sa-lem eight hundred thirty and two persons:

30 In the three and twentieth year of Neb-u-chad-rez'zar Neb'u-zar-a'dan the captain of the guard carried away captive of the Jews seven hundred forty and five persons: all the persons *were* four thousand and six hundred.

31 And it came to pass in the seven and thirtieth year of the captivity of Je-hoi'a-chin king of Ju'dah, in the twelfth month, in the five and twentieth *day* of the month, *that* E'vil-me-ro'dach king of Bab'y-lon in the *first* year of his reign lifted up the head of Je-hoi'a-chin king of Ju'dah, and brought him forth out of prison,

showed favor to

32 And spoke kindly to him, and set his throne above the throne of the kings that *were* with him in Bab'y-lon,

33 And changed his prison garments: and he did continually eat bread before him all the days of his life.

34 And *for* his diet, there was a continual diet given him of the king of Bab'y-lon, every day a portion until the day of his death, all the days of his life.

allowance

LAMENTATIONS

OUTLINE

SURVEY

Lamentations has one main theme: the suffering that befell Jerusalem when Nebuchadrezzar captured the city in 586 B.C. In a series of elegies, the author expresses his inconsolable grief over the city's agony and anguish.

The first lament describes and explains Jerusalem's afflictions in general terms. The second describes the disaster in greater detail. It emphasizes that the city's destruction is a divine judgment upon sin. Some underlying factors in this judgment are elucidated in the third lament. The fourth underlines some lessons which Jerusalem has learned from the judgment. The fifth and final lament (more accurately, a prayer) describes how Jerusalem's sufferings have led her to cast herself upon divine mercy, and to hope that the Lord will again be gracious to Israel, now purified in the crucible of affliction. Because Lamentations deals with suffering as judgment upon sin, the afflicted believer has found in it the language of his confession, self-humiliation, and invocation.

AUTHOR

From earliest times Jews, and then Christians, have ascribed Lamentations to Jeremiah. The Septuagint makes this ascription from the second century B.C., and the Vulgate from the fourth century A.D.

Cogent arguments from the Jewish-Christian tradition of Jeremianic authorship have been put forward. Assuming Jeremiah's authorship, Lamentations becomes "a supplement to the Book of Jeremiah," which so often predicted a catastrophe such as Lamentations describes. But Jeremiah's laments are entirely free from the "I told you so" attitude of mind. He is concerned only to mourn Jerusalem's sorrows, and to plead with God not to cast her off forever.

J.G.S.S.T.

THE LAMENTATIONS
OF JEREMIAH

CHAPTER 1

HOW does the city sit <u>solitary</u>, *that was* full of people! *how* is she become as a widow! she *that was* great among the nations, *and* princess among the provinces, *how* is she become <u>tributary</u>! empty - a forced laborer

2 She weeps <u>sore</u> in the night, and her tears *are* on her cheeks: among all her lovers she has none to comfort *her*: all her friends have dealt treacherously with her, they are become her enemies. bitterly

3 Ju'dah is gone into captivity <u>because of</u> affliction, and <u>because of</u> great servitude: she dwells among the heathen, she finds no rest: all her persecutors overtook her between the <u>straits</u>. under - distresses

4 The ways of Zi'on do mourn, because none come to the <u>solemn</u> feasts: all her gates are desolate: her priests sigh, her virgins are afflicted, and she *is* in <u>bitterness</u>. appointed - suffers bitterly

5 Her adversaries are the chief, her enemies prosper; for the LORD has afflicted her for the multitude of her transgressions: her children are gone into captivity before the enemy.

6 And from the daughter of Zi'on all her beauty is departed: her princes are become like <u>harts</u> *that* find no pasture, and they are gone without strength before the pursuer. bucks

7 Je-ru'sa-lem remembered in the days of her affliction and of her miseries all her pleasant things that she had in the days of old, when her people fell into the hand of the enemy, and none did help her: the adversaries saw her, *and* did mock at her <u>sabbaths</u>. rest days

8 Je-ru'sa-lem has grievously sinned; therefore she is removed: all that honored her despise her, because they have seen her nakedness: yea, she sighs, and turns backward.

9 Her filthiness *is* in her <u>skirts</u>; she remembers not her last end; therefore she came down wonderfully: she had no comforter. O LORD, behold my affliction: for the enemy has magnified *himself*. garments

10 The adversary has spread out his hand upon all her pleasant things: for she has seen *that* the <u>heathen</u> entered into her sanctuary, whom You did command *that* they should not enter into Your congregation. nations

11 All her people sigh, they seek bread; they have given their pleasant things for meat to relieve the soul: see, O LORD, and consider; for I am become vile.

12 *Is it* nothing to you, all you that pass by? behold, and see if there be any sorrow like to my sorrow, which is done to me, wherewith the LORD has afflicted *me* in the day of His fierce anger.

13 From above has He sent fire into my bones, and it prevails against

them: He has spread a net for my feet, He has turned me back: He has made me <u>desolate</u> *and* faint all the day. _{downhearted}

14 The yoke of my transgressions is bound by His hand: they are wreathed, *and* come up upon my neck: He has made my strength to fall, the Lord has delivered me into *their* hands, *from whom* I am not able to rise up.

15 The Lord has <u>trodden under foot</u> all my mighty *men* in the midst of me: He has called an assembly against me to crush my young men: the Lord has trodden the virgin, the daughter of Ju'dah, *as* in a winepress. _{rejected}

16 For these *things* I weep; my eye, my eye runs down with water, because the <u>comforter</u> that should relieve my soul is far from me: my children are desolate, because the enemy prevailed. _{Holy Spirit}

17 Zi'on <u>spreads</u> forth her hands, *and there is* none to comfort her: the LORD has commanded concerning Ja'cob, *that* his adversaries *should be* round about him: Je-ru'sa-lem is as a menstruous woman among them. _{stretches}

18 The LORD is righteous; for I have rebelled against His commandment: hear, I pray you, all people, and behold my sorrow: my virgins and my young men are gone into captivity.

19 I called for my lovers, *but* they deceived me: my priests and my elders gave up the ghost in the city, while they sought their meat to relieve their souls.

20 Behold, O LORD; for I *am* in distress: my <u>bowels</u> are troubled; my heart is turned within me; for I have grievously rebelled: abroad the sword bereaves, at home *you are* as death. _{emotions}

21 They have heard that I sigh: *there is* none to comfort me: all my enemies have heard of my trouble; they are glad that You have done *it*: You will bring the day *that* You have <u>called</u>, and they shall be like to me. _{proclaimed}

22 Let all their wickedness come before You; and do to them, as You have done to me for all my transgressions: for my sighs *are* many, and my heart *is* faint.

CHAPTER 2

HOW has the Lord covered the daughter of Zi'on with a cloud in His anger, *and* cast down from heaven to the earth the beauty of Is'ra-cl, and remembered not His footstool in the day of His anger!

2 The Lord has <u>swallowed up</u> all the <u>habitations</u> of Ja'cob, and has not pitied: He has thrown down in His wrath the strong holds of the daughter of Ju'dah; He has <u>brought *them* down to</u> the ground: He has polluted the kingdom and the princes thereof.

_{i.e., destroyed - dwellings - made to touch}

3 He has cut off in *His* fierce anger all the <u>horn</u> of Is'ra-el: He has drawn back His right hand from before the enemy, and He burned against Ja'cob like a flaming fire, *which* devours round about. _{i.e., strength}

4 He has bent His bow like an enemy: He stood with His right hand as an adversary, and slew all *that were* pleasant to the eye in the tabernacle of

the daughter of Zi'on: He poured out His fury like fire.

5 The Lord was as an enemy: He has <u>swallowed</u> up Is'ra-el, He has <u>swallowed</u> up all its palaces: He has destroyed its strong holds, and has increased in the daughter of Ju'dah mourning and lamentation.   i.e., destroyed

6 And He has violently taken away His tabernacle, as *if it were of* a garden: He has destroyed His places of the assembly: the LORD has caused the solemn feasts and <u>sabbaths</u> to be forgotten in Zi'on, and has despised in the indignation of His anger the king and the priest.   Lit., booth - rest days

7 The Lord has <u>cast off</u> His altar, He has abhorred His sanctuary, He has <u>given up</u> into the hand of the enemy the walls of her palaces; they have made a noise in the house of the LORD, as in the day of a solemn feast.   rejected - delivered

8 The LORD has <u>purposed</u> to destroy the wall of the daughter of Zi'on: He has stretched out a line, He has not withdrawn His hand from destroying: therefore He made the rampart and the wall to lament; they languished together.   determined

9 Her gates are sunk into the ground; He has destroyed and broken her bars: her king and her princes *are* among the Gen'tiles: the law *is* no *more*; her prophets also find no vision from the LORD.

10 The elders of the daughter of Zi'on sit upon the ground, *and* keep silence: they have cast up dust upon their heads; they have girded themselves with sackcloth: the virgins of Je-ru'sa-lem hang down their heads to the ground.

11 My eyes do fail with tears, my <u>bowels</u> are troubled, my <u>liver</u> is poured upon the earth, for the destruction of the daughter of my people; because the children and the sucklings <u>swoon</u> in the streets of the city.   emotions - heart - faint

12 They say to their mothers, Where *is* corn and wine? when they <u>swooned</u> as the wounded in the streets of the city, when <u>their soul was poured out into</u> their mothers' bosom.   i.e., they expired on

13 What thing shall I take to witness for you? what thing shall I liken to you, O daughter of Je-ru'sa-lem? what shall I equal to you, that I may comfort you, O virgin daughter of Zi'on? for your <u>breach</u> *is* great like the sea: who can heal you?   breaking

14 Your prophets have seen vain and foolish things for you: and they have not discovered your iniquity, to turn away your captivity; but have seen for you false burdens and causes of banishment.

15 All that pass by clap *their* hands at you; they <u>hiss</u> and wag their head at the daughter of Je-ru'sa-lem, *saying, Is* this the city that *men* call the perfection of beauty, The joy of the whole earth?   i.e., whistle

16 All your enemies have opened their mouth against you: they <u>hiss</u> and gnash the teeth: they say, We have <u>swallowed</u> *her* up: certainly this *is* the day that we looked for; we have found, we have seen *it*.   i.e., destroyed

17 The LORD has done *that* which He had devised; He has fulfilled His

word that He had commanded in the days of old: He has thrown down, and has not pitied: and He has caused *your* enemy to rejoice over you, He has set up the <u>horn</u> of your adversaries. *power*

18 Their heart cried to the Lord, O wall of the daughter of Zi'on, let tears run down like a river day and night: give yourself no rest; let not the apple of your eye cease.

19 Arise, cry out in the night: in the beginning of the watches pour out your heart like water before the face of the Lord: lift up your hands toward Him for the life of your young children, that faint for hunger in the top of every street.

20 Behold, O LORD, and consider to whom You have done this. Shall the women eat their <u>fruit</u>, *and* children of a span long? shall the priest and the prophet be slain in the sanctuary of the Lord? *offspring*

21 The young and the old lie on the ground in the streets: my virgins and my young men are fallen by the sword; You have slain *them* in the day of Your anger; You have killed, *and* not pitied.

22 You have called as in a solemn day my terrors round about, so that in the day of the LORD's anger none escaped nor remained: those that I <u>have swaddled</u> and brought up has my enemy consumed. *bore*

CHAPTER 3

I AM the man *that* has seen affliction by the rod of His wrath.

2 He has led me, and brought *me into* darkness, but not *into* light.

3 Surely against me is He turned; He turns His hand *against me* all the day.

4 My flesh and my skin has He made old; He has broken my bones.

5 He has builded against me, and <u>compassed</u> *me* with gall and travail. *surrounded*

6 He has set me in dark places, as *they that be* dead of old.

7 He has <u>hedged me about</u>, that I cannot get out: He has made my chain heavy. *walled me in*

8 Also when I cry and shout, He shuts out my prayer.

9 He has inclosed my ways with hewn stone, He has made my paths crooked.

10 He *was* to me *as* a bear lying in wait, *and as* a lion in secret places.

11 He has turned aside my ways, and pulled me in pieces: He has <u>made me desolate</u>. *left me without help*

12 He has bent His bow, and set me as a <u>mark</u> for the arrow. *target*

13 He has caused the arrows of His quiver to enter into my <u>reins</u>. *i.e., most sensitive parts*

14 I was a derision to all my people; *and* their song all the day.

15 He has filled me with bitterness, He has made me drunken with <u>wormwood</u>. *i.e., bitterness*

16 He has also broken my teeth with gravel stones, He has covered me with ashes.

17 And You have removed my soul far off from peace: I forgot prosperity.

18 And I said, My strength and my hope is perished from the LORD:

19 Remembering my affliction and my misery, the <u>wormwood and the gall</u>.   i.e., bitterness

20 My soul has *them* still in remembrance, and is humbled in me.

21 This I recall to my mind, therefore have I hope.

22 *It is of* the LORD's mercies that we are not consumed, because His compassions fail not.

23 *They are* new every morning: great *is* your faithfulness.

24 The LORD *is* my portion, says my soul; therefore will I hope in Him.

25 The LORD *is* good to them that wait for Him, to the soul *that* seeks Him.

26 *It is* good that *a man* should both hope and quietly wait for the salvation of the LORD.

27 *It is* good for a man that he bear the yoke in his youth.

28 He sits alone and keeps silence, because he has borne *it* upon him.

29 He <u>puts his mouth in the dust</u>; if so be there may be hope.   i.e., speaks humbly

30 He gives *his* cheek to him that smites him: he is filled full with reproach.

31 For the Lord will not cast off for ever:

32 But though He cause grief, yet will He have compassion according to the multitude of His mercies.

33 For He does not afflict willingly nor grieve the children of men.

34 To crush under His feet all the prisoners of the earth,

35 To turn aside the right of a man before the face of the Most High,

36 To subvert a man in his cause, the Lord approves not.

37 Who *is* he *that* says, and it comes to pass, *when* the Lord commands *it* not?

38 Out of the mouth of the Most High proceeds not evil and good?

39 Wherefore does a living man complain, a man for the punishment of his sins?

40 Let us <u>search</u> and try our ways, and turn again to the LORD.   examine

41 Let us lift up our heart with *our* hands to God in the heavens.

42 We have transgressed and have rebelled: You have not pardoned.

43 You have covered with anger, and persecuted us: You have slain, You have not pitied.

44 You have covered Yourself with a cloud, that *our* prayer should not pass through.

45 You have made us *as* the <u>offscouring</u> and refuse in the midst of the people.   scum

46 All our enemies have opened their mouths against us

47 <u>Fear</u> and a <u>snare</u> is come upon us, desolation and destruction.   Panic - pitfall

48 My eye runs down with rivers of water for the destruction of the daughter of my people.

49 My eye trickles down, and ceases not, without any intermission,

50 Till the LORD look down, and behold from heaven.

51 My eye affects my heart because of all the daughters of my city.

52 My enemies chased me <u>sore</u>, like a bird, without cause. *much*

53 They have cut off my life in the dungeon, and cast a stone upon me.

54 Waters flowed over my head; *then* I said, I am cut off.

55 I called upon Your name, O LORD, out of the low dungeon.

56 You have heard my voice: hide not Your ear at my breathing, at my cry.

57 You drew near in the day *that* I called upon You: You said, Fear not.

58 O Lord, You have pleaded the causes of my soul; You have redeemed my life.

59 O LORD, You have seen my wrong: judge You my cause.

60 You have seen all their vengeance *and* all their <u>imaginations</u> against me. *schemes*

61 You have heard their reproach, O LORD, *and* all their <u>imaginations</u> against me;

62 The lips of those that rose up against me, and their device against me all the day.

63 Behold their sitting down, and their rising up; I *am* their music.

64 Render to them a <u>recompence</u>, O LORD, according to the work of their hands. *payment*

65 Give them sorrow of heart, Your curse to them.

66 Persecute and destroy them in anger from under the heavens of the LORD.

CHAPTER 4

HOW is the gold become dim! *how* is the most fine gold changed! the stones of the sanctuary are poured out in the top of every street.

2 The precious sons of Zi'on, comparable to fine gold, how are they esteemed as earthen pitchers, the work of the hands of the potter!

3 Even the <u>sea monsters</u> draw out the breast, they give suck to their young ones: the daughter of my people *is become* cruel, like the ostriches in the wilderness. *jackals*

4 The tongue of the sucking child clings to the roof of his mouth for thirst: the young children ask bread, *and* no man breaks *it* to them.

5 They that did feed delicately are desolate in the streets: they that were brought up in scarlet embrace dunghills.

6 For the punishment of the iniquity of the daughter of my people is greater than the punishment of the sin of Sod'om, that was overthrown as in a moment, and no hands <u>stayed on</u> her. *turned toward*

7 Her <u>Naz'a-rites</u> were purer than snow, they were whiter than milk, they were more ruddy in body than rubies, their polishing was of sapphire: *consecrated ones*

8 Their visage is blacker than a coal; they are not known in the streets: their skin clings to their bones; it is withered, it is become like a stick.

9 *They that be* slain with the sword are better than *they that be* slain with

hunger: for these pine away, stricken through for *want of* the fruits of the field.

10 The hands of the pitiful women have <u>sodden</u> their own children: they were their <u>meat</u> in the destruction of the daughter of my people. <small>boiled - food</small>

11 The LORD has accomplished His fury; He has poured out His fierce anger, and has kindled a fire in Zi'on, and it has devoured the foundations thereof.

12 The kings of the earth, and all the inhabitants of the world, would not have believed that the adversary and the enemy should have entered into the gates of Je-ru'sa-lem.

13 For the sins of her prophets, *and* the iniquities of her priests, that have shed the blood of the just in the midst of her,

14 They have wandered *as* blind *men* in the streets, they have polluted themselves with blood, so that men could not touch their garments.

15 They cried to them, Depart you; *it is* <u>unclean</u>; depart, depart, touch not: when they fled away and wandered, they said among the heathen, They shall no more <u>sojourn</u> *there*. <small>unfit - dwell</small>

16 The anger of the LORD has divided them; He will no more regard them: they respected not the persons of the priests, they favored not the elders.

17 As for us, our eyes as yet failed for our vain help: in our watching we have watched for a nation *that* could not save *us*.

18 They hunt our steps, that we can-not go in our streets: our end is near, our days are fulfilled; for our end is come.

19 Our persecutors are swifter than the eagles of the heaven: they pursued us upon the mountains, they laid wait for us in the wilderness.

20 The breath of our nostrils, the anointed of the LORD, was taken in their pits, of whom we said, Under his shadow we shall live among the heathen.

21 Rejoice and be glad, O daughter of E'dom, that dwell in the land of Uz; the cup also shall pass through to you: you shall be drunken, and shall make yourself naked.

22 The punishment of your <u>iniquity</u> is <u>accomplished</u>, O daughter of Zi'on; He will no more carry you away into captivity: He will visit your <u>iniquity</u>, O daughter of E'dom; He will <u>discover</u> your sins. <small>sin - completed - expose</small>

CHAPTER 5

REMEMBER, O LORD, what is come upon us: consider, and behold our reproach.

2 Our inheritance is turned to strangers, our houses to aliens.

3 We are orphans and fatherless, our mothers *are* as widows.

4 We have drunken our water for money; our wood is sold to us.

5 <u>Our necks *are*</u> under persecution: we labor, *and* have no rest. <small>We suffer</small>

6 We have given the hand to the E-gyp'tians, *and to* the As-syr'i-ans, to be satisfied with bread.

7 Our fathers have sinned, *and are* not; and we have borne their iniquities.

8 Servants have ruled over us: *there is* none that does deliver *us* out of their hand.

9 We got our bread with *the peril of* our lives because of the sword of the wilderness.

10 Our skin was black like an oven because of the terrible famine. ^(fever heat of)

11 They ravished the women in Zi'on, *and* the maids in the cities of Ju'dah.

12 Princes are hanged up by their hand: the faces of elders were not honored.

13 They took the young men to grind, and the children fell under the wood.

14 The elders have ceased from the gate, the young men from their music.

15 The joy of our heart is ceased; our dance is turned into mourning.

16 The crown is fallen *from* our head: woe to us, that we have sinned!

17 For this our heart is faint; for these *things* our eyes are dim.

18 Because of the mountain of Zi'on, which is desolate, the foxes walk upon it.

19 You, O LORD, remain for ever; Your throne from generation to generation.

20 Wherefore do You forget us for ever, *and* forsake us so long time?

21 Turn You us to You, O LORD, and we shall be turned; renew our days as of old.

22 But You have utterly rejected us; You are very angry against us.

EZEKIEL

OUTLINE

SURVEY

The Book of Ezekiel records the activity of a prophet during the Exile in Babylonia. His message was directed to his fellow-captives and also to the Hebrew people still at home in Palestine. Both groups remained obstinate and impenitent even after the capture of Jerusalem by the Babylonian king, Nebuchadrezzar, and the exiling of Jehoiachin, king of Judah, together with a large segment of the population in 597 B.C. God therefore assigned to Ezekiel the task of denouncing the rebellious house of Israel and of foretelling the destruction of Jerusalem and the deportation of still greater numbers. Six years after Ezekiel had begun to preach, his words came true. In 586 B.C. Nebuchadrezzar destroyed Jerusalem and brought all but a few of the survivors to Babylonia. But Israel's unfaithfulness did not exhaust God's mercy. Ezekiel was also directed to proclaim the good news

that the Exile would end and that Israel would be restored to her position as the instrument of God's salvation to all men.

The manner in which the Book of Ezekiel presents this message of judgment and promise distinguishes it from other prophetic books of the Old Testament. Its first unique feature is the systematic arrangement of the contents. The first twenty-four chapters set forth Israel's arraignment and condemnation with terrifying consistency. This prospect of doom, relieved by only incidental rays of light, is balanced in the last section (chs. 33 through 48) by an equally consistent portrayal of the bright future that God has in store for His people. Dividing these solid blocks of threat and promise to Israel, there is a series of addresses to foreign nations which have a double aspect: they pronounce doom upon the wicked neighbors of Israel, but the destruction of Israel's enemies also constitutes an assurance that they will not be able to hinder the fulfilment of God's promise to redeem and restore His chosen people.

Another unique feature of the Book of Ezekiel is the form in which both threat and promise are expressed. It abounds in mysterious visions, daring allegories, and weird symbolic actions. These media of God's relevation occur here more frequently than in any other prophetic book and are presented with an equally unusual elaboration of descriptive detail. The visions, in particular, are bizarre, almost grotesque in form, and therefore difficult to interpret.

But the basic meaning of the Book of Ezekiel will not elude the reader if he keeps in mind that God's glory and His great acts of judgment and salvation are portrayed in symbolic language and form. What Ezekiel sees in visions, describes in allegories, and acts out in a manner resembling charades, is designed to contribute to the assurance that God is carrying forward His plan of salvation for all men that He initiated in His covenant with Israel centuries ago. Purified by God's judgment in the Babylonian exile, Israel will again become the bearer of the promises to be fulfilled in the New Covenant and to the end of time. All of this Ezekiel sees in prophetic perspective in which scenes of the immediate and of the distant future are at times superimposed on the same picture of the coming and enduring Kingdom of God.

AUTHOR

So completely is the person of Ezekiel submerged in his message that beyond his name we know little regarding him. Only two biographical facts can be gleaned from the book: he was the son of Buzi, the priest, and unlike his contemporary, Jeremiah, Ezekiel was married, but this "delight of his eyes" was taken from him while he was carrying out his God-given mission.

Quite often Ezekiel is regarded as a stern, heartless individual. He is said to be impersonal in his detachment from his hearers, and is concerned only with the vindication of God's glory even in the proclamation of mercy. While his feelings do not in fact come to the surface as in the case of Jeremiah, to assert that he lacks sympathy is, however, to go beyond the evidence. Nor can radical critics sustain their theories that he was subject to cataleptic seizures and afflicted with schizophrenic paranoia. The symbolic actions he performs and the visions he receives are not essentially different from those recorded by other prophets.

Ezekiel was taken to Babylon in 597 B.C. and called to prophetic service five years later. He was active for at least twenty-two years (29.17).

W.B.R.

THE BOOK OF
EZEKIEL

CHAPTER 1

NOW it came to pass in the thirtieth year, in the fourth *month*, in the fifth *day* of the month, as I *was* among the <u>captives</u> by the river of Che'bar, *that* the heavens were opened, and I saw visions of <u>God</u>.   exiles - Elohim[p.f.]

2 In the fifth *day* of the month, which *was* the fifth year of king Je-hoi'a-chin's captivity,

3 The word of the LORD came expressly to E-ze'ki-el the priest, the son of Bu'zi, in the land of the Chal-de'ans by the river Che'bar; and the hand of the LORD was there upon him.

4 And I looked, and, behold, a whirlwind came out of the north, a great cloud, and a fire <u>infolding itself</u>, and a brightness *was* about it, and out of the midst thereof as the color of amber, out of the midst of the fire.   flashing forth

5 Also out of the midst thereof *came* the likeness of four living creatures. And this *was* their appearance; they had the likeness of a man.   REV. 4:6

6 And every one had four faces, and every one had four wings.

7 And their feet *were* straight feet; and the sole of their feet *was* like the sole of a calf's foot: and they sparkled like the color of burnished brass.

8 And *they had* the hands of a man under their wings on their four sides; and they four had their faces and their wings.

9 Their wings *were* joined one to another; they turned not when they went; they went every one straight forward.

10 As for the likeness of their faces, they four had the face of a man, and the face of a lion, on the right side: and they four had the face of an ox on the left side; they four also had the face of an eagle.   REV. 4:7

11 Thus *were* their faces: and their wings *were* <u>stretched upward</u>; two *wings* of every one *were* joined one to another, and two covered their bodies.   spread out above

12 And they went every one straight forward: where the spirit was to go, they went; *and* they turned not when they went.

13 As for the likeness of the living creatures, their appearance *was* like burning coals of fire, *and* like the appearance of lamps: it went up and down among the living creatures; and the fire was bright, and out of the fire went forth lightning.

14 And the living creatures ran and returned as the appearance of a flash of lightning.

15 Now as I beheld the living creatures, behold one wheel upon the earth by the living creatures, with its four faces.

16 The appearance of the wheels and their work *was* like to the color of a beryl: and they four had one likeness: and their appearance and their work

was as it were a wheel in the middle of a wheel.

17 When they went, they went upon their four sides: *and* they turned not when they went.

18 As for their rings, they were so high that they were dreadful; and their rings *were* full of eyes round about them four.

19 And when the living creatures went, the wheels went by them: and when the living creatures were lifted up from the earth, the wheels were lifted up.

20 Wherever the spirit was to go, they went, there *was their* spirit to go; and the wheels were lifted up opposite them: for the spirit of the living creature *was* in the wheels.

21 When those went, *these* went; and when those stood, *these* stood; and when those were lifted up from the earth, the wheels were lifted opposite them: for the spirit of the living creature *was* in the wheels.

22 And the likeness of the firmament upon the heads of the living creature *was* as the color of the <u>terrible</u> crystal, stretched forth over their heads above.   ^{awesome}

23 And under the firmament *were* their wings straight, the one toward the other: every one had two, which covered on this side, and every one had two, which covered on that side, their bodies.

24 And when they went, I heard the noise of their wings, like the noise of great waters, as the voice of the Al-mighty, the voice of speech, as the noise of an host: when they stood, they <u>let down</u> their wings.   ^{dropped}

25 And there was a voice <u>from</u> the firmament that *was* over their heads, when they stood, *and* had let down their wings.   ^{from above}

26 And above the firmament that *was* over their heads *was* the likeness of a throne, as the appearance of a sapphire stone: and upon the likeness of the throne *was* the likeness as the appearance of a man above upon it.

27 And I saw as the color of amber, as the appearance of fire round about inside it, from the appearance of His loins even upward, and from the appearance of His loins even downward, I saw as it were the appearance of fire, and it had brightness round about.

28 As the appearance of the bow that is in the cloud in the day of rain, so *was* the appearance of the brightness round about. This *was* the appearance of the likeness of the glory of the LORD. And when I saw *it*, I fell upon my face, and I heard a voice of one that spoke. REV. 4:2

CHAPTER 2

AND He said to me, Son of man, stand upon your feet, and I will speak to you.

2 And the Spirit entered into me when He spoke to me, and set me upon my feet, that I heard Him that spoke to me.

3 And He said to me, Son of man, I send you to the children of Is'ra-el, to a rebellious nation that has rebelled against Me: they and their fathers have

transgressed against Me, *even* to this very day.

4 For *they are* impudent children and stiffhearted. I do send you to them; and you shall say to them, Thus says the Lord GOD.

obstinate - stubborn - Adonay[p.f.] Jehovah

5 And they, whether they will hear, or whether they will forbear, (for they *are* a rebellious house,) yet shall know that there has been a prophet among them.

6 And you, son of man, be not afraid of them, neither be afraid of their words, though briers and thorns *be* with you, and you do dwell among scorpions: be not afraid of their words, nor be dismayed at their looks, though they *be* a rebellious house.

7 And you shall speak My words to them, whether they will hear, or whether they will forbear: for they *are* most rebellious.

they listen or not

8 But you, son of man, hear what I say to you; Be not you rebellious like that rebellious house: open your mouth, and eat that I give you.

REV. 10:8-9

9 And when I looked, behold, an hand *was* sent to me; and, lo, a roll of a book *was* therein;

REV. 5:1 extended - scroll

10 And He spread it before me; and it *was* written inside and outside: and *there was* written therein lamentations, and mourning, and woe. both sides

CHAPTER 3

MOREOVER He said to me, Son of man, eat that you find; eat this roll, and go speak to the house of Is'ra-el.

2 So I opened my mouth, and he caused me to eat that roll.

scroll

3 And He said to me, Son of man, cause your belly to eat, and fill your bowels with this roll that I give you. Then did I eat *it*; and it was in my mouth as honey for sweetness.

REV. 10:10   i.e., mind

4 And He said to me, Son of man, go, get you to the house of Is'ra-el, and speak with My words to them.

5 For you *are* not sent to a people of a strange speech and of an hard language, *but* to the house of Is'ra-el;

foreign

6 Not to many people of a strange speech and of an hard language, whose words you can not understand. Surely, had I sent you to them, they would have hearkened to you.

7 But the house of Is'ra-el will not hearken to you; for they will not hearken to Me: for all the house of Is'ra-el *are* impudent and hardhearted.

listen

8 Behold, I have made your face strong against their faces, and your forehead strong against their foreheads.

as hard as

9 As an adamant harder than flint have I made your forehead: fear them not, neither be dismayed at their looks, though they *be* a rebellious house. emery

10 Moreover He said to me, Son of man, all My words that I shall speak to you receive in your heart, and hear with your ears.

11 And go, get you to them of the captivity, to the children of your people, and speak to them, and tell them, Thus says the Lord GOD;

whether they will hear, or whether they will forbear.   Adonay^{a.t.} Jehovah

12 Then the Spirit took me up, and I heard behind me a voice of a great rushing, *saying*, Blessed *be* the glory of the LORD from His place.

13 *I heard* also the noise of the wings of the living creatures that touched one another, and the noise of the wheels over against them, and a noise of a great rushing.

14 So the Spirit lifted me up, and took me away, and I went in bitterness, in the <u>heat</u> of my spirit; but the hand of the LORD was strong upon me. rage

15 Then I came to them of the captivity at Tel-a'bib, that dwelled by the river of Che'bar, and I sat where they sat, and remained there astonished among them seven days.

16 And it came to pass at the end of seven days, that the word of the LORD came to me, saying,

17 Son of man, I have made you a watchman to the house of Is'ra-el: therefore hear the word at My mouth, and give them warning from Me.

18 When I say to the wicked, You shall surely die; and you give him not warning, nor speak to warn the wicked from his wicked way, to save his life; the same wicked *man* shall die in his <u>iniquity</u>; but his blood will I require at your hand.   JOHN 8:24 sin

19 Yet if you warn the wicked, and he turn not from his wickedness, nor from his wicked way, he shall die in his <u>iniquity</u>; but you have delivered your soul.

20 Again, When a righteous *man* does turn from his righteousness, and commit <u>iniquity</u>, and I lay a <u>stumblingblock</u> before him, he shall die: because you have not given him warning, he shall die in his sin, and his righteousness which he has done shall not be remembered; but his blood will I require at your hand.

sin - obstacle

21 Nevertheless if you warn the righteous *man*, that the righteous sin not, and he does not sin, he shall surely live, because he is warned; also you have delivered your soul.

22 And the hand of the LORD was there upon me; and He said to me, Arise, go forth into the plain, and I will there talk with you.

23 Then I arose, and went forth into the plain: and, behold, the glory of the LORD stood there, as the glory which I saw by the river of Che'bar: and I fell on my face.

24 Then the Spirit entered into me, and set me upon my feet, and spoke with me, and said to me, Go, shut yourself inside your house.

25 But you, O son of man, behold, they shall put <u>bands</u> upon you, and shall bind you with them, and you shall not go out among them: ropes

26 And I will make your tongue cling to the roof of your mouth, that you shall be dumb, and shall not be to them a reprover: for they *are* a rebellious house.

27 But when I speak with you, I will open your mouth, and you shall say to them, Thus says the <u>Lord GOD</u>; He that hears, let him hear; and he

that forbears, let him forbear: for they *are* a rebellious house. Adonay[p.f.] Jehovah

CHAPTER 4

YOU also, son of man, take you a <u>tile</u>, and lay it before you, and portray upon it the city, *even* Je-ru'sa-lem: brick

2 And lay siege against it, and build a fort against it, and cast a mount against it; set the camp also against it, and set *battering* rams against it round about.

3 Moreover take you to you an iron <u>pan</u>, and set it *for* a wall of iron between you and the city: and set your face against it, and it shall be besieged, and you shall lay siege against it. This *shall be* a sign to the house of Is'ra-el.   plate

4 Lie you also upon your left side, and lay the <u>iniquity</u> of the house of Is'ra-el upon it: *according* to the number of the days that you shall lie upon it you shall bear their <u>iniquity</u>.   sin

5 For I have laid upon you the years of their <u>iniquity</u>, according to the number of the days, three hundred and ninety days: so shall you bear the <u>iniquity</u> of the house of Is'ra-el.

6 And when you have accomplished them, lie again on your right side, and you shall bear the <u>iniquity</u> of the house of Ju'dah forty days: I have appointed you each day for a year.

7 Therefore you shall <u>set</u> your face toward the siege of Je-ru'sa-lem, and your arm *shall be* uncovered, and you shall prophesy against it.   turn

8 And, behold, I will <u>lay bands</u> upon you, and you shall not turn you from one side to another, till you have ended the days of your siege.   put ropes

9 Take you also to you wheat, and barley, and beans, and lentils, and millet, and <u>fitches</u>, and put them in one vessel, and make you bread thereof, *according* to the number of the days that you shall lie upon your side, three hundred and ninety days shall you eat thereof.   rye

10 And your meat which you shall eat *shall be* by weight, twenty shek-els a day: from time to time shall you eat it.

11 You shall drink also water by mea-sure, the sixth part of an hin: from time to time shall you drink.

12 And you shall eat it *as* barley cakes, and you shall bake it with <u>dung</u> that comes out of man, in their sight.   manure

13 And the LORD said, Even thus shall the children of Is'ra-el eat their de-filed bread among the Gen'tiles, where I will drive them.

14 Then said I, Ah <u>Lord GOD</u>! be-hold, my soul has not been polluted: for from my youth up even till now have I not eaten of that which dies of itself, or is torn in pieces; neither came there <u>abominable flesh</u> into my mouth.   Adonay[p.f.] Jehovah - unclean meat

15 Then He said to me, Lo, I have given you cow's dung for man's dung, and you shall prepare your bread therewith.

16 Moreover He said to me, Son of man, behold, I will break the staff of bread in Je-ru'sa-lem: and they shall eat bread <u>by weight</u>, and with <u>care</u>; and

they shall drink water by measure, and with astonishment:

<small>measured out to them - anxiety - horror</small>

17 That they may want bread and water, and be astonished one with another, and consume away for their iniquity.   <small>horrified - waste - in - sin</small>

CHAPTER 5

AND you, son of man, take you a sharp knife, take you a barber's razor, and cause *it* to pass upon your head and upon your beard: then take you balances to weigh, and divide the *hair*.

2 You shall burn with fire a third part in the midst of the city, when the days of the siege are fulfilled: and you shall take a third part, *and smite* about it with a knife: and a third part you shall scatter in the wind; and I will draw out a sword after them.   <small>sword</small>

3 You shall also take thereof a few in number, and bind them in your skirts.

4 Then take of them again, and cast them into the midst of the fire, and burn them in the fire; *for* thereof shall a fire come forth into all the house of Is'ra-el.

5 Thus says the Lord GOD; This *is* Je-ru'sa-lem: I have set it in the midst of the nations and countries *that are* round about her.   <small>Adonay^{p.f.} Jehovah</small>

6 And she has changed My judgments into wickedness more than the nations, and My statutes more than the countries that *are* round about her: for they have refused My judgments and My statutes, they have not walked in them.   <small>in doing - decrees</small>

7 Therefore thus says the Lord GOD; Because you multiplied more than the nations that *are* round about you, *and* have not walked in My statutes, neither have kept My judgments, neither have done according to the judgments of the nations that *are* round about you;   <small>Adonay^{p.f.} Jehovah - have more turmoil - decrees</small>

8 Therefore thus says the Lord GOD; Behold, I, even I, *am* against you, and will execute judgments in the midst of you in the sight of the nations.

9 And I will do in you that which I have not done, and whereto I will not do any more the like, because of all your abominations.   <small>detestable idols</small>

10 Therefore the fathers shall eat the sons in the midst of you, and the sons shall eat their fathers; and I will execute judgments in you, and the whole remnant of you will I scatter into all the winds.

11 Wherefore, *as* I live, says the Lord GOD; Surely, because you have defiled My sanctuary with all your detestable things, and with all your abominations, therefore will I also diminish *you*; neither shall My eye spare, neither will I have any pity.

<small>Adonay^{p.f.} Jehovah - holy place - idols - detestable practices</small>

12 A third part of you shall die with the pestilence, and with famine shall they be consumed in the midst of you: and a third part shall fall by the sword round about you; and I will scatter a third part into all the winds, and I will draw out a sword after them.

13 Thus shall My anger be accomplished, and I will cause My fury to rest upon them, and I will be comforted:

and they shall know that I the LORD have spoken *it* in My zeal, when I have accomplished My <u>fury</u> in them.   anger

14 Moreover I will make you waste, and a reproach among the nations that *are* round about you, in the sight of all that pass by.

15 So it shall be a reproach and a taunt, an instruction and an astonishment to the nations that *are* round about you, when I shall execute judgments in you in anger and in fury and in furious rebukes. I the LORD have spoken *it.*

16 When I shall send upon them the evil arrows of famine, which shall be for *their* destruction, *and* which I will send to destroy you: and I will increase the famine upon you, and will break your staff of bread:

17 So will I send upon you famine and evil beasts, and they shall bereave you; and pestilence and blood shall pass through you; and I will bring the sword upon you. I the LORD have spoken *it.*

CHAPTER 6

AND the word of the LORD came to me, saying,

2 Son of man, set your face toward the mountains of Is'ra-el, and prophesy against them,

3 And say, You mountains of Is'ra-el, hear the word of the <u>Lord God</u>; Thus says the <u>Lord God</u> to the mountains, and to the hills, to the rivers, and to the valleys; Behold, I, *even* I, will bring a sword upon you, and I will destroy your high places.   Adonay^p.f. Jehovah

4 And your altars shall be desolate, and your images shall be broken: and I will cast down your slain *men* before your idols.

5 And I will lay the dead <u>carcases</u> of the children of Is'ra-el before their idols; and I will scatter your bones round about your altars.   bodies

6 In all your dwelling places the cities shall be laid waste, and the <u>high places</u> shall be desolate; that your altars may be laid waste and made desolate, and your idols may be broken and cease, and your <u>images</u> may be cut down, and your works may be abolished.   shrines - idols

7 And the slain shall fall in the midst of you, and you shall know that I *am* the LORD.

8 Yet will I leave a remnant, that you may have *some* that shall escape the sword among the nations, when you shall be scattered through the countries.

9 And they that escape of you shall remember Me among the nations where they shall be carried captives, because I am broken with their <u>whorish</u> heart, which has departed from Me, and with their eyes, which go a <u>whoring</u> after their idols: and they shall loathe themselves for the evils which they have committed in all their <u>abominations</u>.

adulterous - lusting - detestable practices

10 And they shall know that I *am* the LORD, *and that* I have not said in vain that I would do this evil to them.

11 Thus says the Lord GOD; <u>Smite with your hand,</u> and stamp with your foot, and say, Alas for all the evil <u>abominations</u> of the house of Is'ra-el!

for they shall fall by the sword, by the famine, and by the pestilence. clap your hand
12 He that is far off shall die of the pestilence; and he that is near shall fall by the sword; and he that remains and is besieged shall die by the famine: thus will I accomplish My fury upon them.
13 Then shall you know that I *am* the LORD, when their slain *men* shall be among their idols round about their altars, upon every high hill, in all the tops of the mountains, and under every green tree, and under every thick oak, the place where they did offer sweet savor to all their idols.
14 So will I stretch out My hand upon them, and make the land desolate, yea, more desolate than the wilderness toward Dib'lath, in all their habitations: and they shall know that I *am* the LORD.

CHAPTER 7

MOREOVER the word of the LORD came to me, saying,
2 Also, you son of man, thus says the Lord GOD to the land of Is'ra-el; An end, the end is come upon the four corners of the land. Adonay^p.f. Jehovah
3 Now *is* the end *come* upon you, and I will send My anger upon you, and will judge you according to your ways, and will recompense upon you all your abominations. repay - detestable practices
4 And My eye shall not spare you, neither will I have pity: but I will recompense your ways upon you, and your abominations shall be in the midst of

you: and you shall know that I *am* the LORD.
5 Thus says the Lord GOD; An evil, an only evil, behold, is come. Adonay^p.f. Jehovah
6 An end is come, the end is come: it watches for you; behold, it is come.
7 The morning is come to you, O you that dwells in the land: the time is come, the day of trouble *is* near, and not the sounding again of the mountains.
8 Now will I shortly pour out My fury upon you, and accomplish My anger upon you: and I will judge you according to your ways, and will recompense you for all your abominations. detestable practices
9 And My eye shall not spare, neither will I have pity: I will recompense you according to your ways and your abominations *that* are in the midst of you; and you shall know that I *am* the LORD that smites. repay
10 Behold the day, behold, it is come: the morning is gone forth; the rod has blossomed, pride has budded.
11 Violence is risen up into a rod of wickedness: none of them *shall remain*, nor of their multitude, nor of any of theirs: neither *shall there be* wailing for them.
12 The time is come, the day draws near: let not the buyer rejoice, nor the seller mourn: for wrath *is* upon all the multitude thereof.
13 For the seller shall not return to that which is sold, although they were yet alive: for the vision *is* touching the whole multitude thereof, *which* shall not

return; neither shall any strengthen himself in the <u>iniquity</u> of his life. _{sin}

14 They have blown the trumpet, even to make all ready; but none goes to the battle: for My anger *is* upon all the multitude thereof.

15 The sword *is* without, and the pestilence and the famine within: he that *is* in the field shall die with the sword; and he that *is* in the city, famine and pestilence shall devour him.

16 But they that escape of them shall escape, and shall be on the mountains like doves of the valleys, all of them mourning, every one for his <u>iniquity</u>. _{sins}

17 All hands shall be feeble, and all knees shall be weak *as* water.

18 They shall also gird *themselves* with sackcloth, and horror shall cover them; and shame *shall be* upon all faces, and baldness upon all their heads.

19 They shall cast their silver in the streets, and their gold shall be removed: their silver and their gold shall not be able to deliver them in the day of the wrath of the LORD: they shall not satisfy their souls, neither fill their <u>bowels</u>: because it is the stumblingblock of their <u>iniq</u>-uity. _{stomachs - sins}

20 As for the beauty of His ornament, He set it in majesty: but they made the <u>images of their abominations</u> *and* of their detestable things therein: therefore have I set <u>it far from</u> them.
      _{detestable idols - made it an abhorrent thing to}

21 And I will give it into the hands of the <u>strangers for a prey</u>, and to the wicked of the earth for <u>a spoil</u>; and they shall pollute it. _{foreigners for plunder - loot}

22 My face will I turn also from them, and they shall pollute My secret *place*: for the robbers shall enter into it, and defile it.

23 Make a chain: for the land is full of bloody crimes, and the city is full of violence.

24 Wherefore I will bring the worst of the heathen, and they shall possess their houses: I will also make the pomp of the strong to cease; and their <u>holy places</u> shall be defiled. _{sanctuaries}

25 <u>Destruction</u> comes; and they shall seek peace, and *there shall be* none. _{Terror}

26 Mischief shall come upon mischief, and rumor shall be upon rumor; then shall they seek a vision of the prophet; but the law shall perish from the priest, and counsel from the <u>ancients</u>. _{elders}

27 The king shall mourn, and the prince shall be clothed with desolation, and the hands of the people of the land shall be troubled: I will do to them after their way, and according to their deserts will I judge them; and they shall know that I *am* the LORD.

CHAPTER 8

AND it came to pass in the sixth year, in the sixth *month*, in the fifth *day* of the month, *as* I sat in my house, and the elders of Ju'dah sat before me, that the hand of the Lord GOD fell there upon me. _{Adonay^{p.f.} Jehovah}

2 Then I beheld, and lo a likeness as the appearance of fire: from the ap-

pearance of His loins even downward, fire; and from His loins even upward, as the appearance of brightness, as the color of amber.

3 And He put forth the form of an hand, and took me by a lock of my head; and the Spirit lifted me up between the earth and the heaven, and brought me in the visions of <u>God</u> to Je-ru'sa-lem, to the door of the inner gate that looks toward the north; where *was* the seat of the image of jealousy, which provokes to jealousy.   Elohim p.f.

4 And, behold, the glory of the <u>God</u> of Is'ra-el *was* there, according to the vision that I saw in the plain.

5 Then said He to me, Son of man, lift up your eyes now the way toward the north. So I lifted up my eyes the way toward the north, and behold northward at the gate of the altar this image of jealousy in the <u>entry</u>.   entrance

6 He said furthermore to me, Son of man, see you what they do? *even* the great <u>abominations</u> that the house of Is'ra-el commits here, that I should go far off from My <u>sanctuary</u>? but turn you yet again, *and* you shall see greater <u>abominations</u>.   detestable things - holy place

7 And He brought me to the door of the court; and when I looked, behold a hole in the wall.

8 Then said He to me, Son of man, dig now in the wall: and when I had dug in the wall, behold a door.

9 And He said to me, Go in, and behold the wicked <u>abominations</u> that they do here.

10 So I went in and saw; and behold every form of creeping things, and <u>abominable beasts</u>, and all the idols of the house of Is'ra-el, <u>portrayed</u> upon the wall round about.   detestable animals - were carved

11 And there stood before them seventy men of the <u>ancients</u> of the house of Is'ra-el, and in the midst of them stood Ja-az-a-ni'ah the son of Sha'phan, with every man his censer in his hand; and a thick cloud of incense went up.   elders

12 Then said He to me, Son of man, have you seen what the <u>ancients</u> of the house of Is'ra-el do in the dark, every man in the chambers of his <u>imagery</u>? for they say, The LORD sees us not; the LORD has forsaken the earth.   own idol

13 He said also to me, Turn you yet again, *and* you shall see <u>greater abominations</u> that they do.   things more detestable

14 Then He brought me to the door of the gate of the LORD's house which *was* toward the north; and, behold, there sat women weeping for Tam'muz.

15 Then said He to me, Have you seen *this*, O son of man? turn you yet again, *and* you shall see greater abominations than these.

16 And He brought me into the inner court of the LORD's house, and, behold, at the door of the temple of the LORD, between the porch and the altar, *were* about five and twenty men, with their backs toward the temple of the LORD, and their faces toward the east; and they worshiped the sun toward the east.

17 Then He said to me, Have you seen *this*, O son of man? Is it a light thing to the house of Ju'dah that

they commit the <u>abominations</u> which they commit here? for they have filled the land with violence, and have returned to provoke Me to anger: and, lo, they put the branch to their nose.   detestable things

18 Therefore will I also deal in fury: My eye shall not spare, neither will I have pity: and though they cry in My ears with a loud voice, *yet* will I not hear them.

CHAPTER 9

HE cried also in my ears with a loud voice, saying, Cause them that have charge over the city to draw near, even every man *with* his destroying weapon in his hand.

2 And, behold, six men came from the way of the higher gate, which lies toward the north, and every man a slaughter weapon in his hand; and one man among them *was* clothed with linen, with a writer's inkhorn by his side: and they went in, and stood beside the brazen altar.

3 And the glory of the <u>God</u> of Is'ra-el was gone up from the cherub, where-upon He was, of the threshold of the house. And He called to the man clothed with linen, which *had* the writer's inkhorn by his side;   Elohim^{p.f.}

4 And the LORD said to him, Go through the midst of the city, through the midst of Je-ru'sa-lem, and <u>set</u> a mark upon the foreheads of the men that sigh and that cry for all the <u>abominations</u> that be done in the midst thereof.   REV. 7:3 REV. 9:4 put - detestable things

5 And to the others He said in my hearing, Go you after him through the city, and smite: let not your eye spare, neither have you pity:

6 Slay <u>utterly</u> old *and* young, both maids, and little children, and women: but come not near any man upon whom *is* the mark; and begin at My <u>sanctuary</u>. Then they began at the <u>ancient men</u> which *were* before the house.   completely - holy place - elders

7 And He said to them, Defile the house, and fill the courts with the slain: go you forth. And they went forth, and slew in the city.

8 And it came to pass, while they were slaying them, and I was left, that I fell upon my face, and cried, and said, Ah <u>Lord GOD</u>! will You destroy <u>all the residue</u> of Is'ra-el in Your pouring out of Your fury upon Je-ru'sa-lem?   Adonay^{p.f.} Jehovah - the whole remnant

9 Then said He to me, The iniquity of the house of Is'ra-el and Ju'dah *is* exceeding great, and the land is full of blood, and the city full of <u>perverseness</u>: for they say, The LORD has forsaken the earth, and the LORD sees not.   injustice

10 And as for Me also, My eye shall not spare, neither will I have pity, *but* I will recompense their way upon their head.

11 And, behold, the man clothed with linen, which *had* the inkhorn by his side, reported the matter, saying, I have done as You have commanded me.

CHAPTER 10

THEN I looked, and, behold, in the firmament that was above the head

of the cherubims there appeared over them as it were a sapphire stone, as the appearance of the likeness of a throne.

2 And He spoke to the man clothed with linen, and said, Go in between the wheels, *even* under the cherub, and fill your hand with coals of fire from between the cherubims, and scatter *them* over the city. And he went in in my sight.

3 Now the cherubims stood on the right side of the house, when the man went in; and the cloud filled the inner court.

4 Then the glory of the LORD went up from the cherub, *and stood* over the threshold of the house; and the house was filled with the cloud, and the court was full of the brightness of the LORD's glory.

5 And the sound of the cherubims' wings was heard *even* to the outer court, as the voice of the <u>Almighty God</u> when He speaks.   El^{s.f.} Shaddai

6 And it came to pass, *that* when He had commanded the man clothed with linen, saying, Take fire from between the wheels, from between the cherubims; then he went in, and stood beside the wheels.

7 And *one* cherub stretched forth his hand from between the cherubims to the fire that *was* between the cherubims, and took *thereof*, and put *it* into the hands of *him that was* clothed with linen: who took *it*, and went out.

8 And there appeared in the cherubims the form of a man's hand under their wings.

9 And when I looked, behold the four wheels by the cherubims, one wheel by one cherub, and another wheel by another cherub: and the appearance of the wheels *was* as the color of a beryl stone.

10 And *as for* their appearances, they four had <u>one</u> likeness, as if a wheel had been in the midst of a wheel.   the same

11 When they went, they went upon their four sides; they turned not as they went, but to the place where the head looked they followed it; they turned not as they went.

12 And their whole body, and their backs, and their hands, and their wings, and the wheels, *were* full of eyes round about, *even* the wheels that they four had.

13 As for the wheels, <u>it was cried</u> to them in my hearing, O wheel.   they were called

14 And every one had four faces: the first face *was* the face of a cherub, and the second face *was* the face of a man, and the third the face of a lion, and the fourth the face of an eagle.

15 And the cherubims were lifted up. This *is* the living creature that I saw by the river of Che'bar.

16 And when the cherubims went, the wheels went by them: and when the cherubims lifted up their wings to mount up from the earth, the same wheels also turned not from beside them.

17 When they stood, *these* stood; and when they were lifted up, *these* lifted up themselves *also*: for the spirit <u>of the living creature</u> *was* in them.   of life

18 Then the glory of the LORD departed from off the threshold of the

house, and stood over the cherubims. 19 And the cherubims lifted up their wings, and mounted up from the earth in my sight: when they went out, the wheels also *were* beside them, and *every one* stood at the door of the east gate of the LORD's house; and the glory of the <u>God</u> of Is'ra-el *was* over them above. Elohim^{p.f.}

20 This *is* the living creature that I saw under the <u>God</u> of Is'ra-el by the river of Che'bar; and I knew that they *were* the cherubims.

21 Every one had four faces apiece, and every one four wings; and the likeness of the hands of a man *was* under their wings.

22 And the likeness of their faces *was* the same faces which I saw by the river of Che'bar, their appearances and themselves: they went every one straight forward.

CHAPTER 11

MOREOVER the Spirit lifted me up, and brought me to the east gate of the LORD's house, which looks eastward: and behold at the door of the gate five and twenty men; among whom I saw Ja-az-a-ni'ah the son of A'zur, and Pel-a-ti'ah the son of Be-na'iah, princes of the people.

2 Then said He to me, Son of man, these *are* the men that devise mischief, and give wicked counsel in this city:

3 Which say, *It is* not <u>near</u>; let us build houses: this *city is* the <u>cal-dron</u>, and we *be* the <u>flesh</u>.

i.e., the time to build houses - pot - meat

4 Therefore prophesy against them, prophesy, O son of man.

5 And the Spirit of the LORD fell upon me, and said to me, Speak; Thus says the LORD; Thus have you said, O house of Is'ra-el: for I know the things that come into your mind, *every one of* them.

6 You have multiplied your slain in this city, and you have filled the streets thereof with the slain.

7 Therefore thus says the <u>Lord</u> <u>GOD</u>; Your slain whom you have laid in the midst of it, they *are* the flesh, and this *city is* the caldron: but I will bring you forth out of the midst of it. Adonay^{p.f.} Jehovah

8 You have feared the sword; and I will bring a sword upon you, says the <u>Lord</u> <u>GOD</u>.

9 And I will bring you out of the midst thereof, and deliver you into the hands of strangers, and will execute judgments among you.

10 You shall fall by the sword; I will judge you in the border of Is'ra-el; and you shall know that I *am* the LORD.

11 This *city* shall not be your caldron, neither shall you be the flesh in the midst thereof; *but* I will judge you in the border of Is'ra-el:

12 And you shall know that I *am* the LORD: for you have not walked in My <u>statutes</u>, neither executed My judgments, but have done after the manners of the heathen that *are* round about you. decrees

13 And it came to pass, when I prophesied, that Pel-a-ti'ah the son of Be-na'iah died. Then fell I down upon my face, and cried with a loud voice,

and said, Ah Lord GOD! will You make a full end of the remnant of Is'ra-el? Adonay^{p.f.} Jehovah

14 Again the word of the LORD came to me, saying,

15 Son of man, your brethren, *even* your brethren, the men of your kindred, and all the house of Is'ra-el wholly, *are* they to whom the inhabitants of Je-ru'sa-lem have said, Get you far from the LORD: to us is this land given in possession.

16 Therefore say, Thus says the Lord GOD; Although I have cast them far off among the heathen, and although I have scattered them among the countries, yet will I be to them as a little sanctuary in the countries where they shall come. Adonay^{p.f.} Jehovah

17 Therefore say, Thus says the Lord GOD; I will even gather you from the people, and assemble you out of the countries where you have been scattered, and I will give you the land of Is'ra-el.

18 And they shall come there, and they shall take away all the detestable things thereof and all the abominations thereof from there. detestable idols

19 And I will give them one heart, and I will put a new spirit within you; and I will take the stony heart out of their flesh, and will give them an heart of flesh:

20 That they may walk in My statutes, and keep My ordinances, and do them: and they shall be My people, and I will be their God. decrees - Elohim^{p.f.}

21 But *as for them* whose heart walks after the heart of their detestable things and their abominations, I will recompense their way upon their own heads, says the Lord GOD. Adonay^{p.f.} Jehovah

22 Then did the cherubims lift up their wings, and the wheels beside them; and the glory of the God of Is'ra-el *was* over them above. Elohim^{p.f.}

23 And the glory of the LORD went up from the midst of the city, and stood upon the mountain which *is* on the east side of the city.

24 Afterwards the Spirit took me up, and brought me in a vision by the Spirit of God into Chal-de'a, to them of the captivity. So the vision that I had seen went up from me. Elohim^{p.f.}

25 Then I spoke to them of the captivity all the things that the LORD had showed me.

CHAPTER 12

THE word of the LORD also came to me, saying,

2 Son of man, you dwell in the midst of a rebellious house, which have eyes to see, and see not; they have ears to hear, and hear not: for they *are* a rebellious house.

3 Therefore, you son of man, prepare you stuff for removing, and remove by day in their sight; and you shall remove from your place to another place in their sight: it may be they will consider, though they *be* a rebellious house. baggage for exile

4 Then shall you bring forth your stuff by day in their sight, as stuff for removing: and you shall go forth at even in their sight, as they that go forth into captivity. baggage - evening

5 Dig you through the wall in their sight, and carry out thereby.

6 In their sight shall you bear *it* upon *thy* shoulders, *and* carry *it* forth in the twilight: you shall cover your face, that you see not the ground: for I have set you *for* a sign to the house of Is'ra-el.

7 And I did so as I was commanded: I brought forth my stuff by day, as stuff for captivity, and in the even I dug through the wall with my hand; I brought *it* forth in the twilight, *and* I bare *it* upon *my* shoulder in their sight.   baggage - exile

8 And in the morning came the word of the LORD to me, saying,

9 Son of man, has not the house of Is'ra-el, the rebellious house, said to you, What do you?

10 Say you to them, Thus says the Lord GOD; This burden *concerns* the prince in Je-ru'sa-lem, and all the house of Is'ra-el that *are* among them.   Adonay[p.f.] Jehovah

11 Say, I *am* your sign: like as I have done, so shall it be done to them: they shall remove *and* go into captivity.

12 And the prince that *is* among them shall bear upon *his* shoulder in the twilight, and shall go forth: they shall dig through the wall to carry out thereby: he shall cover his face, that he see not the ground with *his* eyes.

13 My net also will I spread upon him, and he shall be taken in My snare: and I will bring him *to* Bab'y-lon to the land of the Chal-de'ans; yet shall he not see it, though he shall die there.   trap

14 And I will scatter toward every wind all that *are* about him to help him, and all his bands; and I will draw out the sword after them.   troops

15 And they shall know that I *am* the LORD, when I shall scatter them among the nations, and disperse them in the countries.

16 But I will leave a few men of them from the sword, from the famine, and from the pestilence; that they may declare all their abominations among the heathen where they come; and they shall know that I *am* the LORD.   tell - detestable practices - nations

17 Moreover the word of the LORD came to me, saying,

18 Son of man, eat your bread with quaking, and drink your water with trembling and with carefulness;   quivering - anxiety

19 And say to the people of the land, Thus says the Lord GOD of the inhabitants of Je-ru'sa-lem, *and* of the land of Is'ra-el; They shall eat their bread with carefulness, and drink their water with astonishment, that her land may be desolate from all that is therein, because of the violence of all them that dwell therein.   Adonay[p.f.] Jehovah - horror

20 And the cities that are inhabited shall be laid waste, and the land shall be desolate; and you shall know that I *am* the LORD.

21 And the word of the LORD came to me, saying,

22 Son of man, what *is* that proverb *that* you have in the land of Is'ra-el, saying, The days are prolonged, and every vision fails?

23 Tell them therefore, Thus says the

<u>Lord G</u>OD; I will make this proverb to cease, and they shall no more use it as a proverb in Is'ra-el; but say to them, The days are at hand, and the <u>effect</u> of every vision.

Adonay[p.f.] Jehovah - fulfillment

24 For there shall be no more any <u>vain</u> vision nor flattering <u>divination</u> within the house of Is'ra-el.

false - i.e., prediction

25 For I *am* the LORD: I will speak, and the word that I shall speak shall come to pass; it shall be no more prolonged: for in your days, O rebellious house, will I say the word, and will perform it, says the <u>Lord G</u>OD.

Adonay[p.f.] - Jehovah

26 Again the word of the LORD came to me, saying,

27 Son of man, behold, *they of* the house of Is'ra-el say, The vision that he sees *is* for many days *to come*, and he prophesies of the times *that are* far off.

28 Therefore say to them, Thus says the <u>Lord G</u>OD; There shall none of My words be <u>prolonged</u> any more, but the word which I have spoken shall be done, says the <u>Lord G</u>OD.

Adonay[p.f.] Jehovah - delayed

CHAPTER 13

AND the word of the LORD came to me, saying,

2 Son of man, prophesy against the prophets of Is'ra-el that prophesy, and say you to them that prophesy <u>out of their own hearts</u>, Hear you the word of the LORD;

following their own spirit

3 Thus says the <u>Lord G</u>OD; Woe to the foolish prophets, that follow their own spirit, and have seen nothing!

Adonay[p.f.] Jehovah

4 O Is'ra-el, your prophets are like the foxes <u>in the deserts</u>.

among ruins

5 You have not gone up into the <u>gaps,</u> neither <u>made up the hedge</u> for the house of Is'ra-el to stand in the battle in the day of the LORD.

breaks - did you build the wall

6 They have seen <u>vanity</u> and lying <u>divination</u>, saying, The LORD says: and the LORD has not sent them: and they have made *others* to hope that they would confirm the word.

falsehood - predictions

7 Have you not seen a vain vision, and have you not spoken a lying <u>divination</u>, whereas you say, The LORD says *it*; <u>albeit</u> I have not spoken? although

8 Therefore thus says the <u>Lord G</u>OD; Because you have spoken <u>vanity</u>, and seen lies, therefore, behold, I *am* against you, says the <u>Lord G</u>OD.

Adonay[p.f.] Jehovah

9 And My hand shall be upon the prophets that see <u>vanity</u>, and that divine lies: they shall not be in the assembly of My people, neither shall they be written in the writing of the house of Is'ra-el, neither shall they enter into the land of Is'ra-el; and you shall know that I *am* the <u>Lord G</u>OD. falsehood

10 Because, even because they have seduced My people, saying, Peace; and *there was* no peace; and one built up a wall, and, lo, others <u>daubed</u> it with <u>untempered</u> *mortar*:

plastered - white-wash

11 Say to them which <u>daub</u> *it* with <u>untempered</u> *mortar*, that it shall fall: there shall be an overflowing shower; and you, O great hailstones, shall fall; and a stormy wind shall rend *it*.

12 Lo, when the wall is fallen, shall it

not be said to you, Where *is* the <u>daubing</u> wherewith you have <u>daubed</u> *it*?   plaster

13 Therefore thus says the <u>Lord</u> <u>God</u>; I will even rend *it* with a stormy wind in My fury; and there shall be an overflowing shower in My anger, and great hailstones in *My* fury to consume *it*.   Adonay^{p.f.} Jehovah

14 So will I break down the wall that you have <u>daubed</u> <u>with untempered</u> <u>mortar</u>, and bring it down to the ground, so that the foundation thereof shall be discovered, and it shall fall, and you shall be consumed in the midst thereof: and you shall know that I *am* the LORD.   plastered - white-wash

15 Thus will I <u>accomplish</u> My anger upon the wall, and upon them that have <u>daubed</u> it <u>with untempered</u> *mortar*, and will say to you, The wall *is* no *more*, neither they that <u>daubed</u> it;   spend

16 That is, the prophets of Is'ra-el which prophesy concerning Je-ru'sa-lem, and which see visions of peace for her, and *there is* no peace, says the <u>Lord</u> GOD.   Adonay^{p.f.} Jehovah

17 Likewise, you son of man, set your face against the daughters of your people, which prophesy out of their own heart; and prophesy you against them,

18 And say, Thus says the <u>Lord</u> GOD; Woe to the *women* that sew pillows to all armholes, and make kerchiefs upon the head of every stature to hunt <u>souls</u>! Will you hunt the souls of My people, and will you save the <u>souls</u> alive *that come* to you?   persons - lives

19 And will you pollute Me among My people for handfuls of barley and for pieces of bread, to slay the souls that should not die, and to save the souls alive that should not live, by your lying to My people that hear *your* lies?

20 Wherefore thus says the <u>Lord</u> GOD; Behold, I *am* against your pillows, wherewith you there hunt the souls to make *them* fly, and I will tear them from your arms, and will let the souls go, *even* the souls that you hunt to make *them* fly.   Adonay^{p.f.} Jehovah

21 Your kerchiefs also will I tear, and deliver My people out of your hand, and they shall be no more in your hand to be hunted; and you shall know that I *am* the LORD.

22 Because with <u>lies</u> you have made the heart of the righteous sad, whom I have not made sad; and strengthened the hands of the wicked, that he should not return from his wicked way, by promising him life: falsehood

23 Therefore you shall see no more <u>vanity</u>, nor <u>divine divinations</u>: for I will deliver My people out of your hand: and you shall know that I *am* the LORD.   false visions - practice insights

CHAPTER 14

THEN came certain of the elders of Is'ra-el to me, and sat before me.

2 And the word of the LORD came to me, saying,

3 Son of man, these men have set up their idols in their heart, and put the stumblingblock of their <u>iniquity</u> before their face: should I be enquired of at all by them?   wickedness

4 Therefore speak to them, and say to them, Thus says the Lord GOD; Every man of the house of Is'ra-el that sets up his idols in his heart, and puts the stumblingblock of his iniquity before his face, and comes to the prophet; I the LORD will answer him that comes according to the multitude of his idols; Adonay^p.f. Jehovah - wickedness

5 That I may take the house of Is'ra-el in their own heart, because they are all estranged from Me through their idols.

6 Therefore say to the house of Is'ra-el, Thus says the Lord GOD; Repent, and turn *yourselves* from your idols; and turn away your faces from all your abominations. Adonay^p.f. Jehovah - detestable practices

7 For every one of the house of Is'ra-el, or of the stranger that sojourns in Is'ra-el, which separates himself from Me, and sets up his idols in his heart, and puts the stumblingblock of his iniquity before his face, and come to a prophet to enquire of him concerning Me; I the LORD will answer him by Myself: dwells temporarily - wickedness

8 And I will set My face against that man, and will make him a sign and a proverb, and I will cut him off from the midst of My people; and you shall know that I *am* the LORD.

9 And if the prophet be deceived when he has spoken a thing, I the LORD have deceived that prophet, and I will stretch out My hand upon him, and will destroy him from the midst of My people Is'ra-el.

10 And they shall bear the punishment of their iniquity: the punishment of the prophet shall be even as the punishment of him that seeks *to him*; guilt

11 That the house of Is'ra-el may go no more astray from Me, neither be polluted any more with all their transgressions; but that they may be My people, and I may be their God, says the Lord GOD. defiled - Elohim^p.f. - Adonay^p.f. Jehovah

12 The word of the LORD came again to me, saying,

13 Son of man, when the land sins against Me by trespassing grievously, then will I stretch out My hand upon it, and will break the staff of the bread thereof, and will send famine upon it, and will cut off man and beast from it: committing unfaithfulness

14 Though these three men, No'ah, Dan'iel, and Job, were in it, they should deliver *but* their own souls by their righteousness, says the Lord GOD. Adonay^p.f. Jehovah

15 If I cause noisome beasts to pass through the land, and they spoil it, so that it be desolate, that no man may pass through because of the beasts: wild - ravage

16 *Though* these three men *were* in it, *as* I live, says the Lord GOD, they shall deliver neither sons nor daughters; they only shall be delivered, but the land shall be desolate. its midst

17 Or *if* I bring a sword upon that land, and say, Sword, go through the land; so that I cut off man and beast from it:

18 Though these three men *were* in it, *as* I live, says the Lord GOD, they shall

deliver neither sons nor daughters, but they only shall be delivered themselves.   Adonay^{p.f.} Jehovah

19 Or *if* I send a pestilence into that land, and pour out My fury upon it in blood, to cut off from it man and beast: 20 Though No'ah, Dan'iel, and Job, *were* in it, *as* I live, says the Lord GOD, they shall deliver neither son nor daughter; they shall *but* deliver their own souls by their righteousness.

21 For thus says the Lord GOD; How much more when I send My four sore judgments upon Je-ru'sa-lem, the sword, and the famine, and the noisome beast, and the pestilence, to cut off from it man and beast?

    Adonay^{p.f.} Jehovah - severe - wild

22 Yet, behold, therein shall be left a remnant that shall be brought forth, *both* sons and daughters: behold, they shall come forth to you, and you shall see their way and their doings: and you shall be comforted concerning the evil that I have brought upon Je-ru'sa-lem, *even* concerning all that I have brought upon it.

23 And they shall comfort you, when you see their ways and their doings: and you shall know that I have not done without cause all that I have done in it, says the Lord GOD.   Adonay^{p.f.} Jehovah

CHAPTER 15

AND the word of the LORD came to me, saying,

2 Son of man, What is the vine tree more than any tree, *or than* a branch which is among the trees of the forest?

3 Shall wood be taken thereof to do any work? or will *men* take a pin of it to hang any vessel thereon?

4 Behold, it is cast into the fire for fuel; the fire devours both the ends of it, and the midst of it is burned. Is it meet for *any* work?   useful

5 Behold, when it was whole, it was meet for no work: how much less shall it be meet yet for *any* work, when the fire has devoured it, and it is burned?

6 Therefore thus says the Lord GOD; As the vine tree among the trees of the forest, which I have given to the fire for fuel, so will I give the inhabitants of Je-ru'sa-lem.   Adonay^{p.f.} Jehovah

7 And I will set My face against them; they shall go out from *one* fire, and *another* fire shall devour them; and you shall know that I *am* the LORD, when I set My face against them.

8 And I will make the land desolate, because they have committed a trespass, says the Lord GOD.   uninhabited - been unfaithful

CHAPTER 16

AGAIN the word of the LORD came to me, saying,

2 Son of man, cause Je-ru'sa-lem to know her abominations,

    realize - detestable practices

3 And say, Thus says the Lord GOD to Je-ru'sa-lem; Your birth and your nativity *is* of the land of Ca'naan; your father *was* an Am'or-ite, and your mother an Hit'tite.

    Adonay^{p.f.} Jehovah - origin - birth

4 And *as for* your nativity, in the day you were born your navel was not cut, neither were you washed in water to

supple *you*; you were not <u>salted</u> at all, nor <u>swaddled</u> at all.

for cleaning - i.e., rubbed with salt - i.e., wrapped in cloths

5 None eye pitied you, to do any of these to you, to have compassion upon you; but you were cast out in the open field, to the <u>loathing</u> of your person, in the day that you were born. abhorrence

6 And when I passed by you, and saw you <u>polluted</u> in your own blood, I said to you *when you were* in your blood, Live; yea, I said to you *when you were* in your blood, Live. squirming

7 I have caused you to multiply as the bud of the field, and you have increased and <u>waxen</u> great, and you <u>are come to excellent ornaments:</u> *your* breasts are fashioned, and your hair is grown, whereas you *were* naked and bare. grown - became the most beautiful of jewels

8 Now when I passed by you, and looked upon you, behold, your time *was* the time of love; and I <u>spread My skirt over you, and covered</u> your nakedness: yea, I swear to you, and entered into a <u>covenant</u> with you, says the <u>Lord God</u>, and you became Mine. i.e., took you to be my wife - agreement - Adonay^{p.f.} Jehovah

9 Then washed I you with water; yea, I thoroughly washed away your blood from you, and I anointed you with oil.

10 I clothed you also with embroidered <u>work</u>, and shod you with <u>badgers' skin</u>, and I girded you about with fine linen, and I covered you with silk. cloth - i.e., leather

11 I decked you also with ornaments, and I put bracelets upon your hands, and a chain on your neck.

12 And I put a <u>jewel on your forehead,</u> and earrings in your ears, and a beautiful crown upon your head.

golden ring in your nostril

13 Thus were you decked with gold and silver; and your <u>raiment</u> *was of* fine linen, and silk, and broidered work; you did eat fine flour, and honey, and oil: and you were exceeding beautiful, and you did prosper into a kingdom. dress

14 And your <u>renown</u> went forth among the heathen for your beauty: for it *was* perfect through My comeliness, which I had put upon you, says the <u>Lord God</u>. fame - Adonay^{p.f.} Jehovah

15 But you did trust in your own beauty, and played the harlot because of your <u>renown</u>, and poured out your fornications on every one that passed by; his it was. fame

16 And of your garments you did take, and decked your <u>high places</u> with divers colors, and played the harlot thereupon: *the like things* shall not come, neither shall it be *so*. shrines

17 You have also taken your fair jewels of My gold and of My silver, which I had given you, and made to yourself images of men, and did commit whoredom with them,

18 And took your embroidered garments, and covered them: and you have set My oil and My incense before them.

19 My <u>meat</u> also which I gave you, fine flour, and oil, and honey, *wherewith* I fed you, you have even set it before them for a <u>sweet savor</u>: and *thus* it was, says the <u>Lord God</u>. food - soothing aroma - Adonay^{p.f.} Jehovah

20 Moreover you have taken your sons and your daughters, whom you have borne to Me, and these have you sacrificed to them <u>to be devoured</u>. *Is this* of your <u>whoredoms</u> a small matter,   as food to idols - i.e., faithlessness
21 That you have slain My children, and delivered them to cause them to pass through *the fire* for them?
22 And in all your <u>abominations</u> and your <u>whoredoms</u> you have not remembered the days of your youth, when you were naked and bare, and *were* polluted in your blood.

detestable practices - i.e., faithlessness

23 And it came to pass after all your wickedness, (woe, woe to you! **says the** <u>Lord God</u>;)   Adonay^{p.f.} Jehovah
24 *That* you have also built to you an eminent place, and have made you an <u>high place</u> in every street.   shrines
25 You have built your <u>high place</u> at every head of the way, and have made your beauty to be <u>abhorred</u>, and have opened your feet to every one that passed by, and multiplied your <u>whoredoms</u>.   despised
26 You have also committed fornication with the E-gyp'tians your neighbors, great of flesh; and have increased your <u>whoredoms</u>, to provoke Me to anger.   i.e., unfaithfulness
27 Behold, therefore I have stretched out My hand over you, and have diminished your ordinary *food*, and delivered you to the will of them that <u>hate</u> you, the daughters of the Phi-lis'tines, which are <u>ashamed</u> of your lewd way.   despise - shocked
28 You have played the <u>whore</u> also with the As-syr'i-ans, because you were unsatiable; yea, you have played the harlot with them, and yet could not be satisfied.   prostitute
29 You have moreover multiplied your fornication in the land of Ca'naan to Chal-de'a; and yet you were not satisfied herewith.
30 How weak is your heart, **says the** <u>Lord God</u>, seeing you do all these *things*, the work of an <u>imperious</u> whorish woman;

Adonay^{p.f.} Jehovah - brazen

31 In that you built your <u>eminent</u> place in the head of every way, and make your <u>high place</u> in every street; and have not been as an harlot, in that you scorn hire;   special - shrine
32 *But as* a wife that commits adultery, *which* takes strangers instead of her husband!
33 They give gifts to all whores: but you give your gifts to all your lovers, and hire them, that they may come to you on every side for your <u>whoredom</u>.   i.e., faithlessness
34 And the contrary is in you from *other* women in your <u>whoredoms</u>, whereas none follow you to commit <u>whoredoms:</u> and in that you give a reward, and no reward is given to you, therefore you are contrary.
35 Wherefore, O harlot, **hear the word of the** Lord:
36 Thus says the <u>Lord God</u>; Because your filthiness was poured out, and your nakedness <u>discovered</u> through your <u>whoredoms</u> with your lovers, and with all the <u>idols of your abominations</u>, and

by the blood of your children, which you did give to them;

<small>Adonayp.f. Jehovah - uncovered - detestable idols</small>

37 Behold, therefore I will gather all your lovers, with whom you have taken pleasure, and all *them* that you have loved, with all *them* that you have <u>hated</u>; I will even gather them round about against you, and will discover your nakedness to them, that they may see all your nakedness. <small>despised</small>

38 And I will judge you, as women that break wedlock and shed blood are judged; and I will give you blood in fury and jealousy.

39 And I will also give you into their hand, and they shall throw down your <u>eminent</u> place, and shall break down your <u>high places</u>: they shall strip you also of your clothes, and shall take your fair jewels, and leave you naked and bare. <small>special - shrine</small>

40 They shall also bring up a company against you, and they shall stone you with stones, and thrust you through with their swords.

41 And they shall burn your houses with fire, and execute judgments upon you in the sight of many women: and I will cause you to cease from playing the harlot, and you also shall give no hire any more.

42 So will I make My fury toward you to rest, and My jealousy shall depart from you, and I will be quiet, and will be no more angry.

43 Because you have not remembered the days of your youth, but have <u>fretted</u> Me in all these *things*; behold, therefore I also will recompense your way upon your head, says the <u>Lord God</u>: and you shall not commit this lewdness above all your <u>abominations.</u>

<small>enraged - Adonayp.f. Jehovah - detestable practices</small>

44 Behold, every one that uses proverbs shall use *this* proverb against you, saying, As *is* the mother, *so is* her daughter.

45 You *are* your mother's daughter, that <u>loaths</u> her husband and her children; and you *are* the sister of your sisters, which <u>loath</u> their husbands and their children: your mother *was* an Hit'tite, and your father an Am'or-ite. <small>despised</small>

46 And your elder sister *is* Sa-ma'ri-a, she and her daughters that dwell at your left hand: and your younger sister, that dwells at your right hand, *is* Sod'om and her daughters.

47 Yet have you not walked after their ways, nor done after their <u>abominations</u>: but, as *if that were* a very little *thing*, you were corrupted more than they in all your ways. <small>detestable practices</small>

48 *As* I live, says the <u>Lord God</u>, Sod'om your sister has not done, she nor her daughters, as you have done, you and your daughters. <small>Adonayp.f. Jehovah</small>

49 Behold, this was the iniquity of your sister Sod'om, pride, fulness of bread, and abundance of idleness was in her and in her daughters, neither did she strengthen the hand of the poor and needy.

50 And they were haughty, and committed <u>abomination</u> before Me: therefore I took them away as I saw *good*.

51 Neither has Sa-ma'ri-a committed half of your sins; but you have multiplied your <u>abominations</u> more than

they, and have <u>justified your sis</u>-ters in all your <u>abominations</u> which you have done.   i.e., made them seem just
52 You also, which have judged your sisters, bear your own shame for your sins that you have committed more <u>abominable</u> than they: they are more righteous than you: yea, be you confounded also, and bear your shame, in that you have justi-fied your sisters.   detestable practices
53 When I shall bring again their cap-tivity, the captivity of Sod'om and her daughters, and the captivity of Sa-ma'ri-a and her daughters, then *will I bring again* the captivity of your captives in the midst of them:
54 That you may bear your own shame, and may be confounded in all that you have done, in that you are a comfort to them.
55 When your sisters, Sod'om and her daughters, shall return to their former estate, and Sa-ma'ri-a and her daughters shall return to their former estate, then you and your daughters shall return to your former estate.
56 For your sister Sod'om was not mentioned by your mouth in the day of your pride,
57 Before your wickedness was dis-covered, as at the time of *your* re-proach of the daughters of Syr'i-a, and all *that are* round about her, the daughters of the Phi-lis'tines, which despise thee round about.
58 You have borne your lewdness and your <u>abominations</u>, says the LORD.
59 For thus says the <u>Lord God</u>; I will even deal with you as you have

done, which have despised the oath in breaking the <u>covenant</u>.
          Adonay[p.f.] Jehovah - agreement
60 Nevertheless I will remember My <u>covenant</u> with you in the days of your youth, and I will establish to you an everlasting <u>covenant.</u>
61 Then you shall remember your ways, and be ashamed, when you shall receive your sisters, your elder and your younger: and I will give them to you for daughters, but not by your <u>covenant.</u>
62 And I will establish My <u>covenant</u> with you; and you shall know that I *am* the LORD:
63 That you may remember, and be confounded, and never open your mouth any more because of your shame, when I <u>am pacified toward</u> you for all that you has done, says the <u>Lord GOD</u>.   have forgiven - Adonay[p.f.] Jehovah

CHAPTER 17

AND the word of the LORD came to me, saying,
2 Son of man, put forth a riddle, and speak a parable to the house of Is'ra-el;
3 And say, Thus says the <u>Lord GOD</u>; A great eagle with great wings, longwinged, full of feathers, which had <u>divers</u> colors, came to Leb'a-non, and took the highest branch of the cedar: Adonay[p.f.] Jehovah - many
4 He cropped off the top of its young twigs, and carried it into a land of <u>traffic</u>; he set it in a city of merchants.   traders
5 He took also of the seed of the land, and planted it in a <u>fruitful</u> field; he

placed *it* by great waters, *and* set it *as* a willow tree. _{fertile}

6 And it grew, and became a spreading vine of low stature, whose branches turned toward him, and the roots thereof were under him: so it became a vine, and brought forth branches, and shot forth sprigs.

7 There was also another great eagle with great wings and many feathers: and, behold, this vine did bend her roots toward him, and shot forth her branches toward him, that he might water it by the furrows of her plantation.

8 It was planted in a good <u>soil</u> by great waters, that it might bring forth branches, and that it might bear fruit, that it might be a goodly vine. Lit. field

9 Say you, Thus says the <u>Lord God</u>; Shall it prosper? shall he not pull up the roots thereof, and cut off the fruit thereof, that it wither? it shall wither in all the leaves of her spring, even without great power or many people to pluck it up by the roots thereof.

Adonay^{p.f.} Jehovah

10 Yea, behold, *being* planted, shall it prosper? shall it not utterly wither, when the east wind touches it? it shall wither in the furrows where it grew.

11 Moreover the word of the Lord came to me, saying,

12 Say now to the rebellious house, Know you not what these *things mean*? tell *them*, Behold, the king of Bab'y-lon is come to Je-ru'sa-lem, and has taken the king thereof, and the princes thereof, and led them with him to Bab'y-lon;

13 And has taken of the king's *seed*, and made a <u>covenant</u> with him, and <u>has taken an oath of him</u>: he has also taken the mighty of the land: offspring - agreement - putting him under oath

14 That the kingdom might be base, that it might not lift itself up, *but* that by keeping of his <u>covenant</u> it might stand.

15 But he rebelled against him in sending his ambassadors into E'gypt, that they might give him horses and much people. Shall he prosper? shall he escape that does such *things*? or shall he break the covenant, and be delivered?

16 *As* I live, says the <u>Lord God</u>, surely in the place *where* the king *dwell* that made him king, whose oath he despised, and whose covenant he brake, *even* with him in the midst of Bab'y-lon he shall die.

Adonay^{p.f.} Jehovah

17 Neither shall Pha'raoh with *his* mighty army and great company make for him in the war, by casting up mounts, and building forts, to cut off many persons:

18 Seeing he despised the oath by breaking the <u>covenant</u>, when, lo, he <u>had given his hand</u>, and has done all these *things*, he shall not escape. agreement - pledged his allegiance

19 Therefore thus says the <u>Lord God</u>: *As* I live, surely My oath that he has despised, and My <u>covenant</u> that he has broken, even it will I recompense upon his own head. Adonay^{p.f.} Jehovah

20 And I will spread My net upon him, and he shall be taken in My <u>snare</u>, and I will bring him to Bab'y-lon, and

will plead with him there for his trespass that he has trespassed against Me.   trap

21 And all his fugitives with all his <u>bands</u> shall fall by the sword, and they that remain shall be scattered toward all winds: and you shall know that I the Lord have spoken *it*.   troops

22 Thus says the <u>Lord God</u>; I will also take of the highest branch of the high cedar, and will set *it*; I will crop off from the top of its young twigs a tender one, and will plant *it* upon an high mountain and eminent: Adonay[p.f.] Jehovah

23 In the mountain of the height of Is'ra-el will I plant it: and it shall bring forth boughs, and bear fruit, and be a goodly cedar: and under it shall dwell all fowl of every wing; in the shadow of the branches thereof shall they dwell.

24 And all the trees of the field shall know that I the Lord have brought down the high tree, have exalted the low tree, have dried up the green tree, and have made the dry tree to flourish: I the Lord have spoken and have done *it*.

CHAPTER 18

THE word of the Lord came to me again, saying,

2 What mean you, that you use this proverb concerning the land of Is'ra-el, saying, The fathers have eaten sour grapes, and the children's teeth are set on edge?

3 *As* I live, says the <u>Lord God</u>, you shall not have *occasion* any more to use this proverb in Is'ra-el.   Adonay[p.f.] Jehovah

4 Behold, all souls are Mine; as the soul of the father, so also the soul of the son is Mine: the soul that sins, it shall die.   ROM. 6:23   M10 | 1211

5 But if a man be just, and do that which is lawful and right,

6 *And* has not eaten upon the mountains, neither has lifted up his eyes to the idols of the house of Is'ra-el, neither has defiled his neighbor's wife, neither has come near to a menstruous woman,

7 And has not oppressed any, *but* has restored to the debtor his pledge, has <u>spoiled</u> none by violence, has given his bread to the hungry, and has covered the naked with a garment;   robbed

8 He *that* has not given forth upon <u>usury</u>, neither has taken any increase, *that* has withdrawn his hand from <u>iniquity</u>, has executed true judgment between man and man,   interest - doing wrong

9 Has walked in My <u>statutes</u>, and has kept My judgments, to deal truly; he *is* just, he shall surely live, says the <u>Lord God</u>.   decrees - Adonay[p.f.] Jehovah   M03 | 1211

10 If he father a son *that is* a robber, a shedder of blood, and *that* does the like to *any* one of these *things*,

11 And that does not any of those *duties*, but even has eaten upon the mountains, and defiled his neighbor's wife,

12 Has oppressed the poor and needy, has spoiled by violence, has not restored the pledge, and has lifted up his eyes to the idols, has committed <u>abomination</u>,   detestable things

13 <u>Has given forth upon usury</u>, and has taken increase: shall he then live?

he shall not live: he has done all these <u>abominations</u>; he shall surely die; his blood shall be upon him.   lends on interest - detestable things

14 Now, lo, *if* he father a son, that sees all his father's sins which he has done, and considers, and does not such like,

15 *That* has not eaten <u>upon the mountains</u>, neither has lifted up his eyes to the idols of the house of Is'ra-el, has not defiled his neighbor's wife,   at the mountain shrines

16 Neither has oppressed any, has not withholden the pledge, neither has <u>spoiled</u> by violence, *but* has given his bread to the hungry, and has covered the naked with a garment,   robbed

17 *That* has taken off his hand from the poor, *that* has not received <u>usury</u> nor increase, has executed My judgments, has walked in My <u>statutes</u>; he shall not die for the <u>iniquity</u> of his father, he shall surely live.   interest - decrees - sin

18 *As for* his father, because he cruelly oppressed, spoiled his brother by violence, and did *that* which *is* not good among his people, lo, even he shall die in his <u>iniquity</u>.

19 Yet say you, Why? does not the son bear the <u>iniquity</u> of the father? When the son has done that which is lawful and right, *and* has kept all My <u>statutes</u>, and has done them, he shall surely live.   decrees

20 The <u>soul</u> that sins, it shall die. The son shall not bear the <u>iniquity</u> of the father, neither shall the father bear the <u>iniquity</u> of the son: the righteousness of the righteous shall be upon him,

and the wickedness of the wicked shall be upon him.   JOHN 9:2 person - guilt

21 But if the wicked will turn from all his sins that he has committed, and keep all My <u>statutes</u>, and do that which is lawful and right, he shall surely live, he shall not die.   decrees

22 All his transgressions that he has committed, they shall not be mentioned to him in his righteousness that he has done he shall live.

23 Have I any pleasure at all that the wicked should die? says the <u>Lord God</u>: *and* not that he should return from his ways, and live?   Adonay[P.f.] Jehovah

24 But when the righteous turns away from his righteousness, and commits <u>iniquity</u>, *and* does according to all the <u>abominations</u> that the wicked *man* does, shall he live? All his righteousness that he has done shall not be mentioned: in his trespass that he has trespassed, and in his sin that he has sinned, in them shall he die.   sin - detestable things

25 Yet you say, The way of the Lord is not <u>equal</u>. Hear now, O house of Is'ra-el; Is not My way <u>equal</u>? are not your ways <u>unequal</u>?   just - unjust

26 When a righteous *man* turns away from his righteousness, and commits <u>iniquity</u>, and dies in them; for his <u>iniquity</u> that he has done shall he die.

27 Again, when the wicked *man* turns away from his wickedness that he has committed, and does that which is lawful and right, he shall save his <u>soul alive</u>.   life

28 Because he considers, and turns

away from all his transgressions that he has committed, he shall surely live, he shall not die.

29 Yet says the house of Is′ra-el, The way of the Lord is not <u>equal</u>. O house of Is′ra-el, are not My ways <u>equal</u>? are not your ways <u>unequal</u>? _{just}

30 Therefore I will judge you, O house of Is′ra-el, every one according to his ways, says the <u>Lord G</u>OD. Repent, and turn *yourselves* from all your transgressions; so <u>iniquity</u> shall not be your ruin. _{Adonay^{p.f.} Jehovah - sin}

31 Cast away from you all your transgressions, whereby you have transgressed; and make you a new heart and a new spirit: for why will you die, O house of Is′ra-el?

32 For I have no pleasure in the death of him that dies says the <u>Lord G</u>OD: wherefore turn *your-selves*, and live you. _{Adonay^{p.f.} Jehovah}

CHAPTER 19

MOREOVER take you up a lamentation for the princes of Is′ra-el, 2 And say, What *is* your mother? A lioness: she lay down among lions, she nourished her <u>whelps</u> among young lions. _{cubs}

3 And she brought up one of her <u>whelps</u>: it became a young lion, and it learned to catch the prey; it devoured men.

4 The nations also heard of him; he was taken in their pit, and they brought him with chains to the land of E′gypt.

5 Now when she saw that she had waited, *and* her hope was lost, then she took another of her <u>whelps</u>, *and* made him a young lion. _{cubs}

6 And he went up and down among the lions, he became a young lion, and learned to catch the prey, *and* devoured men.

7 And he knew their desolate palaces, and he laid waste their cities; and the land was desolate, and the fulness thereof, by the noise of his roaring.

8 Then the nations <u>set</u> against him on every side from the provinces, and spread their net over him: he was taken in their pit. _{came}

9 And they put him in <u>ward in chains</u>, and brought him to the king of Bab′y-lon: they brought him into holds, that his voice should no more be heard upon the mountains of Is′ra-el. _{a cage with hooks}

10 Your mother *is* like a vine in your blood, planted by the waters: she was fruitful and full of branches by reason of many waters.

11 And she had strong rods for the scepters of them that bare rule, and her stature was exalted among the thick branches, and she appeared in her height with the multitude of her branches.

12 But she was plucked up in fury, she was cast down to the ground, and the east wind dried up her fruit: her strong rods were broken and withered; the fire consumed them.

13 And now she *is* planted in the wilderness, in a dry and thirsty ground.

14 And fire is gone out of a rod of her branches, *which* has devoured her fruit, so that she has no strong rod *to*

be a scepter to rule. This *is* a lamentation, and shall be for a lamentation.

CHAPTER 20

AND it came to pass in the seventh year, in the fifth *month*, the tenth *day* of the month, *that* certain of the elders of Is'ra-el came to enquire of the LORD, and sat before me.   i.e., ask for guidance

2 Then came the word of the LORD to me, saying,

3 Son of man, speak to the elders of Is'ra-el, and say to them, Thus says the Lord GOD; Are you come to enquire of Me? *As* I live, says the Lord GOD, I will not be enquired of by you.   Adonay[p.f.] Jehovah

4 Will you judge them, son of man, will you judge *them*? cause them to know the abominations of their fathers: detestable practices

5 And say to them, Thus says the Lord GOD; In the day when I chose Is'ra-el, and lifted up My hand to the seed of the house of Ja'cob, and made Myself known to them in the land of E'gypt, when I lifted up My hand to them, saying, I *am* the LORD your God;

Adonay[p.f.] Jehovah - promised - descendants - Elohim[p.f.]

6 In the day *that* I lifted up My hand to them, to bring them forth of the land of E'gypt into a land that I had espied for them, flowing with milk and honey, which *is* the glory of all lands: selected

7 Then said I to them, Cast you away every man the abominations of his eyes, and defile not yourselves with the idols of E'gypt: I *am* the LORD your God.   vile things - Elohim[p.f.]

8 But they rebelled against Me, and would not hearken to Me: they did not every man cast away the abominations of their eyes, neither did they forsake the idols of E'gypt: then I said, I will pour out My fury upon them, to accomplish My anger against them in the midst of the land of E'gypt.

9 But I wrought for My name's sake, that it should not be polluted before the heathen, among whom they *were*, in whose sight I made Myself known to them, in bringing them forth out of the land of E'gypt.   profaned - nations

10 Wherefore I caused them to go forth out of the land of E'gypt, and brought them into the wilderness.

11 And I gave them My statutes, and showed them My judgments, which *if* a man do, he shall even live in them.   decrees - informed

12 Moreover also I gave them My sabbaths, to be a sign between Me and them, that they might know that I am the LORD that sanctify them.   rest days - made them holy

13 But the house of Is'ra-el rebelled against Me in the wilderness: they walked not in My statutes, and they despised My judgments, which *if* a man do, he shall even live in them; and My sabbaths they greatly polluted: then I said, I would pour out My fury upon them in the wilderness, to consume them.   decrees - profaned

14 But I wrought for My name's sake, that it should not be polluted before the

heathen, in whose sight I brought them out. _{acted - profaned}

15 Yet also I <u>lifted up my hand</u> to them in the wilderness, that I would not bring them into the land which I had given *them*, flowing with milk and honey, which *is* the glory of all lands; _{promised}

16 Because they despised My judgments, and walked not in My <u>statutes</u>, but <u>polluted</u> My <u>sabbaths</u>: for their heart went after their idols. _{decrees - rest days}

17 Nevertheless My eye spared them from destroying them, neither did I make an end of them in the wilderness.

18 But I said to their children in the wilderness, Walk you not in the <u>statutes</u> of your fathers, neither observe their judgments, nor defile yourselves with their idols:

19 I *am* the LORD your <u>God</u>; walk in My <u>statutes</u>, and keep My judgments, and do them; _{Elohim^{p.f.}}

20 And hallow My <u>sabbaths</u>; and they shall be a sign between Me and you, that you may know that I *am* the LORD your <u>God</u>. _{rest days}

21 Notwithstanding the children rebelled against Me: they walked not in My <u>statutes</u>, neither kept My judgments to do them, which *if* a man do, he shall even live in them; they <u>polluted</u> My <u>sabbaths</u>: then I said, I would pour out My fury upon them, to accomplish My anger against them in the wilderness. _{decrees - profaned - rest days}

22 Nevertheless I <u>withdrew</u> My hand, and <u>wrought</u> for My name's sake, that it should not be <u>polluted</u> in the sight of the heathen, in whose sight I brought them forth. _{withheld - acted}

23 I <u>lifted up My hand</u> to them also in the wilderness, that I would scatter them among the heathen, and disperse them through the countries; _{promised}

24 Because they had not executed My judgments, but had despised My <u>statutes</u>, and had <u>polluted</u> My <u>sabbaths</u>, and their eyes were after their fathers' idols. _{decrees - profaned - rest days}

25 Wherefore I gave them also <u>statutes</u> *that were* not good, and judgments whereby they should not live; ROM. 1:24

26 And I <u>polluted</u> them in their own gifts, in that they caused to pass through *the fire* all that opens the womb, that I might make them desolate, to the end that they might know that I *am* the LORD.

27 Therefore, son of man, speak to the house of Is'ra-el, and say to them, Thus says the <u>Lord God</u>; Yet in this your fathers <u>have blasphemed</u> Me, in that they have committed a trespass against Me. _{Adonay^{p.f.} Jehovah - defiled}

28 *For* when I had brought them into the land, *for* the which I <u>lifted up My hand</u> to give it to them, then they saw every <u>high hill</u>, and all the thick trees, and they offered there their sacrifices, and there they presented the provocation of their offering: there also they made their sweet savor, and poured out there their drink offerings. _{promised}

29 Then I said to them, What *is* the <u>high place</u> whereto you go? And the name thereof is called Ba'mah to this day. _{shrine}

30 Why say to the house of Is'ra-el, Thus says the Lord GOD; Are you polluted after the manner of your fathers? and commit you whoredom after their abominations?

Adonay^p.f. Jehovah - i.e., unfaithfulness -defiled - detestable things

31 For when you offer your gifts, when you make your sons to pass through the fire, you pollute your-selves with all your idols, even to this day: and shall I be enquired of by you, O house of Is'ra-el? *As* I live, says the Lord GOD, I will not be enquired of by you. Adonay^p.f. Jehovah

32 And that which comes into your mind shall not be at all, that you say, We will be as the heathen, as the families of the countries, to serve wood and stone.

33 *As* I live, says the Lord GOD, surely with a mighty hand, and with a stretched out arm, and with fury poured out, will I rule over you:

34 And I will bring you out from the people, and will gather you out of the countries wherein you are scattered, with a mighty hand, and with a stretched out arm, and with fury poured out. 2 COR. 6:17

35 And I will bring you into the wil-derness of the people, and there will I plead with you face to face.

36 Like as I pleaded with your fa-thers in the wilderness of the land of E'gypt, so will I plead with you, says the Lord GOD. Adonay^p.f. Jehovah

37 And I will cause you to pass under the rod, and I will bring you into the bond of the covenant: obligation - agreement

38 And I will purge out from among you the rebels, and them that transgress against Me: I will bring them forth out of the country where they sojourn, and they shall not enter into the land of Is'ra-el: and you shall know that I *am* the LORD.

39 As for you, O house of Is'ra-el, thus says the Lord GOD; Go you, serve you every one his idols, and hereafter *also*, if you will not hear-ken to Me: but pollute you My holy name no more with your gifts, and with your idols. Adonay^p.f. Jehovah - profane

40 For in My holy mountain, in the mountain of the height of Is'ra-el, **says** the Lord GOD, there shall all the house of Is'ra-el, all of them in the land, serve Me: there will I accept them, and there will I require your offerings, and the firstfruits of your oblations, with all your holy things. choicest - gifts

41 I will accept you with your sweet savor, when I bring you out from the people, and gather you out of the countries wherein you have been scattered; and I will be sanctified in you before the heathen.

EPH. 5:2 2 COR. 6:17 holy - nations

42 And you shall know that I *am* the LORD, when I shall bring you into the land of Is'ra-el, into the country *for* the which I lifted up My hand to give it to your fathers. promised

43 And there shall you remember your ways, and all your doings, wherein you have been defiled; and you shall loathe yourselves in your own sight for all your evils that you have com-mitted. despise

44 And you shall know that I *am* the LORD, when I have wrought with you for My name's sake, not according to your wicked ways, nor according to

your corrupt doings, O you house of Is'ra-el, says the Lord GOD.

dealt - Adonay^{p.f.} Jehovah

45 Moreover the word of the LORD came to me, saying,

46 Son of man, set your face toward the south, and drop *your word* to-ward the south, and prophesy against the forest of the south field; speak out against

47 And say to the forest of the south, Hear the word of the LORD; Thus says the Lord GOD; Behold, I will kindle a fire in you, and it shall de-vour every green tree in you, and ev-ery dry tree: the flaming flame shall not be quenched, and all faces from the south to the north shall be burned therein. consume - put out

48 And all flesh shall see that I the LORD have kindled it: it shall not be quenched.

49 Then said I, Ah Lord GOD! they say of me, Does he not speak parables? Adonay^{p.f.} Jehovah

CHAPTER 21

AND the word of the LORD came to me, saying,

2 Son of man, set your face toward Je-ru'sa-lem, and drop *your word* to-ward the holy places, and prophesy against the land of Is'ra-el, speak out against

3 And say to the land of Is'ra-el, Thus says the LORD; Behold, I *am* against you, and will draw forth My sword out of its sheath, and will cut off from you the righteous and the wicked.

4 Seeing then that I will cut off from you the righteous and the wicked, therefore shall My sword go forth out of its sheath against all flesh from the south to the north:

5 That all flesh may know that I the LORD have drawn forth My sword out of its sheath: it shall not return any more.

6 Sigh therefore, you son of man, with the breaking of *your* loins; and with bitterness sigh before their eyes. broken heart - bitter grief

7 And it shall be, when they say to you, Why sigh you? that you shall answer, For the tidings; be-cause it comes: and every heart shall melt, and all hands shall be feeble, and every spirit shall faint, and all knees shall be weak *as* water: behold, it comes, and shall be brought to pass, says the Lord GOD. Adonay^{p.f.} Jehovah

8 Again the word of the LORD came to me, saying,

9 Son of man, prophesy, and say, Thus says the LORD; Say, A sword, a sword is sharpened, and also fur-bished: polished

10 It is sharpened to make a sore slaughter; it is furbished that it may glitter: should we then make mirth? it contempts the rod of My son, *as* every tree. great - despising

11 And he has given it to be fur-bished, that it may be handled: this sword is sharpened, and it is fur-bished, to give it into the hand of the slayer. shined

12 Cry and howl, son of man: for it shall be upon My people, it *shall be* upon all the princes of Is'ra-el: terrors by reason of the sword shall be upon

My people: smite therefore upon *your* thigh.   _{it is against}

13 Because *it is* a trial, and what if *the sword* <u>contemn</u> even the rod? it shall be no *more*, says the <u>Lord</u> <u>G</u>OD.   _{despise - Adonay^{p.f.} Jehovah}

14 You therefore, son of man, prophesy, and smite *your* hands together, and let the sword be doubled the third time, the sword of the slain: it *is* the sword of the great *men that are* slain, which enter into their <u>privy</u> <u>chambers</u>.   _{private}

15 I have set the point of the sword against all their gates, that *their* heart may faint, and *their* ruins be multiplied: ah! *it is* made bright, *it is* <u>wrapped up</u> for the slaughter.   _{prepared}

16 Go you one way or other, *either* on the right hand, *or* on the left, wherever your face *is* set.

17 I will also smite My hands together, and I will cause My fury to rest: I the LORD have said *it*.

18 The word of the LORD came to me again, saying,

19 Also, you son of man, appoint you two ways, that the sword of the king of Bab'y-lon may come: both the two shall come forth out of one land: and choose you a place, choose *it* at the head of the way to the city.

20 Appoint a way, that the sword may come to Rab'bath of the Am'mon-ites, and to Ju'dah in Je-ru'sa-lem the <u>defenced</u>.   _{unfortified}

21 For the king of Bab'y-lon stood at the parting of the way, at the head of the two ways, to use <u>divination</u>: he made *his* arrows bright, he consulted with <u>images</u>, he <u>looked in the</u> <u>liver</u>.   _{seek an omen - idols - i.e., to foretell the future}

22 At his right hand was the <u>divination</u> for Je-ru'sa-lem, to appoint captains, to open the mouth in the slaughter, to lift up the voice with shouting, to appoint *battering* rams against the gates, to <u>cast a mount</u>, *and* to build a fort.   _{build a ramp}

23 And it shall be to them as a false <u>divination</u> in their sight, to them that have sworn oaths: but he will call to remembrance the iniquity, that they may be taken.   _{omen}

24 Therefore thus says the <u>Lord</u> <u>G</u>OD; Because you have made your <u>iniquity</u> to be remembered, in that your transgressions are <u>discovered</u>, so that in all your doings your sins do appear; because, *I say*, that you are come to remembrance, you shall be taken with the hand.

_{Adonay^{p.f.} Jehovah - guilt - uncovered}

25 And you, profane wicked prince of Is'ra-el, whose day is come, when <u>iniquity</u> *shall have* an end,   _{punishment}

26 Thus says the <u>Lord</u> <u>G</u>OD; Remove the <u>diadem</u>, and take off the crown: this *shall* not *be* the same: exalt *him that is* low, and abase *him that is* high.   _{Adonay^{p.f.} Jehovah - turban}

27 I will overturn, overturn, overturn, it: and it shall be no *more*, until He come whose right it is; and I will give it *Him*.

28 And you, son of man, prophesy and say, Thus says the <u>Lord</u> <u>G</u>OD concerning the Am'mon-ites, and concerning their reproach; even say you, The sword, the sword *is* drawn: for the

slaughter *it is* <u>furbished</u>, to consume <u>because of the glittering</u>:

Adonay^{p.f.} Jehovah - polished - that it may be like lightning

29 Whiles they see vanity to you, whiles they divine a lie to you, to bring you upon the necks of *them that are* slain, of the wicked, whose day is come, when their <u>iniquity</u> *shall have* an end.   punishment

30 Shall I cause *it* to return into its sheath? I will judge you in the place where you were created, in the land of your <u>nativity</u>.   birth

31 And I will pour out My indignation upon you, I will blow against you in the fire of My anger, and deliver you into the hand of <u>brutish</u> men, *and* skilful to destroy.   brutal

32 You shall be for fuel to the fire; your blood shall be in the midst of the land; you shall be no *more* remembered: for I the LORD have spoken *it*.

CHAPTER 22

MOREOVER the word of the LORD came to me, saying,

2 Now, you son of man, will you judge, will you judge the <u>bloody</u> city? yea, you shall show her all her <u>abominations</u>.   i.e., sinful - detestable practices

3 Then say you, Thus says the LORD GOD, The city sheds blood in the midst of it, that her time may come, and makes idols against herself to defile herself.   Adonay^{p.f.} Jehovah

4 You are become guilty in your blood that you have shed; and have defiled yourself in your idols which you have made; and you have caused your days to draw near, and are come *even* to your years: therefore have I made you a reproach to the heathen, and a <u>mocking</u> to all countries.   laughing stock

5 *Those that be* near, and *those that be* far from thee, shall mock you, *which are* infamous *and* <u>much vexed</u>.   in turmoil

6 Behold, the princes of Is'ra-el, every one were in you to their power to shed blood.

7 In you have they set light by father and mother: in the midst of you have they dealt by <u>oppression</u> with the stranger: in you have they <u>vexed</u> the fatherless and the widow.   extortion - mistreated

8 You have despised My holy things, and have profaned My <u>sabbaths</u>.   rest days

9 In you are men that carry tales to shed blood: and in you they eat upon the mountains: in the midst of you they commit lewdness.

10 In you have they <u>discovered</u> their fathers' nakedness: in you have they humbled her that was set apart for <u>pollution</u>.   uncovered - menstrual impurity

11 And one has committed <u>abomination</u> with his neighbor's wife; and another has <u>lewdly</u> defiled his daughter in law; and another in you has humbled his sister, his father's daughter.   detestable offense - shamefully

12 In you have they taken gifts to shed blood; you have taken usury and increase, and you have <u>greedily</u> gained of your neighbors by extortion, and have forgotten Me, says the <u>Lord</u> GOD.   unjustly - Adonay^{p.f.} Jehovah

13 Behold, therefore I have smitten My hand at your dishonest gain which

you have made, and at your blood which has been in the midst of you.

14 Can your heart endure, or can your hands be strong, in the days that I shall deal with you? I the LORD have spoken *it*, and will do *it*.

15 And I will scatter you among the heathen, and disperse you in the countries, and will <u>consume</u> your filthiness out of you.   put an end to

16 And you shall take your inheritance in yourself in the sight of the heathen, and you shall know that I *am* the LORD.

17 And the word of the LORD came to me, saying,

18 Son of man, the house of Is'rael is to Me become dross: all they *are* brass, and tin, and iron, and lead, in the midst of the furnace; they are *even* the dross of silver.

19 Therefore thus says the <u>Lord GOD</u>; Because you are all become dross, behold, therefore I will gather you into the midst of Je-ru'sa-lem.   Adonay^{p.f.} Jehovah

20 *As* they gather silver, and brass, and iron, and lead, and tin, into the midst of the furnace, to blow the fire upon it, to melt *it*; so will I gather *you* in My anger and in My fury, and I will leave *you there*, and melt you.

21 Yea, I will gather you, and blow upon you in the fire of My anger, and you shall be melted in the midst thereof.

22 As silver is melted in the midst of the furnace, so shall you be melted in the midst thereof; and you shall know that I the LORD have poured out My fury upon you.

23 And the word of the LORD came to me, saying,

24 Son of man, say to her, You *are* the land that is not cleansed, nor rained upon in the day of indignation.

25 *There is* a conspiracy of her prophets in the midst thereof, like a roaring lion ravening the prey; they have devoured souls; they have taken the treasure and precious things; they have made her many widows in the midst thereof.

26 Her priests have violated My law, and have profaned My holy things: they have put no difference between the holy and profane, neither have they showed *difference* between the unclean and the clean, and have hid their eyes from My <u>sabbaths</u>, and I am profaned among them.   rest days

27 Her princes in the midst thereof *are* like wolves <u>ravening</u> the prey, to shed blood, *and* to destroy souls, to get dishonest gain.   tearing

28 And her prophets have <u>daubed</u> them with <u>untempered *mortar*</u>, seeing vanity, and divining lies to them, saying, Thus says the <u>Lord GOD,</u> when the LORD has not spoken.

smeared - whitewash - Adonay^{p.f.} Jehovah

29 The people of the land have used <u>*oppression*</u>, and exercised robbery, and have <u>vexed</u> the poor and needy: yea, they have oppressed the stranger wrongfully.   extortion - wronged

30 And I sought for a man among them, that should make up the hedge, and stand in the gap before Me for the land, that I should not destroy it: but I found none.

31 Therefore have I poured out My indignation upon them; I have consumed them with the fire of My anger: their own way have I recompensed upon their heads, says the Lord GOD. Adonay$^{p.f.}$ Jehovah

CHAPTER 23

THE word of the LORD came again to me, saying,

2 Son of man, there were two women, the daughters of one mother:

3 And they committed whoredoms in E'gypt; they committed whoredoms in their youth: there were their breasts pressed, and there they bruised the teats of their virginity. i.e., were unfaithful

4 And the names of them *were* A-ho'lah the elder, and A-hol'i-bah her sister: and they were Mine, and they bare sons and daughters. Thus *were* their names; Sa-ma'ri-a *is* A-ho'lah, and Je-ru'sa-lem A-hol'i-bah.

5 And A-ho'lah played the harlot when she was Mine; and she doted on her lovers, on the As-syr'i-ans *her* neighbors,

6 *Which were* clothed with blue, captains and rulers, all of them desirable young men, horsemen riding upon horses.

7 Thus she committed her whoredoms with them, with all them *that were* the chosen men of As-syr'i-a, and with all on whom she doted: with all their idols she defiled herself. harlotries

8 Neither left she her whoredoms brought from E'gypt: for in her youth they lay with her, and they bruised the breasts of her virginity, and poured their whoredom upon her. from the time in

9 Wherefore I have delivered her into the hand of her lovers, into the hand of the As-syr'i-ans, upon whom she doted. lusted after

10 These discovered her nakedness: they took her sons and her daughters, and slew her with the sword: and she became famous among women; for they had executed judgment upon her. uncovered - a byword

11 And when her sister A-hol'i-bah saw *this*, she was more corrupt in her inordinate love than she, and in her whoredoms more than her sister in *her* whoredoms. harlotries

12 She doted upon the As-syr'i-ans *her* neighbors, captains and rulers clothed most gorgeously, horsemen riding upon horses, all of them desirable young men.

13 Then I saw that she was defiled, *that* they *took* both one way,

14 And *that* she increased her whoredoms: for when she saw men portrayed upon the wall, the images of the Chal-de'ans portrayed with vermilion,

15 Girded with girdles upon their loins, exceeding in dyed attire upon their heads, all of them princes to look to, after the manner of the Bab-y-lo'ni-ans of Chal-de'a, the land of their nativity: belt

16 And as soon as she saw them with her eyes, she doted upon them, and sent messengers to them into Chal-de'a. lusted after

17 And the Bab-y-lo'ni-ans came to her into the bed of love, and they de-

filed her with their <u>whoredom</u>, and she was polluted with them, and her mind was <u>alienated from</u> them.   Lit., sons of Babel - harlortry - disgusted with

18 So she discovered her <u>whoredoms</u>, and discovered her nakedness: then My mind was alienated from her, like as My mind was alienated from her sister.

19 Yet she multiplied her <u>whoredoms</u>, in calling to remembrance the days of her youth, wherein she had played the harlot in the land of E'gypt.

20 For she <u>doted upon</u> their <u>par-amours</u>, whose flesh *is as* the flesh of asses, and whose issue *is like* the issue of horses.   lusted after - lovers

21 Thus you called to remembrance the <u>lewdness</u> of your youth, in bruising your teats by the E-gyp'tians for the paps of your youth.   immoral conduct

22 Therefore, O A-hol'i-bah, thus says the Lord God; Behold, I will raise up your lovers against you, from whom your mind is alienated, and I will bring them against you on every side;   Adonay^{p.f.} Jehovah

23 The Bab-y-lo'ni-ans, and all the Chal-de'ans, Pe'kod, and Sho'a, and Ko'a, *and* all the As-syr'i-ans with them: all of them desirable young men, captains and rulers, great lords and renowned, all of them riding upon horses.

24 And they shall come against you with chariots, wagons, and wheels, and with an assembly of people, *which* shall set against you <u>buckler</u> and shield and helmet round about: and I will set judgment before them, and they shall judge you according to their judgments.   large shield

25 And I will set My jealousy against you, and they shall deal furiously with you: they shall take away your nose and your ears; and your remnant shall fall by the sword: they shall take your sons and your daughters; and your <u>residue</u> shall be devoured by the fire.   survivors

26 They shall also strip you out of your clothes, and take away your fair jewels.

27 Thus will I make your lewdness to cease from you, and your <u>whoredom</u> *brought* from the land of E'gypt: so that you shall; not lift up your eyes to them, nor remember E'gypt any more.   harlotry

28 For thus says the Lord God; Behold, I will deliver you into the hand *of them* whom you <u>hate</u>, into the hand *of them* from whom your mind is alienated: Adonay^{p.f.} Jehovah -despised

29 And they shall deal with you <u>hatefully</u>, and shall take away all your labor, and shall leave you naked and bare: and the nakedness of your <u>whoredoms</u> shall be <u>discovered</u>, both your <u>lewdness</u> and your <u>whoredoms</u>.

despitefully - uncovered - immoral conduct

30 I will do these *things* to you, because you have gone a whoring after the heathen, *and* because you are polluted with their idols.

31 You have walked in the way of your sister; therefore will I give her cup into your hand.

32 Thus says the Lord God; You shall drink of your sister's cup deep and large: you shall be laughed to scorn and had in derision; it contains much.   Adonay^{p.f.} Jehovah

33 You shall be filled with drunken-ness and sorrow, with the cup of as-tonishment and desolation, with the cup of your sister Sa-ma'ri-a. horror
34 You shall even drink it and suck *it* out, and you shall break the sherds thereof, and pluck off your own breasts: for I have spoken *it*, says the Lord GOD. Adonay^p.f. Jehovah
35 Therefore thus says the Lord GOD; Because you have forgotten Me, and cast Me behind your back, therefore bear you also your lewdness and your whoredoms. immoral conduct - unfaithfulness
36 The LORD said moreover to me; Son of man, will you judge A-ho'lah and A-hol'i-bah? yea, declare to them their abominations; detestable practices
37 That they have committed adul-tery, and blood *is* in their hands, and with their idols have they com-mitted adultery, and have also caused their sons, whom they bare to Me, to pass for them through *the fire*, to devour *them*. unfaithfulness
38 Moreover this they have done to Me: they have defiled My sanc-tuary in the same day, and have profaned My sabbaths. rest days
39 For when they had slain their chil-dren to their idols, then they came the same day into My sanctuary to profane it; and, lo, thus have they done in the midst of My house.
40 And furthermore, that you have sent for men to come from far, to whom a messenger *was* sent; and, lo, they came: for whom you did wash yourself, painted your eyes, and decked yourself with ornaments,

41 And sat upon a stately bed, and a table prepared before it, where-upon you have set My incense and My oil.
42 And a voice of a multitude being at ease *was* with her: and with the men of the common sort *were* brought Sa-be'ans from the wilder-ness, which put bracelets upon their hands, and beautiful crowns upon their heads. Lit., multitude of mankind - drunkards
43 Then said I to *her that was* old in adulteries, Will they now commit whoredoms with her, and she *with them*? unfaithfulness
44 Yet they went in to her, as they go in to a woman that plays the harlot: so went they in to A-ho'lah and to A-hol'i-bah, the lewd women. immoral
45 And the righteous men, they shall judge them after the manner of adul-teresses, and after the manner of women that shed blood; because they *are* adulteresses, and blood *is* in their hands.
46 For thus says the Lord GOD; I will bring up a company upon them, and will give them to be removed and spoiled. Adonay^p.f. Jehovah - plundered
47 And the company shall stone them with stones, and dispatch them with their swords; they shall slay their sons and their daughters, and burn up their houses with fire.
48 Thus will I cause lewdness to cease out of the land, that all women may be taught not to do after your lewdness.
49 And they shall recompense your lewdness upon you, and you shall bear

the sins of your idols: and you shall know that I *am* the Lord God. Adonay^{p.f.} Jehovah

CHAPTER 24

AGAIN in the ninth year, in the tenth month, in the tenth *day* of the month, the word of the Lord came to me, saying,

2 Son of man, write you the name of the day, *even* of this same day: the king of Bab'y-lon set himself against Je-ru'sa-lem this same day.

3 And utter a parable to the rebellious house, and say to them, Thus says the Lord God; Set on a pot, set *it* on, and also pour water into it:

4 Gather the pieces thereof into it, *even* every good piece, the thigh, and the shoulder; fill *it* with the choice bones.

5 Take the choice of the flock, and burn also the bones under it, *and* make it boil well, and let them seethe the bones of it therein. boil

6 Why thus says the Lord God; Woe to the bloody city, to the pot whose scum *is* therein, and whose scum is not gone out of it! bring it out piece by piece; let no lot fall upon it.

7 For her blood is in the midst of her; she set it upon the top of a rock; she poured it not upon the ground, to cover it with dust;

8 That it might cause fury to come up to take vengeance; I have set her blood upon the top of a rock, that it should not be covered.

9 Therefore thus says the Lord God;

Woe to the bloody city! I will even make the pile for fire great. Adonay^{p.f.} Jehovah

10 Heap on wood, kindle the fire, consume the flesh, and spice it well, and let the bones be burned. cook

11 Then set it empty upon the coals thereof, that the brass of it may be hot, and may burn, and *that* the filthiness of it may be molten in it, *that* the scum of it may be consumed. rust - burned away

12 She has wearied *herself* with lies, and her great scum went not forth out of her: her scum *shall be* in the fire. toil

13 In your filthiness *is* lewdness: because I have purged you, and you were not purged, you shall not be purged from your filthiness any more, till I have caused My fury to rest upon you. immorality

14 I the Lord have spoken *it*: it shall come to pass, and I will do *it*; I will not go back, neither will I spare, neither will I repent; according to your ways, and according to your doings, shall they judge you, says the Lord God. grieve - Adonay^{p.f.} Jehovah

15 Also the word of the Lord came to me, saying,

16 Son of man, behold, I take away from you the desire of your eyes with a stroke: yet neither shall you mourn nor weep, neither shall your tears run down. delight

17 Forbear to cry, make no mourning for the dead, bind the tire of your head upon you, and put on your shoes upon your feet, and cover not *your* lips, and eat not the bread of men. Groan silently - turban

18 So I spoke to the people in the morning: and at even my wife died;

and I did in the morning as I was commanded.

19 And the people said to me, Will you not tell us what these *things are* to us, that you do *so?*

20 Then I answered them, The word of the LORD came to me, saying,

21 Speak to the house of Is'ra-el, Thus says the Lord GOD; Behold, I will profane My sanctuary, the excellency of your strength, the desire of your eyes, and that which your soul pities; and your sons and your daughters whom you have left shall fall by the sword   Adonay^p.f. Jehovah - delights

22 And you shall do as I have done: you shall not cover *your* lips, nor eat the bread of men.

23 And your tires *shall be* upon your heads, and your shoes upon your feet: you shall not mourn nor weep; but you shall pine away for your iniquities, and mourn one toward another.   turbans - sins

24 Thus E-ze'ki-el is to you a sign: according to all that he has done shall you do: and when this comes, you shall know that I *am* the Lord GOD.   Adonay^p.f. Jehovah

25 Also, you son of man, *shall it not be* in the day when I take from them their strength, the joy of their glory, the desire of their eyes, and that whereupon they set their minds, their sons and their daughters,

26 *That* he that escapes in that day shall come to you, to cause *you* to hear *it* with *your* ears?

27 In that day shall your mouth be opened to him which is escaped, and you shall speak, and be no more dumb: and you shall be a sign to them; and they shall know that I *am* the LORD.

CHAPTER 25

THE word of the LORD came again to me, saying,

2 Son of man, set your face against the Am'mon-ites, and prophesy against them;

3 And say to the Am'mon-ites, Hear the word of the Lord GOD; Thus says the Lord GOD; Because you said, Aha, against My sanctuary, when it was profaned; and against the land of Is'ra-el, when it was desolate; and against the house of Ju'dah, when they went into captivity;   Adonay^p.f. Jehovah

4 Behold, therefore I will deliver you to the men of the east for a possession, and they shall set their palaces in you, and make their dwellings in you: they shall eat your fruit, and they shall drink your milk.

5 And I will make Rab'bah a stable for camels, and the Am'mon-ites a couching place for flocks: and you shall know that I *am* the LORD.   resting

6 For thus says the Lord GOD; Because you have clapped *your* hands, and stamped with the feet, and rejoiced in heart with all your despite against the land of Is'ra-el;   scorn

7 Behold, therefore I will stretch out My hand upon you, and will deliver you for a spoil to the heathen; and I will cut you off from the people, and I will cause you to perish out of the

countries: I will destroy you; and you shall know that I *am* the LORD. _{plunder - nations}

8 Thus says the Lord GOD; Because that Mo'ab and Se'ir do say, Behold, the house of Ju'dah *is* like to all the heathen; _{Adonay^{p.f.} Jehovah}

9 Therefore, behold, I will open the side of Mo'ab from the cities, from its cities *which are* on its frontiers, the glory of the country, Beth-jesh'i-moth, Ba'al-me'on, and Kir-i-a-tha'im,

10 To the men of the east with the Am'mon-ites, and will give them in possession, that the Am'mon-ites may not be remembered among the nations.

11 And I will execute judgments upon Mo'ab; and they shall know that I *am* the LORD.

12 Thus says the Lord GOD; Because that E'dom has dealt against the house of Ju'dah by taking vengeance, and has greatly offended, and revenged himself upon them; _{Adonay^{p.f.} Jehovah}

13 Therefore thus says the Lord GOD; I will also stretch out My hand upon E'dom, and will cut off man and beast from it; and I will make it desolate from Te'man; and they of De'dan shall fall by the sword.

14 And I will lay My vengeance upon E'dom by the hand of My people Is'ra-el: and they shall do in E'dom according to My anger and according to My fury; and they shall know My vengeance, says the Lord GOD.

15 Thus says the Lord GOD; Because the Phi-lis'tines have dealt by revenge, and have taken vengeance with a despiteful heart, to destroy *it* for the old hatred; _{Adonay^{p.f.} Jehovah - enmity}

16 Therefore thus says the Lord GOD; Behold, I will stretch out My hand upon the Phi-lis'tines, and I will cut off the Cher'eth-ims, and destroy the remnant of the sea coast.

17 And I will execute great vengeance upon them with furious rebukes; and they shall know that I *am* the LORD, when I shall lay My vengeance upon them.

CHAPTER 26

AND it came to pass in the eleventh year, in the first *day* of the month, *that* the word of the LORD came to me, saying,

2 Son of man, because that Ty'rus has said against Je-ru'sa-lem, Aha, she is broken *that was* the gates of the people: she is turned to me: I shall be replenished, *now* she is laid waste: _{filled}

3 Therefore thus says the Lord GOD; Behold, I *am* against you, O Ty'rus, and will cause many nations to come up against you, as the sea causes its waves to come up. _{Adonay^{p.f.} Jehovah}

4 And they shall destroy the walls of Ty'rus, and break down her towers: I will also scrape her dust from her, and make her like the top of a rock.

5 It shall be *a place for* the spreading of nets in the midst of the sea: for I have spoken *it*, says the Lord GOD: and it shall become a spoil to the nations. _{plunder}

6 And her daughters which *are* in the field shall be slain by the sword; and they shall know that I *am* the LORD.

7 For thus says the Lord God; Behold, I will bring upon Ty'rus Neb-u-chad-rez'zar king of Bab'y-lon, a king of kings, from the north, with horses, and with chariots, and with horsemen, and companies, and much people. Adonay[p.f.] Jehovah

8 He shall slay with the sword your daughters in the field: and he shall make a fort against you, and cast a mount against you, and lift up the <u>buckler</u> against you. shield

9 And he shall set engines of war against your walls, and with his axes he shall break down your towers.

10 By reason of the abundance of his horses their dust shall cover you: your walls shall shake at the noise of the horsemen, and of the wheels, and of the chariots, when he shall enter into your gates, as men enter into a city wherein is made a breach.

11 With the hoofs of his horses shall he tread down all your streets: he shall slay your people by the sword, and your strong garrisons shall go down to the ground.

12 And they shall <u>make a spoil of</u> your riches, and make a prey of your merchandise: and they shall break down your walls, and destroy your <u>pleasant</u> houses: and they shall lay your stones and your timber and your dust in the midst of the water. plunder - fine

13 And I will cause the noise of your songs to cease; and the sound of your harps shall be no more heard. REV. 18:22

14 And I will make you like the top of a rock: you shall be *a place* to spread nets upon; you shall be built no more: for I the Lord have spoken *it*, says the Lord God. Adonay[p.f.] Jehovah

15 Thus says the Lord God to Ty'rus; Shall not the <u>isles</u> shake at the sound of your fall, when the wounded cry, when the slaughter is made in the midst of you?

16 Then all the princes of the sea shall come down from their thrones, and lay away their robes, and put off their broidered garments: they shall clothe themselves with trembling; they shall sit upon the ground, and shall tremble at *every* moment, and be astonished at you. REV. 18:9

17 And they shall take up a lamentation for you, and say to you, How are you destroyed, *that were* inhabited of seafaring men, the renowned city, which were strong in the sea, she and her inhabitants, which cause their terror *to be* on all that <u>haunt</u> it! lived there

18 Now shall the <u>isles</u> tremble in the day of your fall; yea, the <u>isles</u> that *are* in the sea shall be troubled at your departure. coastlands

19 For thus says the Lord God; When I shall make you a desolate city, like the cities that are not inhabited; when I shall bring up the deep upon you, and great waters shall cover you; Adonay[p.f.] Jehovah

20 When I shall bring you down with them that descend into the pit, with the people of old time, and shall set you in the low parts of the earth, in places desolate of old, with them that go down to the pit, that you be not inhabited; and I shall set glory in the land of the living;

21 I will make you a terror, and you *shall be* no *more*: though you be sought for, yet shall you never be found again, says the Lord GOD. _{Adonay^{P.f.} Jehovah}

CHAPTER 27

THE word of the LORD came again to me, saying,

2 Now, you son of man, take up a lamentation for Ty'rus;

3 And say to Ty'rus, O you that are situate at the entry of the sea, *which are* a merchant of the people for many isles, Thus says the Lord GOD; O Ty'rus, you have said, I *am* of perfect beauty. coastlands

4 Your borders *are* in the midst of the seas, your builders have perfected your beauty.

5 They have made all your *ship* boards of fir trees of Se'nir: they have taken cedars from Leb'a-non to make masts for you.

6 *Of* the oaks of Ba'shan have they made your oars; the company of the Ash'ur-ites have made your benches *of* ivory, *brought* out of the isles of Chit'tim.

7 Fine linen with broidered work from E'gypt was that which you spread forth to be your sail; blue and purple from the isles of E-li'shah was that which covered you. coastlands-covering

8 The inhabitants of Zi'don and Ar'vad were your mariners: your wise *men*, O Ty'rus, *that* were in you, were your pilots.

9 The ancients of Ge'bal and the wise *men* thereof were in you your calkers: all the ships of the sea with their mariners were in you to occupy your merchandise. barter in

10 They of Per'sia and of Lud and of Phut were in your army, your men of war: they hanged the shield and helmet in you; they set forth your comeliness.

11 The men of Ar'vad with your army *were* upon your walls round about, and the Gam'ma-dims were in your towers: they hanged their shields upon your walls round about; they have made your beauty perfect.

12 Tar'shish *was* your merchant by reason of the multitude of all *kind of* riches; with silver, iron, tin, and lead, they traded in your fairs.

13 Ja'van, Tu'bal, and Me'shech, they *were* your merchants: they traded the persons of men and vessels of brass in your market.

14 They of the house of To-gar'mah traded in your fairs with horses and horsemen and mules.

15 The men of De'dan *were* your merchants; many isles *were* the merchandise of your hand: they brought you *for* a present horns of ivory and ebony. coastlands

16 Syr'i-a *was* your merchant by reason of the multitude of the wares of your making: they occupied in your fairs with emeralds, purple, and broidered work, and fine linen, and coral, and agate. your goods - rubies

17 Ju'dah, and the land of Is'ra-el, they *were* your merchants: they traded in your market wheat of Min'nith, and Pan'nag, and honey, and oil, and balm. resin

18 Da-mas'cus *was* your merchant in

the multitude of the wares of your making, for the multitude of all riches; in the wine of Hel'bon, and white wool.

19 Dan also and Ja'van going to and fro <u>occupied in your fairs</u>: bright iron, cassia, and calamus, were in your <u>market</u>.   <small>bartered your wares - merchandise</small>

20 De'dan *was* your merchant in <u>precious clothes</u> for chariots.   <small>saddlecloths</small>

21 A-ra'bi-a, and all the princes of Ke'dar, they <u>occupied with you</u> in lambs, and rams, and goats: in these *were they* your merchants.   <small>were your customers</small>

22 The merchants of She'ba and Ra'a-mah, they *were* your merchants: they <u>occupied</u> in your fairs with chief of all spices, and with all precious stones, and gold.   <small>REV. 18:12</small>

23 Ha'ran, and Can'neh, and E'den, the merchants of She'ba, Assh'ur, *and* Chil'mad, *were* your merchants.

24 These *were* your merchants in <u>all sorts *of things*</u>, in blue clothes, and broidered work, and in chests of rich apparel, bound with cords, and made of cedar, among your merchandise.   <small>choice garments</small>

25 The ships of Tar'shish did sing of you in your market: and you were replenished, and made very glorious in the midst of the seas.

26 Your <u>rowers</u> have brought you into great waters: the east wind has broken you in the midst of the seas.   <small>oarsmen</small>

27 Your riches, and your fairs, your merchandise, your mariners, and your pilots, your calkers, and the <u>occupiers</u> of your merchandise, and all your men of war, that *are* in you, and in all your company which *is* in the midst of you, shall fall into the midst of the seas in the day of your ruin.   <small>dealers</small>

28 The <u>suburbs</u> shall shake at the sound of the cry of your pilots.   <small>pasture lands</small>

29 And all that handle the oar, the mariners, *and* all the pilots of the sea, shall come down from their ships, they shall stand upon the land;

30 And shall cause their voice to be heard against you, and shall cry bitterly, and shall cast up dust upon their heads, they shall wallow themselves in the ashes: <small>REV. 18:19</small>

31 And they shall make themselves utterly bald for you, and gird them with sackcloth, and they shall weep for you with bitterness of heart *and* bitter wailing.

32 And in their wailing they shall take up a lamentation for you, and lament over you, *saying*, What *city* is like Ty'rus, like <u>the destroyed</u> in the midst of the sea?   <small>the one destroyed</small>

33 When your wares went forth out of the seas, you filled many people; you did enrich the kings of the earth with the multitude of your riches and of your merchandise.

34 In the time *when* you shall be broken by the seas in the depths of the waters your merchandise and all your company in the midst of you shall fall.

35 All the inhabitants of the <u>isles</u> shall be astonished at you, and their kings shall be <u>sore</u> afraid, they shall be troubled in *their* countenance.   <small>coastlands - horribly</small>

36 The merchants among the people

shall <u>hiss</u> at you; you shall be a terror, and never *shall be* any more.   REV. 18:11,15   whistle i.e., scoff

CHAPTER 28

THE word of the Lord came again to me, saying,

2 Son of man, say to the prince of Ty'rus, Thus says the <u>Lord</u> <u>God</u>; Because your heart *is* <u>lifted up</u>, and you have said, I *am* a <u>God</u>, I sit *in* the seat of <u>God</u>, in the midst of the seas; yet you *are* a man, and not <u>God</u>, though you set your heart as the heart of God:

Adonay^{p.f.} Jehovah - full of pride - El^{s.f.} - Elohim^{p.f.} - El^{s.f.}

3 Behold, you *are* wiser than Dan'iel; there is no secret that they can hide from you:

4 With your wisdom and with your understanding you have gotten you riches, and have gotten gold and silver into your treasures:

5 By your great wisdom *and* by your <u>traffic</u> have you increased your riches, and your heart is <u>lifted up</u> because of your riches: trade - full of pride

6 Therefore thus says the <u>Lord</u> <u>God</u>; Because you have set your heart as the heart of <u>God</u>;   Adonay^{p.f.} Jehovah - Elohim^{p.f.}

7 Behold, therefore I will bring strangers upon you, the <u>terrible</u> of the nations: and they shall draw their swords against the beauty of your wisdom, and they shall defile your brightness. ruthless

8 They shall bring you down to the pit, and you shall die the deaths of *them that are* slain in the midst of the seas.

9 Will you yet say before him that slays you, I *am* God? but you *shall* be a man, and <u>no God</u>, in the hand of him that <u>slays</u> you.   not - Elohim^{p.f.} wound

10 You shall die the deaths of the <u>uncircumcised</u> by the hand of strangers: for I have spoken *it*, says the <u>Lord</u> <u>God</u>.   ungodly - Adonay^{p.f.} Jehovah

11 Moreover the word of the Lord came to me, saying,

12 Son of man, take up a lamentation upon the king of Ty'rus, and say to him, Thus says the <u>Lord</u> <u>God</u>; You seal up the sum, full of wisdom, and perfect in beauty.

13 You have been in E'den the garden of God; every precious stone *was* your covering, the <u>sardius</u>, topaz, and the diamond, the beryl, the onyx, and the jasper, the sapphire, the emerald, and the carbuncle, and gold: the workmanship of your <u>tabrets</u> and of your pipes was prepared in you in the day that you were created.   ruby - settings

14 You *are* the anointed cherub that covers; and I have set you *so*: you were upon the holy mountain of <u>God</u>; you have walked up and down in the midst of the stones of fire.   Elohim^{p.f.}

15 You *were* perfect in your ways from the day that you were created, till *<u>iniquity</u>* was found in you.   unrighteousness

16 By the <u>multitude of your merchandise</u> they have filled the midst of you with violence, and you have sinned: therefore I will cast you as profane out of the mountain of God: and I will destroy you, O covering cherub, from the midst of the stones of fire.   abundance of your trade

17 Your heart was lifted up because of your beauty, you have corrupted your

wisdom by reason of your bright-ness: I will cast you to the ground, I will lay you before kings, that they may behold you.

18 You have defiled your sanctuaries by the multitude of your <u>iniquities, by the iniquity of your traffic</u>; therefore will I bring forth a fire from the midst of you, it shall devour you, and I will bring you to ashes upon the earth in the sight of all them that behold you.   _{dishonest trade}

19 All they that know you among the people shall be astonished at you: you shall be a terror, and never *shall* you *be* any more.

20 Again the word of the LORD came to me, saying,

21 Son of man, set your face against Zi'don, and prophesy against it,

22 And say, Thus says the <u>Lord GOD</u>; Behold, I *am* against you, O Zi'don; and I will be glorified in the midst of you: and they shall know that I *am* the LORD, when I shall have executed judgments in her, and shall <u>be sanctified</u> in her.

Adonay^{p.f.} Jehovah - manifest My holiness

23 For I will send into her <u>pesti-lence</u>, and blood into her streets; and the wounded shall be judged in the midst of her by <u>the sword</u> upon her on every side; and they shall know that I *am* the LORD.   _{epidemics - war}

24 And there shall be no more a <u>pricking</u> brier to the house of Is'ra-el, nor *any* grieving thorn of all *that are* round about them, that despised them; and they shall know that I *am* the <u>Lord GOD</u>.   _{painful - Adonay^{p.f.} Jehovah}

25 Thus says the <u>Lord GOD</u>; When I shall have gathered the house of Is'ra-el from the people among whom they are scattered, and shall be <u>sanctified</u> in them in the sight of the heathen, then shall they dwell in their land that I have given to My servant Ja'cob.   _{set apart}

26 And they shall dwell safely therein, and shall build houses, and plant vineyards; yea, they shall dwell with confidence, when I have executed judgments upon all those that despise them round about them; and they shall know that I *am* the LORD their <u>God</u>.   Elohim^{p.f.}

CHAPTER 29

IN the tenth year, in the tenth *month*, in the twelfth *day* of the month, the word of the LORD came to me, saying,

2 Son of man, set your face against Pha'raoh king of E'gypt, and <u>prophesy</u> against him, and against all E'gypt: _{preach}

3 Speak, and say, Thus says the <u>Lord GOD</u>; Behold, I *am* against you, Pha'raoh king of E'gypt, the great <u>dragon</u> that lies in the midst of its rivers, which has said, my river *is* my own, and I have made *it* for my-self.   _{Adonay^{p.f.} Jehovah - i.e., crocodile}

4 But I will put hooks in your jaws, and I will cause the fish of your riv-ers to stick to your scales, and I will bring you up out of the midst of your rivers, and all the fish of your rivers shall stick to your scales.

5 And I will leave you *thrown* into the wilderness, you and all the fish of your rivers: you shall fall upon the open fields; you shall not be brought to-gether, nor gathered: I have given you

for <u>meat</u> to the beasts of the field and to the fowls of the heaven.   food
6 And all the inhabitants of E'gypt shall know that I *am* the LORD, because they have been a <u>staff of reed</u> to the house of Is'ra-el.   i.e., weak support
7 When they took hold of you by your hand, you did break, and <u>rend</u> all their shoulder: and when they leaned upon you, you broke, and made all their loins to be at a stand.   tear
8 Therefore thus says the <u>Lord</u> <u>GOD</u>; Behold, I will bring a sword upon you, and cut off man and beast out of you.   Adonay^{p.f.} Jehovah
9 And the land of E'gypt shall be desolate and waste; and they shall know that I *am* the LORD: because he has said, The river *is* mine, and I have made *it*.
10 Behold, therefore I *am* against you, and against your rivers, and I will make the land of E'gypt utterly waste *and* desolate, from the tower of Sy-e'ne even to the border of E-thi-o'pi-a.
11 No foot of man shall pass through it, nor foot of beast shall pass through it, neither shall it be inhabited forty years.
12 And I will make the land of E'gypt desolate in the midst of the countries *that are* <u>desolate</u>, and her cities among the cities *that are* laid waste shall be desolate forty years: and I will scatter the E-gyp'tians among the nations, and will disperse them through the countries.   empty
13 Yet thus says the <u>Lord GOD</u>; At the end of forty years will I gather the E-gyp'tians from the people where they were scattered: Adonay^{p.f.} Jehovah
14 And I will bring <u>again</u> the captivity of E'gypt, and will cause them to return *into* the land of Path'ros, into the land of their <u>habitation</u>; and they shall be there a <u>base</u> kingdom.   them back from - origin - lowly
15 It shall be the basest of the kingdoms; neither shall it exalt itself any more above the nations: for I will diminish them, that they shall no more rule over the nations.
16 And it shall be no more the confidence of the house of Is'ra-el, which brings *their* iniquity to remembrance, when they shall look after them: but they shall know that I *am* the <u>Lord GOD</u>.   Adonay^{p.f.} Jehovah
17 And it came to pass in the seven and twentieth year, in the first *month*, in the first *day* of the month, the word of the LORD came to me, saying,
18 Son of man, Neb-u-chad-rez'zar king of Bab'y-lon caused his army to serve a great service against Ty'rus: every head *was* made bald, and every shoulder *was* peeled: yet had he no <u>wages</u>, nor his army, for Ty'rus, for the service that he had served against it: reward
19 Therefore thus says the <u>Lord</u> <u>GOD</u>; Behold, I will give the land of E'gypt to Neb-u-chad-rez'zar king of Bab'y-lon; and he shall take her multitude, and take her spoil, and take her prey; and it shall be the wages for his army.   Adonay^{p.f.} Jehovah
20 I have given him the land of E'gypt *for* his <u>labor</u> wherewith he served

against it, because they wrought for Me, says the Lord GOD. reward

21 In that day will I cause the <u>horn</u> of the house of Is'ra-el to bud forth, and I will give you the opening of the mouth in the midst of them; and they shall know that I *am* the LORD. i.e., strength

CHAPTER 30

THE word of the LORD came again to me, saying,

2 Son of man, prophesy and say, Thus says the <u>Lord GOD</u>; <u>Howl</u> you, <u>Woe worth</u> the day!

Adonay^{p.f.} Jehovah - Wail - Alas for

3 For the day *is* near, even the day of the LORD *is* near, a cloudy day; it shall be the time of the heathen.

4 And the sword shall come upon E'gypt, and great <u>pain</u> shall be in E-thi-o'pi-a, when the slain shall fall in E'gypt, and they shall take away her multitude, and her foundations shall be broken down. anguish

5 E-thi-o'pi-a, and Lib'y-a, and Lyd'i-a, and all the mingled people, and Chub, and the men of the land that is in league, shall fall with them by the sword.

6 Thus says the LORD; They also that uphold E'gypt shall fall; and the pride of her power shall come down: from the tower of Sy-e'ne shall they fall in it by the sword, says the <u>Lord GOD</u>. Adonay^{p.f.} Jehovah

7 And they shall be <u>desolate</u> in the midst of the countries *that are* desolate, and her cities shall be in the midst of the cities *that are* wasted. empty

8 And they shall know that I *am* the LORD, when I have set a fire in E'gypt, and *when* all her helpers shall be destroyed.

9 In that day shall messengers go forth from Me in ships to make the <u>careless</u> E-thi-o'pi-ans afraid, and great pain shall come upon them, as in the day of E'gypt: for, <u>lo</u>, it comes. complacent - behold

10 Thus says the <u>Lord GOD</u>; I will also make the multitude of E'gypt to cease by the hand of Neb-u-chad-rez'zar king of Bab'y-lon. Adonay^{p.f.} Jehovah

11 He and his people with him, the <u>terrible</u> of the nations, shall be brought to destroy the land: and they shall draw their swords against E'gypt, and fill the land with the slain. most ruthless

12 And I will make the rivers dry, and sell the land into the hand of the wicked: and I will make the land waste, and all that is therein, by the hand of strangers: I the LORD have spoken *it*.

13 Thus says the <u>Lord GOD</u>; I will also destroy the idols, and I will cause *their* images to cease out of <u>Noph</u>; and there shall be no more a prince of the land of E'gypt: and I will put a <u>fear</u> in the land of E'gypt.

Adonay^{p.f.} Jehovah - Memphis - dread

14 And I will make Path'ros <u>desolate</u>, and will set fire in Zo'an, and will execute judgments in <u>No</u>. empty - Thebes

15 And I will pour My fury upon <u>Sin,</u> the strength of E'gypt; and I will <u>cut off</u> the multitude of <u>No</u>. Pelusium - destroy - Thebes

16 And I will set fire in E'gypt: <u>Sin</u> shall have great pain, and <u>No</u> shall be <u>rent asunder</u>, and <u>Noph</u> *shall have* distresses daily.

or Pelusium - Thebes - torn apart - Memphis

17 The young men of A'ven and of Pi-

be'seth shall fall by the sword: and these *cities* shall go into captivity.

18 At Te-haph'ne-hes also the day shall be darkened, when I shall break there the yokes of E'gypt: and the pomp of her strength shall cease in her: as for her, a cloud shall cover her, and her daughters shall go into captivity.

19 Thus will I execute judgments in E'gypt: and they shall know that I *am* the LORD.

20 And it came to pass in the eleventh year, in the first *month*, in the seventh *day* of the month, *that* the word of the LORD came to me, saying,

21 Son of man, I have broken the arm of Pha'raoh king of E'gypt; and, lo, it shall not be bound up to be healed, to put a roller to bind it, to make it strong to hold the sword. ^{behold}

22 Therefore thus says the <u>Lord GOD</u>; Behold, I *am* against Pha'raoh king of E'gypt, and will break his arms, the strong, and that which was broken; and I will cause the sword to fall out of his hand. ^{Adonay^{p.f.} Jehovah}

23 And I will scatter the E-gyp'tians among the nations, and will disperse them through the countries.

24 And I will strengthen the arms of the king of Bab'y-lon, and put My sword in his hand: but I will break Pha'raoh's arms, and he shall groan before him with the groanings of a <u>deadly</u> wounded *man*. ^{mortally}

25 But I will strengthen the arms of the king of Bab'y-lon, and the arms of Pha'raoh shall fall down; and they shall know that I *am* the LORD, when I shall put My sword into the hand of the king of Bab'y-lon, and he shall stretch it out upon the land of E'gypt.

26 And I will scatter the E-gyp'tians among the nations, and disperse them among the countries; and they shall know that I *am* the LORD.

CHAPTER 31

AND it came to pass in the eleventh year, in the third *month*, in the first *day* of the month, *that* the word of the LORD came to me, saying,

2 Son of man, speak to Pha'raoh king of E'gypt, and to his multitude; Whom are you like in your greatness?

3 Behold, the As-syr'i-an *was* a cedar in Leb'a-non with fair branches, and with a shadowing shroud, and of an high stature; and its top was among the thick boughs.

4 The waters made him great, the deep set him up on high with its rivers running round about its plants, and sent out its little rivers to all the trees of the field.

5 Therefore its height was exalted above all the trees of the field, and its boughs were multiplied, and its branches became long because of the multitude of waters, <u>when he shot forth</u>. ^{as it spread them out}

6 All the fowls of heaven made their nests in its boughs, and under its branches did all the beasts of the field bring forth their young, and under its shadow dwelled all great nations.

7 Thus was he fair in its greatness, in the length of its branches: for its root was by great waters.

8 The cedars in the garden of <u>God</u>

could not hide him: the fir trees were not like its boughs, and the chestnut trees were not like its branches; nor any tree in the garden of God was like to him in its beauty. Elohim^p.f. - it

9 I have made him fair by the multitude of its branches: so that all the trees of E'den, that *were* in the garden of God, envied him. it

10 Therefore thus says the Lord GOD; Because you have lifted up yourself in height, and he has shot up its top among the thick boughs, and its heart is lifted up in its height; Adonay^p.f. Jehovah - stature - haughty

11 I have therefore delivered him into the hand of the mighty one of the heathen; he shall surely deal with him: I have driven him out for his wickedness.

12 And strangers, the terrible of the nations, have cut him off, and have left him: upon the mountains and in all the valleys its branches are fallen, and its boughs are broken by all the rivers of the land; and all the people of the earth are gone down from its shadow, and have left him. foreigners - tyrants

13 Upon its ruin shall all the fowls of the heaven remain, and all the beasts of the field shall be upon its branches:

14 To the end that none of all the trees by the waters exalt themselves for their height, neither shoot up their top among the thick boughs, neither their trees stand up in their height, all that drink water: for they are all delivered to death, to the nether parts of the earth, in the midst of the children of men, with them that go down to the pit. lower

15 Thus says the Lord GOD; In the day when he went down to the grave I caused a mourning: I covered the deep for him, and I restrained the floods thereof, and the great waters were stayed: and I caused Leb'a-non to mourn for him, and all the trees of the field fainted for him. Adonay^p.f. Jehovah - i.e., subterranean waters

16 I made the nations to shake at the sound of his fall, when I cast him down to hell with them that descend into the pit: and all the trees of E'den, the choice and best of Leb'a-non, all that drink water, shall be comforted in the nether parts of the earth. consoled - lower

17 They also went down into hell with him to *them that be* slain with the sword; and *they that were* his arm, *that* dwelled under his shadow in the midst of the heathen.

18 To whom are you thus like in glory and in greatness among the trees of E'den? yet shall you be brought down with the trees of E'den to the nether parts of the earth: you shall lie in the midst of the uncircumcised with *them that be* slain by the sword. This is Pha'raoh and all his multitude, says the Lord GOD. Adonay^p.f. Jehovah

CHAPTER 32

AND it came to pass in the twelfth year, in the twelfth month, in the first *day* of the month, *that* the word of the LORD came to me, saying,

2 Son of man, take up a lamentation for Pha'raoh king of E'gypt, and say to him, You are like a young lion of the nations, and you *are* as a whale in

the seas: and you came forth with your rivers, and troubled the waters with your feet, and fouled their rivers.

3 Thus says the Lord GOD; I will therefore spread out My net over you with a company of many people; and they shall bring you up in My net. Adonay[p.f.] Jehovah

4 Then will I leave you upon the land, I will cast you forth upon the open field, and will cause all the fowls of the heaven to remain upon you, and I will fill the beasts of the whole earth with you.

5 And I will lay your flesh upon the mountains, and fill the valleys with your height.

6 I will also water with your blood the land wherein you swim, *even* to the mountains; and the rivers shall be full of you.

7 And when I shall put you out, I will cover the heaven, and make the stars thereof dark; I will cover the sun with a cloud, and the moon shall not give her light.

8 All the bright lights of heaven will I make dark over you, and set darkness upon your land, says the Lord GOD.

9 I will also vex the hearts of many people, when I shall bring your destruction among the nations, into the countries which you have not known. trouble

10 Yea, I will make many people amazed at you, and their kings shall be horribly afraid for you, when I shall brandish My sword before them; and they shall tremble at *every* moment, every man for his own life, in the day of your fall.

11 For thus says the Lord GOD; The sword of the king of Bab'y-lon shall come upon you. Adonay[p.f.] Jehovah

12 By the swords of the mighty will I cause your multitude to fall, the terrible of the nations, all of them: and they shall spoil the pomp of E'gypt, and all the multitude thereof shall be destroyed. shatter the pride

13 I will destroy also all the beasts thereof from beside the great waters; neither shall the foot of man trouble them any more, nor the hoofs of beasts trouble them.

14 Then will I make their waters deep, and cause their rivers to run like oil, says the Lord GOD. settle - Adonay[p.f.] Jehovah

15 When I shall make the land of E'gypt desolate, and the country shall be destitute of that whereof it was full, when I shall smite all them that dwell therein, then shall they know that I *am* the LORD.

16 This *is* the lamentation wherewith they shall lament her: the daughters of the nations shall lament her: they shall lament for her, *even* for E'gypt, and for all her multitude, says the Lord GOD. Adonay[p.f.] Jehovah

17 It came to pass also in the twelfth year, in the fifteenth *day* of the month, *that* the word of the LORD came to me, saying,

18 Son of man, wail for the multitude of E'gypt, and cast them down, *even* her, and the daughters of the famous nations, to the nether parts of the earth, with them that go down into the pit. lower

19 Whom do you pass in beauty?

go down, and be you laid with the <u>uncircumcised</u>.   ungodly

20 They shall fall in the midst of *them that are* slain by the sword: she is delivered to the sword: draw her and all her multitudes.

21 The strong among the mighty shall speak to him out of the midst of hell with them that help him: they are gone down, they lie uncircumcised, slain by the sword.

22 Assh'ur *is* there and all her company: his graves *are* about him: all of them slain, fallen by the sword:

23 Whose graves are set in the sides of the pit, and her company is round about her grave: all of them slain, fallen by the sword, which caused terror in the land of the living.

24 There *is* E'lam and all her multitude round about her grave, all of them slain, fallen by the sword, which are gone down uncircumcised into the <u>nether</u> parts of the earth, which caused their terror in the land of the living; yet have they borne their shame with them that go down to the pit.   lower

25 They have set her a bed in the midst of the slain with all her multitude: her graves *are* round about him: all of them uncircumcised, slain by the sword: though their terror was caused in the land of the living, yet have they borne their shame with them that go down to the pit: he is put in the midst of *them that be* slain.

26 There *is* Me'shech, Tu'bal, and all her multitude: her graves *are* round about him: all of them uncircumcised, slain by the sword, though they caused their terror in the land of the living.

27 And they shall not lie with the mighty *that are* fallen of the <u>uncircumcised</u>, which are gone down to hell with their weapons of war: and they have laid their swords under their heads, but <u>their iniquities</u> shall be upon their bones, though *they were* the terror of the mighty in the land of the living.   ungodly - the punishment for their sins

28 Yea, you shall be broken in the midst of the uncircumcised, and shall lie with *them that are* slain with the sword.

29 There *is* E'dom, her kings, and all her princes, which with their might are laid by *them that were* slain by the sword: they shall lie with the uncircumcised, and with them that go down to the pit.

30 There *be* the princes of the north, all of them, and all the Zi-do'ni-ans, which are gone down with the slain; with their terror they are ashamed of their might; and they lie <u>uncircumcised</u> with *them that be* slain by the sword, and bear their shame with them that go down to the pit.   ungodly

31 Pha'raoh shall see them, and shall be comforted over all his multitude, *even* Pha'raoh and all his army slain by the sword, says the <u>Lord God</u>.   Adonay[p.f.] Jehovah

32 For I have caused My terror in the land of the living: and he shall be laid in the midst of the <u>uncircumcised</u> with *them that are* slain with the sword, *even* Pha'raoh and all his multitude, says the <u>Lord God</u>.

CHAPTER 33

AGAIN the word of the LORD came to me, saying,

2 Son of man, speak to the children of your people, and say to them, When I bring the sword upon a land, if the people of the land take a man of their coasts, and set him for their watchman: from among them

3 If when he sees the sword come upon the land, he blow the trumpet, and warn the people;

4 Then whosoever hears the sound of the trumpet, and takes not warning; if the sword come, and take him away, his blood shall be upon his own head.

5 He heard the sound of the trumpet, and took not warning; his blood shall be upon him. But he that takes warning shall deliver his soul.   save

6 But if the watchman see the sword come, and blow not the trumpet, and the people be not warned; if the sword come, and take *any* person from among them, he is taken away in his iniquity; but his blood will I require at the watchman's hand.   sin

7 So you, O son of man, I have set you a watchman to the house of Is'ra-el; therefore you shall hear the word at My mouth, and warn them from Me.

8 When I say to the wicked, O wicked *man*, you shall surely die; if you do not speak to warn the wicked from his way, that wicked *man* shall die in his iniquity; but his blood will I require at your hand.

9 Nevertheless, if you warn the wicked of his way to turn from it; if he do not turn from his way, he shall die in his iniquity; but you have delivered your soul.   sin

10 Therefore, O you son of man, speak to the house of Is'ra-el; Thus you speak, saying, If our transgressions and our sins *be* upon us, and we pine away in them, how should we then live?   rot

11 Say to them, *As* I live, says the Lord GOD, I have no pleasure in the death of the wicked; but that the wicked turn from his way and live: turn you, turn you from your evil ways; for why will you die, O house of Is'ra-el?   Adonay[p.f.] Jehovah

12 Therefore, you son of man, say to the children of your people, The righteousness of the righteous shall not deliver him in the day of his transgression: as for the wickedness of the wicked, he shall not fall thereby in the day that he turns from his wickedness; neither shall the righteous be able to live for his *righteousness* in the day that he sins.

13 When I shall say to the righteous, *that* he shall surely live; if he trust to his own righteousness, and commit iniquity, all his righteousnesses shall not be remembered; but for his iniquity that he has committed, he shall die for it.   evil

14 Again, when I say to the wicked, You shall surely die; if he turn from his sin, and do that which is lawful and right;

15 *If* the wicked restore the pledge, give again that he had robbed, walk in the statutes of life, without committing

iniquity; he shall surely live, he shall not die. decrees - sin

16 None of his sins that he has committed shall be mentioned to him: he has done that which is lawful and right; he shall surely live.

17 Yet the children of your people say, The way of the Lord is not equal: but as for them, their way is not equal. right

18 When the righteous turns from his righteousness, and commits iniquity, he shall even die thereby.

19 But if the wicked turn from his wickedness, and do that which is lawful and right, he shall live thereby.

20 Yet you say, The way of the Lord is not equal. O you house of Is'ra-el, I will judge you every one after his ways.

21 And it came to pass in the twelfth year of our captivity, in the tenth *month*, in the fifth *day* of the month, *that* one that had escaped out of Je-ru'sa-lem came to me, saying, The city is smitten.

22 Now the hand of the LORD was upon me in the evening, afore he that was escaped came; and had opened my mouth, until He came to me in the morning; and my mouth was opened, and I was no more dumb. before - given me a message

23 Then the word of the LORD came to me, saying,

24 Son of man, they that inhabit those wastes of the land of Is'ra-el speak, saying, A'bra-ham was one, and he inherited the land: but we *are* many; the land is given us for inheritance.

25 Wherefore say to them, Thus says the LORD GOD; You eat with the blood, and lift up your eyes toward your idols, and shed blood: and shall you possess the land? Adonay^{p.r.} Jehovah

26 You stand upon your sword, you work abomination, and you defile every one his neighbor's wife: and shall you possess the land? do detestable things

27 Say you thus to them, Thus says the LORD GOD; *As* I live, surely they that *are* in the wastes shall fall by the sword, and him that *is* in the open field will I give to the beasts to be devoured, and they that *be* in the forts and in the caves shall die of the pestilence. ruins

28 For I will lay the land most desolate, and the pomp of her strength shall cease; and the mountains of Is'ra-el shall be desolate, that none shall pass through.

29 Then shall they know that I *am* the LORD, when I have laid the land most desolate because of all their abominations which they have committed. detestable acts

30 Also, you son of man, the children of your people still are talking against you by the walls and in the doors of the houses, and speak one to another, every one to his brother, saying, Come, I pray you, and hear what is the word that comes forth from the LORD. talk about

31 And they come to you as the people come, and they sit before you *as* My people, and they hear your words, but they will not do them: for with their mouth they show much love, *but* their heart goes after their covetousness.

32 And, lo, you *are* to them as a very lovely song of one that has a pleasant voice, and can play well on an instrument: for they hear your words, but they do them not. _{behold - a singer}
33 And when this comes to pass, (lo, it will come,) then shall they know that a prophet has been among them.

CHAPTER 34

AND the word of the LORD came to me, saying,
2 Son of man, prophesy against the shepherds of Is'ra-el, prophesy, and say to them, Thus says the Lord GOD to the shepherds; Woe *be* to the shepherds of Is'ra-el that do feed themselves! should not the shepherds feed the flocks? _{preach - Adonay^{p.f.} Jehovah}
3 You eat the fat, and you clothe you with the wool, you kill them that are fed. *but* you feed not the flock.
4 The diseased have you not strengthened, neither have you healed that which was sick, neither have you bound up *that which was* broken, neither have you brought again that which was driven away, neither have you sought that which was lost; but with force and with cruelty have you ruled them. _{severity}
5 And they were scattered, because *there is* no shepherd: and they became meat to all the beasts of the field, when they were scattered. _{food}
6 My sheep wandered through all the mountains, and upon every high hill: yea, My flock was scattered upon all the face of the earth, and none did search or seek *after them*.

7 Therefore, you shepherds, hear the word of the LORD;
8 *As* I live, says the Lord GOD, surely because My flock became a prey, and My flock became meat to every beast of the field, because *there was* no shepherd, neither did My shepherds search for My flock, but the shepherds fed themselves, and fed not My flock; _{Adonay^{p.f.} Jehovah - food}
9 Therefore, O you shepherds, hear the word of the LORD;
10 Thus says the Lord GOD; Behold, I *am* against the shepherds; and I will require My flock at their hand, and cause them to cease from feeding the flock; neither shall the shepherds feed themselves any more; for I will deliver My flock from their mouth, that they may not be meat for them.
11 For thus says the Lord GOD; Behold, I, *even* I, will both search My sheep, and seek them out.
12 As a shepherd seeks out his flock in the day that he is among his sheep *that are* scattered; so will I seek out My sheep, and will deliver them out of all places where they have been scattered in the cloudy and dark day. _{JOHN 10:9}
13 And I will bring them out from the people, and gather them from the countries, and will bring them to their own land, and feed them upon the mountains of Is'ra-el by the rivers, and in all the inhabited places of the country.
14 I will feed them in a good pasture, and upon the high mountains of Is'ra-el shall their fold be: there shall they lie in a good fold, and *in* a fat pasture shall

they feed upon the mountains of Is'ra-el.   rich

15 I will feed My flock, and I will cause them to lie down, says the Lord GOD.   Adonay^p.f. Jehovah

16 I will seek that which was lost, and bring again that which was driven away, and will bind up *that which was* broken, and will strengthen that which was sick: but I will destroy the fat and the strong; I will feed them with judgment.   rich

17 And *as for* you, O My flock, thus says the Lord GOD; Behold, I judge between cattle and cattle, between the rams and the he goats.   MATT. 25:32

18 *Seems it* a small thing to you to have eaten up the good pasture, but you must tread down with your feet the residue of your pastures? and to have drunk of the deep waters, but you must foul the residue with your feet?   rest

19 And *as for* My flock, they eat that which you have trodden with your feet; and they drink that which you have fouled with your feet.

20 Therefore thus says the Lord GOD to them; Behold, I, *even* I, will judge between the fat cattle and between the lean cattle.   Adonay^p.f. Jehovah

21 Because you have thrust with side and with shoulder, and pushed all the diseased with your horns, till you have scattered them abroad;   driven them away

22 Therefore will I save My flock, and they shall no more be a prey; and I will judge between cattle and cattle.

23 And I will set up one shepherd over them, and he shall feed them, *even* My servant Da'vid; he shall feed them, and he shall be their shepherd.   REV. 7:17

24 And I the LORD will be their God, and My servant Da'vid a prince among them; I the LORD have spoken *it*.   Elohim^p.f.

25 And I will make with them a covenant of peace, and will cause the evil beasts to cease out of the land: and they shall dwell safely in the wilderness, and sleep in the woods.   agreement

26 And I will make them and the places round about My hill a blessing; and I will cause the shower to come down in its season; there shall be showers of blessing.

27 And the tree of the field shall yield her fruit, and the earth shall yield her increase, and they shall be safe in their land, and shall know that I *am* the LORD, when I have broken the bands of their yoke, and delivered them out of the hand of those that served themselves of them.   enslaved

28 And they shall no more be a prey to the heathen, neither shall the beast of the land devour them; but they shall dwell safely, and none shall make *them* afraid.

29 And I will raise up for them a plant of renown, and they shall be no more consumed with hunger in the land, neither bear the shame of the heathen any more.

30 Thus shall they know that I the LORD their God *am* with them, and *that* they, *even* the house of Is'ra-el, *are* My people, says the Lord GOD.   Elohim^p.f. - Adonay^p.f. Jehovah

31 And you My flock, the flock of My

pasture, *are* men, *and* I *am* your God, says the LORD GOD. Adonay^{p.f.} Jehovah

CHAPTER 35

MOREOVER the word of the LORD came to me, saying,

2 Son of man, set your face against mount Se'ir, and prophesy against it,

3 And say to it, Thus says the LORD GOD; Behold, O mount Se'ir, I *am* against you, and I will stretch out My hand against you, and I will make you most desolate.　　strip you bare

4 I will lay your cities waste, and you shall be desolate, and you shall know that I *am* the LORD.　　empty

5 Because you have had a perpetual hatred, and have shed *the blood of* the children of Is'ra-el by the force of the sword in the time of their calamity, in the time *that their* iniquity *had* an end: everlasting enmity - punishment

6 Therefore, *as* I live, says the LORD GOD, I will prepare you to blood, and blood shall pursue you: since you have not hated blood, even blood shall pursue you.　　Adonay^{p.f.} Jehovah

7 Thus will I make mount Se'ir most desolate, and cut off from it him that passes out and him that returns.

8 And I will fill his mountains with its slain *men*: in your hills, and in your valleys, and in all your rivers, shall they fall that are slain with the sword.　　fall in them

9 I will make you perpetual desolations, and your cities shall not return: and you shall know that I *am* the LORD.

10 Because you have said, These two nations and these two countries shall be mine, and we will possess it; whereas the LORD was there:　　although

11 Therefore, *as* I live, says the LORD GOD, I will even do according to your anger, and according to your envy which you have used out of your hatred against them; and I will make Myself known among them, when I have judged you.　　Adonay^{p.f.} Jehovah - enmity

12 And you shall know that I *am* the LORD, *and that* I have heard all your blasphemies which you have spoken against the mountains of Is'ra-el, saying, They are laid desolate, they are given us to consume.　contemptible things - waste

13 Thus with your mouth you have boasted against Me, and have multiplied your words against Me: I have heard *them*.

14 Thus says the LORD GOD; When the whole earth rejoices, I will make you desolate.　Adonay^{p.f.} Jehovah - a ruin

15 As you did rejoice at the inheritance of the house of Is'ra-el, because it was desolate, so will I do to you: you shall be desolate, O mount Se'ir, and all I-du-me'a, *even* all of it: and they shall know that I *am* the LORD.　　Edom

CHAPTER 36

ALSO you son of man, prophesy to the mountains of Is'ra-el, and say, You mountains of Is'ra-el, hear the word of the LORD:

2 Thus says the LORD GOD; Because the enemy has said against you, Aha, even the ancient high places are ours in possession:　Adonay^{p.f.} Jehovah - old shrines

3 Therefore prophesy and say, Thus

says the Lord GOD; Because they have made *you* desolate, and swallowed you up on every side, that you might be a possession to the residue of the heathen, and you are taken up in the lips of talkers, and *are* an infamy of the people:

Adonay^{p.f.} Jehovah - rest - nations - the object of malicious slander

4 Therefore, you mountains of Is'ra-el, hear the word of the Lord GOD; Thus says the Lord GOD to the mountains, and to the hills, to the rivers, and to the valleys, to the desolate wastes, and to the cities that are forsaken, which became a prey and derision to the residue of the heathen that *are* round about;

5 Therefore thus says the Lord GOD; Surely in the fire of My jealousy have I spoken against the residue of the heathen, and against all I-du-me'a, which have appointed My land into their possession with the joy of all *their* heart, with despiteful minds, to cast it out for a prey.   Adonay^{p.f.} Jehovah

6 Prophesy therefore concerning the land of Is'ra-el, and say to the mountains, and to the hills, to the rivers, and to the valleys, Thus says the Lord GOD; Behold, I have spoken in My jealousy and in My fury, because you have borne the shame of the heathen: Preach - nations

7 Therefore thus says the Lord GOD; I have lifted up My hand, Surely the heathen that *are* about you, they shall bear their shame.

8 But you, O mountains of Is'ra-el, you shall shoot forth your branches, and yield your fruit to My people of Is'ra-el; for they are at hand to come.

9 For, behold, I *am* for you, and I will turn to you, and you shall be tilled and sown:

10 And I will multiply men upon you, all the house of Is'ra-el, *even* all of it: and the cities shall be inhabited, and the wastes shall be builded:

11 And I will multiply upon you man and beast; and they shall increase and bring fruit: and I will settle you after your old estates, and will do better *to you* than at your beginnings: and you shall know that I *am* the LORD.

12 Yea, I will cause men to walk upon you, *even* My people Is'ra-el; and they shall possess you, and you shall be their inheritance, and you shall no more here after bereave them *of men*.

13 Thus says the Lord GOD; Because they say to you, You *land* devour up men, and have bereaved your nations;   Adonay^{p.f.} Jehovah

14 Therefore you shall devour men no more, neither bereave your nations any more, says the Lord GOD.

15 Neither will I cause *men* to hear in you the shame of the heathen any more, neither shall you bear the reproach of the people any more, neither shall you cause your nations to fall any more, says the Lord GOD.

16 Moreover the word of the LORD came to me, saying,

17 Son of man, when the house of Is'ra-el dwelled in their own land, they defiled it by their own way and by their doings: their way was before Me as the uncleanness of a removed woman.   impure

18 Wherefore I poured My fury upon them for the blood that they had shed

upon the land, and for their idols *wherewith* they had polluted it:

19 And I scattered them among the heathen, and they were dispersed through the countries: according to their way and according to their doings I judged them.

20 And when they entered to the heathen, where they went, they profaned My holy name, when they said to them, These *are* the people of the LORD, and are gone forth out of His land.

21 But I had pity for My holy name, which the house of Is'ra-el had profaned among the heathen, where they went.

22 Therefore say to the house of Is'ra-el, Thus says the Lord GOD; I do not *this* for your sakes, O house of Is'ra-el, but for My holy name's sake, which you have profaned among the heathen, where you went. ROM. 2:24 Adonay[p.f.] Jehovah

23 And I will sanctify My great name, which was profaned among the heathen, which you have profaned in the midst of them; and the heathen shall know that I *am* the LORD, says the Lord GOD, when I shall be sanctified in you before their eyes.

set apart - nations - Adonay[p.f.] Jehovah - in public

24 For I will take you from among the heathen, and gather you out of all countries, and will bring you into your own land.

25 Then will I sprinkle clean water upon you, and you shall be clean: from all your filthiness, and from all your idols, will I cleanse you.

26 A new heart also will I give you, and a new Spirit will I put within you: and I will take away the stony heart out of your flesh, and I will give you an heart of flesh. JOHN 3:5

27 And I will put My Spirit within you, and cause you to walk in My statutes, and you shall keep My judgments, and do *them*. decrees

28 And you shall dwell in the land that I gave to your fathers; and you shall be My people, and I will be your God. Elohim[p.f.]

29 I will also save you from all your uncleannesses: and I will call for the corn, and will increase it, and lay no famine upon you. grain

30 And I will multiply the fruit of the tree, and the increase of the field, that you shall receive no more reproach of famine among the heathen.

31 Then shall you remember your own evil ways, and your doings that *were* not good, and shall loathe yourselves in your own sight for your iniquities and for your abominations. despise - sins - detestable practices

32 Not for your sakes do I *this*, says the Lord GOD, be it known to you: be ashamed and confounded for your own ways, O house of Is'ra-el. Adonay[p.f.] Jehovah

33 Thus says the Lord GOD; In the day that I shall have cleansed you from all your iniquities I will also cause *you* to dwell in the cities, and the wastes shall be builded. sins

34 And the desolate land shall be tilled, whereas it lay desolate in the sight of all that passed by. forsaken

35 And they shall say, This land that was desolate is become like the garden

of E'den; and the waste and deso-late and ruined cities *are become fenced, and* are inhabited.   fortified

36 Then the heathen that are left round about you shall know that I the LORD build the ruined *places, and* plant that that was <u>desolate</u>: I the LORD have spo-ken *it*, and I will do *it*.   forsaken

37 Thus says the <u>Lord GOD</u>; I will yet *for* this be enquired of by the house of Is'ra-el, to do *it* for them; I will increase them with men like a flock. Adonay^{p.f.} Jehovah

38 As the holy flock, as the flock of Je-ru'sa-lem in her solemn feasts; so shall the waste cities be filled with flocks of men: and they shall know that I *am* the LORD.

CHAPTER 37

THE hand of the LORD was upon me, and carried me out in the Spirit of the LORD, and set me down in the midst of the valley which *was* full of bones,

2 And caused me to pass by them round about: and, behold, *there were* very many in the open valley; and, lo, *they were* very dry.

3 And He said to me, Son of man, can these bones live? And I an-swered, O <u>Lord GOD</u>, You know

.   Adonay^{p.f.} Jehovah

4 Again He said to me, <u>Proph-esy</u> upon these bones, and say to them, O you dry bones, hear the word of the LORD.   preach

5 Thus says the <u>Lord GOD</u> to these bones; Behold, I will cause breath to enter into you, and you shall live: REV. 11:11

6 And I will lay sinews upon you, and will bring up flesh upon you, and cover you with skin, and put breath in you, and you shall live; and you shall know that I *am* the LORD.

7 So I <u>prophesied</u> as I was com-manded: and as I <u>prophesied</u>, there was a noise, and behold a shaking, and the bones came together, bone to his bone.

8 And when I beheld, <u>lo</u>, the sinews and the flesh came up upon them, and the skin covered them above: but *there was* no breath in them.   behold

9 Then said He to me, <u>Prophesy</u> to the wind, <u>prophesy</u>, son of man, and say to the wind, Thus says the <u>Lord GOD</u>; Come from the four winds, O breath, and breathe upon these slain, that they may live.   Preach - Adonay^{p.f.} Jehovah

10 So I <u>prophesied</u> as He commanded me, and the breath came into them, and they lived, and stood up upon their feet, an exceeding great army.

11 Then He said to me, Son of man, these bones are the whole house of Is'ra-el: behold, they say, Our bones are dried, and our hope is lost: we are cut off for our parts.

12 Therefore <u>prophesy</u> and say to them, Thus says the <u>Lord GOD</u>; Be-hold, O My people, I will open your graves, and cause you to come up out of your graves, and bring you into the land of Is'ra-el. Adonay^{p.f.} Jehovah

13 And you shall know that I *am* the LORD, when I have opened your graves, O My people, and brought you up out of your graves,

14 And shall put My Spirit in you, and you shall live, and I shall place you in your own land: then shall you know

that I the LORD have spoken *it*, and performed *it*, says the LORD.

15 The word of the LORD came again to me, saying,

16 Moreover, you son of man, take you one stick, and write upon it, For Ju'dah, and for the children of Is'ra-el his companions: then take another stick, and write upon it, For Jo'seph, the stick of E'phra-im, and *for* all the house of Is'ra-el his companions:

17 And join them one to another into one stick; and they shall become one in your hand.

18 And when the children of your people shall speak to you, saying, Will you not show us what you *mean* by these?

19 Say to them, Thus says the Lord GOD; Behold, I will take the stick of Jo'seph, which *is* in the hand of E'phra-im, and the tribes of Is'ra-el his fellows, and will put them with him, *even* with the stick of Ju'dah, and make them one stick, and they shall be one in My hand.   Adonay[p.f.] Jehovah

20 And the sticks whereon you write shall be in your hand before their eyes.

21 And say to them, Thus says the Lord GOD; Behold, I will take the children of Is'ra-el from among the <u>heathen</u>, where they be gone, and will gather them on every side, and bring them into their own land: nations

22 And I will make them one nation in the land upon the mountains of Is'ra-el; and one king shall be king to them all: and they shall be no more two nations, neither shall they be divided into two kingdoms any more at all:

23 Neither shall they defile themselves any more with their idols, nor with their detestable things, nor with any of their transgressions: but I will save them out of all their <u>dwellingplaces</u>, wherein they have sinned, and will cleanse them: so shall they be My people, and I will be their <u>God</u>.   sinful backsliding - Elohim[p.f.]

24 And Da'vid My servant *shall be* king over them; and they all shall have one shepherd: they shall also walk in My judgments, and observe My <u>statutes</u>, and do them.   decrees

25 And they shall dwell in the land that I have given to Ja'cob My servant, wherein your fathers have dwelled; and they shall dwell therein, *even* they, and their children, and their children's children for ever: and My servant Da'vid *shall be* their prince for ever.

26 Moreover I will make a <u>covenant</u> of peace with them; it shall be an everlasting <u>covenant</u> with them: and I will place them, and multiply them, and will set My sanctuary in the midst of them for evermore.   agreement

27 My <u>tabernacle</u> also shall be with them: yea, I will be their <u>God</u>, and they shall be My people. 2 COR. 6:16 REV. 21:3 dwelling place - Elohim[p.f.]

28 And the <u>heathen</u> shall know that I the LORD do <u>sanctify</u> Is'ra-el, when My sanctuary shall be in the midst of them for evermore.   nations - make Israel holy

CHAPTER 38

AND the word of the LORD came to me, saying,

2 Son of man, set your face against Gog, the land of Ma'gog, the chief prince of Me'shech and Tu'bal, and prophesy against him,   REV. 20:8

3 And say, Thus says the <u>Lord</u> <u>God</u>; Behold, I *am* against you, O Gog, the chief prince of Me'shech and Tu'bal: Adonay^{p.f.} Jehovah

4 And I will turn you back, and put hooks into your jaws, and I will bring you forth, and all your army, horses and horsemen, all of them clothed with all sorts *of armor, even* a great company *with* bucklers and shields, all of them handling swords:

5 Per'sia, E-thi-o'pi-a, and Lib'y-a with them; all of them with shield and helmet:

6 Go'mer, and all his bands; the house of To-gar'mah of the north quarters, and all his bands: *and* many people with you.

7 Be you prepared, and prepare for yourself, you, and all your company that are assembled to you, and be you a guard to them.

8 After many days you shall be visited: in the latter years you shall come into the land *that is* brought back from the sword, *and is* gathered out of many people, against the mountains of Is'ra-el, which have been always waste: but it is brought forth out of the nations, and they shall dwell safely all of them.

9 You shall ascend and come like a storm, you shall be like a cloud to cover the land, you, and all your bands, and many people with you.

10 Thus says the <u>Lord God</u>; It shall also come to pass, *that* at the same time shall things come into your mind, and you shall think an evil thought: Adonay^{p.f.} Jehovah

11 And you shall say, I will go up to the land of unwalled villages; I will go to them that are at rest, that dwell safely, all of them dwelling without walls, and having neither bars nor gates,

12 To take <u>a spoil</u>, and to take <u>a prey</u>; to turn your hand upon the desolate places *that are now* inhabited, and upon the people *that are* gathered out of the nations, which have gotten cattle and goods, that dwell in the midst of the land.   plunder - loot

13 She'ba, and De'dan, and the merchants of Tar'shish, with all the young lions thereof, shall say to you, Are you come to take a <u>spoil</u>? have you gathered your company to take a prey? to carry away silver and gold, to take away cattle and goods, to take a great spoil?

14 Therefore, son of man, prophesy and say to Gog, Thus says the <u>Lord God</u>; In that day when My people of Is'ra-el dwell safely, shall you not know *it*?   Adonay^{p.f.} Jehovah

15 And you shall come from your place out of the north parts, you, and many people with you, all of them riding upon horses, a great company, and a mighty army: REV. 20:8

16 And you shall come up against My people of Is'ra-el, as a cloud to cover the land; it shall be in the latter days, and I will bring you against My land, that the <u>heathen</u> may know Me, when I

shall be sanctified in you, O Gog, before their eyes.   nations - show Myself holy

17 Thus says the Lord GOD; *Are* you he of whom I have spoken in old time by My servants the prophets of Is'ra-el, which prophesied in those days *many* years that I would bring you against them?   Adonay^{p.f.} Jehovah

18 And it shall come to pass at the same time when Gog shall come against the land of Is'ra-el, says the Lord GOD, *that* My fury shall come up in My face.

19 For in My jealousy *and* in the fire of My anger have I spoken, Surely in that day there shall be a great shaking in the land of Is'ra-el;

20 So that the fishes of the sea, and the fowls of the heaven, and the beasts of the field, and all creeping things that creep upon the earth, and all the men that *are* upon the face of the earth, shall shake at My presence, and the mountains shall be thrown down, and the steep places shall fall, and every wall shall fall to the ground.

21 And I will call for a sword against him throughout all My mountains, says the Lord GOD: every man's sword shall be against his brother.   Adonay^{p.f.} Jehovah

22 And I will plead against him with pestilence and with blood; and I will rain upon him, and upon his bands, and upon the many people that *are* with him, an overflowing rain, and great hailstones, fire, and brimstone.

23 Thus will I magnify Myself, and sanctify Myself; and I will be known in the eyes of many nations, and they shall know that I *am* the LORD.

CHAPTER 39

THEREFORE, you son of man, prophesy against Gog, and say, Thus says the Lord GOD; Behold, I *am* against you, O Gog, the chief prince of Me'shech and Tu'bal: Adonay^{p.f.} Jehovah

2 And I will turn you back, and leave but the sixth part of you, and will cause you to come up from the north parts, and will bring you upon the mountains of Is'ra-el:

3 And I will smite your bow out of your left hand, and will cause your arrows to fall out of your right hand.

4 You shall fall upon the mountains of Is'ra-el, you, and all your bands, and the people that *is* with you: I will give you to the ravenous birds of every sort, and *to* the beasts of the field to be devoured.   REV. 19:17

5 You shall fall upon the open field: for I have spoken *it*, says the Lord GOD.   Adonay^{p.f.} Jehovah

6 And I will send a fire on Ma'gog, and among them that dwell carelessly in the isles: and they shall know that I *am* the LORD.   safely - coastlands

7 So will I make My holy name known in the midst of My people Is'ra-el; and I will not *let them* pollute My holy name any more: and the heathen shall know that I *am* the LORD, the Holy One in Is'ra-el.   profane

8 Behold, it is come, and it is done, says the Lord GOD; this *is* the day whereof I have spoken.

9 And they that dwell in the cities of Is'ra-el shall go forth, and shall set on fire and burn the weapons, both the

shields and the <u>bucklers</u>, the bows and the arrows, and the <u>handstaves,</u> and the spears, and they shall burn them with fire seven years:

large shields - war clubs

10 So that they shall take no wood out of the field, neither cut down *any* out of the forests; for they shall burn the weapons with fire: and they shall <u>spoil</u> those that <u>spoiled</u> them, and rob those that robbed them, says the Lord GOD.

plunder - Adonay^{p.f.} Jehovah

11 And it shall come to pass in *that* day, that I will give to Gog a place there of graves in Is'ra-el, the valley of the passengers on the east of the sea: and it shall stop the *noses* of the passengers: and there shall they bury Gog and all his multitude: and they shall call *it* The valley of Ha'mon-gog.

12 And seven months shall the house of Is'ra-el be burying of them, that they may cleanse the land.

13 Yea, all the people of the land shall bury *them*; and it shall be to them a <u>renown the day that</u> I shall be glorified, says the Lord GOD.

memorable day when

14 And they shall <u>sever out</u> men of continual employment, passing through the land to bury with the <u>passengers</u> those that remain upon the face of the earth, to cleanse it: after the end of seven months shall they search.

set apart - travelers

15 And the <u>passengers</u> *that* pass through the land, when *any* sees a man's bone, then shall he set up a <u>sign</u> by it, till the buriers have buried it in the valley of Ha'mon-gog. *marker*

16 And also the name of the city *shall* be Ha-mo'nah. Thus shall they cleanse the land.

17 And, you son of man, thus says the <u>Lord</u> GOD; Speak to every feathered fowl, and to every beast of the field, Assemble yourselves, and come; gather yourselves on every side to My sacrifice that I do sacrifice for you, *even* a great sacrifice upon the mountains of Is'ra-el, that you may eat flesh, and drink blood. *Adonay^{p.f.} Jehovah*

18 You shall eat the flesh of the mighty, and drink the blood of the princes of the earth, of rams, of lambs, and of goats, of bullocks, all of them fatlings of Ba'shan. REV. 19:18

19 And you shall eat fat till you be full, and drink blood till you be drunken, of My sacrifice which I have sacrificed for you.

20 Thus you shall be filled at My table with horses and chariots, with mighty men, and with all men of war, says the <u>Lord</u> GOD. *Adonay^{p.f.} Jehovah*

21 And I will set My glory among the <u>heathen,</u> and all the <u>heathen</u> shall see My judgment that I have executed, and My hand that I have laid upon them. *nations*

22 So the house of Is'ra-el shall know that I *am* the LORD their <u>God</u> from that day and forward. *Elohim^{p.f.}*

23 And the heathen shall know that the house of Is'ra-el went into captivity for their <u>iniquity</u>: because they trespassed against Me, therefore hid I My face from them, and gave them into the hand of their enemies: so fell they all by the sword. *sin*

24 According to their uncleanness

and according to their transgressions have I done to them, and hid My face from them.

25 Therefore thus says the <u>Lord</u> <u>God</u>; Now will I <u>bring again the captivity</u> of Ja'cob, and have mercy upon the whole house of Is'ra-el, and will be <u>jealous</u> for My holy name;   Adonay[p.f.] Jehovah - restore the fortunes - zealous

26 After that they have borne their shame, and all their trespasses whereby they have trespassed against Me, when they dwelled safely in their land, and none made *them* afraid.

27 When I have brought them again from the people, and gathered them out of their enemies' lands, and am <u>sanctified in</u> them in the sight of many nations;   show Myself holy through

28 Then shall they know that I *am* the Lord their <u>God</u>, which caused them to be led into captivity among the heathen: but I have gathered them to their own land, and have left none of them any more there.   Elohim[p.f.]

29 Neither will I hide My face any more from them: for I have poured out My Spirit upon the house of Is'ra-el, says the <u>Lord</u> <u>God</u>.   Adonay[p.f.] Jehovah

CHAPTER 40

IN the five and twentieth year of our captivity, in the beginning of the year, in the tenth *day* of the month, in the fourteenth year after that the city was smitten, in the selfsame day the hand of the Lord was upon me, and brought me there.

2 In the visions of <u>God</u> brought He me into the land of Is'ra-el, and set me upon a very high mountain, by which *was* as the <u>frame</u> of a city on the south.   Elohim[p.f.] - structure

3 And He brought me there, and, behold, *there was* a man, whose appearance *was* like the appearance of brass, with a line of flax in his hand, and a measuring reed; and he stood in the gate.

4 And the man said to me, Son of man, behold with your eyes, and hear with your ears, and <u>set your heart</u> upon all that I shall show you; for to the intent that I might show *them* to you *are* you brought here: declare all that you see to the house of Is'ra-el.   give attention to

5 And behold a wall on the outside of the house round about, and in the man's hand a measuring reed of six cubits *long* by the cubit and an hand breadth: so he measured the breadth of the building, one reed; and the height, one reed.

6 Then came he to the gate which looks toward the east, and went up the stairs thereof, and measured the threshold of the gate, *which was* one reed broad; and the other threshold *of the gate, which was* one reed broad.

7 And *every* little <u>chamber</u> *was* one reed long, and one reed broad; and between the little chambers *were* five cubits; and the threshold of the gate by the porch of the gate inside *was* one reed.   alcoves

8 He measured also the porch of the gate inside, one reed.

9 Then measured he the porch of the

gate, eight cubits; and the posts thereof, two cubits; and the porch of the gate *was* inward.

10 And the little <u>chambers</u> of the gate eastward *were* three on this side, and three on that side; they three *were* of one measure: and the posts had one measure on this side and on that side.

11 And he measured the breadth of the entry of the gate, ten cubits; *and* the length of the gate, thirteen cubits.

12 The space also before the little <u>chambers</u> *was* one cubit *on this side*, and the space *was* one cubit on that side: and the little <u>chambers</u> *were* six cubits on this side, and six cubits on that side.   alcove

13 He measured then the gate from the roof of *one* little <u>chamber</u> to the roof of another: the breadth *was* five and twenty cubits, door against door.   room

14 He made also posts of threescore cubits, even unto the post of the court round about the gate.

15 And from the face of the gate of the entrance to the face of the porch of the inner gate *were* fifty cubits.

16 And *there were* narrow windows to the little <u>chambers</u>, and to their posts within the gate round about, and likewise to the arches: and windows *were* round about inward: and upon *each* post *were* palm trees.

17 Then brought he me into the outward court, and, lo, *there were* <u>chambers</u>, and a pavement made for the court round about: thirty <u>chambers</u> *were* upon the pavement.   rooms

18 And the pavement by the side of the gates opposite the length of the gates *was* the lower pavement.

19 Then he measured the breadth from the forefront of the lower gate to the forefront of the inner court outside, an hundred cubits eastward and northward.

20 And the gate of the outward court that looked toward the north, he measured the length thereof, and the breadth thereof.

21 And the little <u>chambers</u> thereof *were* three on this side and three on that side; and the posts thereof and the arches thereof were after the measure of the first gate: the length thereof *was* fifty cubits, and the breadth five and twenty cubits. alcoves

22 And their windows, and their arches, and their palm trees, *were* after the measure of the gate that looks toward the east; and they went up to it by seven steps; and the arches thereof *were* before them.

23 And the gate of the inner court *was* opposite the gate toward the north, and toward the east; and he measured from gate to gate an hundred cubits.

24 After that he brought me toward the south, and behold a gate toward the south: and he measured the posts thereof and the arches thereof according to these measures.

25 And *there were* windows in it and in the arches thereof round about, like those windows: the length *was* fifty cubits, and the breadth five and twenty cubits.

26 And *there were* seven steps to go

up to it, and the arches thereof *were* before them: and it had palm trees, one on this side, and another on that side, upon the posts thereof.

27 And *there was* a gate in the inner court toward the south: and he measured from gate to gate toward the south an hundred cubits.

28 And he brought me to the inner court by the south gate: and he measured the south gate according to these measures;

29 And the little <u>chambers</u> thereof, and the posts thereof, and the arches thereof, according to these measures: and *there were* windows in it and in the arches thereof round about: *it was* fifty cubits long, and five and twenty cubits broad. _{alcoves}

30 And the arches round about *were* five and twenty cubits long, and five cubits broad.

31 And the arches thereof *were* toward the utter court; and palm trees *were* upon the posts thereof: and the going up to it *had* eight steps.

32 And he brought me into the inner court toward the east: and he measured the gate according to these measures.

33 And the little <u>chambers</u> thereof, and the posts thereof, and the arches thereof, *were* according to these measures: and *there were* windows therein and in the arches thereof round about: *it was* fifty cubits long, and five and twenty cubits broad. _{alcoves}

34 And the arches thereof *were* toward the outward court; and palm trees *were* upon the posts thereof, on this side, and on that side: and the going up to it *had* eight steps.

35 And he brought me to the north gate, and measured *it* according to these measures;

36 The little <u>chambers</u> thereof, the posts thereof, and the arches thereof, and the windows to it round about: the length *was* fifty cubits, and the breadth five and twenty cubits. _{alcoves}

37 And the posts thereof *were* toward the outer court; and palm trees *were* upon the posts thereof, on this side, and on that side: and the going up to it *had* eight steps.

38 And the <u>chambers</u> and the entries thereof *were* by the posts of the gates, where they washed the burned offering.

39 And in the porch of the gate *were* two tables on this side, and two tables on that side, to slay thereon the burned offering and the sin offering and the trespass offering.

40 And at the side outside, as one goes up to the entry of the north gate, *were* two tables; and on the other side, which *was* at the porch of the gate, *were* two tables.

41 Four tables *were* on this side, and four tables on that side, by the side of the gate; eight tables, whereupon they slew *their sacrifices*.

42 And the four tables *were* of <u>hewn</u> stone for the burned offering, of a cubit and an half long, and a cubit and an half broad, and one cubit high: whereupon also they laid the instruments wherewith they slew the burnt offering and the sacrifice. _{dressed}

43 And inside *were* hooks, an hand

broad, fastened round about: and upon the tables *was* the flesh of the offering. _{inside}

44 And outside the inner gate *were* the <u>chambers</u> of the singers in the inner court, which *was* at the side of the north gate; and their prospect *was* toward the south: one at the side of the east gate *having* the prospect toward the north.

45 And he said to me, This <u>chamber</u>, whose prospect *is* toward the south, *is* for the priests, the keepers of the <u>charge</u> of the house. _{room - rule}

46 And the <u>chamber</u> <u>whose prospect *is*</u> toward the north *is* for the priests, the keepers of the charge of the altar: these *are* the sons of Za'dok among the sons of Le'vi, which come near to the LORD to minister to Him. _{room - which faces}

47 So he measured the court, an hundred cubits long, and an hundred cubits broad, foursquare; and the altar *that was* before the house.

48 And he brought me to the porch of the house, and measured *each* post of the porch, five cubits on this side, and five cubits on that side: and the breadth of the gate *was* three cubits on this side, and three cubits on that side.

49 The length of the porch *was* twenty cubits, and the breadth eleven cubits; and *he brought me* by the steps whereby they went up to it: and *there were* pillars by the posts, one on this side, and another on that side.

CHAPTER 41

AFTERWARD he brought me to the temple, and measured the posts, six cubits broad on the one side, and six cubits broad on the other side, *which* was the breadth of the tabernacle.

2 And the breadth of the door *was* ten cubits; and the sides of the door *were* five cubits on the one side, and five cubits on the other side: and he measured the length thereof, forty cubits: and the breadth, twenty cubits.

3 Then went he <u>inward</u>, and measured the post of the door, two cubits; and the door, six cubits; and the breadth of the door, seven cubits. _{inside}

4 So he measured the length thereof, twenty cubits; and the breadth, twenty cubits, before the temple: and he said to me, This *is* the most holy *place*.

5 After he measured the wall of the house, six cubits; and the breadth of *every* side <u>chamber</u>, four cubits, round about the house on every side. _{rooms}

6 And the side <u>chambers</u> *were* three, one over another, and thirty in order; and they entered into the wall which *was* of the house for the side <u>chambers</u> round about, that they might have hold, but they had not hold in the wall of the house.

7 And *there was* an enlarging, and a winding about still upward to the side <u>chambers</u>: for the winding about of the house went still upward round about the house: therefore the breadth of the house *was still* upward, and so increased *from* the lowest <u>chamber</u> to the highest by the midst. _{rooms - floor}

8 I saw also the height of the house round about: the foundations of the side <u>chambers</u> *were* a full reed of six great cubits.

9 The thickness of the wall, which *was*

for the side *chamber* without, *was* five cubits: and *that* which *was* left *was* the place of the side <u>chambers</u> that *were* inside. _{room}

10 And between the <u>chambers</u> *was* the wideness of twenty cubits round about the house on every side.

11 And the doors of the side <u>cham-bers</u> *were* toward *the place that was* left, one door toward the north, and another door toward the south: and the breadth of the place that was left *was* five cubits round about.

12 Now the building that *was* before the separate <u>place</u> at the end toward the west *was* seventy cubits broad; and the wall of the building *was* five cubits thick round about, and the length thereof ninety cubits. _{area}

13 So he measured the house, an hundred cubits long; and the separate place, and the building, with the walls thereof, an hundred cubits long;

14 Also the breadth of the face of the house, and of the separate place toward the east, an hundred cubits.

15 And he measured the length of the building opposite the separate place which *was* behind it, and the galleries thereof on the one side and on the other side, an hundred cubits, with the inner temple, and the porches of the court;

16 The door posts, and the narrow windows, and the galleries round about on their three stories, opposite the door, <u>ceiled</u> with wood round about, and from the ground up to the windows, and the windows *were* covered; _{paneled}

17 To that above the door, even to the inner house, and outside, and by all the wall round about inside and outside, by measure.

18 And *it was* made with cherubims and palm trees, so that a palm tree *was* between a cherub and a cherub; and *every* cherub had two faces;

19 So that the face of a man *was* toward the palm tree on the one side, and the face of a young lion toward the palm tree on the other side: *it was* made through all the house round about.

20 From the ground to above the door *were* cherubims and palm trees made, and *on* the wall of the temple.

21 The <u>posts</u> of the temple *were* squared, *and* the face of the sanctuary; the appearance *of the one* as the appearance *of the other*. _{doorposts}

22 The altar of wood *was* three cubits high, and the length thereof two cubits; and the corners thereof, and the length thereof, and the walls thereof, *were* of wood: and he said to me, This *is* the table that *is* before the Lord.

23 And the temple and the sanctuary had two doors.

24 And the doors had two leaves *apiece*, two turning *leaves*; two leaves for the one door, and two leaves for the other *door*.

25 And *there were* made on them, on the doors of the temple, cherubims and palm trees, like as *were* made upon the walls; and *there were* thick planks upon the face of the porch outside.

26 And *there were* narrow windows and palm trees on the one side and on the other side, on the sides of the porch,

and *upon* the side <u>chambers</u> of the house, and thick planks.   <small>rooms</small>

CHAPTER 42

THEN he brought me forth into the outer court, the way toward the north: and he brought me into the <u>chamber</u> that *was* opposite the separate place, and which *was* before the building toward the north.

2 Before the length of an hundred cubits *was* the north door, and the breadth *was* fifty cubits.

3 Opposite the twenty *cubits* which *were* for the inner court, and opposite the pavement which *was* for the outer court, *was* gallery against gallery in three *stories*.

4 And before the <u>chambers</u> *was* a walk of ten cubits breadth inward, a way of one cubit; and their doors toward the north.   <small>rooms</small>

5 Now the upper <u>chambers</u> *were* shorter: for the galleries were higher than these, than the lower, and than the middlemost of the building.

6 For they *were* in three *stories*, but had not pillars as the pillars of the courts: therefore *the <u>building</u> <u>was straitened</u>* more than the lowest and the middlemost from the ground.   <small>upper rooms were set back</small>

7 And the wall that *was* outside opposite the <u>chambers</u>, toward the outer court on the forepart of the <u>chambers</u>, the length thereof *was* fifty cubits.   <small>rooms</small>

8 For the length of the <u>chambers</u> that *were* in the outer court *was* fifty cubits: and, lo, before the temple *were* an hundred cubits.

9 And from under these <u>chambers</u> *was* the entry on the east side, as one goes into them from the outer court.

10 The <u>chambers</u> *were* in the thickness of the wall of the court toward the east, <u>opposite the separate place</u>, and opposite the building.   <small>rooms - opposite the temple courtyard</small>

11 And the way before them *was* like the appearance of the <u>chambers</u> which *were* toward the north, as long as they, *and* as broad as they: and all their goings out *were* both according to their fashions, and according to their doors.

12 And according to the doors of the <u>chambers</u> that *were* toward the south *was* a door in the head of the way, *even* the way directly before the wall toward the east, as one enters into them.

13 Then said he to me, The north <u>chambers</u> *and* the south <u>chambers</u>, which *are* before the <u>separate place</u>, they *be* holy <u>chambers</u>, where the priests that approach to the LORD shall eat the most holy things: there shall they lay the most holy things, and the meat offering, and the sin offering, and the trespass offering; for the place *is* holy.   <small>temple courtyard</small>

14 When the priests enter therein, then shall they not go out of the holy *place* into the outer court, but there they shall lay their garments wherein they minister; for they *are* holy; and shall put on other garments, and shall approach to *those things* which *are* for the people.

15 Now when he had made an end of measuring the inner house, he brought me forth toward the gate whose pros-

pect *is* toward the east, and measured it round about.

16 He measured the east side with the measuring reed, five hundred reeds, with the measuring reed round about.

17 He measured the north side, five hundred reeds, with the measuring reed round about.

18 He measured the south side, five hundred reeds, with the measuring reed.

19 He turned about to the west side, *and* measured five hundred reeds with the measuring reed.

20 He measured it by the four sides: it had a wall round about, five hundred *reeds* long, and five hundred broad, to make a separation between the sanctuary and the profane place.   common

CHAPTER 43

AFTERWARD he brought me to the gate, *even* the gate that looks toward the east:

2 And, behold, the glory of the God of Is'ra-el came from the way of the east: and His voice *was* like a noise of many waters: and the earth shined with His glory.   Elohim[p.f.]

3 And *it was* according to the appearance of the vision which I saw, *even* according to the vision that I saw when I came to destroy the city: and the visions *were* like the vision that I saw by the river Che'bar; and I fell upon my face.

4 And the glory of the LORD came into the house by the way of the gate whose prospect *is* toward the east.

5 So the Spirit took me up, and brought me into the inner court; and, behold, the glory of the LORD filled the house.

6 And I heard *Him* speaking to me out of the house; and the man stood by me.

7 And He said to me, Son of man, the place of My throne, and the place of the soles of My feet, where I will dwell in the midst of the children of Is'ra-el for ever, and My holy name, shall the house of Is'ra-el no more defile, *neither* they, nor their kings, by their whoredom, nor by the carcases of their kings in their high places.   unfaithfulness

8 In their setting of their threshold by My thresholds, and their post by My posts, and the wall between Me and them, they have even defiled My holy name by their abominations that they have committed: wherefore I have consumed them in My anger.   detestable practices

9 Now let them put away their whoredom, and the carcases of their kings, far from Me, and I will dwell in the midst of them for ever.

10 You son of man, show the house to the house of Is'ra-el, that they may be ashamed of their iniquities: and let them measure the pattern. sins

11 And if they be ashamed of all that they have done, show them the form of the house, and the fashion thereof, and the goings out thereof, and the comings in thereof, and all the forms thereof, and all the ordinances thereof, and all the forms thereof, and all the laws thereof: and write *it* in their sight, that they may keep the whole form thereof,

and all the <u>ordinances</u> thereof, and do them. _{regulations}

12 This *is* the law of the house; Upon the top of the mountain the whole limit thereof round about *shall be* most holy. Behold, this *is* the law of the house.

13 And these *are* the measures of the altar after the cubits: The cubit *is* a cubit and an hand breadth; even the bottom *shall be* a cubit, and the breadth a cubit, and the border thereof by the edge thereof round about *shall be* a span: and this *shall be* the higher place of the altar.

14 And from the bottom *upon* the ground *even* to the lower <u>settle</u> *shall be* two cubits, and the breadth one cubit; and from the lesser <u>settle</u> *even* to the greater <u>settle</u> *shall be* four cubits, and the breadth *one* cubit. _{ledge}

15 So the altar *shall be* four cubits; and from the altar and upward *shall be* four horns.

16 And the altar *shall be* twelve *cubits* long, twelve broad, square in the four squares thereof.

17 And the <u>settle</u> *shall be* fourteen *cubits* long and fourteen broad in the four squares thereof; and the border about it *shall be* half a cubit; and the bottom thereof *shall be* a cubit about; and his stairs shall look toward the east. _{ledge}

18 And He said to me, Son of man, thus says the <u>Lord G</u>od; These *are* the ordinances of the altar in the day when they shall make it, to offer burned offerings thereon, and to sprinkle blood thereon. _{Adonay^{p.f.} Jehovah}

19 And you shall give to the priests the Le'vites that be of the <u>seed</u> of Za'- dok, which approach to Me, to minister to Me, says the <u>Lord G</u>od, a young bullock for a sin offering. _{offspring - Adonay^{p.f.} Jehovah}

20 And you shall take of the blood thereof, and put *it* on the four horns of it, and on the four corners of the <u>settle</u>, and upon the border round about: thus shall you cleanse and purge it. _{ledge}

21 You shall take the bullock also of the sin offering, and he shall burn it in the appointed place of the house, outside the sanctuary.

22 And on the second day you shall offer a <u>kid of the goats</u> without <u>blemish</u> for a sin offering; and they shall cleanse the altar, as they did cleanse *it* with the bullock. _{male goat - defect}

23 When you have made an end of cleansing *it*, you shall offer a young bullock without <u>blemish</u>, and a ram out of the flock without <u>blemish</u>.

24 And you shall offer them before the Lord, and the priests shall cast salt upon them, and they shall offer them up *for* a burned offering to the Lord.

25 Seven days shall you prepare every day a goat *for* a sin offering: they shall also prepare a young bullock, and a ram out of the flock, without <u>blemish</u>.

26 Seven days shall they <u>purge</u> the altar and purify it; and they shall <u>conse-crate</u> themselves. _{make atonement for - dedicate}

27 And when these days are expired, it shall be, *that* upon the eighth day, and *so* forward, the priests shall make your burned offerings upon the altar, and your <u>peace</u> offerings; and I will accept you, says the <u>Lord G</u>od. _{thank - Adonay^{p.f.} Jehovah}

CHAPTER 44

THEN He brought me back the way of the <u>gate of the outward</u> sanctuary which looks toward the east; and it *was* shut.   outer gate of the

2 Then said the LORD to me; This gate shall be shut, it shall not be opened, and no man shall enter in by it; because the LORD, the <u>God</u> of Is'ra-el, has entered in by it, therefore it shall be shut.   Elohim^{p.f.}

3 *It is* for the prince; the prince, he shall sit in it to eat bread before the LORD; he shall enter by the way of the porch of *that* gate, and shall go out by the way of the same.

4 Then brought He me the way of the north gate before the house: and I looked, and, behold, the glory of the LORD filled the house of the LORD: and I fell upon my face.

5 And the LORD said to me, Son of man, <u>mark well</u>, and behold with your eyes, and hear with your ears all that I say to you concerning all the <u>ordinances</u> of the house of the LORD, and all the laws thereof; and <u>mark well</u> the entering in of the house, with every going forth of the sanctuary.   give attention - regulations

6 And you shall say to the rebellious, *even* to the house of Is'ra-el, Thus says the <u>Lord GOD</u>; O you house of Is'ra-el, let it suffice you of all your <u>abominations</u>,   Adonay^{p.f.} Jehovah - detestable practices

7 In that you have brought *into My sanctuary* strangers, uncircumcised in heart, and uncircumcised in flesh, to be in My sanctuary, to pollute it, *even* My house, when you offer My bread, the fat and the blood, and they have broken My <u>covenant</u> because of all your <u>abominations</u>.   agreement - detestable practices

8 And you have not kept the <u>charge</u> of My holy things: but you have set keepers of My charge in My sanctuary for yourselves.   rules

9 Thus says the <u>Lord GOD</u>; No <u>stranger</u>, <u>uncircumcised</u> in heart, nor <u>uncircumcised</u> in flesh, shall enter into My sanctuary, of any <u>stranger</u> that *is* among the children of Is'ra-el.   Adonay^{p.f.} Jehovah - foreigner - ungodly

10 And the Le'vites that are gone away far from Me, when Is'ra-el went astray, which went astray away from Me after their idols; they shall even bear their <u>iniquity</u>.   sin

11 Yet they shall be ministers in My sanctuary, *having* charge at the gates of the house, and ministering to the house: they shall slay the burned offering and the sacrifice for the people, and they shall stand before them to minister to them.

12 Because they ministered to them before their idols, and <u>caused the house</u> of Is'ra-el to fall into <u>iniquity</u>; therefore have I lifted up My hand against them, says the <u>Lord GOD</u>, and they shall bear their iniquity.   become a stumbling block for - Adonay^{p.f.} Jehovah

13 And they shall not come near to Me, to do the office of a priest to Me, nor to come near to any of My holy things, in the most holy *place*: but they shall bear their shame, and their <u>abominations</u> which they have committed.   detestable practices

14 But I will make them keepers of the underline{charge} of the house, for all the service thereof, and for all that shall be done therein. _{rules}
15 But the priests the Le'vites, the sons of Za'dok, that kept the charge of My sanctuary when the children of Is'ra-el went astray from Me, they shall come near to Me to minister to Me, and they shall stand before Me to offer to me the fat and the blood, says the Lord GOD: _{Adonay^{p.f.} Jehovah}
16 They shall enter into My sanctuary, and they shall come near to My table, to minister to Me, and they shall keep My charge. _{holy place - rules}
17 And it shall come to pass, *that* when they enter in at the gates of the inner court, they shall be clothed with linen garments; and no wool shall come upon them, while they minister in the gates of the inner court, and within.
18 They shall have linen bonnets upon their heads, and shall have linen breeches upon their loins; they shall not gird *themselves* with any thing that causes sweat.
19 And when they go forth into the outer court, *even* into the outer court to the people, they shall put off their garments wherein they ministered, and lay them in the holy chambers, and they shall put on other garments; and they shall not sanctify the people with their garments. _{sacred rooms - consecrate}
20 Neither shall they shave their heads, nor permit their locks to grow long; they shall only poll their heads. _{trim}
21 Neither shall any priest drink wine, when they enter into the inner court.
22 Neither shall they take for their wives a widow, nor her that is put away: but they shall take maidens of the seed of the house of Is'ra-el, or a widow that had a priest before. _{divorced - offspring}
23 And they shall teach My people *the difference* between the holy and profane, and cause them to discern between the unclean and the clean. _{common}
24 And in controversy they shall stand in judgment; *and* they shall judge it according to My judgments: and they shall keep My laws and My statutes in all My assemblies; and they shall hallow My sabbaths. _{decrees - rest days}
25 And they shall come at no dead person to defile themselves: but for father, or for mother, or for son, or for daughter, for brother, or for sister that has had no husband, they may defile themselves. _{go to}
26 And after he is cleansed, they shall reckon to him seven days.
27 And in the day that he goes into the sanctuary, to the inner court, to minister in the sanctuary, he shall offer his sin offering, says the Lord GOD. _{Adonay^{p.f.} Jehovah}
28 And it shall be to them for an inheritance: I *am* their inheritance: and you shall give them no possession in Is'ra-el: I *am* their possession.
29 They shall eat the meat offering, and the sin offering, and the trespass offering; and every dedicated thing in Is'ra-el shall be theirs. _{all offerings}

30 And the <u>first</u> of all the firstfruits of all *things*, and every <u>oblation</u> of all, of every *sort* of your <u>oblations</u>, shall be the priest's: you shall also give to the priest the first of your dough, that he may cause the blessing to rest in your house. _{best - contribution}
31 The priests shall not eat of any thing that is dead of itself, or torn, whether it be fowl or beast.

CHAPTER 45

MOREOVER, when you shall divide by lot the land for inheritance, you shall offer an <u>oblation</u> to the LORD, an holy portion of the land: the length *shall be* the length of five and twenty thousand *reeds*, and the breadth *shall be* ten thousand. This *shall be* holy in all the borders thereof round about. _{contribution}
2 Of this there shall be for the sanctuary five hundred *in length*, with five hundred *in breadth*, square round about; and fifty cubits round about for the <u>suburbs</u> thereof. _{open space}
3 And of this measure shall you measure the length of five and twenty thousand, and the breadth of ten thousand: and in it shall be the sanctuary *and* the most holy *place*.
4 The <u>holy</u> *portion* of the land shall be for the priests the ministers of the sanctuary, which shall come near to minister to the LORD: and it shall be a place for their houses, and an <u>holy</u> place for the sanctuary. _{separated}
5 And the <u>five</u> and twenty thousand of length, and the ten thousand of breadth, shall also the Le'vites, the ministers of the house, have for themselves, for a possession for twenty <u>chambers</u>. _{towns to live in}
6 And you shall appoint the possession of the city five thousand broad, and five and twenty thousand long, opposite the <u>oblation</u> of the holy *portion*: it shall be for the whole house of Is'ra-el. _{contribution}
7 And a *portion shall be* for the prince on the one side and on the other side of the <u>oblation</u> of the holy *portion*, and of the possession of the city, before the <u>oblation</u> of the holy *portion*, and before the possession of the city, from the west side westward, and from the east side eastward: and the length *shall be* over against one of the portions, from the west border to the east border.
8 In the land shall be his possession in Is'ra-el: and My princes shall no more oppress My people; and *the rest of* the land shall they give to the house of Is'ra-el according to their tribes.
9 Thus says the <u>Lord</u> GOD; Let it suffice you, O princes of Is'ra-el: remove violence and <u>spoil</u>, and execute judgment and justice, take away your <u>exactions</u> from My people, says the Lord GOD. _{Adonay^{p.f.} Jehovah - destruction - dispossessing}
10 You shall have just balances, and a just ephah, and a just bath.
11 The ephah and the bath shall be of one measure, that the bath may contain the tenth part of an homer, and the ephah the tenth part of an homer: the measure thereof shall be after the homer.
12 And the shekel *shall be* twenty gerahs: twenty shekels, five and twenty

shekels, fifteen shekels, shall be your <u>maneh</u>.   fixed weight

13 This *is* the <u>oblation</u> that you shall offer; the sixth part of an ephah of an homer of wheat, and you shall give the sixth part of an ephah of an homer of barley: offering

14 Concerning the ordinance of oil, the bath of oil, *you shall offer* the tenth part of a bath out of the cor, *which is* an homer of ten baths; for ten baths *are* an homer:

15 And one lamb out of the flock, out of two hundred, out of the <u>fat</u> pastures of Is'ra-el; for a <u>meat</u> offering, and for a burned offering, and for <u>peace</u> offerings, to make reconciliation for them, says the <u>Lord</u> <u>God</u>.   well-watered - grain - thank - Adonay^{p.f.} Jehovah

16 All the people of the land shall give this <u>oblation</u> for the prince in Is'ra-el.   offering

17 And it shall be the prince's part *to give* burned offerings, and meat offerings, and drink offerings, in the feasts, and in the new moons, and in the <u>sabbaths</u>, in all solemnities of the house of Is'ra-el: he shall prepare the sin offering, and the meat offering, and the burned offering, and the peace offerings, to make reconciliation for the house of Is'ra-el.   rest days

18 Thus says the <u>Lord God</u>; In the first *month*, in the first *day* of the month, you shall take a young bullock without <u>blemish</u>, and cleanse the sanctuary: Adonay^{p.f.} Jehovah - defect

19 And the priest shall take of the blood of the sin offering, and put *it* upon the posts of the house, and upon the four corners of the settle of the altar, and upon the posts of the gate of the inner court.

20 And so you shall do the seventh *day* of the month for every one that <u>errs</u>, and for *him that is* <u>simple</u>: so shall you reconcile the house.   goes astray - ignorant

21 In the first *month*, in the fourteenth day of the month, you shall have the passover, a feast of seven days; <u>unleavened</u> bread shall be eaten. without yeast

22 And upon that day shall the prince prepare for himself and for all the people of the land a bullock *for* a sin offering.

23 And seven days of the feast he shall prepare a burned offering to the Lord, seven bullocks and seven rams without <u>blemish</u> daily the seven days; and a kid of the goats daily *for* a sin offering.   defect

24 And he shall prepare a <u>meat</u> offering of an ephah for a bullock, and an ephah for a ram, and an hin of oil for an ephah.   grain

25 In the seventh *month*, in the fifteenth day of the month, shall he do the like in the feast of the seven days, according to the sin offering, according to the burnt offering, and according to the meat offering, and according to the oil.

CHAPTER 46

THUS says the <u>Lord God</u>; The gate of the inner court that looks toward the east shall be shut the six working days; but on the <u>sabbath</u> it shall be opened, and in the day of the new moon it shall be opened.   Adonay^{p.f.} Jehovah - rest day

2 And the prince shall enter by the way of the porch of *that* gate outside, and shall stand by the post of the gate, and the priests shall prepare his burned offering and his peace offerings, and he shall worship at the threshold of the gate: then he shall go forth; but the gate shall not be shut until the evening.

3 Likewise the people of the land shall worship at the door of this gate before the Lord in the <u>sabbaths</u> and in the new moons. rest days

4 And the burned offering that the prince shall offer to the Lord in the <u>sabbath</u> day *shall be* six lambs without <u>blemish</u>, and a ram without <u>blemish</u>. defect

5 And the meat offering *shall be* an ephah for a ram, and the <u>meat</u> offering for the lambs as he shall be able to give, and an hin of oil to an ephah. grain

6 And in the day of the new moon *it shall be* a young bullock without <u>blemish</u>, and six lambs, and a ram: they shall be without <u>blemish</u>.

7 And he shall prepare a meat offering, an ephah for a bullock, and an ephah for a ram, and for the lambs according as <u>his hand shall attain to</u>, and an hin of oil to an ephah. as he is able

8 And when the prince shall enter, he shall go in by the way of the porch of *that* gate, and he shall go forth by the way thereof.

9 But when the people of the land shall come before the Lord in the solemn feasts, he that enters in by the way of the north gate to worship shall go out by the way of the south gate; and he that enters by the way of the south gate shall go forth by the way of the north gate: he shall not return by the way of the gate whereby he came in, but shall go <u>forth against it</u>. straight out

10 And the prince in the midst of them, when they go in, shall go in; and when they go forth, shall go forth.

11 And in the feasts and in the solemnities the meat offering shall be an ephah to a bullock, and ephah to a ram, and to the lambs as he is able to give, and an hin of oil to an ephah.

12 Now when the prince shall prepare a voluntary burned offering or peace offerings voluntarily to the Lord, *one* shall then open him the gate that <u>looks</u> toward the east, and he shall prepare his burned offering and his peace offerings, as he did on the <u>sabbath</u> day: then he shall go forth; and after his going forth *one* shall shut the gate. faces - rest

13 You shall daily prepare a burned offering to the Lord *of* a lamb of the first year without blemish: you shall prepare it every morning.

14 And you shall prepare a meat offering for it every morning, the sixth part of an ephah, and the third part of an hin of oil, to temper with the fine flour; a meat offering continually by a perpetual ordinance to the Lord.

15 Thus shall they prepare the lamb, and the meat offering, and the oil, every morning *for* a continual burned offering.

16 Thus says the <u>Lord God</u>; If the prince give a gift to any of his sons, the inheritance thereof shall be his sons'; it *shall be* their possession by inheritance. Adonay^{p.f.} Jehovah

17 But if he give a gift of his inheritance to one of his servants, then it shall be his to the year of liberty; after it shall return to the prince: but his inheritance shall be his sons' for them.
18 Moreover the prince shall not take of the people's inheritance by oppression, to thrust them out of their possession; *but* he shall give his sons inheritance out of his own possession: that My people be not scattered every man from his possession.
19 After He brought me through the entry, which *was* at the side of the gate, into the holy chambers of the priests, which looked toward the north: and, behold, there *was* a place on the two sides westward. entrance - sacred rooms
20 Then said He to me, This *is* the place where the priests shall boil the trespass offering and the sin offering, where they shall bake the meat offering; that they bear *them* not out into the utter court, to sanctify the people.
21 Then He brought me forth into the outer court, and caused me to pass by the four corners of the court; and, behold, in every corner of the court *there was* a court.
22 In the four corners of the court *there were* courts joined of forty *cubits* long and thirty broad: these four corners *were* of one measure. the same size
23 And *there was* a row *of building* round about in them, round about them four, and *it was* made with boiling places under the rows round about. places for fire
24 Then said He to me, These *are* the places of them that boil, where the

ministers of the house shall boil the sacrifice of the people. cooking houses

CHAPTER 47

AFTERWARD he brought me again to the door of the house; and, behold, waters issued out from under the threshold of the house eastward: for the forefront of the house *stood toward* the east, and the waters came down from under from the right side of the house, at the south *side* of the altar. doorway
2 Then brought he me out of the way of the gate northward, and led me about the way outside to the outer gate by the way that look eastward; and, behold, there ran out waters on the right side.
3 And when the man that had the line in his hand went forth eastward, he measured a thousand cubits, and he brought me through the waters; the waters *were* to the ankles.
4 Again he measured a thousand, and brought me through the waters; the waters *were* to the knees. Again he measured a thousand, and brought me through; the waters *were* to the loins.
5 Afterward he measured a thousand; *and it was* a river that I could not pass over: for the waters were risen, waters to swim in, a river that could not be passed over. enough water - forded
6 And He said to me, Son of man, have you seen *this*? Then He brought me, and caused me to return to the brink of the river.
7 Now when I had returned, behold, at the bank of the river *were* very many

trees on the one side and on the other. 8 Then said He to me, These waters issue out toward the east country, and go down into the desert, and go into the sea: *which being* brought forth into the sea, the waters shall be healed.

9 And it shall come to pass, *that* every thing that lives, which moves, wherever the rivers shall come, shall live: and there shall be a very great multitude of fish, because these waters shall come there: for they shall be healed; and every thing shall live where the river comes.

10 And it shall come to pass, *that* the fishers shall stand upon it from En-ge'di even to En-eg'la-im; they shall be a *place* to spread forth nets; their fish shall be according to their kinds, as the fish of the great sea, exceeding many.

11 But the miry places thereof and the marshes thereof shall not be healed; they shall be given to salt. _{swamps}

12 And by the river upon the bank thereof, on this side and on that side, shall grow all trees for meat, whose leaf shall not fade, neither shall the fruit thereof be consumed: it shall bring forth new fruit according to its months, because their waters they issued out of the sanctuary: and the fruit thereof shall be for meat, and the leaf thereof for medicine. REV. 22:2 food - fail - every month

13 Thus says the Lord GOD; This *shall be* the border, whereby you shall inherit the land according to the twelve tribes of Is'ra-el: Jo'seph *shall have two* portions. Adonay^{p.f.} Jehovah

14 And you shall inherit it, one as well as another: *concerning* the which I lifted up My hand to give it to your fathers: and this land shall fall to you for inheritance. promised

15 And this *shall be* the border of the land toward the north side, from the great sea, the way of Heth"lon, as men go to Ze'dad;

16 Ha'math, Be-ro'thah, Sib'ra-im, which *is* between the border of Da-mas'cus and the border of Ha'math; Ha'zar-hat'ti-con, which *is* by the coast of Hau'ran.

17 And the border from the sea shall be Ha'zar-e'nan, the border of Da-mas'cus, and the north northward, and the border of Ha'math. And *this is* the north side.

18 And the east side you shall measure from Hau'ran, and from Da-mas'cus, and from Gil'e-ad, and from the land of Is'ra-el *by* Jor'dan, from the border to the east sea. And *this is* the east side.

19 And the south side southward, from Ta'mar *even* to the waters of strife *in* Ka'desh, the river to the great sea. And *this is* the south side southward. i.e., Mediterranean

20 The west side also *shall be* the great sea from the border, till a man come opposite Ha'math. This *is* the west side.

21 So shall you divide this land to you according to the tribes of Is'ra-el.

22 And it shall come to pass, *that* you shall divide it by lot for an inheritance to you, and to the strangers

that <u>sojourn</u> among you, which shall father children among you: and they shall be to you as born in the country among the children of Is'ra-el; they shall have inheritance with you among the tribes of Is'ra-el. _{settle}

23 And it shall come to pass, *that* in what tribe the stranger sojourns, there shall you give *him* his inheritance, says the <u>Lord G</u>OD. _{Adonay[p.f.] Jehovah}

CHAPTER 48

NOW these *are* the names of the tribes. From the north end to the coast of the way of Heth'lon, as one goes to Ha'math, Ha'zar-e'nan, the border of Da-mas'cus northward, to the coast of Ha'math; for these are his sides east *and* west; a *portion for* Dan.

2 And by the border of Dan, from the east side to the west side, a *portion for* Ash'er.

3 And by the border of Ash'er, from the east side even to the west side, a *portion for* Naph'ta-li.

4 And by the border of Naph'ta-li, from the east side to the west side, a *portion for* Ma-nas'seh.

5 And by the border of Ma-nas'seh, from the east side to the west side, a *portion for* E'phra-im.

6 And by the border of E'phra-im, from the east side even to the west side, a *portion for* Reu'ben.

7 And by the border of Reu'ben, from the east side to the west side, a *portion for* Ju'dah.

8 And by the border of Ju'dah, from the east side to the west side,

shall be the offering which you shall offer of five and twenty thousand *reeds in* breadth, and *in* length as one of the *other* parts, from the east side to the west side: and the sanctuary shall be in the midst of it.

9 The <u>oblation</u> that you shall offer to the LORD *shall be* of five and twenty thousand in length, and of ten thousand in breadth. _{allotment}

10 And for them, *even* for the priests, shall be *this* holy <u>oblation</u>; toward the north five and twenty thousand *in length*, and toward the west ten thousand in breadth, and toward the east ten thousand in breadth, and toward the south five and twenty thousand in length: and the sanctuary of the LORD shall be in the midst thereof.

11 It *shall be* for the priests that are sanctified of the sons of Za'dok; which have <u>kept My charge</u>, which went not astray when the children of Is'ra-el went astray, as the Le'vites went astray. _{served Me}

12 And *this* <u>oblation</u> of the land that is offered shall be to them a thing most holy by the border of the Le'vites. _{allotment}

13 And opposite the border of the priests the Le'vites *shall have* five and twenty thousand in length, and ten thousand in breadth: all the length *shall be* five and twenty thousand, and the breadth ten thousand.

14 And they shall not sell of it, neither exchange, nor alienate the firstfruits of the land: for *it is* holy to the LORD.

15 And the five thousand, that are

left in the breadth opposite the five and twenty thousand, shall be a profane *place* for the city, for dwelling, and for suburbs: and the city shall be in the midst thereof.

16 And these *shall be* the measures thereof; the north side four thousand and five hundred, and the south side four thousand and five hundred, and on the east side four thousand and five hundred, and the west side four thousand and five hundred.

17 And the suburbs of the city shall be toward the north two hundred and fifty, and toward the south two hundred and fifty, and toward the east two hundred and fifty, and toward the west two hundred and fifty.

18 And the residue in length opposite the <u>oblation</u> of the holy *portion shall be* ten thousand eastward, and ten thousand westward: and it shall be opposite the <u>oblation</u> of the holy *portion*; and the increase thereof shall be for food to them that serve the city._{allotment}

19 And they that serve the city shall serve it out of all the tribes of Is'ra-el.

20 All the <u>oblation</u> *shall be* five and twenty thousand by five and twenty thousand: you shall offer the holy <u>oblation</u> foursquare, with the possession of the city.

21 And the <u>residue</u> *shall be* for the prince, on the one side and on the other of the holy <u>oblation</u>, and of the possession of the city, opposite the five and twenty thousand of the <u>oblation</u> toward the east border, and westward opposite the five and twenty thou-

sand toward the west border, opposite the portions for the prince: and it shall be the holy <u>oblation</u>; and the sanctuary of the house *shall be* in the midst thereof.   balance - allotment

22 Moreover from the possession of the Le'vites, and from the possession of the city, *being* in the midst *of that* which is the prince's, between the border of Ju'dah and the border of Ben'ja-min, shall be for the prince.

23 As for the rest of the tribes, from the east side to the west side, Ben'ja-min *shall have a portion*.   one

24 And by the border of Ben'ja-min, from the east side to the west side, Sim'e-on *shall have* a *portion*.

25 And by the border of Sim'e-on, from the east side to the west side, Is'sa-char a *portion*.

26 And by the border of Is'sa-char, from the east side to the west side, Zeb'u-lun a *portion*.

27 And by the border of Zeb'u-lun, from the east side to the west side, Gad a *portion*.

28 And by the border of Gad, at the south side southward, the border shall be even from Ta'mar *to* the waters of strife *in* Ka'desh, *and* to the river toward the <u>great</u> sea.   i.e., Mediterranean

29 This *is* the land which you shall divide by lot to the tribes of Is'ra-el for inheritance, and these *are* their portions, says the <u>Lord God</u>.   Adonay^{p.f.} Jehovah

30 And these *are* the goings out of the city on the north side, four thousand and five hundred measures.   REV. 21:12

31 And the gates of the city *shall be* after the names of the tribes of Is'ra-el:

three gates northward; one gate of Reu'ben, one gate of Ju'dah, one gate of Le'vi.   REV. 21:14

32 And at the east side four thousand and five hundred: and three gates; and one gate of Jo'seph, one gate of Ben'ja-min, one gate of Dan.

33 And at the south side four thousand and five hundred measures: and three gates; one gate of Sim'e-on, one gate of Is'sa-char, one gate of Zeb'u-lun.

34 At the west side four thousand and five hundred, *with* their three gates; one gate of Gad, one gate of Ash'er, one gate of Naph'ta-li.

35 *It was* round about eighteen thousand *measures*: and the name of the city from *that* day *shall be*, The LORD *is* there.

DANIEL

OUTLINE

SURVEY

The Book of Daniel is one that has never failed to excite interest and provoke controversy in theological circles. At the same time, it has captivated readers with accounts of heroism in time of critical danger and comforted multitudes of God's faithful followers as they read stirring accounts of His presence and blessing.

The first chapters of Daniel relate certain experiences of Jewish youths, Daniel and his three friends, who are part of the Jewish captivity in Babylon in the sixth century B.C. Their refusal to be seduced by the pagan world in which they live and the dangers that threaten them because of their faithfulness are the essence of drama. Their deliverances—Daniel from the lions' den and Shadrach, Meshach and Abednego from the fiery furnace—demonstrate the power and love of God. Nebuchadrezzar, proud and secure in his despotism, is brought low until he comes to recognize that God's providence rules even a monarch's life. The drama of "the handwriting on the wall" has made that phrase a proverbial part of our language to this very day. The dreadful sin of arrogance toward God, of which Belshazzar was guilty, brings certain death and defeat. The narrative sections of the book, among the most famous in literature, hold our interest not only because of their drama, but also because of their relevance whenever materialism and paganism threaten to engulf the children of God.

The visions given in the Book of Daniel, either to pagan rulers or to Daniel himself, are accounted by earnest Bible students to be a preview of the world throughout history and to the last days. The prophecies of four kingdoms and the great fifth kingdom, the Kingdom of God, are a picture of the march of empire. Four kingdoms came as predicted, and the fifth awaits its fulfilment in the Second Coming of our Lord.

The great themes of prophecy in Daniel are matters of vital concern to the Church today: the apostasy of God's people; the revelation of the man of sin; the tribulation, the Second Coming, the Millennium, and the Day of Judgment. As we open the Book of Daniel, we come upon an interpretation of history that not only has been fulfilled in great part but will be entirely fulfilled. It is this assurance that makes Daniel vital and significant in our own time.

AUTHOR

Historically both Judaism and Christendom have received Daniel into the Canon as a genuine work of the period from which it alleges to speak, the sixth century B.C. written by Daniel. Most modern scholars believe that the Book of Daniel, as we have it, comes from the time of the Maccabees, approximately 165 B.C., author(s) unknown. They believe it was issued to strengthen the faith of the people in those days of persecution under a pseudonym, the author(s) creating the impression that a sixth century Jew, Daniel, was the real author. But there is no evidence in history that the Jews issued under a pseudonym a book claiming to be a revelation from God and set centuries earlier than the time when it is alleged to be presented to the public. In the absence of such historic evidence, there is no scientific basis for departing from the accepted Judeo-Christian tradition of a sixth century B.C. date and authorship by Daniel.

G.D.Y.

THE BOOK OF

DANIEL

CHAPTER 1

IN the third year of the reign of Je-hoi'a-kim king of Ju'dah came Neb-u-chad-nez'zar king of Bab'y-lon to Je-ru'sa-lem, and besieged it.

2 And the Lord gave Je-hoi'a-kim king of Ju'dah into his hand, with part of the vessels of the house of God: which he carried into the land of Shi'nar to the house of his god; and he brought the vessels into the treasure house of his god. Adonahy p.f. - Elohim p.f.

3 And the king spoke to Ash'pe-naz the master of his eunuchs, that he should bring certain of the children of Is'ra-el, and of the king's seed, and of the princes; royal family

4 Children in whom was no blemish, but well favored, and skilful in all wisdom, and cunning in knowledge, and understanding science, and such as had ability in them to stand in the king's palace, and whom they might teach the learning and the tongue of the Chal-de'ans. defect - handsome - serve

5 And the king appointed them a daily provision of the king's meat, and of the wine which he drank: so nourishing them three years, that at the end thereof they might stand before the king. food - i.e., serve

6 Now among these were of the children of Ju'dah, Dan'iel, Han-a-ni'ah, Mish'a-el, and Az-a-ri'ah:

7 To whom the prince of the eu-nuchs gave names: for he gave to Dan'iel the name of Bel-te-shaz'zar; and to Han-a-ni'ah, of Sha'drach; and to Mish'a-el, of Me'shach; and to Az-a-ri'ah, of A-bed'-ne-go.

8 But Dan'iel purposed in his heart that he would not defile himself with the portion of the king's meat, nor with the wine which he drank: therefore he requested of the prince of the eunuchs that he might not defile himself. ration - food

9 Now God had brought Dan'iel into favor and tender love with the prince of the eunuchs. Elohim p.f.

10 And the prince of the eunuchs said to Dan'iel, I fear my lord the king, who has appointed your meat and your drink: for why should he see your faces worse liking than the children which are of your sort? then shall you make me endanger my head to the king. food - looking more haggard - age

11 Then said Dan'iel to Mel'zar, whom the prince of the eunuchs had set over Dan'iel, Han-a-ni'ah, Mish'a-el, and Az-a-ri'ah,

12 Prove your servants, I beseech you, ten days; and let them give us pulse to eat, and water to drink. Test - beg - vegetables

13 Then let our countenances be looked upon before you, and the countenance of the children that eat of the portion of the king's meat: and as you see, deal with your servants. food

14 So he consented to them in this

matter, and <u>proved</u> them ten days. _{tested}
15 And at the end of ten days their countenances appeared fairer and <u>fatter in flesh</u> than all the children which did eat the portion of the king's <u>meat</u>.   _{better nourished - food}
16 Thus Mel'zar took away the portion of their <u>meat</u>, and the wine that they should drink; and gave them <u>pulse</u>.   _{vegetables}
17 As for these four children, <u>God</u> gave them knowledge and skill in all learning and wisdom: and Dan'iel had understanding in all visions and dreams.   _{Elohim}^{p.f.}
18 Now at the end of the days that the king had said he should bring them in, then the prince of the eunuchs brought them in before Neb-u-chad-nez'zar.
19 And the king <u>communed</u> with them; and among them all was found none like Dan'iel, Han-a-ni'ah, Mish'a-el, and Az-a-ri'ah: therefore <u>stood</u> they before the king.   _{spoke - i.e., served}
20 And in all matters of wisdom *and* understanding, that the king enquired of them, he found them ten times better than all the magicians *and* <u>astrologers</u> that *were* in all his realm.   _{conjurers}
21 And Dan'iel continued *even* to the first year of king Cy'rus.

CHAPTER 2

AND in the second year of the reign of Neb-u-chad-nez'zar Neb-u-chad-nez'zar dreamed dreams, wherewith his spirit was troubled, and his sleep <u>broke</u> from him.   _{was gone}
2 Then the king commanded to call the magicians, and the <u>astrologers</u>, and the sorcerers, and the Chal-de'ans, for to show the king his dreams. So they came and stood before the king. _{conjurers}
3 And the king said to them, I have dreamed a dream, and my spirit was troubled to <u>know</u> the dream.   _{understand}
4 Then spoke the Chal-de'ans to the king in <u>Syr'i-ack</u>, O king, live for ever: tell your servants the dream, and we will show the interpretation. _{Aramaic}
5 The king answered and said to the Chal-de'ans, The thing is gone from me: if you will not make known to me the dream, with the interpretation thereof, you shall be cut in pieces, and your houses shall be made a dunghill.
6 But if you <u>show</u> the dream, and the interpretation thereof, you shall receive of me gifts and rewards and great honor: therefore show me the dream, and the interpretation thereof.   _{declare}
7 They answered again and said, Let the king tell his servants the dream, and we will show the interpretation of it.
8 The king answered and said, I know of certainty that you would gain the time, because you see the thing is gone from me.   _{dream}
9 But if you will not make known to me the dream, *there is but* one decree for you: for you have prepared lying and corrupt words to speak before me, till the time be changed: therefore tell me the dream, and I shall know that you can show me the interpretation thereof.
10 The Chal-de'ans answered before the king, and said, There is not a man upon the earth that can show the king's matter: therefore *there is* no king,

_{P04}

lord, nor ruler, *that* asked such things at any magician, or astrologer, or Chal-de'an. conjurer

11 And *it is* a rare thing that the king requires and there is none other that can show it before the king, except the gods, whose dwelling is not with flesh. difficult

12 For this cause the king was angry and very furious, and commanded to destroy all the wise *men* of Bab'y-lon.

13 And the decree went forth that the wise *men* should be slain; and they sought Dan'iel and his fellows to be slain.

14 Then Dan'iel answered with counsel and wisdom to A'ri-och the captain of the king's guard, which was gone forth to slay the wise *men* of Bab'y-lon:

15 He answered and said to A'ri-och the king's captain, Why *is* the decree *so* hasty from the king? Then A'ri-och made the thing known to Dan'iel. harsh - explained the matter

16 Then Dan'iel went in, and desired of the king that he would give him time, and that he would show the king the interpretation. declare

17 Then Dan'iel went to his house, and made the thing known to Han-a-ni'ah, Mish'a-el, and Az-a-ri'ah, his companions: dream

18 That they would desire mercies of the God of heaven concerning this secret; that Dan'iel and his fellows should not perish with the rest of the wise *men* of Bab'y-lon. Elah^{s.f.}

19 Then was the secret revealed to Dan'iel in a night vision. Then Dan'iel blessed the God of heaven. Elah^{s.f.}

20 Dan'iel answered and said, Blessed be the name of God for ever and ever: for wisdom and might are His:

21 And He changes the times and the seasons: He removes kings, and sets up kings: He gives wisdom to the wise, and knowledge to them that know understanding: JAMES 1:5

22 He reveals the deep and secret things: He know what *is* in the darkness, and the light dwells with Him.

23 I thank You, and praise You, O You God of my fathers, who have given me wisdom and might, and have made known to me now what we desired of You: for You have *now* made known to us the king's matter. sought

24 Therefore Dan'iel went in to A'ri-och, whom the king had ordained to destroy the wise *men* of Bab'y-lon: he went and said thus to him; Destroy not the wise *men* of Bab'y-lon: bring me in before the king, and I will show to the king the interpretation. appointed - declare

25 Then A'ri-och brought in Dan'iel before the king in haste, and said thus to him, I have found a man of the captives of Ju'dah, that will make known to the king the interpretation. reveal

26 The king answered and said to Dan'iel, whose name *was* Bel-te-shaz'zar, Are you able to make known to me the dream which I have seen, and the interpretation thereof?

27 Dan'iel answered in the presence of the king, and said, The secret which

the king has demanded cannot the wise *men*, the <u>astrologers</u>, the magicians, the soothsayers, <u>show</u> to the king;   conjurers

28 But there is a <u>God</u> in heaven that reveals secrets, and makes known to the king Neb-u-chad-nez'zar what shall be in the latter days. Your dream, and the visions of your head upon your bed, are these;   Elah^{s.f.}

29 As for you, O king, your thoughts came *into your mind* upon your bed, what should come to pass hereafter: and He that reveals secrets makes known to you what shall come to pass.

30 But as for me, this secret is not revealed to me for *any* wisdom that I have more than any living, but for *their* sakes that shall make known the interpretation to the king, and that you might <u>know</u> the thoughts of your <u>heart</u>.   understand - i.e., mind

31 You, O king, saw, and behold a great image. This great <u>image</u>, whose brightness *was* <u>excellent</u>, stood before you; and the form thereof *was* <u>terrible</u>. statue - dazzling - awesome

32 This image's head *was* of fine gold, its breast and its arms of silver, its belly and its thighs of brass,

33 Its legs of iron, its feet part of iron and part of clay.

34 <u>You saw till</u> that a <u>stone</u> was cut out without hands, which <u>smote</u> the image upon its feet *that were* of iron and clay, and broke them to pieces.   You were seeing - rock - struck

35 Then was the iron, the clay, the brass, the silver, and the gold, broken to pieces together, and became like the chaff of the summer threshing-floors; and the wind carried them away, that no place was found for them: and the <u>stone</u> that smote the <u>image</u> became a great mountain, and filled the whole earth.   rock - statue

36 This *is* the dream; and we will tell the interpretation thereof before the king.

37 You, O king, *are* a king of kings: for the God of heaven has given you a kingdom, power, and strength, and glory.   Elah^{s.f.}

38 And wherever the children of men dwell, the beasts of the field and the fowls of the heaven has he given into your hand, and has made you ruler over them all. You *are* this <u>head</u> of gold.   i.e., Kingdom of Babylon

39 And after you shall arise <u>another kingdom</u> inferior to you, and another <u>third kingdom</u> of brass, which shall bear rule over all the earth.   i.e., Medo-Persia - Greece

40 And the <u>fourth kingdom</u> shall be strong as iron: forasmuch as iron breaks in pieces and subdues all *things*: and as iron that breaks all these, shall it break in pieces and bruise.   Roman

41 And whereas you saw the <u>feet and toes</u>, part of potters' clay, and part of iron, the kingdom shall be divided; but there shall be in it of the strength of the iron, forasmuch as you saw the iron mixed with miry clay.

individual nations resulting from Roman empire

42 And *as* the toes of the feet *were* part of iron, and part of clay, *so* the

kingdom shall be partly strong, and partly broken.

43 And whereas you saw iron mixed with miry clay, they shall mingle themselves with the <u>seed</u> of men: but they shall not <u>cleave</u> one to another, even as iron is not mixed with clay. descendants - cling

44 And in the days of these kings shall the <u>God</u> of heaven set up a <u>kingdom</u>, which shall never be destroyed: and the <u>kingdom</u> shall not be left to other people, *but* it shall break in pieces and consume all these kingdoms, and it shall stand for ever. Elah^{s.f.} - Eternal Divine Kingdom

45 Forasmuch as you saw that the <u>stone</u> was cut out of the mountain without hands, and that it broke in pieces the iron, the brass, the clay, the silver, and the gold; the great <u>God</u> has made known to the king what shall come to pass <u>hereafter</u>: and the dream *is* <u>certain</u>, and the interpretation thereof sure. Rock

Christ-Messiah Kingdom of God - in the future - true

46 Then the king Neb-u-chad-nez'zar fell upon his face, and worshiped Dan'iel, and commanded that they should offer an <u>oblation</u> and sweet odors to him. offering

47 The king answered to Dan'iel, and said, Of a truth *it is*, that your <u>God</u> *is* a <u>God</u> of gods, and a Lord of kings, and a revealer of secrets, seeing you could reveal this secret.

REV. 17:14 Elah^{s.f.}

48 Then the king made Dan'iel a great man, and gave him many great gifts, and made him ruler over the whole province of Bab'y-lon, and chief of the governors over all the wise *men* of Bab'y-lon.

49 Then Dan'iel requested of the king, and he set Sha'drach, Me'shach, and A-bed'-ne-go, over the affairs of the province of Bab'y-lon: but Dan'iel *sat* in the <u>gate</u> of the king. i.e., court

CHAPTER 3

NEB-U-CHAD-NEZ'ZAR the king made an image of gold, whose height *was* threescore cubits, *and* the breadth thereof six cubits: he set it up in the plain of Du'ra, in the province of Bab'y-lon.

2 Then Neb-u-chad-nez'zar the king sent to gather together the princes, the governors, and the captains, the judges, the treasurers, the counselors, the sheriffs, and all the rulers of the provinces, to come to the dedication of the image which Neb-u-chad-nez'zar the king had set up.

3 Then the princes, the governors, and captains, the judges, the treasurers, the counselors, the sheriffs, and all the rulers of the provinces, were gathered together to the dedication of the image that Neb-u-chad-nez'zar the king had set up; and they stood before the image that Neb-u-chad-nez'zar had set up.

4 Then an herald cried aloud, To you it is commanded, O people, nations, and languages,

5 *That* at what time you hear the sound of the cornet, flute, harp, sackbut, <u>psaltery</u>, dulcimer, and all kinds of music, you fall down and worship the golden

image that Neb-u-chad-nez'zar the king has set up: lyre

6 And whoso falls not down and worships shall the same hour be cast into the midst of a burning fiery furnace.

7 Therefore at that time, when all the people heard the sound of the cornet, flute, harp, sackbut, <u>psaltery</u>, and all kinds of music, all the people, the nations, and the languages, fell down *and* worshiped the golden image that Neb-u-chad-nez'zar the king had set up.   lyre

8 Wherefore at that time certain Chal-de'ans came near, and accused the Jews.

9 They spoke and said to the king Neb-u-chad-nez'zar, O king, live for ever.

10 You, O king, have made a decree, that every man that shall hear the sound of the cornet, flute, harp, sackbut, <u>psaltery</u>, and dulcimer, and all kinds of music, shall fall down and worship the golden image:

11 And whoso falls not down and worships *that* he should be cast into the midst of a burning fiery furnace.

12 There are certain Jews whom you have set over the affairs of the province of Bab'y-lon, Sha'drach, Me'shach, and A-bed'-ne-go; these men, O king, have not <u>re</u>-<u>garded</u> you: they serve not your gods, nor worship the golden image which you have set up.   obeyed

13 Then Neb-u-chad-nez'zar in *his* rage and fury commanded to bring Sha'drach, Me'shach, and A-bed'-ne-go. Then they brought these men before the king.

14 Neb-u-chad-nez'zar spoke and said to them, *Is it* true, O Sha'drach, Me'shach, and A-bed'-ne-go, do not you serve my gods, nor worship the golden image which I have set up?

15 Now if you be ready that at what time you hear the sound of the cornet, flute, harp, sackbut, <u>psaltery</u>, and dulcimer, and all kinds of music, you fall down and worship the image which I have made; *well*: but if you worship not, you shall be cast the same hour into the midst of a burning fiery furnace; and who *is* that <u>God</u> that shall deliver you out of my hands? lyre - Elah^{s.f.}

16 Sha'drach, Me'shach, and A-bed'-ne-go, answered and said to the king, O Neb-u-chad-nez'zar, we *are* not <u>care</u>-<u>ful</u> to answer you in this matter.   do not need

17 If it be *so*, our God whom we serve is able to deliver us from the burning fiery furnace, and He will deliver *us* out of your hand, O king.   that way

18 But if not, be it known to you, O king, that we will not serve your gods, nor worship the golden image which you have set up.

19 Then was Neb-u-chad-nez'zar full of fury, and <u>the form of his visage</u> was changed against Sha'drach, Me'shach, and A-bed'-ne-go: *therefore* he spoke, and commanded that they should heat the furnace one seven times more than it was <u>wont</u> to be heated.   his facial expression - usually

20 And he commanded the most mighty men that *were* in his army to bind Sha'drach, Me'shach, and A-bed'-ne-go, *and* to cast *them* into the burning fiery furnace.

21 Then these men were bound in their coats, their <u>hosen</u>, and their hats, and their *other* garments, and were cast into the midst of the burning fiery furnace. trousers

22 Therefore because the king's commandment was urgent, and the furnace exceeding hot, the flame of the fire slew those men that took up Sha'-drach, Me'shach, and A-bed'-ne-go.

23 And these three men, Sha'drach, Me'shach, and A-bed'-ne-go, fell down bound into the midst of the burning fiery furnace.

24 Then Neb-u-chad-nez'zar the king was astonished, and rose up in haste, *and* spoke, and said to his counselors, Did not we cast three men bound into the midst of the fire? They answered and said to the king, True, O king.

G4 25 He answered and said, Lo, I see four men loose, walking in the midst of the fire, and they have no hurt; and the form of the fourth is like the Son of God. 1283

26 Then Neb-u-chad-nez'zar came near to the mouth of the burning fiery furnace, *and* spoke, and said, Sha'drach, Me'shach, and A-bed'-ne-go, you servants of the <u>Most High God</u>, come forth, and come here. Then Sha'drach, Me'shach, and A-bed'-ne-go, came forth of the midst of the fire. Elaha Illaya (Aram.)

27 And the princes, governors, and captains, and the king's counselors, being gathered together, saw these men, upon whose bodies the fire had no power, nor was an hair of their head singed, neither were their coats changed, nor the smell of fire had passed on them.

28 *Then* Neb-u-chad-nez'zar spoke, and said, Blessed *be* the <u>God</u> of Sha'drach, Me'shach, and A-bed'-ne-go, who has sent His <u>angel</u>, and delivered His servants that trusted in Him, and have <u>changed</u> the king's word, and yielded their bodies, that they might not serve nor worship any god, except their own <u>God</u>. Elohim^{p.f.} messenger - violated G1G 1281

29 Therefore I make a decree, That every people, nation, and language, which speak any thing <u>amiss</u> against the <u>God</u> of Sha'drach, Me'shach, and A-bed'-ne-go, shall be cut in pieces, and their houses shall be made a <u>dunghill</u>: because there is no other <u>God</u> that can deliver after this sort. offensive - Elohim^{p.f.} - ruin

30 Then the king promoted Sha'drach, Me'shach, and A-bed'-ne-go, in the province of Bab'y-lon.

CHAPTER 4

NEB-U-CHAD-NEZ'ZAR the king, to all people, nations, and languages, that dwell in all the earth; Peace be multiplied to you.

2 I thought it good to show the signs and wonders that the high God has wrought toward me.

3 How great *are* His signs! and how mighty *are* His wonders! His kingdom *is* an everlasting kingdom, and His dominion *is* from generation to generation.

4 I Neb-u-chad-nez'zar was at rest in my house, and flourishing in my palace:

5 I saw a dream which made me afraid, and the thoughts upon my bed and the visions of my head troubled me.

6 Therefore made I a decree to bring in all the wise *men* of Bab'y-lon before me, that they might make known to me the interpretation of the dream.

7 Then came in the magicians, the astrologers, the Chal-de'ans, and the soothsayers: and I told the dream before them; but they did not make known to me the interpretation thereof.   conjurers

8 But at the last Dan'iel came in before me, whose name *was* Bel-te-shaz'zar, according to the name of my god, and in whom *is* the spirit of the holy gods: and before him I told the dream, *saying*,

G5

1279

9 O Bel-te-shaz'zar, master of the magicians, because I know that the spirit of the holy gods *is* in you, and no secret troubles you, tell me the visions of my dream that I have seen, and the interpretation thereof.   i.e., is too difficult for you - explain

10 Thus *were* the visions of my head in my bed; I saw, and behold a tree in the midst of the earth, and the height thereof *was* great.   was looking

11 The tree grew, and was strong, and the height thereof reached to heaven, and the sight thereof to the end of all the earth: visibility

12 The leaves thereof *were* fair, and the fruit thereof much, and in it *was* meat for all: the beasts of the field had shadow under it, and the fowls of the heaven dwell in the boughs thereof, and all flesh was fed of it.   food

13 I saw in the visions of my head upon my bed, and, behold, a watcher and an holy one came down from heaven;

14 He cried aloud, and said thus, Hew down the tree, and cut off its branches, shake off its leaves, and scatter its fruit: let the beasts get away from under it, and the fowls from its branches: Cut

15 Nevertheless leave the stump of its roots in the earth, even with a band of iron and brass, in the tender grass of the field; and let it be wet with the dew of heaven, and *let* his portion *be* with the beasts in the grass of the earth:

16 Let his heart be changed from man's, and let a beast's heart be given to him; and let seven times pass over him.   periods of time

17 This matter *is* by the decree of the watchers, and the demand by the word of the holy ones: to the intent that the living may know that the Most High rules in the kingdom of men, and gives it to whomsoever He will, and sets up over it the basest of men.

18 This dream I king Neb-u-chad-nez'zar have seen. Now you, O Bel-te-shaz'zar, declare the interpretation thereof, forasmuch as all the wise *men* of my kingdom are not able to make known to me the interpretation: but you *are* able; for the spirit of the holy gods *is* in you.

19 Then Dan'iel, whose name *was* Bel-te-shaz'zar, was astonished for one hour, and his thoughts troubled him. The king spoke, and said, Bel-te-shaz'zar, let not the dream, or the interpretation thereof, trouble you. Bel-te-shaz'-

zar answered and said, My lord, the dream *be* to them that <u>hate</u> you, and the interpretation thereof to your enemies.   <small>appalled for a while - despise</small>

20 The tree that you saw, which grew, and was strong, whose height reached to the heaven, and the <u>sight</u> thereof to all the earth;   <small>visibility</small>

21 Whose leaves *were* fair, and the fruit thereof much, and in it *was* meat for all; under which the beasts of the field dwell, and upon whose branches the fowls of the heaven had their habitation:

22 It *is* you, O king, that are grown and become strong: for your greatness is grown, and reaches to heaven, and your dominion to the end of the earth.

23 And whereas the king saw a watcher and an holy one coming down from heaven, and saying, <u>Hew</u> the tree down, and destroy it; yet leave the stump of the roots thereof in the earth, even with a band of iron and brass, in the tender grass of the field; and let it be wet with the dew of heaven, and *let* his portion *be* with the beasts of the field, till seven <u>times</u> pass over him;   <small>Cut - periods of time</small>

24 This *is* the interpretation, O king, and this *is* the decree of the Most High, which is come upon my lord the king:

25 That they shall drive you from men, and your dwelling shall be with the beasts of the field, and they shall make you to eat grass as oxen, and they shall wet you with the dew of heaven, and seven <u>times</u> shall pass over you, till you know that the Most High rules in the kingdom of men, and gives it to whomsoever He will.

26 And whereas they commanded to leave the stump of the tree roots; your kingdom shall be <u>sure</u> to you, after that you shall have known that the heavens do rule.   <small>assured</small>

27 Wherefore, O king, let my counsel be acceptable to you, and break off your sins by righteousness, and your iniquities by showing mercy to the poor; if it may be a lengthening of your tranquillity.

28 All this came upon the king Neb-u-chad-nez'zar.

29 At the end of twelve months he walked in the palace of the kingdom of Bab'y-lon.

30 The king spoke, and said, Is not this great Bab'y-lon, that I have built for the house of the kingdom by the might of my power, and for the honor of my majesty?

31 While the word *was* in the king's mouth, there fell a voice from heaven, *saying*, O king Neb-u-chad-nez'zar, to you it is spoken; The kingdom is <u>departed</u> from you.   <small>removed</small>

32 And they shall drive you from men, and your dwelling *shall be* with the beasts of the field: they shall make you to eat grass as oxen, and seven <u>times</u> shall pass over you, until you know that the Most High rules in the kingdom of men, and gives it to whomsoever He will.   <small>periods of time</small>

33 The same hour was the thing fulfilled upon Neb-u-chad-nez'zar: and he was driven from men, and did eat grass as oxen, and his body was wet with the

dew of heaven, till his hairs were grown like eagles' *feathers*, and his nails like birds' *claws*.

34 And at the end of the days I Neb-u-chad-nez'zar lifted up my eyes to heaven, and my understanding returned to me, and I blessed the Most High, and I praised and honored Him that lives for ever, whose dominion *is* an everlasting dominion, and His kingdom *is* from generation to generation:

35 And all the inhabitants of the earth *are* <u>reputed</u> as nothing: and He does according to His will in the army of heaven, and *among* the inhabitants of the earth: and none can <u>stay</u> His hand, or say to Him, What do You? accounted - stop

36 At the same time my reason returned to me; and for the glory of my kingdom, my honor and brightness returned to me; and my counselors and my lords sought to me; and I was established in my kingdom, and excellent majesty was added to me.

37 Now I Neb-u-chad-nez'zar praise and extol and honor the King of heaven, all whose works *are* truth, and His ways judgment: and those that walk in pride He is able to <u>abase</u>. humble

CHAPTER 5

BEL-SHAZ'ZAR the king made a great feast to a thousand of his lords, and drank wine before the thousand.

2 Bel-shaz'zar, whiles he tasted the wine, commanded to bring the golden and silver vessels which his <u>father</u> Neb-u-chad-nez'zar had taken out of the temple which *was* in Je-ru'sa-lem; that the king, and his princes, his wives, and his concubines, might drink therein. i.e., grandfather

3 Then they brought the golden vessels that were taken out of the temple of the house of God which *was* at Je-ru'sa-lem; and the king, and his princes, his wives, and his concubines, drank in them.

4 They drank wine, and praised the gods of gold, and of silver, of brass, of iron, of wood, and of stone.

5 In the same hour came forth fingers of a man's hand, and wrote opposite the candlestick upon the plaster of the wall of the king's palace: and the king saw the part of the hand that wrote.

6 Then the king's countenance was changed, and his thoughts troubled him, so that the joints of his loins were loosed, and his knees smote one against another.

7 The king cried <u>aloud</u> to bring in the <u>astrologers</u>, the Chal-de'ans, and the soothsayers. *And* the king spoke, and said to the wise *men* of Bab'y-lon, Whosoever shall read this writing, and <u>show</u> me the interpretation thereof, shall be clothed with scarlet, and *have* a chain of gold about his neck, and shall be the <u>third</u> ruler in the kingdom.

urgently - conjurers - declare to - i.e., third in command

8 Then came in all the king's wise *men*: but they could not read the writing, nor make known to the king the interpretation thereof.

9 Then was king Bel-shaz'zar greatly troubled, and his <u>countenance</u> was

changed in him, and his lords were <u>astonished</u>. complexion - perplexed

10 *Now* the queen, by reason of the words of the king and his lords, came into the banquet house: *and* the queen spoke and said, O king, live for ever: let not your thoughts trouble you, nor let your <u>countenance</u> be changed: complexion

G5 11 There is a man in your kingdom, in whom *is* the spirit of the holy gods; and in the days of your <u>father</u> light and understanding and wisdom, like the wisdom of the gods, was found in him; whom the king Neb-u-chad-nez'zar your father, the king, *I say*, your father, made master of the magicians, astrologers, Chal-de'ans, *and* soothsayers; i.e., grandfather

12 Forasmuch as an excellent spirit, and knowledge, and understanding, interpreting of dreams, and showing of hard sentences, and dissolving of doubts, were found in the same Dan'iel, whom the king named Bel-te-shaz'zar: now let Dan'iel be called, and he will show the interpretation.

13 Then was Dan'iel brought in before the king. *And* the king spoke and said to Dan'iel, *Are* you that Dan'iel, which *are* of the children of the captivity of Ju'dah, whom the king my <u>father</u> brought out of Jew'ry?

14 I have even heard of you, that the spirit of the gods *is* in you, and *that* 1280 light and understanding and excellent wisdom is found in you.

15 And now the wise *men*, the <u>astrologers</u>, have been brought in before me, that they should read this writing, and make known to me the interpretation thereof: but they could not show the interpretation of the thing: conjurers

16 And I have heard of you, that you can <u>make</u> interpretations, and dissolve doubts: now if you can read the writing, and make known to me the interpretation thereof, you shall be clothed with scarlet, and *have* a chain of gold about your neck, and shall be the <u>third</u> ruler in the kingdom. give - 1st. Nabonidus, 2nd. BelShazzar, 3rd. Daniel

17 Then Dan'iel answered and said before the king, Let your gifts be to yourself, and give your rewards to another; yet I will read the writing to the king, and make known to him the interpretation.

18 O you king, the <u>Most High God</u> gave Neb-u-chad-nez'zar your <u>father</u> a kingdom, and majesty, and glory, and honor: Elaha^{p.f.} Illaya (Aram.) - i.e., grandfather

19 And for the majesty that He gave him, all people, nations, and languages, trembled and <u>feared</u> before him: whom he would he slew; and whom he would he kept alive; and whom he would he set up; and whom he would he put down. were afraid

20 But when his heart <u>was lifted up</u>, and his mind hardened in pride, he was deposed from his kingly throne, and they took his glory from him: became arrogant

21 And he was driven from the sons of men; and his heart was made like the beasts, and his dwelling *was* with the wild asses: they fed him with grass like oxen, and his body was wet with the dew of heaven; till he <u>knew</u> that the <u>Most High God</u> ruled in the kingdom

of men, and *that* He appoints over it whomsoever He will. _{i.e., recognized}

22 And you his <u>son</u>, O Bel-shaz'zar, have not humbled your heart, though you knew all this; _{i.e., grandson}

23 But have lifted up yourself against the Lord of heaven; and they have brought the vessels of His house before you, and you, and your lords, your wives, and your concubines, have drunk wine in them; and you have praised the gods of silver, and gold, of brass, iron, wood, and stone, which see not, nor hear, nor know: and the <u>God</u> in whose hand your breath *is*, and whose *are* all your ways, have you not glorified: _{Elaha^{s.f.}}

24 Then was the part of the hand sent from Him; and this writing was written.

25 And this *is* the writing that was written, ME'NE, ME'NE, TE'KEL, U-PHAR'SIN.

26 This *is* the interpretation of the <u>thing</u>: ME'NE; <u>God</u> has numbered your kingdom, and finished it. _{message}

27 TE'KEL; You are weighed in the balances, and are found wanting.

28 PE'RES; Your kingdom is divided, and given to the Medes and Per'sians.

29 Then commanded Bel-shaz'zar, and they clothed Dan'iel with scarlet, and *put* a chain of gold about his neck, and made a proclamation concerning him, that he should be the <u>third</u> ruler in the kingdom. _{1st. Nabonidus, 2nd. BelShazzar, 3rd. Daniel}

30 In that night was Bel-shaz'zar the king of the Chal-de'ans slain.

31 And Da-ri'us the Me'di-an took the kingdom, *being* about <u>three-score and two</u> years old. ₆₂

CHAPTER 6

IT pleased Da-ri'us to set over the kingdom an hundred and twenty princes, which should be over the whole kingdom;

2 And over these three presidents; of whom Dan'iel *was* first: that the princes might <u>give accounts</u> to them, and the king should have no <u>damage</u>. _{be accountable - loss}

3 Then this Dan'iel was preferred above the presidents and princes, because an excellent spirit *was* in him; and the king thought to set him over the whole realm. _{G5 1311}

4 Then the presidents and princes sought to find occasion against Dan'iel concerning the kingdom; but they could find none occasion nor fault; forasmuch as he *was* faithful, neither was there any error or fault found in him.

5 Then said these men, We shall not find any occasion against this Dan'iel, except we find *it* against him concerning the law of his <u>God</u>. _{Elah^{s.f.}}

6 Then these presidents and princes assembled together to the king, and said thus to him, King Da-ri'us, live for ever.

7 All the presidents of the kingdom, the governors, and the princes, the counselors, and the captains, have consulted together to establish a royal <u>statute</u>, and to make a firm decree, that whosoever shall ask a petition of any god or man for thirty days, save of you, O king, he shall be cast into the den of lions. _{edict}

8 Now, O king, establish the decree,

and sign the writing, that it be not changed, according to the law of the Medes and Per'sians, which alters not.

9 Wherefore king Da-ri'us signed the writing and the decree.

10 Now when Dan'iel knew that the writing was signed, he went into his house; and his windows being open in his <u>chamber</u> toward Je-ru'sa-lem, he kneeled upon his knees three times a day, and prayed, and gave thanks before his <u>God</u>, as he did aforetime. room - Elah^{s.f.}

11 Then these men assembled, and found Dan'iel praying and making supplication before his <u>God</u>.

12 Then they came near, and spoke before the king concerning the king's decree; Have you not signed a decree, that every man that shall ask *a petition* of any <u>God</u> or man within thirty days, save of you, O king, shall be cast into the den of lions? The king answered and said, The thing *is* true, according to the law of the Medes and Per'sians, which alters not.

13 Then answered they and said before the king, That Dan'iel, which *is* of the children of the captivity of Ju'dah, regards not you, O king, nor the decree that you have signed, but makes his petition three times a day.

14 Then the king, when he heard *these* words, was <u>sore</u> displeased with himself, and set *his* <u>heart</u> on Dan'iel to deliver him: and he <u>labored</u> till the going down of the sun to deliver him. mind - made every effort

15 Then these men assembled to the king, and said to the king, Know, O king, that the law of the Medes and Per'sians *is*, That no decree nor <u>statute</u> which the king established may be changed. edict

16 Then the king commanded, and they brought Dan'iel, and cast *him* into the den of lions. *Now* the king spoke and said to Dan'iel, Your <u>God</u> whom you serve continually, He will deliver you. Elah^{s.f.}

17 And a stone was brought, and laid upon the mouth of the den; and the king sealed it with his own signet, and with the signet of his lords; that the purpose might not be changed concerning Dan'iel.

18 Then the king went to his palace, and passed the night fasting: neither were instruments of music brought before him: and his sleep went from him.

19 Then the king arose very early in the morning, and went in haste to the den of lions.

20 And when he came to the den, he cried with a <u>lamentable</u> voice to Dan'iel: *and* the king spoke and said to Dan'iel, O Dan'iel, servant of the living <u>God</u>, is your <u>God</u>, whom you serve continually, able to deliver you from the lions? pained

21 Then said Dan'iel to the king, O king, live for ever.

22 My <u>God</u> has sent His <u>angel</u>, and has shut the lions' mouths, that they have not hurt me: forasmuch as before Him innocency was found in me; and also before you, O king, have I done no hurt. Elah^{s.f.} - messenger

23 Then was the king exceeding glad for him, and commanded that they should take Dan'iel up out of the den. So Dan'iel was taken up out of the den, and no manner of hurt was found upon him, because he believed in his God.

24 And the king commanded, and they brought those men which had accused Dan'iel, and they cast *them* into the den of lions, them, their children, and their wives; and the lions had the mastery of them, and broke all their bones in pieces or ever they came at the bottom of the den.

25 Then king Da-ri'us wrote to all people, nations, and languages, that dwell in all the earth; Peace be multiplied to you.

26 I make a decree, That in every dominion of my kingdom men tremble and <u>fear</u> before the <u>God</u> of Dan'iel: for He *is* the living <u>God</u>, and steadfast for ever, and His kingdom *that* which shall not be destroyed, and His dominion *shall be even* to the end.   reverence - Elaha^{p.f.}

27 He delivers and rescues, and He works signs and wonders in heaven and in earth, who has delivered Dan'iel from the power of the lions.

28 So this Dan'iel prospered in the reign of Da-ri'us, and in the reign of Cy'rus the Per'sian.

CHAPTER 7

IN the first year of Bel-shaz'zar king of Bab'y-lon Dan'iel had a dream and visions of his head upon his bed: then he wrote the dream, *and* <u>told</u> the sum of the matters.   summarized

2 Dan'iel spoke and said, I saw in my vision by night, and, behold, the four winds of the heaven strove upon the great sea.

3 And four great beasts came up from the sea, diverse one from another.

4 The <u>first</u> *was* like a lion, and had eagle's wings: I beheld till the wings thereof were plucked, and it was lifted up from the earth, and made stand upon the feet as a man, and a man's <u>heart</u> was given to it.   i.e., Babylon - i.e., mind

5 And behold another beast, a <u>second</u>, like to a bear, and it raised up itself on one side, and *it had* three ribs in the mouth of it between the teeth of it: and they said thus to it, Arise, devour much flesh.   i.e., Medo-Persia (v 20)

6 After this I beheld, and lo <u>another</u>, like a leopard, which had upon the back of it four wings of a fowl; the beast had also four <u>heads</u>; and dominion was given to it. i.e., Greece - i.e., officers under Alexander

7 After this I saw in the night visions, and behold a <u>fourth</u> beast, dreadful and <u>terrible</u>, and strong exceedingly; and it had great iron teeth: it devoured and broke in pieces, and stamped the <u>residue</u> with the feet of it: and it *was* diverse from all the beasts that *were* before it; and it had ten <u>horns</u>. i.e.,
Roman - terrifying - remainder - Nations from Roman empire

8 I considered the <u>horns</u>, and, behold, there came up among them another <u>little horn</u>, before whom there were three of the first <u>horns</u> plucked up by the

roots: and, behold, in this <u>horn</u> *were* eyes like the eyes of man, and a mouth speaking great things. REV. 13:1-5 i.e., kings of nations - i.e., king - ruler i.e., antichrist

9 I beheld till the thrones were cast down, and the <u>Ancient of days</u> did sit, whose garment *was* white as snow, and the hair of His head like the pure wool: His throne *was like* the fiery flame, *and* His wheels *as* burning fire. i.e., God Elohim[p.f.] (Father)

10 A fiery stream issued and came forth from before Him: thousand thousands ministered to Him, and ten thousand times ten thousand stood before Him: the judgment was set, and the books were opened. REV. 5:11 - REV. 20:12

11 I beheld then because of the voice of the great words which the <u>horn</u> spoke: I beheld *even* till the beast was slain, and his body destroyed, and given to the burning flame. ruler (antichrist)

12 As concerning the rest of the beasts, they had their dominion taken away: yet their lives were prolonged for a <u>season</u> and time. period of time

13 I saw in the night visions, and, behold, *one* like the Son of man came with the clouds of heaven, and came to the <u>Ancient of days</u>, and they brought Him near before Him. MATT. 24:30 MATT 26:64 MARK 13:26 MARK 14:62 REV. 1:7 i.e., Jesus Christ - God Elohim[p.f.] (Father)

14 And there was given Him dominion, and glory, and a kingdom, that all people, nations, and languages, should serve Him: His dominion *is* an everlasting dominion, which shall not pass away, and His kingdom *that* which shall not be destroyed. JOHN 12:34 REV. 11:15

15 I Dan'iel was grieved in my spirit <u>in the midst of *my* body</u>, and the visions of my head troubled me. i.e., within me

16 I came near to one of them that stood by, and asked him the truth of all this. So he told me, and made me know the interpretation of the things.

17 These great beasts, which are four, *are* four kings, *which* shall arise out of the earth.

18 But the <u>saints</u> of the <u>Most High</u> shall take the kingdom, and possess the kingdom for ever, even for ever and ever. holy ones-believers - "Chal." Heleyonin

19 Then I would know the truth of the <u>fourth</u> beast, which was <u>diverse</u> from all the others, exceeding dreadful, whose teeth *were of* iron, and his nails *of* brass; *which* devoured, broke in pieces, and stamped the residue with his feet; Roman empire - different

20 And of the ten <u>horns</u> that *were* in his head, and *of* the other which came up, and before whom three fell; even *of* that <u>horn</u> that had eyes, and a mouth that spoke very great things, whose look *was* more stout than his fellows. REV. 17:12 nations out of Roman empire - ruler antichrist

21 I beheld, and the same horn made war with the <u>saints</u>, and prevailed against them; holy ones-believers

22 Until the <u>Ancient of days</u> came, and judgment was given to the <u>saints</u> of the <u>Most High</u>; and the time came that the <u>saints</u> possessed the kingdom. God i.e., Elohim[p.f.] (Father) - "Chal." Heleyonin

23 Thus he said, The <u>fourth</u> beast shall be the <u>fourth</u> kingdom upon earth, which shall be diverse from all kingdoms, and shall devour the whole earth,

and shall tread it down, and break it in pieces. Roman empire

24 And the ten horns out of this kingdom *are* ten kings *that* shall arise: and <u>another</u> shall rise after them; and he shall be <u>diverse</u> from the first, and he shall subdue three kings. REV. 17:12 REV. 13:1 ruler-antichrist - different

25 And he shall speak *great* words against the <u>Most High</u>, and shall <u>wear out</u> the <u>saints</u> of the <u>Most High</u>, and think to change times and laws: and they shall be given into his hand until a time and times and the dividing of time. 2 THESS. 2:3 "Chal." Heleyonin (Elohim$^{p.f.}$) - i.e., oppress - holy ones-believers

26 But the <u>judgment</u> shall sit, and they shall take away <u>his</u> dominion, to consume and to destroy *it* to the end. i.e., court - ruler-antichrist

27 And the kingdom and dominion, and the greatness of the kingdom under the whole heaven, shall be given to the people of the <u>saints</u> of the <u>Most High</u>, whose kingdom *is* an everlasting kingdom, and all dominions shall serve and obey Him. believers

28 So far *is* the end of the matter. As for me Dan'iel, my <u>cogitations</u> much troubled me, and my <u>countenance</u> changed in me: but I kept the matter in my heart. thoughts - complexion grew pale

CHAPTER 8

IN the third year of the reign of king Bel-shaz'zar a vision appeared to me, *even to* me Dan'iel, after that which appeared to me at the first.

2 And I saw in a vision; and it came to pass, when I saw, that I *was* at Shu'shan *in* the palace, which *is* in the prov-ince of E'lam; and I saw in a vision, and I was by the river of U'la-i.

3 Then I lifted up my eyes, and saw, and, behold, there stood before the river a <u>ram</u> which had *two* horns: and the *two* horns *were* high; but one *was* higher than the other, and the higher came up last. Medo-Persia - Cyrus, Darius

4 I saw the <u>ram</u> pushing westward, and northward, and southward; so that no beasts might stand before him, neither *was there any* that could deliver out of his hand; but he did according to his will, and <u>became great</u>. magnified himself

5 And as I was considering, behold, an <u>he goat</u> came from the west on the face of the whole earth, and <u>touched not</u> the ground: and the goat *had* a <u>notable</u> horn between his eyes. Alexander of Greece - moved fast - conspicuous

6 And he came to the <u>ram</u> that had *two* horns, which I had seen standing before the river, and ran to him in the fury of his power. Medo-Persia (v 20) - Cyrus, Darius

7 And I saw him come close to the ram, and he was moved with <u>choler</u> against him, and smote the <u>ram</u>, and broke his <u>two horns</u>: and there was no power in the <u>ram</u> to stand before him, but he cast him down to the ground, and <u>stamped</u> upon him: and there was none that could deliver the ram out of his hand. enraged and bitter - defeated them

8 Therefore the <u>he goat</u> <u>waxed</u> very great: and when he was strong, the <u>great horn</u> was broken; and <u>for it</u> came up four <u>notable ones</u> toward the four winds of heaven. Alexander - grew - Alexander, died age 33 - succeeding Alexander - officers under Alexander

9 And out of one of them came forth a <u>little horn</u>, which <u>waxed</u> exceeding great, toward the south, and toward the east, and toward the pleasant *land*. a ruler - grew
10 And it <u>waxed</u> great, *even* to the host of heaven; and it cast down *some* of the host and of the stars to the ground, and <u>stamped</u> upon them. grew - against - defeated
11 Yea, he magnified *himself* even to the prince of the host, and by him the daily *sacrifice* was taken away, and the place of His sanctuary was cast down.
12 And an host was given *him* against the daily *sacrifice* by reason of transgression, and it cast down the truth to the ground; and it practised, and prospered.
13 Then I heard one <u>saint</u> speaking, and another <u>saint</u> said to that certain *saint* which spoke, How long *shall be* the vision *concerning* the daily *sacrifice*, and the transgression of desolation, to <u>give</u> both the sanctuary and the host to be trodden under foot? holy one-believers - allow
14 And he said to me, To two thousand and three hundred days; then shall the sanctuary be <u>cleansed</u>. put right
15 And it came to pass, when I, *even* I Dan'iel, had seen the vision, and sought for the meaning, then, behold, there stood before me as the appearance of a man.
16 And I heard a man's voice between *the banks of* U'la-i, which called, and said, Ga'bri-el, make this *man* to understand the vision. LUKE 1:19
17 So he came near where I stood: and when he came, I was afraid, and

fell upon my face: but he said to me, Understand, O son of man: for at the time of the end *shall be* the vision.
18 Now as he was speaking with me, I was in a deep sleep on my face toward the ground: but he touched me, and <u>set me upright</u>. made me stand
19 And he said, Behold, I will make you know what shall be in the last end of the indignation: for at the time appointed the end *shall be*.
20 The ram which you saw having *two* <u>horns</u> *are* the kings of Me'di-a and Per'sia. Cyrus, Darius
21 And the rough goat *is* the <u>king</u> of Gre'cia: and the <u>great horn</u> that *is* between his eyes *is* the first king. Greece - Alexander
22 Now that being broken, whereas four stood up for it, four kingdoms shall stand up out of the nation, but not in his power.
23 And in the latter time of their kingdom, when the transgressors <u>are come to the full</u>, <u>a king</u> of fierce countenance, and understanding dark sentences, shall stand up. have run their course - antichrist
24 And his power shall be mighty, but not by his own power: and he shall destroy wonderfully, and shall prosper, and practise, and shall destroy the mighty and the holy people.
25 And through his policy also he shall cause craft to prosper in his hand; and he shall magnify *himself* in his heart, and by <u>peace</u> shall destroy many: he shall also stand up against the <u>Prince of princes</u>; but he shall be broken without hand. prosperity - God-Christ

26 And the vision of the evening and the morning which was told *is* true: wherefore <u>shut you up</u> the vision; for it *shall be* for many days. keep to yourself
27 And I Dan'iel fainted, and was sick *certain* days; afterward I rose up, and did the king's business; and I was astonished at the vision, but none understood *it*.

CHAPTER 9

IN the first year of Da-ri'us the son of A-has-u-e'rus, <u>of the seed</u> of the Medes, which was made king over the realm of the Chal-de'ans; descendants
2 In the first year of his reign I Dan'iel understood by books the number of the years, whereof the word of the LORD came to Jer-e-mi'ah the prophet, that He would accomplish seventy years in the <u>desolations</u> of Je-ru'sa-lem. ruin
3 And I set my face to the <u>Lord God</u>, to seek by prayer and supplications, with fasting, and sackcloth, and ashes: Adonay^p.f. Jehovah
4 And I prayed to the <u>LORD</u> my <u>God</u>, and made my confession, and said, O <u>Lord</u>, the great and <u>dreadful God</u>, keeping the <u>covenant</u> and mercy to them that love Him, and to them that keep His commandments;
Jehovah^s.f. - Elohim^p.f. - Adonay^p.f. awesome - El^s.f. agreement
5 We have sinned, and have <u>committed iniquity</u>, and have done wickedly, and have rebelled, even by departing from Your <u>precepts</u> and from Your judgments: done wrong - commands
6 Neither have we hearkened to Your servants the prophets, which spoke in Your name to our kings, our princes, and our fathers, and to all the people of the land.
7 O Lord, righteousness *belongs* to You, but to us <u>confusion</u> of faces, as at this day; to the men of Ju'dah, and to the inhabitants of Je-ru'sa-lem, and to all Is'ra-el, *that are* near, and *that are* far off, through all the countries to which You have driven them, because of their trespass that they have trespassed against You. shame
8 O Lord, to us *belongs* <u>confusion</u> of face, to our kings, to our princes, and to our fathers, because we have sinned against You. shame
9 To the <u>Lord</u> our <u>God</u> *belong* mercies and forgivenesses, though we have rebelled against Him; Adonay^p.f. - Elohim^p.f.
10 Neither have we obeyed the voice of the LORD our <u>God</u>, to walk in His laws, which He set before us by His servants the prophets. Elohim^p.f.
11 Yea, all Is'ra-el have transgressed Your law, even by departing, that they might not obey Your voice; therefore the curse is poured upon us, and the oath that *is* written in the law of Mo'ses the servant of <u>God</u>, because we have sinned against Him.
12 And He has confirmed His words, which He spoke against us, and against our judges that judged us, by bringing upon us a great evil: for under the whole heaven has not been done as has been done upon Je-ru'sa-lem.
13 As *it is* written in the law of Mo'ses, all this evil is come upon us: yet <u>made we not our prayer before</u> the

LORD our God, that we might turn from our iniquities, and understand your truth. we have not sought the favor of - sins

14 Therefore has the LORD watched upon the evil, and brought it upon us: for the LORD our God *is* righteous in all His works which He does: for we obeyed not His voice. Elohim^p.f.

15 And now, O Lord our God, that has brought Your people forth out of the land of E'gypt with a mighty hand, and have gotten You renown, as at this day; we have sinned, we have done wickedly. Adonay^p.f. - Elohim^p.f. made a name for Thyself

16 O Lord, according to all Your righteousness, I beseech You, let Your anger and Your fury be turned away from Your city Je-ru'sa-lem, Your holy mountain: because for our sins, and for the iniquities of our fathers, Je-ru'sa-lem and Your people *are become* a reproach to all *that are* about us. beg

17 Now therefore, O our God, hear the prayer of Your servant, and his supplications, and cause Your face to shine upon Your sanctuary that is desolate, for the Lord's sake. Elohim^p.f. look with favor - in ruins

18 O my God, incline Your ear, and hear; open Your eyes, and behold our desolations, and the city which is called by Your name: for we do not present our supplications before You for our righteousnesses, but for Your great mercies.

19 O Lord, hear; O Lord, forgive; O Lord, hearken and do; defer not, for Your own sake, O my God: for Your city and Your people are called by Your name. Adonay^p.f. - Elohim^p.f.

20 And while I *was* speaking, and praying, and confessing my sin and the sin of my people Is'ra-el, and presenting my supplication before the LORD my God for the holy mountain of my God; Elohim^p.f.

21 Yea, while I *was* speaking in prayer, even the man Ga'bri-el, whom I had seen in the vision at the beginning, being caused to fly swiftly, touched me about the time of the evening oblation. come - offering

22 And he informed *me*, and talked with me, and said, O Dan'iel, I am now come forth to give you skill and understanding.

23 At the beginning of your supplications the commandment came forth, and I am come to show *you*; for you *are* greatly beloved: therefore understand the matter, and consider the vision.

24 Seventy weeks are determined upon your people and upon your holy city, to finish the transgression, and to make an end of sins, and to make reconciliation for iniquity, and to bring in everlasting righteousness, and to seal up the vision and prophecy, and to anoint the most Holy. Or, units of seven

25 Know therefore and understand, *that* from the going forth of the commandment to restore and to build Je-ru'sa-lem to the Mes-si'ah the Prince *shall be* seven weeks, and threescore and two weeks: the street shall be built again, and the wall, even in troublous times. JOHN 1:41 62

26 And after threescore and two weeks shall Mes-si'ah be cut off, but not for Himself: and the people of the

prince that shall come shall destroy the city and the sanctuary; and the end thereof *shall be* with a flood, and to the end of the war desolations are determined. i.e., killed

27 And <u>he</u> shall confirm the <u>covenant</u> with many for <u>one week</u>: and in the <u>midst</u> of the week he shall cause the sacrifice and the <u>oblation</u> to cease, and for the overspreading of <u>abominations</u> he shall make *it* desolate, even until the consummation, and that determined shall be poured upon the desolate. MATT.

24:15 MARK 13:14 i.e., antichrist - agreement - period of 7 years - 42 months-3 ½ years - offering - detestable things

CHAPTER 10

IN the third year of Cy'rus king of Per'sia a <u>thing</u> was revealed to Dan'iel, whose name was called Bel-te-shaz'zar; and the <u>thing</u> *was* true, but the time appointed *was* <u>long</u>: and he understood the thing, and had understanding of the vision. message - one of a great conflict

2 In those days I Dan'iel was mourning three full weeks.

3 I ate no <u>pleasant bread</u>, neither came flesh nor wine in my mouth, neither did I anoint myself at all, till three whole weeks were fulfilled. tasty food

4 And in the four and twentieth day of the first month, as I was by the side of the great river, which *is* Hid'de-kel;

5 Then I lifted up my eyes, and looked, and behold a certain man clothed in linen, whose loins *were* girded with <u>fine</u> gold of U'phaz: pure

6 His body also *was* like the beryl, and his face as the appearance of light-

ning, and his eyes as lamps of fire, and his arms and his feet like in color to polished brass, and the voice of his words like the voice of a multitude.

7 And I Dan'iel alone saw the vision: for the men that were with me saw not the vision; but a great quaking fell upon them, so that they fled to hide themselves.

8 Therefore I was left alone, and saw this great vision, and there remained no strength in me: for my <u>comeliness</u> was turned in me into <u>corruption</u>, and I retained no strength. splendor - deathly pale

9 Yet heard I the voice of his words: and when I heard the voice of his words, then was I in a deep sleep on my face, and my face toward the ground.

10 And, behold, an hand touched me, which set me upon my knees and *upon* the palms of my hands.

11 And he said to me, O Dan'iel, a man greatly beloved, understand the words that I speak to you, and stand upright: for to you am I now sent. And when he had spoken this word to me, I stood trembling.

12 Then said he to me, Fear not, Dan'iel: for from the first day that you did set your heart to understand, and to chasten yourself before your <u>God</u>, your words were heard, and I am come for your words. Elohim^{p.f.}

13 But the <u>prince</u> of the kingdom of Per'sia withstood me one and twenty days: but, lo, <u>Mi'chael</u>, one of the chief princes, came to help me; and I remained there with the kings of Per'sia.

JUDE 9 REV. 12:7 satans representative - prince of God

14 Now I am come to make you understand what shall befall your people in the latter days: for yet the vision *is* for *many* days.

15 And when he had spoken such words to me, I <u>set</u> my face toward the ground, and I became <u>dumb</u>. turned - speechless

16 And, behold, *one* like the similitude of <u>the sons of men</u> touched my lips: then I opened my mouth, and spoke, and said to him that stood before me, O my lord, by the vision my sorrows are turned upon me, and I have retained no strength. a human being

17 For how can the servant of this my lord talk with this my lord? for as for me, immediately there remained no strength in me, neither is there breath left in me.

18 Then there came again and touched me *one* like the appearance of a man, and he strengthened me,

19 And said, O man greatly beloved, fear not: peace *be* to you, be strong, yea, be strong. And when he had spoken to me, I was strengthened, and said, Let my lord speak; for you have strengthened me.

20 Then said he, Know you <u>wherefore</u> I come to you? and now will I return to fight with the prince of Per'sia: and when I am gone forth, lo, the prince of Gre'cia shall come. why

21 But I will show you that which is noted in the scripture of truth: and *there is* none that holds with me in these things, but Mi'chael your <u>prince</u>. i.e., of God

CHAPTER 11

ALSO I in the first year of Da-ri'us the Mede, *even* I, stood to confirm and to strengthen him.

2 And now will I show you the truth. Behold, there shall stand up yet three kings in Per'sia; and the fourth shall be far richer than *they* all: and by his strength through his riches he shall stir up all against the realm of Gre'cia.

3 And a mighty king shall stand up, that shall rule with great dominion, and do according to his will.

4 And when he shall stand up, his kingdom shall be broken, and shall be divided toward the four winds of heaven; and not to his <u>posterity</u>, nor according to his dominion which he ruled: for his kingdom shall be plucked up, even for others beside those. descendants

5 And the king of the south shall be strong, and *one* of his princes; and he shall be strong above him, and have dominion; his dominion *shall be* a great dominion.

6 And in the end of years they shall <u>join themselves together</u>; for the king's daughter of the south shall come to the king of the north to make an agreement: but she shall not retain the power of the arm; neither shall he stand, nor his arm: but she shall be given up, and they that brought her, and he that fathered her, and he that strengthened her in *these* times. form an alliance

7 But out of a branch of her roots shall *one* stand up in his estate, which shall come with an army, and shall enter into the fortress of the king of the

north, and shall deal against them, and shall prevail:

8 And shall also carry captives into E'gypt their gods, with their princes, *and* with their precious vessels of silver and of gold; and he shall continue *more* years than the king of the north.

9 So the king of the south shall come into *his* kingdom, and shall return into his own land.

10 But his sons shall <u>be stirred up</u>, and shall assemble a multitude of great forces: and *one* shall certainly come, and overflow, and pass through: then shall he return, and be stirred up, *even* to his fortress. <small>mobilize</small>

11 And the king of the south shall be <u>moved with choler</u>, and shall come forth and fight with him, *even* with the king of the north: and he shall set forth a great multitude; but the multitude shall be given into his hand. <small>enraged</small>

12 *And* when he has taken away the multitude, his heart shall be lifted up; and he shall cast down *many* ten thousands: but he shall not be strengthened *by it*.

13 For the king of the north shall return, and shall set forth a multitude greater than the former, and shall certainly come after certain years with a great army and with much riches.

14 And in those times there shall many stand up against the king of the south: also the robbers of your people shall exalt themselves to <u>establish</u> the vision; but they shall fall. <small>fulfill</small>

15 So the king of the north shall come, and cast up a mount, and take the most <u>fenced</u> cities: and the <u>arms</u> of the south shall not <u>withstand</u>, neither his chosen people, neither *shall there be any* strength to withstand. <small>fortified - forces - stand their ground</small>

16 But he that comes against him shall do according to his own will, and none shall stand before him: and he shall stand in the <u>glorious land</u>, which by his hand shall be <u>consumed</u>. <small>i.e.Judah - conquered</small>

17 He shall also set his face to enter with the strength of his whole kingdom, and upright ones with him; thus shall he do: and he shall give him the daughter of women, corrupting her: but she shall not stand *on his side*, neither be for him.

18 After this shall he turn his face to the isles, and shall take many: but a prince for his own behalf shall cause the reproach offered by him to cease; without his own reproach he shall cause *it* to turn upon him.

19 Then he shall turn his face toward the fort of his own land: but he shall stumble and fall, and not be found.

20 Then shall stand up in his <u>estate</u> a raiser of taxes *in* the glory of the kingdom: but within few days he shall be destroyed, neither in anger, nor in battle. <small>place</small>

21 And in his <u>estate</u> shall stand up a vile person, to whom they shall not give the honor of the kingdom: but he shall come in <u>peaceably</u>, and obtain the kingdom by flatteries. <small>in a time of tranquillity</small>

22 And with the <u>arms</u> of a flood shall they be overflown from before him, and

shall be broken; yea, also the prince of the <u>covenant</u>. _{forces - agreement}

23 And after the league *made* with him he shall work deceitfully: for he shall come up, and shall become strong with a small people.

24 He shall enter <u>peaceably</u> even upon the <u>fattest</u> places of the province; and he shall do *that* which his fathers have not done, nor his fathers' fathers; he shall scatter among them the prey, and spoil, and riches: *yea*, and he shall <u>forecast his devices</u> against the strong holds, even for a time. _{richest - devise his schemes}

25 And he shall <u>stir</u> up his power and his courage against the king of the south with a great army; and the king of the south shall be <u>stirred</u> up to battle with a very great and mighty army; but he shall not <u>stand</u>: for they shall <u>forecast devices</u> against him. _{call - win - predict}

26 Yea, they that feed of the portion of his <u>meat</u> shall destroy him, and his army shall overflow: and many shall fall down slain. _{food}

27 And both these kings' hearts *shall be* to do mischief, and they shall speak lies at one table; but it shall not prosper: for yet the end *shall be* at the time appointed.

28 Then shall he return into his land with great riches; and his heart *shall be* against the holy <u>covenant</u>; and he shall do *exploits*, and return to his own land. _{agreement}

29 At the time appointed he shall return, and come toward the south; but it shall not be as the former, or as the latter.

30 For the ships of Chit'tim shall come against him: therefore he shall be grieved, and return, and have indignation against the holy <u>covenant</u>: so shall he do; he shall even return, and have intelligence with them that forsake the holy <u>covenant</u>. _{agreement}

31 And <u>arms</u> shall stand on his part, and they shall pollute the sanctuary of strength, and shall take away the daily *sacrifice*, and they shall place the <u>abomination</u> that makes desolate.

_{MATT. 24:15 MARK 13:14 forces - detestable things}

32 And such as do wickedly against the <u>covenant</u> shall he <u>corrupt</u> by flatteries: but the people that do know their <u>God</u> shall be strong, and do *exploits*. _{turn to godlessness - Elohim^{p.f.}}

33 And they that understand among the people shall instruct many: yet they shall fall by the sword, and by flame, by captivity, and by spoil, *many* days.

34 Now when they shall fall, they shall be helped with a little help: but many shall cling to them with flatteries.

35 And *some* of them of understanding shall fall, to <u>try</u> them, and to purge, and to make *them* white, *even* to the time of the end: because *it is* yet for a time appointed. _{test}

36 And the king shall do according to his will; and he shall exalt himself, and magnify himself above every god, and shall speak marvellous things against the God of gods, and shall prosper till the <u>indignation</u> be accomplished: for that that is determined shall be done. _{wrath}

37 Neither shall he regard the God of

his fathers, nor the desire of women, nor regard any god: for he shall magnify himself above all.

38 But in his estate shall he honor the <u>god</u> of forces: and a god whom his fathers knew not shall he honor with gold, and silver, and with precious stones, and <u>pleasant things</u>.   Eloah^{s.f.} - treasures

39 Thus shall he do in the most strong holds with a strange god, whom he shall acknowledge *and* increase with glory: and he shall cause them to rule over many, and shall divide the land for <u>gain</u>. a price

40 And at the time of the end shall the king of the south push at him: and the king of the north shall come against him like a whirlwind, with chariots, and with horsemen, and with many ships; and he shall enter into the countries, and shall overflow and pass over.

41 He shall enter also into the <u>glorious land</u>, and many *countries* shall be overthrown: but these shall escape out of his hand, *even* E'dom, and Mo'ab, and the chief of the children of Am'mon. i.e., Judah

42 He shall <u>stretch forth his hand</u> also upon the countries: and the land of E'gypt shall not escape.   extend his power

43 But he shall have power over the treasures of gold and of silver, and over all the precious things of E'gypt: and the Lib'y-ans and the E-thi-o'pi-ans *shall be* at his steps.

44 But tidings out of the east and out of the north shall trouble him: therefore he shall go forth with great fury <u>to destroy, and utterly to make away</u> many. exterminate

45 And he shall plant the tabernacles of his palace between the seas in the glorious holy mountain; yet he shall come to his end, and none shall help him.

CHAPTER 12

AND at that time shall Mi'chael stand up, the great prince which stands for the children of your people: and there shall be a time of trouble, such as never was since there was a nation *even* to that same time: and at that time your people shall be delivered, every one that shall be found written in the book.   MATT. 24:21

2 And many of them that sleep in the dust of the earth shall awake, some to everlasting life, and some to shame *and* everlasting contempt.   MATT. 25:46   JOHN 5:29   JOHN 11:24

3 And they that <u>be wise</u> shall shine as the brightness of the firmament; and they that turn many to righteousness as the stars for ever and ever. have insights

4 But you, O Dan'iel, shut up the words, and seal the book, *even* to the time of the end: many shall run to and fro, and knowledge shall be increased.

5 Then I Dan'iel looked, and, behold, there stood other two, the one on this side of the bank of the river, and the other on that side of the bank of the river.

6 And *one* said to the man clothed in linen, which *was* upon the waters of the river, How long *shall it be to* the end of these wonders?

7 And I heard the man clothed in linen, which *was* upon the waters of the river, when he held up his right hand and his left hand to heaven, and

swear by Him that lives for ever that *it shall be* for a <u>time, times, and an half</u>; and when He shall have accomplished to scatter the power of the holy people, all these *things* shall be finished.   i.e., 3 ½ years

8 And I heard, but I understood not: then said I, O my Lord, what *shall be* the end of these *things*?

9 And he said, Go your way, Dan'iel: for the words *are* closed up and <u>sealed</u> till the time of the end.   kept secret

10 Many shall be purified, and made white, and tried; but the wicked shall do wickedly: and none of the wicked shall understand; but the wise shall understand.

11 And from the time *that* the daily *sacrifice* shall be taken away, and the <u>abomination</u> that makes desolate set up, *there shall be* a thousand two hundred and ninety days.   detestable things

12 Blessed *is* he that waits, and comes to the thousand three hundred and five and thirty days.

13 But go you your way till the end *be*: for you shall rest, and stand in your lot at the end of the days.

HOSEA

OUTLINE

Hosea's Heartbreaking Home Life, Caused by Gomer's Infidelity, Illustrates Israel's Unfaithfulness to God 1.1—3.5

The Nation Israel, Unfaithful and Unrepentant, is Challenged by the Preacher to Come Home to the Faithful God 4.1—14.9

A Holy God Suffers as He Sees the Foul Sin of Israel 4.1—7.16

A Just God Must Bring Severe Judgment 8.1—10.15

A Loving God Will Provide Restoration, Healing, Forgiveness, and Full Salvation 11.1—14.9

SURVEY

The Book of Hosea gives us the poignant pleadings of a spiritual giant desperately committed to the task of saving a sinful nation. With genuine concern the preacher seeks, over and over again, to bring conviction and repentance, so that God's chosen people may be compelled to come home to find love, forgiveness, and refreshing healing. Faithfully and graphically, Hosea points up the essentials of true religion. With powerful strokes he deals with sin and its tragic results in human lives, judgment that is automatic and disastrous, the lack of knowledge of the Lord and its destructive effect, the unquenchable love of God with its unspeakable treasures for men and women, the true nature of repentance, the certain salvation to be provided, and God's full forgiveness for all who come in genuine repentance and clear faith. The flaming evangelist knows his people. He knows what it is to sob his heart out as his unfaithful wife goes further in sin. He knows the depths of love and the willingness of a loving heart to forgive and welcome and restore. He is aware of the sacred depths of love in the heart of God. Day after day he drives home his personal, penetrating, powerful challenge to wilful sinners who must be drawn back to their God. Through this prophet, the Lord calls His wandering people home. He has mercy and pardon. Grace is plenteous. Salvation awaits them. It is amazing to find in this Old Testament age so much of the New Testament message and to find the basic call of the true evangelist. Every note is there. Every area is uncovered. Every appeal is sounded. It is God's way of doing it.

AUTHOR

The author of the book is Hosea, the son of Beeri, of Israel. Profoundly influenced by the prophet Amos, tragically hurt by the ugly unfaithfulness of his wife Gomer, keenly aware of the foul sins of his own people, sensitive to the voice of God for the sinning people, the prophet comes with poignant pleading as he seeks to call the unfaithful ones back to God. He is the divinely chosen evangelist to persuade callous sinners to come home to a loving God Who is eager to forgive and save. Hosea's ministry extended for several years following 746 B.C.

K.M.Y.

THE BOOK OF

HOSEA

"Salvation"
God Warns, Judges,
and Will Restore

CHAPTER 1

THE word of the LORD that came to Ho-se'a, the son of Be-e'ri, in the days of Uz-zi'ah, Jo'tham, A'haz, *and* Hez-e-ki'ah, kings of Ju'dah, and in the days of Jer-o-bo'am the son of Jo'ash, king of Is'ra-el.

2 The beginning of the word of the LORD by Ho-se'a. And the LORD said to Ho-se'a, Go, take to you a wife of <u>whoredoms</u> and children of <u>whoredoms</u>: for the land has committed great <u>whoredom</u>, *departing* from the LORD.   unfaithfulness

3 So he went and took Go'mer the daughter of Dib'la-im; which conceived, and bare him a son.

4 And the LORD said to him, Call his name Jez're-el; for yet a little *while*, and I will <u>avenge</u> the blood of Jez're-el upon the house of Je'hu, and will cause to cease the kingdom of the house of Is'ra-el.   punish

5 And it shall come to pass at that day, that I will break the bow of Is'ra-el in the valley of Jez're-el.

6 And she conceived again, and bare a daughter. And *God* said to him, Call her name Lo-ru'ha-mah: for I will no more have mercy upon the house of Is'ra-el; but I will utterly take them away.

7 But I will have mercy upon the house of Ju'dah, and will save them by the LORD their <u>God</u>, and will not save them by bow, nor by sword, nor by battle, by horses, nor by horsemen.   Elohim[p.f.]

8 Now when she had weaned Lo-ru'ha-mah, she conceived, and bare a son.

9 Then said *God*, Call his name Lo-am'mi: for you *are* not My people, and I will not be your *God*.

10 Yet the number of the children of Is'ra-el shall be as the sand of the sea, which cannot be measured nor numbered; and it shall come to pass, *that* in the place where it was said to them, You *are* not My people, *there* it shall be said to them, *You are* the sons of the living <u>God</u>.   ROM. 9:26 2 COR. 6:18 El[s.f.]

11 Then shall the children of Ju'dah and the children of Is'ra-el be gathered together, and appoint themselves one head, and they shall come up out of the land: for great *shall be* the day of Jez're-el.

CHAPTER 2

SAY you to your brethren, Am'mi; and to your sisters, Ru'ha-mah.

2 Plead with your mother, plead: for she *is* not My wife, neither *am* I her husband: let her therefore put away her <u>whoredoms</u> out of her sight, and her adulteries from between her breasts;   unfaithfulness

3 Less I strip her naked, and set her as in the day that she was born, and make her as a wilderness, and set her like a dry land, and slay her with thirst.

4 And I will not have mercy upon her children; for they *be* the children of <u>whoredoms</u>.   unfaithfulness

5 For their mother has played the harlot: she that conceived them has done shamefully: for she said, I will go after my lovers, that give *me* my bread and my water, my wool and my flax, mine oil and my drink.

6 Therefore, behold, I will hedge up your way with thorns, and make a <u>wall</u>, that she shall not find her paths. obstruction

7 And she shall follow after her lovers, but she shall not overtake them; and she shall seek them, but shall not find *them*: then shall she say, I will go and return to my first husband; for then *was it* better with me than now.

8 For she did not know that I gave her <u>corn</u>, and wine, and oil, and multiplied her silver and gold, *which* they prepared for Ba'al. grain

9 Therefore will I return, and take away My <u>corn</u> in the time thereof, and My wine in the season thereof, and will <u>recover</u> My wool and My flax *given* to cover her nakedness. take away

10 And now will I <u>discover</u> her <u>lewdness</u> in the sight of her lovers, and none shall deliver her out of My hand.   expose - sin

11 I will also cause all her <u>mirth</u> to cease, her feast days, her new moons, and her <u>sabbaths</u>, and all her solemn feasts.   gayety - rests

12 And I will destroy her vines and her fig trees, whereof she has said, These *are* my rewards that my lovers have given me: and I will make them a forest, and the beasts of the field shall eat them.

13 And I will visit upon her the days of Ba'al-im, wherein she burned incense to them, and she decked herself with her earrings and her jewels, and she went after her lovers, and forgot Me, says the LORD.

14 Therefore, behold, I will allure her, and bring her into the wilderness, and speak comfortably to her.

15 And I will give her her vineyards from there, and the valley of A'chor for a door of hope: and she shall sing there, as in the days of her youth, and as in the day when she came up out of the land of E'gypt.

16 And it shall be at that day, says the LORD, *that* you shall call Me <u>Ish'i</u>; and shall call Me no more <u>Ba'al-i</u>. i.e., my husband - i.e., my lord

17 For I will take away the names of Ba'al-im out of her mouth, and they shall no more be remembered by their name.

18 And in that day will I make a <u>covenant</u> for them with the beasts of the field, and with the fowls of heaven, and *with* the creeping things of the ground: and I will break the bow and the sword and the battle out of the earth, and will make them to lie down safely.   agreement

19 And I will betroth you to Me for ever; yea, I will betroth you to Me in righteousness, and in judgment, and in lovingkindness, and in mercies.

20 I will even betroth you to Me in faithfulness: and you shall know the LORD.   2 COR. 11:2

21 And it shall come to pass in that

day, I will hear, says the LORD, I will hear the heavens, and they shall hear the earth;

22 And the earth shall hear the <u>corn</u>, and the wine, and the oil; and they shall <u>hear</u> Jez`re-el.   grain - respond

23 And I will sow her to Me in the earth; and I will have mercy upon her that had not obtained mercy; and I will say *to them which were* not My people, You *are* My people; and they shall say, *You are* my <u>God</u>.   ROM. 9:25 1 PET. 2:10 Elohim^{p.f.}

CHAPTER 3

THEN said the LORD to me, Go yet, love a woman beloved of *her* friend, yet an adulteress, according to the love of the LORD toward the children of Is'ra-el, who look to other gods, and love flagons of wine.

2 So I bought her to me for fifteen *pieces* of silver, and *for* an homer of barley, and an half homer of barley:

3 And I said to her, You shall abide for me many days; you shall not play the harlot, and you shall not be for *another* man: so *will* I also *be* for you.

4 For the children of Is'ra-el shall abide many days without a king, and without a prince, and without a sacrifice, and without an image, and without an <u>ephod</u>, and *without* <u>teraphim</u>:   priestly robe - household idols

5 Afterward shall the children of Is'ra-el return, and seek the LORD their <u>God</u>, and Da'vid their king; and shall <u>fear</u> the LORD and His goodness in the latter days.   Elohim^{p.f.} - reverence

CHAPTER 4

HEAR the word of the LORD, you children of Is'ra-el: for the LORD has a controversy with the inhabitants of the land, Because *there is* no truth, nor mercy, nor knowledge of <u>God</u> in the land.   Elohim^{p.f.}

2 By swearing, and lying, and killing, and stealing, and committing <u>adultery</u>, they break out, and blood touches blood.   unfaithfulness

3 Therefore shall the land mourn, and every one that dwells therein shall <u>languish</u>, with the beasts of the field, and with the fowls of heaven; yea, the fishes of the sea also shall be taken away.   waste away

4 Yet let no man strive, nor reprove another: for your people *are* as they that strive with the priest.

5 Therefore shall you fall in the day, and the prophet also shall fall with you in the night, and I will destroy your mother.

6 My people are destroyed for lack of knowledge: because you have rejected knowledge, I will also reject you, that you shall be no priest to Me: seeing you have forgotten the law of your <u>God</u>, I will also forget your children. Elohim^{p.f.}

7 As they were increased, so they sinned against Me: *therefore* will I change their glory into shame.

8 They eat up the sin of My people, and they set their heart on their <u>iniquity</u>.   wickedness

9 And there shall be, like people, like

priest: and I will punish them for their ways, and <u>reward</u> them their doings. repay

10 For they shall eat, and not have enough: they shall commit <u>whoredom</u>, and shall not increase: because they have left off to take heed to the Lord. harlotry - unfaithfulness

11 *Whoredom* and wine and new wine take away the heart. Unfaithfulness

12 My people ask counsel at their <u>stocks</u>, and their <u>staff</u> declares to them: for the spirit of <u>whoredoms</u> has caused *them* to err, and they have gone a whoring from under their <u>God</u>. wooden idols - diviner's wand - unfaithfulness - Elohim^{p.f.}

13 They sacrifice upon the <u>tops</u> of the mountains, and burn incense upon the hills, under oaks and poplars and elms, because the shadow thereof *is* good: therefore your daughters shall commit <u>whoredom</u>, and your spouses shall commit <u>adultery</u>. illicit intercourse - harlotry

14 I will not punish your daughters when they commit <u>whoredom</u>, nor your spouses when they commit <u>adultery</u>: for themselves are separated with whores, and they sacrifice with harlots: therefore the people *that* does not understand shall fall.

15 Though you, Is'ra-el, play the harlot, *yet* let not Ju'dah offend; and come not you to Gil'gal, neither go you up to Beth-a'ven, nor swear, The Lord lives.

16 For Is'ra-el slides back as a <u>backsliding</u> heifer: now the Lord will feed them as a lamb in a large place. stubborn

17 E'phra-im *is* joined to idols: let him alone.

18 Their drink is sour: they have committed <u>whoredom</u> continually: her <u>rulers</u> *with* <u>shame do love</u>, Give you. illicit intercourse - leaders love sin

19 The wind has bound her up in her wings, and they shall be ashamed because of their sacrifices.

CHAPTER 5

HEAR you this, O priests; and hearken, you house of Is'ra-el; and give you ear, O house of the king; for judgment *is* toward you, because you have been a <u>snare</u> on Miz'pah, and a net spread upon Ta'bor. trap

2 And the revolters are <u>profound</u> to make slaughter, though I *have been* a rebuker of them all. determined

3 I know E'phra-im, and Is'ra-el is not hid from Me: for now, O E'phra-im, you commit <u>whoredom</u>, *and* Is'ra-el is defiled. unfaithfulness

4 They will not frame their doings to turn to their <u>God</u>: for the spirit of <u>whoredoms</u> *is* in the midst of them, and they have not known the Lord. Elohim^{p.f.} - unfaithfulness

5 And the pride of Is'ra-el does testify to his face: therefore shall Is'ra-el and E'phra-im fall in their iniquity; Ju'dah also shall fall with them.

6 They shall go with their flocks and with their herds to seek the Lord; but they shall not find *Him*; He has withdrawn Himself from them.

7 They have dealt treacherously against the Lord: for they have begotten strange children: now shall a month <u>devour</u> them with their <u>portions</u>. destroy - land

8 Blow you the cornet in Gib'e-ah, *and* the trumpet in Ra'mah: cry aloud *at* Beth-a'ven, after you, O Ben'ja-min.

9 E'phra-im shall be desolate in the day of rebuke: among the tribes of Is'ra-el have I made known that which shall surely be.

10 The princes of Ju'dah were like them that remove the bound: *therefore* I will pour out My <u>wrath</u> upon them like water. _{anger}

11 E'phra-im *is* oppressed *and* broken in judgment, because he willingly walked <u>after</u> the commandment. _{away from}

12 Therefore *will* I *be* to E'phra-im as a moth, and to the house of Ju'dah as rottenness.

13 When E'phra-im saw his sickness, and Ju'dah *saw* his wound, then went E'phra-im to the As-syr'i-an, and sent to king Ja'reb: yet could he not heal you, nor cure you of your wound.

14 For I *will be* to E'phra-im as a lion, and as a young lion to the house of Ju'dah: I, *even* I, will tear and go away; I will take away, and none shall rescue *him*.

15 I will go *and* return to My place, till they acknowledge their offence, and seek My face: in their affliction they will seek Me <u>early</u>. _{earnestly}

CHAPTER 6

COME, and let us return to the LORD: for He has torn, and He will heal us; He has smitten, and He will bind us up.

2 After two days will He revive us: in the third day He will raise us up, and we shall live in His sight. _{1 COR. 15:4 LUKE 24:46}

3 Then shall we know, *if* we follow on to know the LORD: His going forth is prepared as the morning; and He shall come to us as the rain, as the latter *and* former rain to the earth.

4 O E'phra-im, what shall I do to you? O Ju'dah, what shall I do to you? for your <u>goodness</u> *is* as a morning cloud, and as the early dew it goes away. _{loyalty}

5 Therefore have I <u>hewed</u> *them* by the prophets; I have slain them by the words of My mouth: and your judgments *are as* the light *that* goes forth. _{cut down}

6 For I desired mercy, and not sacrifice; and the knowledge of <u>God</u> more than burned offerings. _{MATT. 12:7 Elohim^{p.f.}}

7 But they like <u>men</u> have transgressed the <u>covenant</u>: there have they dealt treacherously against Me. _{Adam - agreement}

8 Gil'e-ad *is* a city of them that work <u>iniquity</u>, *and is* <u>polluted</u> with blood. _{evil - stained}

9 And as troops of robbers wait for a man, *so* the company of priests murder in the way by consent: for they commit <u>lewdness</u>. _{crime}

10 I have seen an horrible thing in the house of Is'ra-el: there *is* the <u>whoredom</u> of E'phra-im, Is'ra-el is defiled. _{unfaithfulness}

11 Also, O Ju'dah, he has set an harvest for you, when I <u>returned</u> the captivity of My people. _{restored the fortunes}

CHAPTER 7

WHEN I would have healed Is'ra-el, then the <u>iniquity</u> of E'phra-im was

discovered, and the wickedness of Sa-ma'ri-a: for they commit falsehood; and the thief comes in, *and* the troop of robbers <u>spoils</u> outside.   sin - raid

2 And they consider not in their hearts *that* I remember all their wickedness: now their own doings have beset them about; they are before My face.

3 They make the king glad with their wickedness, and the princes with their lies.

4 They *are* all <u>adulterers</u>, as an oven heated by the baker, *who* ceases <u>from raising</u> after he has kneaded the dough, until it be <u>leavened</u>.   unfaithful - from stirring fire - rises

5 In the day of our king the princes have made *him* sick with <u>bottles</u> of wine; he stretched out his hand with <u>scorners</u>.   wineskins - scoffers

6 For they have made ready their heart like an oven, while they lie in wait: their baker sleeps all the night; in the morning it burns as a flaming fire.

7 They are all hot as an oven, and have <u>devoured</u> their judges; all their kings are fallen: *there is* none among them that calls to Me.   destroyed

8 E'phra-im, he has mixed himself among the <u>people</u>; E'phra-im is a cake not turned.   nations

9 Strangers have <u>devoured</u> his strength, and he knows *it* not: yea, gray hairs are here and there upon him, yet he knows not.

10 And the <u>pride</u> of Is'ra-el testifies to his face: and they do not return to the Lord their <u>God</u>, nor seek Him for all this.   arrogance - Elohim[p.f.]

11 E'phra-im also is like a silly dove without heart: they call to E'gypt, they go to As-syr'i-a.

12 When they shall go, I will spread My net upon them; I will bring them down as the fowls of the heaven; I will chastise them, as their congregation has heard.

13 Woe to them! for they have fled from Me: destruction to them! because they have transgressed against Me: though I have redeemed them, yet they have spoken lies against Me.

14 And they have not cried to Me with their heart, when they howled upon their beds: they assemble themselves for <u>corn</u> and wine, *and* they rebel against Me.   grain

15 Though I have <u>bound</u> *and* strengthened their arms, yet do they imagine mischief against Me.   trained

16 They return, *but* not to the Most High: they are like a deceitful bow: their princes shall fall by the sword for the rage of their tongue: this *shall be* their derision in the land of E'gypt.

CHAPTER 8

SET the trumpet to your mouth. *He shall come* as an eagle against the house of the Lord, because they have transgressed My <u>covenant</u>, and trespassed against My law.   agreement

2 Is'ra-el shall cry to Me, My <u>God</u>, we know You.   Elohim[p.f.]

3 Is'ra-el has cast off *the thing that is* good: the enemy shall pursue him.

4 They have set up kings, but not by Me: they have made princes, and I

knew *it* not: of their silver and their gold have they made them idols, that they may be cut off.   consented - destroyed

5 Your calf, O Sa-ma'ri-a, has cast *you* off; My anger is kindled against them: how long *will it be* before they attain to innocency?   pagan god

6 For from Is'ra-el *was* it also: the workman made it; therefore it *is* not God: but the calf of Sa-ma'ri-a shall be broken in pieces.   Elohim[p.f.] - pagan god

7 For they have sown the wind, and they shall reap the whirlwind: it has no stalk: the bud shall yield no meal: if so be it yield, the strangers shall swallow it up.

8 Is'ra-el is swallowed up: now shall they be among the Gen'tiles as a vessel wherein *is* no pleasure.   Nations

9 For they are gone up to As-syr'i-a, a wild ass alone by himself: E'phra-im has hired lovers.   paid

10 Yea, though they have hired among the nations, now will I gather them, and they shall sorrow a little for the burden of the king of princes.

11 Because E'phra-im has made many altars to sin, altars shall be to him to sin.

12 I have written to him the great things of My law, *but* they were counted as a strange thing.   alien

13 They sacrifice flesh *for* the sacrifices of My offerings, and eat it; *but* the LORD accepts them not; now will He remember their iniquity, and visit their sins: they shall return to E'gypt.   evil doings

14 For Is'ra-el has forgotten his Maker, and builds temples; and Ju'-dah has multiplied fenced cities: but I will send a fire upon his cities, and it shall devour the palaces thereof.   fortified

CHAPTER 9

REJOICE not, O Is'ra-el, for joy, as *other* people: for you have gone a whoring from your God, you have loved a reward upon every corn floor. an unfaithful way - Elohim[p.f.] - grain

2 The floor and the winepress shall not feed them, and the new wine shall fail in her.

3 They shall not dwell in the LORD's land; but E'phra-im shall return to E'gypt, and they shall eat unclean *things* in As-syr'i-a.

4 They shall not offer wine *offerings* to the LORD, neither shall they be pleasing to Him: their sacrifices *shall be* to them as the bread of mourners; all that eat thereof shall be polluted: for their bread for their soul shall not come into the house of the LORD. defiled

5 What will you do in the solemn day, and in the day of the feast of the LORD?

6 For, lo, they are gone because of destruction: E'gypt shall gather them up, Mem'phis shall bury them: the pleasant *places* for their silver, nettles shall possess them: thorns *shall be* in their tabernacles.   thorns

7 The days of visitation are come, the days of recompence are come; Is'ra-el shall know *it*: the prophet *is* a fool, the spiritual man *is* mad, for the multitude of your iniquity, and the great hatred.   punishment - retribution - sin - hostility

8 The watchman of E'phra-im *was* with my God: *but* the prophet *is* a snare

of a fowler in all his ways, *and* hatred in the house of his God.

Elohim[p.f.] - trap - hostility

9 They have deeply corrupted *themselves*, as in the days of Gib'e-ah: *therefore* He will remember their iniquity, He will visit their sins.   evil ways
10 I found Is'ra-el like grapes in the wilderness; I saw your fathers as the first ripe in the fig tree at her first time: *but* they went to Ba'al-pe'or, and separated themselves to *that* shame; and *their* abominations were according as they loved. devoted - evil ways
11 *As for* E'phra-im, their glory shall fly away like a bird, from the birth, and from the womb, and from the conception.
12 Though they bring up their children, yet will I bereave them, *that there shall* not *be* a man *left*: yea, woe also to them when I depart from them!
13 E'phra-im, as I saw Ty'rus, *is* planted in a pleasant place: but E'phra-im shall bring forth his children to the murderer.
14 Give them, O LORD: what will You give? give them a miscarrying womb and dry breasts.
15 All their wickedness *is* in Gil'gal: for there I hated them: for the wickedness of their doings I will drive them out of My house, I will love them no more: all their princes *are* revolters. despised - leaders - rebels
16 E'phra-im is smitten, their root is dried up, they shall bear no fruit: yea, though they bring forth, yet will I slay *even* the beloved *fruit* of their womb.
17 My God will cast them away, because they did not hearken to Him:

and they shall be wanderers among the nations.   Elohim[p.f.]

CHAPTER 10

IS'RA-EL *is* an empty vine, he brings forth fruit to himself: according to the multitude of his fruit he has increased the altars; according to the goodness of his land they have made goodly images.   degenerate - idols
2 Their heart is divided; now shall they be found faulty: He shall break down their altars, He shall spoil their images.   break down - idols
3 For now they shall say, We have no king, because we feared not the LORD; what then should a king do to us? revered
4 They have spoken words, swearing falsely in making a covenant: thus judgment springs up as hemlock in the furrows of the field.   agreement
5 The inhabitants of Sa-ma'ri-a shall fear because of the calves of Beth-a'ven: for the people thereof shall mourn over it, and the priests thereof *that* rejoiced on it, for the glory thereof, because it is departed from it.   idols
6 It shall be also carried to As-syr'i-a *for* a present to king Ja'reb: E'phra-im shall receive shame, and Is'ra-el shall be ashamed of its own counsel.
7 *As for* Sa-ma'ri-a, her king is cut off as the foam upon the water.
8 The high places also of A'ven, the sin of Is'ra-el, shall be destroyed: the thorn and the thistle shall come up on their altars; and they shall say to the mountains, Cover us; and to the hills, Fall on us.   REV. 6:16 LUKE 23:30

9 O Is'ra-el, you have sinned from the days of Gib'e-ah: there they stood: the battle in Gib'e-ah against the children of <u>iniquity</u> did not overtake them.   _{evil ways}

10 *It is* in My desire that I should chastise them; and the people shall be gathered against them, when they shall bind themselves in their two furrows.

11 And E'phra-im *is as* an heifer *that is* taught, *and* loves to tread out *the* <u>corn</u>; but I passed over upon her fair neck: I will make E'phra-im <u>to ride</u>; Ju'dah shall plow, *and* Ja'cob shall break his clods.   _{grain - be harnessed}

12 Sow to yourselves in righteousness, reap in mercy; break up your fallow ground: for *it is* time to seek the LORD, till He come and rain righteousness upon you.

13 You have plowed wickedness, you have reaped <u>iniquity</u>; you have eaten the fruit of lies: because you did trust in your way, in the multitude of your mighty men.   _{injustice}

14 Therefore shall a tumult arise among your people, and all your fortresses shall be spoiled, as Shal'man spoiled Beth-ar'bel in the day of battle: the mother was dashed in pieces upon *her* children.

15 So shall Beth'-el do to you because of your great wickedness: in a morning shall the king of Is'ra-el utterly be cut off.

CHAPTER 11

WHEN Is'ra-el *was* <u>a child</u>, then I loved him, and called My son out of E'gypt. _{MATT. 2:15 a youth}

2 *As* they called them, so they went from them: they sacrificed to Ba'al-im, and burned incense to <u>graven images</u>.   _{carved idols}

3 I taught E'phra-im also to go, taking them by <u>their</u> arms; but they knew not that I healed them.   _{My}

4 I drew them with cords of a man, with bands of love: and I was to them as they that <u>take</u> off the yoke on their jaws, and I <u>laid meat to</u> them.   _{lift - fed}

5 He shall not return into the land of E'gypt, but the As-syr'i-an shall be his king, because they refused to return.

6 And the sword shall abide on his cities, and shall consume his branches, and devour *them*, because of their own counsels.

7 And My people are bent to backsliding from Me: though they called them to the Most High, none at all would exalt *Him*.

8 How shall I give you up, E'phra-im? *how* shall I deliver you, Is'ra-el? how shall I make you as Ad'-mah? *how* shall I set you as Ze-bo'im? My heart is turned within Me, My <u>repentings</u> are <u>kindled</u> together.   _{compassions - aroused}

9 I will not execute the fierceness of My anger, I will not return to destroy E'phra-im: for I *am* <u>God</u>, and not man; the Holy One in the midst of you: and I will not enter into the city.   _{El^{s.f.}}

10 They shall walk after the LORD: He shall roar like a lion: when He shall roar, then the children shall tremble from the west.

11 They shall tremble as a bird out of E'gypt, and as a dove out of the land of

As-syr'i-a: and I will <u>place</u> them in their houses, says the LORD.   settle

12 E'phra-im <u>compasses</u> Me about with lies, and the house of Is'ra-el with deceit: but Ju'dah yet rules with God, and is faithful with the <u>saints</u>.   surrounds - holy ones

CHAPTER 12

E'PHRA-IM feeds on wind, and follows after the east wind: he daily increases lies and <u>desolation</u>; and they do make a <u>covenant</u> with the As-syr'i-ans, and oil is carried into E'gypt.   violence - agreement

2 The LORD has also a <u>controversy</u> with Ju'dah, and will punish Ja'cob according to his ways; according to his doings will He recompense him.   dispute

3 He took his brother by the heel in the womb, and by his strength he <u>had power</u> with <u>God</u>: contended - Elohim^{p.f.}

4 Yea, he had power over the <u>angel</u>, and prevailed: he wept, and made supplication to Him: he found Him *in* Beth'-el, and there He spoke with us;   messenger

5 Even the LORD God of hosts; the LORD *is* his <u>memorial</u>. Jehovah^{s.f.} Elohe Tsebaoth - name

6 Therefore turn you to your <u>God</u>: keep mercy and judgment, and wait on your <u>God</u> continually.   Elohim^{p.f.}

7 *He is* a merchant, the balances of deceit *are* in his hand: he loves to oppress.

8 And E'phra-im said, Yet I am become rich, I have found me out substance: *in* all my labors they shall find none iniquity in me that *were* sin.   REV. 3:17

G4B

P15B

1342
1376

9 And I *that am* the LORD your <u>God</u> from the land of E'gypt will yet make you to dwell in tabernacles, as in the days of the solemn feast.   Elohim^{p.f.}

10 I have also spoken by the prophets, and I have multiplied visions, and used <u>similitudes</u>, by the ministry of the prophets.   illustrations

11 *Is there* <u>iniquity</u> *in* Gil'e-ad? surely they are vanity: they sacrifice bullocks in Gil'gal; yea, their altars *are* as heaps in the furrows of the fields.   sin

12 And Jacob fled into the country of Syr'i-a, and Is'ra-el served for a wife, and for a wife he kept *sheep*.

13 And by a prophet the LORD brought Is'ra-el out of E'gypt, and by a prophet was he preserved.

14 E'phra-im provoked *Him* to anger most bitterly: therefore shall He leave his blood upon him, and his reproach shall his <u>Lord</u> return to him.   Adonay^{p.f.}

CHAPTER 13

WHEN E'phra-im spoke trembling, he exalted himself in Is'ra-el; but when he offended in Ba'al, he died.

2 And now they sin more and more, and have made them molten <u>images</u> of their silver, *and* idols according to their own understanding, all of it the work of the craftsmen: they say of them, Let the men that sacrifice <u>kiss</u> the calves.   idols - worship

3 Therefore they shall be as the morning cloud, and as the early dew that passes away, as the chaff *that* is driven with the whirlwind out of the floor, and as the smoke out of the chimney.

4 Yet I *am* the LORD your God from the land of E'gypt, and you shall know no god but Me: for *there is* no savior beside Me. Elohim[p.f.]

5 I did know you in the wilderness, in the land of great drought.

6 According to their pasture, so were they filled; they were filled, and their heart was exalted; therefore have they forgotten Me.

7 Therefore I will be to them as a lion: as a leopard by the way will I observe *them*: wait for

8 I will meet them as a bear *that is* bereaved *of her whelps*, and will rend the caul of their heart, and there will I devour them like a lion: the wild beast shall tear them. cut the fat

9 O Is'ra-el, you have destroyed yourself; but in Me *is* your help.

10 I will be your king: where *is any other* that may save you in all your cities? and your judges of whom you said, Give me a king and princes?

11 I gave you a king in My anger, and took *him* away in My wrath. i.e., Saul - anger

12 The iniquity of E'phra-im *is* bound up; his sin *is* hid. evil - stored up

13 The sorrows of a travailing woman shall come upon him: he *is* an unwise son; for he should not stay long in *the place of* the breaking forth of children.

14 I will ransom them from the power of the grave; I will redeem them from death: O death, I will be your plagues; O grave, I will be your destruction: repentance shall be hid from My eyes. 1 COR. 15:55 Sheol - redemption - grieving

15 Though he be fruitful among *his* brethren, an east wind shall come, the wind of the LORD shall come up from the wilderness, and his spring shall become dry, and his fountain shall be dried up: he shall spoil the treasure of all pleasant vessels.

i.e., breath—Holy Spirit - plunder - previous

16 Sa-ma'ri-a shall become desolate; for she has rebelled against her God: they shall fall by the sword: their infants shall be dashed in pieces, and their women with child shall be ripped up. be held guilty - Elohim[p.f.]

CHAPTER 14

O IS'RA-EL, return to the LORD your God; for you have fallen by your iniquity. Elohim[p.f.] - sin

2 Take with you words, and turn to the LORD: say to him, Take away all iniquity, and receive *us* graciously: so will we render the calves of our lips. sin - fruit

3 Assh'ur shall not save us; we will not ride upon horses: neither will we say any more to the work of our hands, *You are* our gods: for in you the fatherless finds mercy.

4 I will heal their backsliding, I will love them freely: for My anger is turned away from him.

5 I will be as the dew to Is'ra-el: he shall grow as the lily, and cast forth his roots as Leb'a-non. blossoms - take

6 His branches shall spread, and his beauty shall be as the olive tree, and his smell as Leb'a-non. grow - fragrance

7 They that dwell under His shadow shall return; they shall revive *as* the <u>corn</u>, and grow as the vine: the <u>scent</u> thereof *shall be* as the wine of Leb'a-non.   grain - fragrance

8 E'phra-im *shall say*, What have I to do any more with idols? I have heard *him*, and observed him: I *am* like a green fir tree. From Me is your fruit found.

9 Who *is* wise, and he shall understand these *things*? prudent, and he shall know them? for the ways of the LORD *are* right, and the just shall walk in them: but the transgressors shall fall therein.   ACTS 13:10

JOEL

OUTLINE

THE LOCUST PLAGUE AND ITS REMOVAL 1.1—2.27
  Plague of Locusts 1.1-20
  The People urged to Repent 2.1-17
  God Pities and Promises Relief 2.18-27

THE FUTURE DAY OF THE LORD 2.28—3.21
  The Spirit of God to be Poured Out 2.28-32
  The Judgment of the Nations 3.1-17
  Blessing upon Israel after the Judgment 3.18-21

SURVEY

A locust invasion had devastated the land of Judah. As Joel, the son of Pethuel, reflected on this calamity, the Word of the Lord came to him. He became a great prophet proclaiming to his people the divine implications of this catastrophe. The book which bears his name records Joel's sermon upon this occasion.

The prophet describes the plague in terms of a human army which, moving on, leaves behind it a scorched earth (1.4-12; 2.2-10). In this attack of insects, Joel knows God is at work. Indeed, this is God's army (2.11), and the day of its invasion is the Day of the Lord—the day of God's judgment upon a sinful people (1.15; 2.1, 11). The prophet urges the people to repent, and extends the hope that God will relent and withdraw the judgment (1.14; 2.12-17).

Evidently Joel's ministry was more successful than that of many of the prophets, for God's relenting (2.18-27) indicates that the people did repent. "I will remove the northern army (that is, the locusts) . . . and I will restore to you the years which the locust hath eaten" (2.20,25) is the prophet's assurance in God's name.

But Joel's sermon was not yet finished. Worse judgments were ahead for the world which did not acknowledge God's sovereignty nor adhere to the common ethical standards of heathen nations (3.2b-8). God will graciously give His Spirit to all His people (2.28,29), but the Gentile nations will be judged and punished (3.1,2, 9-16). From this wrath God's people will be delivered (2.32). Then Judah and Jerusalem will be wonderfully prosperous and be eternally blessed with the divine presence (3.18-21).

In these terms Joel expressed the human hope and the divine promise that God is sovereign in His world, and will yet cause His will to be done on earth as it is in heaven. The kingdoms of this world shall "become the kingdoms of our Lord, and of his Christ, and he shall reign for ever and ever" (Rv 11.15).

AUTHOR

Of Joel, the son of Pethuel, nothing is definitely known. Joel means "the Lord is God" and was a common Hebrew name in Old Testament times. Joel's many references to Jerusalem (1.14;2.1,15,-32:3.1,6,16,17,20,21) seem to indicate that the city was his home.

We cannot date the locust plague which forms the background of this book. Authorities differ widely in their opinions as to the date of composition, some arguing for an early date (perhaps the

reign of Joash, toward the end of the ninth century B.C.); others, a post-Exilic one. The fact that the locust plague is called "the day of the Lord" (a phrase used in later years to designate the final judgment day) and the location of the book near the beginning of the Minor Prophets seem to indicate the early date as more likely. The message of the book is not dependent upon its date, and it remains relevant for men today.

J.B.G.

THE BOOK OF
JOEL

CHAPTER 1

THE word of the LORD that came to Jo'el the son of Pe-thu'el.

2 Hear this, you old men, and give ear, all you inhabitants of the land. Has this been in your days, or even in the days of your fathers?

3 Tell you your children of it, and *let* your children *tell* their children, and their children another generation.

4 That which the palmerworm has left has the locust eaten; and that which the locust has left has the cankerworm eaten; and that which the cankerworm has left has the caterpiller eaten.

5 Awake, you drunkards, and weep; and howl, all you drinkers of wine, because of the new wine; for it is cut off from your mouth.   wail - kept from

6 For a nation is come up upon My land, strong, and without number, whose teeth *are* the teeth of a lion, and he has the cheek teeth of a great lion. REV. 9:8

7 He has laid My vine waste, and barked My fig tree: he has made it clean bare, and cast *it* away; the branches thereof are made white.   cut off the bark

8 Lament like a virgin girded with sackcloth for the husband of her youth.

9 The meat offering and the drink offering is cut off from the house of the LORD; the priests, the LORD's ministers, mourn.

10 The field is wasted, the land mourns; for the corn is wasted: the new wine is dried up, the oil languishes.   destroyed - grain - fails

11 Be you ashamed, O you husbandmen; howl, O you vinedressers, for the wheat and for the barley; because the harvest of the field is perished.   wail

12 The vine is dried up, and the fig tree languishes; the pomegranate tree, the palm tree also, and the apple tree, *even* all the trees of the field, are withered: because joy is withered away from the sons of men.   wastes away - gone

13 Gird yourselves, and lament, you priests: howl, you ministers of the altar: come, lie all night in sackcloth, you ministers of my God: for the meat offering and the drink offering is withholden from the house of your God.   mourning clothes - Elohim^{p.f.} - withheld

14 Sanctify you a fast, call a solemn assembly, gather the elders *and* all the inhabitants of the land *into* the house of the LORD your God, and cry to the LORD,   consecrate

15 Alas for the day! for the day of the LORD *is* at hand, and as a destruction from the Almighty shall it come.

16 Is not the meat cut off before our eyes, *yea*, joy and gladness from the house of our God?   food - Elohim^{p.f.}

17 The seed is rotten under their clods, the garners are laid desolate, the barns are broken down; for the corn is withered.   grain

18 How do the beasts groan! the herds of cattle are <u>perplexed</u>, because they have no pasture; yea, the flocks of sheep are <u>made desolate</u>.   *disturbed mill about - suffering*

19 O LORD, to You will I cry: for the fire has devoured the pastures of the wilderness, and the flame has burned all the trees of the field.

20 The beasts of the field cry also to You: for the rivers of waters are dried up, and the fire has devoured the pastures of the wilderness.

CHAPTER 2

BLOW you the trumpet in Zi'on, and sound an alarm in my holy mountain: let all the inhabitants of the land <u>tremble</u>: for the day of the LORD comes, for *it is* near at hand; *shake*

2 A day of darkness and of gloominess, a day of clouds and of thick darkness, as the morning spread upon the mountains: a great people and a strong; there has not been ever the like, neither shall be any more after it, *even* to the years of many generations. REV. 9:2

3 A fire devoures before them; and behind them a flame burns: the land *is* as the garden of E'den before them, and behind them a desolate wilderness; yea, and nothing shall escape them.

4 The appearance of them *is* as the appearance of horses; and as horsemen, so shall they run. REV 9:7

5 Like the noise of chariots on the tops of mountains shall they leap, like the noise of a flame of fire that devours the stubble, as a strong people set in battle array.

6 Before their face the people shall be much pained: all faces shall <u>gather blackness</u>. *pale*

7 They shall run like mighty men; they shall climb the wall like men of war; and they shall march every one on his ways, and they shall not break their ranks:

8 Neither shall one thrust another; they shall walk every one in his path: and *when* they <u>fall upon the sword</u>, they shall not be wounded. *break through the defenses*

9 They shall run to and fro in the city; they shall run upon the wall, they shall climb up upon the houses; they shall enter in at the windows like a thief.

10 The earth shall quake before them; the heavens shall tremble: the sun and the moon shall be dark, and the stars shall withdraw their shining: REV. 9:2 MATT. 24:29

11 And the LORD shall utter His voice before His army: for His camp *is* very great: for *He is* strong that executes His word: for the day of the LORD *is* great and very <u>terrible</u>; and who can abide it? REV. 6:17 *awesome*

12 Therefore also now, says the LORD, turn you *even* to Me with all your heart, and with fasting, and with weeping, and with mourning:

13 And <u>rend</u> your heart, and not your garments, and turn to the LORD your <u>God</u>: for He *is* gracious and merciful, slow to anger, and of great kindness, and <u>repents</u> Him of the evil. *tear - Elohim^{p.f.} - grieved*

14 Who knows *if* He will return and <u>repent</u>, and leave a blessing behind

Him; *even* a meat offering and a drink offering to the L ORD your <u>God</u>? grieve - Elohim^{p.f.}

15 Blow the trumpet in Zi'on, <u>sanctify</u> a fast, call a solemn assembly: consecrate

16 Gather the people, <u>sanctify</u> the congregation, assemble the elders, gather the children, and those that suck the breasts: let the bridegroom go forth of his chamber, and the bride out of her closet.

17 Let the priests, the ministers of the L ORD, weep between the porch and the altar, and let them say, Spare Your people, O L ORD, and give not Your heritage to reproach, that the <u>heathen</u> should rule over them: wherefore should they say among the people, Where *is* their <u>God</u>? nations - Elohim^{p.f.}

18 Then will the L ORD be jealous for His land, and pity His people.

19 Yea, the L ORD will answer and say to His people, Behold, I will send you <u>corn</u>, and wine, and oil, and you shall be satisfied therewith: and I will no more make you a reproach among the <u>heathen</u>: grain

20 But I will remove far off from you the northern *army*, and will drive him into a land barren and desolate, with his face toward the east sea, and its <u>hinder</u> part toward the <u>utmost</u> sea, and its stink shall come up, and its <u>ill savor</u> shall come up, because it has done great things. back - Mediterranean - foul smell

21 Fear not, O land; be glad and rejoice: for the L ORD will do great things.

22 Be not afraid, you beasts of the field: for the pastures of the wilderness do spring, for the tree bears its fruit, the fig tree and the vine do yield their strength.

23 Be glad then, you children of Zi'on, and rejoice in the L ORD your <u>God</u>: for He has given you the former rain moderately, and He will cause to come down for you the rain, the former rain, and the latter rain in the first *month*. Elohim^{p.f.}

24 And the floors shall be full of wheat, and the vats shall overflow with wine and oil.

25 And I will restore to you the years that the locust has eaten, the cankerworm, and the caterpiller, and the palmerworm, My great army which I sent among you.

26 And you shall eat in plenty, and be satisfied, and praise the name of the L ORD your <u>God</u>, that has dealt wondrously with you: and My people shall never be ashamed. Elohim^{p.f.}

27 And you shall know that I *am* in the midst of Is'ra-el, and *that* I *am* the L ORD your <u>God</u>, and none else: and My people shall never be ashamed.

28 And it shall come to pass afterward, *that* I will pour out My Spirit upon all <u>flesh</u>; and your sons and your daughters shall prophesy, your old men shall dream dreams, your young men shall see visions: ACTS 2:16 people

29 And also upon the servants and upon the handmaids in those days will I pour out My Spirit. ACTS 2:18

30 And I will show wonders in the heavens and in the earth, blood, and fire, and pillars of smoke. ACTS 2:19

31 The sun shall be turned into darkness, and the moon into blood, before the great and the terrible day of the LORD come.

ACTS 2:19,20 REV. 6:12 awesome

32 And it shall come to pass, *that* whosoever shall call on the name of the LORD shall be delivered: for in mount Zi'on and in Je-ru'sa-lem shall be deliverance, as the LORD has said, and in the remnant whom the LORD shall call. ROM. 10:13 saved - salvation

CHAPTER 3

FOR, behold, in those days, and in that time, when I shall bring again the captivity of Ju'dah and Je-ru'sa-lem,

2 I will also gather all nations, and will bring them down into the valley of Je-hosh'a-phat, and will plead with them there for My people and *for* My heritage Is'ra-el, whom they have scattered among the nations, and parted My land.

3 And they have cast lots for My people; and have given a boy for an harlot, and sold a girl for wine, that they might drink.

4 Yea, and what have you to do with Me, O Tyre, and Zi'don, and all the coasts of Pal'es-tine? will you render Me a recompence? and if you recompence Me, swiftly *and* speedily will I return your recompence upon your own head;   repay

5 Because you have taken My silver and My gold, and have carried into your temples My goodly pleasant things: precious

6 The children also of Ju'dah and the children of Je-ru'sa-lem have you sold to the Gre'cians, that you might remove them far from their border.

7 Behold, I will raise them out of the place where you have sold them, and will return your recompence upon your own head: reward

8 And I will sell your sons and your daughters into the hand of the children of Ju'dah, and they shall sell them to the Sa-be'ans, to a people far off: for the LORD has spoken *it*.

9 Proclaim you this among the Gen'tiles; Prepare war, wake up the mighty men, let all the men of war draw near; let them come up: Nations

10 Beat your plowshares into swords, and your pruninghooks into spears: let the weak say, I *am* strong.   farm tools

11 Assemble yourselves, and come, all you heathen, and gather yourselves together round about: there cause Your mighty ones to come down, O LORD.   unbelievers

12 Let the heathen be wakened, and come up to the valley of Je-hosh'a-phat: for there will I sit to judge all the heathen round about.   nations

13 Put you in the sickle, for the harvest is ripe: come, get you down; for the press is full, the fats overflow; for their wickedness *is* great.   REV. 14:15,18,20

14 Multitudes, multitudes in the valley of decision: for the day of the LORD *is* near in the valley of decision.   judgment i.e., God's verdict

15 The sun and the moon shall be darkened, and the stars shall withdraw their shining.

16 The LORD also shall roar out of

Zi'on, and utter His voice from Je-ru'sa-lem; and the heavens and the earth shall shake: but the LORD *will be* the hope of His people, and the strength of the children of Is'ra-el. 17 So shall you know that I *am* the LORD your God dwelling in Zi'on, My holy mountain: then shall Je-ru'sa-lem be holy, and there shall no strangers pass through her any more. Elohim^{p.f.} - set apart 18 And it shall come to pass in that day, *that* the mountains shall drop down new wine, and the hills shall flow with milk, and all the rivers of Ju'dah shall flow with waters, and a fountain shall come forth of the house of the LORD, and shall water the valley of Shit'tim.

19 E'gypt shall be a desolation, and E'dom shall be a desolate wilderness, for the violence *against* the children of Ju'dah, because they have shed innocent blood in their land.

20 But Ju'dah shall dwell for ever, and Je-ru'sa-lem from generation to generation.

21 For I will cleanse their blood *that* I have not cleansed: for the LORD dwells in Zi'on.

AMOS

OUTLINE

SURVEY

The tone of Amos' message is set by the great proclamation at the beginning of his prophecy (1.2). From Zion the Lord's voice, like the roar of a lion, will be heard in judgment. Beneath the respectable surface of material prosperity, Amos uncovers the decaying mass of religious formalism and spiritual corruption (5.12, 21). He points out the total disregard of human rights and personality (2.6), and the deterioration of morality and social justice (2.7,8). The prophet had a remedy for the disease that threatened the life of the nation. Let men seek the Lord, let them repent and establish justice and they might live (5.14,15). But to emphasize the hopelessness of the situation, Amos warns that those responsible for the evil in the land are not "grieved" over the threatened disaster (6.6). Consequently, nothing is left for Israel but destruction (9.1-8). The Day of the Lord will not be a vindication of Israel, as some of the people of the day believed, but an assertion of the claims of God's moral character against those who had repudiated Him. Only when this was recognized would there be established the splendor of the Davidic Kingdom. But that Day was inevitable (9.11-15). Amos' message is largely a "cry for justice."

AUTHOR

A native of Tekoa, about twelve miles south of Jerusalem, Amos was a shepherd and a dresser of sycamore (fig) trees (1.1; 7.14, 15). While he was following the flock, the call of God to the prophetic ministry came to him. He prophesied in the northern kingdom for a brief period in the second half of the reign of Jeroboam II (785-744 B.C.), King of Israel, and during the reign of Uzziah (780-740 B.C.), King of Judah (1.1).

A.C.S.

THE BOOK OF
AMOS

"Burden"
God's Final Warning to
the Northern Kingdom

CHAPTER 1

THE words of A'mos, who was among the herdmen of Te-ko'a, which he saw concerning Is'ra-el in the days of Uz-zi'ah king of Ju'dah, and in the days of Jer-o-bo'am the son of Jo'ash king of Is'ra-el, two years before the earthquake.

2 And he said, The LORD will roar from Zi'on, and utter His voice from Je-ru'sa-lem; and the habitations of the shepherds shall mourn, and the top of Car'mel shall wither.

3 Thus says the LORD; For three transgressions of Da-mas'cus, and for four, I will not turn away *the punishment* thereof; because they have threshed Gil'e-ad with threshing instruments of iron: yea

4 But I will send a fire into the house of Haz'a-el, which shall devour the palaces of Ben-ha'dad. consume

5 I will break also the bar of Da-mas-cus, and cut off the inhabitant from the plain of A'ven, and him that holds the scepter from the house of E'den: and the people of Syr'i-a shall go into captivity to Kir, says the LORD. rules

6 Thus says the LORD; For three transgressions of Ga'za, and for four, I will not turn away *the punishment* thereof; because they carried away captive the whole captivity, to deliver *them* up to E'dom:

7 But I will send a fire on the wall of Ga'za, which shall devour the palaces thereof: consume

8 And I will cut off the inhabitant from Ash'dod, and him that holds the scepter from Ash'ke-lon, and I will turn My hand against Ek'ron: and the remnant of the Phi-lis'tines shall perish, says the Lord GOD. rules - Adonay^{p.f.} Jehovah

9 Thus says the LORD; For three transgressions of Ty'rus, and for four, I will not turn away *the punishment* thereof; because they delivered up the whole captivity to E'dom, and remembered not the brotherly covenant: yea - agreement

10 But I will send a fire on the wall of Ty'rus, which shall devour the palaces thereof.

11 Thus says the LORD; For three transgressions of E'dom, and for four, I will not turn away *the punishment* thereof; because he did pursue his brother with the sword, and did cast off all pity, and his anger did tear perpetually, and he kept his wrath for ever: fear - anger

12 But I will send a fire upon Te'man, which shall devour the palaces of Boz'rah.

13 Thus says the LORD; For three transgressions of the children of Am'mon, and for four, I will not turn away *the punishment* thereof; because they have ripped up the women with child of Gil'e-ad, that they might enlarge their border: yes - mutilated

14 But I will kindle a fire in the wall of Rab'bah, and it shall devour the palaces thereof, with shouting in the day of battle, with a tempest in the day of the whirlwind:

15 And their king shall go into captivity, he and his princes together, says the LORD.

CHAPTER 2

THUS says the LORD; For three transgressions of Mo'ab, and for four, I will not turn away *the punishment* thereof; because he burned the bones of the king of E'dom into lime: yea

2 But I will send a fire upon Mo'ab, and it shall underline{devour} the palaces of Kir'i-oth: and Mo'ab shall die with tumult, with shouting, *and* with the sound of the trumpet: consume

3 And I will cut off the judge from the midst thereof, and will slay all the princes thereof with him, says the LORD.

4 Thus says the LORD; For three transgressions of Ju'dah, and for four, I will not turn away *the punishment* thereof; because they have despised the law of the LORD, and have not kept His commandments, and their lies caused them to err, after the which their fathers have walked: yes

5 But I will send a fire upon Ju'dah, and it shall devour the palaces of Je-ru'sa-lem.

6 Thus says the LORD; For three transgressions of Is'ra-el, and for four, I will not turn away *the punishment* thereof; because they sold the righteous for silver, and the poor for a pair of shoes;   yes

7 That pant after the dust of the earth on the head of the poor, and turn aside the way of the meek: and a man and his father will go in to the *same* maid, to profane My holy name: humble - young woman - degrade

8 And they lay *themselves* down upon clothes laid to pledge by every altar, and they drink the wine of the condemned *in* the house of their god.   judged

9 Yet destroyed I the Am'or-ite before them, whose height *was* like the height of the cedars, and he *was* strong as the oaks; yet I destroyed his fruit from above, and his roots from beneath.

10 Also I brought you up from the land of E'gypt, and led you forty years through the wilderness, to possess the land of the Am'or-ite.

11 And I raised up of your sons for prophets, and of your young men for Naz'a-rites. *Is it* not even thus, O you children of Is'ra-el? says the LORD.   dedicated

12 But you gave the Naz'a-rites wine to drink; and commanded the prophets, saying, Prophesy not.

13 Behold, I am pressed under you, as a cart is pressed *that is* full of sheaves.

14 Therefore the flight shall perish from the swift, and the strong shall not strengthen his force, neither shall the mighty deliver himself: save

15 Neither shall he stand that handles the bow; and *he that is* swift of foot shall not deliver *himself*: neither shall he that rides the horse deliver himself.

16 And *he that is* <u>courageous</u> among the mighty shall flee away naked in that day, says the LORD. <small>bravest</small>

CHAPTER 3

HEAR this word that the LORD has spoken against you, O children of Is'ra-el, against the whole family which I brought up from the land of E'gypt, saying,

2 You only have I known of all the families of the earth: therefore I will punish you for all your <u>iniquities</u>. <small>sins</small>

3 Can two walk together, except they be agreed?

4 Will a lion roar in the forest, when he has no prey? will a young lion cry out of his den, if he have taken nothing?

5 Can a bird fall in a <u>snare</u> upon the earth, where no <u>gin</u> *is* for him? shall *one* take up a <u>snare</u> from the earth, and have taken nothing at all? <small>trap - bait</small>

6 Shall a trumpet be blown in the city, and the people not be afraid? shall there be evil in a city, and the LORD has not <u>done</u> *it*? <small>caused</small>

7 Surely the <u>Lord GOD</u> will do nothing, <u>but</u> He reveals His secret to His servants the prophets

<small>JOHN 15:15 Adonay^{p.f.} Jehovah - unless</small>

8 The lion has roared, who will not fear? the <u>Lord GOD</u> has spoken, who can but prophesy?

9 Publish in the palaces at Ash'dod, and in the palaces in the land of E'gypt, and say, Assemble yourselves upon the mountains of Sa-ma'ri-a, and behold the great tumults in the midst thereof, and the oppressed in the midst thereof.

10 For they know not to do right, says the LORD, who store up violence and <u>robbery</u> in their palaces. <small>loot</small>

11 Therefore thus says the <u>Lord GOD</u>; An adversary *there shall be* even round about the land; and he shall bring down your strength from you, and your palaces shall be <u>spoiled</u>. <small>Adonay^{p.f.} Jehovah - plundered</small>

12 Thus says the LORD; As the shepherd takes out of the mouth of the lion two legs, or a piece of an ear; so shall the children of Is'ra-el be taken out that dwell in Sa-ma'ri-a in the corner of a bed, and in Da-mas'cus *in* a couch.

13 Hear you, and testify in the house of Jacob, says the <u>Lord GOD</u>, the <u>God of hosts</u>, <small>Jehovah^{s.f.} Elohe Tsebaoth</small>

14 That in the day that I shall <u>visit the transgressions</u> of Is'ra-el upon him I will also <u>visit</u> the altars of Beth'-el: and the horns of the altar shall be cut off, and fall to the ground. <small>judge the sins - punish</small>

15 And I will smite the winter house with the summer house; and the houses of ivory shall perish, and the great houses shall have an end, says the LORD.

CHAPTER 4

HEAR this word, you <u>kine</u> of Ba'shan, that *are* in the mountain of Sa-ma'ri-a, which oppress the poor, which crush the needy, which say to their masters, Bring, and let us drink. <small>cows</small>

2 The <u>Lord GOD</u> has sworn by His holiness, that, lo, the days shall come upon you, that He will take you away with hooks, and your posterity with fishhooks. <small>Adonay^{p.f.} Jehovah</small>

3 And you shall go out at the <u>breaches</u>, every *cow at that which is* before her; and you shall <u>cast</u> <u>them</u> into the palace, says the LORD.   breaks in the wall - put them in prison

4 Come to Beth'-el, and transgress; at Gil'gal multiply transgression; and bring your sacrifices every morning, *and* your tithes after three years:

5 And offer a sacrifice of thanksgiving with <u>leaven</u>, and proclaim *and* publish the free offerings: for this likes you, O you children of Israel, says the <u>Lord</u> G<small>OD</small>.   yeast - Adonay^{p.f.} Jehovah

6 And I also have given you cleanness of teeth in all your cities, and want of bread in all your places: yet have you not returned to Me, says the LORD.

7 And also I have withholden the rain from you, when *there were* yet three months to the harvest: and I caused it to rain upon one city, and caused it not to rain upon another city: one piece was rained upon, and the piece whereupon it rained not withered.

8 So two *or* three cities wandered to one city, to drink water; but they were not satisfied: yet have you not returned to Me, says the LORD.

9 I have smitten you with <u>blasting</u> and mildew: when your gardens and your vineyards and your fig trees and your olive trees increased, the palmerworm devoured *them*: yet have you not returned to Me, says the LORD.   wind blown

10 I have sent among you the pestilence after the manner of E'gypt: your young men have I slain with the sword, and have taken away your horses; and I have made the stink of your camps to come up to your nostrils: yet have you not returned to Me, says the LORD.

11 I have overthrown *some* of you, as <u>God</u> overthrew So'dom and Go-mor'rah, and you were as a firebrand plucked out of the burning: yet have you not returned to me, says the LORD.   Elohim^{p.f.}

12 Therefore thus will I do to you, O Is'ra-el: *and* because I will do this to you, prepare to meet your <u>God</u>, O Is'ra-el.

13 For, lo, He that forms the mountains, and creates the wind, and declares to man what *is* His thought, that makes the morning darkness, and treads upon the high places of the earth, <u>The LORD, The God of hosts</u>, *is* His name.   Jehovah^{s.f.} Elohe Tsebaoth

CHAPTER 5

H<small>EAR</small> you this word which I take up against you, *even* a lamentation, O house of Is'ra-el.

2 The virgin of Is'ra-el is fallen; she shall no more rise: she is forsaken upon her land; *there is* none to raise her up.

3 For thus says the <u>Lord</u> G<small>OD</small>; The city that went out *by* a thousand shall leave an hundred, and that which went forth *by* an hundred shall leave ten, to the house of Is'ra-el.   Adonay^{p.f.} Jehovah

4 For thus says the LORD to the house of Is'ra-el, Seek you Me, and you shall live:

5 But seek not Beth'-el, nor enter into Gil'gal, and pass not to Be'er-she'ba: for Gil'gal shall surely go into captivity, and Beth'-el shall come to nothing.

6 Seek the LORD, and you shall live; less He break out like fire in the house of Jo'seph, and <u>devour</u> *it*, and *there be* none to quench *it* in Beth'-el. _{destroy}

7 You who turn judgment to wormwood, and leave off righteousness in the earth,

8 *Seek Him* that makes the seven stars and O-ri'on, and turns the shadow of death into the morning, and makes the day dark with night: that calls for the waters of the sea, and pours them out upon the face of the earth: The LORD *is* His name:

9 That strengthens the <u>spoiled</u> against the strong, so that the <u>spoiled</u> shall come against the fortress. _{robbers}

10 They <u>hate</u> him that rebukes in the gate, and they abhor him that speaks uprightly. _{disrespect}

11 Forasmuch therefore as your treading *is* upon the poor, and you take from him burdens of wheat: you have built houses of <u>hewn</u> stone, but you shall not dwell in them; you have planted pleasant vineyards, but you shall not drink wine of them. _{cut}

12 For I know your manifold transgressions and your mighty sins: they afflict the just, they take a bribe, and they turn aside the poor in the gate *from their right*.

13 Therefore the prudent shall keep silence in that time; for it *is* an evil time.

14 Seek good, and not evil, that you may live: and so the <u>LORD, the God of hosts,</u> shall be with you, as you have spoken. _{Jehovah^s.f. Elohe Tsebaoth}

15 Hate the evil, and love the good, and establish judgment in the gate: it may be that the <u>LORD God of hosts</u> will be gracious to the remnant of Jo'seph. _{Jehovah^s.f. Elohim^p.f. Tsebaoth}

16 Therefore the <u>LORD</u>, the <u>God</u> of hosts, the <u>Lord</u>, says thus; Wailing *shall be* in all streets; and they shall say in all the highways, Alas! alas! and they shall call the husbandman to mourning, and such as are skilful of lamentation to wailing. _{Jehovah^s.f. - Elohim^p.f. - Adonay^p.f.}

17 And in all vineyards *shall be* wailing: for I will pass through you, says the LORD.

18 Woe to you that desire the day of the LORD! to what end *is* it for you? the day of the LORD *is* darkness, and not light.

19 As if a man did flee from a lion, and a bear met him; or went into the house, and leaned his hand on the wall, and a serpent bit him.

20 *Shall* not the day of the LORD *be* darkness, and not light? even very dark, and no brightness in it?

21 I <u>hate</u>, I despise your feast days, and I will not <u>smell</u> in your solemn assemblies. _{abhor - delight}

22 Though you offer Me burned offerings and your <u>meat</u> offerings, I will not accept *them*: neither will I regard the peace offerings of your fat beasts. _{grain}

23 Take you away from Me the noise of your songs; for I will not hear the melody of your viols.

24 But let <u>judgment run</u> down as waters, and righteousness as a mighty stream. _{justice roll}

25 Have you offered to Me sacrifices and offerings in the wilderness forty years, O house of Is'ra-el? ACTS 7:42
26 But you have borne the tabernacle of your Mo'loch and Chi'un your images, the star of your god, which you made to yourselves.
27 Therefore will I cause you to go into captivity beyond Da-mas'cus, says the LORD, whose name *is* The God of hosts. *Jehovah*s.f. *Elohe Tsebaoth*

CHAPTER 6

WOE to them *that are* at ease in Zi'on, and trust in the mountain of Sa-ma'ri-a, *which are* named chief of the nations, to whom the house of Is'ra-el came!
2 Pass you to Cal'neh, and see; and from there go you to Ha'math the great: then go down to Gath of the Phi-lis'tines: *be they* better than these kingdoms? or their border greater than your border?
3 You that put far away the evil day, and <u>cause</u> the seat of violence to come near; encourage
4 That lie upon beds of ivory, and <u>stretch</u> themselves upon their couches, and eat the lambs out of the flock, and the calves out of the midst of the stall; sprawl
5 That chant to the sound of the viol, *and* invent to themselves instruments of music, like Da'vid;
6 That drink wine in bowls, and anoint themselves with the chief ointments: but they are not grieved for the <u>affliction</u> of Jo'seph. ruin

7 Therefore now shall they go captive with the first that go captive, and the banquet of them that <u>stretched</u> themselves shall be removed. sprawled
8 The <u>Lord GOD</u> has sworn by Himself, says the <u>LORD the God of hosts</u>, I abhor the excellency of Ja'cob, and hate his palaces: therefore will I deliver up the city with all that is therein. *Adonay*p.f. *Jehovah - Jehovah*s.f. *Elohe Tsebaoth*
9 And it shall come to pass, if there remain ten men in one house, that they shall die.
10 And a man's uncle shall take him up, and he that burns him, to bring out the bones out of the house, and shall say to him that *is* by the sides of the house, *Is there* yet *any* with you? and he shall say, No. Then shall he say, Hold your tongue: for we may not make mention of the name of the LORD.
11 For, behold, the LORD commands, and He will smite the great house with <u>breaches</u>, and the little house with clefts. broken places
12 Shall horses run upon the rock? will *one* plow *there* with oxen? for you have turned judgment into gall, and the fruit of righteousness into <u>hemlock</u>: i.e., bitterness
13 You which rejoice in a thing of nothing, which say, Have we not taken to us <u>horns</u> by our own strength? i.e., power
14 But, behold, I will raise up against you a nation, O house of Is'ra-el, says the <u>LORD the God of hosts</u>; and they shall afflict you from the entering in of He'math to the river of the wilderness. *Jehovah*s.f. *Elohe Tsebaoth*

CHAPTER 7

THUS has the <u>Lord G</u><small><u>OD</u></small> showed to me; and, behold, He formed grasshoppers in the beginning of the shooting up of the latter growth; and, lo, *it was* the latter growth after the king's mowings. <small>Adonay^{p.f.} Jehovah</small>

2 And it came to pass, *that* when they had made an end of eating the grass of the land, then I said, O <u>Lord G</u><small><u>OD</u></small>, forgive, I <u>beseech</u> You: by whom shall Ja'cob arise? for he *is* small. <small>beg</small>

3 The L<small>ORD</small> <u>repented</u> for this: It shall not be, says the L<small>ORD</small>. <small>grieved</small>

4 Thus has the <u>Lord G</u><small><u>OD</u></small> showed to me: and, behold, the <u>Lord G</u><small><u>OD</u></small> called <u>to contend</u> by fire, and it devoured the great deep, and did eat up a part. <small>for judgment</small>

5 Then said I, O <u>Lord G</u><small><u>OD</u></small>, cease, I <u>beseech</u> You: by whom shall Ja'cob arise? for he *is* small.

<small>Adonay^{p.f.} Jehovah - beg</small>

6 The L<small>ORD</small> <u>repented</u> for this: This also shall not be, says the <u>Lord G</u><small><u>OD</u></small>. <small>grieved</small>

7 Thus He showed me: and, behold, the Lord stood upon a wall *made* by a plumbline, with a plumbline in His hand.

8 And the L<small>ORD</small> said to me, A'mos, what see you? And I said, A plumbline. Then said the <u>Lord</u>, Behold, I will set a plumbline in the midst of My people Is'ra-el: I will not again pass by them any more:

<small>Jehovah^{s.f.} - Adonay^{p.f.}</small>

9 And the high places of I'saac shall be desolate, and the sanctuaries of Is'ra-el shall be laid waste; and I will rise against the house of Jer-o-bo'am with the sword.

10 Then Am-a-zi'ah the priest of Beth'-el sent to Jer-o-bo'am king of Is'ra-el, saying, A'mos has conspired against you in the midst of the house of Is'ra-el: the land is not able to <u>bear</u> all his words. <small>endure</small>

11 For thus A'mos says, Jer-o-bo'am shall die by the sword, and Is'ra-el shall surely be led away captive out of their own land.

12 Also Am-a-zi'ah said to A'mos, O you seer, go, flee you away into the land of Ju'dah, and there eat bread, and prophesy there:

13 But prophesy not again any more at Beth'-el: for it *is* the king's <u>chapel</u>, and it *is* the king's <u>court</u>. <small>sanctuary - residence</small>

14 Then answered A'mos, and said to Am-a-zi'ah, I *was* no prophet, neither *was* I a prophet's son; but I *was* an herdman, and a gatherer of <u>sycamore</u> fruit: <small>wild figs</small>

15 And the L<small>ORD</small> took me as I followed the flock, and the L<small>ORD</small> said to me, Go, prophesy to My people Is'ra-el.

16 Now therefore hear you the word of the L<small>ORD</small>: You say, Prophesy not against Is'ra-el, and drop not *your word* against the house of I'saac.

17 Therefore thus says the L<small>ORD</small>; Your wife shall be an harlot in the city, and your sons and your daughters shall fall by the sword, and your land shall be divided by line; and you shalt die in a <u>polluted</u> land: and Is'ra-el shall surely go into captivity forth of his land. <small>unclean</small>

CHAPTER 8

THUS has the <u>Lord God</u> showed to me: and behold a basket of summer fruit. _{Adonay^{p.f.} Jehovah}
2 And He said, A'mos, what see you? And I said, A basket of summer fruit. Then said the LORD to me, The end is come upon My people of Is'ra-el; I will not again pass by them any more.
3 And the songs of the temple shall be <u>howlings</u> in that day, says the Lord GOD: *there shall be* many dead bodies in every place; they shall cast *them* forth with silence. _{wailings}
4 Hear this, O you that swallow up the needy, even to make the poor of the land to fail,
5 Saying, When will the new moon be gone, that we may sell <u>corn</u>? and the <u>sabbath</u>, that we may set forth wheat, making the ephah small, and the shekel great, and falsifying the balances by deceit? _{grain - rest day}
6 That we may buy the poor for silver, and the needy for a pair of shoes; *yea*, and sell the refuse of the wheat?
7 The LORD has sworn by the excellency of Ja'cob, Surely I will never forget any of their works.
8 Shall not the land tremble for this, and every one mourn that dwells therein? and it shall rise up wholly as a <u>flood</u>; and it shall be cast out and drowned, as *by* the flood of E'gypt. _{river Nile}
9 And it shall come to pass in that day, says the <u>Lord God,</u> that I will cause the sun to go down at noon, and I will darken the earth in the clear day:

10 And I will turn your feasts into mourning, and all your songs into lamentation; and I will bring up sackcloth upon all loins, and baldness upon every head; and I will make it as the mourning of an only *son*, and the end thereof as a bitter day.
11 Behold, the days come, says the <u>Lord God</u>, that I will send a famine in the land, not a famine of bread, nor a thirst for water, but of hearing the words of the LORD: _{Adonay^{p.f.} Jehovah}
12 And they shall wander from sea to sea, and from the north even to the east, they shall run to and fro to seek the word of the LORD, and shall not find *it*.
13 In that day shall the fair virgins and young men faint for thirst.
14 They that swear by the sin of Sa-ma'ri-a, and say, Your god, O Dan, lives; and, The <u>manner</u> of Be'er-she'ba lives; even they shall fall, and never rise up again. _{way}

CHAPTER 9

I SAW the Lord standing upon the altar: and He said, Smite the <u>lintel</u> of the door, that the posts may shake: and <u>cut</u> them in the head, all of them; and I will slay the last of them with the sword: he that flees of them shall not flee away, and he that escapes of them shall not be delivered. _{top crossbar - break}
2 Though they dig into <u>hell</u>, from there shall My hand take them; though they climb up to heaven, from there will I bring them down: _{Sheol}
3 And though they hide themselves in

the top of Car'mel, I will search and take them out from there; and though they be hid from My sight in the bottom of the sea, from there will I command the serpent, and he shall bite them:

4 And though they go into captivity before their enemies, from there will I command the sword, and it shall slay them: and I will set My eyes upon them for evil, and not for good.

5 And the Lord GOD of hosts *is* He that touches the land, and it shall melt, and all that dwell therein shall mourn: and it shall rise up wholly like a <u>flood</u>; and shall be drowned, as *by* the flood of E'gypt.   Adonay^{p.f.} Jehovah Tsebaoth - river Nile

6 *It is* He that builds His stories in the heaven, and has founded His troop in the earth; He that calls for the waters of the sea, and pours them out upon the face of the earth: The LORD *is* His name.

7 *Are you* not as children of the E-thi-o'pi-ans to Me, O children of Is'ra-el? says the LORD. Have not I brought up Is'ra-el out of the land of E'gypt? and the Phi-lis'tines from Caph'tor, and the Syr'i-ans from Kir?

8 Behold, the eyes of the <u>Lord GOD</u> *are* upon the sinful kingdom, and I will destroy it from off the face of the earth; saving that I will not utterly destroy the house of Jacob, says the LORD.   Adonay^{p.f.} Jehovah

9 For, lo, I will command, and I will <u>sift</u> the house of Is'ra-el among all nations, like as *corn* is sifted in a sieve, yet shall not the least grain fall upon the earth.   shake - grain

10 All the sinners of My people shall die by the sword, which say, The evil shall not overtake nor <u>prevent</u> us.   confront

11 In that day will I raise up the tabernacle of Da'vid that is fallen, and close up the <u>breaches</u> thereof; and I will raise up his ruins, and I will build it as in the days of old: ACTS 15:16 breaks

12 That they may possess the remnant of E'dom, and of all the heathen, which are called by My name, says the LORD that does this.

13 Behold, the days come, says the LORD, that the plowman shall overtake the reaper, and the treader of grapes him that sows seed; and the mountains shall drop sweet wine, and all the hills shall melt.

14 And I will bring again the captivity of My people of Is'ra-el, and they shall build the waste cities, and inhabit *them*; and they shall plant vineyards, and drink the wine thereof; they shall also make gardens, and eat the fruit of them.

15 And I will plant them upon their land, and they shall no more be pulled up out of their land which I have given them, says the LORD your <u>God</u>.   Elohim^{p.f.}

OBADIAH

OUTLINE

An Oracle of the Lord Against Edom vv. 1-4

The Awful Fulfilment vv. 5-9

Esau's Sin Against His Brother Jacob vv. 10-14

The Wider Context: The Day of the Lord vv. 15-18

House of Jacob to "Possess Their Possessions" vv. 19-21

SURVEY

This little book sums up the meaning of the relationship of Edom and Israel (Esau and Jacob) in the history of salvation, and in so doing reveals an aspect of the Day of the Lord and the Kingdom of God.

Edom, the nation sprung from Esau, always proved antagonistic to Israel, despite their brotherhood as sons of Isaac. Many prophets were entrusted with messages of condemnation directed against Edom (Amos, Isaiah, Jeremiah, Ezekiel, Malachi), which often drew attention to Edom's self-sufficiency and pride as the root of his sin. In Obadiah, the prophet seems to take up an existing prophecy of doom against Edom (vv. 1b-4 and phrases within vv. 5-9)—perhaps the same oracle as appears in Jeremiah 49.7-22—and notes how terribly it was being fulfilled and with what just retribution. Obadiah then relates this particular doom to the judgment of all the nations in the imminent Day of the Lord, when the escaped remnant of Israel will be alike the sphere of salvation and the instrument of the Lord's rule over all the nations.

Short as it is, this prophecy sets out and illustrates the foundation truths of Biblical revelation: the sovereign rule of God, which will be universally acknowledged (v. 21); the election to blessing of Israel, the people of God (v. 17b); this election fulfilled through a remnant (v. 17a) who will be the arm of God's strength from Mount Zion; the culmination of God's purposes in "the Day of the Lord" which, while bringing vindication to His own and a proper enjoyment of their promised land of rest, will bring condemnation to the enemy and the oppressor, of whom Edom is here the type (v. 15).

Although the Book of Obadiah is only one among many prophetic utterances concerning Edom, it is convenient to take it as the focus for all the Old Testament Edom references, since it is not possible in a commentary of this nature to treat any of the other passages in detail. We therefore list here the main references to Edom: *Historical:* Genesis 25 to 36 (Jacob and Esau); Numbers 20.14-21, Deuteronomy 2.1-8 (the Exodus period); 1 Samuel 14.47 (under Saul); 2 Samuel 8.14 (under David); 2 Kings 8.20-22 (under Jehoram); 2 Chronicles 20.10-23 (under Jehoshaphat); 2 Kings 14.7, 2 Chronicles 25.11-13 (under Amaziah); 2 Chronicles 28.17 (under Ahaz); Psalm 137.7, Lamentations 4.22 (fall of Jerusalem); Psalm 83.1-6 (general). *Prophecies:* Isaiah 11.14; 34; 63.1-6; Jeremiah 49.7-22, Ezekiel 25.12-14; 35; Joel 3.19; Amos 1.11-12; Malachi 1.2-5.

AUTHOR

Beyond his name (which is not uncommon in the Old Testament), nothing is known of the author of this, the shortest book in the Old Testament. Nor is the period of writing a matter of certainty. While some conservative scholars refer the prophecy to a time before the fall of Jerusalem (586 B.C.), the

description of the destruction of the city given in verses 11 to 14 most aptly fits the destruction under Nebuchadrezzar when it is known (from Ps 137.7; Ezk 35.5; Lm 4.21, and so forth) that the Edomites participated. Obadiah seems also to describe a disaster to Edom subsequent to the fall of Jerusalem (vv. 5–7). This was perhaps the first of the Nabatean attacks on Mount Seir which dispossessed the Edomites sometime in the course of the sixth to the fourth centuries (compare Ml 1.3,4). The prophecy would then belong to the time of the Exile or soon after the return.

D.W.B.R.

THE BOOK OF

OBADIAH

THE vision of O-ba-di'ah. Thus says the Lord GOD concerning E'dom; We have heard a rumor from the LORD, and an ambassador is sent among the heathen, Arise you, and let us rise up against her in battle. *Adonay*^{p.f.} *Jehovah - report*

2 Behold, I have made you small among the heathen: you are greatly despised.

3 The pride of your heart has deceived you, you that dwell in the clefts of the rock, whose habitation *is* high; that says in his heart, Who shall bring me down to the ground?

4 Though you exalt *yourself* as the eagle, and though you set your nest among the stars, from there will I bring you down, says the LORD.

5 If thieves came to you, if robbers by night, (how are you cut off!) would they not have stolen till they had enough? if the grapegatherers came to you, would they not leave *some* grapes?

6 How are *the things* of E'sau searched out! *how* are his hidden things sought up!

7 All the men of your confederacy have brought you *even* to the border: the men that were at peace with you have deceived you, *and* prevailed against you; *they that eat* your bread have laid a wound under you: *there is* none understanding in him. *an ambush for - no*

8 Shall I not in that day, says the LORD, even destroy the wise *men* out of E'dom, and understanding out of the mount of E'sau?

9 And your mighty *men*, O Te'man, shall be dismayed, to the end that every one of the mount of E'sau may be cut off by slaughter. *destroyed*

10 For *your* violence against your brother Ja'cob shame shall cover you, and you shall be cut off for ever.

11 In the day that you stood on the other side, in the day that the strangers carried away captive his forces, and foreigners entered into his gates, and cast lots upon Je-ru'sa-lem, even you *were* as one of them. *substance*

12 But you should not have looked on the day of your brother in the day that he became a stranger; neither should you have rejoiced over the children of Ju'dah in the day of their destruction; neither should you have spoken proudly in the day of distress. *gloated over*

13 You should not have entered into the gate of My people in the day of their calamity; yea, you should not have looked on their affliction in the day of their calamity, nor have laid *hands* on their substance in the day of their calamity;

14 Neither should you have stood in the crossway, to cut off those of his that did escape; neither should you have delivered up those of his that did remain in the day of distress. *imprisoned*

15 For the day of the LORD *is* near

upon all the heathen: as you have done, it shall be done to you: your reward shall return upon your own head.

16 For as you have drunk upon My holy mountain, *so* shall all the heathen drink continually, yea, they shall drink, and they shall swallow down, and they shall be as though they had not been.

17 But upon mount Zi'on shall be <u>deliverance</u>, and there shall be holiness; and the house of Ja'cob shall possess their possessions. those who escape

18 And the house of Ja'cob shall be a fire, and the house of Jo'seph a flame, and the house of E'sau for stubble, and they shall kindle in them, and <u>devour</u> them; and there shall not be *any* re-maining of the house of E'sau; for the LORD has spoken *it*. destroy

19 And *they* of the south shall possess the mount of E'sau; and *they of* the plain the Phi-lis'tines: and they shall possess the fields of E'phra-im, and the fields of Sa-ma'ri-a: and Ben'ja-min *shall possess* Gil'e-ad.

20 And the captivity of this host of the children of Is'ra-el *shall possess* that of the Ca'naan-ites, *even* to Zar'e-phath; and the captivity of Je-ru'sa-lem, which *is* in Seph'a-rad, shall possess the cities of the south.

21 And <u>saviors</u> shall come up on mount Zi'on to judge the mount of E'sau; and the kingdom shall be the LORD's. deliverers

JONAH

OUTLINE

THE REBELLIOUS PROPHET 1.1–17
    The Lord Calls, Jonah Rebels 1.1–3
    The Lord Interposes a Storm 1.4–6
    The Sailors Intervene 1.7–16
    The Lord Interposes a Big Fish 1.17

THE REINSTATED PROPHET 2.1—3.10
    Jonah Prays 2.1–9
    The Lord Delivers Jonah 2.10
    Jonah Obeys the Call 3.1–4
    King and Ninevites Repent 3.5–9
    The Lord Withholds Judgment 3.10

THE RETIRED PROPHET 4.1–11
    The Lord Displeases Jonah 4.1–5
    Jonah Displeases the Lord 4.6–10
    The Lord Shows Great Pity 4.11

SURVEY

By its content and spirit, the Book of Jonah reveals the universality and compassion of God's grace. This is hinted in 3.10 and broadly stated in 4.11.

This book is biographical. It begins and ends with the Lord speaking to Jonah. First, Jonah is given a commission of judgment; finally, the Lord portrays His mercy and compassion. Between these two depictions of the Lord's character lies Jonah's response to God's justice and compassion. Jonah refuses to accept the Lord's commission lest the heathen repent and God show mercy. The magnanimous heart of God, forgiving the repentant heathen, appears in strong contrast to the narrow, bigoted and unforgiving spirit of Jonah.

AUTHOR

Since the book makes no assertion abouts its author, it may be fairly conjectured that the author is Jonah himself. He is the son of Amittai (1.1), and doubtless the same son of Amittai who prophesied during the reign of Jeroboam II (cf. 2 K 14.25).

C.A.R.

THE BOOK OF

JONAH

CHAPTER 1

"Dove"
The Reluctant Messenger

NOW the word of the LORD came to Jo'nah the son of A-mit'ta-i, saying,

2 Arise, go to Nin'e-veh, that great city, and cry against it; for their wickedness is come up before Me. **preach**

3 But Jo'nah rose up to flee to Tar'shish from the presence of the LORD, and went down to Jop'pa; and he found a ship going to Tar'shish: so he paid the fare thereof, and went down into it, to go with them to Tar'shish from the presence of the LORD. **?Spain - will**

4 But the LORD sent out a great wind into the sea, and there was a mighty tempest in the sea, so that the ship was like to be broken. **shipwrecked**

5 Then the mariners were afraid, and cried every man to his god, and cast forth the wares that *were* in the ship into the sea, to lighten *it* of them. But Jo'nah was gone down into the sides of the ship; and he lay, and was fast asleep.

6 So the shipmaster came to him, and said to him, What mean you, O sleeper? arise, call upon your God, if so be that God will think upon us, that we perish not.

Elohimp.f.

7 And they said every one to his fellow, Come, and let us cast lots, that we may know for whose cause this evil *is* upon us. So they cast lots, and the lot fell upon Jo'nah.

8 Then said they to him, Tell us, we pray you, for whose cause this evil *is* upon us; What *is* your occupation? and from where come you? what *is* your country? and of what people *are* you? **beg**

9 And he said to them, I *am* an He'brew; and I fear the LORD, the God of heaven, which has made the sea and the dry *land*. **revere - Elohim**p.f.

10 Then were the men exceedingly afraid, and said to him, Why have you done this? For the men knew that he fled from the presence of the LORD, because he had told them.

11 Then said they to him, What shall we do to you, that the sea may be calm to us? for the sea wrought, and was tempestuous. **churned**

12 And he said to them, Take me up, and cast me forth into the sea; so shall the sea be calm to you: for I know that for my sake this great tempest *is* upon you.

13 Nevertheless the men rowed hard to bring *it* to the land; but they could not: for the sea wrought, and was tempestuous against them.

14 Wherefore they cried to the LORD, and said, We beseech you, O LORD, we beseech You, let us not perish for this man's life, and lay not upon us innocent blood: for You, O LORD, have done as it pleased You. **pray**

15 So they took up Jo'nah, and cast

him forth into the sea: and the sea ceased from its raging.

16 Then the men <u>feared</u> the LORD exceedingly, and offered a sacrifice to the LORD, and made <u>vows</u>.

respected - pledges

17 Now the LORD had prepared a great fish to swallow up Jo'nah. And Jo'nah was in the belly of the fish <u>three days and three nights</u>.   MATT. 12:40 (Jesus in tomb)

CHAPTER 2

THEN Jo'nah prayed to the LORD his <u>God</u> out of the fish's belly. Elohim p.f.

2 And said, I cried by reason of my affliction to the LORD, and He heard me; out of the belly of <u>hell</u> cried I, *and* You heard my voice.   sheol

3 For You had cast me into the deep, in the midst of the seas; and the floods compassed me about: all Your billows and Your waves passed over me.

4 Then I said, I am cast out of Your sight; yet I will look again toward Your holy temple.

5 The waters compassed me about, *even* to the soul: the depth closed me round about, the weeds were wrapped about my head.

6 I went down to the bottoms of the mountains; the earth with her bars *was* about me for ever: yet have You brought up my life from <u>corruption</u>, O LORD my <u>God</u>.   the pit - Elohim p.f.

7 When my soul fainted within me I remembered the LORD: and my prayer came in to You, into Your holy temple.

8 They that observe lying vanities forsake their own mercy.

9 But I will sacrifice to You with the voice of thanksgiving; I will pay *that* that I have vowed. <u>Salvation</u> *is* of the LORD.   i.e., Heb. Jeshua

10 And the LORD spoke to the fish, and it vomited out Jo'nah upon the dry *land*.

CHAPTER 3

AND the word of the LORD came to Jo'nah the second time, saying,

2 Arise, go to Nin'e-veh, that great city, and preach to it the preaching that I bid thee.

3 So Jo'nah arose, and went to Nin'e-veh, according to the word of the LORD. Now Nin'e-veh was an exceeding great city of three days' journey.

4 And Jo'nah began to enter into the city a day's journey, and he cried, and said, Yet forty days, and Nin'e-veh shall be overthrown.

5 So the people of Nin'e-veh believed <u>God</u>, and proclaimed a fast, and put on sackcloth, from the greatest of them even to the least of them.   MATT. 16:4 - Elohim p.f.

6 For word came to the king of Nin'e-veh, and he arose from his throne, and he laid his robe from him, and covered *him* with sackcloth, and sat in ashes.

7 And he caused *it* to be proclaimed and published through Nin'e-veh by the decree of the king and his <u>nobles</u>, saying, Let neither man nor beast, herd nor flock, taste any thing: let them not feed, nor drink water: chief men

8 But let man and beast be covered with sackcloth, and cry mightily to

God: yea, let them turn every one from his evil way, and from the violence that *is* in their hands.   Elohim[p.f.]

9 Who can tell *if* God will turn and repent, and turn away from His fierce anger, that we perish not?

10 And God saw their works, that they turned from their evil way; and God repented of the evil, that He had said that He would do to them; and He did *it* not.   grieved

CHAPTER 4

BUT it displeased Jo'nah exceedingly, and he was very angry.

2 And he prayed to the LORD, and said, I pray You, O LORD, *was* not this my saying, when I was yet in my country? Therefore I fled before to Tar'shish: for I knew that You *are* a gracious God, and merciful, slow to anger, and of great kindness, and repentest You of the evil.

?Spain - El[s.f.] - Relented

3 Therefore now, O LORD, take, I beseech You, my life from me; for *it is* better for me to die than to live.   beg

4 Then said the LORD, Do you well to be angry?

5 So Jo'nah went out of the city, and sat on the east side of the city, and there made him a booth, and sat under it in the shadow, till he might see what would become of the city.   shelter

6 And the LORD God prepared a gourd, and made *it* to come up over Jo'nah, that it might be a shadow over his head, to deliver him from his grief. So Jo'nah was exceeding glad of the gourd.   Jehovah[s.f.] Elohim[p.f.] - save - discomfort

7 But God prepared a worm when the morning rose the next day, and it smote the gourd that it withered.   Elohim[p.f.] - attacked - plant

8 And it came to pass, when the sun did arise, that God prepared a vehement east wind; and the sun beat upon the head of Jo'nah, that he fainted, and wished in himself to die, and said, *It is* better for me to die than to live.   scorching

9 And God said to Jo'nah, Do you well to be angry for the gourd? And he said, I do well to be angry, *even* to death.   plant

10 Then said the LORD, You have had pity on the gourd, for the which you have not labored, neither made it grow; which came up in a night, and perished in a night:

11 And should not I spare Nin'eveh, that great city, wherein are more than sixscore thousand persons that cannot discern between their right hand and their left hand; and *also* much cattle?

MICAH

OUTLINE

IDENTIFICATION 1.1

THE REPROOF OF SAMARIA AND JUDAH 1.2—3.12
  Appearance of the Lord in Judgment 1.2—2.13
  The Lord's Denunciation of the Rulers, False Prophets, and Priests 3.1-12

THE COMFORTING HOPE OF A REDEMPTIVE FUTURE 4.1—5.15
  The Issue of Days to Come 4.1—5.1
  The Rise of the Deliverer from Bethlehem and the Victories of His Righteous Remnant 5.2-15

THE LORD'S GREAT LAWSUIT WITH ISRAEL 6.1—7.20
  The Lord's Plea and Indictment 6.1-16
  Israel's Confession of Guilt and Her Complaint Before the Lord 7.1-17
  Who is Like Unto the Lord? The Final Verdict 7.18-20

SURVEY

The first three chapters of Micah's prophecy set forth the Lord's judgments upon Israel and Judah, and the impending doom awaiting these nations. Chapters 4 and 5 offer comfort and hope in view of the issue of days to come when the Lord's house will be established upon the mountain of enduring peace; a remnant will return to Zion, rescued from captivity in Babylon; a deliverer from Bethlehem will cause His righteous remnant to be a blessing in the earth; and the land will be purged of its idolatry and oppression. Chapters 6 and 7 declare the way of salvation by means of the analogy of a great lawsuit: the Lord is the plaintiff and Israel the defendant. Reminding His people of their deliverance from Egypt, and speaking to them of the nature of true worship, the Lord deplores their treasures of wickedness and oppression. This is followed by Israel's confession of guilt and a prayer that the Lord will return and shepherd His flock as of old. Micah concludes with a play upon the meaning of his own name, "Who is like unto the Lord?" He alone can pardon and show compassion to the people of His covenant.

AUTHOR

Micah refers to himself as the Morasthite. He was a native of Moresheth, near Gath in northern Philistia, about twenty miles southwest of Jerusalem. He was probably a peasant farmer. His activity as a prophet covers the reign of three kings from approximately 738 to 698 B.C. His father's name is not mentioned, so scholars conclude that his family was of insignificant and humble status. Micah is a master in his use of classical Hebrew poetry. He champions the cause of the oppressed peasants against the arrogant rich. His plea for true religion is equaled only by James (cf 6.6-8 with Ja 1.27).

R.E.P.

THE BOOK OF MICAH

CHAPTER 1

THE word of the LORD that came to Mi'cah the Mo'ras-thite in the days of Jo'tham, A'haz, *and* Hez-e-ki'ah, kings of Ju'dah, which he saw concerning Sa-ma'ri-a and Je-ru'sa-lem.

2 Hear, all you people; <u>hearken</u>, O earth, and all that therein is: and let the <u>Lord GOD</u> be witness against you, the Lord from His holy temple. listen - Jehovah Elohim p.f.

3 For, behold, the LORD comes forth out of His place, and will come down, and tread upon the high places of the earth.

4 And the mountains shall be molten under Him, and the valleys shall be cleft, as wax before the fire, *and* as the waters *that are* poured down a steep place.

5 For the transgression of Ja'cob *is* all this, and for the sins of the house of Is'ra-el. What *is* the transgression of Ja'cob? *is it* not Sa-ma'ri-a? and what *are* the high places of Ju'dah? *are they* not Je-ru'sa-lem?

6 Therefore I will make Sa-ma'ri-a as an heap of the field, *and* as plantings of a vineyard: and I will pour down the stones thereof into the valley, and I will <u>discover</u> the foundations thereof. reveal

7 And all the <u>graven</u> images thereof shall be beaten to pieces, and all the <u>hires</u> thereof shall be burned with the fire, and all the idols thereof will I lay desolate: for she gathered *it* of the <u>hire</u> of an harlot, and they shall return to the <u>hire</u> of an harlot. carved - earnings

8 Therefore I will wail and howl, I will go stripped and naked: I will make a wailing like the dragons, and mourning as the owls.

9 For her wound *is* incurable; for it is come to Ju'dah; he is come to the gate of My people, *even* to Je-ru'sa-lem.

10 Declare you *it* not at Gath, weep you not at all: in the house of Aph'rah roll yourself in the dust.

11 Pass you away, you inhabitant of Saph'ir, having your shame naked: the inhabitant of Za'a-nan came not forth in the mourning of Beth-e'zel; he shall receive of you his standing.

12 For the inhabitant of Ma'roth waited carefully for good: but evil came down from the LORD to the gate of Je-ru'sa-lem.

13 O you inhabitant of La'chish, bind the chariot to the swift beast: she *is* the beginning of the sin to the daughter of Zi'on: for the transgressions of Is'ra-el were found in you.

14 Therefore shall you give presents to Mor'esh-eth-gath: the houses of Ach'zib *shall be* a <u>lie</u> to the kings of Is'ra-el. deception

15 Yet will I bring an heir to you, O inhabitant of Ma-re'shah: he shall come to A-dul'lam the glory of Is'ra-el.

16 Make you bald, and poll you for your delicate children; enlarge your baldness as the eagle; for they are gone into captivity from you.

shave head - cut hair - in whom delight

CHAPTER 2

WOE to them that devise iniquity, and work evil upon their beds! when the morning is light, they practice it, because it is in the power of their hand.   sin

2 And they covet fields, and take *them* by violence; and houses, and take *them* away: so they oppress a man and his house, even a man and his heritage.   rob

3 Therefore thus says the LORD; Behold, against this family do I devise an evil, from which you shall not remove your necks; neither shall you go haughtily: for this time *is* evil. plan

4 In that day shall *one* take up a parable against you, and lament with a doleful lamentation, *and* say, We be utterly spoiled: He has changed the portion of My people: how has He removed *it* from me! turning away He has divided our fields.   bitter - destroyed

5 Therefore you shall have none that shall cast a cord by lot in the congregation of the LORD.

6 Prophesy you not, *say they to them that* prophesy: they shall not prophesy to them, *that* they shall not take shame.

7 O *you that are* named the house of Ja'cob, is the Spirit of the LORD straitened? *are* these His doings? do not My words do good to him that walks uprightly?   impatient

8 Even of late My people is risen up as an enemy: you pull off the robe with the garment from them that pass by securely as men averse from war. peaceably - returning

9 The women of My people have you cast out from their pleasant houses; from their children have you taken away My glory for ever.

10 Arise you, and depart; for this *is* not *your* rest: because it is polluted, it shall destroy *you*, even with a sore destruction.   grievous

11 If a man walking in the spirit and falsehood do lie, *saying*, I will prophesy to you of wine and of strong drink; he shall even be the prophet of this people.

12 I will surely assemble, O Ja'cob, all of you; I will surely gather the remnant of Is'ra-el; I will put them together as the sheep of Boz'rah, as the flock in the midst of their fold: they shall make great noise by reason of *the multitude of* men.

13 The breaker is come up before them: they have broken up, and have passed through the gate, and are gone out by it: and their king shall pass before them, and the LORD on the head of them.   destroyer

CHAPTER 3

AND I said, Hear, I pray you, O heads of Ja'cob, and you princes of the house of Is'ra-el; *Is it* not for you to know judgment? justice

2 Who hate the good, and love the evil; who pluck off their skin from off them, and their flesh from off their bones;

3 Who also eat the flesh of My people, and flay their skin from off them; and they break their bones, and chop them in pieces, as for the pot, and as flesh within the caldron.

4 Then shall they cry to the LORD, but He will not hear them: He will even hide His face from them at that time, as they have behaved themselves ill in their doings.

5 Thus says the LORD concerning the prophets that make My people err, that bite with their teeth, and cry, Peace; and he that puts not into their mouths, they even prepare war against him.

6 Therefore night *shall be* to you, that you shall not have a vision; and it shall be dark to you, that you shall not divine; and the sun shall go down over the prophets, and the day shall be dark over them.

7 Then shall the seers be ashamed, and the diviners confounded: yea, they shall all cover their lips; for *there is* no answer of God. Elohim^p.f.

8 But truly I am full of power by the Spirit of the LORD, and of judgment, and of might, to declare to Ja'cob his transgression, and to Is'ra-el his sin.

9 Hear this, I pray you, you heads of the house of Ja'cob, and princes of the house of Is'ra-el, that abhor judgment, and pervert all equity. despise - miscarry justice

10 They build up Zi'on with blood, and Je-ru'sa-lem with iniquity. bloodshed

11 The heads thereof judge for reward, and the priests thereof teach for hire, and the prophets thereof divine for money: yet will they lean upon the LORD, and say, *Is* not the LORD among us? none evil can come upon us. wages - instruct

12 Therefore shall Zi'on for your sake be plowed *as* a field, and Je-ru'sa-lem shall become heaps, and the mountain of the house as the high places of the forest. rubble

CHAPTER 4

BUT in the last days it shall come to pass, *that* the mountain of the house of the LORD shall be established in the top of the mountains, and it shall be exalted above the hills; and people shall flow to it.

2 And many nations shall come, and say, Come, and let us go up to the mountain of the LORD, and to the house of the God of Ja'cob; and He will teach us of His ways, and we will walk in His paths: for the law shall go forth of Zi'on, and the word of the LORD from Je-ru'sa-lem. Elohim^p.f.

3 And He shall judge among many people, and rebuke strong nations afar off; and they shall beat their swords into plowshares, and their spears into pruninghooks: nation shall not lift up a sword against nation, neither shall they learn war any more. farm tools

4 But they shall sit every man under his vine and under his fig tree; and none shall make *them* afraid: for the mouth of the LORD of hosts has spoken *it*. Jehovah^s.f. Tsebaoth

5 For all people will walk every one in the name of his god, and we will walk

in the name of the LORD our God for ever and ever. Elohim^{p.f.}

6 In that day, says the LORD, will I assemble her that <u>halt</u>, and I will gather her that is driven out, and her that I have afflicted; is lame

7 And I will make her that halted a remnant, and her that was cast far off a strong nation: and the LORD shall reign over them in mount Zi'on from hereafter, even for ever.

8 And you, O tower of the flock, the strong hold of the daughter of Zi'on, to you shall it come, even the first dominion; the kingdom shall come to the daughter of Je-ru'sa-lem.

9 Now why do you cry out aloud? *is there* no king in you? is your counselor perished? for pangs have taken you as a woman in travail.

10 Be in pain, and labor to bring forth, O daughter of Zi'on, like a woman in travail: for now shall you go forth out of the city, and you shall dwell in the field, and you shall go *even* to Bab'y-lon; there shall you be delivered; there the LORD shall redeem you from the hand of your enemies. REV. 12:2

11 Now also many nations are gathered against you, that say, Let her be defiled, and let our eye look upon Zi'on.

12 But they know not the thoughts of the LORD, neither understand they His <u>counsel</u>: for He shall gather them as the sheaves into the floor. purpose

13 Arise and thresh, O daughter of Zi'on: for I will make your horn iron, and I will make your hoofs brass: and you shall beat in pieces many people:

and I will consecrate their gain to the LORD, and their substance to the Lord of the whole earth. Jehovah^{s.f.} - Adon^{s.f.}

CHAPTER 5

NOW gather yourself in troops, O daughter of troops: he has laid siege against us: they shall smite the judge of Is'ra-el with a rod upon the cheek.

2 But you, Beth'-le-hem Eph'ra-tah, *though* you be little among the thousands of Ju'dah, *yet* out of you shall He come forth to Me *that is* to be ruler in Is'ra-el; whose goings forth *have been* from of old, from <u>everlasting</u>. MATT. 2:6   JOHN 7:42 eternity

3 Therefore will He give them up, until the time *that* she which <u>travails</u> has brought forth: then the remnant of His brethren shall return to the children of Is'ra-el. is in labor

4 And He shall stand and <u>feed</u> in the strength of the LORD, in the majesty of the name of the LORD His <u>God</u>; and they shall abide: for now shall He be great to the ends of the earth. feed the flock - Elohim^{p.f.}

5 And this <u>man</u> shall be the peace, when the As-syr'i-an shall come into our land: and when he shall tread in our palaces, then shall we raise against him seven shepherds, and eight principal men. One (i.e., Jesus)

6 And they shall <u>waste</u> the land of As-syr'i-a with the sword, and the land of Nim'rod in the entrances thereof: thus shall He deliver *us* from the As-syr'i-an, when he comes into our land, and when he treads inside our borders. ruin

7 And the remnant of Ja'cob shall be

in the midst of many people as a dew from the LORD, as the showers upon the grass, that tarries not for man, nor waits for the sons of men.

8 And the remnant of Ja'cob shall be among the Gen'tiles in the midst of many people as a lion among the beasts of the forest, as a young lion among the flocks of sheep: who, if he go through, both treads down, and tears in pieces, and none can deliver.

9 Your hand shall be lifted up upon your adversaries, and all your enemies shall be cut off.

10 And it shall come to pass in that day, says the LORD, that I will cut off your horses out of the midst of you, and I will destroy your chariots: destroy

11 And I will cut off the cities of your land, and throw down all your strong holds:

12 And I will cut off witchcrafts out of your hand; and you shall have no more soothsayers:

13 Your graven images also will I cut off, and your standing images out of the midst of you; and you shall no more worship the work of your hands. idols

14 And I will pluck up your groves out of the midst of you: so will I destroy your cities. idols

15 And I will execute vengeance in anger and fury upon the heathen, such as they have not heard. not obeyed

CHAPTER 6

HEAR you now what the LORD says; Arise, contend you before the mountains, and let the hills hear your voice.

2 Hear you, O mountains, the LORD's controversy, and your strong foundations of the earth: for the LORD has a controversy with His people, and He will plead with Is'ra-el. law suit - dispute

3 O My people, what have I done to you? and wherein have I wearied you? testify against Me.

4 For I brought you up out of the land of E'gypt, and redeemed you out of the house of servants; and I sent before you Mo'ses, Aar'on, and Mir'i-am.

5 O My people, remember now what Ba'lak king of Mo'ab consulted, and what Ba'laam the son of Be'or answered him from Shit'tim to Gil'gal; that you may know the righteousness of the LORD.

6 Wherewith shall I come before the LORD, and bow myself before the high God? shall I come before Him with burned offerings, with calves of a year old? Elohim^p.f.

7 Will the LORD be pleased with thousands of rams, or with ten thousands of rivers of oil? shall I give my firstborn for my transgression, the fruit of my body for the sin of my soul? offspring

8 He has showed you, O man, what is good; and what does the LORD require of you, but to do justly, and to love mercy, and to walk humbly with your God? Elohim^p.f.

9 The LORD's voice cries to the city, and the man of wisdom shall see your name: hear you the rod, and who has appointed it. be afraid of - obey

10 Are there yet the treasures of wickedness in the house of the wicked,

and the <u>scant</u> measure *that is* abominable? _{short}

11 Shall I count *them* pure with the wicked balances, and with the bag of deceitful weights?

12 For the rich men thereof are full of violence, and the inhabitants thereof have spoken lies, and their tongue *is* deceitful in their mouth.

13 Therefore also will I make *you* sick in smiting you, in making *you* desolate because of your sins.

14 You shall eat, but not be satisfied; and your casting down *shall be* in the midst of you; and you shall take hold, but shall not deliver; and *that* which you deliver will I give up to the sword.

15 You shall sow, but you shall not reap; you shall tread the olives, but you shall not anoint you with oil; and sweet wine, but shall not drink wine.   JOHN 4:37

16 For the statutes of Om'ri are kept, and all the works of the house of A'hab, and you walk in their counsels; that I should make you a desolation, and the inhabitants thereof an <u>hissing</u>: therefore you shall bear the reproach of My people.   derision

CHAPTER 7

WOE is me! for I am as when they have gathered the summer fruits, as the grapegleanings of the vintage: *there is* no cluster to eat: my soul desired the first ripe fruit.

2 The good *man* is perished out of the earth: and *there is* none upright among men: they all lie in wait for blood; they hunt every man his brother with a net.

3 That they may do evil with both hands earnestly, the prince asks and the judge *asks* for a reward; and the great *man*, he utters his mischievous desire: so they <u>wrap it up</u>.   weave together

4 The best of them *is* as a brier: the most upright *is sharper* than a thorn hedge: the day of your watchmen *and* your visitation comes; now shall be their perplexity.

5 Trust you not in a friend, put you not confidence in a guide: keep the doors of your mouth from her that lies in your bosom.

6 For the son dishonors the father, the daughter rises up against her mother, the daughter in law against her mother in law; a man's enemies *are* the men of his own house.   MATT. 10:35 LUKE 12:53

7 Therefore I will look to the LORD; I will wait for the <u>God</u> of my salvation: my <u>God</u> will hear me.   Elohim^{p.f.}

8 Rejoice not against me, O my enemy: when I fall, I shall arise; when I sit in darkness, the LORD *shall be* a light to me.

9 I will bear the indignation of the LORD, because I have sinned against Him, until He plead my cause, and execute judgment for me: He will bring me forth to the light, *and* I shall behold His righteousness.

10 Then *she that is* my enemy shall see *it*, and shame shall cover her which said to me, Where is the LORD your <u>God</u>? my eyes shall behold her: now shall she be trodden down as the mire of the streets.   Elohim^{p.f.}

11 *In* the day that your walls are to be

built, *in* that day shall the <u>decree</u>
be far removed. boundary

12 *In* that day *also* he shall come
even to you from As-syr'i-a, and
from the <u>fortified</u> cities, and from
the fortress even to the river, and
from sea to sea, and *from* mountain to mountain. cities of Egypt

13 Notwithstanding the land shall
be desolate because of them that
dwell therein, for the fruit of their
doings.

14 <u>Feed</u> Your people with Your
rod, the flock of Your heritage,
which dwell <u>solitarily</u> *in* the
wood, in the midst of Car'mel:
let them feed *in* Ba'shan and
Gil'e-ad, as in the days of old.

shepherd - alone

15 According to the days of your
coming out of the land of E'gypt will
I show to him marvellous *things*.

16 The nations shall see and be confounded at all their might: they
shall lay *their* hand upon *their*
mouth, their ears shall be deaf.

17 They shall lick the dust like a
serpent, they shall move out of
their holes like worms of the earth:
they shall be afraid of the LORD our
<u>God</u>, and shall fear because of
You. Elohim^{p.f.}

18 Who *is* a God like to You, that
pardons iniquity, and passes by the
transgression of the remnant of His
heritage? He retains not His anger
for ever, because He delights *in*
mercy.

19 He will turn again, He will
have compassion upon us; He
will subdue our <u>iniquities</u>; and
You will cast all their sins into
the depths of the sea. wrong ways

20 You will perform the truth to
Ja'cob, *and* the mercy to A'bra-
ham, which You have sworn to our
fathers from the days of old.

G1
G4

1342

1342

NAHUM

OUTLINE

SURVEY

Nahum, a book of contrast, depicts the powerful imperialism of a despotic, pagan nation and declares the ultimate and certain triumph of God's justice and sovereignty.

The immediate occasion of the prophecy was the pressing question of God's justice and of His faithfulness to His promises. A powerful nation of military might and economic wealth, Assyria had dominated the destinies of her neighboring nations, including Judah. Extracting oppressive tribute and inflicting grievous slavery, she had made Judah almost a vassal state. To protect herself, Judah had entered into alliances with other nations, forsaking God's promise to sustain and protect His people.

The national life of Judah was, therefore, tenuous. Her spiritual life was waning, and her safety was constantly imperiled by pillaging hordes from Nineveh. The question arose, "Has God forsaken Judah? Why does evil Assyria prosper, while we suffer? Are God's promises empty?" Judah lacked a sure answer to these questions, and great despair prevailed in the land.

Suddenly the voice of Nahum thundered, "Nineveh will fall. God will preserve His people." His prophecy seemed incredible to those of limited spiritual understanding. Its purpose was twofold: to foretell Nineveh's destruction because of sin; and to assuage Judah's forlorn hopelessness by reassurance that God's promises are true. The prophecy has but one theme: Nineveh will fall, Judah will be vindicated.

In literary style, it is both poetic and prophetic, combining lively pictorial imagery with the blunt

directness of prophetic utterance. Chapter 1 is primarily a psalm, while chapters 2 and 3 are prophetic.

The message of Nahum opens with a bold declaration of God's nature, the premise on which the prophecy is based. "God *is* jealous, and the LORD revengeth; the LORD revengeth, and *is* furious; the LORD will take vengeance on his adversaries, and he reserveth *wrath* for his enemies." (1.2). This theme pervades the book. Because Assyria has sinned in ignoring God, she will be utterly destroyed. Judah has been unfaithful in distrusting God and making alliances. She should be warned by the doom of Nineveh.

The message of Nahum is pertinent to all ages. Those who arrogantly resist God and do not humbly trust Him for provision and care will inevitably feel his wrath; those who put their faith in Him will be preserved in His love.

AUTHOR

Little is known of Nahum apart from this brief book. He is nowhere else referred to in the Scriptures, except possibly in the genealogical table of Luke. All we know about him is that he lived in Judah, probably at Elkosh, the location of which cannot be determined with certainty, and that he was a contemporary of Jeremiah. The name "Nahum" means "consolation," "full of comfort."

The date of the book is predicated upon internal evidence and known historical facts. There are two fixed dates between which it must be established. Nahum refers to the capture of Thebes (No-Amon, 3.8) and forecasts the doom of Nineveh. Thebes fell to the Assyrians in 661 B.C. so it must be dated somewhere between that date and the subsequent fall of Nineveh in 612 B.C. (604, alternate date). The best estimate places the book about 620 B.C.

C.B.B.

THE BOOK OF
NAHUM

CHAPTER 1

THE burden of Nin'e-veh. The book of the vision of Na'hum the El'koshite.

2 God *is* jealous, and the LORD revenges; the LORD revenges, and *is* furious; the LORD will take vengeance on His adversaries, and He reserves *wrath* for His enemies. El^s.f. - Jehovah^s.f.

3 The LORD *is* slow to anger, and great in power, and will not at all acquit *the wicked*: the LORD *has* His way in the whirlwind and in the storm, and the clouds *are* the dust of His feet.

4 He rebukes the sea, and makes it dry, and dries up all the rivers: Ba'shan languishes, and Car'mel, and the flower of Leb'a-non languishes.

5 The mountains quake at Him, and the hills melt, and the earth is burned at His presence, yea, the world, and all that dwell therein.

6 Who can stand before His indignation? and who can abide in the fierceness of His anger? His fury is poured out like fire, and the rocks are thrown down by Him.

7 The LORD *is* good, a strong hold in the day of trouble; and He knows them that trust in Him. refuge - loves

8 But with an overrunning flood He will make an utter end of the place thereof, and darkness shall pursue His enemies.

9 What do you imagine against the LORD? He will make an utter end: affliction shall not rise up the second time.

10 For while *they be* folden together *as* thorns, and while they are drunken *as* drunkards, they shall be devoured as stubble fully dry. tangled

11 There is *one* come out of you, that imagines evil against the LORD, a wicked counselor. plans

12 Thus says the LORD; Though *they be* quiet, and likewise many, yet thus shall they be cut down, when he shall pass through. Though I have afflicted you, I will afflict you no more. strong

13 For now will I break his yoke from off you, and will burst your bonds in sunder.

14 And the LORD has given a commandment concerning you, *that* no more of your name be sown: out of the house of your gods will I cut off the graven image and the molten image: I will make your grave; for you are vile. perpetuate - destroy - idol

15 Behold upon the mountains the feet of him that brings good tidings, that publishes peace! O Ju'dah, keep your solemn feasts, perform your vows: for the wicked shall no more pass through you; he is utterly cut off. celebrate your

CHAPTER 2

HE that dashes in pieces is come up before your face: keep the muni-

tion, watch the way, make *your* loins strong, fortify *your* power mightily.   _{Satan}

2 For the LORD has turned away the excellency of Ja'cob, as the excellency of Is'ra-el: for the emptiers have emptied them out, and marred their vine branches.

3 The shield of his mighty men is made <u>red</u>, the valiant men *are* in scarlet: the chariots *shall be* with flaming torches in the day of his preparation, and the fir trees shall be terribly shaken.   _{i.e., bloody}

4 The chariots shall rage in the streets, they shall justle one against another in the broad ways: they shall seem like torches, they shall run like the lightnings.

5 He shall recount his <u>worthies</u>: they shall stumble in their walk; they shall make haste to the wall thereof, and the defence shall be prepared.   _{nobles}

6 The gates of the rivers shall be opened, and the palace shall be <u>dissolved</u>.   _{destroyed}

7 And Huz'zab shall be led away captive, she shall be brought up, and her maids shall <u>lead</u> *her* as with the voice of doves, <u>tabering</u> upon their breasts.   _{sob for - beating}

8 But Nin'e-veh *is* of old like a pool of water: yet they shall flee away. Stand, stand, *shall they cry*; but none shall <u>look</u> back.   _{turn}

9 Take you the <u>spoil</u> of silver, take the <u>spoil</u> of gold: for *there is* no end of the store *and* glory out of all the <u>pleasant</u> furniture.   _{plunder - desirable}

10 She is empty, and void, and waste: and the heart melts, and the knees smite together, and much pain *is* in all loins, and the faces of them all gather <u>blackness</u>.   _{pale}

11 Where *is* the dwelling of the lions, and the feedingplace of the young lions, where the lion, *even* the old lion, walked, *and* the lion's whelp, and none made *them* afraid?

12 The lion did tear in pieces enough for his whelps, and strangled for his lionesses, and filled his holes with prey, and his dens with ravin.

13 Behold, I *am* against you, says the <u>LORD of hosts</u>, and I will burn her chariots in the smoke, and the sword shall devour your young lions: and I will cut off your prey from the earth, and the voice of your messengers shall no more be heard.   _{Jehovah^{s.f.} Elohim^{p.f.}}

CHAPTER 3

WOE to the bloody city! it *is* all full of lies *and* robbery; the prey departs not;

2 The noise of a whip, and the noise of the rattling of the wheels, and of the prancing horses, and of the jumping chariots.

3 The horseman lifts up both the bright sword and the glittering spear: and *there is* a multitude of slain, and a great number of <u>carcases</u>; and *there is* no end of *their* corpses; they stumble upon their corpses: _{dead bodies}

4 Because of the multitude of the whoredoms of the well favored harlot, the mistress of <u>witchcrafts</u>, that sells nations through her whoredoms, and families through her <u>witchcrafts</u>.   _{sorceries}

5 Behold, I *am* against you, says the L̟ord of hosts; and I will discover your <u>skirts</u> upon your face, and I will show the nations your nakedness, and the kingdoms your shame.   Jehovah^{s.f.} Elohim^{p.f.} - shame

6 And I will cast abominable filth upon you, and make you <u>vile</u>, and will set you as a <u>gazingstock</u>.

     evil - spectacle

7 And it shall come to pass, *that* all they that look upon you shall flee from you, and say, Nin'e-veh is laid waste: who will bemoan her? where shall I seek comforters for you?

8 Are you better than populous <u>No</u>, that was <u>situate</u> among the rivers, *that had* the waters round about it, whose rampart *was* the sea, *and* her wall *was* from the sea?

     Thought to be Thebes - located

9 E-thi-o'pi-a and E'gypt *were* her strength, and *it was* infinite; Put and Lu'bim were your helpers.

10 Yet *was* she carried away, she went into captivity: her young children also were dashed in pieces at the top of all the streets: and they <u>cast lots</u> for her honorable men, and all her great men were bound in chains.   threw dice?

11 You also shall be drunk: you shall be hid, you also shall seek strength because of the enemy.

12 All your <u>strong holds</u> *shall be like* fig trees with the firstripe figs: if they be shaken, they shall even fall into the mouth of the eater. fortifications

13 Behold, your people in the midst of you *are* <u>women</u>: the gates of your land shall be set wide open to your enemies: the fire shall devour your bars.   i.e., weak

14 Draw you waters for the siege, fortify your strong holds: go into clay, and tread the mortar, make strong the brickkiln.

15 There shall the fire devour you; the sword shall cut you off, it shall eat you up like the cankerworm: make yourself many as the cankerworm, make yourself many as the locusts.

16 You have multiplied your merchants above the stars of heaven: the cankerworm <u>spoils</u>, and flies away.   strips

17 Your <u>crowned</u> *are* as the locusts, and your captains as the great grasshoppers, which camp in the hedges in the cold day, *but* when the sun arises they flee away, and their place is not known where they *are*.   officials

18 Your shepherds slumber, O king of As-syr'i-a: you nobles shall dwell *in the dust*: your people is scattered upon the mountains, and no man gathers *them*.

19 *There is* no healing of your bruise; your wound is grievous: all that hear the <u>bruit</u> of you shall clap the hands over you: for upon whom has not your wickedness passed continually?   report

HABAKKUK

OUTLINE

SURVEY

The prophet-philosopher, Habakkuk, is disturbed about the intense wickedness of Judah. But, in contrast to his contemporary, Jeremiah, he is more concerned with God's seeming reluctance to judge than with the failure of his people to repent. Destruction, violence, and disregard of God's law flourish unchecked (1.2-4), despite the prophet's ardent pleas for God to intervene.

God replies to Habakkuk that he need not wait long for his answer: the fierce, ruthless Chaldeans (Babylonians) will be God's chastening rod to scourge Judah before Habakkuk's very eyes (1.5, 6).

Rather than lifting the prophet's burden, this answer adds to it, for Habakkuk is vexed by a second, even more thorny, problem: How can God, whose eyes are too pure to look on wrong, stand by silently while a wicked, bloodthirsty nation swallows up a more righteous people (1.13)? The prophet seeks a place of solitude to await God's answer (2.1).

The answer comes in one of the grandest declarations in Scripture: The just shall live by his faith (or faithfulness); The righteous will be preserved in the day of trouble, because they have depended upon God and are, in turn, dependable; Certain and swift retribution will be the lot of the haughty invaders, who will learn the emptiness of tyranny and the vanity of idolatry (2.6-19). The answer concludes with a command for universal silence before the sovereign Lord (2.20).

Assured that righteousness will triumph, the prophet lifts his heart in prayer that God will again do a mighty work as He had done in the Exodus and at Mount Sinai (3.2-15). After picturing the majestic splendor of the Omnipotent, Habakkuk reaffirms his confidence in the God of his salvation in one of the most moving confessions in Holy Writ (3.17-19).

AUTHOR

Nothing is known about the prophet Habakkuk except the personal qualities discernible in his writing. He alone in Scripture bears this name, which may mean "embraced" but more probably is

derived from the name of a plant. Various dates from 700 to 300 B.C. have been suggested for this book, but the most likely period is that between 605 B.C., the date of Nebuchadrezzar's victory over the Egyptians at Carchemish in Syria, and 597 B.C., when the Babylonians invaded Judah.

D.A.H.

THE BOOK OF
HABAKKUK

CHAPTER 1

THE burden which Ha-bak'kuk the prophet did see.
2 O LORD, how long shall I cry, and You will not hear! *even* cry out to You *of* violence, and You will not save!
3 Why do You show me iniquity, and cause *me* to behold grievance? for spoiling and violence *are* before me: and there arc *that* raise up strife and contention. destruction
4 Therefore the law is slacked, and judgment does never go forth: for the wicked does compass about the righteous; therefore wrong judgment proceeds. ignored - surround
5 Behold you among the heathen, and regard, and wonder marvel-lously: for *I* will work a work in your days, *which* you will not be-lieve, though it be told *you*. ACTS 13:41
6 For, lo, I raise up the Chal-de'ans, *that* bitter and hasty nation, which shall march through the breadth of the land, to possess the dwelling places *that are* not theirs.
7 They *are* terrible and dreadful: their judgment and their dignity shall proceed of themselves.
8 Their horses also are swifter than the leopards, and are more fierce than the evening wolves: and their horsemen shall spread themselves, and their horse-men shall come from far; they shall fly as the eagle *that* hastes to eat.
9 They shall come all for violence: their faces shall sup up *as* the east wind, and they shall gather the captivity as the sand.
10 And they shall scoff at the kings, and the princes shall be a scorn to them: they shall deride every strong hold; for they shall heap dust, and take it.
11 Then shall *his* mind change, and he shall pass over, and of-fend, *imputing* this his power to his god. transferring
12 *Are* you not from everlasting, O LORD my God, my Holy One? we shall not die. O LORD, You have or-dained them for judgment; and, O mighty God, You have established them for correction. Elohim^p.f. - ordained
13 *You are* of purer eyes than to be-hold evil, and can not look on iniq-uity: wherefore look You upon them that deal treacherously, *and* hold Your tongue when the wicked de-vours *the man that is* more righ-teous than he? sin - i.e., be silent
14 And make men as the fishes of the sea, as the creeping things, *that have* no ruler over them? insects
15 They take up all of them with the angle, they catch them in their net, and gather them in their drag: therefore they rejoice and are glad. hook - fishing net
16 Therefore they sacrifice to their net, and burn incense to their drag;

because by them their portion *is* fat, and their meat plenteous. *fishing net*

17 Shall they therefore empty their net, and not spare continually to slay the nations?

CHAPTER 2

I WILL stand upon my watch, and set me upon the tower, and will watch to see what He will say to me, and what I shall answer when I am reproved.

2 And the LORD answered me, and said, Write the vision, and make *it* plain upon tables, that he may run that read it.

3 For the vision *is* yet for an appointed time, but at the end it shall speak, and not lie: though it tarry, wait for it; because it will surely come, it will not tarry.

4 Behold, his soul *which* is lifted up is not upright in him: but the just shall live by his faith.

GAL. 3:11 ROM 1:16 HEB. 10:38 *puffed up*

5 Yea also, because he transgresses by wine, *he is* a proud man, neither keeps at home, who enlarges his desire as hell, and *is* as death, and cannot be satisfied, but gathers to him all nations, and heaps to him all people:

6 Shall not all these take up a parable against him, and a taunting proverb against him, and say, Woe to him that increases *that which is* not his! how long? and to him that lords himself with thick clay! *pledges*

7 Shall they not rise up suddenly that shall bite you, and awake that shall vex

you, and you shall be for booties to them? *trouble*

8 Because you have spoiled many nations, all the remnant of the people shall spoil you; because of men's blood, and *for* the violence of the land, of the city, and of all that dwell therein. *looted*

9 Woe to him that covets an evil covetousness to his house, that he may set his nest on high, that he may be delivered from the power of evil! *wrong*

10 You have consulted shame to your house by cutting off many people, and have sinned *against* your soul.

11 For the stone shall cry out of the wall, and the beam out of the timber shall answer it.

12 Woe to him that builds a town with blood, and stablishes a city by iniquity!

13 Behold, *is it* not of the LORD of hosts that the people shall labor in the very fire, and the people shall weary themselves for very vanity? *Jehovah*^{s.f.} *Elohim*^{p.f.} *- nothing*

14 For the earth shall be filled with the knowledge of the glory of the LORD, as the waters cover the sea.

15 Woe to him that gives his neighbor drink, that puts your bottle to *him*, and makes *him* drunk also, that you may look on their nakedness!

16 You are filled with shame for glory: drink you also, and let your foreskin be uncovered: the cup of the LORD's right hand shall be turned to you, and shameful spewing *shall be* on your glory.

17 For the violence of Leb'a-non shall cover you, and the spoil of beasts, *which* made them afraid, because of men's blood, and for the violence of the land, of the city, and of all that dwell therein.

18 What profits the graven <u>image</u> that the maker thereof has graven it; the molten <u>image</u>, and a teacher of lies, that the maker of his work trusts therein, to make dumb idols? idol

19 Woe to him that says to the wood, Awake; to the dumb stone, Arise, it shall teach! Behold, it *is* laid over with gold and silver, and *there is* no <u>breath</u> at all in the midst of it. life

20 But the LORD *is* in His holy temple: let all the earth keep silence before Him.

CHAPTER 3

A PRAYER of Ha-bak'kuk the prophet upon Shi-gi'o-noth.

2 O LORD, I have heard Your speech, *and* was afraid: O LORD, <u>revive</u> Your work in the midst of the years, in the midst of the years make known; in wrath remember mercy. make alive

3 <u>God</u> came from Te'man, and the Holy One from mount Pa'ran. Se'lah. His glory covered the heavens, and the earth was full of His praise. Eloah^{s.f.}

4 And *His* brightness was as the light; He had horns *coming* out of His hand: and there *was* the hiding of His power.

5 Before Him went the pestilence, and burning coals went forth at His feet.

6 He stood, and measured the earth: He beheld, and drove asunder the nations; and the everlasting mountains were scattered, the perpetual hills did <u>bow</u>: His ways *are* everlasting. collapse

7 I saw the tents of Cu'shan in <u>affliction</u>: *and* the curtains of the land of Mid'i-an did tremble distress

8 Was the LORD displeased against the rivers? *was* Your anger against the rivers? *was* Your wrath against the sea, that You did ride upon Your horses *and* Your chariots of <u>salvation</u>? escape

9 Your bow was made quite naked, *according* to the oaths of the tribes, *even your* word. Se'lah. You did cleave the earth with rivers.

10 The mountains saw You, *and* they trembled: the overflowing of the water passed by: the deep uttered its voice, *and* lifted up its hands on high.

11 The sun *and* moon stood still in their habitation: at the light of Your arrows they went, *and* at the shining of Your glittering spear.

12 You did march through the land in indignation, You did thresh the heathen in anger.

13 You went forth for the salvation of Your people, *even* for salvation with Your anointed; You wounded the head out of the house of the wicked, by discovering the foundation to the neck. Se'lah.

14 You did strike through with his <u>staves</u> the head of his villages: they came out as a whirlwind to scatter me: their rejoicing was as to devour the poor secretly. poles

15 You did walk through the sea with Your horses, *through* the <u>heap</u> of great waters. surge

16 When I heard, my belly trembled; my lips quivered at the voice: rottenness entered into my bones, and I trembled in myself, that I might rest in the day of trouble: when he comes up to the people, he will <u>invade</u> them with his troops.

^{strike}

17 Although the fig tree shall not blossom, neither *shall* fruit *be* in the vines; the labor of the olive shall fail, and the fields shall yield no meat; the flock shall be cut off from the fold, and *there shall be* no herd in the stalls:

^{produce}

18 Yet I will rejoice in the LORD, I will joy in the <u>God</u> of my salvation.

^{Elohim^{p.f.}}

19 The <u>LORD God</u> *is* my strength, and He will make my feet like <u>hinds' *feet*</u>, and He will make me to walk upon my high places.

^{Jehovah^{s.f.} Adonahy^{p.f.} - deer}

ZEPHANIAH

OUTLINE

SURVEY

Zephaniah, a true prophet of the Lord, faced a corrupt and godless nation, Judah. Though identified with the chosen people, such a nation could not endure, for the Lord is a just God Who is no respecter of persons. Far to the northeast was mighty Assyria, which was to be used of the Lord as His instrument to bring about Judah's destruction. This destruction would be a day in which the Lord's righteousness would be vindicated. It would truly be a Day of the Lord.

Zephaniah rightly seeks to inspire fear of that day in his hearers, and appeals for repentance. He points out that through such judgment mercy will come to those whom God truly intends to deliver. The pure remnant, when it has been delivered, will sing the praises of the just Lord Who dwells in her midst.

AUTHOR

This little prophecy claims to be a revelation to Zephaniah, who prophesied after the destruction of Israel during the days of Josiah. Probably his messages were spoken before Josiah's reformation, for they picture a desperately wicked people who do not seek the Lord.

E.J.Y.

THE BOOK OF
ZEPHANIAH

"Jehovah Hides"
He Hides His People
from His Judgments

CHAPTER 1

THE word of the LORD which came to Zeph-a-ni'ah the son of Cu'shi, the son of Ged-a-li'ah, the son of Am-a-ri'ah, the son of Hiz-ki'ah, in the days of Jo-si'ah the son of A'mon, king of Ju'dah.

2 I will utterly consume all *things* from off the land, says the LORD. destroy

3 I will consume man and beast; I will consume the fowls of the heaven, and the fishes of the sea, and the stumblingblocks with the wicked; and I will cut off man from off the land, says the LORD. ruins - destroy

4 I will also stretch out My hand upon Ju'dah, and upon all the inhabitants of Je-ru'sa-lem; and I will cut off the remnant of Ba'al from this place, *and* the name of the Chem'a-rims with the priests;

5 And them that worship the host of heaven upon the house tops; and them that worship *and* that swear by the LORD, and that swear by Mal'cham;

6 And them that are turned back from the LORD; and *those* that have not sought the LORD, nor enquired for Him. away

7 Hold your peace at the presence of the Lord GOD: for the day of the LORD *is* at hand: for the LORD has prepared a sacrifice, He has bid His guests. Jehovah[s.f.] Elohim[p.f.] - consecrated

8 And it shall come to pass in the day of the LORD's sacrifice, that I will punish the princes, and the king's children, and all such as are clothed with strange apparel.

9 In the same day also will I punish all those that leap on the threshold, which fill their masters' houses with violence and deceit. jump over

10 And it shall come to pass in that day, says the LORD, *that there shall be* the noise of a cry from the fish gate, and an howling from the second, and a great crashing from the hills.

11 Howl, you inhabitants of Mak'tesh, for all the merchant people are cut down; all they that bear silver are cut off.

12 And it shall come to pass at that time, *that* I will search Je-ru'sa-lem with candles, and punish the men that are settled on their lees: that say in their heart, The LORD will not do good, neither will He do evil.

strong wine i.e., dregs

13 Therefore their goods shall become a booty, and their houses a desolation: they shall also build houses, but not inhabit *them*; and they shall plant vineyards, but not drink the wine thereof. plunder

14 The great day of the LORD *is* near, *it is* near, and hastes greatly, *even* the voice of the day of the LORD: the mighty man shall cry there bitterly. comes quickly

15 That day *is* a day of wrath, a day of trouble and distress, a day of waste-

ness and desolation, a day of darkness and gloominess, a day of clouds and thick darkness, _{anger}

16 A day of the trumpet and alarm against the <u>fenced</u> cities, and against the high towers. _{fortified}

17 And I will bring distress upon men, that they shall walk like blind men, because they have sinned against the LORD: and their blood shall be poured out as dust, and their flesh as the dung.

18 Neither their silver nor their gold shall be able to deliver them in the day of the LORD's wrath; but the whole land shall be devoured by the fire of His jealousy: for He shall make even a speedy riddance of all them that dwell in the land.

CHAPTER 2

GATHER yourselves together, yea, gather together, O nation not desired;

2 Before the decree <u>bring forth</u>, *before* the day pass as the chaff, before the fierce anger of the LORD come upon you, before the day of the LORD's anger come upon you. _{takes effect}

3 Seek you the LORD, all you <u>meek</u> of the earth, which have <u>wrought</u> His judgment; seek righteousness, seek <u>meekness</u>: it may be you shall be <u>hid</u> in the day of the LORD's anger. _{humble - carried out - humility - safe from anger}

4 For Ga'za shall be forsaken, and Ash'ke-lon a desolation: they shall drive out Ash'dod at the noon day, and Ek'ron shall be rooted up.

5 Woe to the inhabitants of the sea coast, the nation of the Cher'eth-ites! the word of the LORD *is* against you; O Ca'naan, the land of the Phi-lis'tines, I will even destroy you, that there shall be no inhabitant.

6 And the sea coast shall be <u>dwellings *and* cottages</u> for shepherds, and folds for flocks. _{pastures and wells}

7 And the coast shall be for the remnant of the house of Ju'dah; they shall feed thereupon: in the houses of Ash'ke-lon shall they lie down in the evening: for the LORD their <u>God</u> shall visit them, and turn away their captivity. _{Elohim^{p.f.}}

8 I have heard the reproach of Mo'ab, and the revilings of the children of Am'mon, whereby they have reproached My people, and magnified *themselves* against their border.

9 Therefore *as* I live, says the LORD of hosts, the <u>God</u> of Is'ra-el, Surely Mo'ab shall be as Sod'om, and the children of Am'mon as Go-mor'rah, *even* the <u>breeding</u> of <u>nettles</u>, and <u>saltpits</u>, and a perpetual desolation: the residue of My people shall <u>spoil</u> them, and the remnant of My people shall possess them.

_{Jehovah^{s.f.} Tsebaoth - Elohim^{p.f.} - growing weeds - i.e., pool where water has evaporated - plunder}

10 This shall they have for their pride, because they have reproached and magnified *themselves* against the people of the <u>LORD of hosts</u>.

11 The LORD *will be* terrible to them: for He will <u>famish</u> all the gods of the earth; and *men* shall worship Him, every one from his place, *even* all the isles of the heathen. _{starve}

12 You E-thi-o'pi-ans also, you *shall be* slain by My sword.

13 And He will stretch out His hand against the north, and destroy As-syr'i-a; and will make Nin'e-veh a desolation, *and* dry like a wilderness.

14 And flocks shall lie down in the midst of her, all the beasts of the nations: both the cormorant and the bittern shall lodge in the upper lintels of it; *their* voice shall sing in the windows; desolation *shall be* in the thresholds; for He shall uncover the cedar work. owl - pillars - reveal

15 This *is* the rejoicing city that dwelled carelessly, that said in her heart, I *am*, and *there is* none beside me: how is she become a desolation, a place for beasts to lie down in! every one that passes by her shall hiss, *and* wag his hand.

CHAPTER 3

WOE to her that is filthy and polluted, to the oppressing city! rebellious

2 She obeyed not the voice; she received not correction; she trusted not in the LORD; she drew not near to her God. Elohim^p.f.

3 Her princes within her *are* roaring lions; her judges *are* evening wolves; they gnaw not the bones till the morrow.

4 Her prophets *are* light *and* treacherous persons: her priests have polluted the sanctuary, they have done violence to the law. defiled

5 The just LORD *is* in the midst thereof; He will not do iniquity: every morning does He bring His judgment to light, He fails not; but the unjust knows no shame. evil - love

6 I have cut off the nations: their towers are desolate; I made their streets waste, that none passes by: their cities are destroyed, so that there is no man, that there is none inhabitant. fortifications

7 I said, Surely you will fear Me, yu will receive instruction; so their dwelling should not be cut off, howsoever I punished them: but they rose early, *and* corrupted all their doings. reverence - my decrees

8 Therefore wait you upon Me, says the LORD, until the day that I rise up to the prey: for My determination *is* to gather the nations, that I may assemble the kingdoms, to pour upon them My indignation, *even* all My fierce anger: for all the earth shall be devoured with the fire of My jealousy. anger

9 For then will I turn to the people a pure language, that they may all call upon the name of the LORD, to serve Him with one consent.

10 From beyond the rivers of E-thi-o'pi-a My suppliants, *even* the daughter of My dispersed, shall bring My offering. worshipers - scattered

11 In that day shall you not be ashamed for all your doings, wherein you have transgressed against Me: for then I will take away out of the midst of you them that rejoice in your pride, and you shall no more be haughty because of My holy mountain.

12 I will also leave in the midst of you an afflicted and poor people, and they shall trust in the name of the LORD.

13 The remnant of Is'ra-el shall not do <u>iniquity</u>, nor speak lies; neither shall a deceitful tongue be found in their mouth: for they shall feed and lie down, and <u>none</u> shall make *them* afraid.   <small>REV. 14:5 evil - no one</small>

14 Sing, O daughter of Zi'on; shout, O Is'ra-el; be glad and rejoice with all the heart, O daughter of Je-ru'sa-lem.

15 The LORD has taken away your judgments, He has cast out your enemy: the king of Is'ra-el, *even* the LORD, *is* in the midst of you: you shall not see evil any more.

16 In that day it shall be said to Je-ru'sa-lem, Fear you not: *and to* Zi'on, Let not your hands be <u>slack</u>.

<small>limp</small>

17 The LORD your <u>God</u> in the midst of you *is* mighty; He will save, He will rejoice over you with joy; He will rest in His love, He will joy over you with singing.   <small>Elohim^{p.f.}</small>

18 I will gather *them that are* sorrowful for the solemn assembly, *who* are of you, *to whom* the reproach of it *was* a burden.

19 Behold, at that time I will undo all that afflict you: and I will save her that <u>halts</u>, and gather her that was driven out; and I will <u>get</u> them praise and <u>fame</u> in every land where they have been put to shame.   <small>is lame - bring - renown</small>

20 At that time will I bring you *again*, even in the time that I gather you: for I will make you a name and a praise among all people of the earth, when I <u>turn back</u> your captivity before your eyes, says the LORD.   <small>release</small>

HAGGAI

OUTLINE

SURVEY

The prophecy of Haggai, which belongs to the post-Exilic period, is a call to the rulers and people to resume the rebuilding of the temple after sixteen years of interruption and delay. The prophet ruthlessly exposes the false but prevalent view that God's work is secondary and must wait the solution of economic problems. He shows that the latter are a judgment upon neglect of the former. When the leaders and people respond to his appeal, he assures them of the help of God, encourages them in face of disparaging comparisons, and promises an improvement in material circumstances now that the will and work of God are done. He concludes his message by confirming the divine choice of the governor Zerubbabel and indicating his messianic significance.

AUTHOR

The prophecy is carefully dated (520 B.C.) and undoubtedly is the work of the Haggai whose name it bears and who is referred to in association with Zechariah in Ezra 5.1 and 6.14. Beyond his part in rebuilding the temple, we know nothing of his life or character. His direct, straightforward style is admirably suited to his practical mission of rebuke and encouragement.

G.W.B.

THE BOOK OF
HAGGAI
CHAPTER 1

IN the second year of Da-ri'us the king, in the sixth month, in the first day of the month, came the word of the LORD by Hag'ga-i the prophet to Ze-rub'ba-bel the son of She-al'ti-el, governor of Ju'dah, and to Josh'u-a the son of Jos'e-dech, the high priest, saying,

2 Thus speaks the LORD of hosts, saying, This people say, The time is not come, the time that the LORD's house should be built. Jehovah[s.f.] Tsebaoth

3 Then came the word of the LORD by Hag'ga-i the prophet, saying,

4 *Is it* time for you, O you, to dwell in your ceiled houses, and this house *lie waste*? paneled - desolate

5 Now therefore thus says the LORD of hosts; Consider your ways.

6 You have sown much, and bring in little; you eat, but you have not enough; you drink, but you are not filled with drink; you clothe you, but there is none warm; and he that earns wages earns wages *to put it* into a bag with holes.

7 Thus says the LORD of hosts; Consider your ways. Jehovah[s.f.] Tsebaoth

8 Go up to the mountain, and bring wood, and build the house; and I will take pleasure in it, and I will be glorified, says the LORD.

9 You looked for much, and, lo, *it came* to little; and when you brought *it* home, I did blow upon it. Why? says the LORD of hosts. Because of My house

"Festive"
Time to Rebuild
the Temple

that *is* waste, and you run every man to his own house. Jehovah[s.f.] Tsebaoth - desolate

10 Therefore the heaven over you is stayed from dew, and the earth is stayed *from* her fruit. withholds

11 And I called for a drought upon the land, and upon the mountains, and upon the corn, and upon the new wine, and upon the oil, and upon *that* which the ground brings forth, and upon men, and upon cattle, and upon all the labor of the hands. grain

12 Then Ze-rub'ba-bel the son of She-al'ti-el, and Josh'u-a the son of Jos'e-dech, the high priest, with all the remnant of the people, obeyed the voice of the LORD their God, and the words of Hag'ga-i the prophet, as the LORD their God had sent him, and the people did fear before the LORD. Elohim[p.f.] - reverence

13 Then spoke Hag'ga-i the LORD's messenger in the LORD's message to the people, saying, I *am* with you, says the LORD.

14 And the LORD stirred up the spirit of Ze-rub'ba-bel the son of She-al'ti-el, governor of Ju'dah, and the spirit of Josh'u-a the son of Jos'e-dech, the high priest, and the spirit of all the remnant of the people; and they came and did work in the house of the LORD of hosts, their God, Jehovah[s.f.] Tsebaoth - Elohim[p.f.]

15 In the four and twentieth day of the sixth month, in the second year of Da-ri'us the king.

CHAPTER 2

IN the seventh *month*, in the one and twentieth *day* of the month, came the word of the LORD by the prophet Hag'ga-i, saying,

2 Speak now to Ze-rub'ba-bel the son of She-al'ti-el, governor of Ju'dah, and to Josh'u-a the son of Jos'e-dech, the high priest, and to the resi-due of the people, saying,   balance

3 Who *is* left among you that saw this house in her first glory? and how do you see it now? *is it* not in your eyes in comparison of it as nothing?

4 Yet now be strong, O Ze-rub'ba-bel, says the LORD; and be strong, O Josh'u-a, son of Jos'e-dech, the high priest; and be strong, all you people of the land, says the LORD, and work: for I *am* with you, says the LORD of hosts: Jehovah^s.f. - Jehovah^s.f. Tsebaoth

5 *According to* the word that I covenanted with you when you came out of E'gypt, so My Spirit remains among you: fear you not.   agreement

6 For thus says the LORD of hosts; Yet once, it *is* a little while, and I will shake the heavens, and the earth, and the sea, and the dry *land*;   HEB. 12:26

7 And I will shake all nations, and the desire of all nations shall come: and I will fill this house with glory, says the LORD of hosts.   wealth

8 The silver *is* Mine, and the gold *is* Mine, says the LORD of hosts.

9 The glory of this latter house shall be greater than of the former, says the LORD of hosts: and in this place will I give peace, says the LORD of hosts.   Jehovah^s.f. Tsebaoth

10 In the four and twentieth *day* of the ninth *month*, in the second year of Da-ri'us, came the word of the LORD by Hag'ga-i the prophet, saying,

11 Thus says the LORD of hosts; Ask now the priests *concerning* the law, saying,   Jehovah^s.f. Tsebaoth

12 If one bear holy flesh in the skirt of his garment, and with his skirt do touch bread, or pottage, or wine, or oil, or any meat, shall it be holy? And the priests answered and said, No.

13 Then said Hag'ga-i, If *one that is* unclean by a dead body touch any of these, shall it be unclean? And the priests answered and said, It shall be unclean.

14 Then answered Hag'ga-i, and said, So *is* this people, and so *is* this nation before Me, says the LORD; and so *is* every work of their hands; and that which they offer there *is* unclean.

15 And now, I pray you, consider from this day and upward, from before a stone was laid upon a stone in the temple of the LORD: onward

16 Since those *days* were, when *one* came to an heap of twenty *measures*, there were *but* ten: when *one* came to the pressfat for to draw out fifty *vessels* out of the press, there were *but* twenty.

17 I smote you with blasting and with mildew and with hail in all the labors of your hands; yet you *turned* not to Me, says the LORD.   scorching

18 Consider now from this day and upward, from the four and twentieth day of the ninth *month*, *even* from the day that the foundation of the LORD's temple was laid, consider *it*.   onward

19 Is the seed yet in the barn? yea, as yet the vine, and the fig tree, and the pomegranate, and the olive tree, has not brought forth: from this day will I bless *you*.

20 And again the word of the LORD came to Hag'ga-i in the four and twentieth *day* of the month, saying,

21 Speak to Ze-rub'ba-bel, governor of Ju'dah, saying, I will shake the heavens and the earth;

22 And I will overthrow the throne of kingdoms, and I will destroy the strength of the kingdoms of the heathen; and I will overthrow the chariots, and those that ride in them; and the horses and their riders shall come down, every one by the sword of his brother.

23 In that day, says the LORD of hosts, will I take you, O Ze-rub'ba-bel, my servant, the son of She-al'ti-el, says the LORD, and will make you as a signet: for I have chosen you, says the LORD of hosts.

seal - Jehovah$^{s.f.}$ Tsebaoth

ZECHARIAH

OUTLINE

SURVEY

Zechariah, a younger contemporary of the prophet Haggai, addressed himself to the same task as Haggai, that of inducing the people to rebuild the temple. His written message forms a significant link between the earlier prophets to whose ministry he makes reference (1.6) and the later phases of God's redemptive work to which his book bears such eloquent testimony. Thus he helps us to look forward to the day when the completed Kingdom of God will be established and to fill our joyful expectation regarding that day with rich scriptural content.

AUTHOR

While the first eight chapters of the book are ascribed to Zechariah in 520 B.C., the date of chapters 9-14 is widely disputed, and many deny that Zechariah wrote them. Some have argued pre-Zecharian authorship; others defend a date later than the prophet's time, the latter view being at present the dominant one. Absolute certainty is not easily obtained. Although differences should be recognized, similarity in attitude between the two parts would suggest their unity of origin. To assign the second part to Macedonian times because of the reference to Greece in 9.13 is to assume that Zechariah, as a true prophet of God to whom future things are revealed, could not have foreseen Greece's future prominence. Moreover, Zechariah, who started his ministry in 520 B.C., may well have lived to witness the important victories gained by Greece over the Persians in 490 and 480 B.C. These could point to future Greek domination.

M.H.W.

THE BOOK OF
ZECHARIAH

CHAPTER 1

IN the eighth month, in the second year of Da-ri'us, came the word of the LORD to Zech-a-ri'ah, the son of Ber-e-chi'ah, the son of Id'do the prophet, saying,

2 The LORD has been <u>sore</u> displeased with your fathers. very

3 Therefore say you to them, Thus says the LORD of hosts; Turn you to Me, says the LORD of hosts, and I will turn to you, says the LORD of hosts. Jehovah^s.f. Tsebaoth

4 Be you not as your fathers, to whom the former prophets have cried, saying, Thus says the LORD of hosts; Turn you now from your evil ways, and *from* your evil doings: but they did not hear, nor hearken to Me, says the LORD.

5 Your fathers, where *are* they? and the prophets, do they live for ever?

6 But My words and My <u>statutes</u>, which I commanded My servants the prophets, did they not take hold of your fathers? and they returned and said, Like as the LORD of hosts thought to do to us, according to our ways, and according to our doings, so has He dealt with us. laws - Jehovah^s.f. Tsebaoth

7 Upon the four and twentieth day of the eleventh month, which *is* the month Se'bat, in the second year of Da-ri'us, came the word of the LORD to Zech-a-ri'ah, the son of Ber-e-chi'ah, the son of Id'do the prophet, saying,

8 I saw by night, and behold a man riding upon a red horse, and he stood among the myrtle trees that *were* in the bottom; and behind him *were there* red horses, speckled, and white. REV. 6:2

9 Then said I, O my lord, what *are* these? And the <u>angel</u> that talked with me said to me, I will show you what these *be*. messenger

10 And the man that stood among the myrtle trees answered and said, These *are they* whom the LORD has sent to walk to and fro through the earth.

11 And they answered the <u>angel</u> of the LORD that stood among the myrtle trees, and said, We have walked to and fro through the earth, and, behold, all the earth sits still, and is at rest.

12 Then the angel of the LORD answered and said, O LORD of hosts, how long will You not have mercy on Je-ru'sa-lem and on the cities of Ju'dah, against which You have had indignation these <u>threescore and ten</u> years? REV. 6:10 Jehovah^s.f. Tsebaoth - 70

13 And the LORD answered the <u>angel</u> that talked with me *with* good words *and* <u>comfortable</u> words. messenger - soothing

14 So the <u>angel</u> that <u>communed</u> with me said to me, Cry you, saying, Thus says the LORD of hosts; I am jealous for Je-ru'sa-lem and for Zi'on with a great jealousy. messenger - talked - Jehovah^s.f. Tsebaoth

15 And I am very <u>sore</u> displeased with

the heathen *that are* at ease: for I was but a little displeased, and they <u>helped forward the affliction</u>. _{very - furthered the disaster}

16 Therefore thus says the LORD; I am returned to Je-ru'sa-lem with mercies: My house shall be built in it, says the LORD of hosts, and a line shall be stretched forth upon Je-ru'sa-lem.

17 Cry yet, saying, Thus says the LORD of hosts; My cities through prosperity shall yet be spread abroad; and the LORD shall yet comfort Zi'on, and shall yet choose Je-ru'sa-lem.   Jehovah^{s.f.} Tsebaoth

18 Then lifted I up mine eyes, and saw, and behold four <u>horns</u>.   i.e., rulers

19 And I said to the <u>angel</u> that talked with me, What *be* these? And he answered me, These *are* the <u>horns</u> which have scattered Ju'dah, Is'ra-el, and Je-ru'sa-lem.   messenger

20 And the LORD showed me four <u>carpenters</u>.   craftsmen

21 Then said I, What come these to do? And He spoke, saying, These *are* the <u>horns</u> which have scattered Ju'dah, so that no man did lift up his head: but these are come to <u>fray</u> them, to cast out the <u>horns</u> of the Gen'tiles, which lifted up *their* <u>horn</u> over the land of Ju'dah to scatter it.   rulers - terrify - ruler

CHAPTER 2

I LIFTED up my eyes again, and looked, and behold a man with a measuring line in his hand.

2 Then said I, Where go you? And he said to me, To measure Je-ru'sa-lem, to see what *is* the breadth thereof, and what *is* the length thereof.

3 And, behold, the <u>angel</u> that talked with me went forth, and another <u>angel</u> went out to meet him,   messenger

4 And said to him, Run, speak to this young man, saying, Je-ru'sa-lem shall be inhabited *as* towns without walls for the multitude of men and cattle therein:

5 For I, says the LORD, will be to her a <u>wall of fire</u> round about, and will be the glory in the midst of her.   i.e., protection

6 Ho, ho, *come forth*, and flee from the land of the north, says the LORD: for I have spread you abroad as the four winds of the heaven, says the LORD.

7 Deliver yourself, O Zi'on, that dwell *with* the daughter of Bab'y-lon.

8 For thus says the LORD of hosts; After the glory has He sent Me to the nations which <u>spoiled</u> you: for he that touches you touches the apple of His eye. Jehovah^{s.f.} Tsebaoth - plundered

9 For, behold, I will shake My hand upon them, and they shall be a <u>spoil</u> to their servants: and you shall know that the LORD of hosts has sent Me.   plunder

10 Sing and rejoice, O daughter of Zi'on: for, lo, I come, and I will dwell in the midst of you, says the LORD.

11 And many nations shall be joined to the LORD in that day, and shall be My people: and I will dwell in the midst of you, and you shall know that the LORD of hosts has sent Me to you.

12 And the LORD shall inherit Ju'dah His portion in the holy land, and shall choose Je-ru'sa-lem again.

13 Be silent, O all <u>flesh</u>, before the LORD: for He is raised up out of His holy <u>habitation</u>.   mankind - dwelling

CHAPTER 3

AND he showed me Josh'u-a the high priest standing before the <u>angel</u> of the LORD, and Sa'tan standing at his right hand to <u>resist</u> him.   messenger - accuse

2 And the LORD said to Sa'tan, The LORD rebuke you, O Sa'tan; even the LORD that has chosen Je-ru'sa-lem rebuke you: *is* not this a <u>brand</u> plucked out of the fire?   JUDE 9   burning stick

3 Now Josh'u-a was clothed with filthy garments, and stood before the <u>angel</u>.

4 And he answered and spoke to those that stood before him, saying, Take away the filthy garments from him. And to him He said, Behold, I have caused your iniquity to pass from you, and I will clothe you with change of <u>raiment</u>.   JUDE 23 clothing

5 And I said, Let them set a fair <u>mitre</u> upon his head. So they set a fair <u>mitre</u> upon his head, and clothed him with garments. And the <u>angel</u> of the LORD stood by.   turban - messenger

6 And the <u>angel</u> of the LORD <u>protested</u> to Josh'u-a, saying,   admonished

7 Thus says the <u>LORD of hosts</u>; If you will walk in My ways, and if you will <u>keep</u> My <u>charge</u>, then you shall also judge My house, and shall also keep My courts, and I will give you places to walk among these that stand by.   Jehovah^s.f. Tsebaoth - perform - service

8 Hear now, O Josh'u-a the high priest, you, and your fellows that sit before you: for they *are* men wondered at: for, behold, I will bring forth My servant the <u>BRANCH</u>.   i.e., Jesus Christ

9 For behold the stone that I have laid before Josh'u-a; upon one stone *shall be* <u>seven</u> eyes: behold, I will engrave the graving thereof, says the <u>LORD of hosts</u>, and I will remove the iniquity of that land in one day.   i.e., perfect

10 In that day, says the <u>LORD of hosts</u>, shall you call every man his neighbor under the vine and under the fig tree.   Jehovah^s.f. Tsebaoth

CHAPTER 4

AND the <u>angel</u> that talked with me came again, and waked me, as a man that is wakened out of his sleep,   messenger

2 And said to me, What see you? And I said, I have looked, and behold a candlestick all *of* gold, with a bowl upon the top of it, and its seven lamps thereon, and seven <u>pipes</u> to the seven lamps, which *are* upon the top thereof: REV. 4:12 spouts

3 And two <u>olive trees</u> by it, one upon the right *side* of the bowl, and the other upon the left *side* thereof.   REV. 11:4 "Judah—Israel"

4 So I answered and spoke to the <u>angel</u> that talked with me, saying, What *are* these, my lord?   messenger

5 Then the <u>angel</u> that talked with me answered and said to me, Know you not what these be? And I said, No, my lord.

6 Then he answered and spoke to me, saying, This *is* the word of the

LORD to Ze-rub'ba-bel, saying, Not by might, nor by power, but by My spirit, says the LORD of hosts.

Jehovah[s.f.] Tsebaoth

7 Who *are* you, O great mountain? before Ze-rub'ba-bel *you shall become* a plain: and he shall bring forth the headstone *thereof with* shoutings, *crying*, Grace, grace to it.   authority

8 Moreover the word of the LORD came to me, saying,

9 The hands of Ze-rub'ba-bel have laid the foundation of this house; his hands shall also finish it; and you shall know that the LORD of hosts has sent me to you.

10 For who has despised the day of small things? for they shall rejoice, and shall see the plummet in the hand of Ze-rub'ba-bel *with* those seven; they *are* the eyes of the LORD, which run to and fro through the whole earth.   plumb line

11 Then answered I, and said to him, What *are* these two olive trees upon the right *side* of the candlestick and upon the left *side* thereof?   i.e., Ju'dah—Israel

12 And I answered again, and said to him, What *be these* two olive branches which through the two golden pipes empty the golden *oil* out of themselves?

REV.11:4-8 i.e., Moses-Elijah? Enoch-Elijah - sprouts

13 And he answered me and said, Know you not what these *be*? And I said, No, my lord.

14 Then said he, These *are* the two anointed ones, that stand by the LORD of the whole earth.

REV.11:4-8 i.e., Moses-Elijah? Enoch-Elijah - Adon[s.f.]

CHAPTER 5

THEN I turned, and lifted up mine eyes, and looked, and behold a flying roll.

2 And he said to me, What see you? And I answered, I see a flying roll; the length thereof *is* twenty cubits, and the breadth thereof ten cubits.

3 Then said he to me, This *is* the curse that goes forth over the face of the whole earth: for every one that steals shall be cut off *as* on this side according to it; and every one that swears shall be cut off *as* on that side according to it.

4 I will bring it forth, says the LORD of hosts, and it shall enter into the house of the thief, and into the house of him that swears falsely by My name: and it shall remain in the midst of his house, and shall consume it with the timber thereof and the stones thereof.   Jehovah[s.f.] Tsebaoth - destroy

5 Then the angel that talked with me went forth, and said to me, Lift up now your eyes, and see what *is* this that goes forth.   messenger

6 And I said, What *is* it? And he said, This *is* an ephah that goes forth. He said moreover, This *is* their resemblance through all the earth.   container - appearance

7 And, behold, there was lifted up a talent of lead: and this *is* a woman that sits in the midst of the ephah.

100 lbs.

8 And he said, This *is* wickedness. And he cast it into the midst of the ephah; and he cast the weight of lead upon the mouth thereof.   opening

9 Then lifted I up my eyes, and looked, and, behold, there came out two women, and the wind *was* in their wings; for they had wings like the wings of a stork: and they lifted up the ephah between the earth and the heaven. container

10 Then said I to the angel that talked with me, Where do these bear the ephah? messenger

11 And he said to me, To build it an house in the land of Shi'nar: and it shall be established, and set there upon her own base. her

CHAPTER 6

AND I turned, and lifted up my eyes, and looked, and, behold, there came four chariots out from between two mountains; and the mountains *were* mountains of brass. i.e., judgment

2 In the first chariot *were* red horses; and in the second chariot black horses;

3 And in the third chariot white horses; and in the fourth chariot grisled and bay horses.

4 Then I answered and said to the angel that talked with me, What *are* these, my lord? messenger

5 And the angel answered and said to me, These *are* the four spirits of the heavens, which go forth from standing before the Lord of all the earth. REV. 7:1 winds - Adon^s.f.

6 The black horses which *are* therein go forth into the north country; and the white go forth after them; and the grisled go forth toward the south country.

7 And the bay went forth, and sought to go that they might walk to and fro through the earth: and He said, Get you from there, walk to and fro through the earth. So they walked to and fro through the earth. patrolled

8 Then cried He upon me, and spoke to me, saying, Behold, these that go toward the north country have quieted My spirit in the north country. appeased

9 And the word of the LORD came to me, saying,

10 Take of *them of* the captivity, *even* of Hel'da-i, of To-bi'jah, and of Je-da'iah, which are come from Bab'y-lon, and come you the same day, and go into the house of Josiah the son of Zeph-a-ni'ah;

11 Then take silver and gold, and make crowns, and set *them* upon the head of Josh'u-a the son of Jos'edech, the high priest;

12 And speak to him, saying, Thus speaks the LORD of hosts, saying, Behold the man whose name *is* The BRANCH; and He shall grow up out of His place, and He shall build the temple of the LORD: G4

Jehovah^s.f. - i.e., Jesus Christ

13 Even He shall build the temple of the LORD; and He shall bear the glory, and shall sit and rule upon His throne; and He shall be a priest upon His throne: and the counsel of peace shall be between them both. 1368

14 And the crowns shall be to He'lem, and to To-bi'jah, and to Je-da'iah, and to Hen the son of Zeph-a-ni'ah, for a memorial in the temple of the LORD.

15 And they *that are* far off shall come and build in the temple of the

LORD, and you shall know that the LORD of hosts has sent Me to you. And *this* shall come to pass, if you will diligently obey the voice of the LORD your God.   Jehovah^{s.f.} Tsebaoth

CHAPTER 7

AND it came to pass in the fourth year of king Da-ri'us, *that* the word of the LORD came to Zech-a-ri'ah in the fourth *day* of the ninth month, *even* in Chis'leu;
2 When they had sent to the house of God She-re'zer and Re'gem-me'lech, and their men, to pray before the LORD,
3 *And* to speak to the priests which *were* in the house of the LORD of hosts, and to the prophets, saying, Should I weep in the fifth month, separating myself, as I have done these so many years?   abstaining
4 Then came the word of the LORD of hosts to me, saying,   Jehovah^{s.f.} Tsebaoth
5 Speak to all the people of the land, and to the priests, saying, When you fasted and mourned in the fifth and seventh *month*, even those seventy years, did you at all fast to Me, *even* to Me?   for
6 And when you did eat, and when you did drink, did not you eat *for yourselves*, and drink *for yourselves*?
7 *Should you* not *hear* the words which the LORD has cried by the former prophets, when Je-ru'sa-lem was inhabited and in prosperity, and the cities thereof round about her, when *men* inhabited the south and the plain?
8 And the word of the LORD came to Zech-a-ri'ah, saying,

9 Thus speaks the LORD of hosts, saying, Execute true judgment, and show mercy and compassions every man to his brother: JOHN 7:24 Jehovah^{s.f.} Tsebaoth - dispense
10 And oppress not the widow, nor the fatherless, the stranger, nor the poor; and let none of you imagine evil against his brother in your heart.
11 But they refused to hearken, and pulled away the shoulder, and stopped their ears, that they should not hear.   closed
12 Yea, they made their hearts *as* an adamant stone, less they should hear the law, and the words which the LORD of hosts has sent in His Spirit by the former prophets: therefore came a great wrath from the LORD of hosts.   hard - anger
13 Therefore it is come to pass, *that* as He cried, and they would not hear; so they cried, and I would not hear, says the LORD of hosts: Jehovah^{s.f.} Tsebaoth
14 But I scattered them with a whirlwind among all the nations whom they knew not. Thus the land was desolate after them, that no man passed through nor returned: for they laid the pleasant land desolate.   precious - empty

CHAPTER 8

AGAIN the word of the LORD of hosts came *to me*, saying,
2 Thus says the LORD of hosts; I was jealous for Zi'on with great jealousy, and I was jealous for her with great fury.
3 Thus says the LORD; I am returned to Zi'on, and will dwell in the midst of Je-ru'sa-lem: and Je-ru'sa-lem shall

be called a city of truth; and the mountain of the LORD of hosts the holy mountain. _{Jehovah} Tsebaoth

4 Thus says the LORD of hosts; There shall yet old men and old women dwell in the streets of Je-ru'sa-lem, and every man with his staff in his hand for very age.

5 And the streets of the city shall be full of boys and girls playing in the streets thereof.

6 Thus says the LORD of hosts; If it be marvellous in the eyes of the remnant of this people in these days, should it also be marvellous in My eyes? says the LORD of hosts. difficult

7 Thus says the LORD of hosts; Behold, I will save My people from the east country, and from the west country;

8 And I will bring them, and they shall dwell in the midst of Je-ru'sa-lem: and they shall be My people, and I will be their God, in truth and in righteousness. Elohim

9 Thus says the LORD of hosts; Let your hands be strong, you that hear in these days these words by the mouth of the prophets, which *were* in the day *that* the foundation of the house of the LORD of hosts was laid, that the temple might be built. _{Jehovah} Tsebaoth

10 For before these days there was no hire for man, nor any hire for beast; neither *was there any* peace to him that went out or came in because of the affliction: for I set all men every one against his neighbor. work

11 But now I *will* not *be* to the res-idue of this people as in the former days, says the LORD of hosts. remainder

12 For the seed *shall be* prosperous; the vine shall give her fruit, and the ground shall give her increase, and the heavens shall give their dew; and I will cause the remnant of this people to possess all these *things*.

13 And it shall come to pass, *that* as you were a curse among the heathen, O house of Ju'dah, and house of Is'ra-el; so will I save you, and you shall be a blessing: fear not, *but* let your hands be strong. nations - respect

14 For thus says the LORD of hosts; As I thought to punish you, when your fathers provoked Me to wrath, says the LORD of hosts, and I repented not: regretted

15 So again have I thought in these days to do well to Je-ru'sa-lem and to the house of Ju'dah: fear you not. respect

16 These *are* the things that you shall do; Speak you every man the truth to his neighbor; execute the judgment of truth and peace in your gates: EPH. 4:25 bring to pass

17 And let none of you imagine evil in your hearts against his neighbor; and love no false oath: for all these *are things* that I hate, says the LORD. despise

18 And the word of the LORD of hosts came to me, saying,

19 Thus says the LORD of hosts; The fast of the fourth *month*, and the fast of the fifth, and the fast of the seventh, and the fast of the tenth, shall be to the house of Ju'dah joy and gladness, and cheerful feasts; therefore love the truth and peace. _{Jehovah} Tsebaoth

20 Thus says the LORD of hosts; *It* shall yet *come to pass*, that there shall

come people, and the inhabitants of many cities:

21 And the inhabitants of one *city* shall go to another, saying, Let us go <u>speedily</u> to pray before the LORD, and to seek the <u>LORD of hosts:</u> I will go also.　　　quickly - Jehovah^s.f. Tsebaoth

22 Yea, many people and strong nations shall come to seek the <u>LORD of hosts</u> in Je-ru'sa-lem, and to pray before the LORD.

23 Thus says the <u>LORD of hosts</u>; In those days *it shall come to pass*, that ten men shall take hold out of all languages of the nations, even shall take hold of the skirt of him that is a Jew, saying, We will go with you: for we have heard *that* God *is* with you.　　　Elohim^p.f.

CHAPTER 9

THE burden of the word of the LORD in the land of Ha'drach, and Da-mas'cus *shall be* the rest thereof: when the eyes of man, as of all the tribes of Is'ra-el, *shall be* toward the LORD.

2 And Ha'math also shall border thereby; Ty'rus, and Zi'don, though it be very wise.

3 And Ty'rus did build herself a strong hold, and heaped up silver as the dust, and fine gold as the mire of the streets.

4 Behold, the Lord will cast her out, and He will smite her power in the sea; and she shall be devoured with fire.

5 Ash'ke-lon shall *see it*, and fear; Ga'za also *shall see it*, and be very sorrowful, and Ek'ron; for her expectation shall be ashamed; and the king shall perish from Ga'za, and Ash'ke-lon shall not be inhabited.　　　die

6 And a <u>bastard</u> shall dwell in Ash'dod, and I will cut off the pride of the Phi-lis'tines.　　　foreigner

7 And I will take away his blood out of his mouth, and his <u>abominations</u> from between his teeth: but he that remains, even he, *shall be* for our <u>God</u>, and he shall be as a <u>governor</u> in Ju'dah, and Ek'ron as a Jeb'u-site.　　　evil ways - Elohim^p.f. - leader

8 And I will encamp about My house because of the army, because of him that passes by, and because of him that returns: and no oppressor shall pass through them any more: for now have I seen with My eyes.

9 Rejoice greatly, O daughter of Zi'on; shout, O daughter of Je-ru'sa-lem: behold, your King comes to you: He *is* just, and <u>having</u> salvation; lowly, and riding upon an ass, and upon a colt the foal of an ass.　　　MATT 21:4-5 JOHN 12:15 endowed with

10 And I will cut off the chariot from E'phra-im, and the horse from Je-ru'sa-lem, and the battle bow shall be cut off: and He shall speak peace to the <u>heathen</u>: and His dominion *shall be* from sea *even* to sea, and from the river *even* to the ends of the earth.　　　nations

11 As for you also, by the blood of your <u>covenant</u> I have sent forth your prisoners out of the pit wherein *is* no water.　　　agreement

12 Turn you to the strong hold, you prisoners of hope: even to day do I declare *that* I will render double to you;

13 <u>When</u> I have bent Ju'dah for Me, filled the bow with E'phra-im, and raised up your sons, O Zi'on, against your sons, O Greece, and made you as the sword of a mighty man. _{For}

14 And the Lord shall be seen over them, and His arrow shall go forth as the lightning: and the <u>Lord G</u>od shall blow the trumpet, and shall go with whirlwinds of the south. _{Adonay^{p.f.} Jehovah}

15 The <u>Lord of hosts</u> shall defend them; and they shall devour, and <u>subdue</u> with sling stones; and they shall drink, *and* make a noise as through wine; and they shall be filled like bowls, *and* as the corners of the altar. _{Jehovah^{s.f.} Tsebaoth - conquer}

16 And the Lord their <u>God</u> shall save them in that day as the flock of His people: for *they shall be as* the stones of a crown, lifted up as an ensign upon His land. _{Elohim^{p.f.}}

17 For how great *is* His goodness, and how great *is* His beauty! <u>corn</u> shall make the young men <u>cheerful</u>, and new wine the maids. _{grain - flourish}

CHAPTER 10

ASK you of the Lord rain in the time of the latter rain; *so* the Lord shall make bright clouds, and give them showers of rain, to every one grass in the field.

2 For the <u>idols</u> have spoken vanity, and the <u>diviners</u> have seen a lie, and have told false dreams; they comfort in vain: therefore they went their way as a flock, they were troubled, because *there was* no shepherd. _{MATT. 9:36 gods - soothsayers}

3 My anger was kindled against the shepherds, and I punished the <u>goats</u>: for the <u>Lord of hosts</u> has visited His flock the house of Ju'dah, and has made them as His goodly horse in the battle. _{i.e., leaders - Jehovah^{s.f.} Tsebaoth}

4 Out of him came forth the corner, out of him the nail, out of him the battle bow, out of him every oppressor together.

5 And they shall be as mighty *men*, which tread down *their enemies* in the mire of the streets in the battle: and they shall fight, because the Lord *is* with them, and the riders on horses shall be confounded.

6 And I will strengthen the house of Ju'dah, and I will save the house of Jo'seph, and I will bring them again to place them; for I have mercy upon them: and they shall be as though I had not cast them off: for I *am* the Lord their <u>God</u>, and will hear them. _{Elohim^{p.f.}}

7 And *they of* E'phra-im shall be like a mighty *man*, and their heart shall rejoice as through wine: yea, their children shall see *it*, and be glad; their heart shall rejoice in the Lord.

8 I will <u>hiss</u> for them, and gather them; for I have redeemed them: and they shall increase as they have increased. _{whistle}

9 And I will <u>sow</u> them among the people: and they shall remember Me in far countries; and they shall live with their children, and turn again. _{scatter}

10 I will bring them again also out of the land of E'gypt, and gather them out of As-syr'i-a; and I will bring them into

the land of Gil'e-ad and Leb'a-non; and *place* shall not be found for them. 11 And He shall pass through the sea with affliction, and shall smite the waves in the sea, and all the deeps of the river shall dry up: and the pride of As-syr'i-a shall be brought down, and the scepter of E'gypt shall depart away. 12 And I will strengthen them in the LORD; and they shall walk up and down in His name, says the LORD.

CHAPTER 11

OPEN your doors, O Leb'a-non, that the fire may devour your cedars.
                              feed on
2 Howl, fir tree; for the cedar is fallen; because the mighty are spoiled: howl, O you oaks of Ba'shan; for the forest of the vintage is come down.
3 *There is* a voice of the howling of the shepherds; for their glory is spoiled: a voice of the roaring of young lions; for the pride of Jor'dan is spoiled.
                              ruined
4 Thus says the LORD my God; Feed the flock of the slaughter;
                    Elohim^p.f.
5 Whose possessors slay them, and hold themselves not guilty: and they that sell them say, Blessed *be* the LORD; for I am rich: and their own shepherds pity them not.
6 For I will no more pity the inhabitants of the land, says the LORD: but, lo, I will deliver the men every one into his neighbor's hand, and into the hand of his king: and they shall smite the land, and out of their hand I will not deliver *them.*
7 And I will feed the flock of slaughter, *even* you, O poor of the flock. And I took to Me two staves; the one I called Beauty, and the other I called Bands; and I fed the flock.
        rods - Jewish Tribes? Favor - Union? Binders?
8 Three shepherds also I cut off in one month; and My soul loathed them, and their soul also abhorred Me.
                destroyed - despised
9 Then said I, I will not feed you: that that dies, let it die; and that that is to be cut off, let it be cut off; and let the rest eat every one the flesh of another.
10 And I took My staff, *even* Beauty, and cut it asunder, that I might break My covenant which I had made with all the people.
    Jewish Tribes? Favor? - in two (Ju'dah-Israel) - agreement
11 And it was broken in that day: and so the poor of the flock that waited upon Me knew that it *was* the word of the LORD.
12 And I said to them, If you think good, give *Me* My price; and if not, forbear. So they weighed for My price thirty *pieces* of silver.   MATT. 27:9
13 And the LORD said to me, Cast it to the potter: a goodly price that I was prized at of them. And I took the thirty *pieces* of silver, and cast them to the potter in the house of the LORD.   value
14 Then I cut asunder My other staff, *even* Bands, that I might break the brotherhood between Ju'dah and Is'ra-el.   in two - Union
15 And the LORD said to me, Take to you yet the instruments of a foolish shepherd.   unwise
16 For, lo, I will raise up a shepherd in the land, *which* shall not visit those

that be <u>cut off</u>, neither shall seek the young one, nor heal that that is broken, nor feed that that stands still: but he shall eat the flesh of the fat, and tear their claws in pieces. perishing

17 Woe to the <u>idle</u> shepherd that leaves the flock! the sword *shall be* upon his arm, and upon his right eye: his arm shall be clean dried up, and his right eye shall be utterly darkened. worthless

CHAPTER 12

THE burden of the word of the LORD for Is'ra-el, says the LORD, which stretches forth the heavens, and lays the foundation of the earth, and forms the spirit of man within him.

2 Behold, I will make Je-ru'sa-lem a cup of trembling to all the people round about, when they shall be in the siege both against Ju'dah *and* against Je-ru'sa-lem.

3 And in that day will I make Je-ru'sa-lem a burdensome stone for all people: all that burden themselves with it shall be cut in pieces, though all the people of the earth be gathered together against it.

4 In that day, says the LORD, I will smite every horse with astonishment, and his rider with madness: and I will open My eyes upon the house of Ju'dah, and will smite every horse of the people with blindness.

5 And the <u>governors</u> of Ju'dah shall say in their heart, The inhabitants of Je-ru'sa-lem *shall be* my strength in the <u>LORD of hosts</u> their <u>God</u>. clans - Jehovah[s.f.] Tsebaoth - Elohim[p.f.]

6 In that day will I make the <u>governors</u> of Ju'dah like an hearth of fire among the wood, and like a torch of fire in a sheaf; and they shall devour all the people round about, on the right hand and on the left: and Je-ru'sa-lem shall be inhabited again in her own place, *even* in Je-ru'sa-lem. leaders

7 The LORD also shall save the tents of Ju'dah first, that the glory of the house of Da'vid and the glory of the inhabitants of Je-ru'sa-lem do not magnify *themselves* against Ju'dah.

8 In that day shall the LORD defend the inhabitants of Je-ru'sa-lem; and he that is feeble among them at that day shall be as Da'vid; and the <u>house</u> of Da'vid *shall be* as <u>God,</u> as the <u>angel</u> of the LORD before them. family - Elohim[p.f.] - messenger

9 And it shall come to pass in that day, *that* I will seek to destroy all the nations that come against Je-ru'sa-lem.

10 And I will pour upon the house of Da'vid, and upon the inhabitants of Je-ru'sa-lem, the spirit of grace and of supplications: and they shall look upon Me whom they have pierced, and they shall mourn for Him, as one mourns for *his* only *son*, and shall be in bitterness for Him, as one that is in bitterness for *his* firstborn. JOHN 19:37 REV 1:7

11 In that day shall there be a great mourning in Je-ru'sa-lem, as the mourning of Ha-dad-rim-mon in the valley of Me-gid'don.

12 And the land shall mourn, every family apart; the family of the house of Da'vid apart, and their wives apart; the

family of the house of Na'than apart, and their wives apart;

13 The family of the house of Le'vi apart, and their wives apart; the family of Shim'e-i apart, and their wives apart;

14 All the families that remain, every family apart, and their wives apart.

CHAPTER 13

IN that day there shall be a fountain opened to the house of Da'vid and to the inhabitants of Je-ru'sa-lem for sin and for uncleanness.

2 And it shall come to pass in that day, says the LORD of hosts, *that* I will cut off the names of the idols out of the land, and they shall no more be remembered: and also I will cause the prophets and the unclean spirit to pass out of the land.   Jehovah^{s.f.} Tsebaoth

3 And it shall come to pass, *that* when any shall yet prophesy, then his father and his mother that gave birth to him shall say to him, You shall not live; for you speak lies in the name of the LORD: and his father and his mother that gave birth to him shall <u>thrust</u> him through when he prophesies.   kill

4 And it shall come to pass in that day, *that* the prophets shall be ashamed every one of his vision, when he has prophesied; neither shall they wear a rough garment to deceive:

5 But he shall say, I *am* no prophet, I *am* an <u>husbandman</u>; for man taught me to keep cattle from my youth.   farmer

6 And *one* shall say to him, What *are* these wounds in your hands? Then he shall answer, *Those* with which I was wounded *in* the house of my friends.

7 Awake, O sword, against My shepherd, and against the man *that is* My fellow, says the Lord of hosts: smite the shepherd, and the sheep shall be scattered: and I will turn My hand upon the little ones. MATT. 26:31 MARK 14:27 JOHN 16:32 Jehovah^{s.f.} Tsebaoth

8 And it shall come to pass, *that* in all the land, says the LORD, two parts therein shall be cut off *and* die; but the third shall be left therein.

9 And I will bring the third part through the fire, and will refine them as silver is refined, and will try them as gold is tried: they shall call on My name, and I will hear them: I will say, It *is* My people: and they shall say, The LORD *is* my <u>God</u>.   REV. 8:12 Elohim^{p.f.}

CHAPTER 14

BEHOLD, the day of the LORD comes, and your <u>spoil</u> shall be divided in the midst of you.   plunder

2 For I will gather all nations against Je-ru'sa-lem to battle; and the city shall be taken, and the houses <u>rifled</u>, and the women ravished; and half of the city shall go forth into captivity, and the <u>residue</u> of the people shall not be cut off from the city. i.e., Christ - plundered - rest

3 Then shall the LORD go forth, and fight against those nations, as when He fought in the day of battle.

4 And His feet shall stand in that day upon the mount of Ol'ives, which *is* before Je-ru'sa-lem on the east, and the mount of Ol'ives shall <u>cleave</u> in the midst thereof toward the east and

toward the west, *and there shall be* a very great valley; and half of the mountain shall remove toward the north, and half of it toward the south.   split

5 And you shall flee *to* the valley of the mountains; for the valley of the mountains shall reach to A'zal: yea, you shall flee, like as you fled from before the earthquake in the days of Uz-zi'ah king of Ju'dah: and the LORD my God shall come, *and* all the saints with You.   Elohim p.f. -holy ones

6 And it shall come to pass in that day, *that* the light shall not be clear, *nor* dark:

7 But it shall be one day which shall be known to the LORD, not day, nor night: but it shall come to pass, *that* at evening time it shall be light.   MATT. 24:36

8 And it shall be in that day, *that* living waters shall go out from Je-ru'sa-lem; half of them toward the former sea, and half of them toward the hinder sea: in summer and in winter shall it be.   Eastern - Western

9 And the LORD shall be king over all the earth: in that day shall there be one LORD, and His name one.   i.e., Jesus-God

10 All the land shall be turned as a plain from Ge'ba to Rim'mon south of Je-ru'sa-lem: and it shall be lifted up, and inhabited in her place, from Ben'ja-min's gate to the place of the first gate, to the corner gate, and *from* the tower of Ha-nan'e-el to the king's winepresses.

11 And *men* shall dwell in it, and there shall be no more utter destruction; but Je-ru'sa-lem shall be safely inhabited.   REV. 22:3

12 And this shall be the plague wherewith the LORD will smite all the people that have fought against Je-ru'sa-lem; Their flesh shall consume away while they stand upon their feet, and their eyes shall consume away in their holes, and their tongue shall consume away in their mouth.   sickness

13 And it shall come to pass in that day, *that* a great tumult from the LORD shall be among them; and they shall lay hold every one on the hand of his neighbor, and his hand shall rise up against the hand of his neighbor.   panic

14 And Ju'dah also shall fight at Je-ru'sa-lem; and the wealth of all the heathen round about shall be gathered together, gold, and silver, and apparel, in great abundance. against - nations

15 And so shall be the plague of the horse, of the mule, of the camel, and of the ass, and of all the beasts that shall be in these tents, as this plague.   sickness - those camps

16 And it shall come to pass, *that* every one that is left of all the nations which came against Je-ru'sa-lem shall even go up from year to year to worship the King, the LORD of hosts, and to keep the feast of tabernacles.   Jehovah s.f. Tsebaoth

17 And it shall be, *that* whoso will not come up of *all* the families of the earth to Je-ru'sa-lem to worship the King, the LORD of hosts, even upon them shall be no rain.

18 And if the family of E'gypt go not up, and come not, that *have* no *rain*; there shall be the plague, wherewith the

LORD will smite the <u>heathen</u> that come not up to keep the feast of tabernacles.

sickness - nations

19 This shall be the punishment of E'gypt, and the punishment of all nations that come not up to keep the feast of tabernacles.

20 In that day shall there be upon the bells of the horses, HOLINESS TO THE LORD; and the pots in the LORD's house shall be like the bowls before the altar.

21 Yea, every pot in Je-ru'sa-lem and in Ju'dah shall be holiness to the <u>LORD of hosts</u>: and all they that sacrifice shall come and take of them, and <u>seethe</u> therein: and in that day there shall be no more the Ca'naan-ite in the house of the <u>LORD of hosts</u>.

Jehovah^{s.f.} Tsebaoth - boil

MALACHI

OUTLINE

UNDENIABLE LOVE: God's Love for Israel 1.1-5

UNACCEPTABLE SACRIFICES: Corrupt Offerings by Corrupt Priests 1.6-14

UNKEPT OBLIGATIONS: The Priests' Neglect of the Covenant 2.1-9

UNTRUE HUSBANDS: Rebuke for Idolatry and Divorce 2.10-16

UNEXPECTED JUDGMENT: The Coming of the Lord 2.17—3.6

UNMEASURED BLESSING: God's Promise if Tithes are Forthcoming 3.7-12

UNWARRANTED ASSERTIONS: Sure Meting Out of Justice 3.13—4.3

UNFORGETTABLE FAREWELL: An Admonition, a Promise, a Threat 4.4-6

SURVEY

Speaking for God, Malachi stood at one of the most significant dividing points in history. Prophets had come and gone, but the culture about him did not bear the impress of their labors. The priests were corrupt (1.6—2.9), and the people, with some exceptions, were no better (2.10—4.3). But God was still on the throne—sovereign. He was the father (1.6), the master (1.6), a great king (1.14), the heavenly governor (implied in 1.8), the giver of covenants and commandments (2.5; 4.4). As the God of judgment, He had brought about the doom of Edom (1.3, 4). His curse was upon the unfaithful priests (1.14; 2.2, 3, 9) and those who had robbed Him (3.9). He would cut off those who intermarried with the heathen (2.12). There would be swift judgment (2.17—3.5). The Day of the Lord would consume the wicked (4.1, 3).

Yet as the God of grace He would bless the faithful remnant, for a story of grace lay behind His love for Jacob (1.2), His covenant with Levi (2.4, 5), His forbearance with the sons of Jacob (3.6), His offer to those who had been unfaithful stewards (3.10), the book of remembrance (3.16), the rising of the sun of righteousness (4.2), and the promised coming of Elijah (4.5, 6). The Day of the Lord was coming, said Malachi. It would be a glorious day for the righteous (3.16, 17; 4.2, 3), but a day of destruction for the wicked (4.1, 3). Yet between the lines can be read these words of grace: "Turn ye, turn ye from your evil ways; for why will ye die, O house of Israel?" (Ezk 33.11).

AUTHOR

Whether Malachi is a man's name, or means, rather, "my messenger" or "a missionary," is disputed. Since all the other Old Testament books of prophecy are authenticated by the presence of the authors' names, however, and since the name "Malachi" is formed like certain other Hebrew proper names, it probably is the name of the prophet who wrote the book. In any event, history has preserved for us no certain information about the author. Malachi was probably written sometime in the quarter century following 450 B.C., since it mirrors conditions existing at the time of Nehemiah's second arrival in Jerusalem in 432 B.C.

B.L.G.

THE BOOK OF
MALACHI

"My Messenger"
Jehovah's Messenger
Is Coming Soon

CHAPTER 1

THE burden of the word of the LORD to Is'ra-el by Mal'a-chi.message

2 I have loved you, says the LORD. Yet you say, Wherein have You loved us? *Was* not E'sau Ja'cob's brother? says the LORD: yet I loved Ja'cob,

3 And I hated E'sau, and laid his mountains and his heritage waste for the dragons of the wilderness.

ROM. 9:13 thought less of - inheritance - jackels

4 Whereas E'dom says, We are impoverished, but we will return and build the desolate places; thus says the LORD of hosts, They shall build, but I will throw down; and they shall call them, The border of wickedness, and, The people against whom the LORD has indignation for ever. Jehovah^{s.f.} Tsebaoth

5 And your eyes shall see, and you shall say, The LORD will be magnified from the border of Is'ra-el. honored

6 A son honors *his* father, and a servant his master: if then I *be* a father, where *is* My honor? and if I *be* a master, where *is* My fear? says the LORD of hosts to you, O priests, that despise My name. And you say, Wherein have we despised Your name? respect

7 You offer polluted bread upon My altar; and you say, Wherein have we polluted You? In that you say, The table of the LORD *is* contemptible. defiled

8 And if you offer the blind for sacrifice, *is it* not evil? and if you offer the lame and sick, *is it* not evil? offer it now to your governor; will he be pleased with you, or accept your person? says the LORD of hosts. as a - Jehovah^{s.f.} Tsebaoth

9 And now, I pray you, beseech God that He will be gracious to us: this has been by your means: will He regard your persons? says the LORD of hosts. beg - El ^{s.f.} - work

10 Who *is there* even among you that would shut the doors *for nothing*? neither do you kindle *fire* on My altar for nothing. I have no pleasure in you, says the LORD of hosts, neither will I accept an offering at your hand.

11 For from the rising of the sun even to the going down of the same My name *shall be* great among the Gen'tiles; and in every place incense *shall be* offered to My name, and a pure offering: for My name *shall be* great among the heathen, says the LORD of hosts. is - sincere - Nations

12 But you have profaned it, in that you say, The table of the LORD *is* polluted; and the fruit thereof, *even* its meat, *is* contemptible. defiled - defiled - food

13 You said also, Behold, what a weariness *is it*! and you have snuffed at it, says the LORD of hosts; and you brought *that which was* torn, and the lame, and the sick; thus you brought an offering: should I accept this of your hand? says the LORD. Jehovah^{s.f.} Tsebaoth

14 But cursed *be* the deceiver, which has in his flock a male, and vows,

and sacrifices to the L<small>ORD</small> a cor-rupt thing: for I *am* a great King, says the L<small>ORD</small> of hosts, and My name *is* dreadful among the hea-then.   <small>Adonay^{p.f.} - blemished - Jehovah^{s.f.} nations</small>

CHAPTER 2

A<small>ND</small> now, O you priests, this com-mandment *is* for you.

2 If you will not hear, and if you will not lay *it* to heart, to give glory to My name, says the L<small>ORD</small> of hosts, I will even send a curse upon you, and I will curse your blessings: yea, I have cursed them already, because you do not lay *it* to heart. <small>Jehovah^{s.f.} Tsebaoth</small>

3 Behold, I will corrupt your seed, and spread dung upon your faces, *even* the dung of your solemn feasts; and *one* shall take you away with it.   <small>rebuke - offspring - refuse</small>

4 And you shall know that I have sent this commandment to you, that My covenant might be with Le'vi, says the L<small>ORD</small> of hosts   <small>agreement - Jehovah^{s.f.} Tsebaoth</small>

5 My covenant was with him of life and peace; and I gave them to him *for* the fear wherewith he feared Me, and was afraid before My name.   <small>reverence - revered</small>

6 The law of truth was in his mouth, and iniquity was not found in his lips: he walked with Me in peace and equity, and did turn many away from iniquity.   <small>evil - upright - sin</small>

7 For the priest's lips should keep knowledge, and they should seek the law at his mouth: for he *is* the messen-ger of the L<small>ORD</small> of hosts.   <small>Jehovah^{s.f.} Tsebaoth</small>

8 But you are departed out of the way; you have caused many to stumble at the law; you have corrupted the covenant of Le'vi, says the L<small>ORD</small> of hosts.   <small>agreement</small>

9 Therefore have I also made you contemptible and base before all the people, according as you have not kept My ways, but have been partial in the law.

10 Have we not all one father? has not one God created us? why do we deal treacherously every man against his brother, by profaning the cov-enant of our fathers?   <small>1 COR. 8:6 making useless - agreement</small>

11 Ju'dah has dealt treacherously, and an abomination is committed in Is'ra-el and in Je-ru'sa-lem; for Ju'dah has profaned the holiness of the L<small>ORD</small> which He loved, and has married the daughter of a strange god.   <small>evil thing</small>

12 The L<small>ORD</small> will cut off the man that does this, the master and the scholar, out of the tabernacles of Ja'cob, and him that offers an of-fering to the L<small>ORD</small> of hosts.   <small>witness - respondent - Jehovah^{s.f.} Tsebaoth</small>

13 And this have you done again, covering the altar of the L<small>ORD</small> with tears, with weeping, and with crying out, insomuch that He regards not the offering any more, or receives *it* with good will at your hand.

14 Yet you say, Wherefore? Because the L<small>ORD</small> has been witness between you and the wife of your youth, against whom you have dealt treach-erously: yet *is* she your companion, and the wife of your covenant. <small>agreement</small>

15 And did not he make one? Yet had he the residue of the Spirit. And where-fore one? That he might seek a godly seed. Therefore take heed to your spirit,

and let none deal treacherously against the wife of his youth. offspring

16 For the L<small>ORD</small>, the God of Is'ra-el, says that He hates putting away: for *one* covers violence with his garment, says the L<small>ORD</small> of hosts: therefore take heed to your spirit, that you deal not treacherously. Jehovah<small>s.f.</small> - Elohim<small>p.f.</small> - despised

17 You have wearied the L<small>ORD</small> with your words. Yet you say, Wherein have we wearied *Him*? When you say, Every one that does evil *is* good in the sight of the L<small>ORD</small>, and He delights in them; or, Where *is* the God of judgment? Elohim<small>p.f.</small>

CHAPTER 3

BEHOLD, I will send My messenger, and he shall prepare the way before Me: and the L<small>ORD</small>, whom you seek, shall suddenly come to His temple, even the messenger of the covenant, whom you delight in: behold, He shall come, says the L<small>ORD</small> of hosts. MATT. 11:10 MARK 1:2 LUKE 7:27 LUKE 1:76 Adon<small>s.f.</small> - agreement - Jehovah<small>s.f.</small> Tsebaoth

2 But who may abide the day of His coming? and who shall stand when He appears? for He *is* like a refiner's fire, and like fullers' soap:

3 And He shall sit *as* a refiner and purifier of silver: and He shall purify the sons of Le'vi, and purge them as gold and silver, that they may offer to the L<small>ORD</small> an offering in righteousness. refine

4 Then shall the offering of Ju'dah and Je-ru'sa-lem be pleasant to the L<small>ORD</small>, as in the days of old, and as in former years.

5 And I will come near to you to judgment; and I will be a swift witness against the sorcerers, and against the adulterers, and against false swearers, and against those that oppress the hireling in *his* wages, the widow, and the fatherless, and that turn aside the stranger *from his right*, and fear not Me, says the L<small>ORD</small> of hosts. unfaithful - reverence - Jehovah<small>s.f.</small> Tsebaoth

6 For I *am* the L<small>ORD</small>, I change not; therefore you sons of Ja'cob are not consumed.

7 Even from the days of your fathers you are gone away from My ordinances, and have not kept *them*. Return to Me, and I will return to you, says the L<small>ORD</small> of hosts. But you said, Wherein shall we return? turned aside - Jehovah<small>s.f.</small> Tsebaoth

8 Will a man rob God? Yet you have robbed Me. But you say, Wherein have we robbed You? In tithes and offerings. Elohim<small>p.f.</small>

9 You *are* cursed with a curse: for you have robbed me, *even* this whole nation.

10 Bring you all the tithes into the storehouse, that there may be meat in My house, and prove Me now herewith, says the L<small>ORD</small> of hosts, if I will not open you the windows of heaven, and pour you out a blessing, that *there shall* not *be room* enough *to receive it*. food - test

11 And I will rebuke the devourer for your sakes, and he shall not destroy the fruits of your ground; neither shall your vine cast her fruit before the time in the field, says the L<small>ORD</small> of hosts. i.e., Satan - Jehovah<small>s.f.</small> Tsebaoth

12 And all nations shall call you blessed: for you shall be a <u>delight-some</u> land, says the Lord of hosts.

delightful - Jehovah[s.f.] Tsebaoth

13 Your words have been <u>stout</u> against Me, says the Lord. Yet you say, What have we spoken *so much* against You?

arrogant

14 You have said, It *is* vain to serve <u>God</u>: and what profit *is it* that we have kept His <u>ordinance</u>, and that we have walked mournfully before the Lord of hosts?

Elohim[p.f.] - charge

15 And now we call the proud happy; yea, they that work wickedness are set up; yea, *they that* <u>tempt</u> God are even delivered.

test - Elohim[p.f.]

16 Then they that <u>feared</u> the Lord spoke often one to another: and the Lord hearkened, and heard *it*, and a book of remembrance was written before Him for them that <u>feared</u> the Lord, and that thought upon His name.

revered - reverenced

17 And they shall be Mine, says the Lord of hosts, in that day when I make up My jewels; and I will spare them, as a man spares his own son that serves him.

Jehovah[s.f.] Tsebaoth

18 Then shall you return, and discern between the righteous and the wicked, between him that serves <u>God</u> and him that serves Him not.

Elohim[p.f.]

CHAPTER 4

FOR, behold, the day comes, that shall burn as an oven; and all the proud, yea, and all that do wickedly, shall be stubble: and the day that comes shall burn them up, says the Lord of hosts, that it shall leave them neither root nor branch.

Jehovah[s.f.] Tsebaoth

2 But to you that <u>fear</u> My name shall the Sun of righteousness arise with healing in His wings; and you shall go forth, and grow up as calves of the stall.

LUKE 1:78 reverence

3 And you shall tread down the wicked; for they shall be ashes under the soles of your feet in the day that I shall do *this*, says the Lord of hosts.

Jehovah[s.f.] Tsebaoth

4 Remember you the law of Mo'ses My servant, which I commanded to him in Ho'reb for all Is'ra-el, *with* the <u>statutes</u> and judgments.

laws

5 Behold, I will send you E-li'jah the prophet before the coming of the great and dreadful day of the Lord:

MATT. 11:14

6 And he shall turn the heart of the fathers to the children, and the heart of the children to their fathers, less I come and smite the earth with a curse.

LUKE 1:6

THE END OF THE OLD TESTAMENT

BETWEEN
THE
TESTAMENTS

(420 B.C.—A.D.)

A BASIC OUTLINE OF INTERTESTAMENT HISTORY

THE PERIOD: 420 B.C.—4 B.C.

420 B.C.	Close of the Old Testament canon (Malachi, last book in the O.T. completed).
(639)–337	Period of Persian Rule.
336–323	Alexander the Great conquers the world for Greece.
323	Alexander dies and world is divided among his generals. Civil wars follow.
200±	Rome overshadows Greek Kingdoms.
168–165	Syrian Persecution under Antiochus IV fought off by Judas and the other Maccabees.
66	Pompey conquers Israel for Rome.
4 B.C.	Christ born in Bethlehem.
4 B.C.	Herod the Great dies.

G. Cohen

BETWEEN THE TESTAMENTS

William L. Lane, Th.D.

(420 B.C.- A.D.)

The period between the Old and New Testaments consists of "years of silence" with respect to an authoritative new revelation from God. After the ministries of Haggai, Zechariah, and Malachi, the prophetic voice was silenced until the Word of God came to John the Baptist in the wilderness of Judea. Yet it is impossible to move from the Old to the New Testament without noticing significant differences. At the close of the Old Testament the dominant world empire is Persia, ruled by a king and administered by provincial governors. The international language is Aramaic. The high priest functions essentially as a religious authority. The primary institution of the Jews is the Temple, only recently rebuilt. Prophet and priest ground their ministry in a new awareness of the law of God. The dispersion of the Jewish people is limited to communities in Babylon and Egypt.

When the New Testament opens, Rome is the sole world power, governed by an emperor who delegates authority to proconsuls and procurators. The international language is Greek. The high priest functions in the secular sphere. While the Temple remains central in Jewish life, synagogue and sanhedrin assume their place among the significant institutions of the Jewish people. A plurality of parties and sects unknown in the Persian period demonstrate the heterogeneous character of Jewish piety. The totality of Scripture is familiar to the people. An extensive dispersion accounts for Jewish communities throughout the vast Roman Empire. Nearly every aspect of Jewish life has been subjected to change. Like ancient Israel, Judaea has been the pawn of empires, the buffer between hostile states. Influences from Persia, from the Macedonian empires of Alexander, the Ptolemies and the Seleucids, and from Rome informed and molded its existence. It is impossible to appreciate the complex shaping of faith and culture which furnishes the backdrop to the New Testament record without a knowledge of the period between the Testaments.

I. THE LEGACY OF THE PERSIAN PERIOD
(639 B.C.-336 B.C.)

Our knowledge of the first segment of the intertestamental era, the Persian period, is limited. Apart from the later books of the Old Testament and the few witnesses to Jewish life in Mesopotamia and Egypt provided by Aramaic inscriptions, commercial tablets, and papyri, there is no documentary evidence to illumine the history of this period. Josephus is able to add nothing to these few sources. The literary texts and archaeological research permit one significant conclusion, however: throughout the two centuries of Persian domination the province of Judaea experienced no devastation by war or invasion. Although Persia was involved in both foreign and civil conflicts, none of these took place on Palestinian soil. Two hundred years of undisturbed peace was rare in the ancient world; it provided the climate in which Judaea could mature from a small agrarian state to a province prepared for the encounter with Hellenism.

There were important religious developments in the Persian period. The House of David, which had provided leadership in Israel for more than five centuries, was displaced from political and religious prominence. The last lineal descendant of David to function in a position of leadership in the post-Exilic age, apparently, was Zerubbabel (cf. Zec 4:6-10). The Persians may have insisted that no member of the Judaean royal family be allowed to participate in the government of the province. The House of David fell into complete obscurity. During the brief period when the Jewish people enjoyed independence under the Hasmonaeans, they failed to recall the covenant that God had made with the line of David, but were satisfied with other leaders. By the first century, the heir to the throne is a village carpenter who does not even live in Judaea.

1385

Political authority was now conferred on the high priest. The extent of the power delegated to him may be estimated from Ezra's commission as governor and priest (Ez 7:11-26). The appointment of judges, the instruction of the people, and the exercise of the powers of confiscation, imprisonment, and capital punishment in the enforcement of the laws of God or the king fall within his jurisdiction. The authority of the high priestly office was confirmed by the later kings of Persia and by the Ptolemies of Egypt and the Seleucids of Syria in the Hellenistic age. From the time of the restoration of the Jews exiled in Babylon until the period of the successors of Alexander the Great, the high priest was the religious and civil leader of Judaea and of the scattered Jewish communities outside of Palestine. The office became decidedly secular in orientation as political considerations increasingly commanded attention. The conferral of broad powers on the high priesthood explains why later, within the context of a crucial power struggle, the question emerges, "Which is the legitimate high-priestly line?"

Another significant development was a growing concern for the written law of God and its oral interpretation. Confronted with situations vastly different from those which had prevailed in Judaea under the monarchy, the Jews in Babylon had to concern themselves with the application of the written law. The result was oral law designed to apply Biblical law to new situations and to keep the people a safe distance from transgressing the revealed will of God. On the foundations of the oral law worked out in Babylon the returning exiles erected the first levels of what would become a vast and complex system. Concern for the law of God is expressed in the Biblical account of Ezra reading the law in public, supplying an interpretation in the vernacular of the people (Neh 8:8). In the Persian period the Mosaic laws and other writings were collected into a body of canonical Scripture, acknowledged to be divinely authoritative. The translation of the Pentateuch into Greek, in the version known as the Septuagint, shortly after the close of the Persian era indicates that even in communities removed from Palestine the law was the most prized possession of the Jewish people.

Finally, it is in this period that the Samaritan schism occurred. The breach between the Jews and the Samaritans did not occur in the area of worship or interpretation of the law, but over the site where God had ordained that He should be worshiped. The Samaritans claimed that Mount Gerizim, not Zion, was the sole place where sacrifice could be offered, vows absolved, and festivals observed (cf. Jn 4:20). Tension between the Judaeans and the Samaritans persisted throughout the Persian, Hellenistic, and Roman eras. Josephus tells of a famous debate conducted before Ptolemy I early in the Hellenistic period. Spokesmen for the Temple in Jerusalem and for the temple on Mount Gerizim presented elaborate arguments supported by appeals to Scripture and to the legitimacy of the appointed high-priestly line. Deep resentment and bitterness were shown in both sides of the continuing debate. In the days of Antiochus IV Epiphanes the Samaritans supported the repressive measures of the Seleucids against the Judaeans. When the struggle had been resolved in favor of Israel, the Jewish king John Hyrcanus I burned the Samaritan temple to the ground. It is against a background of four centuries of hostility that the startling note of offense can be understood when Jesus describes as a compassionate and true neighbor not a priest or a Levite, but a Samaritan (Lk 10:29-37).

Questions of legitimate leadership, of law and its application, of authority and worship remain as the legacy of the Persian period. They become of central concern to the Jewish and early Christian communities in the period of which the New Testament speaks.

II. THE ENCOUNTER WITH HELLENISM
(336 B.C.–200 B.C.)

The power of Persia was broken by Alexander of Macedon (conquered: 336 B.C.–323 B.C.), one of the great giants of all mankind. In 334 B.C., at the age of twenty-two, he crossed over to Asia with an army of 32,000 infantry and 5,000 cavalry supported by 160 ships. Victories at the River Granicus (334) and at Issus (333), the conquest of Tyre and Gaza (332), the expedition into Egypt (332-31), and the victory of Gaugemela near Arbela gave Alexander mastery over the vast Persian empire of Darius III. A second-century Jewish writer observed that Alexander "advanced to the ends of the earth and plundered many nations, and the earth was quiet before him" (1 Macc 1:3). His own genius was the greatest single factor in his success. Although he ruled an empire only twelve years, in that time he changed the course of world history.

Alexander may be regarded as the Apostle of Hellenism. He considered himself charged with the task of uniting a disjointed world; his dream was to unify the peoples of Greece and Asia under a common Hellenic culture. Alexander had been a pupil of Aristotle, and he attached to his general staff several Greek scholars and scientists whom Aristotle had trained. Under Alexander the Greeks came to regard the spread of their civilization as a divine mission, and they regarded language as a primary factor in culture. These convictions were new in the history of ideas. It was inevitable that the culture of Greece should make its impact on the peoples reached by the armies of the conqueror. Concurrently, Alexander recognized the value in the foreign culture he encountered in Asia. The fusion of Greek thought with elements of eastern culture produced what is called the Hellenistic, as distinguished from the Hellenic, world. By introducing Greek culture into Syria and Egypt, Alexander probably had more influence on the development of Judaism than any other individual who was not a Jew by birth.

Alexander's empire was the largest the world had known to that time. At his death in 323 B.C. it quickly disintegrated. The commander of the fleet, Ptolemy I Soter, seized Egypt and Palestine for himself. Syria and the eastern portions of the empire fell to Seleucus I. Each of these rulers began dynasties that were involved in almost constant intrigue and aggression to secure control of Palestine as a buffer state to protect their respective kingdoms. For more than a century (323-198 B.C.) Palestine remained under Ptolemaic control.

The policy of the Ptolemies was not to introduce any revolutionary changes in government or customs in Judaea. Consequently, Judaism first encountered Hellenism within a climate of tolerance. The importance of this encounter may be estimated from Sirach (or Ecclesiasticus), a book of the Apocrypha written in Hebrew about 190 B.C. The author of this work was Jesus, the son of Sirach (Sir 50:27). His collection of proverbs and counsel reflects years of involvement as a student and teacher of wisdom. In his academy in Jerusalem he lectured before young men of the upper classes on Scripture, jurisprudence, ethics, and the social graces (51:23). He was a scribe who combined an awareness of Israel's distinctive position and role among the nations with a broad and tolerant appreciation for life in all its expressions. He may have served on diplomatic missions to the Ptolemaic court; he had traveled much and had benefited from his experiences in other lands (34:9-12). He had a thorough knowledge of the strengths and weaknesses of human nature and a frank appreciation for the kind of social life Hellenism had encouraged. Sirach provides an intellectual portrait of the cultured, liberal-spirited Jew who has thought seriously about the greater and lesser questions of this day. His piety is typical of a type current at the close of the third century B.C., a piety characterized by a cosmopolitan spirit and moderation, but opposed to any radical Hellenization of Judaism. Concern with the law of God remains dominant: the true response to divine wisdom is a disciplined life lived in accordance with the commandments of God; the crown and root of wisdom is the fear of the Lord (1:18, 20). This is a Palestinian, rather than a Hellenistic, emphasis.

While the impact of Hellenism on Palestinian Judaism was moderate during the Ptolemaic era, within the Jewish community at Alexandria its influence was far more pervasive. Evidence is provided by a theological treatise contained in the Apocrypha, the Wisdom of Solomon. While this document can scarcely be dated earlier than 140 B.C., it reflects a modification of Jewish thinking at significant points by Hellenistic philosophical ideas current in Alexandria as early as the third century B.C. The creation of the earth "out of formless matter" (11:17) was a Platonic commonplace which implied that this unformed matter was itself uncreated. Platonism also contributed the teaching that the body was a weight to the soul (9:14 f.), the conception of the pre-existent soul (8:19 f.), and the doctrine of the immortality of the soul, which in this document totally supplants the Biblical doctrine of the resurrection of the body. The conception of the world soul (1:7; 7:24; 8:1) and of the transmutation of the elements (19:18-22) in Stoic, while the message of divine wisdom is summarized in terms of the four cardinal virtues of Stoicism (8:7). These ideas were in the air at Alexandria throughout the Hellenistic period and represent no more than an acquaintance with popular philosophy; but they mark a departure from certain Old Testament concepts and furnish an index to the degree of Hellenization which Judaism outside of Palestine experienced under the Ptolemies.

A decisive battle in 198 B.C. brought Judaea under Seleucid control. For three decades there was no indication that this would

mean any radical change in the life and thought of Judaism. The continuing moderate Hellenization of Jewish life and manners, especially among the upper classes, appeared no different in character than that which had taken place under the Ptolemies. It could not be foreseen that the coming of Seleucid rule unleashed forces that would soon result in open conflict between Judaism and Hellenism in which the life or death of Biblical faith was at stake.

The tension between Judaism and Hellenism erupted in the reign of Antiochus IV Epiphanes, a fanatic for Hellenism. He was determined to frustrate Roman intentions of controlling the eastern Mediterranean coast by the bold plan of uniting Egypt and Syria, the only two remaining independent realms, into a single Seleucid state. To accomplish this design, he contemplated war on Egypt and the unification of the heterogeneous populations of Syria by a process of Hellenization. Judaea was crucial to his plan because it provided him with a base for offensive action against Egypt and gave him an outlet to the sea. He was confident of support in high Jewish circles, since the initiative for a more pervasive Hellenization had actually come from certain Jews themselves who built a Greek gymnasium in Jerusalem and repudiated circumcision and the covenant (1 Macc 1:11-15). In 168-67 B.C. a bitter and shameless struggle between two rival claimants to the high priesthood embroiled the city in civil strife. This Antiochus regarded as a repudiation of his rule, an act of treason. He sacked Jerusalem and desecrated the Temple by sacrificing swine on the altar of burnt-offering. By royal edict the worship and practices of Judaism were forbidden. All known copies of the Scripture were destroyed. Sabbath observance, circumcision, and other religious practices were made capital offenses (1 Macc 1:41-64). Pagan sacrifices were commanded, and altars for this purpose were erected throughout the province. Those who refused to transgress the commandments of God were executed without mercy.

A decisive reaction to these detestable measures came from an aged priest named Mattathias in the village of Modin, northwest of Jerusalem. He openly defied the king's emissaries by refusing to participate in idolatry and slew the first Jew who sought to comply with the royal edict. He then fled to the mountains with his five sons. Under the leadership of the eldest, Judas the Maccabee, Jews who were zealous for their traditions began to wage guerrilla warfare, with spectacular results. Judas' strategy was a blockade of Jerusalem by the occupation of the surrounding countryside. Sealing Jerusalem from contact with the Gentile world would force the Seleucid garrison in control of the city to capitulate. Four times the armies of Antiochus tried unsuccessfully to break the blockade. On each occasion the superior strategy, discipline, and valor of the Jewish forces prevailed over the superior numbers of the enemy. In 165 B.C. the Syrian regent was forced to concede religious freedom to the Jews; the edict proscribing Judaism was rescinded. Judas and his jubilant men took possession of Mount Zion and reconsecrated the Temple, an event celebrated in the feast of Hannukah.

In spite of this achievement, Judaea was still under Seleucid rule, and in many cities the Jews remained a persecuted minority. Even in Jerusalem a citadel known as the Acra, occupied by Seleucid troops, stood over against the Temple as an irritating symbol of Gentile intrusion. The decision was made to continue to fight in order to break the yoke of foreign domination. The struggle continued under the leadership of Judas and later of his brothers Jonathan and Simon from 165 to 142 B.C. With the capture of the Acra by Simon, the last surviving son of Mattathias, independence was achieved.

The triumph was costly. Once the Maccabees had established themselves as a significant military power, rival claimants to the Seleucid throne began to outbid one another for their support. Jonathan and Simon became involved in the internal politics of the Seleucid empire and advanced their cause at crucial points by alliances with certain of these pretenders. From Alexander Balas, Jonathan received the appointment as high priest in Jerusalem (1 Macc 10:20), although he was not of the legitimate Zadokite line. When independence came, a grateful nation conferred on Simon and his descendants, now known as the Hasmonaeans, permanent authority as ruling high priests (1 Macc 14:25-49). No inclination was shown to remember the covenant God had made with David or to restore the Zadokite priests to a position of authority. The Biblical injunctions against priest-kings were forgotten (1 S 13:8-14; 1 K 13:1-4; 2 Ch 26:16-18; cf. Nu 16:39 f.; 18:6 f.). The secularization of the priesthood and the displacement of the Zadokite line were undoubtedly responsible for the withdrawal of a significant community of priests from Jerusalem to the wilderness of Judaea,

where they established a center at Khirbet Qumran.

Under Simon's son John Hyrcanus (135–104 B.C.) the Hasmonaean state attained the height of its political power and geographical extent. The hiring of mercenaries and a massive troop build-up produced the most powerful military force in Syria. Hyrcanus fought successfully in the east, capturing key centers in Transjordan; in the north he subdued the Samaritans and destroyed their temple; in the south he conquered the Idumeans and forced them to adopt Judaism. By the end of his reign the new independent state of Israel almost equaled in extent the original kingdom of David and Solomon. It was amply clear that what had originated as a struggle for religious liberty had degenerated into just another Hellenistic struggle for political power.

While Hyrcanus' son Aristobulus (104–103 B.C.) was the first Hasmonaean to assume the title of king, the practice was continued by his brother and successor, Alexander Jannaeus (103–76 B.C.). Jannaeus had a passion for besieging cities and kept the nation embroiled in wars of expansion, with disappointing results. Ironically, the people wearied with the politics of violence, turned to the Seleucid ruler Demetrius III to depose their king. Jannaeus was decisively defeated, but then succeeded in regaining his throne and ruthlessly suppressed the uprising.

His successor was his widow, Salome Alexandra, who reigned as queen for nine years with her son Hyrcanus II serving as high priest without civil authority (76–67 B.C.). Alexandra brought an end to the policy of expansion and introduced a measure of stability to the land. Her peaceful and prosperous reign, however, was only the prelude to another major turning point in Jewish history. The cloud on the horizon was Rome. The outcome of a new crisis would be political collapse. As it turned out, the independent state of Israel lasted less than eighty years.

III. THE INTRUSION OF ROME
(200 B.C.—ONWARD)

The crisis which invited Roman intervention in the affairs of Judaea was civil war between the two sons of Queen Salome Alexandra, Aristobulus II and Hyrcanus II. Rome had gradually extended its control eastward over Asia, North Africa, and the entire Mediterranean Sea. In the time of Antiochus IV Epiphanes Rome was sufficiently entrenched in the eastern Mediterranean to frustrate his plans to annex the Ptolemaic empire in Egypt. It may have been the alliance which Judaea had made with Rome when Jonathan was high priest (1 Macc 12:1) which now permitted Roman intrusion into Judaean affairs.

Pompey, chief of the Roman forces in the Near East, had just broken the power of two ambitious kings in Pontus and Armenia. In the spring of 63 B.C. he came to Damascus and summoned the two brothers to explain their conflict. He also received a delegation of the Jewish people who were weary with civil strife and pleaded for the abolition of the monarchy and a return to the high-priestly rule of the Persian and early Hellenistic periods. Pompey took the dispute under advisement and dispatched a Roman legion to Jerusalem to keep order in the city. When the Romans arrived and found the city gates locked against them by the supporters of Aristobulus, Jerusalem was subjected to a three-month siege and bitter fighting in the Temple area. The end came with the breaching of the northern fortifications; the forces of Aristobulus were butchered, the Jewish community was placed under Roman proconsular rule, and the Hasmonaean state was greatly reduced in size. Numerous Jews were enslaved and brought to Rome, where they became the nucleus of a large Jewish community in the capital after their release. These events inaugurated an era of Roman rule or supervision of Judaea which lasted, with few interruptions, for nearly seven centuries.

Turbulent years followed in which the dispossessed princes of Aristobulus' line tried repeatedly to wrench Jerusalem from the firm grip of Rome and their vassals, Hyrcanus II and Antipater of Idumea. Each attempt was abortive. Judaea remained firmly under Roman control. For supporting Julius Caesar in his successful conflict with Pompey, Hyrcanus was confirmed as hereditary high priest and ethnarch of the Jews while Antipater was made a Roman citizen and governor of Judaea. Not until Persia threw its support on the side of Mattathias Antigonus II, the last surviving son of Aristobulus, did Judaea return to Hasmonaean rule for three brief years (40–37 B.C.). The die, however, was already cast. Herod, the son of Antipater, had been appointed king of Judaea by the Roman Senate and was supported by the armies of Mark Antony. It took three years to defeat the Persians, but when Herod finally entered the city it marked the end of an era; practically all

the old Hasmonaean aristocracy were executed. From that time until the New Testament opens in the closing years of Herod's life, the will of an Idumean determined the destiny of the Jewish people.

Herod never succeeded in gaining the respect and affection of the Jews. Though he was a ruler of ability and energy, whose strong hand kept peace in his dominions, to the Jews he appeared little more than an Arab usurper with purely secular ambitions and goals, whose record was marred by savage murders prompted by insane jealously and suspicion. He had not hesitated to slay members of his own family who had come under suspicion of conspiring for the throne. So well was this fact known that the emperor Octavian (the Caesar Augustus of Lk 2:1) coined the Greek pun, "It is better to be Herod's swine [*hun*] than his son [*huion*]"—because as a Jewish king Herod was not supposed to eat pork, but his sons had fallen victims of his wrath. This climate of suspicion is presumed by the opening chapters of the Gospel of Matthew, with its account of Herod's attempt to kill the child Jesus, whom he feared as a potential king of the Jews from the line of David (Mt 2:16-18). It was only from a Roman point of view that he was "Herod the Great," a capable ruler who was public-spirited in his liberality, a patron of the arts and literature, who advanced in his corner of the empire the great plans of Augustus. Herod was thoroughly aware of the popular opinion. His final decree was that an entire town should be put to the sword to guarantee that there would be weeping in Judea when he died. This ruthless order was not carried out. Herod's death was the signal not for weeping, but for revolt, swift intervention by Rome and, after a brief respite, continued Herodian rule supported by the legions of Rome.

IV. STRUCTURES OF PIETY

In the later phases of the period between the Testaments there are evident two alternatives to the problem of devout religious commitment: party life or sect life. The basic distinction between a party and a sect was the attitude that each took toward society. In a party a group of men joined forces to reshape society in the conviction that it needed to be reformed and was worth reformation. The purpose of the party was to restore sound life to Israel by being the leaven among the people. Goals were achieved through organiza-

tion, education, and party discipline. The basic attitude toward society was optimistic. The attitude toward society in a sect was very different: society is corrupt to the core and beyond redemption; the judgment of God will surely fall on it. With this conviction the members of the sect withdrew from society to the wilderness, where they waited for God's intervention and vindication. Members of the sect submitted to rites of initiation and acute discipline and possessed the certainty that participation in the corporate life of the sect was necessary for admission to the New Covenant.

The most vital Jewish party in the first century was the Pharisees (Hebrew: "Separated ones"), a group that emerged into the light of history during the reign of John Hyrcanus. The roots of Pharisaism can be traced to the fierce pietism of the Hasidim, who chose to perish rather than violate the law of God when Judaism was proscribed by Antiochus. Though never a large group, their earnestness and dedication won them wide respect and influence. Deep concern with separation from defilement led them to develop an extensive oral tradition by which the Mosaic law was applied to every detail of life. Under lay leadership the synagogue became a center of instruction in the law with the Pharisees as the teachers of the people. In contrast to the Sadducees (Hebrew: "Righteous ones"), representing the Temple aristocracy, the Pharisees created an aristocracy of learning committed to the study and interpretation of the law. The purpose of new restrictions added to Biblical law was to keep the people at a safe distance from transgressing the commandments of God; by "putting a fence around the law," oral tradition prepared for the day when the law would be perfectly kept. Casuistry and a confidence in their own righteousness led to abuses, but the Pharisaic ideal was worthy of emulation, the consecration of life to the service of God. A second-century commentary on Deuteronomy expresses this ideal: "The law preaches: Take upon yourself the yoke of God's Kingdom; let the fear of God be your judge and arbiter, and deal with one another according to the dictates of love" (Sifré §323).

The discovery of the Dead Sea Scrolls in 1948 A.D. in eleven caves in the vicinity of Khirbet Qumran provided extensive evidence for the existence of a priestly sect that withdrew into the Judaean wilderness in the late second century B.C. The founder of the sect appears to have been an anonymous figure designated "the legitimate Teacher," a man

with revelatory insights. He saw in the ascendancy of the Hasmonaeans the fulfillment of Scripture heralding an age of apostasy and a time of testing for "the sons of light," the displaced Zadokite priests and their lay supporters. The way of deliverance was withdrawal to the wilderness to prepare the way for the Lord. The task of the wilderness community was the faithful study and observance of the law until the day when God would intervene to punish the wicked and establish "the men of the New Covenant" as the legitimate priesthood and the true Israel. Full membership in the sect entailed total commitment of wealth, strength, and heart demonstrated over a two- or three-year probationary period in which the community submitted to a stringent discipline and a structured existence. Within the communal center, work, study, and devotion were conducted under priestly supervision. In the apocalyptic expectations of the sect an anointed Priest takes precedence over a royal Messiah. By assuming the posture of a holy priesthood in the wilderness, the place where God prepared Israel of old to enter the land to promise, the Covenanters of Qumran prepared themselves for a new exodus and an age of blessedness.

It is undoubtedly true that the vast number of Jews did not commit themselves toward a party or a sectarian way of life. They satisfied themselves with participation in the life of the synagogue or Temple of the Sabbath on special occasions and shared a common grass-roots type of piety consisting of public and private prayer and the observance of certain traditions learned within the family. Few persons kept alive the prophetic faith of the Old Testament pure and undefiled. On opening the pages of the New Testament, we find such a piety in people like Zachariah and Elizabeth, the old man Simeon, the widow Anna, the carpenter Joseph, and Mary, the mother of Jesus. It is expressed particularly in the Magnificat, the Benedictus, and other hymns of Luke 1-2, but what remains is only an echo of what had been loudly proclaimed in an earlier day. A new era begins with the ministry of John the Baptist, to whom the prophetic word comes once more, signaling the end of the period between the Testaments.

THE
NEW TESTAMENT

A BASIC OUTLINE OF NEW TESTAMENT HISTORY

Christ born in Bethlehem

Herod the Great dies.

John the Baptist appears.

Ministry of Christ
   1st Year: Year of Beginnings.
   2nd Year: Year of Popularity in Galilee.
   3rd Year: Year of Opposition in Judea.
   Final months.

Crucifixion of Christ.

Ministry of Paul:
   1st. Missionary Journey   47–48
   Jerusalem Council   49
   2nd. Missionary   49–51
   3rd. Missionary   52–56
   Martyrdom under Nero   64(68)

First Jewish Rebellion against Rome.

Nero persecutes Christians in Rome.

Jerusalem and Second Temple destroyed by Titus and Romans.

John sees Revelation Vision on Patmos (Rev. 1:9).

G. Cohen

MATTHEW

OUTLINE

SURVEY

The purpose of Matthew's Gospel is to witness that Jesus was the Messiah of Old Testament promise and that His messianic mission was to bring the Kingdom of God to men. These two themes—Jesus' Messiahship and the presence of the Kingdom of God—are inseparably linked together and each embodies a "mystery"—a new disclosure of the divine, redemptive purpose (see Ro 16.25, 26).

The mystery of the *messianic mission* is that before Messiah comes as the heavenly Son of Man with the clouds of heaven to establish the Kingdom over all the earth, He must first come in humility among men as the suffering Servant to die. This was unheard of to the first century Jew. To the Christian today Isaiah 53 clearly predicts the sufferings of Messiah. However, Messiah is not named in this passage, and the context (Is 48.20; 49.3) specifically names Israel as God's servant. It is not surprising, therefore, to learn that the Jews did not understand that Isiah 53 referred to Messiah. They looked for a Messiah who would come in power and victory, and the Old Testament does indeed promise such a Messiah.

The Son of David is a divine King Who will rule in the messianic Kingdom (Is 9, 11; Jr 33), when all sin and evil will be taken away and peace and righteousness will prevail. The Son of Man is a heavenly being to Whom the rule over all nations and kingdoms of the earth is to be committed. The Old Testament does not indicate how these two prophetic concepts of the Davidic King and the heavenly Son of Man are related to each other, or how either of them can be identified with the suffering Servant of Isaiah 53. Therefore, first century Jews looked for a conquering Davidic Messiah or a heavenly Son of Man, not for a humble Servant of the Lord Who would suffer and die. The messianic mystery—the new disclosure of the divine purpose—is that the heavenly Son of Man must first suffer and die in fulfilment of His redemptive, messianic mission as the suffering Servant before He comes in power and glory.

The mystery of the Kingdom is similar and closely associated with the messianic mystery. Daniel

2 describes the coming of God's Kingdom vividly in terms of the destruction of every power which resists God and opposes the divine will. The Kingdom is to come in power, sweeping before it all evil and every hostile rule, transforming the earth and ushering in a new universal order of perfect peace and righteousness. However, Jesus offered no such Kingdom of mighty power. Therefore, His message as well as His person was utterly perplexing to His contemporaries including His disciples. He was a carpenter's son; His family was known in Nazareth; He looked like little more than a Jewish rabbi. His works were gentle deeds of kindness and love, yet He claimed that in His words and deeds and in His person the Kingdom of God had come near. However, the kingdoms of men and of the world were undisturbed, and the hated rule of Rome over God's people was not challenged. How could this be the Kingdom of God if it did not break asunder all other kingdoms and grind them to powder? That the Kingdom was to come in spiritual power before it should come in glory was a new revelation of the divine purpose.

AUTHOR

The unchallenged testimony of the early church (Barnabas, Clement of Rome, Polycarp, Justin Martyr, Papias, etc.) declares it to have been written by Mathew, one of the twelve. Papias said that Mathew first wrote the Lord's sayings in Aramaic and then enlarged the work into the gospel, written in Greek.

G. Cohen

4

THE GOSPEL ACCORDING TO

MATTHEW

Matthew presents Jesus as the long awaited King

CHAPTER 1

THE book of the generation of Je'sus Christ, the son of Da'vid, the son of A'bra-ham.

2 A'bra-ham fathered I'saac; and I'saac fathered Ja'cob; and Ja'cob fathered Ju'das and his brethren;

3 And Ju'das fathered Pha'res and Za'ra of Tha'mar; and Pha'res fathered Es'rom; and Es'rom fathered A'ram;

4 And A'ram fathered A-min'a-dab; and A-min'a-dab fathered Na-as'son; and Na-as'son fathered Sal'mon;

5 And Sa'lmon fathered Bo'oz of Ra'chab; and Bo'oz fathered O'bed of Ruth; and O'bed fathered Jes'se;

6 And Jes'se fathered Da'vid the king; and Da'vid the king fathered Sol'o-mon of her *that had been the wife* of U-ri'as;

7 And Sol'o-mon fathered Ro-bo'am; and Ro-bo'am fathered A-bi'a; and A-bi'a fathered A'sa;

8 And A'sa fathered Jos'a-phat; and Jos-a'phat fathered Jo'ram; and Jo'ram fathered O-zi'as;

9 And O-zi'as fathered Jo'a-tham; and Jo'a-tham fathered A'chaz; and A'chaz fathered Ez-e-ki'as;

10 And Ez-e-ki'as fathered Ma-nas'ses; and Ma-nas'ses fathered A'mon; and A'mon fathered Jo-si'as;

11 And Jo-si'as fathered Jech-o-ni'as and his brethren, about the time they were carried away to Bab'y-lon:

12 And after they were brought to Bab'y-lon, Jech-o-ni'as fathered Sa-la'thi-el; and Sa-la'thi-el fathered Zo-rob'a-bel;

13 And Zo-rob'a-bel fathered A-bi'ud; and A-bi'ud fathered E-li'a-kim; and E-li'a-kim fathered A'zor;

14 And A'zor fathered Sa'doc; and Sa'doc fathered A'chim; and A'chim fathered E-li'ud;

15 And E-li'ud fathered E-le-a'zar; and E-le-a'zar fathered Mat'than; and Mat'than fathered Ja'cob;

16 And Ja'cob fathered Jo'seph the husband of Ma'ry, of whom was born Je'sus, who is called Christ.

17 So all the generations from A'bra-ham to Da'vid *are* fourteen generations; and from Da'vid until the carrying away into Bab'y-lon *are* fourteen generations; and from the carrying away into Bab'y-lon to Christ *are* fourteen generations.

18 Now the birth of Je'sus Christ was on this wise: When as His mother Ma'ry was engaged to Jo'seph, before they came together, she was found with child of the Ho'ly Ghost.   Spirit

19 Then Jo'seph her husband, being a just *man*, and not willing to make her a public example, was minded to put her away privily.   fair - secretly

20 But while he thought on these things, behold, the angel of the Lord appeared to him in a dream, saying, Jo'seph, you son of Da'vid, fear not to take to you Ma'ry your wife: for that

which is <u>conceived</u> in her is of the Ho'ly <u>Ghost</u>.   *messenger - begotten - Spirit*

21 And she shall bring forth a son, and you shall call His name <u>JE'SUS</u>: for He shall save His people from their sins.   *Savior*

22 Now all this was done, that it might be fulfilled which was spoken of the Lord by the prophet, saying,

23 Behold, a virgin shall be with child, and shall bring forth a Son, and they shall call His name Im-man'u-el, which being interpreted is, God with us.   ISA. 7:14

24 Then Joseph being raised from sleep did as the <u>angel</u> of the Lord had <u>bidden</u> him, and took to him his wife: *messenger - directed*

25 And <u>knew her not</u> till she had brought forth her firstborn Son: and he called His name JE'SUS.   *had no intercourse*

CHAPTER 2

NOW when Je'sus was born in Beth'le-hem of Ju-dae'a in the days of Her'od the king, behold, there came wise men from the east to Je-ru'sa-lem,

2 Saying, Where is He that is born King of the Jews? for we have seen His star in the east, and are come to worship Him.   NUM. 24:17 JER. 23:5

3 When Her'od the king had heard *these things*, he was troubled, and all Je-ru'sa-lem with him.

4 And when he had gathered all the chief priests and scribes of the people together, he demanded of them where Christ should be born.

5 And they said to him, In Beth'le-hem of Ju-dae'a: for thus it is written by the prophet,

6 And you Beth'le-hem, *in* the land of Ju'da, are not the least among the princes of Ju'da: for out of you shall come a Governor, that shall rule My people Is'ra-el.   MIC. 5:2

7 Then Her'od, when he had <u>privily</u> called the wise men, enquired of them diligently what time the star appeared.   *secretly*

8 And he sent them to Beth'le-hem, and said, Go and search diligently for the young child; and when you have found *Him*, bring me word again, that I may come and worship Him also.

9 When they had heard the king, they departed; and, lo, the star, which they saw in the east, went before them, till it came and stood over where the young Child was.

10 When they saw the star, they rejoiced with exceeding great joy.

11 And when they were come into the house, they saw the young Child with Ma'ry His mother, and fell down, and worshiped Him: and when they had opened their treasures, they presented to Him gifts; gold, frankincense, and myrrh.

12 And being warned of God in a dream that they should not return to Her'od, they departed into their own country another way.

13 And when they were departed, behold, the <u>angel</u> of the Lord appeared to Jo'seph in a dream, saying, Arise, and take <u>the young Child</u> and His mother, and flee into E'gypt, and be you there

until I bring you word: for Her'od will seek the young child to destroy Him.   messenger - Jesus

14 When he arose, he took <u>the young Child</u> and His mother by night, and departed into E'gypt: Jesus

15 And was there until the death of Her'od: that it might be fulfilled which was spoken of the Lord by the prophet, saying, Out of E'gypt have I called My Son.   EX. 4:22 HOS. 11:1

16 Then Her'od, when he saw that he was <u>mocked of</u> the wise men, was exceeding angry, and sent forth, and slew all the <u>children</u> that were in Beth'le-hem, and in all the <u>coasts</u> thereof, from two years old and under, according to the time which he had diligently enquired of the wise men.   tricked by- boys - area

17 Then was fulfilled that which was spoken by Jeremiah the prophet, saying,

18 In Ra'ma was there a voice heard, lamentation, and weeping, and great mourning, Ra'chel weeping *for* her children, and would not be comforted, because they are not.   JER. 31:15

19 But when Her'od was dead, behold, an <u>angel</u> of the Lord appeared in a dream to Jo'seph in E'gypt, messenger

20 Saying, Arise, and take the <u>young Child</u> and His mother, and go into the land of Is'ra-el: for they are dead which sought the young <u>child's life</u>.   Jesus

21 And he arose, and took the <u>young Child</u> and His mother, and <u>came</u> into the land of Is'ra-el.   went back

22 But when he heard that Ar-che-la'-us did reign in Ju-dae'a in the room of his father Her'od, he was afraid to go there: notwithstanding, being warned of God in a dream, he turned aside into the parts of Gal'i-lee:

23 And he came and dwelled in a city called Naz'a-reth: that it might be fulfilled which was spoken by the prophets, He shall be called a Naz'a-rene.

CHAPTER 3

IN those days came John the Bap'tist, preaching in the wilderness of Ju-dae'a,

2 And saying, Repent you: for the kingdom of heaven is at hand.

3 For this is he that was spoken of by the prophet I-sa'iah, saying, The voice of one crying in the wilderness, Prepare you the way of the Lord, make his paths straight. ISA. 40:3

4 And the same John had his <u>raiment</u> of camel's hair, and a leathern girdle about his loins; and his <u>meat</u> was locusts and wild honey.   clothing - food

5 Then <u>went out</u> to him Je-ru'sa-lem, and all Ju-dae'a, and all the region round about Jor'dan,   came

6 And were baptized of him in Jor'dan, confessing their sins.

7 But when he saw many of the Phar'i-sees and Sad'du-cees come to his baptism, he said to them, O generation of vipers, who has warned you to flee from the wrath to come?

8 Bring forth therefore fruits <u>meet</u> for repentance: fitting

9 And think not to say within yourselves, We have A'bra-ham to *our* father: for I say to you, that God is able of these stones to raise up children to A'bra-ham.

10 And now also the ax is laid to the root of the trees: therefore every tree which brings not forth good fruit is hewn down, and cast into the fire.

11 I indeed baptize you with water to repentance: but He that comes after me is mightier than I, whose shoes I am not worthy to bear: He shall baptize you with the Ho'ly Ghost, and *with* fire: Spirit

12 Whose fan *is* in His hand, and He will throughly purge His floor, and gather His wheat into the garner; but He will burn up the chaff with unquenchable fire. clear - barn

13 Then comes Je'sus from Gal'i-lee to Jor'dan to John, to be baptized of him.

14 But John forbad Him, saying, I have need to be baptized of You, and come You to me?

15 And Je'sus answering said to him, allow *it to be so* now: for thus it becomes us to fulfill all righteousness. Then he Allowed Him.

16 And Je'sus, when He was baptized, went up immediately out of the water: and, lo, the heavens were opened to Him, and he saw the Spirit of God descending like a dove, and lighting upon Him: as

17 And lo a voice from heaven, saying, This is My beloved Son, in whom I am well pleased. PS. 2:7 ISA. 42:1

CHAPTER 4

THEN was Je'sus led up of the spirit into the wilderness to be tempted of the devil. Satan

2 And when He had fasted forty days and forty nights, He was afterward hungry. EX. 34:28 1 KGS. 19:8

3 And when the tempter came to Him, he said, If You be the Son of God, command that these stones be made bread. Satan

4 But He answered and said, It is written, Man shall not live by bread alone, but by every word that proceeds out of the mouth of God. DEU. 8:3

5 Then the devil takes Him up into the holy city, and sets Him on a pinnacle of the temple, Satan - highest part

6 And says to Him, If You be the Son of God, cast Yourself down: for it is written, He shall give His angels charge concerning You: and in *their* hands they shall bear You up, less at any time You dash Your foot against a stone. PS. 91:11

7 Je'sus said to him, It is written again, You shall not tempt the Lord your God. DEU. 6:16

8 Again, the devil takes Him up into an exceeding high mountain, and shows Him all the kingdoms of the world, and the glory of them;

9 And says to Him, All these things will I give You, if You will fall down and worship me.

10 Then says Je'sus to him, Get you from here, Sa'tan: for it is written, You shall worship the Lord your God, and Him only shall you serve. DEU. 6:13

11 Then the devil leaves Him, and, behold, angels came and ministered to Him. Satan - left

12 Now when Je'sus had heard that John was cast into prison, He departed into Gal'i-lee; put

13 And leaving Naz'a-reth, He came and dwelled in Ca-per'na-um, which is upon the sea coast, in the borders of Zab'u-lon and Neph'tha-lim:
14 That it might be fulfilled which was spoken by I-sa'iah the prophet, saying,
15 The land of Zab'u-lon, and the land of Neph'tha-lim, *by* the way of the sea, beyond Jor'dan, Gal'i-lee of the Gen'tiles;
16 The people which sat in darkness saw great light; and to them which sat in the region and shadow of death light <u>is sprung up</u>.   has dawned
17 From that time Je'sus began to preach, and to say, Repent: for the kingdom of heaven is <u>at hand</u>.   near
18 And Je'sus, walking by the sea of Gal'i-lee, saw two brethren, Si'mon called Pe'ter, and Andrew his brother, casting a net into the sea: for they were fishers.
19 And He says to them, Follow Me, and I will make you fishers of men.
20 And they immediately left *their* nets, and followed Him.
21 And going on from there, He saw other two brethren, James *the son* of Zeb'e-dee, and John his brother, in a ship with Zeb'e-dee their father, mending their nets; and He called them.
22 And they immediately left the ship and their father, and followed Him.
23 And Je'sus went about all Gal'i-lee, teaching in their synagogues, and preaching the gospel of the kingdom, and healing all <u>manner</u> of sickness and all manner of disease among the people.   kinds

24 And His fame went throughout all Syr'i-a: and they brought to Him all sick people that were taken with <u>divers</u> diseases and torments, and those which were possessed with <u>devils</u>, and those which were <u>luna-tic</u>, and those that had the palsy; and He healed them.   different - demons - crazy
25 And there followed Him great multitudes of people from Gal'i-lee, and *from* De-cap'o-lis, and *from* Je-ru'sa-lem, and *from* Ju-dae'a, and *from* beyond Jor'dan.

CHAPTER 5

AND seeing the multitudes, He went up into a mountain: and when He was set, His disciples came to Him:
2 And He opened His mouth, and taught them, saying,
3 <u>Blessed</u> *are* the <u>poor</u> in spirit: for theirs is the kingdom of heaven.   Happy-Fortunate - meek-humble
4 <u>Blessed</u> *are* they that mourn: for they shall be comforted.   ISA. 61:2
5 <u>Blessed</u> *are* the <u>meek</u>: for they shall inherit the <u>earth</u>.   PS. 37:11 humble - land
6 <u>Blessed</u> *are* they which do hunger and thirst after righteousness: for they shall be filled.   ISA. 55:1-2
7 <u>Blessed</u> *are* the merciful: for they shall obtain mercy.   2 SAM. 22:26
8 <u>Blessed</u> *are* the <u>pure</u> in heart: for they shall see God.   sincere
9 <u>Blessed</u> *are* the peacemakers: for they shall be called the children of God.   Happy-Fortunate
10 <u>Blessed</u> *are* they which are persecuted for righteousness' sake: for theirs is the kingdom of heaven.

11 Blessed *are* you, when *men* shall revile you, and persecute *you*, and shall say all manner of evil against you falsely, for My sake. Happy-Fortunate

12 Rejoice, and be exceeding glad: for great *is* your reward in heaven: for so persecuted they the prophets which were before you. 2 CHRON. 36:16

13 You are the salt of the earth: but if the salt have lost its savor, wherewith shall it be salted? it is therefore good for nothing, but to be cast out, and to be trodden under foot of men.

14 You are the light of the world. A city that is set on an hill cannot be hid.

15 Neither do men light a candle, and put it under a bushel, but on a candlestick; and it gives light to all that are in the house. basket

16 Let your light so shine before men, that they may see your good works, and glorify your Father which is in heaven.

17 Think not that I am come to destroy the law, or the prophets: I am not come to destroy, but to fulfill.

18 For verily I say to you, Till heaven and earth pass, one jot or one tittle shall in no wise pass from the law, till all be fulfilled. truly - small letter or mark

19 Whosoever therefore shall break one of these least commandments, and shall teach men so, he shall be called the least in the kingdom of heaven: but whosoever shall do and teach *them*, the same shall be called great in the kingdom of heaven.

20 For I say to you, That except your righteousness shall exceed *the righteousness* of the scribes and Phar'i-sees, you shall in no case enter into the kingdom of heaven. faithfulness

21 You have heard that it was said by them of old time, You shall not kill; and whosoever shall kill shall be in danger of the judgment: EX. 20:13 DEU. 5:17

22 But I say to you, That whosoever is angry with his brother without a cause shall be in danger of the judgment: and whosoever shall say to his brother, Raca, shall be in danger of the council: but whosoever shall say, you fool, shall be in danger of hell fire. vain fellow

23 Therefore if you bring your gift to the altar, and there remember that your brother has anything against you;

24 Leave there your gift before the altar, and go your way; first be reconciled to your brother, and then come and offer your gift.

25 Agree with your adversary quickly, while you are in the way with him; less at any time the adversary deliver you to the judge, and the judge deliver you to the officer, and you be cast into prison.

26 Verily I say to you, you shall by no means come out there, till you have paid the uttermost farthing. Truly

27 You have heard that it was said by them of old time, you shall not commit adultery: EX.. 20:14 DEU. 5:18

28 But I say to you, That whosoever looks on a woman to lust after her has committed adultery with her already in his heart. PROV. 6:25

29 And if your right eye offend you,

pluck it out, and cast *it* from you: for it is profitable for you that one of your members should perish, and not *that* your whole body should be cast into hell.

30 And if your right hand offend you, cut it off, and cast *it* from you: for it is profitable for you that one of your members should perish, and not *that* your whole body should be cast into hell.

31 It has been said, Whosoever shall put away his wife, let him give her a writing of divorcement: divorce

32 But I say to you, That whosoever shall put away his wife, saving for the cause of fornication, causes her to commit adultery: and whosoever shall marry her that is divorced commits adultery.   except

33 Again, you have heard that it has been said by them of old time, you shall not forswear yourself, but shall perform to the Lord your oaths: commit perjury

34 But I say to you, Swear not at all; neither by heaven; for it is God's throne: LEV. 19:12

35 Nor by the earth; for it is His footstool: neither by Je-ru'sa-lem; for it is the city of the great King.   ISA. 66:1

36 Neither shall you swear by your head, because you can not make one hair white or black.

37 But let your communication be, Yea, yea; Nay, nay: for whatsoever is more than these comes of evil.   Yes, yes - No, no

38 You have heard that it has been said, An eye for an eye, and a tooth for a tooth: EX. 21:24 DEU. 19:21

39 But I say to you, That you resist not evil: but whosoever shall smite you on your right cheek, turn to him the other also.   strike

40 And if any man will sue you at the law, and take away your coat, let him have *your* cloke also.

41 And whosoever shall compel you to go a mile, go with him two.

42 Give to him that asks you, and from him that would borrow of you turn not you away.   DEU. 15:8

43 You have heard that it has been said, you shall love your neighbor, and hate your enemy.   LEV. 19:18

44 But I say to you, Love your enemies, bless them that curse you, do good to them that hate you, and pray for them which despitefully use you, and persecute you;

45 That you may be the children of your Father which is in heaven: for He makes His sun to rise on the evil and on the good, and sends rain on the just and on the unjust.   shine - good

46 For if you love them which love you, what reward have you? do not even the publicans the same?   tax gathers

47 And if you salute your brethren only, what do you more *than others*? do not even the publicans so?   greet

48 Be you therefore perfect, even as your Father which is in heaven is perfect.

CHAPTER 6

TAKE heed that you do not your alms before men, to be seen of them: otherwise you have no reward of your Father which is in heaven.   gift giving

2 Therefore when you do *your* alms, do not sound a trumpet before you, as the hypocrites do in the synagogues and in the streets, that they may have glory of men. Verily I say to you, They have their reward. _{insincere - truly}

3 But when you do alms, let not your left hand know what your right hand does:

4 That your alms may be in secret: and your Father which sees in secret Himself shall reward you openly. _{gift giving}

5 And when you pray, you shall not be as the hypocrites *are*: for they love to pray standing in the synagogues and in the corners of the streets, that they may be seen of men. Verily I say to you, They have their reward. _{insincere - truly}

6 But you, when you pray, enter into your closet, and when you have shut your door, pray to your Father which is in secret; and your Father which sees in secret shall reward you openly.

7 But when you pray, use not vain repetitions, as the heathen *do*: for they think that they shall be heard for their much speaking. _{meaningless}

8 Be not you therefore like to them: for your Father knows what things you have need of, before you ask Him.

9 After this manner therefore pray you: Our Father which art in heaven, Hallowed be Your name.

10 Your kingdom come. Your will be done in earth, as *it is* in heaven.

11 Give us this day our daily bread.

12 And forgive us our debts, as we forgive our debtors.

13 And lead us not into temptation,

but deliver us from evil: For Yours is the kingdom, and the power, and the glory, for ever. Amen.

14 For if you forgive men their trespasses, your heavenly Father will also forgive you:

15 But if you forgive not men their trespasses, neither will your Father forgive your trespasses.

16 Moreover when you fast, be not, as the hypocrites, of a sad countenance: for they disfigure their faces, that they may appear to men to fast. Verily I say to you, They have their reward. _{insincere - truly}

17 But you, when you fast, anoint your head, and wash your face;

18 That you appear not to men to fast, but to your Father which is in secret: and your Father, which sees in secret, shall reward you openly. _{private}

19 Lay not up for yourselves treasures upon earth, where moth and rust does corrupt, and where thieves break through and steal: _{destroy}

20 But lay up for yourselves treasures in heaven, where neither moth nor rust does corrupt, and where thieves do not break through nor steal:

21 For where your treasure is, there will your heart be also.

22 The light of the body is the eye: if therefore your eye be single, your whole body shall be full of light. _{clear}

23 But if your eye be evil, your whole body shall be full of darkness. If therefore the light that is in you be darkness, how great *is* that darkness! _{bad - terrible}

24 No man can serve two masters: for either he will hate the one, and love

the other; or else he will hold to the one, and despise the other. You cannot serve God and <u>mammon</u>.   dislike - worldly riches

25 Therefore I say to you, <u>Take no thought</u> for your life, what you shall eat, or what you shall drink; nor yet for your body, what you shall put on. Is not the life more than <u>meat</u>, and the body than <u>raiment</u>?   be not anxious - food - clothing

26 Behold the fowls of the air: for they sow not, neither do they reap, nor gather into barns; yet your heavenly Father feeds them. Are you not <u>much better</u> than they?   worth more

27 Which of you by <u>taking thought</u> can add one cubit to his <u>stature</u>?   thinking - height

28 And why <u>take you thought</u> for <u>raiment</u>? Consider the lilies of the field, how they grow; they toil not, neither do they spin: are you concerned - clothing

29 And yet I say to you, That even Sol'o-mon in all his glory was not <u>arrayed</u> like one of these.   dressed

30 Wherefore, if God so clothe the grass of the field, which to day is, and to morrow is cast into the oven, *shall He* not much more *clothe* you, O you of little faith?

31 Therefore take no thought, saying, What shall we eat? or, What shall we drink? or, Wherewithal shall we be clothed?

32 (For after all these things do the Gen'tiles seek:) for your heavenly Father knows that you have need of all these things.

33 But seek you first the kingdom of God, and His righteousness; and all these things shall be added to you.   I CHRON. 16:11

34 Take therefore no <u>thought</u> for the morrow: for the morrow shall take thought for the things of itself. Sufficient to the day *is* the evil thereof.   concern; worry

CHAPTER 7

JUDGE not, that you be not judged.
2 For with what <u>judgment</u> you judge, you shall be judged: and with what measure you <u>mete</u>, it shall be measured to you again.   criticism - give

3 And why behold you the <u>mote</u> that is in your brother's eye, but consider not the <u>beam</u> that is in your own eye?   speck - log

4 Or how will you say to your brother, Let me pull out the <u>mote</u> out of your eye; and, behold, a <u>beam</u> *is* in your own eye?

5 You <u>hypocrite</u>, first cast out the <u>beam</u> out of your own eye; and then shall you see clearly to cast out the <u>mote</u> out of your brother's eye.   insincere fool - log - speck

6 Give not that which is holy to the dogs, neither cast you your <u>pearls</u> before swine, less they trample them under their feet, and turn again and <u>rend</u> you.   precious jewels - harm

7 Ask, and it shall be given you; seek, and you shall find; knock, and it shall be opened to you:

8 For every one that asks receives; and he that seeks finds; and to him that knocks it shall be opened.

9 Or what man is there of you, whom if his son ask bread, will he give him a stone?

10 Or if he ask a fish, will he give him a serpent?

11 If you then, being evil, know how to give good gifts to your children, how much more shall your Father which is in heaven give good things to them that ask Him?

12 Therefore all things whatsoever you would that men should do to you, do you even so to them: for this is the law and the prophets.

13 Enter you in at the strait gate: for wide *is* the gate, and broad *is* the way, that leads to destruction, and many there be which go in thereat: narrow

14 Because strait *is* the gate, and narrow *is* the way, which leads to life, and few there be that find it.

15 Beware of false prophets, which come to you in sheep's clothing, but inwardly they are ravening wolves.   hungry

16 You shall know them by their fruits. Do men gather grapes of thorns, or figs of thistles?   actions

17 Even so every good tree brings forth good fruit; but a corrupt tree brings forth evil fruit.   bad

18 A good tree cannot bring forth evil fruit, neither *can* a corrupt tree bring forth good fruit.   worthless

19 Every tree that brings not forth good fruit is hewn down, and cast into the fire.

20 Wherefore by their fruits you shall know them.

21 Not every one that says to Me, Lord, Lord, shall enter into the kingdom of heaven; but he that does the will of My Father which is in heaven.

22 Many will say to Me in that day, Lord, Lord, have we not prophesied in Your name? and in Your name have cast out devils? and in Your name done many wonderful works?   spoken - demons

23 And then will I profess to them, I never knew you: depart from Me, you that work iniquity.   sinful

24 Therefore whosoever hears these sayings of Mine, and does them, I will liken him to a wise man, which built his house upon a rock:

25 And the rain descended, and the floods came, and the winds blew, and beat upon that house; and it fell not: for it was founded upon a rock.

26 And every one that hears these sayings of Mine, and does them not, shall be likened to a foolish man, which built his house upon the sand: words - compared

27 And the rain descended, and the floods came, and the winds blew, and beat upon that house; and it fell: and great was the fall of it.   awesome

28 And it came to pass, when Je'sus had ended these sayings, the people were astonished at His doctrine: teaching

29 For He taught them as *one* having authority, and not as the scribes.

CHAPTER 8

WHEN He was come down from the mountain, great multitudes followed Him.   crowds

2 And, behold, there came a leper and worshiped Him, saying, Lord, if You will, You can make me clean.

3 And Je'sus put forth *His* hand, and touched him, saying, I will; be you

clean. And immediately his leprosy was cleansed.

4 And Je'sus says to him, See you tell no man; but go your way, show yourself to the priest, and offer the gift that Mo'ses commanded, for a testimony to them.

5 And when Je'sus was entered into Ca-per'na-um, there came to Him a centurion, <u>beseeching</u> Him,   begging

6 And saying, Lord, my servant lies at home sick of the palsy, <u>grievously</u> tormented.   much

7 And Je'sus says to him, I will come and heal him.

8 The centurion answered and said, Lord, I am not worthy that You should come under my roof: but speak the word only, and my servant shall be healed.

9 For I am a man under authority, having soldiers under me: and I say to this *man*, Go, and he goes; and to another, Come, and he comes; and to my servant, Do this, and he does *it*.

10 When Je'sus heard *it*, He marveled, and said to them that followed, Verily I say to you, I have not found so great faith, no, not in Is'ra-el.

11 And I say to you, That many shall come from the east and west, and shall sit down with A'bra-ham, and I'saac, and Ja'cob, in the kingdom of heaven.

12 But the children of the kingdom shall be cast out into outer darkness: there shall be weeping and gnashing of teeth.

13 And Je'sus said to the centurion, Go your way; and as you have believed, *so* be it done to you. And his servant was healed in the selfsame hour.

14 And when Je'sus was come into Pe'ter's house, He saw his wife's mother laid, and sick of a fever.

15 And He touched her hand, and the fever left her: and she arose, and <u>ministered</u> to them.   served

16 When the even was come, they brought to Him many that were possessed with <u>devils</u>: and He cast out the spirits with *His* word, and healed all that were sick: demons

17 That it might <u>be fulfilled</u> which was spoken by I-sa'iah the prophet, saying, Himself took our infirmities, and bare *our* sicknesses.   ISA. 53:4   come true

18 Now when Je'sus saw great multitudes about Him, He gave <u>commandment</u> to depart to the other side.   instruction

19 And a certain scribe came, and said to Him, Master, I will follow You wherever You go.

20 And Je'sus says to him, The foxes have holes, and the birds of the air *have* nests; but the Son of Man has <u>not where</u> to lay *His* head.   no place

21 And another of His disciples said to Him, Lord, allow me first to go and bury my father.   I KGS. 19:20

22 But Je'sus said to him, Follow Me; and let the <u>dead</u> bury their <u>dead</u>.   unbelievers

23 And when He was entered into a ship, His disciples followed Him.

24 And, behold, there arose a great <u>tempest</u> in the sea, insomuch that the ship was covered with the waves: but He was asleep.   storm

25 And His disciples came to *Him*, and awoke Him, saying, Lord, save us: we perish. lest we die

26 And He says to them, Why are you fearful, O you of little faith? Then He arose, and rebuked the winds and the sea; and there was a great calm.

27 But the men marveled, saying, What manner of man is this, that even the winds and the sea obey Him!

28 And when He was come to the other side into the country of the Ger'ge-senes, there met Him two possessed with devils, coming out of the tombs, exceeding fierce, so that no man might pass by that way. demons

29 And, behold, they cried out, saying, What have we to do with You, Je'sus, You Son of God? are You come here to torment us before the time?

30 And there was a good way off from them an herd of many swine feeding. pigs

31 So the devils besought Him, saying, If You cast us out, allow us to go away into the herd of swine.
demons begged

32 And He said to them, Go. And when they were come out, they went into the herd of swine: and, behold, the whole herd of swine ran violently down a steep place into the sea, and perished in the waters. pigs

33 And they that kept them fled, and went their ways into the city, and told every thing, and what was befallen to the possessed of the devils.
them that were - demons

34 And, behold, the whole city came out to meet Je'sus: and when they saw Him, they besought *Him* that He would depart out of their coasts. region

CHAPTER 9

AND He entered into a ship, and passed over, and came into His own city.

2 And, behold, they brought to Him a man sick of the palsy, lying on a bed: and Je'sus seeing their faith said to the sick of the palsy; Son, be of good cheer; your sins be forgiven you.

3 And, behold, certain of the scribes said within themselves, This *man* blasphemes. tells lies

4 And Je'sus knowing their thoughts said, Why think you evil in your hearts?

5 For which is easier, to say, *Your* sins be forgiven you; or to say, Arise, and walk? are

6 But that you may know that the Son of Man has power on earth to forgive sins, (then says He to the sick of the palsy,) Arise, take up your bed, and go to your house. authority

7 And he arose, and departed to his house.

8 But when the multitudes saw *it*, they marveled, and glorified God, which had given such power to men.
filled with awe

9 And as Je'sus passed forth from there, He saw a man, named Mat'thew, sitting at the receipt of custom: and He says to him, Follow Me. And he arose, and followed Him. tax office

10 And it came to pass, as Je'sus sat at meat in the house, behold, many

publicans and sinners came and sat down with Him and His disciples.

eating - tax men

11 And when the Phar'i-sees saw *it*, they said to His disciples, Why eat your Master with publicans and sinners?

12 But when Je'sus heard *that*, He said to them, They that be whole need not a physician, but they that are sick.

healthy

13 But go you and learn what *that* means, I will have mercy, and not sacrifice: for I am not come to call the righteous, but sinners to repentance.

14 Then came to Him the disciples of John, saying, Why do we and the Phar'i-sees fast oft, but Your disciples fast not?

15 And Je'sus said to them, Can the children of the bridechamber mourn, as long as the bridegroom is with them? but the days will come, when the bridegroom shall be taken from them, and then shall they fast.

16 No man puts a piece of new cloth to an old garment, for that which is put in to fill it up takes from the garment, and the rent is made worse.

unshrunk - tear

17 Neither do men put new wine into old bottles: else the bottles break, and the wine runs out, and the bottles : but they put new wine into new bottles, and both are preserved.

wineskins

18 While He spoke these things to them, behold, there came a certain ruler, and worshiped Him, saying, My daughter is even now dead: but come and lay Your hand upon her, and she shall live.

19 And Je'sus arose, and followed him, and *so did* His disciples.

20 And, behold, a woman, which was diseased with an issue of blood twelve years, came behind *Him*, and touched the hem of His garment:

LEV. 15:25 flow

21 For she said within herself, If I may but touch His garment, I shall be whole.

well

22 But Je'sus turned Him about, and when He saw her, He said, Daughter, be of good comfort; your faith has made you whole. And the woman was made whole from that hour.

23 And when Je'sus came into the ruler's house, and saw the minstrels and the people making a noise,

flute players

24 He said to them, Give place: for the maid is not dead, but sleeps. And they laughed Him to scorn.

25 But when the people were put forth, He went in, and took her by the hand, and the maid arose.

out

26 And the fame hereof went abroad into all that land.

of this thing

27 And when Je'sus departed from there, two blind men followed Him, crying, and saying, *You* son of Da'vid, have mercy on us.

28 And when He was come into the house, the blind men came to Him: and Je'sus says to them, Believe you that I am able to do this? They said to Him, Yea, Lord.

29 Then touched He their eyes, saying, According to your faith be it to you.

30 And their eyes were opened; and

Je'sus strictly charged them, saying, See *that* no man know *it*.　PSA. 146:8

31 But they, when they were departed, spread abroad His <u>fame</u> in all that <u>country</u>.　news - land

32 As they went out, behold, they brought to Him a dumb man possessed with a <u>devil</u>.　demon

33 And when the <u>devil</u> was <u>cast</u> out, the dumb spoke: and the multitudes marveled, saying, It was never so seen in Is'ra-el.　put

34 But the Phar'i-sees said, He casts out <u>devils</u> through the <u>prince of the devils</u>.　Satan

35 And Je'sus went about all the cities and villages, teaching in their synagogues, and preaching the gospel of the kingdom, and healing every sickness and <u>every</u> disease among the people.　all kinds of

36 But when He saw the multitudes, He was moved with compassion on them, because they fainted, and were scattered abroad, as sheep having no shepherd.　ZEC. 10:2　1 KGS. 22:17

37 Then says He to His disciples, The harvest truly *is* <u>plenteous</u>, but the laborers *are* few;　plentiful

38 Pray you therefore the Lord of the harvest, that He will send <u>forth</u> laborers into His harvest.　out

M27- - 38

CHAPTER 10

AND when He had called to *Him* His twelve disciples, He gave them power *against* unclean spirits, to cast them out, and to heal all manner of sickness and all manner of disease.

2 Now the names of the twelve apostles are these; The first, Si'mon, who is called Pe'ter, and Andrew his brother; James *the son* of Zeb'e-dee, and John his brother;

3 Phil'ip, and Bar-thol'o-mew; Thom'as, and Mat'thew the publican; James *the son* of Al-phae'us, and Leb-bae'us, whose surname was Thad-dae'us;

4 Si'mon the Ca'naan-ite, and Ju'das Is-car'i-ot, who also betrayed Him.

5 These twelve Je'sus sent forth, and commanded them, saying, Go not into the way of the Gen'tiles, and into *any* city of the Sa-mar'i-tans enter you not:

6 But go rather to the lost sheep of the house of Is'ra-el.

7 And as you go, preach, saying, The kingdom of heaven is <u>at hand</u>.　near

8 Heal the sick, cleanse the lepers, raise the dead, cast out <u>devils</u>: freely you have received, freely give.　demons

9 Provide neither gold, nor silver, nor brass in your purses,

10 Nor <u>scrip</u> for *your* journey, neither two coats, neither shoes, nor yet <u>staves</u>: for the workman is worthy of his <u>meat</u>.　bag - staff - food

11 And into whatsoever city or town you shall enter, enquire who in it is worthy; and there abide till you go there.

12 And when you come into an house, <u>salute</u> it.　greet

13 And if the house be worthy, let your peace come upon it: but if it be not worthy, let your peace return to you.

14 And whosoever shall not receive

GIA - 19

you, nor hear your words, when you depart out of that house or city, shake off the dust of your feet.

15 <u>Verily</u> I say to you, It shall be more tolerable for the land of Sod'om and Go-mor'rha in the day of judgment, than for that city.   truly

16 Behold, I send you forth as sheep in the midst of wolves: be you therefore wise as serpents, and <u>harmless</u> as doves.   innocent

17 But beware of men: for they will deliver you up to the councils, and they will scourge you in their synagogues;

18 And you shall be brought before governors and kings for My sake, for a <u>testimony</u> against them and the Gen'tiles.   PSA. 119:46   witness

19 But when they deliver you up, <u>take no thought</u> how or what you shall speak: for it shall be given you in that same hour what you shall speak.   not anxious

20 For it is not you that speak, but the Spirit of your Father which speaks in you.

21 And the brother shall deliver up the brother to death, and the father the child: and the children <u>shall</u> rise up against *their* parents, and cause them to be put to death.

22 And you shall be <u>hated</u> of all *men* for My name's sake: but he that <u>endures</u> to the end shall be saved.   thought less - persists

23 But when they persecute you in this city, flee you into another: for <u>verily</u> I say to you, You shall not have gone <u>over</u> the cities of Is'ra-el, till the Son of Man be come.   truly - finished

24 The disciple is not above *his* master, nor the servant above his lord.

25 It is enough for the disciple that he be as his master, and the servant as his lord. If they have called the master of the house <u>Be'el'ze-bub</u>, how much more *shall they call* them of his household?   2 KGS. 1:2   Satan

26 <u>Fear</u> them not therefore: for there is nothing covered, that shall not be revealed; and hid, that shall not be known.   regard

27 What I tell you in darkness, *that* speak you in light: and what you hear in the ear, *that* preach you upon the housetops.

28 And <u>fear</u> not them which kill the body, but are not able to kill the soul: but rather <u>fear</u> Him which is able to destroy both soul and body in hell.

29 Are not two sparrows sold for a farthing? and one of them shall not fall on the ground without your Father.

30 But the very hairs of your head are all numbered.

31 <u>Fear you not</u> therefore, you are of more value than many sparrows.   be not afraid

32 Whosoever therefore shall confess Me before men, him will I confess also before My Father which is in heaven.

33 But whosoever shall deny Me before men, him will I also deny before My Father which is in heaven.

34 Think not that I am come to <u>send</u> peace on earth: I came not to <u>send</u> peace, but a sword.   bring

35 For I am come to set a man <u>at variance</u> against his father, and the daughter against her mother, and the

daughter in law against her mother in law.   MIC. 7:6 in conflict

36 And a man's foes *shall be* they of his own <u>household</u>.   family

37 He that loves father or mother more than Me is not worthy of Me: and he that loves son or daughter more than Me is not worthy of Me.

38 And he that takes not his cross, and follows after Me, is not worthy of Me.

39 He that finds his life shall lose it: and he that loses his life for My sake shall find it.

40 He that receives you receives Me, and he that receives Me receives Him that sent Me.

41 He that receives a prophet in the name of a prophet shall receive a prophet's reward; and he that receives a righteous man in the name of a righteous man shall receive a righteous man's reward.

42 And whosoever shall give to drink to one of these little ones a cup of cold *water* only in the name of a disciple, <u>verily</u> I say to you, he shall in no wise lose his reward.   truly

CHAPTER 11

AND it came to pass, when Je'sus had made an end of commanding His twelve disciples, He departed there to teach and to preach in their cities.

2 Now when John had heard in the prison the works of Christ, he sent two of his disciples,

3 And said to Him, Are You He that should come, or do we look for another?

4 Je'sus answered and said to them, Go and show John again those things which you do hear and see:

5 The blind receive their sight, and the lame walk, the lepers are cleansed, and the deaf hear, the dead are raised up, and the poor have the gospel preached to them.   ISA. 35:5

6 And blessed is *he*, whosoever shall not <u>be offended in</u> Me. stumble over

7 And as they departed, Je'sus began to say to the multitudes concerning John, What went you out into the wilderness to see? A reed shaken with the wind?

8 But what went you out for to see? A man clothed in soft <u>raiment</u>? behold, they that wear soft *clothing* are in kings' houses.   clothing

9 But what went you out for to see? A prophet? yea, I say to you, and more than a prophet.

10 For this is *he*, of whom it is written, Behold, I send My messenger before your face, which shall prepare your way before you.   ISA. 40:3 MAL. 3:1

11 <u>Verily</u> I say to you, Among them that are born of women there has not risen a greater than John the Bap'tist: notwithstanding he that is least in the kingdom of heaven is greater than he.   truly

12 And from the days of John the Bap'tist until now the kingdom of heaven suffers violence, and the violent take it by force.

13 For all the prophets and the law prophesied until John.

14 And if you will receive *it*, this is E-li'jah, which was for to come.   MAL. 4:5

15 He that has ears to hear, let him hear.
16 But whereto shall I liken this generation? It is like to children sitting in the markets, and calling to their fellows,
17 And saying, We have <u>piped</u> to you, and you have not danced; we have mourned to you, and you have not lamented.   <small>played music</small>
18 For John came neither eating nor drinking, and they say, he has a <u>devil</u>.   <small>demon</small>
19 The Son of Man came eating and drinking, and they say, Behold a man gluttonous, and a <u>winebibber</u>, a friend of <u>publicans</u> and sinners. But wisdom is justified of her children.   <small>drunkard - tax collectors</small>
20 Then began He to <u>upbraid</u> the cities wherein most of His mighty works were done, because they repented not: <small>reproach</small>
21 Woe to you, Cho-ra'zin! woe to you, Beth-sa'i-da! for if the mighty works, which were done in you, had been done in Tyre and Si'don, they would have repented long ago in sackcloth and ashes.
22 But I say to you, It shall be more tolerable for Tyre and Si'don at the day of judgment, than for you.
23 And you, Ca-per'na-um, which are exalted to heaven, shall be brought down to hell: for if the <u>mighty works</u>, which have been done in you, had been done in Sod'om, it would have remained until this day.   <small>miracles</small>
24 But I say to you, That it shall be more tolerable for the land of Sod'om in the day of judgment, than for you.

25 At that time Je'sus answered and said, I thank You, O Father, Lord of heaven and earth, because You have hid these things from the wise and prudent, and have revealed them to babes.
26 Even so, Father: for so it seemed good in Your sight.
27 All things are delivered to Me of My Father: and no man knows the Son, but the Father; neither knows any man the Father, <u>save</u> the Son, and *he* to whomsoever the Son will reveal *Him*.   <small>except</small>
28 Come to Me, all *you* that labor and are heavy laden, and I will give you rest.
29 Take My <u>yoke</u> upon you, and learn of Me; for I am <u>meek</u> and lowly in heart: and you shall find rest to your souls.   <small>burden - humble</small>
30 For My <u>yoke</u> *is* easy, and My burden is light.   <small>load</small>

CHAPTER 12

AT that time Je'sus went on the <u>sabbath</u> day through the <u>corn</u>; and His disciples were an hungry, and began to pluck the ears of <u>corn</u>, and to eat.   <small>DEU. 23:25 day of rest - grain</small>
2 But when the Phar'i-sees saw *it*, they said to Him, Behold, Your disciples do that which is not lawful to do upon the <u>sabbath</u> day.
3 But He said to them, Have you not read what Da'vid did, when he was an hungry, and they that were with him;
4 How he entered into the house of God, and did eat the <u>showbread</u>, which

was not lawful for him to eat, neither for them which were with him, but only for the priests?   _{consecrated bread}

5 Or have you not read in the law, how that on the sabbath days the priests in the temple profane the sabbath, and are blameless? _{days of rest - break}

6 But I say to you, That in this place is *One* greater than the temple.

7 But if you had known what *this* means, I will have mercy, and not sacrifice, you would not have condemned the guiltless.   _{HOS. 6:6}

8 For the Son of Man is Lord even of the sabbath day.

9 And when He was departed from there, He went into their synagogue:

10 And, behold, there was a man which had *his* hand withered. And they asked Him, saying, Is it lawful to heal on the sabbath days? that they might accuse Him.

11 And He said to them, What man shall there be among you, that shall have one sheep, and if it fall into a pit on the sabbath day, will he not lay hold on it, and lift *it* out? _{day of rest - take}

12 How much then is a man better than a sheep? Wherefore it is lawful to do well on the sabbath days.   _{more valuable - good}

13 Then says He to the man, Stretch forth your hand. And he stretched *it* forth; and it was restored whole, like as the other.

14 Then the Phar'i-sees went out, and held a council against Him, how they might destroy Him.

15 But when Je'sus knew *it*, He withdrew Himself from there: and great multitudes followed Him, and He healed them all;

16 And charged them that they should not make Him known: _{instructed}

17 That it might be fulfilled which was spoken by I-sa'iah the prophet, saying,   _{ISA. 42:1-2}

18 Behold My servant, whom I have chosen; My beloved, in whom My soul is well pleased: I will put My spirit upon him, and He shall show judgment to the Gen'tiles.

19 He shall not strive, nor cry; neither shall any man hear His voice in the streets.

20 A bruised reed shall He not break, and smoking flax shall He not quench, till He send forth judgment to victory.

21 And in His name shall the Gen'tiles trust.

22 Then was brought to Him one possessed with a devil, blind, and dumb: and He healed him, insomuch that the blind and dumb both spoke and saw.   _{demon}

23 And all the people were amazed, and said, Is not this the son of Da'vid?

24 But when the Phar'i-sees heard *it*, they said, This *fellow* does not cast out devils, but by Be'el'ze-bub the prince of the devils.   _{Satan - chief}

25 And Je'sus knew their thoughts, and said to them, Every kingdom divided against itself is brought to desolation; and every city or house divided against itself shall not stand: _{waste}

26 And if Sa'tan cast out Sa'tan, he is divided against himself; how shall then his kingdom stand?   _{fights}

27 And if I by <u>Be'el'ze-bub</u> cast out <u>devils</u>, by whom do your <u>children</u> cast *them* out? therefore they shall be your judges.   Satan - demons - sons

28 But if I cast out <u>devils</u> by the Spirit of God, then the kingdom of God is come to you.

29 Or else how can one enter into a strong man's house, and <u>spoil</u> his goods, except he first bind the strong man? and then he will <u>spoil</u> his house.   steal - plunder

30 He that is not with Me is against Me; and he that <u>gathers not</u> with Me scatters abroad.   does not help

31 Wherefore I say to you, All manner of sin and blasphemy shall be forgiven to men: but the <u>blasphemy</u> *against* the *Ho'ly* <u>Ghost</u> shall not be forgiven to men.   evil spoken - Spirit

32 And whosoever speaks a word against the Son of Man, it shall be forgiven him: but whosoever speaks against the Ho'ly <u>Ghost</u>, it shall not be forgiven him, neither in this world, neither in the *world* to come.

33 Either make the tree good, and its fruit good; or else make the tree <u>corrupt</u>, and its fruit <u>corrupt</u>: for the tree is known by *its* fruit.   bad

34 O <u>generation</u> of vipers, how can you, being evil, speak good things? for out of the abundance of the heart the mouth speaks.   brood

35 A good man out of the good treasure of the heart brings forth good things: and an evil man out of the evil treasure brings forth evil things.

36 But I say to you, That every idle word that men shall speak, they shall give account thereof in the day of judgment.

37 For by your words you shall be justified, and by your words you shall be condemned.

38 Then certain of the scribes and of the Phar'i-sees answered, saying, Master, we would see a sign from You.

39 But He answered and said to them, An evil and adulterous generation seeks after a sign; and there shall no sign be given to it, but the sign of the prophet Jo'nah:

40 For as Jo'nah was three days and three nights in the whale's belly; so shall the Son of Man be three days and three nights in the heart of the earth.   JON. 1:17

41 The men of Nin'e-veh shall rise in judgment with this generation, and shall condemn it: because they repented at the preaching of Jo'nah; and, behold, a greater than Jo'nah *is* here.

42 The <u>queen of the south</u> shall rise up in the judgment with this generation, and shall condemn it: for she came from the uttermost parts of the earth to hear the wisdom of Sol'o-mon; and, behold, a greater than Sol'o-mon *is* here.   2 CHRON. 9:1   1 KGS 10:1   Queen of Sheba

43 When the <u>unclean</u> spirit is gone out of a man, he walks through dry places, seeking rest, and finds none.   evil

44 Then he says, I will return into my house from where I came out; and when he is come, he finds *it* empty, swept, and <u>garnished</u>.   which - in order

45 Then goes he, and takes with himself seven other spirits more wicked than himself, and they enter in and

dwell there: and the last *state* of that man is worse than the first. Even so shall it be also to this wicked generation.

46 While He yet talked to the people, behold, *His* mother and His brethren stood outside, desiring to speak with Him.

47 Then one said to Him, Behold, Your mother and Your brethren stand outside desiring to speak with You.

48 But He answered and said to him that told Him, Who is My mother? and who are My brethren?

49 And He stretched forth His hand toward His disciples, and said, Behold My mother and My brethren!   see

50 For whosoever shall do the will of My Father which is in heaven, the same is My brother, and sister, and mother.

CHAPTER 13

THE same day went Je'sus out of the house, and sat by the sea side.

2 And great multitudes were gathered together to Him, so that He went into a ship, and sat; and the whole multitude stood on the shore.

3 And He spoke many things to them in parables, saying, Behold, a sower went forth to sow;   story examples

4 And when he sowed, some *seeds* fell by the way side, and the fowls came and devoured them up: birds

5 Some fell upon stony places, where they had not much earth: and immediately they sprung up, because they had no deepness of earth:

MARK 4:3-9,14-21 LUKE 8:5 rocky

6 And when the sun was up, they were scorched; and because they had no root, they withered away.

7 And some fell among thorns; and the thorns sprung up, and choked them:

8 But other fell into good ground, and brought forth fruit, some an hundredfold, some sixtyfold, some thirtyfold.

9 Who has ears to hear, let him hear.

10 And the disciples came, and said to Him, Why speak You to them in parables?   story examples

11 He answered and said to them, Because it is given to you to know the mysteries of the kingdom of heaven, but to them it is not given.   truths

12 For whosoever has, to him shall be given, and he shall have more abundance: but whosoever has not, from him shall be taken away even that he has.

13 Therefore speak I to them in parables: because they seeing see not; and hearing they hear not, neither do they understand.

14 And in them is fulfilled the prophecy of I-sa'iah, which says, By hearing you shall hear, and shall not understand; and seeing you shall see, and shall not perceive: ISA. 6:10

15 For this people's heart is waxed gross, and *their ears* are dull of hearing, and their eyes they have closed; less at any time they should see with *their* eyes, and hear with *their* ears, and should understand with *their* heart, and should be converted, and I should heal them.   grown - dull

16 But blessed *are* your eyes, for they see: and your ears, for they hear.

17 For <u>verily</u> I say to you, That many prophets and righteous *men* have desired to see *those things* which you see, and have not seen *them*; and to hear *those things* which you hear, and have not heard *them*.   truly

18 Hear you therefore the <u>parable</u> of the sower.   story

19 When any one hears the word of the kingdom, and understands *it* not, then comes the <u>wicked *one*</u>, and catches away that which was sown in his heart. This is he which received seed by the way side.   Satan

20 But he that received the seed into stony places, the same is he that hears the word, and <u>anon</u> with joy receives it;   immediately

21 Yet has he not root in himself, but endures for a while: for when tribulation or persecution arises because of the word, by and by he is offended.

22 He also that received seed among the thorns is he that hears the word; and the care of this world, and the deceitfulness of riches, choke the word, and he becomes unfruitful.

23 But he that received seed into the good ground is he that hears the word, and understands *it*; which also bears fruit, and brings forth, some an hundredfold, some sixty, some thirty.

24 Another parable put He forth to them, saying, The kingdom of heaven is likened to a man which sowed good seed in his field:

25 But while men slept, his enemy came and sowed <u>tares</u> among the wheat, and went his way.   weeds

26 But when the <u>blade</u> was sprung up, and brought forth fruit, then appeared the <u>tares</u> also.   wheat

27 So the servants of the householder came and said to him, Sir, did not you sow good seed in your field? from where then has it <u>tares</u>?

28 He said to them, An enemy has done this. The servants said to him, Will you then that we go and gather them up?

29 But he said, Nay; less while you gather up the <u>tares,</u> you root up also the wheat with them.

30 Let both grow together until the harvest: and in the time of harvest I will say to the reapers, Gather you together first the <u>tares</u>, and bind them in bundles to burn them: but gather the wheat into my barn.

31 Another parable put He forth to them, saying, The kingdom of heaven is like to a grain of mustard seed, which a man took, and sowed in his field:

32 Which indeed is the <u>least</u> of all seeds: but when it is grown, it is the <u>greatest</u> among herbs, and becomes a tree, so that the birds of the air come and lodge in the branches thereof.   smaller - largest

33 Another <u>parable</u> spoke He to them; The kingdom of heaven is like to <u>leaven</u>, which a woman took, and hid in three measures of meal, till the whole was <u>leavened</u>.   without yeast - with yeast

34 All these things spoke Je'sus to

the multitude in parables; and without a parable spoke He not to them:

35 That it might be fulfilled which was spoken by the prophet, saying, I will open my mouth in parables; I will utter things which have been kept secret from the foundation of the world.   PS. 78:2-3

36 Then Je'sus sent the multitude away, and went into the house: and His disciples came to Him, saying, Declare to us the parable of the tares of the field.   weeds

37 He answered and said to them, He that sows the good seed is the Son of Man;

38 The field is the world; the good seed are the children of the kingdom; but the tares are the children of the wicked *one*;

39 The enemy that sowed them is the devil; the harvest is the end of the world; and the reapers are the angels.   messengers

40 As therefore the tares are gathered and burned in the fire; so shall it be in the end of this world.

41 The Son of Man shall send forth His angels, and they shall gather out of His kingdom all things that offend, and them which do iniquity;   messengers - lawlessness

42 And shall cast them into a furnace of fire: there shall be wailing and gnashing of teeth.

43 Then shall the righteous shine forth as the sun in the kingdom of their Father. Who has ears to hear, let him hear.

44 Again, the kingdom of heaven is like to treasure hid in a field; the which when a man has found, he hides, and for joy thereof goes and sells all that he has, and buys that field.

45 Again, the kingdom of heaven is like to a merchant man, seeking goodly pearls: valuable

46 Who, when he had found one pearl of great price, went and sold all that he had, and bought it.

47 Again, the kingdom of heaven is like to a net, that was cast into the sea, and gathered of every kind:

48 Which, when it was full, they drew to shore, and sat down, and gathered the good into vessels, but cast the bad away.

49 So shall it be at the end of the world: the angels shall come forth, and sever the wicked from among the just,   messengers - take

50 And shall cast them into the furnace of fire: there shall be wailing and gnashing of teeth.

51 Je'sus says to them, Have you understood all these things? They say to Him, Yea, Lord.   yes

52 Then said He to them, Therefore every scribe *which is* instructed to the kingdom of heaven is like to a man *that is* an householder, which brings forth out of his treasure *things* new and old.   writer

53 And it came to pass, *that* when Je'sus had finished these parables, He departed from there.

54 And when He was come into His own country, He taught them in their synagogue, insomuch that they were astonished, and said, Where has this

man this wisdom, and *these* mighty works?

55 Is not this the carpenter's son? is not His mother called Ma'ry? and His brethren, James, and Jo'ses, and Si'mon, and Ju'das?

56 And His sisters, are they not all with us? Where then has this *man* all these things?   living here

57 And they were offended in Him. But Je'sus said to them, A prophet is not without honor, save in his own country, and in his own house. 1 SAM. 10:11

58 And He did not many mighty works there because of their unbelief.

CHAPTER 14

AT that time Her'od the tetrarch heard of the fame of Je'sus,

2 And said to his servants, This is John the Bap'tist; he is risen from the dead; and therefore mighty works do show forth themselves in him.   are done by

3 For Her'od had laid hold on John, and bound him, and put *him* in prison for He-ro'di-as' sake, his brother Phil'ip's wife.

4 For John said to him, It is not lawful for you to have her.

5 And when he would have put him to death, he feared the multitude, because they counted him as a prophet.

6 But when Her'od's birthday was kept, the daughter of He-ro'di-as danced before them, and pleased Her'od.

7 Whereupon he promised with an oath to give her whatsoever she would ask.

8 And she, being before instructed of her mother, said, Give me here John Bap'tist's head in a charger.   platter

9 And the king was sorry: nevertheless for the oath's sake, and them which sat with him at meat, he commanded *it* to be given *her*.   dinner guests

10 And he sent, and beheaded John in the prison.

11 And his head was brought in a charger, and given to the damsel: and she brought *it* to her mother.   girl

12 And his disciples came, and took up the body, and buried it, and went and told Je'sus.

13 When Je'sus heard *of it*, He departed from there by ship into a desert place apart: and when the people had heard *thereof*, they followed Him on foot out of the cities.

14 And Je'sus went forth, and saw a great multitude, and was moved with compassion toward them, and He healed their sick.

15 And when it was evening, His disciples came to Him, saying, This is a desert place, and the time is now past; send the multitude away, that they may go into the villages, and buy themselves victuals.   food

16 But Je'sus said to them, They need not depart; give you them to eat.

17 And they say to Him, We have here but five loaves, and two fishes.

18 He said, Bring them here to Me.

19 And He commanded the multitude to sit down on the grass, and took the five loaves, and the two fishes, and looking up to heaven, He blessed, and

broke, and gave the loaves to *His* disciples, and the disciples to the multitude. thanked God

20 And they did all eat, and were filled: and they took up of the <u>fragments</u> that remained twelve baskets full. leftovers

21 And they that had eaten were about five thousand men, <u>beside</u> women and children.   PROV. 8:17 without

22 And immediately Je'sus <u>con-strained</u> His disciples to get into a ship, and to go before Him to the other side, while He sent the multitudes away. made

23 And when He had sent the multitudes away, He went up into a mountain apart to pray: and when the evening was come, He was there alone.

24 But the ship was now in the midst of the sea, tossed with waves: for the wind was <u>contrary</u>. blowing

25 And in the <u>fourth watch</u> of the night Je'sus went to them, walking on the sea.   3 AM to 6 AM

26 And when the disciples saw Him walking on the sea, they were troubled, saying, It is a <u>spirit</u>; and they cried out for fear.   ISA. 50:6 ghost

27 But immediately Je'sus spoke to them, saying, <u>Be of good cheer</u>; it is I; be not afraid. take courage

28 And Pe'ter answered Him and said, Lord, if it be You, <u>bid</u> me come to You on the water. command

29 And He said, Come. And when Pe'ter was come down out of the ship, he walked on the water, to go to Je'sus.

30 But when he saw the wind <u>boister-</u> ous, he was afraid; and beginning to sink, he cried, saying, Lord, save me. strong

31 And immediately Je'sus stretched forth *His* hand, and caught him, and said to him, O you of little faith, wherefore did you doubt?

32 And when they <u>were come</u> into the ship, the wind <u>ceased</u>. got - stopped

33 Then they that were in the ship came and worshiped Him, saying, Of a truth You are the Son of God.

34 And when they were gone over, they came into the land of Gen-nes'a-ret.

35 And when the men of that place had <u>knowledge of</u> Him, they sent out into all that country round about, and brought to Him all that were diseased; recognized

36 And besought Him that they might only touch the hem of His garment: and as many as touched were made perfectly <u>whole</u>. well

CHAPTER 15

THEN came to Je'sus scribes and Phar'i-sees, which were of Je-ru'sa-lem, saying,

2 Why do your disciples transgress the tradition of the elders? for they wash not their hands when they eat bread.

3 But He answered and said to them, Why do you also <u>transgress</u> the commandment of God by your tradition? disobey

4 For God commanded, saying, Honor your father and mother: and, He that curses father or mother, let him die the death.   EX. 21:17 EX. 20:12

5 But you say, Whosoever shall say to *his* father or *his* mother, *It is* a gift, by whatsoever you might be profited by me;

6 And honor not his father or his mother, *he shall be free*. Thus have you made the commandment of God of none effect by your tradition.

7 You hypocrites, well did I-sa'iah prophesy of you, saying,   insincere - rightly

8 This people draw near to Me with their mouth, and honor Me with *their* lips; but their heart is far from Me.   ISA. 29:13 JER. 12:2

9 But in vain they do worship Me, teaching *for* doctrines the commandments of men.   facts

10 And He called the multitude, and said to them, Hear, and understand:

11 Not that which goes into the mouth defiles a man; but that which comes out of the mouth, this defiles a man.

12 Then came His disciples, and said to Him, Know You that the Phar'i-sees were offended, after they heard this saying?

13 But He answered and said, Every plant, which My heavenly Father has not planted, shall be rooted up. ISA. 60:21

14 Let them alone: they be blind leaders of the blind. And if the blind lead the blind, both shall fall into the ditch.

15 Then answered Pe'ter and said to Him, Declare to us this parable.

       explain - story

16 And Je'sus said, Are you also yet without understanding?

17 Do not you yet understand, that whatsoever enters in at the mouth goes into the belly, and is cast out into the draught?

18 But those things which proceed out of the mouth come forth from the heart; and they defile the man.

19 For out of the heart proceed evil thoughts, murders, adulteries, fornications, thefts, false witness, blasphemies:

20 These are *the things* which defile a man: but to eat with unwashen hands defiles not a man.   make unclean

21 Then Je'sus went from there, and departed into the coasts of Tyre and Si'don.

22 And, behold, a woman of Ca'naan came out of the same coasts, and cried to Him, saying, Have mercy on me, O Lord, *You* Son of Da'vid; my daughter is grievously vexed with a devil.   demon possessed

23 But He answered her not a word. And His disciples came and besought Him, saying, Send her away; for she cries after us.

24 But He answered and said, I am not sent but to the lost sheep of the house of Is'ra-el.   only

25 Then came she and worshiped Him, saying, Lord, help me.   bowed before

26 But He answered and said, It is not meet to take the children's bread, and to cast *it* to dogs.   fit - symbolic of Israel and Gentiles

27 And she said, Truth, Lord: yet the dogs eat of the crumbs which fall from their masters' table.

28 Then Je'sus answered and said to her, O woman, great *is* your faith: be it to you even as you will. And

her daughter was made <u>whole</u> from that very hour. ⟨healed⟩

29 And Je'sus departed from thcre, and came near to the sea of Gal'i-lee; and went up into a mountain, and sat down there.

30 And great multitudes came to Him, having with them *those that were* lame, blind, dumb, <u>maimed</u>, and many others, and cast them down at Je'sus' feet; and He healed them: ⟨crippled⟩

31 Insomuch that the multitude wondered, when they saw the dumb to speak, the <u>maimed</u> to be <u>whole</u>, the lame to walk, and the blind to see: and they <u>glorified</u> the God of Is'ra-el. ⟨hcaled - praised⟩

32 Then Je'sus called His disciples *to Him*, and said, I have compassion on the multitude, because they continue with Me now three days, and have nothing to eat: and I will not send them away fasting, less they faint in the way.

33 And His disciples say to Him, Where would we have so much bread in the wilderness, as to <u>fill</u> so great a multitude? ⟨satisfy⟩

34 And Je'sus says to them, How many loaves have you? And they said, Seven, and a few little fishes.

35 And He <u>commanded</u> the multitude to sit down on the ground. ⟨directed⟩

36 And He took the seven loaves and the fishes, and gave thanks, and broke *them*, and gave to His disciples, and the disciples to the multitude.

37 And they did all eat, and were filled: and they took up of the broken *meat* that was left seven baskets full. ⟨pieces⟩

38 And they that did eat were four thousand men, beside women and children.

39 And He sent away the multitude, and took ship, and came into the coasts of Mag'da-la.

CHAPTER 16

THE Phar'i-sees also with the Sad'du-cees came, and <u>tempting</u> <u>desired</u> Him that He would show them a sign from heaven. ⟨testing - asked⟩

2 He answered and said to them, When it is <u>evening</u>, you say, *It will be* fair weather: for the sky is red. ⟨sunset⟩

3 And in the morning, *It will be* foul weather to day: for the sky is red and <u>lowring</u>. O *you* <u>hypocrites</u>, you can discern the face of the sky; but can you not *discern* the signs of the times? ⟨threatening - insincere⟩

4 A <u>wicked and adulterous</u> generation seeks after a <u>sign;</u> and there shall no <u>sign</u> be given to it, but the <u>sign</u> of the prophet Jo'nah. And He left them, and departed. ⟨JON. 3:5 evil and unfaithful - miracle⟩

5 And when His disciples were come to the other side, they had forgotten to take bread.

6 Then Je'sus said to them, Take heed and beware of the <u>leaven</u> of the Phar'i-sees and of the Sad'du-cees. ⟨evil teaching⟩

7 And they <u>reasoned</u> among themselves, saying, *It is* because we have taken no bread. ⟨discussed⟩

8 *Which* when Je'sus perceived, He said to them, O you of little faith, why reason you among yourselves, because you have brought no bread?

9 Do you not yet understand, neither remember the five loaves of the five thousand, and how many baskets you <u>took</u> up? _{gathered}

10 Neither the seven loaves of the four thousand, and how many baskets you took up?

11 How is it that you do not understand that I spoke *it* not to you concerning bread, that you should beware of the <u>leaven</u> of the Phar'i-sees and of the Sad'du-cees? _{evil}

12 Then understood they how that He bade *them* not beware of the <u>leaven</u> of bread, but of the <u>doctrine</u> of the Phar'i-sees and of the Sad'du-cees. _{yeast - teaching}

13 When Je'sus came into the coasts of Caes-a-re'a Phi-lip'pi, He asked His disciples, saying, Whom do men say that I the Son of man am?

14 And they said, Some *say that You are* John the Bap'tist: some, Elijah; and others, Jeremiah, or one of the prophets.

15 He says to them, But whom say you that I am?

16 And Si'mon Pe'ter answered and said, You are the Christ, the Son of the living God.

17 And Je'sus answered and said to him, Blessed are you, Si'mon <u>Bar-jo'na</u>: for flesh and blood has not revealed *it* to you, but My Father which is in heaven. _{Son of John}

18 And I say also to you, That you are <u>Pe'ter</u>, and upon this <u>rock</u> I will build My church; and the gates of hell shall not <u>prevail</u> against it. _{Petros-little stone - Rock - succeed}

19 And I will give to you the keys of the kingdom of heaven: and whatsoever you shall bind on earth shall be bound in heaven: and whatsoever you shall <u>loose</u> on earth shall be loosed in heaven. _{do - done}

20 Then <u>charged</u> He His disciples that they should tell no man that He was Je'sus the <u>Christ</u>. _{instructed - Messiah}

21 From that time forth began Je'sus to show to His disciples, how that He must go to Je-ru'sa-lem, and suffer many things of the elders and chief priests and scribes, and be killed, and be raised again the third day.

22 Then Pe'ter took Him, and began to rebuke Him, saying, Be it far from You, Lord: this shall not be to You.

23 But He turned, and said to Pe'ter, Get you behind Me, Sa'tan: you are an <u>offence</u> to Me: for you <u>savor</u> not the things that be of God, but those that be of men. _{obstruction - understand}

24 Then said Je'sus to His disciples, If any *man* will come after Me, let him deny himself, and take up his cross, and follow Me.

25 For whosoever will save his life shall lose it: and whosoever will lose his life for My sake shall find it.

26 For what is a man profited, if he shall gain the whole world, and lose his own <u>soul</u>? or what shall a man give in exchange for his <u>soul</u>? _{JOB 27:8 life}

27 For the Son of man shall come in the glory of His Father with His <u>angels</u>; and then He shall reward every man according to his works. _{messengers}

28 <u>Verily</u> I say to you, There be some standing here, which shall not

taste of death, till they see the Son of man coming in His kingdom.　*truly*

CHAPTER 17

AND after six days Je'sus takes Pe'ter, James, and John his brother, and brings them up into an high mountain apart,

2 And was <u>transfigured</u> before them: and His face did shine as the sun, and His <u>raiment</u> was white as the light.　*changed - clothes*

3 And, behold, there appeared to them Mo'ses and Elijah talking with Him.

4 Then answered Pe'ter, and said to Je'sus, Lord, it is good for us to be here: if You will, let us make here three <u>tabernacles</u>; one for You, and one for Mo'ses, and one for Elijah.　*monuments*

5 While he yet spoke, behold, a bright cloud overshadowed them: and behold a voice out of the cloud, which said, This is My <u>beloved Son, in whom I am well pleased; hear you Him.</u>　*PS. 2:7 Jesus*

6 And when the disciples heard *it*, they fell on their face, and were <u>sore</u> afraid.　*much*

7 And Je'sus came and touched them, and said, Arise, and be not afraid.

8 And when they had lifted up their eyes, they saw no man, <u>save</u> Je'sus only.　*except*

9 And as they came down from the mountain, Je'sus <u>charged</u> them, saying, Tell the vision to no man, until the Son of man be risen again from the dead.　*instructed*

10 And His disciples asked Him, saying, Why then say the scribes that Elijah must first come?

11 And Je'sus answered and said to them, Elijah truly shall first come, and restore all things.

12 But I say to you, That Elijah is come already, and they knew him not, but have done to him whatsoever they <u>listed</u>. Likewise shall also the Son of man suffer of them.　*wanted*

13 Then the disciples understood that He spoke to them of John the Bap'tist.

14 And when they were come to the multitude, there came to Him a *certain* man, kneeling down to Him, and saying,

15 Lord, have mercy on my son: for he is lunatic, and <u>sore vexed</u>: for often he falls into the fire, and <u>oft</u> into the water.　*much troubled - often*

16 And I brought him to Your disciples, and they could not cure him.

17 Then Je'sus answered and said, O faithless and <u>perverse</u> generation, how long shall I be with you? how long shall I <u>suffer</u> you? bring him here to Me.　*perverted - allow*

18 And Je'sus rebuked the <u>devil</u>; and he departed out of him: and the child was cured from that very hour.　*demon*

19 Then came the disciples to Je'sus apart, and said, Why could not we cast him out?

20 And Je'sus said to them, Because of your unbelief: for <u>verily</u> I say to you, If you have faith as a grain of mustard seed, you shall say to this mountain, Remove here to yonder

place; and it shall remove; and nothing shall be impossible to you.   truly

21 However this kind goes not out but by prayer and fasting.

22 And while they abode in Gal'i-lee, Je'sus said to them, The Son of man shall be betrayed into the hands of men:

23 And they shall kill Him, and the third day He shall be raised again. And they were exceeding <u>sorry</u>.   grieved

24 And when they were come to Ca-per'na-um, they that received <u>tribute</u> *money* came to Pe'ter, and said, Does not your master pay <u>tribute</u>?   tax

25 He says, Yes. And when he was come into the house, Je'sus prevented him, saying, What think you, Si'mon? of whom do the kings of the earth <u>take</u> custom or <u>tribute</u>? of their own children, or of <u>strangers</u>?   collect - foreigners

26 Pe'ter says to Him, Of <u>strangers</u>. Je'sus says to him, Then are the <u>children</u> free.   citizens

27 Notwithstanding, less we should offend them, go you to the sea, and cast an hook, and take up the fish that first comes up; and when you have opened its mouth, you shall find a piece of money: that take, and give to them for Me and you.

CHAPTER 18

AT the same time came the disciples to Je'sus, saying, Who is the greatest in the kingdom of heaven?

2 And Je'sus called a little child to Him, and set him in the midst of them,

3 And said, <u>Verily</u> I say to you, Ex-cept you be <u>converted</u>, and become as little children, you shall not enter into the kingdom of heaven.   truly - changed

4 Whosoever therefore shall humble himself as this little child, the same is greatest in the kingdom of heaven.

5 And whoso shall receive one such little child in My name receives Me.

6 But whoso shall <u>offend</u> one of these little ones which believe in Me, it were better for him that a millstone were hanged about his neck, and *that* he were drowned in the depth of the sea.   cause

7 Woe to the world because of <u>offences</u>! for it <u>must needs</u> be that offences come; but woe to that man by whom the offence comes.   wrongs done - is natural

8 Wherefore if your hand or your foot offend you, cut them off, and cast *them* from you: it is better for you to enter into life <u>halt</u> or <u>maimed</u>, rather than having two hands or two feet to be cast into everlasting fire.   lame - crippled

9 And if your eye <u>offend</u> you, pluck it out, and cast *it* from you: it is better for you to enter into life with one eye, rather than having two eyes to be cast into hell fire.   trouble

10 Take heed that you despise not one of these little ones; for I say to you, That in heaven their <u>angels</u> do always behold the face of My Father which is in heaven.   messengers

11 For the Son of man is come to save that which was lost.

12 How think you? if a man have an hundred sheep, and one of them be gone astray, does he not leave the

ninety and nine, and goes into the mountains, and seeks that which is gone astray?

13 And if so be that he find it, <u>verily</u> I say to you, he rejoices more of that *sheep*, than of the ninety and nine which went not astray. truly

14 Even so it is not the will of your Father which is in heaven, that one of these little ones should perish.

15 Moreover if your brother shall <u>trespass</u> against you, go and tell him his fault between you and him alone: if he shall hear you, you have gained your brother. sin

16 But if he will not hear *you*, *then* take with you one or two more, that in the mouth of two or three witnesses every word may be established.

17 And if he shall neglect to hear them, tell *it* to the church: but if he neglect to hear the church, let him be to you as an <u>heathen</u> man and a <u>publican</u>. unbeliever - tax gatherer

18 <u>Verily</u> I say to you, Whatsoever you shall bind on earth shall be bound in heaven: and whatsoever you shall <u>loose</u> on earth shall be <u>loosed</u> in heaven. Truly - do - done

19 Again I say to you, That if two of you shall agree on earth as touching any thing that they shall ask, it shall be done for them of My Father which is in heaven.

20 For where two or three are gathered together in My name, there am I in the midst of them.

21 Then came Pe'ter to Him, and said, Lord, how oft shall my brother sin against me, and I forgive him? till seven times?

22 Je'sus says to him, I say not to you, Until seven times: but, Until seventy times seven.

23 Therefore is the kingdom of heaven likened to a certain king, which would <u>take account of</u> his servants settled accounts with

24 And when he had begun to reckon, one was brought to him, which owed him ten thousand talents.

25 But forasmuch as he had not to pay, his lord commanded him to be sold, and his wife, and children, and all that he had, and payment to be made.

26 The servant therefore fell down, and worshiped him, saying, Lord, have patience with me, and I will pay you all.

27 Then the lord of that servant was moved with <u>compassion</u>, and <u>loosed</u> him, and forgave him the debt. pity - released

28 But the same servant went out, and found one of his fellowservants, which owed him an hundred pence: and he laid hands on him, and took *him* by the throat, saying, Pay me <u>that</u> you owe. what

29 And his fellowservant fell down at his feet, and besought him, saying, Have patience with me, and I will pay you all.

30 And he would not: but went and cast him into prison, till he should pay the debt.

31 So when his fellowservants saw what was done, they were very sorry, and came and told to their lord all that was done.

32 Then his lord, after that he had called him, said to him, O you wicked servant, I forgave you all that debt, because you <u>desire</u> me: entreated

33 Should not you also have had <u>compassion</u> on your fellowservant, even as I had pity on you?   pity

34 And his lord was angry, and <u>delivered</u> him to the tormentors, till he should pay all that was due to him.   transferred

35 So likewise shall My heavenly Father do also to you, if you from your hearts forgive not every one his brother their trespasses.

CHAPTER 19

AND it came to pass, *that* when Je'sus had finished these sayings, He departed from Gal'i-lee, and came into the coasts of Ju-dae'a beyond Jor'dan;

2 And great multitudes followed Him; and He healed them there.

3 The Phar'i-sees also came to Him, <u>tempting</u> Him, and saying to Him, Is it lawful for a man to <u>put away his wife</u> for <u>every</u> cause?   testing - divorce - any

4 And He answered and said to them, Have you not read, that He which made *them* at the beginning made them male and female,   GEN. 1:26 GEN. 5:2

5 And said, For this cause shall a man leave father and mother, and shall cling to his wife: and they two shall be one flesh?   GEN. 2:24

6 Wherefore they are no more two, but one flesh. What therefore God has joined together, let not man <u>put</u> <u>asunder</u>.   separate

7 They say to Him, Why did Mo'-ses then command to give a writing of divorcement, and to put her away?

8 He says to them, Mo'ses because of the hardness of your hearts permitted you to put away your wives: but from the beginning it was not so.

9 And I say to you, Whosoever shall put away his wife, except *it be* for fornication, and shall marry another, commits adultery: and whoso marries her which is put away does commit adultery.

10 His disciples say to Him, If the case of the man be so with *his* wife, it is not good to marry.

11 But He said to them, All *men* cannot <u>receive</u> this saying, save *they* to whom it is given.   accept

12 For there are some <u>eunuchs</u>, which were so born from *their* mother's womb: and there are some <u>eunuchs</u>, which were made <u>eunuchs</u> of men: and there be <u>eunuchs</u>, which have made themselves <u>eunuchs</u> for the kingdom of heaven's sake. He that is able to receive *it*, let him receive *it*.   castrated men

13 Then were there brought to Him little children, that He should put *His* hands on them, and pray: and the disciples <u>rebuked</u> them.   censored

14 But Je'sus said, Permit little children, and forbid them not, to come to Me: for of such is the kingdom of heaven.

15 And He <u>laid</u> *His* hands on them, and departed from there.   placed

16 And, behold, one came and said to Him, Good Master, what good thing shall I do, that I may have eternal life?

17 And He said to him, Why call you Me <u>good</u>? *there is* none <u>good</u> but one, *that is*, God: but if you will enter into life, keep the commandments.

perfect-Godly

18 He says to Him, Which? Je'sus said, you shall do no murder, you shall not commit adultery, you shall not steal, you shall not bear false witness,   EX. 20:13-16

19 Honor your father and *your* mother: and, you shall love your neighbor as yourself.   LEV. 19:18

20 The young man said to Him, All these things have I kept from my youth up: what <u>lack I yet</u>?   must I do

21 Je'sus said to him, If you will be perfect, go *and* sell that you have, and give to the poor, and you shall have treasure in heaven: and come *and* follow Me.

22 But when the young man heard that saying, he went away sorrowful: for he had great <u>possessions</u>.   riches

23 Then said Je'sus to His disciples, <u>Verily</u> I say to you, That a rich man shall hardly enter into the kingdom of heaven.   truly

24 And again I say to you, It is easier for a camel to go through the eye of a needle, than for a rich man to enter into the kingdom of God.

25 When His disciples heard *it*, they were exceedingly amazed, saying, Who then can be saved?

26 But Je'sus beheld *them*, and said to them, With men this is impossible; but with God all things are possible. GEN. 18:14

27 Then answered Pe'ter and said to Him, Behold, we have forsaken all, and followed You; what shall we have therefore?

28 And Je'sus said to them, <u>Verily</u> I say to you, That you which have followed Me, in the regeneration when the Son of Man shall sit in the throne of His glory, you also shall sit upon twelve thrones, judging the twelve tribes of Is'ra-el.   2 SAM. 7:25 truly

29 And every one that has forsaken houses, or brethren, or sisters, or father, or mother, or wife, or children, or lands, for My name's sake, shall receive an hundredfold, and shall inherit everlasting life.

30 But many *that are* first shall be last; and the last *shall be* first.

CHAPTER 20

FOR the kingdom of heaven is like to a man *that* is an householder, which went out early in the morning to hire laborers into his vineyard.

2 And when he had agreed with the laborers for a penny a day, he sent them into his vineyard.

3 And he went out about the <u>third hour</u>, and saw others standing idle in the marketplace,   9 AM

4 And said to them; Go you also into the vineyard, and whatsoever is right I will give you. And they went their way.

5 Again he went out about the <u>sixth</u> and <u>ninth</u> hour, and did likewise.

12 noon - 3PM

6 And about the <u>eleventh</u> hour he went out, and found others standing idle, and says to them, Why stand you here all the day idle?   5 PM

7 They say to him, Because no man has hired us. He says to them, Go you also into the vineyard; and whatsoever is right, *that* shall you receive.

8 So when even was come, the lord of the vineyard says to his steward, Call the laborers, and give them *their* hire, beginning from the last to the first.   LEV. 19:13

9 And when they came that *were hired* about the eleventh hour, they received every man a penny.

10 But when the first came, they supposed that they should have received more; and they likewise received every man a penny.

11 And when they had received *it*, they murmured against the goodman of the house,   complained - landowner

12 Saying, These last have wrought *but* one hour, and you have made them equal to us, which have borne the burden and heat of the day.   worked

13 But he answered one of them, and said, Friend, I do you no wrong: did not you agree with me for a penny?

14 Take *that* yours *is*, and go your way: I will give to this last, even as to you.

15 Is it not lawful for me to do what I will with my own? Is your eye evil, because I am good?   envious

16 So the last shall be first, and the first last: for many be called, but few chosen.

17 And Je'sus going up to Je-ru'sa-lem took the twelve disciples apart in the way, and said to them,

18 Behold, we go up to Je-ru'sa-lem; and the Son of man shall be betrayed to the chief priests and to the scribes, and they shall condemn Him to death,

19 And shall deliver Him to the Gen'tiles to mock, and to scourge, and to crucify *Him*: and the third day He shall rise again.   ridicule

20 Then came to Him the mother of Zeb'e-dee's children with her sons, worshipping *Him*, and desiring a certain thing of Him.   wanting

21 And He said to her, What will you? She says to Him, Grant that these my two sons may sit, the one on Your right hand, and the other on the left, in Your kingdom.   Permit

22 But Je'sus answered and said, You know not what you ask. Are you able to drink of the cup that I shall drink of, and to be baptized with the baptism that I am baptized with? They say to Him, We are able.

23 And He says to them, You shall drink indeed of My cup, and be baptized with the baptism that I am baptized with: but to sit on My right hand, and on My left, is not Mine to give, but *it shall be given to them* for whom it is prepared of My Father.

24 And when the ten heard *it*, they were moved with indignation against the two brethren.

25 But Je'sus called them *to Him*, and said, You know that the princes of the Gen'tiles exercise dominion over them, and they that are great exercise authority upon them.   chiefs - authority

26 But it shall not be so among you: but whosoever will be great among you, let him be your minister;   servant

27 And whosoever will be chief among you, let him be your servant:
28 Even as the Son of man came not to be ministered to, but to minister, and to give His life a ransom for many.
29 And as they departed from Jer'i-cho, a great multitude followed Him.
30 And, behold, two blind men sitting by the way side, when they heard that Je'sus passed by, cried out, saying, Have mercy on us, O Lord, *You* Son of Da'vid.
31 And the multitude rebuked them, because they should <u>hold their peace</u>: but they cried the more, saying, Have mercy on us, O Lord, *You* Son of Da'vid. be quiet
32 And Je'sus stood still, and called them, and said, What <u>will</u> you that I shall do <u>to</u> you? would - for
33 They say to Him, Lord, that our eyes may be opened.
34 So Je'sus had <u>compassion</u> *on them*, and touched their eyes: and immediately their eyes received sight, and they followed Him. pity

CHAPTER 21

AND when they drew near to Je-ru'sa-lem, and were come to Beth'-pha-ge, to the mount of Ol'ives, then sent Je'sus two disciples,
2 Saying to them, Go into the village opposite you, and immediately you shall find an ass tied, and a colt with her: loose *them*, and bring *them* to Me.
3 And if any *man* say anything to you, you shall say, The Lord has need of them; and immediately he will send them.
4 All this was done, that it might <u>be fulfilled</u> which was spoken by the prophet, saying, ZEC. 9:9 come true

5 Tell you the daughter of Zi'on, Behold, your King comes to you, <u>meek</u>, and sitting upon an ass, and a colt the foal of an ass. ISA. 62:11 ZEC. 9:9 humble

6 And the disciples went, and did as Je'sus commanded them,
7 And brought the ass, and the colt, and put on them their clothes, and they set *Him* thereon.
8 And a very great multitude spread their garments in the way; others cut down branches from the trees, and spread *them* in the <u>way</u>. road
9 And the multitudes that went before, and that followed, cried, saying, Ho-san'na to the son of Da'vid: Blessed *is* He that comes in the name of the Lord; <u>Ho-san'na</u> in the highest. PS. 118:26 i.e., Save, we pray
10 And when He was come into Je-ru'sa-lem, all the city was moved, saying, Who is this?
11 And the multitude said, This is Je'sus the prophet of Naz'a-reth of Gal'i-lee.
12 And Je'sus went into the temple of God, and cast out all them that sold and bought in the temple, and overthrew the tables of the moneychangers, and the seats of them that sold doves,
13 And said to them, It is written, My house shall be called the house of prayer; but you have made it a den of thieves. ISA. 56:7 JER. 7:11
14 And the blind and the lame came

to Him in the temple; and He healed them.

15 And when the chief priests and scribes saw the wonderful things that He did, and the children crying in the temple, and saying, Ho-san'na to the Son of Da'vid; they were <u>sore</u> displeased, _i.e., Save, we pray - very_

16 And said to Him, Hear You what these say? And Je'sus says to them, Yea; have you never read, Out of the mouth of babes and sucklings you have perfected praise? PS. 8:2

17 And He left them, and went out of the city into Beth'a-ny; and He lodged there.

18 Now in the morning as He returned into the city, He <u>hungered</u>. wanted food

19 And when He saw a fig tree in the way, He came to it, and found nothing thereon, but leaves only, and said to it, Let no fruit grow on you from now on for ever. And <u>presently</u> the fig tree withered away. JER. 8:13 at once

20 And when the disciples saw *it*, they marveled, saying, How soon is the fig tree withered away!

21 Je'sus answered and said to them, <u>Verily</u> I say to you, If you have faith, and doubt not, you shall not only do this *which is done* to the fig tree, but also if you shall say to this mountain, Be you removed, and be you cast into the sea; it shall be done. truly

22 And all things, whatsoever you shall ask in prayer, believing, you shall receive.

23 And when He was come into the temple, the chief priests and the elders of the people came to Him as He was teaching, and said, By what authority do You these things? and who gave You this authority?

24 And Je'sus answered and said to them, I also will ask you one thing, which if you tell Me, I in like wise will tell you by what authority I do these things.

25 The baptism of John, from where was it? from heaven, or of men? And they reasoned with themselves, saying, If we shall say, From heaven; He will say to us, Why did you not then believe him?

26 But if we shall say, Of men; we fear the people; for all <u>hold</u> John as a <u>prophet</u>. believe - God's representative

27 And they answered Je'sus, and said, We <u>cannot tell</u>. And He said to them, Neither tell I you by what authority I do these things. don't know

28 But what think you? A *certain* man had two sons; and he came to the first, and said, Son, go work to day in my vineyard.

29 He answered and said, I will not: but afterward he <u>repented</u>, and went. relented

30 And he came to the second, and said likewise. And he answered and said, I *go*, sir: and went not.

31 Whether of them two did the will of *his* father? They say to Him, The first. Je'sus says to them, <u>Verily</u> I say to you, That the <u>publicans</u> and the harlots go into the kingdom of God before you. truly - tax gatherers

32 For John came to you in the way of righteousness, and you believed

him not: but the <u>publicans</u> and the harlots believed him: and you, when you had seen *it*, <u>repented not</u> afterward, that you might believe him. tax gatherers - had no remorse

33 Hear another parable: There was a certain householder, which planted a vineyard, and hedged it round about, and digged a winepress in it, and built a tower, and <u>let it out</u> to <u>husbandmen</u>, and went into a far country: rented-leased - farmers

34 And when the <u>time</u> of the fruit drew near, he sent his servants to the husbandmen, that they might receive the fruits of it. harvest time

35 And the husbandmen took his servants, and beat one, and killed another, and stoned another.

36 Again, he sent other servants more than the first: and they did to them <u>likewise</u>. the same

37 But last of all he sent to them his son, saying, They will reverence my son.

38 But when the <u>husbandmen</u> saw the son, they said among themselves, This is the heir; come, let us kill him, and let us seize on his inheritance. vine growers

39 And they caught him, and cast *him* out of the vineyard, and slew *him*.

40 When the lord therefore of the vineyard comes, what will he do to those <u>husbandmen</u>?

41 They say to Him, He will miserably destroy those wicked men, and will let out *his* vineyard to other <u>husbandmen</u>, which shall <u>render</u> him the fruits in their seasons. pay

42 Je'sus says to them, Did you never read in the scriptures, The stone which the builders rejected, the same is become the head of the corner: this is the Lord's doing, and it is marvellous in our eyes? PS. 118:22 ISA. 28:16

43 Therefore say I to you, The kingdom of God shall be taken from you, and given to a <u>nation</u> bringing forth the fruits thereof. group

44 And whosoever shall fall on this stone shall be broken: but on whomsoever it shall fall, it will grind him to powder.

45 And when the chief priests and Phar'i-sees had heard His parables, they <u>perceived</u> that He spoke of them. understood

46 But when they sought to lay hands on Him, they feared the multitude, because they took Him for a prophet.

CHAPTER 22

AND Je'sus answered and spoke to them again by <u>parables</u>, and said, story examples

2 The kingdom of heaven is like to a certain king, which made a marriage for his son,

3 And sent forth his servants to call them that were <u>bidden</u> to the wedding: and they would not come.

4 Again, he sent forth other servants, saying, Tell them which are <u>bidden</u>, Behold, I have prepared my dinner: my oxen and *my* fatlings *are* killed, and all things *are* ready: come to the marriage.

5 But they <u>made light of</u> *it*, and went their ways, one to his farm, another to his merchandise: paid no attention

6 And the <u>remnant</u> took his servants,

and <u>entreated</u> *them* <u>spitefully</u>, and slew *them*.   rest - treated - roughly

7 But when the king heard *thereof*, he was angry: and he sent forth his armies, and destroyed those murderers, and burned up their city.

8 Then says he to his servants, The wedding is ready, but they which were bidden were not worthy.

9 Go you therefore into the highways, and as many as you shall find, bid to the marriage.

10 So those servants went out into the highways, and gathered together all as many as they found, both bad and good: and the wedding was <u>furnished</u> with guests.   filled

11 And when the king came in to see the guests, he saw there a man which had not on a wedding garment:

12 And he says to him, Friend, how came you in here not having a wedding garment? And he was speechless.

13 Then said the king to the servants, Bind him hand and foot, and take him away, and cast *him* into outer darkness; there shall be weeping and gnashing of teeth.

14 For many are called, but few *are* chosen.

15 Then went the Phar'i-sees, and took counsel how they might entangle Him in *His* talk.

16 And they sent out to Him their disciples with the He-ro'di-ans, say-ing, Master, we know that You are true, and teaches the way of God in truth,

neither care You for any *man*: for You <u>regard not</u> the person of men.   are not partial to

17 Tell us therefore, What think You? Is it <u>lawful</u> to give <u>tribute</u> to Cae'sar, or not?   proper - tax money

18 But Je'sus <u>perceived</u> their wickedness, and said, Why <u>tempt</u> you Me, *you* hypocrites?   knew - test

19 Show Me the <u>tribute</u> money. And they brought to Him a penny.

20 And He says to them, Whose *is* this image and <u>superscription</u>?   writing

21 They say to Him, Cae'sar's. Then says He to them, <u>Render</u> therefore to Cae'sar the things which are Cae'sar's; and to God the things that are God's.   give

22 When they had heard *these words*, they <u>marveled</u>, and left Him, and went their way.   were surprised

23 The same day came to Him the Sad'du-cees, which say that there is no resurrection, and asked Him,

24 Saying, Master, Mo'ses said, If a man die, having no children, his brother shall marry his wife, and raise up <u>seed</u> to his brother.   DEU. 25:5 descendants

25 Now there were with us seven brethren: and the first, when he had married a wife, <u>deceased</u>, and, having no <u>issue</u>, left his wife to his brother: dead - children

26 Likewise the second also, and the third, to the seventh.

27 And last of all the woman died also.

28 Therefore in the resurrection whose wife shall she be of the seven? for they all had her.

29 Je'sus answered and said to them, You <u>do err</u>, not <u>knowing</u> the scriptures, nor the power of God.

think wrong - understanding

30 For in the resurrection they neither marry, nor are given in marriage, but are as the angels of God in heaven.

31 But as <u>touching</u> the resurrection of the dead, have you not read that which was spoken to you by God, saying,

regarding

32 I am the God of A'bra-ham, and the God of I'saac, and the God of Ja'cob? God is not the God of the dead, but of the living.

EX. 3:6

33 And when the multitude heard *this*, they were astonished at His <u>doctrine</u>.

teaching

34 But when the Phar'i-sees had heard that He had put the Sad'du-cees to silence, they were gathered together.

35 Then one of them, *which was* a lawyer, asked *Him a question*, <u>tempting</u> Him, and saying,

testing

36 Master, which *is* the great commandment in the law?

37 Je'sus said to him, You shall love the Lord your God with all your heart, and with all your soul, and with all your mind.

DEU. 6:5

38 This is the first and <u>great</u> commandment.

important

39 And the second *is* like to it, You shall love your neighbor as yourself.

40 On these two commandments hang all the law and the prophets.

LEV. 19:18

41 While the Phar'i-sees were gathered together, Je'sus asked them,

42 Saying, What think you of Christ?

whose son is He? They say to Him, *The Son* of Da'vid.

43 He says to them, How then does Da'vid in spirit call Him Lord, saying,

44 The LORD said to My Lord, Sit You on My right hand, till I make Your enemies your footstool?

PS. 110:1

45 If Da'vid then call Him Lord, how is He his son?

46 And no man was able to answer Him a word, neither dare any *man* from that day forth ask Him any more *questions*.

CHAPTER 23

THEN spoke Je'sus to the multitude, and to His disciples,

2 Saying, The scribes and the Phar'i-sees sit in Mo'ses' seat:

3 All therefore whatsoever they bid you observe, *that* observe and do; but do not you <u>after their works</u>: for they say, and do not.

in the same way

4 For they bind heavy burdens and grievous to be borne, and lay *them* on men's shoulders; but they *themselves* will not move them with one of their fingers.

5 But all their works they do for to be seen of men: they make broad their <u>phylacteries</u>, and enlarge the borders of their garments,

boxes with old Testament scriptures

6 And love the uppermost rooms at feasts, and the chief seats in the synagogues,

7 And greetings in the markets, and to be called of men, <u>Rab'bi</u>, <u>Rab'bi</u>.

Teacher, Teacher

8 But be not you called <u>Rab'bi</u>: for One

is your Master, *even* Christ; and all you are brethren.

9 And call no *man* your father upon the earth: for One is your Father, which is in heaven.

10 Neither be you called <u>masters</u>: for One is your Master, *even* Christ. leaders

11 But he that is greatest among you shall be your servant.

12 And whosoever shall exalt himself shall be <u>abased</u>; and he that shall humble himself shall be exalted.   humbled

13 But woe to you, scribes and Phar'i-sees, <u>hypocrites</u>! for you <u>shut</u> up the kingdom of heaven against men: for you neither go in *yourselves*, neither allow you them that are entering to go in. insincere - close

14 Woe to you, scribes and Phar'i-sees, <u>hypocrites</u>! for you <u>devour</u> widows' houses, and for a pretence make long prayer: therefore you shall receive the greater <u>damnation</u>. take away - censure

15 Woe to you, scribes and Phar'i-sees, <u>hypocrites</u>! for you <u>compass</u> sea and land to make one <u>proselyte</u>, and when he is made, you make him twofold more the child of hell than yourselves.   travel - follower

16 Woe to you, you blind guides, which say, Whosoever shall swear by the temple, it is nothing; but whosoever shall swear by the gold of the temple, he is a <u>debtor</u>!   obligated

17 *You* fools and blind: for whether is greater, the gold, or the temple that <u>sanctifies</u> the gold?   sets apart

18 And, Whosoever shall swear by the altar, it is nothing; but whosoever

swears by the gift that is upon it, he is guilty.

19 *You* fools and blind: for whether *is* greater, the gift, or the altar that sanctifies the gift?

20 Whoso therefore shall <u>swear</u> by the altar, swears by it, and by all <u>things</u> thereon.   pledge - gifts

21 And whoso shall swear by the temple, swears by it, and by Him that dwelled therein.

22 And he that shall swear by heaven, swears by the throne of God, and by Him that sits thereon.

23 Woe to you, scribes and Phar'i-sees, <u>hypocrites</u>! for you pay tithe of mint and anise and cummin, and have omitted the weightier *matters* of the law, judgment, mercy, and faith: these ought you to have done, and not to leave the other undone.   insincere

24 *You* blind guides, which strain at a gnat, and swallow a camel.

25 Woe to you, scribes and Phar'i-sees, <u>hypocrites</u>! for you make clean the outside of the cup and of the platter, but within they are full of extortion and excess.

26 *You* blind Phar'i-see, cleanse first that *which* is within the cup and platter, that the outside of them may be clean also.

27 Woe to you, scribes and Phar'i-sees, <u>hypocrites</u>! for you are <u>like to</u> whited <u>sepulchers</u>, which indeed appear beautiful outward, but are within full of dead *men's* bones, and of all uncleanness.   insincere - same as - cave graves

28 Even so you also outwardly appear

righteous to men, but within you are full of hypocrisy and iniquity.

good - insincerity - sin

29 Woe to you, scribes and Phar'i-sees, hypocrites! because you build the tombs of the prophets, and garnish the sepulchers of the righteous,

adorn - cave graves

30 And say, If we had been in the days of our fathers, we would not have been partakers with them in the blood of the prophets. lived - ancestors - death

31 Wherefore you be witnesses to yourselves, that you are the children of them which killed the prophets.

32 Fill you up then the measure of your fathers.

33 *You* serpents, *you* generation of vipers, how can you escape the damnation of hell?

34 Wherefore, behold, I send to you prophets, and wise men, and scribes: and *some* of them you shall kill and crucify; and *some* of them shall you scourge in your synagogues, and persecute *them* from city to city: 2 CHRON. 36:16

35 That upon you may come all the righteous blood shed upon the earth, from the blood of righteous A'bel to the blood of Zech'a-ri'ah son of Bara-chi'as, whom you slew between the temple and the altar. GEN. 4:8

36 Verily I say to you, All these things shall come upon this generation. truly

37 O Je-ru'sa-lem, Je-ru'sa-lem, *you* that kill the prophets, and stone them which are sent to you, how often would I have gathered your children together, even as a hen gathers her chickens under *her* wings, and you would not!

38 Behold, your house is left to you desolate. PSA. 69:25 JER. 22:5 empty

39 For I say to you, You shall not see Me hereafter, till you shall say, Blessed *is* He that comes in the name of the Lord. PS 118:26

CHAPTER 24

AND Je'sus went out, and departed from the temple: and His disciples came to *Him* for to show Him the buildings of the temple.

2 And Je'sus said to them, See you not all these things? verily I say to you, There shall not be left here one stone upon another, that shall not be thrown down. truly

3 And as He sat upon the mount of Ol'ives, the disciples came to Him privately, saying, Tell us, when shall these things be? and what *shall be* the sign of Your coming, and of the end of the world? LUKE 21

4 And Je'sus answered and said to them, Take heed that no man deceive you.

5 For many shall come in My name, saying, I am Christ; and shall deceive many.

6 And you shall hear of wars and rumors of wars: see that you be not troubled: for all *these things* must come to pass, but the end is not yet.

7 For nation shall rise against nation, and kingdom against kingdom: and there shall be famines, and pestilences, and earthquakes, in divers places. REV. 8 various

8 All these *are* the beginning of sorrows.

9 Then shall they deliver you up to be afflicted, and shall kill you: and you shall be hated of all nations for My name's sake.

10 And then shall many be <u>offended</u>, and shall betray one another, and shall <u>hate</u> one another.   affected - not trust

11 And many false prophets shall rise, and shall deceive many.

12 And because <u>iniquity</u> shall abound, the love of many shall <u>wax</u> cold.

sin - become

13 But he that shall endure to the end, the same shall be saved.

14 And this gospel of the kingdom shall be preached in all the world for a witness to all nations; and then shall the end come.

15 When you therefore shall see the <u>abomination</u> of desolation, spoken of by Dan'iel the prophet, stand in the holy place, (whoso reads, let him understand:)   DAN. 9:7 DAN. 11:31 evil ways

16 Then let them which be in Ju-dae'a flee into the mountains:

17 Let him which is on the house-top not come down to take any thing out of his house:

18 Neither let him which is in the field return back to take his clothes.

19 And woe to them that are with child, and to them that <u>give suck</u> in those days!   nurse

20 But pray you that your flight be not in the winter, neither on the <u>sab-bath day</u>:   rest day

21 For then shall be great <u>tribulation</u>, such as was not since the beginning of the world to this time, no, nor ever shall be.   DAN. 12:1 trials

22 And except those days should be shortened, there should no flesh be saved: but for the <u>elect's</u> sake those days shall be shortened.   chosen's

23 Then if any man shall say to you, Lo, here *is* Christ, or there; believe *it* not.

24 For there shall arise false Christs, and false prophets, and shall show great signs and wonders; insomuch that, if *it were* possible, they shall deceive the very elect.   DEU. 13:1

25 Behold, I have told you before.

26 Wherefore if they shall say to you, Behold, He is in the desert; go not forth: behold, *He is* in the <u>secret cham-bers</u>; believe *it* not.   inner rooms

27 For as the lightning comes out of the east, and shines even to the west; so shall also the coming of the Son of man be.

28 For wheresoever the carcase is, there will the eagles be gathered together.

29 Immediately after the <u>tribulation</u> of those days shall the sun be darkened, and the moon shall not give her light, and the stars shall fall from heaven, and the powers of the heavens shall be shaken: ISA. 13:10 JOEL 2:10 trials

30 And then shall appear the sign of the Son of man in heaven: and then shall all the tribes of the earth mourn, and they shall see the Son of man coming in the clouds of heaven with power and great glory.   DAN. 7:13

31 And He shall send His <u>angels</u> with a great sound of a trumpet, and they

shall gather together His elect from the four winds, from one end of heaven to the other. _{messengers}

32 Now learn a parable of the fig tree; When its branch is yet tender, and puts forth leaves, you know that summer *is* near:

33 So likewise you, when you shall see all these things, know that it is near, *even* at the doors. _{He}

34 <u>Verily</u> I say to you, This generation shall not pass, till all these things be fulfilled. _{truly}

35 Heaven and earth shall pass away, but My words shall not pass away.

36 But of that day and hour knows no *man*, no, not the <u>angels</u> of heaven, but My Father only. _{ZEC. 14:7 messengers}

37 But as the days of No'ah *were*, so shall also the coming of the Son of man be.

38 For as in the days that were before the flood they were eating and drinking, marrying and giving in marriage, until the day that No'ah entered into the ark, _{GEN. 7:7}

39 And <u>knew</u> not until the flood came, and took them all away; so shall also the coming of the Son of man be. _{understood}

40 Then shall two be in the field; the one shall be taken, and the other left.

41 Two *women shall be* grinding at the mill; the one shall be taken, and the other left.

42 Watch therefore: for you know not what hour your Lord do come.

43 But know this, that if the goodman of the house had known in what watch the thief would come, he would have watched, and would not have allowed his house to be broken <u>up</u>. _{into}

44 Therefore be you also ready: for in such an hour as you think not the Son of man comes.

45 Who then is a faithful and wise servant, whom his lord has made ruler over his household, to give them meat in due season?

46 <u>Blessed</u> *is* that servant, whom his lord when he comes shall find so doing. _{Happy}

47 <u>Verily</u> I say to you, That he shall make him ruler over all his goods. _{Truly}

48 But and if that evil servant shall say in his heart, My lord delays his coming;

49 And shall begin to <u>smite</u> *his* fellowservants, and to eat and drink with the drunken; _{beat}

50 The lord of that servant shall come in a day when he looks not for *him*, and in an hour that he is not aware of,

51 And shall cut him <u>asunder</u>, and appoint *him* his portion with the <u>hypocrites</u>: there shall be weeping and gnashing of teeth. _{into pieces - insincere}

CHAPTER 25

THEN shall the kingdom of heaven be likened to ten virgins, which took their lamps, and went forth to meet the bridegroom.

2 And five of them were wise, and five *were* foolish.

3 They that *were* foolish took their lamps, and took no oil with them:

4 But the wise took oil in their <u>vessels</u> with their lamps. _{flasks}

5 While the bridegroom <u>tarried</u>, they all slumbered and slept.   _{delayed}

6 And at midnight there was a cry made, Behold, the bridegroom comes; go you out to meet him.

7 Then all those virgins arose, and trimmed their lamps.   REV. 8

8 And the foolish said to the wise, Give us of your oil; for our lamps are gone out.

9 But the wise answered, saying, *Not so*; less there be not enough for us and you: but go you rather to them that sell, and buy for yourselves.

10 And while they went to buy, the bridegroom came; and they that were ready went in with him to the <u>marriage</u>: and the door was shut.   _{marriage feast}

11 Afterward came also the other virgins, saying, lord, lord, open to us.

12 But he answered and said, <u>Verily</u> I say to you, I know you not.   _{Truly}

13 Watch therefore, for you know neither the day nor the hour wherein the Son of Man comes.

14 For *the kingdom of heaven is* as a man travelling into a far country, *who* called his own servants, and delivered to them his goods.

15 And to one he gave five talents, to another two, and to another one; to every man according to his <u>several</u> ability; and immediately took his journey.   _{own}

16 Then he that had received the five talents went and traded with the same, and <u>made</u> *them* other five talents. _{gained}

17 And likewise he that *had received* two, he also gained other two.

18 But he that had received one went and dug in the earth, and hid his <u>lord's</u> money.   _{master's}

19 After a long time the <u>lord</u> of those servants comes, and <u>reckons</u> with them.   _{settled}

20 And so he that had received five talents came and brought other five talents, saying, lord, you delivered to me five talents: behold, I have gained beside them five talents more.

21 His lord said to him, Well done, *you* good and faithful servant: you have been faithful over a few things, I will make you ruler over many things: enter you into the joy of your lord.

22 He also that had received two talents came and said, lord, you delivered to me two talents: behold, I have gained two other talents beside them.

23 His lord said to him, Well done, good and faithful servant; you have been faithful over a few things, I will make you ruler over many things: enter you into the joy of your lord.

24 Then he which had received the one talent came and said, lord, I knew you that you are an hard man, reaping where you have not sown, and gathering where you have not spread:

25 And I was afraid, and went and hid your talent in the earth: lo, *there* you have *that is* yours.

26 His lord answered and said to him, *you* wicked and <u>slothful</u> servant, you knew that I reap where I sowed not, and gather where I have not scattered.   _{lazy}

27 You ought therefore to have put my money to the <u>exchangers,</u> and

then at my coming I should have received mine own with <u>usury</u>.

bankers - interest

28 Take therefore the <u>talent</u> from him, and give *it* to him which has ten <u>talents</u>.

coin

29 For to every one that has shall be given, and he shall have abundance: but from him that has not shall be taken away even that which he has.

30 And cast you the unprofitable servant into outer darkness: there shall be weeping and gnashing of teeth.

31 When the Son of man shall come in His glory, and all the holy angels with Him, then shall He sit upon the throne of His glory:

32 And before Him shall be gathered all nations: and He shall separate them one from another, as a shepherd divides *his* sheep from the goats:

EZE. 34:17

33 And He shall set the <u>sheep</u> on His right hand, but the <u>goats</u> on the left.

believers - unbelievers

34 Then shall the King say to them on His right hand, Come, you blessed of My Father, inherit the kingdom prepared for you from the foundation of the world:

35 For I was an hungry, and you gave Me <u>meat</u>: I was thirsty, and you gave Me drink: I was a stranger, and you took Me in:

food

36 Naked, and you clothed Me: I was sick, and you visited Me: I was in prison, and you came to Me.

37 Then shall the righteous answer Him, saying, Lord, when saw we You an hungry, and fed *You*? or thirsty, and gave *You* drink?

38 When saw we You a stranger, and took *You* in? or naked, and clothed *You*?

39 Or when saw we You sick, or in prison, and came to You?

40 And the King shall answer and say to them, <u>Verily</u> I say to you, Inasmuch as you have done *it* to one of the least of these My brethren, you have done *it* to Me.

PROV. 19:17 Truly

41 Then shall He say also to them on the left hand, Depart from Me, you cursed, into everlasting <u>fire</u>, prepared for the <u>devil</u> and his angels: PS. 6:8 hell - Satan

42 For I was an hungry, and you gave Me no <u>meat</u>: I was thirsty, and you gave Me no drink:

food

43 I was a stranger, and you took Me not in: naked, and you clothed Me not: sick, and in prison, and you visited Me not.

44 Then shall they also answer Him, saying, Lord, when saw we You an hungry, or <u>athirst</u>, or a stranger, or naked, or sick, or in prison, and did not <u>minister to</u> You?

thirsty - care for

45 Then shall He answer them, saying, <u>Verily</u> I say to you, Inasmuch as you did *it* not to one of the least of these, you did *it* not to Me.

Truly

46 And these shall go away into everlasting punishment: but the righteous into life eternal.

DAN. 12:2

CHAPTER 26

AND it came to pass, when Je'sus had finished all these sayings, He said to His disciples,

2 You know that after two days is *the feast of* the passover, and the Son of man is betrayed to be crucified.

3 Then assembled together the chief priests, and the scribes, and the elders of the people, to the palace of the high priest, who was called Ca'ia-phas,

4 And consulted that they might take Je'sus by underlined subtilty, and kill *Him*.   stealth

5 But they said, Not on the feast *day*, less there be an uproar among the people.

6 Now when Je'sus was in Beth'a-ny, in the house of Si'mon the leper,

7 There came to Him a woman having an alabaster box of very precious ointment, and poured it on His head, as He sat *at meat*.   costly - eating

8 But when His disciples saw *it*, they had indignation, saying, To what purpose *is* this waste?   were indignant

9 For this ointment might have been sold for much, and given to the poor.

10 When Je'sus understood *it*, He said to them, Why trouble you the woman? for she has wrought a good work upon Me.   worked

11 For you have the poor always with you; but Me you have not always.   DEU. 15:11

12 For in that she has poured this ointment on My body, she did *it* for My burial.

13 Verily I say to you, Wheresoever this gospel shall be preached in the whole world, *there* shall also this, that this woman has done, be told for a memorial of her.   Truly

14 Then one of the twelve, called Ju'das Is-car'i-ot, went to the chief priests,

15 And said *to them*, What will you give me, and I will deliver Him to you? And they covenanted with him for thirty pieces of silver.   EX. 21:32 agreed

16 And from that time he sought opportunity to betray Him.

17 Now the first *day* of the *feast of* unleavened bread the disciples came to Je'sus, saying to Him, Where will You that we prepare for You to eat the passover?   without yeast

18 And He said, Go into the city to such a man, and say to him, The Master says, My time is at hand; I will keep the passover at your house with My disciples.

19 And the disciples did as Je'sus had appointed them; and they made ready the passover.   prepared

20 Now when the even was come, He sat down with the twelve.

21 And as they did eat, He said, Verily I say to you, that one of you shall betray Me.   ZEC. 13:7 truly

22 And they were exceeding sorrowful, and began every one of them to say to Him, Lord, is it I?   very

23 And He answered and said, He that dips *his* hand with Me in the dish, the same shall betray Me.

24 The Son of Man goes as it is written of Him: but woe to that man by whom the Son of Man is betrayed! it had been good for that man if he had not been born.

25 Then Ju'das, which betrayed Him, answered and said, Master, is it I? He said to him, you have said.

26 And as they were eating, Je'sus took bread, and blessed *it*, and broke *it*,

and gave *it* to the disciples, and said, Take, eat; this is My body.

gave thanks to God for

27 And He took the cup, and gave thanks, and gave *it* to them, saying, Drink you all of it;

28 For this is My blood of the new testament, which is shed for many for the <u>remission</u> of sins.   EX. 24:8 *forgiveness*

29 But I say to you, I will not drink hereafter of this fruit of the vine, until that day when I drink it new with you in My Father's kingdom.

30 And when they had sung an hymn, they went out into the mount of Ol'ives.

31 Then says Je'sus to them, All you shall be <u>offended</u> because of Me this night: for it is written, I will smite the shepherd, and the <u>sheep</u> of the flock shall be scattered abroad.

ZEC. 13:7 *upset - believers*

32 But after I am risen again, I will go before you into Gal'i-lee.

33 Pe'ter answered and said to Him, Though all *men* shall be <u>offended</u> because of You, *yet* will I never be <u>offended</u>.   *fallen away*

34 Je'sus said to him, <u>Verily</u> I say to you, That this night, before the cock crow, you shall deny Me thrice.   *truly*

35 Pe'ter said to Him, Though I should die with You, yet will I not deny You. Likewise also said all the disciples.

36 Then comes Je'sus with them to a place called Geth-sem'a-ne, and says to the disciples, Sit you here, while I go and pray yonder.

37 And he took with Him Pe'ter and the two sons of Zeb'e-dee, and began to be sorrowful and very <u>heavy</u>.   *distressed*

38 Then says He to them, My soul is exceeding sorrowful, even to death: tarry you here, and watch with Me.

39 And He went a little farther, and fell on His face, and prayed, saying, O My Father, if it be possible, let this cup pass from Me: nevertheless not as I will, but as You *will*.

40 And He comes to the disciples, and finds them asleep, and says to Pe'ter, What, could you not watch with Me one hour?

41 Watch and pray, that you enter not into temptation: the spirit indeed *is* willing, but the flesh *is* weak.

42 He went away again the second time, and prayed, saying, O My Father, if this cup may not pass away from Me , except I drink it, Your will be done.

43 And He came and found them asleep again: for their eyes were <u>heavy</u>.   *sleepy*

44 And He left them, and went away again, and prayed the third time, saying the same words.

45 Then comes He to His disciples, and says to them, Sleep on now, and take *your* rest: behold, the hour is at hand, and the Son of man is betrayed into the hands of sinners.

46 Rise, let us be going: behold, he is at hand that do betray Me.

47 And while He yet spoke, lo, Ju'das, one of the twelve, came, and with him a great multitude with swords and <u>staves</u>, from the chief priests and elders of the people.   *poles*

48 Now he that betrayed Him gave them a sign, saying, Whomsoever I shall kiss, that same is He: hold Him <u>fast</u>.   firmly

49 And immediately he came to Je'sus, and said, Hail, master; and kissed Him.

50 And Je'sus said to him, Friend, wherefore are you come? Then came they, and laid hands on Jesus, and took Him.

51 And, behold, one of them which were with Je'sus stretched out *his* hand, and drew his sword, and struck a servant of the high priest's, and smote off his ear.

52 Then said Je'sus to him, Put up again your sword into its place: for all they that take the sword shall perish with the sword.   GEN. 9:6

53 Think you that I cannot now pray to My Father, and He shall presently give Me more than <u>twelve legions</u> of <u>angels</u>?   72,000 - messengers

54 But how then shall the scriptures be fulfilled, that thus it must be?   DAN. 7:13

55 In that same hour said Je'sus to the multitudes, Are you come out as against a thief with swords and <u>staves</u> for to take Me? I sat daily with you teaching in the temple, and you laid no hold on Me.   poles

56 But all this was done, that the scriptures of the prophets might be fulfilled. Then all the disciples <u>forsook</u> Him, and fled.   left

57 And they that had laid hold on Je'sus led Him away to Ca'ia-phas the high priest, where the scribes and the elders were assembled.

58 But Pe'ter followed Him afar off to the high priest's palace, and went in, and sat with the servants, to see the end.

59 Now the chief priests, and elders, and all the council, sought false <u>witness</u> against Je'sus, to put Him to death;   testimony

60 But found none: yea, though many false witnesses came, *yet* found they none. At the last came two false witnesses,   PSA. 27:12

61 And said, This *fellow* said, I am able to destroy the temple of God, and to build it in three days.

62 And the high priest arose, and said to Him, Answer You nothing? what *is it which* these witness against You?

63 But Je'sus held His peace. And the high priest answered and said to Him, I <u>adjure</u> You by the living God, that You tell us whether You be the Christ, the Son of God.   command

64 Je'sus says to him, You have said: nevertheless I say to you, Hereafter shall you see the Son of man sitting on the right hand of power, and coming in the clouds of heaven.   DAN. 7:13

65 Then the high priest <u>rent</u> his clothes, saying, He has spoken <u>blasphemy</u>; what further need have we of witnesses? behold, now you have heard His <u>blasphemy</u>.LEV. 24:16   tore - evil things - wrong words

66 What think you? They answered and said, He is guilty of death.

67 Then did they spit in His face, and buffeted Him; and others <u>smote</u> *Him* with the palms of their hands,   struck

68 Saying, <u>Prophesy</u> to us, You Christ, Who is he that <u>smote</u> You?

Speak - struck

69 Now Pe'ter sat outside in the palace: and a <u>damsel</u> came to him, saying, You also were with Je'sus of Gal'i-lee.

young girl

70 But he denied before *them* all, saying, I know not what you say.

71 And when he was gone out into the porch, another *maid* saw him, and said to them that were there, This *fellow* was also with Je'sus of Naz'a-reth.

72 And again he denied with an oath, I do not know the man.

73 And after a while came to *him* they that stood by, and said to Pe'ter, Surely you also are *one* of them; for your speech <u>bewray</u> you.

identifies

74 Then began he to curse and to swear, *saying*, I know not the man. And immediately the cock crew.

75 And Pe'ter remembered the word of Je'sus, which said to him, Before the cock crow, you shall deny Me thrice. And he went out, and wept bitterly.

CHAPTER 27

WHEN the morning was come, all the chief priests and elders of the people <u>took counsel</u> against Je'sus to put Him to death:

PSA. 31:13 talked together

2 And when they had bound Him, they led *Him* away, and delivered Him to Pon'ti-us Pi'late the governor.

3 Then Ju'das, which had betrayed Him, when he saw that He was condemned, <u>repented himself</u>, and brought again the thirty pieces of silver to the chief priests and elders,

felt remorse

4 Saying, I have sinned in that I have betrayed the innocent blood. And they said, What *is that* to us? see you *to that*.

5 And he <u>cast</u> down the pieces of silver in the temple, and departed, and went and hanged himself.

threw

6 And the chief priests took the silver pieces, and said, It is not <u>lawful</u> for to put them into the treasury, because it is the <u>price of blood</u>.

DEU. 23:18 right - blood money

7 And they <u>took counsel</u>, and bought with <u>them</u> the potter's field, to bury strangers in.

talked together - i.e., the money

8 Wherefore that field was called, The field of blood, to this day.

9 Then was fulfilled that which was spoken by Jeremiah the prophet, saying, And they took the thirty pieces of silver, the price of him that was valued, whom they of the children of Is'ra-el did value;

ZEC. 11:12-13

10 And gave them for the potter's field, as the Lord appointed me.

11 And Je'sus stood before the governor: and the governor asked Him, saying, Are you the King of the Jews? And Je'sus said to him, You say.

12 And when He was accused of the chief priests and elders, He answered nothing.

ISA. 53:7

13 Then said Pi'late to Him, Hear You not how many things they witness against You?

14 And He answered him to never a word; insomuch that the governor <u>marveled greatly</u>.

was amazed

15 Now at *that* feast the governor was <u>wont</u> to release to the people a prisoner, whom they would. _{accustomed}

16 And they had then a <u>notable</u> prisoner, called Ba-rab'bas.   _{notorious}

17 Therefore when they were gathered together, Pi'late said to them, Whom will you that I release to you? Ba-rab'bas, or Je'sus which is called Christ?

18 For he knew that for envy they had <u>delivered</u> Him.   _{secured}

19 When he was set down on the judgment seat, his wife sent to him, saying, Have you nothing to do with that just man: for I have suffered many things this day in a dream because of Him.

20 But the chief priests and elders persuaded the multitude that they should ask Ba-rab'bas, and destroy Je'sus.

21 The governor answered and said to them, Whether of the two will you that I release to you? They said, Ba-rab'bas.

22 Pi'late says to them, What shall I do then with Je'sus which is called Christ? *They* all say to him, Let Him be <u>crucified</u>.   _{nailed to a cross}

23 And the governor said, Why, what evil has He done? But they cried out the more, saying, Let Him be crucified.

24 When Pi'late saw that he could prevail nothing, but *that* rather a <u>tumult</u> was made, he took water, and washed *his* hands before the multitude, saying, I am innocent of the blood of this just person: see you *to it*.   _{PS. 26:6 riot}

25 Then answered all the people, and said, His blood *be* on us, and on our children.   _{JOS. 2:19}

26 Then released he Ba-rab'bas to them: and when he had <u>scourged</u> Je'sus, he delivered *Him* to be crucified.   _{ISA. 50:6 flogged}

27 Then the soldiers of the governor took Je'sus into the common hall, and gathered to Him the whole band *of soldiers*.

28 And they stripped Him, and put on Him a scarlet robe.

29 And when they had platted a crown of thorns, they put *it* upon His head, and a reed in His right hand: and they bowed the knee before Him, and mocked Him, saying, Hail, King of the Jews!

30 And they spit upon Him, and took the reed, and <u>smote</u> Him on the head.   _{struck}

31 And after that they had <u>mocked</u> Him, they took the robe off from Him, and put His own <u>raiment</u> on Him, and led Him away to crucify *Him*.   _{ridiculed - clothes}

32 And as they came out, they found a man of Cy-re'ne, Si'mon by name: him they compelled to bear His cross.

33 And when they were come to a place called Gol'go-tha, that is to say, a place of a skull,

34 They gave Him <u>vinegar</u> to drink mingled with gall: and when He had tasted *thereof*, He would not drink.   _{wine}

35 And they crucified Him, and <u>parted</u> His garments, casting lots: that it might be fulfilled which was spoken by the prophet, They parted My gar-

ments among them, and upon my vesture did they cast lots. Ps. 22:18 divided

36 And sitting down they watched Him there;

37 And set up over His head His accusation written, THIS IS JE'SUS THE KING OF THE JEWS.

38 Then were there two thieves crucified with Him, one on the right hand, and another on the left.

39 And they that passed by reviled Him, wagging their heads, PSA. 109:25 ridiculed

40 And saying, You that destroys the temple, and builds it in three days, save Yourself. If You be the Son of God, come down from the cross.

41 Likewise also the chief priests mocking Him, with the scribes and elders, said, taunting

42 He saved others; Himself He cannot save. If He be the King of Is'rael, let Him now come down from the cross, and we will believe Him. Jesus

43 He trusted in God; let Him deliver Him now, if He will have Him: for He said, I am the Son of God. PSA. 22:8

44 The thieves also, which were crucified with Him, cast the same in His teeth. insult

45 Now from the sixth hour there was darkness over all the land to the ninth hour. 12:00 Noon - 3:00 PM

46 And about the ninth hour Je'sus cried with a loud voice, saying, E'li, E'li, la'ma sa-bach-tha'ni? that is to say, My God, My God, why have You forsaken Me? PS. 22:1 PS 22:11

47 Some of them that stood there, when they heard that, said, This man calls for Elijah.

48 And immediately one of them ran, and took a sponge, and filled it with vinegar, and put it on a reed, and gave Him to drink. PS. 69:21

49 The rest said, Let be, let us see whether Elijah will come to save Him.

50 Je'sus, when He had cried again with a loud voice, yielded up the ghost.

51 And, behold, the veil of the temple was rent in two from the top to the bottom; and the earth did quake, and the rocks rent; torn - split

52 And the graves were opened; and many bodies of the saints which slept arose, were dead

53 And came out of the graves after His resurrection, and went into the holy city, and appeared to many. rising

54 Now when the centurion, and they that were with him, watching Je'sus, saw the earthquake, and those things that were done, they feared greatly, saying, Truly this was the Son of God. were terrified

55 And many women were there beholding afar off, which followed Je'sus from Gal'i-lee, ministering to Him:

56 Among which was Ma'ry Mag-da-le'ne, and Ma'ry the mother of James and Jo'ses, and the mother of Zeb'e-dee's children.

57 When the even was come, there came a rich man of Ar-i-ma-thae'a, named Jo'seph, who also himself was Je'sus' disciple: ISA. 53:9

58 He went to Pi'late, and begged the body of Je'sus. Then Pi'late commanded the body to be delivered. asked for

59 And when Jo'seph had taken the

body, he wrapped it in a clean linen cloth,

60 And laid it in his own new tomb, which he had <u>hewn</u> out in the rock: and he rolled a great stone to the door of the <u>sepulcher</u>, and departed.   cut - grave

61 And there was Ma'ry Mag-da-le'ne, and the other Ma'ry, sitting opposite the <u>sepulcher</u>.

62 Now the next day, that followed the day of the preparation, the chief priests and Phar'i-sees came to-gether to Pi'late,

63 Saying, Sir, we remember that that <u>deceiver</u> said, while He was yet alive, After three days I will rise again.   impostor

64 Command therefore that the <u>sep-ulcher</u> be made <u>sure</u> until the third day, less His disciples come by night, and steal Him away, and say to the people, He is risen from the dead: so the last error shall be worse than the first.   secure

65 Pi'late said to them, You have a <u>watch</u>: go your way, make *it* as sure as you can.   guard

66 So they went, and made the <u>sep-ulcher sure</u>, <u>sealing</u> the stone, and set-ting a <u>watch</u>.   grave - securing

CHAPTER 28

IN the end of the <u>sabbath</u>, as it began to dawn toward the first *day* of the week, came Ma'ry Mag-da-le'ne and the other Ma'ry to see the sepulcher.   rest day

2 And, behold, there was a great earth-quake: for the <u>angel</u> of the Lord de-scended from heaven, and came and rolled back the stone from the door, and sat upon it.   messenger

3 His countenance was like light-ning, and his <u>raiment</u> white as snow: garment

4 And for fear of him the keepers did shake, and became as dead *men*.

5 And the <u>angel</u> answered and said to the women, Fear not you: for I know that you seek Je'sus, which was crucified.   messenger

6 He is not here: for He is risen, as He said. Come, see the place where the Lord lay.

7 And go quickly, and tell His dis-ciples that He is risen from the dead; and, behold, He goes before you into Gal'i-lee; there shall you see Him: lo, I have told you.

8 And they departed quickly from the <u>sepulcher</u> with <u>fear</u> and great joy; and did run to bring His disciples word.   grave - reverence

9 And as they went to tell His dis-ciples, behold, Je'sus met them, saying, All hail. And they came and held Him by the feet, and worshiped Him.

10 Then said Je'sus to them, Be not afraid: go tell My brethren that they go into Gal'i-lee, and there shall they see Me.

11 Now when they were going, be-hold, some of the <u>watch</u> came into the city, and showed to the chief priests all the things that were done.   guard

12 And when they were assembled with the elders, and had taken coun-sel, they gave large money to the sol-diers,

13 Saying, Say you, His disciples came by night, and stole Him *away* while we slept.

14 And if this come to the governor's ears, we will persuade him, and <u>secure</u> you. protect

15 So they took the money, and did as they were taught: and this saying is commonly <u>reported</u> among the Jews until this day. believed

16 Then the eleven disciples went away into Gal'i-lee, into a mountain where Je'sus had appointed them.

17 And when they saw Him, they worshiped Him: but some doubted.

18 And Je'sus came and spoke to them, saying, All power is given to Me in heaven and in earth.

19 Go you therefore, and <u>teach</u> all nations, baptizing them in the name of the Father, and of the Son, and of the Ho'ly Ghost: tell

20 Teaching them to observe all things whatsoever I have commanded you: and, lo, I am with you always, *even* to the end of the <u>world</u>. Amen.   JER. 26:2   age

MARK

OUTLINE

Friday: Jesus in Gethsemane 14.26–52
               The Jewish Trials 14.53–72
               The Roman Trial 15.1–20
               The Crucifixion and Burial 15.21–47

THE RESURRECTION 16.1–20

SURVEY

The Second Gospel is very distinctive in character. The personality of Peter is reflected on almost every page. Like him it is quick in movement, active, impulsive. *Rapidity of action* is its main characteristic. Swiftly the narrative moves from one event to another. The Gospel of Mark has well been called a moving picture of the ministry of Jesus.

Vividness of detail is another outstanding characteristic. Though Mark is the shortest of the Four Gospels, it often incorporates vivid details not to be found in Matthew's or Luke's account of the same event. Considerable attention is given to the looks and gestures of Jesus.

A third prominent characteristic is *picturesqueness of description*. In Mark's account of the feeding of the five thousand, he tells us that the people sat down in "ranks" on the green grass. The Greek word means "flower beds" and reflects the beautiful sight of groups of people in bright red and oriental garments sitting on the green grass of the hillside.

Mark's Gospel is pre pre-eminently the Gospel of action. It includes only one long discourse of Jesus (the Olivet Discourse). But majors on His deeds. It gives us the works, rather than the words, of Christ. Mark records eighteen of the miracles of Jesus but only four of His parables.

This emphasis on action is appropriate in a Gospel written probably at Rome and primarily for the Romans. Mark uses Latinisms and has fewer references to the Old Testament than the others gospel writers. He explains Jewish customs for his Roman readers. He does not even use the word "law," which occurs eight times in Matthew, nine times in Luke, and fifteen times in John.

Because he is writing for Romans, he omits all reference to Jesus' genealogy and childhood. The Romans were more interested in power than pedigree. So here we find Jesus presented as the great Conqueror—of storm, demons, disease and death. He is the *Servant of the Lord* (cf. Isaiah): first the *conquering* Servant, then the *suffering* Servant, and finally the *triumphant* servant in His resurrection.

Though Mark's Gospel is primarily historical, it also has strong theological emphasis. The first verse strikes the keynote: "The gospel of Jesus Christ, the Son of God." Over and over again the deity of Jesus is underscored, either explicitly or implicitly. He is the Son of Man, the Messiah, the One for Whom long centuries have waited. In one of the strongest theological passages of the Synoptic Gospels, Jesus is quoted as declaring that the Son of Man came to "give his life a ransom for may" (10:45). As the first verse of the book indicates, this primarily the *Gospel* of Jesus Christ, the good news of salvation through His anointing death.

AUTHOR

The Early Church is practically unanimous in ascribing the Second Gospel to Mark, the cousin of Barnabas and associate of Paul and Peter. Strong tradition also supports the assertion that in this Gospel we have the preaching of Peter, who calls Mark "my son" (1 P 5.13). The characteristics of this Gospel fit well the personality of Peter. Most scholars hold that this is the earliest of the Four Gospels. It can safely be dated between A.D. 50 and A.D. 70.

R.E.

THE GOSPEL ACCORDING TO
MARK

Mark presents Jesus
as the perfect
Servant of God the Father

CHAPTER 1

THE beginning of the gospel of Je'sus Christ, the Son of God;
2 As it is written in the prophets, Behold, I send My messenger before your face, which shall prepare your way before you. MAL. 3:1
3 The voice of one crying in the wilderness, Prepare you the way of the Lord, make His paths straight. ISA. 40:3
4 John did baptize in the wilderness, and preach the baptism of repentance for the remission of sins.
5 And there went out to him all the land of Ju-dae'a, and they of Je-ru'sa-lem, and were all baptized of him in the river of Jor'dan, confessing their sins.
6 And John was clothed with camel's hair, and with a girdle of a skin about his loins; and he did eat locusts and wild honey; waist
7 And preached, saying, There comes One mightier than I after me, the latchet of whose shoes I am not worthy to stoop down and unloose. throng
8 I indeed have baptized you with water: but He shall baptize you with the Ho'ly Ghost. Spirit
9 And it came to pass in those days, that Je'sus came from Naz'a-reth of Gal'i-lee, and was baptized of John in Jor'dan.
10 And immediately coming up out of the water, he saw the heavens opened, and the Spirit like a dove descending upon Him:
11 And there came a voice from heaven, saying, You are My beloved Son, in whom I am well pleased. ISA. 42:1
12 And immediately the Spirit drives Him into the wilderness. sent
13 And He was there in the wilderness forty days, tempted of Sa'tan; and was with the wild beasts; and the angels ministered to Him. tested - attended
14 Now after that John was put in prison, Je'sus came into Gal'i-lee, preaching the gospel of the kingdom of God,
15 And saying, The time is fulfilled, and the kingdom of God is at hand: repent you, and believe the gospel.
16 Now as He walked by the sea of Gal'i-lee, He saw Si'mon and Andrew his brother casting a net into the sea: for they were fishers. fishermen
17 And Je'sus said to them, Come you after Me, and I will make you to become fishers of men.
18 And immediately they forsook their nets, and followed Him. left
19 And when He had gone a little farther from there, he saw James the son of Zeb'e-dee, and John his brother, who also were in the ship mending their nets.
20 And immediately He called them: and they left their father Zeb'e-dee in the ship with the hired servants, and went after Him. with

21 And they went into Ca-per'na-um; and immediately on the sabbath day He entered into the synagogue, and taught.

22 And they were astonished at His <u>doctrine</u>: for He taught them as one that had authority, and not as the scribes. _{teaching}

23 And there was in their synagogue a man with an <u>unclean</u> spirit; and he cried out, _{evil}

24 Saying, Let *us* alone; what have we to do with You, You Je'sus of Naz'a-reth? are You come to destroy us? I know You who You are, the Holy One of God.

25 And Je'sus <u>rebuked</u> him, saying, Hold your peace, and come out of him. _{admonished}

26 And when the unclean spirit had <u>torn</u> him, and cried with a loud voice, he came out of him. _{violently shook}

27 And they were all amazed, insomuch that they questioned among themselves, saying, What thing is this? what new <u>doctrine</u> *is* this? for with authority commands He even the unclean spirits, and they do obey Him. _{teaching}

28 And immediately His <u>fame</u> spread abroad throughout all the region round about Gal'i-lee. _{news}

29 And forthwith, when they were come out of the synagogue, they entered into the house of Si'mon and Andrew, with James and John.

30 But Si'mon's wife's mother lay sick of a fever, and <u>anon</u> they tell Him of her. _{immediately}

31 And He came and took her by the hand, and lifted her up; and immediately the fever left her, and she <u>ministered</u> to them. _{waited}

32 And at even, when the sun did set, they brought to Him all that were diseased, and them that were possessed with <u>devils</u>. _{demons}

33 And all the city was gathered together at the door.

34 And He healed many that were sick of <u>divers</u> diseases, and cast out many <u>devils</u>; and allowed not the <u>devils</u> to speak, because they knew Him. _{various}

35 And in the morning, rising up a great while before day, He went out, and departed into a <u>solitary</u> place, and there prayed. _{lonely}

36 And Si'mon and they that were with Him <u>followed after</u> Him. _{hunted for}

37 And when they had found Him, they said to Him, All *men* seek for You.

38 And He said to them, Let us go into the next towns, that I may preach there also: for therefore came I forth.

39 And He preached in their synagogues throughout all Gal'i-lee, and cast out <u>devils</u>. _{demons}

40 And there came a leper to Him, <u>beseeching</u> Him, and kneeling down to Him, and saying to Him, If You will, You can make me clean. _{begging}

41 And Je'sus, moved with compassion, put forth *His* hand, and touched him, and said to him, I will; be you clean.

42 And as soon as He had spoken, immediately the leprosy departed from him, and he was cleansed.

43 And He <u>straitly charged</u> him, and forthwith sent him away;   sternly warned
44 And said to him, See you say nothing to any man: but go your way, show yourself to the priest, and offer for your cleansing those things which Mo'ses commanded, for a testimony to them.   LEV. 13:49
45 But he went out, and began to publish *it* much, and to blaze abroad the matter, insomuch that Je'sus could no more openly enter into the city, but was outside in desert places: and they came to Him from every <u>quarter</u>.   everywhere

CHAPTER 2

A ND again He entered into Ca-per'na-um, after *some* days; and it was <u>noised</u> that He was in the house. heard
2 And immediately many were gathered together, insomuch that there was no room to receive *them*, no, not so much as about the door: and He preached the word to them.
3 And they come to Him, bringing one sick of the palsy, which was borne of four.
4 And when they could not come near to Him for the <u>press</u>, they uncovered the roof where He was: and when they had broken *it* up, they let down the bed wherein the sick of the palsy lay.   crowd
5 When Je'sus saw their faith, He said to the sick of the palsy, Son, your sins be forgiven you.
6 But there were certain of the scribes sitting there, and reasoning in their hearts,
7 Why does this *man* thus speak <u>blas-</u>phemies? who can forgive sins but God only?   evilly
8 And immediately when Je'sus perceived in His Spirit that they so reasoned inside themselves, He said to them, Why reason you these things in your hearts?
9 Whether is it easier to say to the sick of the palsy, *Your* sins be forgiven you; or to say, Arise, and take up your <u>bed</u>, and walk?
10 But that you may know that the Son of man has power on earth to forgive sins, (He says to the sick of the palsy,)
11 I say to you, Arise, and take up your <u>bed</u>, and go your way into your house.   pallet
12 And immediately he arose, took up the <u>bed</u>, and went forth <u>before them</u> all; insomuch that they were all amazed, and glorified God, saying, We never saw it on this fashion.   in sight of
13 And He went forth again by the sea side; and all the multitude resorted to Him, and He taught them.
14 And as He passed by, He saw Le'vi the *son* of Al-phae'us sitting at the <u>receipt of custom</u>, and said to him, Follow Me. And he arose and followed Him.   tax office
15 And it came to pass, that, as Je'sus sat at <u>meat</u> in his house, many <u>publicans</u> and sinners sat also together with Je'sus and His disciples: for there were many, and they followed Him.   dining - tax gatherers
16 And when the scribes and Phar'i-sees saw Him eat with <u>publicans</u> and sinners, they said to His disciples,

How is it that He eats and drinks with <u>publicans</u> and sinners?

17 When Je'sus heard *it*, He said to them, They that are whole have no need of the physician, but they that are sick: I came not to call the righteous, but sinners to repentance.

18 And the disciples of John and of the Phar'i-sees <u>used to fast</u>: and they come and say to Him, Why do the disciples of John and of the Phar'i-sees fast, but Your disciples fast not?   *were fasting*

19 And Je'sus said to them, Can the <u>children</u> of the bride chamber <u>fast</u>, while the bridegroom is with them? as long as they have the bridegroom with them, they cannot <u>fast</u>.   *attendants - do without food*

20 But the days will come, when the bridegroom shall be taken away from them, and then shall they fast in those days.

21 No man also sews a piece of new <u>cloth</u> on an old garment: else the new piece that filled it up takes away from the old, and the rent is made worse.   *unshrunk*

22 And no man puts new wine into old <u>bottles</u>: else the new wine does burst the <u>bottles</u>, and the wine is spilled, and the bottles will <u>be marred</u>: but new wine must be put into new <u>bottles</u>.   *wineskins - burst*

23 And it came to pass, that He went through the <u>corn</u> fields on the <u>sabbath</u> day; and His disciples began, as they went, to pluck the ears of <u>corn</u>.   DEU. 23:25 *grain - rest day*

24 And the Phar'i-sees said to Him, Behold, why do they on the <u>sabbath</u> day that which is not lawful?

25 And He said to them, Have you never read what Da'vid did, when he had need, and was an hungry he, and they that were with him?   *hungry*

26 How he went into the house of God in the days of A-bi'a-thar the high priest, and did eat the <u>showbread</u>, which is not lawful to eat but for the priests, and gave also to them which were with him?   *sacred*

27 And He said to them, The <u>sabbath</u> was made for man, and not man for the <u>sabbath</u>:   EX. 23:12 *rest day*

28 Therefore the Son of man is Lord <u>also</u> of the <u>sabbath.</u>   *even*

CHAPTER 3

AND He entered again into the synagogue; and there was a man there which had a withered hand.

2 And they watched Him, whether He would heal him on the <u>sabbath</u> day; that they might accuse Him.

3 And He said to the man which had the withered hand, Stand forth.

4 And He said to them, Is it lawful to do good on the <u>sabbath</u> days, or to do evil? to save life, or to kill? But they <u>held their peace</u>.   *kept silent*

5 And when He had looked round about on them with anger, being grieved for the hardness of their hearts, He said to the man, Stretch forth your hand. And he stretched *it* out: and his hand <u>was restored whole</u> as the other.   *became well*

6 And the Phar'i-sees went forth, and

immediately took counsel with the He-ro'di-ans against Him, how they might destroy Him.

7 But Je'sus withdrew Himself with His disciples to the sea: and a great multitude from Gal'i-lee followed Him, and from Ju-dae'a,

8 And from Je-ru'sa-lem, and from I-du-mae'a, and *from* beyond Jor'dan; and they about Tyre and Si'don, a great multitude, when they had heard what great things He did, came to Him.

9 And He spoke to His disciples, that a small ship should wait on Him because of the multitude, less they should throng Him.   boat - crowd

10 For He had healed many; insomuch that they pressed upon Him for to touch Him, as many as had plagues.   crowded - afflictions

11 And unclean spirits, when they saw Him, fell down before Him, and cried, saying, You are the Son of God.

12 And He straitly charged them that they should not make Him known. sternly

13 And He goes up into a mountain, and calls *to Him* whom He would: and they came to Him.   those he wanted

14 And He ordained twelve, that they should be with Him, and that He might send them forth to preach,   appointed

15 And to have power to heal sicknesses, and to cast out devils: authority - demons

16 And Si'mon He surnamed Pe'ter;

17 And James the *son* of Zeb'e-dee, and John the brother of James; and He surnamed them Bo-an-er'ges, which is, The sons of thunder:

18 And Andrew, and Phil'ip, and Bar-thol'o-mew, and Mat'thew, and Thom'as, and James the *son* of Al-phae'us, and Thad-dae'us, and Si'mon the Ca'naan-ite,

19 And Ju'das Is-car'i-ot, which also betrayed Him: and they went into an house.

20 And the multitude comes together again, so that they could not so much as eat bread.

21 And when His friends heard *of it*, they went out to lay hold on Him: for they said, He is beside Himself.

    take custody - lost his balance

22 And the scribes which came down from Je-ru'sa-lem said, He has Beel'ze-bub, and by the prince of the devils casts He out devils.

    i.e., Satan - demons

23 And He called them *to Him*, and said to them in parables, How can Sa'tan cast out Sa'tan?

24 And if a kingdom be divided against itself, that kingdom cannot stand.

25 And if a house be divided against itself, that house cannot stand.

26 And if Sa'tan rise up against himself, and be divided, he cannot stand, but has an end.   he is finished

27 No man can enter into a strong man's house, and spoil his goods, except he will first bind the strong man; and then he will spoil his house. plunder

28 Verily I say to you, All sins shall be forgiven to the sons of men, and blasphemies wherewith soever they shall blaspheme: Truly

29 But he that shall blaspheme against the Ho'ly Ghost has never forgiveness,

but is in danger of eternal damnation: Spirit

30 Because they said, He has an un-clean spirit.   evil

31 There came then His brethren and His mother, and, standing outside, sent to Him, calling Him.

32 And the multitude sat about Him, and they said to Him, Behold, Your mother and Your brethren outside seek for You.

33 And He answered them, saying, Who is My mother, or My brethren?

34 And He looked round about on them which sat about Him, and said, Behold My mother and My brethren!

35 For whosoever shall do the will of God, the same is My brother, and My sister, and mother.

G4T - 178

CHAPTER 4

AND He began again to teach by the sea side: and there was gathered to Him a great multitude, so that He entered into a ship, and sat in the sea; and the whole multitude was by the sea on the land.   boat - in a boat offshore

2 And He taught them many things by parables, and said to them in His doctrine,   teaching

3 Hearken; Behold, there went out a sower to sow: Listen

4 And it came to pass, as he sowed, some fell by the way side, and the fowls of the air came and devoured it up.

5 And some fell on stony ground, where it had not much earth; and immediately it sprang up, because it had no depth of earth: soil

6 But when the sun was up, it was scorched; and because it had no root, it withered away.

7 And some fell among thorns, and the thorns grew up, and choked it, and it yielded no fruit.   crop

8 And other fell on good ground, and did yield fruit that sprang up and increased; and brought forth, some thirty, and some sixty, and some an hundred.

9 And He said to them, He that has ears to hear, let him hear.

10 And when He was alone, they that were about Him with the twelve asked of Him the parable.

11 And He said to them, To you it is given to know the mystery of the kingdom of God: but to them that are outside, all *these* things are done in parables: hidden truth

12 That seeing they may see, and not perceive; and hearing they may hear, and not understand; less at any time they should be converted, and *their* sins should be forgiven them.   ISA. 6:10 understand

13 And He said to them, Know you not this parable? and how then will you know all parables?   understand

14 The sower sows the word.

15 And these are they by the way side, where the word is sown; but when they have heard, Sa'tan comes immediately, and takes away the word that was sown in their hearts.

16 And these are they likewise which are sown on stony ground; who, when they have heard the word, immediately receive it with gladness;

17 And have no root in themselves,

M07

74

P09
G1H

101
65

and so endure but for a time: afterward, when affliction or persecution arises <u>for</u> the word's sake, immediately they <u>are offended</u>. because of - fall away

18 And these are they which are sown among thorns; such as hear the word,

19 And the <u>cares</u> of this world, and the deceitfulness of riches, and the lusts of other things entering in, choke the word, and it becomes unfruitful. worries

20 And these are they which are sown on good ground; such as hear the word, and receive *it*, and bring forth fruit, some thirtyfold, some sixty, and some an hundred.

21 And He said to them, Is a candle brought to be put under a bushel, or under a bed? and not to set on a candlestick?

22 For there is nothing hid, which shall not be <u>manifested</u>; neither was any thing kept secret, but that it should come <u>abroad</u>. revealed - to light

23 If any man have ears to hear, let him hear.

24 And He said to them, Take heed what you hear: with what measure you <u>mete</u>, it shall be measured to you: and to you that hear shall more be given. measure

25 For he that has, to him shall be given: and he that has not, from him shall be taken even that which he has.

26 And He said, So is the kingdom of God, as if a man should <u>cast</u> seed into the ground; scatters

27 And should sleep, and rise night and day, and the seed should spring and grow up, he knows not how.

28 For the earth brings forth fruit of itself; first the blade, then the ear, after that the full corn in the ear.

29 But when the fruit is <u>brought forth</u>, immediately he puts in the sickle, because the harvest is come. ripe

30 And He said, Whereto shall we liken the kingdom of God? or with what comparison shall we compare it?

31 *It is* like a grain of mustard seed, which, when it is sown in the earth, is less than all the seeds that be in the earth:

32 But when it is sown, it grows up, and becomes <u>greater</u> than all herbs, and shoots out great branches; so that the fowls of the air may lodge under the shadow of it. larger

33 And with many such <u>parables</u> spoke He the word to them, as they were able to hear *it*. illustrations

34 But without a <u>parable</u> spoke He not to them: and when they were alone, He expounded all things to His disciples.

35 And the same day, when the even was come, He said to them, Let us pass over to the other side.

36 And when they had sent away the multitude, they took Him even as He was in the <u>ship</u>. And there were also with Him other little <u>ships</u>. boats

37 And there arose a great storm of wind, and the waves beat into the ship, so that it was now full.

38 And He was in the <u>hinder</u> part of the <u>ship</u>, asleep on a pillow: and they awake Him, and say to Him, <u>Master</u>, care You not that we perish? stern - Teacher

39 And He arose, and rebuked the

wind, and said to the sea, Peace, be still. And the wind ceased, and there was a great calm.

40 And He said to them, Why are you so fearful? how is it that you have no faith?

41 And they feared exceedingly, and said one to another, What <u>manner</u> of man is this, that even the wind and the sea obey Him?   kind

CHAPTER 5

AND they came over to the other side of the sea, into the country of the Gad'a-renes.

2 And when He was come out of the ship, immediately there met Him out of the tombs a man with an unclean spirit,

3 Who had *his* dwelling among the <u>tombs</u>; and no man could bind him, no, not with chains:

4 Because that he had been often bound with <u>fetters</u> and chains, and the chains had been <u>plucked asunder</u> by him, and the <u>fetters</u> broken in pieces: neither could any *man* <u>tame</u> him.   shackles - torn apart - subdue

5 And always, night and day, he was in the mountains, and in the tombs, crying, and cutting himself with stones.

6 But when he saw Je'sus afar off, he ran and <u>worshiped</u> Him,   bowed down

7 And cried with a loud voice, and said, What have I to do with You, Je'sus, *You* Son of the Most High God? I <u>adjure</u> You by God, that You torment me not.   implore

8 For He said to him, Come out of the man, *you* unclean spirit.

9 And He asked him, What *is* your name? And he answered, saying, My name *is* Legion: for we are many.

10 And he <u>besought</u> Him much that He would not send them away out of the country.   entreated

11 Now there was there near to the mountains a great herd of <u>swine</u> feeding.   pigs

12 And all the <u>devils</u> besought Him, saying, Send us into the <u>swine</u>, that we may enter into them.   demons

13 And forthwith Je'sus gave them leave. And the unclean spirits went out, and entered into the <u>swine</u>: and the herd ran violently down a steep place into the sea, (they were about two thousand;) and were <u>choked</u> in the sea.   drowned

14 And they that fed the <u>swine</u> fled, and told *it* in the city, and in the country. And they went out to see what it was that was <u>done</u>.   happening

15 And they come to Je'sus, and see him that was possessed with the <u>devil</u>, and had the legion, sitting, and clothed, and in his right mind: and they were afraid.   demons

16 And they that saw *it* told them how it befell to him that was possessed with the <u>devil</u>, and *also* concerning the <u>swine</u>.

17 And they began to <u>pray</u> Him to depart out of their coasts.   entreat

18 And when He was come into the ship, he that had been possessed with the <u>devil prayed</u> Him that he might be with Him.   demon entreated

19 However Je'sus allowed him not, but said to him, Go home to your

friends, and tell them how great things the Lord has done for you, and has had compassion on you.

20 And he departed, and began to publish in De-cap'o-lis how great things Je'sus had done for him: and all *men* did marvel.

21 And when Je'sus was passed over again by ship to the other side, much people gathered to Him: and He was near to the sea.

22 And, behold, there comes one of the rulers of the synagogue, Ja-i'rus by name; and when he saw Him, he fell at His feet,

23 And <u>besought</u> Him greatly, saying, My little daughter lies at the point of death: *I pray You*, come and lay Your hands on her, that she may be healed; and she shall live   _{entreated}

24 And *Jesus* went with him; and much people followed Him, and thronged Him.

25 And a certain woman, which had an <u>issue</u> of blood twelve years,   _{flow}

26 And had suffered many <u>things</u> of many physicians, and had spent all that she had, and was <u>nothing bettered</u>, but rather grew worse,   _{treatments - not helped}

27 When she had heard of Je'sus, came in the <u>press</u> behind, and touched His garment.   _{crowd}

28 For she said, If I may touch but His clothes, I shall be <u>whole</u>.   _{well}

29 And immediately the fountain of her blood was dried up; and she felt in *her* body that she was healed of that <u>plague</u>.   _{affliction}

30 And Je'sus, immediately knowing in Himself that <u>virtue</u> had gone out of Him, turned Him about in the <u>press</u>, and said, Who touched My clothes?   _{power}

31 And His disciples said to Him, You see the <u>multitude thronging You</u>, and say You, Who touched Me?

32 And He looked round about to see her that had done this thing.

33 But the woman <u>fearing</u> and trembling, <u>knowing</u> what was done <u>in</u> her, came and fell down before Him, and told Him all the truth. _{afraid - aware - to}

34 And He said to her, Daughter, your faith has made you whole; go in peace, and be whole of your <u>plague</u>.   _{afflictions}

35 While He yet spoke, there came from the ruler of the synagogue's *house certain* which said, Your daughter is dead: why trouble you the Master any further?

36 As soon as Je'sus heard the word that was spoken, He said to the ruler of the synagogue, Be not afraid, only believe.

37 And He allowed no man to follow Him, save Pe'ter, and James, and John the brother of James.

38 And He comes to the house of the ruler of the synagogue, and sees the <u>tumult</u>, and them that wept and wailed greatly.   _{commotion}

39 And when He <u>was come</u> in, He said to them, Why make you this <u>ado</u>, and weep? the <u>damsel</u> is not dead, but sleeps.

_{entered - commotion - young girl}

40 And they laughed Him to scorn. But when He had put them all out, He takes the father and the mother of the <u>damsel</u>, and them that were with Him,

and enters in where the <u>damsel</u> was lying.

41 And He took the <u>damsel</u> by the hand, and said to her, Tal'i-tha cu'mi; which is, being interpreted, <u>Damsel</u>, I say to you, arise.

42 And immediately the <u>damsel</u> arose, and walked; for she was *of the age* of twelve years. And they were astonished with a great astonishment.

43 And He charged them <u>straitly</u> that no man should know it; and commanded that something should be given her to eat. strictly

CHAPTER 6

AND He went out from there, and came into His own country; and His disciples follow Him.

2 And when the <u>sabbath</u> day was come, He began to teach in the synagogue: and many hearing *Him* were astonished, saying, From where has this *man* these things? and what wisdom *is* this which is given to Him, that even such mighty works are wrought by His hands? rest day

3 Is not this the carpenter, the son of Ma'ry, the brother of James, and Jo'ses, and of Ju'da, and Si'mon? and are not His sisters here with us? And they were offended at Him.

4 But Je'sus said to them, A prophet is not without honor, but in His own country, and among His own <u>kin</u>, and in His own <u>house</u>. relatives - family

5 And He could there do no mighty work, save that He laid his hands upon a few sick folk, and healed *them*.

6 And He marveled because of their unbelief. And He went round about the villages, teaching.

7 And He called *to Him* the twelve, and began to send them forth by two and two; and gave them <u>power</u> over unclean spirits; authority

8 And commanded them that they should take nothing for *their* journey, save a staff only; no <u>scrip</u>, no bread, no money in *their* purse: bag

9 But *be* shod with sandals; and not put on two coats.

10 And He said to them, In what place soever you enter into an house, there abide till you depart from that place.

11 And whosoever shall not receive you, nor hear you, when you depart from there, shake off the dust under your feet for a <u>testimony</u> against them. <u>Verily</u> I say to you, It shall be more tolerable for Sod'om and Go-mor'rha in the day of judgment, than for that city. witness - truly

12 And they went out, and preached that men should <u>repent</u>. turn from sin

13 And they cast out many <u>devils</u>, and anointed with oil many that were sick, and healed *them*. demons

14 And king Her'od heard *of Him*; (for His name was spread abroad:) and he said, That John the Bap'tist was risen from the dead, and therefore mighty works do show forth themselves in Him.

15 Others said, That it is Elijah And others said, That it is a <u>prophet</u>, or as one of the <u>prophets</u>. spokesman of God

16 But when Her'od heard *thereof*, he

said, It is John, whom I beheaded: he is risen from the dead.

17 For Her'od himself had sent forth and laid hold upon John, and bound him in prison for He-ro'di-as' sake, his brother Phil'ip's wife: for he had married her.

18 For John had said to Her'od, It is not <u>lawful</u> for you to have your brother's wife.   right

19 Therefore He-ro'di-as had a quarrel <u>against</u> him, and would have killed him; but she could not: with

20 For Her'od feared John, knowing that he was a just man and an holy, and <u>observed</u> him; and when he heard him, he did many things, and heard him gladly.   watched

21 And when a convenient day was come, that Her'od on his birthday made a supper to his lords, high captains, and chief *estates* of Gal'i-lee;

22 And when the daughter of the said He-ro'di-as came in, and danced, and pleased Her'od and them that sat with him, the king said to the <u>damsel</u>, Ask of me whatsoever you will, and I will give *it* you.   young girl

23 And he swear to her, Whatsoever you shall ask of me, I will give *it* you, to the half of my kingdom. EST. 5:3

24 And she went forth, and said to her mother, What shall I ask? And she said, The head of John the Bap'tist.

25 And she came in immediately with haste to the king, and asked, saying, I will that you give me by and by in a <u>charger</u> the head of John the Bap'tist.   platter

26 And the king was exceeding sorry; *yet* for his oath's sake, and for their sakes which sat with him, he would not <u>reject</u> her.   refuse

27 And immediately the king sent an executioner, and commanded his head to be brought: and he went and beheaded him in the prison,

28 And brought his head in a <u>charger</u>, and gave it to the <u>damsel</u>: and the <u>damsel</u> gave it to her mother.   young girl

29 And when his disciples heard *of it*, they came and took up his corpse, and laid it in a tomb.

30 And the apostles <u>gathered</u> themselves together to Je'sus, and told Him all things, both what they had done, and what they had taught.   assembled

31 And He said to them, Come you yourselves apart into a <u>desert</u> place, and rest a while: for there were many coming and going, and they had no <u>leisure</u> so much as to eat.   lonely - time

32 And they departed into a <u>desert</u> place by <u>ship</u> privately.   boat

33 And the people saw them departing, and many knew Him, and ran afoot there out of all cities, and <u>outwent</u> them, and came together to Him.   ran ahead

34 And Je'sus, when He came out, saw much people, and was moved with compassion toward them, because they were as sheep not having a shepherd: and He began to teach them many things.

35 And when the day was now far spent, His disciples came to Him, and said, This is a <u>desert</u> place, and now the time *is* <u>far passed</u>:   quite late

36 Send them away, that they may go into the country round about, and into the villages, and buy themselves bread: for they have nothing to eat.
37 He answered and said to them, Give you them to eat. And they say to Him, Shall we go and buy two hundred pennyworth of bread, and give them to eat?   2KGS 4:42
38 He said to them, How many loaves have you? go and see. And when they knew, they say, Five, and two fishes.
39 And He commanded them to make all sit down by <u>companies</u> upon the green grass.   groups
40 And they sat down in <u>ranks</u>, by hundreds, and by fifties.   companies
41 And when He had taken the five loaves and the two fishes, He looked up to heaven, and blessed, and broke the loaves, and gave *them* to IIis disciples to set before them; and the two fishes divided He among thcm all.
42 And they did all eat, and were filled.
43 And they took up twelve baskets full of the <u>fragments</u>, and of the fishes.   pieces
44 And they that did eat of the loaves were about five thousand men.
45 And immediately He constrained His disciples to get into the ship, and to go to the other side before to Beth-sa'i-da, while He sent away the people.
46 And when He had sent them away, He departed into a mountain to pray.
47 And when <u>even</u> was come, the <u>ship</u> was in the midst of the sea, and He alone on the land.   evening - boat
48 And He saw them toiling in rowing; for the wind was <u>contrary</u> to them: and about the <u>fourth</u> watch of the night He comes to them, walking upon the sea, and would have passed by them.   against - 3-6 AM
49 But when they saw Him walking upon the sea, they supposed it had been a <u>spirit</u>, and cried out: ghost
50 For they all saw Him, and were <u>troubled</u>. And immediately He talked with them, and said to them, Be of good cheer: it is I; be not afraid.   frightened
51 And He went up to them into the ship; and the wind ceased: and they were <u>sore amazed</u> in themselves beyond measure, and wondered.   very surprised
52 For they considered not *the miracle* of the loaves: for their heart was hardened.
53 And when they had <u>passed</u> over, they came into the land of Gen-nes'a-ret, and drew to the shore.   crossed
54 And when they were come out of the ship, immediately they knew Him,
55 And ran through that whole region round about, and began to carry about in <u>beds</u> those that were sick, where they heard He was.   pallets
56 And wherever He entered, into villages, or cities, or country, they laid the sick in the streets, and <u>besought</u> Him that they might touch if it were but the border of His garment: and as many as touched Him were made whole.   entreated - Him—Jesus

CHAPTER 7

THEN came together to Him the Phar'i-sees, and certain of the scribes, which came from Je-ru'sa-lem. 2 And when they saw some of His disciples eat bread with defiled, that is to say, with unwashed, hands, they found fault. 3 For the Phar'i-sees, and all the Jews, except they wash *their* hands oft, eat not, holding the tradition of the elders. _{often}
4 And *when they come* from the market, except they wash, they eat not. And many other things there be, which they have received to hold, *as* the washing of cups, and pots, brazen vessels, and of tables. _{copper}
5 Then the Phar'i-sees and scribes asked Him, Why walk not Your disciples according to the tradition of the elders, but eat bread with unwashed hands? _{impure}
6 He answered and said to them, Well has I-sa'iah prophesied of you hypocrites, as it is written, This people honor Me with *their* lips, but their heart is far from Me. _{insincere}
7 However in vain do they worship Me, teaching *for* doctrines the commandments of men. _{i.e., ways}
8 For laying aside the commandment of God, you hold the tradition of men, *as* the washing of pots and cups: and many other such like things you do.
9 And He said to them, Full well you reject the commandment of God, that you may keep your own tradition. _{set aside}
10 For Mo'ses said, Honor your father and your mother; and, Whoso curses father or mother, let him die the death: _{EX 20:12 - EX. 21:17}
11 But you say, If a man shall say to his father or mother, *It is* Corban, that is to say, a gift, by whatsoever you might be profited by me; *he shall be free.*
12 And you permit him no more to do anything for his father or his mother;
13 Making the word of God of none effect through your tradition, which you have delivered: and many such like things do you. _{no use - handed down}
14 And when He had called all the people *to Him*, He said to them, Hearken to Me every one *of you*, and understand:
15 There is nothing from outside a man, that entering into him can defile him: but the things which come out of him, those are they that defile the man. _{make unclean}
16 If any man have ears to hear, let him hear.
17 And when He was entered into the house from the people, His disciples asked Him concerning the parable.
18 And He said to them, Are you so without understanding also? Do you not perceive, that whatsoever thing from outside enters into the man, *it* cannot defile him; _{understand}
19 Because it enters not into his heart, but into the belly, and goes out into the draught, purging all meats? _{eliminating - food}
20 And He said, That which comes out of the man, that defiles the man. _{makes unclean}

21 For from inside, out of the heart of men, proceed evil thoughts, adulteries, fornications, murders,

22 Thefts, covetousness, wickedness, deceit, <u>lasciviousness</u>, an evil eye, <u>blasphemy</u>, pride, foolishness: _{sensuality - slander}

sensuality - slander

23 All these evil things come from inside, and <u>defile</u> the man.

24 And from there He arose, and went into the borders of Tyre and Si'don, and entered into an house, and <u>would</u> have no man know *it*: but He could not be hid. _{wanted}

wanted

25 For a *certain* woman, whose young daughter had an unclean spirit, heard of Him, and came and fell at His feet:

26 The woman was a Greek, a Sy-ro-phe-ni'-cian by nation; and she <u>besought</u> Him that He would cast forth the <u>devil</u> out of her daughter. begged - demon

27 But Je'sus said to her, Let the children first be <u>filled</u>: for it is not <u>meet</u> to take the children's bread, and to cast *it* to the dogs. satisfied - good

28 And she answered and said to Him, Yes, Lord: yet the dogs under the table eat of the children's <u>crumbs</u>. leftovers

29 And He said to her, For this saying go your way; the <u>devil</u> is gone out of your daughter. demon

30 And when she was come to her house, she found the <u>devil</u> gone out, and her daughter laid upon the bed.

31 And again, departing from the coasts of Tyre and Si'don, He came to the sea of Gal'i-lee, through the midst of the coasts of De-cap'o-lis.

32 And they bring to Him one that was deaf, and had an impediment in his speech; and they <u>beseech</u> Him to put His hand upon him. beg

33 And He took him aside from the multitude, and put His fingers into his ears, and He spit, and touched his tongue;

34 And looking up to heaven, *he* sighed, and said to him, Eph'pha-tha, that is, Be opened.

35 And immediately his ears were opened, and the <u>string</u> of his tongue was loosed, and he spoke plain. impediment

36 And He <u>charged</u> them that they should tell no man: but the more He <u>charged</u> them, so much the more a great deal they published *it*; ordered

37 And were beyond measure astonished, saying, He has done all things well: He makes both the deaf to hear, and the dumb to speak.

CHAPTER 8

IN those days the multitude being very great, and having nothing to eat, Je'sus called His disciples *to Him*, and says to them,

2 I have compassion on the multitude, because they have now been with Me three days, and have nothing to eat:

3 And if I send them away fasting to their own houses, they will faint by the way: for <u>divers</u> of them came from far. some

4 And His disciples <u>answered</u> Him, From where can a man satisfy these *men* with bread here in the wilderness? asked

5 And He asked them, How many loaves have you? And they said, Seven.

6 And He commanded the people to sit down on the ground: and He took the seven loaves, and gave thanks, and broke, and gave to His disciples to set before *them*; and they did set *them* before the people.

7 And they had a few small fishes: and He blessed, and commanded to set them also before *them*.

8 So they did eat, and <u>were filled</u>: and they took up of the broken *meat* that was left seven baskets. _{satisfied}

9 And they that had eaten were about four thousand: and He sent them away.

10 And immediately He entered into a ship with His disciples, and came into the parts of Dal-ma-nu'tha.

11 And the Phar'i-sees came forth, and began to question with Him, seeking of Him a sign from heaven, <u>tempting</u> Him. _{testing}

12 And He sighed deeply in His spirit, and says, Why does this generation seek after a sign? <u>verily</u> I say to you, There shall no sign be given to this generation. _{truly}

13 And He left them, and entering into the ship again departed to the other side.

14 Now *the disciples* had forgotten to take bread, neither had they in the ship with them more than one loaf.

15 And He <u>charged</u> them, saying, Take heed, beware of the <u>leaven</u> of the Phar'i-sees, and *of* the <u>leaven</u> of Her'od. _{instructed - i.e., false teaching}

16 And they <u>reasoned</u> among themselves, saying, *It is* because we have no bread. _{discussed}

17 And when Je'sus knew *it*, He says to them, Why reason you, because you have no bread? <u>perceive</u> you not yet, neither understand? have you your heart yet hardened? _{understand}

18 Having eyes, see you not? and having ears, hear you not? and do you not remember?

19 When I broke the five loaves among five thousand, how many baskets full of fragments took you up? They say to Him, Twelve.

20 And when the seven among four thousand, how many baskets full of fragments took you up? And they said, Seven.

21 And He said to them, How is it that you do not understand?

22 And He comes to Beth-sa'i-da; and they bring a blind man to Him, and <u>besought</u> Him to touch him. _{entreated}

23 And He took the blind man by the hand, and led him out of the town; and when He had spit on his eyes, and put His hands upon him, He asked him if he saw anything.

24 And he looked up, and said, I see men <u>as</u> trees, walking. _{like}

25 After that He put *His* hands again upon his eyes, and made him look up: and he was restored, and saw every man clearly.

26 And He sent him away to his house, saying, Neither go into the town, nor tell *it* to any in the town.

27 And Je'sus went out, and His disciples, into the towns of Caes-a-re'a Phi-lip'pi: and by the way He asked His disciples, saying to them, Whom do men say that I am?

28 And they answered, John the Bap'tist: but some *say*, Elijah; and others, One of the prophets.

29 And He says to them, But whom say you that I am? And Pe'ter answered and says to Him, You are the Christ.

30 And He charged them that they should tell no man of Him.　warned

31 And He began to teach them, that the Son of man must suffer many things, and be rejected *of* the elders, and of the chief priests, and scribes, and be killed, and after three days rise again.

32 And He spoke that saying openly. And Pe'ter took Him, and began to rebuke Him.

33 But when He had turned about and looked on His disciples, He rebuked Pe'ter, saying, Get you behind Me, Sa'tan: for you savor not the things that be of God, but the things that be of men.　mind

34 And when He had called the people *to Him* with His disciples also, He said to them, Whosoever will come after Me, let him deny himself, and take up his cross, and follow Me.

35 For whosoever will save his life shall lose it; but whosoever shall lose his life for My sake and the gospel's, the same shall save it.　i.e., Jesus

36 For what shall it profit a man, if he shall gain the whole world, and lose his own soul?　gain

37 Or what shall a man give in exchange for his soul?

38 Whosoever therefore shall be ashamed of Me and of My words in this adulterous and sinful generation; of him also shall the Son of man be ashamed, when He comes in the glory of His Father with the holy angels.

CHAPTER 9

AND He said to them, Verily I say to you, That there be some of them that stand here, which shall not taste of death, till they have seen the kingdom of God come with power.　Truly

2 And after six days Je'sus takes *with Him* Pe'ter, and James, and John, and leads them up into an high mountain apart by themselves: and He was transfigured before them.　changed

3 And His raiment became shining, exceeding white as snow; so as no fuller on earth can white them.　garment - launderer

4 And there appeared to them Elijah with Mo'ses: and they were talking with Je'sus.

5 And Pe'ter answered and said to Je'sus, Master, it is good for us to be here: and let us make three tabernacles; one for You, and one for Mo'ses, and one for Elijah.　sacred tents

6 For he knew not what to say; for they were sore afraid.　very

7 And there was a cloud that overshadowed them: and a voice came out of the cloud, saying, This is My beloved Son: hear Him.

8 And suddenly, when they had looked round about, they saw no man any more, save Je'sus only with themselves.　except

9 And as they came down from the mountain, He charged them that they

should tell no man what things they had seen, till the Son of man were risen from the dead. _{ordered}

10 And they kept that saying with themselves, questioning one with another what the rising from the dead should mean.

11 And they asked Him, saying, Why say the scribes that Elijah must first come?

12 And He answered and told them, Elijah <u>verily</u> comes first, and restores all things; and how it is written of the Son of man, that He must suffer many things, and be <u>set at nothing</u>. _{truly - destroyed}

13 But I say to you, That Elijah is indeed come, and they have done to him whatsoever they <u>listed</u>, as it is written of him. _{wished}

14 And when He came to *His* disciples, He saw a great multitude about them, and the scribes questioning with them.

15 And immediately all the people, when they beheld Him, were greatly amazed, and running to *Him* <u>saluted</u> Him. _{greeted}

16 And He asked the scribes, What question you with them?

17 And one of the multitude answered and said, Master, I have brought to You my son, which has a dumb spirit;

18 And wherever he takes him, he tears him: and he foams, and gnashes with his teeth, and <u>pines</u> away: and I spoke to Your disciples that they should cast him out; and they could not. _{stiffens out}

19 He answered him, and said, O <u>faithless</u> generation, how long shall I be with you? how long shall I <u>suffer</u> you? bring him to Me. _{unbelieving - put up with}

20 And they brought him to Him: and when He saw him, immediately the spirit <u>tare him</u>; and he fell on the ground, and wallowed foaming. _{convulsed}

21 And He asked his father, How long is it ago since this came to him? And he said, Of a child.

22 And often it has cast him into the fire, and into the waters, to destroy him: but if You can do any thing, have compassion on us, and help us.

23 Je'sus said to him, If you can believe, all things *are* possible to him that believes.

24 And immediately the father of the child cried out, and said with tears, Lord, I believe; help You mine unbelief.

25 When Je'sus saw that the people came running together, He rebuked the foul spirit, saying to him, *You* dumb and deaf spirit, I <u>charge</u> you, come out of him, and enter no more into him. _{command}

26 And *the spirit* cried, and <u>rent him sore</u>, and came out of him: and he was as one dead; insomuch that many said, He is dead. _{convulsed - terribly}

27 But Je'sus took him by the hand, and lifted him up; and he arose.

28 And when He was come into the house, His disciples asked Him privately, Why could not we cast him out?

29 And He said to them, This kind

M41 - - 79
M07 - - 75

can come <u>forth</u> by nothing, but by prayer and fasting. _{out}

30 And they departed there, and passed through Gal'i-lee; and He <u>would not</u> that any man should know *it*. _{was unwilling}

31 For He taught His disciples, and said to them, The Son of man is delivered into the hands of men, and they shall kill Him; and after that He is killed, He shall rise the third day.

32 But they understood not that saying, and were afraid to ask Him.

33 And He came to Ca-per'na-um: and being in the house He asked them, What was it that you <u>disputed</u> among yourselves by the way? _{discussed}

34 But they <u>held their peace</u>: for by the way they had <u>disputed</u> among themselves, who *should be* the greatest. _{kept silent}

35 And He sat down, and called the twelve, and says to them, If any man desire to be first, *the same* shall be last of all, and servant of all.

36 And He took a child, and set him in the midst of them: and when He had taken him in His arms, He said to them,

37 Whosoever shall receive one of such children in My name, receives Me: and whosoever shall receive Me, receives not Me, but Him that sent Me.

38 And John answered Him, saying, Master, we saw one casting out <u>devils</u> in Your name, and he follows not us: and we forbad him, because he follows not us. _{demons}

39 But Je'us said, Forbid him not: for there is no man which shall do a miracle in My name, that can lightly speak evil of Me. _{NUM. 11:29}

40 For he that is not against us is on <u>our part</u>. _{for us}

41 For whosoever shall give you a cup of water to drink in My name, because you belong to Christ, <u>verily</u> I say to you, he shall not lose his reward. _{truly}

42 And whosoever shall <u>offend</u> one of *these* little ones that believe in Me, it is better for him that a millstone were hanged about his neck, and he were cast into the sea. _{make stumble}

43 And if your hand offend you, cut it off: it is better for you to enter into life <u>maimed</u>, than having two hands to go into hell, into the fire that never shall be quenched: _{crippled}

44 Where their <u>worm</u> dies not, and the fire is not <u>quenched</u>. _{torment - put out}

45 And if your foot offend you, cut it off: it is better for you to enter <u>halt</u> into life, than having two feet to be cast into hell, into the fire that never shall be <u>quenched</u>: _{lame}

46 Where their <u>worm</u> dies not, and the fire is not <u>quenched</u>. _{ISA. 66:24 Put out - ended}

47 And if your eye <u>offend</u> you, pluck it out: it is better for you to enter into the kingdom of God with one eye, than having two eyes to be cast into hell fire: _{cause to stumble}

48 Where their <u>worm</u> dies not, and the fire is not <u>quenched</u>.

49 For every one shall be salted with fire, and every sacrifice shall be salted with salt.

50 Salt *is* good: but if the salt have

lost its saltness, wherewith will you season it? Have salt in yourselves, and have peace one with another.

CHAPTER 10

AND He arose from there, and comes into the coasts of Ju-dae'a by the farther side of Jor'dan: and the people resort to Him again; and, as He was <u>wont</u>, He taught them again. accustomed

2 And the Phar'i-sees came to Him, and asked Him, Is it lawful for a man to put away *his* wife? tempting Him.

3 And He answered and said to them, What did Mo'ses command you?

4 And they said, Mo'ses <u>suffered</u> to write a bill of divorcement, and to put *her* away.   DEU. 24:1-3 permitted

5 And Je'sus answered and said to them, For the hardness of your heart he wrote you this <u>precept</u>.   commandment

6 But from the beginning of the creation God made them male and female.   GEN. 1:27

7 For this cause shall a man leave his father and mother, and cleave to his wife;

8 And they two shall be one flesh: so then they are no more two, but one flesh.   GEN. 2:24

9 What therefore God has joined to-gether, let not man put <u>asunder</u>. separate

10 And in the house His disciples asked Him again of the same *matter*.

11 And He said to them, Whosoever shall put away his wife, and marry another, commits adultery against her.

12 And if a woman shall put away her husband, and be married to another, she commits adultery.

13 And they brought young child-ren to Him, that He should touch them: and *His* disciples <u>rebuked</u> those that brought *them*. chided

14 But when Je'sus saw *it*, He was <u>much displeased</u>, and said to them, Allow the little children to come to Me, and forbid them not: for of such is the kingdom of God. indignant

15 <u>Verily</u> I say to you, Whosoever shall not receive the kingdom of God as a little child, he shall not enter therein. Truly

16 And He took them up in His arms, put *His* hands upon them, and blessed them.

17 And when He was gone forth into the way, there came one running, and kneeled to Him, and asked Him, Good Master, what shall I do that I may inherit eternal life?

18 And Je'sus said to him, Why call you Me good? *there is* none good but one, *that is*, God.

19 You know the commandments, Do not commit adultery, Do not kill, Do not steal, Do not bear false wit-ness, Defraud not, Honor your fa-ther and mother. EX. 20:13-16 DEU. 5:16

20 And he answered and said to Him, Master, all these have I <u>observed</u> from my youth. kept

21 Then Je'sus beholding him loved him, and said to him, One thing you lack: go your way, sell whatsoever you have, and give to the poor, and you shall have treasure in heaven: and come, take up the cross, and follow Me.

22 And he was sad at that saying, and went away grieved: for he had great <u>possessions</u>.
riches

23 And Je'sus looked round about, and said to His disciples, <u>How hardly</u> shall they that have riches enter into the kingdom of God!   with what difficulty

24 And the disciples were astonished at His words. But Je'sus answered again, and says to them, Children, how hard is it for them that trust in riches to enter into the kingdom of God!

25 It is easier for a camel to go through the eye of a needle, than for a rich man to enter into the kingdom of God.

26 And they were astonished <u>out of</u> measure, saying among themselves, Who then can be saved? beyond

27 And Je'sus looking upon them says, With men *it is* impossible, but not with God: for with God all things are possible.

28 Then Pe'ter began to say to Him, <u>Lo</u>, we have left all, and have followed You.   Behold

29 And Je'sus answered and said, <u>Verily</u> I say to you, There is no man that has left house, or brethren, or sisters, or father, or mother, or wife, or children, or lands, for My sake, and the gospel's,   Truly

30 But he shall receive an hundredfold now in this time, houses, and brethren, and sisters, and mothers, and children, and lands, with persecutions; and in the world to come eternal life.

31 But many *that are* first shall be last; and the last first.

32 And they were in the way going up to Je-ru'sa-lem; and Je'sus went before them: and they were amazed; and as they followed, they were afraid. And He took again the twelve, and began to tell them what things should happen to Him,

33 *Saying*, Behold, we go up to Je-ru'sa-lem; and the Son of man shall be <u>delivered to</u> the chief priests, and to the scribes; and they shall condemn Him to death, and shall deliver Him to the Gen'tiles: turned over

34 And they shall <u>mock</u> Him, and shall <u>scourge</u> Him, and shall spit upon Him, and shall kill Him: and the third day He shall rise again. ridicule - whip

35 And James and John, the sons of Zeb'e-dee, come to Him, saying, Master, we would that You should do for us whatsoever we shall desire.

36 And He said to them, What <u>would you</u> that I should do for you?   do you want

37 They said to Him, Grant to us that we may sit, one on Your right hand, and the other on Your left hand, in Your glory.

38 But Je'sus said to them, You know not what you ask: can you drink of the cup that I drink of? and be baptized with the baptism that I am baptized with?

39 And they said to Him, We can. And Je'sus said to them, You shall indeed drink of the cup that I drink of; and with the baptism that I am baptized with shall you be baptized:

40 But to sit on My right hand and on My left hand is not Mine to give; but *it*

shall be given to them for whom it is prepared.

41 And when the ten heard *it*, they began to be <u>much displeased</u> with James and John. very indignant

42 But Je'sus called them *to Him*, and says to them, You know that they which are accounted to rule over the Gen'tiles exercise lordship over them; and their great ones exercise authority upon them.

43 But so shall it not be among you: but whosoever will be great among you, shall be your <u>minister</u>: servant

44 And whosoever of you will be the chiefest, shall be servant of all.

45 For even the Son of man came not to be <u>ministered</u> to, but to <u>minister</u>, and to give His life a ransom for many. served

46 And they came to Jer'i-cho: and as He went out of Jer'i-cho with His disciples and a great number of people, blind Bar-ti-mae'us, the son of Ti-mae'us, sat by the <u>highway</u> side begging.

47 And when he heard that it was Je'sus of Naz'a-reth, he began to cry out, and say, Je'sus, *You* Son of Da'vid, have mercy on me.

48 And many <u>charged</u> him that he should <u>hold his peace</u>: but he cried the more <u>a great deal</u>, *You* Son of Da'vid, have mercy on me. sternly told - be quiet - loudly

49 And Je'sus stood still, and commanded him to be called. And they call the blind man, saying to him, <u>Be of good comfort</u>, rise; He calls you. take courage

50 And he, casting away his garment, <u>rose</u>, and came to Je'sus. jumped up

51 And Je'sus answered and said to him, What will you that I should do to you? The blind man said to Him, <u>Lord</u>, that I might receive my sight. Master

52 And Je'sus said to him, Go your way; your faith has made you <u>whole</u>. And immediately he received his sight, and followed Je'sus in the way. well

CHAPTER 11

AND when they came near to Je-ru'sa-lem, to Beth'pha-ge and Beth'a-ny, at the mount of Ol'ives, He sends forth two of His disciples,

2 And says to them, Go your way into the village opposite you: and as soon as you be entered into it, you shall find a colt tied, whereon never man sat; loose him, and bring *him*.

3 And if any man say to you, Why do you this? say you that the Lord has need of him; and immediately he will send him here.

4 And they went their way, and found the colt tied by the door outside in a place where two ways met; and they <u>loose</u> him. untied

5 And certain of them that stood there said to them, What do you, <u>loosing</u> the colt?

6 And they said to them even as Je'sus had commanded: and they let them go.

7 And they brought the colt to Je'sus, and <u>cast</u> their garments on him; and He sat upon him. put

8 And many spread their garments in the <u>way</u>: and others cut down branches

off the trees, and <u>strawed</u> *them* in the way. road - spread

9 And they that went before, and they that followed, cried, saying, Ho-san'na; Blessed *is* He that comes in the name of the Lord: PS. 118:26

10 Blessed *be* the kingdom of our father Da'vid, that comes in the name of the Lord: Ho-san'na in the highest.

11 And Je'sus entered into Je-ru'sa-lem, and into the temple: and when He had looked round about upon all things, and now the eventide was come, He went out to Beth'a-ny with the twelve.

12 And on the <u>morrow</u>, when they were come from Beth'a-ny, He was hungry: next day

13 And seeing a fig tree afar off having leaves, He came, if <u>haply</u> He might find any thing thereon: and when He came to it, He found nothing but leaves; for the time of figs was not *yet*. perhaps

14 And Je'sus answered and said to it, No man eat fruit of you hereafter for ever. And His disciples heard *it*.

15 And they come to Je-ru'sa-lem: and Je'sus went into the temple, and began to cast out them that sold and bought in the temple, and overthrew the tables of the moneychangers, and the seats of them that sold doves;

16 And would not permit that any man should carry *any* vessel through the temple.

17 And He taught, saying to them, Is it not written, My house shall be called of all <u>nations</u> the house of prayer? but you have made it a den of thieves. ISA. 56:7 JER. 7:11 - peoples, nationalities

18 And the scribes and chief priests heard *it*, and sought how they might destroy Him: for they feared Him, because all the people was astonished at His <u>doctrine</u>. teaching

19 And when <u>even</u> was come, He went out of the city. evening

20 And in the morning, as they passed by, they saw the fig tree dried up from the roots.

21 And Pe'ter calling to remembrance said to Him, Master, behold, the fig tree which You cursed is withered away.

22 And Je'sus answering said to them, Have faith in God.

23 For <u>verily</u> I say to you, That whosoever shall say to this mountain, Be you removed, and be you cast into the sea; and shall not doubt in his heart, but shall believe that those things which he says shall come to pass; he shall have whatsoever he says. truly

24 Therefore I say to you, What things soever you desire, when you pray, believe that you receive *them*, and you shall have *them*.

25 And when you stand praying, forgive, if you have anything against any: that your Father also which is in heaven may forgive you your trespasses.

26 But if you do not forgive, neither will your Father which is in heaven forgive your trespasses.

27 And they come again to Je-ru'sa-lem: and as He was walking in the temple, there come to Him the chief priests, and the scribes, and the elders,

28 And say to Him, By what author-ity do You these things? and who gave You this authority to do these things?

29 And Je'sus answered and said to them, I will also ask of you one ques-tion, and answer Me, and I will tell you by what authority I do these things.

30 The baptism of John, was *it* from heaven, or of men? answer Me.

31 And they reasoned with them-selves, saying, If we shall say, From heaven; He will say, Why then did you not believe him?

32 But if we shall say, Of men; they feared the people: for all *men* counted John, that he was a prophet indeed.

33 And they answered and said to Je'sus, We cannot tell. And Je'sus answering says to them, Neither do I tell you by what authority I do these things.

CHAPTER 12

AND He began to speak to them by parables. A *certain* man planted a vineyard, and set an hedge about *it*, and digged *a place for* the winefat, and built a tower, and let it out to husbandmen, and went into a far country.   rented - tenant farmers

2 And at the season he sent to the husbandmen a servant, that he might receive from the husbandmen of the fruit of the vineyard.   harvest

3 And they caught *him*, and beat him, and sent *him* away empty.   empty handed

4 And again he sent to them an-other servant; and at him they cast stones, and wounded *him* in the head, and sent *him* away shamefully handled.   treated

5 And again he sent another; and him they killed, and many others; beating some, and killing some.

6 Having yet therefore one son, his wellbeloved, he sent him also last to them, saying, They will reverence my son.

7 But those husbandmen said among themselves, This is the heir; come, let us kill him, and the inher-itance shall be ours.   tenant farmers

8 And they took him, and killed *him*, and cast *him* out of the vineyard.

9 What shall therefore the lord of the vineyard do? he will come and de-stroy the husbandmen, and will give the vineyard to others.   owner

10 And have you not read this scrip-ture; The stone which the builders re-jected is become the head of the corner:

11 This was the Lord's doing, and it is marvellous in our eyes? PS. 118:23

12 And they sought to lay hold on Him, but feared the people: for they knew that He had spoken the par-able against them: and they left Him, and went their way.

13 And they send to Him certain of the Phar'i-sees and of the He-ro'di-ans, to catch Him in *His* words.   trap

14 And when they were come, they say to Him, Master, we know that You are true, and care for no man: for You regard not the person of men, but teach the way of God in truth: Is it lawful to give tribute to Cae'sar, or not?   have regard - right - tax

15 Shall we give, or shall we not give? But He, knowing their hypocrisy, said to them, Why tempt you Me? bring Me a penny, that I may see it. insincerity - test
16 And they brought *it*. And He says to them, Whose *is* this image and superscription? And they said to him, Cae'sar's.   inscription
17 And Je'sus answering said to them, Render to Cae'sar the things that are Cae'sar's, and to God the things that are God's. And they marveled at Him. Give
18 Then come to Him the Sad'ducees, which say there is no resurrection; and they asked Him, saying,
19 Master, Mo'ses wrote to us, If a man's brother die, and leave *his* wife *behind him*, and leave no children, that his brother should take his wife, and raise up seed to his brother.   DEU. 25:5 offspring
20 Now there were seven brethren: and the first took a wife, and dying left no seed.   brothers
21 And the second took her, and died, neither left he any seed: and the third likewise.
22 And the seven had her, and left no seed: last of all the woman died also.
23 In the resurrection therefore, when they shall rise, whose wife shall she be of them? for the seven had her to wife.
24 And Je'sus answering said to them, Do you not therefore err, because you know not the scriptures, neither the power of God? make mistakes
25 For when they shall rise from the dead, they neither marry, nor are given in marriage; but are as the angels which are in heaven.
26 And as touching the dead, that they rise: have you not read in the book of Mo'ses, how in the bush God spoke to him, saying, I *am* the God of A'bra-ham, and the God of I'saac, and the God of Ja'cob? EX. 3:6
27 He is not the God of the dead, but the God of the living: you therefore do greatly err.   big mistake
28 And one of the scribes came, and having heard them reasoning together, and perceiving that He had answered them well, asked Him, Which is the first commandment of all?   arguing - seeing - foremost
29 And Je'sus answered him, The first of all the commandments *is*, Hear, O Is'ra-el; The Lord our God is one Lord: DEU. 6:4
30 And you shall love the Lord your God with all your heart, and with all your soul, and with all your mind, and with all your strength: this *is* the first commandment.
31 And the second *is* like, *namely this*, You shall love your neighbor as yourself. There is none other commandment greater than these. LEV. 19:18
32 And the scribe said to Him, Well, Master, You have said the truth: for there is one God; and there is none other but He:
33 And to love Him with all the heart, and with all the understanding, and with all the soul, and with all the strength, and to love *his* neighbor as himself, is more than all whole burned offerings and sacrifices.   1 SAM. 15:22
34 And when Je'sus saw that he answered discreetly, He said to him, You are not far from the kingdom of

God. And no man after that dare ask him *any question*.

35 And Je'sus answered and said, while He taught in the temple, How say the scribes that Christ is the Son of Da'vid?   PS. 110:1

36 For Da'vid himself said by the Ho'ly Ghost, The LORD said to my Lord, Sit You on My right hand, till I make Your enemies Your footstool.   Spirit

37 Da'vid therefore himself calls Him Lord; and where is He *then* his son? And the common people heard Him gladly.

38 And He said to them in His doctrine, Beware of the scribes, which *love* to go in long clothing, and love salutations in the market-places,   teaching

39 And the chief seats in the synagogues, and the uppermost rooms at feasts: chief

40 Which devour widows' houses, and for a pretence make long prayers: these shall receive greater damnation.   consumed - appearance sake

41 And Je'sus sat opposite the treasury, and beheld how the people cast money into the treasury: and many that were rich cast in much.   observed

42 And there came a certain poor widow, and she threw in two mites, which make a farthing.

43 And He called *to Him* His disciples, and says to them, Verily I say to you, That this poor widow has cast more in, than all they which have cast into the treasury: Truly - put - others

44 For all *they* did cast in of their abundance; but she of her want did cast in all that she had, *even* all her living.

CHAPTER 13

AND as He went out of the temple, one of His disciples says to Him, Master, see what manner of stones and what buildings *are here*!

2 And Je'sus answering said to him, See you these great buildings? there shall not be left one stone upon another, that shall not be thrown down.

3 And as He sat upon the mount of Ol'ives opposite the temple, Pe'ter and James and John and An'drew asked Him privately,

4 Tell us, when shall these things be? and what *shall be* the sign when all these things shall be fulfilled?

5 And Je'sus answering them began to say, Take heed less any *man* deceive you:

6 For many shall come in My name, saying, I am *Christ*; and shall deceive many.

7 And when you shall hear of wars and rumors of wars, be you not troubled: for *such things* must needs be; but the end *shall* not *be* yet.

8 For nation shall rise against nation, and kingdom against kingdom: and there shall be earthquakes in divers places, and there shall be famines and troubles: these *are* the beginnings of sorrows.   various

9 But take heed to yourselves: for they shall deliver you up to councils; and in the synagogues you shall be beaten: and you shall be brought before

rulers and kings for My sake, for a testimony against them.

10 And the gospel must first be published among all nations.

11 But when they shall lead *you*, and deliver you up, take no thought beforehand what you shall speak, neither do you premeditate: but whatsoever shall be given you in that hour, that speak you: for it is not you that speak, but the Ho'ly Ghost.   Spirit

12 Now the brother shall betray the brother to death, and the father the son; and children shall rise up against *their* parents, and shall cause them to be put to death.

13 And you shall be hated of all *men* for My name's sake: but he that shall endure to the end, the same shall be saved.

P17 14 But when you shall see the abomination of desolation, spoken of by Dan'iel the prophet, standing where it ought not, (let him that reads understand,) then let them that be in Judae'a flee to the mountains:

DAN 9:27 DAN. 11:31

15 And let him that is on the housetop not go down into the house, neither enter *therein*, to take any thing out of his house:

16 And let him that is in the field not turn back again for to take up his garment.

17 But woe to them that are with child, and to them that give suck in those days!

18 And pray you that your flight be not in the winter.

19 For *in* those days shall be affliction, such as was not from the beginning of the creation which God created to this time, neither shall be.   tribulation

20 And except that the Lord had shortened those days, no flesh should be saved: but for the elect's sake, whom He has chosen, He has shortened the days.

21 And then if any man shall say to you, Lo, here *is* Christ; or, lo, *He is* there; believe *him* not:

22 For false Christs and false prophets shall rise, and shall show signs and wonders, to seduce, if *it were* possible, even the elect.   lead astray - chosen

23 But take you heed: behold, I have foretold you all things.

24 But in those days, after that tribulation, the sun shall be darkened, and the moon shall not give her light,

25 And the stars of heaven shall fall, and the powers that are in heaven shall be shaken.

26 And then shall they see the Son of man coming in the clouds with great power and glory.   DAN. 7:13

27 And then shall He send His angels, and shall gather together His elect from the four winds, from the uttermost part of the earth to the uttermost part of heaven.   farthest

28 Now learn a parable of the fig tree; When her branch is yet tender, and puts forth leaves, you know that summer is near: illustration

29 So you in like manner, when you shall see these things come to pass, know that it is near, *even* at the doors.

30 Verily I say to you, that this generation shall not pass, till all these things be done.   Truly

POI-101
P17-114

31 Heaven and earth shall pass away: but My words shall not pass away.

32 But of that day and *that* hour knows no man, no, not the <u>angels</u> which are in heaven, neither the Son, but the Father.   messengers

33 Take you heed, watch and pray: for you know not when the time is.

34 *For the Son of man is* as a man taking a <u>far</u> journey, who left his house, and gave authority to his servants, and to every man his work, and commanded the porter to watch.   long

35 Watch you therefore: for you know not when the master of the house comes, at even, or at midnight, or at the cockcrowing, or in the morning:

36 Less coming suddenly he find you sleeping.

37 And what I say to you I say to all, Watch.

CHAPTER 14

AFTER two days was *the feast of* the passover, and of <u>un-leavened</u> bread: and the chief priests and the scribes sought how they might take Him by <u>craft</u>, and put Him to death.   without yeast - stealth

2 But they said, Not on the feast *day*, less there be an uproar of the people.

3 And being in Beth'a-ny in the house of Si'mon the leper, as He sat at <u>meat</u>, there came a woman having an alabaster box of ointment of <u>spikenard</u> very <u>precious</u>; and she broke the box, and poured *it* on his head.   food - perfume - costly

4 And there were some that had indignation inside themselves, and said, Why was this waste of the ointment made?

5 For it might have been sold for more than three hundred pence, and have been given to the poor. And they <u>murmured</u> against her.   scolded

6 And Je'sus said, Let her alone; why trouble you her? she has wrought a good <u>work</u> on Me.   deed

7 For you have the poor with you always, and whensoever you will you may do them good: but Me you have not always.   DEU. 15:11

8 She has done what she could: she is come <u>beforehand</u> to anoint My body to <u>the burying</u>.   before time - its burial

9 <u>Verily</u> I say to you, Whenever this gospel shall be preached throughout the whole world, *this* also that she has done shall be spoken of for a memorial of her.   Truly

10 And Ju'das Is-car'i-ot, one of the twelve, went to the chief priests, to betray Him to them.

11 And when they heard *it*, they were glad, and promised to give him money. And he sought how he might conveniently betray Him.

12 And the first day of <u>unleavened</u> bread, when they <u>killed</u> the passover, His disciples said to Him, Where will You that we go and prepare that You may eat the passover?   without yeast - sacrificed

13 And He sends forth two of His disciples, and says to them, Go you into the city, and there shall meet you a man bearing a pitcher of water: follow him

14 And wherever he shall go in, say you to the goodman of the house,

The Master says, Where is the guestchamber, where I shall eat the passover with My disciples? room

15 And he will show you a large upper room furnished *and* prepared: there make ready for us.

16 And His disciples went forth, and came into the city, and found as He had said to them: and they made ready the passover.

17 And in the evening He comes with the twelve.

18 And as they sat and did eat, Je'sus said, Verily I say to you, One of you which eats with Me shall betray Me. PS 41:9 Truly

19 And they began to be sorrowful, and to say to Him one by one, *Is it I?* and another *said, Is it I?*

20 And He answered and said to them, *It is* one of the twelve, that dips with Me in the dish.

21 The Son of man indeed goes, as it is written of Him: but woe to that man by whom the Son of man is betrayed! good were it for that man if he had never been born.

22 And as they did eat, Je'sus took bread, and blessed, and broke *it*, and gave to them, and said, Take, eat: this is My body.

23 And He took the cup, and when He had given thanks, He gave *it* to them: and they all drank of it.

24 And He said to them, This is My blood of the new testament, which is shed for many. EX. 24:8 poured out

25 Verily I say to you, I will drink no more of the fruit of the vine, until that day that I drink it new in the kingdom of God. Truly

26 And when they had sung an hymn, they went out into the mount of Ol'ives.

27 And Je'sus says to them, All you shall be offended because of Me this night: for it is written, I will smite the shepherd, and the sheep shall be scattered. ZEC. 13:7 scattered

28 But after that I am risen, I will go before you into Gal'i-lee.

29 But Pe'ter said to Him, Although all shall be offended, yet *will* not I.

30 And Je'sus says to him, Verily I say to you, That this day, *even* in this night, before the cock crow twice, you shall deny Me thrice. Truly - deny knowing

31 But he spoke the more vehemently, If I should die with You, I will not deny You in any wise. Likewise also said they all. insistently - way

32 And they came to a place which was named Geth'sem'a-nc: and He says to His disciples, Sit you here, while I shall pray.

33 And He takes with him Pe'ter and James and John, and began to be sore amazed, and to be very heavy; very distressed - troubled

34 And says to them, My soul is exceeding sorrowful to death: tarry you here, and watch.

35 And He went forward a little, and fell on the ground, and prayed that, if it were possible, the hour might pass from Him.

36 And He said, Ab'ba, Father, all things *are* possible to You; take

away this cup from Me: nevertheless not what I will, but what You will.

37 And He <u>comes</u>, and finds them sleeping, and says to Pe'ter, Si'mon, sleep you? could not you <u>watch</u> one hour? _{came - stay awake}

38 Watch you and pray, less you enter into temptation. The spirit truly *is* ready, but the flesh *is* weak.

39 And again He went away, and prayed, and spoke the same words.

40 And when He returned, He found them asleep again, (for their eyes were heavy,) neither knew they what to answer Him.

41 And He comes the third time, and says to them, Sleep on now, and take *your* rest: it is enough, the <u>hour</u> is come; behold, the Son of man is betrayed into the hands of sinners. _{time}

42 Rise up, let us go; lo, he that betrays Me is at hand.

43 And immediately, while He yet spoke, comes Ju'das, one of the twelve, and with him a great multitude with swords and <u>staves</u>, from the chief priests and the scribes and the elders. _{clubs}

44 And he that betrayed Him had given them a <u>token</u>, saying, Whomsoever I shall kiss, that same is He; take Him, and lead *Him* away <u>safely</u>. _{signal - under guard}

45 And as soon as he <u>was come</u>, he goes immediatly to Him, and says, Master, master; and kissed Him. _{arrived}

46 And they laid their hands on Him, and took Him.

47 And one of them that stood by drew a sword, and <u>smote</u> a servant of the high priest, and cut off his ear. _{struck}

48 And Je'sus answered and said to them, Are you come out, as against a thief, with swords and *with* <u>staves</u> to take Me? _{clubs}

49 I was daily with you in the temple teaching, and you took Me not: but the scriptures must be fulfilled.

50 And they all <u>forsook</u> Him, and fled. _{left}

51 And there followed Him a certain young man, having a linen cloth cast about *his* naked *body*; and the young men <u>laid hold on</u> him: _{seized}

52 And he left the linen cloth, and fled from them naked.

53 And they led Je'sus away to the high priest: and with Him were assembled all the chief priests and the elders and the scribes.

54 And Pe'ter followed Him <u>afar off</u>, even into the palace of the high priest: and he sat with the servants, and warmed himself at the fire. _{at a distance}

55 And the chief priests and all the council <u>sought</u> for witness against Je'sus to put Him to death; and found none. _{kept trying}

56 For many bare false witness against Him, but their witness agreed not together.

57 And there arose <u>certain</u>, and bare false witness against Him, saying, _{certain men}

58 We heard Him say, I will destroy this temple that is made with hands, and within three days I will build another made without hands.

59 But neither so did their <u>witness</u> agree together.   testimony

60 And the high priest stood up in the midst, and asked Je'sus, saying, Answer You nothing? what *is it which* these <u>witness</u> against You?   testify

61 But He held His peace, and answered nothing. Again the high priest asked Him, and said to Him, Are You the Christ, the Son of the Blessed?

62 And Je'sus said, I am: and you shall see the Son of man sitting on the right hand of power, and coming in the clouds of heaven.   DAN. 7:13

63 Then the high priest <u>rent</u> his clothes, and says, What need we any further witnesses?   tore

64 You have heard the <u>blasphemy</u>: what think you? And they all condemned Him to be <u>guilty</u> of death.

                    LEV. 24:16 slander - deserving

65 And some began to spit on Him, and to cover His face, and to <u>buffet</u> Him, and to say to Him, Prophesy: and the <u>servants</u> did strike Him with the palms of their hands.   beat - officers

66 And as Pe'ter was beneath in the palace, there comes one of the maids of the high priest:

67 And when she saw Pe'ter warming himself, she looked <u>upon</u> him, and said, And you also were with Je'sus of Naz'a-reth.   at

68 But he denied, saying, I know not, neither understand I what you say. And he went out into the porch; and the cock crew.

69 And a maid saw him again, and began to say to them that stood by, This is *one* of them.

70 And he denied it again. And a little after, they that stood by said again to Pe'ter, Surely you are *one* of them: for you are a Gal-i-lae'an, and your <u>speech</u> agrees *thereto*.   accent

71 But he began to curse and <u>to</u> <u>swear</u>, *saying*, I know not this man of whom you speak.   curse

72 And the second time the cock crew. And Pe'ter called to mind the word that Je'sus said to him, Before the cock crow twice, you shall deny Me thrice. And when he thought thereon, he wept.

CHAPTER 15

AND immediatly in the morning the chief priests held a consultation with the elders and scribes and the whole council, and bound Je'sus, and carried *Him* away, and delivered *Him* to Pi'late.

2 And Pi'late asked Him, Are you the King of the Jews? And He answering said to him, you say *it*.

3 And the chief priests accused Him of many things: but He answered nothing.

4 And Pi'late asked Him again, saying, Answer You nothing? behold how many things they witness against You.

5 But Je'sus yet answered nothing; so that Pi'late marveled.

6 Now at *that* feast he released to them one prisoner, whomsoever they <u>desired</u>.   requested

7 And there was *one* named Ba-rab'-bas, *which* <u>lay</u> <u>bound</u> with them that

G4 had made insurrection with him, who had committed murder in the insurrection. _{was imprisoned}

8 And the multitude crying aloud began <u>to desire</u> *him to do* as he had ever done to them. _{asking}

9 But Pi'late answered them, saying, Will you that I release to you the King of the Jews?

10 For he knew that the chief priests had delivered Him for envy.

11 But the chief priests <u>moved</u> the people, that he should rather release Ba-rab'bas to them. _{stirred up}

12 And Pi'late answered and said again to them, What will you then that I shall do *to Him* whom you call the King of the Jews?

13 And they cried out again, Crucify Him.

14 Then Pi'late said to them, Why, what evil has He done? And they cried out the more exceedingly, Crucify Him.

15 And *so* Pi'late, willing to <u>content</u> the people, released Ba-rab'bas to them, and delivered Je'sus, when he had scourged *Him*, to be crucified. _{satisfy}

16 And the soldiers led Him away into the hall, called Prae-to'ri-um; and they call together the whole band.

17 And they clothed Him with purple, and platted a crown of thorns, and put it about His *head*,

18 And began to <u>salute</u> Him, Hail, King of the Jews! _{acclaim}

19 And they <u>smote</u> Him on the head with a <u>reed</u>, and did spit upon Him, and bowing *their* knees worshiped Him. _{struck - cane stick}

20 And when they had <u>mocked</u> Him, G4 they took off the purple from Him, and put His own clothes on Him, and led Him out to crucify Him. _{ridiculed}

21 And they compel one Si'mon a Cy-re'ni-an, who passed by, coming out of the country, the father of Al-ex-an'der and Ru'fus, to bear His cross.

22 And they bring Him to the place Gol'go-tha, which is, being interpreted, The place of a skull.

23 And they gave Him to drink wine mingled with myrrh: but He <u>received</u> *it* not. _{took}

24 And when they had crucified Him, they parted His garments, casting lots upon them, what every man should take. _{PS. 22:18}

25 And it was the <u>third</u> hour, and they crucified Him. _{9 A.M.}

26 And the <u>superscription</u> of His accusation was written over, THE KING OF THE JEWS. _{inscription}

27 And with Him they crucify two thieves; the one on His right hand, and the other on His left.

28 And the scripture was fulfilled, which says, And He was num- bered with the transgressors ISA. 53:12

29 And they that passed by <u>railed on</u> Him, wagging their heads, and saying, Ah, You that destroy the temple, and build *it* in three days, _{shouted to}

30 Save Yourself, and come down from the cross.

31 Likewise also the chief priests mocking said among themselves with the scribes, He saved others; Himself He cannot save. _{PS. 22:8}

32 Let Christ the King of Is'ra-el descend now from the cross, that we may see and believe. And they that were crucified with Him reviled Him. insulted

33 And when the sixth hour was come, there was darkness over the whole land until the ninth hour. 12 noon - 3 PM

34 And at the ninth hour Je'sus cried with a loud voice, saying, E-lo'i, E-lo'i, la'ma sa-bach-tha'ni? which is, being interpreted, My God, My God, why have You forsaken Me? PS. 22:1

35 And some of them that stood by, when they heard *it*, said, Behold, he calls Elijah.

36 And one ran and filled a sponge full of vinegar, and put *it* on a reed, and gave Him to drink, saying, Let alone; let us see whether Elijah will come to take Him down.

37 And Je'sus cried with a loud voice, and gave up the ghost.

38 And the veil of the temple was rent in two from the top to the bottom. torn

39 And when the centurion, which stood opposite Him, saw that He so cried out, and gave up the ghost, he said, Truly this man was the Son of God.

40 There were also women looking on afar off: among whom was Ma'ry Mag-da-le'ne, and Ma'ry the mother of James the less and of Jo'ses, and Sa-lo'me;

41 (Who also, when He was in Gali'lee, followed Him, and ministered to Him;) and many other women which came up with Him to Je-ru'sa-lem.

42 And now when the even was come, because it was the preparation, that is, the day before the sabbath, DEU. 21:25

43 Jo'seph of Ar-i-ma-thae'a, an honorable counselor, which also waited for the kingdom of God, came, and went in boldly to Pi'late, and craved the body of Je'sus. asked for

44 And Pi'late marveled if He were already dead: and calling *to him* the centurion, he asked him whether He had been any while dead.

wondered - dead a long time

45 And when he knew *it* of the centurion, he gave the body to Jo'seph. heard

46 And he bought fine linen, and took Him down, and wrapped Him in the linen, and laid Him in a sepulcher which was hewn out of a rock, and rolled a stone to the door of the sepulcher. cave grave - cut - tomb

47 And Ma'ry Mag-da-le'ne and Ma'ry the mother of Jo'ses beheld where He was laid. saw

CHAPTER 16

AND when the sabbath was past, Ma'ry Mag-da-le'ne, and Ma'ry the *mother* of James, and Sa-lo'me, had bought sweet spices, that they might come and anoint Him. rest day

2 And very early in the morning the first *day* of the week, they came to the sepulcher at the rising of the sun. (Sunday) - tomb

3 And they said among themselves, Who shall roll away the stone from the door of the sepulcher?

4 And when they looked, they saw

that the stone was rolled away; for it was very <u>great</u>. _{large}

5 And entering into the <u>sepulcher</u>, they saw a young man sitting on the right side, clothed in a long white garment; and they were <u>affrighted</u>. _{amazed}

6 And he says to them, Be not affrighted: You seek Je'sus of Naz'a-reth, which was crucified: He is risen; He is not here: behold the place where they laid Him.

7 But go your way, tell His disciples and Pe'ter that He goes <u>before</u> you into Gal'i-lee: there shall you see Him, as He said to you. _{ahead of}

8 And they went out quickly, and fled from the <u>sepulcher</u>; for they trembled and were amazed: neither said they any thing to any *man*; for they were afraid. _{tomb}

9 Now when *Jesus* was risen early the <u>first</u> *day* of the week, He appeared first to Ma'ry Mag-da-le'ne, out of whom He had cast seven devils. _(Sunday)

10 *And* she went and told them that had been with Him, as they mourned and wept.

11 And they, when they had heard that He was alive, and had been seen of her, <u>believed not</u>. _{refused to believe}

12 After that He appeared in another form to two of them, as they walked, and went into the country

13 And they went and told *it* to the <u>residue</u>: neither believed they them _{others}

14 Afterward He appeared to the eleven as they sat at <u>meat,</u> and upbraided them with their unbelief and hardness of heart, because they believed not them which had seen Him after He was risen. _{eating}

15 And He said to them, Go you into all the world, and preach the gospel to every creature.

16 He that believes and is baptized shall be saved: but he that believes not shall be <u>damned</u>. _{condemned}

17 And these signs shall follow them that believe; In My name shall they cast out <u>devils</u>; they shall speak with new <u>tongues</u>; _{demon - languages}

18 They shall take up serpents; and if they drink any deadly thing, it shall not hurt them; they shall lay hands on the sick, and they shall recover.

19 So then after the Lord had spoken to them, He was received up into heaven, and sat on the right hand of God

20 And they went forth, and preached every where, the Lord working with *them*, and confirming the word with signs following. Amen.

LUKE

OUTLINE

SURVEY

The great theme of the Gospel of Luke is: Jesus Christ is the Divine Savior. From the very beginning everything is focused on this supreme fact. Even before His birth, the angel as messenger of God commands Mary to call Him Jesus (which means "the Lord saves," 1.31). To the shepherds the angel brought the "good tidings of great joy" (2.10) that in the city of David is born "a Savior which

is Christ the Lord" (2.11). And in the first public announcement which Jesus made regarding His mission, He explicitly taught that He is the Divine Savior of Whom the Old Testament Scriptures wrote (4.17–21).

From that moment we see how Jesus reveals Himself as the Divine Redeemer Who came to save those that are lost. He saves from the power of evil spirits (4.33–36), from severe illness (4.38–40), from leprosy (5.12, 13) and even from the power and consequences of sin (5.20–26). Luke further shows that Jesus as the Almighty Savior has the power and divine authority to raise the dead (7.12–17). Being one with God the Father, He also has the power over nature to be able to save His disciples from a raging storm (8.22–25) and the multitudes from hunger (9.11–17).

After Jesus had revealed Himself as the Almighty Savior and after the apostles confessed Him as the Christ (9.18–20), our Lord began to teach His followers that in order to be their Divine Savior He must suffer and die (9.22).

The words of Jesus in 19.10, "the Son of man is come to seek and to save that which was lost," crystallize the wonderful message of the Gospel of Luke.

He shows that Jesus came as Savior in a universal sense—for people of all ages and conditions, for Jews (1.13; 2.10), for Samaritans (9.51–56), for heathen (2.32; 3.6, 38), for publicans, sinners and outcasts (7.37–50) as well as for respectable people (7.36), for the poor (1.53), as well as for the rich (19.2; 23.50).

At the same time, our Lord urgently warned people that, although He came to save and not to destroy, all those who refuse to be saved by Him will bring terrible suffering upon themselves (19.27, 41–44).

The Gospel of Luke proclaims the glad tidings that Jesus not only claimed to be the Divine Savior, but that He revealed Himself as the Almighty Redeemer who is the only begotten Son of the Father. Through His resurrection and ascension (24.50–53), He finally proved the truth of His claims and the genuineness of His self-revelation as the Savior of the world, sent, approved and equipped by God (4.17–21; 10.22).

AUTHOR

There can be no doubt that tradition is correct in stating that Luke, the beloved physician (Cl 4.14) is the author of this Gospel. As a companion of Paul (Phm 24; 2 Tm 4.11; Cl 4.10–14; Ac 1.1; 20.5—21.17; 27.2—28.16), Luke had many personal contacts with apostles and other witnesses of the gospel history. This, together with his Greek cultural background, his intellectual training and his intimate contact with men like Mark (who also wrote a Gospel), enabled him to write a trustworthy, comprehensive and beautiful Gospel. He probably wrote the Gospel between A.D. 64 and 70. Soon afterwards he also wrote Acts.

J.N.G.

THE GOSPEL ACCORDING TO

LUKE

CHAPTER 1

FORASMUCH as many have taken in hand to set forth in order a declaration of those things which are most surely believed among us,

2 Even as they delivered them to us, which from the beginning were eye-witnesses, and ministers of the word; *Jesus' teaching*

3 It seemed good to me also, having had perfect understanding of all things from the very first, to write to you in order, most excellent The-oph'i-lus,

4 That you might know the certainty of those things, wherein you have been instructed.

5 There was in the days of Her'od, the king of Ju-dae'a, a certain priest named Zech'a-ri'ah, of the course of A-bi'a: and his wife *was* of the daughters of Aar'on, and her name *was* E-lis'a-beth. *lineage*

6 And they were both righteous before God, walking in all the commandments and ordinances of the Lord blameless. *MAL. 4:6*

7 And they had no child, because that E-lis'a-beth was barren, and they both were *now* well stricken in years. *advanced*

8 And it came to pass, that while he executed the priest's office before God in the order of his course. *performed*

9 According to the custom of the priest's office, his lot was to burn in-cense when he went into the temple of the Lord.

10 And the whole multitude of the people were praying outside at the time of incense. *turn*

11 And there appeared to him an angel of the Lord standing on the right side of the altar of incense. *messenger*

12 And when Zech'a-ri'ah saw *him*, he was troubled, and fear fell upon him. *anxiety*

13 But the angel said to him, Fear not, Zech'a-ri'ah: for your prayer is heard; and your wife E-lis'a-beth shall bear you a son, and you shall call his name John.

14 And you shall have joy and gladness; and many shall rejoice at his birth.

15 For he shall be great in the sight of the Lord, and shall drink neither wine nor strong drink; and he shall be filled with the Ho'ly Ghost, even from his mother's womb. *NUM. 6:3 Spirit*

16 And many of the children of Is'ra-el shall he turn to the Lord their God.

17 And he shall go before Him in the spirit and power of Elijah, to turn the hearts of the fathers to the children, and the disobedient to the wisdom of the just; to make ready a people prepared for the Lord.

18 And Zech'a-ri'ah said to the angel, Whereby shall I know this? for I

am an old man, and my wife well stricken in years. messenger - advanced

19 And the <u>angel</u> answering said to him, I am Ga'bri-el, that stand in the presence of God; and am sent to speak to you, and to show you these glad tidings. DAN. 8:16 messenger

20 And, behold, you shall be dumb, and not able to speak, until the day that these things shall be performed, because you believe not my words, which shall be fulfilled in their season.

21 And the people waited for Zech'a-ri'ah, and marveled that he tarried so long in the temple.

22 And when he came out, he could not speak to them: and they perceived that he had seen a vision in the temple: for he <u>beckoned</u> to them, and remained speechless. made signs

23 And it came to pass, that, as soon as the days of his ministration were accomplished, he departed to his own house.

24 And after those days his wife E-lis'a-beth conceived, and hid herself five months, saying,

25 Thus has the Lord dealt with me in the days wherein He looked on *me*, to take away my reproach among men. ISA. 4:1

26 And in the sixth month the angel Ga'bri-el was sent from God to a city of Gal'i-lee, named Naz'a-reth,

27 To a virgin <u>espoused</u> to a man whose name was Jo'seph, of the house of Da'vid; and the virgin's name was Ma'ry. engaged

28 And the <u>angel</u> came in to her, and said, Hail, *you that are* highly fa-vored, the Lord *is* with you: blessed *are* you among women. i.e., Gabriel

29 And when she saw *him*, she was troubled at his saying, and cast in her mind what manner of <u>salutation</u> this should be. greeting

30 And the <u>angel</u> said to her, Fear not, Ma'ry: for you have found favor with God.

31 And, behold, you shall conceive in your womb, and bring forth a son, and shall call His name JE'SUS.

32 He shall be great, and shall be called the Son of the Highest: and the Lord God shall give to Him the throne of His father Da'vid:

33 And He shall reign over the house of Ja'cob for ever; and of His kingdom there shall be no end. GEN. 49:10 2 SAM 7:16

34 Then said Ma'ry to the <u>angel</u>, How shall this be, seeing I know not a man?

35 And the <u>angel</u> answered and said to her, The Ho'ly <u>Ghost</u> shall come upon you, and the power of the Highest shall overshadow you: therefore also that holy thing which shall be born of you shall be called the Son of God. i.e., Gabriel - Spirit

36 And, behold, your cousin E-lis'a-beth, she has also conceived a son in her old age: and this is the sixth month with her, who was called <u>barren</u>. childless

37 For with God nothing shall be impossible. GEN. 18:14

38 And Ma'ry said, Behold the <u>handmaid</u> of the Lord; be it to me according to your word. And the <u>angel</u> departed from her. servant

39 And Ma'ry arose in those days, and went into the hill country with haste, into a city of Ju'da;

40 And entered into the house of Zech'a-ri'ah, and saluted <u>E-lis'a-beth</u>. _{greeted}

41 And it came to pass, that, when E-lis'a-beth heard the <u>salutation</u> of Ma'ry, the babe leaped in her womb; and E-lis'a-beth was filled with the Ho'ly <u>Ghost</u>: _{Spirit}

42 And she spoke out with a loud voice, and said, Blessed *are* you among women, and blessed *is* the fruit of your womb.

43 And what *is* this to me, that the mother of my Lord should come to me?

44 For, lo, as soon as the voice of your <u>salutation</u> sounded in mine ears, the babe leaped in my womb for joy. _{greeting}

45 And blessed *is* she that believed: for there shall be a performance of those things which were told her from the Lord.

46 And Ma'ry said, My soul does magnify the Lord,

47 And my spirit has rejoiced in God my Savior.

48 For He has regarded the low estate of His handmaiden: for, behold, from hereafter all generations shall call me blessed.

49 For He that is mighty has done to me great things; and holy *is* His name.

50 And His mercy *is* on them that <u>fear</u> Him from generation to generation. _{reverence}

51 He has showed strength with His arm; He has scattered the proud in the imagination of their hearts.

52 He has put down the mighty from *their* seats, and exalted them of <u>low degree</u>. _{humility}

53 He has filled the hungry with good things; and the rich He has sent empty away.

54 He has helped His servant Is'ra-el, in remembrance of *His* mercy;

55 As He spoke to our fathers, to A'bra-ham, and to His <u>seed</u> for ever. _{GEN. 17:7 descendants}

56 And Ma'ry <u>abode</u> with her about three months, and returned to her own house. _{lived}

57 Now E-lis'a-beth's full time came that she should be delivered; and she brought forth a son.

58 And her neighbors and her cousins heard how the Lord had showed great mercy upon her; and they rejoiced with her.

59 And it came to pass, that on the eighth day they came to circumcise the child; and they called him Zech'a-ri'ah, after the name of his father. _{GEN. 17:12}

60 And his mother answered and said, Not *so*; but he shall be called John.

61 And they said to her, There is none of your <u>kindred</u> that is called by this name. _{relatives}

62 And they made signs to his father, how he would have him <u>called</u>. _{named}

63 And he asked for a writing table, and wrote, saying, his name is John. And they <u>marveled</u> all. _{were astonished}

64 And his mouth was opened immediately, and his tongue *loosed*, and he spoke, and praised God.

65 And fear came on all that dwelt round about them: and all these <u>sayings</u> were <u>noised</u> abroad throughout all the hill country of Ju-dae'a.

things - talked

66 And all they that heard *them* laid *them* up in their hearts, saying, What manner of child shall this be! And the hand of the Lord was with him.

67 And his father Zech'a-ri'ah was filled with the Ho'ly <u>Ghost</u>, and <u>prophesied</u>, saying,

Spirit - spoke

68 Blessed *be* the Lord God of Is'ra-el; for He has visited and redeemed His people,

1 SAM. 25:32

69 And has raised up an <u>horn</u> of salvation for us in the house of His servant Da'vid;

ruler

70 As He spoke by the mouth of His holy prophets, which have been since the world began:

71 That we should be saved from our enemies, and from the hand of all that <u>hate</u> us;

abhor

72 To perform the mercy *promised* to our fathers, and to remember His holy <u>covenant</u>;

agreement

73 The oath which He sware to our father A'bra-ham,

74 That He would grant to us, that we being delivered out of the hand of our enemies might serve Him without fear,

75 In holiness and righteousness before Him, all the days of our life.

76 And you, child, shall be called the prophet of the Highest: for you shall go before the face of the Lord to prepare his ways;

MAL 3:1

77 To give knowledge of salvation to His people by the remission of their sins,

78 Through the tender mercy of our God; <u>whereby the dayspring</u> from on high has visited us, MAL. 4:2 light i.e., Jesus

79 To give light to them that sit in darkness and *in* the shadow of death, to guide our feet into the way of peace.

ISA. 9:2

80 And the child grew, and <u>waxed</u> strong in spirit, and was in the deserts till the day of his showing to Is'ra-el.

grew

CHAPTER 2

AND it came to pass in those days, that there went out a decree from Cae'sar Au-gus'tus, that all the world should be <u>taxed</u>.

registered

2 (*And* this taxing was first made when Cy-re'ni-us was governor of Syr'i-a.)

3 And all went to be <u>taxed</u>, every one into his own city.

4 And Jo'seph also went up from Gal'i-lee, out of the city of Naz'a-reth, into Ju-dae'a, to the city of Da'vid, which is called Beth'le-hem; (because he was of the <u>house</u> and <u>lineage</u> of Da'vid:)

family - descendants

5 To be taxed with Ma'ry his <u>espoused</u> wife, being great with child.

engaged

6 And so it was, that, while they were there, the days were accomplished that she should be delivered.

7 And she brought forth her firstborn son, and wrapped Him in swaddling

clothes, and laid Him in a manger; because there was no room for them in the inn.

8 And there were in the same country shepherds <u>abiding</u> in the field, keeping watch over their flock by night.   living

9 And, lo, the <u>angel</u> of the Lord came upon them, and the glory of the Lord shone round about them: and they were <u>sore</u> afraid. messenger - very

10 And the <u>angel</u> said to them, Fear not: for, behold, I bring you good <u>tidings</u> of great joy, which shall be to all people.   news

11 For to you is born this day in the <u>city of Da'vid</u> a Savior, which is Christ the Lord.   ISA. 9:6 Jerusalem

12 And this *shall be* a sign to you; You shall find the babe wrapped in swaddling clothes, lying in a manger.   1 TIM. 1:15

13 And suddenly there was with the <u>angel</u> a multitude of the heavenly host praising God, and saying messenger

14 Glory to God in the highest, and on earth peace, good will toward men.

15 And it came to pass, as the <u>angels</u> were gone away from them into heaven, the shepherds said one to another, Let us now go even to Beth'le-hem, and see this thing which is come to pass, which the Lord has made known to us.

16 And they came with haste, and found Ma'ry, and Jo'seph, and the babe lying in a manger.

17 And when they had seen *it*, they made known abroad the saying which was told them concerning this Child.

18 And all they that heard *it* wondered at those things which were told them by the shepherds.

19 But Ma'ry kept all these things, and <u>pondered</u> *them* in her heart.   thought of

20 And the shepherds returned, glorifying and praising God for all the things that they had heard and seen, as it was told to them.

21 And when eight days were accomplished for the circumcising of the Child, His name was called JE'SUS, which was so named of the <u>angel</u> before He was conceived in the womb.   messenger

22 And when the days of her purification according to the law of Mo'ses were <u>accomplished</u>, they brought Him to Je-ru'sa-lem, to present *Him* to the Lord;   fulfilled

23 (As it is written in the law of the Lord, Every male that opens the womb shall be called holy to the Lord;)   EX. 13:12

24 And to offer a sacrifice according to that which is said in the law of the Lord, A pair of turtledoves, or two young pigeons.   LEV. 12:8

25 And, behold, there was a man in Je-ru'sa-lem, whose name *was* Sim'e-on; and the same man *was* just and devout, waiting for the consolation of Is'ra-el: and the Ho'ly <u>Ghost</u> was upon him.   Spirit

26 And it was revealed to him by the Ho'ly <u>Ghost</u>, that he should not see death, before he had seen the Lord's Christ.

27 And he came <u>by</u> the Spirit into the temple: and when the parents brought in the child Je'sus, to do for Him after the custom of the law, in

28 Then took he Him up in his arms, and blessed God, and said,

29 Lord, now let You Your servant depart in peace, according to Your word:

30 For my eyes have seen Your salvation,   ISA. 52:10

31 Which You have prepared before the face of all people;

32 A light to lighten the Gen'tiles, and the glory of Your people Is'rael.   ISA. 42:6 guide

33 And Jo'seph and His mother marveled at those things which were spoken of Him.   wondered

34 And Sim'e-on blessed them, and said to Ma'ry His mother, Behold, this *Child* is set for the fall and rising again of many in Is'ra-el; and for a sign which shall be spoken against;

35 (Yea, a sword shall pierce through your own soul also,) that the thoughts of many hearts may be revealed.

36 And there was one An'na, a prophetess, the daughter of Phan-u'el, of the tribe of A'ser: she was of a great age, and had lived with an husband seven years from her virginity;

37 And she *was* a widow of about fourscore and four years, which departed not from the temple, but served *God* with fastings and prayers night and day.

38 And she coming in that instant gave thanks likewise to the Lord, and spoke of Him to all them that looked for redemption in Je-ru'sa-lem.

39 And when they had performed all things according to the law of the Lord, they returned into Gal'i-lee, to their own city Naz'a-reth.   done

40 And the Child grew, and waxed strong in spirit, filled with wisdom: and the grace of God was upon Him.   grew

41 Now His parents went to Je-ru'sa-lem every year at the feast of the passover.

42 And when He was twelve years old, they went up to Je-ru'sa-lem after the custom of the feast.

43 And when they had fulfilled the days, as they returned, the child Je'sus tarried behind in Je-ru'sa-lem; and Jo'seph and His mother knew not *of it*.

44 But they, supposing Him to have been in the company, went a day's journey; and they sought Him among *their* kinsfolk and acquaintance.   group - re;atives

45 And when they found Him not, they turned back again to Je-ru'sa-lem, seeking Him.

46 And it came to pass, that after three days they found Him in the temple, sitting in the midst of the doctors, both hearing them, and asking them questions.   teachers

47 And all that heard Him were astonished at His understanding and answers.

48 And when they saw Him, they were amazed: and His mother said to Him, Son, why have You thus dealt with us? behold, Your father and I have sought You sorrowing.

49 And He said to them, How is it that you sought Me? knew you not that I must be about My Father's business?

50 And they understood not the saying which He spoke to them.

51 And He went down with them, and came to Naz'a-reth, and was sub-

ject to them: but His mother kept all these sayings in her heart. _{obedient}

52 And Je'sus increased in wisdom and stature, and in favor with God and man.

CHAPTER 3

NOW in the fifteenth year of the reign of Ti-be'ri-us Cae'sar, Pon'ti-us Pi'late being governor of Ju-dae'a, and Her'od being tetrarch of Gal'i-lee, and his brother Phil'ip tetrarch of I-tu-rae'a and of the region of Trach-o-ni'tis, and Ly-sa'ni-as the tetrarch of Ab-i-le'ne,

2 An'nas and Ca'ia-phas being the high priests, the word of God came to John the son of Zech'a-ri'ah in the wilderness.

3 And he came into all the country about Jor'dan, preaching the baptism of repentance for the remission of sins;

4 As it is written in the book of the words of I-sa'iah the prophet, saying, The voice of one crying in the wilderness, Prepare you the way of the Lord, make His paths straight. ISA. 40:3

5 Every valley shall be filled, and every mountain and hill shall be brought low; and the crooked shall be made straight, and the rough ways *shall be* made smooth;

6 And all flesh shall see the salvation of God. PSA. 98:3 ISA. 52:10

7 Then said he to the multitude that came forth to be baptized of him, O generation of <u>vipers</u>, who has warned you to flee from the wrath to come? _{serpants—i.e., deceivers}

8 Bring forth therefore fruits worthy of repentance, and begin not to say within yourselves, We have A'braham to *our* father: for I say to you, That God is able of these stones to raise up children to A'bra-ham.

9 And now also the ax is laid to the root of the trees: every tree therefore which brings not forth good fruit is hewn down, and cast into the fire.

10 And the people asked him, saying, What shall we do then?

11 He answers and says to them, He that has two coats, let him <u>impart</u> to him that has none; and he that has <u>meat</u>, let him do likewise. _{give - food}

12 Then came also <u>publicans</u> to be baptized, and said to him, Master, what shall we do? _{tax gatherers}

13 And he said to them, <u>Exact</u> no more than that which is <u>appointed</u> you. _{collect - due}

14 And the soldiers likewise demanded of him, saying, And what shall we do? And he said to them, Do violence to no man, neither accuse *any* falsely; and be content with your wages.

15 And as the people were in expectation, and all men mused in their hearts of John, whether he were the Christ, or not;

16 John answered, saying to *them* all, I indeed baptize you <u>with</u> water; but one mightier than I comes, the <u>latchet</u> of whose shoes I am not worthy to unloose: He shall baptize you with the Ho'ly <u>Ghost</u> and with fire: _{in - thong - Spirit}

17 Whose fan *is* in His hand, and He will throughly purge His floor, and will

gather the wheat into His garner; but the chaff He will burn with fire unquenchable.

18 And many other things in his exhortation preached he to the people.

19 But Her'od the tetrarch, being re-proved by him for He-ro'di-as his brother Phil'ip's wife, and for all the evils which Her'od had done, criticized

20 Added yet this above all, that he shut up John in prison.

21 Now when all the people were baptized, it came to pass, that Je'sus also being baptized, and praying, the heaven was opened,

22 And the Ho'ly Ghost descended in a bodily shape like a dove upon Him, and a voice came from heaven, which said, You are My beloved Son; in You I am well pleased. Spirit - came down

23 And Je'sus Himself began to be about thirty years of age, being (as was supposed) the son of Jo'seph, which was *the son* of He'li,

24 Which was *the son* of Mat'that, which was *the son* of Le'vi, which was *the son* of Mel'chi, which was *the son* of Jan'na, which was *the son* of Jo'seph,

25 Which was *the son* of Mat-ta-thi'as, which was *the son* of A'mos, which was *the son* of Na'um, which was *the son* of Es'li, which was *the son* of Nag'ge,

26 Which was *the son* of Ma'ath, which was *the son* of Mat-ta-thi'as, which was *the son* of Sem'e-i, which was *the son* of Jo'seph, which was *the son* of Ju'da,

27 Which was *the son* of Jo-an'na, which was *the son* of Rhe'sa, which was *the son* of Zo-rob'a-bel, which was *the son* of Sa-la'thi-el, which was *the son* of Ne'ri,

28 Which was *the son* of Mel'chi, which was *the son* of Ad'di, which was *the son* of Co'sam, which was *the son* of El-mo'dam, which was *the son* of Er,

29 Which was *the son* of Jo'se, which was *the son* of E-li-e'zer, which was *the son* of Jo'rim, which was *the son* of Mat'that, which was *the son* of Le'vi,

30 Which was *the son* of Sim'e-on, which was *the son* of Ju'da, which was *the son* of Jo'seph, which was *the son* of Jo'nan, which was *the son* of E-li'a-kim,

31 Which was *the son* of Me'le-a, which was *the son* of Me'nan, which was *the son* of Mat'ta-tha, which was *the son* of Na'than, which was *the son* of Da'vid,

32 Which was *the son* of Jes'se, which was *the son* of O'bed, which was *the son* of Bo'oz, which was *the son* of Sal'mon, which was *the son* of Na-as'son,

33 Which was *the son* of A-min'a-dab, which was *the son* of A'ram, which was *the son* of Es'rom, which was *the son* of Pha'res, which was *the son* of Ju'da,

34 Which was *the son* of Ja'cob, which was *the son* of I'saac, which was *the son* of A'bra-ham, which was *the son* of Tha'ra, which was *the son* of Na'chor,

35 Which was *the son* of Sa'ruch, which was *the son* of Ra'gau, which was *the son* of Pha'lec, which was *the son* of He'ber, which was *the son* of Sa'la,

36 Which was *the son* of Ca-i'nan, which was *the son* of Ar-phax'ad, which was *the son* of Sem, which was *the son*

of No'ah, which was *the son* of La'mech,

37 Which was *the son* of Ma-thu'sa-la, which was *the son* of E'noch, which was *the son* of Ja'red, which was *the son* of Ma-le'le-el, which was *the son* of Ca-i'nan,

38 Which was *the son* of E'nos, which was *the son* of Seth, which was *the son* of Ad'am, which was *the son* of God.

CHAPTER 4

AND Je'sus being full of the Ho'ly Ghost returned from Jor'dan, and was led by the Spirit into the wilderness,   Spirit

2 Being forty days tempted of the devil. And in those days He did eat nothing: and when they were ended, He afterward hungered. DEU. 9:9 tested - Satan

3 And the devil said to Him, If You be the Son of God, command this stone that it be made bread.

4 And Je'sus answered him, saying, It is written, That man shall not live by bread alone, but by every word of God.

5 And the devil, taking Him up into an high mountain, showed to Him all the kingdoms of the world in a moment of time.   all nations

6 And the devil said to Him, All this power will I give You, and the glory of them: for that is delivered to me; and to whomsoever I will I give it.   Satan

7 If You therefore will worship me, all shall be Yours.   honor

8 And Je'sus answered and said to him, Get you behind Me, Sa'tan: for it is written, You shall worship the Lord your God, and Him only shall you serve.   DEU. 6:13

9 And he brought Him to Je-ru'sa-lem, and set Him on a pinnacle of the temple, and said to Him, If You be the Son of God, cast Yourself down from here:

10 For it is written, He shall give His angels charge over You, to keep You: PS.91:11-12 - messengers

11 And in *their* hands they shall bear You up, less at any time You dash your foot against a stone.

12 And Je'sus answering said to him, It is said, You shall not tempt the Lord your God.   DEU. 6:16 - test

13 And when the devil had ended all the temptation, he departed from Him for a season.   Satan - time

14 And Je'sus returned in the power of the Spirit into Gal'i-lee: and there went out a fame of Him through all the region round about.   news

15 And He taught in their synagogues, being glorified of all.

16 And He came to Naz'a-reth, where He had been brought up: and, as His custom was, He went into the synagogue on the sabbath day, and stood up for to read.

17 And there was delivered to Him the book of the prophet I-sa'iah. And when He had opened the book, He found the place where it was written,   scroll

18 The Spirit of the Lord *is* upon Me, because He has anointed Me to preach the gospel to the poor; He has sent Me to heal the brokenhearted, to

preach deliverance to the captives, and recovering of sight to the blind, to set at liberty them that are bruised,   ISA. 61:1-3

19 To preach the acceptable year of the Lord.

20 And He closed the book, and He gave *it* again to the <u>minister</u>, and sat down. And the eyes of all them that were in the synagogue were fastened on Him.   Rabbi

21 And He began to say to them, This day is this scripture fulfilled in your ears.   ISA. 61: 1-3

22 And all bare Him witness, and wondered at the gracious words which proceeded out of His mouth. And they said, Is not this Jo'seph's son?

23 And He said to them, You will surely say to Me this proverb, Physician, heal yourself: whatsoever we have heard done in Ca-per'na-um, do also here in your country.

24 And He said, <u>Verily</u> I say to you, No prophet is accepted in his own country.   Truly

25 But I tell you of a truth, many widows were in Is'ra-el in the days of Elijah, when the heaven was shut up three years and six months, when great famine was throughout all the land ;   1 KGS. 17:1

26 But to none of them was Elijah sent, <u>save</u> to Sa-rep'ta, a *city* of Si'don, to a woman *that was* a widow.   except

27 And many lepers were in Is'ra-el in the time of Elisha the prophet; and none of them was <u>cleansed</u>, saving Na'a-man the Syr'i-an.   2 KGS 5:14 made fit

28 And all they in the synagogue, when they heard these things, were filled with <u>wrath</u>,   anger

29 And rose up, and thrust Him out of the city, and led Him to the <u>brow</u> of the hill whereon their city was built, that they might cast Him down headlong.   crest

30 But He passing through the midst of them went His way,

31 And came down to Ca-per'na-um, a city of Gal'i-lee, and taught them on the sabbath days.

32 And they were <u>astonished</u> at His <u>doctrine</u>: for His word was with power.   surprised - teaching

33 And in the synagogue there was a man, which had a spirit of an unclean <u>devil</u>, and cried out with a loud voice,   demon

34 Saying, Let *us* alone; what have we to do with You, *You* Je'sus of Naz'a-reth? are You come to destroy us? I know You who You are; the Holy One of God.

35 And Je'sus <u>rebuked</u> him, saying, Hold your peace, and come out of him. And when the <u>devil</u> had thrown him in the midst, he came out of him, and hurt him not.   admonished

36 And they were all amazed, and spoke among themselves, saying, What a word *is* this! for with authority and power He commands the <u>unclean</u> spirits, and they come out.   unfit

37 And the <u>fame</u> of Him went out into every place of the country round about.   knowledge

38 And He arose out of the synagogue, and entered into Si'mon's house. And Si'mon's wife's mother was taken

with a great fever; and they <u>be-sought</u> Him for her. _{requested}

39 And He stood over her, and re-buked the fever; and it left her: and immediately she arose and minis-tered to them.

40 Now when the sun was setting, all they that had any sick with <u>divers</u> diseases brought them to Him; and He laid His hands on every one of them, and healed them. _{various}

41 And <u>devils</u> also came out of many, crying out, and saying, You are Christ the Son of God. And He rebuking *them* permitted them not to speak: for they knew that He was Christ. _{demons}

42 And when it was day, He departed and went into a desert place: and the people sought Him, and came to Him, and <u>stayed</u> Him, that He should not depart from them. _{delayed}

43 And He said to them, I must preach the kingdom of God to other cities also: for <u>therefore</u> am I sent. _{this reason}

44 And He preached in the syna-gogues of Gal'i-lee.

CHAPTER 5

AND it came to pass, that, as the people pressed upon Him to hear the word of God, He stood by the lake of Gen-nes'a-ret,

2 And saw two <u>ships</u> <u>standing</u> by the lake: but the fishermen were gone out of them, and were wash-ing *their* nets. _{boats - alone}

3 And He entered into one of the <u>ships</u>, which was Si'mon's, and <u>pray-ed</u> him that he would <u>thrust</u> out a little from the land. And He sat down, and taught the people out of the ship. _{asked-put}

4 Now when He had left speaking, He said to Si'mon, Launch out into the deep, and let down your nets for a <u>draught</u>. _{catch}

5 And Si'mon answering said to Him, Master, we have <u>toiled</u> all the night, and have taken nothing: nevertheless at Your word I will let down the net. _{worked}

6 And when they had this done, they <u>inclosed</u> a great multitude of fishes: and their net broke. _{caught}

7 And they <u>beckoned</u> to *their* part-ners, which were in the other ship, that they should come and help them. And they came, and filled both the ships, so that they began to sink. _{signaled}

8 When Si'mon Pe'ter saw *it*, he fell down at Je'sus' knees, saying, Depart from me; for I am a sinful man, O Lord.

9 For he was astonished, and all that were with him, at the <u>draught</u> of the fishes which they had taken: _{catch}

10 And so *was* also James, and John, the sons of Zeb'e-dee, which were partners with Si'mon. And Je'sus said to Si'mon, Fear not; from hereaf-ter you shall catch men.

11 And when they had brought their ships to land, they <u>forsook</u> all, and followed Him. _{left}

12 And it came to pass, when He was in a certain city, behold a man full of leprosy: who seeing Je'sus fell on *his* face, and <u>besought</u> Him, saying, Lord, if You will, you can make me clean. _{requested}

13 And He put forth *His* hand, and touched him, saying, I will: be you clean. And immediately the leprosy departed from him.

14 And He charged him to tell no man: but go, and show yourself to the priest, and offer for your cleansing, according as Mo'ses commanded, for a testimony to them.   LEV. 13:49 instructed

15 But so much the more went there a fame abroad of Him: and great multitudes came together to hear, and to be healed by Him of their infirmities.   knowledge

16 And He withdrew Himself into the wilderness, and prayed.

17 And it came to pass on a certain day, as He was teaching, that there were Phar'i-sees and doctors of the law sitting by, which were come out of every town of Gal'i-lee, and Ju-dae'a, and Je-ru'sa-lem: and the power of the Lord was *present* to heal them.   teachers

18 And, behold, men brought in a bed a man which was taken with a palsy: and they sought *means* to bring him in, and to *lay* him before Him   sick

19 And when they could not find by what *way* they might bring him in because of the multitude, they went upon the housetop, and let him down through the tiling with *his* couch into the midst before Je'sus.   big crowd - pallet

20 And when He saw their faith, He said to him, Man, your sins are forgiven you.

21 And the scribes and the Phar'i-sees began to reason, saying, Who is this which speaks blasphemies? Who can forgive sins, but God alone?   talk

22 But when Je'sus perceived their thoughts, He answering said to them, What reason you in your hearts?   understood - think

23 Whether is easier, to say, Your sins be forgiven you; or to say, Rise up and walk?

24 But that you may know that the Son of man has power upon earth to forgive sins, (He said to the sick of the palsy,) I say to you, Arise, and take up your couch, and go into your house.   pallet

25 And immediately he rose up before them, and took up that whereon he lay, and departed to his own house, glorifying God.

26 And they were all amazed, and they glorified God, and were filled with fear, saying, We have seen strange things to day.   reverence

27 And after these things He went forth, and saw a publican, named Le'vi, sitting at the receipt of custom: and He said to him, Follow Me.   tax gatherer

28 And he left all, rose up, and followed Him.

29 And Le'vi made Him a great feast in his own house: and there was a great company of publicans and of others that sat down with them.

30 But their scribes and Phar'i-sees murmured against His disciples, saying, Why do you eat and drink with publicans and sinners?   grumbled

31 And Je'sus answering said to them, They that are whole need not a physician; but they that are sick.   well

32 I came not to call the righteous, but sinners to repentance.

33 And they said to Him, Why do the disciples of John fast often, and make prayers, and likewise *the disciples* of the Phar'i-sees; but yours eat and drink?

34 And He said to them, Can you make the children of the bridechamber fast, while the bridegroom is with them?

35 But the days will come, when the bridegroom shall be taken away from them, and then shall they fast in those days.

36 And He spoke also a parable to them; No man puts a piece of a new garment upon an old; if otherwise, then both the new <u>makes a rent,</u> and the piece that was *taken* out of the new <u>agrees not</u> with the old.   is torn - - doesn't match

37 And no man puts new wine into old <u>bottles</u>; else the new wine will burst the <u>bottles</u>, and be spilled, and the <u>bottles</u> shall <u>perish</u>. wineskins - be of no use

38 But new wine must be put into new <u>bottles</u>; and both are preserved.

39 No man also having drunk old *wine* immediately desires new: for he says, The old is better.

CHAPTER 6

AND it came to pass on the second <u>sabbath</u> after the first that He went through the <u>corn</u> fields; and His disciples plucked the ears of <u>corn</u>, and did eat, rubbing *them* in *their* hands.   DEU. 23:25 rest day - grain

2 And certain of the Phar'i-sees said to them, Why do you that which is not <u>lawful</u> to do on the <u>sabbath</u> days?   proper

3 And Je'sus answering them said, Have you not read so much as this, what Da'vid did, when himself was an hungry, and they which were with him;

4 How he went into the house of God, and did take and eat the <u>showbread</u>, and gave also to them that were with him; which it is not <u>lawful</u> to eat but for the priests alone? consecrated bread - proper

5 And He said to them, That the Son of man is Lord also of the <u>sabbath</u>.   rest day

6 And it came to pass also on another <u>sabbath</u>, that He entered into the synagogue and taught: and there was a man whose right hand was withered.

7 And the scribes and Phar'i-sees watched Him, whether He would heal on the <u>sabbath</u> day; that they might find an accusation against Him.

8 But He knew their thoughts, and said to the man which had the withered hand, Rise up, and <u>stand</u> forth in the midst. And he arose and stood forth.   come

9 Then said Je'sus to them, I will ask you one thing; Is it lawful on the <u>sabbath</u> days to do good, or to do evil? to save life, or to destroy *it*?   proper

10 And looking round about upon them all, He said to the man, Stretch forth your hand. And he did so: and his hand was <u>restored whole</u> as the other.   made well

11 And they were filled with madness; and <u>communed</u> one with another what they might do to Je'sus. talked

12 And it came to pass in those days, that He went out into a mountain to

pray, and continued all night in prayer to God.

13 And when it was day, He called *to Him* His disciples: and of them He chose twelve, whom also He named apostles;

14 Si'mon, (whom He also named Pe'ter,) and Andrew his brother, James and John, Phil'ip and Bar-thol'o-mew,

15 Mat'thew and Thom'as, James the son of Al-phae'us, and Si'mon called Ze-lo'tes,

16 And Ju'das *the brother* of James, and Ju'das Is-car'i-ot, which also was the traitor.

17 And He came down with them, and stood in the plain, and the company of His disciples, and a great multitude of people out of all Ju-dae'a and Je-ru'sa-lem, and from the sea coast of Tyre and Si'don, which came to hear Him, and to be healed of their diseases;

18 And they that were <u>vexed</u> with unclean spirits: and they were healed.   troubled

19 And the whole multitude sought to touch Him: for there went virtue out of Him, and healed *them* all.

20 And He lifted up His eyes on His disciples, and said, <u>Blessed</u> *be you* poor: for yours is the kingdom of God.   happy

21 <u>Blessed</u> *are you* that hunger now: for you shall be <u>filled</u>. <u>Blessed</u> *are you* that weep now: for you shall laugh.   satisified

22 <u>Blessed</u> are you, when men shall <u>hate</u> you, and when they shall separate you *from their company*, and shall reproach *you*, and cast out your name as evil, for the Son of man's sake.   revile

23 Rejoice you in that day, and leap for joy: for, behold, your reward *is* great in heaven: for in the like manner did their fathers to the prophets.

24 But woe to you that are rich! for you have received your consolation.

25 Woe to you that are full! for you shall hunger. Woe to you that laugh now! for you shall mourn and weep.

26 Woe to you, when all men shall speak well of you! for so did their fathers to the false prophets.

27 But I say to you which hear, Love your enemies, do good to them which hate you.

28 Bless them that curse you, and pray for them which despitefully use you.

29 And to him that smite you on the *one* cheek offer also the other; and him that takes away your cloak forbid not *to take your* coat also.

30 Give to every man that asks of you; and of him that takes away your goods ask *them* not again.

31 And as you would that men should do to you, do you also to them likewise.

32 For if you love them which love you, what thank have you? for sinners also love those that love them.

33 And if you do good to them which do good to you, what thank have you? for sinners also do even the same.

34 And if you lend *to them* of whom you hope to receive, what thank have you? for sinners also lend to sinners, to receive as much again.

35 But love you your enemies, and do good, and lend, hoping for nothing again; and your reward shall be great,

M29 - 202

and you shall be the children of the Highest: for He is <u>kind</u> to the unthankful and *to* the evil. in return

36 Be you therefore merciful, as your Father also is merciful.

37 Judge not, and you shall not be judged: condemn not, and you shall not be condemned: forgive, and you shall be forgiven:

38 Give, and it shall be given to you; good measure, pressed down, and shaken together, and running over, shall men give into your bosom. For with the same measure that you <u>mete withal</u> it shall be measured to you again. measure anything

39 And He spoke a parable to them, Can the blind lead the blind? shall they not both fall into the ditch?

40 The disciple is not above his master: but every one that is perfect shall be as his master.

41 And why behold you the <u>mote</u> that is in your brother's eye, but <u>perceive</u> not the *beam* that is in your own eye? speck - see - log

42 Either how can you say to your brother, Brother, let me pull out the <u>mote</u> that is in your eye, when you yourself behold not the <u>beam</u> that is in your own eye? You <u>hypocrite</u>, cast out first the <u>beam</u> out of your own eye, and then shall you see clearly to pull out the <u>mote</u> that is in your brother's eye. insincere

43 For a good tree brings not forth <u>corrupt</u> fruit; neither does a <u>corrupt</u> tree bring forth good fruit. bad

44 For every tree is known by its own fruit. For of thorns men do not gather figs, nor of a <u>bramble</u> bush gather they grapes. thorn

45 A good man out of the good treasure of his heart brings forth that which is good; and an evil man out of the evil treasure of his heart brings forth that which is evil: for of the abundance of the heart his mouth speaks.

46 And why call you Me, Lord, Lord, and do not the things which I say?

47 Whosoever comes to Me, and hears My sayings, and does them, I will show you to whom he is like:

48 He is like a man which built an house, and dig deep, and laid the foundation on a rock: and when the flood arose, the stream beat <u>vehemently</u> upon that house, and could not shake it: for it was founded upon a rock. strongly

49 But he that hears, and does not, is like a man that without a foundation built an house upon the earth; against which the stream did beat <u>vehemently</u>, and immediately it fell; and the ruin of that house was great.

G4B - 139

CHAPTER 7

NOW when He had ended all His sayings in the audience of the people, He entered into Ca-per'na-um.

2 And a certain <u>centurion's</u> servant, who was dear to him, was sick, and <u>ready</u> to die. Roman officer - about

3 And when he heard of Je'sus, he sent to Him the elders of the Jews, <u>beseeching</u> Him that He would come and heal his servant. asking

4 And when they came to Je'sus, they

besought Him instantly, saying, That he was worthy for whom He should do this:

5 For he loves our <u>nation</u>, and he has built us a synagogue.   people

6 Then Je'sus went with them. And when He was now not far from the house, the centurion sent friends to Him, saying to Him, Lord, trouble not Yourself: for I am not worthy that You should <u>enter under my roof</u>:   i.e., enter my house

7 Wherefore neither thought I myself worthy to come to You but say in a word, and my servant shall be healed.

8 For I also am a man <u>set</u> under authority, having under me soldiers, and I say to one, Go, and he goes; and to another, Come, and he comes; and to my servant, Do this, and he does *it*.   placed

9 When Je'sus heard these things, He marveled at him, and turned Him about, and said to the people that followed Him, I say to you, I have not found so great faith, no, not in Is'ra-el.

10 And they that were sent, returning to the house, found the servant <u>whole</u> that had been sick.   well

11 And it came to pass the day after, that He went into a city called Na'-in; and many of His disciples went with Him, and <u>much</u> people.   many

12 Now when He came near to the gate of the city, behold, there was a dead man carried out, the only son of his mother, and she was a widow: and much people of the city was with her.

13 And when the Lord saw her, He had <u>compassion</u> on her, and said to her, <u>Weep</u> not.   pity - Cry

14 And He came and touched the <u>bier</u>: and they that bare *him* stood still. And He said, Young man, I say to you, Arise.   coffin

15 And he that was dead sat up, and began to speak. And He delivered him to his mother.

16 And there came a <u>fear</u> on all: and they glorified God, saying, That a great prophet is risen up among us; and, That God has visited His people.   reverence

17 And this <u>rumor</u> of Him went forth throughout all Ju-dae'a, and throughout all the region round about.   knowledge

18 And the disciples of John <u>showed</u> him of all these things.   told

19 And John calling *to him* two of his disciples sent *them* to Je'sus, saying, Are You He that should come? or look we for <u>another</u>?   someone else

20 When the men were come to Him, they said, John Bap'tist has sent us to You, saying, Are You He that should come? or look we for another?

21 And in that same hour He cured many of *their* <u>infirmities</u> and <u>plagues</u>, and of evil spirits; and to many *that were* blind He gave sight.   diseases - afflictions

22 Then Je'sus answering said to them, Go your way, and tell John what things you have seen and heard; how that the blind see, the lame walk, the lepers are cleansed, the deaf hear, the dead are raised, to the poor the <u>gospel</u> is preached.   ISA. 29:18 good news

23 And <u>blessed</u> is *he*, whosoever shall not be <u>offended</u> in Me.   happy - doubtful of

24 And when the messengers of John were departed, He began to speak to the people concerning John, What went you out into the wilderness for to see? A reed shaken with the wind?

25 But what went you out for to see? A man clothed in soft <u>raiment</u>? Behold, they which are gorgeously <u>appareled</u>, and live delicately, are in kings' courts. clothing - arrayed

26 But what went you out for to see? A prophet? Yea, I say to you, and much more than a prophet.

27 This is *he*, of whom it is written, Behold, I send My messenger before your face, which shall prepare your way before you. MAL. 3:1

28 For I say to you, Among those that are born of women there is not a greater prophet than John the Bap'tist: but he that is <u>least</u> in the kingdom of God is greater than he. smallest

29 And all the people that heard *Him*, and the <u>publicans</u>, justified God, being baptized with the baptism of John. tax gatherers

30 But the Phar'i-sees and lawyers <u>rejected</u> the counsel of God against themselves, being not baptized of him. refused

31 And the Lord said, Whereto then shall I liken the men of this generation? and to what are they like?

32 They are like to children sitting in the marketplace, and calling one to another, and saying, We have <u>piped</u> to you, and you have not danced; we have <u>mourned</u> to you, and you have not wept. played wedding music - played funeral music

33 For John the Bap'tist came neither eating bread nor drinking wine; and you say, He has a <u>devil</u>. demon

34 The Son of man is come eating and drinking; and you say, Behold a <u>gluttonous</u> man, and a <u>wine-bibber</u>, a friend of <u>publicans</u> and <u>sinners</u>! excessive eating - i.e., drunkard - tax men - rebellious to God

35 But wisdom is <u>justified</u> of all her children. show true

36 And one of the Phar'i-sees <u>desired</u> Him that He would eat with him. And He went into the Phar'i-see's house, and sat down to <u>meat</u>. asked - eat

37 And, behold, a woman in the city, which was a sinner, when she knew that *Je'sus* sat at meat in the Phar'i-see's house, brought an alabaster box of ointment,

38 And stood at His feet behind *Him* weeping, and began to wash His feet with tears, and did wipe *them* with the hairs of her head, and kissed His feet, and <u>anointed</u> *them* with the <u>ointment</u>. 1 SAM. 25:41 - bathed - perfume

39 Now when the Phar'i-see which had <u>bidden</u> Him saw *it*, he spoke within himself, saying, This man, if He were a <u>prophet</u>, would have known who and what manner of woman *this is* that touches Him: for she is a sinner. asked - teacher

40 And Je'sus answering said to him, Si'mon, I have somewhat to say to you. And he says, Master, say on.

41 There was a certain creditor which had two debtors: the one owed five hundred pence, and the other fifty.

42 And when they had nothing to pay, he frankly forgave them both. Tell

me therefore, which of them will love him most?

43 Si'mon answered and said, I suppose that *he*, to whom he forgave most. And He said to him, You have rightly judged.

44 And He turned to the woman, and said to Si'mon, See you this woman? I entered into your house, you gave Me no water for My feet: but she has washed My feet with tears, and wiped *them* with the hairs of her head.

45 You gave Me no kiss: but this woman since the time I came in has not <u>ceased</u> to kiss My feet.   stopped kissing

46 My head with oil you did not anoint: but this woman has anointed My feet with <u>ointment</u>.   perfume

47 Wherefore I say to you, Her sins, which are many, are forgiven; for she loved much: but to whom little is forgiven, *the same* loves little.

48 And He said to her, Your sins are forgiven.

49 And they that sat at <u>meat</u> with Him began to say within themselves, Who is this that forgives sins also?   food

50 And He said to the woman, Your faith has saved you; go in peace.

CHAPTER 8

A ND it came to pass afterward, that He went throughout every city and village, preaching and showing the glad tidings of the kingdom of God: and the twelve *were* with Him,

2 And certain women, which had been healed of evil spirits and <u>infirmi</u>-ties, Ma'ry called Mag-da-le'ne, out of whom went seven <u>devils</u>,

   diseases - demons

3 And Jo-an'na the wife of Chu'za Her'od's steward, and Su-san'na, and many others, which <u>ministered</u> to Him of their <u>substance</u>.   served - things

4 And when much people were gathered together, and were come to Him out of every city, He spoke by a <u>parable</u>:   illustrations

5 A sower went out to sow his seed: and as he sowed, some fell by the way side; and it was trodden down, and the fowls of the air devoured it.

6 And some fell upon a rock; and as soon as it was sprung up, it withered away, because it lacked moisture.

7 And some fell among thorns; and the thorns sprang up with it, and choked it.

8 And other fell on good ground, and sprang up, and bare fruit an hundredfold. And when he had said these things, he cried, He that has ears to <u>hear</u>, let him hear.   listen

9 And His disciples asked Him, saying, What might this <u>parable be</u>?

   illustration mean

10 And He said, To you it is given to know the <u>mysteries</u> of the kingdom of God: but to others in <u>parables</u>; that seeing they might not see, and hearing they might not understand.

   ISA. 6:9 JER. 5:21 full understanding - illustrations

11 Now the <u>parable</u> is this: The seed is the word of God.

12 Those by the way side are they that hear; then comes the devil, and takes away the word out of their

hearts, less they should believe and be saved.

13 They on the <u>rock</u> *are they*, which, when they hear, receive the word with joy; and these have no root, which for a while believe, and in time of <u>temptation</u> fall away. *solid foundation - testing*

14 And that which fell among thorns are they, which, when they have heard, go forth, and are choked with cares and riches and pleasures of *this* life, and bring no fruit to <u>perfection</u>. *harvest*

15 But that on the good ground are they, which in an honest and good heart, having heard the word, keep *it,* and bring forth fruit <u>with patience</u>. *after a time*

16 No man, when he has lighted a candle, covers it with a vessel, or puts *it* under a bed; but sets *it* on a candlestick, that they which enter in may see the light.

17 For nothing is secret, that shall not be made <u>manifest</u>; neither *any thing* hid, that shall not be known and come abroad. *known*

18 Take <u>heed</u> therefore how you hear: for whosoever has, to him shall be given; and whosoever has not, from him shall be taken even that which he seems to have. *care*

19 Then came to Him *His* mother and His brethren, and could not come at Him for the <u>press</u>. *many people*

20 And it was told Him *by certain* which said, Your mother and Your brethren stand outside, desiring to see You.

21 And He answered and said to them, My mother and My brethren are these which hear the word of God, and do it.

22 Now it came to pass on a certain day, that He went into a ship with His disciples: and He said to them, Let us go over to the other side of the lake. And they launched forth.

23 But as they sailed He fell asleep: and there came down a storm of wind on the lake; and <u>they were</u> filled *with water,* and were in <u>jeopardy</u>. *i.e., boat was - danger*

24 And they came to Him, and awoke Him, saying, Master, master, we perish. Then He arose, and <u>rebuked</u> the wind and the raging of the water: and they ceased, and there was a calm. *spoke to*

25 And He said to them, Where is your faith? And they being afraid wondered, saying one to another, What manner of man is this! for He commands even the winds and water, and they obey Him.

26 And they arrived at the country of the Gad'a-renes, which is opposite Gal'i-lee.

27 And when He went forth to land, there met Him out of the city a certain man, which had <u>devils</u> long time, and <u>ware</u> no clothes, neither <u>abode</u> in *any* house, but in the tombs. *demons - wore - lived*

28 When he saw Je'sus, he cried out, and fell down before Him, and with a loud voice said, What have I to do with You, Je'sus, *You* Son of God Most High? I <u>beseech</u> You, torment me not. *beg*

29 (For He had commanded the unclean spirit to come out of the man. For oftentimes it had caught him: and he

was kept bound with chains and in <u>fetters</u>; and he broke the bands, and was driven of the <u>devil</u> into the wilderness.)   shackles - demons

30 And Je'sus asked him, saying, What is your name? And he said, Legion: because many <u>devils</u> were entered into him.

31 And they <u>besought</u> Him that He would not command them to go out into the <u>deep</u>.   pleaded with - abyss

32 And there was there an herd of many <u>swine</u> feeding on the mountain: and they besought Him that He would allow them to enter into them. And He permitted them.   pigs

33 Then went the <u>devils</u> out of the man, and entered into the <u>swine</u>: and the herd ran violently down a steep place into the lake, and were <u>choked</u>.   demons - drowned

34 When they that fed *them* saw what was done, they fled, and went and told *it* in the city and in the country.

35 Then they went out to see what was done; and came to Je'sus, and found the man, out of whom the <u>devils</u> departed, sitting at the feet of Je'sus, clothed, and in his right mind: and they were afraid.

36 They also which saw *it* told them by what means he that was possessed of the <u>devils</u> was <u>healed</u>.made well

37 Then the whole multitude of the country of the Gad'a-renes round about <u>besought</u> Him to depart from them; for they were taken with great fear: and He went up into the ship, and returned back again.   pleaded with

38 Now the man out of whom the devils were departed <u>besought</u> Him that he might be with Him: but Je'sus sent him away, saying,   demons - asked

39 Return to your own house, and show how great things God has done to you. And he went his way, and <u>published</u> throughout the whole city how great things Je'sus had done to him.   told

40 And it came to pass, that, when Je'sus was returned, the people *gladly* received Him: for they were all waiting for Him.

41 And, behold, there came a man named Ja-irus, and he was a ruler of the synagogue: and he fell down at Je'sus' feet, and <u>besought</u> Him that He would come into his house:

42 For he had one only daughter, about twelve years of age, and she lay a dying. But as He went the people thronged Him.

43 And a woman having an <u>issue</u> of blood twelve years, which had spent all her living upon physicians, neither could be <u>healed</u> of any,   flow - cured

44 Came behind *Him*, and touched the border of His garment: and immediately her <u>issue</u> of blood <u>stanched</u>.   stopped

45 And Je'sus said, Who touched Me? When all denied, Pe'ter and they that were with Him said, Master, the multitude throng You and <u>press</u> *You*, and say You, Who touched Me?   crowd

46 And Je'sus said, Somebody has touched Me: for I perceive that <u>virtue</u> is gone out of Me.   strength

47 And when the woman saw that she was not <u>hid</u>, she came trembling, and

falling down before Him, she declared to Him before all the people for what cause she had touched Him, and how she was healed immediately.   unknown

48 And He said to her, Daughter, be of good comfort: your faith has made you whole; go in peace.   well

49 While He yet spoke, there comes one from the ruler of the synagogue's *house*, saying to him, Your daughter is dead; trouble not the Master.

50 But when Je'sus heard *it*, He answered him, saying, Fear not: believe only, and she shall be made whole.

51 And when He came into the house, He permitted no man to go in, save Pe'ter, and James, and John, and the father and the mother of the maiden.   except

52 And all wept, and bewailed her: but He said, Weep not; she is not dead, but sleeps.   mourned

53 And they laughed Him to scorn, knowing that she was dead.

54 And He put them all out, and took her by the hand, and called, saying, Maid, arise.

55 And her spirit came again, and she arose immediately: and He commanded to give her meat.   victuals

56 And her parents were astonished: but He charged them that they should tell no man what was done.   instructed

CHAPTER 9

THEN He called His twelve disciples together, and gave them power and authority over all devils, and to cure diseases.   demons

2 And He sent them to preach the kingdom of God, and to heal the sick.

3 And He said to them, Take nothing for *your* journey, neither staves, nor scrip, neither bread, neither money; neither have two coats apiece.   staff - bag

4 And whatsoever house you enter into, there abide, and then depart.   stay

5 And whosoever will not receive you, when you go out of that city, shake off the very dust from your feet for a testimony against them.

6 And they departed, and went through the towns, preaching the gospel, and healing every where.   good news

7 Now Her'od the tetrarch heard of all that was done by Him: and he was perplexed, because that it was said of some, that John was risen from the dead;   troubled

8 And of some, that Elijah had appeared; and of others, that one of the old prophets was risen again.

9 And Her'od said, John have I beheaded: but who is this, of whom I hear such things? And he desired to see Him.   wished

10 And the apostles, when they were returned, told Him all that they had done. And He took them, and went aside privately into a desert place belonging to the city called Beth-sa'i-da.   lonely

11 And the people, when they knew *it*, followed Him: and He received them, and spoke to them of the kingdom of God, and healed them that had need of healing.

12 And when the day began to wear away, then came the twelve, and said

to Him, Send the multitude away, that they may go into the towns and country round about, and lodge, and get victuals: for we are here in a <u>desert</u> place.   get late - lonely

13 But He said to them, Give you them to eat. And they said, We have no more but five loaves and two fishes; <u>except</u> we should go and buy <u>meat</u> for all this people.

      2 KGS. 4:42 unless - food

14 For they were about five thousand men. And He said to His disciples, Make them sit down by fifties in a company.

15 And they did so, and made them all sit down.

16 Then He took the five loaves and the two fishes, and looking up to heaven, He blessed them, and broke, and gave to the disciples to set before the multitude.

17 And they did eat, and were all <u>filled</u>: and there was taken up of fragments that remained to them twelve baskets.   2 KGS. 4:43 satisfied

18 And it came to pass, as He was alone praying, His disciples were with Him: and He asked them, saying, Whom say the people that I am?

19 They answering said, John the Bap'tist; but some *say*, Elijah; and others *say*, that one of the old prophets is risen again.

20 He said to them, But whom say you that I am? Pe'ter answering said, The Christ of God.

21 And He <u>straitly charged</u> them, and commanded *them* to tell no man that thing;   firmly told

22 Saying, The Son of man must <u>suffer</u> many things, and be rejected of the elders and chief priests and scribes, and be slain, and be raised the third day.   endure

23 And He said to *them* all, If any *man* will come after Me, let him deny himself, and take up his cross daily, and follow Me.

24 For whosoever will save his life shall lose it: but whosoever will lose his life for My sake, the same shall save it.

25 For what is a man advantaged, if he gain the whole world, and lose himself, or be cast away?

26 For whosoever shall be ashamed of Me and of My words, of him shall the Son of man be ashamed, when He shall come in His own glory, and *in* His Father's, and of the Holy angels.

27 But I tell you of a truth, there be some standing here, which shall not taste of death, till they see the kingdom of God.

28 And it came to pass about an eight days after these <u>sayings</u>, He took Pe'ter and John and James, and went up into a mountain to pray.   words

29 And as He prayed, the fashion of His countenance was altered, and His <u>raiment</u> *was* white *and* <u>glistering</u>.   garments - glowing

30 And, behold, there talked with Him two men, which were Mo'ses and Elijah:

31 Who appeared in glory, and spoke of His <u>decease</u> which He should accomplish at Je-ru'sa-lem.   dying

32 But Pe'ter and they that were with Him were heavy with sleep: and when

they were awake, they saw His glory, and the two men that stood with Him.

33 And it came to pass, as they departed from Him, Pe'ter said to Je'sus, Master, it is good for us to be here: and let us make three <u>tabernacles</u>; one for You, and one for Mo'ses, and one for Elijah: not <u>knowing</u> what he said. tents - really understanding

34 While he thus spoke, there came a cloud, and overshadowed them: and they <u>feared</u> as they entered into the cloud. were afraid

35 And there came a voice out of the cloud, saying, This is My beloved Son: hear Him.

36 And when the voice was past, Je'sus was found alone. And they kept *it* <u>close</u>, and told no man in those days any of those things which they had seen. a secret

37 And it came to pass, that on the next day, when they were come down from the hill, much people met Him.

38 And, behold, a man of the company cried out, saying, Master, I <u>beseech</u> You, look upon my son: for he is mine only child. beg

39 And, lo, a spirit takes him, and he suddenly cried out; and it tears him that he foams again, and bruising him <u>hardly</u> departs from him. very little

40 And I <u>besought</u> Your disciples to cast him out; and they could not. pleaded with

41 And Je'sus answering said, O <u>faithless</u> and <u>perverse</u> generation, how long shall I be with you, and <u>suffer</u> you? Bring your son here. unbelieving - rebellious - endure

42 And as he was yet a coming, the <u>devil</u> threw him down, and <u>tare</u> *him*. And Je'sus <u>rebuked</u> the unclean spirit, and healed the child, and delivered him again to his father. demon - tore - spoke sharply to

43 And they were all amazed at the mighty power of God. But while they wondered every one at all things which Je'sus did, He said to His disciples,

44 Let these sayings sink down into your ears: for the Son of man shall be delivered into the <u>hands</u> of men. power

45 But they understood not this saying, and it was <u>hid</u> from them, that they perceived it not: and they <u>feared</u> to ask Him of that saying. understanding kept - were afraid

46 Then there arose a <u>reasoning</u> among them, which of them should be greatest. argument

47 And Je'sus, <u>perceiving</u> the thought of their heart, took a child, and set him by Him, knowing

48 And said to them, Whosoever shall receive this child in My name receives Me: and whosoever shall receive Me receives Him that sent Me: for he that is least among you all, the same shall be great.

49 And John answered and said, Master, we saw one casting out <u>devils</u> in Your name; and we forbad him, because he follows not with us. demons

50 And Je'sus said to him, Forbid *him* not: for he that is not against us is for us.

51 And it came to pass, when the time was come that He should be received up, He <u>steadfastly</u> <u>set</u> His <u>face</u> to go to Je-ru'sa-lem, firmly - i.e., decided

52 And sent messengers before <u>His face</u>: and they went, and entered into a village of the Sa-mar'i-tans, to make ready for Him. Him

53 And they did not receive Him, because His <u>face</u> was as though He would go to Je-ru'sa-lem. action

54 And when His disciples James and John saw *this*, they said, Lord, will You that we command fire to come down from heaven, and <u>consume</u> them, even as Elijah did? destroy

55 But He turned, and <u>rebuked</u> them, and said, You know not what manner of spirit you are of. chided

56 For the Son of man is not come to destroy men's lives, but to save *them*. And they went to another village.

57 And it came to pass, that, as they went in the way, a certain *man* said to Him, Lord, I will follow You whersoever You go.

58 And Je'sus said to him, Foxes have holes, and birds of the air *have* nests; but the Son of man <u>has not where to lay *His* head</u>. i.e., no place to sleep

59 And He said to another, Follow Me. But he said, Lord, permit me first to go and bury my father.

60 Je'sus said to him, Let the dead bury their dead: but go you and preach the kingdom of God.

61 And another also said, Lord, I will follow You; but let me first go bid them farewell, which are at home at my house. 1 KGS 19:20

62 And Je'sus said to him, No man, having put his hand to the plow, and looking back, is fit for the kingdom of God.

CHAPTER 10

AFTER these things the Lord appointed other seventy also, and sent them two and two before His face into every city and place, where He Himself would come.

2 Therefore said He to them, The harvest truly *is* great, but the laborers are few: pray you therefore the Lord of the harvest, that He would send forth laborers into His harvest.

3 Go your ways: behold, I send you forth as lambs among wolves.

4 Carry neither <u>purse</u>, nor <u>scrip</u>, nor shoes: and <u>salute</u> no man by the way. money - bag - greet

5 And into whatsoever house you enter, first say, Peace *be* to this house. 1 SAM. 25:6

6 And if <u>the son of peace be there</u>, your peace shall rest upon it: if not, it shall turn to you again. i.e., a welcome spirit

7 And in the same house remain, eating and drinking such things as they give: for the laborer is worthy of his hire. Go not from house to house.

8 And into whatsoever city you enter, and they <u>receive</u> you, eat such things as are set before you: welome

9 And heal the sick that are therein, and say to them, The kingdom of God is come near to you.

10 But into whatsoever city you enter, and they receive you not, go your ways out into the streets of the same, and say,

11 Even the very dust of your city, which cling on us, we do wipe off against you: <u>notwithstanding</u> be you sure of this, that the kingdom of God is come near to you. nevertheless

12 But I say to you, that it shall be more <u>tolerable</u> in that day for Sod'om, than for that city. merciful
13 Woe to you, Cho-ra'zin! woe to you, Beth-sa'i-da! for if the mighty works had been done in Tyre and Si'don, which have been done in you, they had a great while ago repented, sitting in sackcloth and ashes.
14 But it shall be more <u>tolerable</u> for Tyre and Si'don at the judgment, than for you.
15 And you, Ca-per'na-um, which are exalted to heaven, shall be thrust down to hell.
16 He that hears you hears Me; and he that despises you despises Me; and he that despises Me despises Him that sent Me.
17 And the seventy returned again with joy, saying, Lord, even the <u>dev-ils</u> are subject to us through Your name. demons
18 And He said to them, I beheld Sa'tan as lightning fall from heaven.
19 Behold, I give to you power to tread on serpents and scorpions, and over all the power of the enemy: and nothing shall by any means hurt you.
20 Notwithstanding in this rejoice not, that the spirits are subject to you; but rather rejoice, because your names are written in heaven. EX. 32:32
21 In that hour Je'sus rejoiced in spirit, and said, I thank You, O Father, Lord of heaven and earth, that You have hid these things from the wise and prudent, and have revealed them to babes: even so, Father; for so it seemed good in Your sight.

22 All things are delivered to Me of My Father: and no man knows who the Son is, but the Father; and who the Father is, but the Son, and *he* to whom the Son will reveal *Him*.
23 And He turned Him to *His* disciples, and said privately, <u>Blessed</u> *are* the eyes which see the things that you see: happy
24 For I tell you, that many prophets and kings have desired to see those things which you see, and have not seen *them*; and to hear those things which you hear, and have not heard *them*.
25 And, behold, a certain lawyer stood up, and <u>tempted</u> Him, saying, Master, what shall I do to inherit eternal life? DEU. 6:5 tested
26 He said to him, What is written in the law? how read you?
27 And he answering said, You shall love the Lord your God with all your heart, and with all your soul, and with all your strength, and with all your mind; and your neighbor as yourself. LEV. 19:18 DEU. 6:5
28 And He said to him, You have answered right: this do, and you shall live.
29 But he, willing to justify himself, said to Je'sus, And who is my neighbor?
30 And Je'sus answering said, A certain *man* went down from Je-ru'sa-lem to Jer'i-cho, and fell among thieves, which stripped him of his <u>raiment</u>, and wounded *him*, and departed, leaving *him* half dead. thing
31 And by chance there came down a certain priest that way: and when he saw him, he passed by on the other side.

32 And likewise a Le'vite, when he was at the place, came and looked *on him*, and passed by on the other side.

33 But a certain Sa-mar'i-tan, as he journeyed, came where he was: and when he saw him, he had <u>compassion</u> *on him*,   pity

34 And went to *him*, and bound up his wounds, pouring in oil and wine, and set him on his own beast, and brought him to an inn, and took care of him.

35 And on the morrow when he departed, he took out two pence, and gave *them* to the host, and said to him, Take care of him; and whatsoever you spend more, when I come again, I will repay you.

36 Which now of these three, thinks you, was neighbor to him that fell among the thieves?

37 And he said, He that showed mercy on him. Then said Je'sus to him, Go, and do you likewise.

38 Now it came to pass, as they went, that He entered into a certain village: and a certain woman named Mar'tha received Him into her house.

39 And she had a sister called Ma'ry, which also sat at Je'sus' feet, and heard His word.

40 But Mar'tha was <u>cumbered</u> about much serving, and came to Him, and said, Lord, do You not care that my sister has left me to serve alone? bid her therefore that she help me.   burdened with

41 And Je'sus answered and said to her, Mar'tha, Mar'tha, you are <u>careful</u> and troubled about many things: concerned

42 But one thing is needful: and Ma'ry has chosen that good part, which shall not be taken away from her.

CHAPTER 11

AND it came to pass, that, as He was praying in a certain place, when He <u>ceased</u>, one of His disciples said to Him, Lord, teach us to pray, as John also taught his disciples.   stopped

2 And He said to them, When you pray, say, Our Father which are in heaven, Hallowed be Your name. Your kingdom come. Your will be done, as in heaven, so in earth.

3 Give us day by day our daily bread.

4 And forgive us our sins; for we also forgive every one that is indebted to us. And <u>lead</u> us not into <u>temptation</u>; but deliver us from evil.   bring - testing

5 And He said to them, Which of you shall have a friend, and shall go to him at midnight, and say to him, Friend, lend me three loaves;

6 For a friend of mine in his journey is come to me, and I have nothing to <u>set</u> before him?   no foods for him

7 And he from within shall answer and say, Trouble me not: the door is now shut, and my children are with me in bed; I cannot rise and give you.

8 I say to you, Though he will not rise and give him, because he is his friend, yet because of his importunity he will rise and give him as many as he needs.

9 And I say to you, Ask, and it shall be given you; seek, and you shall

find; knock, and it shall be opened to you.

10 For every one that asks receives; and he that seeks finds; and to him that knocks it shall be opened.

11 If a son shall ask bread of any of you that is a father, will he give him a stone? or if *he ask* a fish, will he for a fish give him a serpent?

12 Or if he shall ask an egg, will he offer him a scorpion?

13 If you then, being evil, know how to give good gifts to your children: how much more shall *your* heavenly Father give the Ho'ly Spir'it to them that ask Him?

14 And He was casting out a devil, and it was dumb. And it came to pass, when the devil was gone out, the dumb spoke; and the people wondered. demons

15 But some of them said, He casts out devils through Be'el'ze-bub the chief of the devils. i.e., Satan

16 And others, tempting *Him*, sought of Him a sign from heaven. testing - begged

17 But He, knowing their thoughts, said to them, Every kingdom divided against itself is brought to desolation; and a house *divided* against a house falls. nothing

18 If Sa'tan also be divided against himself, how shall his kingdom stand? because you say that I cast out devils through Be'el'ze-bub. i.e., Satan

19 And if I by Be'el'ze-bub cast out devils, by whom do your sons cast *them* out? therefore shall they be your judges. demons

20 But if I with the finger of God cast out devils, no doubt the kingdom of God is come upon you. power - demons - i.e., proving

21 When a strong man armed keeps his palace, his goods are in peace:

22 But when a stronger than he shall come upon him, and overcome him, he takes from him all his armor wherein he trusted, and divides his spoils. booty

23 He that is not with Me is against Me: and he that gathers not with Me scatters. for

24 When the unclean spirit is gone out of a man, he walks through dry places, seeking rest; and finding none, he says, I will return to my house where I came out. unfit - evil, i.e., the evil spirit

25 And when he comes, he finds *it* swept and garnished. furnished

26 Then goes he, and takes *to him* seven other spirits more wicked than himself; and they enter in, and dwell there: and the last *state* of that man is worse than the first. evil spirit

27 And it came to pass, as He spoke these things, a certain woman of the company lifted up her voice, and said to Him, Blessed *is* the womb that bare You, and the paps which You have sucked. happy

28 But He said, Yea rather, blessed *are* they that hear the word of God, and keep it. PROV. 8:32

29 And when the people were gathered thick together, He began to say, This is an evil generation: they seek a sign; and there shall no sign be given it, but the sign of Jo'nah the prophet.

30 For as Jo'nah was a sign to the

Nin'e-vites, so shall also the Son of man be to this generation.

31 The <u>queen</u> of the south shall rise up in the judgment with the men of this generation, and condemn them: for she came from the utmost parts of the earth to hear the wisdom of Sol'o-mon; and, behold, a greater than Sol'o-mon *is* here. queen of Sheba

32 The men of Ninevah shall rise up in the judgment with this generation, and shall condemn it: for they repented at the preaching of Jo'nah; and, behold, a greater than Jo'nah *is* here.

33 No man, when he has lighted a candle, puts *it* in a secret place, neither under a bushel, but on a candlestick, that they which come in may see the light.

34 The light of the body is the eye: therefore when your eye is <u>single</u>, your whole body also is full of light; but when *your eye* is <u>evil</u>, your body also *is* full of darkness. seeing good-truth - bad-seeing evil

35 Take <u>heed</u> therefore that the light which is in you be not darkness. care

36 If your whole body therefore *be* full of light, having no part dark, the whole shall be full of light, as when the bright shining of a candle does give you light.

37 And as He spoke, a certain Phar'i-see <u>besought</u> Him to dine with him: and He went in, and sat down to <u>meat</u>. asked - food

38 And when the Phar'i-see saw *it*, he <u>marveled</u> that He had not first washed before dinner. was astonished

39 And the Lord said to him, Now do you Phar'i-sees make clean the outside of the cup and the platter; but your inward part is full of <u>ravening</u> and wickedness. robbery

40 *You* fools, did not He that made that which is outside make that which is within also?

41 But rather give alms of such things as you have; and, behold, all things are clean to you.

42 But woe to you, Phar'i-sees! for you tithe mint and rue and all manner of herbs, and pass over judgment and the love of God: these ought you to have done, and not to leave the other undone.

43 Woe to you, Phar'i-sees! for you love the <u>uppermost</u> seats in the synagogues, and greetings in the markets. choice

44 Woe to you, scribes and Phar'i-sees, hypocrites! for you are as graves which <u>appear not</u>, and the men that walk over *them* are not aware *of them*. don't show

45 Then answered one of the lawyers, and said to Him, Master, thus saying You <u>reproachest</u> us also. insult

46 And He said, Woe to you also, *you* lawyers! for you <u>lade</u> men with burdens grievous to be borne, and you yourselves touch not the burdens with one of your fingers. weighed down

47 Woe to you! for you build the <u>sepulchers</u> of the prophets, and your fathers killed them. graves

48 Truly you bear witness that you allow the deeds of your fathers: for they indeed killed them, and you build their <u>sepulchers</u>.

49 Therefore also said the wisdom of God, I will send them prophets and

apostles, and *some* of them they shall slay and persecute:

50 That the blood of all the prophets, which was shed from the foundation of the world, may be required of this generation;

51 From the blood of A'bel to the blood of Zech'a-ri'ah, which perished between the altar and the temple: <u>verily</u> I say to you, It shall be required of this generation. truly

52 Woe to you, lawyers! for you have taken away the key of knowledge: you entered not in yourselves, and them that were entering in you hindered.

53 And as He said these things to them, the scribes and the Phar'i-sees began to <u>urge</u> *Him* vehemently, and to provoke Him to speak of many things: be hostile to

54 Laying wait for Him, and seeking to catch something out of His mouth, that they might accuse Him.

CHAPTER 12

IN the mean time, when there were gathered together an innumerable multitude of people, insomuch that they trode one upon another, He began to say to His disciples first of all, Beware you of the <u>leaven</u> of the Phar'i-sees, which is hypocrisy. i.e., false teaching

2 For there is nothing covered, that shall not be revealed; neither hid, that shall not be known.

3 Therefore whatsoever you have spoken in darkness shall be heard in the light; and that which you have spoken in the ear in <u>closets</u> shall be proclaimed upon the house tops. inner rooms

4 And I say to you My friends, Be not afraid of them that kill the body, and after that have no more that they can do.

5 But I will forewarn you whom you shall <u>fear</u>: <u>Fear</u> him, which after he has killed has power to cast into <u>hell</u>; yea, I say to you, <u>Fear</u> him. be afraid of - Lake of Fire

6 Are not five sparrows sold for two farthings, and not one of them is forgotten before God?

7 But even the very hairs of your head are all numbered. <u>Fear not</u> therefore: you are of more value than many sparrows. respect not

8 Also I say to you, Whosoever shall confess Me before men, him shall the Son of man also confess before the angels of God:

9 But he that denies Me before men shall be denied before the angels of God.

10 And whosoever shall speak a word against the Son of man, it shall be forgiven him: but to him that <u>blasphemes</u> against the Ho'ly <u>Ghost</u> it shall not be forgiven. speaks evil - Spirit

11 And when they bring you to the synagogues, and *to* magistrates, and powers, take you no thought how or what thing you shall answer, or what you shall say:

12 For the Ho'ly <u>Ghost</u> shall teach you in the same hour what you ought to say.

13 And one of the company said to Him, Master, <u>speak</u> to my brother, that he divide the inheritance with me. tell

14 And He said to him, Man, who made Me a judge or a divider over you?

15 And He said to them, Take heed, and beware of covetousness: for a man's life consists not in the abundance of the things which he possesses.   PSA. 62:10 greed

16 And He spoke a parable to them, saying, The ground of a certain rich man brought forth plentifully:

17 And he thought within himself, saying, What shall I do, because I have no room where to bestow my fruits?

18 And he said, This will I do: I will pull down my barns, and build greater; and there will I bestow all my fruits and my goods.   larger - store

19 And I will say to my soul, Soul, you have much goods laid up for many years; take your ease, eat, drink, *and* be merry.

20 But God said to him, *You* fool, this night your soul shall be required of you: then whose shall those things be, which you have provided?

21 So *is* he that lays up treasure for himself, and is not rich toward God.

22 And He said to His disciples, Therefore I say to you, Take no thought for your life, what you shall eat; neither for the body, what you shall put on.   be not anxious

23 The life is more than meat, and the body *is more* than raiment.   food - clothing

24 Consider the ravens: for they neither sow nor reap; which neither have storehouse nor barn; and God feeds them: how much more are you better than the fowls?   worth

25 And which of you with taking thought can add to his stature one cubit?

26 If you then be not able to do that thing which is least, why take you thought for the rest?   be anxious

27 Consider the lilies how they grow: they toil not, they spin not; and yet I say to you, that Sol'o-mon in all his glory was not arrayed like one of these.   clothed

28 If then God so clothe the grass, which is to day in the field, and to morrow is cast into the oven; how much more *will he clothe* you, O you of little faith?

29 And seek not you what you shall eat, or what you shall drink, neither be you of doubtful mind.   worrying

30 For all these things do the nations of the world seek after: and your Father knows that you have need of these things.

31 But rather seek you the kingdom of God; and all these things shall be added to you.   desire

32 Fear not, little flock; for it is your Father's good pleasure to give you the kingdom.   be not afraid

33 Sell that you have, and give alms; provide yourselves bags which wax not old, a treasure in the heavens that fails not, where no thief approaches, neither moth corrupts.   grow - destroys

34 For where your treasure is, there will your heart be also.

35 Let your loins be girded about, and *your* lights burning;   body clothed

36 And you yourselves like to men that wait for their lord, when he will return from the wedding; that when he

comes and knocks they may open to him immediately.   *i.e., wedding feast*

37 <u>Blessed</u> *are* those servants, whom the lord when he comes shall find watching: <u>verily</u> I say to you, that he shall gird himself, and make them to sit down to <u>meat</u>, and will come forth and serve them.   *happy - truly - eat*

38 And if he shall come in the <u>second</u> watch, or come in the <u>third</u> watch, and find *them* so, <u>blessed</u> are those servants.   *9 to 12 - 12 to 3*

39 And this know, that if the <u>goodman</u> of the house had known what hour the thief would come, he would have watched, and not have permitted his house to be broken <u>through</u>.   *head - into*

40 Be you therefore ready also: for the Son of man comes at an hour when you think not.

41 Then Pe'ter said to Him, Lord, speak You this parable to us, or even to all?

42 And the Lord said, Who then is that faithful and wise steward, whom *his* lord shall make ruler over his household, to give *them their* portion of <u>meat</u> in due season?   *food*

43 <u>Blessed</u> *is* that servant, whom his lord when he comes shall find so doing.   *happy*

44 Of a truth I say to you, that he will make him ruler over all that he has.

45 But and if that servant say in his heart, My <u>lord</u> delays his coming; and shall begin to beat the menservants and maidens, and to eat and drink, and to be drunken;   *master*

46 The lord of that servant will come in a day when he looks not for *him*, and at an hour when he is not aware, and will cut him in <u>asunder</u>, and will appoint him his portion with the unbelievers.   *pieces*

47 And that servant, which knew his lord's will, and prepared not *himself*, neither did according to his will, shall be beaten with many *stripes*.

48 But he that knew not, and did commit things worthy of <u>stripes</u>, shall be beaten with few *stripes*. For to whomsoever much is given, of him shall be much required: and to whom men have committed much, of him they will ask the more. DEU. 25:2-3 *flogging*

49 I am come to send fire on the earth; and what will I, if it be already kindled?

50 But I have a baptism to be baptized with; and how am I distressed till it be accomplished!

51 Suppose you that I am come to give peace on earth? I tell you, Nay; but rather division:

52 For from hereafter there shall be in one house divided, three against two, and two against three.

53 The father shall be divided against the son, and the son against the father; the mother against the daughter, and the daughter against the mother; the mother in law against her daughter in law, and the daughter in law against her mother in law. MIC. 7:6

54 And He said also to the people, When you see a cloud rise out of the west, immediately you say, There comes a shower; and so it is.

55 And when *you* <u>see</u> the south wind blow, you say, There will be heat; and it comes to pass. _{feel}

56 *You* <u>hypocrites</u>, you can discern the face of the sky and of the earth; but how is it that you do not discern this time? _{insincere}

57 Yea, and why even of yourselves judge you not what is right?

58 When you go with your adversary to the magistrate, *as you are* in the way, give diligence that you may be delivered from him; less he <u>hale</u> you to the judge, and the judge deliver you to the officer, and the officer cast you into prison. _{drag}

59 I tell you, you shall not depart there, till you have paid the very last mite.

CHAPTER 13

THERE were present at that season some that told him of the Gal-i-lae'ans, whose blood Pi'late had mingled with their sacrifices.

2 And Je'sus answering said to them, <u>Suppose</u> you that these Gal-i-lae'ans were sinners above all the Gal-i-lae'ans, because they suffered such things? _{think}

3 I tell you, Nay: but, except you repent, you shall all likewise perish. NUM. 21:7

4 Or those eighteen, upon whom the tower in Si-lo'am fell, and slew them, think you that they were sinners above all men that dwelt in Je-ru'sa-lem?

5 I tell you, Nay: but, <u>except</u> you repent, you shall all likewise perish. _{unless}

6 He spoke also this parable; A certain *man* had a fig tree planted in his vineyard; and he came and sought fruit thereon, and found none.

7 Then said he to the dresser of his vineyard, Behold, these three years I come seeking fruit on this fig tree, and find none: cut it down; why <u>cumber</u> it the ground? _{let it use}

8 And he answering said to him, Lord, let it alone this year also, till I shall dig about it, and <u>dung *it*</u>: _{fertilize}

9 And if it bear fruit, *well*: and if not, *then* after that you shall cut it down.

10 And He was teaching in one of the synagogues on the <u>sabbath</u>. _{rest day}

11 And, behold, there was a woman which had <u>a spirit of infirmity</u> eighteen years, and was bowed together, and could in no wise lift up *herself*. _{sickness caused by a spirit}

12 And when Je'sus saw her, He called *her to Him*, and said to her, Woman, you are <u>loosed</u> from your <u>infirmity</u>. _{released - sickness}

13 And He laid *His* hands on her: and immediately she was made straight, and glorified God.

14 And the ruler of the synagogue answered with indignation, because that Je'sus had healed on the <u>sabbath</u> day, and said to the people, There are six days in which men ought to work: in them therefore come and be healed, and not on the <u>sabbath</u> day. LEV. 23:3 EX. 20:10

15 The Lord then answered him, and said, *You* <u>hypocrite</u>, do not each one of you on the <u>sabbath</u> loose his ox or *his* ass from the stall, and lead *him* away to watering? _{insincere - rest day}

16 And ought not this woman, being a daughter of A'bra-ham, whom Sa'tan

has bound, lo, these eighteen years, be loosed from this bond on the sabbath day?   rest

17 And when He had said these things, all His adversaries were ashamed: and all the people rejoiced for all the glorious things that were done by Him.

18 Then said He, To what is the kingdom of God like? and whereto shall I resemble it?

19 It is like a grain of mustard seed, which a man took, and cast into his garden; and it grew, and <u>waxed</u> a great tree; and the fowls of the air lodged in the branches of it.   became

20 And again He said, Whereto shall I liken the kingdom of God?

21 It is like <u>leaven</u>, which a woman took and hid in three measures of meal, till the whole was <u>leavened</u>.

yeast - with yeast

22 And He went through the cities and villages, teaching, and journeying toward Je-ru'sa-lem.

23 Then said one to Him, Lord, are there few that be saved? And He said to them,

24 Strive to enter in at the <u>strait</u> gate: for many, I say to you, will seek to enter in, and shall not be able.   narrow

25 When once the master of the house is risen up, and has shut to the door, and you begin to stand outside, and to knock at the door, saying, Lord, Lord, open to us; and He shall answer and say to you, I know you not from where you are:

26 Then shall you begin to say, We have eaten and drunk in Your presence, and You have taught in our streets.

27 But He shall say, I tell you, I know you not where you are; depart from Me, all *you* workers of iniquity.

28 There shall be weeping and gnashing of teeth, when you shall see A'bra-ham, and I'saac, and Ja'cob, and all the prophets, in the kingdom of God, and you *yourselves* thrust out.

29 And they shall come from the east, and *from* the west, and from the north, and *from* the south, and shall sit <u>down</u> in the kingdom of God.   at the table

30 And, behold, there are last which shall be first, and there are first which shall be last.

31 The same day there came certain of the Phar'i-sees, saying to Him, Get You out, and depart from here: for Her'od <u>will</u> kill you.

wants to

32 And He said to them, Go you, and tell that fox, Behold, I cast out <u>devils</u>, and I do <u>cures</u> to day and to morrow, and the third *day* I shall be perfected.   demons - heal

33 Nevertheless I must walk to day, and to morrow, and the *day* following: for it cannot be that a prophet perish out of Je-ru'sa-lem.

34 O Je-ru'sa-lem, Je-ru'sa-lem, which kills the prophets, and stones them that are sent to you; how often would I have gathered your children together, as a hen *does gather* her brood under *her* wings, and you would not!

35 Behold, your house is left to you <u>desolate</u>: and <u>verily</u> I say to you, You shall not see Me, until *the time* come

when you shall say, <u>Blessed</u> *is* He that comes in the name of the Lord.

PS. 118:26   alone-empty - truly - happy

CHAPTER 14

AND it came to pass, as He went into the house of one of the chief Phar'i-sees to eat bread on the <u>sabbath</u> day, that they watched Him. rest
2 And, behold, there was a certain man before Him which had the dropsy.
3 And Je'sus answering spoke to the lawyers and Phar'i-sees, saying, Is it <u>lawful</u> to heal on the <u>sabbath</u> day?

proper - rest

4 And they held their peace. And He took *him*, and healed him, and let him go;
5 And answered them, saying, Which of you shall have an ass or an ox fallen into a pit, and will not immediately pull him out on the <u>sabbath</u> day?
6 And they could <u>not</u> answer Him again to these things.
7 And He put forth a parable to those which were bidden, when He marked how they chose out the <u>chief rooms</u>; saying to them, best places
8 When you are bidden of any *man* to a wedding, sit not down in the <u>highest room</u>; less a more honorable man than you be bidden of him; PROV. 25:7 choice place
9 And he that bade you and him come and say to you, Give this man place; and you begin with shame to take the lowest <u>room</u>. i.e., the host - place
10 But when you are bidden, go and sit down in the lowest room; that when he that bade you come, he may say to you, Friend, go up higher: then

shall you have <u>worship</u> in the presence of them that sit at meat with you. honor
11 For whosoever exalts himself shall be <u>abased</u>; and he that humbles himself shall be exalted. humbled
12 Then said He also to him that <u>bade</u> Him, When you make a dinner or a supper, call not your friends, nor your brethren, neither your kinsmen, nor *your* rich neighbors; less they also bid you again, and a <u>recompence</u> be made you. invited - repayment
13 But when you make a feast, call the poor, the <u>maimed</u>, the lame, the blind: crippled
14 And you shall be <u>blessed</u>; for they cannot <u>recompense</u> you: for you shall be <u>recompensed</u> at the resurrection of the <u>just</u>. happy - righteous
15 And when one of them that sat at <u>meat</u> with Him heard these things, He said to him, <u>Blessed</u> *is* he that shall eat bread in the kingdom of God. the table
16 Then said He to him, A certain man made a great supper, and <u>bade</u> many: invited
17 And sent his servant at supper time to say to them that were <u>bidden</u>, Come; for all things are now ready.
18 And they all with one *consent* began to make excuse. The first said to him, I have bought a piece of ground, and I must needs go and see it: I pray you have me excused.
19 And another said, I have bought five yoke of oxen, and I go to <u>prove</u> them: I pray you have me excused. try
20 And another said, I have married a wife, and therefore I cannot come. DEU. 24:5

M09 - - - - 128   GIA — 131

21 So that servant came, and showed his lord these things. Then the master of the house being angry said to his servant, Go out quickly into the streets and lanes of the city, and bring in here the poor, and the <u>maimed</u>, and the <u>halt</u>, and the blind.

<small>crippled - lame</small>

22 And the servant said, Lord, it is done as you have commanded, and yet there is room.

23 And the lord said to the servant, Go out into the highways and hedges, and <u>compel</u> *them* to come in, that my house may be filled. <small>urge</small>

24 For I say to you, That none of those men which were <u>bidden</u> shall taste of my supper. <small>invited</small>

25 And there went great multitudes with Him: and He turned, and said to them,

26 If any *man* come to Me, and <u>hate not</u> his father, and mother, and wife, and children, and brethren, and sisters, yea, and his own life also, he cannot be My disciple. <small>think less of</small>

27 And whosoever does not bear his cross, and come after Me, cannot be My disciple.

28 For which of you, intending to build a tower, sits not down first, and <u>count</u> the cost, whether he have *sufficient* to finish *it*? <small>calculates</small>

29 Less haply, after he has laid the foundation, and is not able to finish *it*, all that behold *it* begin to <u>mock</u> him, <small>ridicule</small>

30 Saying, This man began to build, and was not able to finish.

31 Or what king, going to make war against another king, sits not down first, and <u>consults</u> whether he be able with ten thousand to meet him that comes against him with twenty thousand? <small>considers</small>

32 Or else, while the other is yet a great way off, he sends an <u>ambassage</u>, and desires conditions of peace. <small>representative</small>

33 So likewise, whosoever he be of you that <u>forsake</u> not all that he has, he cannot be My disciple. <small>gives</small>

34 Salt *is* good: but if the salt have lost his <u>savor</u>, wherewith shall it be seasoned? <small>flavor</small>

35 It is neither fit for the land, nor yet for the <u>dunghill</u>; *but* men cast it out. He that has ears to hear, let him hear. <small>manure pile</small>

CHAPTER 15

THEN drew near to him all the <u>publicans</u> and sinners for to hear Him. <small>tax gatherers</small>

2 And the Phar'i-sees and scribes murmured, saying, This man <u>receives</u> sinners, and eats with them. <small>is friendly with</small>

3 And He spoke this <u>parable</u> to them, saying, <small>illustration</small>

4 What man of you, having an hundred sheep, if he lose one of them, does not leave the ninety and nine in the wilderness, and go after that which is lost, until he find it?

5 And when he has found *it*, he lays *it* on his shoulders, rejoicing.

6 And when he comes home, he call together *his* friends and neighbors, saying to them, Rejoice with me; for I have found my sheep which was lost.

7 I say to you, that likewise joy

shall be in heaven over one sinner that repents, more than over ninety and nine <u>just</u> persons, which need no repentance.   righteous

8 Either what woman having ten pieces of silver, if she lose one piece, does not light a candle, and sweep the house, and seek diligently till she find *it*?

9 And when she has found *it*, she calls *her* friends and her neighbors together, saying, Rejoice with me; for I have found the <u>piece</u> which I had lost.   coin

10 Likewise, I say to you, there is joy in the presence of the <u>angels</u> of God over one sinner that repents.   messengers

11 And He said, A certain man had two sons:

12 And the younger of them said to *his* father, Father, give me the <u>portion</u> of goods that falls *to me*. And he divided to them *his* <u>living</u>.   share - wealth

13 And not many days after the younger son gathered all together, and took his journey into a far country, and there wasted his substance with riotous living.

14 And when he had spent all, there arose a <u>mighty</u> famine in that land; and he began to be in <u>want</u>.   severe- need

15 And he went and <u>joined</u> himself to a citizen of that country; and he sent him into his fields to feed <u>swine</u>.   attached - pigs

16 And he <u>would fain</u> have filled his belly with the husks that the <u>swine</u> did eat: and no man gave to him.   longed to

17 And when he came to himself, he said, How many hired servants of my father's have bread enough and to spare, and I <u>perish</u> with hunger!   die

18 I will arise and go to my father, and will say to him, Father, I have sinned against heaven, and <u>before</u> you,   against

19 And am no more worthy to be called your son: make me as one of your hired <u>servant</u>s.   men

20 And he arose, and came to his father. But when he was yet a great way off, his father saw him, and had <u>compassion</u>, and ran, and fell on his neck, and kissed him.   pity

21 And the son said to him, Father, I have sinned against heaven, and in your sight, and am no more worthy to be called your son.   JOB 33:27

22 But the father said to his servants, Bring forth the best robe, and put *it* on him; and put a ring on his <u>hand</u>, and shoes on *his* feet: finger

23 And bring here the fatted calf, and kill *it*; and let us eat, and be merry:

24 For this my son was dead, and is alive again; he was lost, and is found. And they began to be merry.

25 Now his elder son was in the field: and as he came and drew near to the house, he heard music and dancing.

26 And he called one of the servants, and asked what these things meant.

27 And he said to him, Your brother is <u>come;</u> and your father has killed the fatted calf, because he has <u>received</u> him safe and sound.   here - returned

28 And he was angry, and would not go in: therefore came his father out, and <u>entreated</u> him. pleaded with

29 And he answering said to *his* father, Lo, these many years do I serve you, neither <u>transgressed</u> I at any time your commandment: and yet you never gave me a <u>kid</u>, that I might make merry with my friends:

disobeyed - i.e., feast

30 But as soon as this your son was come, which has <u>devoured</u> your <u>living</u> with harlots, you have killed for him the fatted calf.

wasted - wealth

31 And he said to him, Son, you are ever with me, and all that I have is yours.

32 It was <u>meet</u> that we should make merry, and be glad: for this your brother was dead, and is alive again; and was lost, and is found.

fitting

CHAPTER 16

AND he said also to His disciples, There was a certain rich man, which had a steward; and the same was accused to him that he had wasted his goods.

2 And he called him, and said to him, How is it that I hear this of you? give an account of your <u>stewardship</u>; for you may be no longer steward.

management

3 Then the steward said within himself, What shall I do? for my lord takes away from me the <u>stewardship</u>: I cannot dig; to beg I am ashamed.

4 I <u>am resolved</u> what to do, that, when I am put out of the <u>stewardship</u>, they may receive me into their houses. know

5 So he called every one of his lord's debtors *to him*, and said to the first, How much owe you to my lord?

6 And he said, An hundred measures of oil. And he said to him, Take your bill, and sit down quickly, and write fifty.

7 Then said he to another, And how much owe you? And he said, An hundred measures of wheat. And he said to him, Take your bill, and write <u>fourscore</u>.

80

8 And the lord commended the unjust steward, because he had done wisely: for the children of this world are in their generation wiser than the children of light.

9 And I say to you, Make to yourselves friends of the <u>mammon</u> of unrighteousness; that, when you fail, they may receive you into everlasting habitations.

wealth

10 He that is faithful in that which is least is faithful also in much: and he that is unjust in the least is unjust also in much.

11 If therefore you have not been faithful in the unrighteous <u>mammon</u>, who will commit to your trust the true *riches*?

12 And if you have not been faithful in that which is another man's, who shall give you that which is your own?

13 No servant can serve two masters: for either he will <u>hate</u> the one, and love the other; or else he will hold to the one, and despise the other. You cannot serve God and <u>mammon</u>.

disrespect - wealth

14 And the Phar'i-sees also, who were

M40

159

covetous, heard all these things: and they derided Him. money lovers - scoffed at

15 And He said to them, You are they which justify yourselves before men; but God knows your hearts: for that which is highly esteemed among men is abomination in the sight of God.

1 SAM. 16:7　understands - evil

16 The law and the prophets *were* until John: since that time the kingdom of God is preached, and every man presses into it.

17 And it is easier for heaven and earth to pass, than one tittle of the law to fail. small mark

18 Whosoever puts away his wife, and marries another, commits adultery: and whosoever marries her that is put away from *her* husband commits adultery.

19 There was a certain rich man, which was clothed in purple and fine linen, and fared sumptuously every day: lavishly

20 And there was a certain beggar named Laz'a-rus, which was laid at his gate, full of sores,

21 And desiring to be fed with the crumbs which fell from the rich man's table: moreover the dogs came and licked his sores.

22 And it came to pass, that the beggar died, and was carried by the angels into A'bra-ham's bosom: the rich man also died, and was buried; messengers

23 And in hell he lift up his eyes, being in torments, and sees A'braham afar off, and Laz'a-rus in his bosom. tormented

24 And he cried and said, Father A'- bra-ham, have mercy on me, and send Laz'a-rus, that he may dip the tip of his finger in water, and cool my tongue; for I am tormented in this flame.

25 But A'bra-ham said, Son, remember that you in your lifetime received your good things, and likewise Laz'a-rus evil things: but now he is comforted, and you are tormented.

26 And beside all this, between us and you there is a great gulf fixed: so that they which would pass from here to you cannot; neither can they pass to us, that *would come* from there.

27 Then he said, I pray you therefore, father, that you would send him to my father's house: i.e., Lazarus

28 For I have five brethren; that he may testify to them, less they also come into this place of torment. warn

29 A'bra-ham says to him, They have Mo'ses and the prophets; let them hear them.

30 And he said, Nay, father A'braham: but if one went to them from the dead, they will repent. no

31 And he said to him, If they hear not Mo'ses and the prophets, neither will they be persuaded, though one rose from the dead.

CHAPTER 17

THEN said He to the disciples, It is impossible but that offences will come: but woe *to him*, through whom they come!

2 It were better for him that a millstone were hanged about his neck, and be cast into the sea, than that he should offend one of these little ones. injure

3 Take heed to yourselves: If your brother trespass against you, <u>rebuke</u> him; and if he repent, forgive him. _{speak to}

4 And if he <u>trespass</u> against you seven times in a day, and seven times in a day turn again to you, saying, I repent; you shall forgive him. _{sins}

5 And the apostles said to the Lord, Increase our faith.

6 And the Lord said, If you had faith as a grain of mustard seed, you might say to this sycamine tree, Be you plucked up by the root, and be you planted in the sea; and it should obey you.

7 But which of you, having a servant plowing or feeding cattle, will say to him by and by, when he is come from the field, Go and sit down to <u>meat</u>? _{eat}

8 And will not rather say to him, Make ready wherewith I may <u>sup</u>, and <u>gird</u> yourself, and serve me, till I have eaten and drunken; and afterward you shall eat and drink? _{eat - prepare}

9 Does he thank that servant because he did the things that were commanded him? I <u>trow</u> not. _{think}

10 So likewise you, when you shall have done all those things which are commanded you, say, We are unprofitable servants: we have done that which was our duty to do.

11 And it came to pass, as He went to Je-ru'sa-lem, that He passed through the midst of Sa-ma'ri-a and Gal'i-lee.

12 And as He entered into a certain village, there met Him ten men that were lepers, which stood afar off:

13 And they lifted up *their* voices, and said, Je'sus, Master, have mercy on us.

14 And when He saw *them*, He said to them, Go show yourselves to the priests. And it came to pass, that, as they went, they were cleansed.

15 And one of them, when he saw that he was healed, turned back, and with a loud voice glorified God,

16 And fell down <u>on *his* face</u> at His feet, giving Him thanks: and he was a Sa-mar'i-tan. _{to the ground}

17 And Je'sus answering said, Were there not ten cleansed? but where are the nine?

18 There are not found that returned to give glory to God, <u>save</u> this stranger. _{except}

19 And He said to him, Arise, go your way: your faith has made you <u>whole</u>. _{well}

20 And when He was <u>demanded</u> of the Phar'i-sees, when the kingdom of God should come, He answered them and said, The kingdom of God comes not with observation: _{questioned}

21 Neither shall they say, Lo here! or, lo there! for, behold, the kingdom of God is within you.

22 And He said to the disciples, The days will come, when you shall desire to see one of the days of the Son of man, and you shall not see *it*.

23 And they shall say to you, See here; or, see there: go not after *them*, nor follow *them*.

24 For as the lightning, that lightens out of the one *part* under heaven, shines to the other *part* under heaven; so shall also the Son of Man be in His day.

25 But first must He suffer many

things, and be rejected of this generation.

26 And as it was in the days of No'ah, so shall it be also in the days of the Son of Man.

27 They did eat, they drank, they married wives, they were given in marriage, until the day that No'ah entered into the ark, and the flood came, and destroyed them all.

28 Likewise also as it was in the days of Lot; they did eat, they drank, they bought, they sold, they planted, they built;

29 But the same day that Lot went out of Sod'om it rained fire and brimstone from heaven, and destroyed *them* all.

30 Even thus shall it be in the day when the Son of Man is revealed.

31 In that day, he which shall be upon the housetop, and his stuff in the house, let him not come down to take it away: and he that is in the field, let him likewise not return back.   goods

32 Remember Lot's wife.   GEN. 19:26

33 Whosoever shall seek to save his life shall lose it; and whosoever shall lose his life shall preserve it.   save

34 I tell you, in that night there shall be two *men* in one bed; the one shall be taken, and the other shall be left.

35 Two *women* shall be grinding together; the one shall be taken, and the other left.

36 Two *men* shall be in the field; the one shall be taken, and the other left.

37 And they answered and said to Him, Where, Lord? And He said to them, Wheresoever the body *is*, there will the eagles be gathered together.   vultures

CHAPTER 18

AND He spoke a parable to them *to this end*, that men ought always to pray, and not to faint;   lose heart

2 Saying, There was in a city a judge, which feared not God, neither regarded man: respected

3 And there was a widow in that city; and she came to him, saying, Avenge me of mine adversary.   protect

4 And he would not for a while: but afterward he said within himself, Though I fear not God, nor regard man;   revere

5 Yet because this widow troubles me, I will avenge her, less by her continual coming she weary me.

6 And the Lord said, Hear what the unjust judge says.   unrighteous

7 And shall not God avenge His own elect, which cry day and night to Him, though He bear long with them?   protect

8 I tell you that He will avenge them speedily. Nevertheless when the Son of Man comes, shall He find faith on the earth?

9 And He spoke this parable to certain which trusted in themselves that they were righteous, and despised others:

10 Two men went up into the temple to pray; the one a Phar'i-see, and the other a publican.   tax gatherer

11 The Phar'i-see stood and prayed thus with himself, God, I thank You,

that I am not as other men *are*, extortioners, unjust, adulterers, or even as this <u>publican</u>. tax gatherer

12 I fast twice in the week, I give <u>tithes</u> of all that I possess. one tenth

13 And the <u>publican</u>, standing afar off, would not lift up so much as *his* eyes to heaven, but smote upon his breast, saying, God be merciful to me a sinner.

14 I tell you, this man went down to his house justified *rather* than the other: for every one that exalts himself shall be abased; and he that humbles himself shall be exalted.

15 And they brought to Him also infants, that He would touch them: but when *His* disciples saw *it*, they rebuked them.

16 But Je'sus called them *to Him*, and said, Permit little children to come to Me, and forbid them not: for of such is the kingdom of God.

17 <u>Verily</u> I say to you, Whosoever shall not receive the kingdom of God as a little child shall in no wise enter therein. Truly

18 And a certain ruler asked Him, saying, Good Master, what shall I do to <u>inherit</u> eternal life? secure

19 And Je'sus said to him, Why call you Me good? none *is* good, save One, *that is*, God.

20 You know the commandments, Do not commit adultery, Do not kill, Do not steal, Do not bear false witness, Honor your father and your mother.

21 And he said, All these have I kept from my youth up.

22 Now when Je'sus heard these things, He said to him, Yet lack you one thing: sell all that you have, and distribute to the poor, and you shall have treasure in heaven: and come, follow Me.

23 And when he heard this, he was very <u>sorrowful</u>: for he was very rich. sad

24 And when Je'sus saw that he was very <u>sorrowful</u>, He said, How hardly shall they that have riches enter into the kingdom of God!

25 For it is easier for a camel to go through a needle's eye, than for a rich man to enter into the kingdom of God.

26 And they that heard *it* said, Who then can be saved?

27 And He said, The things which are impossible with men are possible with God. JER. 32:17

28 Then Pe'ter said, Lo, we have left <u>all</u>, and followed You. our home

29 And He said to them, <u>Verily</u> I say to you, There is no man that has left house, or parents, or brethren, or wife, or children, for the kingdom of God's sake, Truly

30 Who shall not receive <u>manifold</u> more in this present time, and in the world to come life everlasting. many times

31 Then He took *to Him* the twelve, and said to them, Behold, we go up to Je-ru'sa-lem, and all things that are written by the prophets concerning the Son of man shall be accomplished.

32 For He shall be delivered to the Gen'tiles, and shall be <u>mocked</u>, and spitefully <u>entreated</u>, and spitted on: ridiculed - mistreated

33 And they shall <u>scourge</u> *Him*, and put Him to death: and the third day He shall rise again. <small>whip</small>

34 And they understood none of these things: and this saying was <u>hid from</u> them, neither knew they the things which were spoken. <small>unknown to</small>

35 And it came to pass, that as He was come near to Jer'i-cho, a certain blind man sat by the way side begging:

36 And hearing the multitude pass by, he asked what it meant.

37 And they told him, that Je'sus of Naz'a-reth passes by.

38 And he cried, saying, Je'sus, *You* Son of Da'vid, have mercy on me.

39 And they which went before <u>rebuked</u> him, that he should hold his peace: but he cried so much the more, *You* Son of Da'vid, have mercy on me. <small>sternly told</small>

40 And Je'sus <u>stood</u>, and commanded Him to be brought to Him: and when he was come near, He asked him, <small>stopped</small>

41 Saying, What will you that I shall do to you? And he said, Lord, that I may receive my sight.

42 And Je'sus said to him, Receive your sight: your faith has saved you.

43 And immediately he received his sight, and followed Him, glorifying God: and all the people, when they saw *it*, gave praise to God.

CHAPTER 19

AND *Je'sus* entered and passed through Jer'i-cho.

2 And, behold, *there was* a man named Zac-chae'us, which was the chief among the <u>publicans</u>, and he was rich. <small>tax gatherers</small>

3 And he sought to see Je'sus who he was; and could not for the <u>press</u>, because he was <u>little of stature</u>. <small>crowd - short</small>

4 And he ran before, and climbed up into a sycamore tree to see Him: for He was to pass that *way*.

5 And when Je'sus came to the place, He looked up, and saw him, and said to him, Zac-chae'us, <u>make haste</u>, and come down; for to day I must abide at your house. <small>hurry</small>

6 And he <u>made haste</u>, and came down, and received Him joyfully.

7 And when they saw *it*, they all <u>murmured</u>, saying, That He was gone to be guest with a man that is a sinner. <small>grumbled</small>

8 And Zac-chae'us stood, and said to the Lord; Behold, Lord, the half of my goods I give to the poor; and if I have taken any thing from any man by false accusation, I restore *him* fourfold.

9 And Je'sus said to him, This day is salvation come to this house, forsomuch as he also is a son of A'bra-ham.

10 For the Son of man is come to seek and to save that which was lost.

11 And as they heard these things, He added and spoke a parable, because He was near to Je-ru'sa-lem, and because they thought that the kingdom of God should immediately appear.

12 He said therefore, A certain nobleman went into a far country to receive for himself a kingdom, and to return.

13 And he called his ten servants, and delivered them ten pounds, and said to them, <u>Occupy</u> till I come. <small>Do business</small>

14 But his citizens <u>hated</u> him, and sent a message after him, saying, We will not have this *man* to reign over us. disliked
15 And it came to pass, that when he was returned, having received the kingdom, then he commanded these servants to be called to him, to whom he had given the money, that he might know how much every man had gained by trading.
16 Then came the first, saying, Lord, your pound has gained ten pounds.
17 And he said to him, <u>Well</u>, you good servant: because you have been faithful in a very little, have you authority over ten cities. well done
18 And the second came, saying, Lord, your pound has gained five pounds.
19 And he said likewise to him, Be you also <u>over</u> five cities. in charge of
20 And another came, saying, Lord, behold, *here is* your pound, which I have kept <u>laid</u> up in a napkin: wrapped
21 For I feared you, because you are an <u>austere</u> man: you take up that you lay not down, and reap that you did not sow. exacting
22 And he says to him, Out of your own mouth will I judge you, *you* wicked servant. You knew that I was an <u>austere</u> man, taking up that I laid not down, and reaping that I did not sow: JOB 15:6
23 Wherefore then gave not you my money into the bank, that at my coming I might have required mine own with <u>usury</u>? interest
24 And he said to them that stood by, Take from him the pound, and give *it* to him that has ten pounds.
25 (And they said to him, Lord, he has ten pounds.)
26 For I say to you, That to every one which has shall be given; and from him that has not, even that he has shall be taken away from him.
27 But those mine enemies, which would not that I should reign over them, bring here, and slay *them* before me.
28 And when He had thus spoken, He went before, ascending up to Je-ru'sa-lem.
29 And it came to pass, when He was come near to Beth'pha-ge and Beth'a-ny, at the mount called *the mount* of Ol'ives, He sent two of His disciples,
30 Saying, Go you into the village opposite *you*; in the which at your entering you shall find a colt tied, whereon yet never man sat: loose him, and bring *him here*.
31 And if any man ask you, Why do you loose *him*? thus shall you say to him, Because the Lord has need of him.
32 And they that were sent went their way, and found <u>even</u> as He had said to them. everything
33 And as they were <u>loosing</u> the colt, the owners thereof said to them, Why <u>loose</u> you the colt? untying - untie
34 And they said, The Lord has need of him.
35 And they brought him to Je'sus: and they cast their garments upon the colt, and they set Je'sus thereon.

36 And as He went, they spread their clothes in the <u>way</u>.   road

37 And when He was come near, even now at the descent of the mount of Ol'ives, the whole multitude of the disciples began to rejoice and praise God with a loud voice for all the <u>mighty works</u> that they had seen;   miracles

38 Saying, Blessed *be* the King that comes in the name of the Lord: peace in heaven, and glory in the highest.   PSA. 118:26

39 And some of the Phar'i-sees from among the multitude said to Him, Master, <u>rebuke</u> Your disciples.   correct

40 And He answered and said to them, I tell you that, if these should <u>hold their peace</u>, the stones would immediately cry out.   become silent

41 And when He was come near, He beheld the city, and wept over it,

42 Saying, If you had known, even you, at least in this your day, the things *which* <u>belong</u> to your peace! but now they are hid from your eyes.   are needed for

43 For the days shall come upon you, that your enemies shall cast a trench about you, and <u>compass you round,</u> and <u>keep</u> you in on every side,   surround you - hem

44 And shall <u>lay you</u> even with the ground, and your children within you; and they shall not leave in you one stone upon another; because you knew not the time of your visitation.   level you

45 And He went into the temple, and began to cast out them that sold therein, and them that bought;

46 Saying to them, It is written, My house is the house of prayer: but you have made it a den of thieves.

47 And He taught daily in the temple. But the chief priests and the scribes and the chief of the people <u>sought</u> to destroy Him,   were trying

48 And could not find what they might do: for all the people were very attentive to hear Him.

CHAPTER 20

AND it came to pass, *that* on one of those days, as He taught the people in the temple, and preached the gospel, the chief priests and the scribes came upon *Him* with the elders,

2 And spoke to Him, saying, Tell us, by what <u>authority</u> do You these things? or who is he that gave You this <u>authority</u>?   right

3 And He answered and said to them, I will also ask you one thing; and answer Me:

4 The baptism of John, was it from heaven, or of men?

5 And they reasoned with themselves, saying, If we shall say, From heaven; He will say, Why then believed you him not?

6 But and if we say, Of men; all the people will stone us: for they be persuaded that John was a prophet.

7 And they answered, that they could not tell from where *it was*.

8 And Je'sus said to them, Neither tell I you by what authority I do these things.

9 Then began He to speak to the people this parable; A certain man planted

a vineyard, and let it forth to <u>hus-bandmen,</u> and went into a far country for a long time.   ISA. 5:4 vine growers

10 And at the season he sent a servant to the <u>husbandmen</u>, that they should give him of the <u>fruit</u> of the vineyard: but the <u>husbandmen</u> beat him, and sent *him* away <u>empty</u>. produce - empty handed

11 And again he sent another servant: and they beat him also, and <u>entreated</u> *him* shamefully, and sent *him* away <u>empty</u>.   treated - empty handed

12 And again he sent a third: and they wounded him also, and cast *him* out.

13 Then said the lord of the vineyard, What shall I do? I will send my beloved son: it may be they will reverence *him* when they see him.

14 But when the <u>husbandmen</u> saw him, they reasoned among themselves, saying, This is the heir: come, let us kill him, that the inheritance may be ours.   vine growers

15 So they cast him out of the vineyard, and killed *him*. What therefore shall the lord of the vineyard do to them?

16 He shall come and destroy these <u>husbandmen</u>, and shall give the vineyard to others. And when they heard *it*, they said, God forbid.

17 And He beheld them, and said, What is this then that is written, The stone which the builders rejected, the same is become the head of the corner?   PSA 118:22

18 Whosoever shall fall upon that stone shall be broken; but on whomsoever it shall fall, it will grind him to <u>powder</u>.   ISA. 8:14 dust

19 And the chief priests and the scribes the same hour <u>sought</u> to lay hands on Him; and they feared the people: for they perceived that He had spoken this parable against them. tried

20 And they watched *Him*, and sent forth spies, which should <u>feign</u> themselves <u>just</u> men, that they might take hold of His words, that so they might deliver Him to the power and authority of the governor.   pretend-good

21 And they asked Him, saying, Master, we know that You say and teach rightly, neither accept You the person *of any*, but teach the way of God truly:

22 Is it lawful for us to give <u>tribute</u> to Cae'sar, or no?   taxes

23 But He perceived their craftiness, and said to them, Why tempt you Me?

24 Show Me a penny. Whose image and <u>superscription</u> has it? They answered and said, Cae'sar's.   inscription

25 And He said to them, <u>Render</u> therefore to Cae'sar the things which be Cae'sar's, and to God the things which be God's.   give

26 And they could not take hold of His words before the people: and they marveled at His answer, and held their peace.

27 Then came to *Him* certain of the Sad'du-cees, which deny that there is any resurrection; and they asked Him,

28 Saying, Master, Mo'ses wrote to us, If any man's brother die, having a wife, and he die without children, that his brother should take his wife, and raise up seed to his brother.

29 There were therefore seven <u>breth-ren</u>: and the first took a wife, and died without children. _{brothers}

30 And the second took her to wife, and he died childless.

31 And the third took her; and in like manner the seven also: and they left no children, and died.

32 Last of all the woman died also.

33 Therefore in the <u>resurrection</u> whose wife of them is she? for seven had her to wife. _{i.e., at the second coming of Christ}

34 And Je'sus answering said to them, The children of this <u>world</u> marry, and are given in marriage:_{this age}

35 But they which shall be accounted worthy to obtain that world, and <u>the resurrection</u> from the dead, neither marry, nor are given in marriage:

36 Neither can they die any more: for they are equal to the angels; and are the children of God, being the children of the resurrection.

37 Now that the dead are raised, even Mo'ses showed at the bush, when he call the Lord the God of A'bra-ham, and the God of I'saac, and the God of Ja'cob. EX. 3:6

38 For He is not <u>a</u> God of the dead, but of the living: for all live to Him. _{the}

39 Then certain of the scribes answering said, Master, You have well said.

40 And after that they dare not ask him any *question at all*.

41 And He said to them, How say they that Christ is Da'vid's son?

42 And Da'vid himself says in the book of Psalms, The LORD said to my Lord, Sit You on My right hand,

43 Till I make Your enemies Your footstool. PS. 110:1

44 Da'vid therefore call Him Lord, how is He then his son?

45 Then in the audience of all the people He said to His disciples,

46 Beware of the scribes, which desire to walk in long robes, and love greetings in the markets, and the highest seats in the synagogues, and the chief rooms at feasts;

47 Which devour widows' houses, and for <u>a show</u> make long prayers: the same shall receive greater damnation. _{appearance sake}

CHAPTER 21

And He looked up, and saw the rich men <u>casting</u> their gifts into the treasury. _{putting}

2 And He saw also a certain poor widow casting in there two mites.

3 And He said, Of a truth I say to you, that this poor widow has cast in more than they all:

4 For all these have of their abundance <u>cast</u> in to the offerings of God: but she of her <u>penury</u> has <u>cast</u> in all the living that she had. _{put - poverty}

5 And as some spoke of the temple, how it was adorned with goodly stones and gifts, He said,

6 *As for* these things which you behold, the days will come, in the which there shall not be left one stone upon another, that shall not be thrown down.

7 And they asked Him, saying, Mas-

ter, but when shall these things be? and what sign *will there be* when these things shall come to pass?

8 And He said, Take heed that you be not deceived: for many shall come in My name, saying, I am *Christ*; and the time draws near: go you not therefore after them. follow

9 But when you shall hear of wars and commotions, be not terrified: for these things must first <u>come</u> to pass; but the end is not <u>by and by</u>. take place - just yet

10 Then said He to them, Nation shall rise against nation, and kingdom against kingdom: 2 CHRON. 15:6

11 And great earthquakes shall be in <u>divers</u> places, and famines, and pestilences; and fearful sights and great signs shall there be from heaven. various

12 But before all these, they shall lay their hands on you, and persecute *you*, delivering *you* up to the synagogues, and into prisons, being brought before kings and rulers for My name's sake.

13 And it shall turn to you for a testimony.

14 Settle *it* therefore in your hearts, not to meditate before what you shall answer:

15 For I will give you a mouth and wisdom, which all your adversaries shall not be able to <u>gainsay</u> nor resist. contradict

16 And you shall be betrayed both by parents, and brethren, and kinsfolks, and friends; and *some* of you shall they cause to be put to death.

17 And you shall be hated of all *men* <u>for</u> My name's sake. on account of

18 But there shall not an hair of your head <u>perish</u>. 1 SAM. 14:45 be lost

19 In your patience possess you your souls.

20 And when you shall see Je-ru'sa-lem compassed with armies, then <u>know</u> that the desolation thereof is near. recognize

21 Then let them which are in Ju-dae'a flee to the mountains; and let them which are in the midst of it depart out; and let not them that are in the <u>countries</u> enter thereto. country

22 For these be the days of <u>vengeance</u>, that all things which are written may be fulfilled. justice

23 But woe to them that are with child, and to them that <u>give suck</u>, in those days! for there shall be great distress in the land, and wrath upon this people. are nursing

24 And they shall fall by the edge of the sword, and shall be led away captive into all nations: and Je-ru'sa-lem shall be trodden down of the Gen'tiles, until the times of the Gen'tiles be fulfilled. ISA. 63:18

25 And there shall be signs in the sun, and in the moon, and in the stars; and upon the earth distress of nations, with perplexity; the sea and the waves roaring; ISA. 13:10

26 Men's hearts failing them for fear, and for looking after those things which are coming on the earth: for the powers of heaven shall be shaken.

27 And then shall they see the Son of man coming in a cloud with power and great glory.

28 And when these things begin to <u>come</u> to pass, then look up, and lift up your heads; for your redemption draws near. take place

29 And He spoke to them a parable; Behold the fig tree, and all the trees;

30 When they now shoot forth, you see and know of your own selves that summer is now near at hand.

31 So likewise you, when you see these things come to pass, know you that the kingdom of God is near at hand.   happening

32 Verily I say to you, This generation shall not pass away, till all be fulfilled.   Truly

33 Heaven and earth shall pass away: but My words shall not pass away.

34 And take heed to yourselves, less at any time your hearts be overcharged with surfeiting, and drunkenness, and cares of this life, and *so* that day come upon you unawares.   dissipation - suddenly

35 For as a snare shall it come on all them that dwell on the face of the whole earth.   lure

36 Watch you therefore, and pray always, that you may be accounted worthy to escape all these things that shall come to pass, and to stand before the Son of man.

37 And in the day time He was teaching in the temple; and at night He went out, and abode in the mount that is called *the mount* of Ol'ives.   stayed

38 And all the people came early in the morning to Him in the temple, for to hear Him.

CHAPTER 22

NOW the feast of unleavened bread drew near, which is called the Passover.   without yeast

2 And the chief priests and scribes sought how they might kill Him; for they feared the people.   planned

3 Then entered Sa'tan into Ju'das surnamed Is-car'i-ot, being of the number of the twelve.

4 And he went his way, and communed with the chief priests and captains, how he might betray Him to them.   discussed

5 And they were glad, and covenanted to give him money.   agreed

6 And he promised, and sought opportunity to betray Him to them in the absence of the multitude.   people

7 Then came the day of unleavened bread, when the passover must be killed.   without yeast

8 And He sent Pe'ter and John, saying, Go and prepare us the passover, that we may eat.   i.e., passover lamb

9 And they said to Him, Where will You that we prepare?

10 And He said to them, Behold, when you are entered into the city, there shall a man meet you, bearing a pitcher of water; follow him into the house where he enters in.   carrying

11 And you shall say to the goodman of the house, The Master says to you, Where is the guestchamber, where I shall eat the passover with My disciples?   owner

12 And he shall show you a large upper room furnished: there make ready.

13 And they went, and found as He had said to them: and they made ready the passover.   everything

14 And when the hour was come, He sat down, and the twelve apostles with Him.

15 And He said to them, <u>With desire I have desired</u> to eat this passover with you before I suffer: earnestly desired

16 For I say to you, I will not any more eat thereof, until it be fulfilled in the kingdom of God.

17 And He took the cup, and gave thanks, and said, Take this, and divide *it* among yourselves:

18 For I say to you, I will not drink of the fruit of the vine, until the kingdom of God shall come.

19 And He took bread, and gave thanks, and broke *it*, and gave to them, saying, This is My body which is given for you: this do in remembrance of Me.

20 Likewise also the cup after supper, saying, This cup *is* the new testament in My blood, which is shed for you.

21 But, behold, the hand of him that betrays Me *is* with Me on the table.

22 And truly the Son of man goes, as it was <u>determined</u>: but woe to that man by whom He is betrayed!   planned

23 And they began to enquire among themselves, which of them it was that should do this thing.

24 And there was also a strife among them, which of them should be <u>accounted</u> the greatest.   regarded

25 And He said to them, The kings of the Gen'tiles exercise lordship over them; and they that exercise authority upon them are called benefactors.

26 But you *shall* not *be* so: but he that is greatest among you, let him be as the younger; and he that is chief, as he that does serve.

27 For <u>whether</u> *is* greater, he that sits at <u>meat</u>, or he that serves? *is* not he that sits at <u>meat</u>? but I am among you as he that serves.   who - to eat

28 You are they which have <u>continued</u> with Me in My <u>temptations</u>.   stood - trials

29 And I appoint to you a kingdom, as My Father has appointed to Me;

30 That you may eat and drink at My table in My kingdom, and sit on thrones judging the twelve tribes of Is'ra-el.

31 And the Lord said, Si'mon, Si'mon, behold, Sa'tan has desired *to have* you, that he may sift *you* as wheat:

32 But I have prayed for you, that your faith fail not: and when you are converted, strengthen your brethren.

33 And he said to Him, Lord, I am ready to go with You, both into prison, and to death.

34 And He said, I tell you, Pe'ter, the cock shall not crow this day, before that you shall thrice deny that you know Me.

35 And He said to them, When I sent you without purse, and <u>scrip</u>, and shoes, lacked you any thing? And they said, Nothing.   bag

36 Then said He to them, But now, he that has a purse, let him take *it*, and likewise *his* <u>scrip</u>: and he that has no sword, let him sell his garment, and buy one.

37 For I say to you, that this that is written must yet be <u>accomplished</u> in Me, And He was reckoned among the transgressors: for the things concerning Me <u>have an end</u>.

ISA. 53:12   fulfilled - has its fulfillment

38 And they said, Lord, behold, here *are* two swords. And He said to them, It is enough.

39 And He came out, and went, as He was <u>wont</u>, to the mount of Ol'ives; and His disciples also followed Him. _{customed}

40 And when He was at the place, He said to them, Pray that you enter not into temptation.

41 And He <u>was withdrawn</u> from them about a stone's <u>cast</u>, and kneeled down, and prayed, _{withdrew - throw}

42 Saying, Father, if You be willing, remove this cup from Me: nevertheless not My will, but Yours, be done.

43 And there appeared an <u>angel</u> to Him from heaven, strengthening Him. _{messenger}

44 And being in an agony He prayed more earnestly: and His sweat was as it were great drops of blood falling down to the ground.

45 And when He rose up from prayer, and was come to His disciples, He found them sleeping for sorrow,

46 And said to them, Why sleep you? rise and pray, less you enter into <u>temptation</u>. _{testing}

47 And while He yet spoke, behold a multitude, and he that was called Ju'das, one of the twelve, went before them, and drew near to Je'sus to kiss Him.

48 But Je'sus said to him, Ju'das, betrays you the Son of MAN with a kiss?

49 When they which were about Him saw what would follow, they said to Him, Lord, shall we <u>smite</u> with the sword? _{strike}

50 And one of them smote the servant of the high priest, and cut off his right ear.

51 And Je'sus answered and said, <u>Suffer you thus far</u>. And He touched his ear, and healed him. _{stop no more of this}

52 Then Je'sus said to the chief priests, and captains of the temple, and the elders, which were come to Him, Be you come out, as against a thief, with swords and <u>staves</u>? _{clubs}

53 When I was daily with you in the temple, you stretched forth no hands against Me: but this is your hour, and the power of darkness.

54 Then took they Him, and led *Him*, and brought Him into the high priest's house. And Pe'ter followed afar off.

55 And when they had kindled a fire in the midst of the hall, and were set down together, Pe'ter sat down among them.

56 But a certain maid beheld him as he sat by the fire, and earnestly looked upon him, and said, This man was also with Him.

57 And he denied Him, saying, Woman, I know Him not.

58 And after a little while another saw him, and said, You are also of them. And Pe'ter said, Man, I am not.

59 And about the space of one hour after another confidently <u>affirmed</u>, saying, Of a truth this *fellow* also was with Him: for he is a Gal-i-lae'an. _{insisted}

60 And Pe'ter said, Man, I know not

what you say. And immediately, while he yet spoke, the cock crew.

61 And the Lord turned, and looked upon Pe'ter. And Pe'ter remembered the word of the Lord, how He had said to him, Before the cock crow, you shall deny Me thrice.

62 And Pe'ter went out, and wept bitterly.

63 And the men that held Je'sus <u>mocked</u> Him, and <u>smote</u> *Him*.   ridiculed - struck

64 And when they had blindfolded Him, they struck Him on the face, and asked Him, saying, <u>Prophesy</u>, who is it that <u>smote</u> You?   speak now

65 And many other things <u>blasphemously</u> spoke they against Him. wickedly

66 And as soon as it was day, the elders of the people and the chief priests and the scribes came together, and led Him into their council, saying,

67 Are you the <u>Christ</u>? tell us. And He said to them, If I tell you, you will not believe: Messiah

68 And if I also ask *you*, you will not answer Me, nor let *Me* go.

69 Hereafter shall the Son of MAN sit on the right hand of the power of God.

70 Then said they all, Are You then the Son of God? And He said to them, You say that I am.

71 And they said, What need we any further witness? for we ourselves have heard of His own mouth.

CHAPTER 23

AND the whole multitude of them arose, and led Him to Pi'late.

2 And they began to accuse Him, saying, We found this *fellow* <u>perverting</u> the nation, and forbidding to give <u>tribute</u> to Cae'sar, saying that He Himself is Christ a King.   misleading - tax

3 And Pi'late asked Him, saying, Are You the King of the Jews? And He answered him and said, You say *it*.

4 Then said Pi'late to the chief priests and *to* the people, I find no fault in this man.

5 And they were the more <u>fierce</u>, saying, He stirs up the people, teaching throughout all Jew'ry, beginning from Gal'i-lee to this place.   insisting

6 When Pi'late heard of Gal'i-lee, he asked whether the man were a Gal-i-lae'an.

7 And as soon as he knew that He belonged to Her'od's jurisdiction, he sent Him to Her'od, who himself also was at Je-ru'sa-lem at that time.

8 And when Her'od saw Je'sus, he was exceeding glad: for he was desirous to see him of a long *season*, because he had heard many things of Him; and he hoped to have seen some miracle done by Him.   long time

9 Then he questioned with Him in many words; but He answered him nothing.

10 And the chief priests and scribes stood and <u>vehemently</u> accused Him.   strongly

11 And Her'od with his <u>men</u> of war <u>set</u> <u>Him at nothing</u>, and mocked *Him*, and arrayed Him in a gorgeous robe, and sent Him again to Pi'late.   soldiers - i,e,. belittled - treated Him with contempt

12 And the same day Pi'late and

Her'od were made friends together: for before they were at enmity between themselves.

13 And Pi'late, when he had called together the chief priests and the rulers and the people,

14 Said to them, You have brought this man to me, as one that <u>perverts</u> the people: and, behold, I, having examined *Him* before you, have found no <u>fault</u> in this man touching those things whereof you accuse Him: incites - guilt

15 No, nor yet Her'od: for I sent you to him; and, lo, nothing worthy of death is done to Him.

16 I will therefore <u>chastise</u> Him, and release *Him*.   punish

17 (For of necessity he must release one to them at the feast.)

18 And they cried out all at once, saying, Away with this *man*, and release to us Ba-rab'bas:

19 (Who for a certain <u>sedition</u> made in the city, and for murder, was cast into prison.)   insurrection

20 Pi'late therefore, <u>willing</u> to release Je'sus, spoke again to them.   wanting

21 But they cried, saying, Crucify *Him*, crucify Him.

22 And he said to them the third time, Why, what <u>evil</u> has He done? I have found no cause of death in Him: I will therefore chastise Him, and let *Him* go.   crime

23 And they were <u>instant</u> with loud voices, requiring that He might be <u>crucified</u>. And the voices of them and of the chief priests prevailed.   insistent - nailed to cross

24 And Pi'late gave <u>sentence</u> that it should be as they required. pronounced

25 And he released to them him that for <u>sedition</u> and murder was cast into prison, whom they had desired; but he delivered Je'sus to their will.   insurrection

26 And as they led Him away, they laid hold upon one Si'mon, a Cy-re'ni-an, coming out of the country, and on him they laid the cross, that he might bear *it* after Je'sus.

27 And there followed Him a great company of people, and of women, which also <u>bewailed and lamented</u> Him.   wailing and weeping

28 But Je'sus turning to them said, Daughters of Je-ru'sa-lem, <u>weep</u> not for Me, but <u>weep</u> for yourselves, and for your children.   cry

29 For, behold, the days are coming, in the which they shall say, <u>Blessed</u> *are* the barren, and the wombs that never bare, and the paps which never <u>gave suck</u>.   happy - nursed

30 Then shall they begin to say to the mountains, Fall on us; and to the hills, Cover us.   HOS. 10:8

31 For if they do these things in a green tree, what shall be done in the dry?

32 And there were also two other, malefactors, led with Him to be put to death.

33 And when they were come to the place, which is called Cal'va-ry, there they <u>crucified</u> Him, and the malefactors, one on the right hand, and the other on the left.

                     nailed to the cross

34 Then said Je'sus, Father, forgive them; for they know not what they do. And they <u>parted His raiment</u>, and cast lots. ISA. 53:11 divided His clothes

35 And the people stood beholding. And the rulers also with them derided *Him*, saying, He saved others; let Him save Himself, if He be Christ, the chosen of God.

36 And the soldiers also <u>mocked</u> Him, coming to Him, and offering Him vinegar,   ridiculed

37 And saying, If You be the king of the Jews, save Yourelf.

38 And a superscription also was written over Him in letters of Greek, and Lat'in, and He'brew, THIS IS THE KING OF THE JEWS.

39 And one of the <u>malefactors</u> which were hanged railed on Him, saying, If You be Christ, save Yourself and us.   criminals

40 But the other answering rebuked him, saying, Do not you fear God, seeing you are in the same condemnation?

41 And we indeed justly; for we receive the due reward of our deeds: but this man has done nothing <u>amiss</u>.   wrong

42 And he said to Je'sus, Lord, remember me when You come into Your kingdom.

43 And Je'sus said to him, <u>Verily</u> I say to you, To day shall you be with Me in paradise.   Truly

44 And it was about the <u>sixth</u> hour, and there was a darkness over all the <u>earth</u> until the <u>ninth</u> hour.   12 noon - land - 3 PM

45 And the sun was darkened, and the veil of the temple was rent in the midst.

46 And when Je'sus had cried with a loud voice, He said, Father, into Your hands I commend My spirit: and having said thus, He gave up the ghost. PS. 31:5

47 Now when the centurion saw what was done, he glorified God, saying, Certainly this was a righteous man.

48 And all the people that came together to that <u>sight</u>, beholding the things which <u>were done</u>, smote their breasts, and <u>returned</u>.   spectacle - happened - went home

49 And all His acquaintance, and the women that followed Him from Gal'i-lee, stood afar off, beholding these things.

50 And, behold, *there was* a man named Jo'seph, a counselor; *and he was* a good man, and a just:

51 (The same had not consented to the counsel and deed of them;) *he was* of Ar-i-ma-thae'a, a city of the Jews: who also himself waited for the kingdom of God.

52 This *man* went to Pi'late, and <u>begged</u> the body of Je'sus.   asked for

53 And he took it down, and wrapped it in linen, and laid it in a <u>sepulcher</u> that was <u>hewn</u> in stone, wherein never man before was laid.   cave grave - cut

54 And that day was the preparation, and the <u>sabbath</u> drew on. rest day

55 And the women also, which came with Him from Gal'i-lee, followed after, and beheld the <u>sepulcher</u>, and how His body was laid.

56 And they returned, and prepared spices and ointments; and rested the

sabbath day according to the commandment.   EX. 12:16 rest

CHAPTER 24

NOW upon the first *day* of the week, very early in the morning, they came to the sepulcher, bringing the spices which they had prepared, and certain *others* with them.   Sunday - cave grave
2 And they found the stone rolled away from the sepulcher.
3 And they entered in, and found not the body of the Lord Je'sus.
4 And it came to pass, as they were much perplexed thereabout, behold, two men stood by them in shining garments:
5 And as they were afraid, and bowed down *their* faces to the earth, they said to them, Why seek you the living among the dead?   living One
6 He is not here, but is risen: remember how He spoke to you when He was yet in Gal'i-lee,
7 Saying, The Son of man must be delivered into the hands of sinful men, and be crucified, and the third day rise again.
8 And they remembered His words,
9 And returned from the sepulcher, and told all these things to the eleven, and to all the rest.   cave grave
10 It was Ma'ry Mag-da-le'ne, and Jo-an'na, and Ma'ry *the mother* of James, and other *women that were* with them, which told these things to the apostles.
11 And their words seemed to them as idle tales, and they believed them not.

12 Then arose Pe'ter, and ran to the sepulcher; and stooping down, he beheld the linen clothes laid by themselves, and departed, wondering in himself at that which was come to pass.
13 And, behold, two of them went that same day to a village called Em'ma-us, which was from Je-ru'sa-lem *about* threescore furlongs.   60
14 And they talked together of all these things which had happened.
15 And it came to pass, that, while they communed *together* and reasoned, Je'sus Himself drew near, and went with them.   talked
16 But their eyes were holden that they should not know Him.   heavy-cloud
17 And He said to them, What manner of communications *are* these that you have one to another, as you walk, and are sad?
18 And the one of them, whose name was Cle'-o-pas, answering said to him, Are you only a stranger in Je-ru'sa-lem, and have not known the things which are come to pass there in these days?
19 And He said to them, What things? And they said to Him, Concerning Je'sus of Naz'a-reth, which was a prophet mighty in deed and word before God and all the people:
20 And how the chief priests and our rulers delivered Him to be condemned to death, and have crucified Him.
21 But we trusted that it had been He which should have redeemed Is'ra-el: and beside all this, to day is the third day since these things were done.
22 Yea, and certain women also of

our company made us astonished, which were early at the sepulcher;   cave grave

23 And when they found not His body, they came, saying, that they had also seen a vision of angels, which said that He was alive.   messengers

24 And certain of them which were with us went to the sepulcher, and found *it* even so as the women had said: but Him they saw not.   exactly

25 Then He said to them, O fools, and slow of heart to believe all that the prophets have spoken: foolish men

26 Ought not Christ to have suffered these things, and to enter into His glory?

27 And beginning at Mo'ses and all the prophets, He expounded to them in all the scriptures the things concerning Himself.   explained

28 And they drew near to the village, where they went: and He made as though He would have gone further.

29 But they constrained Him, saying, Abide with us: for it is toward evening, and the day is far spent. And He went in to tarry with them.

30 And it came to pass, as He sat at meat with them, He took bread, and blessed *it*, and broke, and gave to them.   to eat

31 And their eyes were opened, and they knew Him; and He vanished out of their sight.   recognized

32 And they said one to another, Did not our heart burn within us, while He talked with us by the way, and while He opened to us the scriptures?   road - explained

33 And they rose up the same hour, and returned to Je-ru'sa-lem, and found the eleven gathered together, and them that were with them,

34 Saying, The Lord is risen indeed, and has appeared to Si'mon.

35 And they told what things *were done* in the way, and how He was known of them in breaking of bread.   recognized

36 And as they thus spoke, Je'sus Himself stood in the midst of them, and says to them, Peace *be* to you.

37 But they were terrified and affrighted, and supposed that they had seen a spirit.

38 And He said to them, Why are you troubled? and why do thoughts arise in your hearts?   doubts - mind

39 Behold My hands and My feet, that it is I Myself: handle Me, and see; for a spirit has not flesh and bones, as you see Me have.   feel

40 And when He had thus spoken, He showed them *His* hands and *His* feet.

41 And while they yet believed not for joy, and wondered, He said to them, Have you here any meat?   food

42 And they gave him a piece of a broiled fish, and of an honeycomb.

43 And he took *it*, and did eat before them.

44 And he said to them, These *are* the words which I spoke to you, while I was yet with you, that all things must be fulfilled, which were written in the law of Mo'ses, and *in* the prophets, and *in* the psalms, concerning Me.

45 Then opened He their understanding, that they might understand the scriptures,

46 And said to them, Thus it is written, and thus it behoved Christ to suffer, and to rise from the dead the third day: HOS. 6:2

47 And that repentance and remission of sins should be preached in His name among all nations, beginning at Je-ru'sa-lem.

48 And you are witnesses of these things.

49 And, behold, I send the promise of My Father upon you: but <u>tarry</u> you in the city of Je-ru'sa-lem, until you be endued with power from on high.   stay

50 And He led them out as far as to Beth'a-ny, and He lifted up His hands, and blessed them.

51 And it came to pass, while He blessed them, He was parted from them, and carried up into heaven.

52 And they worshiped Him, and returned to Je-ru'sa-lem with great joy:

53 And were continually in the temple, praising and blessing God. Amen.

JOHN

OUTLINE

SURVEY

The Fourth Gospel clearly states the aim of the book: "Many other signs . . . did Jesus . . . but these are written that ye may believe that Jesus is the Christ, the Son of God; and that believing ye may have life in his name" (20.30, 31).

From the prologue (1.1-18) with its grand climax: "We beheld his glory" (v.14) to the conclusion's confession by Thomas: "My Lord and my God" (20.28), the reader is constantly driven to his knees in worship. Jesus Christ stands forth as more than a man; indeed, even as more than a supernatural envoy or representative of Deity. He is very God come in the flesh.

The Hebrews, looking for their coming Redeemer, however (1.19-26), need proof of Jesus' claim to be the promised Old Testament Messiah. John presents these verifications. Miracles and discourses selected from but twenty days in Jesus' three-year public ministry dramatically validate Him as the Christ, the Son of God. Eight *signs* or works reveal not only His power but attest His glory as the divine bearer of redemptive grace. Jesus is the great "I am," the only hope of an otherwise hopeless race. Water turned to wine; merchants and sacrificial animals driven from the temple; the nobleman's son healed afar off; the impotent man healed on the Sabbath; the multiplied loaves; Jesus' walking on the sea; sight restored to the man born blind; Lazarus recalled from death: these miracles reveal who Jesus Christ is and what He does. Progressively, John portrays Him as the source of new life, the water of life, and the bread of life. Even His enemies finally fall back before the "I am" Who yields Himself voluntarily to the suffering of the cross (18.5, 6).

Seeking to rescue man from sin and doom, and to restore him to divine fellowship and holiness, the eternal Logos makes this world His temporary dwelling place (1.14). Through His grace, fallen man becomes qualified to abide in God (14.20) and finally in the eternal mansions (14.2, 3). In His own person, Jesus fulfills the meaning of the Old Testament prophecies and feasts. He triumphs at last even over death and the grave, and leaves to His followers a remarkable legacy for carrying forward history's unique mission of mercy.

Sweeping from eternity to eternity, the Fourth Gospel links the destiny of both Jew and Gentile as part of the entire creation to the resurrection of the incarnate, crucified Logos.

AUTHOR

Although the Fourth Gospel nowhere definitely names its writer, there is little doubt of John "the beloved's" authorship. Only an eyewitness in the inner circle of our Lord's followers (cf. 12.16; 13.29) could furnish the book's intimate details. Moreover, the special and sometimes indirect report of John's participation would likewise confirm his authorship (1.37-40; 19.26; 20.2, 4, 8; 21.20, 23, 24). Fragment of an ancient copy dating to the beginning of the second century indicates the original is, of course, older and within John's lifetime. Conservative scholars place its date after the other Gospels were written, hence somewhere between A.D. 69 (before the fall of Jerusalem) and A.D. 90.

C.F.H.H.

THE GOSPEL ACCORDING TO

JOHN

John presents Jesus in His Deity

CHAPTER 1

IN the beginning was the Word, and the Word was with God, and the Word was God. GEN. 1:1 Christ

2 The Same was in the beginning with God.

3 All things were made by Him; and without Him was not any thing made that was made.

4 In Him was life; and the life was the light of men.

5 And the light shines in darkness; and the darkness comprehended it not. understood

6 There was a man sent from God, whose name *was* John.

7 The same came for a witness, to bear witness of the Light, that all *men* through Him might believe. i.e., tell about - Jesus

8 He was not that Light, but *was sent* to bear witness of that Light. came

9 *That was* the true Light, which lights every man that comes into the world.

10 He was in the world, and the world was made by Him, and the world knew Him not. Jesus - i.e., did not recognize

11 He came to His own, and His own received Him not. i.e. own people

12 But as many as received Him, to them gave He power to become the sons of God, *even* to them that believe on His name:

13 Which were born, not of blood, nor of the will of the flesh, nor of the will of man, but of God.

14 And the Word was made flesh, and dwelt among us, (and we beheld His glory, the glory as of the only begotten of the Father,) full of grace and truth. Jesus Christ - became

15 John bare witness of Him, and cried, saying, This was He of whom I spoke, He that comes after me is preferred before me: for He was before me. existed

16 And of His fulness have all we received, and grace for grace. upon

17 For the law was given by Mo'ses, *but* grace and truth came by Je'sus Christ.

18 No man has seen God at any time; the only begotten Son, which is in the bosom of the Father, He has declared *Him*. EX. 33:20

19 And this is the record of John, when the Jews sent priests and Le'vites from Je-ru'sa-lem to ask him, Who are you?

20 And he confessed, and denied not; but confessed, I am not the Christ. admitted

21 And they asked him, What then? Are you Elijah? And he said, I am not. Are you that prophet? And he answered, No. DEU. 18:15,18

22 Then said they to him, Who are you? that we may give an answer to them that sent us. What say you of yourself?

23 He said, I *am* the voice of one crying in the wilderness, Make straight the way of the Lord, as said the prophet I-sa'iah.   ISA. 40:3

24 And they which were sent were of the Phar'i-sees.

25 And they asked him, and said to him, Why baptize you then, if you be not that <u>Christ</u>, nor Elijah, neither that prophet?   i.e., the Messiah

26 John answered them, saying, I baptize with water: but there stands One among you, whom you know not;

27 He it is, who coming after me is preferred before me, whose shoe's <u>latchet</u> I am not worthy to <u>unloose</u>.   thong - untie

28 These things were done in <u>Beth-ab'a-ra</u> beyond Jor'dan, where John was baptizing.   Bethany

29 The next day John sees Je'sus coming to him, and said, Behold the Lamb of God, which takes away the sin of the world.

30 This is He of whom I said, After me comes a Man which is preferred before me: for He was before me.

31 And I knew Him not: but that He should be made manifest to Is'ra-el, therefore am I come baptizing with water.

32 And John bare record, saying, I saw the Spirit descending from heaven like a dove, and It abode upon Him.

33 And I knew Him not: but He that sent me to baptize with water, the same said to me, Upon whom you shall see the Spirit descending, and remaining on Him, the same is He which baptizes with the Ho'ly <u>Ghost</u>.   Spirit

34 And I saw, and <u>bare record</u> that this is the Son of God.   gave witness

35 Again the next day after John stood, and two of his disciples;

36 And looking upon Je'sus as He walked, he said, Behold the Lamb of God!

37 And the two disciples heard him speak, and they followed Je'sus.

38 Then Je'sus turned, and saw them following, and said to them, What seek you? They said to Him, Rab'bi, (which is to say, being interpreted, Master,) where <u>dwell</u> You?   live

39 He said to them, Come and see. They came and saw where He dwelt, and abode with Him that day: for it was <u>about the tenth hour</u>.   4 P.M.

40 One of the two which heard John *speak*, and followed *Him*, was Andrew, Si'mon Pe'ter's brother.   Jesus

41 He first finds his own brother Si'mon, and said to him, We have found the Mes-si'as, which is, being interpreted, the Christ.   DAN. 9:25

42 And he brought him to Je'sus. And when Je'sus beheld him, He said, You are Si'mon the son of <u>Jo'na</u>: you shall be called Ce'phas, which is by interpretation, <u>A stone</u>.   John - petros

43 The day following Je'sus <u>would</u> go forth into Gal'i-lee, and finds Phil'ip, and said to him, Follow Me.   planned to

44 Now Phil'ip was of Beth-sa'i-da, the city of Andrew and Pe'ter.

45 Phil'ip finds Na-than'a-el, and said to him, We have found Him, of whom Mo'ses in the law, and the

prophets, did write, Je'sus of Naz'a-reth, the son of Jo'seph.   DEU. 18:15

46 And Na-than'a-el said to him, Can there any good thing come out of Naz'a-reth? Phil'ip said to him, Come and see.

47 Je'sus saw Na-than'a-el coming to Him, and said of him, Behold an Is'-ra-el-ite indeed, in whom is no guile!deceit

48 Na-than'a-el said to Him, From where know You me? Je'sus answered and said to him, Before that Phil'ip called you, when you were under the fig tree, I saw you.

49 Na-than'a-el answered and said to Him, Rab'bi, You are the Son of God; You are the King of Is'ra-el.

50 Je'sus answered and said to him, Because I said to you, I saw you under the fig tree, believe you? you shall see greater things than these.

51 And He said to him, Verily, verily, I say to you, Hereafter you shall see heaven open, and the angels of God ascending and descending upon the Son of Man.   GEN. 28:12 Truly - messengers

CHAPTER 2

AND the third day there was a marriage in Ca'na of Gal'i-lee; and the mother of Je'sus was there:

2 And both Je'sus was called, and His disciples, to the marriage.   invited

3 And when they wanted wine, the mother of Je'sus said to Him, They have no wine.   needed

4 Je'sus said to her, Woman, what have I to do with you? My hour is not yet come.

5 His mother said to the servants, Whatsoever He said to you, do *it*.

6 And there were set there six water-pots of stone, after the manner of the purifying of the Jews, containing two or three firkins apiece.   20-30 gallons

7 Je'sus said to them, Fill the waterpots with water. And they filled them up to the brim.

8 And He said to them, Draw out now, and bear to the governor of the feast. And they bare *it*.   stewart

9 When the ruler of the feast had tasted the water that was made wine, and knew not where it was: (but the servants which drew the water knew;) the governor of the feast called the bridegroom,

10 And said to him, Every man at the beginning does set forth good wine; and when men have well drunk, then that which is worse: *but* you have kept the good wine until now.   drunk freely

11 This beginning of miracles did Je'sus in Ca'na of Gal'i-lee, and manifested forth His glory; and His disciples believed on Him.
EXO. 14:31 His signs - made known

12 After this He went down to Ca-per'na-um, He, and His mother, and His brethren, and His disciples: and they continued there not many days.

13 And the Jews' passover was at hand, and Je'sus went up to Je-ru'sa-lem,

14 And found in the temple those that sold oxen and sheep and doves, and the changers of money sitting:

15 And when He had made a scourge of small cords, He drove them all out of the temple, and the sheep, and the

oxen; and poured out the changers' money, and overthrew the tables;   whip

16 And said to them that sold doves, Take these things from here; make not My Father's house an house of merchandise.

17 And His disciples remembered that it was written, The zeal of Your house has eaten me up.   PS. 69:9

18 Then answered the Jews and said to Him, What sign show You to us, seeing that You do these things?

19 Je'sus answered and said to them, Destroy this temple, and in three days I will raise it up.

20 Then said the Jews, Forty and six years was this temple in building, and will You rear it up in three days?   build

21 But He spoke of the temple of His body.

22 When therefore He was risen from the dead, His disciples remembered that He had said this to them; and they believed the scripture, and the word which Je'sus had said.

23 Now when He was in Je-ru'sa-lem at the passover, in the feast *day*, many believed in His name, when they saw the miracles which He did.

24 But Je'sus did not commit Himself to them, because He knew all *men*,   entrust

25 And needed not that any should testify of man: for He knew what was in man.

CHAPTER 3

THERE was a man of the Phar'i-sees, named Nic-o-de'mus, a ruler of the Jews:

2 The same came to Je'sus by night, and said to Him, Rab'bi, we know that You are a teacher come from God: for no man can do these miracles that You do except God be with Him.   1 KGS. 17:24

3 Je'sus answered and said to him, Verily, verily, I say to you, Except a man be born again, he cannot see the kingdom of God.   JER. 32:40 Truly

4 Nic-o-de'mus said to Him, How can a man be born when he is old? can he enter the second time into his mother's womb, and be born?

5 Je'sus answered, Verily, verily, I say to you, Except a man be born of water and *of* the Spirit, he cannot enter into the kingdom of God.   EZE. 36:25-27

6 That which is born of the flesh is flesh; and that which is born of the Spirit is spirit.   human parents - human

7 Marvel not that I said to you, You must be born again.   anew

8 The wind blows where it lists, and you hear the sound thereof, but can not tell from where it comes, and where it goes: so is every one that is born of the Spirit.   ECC. 1:6

9 Nic-o-de'mus answered and said to Him, How can these things be?

10 Je'sus answered and said to him, Are you a master of Is'ra-el, and know not these things?   teacher

11 Verily, verily, I say to you, We speak that we do know, and testify that we have seen; and you receive not our witness.   Truly - believe

12 If I have told you earthly things, and you believe not, how shall you believe, if I tell you *of* heavenly things?   worldly

13 And no man has ascended up to heaven, but He that came down from heaven, *even* the Son of man which is in heaven. PROV 30:4

14 And as Mo'ses lifted up the serpent in the wilderness, even so must the Son of man be lifted up: NUM 21:9

15 That whosoever believes in Him should not perish, but have eternal life.

16 For God so loved the world, that He gave His only begotten Son, that whosoever believes in Him should not perish, but have everlasting life. ACTS 16:31 i.e., all people - Jesus

17 For God sent not His Son into the world to condemn the world; but that the world through Him might be saved. judge

18 He that believes on Him is not condemned: but he that believes not is condemned already, because he has not believed in the name of the only begotten Son of God.

19 And this is the condemnation, that light is come into the world, and men loved darkness rather than light, because their deeds were evil. judgment

20 For every one that does evil hates the light, neither comes to the light, less his deeds should be reproved.

exposed

21 But he that does truth comes to the light, that his deeds may be made manifest, that they are wrought in God. known

22 After these things came Je'sus and His disciples into the land of Ju-dae'a; and there He tarried with them, and baptized. stayed

23 And John also was baptizing in AE'non near to Sa'lim, because there was much water there: and they came, and were baptized.

24 For John was not yet cast into prison.

25 Then there arose a question between *some* of John's disciples and the Jews about purifying.

26 And they came to John, and said to him, Rab'bi, He that was with you beyond Jor'dan, to whom you bare witness, behold, the same baptizes, and all *men* come to Him.

27 John answered and said, A man can receive nothing, except it be given him from heaven.

28 You yourselves bear me witness, that I said, I am not the Christ, but that I am sent before Him.

29 He that has the bride is the bridegroom: but the friend of the bridegroom, which stands and hears Him, rejoices greatly because of the bridegroom's voice: this my joy therefore is fulfilled.

30 He must increase, but I *must* decrease. i.e., more important

31 He that comes from above is above all: he that is of the earth is earthly, and speaks of the earth: He that comes from heaven is above all.

32 And what He has seen and heard, that He testifies; and no man receives His testimony. told about - statements

33 He that has received His testimony has set to his seal that God is true.

34 For He whom God has sent speaks the words of God: for God

gives not the Spirit <u>by measure</u> to *Him*. _{part}

35 The Father loves the Son, and has given all things into His hand.

36 He that believes on the Son has everlasting life: and he that believes not the Son shall not see life; but the <u>wrath</u> of God <u>abides</u> on him._{anger - rests}

CHAPTER 4

WHEN therefore the Lord knew how the Phar'i-sees had heard that Je'sus made and baptized more disciples than John,

2 (Though Je'sus Himself baptized not, but His disciples,)

3 He left Ju-dae'a, and <u>departed</u> again into Gal'i-lee. _{returned}

4 And He must <u>needs</u> go through Sa-ma'ri-a. _{necessarily}

5 Then comes He to a city of Sa-ma'ri-a, which is called Sy'char, near to the <u>parcel</u> of ground that Ja'cob gave to his son Jo'seph._{section}

6 Now Ja'cob's well was there. Je'sus therefore, being <u>wearied</u> with *His* journey, sat thus on the well: *and* it was about the <u>sixth</u> hour. _{tired - 12 noon}

7 There comes a woman of Sa-ma'ri-a to draw water: Je'sus said to her, Give Me to drink.

8 (For His disciples were gone away to the city to buy <u>meat</u>.) _{food}

9 Then said the woman of Sa-ma'ri-a to Him, How is it that You, being a Jew, ask drink of me, which am a woman of Sa-ma'ri-a? for the Jews have no dealings with the Sa-mar'i-tans.

10 Je'sus answered and said to her, If you knew the gift of God, and who it is that said to you, Give Me to drink; you would have asked of Him, and He would have given you living water.

11 The woman said to Him, Sir, You have nothing to draw with, and the well is deep: from where then have You that living water?

12 Are You greater than our father Ja'cob, which gave us the well, and drank <u>thereof</u> himself, and his children, and his cattle? _{there}

13 Je'sus answered and said to her, Whosoever drinks of this water shall thirst again:

14 But whosoever drinks of the water that I shall give him shall never thirst; but the water that I shall give him shall be in him a well of water springing up into everlasting life. _{JOHN 7:37}

15 The woman said to Him, Sir, give me this water, that I thirst not, neither come here to draw.

16 Je'sus said to her, Go, call your husband, and come here.

17 The woman answered and said, I have no husband. Je'sus said to her, You have well said, I have no husband:

18 For you have had five husbands; and he whom you now have is not your husband: in that said you truly.

19 The woman said to Him, Sir, I <u>perceive</u> that You are a prophet. _{can see}

20 Our fathers worshiped in this mountain; and you say, that in Je-ru'sa-lem is the place where men ought to worship.

21 Je'sus said to her, Woman, believe Me, the hour comes, when you shall neither in this mountain, nor yet at Je-ru'sa-lem, worship the Father.

22 You worship you know not what: we know what we worship: for salvation is of the Jews.

23 But the hour comes, and now is, when the true worshippers shall worship the Father in spirit and in truth: for the Father seeks such to worship him.

24 God *is* a Spirit: and they that worship Him must worship *Him* in spirit and in truth.

25 The woman said to Him, I know that Mes-si'as comes, which is called Christ: when He is come, He will tell us all things.   DEU. 18:15-18

26 Je'sus said to her, I that speak to you am *He*.

27 And upon this came His disciples, and <u>marveled</u> that He talked with the woman: yet no man said, What seek You? or, Why talk You with her?   were surprised

28 The woman then left her waterpot, and went her way into the city, and said to the men,

29 Come, see a man, which told me all things that ever I did: is not this the Christ?

30 Then they went out of the city, and came to Him.

31 In the mean while His disciples <u>prayed</u> Him, saying, Master, eat. urged

32 But He said to them, I have <u>meat</u> to eat that you know not of.   food

33 Therefore said the disciples one to another, Has any man brought Him *anything* to eat?

34 Je'sus said to them, My meat is to do the will of Him that sent Me, and to finish His work.

35 Say not you, There are yet four months, and *then* comes harvest? behold, I say to you, Lift up your eyes, and look on the fields; for they are white already to harvest.

36 And he that reaps receives wages, and gathers fruit to life eternal: that both he that sows and he that reaps may rejoice together.

37 And herein is that saying true, One sows, and another reaps.   MIC. 6:15

38 I sent you to reap that whereon you <u>bestowed</u> no labor: other men labored, and you are entered into their labors.   put

39 And many of the Sa-mar'i-tans of that city believed on Him for the saying of the woman, which testified, He told me all that ever I did.

40 So when the Sa-mar'i-tans were come to Him, they besought Him that He would <u>tarry</u> with them: and He abode there two days.   stay

41 And many more believed because of His own word;

42 And said to the woman, Now we believe, not because of your saying: for we have heard *Him* ourselves, and know that this is indeed the Christ, the Savior of the world.

43 Now after two days He departed from there, and went into Gal'i-lee.

44 For Je'sus Himself testified, that a prophet has no honor in his own country.

45 Then when He was come into Gal'i-lee, the Gal-i-lae'ans received Him, having seen all the things that He did at Je-ru'sa-lem at the feast: for they also went to the feast.

46 So Je'sus came again into Ca'na of Gal'i-lee, where He made the water wine. And there was a certain <u>nobleman</u>, whose son was sick at Ca-per'na-um. _{official}

47 When he heard that Je'sus was come out of Ju-dae'a into Gal'i-lee, he went to Him, and <u>besought</u> Him that He would come down, and heal his son: for he was at the point of death. _{asked}

48 Then said Je'sus to him, <u>Except</u> you see signs and wonders, you will not believe. _{unless}

49 The nobleman said to Him, Sir, come down before my child die.

50 Je'sus said to him, Go your way; your son lives. And the man believed the word that Je'sus had spoken to him, and he went his way.

51 And as he was now going down, his servants met him, and told him, saying, Your son lives.

52 Then enquired he of them the hour when he began to <u>amend</u>. And they said to him, Yesterday at the <u>seventh</u> hour the fever left him. _{get better - 1 P.M.}

53 So the father knew that *it was* at the same hour, in the which Je'sus said to him, Your son lives: and himself believed, and his whole house.

54 This *is* again the second miracle *that* Je'sus did, when He was come out of Ju-dae'a into Gal'i-lee.

CHAPTER 5

AFTER this there was a feast of the Jews; and Je'sus went up to Je-ru'sa-lem.

2 Now there is at Je-ru'sa-lem by the sheep *market* a pool, which is called in the He'brew tongue Be-thes'da, having five porches. _{gate}

3 In these lay a great multitude of <u>impotent</u> folk, of blind, <u>halt</u>, <u>withered</u>, waiting for the moving of the water. _{invalid - lame - paralyzed}

4 For an <u>angel</u> went down at a certain season into the pool, and <u>troubled</u> the water: whosoever then first after the troubling of the water stepped in was made <u>whole</u> of whatsoever disease he had. _{messenger - stirred - well}

5 And a certain man was there, which had an <u>infirmity</u> thirty and eight years. _{sickness}

6 When Je'sus saw him lie, and knew that he had been now a long time *in that case*, He said to him, Will you be made <u>whole</u>?

7 The <u>impotent</u> man answered Him, Sir, I have no man, when the water is troubled, to put me into the pool: but while I am coming, another steps down before me. _{invalid}

8 Je'sus said to him, Rise, take up your bed, and walk.

9 And immediately the man was made <u>whole</u>, and took up his bed, and walked: and on the same day was the <u>sabbath</u>. _{rest day}

10 The Jews therefore said to him that was cured, It is the <u>sabbath</u> day: it is not <u>lawful</u> for you to carry *your* <u>bed</u>. _{JER 17:21 proper - pallet}

11 He answered them, He that made me <u>whole</u>, the same said to me, Take up your <u>bed</u>, and walk. *well - pallet*

12 Then asked they him, What man is that which said to you, Take up your <u>bed</u>, and walk?

13 And he that was healed knew not who it was: for Je'sus had conveyed Himself away, a multitude being in *that* place.

14 Afterward Je'sus finds him in the temple, and said to him, Behold, you are made <u>whole</u>: sin no more, less a worse thing come to you.

15 The man departed, and told the Jews that it was Je'sus, which had made him <u>whole</u>. *well*

16 And therefore did the Jews persecute Je'sus, and sought to slay Him, because He had done these things on the <u>sabbath</u> day. *rest*

17 But Je'sus answered them, My Father works until now, and I work. *GEN. 2:2*

18 Therefore the Jews sought the more to kill Him, because He not only had broken the <u>sabbath</u>, but said also that God was His Father, making Himself equal with God. *rest day*

19 Then answered Je'sus and said to them, <u>Verily, verily</u>, I say to you, The Son can do nothing of Himself, but what He sees the Father do: for what things soever He does, these also does the Son likewise. *Truly*

20 For the Father loves the Son, and shows Him all things that Himself does: and He will show Him greater works than these, that you may <u>marvel</u>. *be amazed*

21 For as the Father raises up the dead, and makes *them alive*; even so the Son makes alive whom He will.

22 For the Father judges no man, but has committed all judgment to the Son:

23 That all *men* should honor the Son, even as they honor the Father. He that honors not the Son honors not the Father which has sent Him.

24 <u>Verily, verily</u>, I say to you, He that hears My word, and believes on Him that sent Me, has everlasting life, and shall not come into condemnation; but is passed from death to life. *Truly*

25 <u>Verily, verily</u>, I say to you, The hour is coming, and now is, when the dead shall hear the voice of the Son of God: and they that hear shall live.

26 For as the Father has life in Himself; so has He given to the Son to <u>have life in Himself</u>; *i.e., source of life*

27 And has given Him authority to <u>execute</u> judgment also, because He is the Son of Man. *make*

28 Marvel not at this: for the hour is coming, in the which all <u>that</u> are in the graves shall hear His voice, *the dead*

29 And shall come forth; they that have done good, to the resurrection to of life; and they that have done evil, to the resurrection of <u>damnation</u>. *DAN. 12:2 judgment*

30 I can of My own self do nothing: as I hear, I judge: and My judgment is just; because I seek not My own will, but the will of the Father which has sent Me. *NUM. 16:28*

31 If I bear witness of Myself, My witness is not true.

32 There is another that bears witness of Me; and I know that the witness which he witnesses of Me is true.

33 You sent to John, and he bare witness to the truth.

34 But I receive not <u>testimony</u> from man: but these things I say, that you might be saved. witness

35 He was a burning and a shining light: and you were willing for a <u>season</u> to rejoice in his light. while

36 But I have greater witness than *that* of John: for the works which the Father has given Me to finish, the same works that I do, bear witness of Me, that the Father has sent Me.

37 And the Father Himself, which has sent Me, has borne witness of Me. You have neither heard His voice at any time, nor seen His shape.

38 And you have <u>not</u> His word abiding in you: for whom He has sent, Him you believe not. not honored

39 <u>Search</u> the scriptures; <u>for</u> in them you think you have eternal life: and they are they which testify of Me. i.e., you search - because

40 And you will not come to Me, that you might have life.

41 I receive not <u>honor</u> from men. respect

42 But I know you, that you have not the love of God in you.

43 I am come in My Father's name, and you receive Me not: if another shall come in his own name, him you will receive.

44 How can you believe, which receive honor one of another, and seek not the honor that *comes* from God only?

45 Do not think that I will accuse you to the Father: there is *one* that accuses you, *even* Mo'ses, in whom you <u>trust</u>. hope

46 For had you believed Mo'ses, you would have believed Me: for he wrote of Me.

47 But if you believe not his <u>writings</u>, how shall you believe My words? Genesis-Deuteronomy

CHAPTER 6

AFTER these things Je'sus went over the sea of Gal'i-lee, which is *the sea* of Ti-be'ri-as.

2 And a great multitude followed Him, because they saw His miracles which He did on them that were diseased.

3 And Je'sus went up into a mountain, and there He sat with His disciples.

4 And the passover, a feast of the Jews, was near.

5 When Je'sus then lifted up *His* eyes, and saw a great company come to Him, He said to Phil'ip, Where shall we buy bread, that these may eat?

6 And this He said to <u>prove</u> him: for He Himself knew what He would do. test

7 Phil'ip answered Him, Two hundred pennyworth of bread is not sufficient for them, that every one of them may take a little.

8 One of His disciples, Andrew, Si'mon Pe'ter's brother, said to Him,

9 There is a lad here, which has five

barley loaves, and two small fishes: but what are they among so many?

10 And Je'sus said, Make the men sit down. Now there was much grass in the place. So the men sat down, in number about five thousand.

11 And Je'sus took the loaves; and when He had given thanks, He distributed to the disciples, and the disciples to them that were set down; and likewise of the fishes as much as they <u>would</u>.   wanted

12 When they were filled, He said to His disciples, Gather up the <u>fragments</u> that remain, that nothing be lost.   pieces

13 Therefore they gathered *them* together, and filled twelve baskets with the <u>fragments</u> of the five barley loaves, which remained over and above <u>to them that</u> had eaten.
     that which the people

14 Then those men, when they had seen the miracle that Je'sus did, said, This is of a truth that prophet that should come into the world. DEU. 18:18

15 When Je'sus therefore <u>perceived</u> that they would come and take Him by force, to make Him a king, He departed again into a mountain Himself alone.   knew

16 And when <u>even</u> was *now* come, His disciples went down to the sea,   evening

17 And entered into a <u>ship</u>, and went over the sea toward Ca-per'-na-um. And it was now dark, and Je'sus was not come to them.   boat

18 And the sea arose by reason of a great wind that blew.

19 So when they had rowed about five and twenty or thirty furlongs, they see Je'sus walking on the sea, and drawing near to the ship: and they were afraid.

20 But He said to them, It is I; be not afraid.

21 Then they willingly <u>received</u> Him into the ship: and immediately the ship was at the land where they went.   took

22 The day following, when the people which stood on the other side of the sea saw that there was <u>none</u> other boat there, save that one whereinto His disciples were entered, and that Je'sus went not with His disciples into the boat, but *that* His disciples were gone away alone;   no

23 (<u>However</u> there came other boats from Ti-be'ri-as near to the place where they did eat bread, after that the Lord had given thanks:)

24 When the people therefore saw that Je'sus was not there, neither His disciples, they also took <u>shipping</u>, and came to Ca-per'na-um, seeking for Je'sus.   to the boats

25 And when they had found Him on the other side of the sea, they said to Him, Rab'bi, when came You here?

26 Je'sus answered them and said, <u>Verily</u>, <u>verily,</u> I say to you, You seek Me, not because you saw the miracles, but because you did eat of the loaves, and were filled.   Truly

27 <u>Labor</u> not for the <u>meat</u> which perishes, but for that <u>meat</u> which endures to everlasting life, which the

Son of man shall give to you: for Him has God the Father sealed.

ISA. 55:2 work - food

28 Then said they to Him, What shall we do, that we might <u>work</u> the works of God?　　　　　　　　　　do

29 Je'sus answered and said to them, This is the work of God, that you believe on Him whom He has sent.

30 They said therefore to Him, What sign show You then, that we may see, and believe You? what do You work?

31 Our fathers did eat manna in the desert; as it is written, He gave them bread from heaven to eat. EX. 16:4

32 Then Je'sus said to them, <u>Verily</u>, <u>verily</u>, I say to you, Mo'ses gave you not that bread from heaven; but My Father gives you the true bread from heaven.　　　　　　Truly

33 For the bread of God is He which comes down from heaven, and gives life to the world.

34 Then said they to Him, Lord, <u>evermore</u> give us this bread.　　forever

35 And Je'sus said to them, I am the bread of life: he that comes to Me shall never hunger; and he that believes on Me shall never thirst.

36 But I said to you, That you also have seen Me, and believe not.

37 All that the Father gives Me shall come to Me; and him that comes to Me I will in no wise cast out.

38 For I came down from heaven, not to do Mine own will, but the will of Him that sent Me.

39 And this is the Father's will which has sent Me, that of all which He has given Me I should lose nothing, but should raise it up again at the last day.

40 And this is the will of <u>Him</u> that sent Me, that every one which sees the Son, and believes on Him, may have everlasting life: and I will raise him up at the last day.　　God the father

41 The Jews then <u>murmured</u> at Him, because He said, I am the bread which came down from heaven. grumbled

42 And they said, Is not this Je'sus, the son of Jo'seph, whose father and mother we know? how is it then that He said, I came down from heaven?

43 Je'sus therefore answered and said to them, <u>Murmur</u> not among yourselves.

44 No man can come to Me, except the Father which has sent Me draw him: and I will raise him up at the last day.　　JER. 31:3

45 It is written in the prophets, And they shall be all taught of God. Every man therefore that has heard, and has learned of the Father, comes to Me.　　ISA. 54:13

46 Not that any man has seen the Father, save He which is of God, He has seen the Father.

47 <u>Verily</u>, <u>verily</u>, I say to you, He that believes on Me has everlasting life.　　Truly

48 I am that bread of life.

49 Your fathers did eat manna in the wilderness, and are dead.

50 This is the bread which comes down from heaven, that a man may eat thereof, and not die.

51 I am the living bread which came down from heaven: if any man eat of

this bread, he shall live for ever: and the bread that I will give is My flesh, which I will give for the life of the world.

52 The Jews therefore <u>strove</u> among themselves, saying, How can this man give us *His* flesh to eat? _{argued}

53 Then Je'sus said to them, <u>Verily, verily</u>, I say to you, Except you eat the flesh of the Son of Man, and drink His blood, you have no life in you. _{Truly}

54 Whoso eats My flesh, and drinks My blood, has eternal life; and I will raise him up at the last day.

55 For My flesh is <u>meat</u> indeed, and My blood is drink indeed. _{food}

56 He that eats My flesh, and drinks My blood, <u>dwells</u> in Me, and I in him. _{abides}

57 As the living Father has sent Me, and I live by the Father: so he that eats Me, even he shall live by Me. _{because of}

58 This is that bread which came down from heaven: not as your fathers did eat manna, and are dead: he that eats of this bread shall live for ever.

59 These things said He in the synagogue, as He taught in Ca-per'na-um.

60 Many therefore of His disciples, when they had heard *this*, said, This is an <u>hard</u> saying; who can <u>hear</u> *it*? _{difficult - understand}

61 When Je'sus knew in Himself that His disciples <u>murmured</u> at it, He said to them, Does this offend you? _{complained}

62 *What* and if you shall see the Son of man ascend up where He was before?

63 It is the spirit that <u>quickens</u>; the flesh profits nothing: the words that I speak to you, *they* are spirit, and *they* are life. _{gives life}

64 But there are some of you that believe not. For Je'sus knew from the beginning who they were that believed not, and who should betray Him.

65 And He said, Therefore said I to you, that no man can come to Me, except it were given to him of My Father.

66 From that *time* many of His disciples went back, and walked no more with Him.

67 Then said Je'sus to the twelve, Will you also go away?

68 Then Si'mon Pe'ter answered Him, Lord, to whom shall we go? You have the words of eternal life.

69 And we believe and are sure that You are that Christ, the Son of the living God.

70 Je'sus answered them, Have not I chosen you twelve, and one of you is <u>a devil</u>? _{evil}

71 He spoke of Ju'das Is-car'i-ot *the son* of Si'mon: for he it was that should betray Him, being one of the twelve.

CHAPTER 7

AFTER these things Je'sus walked in Gal'i-lee: for He would not walk in <u>Jew'ry</u>, because the Jews <u>sought</u> to kill Him. _{i.e., Judea - wanted}

2 Now the Jews' feast of tabernacles was at hand.

3 His brethren therefore said to Him, Depart from here, and go into Judae'a, that Your disciples also may see the works that You do.

4 For *there is* no man *that* does any thing in secret, and he himself seeks to be known openly. If You do these things, show Yourself to the world.

5 For <u>neither</u> did His brethren believe in Him.   not even

6 Then Je'sus said to them, My time is not yet come: but your time is always ready.

7 The world cannot <u>hate</u> you; but Me it <u>hates</u>, because I testify of it, that the works thereof are evil.   dislike - abhors

8 Go you up to this feast: I go not up yet to this feast; for My time is not yet full come.

9 When He had said these words to them, He <u>abode</u> *still* in Gal'i-lee. stayed

10 But when His brethren were gone up, then went He also up to the feast, not openly, but as it were in secret.

11 Then the Jews sought Him at the feast, and said, Where is He?

12 And there was much <u>murmuring</u> among the people concerning Him: for some said, He is a good man: others said, Nay; but He deceives the people.   talking

13 However no man spoke openly of Him <u>for fear</u> of the Jews.   being afraid

14 Now about the midst of the feast Je'sus went up into the temple, and taught.

15 And the Jews marveled, saying, How knows this man letters, having never learned?

16 Je'sus answered them, and said, My <u>doctrine</u> is not Mine, but His that sent Me.   teaching

17 If any man will do His will, he shall know of the <u>doctrine</u>, whether it be of God, or *whether* I speak of Myself.

18 He that speaks of himself seeks his own glory: but he that seeks His glory that sent Him, the same is true, and no <u>unrighteousness</u> is in him.   falsehood

19 Did not Mo'ses give you the law, and *yet* none of you keeps the law? Why go you about to kill Me?

20 The people answered and said, You have a <u>devil</u>: who goes about to kill You?   demon

21 Je'sus answered and said to them, I have done one work, and you all marvel.

22 Mo'ses therefore gave to you circumcision; (not because it is of Mo'ses, but of the fathers;) and you on the <u>sabbath</u> day circumcise a man.   rest

23 If a man on the <u>sabbath</u> day receive circumcision, that the law of Mo'ses should not be broken; are you angry at Me, because I have made a man every <u>whit whole</u> on the <u>sabbath</u> day?   bit well

24 Judge not according to the appearance, but judge righteous judgment.   ZEC. 7:9

25 Then said some of them of Je-ru'sa-lem, Is not this He, whom they seek to kill?

26 But, lo, He speaks boldly, and they say nothing to Him. Do the rulers know indeed that this is the very Christ?

27 However we know this man where He is: but when Christ come, no man knows where He is.

28 Then cried Je'sus in the temple as He taught, saying, You both know Me, and you know from where I am: and I am not come of My-self, but He that sent Me is true, whom you know not.

29 But I <u>know</u> Him: for I am from Him, and He has sent Me.   revere

30 Then they <u>sought</u> to take Him: but no man laid hands on Him, because His hour was not yet come.   wanted

31 And many of the people believed on Him, and said, When Christ comes, will He do more miracles than these which this *man* has done?

32 The Phar'i-sees heard that the people <u>murmured</u> such things con-cerning Him; and the Phar'i-sees and the chief priests sent officers to take Him.   muttered

33 Then said Je'sus to them, Yet a little while am I with you, and *then* I go to Him that sent Me.

34 You shall seek Me, and shall not find *Me*: and where I am, *there* you cannot <u>come</u>.   go

35 Then said the Jews among them-selves, Where will He go, that we shall not find Him? will He go to the <u>dis-persed</u> among the <u>Gen'tiles</u>, and teach the <u>Gen'tiles</u>?   scattered - Greeks

36 What *manner of* saying is this that He said, You shall seek Me, and shall not find *Me*: and where I am, *there* you cannot <u>come</u>?   go

37 In the last day, that great *day* of the feast, Je'sus stood and cried, saying, If any man thirst, let him come to Me, and drink.   JOHN 4:14

38 He that believes on Me, as the scripture has said, out of his belly shall flow rivers of living water. ISA. 44:3

39 (But this spoke He of the Spirit, which they that believe on Him should receive: for the Ho'ly <u>Ghost</u> was not yet *given*; because that Je'sus was not yet glorified.)   Spirit

40 Many of the people therefore, when they heard this saying, said, Of a truth this is the Prophet.

41 Others said, This is the Christ. But some said, Shall Christ come out of Gal'i-lee?

42 Has not the scripture said, That Christ comes of the seed of Da'vid, and out of the town of Beth'le-hem, where Da'vid was?   MIC. 5:2

43 So there was a division among the people because of Him.

44 And some of them would have taken Him; but no man laid hands on Him.

45 Then came the officers to the chief priests and Phar'i-sees; and they said to them, Why have you not brought Him?

46 The officers answered, Never man <u>spoke</u> like this man.   talked

47 Then answered them the Phar'i-sees, Are you also <u>deceived</u>?   fooled

48 Have any of the rulers or of the Phar'i-sees believed on Him?

49 But this people who <u>knows</u> not the <u>law</u> are cursed.   understands - i.e., law of Moses

50 Nic-o-de'mus said to them, (he that came to Je'sus by night, being one of them,)

51 Does our law judge *any* man, before it hear him, and know what he does?   DEU. 17:6

52 They answered and said to him, Are you also of Gal'i-lee? Search, and look: for out of Gal'i-lee arises no prophet.

53 And every man went to his own house.

CHAPTER 8

JE'SUS went to the mount of Ol'ives.

2 And early in the morning He came <u>again</u> into the temple, and all the people came to Him; and He sat down, and taught them.   back

3 And the scribes and Phar'i-sees brought to Him a woman taken in adultery; and when they had set her in the midst,

4 They say to Him, Master, this woman was taken in adultery, in the very act.

5 Now Mo'ses in the law commanded us, that such should be <u>stoned</u>: but what say You?   killed

6 This they said, <u>tempting</u> Him, that they might have to accuse Him. But Je'sus stooped down, and with *His* finger wrote on the ground, *as though he heard them not*.   testing

7 So when they continued asking Him, He lifted up Himself, and said to them, He that is without sin among you, let him first cast a stone at her.

8 And again He stooped down, and wrote on the ground.

9 And they which heard *it*, being convicted by *their own* conscience, went out one by one, beginning at the eldest, *even* to the last: and Je'sus was left alone, and the woman standing in the midst.

10 When Je'sus had lifted up Himself, and saw none but the woman, He said to her, Woman, where are those your accusers? <u>has</u> no man condemned you?   did

11 She said, No man, Lord. And Je'sus said to her, Neither do I condemn you: go, and sin no more.

12 Then spoke Je'sus again to them, saying, I am the light of the world: he that follows Me shall not walk in darkness, but shall have the light of life.

13 The Phar'i-sees therefore said to Him, You bear <u>record</u> of Yourself; Your <u>record</u> is not true.   witness

14 Je'sus answered and said to them, Though I bear record of Myself, *yet* My record is true: for I know from where I came, and where I go; but you cannot tell from where I come, and where I go.

15 You judge after the flesh; I judge no man.

16 And yet if I judge, My judgment is true: for I am not alone, but I and the Father that sent Me.

17 It is also written in your law, that the testimony of two men is true.   DEU. 19:15

18 I am one that bear witness of Myself, and the Father that sent Me <u>bears</u> witness of Me.   gives

19 Then said they to Him, Where is Your Father? Je'sus answered, You neither know Me, nor My Father: if you had known Me, you should have known My Father also.

20 These words spoke Je'sus in the

treasury, as He taught in the temple: and no man laid hands on Him; for His hour was not yet come.

21 Then said Je'sus again to them, I go My way, and you shall seek me, and shall die in your sins: where I go, you cannot come.

22 Then said the Jews, Will He kill Himself? because He said Where I go, you cannot come.

23 And He said to them, You are from beneath; I am from above: you are of this world; I am not of this world.

24 I said therefore to you, that you shall die in your sins: for if you believe not that I am *He*, you shall die in your sins. EZE. 3:18

25 Then said they to Him, Who are You? And Je'sus said to them, Even *the same* that I said to you from the beginning.

26 I have many things to say and to judge of you: but He that sent Me is true; and I speak to the world those things which I have heard of Him. worthy

27 They understood not that He spoke to them of the Father.

28 Then said Je'sus to them, When you have lifted up the Son of Man, then shall you know that I am *He*, and *that* I do nothing of Myself; but as My Father has taught Me, I speak these things. crucified

29 And He that sent Me is with Me: the Father has not left Me alone; for I do always those things that please Him.

30 As He spoke these words, many believed on Him. in

31 Then said Je'sus to those Jews which believed on Him, If you continue in My word, *then* are you My disciples indeed;

32 And you shall know the truth, and the truth shall make you free.

33 They answered Him, We be A'braham's seed, and were never in bondage to any man: how say You, You shall be made free? descendants - slavery

34 Je'sus answered them, Verily, verily, I say to you, Whosoever commits sin is the servant of sin. truly

35 And the servant abides not in the house for ever: *but* the Son abides ever.

36 If the Son therefore shall make you free, you shall be free indeed.

37 I know that you are A'bra-ham's seed; but you seek to kill Me, because My word has no place in you.

38 I speak that which I have seen with My Father: and you do that which you have seen with your father.

39 They answered and said to Him, A'bra-ham is our father. Je'sus said to them, If you were A'bra-ham's children, you would do the works of A'bra-ham.

40 But now you seek to kill Me, a man that had told you the truth, which I have heard of God: this did not A'bra-ham.

41 You do the deeds of your father. Then said they to Him, We be not born of fornication; we have one Father, *even* God. DEU. 32:6

42 Je'sus said to them, If God were your Father, you would love Me: for I proceeded forth and came from God; neither came I of Myself, but He sent Me.

43 Why do you not understand My speech? even because you cannot <u>hear</u> My word. understand

44 You are of *your* father the devil, and the <u>lusts</u> of your father you will do. He was a murderer from the beginning, and <u>abode</u> not in the truth, because there is no truth in him. When he speaks a lie, he speaks of his own: for he is a liar, and the father of it. desires - stands

45 And because I tell *you* the truth, you believe Me not.

46 Which of you <u>convinces</u> Me of sin? And if I say the truth, why do you not believe Me? convicts

47 He that is of God hears God's words: you therefore hear *them* not, because you are not of God.

48 Then answered the Jews, and said to Him, Say we not well that You are a Sa-mar'i-tan, and have a <u>devil</u>? demon

49 Je'sus answered, I have not a devil; but I honor My Father, and you do dishonor Me.

50 And I seek not Mine own glory: there is One that seeks and judges.

51 <u>Verily</u>, <u>verily</u>, I say to you, If a man <u>keep</u> My saying, he shall never see death. Truly - obeys

52 Then said the Jews to Him, Now we know that You have a <u>devil</u>. A'bra-ham is dead, and the prophets; and You say, If a man keep My saying, he shall never <u>taste</u> of death.

demon - experience

53 Are You greater than our father A'bra-ham, which is dead? and the prophets are dead: whom make You Yourself?

54 Je'sus answered, If I honor Myself, My honor is nothing: it is My Father that honors Me; of whom you say, that He is your God:

55 Yet you have not known Him; but I know Him: and if I should say, I know Him not, I shall be a liar like to you: but I know Him, and keep His saying.

56 Your father A'bra-ham rejoiced to see My day: and he saw *it*, and was glad.

57 Then said the Jews to Him, You are not yet fifty years old, and have You seen A'bra-ham?

58 Je'sus said to them, <u>Verily</u>, <u>verily</u>, I say to you, Before A'bra-ham was, I am. Truly

59 Then took they up stones to cast at Him: but Je'sus hid Himself, and went out of the temple, going through the midst of them, and so passed by. EXO. 17:4

CHAPTER 9

AND as *Je'sus* passed by, He saw a man which was blind from *his* birth.

2 And His disciples asked Him, saying, Master, who did sin, this man, or his parents, that he was born blind? EZE. 18:20

3 Je'sus answered, Neither has this man sinned, nor his parents: but <u>that</u> the works of God should be made <u>manifest</u> in him. so - known

4 I must <u>work</u> the works of Him that sent Me, while it is day: the night comes, when no man can work. do

5 As long as I am in the world, I am the light of the world.

6 When He had thus spoken, He spat on the ground, and made clay of the spittle, and He <u>anointed</u> the eyes of the blind man with the clay,   rubbed

7 And said to him, Go, wash in the pool of Si-lo'am, (which is by interpretation, Sent.) He went his way therefore, and washed, and came seeing.

8 The neighbors therefore, and they which before had seen him that he was blind, said, Is not this he <u>that</u> sat and begged?   who

9 Some said, This is he: others *said*, He is like him: *but* he said, I am *he*.

10 Therefore said they to him, How were your eyes opened?

11 He answered and said, A man that is called Je'sus made clay, and <u>anointed</u> my eyes, and said to me, Go to the pool of Si-lo'am, and wash: and I went and washed, and I received sight.   rubbed

12 Then said they to him, Where is he? He said, I know not.

13 They brought to the Phar'i-sees him that before was blind.

14 And it was the <u>sabbath</u> day when Je'sus made the clay, and opened his eyes.   rest

15 Then again the Phar'i-sees also asked him how he had received his sight. He said to them, He put clay upon my eyes, and I washed, and do see.

16 Therefore said some of the Phar'i-sees, This man is not of God, because He <u>keeps</u> not the <u>sabbath</u> day. Others said, How can a man that is a sinner do such miracles? And there was a <u>division</u> among them.   respects - rest - difference of opinion

17 They say to the blind man again, What say you of Him, that He has opened your eyes? he said, He is a prophet.

18 But the Jews did not believe concerning him, that he had been blind, and received his sight, until they called the parents of him that had received his sight.

19 And they asked them, saying, Is this your son, who you say was born blind? how then does he now see?

20 His parents answered them and said, We know that this is our son, and that he was born blind:

21 But by what means he now sees, we know not; or who has opened his eyes, we know not: he is of age; ask him: he shall speak for himself.

22 These *words* spoke his parents, because they <u>feared</u> the Jews: for the Jews had agreed already, that if any man did confess that He was Christ, he should be put out of the synagogue.   were afraid of

23 Therefore said his parents, He is of age; ask him.

24 Then again called they the man that was blind, and said to him, Give God the praise: we know that this man is a sinner.

25 He answered and said, Whether He be a sinner *or no*, I know not: one thing I know, that, whereas I was blind, now I see.

26 Then said they to him again, What did He to you? how opened He your eyes?

27 He answered them, I have told you already, and you did not hear: wherefore would you hear *it* again? will you also be His disciples?

28 Then they reviled him, and said, You are His disciple; but we are Mo'ses' disciples. ridiculed

29 We know that God spoke to Mo'ses: *as for* this *fellow*, we know not from where He is.

30 The man answered and said to them, Why herein is a marvellous thing, that you know not from where He is, and *yet* He has opened my eyes.

31 Now we know that God hears not sinners: but if any man be a worshipper of God, and does His will, him He hears.

32 Since the world began was it not heard that any man opened the eyes of one that was born blind. that no

33 If this man were not of God, He could do nothing.

34 They answered and said to him, You were altogether born in sins, and do you teach us? And they cast him out. i.e., show us truth

35 Je'sus heard that they had cast him out; and when He had found him, He said to him, Do you believe on the Son of God?

36 He answered and said, Who is He, Lord, that I might believe on Him?

37 And Je'sus said to him, You have both seen Him, and it is He that talks with you.

38 And he said, Lord, I believe. And he worshiped Him.

39 And Je'sus said, For judgment I am come into this world, that they which see not might see; and that they which see might be made blind.

40 And *some* of the Phar'i-sees which were with Him heard these words, and said to Him, Are we blind also?

41 Je'sus said to them, If you were blind, you should have no sin: but now you say, We see; therefore your sin remains.

CHAPTER 10

VERILY, verily, I say to you, He that enters not by the door into the sheepfold, but climbs up some other way, the same is a thief and a robber. Truly

2 But he that enters in by the door is the shepherd of the sheep.

3 To him the porter opens; and the sheep hear his voice: and he calls his own sheep by name, and leads them out.

4 And when he puts forth his own sheep, he goes before them, and the sheep follow him: for they know his voice.

5 And a stranger will they not follow, but will flee from him: for they know not the voice of strangers.

6 This parable spoke Je'sus to them: but they understood not what things they were which He spoke to them. illustration

7 Then said Je'sus to them again, Verily, verily, I say to you, I am the door of the sheep. Truly - for

8 All that ever came before Me are thieves and robbers: but the sheep did not hear them. JER. 23:1 listen to

9 I am the door: by Me if any man enter in, he shall be saved, and shall go in and out, and find pasture.EZE. 34:12

10 The thief comes not, but for to steal, and to kill, and to destroy: I am come that they might have life, and that they might have *it* more abundantly.

11 I am the good shepherd: the good shepherd gives His life for the sheep. ISA. 40:11 EZE. 34:12

12 But he that is an hireling, and not the shepherd, whose own the sheep are not, sees the wolf coming, and leaves the sheep, and flees: and the wolf catches them, and scatters the sheep.

13 The hireling flees, because he is an hireling, and cares not for the sheep.

14 I am the good shepherd, and know My *sheep*, and am known of Mine.

15 As the Father knows Me, even so know I the Father: and I lay down My life for the sheep.

16 And other sheep I have, which are not of this fold: them also I must bring, and they shall hear My voice; and there shall be one fold, *and* one shepherd. ISA. 56:8

17 Therefore does My Father love Me, because I lay down My life, that I might take it again. give up

18 No man takes it from Me, but I lay it down of Myself. I have power to lay it down, and I have power to take it again. This commandment have I received of My Father.

19 There was a division therefore again among the Jews for these sayings. words of Jesus

20 And many of them said, He has a devil, and is mad; why hear you Him? demon - insane

21 Others said, These are not the words of him that has a devil. Can a devil open the eyes of the blind?

22 And it was at Je-ru'sa-lem the feast of the dedication, and it was winter.

23 And Je'sus walked in the temple in Sol'o-mon's porch.

24 Then came the Jews round about Him, and said to Him, How long do You make us to doubt? If You be the Christ, tell us plainly. keep us in suspense

25 Je'sus answered them, I told you, and you believed not: the works that I do in My Father's name, they bear witness of Me.

26 But you believe not, because you are not of My sheep, as I said to you.

27 My sheep hear My voice, and I know them, and they follow Me:

28 And I give to them eternal life; and they shall never perish, neither shall any *man* pluck them out of My hand.

29 My Father, which gave *them* Me, is greater than all; and no *man* is able to pluck *them* out of My Father's hand.

30 I and *My* Father are one.

31 Then the Jews took up stones again to stone Him. kill

32 Je'sus answered them, Many good works have I showed you from My Father; for which of those works do you stone Me?

33 The Jews answered Him, saying, For a good work we stone You not; but for blasphemy; and because that

You, being a man, make Yourself God.   LEV. 24:16 PSA. 82:6 evil

34 Je'sus answered them, Is it not written in your law, I said, You are gods?

35 If He called them gods, to whom the word of God came, and the scripture cannot be broken;

36 Say you of Him, whom the Father has sanctified, and sent into the world, You blaspheme; because I said, I am the Son of God?   speak evil

37 If I do not the works of My Father, believe Me not.

38 But if I do, though you believe not Me, believe the works: that you may know, and believe, that the Father *is* in Me, and I in Him.

39 Therefore they sought again to take Him: but He escaped out of their hand,   tried

40 And went away again beyond Jor'dan into the place where John at first baptized; and there He abode. stayed

41 And many resorted to Him, and said, John did no miracle: but all things that John spoke of this man were true.

42 And many believed on Him there.

CHAPTER 11

NOW a certain *man* was sick, *named* Laz'a-rus, of Beth'a-ny, the town of Ma'ry and her sister Mar'tha.

2 (It was *that* Ma'ry which anointed the Lord with ointment, and wiped His feet with her hair, whose brother Laz'a-rus was sick.)   perfume - dried

3 Therefore his sisters sent to Him, saying, Lord, behold, he whom You love is sick.

4 When Je'sus heard *that*, He said, This sickness is not to death, but for the glory of God, that the Son of God might be glorified thereby.   honored

5 Now Je'sus loved Mar'tha, and her sister, and Laz'a-rus.

6 When He had heard therefore that he was sick, He abode two days still in the same place where He was. stayed

7 Then after that said He to *His* disciples, Let us go into Ju-dae'a again.

8 *His* disciples say to Him, Master, the Jews of late sought to stone You; and go You there again?   wanted

9 Je'sus answered, Are there not twelve hours in the day? If any man walk in the day, he stumbles not, because he sees the light of this world.

10 But if a man walk in the night, he stumbles, because there is no light in him.

11 These things said He: and after that He said to them, Our friend Laz'a-rus sleeps; but I go, that I may awake him out of sleep.

12 Then said His disciples, Lord, if he sleep, he shall do well.   will recover

13 However Je'sus spoke of his death: but they thought that He had spoken of taking of rest in sleep.   however

14 Then said Je'sus to them plainly, Laz'a-rus is dead.

15 And I am glad for your sakes that I was not there, to the intent you may believe; nevertheless let us go to him.

16 Then said Thom'as, which is called Did'y-mus, to his fellow disciples, Let us also go, that we may die with Him. twin

17 Then when Je'sus came, He found

that he had *lain* in the grave four days already.

18 Now Beth'a-ny was near to Je-ru'sa-lem, about fifteen furlongs off:

19 And many of the Jews came to Mar'tha and Ma'ry, to comfort them concerning their brother.

20 Then Mar'tha, as soon as she heard that Je'sus was coming, went and met Him: but Ma'ry sat *still* in the house.

21 Then said Mar'tha to Je'sus, Lord, if You had been here, my brother <u>had not</u> died.   would not have

22 But I know, that even now, whatsoever You will ask of God, God will give *it* You.

23 Je'sus said to her, Your brother shall rise again.

24 Mar'tha said to Him, I know that he shall rise again in the resurrection at the last day.   DAN. 12:2

25 Je'sus said to her, I am the resurrection, and the life: he that believes in Me, though he were dead, yet shall he live:

26 And whosoever lives and believes in Me shall never die. Believe you this?

27 She said to him, Yea, Lord: I believe that You are the Christ, the Son of God, which should come into the world.

28 And when she had so said, she went her way, and called Ma'ry her sister secretly, saying, The Master is come, and calls for you.

29 As soon as she heard *that*, she arose quickly, and came to Him.

30 Now Je'sus was not yet come into the town, but was in that place where Mar'tha met Him.

31 The Jews then which were with her in the house, and comforted her, when they saw Ma'ry, that she rose up <u>hastily</u> and went out, followed her, saying, She goes to the grave to weep there.   quickly

32 Then when Ma'ry was come where Je'sus was, and saw Him, she fell down at His feet, saying to Him, Lord, if You had been here, my brother had not died.

33 When Je'sus therefore saw her weeping, and the Jews also weeping which came with her, He groaned in the spirit, and was <u>troubled</u>,   concerned

34 And said, Where have you laid him? They said to Him, Lord, come and see.

35 Je'sus wept.

36 Then said the Jews, Behold how He loved him!

37 And some of them said, Could not this man, which opened the eyes of the blind, have caused that even this man should not have died?

38 Je'sus therefore again <u>groaning</u> in Himself comes to the grave. It was a cave, and a stone lay upon it.   deeply moved

39 Je'sus said, Take you away the stone. Mar'tha, the sister of him that was dead, said to Him, Lord, by this time he stinks: for he has been *dead* four days.

40 Je'sus said to her, Said I not to you, that, if you would believe, you should see the glory of God?

41 Then they took away the stone *from the place* where the dead was laid. And Je'sus lifted up *His* eyes, and said, Father, I thank You that You have heard Me.

42 And I knew that You hear Me always: but because of the people which stand by I said *it*, that they may believe that You have sent Me.

43 And when He thus had spoken, He cried with a loud voice, Laz'a-rus, come <u>forth</u>. ₒᵤₜ out

44 And he that was dead came forth, bound hand and foot with graveclothes: and his face was bound about with a napkin. Je'sus said to them, <u>Loose</u> him, and let him go. unbind

45 Then many of the Jews which came to Ma'ry, and had seen the things which Je'sus did, believed on Him.

46 But some of them <u>went their ways</u> to the Phar'i-sees, and told them what things Je'sus had done. returned

47 Then gathered the chief priests and the Phar'i-sees a council, and said, What do we? for this man does many miracles.

48 If we let Him <u>thus alone</u>, all *men* will believe on Him: and the Ro'mans shall come and take away both our place and nation. go this way

49 And one of them, *named* Ca'ia-phas, being the high priest that same year, said to them, You know nothing at all,

50 Nor consider that it is expedient for us, that one man should die for the people, and that the whole nation perish not.

51 And this spoke he not of himself: but being high priest that year, he prophesied that Je'sus should die for that nation;

52 And not for that nation only, but that also He should gather together in one the children of God that were scattered abroad.

53 Then from that day forth they took counsel together for to put Him to death.

54 Je'sus therefore walked no more openly among the Jews; but went from there to a country near to the wilderness, into a city called E'phra-im, and there continued with His disciples.

55 And the Jews' passover was near at hand: and many went out of the country up to Je-ru'sa-lem before the passover, to <u>purify</u> themselves. cleanse

56 Then <u>sought</u> they for Je'sus, and spoke among themselves, as they stood in the temple, What think you, that He will not come to the feast? they looked

57 Now both the chief priests and the Phar'i-sees had given a commandment, that, if any man knew where He were, he should show *it*, that they might take Him.

CHAPTER 12

THEN Je'sus six days before the passover came to Beth'a-ny, where Laz'a-rus was which had been dead, whom He raised from the dead.

2 There they made Him a supper; and Mar'tha served: but Laz'a-rus was one of them that sat at the table with Him.

3 Then took Ma'ry a pound of ointment of spikenard, very costly, and anointed the feet of Je'sus, and wiped His feet with her hair: and the house was filled with the odor of the ointment.

4 Then said one of His disciples, Ju'das Is-car'i-ot, Si'mon's *son*, <u>which should</u> betray Him, _{who would}

5 Why was not this <u>ointment</u> sold for three hundred pence, and given to the poor? _{perfume}

6 This he said, not that he cared for the poor; but because he was a thief, and had the <u>bag</u>, and bare what was put therein. _{money purse}

7 Then said Je'sus, Let her alone: against the day of My burying has she kept this.

8 For the poor always you have with you; but Me you have not always.

9 Much people of the Jews therefore knew that He was there: and they came not for Je'sus' sake only, but that they might see Laz'a-rus also, whom He had raised from the dead.

10 But the chief priests consulted that they might put Laz'a-rus also to death;

11 Because that by reason of him many of the Jews went <u>away</u>, and believed on Je'sus. _{i.e., away from the leaders}

12 On the next day <u>much</u> people that were come to the feast, when they heard that Je'sus was coming to Je-ru'sa-lem, _{many}

13 Took branches of palm trees, and went forth to meet Him, and cried, Ho-san'na: Blessed *is* the King of Is'ra-el that comes in the name of the Lord. _{PSA. 118:26}

14 And Je'sus, when He had found a young ass, sat thereon; as it is written,

15 Fear not, daughter of Zi'on: behold, Your King comes, sitting on an ass's colt. _{ZEC. 9:9}

16 These things understood not His disciples at the first: but when Je'sus was <u>glorified</u>, then remembered they that these things were written of Him, and *that* they had done these things to Him. _{honored}

17 The people therefore that was with Him when He called Laz'a-rus out of his grave, and raised him from the dead, <u>bare record</u>. _{reported the actions}

18 For this cause the people also met Him, for that they heard that He had done this miracle.

19 The Phar'i-sees therefore said among themselves, <u>Perceive</u> you how you prevail nothing? behold, the world <u>is gone</u> after Him. _{Look - has gone}

20 And there were certain Greeks among them that came up to worship at the feast:

21 The same came therefore to Phil'ip, which was of Beth-sa'i-da of Gal'i-lee, and <u>desired</u> him, saying, Sir, we <u>would</u> see Je'sus. _{asked - want to}

22 Phil'ip comes and tells An'drew: and again An'drew and Phil'ip tell Je'sus.

23 And Je'sus answered them, saying, The hour is come, that the Son of man should be <u>glorified</u>. _{honored}

24 <u>Verily</u>, <u>verily</u>, I say to you, Except a corn of wheat fall into the ground and die, it abides alone: but if it die, it brings forth much fruit. _{Truly}

25 He that loves his life shall lose it; and he that <u>hates</u> his life in this world shall keep it to life eternal.   disregards

26 If any man serve Me, let him follow Me; and where I am, there shall also My servant be: if any man serve Me, him will *My* Father honor.

27 Now is My soul troubled; and what shall I say? Father, save Me from this hour: but for this cause came I to this hour.

28 Father, glorify Your name. Then came there a voice from heaven, *saying*, I have both glorified *it*, and will glorify *it* again.

29 The people therefore, that stood by, and heard *it*, said that it thundered: others said, An <u>angel</u> spoke to Him.   messenger

30 Je'sus answered and said, This voice came not because of Me, but for your sakes.

31 Now is the judgment of this world: now shall the <u>prince</u> of this world be cast out.   i.e., Satan

32 And I, if I be lifted up from the earth, will draw all *men* to Me.

33 This He said, signifying what <u>death</u> He should die.   i.e., type death

34 The people answered Him, We have heard out of the law that Christ <u>abides</u> for ever: and how say You, The Son of Man must be <u>lifted up</u>? who is this Son of Man?   DAN. 7:14   lives - i.e., put to death

35 Then Je'sus said to them, Yet a little while is the light with you. Walk while you have the light, less darkness come upon you: for he that walks in darkness knows not where he goes.

36 While you have light, believe in the light, that you may be the children of light. These things spoke Je'sus, and departed, and did hide Himself from them.

37 But though He had done so many miracles before them, yet they believed not on Him:

38 That the saying of I-sa'iah the prophet might be fulfilled, which he spoke, Lord, who has believed our report? and to whom has the arm of the Lord been revealed?   ISA. 53:1

39 Therefore they could not believe, because that I-sa'iah said again,

40 He has blinded their eyes, and hardened their heart; that they should not see with *their* eyes, nor understand with *their* heart, and be converted, and I should heal them.   ISA. 6:10   EXO. 4:21

41 These things said I-sa'iah, when he saw His glory, and spoke of Him.   ISA. 6:1

42 Nevertheless among the chief rulers also many believed on Him; but because of the Phar'i-sees they did not confess *Him*, less they should be put out of the synagogue:

43 For they loved the praise of men more than the praise of God.

44 Je'sus cried and said, he that believes on Me, believes not on Me, but on Him that sent Me.

45 And he that sees Me sees Him that sent Me.

46 I am come a <u>light</u> into the world, that whosoever believes on Me should not <u>abide</u> in darkness.   i.e., as a light to show truth - live

47 And if any man hear My words, and <u>believe</u> not, I judge him not: for I

came not to judge the world, but to save the world.   *obeys*

48 He that rejects Me, and receives not My words, has one that judges him: the word that I have spoken, the same shall judge him in the last day.

49 For I have not spoken of Myself; but the Father which sent Me, He gave Me a commandment, what I should say, and what I should speak.

50 And I know that His commandment is life everlasting: whatsoever I speak therefore, even as the Father said to Me, so I speak.   *eternal*

CHAPTER 13

NOW before the feast of the passover, when Je'sus knew that His hour was come that He should depart out of this world to the Father, having loved His own which were in the world, He loved them to the end.

2 And supper being ended, the devil having now put into the heart of Ju'das Is-car'i-ot, Si'mon's *son*, to betray Him;   *Satan*

3 Je'sus knowing that the Father had given all things into His hands, and that He was come from God, and went to God;

4 He rises from supper, and laid aside His garments; and took a towel, and girded Himself.

5 After that He pours water into a basin, and began to wash the disciples' feet, and to wipe *them* with the towel wherewith He was girded.   *dry*

6 Then comes He to Si'mon Pe'ter: and Pe'ter said to Him, Lord, do You wash my feet?

7 Je'sus answered and said to him, What I do you know not now; but you shall know hereafter.   *i.e., you understand*

8 Pe'ter said to Him, You shall never wash my feet. Je'sus answered him, If I wash you not, you have no part with Me.

9 Si'mon Pe'ter said to Him, Lord, not my feet only, but also *my* hands and *my* head.

10 Je'sus said to him, he that is washed need not save to wash *his* feet, but is clean every whit: and you are clean, but not all.   *except - bit - i.e., except Judas*

11 For He knew who should betray Him; therefore said He, You are not all clean.

12 So after He had washed their feet, and had taken His garments, and was set down again, He said to them, Know you what I have done to you?   *understand*

13 You call Me Master and Lord: and you say well; for *so* I am.   *correctly*

14 If I then, *your* Lord and Master, have washed your feet; you also ought to wash one another's feet.

15 For I have given you an example, that you should do as I have done to you.

16 Verily, verily, I say to you, The servant is not greater than his lord; neither he that is sent greater than he that sent him.   *truly*

17 If you know these things, happy are you if you do them.   *understand*

18 I speak not of you all: I know whom I have chosen: but that the scripture may be fulfilled, He that eats bread with Me has lifted up his heel against Me.   PS.41:9

19 Now I tell you before it come, that, when it is come to pass, you may believe that I am *He*.

20 Verily, verily, I say to you, he that receives whomsoever I send receives Me; and he that receives Me receives Him that sent Me.   truly

21 When Je'sus had thus said, He was troubled in spirit, and testified, and said, Verily, verily, I say to you, that one of you shall betray Me.   PS. 41:9

22 Then the disciples looked one on another, doubting of whom He spoke.   uncertain

23 Now there was leaning on Je'sus' bosom one of His disciples, whom Je'sus loved.   sitting next to

24 Si'mon Pe'ter therefore beckoned to him, that he should ask who it should be of whom He spoke.   gestured - is

25 He then lying on Je'sus' breast said to Him, Lord, who is it?   sitting next to

26 Je'sus answered, he it is, to whom I shall give a sop, when I have dipped *it*. And when He had dipped the sop, He gave *it* to Ju'das Is-car'i-ot, *the son* of Si'mon.   morsel

27 And after the sop Sa'tan entered into him. Then said Je'sus to him, That you do, do quickly.

28 Now no man at the table knew for what intent He spoke this to him.   what reason

29 For some *of them* thought, because Ju'das had the bag, that Je'sus had said to him, Buy *those things* that we have need of against the feast; or, that he should give something to the poor.   money bag

30 He then having received the sop went immediately out: and it was night .   morsel

31 Therefore, when he was gone out, Je'sus said, Now is the Son of Man glorified, and God is glorified in Him.   honored

32 If God be glorified in Him, God shall also glorify Him in Himself, and shall immediately glorify Him.   honored

33 Little children, yet a little while I am with you. You shall seek Me: and as I said to the Jews, Where I go, you cannot come; so now I say to you.

34 A new commandment I give to you, That you love one another; as I have loved you, that you also love one another.   LEV. 19:18

35 By this shall all *men* know that you are My disciples, if you have love one to another.   for

36 Si'mon Pe'ter said to Him, Lord, where go You? Je'sus answered him, Where I go, you cannot follow Me now; but you shall follow Me afterwards.

37 Pe'ter said to Him, Lord, why cannot I follow You now? I will lay down my life for Your sake.

38 Je'sus answered him, Will you lay down your life for My sake? Verily, verily, I say to you, The cock shall not crow, till you have denied Me thrice.   truly - i.e., denied knowing

CHAPTER 14

LET not your heart be troubled: you believe in God, believe also in Me.

2 In My Father's house are many

mansions: if *it were* not *so*, I would have told you. I go to prepare a place for you.

3 And if I go and prepare a place for you, I will come again, and receive you to Myself; that where I am, *there* you may be also.

4 And where I go you know, and the way you know.

5 Thom'as said to Him, Lord, we know not where You go; and how can we know the way?

6 Je'sus said to him, I am the way, the truth, and the life: no man comes to the Father, but by Me.

7 If you had known Me, you should have known My Father also: and from hereafter you know Him, and have seen Him.

8 Phil'ip said to Him, Lord, show us the Father, and it suffced us.

is enough for

9 Je'sus said to him, Have I been so long time with you, and yet have you not known Me, Phil'ip? he that has seen Me has seen the Father; and how say you *then*, Show us the Father?

10 Believe you not that I am in the Father, and the Father in Me? the words that I speak to you I speak not of Myself: but the Father that dwells in Me, He does the works.

11 Believe Me that I *am* in the Father, and the Father in Me: or else believe Me for the very works' sake.

12 Verily, verily, I say to you, he that believes on Me, the works that I do shall he do also; and greater *works*

than these shall he do; because I go to My Father. Truly

13 And whatsoever you shall ask in My name, that will I do, that the Father may be glorified in the Son. honored

14 If you shall ask any thing in My name, I will do *it*.

15 If you love Me, keep My commandments.

16 And I will pray the Father, and He shall give you another Comforter, that He may abide with you for ever; be

17 *Even* the Spirit of truth; whom the world cannot receive, because it sees Him not, neither knows Him: but you know Him; for He dwells with you, and shall be in you.

18 I will not leave you comfortless: I will come to you. as orphans

19 Yet a little while, and the world see Me no more; but you see Me: because I live, you shall live also.

20 At that day you shall know that I *am* in My Father, and you in Me, and I in you.

21 He that has My commandments, and keeps them, he it is that loves Me: and he that loves Me shall be loved of My Father, and I will love him, and will manifest Myself to him. obeys - disclose

22 Ju'das said to Him, not Is-car'i-ot, Lord, how is it that You will manifest Yourself to us, and not to the world?

23 Je'sus answered and said to him, If a man love Me, he will keep My words: and My Father will love him, and We will come to him, and make Our abode with him. i.e., live within

24 He that loves Me not keeps not My sayings: and the word which you hear is not Mine, but the Father's which sent Me.

25 These things have I spoken to you, being *yet* present with you.

26 But the Comforter, *which is* the Ho'ly Ghost, whom the Father will send in My name, He shall teach you all things, and bring all things to your remembrance, whatsoever I have said to you.   Spirit

27 Peace I leave with you, My peace I give to you: not as the world gives, give I to you. Let not your heart be troubled, neither let it be afraid.

28 You have heard how I said to you, I go away, and come *again* to you. If you loved Me, you would rejoice, because I said, I go to the Father: for My Father is greater than I.

29 And now I have told you before it come to pass, that, when it is come to pass, you might believe.

30 Hereafter I will not talk much with you: for the prince of this world comes, and has nothing in Me.   Satan - has no power with

31 But that the world may know that I love the Father; and as the Father gave Me commandment, even so I do. Arise, let us go there.

CHAPTER 15

I AM the true vine, and My Father is the husbandman.   ISA. 5:5 vine dresser

2 Every branch in Me that bears not fruit He takes away: and every *branch* that bears fruit, He purges it, that it may bring forth more fruit.   prunes

3 Now you are clean through the word which I have spoken to you.

4 Abide in Me, and I in you. As the branch cannot bear fruit of itself, except it abide in the vine; no more can you, except you abide in Me.   lives

5 I am the vine, you *are* the branches: He that abides in Me, and I in him, the same brings forth much fruit: for without Me you can do nothing.   apart

6 If a man abide not in Me, he is cast forth as a branch, and is withered; and men gather them, and cast *them* into the fire, and they are burned.

7 If you abide in Me, and My words abide in you, you shall ask what you will, and it shall be done to you.   live

8 Herein is My Father glorified, that you bear much fruit; so shall you be My disciples.   honored

9 As the Father has loved Me, so have I loved you: continue you in My love.

10 If you keep My commandments, you shall abide in My love; even as I have kept My Father's commandments, and abide in His love.   obey

11 These things have I spoken to you, that My joy might remain in you, and *that* your joy might be full.

12 This is My commandment, That you love one another, as I have loved you.

13 Greater love has no man than this, that a man lay down his life for his friends.

14 You are My friends, if you do whatsoever I command you.

15 Hereafter I call you not servants; for the servant knows not what his

lord does: but I have called you friends; for all things that I have heard of My Father I have made known to you.   AMOS 3:7

16 You have not chosen Me, but I have chosen you, and <u>ordained</u> you, that you should go and bring forth fruit, and *that* your fruit should remain: that whatsoever you shall ask of the Father in My name, He may give it you.   appointed

17 These things I command you, that you love one another.

18 If the world <u>hate</u> you, you know that it <u>hated</u> Me before *it hated* you.   disrespect

19 If you <u>were</u> of the world, the world would love his own: but because you are not of the world, but I have chosen you out of the world, therefore the world hates you.   belonged to

20 Remember the word that I said to you, The servant is not greater than his lord. If they have persecuted Me, they will also persecute you; if they have kept My saying, they will keep yours also.

21 But all these things will they do to you for My name's sake, because they know not Him that sent Me.

22 If I had not come and spoken to them, they had not had sin: but now they have no <u>cloak</u> for their sin.   covering

23 He that <u>hates</u> Me <u>hates</u> My Father also.   abhorred

24 If I had not done among them the works which none other man did, they had not had sin: but now have they both seen and <u>hated</u> both Me and My Father.

25 But *this comes to pass*, that the word might be fulfilled that is written in their law, They <u>hated</u> Me without a cause.   PS. 69:4

26 But when the <u>Comforter</u> is come, whom I will send to you from the Father, *even* the Spirit of truth, which proceeds from the Father, He shall testify of Me: i.e., Holy Spirit

27 And you also shall bear witness, because you have been with Me from the beginning.

CHAPTER 16

THESE things have I spoken to you, that you should not <u>be offended</u>.   stumble

2 They shall put you out of the synagogues: yea, the time comes, that whosoever kills you will think that he does God service.

3 And these things will they do to you, because they have not known the Father, nor Me.

4 But these things have I told you, that when the time shall come, you may remember that I told you of them. And these things I said not to you at the beginning, because I was with you.

5 But now I go my way to Him that sent Me; and none of you asks Me, Where go You?

6 But because I have said these things to you, sorrow has filled your heart.

7 Nevertheless I tell you the truth; It is <u>expedient</u> for you that I go away: for if I go not away, the <u>Comforter</u> will not come to you; but if I depart, I will send Him to you.   advisable - Holy Spirit

8 And when He is come, He will <u>reprove</u> the world of sin, and of righteousness, and of <u>judgment</u>:

convict - i.e., God's judgment

9 Of sin, because they believe not on Me;

10 Of righteousness, because I go to My Father, and you see Me no more;

11 Of judgment, because the <u>prince</u> of this world is judged.   Satan

12 I have yet many things to say to you, but you cannot <u>bear</u> them now.

understand

13 However when He, the Spirit of truth, is come, He will guide you into all truth: for He shall not speak of Himself; but whatsoever He shall hear, *that* shall He speak: and He will show you things to come.

14 He shall glorify Me: for He shall receive of Mine, and shall show *it* to you.

15 All things that the Father has are Mine: therefore said I, that He shall take of Mine, and shall show *it* to you.

16 A little while, and you shall not see Me: and again, a little while, and you shall see Me, because I go to the Father.

17 Then said *some* of His disciples among themselves, What is this that He said to us, A little while, and you shall not see Me: and again, a little while, and you shall see Me: and, Because I go to the Father?

18 They said therefore, What is this that He said, A little while? we <u>cannot tell</u> what He said.   do not understand

19 Now Je′sus knew that they were desirous to ask Him, and said to them, Do you enquire among yourselves of that I said, A little <u>while</u>, and you shall not see Me: and again, a little <u>while</u>, and you shall see Me?   wait a bit

20 <u>Verily</u>, <u>verily</u>, I say to you, That you shall weep and lament, but the world shall rejoice: and you shall be sorrowful, but your sorrow shall be turned into joy.   ISA. 13:8 Truly

21 A woman when she is in <u>travail</u> has sorrow, because her hour is come: but as soon as she is delivered of the child, she remembers no more the anguish, for joy that a man is born into the world.   ISA. 13:8 birth pains

22 And you now therefore have sorrow: but I will see you again, and your heart shall rejoice, and your joy no man takes from you.

23 And in that day you shall ask Me nothing. <u>Verily</u>, <u>verily</u>, I say to you, Whatsoever you shall ask the Father in My name, He will give *it* you.   Truly

24 Here before to have you asked nothing in My name: ask, and you shall receive, that your <u>joy</u> may be full.   contentment

25 These things have I spoken to you in <u>proverbs</u>: but the time comes, when I shall no more speak to you in <u>proverbs</u>, but I shall show you plainly of the Father.   example stories

26 At that day you shall ask in My name: and I say not to you, that I will pray the Father <u>for you</u>:   on your behalf

27 For the Father Himself loves you, because you have loved Me, and have believed that I came out from God.

28 I came forth from the Father, and

am come into the world: again, I leave the world, and go to the Father.

29 His disciples said to Him, Lo, now speak You plainly, and speak no <u>proverb</u>.   example story

30 Now are we sure that You know all things, and need not that any man should ask You: by this we believe that You came forth from God.

31 Je'sus answered them, Do you now believe?

32 Behold, the hour comes, yea, is now come, that you shall be scattered, every man to his <u>own</u>, and shall leave Me alone: and yet I am not alone, because the Father is with Me.   ZEC. 13:7   own home

33 These things I have spoken to you, that in Me you might have peace. In the world you shall have <u>tribulation</u>: but be of good cheer; I have overcome the world.   troubles

CHAPTER 17

THESE words spoke Je'sus, and lifted up His eyes to heaven, and said, Father, the hour is come; <u>glorify</u> Your Son, that Your Son also may <u>glorify</u> You: honor

2 As You have given Him power over all flesh, that He should give eternal life to as many as You have given Him.

3 And this is life eternal, that they might know You the only true God, and Je'sus Christ, whom You have sent.

4 I have <u>glorified</u> You on the earth: I have finished the work which You gave Me to do.   ISA. 42:1

5 And now, O Father, glorify You Me with Your own self with the glory which I had with You before the world was.

6 I have <u>manifested</u> Your name to the men which You gave Me out of the world: Yours they were, and You gave them Me; and they have kept Your word.   made known

7 Now they have known that all things whatsoever you have given Me are of You.

8 For I have given to them the words which You gave Me; and they have received *them*, and have known surely that I came out from You, and they have believed that You did send Me.

9 I pray for them: I pray not for the world, but for them which You have given Me; for they are Yours.

10 And all Mine are Yours, and Yours are Mine; and I am <u>glorified</u> in them.   honored

11 And now I am no more in the world, but these are in the world, and I come to You. Holy Father, keep through Your own name those whom You have given Me, that they may be one, as We *are*.

12 While I was with them in the world, I kept them in Your name: those that You gave Me I have kept, and none of them is lost, but the <u>son of perdition</u>; that the scripture might be fulfilled.   PS. 41;9 Judas

13 And now come I to You; and these things I speak in the world, that they might have My joy fulfilled in themselves.

14 I have given them Your word; and the world has <u>hated</u> them, because

they <u>are</u> <u>not</u> of the world, even as I am not of the world.   abhorred - i.e., are spiritual

15 I pray not that You should take them out of the world, but that You should <u>keep</u> them from the evil.

protect

16 They are not of the world, even as I am not of the world.

17 <u>Sanctify</u> them through Your truth: Your word is truth.   PS. 119:142 make holy

18 As You have sent Me into the world, even so have I also sent them into the world.

19 And for their sakes I <u>sanctify</u> Myself, that they also might be <u>sanctified</u> through the truth.   set apart

20 Neither pray I for these alone, but for them also which shall believe on Me through their word;

21 That they all may be one; as You, Father, *are* in Me, and I in You, that they also may be one in Us: that the world may believe that You have sent Me.

22 And the glory which You gave Me I have given them; that they may be one, even as We are one:

23 I in them, and You in Me, that they may be made <u>perfect</u> in one; and that the world may know that You have sent Me, and have loved them, as You have loved Me.   complete

24 Father, I will that they also, whom You have given Me, be with Me where I am; that they may behold My glory, which You have given Me: for You loved Me before the foundation of the world.

25 O righteous Father, the world has not known You: but I have known You, and these have known that You have sent Me.

26 And I have <u>declared</u> to them Your name, and will declare *it*: that the love wherewith You have loved Me may be in them, and I in them.   made known

CHAPTER 18

WHEN Je'sus had spoken these words, He went forth with His disciples over the brook Ce'dron, where was a garden, into the which He entered, and His disciples.

2 And Ju'das also, which betrayed Him, knew the place: for Je'sus often <u>resorted there</u> with His disciples.

met there

3 Ju'das then, having received a band *of men* and officers from the chief priests and Phar'i-sees, came there with lanterns and torches and weapons.

4 Je'sus therefore, knowing all things that should <u>come upon</u> Him, went forth, and said to them, Whom seek you?

happen to

5 They answered Him, Je'sus of Naz'a-reth. Je'sus said to them, I am *He*. And Ju'das also, which betrayed Him, stood with them.

6 As soon then as He had said to them, I am *He*, they went backward, and fell to the ground.

7 Then asked He them again, Whom seek you? And they said, Je'sus of Naz'a-reth.

8 Je'sus answered, I have told you that I am *He*: if therefore you seek Me, let these go their way:

9 That the saying might be fulfilled,

which He spoke, Of them which You gave Me have I lost none.

10 Then Si'mon Pe'ter having a sword drew it, and smote the high priest's servant, and cut off his right ear. The servant's name was Mal'chus.

11 Then said Je'sus to Pe'ter, Put up your sword into the sheath: the cup which My Father has given Me, shall I not drink it?

12 Then the <u>band</u> and the captain and officers of the Jews took Je'sus, and bound Him,   soldiers

13 And led Him away to An'nas first; for he was father in law to Ca'ia-phas, which was the high priest that same year.

14 Now Ca'ia-phas was he, which gave counsel to the Jews, that it was expedient that one man should die for the people.

15 And Si'mon Pe'ter followed Je'sus, and *so did* another disciple: that disciple was known to the high priest, and went in with Je'sus into the <u>palace</u> of the high priest.   court

16 But Pe'ter stood at the door outside. Then went out that other disciple, which was known to the high priest, and spoke to her that kept the door, and brought in Pe'ter.

17 Then said the <u>damsel</u> that kept the door to Pe'ter, Are not you also *one* of this man's disciples? He said, I am not.   young woman

18 And the servants and officers stood there, who had made a fire of coals; for it was cold: and they warmed themselves: and Pe'ter stood with them, and warmed himself.

19 The high priest then asked Je'sus of His disciples, and of His <u>doc-trine</u>.   teaching

20 Je'sus answered him, I spoke openly to the world; I ever taught in the synagogue, and in the temple, where the Jews always <u>resort</u>; and in secret have I said nothing.   gather

21 Why ask you Me? ask them which heard Me, what I have said to them: behold, they know what I said.

22 And when He had thus spoken, one of the officers which stood by struck Je'sus with the palm of his hand, saying, Answer You the high priest so?

23 Je'sus answered him, If I have spoken <u>evil</u>, <u>bear witness</u> of the evil: but if well, why <u>smite</u> you Me?

                    wrongly - show proof - strike

24 Now An'nas had sent Him bound to Ca'ia-phas the high priest.

25 And Si'mon Pe'ter stood and warmed himself. They said therefore to him, Are not you also *one* of His disciples? He denied *it*, and said, I am not.

26 One of the servants of the high priest, being *his* kinsman whose ear Pe'ter cut off, said, Did not I see you in the garden with Him?

27 Pe'ter then denied again: and immediately the cock crew.

28 Then led they Je'sus from Ca'ia-phas to the hall of judgment: and it was early; and they themselves went not into the judgment hall, less they should be defiled; but that they might eat the passover.

29 Pi'late then went out to them,

and said, What accusation bring you against this man?

30 They answered and said to him, If He were not a <u>malefactor</u>, we would not have delivered Him up to you.   wrong doer

31 Then said Pi'late to them, Take you Him, and judge Him according to your law. The Jews therefore said to Him, It is not lawful for us to put any man to death:

32 That the saying of Je'sus might be fulfilled, which He spoke, signifying what death He should die.

33 Then Pi'late entered into the judgment hall again, and called Je'sus, and said to Him, Are You the King of the Jews?

34 Je'sus answered him, Say you this <u>thing</u> of yourself, or did others tell it you of Me?   question

35 Pi'late answered, Am I a Jew? Your own nation and the chief priests have delivered You to me: what have You done?

36 Je'sus answered, My kingdom is not of this world: if My kingdom were of this world, then would My servants fight, that I should not be delivered to the Jews: but now is My kingdom not from here.

37 Pi'late therefore said to Him, Are You a king then? Je'sus answered, You say that I am a king. To this end was I born, and for this cause came I into the world, that I should <u>bear witness</u> <u>to</u> the truth. Every one that is of the truth <u>hears</u> My voice.   tell - knows

38 Pi'late said to Him, What is truth? And when he had said this, he went out again to the Jews, and said to them, I find in Him no fault *at all*.

39 But you have a custom, that I should <u>release</u> to you one at the passover: will you therefore that I <u>release</u> to you the King of the Jews?   set free

40 Then cried they all again, saying, Not this man, but Ba-rab'bas. Now Ba-rab'bas was a robber.

CHAPTER 19

THEN Pi'late therefore took Je'sus, and scourged *Him*.

2 And the soldiers <u>platted</u> a crown of thorns, and put *it* on His head, and they put on Him a purple robe,   wove

3 And said, Hail, King of the Jews! and they <u>smote</u> Him with their hands.   struck

4 Pi'late therefore went forth again, and said to them, Behold, I bring Him forth to you, that you may know that I find no <u>fault</u> in Him.   guilt

5 Then came Je'sus forth, wearing the crown of thorns, and the purple robe. And *Pi'late* said to them, Behold the Man!

6 When the chief priests therefore and officers saw Him, they cried out, saying, Crucify *Him*, crucify *Him*. Pi'late said to them, Take you Him, and crucify *Him*: for I find no <u>fault</u> in Him.

7 The Jews answered him, We have a law, and by our law He ought to die, because He made Himself the Son of God.   LEV. 24:16

8 When Pi'late therefore heard that saying, he was the more afraid;

9 And went again into the judgment

hall, and said to Je'sus, From where are You? But Je'sus gave him no answer.

10 Then said Pi'late to Him, Speak You not to me? know You not that I have <u>power</u> to crucify You, and have power to release You?   authority

11 Je'sus answered, You could have no power *at all* against Me, except it were given you from above: therefore he that delivered Me to you have the greater sin.

12 And from thereafter Pi'late sought to release Him: but the Jews cried out, saying, If you let this man go, you are not Cae'sar's friend: whosoever makes himself a king speaks against Cae'sar.

13 When Pi'late therefore heard that saying, he brought Je'sus forth, and sat down in the judgment seat in a place that is called the Pavement, but in the He'brew, Gab'ba-tha.

14 And it was the preparation of the passover, and about <u>the sixth hour</u>: and he said to the Jews, Behold your King!   12 noon

15 But they cried out, Away with *Him*, away with *Him*, crucify Him. Pi'late said to them, Shall I crucify your King? The chief priests answered, We have no king but Cae'sar.

16 Then delivered he Him therefore to them to be crucified. And they took Je'sus, and led *Him* away.

17 And He bearing His cross went forth into a place called *the place* of a skull, which is called in the He'brew Gol'go-tha:

18 Where they crucified Him, and two other with Him, on either side one, and Je'sus <u>in the midst</u>.   in between

19 And Pi'late wrote a title, and put *it* on the cross. And the writing was, JE'SUS OF NAZ'A-RETH THE KING OF THE JEWS.

20 This title then read many of the Jews: for the place where Je'sus was crucified was near to the city: and it was written in He'brew, *and* Greek, *and* Lat'in.

21 Then said the chief priests of the Jews to Pi'late, Write not, The King of the Jews; but that He said, I am King of the Jews.

22 Pi'late answered, What I have written I have written.

23 Then the soldiers, when they had crucified Je'sus, took His garments, and made four parts, to every soldier a part; and also *His* coat: now the coat was without seam, woven from the top throughout.

24 They said therefore among themselves, Let us not <u>rend</u> it, but cast lots for it, whose it shall be: that the scripture might be fulfilled, which said, They parted My <u>raiment</u> among them, and for My <u>vesture</u> they did cast lots. These things therefore the soldiers did.

EX. 28:32   PS. 22:18   tear - out garments - clothing

25 Now there stood by the cross of Je'sus His mother, and His mother's sister, Ma'ry the *wife* of Cle'o-phas, and Ma'ry Mag-da-le'ne.

26 When Je'sus therefore saw His mother, and the disciple standing by, whom He loved, He said to His mother, Woman, behold your son!

27 Then said He to the disciple, Behold your mother! And from that hour that disciple took her to his own *home*.

28 After this, Je'sus knowing that all things were now accomplished, that the scripture might be fulfilled, said, I thirst.   PS. 69:21

29 Now there was set a vessel full of <u>vinegar</u>: and they filled a sponge with <u>vinegar</u>, and put *it* upon <u>hyssop</u>, and put *it* to His mouth. <small>sour wine - a branch</small>

30 When Je'sus therefore had received the <u>vinegar</u>, He said, <u>It</u> is finished: and He bowed His head, and gave up the ghost.   J OS. 4:10 way of salvation

31 The Jews therefore, because it was the preparation, that the bodies should not remain upon the cross on the <u>sabbath</u> day, (for that <u>sabbath</u> day was an <u>high</u> day,) <u>besought</u> Pi'late that their legs might be broken, and *that* they might be taken away. DEU. 21:23 EX. 12:46 rest - special - asked

32 Then came the soldiers, and broke the legs of the first, and of the other which was crucified with Him.

33 But when they came to Je'sus, and *saw* that He was dead already, they broke not His legs: knew

34 But one of the soldiers with a spear pierced His side, and <u>forthwith</u> came there out blood and water.   immediately

35 And he that saw *it* bare record, and his record is true: and he know that he <u>said true</u>, that you might believe.   tells truth

36 For these things were done, that the scripture should be fulfilled, A bone of Him shall not be broken. EXO.12:46PS. 34:20

37 And again another scripture said, They shall look on Him whom they pierced.   ZEC. 12:10

38 And after this Jo'seph of Ar-i-ma-thae'a, being a disciple of Je'sus, but secretly for <u>fear</u> of the Jews, <u>besought</u> Pi'late that he might take away the body of Je'sus: and Pi'late gave *him* leave. He came therefore, and took the body of Je'sus.   being afraid - asked

39 And there came also Nic-o-de'mus, which at the first came to Je'sus by night, and brought a mixture of myrrh and aloes, about an hundred pound *weight*.

40 Then took they the body of Je'sus, and <u>wound</u> it in linen clothes with the spices, as the manner of the Jews is to bury.   wrapped

41 Now in the place where He was crucified there was a garden; and in the garden a new <u>sepulcher</u>, wherein was never man yet laid.   grave

42 There laid they Je'sus therefore because of the Jews' preparation *day*; for the <u>sepulcher</u> was near at hand.

CHAPTER 20

THE first *day* of the week comes Ma'ry Mag-da-le'ne early, when it was yet dark, to the <u>sepulcher</u>, and sees the stone taken away from the <u>sepulcher</u>.   grave

2 Then she ran, and came to Si'mon Pe'ter, and to the other disciple, whom Je'sus loved, and said to them, They have taken away the Lord out of the <u>sepulcher</u>, and we know not where they have laid Him.

3 Pe'ter therefore went forth, and that other disciple, and came to the <u>sepulcher</u>.

4 So they ran both together: and the other disciple did outrun Pe'ter, and came first to the <u>sepulcher</u>.   grave

5 And he stooping down, *and looking in*, saw the linen clothes lying; yet went he not in.

6 Then came Si'mon Pe'ter following him, and went into the <u>sepulcher</u>, and saw the linen clothes lie,

7 And the napkin, that was about His head, not lying with the linen clothes, but wrapped together in a place by itself.

8 Then went in also that other disciple, which came first to the <u>sepulcher</u>, and he saw, and believed.

9 For as yet they <u>knew</u> not the scripture, that He must rise again from the dead.   understood

10 Then the disciples went away again to their own home.

11 But Ma'ry stood outside at the <u>sepulcher</u> weeping: and as she wept, she stooped down, *and looked* into the <u>sepulcher</u>,   grave

12 And sees two <u>angels</u> in white sitting, the one at the head, and the other at the feet, where the body of Je'sus had lain.   messengers

13 And they say to her, Woman, why weep you? She said to them, Because they have taken away my Lord, and I know not where they have laid Him.

14 And when she had thus said, she turned herself back, and saw Je'sus standing, and knew not that it was Je'sus.

15 Je'sus said to her, Woman, why weep you? whom seek you? She, supposing Him to be the gardener, said to Him, Sir, if you have borne Him away, tell me where you have laid Him, and I will take Him away.

16 Je'sus said to her, Ma'ry. She turned herself, and said to Him, Rabbo'ni; which is to say, Master.

17 Je'sus said to her, Touch Me not; for I am not yet ascended to My Father: but go to My brethren, and say to them, I ascend to My Father, and your Father; and *to* My God, and your God.

18 Ma'ry Mag-da-le'ne came and told the disciples that she had seen the Lord, and *that* He had spoken these things to her.

19 Then the same day at evening, being the first *day* <u>of the week</u>, when the doors were shut where the disciples were assembled <u>for fear</u> of the Jews, came Je'sus and stood in the midst, and said to them, Peace *be* to you.   Sunday - being afraid

20 And when He had so said, He showed to them *His* hands and His side. Then were the disciples <u>glad</u>, when they saw the Lord.   happy

21 Then said Je'sus to them again, Peace *be* to you: as *My* Father has sent Me, even so send I you.

22 And when He had said this, He breathed on *them*, and said to them, Receive you the Ho'ly <u>Ghost</u>:   Spirit

23 Whose soever sins you remit, they

are remitted to them; *and* whose soever *sins* you retain, they are retained.

24 But Thom'as, one of the twelve, called Did'y-mus, was not with them when Je'sus came.

25 The other disciples therefore said to him, We have seen the Lord. But he said to them, Except I shall see in His hands the print of the nails, and put my finger into the print of the nails, and thrust my hand into His side, I will not believe.

26 And after eight days again His disciples were within, and Thom'as with them: *then* came Je'sus, the doors being shut, and stood in the midst, and said, Peace *be* to you. with

27 Then said He to Thom'as, Reach here your finger, and behold My hands; and reach here your hand, and thrust *it* into My side: and be not faithless, but believing. unbelieving

28 And Thom'as answered and said to Him, My Lord and My God.

29 Je'sus said to him, Thom'as, because you have seen Me, you have believed: blessed *are* they that have not seen, and *yet* have believed.

30 And many other signs truly did Je'sus in the presence of His disciples, which are not written in this book:

31 But these are written, that you might believe that Je'sus is the Christ, the Son of God; and that believing you might have life through His name. authority

CHAPTER 21

AFTER these things Je'sus showed Himself again to the disciples at the sea of Ti-be'ri-as; and on this wise showed He *Himself*. fashion

2 There were together Si'mon Pe'ter, and Thom'as called Did'y-mus, and Na-than'a-el of Ca'na in Gal'i-lee, and the *sons* of Zeb'e-dee, and two other of His disciples.

3 Si'mon Pe'ter said to them, I go a fishing. They say to him, We also go with you. They went forth, and entered into a ship immediately; and that night they caught nothing. boat

4 But when the morning was now come, Je'sus stood on the shore: but the disciples knew not that it was Je'sus.

5 Then Je'sus said to them, Children, have you any meat? They answered Him, No. food

6 And He said to them, Cast the net on the right side of the ship, and you shall find. They cast therefore, and now they were not able to draw it for the multitude of fishes. make a catch

7 Therefore that disciple whom Je'sus loved said to Pe'ter, It is the Lord. Now when Si'mon Pe'ter heard that it was the Lord, he girt *his* fisher's coat *to him*, (for he was naked,) and did cast himself into the sea. put

8 And the other disciples came in a little ship; (for they were not far from land, but as it were two hundred cubits,) dragging the net with fishes. full of

9 As soon then as they were come to land, they saw a fire of coals there, and fish laid thereon, and bread. charcoal

10 Je'sus said to them, Bring of the fish which you have now caught. i.e., some of

11 Si'mon Pe'ter went up, and drew the net to land full of great fishes, an

hundred and fifty and three: and for all there were so many, yet was not the net broken.

12 Je'sus said to them, Come *and* dine. And none of the disciples dare ask Him, Who are You? knowing that it was the Lord.

13 Je'sus then comes, and takes bread, and gives them, and fish likewise.

14 This is now the third time that Je'sus showed Himself to His disciples, after that He was risen from the dead.

15 So when they had dined, Je'sus said to Si'mon Pe'ter, Si'mon, *son* of Jo'nah, love you Me more than these? He said to Him, Yea, Lord; You know that I love You. He said to him, Feed My lambs.

agape - phileo

16 He said to him again the second time, Si'mon, son of Jo'nah, love you Me? He said to Him, Yea, Lord; You know that I love You. He said to him, Feed My sheep.

17 He said to him the third time, Si'mon, *son* of Jo'nah, love you Me? Pe'ter was grieved because He said to him the third time, Love you Me? And he said to Him, Lord, You know all things; You know that I love You. Je'sus said to him, Feed My sheep.

agape

18 Verily, verily, I say to you, When you were young, you girded yourself, and walked where you would: but when you shall be old, you shall stretch forth your hands, and another shall gird you, and carry *you* where you would not.

Truly - wrapped

19 This spoke He, signifying by what death he should glorify God. And when He had spoken this, He said to him, Follow Me.

Peter - honor

20 Then Pe'ter, turning about, sees the disciple whom Je'sus loved following; which also leaned on His breast at supper, and said, Lord, which is he that betrays You?

21 Pe'ter seeing him said to Je'sus, Lord, and what *shall* this man *do*?

22 Je'sus said to him, If I will that he tarry till I come, what *is that* to you? follow you Me.

wait

23 Then went this saying abroad among the brethren, that that disciple should not die: yet Je'sus said not to him, He shall not die; but, If I will that he tarry till I come, what *is that* to you?

want

24 This is the disciple which testifies of these things, and wrote these things: and we know that his testimony is true.

25 And there are also many other things which Je'sus did, the which, if they should be written every one, I suppose that even the world itself could not contain the books that should be written. Amen.

ACTS

OUTLINE

Before Festus 25.1-22
Before Agrippa 25.23—26.32
Voyage to Rome 27.1—28.15
Ministry at Rome 28.16-31

SURVEY

In Acts 1.8 the Risen Christ states the purpose of the baptism with the Holy Spirit: "But ye shall receive power, after that the Holy Ghost is come upon you: and ye shall be witnesses unto me both in Jerusalem, and in all Ju-dæ´a, and in Sa-ma´ri-a, and unto the uttermost part of the earth." By location and emphasis this verse seems clearly to designate the purpose of this Book of the Acts of the Apostles. The book is a special history of the establishment and extension of the Church among Jews and Gentiles by the gradual location of centers of influence at salient points in the Roman Empire, from Jerusalem to Rome. Furthermore, Luke arranges this historic material in such a way that the progress of the Gospel is immediately evident. It is distinctly a schematic history—designed to edify no less than to narrate. Hence, we may view the Acts as an historical sermon on Christian power: its source and its effects. The source is Pentecost-given baptism with the Holy Spirit, and the effect is the power to witness to Christ in the world. This witness is presented in epitome in Peter's pentecostal sermon to the members of the Dispersion gathered at Jerusalem and in progressive detail throughout the remainder of the book.

AUTHOR

The almost universally accepted opinion is that Luke and Acts had a common authorship. The author of Acts begins by referring to a "former treatise" which is taken to indicate a first installment of the same historical volume, addressed to the same person "Theophilus." The expression "Luke-Acts" is used by modern scholars to indicate the singleness of the work. Furthermore, the preponderance of opinion has favored the view that Luke must have been the author of Acts because he was the author of Luke. There are at least three corroborating arguments for Lukan authorship. First, there is the evidence of the "we" sections 16.10-17; 20.5-15; 21.1-18; 27.1—28.16, which suggests that the author was an eyewitness, as Luke was. Second, there is evidence that the writer was a physician. And third, an extensive and convincing tradition supports Lukan authorship.

The Book of Acts seems to have been written about the time of Paul's first imprisonment, with the account of which the narrative closes. Nor does it anticipate a second imprisonment or Paul's martyrdom. The possibility that it was written by Luke while with Paul in Rome, as the "we" section indicates, seems more than likely. The currently prevailing opinion that the book was written about A.D. 90 seems to be contradicted by the silence of the author concerning the death of Paul, plus the absence of cross references to other Pauline writings which would have been widely circulated by that time.

J.H.G.

THE ACTS OF THE

APOSTLES

CHAPTER 1

THE former treatise have I made, O The-oph'i-lus, of all that Je'sus began both to do and teach, <small>writing</small>

2 Until the day in which He was taken up, after that He through the Ho'ly Ghost had given commandments to the apostles whom He had chosen: <small>to heaven - Spirit</small>

3 To whom also He showed Himself alive after His passion by many infallible proofs, being seen of them forty days, and speaking of the things pertaining to the kingdom of God: <small>suffering</small>

4 And, being assembled together with *them*, commanded them that they should not depart from Je-ru'sa-lem, but wait for the promise of the Father, which, *says He*, you have heard of Me. <small>gathered</small>

5 For John truly baptized with water; but you shall be baptized with the Ho'ly Ghost not many days from here.

6 When they therefore were come together, they asked of Him, saying, Lord, will You at this time restore again the kingdom to Is'ra-el?

7 And He said to them, It is not for you to know the times or the seasons, which the Father has put in His own power. <small>happenings</small>

8 But you shall receive power, after that the Ho'ly Ghost is come upon you: and you shall be witnesses to Me both in Je-ru'sa-lem, and in all Ju-dae'a, and in Sa-ma'ri-a, and to the uttermost part of the earth. <small>Spirit - farthest</small>

9 And when He had spoken these things, while they beheld, He was taken up; and a cloud received Him out of their sight. <small>looked</small>

10 And while they looked steadfastly toward heaven as He went up, behold, two men stood by them in white apparel;

11 Which also said, You men of Gal'i-lee, why stand you gazing up into heaven? this same Je'sus, which is taken up from you into heaven, shall so come in like manner as you have seen Him go into heaven.

12 Then returned they to Je-ru'sa-lem from the mount called Ol'i-vet, which is from Je-ru'sa-lem a sabbath day's journey. <small>about half mile</small>

13 And when they were come in, they went up into an upper room, where abode both Pe'ter, and James, and John, and Andrew, Phil'ip, and Thom'as, Bar-thol'o-mew, and Mat'thew, James *the son* of Al-phae'us, and Si'mon Ze-lo'tes, and Ju'das *the brother* of James.

14 These all continued with one accord in prayer and supplication, with the women, and Ma'ry the mother of Je'sus, and with His brethren. <small>united</small>

15 And in those days Pe'ter stood up in the midst of the disciples, and

said, (the number of names together were about an hundred and twenty,)

16 Men *and* brethren, this scripture must needs have been fulfilled, which the Ho'ly <u>Ghost</u> by the mouth of Da'vid spoke before concerning Ju'das, which was guide to them that took Je'sus.   Spirit

17 For he was numbered with us, and had obtained part of this ministry.

18 Now this man purchased a field with the reward of iniquity; and falling headlong, he burst asunder in the midst, and all his bowels gushed out.

19 And it was known to all the <u>dwellers</u> at Je-ru'sa-lem; insomuch as that field is called in their proper tongue, A-cel'da-ma, that is to say, The field of blood.   people

20 For it is written in the book of Psalms, Let his habitation be desolate, and let no man dwell therein: and his bishoprick let another take.   PSA. 69:25 PSA. 109:8

21 Wherefore of these men which have companied with us all the time that the Lord Je'sus went in and out among us,

22 Beginning from the baptism of John, to that same day that He was taken up from us, must one be <u>ordained</u> to be a witness with us of His resurrection.   chosen

23 And they <u>appointed</u> two, Jo'seph called Bar'sa-bas, who was surnamed Jus'tus, and Mat-thi'as.   selected

24 And they prayed, and said, You, Lord, which know the hearts of all *men*, show which of these two You have chosen,

25 That he may take part of this ministry and apostleship, from which Ju'das by transgression fell, that he might go to his own place.

26 And they gave forth their lots; and the lot fell upon Mat-thi'as; and he was <u>numbered with</u> the eleven apostles.   added to

CHAPTER 2

AND when the day of Pen'te-cost was fully come, they were all with one accord in one place.

2 And suddenly there came a sound from heaven as of a rushing mighty wind, and it filled all the house where they were sitting.

3 And there appeared to them cloven tongues <u>like</u> as of fire, and it <u>sat</u> upon each of them.   i.e., looked like fire - rested

4 And they were all filled with the Ho'ly <u>Ghost</u>, and began to speak with other <u>tongues</u>, as the Spirit gave them utterance.   Spirit - languages

5 And there were dwelling at Je-ru'sa-lem Jews, devout men, out of every nation under heaven.

6 Now when this was noised abroad, the multitude came together, and were <u>confounded</u>, because that every man heard them speak in his own language.   amazed

7 And they were all amazed and marveled, saying one to another, Behold, are not all these which speak Gal-i-lae'ans?

8 And how hear we every man in our own <u>tongue</u>, wherein we were born?   language

9 Par'thi-ans, and Medes, and E'lam-ites, and the <u>dwellers</u> in Mes-o-po-ta'mi-a, and in Ju-dae'a, and Cap-pa-do'ci-a, in Pon'tus, and A'sia, people of
10 Phryg'i-a, and Pam-phyl'i-a, in E'gypt, and in the parts of Lib'y-a about Cy-re'ne, and strangers of Rome, Jews and <u>proselytes</u>,   followers
11 Cretes and A-ra'bi-ans, we do hear them speak in our <u>tongues</u> the wonderful <u>works</u> of God. languages - deeds
12 And they were all amazed, and were in doubt, saying one to another, What means this?
13 Others <u>mocking</u> said, These men are full of new wine.   ridiculing
14 But Pe'ter, standing up with the eleven, lifted up his voice, and said to them, You men of Ju-dae'a, and all you that <u>dwell</u> at Je-ru'sa-lem, be this known to you, and <u>hearken</u> to my words: live - listen
15 For these are not drunken, as you suppose, seeing it is *but* the <u>third</u> <u>hour</u> of the day.   9 A.M.
16 But this is that which was spoken by the prophet Jo'el;   JOEL 2:28
17 And it shall come to pass in the last days, says God, I will pour out of My Spirit upon all flesh: and your sons and your daughters shall <u>proph-esy</u>, and your young men shall see visions, and your old men shall dream dreams: speak out
18 And on My servants and on My handmaidens I will pour out in those days of My Spirit; and they shall <u>prophesy</u>:   JOEL 2:29
19 And I will show wonders in heaven above, and signs in the earth beneath; blood, and fire, and vapor of smoke: JOEL 2:30
20 The sun shall be turned into darkness, and the moon into blood, before that great and notable day of the Lord come: JOEL 2:30,31
21 And it shall come to pass, *that* whosoever shall call on the name of the Lord shall be saved.   JOEL 2:32 Jesus
22 You men of Is'ra-el, hear these words; Je'sus of Naz'a-reth, a man approved of God among you by miracles and wonders and signs, which God did by Him in the midst of you, as you yourselves also know: DEU. 18:15
23 Him, being delivered by the determinate counsel and foreknowledge of God, you have taken, and by wicked hands have crucified and slain:
24 Whom God has raised up, having loosed the pains of death: because it was not possible that He should be <u>holden</u> of it.   held
25 For Da'vid speaks concerning Him, I foresaw the Lord always before my face, for He is on my right hand, that I should not be <u>moved</u>:   PSA. 16:8 shaken
26 Therefore did my heart rejoice, and my tongue was glad; moreover also my flesh shall rest in hope:
27 Because You will not <u>leave</u> my soul in hell, neither will You allow Your Holy One to <u>see corruption</u>.   abandon - undergo decay
28 You have made known to me the ways of life; You shall make me full of joy with Your <u>countenance</u>.   presence
29 Men *and* brethren, let me freely speak to you of the patriarch Da'vid,

that he is both dead and buried, and his <u>sepulcher</u> is with us to this day.   grave

30 Therefore being a <u>prophet</u>, and knowing that God had sworn with an oath to Him, that of the fruit of His loins, according to the flesh, He would raise up Christ to sit on His throne;   1 CHRON. 17:14 PS. 132:11 God's spokesman

31 <u>He</u> seeing this before spoke of the resurrection of Christ, that His soul was not left in hell, neither His flesh did see corruption.   PSA. 49:15 PS 16:10 David

32 This Je'sus has God raised up, whereof we all are witnesses.

33 Therefore being by the right hand of God exalted, and having received of the Father the promise of the Ho'ly <u>Ghost</u>, He has shed forth this, which you now see and hear.   Spirit

34 For Da'vid is not ascended into the heavens: but he says himself, The Lord said to my Lord, Sit You on My right hand,   PS. 110:1

35 Until I make Your foes Your footstool.

36 Therefore let all the house of Is'ra-el know <u>assuredly</u>, that God has made that same Je'sus, whom you have crucified, both Lord and <u>Christ</u>.   for certain - Messiah

37 Now when they heard *this*, they were pricked in their heart, and said to Pe'ter and to the rest of the apostles, Men *and* brethren, what shall we do?

38 Then Pe'ter said to them, Repent, and be baptized every one of you in the <u>name</u> of Je'sus Christ for the remission of sins, and you shall receive the gift of the Ho'ly <u>Ghost</u>.   authority - Spirit

39 For the promise is to you, and to your children, and to all that are afar off, *even* as many as the Lord our God shall <u>call</u>.   ISA. 57:19 i.e., to salvation

40 And with many other words did he testify and exhort, saying, Save yourselves from this <u>toward</u> generation.   perverse

41 Then they that gladly received his word were baptized: and the same day there were added *to them* about three thousand souls.

42 And they continued steadfastly in the apostles' <u>doctrine</u> and fellowship, and in breaking of bread, and in prayers.   HEB. 10:25 teaching

43 And fear came upon every soul: and many wonders and signs were done by the apostles.

44 And all that believed were together, and had all things common;

45 And sold their possessions and goods, and <u>parted</u> them to all men, as every man had need.   divided

46 And they, continuing daily with one accord in the temple, and breaking bread from house to house, did eat their <u>meat</u> with gladness and singleness of heart,   food

47 Praising God, and having favor with all the people. And the Lord added to the church daily such as should be saved.

CHAPTER 3

NOW Pe'ter and John went up together into the temple at the hour of prayer, *being* <u>the ninth *hour*</u>.   3 P.M

2 And a certain man lame from his

mother's womb was carried, whom they laid daily at the gate of the temple which is called Beautiful, to <u>ask</u> alms of them that entered into the temple; beg

3 Who seeing Pe'ter and John about to go into the temple asked <u>an alms</u>.   a gift

4 And Pe'ter, fastening his eyes upon him with John, said, Look <u>on</u> us.   at

5 And he gave <u>heed</u> to them, expecting to receive something of them.   attention

6 Then Pe'ter said, Silver and gold have I none; but such as I have give I you: In the name of Je'sus Christ of Naz'a-reth rise up and walk.

7 And he took him by the right hand, and lifted *him* up: and immediately his feet and ankle bones received strength.

8 And he leaping up stood, and walked, and entered with them into the temple, walking, and leaping, and praising God.

9 And all the people saw him walking and praising God:

10 And they knew that it was he which sat for <u>alms</u> at the Beautiful gate of the temple: and they were filled with wonder and amazement at that which had happened to him.   charity

11 And as the lame man which was healed held Pe'ter and John, all the people ran together to them in the porch that is called Sol'o-mon's, greatly wondering.

12 And when Pe'ter saw *it*, he answered to the people, You men of Is'ra-el, why <u>marvel you</u> at this? or why look you so earnestly on us, as though by our own power or holiness we had made this man to walk?   be surprised

13 The God of A'bra-ham, and of I'saac, and of Ja'cob, the God of our fathers, has glorified His Son Je'sus; whom you delivered up, and denied Him in the presence of Pi'late, when he was determined to let *Him* go.

14 But you denied the Holy One and the Just, and desired a murderer to be granted to you;

15 And killed the <u>Prince</u> of life, whom God has raised from the dead; whereof we are witnesses.   Jesus the Son-God

16 And His name through faith in His name has made this man strong, whom you see and know: yea, the faith which is by Him has given him this perfect soundness in the presence of you all.

17 And now, brethren, I know that through ignorance you did *it*, as *did* also your rulers.

18 But those things, which God before had showed by the mouth of all His prophets, that Christ should suffer, He has so fulfilled.

19 Repent you therefore, and be converted, that your sins may be blotted out, when the times of refreshing shall come from the presence of the Lord;

20 And He shall send Je'sus Christ, which before was preached to you:

21 Whom the heaven must receive until the times of <u>restitution</u> of all things, which God has spoken by the mouth of all His holy prophets since the world began.   restoration

22 For Mo'ses truly said to the fathers, A prophet shall the Lord your God raise up to you of your brethren, like to me; Him shall you hear in

G4 | 199 | M19 - - - 226 | P15 | 206

all things whatsoever He shall say to you. DEU. 18:15

23 And it shall come to pass, *that* every soul, which will not hear that prophet, shall be destroyed from among the people. DEU. 18:19

24 Yea, and all the prophets from Sam'u-el and those that follow after, as many as have spoken, have likewise foretold of these days.

25 You are the children of the prophets, and of the covenant which God made with our fathers, saying to A'bra-ham, And in your seed shall all the kindreds of the earth be blessed. GEN. 22:18 sons - agreement - descendants - families

26 To you first God, having raised up His Son Je'sus, sent Him to bless you, in turning away every one of you from his iniquities. i.e., as servant

CHAPTER 4

AND as they spoke to the people, the priests, and the captain of the temple, and the Sad'du-cees, came upon them,

2 Being grieved that they taught the people, and preached through Je'sus the resurrection from the dead. disturbed

3 And they laid hands on them, and put *them* in hold to the next day: for it was now eventide. prison - evening

4 However many of them which heard the word believed; and the number of the men was about five thousand.

5 And it came to pass on the morrow, that their rulers, and elders, and scribes,

6 And An'nas the high priest, and Ca'ia-phas, and John, and Al-ex-an'der,

and as many as were of the kindred of the high priest, were gathered together at Je-ru'sa-lem.

7 And when they had set them in the midst, they asked, By what power, or by what name, have you done this?

8 Then Pe'ter, filled with the Ho'ly Ghost, said to them, You rulers of the people, and elders of Is'ra-el, Spirit

9 If we this day be examined of the good deed done to the impotent man, by what means he is made whole; helpless - well

10 Be it known to you all, and to all the people of Is'ra-el, that by the name of Je'sus Christ of Naz'a-reth, whom you crucified, whom God raised from the dead, *even* by Him does this man stand here before you whole.

11 This is the stone which was set at nothing of you builders, which is become the head of the corner. PS. 118:22

12 Neither is there salvation in any other: for there is none other name under heaven given among men, whereby we must be saved.

13 Now when they saw the boldness of Pe'ter and John, and perceived that they were unlearned and ignorant men, they marveled; and they took knowledge of them, that they had been with Je'sus.

14 And beholding the man which was healed standing with them, they could say nothing against it.

15 But when they had commanded them to go aside out of the council, they conferred among themselves, leave - discussed it

16 Saying, What shall we do to these

men? for that indeed a <u>notable</u> miracle has been done by them *is* <u>manifest</u> to all them that dwell in Je-ru'sa-lem; and we cannot deny *it*.

noteworthy - known

17 But that it spread no further among the people, let us strictly threaten them, that they speak hereafter to no man in <u>this name</u>.

Jesus

18 And they called them, and commanded them not to speak at all nor teach in the name of Je'sus.

19 But Pe'ter and John answered and said to them, Whether it be right in the sight of God to hearken to you more than to God, judge you.

20 For we cannot but speak the things which we have seen and heard.

21 So when they had further threatened them, they let them go, finding nothing how they might punish them, because of the people: for all *men* <u>glorified</u> God for that which was done.

honored

22 For the man was <u>above</u> forty years old, on whom this miracle of healing was <u>showed</u>.

over - seen

23 And being <u>let go</u>, they went to their own company, and reported all that the chief priests and elders had said to them.

released

24 And when they heard that, they <u>lifted up their voice</u> to God with one accord, and said, Lord, You *are* God, which has made heaven, and earth, and the sea, and all that in them is:

PS. 146:6 i.e., prayed

25 Who by the mouth of Your servant Da'vid has said, Why did the heathen rage, and the people imagine vain things?

PS. 2:1-2

26 The kings of the earth stood up, and the rulers were gathered together against the Lord, and against His Christ.

27 For of a truth against Your Holy <u>child</u> Je'sus, whom You have anointed, both Her'od, and Pon'ti-us Pi'late, with the Gen'tiles, and the people of Is'ra-el, were gathered together,

PS. 2:2 servant

28 For to do whatsoever Your hand and Your counsel determined before to be done.

29 And now, Lord, behold their threatenings: and grant to Your servants, that with all boldness they may speak Your word,

30 By stretching forth Your hand to heal; and that signs and wonders may be done by the name of Your holy child Je'sus.

31 And when they had prayed, the place was shaken where they were assembled together; and they were all filled with the Ho'ly <u>Ghost</u>, and they spoke the word of God with boldness.

Spirit

32 And the multitude of them that believed were of one heart and of one soul: neither said any *of them* that <u>ought</u> of the things which he possessed was his own; but they had all things common.

nothing

33 And with great power gave the apostles witness of the resurrection of the Lord Je'sus: and great grace was upon them all.

34 Neither was there any among them that <u>lacked</u>: for as many as were <u>possessors</u> of lands or houses sold them, and

G5
201
GIL — 214

brought the <u>prices</u> of the things that were sold, _{were in need - owners - proceeds}

35 And laid *them* down at the apostles' feet: and distribution was made to every man according as he had need.

36 And Jo'ses, who by the apostles was surnamed Bar'na-bas, (which is, being interpreted, The son of consolation,) a Le'vite, *and* of the country of Cy'prus,

37 Having land, sold *it*, and brought the money, and laid *it* at the apostles' feet.

CHAPTER 5

BUT a certain man named An-a-ni'as, with Sap-phi'ra his wife, sold a possession,

2 And kept back *part* of the price, his wife also <u>being privy *to it*</u>, and brought a certain part, and laid *it* at the apostles' feet. _{knowing of}

3 But Pe'ter said, An-a-ni'as, why has Sa'tan <u>filled</u> your heart to lie to the Ho'ly <u>Ghost</u>, and to keep back *part* of the price of the land? _{controlled - Spirit}

4 While it remained, was it not your own? and after it was sold, was it not in your own power? why have you <u>conceived</u> this thing in your heart? you have not lied to men, but to God. _{ECC. 5:5 thought}

5 And An-a-ni'as hearing these words fell down, and <u>gave up the ghost</u>: and great fear came on all them that heard these things. _{died}

6 And the young men arose, wound him up, and carried *him* out, and buried *him*.

7 And it was about the space of three hours after, when his wife, not knowing what <u>was done</u>, came in. _{had happened}

8 And Pe'ter answered to her, Tell me whether you sold the land for so much? And she said, Yea, for so much.

9 Then Pe'ter said to her, How is it that you have agreed together to <u>tempt</u> the Spirit of the Lord? behold, the feet of them which have buried your husband *are* at the door, and shall carry you out. _{test}

10 Then fell she down immediately at his feet, and <u>yielded up the ghost</u>: and the young men came in, and found her dead, and, carrying *her* forth, buried *her* by her husband. _{died}

11 And great fear came upon all the church, and upon as many as heard these things.

12 And by the hands of the apostles were many signs and wonders <u>wrought</u> among the people; (and they were all with one accord in Sol'o-mon's porch. _{worked}

13 And of the rest dare no man join himself to them: but the people magnified them.

14 And believers were the more added to the Lord, multitudes both of men and women.)

15 Insomuch that they brought forth the sick into the streets, and laid *them* on beds and couches, that at the least the shadow of Pe'ter passing by might overshadow some of them.

16 There came also a multitude *out* of the cities round about to Je-ru'sa-lem, bringing sick folks, and them

which were <u>vexed</u> with unclean spirits: and they were healed every one. _{troubled}

17 Then the high priest rose up, and all they that were with him, (which is the sect of the Sad'du-cees,) and were filled with indignation,

18 And laid their hands on the apostles, and put them in the common prison.

19 But the <u>angel</u> of the Lord by night opened the prison doors, and brought them forth, and said, _{messenger}

20 Go, stand and speak in the temple to the people all the words of this life.

21 And when they heard *that*, they entered into the temple early in the morning, and taught. But the high priest came, and they that were with him, and called the council together, and all the senate of the children of Is'ra-el, and sent to the prison to have them brought.

22 But when the officers came, and found them not in the prison, they returned, and <u>told</u>, _{reported}

23 Saying, The prison truly found we shut with all safety, and the <u>keepers</u> standing outside before the doors: but when we had opened, we found no man within. _{guards}

24 Now when the high priest and the captain of the temple and the chief priests heard these things, they <u>doubted</u> of them whereto this would grow. _{were uncertain}

25 Then came one and told them, saying, Behold, the men whom you put in prison are standing in the temple, and teaching the people.

26 Then went the captain with the officers, and brought them without violence: for they feared the people, less they should have been stoned.

27 And when they had brought them, they <u>set</u> *them* before the council: and the high priest asked them, _{brought}

28 Saying, Did not we strictly command you that you should not teach in this name? and, behold, you have filled Je-ru'sa-lem with your <u>doc-trine</u>, and intend to bring this man's blood upon us. _{teaching}

29 Then Pe'ter and the *other* apostles answered and said, We ought to obey God rather than men.

30 The God of our fathers raised up Je'sus, whom you slew and hanged on a tree. _{DEU. 21:22}

31 Him has God exalted with His right hand *to be* a Prince and a Sav-ior, for to give repentance to Is'ra-el, and forgiveness of sins.

32 And we are His witnesses of these things; and *so is* also the Ho'ly <u>Ghost</u>, whom God has given to them that obey Him. _{Spirit}

33 When they heard *that*, they were <u>cut</u> *to the heart*, and <u>took counsel</u> to slay them. _{angry - talked about}

34 Then stood there up one in the council, a Phar'i-see, named Ga-ma'li-el, a doctor of the law, had in reputation among all the people, and commanded to put the apostles forth a little space;

35 And said to them, You men of Is'-ra-el, take <u>heed</u> to yourselves what you intend to do as touching these men. _{care}

36 For before these days rose up

Theu'das, boasting himself to be somebody; to whom a number of men, about four hundred, joined themselves: who was slain; and all, as many as obeyed him, were scattered, and <u>brought to nought</u> _{came to nothing}

37 After this man rose up Ju'das of Gal'i-lee in the days of the <u>tax-ing</u>, and drew away much people after him: he also perished; and all, *even* as many as obeyed him, were <u>dispersed</u>. _{census taking - scattered}

38 And now I say to you, <u>Refrain</u> from these men, and let them alone: for if this <u>counsel</u> or this work be of men, it will come to nothing: _{Stay - talking}

39 But if it be of God, you cannot overthrow it; less <u>haply</u> you be found even to fight against God. _{perhaps}

40 And to him they agreed: and when they had called the apostles, and beaten *them*, they commanded that they should not speak in the name of Je'sus, and let them go.

41 And they departed from the presence of the council, rejoicing that they were counted worthy to suffer shame for His name.

42 And daily in the temple, and in every house, they ceased not to teach and preach Je'sus Christ.

CHAPTER 6

AND in those days, when the number of the disciples was multiplied, there arose a murmuring of the Gre'cians against the He'brews, because their widows were neglected in the daily <u>ministration</u>. _{serving of food}

2 Then the twelve called the multitude of the disciples *to them*, and said, It is not <u>reason</u> that we should leave the word of God, and serve tables. _{desirable}

3 Wherefore, brethren, look you out among you seven men of honest report, full of the Ho'ly <u>Ghost</u> and wisdom, whom we may appoint over this business. _{EXO. 18:21 Spirit}

4 But we will give ourselves continually to prayer, and to the ministry of the word.

5 And the saying pleased the whole multitude: and they chose Ste'phen, a man full of faith and of the Ho'ly <u>Ghost</u>, and Phil'ip, and Proch'o-rus, and Ni-ca'nor, and Ti'mon, and Par'me-nas, and Nic'o-las a proselyte of An'ti-och:

6 Whom they set before the apostles: and when they had prayed, they laid *their* hands on them.

7 And the word of God increased; and the number of the disciples multiplied in Je-ru'sa-lem greatly; and a great company of the priests were obedient to the faith.

8 And Ste'phen, full of faith and power, <u>did</u> great wonders and miracles among the people. _{performed}

9 Then there arose certain of the synagogue, which is called *the synagogue* of the Lib'er-tines, and Cy-re'ni-ans, and Al-ex-an'dri-ans, and of them of Ci-li'cia and of A'sia, <u>disputing</u> with Ste'phen. _{arguing}

10 And they were not able to resist the wisdom and the Spirit by which he spoke.

11 Then they <u>suborned</u> men, which said, We have heard him speak blasphemous words against Mo'-ses, and *against* God.   bribed

12 And they <u>stirred up</u> the people, and the elders, and the scribes, and came upon *him*, and caught him, and brought *him* to the council,   aroused

13 And set up false witnesses, which said, This man ceases not to speak <u>blasphemous</u> words against this holy <u>place</u>, and the law: evil - temple

14 For we have heard him say, that this Je'sus of Naz'a-reth shall destroy this place, and shall change the <u>cus-toms</u> which Mo'ses delivered us.   teachings

15 And all that sat in the council, looking steadfastly on him, saw his face as it had been the face of an <u>angel</u>.   messenger

CHAPTER 7

THEN <u>said</u> the high priest, Are these things so?   asked

2 And he said, Men, brethren, and fathers, <u>hearken</u>; The God of glory appeared to our father A'bra-ham, when he was in Mes-o-po-ta'mi-a, before he dwelled in Char'ran,   Gen. 11:31 listen

3 And said to him, Get you out of your country, and from your <u>kindred</u>, and come into the land which I shall show you.   GEN. 12:1 relatives

4 Then came he out of the land of the Chal-dae'ans, and dwelled in Char'-ran: and from there, when his father was dead, <u>He</u> removed him into this land, wherein you now dwell.   God

5 And He gave him none inheritance in it, no, not *so much as* to set his foot on: yet He promised that He would give it to him for a possession, and to his <u>seed</u> after him, when *as yet* he had no child.   GEN. 12:7 descendants

6 And God spoke on this wise, That his <u>seed</u> should <u>sojourn</u> in a strange land; and that they should bring them into bondage, and <u>entreat</u> *them* <u>evil</u> <u>four hundred years</u>.   live - deal harshly with them for

7 And the nation to whom they shall be in bondage will I judge, said God: and after that shall they come forth, and serve Me in this place.   GEN. 15:13 GEN 15:14

8 And He gave him the <u>covenant</u> of circumcision: and so *A'bra-ham* fathered I'saac, and circumcised him the eighth day; and I'saac *fathered* Ja'cob; and Ja'cob *fathered* the twelve patriarchs.   GEN. 17:10 agreement

9 And the patriarchs, moved with envy, sold Jo'seph into E'gypt: but God was with him,

10 And delivered him out of all his <u>afflictions</u>, and gave him favor and wisdom in the sight of Pha'raoh king of E'gypt; and he made him governor over E'gypt and all his house.   GEN. 41:41 troubles

11 Now there came a <u>dearth</u> over all the land of E'gypt and Cha'naan, and great <u>affliction</u>: and our fathers found <u>no sustenance</u>.   famine - food

12 But when Ja'cob heard that there was <u>corn</u> in E'gypt, he sent out our fathers first.   grain

13 And at the second *time* Jo'seph was made known to his brethren; and Jo'seph's kindred was made known to Pha'raoh.   GEN. 45:3

14 Then sent Jo'seph, and called his

father Ja'cob to *him*, and all his kindred, <u>threescore and fifteen</u> souls. DEU. 10:22 75

15 So Ja'cob went down into E'-gypt, and died, he, and our fathers,

16 And were carried over into Sy'chem, and laid in the <u>sepulcher</u> that A'bra-ham bought for a sum of money of the sons of Em'mor *the father* of Sy'chem. JOS. 24:32 grave

17 But when the time of the promise drew near, which God had sworn to A'bra-ham, the people grew and multiplied in E'gypt,

18 Till another king <u>arose</u>, which knew not Jo'seph. EX. 1:8 i.e., came to power

19 The same dealt <u>subtlety</u> with our <u>kindred</u>, and evil entreated our fathers, so that they cast out their young children, to the end they might not live. shrewdly - family

20 In which time Mo'ses was born, and was exceeding fair, and <u>nourished</u> up in his father's house three months: EX. 2:2 brought

21 And when he was cast out, Pha'raoh's daughter took him up, and nourished him for her own son.

22 And Mo'ses was <u>learned</u> in all the wisdom of the E-gyp'tians, and was mighty in words and in deeds. educated

23 And when he was full forty years old, it came into his heart to visit his brethren the children of Is'ra-el.

24 And seeing one *of them* suffer wrong, he defended *him*, and avenged him that was oppressed, and smote the E-gyp'tian:

25 For he supposed his brethren would have understood how that God

<u>by his hand</u> would deliver them: but they understood not. i.e., through Moses

26 And the next day he showed himself to them as they <u>strove</u>, and would have set them at one again, saying, Sirs, you are brethren; why do you wrong one to another? were fighting

27 But he that did his neighbor wrong thrust him away, saying, Who made you a ruler and a judge over us? EX. 2:14

28 Will you kill me, as you did the E-gyp'tian yesterday?

29 Then fled Mo'ses at this saying, and was a stranger in the land of Ma'di-an, where he fathered two sons.

30 And when forty years were <u>expired</u>, there appeared to him in the wilderness of mount Si'na an <u>angel</u> of the Lord in a flame of fire in a bush. passed - messenger

31 When Mo'ses saw *it*, he wondered at the sight: and as he drew near to behold *it*, the voice of the Lord came to him, EX. 3:3

32 *Saying*, I *am* the God of your fathers, the God of A'bra-ham, and the God of I'saac, and the God of Ja'cob. Then Mo'ses trembled, and dare not behold. EX. 3:15

33 Then said the Lord to him, Put off your shoes from your feet: for the place where you stand is holy ground.

34 I have seen, I have seen the affliction of My people which is in E'gypt, and I have heard their groaning, and am come down to deliver them. And now come, I will send you into E'gypt.

35 This Mo'ses whom they refused, saying, Who made you a ruler and a judge? the same did God send *to be* a

ruler and a deliverer by the hand of the <u>angel</u> which appeared to him in the bush.   messenger

36 He brought them out, after that he had showed wonders and signs in the land of E'gypt, and in the Red sea, and in the wilderness forty years.   EX. 7:3

37 This is that Mo'ses, which said to the children of Is'ra-el, A prophet shall the Lord your God raise up to you of your brethren, like to me; him shall you hear.   DEU. 18:15

38 This is he, that was in the church in the wilderness with the angel which spoke to him in the mount Si'na, and *with* our fathers: who received the lively oracles to give to us:

39 To whom our fathers would not obey, but thrust *him* from them, and in their hearts turned back again into E'gypt,   NUM. 14:4

40 Saying to Aar'on, Make us gods to go before us: for *as for* this Mo'ses, which brought us out of the land of E'gypt, we know not what is become of him.   EX. 32:1

41 And they made a calf in those days, and offered sacrifice to the idol, and rejoiced in the works of their own hands.   EX. 32:6

42 Then God turned, and gave them up to worship the host of heaven; as it is written in the book of the prophets, O you house of Is'ra-el, have you offered to Me slain beasts and sacrifices *by the space of* forty years in the wilderness?   AMOS 5:25

43 Yea, you took up the tabernacle of Mo'loch, and the star of your god Rem'phan, figures which you made to worship them: and I will carry you away beyond Bab'y-lon.   JOS. 24:20   JER 20:6

44 Our fathers had the tabernacle of <u>witness</u> in the wilderness, as He had appointed, speaking to Mo'ses, that he should make it according to the fashion that he had seen.   JOS. 3:14   i.e., God's presence

45 Which also our fathers that came after brought in with Je'sus into the possession of the Gen'tiles, whom God drove out before the face of our fathers, to the days of Da'vid;

46 Who found favor before God, and desired to find a tabernacle for the God of Ja'cob.   PSA. 132:5

47 But Sol'o-mon built Him an house.

48 However the Most High dwells not in temples made with hands; as says the prophet,   1 KGS. 6:

49 Heaven *is* My throne, and earth *is* My footstool: what house will you build Me? says the Lord: or what *is* the place of My rest?   ISA. 66:1-2

50 Has not My hand made all these things?

51 You <u>stiffnecked</u> and uncircumcised in heart and ears, you do always resist the Ho'ly <u>Ghost</u>: as your fathers *did*, so *do* you.   2 KGS. 17:14   EX. 33:3   stubborn - Spirit

52 Which of the prophets have not your fathers persecuted? and they have slain them which showed before of the coming of the Just One; of whom you have been now the betrayers and murderers:

53 Who have received the law by the disposition of <u>angels</u>, and have not <u>kept</u> it.   messengers - obeyed

54 When they heard these things,

they were <u>cut</u> to the heart, and they gnashed on him with *their* teeth. _{hurt}

55 But he, being full of the Ho'ly <u>Ghost</u>, looked up <u>steadfastly</u> into heaven, and saw the glory of God, and Je'sus standing on the right hand of God, _{Spirit - intently}

56 And said, Behold, I see the heavens opened, and the Son of Man standing on the right hand of God.

57 Then they cried out with a loud voice, and stopped their ears, and ran upon him <u>with one accord</u>, _{on impulse}

58 And cast *him* out of the city, and stoned *him*: and the witnesses laid down their clothcs at a young man's feet, whose name was Saul.

59 And they stoned Ste'phen, <u>calling</u> upon *God*, and saying, Lord Je'sus, receive my spirit. _{i.e., Stephen calling}

60 And he kneeled down, and cried with a loud voice, Lord, lay not this sin to their charge. And when he had said this, he fell <u>asleep</u>. _{i.e., in Christ}

CHAPTER 8

AND Saul was <u>consenting</u> to his death. And at that time there was a great persecution against the church which was at Je-ru'sa-lem; and they were all scattered abroad throughout the regions of Ju-dae'a and Sa-ma'ri-a, except the apostles. _{agreeing}

2 And devout men carried Ste'phen *to his burial*, and made great <u>lamentation</u> over him. _{sorrowing}

3 As for Saul, he <u>made havoc</u> of the church, entering into every house, and

haling men and women committed *them* to prison. _{began ravaging - arresting}

4 Therefore <u>they</u> that were scattered abroad went every where preaching the <u>word</u>. _{i.e., believers - i.e., the gospel}

5 Then Phil'ip went down to the city of Sa-ma'ri-a, and preached Christ to them.

6 And the people with one accord gave <u>heed</u> to those things which Phil'ip spoke, hearing and seeing the miracles which he <u>did</u>. _{attention - performed}

7 For unclean spirits, crying with loud voice, came out of many that were possessed *with them*: and many <u>taken</u> with palsies, and that were lame, were healed. _{stricken}

8 And there was great joy in that city.

9 But there was a certain man, called Si'mon, which beforetime in the same city used <u>sorcery</u>, and <u>bewitched</u> the people of Sa-ma'ri-a, giving out that himself was some great one: _{magic - confused}

10 To whom they all gave heed, from the least to the greatest, saying, This man is the great power of God.

11 And to him they had <u>regard</u>, because that of long time he had <u>bewitched</u> them with <u>sorceries</u>. _{respect - confused - magic}

12 But when they believed Phil'ip preaching the things concerning the kingdom of God, and the name of Je'sus Christ, they were baptized, both men and women.

13 Then Si'mon himself believed also: and when he was baptized, he continued with Phil'ip, and wondered, beholding the miracles and signs which were done.

14 Now when the apostles which were at Je-ru'sa-lem heard that Sa-ma'ri-a had received the word of God, they sent to them Pe'ter and John:

15 Who, when they were come down, prayed for them, that they might receive the Ho'ly <u>Ghost</u>: Spirit

16 (For as yet He was fallen upon none of them: only they were baptized in the name of the Lord Je'sus.)

17 Then laid they *their* hands on them, and they received the Ho'ly <u>Ghost</u>.

18 And when Si'mon saw that through laying on of the apostles' hands the Ho'ly <u>Ghost</u> was given, he offered them money,

19 Saying, Give me also this power, that on whomsoever I lay hands, he may receive the Ho'ly <u>Ghost</u>. Spirit

20 But Pe'ter said to him, Your money perish with you, because you have thought that the gift of God may be purchased with money.

21 You have neither part nor <u>lot</u> in this matter: for your heart is not right in the sight of God. P.S. 78:37 portion

22 Repent therefore of this your wickedness, and pray God, if perhaps the thought of your heart may be forgiven you.

23 For I perceive that you are in the gall of bitterness, and *in* the bond of <u>iniquity</u>. sin

24 Then answered Si'mon, and said, Pray you to the Lord for me, that none of these things which you have spoken come upon me.

25 And they, when they had testified and preached the word of the Lord, returned to Je-ru'sa-lem, and preached the gospel in many villages of the Sa-mar'i-tans.

26 And the <u>angel</u> of the Lord spoke to Phil'ip, saying, Arise, and go toward the south to the way that goes down from Je-ru'sa-lem to Ga'za, which is desert. messenger

27 And he arose and went: and, behold, a man of E-thi'o-pi-a, an eunuch of great authority under Can'da-ce queen of the E-thi-o'pi-ans, who had the charge of all her treasure, and had come to Je-ru'sa-lem for to worship,

28 Was returning, and sitting in his chariot read I-sa'iah the prophet.

29 Then the Spirit said to Phil'ip, Go near, and join yourself to this chariot.

30 And Phil'ip ran there to *him*, and heard him read the prophet I-sa'iah, and said, Understand you what you read?

31 And he said, How can I, except some man should <u>guide</u> me? And he <u>desired</u> Phil'ip that he would come up and sit with him. instruct - asked

32 The place of the scripture which he read was this, He was led as a sheep to the slaughter; and like a lamb dumb before his shearer, so opened He not His mouth: ISA. 53:7

33 In His humiliation His judgment was taken away: and who shall declare His generation? for His life is taken from the earth.

34 And the eunuch <u>answered</u> Phil'ip, and said, I pray you, of whom speaks the prophet this? of himself, or of some other man? asked

35 Then Phil'ip opened his mouth,

and began at the same scripture, and preached to him Je'sus.

36 And as they went on *their* way, they came to a certain water: and the eunuch said, <u>See</u>, *here is* water; what does hinder me to be baptized?   Look

37 And Phil'ip said, If you believe with all your heart, you may. And he answered and said, I believe that Je'sus Christ is the Son of God.

38 And he commanded the chariot to stand still: and they went down both into the water, both Phil'ip and the eunuch; and he baptized him.

39 And when they were come up out of the water, the Spirit of the Lord caught away Phil'ip, that the eunuch saw him no more: and he went on his way rejoicing.

40 But Phil'ip was found at A-zo'tus: and passing through he preached in all the cities, till he came to Caes-a-re'a.

CHAPTER 9

AND Saul, <u>yet</u> breathing out threatenings and slaughter against the disciples of the Lord, went to the high priest,   still

2 And <u>desired</u> of him letters to Da-mas'cus to the synagogues, that if he found any <u>of this way</u>, whether they were men or women, he might bring them bound to Je-ru'sa-lem.

asked - i.e., knowing Jesus-Messiah

3 And as he journeyed, he came near Da-mas'cus: and suddenly there shined round about him a light from heaven:

4 And he fell to the earth, and heard a voice saying to him, Saul, Saul, why persecute you Me?

5 And he said, Who are You, Lord? And the Lord said, I am Je'sus whom you persecute: *it is* hard for you to kick against the pricks.

6 And he trembling and astonished said, Lord, what will You have me to do? And the Lord *said* to him, Arise, and go into the city, and it shall be told you what you must do.

7 And the men which journeyed with him stood speechless, hearing a voice, but seeing no man.

8 And Saul arose from the earth; and when his eyes were opened, he saw <u>no man</u>: but they led him by the hand, and brought *him* into Da-mas'cus.   nothing

9 And he was three days without sight, and neither did eat nor drink.

10 And there was a certain disciple at Da-mas'cus, named An-a-ni'as; and to him said the Lord in a vision, An-a-ni'as. And he said, Behold, I *am here*, Lord.

11 And the Lord *said* to him, Arise, and go into the street which is called Straight, and enquire in the house of Ju'das for one called Saul, of Tar'sus: for, behold, he prays,

12 And has seen in a vision a man named An-a-ni'as coming in, and putting *his* hand on him, that he might receive his sight.

13 Then An-a-ni'as answered, Lord, I have heard by many of this man, how much <u>evil</u> he has done to Your saints at Je-ru'sa-lem: wrong - followers

14 And here he has authority from the chief priests to <u>bind</u> all that call on Your name.   arrest

15 But the Lord said to him, Go

your way: for he is a chosen vessel to Me, to bear My name before the Gen'tiles, and kings, and the children of Is'ra-el:

16 For I will show him how <u>great</u> things he must suffer for My name's sake. ^{many}

17 And An-a-ni;as went his way, and entered into the house; and putting his hands on him said, Brother Saul, the Lord, *even* Je'sus, that appeared to you in the way as you came, has sent me, that you might receive your sight, and be filled with the Ho'ly <u>Ghost</u>. ^{Spirit}

18 And immediately there fell from his eyes as it had been scales: and he received sight forthwith, and arose, and was baptized.

19 And when he had <u>received meat</u>, he was strengthened. Then was Saul <u>certain</u> days with the disciples which were at Da-mas'cus. ^{eaten food - several}

20 And immediately he preached Christ in the synagogues, that He is the Son of God.

21 But all that heard *him* were amazed, and said; Is not this he that destroyed them which called on this name in Je-ru'sa-lem, and came here for that intent, that he might bring them bound to the chief priests?

22 But Saul increased the more in strength, and confounded the Jews which dwelled at Da-mas'cus, proving that this is very Christ.

23 And after that many days were fulfilled, the Jews <u>took counsel</u> to kill him: ^{made plans}

24 But their <u>laying await</u> was known of Saul. And they watched the gates day and night to kill him. ^{plot}

25 Then the disciples took him by night, and let *him* down by the wall in a basket.

26 And when Saul was come to Je-ru'sa-lem, he assayed to join himself to the disciples: but they were all afraid of him, and believed not that he was a disciple.

27 But Bar'na-bas took him, and brought *him* to the apostles, and declared to them how he had seen the Lord in the way, and that He had spoken to him, and how he had preached boldly at Da-mas'cus in the name of Je'sus.

28 And he was with them coming in and going out at Je-ru'sa-lem.

29 And he spoke boldly in the name of the Lord Je'sus, and <u>disputed</u> against the Gre'cians: but they went about to slay him. ^{argued}

30 *Which* when the brethren knew, they brought him down to Caes-a-re'a, and sent him forth to Tar'sus.

31 Then had the <u>churches</u> rest throughout all Ju-dae'a and Gal'i-lee and Sa-ma'ri-a, and were <u>edified</u>; and walking in the <u>fear</u> of the Lord, and in the comfort of the Ho'ly <u>Ghost</u>, were multiplied. ^{church - built up - reverence - Spirit}

32 And it came to pass, as Pe'ter passed throughout all quarters, he came down also to the saints which dwelled at Lyd'da.

33 And there he found a certain man named AE'ne-as, which had kept his bed eight years, and was sick of the palsy.

34 And Pe'ter said to him, AE'ne-as,

Je'sus Christ make you <u>whole</u>: arise, and make your bed. And he arose immediately. _{well}

35 And all that dwelled at Lyd'da and Sa'ron saw him, and turned to the Lord.

36 Now there was at Jop'pa a certain disciple named Tab'i-tha, which by interpretation is called Dor'cas: this woman was full of good works and <u>almsdeeds</u> which she did.   charity works

37 And it came to pass in those days, that she was sick, and died: whom when they had <u>washed</u>, they laid *her* in an upper chamber.   i.e., prepared her body

38 And forasmuch as Lyd'da was near to Jop'pa, and the disciples had heard that Pe'ter was there, they sent to him two men, <u>desiring</u> *him* that he would not delay to come to them.   requesting

39 Then Pe'ter arose and went with them. When he was come, they brought him into the upper chamber: and all the widows stood <u>by</u> him weeping, and showing the coats and garments which Dor'cas made, while she was with them.   around

40 But Pe'ter put them all forth, and kneeled down, and prayed; and turning *him* to the body said, Tab'i-tha, arise. And she opened her eyes: and when she saw Pe'ter, she sat up.

41 And he gave her *his* hand, and lifted her up, and when he had called the <u>saints</u> and widows, presented her alive.   believers

42 And it was known throughout all Jop'pa; and many believed in the Lord.

43 And it came to pass, that he tar-ried many days in Jop'pa with one Si'mon a tanner.

CHAPTER 10

THERE was a certain man in Caes-a-re'a called Cor-ne'lius, a <u>centurion</u> of the band called the Ital'ian *band*,   officer

2 A devout *man*, and one that <u>feared</u> God with all his house, which gave much <u>alms</u> to the people, and prayed to God always.   revered - charity

3 He saw in a vision evidently about the <u>ninth hour of the day</u> an <u>angel</u> of God coming in to him, and saying to him, Cor-ne'lius.   3 P.M. - messenger

4 And when he looked on him, he was afraid, and said, What is it, Lord? And he said to him, Your prayers and your alms are come up for a memorial before God.

5 And now send men to Jop'pa, and call for one Si'mon, whose surname is Pe'ter:

6 He lodges with one Si'mon a tanner, whose house is by the sea side: he shall tell you what you ought to do.

7 And when the <u>angel</u> which spoke to Cor-ne'lius was departed, he called two of his household servants, and a devout soldier of them that waited on him continually;

8 And when he had declared all *these* things to them, he sent them to Jop'pa.

9 On the morrow, as they went on their journey, and drew near to the city, Pe'ter went up upon the house-top to pray about <u>the sixth hour</u>: 12 noon

10 And he became very hungry, and

would have eaten: but while they made ready, he fell into a trance,

11 And saw heaven opened, and a certain vessel descending to him, as it had been a great sheet knit at the four corners, and let down to the earth:

12 Wherein were all manner of fourfooted beasts of the earth, and wild beasts, and creeping things, and fowls of the air.

13 And there came a voice to him, Rise, Pe'ter; kill, and eat.

14 But Pe'ter said, Not so, Lord; for I have never eaten any thing that is common or unclean.   LEV. 11:4

15 And the voice *spoke* to him again the second time, What God has cleansed, *that* call not you common.

16 This was done thrice: and the vessel was received up again into heaven.

17 Now while Pe'ter doubted in himself what this vision which he had seen should mean, behold, the men which were sent from Cor-ne'lius had made enquiry for Si'mon's house, and stood before the gate,   questioned

18 And called, and asked whether Si'mon, which was surnamed Pe'ter, were lodged there.   was staying

19 While Pe'ter thought on the vision, the Spirit said to him, Behold, three men seek you.   look for you

20 Arise therefore, and get you down, and go with them, doubting nothing: for I have sent them.

21 Then Pe'ter went down to the men which were sent to him from Cor-ne'lius; and said, Behold, I am he whom you seek: what *is* the cause why you are come?

22 And they said, Cor-ne'lius the centurion, a just man, and one that fears God, and of good report among all the nation of the Jews, was warned from God by an holy angel to send for you into his house, and to hear words of you.   honors - messenger

23 Then called he them in, and lodged *them*. And on the morrow Pe'ter went away with them, and certain brethren from Jop'pa accompanied him.

24 And the morrow after they entered into Caes-a-re'a. And Cor-ne'lius waited for them, and had called together his kinsmen and near friends.

25 And as Pe'ter was coming in, Cor-ne'lius met him, and fell down at his feet, and worshiped *him*.

26 But Pe'ter took him up, saying, Stand up; I myself also am a man.

27 And as he talked with him, he went in, and found many that were come together.

28 And he said to them, You know how that it is an unlawful thing for a man that is a Jew to keep company, or come to one of another nation; but God has showed me that I should not call any man common or unclean.   unholy

29 Therefore came I *to you* without gainsaying, as soon as I was sent for: I ask therefore for what intent you have sent for me?   any objection - purpose

30 And Cor-ne'lius said, Four days ago I was fasting until this hour; and at the ninth hour I prayed in my house, and, behold, a man stood before me in bright clothing,   3 P.M.

31 And said, Cor-ne′lius, your prayer is heard, and your <u>alms</u> are had in remembrance in the sight of God. _{gifts}

32 Send therefore to Jop′pa, and call here Si′mon, whose surname is Pe′ter; he is lodged in the house of *one* Si′mon a tanner by the sea side: who, when he come, shall speak to you.

33 Immediately therefore I sent to you; and you have well done that you are come. Now therefore are we all here present before God, to hear all things that are commanded you of God.

34 Then Pe′ter opened *his* mouth, and said, Of a truth I perceive that God is no respecter of persons:

35 But in every nation he that <u>fears</u> Him, and <u>works</u> righteousness, is accepted with Him. _{revered - does}

36 The word which *God* sent to the children of Is′ra-el, preaching peace by Je′sus Christ: (He is Lord of all:)

37 That word, *I say*, you know, which was published throughout all Ju-dae′a, and began from Gal′i-lee, after the baptism which John preached;

38 How God anointed Je′sus of Naz′a-reth with the Ho′ly <u>Ghost</u> and with power: who went about doing good, and healing all that were <u>oppressed</u> of the devil; for God was with Him. _{Spirit - dominated by}

39 And we are witnesses of all things which He did both in the land of the Jews, and in Je-ru′sa-lem; whom they slew and hanged on a tree:

40 Him God raised up the third day, and showed Him <u>openly</u>; _{visible-alive}

41 Not to all the people, but to witnesses chosen before of God, *even* to us, who did eat and drink with Him after He rose from the dead.

42 And He commanded us to preach to the people, and to testify that it is He which was ordained of God *to be* the Judge of living and dead.

43 To Him give all the prophets witness, that through His name whosoever believe in Him shall receive remission of sins.

44 While Pe′ter yet spoke these words, the Ho′ly <u>Ghost</u> fell on all them which heard the word. _{Spirit}

45 And they of the circumcision which believed were astonished, as many as came with Pe′ter, because that on the Gen′tiles also was poured out the gift of the Ho′ly <u>Ghost</u>.

46 For they heard them speak with <u>tongues</u>, and <u>magnify</u> God. Then answered Pe′ter, _{strange languages - exalting}

47 Can any man forbid water, that these should not be baptized, which have received the Ho′ly <u>Ghost</u> as well as we?

48 And he commanded them to be baptized in the name of the Lord. Then prayed they him to <u>tarry</u> certain days. _{stay}

CHAPTER 11

AND the apostles and brethren that were in Ju-dae′a heard that the Gen′tiles had also received the word of God.

2 And when Pe′ter was come up to Je-ru′sa-lem, they that were of the circumcision <u>contended</u> with him, _{took issue}

3 Saying, You went in to men uncircumcised, and did eat with them.

4 But Pe'ter rehearsed *the matter* from the beginning, and expounded *it* by order to them, saying,　explained

5 I was in the city of Jop'pa praying: and in a trance I saw a vision, A certain vessel descend, as it had been a great sheet, let down from heaven by four corners; and it came even to me:　down

6 Upon the which when I had fastened mine eyes, I considered, and saw fourfooted beasts of the earth, and wild beasts, and creeping things, and fowls of the air.　birds

7 And I heard a voice saying to me, Arise, Pe'ter; slay and eat.

8 But I said, Not so, Lord: for nothing common or unclean has at any time entered into my mouth.　unholy

9 But the voice answered me again from heaven, What God has cleansed, *that* call not you common.

10 And this was done three times: and all were drawn up again into heaven.

11 And, behold, immediately there were three men already come to the house where I was, sent from Caes-a-re'a to me.

12 And the spirit bade me go with them, nothing doubting. Moreover these six brethren accompanied me, and we entered into the man's house:

13 And he showed us how he had seen an angel in his house, which stood and said to him, Send men to Jop'pa, and call for Si'mon, whose surname is Pe'ter;　messenger

14 Who shall tell you words, whereby you and all your house shall be saved.

15 And as I began to speak, the Ho'ly Ghost fell on them, as on us at the beginning.　Spirit

16 Then remembered I the word of the Lord, how that He said, John indeed baptized with water; but you shall be baptized with the Ho'ly Ghost.

17 Forasmuch then as God gave them the like gift as *He did* to us, who believed on the Lord Je'sus Christ; what was I, that I could withstand God?

18 When they heard these things, they held their peace, and glorified God, saying, Then has God also to the Gen'tiles granted repentance to life.　praised

19 Now they which were scattered abroad upon the persecution that arose about Ste'phen travelled as far as Phe-ni'ce, and Cy'prus, and An'ti-och, preaching the word to none but to the Jews only.

20 And some of them were men of Cy'prus and Cy-re'ne, which, when they were come to An'ti-och, spoke to the Gre'cians, preaching the Lord Je'sus.

21 And the hand of the Lord was with them: and a great number believed, and turned to the Lord.

22 Then tidings of these things came to the ears of the church which was in Je-ru'sa-lem: and they sent forth Bar'na-bas, that he should go as far as An'ti-och.　news

23 Who, when he came, and had seen the grace of God, was glad, and exhorted them all, that with purpose of heart they would cling to the Lord.　encouraged

24 For he was a good man, and full of

the Ho'ly Ghost and of faith: and much people was added to the Lord. Spirit

25 Then departed Bar'na-bas to Tar'sus, for to seek Saul:

26 And when he had found him, he brought him to An'ti-och. And it came to pass, that a whole year they assembled themselves with the church, and taught much people. And the disciples were called Chris'tians first in An'ti-och.

27 And in these days came prophets from Je-ru'sa-lem to An'ti-och. teachers

28 And there stood up one of them named Ag'a-bus, and signified by the spirit that there should be great dearth throughout all the world: which came to pass in the days of Clau'di-us Cae'sar. indicated - famine

29 Then the disciples, every man according to his ability, determined to send relief to the brethren which dwelled in Ju-dae'a:

30 Which also they did, and sent it to the elders by the hands of Bar'na-bas and Saul. i.e., the money

CHAPTER 12

NOW about that time Her'od the king stretched forth *his* hands to vex certain of the church. trouble

2 And he killed James the brother of John with the sword.

3 And because he saw it pleased the Jews, he proceeded further to take Pe'ter also. (Then were the days of unleavened bread.) arrest - without yeast

4 And when he had apprehended him, he put *him* in prison, and delivered *him* to four quaternions of soldiers to keep him; intending after Eas-ter to bring him forth to the people. seized - squads - i.e., the Passover

5 Pe'ter therefore was kept in prison: but prayer was made without ceasing of the church to God for him. believers

6 And when Her'od would have brought him forth, the same night Pe'ter was sleeping between two soldiers, bound with two chains: and the keepers before the door kept the prison. guarded

7 And, behold, the angel of the Lord came upon *him*, and a light shined in the prison: and he smote Pe'ter on the side, and raised him up, saying, Arise up quickly. And his chains fell off from *his* hands. messenger - cell - struck - aroused

8 And the angel said to him, Gird your-self, and bind on your sandals. And so he did. And he says to him, Cast your garment about you, and follow me.

9 And he went out, and followed him; and knew not that it was true which was done by the angel; but thought he saw a vision. real

10 When they were past the first and the second ward, they came to the iron gate that leads to the city; which opened to them of its own accord: and they went out, and passed on through one street; and immediately the angel departed from him. guard - walked

11 And when Pe'ter was come to him-self, he said, Now I know of a surety, that the Lord has sent His angel, and has delivered me out of the hand of Her'od, and *from* all the expectation of the people of the Jews. for sure - messenger

P12 - 220 GIG 216

12 And when he had considered *the thing*, he came to the house of Ma'ry the mother of John, whose surname was Mark; where many were gathered together praying.

13 And as Pe'ter knocked at the door of the gate, a <u>damsel</u> came to <u>hearken</u>, named Rho'da_{servant girl - answer}

14 And when she knew Pe'ter's voice, she opened not the gate for gladness, but ran in, and told how Pe'ter stood before the gate.

15 And they said to her, You are <u>mad</u>. But she <u>constantly</u> affirmed that it was even so. Then said they, It is his <u>angel</u>.   insane - stoutly - messenger

16 But Pe'ter continued knocking: and when they had opened *the door*, and saw him, they were <u>astonished</u>.   amazed

17 But he, beckoning to them with the hand to <u>hold their peace</u>, declared to them how the Lord had brought him out of the prison. And he said, Go show these things to James, and to the brethren. And he departed, and went into another place.   i.e., be silent

18 Now as soon as it was day, there was no small <u>stir</u> among the soldiers, what was become of Pe'ter.   disturbance

19 And when Her'od had sought for him, and found him not, he examined the keepers, and commanded that *they* should be put to death. And he went down from Ju-dae'a to Caes-a-re'a, and *there* abode.

20 And Her'od was highly displeased with them of Tyre and Si'don: but they came with one accord to him, and, having made Blas'tus the king's chamberlain their friend, desired peace; because their country was nourished by the king's *country*.

21 And upon a set day Her'od, <u>arrayed</u> in royal apparel, sat upon his throne, and made an <u>oration</u> to them.   dressed - speech

22 And the people gave a shout, *saying*, *It is* the voice of a god, and not of a man.

23 And immediately the <u>angel</u> of the Lord smote him, because he gave not God the glory: and he was eaten of worms, and <u>gave up the ghost</u>.   messenger - died

24 But the word of God grew and multiplied.

25 And Bar'na-bas and Saul returned from Je-ru'sa-lem, when they had fulfilled *their* <u>ministry</u>, and took with them John, whose surname was Mark.   mission

CHAPTER 13

NOW there were in the church that was at An'ti-och certain prophets and teachers; as Bar'na-bas, and Sim'e-on that was called Ni'ger, and Lu'cius of Cy-re'ne, and Man'a-en, which had been brought up with Her'od the tetrarch, and Saul.

2 As they ministered to the Lord, and fasted, the Ho'ly <u>Ghost</u> said, Separate Me Bar'na-bas and Saul for the work whereto I have called them.   Spirit

3 And when they had fasted and prayed, and laid *their* hands on them, they sent *them* away.

4 So they, being sent forth by the

Ho'ly <u>Ghost</u>, departed to Se-leu'ci-a; and from there they sailed to Cy'prus.   _{Spirit}

5 And when they were at Sal'a-mis, they preached the word of God in the synagogues of the Jews: and they had also John <u>to *their* minister</u>.   _{i.e., as their helper}

6 And when they had gone through the isle to Pa'phos, they found a certain sorcerer, a false prophet, a Jew, whose name *was* Bar-je'sus:

7 Which was with the <u>deputy</u> of the country, Ser'gi-us Pau'lus, a <u>prudent</u> man; who called for Bar'na-bas and Saul, and desired to hear the word of God._{procounsel - wise}

8 But El'y-mas the sorcerer (for so is his name by interpretation) <u>withstood</u> them, seeking to turn away the deputy from the faith.   _{opposed}

9 Then Saul, (who also *is called* Paul,) filled with the Ho'ly <u>Ghost</u>, set his eyes on <u>him</u>,   _{Spirit - Elymas}

10 And said, O full of all <u>subtilty</u> and all mischief, *you* child of the <u>devil</u>, *you* enemy of all righteousness, will you not cease to <u>pervert</u> the right ways of the Lord?   _{HOS. 14:9 deceit - Satan - corrupt}

11 And now, behold, the hand of the Lord *is* upon you, and you shall be blind, not seeing the sun for a <u>season</u>. And immediately there fell on him a mist and a darkness; and he went about seeking some to lead him by the hand.   _{time}

12 Then the deputy, when he saw what was done, believed, being astonished at the <u>doctrine of</u> the Lord.   _{teaching about}

13 Now when Paul and his company loosed from Pa'phos, they came to Per'ga in Pam-phyl'i-a: and John departing from them returned to Je-ru'sa-lem.   _{left}

14 But when they departed from Per'ga, they came to An'ti-och in Pi-sid'i-a, and went into the synagogue on the <u>sabbath</u> day, and sat down. _{rest}

15 And after the reading of the law and the prophets the rulers of the synagogue sent to them, saying, *You* men *and* brethren, if you have any word of exhortation for the people, say on.

16 Then Paul stood up, and beckoning with *his* hand said, Men of Is'ra-el, and you that <u>fear</u> God, give audience.   _{honor}

17 The God of this people of Is'ra-el chose our fathers, and exalted the people when they dwelled as strangers in the land of E'gypt, and with <u>an high arm</u> brought He them out of it._{EX. 6:1,6 i.e., power}

18 And about the time of forty years <u>suffered</u> He their <u>manners</u> in the wilderness.   _{allowed - false ways}

19 And when He had destroyed seven nations in the land of Cha'naan, He divided their land to them by lot.

20 And after that He gave *to them* judges about the space of four hundred and fifty years, until Sam'u-el the prophet.

21 And afterward they desired a king: and God gave to them Saul the son of Cis, a man of the tribe of Ben'-ja-min, by the space of forty years.

22 And when He had removed him, He raised up to them Da'vid to be their king; to whom also He gave testimony, and said, I have found Da'vid the *son* of Jes'se, a man after My own heart, which shall fulfill all My will. 1 SAM 13:14 PSA. 89:20

23 Of this man's <u>seed</u> has God according to *His* promise raised to Is'ra-el a Savior, Je'sus: offspring

24 When John had first preached before His coming the baptism of repentance to all the people of Is'ra-el.

25 And as John fulfilled his course, he said, Whom think you that I am? I am not *He*. But, behold, there comes one after me, whose shoes of *His* feet I am not worthy to <u>loose</u>.   untie

26 Men *and* brethren, children of the stock of A'bra-ham, and whosoever among you <u>fears</u> God, to you is the word of this salvation sent.   reverence

27 For they that dwell at Je-ru'sa-lem, and their rulers, because they knew Him not, nor yet the voices of the prophets which are read every <u>sabbath</u> day, they have fulfilled *them* in condemning *Him*.   rest

28 And though they found no <u>cause</u> of death *in Him*, yet desired they Pi'late that He should be slain.   reason

29 And when they had fulfilled all that was written of Him, they took *Him* down from the tree, and laid *Him* in a <u>sepulcher</u>.   grave

30 But God raised Him from the dead:

31 And He was seen many days of them which came up with Him from Gal'i-lee to Je-ru'sa-lem, who are His witnesses to the people.

32 And we declare to you glad tidings, how that the promise which was made to the fathers,

33 God has fulfilled the same to us their children, in that He has raised up Je'sus again; as it is also written in the second psalm, You are My Son, this day have I begotten You.   PS. 2:7

34 And as concerning that He raised Him up from the dead, *now* no more to return to corruption, He said on this wise, I will give you the sure mercies of Da'vid.   ISA. 55:3

35 Wherefore He says also in another *psalm*, You shall not allow Your Holy One to see corruption.   PS. 16:10

36 For Da'vid, after he had served his own generation by the will of God, fell <u>on sleep</u>, and was laid to his fathers, and <u>saw corruption</u>:   i.e., death - decayed

37 But He, whom God raised again, saw no <u>corruption</u>.

38 Be it known to you therefore, men *and* brethren, that through this man is preached to you the forgiveness of sins:

39 And by Him all that believe are justified from all things, from which you could not be justified by the law of Mo'ses.

40 Beware therefore, <u>less that</u> come upon you, which is spoken of in the prophets;   that it might

41 Behold, you despisers, and wonder, and perish: for I work a work in your days, a work which you shall in no wise believe, though a man declare it to you.   HAB. 1:5

42 And when the Jews were gone out of the synagogue, the Gen'tiles <u>besought</u> that these words might be preached to them the next <u>sabbath</u>.   begged - rest day

43 Now when the congregation was broken up, many of the Jews and reli-

M32 - - - - - 253
M41 - - - - 224

gious proselytes followed Paul and Bar'na-bas: who, speaking to them, persuaded them to continue in the grace of God. _{converts}

44 And the next sabbath day came almost the whole city together to hear the word of God. _{rest}

45 But when the Jews saw the multitudes, they were filled with envy, and spoke against those things which were spoken by Paul, contradicting and blaspheming. _{contradicted}

46 Then Paul and Bar'na-bas waxed bold, and said, It was necessary that the word of God should first have been spoken to you: but seeing you put it from you, and judge yourselves unworthy of everlasting life, lo, we turn to the Gen'tiles. _{grew}

47 For so has the Lord commanded us, *saying,* I have set you to be a light of the Gen'tiles, that you should be for salvation to the ends of the earth. ISA. 49:6

48 And when the Gen'tiles heard this, they were glad, and glorified the word of the Lord: and as many as were ordained to eternal life believed. _{praised}

49 And the word of the Lord was published throughout all the region.

50 But the Jews stirred up the devout and honorable women, and the chief men of the city, and raised persecution against Paul and Bar'na-bas, and expelled them out of their coasts. _{districts}

51 But they shook off the dust of their feet against them, and came to I-co'ni-um.

52 And the disciples were filled with joy, and with the Ho'ly Ghost. _{Spirit}

CHAPTER 14

AND came to pass in I-co'ni-um, that they went both together into the synagogue of the Jews, and so spoke, that a great multitude both of the Jews and also of the Greeks believed.

2 But the unbelieving Jews stirred up the Gen'tiles, and made their minds evil affected against the brethren. _{bitter}

3 Long time therefore abode they speaking boldly in the Lord, which gave testimony to the word of His grace, and granted signs and wonders to be done by their hands.

4 But the multitude of the city was divided: and part held with the Jews, and part with the apostles.

5 And when there was an assault made both of the Gen'tiles, and also of the Jews with their rulers, to use *them* despitefully, and to stone them, _{wrongfully}

6 They were ware of *it*, and fled to Lys'tra and Der'be, cities of Lyc-a-o'ni-a, and to the region that lie round about: _{knew about}

7 And there they preached the gospel.

8 And there sat a certain man at Lys'tra, impotent in his feet, being a cripple from his mother's womb, who never had walked: _{weak}

9 The same heard Paul speak: who steadfastly beholding him, and perceiving that he had faith to be healed, _{feeling}

10 Said with a loud voice, Stand upright on your feet. And he leaped and walked.

11 And when the people saw what Paul had done, they lifted up their

voices, saying in the speech of Lyc-a-o'ni-a, The gods <u>are</u> come down to us in the likeness of men.   have

12 And they called Bar'na-bas, Ju'pi-ter; and Paul, Mer-cu'ri-us, because he was the chief speaker.

13 Then the priest of Ju'pi-ter, which was before their city, brought oxen and garlands to the gates, and would have <u>done sacrifice</u> with the people.   worshipped

14 *Which* when the apostles, Bar'na-bas and Paul, heard *of*, they <u>rent</u> their clothes, and ran in among the people, crying out,   tore

15 And saying, Sirs, why do you these things? We also are men of like <u>pas-sions</u> with you, and preach to you that you should turn from these vanities to the living God, which made heaven, and earth, and the sea, and all things that are therein: EX. 20:11 feelings

16 Who in times past permitted all nations to walk in their own ways.

17 Nevertheless He left not Himself without witness, in that He did good, and gave us rain from heaven, and fruitful seasons, filling our hearts with food and gladness.

18 And with these sayings scarce restrained they the people, that they had not <u>done sacrifice</u> to them.   worshipped

19 And there came there *certain* Jews from An'ti-och and I-co'ni-um, who persuaded the people, and, having stoned Paul, drew *him* out of the city, <u>supposing</u> he had been dead.   thinking

20 However, as the disciples stood round about him, he <u>rose up</u>, and came into the city: and the next day he departed with Bar'na-bas to Der'be.   revived

21 And when they had preached the gospel to that city, and had taught many, they returned again to Lys'tra, and *to* I-co'ni-um, and An'ti-och,

22 Confirming the souls of the disciples, *and* <u>exhorting</u> them to continue in the faith, and that we must through much tribulation enter into the kingdom of God.   encouraging

23 And when they had ordained them elders in every church, and had prayed with fasting, they commended them to the Lord, on whom they believed.

24 And after they had passed throughout Pi'sid'i-a, they came to Pam-phyl'i-a.

25 And when they had preached the word in Per'ga, they went down into At'ta'li-a:

26 And from there sailed to An'ti-och, from where they had been <u>recommended</u> to the grace of God for the work which they <u>fulfilled</u>.

commended - accomplished

27 And when they were come, and had gathered the church together, they <u>rehearsed</u> all that God had done with them, and how He had opened the door of faith to the Gen'tiles.   talked over

28 And there they abode long time with the <u>disciples</u>.   believers

CHAPTER 15

AND certain men which came down from Ju-dae'a taught the brethren, *and said*, Except you be circumcised after

the manner of Mo'ses, you cannot be saved.

2 When therefore Paul and Bar'na-bas had no small dissension and dis-putation with them, they determined that Paul and Bar'na-bas, and certain other of them, should go up to Je-ru'sa-lem to the apostles and elders about this question. debate

3 And being brought on their way by the church, they passed through Phe-ni'ce and Sa-ma'ri-a, declaring the conversion of the Gen'tiles: and they caused great joy to all the brethren. sent

4 And when they were come to Je-ru'sa-lem, they were received of the church, and *of* the apostles and elders, and they declared all things that God had done with them. reported

5 But there rose up certain of the sect of the Phar'i-sees which believed, saying, That it was needful to circumcise them, and to command *them* to keep the law of Mo'ses. necessary - obey

6 And the apostles and elders came together for to consider of this matter.

7 And when there had been much disputing, Pe'ter rose up, and said to them, Men *and* brethren, you know how that a good while ago God made choice among us, that the Gen'tiles by my mouth should hear the word of the gospel, and believe.

8 And God, which know the hearts, bare them witness, giving them the Ho'ly Ghost, even as *He did* to us; Spirit

9 And put no difference between us and them, purifying their hearts by faith.

10 Now therefore why tempt you God, to put a yoke upon the neck of the disciples, which neither our fathers nor we were able to bear? test - burden

11 But we believe that through the grace of the Lord Je'sus Christ we shall be saved, even as they.

12 Then all the multitude kept silence, and gave audience to Bar'na-bas and Paul, declaring what miracles and wonders God had wrought among the Gen'tiles by them. relating - worked

13 And after they had held their peace, James answered, saying, Men *and* brethren, hearken to me: stopped speaking

14 Sim'e-on has declared how God at the first did visit the Gen'tiles, to take out of them a people for His name.

15 And to this agree the words of the prophets; as it is written,

16 After this I will return, and will build again the tabernacle of Da'vid, which is fallen down; and I will build again the ruins thereof, and I will set it up: AMOS 9:11-12

17 That the residue of men might seek after the Lord, and all the Gen'tiles, upon whom My name is called, says the Lord, who does all these things.

18 Known to God are all His works from the beginning of the world.

19 Wherefore my sentence is, that we trouble not them, which from among the Gen'tiles are turned to God: judgment

20 But that we write to them, that they abstain from pollutions of idols,

and *from* fornication, and *from* things strangled, and *from* blood.

21 For Mo'ses of old time has in every city them that preach him, being read in the synagogues every sabbath day.

22 Then pleased it the apostles and elders, with the whole church, to send chosen men of their own company to An'ti-och with Paul and Bar'na-bas; *namely*, Ju'das surnamed Bar'sa-bas, and Si'las, chief men among the brethren: leading

23 And they wrote *letters* by them after this manner; The apostles and elders and brethren *send* greeting to the brethren which are of the Gen'tiles in An'ti-och and Syr'i-a and Ci-li'cia: i.e., Gentile birth

24 Forasmuch as we have heard, that certain which went out from us have troubled you with words, subverting your souls, saying, *You must* be circumcised, and keep the law: to whom we gave no *such* commandment: unsettling

25 It seemed good to us, being assembled with one accord, to send chosen men to you with our beloved Bar'na-bas and Paul,   i.e., as one

26 Men that have hazarded their lives for the name of our Lord Je'sus Christ.   risked

27 We have sent therefore Ju'das and Si'las, who shall also tell *you* the same things by mouth. i.e., face to face

28 For it seemed good to the Ho'ly Ghost, and to us, to lay upon you no greater burden than these necessary things;   Spirit

29 That you abstain from meats offered to idols, and from blood, and from things strangled, and from fornication: from which if you keep yourselves, you shall do well. Fare you well.

30 So when they were dismissed, they came to An'ti-och: and when they had gathered the multitude together, they delivered the epistle: group - letter

31 *Which* when they had read, they rejoiced for the consolation. encouragement

32 And Ju'das and Si'las, being prophets also themselves, exhorted the brethren with many words, and confirmed *them*.

33 And after they had tarried *there* a space, they were let go in peace from the brethren to the apostles.   stayed

34 Notwithstanding it pleased Si'las to abide there still.   awhile

35 Paul also and Bar'na-bas continued in An'ti-och, teaching and preaching the word of the Lord, with many others also.

36 And some days after Paul said to Bar'na-bas, Let us go again and visit our brethren in every city where we have preached the word of the Lord, *and see* how they do.

37 And Bar'na-bas determined to take with them John, whose surname was Mark.

38 But Paul thought not good to take him with them, who departed from them from Pam-phyl'i-a, and went not with them to the work.   deserted

39 And the contention was so sharp between them, that they departed asunder one from the other: and so Bar'na-bas took Mark, and sailed to Cy'prus;   divided in two

40 And Paul chose Si'las, and departed, being <u>recommended</u> by the brethren to the grace of God. committed

41 And he went through Syr'i-a and Ci-li'cia, <u>confirming</u> the churches.

strengthening

CHAPTER 16

THEN came he to Der'be and Lys'tra: and, behold, a certain disciple was there, named Tim'o-thy, the son of a certain woman, which was a Jew'ess, <u>and</u> believed; but his father *was* a Greek:

who

2 Which was well reported of by the brethren that were at Lys'tra and I-co'ni-um.

3 Him would Paul have to go forth with him; and took and circumcised him because of the Jews which were in those quarters: for they knew all that his father was a Greek.

4 And as they went through the cities, they delivered them the decrees for to keep, that were ordained of the apostles and elders which were at Je-ru'sa-lem.

5 And so were the churches established in the faith, and increased in number daily.

6 Now when they had gone throughout Phryg'i-a and the region of Ga-la'-tia, and were forbidden of the Ho'ly <u>Ghost</u> to preach the word in A'sia, Spirit

7 After they were come to Mys'ia, they <u>assayed</u> to go into Bi-thyn'i-a: but the Spirit permitted them not. were trying

8 And they passing by Mys'ia came down to Tro'as.

9 And a vision appeared to Paul in the night; There stood a man of Mac-e-do'ni-a, and prayed him, saying, Come over into Mac-e-do'ni-a, and help us.

10 And after he had seen the vision, immediately we endeavored to go into Mac-e-do'ni-a, <u>assuredly gathering</u> that the Lord had called us for to preach the gospel to them. concluding

11 Therefore <u>loosing</u> from Tro'as, we came with a straight course to Sam-o-thra'cia, and the next *day* to Ne-ap'o-lis; putting out

12 And from there to Phi-lip'pi, which is the <u>chief</u> city of that part of Mac-e-do'ni-a, *and* a colony: and we were in that city abiding certain days. leading

13 And on the <u>sabbath</u> we went out of the city by a river side, where prayer was <u>wont</u> to be made; and we sat down, and spoke to the women which <u>resorted</u> *there*. rest day - generally - gathered

14 And a certain woman named Lyd'i-a, a seller of purple, of the city of Thy-a-ti'ra, which worshiped God, heard *us*: whose heart the Lord opened, that she attended to the things which were spoken of Paul.

15 And when she was baptized, and her household, she besought *us*, saying, If you have judged me to be faithful to the Lord, come into my house, and abide *there*. And she <u>constrained</u> us. prevailed upon

16 And it came to pass, as we went to prayer, a certain <u>damsel</u> possessed with a spirit of divination met us, which brought her masters much <u>gain</u> by <u>soothsaying</u>: young girl - profit - fortune telling

17 The same followed Paul and us,

and cried, saying, These men are the servants of the Most High God, which show to us the way of salvation.

18 And this did she many days. But Paul, being <u>grieved</u>, turned and said to the spirit, I command you in the name of Je'sus Christ to come out of her. And he came out the same hour. _{annoyed}

19 And when her masters saw that the hope of their gains was gone, they caught Paul and Si'las, and drew *them* into the <u>marketplace</u> to the rulers, _{court}

20 And brought them to the magistrates, saying, These men, being Jews, do exceedingly trouble our city,

21 And teach customs, which are not lawful for us to receive, neither to observe, being Ro'mans.

22 And the multitude rose up together against them: and the magistrates <u>rent</u> off their clothes, and commanded to beat *them*. _{tore}

23 And when they had laid many <u>stripes</u> upon them, they cast *them* into prison, <u>charging</u> the jailor to keep them safely: _{blows - commanding}

24 Who, having received such a <u>charge</u>, thrust them into the inner prison, and made their feet <u>fast</u> in the stocks. _{instruction - lock}

25 And at midnight Paul and Si'las prayed, and sang praises to God: and the prisoners heard them.

26 And suddenly there was a great earthquake, so that the foundations of the prison were shaken: and immediately all the doors were opened, and every one's bands were loosed.

27 And the keeper of the prison awaking out of his sleep, and seeing the prison doors open, he drew out his sword, and would have killed himself, supposing that the prisoners had <u>been fled</u>. _{escaped}

28 But Paul cried with a loud voice, saying, Do yourself no harm: for we are all here.

29 Then he called for a light, and <u>sprang</u> in, and came trembling, and fell down before Paul and Si'las, _{rushed}

30 And brought them out, and said, Sirs, what must I do to be saved?

31 And they said, Believe on the Lord Je'sus Christ, and you shall be saved, and your house. _{JOHN 3:16 EPH. 2:8-9}

32 And they spoke to him the word of the Lord, and to all that were in his house.

33 And he took them the same hour of the night, and washed *their* <u>stripes</u>; and was baptized, he and all his, immediately. _{lash wounds}

34 And when he had brought them into his house, he set <u>meat</u> before them, and rejoiced, believing in God with all his house. _{food}

35 And when it was day, the magistrates sent the sergeants, saying, Let those men go.

36 And the keeper of the prison told this saying to Paul, The magistrates have <u>sent</u> to let you go: now therefore depart, and go in peace. _{instructed}

37 But Paul said to them, They have beaten us openly uncondemned, being Ro'mans, and have cast *us* into prison; and now do they <u>thrust</u> us out <u>privily</u>? nay <u>verily</u>; but let them come themselves and bring us out. _{put - secretly - truly}

38 And the sergeants told these words to the magistrates: and they feared, when they heard that they were Ro'mans.

39 And they came and besought them, and brought *them* out, and desired *them* to depart out of the city.

40 And they went out of the prison, and entered into *the house of* Lyd'i-a: and when they had seen the brethren, they comforted them, and departed.

CHAPTER 17

NOW when they had passed through Am-phip'o-lis and Ap-ol-lo-'ni-a, they came to Thes-sa-lo-ni'ca, where was a synagogue of the Jews:

2 And Paul, as his manner was, went in to them, and three sabbath days reasoned with them out of the scriptures,   rest

3 Opening and alleging, that Christ must needs have suffered, and risen again from the dead; and that this Je'sus, whom I preach to you, is Christ.   giving evidence

4 And some of them believed, and consorted with Paul and Si'las; and of the devout Greeks a great multitude, and of the chief women not a few.   joined - God honoring

5 But the Jews which believed not, moved with envy, took to them certain lewd fellows of the baser sort, and gathered a company, and set all the city on an uproar, and assaulted the house of Ja'son, and sought to bring them out to the people. wicked - lower - attacked

6 And when they found them not, they drew Ja'son and certain brethren to the rulers of the city, crying, These that have turned the world upside down are come here also;

7 Whom Ja'son has received: and these all do contrary to the decrees of Cae'sar, saying that there is another king, *one* Je'sus.

8 And they troubled the people and the rulers of the city, when they heard these things.   stirred up

9 And when they had taken security of Ja'son, and of the other, they let them go.

10 And the brethren immediately sent away Paul and Si'las by night to Be-re'a: who coming *there* went into the synagogue of the Jews.

11 These were more noble than those in Thes-sa-lo-ni'ca, in that they received the word with all readiness of mind, and searched the scriptures daily, whether those things were so.

12 Therefore many of them believed; also of honorable women which were Greeks, and of men, not a few. prominent

13 But when the Jews of Thes-sa-lo-ni'ca had knowledge that the word of God was preached of Paul at Be-re'a, they came there also, and stirred up the people.

14 And then immediately the brethren sent away Paul to go as it were to the sea: but Si'las and Tim'o-thy abode there still.

15 And they that conducted Paul brought him to Ath'ens: and receiving a commandment to Si'las and Tim'o-thy for to come to him with all speed, they departed.   for

P01

228

16 Now while Paul waited for them at Ath'ens, his spirit was <u>stirred</u> in him, when he saw the city <u>wholly</u> given to idolatry.   provoked - completely

17 Therefore <u>disputed he</u> in the synagogue with the Jews, and with the <u>devout</u> persons, and in the market daily with them that met with him.   he argued - God honoring

18 Then certain philosophers of the Ep-i-cu-re'ans, and of the Sto'icks, <u>encountered</u> him. And some said, What will this babbler say? other some, he seems to be a setter forth of strange gods: because he preached to them Je'sus, and the resurrection.   talked to

19 And they took him, and brought him to Ar-e-op'a-gus, saying, May we know what this new <u>doctrine</u>, <u>whereof</u> you speak, *is*?   teaching - which

20 For you bring certain strange things to our ears: we would know therefore what these things mean.

21 (For all the Ath-e'ni-ans and strangers which were there spent their time in nothing else, but either to tell, or to hear some new thing.)

22 Then Paul stood in the midst of Mars' hill, and said, *You* men of Ath'ens, I perceive that in all things you are too superstitious.

23 For as I passed by, and beheld <u>your devotions</u>, I found an altar with this inscription, TO THE UN-KNOWN GOD. Whom therefore you ignorantly worship, him declare I to you.   i.e., worship objects

24 God that made the world and all things therein, seeing that he is Lord of heaven and earth, dwells not in temples made with hands;   GEN. 1:1

25 Neither is worshiped with men's hands, as though He needed any thing, seeing He gives to all life, and breath, and all things;   ISA. 42:5

26 And has made of one blood all nations of men for to dwell on all the face of the earth, and has determined the times before appointed, and the bounds of their habitation;

27 That they should seek the Lord, if <u>haply</u> they might feel after Him, and find Him, though He be not far from every one of us: perhaps

28 For in Him we live, and move, and have our being; as certain also of your own poets have said, For we are also His <u>offspring</u>.   children

29 Forasmuch then as we are the offspring of God, we ought not to think that the Godhead is like to gold, or silver, or stone, graven by art and man's device.

30 And the times of this ignorance God <u>winked at</u>; but now commands all men every where to repent: overlooked

31 Because He has appointed a day, in the which He will judge the world in righteousness by *that* Man whom He has <u>ordained</u>; *whereof* He has given assurance to all *men*, in that He has raised Him from the dead.   PS. 9:8 appointed

32 And when they heard of the <u>res</u>-urrection of the dead, some <u>mocked</u>: and others said, We will hear you again of this *matter*.   rising - ridiculed

33 So Paul departed from among them.

34 However certain men <u>clung</u> to

him, and believed: among the which *was* Di-o-nys'ius the Ar-e-op'a-gite, and a woman named Dam'a-ris, and others with them.   joined

CHAPTER 18

AFTER these things Paul departed from Ath'ens, and came to Cor'inth;

2 And found a certain Jew named A'qui-la, born in Pon'tus, lately come from It'a-ly, with his wife Pris-cil'la; (because that Clau'di-us had commanded all Jews to depart from Rome:) and came to them.

3 And because he was of the same craft, he abode with them, and wrought: for by their occupation they were tentmakers.   trade - worked

4 And he reasoned in the synagogue every sabbath, and persuaded the Jews and the Greeks.   rest day

5 And when Si'las and Tim'o-thy were come from Mac-e-do'ni-a, Paul was pressed in the spirit, and testified to the Jews *that* Je'sus *was* Christ.

6 And when they opposed themselves, and blasphemed, he shook *his* raiment, and said to them, Your blood *be* upon your own heads; I *am* clean: from hereafter I will go to the Gen'tiles.   clothes

7 And he departed from there, and entered into a certain *man's* house, named Jus'tus, *one* that worshiped God, whose house joined hard to the synagogue.   was next

8 And Cris'pus, the chief ruler of the synagogue, believed on the Lord with all his house; and many of the Co-rin'-thi-ans hearing believed, and were baptized.

9 Then spoke the Lord to Paul in the night by a vision, Be not afraid, but speak, and hold not your peace: do not keep quiet

10 For I am with you, and no man shall set on you to hurt you: for I have much people in this city.   ISA. 43:5 attack

11 And he continued *there* a year and six months, teaching the word of God among them.   stayed

12 And when Gal'li-o was the deputy of A-cha'ia, the Jews made insurrection with one accord against Paul, and brought him to the judgment seat,   rose up

13 Saying, This *fellow* persuades men to worship God contrary to the law.

14 And when Paul was now about to open *his* mouth, Gal'li-o said to the Jews, If it were a matter of wrong or wicked lewdness, O *you* Jews, reason would that I should bear with you.

15 But if it be a question of words and names, and *of* your law, look you *to it*; for I will be no judge of such *matters*.

16 And he drove them from the judgment seat.

17 Then all the Greeks took Sos'thenes, the chief ruler of the synagogue, and beat *him* before the judgment seat. And Gal'l-io cared for none of those things.   was concerned

18 And Paul *after this* tarried *there* yet a good while, and then took his leave of the brethren, and sailed from there into Syr'i-a, and with him Pris-cil'la

and A'qui-la; having shorn *his* head in Cen'-chre-a: for he had a vow. _{stayed}

19 And he came to Eph'e-sus, and left them there: but he himself entered into the synagogue, and reasoned with the Jews.

20 When they desired *him* to tarry longer time with them, he consented not; _{stay}

21 But bade them farewell, saying, I must by all means keep this feast that comes in Je-ru'sa-lem: but I will return again to you, if God will. And he sailed from Eph'e-sus. _{told}

22 And when he had landed at Caes-a-re'a, and gone up, and saluted the church, he went down to An'ti-och. _{greeted}

23 And after he had spent some time *there*, he departed, and went over *all* the country of Ga-la'tia and Phryg'i-a in order, strengthening all the disciples.

24 And a certain Jew named A-pol'los, born at Al-ex-an'dri-a, an eloquent man, *and* mighty in the scriptures, came to Eph'e-sus.

25 This man was instructed in the way of the Lord; and being fervent in the spirit, he spoke and taught diligently the things of the Lord, knowing only the baptism of John.

_{ardent - understanding}

26 And he began to speak boldly in the synagogue: whom when A'qui-la and Pris-cil'la had heard, they took him to *them*, and expounded to him the way of God more perfectly. _{explained - accurately}

27 And when he was disposed to pass into A-cha'ia, the brethren wrote, exhorting the disciples to receive him: who, when he was come, helped them much which had believed through grace:

28 For he mightily convinced the Jews, *and that* publicly, showing by the scriptures that Je'sus was Christ.

_{i.e., Old Testament}

CHAPTER 19

AND it came to pass, that, while A-pol'los was at Cor'inth, Paul having passed through the upper coasts came to Eph'e-sus: and finding certain disciples,

2 He said to them, Have you received the Ho'ly Ghost since you believed? And they said to him, We have not so much as heard whether there be any Ho'ly Ghost. _{Spirit}

3 And he said to them, To what then were you baptized? And they said, To John's baptism. _{Into}

4 Then said Paul, John verily baptized with the baptism of repentance, saying to the people, that they should believe on Him which should come after him, that is, on Christ Je'sus.

5 When they heard *this*, they were baptized in the name of the Lord Je'sus.

6 And when Paul had laid *his* hands upon them, the Ho'ly Ghost came on them; and they spoke with tongues, and prophesied. _{different languages - taught}

7 And all the men were about twelve.

8 And he went into the synagogue, and spoke boldly for the space of three months, disputing and persuading the things concerning the kingdom of God.

9 But when <u>divers</u> were hardened, and believed not, but spoke evil of that way before the multitude, he departed from them, and separated the disciples, <u>disputing</u> daily in the school of one Ty-ran'nus. some - reasoning

10 And this continued by the space of two years; so that all they which <u>dwelled</u> in A'sia heard the word of the Lord Je'sus, both Jews and Greeks. lived

11 And God wrought special miracles by the hands of Paul:

12 So that from his body were brought to the sick handkerchiefs or aprons, and the diseases departed from them, and the evil spirits went out of them.

13 Then certain of the vagabond Jews, <u>exorcists</u>, took upon them to call over them which had evil spirits the name of the Lord Je'sus, saying, We adjure you by Je'sus whom Paul preaches. i.e., a spellbinder

14 And there were seven sons of *one* Sce'va, a Jew, *and* chief of the priests, which did so.

15 And the evil spirit answered and said, Je'sus I know, and Paul I know; but who are you?

16 And the man in whom the evil spirit was leaped on them, and overcame them, and <u>prevailed against</u> them, so that they fled out of that house naked and wounded. subdued all

17 And this was known to all the Jews and Greeks also dwelling at Eph'e-sus; and <u>fear</u> fell on them all, and the name of the Lord Je'sus was magnified. respect

18 And many that believed came, and confessed, and showed their deeds.

19 Many of them also which used <u>curious arts</u> brought their books together, and burned them before all *men*: and they counted the price of them, and found *it* fifty thousand *pieces* of silver. magic

20 So mightily <u>grew</u> the word of God and <u>prevailed</u>. spread - had power

21 After these things were ended, Paul purposed in the spirit, when he had passed through Mac-e-do'ni-a and A-cha'ia, to go to Je-ru'sa-lem, saying, After I have been there, I must also see Rome.

22 So he sent into Mac-e-do'ni-a two of them that ministered to him, Tim'o-thy and E-ras'tus; but he himself stayed in A'sia for a <u>season</u>. while

23 And the same time there arose no small stir about that way.

24 For a certain *man* named De-me'tri-us, a silversmith, which made silver shrines for Di-an'a, brought <u>no small gain</u> to the craftsmen; a good profit

25 Whom he called together with the workmen of like occupation, and said, Sirs, you know that by this craft we have our wealth.

26 Moreover you see and hear, that not alone at Eph'e-sus, but almost throughout all A'sia, this Paul has persuaded and turned away much people, saying that they be no gods, which are made with hands:

27 So that not only this our craft is in danger to <u>be set at nothing</u>; but also that the temple of the great goddess Di-an'a

should be despised, and her magnificence should be destroyed, whom all A'sia and the world worships.

become worthless

28 And when they heard *these sayings*, they were full of wrath, and cried out, saying, Great *is* Di-an'a of the E-phe'sians.

M28—
255

29 And the whole city was filled with confusion: and having caught Ga'ius and Ar-is-tar'chus, men of Mac-e-do'ni-a, Paul's companions in travel, they rushed with one accord into the theatre.

30 And when Paul would have entered in to the people, the disciples permitted him not.

31 And certain of the chief of A'sia, which were his friends, sent to him, desiring *him* that he would not ad-venture himself into the theatre. risk

32 Some therefore cried one thing, and some another: for the assembly was confused; and the more part knew not wherefore they were come together.

33 And they drew Al-ex-an'der out of the multitude, the Jews putting him forward. And Al-ex-an'der beckoned with the hand, and would have made his defence to the people.

34 But when they knew that he was a Jew, all with one voice about the space of two hours cried out, Great *is* Di-an'a of the E-phe'sians.

35 And when the townclerk had ap-peased the people, he said, *You* men of Eph'e-sus, what man is there that knows not how that the city of the E-phe'sians is a worshipper of the great goddess Di-an'a, and of the *image* which fell down from Ju'pi-ter? quieted

36 Seeing then that these things cannot be spoken against, you ought to be quiet, and to do nothing rashly.

37 For you have brought here these men, which are neither robbers of churches, nor yet blasphemers of your goddess.

38 Wherefore if De-me'tri-us, and the craftsmen which are with him, have a matter against any man, the law is open, and there are deputies: let them implead one another. complaint - available - accuse

39 But if you inquire any thing concerning other matters, it shall be de-termined in a lawful assembly. settled

40 For we are in danger to be call-ed in question for this day's up-roar, there being no cause whereby we may give an account of this con-course. accused - disorder - disorderly gathering

41 And when he had thus spoken, he dismissed the assembly. groups

CHAPTER 20

AND after the uproar was ceased, Paul called to *him* the disciples, and embraced *them*, and departed for to go into Mac-e-do'ni-a. quieted

2 And when he had gone over those parts, and had given them much exhor-tation, he came into Greece, encouragement

3 And *there* abode three months. And when the Jews laid wait for him, as he was about to sail into Syr'i-a, he purposed to return through Mac-e-do'ni-a. stayed

4 And there accompanied him into A'sia Sop'a-ter of Be-re'a; and of the Thessa-lo'ni-ans, Ar-is-tar'chus and Se-cun'dus; and Ga'ius of Der'be, and

Tim'o-thy; and of A'sia, Tych'i-cus and Troph'i-mus.

5 These going before <u>tarried</u> for us at Tro'as. waited

6 And we sailed away from Phi-lip'pi after the days of <u>unleavened</u> bread, and came to them to Tro'as in five days; where we abode seven days. without yeast

7 And upon <u>the first *day* of the week</u>, when the disciples came together to break bread, Paul preached to them, ready to depart on the morrow; and continued his speech until midnight. Sunday

8 And there were many lights in the upper chamber, where they were <u>gathered</u> together. meeting

9 And there sat in a window a certain young man named Eu'ty-chus, being fallen into a deep sleep: and as Paul was long preaching, he sunk down with sleep, and fell down from the third <u>loft</u>, and was taken up dead. story

10 And Paul went down, and fell on him, and embracing *him* said, Trouble not yourselves; for his life is in him.

11 When he therefore was come up again, and had broken bread, and eaten, and talked a long while, even till break of day, so he departed.

12 And they brought the young man alive, and were <u>not a little</u> comforted. greatly

13 And we went before to ship, and sailed to As'sos, there intending to take in Paul: for so had he <u>appointed</u>, minding himself to go <u>afoot</u>. arranged - by land

14 And when he met with us at As'sos, we took him in, and came to Mit-y-le'ne.

15 And we sailed from there, and came the next *day* opposite Chi'os; and the next *day* we arrived at Sa'mos, and <u>tarried</u> at Tro-gyl'li-um; and the next *day* we came to Mi-le'tus. stayed

16 For Paul had determined to sail by Eph'e-sus, because he would not spend the time in A'sia: for he <u>hasted</u>, if it were possible for him, to be at Je-ru'sa-lem the day of Pen'te-cost. hurried

17 And from Mi-le'tus he sent to Eph'e-sus, and called the elders of the church.

18 And when they were come to him, he said to them, You know, from the first day that I came into A'sia, after what manner I have been with you at all <u>seasons</u>, times

19 Serving the Lord with all humility of mind, and with many tears, and temptations, which befell me by the <u>lying in wait</u> of the Jews: plots

20 *And* how I kept back nothing that was profitable *to you*, but have showed you, and have taught you publicly, and from house to house, PSA. 40:10

21 Testifying both to the Jews, and also to the Greeks, repentance toward God, and faith toward our Lord Je'sus Christ.

22 And now, behold, I go bound in the spirit to Je-ru'sa-lem, not knowing the things that shall <u>befall</u> me there: happen to

23 Save that the Ho'ly <u>Ghost</u> witnessed in every city, saying that bonds and afflictions <u>abide</u> me. Spirit - await

24 But none of these things move me,

neither count I my life dear to myself, so that I might finish my course with joy, and the ministry, which I have received of the Lord Je'sus, to <u>testify</u> the gospel of the grace of God.   tell

25 And now, behold, I know that you all, among whom I have gone preaching the kingdom of God, shall see my face no more.

26 Wherefore I take you to record this day, that I *am* pure from the blood of all *men*.

27 For I have not <u>shunned</u> to declare to you all the counsel of God.   hesitated

28 Take heed therefore to yourselves, and to all the flock, over the which the Ho'ly <u>Ghost</u> has made you overseers, to feed the church of God, which He has purchased with His own blood.   Spirit

29 For I know this, that after my departing shall <u>grievous</u> wolves enter in among you, not sparing the flock.   savage

30 Also of your own selves shall men arise, speaking <u>perverse</u> things, to draw away disciples after them. distorted

31 Therefore watch, and remember, that by the space of three years I ceased not to warn every one night and day with tears.

32 And now, brethren, I commend you to God, and to the word of His grace, which is able to build you up, and to give you an inheritance among all them which are sanctified.

33 I have coveted no man's silver, or gold, or apparel.

34 Yea, you yourselves know, that these hands have ministered to my necessities, and to them that were with me.

35 I have showed you all things, how that so laboring you ought to support the weak, and to remember the words of the Lord Je'sus, how He said, It is more blessed to give than to receive.

36 And when he had thus spoken, he kneeled down, and prayed with them all.

37 And they all wept sore, and fell on Paul's neck, and kissed him,

38 Sorrowing most of all for the words which he spoke, that they should see his face no more. And they accompanied him to the ship.

CHAPTER 21

AND it came to pass, that after we were gotten from them, and had launched, we came with a straight course to Co'os, and the *day* following to Rhodes, and from there to Pat'a-ra:

2 And finding a ship sailing over to Phe-ni'cia, we went aboard, and set <u>forth</u>.   sail

3 Now when we had <u>discovered</u> Cy'prus, we left it on the left hand, and sailed into Syr'i-a, and landed at Tyre: for there the ship was to <u>unlade</u> her burden.   sighting - unload

4 And finding disciples, we <u>tarried</u> there seven days: who said to Paul through the Spirit, that he should not go up to Je-ru'sa-lem.   delayed

5 And when we had <u>accomplished</u> those days, we departed and went our way; and they all brought us on our

way, with wives and children, till *we were* out of the city: and we kneeled down on the shore, and prayed. finished

6 And when we had taken our leave one of another, we took ship; and they returned home again.

7 And when we had finished *our* course from Tyre, we came to Ptol-e-ma'is, and saluted the brethren, and abode with them one day. trip - greeted - stayed

8 And the next *day* we that were of Paul's company departed, and came to Caes-a-re'a: and we entered into the house of Phil'ip the evangelist, which was *one* of the seven; and abode with him.

9 And the same man had four daughters, virgins, which did prophesy. teach

10 And as we tarried *there* many days, there came down from Ju-dae'a a certain prophet, named Ag'a-bus. stayed

11 And when he was come to us, he took Paul's girdle, and bound his own hands and feet, and said, Thus says the Ho'ly Ghost, So shall the Jews at Je-ru'sa-lem bind the man that owns this girdle, and shall deliver *him* into the hands of the Gen'tiles. belt - Spirit

12 And when we heard these things, both we, and they of that place, besought him not to go up to Je-ru'sa-lem. begged

13 Then Paul answered, What mean you to weep and to break mine heart? for I am ready not to be bound only, but also to die at Je-ru'sa-lem for the name of the Lord Je'sus.

14 And when he would not be persuaded, we ceased, saying, The will of the Lord be done.

15 And after those days we took up our carriages, and went up to Je-ru'sa-lem. baggage

16 There went with us also *certain* of the disciples of Caes-a-re'a, and brought with them one Mna'son of Cy'prus, an old disciple, with whom we should lodge. early

17 And when we were come to Je-ru'sa-lem, the brethren received us gladly.

18 And the *day* following Paul went in with us to James; and all the elders were present.

19 And when he had saluted them, he declared particularly what things God had wrought among the Gen'tiles by his ministry. greeted - told

20 And when they heard *it*, they glorified the Lord, and said to him, You see, brother, how many thousands of Jews there are which believe; and they are all zealous of the law:

21 And they are informed of you, that you teach all the Jews which are among the Gen'tiles to forsake Mo'ses, saying that they ought not to circumcise *their* children, neither to walk after the customs.

22 What is it therefore? the multitude must needs come together: for they will hear that you are come. will certainly

23 Do therefore this that we say to you: We have four men which have a vow on them; pledge

24 Them take, and purify yourself with them, and be at charges with them, that they may shave *their* heads: and all may know that those things, whereof they were informed concerning you,

are nothing; but *that* you yourself also walk orderly, and keep the law.

pay expenses

25 As underline{touching} the Gen'tiles which believe, we have written *and* concluded that they observe no such thing, save only that they keep themselves from *things* offered to idols, and from blood, and from strangled, and from fornication.

concerning

26 Then Paul took the men, and the next day purifying himself with them entered into the temple, to signify the underline{accomplishment} of the days of purification, until that an offering should be offered for every one of them. completion

27 And when the seven days were almost ended, the Jews which were of A'sia, when they saw him in the temple, stirred up all the people, and laid hands on him,

28 Crying out, Men of Is'ra-el, help: This is the man, that teaches all *men* every where against the people, and the law, and this place: and further brought Greeks also into the temple, and has underline{polluted} this holy place. defiled

29 (For they had seen before with him in the city Troph'i-mus an E-phe'sian, whom they supposed that Paul had brought into the temple.)

30 And all the city was underline{moved}, and the people ran together: and they took Paul, and drew him out of the temple: and forthwith the doors were shut. aroused

31 And as they went about to kill him, tidings came to the chief captain of the band, that all Je-ru'salem was in an uproar.

32 Who immediately took soldiers and centurions, and ran down to them: and when they saw the chief captain and the soldiers, they underline{left} beating of Paul. stopped

33 Then the chief captain came near, and took him, and commanded *him* to be bound with two chains; and underline{demanded} who he was, and what he had done. asked

34 And some cried one thing, some another, among the multitude: and when he could not know underline{the certainty} for the tumult, he commanded him to be carried into the castle. for sure

35 And when he came upon the stairs, so it was, that he was borne of the soldiers underline{for} the violence of the people. because of

36 For the multitude of the people followed after, crying, Away with him.

37 And as Paul was to be led into the castle, he said to the chief captain, May I speak to You? Who said, Can you speak Greek?

38 Are not you that E-gyp'tian, which before these days underline{made an uproar}, and led out into the wilderness four thousand men that were murderers? called a revolt

39 But Paul said, I am a man *which am* a Jew of Tar'sus, *a city* in Ci-li'cia, a citizen of no mean city: and, I underline{beseech} you, allow me to speak to the people. beg

40 And when he had given him underline{licence}, Paul stood on the stairs, and beckoned with the hand to the people. And when there was made a great silence, he spoke to *them* in the He'brew underline{tongue}, saying,

permission - language

CHAPTER 22

MEN, brethren, and fathers, hear you my defence *which I make* now to you.

2 (And when they heard that he spoke in the He'brew <u>tongue</u> to them, they kept the more silence: and he says,) ^{language}

3 I am <u>verily</u> a man *which am* a Jew, born in Tar'sus, *a city* in Ci-li'cia, yet brought up in this city at the feet of Ga-ma'li-el, *and* taught according to the perfect manner of the law of the fathers, and was zealous toward God, as you all are this day. ^{truly}

4 And I persecuted this way to the death, binding and delivering into prisons both men and women.

5 As also the high priest does bear me witness, and all the <u>estate</u> of the elders: from whom also I received letters to the brethren, and went to Da-mas'cus, to bring them which were there bound to Je-ru'sa-lem, for to be punished. ^{council}

6 And it came to pass, that, as I made my journey, and was come near to Da-mas'cus about noon, suddenly there shone from heaven a great light round about me.

7 And I fell to the ground, and heard a voice saying to me, Saul, Saul, why persecute you Me?

8 And I answered, Who are You, Lord? And He said to me, I am Je'sus of Naz'a-reth, whom you persecute.

9 And they that were with me saw indeed the light, and were afraid; but they heard not the voice of Him that spoke to me.

10 And I said, What shall I do, Lord? And the Lord said to me, Arise, and go into Da-mas'cus; and there it shall be told you of all things which are <u>appointed</u> for you to do. ^{assigned}

11 And when <u>I could not see</u> for the glory of that light, being led by the hand of them that were with me, I came into Da-mas'cus.

^{i.e., was blind}

12 And one An-a-ni'as, a devout man according to the law, having a good report of all the Jews which <u>dwelled</u> *there*, ^{lived}

13 Came to me, and stood, and said to me, Brother Saul, receive your sight. And the same hour I looked up upon him.

14 And he said, The God of our fathers has chosen you, that you should know His will, and see that Just One, and should hear the voice of His mouth.

15 For you shall be His witness to all men of what you have seen and heard.

16 And now why <u>tarriest</u> you? arise, and be baptized, and wash away your sins, calling on the name of the Lord. ^{delay}

17 And it came to pass, that, when I was come again to Je-ru'sa-lem, even while I prayed in the temple, I was in a trance;

18 And saw Him saying to me, Make haste, and get you quickly out of Je-ru'sa-lem: for they will not receive your testimony concerning Me.

19 And I said, Lord, they know that I imprisoned and beat in every synagogue them that believed on You:

20 And when the blood of Your martyr Ste'phen was shed, I also was standing by, and consenting to his death, and kept the <u>raiment</u> of them that slew him. _{clothes}
21 And he said to me, Depart: for I will send you far from here to the Gen'tiles.
22 And they gave him audience to this word, and *then* lifted up their voices, and said Away with such a *fellow* from the earth: for it is not fit that he should live.
23 And as they cried out, and cast off *their* clothes, and threw dust into the air,
24 The chief captain commanded him to be brought into the castle, and bade that he should be examined by <u>scourging</u>; that he might know wherefore they cried so against him. _{whipping}
25 And as they bound him with thongs, Paul said to the centurion that stood by, Is it lawful for you to <u>scourge</u> a man that is a Ro'man, and uncondemned?
26 When the centurion heard *that*, he went and told the chief captain, saying, Take <u>heed</u> what you do: for this man is a Ro'man. _{care}
27 Then the chief captain came, and said to him, Tell me, are you a Ro'man? He said, Yea.
28 And the chief captain answered, With a great sum obtained I this freedom. And Paul said, But I was *free born*. _{a Roman citizen}
29 Then immediately they departed from him which should have examined him: and the chief captain also was afraid, after he knew that he was a Ro'man, and because he had bound him.
30 On the morrow, because he would have known the certainty wherefore he was accused of the Jews, he loosed him from *his* bands, and commanded the chief priests and all their council to appear, and brought Paul down, and set him before them.

CHAPTER 23

AND Paul, earnestly beholding the council, said, Men *and* brethren, I have lived in all good conscience before God until this day.
2 And the high priest An-a-ni'as commanded them that stood by him to <u>smite</u> him on the mouth. _{strike}
3 Then said Paul to him, God shall smite you, *you* <u>whited</u> wall: for sit you to judge me after the law, and command me to be smitten contrary to the law? _{whitewashed}
4 And they that stood by said, <u>Revile</u> you God's high priest? _{Insult}
5 Then said Paul, I knew not, brethren, that he was the high priest: for it is written, You shall not speak evil of the ruler of your people. _{EX. 22:28 ECC. 10:20}
6 But when Paul perceived that the one part were Sad'du-cees, and the other Phar'i-sees, he cried out in the council, Men *and* brethren, I am a Phar'i-see, the son of a Phar'i-see: of the hope and resurrection of the dead I am called in question.
7 And when he had so said, there arose a <u>dissension</u> between the Phar'i-

sees and the Sad'du-cees: and the multitude was divided. _{dispute}

8 For the Sad'du-cees say that there is no resurrection, neither angel, nor spirit: but the Phar'i-sees confess both.

9 And there arose a great cry: and the scribes *that were* of the Phar'i-sees' part arose, and <u>strove</u>, saying, We find no evil in this man: but if a spirit or an angel has spoken to him, let us not fight against God. _{argued}

10 And when there arose a great <u>dissension</u>, the chief captain, fearing less Paul should have been pulled in pieces of them, commanded the soldiers to go down, and to take him by force from among them, and to bring *him* into the castle. _{dispute}

11 And the night following the Lord stood by him, and said, Be of good <u>cheer</u>, Paul: for as you have testified of Me in Je-ru'sa-lem, so must you bear witness also at Rome. _{courage}

12 And when it was day, certain of the Jews banded together, and <u>bound</u> themselves under <u>a curse</u>, saying that they would neither eat nor drink till they had killed Paul. _{pledged - an oath}

13 And they were more than forty which had made this conspiracy.

14 And they came to the chief priests and elders, and said, We have bound ourselves under a great <u>curse</u>, that we will eat nothing until we have slain Paul.

15 Now therefore you with the council signify to the chief captain that he bring him down to you to morrow, as though you would enquire <u>something</u> <u>more perfectly</u> concerning him: and we, or ever he come near, are ready to kill him. _{thoroughly}

16 And when Paul's sister's son heard of their lying in wait, he went and entered into the castle, and told Paul.

17 Then Paul called one of the centurions to *him*, and said, Bring this young man to the chief captain: for he has a certain thing to tell him.

18 So he took him, and brought *him* to the chief captain, and said, Paul the prisoner called me to *him*, and prayed me to bring this young man to you, who has something to say to you.

19 Then the chief captain took him by the hand, and went *with him* aside privately, and asked *him*, What is that you have to tell me?

20 And he said, The Jews have agreed to desire you that you would bring down Paul to morrow into the council, as though they would enquire somewhat of him more <u>perfectly</u>. _{thoroughly}

21 But do not you yield to them: for there lie in wait for him of them more than forty men, which have <u>bound</u> themselves with an oath, that they will neither eat nor drink till they have killed him: and now are they ready, looking for a promise from you. _{promised}

22 So the chief captain *then* let the young man depart, and <u>charged</u> *him*, *See you* tell no man that you have <u>showed</u> these things to me. _{instruct - told}

23 And he called to *him* two centurions, saying, Make ready two hundred

soldiers to go to Caes-a-re'a, and horsemen threescore and ten, and spearmen two hundred, at the <u>third hour of the night</u>;   9 P.M.

24 And provide *them* <u>beasts</u>, that they may set Paul on, and bring *him* safe to Fe'lix the governor.   horses

25 And he wrote a letter after this manner:

26 Clau'di-us Lys'ias to the most excellent governor Fe'lix *sends* greeting.

27 This man was taken of the Jews, and should have been killed of them: then came I with an army, and rescued him, having understood that he was a Ro'man.

28 And when I would have known the cause wherefore they accused him, I brought him forth into their council:

29 Whom I perceived to be accused of questions of their law, but to have nothing laid to his charge worthy of death or of bonds.

30 And when it was told me how that the Jews laid wait for the man, I sent immediately to you, and gave commandment to his accusers also to say before you what *they had* against him. Farewell.

31 Then the soldiers, as it was commanded them, took Paul, and brought *him* by night to An-tip'a-tris.

32 On the <u>morrow</u> they left the horsemen to go with him, and returned to the castle: next day

33 Who, when they came to Caes-a-re'a, and delivered the <u>epistle</u> to the governor, presented Paul also before him. letter

34 And when the governor had read *the letter*, he asked of what province he was. And when he understood that *he was* of Ci-li'cia;

35 I will hear you, said he, when your accusers are also come. And he commanded him to be kept in Her'od's judgment hall.

CHAPTER 24

AND after five days An-a-ni'as the high priest descended with the elders, and *with* a certain orator *named* Ter-tul'lus, who informed the governor against Paul.

2 And when he was called forth, Ter-tul'lus began to accuse *him*, saying, Seeing that by you we enjoy great quietness, and that very worthy deeds are done to this nation by your <u>providence</u>,   will

3 We accept *it* always, and in all places, most noble Fe'lix, with all thankfulness.

4 Notwithstanding, that I be not further <u>tedious</u> to you, I pray you that you would hear us of your <u>clemency</u> a few words.   worrying - kindness

5 For we have found this man *a* pestilent *fellow*, and a mover of sedition among all the Jews throughout the world, and a ringleader of the sect of the Naz'a-renes:

6 Who also has gone about to <u>profane</u> the temple: whom we took, and would have judged according to our law.   desecrate

7 But the chief captain Lys'ias came *upon us*, and with great violence took *him* away out of our hands,

8 Commanding his accusers to come to you: by examining of whom yourself may take knowledge of all these things, whereof we accuse him.

9 And the Jews also <u>assented</u>, saying that these things were so.   agreed

10 Then Paul, after that the governor had beckoned to him to speak, answered, Forasmuch as I know that you have been of many years a judge to this nation, I do the more cheerfully answer for myself:

11 Because that you may understand, that there are yet but twelve days since I went up to Je-ru'sa-lem for to worship.

12 And they neither found me in the temple disputing with any man, neither raising up the people, neither in the synagogues, nor in the city:

13 Neither can they prove the things whereof they now accuse me.

14 But this I confess to you, that after the way which they call <u>heresy</u>, so worship I the God of my fathers, believing all things which are written in the law and in the prophets: a sect

15 And have hope toward God, which they themselves also <u>allow</u>, that there shall be a resurrection of the dead, both of the just and unjust.   cherish

16 And herein do I exercise myself, to have always a conscience <u>void</u> of offence toward God, and *toward* men.   blameless

17 Now after many years I came to bring <u>alms</u> to my nation, and offerings.   gifts

18 Whereupon certain Jews from A'- sia found me purified in the temple, neither with multitude, nor with <u>tumult</u>.   disturbance

19 Who ought to have been here before you, and object, if they had anything against me.

20 Or else let these same *here* say, if they have found any <u>evil</u> doing in me, while I stood before the council,   wrong

21 Except it be for this one voice, that I cried standing among them, Touching the resurrection of the dead I am called in question by you this day.

22 And when Fe'lix heard these things, having more <u>perfect</u> knowledge of *that* way, he deferred them, and said, When Lys'ias the chief captain shall come down, I will <u>know</u> the uttermost of your matter.   complete - decide

23 And he commanded a centurion to keep Paul, and to let *him* have liberty, and that he should forbid none of his acquaintance to minister or come to him.

24 And after certain days, when Fe'lix came with his wife Dru-sil'la, which was a Jew'ess, he sent for Paul, and heard him concerning the faith in Christ.

25 And as he reasoned of righteousness, <u>temperance</u>, and judgment to come, Fe'lix trembled, and answered, Go your way for this time; when I have a convenient <u>season</u>, I will call for you.   self control - time

26 He hoped also that money should have been given him of Paul, that he might loose him: wherefore he sent for him the oftener, and communed with him.

27 But after two years Por'ci-us Fes'tus came into Fe'lix' room: and Fe'lix, willing to show the Jews a pleasure, left Paul bound.

CHAPTER 25

NOW when Fes'tus was come into the province, after three days he ascended from Caes-a-re'a to Je-ru'sa-lem.

2 Then the high priest and the chief of the Jews informed him against Paul, and <u>besought</u> him,   begged

3 And desired favor against him, that he would send for him to Je-ru'sa-lem, laying wait in the way to kill him.

4 But Fes'tus answered, that Paul should be kept at Caes-a-re'a, and that he himself would depart shortly from there.

5 Let them therefore, said he, which among you are able, go down with *me*, and accuse this man, if there be any wickedness in him.

6 And when he had tarried among them more than ten days, he went down to Caes-a-re'a; and the next day sitting on the judgment seat commanded Paul to be brought.

7 And when he was come, the Jews which came down from Je-ru'sa-lem stood round about, and laid many and <u>grievous</u> complaints against Paul, which they could not prove.   serious

8 While he answered for himself, Neither against the law of the Jews, neither against the temple, nor yet against Cae'sar, have I offended any thing at all.

9 But Fes'tus, willing to do the Jews a pleasure, answered Paul, and said, Will you go up to Je-ru'sa-lem, and there be judged of these things before me?

10 Then said Paul, I stand at Cae'sar's judgment seat, where I ought to be <u>judged</u>: to the Jews have I done no wrong, as you very well know.   tried

11 For if I be an offender, or have committed any thing worthy of death, I refuse not to die: but if there be none of these things whereof these accuse me, no man may deliver me to them. I appeal to Cae'sar.

12 Then Fes'tus, when he had <u>conferred</u> with the council, answered, Have you appealed to Cae'sar? to Cae'sar shall you go.   checked

13 And after certain days king A-grip'pa and Ber-ni'ce came to Caes-a-re'a to <u>salute</u> Fes'tus.   greet

14 And when they had been there many days, Fes'tus declared Paul's cause to the king, saying, There is a certain man left in bonds by Fe'lix:

15 About whom, when I was at Je-ru'sa-lem, the chief priests and the elders of the Jews informed *me*, desiring *to have* judgment against him.

16 To whom I answered, It is not the manner of the Ro'mans to deliver any man to die, before that he which is accused have the accusers face to face, and have <u>licence</u> to answer for himself concerning the crime laid against him.   permission

17 Therefore, when they were come here, without any delay on the morrow I sat on the judgment seat, and commanded the man to be brought forth.

18 Against whom when the accusers stood up, they brought none accusation of such things as I <u>supposed</u>:   expected

19 But had certain questions against him of their own <u>superstition</u>, and of one Je'sus, which was dead, whom Paul affirmed to be alive. religion

20 And because I <u>doubted of</u> such manner of questions, I asked *him* whether he would go to Je-ru'sa-lem, and there be judged of these matters. questioned

21 But when Paul had appealed to be reserved to the hearing of Au-gus'tus, I commanded him to be kept till I might send him to Cae'sar.

22 Then A-grip'pa said to Fes'tus, I would also hear the man myself. To morrow, said he, you shall hear him.

23 And on the morrow, when A-grip'pa was come, and Ber-ni'ce, with great <u>pomp</u>, and was entered into the place of hearing, with the chief captains, and principal men of the city, at Fes'tus' commandment Paul was brought forth.   ceremony

24 And Fes'tus said, King A-grip'pa, and all men which are here present with us, you see this man, about whom all the multitude of the Jews have dealt with me, both at Je-ru'sa-lem, and *also* here, crying that he ought not to live any longer.

25 But when I found that he had committed nothing worthy of death, and that he himself has appealed to Au-gus'tus, I have determined to send him.

26 Of whom I have no <u>certain</u> thing to write to my lord. Wherefore I have brought him forth before you, and specially before you, O king A-grip'-pa, that, after examination <u>had</u>, I might have somewhat to write.   exact - had finished

27 For it seems to me unreasonable to send a prisoner, and not <u>withal to signify</u> the crimes *laid* against him.   indicate

CHAPTER 26

THEN A-grip'pa said to Paul, You are permitted to speak for yourself. Then Paul stretched forth the hand, and answered for himself:

2 I think myself happy, king A-grip'pa, because I shall answer for myself this day before you touching all the things whereof I am accused of the Jews:

3 Especially *because I know* you to be expert in all customs and questions which are among the Jews: wherefore I <u>beseech</u> you to hear me patiently.   ask

4 My manner of life from my youth, which was at the first among mine own nation at Je-ru'sa-lem, know all the Jews;

5 Which knew me from the beginning, if they would testify, that after the most strict sect of our religion I lived a Phar'i-see.

6 And now I stand and am judged for the hope of the promise made of God to our fathers:

7 To which *promise* our twelve tribes, instantly serving *God* day and night, hope to come. For which hope's sake, king A-grip'pa, I am accused of the Jews.

8 Why should it be thought a thing

incredible with you, that God should raise the dead?

9 I <u>verily</u> thought with myself, that I ought to do many things <u>contrary</u> to the name of Je'sus of Naz'a-reth. truly - hostile

10 Which thing I also did in Je-ru'sa-lem: and many of the saints did I shut up in prison, having received authority from the chief priests; and when they were put to death, I gave my voice against *them*.

11 And I punished them oft in every synagogue, and <u>compelled</u> *them* to blaspheme; and being exceedingly mad against them, I persecuted *them* even to <u>strange</u> cities.   forced - foreign

12 Whereupon as I went to Da-mas'cus with authority and commission from the chief priests,

13 At midday, O king, I saw in the way a light from heaven, above the brightness of the sun, shining round about me and them which journeyed with me.

14 And when we were all fallen to the earth, I heard a voice speaking to me, and saying in the He'brew <u>tongue</u>, Saul, Saul, why persecute you Me? *it is* hard for you to kick against the <u>pricks</u>.   language - goads

15 And I said, Who are You, Lord? And He said, I am Je'sus whom you persecute.

16 But rise, and stand upon your feet: for I have appeared to you for this purpose, to make you a minister and a witness both of these things which you have seen, and of those things in the which I will appear to you;

17 Delivering you from the people, and *from* the Gen'tiles, to whom now I send you,

18 To open their eyes, *and* to turn *them* from darkness to light, and *from* the power of Sa'tan to God, that they may receive forgiveness of sins, and inheritance among them which are <u>sanctified</u> by faith that is in Me.   ISA. 42:7 set apart

19 Whereupon, O king A-grip'pa, I was not disobedient to the heavenly vision:

20 But showed first to them of Da-mas'cus, and at Je-ru'sa-lem, and throughout all the coasts of Ju-dae'a, and *then* to the Gen'tiles, that they should repent and turn to God, and do works <u>meet</u> for repentance.   fit

21 For these causes the Jews caught me in the temple, and went about to kill *me*.

22 Having therefore obtained help of God, I continue to this day, <u>witnessing</u> both to small and great, saying none other things than those which the prophets and Mo'ses did say should come: talking

23 That Christ should suffer, *and* that He should be the first that should rise from the dead, and should show light to the people, and to the Gen'tiles.

24 And as he thus spoke for himself, Fes'tus said with a loud voice, Paul, you are beside yourself; much learning does make you mad.

25 But he said, I am not mad, most <u>noble</u> Fes'tus; but speak forth the words of truth and soberness.   excellent

26 For the king know of these things, before whom also I speak freely: for I am persuaded that none of these

things are hidden from him; for this thing was not done in a corner.

27 King A-grip'pa, believe you the prophets? I know that you believe.

28 Then A-grip'pa said to Paul, Almost you persuade me to be a Chris'tian.

29 And Paul said, I would to God, that not only you, but also all that hear me this day, were both almost, and altogether such as I am, except these bonds.

30 And when he had thus spoken, the king rose up, and the governor, and Ber-ni'ce, and they that sat with them:

31 And when they were gone aside, they talked between themselves, saying, This man does nothing worthy of death or of bonds.

32 Then said A-grip'pa to Fes'tus, This man might have been set at liberty, if he had not appealed to Cae'sar.

CHAPTER 27

AND when it was determined that we should sail into It'a-ly, they delivered Paul and certain other prisoners to *one* named Ju'lius, a centurion of Au-gus'tus' band.

2 And entering into a ship of Ad-ra-myt'ti-um, we launched, meaning to sail by the coasts of A'sia; *one* Ar-is-tar'chus, a Mac-e-do'ni-an of Thes-sa-lo-ni'ca, being with us. set sail

3 And the next *day* we touched at Si'don. And Ju'lius courteously entreated Paul, and gave *him* liberty to go to his friends to refresh himself.

4 And when we had launched from there, we sailed under Cy'prus, because the winds were contrary. set sail

5 And when we had sailed over the sea of Ci-li'cia and Pam-phyl'i-a, we came to My'ra, *a city* of Ly'cia.

6 And there the centurion found a ship of Al-ex-an'dri-a sailing into It'a-ly; and he put us therein.

7 And when we had sailed slowly many days, and scarce were come over against Cni'dus, the wind not allowing us, we sailed under Crete, over against Sal-mo'ne; near

8 And, hardly passing it, came to a place which is called The Fair Havens; near whereto was the city *of* La-se'a.

9 Now when much time was spent, and when sailing was now dangerous, because the fast was now already past, Paul admonished *them,*

10 And said to them, Sirs, I perceive that this voyage will be with hurt and much damage, not only of the lading and ship, but also of our lives. danger - cargo

11 Nevertheless the centurion believed the master and the owner of the ship, more than those things which were spoken by Paul.

12 And because the haven was not commodious to winter in, the more part advised to depart from there also, if by any means they might attain to Phe-ni'ce, *and there* to winter; *which is* an haven of Crete, and lie toward the south west and north west. suitable - majority - harbor

13 And when the south wind blew

softly, supposing that they had ob-tained *their* purpose, <u>loosing</u> there, they sailed close by Crete.   lifting anchor

14 But not long after there arose against it a tempestuous wind, called Eu-roc'ly-don.

15 And when the ship was caught, and could not bear up into the wind, we let *her* drive.

16 And running <u>under</u> a certain island which is called Clau'da, we had much work to <u>come by</u> the boat: near - secure

17 Which when they had taken up, they used helps, undergirding the ship; and, fearing less they should fall into the quicksands, struck sail, and so were driven.

18 And we being exceedingly tossed with a tempest, the next *day* they <u>lightened</u> the ship; i.e., cargo overboard

19 And the third *day* we cast out with our own hands the tackling of the ship.

20 And when neither sun nor stars in many days appeared, and no small tempest lay on *us*, all hope that we should be saved was then <u>taken away</u>.   abandoned

21 But after long abstinence Paul stood forth in the midst of them, and said, Sirs, you should have hearkened to me, and not have loosed from Crete, and to have gained this harm and loss.

22 And now I <u>exhort</u> you to be of good cheer: for there shall be no loss of *any man's* life among you, but of the ship.   urge

23 For there stood by me this night the <u>angel</u> of God, whose I am, and whom I serve,   messenger

24 Saying, Fear not, Paul; you must be brought before Cae'sar: and, lo, God has given you all them that sail with you.

25 Wherefore, sirs, be of good cheer: for I believe God, that it shall be even as it was told me.

26 However we must be cast upon a certain island.

27 But when the fourteenth night was come, as we were driven <u>up and down</u> in A'dri-a, about midnight the shipmen <u>deemed</u> that they drew near to some <u>country</u>;   back and forth - knew - land

28 And sounded, and found *it* twenty fathoms: and when they had gone a little further, they sounded again, and found *it* fifteen fathoms.

29 Then fearing less we should have fallen upon rocks, they cast four anchors out of the stern, and wished for the day.

30 And as the shipmen were about to flee out of the ship, when they had let down the boat into the sea, under <u>color</u> as though they would have cast anchors out of the foreship,   pretense

31 Paul said to the centurion and to the soldiers, Except these <u>abide</u> in the ship, you cannot be saved.   stay

32 Then the soldiers cut off the ropes of the boat, and let her fall off.

33 And while the day was coming on, Paul <u>besought</u> *them* all to take <u>meat</u>, saying, This day is the fourteenth day that you have <u>tarried</u> and continued fasting, having taken nothing.   begged - food - waited

34 Wherefore I pray you to take *some* <u>meat</u>: for this is for your health: for

there shall not an hair fall from the head of any of you.

35 And when he had thus spoken, he took bread, and gave thanks to God in presence of them all: and when he had broken *it*, he began to eat.

36 Then were they all of good cheer, and they also took *some* meat. food

37 And we were in all in the ship two hundred threescore and sixteen souls. 276

38 And when they had eaten enough, they lightened the ship, and cast out the wheat into the sea.

39 And when it was day, they knew not the land: but they discovered a certain creek with a shore, into the which they were minded, if it were possible, to thrust in the ship. did not recognize - bay

40 And when they had taken up the anchors, they committed *themselves* to the sea, and loosed the rudder bands, and hoised up the mainsail to the wind, and made toward shore.

41 And falling into a placc where two seas met, they ran the ship aground; and the forepart stuck fast, and remained unmoveable, but the hinder part was broken with the violence of the waves.

42 And the soldiers' counsel was to kill the prisoners, less any of them should swim out, and escape. plan

43 But the centurion, willing to save Paul, kept them from *their* purpose; and commanded that they which could swim should cast *themselves* first *into the sea*, and get to land:

44 And the rest, some on boards, and some on *broken pieces* of the ship. And so it came to pass, that they escaped all safe to land.

CHAPTER 28

AND when they were escaped, then they knew that the island was called Mel'i-ta. Malta

2 And the barbarous people showed us no little kindness: for they kindled a fire, and received us every one, because of the present rain, and because of the cold.

3 And when Paul had gathered a bundle of sticks, and laid *them* on the fire, there came a viper out of the heat, and fastened on his hand.

4 And when the barbarians saw the *venomous* beast hang on his hand, they said among themselves, No doubt this man is a murderer, whom, though he has escapcd the sea, yet vengeance allows not to live. justice

5 And hc shook off the beast into the fire, and felt no harm.

6 However they looked when he should have swollen, or fallen down dead suddenly: but after they had looked a great while, and saw no harm come to him, they changed their minds, and said that he was a god.

7 In the same quarters were possessions of the chief man of the island, whose name was Pub'li-us; who received us, and lodged us three days courteously.

8 And it came to pass, that the father of Pub'li-us lay sick of a fever and of a bloody flux: to whom Paul entered in, and prayed, and laid his hands on him, and healed him. dysentery

9 So when this was done, others also, which had diseases in the island, came, and were healed:

10 Who also honored us with many honors; and when we departed, they laded *us* with such things as were necessary.

11 And after three months we departed in a ship of Al-ex-an'dri-a, which had wintered in the isle, whose sign was Cas'tor and Pol'lux.

12 And landing at Syr'a-cuse, we tarried *there* three days.   stayed

13 And from there we brought a compass, and came to Rhe'gi-um: and after one day the south wind blew, and we came the next day to Pu-te'o-li: sailed around

14 There we found brethren, and were desired to tarry with them seven days: and so we went toward Rome.   stay

15 And from there, when the brethren heard of us, they came to meet us as far as Ap'pi-i forum, and the three taverns: whom when Paul saw, he thanked God, and took courage.

16 And when we came to Rome, the centurion delivered the prisoners to the captain of the guard: but Paul was allowed to dwell by himself with a soldier that kept him.

17 And it came to pass, that after three days Paul called the chief of the Jews together: and when they were come together, he said to them, Men *and* brethren, though I have committed nothing against the people, or customs of our fathers, yet was I delivered prisoner from Je-ru'sa-lem into the hands of the Ro'mans.

18 Who, when they had examined me, would have let *me* go, because there was no cause of death in me.

19 But when the Jews spoke against *it*, I was constrained to appeal to Cae'sar; not that I had ought to accuse my nation of.   forced - anything

20 For this cause therefore have I called for you, to see *you*, and to speak with *you*: because that for the hope of Is'ra-el I am bound with this chain.

21 And they said to him, We neither received letters out of Ju-dae'a concerning you, neither any of the brethren that came showed or spoke any harm of you.

22 But we desire to hear of you what you think: for as concerning this sect, we know that every where it is spoken against.

23 And when they had appointed him a day, there came many to him into *his* lodging; to whom he expounded and testified the kingdom of God, persuading them concerning Je'sus, both out of the law of Mo'ses, and *out of* the prophets, from morning till evening.

24 And some believed the things which were spoken, and some believed not.

25 And when they agreed not among themselves, they departed, after that Paul had spoken one word, Well spoke the Ho'ly Ghost by I-sa'iah the prophet to our fathers,   Spirit   G5   250

26 Saying, Go to this people, and say, Hearing you shall hear, and shall not understand; and seeing you shall see, and not perceive: ISA. 6:9

27 For the heart of this people is

waxed gross, and their ears are dull of hearing, and their eyes have they closed; less they should see with *their* eyes, and hear with *their* ears, and understand with *their* heart, and should be <u>converted</u>, and I should heal them.

turned

28 Be it known therefore to you, that the salvation of God is sent to the Gen'tiles, and *that* they will hear it.

29 And when he had said these words, the Jews departed and had great <u>reasoning</u> amoung themselves.

disputes

30 And Paul dwelt two whole years in his own hired house, and <u>received</u> all that came in to him,

welcomed

31 Preaching the kingdom of God and teaching those things which concern the Lord Je'sus Christ with all confidence, no man forbidding him.

ROMANS

OUTLINE

SURVEY

After a proper salutation and thanksgiving, the Apostle Paul, appealing to a text of the Old Testament (Hab. 2.4), introduces the theme from his epistle as justification by faith

The opening three chapters establish the first main point: that all men are sinners. Paul begins with a description of the gross idolatry and immorality of the Gentiles; yet by reason of the display of God's power in nature and the witness of their own consciences that "they which commit such things are worthy of death," the Gentiles are held responsible.

At the same time the Jews, though they are the favored recipients of God's oracles, are equally sinners. The Gentiles sinned without the law—they shall perish without the law; the Jews sinned under the law—they shall be judged by the law. "For not the hearers of the law are just before God, but the doers of the law shall be justified" (2.13).

However, there are no doers of the law, either Jew or Gentile; for "there is none righteous, no, not one" (3.10). "Therefore by the deeds of the law there shall no flesh be justified in his sight" (3.20).

If, then, anyone is to be justified, God himself must graciously supply the righteousness needed for

acquittal. This is accomplished in virtue of Christ's propitiatory sacrifice. His shed blood satisfies the justice of His Father, so that God may be *just* as well as *justifier* of him who has faith in Jesus.

Chapter 4 with Abraham as the chief example further explains how God imputes righteousness apart from works. Then chapter 5 compares Adam and Christ. All whom Adam represented were made sinners by his single offense; all who are in Christ are made righteous by His obedience.

In reply to the accusation that justification by faith encourages sin—"shall we continue in sin that grace may abound?" (6.1)—Paul explains that the sincere believer has come to Christ in order to escape sin. Justification produces sanctification; and the sanctifying struggle itself (7.14-25) is evidence that we have escaped condemnation. Therefore, depending on predestination (8.29) and God's immutable love (8.39), we can have assurance of salvation.

Justification by faith, the rejection of the Jews, and the inclusion of the Gentiles are not inconsistent with God's promises to Israel. The promises were made, not to the physical, but to the spiritual descendants of Abraham. God chose Isaac and rejected Ishmael; God chose Jacob and rejected Esau. These choices and exclusions are inherent in the promises themselves. God's choice is sovereign. He is like a potter who makes vessels to suit his purpose.

However, there will come a day when the Jews as a whole, who now have been cut out of the Church in order to make place for the Gentiles, will be grafted back in again. And if the casting away of the Jews has effected the reconciling of the world, their future reception will be like life from the dead (11.15).

Because of these divine mercies, each Christian should fulfil his particular function in the Church with diligence and simplicity. Similarly in the State each believer should be a good citizen. And in social affairs the more mature Christian must accommodate himself to the weaker brethren who are still held by superstitious scruples.

Finally Paul expresses his hope of visiting the Romans on his way to Spain and concludes the letter with a score of personal greetings.

AUTHOR

The Epistle to the Romans, the longest, the most systematic, and the most profound of all the epistles, and perhaps the most important book in the Bible, was written by the Apostle Paul (1.1, 5). He was in Corinth at the time (15.26; 16.1, 2). The careful composition of the letter suggests that after some tempestuous experiences there he had a period of leisure before he took relief money to the saints in Jerusalem. This puts the date early in A.D. 58. Unlike the other epistles, Romans was written to a church he had never visited (1.10, 11, 15). All the ingenuity of destructive criticism has never been able to impugn the authenticity of the epistle.

G.H.C.

THE LETTER OF PAUL TO THE
ROMANS

The Systematic Theology
Manual of the NT

CHAPTER 1

PAUL, a servant of Je'sus Christ, called *to be* an apostle, separated to the gospel of God,

2 (Which He had promised before by His prophets in the Holy Scriptures,)

3 Concerning His Son Je'sus Christ our Lord, which was made of the seed of Da'vid according to the flesh;   descendants

4 And declared *to be* the Son of God with power, according to the Spirit of holiness, by the resurrection from the dead:

5 By whom we have received grace and apostleship, for obedience to the faith among all nations, for His name:

6 Among whom are you also the called of Je'sus Christ: chosen

7 To all that be in Rome, beloved of God, called *to be* saints: Grace to you and peace from God our Father, and the Lord Je'sus Christ.   believers

8 First, I thank my God through Je'sus Christ for you all, that your faith is spoken of throughout the whole world.

9 For God is my witness, whom I serve with my spirit in the gospel of His Son, that without ceasing I make mention of you always in my prayers;

10 Making request, if by any means now at length I might have a prosperous journey by the will of God to come to you.

11 For I long to see you, that I may impart to you some spiritual gift, to the end you may be established;   give - strengthened

12 That is, that I may be comforted together with you by the mutual faith both of you and me.

13 Now I would not have you ignorant, brethren, that oftentimes I purposed to come to you, (but was prevented,) that I might have some fruit among you also, even as among other Gen'tiles.

14 I am debtor both to the Greeks, and to the Bar-ba'ri-ans; both to the wise, and to the unwise.   under obligation

15 So, as much as in me is, I am ready to preach the gospel to you that are at Rome also.

16 For I am not ashamed of the gospel of Christ: for it is the power of God to salvation to every one that believes; to the Jew first, and also to the Greek.   HAB. 2:4

17 For therein is the righteousness of God revealed from faith to faith: as it is written, The just shall live by faith.

18 For the wrath of God is revealed from heaven against all ungodliness and unrighteousness of men, who hold the truth in unrighteousness;   suppress

19 Because that which may be known of God is manifest in them; for God has showed *it* to them.   known to

20 For the invisible things of Him from the creation of the world are

clearly seen, clearly seen being understood by the things that are made, *even* His eternal power and Godhead; so that they are without excuse:

21 Because that, when they knew God, they glorified *Him* not as God, neither were thankful; but became vain in their imaginations, and their foolish heart was darkened.

honored - conceited

22 Professing themselves to be wise, they became fools,

ISA. 5:21

23 And changed the glory of the uncorruptible God into an image made like to corruptible man, and to birds, and fourfooted beasts, and creeping things.

PSA. 106:20

24 Wherefore God also gave them up to uncleanness through the lusts of their own hearts, to dishonor their own bodies between themselves:

EZE. 20:25

25 Who changed the truth of God into a lie, and worshiped and served the creature more than the Creator, who is blessed for ever. Amen.

rather

26 For this cause God gave them up to vile affections: for even their women did change the natural use into that which is against nature:

degrading passions

27 And likewise also the men, leaving the natural use of the woman, burned in their lust one toward another; men with men working that which is unseemly, and receiving in themselves that recompence of their error which was meet.

penalty - fit

28 And even as they did not like to retain God in *their* knowledge, God gave them over to a reprobate mind, to do those things which are not convenient;

29 Being filled with all unrighteousness, fornication, wickedness, covetousness, maliciousness; full of envy, murder, debate, deceit, malignity; whisperers

strife - malice

30 Backbiters, haters of God, despiteful, proud, boasters, inventors of evil things, disobedient to parents,

insolent

31 Without understanding, covenant-breakers, without natural affection, implacable, unmerciful:

agreement - unloving

32 Who knowing the judgment of God, that they which commit such things are worthy of death, not only do the same, but have pleasure in them that do them.

CHAPTER 2

THEREFORE you are inexcusable, O man, whosoever you are that judge: for wherein you judge another, you condem yourself; for you that judge do the same things.

2 But we are sure that the judgment of God is according to truth against them which commit such things.

3 And think you this, O man, that judge them which do such things, and do the same, that you shall escape the judgment of God?

4 Or despise you the riches of His goodness and forbearance and longsuffering; not knowing that the goodness of God leads you to repentance?

patience

5 But after your hardness and impenitent heart treasure up to yourself

wrath against the day of wrath and revelation of the righteous judgment of God;

6 Who will render to every man according to his deeds: PSA. 62:12 JER. 17:10 ECC. 12:14

7 To them who by patient continuance in well doing seek for glory and honor and immortality, eternal life:

8 But to them that are <u>contentious</u>, and do not obey the truth, but obey unrighteousness, indignation and wrath,   selfish

9 <u>Tribulation</u> and anguish, upon every soul of man that does evil, of the Jew first, and also of the Gen'tile;   trouble

10 But glory, honor, and peace, to every man that works good, to the Jew first, and also to the Gen'tile:

11 For there is no respect of persons with God.   DEU. 10:17

12 For as many as have sinned without law shall also perish without law: and as many as have sinned in the law shall be judged by the law;

13 (For not the hearers of the law *are* just before God, but the doers of the law shall be justified.

14 For when the Gen'tiles, which have not the law, do by nature the things contained in the law, these, having not the law, are a law to themselves:

15 <u>Which</u> show the work of the law written in their hearts, their conscience also bearing witness, and *their* thoughts <u>the mean</u> while accusing or else excusing one another;)   Who - bearing witness

16 In the day when God shall judge the secrets of men by Je'sus Christ according to my gospel.   ECC. 12:14

17 Behold, you are called a Jew, and <u>rest</u> in the law, and make your boast of God,   rely on

18 And know *His* will, and approve the things that are more excellent, being instructed out of the law;

19 And are confident that you yourself are a guide of the blind, a light of them which are in darkness,

20 An instructor of the foolish, a teacher of babes, which have the form of knowledge and of the truth in the law.

21 You therefore which teach another, teach you not yourself? you that preaches a man should not steal, do you steal?

22 You that say a man should not commit adultery, do you commit adultery? you that <u>abhor</u> idols, do you <u>commit sacrilege</u>?   detests - rob temples

23 You that make your boast of the law, through breaking the law dishonor you God?

24 For the name of God is blasphemed among the Gen'tiles through you, as it is written.   ISA. 52:5 EZE. 36:22

25 For circumcision <u>verily</u> profits, if you keep the law: but if you be a breaker of the law, your circumcision is made uncircumcision.   JER. 9:25 truly

26 Therefore if the uncircumcision keep the <u>righteousness</u> of the law, shall not his uncircumcision be counted for circumcision? requirements

27 And shall not uncircumcision which is by nature, if it fulfill the law, judge you, who by the letter and circumcision do transgress the law?

28 For he is not a Jew, which is one outwardly; neither *is that* circumcision, which is outward in the flesh: 29 But he *is* a Jew, which is one inwardly; and circumcision *is that* of the heart, in the spirit, *and* not in the letter; whose praise *is* not of men, but of God.

CHAPTER 3

WHAT advantage then has the Jew? or what profit *is there* of circumcision?

2 Much every way: chiefly, because that to them were committed the oracles of God. PS. 147:19 words

3 For what if some did not believe? shall their unbelief make the faith of God without effect? faithfulness

4 God forbid: yea, let God be true, but every man a liar; as it is written, That You might be justified in Your sayings, and might overcome when You are judged. PS. 51:4 PS. 116:11

5 But if our unrighteousness commend the righteousness of God, what shall we say? *Is* God unrighteous who takes vengeance? (I speak as a man)

6 God forbid: for then how shall God judge the world?

7 For if the truth of God has more abounded through my lie to His glory; why yet am I also judged as a sinner?

8 And not *rather*, (as we be slanderously reported, and as some affirm that we say,) Let us do evil, that good may come? whose damnation is just.

9 What then? are we better *than they*? No, in no wise: for we have before proved both Jews and Gen'tiles, that they are all under sin;

10 As it is written, There is none righteous, no, not one: PS. 5:9 ISA 59:7-8

11 There is none that understands, there is none that seeks after God.

12 They are all gone out of the way, they are together become unprofitable; there is none that does good, no, not one. PS. 14:3

13 Their throat *is* an open sepulcher; with their tongues they have used deceit; the poison of asps *is* under their lips: PSA. 5:9 PSA. 140:3 grave

14 Whose mouth *is* full of cursing and bitterness: PS. 10:7

15 Their feet *are* swift to shed blood:

16 Destruction and misery *are* in their ways: ISA. 59:7

17 And the way of peace have they not known:

18 There is no fear of God before their eyes. PS. 36:1 respect

19 Now we know that what things soever the law says, it says to them who are under the law: that every mouth may be stopped, and all the world may become guilty before God.

accountable

20 Therefore by the deeds of the law there shall no flesh be justified in His sight: for by the law *is* the knowledge of sin. man

21 But now the righteousness of God without the law is manifested, being witnessed by the law and the prophets;

known

22 Even the righteousness of God *which is* by faith of Je'sus Christ to all and upon all them that believe: for there is no difference: distinction

23 For all have sinned, and <u>come</u> short of the glory of God; _{fall}

24 Being justified freely by His grace through the redemption that is in Christ Je'sus:

25 Whom God has set forth *to be* a <u>propitiation</u> through faith in His blood, to declare His righteousness for the <u>remission</u> of sins that are past, through the forbearance of God;

substitution - forgiveness

26 To declare, *I say*, at this time His righteousness: that He might be just, and the justifier of him which believes in Je'sus.

27 Where *is* boasting then? It is excluded. By what law? of works? Nay: but by the law of faith.

28 Therefore we conclude that a man is justified by faith <u>without</u> the deeds of the law. _{apart from}

29 *Is He* the God of the Jews only? *is He* not also of the Gen'tiles? Yes, of the Gen'tiles also:

30 Seeing *it is* one God, which shall justify the circumcision by faith, and uncircumcision through faith.

31 Do we then <u>make void</u> the law through faith? God forbid: yea, we establish the law. _{nullify}

CHAPTER 4

WHAT shall we say then that A'bra-ham our father, as pertaining to the flesh, has found?

2 For if A'bra-ham were justified by works, he has *whereof* to glory; but not before God.

3 For what says the scripture? A'bra-ham believed God, and it was counted to him for righteousness. _{GEN. 15:6}

4 Now to him that works is the reward not reckoned of grace, but of debt.

5 But to him that works not, but believes on Him that justifies the ungodly, his faith is counted for righteousness.

6 Even as Da'vid also describes the blessedness of the man, to whom God <u>imputes</u> righteousness without works, _{transfers}

7 *Saying*, <u>Blessed</u> *are* they whose iniquities are forgiven, and whose sins are covered. _{PS. 32:1 Fortunate}

8 <u>Blessed</u> *is* the man to whom the Lord will not <u>impute</u> sin. _{count}

9 *Comes* this blessedness then upon the circumcision *only*, or upon the uncircumcision also? for we say that faith was reckoned to A'bra-ham for righteousness.

10 How was it then reckoned? when he was in circumcision, or in uncircumcision? Not in circumcision, but in uncircumcision.

11 And he received the sign of circumcision, a seal of the righteousness of the faith which *he had yet* being uncircumcised: that he might be the father of all them that believe, though they be not circumcised; that righteousness might be <u>imputed</u> to them also: _{GEN. 17:10 - transfers}

12 And the father of circumcision to them who are not of the circumcision only, but who also walk in the steps of that faith of our father A'bra-ham, which *he had* being *yet* uncircumcised.

13 For the promise, that he should be the heir of the world, *was* not to A'bra-ham, or to his seed, through the law, but through the righteousness of faith.   GEN. 17:4-6 offspring

14 For if they which are of the law *be* heirs, faith is made void, and the promise made of none effect: worthless - no

15 Because the law works wrath: for where no law is, *there is* no transgression.

16 Therefore *it is* of faith, that *it might be* by grace; to the end the promise might be sure to all the seed; not to that only which is of the law, but to that also which is of the faith of A'bra-ham; who is the father of us all,   certain - descendants

17 (As it is written, I have made you a father of many nations,) before Him whom he believed, *even* God, who *makes alive* the dead, and calls those things which be not as though they were.   GEN. 17:5

18 Who against hope believed in hope, that he might become the father of many nations; according to that which was spoken, So shall your seed be.   descendants

19 And being not weak in faith, he considered not his own body now dead, when he was about an hundred years old, neither yet the deadness of Sa'rah's womb: GEN. 17:17

20 He staggered not at the promise of God through unbelief; but was strong in faith, giving glory to God;   wavered

21 And being fully persuaded that, what He had promised, He was able also to perform.

22 And therefore it was imputed to him for righteousness.   transferred

23 Now it was not written for his sake alone, that it was imputed to him;

24 But for us also, to whom it shall be imputed, if we believe on Him that raised up Je'sus our Lord from the dead;

25 Who was delivered for our offences, and was raised again for our justification.   ISA. 53:5 put to death

CHAPTER 5

THEREFORE being justified by faith, we have peace with God through our Lord Je'sus Christ:

2 By whom also we have access by faith into this grace wherein we stand, and rejoice in hope of the glory of God.

3 And not only *so*, but we glory in tribulations also: knowing that tribulation works patience;   troubles

4 And patience, experience; and experience, hope:

5 And hope makes not ashamed; because the love of God is shed abroad in our hearts by the Ho'ly Ghost which is given to us.   PS. 119:116

6 For when we were yet without strength, in due time Christ died for the ungodly.   still

7 For scarcely for a righteous man will one die: yet perhaps for a good man some would even dare to die.

8 But God commends His love toward us, in that, while we were yet sinners, Christ died for us.

9 Much more then, being now justi-

fied by His blood, we shall be saved from wrath through Him.

10 For if, when we were enemies, we were reconciled to God by the death of His Son, much more, being reconciled, we shall be saved by His life.

11 And not only *so*, but we also joy in God through our Lord Je'sus Christ, by whom we have now received the <u>atonement.</u>   reconciliation

12 Wherefore, as by <u>one man</u> sin entered into the world, and death by sin; and so death passed upon all men, for that all have sinned: i.e., Adam

13 (For until the law sin was in the world: but sin is not <u>imputed</u> when there is no law.   transferred

14 Nevertheless death reigned from Ad'am to Mo'ses, even over them that had not sinned after the <u>simili-tude</u> of Ad'am's transgression, who is the figure of Him that was to come.likeness

15 But not as the offence, so also *is* the free gift. For if through the offence of one many be dead, much more the grace of God, and the gift by grace, *which is* by one man, Je'-sus Christ, has abounded to many.

16 And not as *it was* by one that sinned, *so is* the gift: for the judgment *was* by one to condemnation, but the free gift *is* of many offences to justification.

17 For if by one man's offence death reigned by one; much more they which receive abundance of grace and of the gift of righteousness shall reign in life by One, Je'sus Christ.)

18 Therefore as by the offence of one judgment came upon all men to condemnation; even so by the righteousness of One *the free gift came* upon all men to justification of life.

19 For as by <u>one man's</u> disobedience many were made sinners, so by the obedience of One shall many be made righteous.   i.e., Adam

20 Moreover the law entered, that the offence might abound. But where sin abounded, grace did much more abound:

21 That as sin has reigned to death, even so might grace reign through righteousness to eternal life by Je'sus Christ our Lord.

CHAPTER 6

WHAT shall we say then? Shall we continue in sin, that grace may abound?

2 God forbid. How shall we, that are dead to sin, live any longer therein?

3 Know you not, that so many of us as were baptized into Je'sus Christ <u>were</u> baptized into His death?   have been

4 Therefore we are buried with Him by baptism into death: that like as Christ was raised up from the dead by the glory of the Father, even so we also should walk in newness of life.

5 For if we have been planted together in the likeness of His death, we shall be also *in the likeness* of *His* resurrection:

6 Knowing this, that our old man is crucified with *Him*, that the body of sin might be destroyed, that hereafter we should not serve sin.

7 For he that is dead is freed from sin.

8 Now if we be dead with Christ, we believe that we shall also live with Him:

9 Knowing that Christ being raised from the dead dies no more; death has no more <u>dominion</u> over Him.   control

10 For in that He died, He died to sin once: but in that He lives, He lives to God.

11 Likewise reckon you also yourselves to be dead indeed to sin, but alive to God through Je'sus Christ our Lord.

12 Let not sin therefore <u>reign</u> in your mortal body, that you should obey it in the <u>lusts</u> thereof.   PSA. 119:133 rule - evil desires

13 Neither yield you your members *as* instruments of unrighteousness to sin: but yield yourselves to God, as those that are alive from the dead, and your members *as* instruments of righteousness to God.

14 For sin shall not have <u>dominion</u> over you: for you are not under the law, but under grace.   control

15 What then? shall we sin, because we are not under the law, but under grace? God forbid.

16 Know you not, that to whom you yield yourselves servants to obey, his servants you are to whom you obey; whether of sin to death, or of obedience to righteousness?

17 But God be thanked, that you were the servants of sin, but you have obeyed from the heart that form of <u>doctrine</u> which was delivered you.   teachings

18 Being then made free from sin, you became the servants of righteousness.

19 I speak after the manner of men because of the infirmity of your flesh:

for as you have yielded your <u>members</u> servants to uncleanness and to iniquity to iniquity; even so now yield your <u>members</u> servants to righteousness to <u>holiness</u>.   body - sanctification

20 For when you were the servants of sin, you were free from righteousness.

21 What fruit had you then in those things whereof you are now ashamed? for the end of those things *is* death.

22 But now being made free from sin, and become servants to God, you have your fruit to holiness, and the end everlasting life.   LEV. 25:42

23 For the <u>wages</u> of sin *is* <u>death</u>; but the gift of God *is* eternal <u>life</u> through Je'sus Christ our Lord.

EZE. 18:4 cost - separation (from God) - union (with God)

CHAPTER 7

KNOW you not, brethren, (for I speak to them that know the law,) how that the law has <u>dominion</u> over a man as long as he lives?   control

2 For the woman which has an husband is bound by the law to *her* husband so long as he lives; but if the husband be dead, she is <u>loosed</u> from the law of *her* husband.   released

3 So then if, while *her* husband lives, she be <u>married</u> to another man, she shall be called an adulteress: but if her husband be dead, she is free from that law; so that she is no adulteress, though she be <u>married</u> to another man.   joined

4 Wherefore, my brethren, you also are become dead to the law by the body of Christ; that you should be <u>married</u> to an-

other, *even* to Him who is raised from the dead, that we should bring forth fruit to God.

5 For when we were in the flesh, the <u>motions</u> of sins, which were by the law, did work in our <u>members</u> to bring forth fruit to death.   <small>desire - body</small>

6 But now we are delivered from the law, that being dead wherein we were held; that we should serve in newness of spirit, and not *in* the oldness of the letter.

7 What shall we say then? *Is* the law sin? God forbid. Nay, I had not known sin, but by the law: for I had not known <u>lust,</u> except the law had said, You shall not covet.   <small>EX. 20:17 DEU. 5:21 evil desires</small>

8 But sin, taking <u>occasion</u> by the commandment, <u>wrought</u> in me all manner of <u>concupiscence</u>. For <u>without</u> the law sin *was* dead.

<small>opportunity - worked - sin - apart from</small>

9 For I was alive without the law once: but when the commandment came, sin revived, and I died.

10 And the commandment, which *was* ordained to life, I found *to be* to death.

11 For sin, taking <u>occasion</u> by the commandment, deceived me, and by it slew *me.*

12 Wherefore the law *is* holy, and the commandment holy, and just, and good.

13 Was then that which is good made death to me? God forbid. But sin, that it might appear sin, working death in me by that which is good; that sin by the commandment might become exceeding sinful.

14 For we know that the law is spiritual: but I am <u>carnal,</u> sold under sin.   <small>worldly</small>

15 For that which I do I <u>allow</u> not: for what I <u>would,</u> that do I not; but what I <u>hate,</u> that do I.   <small>approve - want - dislike</small>

16 If then I do that which I would not, I <u>consent</u> to the law that *it is* good.   <small>agree</small>

17 Now then it is no more I that do it, but sin that dwells in me.

18 For I know that in me (that is, in my flesh,) dwells no good thing: for to will is present with me; but *how* to perform that which is good I find not.

19 For the good that I <u>would</u> I do not: but the evil which I <u>would</u> not, that I do.   <small>wish</small>

20 Now if I do that I <u>would</u> not, it is no more I that do it, but sin that dwells in me.

21 I find then a law, that, when I would do good, evil is present with me.

22 For I delight in the law of God after the inward man: <small>PS. 1:2</small>

23 But I see another law in my members, warring against the law of my mind, and bringing me into captivity to the law of sin which is in my members.

24 O wretched man that I am! who shall deliver me from the body of this death?

25 I thank God through Je'sus Christ our Lord. So then with the mind I myself serve the law of God; but with the flesh the law of sin.

CHAPTER 8

THERE *is* therefore now no condemnation to them which are in Christ

Je'sus, who walk not after the flesh, but after the Spirit.

2 For the law of the Spirit of life in Christ Je'sus has made me free from the law of sin and death.

3 For what the law could not do, in that it was weak through the flesh, God sending His own Son in the likeness of sinful flesh, and <u>for</u> sin, condemned sin in the flesh: *as a sacrifice for*

4 That the <u>righteousness</u> of the law might be fulfilled in us, who walk not after the flesh, but after the Spirit. *requirement*

5 For they that are after the flesh do mind the things of the flesh; but they that are after the Spirit the things of the Spirit.

6 For to be <u>carnally</u> minded *is* death; but to be spiritually minded *is* life and peace. *worldly*

7 Because the <u>carnal</u> mind *is* <u>enmity</u> against God: for it is not subject to the law of God, neither indeed can be. *hostile*

8 So then they that are <u>in the flesh</u> cannot please God. *controlled by the world*

9 But you are not in the flesh, but in the Spirit, if so be that the Spirit of God dwell in you. Now if any man have not the Spirit of Christ, he is none of His.

10 And if Christ *be* in you, the body *is* dead because of sin; but the Spirit *is* life because of righteousness.

11 But if the Spirit of Him that raised up Je'sus from the dead dwell in you, He that raised up Christ from the dead shall also <u>quicken your mortal</u> bodies by His Spirit that dwells in you. *make alive your*

12 Therefore, brethren, we are <u>debtors</u>, not to the flesh, to live after the flesh. *under obligation*

13 For if you live after the flesh, you shall die: but if you through the Spirit do <u>mortify</u> the deeds of the body, you shall live. *reject*

14 For as many as are led by the Spirit of God, they are the sons of God.

15 For you have not received the spirit of bondage again to fear; but you have received the Spirit of adoption, whereby we cry, Ab'ba, Father.

16 The Spirit Itself bears witness with our spirit, that we are the children of God:

17 And if children, then heirs; heirs of God, and joint-heirs with Christ; if so be that we suffer with *Him*, that we may be also glorified together.

18 For I reckon that the sufferings of this present time *are* not worthy *to be compared* with the glory which shall be revealed in us.

19 For the <u>earnest expectation</u> of the creature waits for the <u>manifestation</u> of the sons of God. *anxious longing - revelation*

20 For the creature was made subject to vanity, not willingly, but by reason of Him who has subjected *the same* in hope, *ECC. 1:2*

21 Because the creature itself also shall be delivered from the bondage of <u>corruption</u> into the glorious liberty of the children of God. *deadly decay*

22 For we know that the whole creation groans and <u>travails</u> in pain together until now. *suffers*

23 And not only *they*, but ourselves also, which have the firstfruits of the

Spirit, even we ourselves groan inside ourselves, waiting for the adoption, *to wit*, the redemption of our body.

24 For we are saved by hope: but hope that is seen is not hope: for what a man sees, why does he yet hope for? HEB. 11:1

25 But if we hope for that we see not, *then* do we with patience wait for *it*.

26 Likewise the Spirit also helps our infirmities: for we know not what we should pray for as we ought: but the Spirit Itself makes intercession for us with groanings which cannot be uttered.

27 And He that searches the hearts knows what *is* the mind of the Spirit, because He makes intercession for the saints according to *the will of* God. PS. 139:1-2 believers

28 And we know that all things work together for good to them that love God, to them who are the called according to *His* purpose. EPH. 2:8

29 For whom He did foreknow, He also did predestinate *to be* conformed to the image of His Son, that He might be the firstborn among many brethren.

30 Moreover whom He did predestinate, them He also called: and whom He called, them He also justified: and whom He justified, them He also glorified.

31 What shall we then say to these things? If God *be* for us, who *can be* against us? PS. 118:6 2 KGS 6:16

32 He that spared not His own Son, but delivered Him up for us all, how shall He not with Him also freely give us all things?

33 Who shall lay any thing to the charge of God's elect? *It is* God that justifies.

34 Who *is* he that condemns? *It is* Christ that died, yea rather, that is risen again, who is even at the right hand of God, who also makes intercession for us.

35 Who shall separate us from the love of Christ? *shall* tribulation, or distress, or persecution, or famine, or nakedness, or peril, or sword? trouble - war

36 As it is written, For Your sake we are killed all the day long; we are accounted as sheep for the slaughter. PS. 42:22

37 Nay, in all these things we are more than conquerors through Him that loved us.

38 For I am persuaded, that neither death, nor life, nor angels, nor principalities, nor powers, nor things present, nor things to come, convinced

39 Nor height, nor depth, nor any other creature, shall be able to separate us from the love of God, which is in Christ Je'sus our Lord.

CHAPTER 9

I SAY the truth in Christ, I lie not, my conscience also bearing me witness in the Ho'ly Ghost, Spirit

2 That I have great heaviness and continual sorrow in my heart.

3 For I could wish that myself were accursed from Christ for my brethren, my kinsmen according to the flesh: separated

4 Who are Is'ra-el-ites; to whom *pertains* the adoption, and the glory, and the covenants, and the giving of the

law, and the service *of God*, and the promises; agreements

5 Whose *are* the fathers, and of whom as concerning the flesh Christ *came*, who is over all, God blessed for ever. Amen.

6 Not as though the word of God has taken none effect. For they *are* not all Is'ra-el, which are of Is'ra-el:

7 Neither, because they are the seed of A'bra-ham, *are they* all children: but, In I'saac shall your seed be called. GEN. 21:12 offspring

8 That is, They which are the children of the flesh, these *are* not the children of God: but the children of the promise are counted for the seed. regarded

9 For this *is* the word of promise, At this time will I come, and Sa'rah shall have a son. GEN. 18:10

10 And not only *this*; but when Re-bec'ca also had conceived by one, *even* by our father I'saac; GEN. 25:21

11 (For *the children* being not yet born, neither having done any good or evil, that the purpose of God according to election might stand, not of works, but of Him that calls;)

12 It was said to her, The elder shall serve the younger. GEN. 25:23

13 As it is written, Ja'cob have I loved, but E'sau have I hated. MAL. 1:3 loved less

14 What shall we say then? *Is there* unrighteousness with God? God forbid.

15 For He says to Mo'ses, I will have mercy on whom I will have mercy, and I will have compassion on whom I will have compassion. EX. 33:19 mercy

16 So then *it is* not of him that wills, nor of him that runs, but of God that shows mercy.

17 For the scripture says to Pha'raoh, Even for this same purpose have I raised you up, that I might show My power in you, and that My name might be declared throughout all the earth. EX. 9:16

18 Therefore has He mercy on whom He will *have mercy*, and whom He will He hardens. makes stubborn

19 You will say then to me, Why does He yet find fault? For who has resisted His will?

20 Nay but, O man, who are you that replies against God? Shall the thing formed say to Him that formed *it*, Why have you made me thus? ISA. 45:9 answers

21 Has not the potter power over the clay, of the same lump to make one vessel to honor, and another to dishonor?

22 *What* if God, willing to show *His* wrath, and to make His power known, endured with much longsuffering the vessels of wrath fitted to destruction: PROV. 16:4

23 And that He might make known the riches of His glory on the vessels of mercy, which He had afore prepared to glory,

24 Even us, whom He has called, not of the Jews only, but also of the Gen'tiles?

25 As He says also in Ho-se'a, I will call them My people, which were not My people; and her beloved, which was not beloved. HOS. 2:23

26 And it shall come to pass, *that* in the place where it was said to them, You *are* not My people; there shall they be called the children of the living God. HOS. 1:10

27 I-sa'iah also cries concerning Is-ra-el, Though the number of the chil-

dren of Is'ra-el be as the sand of the sea, a remnant shall be saved: ISA. 10:22

28 For He will finish <u>the work</u>, and cut *it* short in righteousness: because a short work will the Lord make upon the earth.   His Word

29 And as I-sa'iah said before, Except the Lord of Sab'a-oth had left us a <u>seed</u>, we had been as Sod'om-a, and been made like to Go-mor'rha.   ISA. 1:9 descendants

30 What shall we say then? That the Gen'tiles, which followed not after righteousness, have attained to righteousness, even the righteousness which is of faith.

31 But Is'ra-el, which followed after the law of righteousness, has not attained to the law of righteousness.

32 <u>Wherefore</u>? Because *they sought it* not by faith, but as it were by the works of the law. For they stumbled at that stumblingstone;   Why

33 As it is written, Behold, I lay in Zi'on a stumblingstone and rock of offence: and whosoever believes on Him shall not be <u>ashamed</u>.

ISA. 28:16   disappointed

CHAPTER 10

BRETHERN, my heart's desire and prayer to God for Is'ra-el is, that they might be saved.

2 For I bear them record that they have a <u>zeal</u> of God, but not according to knowledge.   desire

3 For they being ignorant of God's righteousness, and going about to <u>establish</u> their own righteousness, have not submitted themselves to the righteousness of God.   make certain

4 For Christ *is* the end of the law for righteousness to every one that believes.

5 For Mo'ses describes the righteousness which is of the law, That the man which does those things shall live by them.   LEV. 18:5

6 But the righteousness which is of faith speaks on this wise, Say not in your heart, Who shall ascend into heaven? (that is, to bring Christ down *from above*:)   DEU. 30:12-14

7 Or, Who shall descend into the deep? (that is, to bring up Christ again from the dead.)

8 But what says it? The word is near you, *even* in your mouth, and in your heart: that is, the word of faith, which we preach;   DEU. 30:14

9 That if you shall confess with your mouth the Lord Je'sus, and shall believe in your heart that God has raised Him from the dead, you shall be saved.

10 For with the heart man believes to righteousness; and with the mouth confession is made to salvation.

11 For the scripture says, Whosoever believes on Him shall not be ashamed.   ISA. 49:23

12 For there is no difference between the Jew and the Greek: for the same Lord over all is rich to all that call upon Him.

13 For <u>whosoever</u> shall call upon the name of the Lord shall be saved.   JOEL 2:32 whoever

14 How then shall they call on Him in whom they have not believed? and how shall they believe in Him of whom they have not heard? and how shall they hear without a preacher?

15 And how shall they preach, except they be sent? as it is written, How beautiful are the feet of them that preach the gospel of peace, and bring glad tidings of good things! ISA. 52:7

16 But they have not all obeyed the gospel. For I-sa'iah says, Lord, who has believed our report. ISA. 53:1 message

17 So then faith comes by hearing, and hearing by the word of God. Christ

18 But I say, Have they not heard? Yes verily, their sound went into all the earth, and their words to the ends of the world. PS. 19:4 truly

19 But I say, Did not Is'ra-el know? First Mo'ses says, I will provoke you to jealousy by *them that are* no people, *and* by a foolish nation I will anger you. DEU. 32:21

20 But I-sa'iah is very bold, and says, I was found of them that sought Me not; I was made manifest to them that asked not after Me. ISA. 65:1-2 known

21 But to Is'ra-el He says, All day long I have stretched forth My hands to a disobedient and gainsaying people. ISA 65:2 obstinate

CHAPTER 11

I SAY then, Has God cast away His people? God forbid. For I also am an Is'ra-el-ite, of the seed of A'bra-ham, *of* the tribe of Ben'ja-min. 1 SAM. 12:22 may it never be - offspring

2 God has not cast away His people which He foreknew. Know you not what the scripture says of E-li'jah? how he makes intercession to God against Is'ra-el, saying, PS. 94:14 ISA. 41:17 pleads

3 Lord, they have killed Your proph-ets, and digged down Your altars; and I am left alone, and they seek my life. 1 KGS. 19:10 torn down

4 But what says the answer of God to him? I have reserved to My-self seven thousand men, who have not bowed the knee to *the image of* Ba'al. 1 KGS. 19:18 i.e., in worship

5 Even so then at this present time also there is a remnant according to the election of grace. 2 KGS 19:4

6 And if by grace, then *is it* no more of works: otherwise grace is no more grace. But if *it be* of works, then is it no more grace: otherwise work is no more work.

7 What then? Is'ra-el has not ob-tained that which he seeks for; but the election has obtained it, and the rest were blinded sought - looked - hardened

8 (According as it is written, God has given them the spirit of slum-ber, eyes that they should not see, and ears that they should not hear;) to this day. DEU. 29:4 ISA. 29:10 stupor

9 And Da'vid says, Let their table be made a snare, and a trap, and a stumblingblock, and a recompence to them: PS. 69:22-23 reward

10 Let their eyes be darkened, that they may not see, and bow down their back alway.

11 I say then, Have they stumbled that they should fall? God forbid: but *rather* through their fall salvation *is come* to the Gen'tiles, for to pro-voke them to jealousy. i.e., by no means - to be envious

12 Now if the fall of them *be* the riches of the world, and the diminishing

of them the riches of the Gen'tiles; how much more their fulness? loss

13 For I speak to you Gen'tiles, inasmuch as I am the apostle of the Gen'tiles, I magnify mine office: my ministry

14 If by any means I may provoke to emulation *them which are* my flesh, and might save some of them. jealousy

15 For if the casting away of them *be* the reconciling of the world, what *shall* the receiving *of them be*, but life from the dead? rejection - acceptance

16 For if the firstfruit *be* holy, the lump *is* also *holy*: and if the root *be* holy, so *are* the branches.

17 And if some of the branches be broken off, and you, being a wild olive tree, were grafted in among them, and with them partakes of the root and fatness of the olive tree; richness

18 Boast not against the branches. But if you boast, you bear not the root, but the root you. you support

19 You will say then, The branches were broken off, that I might be grafted in. i.e. made a part

20 Well; because of unbelief they were broken off, and you stand by faith. Be not highminded, but fear:

conceited - respectful—humble

21 For if God spared not the natural branches, *take heed* less he also spare not you. i.e., the Jews - care

22 Behold therefore the goodness and severity of God: on them which fell, severity; but toward you, goodness, if you continue in *His* goodness: otherwise you also shall be cut off.

23 And they also, if they abide not still in unbelief, shall be grafted in: for God is able to graft them in again.

24 For if you were cut out of the olive tree which is wild by nature, and were grafted contrary to nature into a good olive tree: how much more shall these, which be the natural *branches*, be grafted into their own olive tree? easier

25 For I would not, brethren, that you should be ignorant of this mystery, less you should be wise in your own conceits; that blindness in part is happened to Is'ra-el, until the fulness of the Gen'tiles be come in.

hidden truth - thoughts - hardness

26 And so all Is'ra-el shall be saved: as it is written, There shall come out of Zi'on the Deliverer, and shall turn away ungodliness from Ja'cob: ISA. 59:20-21

27 For this *is* My covenant to them, when I shall take away their sins.

JER. 31:33 agreement

28 As concerning the gospel, *they are* enemies for your sakes: but as touching the election, *they are* beloved for the fathers' sakes. from the standpoint of - God's chosen

29 For the gifts and calling of God *are* without repentance.

30 For as you in times past have not believed God, yet have now obtained mercy through their unbelief: obeyed - received

31 Even so have these also now not believed, that through your mercy they also may obtain mercy.

32 For God has concluded them all in unbelief, that He might have mercy upon all. shut up

33 O the depth of the riches both of the wisdom and knowledge of God!

how unsearchable *are* His judgments, and His ways past finding out!

34 For who has known the mind of the Lord? or who has been His counselor? ISA. 40:13 ISA. 40:14 advisor

35 Or who has first given to Him, and it shall be recompensed to him again? JOB 35:7 JOB 41:11 rewarded

36 For of Him, and through Him, and to Him, *are* all things: to whom *be* glory for ever. Amen. 1 CHRON. 29:12 Him

CHAPTER 12

I BESEECH you therefore, brethren, by the mercies of God, that you present your bodies a living sacrifice, holy, acceptable to God, *which is* your reasonable service. beg - offer

2 And be not conformed to this world: but be you transformed by the renewing of your mind, that you may prove what *is* that good, and acceptable, and perfect, will of God. show

3 For I say, through the grace given to me, to every man that is among you, not to think *of himself* more highly than he ought to think; but to think soberly, according as God has dealt to every man the measure of faith. ECC. 7:16

4 For as we have many members in one body, and all members have not the same office: parts

5 So we, *being* many, are one body in Christ, and every one members one of another.

6 Having then gifts differing according to the grace that is given to us, whether prophecy, *let us prophesy* according to the proportion of faith;

7 Or ministry, *let us wait* on *our* ministering: or he that teaches, on teaching;

8 Or he that exhorts, on exhortation: he that gives, *let him do it* with simplicity; he that rules, with diligence; he that shows mercy, with cheerfulness.

9 *Let* love be without dissimulation. Abhor that which is evil; cling to that which is good. ISA. 1:16 hypocrisy

10 *Be* kindly affectioned one to another with brotherly love; in honor preferring one another;

11 Not slothful in business; fervent in spirit; serving the Lord; lazy

12 Rejoicing in hope; patient in tribulation; continuing instant in prayer; always

13 Distributing to the necessity of saints; given to hospitality. giving - needs

14 Bless them which persecute you: bless, and curse not.

15 Rejoice with them that do rejoice, and weep with them that weep.

16 *Be* of the same mind one toward another. Mind not high things, but condescend to men of low estate. Be not wise in your own conceits. estimation

17 Recompense to no man evil for evil. Provide things honest in the sight of all men. PROV. 20:22 Give

18 If it be possible, as much as lies in you, live peaceably with all men. it depends on

19 Dearly beloved, avenge not yourselves, but *rather* give place to wrath: for it is written, Vengeance *is* Mine; I will repay, says the Lord. DEU. 32:35 i.e., don't take revenge

20 Therefore if your enemy hunger, feed him; if he thirst, give him drink:

for in so doing you shall heap coals of fire on his head. PROV. 25:22 2 KGS. 6:22
21 Be not overcome of evil, but overcome evil with good.

CHAPTER 13

LET every soul be subject to the higher powers. For there is no power but of God: the powers that be are ordained of God. PROV. 8:15 person - i.e., governmental authorities - established by

2 Whosoever therefore resists the power, resists the ordinance of God: and they that resist shall receive to themselves damnation. condemnation

3 For rulers are not a terror to good works, but to the evil. Will you then not be afraid of the power? do that which is good, and you shall have praise of the same:

4 For he is the minister of God to you for good. But if you do that which is evil, be afraid; for he bears not the sword in vain: for he is the minister of God, a revenger to *execute* wrath upon him that does evil. servant

5 Wherefore *you* must needs be subject, not only for wrath, but also for conscience sake.

6 For for this cause pay you tribute also: for they are God's ministers, attending continually upon this very thing. taxes

7 Render therefore to all their dues: tribute to whom tribute *is due*; custom to whom custom; fear to whom fear; honor to whom honor.

8 Owe no man any thing, but to love one another: for he that loves another has fulfilled the law.

9 For this, You shall not commit adultery, You shall not kill, You shall not steal, You shall not bear false witness, You shall not covet; and if *there be* any other commandment, it is briefly comprehended in this saying, namely, You shall love your neighbor as yourself. EX. 20:13-14 LEV. 19:18

10 Love works no ill to his neighbor: therefore love *is* the fulfilling of the law. wrong

11 And that, knowing the time, that now *it is* high time to awake out of sleep: for now *is* our salvation nearer than when we believed.

12 The night is far spent, the day is at hand: let us therefore cast off the works of darkness, and let us put on the armor of light. almost gone

13 Let us walk honestly, as in the day; not in rioting and drunkenness, not in chambering and wantonness, not in strife and envying. properly - carousing - drunkenness

14 But put you on the Lord Je'sus Christ, and make not provision for the flesh, to *fulfil* the lusts *thereof*. evil desires

CHAPTER 14

HIM that is weak in the faith receive you, *but* not to doubtful disputations. questionable opinions

2 For one believes that he may eat all things: another, who is weak, eats herbs.

3 Let not him that eats despise him that eats not; and let not him which eats not judge him that eats: for God has received him.

4 Who are you that judge another

man's servant? to his own master he stands or falls. Yea, he shall be helped up: for God is able to make him stand.

5 One man esteems one day above another: another esteems every day *alike*. Let every man be fully <u>per-suaded</u> in his own mind.   convinced

6 He that <u>regards</u> the day, <u>regards</u> *it* to the Lord; and he that <u>regards</u> not the day, to the Lord he does not <u>re-gard</u> *it*. He that eats, eats to the Lord, for he gives God thanks; and he that eats not, to the Lord he eats not, and gives God thanks.   observes

7 For none of us lives to himself, and no man dies to himself.

8 For whether we live, we live to the Lord; and whether we die, we die to the Lord: whether we live therefore, or die, we are the Lord's.

9 For to this end Christ both died, and rose, and <u>revived</u>, that He might be Lord both of the dead and living.   lives still

10 But why do you judge your brother? or why do you set at nothing your brother? for we shall all stand before the judgment seat of Christ.   2 COR. 5:10

11 For it is written, As I live, says the Lord, every knee shall bow to Me, and every tongue shall confess to God.   ISA. 45:23

12 So then every one of us shall give account of himself to God.

13 Let us not therefore judge one another any more: but judge this rather, that no man put a stumbling-block or an occasion to fall in *his* brother's way.

14 I know, and am persuaded by the Lord Je'sus, that *there is* nothing un-

clean of itself: but to him that esteems any thing to be unclean, to him *it is* unclean.

15 But if your brother be grieved with *your* <u>meat</u>, now walk you not <u>chari-tably</u>. Destroy not him with your meat, for whom Christ died.   food - in love

16 Let not then your good be <u>evil spo-ken of</u>:   be given a bad name

17 For the kingdom of God is not <u>meat</u> and drink; but righteousness, and peace, and joy in the Ho'ly <u>Ghost</u>. Spirit

18 For he that in these things serves Christ *is* <u>acceptable</u> to God, and ap-proved of men.   pleasing

19 Let us therefore follow after the things which make for peace, and things wherewith one may <u>edify</u> an-other.   build up

20 For <u>meat</u> destroy not the work of God. All things indeed *are* pure; but *it* is evil for that man who eats with of-fence.

21 *It is* good neither to eat flesh, nor to drink wine, *nor <u>any</u>* thing whereby your brother stumbles, or is of-fended, or is made weak.   do anything

22 Have you faith? have *it* to your-self before God. Happy *is* he that <u>condemns</u> not himself in that thing which he <u>allows</u>.   judges - approves

23 And he that doubts is <u>damned</u> if he eat, because *he eats* not of faith: for whatsoever *is* not of faith is sin.   condemned

CHAPTER 15

WE then that are strong ought to bear the <u>infirmities</u> of the weak, and not to please ourselves.   weaknesses

M21
267

M03

G40 — 270

M06
291
267

G4B

G4K

G4B
GIN — 359
G40

276 275
267

M10 — 277
267

M03 - - 286
M21

2 Let every one of us please *his* neighbor for *his* good to <u>edification</u>.   being built up

3 For even Christ pleased not Himself; but, as it is written, The reproaches of them that reproached you fell on Me.   PS. 69:9

4 For whatsoever things were written aforetime were written for our learning, that we through patience and comfort of the scriptures might have hope.

5 Now the God of patience and <u>consolation</u> grant you to be likeminded one toward another according to Christ Je'sus: encouragement

6 That you may with one mind *and* one mouth <u>glorify</u> God, even the Father of our Lord Je'sus Christ.   honor

7 Wherefore receive you one another, as Christ also received us to the glory of God.

8 Now I say that Je'sus Christ was a minister of the circumcision for the truth of God, to confirm the promises *made* to the fathers:

9 And that the Gen'tiles might <u>glorify</u> God for *His* mercy; as it is written, For this cause I will confess to You among the Gen'tiles, and sing to Your name.   PS. 18:49 PS. 117:1 honor

10 And again He says, Rejoice, ye Gen'tiles, with His people.   DEU. 32:43

11 And again, Praise the Lord, all you Gen'tiles; and <u>laud</u> Him, all you people.   PS. 117:1 praise

12 And again, I-sa'iah says, There shall be a root of Jes'se, and He that shall rise to reign over the Gen'tiles; in Him shall the Gen'tiles <u>trust</u>.   ISA. 11:10 hope

13 Now the God of hope fill you with all joy and peace in believing, that you may abound in hope, through the power of the Ho'ly <u>Ghost</u>.   Spirit

14 And I myself also am persuaded of you, my brethren, that you also are full of goodness, filled with all knowledge, able also to <u>admonish</u> one another.   instruct

15 Nevertheless, brethren, I have written the more boldly to you in some <u>sort</u>, as putting you in mind, because of the grace that is given to me of God,   points

16 That I should be the minister of Je'sus Christ to the Gen'tiles, ministering the gospel of God, that the offering up of the Gen'tiles might be acceptable, being sanctified by the Ho'ly <u>Ghost</u>.   Spirit

17 I have therefore whereof I may <u>glory</u> through Je'sus Christ in those things which pertain to God.   rejoice

18 For I will not dare to speak of any of those things which Christ has not wrought by me, to make the Gen'tiles obedient, by word and deed,

19 Through mighty signs and wonders, by the power of the Spirit of God; so that from Je-ru'sa-lem, and round about to Il-lyr'i-cum, I have fully preached the gospel of Christ.

20 Yea, so have I strived to preach the gospel, not where Christ was named, less I should build upon another man's foundation:

21 But as it is written, To whom He was not spoken of, they shall see: and they that have not heard shall understand.   ISA. 52:15

22 For which cause also I have been much <u>hindered from</u> coming to you.   delayed in

23 But now having no more place in

these parts, and having a great desire these many years to come to you;

24 Whensoever I take my journey into Spain, I will come to you: for I trust to see you in my journey, and to be brought on my way there by you, if first I be somewhat filled with your *company*.

25 But now I go to Je-ru'sa-lem to <u>minister</u> to the saints.   serve

26 For it has pleased them of Mac-e-do'ni-a and A-cha'ia to make a certain contribution for the poor <u>saints</u> which are at Je-ru'sa-lem.

                    followers—believers

27 It has pleased them <u>verily</u>; and their debtors they are. For if the Gen'tiles have been made partakers of their spiritual things, their duty is also to minister to them in <u>carnal</u> things.

                    truly - material

28 When therefore I have performed this, and have sealed to them this fruit, I will come by you into Spain.

29 And I am sure that, when I come to you, I shall come in the fulness of the blessing of the gospel of Christ.

30 Now I <u>beseech</u> you, brethren, for the Lord Je'sus Christ's sake, and for the love of the Spirit, that you strive together with me in *your* prayers to God for me;   beg

31 That I may be delivered from them that do not believe in Ju-dae'a; and that my service which *I have* for Je-ru'sa-lem may be <u>accepted</u> of the saints;   acceptable

32 That I may come to you with joy by the will of God, and may with you be refreshed.

33 Now the God of peace *be* with you all. Amen.

CHAPTER 16

I COMMAND to you Phe'be our sister, which is a servant of the church which is at Cenchre-a:

2 That you receive her in the Lord, as <u>becomes</u> saints, and that you assist her in whatsoever <u>business</u> she has need of you: for she has been a <u>succorer</u> of many, and of myself also.   worthy manner of - manner - helper

3 Greet Pris-cil'la and A'qui-la my helpers in Christ Jesus:

4 Who have for my life <u>laid down</u> their own necks: to whom not only I give thanks, but also all the churches of the Gen'tiles.   risked

5 Likewise *greet* the church that is in their house. <u>Salute</u> my wellbeloved E-paen'e-tus, who is the firstfruits of A-cha'ia to Christ.   greet

6 Greet Ma'ry, who bestowed much labor on <u>us</u>.   you

7 <u>Salute</u> An-dro-ni'cus and Ju'nia, my kinsmen, and my fellow-prisoners, who are of note among the apostles, who also were in Christ before me.

8 Greet Am'pli-as my beloved in the Lord.

9 <u>Salute</u> Ur'bane, our helper in Christ, and Sta'chys my beloved.

10 <u>Salute</u> A-pelles <u>approved in</u> Christ. <u>Salute</u> them which are of Ar-is-to-bu'lus' *household*.   loyal to - family

11 <u>Salute</u> He-ro'di-on my kinsman. Greet them that be of the *household* of Nar-cis'sus, which are in the Lord.

12 Salute Try-phe'na and Try-pho'sa, who labor in the Lord. Salute the beloved Per'sis, which labored much in the Lord. _{Greet}

13 Salute Ru'fus chosen in the Lord, and his mother and mine.

14 Salute A-syn'cri-tus, Phle'gon, Her'mas, Pat'ro-bas, Her'mes, and the brethren which are with them.

15 Salute Phi-lolo'-gus, and Ju'lia, Ne're-us, and his sister, and O-lym'pas, and all the saints which are with them. _{i.e., believer—followers}

16 Salute one another with an holy kiss. The churches of Christ salute you.

17 Now I beseech you, brethren, mark them which cause divisions and offences contrary to the doctrine which you have learned; and avoid them. _{beg - teaching}

18 For they that are such serve not our Lord Je'sus Christ, but their own belly; and by good words and fair speeches deceive the hearts of the simple. _{unsuspecting}

19 For your obedience is come abroad to all *men*. I am glad therefore on your behalf: but yet I would have you wise to that which is good, and simple concerning evil. _{harmless}

20 And the God of peace shall bruise Sa'tan under your feet shortly. The grace of our Lord Je'sus Christ *be* with you. Amen. _{GEN. 3:15 crush}

21 Tim'o-thy my workfellow, and Lu'cius, and Ja'son, and So-sip'a-ter, my kinsmen, salute you. _{greet}

22 I Ter'tius, who wrote *this* epistle, salute you in the Lord. _{letter}

23 Ga'ius my host, and of the whole church, salutes you. E-ras'tus the chamberlain of the city salutes you, and Quar'tus a brother. _{treasurer}

24 The grace of our Lord Je'sus Christ *be* with you all. Amen.

25 Now to Him that is of power to stablish you according to my gospel, and the preaching of Jesus Christ, according to the revelation of the mystery, which was kept secret since the world began, _{establish - i.e., knowledge of the church}

26 But now is made manifest, and by the scriptures of the prophets, according to the commandment of the everlasting God, made known to all nations for the obedience of faith: _{known}

27 To God only wise, *be* glory through Je'sus Christ for ever. Amen.

1 CORINTHIANS

OUTLINE

SURVEY

Not only is 1 Corinthians a letter in which the Apostle Paul gives counsel and instruction on important issues of Christian faith and conduct, but it also throws a revealing light on the serious problems facing a young church not long after its foundation in the middle of the first century. Paul had brought the message of Christ to Corinth during the course of his second missionary journey. This city presented a tremendous challenge to the Gospel, both as one of the great cosmopolitan centers of commerce in the ancient world and as a place notorious for profligacy and licentiousness. If the message of the Cross had power to reach and transform the lives of men and women in such a setting, then it was powerful indeed! And this is precisely what happened. Moreover, the members of this young church had been enriched with a variety of spiritual gifts—a confirmation to them, and to the world, that God was present and working powerfully in their midst.

But it was not long before serious errors of doctrine and practice, which threatened the well-being and even the survival of the Christian community there, arose within the ranks of the believers. To the correction of these errors 1 Corinthians is mainly devoted. In the first place, deplorable divisions had split the church into hostile factions, shattering the unity in which all who profess to be brothers in Christ should be bound together. Secondly, one of their number had been guilty of gross immorality, of a kind which even the profligate society of that pagan city would have condemned, and yet the congregation had failed to impose discipline upon the offender by expelling him from their fellowship. Thirdly, members of the church had been dragging each other before pagan secular courts for the settlement of disputes that had arisen between them, instead of resolving their quarrels in a spirit of Christian love within the community of the church, or being willing, after Christ's example, to endure wrongs without retaliation. Fourthly, some had been committing fornication with prostitutes and attempting to justify their conduct by arguing that the body only was involved and that the deeds of the body were of no consequence. Fifthly, the Supper of the Lord, which should have been an expression of loving harmony, had degenerated into an occasion for irreverence, gluttony, and uncharitable behavior. Sixthly, there were disorderly and unedifying scenes when they met together for public worship, especially in the exercise of the spiritual gifts with which they had been endowed. Paul finds it necessary to remind them that the gift which is best of all and most to be coveted is the gift of love, apart from which all other gifts are worthless. Seventhly, heretical teaching, which, by its denial of the fact of Christ's resurrection and indeed of the possibility of any resurrection from the dead, struck at the very cornerstone of the Christian faith, had gained a footing in the Corinthian church. These matters, every one of them scandalous, receive careful and urgent attention in this letter.

The Apostle Paul also offers instruction on certain other questions which had been raised by the Corinthians in a letter they had sent to him. These questions may be summed up as follows: Was it advisable for Christians to enter into the married state? Should a husband or wife after being converted continue to live with an unconverted partner? What should be the attitude of a Christian toward the eating of meat which had previously been offered in sacrifice to idols? Should women have their heads covered when attending public worship? What is the significance of the variety of spiritual gifts? What arrangements should be made with regard to the collection for the relief of the poverty-stricken Christians at Jerusalem?

It would be a mistake to imagine that the contents of this epistle are relevant only to the particular situation of the Church in Corinth of the first century, for, although in circumstance and outward form the problems of the Church vary from age to age, yet in essence they remain the same, and the principles which the apostle has laid down are applicable to our day and situation no less than to his own.

AUTHOR

The internal as well as external evidence that the Apostle Paul was the author of this epistle is so strong as to be conclusive. It is not possible to fix the date of composition with certainty, but it was probably in the spring of A.D. 55, 56, or 57. Paul was in Ephesus at the time, during the course of his third missionary journey.

P.E.H.

THE FIRST LETTER OF PAUL TO THE
CORINTHIANS
CHAPTER 1

Vital Questions
Answered

PAUL, called *to be* an apostle of Je'sus Christ through the will of God, and Sos'the-nes *our* brother,

2 To the church of God which is at Cor'inth, to them that are <u>sanctified</u> in Christ Je'sus, called *to be* <u>saints</u>, with all that in every place call upon the name of Je'sus Christ our Lord, both theirs and ours: set apart - believers

3 Grace *be* to you, and peace, from God our Father, and *from* the Lord Je'sus Christ.

4 I thank my God always <u>on your be-half</u>, for the grace of God which is given you by Je'sus Christ; concerning you

5 That in every thing you are en-riched by Him, in all <u>utterance</u>, and *in* all knowledge;   speech

6 Even as the testimony of Christ was <u>confirmed</u> in you: made known

7 So that you come behind in no gift; waiting for the coming of our Lord Je'sus Christ:

8 Who shall also <u>confirm</u> you to the end, *that you may be* blameless in the day of our Lord Je'sus Christ.   keep you strong

9 God *is* faithful, by whom you were called to the fellowship of His Son Je'sus Christ our Lord.

10 Now I <u>beseech</u> you, brethren, by the name of our Lord Je'sus Christ, that you all speak the same thing, and *that* there be no divisions among you; but *that* you be perfectly joined together in the same mind and in the same judgment.   beg

11 For it has been <u>declared</u> to me of you, my brethren, by them *which are of the house* of Chlo'e, that there are <u>contentions</u> among you.   told - quarrels

12 Now this I say, that every one of you says, I am of Paul; and I of A-pol'los; and I of Ce'phas; and I of Christ.

13 Is Christ divided? was Paul cruci-fied for you? or were you baptized in the name of Paul?

14 I thank God that I baptized none of you, but Cris'pus and Ga'ius;

15 Less any should say that I had bap-tized <u>in mine own name</u>.   as my disciples

16 And I baptized also the house-hold of Steph'a-nas: besides, I know not whether I baptized any other.

17 For Christ sent me not to bap-tize, but to preach the gospel: not with wisdom of words, less the cross of Christ should be made of <u>none effect</u>.   no power

18 For the preaching of the cross is to them that perish foolishness; but to us which are saved it is the power of God.

19 For it is written, I will destroy the wisdom of the wise, and will bring to nothing the understanding of the prudent.   ISA. 29:14

20 Where *is* the wise? where *is* the scribe? where *is* the disputer of this

world? has not God made foolish the wisdom of this world?   ISA. 33:18 knowledge

21 For after that in the wisdom of God the world by wisdom knew not God, it pleased God by the foolishness of preaching to save them that believe.

22 For the Jews require a sign, and the Greeks seek after wisdom:

23 But we preach Christ crucified, to the Jews a stumblingblock, and to the Greeks foolishness;

24 But to them which are called, both Jews and Greeks, Christ the power of God, and the wisdom of God.

25 Because the foolishness of God is wiser than men; and the weakness of God is stronger than men.

26 For you see your calling, brethren, how that not many wise men after the flesh, not many mighty, not many noble, *are called*:   consider

27 But God has chosen the foolish things of the world to confound the wise; and God has chosen the weak things of the world to confound the things which are mighty;   shame

28 And base things of the world, and things which are despised, has God chosen, *yea*, and things which are not, to bring to nought things that are: lowly

29 That no flesh should glory in His presence.

30 But of Him are you in Christ Je'sus, who of God is made to us wisdom, and righteousness, and sanctification, and redemption:

31 That, according as it is written, he that glories, let him glory in the Lord.   JER. 9:24 boasts

CHAPTER 2

AND I, brethren, when I came to you, came not with excellency of speech or of wisdom, declaring to you the testimony of God.   superiority

2 For I determined not to know any thing among you, save Je'sus Christ, and Him crucified.

3 And I was with you in weakness, and in fear, and in much trembling.

4 And my speech and my preaching *was* not with enticing words of man's wisdom, but in demonstration of the Spirit and of power: persuasive - knowledge

5 That your faith should not stand in the wisdom of men, but in the power of God.

6 However we speak wisdom among them that are perfect: yet not the wisdom of this world, nor of the princes of this world, that come to nought: knowledge - mature

7 But we speak the wisdom of God in a mystery, *even* the hidden *wisdom*, which God ordained before the world to our glory: veiled - planned

8 Which none of the princes of this world knew: for had they known *it*, they would not have crucified the Lord of glory.

9 But as it is written, Eye has not seen, nor ear heard, neither have entered into the heart of man, the things which God has prepared for them that love Him.   ISA. 64:4

10 But God has revealed *them* to us by His Spirit: for the Spirit searches all things, yea, the deep things of God.

11 For what man knows the things

of a man, save the spirit of man which is in him? even so the things of God knows no man, but the Spirit of God.

12 Now we have received, not the spirit of the world, but the Spirit which is of God; that we might know the things that are freely given to us of God.

13 Which things also we speak, not in the words which man's <u>wisdom</u> teaches, but which the Ho'ly <u>Ghost</u> teaches; comparing spiritual things with spiritual. knowledge - Spirit

14 But the natural man <u>receives</u> not the things of the Spirit of God: for they are foolishness to him: neither can he know *them*, because they are spiritually <u>discerned</u>. 2 PET. 3:9 accepts - understood

15 But he that is spiritual judges all things, yet he himself is judged of no man. ISA. 40:13

16 For who has known the mind of the Lord, that he may instruct Him? But we have the mind of Christ. ISA. 40:13

CHAPTER 3

AND I, brethren, could not speak to you as to spiritual, but as to <u>carnal</u>, *even* as to babes in Christ.
the worldly

2 I have fed you with milk, and not with meat: for before you were not able *to bear it*, neither yet now are you able.

3 For you are yet <u>carnal</u>: for whereas *there is* among you <u>envying</u>, and strife, and divisions, are you not <u>carnal</u>, and walk as men? jealousy

4 For while one says, I am of Paul; and another, I *am* of A-pol'los; are you not <u>carnal</u>? worldly

5 Who then is Paul, and who *is* A-pol'los, but ministers by whom you believed, even as the Lord gave to every man?

6 I have planted, A-pol'los watered; but God gave the increase.

7 So then neither is he that plants any thing, neither he that waters; but God that gives the increase.

8 Now he that plants and he that waters are one: and every man shall receive his own reward according to his own labor.

9 For we are laborers together with God: you are God's <u>husbandry</u>, *you are* God's building. ISA 61:3 garden

10 According to the grace of God which is given to me, as a wise masterbuilder, I have laid the foundation, and another builds thereon. But let every man take heed how he builds thereupon.

11 For other foundation can no man lay than that is laid, which is Je'sus Christ.

12 Now if any man build upon this foundation gold, silver, precious stones, wood, hay, stubble;

13 Every man's work shall be made <u>manifest</u>: for the day shall declare it, because it shall be revealed by fire; and the fire shall <u>try</u> every man's work of what sort it is. known - test

14 If any man's work abide which he has built thereupon, he shall receive a reward.

15 If any man's work shall be burned, he shall suffer loss: but he himself shall be saved; yet <u>so as</u> by fire. as tried

16 Know you not that you are the tem-

ple of God, and *that* the Spirit of God dwells in you?

17 If any man <u>defile</u> the temple of God, him shall God destroy; for the temple of God is holy, which *temple* you are. destroys

18 Let no man deceive himself. If any man among you seems to be wise in this world, let him become a fool, that he may be wise.

19 For the wisdom of this world is foolishness with God. For it is written, He takes the wise in their own craftiness. JOB 5:13

20 And again, The Lord knows the thoughts of the wise, that they are <u>vain</u>. PS. 94: 11 foolish

21 Therefore let no man glory in men. For all things are yours;

22 Whether Paul, or A-pol'los, or Ce'phas, or the world, or life, or death, or things present, or things to come; all are yours;

23 And you are Christ's; and Christ *is* God's.

CHAPTER 4

LET a man so account of us, as of the <u>ministers</u> of Christ, and stewards of the <u>mysteries</u> of God. servants - hidden truths

2 Moreover it is required in stewards, that a man be found faithful.

3 But with me it is a very small thing that I should be judged of you, or of man's judgment: yea, I judge not mine own self.

4 For I know nothing <u>by</u> myself; yet am I not hereby justified: but He that judges me is the Lord. against

5 Therefore judge nothing before the time, until the Lord come, who both will bring to light the hidden things of darkness, and will make <u>manifest</u> the <u>counsels</u> of the hearts: and then shall every man have praise of God. known - thoughts

6 And these things, brethren, I have in a figure transferred to myself and *to* A-pol'los for your sakes; that you might learn in us not to think *of men* above that which is written, that no one of you be puffed up for one against another.

7 For who make you to differ *from another*? and what have you that you did not receive? now if you did receive *it*, why do you glory, as if you had not received *it*?

8 Now you are full, now you are rich, you have reigned as kings without us: and I <u>would</u> to God you did reign, that we also might reign with you. desire

9 For I think that God has set forth us the apostles last, as <u>it were</u> appointed to death: for we are made a spectacle to the world, and to angels, and to men. men

10 We *are* fools for Christ's sake, but you *are* wise in Christ; we *are* weak, but you *are* strong; you *are* honorable, but we *are* <u>despised</u>. without honor

11 Even to this present hour we both hunger, and thirst, and are naked, and are <u>buffeted</u>, and have no certain <u>dwelling place</u>; roughly treated - home

12 And labor, working with our own hands: being <u>reviled</u>, we bless; being persecuted, we suffer it: cursed

13 Being defamed, we entreat: we are made as the filth of the world, *and are*

the offscouring of all things to this day.

14 I write not these things to shame you, but as my beloved sons I warn *you*.

15 For though you have ten thousand instructors in Christ, yet *have you* not many fathers: for in Christ Je'sus I have begotten you through the gospel.

16 Wherefore I <u>beseech</u> you, be you <u>followers</u> of me.   beg - imitators

17 For this cause have I sent to you Tim'o-thy, who is my beloved son, and faithful in the Lord, who shall bring you into remembrance of my ways which be in Christ, as I teach every where in every church.

18 Now some are <u>puffed up</u>, as though I would not come to you.   arrogant

19 But I will come to you shortly, if the Lord will, and will know, not the speech of them which are <u>puffed up</u>, but the power.

20 For the kingdom of God *is* not in word, but in power.

21 What will you? shall I come to you with a rod, or in love, and *in* the spirit of meekness?

CHAPTER 5

IT is reported commonly *that there is* fornication among you, and such fornication as is not so much as named among the Gen'tiles, that one should have his father's wife.   DEU. 22:30

2 And you are <u>puffed up</u>, and have not rather mourned, that he that has done this deed might be taken away from among you.   arrogant

3 For I <u>verily</u>, as absent in body, but present in spirit, have judged already, as though I were present, *concerning* him that has so done this deed,   truly

4 In the name of our Lord Je'sus Christ, when you are gathered together, and my spirit, with the power of our Lord Je'sus Christ,

5 To deliver such an one to Sa'tan for the destruction of the flesh, that the spirit may be saved in the day of the Lord Je'sus.

6 Your <u>glorying</u> *is* not good. Know you not that a little <u>leaven</u> <u>leavens</u> the whole lump?   boasting - yeast - puffs up

7 <u>Purge</u> out therefore the <u>old</u> <u>leaven</u>, that you may be a new lump, as you are unleavened. For even Christ our passover is sacrificed for us: Clean - i.e., sinful person

8 Therefore let us keep the feast, not with <u>old leaven</u>, neither with the <u>leaven</u> of malice and wickedness; but with the <u>unleavened</u> *bread* of sincerity and truth.   EX. 12:19 teachings - i.e., pure ways

9 I wrote to you in an epistle not to <u>company</u> with fornicators: associate

10 Yet not altogether with the fornicators of this world, or with the covetous, or extortioners, or with idolaters; for then must you needs go out of the world.

11 But now I have written to you not to keep company, if any man that is called a brother be a fornicator, or covetous, or an idolater, or a <u>railer</u>, or a drunkard, or an extortioner; with such an one no not to <u>eat</u>.   reviler - mix with

12 For what have I to do to judge them also that are outside? do not you judge them that are inside?

13 But them that are outside God

judges. Therefore put away from among yourselves that wicked person.   DEU. 17:7

CHAPTER 6

DARE any of you, having a matter against another, go to law before the <u>unjust</u>, and not before the saints?   unrighteous

2 Do you not know that the <u>saints</u> shall judge the world? and if the world shall be judged by you, are you unworthy to judge the smallest matters?   believers

3 Know you not that we shall judge angels? how much more things that pertain to this life?

4 If then you have judgments of things pertaining to this life, set them to judge who are <u>least esteemed</u> in the church.   of no account

5 I speak to your shame. Is it so, that there is not a wise man among you? no, not one that shall be able to judge between his brethren?

6 But brother goes to law with brother, and that before the unbelievers.

7 Now therefore there is utterly a fault among you, because you go to law one with another. Why do you not rather take wrong? why do you not rather *suffer yourselves to* be defrauded?

8 Nay, you do wrong, and defraud, and that *your* brethren.   to your

9 Know you not that the unrighteous shall not inherit the kingdom of God? Be not deceived: neither fornicators, nor idolaters, nor adulterers, nor effeminate, nor abusers of themselves with mankind,

10 Nor thieves, nor covetous, nor drunkards, nor revilers, nor extortioners, shall inherit the kingdom of God.

11 And such were some of you: but you are washed, but you are <u>sanctified</u>, but you are justified in the name of the Lord Je'sus, and by the Spirit of our God.   set apart

12 All things are lawful to me, but all things are not <u>expedient</u>: all things are lawful for me, but I will not be brought under the power of any.   profitable

13 <u>Meats</u> for the belly, and the belly for <u>meats</u>: but God shall destroy both it and them. Now the body *is* not for fornication, but for the Lord; and the Lord for the body.   foods

14 And God has both raised up the Lord, and will also raise up us by His own power.

15 Know you not that your bodies are the members of Christ? shall I then take the members of Christ, and make *them* the members of an harlot? God forbid.

16 What? know you not that he which is joined to an harlot is one body? for two, says He, shall be one flesh.   GEN. 2:24

17 But he that is joined to the Lord is one spirit.

18 <u>Flee</u> fornication. Every sin that a man does is outside the body; but he that commits fornication sins against his own body.   Avoid

19 What? know you not that your body is the temple of the Ho'ly <u>Ghost</u> *which is* in you, which you have of God, and you are not your own?   Spirit

20 For you are bought with a price: therefore glorify God in your body, and in your spirit, which are God's.   ISA. 44:22

CHAPTER 7

NOW concerning the things whereof you wrote to me: *It is* good for a man not to touch a woman, i.e., like in marriage

2 Nevertheless, *to avoid* fornication, let every man have his own wife, and let every woman have her own husband.

3 Let the husband render to the wife due benevolence: and likewise also the wife to the husband.   fulfill - his duty

4 The wife has not power of her own body, but the husband: and likewise also the husband has not power of his own body, but the wife.   over

5 Defraud you not one the other, except *it be* with consent for a time, that you may give yourselves to fasting and prayer; and come together again, that Sa'tan tempt you not for your incontinency.   EX. 19:15 Deprive - lack of self control

6 But I speak this by permission, *and* not of commandment.

7 For I would that all men were even as I myself. But every man has his proper gift of God, one after this manner, and another after that.   own

8 I say therefore to the unmarried and widows, It is good for them if they abide even as I.   better - live

9 But if they cannot contain, let them marry: for it is better to marry than to burn.   control themselves - i.e., passion without control

10 And to the married I command, *yet* not I, but the Lord, Let not the wife depart from *her* husband:

11 But and if she depart, let her remain unmarried, or be reconciled to *her* husband: and let not the husband put away *his* wife.   send

12 But to the rest speak I, not the Lord: If any brother has a wife that believes not, and she be pleased to dwell with him, let him not put her away.   send

13 And the woman which has an husband that believes not, and if he be pleased to dwell with her, let her not leave him.

14 For the unbelieving husband is sanctified by the wife, and the unbelieving wife is sanctified by the husband: else were your children unclean; but now are they holy.

set apart - illegitimate - legitimate

15 But if the unbelieving depart, let him depart. A brother or a sister is not under bondage in such *cases*: but God has called us to peace.

16 For what know you, O wife, whether you shall save *your* husband? or how know you, O man, whether you shall save *your* wife?

17 But as God has distributed to every man, as the Lord has called every one, so let him walk. And so ordain I in all churches.   assigned - direct

18 Is any man called being circumcised? let him not become uncircumcised. Is any called in uncircumcision? let him not be circumcised.

19 Circumcision is nothing, and uncircumcision is nothing, but the keeping of the commandments of God.   obeying

20 Let every man abide in the same calling wherein he was called.   remain

21 Are you called *being* a servant? care not for it: but if you may be made free, use *it* rather.   Were - are able

22 For he that is called in the Lord, *being* a servant, is the Lord's freeman:

likewise also he that is called, *being* free, is Christ's <u>servant</u>. bond slave
23 You are bought with a price; be not you the <u>servants</u> of men. slaves
24 Brethren, let every man, wherein he is called, therein <u>abide</u> with God. remain
25 Now concerning virgins I have no commandment of the Lord: yet I give my judgment, as one that has obtained mercy of the Lord to be faithful.
26 I suppose therefore that this is good for the present distress, *I say*, that *it is* good for a man so to be.
27 Are you bound to a wife? seek not to be <u>loosed</u>. Are you <u>loosed</u> from a wife? seek not a wife. released
28 But and if you marry, you have not sinned; and if a virgin marry, she has not sinned. Nevertheless such shall have trouble in the flesh: but I spare you.
29 But this I say, brethren, the time *is* short: it remains, that both they that have wives be as though they had none;
30 And they that weep, as though they wept not; and they that rejoice, as though they rejoiced not; and they that buy, as though they possessed not;
31 And they that use this world, as not abusing *it*: for the <u>fashion</u> of this world passes away. structure
32 But I would have you without <u>carefulness</u>. He that is unmarried <u>cares</u> for the things that belong to the Lord, how he may please the Lord: being concerned - is concerned
33 But he that is married <u>cares</u> for the things that are of the world, how he may please *his* wife.
34 There is difference *also* between a wife and a virgin. The unmarried woman <u>cares</u> for the things of the Lord, that she may be holy both in body and in spirit: but she that is married <u>cares</u> for the things of the world, how she may please *her* husband. is concerned
35 And this I speak for your own profit; not that I may cast a <u>snare</u> upon you, but for that which is comely, and that you may attend upon the Lord without distraction. restraint
36 But if any man think that he behaves himself <u>uncomely</u> toward his virgin, if she pass <u>the flower of *her* age</u>, and need so require, let him do what he will, he sins not: let them marry. unbecomingly - i.e., of older age
37 Nevertheless he that stands steadfast in his heart, having no necessity, but has power over his own will, and has so decreed in his heart that he will keep his virgin, does well.
38 So then he that gives *her* in marriage does well; but hc that gives *her* not in marriage does better.
39 The wife is bound by the law as long as her husband lives; but if her husband be dead, she is at liberty to be married to whom she will; only in the Lord.
40 But she is happier if she so abide, after my judgment: and I think also that I have the Spirit of God.

CHAPTER 8

NOW as touching things offered to idols, we know that we all have knowledge. Knowledge <u>puffs up</u>, but <u>charity edifies</u>. exalts one - love builds one

2 And if any man think that he knows any thing, he knows nothing yet as he ought to know.

3 But if any man love God, the same is known of Him.

4 As concerning therefore the eating of those things that are offered in sacrifice to idols, we know that an idol *is* nothing in the world, and that *there is* none other God but one. DEU. 6:4 EXO. 34:15

5 For though there be that are called gods, whether in heaven or in earth, (as there be gods many, and lords many,)

6 But to us *there is but* one God, the Father, of whom *are* all things, and we in Him; and one Lord Je'sus Christ, by whom *are* all things, and we by Him. MAL. 2:10

7 However *there is* not in every man that knowledge: for some with conscience of the idol to this hour eat *it* as a thing offered to an idol; and their conscience being weak is defiled. understanding

8 But meat commends us not to God: for neither, if we eat, are we the better; neither, if we eat not, are we the worse. food

9 But take heed less by any means this liberty of yours become a stumbling-block to them that are weak. care - freedom

10 For if any man see you which has knowledge sit at meat in the idol's temple, shall not the conscience of him which is weak be emboldened to eat those things which are offered to idols; strengthened

11 And through your knowledge shall the weak brother perish, for whom Christ died? understanding

12 But when you sin so against the brethren, and wound their weak conscience, you sin against Christ.

13 Wherefore, if meat make my brother to offend, I will eat no flesh while the world stands, less I make my brother to offend. stumble

CHAPTER 9

AM I not an apostle? am I not free? have I not seen Je'sus Christ our Lord? are not you my work in the Lord?

2 If I be not an apostle to others, yet doubtless I am to you: for the seal of mine apostleship are you in the Lord. proof

3 Mine answer to them that do examine me is this, defense

4 Have we not power to eat and to drink? no right

5 Have we not power to lead about a sister, a wife, as well as other apostles, and *as* the brethren of the Lord, and Ce'phas?

6 Or I only and Bar'na-bas, have not we power to forbear working? right - refrain from

7 Who goes a warfare any time at his own charges? who plants a vineyard, and eats not of the fruit thereof? or who feeds a flock, and eats not of the milk of the flock? expenses

8 Say I these things as a man? or says not the law the same also?

9 For it is written in the law of Mo'ses, You shall not muzzle the mouth of the ox that treads out the corn. Does God take care for oxen? DEU. 25:4 1 TIM. 5:18

10 Or says He *it* altogether for our sakes? For our sakes, no doubt, *this* is written: that he that plows should

plow in hope; and that he that threshes in hope should be partaker of his hope.

11 If we have sown to you spiritual things, *is it* a great thing if we shall reap your <u>carnal</u> things?   _{material}

12 If others be partakers of *this* <u>power</u> over you, *are* not we rather? Nevertheless we have not used this power; but <u>suffer</u> all things, less we should hinder the gospel of Christ.   _{right - endure}

13 Do you not know that they which minister about holy things live *of the things* of the temple? and they which wait at the altar are partakers with the altar?   _{DEU. 18:1}

14 Even so has the Lord ordained that they which preach the gospel should live of the gospel.

15 But I have used none of these things: neither have I written these things, that it should be so done to me: for *it were* better for me to die, than that any man should make my glorying <u>void</u>.   _{empty}

16 For though I preach the gospel, I have nothing to glory of: for necessity is laid upon me; yea, woe is to me, if I preach not the gospel!

17 For if I do this thing willingly, I have a reward: but if against my will, a <u>dispensation</u> *of the gospel* is committed to me.   _{stewartship}

18 What is my reward then? *<u>Verily</u>* that, when I preach the gospel, I may make the gospel of Christ without <u>charge</u>, that I abuse not my <u>power</u> in the gospel.   _{Truly - expense - right}

19 For though I be free from all *men*,

yet have I made myself servant to all, that I might <u>gain</u> the more.   _{win}

20 And to the Jews I became as a Jew, that I might <u>gain</u> the Jews; to them that are under the law, as under the law, that I might <u>gain</u> them that are under the law;

21 To them that are without law, as without law, (being not without law to God, but under the law to Christ,) that I might <u>gain</u> them that are without law.

22 To the weak became I as weak, that I might gain the weak: I am made all things to all *men*, that I might by all means save some.

23 And this I do for the gospel's sake, that I might <u>be partaker</u> thereof with *you*.   _{share}

24 Know you not that they which run in a race run all, but one receives the prize? So run, that you may <u>obtain</u>. _{win}

25 And every man that strives for <u>the mastery</u> is temperate in all things. Now they *do it* to obtain a corruptible crown; but we an incorruptible. _{self control}

26 I therefore so run, not as <u>uncertainly</u>; so fight I, not as one that beats the air: _{without aim}

27 But I keep under my body, and bring *it* <u>into subjection</u>: less that by any means, when I have preached to others, I myself should be <u>a castaway</u>.   _{under control - disqualified}

CHAPTER 10

MOREOVER, brethren, I would not that you should be ignorant, how that all our fathers were under the cloud, and all passed through the sea;   _{not knowing}

2 And were all baptized <u>to</u> Mo'ses in the cloud and in the sea;   into

3 And did all eat the same spiritual <u>meat</u>;   EXO. 16:15 food

4 And did all drink the same spiritual drink: for they drank of that spiritual <u>Rock</u> that <u>followed</u> them: and that <u>Rock</u> was Christ.

EX. 17:6 Gr. Petras - accompanied

5 But with many of them God was not well pleased: for they were <u>overthrown</u> in the wilderness.   NUM. 14:29 destroyed

6 Now these things were our examples, to the intent we should not <u>lust</u> after evil things, as they also <u>lusted</u>.   NUM. 11:4 DEU. 7:4 crave

7 Neither be you idolaters, as *were* some of them; as it is written, The people sat down to eat and drink, and rose up to play   EX. 32:6.

8 Neither let us commit fornication, as some of them committed, and fell in one day three and twenty thousand.

9 Neither let us <u>tempt</u> Christ, as some of them also <u>tempted</u>, and were destroyed of serpents.   test

10 Neither <u>murmur</u> you, as some of them also <u>murmured</u>, and were destroyed of the destroyer. NUM. 16:41 grumble

11 Now all these things happened to them for examples: and they are written for our <u>admonition</u>, upon whom the ends of the world are come.   instruction

12 Wherefore let him that thinks he stands take <u>heed</u> less he fall.   care

13 There has no temptation taken you but such as is common to man: but God *is* faithful, who will not <u>suffer</u> you to be tempted above that you are able; but will with the temptation also make a way to escape, that you may be able to bear *it*.   permit

14 Wherefore, my dearly beloved, flee from idolatry.   EX. 17:6

15 I speak as to wise men; judge you what I say.

16 The cup of blessing which we bless, is it not the communion of the blood of Christ? The bread which we break, is it not the communion of the body of Christ?

17 For we *being* many are one bread, *and* one body: for we are all partakers of <u>that</u> one bread.   the

18 Behold Is'ra-el after the flesh: are not they which eat of the sacrifices <u>partakers</u> of the altar?   sharers

19 What say I then? that the idol is any thing, or that which is offered in sacrifice to idols is any thing?

20 But *I say*, that the things which the Gen'tiles sacrifice, they sacrifice to <u>devils</u>, and not to God: and I would not that you should have fellowship with <u>devils</u>.   DEU. 32:17 demons

21 You cannot drink the cup of the Lord, and the cup of devils: you cannot be partakers of the Lord's table, and of the table of devils.

22 Do we provoke the Lord to jealousy? are we stronger than He? DEU. 32:21

23 All things are lawful for me, but all things are not expedient: all things are lawful for me, but all things <u>edify</u> not.   build

24 Let no man seek his own, but every man another's <u>wealth</u>.   good

25 Whatsoever is sold in the <u>shambles</u>, *that* eat, asking no question for conscience sake: meat market

26 For the earth *is* the Lord's, and the fulness thereof.   PS. 24:1

27 If any of them that believe not bid you *to a feast*, and you be disposed to go; whatsoever is set before you, eat, asking no question for conscience sake.

28 But if any man say to you, This is offered in sacrifice to idols, eat not for his sake that showed it, and for conscience sake: for the earth *is* the Lord's, and the fulness thereof:

29 Conscience, I say, not your own, but of the other: for why is my liberty judged of another *man's* conscience?

30 For if I by grace be a partaker, why am I evil spoken of for that for which I give thanks? thanksgiving - sharer

31 Whether therefore you eat, or drink, or whatsoever you do, do all to the glory of God.

32 Give none offence, neither to the Jews, nor to the Gen'tiles, nor to the church of God: no - Greeks

33 Even as I please all *men* in all *things*, not seeking mine own profit, but the *profit* of many, that they may be saved.

CHAPTER 11

BE you followers of me, even as I also *am* of Christ.   imitators

2 Now I praise you, brethren, that you remember me in all things, and keep the ordinances, as I delivered *them* to you.

3 But I would have you know, that the head of every man is Christ; and the head of the woman *is* the man; and the head of Christ *is* God.

4 Every man praying or prophesying, having *his* head covered, dishonors his head.   preaching

5 But every woman that prays or prophesies with *her* head uncovered dishonors her head: for that is even all one as if she were shaven.

6 For if the woman be not covered, let her also be shorn: but if it be a shame for a woman to be shorn or shaven, let her be covered.

7 For a man indeed ought not to cover *his* head, forasmuch as he is the image and glory of God: but the woman is the glory of the man.

8 For the man is not of the woman; but the woman of the man.   GEN. 2:21

9 Neither was the man created for the woman; but the woman for the man.   GEN. 2:18

10 For this cause ought the woman to have power on *her* head because of the angels.

11 Nevertheless neither is the man without the woman, neither the woman without the man, in the Lord.

12 For as the woman *is* of the man, even so *is* the man also by the woman; but all things of God.   originate from

13 Judge in yourselves: is it comely that a woman pray to God uncovered?   proper

14 Does not even nature itself teach you, that, if a man have long hair, it is a shame to him?   dishonor

15 But if a woman have long hair, it is a glory to her: for *her* hair is given her for a covering.

16 But if any man seem to be contentious, we have no such custom, neither the churches of God.

17 Now in this that I declare *to you* I praise *you* not, that you come together not for the better, but for the worse.

18 For first of all, when you come together in the church, I hear that there be divisions among you; and I partly believe it.

19 For there must be also <u>heresies</u> among you, that they which are approved may be made <u>manifest</u> among you.   factions - known

20 When you come together therefore into one place, *this* is not to eat the Lord's supper.

21 For in eating every one takes before *other* his own supper: and one is hungry, and another is drunken.

22 What? have you not houses to eat and to drink in? or despise you the church of God, and shame them that <u>have not</u>? What shall I say to you? shall I praise you in this? I praise *you* not.   are poor

23 For I have received of the Lord that which also I delivered to you, That the Lord Je'sus the *same* night in which He was betrayed took bread:

24 And when He had given thanks, He broke *it*, and said, Take, eat: this is My body, which is broken for you: this do in remembrance of Me.

25 After the same manner also *He took* the cup, when He had <u>supped</u>, saying, This cup is the new <u>testament</u> in My blood: this do you, as oft as you drink *it*, in remembrance of Me.   finished eating - agreement

26 For as often as you eat this bread, and drink this cup, you do <u>show</u> the Lord's death till He come.   proclaim

27 Wherefore whosoever shall eat this bread, and drink *this* cup of the Lord, unworthily, shall be guilty of the body and blood of the Lord.

28 But let a man examine himself, and so let him eat of *that* bread, and drink of *that* cup.

29 For he that eats and drinks unworthily, eats and drinks damnation to himself, not discerning the Lord's body.

30 For this cause many *are* weak and sickly among you, and many sleep.

31 For if we would judge ourselves, we should not be judged.

32 But when we are judged, we are chastened of the Lord, that we should not be condemned with the world.

33 Wherefore, my brethren, when you come together to eat, <u>tarry</u> one for another.   wait

34 And if any man hunger, let him eat at home; that you come not together to <u>condemnation</u>. And the rest will I set in order when I come.   judgment

CHAPTER 12

NOW concerning spiritual *gifts*, brethren, I would not have you <u>ignorant</u>.   not knowing

2 You know that you were Gen'tiles, carried away to these dumb idols, even as you were led.

3 Wherefore I give you to understand, that no man speaking by the Spirit of God calls Je'sus accursed: and *that* no man can say that Je'sus is the Lord, but by the Ho'ly <u>Ghost</u>.   Spirit

4 Now there are diversities of gifts, but the same Spirit.

5 And there are differences of administrations, but the same Lord. varieties - ministries

6 And there are diversities of operations, but it is the same God which works all in all. varieties

7 But the manifestation of the Spirit is given to every man to profit withal. by

8 For to one is given by the Spirit the word of wisdom; to another the word of knowledge by the same Spirit;

9 To another faith by the same Spirit; to another the gifts of healing by the same Spirit;

10 To another the working of miracles; to another prophecy; to another discerning of spirits; to another *divers* kinds of tongues; to another the interpretation of tongues: various

11 But all these works that one and the selfsame Spirit, dividing to every man severally as He will. distributing individually

12 For as the body is one, and has many members, and all the members of that one body, being many, are one body: so also *is* Christ.

13 For by one Spirit are we all baptized into one body, whether *we be* Jews or Gen'tiles, whether *we be* bond or free; and have been all made to drink into one Spirit. Greeks

14 For the body is not one member, but many.

15 If the foot shall say, Because I am not the hand, I am not of the body; is it therefore not of the body?

16 And if the ear shall say, Because I am not the eye, I am not of the body; is it therefore not of the body?

17 If the whole body *were* an eye, where *were* the hearing? If the whole *were* hearing, where *were* the smelling?

18 But now has God set the members every one of them in the body, as it has pleased Him.

19 And if they were all one member, where *were* the body?

20 But now *are they* many members, yet but one body.

21 And the eye cannot say to the hand, I have no need of you: nor again the head to the feet, I have no need of you.

22 Nay, much more those members of the body, which seem to be more feeble, are necessary: On the contrary - weaker

23 And those *members* of the body, which we think to be less honorable, upon these we bestow more abundant honor; and our uncomely *parts* have more abundant comeliness. parts - give

24 For our comely *parts* have no need: but God has tempered the body together, having given more abundant honor to that *part* which lacked: assembled

25 That there should be no schism in the body; but *that* the members should have the same care one for another. division

26 And whether one member suffer, all the members suffer with it; or one member be honored, all the members rejoice with it.

27 Now you are the body of Christ, and members in particular.

28 And God has set some in the church, first apostles, secondarily

prophets, thirdly teachers, after that miracles, then gifts of healings, helps, governments, <u>diversities</u> of <u>tongues</u>. <small>different kinds - languages</small>

29 *Are* all apostles? *are* all prophets? *are* all teachers? are all workers of miracles?

30 Have all the gifts of healing? do all speak with <u>tongues</u>? do all interpret?

31 But <u>covet</u> earnestly the best gifts: and yet show I to you a more excellent way. <small>seek</small>

CHAPTER 13

THOUGH I speak with the <u>tongues</u> of men and of angels, and have not <u>charity</u>, I am become *as* sounding brass, or a tinkling cymbal.<small>love</small>

2 And though I have *the gift of* <u>prophecy</u>, and understand all mysteries, and all knowledge; and though I have all faith, so that I could remove mountains, and have not <u>charity</u>, I am nothing. <small>understanding</small>

3 And though I <u>bestow</u> all my goods to feed *the poor*, and though I give my body to be burned, and have not <u>charity</u>, it profits me nothing. <small>give</small>

4 <u>Charity</u> suffers long, *and* is kind; <u>charity</u> envies not; <u>charity</u> <u>vaunts not itself</u>, is not <u>puffed</u> up, <small>love - does not brag - arrogant</small>

5 Does not behave itself unseemly, seeks not her own, is not easily provoked, <u>thinks no evil</u>; <small>thinks no wrong</small>

6 Rejoices not in iniquity, but rejoices in the truth; <small>with</small>

7 Bears all things, believes all things, hopes all things, endures all things.

8 <u>Charity</u> never fails: but whether *there be* prophecies, they shall fail; whether *there be* <u>tongues</u>, they shall cease; whether *there be* knowledge, it shall vanish away.<small>love - languages</small>

9 For we <u>know in part</u>, and we <u>prophesy</u> in part. <small>i.e., limited knowledge - speak</small>

10 But when that which is perfect is come, then that which is in part shall be done away.

11 When I was a child, I spoke as a child, I <u>understood</u> as a child, I <u>thought</u> as a child: but when I became a man, I put away childish things. <small>spoke - reasoned</small>

12 For now we see through a glass, darkly; but then face to face: now I know in part; but then shall I know even as also I am known.

13 And now abides faith, hope, <u>charity</u>, these three; but the greatest of these *is* <u>charity</u>. <small>love</small>

CHAPTER 14

FOLLOW after <u>charity</u>, and desire spiritual *gifts*, but rather that you may <u>prophesy</u> <small>love - teach</small>

2 For he that speaks in an *unknown* <u>tongue</u> speaks not to men, but to God: for no man understands *him*; however in the spirit he speaks mysteries. <small>languages</small>

3 But he that <u>prophesies</u> speaks to men *to* <u>edification</u>, and exhortation, and comfort. <small>speaks - greater knowledge</small>

4 He that speaks in an *unknown* <u>tongue</u> <u>edifies</u> himself; but he that <u>prophesies</u> <u>edifies</u> the church. <small>strange language - builds up</small>

5 I would that you all spoke with <u>tongues</u>, but rather that you <u>prophesied</u>:

for greater *is* he that <u>prophesies</u> than he that speaks with <u>tongues</u>, except he interpret, that the church may receive <u>edifying</u>. speaks - languages - building up

6 Now, brethren, if I come to you speaking with <u>tongues</u>, what shall I profit you, except I shall speak to you either by revelation, or by knowledge, or by prophesying, or by <u>doctrine</u>? teaching

7 And even things without life giving <u>sound</u>, whether pipe or harp, except they give a distinction in the <u>sounds</u>, how shall it be known what is piped or harped? tones

8 For if the trumpet give an <u>uncertain</u> sound, who shall prepare himself to <u>the battle</u>? indistinct - war

9 So likewise you, except you utter by the tongue words easy to be understood, how shall it be known what is spoken? for you shall speak <u>into the air</u>. i.e., to no advantage

10 There are, it may be, so many kinds of voices in the world, and none of them *is* without <u>signification</u>. meaning

11 Therefore if I know not the meaning of the <u>voice</u>, I shall be to him that speaks a barbarian, and he that speaks *shall be* a barbarian to me. language

12 Even so you, forasmuch as you are zealous of spiritual *gifts*, seek that you may excel to the <u>edifying</u> of the church. building up

13 Wherefore let him that speaks in an *unknown* <u>tongue</u> pray that he may interpret. language

14 For if I pray in an *unknown* <u>tongue</u>, my spirit prays, but my understanding is unfruitful.

15 What is it then? I will pray with the spirit, and I will pray with the understanding also: I will sing with the spirit, and I will sing with the understanding also.

16 Else when you shall bless with the spirit, how shall he that occupies the room of the <u>unlearned</u> say Amen at your giving of thanks, seeing he understands not what you say? uneducated

17 For you <u>verily</u> give thanks well, but the other is not <u>edified</u>. truly - helped

18 I thank my God, I speak with <u>tongues</u> more than you all: languages

19 Yet in the church I had rather speak five words with my understanding, that *by my voice* I might teach others also, than ten thousand words in an *unknown* <u>tongue</u>.

20 Brethren, be not children in understanding: however in <u>malice</u> be you children, but in understanding be men. evil

21 In the law it is written, With *men of* other <u>tongues</u> and other lips will I speak to this people; and yet for all that will they not hear Me, says the Lord. ISA. 28:11

22 Wherefore <u>tongues</u> are for a sign, not to them that believe, but to them that believe not: but <u>prophesying</u> *serves* not for them that believe not, but for them which believe. languages - speaking

23 If therefore the whole church be come together into one place, and all speak with <u>tongues</u>, and there come in *those that are* <u>unlearned</u>, or unbelievers, will they not say that you are mad? uneducated

24 But if all prophesy, and there come

in one that believes not, or *one* unlearned, he is convinced of all, he is judged of all:

25 And thus are the secrets of his heart made manifest; and so falling down on *his* face he will worship God, and report that God is in you of a truth.

26 How is it then, brethren? when you come together, every one of you has a psalm, has a <u>doctrine</u>, has a <u>tongue</u>, has a revelation, has an interpretation. Let all things be done to <u>edifying</u>. teaching - language - understanding

27 If any man speak in an *unknown* <u>tongue</u>, *let it be* by two, or at the most *by* three, and *that* <u>by course</u>; and let one interpret. in turn

28 But if there be no interpreter, let him keep silence in the church; and let him speak to himself, and to God.

29 Let the prophets speak two or three, and let the other judge.

30 If *any thing* be revealed to another that sits by, let the first <u>hold</u> his peace. keep

31 For you may all <u>prophesy</u> one by one, that all may learn, and all may be <u>comforted</u>. speak - exhorted

32 And the spirits of the prophets are subject to the prophets.

33 For God is not *the author* of confusion, but of peace, as in all churches of the saints.

34 Let your women keep silence in the churches: for it is not permitted to them to speak; but *they are commanded* to be under obedience, as also says the law.

35 And if they will learn any thing, let them ask their husbands at home: for it is a shame for women to speak in the church.

36 What? came the word of God out from you? or came it to you only?

37 If any man think himself to be a prophet, or spiritual, let him acknowledge that the things that I write to you are the commandments of the Lord.

38 But if any man be <u>ignorant</u>, let him be <u>ignorant</u>. not knowing

39 Wherefore, brethren, <u>covet</u> to prophesy, and forbid not to speak with <u>tongues</u>. desire - languages

40 Let all things be done <u>decently</u> and in order. properly

CHAPTER 15

MOREOVER, brethren, I declare to you the gospel which I preached to you, which also you have received, and wherein you stand;

2 By which also you are saved, if you keep in memory what I preached to you, unless you have believed in vain.

3 For I delivered to you first of all that which I also received, how that Christ died for our sins according to the scriptures; ISA. 53:3-12

4 And that He was buried, and that He rose again the third day according to the scriptures: HOS. 6:2

5 And that He was seen of <u>Ce'phas</u>, then of the twelve: Peter

6 After that, He was seen of above five hundred brethren at once; of whom the greater part remain to this present, but some are <u>fallen asleep</u>. dead

7 After that, He was seen of James; then of all the apostles.

8 And last of all He was seen of me also, as of one born out of due time.

9 For I am the least of the apostles, that am not <u>meet</u> to be called an apostle, because I persecuted the church of God. ^{fit}

10 But by the grace of God I am what I am: and His grace which *was* <u>bestowed</u> upon me was not in vain; but I labored more abundantly than they all: yet not I, but the grace of God which was with me. ^{placed}

11 Therefore whether *it were* I or they, so we preach, and so you believed.

12 Now if Christ be preached that He rose from the dead, how say some among you that there is no resurrection of the dead?

13 But if there be no resurrection of the dead, then is Christ not risen:

14 And if Christ be not risen, then *is* our preaching <u>vain</u>, and your faith *is* also <u>vain</u>. ^{worthless}

15 Yea, and we are found false witnesses of God; because we have testified of God that He raised up Christ: whom He raised not up, if so be that the dead rise not.

16 For if the dead rise not, then is not Christ raised:

17 And if Christ be not <u>raised</u>, your faith *is* <u>vain</u>; you are yet in your sins. ^{i.e., raised from death}

18 Then they also which are <u>fallen asleep</u> in Christ are perished. ^{dead}

19 If in this life only we have hope in Christ, we are of all men most miserable.

20 But now is Christ risen from the dead, *and* become the firstfruits of them that <u>slept</u>. ^{died}

21 For since by man *came* death, by man *came* also the resurrection of the dead.

22 For as in Ad'am all die, even so in Christ shall all be made alive.

23 But every man in his own order: Christ the firstfruits; afterward they that are Christ's at His coming.

24 Then *comes* the end, when He shall have delivered up the kingdom to God, even the Father; when He shall have put down all rule and all authority and power.

25 For He must reign, till He has put all enemies under His feet. ^{PS. 110:1}

26 The last enemy *that* shall be destroyed *is* death.

27 For He has put all things under His feet. But when He says, all things are put under *Him*, *it is* manifest that He is excepted, which did put all things under Him. ^{PS. 8:6}

28 And when all things shall be <u>subdued</u> to Him, then shall the Son also Himself be subject to Him that put all things under Him, that God may be all in all. ^{subjected}

29 Else what shall they do which are baptized for the dead, if the dead rise not at all? why are they then baptized for the dead?

30 And why stand we in <u>jeopardy</u> every hour? ^{danger}

31 I protest by your rejoicing which I have in Christ Jesus our Lord, I die daily.

32 If after the manner of men I have fought with beasts at Eph'e-sus, what

advantage it me, if the dead rise not? let us eat and drink; for to morrow we die.   ISA. 22:13

33 Be not deceived: evil <u>communications</u> corrupt good manners.·company

34 Awake to righteousness, and sin not; for some have not the knowledge of God: I speak *this* to your shame.

35 But some *man* will say, How are the dead raised up? and with what body do they come?

36 *You* fool, that which you sow is not made alive, except it die:

37 And that which you sow, you sow not that body that shall be, but bare grain, it may chance of wheat, or of some other *grain*:

38 But God give it a body as it has pleased him, and to every seed its own body.   GEN. 1:11

39 All flesh *is* not the same flesh: but *there is* one *kind of* flesh of men, another flesh of beasts, another of fishes, *and* another of birds.

40 *There are* also <u>celestial</u> bodies, and bodies <u>terrestrial</u>: but the glory of the <u>celestial</u> *is* one, and the *glory* of the <u>terrestrial</u> *is* another. ·heavenly - earthly

41 *There is* one glory of the sun, and another glory of the moon, and another glory of the stars: for *one* star differs from *another* star in glory.

42 So also *is* the resurrection of the dead. It is sown in corruption; it is raised in incorruption:

43 It is sown in dishonor; it is raised in glory: it is sown in weakness; it is raised in power:

44 It is sown a natural body; it is raised a spiritual body. There is a natural body, and there is a spiritual body.

45 And so it is written, The first man Ad'am was made a living soul; the last Ad'am *was made* a living spirit.   GEN. 2:7

46 However that *was* not first which is spiritual, but that which is natural; and afterward that which is spiritual.

47 The first man *is* of the earth, earthy: the second man *is* the Lord from heaven.

48 As *is* the earthy, such *are* they also that are earthy: and as *is* the heavenly, such *are* they also that are heavenly.

49 And as we have borne the image of the earthy, we shall also bear the image of the heavenly.

50 Now this I say, brethren, that flesh and blood cannot inherit the kingdom of God; neither does corruption inherit incorruption.

51 Behold, I show you a <u>mystery</u>; We shall not all sleep, but we shall all be changed,   ·secret (i.e., of rapture)

52 In a moment, in the twinkling of an eye, at the last trump: for the trumpet shall sound, and the dead shall be raised incorruptible, and we shall be changed.

53 For this <u>corruptible</u> must put on incorruption, and this mortal *must* put on immortality.   ·perishable

54 So when this <u>corruptible</u> shall have put on incorruption, and this mortal shall have put on immortality, then shall be brought to pass the saying that is written, Death is swallowed up in victory.   ISA. 25:8

55 O death, where *is* your sting? O <u>grave</u>, where *is* your victory? HOS.13:14 death

56 The sting of death *is* sin; and the strength of sin *is* the law.

57 But thanks *be* to God, which give us the victory through our Lord Je'sus Christ.

58 Therefore, my beloved brethren, be you steadfast, unmoveable, always abounding in the work of the Lord, forasmuch as you know that your labor is not in vain in the Lord.

CHAPTER 16

NOW concerning the collection for the <u>saints</u>, as I have given order to the churches of Ga-la'tia, even so do you. believers

2 Upon <u>the first</u> *day* of the week let every one of you lay by him in store, as *God* has prospered him, that there be no <u>gatherings</u> when I come. Sunday - collections

3 And when I come, whomsoever you shall approve by *your* letters, them will I send to bring your <u>liberality</u> to Je-ru'sa-lem. gifts

4 And if it be <u>meet</u> that I go also, they shall go with me. fitting

5 Now I will come to you, when I shall pass through Mac-e-do'ni-a: for I do pass through Mac-e-do'ni-a.

6 And it may be that I will abide, yea, and winter with you, that you may bring me on my journey where ever I go.

7 For I will not see you now by the way; but I trust to <u>tarry</u> a while with you, if the Lord permit. stay

8 But I will tarry at Eph'e-sus until Pen'te-cost.

9 For a great door and effectual is opened to me, and *there are* many adversaries.

10 Now if Tim'o-thy come, see that he may be with you without fear: for he works the work of the Lord, as I also *do*.

11 Let no man therefore despise him: but <u>conduct</u> him forth in peace, that he may come to me: for I look for him with the brethren. bring

12 As touching *our* brother A-pol'los, I greatly desired him to come to you with the brethren: but his will was not at all to come at this time; but he will come when he shall have convenient time.

13 Watch you, stand fast in the faith, <u>quit you</u> like men, be strong. PS. 31:24 act

14 Let all your <u>things</u> be done with <u>charity</u>. doings - love

15 I <u>beseech</u> you, brethren, (you know the house of Steph'a-nas, that it is the firstfruits of A-cha'ia, and *that* they have <u>addicted</u> themselves to the ministry of the <u>saints</u>,) beg - devoted - believers

16 That you submit yourselves to such, and to every one that helps with *us*, and labors.

17 I am glad of the coming of Steph'a-nas and For-tu-na'tus and A-cha'i-cus: for that which was lacking on your part they have supplied.

18 For they have refreshed my spirit and yours: therefore acknowledge you them that are such.

19 The churches of A'sia <u>salute</u> you. A-qui'la and Pris-cil'la <u>salute</u> you much in the Lord, with the church that is in their house. greet

20 All the brethren greet you. Greet you one another with an holy kiss.
21 The salutation of *me* Paul with mine own hand.
22 If any man love not the Lord Je'-sus Christ, let him be <u>An-ath'e-ma Mar'an-a'tha</u>.   accursed - the Lord is coming'
23 The grace of our Lord Je'sus Christ *be* with you.
24 My love *be* with you all in Christ Je'sus. Amen.

2 CORINTHIANS

OUTLINE

SPECIAL GREETINGS 1.1–11
Salutation 1.1, 2
Expression of Thanksgiving and Trust 1.3–11

PAUL'S ANSWER TO HIS CRITICS 1.2—7.16
Variation of His Plan for Visiting Corinth 1.12—2.4
Punishment and Forgiveness of the Serious Offender 2.5–11
Paul's Disappointment at Not Finding Titus in Troas 2.12–16
Paul's Letters of Commendation 2.17—3.5
Comparison of the Old and the New Covenants 3.6–18
Character of Paul's Ministry 4.1–6
Paul's Confidence in the Face of Affliction 4.7—5.10
The Ministry of Reconciliation 5.11—6.10
Paul's Appeal to the Corinthians 6.11—7.4
Meeting with Titus in Macedonia 7.5–16

THE COLLECTION FOR THE POOR CHRISTIANS AT JERUSALEM 8.1—9.15

PAUL AFFIRMS HIS APOSTOLIC AUTHORITY 10.1—13.14
Accusations of Cowardice and Weakness Answered 10.1–11
The Invasion of His Territory by Unauthorized Persons 10.12–18
Vindication of the Authenticity of His Apostleship 11.1—12.18
Warnings to Any Who Continue to Oppose His Authority 12.19—13.10
An Exhortation and Salutation 13.11–14

SURVEY

No brief outline can give any idea of the wealth and warmth of this remarkable epistle. Paul's main object in writing was to vindicate his apostolic authority, especially as the church in Corinth had been invaded by false apostles who were seeking to undermine his authority and to lead the people away from the Gospel which they had received from him. He writes, however, as no mere authoritarian, but rather as the spiritual father of the Corinthian believers, who loves them and yearns that they should reciprocate his love and remain faithful to the truth he has imparted to them. The situation in Corinth was such that it was necessary for Paul to speak about himself. Although appealing to their own personal and intimate knowledge of him and his character, and reminding them of the great sufferings and hardships he had endured in order to bring the message of salvation to them, he does so with transparent humility and sincerity and, indeed, with embarrassment. Throughout the epistle the dignity, the devotion, the serene faith, and the passionate dedication of the Apostle Paul shine forth with an intense glow that warms all but the most wilfully unresponsive hearts. He sets himself before his readers as one who in himself is utterly weak and worthless, but through whose weakness the grace and power of Almighty God are magnified. In contrast to the self-esteem and self-interest of the false apostles is Paul's self-effacement: all is of God and to the glory of God. The keynote sounded sweetly through the whole epistle is that of the divine assurance to him: "And he said unto me, My grace is sufficient for thee: for my strength is made perfect in weakness" (12.9). The rediscovery in our day of this epistle, with its doctrine of reconciliation in

Christ and its theme of glory through suffering, would mean a renewal of the vision and vitality of God's people and, through them, blessing to multitudes who are as yet in spiritual darkness.

AUTHOR

There can be no reasonable doubt concerning Paul's authorship of this epistle. The Second Epistle to the Corinthians was written in the same year as, and probably some six months after, 1 Corinthians.

P.E.H.

THE SECOND LETTER OF PAUL TO THE
CORINTHIANS

Paul Defends
His Apostleship

CHAPTER 1

PAUL, an apostle of Je'sus Christ by the will of God, and Tim'o-thy *our* brother, to the church of God which is at Cor'inth, with all the saints which are in all A-cha'ia: believers

2 Grace *be* to you and peace from God our Father, and *from* the Lord Je'sus Christ.

3 Blessed *be* God, even the Father of our Lord Je'sus Christ, the Father of mercies, and the God of all comfort;

4 Who comforts us in all our tribulation, that we may be able to comfort them which are in any trouble, by the comfort wherewith we ourselves are comforted of God. afflictions

5 For as the sufferings of Christ abound in us, so our consolation also abounds by Christ. comfort

6 And whether we be afflicted, *it is* for your consolation and salvation, which is effectual in the enduring of the same sufferings which we also suffer: or whether we be comforted, *it is* for your consolation and salvation. effective

7 And our hope of you *is* steadfast, knowing, that as you are partakers of the sufferings, so *shall you be* also of the consolation.

8 For we would not, brethren, have you ignorant of our trouble which came to us in A'sia, that we were pressed out of measure, above strength, insomuch that we despaired even of life: not knowing - burdened

9 But we had the sentence of death in ourselves, that we should not trust in ourselves, but in God which raises the dead:

10 Who delivered us from so great a death, and does deliver: in whom we trust that He will yet deliver *us*;

11 You also helping together by prayer for us, that for the gift bestowed upon us by the means of many persons thanks may be given by many on our behalf. given

12 For our rejoicing is this, the testimony of our conscience, that in simplicity and godly sincerity, not with fleshly wisdom, but by the grace of God, we have had our conversation in the world, and more abundantly to you-ward. holiness - conducted ourselves

13 For we write none other things to you, than what you read or acknowledge; and I trust you shall acknowledge even to the end; understand

14 As also you have acknowledged us in part, that we are your rejoicing, even as you also *are* ours in the day of the Lord Je'sus.

15 And in this confidence I was minded to come to you before, that you might have a second benefit;

16 And to pass by you into Mac-e-do'ni-a, and to come again out of Mac-e-do'-ni-a to you, and of you to be <u>brought</u> on my way toward Ju-dae'a. _{helped}

17 When I therefore was thus minded, did I use <u>lightness</u>? or the things that I purpose, do I purpose according to the flesh, that with me there should be <u>yea yea</u>, and <u>nay nay</u>? _{worldly ways - yes - no}

18 But *as* God *is* true, our word toward you was not <u>yea</u> and <u>nay</u>.

19 For the Son of God, Je'sus Christ, who was preached among you by us, *even* by me and Sil-va'nus and Tim'o-thy, was not <u>yea</u> and <u>nay</u>, but in Him was <u>yea</u>.

20 For all the promises of God in Him *are* <u>yea</u>, and in Him Amen, to the glory of God by us.

21 Now He which <u>stablisheth</u> us with you in Christ, and has anointed us, *is* God; _{placed}

22 Who has also sealed us, and given the <u>earnest</u> of the Spirit in our hearts. _{pledge}

23 Moreover I call God for a record upon my soul, that to spare you I came not as yet to Cor'inth.

24 Not for that we have <u>dominion</u> over your faith, but are helpers of your joy: for by faith you stand. _{control}

CHAPTER 2

BUT I determined this with myself, that I would not come again to you in <u>heaviness</u>. _{sorrow}

2 For if I make you sorry, who is he then that makes me glad, but the same which is made by me <u>sorry</u> by me? _{sad}

3 And I wrote this same to you, less, when I came, I should have sorrow from them of whom I ought to rejoice; having confidence in you all, that my joy is *the joy* of you all.

4 For out of much <u>affliction</u> and anguish of heart I wrote to you with many tears; not that you should be grieved, but that you might know the love which I have more abundantly to you. _{distress}

5 But if any have caused grief, he has not grieved me, but in part: that I may not overcharge you all.

6 Sufficient to such a man *is* this punishment, which *was inflicted* of many.

7 So that contrariwise you *ought* rather to forgive *him*, and comfort *him*, less perhaps such a one should be <u>swallowed up</u> with overmuch sorrow. _{overwhelmed}

8 Wherefore I <u>beseech</u> you that you would confirm *your* love toward him. _{beg}

9 For to this end also did I write, that I might know the proof of you, whether you be obedient in all things.

10 To whom you forgive any thing, I *forgive* also: for if I forgave any thing, to whom I forgave *it*, for your sakes *forgave I it* in the <u>person</u> of Christ; _{presence}

11 Less Sa'tan should get an advantage of us: for we are not <u>ignorant</u> of his devices. _{not knowing}

12 Furthermore, when I came to Tro'-as to *preach* Christ's gospel, and a door was opened to me of the Lord,

13 I had no <u>rest</u> in my spirit, because I found not Ti'tus my brother: but taking my leave of them, I went from there into Mac-e-do'ni-a. _{peace}

14 Now thanks *be* to God, which always causes us to triumph in Christ, and makes <u>manifest</u> the <u>savor</u> of His knowledge by us in every place. _{known - fragrance}

15 For we are to God a sweet <u>savor</u> of Christ, in them that are saved, and in them that perish:

16 To the one *we are* the <u>savor</u> of death to death; and to the other the <u>savor</u> of life to life. And who *is* sufficient for these things?

17 For we are not as many, which <u>corrupt</u> the word of God: but as of sincerity, but as of God, in the sight of God speak we in Christ. _{peddle}

CHAPTER 3

DO we begin again to commend ourselves? or need we, as some *others*, epistles of commendation to you, or *letters* of commendation from you?

2 You are our <u>epistle</u> written in our hearts, known and read of all men:_{letter}

3 *Forasmuch as you are* <u>manifestly</u> declared to be the epistle of Christ ministered by us, written not with ink, but with the Spirit of the living God; not in tables of stone, but in fleshy tables of the heart. _{openly}

4 And such <u>trust</u> have we through Christ to Godward: _{confidence}

5 Not that we are sufficient of ourselves to think any thing as of ourselves; but our sufficiency *is* of God;

6 Who also has made us able <u>ministers</u> of the new testament; not of the letter, but of the Spirit: for the letter kills, but the Spirit gives life. _{JER. 31:31 teachers}

7 But if the <u>ministration</u> of death,

written *and* engraven in stones, was glorious, so that the children of Is'ra-el could not steadfastly behold the face of Mo'ses for the glory of his countenance; which *glory* was to be done away: _{EXO. 34:29 ministry}

8 How shall not the <u>ministration</u> of the Spirit be rather glorious?

9 For if the <u>ministration</u> of condemnation *be* glory, much more does the <u>ministration</u> of righteousness exceed in glory.

10 For even that which was made glorious had no glory in this <u>respect</u>, by reason of the glory that <u>excels</u>. _{account - exceeds}

11 For if that which <u>is done</u> away *was* glorious, much more that which remains *is* glorious. _{fades}

12 Seeing then that we have such hope, we use great <u>plainness</u> of speech: _{boldness}

13 And not as Mo'ses, *which* put a veil over his face, that the children of Is'ra-el could not steadfastly look to the end of that which is abolished:

14 But their minds were blinded: for until this day remains the same veil <u>untaken away</u> in the reading of the old testament; which *veil* is done away in Christ. _{unlifted}

15 But even to this day, when Mo'ses is read, the veil is upon their heart.

16 Nevertheless when he shall turn to the Lord, the veil shall be taken away.

17 Now the Lord is that Spirit: and where the Spirit of the Lord *is*, there *is* <u>liberty</u>. _{ISA. 61:1 freedom}

18 But we all, with open face beholding as in a glass the glory of the Lord,

are changed into the same image from glory to glory, *even* as by the Spirit of the Lord. mirror

CHAPTER 4

THEREFORE seeing we have this ministry, as we have received mercy, we <u>faint</u> not; falter
2 But have renounced the hidden things of dishonesty, not walking in craftiness, nor handling the word of God deceitfully; but by <u>manifestation</u> of the truth commending ourselves to every man's conscience in the sight of God. open showing
3 But if our gospel be <u>hid</u>, it is <u>hid</u> to them that are lost: veiled
4 In whom the god of this world has blinded the minds of them which believe not, less the light of the glorious gospel of Christ, who is the image of God, should shine to them.
5 For we preach not ourselves, but Christ Je'sus the Lord; and ourselves your servants for Je'sus' sake.
6 For God, who commanded the light to shine out of darkness, has shined in our hearts, to *give* the light of the knowledge of the glory of God in the face of Je'sus Christ. GEN. 1:4
7 But we have this treasure in earthen vessels, that the excellency of the power may be of God, and not of us.
8 *We are* troubled on every side, yet not distressed; *we are* <u>perplexed</u>, but not in despair; puzzled
9 Persecuted, but not forsaken; cast down, but not destroyed;
'0 Always bearing about in the body

the dying of the Lord Je'sus, that the life also of Je'sus might be made <u>manifest</u> in our body. known
11 For we which live are always delivered to death for Je'sus' sake, that the life also of Je'sus might be made <u>manifest</u> in our mortal flesh.
12 So then death works in us, but life in you.
13 We having the same spirit of faith, according as it is written, I believed, and therefore have I spoken; we also believe, and therefore speak; PS. 116:10
14 Knowing that He which raised up the Lord Je'sus shall raise up us also by Je'sus, and shall present *us* with you.
15 For all things *are* for your sakes, that the abundant grace might through the thanksgiving of many <u>redound</u> to the glory of God. abound
16 For which cause we faint not; but though our outward man <u>perish</u>, yet the inward *man* is renewed day by day. die
17 For our light <u>affliction</u>, which is but for a moment, works for us a far more exceeding *and* eternal weight of glory; troubles
18 While we look not at the things which are seen, but at the things which are not seen: for the things which are seen *are* temporal; but the things which are not seen *are* eternal.

CHAPTER 5

FOR we know that if our earthly house of *this* tabernacle were dissolved, we have a building of God, an house not made with hands, eternal in the heavens.

2 For in this we groan, earnestly desiring to be clothed upon with our house which is from heaven:

3 If so be that being clothed we shall not be found naked.

4 For we that are in *this* tabernacle do groan, being burdened: not for that we would be unclothed, but clothed upon, that mortality might be swallowed up of life. *body*

5 Now He that has wrought us for the selfsame thing *is* God, who also has given to us the earnest of the Spirit. *prepared*

6 Therefore *we are* always confident, knowing that, while we are at home in the body, we are absent from the Lord:

7 (For we walk by faith, not by sight:)

8 We are confident, *I say*, and willing rather to be absent from the body, and to be present with the Lord. *of good courage*

9 Wherefore we labor, that, whether present or absent, we may be accepted of him.

10 For we must all appear before the judgment seat of Christ; that every one may receive the things *done* in *his* body, according to that he has done, whether *it be* good or bad. *ROM. 14:10*

11 Knowing therefore the terror of the Lord, we persuade men; but we are made manifest to God; and I trust also are made manifest in your consciences. *known*

12 For we commend not ourselves again to you, but give you occasion to glory on our behalf, that you may have somewhat to *answer* them which glory in appearance, and not in heart. *be proud*

13 For whether we be beside ourselves, *it is* to God: or whether we be sober, *it is* for your cause. *crazy*

14 For the love of Christ constrains us; because we thus judge, that if one died for all, then were all dead:

15 And *that* He died for all, that they which live should not hereafter live to themselves, but to Him which died for them, and rose again.

16 Wherefore hereafter know we no man after the flesh: yea, though we have known Christ after the flesh, yet now hereafter know we *Him* no more.

17 Therefore if any man *be* in Christ, *he is* a new creature: old things are passed away; behold, all things are become new.

18 And all things *are* of God, who has reconciled us to Himself by Je'sus Christ, and has given to us the ministry of reconciliation;

19 To say, that God was in Christ, reconciling the world to Himself, not imputing their trespasses to them; and has committed to us the word of reconciliation. *counting*

20 Now then we are ambassadors for Christ, as though God did beseech *you* by us: we pray *you* in Christ's stead, be you reconciled to God. *beg*

21 For He has made Him *to be* sin for us, who knew no sin; that we might be made the righteousness of God in Him.

CHAPTER 6

WE then, *as* workers together *with Him*, beseech *you* also that you receive not the grace of God in vain.

2 (For He says, I have heard you in a time accepted, and in the day of salvation have I succoured you: behold, now *is* the accepted time; behold, now *is* the day of salvation.) ISA. 49:8 helped

3 Giving no offence in any thing, that the ministry be not blamed:

4 But in all *things* approving ourselves as the ministers of God, in much patience, in afflictions, in necessities, in distresses,

5 In stripes, in imprisonments, in tumults, in labors, in watchings, in fastings; beatings - riots

6 By pureness, by knowledge, by longsuffering, by kindness, by the Ho'ly Ghost, by love unfeigned, patience - Spirit - genuine love

7 By the word of truth, by the power of God, by the armor of righteousness on the right hand and on the left,

8 By honor and dishonor, by evil report and good report: as deceivers, and *yet* true; imposters

9 As unknown, and *yet* well known; as dying, and, behold, we live; as chastened, and not killed;

10 As sorrowful, yet always rejoicing; as poor, yet making many rich; as having nothing, and *yet* possessing all things.

11 O *you* Co-rin'thi-ans, our mouth is open to you, our heart is enlarged.

12 You are not straitened in us, but you are straitened in your own bowels. LEV. 26:12 restrained - emotions

13 Now for a recompence in the same, (I speak as to *my* children,) be you also enlarged. fair exchange - growing

14 Be you not unequally yoked together with unbelievers: for what fellowship has righteousness with unrighteousness? and what communion has light with darkness? JOS. 9:16 DEU. 6:14 DEU. 22:10 DEU 7:3

15 And what concord has Christ with Be'li-al? or what part has he that believes with an infidel? harmony - Satan - unbeliever

16 And what agreement has the temple of God with idols? for you are the temple of the living God; as God has said, I will dwell in them, and walk in *them*; and I will be their God, and they shall be My people. LEV. 26:12 EZE. 37:27

17 Wherefore come out from among them, and be you separate, says the Lord. and touch not the unclean *thing*; and I will receive you, ISA. 52:11 EZE. 20: 34,41 unfit

18 And will be a Father to you, and you shall be My sons and daughters, says the Lord Almighty. Hos. 1:10

CHAPTER 7

HAVING therefore these promises, dearly beloved, let us cleanse ourselves from all filthiness of the flesh and spirit, perfecting holiness in the fear of God. reverence

2 Receive us; we have wronged no man, we have corrupted no man, we have defrauded no man. wronged - robbed

3 I speak not *this* to condemn *you*: for I have said before, that you are in our hearts to die and live with *you*.

4 Great *is* my boldness of speech toward you, great *is* my glorying of you: I am filled with comfort, I am exceeding joyful in all our tribulation. boasting

5 For, when we were come into Mac-

e-do'ni-a, our flesh had no rest, but we were troubled on every side; outside *were* fightings, inside *were* fears.

6 Nevertheless God, that comforts those that are cast down, comforted us by the coming of Ti'tus;

7 And not by his coming only, but by the consolation wherewith he was comforted in you, when he told us your earnest desire, your mourning, your <u>fervent mind</u> toward me; so that I rejoiced the more. _{concern}

8 For though I made you sorry with a letter, I do not <u>repent</u>, though I did <u>repent</u>: for I perceive that the same <u>epistle</u> has made you sorry, though *it were* but for a <u>season</u>. _{regret it - letter - time}

9 Now I rejoice, not that you were made sorry, but that you sorrowed to repentance: for you were made sorry <u>after</u> a godly manner, that you might <u>receive damage</u> by us in nothing. _{according to - suffer loss}

10 For godly sorrow works repentance to salvation not to be repented of: but the sorrow of the world works death. _{ECC. 7:3}

11 For behold this selfsame thing, that you sorrowed after a godly sort, what carefulness it wrought in you, <u>yea</u>, *what* clearing of yourselves, <u>yea</u>, *what* indignation, <u>yea</u>, *what* fear, <u>yea</u>, *what* vehement desire, <u>yea</u>, *what* zeal, <u>yea</u>, *what* revenge! In all *things* you have <u>approved</u> yourselves to be <u>clear</u> in this matter. _{yes - shown - innocent}

12 Wherefore, though I wrote to you, *I did it* not for his cause that had done the wrong, nor for his cause that suffered wrong, but that our care for you in the sight of God might appear to you.

13 Therefore we were comforted in your comfort: yea, and exceedingly the more joyed we for the joy of Ti'tus, because his spirit was refreshed by you all.

14 For if I have boasted any thing to him of you, I am not <u>ashamed</u>; but as we spoke all things to you in truth, even so our boasting, which *I made* before Ti'tus, is found <u>a</u> truth. _{embarrassed - to be the}

15 And his inward affection is more abundant toward you, until he remembers the obedience of you all, how with fear and trembling you received him.

16 I rejoice therefore that I have confidence in you in all *things*.

CHAPTER 8

MOREOVER, brethren, we <u>do</u> you to know of the grace of God bestowed on the churches of Mac-e-do'ni-a; _{inform}

2 How that in a great trial of <u>affliction</u> the abundance of their joy and their deep poverty abounded to the riches of their liberality. _{trouble}

3 For to *their* power, I bear record, yea, and beyond *their* power *they were* willing <u>of themselves</u>; _{i.e., own accord}

4 Praying us with much entreaty that we would receive the gift, and *take upon us* the fellowship of the <u>ministering</u> to the saints. _{support}

5 And *this they did*, not as we hoped, but first gave their own selves to the Lord, and to us by the will of God.

6 Insomuch that we desired Ti'tus, that as he had begun, so he would also finish in you the same grace also.

7 Therefore, as you <u>abound</u> in every *thing, in* faith, and utterance, and knowledge, and *in* all diligence, and *in* your love to us, *see* that you <u>abound</u> in this grace also.　　excel

8 I speak not by commandment, but by occasion of the forwardness of others, and to prove the sincerity of your love.

9 For you know the grace of our Lord Je'sus Christ, that, though He was rich, yet for your sakes He became poor, that you through His poverty might be rich.

10 And herein I give *my* advice: for this is <u>expedient</u> for you, who have begun before, not only to do, but also to <u>be forward</u> a year ago.　　good - desire it

11 Now therefore perform the doing *of it*; that as *there was* a <u>readiness</u> to will, so *there may be* a performance also out of that which you have. willingness

12 For if there be first a willing mind, *it is* accepted according to that a man has, *and* not according to that he has not.

13 For *I mean* not that other men be eased, and you burdened:

14 But by an equality, *that* now at this time your abundance *may be a supply* for their want, that their abundance also may be *a supply* for your want: that there may be equality:

15 As it is written, He that *had gathered* much had nothing over; and he that *had gathered* little had no lack.　　EX. 16:18

16 But thanks *be* to God, which put the same earnest care into the heart of Ti'tus for you.

17 For indeed he accepted the <u>exhortation</u>; but being more forward, of his own accord he went to you.　　appeal

18 And we have sent with him the brother, whose praise *is* in the gospel throughout all the churches;

19 And not *that* only, but who was also chosen of the churches to travel with us with this grace, which is administered by us to the glory of the same Lord, and *declaration of* your ready mind:

20 Avoiding this, that no man should blame us in this abundance which is administered by us:

21 Providing for honest things, not only in the sight of the Lord, but also in the sight of men.

22 And we have sent with them our brother, whom we have <u>oftentimes</u> proved diligent in many things, but now much more diligent, upon the great confidence which *I have* in you.　　many times

23 Whether *any do enquire* of Ti'tus, *he is* my partner and fellowhelper concerning you: or our brethren *be enquired of, they are* the messengers of the churches, *and* the glory of Christ.

24 Wherefore show you to them, and before the churches, the proof of your love, and of our boasting on your behalf.

CHAPTER 9

FOR as <u>touching the ministering</u> to the saints, it is <u>superfluous</u> for me to write to you: concerning the helping - not necessary

2 For I know the <u>forwardness</u> of your mind, for which I boast of you to them of Mac-e-do'ni-a, that A-cha'i-a was ready a year ago; and your zeal has <u>provoked</u> very many. readiness - stirred

3 Yet have I sent the brethren, less our boasting of you should be in vain in this behalf; that, as I said, you may be ready:

4 Less haply if they of Mac-e-do'ni-a come with me, and find you unprepared, we (that we say not, you) should be ashamed in this same confident boasting.

5 Therefore I thought it necessary to <u>exhort</u> the brethren, that they would go before to you, and make up beforehand your <u>bounty</u>, whereof you had notice before, that the same might be ready, as *a matter of* <u>bounty</u>, and not as *of* covetousness. urge - gift

6 But this *I say*, he which sows sparingly shall reap also sparingly; and he which sows <u>bountifully</u> shall reap also <u>bountifully</u>. i.e., generously

7 Every man according as he purposed in his heart, *so let him give*; not grudgingly, or <u>of necessity</u>: for God loves a cheerful giver. under compulsion

8 And God *is* able to make all grace abound toward you; that you, always having all sufficiency in all *things*, may abound to every good work:

9 (As it is written, He has dispersed abroad; He has given to the poor: His righteousness remains for ever. PS. 112:9

10 Now He that <u>ministers</u> seed to the sower both minister bread for *your* food, and multiply your seed sown, and increase the fruits of your righteousness;) ISA. 55:10 supplies

11 Being enriched in every thing to all <u>bountifulness</u>, which causes through us thanksgiving to God. liberality

12 For the <u>administration</u> of this service not only supplies the <u>want</u> of the <u>saints</u>, but is abundant also by many thanksgivings to God; rendering - need - believers

13 While by the <u>experiment</u> of this <u>ministration</u> they glorify God for your professed subjection to the gospel of Christ, and for *your* liberal distribution to them, and to all *men*; proof - ministry

14 And by their prayer for you, which <u>long</u> after you for the exceeding grace of God in you. yearn

15 Thanks *be* to God for His <u>unspeakable</u> gift. indescribable

CHAPTER 10

NOW I Paul myself <u>beseech</u> you by the meekness and gentleness of Christ, who in presence *am* <u>base</u> among you, but being absent am bold toward you: beg - meek

2 But I <u>beseech</u> *you*, that I may not be bold when I am present with that confidence, wherewith I think to be bold against some, which think of us as if we walked according to the flesh.

3 For though we walk in the flesh, we do not war after the flesh:

4 (For the weapons of our warfare *are* not <u>carnal</u>, but mighty through God to the pulling down of strong holds;) worldly

5 Casting down imaginations, and every <u>high</u> thing that exalts itself against the knowledge of God, and

bringing into captivity every thought to the obedience of Christ;   proud

6 And having in a readiness to re- venge all disobedience, when your obedience is fulfilled.   punish

7 Do you look on things after the out- ward appearance? If any man trust to himself that he is Christ's, let him of himself think this again, that, as he *is* Christ's, even so *are* we Christ's.

8 For though I should boast some- what more of our authority, which the Lord has given us for edifica- tion, and not for your destruction, I should not be ashamed: building up

9 That I may not seem as if I would terrify you by letters.   frighten

10 For *his* letters, say they, *are* weighty and powerful; but *his* bodily presence *is* weak, and *his* speech contemptible.

11 Let such an one think this, that, such as we are in word by letters when we are absent, such *will we be* also in deed when we are present.

12 For we dare not make ourselves of the number, or compare ourselves with some that commend them- selves: but they measuring them- selves by themselves, and compar- ing themselves among themselves, are not wise.   without understanding

13 But we will not boast of things without *our* measure, but according to the measure of the rule which God has distributed to us, a measure to reach even to you.

14 For we stretch not ourselves be- yond *our measure*, as though we reached not to you: for we are come as far as to you also in *preaching* the gospel of Christ:

15 Not boasting of things without *our* measure, *that is*, of other men's labors; but having hope, when your faith is in- creased, that we shall be enlarged by you according to our rule abundantly,

16 To preach the gospel in the re- *gions* beyond you, *and* not to boast in another man's line of things made ready to our hand.   brag about

17 But he that glories, let him glory in the Lord.   JER. 9:24 boasts

18 For not he that commends him- self is approved, but whom the Lord commends.

CHAPTER 11

WOULD to God you could bear with me a little in *my* folly: and indeed bear with me.   foolishness

2 For I am jealous over you with godly jealousy: for I have es- poused you to one husband, that I may present *you as* a chaste vir- gin to Christ.   HOS. 2:19-20 engaged

3 But I fear, less by any means, as the serpent beguiled Eve through his subtilty, so your minds should be corrupted from the simplicity that is in Christ.   GEN. 3:4

4 For if he that comes preaches another Je'sus, whom we have not preached, or *if* you receive another spirit, which you have not received, or another gos- pel, which you have not accepted, you might well bear with *him*.   a different

5 For I suppose I was not a whit be- hind the very chiefest apostles.   inferior to

6 But though *I be* rude in speech, yet not in knowledge; but we have been

throughly made <u>manifest</u> among you in all things.   _{unskilled - known}

7 Have I committed an offence in <u>abasing</u> myself that you might be exalted, because I have preached to you the gospel of God <u>freely</u>?

humbling - without charge

8 I robbed other churches, taking wages *of them*, to do you service.

9 And when I was present with you, and wanted, I was <u>chargeable</u> to no man: for that which was lacking to me the brethren which came from Mac-e-do'ni-a supplied: and in all *things* I have kept myself from being burdensome to you, and *so* will I keep *myself*.   _{not a burden}

10 As the truth of Christ is in me, no man shall stop me of this boasting in the regions of A-cha'ia.

11 Wherefore? because I love you not? God knows.

12 But what I do, that I will do, that I may cut off occasion from them which desire occasion; that wherein they glory, they may be found even as we.

13 For such *are* false apostles, deceitful workers, transforming themselves into the apostles of Christ.

14 And no marvel; for Sa'tan himself is <u>transformed</u> into an angel of light.   _{changed}

15 Therefore *it is* no great thing if his ministers also be <u>transformed</u> as the ministers of righteousness; whose end shall be according to their works.

16 I say again, Let no man think me a fool; if otherwise, yet as a fool <u>receive</u> me, that I may boast myself a little.   _{tolerate}

17 That which I speak, I speak *it* not after the Lord, but as it were foolishly, in this confidence of boasting.

18 Seeing that many <u>glory</u> after the flesh, I will <u>glory</u> also.   _{boast}

19 For you <u>suffer</u> fools gladly, seeing you *yourselves* are wise.   _{endure}

20 For you endure, if a man bring you into bondage, if a man devour *you*, if a man <u>take *of you*</u>, if a man exalt himself, if a man smite you on the face.   _{enslave}

21 I speak as concerning <u>reproach</u>, as though we had been weak. However whereinsoever any is bold, (I speak foolishly,) I am bold also.   _{criticism}

22 Are they He'brews? so *am* I. Are they Is'ra-el-ites? so *am* I. Are they the <u>seed</u> of A'bra-ham? so *am* I._{descendants}

23 Are they ministers of Christ? (I speak as a fool) I *am* more; in labors more abundant, in <u>stripes</u> above measure, in prisons more frequent, in deaths oft.   _{lashes}

24 Of the Jews five times received I forty *stripes* save one.   DEU. 25:3

25 Thrice was I beaten with rods, once was I stoned, thrice I suffered shipwreck, a night and a day I have been in the deep;

26 *In* journeyings often, *in* perils of waters, *in* perils of robbers, *in* perils by *my own* countrymen, *in* perils by the heathen, *in* perils in the city, *in* perils in the wilderness, *in* perils in the sea, *in* perils among false brethren;

27 In weariness and painfulness, in <u>watchings</u> often, in hunger and thirst, in fastings often, in cold and nakedness.   _{sleepless nights}

28 Beside those things that are out-,

side that which comes upon me daily, the <u>care</u> of all the churches _{concern}

29 Who is weak, and I am not weak? who is offended, and I burn not?

30 If I must needs <u>glory</u>, I will <u>glory</u> of the things which concern mine infirmities. _{boast}

31 The God and Father of our Lord Je'sus Christ, which is blessed for evermore, knows that I lie not.

32 In Da-mas'cus the governor under Ar'e-tas the king kept the city of the Da-mas'cenes with a garrison, desirous to <u>apprehend</u> me: _{seize}

33 And through a window in a basket was I let down by the wall, and escaped his hands.

CHAPTER 12

IT is not expedient for me doubtless to <u>glory</u>. I will come to visions and revelations of the Lord.

2 I knew a man in Christ <u>above</u> fourteen years ago, (whether in the body, I cannot tell; or whether out of the body, I cannot tell: God knows;) such an one caught up to the third heaven. _{about}

3 And I knew such a man, (whether in the body, or out of the body, I cannot tell: God knows;)

4 How that he was caught up into paradise, and heard unspeakable words, which it is not <u>lawful</u> for a man to <u>utter</u>. _{permissible - speak}

5 Of such an one will I <u>glory</u>: yet of myself I will not <u>glory</u>, but in mine <u>infirmities</u>. _{boast - weakness}

6 For though I would desire to <u>glory</u>, I shall not be a fool; for I will say the truth: but *now* I <u>forbear</u>, less any man

should think of me above that which he sees me *to be*, or *that* he hears of me. _{boast - stop}

7 And less I should be exalted above measure through the abundance of the revelations, there was given to me a thorn in the flesh, the messenger of Sa'tan to <u>buffet</u> me, less I should be exalted above measure. _{JOB 2:6 torment}

8 For this thing I besought the Lord thrice, that it might depart from me.

9 And He said to me, My grace is sufficient for you: for My <u>strength</u> is made perfect in weakness. Most gladly therefore will I rather <u>glory</u> in my <u>infirmities</u>, that the power of Christ may rest upon me. _{power - boast - weakness}

10 Therefore I take pleasure in infirmities, in reproaches, in necessities, in persecutions, in distresses for Christ's sake: for when I am weak, then am I strong.

11 I am become a fool in <u>glorying</u>; you have compelled me: for I ought to have been commended of you: for in nothing am I behind the very chiefest apostles, though I be nothing.

12 Truly the signs of an apostle were <u>wrought</u> among you in all patience, in signs, and wonders, and mighty deeds. _{performed}

13 For what is it wherein you were inferior to other churches, except *it be* that I myself was not <u>burdensome</u> to you? forgive me this wrong. _{bother}

14 Behold, the third time I am ready to come to you; and I will not be <u>burdensome</u> to you: for I seek not yours, but you: for the children ought not to

lay up for the parents, but the parents for the children. bother

15 And I will very gladly spend and be spent for you; though the more abundantly I love you, the less I be loved.

16 But be it so, I did not burden you: nevertheless, being crafty, I caught you with guile.

17 Did I <u>make a gain</u> of you by any of them whom I sent to you? take advantage

18 I desired Ti'tus, and with *him* I sent a brother. Did Ti'tus <u>make a gain</u> of you? walked we not in the same spirit? *walked we* not in the same steps?

19 Again, think you that we excuse ourselves to you? we speak before God in Christ: but *we do* all things, dearly beloved, for your <u>edifying</u>. up building

20 For I fear, less, when I come, I shall not find you such as I would, and *that* I shall be found to you such as you would not: less *there be* debates, envyings, wraths, strifes, backbitings, whisperings, swellings, <u>tumults</u>: disturbances

21 *And* less, when I come again, my God will humble me among you, and *that* I shall <u>bewail</u> many which have sinned already, and have not repented of the uncleanness and fornication and <u>lasciviousness</u> which they have committed. mourn over - sensuality

CHAPTER 13

THIS *is* the third *time* I am coming to you. In the mouth of two or three witnesses shall every word be established. DEU. 19:15

2 I told you before, and foretell you, as if I were present, the second time; and being absent now I write to them which heretofore have sinned, and to all other, that, if I come again, I will not spare:

3 Since you seek a proof of Christ speaking in me, which to you-ward is not weak, but is mighty in you.

4 For though He was crucified through weakness, yet He lives by the power of God. For we also are weak in Him, but we shall live with Him by the power of God toward you.

5 Examine yourselves, whether you be in the faith; prove your own selves. Know you not your own selves, how that Je'sus Christ is in you, except you be reprobates?

6 But I trust that you shall know that we are not <u>reprobates</u>. failing the test

7 Now I pray to God that you do no evil; not that we should appear approved, but that you should do that which is <u>honest</u>, though we be as <u>reprobates</u>. right

8 For we can do nothing against the truth, but for the truth.

9 For we are glad, when we are weak, and you are strong: and this also we wish, *even* your perfection.

10 Therefore I write these things being absent, less being present I should use sharpness, according to the <u>power</u> which the Lord has given me to <u>edification</u>, and not to destruction. authority - building up

11 Finally, brethren, farewell. Be <u>perfect</u>, be of good comfort, be of one

mind, live in peace; and the God of love and peace shall be with you.   made complete

12 Greet one another with an holy kiss.

13 All the saints salute you. believers - greet

14 The grace of the Lord Je'sus Christ, and the love of God, and the communion of the Ho'ly Ghost, *be* with you all. Amen.   fellowship - Spirit

G5
G4

314
314

GALATIANS

OUTLINE

SURVEY AND AUTHOR

Paul wrote this letter to his Galatian converts some time between A.D. 48 and A.D. 58. Jewish Christian teachers had tried to turn them against him and to convince them that, as Gentiles, they needed to be circumcised (5.2-6; 6.12-15) and to keep the ritual law (4.10) in order to be saved. In the letter Paul vindicates his authority as an expositor of the Gospel, and condemns the Judaizing position as anti-Christian legalism.

Believers, Jew and Gentile alike, Paul argues, enjoy in Christ a complete salvation. They are justified (3.6-9), adopted (4.4-7), renewed (4.6; 6.15), and made God's heirs according to the promises of the Abrahamic Covenant (3.15-18). Faith in the Christ of Calvary thus frees them forever from the need to seek salvation through works of law. This quest is, in any case, hopeless, for the law does not save, nor was it meant to (3.19-24); it can only condemn (3.10-12), and when trusted for salvation it leads only to bondage (4.21-24). Believers must not, therefore, revert to the principle of law-keeping as a ground of salvation, or else they return to slavery (5.1) and forfeit the grace of Christ (5.2-4). Rather, they must hold fast the freedom Christ has given them, and serve God and their fellows in the power of the Spirit as free men (5.13-18), gladly fulfilling the will of their Savior (6.2).

Paul's argument shows that all legalistic versions of the Gospel are perversions of it, and that the enjoyment of Christian liberty depends on seeing that salvation is by grace alone through Christ alone, received by faith alone.

J.I.P.

THE LETTER OF PAUL TO THE

GALATIANS
CHAPTER 1

Beware
of False Gospels

PAUL, an apostle, (not of men, neither by man, but by Je'sus Christ, and God the Father, who raised Him from the dead;)

2 And all the brethren which are with me, to the churches of Ga-la'tia:

3 Grace *be* to you and peace from God the Father, and *from* our Lord Je'sus Christ,

4 Who gave Himself for our sins, that He might deliver us from this present evil world, according to the will of God and our Father: age

5 To whom *be* glory for ever and ever. Amen.

6 I marvel that you are so soon removed from Him that called you into the grace of Christ to another gospel: am amazed - different

7 Which is not another; but there be some that trouble you, and would pervert the gospel of Christ. distort

8 But though we, or an angel from heaven, preach any other gospel to you than that which we have preached to you, let him be accursed. messenger - condemned

9 As we said before, so say I now again, If any *man* preach any other gospel to you than that you have received, let him be accursed.

10 For do I now persuade men, or God? or do I seek to please men? for if I yet pleased men, I should not be the servant of Christ.

11 But I certify you, brethren, that the gospel which was preached of me is not after man. assure - according to

12 For I neither received it of man, neither was I taught *it*, but by the revelation of Je'sus Christ.

13 For you have heard of my conversation in time past in the Jews' religion, how that beyond measure I persecuted the church of God, and wasted it: way of life

14 And profited in the Jews' religion above many my equals in mine own nation, being more exceedingly zealous of the traditions of my fathers. i.e., own age

15 But when it pleased God, who separated me from my mother's womb, and called *me* by His grace, JER. 1:5

16 To reveal His Son in me, that I might preach Him among the heathen; immediately I conferred not with flesh and blood: Gentiles

17 Neither went I up to Je-ru'sa-lem to them which were apostles before me; but I went into A-ra'bi-a, and returned again to Da-mas'cus.

18 Then after three years I went up to Je-ru'sa-lem to see Pe'ter, and abode with him fifteen days. stayed

19 But other of the apostles saw I none, save James the Lord's brother.

20 Now the things which I write to you, behold, before God, I lie not.

21 Afterwards I came into the regions of Syr'i-a and Ci-li'cia;

22 And was unknown by face to the churches of Ju-dae'a which were in Christ:

23 But they had heard only, That he which persecuted us in times past now preaches the faith which once he destroyed.

24 And they glorified God in me. *praised*

CHAPTER 2

THEN fourteen years after I went up again to Je-ru'sa-lem with Bar'-na-bas, and took Ti'tus with *me* also.

2 And I went up by revelation, and communicated to them that gospel which I preach among the Gen'tiles, but privately to them which were of reputation, less by any means I should run, or had run, in vain.

3 But neither Ti'tus, who was with me, being a Greek, was compelled to be circumcised:

4 And that because of false brethren unawares brought in, who came in privily to spy out our liberty which we have in Christ Je'sus, that they might bring us into bondage:

JUDE 4 without notice - secretly

5 To whom we gave place by subjection, no, not for an hour; that the truth of the gospel might continue with you.

6 But of these who seemed to be somewhat, (whatsoever they were, it makes no matter to me: God accepts no man's person:) for they who seemed *to be somewhat* in conference added nothing to me:

7 But contrariwise, when they saw that the gospel of the uncircumcision was committed to me, as *the gospel* of the circumcision *was* to Pe'ter;

8 (For He that wrought effectually in Pe'ter to the apostleship of the circumcision, the same was mighty in me toward the Gen'tiles:) *worked*

9 And when James, Ce'phas, and John, who seemed to be pillars, perceived the grace that was given to me, they gave to me and Bar'na-bas the right hands of fellowship; that we *should go* to the heathen, and they to the circumcision. *Gentiles*

10 Only *they would* that we should remember the poor; the same which I also was forward to do. *anxious*

11 But when Pe'ter was come to An'ti-och, I withstood him to the face, because he was to be blamed.

12 For before that certain came from James, he did eat with the Gen'tiles: but when they were come, he withdrew and separated himself, fearing them which were of the circumcision.

13 And the other Jews dissembled likewise with him; insomuch that Bar'na-bas also was carried away with their dissimulation. *hypocrisy*

14 But when I saw that they walked not uprightly according to the truth of the gospel, I said to Pe'ter before *them* all, If you, being a Jew, live after the manner of Gen'tiles, and not as do the Jews, why compel you the Gen'tiles to live as do the Jews?

15 We *who are* Jews by nature, and not sinners of the Gen'tiles,

16 Knowing that a man is not justified by the works of the law, but by the faith of Je'sus Christ, even we have believed in Je'sus Christ, that we might be justified by the faith of Christ, and not

by the works of the law: for by the works of the law shall no <u>flesh</u> be justified.   PS. 143:2 man

17 But if, while we seek to be justified by Christ, we ourselves also are found sinners, *is* therefore Christ the minister of sin? God forbid.

18 For if I build again the things which I destroyed, I make myself a transgressor.

19 For I through the law am dead to the law, that I might live to God.

20 I am crucified with Christ: nevertheless I live; yet not I, but Christ lives in me: and the life which I now live in the flesh I live by the faith of the Son of God, who loved me, and gave Himself for me.

21 I do not frustrate the grace of God: for if righteousness *come* by the law, then Christ is dead <u>in vain</u>.   needlessly

CHAPTER 3

O FOOLISH Ga-la'tians, who has bewitched you, that you should not obey the truth, before whose eyes Je'sus Christ has been <u>evidently set forth</u>, crucified among you?   clearly portrayed

2 This only would I learn of you, Received you the Spirit by the works of the law, or by the hearing of faith?

3 Are you so foolish? having begun in the Spirit, are you now made perfect by the flesh?

4 Have you suffered so <u>many things</u> in vain? if *it be* yet <u>in vain</u>.   much

5 He therefore that <u>ministers</u> to you the Spirit, and works miracles among you, *does He it* by the works of the law, or by the hearing of faith?   provides

6 Even as A'bra-ham believed God, and it was <u>accounted</u> to him for righteousness.   reckoned

7 Know you therefore that they <u>which are of</u> faith, the same are the children of A'bra-ham.   who have

8 And the scripture, foreseeing that God would justify the <u>heathen</u> through faith, preached before the gospel to A'bra-ham, *saying,* In you shall all nations be blessed.   GEN. 12:3 GEN. 22:18 unbeliever

9 So then they which be of faith are blessed with <u>faithful</u> A'bra-ham.   believer

10 For as many as are of the works of the law are under the curse: for it is written, Cursed *is* every one that continues not in all things which are written in the book of the law to do them.   DEU. 27:26

11 But that no man is justified by the law in the sight of God, *it is* evident: for, The just shall live by faith.   HAB. 2:4

12 And the law is not of faith: but, The man that does them shall live in them.   LEV. 18:5

13 Christ has redeemed us from the curse of the law, being made a curse for us: for it is written, Cursed *is* every one that hangs on a tree: DEU. 21:23

14 That the blessing of A'bra-ham might come on the Gen'tiles through Je'sus Christ; that we might receive the promise of the Spirit through faith.

15 Brethren, I speak after the manner of men; Though *it be* but a man's <u>covenant</u>, yet *if it be* <u>confirmed</u>, no man disannuls, or adds thereto.   agreement - ratified

16 Now to A'bra-ham and his <u>seed</u> were the promises made. He said not,

And to <u>seeds</u>, as of many; but as of one, And to your <u>seed</u>, which is Christ. GEN. 12:7 descendants

17 And this I say, *that* the <u>covenant</u>, that was confirmed before of God in Christ, the law, which was four hundred and thirty years after, cannot disannul, that it should make the promise of <u>none</u> effect. GEN. 15:18 EX. 12:40 no

18 For if the inheritance *be* of the law, *it is* no more of promise: but God gave *it* to A'bra-ham by promise.

19 Wherefore then *serves* the law? It was added because of transgressions, till the <u>seed</u> should come to whom the promise was made; *and it was* ordained by angels in the hand of a mediator.

20 Now a mediator is not a *mediator* of one, but God is one.

21 *Is* the law then against the promises of God? God forbid: for if there had been a law given which could have given life, verily righteousness should have been by the law.

22 But the scripture has <u>concluded</u> all under sin, that the promise by faith of Je'sus Christ might be given to them that believe. shut up

23 But before faith came, we were kept under the law, shut up to the faith which should afterwards be revealed.

24 Wherefore the law was our schoolmaster *to bring us* to Christ, that we might be justified by faith.

25 But after that faith is come, we are no longer under a schoolmaster.

26 For you are all the children of God by faith in Christ Je'sus.

27 For as many of you as have been baptized into Christ have put on Christ.

28 There is neither Jew nor Greek, there is neither bond nor free, there is neither male nor female: for you are all one in Christ Je'sus.

29 And if you *be* Christ's, then are you A'bra-ham's <u>seed</u>, and heirs according to the promise. offspring

CHAPTER 4

NOW I say, *That* the heir, as long as he is a child, differs nothing from a <u>servant</u>, though he be lord of all; slave

2 But is under <u>tutors</u> and <u>governors</u> until the time appointed of the father. guardians - managers

3 Even so we, when we were children, were in bondage under the <u>elements</u> of the world: principles

4 But when the fulness of the time was come, God sent forth His Son, made of a woman, <u>made</u> under the law, born

5 To redeem them that were under the law, that we might <u>receive the adoption</u> of sons. have the rights

6 And because you are sons, God has sent forth the Spirit of His Son into your hearts, crying, <u>Ab'ba</u>, Father. Father

7 Wherefore you are no more a <u>servant</u>, but a son; and if a son, then an heir of God through Christ. slave

8 However then, when you knew not God, you did service to them which by nature are no gods.

9 But now, after that you have known God, or rather are known of God, how turn you again to the weak and beggarly elements, whereto you desire again to be in bondage?

10 You observe days, and months, and times, and years.

11 I am afraid of you, less I have bestowed upon you labor in vain.

12 Brethren, I <u>beseech</u> you, be as I *am*; for I *am* as you *are*: you have not <u>injured</u> me at all.   beg - wronged

13 You know <u>how through</u> infirmity of the flesh I preached the gospel to you at the first.   because of

14 And my <u>temptation</u> which was in my flesh you despised not, nor rejected; but received me as an <u>angel</u> of God, *even* as Christ Je'sus.   trial - messenger

15 Where is then the blessedness you spoke of? for I bear you record, that, if *it had been* possible, you would have plucked out your own eyes, and have given them to me.

16 Am I therefore become your enemy, because I tell you the truth?

17 They <u>zealously</u> affect you, *but* not <u>well</u>; yea, they would exclude you, that you might <u>affect</u> them.

eagerly - for good - seek

18 But *it is* good to be <u>zealously</u> affected always in *a* good *thing*, and not only when I am present with you.

19 My little children, of whom I <u>travail</u> in birth again until Christ be formed in you,   suffer

20 I desire to be present with you now, and to change my <u>voice</u>; for I stand in doubt of you.   tone

21 Tell me, you that desire to be under the law, do you not hear the law?

22 For it is written, that A'bra-ham had two sons, the one by a bondmaid, the other by a freewoman.   GEN. 16:15

23 But he *who was* of the bondwoman was born after the flesh; but he of the freewoman *was* by promise.

24 Which things are an allegory: for these are the two <u>covenants</u>; the one from the mount Si'nai, which <u>genders</u> to bondage, which is A'gar.   agreements - leads

25 For this A'gar is mount Si'nai in A-ra'bi-a, and <u>answers</u> to Je-ru'sa-lem which now is, and is in bondage with her children.   corresponds

26 But Je-ru'sa-lem which is above is free, which is the mother of us all.

27 For it is written, Rejoice, *you* barren that bear not; break forth and cry, you that travails not: for the desolate has many more children than she which has an husband.   ISA 54:1

28 Now we, brethren, as I'saac was, are the children of promise.

29 But as then he that was born after the flesh persecuted him *that was born* after the Spirit, even so *it is* now.

30 Nevertheless what says the scripture? Cast out the bondwoman and her son: for the son of the bondwoman shall not be heir with the son of the freewoman.   GEN. 21:10

31 So then, brethren, we are not children of the bondwoman, but of the free.

CHAPTER 5

STAND fast therefore in the liberty wherewith Christ has made us free, and be not entangled again with the yoke of bondage.

2 Behold, I Paul say to you, that if you be circumcised, Christ shall <u>profit</u> you nothing.   benefit

3 For I testify again to every man that

is circumcised, that he is a <u>debtor</u> to do the whole law.   under obligation

4 Christ is become of no effect to you, whosoever of you are justified by the law; you are fallen from grace.

5 For we through the Spirit wait for the hope of righteousness by faith.

6 For in Je'sus Christ neither circumcision avails any thing, nor uncircumcision; but faith which works by love.

7 You did run well; who did hinder you that you should not obey the truth?

8 This <u>persuasion</u> *comes* not of Him that calls you.   leading

9 A little <u>leaven leavens</u> the whole lump.   i.e., wrong doctrine mixes in

10 I have confidence in you through the Lord, that you will be none otherwise minded: but he that troubles you shall bear his judgment, whosoever he be.

11 And I, brethren, if I yet preach circumcision, why do I yet suffer persecution? then is <u>the offence</u> of the cross <u>ceased</u>.   stumbling block - removed

12 I would they were <u>even cut off</u> which trouble you.   removed

13 For, brethren, you have been called to liberty; only *use* not liberty for an occasion to the flesh, but by love serve one another.

14 For all the law is <u>fulfilled in one</u> word, *even* in this; You shall love your neighbor as yourself   LEV. 19:18

15 But if you <u>bite</u> and devour one another, take heed that you be not <u>consumed</u> one of another.   fight - destroyed

16 *This* I say then, Walk in the Spirit, and you shall not fulfill the lust of the flesh.

17 For the flesh lusts against the Spirit, and the Spirit against the flesh: and these are <u>contrary</u> the one to the other: so that you cannot do the things that you would.   in opposition

18 But if you be led of the Spirit, you are not under the law.

19 Now the works of the flesh are <u>manifest</u>, which are *these*; Adultery, fornication, uncleanness, <u>lasciviousness</u>,   evident - sensuality

20 Idolatry, witchcraft, hatred, <u>variance</u>, <u>emulations</u>, wrath, strife, <u>seditions</u>, heresies,   discord - jealousy - dissensions

21 Envyings, murders, drunkenness, revellings, and such like: of the which I tell you before, as I have also told *you* in time past, that they which do such things shall not inherit the kingdom of God.

22 But the fruit of the Spirit is love, joy, peace, longsuffering, gentleness, goodness, faith,

23 Meekness, temperance: against such there is no law.

24 And they that are Christ's have crucified the flesh with the <u>affections</u> and lusts.   passions

25 If we live in the Spirit, let us also walk in the Spirit.

26 Let us not be desirous of <u>vain glory</u>, provoking one another, envying one another.   boasting

CHAPTER 6

BRETHERN, if a man be overtaken in a <u>fault</u>, you which are spiritual, restore such an one in the spirit of meekness; considering yourself, less you also be tempted.   trespass

M21 - 331 M20 - 355
M30 - 346

2 Bear you one another's burdens, and so fulfill the law of Christ.

3 For if a man think himself to be something, when he is nothing, he deceives himself.

4 But let every man prove his own work, and then shall he have rejoicing in himself alone, and not in another.

5 For every man shall bear his own burden.   *load*

6 Let him that is taught in the word communicate to him that teaches in all good things.   *share*

M10
M18 - 332

7 Be not deceived; God is not mocked: for whatsoever a man sows, that shall he also reap.

8 For he that sows to his flesh shall of the flesh reap corruption; but he that sows to the Spirit shall of the Spirit reap life everlasting.   *destruction*

325 M24 - 343

9 And let us not be weary in well doing: for in due season we shall reap, if we faint not.   *tire*

10 As we have therefore opportunity, let us do good to all *men*, especially to them who are of the household of faith.

11 You see how large a letter I have written to you with mine own hand.

12 As many as desire to make a fair show in the flesh, they constrain you to be circumcised; only less they should suffer persecution for the cross of Christ.   *compel*

13 For neither they themselves who are circumcised keep the law; but desire to have you circumcised, that they may glory in your flesh.   *obey - boast*

14 But God forbid that I should glory, save in the cross of our Lord Je'sus Christ, by whom the world is crucified to me, and I to the world.

15 For in Christ Je'sus neither circumcision avails any thing, nor uncircumcision, but a new creature.

16 And as many as walk according to this rule, peace *be* on them, and mercy, and upon the Is'ra-el of God.   PS. 125:5

17 From hereafter let no man trouble me: for I bear in my body the marks of the Lord Je'sus.   *on*

18 Brethren, the grace of our Lord Je'sus Christ *be* with your spirit. Amen.

EPHESIANS

OUTLINE

SALUTATION 1.1, 2

THANKSGIVING FOR THE GLORIOUS PLAN OF SALVATION 1.3-14
 God's Purpose for the Church in Holiness, Grace, and Glory 1.3-6
 Christ's Redemption, Uniting All in Him 1.7-12
 The Holy Spirit's Seal, Sample and Pledge of Inheritance 1.13, 14

PRAYER THAT CHRISTIAN LIFE CORRESPOND TO DIVINE PROVISION 1.15-23

THE UNITY OF ALL BELIEVERS IN CHRIST 2.1—3.21
 Release from Death and Sin to Union with Christ 2.1-10
 Privileges of the Gospel Equally Shared by Gentiles 2.11-22
 Mystery of the Union of All Saints in Christ Revealed to Paul 3.1-13
 Prayer that this Reality be Truly and Fully Experienced 3.14-19
 Doxology to God for Abundant Grace 3.20, 21

EXHORTATION TO WALK AS CHRISTIANS 4.1—6.9
 A Walk in Unity of the Spirit 4.1-16
 A Walk in Newness of Life 4.17-32
 A Walk in Love 5.1-21
 A Walk of Humility and Justice in Human Relations 5.22—6.9

EXHORTATION TO BE STRONG IN THE LORD 6.10-17
 Firm Stand against the Enemy 6.10-13
 Full Equipment for Defense and Offense 6.14-17

EXHORTATION TO PRAY: BENEDICTORY REMARKS 6.18-24

SURVEY

The Ephesian letter generally presents doctrine in the first half and exhortation in the last; yet the line cannot be drawn absolutely. The doctrinal discourse is occasioned by the practical situation, and the exhortations are studded with gems of truth.

Opening praise swells to exultation over the plan of God for His saints through redemption by Jesus Christ and the work of the Holy Spirit. Pausing only for two prayers (1.15-23 and 3.14-19), Paul elaborates the implications of redemption in deliverance from sin, the new life of victory, the mystery of the unity of all saints, and their union with Christ.

In the last half, the ethical implications are set forth in terms of Christian unity, the new walk, love, humility, constructive human relations, and victorious warfare against evil through full reliance on spiritual realities.

AUTHOR

Paul is clearly the author of this epistle. No ancient scholar appears to have dissented from this view, and modern objectors have had to proceed against overwhelming historical and internal evidence. Though the epistle may also have been intended as a circular letter to other churches of Asia, there is little room for doubt that the writer had in mind the church which he had founded in the great

metropolis of Ephesus. Both manuscript and doctrinal evidence indicate that the epistle has been associated with the church in Ephesus from very ancient times. Paul seems to have written the epistle from a prison in Rome at about the same time as Philemon and Colossians and to have sent it by the same friend, Tychicus, who had been visiting him (A.D. 62 or 63).

W.T.D.

THE LETTER OF PAUL TO THE
EPHESIANS

| The Position |
| Walk, and Warfare |
| of the Believer |

CHAPTER 1

PAUL, an apostle of Je'sus Christ by the will of God, to the saints which are at Eph'e-sus, and to the faithful in Christ Je'sus: believers

2 Grace *be* to you, and peace, from God our Father, and *from* the Lord Je'sus Christ.

3 Blessed *be* the God and Father of our Lord Je'sus Christ, who has blessed us with all spiritual blessings in heavenly *places* in Christ:

4 According as He has chosen us in Him before the foundation of the world, that we should be holy and without blame before Him in love: beginning

5 Having predestinated us to the adoption of children by Je'sus Christ to Himself, according to the good pleasure of His will,

6 To the praise of the glory of His grace, wherein He has made us accepted in the beloved.

7 In whom we have redemption through His blood, the forgiveness of sins, according to the riches of His grace;

8 Wherein He has abounded toward us in all wisdom and prudence;   insight

9 Having made known to us the mystery of His will, according to His good pleasure which He has purposed in Himself:

10 That in the dispensation of the fulness of times He might gather together in one all things in Christ, both which are in heaven, and which are on earth; *even* in Him: era

11 In whom also we have obtained an inheritance, being predestinated according to the purpose of Him who works all things after the counsel of His own will:

12 That we should be to the praise of His glory, who first trusted in Christ.

13 In whom you also *trusted*, after that you heard the word of truth, the gospel of your salvation: in whom also after that you believed, you were sealed with that holy Spirit of promise,   good news

14 Which is the earnest of our inheritance until the redemption of the purchased possession, to the praise of His glory.   promise

15 Wherefore I also, after I heard of your faith in the Lord Je'sus, and love to all the saints,   believers

16 Cease not to give thanks for you, making mention of you in my prayers;

17 That the God of our Lord Je'sus Christ, the Father of glory, may give to you the spirit of wisdom and revelation in the knowledge of Him:

18 The eyes of your understanding being enlightened; that you may know what is the hope of His calling, and what the riches of the glory of His inheritance in the saints,   heart

19 And what *is* the exceeding greatness of His power to us-ward who be-

lieve, according to the working of His mighty power,   *toward us*

20 Which He wrought in Christ, when He raised Him from the dead, and set *Him* at His own right hand in the heavenly *places*,   PS. 110:1

21 Far above all principality, and power, and might, and dominion, and every name that is named, not only in this world, but also in that which is to come:

22 And has put all *things* under His feet, and gave Him *to be* the head over all *things* to the church,   PS. 8:6

23 Which is His body, the fulness of Him that fills all in all.

CHAPTER 2

AND you *has He quickened*, who were dead in trespasses and sins;   *made alive*

2 Wherein in time past you walked according to the course of this world, according to the <u>prince</u> of the power of the air, the spirit that now works in the children of disobedience: *i.e., Satan*

3 Among whom also we all had our conversation in times past in the lusts of our flesh, fulfilling the desires of the flesh and of the mind; and were by nature the children of wrath, even as others.

4 But God, who is rich in mercy, for His great love <u>wherewith</u> He loved us,   *because*

5 Even when we were dead in sins, has <u>quickened us</u> together with Christ, (by grace you are saved;)   *made us alive*

6 And has raised *us* up together, and

made *us* sit together in heavenly *places* in Christ Je'sus:

7 That in the ages to come He might show the exceeding riches of His grace in *His* kindness toward us through Christ Je'sus.

8 For by grace are you saved through faith; and that not of yourselves: *it is* the gift of God: ROM. 8:28-30 ACTS 16:31

9 Not of works, less any man should boast.

10 For we are His workmanship, created in Christ Je'sus to good works, which God has before <u>ordained</u> that we should walk in them.   PSA. 100:3 *planned*

11 Wherefore remember, that you *being* in time past Gen'tiles in the flesh, who are called Uncircumcision by that which is called the Circumcision in the flesh made by hands;

12 That at that time you were without Christ, being aliens from the commonwealth of Is'ra-el, and strangers from the <u>covenants</u> of promise, having no hope, and without God in the world: *agreements*

13 But now in Christ Je'sus you who sometimes were far off are made near by the blood of Christ.

14 For He is our peace, who has made both one, and has broken down the middle wall of <u>partition</u> *between us*;   *i.e., a barrier*

15 Having abolished in His flesh the enmity, *even* the law of commandments *contained* in ordinances; for to make in Himself of two one new man, *so* making peace;

16 And that He might reconcile both

to God in one body by the cross, having slain the enmity thereby:

17 And came and preached peace to you which were afar off, and to them that were near.

18 For through Him we both have access by one Spirit to the Father.

19 Now therefore you are no more strangers and foreigners, but fellowcitizens with the saints, and of the household of God; ISA. 57:19 believers

20 And are built upon the foundation of the apostles and prophets, Je'sus Christ Himself being the chief corner *stone*;

21 In whom all the building fitly framed together grows to an holy temple in the Lord:

22 In whom you also are built together for an habitation of God through the Spirit. dwelling

CHAPTER 3

FOR this cause I Paul, the prisoner of Je'sus Christ for you Gen'tiles,

2 If you have heard of the dispensation of the grace of God which is given me to you-ward: stewartship

3 How that by revelation He made known to me the mystery; (as I wrote afore in few words, secret - before

4 Whereby, when you read, you may understand my knowledge in the mystery of Christ)

5 Which in other ages was not made known to the sons of men, as it is now revealed to His holy apostles and prophets by the Spirit;

6 That the Gen'tiles should be fellow-heirs, and of the same body, and partakers of His promise in Christ by the gospel:

7 Whereof I was made a minister, according to the gift of the grace of God given to me by the effectual working of His power. servant

8 To me, who am less than the least of all saints, is this grace given, that I should preach among the Gen'tiles the unsearchable riches of Christ; believers

9 And to make all *men* see what *is* the fellowship of the mystery, which from the beginning of the world has been hid in God, who created all things by Je'sus Christ: secret

10 To the intent that now to the principalities and powers in heavenly *places* might be known by the church the manifold wisdom of God,

11 According to the eternal purpose which He purposed in Christ Je'sus our Lord: planned

12 In whom we have boldness and access with confidence by the faith of Him.

13 Wherefore I desire that you faint not at my tribulations for you, which is your glory. not lose heart - sufferings

14 For this cause I bow my knees to the Father of our Lord Je'sus Christ,

15 Of whom the whole family in heaven and earth is named,

16 That He would grant you, according to the riches of His glory, to be strengthened with might by His Spirit in the inner man;

17 That Christ may dwell in your

hearts by faith; that you, being rooted and grounded in love,

18 May be able to <u>comprehend</u> with all <u>saints</u> what *is* the breadth, and length, and depth, and height; understand - believers

19 And to know the love of Christ, which passes knowledge, that you might be filled with all the fulness of God.

20 Now to Him that is able to do exceeding abundantly <u>above</u> all that we ask or think, according to the power that works in us, beyond

21 To Him *be* <u>glory</u> in the church by Christ Je'sus throughout all ages, world without end. Amen. honor

CHAPTER 4

I THEREFORE, the prisoner of the Lord, <u>beseech</u> you that you walk worthy of the vocation wherewith you are called, beg

2 With all lowliness and meekness, with longsuffering, forbearing one another in love;

3 <u>Endeavoring</u> to keep the unity of the Spirit in the bond of peace.

Making every effort

4 *There is* one body, and one Spirit, <u>even</u> as you are called in one hope of your calling; just

5 One Lord, one faith, one baptism,

6 One God and Father of all, who *is* above all, and through all, and in you all.

7 But to every one of us is given grace according to the measure of the gift of Christ.

8 Wherefore He says, When He as-cended up on high, He led captivity captive, and gave gifts to men. PS. 68:18

9 (Now that He ascended, what is it but that He also descended first into the lower parts of the earth?

10 He that descended is the same also that ascended up far above all heavens, that He might fill all things.)

11 And He gave some, apostles; and some, prophets; and some, evangelists; and some, pastors and teachers;

12 For the <u>perfecting</u> of the <u>saints</u>, for the work of the ministry, for the <u>edifying</u> of the body of Christ: equipping - believers - building up

13 Till we all come <u>in</u> the unity of the faith, and of the knowledge of the Son of God, to a <u>perfect</u> man, to the measure of the stature of the fulness of Christ: to - mature

14 That we *hereafter* be no more children, tossed to and fro, and carried about with every wind of <u>doctrine</u>, by the <u>sleight</u> of men, *and* cunning <u>craftiness</u>, whereby they lie in wait to deceive; teaching - trickery - cleverness

15 But speaking the truth in love, may grow up into Him in all things, which is the head, *even* Christ:

16 From whom the whole body fitly joined together and <u>compacted</u> by that which every joint supplies, according to the effectual working in the measure of every part, makes increase of the body to the <u>edifying</u> of itself in love. held together - building up

17 This I say therefore, and testify in the Lord, that you hereafter walk not as other Gen'tiles walk, in the <u>vanity</u> of their mind, futility

18 Having the understanding darkened, being alienated from the life of God through the ignorance that is in them, because of the blindness of their heart:

19 Who being past feeling have given themselves over to lasciviousness, to work all uncleanness with greediness.

20 But you have not so learned Christ;

21 If so be that you have heard Him, and have been taught by Him, as the truth is in Je'sus:

22 That you put off concerning the former <u>conversation the old man</u>, which is corrupt according to the deceitful lusts; ^{life manner}

23 And be renewed in the spirit of your mind;

24 And that you put on the new man, which after God is created in righteousness and true holiness.

25 Wherefore putting away lying, speak every man truth with his neighbor: for we are members one of another. ZEC. 8:16

26 Be you angry, and sin not: let not the sun go down upon your <u>wrath</u>: anger

27 Neither give place to the devil.

28 Let him that stole steal no more: but rather let him labor, working with *his* hands the thing which is good, that he may have to give to him that needs.

29 Let no <u>corrupt communication</u> proceed out of your mouth, but that which is good to the use of <u>edifying</u>, that it may minister grace to the hearers. unwholesome word - building up

30 And grieve not the Holy Spirit of God, whereby you are sealed to the day of redemption.

31 Let all bitterness, and wrath, and anger, and clamor, and evil speaking, be put away from you, with all malice:

32 And be you kind one to another, tenderhearted, forgiving one another, even as God for Christ's sake has forgiven you.

CHAPTER 5

BE you therefore <u>followers</u> of God, as dear children; imitators

2 And walk in love, as Christ also has loved us, and has given Himself for us an offering and a sacrifice to God for a sweetsmelling savor. EZE. 20:41

3 But fornication, and all uncleanness, or covetousness, let it not be once named among you, as becomes <u>saints</u>; believers

4 Neither filthiness, nor foolish talking, nor jesting, which are not <u>convenient</u>: but rather giving of thanks. fitting

5 For this you know, that no whoremonger, nor unclean person, nor covetous man, who is an idolater, has any inheritance in the kingdom of Christ and of God.

6 Let no man deceive you with <u>vain</u> words: for because of these things comes the wrath of God upon the children of disobedience. empty

7 Be not you therefore <u>partakers</u> with them. partners

8 For you were <u>sometimes</u> darkness, but now *are you* light in the Lord: walk as children of light: ISA. 2:5 formerly

9 (For the fruit of the Spirit *is* in all goodness and righteousness and truth;)

10 Proving what is <u>acceptable</u> to the Lord. pleasing

11 And have no fellowship with the unfruitful works of darkness, but rather <u>reprove</u> *them*. expose

12 For it is a shame even to speak of those things which are done of them in secret.

13 But all things that are <u>reproved</u> are made <u>manifest</u> by the light: for whatsoever does make <u>manifest</u> is light. known

14 Wherefore He says, Awake you that sleep, and arise from the dead, and Christ shall give you light.

15 See then that you walk <u>circumspectly</u>, not as fools, but as wise, PROV. 15:21 wisely

16 Redeeming the time, because the days are evil.

17 Wherefore be you not unwise, but understanding what the will of the Lord *is*.

18 And be not drunk with wine, wherein is excess; but be <u>filled</u> with the Spirit; controlled

19 Speaking to yourselves in psalms and hymns and spiritual songs, singing and making melody in your heart to the Lord;

20 Giving thanks always for all things to God and the Father in the name of our Lord Je'sus Christ; PSA. 34:1

21 <u>Submitting</u> yourselves one to another in the <u>fear</u> of God. harmonizing - reverence

22 Wives, <u>submit yourselves</u> to your own husbands, as to the Lord. be in harmony

23 For the husband is the head of the wife, even as Christ is the head of the church: and He is the Savior of the body.

24 Therefore as the church is subject to Christ, so *let* the wives *be* to their own husbands in every thing.

25 Husbands, love your wives, even as Christ also loved the church, and gave Himself for it;

26 That He might <u>sanctify</u> and cleanse it with the washing of water by the word, make holy

27 That He might present it to Himself a glorious church, not having spot, or wrinkle, or any such thing; but that it should be holy and without <u>blemish</u>. SONG 4:7 LEV. 1:3 blame

28 So ought men to love their wives as their own bodies. He that loves his wife loves himself.

29 For no man ever yet <u>hated</u> his own flesh; but <u>nourishes</u> and <u>cherishes</u> it, even as the Lord the church: disrespects - feeds - cares for

30 For we are members of His body, of His flesh, and of His bones.

31 For this <u>cause</u> shall a man leave his father and mother, and shall be joined to his wife, and they two shall be one flesh. GEN. 2:24 reason

32 This is a great <u>mystery</u>: but I speak concerning Christ and the church. secret

33 Nevertheless let every one of you <u>in particular</u> so love his wife even as himself; and the wife *see* that she <u>reverence</u> *her* husband. individually - honor

CHAPTER 6

CHILDREN, obey your parents in the Lord: for this is right. PROV. 6:20

2 Honor your father and mother; (which is the first commandment with promise;) EXO. 20:12

3 That it may be well with you, and you may live long on the earth.

DEU. 5:16

4 And, you fathers, provoke not your children to wrath: but bring them up in the <u>nurture</u> and admonition of the Lord. PS. 127:3 PROV. 22:6 discipline

5 Servants, be obedient to them that are *your* masters according to the flesh, with <u>fear</u> and trembling, in <u>singleness</u> of your heart, as to Christ;   respect - sincerity

6 Not with eyeservice, as menpleasers; but as the servants of Christ, doing the will of God from the heart;

7 With good will doing service, as to the Lord, and not to men:

8 Knowing that whatsoever good thing any man does, the same shall he receive of the Lord, whether *he be* bond or free.

9 And, you masters, do the same things to them, <u>forbearing</u> threatening: knowing that your <u>Master</u> also is in heaven; neither is there respect of persons with him.   give up - Lord

10 Finally, my brethren, be strong in the Lord, and in the power of His might.

11 Put on the whole armor of God, that you may be able to stand against the <u>wiles</u> of the devil. schemes

12 For we wrestle not against flesh and blood, but against principalities, against powers, against the rulers of the darkness of this world, against spiritual wickedness in high *places*.

13 Wherefore take to you the whole armor of God, that you may be able to withstand in the evil day, and having <u>done</u> all, to stand.   overcome

14 Stand therefore, having your loins girt about with truth, and having on the breastplate of righteousness; ISA. 11:5 belted

15 And your feet shod with the preparation of the gospel of peace;

16 Above all, taking the shield of faith, wherewith you shall be able to <u>quench</u> all the fiery <u>darts</u> of the wicked.   put out - arrows-i.e., shots

17 And take the helmet of salvation, and the sword of the Spirit, which is the word of God:

18 Praying always with all prayer and supplication in the Spirit, and watching thereto with all perseverance and supplication for all saints;

19 And for me, that <u>utterance</u> may be given to me, that I may open my mouth boldly, to make known the <u>mystery</u> of the <u>gospel</u>,   speech - secret - good news

20 For which I am an ambassador in <u>bonds</u>: that therein I may speak boldly, as I ought to speak.   chains

21 But that you also may know my affairs, *and* how I do, Tych'i-cus, a beloved brother and faithful minister in the Lord, shall make known to you all things:

22 Whom I have sent to you for the same purpose, that you might know our affairs, and *that* he might comfort your hearts.

23 Peace *be* to the brethren, and love with faith, from God the Father and the Lord Je'sus Christ.

24 Grace *be* with all them that love our Lord Je'sus Christ in sincerity. Amen.

PHILIPPIANS

OUTLINE

SURVEY

This is one of Paul's most personal letters. One needs but to note throughout the frequency of the first personal pronoun. The apostle was writing to a group of friends whom he deeply loved. Such a letter does not lend itself readily to systematic outline. In the letter Paul's concern for these Christians stands out clearly. He writes to them not so much as the apostle who established the church in Philippi as their father in Christ. This difference is evident in the salutation: not, "Paul an apostle . . . ," his customary opening; rather, "Paul and Timothy, slaves of Christ Jesus. . ."

The dominant note of this short letter is joy. This is the more remarkable in view of the fact that Paul was writing from prison. The immediate circumstances surrounding a believer are not the factors which should determine his attitude toward life.

The twin notes of humility and concern for others are also very evident. In view of what Christ did, no room for pride remains to the child of God. In view of Christ's great example, His followers dare not be self-centered.

This letter has little of theology in the usual sense. A notable exception, however, is the great passage on the humiliation and exaltation of Christ (2.5-11). Similarly, the letter has little in the way of specific ethical instruction. Short, sharp warnings flash out regarding those who had caused Paul so much difficulty in other places (3.2), but there is no refutation of theological error, no strong rebuke of faults within the church.

AUTHOR

This letter is almost universally accepted today as from the hand of Paul. It was written from prison, but the location of the prison is not given. The possibilities that have been suggested are Rome,

Caesarea and Ephesus. The traditional position is that Paul wrote this letter from Rome. The arguments for this position still outweigh the arguments which favor Caesarea or Ephesus. If we place the writing of this letter near the close of this imprisonment, the date would be about A.D. 62.

R.A.G.

THE LETTER OF PAUL TO THE

PHILIPPIANS

CHAPTER 1

Loveliest Thank You Note Ever Written

PAUL and Tim'o-thy, the servants of Je'sus Christ, to all the <u>saints</u> in Christ Je'sus which are at Phi-lip'pi, with the bishops and deacons: _{believers}

2 Grace *be* to you, and peace, from God our Father, and *from* the Lord Je'sus Christ.

3 I thank my God upon every remembrance of you,

4 Always in every prayer of mine for you all making request with joy,

5 For your fellowship in the gospel from the first day until now;

6 Being confident of this very thing, that He which has begun a good work in you will <u>perform</u> *it* until the day of Je'sus Christ: continue

7 Even as it is <u>meet</u> for me to think this of you all, because I have you in my heart; inasmuch as both in my bonds, and in the defence and confirmation of the gospel, you all are <u>partakers</u> of my grace. right - partners

8 For God is my <u>record</u>, how greatly I long after you all in the <u>bowels</u> of Je'sus Christ witness - affections

9 And this I pray, that your love may abound yet more and more in knowledge and *in* all <u>judgment</u>; discernment

10 That you may approve things that are excellent; that you may be sincere and without offence till the day of Christ;

11 Being filled with the fruits of righteousness, which are by Je'sus Christ, to the glory and praise of God.

12 But I would you should understand, brethren, that the things *which happened* to me have <u>fallen</u> out rather to the furtherance of the gospel; turned

13 So that my bonds in Christ are <u>manifest</u> in all <u>the palace</u>, and in all other <u>places</u>; known - i.e., palace people - i.e., people

14 And many of the brethren in the Lord, <u>waxing</u> confident by my bonds, are much more bold to speak the word without fear. growing

15 Some indeed preach Christ even of envy and strife; and some also of good will:

16 The one preach Christ of <u>contention</u>, not sincerely, supposing to add affliction to my bonds: faction

17 But the other of love, knowing that I am set for the defence of the gospel.

18 What then? notwithstanding, every way, whether in pretence, or in truth, Christ is preached; and I therein do rejoice, yea, and will rejoice.

19 For I know that this shall turn to my salvation through your prayer, and the <u>supply</u> of the Spirit of Je'sus Christ, provision

20 According to my earnest expectation and *my* hope, that in nothing I shall be ashamed, but *that* with all boldness, as always, *so* now also Christ shall be magnified in my body, whether *it be* by life, or by death.

21 For to me to live *is* Christ, and to die *is* gain.

22 But if I live in the flesh, this *is* the fruit of my labor: yet what I shall choose I know not.

23 For I am in a <u>strait</u> between two, having a desire to depart, and to be with Christ; which is far better: position

24 Nevertheless to abide in the flesh *is* more <u>needful</u> for you.   necessary

25 And having this confidence, I know that I shall abide and continue with you all for your furtherance and joy of faith;

26 That your rejoicing may be more abundant in Je'sus Christ for me by my coming to you again.

27 Only let your conversation be as it becomes the gospel of Christ: that whether I come and see you, or else be absent, I may hear of your affairs, that you stand <u>fast</u> in one spirit, with one mind striving together for the faith of the gospel;   firm

28 And in nothing <u>terrified</u> by your adversaries: which is to them an evident <u>token</u> of perdition, but to you of salvation, and that of God.   alarmed - sign

29 For to you it is given in the behalf of Christ, not only to believe on Him, but also to suffer for His sake;

30 Having the same conflict which you saw in me, and now hear *to be* in me.

CHAPTER 2

IF *there be* therefore any consolation in Christ, if any comfort of love, if any fellowship of the Spirit, if any <u>bowels</u> and mercies,   compassion

2 Fulfil you my joy, that you be likeminded, having the same love, *being* of one accord, of one mind.

3 *Let* nothing *be done* through strife or <u>vainglory</u>; but in lowliness of mind let each esteem other better than themselves.   empty conceit

4 Look not every man on his own things, but every man also on the things of others.

5 Let this mind be in you, which was also in Christ Je'sus:

6 Who, being in the form of God, thought it not robbery to be equal with God:

7 But made Himself of no reputation, and took upon Him the form of a servant, and was made in the likeness of men:

8 And being found in fashion as a man, He humbled Himself, and became obedient to death, even the death of the cross.

9 Wherefore God also has highly exalted Him, and given Him a name which is above every name:

10 That at the name of Je'sus every knee should bow, of *things* in heaven, and *things* in earth, and *things* under the earth;   PSA. 95:6

11 And *that* every tongue should confess that Je'sus Christ *is* Lord, to the glory of God the Father.

12 Wherefore, my beloved, as you have always obeyed, not as in my presence only, but now much more in my absence, work out your own salvation with <u>fear</u> and trembling.   respect

13 For it is God which works in

you both to will and to do of *His* good pleasure.

14 Do all things without <u>murmurings</u> and disputings: grumblings

15 That you may be blameless and <u>harmless</u>, the sons of God, without rebuke, in the midst of a crooked and perverse nation, among whom you shine as lights in the world; innocent

16 Holding forth the word of life; that I may rejoice in the day of Christ, that I have not run in vain, neither labored in vain.

17 Yea, and if I be offered upon the sacrifice and service of your faith, I joy, and rejoice with you all.

18 For the same cause also do you joy, and rejoice with me.

19 But I trust in the Lord Je'sus to send Tim'o-thy shortly to you, that I also may be of good comfort, when I know your <u>state</u>. condition

20 For I have no man <u>likeminded</u>, who will naturally care for your <u>state</u>. of kindred spirit - welfare

21 For all seek their own, not the things which are Je'sus Christ's.

22 But you know the <u>proof</u> of him, that, as a son with the father, he has served with me in the gospel. worth

23 Him therefore I hope to send <u>presently</u>, so soon as I shall see how it will go with me. immediately

24 But I trust in the Lord that I also myself shall come shortly.

25 Yet I supposed it necessary to send to you E-paph-ro-di'tus, my brother, and companion in labor, and fellowsoldier, but your messenger, and he that <u>ministered to</u> my wants. helps with

26 For he longed after you all, and was <u>full of heaviness,</u> because that you had heard that he had been sick. distressed

27 For indeed he was sick near to death: but God had mercy on him; and not on him only, but on me also, less I should have sorrow upon sorrow.

28 I sent him therefore the more <u>carefully</u>, that, when you see him again, you may rejoice, and that I may be the less sorrowful. eagerly

29 Receive him therefore in the Lord with all gladness; and hold such in <u>reputation</u>: high regard

30 Because for the work of Christ he was near to death, not regarding his life, to supply your lack of service toward me.

CHAPTER 3

FINALLY, my brethren, rejoice in the Lord. To write the same things to you, to me indeed *is* not <u>grievous</u>, but for you *it is* safe. troublesome

2 Beware of <u>dogs</u>, beware of evil workers, beware of the <u>concision</u>.

i.e., Gentiles (unbelievers) false circumcision

3 For we are the circumcision, which worship God in the Spirit, and rejoice in Christ Je'sus, and have no confidence in the flesh.

4 Though I might also have confidence in the flesh. If any other man thinks that he has whereof he might trust in the flesh, I more:

5 Circumcised the eighth day, of the stock of Is'ra-el, *of* the tribe of Ben'ja-min, an He'brew of the He'brews; as touching the law, a Phar'i-see;

6 Concerning zeal, persecuting the

church; touching the righteousness which is in the law, blameless.

7 But what things were gain to me, those I counted loss for Christ.

8 Yea doubtless, and I count all things *but* loss for the excellency of the knowledge of Christ Je'sus my Lord: for whom I have suffered the loss of all things, and do count them *but* <u>dung</u>, that I may win Christ, _{rubbish}

9 And be found in Him, not having mine own righteousness, which is <u>of</u> the law, but that which is through the faith of Christ, the righteousness which is <u>of</u> God by faith: _{from}

10 That I may know Him, and the power of His resurrection, and the fellowship of His sufferings, being made conformable to His death;

11 If by any means I might attain to the resurrection <u>of</u> the dead.

12 Not as though I had already attained, either were already perfect: but I follow after, if that I may <u>apprehend</u> that for which also I am <u>apprehended</u> of Christ Je'sus. _{understand}

13 Brethren, I <u>count</u> not myself to have apprehended: but *this* one thing *I do*, forgetting those things which are behind, and reaching forth to those things which are before, _{regard}

14 I press toward the <u>mark</u> for the prize of the high calling of God in Christ Je'sus. _{goal}

15 Let us therefore, as many as be perfect, be thus minded: and if in any thing you be otherwise minded, God shall reveal even this to you.

16 Nevertheless, whereto we have already attained, let us walk by the same rule, let us mind the same thing.

17 Brethren, be followers together of me, and mark them which walk so as you have us for an example.

18 (For many walk, of whom I have told you often, and now tell you even weeping, *that they are* the enemies of the cross of Christ:

19 Whose end *is* destruction, whose God *is their* belly, and *whose* glory *is* in their shame, who mind earthly things.)

20 For our <u>conversation</u> is in heaven; from where also we look for the Savior, the Lord Je'sus Christ: _{citizenship}

21 Who shall change our vile body, that it may be fashioned like to His glorious body, according to the working whereby He is able even to subdue all things to Himself.

CHAPTER 4

THEREFORE, my brethren dearly beloved and longed for, my joy and crown, so stand fast in the Lord, *my* dearly beloved.

2 I <u>beseech</u> Eu-o'di-as, and <u>beseech</u> Syn'ty-che, that they be of the same mind in the Lord. _{beg}

3 And I <u>entreat</u> you also, true <u>yokefellow</u>, help those women which labored with me in the gospel, with Clem'ent also, and *with* other my fellowlaborers, whose names *are* in the book of life. _{ask - fellow men}

4 Rejoice in the Lord always: *and* again I say, Rejoice.

5 Let your <u>moderation</u> be known to all men. The Lord *is* at hand. _{gentleness}

6 Be <u>careful</u> for nothing; but in every thing by prayer and supplication with thanksgiving let your requests be made known to God.   anxious

7 And the peace of God, which passes all understanding, shall keep your hearts and minds through Christ Je'sus.

8 Finally, brethren, whatsoever things are true, whatsoever things *are* <u>honest</u>, whatsoever things *are* just, whatsoever things *are* pure, whatsoever things *are* lovely, whatsoever things *are* of good report; if *there be* any virtue, and if *there be* any praise, think on these things. honorable

9 Those things, which you have both learned, and received, and heard, and seen in me, do: and the God of peace shall be with you.

10 But I rejoiced in the Lord greatly, that now at the last your care of me has flourished again; wherein you were also careful, but you lacked opportunity.

11 Not that I speak in respect of want: for I have learned, in whatsoever state I am, *therewith* to be content.

12 I know both how to be <u>abased</u>, and I know how to <u>abound</u>: every where and in all things I am instructed both to be full and to be hungry, both to <u>abound</u> and to suffer need.   made low - be prosperous

13 I can do all things through Christ which strengthens me.

14 Notwithstanding you have well done, that you did <u>communicate</u> with my <u>affliction</u>.   share - troubles

15 Now you Phi-lip'pi-ans know also, that in the beginning of the gospel, when I departed from Mac-e-do'ni-a, no church communicated with me as concerning giving and receiving, but you only.

16 For even in Thes-sa-lo-ni'ca you sent once and again to my necessity.

17 Not because I desire a gift: but I desire fruit that may <u>abound</u> to your account.   increase

18 But I have all, and abound: I am full, having received of E-paph-ro-di'-tus the things *which were sent* from you, an <u>odor</u> of a sweet smell, a sacrifice acceptable, well pleasing to God.   fragrance

19 But my God shall supply all your need according to His riches in glory by Christ Je'sus.

20 Now to God and our Father *be* glory for ever and ever. Amen.

21 <u>Salute</u> every <u>saint</u> in Christ Je'sus. The brethren which are with me greet you.   Greet - believer

22 All the <u>saints</u> <u>salute</u> you, chiefly they that are of Cae'sar's household.

23 The grace of our Lord Je'sus Christ *be* with you all. Amen.

COLOSSIANS

OUTLINE

SURVEY

The Colossians had an exaggerated regard for the observance of rites and ceremonies, and they also indulged in some form of worshipping of angels. They were infected, therefore, with a heresy which seems to have had both Jewish and Gnostic elements. Paul deals with their problem by setting before them the incomparableness of Christ. In a notable passage he speaks of what the Lord accomplished in redemption and reconciliation and of His pre-eminence. Christ is "the image of the invisible God." Through Him all things were created. He is the Head of the Church. Thus Paul presents to them the Christ he preached. Because Christ is of such surpassing excellence, and because He has fully won their salvation, Paul can beseech them to abstain from the fancies they have been pursuing. He contrasts the new life in Christ with their former sinful manner of life and urges them to practice Christian virtues. Because they are Christians they must regulate all their relationships in terms of their Christian faith. So he speaks of the way wives and husbands, children and parents, slaves and masters, should behave towards one another. He reminds them that Christians should behave wisely before unbelievers. The letter comes to an end with a series of greetings.

AUTHOR

The letter claims to be written by Paul (1.1). It is in the Pauline style and expresses Pauline ideas. There is no reasonable doubt that the letter was written by the great apostle. It was written from prison (4.18), which most take to be the imprisonment at Rome towards the end of his life.

L.M.

THE LETTER OF PAUL TO THE

COLOSSIANS

Christ
Is All You Need

CHAPTER 1

PAUL, an apostle of Je'sus Christ by the will of God, and Tim'o-thy *our* brother,

2 To the saints and faithful brethren in Christ which are at Co-los'se: Grace *be* to you, and peace, from God our Father and the Lord Je'sus Christ. believers

3 We give thanks to God and the Father of our Lord Je'sus Christ, praying always for you,

4 Since we heard of your faith in Christ Je'sus, and of the love *which you have* to all the saints,

5 For the hope which is laid up for you in heaven, whereof you heard before in the word of the truth of the gospel;

6 Which is come to you, as *it is* in all the world; and brings forth fruit, as *it does* also in you, since the day you heard *of it*, and knew the grace of God in truth:

7 As you also learned of Ep'a-phras our dear fellowservant, who is for you a faithful minister of Christ;

8 Who also declared to us your love in the Spirit.

9 For this cause we also, since the day we heard *it*, do not cease to pray for you, and to desire that you might be filled with the knowledge of His will in all wisdom and spiritual understanding;

10 That you might walk worthy of the Lord to all pleasing, being fruitful in every good work, and increasing in the knowledge of God;

11 Strengthened with all might, according to His glorious power, to all patience and longsuffering with joyfulness;

12 Giving thanks to the Father, which has made us meet to be partakers of the inheritance of the saints in light: qualified - believers

13 Who has delivered us from the power of darkness, and has translated *us* into the kingdom of His dear Son:

14 In whom we have redemption through His blood, *even* the forgiveness of sins:

15 Who is the image of the invisible God, the firstborn of every creature:

16 For by Him were all things created, that are in heaven, and that are in earth, visible and invisible, whether *they be* thrones, or dominions, or principalities, or powers: all things were created by Him, and for Him:

17 And He is before all things, and by Him all things consist. PROV. 8:22

18 And He is the head of the body, the church: who is the beginning, the firstborn from the dead; that in all *things* He might have the preeminence. first place

19 For it pleased *the Father* that in Him should all fulness dwell;

20 And, having made peace through the blood of His cross, by Him to reconcile all things to Himself; by Him,

I say, whether *they be* things in earth, or things in heaven. _{adjust}

21 And you, that were sometime alienated and enemies in *your* mind by wicked works, yet now has He reconciled

22 In the body of His flesh through death, to present you holy and unblameable and unreproveable in His sight:

23 If you continue in the faith grounded and settled, and *be* not moved away from the hope of the gospel, which you have heard, *and* which was preached to every creature which is under heaven; whereof I Paul am made a minister; _{established}

24 Who now rejoice in my sufferings for you, and fill up that which is behind of the afflictions of Christ in my flesh for His body's sake, which is the church:

25 Whereof I am made a minister, according to the dispensation of God which is given to me for you, to fulfill the word of God; _{servant - commission - fully preach}

26 *Even* the mystery which has been hid from ages and from generations, but now is made manifest to His saints: _{secret - known - believers}

27 To whom God would make known what *is* the riches of the glory of this mystery among the Gen'tiles; which is Christ in you, the hope of glory:

28 Whom we preach, warning every man, and teaching every man in all wisdom; that we may present every man perfect in Christ Je'sus: _{complete}

29 Whereto I also labor, striving according to His working, which works in me mightily.

CHAPTER 2

FOR I would that you knew what great conflict I have for you, and *for* them at La-od-i-ce'a, and *for* as many as have not seen my face in the flesh;

2 That their hearts might be comforted, being knit together in love, and to all riches of the full assurance of understanding, to the acknowledgement of the mystery of God, and of the Father, and of Christ; _{secret}

3 In whom are hid all the treasures of wisdom and knowledge.   ISA. 45:3

4 And this I say, less any man should beguile you with enticing words. _{deceive - persuasive}

5 For though I be absent in the flesh, yet am I with you in the spirit, joying and beholding your order, and the steadfastness of your faith in Christ. _{good discipline}

6 As you have therefore received Christ Je'sus the Lord, *so* walk you in Him:

7 Rooted and built up in Him, and stablished in the faith, as you have been taught, abounding therein with thanksgiving.

8 Beware less any man spoil you through philosophy and vain deceit, after the tradition of men, after the rudiments of the world, and not after Christ. _{captures - principles}

9 For in Him dwells all the fulness of the Godhead bodily.

10 And you are complete in Him, which is the head of all principality and power: _{rule}

11 In whom also you are circumcised with the circumcision made without

hands, in putting off the body of the sins of the flesh by the circumcision of Christ:

12 Buried with Him in baptism, wherein also you are risen with *Him* through the faith of the operation of God, who has raised Him from the dead.

13 And you, being dead in your sins and the uncircumcision of your flesh, has He quickened together with Him, having forgiven you all trespasses; made alive

14 Blotting out the handwriting of ordinances that was against us, which was contrary to us, and took it out of the way, nailing it to His cross;

15 *And* having spoiled principalities and powers, He made a show of them openly, triumphing over them in it.

16 Let no man therefore judge you in meat, or in drink, or in respect of an holyday, or of the new moon, or of the sabbath *days*: food - a festival - rest

17 Which are a shadow of things to come; but the body *is* of Christ.

18 Let no man beguile you of your reward in a voluntary humility and worshipping of angels, intruding into those things which he has not seen, vainly puffed up by his fleshly mind, trick - inflated

19 And not holding the Head, from which all the body by joints and bands having nourishment ministered, and knit together, increases with the increase of God. Christ - whom - grows

20 Wherefore if you be dead with Christ from the rudiments of the world, why, as though living in the world, are you subject to ordinances, base principles - rules

21 (Touch not; taste not; handle not;

22 Which all are to perish with the using;) after the commandments and doctrines of men? teachings

23 Which things have indeed a show of wisdom in will worship, and humility, and neglecting of the body; not in any honor to the satisfying of the flesh.

CHAPTER 3

IF you then be risen with Christ, seek those things which are above, where Christ sits on the right hand of God.

2 Set your affection on things above, not on things on the earth. mind

3 For you are dead, and your life is hid with Christ in God.

4 When Christ, *who is* our life, shall appear, then shall you also appear with Him in glory.

5 Mortify therefore your members which are upon the earth; fornication, uncleanness, inordinate affection, evil concupiscence, and covetousness, which is idolatry: Put to death - unnatural - desire

6 For which things' sake the wrath of God comes on the children of disobedience:

7 In the which you also walked some time, when you lived in them.

8 But now you also put off all these; anger, wrath, malice, blasphemy, filthy communication out of your mouth. slander

9 Lie not one to another, seeing that you have put off the old man with his deeds;

10 And have put on the new *man*, which is renewed in knowledge after the image of Him that created him: GEN. 1:26

11 Where there is neither Greek nor Jew, circumcision nor uncircumcision, Bar-ba'ri-an, Scyth'i-an, bond *nor* free: but Christ *is* all, and in all.

12 Put on therefore, as the elect of God, holy and beloved, bowels of mercies, kindness, humbleness of mind, meekness, longsuffering;   chosen - i.e., compassion

13 Forbearing one another, and forgiving one another, if any man have a quarrel against any: even as Christ forgave you, so also *do* you.   complaint

14 And above all these things *put on* charity, which is the bond of perfectness.   love

15 And let the peace of God rule in your hearts, to the which also you are called in one body; and be you thankful.

16 Let the word of Christ dwell in you richly in all wisdom; teaching and admonishing one another in psalms and hymns and spiritual songs, singing with grace in your hearts to the Lord.   urging

17 And whatsoever you do in word or deed, *do* all in the name of the Lord Je'sus, giving thanks to God and the Father by Him.

18 Wives, submit yourselves to your own husbands, as it is fit in the Lord.   be in harmony

19 Husbands, love *your* wives, and be not bitter against them.

20 Children, obey *your* parents in all things: for this is well pleasing to the Lord.

21 Fathers, provoke not your children *to anger*, less they be discouraged.

22 Servants, obey in all things *your* masters according to the flesh; not with eyeservice, as menpleasers; but in singleness of heart, fearing God: sincerity - revering

23 And whatsoever you do, do *it* heartily, as to the Lord, and not to men;

24 Knowing that of the Lord you shall receive the reward of the inheritance: for you serve the Lord Christ.

25 But he that does wrong shall receive for the wrong which he has done: and there is no respect of persons.

CHAPTER 4

MASTERS, give to *your* servants that which is just and equal; knowing that you also have a Master in heaven.   LEV. 25:43

2 Continue in prayer, and watch in the same with thanksgiving;

3 Meanwhile praying also for us, that God would open to us a door of utterance, to speak the mystery of Christ, for which I am also in bonds: speech - secret

4 That I may make it manifest, as I ought to speak.   known

5 Walk in wisdom toward them that are without, redeeming the time.

6 Let your speech *be* always with grace, seasoned with salt, that you may know how you ought to answer every man.

7 All my state shall Tych'i-cus declare to you, *who is* a beloved brother, and a faithful minister and fellowservant in the Lord: affairs

8 Whom I have sent to you for the same purpose, that he might know your estate, and comfort your hearts;   circumstances

9 With O'nes'i-mus, a faithful and beloved brother, who is *one* of you. They shall make known to you all things which *are done* here.

10 Ar-is-tar'chus my fellowprisoner <u>salutes</u> you, and Mar'cus, sister's son to Bar'na-bas, (touching whom you received commandments: if he come to you, receive him;) _{greets}

11 And Je'sus, which is called Jus'tus, who are of the circumcision. These only *are my* fellowworkers to the kingdom of God, which have been a comfort to me.

12 Ep'a-phras, who is *one* of you, a servant of Christ, salutes you, always laboring fervently for you in prayers, that you may stand perfect and <u>complete</u> in all the will of God. _{assured}

13 For I bear him record, that he has a great zeal for you, and them *that are* in La-od-i-ce'a, and them in Hi-e-rap'o-lis.

14 Luke, the beloved physician, and De'mas, greet you.

15 <u>Salute</u> the brethren which are in La-od-i-ce'a, and Nym'phas, and the church which is in his house. _{Greet}

16 And when this epistle is read among you, cause that it be read also in the church of the La-od-i-ce'ans; and that you likewise read the *epistle* from La-od-i-ce'a.

17 And say to Ar-chip'pus, Take <u>heed</u> to the ministry which you have received in the Lord, that you fulfill it. _{care}

18 The <u>salutation</u> by the hand of me Paul. Remember my bonds. Grace *be* with you. Amen. _{greeting}

1 THESSALONIANS

OUTLINE

RELATION OF PAUL TO THE THESSALONIAN CHURCH 1.1—3.13
  Response of the Thessalonians to the Gospel 1.2-10
    Prayer of Thanksgiving 1.2-4
    Proofs of Election 1.5-10
  Recounting of the Character of Paul's Ministry 2.1-12
    Purity of His Motives 2.1-6
    Purity of His Emotions 2.7, 8
    Purity of His Life 2.9-12
  Reception by the Thessalonians 2.13-16
    Reception of the Word of God 2.13
    Persecution for the Word of God 2.14-16
  Relation of Paul to the Thessalonians 2.17—3.13
    Intention of Paul 2.17-20
    Mission of Timothy 3.1-10
    Prayer for Reunion 3.11-13

EXHORTATION OF PAUL TO THE THESSALONIAN CHURCH 4.1—5.28
  Concerning the Conduct of the Believer 4.1-12
    Laxity in Morals 4.1-8
    Love of the Brethren 4.9-12
  Concerning the Consolation of the Believer 4.13—5.11
    The Rapture of the Saints 4.13-18
    The Day of the Lord 5.1-11
  Concerning Conduct in the Church 5.12-22
  Concluding Prayer 5.23, 24
  Final Requests 5.25-28

SURVEY

The church at Thessalonica, founded by Paul on his second missionary journey (Ac 17), was composed of converts from among the Jews, devout Greeks, noble women (Ac 17.4), and many from Gentile heathenism. After leaving Thessalonica (Ac 17.10), Paul sent Timothy to them (1 Th 3.1-3), and he later brought a report to Paul in Corinth. Many Thessalonians were disconsolate over departed loved ones (4.13-17); some were idle (4.11) and even disorderly (5.14). Some were tempted to return to heathen vices (4.1-18). Persecution was strong (3.3, 4). Some maligned the motives and character of Paul (2.1-12), others longed for his presence (3.6). In response to the report of Timothy, Paul writes from Corinth to commend the believers for their faith (1.2-10); to defend his apostleship (2.1-12) and to unite himself to the church in closer ties (2.17—3.10); to exhort to moral purity, brotherly love, and diligence in daily work (4.1-12); to comfort them in their concern for their departed loved ones (4.13-17) and to assure them of their deliverance from the coming judgment of the Day of the Lord (5.1-5); to exhort them to watchfulness (5.6-11) and orderly conduct in the assembly and in daily life (5.12-23).

AUTHOR

The Thessalonian epistles are important, not only because they are among Paul's first letters, and reveal much about the character of Paul's ministry and conditions in the church, but because they contain so much teaching concerning the second coming of Christ. 1 Thessalonians was written from Corinth in A.D. 51.

J.D.P.

THE FIRST LETTER OF PAUL TO THE
THESSALONIANS

Christ Will Return
His Church

CHAPTER 1

PAUL, and Sil-va'nus, and Tim'o-thy, to the church of the Thes-sa-lo'nians *which is* in God the Father and *in* the Lord Je'sus Christ: Grace *be* with you, and peace, from God our Father, and the Lord Je'sus Christ.

2 We give thanks to God always for you all, making mention of you in our prayers;

3 Remembering without ceasing your work of faith, and labor of love, and patience of hope in our Lord Je'sus Christ, in the sight of God and our Father;

4 Knowing, brethren beloved, your underline{election} of God. being chosen

5 For our gospel came not to you in word only, but also in power, and in the Ho'ly Ghost, and in much assurance; as you know what manner of men we were among you for your sake. Spirit

6 And you became followers of us, and of the Lord, having received the word in much affliction, with joy of the Ho'ly Ghost: imitators

7 So that you were examples to all that believe in Mac-e-do'ni-a and A-cha'ia.

8 For from you sounded out the word of the Lord not only in Mac-e-do'ni-a and A-cha'ia, but also in every place your faith to God-ward is spread abroad; so that we need not to speak any thing.

9 For they themselves show of us what manner of entering in we had to you, and how you turned to God from idols to serve the living and true God;

10 And to wait for His Son from heaven, whom He raised from the dead, *even* Je'sus, which delivered us from the wrath to come. judgment

CHAPTER 2

FOR yourselves, brethren, know our entrance in to you, that it was not in vain: coming - a failure

2 But even after that we had suffered before, and were shamefully en-treated, as you know, at Phi-lip'pi, we were bold in our God to speak to you the gospel of God with much contention. mistreated

3 For our exhortation *was* not of de-ceit, nor of uncleanness, nor in guile: error

4 But as we were allowed of God to be put in trust with the gospel, even so we speak; not as pleasing men, but God, which tries our hearts.
approved - examines

5 For neither at any time used we flat-tering words, as you know, nor a cloke of covetousness; God *is* witness: greed

6 Nor of men sought we glory, neither of you, nor *yet* of others, when we might have been burdensome, as the apostles of Christ. praise - expensive

7 But we were gentle among you, even as a nurse <u>cherishes</u> her children:

tenderly cares for

8 So being affectionately desirous of you, we were willing to have <u>imparted</u> to you, not the gospel of God only, but also our own souls, because you were dear to us. shared

9 For you remember, brethren, our labor and <u>travail</u>: for laboring night and day, because we would not be <u>chargeable</u> to any of you, we preached to you the gospel of God. hardship - a burden

10 You *are* witnesses, and God *also*, how holy and justly and unblameably we behaved ourselves among you that believe:

11 As you know how we <u>exhorted</u> and comforted and <u>charged</u> every one of you, as a father *does* his children,

urged - imploring

12 That you would walk worthy of God, who has called you to His kingdom and glory.

13 For this <u>cause</u> also thank we God without ceasing, because, when you received the word of God which you heard of us, you received *it* not *as* the word of men, but as it is in truth, the word of God, which effectually works also in you that believe. reason

14 For you, brethren, became followers of the churches of God which in Ju-dae'a are in Christ Je'sus: for you also have suffered like things of your own countrymen, even as they *have* of the Jews:

15 Who both killed the Lord Je'sus, and their own prophets, and have per-secuted us; and they please not God, and are <u>contrary</u> to all men: hostile

16 Forbidding us to speak to the Gen'tiles that they might be saved, to <u>fill</u> up their sins alway: for the wrath is come upon them to the <u>uttermost</u>. heap - last

17 But we, brethren, being taken from you for a short time in presence, not in heart, endeavored the more abundantly to see your face with great desire.

18 Wherefore we would have come to you, even I Paul, once and again; but Sa'tan hindered us.

19 For what *is* our hope, or joy, or crown of rejoicing? *Are* not even you in the presence of our Lord Je'sus Christ at His coming?

20 For you are our glory and joy.

CHAPTER 3

WHEREFORE when we could no longer <u>forbear</u>, we thought it good to be left at Ath'ens alone; endure

2 And sent Tim'o-thy, our brother, and minister of God, and our fellowlaborer in the gospel of Christ, to establish you, and to comfort you concerning your faith:

3 That no man should be moved by these afflictions: for yourselves know that we are appointed <u>thereunto</u>. for this

4 For <u>verily</u>, when we were with you, we told you before that we should suffer <u>tribulation</u>; even as it came to pass, and you know. truly - affliction

5 For this cause, when I could no longer <u>forbear</u>, I sent to know your faith, less by some means the <u>tempter</u>

have tempted you, and our labor be in vain. *i.e., Satan*

6 But now when Tim'o-thy came from you to us, and brought us good <u>tidings</u> of your faith and <u>charity</u>, and that you have good remembrance of us always, desiring greatly to see us, as we also *to see* you: *news - love*

7 Therefore, brethren, we were comforted over you in all our affliction and distress by your faith:

8 For now we live, if you stand <u>fast</u> in the Lord. *firm*

9 For what thanks can we <u>render</u> to God again for you, for all the joy wherewith we joy for your sakes before our God; *give*

10 Night and day praying exceedingly that we might see your face, and might perfect that which is lacking in your faith?

11 Now God Himself and our Father, and our Lord Je'sus Christ, <u>direct</u> our way to you. *guide*

12 And the Lord make you to increase and <u>abound</u> in love one toward another, and toward all *men*, even as we *do* toward you: *overflow*

13 To the end He may stablish your hearts unblameable in holiness before God, even our Father, at the coming of our Lord Je'sus Christ with all His <u>saints</u>. *believers*

CHAPTER 4

FURTHERMORE then we <u>beseech</u> you, brethren, and exhort *you* by the Lord Je'sus, that as you have received of us how you ought to walk and to please God, so you would abound more and more. *beg*

2 For you know what <u>commandments</u> we gave you by the Lord Je'sus. *instructions*

3 For this is the will of God, *even* your <u>sanctification</u>, that you should abstain from fornication: *holiness*

4 That every one of you should know how to <u>possess his vessel</u> in <u>sanctification</u> and honor; *control his body*

5 Not in the lust of <u>concupiscence</u>, even as the <u>Gen'tiles</u> which know not God: *passion - heathens*

6 That no *man* go beyond and defraud his brother in *any* matter: because that the Lord *is* the avenger of all such, as we also have forewarned you and <u>testified</u>. *spoken*

7 For God has not called us to uncleanness, but to holiness.

8 He therefore that <u>despises</u>, <u>despises</u> not man, but God, who has also given to us His Holy Spirit. *rejects*

9 But as touching brotherly love you need not that I write to you: for you yourselves are taught of God to love one another.

10 And indeed you do it toward all the brethren which are in all Mac-e-do'-ni-a: but we <u>beseech</u> you, brethren, that you increase more and more; *beg*

11 And that you <u>study</u> to be quiet, and to do your own business, and to work with your own hands, as we <u>commanded</u> you; *try - instructed*

12 That you may walk honestly toward them that are outside, and *that* you may have <u>lack of nothing</u>. *all you need*

13 But I would not have you to be <u>ignorant</u>, brethren, concerning them *not knowing*

which are <u>asleep</u>, that you sorrow not, even as others which have no hope.   dead

14 For if we believe that Je'sus died and rose again, even so them also which <u>sleep</u> in Je'sus will God bring with Him.   die

15 For this we say to you by the word of the Lord, that we which are alive *and* remain to the coming of the Lord shall not <u>prevent</u> them which are <u>asleep</u>.   precede

16 For the Lord Himself shall descend from heaven with a shout, with the voice of the archangel, and with the trump of God: and the dead in Christ shall rise first:

17 Then we which are alive *and* remain shall be caught up together with them in the clouds, to meet the Lord in the air: and so shall we ever be with the Lord.

18 Wherefore <u>comfort</u> one another with these words.   encourage

CHAPTER 5

BUT of the times and the <u>seasons</u>, brethren, you have no need that I write to you.   dates

2 For yourselves know <u>perfectly</u> that the day of the Lord so comes as a thief in the night.   full well

3 For when they shall say, Peace and safety; then sudden destruction comes upon them, as <u>travail</u> upon a woman with child; and they shall not escape.   birth pains

4 But you, brethren, are not in darkness, that that day should <u>overtake</u> you as a thief.   ISA. 35:4 surprise

5 You are all the children of light, and the children of the day: we are not of the night, nor of darkness.

6 Therefore let us not sleep, as *do* others; but let us watch and be sober.

7 For they that sleep sleep in the night; and they that be drunken are drunken in the night.

8 But let us, who are of the day, be sober, putting on the breastplate of faith and love; and for an helmet, the hope of salvation.

9 For God has not appointed us to wrath, but to obtain salvation by our Lord Je'sus Christ,

10 Who died for us, that, whether we wake or sleep, we <u>should</u> live together with Him.   may

11 Wherefore <u>comfort</u> yourselves together, and <u>edify</u> one another, even as also you do.   encourage - build up

12 And we <u>beseech</u> you, brethren, to know them which <u>labor</u> among you, and are over you in the Lord, and <u>admonish</u> you;   beg - work - instruct

13 And to <u>esteem</u> them very highly in love for their work's sake. *And* be at peace among yourselves.   hold

14 Now we exhort you, brethren, warn them that are unruly, comfort the <u>feebleminded</u>, support the weak, be patient toward all *men*.   faint hearted

15 See that none render <u>evil for evil</u> to any *man*; but ever follow that which is good, both among yourselves, and to all *men*.   wrong for wrong

16 Rejoice <u>evermore</u>.   always

17 Pray without ceasing.

18 In every thing give thanks: for this

is the will of God in Christ Je'sus concerning you.

19 Quench not the Spirit. _{Put out}

20 Despise not prophesyings.

21 Prove all things; hold fast that which is good. _{firm}

22 Abstain from all appearance of evil.

23 And the very God of peace sanctify you wholly; and *I pray God* your whole spirit and soul and body be preserved blameless to the coming of our Lord Je'sus Christ. _{kept}

24 Faithful *is* He that calls you, who also will do *it*.

25 Brethren, pray for us.

26 Greet all the brethren with an holy kiss.

27 I charge you by the Lord that this epistle be read to all the holy brethren. _{instruct}

28 The grace of our Lord Je'sus Christ *be* with you. Amen.

2 THESSALONIANS

OUTLINE

SURVEY

The bearer of the First Epistle to the Thessalonians brought Paul word concerning the spiritual growth of these believers. Paul was greatly comforted by the report. In addition, the report to the apostle indicated that erroneous teaching, purporting to come from Paul, had reached Thessalonica either through a forged letter or through oral and written reports of his teaching. Some held that the tribulations and persecutions they were enduring were the tribulations of the Day of the Lord and consequently that they had either missed the translation or Paul had been wrong in his teaching (1 Th 4.13—5.10). Paul writes the Second Epistle to commend them for their spiritual growth (1.3, 4); to comfort them in their persecutions (1.5–10); to correct their misinformation and misapprehension concerning the Day of the Lord (2.1–12); and to correct disorderliness in the church (3.6–15).

AUTHOR

From the similarity of the conditions reflected by the two epistles, it is concluded that Paul wrote the second letter shortly after the first, probably within a few months. It was written from Corinth in A.D. 51.

J.D.P.

THE SECOND LETTER OF PAUL TO THE
THESSALONIANS

CHAPTER 1

The Man of Sin
Will Be Revealed

PAUL, and Sil-va'nus, and Tim'o-thy to the church of the Thes-sa-lo'ni-ans in God our Father and the Lord Je'sus Christ:

2 Grace to you, and peace, from God our Father and the Lord Je'sus Christ.

3 We are bound to thank God always for you, brethren, as it is <u>meet</u>, be-cause that your faith grows exceed-ingly, and the <u>charity</u> of every one of you all toward each other <u>abounds</u>;

fitting - love - grow

4 So that we ourselves <u>glory in</u> you in the churches of God for your pa-tience and faith in all your persecu-tions and <u>tribulations</u> that you en-dure:

speak proudly of - afflictions

5 *Which is* a <u>manifest</u> token of the righteous judgment of God, that you may be counted worthy of the king-dom of God, for which you also suf-fer:

known

6 Seeing *it is* a righteous thing with God to <u>recompense tribulation</u> to them that trouble you;

repay with affliction

7 And to you who are troubled rest with us, when the Lord Je'sus shall be revealed from heaven with His mighty angels,

8 In flaming fire taking vengeance on them that know not God, and that obey not the gospel of our Lord Je'sus Christ:

ISA. 1:28

9 Who shall be punished with ever-lasting destruction from the presence of the Lord, and from the glory of His power;

10 When He shall come to be glori-fied in His <u>saints</u>, and to be admired in all them that believe (because our testimony among you was believed) in that day.

believers

11 Wherefore also we pray always for you, that our God would count you worthy of *this* calling, and fulfill all the good pleasure of *His* goodness, and the work of faith with power:

12 That the name of our Lord Je'sus Christ may be glorified in you, and you in Him, according to the grace of our God and the Lord Je'sus Christ.

CHAPTER 2

NOW we <u>beseech</u> you, brethren, by the coming of our Lord Je'sus Christ, and *by* our gathering together to Him,

beg

2 That you be not soon <u>shaken</u> in mind, or be troubled, neither by spirit, nor by word, nor by letter as from us, as that the day of Christ is at hand.

unsettled

3 Let no man deceive you by any means: for *that day shall not come*, except there come a falling away first, and that man of sin be revealed, the son of perdition;

DAN. 7:25

4 Who opposes and exalts himself above all that is called god, or that is worshiped; so that he as god sits in

the temple of God, showing himself that he is god.   EZE. 28:2

5 Remember you not, that, when I was yet with you, I told you these things?

6 And now you know what withholds that he might be revealed in his time.

7 For the mystery of <u>iniquity</u> does already work: only He who now <u>lets</u> *will* <u>let</u>, until <u>He</u> be taken out of the way.   lawlessness - restrains - Holy Spirit

8 And then shall that <u>wicked one</u> be revealed, whom the Lord shall <u>con-sume</u> with the spirit of His mouth, and shall destroy with the brightness of His coming: ISA. 11:4 Satan - slay

9 *Even him*, whose coming is after the working of Sa'tan with all power and signs and lying wonders, anti-christ

10 And with all <u>deceivableness</u> of unrighteousness in them that perish; because they received not the love of the truth, that <u>they</u> might be saved.   deception

11 And for this cause God shall send them strong <u>delusion</u>, that <u>they</u> should believe <u>a lie</u>:   unbelief i.e., unbelievers - what is false

12 That <u>they</u> all might be <u>damned</u> who believed not the truth, but had pleasure in unrighteousness.   judged

13 But we are <u>bound</u> to give thanks always to God for you, brethren beloved of the Lord, because God has from the beginning chosen you to salvation through sanctification of the Spirit and belief of the truth: obliged

14 Whereto He called you by our gospel, to the <u>obtaining</u> of the glory of our Lord Je'sus Christ.   gaining

15 Therefore, brethren, stand <u>fast</u>, and hold the traditions which you have been taught, whether by word, or our epistle.   firm

16 Now our Lord Je'sus Christ Himself, and God, even our Father, which has loved us, and has given *us* everlasting <u>consolation</u> and good hope through grace,   comfort

17 Comfort your hearts, and <u>stablish</u> you in every good word and work.   strengthen

CHAPTER 3

FINALLY, brethren, pray for us, that the word of the Lord may <u>have</u> *free* course, and be <u>glorified</u>, even as *it is* with you: spread rapidly - honored

2 And that we may be delivered from unreasonable and wicked men: for all *men* have not faith.

3 But the Lord is faithful, who shall <u>stablish</u> you, and keep *you* from evil.   strengthen

4 And we have confidence in the Lord <u>touching</u> you, that you both do and will do the things which we command you.   concerning

5 And the Lord direct your hearts into the love of God, and into the patient waiting for Christ.

6 Now we command you, brethren, in the name of our Lord Je'sus Christ, that you withdraw yourselves from every brother that walks disorderly, and not after the <u>tradition</u> which he received of us.   teaching

7 For yourselves know how you ought to <u>follow us</u>: for we behaved not ourselves <u>disorderly</u> among you;

8 Neither did we eat any man's bread

i.e., our example - undisciplined

for nought; but wrought with labor and travail night and day, that we might not be chargeable to any of you:

worked - hardship - a burden

9 Not because we have not power, but to make ourselves an example to you to follow us.

the right

10 For even when we were with you, this we commanded you, that if any would not work, neither should he eat.

11 For we hear that there are some which walk among you disorderly, working not at all, but are busybodies.

live

12 Now them that are such we command and exhort by our Lord Je'sus Christ, that with quietness they work, and eat their own bread.

urge

13 But you, brethren, be not weary in well doing.

14 And if any man obey not our word by this epistle, note that man, and have no company with him, that he may be ashamed.

instruction - association

15 Yet count *him* not as an enemy, but admonish *him* as a brother. *warn*

16 Now the Lord of peace Himself give you peace always by all means. The Lord *be* with you all.

in every way

17 The salutation of Paul with my own hand, which is the token in every epistle: so I write.

greeting - sign

18 The grace of our Lord Je'sus Christ *be* with you all. Amen.

1 TIMOTHY

OUTLINE

SALUTATION 1.2

THE SITUATION AT EPHESUS 1.3-17

THE CHARGE TO TIMOTHY 1.18-20

INSTRUCTIONS CONCERNING PUBLIC WORSHIP 2.1-15
    Prayers 2.1-8
    Conduct of Women 2.9-15

QUALIFICATIONS OF CHURCH OFFICERS 3.1-13
    Bishops 3.1-7
    Deacons 3.8-13

PURPOSE OF THE CHARGE 3.14-16

INSTRUCTIONS CONCERNING APOSTASY 4.1-16
    Apostasy Described 4.1-5
    Methods of Dealing with Apostasy 4.6-16

INSTRUCTIONS CONCERNING GROUPS AND INDIVIDUALS IN THE CHURCH 5.1—6.21
    Older and Younger Men and Women 5.1, 2
    Widows 5.3-16
    Elders and Prospective Elders 5.17-25
    Slaves 6.1, 2
    False Teachers 6.3-10
    Timothy 6.11-21
        A Charge to Timothy Himself 6.11-16
        Through Him to the Rich 6.17-19
        A Concluding Appeal 6.20, 21

SURVEY

Since the early eighteenth century, 1 and 2 Timothy and Titus have been designated the Pastoral Epistles. Though not completely adequate, this designation indicates the practical nature of the subject matter treated in these letters. Timothy, an inexperienced pastor, was left in charge of the important church at Ephesus. Paul, his spiritual father, writes to encourage and to instruct him in relation to such practical subjects as public worship, qualifications for church officials, and confrontation of false teaching in the church. He also instructs Timothy about relations to various groups in the church including widows, elders, slaves and false teachers. 1 Timothy therefore contains much information about the problems of the developing church in the third quarter of the first Christian century. The letter reveals throughout the personal warmth of the great apostle for his son in the faith and his emphasis on the one great qualification for Christ's minister, godliness.

AUTHOR

Pauline authorship of the Pastorals has been widely denied by modern scholarship, based largely on linguistic phenomena and the "advanced theology" of these letters. However, the arguments against

the traditional view of Paul's authorship are not conclusive. 1 Timothy was written from Macedonia (probably Philippi) about A.D. 63, during the interval between Paul's first and second Roman imprisonments.

W.W.W.

THE FIRST LETTER OF PAUL TO

TIMOTHY

CHAPTER 1

PAUL, an apostle of Je'sus Christ by the commandment of God our Savior, and Lord Je'sus Christ, *which is* our hope;

2 To Tim'o-thy, *my* own son in the faith: Grace, mercy, *and* peace, from God our Father and Je'sus Christ our Lord.

3 As I <u>besought</u> you to abide still at Eph'e-sus, when I went into Mac-e-do'ni-a, that you might <u>charge</u> some that they teach no other doctrine, urged - command

4 Neither give heed to fables and endless <u>genealogies</u>, which <u>minister</u> questions, rather than godly <u>edifying</u> which is in faith: *so do.* history - cause - building up

5 Now the <u>end</u> of the commandment is <u>charity</u> out of a pure heart, and *of* a good conscience, and *of* faith unfeigned: goal - love

6 From which some having swerved have turned aside to <u>vain jangling</u>; meaningless talk

7 Desiring to be teachers of the law; understanding neither what they say, nor whereof they <u>affirm</u>. speak positively

8 But we know that the law *is* good, if a man use it lawfully;

9 Knowing this, that the law is not made for a righteous man, but for the lawless and <u>disobedient</u>, for the ungodly and for sinners, for unholy and profane, for murderers of fathers and murderers of mothers, for <u>manslayers</u>, rebellious - murderers

10 For <u>whoremongers</u>, for them that defile themselves with <u>mankind</u>, for <u>menstealers</u>, for liars, for perjured persons, and if there be any other thing that is contrary to sound doctrine; adulterers - i.e., homosexuals - kidnappers

11 According to the glorious gospel of the blessed God, which was committed to my trust.

12 And I thank Christ Je'sus our Lord, who has enabled me, for that He counted me faithful, putting me into the ministry;

13 Who was before a <u>blasphemer</u>, and a persecutor, and <u>injurious</u>: but I obtained mercy, because I did *it* ignorantly in unbelief. evil speaker - violent

14 And the grace of our Lord was exceeding abundant with faith and love which is in Christ Je'sus.

15 This *is* a <u>faithful</u> saying, and worthy of all acceptation, that Christ Je'sus came into the world to save sinners; of whom I am chief. LUKE 2:12 trustworthy

16 However for this cause I obtained mercy, that in me first Je'sus Christ might show forth all longsuffering, for a pattern to them which should hereafter believe on Him to life everlasting.

17 Now to the King eternal, immortal, invisible, the only wise God, *be* honor and glory for ever and ever. Amen.

18 This charge I commit to you, son Tim'o-thy, according to the prophecies which went before on you, that you by them might <u>war</u> a good warfare; fight

19 <u>Holding</u> faith, and a good conscience; which some having put away concerning faith have made <u>ship-wreck</u>: Keeping - i.e., their faith

20 Of whom is Hy-me-nae'us and Alex-an'der; whom I have delivered to Sa'tan, that they may learn not to blaspheme.

CHAPTER 2

I EXHORT therefore, that, first of all, supplications, prayers, intercessions, *and* giving of thanks, be made for all men;

2 For kings, and *for* all that are in authority; that we may lead a quiet and peaceable life in all godliness and honesty.

3 For this *is* good and acceptable in the sight of God our Savior;

4 Who <u>will have</u> all men to be saved, and to come to the knowledge of the truth. desires

5 For *there is* one God, and one <u>mediator</u> between God and men, the man Christ Je'sus; i.e., who speak

6 Who gave Himself a ransom for all, to be <u>testified</u> in due time. witnessed of

7 Whereto I am ordained a preacher, and an apostle, (I speak the truth in Christ, *and* lie not;) a teacher of the Gen'tiles in faith and <u>verity</u>. truth

8 I will therefore that men pray every where, lifting up holy hands, without wrath and doubting.

9 In like manner also, that women adorn themselves in modest apparel, with shamefacedness and sobriety; not with braided hair, or gold, or pearls, or costly array;

10 But (which becomes women professing godliness) with good works.

11 Let the woman learn <u>in silence</u> with all <u>subjection</u>. quietly - submission

12 But I <u>suffer</u> not a woman to teach, nor to <u>usurp</u> authority over the man, but to be in silence. permit - exercise

13 For Ad'am was first <u>formed</u>, then Eve. GEN. 2:7 created

14 And Ad'am was not deceived, but the woman being deceived was <u>in the transgression</u>. GEN. 3:6 sinful

15 Notwithstanding she shall be saved in childbearing, if they continue in faith and <u>charity</u> and holiness with sobriety. love

CHAPTER 3

THIS *is* a true saying, If a man desire the office of a bishop, he desires a good work.

2 A bishop then must be <u>blameless</u>, the husband of one wife, vigilant, sober, of good behavior, given to hospitality, apt to teach; above reproach

3 Not <u>given</u> to wine, no <u>striker</u>, not greedy of filthy <u>lucre</u>; but patient, not a brawler, not covetous; addicted - fighter - money

4 One that <u>rules</u> well his own house, having his children in <u>subjection</u> with all gravity; manages - control

5 (For if a man know not how to rule his own <u>house</u>, how shall he take care of the church of God?) family

6 Not a <u>novice</u>, less being <u>lifted up</u> with pride he fall into the condemnation of the devil. <small>new convert - filled</small>

7 Moreover he must have a good report of them which are outside; less he fall into <u>reproach</u> and the <u>snare</u> of the <u>devil</u>. <small>disgrace - trap - Satan</small>

8 Likewise *must* the deacons *be* grave, not <u>doubletongued</u>, not given to much wine, not greedy of filthy <u>lucre</u>; <small>i.e., double talking to please - money</small>

9 Holding the <u>mystery</u> of the faith in a pure conscience. <small>secret</small>

10 And let these also first be <u>proved</u>; then let them use the office of a deacon, being *found* blameless. <small>tested</small>

11 Even so *must their* wives *be* grave, not slanderers, sober, faithful in all things.

12 Let the deacons be the husbands of one wife, ruling their children and their own houses well.

13 For they that have <u>used</u> the office of a deacon well purchase to themselves a good <u>degree</u>, and great boldness in the faith which is in Christ Je'sus. <small>served - standing</small>

14 These things write I to you, hoping to come to you shortly:

15 But if I tarry long, that <u>you</u> may know how <u>you</u> ought to behave <u>yourself</u> in the house of God, which is the church of the living God, the pillar and ground of the truth. <small>one - himself</small>

16 And without controversy great is the <u>mystery</u> of godliness: God was <u>manifest</u> in the flesh, justified in the Spirit, seen of angels, preached to the Gen'tiles, believed on in the world, received up into glory. <small>secret - made known</small>

CHAPTER 4

NOW the Spirit speaks expressly, that in the latter times some shall depart from the faith, giving heed to seducing spirits, and <u>doctrines</u> of devils; <small>teachings</small>

2 Speaking lies in hypocrisy; having their conscience seared with a hot iron;

3 Forbidding to marry, *and commanding* to abstain from <u>meats</u>, which God has created to be received with thanksgiving of them which believe and know the truth. <small>food</small>

4 For every creature of God *is* good, and nothing to be refused, if it be received with thanksgiving:

5 For it is <u>sanctified</u> by the word of God and prayer. <small>set apart</small>

6 If you put the brethren in remembrance of these things, you shall be a good <u>minister</u> of Je'sus Christ, nourished up in the words of faith and of good <u>doctrine</u>, whereto you have attained. <small>servant - teaching</small>

7 But refuse profane and old wives' fables, and <u>exercise</u> yourself *rather* to godliness. <small>train</small>

8 For bodily exercise profits little: but godliness is profitable to all things, having promise of the life that now is, and of that which is to come.

9 This *is* a <u>faithful</u> saying and worthy of all acceptation. <small>trustworthy</small>

10 For therefore we both labor and suffer reproach, because we trust in the living God, who is the Savior of all men, specially of those that believe.

11 These things command and teach.

12 Let no man <u>despise</u> your youth; but

be you an example of the believers, in word, in <u>conversation</u>, in <u>charity</u>, in spirit, in faith, in purity.

look down on - conduct - love

13 Till I come, give <u>attendance</u> to reading, to <u>exhortation</u>, to <u>doctrine</u>.

attention - preaching - teaching

14 Neglect not the gift that is in you, which was given you <u>by prophecy</u>, with the laying on of the hands of the <u>presbytery</u>.

for speaking - elders

15 <u>Meditate</u> upon these things; give yourself wholly to them; that your <u>profiting</u> may appear to all. Think - progress

16 Take <u>heed</u> to yourself, and to the <u>doctrine</u>; continue in them: for in doing this you shall both save yourself, and them that hear you. care

CHAPTER 5

REBUKE not an elder, but <u>entreat</u> him as a father; *and* the younger men as brethren; appeal to

2 The elder women as mothers; the younger as sisters, with all purity.

3 Honor widows that are widows indeed.

4 But if any widow have children or nephews, let them learn first to show piety at home, and to requite their parents: for that is good and acceptable before God.

5 Now she that is a widow indeed, and <u>desolate</u>, trusts in God, and continues in <u>supplications</u> and prayers night and day. lonely - requests

6 But she that lives in pleasure is dead while she lives.

7 And these things give in <u>charge</u>, that they may be blameless. instruction

8 But if any provide not for his own, and specially for those of his own <u>house</u>, he has denied the faith, and is worse than an <u>infidel</u>. family - unbeliever

9 Let not a widow be <u>taken into the number</u> under threescore years old, having been the wife of one man, put on a list

10 Well reported of for good works; if she have brought up children, if she have lodged strangers, if she have washed the saints' feet, if she have relieved the afflicted, if she have diligently followed every good work.

11 But the younger widows refuse: for when they have begun to <u>wax wanton</u> against Christ, they will marry; grow careless

12 Having damnation, because they have cast off their first <u>faith</u>. pledge

13 And besides they learn *to be* idle, wandering about from house to house; and not only idle, but <u>tattlers</u> also and busybodies, speaking things which they ought not. gossip

14 I will therefore that the younger women marry, bear children, <u>guide</u> the house, give none occasion to the <u>adversary</u> to speak reproachfully. keep - enemy

15 For some are already turned <u>aside after</u> Sa'tan. to follow

16 If any man or woman that believes have widows, let them relieve them, and let not the church be <u>charged</u>; that it may relieve them that are widows indeed. burdened

17 Let the elders that rule well be counted worthy of double honor, especially they who labor in the <u>word</u> and <u>doctrine</u>. preaching - teaching

18 For the scripture says, You shall

not muzzle the ox that treads out the corn. And, The laborer *is* worthy of his reward. DEU. 25:4 1 COR. 9:9

19 Against an elder <u>receive</u> not an accusation, but before two or three witnesses. listen

20 Them that sin <u>rebuke</u> before all, that others also may fear. speak against

21 I <u>charge</u> *you* before God, and the Lord Je'sus Christ, and the <u>elect</u> angels, that you observe these things without <u>preferring</u> one before another, doing nothing by <u>partiality</u>.

instruct - chosen - bias - favoritism

22 Lay hands suddenly on no man, neither be <u>partaker</u> of other men's sins: keep yourself pure. a partner

23 Drink no longer water, but use a little wine for your stomach's sake and your <u>often infirmities</u>. frequent ailments

24 Some men's sins are open beforehand, going before to judgment; and some *men* <u>they follow after</u>. i.e., sins show later

25 Likewise also the good works *of some* are <u>manifest</u> beforehand; and they that are otherwise cannot be hid. known

CHAPTER 6

LET as many servants as are <u>under the yoke</u> count their own masters worthy of all honor, that the name of God and *His* <u>doctrine</u> be not <u>blasphemed</u>. i.e. as slaves - teaching - spoken against

2 And they that have believing masters, let them not <u>despise</u> *them*, because they are brethren; but rather do *them* service, because they are <u>faithful</u> and beloved, partakers of the benefit. These things teach and <u>exhort</u>. belittle - believers - urge

3 If any man teach otherwise, and <u>consent</u> not to wholesome words, *even* the words of our Lord Je'sus Christ, and to the doctrine which is according to godliness; agrees

4 He is <u>proud</u>, knowing nothing, but <u>doting about</u> questions and strifes of words, whereof comes envy, strife, <u>railings</u>, evil <u>surmisings</u>,

conceited - dwelling on - abusive talk - suspicions

5 <u>Perverse disputings</u> of men of corrupt minds, and <u>destitute</u> of the truth, supposing that gain is godliness: from such withdraw yourself. constant frictions - deprived

6 But godliness with contentment is great gain.

7 For we brought nothing into *this* world, *and it is* certain we can carry nothing out.

8 And having food and <u>raiment</u> let us be therewith content. clothing

9 But they that will be rich fall into temptation and a <u>snare</u>, and *into* many foolish and hurtful lusts, which drown men in destruction and perdition. trap

10 For the love of money is the root of all evil: which while some coveted after, they have <u>erred</u> from the faith, and pierced themselves through with many sorrows. turned

11 But you, O man of God, flee these things; and follow after righteousness, godliness, faith, love, patience, <u>meekness</u>. gentleness

12 Fight the good fight of faith, <u>lay</u> hold on eternal life, whereto you are also called, and have professed a good profession before many witnesses. take

13 I give you <u>charge</u> in the sight of

God, who makes alive all things, and *before* Christ Je'sus, who before Pon'ti-us Pi'late witnessed a good confession; instruction

14 That you keep *this* commandment without spot, unrebukeable, until the appearing of our Lord Je'sus Christ:

15 Which in His times He shall show, *who is* the blessed and only Potentate, the King of kings, and Lord of lords; Ruler

16 Who only has immortality, dwelling in the light which no man can approach to; whom no man has seen, nor can see: to whom *be* honor and power everlasting. Amen. PROV. 29:25

17 Charge them that are rich in this world, that they be not highminded, nor trust in uncertain riches, but in the living God, who gives us richly all things to enjoy; Instruct - conceited

18 That they do good, that they be rich in good works, ready to distribute, willing to communicate; ready - share

19 Laying up in store for themselves a good foundation against the time to come, that they may lay hold on eternal life.

20 O Tim'o-thy, keep that which is committed to your trust, avoiding profane *and* vain babblings, and oppositions of science falsely so called: worldly - empty

21 Which some professing have erred concerning the faith. Grace *be* with you. Amen. strayed

2 TIMOTHY

OUTLINE

SURVEY

2 Timothy is chronologically last in order of the three Pastoral Epistles. It breathes a different atmosphere than the other two. In 1 Timothy and Titus, Paul is free to make travel plans and to move about at will. In this epistle, he is a prisoner and the end is rapidly approaching (4.6). Where Paul was arrested the second time and for what reason are not known. He writes 2 Timothy apparently from Rome where he is awaiting execution. All have forsaken him but Luke. He is anxious for Timothy, who is probably at Ephesus, to come to Rome before winter. However, he is even more concerned, in view of his own circumstances, that Timothy fulfil the ministry to which he was called. The content of the letter is rich and varied and includes a number of touching appeals, especially in view of Paul's situation. Four specific charges are addressed to Timothy that have to do primarily with his personal life as a minister. The threat of false teaching looms large in this letter as in 1 Timothy.

AUTHOR

The problem of authorship is discussed in the introduction to 1 Timothy. The circumstances of the writer, the theology, vocabulary, and style reveal that all three Pastorals were written by the same individual. If Paul wrote 1 Timothy, he is also the author of 2 Timothy. Since this epistle was written shortly before his death, A.D. 64 is the probable date.

W.W.W.

THE SECOND LETTER OF PAUL TO

TIMOTHY

CHAPTER 1

PAUL, an apostle of Je'sus Christ by the will of God, according to the promise of life which is in Christ Je'sus,

2 To Tim'o-thy, *my* dearly beloved son: Grace, mercy, *and* peace, from God the Father and Christ Je'sus our Lord.

3 I thank God, whom I serve from *my* forefathers with <u>pure</u> conscience, that without ceasing I have remembrance of you in my prayers night and day; _{clear}

4 Greatly desiring to see you, being mindful of your tears, that I may be filled with joy;

5 When I call to remembrance the <u>unfeigned</u> faith that is in you, which dwelled first in your grandmother Lo'is, and your mother Eu'nice; and I am persuaded that in you also._{sincere}

6 Wherefore I put you in remembrance that you stir up the gift of God, which is in you by the putting on of my hands.

7 For God has not given us the spirit of <u>fear</u>; but of power, and of love, and of a <u>sound mind</u>. timidity - self discipline

8 Be not you therefore ashamed of the testimony of our Lord, nor of me His prisoner: but be you <u>partaker</u> of the afflictions of the gospel according to the power of God; a sharer

9 Who has saved us, and called *us* with an holy calling, not according to our works, but according to His own purpose and grace, which was given us in Christ Je'sus before the world began,

10 But is now made <u>manifest</u> by the appearing of our Savior Je'sus Christ, who has abolished death, and has brought life and immortality to light through the <u>gospel</u>: known - good news

11 Whereto I am appointed a preacher, and an apostle, and a teacher of the Gen'tiles.

12 For the which <u>cause</u> I also suffer these things: nevertheless I am not ashamed: for I know whom I have believed, and am persuaded that He is able to keep that which I have committed to Him against that day. reason

13 Hold <u>fast</u> the form of sound words, which you have heard of me, in faith and love which is in Christ Je'sus. firm

14 That good thing which was <u>committed</u> to you keep by the Ho'ly <u>Ghost</u> which dwells in us. entrusted - Spirit

15 This you know, that all they which are in A'sia <u>be turned away from</u> me; of whom are Phy-gel'lus and Her-mog'e-nes. have deserted

16 The Lord give mercy to the house of On-e-siph'o-rus; for he <u>oft</u> refreshed me, and was not ashamed of my chain: often

17 But, when he was in Rome, he <u>sought</u> me out very <u>diligently</u>, and found *me*. searched - eagerly

18 The Lord grant to him that he may find mercy of the Lord in that day:

and in how many things he <u>minis-tered</u> to me at Eph'e-sus, you know very well. rendered

CHAPTER 2

YOU therefore, my son, be strong in the grace that is in Christ Je'sus.
2 And the things that you have heard of me among many witnesses, the same commit you to faithful men, who shall be able to teach others also.
3 You therefore endure hardness, as a good soldier of Je'sus Christ.
4 No man that goes to war entangles himself with the affairs of *this* life; that he may please him who has chosen him to be a soldier.
5 And if a man also strive for <u>masteries</u>, *yet* is he not crowned, except he strive lawfully. victories
6 The <u>husbandman</u> that labors must be first <u>partaker</u> of the fruits.
farmer - in sharing
7 Consider what I say; and the Lord give you understanding in all things.
8 Remember that Je'sus Christ of the <u>seed</u> of Da'vid was raised from the dead according to my gospel: offspring
9 Wherein I suffer trouble, as an evil doer, *even* to <u>bonds</u>; but the word of God is not bound. imprisonment
10 Therefore I endure all things for the <u>elect's</u> sakes, that they may also obtain the salvation which is in Christ Je'sus with eternal glory. chosen's
11 *It is* a <u>faithful</u> saying: For if we <u>be dead</u> with *Him*, we shall also live with *Him*: trustworthy - died

12 If we suffer, we shall also <u>reign</u> with *Him*: if we deny *Him*, He also will deny us: rule
13 If we <u>believe</u> not, *yet* He <u>abides</u> faithful: He cannot deny Himself.
are faithless - remains
14 Of these things put *them* in remembrance, <u>charging</u> *them* before the Lord that they strive not about words to no profit, *but* to the subverting of the hearers. warning
15 Study to show yourself approved to God, a workman that needs not to be ashamed, rightly dividing the word of truth.
16 But shun <u>profane *and*</u> <u>vain bab-blings</u>: for they will increase to more ungodliness. worldly and empty chattering
17 And their word will eat as does a <u>canker</u>: of whom is Hy-me-nae'us and Phi-le'tus; gangrene
18 Who concerning the truth have erred, saying that the resurrection is past already; and overthrow the faith of some.
19 Nevertheless the foundation of God stands <u>sure</u>, having this seal, The Lord knows them that are His. And, Let every one that names the name of Christ depart from <u>in-iquity</u>. NUM. 16.5 firm - wickedness
20 But in a great house there are not only vessels of gold and of silver, but also of wood and of earth; and some to honor, and some to dishonor.
21 If a man therefore <u>purge</u> himself from these, he shall be a vessel to honor, sanctified, and <u>meet</u> for the master's use, *and* prepared to every good work. cleanse - fit

22 Flee also youthful <u>lusts</u>: but follow righteousness, faith, <u>charity</u>, peace, with them that call on the Lord out of a pure heart. *passions - love*

23 But foolish and <u>unlearned</u> questions avoid, knowing that they do <u>gender strifes</u>. *ignorant - produce strife*

24 And the servant of the Lord must not <u>strive</u>; but be gentle to all *men*, apt to teach, patient, *struggle*

25 In meekness instructing those that oppose themselves; if God perhaps will give them repentance to the acknowledging of the truth;

26 And *that* they may recover themselves out of the <u>snare</u> of the devil, who are taken captive by him at his will. *trap*

CHAPTER 3

THIS know also, that in the last days <u>perilous</u> times shall come. *difficult*

2 For men shall be lovers of their own selves, covetous, boasters, proud, <u>blasphemers</u>, disobedient to parents, unthankful, unholy, *revilers*

3 Without natural affection, trucebreakers, false accusers, <u>incontinent</u>, fierce, despisers of those that are good, *without self control*

4 Traitors, heady, <u>highminded</u>, lovers of pleasures more than lovers of God; *conceited*

5 Having a form of godliness, but denying the power thereof: from such turn away.

6 For of this sort are they which creep into houses, and lead captive silly women laden with sins, led away with <u>divers</u> lusts, *various*

7 Ever learning, and never able to come to the knowledge of the truth.

8 Now as Jan'nes and Jam'bres withstood Mo'ses, so do these also resist the truth: men of corrupt minds, <u>reprobate</u> concerning the faith. *rejected*

9 But they shall proceed no further: for their folly shall be <u>manifest</u> to all *men*, as theirs also was. *known*

10 But you have fully known my <u>doctrine</u>, manner of life, purpose, faith, longsuffering, <u>charity</u>, patience, *teaching - love*

11 Persecutions, afflictions, which came to me at An'ti-och, at I-co'ni-um, at Lys'tra; what persecutions I endured: but out of *them* all the Lord delivered me.

12 Yea, and all that will live godly in Christ Je'sus shall suffer persecution.

13 But evil men and <u>seducers</u> shall <u>wax worse and worse</u>, deceiving, and being deceived. *imposters - proceed bad to worse*

14 But continue you in the things which you have learned and have been assured of, knowing of whom you have learned *them*;

15 And that from a child you have known the holy scriptures, which are able to make you wise to salvation through faith which is in Christ Je'sus.

16 All scripture *is* given by inspiration of God, and *is* profitable for <u>doctrine</u>, for reproof, for correction, for instruction in righteousness: *teaching*

17 That the man of God may be <u>perfect</u>, throughly furnished to all good works. *adequate*

CHAPTER 4

I CHARGE *you* therefore before God, and the Lord Je'sus Christ, who shall judge the quick and the dead at His appearing and His kingdom; instruct - living

2 Preach the word; be instant in season, out of season; reprove, rebuke, exhort with all longsuffering and doctrine. ready - encourage - teaching

3 For the time will come when they will not endure sound doctrine; but after their own lusts shall they heap to themselves teachers, having itching ears; teaching

4 And they shall turn away *their* ears from the truth, and shall be turned to fables. myths

5 But watch you in all things, endure afflictions, do the work of an evangelist, make full proof of your ministry. discharge all duties

6 For I am now ready to be offered, and the time of my departure is at hand. dying

7 I have fought a good fight, I have finished *my* course, I have kept the faith: race

8 Hereafter there is laid up for me a crown of righteousness, which the Lord, the righteous judge, shall give me at that day: and not to me only, but to all them also that love His appearing.

9 Do your diligence to come shortly to me: best

10 For De'mas has forsaken me, having loved this present world, and is departed to Thes-sa-lo-ni'ca; Cres'cens to Ga-la'tia, Ti'tus to Dal-ma'ti-a.

11 Only Luke is with me. Take Mark, and bring him with you: for he is profitable to me for the ministry. useful

12 And Tych'i-cus have I sent to Eph'e-sus.

13 The cloke that I left at Tro'as with Car'pus, when you come, bring *with you*, and the books, *but* especially the parchments.

14 Al-ex-an'der the coppersmith did me much evil: the Lord reward him according to his works: repay

15 Of whom be you ware also; for he has greatly withstood our words. on guard - opposed

16 At my first answer no man stood with me, but all *men* forsook me: *I pray God* that it may not be laid to their charge.

17 Notwithstanding the Lord stood with me, and strengthened me; that by me the preaching might be fully known, and *that* all the Gen'tiles might hear: and I was delivered out of the mouth of the lion. PSA.22:21 Nevertheless

18 And the Lord shall deliver me from every evil work, and will preserve *me* to His heavenly kingdom: to whom *be* glory for ever and ever. Amen.

19 Salute Pris'ca and A'qui-la, and the household of On-e-siph'o-rus. Greet

20 E-ras'tus abode at Cor'inth: but Troph'i-mus have I left at Mi-le'tum sick. stayed

21 Do your diligence to come before winter. Eu-bu'lus greets you, and

Pu'dens, and Li'nus, and Clau'di-a, and all the brethren.

your best

22 The Lord Je'sus Christ *be* with your spirit. Grace *be* with you. Amen.

TITUS

OUTLINE

SALUTATION TO TITUS, APOSTOLIC DELEGATE TO CHURCHES OF CRETE 1.1-4

GENERAL INSTRUCTIONS FOR REFORMING CHURCH LIFE IN CRETE 1.5-16
   Qualifications for Elder Leadership 1.5-9
   Special Warnings against Unhealthy Judaizing Influences 1.10-16

SPECIFIC INSTRUCTIONS FOR PREACHING TO THE PEOPLE 2.1-15
   Moral Responsibilities of Christians 2.1-10
      For Older Men and Women of the Congregations 2.2-5
      For Young Men 2.6-8
      For the Slaves 2.9, 10
   The Necessary Relationship of Salvation to Personal Ethics 2.11-15

CONCLUDING INSTRUCTION FOR CHRISTIANS IN THE WORLD 3.1-15
   Civil and Social Responsibilities of Christians 3.1, 2
   A Personal Witness to God's Power to Save Any Sinner through Christ 3.3-7
   Final Advice to Preach the Gospel and not Argue with Legalists 3.8-11
   Closing Personal Requests 3.12-15

SURVEY

Paul salutes Titus, his apostolic delegate to the churches of Crete, with affection as his "true son in respect to [their] common faith." He associates his own apostleship with the promotion of "the faith of God's elect and knowledge of divine truth" (1.1-4).

Paul had left Titus in Crete to reform a weak, corrupt church. He writes this letter to reaffirm the objectives which he is to promote (1.5). This requires the inclusion of general directions for installing fit elder leadership in the parishes (1.6-9) and for dealing with unwholesome influences of Jewish legalism and mythologizing as found in the Talmud and the Midrashim (1.10-16).

In view of these problems, Paul outlines specific areas of Christian moral responsibility for Titus' ministry to each age group and class, free and slave, that they may fulfil the obligations of true faith (2.1-10; 3.1, 2). In two beautiful passages, Paul reminds Titus of important aspects of the Gospel. In the first (2.11-15) he explains the necessary relevance of God's saving grace in Christ to Christian behavior. In the second (3.3-7) he gives humble testimony to what God has done in his own life through Christ, and can do also in the life of the basest Cretan who believes. He urges the preaching of the Gospel and the avoidance of argument with Jewish legalism (3.8-11). Paul closes with two requests (3.12-15).

AUTHOR

We cannot be sure from where Paul wrote this letter to Titus. Probably Paul is somewhere in Asia (Ephesus?), where he went from Rome after his release from the first imprisonment around A.D. 63. Going east he left Titus in Crete. He sends this letter, probably by Zenas and Apollos, who may be on their way to Alexandria. There is no internal linguistic evidence to support conclusively the claims that this letter is not genuine; from its contents there is every reason to believe that it is genuine. It must have been written around the summer of A.D. 65, shortly before 1 Timothy.

Titus is a prominent young Christian associate of Paul. Some suspect he was the brother of Luke. He is usually regarded as the Titus of Galatians 2, a Gentile Christian from the Antioch church (in Syria) who became the test case in the circumcision controversy at the Jerusalem conference about A.D. 48. Titus later rendered Paul distinguished service in reconciling the Corinthian church torn with dissension. So he came to assist the Cretan Christians as an experienced leader.

R.M.S.

THE LETTER OF PAUL TO
TITUS

CHAPTER 1

PAUL, a servant of God, and an apostle of Je'sus Christ, according to the faith of God's underline{elect}, and the acknowledging of the truth which is after godliness; chosen

2 In hope of eternal life, which God, that cannot lie, promised before the world began;

3 But has in due times underline{manifested} His word through preaching, which is committed to me according to the commandment of God our Savior; made known

4 To Ti'tus, *mine* own son after the common faith: Grace, mercy, *and* peace, from God the Father and the Lord Je'sus Christ our Savior.

5 For this cause left I you in Crete, that you should set in order the things that are wanting, and underline{ordain} elders in every city, as I had appointed you: appoint

6 If any be underline{blameless}, the husband of one wife, having underline{faithful} children not accused of riot or unruly.

above reproach - believing

7 For a bishop must be blameless, as the steward of God; not selfwilled, not soon angry, not given to wine, underline{no striker}, not given to underline{filthy lucre}.

not violent - dishonest money

8 But a lover of hospitality, a lover of good men, sober, just, holy, underline{temperate}; disciplined

9 Holding fast the faithful word as he has been taught, that he may be able by sound underline{doctrine} both to exhort and to convince the underline{gainsayers}. teaching - opposition

10 For there are many unruly and vain talkers and deceivers, specially underline{they of the circumcision}: i.e. Jews

11 Whose mouths must be stopped, who underline{subvert} whole houses, teaching things which they ought not, for underline{filthy lucre's} sake. ruining

12 One of themselves, *even* a prophet of their own, said, The Cre'ti-ans *are* alway liars, evil beasts, underline{slow bellies}. lazy gluttons

13 This witness is true. Wherefore rebuke them sharply, that they may be sound in the faith;

14 Not giving heed to Jew'ish underline{fables}, and commandments of men, that turn from the truth. myths

15 To the pure all things *are* pure: but to them that are defiled and unbelieving *is* nothing pure; but even their mind and conscience is defiled.

16 They profess that they know God; but in works they deny *Him*, being underline{abominable}, and disobedient, and to every good work underline{reprobate}. detestable - worthless

CHAPTER 2

BUT speak you the things which underline{become} sound underline{doctrine}: are fitting - teaching

2 That the aged men be underline{sober}, grave, temperate, sound in faith, in underline{charity}, in patience. temperate - love

3 The aged women likewise, that *they be* in behavior as becomes holiness, not false accusers, not given to much wine, teachers of good things;

4 That they may teach the young women to be <u>sober</u>, to love their husbands, to love their children,　temperate

5 *To be* <u>discreet</u>, chaste, keepers at home, good, obedient to their own husbands, that the word of God be not <u>blasphemed</u>.　sensible - dishonored

6 Young men likewise <u>exhort</u> to be <u>sober minded</u>.　urge - self controlled

7 In all things showing yourself a pattern of good works: in doctrine *showing* <u>uncorruptness</u>, <u>gravity</u>, sincerity,

good deeds - purity

8 Sound speech, that cannot be condemned; that he that is of the <u>contrary</u> part may be ashamed, having no evil thing to say of you.　opposite

9 *Exhort* servants to be obedient to their own masters, *and* to please *them* well in all things; not answering again;　Urge

10 Not <u>purloining</u>, but showing all good <u>fidelity</u>; that they may adorn the doctrine of God our Savior in all things.　stealing - faith

11 For the grace of God that brings salvation has appeared to all men,

12 Teaching us that, denying ungodliness and worldly lusts, we should live <u>soberly</u>, righteously, and godly, in this present world;　sensibly

13 Looking for that blessed hope, and the glorious appearing of the great God and our Savior Jesus Christ;

14 Who gave Himself for us, that He might redeem us from all <u>iniquity</u>, and

purify to Himself a <u>peculiar</u> people, zealous of good works.

PS. 130:8 lawlessness - special

15 These things speak, and <u>exhort</u>, and <u>rebuke</u> with all authority. Let no man despise you.　urge - reprove

CHAPTER 3

PUT them in mind to be subject to <u>principalities</u> and <u>powers</u>, to obey magistrates, to be ready to every good work,　rulers - authorities

2 To speak evil of no man, to be no <u>brawlers</u>, *but* gentle, showing all <u>meekness</u> to all men. uncontentious - gentleness

3 For we ourselves also were sometimes foolish, disobedient, deceived, <u>serving divers lusts</u> and pleasures, living in malice and envy, hateful, *and* hating one another.　enslaved to various desires

4 But after that the kindness and love of God our Savior toward man appeared,

5 Not by works of righteousness which we have done, but according to His mercy He saved us, by the washing of regeneration, and renewing of the Ho'ly <u>Ghost</u>;　Spirit

6 Which He shed on us abundantly through Je'sus Christ our Savior;

7 That being justified by His grace, we should be made heirs according to the hope of eternal life.

8 *This is* a faithful saying, and these things I will that you <u>affirm constantly</u>, that they which have believed in God might be careful to maintain good works. These things are good and profitable to men.　speak confidently

9 But avoid foolish questions, and genealogies, and contentions, and <u>strivings</u> about the law; for they are unprofitable and <u>vain</u>. <small>disputes - worthless</small>

10 A man that is <u>an heretic</u> after the first and second admonition reject; <small>divisive</small>

11 Knowing that he that is such is <u>subverted</u>, and sinning, being condemned of himself. <small>perverted</small>

12 When I shall send Ar'te-mas to you, or Tych'i-cus, be diligent to come to me to Ni-cop'o-lis: for I have <u>determined</u> there to winter. <small>decided</small>

13 Bring Ze'nas the lawyer and A-pol'los on their journey diligently, that nothing be <u>wanting</u> to them. <small>lacking</small>

14 And let <u>ours</u> also learn to <u>maintain</u> good works for necessary uses, that they be not unfruitful. <small>i.e., our people - do</small>

15 All that are with me <u>salute</u> you. Greet them that love us in the faith. Grace *be* with you all. Amen. <small>greet</small>

PHILEMON

OUTLINE

SURVEY

After the salutation and thanksgiving to God for Philemon's faith and love, and prayer for his further growth in grace, Paul comes to the central theme of the letter. Onesimus, a slave belonging to Philemon, ran away from his master at Colossae, after having apparently committed theft. He found his way to the metropolis Rome, where he came in contact with Paul and was converted to Christ under his influence and ministry. Paul thereupon sends him back to his lawful owner with this personal letter of recommendation in his favor to be delivered to Philemon. He pleads with Philemon to receive back the penitent (and meanwhile converted) slave with good will, and to forgive and rehabilitate him because he would no longer be only a slave to him, but "above a servant, a brother beloved" (KJV). Paul himself would make good any loss which Onesimus had caused him, and expected Philemon to yield to the urge of Christian love and Christian duty. The whole affords a striking analogy to the gospel story of redemption.

AUTHOR

The author of the letter on three occasions identifies himself as Paul (vv. 1, 9, 19), and the letter is furthermore closely connected with Paul's letter to the Colossians (cf. Cl 4.10–17, with Phm 2, 23, 24). Its authenticity is generally accepted. The letter was probably written towards the end of Paul's first imprisonment at Rome, most likely in the year A.D. 61 or 62.

J.J.M.

THE LETTER OF PAUL TO

PHILEMON

> A Personal Letter
> on Behalf of a Friend

PAUL, a prisoner of Je'sus Christ, and Tim'o-thy *our* brother, to Phi-le'mon our dearly beloved, and fellowlaborer,

2 And to *our* beloved Apph'i-a, and Ar-chip'pus our fellowsoldier, and to the church in your house:

3 Grace to you, and peace, from God our Father and the Lord Je'sus Christ.

4 I thank my God, making mention of you always in my prayers,

5 Hearing of your love and faith, which you have toward the Lord Je'sus, and toward all saints; _{believers}

6 That the communication of your faith may become effectual by the acknowledging of every good thing which is in you in Christ Je'sus. _{fellowship}

7 For we have great joy and consolation in your love, because the bowels of the saints are refreshed by you, brother. _{comfort - hearts}

8 Wherefore, though I might be much bold in Christ to enjoin you that which is convenient, _{order - proper}

9 Yet for love's sake I rather beseech *you*, being such an one as Paul the aged, and now also a prisoner of Je'sus Christ. _{beg}

10 I beseech you for my son O'nes'i-mus, whom I have begotten in my bonds: _{imprisonment}

11 Which in time past was to you unprofitable, but now profitable to you and to me: _{unuseful}

12 Whom I have sent again: you therefore receive him, that is, mine own bowels:

13 Whom I would have retained with me, that in your stead he might have ministered to me in the bonds of the gospel: _{behalf}

14 But without your mind would I do nothing; that your benefit should not be as it were of necessity, but willingly.

15 For perhaps he therefore departed for a season, that you should receive him for ever;

16 Not now as a servant, but above a servant, a brother beloved, specially to me, but how much more to you, both in the flesh, and in the Lord?

17 If you count me therefore a partner, receive him as myself. _{welcome}

18 If he has wronged you, or owes *you* anything, put that on mine account;

19 I Paul have written *it* with mine own hand, I will repay *it*: albeit I do not say to you how you owe to me even your own self besides.

20 Yea, brother, let me have joy of you in the Lord: refresh my bowels in the Lord. _{benefit - heart}

21 Having confidence in your obedience I wrote to you, knowing that you will also do more than I say.

22 But meanwhile prepare me also a lodg-

ing: for I trust that through your prayers I shall be <u>given</u> to you.

^{restored}

23 There <u>salute</u> you Ep'a-phras, my fellowprisoner in Christ Je'sus; ^{greet}

24 Mar'cus, Ar-is-tar'chus, De'mas, Lu'cas, my fellowlaborers.

25 The grace of our Lord Je'sus Christ *be* with your spirit. Amen.

HEBREWS

OUTLINE

SURVEY

Although God spoke to the fathers by the prophets, He has now spoken by His Son. The prologue affirms the distinctiveness of the Son. He is before history, in history, above history, the goal of history, and the agent who brings about a cleansing of men from the sins committed in history. He shares the essence of deity and radiates the glory of deity. He is the supreme revelation of God (1.1-3).

The next passage (1.4-14) makes clear the pre-eminence of Christ. He is superior to angels. They assist those who will be heirs of salvation. Christ, by virtue of Who He is, of God's appointment, and

of what He has done, stands exalted far above them. How tragic to be careless of the great salvation He proclaimed. He will achieve for man the promise that all things will be in harmonious subjection to man. He can do this because He is fully man and has provided the expiation for sins. He is superior to Moses. Moses was a servant among the people of God. Christ is a son over the people of God. How tragic to cease trusting Him! Unbelief kept one entire generation of Israelites from Canaan. Christians are warned of such unbelief. Faith is emphasized as well as zeal to enter into the eternal rest of God. The Gospel of God and God Himself scrutinizes men.

The priesthood of Christ is also developed by comparison (4.14—10.18). Qualifications, conditions, and experiences of the Aaronic priesthood are listed in comparison to Christ as a priest. Before further developing this theme, the writer warns his readers of their unpreparedness for advanced teaching. Only earnest diligence in things of God will bring them out of immaturity. Christ as a priest, like Melchizedek, is superior to the Levitical priesthood because His life is indestructible; He was both priest and sacrifice; His priesthood is eternal. His sanctuary is in heaven and His blood establishes the validity of the New Covenant that is also an eternal covenant.

The perseverance of Christians springs out of fellowship with God, activity for God, faith in God, and a consciousness of what lies ahead (10.19—12.29).

The cross as the Christian altar and the resurrection of the great shepherd are the basis for God's action. These redemptive, historical events move the believer to action (13.1-25).

AUTHOR

The author is not named. Except for Hebrews and 1 John, every epistle of the New Testament designates its author by name and by title.

Ever since the first century the question of who wrote Hebrews has attracted much discussion. The answers of the early Christians varied. On the eastern shore of the Mediterranean and around Alexandria, they associated the book with Paul. Origen (A.D. 185-254) felt that the thoughts of the book are Paul's, but that the language and composition are someone else's. In North Africa, Tertullian (A.D. 155-225) held that Barnabas wrote Hebrews. Although the epistle was known first in Rome and the West (1 Clement, dated about A.D. 95, cites Hebrews frequently), the unanimous opinion in this area for 200 years was that Paul did not write Hebrews. These early Christians did not state who they thought wrote it. They just did not know.

Christians today should not be dogmatic about an issue which has long been uncertain. However, students of Scripture should look at the book of Hebrews for themselves. A careful study in the Greek text tells many things about the author. The book has a polished Greek style, like that of a master rhetorician. This is unlike Paul. Paul frequently picks up a new stream of thought before he finishes the one he is treating. The writer of Hebrews never does this. The vocabulary, figures of speech, and manner of argument show an Alexandrian and Philonic influence (Philo, 20 B.C. to A.D. 50 or 60). Paul had no such background. The writer of Hebrews quotes the Old Testament differently from Paul. Paul's phrases—"just as it has been written" (nineteen times), "it has been written" (ten times), "the scripture says" (six times), "the scripture proclaims good tidings beforehand" (one time)—never occur in Hebrews although the writer quotes the Old Testament profusely.

If Paul is not the author, who is? Apollos fits the evidence found in the book. He came from Alexandria. He was an eloquent and learned man. He was powerful in the Scriptures. The following New Testament passages tell us about Apollos: Acts 18.24-28; 19.1; 1 Corinthians 1.12; 3.4-6, 22; 4.6; 16.12; Titus 3.13. We may never be sure of the author's name, but if we read the epistle carefully, we will really get to know him.

The best date for the epistle is between A.D. 68 and 70.

A.B.M.

THE LETTER TO THE

HEBREWS

CHAPTER 1

Christ
Is a Better Highpriest

GOD, who at sundry times and in divers manners spoke in time past to the fathers by the prophets, various

2 Has in these last days spoken to us by *His* Son, whom He has appointed heir of all things, by whom also He made the worlds;

3 Who being the brightness of *His* glory, and the express image of His person, and upholding all things by the word of His power, when He had by Himself purged our sins, sat down on the right hand of the Majesty on high; PS. 110.1 cleansed

4 Being made so much better than the angels, as He has by inheritance obtained a more excellent name than they. messengers

5 For to which of the angels said He at any time, You are My Son, this day have I begotten you? And again, I will be to Him a Father, and He shall be to Me a Son? PS. 2:7 2SAM. 7:14

6 And again, when He brings in the First Begotten into the world, He says, And let all the angels of God worship Him.

7 And of the angels He says, Who makes His angels spirits, and His ministers a flame of fire. PS. 104:4

8 But to the Son *He says,* Your throne, O God, *is* for ever and ever: a scepter of righteousness *is* the scepter of Your kingdom. PS. 45:6 about

9 You have loved righteousness, and hated iniquity; therefore God, *even* Your God, has anointed You with the oil of gladness above Your fellows. PS. 45:7

10 And, You, Lord, in the beginning have laid the foundation of the earth; and the heavens are the works of Your hands: PS. 102:25

11 They shall perish; but You remain; and they all shall wax old as does a garment; PS. 102:26 grow

12 And as a vesture shall You fold them up, and they shall be changed: but You are the same, and Your years shall not fail. PS. 102:27 robe

13 But to which of the angels said He at any time, Sit on My right hand, until I make Your enemies Your footstool? Ps. 110:1

14 Are they not all ministering spirits, sent forth to minister for them who shall be heirs of salvation? serving

CHAPTER 2

THEREFORE we ought to give the more earnest heed to the things which we have heard, less at any time we should let *them* slip. drift away

2 For if the word spoken by angels was steadfast, and every transgression and disobedience received a just recompence of reward; messengers - binding - payment

3 How shall we escape, if we neglect so great salvation; which at the first began to be spoken by the Lord, and was

confirmed to us by them that heard *Him*;

4 God also bearing *them* witness, both with signs and wonders, and with divers miracles, and gifts of the Ho'ly Ghost, according to His own will? various - Spirit

5 For to the angels has He not put in subjection the world to come, whereof we speak. control

6 But one in a certain place testified, saying, What is man, that You are mindful of him? or the son of man, that You visit him? PS. 8:4 care for

7 You made him a little lower than the angels; You crowned him with glory and honor, and did set him over the works of Your hands: PS. 8:5

8 You have put all things in subjection under his feet. For in that He put all in subjection under him, He left nothing *that is* not put under him. But now we see not yet all things put under him. PS.8:6

9 But we see Je'sus, who was made a little lower than the angels for the suffering of death, crowned with glory and honor; that He by the grace of God should taste death for every man.

10 For it became Him, for whom *are* all things, and by whom *are* all things, in bringing many sons to glory, to make the captain of their salvation perfect through sufferings. author - mature

11 For both He that sanctifies and they who are sanctified *are* all of one: for which cause He is not ashamed to call them brethren, makes holy

12 Saying, I will declare Your name to My brethren, in the midst of the church will I sing praise to You. PS. 22:22 congregation

13 And again, I will put My trust in Him. And again, Behold I and the children which God has given Me. ISA. 8:18

14 Forasmuch then as the children are partakers of flesh and blood, He also Himself likewise took part of the same; that through death He might destroy him that had the power of death, that is, the devil; Since

15 And deliver them who through fear of death were all their lifetime subject to bondage. free

16 For verily He took not on *Him the nature of* angels; but He took on *Him* the seed of A'bra-ham.

ISA. 41:8 truly - angels to help - offspring

17 Wherefore in all things it behooved Him to be made like to *His* brethren, that He might be a merciful and faithful high priest in things *pertaining* to God, to make reconciliation for the sins of the people. was best for

18 For in that He Himself has suffered being tempted, He is able to succour them that are tempted. tested - help

CHAPTER 3

WHEREFORE, holy brethren, partakers of the heavenly calling, consider the Apostle and High Priest of our profession, Christ Je'sus; sharers - confession

2 Who was faithful to Him that appointed Him, as also Mo'ses *was faithful* in all his house. NUM. 12:7

3 For this *man* was counted worthy of more glory than Mo'ses, inasmuch as

He who has built the house has more honor than the house.   honor

4 For every house is built by some *man*; but He that built all things *is* God.

5 And Mo'ses verily *was* faithful in all His house, as a servant, for a testimony of those things which were to be spoken after;   truly

6 But Christ as a son over His own house; whose house are we, if we hold fast the confidence and the rejoicing of the hope firm to the end.

7 Wherefore (as the Ho'ly Ghost says, Today if you will hear His voice,

8 Harden not your hearts, as in the provocation, in the day of temptation in the wilderness: testing

9 When your fathers tempted Me, proved Me, and saw My works forty years.

10 Wherefore I was grieved with that generation, and said, They do alway err in *their* heart; and they have not known My ways.

11 So I swear in My wrath, They shall not enter into My rest.)   PS. 95:11

12 Take heed, brethren, less there be in any of you an evil heart of unbelief, in departing from the living God.   turning away

13 But exhort one another daily, while it is called Today; less any of you be hardened through the deceitfulness of sin.   urge

14 For we are made partakers of Christ, if we hold the beginning of our confidence steadfast to the end;   partners - firm

15 While it is said, Today if you will hear His voice, harden not your hearts, as in the provocation.   rebellion

16 For some, when they had heard, did provoke: however not all that came out of E'gypt by Mo'ses.

17 But with whom was He grieved forty years? *was it* not with them that had sinned, whose carcases fell in the wilderness?   angry with for - bodies

18 And to whom swear He that they should not enter into His rest, but to them that believed not?   were disobedient

19 So we see that they could not enter in because of unbelief.   NUM. 14:1-35

CHAPTER 4

LET us therefore fear, less, a promise being left *us* of entering into His rest, any of you should seem to come short of it.   be careful

2 For to us was the gospel preached, as well as to them: but the word preached did not profit them, not being mixed with faith in them that heard *it*.   good news - combined

3 For we which have believed do enter into rest, as He said, As I have sworn in My wrath, if they shall enter into My rest: although the works were finished from the foundation of the world.   PS. 95:11 they shall not

4 For He spoke in a certain place of the seventh *day* on this wise, And God did rest the seventh day from all His works.

5 And in this *place* again, If they shall enter into My rest.   PS. 95:11

6 Seeing therefore it remains that some must enter therein, and they to

whom it was first preached entered not in because of <u>unbelief</u>:

i.e., good news - disobedience

7 Again, He limits a certain day, saying in David, To day, after so long a time; as it is said, To day if you will hear His voice, harden not your hearts.

8 For if Je'sus had given them rest, then would He not afterward have spoken of another day.   PS. 95:7

9 There remains therefore a rest to the people of God.

10 For he that is entered into His rest, he also has <u>ceased</u> from his own works, as God *did* from His.

GEN. 2:2   rested

11 Let us labor therefore to enter into that rest, less any man fall after the same example of <u>unbelief</u>.

12 For the word of God *is* <u>quick</u>, and powerful, and sharper than any twoedged sword, piercing even to the dividing <u>asunder</u> of soul and spirit, and of the joints and marrow, and *is* a <u>discerner</u> of the thoughts and intents of the heart. living - in two - judge

13 Neither is there any creature that is <u>not manifest</u> in His sight: but all things *are* naked and opened to the eyes of Him with whom we have to do.   hidden

14 Seeing then that we have a great high priest, that is passed into the heavens, Je'sus the Son of God, let us hold <u>fast</u> *our* <u>profession</u>.   firm - confession

15 For we have not an high priest which cannot be touched with the feeling of our <u>infirmities</u>; but was in all points tempted like as *we are*, *yet* without sin.   weaknesses

16 Let us therefore come boldly to the throne of grace, that we may obtain mercy, and find grace to help in time of need.

CHAPTER 5

FOR every high priest taken from among men is <u>ordained</u> for men in things *pertaining* to God, that he may offer both gifts and sacrifices for sins: appointed

2 Who can have compassion on the ignorant, and on them that are <u>out of the way</u>; for that he himself also is <u>compassed with infirmity</u>.

wayward - beset with weakness

3 And by reason hereof he should, as for the people, so also for himself, to offer for sins.

4 And no man <u>takes</u> this honor to himself, but he that is called of God, as *was* Aar'on.   chooses

5 So also Christ <u>glorified</u> not Himself to be made an high priest; but He that said to Him, You are My Son, to day have I begotten You.   PS. 2:7 JOB 2:7 honored

6 As He says also in another *place*, You *are* a priest for ever after the order of Mel-chis'e-dec.   PS. 110:4

7 Who in the days of His flesh, when He had offered up prayers and supplications with strong crying and tears to Him that was able to save Him from death, and was heard in that He <u>feared</u>;   respected

8 Though He were a Son, yet learned He obedience by the things which He suffered;

9 And being made perfect, He became the author of eternal salvation to all them that obey Him;

10 Called of God an high priest after the order of Mel-chis'e-dec.

11 Of whom we have many things to say, and hard to be <u>uttered</u>, seeing you are <u>dull</u> of hearing. explained - slow

12 For when for the time you ought to be teachers, you have need that one teach you again which *be* the first principles of the <u>oracles</u> of God; and are become such as have need of milk, and not of strong meat.   words

13 For every one that uses milk *is* <u>unskillful</u> in the word of righteousness: for he is a babe.   not acquainted

14 But strong meat belongs to them that are of full age, *even* those who by reason of use have their senses <u>exercised</u> to discern both good and evil.   1 KGS. 3:9   trained

CHAPTER 6

THEREFORE leaving the principles of the <u>doctrine</u> of Christ, let us go on to <u>perfection</u>; not laying again the foundation of repentance from dead works, and of faith toward God,   teaching - maturity

2 Of the <u>doctrine</u> of baptisms, and of laying on of hands, and of resurrection of the dead, and of eternal judgment.

3 And this will we do, if God permit.

4 For *it is* impossible for those who were once enlightened, and have tasted of the heavenly gift, and were made partakers of the Ho'ly Ghost,

5 And have tasted the good word of God, and the powers of the <u>world</u> to come,   age

6 If they shall fall away, to <u>renew</u> them again to repentance; seeing they crucify to themselves the Son of God afresh, and put *Him* to an open shame.   revive

7 For the earth which drinks in the rain that comes oft upon it, and brings forth herbs <u>meet</u> for them by whom it is dressed, receives blessing from God: useful

8 But that which bears thorns and briers *is* rejected, and *is* near to cursing; whose end *is* to be burned.

9 But, beloved, we are <u>persuaded</u> better things of you, and things that <u>accompany</u> salvation, though we thus speak.   convinced - go with

10 For God *is* not unrighteous to forget your work and labor of love, which you have showed toward His name, in that you have <u>ministered</u> to the saints, and do minister.   given help

11 And we desire that every one of you do show the same diligence to the full assurance of hope to the end:

12 That you be not <u>slothful</u>, but <u>followers</u> of them who through faith and patience inherit the promises. lazy - imitators

13 For when God made promise to A'bra-ham, because He could swear by no greater, He swear by Himself, JER. 44:26

14 Saying, Surely blessing I will bless you, and multiplying I will multiply you.   GEN. 22:16-17

15 And so, after he had patiently <u>endured</u>, he obtained the promise.   waited

16 For men <u>verily</u> swear by the greater: and an oath for confirmation *is* to them an end of all strife.   truly

17 Wherein God, willing more abundantly to show to the heirs of promise the <u>immutability</u> of His counsel, confirmed *it* by an oath: unchangeableness

18 That by two <u>immutable</u> things, in which *it was* impossible for God to lie, we might have a strong consolation, who have fled for refuge to lay hold upon the hope set before us: <small>unchangeable</small>

19 Which *hope* we have as an anchor of the soul, both sure and <u>steadfast</u>, and which enters into that inside the veil; <small>LEV. 16:2 firm</small>

20 Where the <u>forerunner</u> is for us entered, *even* Je'sus, made an high priest for ever after the order of Mel-chis'e-dec. <small>PS. 110:4 advance one</small>

CHAPTER 7

FOR this Mel-chis'e-dec, king of Sa'lem, priest of the Most High God, who met A'bra-ham returning from the slaughter of the kings, and blessed him;

2 To whom also A'bra-ham gave a tenth part of all; first being by interpretation King of righteousness, and after that also King of Sa'lem, which is, King of peace; <small>GEN. 14:17-20</small>

3 Without father, without mother, without <u>descent</u>, having neither beginning of days, nor end of life; but made like to the Son of God; <u>abides</u> a priest continually. <small>genealogy - remains</small>

4 Now consider how great this man *was*, to whom even the <u>patriarch</u> A'bra-ham gave the tenth of the <u>spoils</u>. <small>father - plunder</small>

5 And <u>verily</u> they that are of the sons of Le'vi, who receive the office of the priesthood, have a commandment to take tithes of the people according to the law, that is, of their brethren, though they come out of the loins of A'bra-ham: <small>truly</small>

6 But he whose descent is not <u>counted</u> from them received tithes of A'bra-ham, and blessed him that had the promises. <small>known</small>

7 And without all contradiction the less is blessed of the <u>better</u>. <small>greater</small>

8 And here men that die receive tithes; but there he *receives them*, of whom it is <u>witnessed</u> that he lives. <small>declared</small>

9 And as I may so say, Le'vi also, who receives tithes, payed tithes in A'bra-ham.

10 For he was <u>yet</u> in the loins of his father, when Mel-chis'e-dec met him. <small>still</small>

11 If therefore perfection were by the Le-vit'i-cal priesthood, (for under it the people received the law,) what further need *was there* that another priest should rise after the order of Mel-chis'e-dec, and not be called after the order of Aar'on?

12 For the priesthood being changed, there is made of necessity a change also of the law.

13 For he of whom these things are spoken <u>pertains</u> to another tribe, of which no man <u>gave attendance</u> at the altar. <small>belongs - ever served</small>

14 For *it is* evident that our Lord sprang out of Ju'da; of which tribe Mo'ses spoke nothing concerning priesthood.

15 And it is yet far more evident: for that after the <u>similitude</u> of Mel-chis'e-dec there arises another priest, <small>likeness</small>

16 Who is made, not after the law of a <u>carnal commandment</u>, but after the power of an endless life. <small>physical requirements</small>

17 For He testifies, You *are* a priest for ever after the order of Mel-chis'e-dec.

18 For there is verily a disannulling of the commandment going before for the weakness and unprofitableness thereof.   truly - setting aside

19 For the law made nothing perfect, but the bringing in of a better hope *did*; by the which we draw near to God.

20 And inasmuch as not without an oath *He was made priest*:   a vow

21 (For those priests were made without an oath; but this with an oath by Him that said to Him, The Lord swear and will not repent, You *are* a priest for ever after the order of Mel-chis'e-dec:)   PS. 110:4 grieve

22 By so much was Je'sus made a surety of a better testament.   guarantee -agreement

23 And they truly were many priests, because they were not permitted to continue by reason of death:

G1D
G4
24 But this *man*, because He continues ever, has an unchangeable priesthood.

25 Wherefore He is able also to save them to the uttermost that come to God by Him, seeing He ever lives to make intercession for them.

383
26 For such an high priest became us, *who is* holy, harmless, undefiled, separate from sinners, and made higher than the heavens;

27 Who needs not daily, as those high priests, to offer up sacrifice, first for His own sins, and then for the people's: for this He did once, when He offered
390
up Himself.   i.e., once for all

28 For the law makes men high priests which have infirmity; but the word of the oath, which was since the law, *makes* the Son, who is consecrated for evermore.   are weak - appoints

CHAPTER 8

NOW of the things which we have spoken *this is* the sum: We have such an high priest, who is set on the right hand of the throne of the Majesty in the heavens;

2 A minister of the sanctuary, and of the true tabernacle, which the Lord pitched, and not man.

3 For every high priest is ordained to offer gifts and sacrifices: wherefore *it is* of necessity that this man have somewhat also to offer.   appointed

4 For if He were on earth, He should not be a priest, seeing that there are priests that offer gifts according to the law:

5 Who serve to the example and shadow of heavenly things, as Mo'ses was admonished of God when he was about to make the tabernacle: for, See, says He, *that* you make all things according to the pattern showed to you in the mount.   EX. 25:40 copy

P02
6 But now has He obtained a more excellent ministry, by how much also He is the mediator of a better covenant, which was established upon better promises.   JER. 31:31 superior - agreement
382

7 For if that first *covenant* had been faultless, then should no place have been sought for the second.

P02
8 For finding fault with them, He says, Behold, the days come, says the

Lord, when I will make a new covenant with the house of Is'ra-el and with the house of Ju'dah: JER. 31:31 agreement
9 Not according to the covenant that I made with their fathers in the day when I took them by the hand to lead them out of the land of E'gypt; because they continued not in My covenant, and I regarded them not, says the Lord.
10 For this *is* the covenant that I will make with the house of Is'ra-el after those days, says the Lord; I will put My laws into their mind, and write them in their hearts: and I will be to them a God, and they shall be to Me a people: JER. 31:31-34 2 COR. 3:6 HEB. 8:6
11 And they shall not teach every man his neighbor, and every man his brother, saying, Know the Lord: for all shall know Me, from the least to the greatest.
12 For I will be merciful to their unrighteousness, and their sins and their iniquities will I remember no more. wrongs
13 In that He says, A new *covenant*, He has made the first old. Now that which decays and waxes old *is* ready to vanish away. grows - disappear

CHAPTER 9

THEN verily the first *covenant* had also ordinances of divine service, and a worldly sanctuary. truly - agreement - regulations - earthly
2 For there was a tabernacle made; the first, wherein *was* the candlestick, and the table, and the showbread; which is called the sanctuary. EXO. 26:33 temple - sacred bread - holy place

3 And after the second veil, the tabernacle which is called the Holiest of all; temple
4 Which had the golden censer, and the ark of the covenant overlaid round about with gold, wherein *was* the golden pot that had manna, and Aar'on's rod that budded, and the tables of the covenant; NUM. 17:8 agreement
5 And over it the cherubims of glory shadowing the mercy seat; of which we cannot now speak particularly. in detail
6 Now when these things were thus ordained, the priests went always into the first tabernacle, accomplishing the service *of God*. prepared - performing
7 But into the second *went* the high priest alone once every year, not without blood, which he offered for himself, and *for* the errors of the people:
8 The Ho'ly Ghost this signifying, that the way into the holiest of all was not yet made manifest, while as the first tabernacle was yet standing: Spirit thus showing - disclosed
9 Which *was* a figure for the time then present, in which were offered both gifts and sacrifices, that could not make him that did the service perfect, as pertaining to the conscience;
10 *Which stood* only in meats and drinks, and divers washings, and carnal ordinances, imposed *on them* until the time of reformation. food - various - fleshly laws
11 But Christ being come an high priest of good things to come, by a greater and more perfect tabernacle, not made with hands, that is to say, not of this building;
12 Neither by the blood of goats and

calves, but by His own blood He entered in once into the holy place, having obtained eternal redemption *for us*.
13 For if the blood of bulls and of goats, and the ashes of an heifer sprinkling the unclean, <u>sanctifies</u> to the <u>purifying</u> of the flesh: set apart - cleansing
14 How much more shall the blood of Christ, who through the eternal Spirit offered Himself without <u>spot</u> to God, <u>purge</u> your conscience from dead works to serve the living God? defect - cleanse
15 And for this cause He is the mediator of the new testament, that by means of death, for the redemption of the <u>transgressions</u> *that were* under the first testament, they which are called might receive the promise of eternal inheritance.   sins committed
16 For where a <u>testament</u> *is*, there must also of necessity be the death of <u>the testator</u>.   will - maker of will
17 For a <u>testament</u> *is* of force after men are dead: otherwise it is of no strength at all while the <u>testator</u> lives.
18 Whereupon neither the first *testament* was <u>dedicated</u> without blood.   EXO. 24:6 confirmed
19 For when Mo'ses had spoken every <u>precept</u> to all the people according to the law, he took the blood of calves and of goats, with water, and scarlet wool, and hyssop, and sprinkled both the book, and all the people, EXO. 24:6-8 commandment
20 Saying, This *is* the blood *of* the <u>testament</u> which God has <u>enjoined</u> to you.   which seals - covenant-agreement - commanded
21 Moreover he sprinkled with blood both the tabernacle, and all the vessels *of* the ministry.   i.e., used in

22 And almost all things are by the law purged with blood; and without shedding of blood is no <u>remission</u>.   forgiveness
23 *It was* therefore necessary that the <u>patterns</u> of things in the heavens should be <u>purified</u> with these; but the heavenly things themselves with better sacrifices than these.   copies - cleansed
24 For Christ is not entered into the holy places made with hands, *which are* the <u>figures</u> of the true; but into heaven itself, now to appear in the presence of God for us: representatives
25 Nor yet that He should offer Himself often, as the high priest enters into the holy place every year with blood of others;
26 For then must He often have suffered since the foundation of the <u>world</u>: but now once in the end of the world has He appeared to put away sin by the sacrifice of Himself.   ages
27 And as it is appointed to men once to die, but after this the judgment: ECC. 3:2
28 So Christ was once offered to bear the sins of many; and to them that look for Him shall He appear the second time without sin to salvation.

CHAPTER 10

FOR the law having a <u>shadow</u> of good things to come, *and* not the very <u>image</u> of the things, can never with those sacrifices which they offered year by year continually make the comers thereunto perfect.   appearance - form
2 For then would they not have ceased to be offered? because that the

worshippers once <u>purged</u> should have had no more <u>conscience</u> of sins.

cleansed - awareness

3 But in those *sacrifices there is* a <u>remembrance</u> again *made* of sins every year.

reminder

4 For *it is* not possible that the blood of bulls and of goats should take away sins.

5 Wherefore when He comes into the world, He says, Sacrifice and offering You <u>would</u> not, but a body have You prepared Me:

PS. 40:6 desired

6 In burnt offerings and *sacrifices* for sin You have had no pleasure.

7 Then said I, Lo, I come (in the volume of the book it is written of Me,) to do Your will, O God.

PS. 40:7-8

8 Above when He said, Sacrifice and offering and burnt offerings and *offering* for sin You would not, neither had pleasure *therein*; which are offered by the law;

9 Then said He, Lo, I come to do Your will, O God. He takes away the first, that He may establish the second.

10 By the which will we are <u>sanctified</u> through the offering of the body of Jesus Christ once *for all*.

made holy

11 And every priest stands daily ministering and offering oftentimes the same sacrifices, which can never take away sins:

12 But this <u>man</u>, <u>after</u> He had offered one sacrifice for sins for ever, sat down on the right hand of God;

i.e., Christ - when

13 From hereafter <u>expecting</u> till His enemies be made His footstool.

PS. 110:1 waiting

14 For by one offering He has <u>perfected</u> for ever them that are <u>sanctified</u>.

completed - made holy

15 *Whereof* the Ho'ly <u>Ghost</u> also is a witness to us: for after that He had said before,

Spirit

16 This *is* the <u>covenant</u> that I will <u>make with them</u> after those days, <u>says the Lord,</u> I will put My laws into their hearts, and in their minds will I write them;

JER. 31:33 agreement

17 And their sins and iniquities will I remember no more.

18 Now where <u>remission</u> of these *is*, *there is* no more <u>offering</u> for sin.

forgiveness - sacrifice

19 Having therefore, brethren, <u>boldness</u> to enter into the holiest by the blood of Je'sus,

confidence

20 By a new and living way, which He has <u>consecrated</u> for us, through the veil, that is to say, His flesh;

prepared

21 And *having* an <u>high</u> priest over the house of God;

great

22 Let us draw near with a true heart in full assurance of faith, having our hearts sprinkled from an evil conscience, and our bodies washed with pure water.

PS. 73:28

23 Let us hold <u>fast</u> the profession of *our* faith without wavering; (for He *is* faithful that promised;)

firm

24 And let us consider one another to provoke to love and to good works:

25 Not <u>forsaking</u> the assembling of ourselves together, as the manner of some *is*; but <u>exhorting</u> *one another*: and so much the more, as you see the day approaching.

ACTS 2:42 giving up - encouraging

26 For if we sin willfully after that we

have received the knowledge of the truth, there remains no more sacrifice for sins,

27 But a certain <u>fearful</u> looking for of judgment and fiery indignation, which shall devour the <u>adversaries</u>.

ISA. 26:11 terrifying - enemies

28 He that <u>despised</u> Mo'ses' law died without mercy under two or three witnesses: DEU. 17:6 rejected

29 Of how much sorer punishment, suppose you, shall he be thought worthy, who has trodden under foot the Son of God, and has counted the blood of the <u>covenant</u>, wherewith he was sanctified, an unholy thing, and has <u>done despite to</u> the Spirit of grace?   agreement - insulted

30 For we know Him that has said, Vengeance *belongs* to Me, I will recompense, says the Lord. And again, The Lord shall judge His people.   PS. 135:14 DEU. 32: 35-36

31 *It is* a <u>fearful</u> thing to fall into the hands of the living God.   terrible

32 But call to remembrance the former days, in which, after you were illuminated, you endured a great fight of afflictions;

33 Partly, until you were made a <u>gazingstock</u> both by reproaches and afflictions; and partly, until you became companions of them that were so used.   public spectacle

34 For you had <u>compassion of</u> me in my bonds, and took joyfully the spoiling of your <u>goods</u>, knowing in yourselves that you have in heaven a better and an enduring substance. sympathy on - property

35 Cast not away therefore your con-fidence, which has great <u>recompence</u> of reward.   promise

36 For you have need of <u>patience</u>, that, after you have done the will of God, you might receive the promise.   endurance

37 For yet a little while, and He that shall come will come, and will not <u>tarry</u>.   ISA. 26:20 delay

38 Now the just shall live by faith: but if *any man* draw back, My soul shall have no pleasure in him.   HAB. 2:4

39 But we are not of them who draw back to <u>perdition</u>; but of them that believe to the saving of the soul.

destruction

CHAPTER 11

NOW faith is the <u>substance</u> of things hoped for, the <u>evidence</u> of things not seen. ROM. 8:24 assurance - conviction

2 For by <u>it</u> the elders <u>obtained</u> a good report.   faith - gained

3 Through faith we understand that the worlds were framed by the word of God, so that things which are seen were not made of things which do appear.

4 By faith A'bel offered to God a more excellent sacrifice than Cain, by which he obtained witness that he was righteous, God testifying of his gifts: and by it he being dead yet speaks.   GEN. 4:4

5 By faith E'noch was <u>translated</u> that he should not see death; and was not found, because God had <u>translated</u> him: for before his <u>translation</u> he had this testimony, that he pleased God. GEN. 5:24 taken up

6 But without faith *it is* impossible to please *Him*: for he that comes to God must believe that He is, and *that* He is a

rewarder of them that diligently seek Him.

7 By faith No'ah, being warned of God of things not seen as yet, moved with <u>fear</u>, prepared an ark to the saving of his house; by the which he condemned the world, and became heir of the righteousness which is by faith. GEN. 6:13-22 reverence

8 By faith A'bra-ham, when he was called to go out into a place which he should after receive for an inheritance, obeyed; and he went out, not knowing where he went. GEN. 12:4

9 By faith he sojourned in the land of promise, as *in* a strange country, dwelling in <u>tabernacles</u> with I'saac and Ja'cob, the heirs with him of the same promise: tents

10 For he looked for a city which has foundations, whose builder and maker *is* God.

11 Through faith also Sa'ra herself received strength to conceive seed, and was delivered of a child when she was past age, because she <u>judged</u> Him faithful who had promised. GEN. 17:19 considered

12 Therefore sprang there even of one, and him <u>as good as dead</u>, *so many* as the stars of the sky in multitude, and as the sand which is by the sea shore innumerable. GEN. 15:5 i.e., by age close to death

13 These all died in faith, not having received the promises, but having seen them afar off, and were <u>persuaded</u> of *them*, and embraced *them*, and confessed that they were strangers and <u>pilgrims</u> on the earth. PS. 39:12 convinced - exiles

14 For they that say such things declare <u>plainly</u> that they seek a country. clearly

15 And truly, if they had been <u>mindful</u> of that *country* from where they came out, they might have had opportunity to have returned. thinking

16 But now they desire a better *country*, that is, an heavenly: wherefore God is not ashamed to be called their God: for He has prepared for them a city.

17 By faith A'bra-ham, when he was <u>tried</u>, offered up I'saac: and he that had received the promises offered up his only begotten *son*, GEN. 22:1-10 tested

18 Of whom it was said, That in I'saac shall your <u>seed</u> be called. GEN. 21:12 descendants

19 Accounting that God *was* able to raise *him* up, even from the dead; from where also he received him in a figure.

20 By faith I'saac blessed Ja'cob and E'sau concerning things to come. GEN. 27:29

21 By faith Ja'cob, when he was a dying, blessed both the sons of Jo'seph; and worshiped, *leaning* upon the top of his staff. GEN. 48:14

22 By faith Jo'seph, when he died, <u>made mention</u> of the departing of the children of Is'ra-el; and gave commandment concerning his bones. spoke of

23 By faith Mo'ses, when he was born, was hid three months of his parents, because they saw *he was* a proper child; and they were not afraid of the king's commandment. EX. 2:2

24 By faith Mo'ses, when he was <u>come to years</u>, refused to be called the son of Pha'raoh's daughter; grown

25 Choosing rather to suffer affliction

with the people of God, than to en-joy the pleasures of sin for a sea-son;

short time

26 Esteeming the reproach of Christ greater riches than the treasures in E'gypt: for he had respect to the recompence of the reward.

payment

27 By faith he forsook E'gypt, not fear-ing the wrath of the king: for he endured, as seeing Him who is invisible.

left

28 Through faith he kept the passover, and the sprinkling of blood, less He that destroyed the firstborn should touch them. EX. 12:21

29 By faith they passed through the Red Sea as by dry *land*: which the E-gyp'tians assaying to do were drowned.

EX. 14:26 attempting

30 By faith the walls of Jer'i-cho fell down, after they were compassed about seven days.

JOS. 6:4-8 encircled

31 By faith the harlot Ra'hab per-ished not with them that believed not, when she had received the spies with peace.

JOS. 2:20 died

32 And what shall I more say? for the time would fail me to tell of Ged'e-on, and *of* Ba'rak, and *of* Sam'son, and *of* Jeph'tha-e; *of* Da'vid also, and Sam'uel, and *of* the prophets:

33 Who through faith subdued king-doms, wrought righteousness, obtained promises, stopped the mouths of lions,

34 Quenched the violence of fire, es-caped the edge of the sword, out of weakness were made strong, waxed valiant in fight, turned to flight the armies of the aliens.

Controlled - grew

35 Women received their dead raised to life again: and others were tortured, not accepting deliverance; that they might obtain a better resurrection:

36 And others had trial of *cruel* mock-ings and scourgings, yea, moreover of bonds and imprisonment:

jeers - floggings

37 They were stoned, they were sawn asunder, were tempted, were slain with the sword: they wandered about in sheepskins and goatskins; being destitute, afflicted, tormented;

in two

38 (Of whom the world was not worthy:) they wandered in deserts, and *in* mountains, and *in* dens and caves of the earth.

39 And these all, having obtained a good report through faith, received not the promise:

approval

40 God having provided some better thing for us, that they without us should not be made perfect.

planned - complete

CHAPTER 12

WHEREFORE seeing we also are compassed about with so great a cloud of witnesses, let us lay aside every weight, and the sin which does so easily beset *us*, and let us run with patience the race that is set before us,

surrounding - endurance

2 Looking to Je'sus the author and finisher of *our* faith; who for the joy that was set before Him endured the cross, despising the shame, and is set down at the right hand of the throne of God.

scorning

3 For consider Him that endured such contradiction of sinners against Himself, less you be wea-ried and faint in your minds.

4 You have not yet resisted to blood, striving against sin.

5 And you have forgotten the exhortation which speaks to you as to children, My son, despise not you the <u>chastening</u> of the Lord, nor faint when you are rebuked of Him: PROV. 3:11 discipline

6 For whom the Lord loves He <u>chastens</u>, and scourges every son whom He receives.

7 If you endure <u>chastening</u>, God deals with you as with sons; for what son is he whom the father <u>chastens</u> not?

8 But if you be without chastisement, whereof all are partakers, then are you <u>bastards</u>, and not sons. illegitimate

9 Furthermore we have had fathers of our flesh which corrected *us*, and we gave *them* reverence: shall we not much rather be in <u>subjection</u> to the Father of spirits, and live? submission

10 For they <u>verily</u> for a few days chastened *us* after their own <u>pleasure</u>; but Hc for *our* profit, that *we* might be partakers of His holiness. truly - judgment

11 Now no <u>chastening</u> for the present seems to be joyous, but grievous: nevertheless afterward it yields the peaceable fruit of righteousness to them which are <u>exercised</u> thereby.

discipline - trained

12 Wherefore <u>lift up</u> the hands which hang down, and the feeble knees; strengthen

13 And make straight paths for your feet, less that which is lame be turned out of the way; but let it rather be healed.

14 Follow peace with all *men*, and holiness, without which no man shall see the Lord:

15 Looking <u>diligently</u> less any man fail of the grace of God; less any root of bitterness springing up trouble *you*, and thereby many be defiled; DEU. 29:18 carefully

16 Less there *be* any fornicator, or <u>profane</u> person, as E'sau, who for one morsel of <u>meat</u> sold his birthright. GEN. 25:32 godless - food

17 For you know how that afterward, when he would have inherited the blessing, he was rejected: for he found no place of <u>repentance</u>, though he sought it carefully with tears. GEN. 27:34 forgiveness

18 For you are not come to the mount that might be touched, and that burned with fire, nor to blackness, and darkness, and tempest, EX. 19:12

19 And the sound of a trumpet, and the voice of words; which *voice* they that heard <u>entreated</u> that the word should not be spoken to them any more: begged

20 (For they could not endure that which was commanded, And if so much as a beast touch the mountain, it shall be stoned, or thrust through with a dart: EX. 19:13

21 And so terrible was the sight, *that* Mo'ses said, I exceedingly fear and quake:) DEU. 9:19

22 But you are come to mount Zi'on, and to the city of the living God, the heavenly Je-ru'sa-lem, and to an innumerable company of angels,

23 To the general assembly and church of the firstborn, which are written in heaven, and to God the Judge of all, and to the spirits of just men made perfect,

24 And to Je'sus the mediator of the

new <u>covenant</u>, and to the blood of sprinkling, that speaks better things than *that of* A'bel.   GEN. 4:10 agreement

25 See that you refuse not Him that speaks. For if they escaped not who refused Him that spoke on earth, much more *shall not* we *escape*, if we turn away from Him that *speaks* from heaven: EX. 20:19

26 Whose voice then shook the earth: but now He has promised, saying, Yet once more I shake not the earth only, but also heaven.   HAG. 2:6

27 And this *word*, Yet once more, signifies the removing of those things that are shaken, as of things that are made, that those things which cannot be shaken may remain.

28 Wherefore we receiving a kingdom which cannot be moved, let us have grace, whereby we may serve God acceptably with reverence and godly fear:

29 For our God *is* a consuming fire.   DEU. 4:24

CHAPTER 13

LET brotherly love continue. 2 Be not forgetful to <u>entertain</u> strangers: for thereby some have entertained <u>angels unawares</u>.   GEN. 18:2 receive - messengers without knowing it

3 Remember them that are in <u>bonds</u>, as bound with them; *and* them which suffer <u>adversity</u>, as being yourselves also in the body.   prison - trouble

4 Marriage *is* honorable in all, and the bed <u>undefiled</u>: but whoremongers and adulterers God will judge.   kept pure

5 *Let your* conversation *be* without covetousness; *and be* content with such things as you have: for He has said, I will never leave you, nor forsake you.   JOS. 1:5 DEU. 31:6 DEU 31:8

6 So that we may boldly say, The Lord *is* my helper, and I will not fear what man shall do to me.   PS. 118:6

7 Remember them which have the rule over you, who have spoken to you the word of God: whose faith follow, considering the <u>end</u> of *their* conversation.   result - life

8 Je'sus Christ the same yesterday, and to day, and for ever.

9 Be not carried about with <u>divers</u> and strange <u>doctrines</u>. For *it is* a good thing that the heart be established with grace; not with meats, which have not <u>profited</u> them that have been occupied therein.   various - teachings - benefitted

10 We have an altar, whereof they have no right to eat which serve the tabernacle.

11 For the bodies of those beasts, whose blood is brought into the <u>sanctuary</u> by the high priest for sin, are burned outside the camp.   LEV. 16:27 holy place

12 Wherefore Je'sus also, that He might <u>sanctify</u> the people with His own blood, suffered outside the gate. make holy

13 Let us go forth therefore to Him outside the camp, bearing His <u>reproach</u>.   disgrace

14 For here have we no continuing city, but we seek one to come.

15 By Him therefore let us offer the sacrifice of praise to God continually, that is, the <u>fruit</u> of *our* lips giving thanks to His name.   LEV. 7:12 praise

16 But to do good and to <u>communi-</u>

cate forget <u>not</u>: for with such sacrifices God is well pleased. i.e., share with others

P12 17 Obey them that <u>have the rule</u> <u>over you</u>, and submit yourselves: for they watch for your souls, as they that must give account, that they may do it with joy, and not with <u>grief</u>: for that *is* unprofitable for you.

398

i.e., leaders - unhappiness

18 Pray for us: for we trust we have a good conscience, in all things <u>will-</u> ing to live honestly.   desiring

19 But I <u>beseech</u> *you* the rather to do this, that I may be restored to you the sooner.   beg

P02 20 Now the God of peace, that brought again from the dead our Lord Je'sus, that great shepherd of the sheep,

through the blood of the everlasting P02 - 402 <u>covenant</u>,   ISA. 63:11 agreement

21 Make you perfect in every good work to do His will, working in you that which is wellpleasing in His sight, through Je'sus Christ; to whom *be* glory for ever and ever. Amen.

22 And I <u>beseech</u> you, brethren, suffer the word of <u>exhortation</u>: for I have written a letter to you in few words.   beg - urging

23 Know you that *our* brother Tim'o-thy is set at liberty; with whom, if he come shortly, I will see you.

24 <u>Salute</u> all them that <u>have the rule</u> over you, and all the saints. They of It'a-ly <u>salute</u> you.   Greet - i.e., leadership

25 Grace *be* with you all. Amen.

JAMES

OUTLINE

GOD'S PURPOSE FOR THE BELIEVER'S ADVANCEMENT IN PURE RELIGION 1.1–27
  Temptation that Builds: Helpful and Harmful Testing 1.1–12
    The Apostolic Greeting 1.1
    Testing to be Received with Joy 1.2
    Its Use by God towards Holiness of Character 1.3
    Its Requirement of Obedience of Spirit 1.4
    Its Endurance Implies a God-Given Wisdom of Spirit: True and False Wisdom 1.5
    God's Gift of Wisdom Conditioned upon True Faith: True and False Faith 1.6–8
      Lack of Such Faith Reveals a Duality of Life: The Fleshly and the Spiritual Self 1.8
    The Lowly in Circumstances to be Congratulated in this Testing: True and False Confidence 1.9–11
    Key Importance of Personal Attitude under Test 1.12
  Temptation that Destroys: Helpful and Harmful Testing 1.13–16
    God Does not Solicit to Evil 1.13
    Self-centered Desire the Seductive Force of Temptation 1.14–16
  God Himself the Believer's Chief Good: True and False Confidence 1.17, 18
    Originator of Every Blessing 1.17
    His Redemptive Work the Evidence of His Love 1.18
  Consequent Exhortation to Personal Holiness 1.19–27
    Probity of Heart Enjoined: True and False Wisdom 1.19–21
    Heart Probity Results in Practical Righteousness: True and False Faith 1.22–27

TESTS OF PURE RELIGION 2.1—5.20
  Test of Self-seeking Partiality: True and False Confidence; Fleshly and Spiritual Self 2.1–13
  Test of Faith Operative through Love: True and False Faith 2.14–26
  Test of Love as an Approach to Life: True and False Wisdom, 3.1–18
  Test of Selfish Faction: Fleshly and Spiritual Self 4.1–12
  Test of Self-Willed Life Direction: True and False Confidence 4.13–17
  Test of Charity in the Acquisition and Stewardship of Wealth: True and False Confidence 5.1–6
  Test of Patience under Oppression: Helpful and Harmful Testing 5.7–11
  Test of Restraint in Commitments: True and False Confidence 5.12
  Test of Prevailing Prayer: True and False Confidence 5.13–20

SURVEY

Writing much in the style of the Old Testament wisdom literature, though with evident Christian presuppositions, James has for his theme "pure religion" (1.27), the religion of heart-experienced divine love. He shows pure religion as being tested by trial and temptation in the faithful, and as itself testing the carnal and the selfish. These positive and negative tests of pure religion reveal contrasting spiritual and fleshly qualities. For example, there are recurring accounts of helpful and harmful temptation (testing), true and false wisdom, true and false faith, a fleshly and a spiritual self, true and false confidence. These contrasts are suggested parenthetically where they occur in the outline.

Clearly Christian in its acknowledgment of the claims of Christ (1.1; 2.1, 7), and in its reference to the Second Coming (1.12; 5.7, 8), and to personal regeneration through faith (1.18, 21), the epistle is reminiscent of the teaching in the so-called "wisdom literature" of the Old Testament as seen in Job, in some of the Psalms, and in Proverbs and Ecclesiastes. It places the good and the evil in juxtaposition, and speaks basically on the theme of "pure religion" and false.

The author has in view the faithful believers who are an example of "pure religion" under test and trial. These he encourages. James also has in view the more fleshly and self-seeking, whose conduct shows them as failing the test of "pure religion." These he rebukes. But throughout the epistle, true heart-religion, whether as *tested* in the lives of the faithful or as *testing* and judging the lives of the carnal, is the theme of this book.

James makes repeated use of paradox as he asserts the superiority of the spiritual values so commonly unrealized. Thus James tells of two kinds of faith, two kinds of wisdom, two kinds of temptation, two kinds of confidence, two kinds of self. These will be noted as they occur in the development of the theme. James is practical and nontheological in emphasis. His first chapter, which speaks of God's program of actual sanctification in the believer, introduces and sets forth in miniature the topics to be treated more fully in the remaining chapters.

AUTHOR

The epistle declares itself to be the writing of James. Three persons of this name are mentioned in the New Testament. However, James the son of Joseph and Mary, and half brother of the Lord Jesus, is accredited by the Christian Church as the author of this epistle. James in his teaching presents a striking resemblance to our Lord. A comparison of this epistle with the Sermon on the Mount reveals at least a dozen clear parallelisms. Chosen as the moderator of the Jerusalem church subsequent to Pentecost, James gave to his epistle a note of unassuming authority. Devoid of all apology, its 108 verses contain fifty-four commands.

S.W.P.

THE LETTER OF
JAMES

CHAPTER 1

JAMES, a servant of God and of the Lord Je'sus Christ, to the twelve tribes which are scattered abroad, greeting.

2 My brethren, count it all joy when you fall into <u>divers temptations</u>; *various trials*

3 Knowing *this*, that the trying of your faith <u>works</u> patience. *produces*

4 But let patience have *her* perfect work, that you may be perfect and <u>entire</u>, <u>wanting</u> nothing. *complete - lacking*

5 If any of you lack wisdom, let him ask of God, that gives to all *men* liberally, and upbraids not; and it shall be given him. DAN 2:21

6 But let him ask in faith, nothing <u>wavering</u>. For he that <u>wavers</u> is like a wave of the sea driven with the wind and tossed. ISA 40:7 *doubting*

7 For let not that man think that he shall receive any thing of the Lord.

8 A double minded man *is* unstable in all his ways.

9 Let the brother of <u>low degree</u> rejoice in that he is exalted: *humble circumstances*

10 But the rich, in that he is made low: because as the flower of the grass he shall pass away.

11 For the sun is no sooner risen with a burning heat, but it withers the grass, and the flower thereof falls, and the grace of the fashion of it perishes: so also shall the rich man fade away in his ways.

12 Blessed *is* the man that endures <u>temptation</u>: for when he is tried, he shall receive the crown of life, which the Lord has promised to them that love Him *trials*

13 Let no man say when he is <u>tempted</u>, I am <u>tempted</u> of God: for God cannot be <u>tempted</u> <u>with</u> evil, neither <u>tempts</u> He any man: *tested - by*

14 But every man is <u>tempted</u>, when he is drawn away of his own lust, and enticed.

15 Then when lust has conceived, it brings forth sin: and sin, when it is finished, brings forth death.

16 Do not <u>err</u>, my beloved brethren. *be deceived*

17 Every good gift and every perfect gift is from above, and comes down from the Father of lights, with whom is no variableness, neither shadow of turning.

18 Of His own will fathered He us with the word of truth, that we should be a kind of firstfruits of His creatures.

19 Wherefore, my beloved brethren, let every man be swift to hear, slow to speak, slow to wrath: PROV. 14:29

20 For the wrath of man <u>works</u> not the righteousness of God. *achieves*

21 Wherefore lay apart all filthiness and <u>superfluity</u> of <u>naughtiness</u>, and receive with meekness the <u>engrafted</u> word, which is able to save your souls. *excess - evil - implanted*

22 But be you doers of the word, and not hearers only, deceiving your own selves.

23 For if any be a hearer of the word, and not a doer, he is like to a man <u>beholding</u> his natural face in a <u>glass</u>:   _{seeing - mirror}

24 For he beholds himself, and goes his way, and immediately forgets what manner of man he was.

25 But whoso looks into the perfect law of liberty, and <u>continues</u> *therein*, he being not a forgetful hearer, but a doer of the work, this man shall be blessed in his deed.   lives

26 If any man among you seem to be religious, and <u>bridles</u> not his tongue, but deceives his own heart, this man's religion *is* <u>vain</u>   controls - worthless

27 Pure religion and <u>undefiled</u> before God and the Father is this, To visit the fatherless and widows in their <u>affliction</u>, *and* to keep himself unspotted from the world.   faultless - distress

CHAPTER 2

MY brethren, have not the faith of our Lord Je'sus Christ, *the Lord* of glory, with respect of persons.

2 For if there come to your <u>assembly</u> a man with a gold ring, in <u>goodly</u> <u>apparel</u>, and there come in also a poor man in <u>vile raiment</u>;

meeting - fine clothes - dirty clothes

3 And you have <u>respect</u> to him that wears the <u>gay</u> clothing, and say to him, Sit you here in a good place; and

say to the poor, Stand you there, or sit here under my footstool:

special attention - nice

4 Are you not then partial in yourselves, and are become judges of evil thoughts?

5 <u>Hearken</u>, my beloved brethren, Has not God chosen the poor of this world rich in faith, and heirs of the kingdom which He has promised to them that love Him?   Listen

6 But you have <u>despised</u> the poor. Do not rich men oppress you, and draw you before the judgment seats?   dishonored

7 Do not they <u>blaspheme</u> that worthy name by the which you are called?   slander

8 If you fulfill the <u>royal law according to the scripture</u>, You shall love your neighbor as yourself, you do well: LEV. 19:18

9 But if you have <u>respect</u> to persons, you commit sin, and are convinced of the law as transgressors.   special attention

10 For whosoever shall keep the whole law, and yet <u>offend</u> in one *point*, he is guilty of all.   stumbles

11 For He that said, Do not commit adultery, said also, Do not kill. Now if you commit no adultery, yet if you kill, you are become a transgressor of the law.   EX. 20:13-14

12 So speak you, and so <u>do</u>, as they that shall be judged by the law of liberty.   act

13 For He shall have judgment without mercy, that has showed no mercy; and mercy <u>rejoices</u> against judgment.   triumphs

14 What *does* it profit, my brethren, though a man say he has faith, and have not works? can faith save him?

15 If a brother or sister be naked, and <u>destitute</u> of daily food,   in need
16 And one of you say to them, Depart in peace, be *you* warmed and filled; notwithstanding you give them not those things which are needful to the body; what *does it* profit?
17 Even so faith, if it has not works, is dead, being <u>alone</u>.   by itself
18 Yea, a man may say, You have faith, and I have works: show me your faith without your works, and I will show you my faith by my works.
19 You believe that there is one God; you do well: the <u>devils</u> also believe, and <u>tremble</u>.   demons - shudder
20 But will you know, O <u>vain</u> man, that faith without works is dead?   foolish
21 Was not A'bra-ham our father justified by works, when he had offered I'saac his son upon the altar?   GEN 22:12
22 See you how faith <u>wrought</u> with his works, and by works was faith made perfect?   working
23 And the scripture was fulfilled which says, A'bra-ham believed God, and it was <u>imputed</u> to him for righteousness: and he was called the Friend of God.   GEN 16:6   reckoned
24 You see then how that by works a man is <u>justified</u>, and not by faith only.   made right
25 Likewise also was not Ra'hab the harlot justified by works, when she had received the messengers, and had sent *them* out another way?   JOS. 2:15
26 For as the body without the spirit is dead, so faith without works is dead also.

CHAPTER 3

MY brethren, be not many <u>masters</u>, knowing that we shall receive the greater condemnation.   teachers
2 For in many things we offend all. If any man offend not in word, the same *is* a perfect man, *and* able also to <u>bridle</u> the whole body.   control
3 Behold, we put bits in the horses' mouths, that they may obey us; and we turn about their whole body.
4 Behold also the ships, which though *they be* so great, and *are* driven of <u>fierce</u> winds, yet are they turned about with a very small helm, wherever the <u>governor lists</u>.   strong - pilot desires
5 Even so the tongue is a little member, and boasts great things. Behold, how great a matter a little fire kindles!
6 And the tongue *is* a fire, a world of <u>iniquity</u>: so is the tongue among our members, that it <u>defiles</u> the whole body, and sets on fire the course of nature; and it is set on fire of hell.   evil - corrupts
7 For every kind of beasts, and of birds, and of serpents, and of things in the sea, is tamed, and has been tamed of mankind:
8 But the tongue can no man tame; *it is* an unruly evil, full of deadly poison.
9 Therewith bless we God, even the Father; and therewith curse we men, which are made after the <u>similitude</u> of God.   likeness
10 Out of the same mouth proceeds blessing and cursing. My brethren, these things ought not so to be.
11 Does a fountain send forth at the same <u>place</u> sweet *water* and bitter? opening

12 Can the fig tree, my brethren, bear olive berries? either a vine, figs? so *can* no fountain both yield salt water and fresh.

13 Who *is* a wise man and <u>endued</u> with knowledge among you? let him show out of a good <u>conversation</u> his works with <u>meekness</u> of wisdom. given - behavior - gentleness

14 But if you have bitter envying and <u>strife</u> in your hearts, <u>glory</u> not, and lie not against the truth.   selfish ambition - boast

15 This wisdom descends not from above, but *is* earthly, sensual, devilish.

16 For where envying and <u>strife</u> *is*, there *is* <u>confusion</u> and every evil work.

disorder

17 But the wisdom that is from above is first pure, then peaceable, gentle, *and* easy to be entreated, full of mercy and good fruits, without <u>partiality</u>, and without hypocrisy. favoritism

18 And the fruit of righteousness is sown in peace of them that make peace.   ISA. 32:17

CHAPTER 4

FROM where *come* wars and fightings among you? *come they* not here, *even* of your lusts that war in your members?

2 You lust, and have not: you kill, and desire to have, and cannot obtain: you fight and war, yet you have not, because you ask not.

3 You ask, and receive not, because you ask amiss, that you may consume *it* upon your <u>lusts</u>.

pleasures

4 You <u>adulterers</u> and <u>adulteresses</u>, know you not that the friendship of the world is enmity with God? whosoever

therefore will be a friend of the world is the enemy of God.   unfaithful

5 Do you think that the scripture says in vain, The spirit that dwells in us lusts to envy?

6 But He gives more grace. Wherefore He says, God resists the proud, but gives grace to the humble. PROV. 3:34

7 Submit yourselves therefore to God. Resist the devil, and he will flee from you.

8 Draw near to God, and He will draw near to you. Cleanse *your* hands, *you* sinners; and purify *your* hearts, *you* <u>double minded</u>.   2 CHRON.15:2 hypocrites

9 Be <u>afflicted</u>, and mourn, and weep: let your laughter be turned to mourning, and *your* joy to <u>heaviness</u>.   miserable - gloom

10 Humble yourselves in the sight of the Lord, and He shall lift you up.

11 Speak not evil one of another, brethren. He that speaks evil of *his* brother, and judges his brother, speaks evil of the law, and judges the law: but if you judge the law, you are not a doer of the law, but a judge.

12 There is One Lawgiver, who is able to save and to destroy: who are you that judge another?

13 <u>Go to</u> now, you that say, To day or to morrow we will go into such a city, and continue there a year, and buy and sell, and get gain: Come now

14 Whereas you know not what *shall be* on the morrow. For what *is* your life? It is <u>even a vapor</u>, that appears for a little time, and then vanishes away.   like a mist

15 For that you *ought* to say, If the

Lord will, we shall live, and do this, or that.

16 But now you rejoice in your <u>boastings</u>: all such rejoicing is evil.   arrogance

17 Therefore to him that knows to do good, and does *it* not, to him it is sin.

CHAPTER 5

GO to now, *you* rich men, weep and howl for your miseries that shall come upon *you*.   Now listen

2 Your riches are <u>corrupted</u>, and your garments are motheaten.   rotted

3 Your gold and silver <u>is cankered</u>; and the rust of them shall be a witness against you, and shall eat your flesh as it were fire. You have <u>heaped</u> treasure together <u>for</u> the last days.

  has rusted - stored up - in

4 Behold, the hire of the laborers who have reaped down your fields, which is of you kept back by fraud, cries: and the cries of them which have reaped are entered into the ears of the Lord of sab'a-oth.   EXO. 2:23

5 You have lived in pleasure on the earth, and been <u>wanton</u>; you have nourished your hearts, as in a day of slaughter.   self indulgence

6 You have condemned *and* killed the <u>just</u>; *and* he does not resist you.

  innocent man

7 Be patient therefore, brethren, to the coming of the Lord. Behold, the <u>husbandman</u> waits for the precious fruit of the earth, and has long patience for it, until he receive the early and latter rain.   farmer

8 Be you also patient; <u>stablish</u> your hearts: for the coming of the Lord draws near.   strengthen

9 <u>Grudge</u> not one against another, brethren, less you be condemned: behold, the judge stands before the door.   Complain

10 Take, my brethren, the prophets, who have spoken in the name of the Lord, for an example of suffering affliction, and of patience.

11 Behold, we count them happy which endure. You have heard of the patience of Job, and have seen the <u>end</u> of the Lord; that the Lord is very pitiful, and of tender mercy.   JOB 1:22 way

12 But above all things, my brethren, swear not, neither by heaven, neither by the earth, neither by any other oath: but let your <u>yea</u> be <u>yea</u>; and *your* <u>nay, nay</u>; less you fall into <u>condemnation</u>.   LEV. 5:4 yes - no - judgment

13 Is any among you afflicted? let him pray. Is any merry? let him sing <u>psalms</u>.   praises

14 Is any sick among you? let him call for the elders of the church; and let them pray over him, anointing him with oil in the name of the Lord:

15 And the prayer of faith shall <u>save</u> the sick, and the Lord shall raise him up; and if he have committed sins, they shall be forgiven him.   make well

16 Confess *your* faults one to another, and pray one for another, that you may be healed. The <u>effectual</u> fervent prayer of a righteous man avails much.   effective

17 E-li'jah was a man subject to <u>like</u>

passions as we are, and he prayed earnestly that it might not rain: and it rained not on the earth by the space of three years and six months.

1KGS.17:1 the same

18 And he prayed again, and the <u>heaven</u> gave rain, and the earth <u>brought</u> forth her fruit.

1 KGS. 18:45   sky - produced

19 Brethren, if any of you do err from the truth, and one convert him;

20 Let him know, that he which <u>converts</u> the sinner from the error of his way shall save a <u>soul</u> from death, and shall <u>hide</u> a multitude of sins.

turns - person - cover

1 PETER

OUTLINE

SURVEY

This beautiful letter was written to Christians in Asia Minor to stimulate in them a joyful hope in the face of coming persecution. It was intended to be circulated among Christians of predominantly Gentile heritage in congregations located in provinces of the Roman Empire where the imperial yoke was apt to be most severe. Persecution was not unknown to the Church. From the early persecution of Stephen and the dispersion that followed, to the constant harassment of Paul wherever he went, the early Christians knew the strain and tension of antagonism. Now the wrath of the demented emperor Nero was about to explode in Rome at the expense of the Church. Therefore, the Apostle Peter tried to prepare the Church in Asia Minor for imminent disaster in these eastern provinces where oppression would undoubtedly spread from its source in Rome. In the spirit of a faithful shepherd and bishop of souls, Peter sent this pastoral letter to confirm his flock in the comforting hope of the Spirit's coming. Being rooted in the passions of Christ, they are to abstain from the passions of the flesh. If they find themselves in a hostile society, their suffering for righteousness' sake will actually be a blessing.

AUTHOR

This letter from Peter was probably sent from Rome to Christians in Asia Minor sometime between A.D. 62 and 69. There is a remarkable affinity of thought between this letter and the Epistle of Paul to the Romans (A.D. 56-57) and the anonymous Epistle to the Hebrews (A.D. 60?). Probably both letters were available to Peter in Rome.

R.P.R.

THE FIRST LETTER OF
PETER

CHAPTER 1

PETER, an apostle of Je'sus Christ, to the <u>strangers</u> scattered throughout Pont'us, Ga-la'tia, Cap-pa-do'ci-a, A'sia, and Bi-thyn'i-a, i.e. strangers in the world

2 <u>Elect</u> according to the foreknowledge of God the Father, through sanctification of the Spirit, to obedience and sprinkling of the blood of Je'sus Christ: Grace to you, and peace be multiplied. chosen

3 Blessed *be* the God and Father of our Lord Je'sus Christ, which according to His abundant mercy has <u>begotten</u> us again to a <u>lively</u> hope by the resurrection of Je'sus Christ from the dead, i.e. spiritual birth - living

4 To an inheritance <u>incorruptible</u>, and undefiled, and that fades not away, reserved in heaven for you, imperishable

5 Who are <u>kept</u> by the power of God through faith to salvation ready to be revealed in the last time. protected

6 Wherein you greatly rejoice, though now for a season, if need be, you are in heaviness through <u>manifold</u> temptations: various

7 That the trial of your faith, being much more precious than of gold that perishes, though it be tried with fire, might be found to praise and honor and glory at the appearing of Je'sus Christ:

8 Whom having not seen, you love; in whom, though now you see *Him* not, yet believing, you rejoice with joy unspeakable and full of glory:

9 Receiving the <u>end</u> of your faith, *even* the salvation of *your* souls. outcome

10 Of which salvation the prophets have enquired and searched diligently, who prophesied of the grace *that should come* to you:

11 Searching what, or what manner of time the Spirit of Christ which was in them did signify, when it testified beforehand the sufferings of Christ, and the glory that should follow. ISA. 53:

12 To whom it was revealed, that not to themselves, but to <u>us</u> they did minister the things, which are now reported to you by them that have preached the gospel to you with the Ho'ly <u>Ghost</u> sent down from heaven; which things the <u>angels</u> desire to look into. you - Spirit - messengers

13 Wherefore gird up the loins of your mind, be sober, and hope to the end for the grace that is to be brought to you at the revelation of Je'sus Christ;

14 As obedient children, not <u>fashioning</u> yourselves according to the former lusts in your ignorance: conforming

15 But as He which has called you is holy, so be you holy in all manner of <u>conversation</u>; behavior

16 Because it is written, Be you holy; for I am holy. LEV. 11:44-45 i.e. the Scriptures

17 And if you call on the Father, who without respect of persons judges according to every man's work, pass the time of your sojourning *here* in fear: living on earth

18 Forasmuch as you know that you were not redeemed with corruptible things, *as* silver and gold, from your vain conversation *received* by tradition from your fathers; foolish ways - inherited

19 But with the precious blood of Christ, as of a lamb without blemish and without spot:

20 Who verily was foreordained before the foundation of the world, but was manifest in these last times for you, truly - revealed

21 Who by Him do believe in God, that raised Him up from the dead, and gave Him glory; that your faith and hope might be in God.

22 Seeing you have purified your souls in obeying the truth through the Spirit to unfeigned love of the brethren, *see that you* love one another with a pure heart fervently: cleansed - sincere

23 Being born again, not of corruptible seed, but of incorruptible, by the word of God, which lives and abides for ever.

24 For all flesh *is* as grass, and all the glory of man as the flower of grass. The grass withers, and the flower thereof falls away: ISA. 40:6

25 But the word of the Lord endures for ever. And this is the word which by the gospel is preached to you.

CHAPTER 2

WHEREFORE laying aside all malice and all guile, and hypocrisies, and envies, and all evil speakings, hypocrisy

2 As newborn babes, desire the sincere milk of the word, that you may grow thereby: want - pure spiritual

3 If so be you have tasted that the Lord *is* gracious. PS. 34:8 good

4 To whom coming, *as to* a living stone, disallowed indeed of men, but chosen of God, *and* precious, rejected

5 You also, as lively stones, are built up a spiritual house, an holy priesthood, to offer up spiritual sacrifices, acceptable to God by Je'sus Christ. EX. 19:5 living

6 Wherefore also it is contained in the scripture, Behold, I lay in Zi'on a chief corner stone, elect, precious: and he that believes on Him shall not be confounded. PSA. 118.22 ISA. 28:16 chosen - disappointed

7 To you therefore which believe *He is* precious: but to them which be disobedient, the stone which the builders disallowed, the same is made the head of the corner,

8 And a stone of stumbling, and a rock of offence, *even to them* which stumble at the word, being disobedient: whereto also they were appointed.

9 But you *are* a chosen generation, a royal priesthood, an holy nation, a peculiar people; that you should show forth the praises of Him who has called you out of darkness into His marvellous light: DEU. 10:15 EX. 19:5 i.e. God's own

10 Which in time past *were* not a people, but *are* now the people of God:

which had not <u>obtained</u> mercy, but now have obtained mercy.HOS. 2:23 received

11 Dearly beloved, I <u>beseech</u> *you* as strangers and pilgrims, abstain from fleshly <u>lusts</u>, which war against the soul; beg - desire

12 Having your conversation honest among the Gen'tiles: that, whereas they speak against you as evildoers, they may by *your* good works, which they shall <u>behold</u>, glorify God in the day of visitation. observe

13 Submit yourselves to every <u>or-dinance</u> of man for the Lord's sake: whether it be to the king, as supreme; law

14 Or to governors, as to them that are sent by him for the punishment of evildoers, and for the praise of them that do well.

15 For so is the will of God, that with well doing you may put to si-lence the ignorance of foolish men:

16 As free, and not using *your* <u>lib-erty</u> for a cloke of <u>maliciousness</u>, but as the servants of God. freedom - evil

17 Honor all *men.* Love the brother-hood. <u>Fear</u> God. Honor the king. revere

18 Servants, *be* subject to *your* masters with all <u>fear</u>; not only to the good and gentle, but also to the <u>froward</u>. respect - unreasonable

19 For this *is* <u>thankworthy</u>, if a man for conscience toward God endure grief, suffering wrongfully. commendable

20 For what glory *is it*, if, when you be <u>buffeted</u> for your faults, you shall take it patiently? but if, when you do well, and suffer *for it*, you take it patiently, this *is* acceptable with God. harshly treated

21 For even hereunto were you called:

because Christ also suffered for <u>us</u>, leaving <u>us</u> an example, that you should follow His steps: you

22 Who <u>did</u> no sin, neither was <u>guile</u> found in His mouth: ISA. 53:9 committed - deceit

23 Who, when He was reviled, re-viled not again; when He suffered, He threatened not; but committed *Him-self* to Him that judges righteously:

24 Who His own self bare our sins in His own body on the tree, that we, being dead to sins, should live to righteousness: by whose <u>stripes</u> you were healed. ISA.53:12 wounds

25 For you were as sheep going astray; but are now returned to the <u>Shepherd</u> and <u>Bishop</u> of your souls. ISA 53:6 i.e. Christ

CHAPTER 3

LIKEWISE, you wives, *be* in <u>subjection</u> to your own husbands; that, if any obey not the word, they also may without the word be won by the <u>conversation</u> of the wives; harmony - behavior

2 While they behold your <u>chaste</u> con-versation *coupled* with <u>fear</u>. pure - respect

3 Whose adorning let it not be that outward *adorning* of <u>plaiting</u> the hair, and of wearing of gold, or <u>of putting on of apparel</u>; braiding - i.e. elaborate dressing

4 But *let it be* the hidden man of the heart, in that which is <u>not corrupt-ible</u>, *even the ornament* of a meek and quiet spirit, which is in the sight of God of great price. imperishable

5 For after this manner in the old time the holy women also, who trusted in God, adorned themselves, being in <u>subjection</u> to their own husbands:

6 Even as Sa'ra obeyed A'bra-ham, calling him lord: whose daughters you are, as long as you do well, and are not afraid with any <u>amazement</u>.   GEN. 18:12 surprise

7 Likewise, you husbands, dwell with *them* <u>according to knowledge</u>, giving honor to the wife, as to the weaker vessel, and as being heirs together of the grace of life; that your prayers be not hindered. treating with respect

8 Finally, *be you* all of one mind, having <u>compassion</u> one of another, love as brethren, *be* <u>pitiful</u>, *be* courteous:

sympathy - humble

9 Not rendering evil for evil, or <u>railing</u> for <u>railing</u>: but contrariwise blessing; knowing that you are thereunto called, that you should inherit a blessing.   insult

10 For he that will love life, and see good days, let him refrain his tongue from evil, and his lips that they speak no <u>guile</u>:   deceit

11 Let him <u>eschew</u> evil, and do good; let him seek peace, and ensue it. turn from

12 For the eyes of the Lord *are* over the righteous, and His ears *are open* to their prayers: but the face of the Lord *is* against them that do evil.   PS. 34:15

13 And who *is* he that will harm you, if you be followers of that which is good?

14 But and if you suffer for righteousness' sake, happy *are you*: and be not afraid of their terror, neither be <u>troubled</u>; frightened

15 But <u>sanctify</u> the Lord God in your hearts: and *be* ready always to *give* an answer to every man that asks you a reason of the hope that is in you with meekness and <u>fear</u>: ISA. 8:13 set apart - reverence

16 Having a good conscience; that, whereas they speak evil of you, as of evildoers, they may be ashamed that falsely accuse your good conversation in Christ.

17 For *it is* better, if the will of God be so, that you suffer for well doing, than for <u>evil</u> doing.   wrong

18 For Christ also has once suffered for sins, the just for the unjust, that He might bring us to God, being put to death in the flesh, but <u>quickened</u> by the Spirit: PROV. 11:31 made alive

19 By which also He went and preached to the spirits in prison;

20 Which <u>sometime</u> were disobedient, when once the longsuffering of God waited in the days of No'ah, while the ark was a preparing, wherein few, that is, eight souls were saved by water. once

21 The like figure whereto *even* baptism does also now save us (not the putting away of the filth of the flesh, but the answer of a good conscience toward God,) by the resurrection of Je'sus Christ:

22 Who is gone into heaven, and is on the right hand of God; angels and authorities and powers being made subject to Him.

CHAPTER 4

FORASMUCH then as Christ has suffered for us in the <u>flesh</u>, arm yourselves likewise with the same mind: for he that has suffered in the flesh has ceased from sin;   body

2 That he no longer should live the rest of *his* time in the <u>flesh</u> to the <u>lusts</u> of men, but to the will of God. evil desires

3 For the time past of *our* life may suffice us to have wrought the will of the Gen'tiles, when we walked in lasciviousness, lusts, excess of wine, revellings, banquetings, and abominable idolatries: 　　sensuality - detestable

4 Wherein they think it strange that you run not with *them* to the same excess of riot, speaking evil of *you*:

5 Who shall give account to Him that is ready to judge the quick and the dead. 　　living (alive)

6 For for this cause was the gospel preached also to them that are dead, that they might be judged according to men in the flesh, but live according to God in the spirit. 　　purpose

7 But the end of all things is at hand: be you therefore sober, and watch to prayer. 　　clear minded

8 And above all things have fervent charity among yourselves: for charity shall cover the multitude of sins. PROV. 10:12 love

9 Use hospitality one to another without grudging. 　　complaint

10 As every man has received the gift, *even so* minister the same one to another, as good stewards of the manifold grace of God. 　　various

11 If any man speak, *let him speak* as the oracles of God; if any man minister, *let him do it* as of the ability which God gives: that God in all things may be glorified through Je'sus Christ, to whom be praise and dominion for ever and ever. Amen. utterances - serves - praised - power

12 Beloved, think it not strange concerning the fiery trial which is to try you, as though some strange thing happened to you: 　　painful ordeal - test

13 But rejoice, inasmuch as you are partakers of Christ's sufferings; that, when His glory shall be revealed, you may be glad also with exceeding joy. 　　sharers

14 If you be reproached for the name of Christ, happy *are you*; for the Spirit of glory and of God rests upon you: on their part He is evil spoken of, but on your part He is glorified.

ISA 11:12　insulted - wrongly - honored

15 But let none of you suffer as a murderer, or *as* a thief, or *as* an evildoer, or as a busybody in other men's matters.

PROV. 11:31

16 Yet if *any man suffer* as a Chris'tian, let him not be ashamed; but let him glorify God on this behalf.

17 For the time *is come* that judgment must begin at the house of God: and if *it* first *begin* at us, what shall the end *be* of them that obey not the gospel of God?

18 And if the righteous scarcely be saved, where shall the ungodly and the sinner appear? 　　PROV. 11:31

19 Wherefore let them that suffer according to the will of God commit the keeping of their souls *to Him* in well doing, as to a faithful Creator.

CHAPTER 5

THE elders which are among you I exhort, who am also an elder, and a witness of the sufferings of Christ, and also a partaker of the glory that shall be revealed: 　　sharer

2 Feed the flock of God which is among you, taking the oversight *thereof*, not by constraint but willingly;

not for <u>filthy lucre</u>, but of a <u>ready</u> mind;

compulsion - sordid gain - willing

3 Neither as being lords over *God's* heritage, but being examples to the flock.

4 And when the chief <u>Shepherd</u> shall appear, you shall receive a crown of glory that fades not away. i.e. Christ

5 Likewise, you younger, <u>submit</u> yourselves to the elder. Yea, all *of you* be subject one to another, and be clothed with humility: for God resists the proud, and gives grace to the humble. PROV. 3:34 subject

6 Humble yourselves therefore under the mighty hand of God, that He may exalt you in due time:

7 Casting all your <u>care</u> upon Him; for He cares for you. PS. 55:22 anxiety

8 Be sober, be vigilant; because your adversary the devil, as a roaring lion, walks about, seeking whom he may devour: JOB 1:7

9 Whom resist <u>steadfast</u> in the faith, knowing that the same afflictions are <u>accomplished in</u> your brethren that are in the world. firm - suffered by

10 But the God of all grace, who has called us to His eternal glory by Christ Je'sus, after that you have suffered a while, make you perfect, <u>stablish</u>, strengthen, settle *you*. firm

11 To Him *be* glory and dominion for ever and ever. Amen.

12 By Sil-va'nus, a faithful brother to you, as I suppose, I have written briefly, exhorting, and testifying that this is the true grace of God wherein you stand.

13 The *church that is* at Bab'y-lon, elected together with *you*, <u>salutes</u> you; and *so does* Mar'cus my son. greets

14 Greet you one another with a kiss of <u>charity</u>. Peace *be* with you all that are in Christ Je'sus. Amen love

2 PETER

OUTLINE

SURVEY

While 1 Peter is an epistle of joyful hope in the face of suffering, 2 Peter is an epistle of faithful truth in the face of falsehood. The latter begins with a forthright statement of the truth of God as it is based upon both the prophetic and the witnessed Word. It warns against false teachers who will try to substitute human words for this divine Word. And it concludes with the assurance that Christ's coming is a future reality that will both destroy the world and bring a new heavens and a new earth.

AUTHOR

The authorship, date, and destination of the second letter of Peter are extremely uncertain. No New Testament writing had a more difficult time establishing itself in the Canon. Scholars, both ancient and modern, have seriously doubted its Petrine composition. Although hints of the letter occur in the second century epistle of the churches of Lyons and Vienne and in a treatise by Theophilus of Antioch, the first time it is definitely mentioned is by Origen, and this is to question it. In the third century Eusebius says, "As for the current second epistle, it has not come down to us as canonical, though it has been studied long with the rest of the scriptures, since it has seemed useful to many people." Following the observation of Jerome, many modern scholars find the Greek style significantly different from 1 Peter. The theory has been advanced that some second century author wrote in the name of Peter so as to gain prestige for his message. We have other writings under the name of Peter and the other apostles which are known to be spurious.

In spite of these scholarly judgments, the Church has traditionally regarded this epistle as of genuine Petrine authorship. The difference in style can be explained: Peter had a different amanuensis; he wrote to a single congregation rather than to a group; he wrote with less urgency because his purpose and the situation were different. When he refers in this second letter to a previous letter, we must not suppose this means our canonical 1 Peter, but rather a lost letter. There is even the possibility that Peter wrote 2 Peter before the canonical 1 Peter. The circumstances of writing reflect a situation in which Gnostic heresies were infecting the Church. This false teaching led to licentious

conduct. Only a proper understanding of the wisdom of God in the light of the return of the Lord at the last day would refute these errors.

Why this letter was so long in gaining recognition by the ancient Church is difficult to answer. Perhaps an explanation lies in the obscurity of the congregation to which he wrote. If this had been stated, as in 1 Peter, the authorship could have been verified.

R.P.R.

THE SECOND LETTER OF
PETER

CHAPTER 1

SI'MON Pe'ter, a servant and an apostle of Je'sus Christ, to them that have <u>obtained</u> like precious faith with us through the righteousness of God and our Savior Je'sus Christ: *received*

2 Grace and peace be multiplied to you through the knowledge of God, and of Je'sus our Lord,

3 According as His divine power has given to us all things that *pertain* to life and godliness, through the knowledge of Him that has called us to glory and virtue:

4 Whereby are given to us exceeding great and precious promises: that by these you might be partakers of the divine nature, having escaped the corruption that is in the world through lust.

M24

5 And beside this, giving all <u>diligence</u>, add to your faith virtue; and to virtue knowledge; *effort*

6 And to knowledge <u>temperance</u>; and to <u>temperance</u> patience; and to patience godliness; *self control*

442

7 And to godliness brotherly kindness; and to brotherly kindness <u>charity</u>. *love*

8 For if these things be in you, and abound, they make *you that you shall* neither *be* <u>barren</u> nor unfruitful in the knowledge of our Lord Je'sus Christ. *useless*

9 But he that lacks these things is blind, and cannot see afar off, and has forgotten that he was <u>purged</u> from his old sins. *cleansed*

10 <u>Wherefore</u> the rather, brethren, give diligence to make your calling and <u>election</u> sure: for if you do these things, you shall never <u>fall</u>: *Therefore - choosing - stumble*

11 For so an entrance shall be <u>ministered</u> to you abundantly into the everlasting kingdom of our Lord and Savior Je'sus Christ. *supplied*

12 Wherefore I will not be negligent to put you always in remembrance of these things, though you know *them*, and be established in the present truth.

13 Yea, I think it <u>meet</u>, as long as I am in this <u>tabernacle</u>, to stir you up by putting *you* in remembrance; *right - earthly body*

M16 - - - - 415
M06 - - - - 434

We Were Eyewitnesses to His Majesty

14 Knowing that shortly I must put off *this* my <u>tabernacle</u>, even as our Lord Je'sus Christ has showed me.

15 Moreover I will endeavor that you may be able after my <u>decease</u> to have these things always in remembrance. *death*

16 For we have not followed cunningly devised fables, when we made known to you the power and coming of our Lord Je'sus Christ, but were eyewitnesses of His majesty.

17 For He received from God the Father honor and glory, when there came such a voice to Him from the <u>excellent glory,</u> This is My beloved Son, in whom I am well pleased. *Majestic Glory*

G3
G4

418

18 And this voice which came from heaven we heard, when we were with Him in the holy mount.

19 We have also a more sure word of prophecy; whereunto you do well that you take heed, as to a light that shines in a dark place, until the day dawn, and the day star arise in your hearts:

20 Knowing this first, that no prophecy of the scripture is of any underline{private} interpretation.   i.e. one man's

21 For the prophecy came not in old time by the will of man: but holy men of God spoke *as they were* moved by the Ho'ly underline{Ghost}.   Spirit

CHAPTER 2

BUT there were false prophets also among the people, even as there shall be false teachers among you, who underline{privily} shall bring in underline{damnable} heresies, even denying the Lord that bought them, and bring upon themselves swift destruction.   JUDE 4   secretly - destructive

2 And many shall follow their underline{pernicious} ways; by reason of whom the way of truth shall be evil spoken of.   shameful

3 And through underline{covetousness} shall they with feigned words make merchandise of you: whose judgment now of a long time lingers not, and their underline{damnation} slumbers not.   greed

4 For if God spared not the angels that sinned, but cast *them* down to hell, and delivered *them* into underline{chains} of darkness, to be reserved to judgment;   pits

5 And spared not the old world, but saved No'ah the eighth *person*, a preacher of righteousness, bringing in the flood upon the world of the ungodly;   GEN. 8:18

6 And turning the cities of Sod'om and Go-mor'rha into ashes condemned *them* with an overthrow, making *them* an example to those that after should live ungodly;   GEN. 19:24

7 And delivered just Lot, underline{vexed} with the filthy conversation of the wicked: GEN. 19:16   troubled

8 (For that righteous man dwelling among them, in seeing and hearing, vexed *his* righteous soul from day to day with *their* unlawful deeds;)

9 The Lord knows how to deliver the godly out of underline{temptations}, and to reserve the unjust unto the day of judgment to be punished: trials

10 But chiefly them that walk after the flesh in the lust of uncleanness, and despise underline{government}. Presumptuous *are they*, selfwilled, they are not afraid to speak evil of dignities.   authority

11 Whereas angels, which are greater in power and might, bring not underline{railing} accusation against them before the Lord.   slanderous

12 But these, underline{as} natural brute beasts, made to be taken and destroyed, speak evil of the things that they understand not; and shall utterly perish in their own corruption;   like

13 And shall receive the reward of unrighteousness, *as* they that count it pleasure to riot in the day time. Spots *they are* and blemishes, underline{sporting} themselves with their own deceivings while they underline{feast} with you;   reveling - share

14 Having eyes full of adultery, and that cannot cease from sin; underline{beguiling}

unstable souls: an heart they have exercised with covetous practices; cursed children: enticing

15 Which have forsaken the right way, and are gone astray, following the way of Ba'laam *the son* of Bo'sor, who loved the wages of unrighteousness;   NUM. 22:5

16 But was rebuked for his iniquity: the dumb ass speaking with man's voice forbad the madness of the prophet.   NUM. 22:23 restrained

17 These are wells without water, clouds that are carried with a tempest; to whom the mist of darkness is reserved for ever.

18 For when they speak great swelling *words* of vanity, they allure through the lusts of the flesh, *through much* wantonness, those that were clean escaped from them who live in error.   boasting - desires - sinfulness - barely

19 While they promise them liberty, they themselves are the servants of corruption: for of whom a man is overcome, of the same is he brought in bondage.   slavery

20 For if after they have escaped the pollutions of the world through the knowledge of the Lord and Savior Je'sus Christ, they are again entangled therein, and overcome, the latter end is worse with them than the beginning.   corruptions

21 For it had been better for them not to have known the way of righteousness, than, after they have known *it*, to turn from the holy commandment delivered to them.

22 But it is happened to them according to the true proverb, The dog *is* turned to his own vomit again; and the sow that was washed to her wallowing in the mire.   PROV. 26:11 mud

CHAPTER 3

THIS second epistle, beloved, I now write to you; in *both* which I stir up your pure minds by way of remembrance: dear friends

2 That you may be mindful of the words which were spoken before by the holy prophets, and of the commandment of us the apostles of the Lord and Savior:

3 Knowing this first, that there shall come in the last days scoffers, walking after their own lusts,   mockers - desires

4 And saying, Where is the promise of His coming? for since the fathers fell asleep, all things continue as *they were* from the beginning of the creation.   died

5 For this they willingly are ignorant of, that by the word of God the heavens were of old, and the earth standing out of the water and in the water: GEN. 1:2,6 formed

6 Whereby the world that then was, being overflowed with water, perished: GEN. 6:17

7 But the heavens and the earth, which are now, by the same word are kept in store, reserved to fire against the day of judgment and perdition of ungodly men.   destruction

8 But, beloved, be not ignorant of this one thing, that one day *is* with the Lord as a thousand years, and a thousand years as one day.   PS. 90:4

9 The Lord is not slack concerning His promise, as some men count slack-

ness; but is longsuffering to us-ward, not willing that any should perish, but that all should come to repentance.

1 COR. 2:14 slow

10 But the day of the Lord will come as a thief in the night; in the which the heavens shall pass away with a great noise, and the elements shall melt with fervent heat, the earth also and the works that are therein shall be burned up.

11 *Seeing* then *that* all these things shall be <u>dissolved</u>, what manner *of persons* ought you to be in *all* holy <u>conversation</u> and godliness,   destroyed - conduct

12 Looking for and hasting to the coming of the day of God, wherein the heavens being on fire shall be dissolved, and the elements shall melt with <u>fervent</u> heat?   ISA. 34:4 intense

13 Nevertheless we, according to His promise, look for new heavens and a new earth, wherein dwells righteousness.   ISA. 65:17

14 Wherefore, beloved, seeing that you look for such things, be diligent that you may be found of Him in peace, without spot, and blameless.

15 And <u>account</u> *that* the longsuffering of our Lord *is* salvation; even as our beloved brother Paul also according to the wisdom given to him has written to you;   bear in mind

16 As also in all *his* epistles, speaking in them of these things; in which are some things hard to be understood, which they that are unlearned and unstable twist, as *they do* also the other scriptures, to their own destruction.

17 You therefore, beloved, seeing you know *these things* before, beware less you also, being led away with the error of the wicked, fall from your own steadfastness.

18 But grow in grace, and *in* the knowledge of our Lord and Savior Je'sus Christ. To Him *be* glory both now and for ever. Amen.

1, 2 AND 3 JOHN

OUTLINE

SECOND JOHN

THIRD JOHN

LEADERS CONTRASTED VV. 9–12
  Apostate Diotrephes vv. 9–11
  Good Demetrius v. 12
CONCLUSION VV. 13, 14

SURVEY

The First Epistle of John was written to a Christian community who faced the Gnostic heresy of the first century. John sought to encourage its members to live the kind of life consistent with fellowship with God and His Christ. It deals with such vital themes as righteousness, love, truth and assured knowledge. The author does not consider these themes merely as ethical requirements, but as religious realities based upon the Christian revelation of God and His Son, the Lord Jesus Christ. Therefore, Christian doctrine lies at the root of the book and one is tempted, at times, to think of it as a doctrinal exposition of the reality of the incarnation of God in Christ. If we are to follow the mind of the writer, however, we must avoid this temptation, since he is primarily concerned with the quality of the Christian life of his readers.

John's second letter was written to warn a Christian woman against indiscriminate fellowship with unbelievers. The leading ideas of the epistle are love, truth and obedience which partly involve and partly supplement one another. Obedience without love is servile; love without obedience is unreal; neither of them can flourish outside the realm of truth.

The letter is addressed to "an elect lady" which probably is exactly what is meant, though many interpreters take this as a figurative expression designating a church. The evidence for such use is weak, and the reason to expect it here is obscure. The epistle seems to be a private note to some Christian woman of John's acquaintance, probably a widow, and was occasioned by his meeting some of her children whom he found to be true to the faith of Christ (cf. v. 4).

The purpose of the third letter is to commend Gaius, a loyal and active layman with considerable property, for his Christian hospitality in entertaining itinerant Christian preachers and helping them on their way, thus participating in their missionary work. The letter also speaks of some internal trouble in that church that involved Gaius and Diotrephes.

AUTHOR

Available evidence indicates that John, the Apostle, was the author not only of the Gospel which bears his name but also of these three epistles. These letters were presumably written between A.D. 85 and 100.

F.L.F.

THE FIRST LETTER OF
JOHN
CHAPTER 1

| If We Walk |
| In the Light |

THAT which was from the beginning, which we have heard, which we have seen with our eyes, which we have looked upon, and our hands have handled, of the Word of life;

2 (For the life was <u>manifested</u>, and we have seen *it*, and bear witness, and show to you that eternal life, which was with the Father, and was <u>manifested</u> to us;)   known

3 That which we have seen and heard <u>declare we</u> to you, that you also may have fellowship with us: and truly our fellowship *is* with the Father, and with His Son Je'sus Christ.   we tell

4 And these things write we to you, that <u>your</u> joy may be full.   our

5 This then is the message which we have heard of Him, and <u>declare</u> to you, that God is light, and in Him is no darkness at all.   tell

6 If we say that we have fellowship with Him, and walk in darkness, we lie, and <u>do</u> not the truth: practice

7 But if we walk in the light, as He is in the light, we have fellowship one with another, and the blood of Je'sus Christ His Son cleanses us from all sin.

8 If we say that we have no sin, we deceive ourselves, and the truth is not in us.   ECC. 7:20

9 If we confess our sins, He is faithful and just to forgive us *our* sins, and to cleanse us from all unrighteousness.

10 If we say that we have not sinned, we make Him a liar, and His word is not in us.

CHAPTER 2

MY little children, these things write I to you, that you sin not. And if any man sin, we have <u>an advocate</u> with the Father, Je'sus Christ the righteous: a friend

2 And He is the <u>propitiation</u> for our sins: and not for ours only, but also for *the sins of* the whole world.   LEV. 16:10   substitution

3 And hereby we do know that we know Him, if we keep His commandments.

4 He that says, I know Him, and keeps not His commandments, is a liar, and the truth is not in him.

5 But whoso keeps His word, in him <u>verily</u> is the love of God perfected: hereby know we that we are in Him.   truly

6 He that says he <u>abides</u> in Him ought himself also so to walk, even as He walked.   lives

7 Brethren, I write no new commandment to you, but an old commandment which you had from the beginning. The old commandment is the word which you have heard from the beginning.

8 Again, a new commandment I write to you, which thing is true in Him and in you: because the darkness is past, and the true light now shines.

9 He that says he is in the light, and <u>hates</u> his brother, is in darkness even until now.   disrespects

10 He that loves his brother <u>abides</u> in the light, and there is none occasion of stumbling in him.

11 But he that <u>hates</u> his brother is in darkness, and walks in darkness, and knows not where he goes, because that darkness has blinded his eyes.

12 I write to you, little children, because your sins are forgiven you for His name's sake.

13 I write to you, fathers, because you have known Him *that is* from the beginning. I write to you, young men, because you have overcome the wicked one. I write to you, little children, because you have known the Father.

14 I have written to you, fathers, because you have known Him *that is* from the beginning. I have written to you, young men, because you are strong, and the word of God <u>abides</u> in you, and you have overcome the wicked one.   lives

15 Love not the world, neither the things *that are* in the world. If any man love the world, the love of the Father is not in him.

16 For all that *is* in the world, the <u>lust</u> of the flesh, and the <u>lust</u> of the eyes, and the pride of life, is not of the Father, but is of the world.   desire

17 And the world passes away, and the <u>lust</u> thereof: but he that does the will of God <u>abides</u> for ever.

18 Little children, it is the last time: and as you have heard that antichrist shall come, even now are there many antichrists; whereby we know that it is the last time.

19 They went out from us, but they were not of us; for if they had been of us, they would *no doubt* have continued with us: but *they went out*, that they might be made <u>manifest</u> that they were not all of us.   known

20 But you have an <u>unction</u> from the Holy One, and you know all things.   anointing

21 I have not written to you because you know not the truth, but because you know it, and that no lie is of the truth.

22 Who is a liar but he that denies that Je'sus is the Christ? He is antichrist, that denies the Father and the Son.

23 Whosoever denies the Son, the same has not the Father: [*but*] *he that acknowledges the Son has the Father also*.

24 Let that therefore <u>abide</u> in you, which you have heard from the beginning. If that which you have heard from the beginning shall remain in you, you also shall continue in the Son, and in the Father.   live

25 And this is the promise that He has promised us, *even* eternal life.

26 These *things* have I written to you concerning them that <u>seduce</u> you.   deceive

27 But the anointing which you have received of Him <u>abides</u> in you, and you need not that any man teach you: but as the same anointing teaches you of all things, and is truth, and is no lie,

and even as it has taught you, you shall <u>abide</u> in Him.

28 And now, little children, abide in Him; that, when He shall appear, we may have confidence, and not be ashamed before Him at His coming.

29 If you know that He is righteous, you know that every one that does righteousness is born of Him.

CHAPTER 3

BEHOLD, what manner of love the Father has bestowed upon us, that we should be called the sons of God: therefore the world knows us not, because it knew Him not.

2 Beloved, now are we the sons of God, and it does not yet appear what we shall be: but we know that, when He shall appear, we shall be like Him; for we shall see Him as He is.

3 And every man that has this hope in Him purifies himself, even as He is pure.

4 Whosoever commits sin transgresses also the law: for sin is the <u>transgression</u> of the law.   *disobedience*

5 And you know that He was <u>manifested</u> to take away our sins; and in Him is no sin.   *made known*

6 Whosoever <u>abides</u> in Him sins not: whosoever sins has not seen Him, neither known Him.   *lives*

7 Little children, let no man deceive you: he that does righteousness is righteous, even as He is righteous.

8 He that commits sin is of the <u>devil</u>; for the <u>devil</u> sinned from the beginning. For this purpose the Son of God was <u>manifested</u>, that He might destroy the works of the <u>devil</u>.   *Satan - known*

9 Whosoever is born of God does not <u>commit</u> sin; for His seed remains in him: and he cannot sin, because he is born of God.   *practice*

10 In this the children of God are <u>manifest</u>, and the children of the <u>devil</u>: whosoever does not righteousness is not of God, neither he that loves not his brother.

11 For this is the <u>message</u> that you heard from the beginning, that we should love one another.   *commandment*

12 Not as Cain, *who* was of that wicked one, and slew his brother. And wherefore slew he him? Because his own works were evil, and his brother's righteous.   GEN. 4:8

13 Marvel not, my brethren, if the world <u>hate</u> you.   *abhors*

14 We know that we have passed from death to life, because we love the brethren. He that loves not *his* brother <u>abides</u> in death.   *lives*

15 Whosoever <u>hates</u> his brother is a murderer: and you know that no murderer has eternal life <u>abiding</u> in him.

16 Hereby perceive we the love *of God*, because He laid down His life for us: and we ought to lay down *our* lives for the brethren.

17 But whoso has this world's good, and sees his brother have need, and shuts up his <u>bowels *of compassion*</u> from him, how dwells the love of God in him?   *heart of mercy*

18 My little children, let us not love in word, neither in <u>tongue</u>; but in <u>deed</u> and in truth.   *talk - action*

19 And hereby we know that we are of the truth, and shall <u>assure</u> our hearts before Him.   set

20 For if our heart condemn us, God is greater than our heart, and knows all things.

21 Beloved, if our heart condemn us not, *then* have we confidence toward God.

22 And whatsoever we ask, we receive of Him, because we <u>keep</u> His commandments, and do those things that are pleasing in His sight.   obey

23 And this is His commandment, That we should believe on the name of His Son Je'sus Christ, and love one another, as He gave us commandment.

24 And he that keeps His commandments dwells in Him, and He in him. And hereby we know that He abides in us, by the Spirit which He has given us.

CHAPTER 4

BELOVED, believe not every spirit, but <u>try</u> the spirits whether they are of God: because many false prophets are gone out into the world. Dear friends - test

2 Hereby know you the Spirit of God: Every spirit that confesses that Je'sus Christ is come in the flesh is of God:

3 And every spirit that confesses not that Je'sus Christ is come in the flesh is not of God: and this is that *spirit* of antichrist, whereof you have heard that it should come; and even now already is it in the world.

4 You are of God, little children, and have overcome them: because greater is He that is in you, than he that is in the world.

5 They are of the world: therefore speak they of the world, and the world <u>hears</u> them.   listens to

6 We are of God: he that knows God hears us; he that is not of God hears not us. Hereby know we the spirit of truth, and the spirit of error.

7 Beloved, let us love one another: for love is of God; and every one that loves is born of God, and knows God.

8 He that loves not knows not God; for God is love.

9 In this was <u>manifested</u> the love of God toward us, because that God sent His only begotten Son into the world, that we might live through Him.   made known

10 Herein is love, not that we loved God, but that He loved us, and sent His Son *to be* the <u>propitiation</u> for our sins.   atoning sacrifice

11 Beloved, if God so loved us, we ought also to love one another.

12 No man has seen God at any time. If we love one another, God dwells in us, and His love is perfected in us.

13 Hereby know we that we dwell in Him, and He in us, because He has given us of His Spirit.

14 And we have seen and do <u>testify</u> that the Father sent the Son *to be* the Savior of the world.   speak

15 Whosoever shall <u>confess</u> that Je'sus is the Son of God, God dwells in him, and he in God.   admit

16 And we have known and believed the love that God has to us. God is

love; and he that dwells in love dwells in God, and God in him.

17 Herein is our love made <u>perfect</u>, that we may have <u>boldness</u> in the day of judgment: because as He is, so are we in this world.   complete - confidence

18 There is no fear in love; but perfect love casts out fear: because fear has <u>torment</u>. He that fears is not made perfect in love.   punishment

19 We love Him, because He first loved us.

20 If a man say, I love God, and hates his brother, he is a liar: for he that loves not his brother whom he has seen, how can he love God whom he has not seen?

21 And this commandment have we from Him, That he who loves God love his brother also.

CHAPTER 5

WHOSOEVER believes that Je'sus is the Christ is born of God: and every one that loves Him that begat loves Him also that is begotten of Him.

2 By this we know that we love the children of God, when we love God, and <u>keep</u> His commandments.   obey

3 For this is the love of God, that we <u>keep</u> His commandments: and His commandments are not <u>grievous</u>.   burdensome

4 For whatsoever is born of God overcomes the world: and this is the victory that overcomes the world, *even* our faith.

5 Who is he that overcomes the world, but he that believes that Je'sus is the Son of God?

6 This is He that came by water and blood, *even* Je'sus Christ; not by water only, but by water and blood. And it is the Spirit that bears witness, because the Spirit is truth.

7 For there are three that bear record in heaven, the Father, the <u>Word</u>, and the Ho'ly <u>Ghost</u>: and these three are one.   Jesus - Spirit

8 And there are three that bear witness in earth, the spirit, and the water, and the blood: and these three agree in one.

9 If we receive the witness of men, the witness of God is greater: for this is the witness of God which He has <u>testified</u> of His Son.   told

10 He that believes on the Son of God has the witness in himself: he that believes not God has made Him a liar; because he believes not the record that God gave of His Son.

11 And this is the record, that God has given to us eternal life, and this life is in His Son.

12 He that has the Son has life; *and* he that has not the Son of God has not life.

13 These things have I written to you that believe on the name of the Son of God; that you may know that you have eternal life, and that you may believe <u>on</u> the name of the Son of God.   in

14 And this is the confidence that we have in Him, that, if we ask any thing according to His will, He hears us:

15 And if we know that He hear us,

whatsoever we ask, we know that we have the petitions that we desired of Him.

16 If any man see his brother sin a sin *which is* not to death, he shall ask, and He shall give him life for them that sin not to death. There is a sin to death: I do not say that he shall pray for it.

17 All <u>unrighteousness</u> is sin: and there is a sin not to death.   wrongdoing

18 We know that whosoever is born of God sins not; but he that is <u>be-gotten</u> of God keeps himself, and that <u>wicked one</u> touches him not.

born - i.e. Satan

19 *And* we know that we are of God, and the whole world lies in wickedness.

20 And we know that the Son of God is come, and has given us an understanding, that we may know Him that is true, and we are in Him that is true, *even* in His Son Je'sus Christ. This is the true God, and eternal life.

21 Little children, <u>keep</u> yourselves from idols. Amen.   guard

THE SECOND LETTER OF

JOHN

THE elder to the <u>elect</u> lady and her children, whom I love in the truth; and not I only, but also all they that have known the truth; chosen

2 For the truth's sake, which <u>dwells</u> in us, and shall be with us for ever. lives

3 Grace be with you, mercy, *and* peace, from God the Father, and from the Lord Je'sus Christ, the Son of the Father, in truth and love.

4 I rejoiced greatly that I found of your children walking in truth, as we have received a commandment from the Father.

5 And now I <u>beseech</u> you, lady, not as though I wrote a new commandment to you, but that which we had from the beginning, that we love one another. beg

6 And this is love, that we walk after His commandments. This is the commandment, That, as you have heard from the beginning, you should walk in it.

7 For many deceivers are entered into the world, who confess not that Je'sus Christ is come in the flesh. This is a deceiver and an antichrist.

8 Look to yourselves, that we lose not those things which we have <u>wrought</u>, but that we receive a full reward worked for

9 Whosoever transgresses, and <u>abides</u> not in the <u>doctrine</u> of Christ, <u>has not</u> God. He that <u>abides</u> in the <u>doctrine</u> of Christ, he has both the Father and the Son. lives - teaching - belongs not to

10 If there come any to you, and bring not this <u>doctrine</u>, receive him not into *your* house, neither bid him God speed:

11 For he that bids him God speed is <u>partaker</u> of his evil deeds. sharing

12 Having many things to write to you, I would not *write* with paper and ink: but I trust to come to you, and speak face to face, that <u>our</u> joy may be full. your

13 The children of your <u>elect</u> sister greet you. Amen.

THE THIRD LETTER OF

JOHN

THE elder to the wellbeloved Ga'ius, whom I love in the truth.

2 Beloved, I wish above all things that you may prosper and be in health, even as your soul prospers.

3 For I rejoiced greatly, when the brethren came and testified of the truth that is in you, even as you walk in the truth.

4 I have no greater joy than to hear that my children walk in truth.

5 Beloved, you do faithfully whatsoever you do to the brethren, and to strangers;

6 Which have borne witness of your underline{charity} before the church: whom if you underline{bring} forward on their journey after a godly sort, you shall do well: love - help

7 Because that for His name's sake they went forth, underline{taking} nothing of the Gen'tiles.   accepting

8 We therefore ought to receive such, that we might be fellow helpers to the truth.

9 I wrote to the church : but Di-ot'-re-phes, who loves to have the pre-eminence among them, receives us not.

10 Wherefore, if I come, I will remember his deeds which he did, underline{prating against} us with underline{malicious} words: and not content therewith, neither did he himself receive the brethren, and forbid them that would, and underline{cast} *them* out of the church.   accusing - wicked - puts

11 Beloved, follow not that which is evil, but that which is good. He that does good is of God: but he that does evil has not seen God.

12 De-me'tri-us has good report of all *men*, and of the truth itself: yea, and we *also* bear underline{record}; and you know that our underline{record} is true.   witness

13 I had many things to write, but I will not with ink and pen write to you:

14 But I trust I shall shortly see you, and we shall speak face to face. Peace *be* to you. *Our* friends underline{salute} you. Greet the friends by name.   greet

JUDE

OUTLINE

SURVEY

The General Epistle of Jude was written as a warning against certain nominal Christians who threatened to undermine and destroy the fellowship of believers by their immoral character and conduct. Those who follow in their path can be certain of God's judgment. Indeed, the Old Testament bears witness to six judgments of God upon just such sins as these persons practice (vv. 5-11). As if to emphasize their ripeness for God's wrath, Jude adds a twelvefold description of their guilt (vv. 12-16).

In contrast to the destructive and worldly attitude of the false teachers, believers are to show a constructive and spiritual love. Remembering the mercy of christ towards them, they are also to show mercy towards those engulfed in these evils. Perhaps some will thus be saved (vv. 12-23).

The beautiful doxology (vv.24, 25) is especially appropriate for those in great temptation.

In addition to his use of the Old Testament, Jude shows a knowledge of current Jewish tradition. (References in Jude 9,14, although not to the Old Testament, are found in other Jewish writings of his day.) The epistle bears a particularly close relationship to 2 Peter, and it is possible that both letters were destined for the same group of Christians. Although a number of scholars believe that 2 Peter made use of Jude, it is more likely the earlier of the two. The evils which 2 Peter (2.1; 3.3) predicts are described in Jude (vv.4,18, 19) as having come in accordance with the apostolic prophecy made to them.

AUTHOR

According to tradition, Jude is the brother of Jesus (Mt. 13.55) who became a believer only after the resurrection (Jn 7.5; Ac 1.14), and whose brother, James, became a leading figure in the early Church (Ac 15.13; Gl 1.19). This accords with Jude's mention of James (v. 1) as though he were widely known and with his exclusion of himself from the apostles. Within this framework a date between A.D. 70 and 80 may be suggested for this letter.

E.E.E.

THE LETTER OF

JUDE

JUDE, the servant of Je'sus Christ, and brother of James, to them that are <u>sanctified</u> by God the Father, and <u>preserved</u> in Je'sus Christ, *and* called: called - kept

2 Mercy to you, and peace, and love, be multiplied.

3 Beloved, when I gave all diligence to write to you of the common salvation, it was needful for me to write to you, and <u>exhort</u> *you* that you should earnestly contend for the faith which was once delivered to the saints. urge

4 For there are certain men crept in <u>unawares</u>, who were before of old <u>ordained to</u> this condemnation, ungodly men, turning the grace of our God into <u>lasciviousness</u>, and denying the only Lord God, and our Lord Je'sus Christ. GAL. 2:4 2 PET. 2:1 unnoticed - known for - immorality

5 I will therefore put you in remembrance, though you once knew this, how that the Lord, having saved the people out of the land of E'gypt, afterward destroyed them that believed not.

6 And the angels which kept not their first <u>estate</u>, but left their own habitation, He has reserved in <u>everlasting</u> <u>chains</u> under darkness to the judgment of the great day. position - eternal bonds

7 Even as Sod'om and Go-mor'rha, and the cities about them in like manner, giving themselves over to fornication, and <u>going after strange flesh</u>, are set forth for an example, suffering the <u>vengeance</u> of eternal fire. GEN. 19:7 unnatural ways - punishment

8 Likewise also these *filthy* dreamers defile the flesh, despise <u>dominion</u>, and speak evil of <u>dignities</u>. authority - celestial beings

9 Yet Mi'chael the archangel, when <u>contending</u> with the <u>devil</u> he disputed about the body of Mo'ses, dare not bring against him a railing <u>accusation</u>, but said, The Lord rebuke you. DAN. 10:13 ZEC. 3:2 disputing - satan - judgment

10 But these speak evil of those things which they know not: but what they know naturally, as brute beasts, in those things they <u>corrupt</u> themselves. destroy

11 Woe to them! for they have gone in the way of Cain, and ran greedily after the error of Ba'laam for reward, and perished in the <u>gainsaying</u> of Co're. NUM. 22:25 rebellion

12 These are spots in your feasts of <u>charity</u>, when they feast with you, feeding themselves without <u>fear</u>: clouds *they are* without water, carried about of winds; trees whose fruit wither, without fruit, twice dead, plucked up by the roots; love - respect

13 Raging waves of the sea, foaming out their own shame; wandering stars, to whom is reserved the blackness of darkness for ever.

14 And E'noch also, the seventh from Ad'am, prophesied of these, saying, Behold, the Lord come with ten thousands of His saints,

15 To execute judgment upon all, and to <u>convince</u> all that are ungodly among

them of all their ungodly deeds which they have ungodly committed, and of all their hard *speeches* which ungodly sinners have spoken against Him.

convict

16 These are <u>murmurers</u>, complainers, walking after their own lusts; and their mouth speak great swelling *words*, having men's persons in admiration <u>because of</u> advantage.

grumblers - to gain an

17 But, beloved, remember you the words which were <u>spoken before</u> of the apostles of our Lord Je'sus Christ;

foretold

18 How that they told you there should be mockers in the last time, who should walk after their own ungodly <u>lusts</u>.

desires

19 These be they who <u>separate</u> themselves, sensual, having not the Spirit.

divide

20 But you, beloved, building up yourselves on your most holy faith, praying in the Ho'ly <u>Ghost</u>,   Spirit

21 Keep yourselves in the love of God, looking for the mercy of our Lord Je'sus Christ to eternal life.

22 And <u>of</u> some have compassion, <u>making</u> a difference: on - who doubt

23 And others save with fear, pulling *them* out of the fire; hating even the garment <u>spotted</u> by the flesh.

ZEC. 3:4   stained

24 Now to Him that is able to keep you from falling, and to present *you* faultless before the presence of His glory with exceeding joy,

25 To the only wise God our Savior, *be* glory and majesty, dominion and power, both now and ever. Amen.

REVELATION

OUTLINE

SURVEY

The key to this book is found in the opening verse: "The Revelation of Jesus Christ." The main purpose is to reveal the person of the Lord Jesus Christ as the Redeemer of the world and as the conqueror of evil, and to present in symbolic form the program by which He will carry out His work.

The structure of Revelation is built on four great visions, each of which contains one aspect of the person of Christ in His capacity as the judge of the world. Each is laid in a different scene and each advances the thought of the book one step.

Revelation begins with letters addressed by the Lord to seven actual churches of the apostolic age which were typical of the churches of all time. In them He voices His commendation and criticism, concluding with a warning and a promise.

Beginning with the fourth chapter, the seer is transferred to heaven and beholds "things which must be hereafter" (4.1). Through a succession of judgments, the seals, the trumpets, and the bowls, the earth is punished for its sin, and the great day of God's wrath is ushered in. No indication is given of the length of the process, though it seems to accelerate toward the end.

In the seventeenth chapter through the twentieth, we are given a detailed view of the consummation of the age. The return of Christ in glory with the armies of heaven (19.11-21), the establishment of the Kingdom and its conclusion in the final judgment of the white throne (20.1-15), and the creation of a new world (21.1-8) are depicted. The last vision continues the third by describing more fully the nature of the city of God (21.9—22.5).

The conclusion of the book is a call to devotion. If Christ is going to return, holiness and industry are obligatory upon His people. The prayer at the end should express the desire of all Christians: "Even so, come, Lord Jesus" (22.20).

AUTHOR

The author of Revelation is plainly named John. He was a prisoner on the island of Patmos, where he had been exiled because of his Christian faith (1.4-9; 22.8). He was well known among the churches of Asia, and was classed as a "prophet" (22.9). Justin Martyr (about A.D. 135) and Irenaeus (about A.D. 180) both quote this book verbatim, and attribute it to John, an apostle of Christ. Conservative thought has through the centuries attributed this book to John, the son of Zebedee, who probably wrote it about A.D. 95 in the reign of Domitian. Even though the subject matter is radically different from that of the Gospel of John, both works exhibit the same straight forward simple Greek style, which is also found in the three General Epistles by John (I, II, III John). The Western church accepted it as canonical; the Eastern church did not receive it until about the year 500. This was due to their hesitance to accept a book whose interpretation seemed so difficult due to its vision-type contents. The grandeur of the book, and its holy contents, give its own internal witness to its supernatural origin, inspiration, and place in the canon.

M.C.T./G.G.C.

THE
REVELATION
TO JOHN
(The Apocalypse)

CHAPTER 1

THE Revelation of Je'sus Christ, which God gave to Him, to show to His servants things which must <u>shortly</u> come to pass; and He sent and signified *it* by His angel to His servant John: soon

2 Who bare record of the word of God, and of the testimony of Je'sus Christ, and of all things that he saw.

3 Blessed *is* he that reads, and they that hear the words of this prophecy, and keep those things which are written therein: for the time *is* at hand.

4 John to the seven churches which are in A'sia: Grace *be* to you, and peace, from Him which is, and which was, and which is to come; and from the seven Spirits which are before His throne;   ISA. 11:2

5 And from Je'sus Christ, *who is* the faithful witness, *and* the First Begotten of the dead, and the Prince of the kings of the earth. To Him that loved us, and washed us from our sins in His own blood,   PS. 89:27

6 And has made us kings and priests to God and His Father; to Him *be* glory and dominion for ever and ever. Amen.   EX. 19:6 ISA. 61:6

7 Behold, He comes with clouds; and every eye shall see Him, and they *also* which pierced Him: and all kindreds of the earth shall <u>wail</u> because of Him. Even so, Amen.   DAN. 7:13 ZEC. 12:10 mourn

8 I am <u>Al'pha and O'me-ga</u>, the beginning and the ending, say the Lord, which is, and which was, and which is to come, the Almighty.   EX. 3:14 Beginning and End

9 I John, who also am your brother, and companion in <u>tribulation</u>, and in the kingdom and patience of Je'sus Christ, was in the isle that is called Pat'mos, for the word of God, and for the <u>testimony</u> of Je'sus Christ. suffering - gospel witness

10 I was in the Spirit on the Lord's day, and heard behind me a great voice, as of a trumpet,

11 Saying, I am Al'pha and O'me-ga, the first and the last: and, What you see, write in a book, and send *it* to the seven churches which are in A'sia; to Eph'e-sus, and to Smyr'na, and to Per'ga-mos, and to Thy-a-ti'ra, and to Sar'dis, and to Phil-a-del'phi-a, and to La-od-i-ce'a.

12 And I turned to see the voice that spoke with me. And being turned, I saw seven golden candlesticks;   ZEC. 4:2

13 And in the midst of the seven candlesticks *one* like to the Son of man, clothed with a garment down to the foot, and <u>girt</u> about the <u>paps</u> with a golden girdle. DAN. 7:13 wrapped - chest

14 His head and *His* hairs *were* white like wool, as white as snow; and His eyes *were* as a flame of fire;

15 And His feet like to fine brass, as if they burned in a furnace; and His voice as the sound of many waters.

16 And He had in His right hand seven stars: and out of His mouth went a sharp two edged sword: and His countenance *was* as the sun shines in His strength.

17 And when I saw Him, I fell at His feet as dead. And He laid His right hand upon me, saying to me, Fear not; I am the First and the Last: ISA. 44:2

18 I *am* He that lives, and was dead; and, behold, I am alive for evermore, Amen; and have the keys of hell and of death.   hades

19 Write the things which you have seen, and the things which are, and the things which shall be hereafter;

20 The mystery of the seven stars which you saw in My right hand, and the seven golden candlesticks. The seven stars are the angels of the seven churches: and the seven candlesticks which you saw are the seven churches.   secret - messengers

CHAPTER 2

TO the angel of the church of Eph'e-sus write; These things says He that holds the seven stars in His right hand, who walks in the midst of the seven golden candlesticks;

2 I know your works, and your labor, and your patience, and how you can not bear them which are evil: and you have tried them which say they are apostles, and are not, and have found them liars: endure

3 And have borne, and have patience, and for My name's sake have labored, and have not fainted.   perserverence - grown weary

4 Nevertheless I have *somewhat* against you, because you have left your first love.

5 Remember therefore from where you are fallen, and repent, and do the first works; or else I will come to you quickly, and will remove your candlestick out of its place, except you repent.   lampstand

6 But this you have, that you hate the deeds of the Nic-o-la'i-tanes, which I also hate.   i.e., make believe christians

7 He that has an ear, let him hear what the Spirit says to the churches; To him that overcomes will I give to eat of the tree of life, which is in the midst of the paradise of God.   GEN. 2:9

8 And to the angel of the church in Smyr'na write; These things says the First and the Last, which was dead, and is alive;   ISA. 44:6 messenger

9 I know your works, and tribulation, and poverty, (but you are rich) and *I know* the blasphemy of them which say they are Jews, and are not, but *are* the synagogue of Sa'tan.   slander

10 Fear none of those things which you shall suffer: behold, the devil shall cast *some* of you into prison, that you may be tried; and you shall have tribulation ten days: be you faithful to death, and I will give you a crown of life.   tested - persecution

11 He that has an ear, let him hear what the Spirit says to the churches; He that overcomes shall not be hurt of the second death.

12 And to the angel of the church in Per'ga-mos write; These things says He

which has the sharp sword with two edges; messenger

13 I know your works, and where you dwell, *even* where Sa'tan's seat *is*: and you hold fast My name, and have not denied My faith, even in those days wherein An'ti-pas *was* My faithful martyr, who was slain among you, where Sa'tan dwell. remain true to

14 But I have a few things against you, because you have there them that hold the doctrine of Ba'laam, who taught Ba'lak to cast a stumbling block before the children of Is'ra-el, to eat things sacrificed to idols, and to commit fornication.

NUM. 31:16 teaching

15 So have you also them that hold the doctrine of the Nic-o-la'i-tanes, which thing I hate. i.e., make believe christians

16 Repent; or else I will come to you quickly, and will fight against them with the sword of My mouth.

17 He that has an ear, let him hear what the Spirit says to the churches; To him that overcomes will I give to eat of the hidden manna, and will give him a white stone, and in the stone a new name written, which no man knows saving he that receives it.

ISA. 62:2

18 And to the angel of the church in Thy-a-ti'ra write; These things says the Son of God, who has His eyes like to a flame of fire, and His feet *are* like fine brass; messenger

19 I know your works, and charity, and service, and faith, and your patience, and your works; and the last *to be* more than the first. deeds - love - perseverance

20 Notwithstanding I have a few things against you, because you permit that woman Jez'e-bel, which calls herself a prophetess, to teach and to seduce My servants to commit fornication, and to eat things sacrificed to idols. mislead

21 And I gave her space to repent of her fornication; and she repented not. time

22 Behold, I will cast her into a bed, and them that commit adultery with her into great tribulation, except they repent of their deeds. unfaithfulness - trouble

23 And I will kill her children with death; and all the churches shall know that I am He which searches the reins and hearts: and I will give to every one of you according to your works. PS. 62:12 JER. 17:10 minds

24 But to you I say, and to the rest in Thy-a-ti'ra, as many as have not this doctrine, and which have not known the depths of Sa'tan, as they speak; I will put upon you none other burden. teaching - deep things - no

25 But that which you have *already* hold fast till I come. firm

26 And he that overcomes, and keeps My works to the end, to him will I give power over the nations: is doing

27 And he shall rule them with a rod of iron; as the vessels of a potter shall they be broken to shivers: even as I received of My Father. PS. 2:9 pieces

28 And I will give him the morning star.

29 He that has an ear, let him hear what the Spirit says to the churches.

CHAPTER 3

AND to the <u>angel</u> of the church in Sar'dis write; These things says He that has the seven Spirits of God, and the seven stars; I know your works, that you have a name that you live, and are dead.   messenger

2 Be watchful, and strengthen the things which remain, that are ready to die: for I have not found your works <u>perfect</u> before God.   complete

3 Remember therefore how you have received and heard, and hold fast, and repent. If therefore you shall not watch, I will come on you as a thief, and you shall not know what hour I will come upon you.

4 You have a few names even in Sar'dis which have not defiled their garments; and they shall walk with Me in white: for they are worthy.

5 He that overcomes, the same shall be clothed in white <u>raiment</u>; and I will not blot out his name out of the book of life, but I will confess his name before My Father, and before His angels.   EX. 32:32   clothes

6 He that has an ear, let him hear what the Spirit says to the churches.

7 And to the <u>angel</u> of the church in Phil-a-del'phi-a write; These things says He that is holy, He that is true, He that has the key of Da'vid, He that opens, and no man shuts; and shuts, and no man opens;   ISA. 22:22   messenger

8 I know your works: behold, I have set before you an open door, and no man can shut it: for you have a little <u>strength</u>, and have kept My word, and have not denied My name.   power

9 Behold, I will make them of the synagogue of Sa'tan, which say they are Jews, and are not, but do lie; behold, I will make them to come and worship before your feet, and to know that I have loved you.   ISA. 60:14

10 Because you have kept the word of My <u>patience</u>, I also will keep you from the hour of <u>temptation</u>, which shall come upon all the world, to <u>try</u> them that dwell upon the earth.   perseverance - testing - test

11 Behold, I come quickly: hold that fast which you have, that no man take your crown.

12 Him that overcomes will I make a pillar in the temple of My God, and he shall go no more out: and I will write upon him the name of My God, and the name of the city of My God, *which is* new Je-ru'sa-lem, which comes down out of heaven from My God: and *I will write upon him* My new name.   ISA. 62:2

13 He that has an ear, let him hear what the Spirit says to the churches.

14 And to the <u>angel</u> of the church of the La-od-i-ce'ans write; These things says the Amen, the faithful and true witness, the beginning of the creation of God;   messenger

15 I know your works, that you are neither cold nor hot: I would you were cold or hot.

16 So then because you are lukewarm, and neither cold nor hot, I will <u>spew</u> you out of My mouth.   spit

17 Because you say, I am rich, and increased with goods, and have need of nothing; and know not that

you are wretched, and miserable, and poor, and blind, and naked: HOS. 12:8

18 I counsel you to buy of Me gold tried in the fire, that you may be rich; and white raiment, that you may be clothed, and *that* the shame of your nakedness do not appear; and anoint your eyes with eye salve, that you may see.   advise - clothes

19 As many as I love, I rebuke and chasten: be zealous therefore, and repent. PROV. 3:12 reprove - discipline - earnest

20 Behold, I stand at the door, and knock: if any man hear My voice, and open the door, I will come in to him, and will sup with him, and he with Me. dine

21 To him that overcomes will I grant to sit with Me in My throne, even as I also overcame, and am set down with My Father in His throne.

22 He that has an ear, let him hear what the Spirit says to the churches.

CHAPTER 4

AFTER this I looked, and, behold, a door *was* opened in heaven: and the first voice which I heard *was* as it were of a trumpet talking with me; which said, Come up here, and I will show you things which must be hereafter.   EX. 19:24-25

2 And immediately I was in the Spirit: and, behold, a throne was set in heaven, and *One* sat on the throne.   EZE. 1:28

3 And He that sat was to look upon like a jasper and a sardine stone: and *there was* a rainbow round about the throne, in sight like to an emerald.

     EZE. 1:28 appearance

4 And round about the throne *were* four and twenty seats: and upon the seats I saw four and twenty elders sitting, clothed in white raiment; and they had on their heads crowns of gold. i.e., could be 12 Jewish tribes and 12 apostles - clothes

5 And out of the throne proceeded lightnings and thunderings and voices: and *there were* seven lamps of fire burning before the throne, which are the seven Spirits of God. ZEC. 4:2

6 And before the throne *there was* a sea of glass like to crystal: and in the midst of the throne, and round about the throne, *were* four beasts full of eyes before and behind.

     EZE. 1:5 living creatures

7 And the first beast *was* like a lion, and the second beast like a calf, and the third beast had a face as a man, and the fourth beast *was* like a flying eagle.   EZE. 1:10

8 And the four beasts had each of them six wings about *him*; and *they were* full of eyes inside: and they rest not day and night, saying, Holy, holy, holy, Lord God Almighty, which was, and is, and is to come.   ISA. 6:2-3 cease

9 And when those beasts give glory and honor and thanks to Him that sat on the throne, who lives for ever and ever,   PS. 47:8 living creatures

10 The four and twenty elders fall down before Him that sat on the throne, and worship Him that lives for ever and ever, and cast their crowns before the throne, saying, ? 12 tribes, 12 apostles

11 You are worthy, O Lord, to receive glory and honor and power: for You have created all things, and for Your pleasure they are and were created.

CHAPTER 5

AND I saw in the right hand of Him that sat on the throne a book written <u>inside and on the backside</u>, sealed with seven seals. EZE. 2:9 *i.e., both sides*

2 And I saw a strong angel proclaiming with a loud voice, Who is worthy to open the book, and to loose the seals thereof?

3 And no man in heaven, nor in earth, neither under the earth, was able to open the book, neither to look thereon.

4 And I wept <u>much</u>, because no man was found worthy to open and to read the book, neither to look <u>thereon</u>. *greatly - on it*

5 And one of the elders says to me, Weep not: behold, the <u>Lion</u> of the tribe of Ju'da, the <u>Root</u> of Da'vid, has <u>prevailed</u> to open the book, and to loose the seven seals thereof. *i.e., Christ - agreed*

6 And I beheld, and, lo, in the midst of the throne and of the four <u>beasts</u>, and in the midst of the elders, stood a <u>Lamb</u> as it had been slain, having seven horns and seven eyes, which are the seven Spirits of God sent forth into all the earth. *living creatures - i.e. Christ*

7 And He came and took the <u>book</u> out of the right hand of Him that sat upon the throne. *scroll*

8 And when He had taken the book, the four <u>beasts</u> and <u>four *and* twenty elders</u> fell down before the Lamb, having every one of them harps, and golden <u>vials</u> full of <u>odors</u>, which are the prayers of saints. *bowls - incense*

9 And they sung a new song, saying, You are worthy to take the book, and to open the seals thereof: for You were slain, and have redeemed us to God by Your blood out of every kindred, and tongue, and people, and nation;

10 And have made us to our God kings and priests: and we shall reign on the earth. EX. 19:6

11 And I beheld, and I heard the voice of many angels round about the throne and the <u>beasts</u> and the elders: and the number of them was ten thousand times ten thousand, and thousands of thousands; DAN. 7:10 *living creatures*

12 Saying with a loud voice, Worthy is the Lamb that was slain to receive power, and riches, and wisdom, and strength, and honor, and glory, and blessing.

13 And every creature which is in heaven, and on the earth, and under the earth, and such as are in the sea, and all that are in them, heard I saying, Blessing, and honor, and glory, and power, *be* to Him that sits upon the throne, and to the Lamb for ever and ever.

14 And the four <u>beasts</u> said, Amen. And the <u>four *and* twenty elders</u> fell down and worshiped him that lives for ever and ever. *living creatures*

CHAPTER 6

AND I saw when the Lamb opened one of the seals, and I heard, as it were the noise of thunder, one of the four <u>beasts</u> saying, Come and see.

2 And I saw, and behold a white horse: and <u>he</u> that sat on him had a bow; and a crown was given to

him: and <u>he</u> went forth conquering, and to conquer.   ZEC. 1:8 anti-christ

3 And when He had opened the second seal, I heard the second <u>beast</u> say, Come and see.   living creature

4 And there went out another horse *that was* <u>red</u>: and *power* was given to him that sat thereon to take peace from the earth, and that they should kill one another: and there was given to him a great sword.   i.e., color of war

5 And when He had opened the third seal, I heard the third <u>beast</u> say, Come and see. And I beheld, and lo a <u>black</u> horse; and he that sat on him had a pair of <u>balances</u> in his hand.   i.e., color of famine - scales

6 And I heard a voice in the midst of the four <u>beasts</u> say, A measure of wheat for a penny, and three measures of barley for a penny; and *see* you hurt not the oil and the wine.

7 And when He had opened the fourth seal, I heard the voice of the fourth <u>beast</u> say, Come and see.   living creature

8 And I looked, and behold a <u>pale</u> horse: and his name that sat on him was Death, and <u>Hell</u> followed with him. And power was given to them over the fourth part of the earth, to kill with sword, and with hunger, and with death, and with the <u>beasts</u> of the earth.   i.e., color of death - Hades - wild animal_s

9 And when He had opened the fifth seal, I saw under the altar the souls of them that were slain for the word of God, and for the <u>testimony</u> which they held: witness

10 And they cried with a loud voice,

saying, How long, O Lord, holy and true, do You not judge and avenge our blood on them that dwell on the earth?   ZEC. 1:12

11 And white robes were given to every one of them; and it was said to them, that they should <u>rest</u> yet for a little <u>season</u>, until their fellowservants also and their brethren, that should be killed as they *were*, should be fulfilled.   wait - while

12 And I beheld when He had opened the sixth seal, and, lo, there was a great earthquake; and the sun <u>became</u> black as sackcloth of hair, and the moon <u>became</u> as <u>blood</u>; JOEL 2:31 turned - red

13 And the stars of <u>heaven</u> fell to the earth, even as a fig tree casts her <u>untimely</u> figs, when she is shaken of a mighty wind.   ISA. 34:4 the sky - unripe

14 And the heaven departed as a scroll when it is rolled together; and every mountain and island were moved out of their places.

15 And the kings of the earth, and the great men, and the rich men, and the chief captains, and the mighty men, and every <u>bondman</u>, and every free man, hid themselves <u>in</u> the dens and in the rocks of the mountains; slave - among

16 And said to the mountains and rocks, Fall on us, and hide us from the face of Him that sits on the throne, and from the <u>wrath</u> of the Lamb: HOS. 10:8 anger

17 For the great day of His <u>wrath</u> is come; and who shall be able to stand?   PS. 76:7 JOEL 2:11

CHAPTER 7

AND after these things I saw four <u>an</u>gels standing on the four corners of

the earth, holding the four winds of the earth, that the wind should not blow on the earth, nor on the sea, nor on any tree. JER. 49:36 ZEC. 6:5 messengers

2 And I saw another <u>angel</u> ascending from the east, having the seal of the living God: and he cried with a loud voice to the four <u>angels</u>, to whom it was given to <u>hurt</u> the earth and the sea,   harm

3 Saying, <u>Hurt</u> not the earth, neither the sea, nor the trees, till we have sealed the servants of our God in their foreheads.   EZE. 9:4

4 And I heard the number of them which were sealed: *and there were* sealed an hundred *and* forty *and* four thousand of all the tribes of the children of Is'ra-el.

5 Of the tribe of Ju'da *were* sealed twelve thousand. Of the tribe of Reu'ben *were* sealed twelve thousand. Of the tribe of Gad *were* sealed twelve thousand.

6 Of the tribe of A'ser *were* sealed twelve thousand. Of the tribe of Nep'tha'lim *were* sealed twelve thousand. Of the tribe of Ma-nas'ses *were* sealed twelve thousand.

7 Of the tribe of Sim'e-on *were* sealed twelve thousand. Of the tribe of Le'vi *were* sealed twelve thousand. Of the tribe of Is'sa-char *were* sealed twelve thousand.

8 Of the tribe of Zab'u-lon *were* sealed twelve thousand. Of the tribe of Jo'seph *were* sealed twelve thousand. Of the tribe of Ben'ja-min *were* sealed twelve thousand.

9 After this I beheld, and, lo, a great multitude, which no man could number, of all nations, and kindreds, and people, and tongues, stood before the throne, and before the <u>Lamb</u>, clothed with white robes, and palms in their hands;   LEV. 23:40 i.e., Christ-God

10 And cried with a loud voice, saying, Salvation to our God which sits upon the throne, and to the Lamb.

11 And all the angels stood round about the throne, and *about* the elders and the four <u>beasts</u>, and fell before the throne on their faces, and worshiped God,   living creatures

12 Saying, Amen: Blessing, and glory, and wisdom, and thanksgiving, and honor, and power, and might, *be* to our God for ever and ever. Amen.

13 And one of the elders <u>answered</u>, saying to me, What are these which are <u>arrayed</u> in white robes? and from where came they?   asked - clothed

14 And I said to him, Sir, you know. And he said to me, These are they which came out of great tribulation, and have washed their robes, and made them white in the blood of the <u>Lamb</u>.   i.e., crucified Jesus

15 Therefore are they before the throne of God, and serve Him day and night in His temple: and He that sits on the throne shall dwell among them.

16 They shall hunger no more, neither thirst any more; neither shall the sun light on them, nor any heat.   PS. 121:6 ISA. 49:10

17 For the <u>Lamb</u> which is in the midst of the throne shall feed them, and shall lead them to living <u>fountains</u> of waters: and God shall wipe away all tears from their eyes.   EZE. 34:23 springs

CHAPTER 8

AND when He had opened the seventh seal, there was silence in heaven about the space of half an hour. 2 And I saw the seven <u>angels</u> which stood before God; and to them were given seven trumpets. _{messengers}

3 And another <u>angel</u> came and stood at the altar, having a golden censer; and there was given to him much incense, that he should offer *it* with the prayers of all <u>saints</u> upon the golden altar which was before the throne.

_{believers}

4 And the smoke of the incense, *which came* with the prayers of the saints, ascended up before God out of the <u>angel's</u> hand. _{went up}

5 And the <u>angel</u> took the censer, and filled it with fire of the altar, and cast *it* <u>into</u> the earth: and there were voices, and thunderings, and lightnings, and an earthquake. _{on}

6 And the seven <u>angels</u> which had the seven trumpets prepared themselves to <u>sound</u>. _{i.e., trumpets}

7 The first <u>angel</u> sounded, and there followed hail and fire mingled with blood, and they were cast upon the earth: and the third part of trees was burned up, and all green grass was burned up. _{messenger}

8 And the second <u>angel</u> sounded, and as it were a great mountain burning with fire was cast into the sea: and the third part of the sea became blood;

9 And the third part of the creatures which were in the sea, and had life, died; and the third part of the ships were destroyed.

10 And the third <u>angel</u> sounded, and there fell a great star from heaven, burning as it were a <u>lamp</u>, and it fell upon the third part of the rivers, and upon the fountains of waters; _{messenger}

11 And the name of the star is called Wormwood: and the third part of the waters became wormwood; and many men died of the waters, because they were made bitter. JER. 9:15

12 And the fourth <u>angel</u> sounded, and the third part of the sun was smitten, and the third part of the moon, and the third part of the stars; so as the third part of them was darkened, and the day shone not for a third part of it, and the night likewise. ZEC. 13:8-9

13 And I beheld, and heard an <u>angel</u> flying through the midst of heaven, saying with a loud voice, Woe, woe, woe, to the <u>inhabiters</u> of the earth by reason of the other voices of the trumpet of the three <u>angels</u>, which are yet to sound! _{messenger - people}

CHAPTER 9

AND the fifth <u>angel</u> sounded, and I saw a star fall from heaven to the earth: and to him was given the key of the bottomless pit.

2 And he opened the bottomless pit; and there arose a smoke out of the pit, as the smoke of a great furnace; and the sun and the air were darkened by reason of the smoke of the pit. JOEL 2:2,10

3 And there came out of the smoke locusts upon the earth: and to them was given power, as the scorpions of the earth have power.

4 And it was commanded them that thcy should not hurt the grass of the earth, neither any green thing, neither any tree; but only those men which have not the seal of God in their foreheads.   EX. 12:23 EZE. 9:4

5 And to them it was given that they should not kill them, but that they should be tormented five months: and their torment *was* as the torment of a scorpion, when he strikes a man.

6 And in those days shall men seek death, and shall not find it; and shall desire to die, and death shall flee from them.

7 And the shapes of the locusts *were* like to horses prepared to battle; and on their heads *were* as it were crowns like gold, and their faces *were* as the faces of men.   JOEL 2:4 looked

8 And they had hair <u>as</u> the hair of women, and their teeth <u>were as</u> *the teeth* of lions. JOEL 1:6 like - i.e., were like

9 And they had breastplates, as it were breastplates of iron; and the sound of their wings *was* as the sound of chariots of many horses running to battle.

10 And they had tails like to scorpions, and there were stings in their tails: and their power *was* to hurt men five months.

11 And they had a king over them, *which is* the angel of the bottomless pit, whose name in the He'brew <u>tongue</u> *is* A-bad'don, but in the Greek <u>tongue</u> has *his* name A-poll'yon.

                 language

12 One woe is past; *and*, behold, there come two woes more hereafter.

13 And the sixth <u>angel</u> sounded, and I heard a voice from the four horns of the golden altar which is before God,   messenger

14 Saying to the sixth <u>angel</u> which had the trumpet, Loose the four <u>angels</u> which are bound in the great river Eu-phra'tes.

15 And the four <u>angels</u> were loosed, which were prepared for an hour, and a day, and a month, and a year, for to slay the third part of men.

16 And the number of the army of the horsemen *were* <u>two hundred thousand thousand</u>: and I heard the number of them.   two hundred million

17 And thus I saw the horses in the vision, and them that sat on them, having breastplates of fire, and of ja-cinth, and <u>brimstone</u>: and the heads of the horses *were* as the heads of li-ons; and out of their mouths issued fire and smoke and brimstone. sulphur

18 By these three was the third part of men killed, by the fire, and by the smoke, and by the <u>brimstone</u>, which <u>issued</u> out of their mouths.   came

19 For their power is in their mouth, and in their tails: for their tails *were* like to serpents, and had heads, and with them they do hurt.

20 And the rest of the men which were not killed by these plagues yet repented not of the works of their hands, that they should not worship <u>devils</u>, and idols of gold, and silver, and brass, and stone, and of wood: which neither can see, nor hear, nor walk: demons

21 Neither repented they of their murders, nor of their sorceries, nor of their fornication, nor of their thefts.

CHAPTER 10

AND I saw another mighty <u>an-gel</u> come down from heaven, clothed with a cloud: and a rainbow *was* upon his head, and his face *was* as it were the sun, and his feet as pillars of fire: messenger

2 And he had in his hand a little book open: and he set his right foot upon the sea, and *his* left *foot* on the earth,

3 And cried with a loud voice, as *when* a lion roars: and when he had cried, seven thunders uttered their voices.

4 And when the seven thunders had <u>uttered</u> their voices, I was about to write: and I heard a voice from heaven saying to me, Seal up those things which the seven thunders uttered, and write them not.   spoke

5 And the <u>angel</u> which I saw stand upon the sea and upon the earth lifted up his hand to heaven,

6 And swear by Him that lives for ever and ever, who created heaven, and the things that therein are, and the earth, and the things that therein are, and the sea, and the things which are therein, that there should be time no longer:

7 But in the days of the voice of the seventh <u>angel</u>, when he shall begin to sound, the <u>mystery</u> of God should be finished, as He has declared to His servants the prophets.

messenger - secret

8 And the voice which I heard from heaven spoke to me again, and said, Go *and* take the little book which is open in the hand of the <u>angel</u> which stands upon the sea and upon the earth.
                    EZE. 2:8-9 messenger

9 And I went to the <u>angel</u>, and said to him, Give me the little book. And he said to me, Take *it*, and eat it up; and it shall make your belly bitter, but it shall be in your mouth sweet as honey.

10 And I took the little book out of the <u>angel's</u> hand, and ate it up; and it was in my mouth sweet as honey: and as soon as I had eaten it, my belly was bitter.   EZE. 3:3

11 And he said to me, You must <u>proph-esy</u> again before many peoples, and nations, and tongues, and kings.   speak

CHAPTER 11

AND there was given me a reed like to a rod: and the <u>angel</u> stood, saying, Rise, and measure the temple of God, and the altar, and them that worship therein.   messenger

2 But the court which is outside the temple <u>leave out</u>, and measure it not; for it is given to the Gen'tiles: and the holy city shall they tread under foot forty *and* two months.   exclude it

3 And I will give *power* to my <u>two wit-nesses</u>, and they shall <u>prophesy a thou-sand two hundred *and* threescore days</u>, clothed in sackcloth. i.e., thought to be

Moses and Elijah? or Enoch-Elijah - Speak - Zec-12:60(3 ½ Years)

4 These are the <u>two olive trees</u>, and the two <u>candlesticks</u> standing before the God of the earth.

ZEC. 4:3 ZEC. 4:12,14 Spirit filled witnesses - lampstands

5 And if any man will hurt them, fire proceeds out of their mouth, and devours their enemies: and if any man

will hurt them, he must in this manner be killed. NUM. 16:29

6 These have power to shut heaven, that it rain not in the days of their prophecy: and have power over waters to turn them to blood, and to smite the earth with all plagues, as often as they will. preaching

7 And when they shall have finished their testimony, the beast that ascends out of the bottomless pit shall make war against them, and shall overcome them, and kill them. i.e., Moses - Elijah witnessing

8 And their dead bodies *shall lie* in the street of the great city, which spiritually is called Sod'om and E'gypt, where also our Lord was crucified. i.e., Jerusalem

9 And they of the people and kindreds and tongues and nations shall see their dead bodies three days and an half, and shall not permit their dead bodies to be put in graves.

10 And they that dwell upon the earth shall rejoice over them, and make merry, and shall send gifts one to another; because these two prophets tormented them that dwelt on the earth. i.e., Moses - Elijah i.e., ?Elijah-Enoch

11 And after three days and an half the Spirit of life from God entered into them, and they stood upon their feet; and great fear fell upon them which saw them. EZE. 37:5

12 And they heard a great voice from heaven saying to them, Come up here. And they ascended up to heaven in a cloud; and their enemies beheld them. 2KGS. 2:11

13 And the same hour was there a great earthquake, and the tenth part of the city fell, and in the earthquake were slain of men seven thousand: and the remnant were affrighted, and gave glory to the God of heaven. terrified

14 The second woe is past; *and*, behold, the third woe comes quickly.

15 And the seventh angel sounded; and there were great voices in heaven, saying, The kingdoms of this world are become *the kingdoms* of our Lord, and of His Christ; and He shall reign for ever and ever. DAN. 7:14 messenger

16 And the four and twenty elders, which sat before God on their seats, fell upon their faces, and worshiped God,

17 Saying, We give You thanks, O Lord God Almighty, which are, and were, and are to come; because You have taken to You Your great power, and have reigned.

18 And the nations were angry, and Your wrath is come, and the time of the dead, that they should be judged, and that You should give reward to Your servants the prophets, and to the saints, and them that fear Your name, small and great; and should destroy them which destroy the earth.

19 And the temple of God was opened in heaven, and there was seen in His temple the ark of His testament: and there were lightnings, and voices, and thunderings, and an earthquake, and great hail.

CHAPTER 12

AND there appeared a great wonder in heaven; a woman clothed with the sun, and the moon under her feet,

and upon her head a crown of twelve stars: <u>i.e., Israel - sign - 12 tribes</u>

2 And she being with child cried, travailing in birth, and pained to be delivered. MIC. 4:10

3 And there appeared another <u>wonder</u> in heaven; and behold a great red <u>dragon</u>, having seven heads and ten horns, and seven crowns upon his heads. i.e., Satan

4 And his tail drew the third part of the stars of heaven, and did cast them to the earth: and the <u>dragon</u> stood before the woman which was ready to be delivered, for to <u>devour</u> her child as soon as it was born. destroy

5 And <u>she</u> brought forth a <u>man child</u>, who was to rule all nations with a rod of iron: and her child was caught up to God, and *to* His throne. ISA. 66:7 i.e., Israel - Messiah-Christ

6 And the <u>woman</u> fled into the <u>wilderness</u>, where she has a place prepared of God, that they should feed her there a <u>thousand two hundred *and* threescore days</u>. Israel - desert - 1260 (3 ½ years)

7 And there was war in heaven: Mi'chael and his angels fought against the <u>dragon</u>; and the <u>dragon</u> fought and his angels, DAN. 10:13 i.e., satan

8 And <u>prevailed not</u>; neither was their place found any more in heaven. did not win

9 And the great <u>dragon</u> was cast out, that old serpent, called the Dev'il, and Sa'tan, which deceives the whole world: he was cast out into the earth, and his <u>angels</u> were cast out with him. GEN. 3:14-15 followers

10 And I heard a loud voice saying in heaven, Now is come salvation, and strength, and the kingdom of our God, and the power of His Christ: for the accuser of our brethren is cast down, which accused them before our God day and night.

11 And they overcame him by the blood of the Lamb, and by the word of their <u>testimony</u>; and they loved not their lives to the death. witness

12 Therefore rejoice, *you* heavens, and you that dwell in them. Woe to the inhabiters of the earth and of the sea! for the devil is come down to you, having great wrath, because he knows that he has but a short time.

13 And when the <u>dragon</u> saw that he was cast to the earth, he persecuted the <u>woman</u> which brought forth the <u>man *child*</u>. satan - i.e., Israel - i.e., Jesus Christ

14 And to the <u>woman</u> were given two wings of a great eagle, that she might fly into the wilderness, into her place, where she is <u>nourished</u> for <u>a time, and times, and half a time</u>, from the face of the serpent. EX. 19:4 Israel - fed - 3 ½ years

15 And the <u>serpent</u> cast out of his mouth water as a flood after the <u>woman</u>, that he might cause her to be carried away of the flood. satan (v.9)

16 And the earth helped the <u>woman</u>, and the earth opened her mouth, and swallowed up the flood which the <u>dragon</u> cast out of his mouth.

17 And the <u>dragon</u> was angry with the woman, and went to make war with the remnant of her <u>seed</u>, which <u>keep</u> the commandments of God, and have the <u>testimony</u> of Je'sus Christ. offspring - obey - gospel

CHAPTER 13

AND I stood upon the sand of the sea, and saw a beast rise up out of the sea, having seven heads and ten horns, and upon his horns ten crowns, and upon his heads the name of blasphemy. DAN. 7:24 DAN. 7:8 anti-christ - nations - kings - evil

2 And the beast which I saw was like to a leopard, and his feet were as *the feet* of a bear, and his mouth as the mouth of a lion: and the dragon gave him his power, and his seat, and great authority.   satan

3 And I saw one of his heads as it were wounded to death; and his deadly wound was healed: and all the world wondered after the beast. followed

4 And they worshiped the dragon which gave power to the beast: and they worshiped the beast, saying, Who *is* like to the beast? who is able to make war with him?   because he - anti-christ

5 And there was given to him a mouth speaking great things and blasphemies; and power was given to him to continue forty *and* two months.   DAN. 7:8 evil works - 3 ½ years

6 And he opened his mouth in blasphemy against God, to blaspheme His name, and His tabernacle, and them that dwell in heaven.   curse - dwelling place

7 And it was given to him to make war with the saints, and to overcome them: and power was given him over all kindreds, and tongues, and nations.

8 And all that dwell upon the earth shall worship him, whose names are not written in the book of life of the Lamb slain from the foundation of the world.

9 If any man have an ear, let him hear.

10 He that leads into captivity shall go into captivity: he that kills with the sword must be killed with the sword. Here is the patience and the faith of the saints.

11 And I beheld another beast coming up out of the earth; and he had two horns like a lamb, and he spoke as a dragon.   false prophet - satan

12 And he exercises all the power of the first beast before him, and causes the earth and them which dwell therein to worship the first beast, whose deadly wound was healed.   false prophet - makes - anti-christ

13 And he does great wonders, so that he makes fire come down from heaven on the earth in the sight of men,

14 And deceives them that dwell on the earth by *the means of* those miracles which he had power to do in the sight of the beast; saying to them that dwell on the earth, that they should make an image to the beast, which had the wound by a sword, and did live.

15 And he had power to give life to the image of the beast, that the image of the beast should both speak, and cause that as many as would not worship the image of the beast should be killed.   false prophet - anti-christ

16 And he causes all, both small and great, rich and poor, free and bond, to receive a mark in their right hand, or in their foreheads:

17 And that no man might buy or sell, save he that had the mark, or the name of the beast, or the number of his name.

18 Here is wisdom. Let him that has

understanding count the number of the beast: for it is the number of a man; and his number *is* Six hundred threescore *and* six.

i.e., 666

CHAPTER 14

A nd I looked, and, lo, a Lamb stood on the mount Zi'on, and with Him an hundred forty *and* four thousand, having His Father's name written in their foreheads. PS. 2:6 the - on

2 And I heard a voice from heaven, as the voice of many waters, and as the voice of a great thunder: and I heard the voice of harpers harping with their harps:

3 And they sung as it were a new song before the throne, and before the four beasts, and the elders: and no man could learn that song but the hundred *and* forty *and* four thousand, which were redeemed from the earth. living creatures

4 These are they which were not defiled with women; for they are virgins. These are they which follow the Lamb wherever He goes. These were redeemed from among men, *being* the firstfruits to God and to the Lamb. Christ-God

5 And in their mouth was found no guile: for they are without fault before the throne of God. ZEP. 3:13 lie - blameless

6 And I saw another angel fly in the midst of heaven, having the everlasting gospel to preach to them that dwell on the earth, and to every nation, and kindred, and tongue, and people, messenger

7 Saying with a loud voice, Fear God, and give glory to Him; for the hour of His judgment is come: and worship Him that made heaven, and earth, and the sea, and the fountains of waters. PSA. 146:6 Reverence

8 And there followed another angel, saying, Bab'y-lon is fallen, is fallen, that great city, because she made all nations drink of the wine of the wrath of her fornication.

JER. 51:7 ISA. 21:9 anger - unfaithfulness

9 And the third angel followed them, saying with a loud voice, If any man worship the beast and his image, and receive *his* mark in his forehead, or in his hand, messenger - anti-christ

10 The same shall drink of the wine of the wrath of God, which is poured out without mixture into the cup of His indignation; and he shall be tormented with fire and brimstone in the presence of the holy angels, and in the presence of the Lamb: JER. 25:15 JER. 51:7 anger - Jesus Christ

11 And the smoke of their torment ascends up for ever and ever: and they have no rest day nor night, who worship the beast and his image, and whosoever receives the mark of his name.

12 Here is the patience of the saints: here *are* they that keep the commandments of God, and the faith of Je'sus. believers - obey

13 And I heard a voice from heaven saying to me, Write, Blessed *are* the dead which die in the Lord from hereafter: Yea, says the Spirit, that they may rest from their labors; and their works do follow them. Fortunate

14 And I looked, and behold a white cloud, and upon the cloud *one* sat like to the Son of man, having on His

head a golden crown, and in His hand a sharp sickle.

15 And another <u>angel</u> came out of the temple, crying with a loud voice to Him that sat on the cloud, Thrust in Your sickle, and reap: for the time is come for You to reap; for the harvest of the earth is ripe. JOEL 3:13 messenger

16 And He that sat on the cloud thrust in His sickle on the earth; and the earth was reaped.

17 And another <u>angel</u> came out of the temple which is in heaven, he also having a sharp sickle.

18 And another <u>angel</u> came out from the altar, which had power over fire; and cried with a loud cry to him that had the sharp sickle, saying, Thrust in your sharp sickle, and gather the clusters of the vine of the earth; for her grapes are fully ripe.   JOEL 3:13

19 And the <u>angel</u> thrust in his sickle into the earth, and gathered the vine of the earth, and cast *it* into the great winepress of the <u>wrath</u> of God.   anger

20 And the winepress was trodden outside the city, and blood came out of the winepress, even to the horse bridles, by the space of a thousand *and* six hundred furlongs.   JOEL 3:13

CHAPTER 15

AND I saw another sign in heaven, great and marvellous, seven <u>angels</u> having the seven last plagues; for in them is filled up the <u>wrath</u> of God.   LEV. 26:21 messengers - anger

2 And I saw as it were a sea of glass mingled with fire: and them that had gotten the victory over the <u>beast</u>, and over his image, and over his mark, *and* over the number of his name, stand on the sea of glass, having the harps of God.   anti-christ

3 And they sing the song of Mo'ses the servant of God, and the song of the Lamb, saying, Great and marvellous *are* Your works, Lord God Almighty; just and true *are* Your ways, You King of <u>saints</u>. EX. 15:1 followers of Jesus

4 Who shall not fear You, O Lord, and glorify Your name? for *You* only *are* holy: for all nations shall come and worship before You; for Your judgments are made manifest.   JER. 10:7

5 And after that I looked, and, behold, the temple of the tabernacle of the testimony in heaven was opened:

6 And the seven <u>angels</u> came out of the temple, having the seven plagues, clothed in pure and white linen, and having their breasts <u>girded</u> with golden girdles.   messengers - wrapped

7 And one of the four <u>beasts</u> gave to the seven <u>angels</u> seven golden <u>vials</u> full of the <u>wrath</u> of God, who lives for ever and ever.   living creatures - bowls - anger

8 And the temple was filled with smoke from the glory of God, and from His power; and no man was able to enter into the temple, till the seven plagues of the seven <u>angels</u> were fulfilled.   1 KGS. 8:10

CHAPTER 16

AND I heard a great voice out of the temple saying to the seven <u>angels</u>, Go your ways, and pour out the <u>vials</u> of the <u>wrath</u> of God upon the earth.   PS.69:24 anger

2 And the first went, and poured out his vial upon the earth; and there fell a <u>noisome</u> and grievous sore upon the men which had the mark of the <u>beast</u>, and *upon* them which worshiped his image.   EX. 9:10-11   loathsome - anti-christ

3 And the second <u>angel</u> poured out his <u>vial</u> upon the sea; and it became as the blood of a dead *man*: and every living soul died in the sea.   EX. 7:18

4 And the third <u>angel</u> poured out his vial upon the rivers and fountains of waters; and they became blood.   EX. 12:23 messenger

5 And I heard the <u>angel</u> of the waters say, You are righteous, O Lord, which are, and were, and shall be, because You have judged thus.

6 For they have shed the blood of saints and prophets, and You have given them blood to drink; for they are worthy.

7 And I heard another out of the altar say, Even so, Lord God Almighty, true and righteous *are* Your judgments.   PS. 119:137

8 And the fourth <u>angel</u> poured out his <u>vial</u> upon the sun; and power was given to him to scorch men with fire.   bowl

9 And men were <u>scorched</u> with great heat, and <u>blasphemed</u> the name of God, which has power over these plagues: and they repented not to give Him glory.   burned - cursed

10 And the fifth <u>angel</u> poured out his vial upon the seat of the <u>beast</u>; and his kingdom was full of darkness; and they gnawed their tongues for pain,   anti-christ

11 And <u>blasphemed</u> the God of heaven because of their pains and their sores, and repented not of their deeds.

12 And the sixth <u>angel</u> poured out his <u>vial</u> upon the great river Euphra'tes; and the water thereof was dried up, that the way of the kings of the east might be prepared. messenger - bowl

13 And I saw three unclean spirits like frogs *come* out of the mouth of the <u>dragon</u>, and out of the mouth of the <u>beast</u>, and out of the mouth of the false prophet. satan - anti-christ

14 For they are the spirits of <u>devils</u>, working miracles, *which* go forth to the kings of the earth and of the whole world, to gather them to the battle of that great day of God Almighty.   demons

15 Behold, I come as a thief. <u>Blessed</u> *is* he that watches, and keeps his garments, less he walk naked, and they see his shame.   Fortunate

16 And he gathered them together into a place called in the He'brew <u>tongue</u> Ar-ma-ged'don.   language

17 And the seventh <u>angel</u> poured out his <u>vial</u> into the air; and there came a great voice out of the temple of <u>heaven</u>, from the throne, saying, It is done.   ISA. 66:6   messenger - bowl

18 And there were voices, and thunders, and lightnings; and there was a great earthquake, such as was not since men were upon the earth, so mighty an earthquake, *and* so great.

19 And the great city was divided into three parts, and the cities of the nations fell: and great Bab'y-lon came in remembrance before God, to give to her the cup of the wine of the fierceness of His wrath.

20 And every island fled away, and the mountains were not found.

21 And there fell upon men a great hail out of heaven, *every stone* about the weight of a talent: and men blasphemed God because of the plague of the hail; for the plague thereof was exceeding great. EX. 9:23 100 lbs. - cursed

CHAPTER 17

AND there came one of the seven angels which had the seven vials, and talked with me, saying to me, Come here; I will show to you the judgment of the great whore that sits upon many waters: messengers - bowls

2 With whom the kings of the earth have committed fornication, and the inhabitants of the earth have been made drunk with the wine of her fornication. ISA. 23:17

3 So he carried me away in the Spirit into the wilderness: and I saw a woman sit upon a scarlet colored beast, full of names of blasphemy, having seven heads and ten horns.

4 And the woman was arrayed in purple and scarlet color, and decked with gold and precious stones and pearls, having a golden cup in her hand full of abominations and filthiness of her fornication:

JER. 51:7 adorned - unclean things - unfaithfulness

5 And upon her forehead *was* a name written, MYSTERY, BAB'Y-LON THE GREAT, THE MOTHER OF HARLOTS AND ABOMINATIONS OF THE EARTH.

6 And I saw the woman drunken with the blood of the saints, and with the blood of the martyrs of Je'sus: and when I saw her, I wondered with great admiration.

7 And the angel said to me, Wherefore did you marvel? I will tell you the mystery of the woman, and of the beast that carries her, which has the seven heads and ten horns.

messenger - secret - anti-christ - nations - kings

8 The beast that you saw was, and is not; and shall ascend out of the bottomless pit, and go into perdition: and they that dwell on the earth shall wonder, whose names were not written in the book of life from the foundation of the world, when they behold the beast that was, and is not, and yet is. destruction

9 And here *is* the mind which has wisdom. The seven heads are seven mountains, on which the woman sits.

10 And there are seven kings: five are fallen, and one is, *and* the other is not yet come; and when he comes, he must continue a short space. remain

11 And the beast that was, and is not, even he is the eighth, and is of the seven, and goes into perdition.

12 And the ten horns which you saw are ten kings, which have received no kingdom as yet; but receive power as kings one hour with the beast.

DAN. 7:20-24 kings - authority - anti-christ

13 These have one mind, and shall give their power and strength to the beast.

14 These shall make war with the Lamb, and the Lamb shall overcome them: for He is Lord of lords, and King of kings: and they that are with Him *are* called, and chosen, and faithful. DAN. 2:47 i.e., Christ-God

15 And he says to me, The waters

which you saw, where the <u>whore</u> sits, are peoples, and multitudes, and nations, and tongues. unfaithful one

16 And the ten <u>horns</u> which you saw upon the <u>beast</u>, these shall hate the <u>whore</u>, and shall make her desolate and naked, and shall eat her flesh, and burn her with fire. kings - anti-christ

17 For God has put in their hearts to fulfill His will, and to agree, and give their kingdom to the <u>beast</u>, until the words of God shall be fulfilled.

18 And the <u>woman</u> which you saw is that <u>great city</u>, which reigns over the kings of the earth. ? Rome-Babylon

CHAPTER 18

AND after these things I saw another angel come down from heaven, having great power; and the earth was <u>lightened</u> with his glory. messenger - illuminated

2 And he cried mightily with a strong voice, saying, Bab'y-lon the great is fallen, is fallen, and is become the habitation of <u>devils</u>, and the hold of every foul spirit, and a cage of every unclean and hateful bird.

JER. 50:39 ISA. 21:9 demons

3 For all nations have drunk of the wine of the wrath of her <u>fornication</u>, and the kings of the earth have committed <u>fornication</u> with her, and the merchants of the earth are <u>waxed</u> rich through the <u>abundance</u> of her <u>delicacies</u>.

JER. 25:27 unfaithfulness - growing - wealth - sensuality

4 And I heard another voice from heaven, saying, Come out of her, my people, that you be not partakers of her sins, and that you receive not of her <u>plagues</u>. sickness

5 For her sins have reached to heaven, and God has remembered her iniquities. JER. 51:9

6 Reward her even as she rewarded you, and double to her double according to her works: in the cup which she has filled fill to her double.

7 How much she has glorified herself, and lived <u>deliciously</u>, so much torment and sorrow give her: for she says in her heart, I sit a queen, and am no widow, and shall see no sorrow. ISA. 47:8-9 sensually

8 Therefore shall her plagues come in one day, death, and mourning, and famine; and she shall be utterly burned with fire: for <u>strong</u> *is* the Lord God who judges her. mighty

9 And the kings of the earth, who have committed <u>fornication</u> and lived deliciously with her, shall bewail her, and lament for her, when they shall see the smoke of her burning, EZE. 26:16-17 unfaithfulness

10 Standing afar off for the fear of her torment, saying, Alas, alas, that great city Bab'y-lon, that mighty city! for in one hour is your judgment come.

11 And the merchants of the earth shall weep and mourn over her; for no man buys their merchandise any more: EZE. 27:36

12 The merchandise of gold, and silver, and precious stones, and of pearls, and fine linen, and purple, and silk, and scarlet, and all thyine wood, and all manner vessels of ivory, and all manner vessels of most precious wood, and of brass, and iron, and marble, EZE. 27:22

13 And cinnamon, and odors, and ointments, and frankincense, and wine, and oil, and fine flour, and wheat, and

beasts, and sheep, and horses, and chariots, and slaves, and souls of men. 14 And the <u>fruits</u> that your soul <u>lusted</u> after are departed from you, and all things which were dainty and goodly are departed from you, and you shall find them no more at all.   things - desired
15 The merchants of these things, which were made rich by her, shall stand afar off for the fear of her torment, weeping and wailing,   EZE. 27:36
16 And saying, Alas, alas, that great city, that was clothed in fine linen, and purple, and scarlet, and decked with gold, and precious stones, and pearls!
17 For in one hour so great riches is come to nothing. And every shipmaster, and all the company in ships, and sailors, and as many as trade by sea, stood afar off,   ISA. 23:14
18 And cried when they saw the smoke of her burning, saying, What *city is* like to this great city!
19 And they cast dust on their heads, and cried, weeping and wailing, saying, Alas, alas, that great city, wherein were made rich all that had ships in the sea by reason of her costliness! for in one hour is she made <u>desolate</u>.EZE. 27:30-34 a ruin
20 Rejoice over her, *you* heaven, and *you* holy apostles and prophets; for God has avenged you on her. ISA. 44:23
21 And a mighty <u>angel</u> took up a stone like a great millstone, and cast *it* into the sea, saying, Thus with violence shall that great city Bab'y-lon be thrown down, and shall be found no more at all.   JER. 51:63 messenger
22 And the voice of harpers, and musicians, and of pipers, and trumpeters,

shall be heard no more at all in you; and no craftsman, of whatsoever craft *he be*, shall be found any more in you; and the sound of a millstone shall be heard no more at all in you;   EZE. 26:13
23 And the light of a candle shall shine no more at all in you; and the voice of the bridegroom and of the bride shall be heard no more at all in you: for your merchants were the great men of the earth; for by your sorceries were all nations deceived.
24 And in her was found the blood of prophets, and of saints, and of all that were slain upon the earth.JER. 51:49

CHAPTER 19

AND after these things I heard a great voice of much people in heaven, saying, Al-le-lu'ia; Salvation, and glory, and honor, and power, to the Lord our God:
2 For true and righteous *are* His judgments: for He has judged the great whore, which did corrupt the earth with her <u>fornication</u>, and has avenged the blood of His servants at her hand.   DEU. 32:43 unfaithfulness
3 And again they said, Al-le-lu'ia. And her smoke rose up for ever and ever.
4 And the <u>four and twenty elders</u> and the four <u>beasts</u> fell down and worshiped God that sat on the throne, saying, Amen; Al-le-lu'ia.

i.e., could be 12 Jewish tribes and 12 apostles - living creatures

5 And a voice came out of the throne, saying, Praise our God, all you His servants, and you that <u>fear</u> Him, both small and great.   PS. 115:13 reverence

6 And I heard as it were the voice of a great multitude, and as the voice of many waters, and as the voice of mighty thunderings, saying, Al-le-lu'ia: for the Lord God <u>om-nipotent</u> reigns.   all powerful

7 Let us be glad and rejoice, and give honor to Him: for the marriage of the Lamb is come, and His wife has made herself ready.   PS. 118:24

8 And to <u>her</u> was granted that <u>she</u> should be <u>arrayed</u> in fine linen, clean and white: for the fine linen is the righteousness of <u>saints</u>.

          i.e., believers of the church - clothed - believers

9 And he says to me, Write, Blessed *are* they which are called to the marriage supper of the Lamb. And he says to me, These are the true sayings of God.

10 And I fell at his feet to worship him. And he said to me, See *you do it* not: I am your fellowservant, and of your brethren that have the testimony of Je'sus: worship God: for the testimony of Je'sus is the spirit of prophecy.

11 And I saw heaven opened, and behold a white horse; and He that sat upon him *was* called <u>Faithful and True</u>, and in righteousness He does judge and make war. PSA. 96:13 i.e., Christ, God

12 His eyes *were* as a flame of fire, and on His head *were* many crowns; and He had a name written, that no man knew, <u>but</u> He Himself.   except

13 And He *was* clothed with a <u>vesture</u> dipped in blood: and His name is called The Word of God.   robe

14 And the armies *which were* in heaven followed Him upon white horses, clothed in fine linen, white and clean.

15 And out of His mouth goes a sharp sword, that with it He should smite the nations: and He shall rule them with a rod of iron: and He treads the winepress of the fierceness and wrath of Almighty God.

16 And He has on *His* <u>vesture</u> and on His thigh a name written, <u>KING OF KINGS, AND LORD OF LORDS</u>.

          DEU. 10:17   robe - Christ, God

17 And I saw an <u>angel</u> standing in the sun; and he cried with a loud voice, saying to all the fowls that fly in the midst of heaven, Come and gather yourselves together to the supper of the great God;   EZE. 39:4 messenger

18 That you may eat the flesh of kings, and the flesh of captains, and the flesh of mighty men, and the flesh of horses, and of them that sit on them, and the flesh of all *men, both* free and <u>bond</u>, both small and great.   EZE. 39:18 slaves

19 And I saw the <u>beast</u>, and the kings of the earth, and their armies, gathered together to make war against Him that sat on the horse, and against His army.   anti-christ

20 And the <u>beast</u> was taken, and with him the <u>false</u> <u>prophet</u> that wrought miracles before him, with which he deceived them that had received the mark of the <u>beast</u>, and them that worshiped his image. These both were cast alive into a lake of fire burning with brimstone.   an imitation of the Holy Spirit

21 And the remnant were slain with the sword of Him that sat upon the horse, which *sword* proceeded out of

His mouth: and all the <u>fowls</u> were filled with their flesh. birds

CHAPTER 20

AND I saw an <u>angel</u> come down from heaven, having the key of the bottomless pit and a great chain in his hand. messenger
2 And he laid hold on the dragon, that old serpent, which is the Dev'il, and Sa'tan, and bound him a thousand years, ISA. 27:1
3 And cast him into the bottomless pit, and <u>shut</u> him up, and set a seal upon him, that he should deceive the nations no more, till the thousand years should be fulfilled: and after that he must be <u>loosed</u> a little <u>season</u>. locked - released - while
4 And I saw thrones, and they sat upon them, and judgment was given to them: and *I saw* the souls of them that were beheaded for the witness of Je'sus, and for the word of God, and which had not worshiped the <u>beast</u>, neither his image, neither had received *his* mark upon their foreheads, or in their hands; and they lived and reigned with Christ a thousand years. anti-christ
5 But the rest of the dead lived not again until the thousand years were finished. This *is* the first resurrection.
6 Blessed and holy *is* he that has part in the first resurrection: on such the second death has no power, but they shall be priests of God and of Christ, and shall reign with Him a thousand years.
7 And when the thousand years are expired, Sa'tan shall be <u>loosed</u> out of his prison, over - released

8 And shall go out to deceive the nations which are in the four <u>quarters</u> of the earth, <u>Gog and Ma'gog</u>, to gather them together to battle: the number of whom *is* as the sand of the sea. EZE. 38:2,15 corners - i.e., thought to be Russia
9 And they went up on the breadth of the earth, and <u>compassed</u> the camp of the <u>saints</u> about, and the beloved city: and fire came down from God out of heaven, and devoured them. 2 KGS. 1:10-11 surrounded - believers
10 And the <u>devil</u> that deceived them was cast into the lake of fire and brimstone, where the <u>beast</u> and the <u>false prophet</u> *are*, and shall be tormented day and night for ever and ever. satan - anti-christ - imitator of Holy Spirit
11 And I saw a great white throne, and Him that sat on it, from whose face the earth and the heaven fled away; and there was found no place for them.
12 And I saw the dead, small and great, stand before God; and the books were opened: and another book was opened, which is *the book* of life: and the dead were judged out of those things which were written in the books according to their works. DAN. 7:10
13 And the sea gave up the dead which were in it; and death and hell delivered up the dead which were in them: and they were judged every man according to their works.
14 And death and hell were cast into the lake of fire. This is the second death.
15 And whosoever was not found written in the book of life was cast into the lake of fire.

CHAPTER 21

AND I saw a new heaven and a new earth: for the first heaven and the first earth were passed away; and there was no more sea. ISA. 66:22

2 And I John saw the holy city, new Je-ru'sa-lem, coming down from God out of heaven, prepared as a bride adorned for her husband.

3 And I heard a great voice out of heaven saying, Behold, the tabernacle of God *is* with men, and He will dwell with them, and they shall be His people, and God Himself shall be with them, *and be* their God. EXO. 29:45 EZE. 37:27

4 And God shall wipe away all tears from their eyes; and there shall be no more death, neither sorrow, nor crying, neither shall there be any more pain: for the former things are passed away. ISA. 25:8

5 And He that sat upon the throne said, Behold, I make all things new. And He said to me, Write: for these words are true and faithful. ISA. 43:19

6 And He said to me, It is done. I am Al'pha and O'me-ga, the beginning and the end. I will give to him that is athirst of the fountain of the water of life freely.

7 He that overcomes shall inherit all things; and I will be his God, and he shall be My son. PS. 89:28

8 But the fearful, and unbelieving, and the abominable, and murderers, and whoremongers, and sorcerers, and idolaters, and all liars, shall have their part in the lake which burns with fire and brimstone: which is the second death.

9 And there came to me one of the seven angels which had the seven vials full of the seven last plagues, and talked with me, saying, Come here, I will show you the bride, the Lamb's wife. *messengers - bowls - the church - Jesus'*

10 And he carried me away in the Spirit to a great and high mountain, and showed me that great city, the holy Je-ru'sa-lem, descending out of heaven from God,

11 Having the glory of God: and her light *was* like to a stone most precious, even like a jasper stone, clear as crystal;

12 And had a wall great and high, *and* had twelve gates, and at the gates twelve angels, and names written thereon, which are *the names* of the twelve tribes of the children of Is'ra-el: EZE. 48:30-34

13 On the east three gates; on the north three gates; on the south three gates; and on the west three gates.

14 And the wall of the city had twelve foundations, and in them the names of the twelve apostles of the Lamb. EZE. 48:31 Jesus

15 And he that talked with me had a golden reed to measure the city, and the gates thereof, and the wall thereof.

16 And the city lies foursquare, and the length is as large as the breadth: and he measured the city with the reed, twelve thousand furlongs. The length and the breadth and the height of it are equal. *1500 miles*

17 And he measured the wall thereof, an hundred *and* forty *and* four cubits, *according to* the measure of a man, that is, of the angel.

18 And the building of the wall of it

was *of* jasper: and the city *was* pure gold, like to clear glass.

19 And the foundations of the wall of the city *were* garnished with all manner of precious stones. The first foundation was jasper; the second, sapphire; the third, a chalcedony; the fourth, an emerald;

20 The fifth, sardonyx; the sixth, sardius; the seventh, chrysolyte; the eighth, beryl; the ninth, a topaz; the tenth, a chrysoprasus; the eleventh, a jacinth; the twelfth, an amethyst.

21 And the twelve gates *were* twelve pearls; every several gate was of one pearl: and the street of the city *was* pure gold, as it were transparent glass.

22 And I saw no temple <u>therein</u>: for the Lord God Almighty and the <u>Lamb</u> are the temple of it.   in it - Jesus

23 And the city had no need of the sun, neither of the moon, to shine in it: for the glory of God did <u>lighten</u> it, and the <u>Lamb</u> *is* the light thereof.   ISA. 24:23   illuminate - Jesus

24 And the nations of them which are saved shall walk in the light of it: and the kings of the earth do bring their glory and honor into it.

25 And the gates of it shall not be shut at all by day: for there shall be no night there.   ISA. 60:11

26 And they shall bring the glory and honor of the nations into it.

27 And there shall in no wise enter into it any thing that defiles, neither *whatsoever* works <u>abomination</u>, or *makes* a lie: but they which are written in the <u>Lamb's</u> book of life.   ISA. 52:1   evil - Jesus

CHAPTER 22

AND he showed me a pure river of water of life, clear as crystal, <u>proceeding</u> out of the throne of God and of the <u>Lamb</u>.   flowing - Jesus

2 In the midst of the street of it, and on either side of the river, *was there* the tree of life, which bare twelve *manner of* fruits, *and* yielded her fruit every month: and the leaves of the tree *were* for the healing of the nations.   EZE. 47:12 GEN 2:9

3 And there shall be no more curse: but the throne of God and of the <u>Lamb</u> shall be in it; and his servants shall serve Him: ZEC. 14:11

4 And they shall see His face; and His name *shall be* in their foreheads.

5 And there shall be no night there; and they need no candle, neither light of the sun; for the Lord God gives them light: and they shall reign for ever and ever.

6 And he said to me, These sayings *are* faithful and true: and the Lord God of the holy prophets sent His <u>angel</u> to show to His servants the things which must shortly be done.   messenger

7 Behold, I come quickly: blessed *is* he that keeps the sayings of the <u>prophecy</u> of this book.   teachings

8 And I John saw these things, and heard *them*. And when I had heard and seen, I fell down to worship before the feet of the angel which showed me these things.

9 Then says he to me, See *you do it* not: for I am your fellowservant, and of your brethren the prophets, and of

them which keep the sayings of this book: worship God.

10 And he says to me, Seal not the sayings of the prophecy of this book: for the time is at hand.   teaching

11 He that is unjust, let him be unjust still: and he which is filthy, let him be filthy still: and he that is righteous, let him be righteous still: and he that is holy, let him be holy still.

12 And, behold, I come quickly; and My reward *is* with Me, to give every man according as his work shall be.   ISA. 40:10

13 I am Al'pha and O'me-ga, the beginning and the end, the First and the Last.   ISA. 44:6 ISA:48:12

14 Blessed *are* they that do His commandments, that they may have right to the tree of life, and may enter in through the gates into the city.

15 For outside *are* dogs, and sorcerers, and whoremongers, and murderers, and idolaters, and whosoever loves and makes a lie.

16 I Je'sus have sent Mine angel to testify to you these things in the churches. I am the Root and the Offspring of Da'vid, *and* the Bright and Morning Star.   ISA. 11:1 messenger - tell

17 And the Spirit and the bride say, Come. And let him that hears say, Come. And let him that is athirst come. And whosoever will, let him take the water of life freely.   ISA. 55:1

18 For I testify to every man that hears the words of the prophecy of this book, If any man shall add to these things, God shall add to him the plagues that are written in this book: DEU. 12:32 teaching

19 And if any man shall take away from the words of the book of this prophecy, God shall take away his part out of the book of life, and out of the holy city, and *from* the things which are written in this book.

20 He which testifies these things says, Surely I come quickly. Amen. Even so, come, Lord Je'sus.   told

21 The grace of our Lord Je'sus Christ *be* with you all. Amen.

THE END OF THE NEW TESTAMENT.

TREASURY
OF
BIBLICAL
INFORMATION

HOW TO INTERPRET THE BIBLE

Paul Danielson

PROBLEM: There seem to be almost as many interpretations of the Bible as there are religious groups or even individuals. Out of this morass comes the legitimate question of the honest seeker after truth—Is it possible to know the right meaning of a given passage of Scripture? Indeed, one's heart cries with the Preacher of Ecclesiastes 8:1, "Who is as the wise man? And who knoweth the interpretation of a thing?"

PROPOSITION: In this article we are going to define one of the key principles of Biblical interpretation. From a proper understanding and application of this key principle the student of the Word will be greatly aided in arriving at the correct interpretation of a given passage of Scripture.

PRINCIPLE STATED: Simply stated, "The Bible interprets the Bible." Please notice that the word, "Bible" is repeated twice. The first mention is with reference to the Word of God as a whole. The second mention is to God's Word in any of its parts. So then, if we are wanting to know the correct interpretation of a particular verse or chapter of Scripture, it must be examined in the light of the other parts or whole of Scripture.

The beauty of this principle is that it is so clearly stated again and again within the Scriptures. For example, in I Corinthians 2:13 we read, "comparing spiritual things with spiritual." Or as another has rendered it, "explaining the things of the Spirit in the words of the Spirit." Then again, we read in Isaiah 28:13, "But the word of the Lord was unto them precept upon precept, precept upon precept; line upon line, line upon line; here a little, and there a little . . ." The context of verses 9-14 indicate that Isaiah is clearly talking about the Word of God. Furthermore, the passage in II Peter 1:20 speaks of God being the ultimate *originator* and writer of Scripture. Thus Peter calls our attention to this principle with the warning that ". . . no prophecy of the Scripture is of any *private* interpretation." The word, "Private" is *idios* in the Greek and means, "One's own." The passage teaches that all Scripture *originates* from God, not from the invention of any individual, and therefore its meaning must be that which God intended it to have—not merely the different understandings that various people may assign to it. See also II Timothy 3:16.

Now just as no individual has the right to interpret Scripture for himself, so also no verse or truth in Scripture stands alone, but finds its illumination from one or more other passages. Yet how easy it is to allow the mind to select certain detached verses of Scripture, and then combine them in the most arbitrary manner. In so doing we are using the very words of Scripture, yet at the same time they are only expressing *our own* thoughts, and not those of the Holy Spirit. So then, care must be taken that no verse ever be explained in a way which will be in conflict with what is clearly taught in the Bible as a whole.

PRINCIPLE APPLIED AND ILLUSTRATED: *First* of all, the principle that the Bible interprets the Bible is seen *in the relationship of the Old Testament to the New*. Or, as is so ably expressed in the well-known saying, "The NEW is within the OLD concealed; the OLD is within the NEW revealed." A few comparative verses should make this clear. The "Lamb" of Isaiah 53:7, 8 is interpreted in Acts 8:32–35 as being none other than Jesus Christ. Now read Genesis 3:15 and see if the enigma of the bruised seed is not explained in Romans 16:20. Now try Malachi 3:1 with Mark 1:2.

Secondly, the principle that the Bible interprets the Bible is seen *in the relationship of one verse to another.* This can be illustrated in a number of ways. (1) Question and answer method—Question, What are the seven Spirits of God mentioned in Revelation 1:4? Answer, Isaiah 11:2. Again, the question, What is meant by being "born of water" in John 3:5? Answer, Compare I Peter 1:23 with Ephesians 5:26. (2) *The identification of personalities* within Scripture can also be clarified by comparing one portion with another. That awesome creature of Isaiah 27:1 is easily identified in Revelation 20:2. The obscure Eliphaz and his son Teman of Genesis 36:11 take on special meaning when compared with Eliphaz the Temanite of Job 4:1 (See Also Obadiah 9)! (3) *Understanding the figurative language* of Scripture is exciting when one verse is compared with another. In Zechariah 13:7 we read that "the SHEPHERD and the SHEEP of the flock shall be scattered abroad." Do we only picture a herdsman and his flock, or do we not thrill

to fulfilled prophecy when in Matthew 26:56 we read, "But all this was done, that the Scriptures of the prophets might be fulfilled. Then all the DISCIPLES forsook HIM, and fled." Now read Daniel 2:32 and see if these "metalic terms" are not explained in the same chapter in verses 36-38. Then, compare the "many waters" of Revelation 17:1 with the Bible's own interpretation in 17:15. (4) This principle can also be illustrated by the help it gives in *understanding individual word meanings.* For example, in I Corinthians 7:26 a key word is "distress." When this word and its context is compared with the same word and its context in Luke 21:23, we begin to understand what Paul is talking about when he advises that, "for the present distress, I say, that it is good for a man so to be." Another such instance is the word, "sin" which first occurs in Genesis 4:7. That the Bible defines and explains its own words is seen in this case in the many synonyms of sin sprinkled throughout Genesis 3 and 4 (e.g. naked, hid, afraid, beguiled, enmity, bruised, sorrow, cursed, thorns, thistles, sweat, wroth, slew, fugitive, and vagabond). Each of these descriptive words aid us in achieving a Scriptural definition of the word sin.

Thirdly, many other illustrations may be given to show that the Bible is its own best interpreter. Here are a few suggestions for the reader who would like to utilize this approach in greater detail.

(1) By comparing Scripture with Scripture, one is able to better understand *the historical setting of a given passage.* Examine Luke 11:51 in relation to II Chronicles 24:20, 21; Psalm 3 in relation to II Samuel 15:14-17, 29; Proverbs 1:8, 10, 15; 2:1; 3:1 (Solomon's exhortation to his son) in the historical light of I Kings 12 (the fateful choice of Rehoboam, Solomon's son).

(2) By comparing Scripture with Scripture, one is able to better understand *the Mosaic Law* and its application in the life of the nation Israel. Compare Deuteronomy 25:9 with Ruth 4:7, 8. The difficulty in understanding the sudden death of Uzzah in II Samuel 6:3-7 is solved when examined in the light of the law given in Numbers 4:15.

(3) By comparing Scripture with Scripture, one is able to understand *prophecy and its fulfillment.* Compare Isaiah 28:16 with I Corinthians 3:11 and I Peter 2:6.

(4) By comparing Scripture with Scripture, one is able to understand *types and antitypes.* For example, compare Jonah 1:17 with Matthew 12:40, 41.

CONCLUSION: For additional help in the use of this principle there are at least three other valuable study tools to recommend: (1) A good study Bible with cross references in the margins or in a special section in the back; (2) a Bible concordance (a book that gives the references for finding the places where any given word is used throughout the Bible); and (3) a topical Bible.

Having said all this, we must bear in mind that this pragmatic principle of Biblical interpretation—Scripture interpreting Scripture—cannot be separated from a living relationship with Jesus Christ by faith and obedience to the very Word of God we have come to understand. Remember, ". . . they that seek the Lord understand all things" (Proverbs 28:5); ". . . a good understanding have all they that do His commandments" (Psalm 111:10); and "I understand more than all the ancients, because I keep thy precepts" (Psalm 119:100).

INTERNATIONAL COUNCIL ON BIBLICAL INERRANCY

P.O. Box 13261, Oakland, California 94661

(following used by permission)

THE CHICAGO STATEMENT ON BIBLICAL INERRANCY

(October 1978)

PREFACE

The authority of Scripture is a key issue for the Christian Church in this and every age. Those who profess faith in Jesus Christ as Lord and Savior are called to show the reality of their discipleship by humbly and faithfully obeying God's written Word. To stray from Scripture in faith or conduct is disloyalty to our Master. Recognition of the total truth and trustworthiness of Holy Scripture is essential to a full grasp and adequate confession of its authority.

The following Statement affirms this inerrancy of Scripture afresh, making clear our understanding of it and warning against its denial. We are persuaded that to deny it is to set aside the witness of Jesus Christ and of the Holy Spirit and to refuse that submission to the claims of God's own Word which marks true Christian faith. We see it as our timely duty to make this affirmation in the face of current lapses from the truth of inerrancy among our fellow Christians and misunderstanding of this doctrine in the world at large.

This Statement consists of three parts: a Summary Statement, Articles of Affirmation and Denial, and an accompanying Exposition. It has been prepared in the course of a three-day consultation in Chicago. Those who have signed the Summary Statement and the Articles wish to affirm their own conviction as to the inerrancy of Scripture and to encourage and challenge one another and all Christians to growing appreciation and understanding of this doctrine. We acknowledge the limitations of a document prepared in a brief, intensive conference and do not propose that this Statement be given creedal weight. Yet we rejoice in the deepening of our own convictions through our discussions together, and we pray that the Statement we have signed may be used to the glory of our God toward a new reformation of the Church in its faith, life, and mission.

We offer this Statement in a spirit, not of contention, but of humility and love, which we purpose by God's grace to maintain in any future dialogue arising out of what we have said. We gladly acknowledge that many who deny the inerrancy of Scripture do not display the consequences of this denial in the rest of their belief and behavior, and we are conscious that we who confess this doctrine often deny it in life by failing to bring our thoughts and deeds, our traditions and habits, into true subjection to the divine Word.

We invite response to this statement from any who see reason to amend its affirmations about Scripture by the light of Scripture itself, under whose infallible authority we stand as we speak. We claim no personal infallibility for the witness we bear, and for any help which enables us to strengthen this testimony to God's Word we shall be grateful.

A SHORT STATEMENT

1. God, who is Himself Truth and speaks truth only, has inspired Holy Scripture in order thereby to reveal Himself to lost mankind through Jesus Christ as Creator and Lord, Redeemer and Judge. Holy Scripture is God's witness to Himself.

2. Holy Scripture, being God's own Word, written by men prepared and superintended by His Spirit, is of infallible divine authority in all matters upon which it touches: it is to be believed, as God's instruction, in all that it affirms; obeyed, as God's command, in all that it requires; embraced, as God's pledge, in all that it promises.

3. The Holy Spirit, Scripture's divine Author, both authenticates it to us by His inward witness and opens our minds to understand its meaning.

4. Being wholly and verbally God-given, Scripture is without error or fault in all its teaching, no less in what it states about God's acts in creation, about the events of world history, and about its own literary origins under God, than in its witness to God's saving grace in individual lives.

5. The authority of Scripture is inescapably impaired if this total divine inerrancy is in any way limited or disregarded, or made relative to a view of truth contrary to the Bible's own; and such lapses bring serious loss to both the individual and the Church.

ARTICLES OF AFFIRMATION AND DENIAL

Article I.	We affirm that the Holy Scriptures are to be received as the authoritative Word of God.
	We deny that the Scriptures receive their authority from the Church, tradition, or any other human source.
Article II.	We affirm that the Scriptures are the supreme written norm by which God binds the conscience, and that the authority of the Church is subordinate to that of Scripture.
	We deny that Church creeds, councils, or declarations have authority greater than or equal to the authority of the Bible.
Article III.	We affirm that the written Word in its entirety is revelation given by God.
	We deny that the Bible is merely a witness to revelation, or only becomes revelation in encounter, or depends on the responses of men for its validity.
Article IV.	We affirm that God who made mankind in His image has used language as a means of revelation.

We deny that human language is so limited by our creatureliness that it is rendered inadequate as a vehicle for divine revelation. We further deny that the corruption of human culture and language through sin has thwarted God's work of inspiration.

Article V.

We affirm that God's revelation within the Holy Scriptures was progressive.

We deny that later revelation, which may fulfill earlier revelation, ever corrects or contradicts it. We further deny that any normative revelation has been given since the completion of the New Testament writings.

Article VI.

We affirm that the whole of Scripture and all its parts, down to the very words of the original, were given by divine inspiration.

We deny that the inspiration of Scripture can rightly be affirmed of the whole without the parts, or of some parts but not the whole.

Article VII.

We affirm that inspiration was the work in which God by His Spirit, through human writers, gave us His Word. The origin of Scripture is divine. The mode of divine inspiration remains largely a mystery to us.

We deny that inspiration can be reduced to human insight, or to heightened states of consciousness of any kind.

Article VIII.

We affirm that God in His work of inspiration utilized the distinctive personalities and literary styles of the writers whom He had chosen and prepared.

We deny that God, in causing these writers to use the very words that He chose, overrode their personalities.

Article IX.

We affirm that inspiration, though not conferring omniscience, guaranteed true and trustworthy utterance on all matters of which the Biblical authors were moved to speak and write.

We deny that the finitude or fallenness of these writers, by necessity or otherwise, introduced distortion or falsehood into God's Word.

Article X.

We affirm that inspiration, strictly speaking, applies only to the autographic text of Scripture, which in the providence of God can be ascertained from available manuscripts with great accuracy. We further affirm that copies and translations of Scripture are the Word of God to the extent that they faithfully represent the original.

We deny that any essential element of the Christian faith is affected by the absence of the autographs. We further deny that this absence renders the assertion of Biblical inerrancy invalid or irrelevant.

Article XI.

We affirm that Scripture, having been given by divine inspiration, is infallible, so that, far from misleading us, it is true and reliable in all the matters it addresses.

We deny that it is possible for the Bible to be at the same time infallible and errant in its assertions. Infallibility and inerrancy may be distinguished, but not separated.

Article XII.

We affirm that Scripture in its entirety is inerrant, being free from all falsehood, fraud, or deceit.

We deny that Biblical infallibility and inerrancy are limited to spiritual, religious, or redemptive themes, exclusive of assertions in the fields of history and science. We further deny that scientific hypotheses about earth history may properly be used to overturn the teaching of Scripture on creation and the flood.

Article XIII. We affirm the propriety of using inerrancy as a theological term with reference to the complete truthfulness of Scripture.

We deny that it is proper to evaluate Scripture according to standards of truth and error that are alien to its usage or purpose. We further deny that inerrancy is negated by Biblical phenomena such as a lack of modern technical precision, irregularities of grammar or spelling, observational descriptions of nature, the reporting of falsehoods, the use of hyperbole and round numbers, the topical arrangement of material, variant selections of material in parallel accounts, or the use of free citations.

Article XIV. We affirm the unity and internal consistency of Scripture.

We deny that alleged errors and discrepancies that have not yet been resolved vitiate the truth claims of the Bible.

Article XV. We affirm that the doctrine of inerrancy is grounded in the teaching of the Bible about inspiration.

We deny that Jesus' teaching about Scripture may be dismissed by appeals to accommodation or to any natural limitation of His humanity.

Article XVI. We affirm that the doctrine of inerrancy has been integral to the Church's faith throughout its history.

We deny that inerrancy is a doctrine invented by scholastic Protestantism, or is a reactionary position postulated in response to negative higher criticism.

Article XVII. We affirm that the Holy Spirit bears witness to the Scriptures, assuring believers of the truthfulness of God's written Word.

We deny that this witness of the Holy Spirit operates in isolation from or against Scripture.

Article XVIII. We affirm that the text of Scripture is to be interpreted by grammatico-historical exegesis, taking account of its literary forms and devices, and that Scripture is to interpret Scripture.

We deny the legitimacy of any treatment of the text or quest for sources lying behind it that leads to relativizing, dehistoricizing, or discounting its teaching, or rejecting its claims to authorship.

Article XIX. We affirm that a confession of the full authority, infallibility, and inerrancy of Scripture is vital to a sound understanding of the whole of the Christian faith. We further affirm that such confession should lead to increasing conformity to the image of Christ.

We deny that such confession is necessary for salvation. However, we further deny that inerrancy can be rejected without grave consequences, both to the individual and to the Church.

EXPOSITION

Our understanding of the doctrine of inerrancy must be set in the context of the broader teachings of the Scripture concerning itself. This exposition gives an account of the outline of doctrine from which our summary statement and articles are drawn.

Creation, Revelation and Inspiration

The Triune God, who formed all things by his creative utterances and governs all things by His Word of decree, made mankind in His own image for a life of communion with Himself, on the model of the eternal fellowship of loving communication within the Godhead. As God's image-bearer, man was to hear God's Word addressed to him and to respond in the joy of adoring obedience. Over and above God's self-disclosure in the created order and the sequence of events within it, human beings from Adam on have received verbal messages from Him, either directly, as stated in Scripture, or indirectly in the form of part or all of Scripture itself.

When Adam fell, the Creator did not abandon mankind to final judgment but promised salvation and began to reveal Himself as Redeemer in a sequence of historical events centering on Abraham's family and culminating in the life, death, resurrection, present heavenly ministry, and promised return of Jesus Christ. Within this frame God has from time to time spoken specific words of judgment and mercy, promise and command, to sinful human beings so drawing them into a covenant relation of mutual commitment between Him and them in which He blesses them with gifts of grace and they bless Him in responsive adoration. Moses, whom God used as mediator to carry His words to His people at the time of the Exodus, stands at the head of a long line of prophets in whose mouths and writings God put His words for delivery to Israel. God's purpose in this succession of messages was to maintain His covenant by causing His people to know His Name—that is, His nature—and His will both of precept and purpose in the present and for the future. This line of prophetic spokesmen from God came to completion in Jesus Christ, God's incarnate Word, who was Himself a prophet—more than a prophet, but not less—and in the apostles and prophets of the first Christian generation. When God's final and climactic message, His word to the world concerning Jesus Christ, had been spoken and elucidated by those in the apostolic circle, the sequence of revealed messages ceased. Henceforth the Church was to live and know God by what He had already said, and said for all time.

At Sinai God wrote the terms of His covenant on tables of stone, as His enduring witness and for lasting accessibility, and throughout the period of prophetic and apostolic revelation He prompted men to write the messages given to and through them, along with celebratory records of His dealings with His people, plus moral reflections on covenant life and forms of praise and prayer for covenant mercy. The theological reality of inspiration in the producing of Biblical documents corresponds to that of spoken prophecies: although the human writers' personalities were expressed in what they wrote, the words were divinely constituted. Thus, what Scripture says, God says; its authority is His authority, for He is its ultimate Author, having given it through the minds and words of chosen and prepared men who in freedom and faithfulness "spoke from God as they were carried along by the Holy Spirit" (1 Pet. 1:21). Holy Scripture must be acknowledged as the Word of God by virtue of its divine origin.

Authority: Christ and the Bible

Jesus Christ, the Son of God who is the Word made flesh, our Prophet, Priest, and King, is the ultimate Mediator of God's communication to man, as He is of all God's gifts of grace. The revela-

tion He gave was more than verbal; He revealed the Father by His presence and His deeds as well. Yet His words were crucially important; for He was God, He spoke from the Father, and His words will judge all men at the last day.

As the prophesied Messiah, Jesus Christ is the central theme of Scripture. The Old Testament looked ahead to Him; the New Testament looks back to His first coming and on to His second. Canonical Scripture is the divinely inspired and therefore normative witness to Christ. No hermeneutic, therefore, of which the historical Christ is not the focal point is acceptable. Holy Scripture must be treated as what it essentially is—the witness of the Father to the incarnate Son.

It appears that the Old Testament canon had been fixed by the time of Jesus. The New Testament canon is likewise now closed inasmuch as no new apostolic witness to the historical Christ can now be borne. No new revelation (as distinct from Spirit-given understanding of existing revelation) will be given until Christ comes again. The canon was created in principle by divine inspiration. The Church's part was to discern the canon which God had created, not to devise one of its own.

The word *canon,* signifying a rule or standard, is a pointer to authority, which means the right to rule and control. Authority in Christianity belongs to God in His revelation, which means, on the one hand, Jesus Christ, the living Word, and, on the other hand, Holy Scripture, the written Word. But the authority of Christ and that of Scripture are one. As our Prophet, Christ testified that Scripture cannot be broken. As our Priest and King, He devoted His earthly life to fulfilling the law and the prophets, even dying in obedience to the words of Messianic prophecy. Thus, as He saw Scripture attesting Him and His authority, so by His own submission to Scripture He attested its authority. As He bowed to His Father's instruction given in His Bible (our Old Testament), so He requires His disciples to do—not, however, in isolation but in conjunction with the apostolic witness to Himself which He undertook to inspire by His gift of the Holy Spirit. So Christians show themselves faithful servants of their Lord by bowing to the divine instruction given in the prophetic and apostolic writings which together make up our Bible.

By authenticating each other's authority, Christ and Scripture coalesce into a single fount of authority. The Biblically-interpreted Christ and the Christ-centered, Christ-proclaiming Bible are from this standpoint one. As from the fact of inspiration we infer that what Scripture says, God says, so from the revealed relation between Jesus Christ and Scripture we may equally declare that what Scripture says, Christ says.

Infallibility, Inerrancy, Interpretation

Holy Scripture, as the inspired Word of God witnessing authoritatively to Jesus Christ, may properly be called *infallible* and *inerrant.* These negative terms have a special value, for they explicitly safeguard crucial positive truths.

Infallible signifies the quality of neither misleading nor being misled and so safeguards in categorical terms the truth that Holy Scripture is a sure, safe, and reliable rule and guide in all matters.

Similarly, *inerrant* signifies the quality of being free from all falsehood or mistake and so safeguards the truth that Holy Scripture is entirely true and trustworthy in all its assertions.

We affirm that canonical Scripture should always be interpreted on the basis that it is infallible and inerrant. However, in determining what the God-taught writer is asserting in each passage, we must pay the most careful attention to its claims and character as a human production. In inspiration, God utilized the culture and conventions of his penman's milieu, a milieu that God controls in His sovereign providence; it is misinterpretation to imagine otherwise.

So history must be treated as history, poetry as poetry, hyperbole and metaphor as hyperbole

and metaphor, generalization and approximation as what they are, and so forth. Differences between literary conventions in Bible times and in ours must also be observed: since, for instance, non-chronological narration and imprecise citation were conventional and acceptable and violated no expectations in those days, we must not regard these things as faults when we find them in Bible writers. When total precision of a particular kind was not expected nor aimed at, it is no error not to have achieved it. Scripture is inerrant, not in the sense of being absolutely precise by modern standards, but in the sense of making good its claims and achieving that measure of focused truth at which its authors aimed.

The truthfulness of Scripture is not negated by the appearance in it of irregularities of grammar or spelling, phenomenal descriptions of nature, reports of false statements (*e.g.*, the lies of Satan), or seeming discrepancies between one passage and another. It is not right to set the so-called "phenomena" of Scripture against the teaching of Scripture about itself. Apparent inconsistencies should not be ignored. Solution of them, where this can be convincingly achieved, will encourage our faith, and where for the present no convincing solution is at hand we shall significantly honor God by trusting His assurance that His Word is true, despite these appearances, and by maintaining our confidence that one day they will be seen to have been illusions.

Inasmuch as all Scripture is the product of a single divine mind, interpretation must stay within the bounds of the analogy of Scripture and eschew hypotheses that would correct one Biblical passage by another, whether in the name of progressive revelation or of the imperfect enlightenment of the inspired writer's mind.

Although Holy Scripture is nowhere culture-bound in the sense that its teaching lacks universal validity, it is sometimes culturally conditioned by the customs and conventional views of a particular period, so that the application of its principles today calls for a different sort of action.

Skepticism and Criticism

Since the Renaissance, and more particularly since the Enlightenment, world-views have been developed which involve skepticism about basic Christian tenets. Such are the agnosticism which denies that God is knowable, the rationalism which denies that He is incomprehensible, the idealism which denies that He is transcendent, and the existentialism which denies rationality in His relationships with us. When these un- and anti-biblical principles seep into men's theologies at presuppositional level, as today they frequently do, faithful interpretation of Holy Scripture becomes impossible.

Transmission and Translation

Since God has nowhere promised an inerrant transmission of Scripture, it is necessary to affirm that only the autographic text of the original documents was inspired and to maintain the need of textual criticism as a means of detecting any slips that may have crept into the text in the course of its transmission. The verdict of this science, however, is that the Hebrew and Greek text appear to be amazingly well preserved, so that we are amply justified in affirming, with the Westminster Confession, a singular providence of God in this matter and in declaring that the authority of Scripture is in no way jeopardized by the fact that the copies we possess are not entirely error-free.

Similarly, no translation is or can be perfect, and all translations are an additional step away from the *autographa*. Yet the verdict of linguistic science is that English-speaking Christians, at least, are exceedingly well served in these days with a host of excellent translations and have no cause for hesitating to conclude that the true Word of God is within their reach. Indeed, in view of the frequent repetition in Scripture of the main matters with which it deals and also of the Holy Spirit's

constant witness to and through the Word, no serious translation of Holy Scripture will so destroy its meaning as to render it unable to make its reader "wise for salvation through faith in Christ Jesus" (2 Tim. 3:15).

Inerrancy and Authority

In our affirmation of the authority of Scripture as involving its total truth, we are consciously standing with Christ and His apostles, indeed with the whole Bible and with the main stream of Church history from the first days until very recently. We are concerned at the casual, inadvertent, and seemingly thoughtless way in which a belief of such far-reaching importance has been given up by so many in our day.

We are conscious too that great and grave confusion results from ceasing to maintain the total truth of the Bible whose authority one professes to acknowledge. The result of taking this step is that the Bible which God gave loses its authority, and what had authority instead is a Bible reduced in content according to the demands of one's critical reasonings and in principle reducible still further once one has started. This means that at bottom independent reason now has authority, as opposed to Scriptural teaching. If this is not seen and if for the time being basic evangelical doctrines are still held, persons denying the full truth of Scripture may claim an evangelical identity while methodologically they have moved away from the evangelical principle of knowledge to an unstable subjectivism, and will find it hard not to move further.

We affirm that what Scripture says, God says. May He be glorified. Amen and Amen.

THE INSPIRATION AND AUTHORITY OF SCRIPTURE

Geoffrey W. Bromiley, D.Litt.

A. THE INSPIRATION OF SCRIPTURE

1. The Fact of Inspiration

Acknowledging the inspiration of Scripture is part of the Christian confession. For Christians inspiration is not just a hypothesis, a theory, or a fancy. Nor is it a logical deduction from something else. It is a fact which is part of the essence of Christianity. To confess it is part of being a Christian.

A first reason why this is so is that Scripture itself proclaims its inspiration. It does so most obviously in the verse 2 Timothy 3:16, which says that all (or every) Scripture is God-breathed. This does not mean that God "breathed into" the text, and perhaps the term "inspiration" is not, strictly, the best term. Yet the verse does speak of "spiration." Connected with Scripture is a breathing of God; in virtue of this we speak of inspiration.

Now 2 Timothy 3:16 is no isolated reference. Though it is the only one to make the direct equation, many other passages speak of the same thing in other ways. Thus 2 Peter 1:21 says that holy men of old spoke as they were moved by the Spirit. Here, of course, it is the men who are inspired, and they speak rather than write. Yet it is a mistake to see any basic difference or contradiction. Writings cannot be artificially separated from authors, and much of the Bible was spoken first, or is a distillation or expansion of what was spoken. The essential point is the work of the Spirit.

2 Peter 1:21 is in line with a basic conviction of both the Old and the New Testament; namely, that the prophets and apostles are taken, filled, and used by the Spirit to speak God's word. This is the constitutive witness of the Bible. God by His Spirit has spoken His own Word of revealing and reconciling truth. He has done so through the men of the Bible—the men about whom it tells us, the men whose words are enshrined in it, the men who wrote it. One can and must speak of the inspiration of Scripture because the divine message given by God Himself is its real content.

Scripture proclaims its inspiration as part of what it says about God the Holy Spirit. Even 2 Timothy 3:16 brings this out, for "breathing" carries a clear reference to the Spirit. Elsewhere the connection is even more direct. It is the Spirit Who comes on men, whether they are Old Testament prophets or New Testament apostles. It is the Spirit Who endows them. It is the Spirit Who gives their words the power and authority of the divine Word. It is the Spirit Whose ministry compels us to say that Scripture is inspired of God.

Confession of the inspiration of Scripture is an integral part of Christian confession precisely because it is confession of the person and ministry of the Holy Spirit. Primarily, then, a statement about inspiration is a statement about God, not Scripture. It says not that Scripture has this or that quality, but that God the Holy Spirit did something. As the early Creed says, "he spake by the prophets." To say that Scripture is inspired is to say that God has given His own revelation, has spoken His own Word, and has embodied it in writing, using human speakers and authors in a work of His Holy Spirit.

This is a basic premise, starting point, and place of decision. If a man believes in the Biblical God—Father, Son, and Spirit—that man also believes in the inspiration of Scripture. On the other hand, if a man does not really believe in the Biblical God, but accepts at best only some of the insights of the Bible into religious truth, that man will not believe in the unique inspiration of Scripture. The converse is also true. Belief in the inspiration of Scripture means commitment to the Biblical God, while rejection of inspiration means at root rejection of this God. The doctrine of Scripture is part and parcel of the doctrine of God. It flows from the divine nature. It is linked with what God has done. With God and His Word and works it is thus confessed or negated.

This means, of course, that we are here in a realm of first principles. There can be no proving of inspiration just as there can be no proving of God. Considerations can be advanced which point this way, whether in characteristics of the Bible or experiences in relation to it. But these considerations have no final cogency except for believers or in the purely negative sense that if, for example, the Bible consisted of nonsense, or taught manifest falsehoods, or recorded events which were palpably untrue, or had either no effects at all or purely injurious effects, one would dismiss its inspiration as groundless. Yet the fact that it does make sense, that it teaches manifest truths, that its events can stand up to investigation, and that it has good effects is inadequate in itself to prove conclusively its inspiration as the revelation of the one true and living God. All this may incline people to faith, or strengthen faith already present. But it cannot be the real ground for accepting and confessing inspiration.

There is a circular aspect to confessing inspiration, as there is to confessing God. One believes in the Biblical God because the Bible is inspired. One believes the Bible is inspired because it is given by the Biblical God. Of these two statements the former seems to have priority. This is why some people feel it necessary to go further and find other reasons

465

why the Bible is to be regarded as inspired. In fact, however, the second statement is the more basic. Any statement about God necessarily takes precedence. God inspired the Bible so that we might know Him in his Word and acts. He uses Scripture to this end. Bringing us to knowledge of Himself, He also brings us to confess the inspiration of Scripture not as a human evaluation, but as a divinely posited fact. Scripture, too, is part of His word and work. Its inspiration is thus a fact. Confessing it through God's work, we know it as God's work. As God's work it is a fact. Knowing God through this fact, the Christian is sure of it as a fact, and his knowledge of God is given the greater assurance thereby. For the Christian the knowledge of inspiration is grounded unshakably and inescapably in the knowledge of God. Its confession is part of his confession of the triune God.

2. The Nature of Inspiration

What is the nature of inspiration? This is a hard question, for Scripture itself does not specifically define the term. The word also has a broad use in relation to many historical phenomena. What we have to do, then, is to observe the work of the Spirit and to compare and contrast it with what goes on in other fields. Or perhaps one might proceed in the opposite direction, showing first what the work of the Spirit is not, and then what it is.

First, this particular work of the Spirit is not the same as the inspiration that can be claimed for works of art, music, and literature, or indeed for many discoveries in the intellectual sphere. It is arguable, of course, that this general inspiration is not just an outburst of man's spirit. The Christian will believe that where it is good the Spirit of God does ultimately lie behind it. This seems to be implied in the doctrines of creation and providence. Even the doctrine of sin cannot ascribe to man the autonomy he vainly seeks. The difference between Biblical and artistic inspiration does not reside in a complete disparity of origin.

It may also be argued that as a great work of literature and religion the Bible too has the inspiration common to higher achievements of the race. Perhaps this is not the main thing and to stress it is to run the risk of confusion and to do a disservice to the proper understanding of Scripture. Yet to deny it is to fly in the face of facts, to make an improper disjunction, and to call in question the real humanity of the Bible. The problem is one of proportion rather than exclusion.

If Scripture is in fact inspired as other books are, it is also inspired as they are not. This inspiration is connected with the special work of God in revelation and reconciliation. If God works in all things and peoples, He works specifically and uniquely in the words and works recorded in Scripture and in the word and work of Scripture itself. Written with a particular theme and for a particular end, Scripture has a particular inspiration. God the Spirit breathes specially here, so that with the inspiration common to other works Scripture has this special inspiration consonant with its special theme and purpose.

Furthermore, inspiration is not mantic ecstaticism such as that found elsewhere in religious history. There might seem to be a close parallel here. The wind had a place in oracles, for example, and the human prophet or interpreter acted as the mouthpiece of deity. The divine inspiration would seem, then, to correspond both in principle and procedure to that of the Bible, the more so as the Bible records such ecstatic phenomena as prophetism in the Old Testament and speaking in tongues in the New.

Nevertheless, the many distinctive features of prophetism and the Bible generally show that its inspiration differs from that of manticism. First, the Bible does not make unintelligible or sporadic pronouncements. Secondly, the divine aspect is not inscrutable providence, fate, or destiny. Thirdly, the Biblical sayings though often oracular in form, are not obscure or devious. Finally, there is an ethical quality about God's Word and work in Scripture. All in all, God is not playing with man. He is actively speaking and working in history for man's salvation. He confronts man with the great truths and issues of good and evil, life and death. While individuals no doubt had ecstatic experiences, the Spirit's work in Scripture differs radically from manticism. It is integrally bound up with the whole work of God of which the Bible is the story.

This involves a further point. Working historically through men and peoples, God takes man seriously. If it is God speaking and working through men, it is men through whom God speaks and works. The men are not passive instruments; they are real men. Their words and works and writings are the stuff of history. God does not manipulate them like puppets. The Biblical authors have their own historical settings, personal experiences, and individual styles. Some are better writers than others. Some write with passion, some reflectively, some even in rapture. God the Spirit breathes on them to speak and write what is needed at this or that point, but for the effecting of His purpose He uses rather than quenches their individualities.

Since inspiration is part of the Spirit's ministry, it does not end with the writing. In an important sense inspiration, like Christ's atonement, is a finished work. The breathing took place in history, on the authors. This historical givenness, as we have seen, is important. It lifts inspiration out of a purely subjective realm of opinion, experience, or fancy. It gives it the absoluteness of objectivity, of fact. The Spirit has set His stamp on these writings, so that no matter how we read them,

or whether we read them, nothing can alter their inspiration.

Yet in another important sense inspiration is an ongoing work too. The Spirit does not cease His work with Scripture when the writing is done. He does not simply put things in writing and then leave everything to human factors. The Spirit Who inspired the authors also works in the readers and hearers. He applies what is written, showing its truth, giving understanding, leading to faith in the God Who has spoken these words and done these deeds of revelation and reconciliation. Strictly, perhaps, this work of the Spirit in readers and hearers is not inspiration, and one must beware of allowing this aspect to crowd out the given inspiring of the writers. Yet any work of the Spirit is a breathing, a "spiration." Furthermore, the emphasis on the ongoing ministry of the Spirit prevents us from regarding inspiration as a mere quality, from ascribing to Scripture a false autonomy or quasi-magical power. The poet was not entirely wide of the mark when he said: "The Spirit breathes upon the word,/And brings its truth to light."

One must stress that this "subjective" side is not in conflict with the "objective." The Spirit does this work of breathing and illuminating by Himself speaking the word which He inspired. The important thing is that we have here not two conflicting views of inspiration, but two complementary aspects of the Spirit's ministry. When this is recognized, there need be no hesitation in confessing that the inspiring of the reader as well as the writer—the inspiration of Scripture read as well as written—forms an integral and indispensable part of the total picture.

3. Verbal Inspiration

The Bible is thus inspired in this unique way. But what is it in Scripture which is inspired? The words? The thought expressed by the words? Or the two in combination? This matter has been much discussed in the last decades. It underlies the pedantic stress of some ministers not on Scripture as God's Word, but on the Word of God contained in Scripture.

Historically the Church has regarded the words as inspired. This rests on the Jewish view which attaches importance to the very letters. In controversy some theologians have even argued that inspiration extends to the Hebrew vowel points. A valuable by-product of this high view has been the great care in transmitting the text. Without the concept of verbal inspiration variations might have been not only more numerous but also much more serious.

The main objection to verbal inspiration is that it implies a mantic or dictation understanding of the composition of Scripture. If the Spirit chooses the very words, the writers must have received them either in a trance (automatic writing) or as secretaries. This is not unjustly felt to be inconsistent with a true view of inspiration. It destroys the real humanity of the authors. It also concentrates on form rather than content.

In contrast, the argument is that what really matters is what is said, not how it is said. The content of Scripture—its ideas, truths, facts, and insights—is what is inspired. For the rest, the writers have complete freedom to state these as best they can according to their own background and literary or linguistic powers. The words are not inspired; what they express is.

Now one may grant that the idea of verbal inspiration sometimes leads to a wooden view of the Bible. The fear of a mantic or dictation view is probably overdone, since few serious thinkers have positively advanced such ideas. On the other hand, it is easy enough to engage in a process of abstraction from history as though the words had little or nothing to do with the real abilities, experiences, and circumstances of the human writers, but were simply transcendent oracles. When this is done, inspiration is in practice reduced to a mantic or dictation process even where no such view is advocated.

Another point is that the work of interpretation assumes that some distinction can be made between words and content. At root, exposition, and preaching too, are attempts to bring out the meaning in different words. It is demanded in the first instance by the fact that words can have various meanings and nuances. But it is demanded too by the fact that the literary, linguistic, or cultural background may change. To get at the true sense, one has to go behind the words used. If this is legitimate, however, it would seem that the words are in fact less important than the content.

All the same, the case against verbal inspiration is not so strong as it looks. To meet the objections first, there is surely no reason why verbal inspiration should entail an ignoring of the personal characteristics of the authors. Indeed, one might say that the more seriously the words are taken, the more significant are the peculiarities of the writers. Stress on content carries with it an even greater danger of abstraction.

Again, the legitimacy of exposition has no real bearing on the matter. Exposition certainly uses other words to try to bring out what is said. But if it is true to itself, it does this by first concentrating on the actual text. It asks not what the author is trying to say, but what he actually does say. It studies the words used, both singly and contextually, in order to get as precise an understanding as possible. Far from justifying a separation of form and content, it presupposes their conjunction.

This leads to the main point about verbal inspiration. What it stands for is not that the words rather than their content are inspired,

but that there is no such thing as the one without the other. The Biblical message does not consist of general abstractions which can come in all kinds of forms. It relates to what is said and done by God in the working out of His purpose of grace and judgment. It has the character of historicity, particularity. The verbal form is part of this particularity. If what is said might have been put in other ways, it is in fact put in this way. This is no accident of history. It is part of the story. The form is not expendable. This content is not to be had without this form.

Verbal inspiration is very important. It reminds us that we are dealing with God's Word and work in history, not with abstract truths or insights. It commits us to a serious reckoning with the humanity of the writers—this man, this style, these circumstances. It thus binds us to the proper work not merely of exposition in general, but more specifically of linguistic study, exegesis, translation, and interpretation. Furthermore, it gives us an objective reference. Ideas put in other forms can surreptitiously change or be changed. The words are a rein. They do not let the preacher or commentator go too far afield. They bear this meaning, no less, no more. They state this content. Fancy must yield to factuality.

Verbal inspiration does not extend, of course, to translations. One must be grateful to scholars for the accuracy they achieve. One may believe that God's providence superintends their labors. But the inspired words are the original words in Greek and Hebrew, not the words of the KJV or the Luther Bible or the Vulgate. This is why Greek and Hebrew studies are so vitally important. Since the autographs are no longer available, it is also understandable that textual work should be essential too, for this leads us as close as possible to the pure and authentic text. The student has his work to do as well as the Spirit.

Incidentally, the fact that the inspired originals are not to hand does not make a mockery of verbal inspiration. To all intents and purposes the words transmitted are the divinely inspired words. They can still act as a reliable control for translation, exposition, and proclamation. Nor is it pointless that inspiration took place in relation to documents which have now perished in their original state. As noted, this is part of the historical singularity of all God's work. Verbal inspiration is no abstraction. It is the inspiring of these words written by these men to convey this message in this situation and this context of God's revealing and reconciling word and work. To know this word and work, one needs to know it in these words and no other.

4. Inspiration and Infallibility

A word which often crops up in relation to inspiration is infallibility, or, more recently, inerrancy. The Bible, by the way, does not explicitly use either term, and discussion tends to be tied up with modern problems rather alien to Scripture itself. Caution is thus demanded when one asks: Does Biblical inspiration imply Biblical infallibility?

Infallibility, too, can mean different things. An older sense was that of reliability in achieving an end. This is undoubtedly a sound Biblical concept. There are many instances in the Bible. When God says, "Let there be light," one may count upon it that light will shine. When Christ says to the leper, "Be clean," cleansing is to be expected. God's Word has the power to accomplish what it says. This kind of infallibility is expressly ascribed to God's Word when Isaiah 55:11 says that it will accomplish what God pleases. Scripture cannot fail in what it is meant to do; it is infallible.

Yet quite naturally, and not unjustifiably, the narrower sense broadens out into that of general reliability. If Scripture can be relied on to achieve certain ends, it can be counted on in other ways too. Its promises (and threats) will be fulfilled. Its account of God's works is authentic. Its teachings are true. The Bible does not mislead its readers. It does not teach what is false or erroneous. It can be relied on implicitly. It is infallible.

This infallibility cannot be finally questioned, for if the Bible is not reliable, if many of its records are untrue and its doctrines false, then, as we have seen, there is little point or sense in being a Biblical Christian. Perhaps one might accept some of the insights of Scripture, or dig out a reliable core, but what is left does not amount to much. Only the non-Christian or pseudo-Christian either deliberately or practically denies the reliability of Scripture.

But how far does this infallibility extend? Literary and historical study of the Bible seems to have put this question acutely. Analysis of the books suggests difficulties of various kinds, and natural science also seems to indicate that many accounts or statements are at odds with scientific findings. Historically it is not always easy to integrate the Biblical narratives with secular data, and archaeology, while generally supporting the Bible, raises a few problems of its own.

Two main lines have been followed in answering these questions. The first is to defend detailed infallibility by meeting every objection, often on the ground that inspiration stands or falls by this, since God would not have inspired an imperfect book. The latter principle is good, and the defenses of Biblical data have been massive and not without success, since many supposed errors do not stand up to close investigation. The final difficulty, however, is that there is no absolute proof, only probability, in these matters, so that one cannot really demonstrate inspiration by demonstrating infallibility. This is the truth in the famous (and by no means infallible) dictum that the eternal truths of reason cannot

rest on the contingent facts of history. The charge of utter unreliability can be met, but historical or literary or scientific demonstration does not have the absolute character which would qualify it as a basis of belief.

The second line is to distinguish between a doctrinal sphere of infallibility and a historical or scientific sphere of fallibility. The argument from purpose is used here. Scripture is meant to teach us about God, not about geology or botany. In some cases a distinction is also made between content and form, as noted in respect of verbal inspiration. Ancient forms, possibly myths, are said to be used to convey truth or to effect existential encounter. These forms are either to be replaced or to be understood for what they are, but in neither case is one to insist on the historical factuality of what belongs to the form. Infallibility extends only to the specific area of teaching about God, not to other areas or to forms. It is not comprehensive.

This plausible position raises its own difficulties. Can one trust the doctrine if the facts are unreliable? As Tertullian remarked in another connection, why should one believe someone in hidden matters if he has been found so false on a plain fact? Again, Scripture does not seem to make the distinctions suggested. Nor does it seem to think of itself as mythological or as a book of nonhistorical truths. In fact, by its very nature the Biblical revelation is historical. Many of the details may be incidental, but the Gospel has to be factually as well as doctrinally true if it is true at all. To make distinctions here is to bring it into jeopardy at a crucial point.

The two main lines seem to involve both truth and difficulty, so that one may well ask whether they do not share a basic error. Are they really asking the right questions? Are they approaching the Bible with true objectivity; i.e., in the light of what it is and purports to be? Are they not perhaps importing alien criteria and then trying to get an answer when obviously no answer is to be had along these lines? Three considerations suggest themselves here, and they may well point us in a more satisfactory direction.

The first is that statements do not have to be precisely scientific to be true. A popular statement (e.g., the sun rises) can also be true in its own terms even if it might not stand up to analysis in other terms. The second is that the Bible is written in many genres; and while there seems to be no evidence of myth, it is obviously nonsensical either to treat poetry as a factual record or to dismiss the truth or even the historicity of poetry because it is not a factual record. The third is that attention must indeed be paid to the Bible's own purpose in this matter of factual as well as doctrinal reliability. If Scripture is not imparting knowledge encyclopedically, it is also not inculcating abstract truths. As the story of God's words and works in history, it contains a great deal of history and includes many incidental data on a wide range of topics. These are not offered as textbook information but within Scripture's own broader context; and according to the literary genres employed, the statements of Scripture are indeed quite reliable.

In other words, when Scripture is taken with true objectivity, and interpreted according to its own nature, criteria, and purpose, one may well say that it is infallible. Most of the problems that suggest themselves to the modern mind are no real problems when approached in this way. The real need is to break the empiricist tyranny that imposes its own narrow view of factuality and that will not let us see the Bible as it really is and in its own terms. The reason why both ordinary lines of approach run into difficulty is that they far too readily accept this tyranny, so that even the true things they say are distorted and can give no final satisfaction.

In conclusion, it must be stressed that infallibility as inerrancy is not to be divorced from infallibility as efficacy, for this is what counts in the final analysis; i.e., in the last judgment. It must also be stressed that infallibility in either sense is not to be divorced from inspiration, for ultimately the infallibility of Scripture is that of the Holy Spirit. Inspiration guarantees infallibility, not vice versa. But it guarantees the infallibility of these documents written in this way and to this end. Once this is appreciated, the false choices in a good deal of modern theology may be dismissed, and the Scripture which was given by the Spirit and is used by the Spirit can do its proper work with its proper authority.

B. THE AUTHORITY OF SCRIPTURE

1. The Basis of Authority

Scripture claims authority for itself. It does so in many ways. "It is written," followed by a quotation, is a frequent argument in the Bible. "According to the scriptures" is the clue to the ministry, death, and Resurrection of Jesus. Not to know Scripture is a cause of error. The Epistles are written not as expressions of opinion, but as authoritative rulings on doctrine and practice. Revelation even has a solemn warning against adding to or subtracting from the book.

For the most part theologians and the Church generally have assented to the supreme authority of Scripture. Even where we find other authorities, the Bible has not been dethroned. Some of the historic confessions state this authority clearly. Scripture is the supreme rule of faith and practice. Everything necessary to salvation is found in it. Things plainly contrary to Scripture are not to be believed or done. Scripture is the final judge in controverted questions.

It should be noted that the authority

claimed for the Bible is not just a historical authority. The Bible does have this kind of authority too. Most of what we know about the story of God's Word and work in Israel, in Jesus Christ, and in the primitive Church comes from the Old and New Testaments. These are our primary and almost exclusive source. They have the peculiar authority of firsthand sources and eyewitness accounts. At the level of knowledge they can claim a position which it is impossible to challenge. What do we really know of Jesus without the New Testament?

In four ways, however, the authority of Scripture has both a deeper basis and a wider range. (1) It is witness to a specific series of events. (2) It is a witness uniquely raised up by God within these events to fulfill this role. (3) It has a distinctive reliability by reason of its distinctive nature, origin, and function. (4) It is God Himself who in all His authority speaks in and through Scripture.

Many books besides the Bible are historical sources. Many can lay claim to special authority, particularly when they present unchallenged data about a specific segment of history. But the persons or events described are of no further interest. They make no demand on the student. No one has to shape his beliefs or conduct according to them. The Bible, however, is testimony to God's Word and acts. If it has supreme historical value, it also raises a claim to faith and obedience. It does not just pass on authoritative information; it makes an authoritative demand.

This ties in with the fact that Scripture was uniquely written within God's words and acts not merely to provide an authentic record but also to present God's message and claim with enduring fidelity and power. Other books and documents have been written as records and are authoritative by virtue of the authors or circumstances of writing. Some—e.g., laws and constitutions—may even raise a limited claim. Formally, then, they are like Scripture. The difference is that the author in this case is God and the claim he makes is of universal relevance and validity. The different quality of the Bible's authority lies precisely in the fact that it comes from God. This works itself out in the next two points.

Scripture has a unique reliability by reason of its nature, function, and origin. Inspired of God, written to tell of His saving words and works, employed by the Spirit, it has a reliability unparalleled among other works. Many books have a high degree of trustworthiness, and yet they still remain within the sphere of human relativity. At the level of its humanity this could be said of the Bible too. But in its divine function the Bible has the absoluteness of the divine authority. This does not mean, as we have seen, that it is an infallible encyclopedia of all knowledge. It does mean that what the Bible tells us about God in His Word and work is absolutely reliable. Even inciden-

tal matters share this reliability within the context and purpose in which they are given.

Nor is the Bible uniquely authoritative merely as a reliable record. It is authoritative as the living voice and act of the God about whom it tells us. Authority, like inspiration, is not a static attribute. It has a static side. It is the authority of the finished work. But it also has a dynamic side. It is the authority of the Holy Spirit using Scripture as a continuing word and work. The voice of Scripture is the voice of God.

In the last analysis, then, Scripture's authority is God's authority. The Bible is no paper pope. It is the writing by which God, Who spoke and acted definitively in Jesus Christ, still speaks and acts by the Holy Spirit. It is the organ by which Christ Himself does His work and rules the Church in a holy continuity of doctrine and practice. One dares to say that Scripture is the supreme, unique, infallible, and absolute norm because it is God Who gave it and God Who uses it in this role. God Himself is the supreme, unique, infallible, and absolute norm. He discharges this normative function through Holy Scripture.

2. Other Authorities

Scripture's authority has been almost universally acknowledged in the Church. But other authorities have been advanced which either rival or qualify that of Scripture. What are these? What claim do they have? Are they to be rejected out of hand? Have they a proper place and function?

Oral tradition is the first. The argument is that the message was spoken before it was written, that the living word has come down alongside the written word, that it has therefore the same authority, and that if it includes teachings or practices not recorded in the written word, these have the same normative status as those that are. The trouble begins with this final point. No one disputes the chronological priority of the spoken word; did Jesus Himself write anything? No one contests that the living word is a valid form alongside Scripture. The point is, however, that Scripture was written as a permanent embodiment of the original prophetic and apostolic Word. Oral transmission is subject to change, development, degeneration, and deviation. It needs a check, a standard, a point of reference. Scripture supplies this. Hence oral tradition which accords with Scripture shares Scripture's authority. This is how it should be. But tradition which proclaims what is nonscriptural cannot have absolute authority. What is proclaimed may be good enough. It may have the authority of antiquity or consent. But it does not have ultimate compulsion or necessity.

The Church also claims authority. The basic argument here is that the Church, too, is divinely instituted, that it preached before Scripture was written, that it produced Scrip-

ture, that it established the Canon, that it expounds Scripture, and that it has certain disciplinary functions. These theses are sound enough. But they do not prove that the Church's authority is equal or superior to that of Scripture. The mistake is a failure to see the uniqueness of the apostolate and its function. The Church has an apostolic ministry, but it does not have the role of the first apostles who were specifically called to be with Christ, who bore the first testimony, and who gave this testimony a permanent form in their writings. The Church may judge and rule. Its authority is not to be treated lightly. But the Church, too, is under the authority Christ exercises through the prophetic and apostolic writings. Where it speaks Biblically, its authority is absolute. Where it does not, it can claim at most only relative authority.

This goes for the Pope as well. On the ground of apostolic or more specifically Petrine succession, absolute authority has been claimed for the Pope. Where the argument is put more generally and the Pope is simply the mouthpiece of the Church, what has been said about the Church applies. Where a unique Petrine authority is alleged, the same difficulties arise with even greater force. As the apostolate was unique, so was Peter's position within it. Even if it had been handed down, it is not clear why it should go to Rome. The idea that Peter was founder or first bishop of the Roman church is precarious, and support for the notion that he handed on headship over the whole Church to the Roman bishops is conspicuous by its absence. Thoughtful Roman Catholics see this, and prefer to see in the Pope's authority an epitome of that of the Church. If so, the rule holds good: The Pope is infallible when he is Biblical; when he is not, his authority even at best is only relative and fallible.

Creeds, confessions, and the fathers come under a similar rule. The Churches have not been wrong to issue official statements on debated issues. Individual Christians also do well to quote such statements, or judgments of the fathers, in favor of particular positions. Such statements and judgments have their authority; but they do not have absolute authority. They are fallible and reformable. They are not to be treated as definitive. They are always open to the question as to whether what they say is really Biblical. This question is not to be put too cavalierly. Much Biblical work lies behind the formulations of gifted minds and learned councils. Nevertheless, they too stand under the one norm which is unique, supreme, and absolute. Where they agree with this they are right. Where they only thought they agreed with it, they must be corrected.

Three important points emerge from this survey. First, nothing but mischief results when other authorities are set up as rivals of Scripture or coequal to it. Their own normativeness is disturbed as well as that of Scrip-

ture. Secondly, and conversely, acknowledgment of the unique authority of Scripture establishes the real authority of other standards rather than shattering or destroying it. The absoluteness of the Bible is not absolutism. The God who set up the supreme norm also established the subsidiary norms. When these are seen in due proportion, they have their proper role and weight. Finally, the fact that subsidiary standards have their own authority is a reminder that we are not their judges. If we may rightly put to them the question as to whether they are Biblical, we too stand under the same question. It is only on Biblical grounds that we have a right to challenge them. Even where we have reason to suspect that they might be in error, we must proceed with due caution and respect, recognizing that in the upshot they might still have the best of the argument. Like tradition, Church, Pope, or confession, the individual Christian is infallible only where he is truly Biblical, and he is not always so Biblical as he thinks. In reminding him of this, the secondary authorities play a role of inestimable value.

3. Authority and Interpretation

The point just made introduces us to one of the most difficult aspects of Biblical authority; namely, that of interpretation. The Bible is infallible and authoritative. But if there are different possibilities of interpretation, where is one to find that which is infallible and absolute? An authoritative Bible is good enough in theory, but how does it work out, and how is it to be worked out, in practice?

The problem arose as soon as heresy arose. Heresy could also appeal to Scripture, and who was to say, by what criteria, that one understanding was right and the other wrong? Answering this question was no academic exercise. It meant truth or error, life or death, for the Church. It still does today. The Bible can exert its authority only if an answer is found.

In fact, the establishment of subsidiary standards was very largely in answer to this question, and they still have a valid function in this respect. Thus the teaching of the Church, handed down from apostolic times, comes down with a specific interpretation which can claim greater legitimacy than false teaching, especially in the immediate postapostolic age. Tradition here is not a rival of Scripture; it provides authentic interpretation which enables Scripture to fulfill its true office.

With tradition one also finds the Church not just as clergy, but as the company of believers who have received the message and pass it on. The message is embodied in the Bible; here it has an objective safeguard against distortion. But the Church in its work of proclamation offers an authentic interpre-

tation of Scripture by which the latter is safeguarded against misinterpretation. The Church does not control the Bible; it simply serves as a check against divergent understanding.

Finally, the creeds have a similar role. They were quickly formulated as confessional expressions of basic facts and doctrines. Naturally they were taken from Scripture, but they could also have a hermeneutical function in relation to it. Biblical interpretation which is in keeping with them is authentic, while that which comes into conflict with them is thereby shown to be erroneous.

Yet there are weaknesses and dangers in these attempted solutions of the problem of interpretation. Oral tradition is notoriously subject to corruption. The Church itself may well fall into error. Many creedal statements were drawn up in specific repudiation of heresies, so that to use them as a guarantee of proper exposition can look like a begging of the question; a majority or official group has decided that this is the right interpretation and has then put it in a creed.

A further difficulty is that once hermeneutical authority is ascribed to something, whether it be tradition, Church, or creed, the supreme normativeness of Scripture is hard to maintain in practice. The teaching office of Rome is a good example; by imposing interpretations it tends to make itself the final authority rather than the Bible. Individuals can play a similar role when they take it for granted that their own understanding is right and is thus the same thing as Scripture.

Is there any way out of this impasse? The answer lies in paying greater attention to the objective entity of the Bible itself. At this point modern disciplines such as textual study, lexical investigation, literary and historical inquiry, and Biblical theology have a significant part to play. If they cannot solve all problems, they do at least try to show with greater precision what the Bible is really saying, not according to an external rule but from within itself.

Thus textual study gives us a reasonably assured text. Lexical investigation handles the terms, their meaning, and the most likely sense in a given passage. Literary and historical inquiry deals with the broader context, the nature and purpose of a book, the time and circumstances of its composition. Biblical theology studies the great themes of Scripture not only in the immediate context but also in historical continuity so that the total picture emerges. Naturally this type of work leaves plenty of room for disagreement. But this is at the more modest level of academic judgment, and the text itself preserves its authority as the object.

In this approach tradition, Church, and creeds still have a place along with the lexicons and commentaries and other scholarly aids. But they are consulted as academic witnesses rather than hermeneutical authorities. As such, they have to take their place with other witnesses. They deserve respect. They may often be right. But they are also open to correction. They cannot get a stranglehold on the text so that it can say only what they say it says.

There is still the difficulty that academic study too can become the victim of non-Biblical preconceptions and lose its professed and required objectivity. There are many examples of this, not only in attempted reconstructions of Biblical thought and history according to current ideas, but also in dissection, demythologizing, and systematic dogmatizing. Nevertheless, the principle that the Bible should be studied for what it is and allowed to say its own piece, whether we like and accept this or not, is at least recognized. Where this is realized, the possibility of objective exposition is present.

Even this objective study, however, does not quite solve the problem of the total interpretation of Scripture. What is the overarching theme? How is the Old Testament related to the New? Does some one book or doctrine underlie a true understanding? Is there a hermeneutical key to the Bible, and if so what is it? Yet here, too, one may best begin with what Scripture itself says. Perhaps the simplest and most basic rule of interpretation is that Christ is the theme and center. This still leaves many possibilities of variation, but so much is involved in Christ in so many ways that the whole Bible makes good sense, and the pieces fall into place, when set in this inner Biblical relation.

A final point is that the Spirit Who gave Scripture and speaks in and through it is also indispensable to sound understanding. The Spirit does not replace the exegetical task. He speaks only through the text. Knowledge of the text and its natural sense is thus demanded. Yet it is possible to have this and still to miss understanding in the deeper sense. This is where the help and guidance of the Spirit are needed. The Spirit is God's Spirit bearing witness to God's Word and work in Jesus Christ. He takes the Scriptural word and makes it clear to heart, mind, will—the whole man—in its total reach and dimension. As the poet said in another connection: "God is his own interpreter,/And he will make it plain."

4. The Range of Authority

How far does the absolute authority of Scripture extend? Do all parts have perpetual authority? Is there some relativity to age and situations? Does precedent have the same weight as precept? Does the Bible leave scope for the Church or reason or current norms? These are hard questions when the principle of authority is put into practice.

One may begin by noting that Scripture's absolute authority does not apply comprehensively to all spheres of life. The Bible impinges

on many things: geography, botany, astronomical data, political and economic conditions, and so forth. In context what Scripture says about these things is reliable, but it is not comprehensive or normative. One does not go to Scripture for a detailed study of the flora and fauna of Palestine or for full information on the reigns of the kings of Israel and Judah. Indeed, great though some of the Biblical literature is, one would not regard the Bible as a textbook of literary composition. Such things are to be learned elsewhere.

As the Bible does not offer us full knowledge on incidental matters, so it does not offer precepts or precedents for action in all areas of life. Civil policies lie outside its authority except insofar as these have theological or ethical implications. So do many of the rules relating to social life. So do modes of warfare or details of legal procedure. Much may be learned about many of these things, and the general demand for righteousness is of universal application. But at the technical level other authorities may well be consulted and followed.

There are also many indifferent matters in everyday life. On some Scripture is silent. The dress and hair styles of the apostles are not described in the Bible. Presumably they followed current modes. Even where incidental information is given, it is surely not a binding rule. Because Paul crossed the sea in sailing vessels, Christians are not committed to this form of transport.

From a different angle the cultic side of the Old Testament has also lost its absolute authority for Christians. This certainly belongs to the true matter of Scripture. It is not an adiaphoron. But Jesus Christ has perfectly and comprehensively fulfilled it as both priest and offering, so that the cultic provisions no longer demand observance in the churches today.

There are thus considerable limits to the Bible's authority. One might summarize these as follows: In secular matters the Bible, while it has a certain authority, does not offer encyclopedic information or present inescapable demands. Where there is a relation of promise (or prefiguring) and fulfillment, the figure serves only a temporary purpose and ceases to have a binding status with the fulfillment. Both points come out in relation to the Old Testament law, for there is fairly general agreement that its social and ceremonial parts applied only in Israel and are not obligatory today.

In contrast, Scripture enjoys full and absolute authority in its own proper sphere, the sphere of the self-revelation of God, and of all that this implies for belief and action. This authority is historical insofar as the acts of God in history are the theme of the Bible; the Biblical account is to be accepted. More deeply, however, it is a theological authority; the Bible is the book about God, and what it tells us about God, about His words and works, about the right relation to Him, is normative. Being theological, this authority is also ethical; what we are told about God includes His will, and the right relationship to God is a living of life in the love and righteousness that He requires. But the authority is liturgical too, for God is the God of grace and glory Whom we are to fear and worship and serve; the fulfilling of the ceremonial law in Christ by no means implies that the authority of Scripture is now irrelevant or purely relative in this sphere.

When all this is added up, its range is considerable. Historical authority covers the data of God's work in history. Theological authority covers the teachings not as human ideas about God, but as God's authentic Word about Himself. Ethical authority covers the whole range of conduct as it falls under the commandments, injunctions, and intentional precedents of the Bible. Liturgical authority covers the practice and worship of the Church; preaching the Word, singing God's praise, prayer, administering the Sacraments. Nor is this all, for since every human relation also involves a relation to God, from its own angle the Bible does have absolute authority in many secular affairs too. We learn this from the prophetic ministry of the Old Testament, where the policy of relying on Egypt is condemned because it betrays a lack of trust in God, or economic developments are castigated because they are at odds with brotherly concern and neighborly love. Technically such things may be decided at other levels, but where there is theological, ethical, or liturgical involvement the Bible still has a normative voice for the people of God.

There are limits, then, to Scripture's authority. All parts of the Bible do not have lasting validity. Some things are relative to time and circumstance. Precedents, often normative, should be handled with care and accepted only where they are fairly plainly meant to be such. Not all things to be done in life, or even in the Church, are laid down in Scripture. We are not told, for example, how to conduct a church business meeting, and excessive literalism should not conclude that there either ought not to be such meetings, or that rules must be found somehow in the Bible.

Nevertheless, in its own sphere the Bible is an absolute norm which is not to be speciously relativized or generalized. This sphere is the big one of God's relation to man in its historical, theological, ethical, and liturgical dimensions. The relation of God to man (and man to God) has implications for all of life, especially its motivations, choices, and ends. To this degree Scripture at its own level and in its own dimensions has a vital bearing even in things which are technically decided according to other authorities. For God is lord of all life. The divine revelation cannot be sealed off in a

compartment all its own. Hence the range of Biblical authority is no less comprehensive than absolute. It is in fact God's own author-

ity. In and through Scripture God is the unique, infallible, and absolute authority in all matters of faith and practice.

IN GOD'S PLAN
MEN AND WOMEN WERE CALLED TO SERVE HIM.
A LIST OF SUCH INDIVIDUALS FOLLOWS
WITH APPROPRIATE HEADINGS SUGGESTED.

ADAM	EVE	ENOCH	NOAH	ABRAM	ABRAHAM
Created	Created	Grace	Grace	Called	Righteous
Gen. 1:26–27	Gen. 1:27	Gen. 5:21–23	Gen. 6:8	Gen. 12:1,3,7	Gen. 17:5
Gen. 5:2	Gen. 5:2			Gen. 15:1,6,7	Heb. 11:8

LOT	ISAAC	JACOB	JOSEPH	MOSES	AARON
Called	Called	Chosen	Mercy	Chosen	Chosen
Gen. 12:5	Gen. 17:20	Gen. 28:13–15	Gen. 39:2,31	Ex. 3:4–14	Ex. 4:14-17
	Gen. 22:12	Gen. 31:11–13	Gen. 41:38		Heb. 5:4
	Gen. 26:3–4	Gen. 35:10–12	Gen. 45:5		
		Gen. 46:2–4			

JOSHUA	GIDEON	RUTH	SAMUEL	SAUL	DAVID
Spirit	Called	Accepted	Called	Chosen	Chosen
Deu. 34:9	Jude 6:14,16	Ruth 1:14,16	1 Sam. 3:4,6	1 Sam. 8:17	1 Sam. 16:12–14
Jos. 1:2–9					
Jos. 3:7–8					

SOLOMON	ELIJAH	ELISHA	JOB	ESTHER
Chosen	Obedient	Spirit-Filled	Blessed	Grace
1 Kg. 3:10–14	1 Kg. 17:3,4,9	1 Kg. 19:19	Job 1:8	Esther 4:16
	2 Kg. 2:1,8	2 Kg. 2:2,9,14		

EZRA	NEHEMIAH	ISAIAH	JEREMIAH	EZEKIEL
Teacher	Leader	Prophet	Spirit-Filled	Spirit-Filled
Ezra 7:6,10,25	Num. 3:18,20	Isa. 6:8–10	Jer. 1:5	Eze. 2:1–8

DANIEL	HOSEA	JOEL	JONAH	MICAH
Favor, Chosen	Prophet	Prophet	Prophet	Prophet
Dan. 1:12–13	Hos. 1:1–2	Joel 1:1	Jon. 1:1–2	Mic. 1:1

ZEPHANIAH	HAGGAI	ZECHARIAH	MATTHEW	MARK
Prophet	Prophet	Prophet	Chosen	Accepted
Zep. 1:1	Hag. 1:1	Zec. 1:1		

LUKE	JOHN	PETER	PAUL	CHURCH
Accepted	Chosen	Chosen	Chosen	Believers
				Faithful
				John 15:16,19

A BRIEF SURVEY OF DANIEL CHAPTER 9: THE PROPHECY OF THE SEVENTY WEEKS OF YEARS

1. This chapter begins with Daniel praying that his nation, Israel, would soon be released from their captivity in Babylon, as the 70 years of captivity prophesied by Jeremiah had almost come to a close (Jer. 25:11,12; 29:10). The Persians had just conquered Babylon in 539 BC and Daniel was praying that the release of the Jews would soon follow (Dan. 9:1). Nebuchadnezzar had invaded Jerusalem three times, first in 606 BC and he then took Daniel and others captive. The third time he besieged the city, he destroyed Solomon's Temple, and took those who were left off of the land. 2 Chron. 36:21 explains that Israel was off of its land for 70 years because it had violated the sabbatical year commandment [Lev. 25:4–7] for seventy sets of seven years (or in King James' language, "seventy weeks of years").

2. In Dan. 9:21–24 the Archangel Gabriel appeared to Daniel and announced that there would yet be *another set of seventy sevens of years* to complete Israel's prophetic history. Verse 24 in the KJV says, "Seventy weeks are determined." The Hebrew for these words are *shavuim shivim* and literally mean, "seventy sevens," with the context clearly being seventy sevens of years.

3. Verse 25 shows that this period of 490 years (70 x 7 = 490) of future history would begin "from the going forth of the commandment to restore and to build Jerusalem." Verse 26 shows that when 483 years would be up the Messiah would be "cut off, but not for Himself" (7 x 7 plus 62 x 7 = 69 x 7 = 483). Taking the end of this period to be 30 AD, the time of Christ's crucifixion, going 483 years backwards would calculate to be at 453 BC. If there is no gap between the first seven sevens and the sixty-two sevens that follows, the proclamation in 454/453 BC by the King Artaxerxes Longimanus of Persia to Ezra (Ezra 7:11–26) would be the start of the time clock of this prophecy.

4. Some, however, suggest that the time clock began in 445 BC, the 20th year of Artaxerxes, when he commanded Nehemiah to go back to Jerusalem to restore the city to a degree of its former glory (Neh. 2:1–8). Thus a century ago Robert Anderson, of Scotland Yard, London, made the following calculation which he published in, *The Coming Prince* (5th edn., London: 1895): He took the initial commandment to have been given in 445 BC and urged that the crucifixion occurred in 31 AD, making some 476 years. He multiplied these 476 years by 365 days in a year = 173,740 days. Adding 116 leap year days = 173,856 days. Then he added 24 days for the partial day of the solar year over 365 = 173,880. He then divided this by 360, the length in days of the calculated year, or the biblical prophetic year = 483, the period of the prophecy through verse 26! In any case this brings us remarkably close to the span of the prophecy, and with some uncertainty of the exact date of the commandment of Artaxerxes we can hardly hope to obtain a closer accuracy at this time.

5. The Julian calendar saw Julius Caesar, upon the advice of the astronomer Sosigenes that the year should be 365.25 days, add 90 days to the year 46/45 BC. Then too, the passover occurs on the 14th of Nisan, which is approximately 90 days into our modern Roman year.

6. The second half of verse 26 says "the people of the prince that shall come shall destroy the city and the sanctuary..." Since "the people" who destroyed the city and sanctuary were the Romans in 70 AD, "the prince that shall come" is commonly interpreted as the antichrist, "the man of sin" of 2 Thessalonians 2:3–4.

7. Verse 27 therefore prophesies that the coming man of sin will (a) make a peace treaty [literally, "will cut a covenant"] with many for the final set of seven years. Then "in the midst of the week," in the middle of the final seven years, he will commit a public blasphemy at the restored Temple area and thus reveal his Satanic character. Matthew 24:15–21 and 2 Thessalonians 2:3–4 confirm this.

G. COHEN

MODERN ISRAEL IN HISTORY AND PROPHECY

1896   Herzl publishes *Der Judenstat* (*The Jewish State*).

1897   First Zionist Congress, Basle, Switzerland.

1917   General Allenby of Britain takes Palestine from Turkey in WWI. Col. T.E. Lawrence leads liberation E of Jordan.

1917   British Balfour Declaration promises "the establishment in Palestine of a National Home for the Jewish People."

1917–1947   Britain occupies Palestine under "Mandate" from League of Nations.

1939   Britain issues "White Paper" promising to end Jewish immigration into Palestine by 1943.

1947   Dead Sea Scrolls discovered in Dead Sea Qumran caves.

1947   United Nations partitions Palestine into Israel and Jordanian territory: West Bank (Old City of Jerusalem included in Jordan; newer west Jerusalem to Israel).

1948   British troops pull out of Palestine (May 14th).

1948   Modern Israel Born (May 14th): Independence declared in wake of attack by Syria, Egypt, and Jordan.

1949   Israel admitted into United Nations (May 11th).

1954   Dead Sea Scrolls purchased by Israel for $250,000. (They had been hidden in the U.S. for safety during the war.)

1956   Israel defeats Egypt in "Sinai Campaign" tank war.

1967   Israel captures Jerusalem in Six Day War (6–11 June) when attacked by Syria, Egypt, and Jordan.

1973   Yom Kippur War: Israel survives attack by Syria & Egypt.

1978   Israel invades S Lebanon in response to PLO attacks. She withdraws after 3 months (March 14th – June).

1978   Camp David Accord: Peace between Egypt & Israel.

1982   Israel invades S Lebanon in response to PLO attacks.

1989   King Hussein of Jordan declares that Jordan, for peace, is giving up its claim to the West Bank area.

1994   West Bank given provisional Palestinian autonomy.

THE NATION OF ISRAEL AS A TYPE OF GOD'S SON IN HISTORY AND PROPHECY

Hos. 11:1   "When Israel was a child, then I loved him, and called my son out of Egypt."

Isa. 11:12   "And He shall set up an ensign for the nations, and shall assemble the outcasts of Israel, and gather together the dispersed of Judah from the four corners of the earth."

Isa. 41:8–9   'But thou, Israel, are My servant, ... Thou whom I have taken from the ends of the earth ... and not cast thee away.:

Jer. 31:31–33 "Behold, the days come, saith the LORD, that I will make a new covenant with the house of Israel, and with the house of 6 will put my law in their inward parts, and...will be their God, and they shall be my people."

Ezek. 37:1–28 "... And He said unto me, Son of man, can these bones live? ... My people, I will open your graves, and bring you into the land of Israel ... And I will make them one nation in the land upon the mountains of Israel ... Neither shall they defile themselves any more ... but I will save them ... and will cleanse them: so shall they be My people, and I will be their God. And David My servant shall be king over them; and they shall have one shepherd: they shall also walk in My judgments...."

Zech. 12:1– "Behold, I will make Jerusalem a cup of trembling unto all the people round about ... In that day shall the LORD defend the inhabitants of Jerusalem ... in that day, I will seek to destroy all the nations that come against Jerusalem. And I will pour out upon the house of David the Spirit of grace ... and they shall look at Me whom they have pierced ... In that day there shall be a fountain opened to the house of David and to the inhabitants of Jerusalem for sin and for uncleanness ... And His feet shall stand in that day upon the Mount of Olives...."

Acts 1:6–8 "... Lord, will Thou at this time restore again the kingdom to Israel? And He said unto them, It is not for you to know the times and seasons, which the Father has put in His own power."

Rom. 11:23,26 "And they also [Israel] if they abide not still in unbelief, shall be grafted in: for God is able to graft them in again. ... And so all Israel shall be saved...."

Rev. 21:12 "... And at the gates [of New Jerusalem] twelve angels, and names written thereon, which are the names of the twelve tribes of the children of Israel."

TYPOLOGICAL COMPARISONS CONCERNING MODERN ISRAEL

Conceived	1947,	United Nations Partition under God's Providence
Born	1948,	Independence & Survival against triple attack
13th Year	1961,	Bar Mitzvah, midway between the Sinai Campaign (1956) and the Six Day War (1967)
20th Year	1968,	Warrior, Recovery of the Old City and Wailing Wall after the 6 Day War (1967)
30th Year	1978,	Life's Work, South Lebanon Struggle continues; Camp David Accord: Peace with Egypt.
40th Year	1988,	Middle Age begins, continued struggle with PLO
50th Year	1998,	Jubilee, "Proclaim liberty throughout all the land to all the inhabitants thereof." (Lev. 25:10)

G. COHEN

The Statue of Daniel 2 is drawn to represent the current times rather than the actual vision of the Statue that was seen in Babylon.

Past History

606 BC

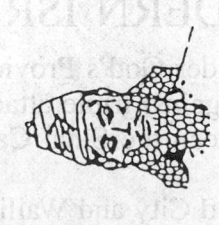

Nebuchadnezzar's Babylon – Pure sovereignty (GOLD)

The head is extremely small and represents the Bablonian Empire which is now old history — Prophecy fulfilled.

Dan. 2:28–31;
Dan. 2:32,38

539 BC

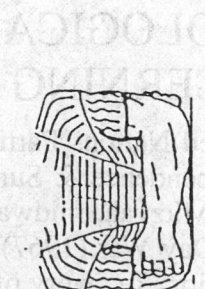

Empire of the Medes and the Persians — 2 Arms represent a dual kingdom (SILVER)

The shoulders, chest, and two arms represent the Medio-Persia Empire and again this represents ancient history and prophecy fulfilled.

Dan. 2:32, 39;
Dan. 8:3–4, 20;
Dan. 10:20;
Dan. 11:2

336 BC

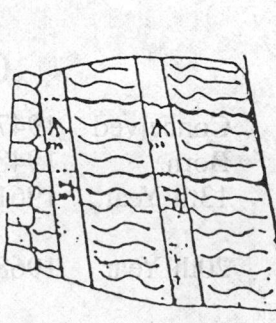

The Greek Empire of Alexander the Great (BRASS)

At his death in 323 his four generals divide the conquests: Thrace, Western Antolla, Syria, and Egypt. 125 years of fighting follows.

Dan. 2:32, 39;
Dan. 7:6;
Dan. 8:5–8;
Dan. 10:20; 11:2
Dan. 7:6;
Dan. 8:8-12

196 BC

Dan. 2:40

The Roman Republic & Empire
(IRON LEGS UNITED)

The abdomen and upper thighs, which are covered by the garment, is also now history.

300 AD

Dan. 2:33, 40

(IRON LEGS DIVIDED)

Rome divided into Western and Eastern Empires.

The Roman Republic and Empire, and the Empire divided into East and West as Emperor Constantine decreed that Christianity was to be legalized in 313 A.D.

The division of the Empire by Diocletian's edict into the two legs represent the eastern Greek Orthodox and the western (Catholic, then Protestant) divisions.

476 AD	1453 AD
Fall of W. Empire	Fall of E. Empire

Dan. 2:41

(IRON LEGS CRACKING)

European Nations: Lawlessness
Modern History and Today

Endtimes (IRON & CLAY)
(TEN TOES: Revived Rome:
European Confederacy)

Dan. 2:34, 41–43;
Dan. 7:19–28

Dan. 2:34–35, 41–45;
Dan. 7:8, 27–28
Rev. 17:12–14, 16–18;
Rev. 18:2, 9

The ten toes represent the modern current times of the division of the Roman Empire — the (European) ten nations that are talked about in Books of Revelation and in other places in biblical prophecy.

We are in the stage now of the ten toes, signifying the formation of a European common union (Common Market) and the many other things that will soon be happening.

481

THE MYSTERY OF MATTHEW'S THREE SETS OF FOURTEEN GENERATIONS!

Matthew 1:17 tells us that there were 14 generations
- (a) from Abraham to David
- (b) from David to the Babylonian Captivity
- (c) from the Babylonian Captivity to Christ

They are listed in Matthew 1:2–16 as follows:

Listed	Listed	Listed
	Omitted	
1 Abraham	Solomon	Jechonias (Jehoiachin)
2 Isaac	Rehoboam	Salathiel
3 Jacob	Abia	Zorobabel
4 Judah*	Asa	Abiud
5 Phares	Jehoshaphat	Eliakim
6 Esrom	Joram	Azor
	Ahaziah	
	Athaliah (Queen)	
	Joash	
	Amaziah	
7 Aram	Uzziah (Azariah)	Sadoc
8 Aminadab	Joatham	Achim
9 Naasson	Ahaz	Eliud
10 Salmon	Hezekiah	Eleazar
11 Booz	Manasses	Matthan
12 Obed	Amon	Jacob
13 Jesse	Josiah	Joseph**
	Jehoahaz	
	Jehoiakim	
14 David	Jechonias (Jehoiachin)	Christ
	"and his brethren"	
	Zedekiah	

*Judah is spelled "Judas" in the New Testament period. The reader will note that the Greek spelling used in the NT often differs from the OT Hebrew spelling for various royal names. The more familiar OT spelling is used at times for some of the more well known kings.

**1:16 speaks of "Joseph the husband of Mary, of whom was born Jesus, who is called Christ." The Greek pronoun for "of-whom" is feminine singular, showing that it refers to Mary only.

Several observations, then several conclusions, must be made:

1. To get the three sets of 14 we must either repeat David's name as both the last name of Set One and the first name of Set Two — or — we must repeat Jechonias' name as the last of Set Two and the first of Set Three, as we have done above. Yet Set Two ideally should end with Jechonias as Josias before him clearly died before the start of the Babylonian Captivity.

2. Three kings are omitted between Joram and Uzziah (who is Azariah), 1 Chron. 3:11–12. This is probably due to rabbinical technical and religious preferences. This is done just as Democrats seem to recite "Our leaders from Washington to Jefferson, Franklin Delano Roosevelt, Truman, Kennedy, Johnson, Carter, Clinton," and Republicans speak of "Our leaders from Washington to Lincoln, Eisenhower, Nixon, Ford, Reagan, Bush."

3. King Zedckiah, who followed Jechonias, is also omitted. His name should have been the last name of Set Two. He was an uncle of Jechonias and the final king of Judah at the time of the Babylonian Captivity. Nevertheless he is in a sense included in the words of Matthew 1:11, "and his brethren" (2 Kings 24:17; 2 Chron. 36:10).

4. From Salmon and his wife "Rachab" (Matt. 1:5) to David, Jamieson, Fausset, & Brown (Zondervan reprint, p. 881) urge would be as many as four centuries. Ruth 4:20–22 & 1 Chron. 2:11–15. Thus a purposeful compression is possible here.

CONCLUSIONS:

1. This list of Matthew is a "genealogy," that is, a true and accurate record of descent; it is not, nor was it meant to be, a complete "chronology" listing every last name in the lineage.

2. Probably for mnemonic reasons, Matthew put it in a list of three fourteens. Fourteen being chosen as just twice the total-cycle number seven.

3. Israelites knew their patriarchs and kings. The omission of the kings would have been noticed immediately. Matthew apparently wanted his genealogy to be memorized in three lists of 14. The first two lists may already have been available to him; perhaps even Mary was the one who compile these three 14's.

4. Certainly our clue of verification is in Matthew 1:1, his first verse, "The book of the generation of Jesus Christ, the son of David, the son of Abraham." Abraham lived across the 2000 BC line and David crossed the 1000 BC line. Jesus in turn crossed the 1 BC-1 AD line, having been born probably at about 4 BC, just before Herod the Great died in that year. Thus Matthew 1:1 is a genealogical trace! We believe the Bible, but is it claiming here that King David was Jesus' father, and that Patriarch Abraham was Jesus' grandfather? Of course not. Matthew 1:1 is not in error, it is an accurate genealogical trace with many omissions. In the same way Matthew 1:2–16 accurately accomplishes the same thing.

5. The genealogies of Genesis chapters 5 and 11 seem also to be genealogical traces, with the addition of siring and length of life data. Both are lists of ten, ending in a set of three brothers. The first begins with Adam and ends with Noah, listing his three sons; the second begins with Noah and ends with Terah and lists his three sons, one of which is Abraham. Symmetrical, accurate, and inspired — a genealogical trace.

G. COHEN

THE LAND AND THE PEOPLE OF THE BIBLE

J. R. Hiles, B.A. (The Rev.)

The technical discipline involved here is Biblical geography. Strictly speaking, the geography of the Bible is concerned with all those lands prominently mentioned in Scripture. Since every inquiry must have its limits, however, this article will in general confine itself to the land and people of Palestine, for the Biblical drama of God's redemptive activity is presented on that stage and is inextricably associated with those participants. Yet the lands and peoples of a given area are also inseparably bound together with the larger context of geography and history in which they are set. This is particularly true of Palestine, for it was located as a bridge between continents and as a crossroad for nations. Hence this survey will necessarily be somewhat concerned with Egypt, Mesopotamia, Asia Minor, Greece, and Rome, Palestine's most immediate and influential neighbors.

THE LAND OF ISRAEL

1. The Name of the Land

At a number of places in the KJV (e.g., Ex 15:14; Isa 14:29; 31; Jl 3:4) appears the territorial designation Palestine or Palestina. In the RSV the same place is always rendered more correctly Philistia. Indeed, the Biblical term "Palestine" originally signified only the land of the Philistines, ancient enemies of Israel. Rather early, however, Herodotus referred to the entire coastal area between Mount Carmel and Gaza as Palestinian Syria, or simply Palestine, and this meaning was then adopted by other Greek and Roman writers. Following the Jewish revolt of A.D. 132-135, the Romans applied the name "Palestine" to their province of Judaea, which extended inland beyond the River Jordan and the Dead Sea. That portion of this territory which lies west of the river and the sea was usually called Canaan by the ancient Hebrews (Gen 11:31; 17:8; et al.), but at times after the conquest it was also referred to as the land of Israel (1 S 13:19), the land of the Lord (Hos 9:3) and the holy land (Zec 2:12). In the New Testament it is spoken of as the land of promise (Heb 11:9). In the Middle Ages the Church displayed a particular fondness for the terms "Holy Land" and "Promised Land."

2. Boundaries

In the course of its history Palestine has been a place of varying size. In general, the Biblical reader understands the land involved as that which was promised to the patriarchs (Gen 12:7; 13:15; 17:8; Ex 6:8; et al.) and within which the Israelites settled according to the tribal distribution outline in Joshua, chapters 13 to 19. Thus understood, Palestine is the southern third of ancient Syria. Its geographical bounds are the Mediterranean Sea in the west, the great desert of Syria and Arabia in the east, the lower border of Lebanon in the north, and the southern extremity of the Dead Sea in the south. Including the land of the Philistines, but not that extending south to the Gulf of Aqabah as in the British mandate of 1923-48, it covers an area of 10,150 square miles, approximately the size of the State of Maryland. According to census figures from 1940, the population of this region numbered 1,466,536, about the same as that of Maryland, but only one third that of Massachusetts, an area one sixth smaller in size. On the basis of Biblical references, secular documents, and numerous ruins of former communities, it can be fairly assumed that the area was formerly more populous.

3. Geology

The underlying rock structure of the land of Palestine consists mainly of horizontal marine deposits of lime and chalk from the Jurassic and Cretaceous periods. The Jura is now visible in only a few places on the sides of the Jordan rift. Immediately above that, from the Early Cretaceous, and also appearing only in the Jordan rift and along the east coast of the Dead Sea, is a dark reddish-brown formation called Nubian sandstone. Above this lies the formations of the Later or Upper Cretaceous, named Cenomanian, Turonian, and Senonian, constituting the main part of the mountains of Palestine. The Cenomanian, a hard crystalline limestone, averages approximately 2,000 feet in depth and is characterized by canyonlike valleys formed from the runoff of rain. Above this and related to it is the Turonian. And on top of the Turonian is the Senonian, a delicate, dazzling white limestone averaging about 660 feet in thickness. Somewhat later a new phase of marine sedimentation developed the Tertiary stratum. The lowest level of this is called Eocene, a white or gray limestone found in the mountains of Palestine. The upper levels of the Tertiary period are known as Oligocene, Miocene, and Pliocene. Finally there was the Quaternary, or Pleistocene, period of marine sedimentation. These latter alluvial deposits constitute the present coastal plain as well as parts of the Jordan rift.

The horizontal rock deposits did not, however, remain undisturbed. After the Cretaceous period folding and warping of that strata occurred, particularly on the eastern

side of the Judaean and Samaritan mountains and in present Transjordan. Between the Miocene and Pliocene periods, hence near the end of the Tertiary, the horizontal strata underwent an even more violent rending from north to south, resulting in the Jordan rift. Another north and south breach took place on the western edge of the west Jordan range. Later still southeast to northwest land ruptures developed, the most significant of which formed the Plain of Jezreel.

Volcanic eruptions began in the mid-Pliocene age following the formation of the Jordan rift. They centered in what is now northern Transjordan and from there spread a mass of lava over the Jordan rift north and south of the Sea of Galilee. Accordingly, the entire southern part of the Galilean mountains is still overspread by a layer of basalt.

4. Topography

The relief features of Palestine are determined by the Jordan rift and its continuation north and south. This immense split in the mainland, resulting from the afore-mentioned geological fault, formed highlands west and east.

West of the Jordan, in what is termed Cisjordan, these highlands consist of the mountains of Judah, Samaria, and Galilee (Jos 20:7). The Judaean range includes the mountains of Hebron, which about 3 miles north of Hebron rise as high as 3,373 feet, and the mountains of Jerusalem, whose highest elevations are modern Mount Scopus and the Mount of Olives (2 S 15:30; Ezk 11:23; Mk 13:3), rising 2,693 and 2,600 feet respectively. On the western side the Judaean hills are bordered by the so-called 'Artuf fault, beyond which a sunken plateau forms rolling foothills 1,000 to 1,300 feet high. The eastern slope of the Judaean hill country lies in what is termed the "rain shadow"; hence, it is extremely low in rainfall and therefore a desert.

The Samaritan hill country begins at the northern edge of the mountains of Jerusalem and extends northwesterly to Mount Carmel (1 K 18:19; et al.) and northeasterly to Mount Gilboa (e.g., 1 S 31:1-6), which in order have elevations of 1,736 and 1,737 feet. The highest elevations, however, are at the ancient city of Baal-Hazor (2 S 13:23), now called Tell Asur; Mount Ebal (Dt 11:29; 27:13); and Mount Gerizim (Dt 27:12; Jos 8:33), rising respectively to 3,333 and 3,085 and 2,890 feet. Since these Samaritan hills do not lie in the "rain shadow" and possess a gentle contour, they are more fertile and habitable than the Judaean ones.

The Galilean range commences north of the great inland Plain of Jezreel (Jos 17:16; Jg 6:33), called also Esdraelon, and falls into two natural parts, lower and upper Galilee. Lower Galilee consists of several east to west mountain ranges of moderate height. With adequate rainfall and an overall land structure similar to that of the Samaritan hill country, this area naturally lends itself to agriculture and a settled life. Its most notable mountain is Tabor (Jg 4:14; et al.), with an elevation of 1,850 feet. The upper Galilean mountains begin their rise, quite abruptly, just above the longitudinal line marking the northern end of the Sea of Galilee and reach their peak at Mount Jermaq, 3,963 feet, easily the highest elevation west of the Jordan. From there highlands of 2,300 to 2,600 feet continue north until they finally terminate at the valley of the River Litani, the natural boundary between Palestine and Syria. Beyond the river lies the rugged, well-watered, and Biblically significant mountains of Lebanon (Jos 13:6; 1 K 5:6; Ez 3:7; Ps 29:5; Isa 14:8), which rise to heights of approximately 6,000 feet.

Between the mountains of Western Palestine and the Mediterranean Sea lie a series of coastal plains formed by the late sedimentation already mentioned. North of the Carmel range is located the relatively small Plain of Accho, named after the ancient city situated in its midst. This plain extends northward to the promontory of Naqurah and eastward to the slopes of the Galilean hill country, but measures just 5 miles in width at its center. Flowing northwesterly through it to the sea is the River Kishon (Jg 4:13-16), now known as Nahr el Muqatta), which drains the whole Plain of Jezreel. A shallow bay, some 10 miles long, is formed between Accho and the foot of Carmel, creating a natural harbor on which is located the currently significant port city of Haifa.

South of Carmel is the great plain generally known as the Palestinian Coastal Plain. In the Old Testament its northern part is referred to as Sharon (e.g., Isa 35:2; Can 2:1) and is celebrated for its beauty and fertility. The whole plain extends southward to the Sinai Desert and eastward to the mountains of Judah and Samaria. Its greatest west to east expanse is at the southwest corner of the Judaean range, where it extends about 25 miles from Beersheba to the sea. Farther north it narrows down to 20 miles in width at Joppa, 7 miles at Caesarea, and less than 2 miles west of Carmel. Numerous small rivers and streams flow through it to the sea; hence the area is very productive. Along the seacoast are almost unbroken dune formations.

The highland formed east of the Jordan rift—that is, Transjordan—has the character of a plateau and indeed is an extension of the great Syro-Arabian Desert tableland still further to the east. It is marked by many small gullies and several great ravines that fall sharply into the Jordan Valley and the Dead Sea. Between the Brook Zered (Dt 2:14), now called Wadi Hesa, to the south and the Arnon (Nu 21:13; Jos 13:16), presently known as Wadi Mojib, to the north, both of which empty into the Dead Sea, lies the land which

was the principal territory of the Moabites.

The area extending from the Arnon northward and approaching the River Jabbok (Dt 3:16; cf. Gen 32:22), now referred to as Nahr Zerqa, is known in Old Testament Hebrew as Mishor, the tableland (Dt 3:10). Its highest elevations, at Mount Nebo (Dt 32:49) and in the peaks just south of the Jabbok, rising to 3,760 and 3,590 feet, offer extensive views of the Jordan Valley and the mountains beyond to the west. Further east was the land of Ammon. Rabbath-ammon, the ancient city and strong fortress of the Ammonites, is modern Ammon, the capital of the present kingdom of Jordan.

Beyond the Jabbok and continuing north to the River Yarmuk lies the region generally referred to in the Old Testament as the land of Gilead (Jg 11:4; ff.; et al.). Such a demarcation is not entirely precise, however, for even today many places south of the Jabbok bear the name, most notably Mount Gilead. In any case, the area between the two rivers is one of the loveliest and most richly forested in all of Palestine; very early in Biblical times it was well known for the valuable gum from its trees called the "balm of Gilead" (Gen 37:25; Jer 8:22). Its highest elevation is Mount Ajlun, 4,138 feet at its peak. Presently the entire region of Gilead is called Ajlun.

Across the Yarmuk to the north is an area composed of a number of extinct volcanic craters, now named the Jolan, probably after the ancient city of Golan (Jos 20:8), which extends to Palestine's northeastern boundary near the ancient city of Dan (Jg 18:29, et al.) and the foothills of Mount Hermon (Dt 3:8). Northwest of the Yarmuk lies a large fertile region, with an altitude of 1,600 to 2,100 feet, now referred to as en-Nuqreh. In the Old Testament both these places are probably included in the name "Bashan," meaning "plain" (Nu 21:33; Isa 2:13; et al.). Two great lava formations are located east of the plain: the rugged desertlike plateau named Lejah, Hellenistic Trachonitis; and the impressive snow-capped mountain called Hauran, probably Biblical Bashan (Ps 68:15), rising to 6,036 feet. Directly north is Damascus (Gen 14:15; Ac 9:2 ff.), the celebrated capital city of ancient and modern Syria.

The Jordan rift itself extends from North Syria to the Gulf of Aqabah. In the center of this rift is the River Jordan, named "the great river" in Arabic. Its main sources are in a series of springs and small streams at the foot of Mount Hermon, near Dan and Caesarea Philippi (Mk 8:27), formerly Paneas, now Baniyas. From there it flows south through the well-watered and fertile area between the upper parts of Galilee and Bashan now called the Huleh Valley, probably the Biblical Valley of Mizpah (Jos 11:3 ff.), which presently lies largely in modern Lebanon. Lake Huleh, about 4 miles long, was once located in the southern part of the valley, but it has now

been drained by an artificial deepening of the Jordan outlet east of the very old city of Hazor (Jos 11:10).

Immediately south of Huleh the river descends suddenly, from 210 feet above to 630 feet below sea level in just 10 miles, to the Sea of Galilee, variously termed Chinnereth, Gennesaret, and Tiberias in the Bible (Mk 7:31; cf. Nu 34:11; Lk 5:1; Jn 6:1). It measures 11 miles in length, 7 miles in width at its broadest, and 160 feet in depth. The waters of the lake are dark blue and drinkable, and abound in fish. Normally they are quite placid, yet sudden and violent storms of the kind frequently mentioned in the New Testament (Mt 8:24; et al.) are not uncommon. Characterized by scenic mountains and fertile valleys, and possessing an agreeably warm climate, this lake region has been, and remains, one of the most popular and densely inhabited in the country. Around the shore were the very ancient and later cities of Chinnereth, Hammath, Capernaum, Tiberias, Bethsaida, and, perhaps, the unknown location of Cana.

From the southern end of the Sea of Galilee to the northern end of the Dead Sea, a distance of approximately 70 miles, the Jordan River cuts a deep, winding, unnavigable course through that section of the great rift which is the Jordan Valley proper, now known as el-Ghor, meaning "the lowland." At the river's edge is an even lower section of ground, in effect a sunken channel through the Ghor extending up to 1 mile in width, called the Zor, with dense junglelike vegetation (Jer 49:19). West and east of the valley are the Cisjordan highlands and the Transjordan mountain plateau. Only one major perennial stream comes down from the west; namely, the River Jalud, which enters the Jordan through the Bethshan Valley, a continuation of the Plain of Jezreel. This broad, level valley has a number of oases and was densely settled in the Canaanite and Israelite periods. It was the location of ancient Beth-shan (Jos 17:11; 1 S 31:10 ff.), very near modern Beisan. Rather more affluents enter the Jordan from the great plateau to the east, the most notable of which are the Yarmuk and the Jabbok. Consequently, on this well-watered side of the valley in very early times were a chain of important communities, such as Zaphon and Succoth (Jos 13:27), linked together by a road called "the way of the plain" (2 S 18:23). South of the Jabbok and continuing down to the Dead Sea the Ghor opens out into a desert plain more than 20 miles long and up to 12 miles wide. Some oases, fed by mountain springs, have been formed on both sides of the Jordan in this section; e.g., the highly significant one at Jericho (Jos 6:1 ff.; et al.), perhaps Palestine's most ancient city. Opposite Jericho across the Jordan is that region of the desert plain called "the plains of Moab" (Nu 33:48 f.).

The Jordan and the desert plain terminate at the Dead Sea. This inland body of water extends approximately 50 miles in length and 10 miles in breadth, and is divided into two parts by the Lisan peninsula. Its surface is 1,290 feet below sea level, and it reaches an interior depth of 1,300 feet in the northern part, the lowest point on earth. The saltiness of the water and the high temperature of the immediate surroundings prevent marine life in the lake or normal vegetation on its shores; hence the common term Dead Sea. It is also known in the Bible as the Salt Sea (e.g., Nu 34:3; Dt 3:17), named thus for its character or location rather than effect. High cliffs and great canyons, entirely devoid of trees, rise abruptly on both sides of the sea, presenting wild and splendid scenery. In 1947 Bedouins discovered large jars containing scrolls in caves on the cliff at the northwest side, near the ruins of a community called Qumran, perhaps the Biblical "city of Salt" (Jos 15:62). It should also be noted here that tradition places the ancient cities of Sodom, Gomorrah, Admah, and Zeboiim (Gen 10:19) at the southern end of the Dead Sea. Some oases are located around the shores, particularly in the eastern gorges. On the western side is the important one at the old city of En-gedi (Jos 15:62; cf. Can 1:14).

Below the Dead Sea the Jordan rift continues between the mountains of the Negeb and Edom down to the Gulf of Aqabah, a distance of about 110 miles. This is the Arabah (Dt 3:17), a desert expanse much coveted by Israel and her neighbors because of its wealth of copper ore and the important main road through it known as "the way to the Reed Sea" (Nu 14:25, et al.). Opposite one another at the southern end of this highway and on the northern tip of the gulf were the strategic old port cities of Eloth and Ezion-geber (Dt 2:8; 1 K 9:26); the former is in modern Israel under the same name and the latter is now Aqabah in the present State of Jordan.

5. Climate

Palestine, together with the entire Mediterranean region, is situated in a zone of subtropical climate. It is therefore characterized by an alternation between a rainy season in the winter and a dry season in the summer, these being influenced in turn by the great sea to the west and the vast desert to the east. The rainy season normally begins in October or November and continues until April or May, with the heaviest falls usually occurring in January. Generally these rains are in the form of periodic heavy cloudbursts during a limited number of days rather than in steady showers extending over many days. Since geographic and associated climatic factors also influence precipitation, there are naturally great variations of rainfall in this small land of sharp

physical contrasts. Only the coastal plains and the western half of the Cisjordan mountains receive an appreciable amount of rainfall, and the transition to arid regions east and south is extreme. For example, according to figures compiled for the decade from 1927 to 1936, the average annual rainfall was 20.7 inches at Haifa, 19.6 inches near Jaffa, 17 inches in Jerusalem, and just 15 inches in the western part of the Bethshan Valley. Inasmuch as rainfall is confined to a relatively small number of days in the rainy season, most of the streams in Palestine are intermittent, particularly those flowing into the Mediterranean. The Bible frequently refers to waters, called wadis, that are torrential on wet days but vanish rapidly in dry periods (e.g., Job 6:15-20). Numerous natural springs offer some compensation, however, especially in the north, and even in Biblical times man-made cisterns were employed to conserve water (2 S 3:26; Jn 4:6). It is also noteworthy that all the perennial streams of Palestine except the Jordan are, according to the terrain, of necessarily short course.

Dew is an important precipitation element in all parts of Palestine. It alone supports even meager vegetation in the desert areas and also furnishes moisture in other areas during the summer dry season. Snow, on the other hand, falls very infrequently, and then only in the hills of Samaria and Judah.

Temperatures in Palestine are likewise subject to great fluctuations according to the season and location. Normally January is the coldest month and August the warmest. In the period between 1927 and 1936 the average January temperature was 55°F. on the coastal plain near Jaffa, and 46.2°F. in Jerusalem; the mean August temperature for the same decade was respectively 83.7° and 75°F. In the southern part of the Jordan Valley, in the vicinity of Jericho, temperatures are even higher in the warm season, ranging to 120°F. or more. Degrees below freezing are very rare.

It must also be noted that winds have a decided climatic effect on Palestine. Westerly winds normally prevail; they arise around noon, bringing with them not only the necessary rains of winter but also the cooling and refreshing summer breezes from the sea. Prominent easterly winds off the desert have an opposite effect, carrying into the land oppressive sultriness in the summer and cool but dry elements in the winter. In late spring and early fall the east wind is called "sirocco," and with its arrival the blossoming landscape quickly dries up and turns desolate.

6. Vegetation

The flora of Palestine is naturally influenced by the fact that the country is located in a subtropical zone and by the sharp variations of altitude, rainfall, and temperature in different parts of the land. Although the

Palestinian mountains were originally heavily forested, and continued partially so in Old Testament times (Jos 17:14-18), in ancient days and until very recently they were periodically denuded by military invaders, economic necessity, or sheer neglect. True forests now exist only on the Carmel ridge and in former Gilead. The most notable forest trees are oak, terebinth, pine, and carob. Cedars continue to flourish in Lebanon. Steppe and desert growth consists of tamarisk, broom, and the so-called Christ's thorn, from which Christ's crown of thorns is legendarily said to have been made. The products of the land are basically as of old, and primitive methods of cultivation are still widely used. Among the cultivated plants, the various types of grain are of primary significance, above all wheat, barley, and kafir. These are common throughout the country but are especially abundant in northern and southern Transjordan. The principal fruit trees are the olive, the fig, the pomegranate, the date palm, and the banana, as well as the grape vine. In recent years orange trees have been imported into Palestine, and now large quantities of this fruit are cultivated on the coastal plain; indeed, it is presently one of the country's main exports.

7. Animals

The fauna of Palestine is unusually varied and substantially the same today as in Biblical times. Among the wild animals, predatory creatures such as wolves, jackals, hyenas, foxes, and wild dogs are still prominent. On the other hand, the lion (Jer 49:19) and the bear (Isa 11:7) have become extinct, except that the latter is still found in the Lebanon range. Game animals include gazelles, rabbits, and groundhogs, as well as wild boars in the dense tropical vegetation along the Jordan and droves of wild goats in the deserts of Judah. There are still some roebuck deer (1 K 4:23) in central Transjordan. Other species such as the red deer and the antelope, however, appear to have died out altogether. Numerous kinds of predatory birds, such as vultures, continue to feed on decaying flesh left in open fields, and the ostrich (Job 39:13), though nearly extinct, still inhabits certain desert sections. Snakes and lizards in great numbers and varieties abound everywhere in the land. Of the host of insects, the migratory locust was and is most notable. As recently as 1915 a great plague, like those alluded to in the Bible (Ex 10:12-15; Jl 2; et al.), literally devastated all green plant life. Among the domesticated animals are donkeys, oxen, horses, and camels, used largely as creatures of burden, and chickens and pigeons for food purposes. Sheep and goats, which are found in flocks everywhere in the country, are now as always of great significance for the food, milk, and clothing material they provide.

8. Mineral Resources

Palestine is very deficient in mineral resources. Scripture does say, nevertheless, that it is "a land whose stones are iron, and out of whose hills you can dig copper" (Dt 8:9). As for iron, however, only a few ancient mines have been discovered, and these are confined to a relatively small area around the Jabbok in central Transjordan. Of course, the text may have meant to include the Lebanon region, where there were numerous mines which belonged for a time to the kingdom of David. Even so, the supply and processing of iron was at best probably very limited (cf. 1 S 13:19-22). There is evidence that copper was extensively mined and smelted in the Arabah from ancient Punon (Nu 33:42-43) south to the Gulf of Aqabah, which apparently was the source of Solomon's supply. On the other hand, Cisjordan is totally lacking in both iron and copper. Although the waters of the Dead Sea are unusually abundant in salt and other minerals, we have no clear indication that they were utilized in the Biblical period. Gold and silver are often mentioned in the Bible, but had to be imported into the country, probably from southern Arabia (1 K 10:21-25).

THE HISTORICAL GEOGRAPHY OF PALESTINE

1. Pre-Israelite Period

Numerous remnants of the various stages of the Stone Age, uncovered at scattered sites throughout the country, attest to human existence in Palestine in very ancient time. From the Old Stone Age there are characteristic flints and even skeletal remains. At this stage man dwelt on the land in caves and obtained his food solely by hunting and foraging. Already in the Middle Stone Age (c. 10000-6000 B.C.), however, Palestine had developed a discernible cultural form, called Natufian after the Wadi en-Natuf, where it was first identified. In the early part of this stage, while still living in caves and employing stone implements, man had learned to till the soil and, apparently, to domesticate animals. Somewhat later the first crude houses of packed mud began to appear. The Late Stone Age, known as Neolithic (c. 6000-4000 B.C.), and usually divided into prepottery and pottery phases, reveals further cultural development thousands of years before the Israelite period. This is particularly evident at the mound of Jericho and in the Yarmuk valley. Rather well developed stone tools and methods of cultivation, clay vessels and statues (perhaps to gods), and less crude dwellings of mud-brick, often in villages surrounded by strong stone walls, are characteristic of this stage.

The Copper-Stone Age, termed Chalco-

lithic (c. 4000-3000 B.C.), which witnesses to a marked cultural flowering everywhere in the ancient East, especially in Mesopotamia, is also visible in Palestine. Of particular importance is the Ghassulian culture, so named for Tuleilat el-Ghassul in the Jordan Valley, where it was first discovered. Stone implements were still employed in this age, but copper was also in use and the houses were more firmly made of brick and stone and were often richly decorated with painted frescoes. It should also be noted that people of this culture buried food with their dead, perhaps indicating an early belief in life after death.

Investigations into the Bronze Age (c. 3000-1200 B.C.) have resulted in the identification of a considerable number of Palestinian city settlements dating from the different phases of that time span. They are generally marked by massive fortifications, extensive drainage, and many fine homes. Among these communities are such later Biblically significant places as Megiddo, Beth-shan, Ai, Shechem, and Gezer.

Additional information about these ancient cities of Palestine has been furnished by Egyptian documents from the Late Bronze Age, especially in the accounts of Pharaoh Thuthmosis III (c. 1490-1435) and in those dealing with the reign of Amenhotep IV (c. 1370-1353), known to us from the famous Amarna letters. They confirm that the land was then indeed divided into unnumerable small city-states. They furthermore clearly indicate that these communities were largely under Egyptian domination for an extended time, although, because of pressing internal affairs and open rebellion in Palestine, this power was substantially reduced in the so-called Amarna Period (c. 1400-1350).

These same Egyptian texts also point, by way of complaint, to the appearance in the land of a troublesome band of wandering people called Habiru. They obviously joined the settled revolutionaries against the Pharaoh. In the light of all available evidence, they seem to have been a low-class social group without citizenship anywhere, who, as opportunity or necessity arose, sold their services as soldiers, laborers, or even slaves. Because of the great similarity in name and their coincidence in time, some have sought to equate the Habiru and the Hebrews. Although discussion of such a thesis is beyond the scope of this article, it may be fairly said that the two probably belonged to a similar Semitic class. In any case, the prominent presence of the Habiru attests to a significant seminomadic movement into Palestine prior to the arrival of the Israelites proper under Joshua and later.

The aggressive foreign policy of Pharaohs Sethos I (c. 1309-1290) and Rameses II (c. 1290-1224), designed to re-establish Egyptian control throughout Asia, was at least successful in restoring a strong hold on the Late Bronze Age cities of Palestine. But that success did not endure long. Literature from the time speaks of continuing turmoil in the land and likewise distinguishes between established and bothersome nomadic peoples there.

Together with such external evidence the Old Testament itself shows that the Israelites were not the first or sole inhabitants of the land of Palestine. Although the information there is uneven (e.g., Gen 15:19-21; Ex 13:5; 23:23, 38; Dt 7:1; Jos 3:10), it clearly points to a great variety of indigenous elements in the land prior to the arrival of the tribes. Among these, Amorites, Canaanites, Hittites, Hurrians, and Philistines seem to have been the most important.

Amorites and Canaanites were apparently of common Semitic culture and probably represent successive waves of the same seminomadic penetration into Palestine from the end of the third millennium B.C. onward. Indeed, the two names are frequently used interchangeably in the Old Testament to designate a substantial portion of the land's residents at the time of Israel's entry.

The Hittites are a people of very obscure origin. It is now known, however, that they had a strong kingdom in Asia Minor (cf. Cappadocia) in the sixteenth century B.C. Racially an admixture, their language and leadership were essentially Indo-European. They possessed a highly developed culture, contested the hegemony of Assyria and Egypt at the peak of their power, and even compelled the latter to enter into a peace treaty in the thirteenth century. Hittites were apparently present in Palestine as early as the time of Abraham, and it is now believed that they had a decisive influence on the land and the whole people (cf. Ezk 16:3, 45).

Horites are frequently mentioned in the Bible (e.g., Gen 14:6; 36:20; Dt 2:12). Once regarded as cave dwellers, they are now widely understood as the Hurrians, an Indo-European directed people whose center was in northern Mesopotamia and one of whose communities was Nuzi. Laban's home was probably located in that region, and texts discovered at Nuzi are especially helpful in understanding many otherwise obscure Old Testament happenings, including aspects of the Laban-Jacob stories in Genesis, chapters 29-31. That the Hurrians were a significant people and prominently present in Palestine by the thirteenth century B.C. is attested by the fact that the Egyptians then called the land Huru. It should furthermore be noted that the name "Hivite" is now generally held to be a corrupt form of Horite.

The Philistines were part of the Sea Peoples who came from the eastern Mediterranean world. They entered Palestine at about the same time as the tribes of Israel, c. 1200 B.C., following an unsuccessful attack on Egypt. They settled mainly in the coastal area known as Philistia but, bearing a strong

military tradition and being skilled in the use of iron, particularly for weaponry, they soon occupied a larger portion of the land. Later they posed a constant threat to the Israelites, only being put down finally by David.

Other peoples connected with early Palestine in the Old Testament (Jebusites, Perizzites, Girgashites, etc.) are of uncertain ethnic nature. It has been suggested that they may have been subgroups within the Hittite and/or Hurrian races. However that may be, all such names other than Amorite and Canaanite, including those discussed above, represent non-Semitic elements in the population of Palestine prior to, or coincident with, the Israelite entry. In due course all these peoples, whatever their origin, adopted that style of cultural life which the Old Testament generally knows as Canaanite.

2. Israelite Era

The ancestors of the Israelites were also present in Palestine in the latter stages of the period just discussed. They are the Biblical patriarchs. They arrived in the land in the late third and early second millennia B.C., as a small part of that great seminomadic Semitic penetration already mentioned. At first they roamed the country in strictly seminomadic fashion (e.g., Gen 37:12 ff.), but, judging from certain Egyptian sources, they apparently made a rapid transition to sedentary life, taking up agricultural pursuits and even in due course establishing towns and cities. While many of these Israelite forefathers went down into Egypt at various times during the mid-second millennium B.C., some doubtless remained in Palestine up to the time of Joshua.

Properly speaking, however, the Israelite era in Palestine begins with the Biblically momentous occupation, or reoccupation, of the land which occurred about 1250 to 1200 B.C. Following the exodus from Egypt under Moses and the reception of a peculiar charter of faith at Sinai, the various Hebrew elements that were once represented in Palestine entered the land again, and in force, as the united people Israel. Whether this occupation took place suddenly and completely, as reported in Joshua, chapters 1-12, or rather slowly and partially over an extended time, as presented in Judges 1:16-31 (cf. 1 K 9:20 f.), cannot be argued here. It is sufficient to say, on the basis of broad Biblical tradition supported by substantial archaeological evidence, that this new people Israel violently and decisively took the land of Palestine in the thirteenth century B.C.

On the other hand, Israel's taking of the land did not mean immediate union of Palestine into a uniform political system. At first the country was divided into twelve tribal areas in confederation. The geographical extent of these regions is rather precisely stated in Joshua, chapters 13-19, and can be generally visualized by consulting a standard map dealing with the subject. Such boundaries are not always clear, however, as is shown, for example, in Simeon's allotment of "an inheritance in the midst of" Judah (19:9). Furthermore, certain of these tribal holdings have to be understood as reflecting theoretical or subsequent situations, for some of the apportioned land in fact remained outside Israelite control well into the period of the Judges and even until the time of the monarchy. Of decisive significance for the geography, economy, and history of Israel is the fact that, whereas the inhabitants were in former times clustered in and around the fertile valleys, now the population was largely scattered across the land.

The tribal confederacy endured about 200 years. Thereafter, as a result of mounting Philistine aggression and the necessity of concerted response to it, the tribes formed themselves into an essentially united monarchy, first under Saul (c. 1020-1000?) and then, more importantly, under David (c. 1000-961). The latter established Jerusalem as a strong national capital, expanded Israel's realm to its maximum limits, and elevated the country to the status of a major world power. Nevertheless, as the Bible well shows, it was Solomon (c. 961-922) who brought Israel into an age of unparalleled military security, economic prosperity, and cultural activity. While Saul and David reigned more or less within the old tribal structure, Solomon, in order to facilitate tax collection, reorganized the land into twelve administrative districts in marked disregard of the former names and boundaries. Notable is the impression that the reorganization involved only the northern realm, perhaps implying that Israel and Judah already had the character of separate and independent units (1 K 4:7-19).

After the death of Solomon, and largely because of his oppressive policies, the monarchy indeed split into two kingdoms, Judah and Israel. Although there were intermittent periods of peace and achievement throughout the land, the history of the two realms in the following 350 years is one of rivalry, warfare, dissipation, and, finally, loss of identity for both.

The boundary between Judah and Israel was vigorously disputed for generations (e.g., 1 K 14:30) and fluctuated according to their relative power. Virtual civil war caused by this and other issues between them so weakened both that they were unable to maintain control over the vast areas conquered under the united monarchy. Theoretically, Transjordan belonged to Israel, but it was effectively held only in times of Syrian weakness and through the particularly energetic efforts of leaders such as Ahab (869-850) and Jeroboam II (786-746). Between 734 and 733 all Israelite holdings in Galilee and Transjordan were substantially lost to Assyria, and in 721,

following the conquest of Samaria by Sargon II (722-705), the remainder of the northern kingdom became an Assyrian province. In accordance with the conqueror's policy, many Israelites were deported (2 K 17:24) and the land was resettled with peoples banished from elsewhere. Israel was finished as an independent political entity. Judah, on the other hand, barely escaped the same fate in 701 when, while systematically destroying its cities and carrying off its people, the forces of Sennacherib (705-681) were suddenly recalled to handle an urgent problem at home. Following the subsequent collapse of the Assyrian Empire, Judah's situation markedly improved, at least temporarily. Capitalizing on the political vacuum in Palestine, Josiah (640-609) took control of a large portion of Israel's former territory, put through a sweeping reform (2 K 22:3-23:25), and thereby restored a measure of national unity and prosperity in the land. In 609, however, Josiah was defeated and killed at Megiddo by the Egyptian forces under Neco II (609-593). Thereafter Judah existed only as a vassal, first of Egypt and then of Babylon, the new great power in the East. Repeated rebellion in Judah against this subjugation provoked Babylon to even more drastic steps: in 598 Jehoiachin and numerous leading citizens were deported, and in 587 the troops of Nebuchadrezzar burned Jerusalem and utterly decimated Judah.

By the middle of the sixth century B.C. Persia, under Cyrus (550-530), was the dominant power in the East. Babylon fell to it in 539, and with this Palestine probably passed automatically to Persian control. In the first year of his rule in Babylon, however, Cyrus decreed the political and religious restoration of Judah in Palestine (Ez 1:2-4; 6:3-5). Accordingly, though with a somewhat diminished area, Judah was granted the status of a Persian province under a native governor, and the exiles, who regarded themselves as the true remnant of Israel, were allowed to return to their land. We know very little about the political division of Palestine in this period. From what information we do have, it appears that four other provinces surrounded Judah; namely, Ammon in the east, Idumaea in the south, Ashdod in the west, and Samaria in the north (cf. Neh 4:1 f). Samaria, inhabited by residual Israelites and those peoples resettled there under the Assyrians, became the center of open and veiled resistance to the new "Jewish" community in Judah.

After about 200 years the vast Persian Empire, including Palestine, was in turn taken over by Alexander the Great (336-323 B.C.). He sought not only the liberation of Greeks from Persian bondage but also the thorough Hellenization of the Orient. On the basis of limited information, it does not appear that the political and administrative structure of Palestine was altered during Alexander's short reign. Following his death, the land became a place of contention between two rival Hellen-powers, the Ptolemies in Egypt and the Seleucids in Syria, until the issue was finally settled by the victory of Antiochus III (223-187) at ancient Paneas in 198. Under the Seleucids Palestine apparently belonged to the larger political area, or satrapy, called Coele Syria and Phonecia, and remained separated into numerous provincial regions on the order of the former Persian structure. In this period, however, the provinces of the land were further divided into smaller administrative units, known as toparchies.

Antiochus IV Epiphanes (175-163 B.C.) pursued a Hellenization policy which utterly threatened Jewish religion and life. It finally resulted in the so-called Maccabean Revolt, thus designated after the third son of a priestly family (later called Hasmonaean), named Judas, but nicknamed Maccabeus, meaning "the hammer." He and certain of his brothers, especially Simon, who thought of himself as both priest and king, gained control of the province of Judah and even extended its frontiers (cf. 1 Macc 14:5) into Samaria and east of the Jordan. John Hyrcanus (135-104), son of Simon, and his successors expanded Judah's borders even further within these areas as well as into Idumaea and Galilee, with the end result that the Hasmonaean monarchy ultimately embraced the whole territory of the old Israelite tribes.

The success of the new kingdom was short-lived. Taking full advantage of the collapse of the Seleucid state and the incompetence of the later Hasmonaean rulers, Pompey conquered Palestine for the Romans in 63 B.C. and thereupon annexed the land to the newly constituted province of Syria. As part of an extensive Roman reorganization, in which the land was divided into a system of vassal states and cities, the Hasmonaeans were denied the title of king and, apart from Galilee, Idumaea, and a strip of land east of the Jordan called Peraea, their conquered regions were liquidated.

3. New Testament Age

After considerable internal dispute and intrigue, Herod succeeded in having himself appointed king of Judah, or Judaea, by the Roman Senate in 40 B.C. Following a series of military campaigns to wrest his kingdom from the control of certain Jewish antagonists, he assumed his royal office in Jerusalem in the year 37. His realm ultimately included all the land west of the Jordan as well as Gaulanitis, Batanaea, Trachonitis, Auranitis, and Peraea to the east, thus taking in virtually the whole of Palestine. Only the regions belonging to the free cities of the so-called Decapolis (Mt 4:25; Mk 5:20; 7:31), established by Pompey, remained beyond his domain. After his death in 4 B.C., and probably in

accord with the emperor's desire, the kingdom was divided among his three younger sons. Archelaus, with the title "ethnarch," was given Judaea, Samaria, and Idumaea; Antipas received Galilee and Peraea, and Philip the territories of Batanea, Auranitis, and Trachonitis (Lk 3:1), both with the designation "tetrarch." But responding to widespread displeasure with despotic Herodian rule, particularly in the central and southern part of the land west of the Jordan, Augustus removed Archelaus from power in A.D. 6 and banished him to Gaul. Thereafter, Judaea, Samaria, and Idumaea became a Roman administrative district, composed of eleven toparchies, under a procurator, the best known of which was Pontius Pilate (26-36).

Under Herod's grandson, Agrippa I (A.D. 37-44), the old monarchy was somewhat restored. Through shrewd support of the emperors, Agrippa successively achieved control of Abilene (Lk 3:1) and the tetrarchy of Philip in the year 37, Galilee in 39, and eventually Judaea, Samaria, and Idumaea in 40, so nearly the entire territory formerly ruled by his grandfather. Yet his kingdom was more a useful device of Caligula and Claudius than a real political entity and, indeed, was practically dissolved after his death in the year 44. Although his son, Agrippa II (53-93), was allowed the title of king and was finally granted certain small consolation holdings in the north by Claudius and Nero, together with supervision of the Temple in Jerusalem, he was in effect denied his father's kingdom, and all of Palestine henceforth became a Roman province under procurators, the whole officially named Judaea.

Tensions between the Roman authorities and the population of the land naturally appeared almost from the beginning of occupation. Subsequent maladministration, religious interference, plundering of the land and even of the Temple, and brutal persecution of the people made matters progressively worse.

Finally, between A.D. 66 to 70, with provocations on both sides, deep-seated hostility broke into violent insurrection. The rebels won a decisive early battle against Cestius and hence were in control throughout the land. Later, however, the mighty Roman legions, first under Vespasian and then Titus, swept through the country from the northwest and, after an epic siege and defense, took Jerusalem in the year 70, burned the Temple, and completely destroyed whatever remained of the city. This was the next to last stage in Israel's final political annihilation. Another great rising of rebellious Jews occurred under Hadrian (117-138), led by a certain Simon bar Cochba (132-135), perhaps the ben Koseba known from documents recently found near the Dead Sea. Even though this rebellion was likewise quite successful at the outset, bringing new independence to Israel, the Romans once more devastated the country. From this point the land became a complete Roman province. On the site of another destroyed Jerusalem was erected the Roman Colonia Aelia Capitolina. In all probability the land was henceforth referred to as Palestine, or Palestina, rather than Judaea.

* * *

The material presented in this article is substantially based on the following standard scholarly works in the field: Yohanan Aharoni, *The Land of the Bible* (1966); Denis Baly, *The Geography of the Bible* (1957) and *Geographical Companion to the Bible* (1963); Martin Noth, *The World of the Old Testament* (1966); and Charles F. Pfeiffer and Howard F. Vos, *The Wycliffe Historical Geography of Bible Lands* (1967). John Bright's *The History of Israel* (1959) was likewise of considerable help. Interested readers are directed to these for further reading and for useful maps, topographical charts, and photographs.

JEWISH CALENDAR.

Year (Sacred)	Year (Civil)	Month	English Month (nearly)	Festivals	Corresponding Dates 1916-1917	Corresponding Dates 1921-1922	Seasons and Productions
1	7	Nisan/Abib — 30 days	April	1 New Moon; 14 The Passover; 15 Unleavened bread; 21	April 4; April 17; April 18-24	April 9; April 22; April 23-29	Spring rains (Deut. 11:14); Floods (Josh. 3:15); Barley ripe at Jericho
2	8	Iyar/Zif — 29 days	May	1 New Moon; 14 Second Passover (for those unable to keep first)	May 4; May 17	May 9; May 22	**Harvest** — Barley Harvest (Ruth 1:22); Wheat Harvest; Summer begins; No rain from April to Sept. (1 Sam. 12:17)
3	9	Sivan — 30 days	June	1 New Moon; 6 Pentecost	June 2; June 7	June 7; June 12	
4	10	Thammuz — 29 days	July	1 New Moon; 17 Fast Taking of Jerusalem	July 2; July 18	July 7; July 23	**Hot Season** — Heat increases
5	11	Ab — 30 days	August	1 New Moon; 9 Fast Destruction of Temple	July 31; August 8	August 5; August 13	The streams dry up; Heat intense; Vintage (Lev. 26:5)
6	12	Elul — 29 days	September	1 New Moon	August 30	September 4	Heat intense (2 Ki. 4:19); Grape harvest (Num. 13:23)
7	1	Tishri/Ethanim — 30 days	October	1 New Year, Day of blowing of Trumpet, Day of Judgment and Memorial (Num. 29:1); 10 Day of Atonement (Lev. 16); 15 Tabernacles; 21 (Lev 23:24); 22 Solemn Assembly	September 28; October 7; October 12-18; October 19	October 3; October 12; October 17-23; October 24	**Seed time** — Former or early rains begin (Joel 2:23); Plowing and sowing begin
8	2	Marchesvan/Bul — 29 days	November	1 New Moon	October 28	November 2	Rain continues; Wheat and barley sown; Vintage in North Palestine
9	3	Kislev(Chislev) — 30 days	December	1 New Moon; 25 Dedication (John 10:22, 29)	November 26; December 20-27 January 4, 1917	December 2; December 26- January 2, 1922	**Winter** — Winter begins; Snow on mountains
10	4	Tebeth — 29 days	January	1 New Moon; 10 Fast Siege of Jerusalem	December 26	January 1, 1922; January 10	Coldest month; Hail and snow (Josh. 10:11)
11	5	Shebat — 30 days	February	1 New Moon	January 24	January 30	Weather gradually warmer
12	6	Adar — 29 days	March	1 New Moon; 13 Fast of Esther; 14-15 Purim	February 23; March 7; March 8-9	March 1; March 13; March 14, 15	Thunder and hail frequent; Almond tree blossoms
13 Leap year		Veadar	March/April	1 New Moon; 13 Fast of Esther; 14-15 Purim	March 10, 1913; March 23, 1913; March 24, 25, 1913		Intercalary Month

Note I. The "corresponding dates" are given to show the variations of the months from the corresponding ones in our year. This data is from the International Bible Dictionary by permission.

Note II. The Jewish year is strictly lunar, being 12 lunations with an average of 29-1/2 days making 354 days in the year.
The Jewish sacred year begins with that new moon of spring which comes between our March 22 and April 25 in cycles of 19 years.
We can understand it best if we imagine our New Year's Day, which now comes on Jan. 1, without regard to the moon, varying each year with Easter, the time of the Passover, at the time of the full moon which, as a new moon had introduced the New Year two weeks before.

Note III. Hence the Jewish calendar contains a 13th month, Veadar, introduced 7 times in every 19 years, to render the average length of the year nearly correct, and to keep the seasons in their proper months.

Note IV. The Jewish day begins at sunset of the previous day.

THE BIBLE AND MODERN SCIENCE

Dr. Carl F. H. Henry

Despite their quarrels of varying intensity, biblical religion and science cannot gainsay their intimate alliance, even kinship. Although they stand today in a broken relationship, revealed religion and the scientific enterprise are mutually related.

I. THE FAITH IN RATIONALITY

The beginnings of modern science center in what Christianity has communicated about the essential character of nature. From the Christian religion Western science derived its conviction of a comprehensively rational universe that everywhere bears evidence of one ultimate principle of explanation. By contrast neither the teachings of Oriental polytheistic religion (with its enormous galaxy of gods) nor of Occidental philosophical speculation (with its compromise of divine sovereignty, and notions of caprice in nature) could have encouraged such scientific spirit. The connection between Christianity and science, therefore, encompasses far more than the oft-debated question of origins. "There seems but one source," Alfred North Whitehead acknowledges, for the "inexpugnable belief that every detailed occurrence can be correlated with its antecedents in a perfectly definite manner, exemplifying general principles. . . . It must come from the medieval insistence on the rationality of God. . . . Every detail was supervised and ordered; the search into nature could only result in the vindication of the faith in rationality" (*Science and the Modern World* [The Macmillan Co., 1946], p. 18).

1. Human Wisdom and Striving

At the same time, biblical religion holds no enthusiastic brief for scientific achievements as symbols of man's best wisdom and striving. This reserve doubtless springs from Scripture's emphasis on the sinful condition of the human race, and the pessimism of redemptive religion toward fallen man's reliance on human schemes for salvation. Scriptural warnings against worldly wisdom are not, of course, specifically directed against modern science as such. Inasmuch, however, as today's world ascribes to science the place of intellectual prestige once enjoyed by philosophy, a passage like Colossians 2.8 has sobering relevance: "Beware lest any man spoil you through philosophy and vain deceit, after the tradition of men, after the rudiments of the world, and not after Christ" (KJV). To apply this apostolic warning to a misplaced trust in constantly changing scientific theories as the final arbiter of truth is not amiss. "See to it that no one makes a prey of you by philoso-

phy and empty deceit, according to human tradition . . . and not according to Christ" (RSV). "Be on your guard," translates *The New English Bible*, "do not let your minds be captured by hollow and delusive speculations based on traditions of man-made teaching and centered on the elemental spirits (*or* rudimentary notions) of the world and not on Christ."

2. The Secularizing of Power

There is more to the Bible's implicit criticism of scientism than this warning against blind trust in the wisdom of this world. The sacred writers fear not only the expansion of secular speculation, but also the awesome increase of human *power,* that only multiplies the prospect of demonic perversion. Antichrist does not merely appropriate false doctrine, but places power in the service of false gods. Totalitarian government no less than the secular world spirit is a manifestation of false religion. Our tense era of nuclear bombs, rockets and missiles should soberly remind us that the prophetic Scriptures characterize Gentile world-government as rapacious and warlike, and as established and maintained by force. Through the centuries expositors of prophetic passages have warned of approaching Armageddon (Rv 16.14) and of this era's terrible termination. Christ is pictured in His second advent or majestic return as coming in might and in great glory (Mt 16.27; 25.31), as smiting and sweeping away this power-proud world-order (Dn 2.45, 7.9-11, Rv 19.11-21), as bringing the nations of earth under judgment (Mt 25.31-46, Rv 20.1-6), and as divinely establishing the messianic age of righteousness and peace.

Swift and spectacular increase of knowledge as the end-time nears is etched in Daniel's well-known prophecy: "O Daniel, shut up the words and seal the book, even to the time of the end; many shall run to and fro, and knowledge shall be increased" (12.4). Not in all the centuries of Christianity has any explosion of knowledge paralleled that of pure and applied science in recent times. Our generation stands in a period of more rapid and radical change than ever confronted in human history. Within a few short decades science has penetrated more barriers than in all preceding centuries. "Technology advanced further in this age than in all man's previous existence. Fission, fusion, radar, television, automation, miniaturization, plastics, jets, rockets, satellites—each fantastic new art separated one year from another as distinctively as stone or bronze separated whole eons of pre-history" (*Life* magazine, December, 1960). Since 1936 atomic research has multiplied the number of known elementary

atomic particles from six to thirty. In 1939 came the splitting of the atom and release of nuclear energy. Then followed new discoveries that probe microcosm and macrocosm. Nuclear submarines for year-round operation in the Arctic; computer systems for automatic calculation; satellites to investigate outer space; rockets reaching for the moon; manned spaceships orbiting the earth; optical and radio telescopes to photograph the heavens and to explore the cosmos by gathering its radio emissions; the new science of space medicine; radio isotopes to label atoms in intricate reactions and to kill cancers; antibiotics to cure dangerous bacterial diseases; synthetic plastic substitutes for parts of the human body—these are but a few of recent scientific achievements. The rapid pace of today's discovery and change makes it increasingly difficult even for scientists to keep up with science.

From man's expanded world-wisdom, however, the Bible expects neither inevitable human progress, nor moral transformation of life and existence. Only the knowledge of God written upon men's hearts (2 Co 3.2 f.), only the regenerating fruit of revealed religion can secure any prospect of enduring peace on earth. Actually, many critics of modern culture now correlate scientific advance with moral paralysis, even though just a generation ago evolutionary speculation assured a scientifically-inaugurated millennium, and scientific method was irreverently hailed as the Spirit-guide into all truth. But now, in the latter half of our century leading scientists even more often than theologians warn of imminent doom.

In our atomic age a passage like 2 Peter 3.10-12 is strangely relevant: "But the day of the Lord will come as a thief in the night; in the which the heavens shall pass away with a great noise, and the elements shall melt with fervent heat, the earth also and the works that are therein shall be burned up. Seeing then that all these things shall be dissolved, what manner of persons ought ye to be in all holy conversation and godliness, looking for and hasting unto the coming of the day of God, wherein the heavens being on fire shall be dissolved, and the elements shall melt with fervent heat?" (KJV). The world weapons race dramatically illustrates that scientific and spiritual advance do not necessarily go hand in hand. The anxious debate over whether the strategic balance of force has passed to the Communist nations, or whether even the non-Communist nations now reflect a secular post-Christian spirit more than the spirit of Christianity, reminds us that power without morality is an obvious trait of our times. The sordid story of the Nazi attempt to destroy the Jews shows that scientific development presented the sadists with their great opportunity to use highly refined techniques for the mass destruction of civilians. As the Scriptures indicate, the power of the Spirit and the forces of this fallen world are disposed to increasing competition. While the science laboratory can produce a mechanical brain, only the Divine Spirit can shape a regenerate heart.

3. Science and Scientism

The interrelation between science and religion, therefore, involves issues deeper than the so-called conflict over the origin of matter, of life, and of mind. When science assumes omnicompetence—thereby becoming *scientism* (exalting its methodology as alone sufficient to solve all man's problems and to answer all his questions)—it in effect establishes a rival religion. This phenomenon that science should promote atheism, rather than subserve spiritual and moral realities, is one of the distressing developments of the twentieth century. Many scientists now speak of "synthesizing life." Others find encouragement in mathematical computers that explain mind in mechanical terms and that duplicate its behavior electronically. Still others think everyone will soon privately control enough energy to be "a sort of God." In such circumstances the conflict between science and religion augurs terrifying complexities.

Two significant developments, however, have limited the bold optimism of *scientism*, and have actually increased a feeling of pessimism over its claims of omnicompetence to provide "salvation" from discomfort and despair. One development is the achievement by science of the atomic bomb, whose mass destruction of Nagasaki and Hiroshima chilled men everywhere to swift awareness that all civilization could vanish in a single night. (Even south of Beersheba in the Negev desert where Abraham heard and obeyed the voice of the Lord, a nuclear reactor is today fashioning atomic power.) Alongside the atomic bomb's destructive potential exists another telling fact. Despite its ability to manipulate and control physical data, scientific methodology cannot provide spiritual judgments nor establish moral criteria. This amorality of science in an age of scientific "omnipotence" can only widen the stream of cynicism in modern life.

On the other hand, Christian confidence that Jesus Christ is Lord of all, and that all realms of culture, including science, are answerable to His lordship, sustains hope both for a renewal of scientific piety and for a fresh, more virile era of Christian faith. If *scientism* has led to frustration, then at least science has disclosed both microcosm and macrocosm to be more awesome than even the most devout men had dreamed. An editorial in *Life* magazine (December, 1960, p. 44) notes that "one result of the scientific revolution may conceivably be a revival of natural piety, perhaps of religion itself. That would be a sign that ours is indeed becoming a great

civilization, for the discovery and spread of religious truth is a great civilization's transcendent purpose. But although Christianity is the religion of the West, it is not so certain that the West is still Christian."

The prestige of science has led scientists themselves along two avenues of hopeful contemplation. One is the promotion of peaceful use of discoveries which may bring about an age of peace. The difficulty here, as noted by Dr. R. M. Page, Director of Research of the U.S. Naval Research Laboratory in Washington, D.C., is the implication that "scientists might accomplish in the realm of human morals, miracles such as they appear to achieve in the realm of physical nature." Dr. Page considers this an unrealistic expectation: "While the human will is capable of accepting from society a thin veneer which makes it look good on the surface, the veneer does not change the base. In human nature can be recognized at least some elements of a foundation for war." Dr. Page indicates it is "the central belief of Christianity that man can be reconciled to God"; in consequence of this spiritual experience human nature can then be transformed. "The 'age of Peace' will come," he says, "only when mankind turns wholeheartedly to God in complete humility and voluntary unconditional surrender." Dr. Page admits that scientists have an important role in respect to the world crisis. But he does not center their responsibility one-sidedly in the research library, with the special hope of there shaping new conditions of life. Instead—at a time when agnosticism or atheism is common among many brilliant younger scientists—he emphasizes the importance of spiritual conviction and of moral influence: "If scientists in fulfilling their responsibilities not as scientists but as world citizens were openly to lead the way in true repentance and personal surrender to God, it would exert a social pressure far out of proportion to their number, simply because they *are* scientists" (in an address on "The Scientist and World Peace" to the American Scientific Affiliation, February, 1961). Yet it is obvious that repentance (at which men of all vocations stumble because of the hardness of the human heart) seems irrelevant especially to the scientific temper. If past errors are pondered, the scientist tends to examine these not so much to uncover a contrite heart as to refine analytical tools and to avoid repeating mistakes.

The second avenue of hopeful inquiry asks whether modern theology, no less than modern science, has lost its power over life by neglecting the eternal biblical verities. The arresting rediscovery of biblical theology once again has set a theistic view of the world and of man in the context of special divine revelation. The conflict between biblical religion and the scientific world view rests on today's tendency to explain everything by the so-called scientific method. While this method is ideal for providing quantitative answers to quantitative questions, it cannot decide the issues of purpose, of providence and of miracle. When the scientific method, therefore, is used to unlock the secrets of being, all reality becomes automatically and artificially limited to only those aspects which this methodology can comprehend. The scientifically trained mind has difficulty therefore, with the biblical doctrines of creation, of providence and of miracle. If every event depends entirely on empirically ascertainable causes verifiable by sense experience alone, then God's activity is reduced to irrelevance by advance definition. Such arbitrary definition itself defies empirical proof and, as a kind of speculative dogmatism, really violates the spirit of science. Dr. William G. Pollard, Executive Director of the Oak Ridge Institute of Nuclear Studies, speaks of this danger in his volume *Chance and Providence: God's Action in a World Governed by Scientific Thought* (1958). He writes: "Among the several key elements of the historic Christian faith which are difficult for the modern mind, there is none so remote from contemporary thought forms as the notion of providence. The central Judeo-Christian apprehension of events in individual life and in history as manifestations of the work of the living God, acting in judgment or in redemption, has lost all meaningful content. It is common to run across the statement that . . . in contrast to men of earlier centuries . . . we can no longer believe . . . in the divine guidance of history or in the hand of God in events. . . . The relation between God and nature, if acknowledged at all, has been reduced to that of . . . having initially brought the world into existence and endowed it with a certain structure regulated by a complete system of scientific law. . . ." Dr. Pollard however, finds in the validity of modern science no reason to doubt the "validity and reality" of the historic revelation of the living God to which the Bible and the Church both bear witness.

II. CREATION AND EVOLUTION

Between scientific truth and Christianity as revealed religion there is not, nor can there be, any final conflict. Nonetheless a wide range of disagreement may surely exist between speculative, investigative theories and private interpretations of the biblical record. In the clash between revealed religion and modern science over the origin and development of the universe and life, for example, the biblical doctrine of creation opposes all evolutionary speculations. Rival explanations of the world are really nothing new, of course; they have existed from ancient times. Only monotheistic religion, however, teaches the fashioning of the universe out of nothing by the creative power of God. The only source of this doctrine is the Bible (Gn

1.1-2.25, Jn 1.3, Cl 1.16-17, He 11.3). Scripture refers to the fact of divine creation not only in the book of Genesis but also in more than 65 other passages. Having no concept of divine creation nor of revelation, Greek philosophers came to assume the eternality of matter in one form or another. In their search for an ultimate explanatory principle the Greeks regarded deity and process as alternative or rival premises and referred all reality either to Being or to Becoming. But even when they ascribed a role both to Being and to Becoming, they avoided merging them into the "god-evolution" principle so commonly found today. By contrast, without careful definition and distinction modern thought often joins theism and evolution to formulate some ultimate explanatory principle. This confusion of ultimate principles is due especially to the influence of Charles Darwin. In *The Origin of Species* (1859), he derived all complex forms from simpler causes by gradual change (chance variation and natural selection). In such a context the only deity is Evolution. In the century since Darwin ideas of the "simplicity" of the lowest forms have had to be modified. Dr. Robert E. D. Clark, Lecturer in Chemistry, at Cambridgeshire Technical College, Cambridge, England, points out the growing awareness among scientists that "the 'lowest' forms of life involve unsuspected complexity, suggestive of immense ingenuity." He indicates that "evidence that early life was, in fact, simpler than later life is lacking" (*Baker's Dictionary of Theology*, 1960, "Evolution"). In a semi-religious moment, even Darwin granted the possibility that God as First Cause stands behind the primal protozoa from which all other forms supposedly developed. This deity, however, is simply the first of a series of evolutionary causes. Darwin and many evolutionists after him retained the term "god"; their speculations about the world and life erase essential features of the scriptural view of the universe, however, and of the biblical revelation of the nature of the living God as well. It is this deletion of spiritual realities, and not the modern scientific attempt to demonstrate the fact and extent of change in nature, that is the central issue in the so-called conflict of science and religion.

The biblical view of creation presupposes several things: (1) a sovereign mind and will; (2) origination by fiat command; (3) graded orders of being and life. In other words, the Bible teaches that the universe owes its existence and continuation to the Will and Word of a transcendent God; that this unique divine activity of creation (Gn 1.1; 2.4; cf. He 11.3) established fixed grades of being and life (cf. "after his kind," Gn 1.11, 12, 21, 24, 25, and 6.20; cf. also Gn 1.26 with Jn 1.4, 9, 14, and 1 Co 15.39). The broad sweep of the biblical teaching may be summarized as follows: "That a sovereign, personal, ethical God is the voluntary creator of the space-time universe; that God created *ex nihilo* by divine fiat; that the stages of creation reflect an orderly rational sequence; that there are divinely graded levels of life; that man is distinguished from the animals by a superior origin and dignity; that the human race is a unity in Adam; that man was divinely assigned the vocation of conforming the created world to the service of the will of God; that the whole creation is a providential and teleological order: the whole front of evangelical theology finds these irreducible truths of revelation in the Genesis creation account. That the word of creation is no mere instrumental word, but rather a personal Word, the Logos, who is the divine agent in creation; that this Logos permanently assumed human nature in Jesus Christ; that the God of creation and of revelation and of redemption and of sanctification and of judgment is one and the same God: these staggering truths evangelical theology unanimously supports on the basis of the larger New Testament disclosure" ("Science and Religion," in *Contemporary Evangelical Thought,* Channel Press, 1957, pp. 258 f.).

By contrast evolutionary theory asserts the following: (1) a simple (unendowed or unactualized) primal entity; (2) temporal origination and development; (3) progressive appearance of new capacities and new forms. In its pure, and most consistent, form, then, evolution as an explanation of origins rules out such principles as God, divine purpose and providence, and man's essential uniqueness. By insisting on a continuing movement toward ever new and higher forms evolution strikes at the very heart of revealed religion. For the divine incarnation of God in Christ implies the permanent significance of human nature.

"Total evolution," as opposed to less severe forms that incorporate religious features, has been championed not alone by the Communists advocating "dialectical materialism," but by such Western philosophers as the late John Dewey and Bertrand Russell. For a generation Dewey's naturalistic philosophy adversely penetrated the theism that had characterized American public education. More recently, Oscar Riddle has designated supernaturalism as an enemy "of science and society . . . more formidable and more durable . . . than Nazism and Communism," and pleads for "unmitigated evolution" not rendered "flat and innocuous" through the introduction of ideas of divinity (*The Unleashing of Evolutionary Thought,* Vantage Press, 1954, pp. 396 ff.). The earlier evasive and confusing tactic of simply exalting the "god" of evolution as the ultimate principle of explanation has now largely fallen into disrepute.

Actually, many Western scientists recognize large, distressing gaps in any attempt to use evolution as the total explanation of the

world and man. Precisely the failure of evolution to solve the so-called "riddles of the universe" has led scientific circles to reassert religious factors, some borrowed from revealed religion and others shaped by imaginative speculation. Modern theories both supplement and contradict each other in what they postulate as spiritual or religious elements alongside their evolutionary interpretations. This fact shows the inability of developmental theories to account adequately for the data of scientific experience. Confusion in what is retained of the biblical view, together with great originality in blending the biblical with modern secular motifs, tells much about the dilemma of evolutionary science today, and also about the modern drift from revealed religion. Only where Marxist dogma is peremptorily dignified as scientific truth, where evolutionary explanation relies first on philosophical determinations and then on scientific evidences, do scientists define a universal and uniform "total evolution."

No conflict could exist between the Bible and science, of course, if one arbitrarily dismissed the scriptural account as simply sublime poetry or mythology; or reduced its truths to mere parabolic symbols; or transposed objective meaning and narrative into mere subjective religious attitude or existential response. Nor would conflict occur were one to say that whatever pronouncements are delivered to our reason by the historical and natural sciences, these judgments cannot really jeopardize the emotional or volitional implications of scriptural teaching.

Even if mediating theologians in recent decades have sometimes been vulnerable to one or another of these unpromising courses, none of these alternatives is truly satisfactory. Actually these options purchase peace between science and religion by surrendering the very heart of the Christian religion, and by denying a meeting place in the mind of man, as well as in nature and in history, for the legitimate claims of both religion and science. Doubtless there are questions which neither theology nor science because of their respective limitations of method is competent to answer. But to preserve the claims of both, even when they conflict, simply by deeding separate territorial rights to each, is more a ruse than a resolution. If Christianity affirms, as indeed it does, that there are graded kinds of life and that human nature is essentially changeless (recall the doctrines of Christ's assumption of human nature in the incarnation and the future resurrection of mankind), then the dogma that all complex forms of life have emerged from a simple primitive form is manifestly false, and likewise its implication that man will be superseded by some more intricate species. If science actually shows, as its spokesmen in earlier decades sometimes rashly asserted, that miracles are impossible, and that every effect results only from some

immediately preceding natural cause, then the biblical miracles, not least among them the virgin birth and bodily resurrection of Christ are, of course, impossible.

Fortunate is the new piety now sometimes discernible among scientists and theologians as they confront the relevant evidence supplied by the space-time universe and by the inspired Scriptures. On the ecclesiastical side, churchmen more readily admit that reactionary positions have sometimes been wrongly dignified with biblical status. On the experimental side, scientists more openly concede that speculative theories have often been pronounced as established fact. The tremendous scientific breakthrough of recent times has forced many scientists to reexamine both the basic assumptions and the details of their theories. Instead of presuming to declare how nature is objectively constituted, contemporary physicists more and more view their theories simply as operational procedures which show what "works" rather than establish what is "true." The exciting rediscovery of biblical theology, accompanied by archaeological confirmations of the sacred records, has meanwhile brought a questioning of long-established critical theories and fresh pursuit of the meaning and content of special divine revelation.

The Bible is studded with supernatural acts that reveal the Living God and His purposes. In His work of creation, God shaped the heavens and the earth and made man in His image. In the mighty miracle of Christ's resurrection, God fashioned a redeemed race and pledged a new heaven and a new earth. Both acts are decisive centers of the scriptural account. Since acceptance or rejection of these miracles involves two vastly different views of reality and of life, it is no wonder that here the so-called conflict between science and the miraculous comes into sharpest focus. From the Christian point of view, to reject either the doctrine of creation or that of the resurrection violates revealed religion which relates man's natural life (Jn 1.3,4) and his spiritual redemption (1 Co 15.22) to the supernatural being and work of the Logos. This is one reason scientism, in trying to explain the existence of all things by natural causes alone, inevitably must tangle with these sacred doctrines. Dr. George K. Schweitzer, Associate Professor of Chemistry in the University of Tennessee, reminds us that speculative accounts, instead of acknowledging that the origin of the universe is outside human observation, often promulgate a bias against the doctrine of creation. He writes: "No person can come to the problem of cosmogony without preconceived ideas. Since one of the basic beliefs of Christianity is its concept of God as Creator, the question of cosmogony is particularly controversial in our society. Attempts to avoid the idea of creation are found in much scientific literature,

indicating the presence of much prejudice. Many writers are not content to leave the idea alone, which would be the strict scientific attitude, since science does not deal with ultimate origins, but instead they take particular pains to set forth and promote belief in possibilities for a universe without an origin" (in *Evolution and Christian Thought Today,* Russell L. Mixter, ed., Eerdmans, 1959, p. 51).

1. The Origin of the Universe

Our statement of "the scientific view" of origins must promptly acknowledge that scientific theories undergo revision constantly and that in every decade scientists themselves disagree over the larger meaning of scientific data. Even if we cannot ask science for final pronouncements, we can survey the dominant scientific convictions now extant concerning origins.

The age of the universe is currently estimated between 6 and 10 billion years. At present, density of galaxy clusters and velocity of galaxial cluster recession are the preferred methods for dating the universe. Assuming that the total amount of matter plus energy has remained unchanged, most contemporary scientists trace the expanding galaxial clusters back (1) to a superdense conglomerate state some 6 to 10 billion years ago, when a mighty explosion hurled matter and radiation into galaxial clusters that are still expanding from this explosive force; or (2) to infinity past, ever since which (as a steady state of events) cloud-forming hydrogen atoms have condensed into planets, stars, galaxies and galaxial clusters. Neither cosmological theory offers a full explanation of origins. The so-called "big bang" theory leaves unanswered the question of the source of the material that originated at the time of the tremendous explosion. The "steady state" theory does not explain where the material comes from that goes into constant creation.

The latter theory (supported by Professors Fred Hoyle and Hermann Bondi, Cambridge University cosmologists, and by Professor Thomas Gold of Cornell University), asserts that the universe is being created continuously out of new matter. The former theory (held by Cambridge Professor Martin Ryle and "orthodox" cosmologists) speaks of a moment of creation when all matter was one mass and of the later outward flight of irregular groups of star kingdoms or galaxies by which the universe is constantly expanding. Both theories come under the category of hypothesis and are subject therefore to revision or replacement. Professor Martin Ryle, in February, 1961, told the Royal Astronomical Society that on the basis of the distribution of radio signals from the outermost space yet probed by man—a distance of 8 to 10 million light years (reckoned to be near the limits of physical observation)—the outward expansion of the galaxies is now confirmed, and the thesis of continuous creation disproved. But these interpretations are also disputed.

The earth as part of the universe is thought to have first appeared as a molten mass of matter that resulted from condensation of the solar system after turbulence in the cloud of dust around the sun. After a few billion years of change (slow cooling, solidifying of surface rocks, shaping of the continents; condensation of water to form the oceans; erosive, thermal, chemical and mechanical processes on the surface), the earth was ready for a major event; the coming of life.

In Scripture the interest in origins is primarily moral and purposive, rather than quantitative and mechanical. The Bible especially stresses the *who* and *why* of creation. God's act of creation reveals his "eternal deity and Godhead" (Ro 1.20); the final purpose of His created universe is to publish His glory (Ps 19.1).

While it is not wholly indifferent to the *how* and *when* of creation, Scripture presents these themes only in a general and nontechnical way. Both Old and New Testaments affirm the fact of a primal divine creation of the universe. "In the beginning God created the heavens and the earth" (Gn 1.1). "By faith we understand that the world was created by the word of God. . . ." (He 11.3). The Genesis account extends the divine activity of creation over separate periods designated as successive days. But no date is stipulated for the origin of the universe.

Noted archaeologist W. F. Albright values the Genesis creation account as a unique phenomenon in ancient literature (H. C. Alleman and E. E. Flack, *Old Testament Commentary,* Muhlenberg, 1948, p. 135). Reflecting an advanced monotheistic viewpoint, the creation narrative has demanded consideration in every age of human thought.

Although modern scientific cosmogonies tend to be swiftly and often replaced, their general espousal of Darwinism has nonetheless made wide inroads into the teaching of the Church. Critical and mediating schools of thought either have dismissed Genesis 1 to 3 *in toto* as legend, or have allowed the creation account and that of the fall only a poetic and allegorical sense, or more recently have assigned it a cryptic mythical meaning. On the other hand, evangelical Christianity has insisted that the creation narrative addresses scientist and historian no less than theologian and moralist, even though the Bible nowhere claims to be a scientific sourcebook for astronomy, geology, physics, anthropology, or psychology. The Bible speaks in everyday nontechnical language. For that very reason its writings have retained relevance for all ages and all peoples from primitive times to the modern era. By contrast, the ever-changing technical vocabulary of philosophy and of

science easily eludes the comprehension of common people. In language of timeless simplicity the Scriptures deal with the loftiest of themes such as the creation, the fall, redemption, incarnation, justification, and sanctification. Absence of scientific vocabulary does not make the book unscientific, however. By the facts it states, the Bible not only excludes false and arbitrary views of existence and life but also supplies certain premises essential to any reliable view of man and the world.

Contemporary critics commonly say that the New Testament universe of three "levels" –heaven, the earth, and hell–upon which supernatural forces act, reflects a mythological view of the universe. Some, like the followers of Rudolf Bultmann, reduce the essence of revealed religion to immediate divine-human confrontation. This dismissal of the heart of the Gospel (the supernatural incarnation, atonement, and bodily resurrection of Christ) depends on assumptions like the nonexistence of the supernatural, the impossibility of miracle, the unreality of heaven and hell, which science has hardly demonstrated and which fall outside the limitations of its method. It should be remembered that–contrary to certain allegations–the Bible nowhere teaches the centrality of the earth in the astronomical system. What Scripture does present is earth as the locus where the divine drama of redemption has been enacted. Scriptural assertions that Christ "came down" from heaven or "ascended" into heaven, or that the wicked are finally consigned by God's wrath to the depths of hell, do not ask the Christian to abandon the assured results of science. The fact is that, despite the rejection by mediating scholars of central features of the biblical view on supposed scientific grounds, contemporary scientists more and more concede that the scientific method does not discover the real nature of things but simply provides operational procedures. Speculative critics, on the other hand, by rejecting biblical miracles and by ascribing finality to modern scientism establish not so much the untenability of historic Christianity as their own revolt against revealed religion.

2. The Species of Life

In recent generations the main problem in harmonizing the Bible and science has been *fixity of the species*. Although both theologians and scientists have had to yield ground, in the aftermath of this debate the biblical record still retains its relevance uncompromised.

When evolutionists denied and evangelicals affirmed the fixity of species conflict between science and religion widened. The English biologist John Rae (1628-1705) had already spoken of all species originating simultaneously through an original divine act of creation. In the nineteenth century (when Darwin came on the scene) most scientists affirmed the constancy of species. Through misplaced reliance on scientific opinion, and not initially through appeal to the Genesis account and its excessive interpretation did fixity of species virtually become an evangelical dogma. The Bible itself, while insisting on divinely graded orders of life, speaks only of the fixity of *kinds*, rather than of species, of life. Genesis neither teaches nor denies that all species of life were specially created (nor explicitly that some forms of life began by secondary means). That God's creative activity embraced natural forces, at least some passages in Genesis imply; we have, for example: "Let the waters . . . be gathered. . . . And it was so" (Gn 1.9). This procedure is not uniform, however. Even in regard to the mention of "bearing seed" after its kind, it is well to recall the parable of the seed growing *of itself* and Jesus' significant emphasis on its supernatural endowment independently of human help and beyond human comprehension (Mk 4.26 ff.). Contemporary science classifies living things into almost a million species, although scientific circles still debate the basic definition of this term. On the premise that modern species are to be identified with the biblical kinds of life the narrative of Noah and the ark would be sheer nonsense ("And of every living thing of all flesh, two of every sort shalt thou bring into the ark, to keep them alive with thee; they shall be male and female. Of fowls after their kind, and of cattle after their kind, of every creeping thing of the earth after his kind, two of every sort shall come unto thee, to keep them alive" Gn 6.19 f.).

Darwin's attempt to derive all species from a single primitive form is today in wide disrepute; science has had to abandon this notion of the fluidity of the forms of life. In the forepart of the century even the naturalistic philosopher Oswald Spengler conceded that absence of transitional types in the paleontological fossil record supports the premise that "the great classes and kinds of living being exist aboriginally, and exist still, without transition types. . . ." (*The Decline of the West*, Knopf, 1932, Vol. III, p. 32).

3. The Origin of Man

In at least one respect the Bible insists on the constancy of species, and that notably in respect to man as a special creation.

We often hear that modern assertions of man's antiquity, and discovery of manlike forms in the fossil record from which the first humans are said to have emerged contradict the biblical view. Here it is important to note the difficulty of comparing any one "scientific view" with the Genesis account, both because of the continual reconstruction of scientific theories and the marked differences among scientists. Some speculative theories of man's origin openly conflict with the Genesis record, but these often also contradict competitive scientific views. Some accounts of

man's origin renounce existence of the supernatural from the outset, and insist man is simply a higher beast whose existence can be explained only in terms of natural forces. In such context inevitable conflict arises with the theological explanation of man. Dr. John Brobeck, Chairman of the Physiology Department of the University of Pennsylvania Medical School, reminds us that the Gospel has a "built-in conflict" with certain modern prejudices. Against mechanism (which asserts that every phenomenon has a discoverable physical cause) the New Testament speaks of the realities of man's spiritual life (1 Co 2.14). Against relativism (which renounces absolute standards of truth and goodness) the New Testament presents ultimates (Mt 5.28). Against humanism (which stresses love of neighbor) the New Testament emphasizes man's prior obligation of love for God with his whole being (Mt 22.37, 38). But such conflict does not really stem from scientific as much as from speculative or philosophical considerations; the limitations of science are such that it cannot, by sustained examination of *natural realities,* decide the existence or non-existence of *supernatural realities.*

The live nerve of the anthropological debate concerns whether or not modern man has a "pre-history." Evolutionary anthropology claims the antiquity of "prehistoric man" on the basis of archaeological, geological, paleontological and morphological evidence. Theistic evolutionists, in contrast with creationists, concede the evolutionary origin of man from some pre-human form. Since the discovery in 1891 of *Pithecanthropos erectus* the Greek term *anthropos* has been applied to these forms one way or another. This development has led some theistic evolutionists to contend that only morphologically human creatures without culture existed before Adam. From the association of such fossil bones with material culture others argue for the antiquity of the human race. Over against these theories the traditional creationist view teaches man was both anatomically and spiritually a new divine creation.

While various humanlike forms are dated in the Pleistocene epoch (100,000 years ago or more) no undisputed anthropoid fossils have been found in the still earlier Pliocene epoch. Ten to fifteen million years of silence here confront the argument for man's animal ancestry. Moreover, scientists like Jan Lever, Professor of Zoology at Free University, Amsterdam, (who in principle is not opposed to supernatural derivation of man "through the animals"), readily concede that the gap from the anthropoids to man has not really been bridged. "The opinion expressed at times, that it has been proved that man descended from anthropoids," he writes, "lacks a scientific basis" (*Creation and Evolution,* Grand Rapids: International Publications, 1958, p. 157). The evolutionary emphasis

rests one-sidedly on strong anatomical and physiological resemblances between the anthropoids and man. But Franz Weidenreich appropriately admonishes scientists to consider also the "most characteristic differences" between the organization of man and of the great apes (*Apes, Giants and Man,* 4th ed., Chicago: University of Chicago Press, 1948, p. 5). Lever in fact acknowledges that "investigators are becoming more and more convinced that upon the basis of the remnants of the skeletons of these old forms it is not possible to decide whether a being is man or animal" (*op. cit.,* p. 158).

Here we come to real grips with the central affirmation of the biblical account in the so-called conflict of science and religion. The crucial declaration of biblical religion, one which modern scientists consider only obliquely if at all, is simply that man's uniqueness in the creature world lies in his bearing the image of God. Nowhere does Genesis affirm man to be anatomically and physiologically wholly dissimilar from the animals. (Does the evolutionary premise "anatomical similarity proves descent" imply that unless a creature is physically dissimilar to other existing finite forms no evidence of divine creation of any being or species is admissible?) Rather the biblical account affirms man's striking dissimilarity by locating his uniqueness in his spiritual nature, particularly in his capacity to know God. While the Bible affirms man's creation by a unique divine act, it does not exclude anatomical similarities between human and non-human forms. Similarly, the Bible's explanation of the different kinds of life by supernatural creation does not wholly rule out all physiological similarities between these various grades of being. What the Scriptures assert, alongside the fact of divinely fixed kinds of life, is the unique creation of man as a bearer of God's image. "And God said, Let us make man in our image, after our likeness: and let them have dominion over the fish of the sea, and over the fowl of the air, and over the cattle, and over all the earth, and over every creeping thing that creepeth upon the earth" (Gn 1.26). "In the beginning was the Word. . . . In him was life; and the life was the light of men" (Jn 1.1,4).

Let the reader attest whether the story of mankind confirms the statement of man's uniqueness in the creation. Let the reader likewise declare whether human history verifies the Bible's affirmations that man's fall into sin sullies this divine image (Gn 3.6-24), that fallen man requires supernatural renewal (Co 3.10), that apart from spiritual regeneration man deteriorates to bestiality (Ro 1.21-32).

It should certainly be clear why "scientism," which explains all existence and life on naturalistic premises alone, is hostile especially to the Christian doctrines of man's creation and of God's incarnation in Jesus of Nazareth.

Because it arbitrarily rules out the reality of the supernatural, naturalism discounts not only the occurrence of isolated miracles, but even the very possibility of miracle. Naturalism heaps special contempt upon man's creation by God and upon Christ's incarnation, however, because once these cardinal truths are admitted, they carry many implications. To concede that man by creation bears the divine image, and that in Jesus Christ deity has permanently assumed our nature, postulates a definitive view not only of human history and destiny, but of God and the world. Therefore the revolt against a spiritual interpretation of human life and experience vents its fury schematically and systematically upon the biblical declaration that the Logos, who from the foundation of the world purposed to assume human nature (Rv 13.8), in the creation furnished the unique light of man's life (Jn 1.4, 9). In John 1.3, Colossians 1.16 and Hebrews 1.2 the second person of the Trinity is specifically identified as the special divine agent in creation.

Although Genesis sets no fixed dates, it begins the history of the human race at a point which, according to Bible chronologists, must be set no more recently than 6,000 and no more remotely than 10,000 years ago. Although early champions of evolution ridiculed so recent a beginning for culture as the biblical concept presents, this view is now widely conceded as credible. Whether civilization dates back more than six to eight thousand years is no longer a matter of debate. Archaeological finds tend to confirm rather than to dispute the biblical picture of man's appearance as the domesticator of nature. Even the historian Arnold J. Toynbee readily concedes that Ussher's speculative and much-lampooned date of 4004 B.C. "approximately marks the first appearance of representatives of the species of human society called civilization" (*The Atlantic Monthly:* "Civilization on Trial," Vol. 179 [June, 1942], p. 35). Biblical expositors, meanwhile, have shown from within the Old Testament narratives that the genealogies preserve a selective rather than a complete chronology; the narratives therefore accommodate a date for civilized man reaching back 8,000 years or so. "The Bible dates man at probably 5-10,000 B.C. and places him in Mesopotamia. It tells us that after his arrival there was a welter of technical invention. If attention is paid, not to man's anatomy, but to his mental endowment, then archaeology confirms both the biblical date and, probably, place: civilization started relatively suddenly and spread rapidly. When God made man in his own image the face of the world was changed and history commenced" (Robert E. D. Clark, *op. cit.*).

4. The Enduring Enigmas

Certain enigmas to which it speaks only in generalities still confound modern science. These very enigmas scriptural revelation refers confidently to the supernatural activity of the Creator. They are the origin of matter; the origin of life; stability of the major graded forms or kinds of plant and animal life; and the origin of man. It is true that some speculative theologians have joined speculative scientists in dismissing the creation story as irrelevant to reconstructing a theory of origins. Nevertheless in this twentieth century the Genesis account still supplies for multitudes of devout men and women the same sense of awe and relevance as it did not only for the ancient prophets but also for the Founder of the Christian religion.

Jesus of Nazareth, the incarnate Son of God, Himself vouches for the Creation story, for Adam and Eve as first parents of the human race, as well as for all "the law and the prophets." While we properly welcome every scientific gain in the conquest of the universe yet we maintain that man's true dominion over nature, and over sin and death and Satan, is comprehended only in a knowledge of the Creator-Redeemer who is both Saviour and Lord.

The danger to which the Church of Christ is exposed is that of coveting the prestige won by science, and of exhausting her own energies to show herself "scientifically acceptable." The fact is that avowedly secular scientific schemes are conquering space and time to an ever greater extent in our century. Such success has given scientism virtually the prestige and power of a new divinity. The Church then has little to gain from constantly declaring the Gospel to be flawlessly compatible with the "latest scientific version." If the Gospel reconciles itself with so many successively revised scientific points of view it might indeed appear to make Christianity "acceptable" to the secular world outlook but only by depriving theologians of the capacity to address scientists and philosophers. Christianity claims the whole being, man's reason included. The Christian message teaches the Living God is Creator, Preserver and Judge of all and that He alone is Lord of time and space. Christianity also teaches that even science owes its origin and success to a rational God, one who created rational creatures for knowledge not only of an intelligible universe, but also of Himself, the Truth.

THE CHRONOLOGY OF THE BIBLE

Donald J. Wiseman, D.Litt.

Biblical events are recorded according to the chronological systems then prevailing, so the purpose of any modern reconstruction of the precise time and order of these ancient happenings is to present them in terms of the Western calendar now in use (that is distinguished as B.C. and A.D.). This can be an important contribution to the understanding and interpretation of Scripture.

The Bible itself contains numerous chronological references, and these data are of themselves sufficient to assure the general reader of the march of events. When this internal evidence is correlated with the increasing volume of extra-Biblical information, much of it from written and archaeological and mainly contemporary sources, differences of opinion may arise. In some instances it is outside the purpose of the Biblical narrative to present precise information on the timing of events which in antiquity may well have been of less importance than to a modern reader. It must be remembered that in the extant manuscripts there are some variants which should warn against the construction of theological theories on so-called infallible chronological systems. There are numerous items of chronological interpretation over which equally devout students of the Bible differ. In our present state of knowledge it is therefore often wise to withhold final judgment on some of these points of disagreement, except where they obviously discredit the explicit statement of Scripture.

In early times the ancients, including the Jews, used more than one method of time reckoning, and systems varied in different places and periods.

The purpose here is to give a summary of those systems in use in Bible times, to outline areas of major agreement, and to indicate some of the points at which scholars now differ.

Some Ancient Chronological Systems

The written records of the earliest peoples of the ancient Near East—the Sumerians—show that time was reckoned by "day" and "night," each of twelve hours, a "day" being used at first also of the twenty hours beginning with sunset. The Hebrews and Greeks largely followed this practice, though by New Testament times this "day" was considered (as in Egypt) to begin at sunrise (Mk 11:11-12; Ac 4:3). The day was divided into twelve periods or "watches" of two hours. Seven days comprised the week, while twenty-nine days (and some hours) were counted to the month, the Egyptians adopting a calendar of twelve solar months and the Mesopotamians one of twelve lunar months. Each of these systems required artificial regulation by intercalating one or two months to keep the "calendar" in relation to the seasons and a year of 365 days. Thus by c. 2900 B.C. Egypt had an artificial schematic, in effect, solar or fixed civil calendar. By the eighth century B.C. the Babylonians had stabilized their year of twelve lunar months (which fell short of the solar year by about eleven days) by intercalating additional months at regular intervals over a nineteen-year period.

In antiquity history was recorded in various modes. Thus before 2100 B.C. in Mesopotamia there was no precise attempt to equate or parallel their own history closely with that of their neighbors. Succession of events was shown in lists which first gave the order of rulers at one city before listing those who, though sometimes their contemporary, ruled at a nearby city. These "genealogical lists" (as perhaps those in Gen 1-11) mark territorial or other lines of succession in general, rather than aiming to provide a strict chronology in the modern sense. Thus down to c. 2000 B.C. there is a degree of uncertainty (even up to a century or more) mainly caused by the lack of continuous evidence for a precise link with later events. Dating in these, as in later, periods may be assigned from archaeological evidence. Successive periods of human occupation at a given site may be distinguished by the types of artifacts discovered and compared with similar finds at other places. This archaeological evidence is useful only for general chronological purposes, though in some periods (e.g., the Israelite occupation of Palestine) a close and accurate relative dating is thus possible. Various other scientific methods of dating are currently being devised but are as yet less precise than cumulative archaeological and written records. One method ("Carbon-14 dating"), which counts the "half life" of carbonized organic matter on the assumption that there is a constant state and decline in radioactivity, has so far proved of value in giving approximate dates ($\pm$ 250 years) where other historical sources are not extant, as in prehistoric eras. It is thus of little practical importance to Biblical chronology.

From about 2100 B.C. increasing precision is possible. In Egypt, king lists, dated inscriptions, astronomical observations, and parallels with records from Mesopotamia and elsewhere enable the dynasties to be closely dated. Thus the 11th and 12th dynasties can be assigned to c. 2134-1786 B.C. and the 18th to 20th to c. 1570-1085 B.C., with a maximum margin of error of four to ten years. The intervening dynasties are themselves subject

503

to a possible error in dating of up to only twenty years. Even within this small compass of disagreement, there is often general accord on the dating of the individual pharaohs.

The Babylonians dated their regnal years by significant events. The formulae sometimes refer to intercity or international happenings, and lists of these year names were kept for reference by later scribes. Unfortunately, gaps still remain in these lists and some relative information is interpreted differently by scholars. Thus for Babylonia there has arisen a "school" favoring the "long" or "higher" chronology which, for example, dates Hammurabi, the sixth king of the First Amorite Dynasty of Babylon, to 1792-1750 B.C. (Sidney Smith). Another "school" of thought favors a "short" chronology by dating the same king to 1728-1686 B.C. (W. F. Albright). Consequently, all Mesopotamian dates before c. 1400 B.C. are subject to a similar variation of approximately sixty years.

Already c. 2000 B.C. the Assyrians marked each year by the name of a specially appointed eponymn (limmu,) or official. Kings and high officials held this office in turn, and since scribes often noted important foreign or domestic events alongside the limmu name, a useful correspondence with other historical sources is readily available. In addition, a reference to an eclipse of the sun in the eponymate of Bur-Sagale can be assigned to June 15, 763 B.C., and thus furnishes the precise equivalent in Julian dating for all the years 892-648 B.C. given in the same list. For the intervening period from c. 1400-900 B.C., and for the same period as the limmu lists, king lists, "synchronous histories" of events in Assyria, Babylonia, and the West provide us with firsthand evidence. As will be seen, there are direct references in some of these sources to individuals or events in Israel and Judah which give a firm link between the individual chronological systems employed.

From at least the ninth century B.C., the Assyrians and Babylonians dated documents by the day, month, and regnal year of the king. These datings can be checked against contemporary records including the Old Testament, Egyptian papyri, and later classical sources (the Canon of Ptolemy of 620 B.C. onward, Manetho, and Berossus). Since regnal years can be readily transposed into the Julian calendar (see R. H. Parker and W. H. Dubberstein, *Babylonian Chronology 626 B.C.-A.D. 75*, 1956) a precise equivalent to within the year can be given or, if the day and month is stated, accurate to within twenty-four hours. From 312 B.C. a continuous "era" system of dating (Seleucid) was in use.

These ancient methods of dating all have their bearing on the Biblical data. The Israelites, like many other ancient peoples, employed more than one system or calendar. One reckoned according to the agricultural seasons, as attested by the Gezer Calendar.

Months named in this way are Abib ("fresh ear of grain": Ex 23:15); Ziv ("spring flowers": 1 K 6:1, 37); Ethanim (7th month), and Bul may be of Canaanite origin and were listed beginning with the fall. At the same time the Babylonian system of numerical equivalents for the months was used (1 K 12:32, etc.), the year beginning in the spring (Est 3:7). The Hebrew names for the months are the direct equivalent of the Babylonian.

Within the sects of Judaism in intertestamental times various calendars were compiled for ritual purposes (the Qumran calendar, and the calendar of Jubilees). We learn from Josephus that, for secular use in Palestine in New Testament times, the Seleucid and "Macedonian calendar" was also used.

I. THE OLD TESTAMENT

1. Creation to Abraham

Until a century and a half ago Old Testament dates followed the literal interpretation advocated by Archbishop James Ussher in his *Annales Veteris et Novi Testamenti* of 1650-1654 inserted by an unknown authority into the margin of reference editions of the KJV in 1703. This computation adds up the successive figures in the Biblical text, assuming them to follow our modern system of consecutive arrangement without overlappings or omissions. It ignores variants in some ancient authorities and the distinct possibility that some of the Biblical data refer to concurrent rather than consecutive events as in the old Babylonian systems. By adding the time between the birth of the patriarchs, 1,656 years are reckoned from the creation to the flood and 290 years from the flood to Abram's birth, thus yielding a total of 1,946 years from the creation. Allowing the two years of Genesis 11:10 and dating Abraham at 2056 B.C. (on which see below), Ussher arrived at 4004 B.C. as the date of creation. This view implies that Shem was not the eldest son of Noah born 100 years before the flood as is stated in Genesis 5:32 (cf. 7:6, 11). This literal interpretation, which pays no regard to ancient systems of chronology, gives a date for creation which results in many difficulties. Many archaeological discoveries in the ancient Near East show that town-dwelling communities (Catal Hüyuk and Jericho) are found as early as the seventh or sixth millennium B.C., with village life even earlier (c. 9000-7000 B.C.). Ussher's chronology requires a date for the flood at 2300 B.C., a time when historical and written records abound without any such reference. It lacks even the corroborating evidence of the various local floods of Mesopotamia dated to c. 3000-2850 B.C. (Kish) and c. 3500-2700 B.C. (Ur).

Others interpret the Genesis "genealogical-histories" (Hebrew *toledoth*) and other data

according to the Babylonian system; i.e., the texts were not intended to provide a continuous chronology. The term "son" is said to denote (as elsewhere in the Old Testament and in contemporary records) either a son, grandson, or remote descendant. Similarly the word "begat" may be used of other than immediate procreation. Some support for this view is found in the genealogy of our Lord in Matthew 1:8 which, by saying that Joram begat Uzziah (Ozias), omits the three kings Ahaziah, Joash, and Amaziah and thus passes over two generations. According to this view, only prominent members of the line are named, sufficient to insure the unbroken link between Adam and Abraham, the father of the Hebrews. In the summary introduction to the history of God's elect people, there may well be no intention or necessity to give a precise date for God's creation of man or of his environment. These abbreviated lists are just as valuable for showing lines of descent as are their modern, and to us more complete, counterparts. The grouping of names by tens (as the groups of seven in Matthew's genealogy) may be accounted for by literary style, or perhaps explained as a memory aid for oral transmission. Recent research shows that in most instances oral tradition was accompanied, or even anticipated, by the written word. Also the earliest style of historiography so far discovered appears in the form of lists. According to this view, the dates of such events as the flood or creation cannot be decided from Biblical evidence alone.

A less likely theory suggests that the names in the Genesis lists denote both the individual ancestor and his collective family in much the same way as the name Israel or David stood for both the man and his descendants (1 K 12:16). Thus the names in Genesis 10 may sometimes be taken to be those of individuals and sometimes to be the places bearing their names. This theory, which stresses the period in which one named family held sway, results in 8,225 years from Adam to the flood and 11,571 years from Adam to the death of Terah (*Westminster Dictionary of the Bible*, 1944, p. 103).

2. Abraham to the Exodus

The time that elapsed between the flood and Abraham is not expressly stated in the Old Testament. He is, however, linked with later events by the statement of Genesis 15:13-16 in which he is told that his descendants would dwell in a land which was not their own for four hundred years and that they would return to Palestine in the fourth generation. The fourth generation (since a generation can scarcely be equated with a century) might refer to Joseph's journey to bury Jacob. Exodus 12:40 states that "the time the people of Israel dwelt in Egypt was four hundred and thirty years." (The Septuagint and Samaritan texts add "and in the land of Canaan" after Egypt.) The sojourn was reckoned to have begun with Jacob's entry into Egypt (Gen 46:6-7). The time between this covenant with Abraham and Jacob's migration into Egypt covers some 215 years (cf. Gen 12:4; 21:5; 25:26; 47:9), so the period of the sojourn could have been "215 years only after Jacob removed into Egypt" (Josephus, *Antiquities* ii. xv. 2). There was thus an interval of 430 years from Jacob's entry to Moses' leading the people out of Egypt. The genealogy of Exodus 6:16-20 can hardly cover the whole 430 years unless it is interpreted, as has been done above for Genesis 6 and 11, as listing some, but not all, of the links in the family chain. Elsewhere Moses is shown as the fourth generation after Jacob (1 Ch 6:1-3), yet his contemporary Bezaleel was considered to be in the seventh generation (1 Ch 2:18-20) and Joshua in the twelfth (1 Ch 7:23-27). Thus Moses' genealogy may be in an ancient abbreviated form.

Different interpretations are also possible concerning the beginning and end of these 430 years between Abraham's entry (Gen 12:14) and that of Jacob into Egypt (Gen 46:6-7). Genesis 15:13-16 could be read as a reference to the stay of any Hebrews in Egypt, and Hebrews were known from Egyptian sources at least as early as the time of Joseph in the seventeenth century B.C. Josephus elsewhere implies that the 400 years were the time of the oppression only (*Antiquities* ii. ix. 1; *cf.* Ac 7). Others suggest that the four "generations" refer to the principal families between Jacob and Moses (through Kohath, Amram, and Aaron). Although Levi, Kohath, and Amram were genealogically consecutive, Moses was hardly the immediate son of Amram and Jochebed, since within a year of the Exodus Amram and his brothers had given rise to 8,600 males (Nu 3:28; 4:36). Exodus 6:20 may mean that Moses was the "descendant" of Amram. On this basis an exact dating for Abraham is not possible. On the other hand, it is to be noted that archaeological evidence, as well as the social conditions portrayed in the patriarchal narratives of Genesis 12-35, clearly point to the Middle Bronze Age (c. 2100-1550). The texts from Mari and Alalah and of the Old Babylonian period reflect many of the patriarchal customs and seem to support the view that the twentieth to nineteenth centuries B.C. were the most likely setting. This fits well with evidence of occupation of places described in Genesis found in archaeological excavations. It should be noted that Ussher, by calculating back from data in the time of the Monarchy, arrived at 1996 B.C. for the birth of Abraham. Contrary to popular theory, the kings of Genesis 14 have not been certainly identified and thus cannot be used as evidence for the present purpose.

From this evidence it is probable that

Abraham is to be placed c. 2000-1850 B.C.; Isaac, c. 1900-1750; Jacob, c. 1800-1700; and Joseph, within the period of the Hykses, c. 1750-1650 B.C. For any more precise dating, additional extra-Biblical evidence would be needed, but for the understanding of this part of Scripture, specific dating is unnecessary.

3. The Exodus and Conquest

There are two main schools of thought about the date of the Exodus. Those who interpret 1 Kings 6:1 as the exact period of years from the Exodus under Moses to the founding of the Temple in Solomon's fourth year (c. 960 B.C., but see below) place the Exodus about 1447 B.C. If this is correct, Moses' flight (Ex 2:15) was from the pharaoh Thuthmosis III (c. 1482 B.C.) and he was the king whose death is recorded in Exodus 2:23. The Exodus itself would then have taken place in the reign of Amenhotep II and the entry into the Promised Land about the year 1400 B.C.

It must, however, be recognized that this view is seriously challenged. Exodus 1:11 tells of the Hebrews, building of Pithom and Ra'amses in the days of Moses. The latter capital was named after Rameses II (c. 1290-1224), who had finished work begun by his father, Seti I, about 1302-1290 B.C. No work in the Delta was undertaken by Thuthmosis or any other pharaoh between the time of Joseph (Hyskos period) and Rameses. The city is unlikely to have been named after Rameses I, who reigned scarcely a year (1203/2 B.C.). Remains at Tanis and Qantir, which are possible sites for Ra'amses, support this. Hence the Exodus would seem to fall after 1300 B.C.

Israel is mentioned as already in the land on triumphal stela of Merneptah's fifth year (c. 1220 B.C.). The entry must, on this ground, be earlier and, with the forty years of desert travel, the Hebrews must then have left Egypt some time before 1260 B.C. A date of c. 1290-1260 for the Exodus, a view once held by most conservative scholars, is thus again possible. The destruction of cities including Bethel, Lachish, Hazor, and Debir (Tell Beit Mirsim) at the end of the Late Bronze Age, but not sooner, would support a date of about 1240 B.C. for the entry of the Israelites. More recent work at Jericho has shown that the supposed date of c. 1407 B.C., for the destruction of the walls there must be revised to c. 2300 B.C. (Early Bronze Age), so can have no bearing on this problem. Another argument once used to support the earlier date of the Exodus was the allusion to *hab/piru* ("semi-nomads") entering Palestine in the fifteenth century B.C. Similar references, however, have now been found in texts throughout Upper Mesopotamia and Palestine in all centuries from the eighteenth to the fourteenth. Thus wandering semi-nomadic

tribes were not uncommon, though Abraham was considered to be a member of such a group (Gen 14:13), and afford no certain clue as to date.

4. The Time of the Judges

This period also poses a problem. According to 1 Kings 6:1 the period from the Exodus to the building of the Temple comprised 480 years. This figure has been thought to be based on twelve periods of forty years each: forty years of the wilderness wanderings (Ex 16:35; Nu 14:33); forty under Joshua's leadership (Jg 2:8); an aggregate of seven periods of forty years for the Judges (though 3:11, 30; 5:31; 8:28; 13:1); Eli's priesthood (1 S 4:18, including perhaps part of Samuel's tenure of office); Saul (Ac 13:21); David (1 K 2:11); and part of Solomon's reign (1 K 11:42), in whose fourth year work on the Temple began. Others interpret 1 Kings 6:1 as representing the twelve generations, including Moses and Joshua, the six major judges, Eli, Samuel, Saul, and David. The chronological data within the Book of Judges itself add up to at least 397 years, and if the judgeship of Samson, Shamgar, and Eli are added, with time for the reign of David (2 S 5:4) and the four years of Solomon's reign, a total of 514 years is reached. With this must be compared the 300 years given by Jephthah for the occupation of Heshbon by the Israelites until his day (Jg 11:26) and Paul's reference to the period of the Judges as 450 years (Ac 13:19-20 KJV, but note also the variants). While this points toward the early dating of the Exodus and entry in Israel, there are problems.

Those who favor the "late" date for the Exodus argue that these narratives of the judges should not necessarily be taken to be consecutive. Thus the oppression by the Philistines and Ammonites could have been contemporaneous (Jg 10:7, 8; 13:1); the administration of Ibzan and Abdon (12:8-13) coincides with the time of Jephthah and Samson in different regions. Abimelech's attempt to rule as king (Jg 9) may have occurred at the same time as Gideon's exploits. Similarly, other overlapping of events could be postulated, as suggested also for the Genesis lists. It is noteworthy that the shorter period agrees well with the genealogies of Ruth 4:18-22. Thus those who support the "later" date for the Exodus assign the Judges to about 1220 to 1050 B.C.; those for the "earlier" date, to 1380 (or earlier) to 1050 B.C. Neither of these views supports the modern tendency to interpret each use of "forty years" as an approximate figure applicable to the duration of one generation. The forty years attributed to Saul (Ac 13:21), for example, could be a precise figure since he was made king while still a "young man" (that is, twenty years of age or less; 1 S 9:2)

THE CHRONOLOGY OF THE BIBLE

and since his fourth son, Ishbosheth, was at least thirty-five years old at the time of his father's death (2 S 2:10). Saul's accession may be dated c. 1050 B.C.

5. The Monarchy

David reigned for exactly forty years, seven at Hebron and thirty-three at Jerusalem (1 K 2:11). Some scholars feel that the variant of seven and a half years for David's rule at Hebron (2 S 5:4,5; 1 Ch 3:4) may indicate a reform in the calendar in use at the time of his move to Jerusalem, whereby the beginning of the year was calculated from the autumn instead of the spring. This calendrical change does indeed cause difficulties to us today, since two systems were in use at different times and places throughout the later divided kingdom. From Biblical evidence it is clear that in Israel the autumn (Tishri) calendar was in use alongside the other (Babylonian) spring (Nisan) reckoning for the commencement of the year.

When examining the chronology of this period, it is important to observe that there were also two methods of calculating the regnal years of any king. In some instances his accession year could be counted as his first while still being counted as the last year of his predecessor's reign (the antedating system). In other instances the Babylonian practice was followed whereby the months that remained of the year in which a ruler dies were included in his total regnal years and at the same time were marked as the "accession year" of the new king. The new king then counted the first year of his own reign as beginning on the following New Year's Day. It should therefore cause no surprise that, pending the discovery of additional evidence, different reconstructions of the chronology of the kings of Israel and Judah will vary within a few years. For this reason the table of dates must be considered as only approximate and must be used with due caution.

One such coregency was of Solomon, who was elevated to the throne while his father David was an old man in an attempt to preserve the dynasty and succession unbroken (1 K 1:37-2:11). It is likely that this practice was customary in Judah and did much to account for the stability of that kingdom compared with that of Israel. Solomon's accession date is related to external events. The Temple was under construction in his fourth year (1 K 6:1) and was completed, according to Josephus, in Hiram's eleventh (*Antiquities* viii. 3) or twelfth (*Contra Apionem* i. 126) year. Josephus also states that the Temple was completed 143 years and 8 months before the founding of Carthage in the seventh year of Pygmalion. Correlating the Tyrian king list with the evidence of the Assyrian annals places this latter event in 815/4 B.C., which therefore gives 959 B.C. for the Temple's

completion—a date which is widely accepted. Solomon's accession accordingly becomes 962/1 B.C. If, however, Josephus is referring to the completion of the Temple, which took seven years to build (1 K 6:38), and not to the founding of Carthage, Solomon's accession year was 971/0 B.C. (K. A. Kitchen, *The New Bible Dictionary*, 1962, p. 219) and the Temple was founded in 968/967. The division of the Monarchy began in 931 B.C.

The chronology of the divided monarchy during the 350 years from Rehoboam's accession in Judah to the fall of its capital, Jerusalem, in 587 B.C. is well attested. The various accounts within the Old Testament itself (Kings, Chronicles, Isaiah, and Jeremiah) can be checked by external references, and E. R. Thiele (*Mysterious Numbers of the Hebrew Kings*, 1965) has demonstrated a number of coregencies including Asa and Jehoshaphat, Jehoshaphat and Jehoram, Amaziah and Uzziah (Azariah), Uzziah and Jotham. Kitchen has argued for further such coregencies between Ahaz and Jotham and Hezekiah with Ahaz. Correlation between the Biblical history and external (mainly Assyrian) sources has given the following "fixed" points:

(1) *The accession of Jehu.* The battle of Qarqar between Shalmaneser III and a Syrian coalition is dated to 853 B.C. on the basis of eponym lists (calculated from the eclipse of 763 B.C.). This was the year in which Ahab ("Ahab, the Israelite") opposed Shalmaneser III in the latter's sixth year. In the Assyrian king's eighteenth year he was opposed by Jehu ("Yaua son of Omri"), whose tribute is pictured on the black obelisk of Shalmaneser. Since the commencement of Jehu's reign was marked by the death of both Joram of Israel and Ahaziah of Judah and occurred twelve years after the death of Ahab (2 K 3:1), this date (841 B.C.), as the first possible year for Jehu's accession, is an important synchronistic dating. Jehu, after reigning twenty-eight years (2 K 10:36), was succeeded by Jehoahaz, whose reign thus dates 814-798. This king could be the "Ia'asu of Samaria" named by Adad-nirari III of Assyria (in the Rimah stela) as paying tribute to him after his first campaign (806/5). (Others believe that the Assyrian is here referring to J(eh)oash, the son of Jehoahaz, in 798 B.C.)

(2) *Azariah of Judah.* In an inscription dated to the third year of Tiglath-pileser III of Assyria (743 B.C.), he claims to have taken tribute from Azariah of Judah. Another of his tests related the exemption bought by Menahem of Israel, and yet another, dated according to the eponym lists in 732 B.C., speaks of the defeat of Rezin (2 K 16:9), thus giving a precise date for his deportation of Israelites, for the change in rule from Pekah to Hoshea (both named in the Assyrian annals), and for Ahaz becoming his vassal.

(3) *The fall of Samaria.* According to a

507

Babylonian Chronicle, Shalmaneser V of Assyria (726-722 B.C.) died in the tenth month of the fifth year of his reign and was immediately succeeded by Sargon II (722/1-705 B.C.). The siege of Samaria took place in the seventh to ninth years of Hoshea of Israel (2 K 17:5), and the city fell in the accession year of Sargon II, who claimed the victory. Shalmaneser V himself claimed to have sacked Shamarain (Samaria), which, according to 2 Kings 17:6, fell in the ninth year of Hoshea. All these pieces of evidence indicate the year 722 B.C., which was also the sixth year of Hezekiah (2 K 18:10), the beginning of whose rule (as coregent with Ahaz) may thus be fixed as 728 B.C.

(4) *The siege of Jerusalem.* According to the royal annals of the Assyrian king Sennacherib (705-681 B.C.), he marched against Judah in his third campaign in 701 B.C. According to 2 Kings 18:13 and Isaiah 36:1, this event took place in Hezekiah's fourteenth year, thus showing a reckoning from the beginning of his reign as sole ruler of Judah (716/15 B.C.).

(5) *The fall of Nineveh.* The Babylonian Chronicle (BM 25127) for the fourteenth year of Nobopolassar and the month Abu records the destruction of Nineveh by a combined force of Babylonians, Medes, and their allies. The Assyrian capital, and with it the whole empire, thus came to an end in July/August, 612 B.C.

(6) *The Battle of Carchemish.* Another chronicle text (BM 21946) relates Nebuchadrezzar's capture of Carchemish in May/June 605 B.C., after which he claimed tribute from all the kings of Syro-Palestine (so 2 K 24:7). In 604 B.C. the Babylonians sacked Ashkelon. The fall of the city seems to have had a profound effect on Judah (Jr 36-9). The chronicle continues with the account of a hitherto unknown defeat of the Babylonians by the Egyptians in 601 B.C., which explains Jehoiakim's motive in withdrawing from his treaty obligations to Nebuchadrezzar after three years as vassal. Two years later the Babylonians reported a raid on the Arab tribes of Kedar, thus giving a date for one of Jeremiah's prophecies (49:28-33).

(7) *The capture of Jerusalem.* The Babylonian Chronicle for Nebuchadrezzar's seventh year records his capture of Jerusalem on the second day of the month Adar (= 15/16 March, 597 B.C.). He captured the king (Jehoiachin) and appointed his own nominee (Mattaniah-Zedekiah) before taking tribute and prisoners to Babylon. Thus we have a precise date for the beginning of the Exile as well as for the reigns of Jehoiakim, Jehoiachin, and Zedekiah. 2 Kings 24:12 puts this episode as in the Babylonian eighth regnal, either referring to the final capture as a fortnight later (i.e., March/April) or, more likely, following a nonaccession year system at this point.

Consequent upon this date the battle of Megiddo, at which Josiah lost his life, must be placed in 609 B.C., and the destruction of Jerusalem in the latter attack on the city by the Babylonians in the eleventh year of Zedekiah must fall in 587 B.C.

(8) *The fall of Babylon.* Cyrus' entry into Babylon seventeen days after its capture by the Persians is chronicled as October 29, 539 B.C., and the return of the exiles followed soon thereafter.

6. Post-Exilic Data

The dates of Babylonian and Persian kings have been established beyond question from contemporary records. It is thus possible to date any direct allusions to their reigns in the Old Testament. The rebuilding of the Jerusalem Temple began in the second year of Darius 1 (Ez 4:24); that is, 520/19 B.C. The stages are given from Haggai's first exhortation to Zerubbabel in that year on the first day of the sixth month (August 29, 520). Work began twenty-four days later (September 21, 520; Hag 1:15). Two months later Zechariah's first speech was recorded (Zec 1:1; October/November 520), and the rebuilding was finished on the third day of Adar in Darius's sixth year (March 12, 515 B.C. Ez 6:15).

Chronological problems sometimes arise from a critical tendency to reverse the traditional order of events. Thus Ezra went to Jerusalem in the seventh year of Artaxerxes I (458/7 B.C.; Ez 7:1, 8-9), leaving Babylon on April 8 and reaching the city on August 4, 458. Nehemiah was given a permit to return in his twentieth year (445/444; Neh 2:1). The wall was completed fifty-two days after the work recommenced (October 2, 445; Neh 6:15). To argue that Ezra must have followed Nehemiah, since he lived in the seventh year of Artaxerxes (taken as the second ruler of that name, 398 B.C.), requires a change of text to assume that Ezra's ministry began in the thirty-seventh (not seventh) year of Artaxerxes I (428 B.C.). Such an emendation has no textual warrant whatever.

II. THE NEW TESTAMENT

The New Testament writers, like those of the Old Testament, add specific chronological data only where it is essential to explain a particular action to their immediate readers. As a result, some of their statements cannot be interpreted easily today, mainly because of the absence at present of corresponding facts from contemporary extra-Biblical sources. Nevertheless, it must always be remembered that a precise appraisal at these points is unnecessary for establishing the authority, or our understanding, of the narratives.

1. The Life of Christ

(1) *His Birth.* The birth of Jesus Christ occurred in the days of Herod, King of Judah (Mt 2:1, Lk 1:5). According to Josephus, Herod the Great died after a reign of thirty-four years or of thirty-seven years "from the date he was proclaimed King of the Romans" (*Antiquities* xvii. 191) shortly after a lunar eclipse (xvii. 167) and possibly just before the Jewish Passover. From this his death is usually dated to the spring (March/April) of 4 B.C.; that is, when he was seventy in the 750th year of Rome. Even allowing time for the Magi to visit Herod en route for Bethlehem, there is no need to assume that the infant Jesus (Mt 2:11) was as old as two (Mt 2:16) at this time. Christ's birth took place while P. Sulpicius Quirinius was governor of Syria (Lk 2:2). His term of office is not precisely known and must have been after his consulship in 12 B.C. and before A.D. 6/7 when his edict for taxing the Jews led to the revolt of Judas the Galilean (Ac 5:37; Josephus, *Antiquities* xviii. 1-26). This has led to suggested dates as early as 11 B.C. for the birth of Jesus. Neither Roman nor other writers mention Quirinius as in Syria in the intervening period, though he was an important Roman official with responsibilities in the East for some years and another term of office in Syria in 6/5 B.C. has been proposed. Therefore, while the year 4 B.C., or shortly before, is at present the most favored date, there can be no certainty.

The star which led the Magi to Bethlehem does not yet help us to fix the date. Argentieri, assuming that Jesus was born on a Sunday and on December 25, found that Halley's comet was seen in the East in 12 B.C.; but such astronomical phenomena were usually interpreted in antiquity as ominous and not fortunate. Another theory is that the star was a rare combination of Jupiter, Saturn, and some other extraordinary star (in Pisces) which, according to contemporary texts checked by modern calculations, did occur in 7 B.C. With all these uncertainties, it should be pointed out that early Christian sources themselves varied between 4 and 1 B.C., though a recent study has again argued powerfully for the year 1 B.C.-A.D. 1 (*Journal of Theological Studies,* xviii, 1966, 283-298)—this on the basis of revised dates for Herod the Great. That the shepherds were feeding their flocks by night (Lk 2:8) probably indicates the winter season. The western tradition of December 25 as the night of Christ's birth dates back only to the second century, and the Eastern Church still observes Christ's birthday on January 6. While the precise date is not yet known (about 7 B.C. seems to best fit the evidence), it is not the date but rather the fact that "Jesus Christ came into the world" that is a vital matter of dogmatic statement and belief.

(2) *The Commencement of Jesus' Public Ministry.* The call to John, son of Zechariah, came in the fifteenth year of the reign of Tiberius Caesar (Lk 3:1ff.), which fell in A.D. 26-29 according to varying calculations, the later date calculated from the death of Augustus (A.D. 14). This is preferable to theories which calculate the time from his association with Tiberius as tribune (A.D. 6) or as Imperator (II). Some variation in assessing the precise year is necessary according to whether the Syrian or, as is more likely, the Jewish calendar, was in mind. This accords with the evidence that "*about* thirty years" elapsed between the birth of our Lord and His baptism by John (Lk 3:23) an unspecified time after the Baptists' call (v. 21). During Jesus' ministry His hearers implied that being "not yet fifty years old" (Jn 8:57), He was in his forties. After His baptism, the forty days in the desert, the call of the disciples, the wedding at Cana, and the visit to Capernaum, Jesus was at Jerusalem in time for the Passover (Jn 2:13). At this time it was said that the Temple had already taken forty-one years to build (Jn 2:20). According to Josephus (*Antiquities* xv. 1), Herod "undertook to build" this in his eighteenth regnal year (20/19 B.C.). It is not known, however, how much time was spent in the preparation of material and men prior to the actual commencement of work. According to Josephus, the main structure was completed in ten years but the Temple was not finished until A.D. 64. Some interpret the statement of John to mean that the temple was then finished, but in either case it does not provide a precise chronological reckoning in our present state of knowledge.

(3) *Duration of the Ministry.* The theory of a one-year ministry rests solely on the belief that Jesus applied to Himself, in a literal and restricted sense of "year," the prophecy of Isaiah of "the acceptable year of the Lord" (61:2; Lk 4:19). This view must be rejected because of the Passover reference in John 6:4. It is more customary to support a ministry of two or three years' length. The mention of three Passovers (Jn 2:13, 6:4; 11:55) and perhaps a fourth (Jn 5:1) requires a ministry of at least two years. The three-year view, following Melito and Eusebius, depends on the length of the interval between the Passovers mentioned in John 2:13 and 6:4. Christ's return to Galilee (Jn 4:43) seems to have been in winter. The "yet four months and then comes the harvest" (of which there were two annually) in John 4:35 would usually point to December/January, since the barley harvest began about April and the wheat harvest in the following month (cf. Ru 1:23). For this reason the interpretation of the unnamed feast of John 5:1 as Purim (celebrated only locally and in February/March) is unlikely. Moreover, "after these things" implies an interval between Christ's return and His next journey south to Jerusalem. The

feast, therefore, is more probably the Passover of the following March/April or a later festival. This Passover can hardly be the one of John 6:4, however, since "nigh" does not mean "just past" and there is an interval between John 5 and 6. It is therefore most probable that a Passover took place between those recorded in John 2:13 and 6:4 and that Jesus' ministry lasted three full years (about A.D. 28/29-30/31).

(4) *The Death of Jesus.* All four Gospels imply that the day of the Crucifixion was on Friday, since the following day was the sabbath (Mt 28:1; Mk 15:42; Lk 23:54; Jn 19:31), and that the next day thereafter was the first day of the week (our Sunday). The month (Nisan = March/April) is also fixed for Passover. In the Synoptic Gospels the passover meal (Mt 26:17; Mk 14:12; Lk 22:7-8) appears to fall on the fifteenth of Nisan, though John (19:14) names the "day of preparation of the Passover" (cf. Jn 18:28). This would be the 14th Nisan but may represent the difference of a day between two calendrical systems, especially as the 15th Nisan places events of Passion Week on a day of holy convocation. In this connection, however, it is interesting to note that astronomical observations of the new moon (Fotheringham and Schoch) of the likely years for this event find 15 Nisan as a Friday in A.D. 27 and Friday, 14 Nisan in 30 or 33. Either Friday 7 April A.D. 30 or 3 April 33 would seem possible. They cannot find a year for the Crucifixion in which 14 Nisan falls on a Thursday.

The year of the Crucifixion must come within the Procuratorship of Judaea held by Pontius Pilate (so also Tacitus and Josephus); that is, between A.D. 26-36. It is unlikely to have been immediately after his appointment (Lk 13:1; 23:12) or in A.D. 29, as given by Hippolytus, since the Paschal full moon was not until later in April that year, which vitiates his other arguments. If the enmity between Herod Antipas and Pilate was that implied by Luke 23:2, it might show that Tiberius was still under the influence of that enemy of the Jews, Serjanus, and this points to a date not earlier than A.D. 32. For the present the astronomical evidence of A.D. 30 or 33 appears to fit best such evidence as is available.

2. The Apostolic Age

Thanks to a number of correlations between the Biblical data (mainly Acts and Epistles) and events recorded elsewhere concerning the Hellenistic-Roman, we may gain several fixed chronological points.

(1) *The Early Church.* Within three years of his conversion (Gal 1:17-18; Ac 9:3), Paul stayed in Damascus, and then in "Arabia," before returning to Syria and thence to Jerusalem. On the occasion of his flight from Damascus, an official, "the ethnarch of King Aretas," tried to seize him (2 Co 11:32). It is unlikely that, as some suppose, this was the leader of the band of Aretas's subjects encamped outside the city, since the reference is to a known official position normally held within a large city. It would seem that he was a local viceroy of the Nabataean Aretas IV rather than a local officer in league with the Romans who, according to the coinage, may have held away in Damascus till A.D. 33. Vitellius seems to have controlled the city in A.D. 37 when he marched on Petra. Aretas died in 40, so that it seems likely that he controlled Damascus within the years 34-37; Paul's conversion could then be assigned to this period.

About 37/38 Paul visited Jerusalem and remained there for fifteen days before returning home to Cilicia, where he awaited the call from Barnabas to go to Antioch. Soon thereafter the two brought famine relief to Jerusalem (Ac 11:29; 12:25). Luke dates this after his account of the death of Agrippa I following his persecution of the Church in A.D. 44 (Josephus, *Antiquities* xix. 2). The famine foretold by Agabus (Ac 11:28) occurred after Herod's death in the reign of Claudius and during the procuratorship of Tiberius Alexander in Judaea (46-48). Josephus records the generosity of Helena, queen of Adiabene, in sending corn from Egypt (*Antiquities* xx. 2-5) even though Egypt itself, according to papyri text, suffered famine late in A.D. 45. It was probably about this time that Barnabas and Paul came up to Jerusalem.

(2) *Missionary Journeys.* On their return from Jerusalem, probably in 46, Paul and Barnabas sailed for Cyprus, where they met the proconsul Sergius Paulus (Ac 13:7), whose period of office, mentioned in an inscription from Soloi in Cyprus, must have fallen before A.D. 51.

Paul attended the Apostolic council of Acts 15 fourteen years after his conversion. Despite the theory that this conference is that referred to in Galatians 2:1-10 and that Paul is unlikely to have omitted any mention of an earlier visit (Ac 11:30, but cf. Gal 1:18; 2:1), it is most likely that this council met in A.D. 48 between the first and second missionary journeys.

On the second tour, after visiting churches in Syria, Silicia, and Asia, Paul "went through the region of Phrygia and Galatia" (Ac 16:6) before crossing into Macedonia and Achaia, where he met the proconsul Gallio (Ac 18:12-17). Gallio is known from inscriptions and from his correspondence with Claudius. These fix his tenure of office at A.D. 51/52. In Corinth Paul met Aquila and Priscilla, who had but recently come from Rome where Claudius in his ninth year (49/50) had expelled the Jews. This confirms A.D. 50-51 for Paul's sojourn in Corinth.

The third journey, begun about a year after the previous one in 52, included at least

three months in Greece (Ac 20:3) followed by a ministry of three years in Ephesus. It cannot, therefore, have terminated before A.D. 55, which would have been the earliest date for Paul's arrest (Ac 21:33). Felix was appointed by Claudius in A.D. 52 (Tacitus, *Annals* xii, 54; Josephus, *Antiquities* xx. 2), two years after Paul's arrest. He continued in office under Nero (*Antiquities* xx. 5) and had occupied office for some time before Paul was brought before him (Ac 24:10). Felix was succeeded by Porcius Festus in 60/61 and died while in office in A.D. 62 (Tacitus). On this basis Paul would have reached Rome, after two years' imprisonment in Caesarea, his appeal to Caesar, and sea journey, about 62. The narrative of Acts would have closed in 64, about the time the Neronian persecutions began.

(3) *The End of the Apostolic Era.* Paul may well have died within the period of Nero's persecutions at Rome. After Peter had been miraculously delivered from Agrippa (Ac 12:3 f.), he visited Antioch (Gal 2:11). His possible visit to Corinth (based on 1 Co 1:12) and to Rome are based only on early church traditions (cf. Jn 21:15 f.). Eusebius dates his arrival to the reign of Claudius (A.D. 41-54; cf. Ac 18:2) and his death to Nero (A.D. 69). Similarly, evidence for death by stoning of James, the Lord's brother, in A.D. 62 rests largely on Josephus (*Antiquities* xx. 200). The Jewish war broke out in 66 and ended with the sack of Jerusalem by the Romans in A.D. 70, a date which is not in dispute. The Jerusalem Christians fled to Pella. Although there were persecutions of Christians under Domitian (A.D. 81-96), there is no evidence that John suffered martyrdom. Indeed, according to Irenaeus (*Adv. Haer,* II. xxii. 5), John lived on into the reign of Trajan and probably died about A.D. 100, a date which would mark the end of the apostolic age.

It will have been observed that, at this long time after the events, it is not always possible for modern scholarship to reconstruct the precise date of certain events in terms of our Western calendar. Though this applies to such central events of the Bible as the birth and death of Jesus Christ, this in no way invalidates the narratives or implies that they were not a true record of God's action in history. The deviation between datings of only a few years for a happening of two or more thousand years ago is itself a testimony to the authenticity of the event. We must concentrate on the facts as given and ensure that we thus grasp the historical and spiritual lessons recorded for our learning.

THREE VIEWS ON THE MILLENNIUM

Definition: "Millennium: is from the Latin <u>Mille</u>, a thousand, and <u>annum</u>, year(s), and it is a term that refers to the thousand year period mentioned six times in Revelation 20:2–7 (once in each verse). The characteristics of this period, as described in Revelation 20:1–9, which see, are:

1. Satan is bound for the 1000 years;
2. Satan is bound and locked inside the bottomless pit for this period;
3. The bottomless pit [not Satan; see the Greek] has the seal of God on it for the 1000 years, meaning no one can open it during this time;
4. Satan cannot and will not deceive the nations on earth during this time;
5. Satan will be loosed for a short time <u>after</u> the 1000 years are expired;
6. Those who were loyal to Christ, who did not accept the Mark of the Beast during the Tribulation Period, will reign with Christ during this 1000 year period;
7. "The rest of the dead," seemingly the lost of the ages, will be raised up after the 1000 years;
8. The saved are raised up in "the first resurrection," at the start of the 1000 years (1 Thess. 4:14–16); these have no part in the "second death";
9. The saved will reign with Christ for the 1000 years;
10. After the 1000 years have expired, Satan will then be let out of his prison. During this time he will deceive many, and these who will follow him will march to Jerusalem to protest against Christ's rule, and there they shall be destroyed by fire from heaven.

VIEW ONE: PREMILLENNIALISM.
[Christ will come and then the Millennial Kingdom will begin]

This view states that the Second Coming of Christ, and all of its attendant events, will occur pre-, <u>before</u>, the 1000 years, <u>millennial</u>. They argue that clearly Satan has not been bound in the total sense described by Revelation chapter 20 ("that he should deceive the nations no more," verse 3), and the first resurrection of the martyred saints (and all of the saints) has not yet occurred. Rather, these things will occur when and after Christ returns and then the earth shall have its golden age, the saved dead shall be raised, and Jerusalem shall be the world capital and holy to the Lord for a 1000 years (Zechariah 14:4,16,21). At the end of this period, Satan will be loosed, a brief rebellion shall occur and be put down, and then the 1000 year kingdom shall go into the perfect and sinless eternal state.

VIEW TWO: POSTMILLENNIALISM.
[The world will be converted by the Gospel, then the Millennial Kingdom will begin]

This view states that the Second Coming of Christ, and all of its attendant events, will occur post-, after, the 1000 year millennium. This view states that the world will yet be converted by the preaching of the Gospel, and that by means of the conversion of the world, the earth shall become that perfect place wherein Satan is bound for the 1000 years. Then, at the end of the perfect 1000 years, Christ shall return and receive to Himself the almost perfect earthly kingdom. After this a short rebellion shall occur, and then the 1000 kingdom shall continue into eternity.

VIEW THREE: AMILLENNIALISM.
[Satan is bound today; the Church is Israel; we are now in the Millennial Kingdom]

This view states that the Second Coming of Christ, and all of its attendant events, will not, (a in Greek means not) occur in any future 1000 years, but rather the 1000 year millennium is taking place right now, and has been taking place during this entire Church Age for the last 2000 years. Modern exponents of this view prefer to call it, "Realized Millennialism." Here it is advocated that Satan is bound throughout our present age, in the sense that he cannot stop the preaching of the Gospel. The future holy Jerusalem of Zechariah 14:21 is the Church of this age, and the nation of Israel will be restored according to the Old Testament prophecies in the sense that the Church is this restoration. Modern Israel is viewed as a political entity of interest, but without any prophetic significance, and without any claims on the Old Testament prophecies.

VARIOUS VIEWS ON THE TRIBULATION

Explanation and definition: The following views on the Tribulation Period are in reality more properly views concerning the time of Christ's coming for His Church. This event is often referred to as the "rapture" of the Church, from the Latin translation of 1 Thessalonians 4:17, rapturo, "to lift up." In the Greek original it is harpadzo, "to grab, to take up."

Here the issue is the time of our Lord's coming for His Church (1 Thess. 4:17) in relation to the final seven years of this age, as described in Daniel 9:27. Strictly speaking, the "Great Tribulation" begins at the middle of this seven year period (Matthew 24:21) when the "Man of Sin" (commonly called, "the Antichrist") commits a great public blasphemous act, the "Abomination of Desolation" (Matthew 24:15: 2 Thessalonians 2:3,4,8,9).

Let all, however, keep in mind that:
  (a) our Lord is coming back for His Church (John 14:1–3; 1 Thess 4:13–18);
  (b) His Church is "not appointed to wrath," i.e., God's wrath (1 Thess 5:9);

(c)   no one knows the exact time of His coming (Matthew 24:36,42,44);

(d)   recent predictors have <u>incorrectly</u> named the day, month, and year of our Lord's Second Coming repeatedly time-after-time during this century. They have claimed to have counted the days of Noah's flood, the day of the blowing of the trumpets of Leviticus 23:24, or some other formula, and many have claimed to have had this revealed to them by the Lord—all incorrectly;

(e)   the commandment of our Lord to His Church has been, "Watch therefore: for ye know not what hour your Lord doth come" (Matthew 24:42). This has been taken to mean that the coming of Christ is <u>imminent</u>, i.e., it may occur at any time, and the basis for our ever being alert is that we cannot know the time of His arrival, and therefore must constantly be on the watch; and

(f)   the sure promise of His second coming is "the blessed hope" of the Church (Titus 2:13). This "blessed hope" is not to be marred by differences among sincere believers as to the precise schedule of end-time events.

The various views on this subject, however, are:

1. <u>THE PRETRIBULATION RAPTURE OF THE CHURCH.</u> — Christ will come before or at the beginning of the seven years, and the Church will be taken up before the suffering of the period of Daniel's final seven years begins. (1 Thess. 5:9; Revelation 3:10)

2. <u>THE MIDTRIBULATION RAPTURE OF THE CHURCH.</u> — Christ will come for His Church at the midpoint of the seven years and lift the believers out of this period of suffering. (Matthew 24:26–28; Revelation 12:6)

3. <u>THE POSTTRIBULATION RAPTURE OF THE CHURCH.</u> — Christ will come for His Church at the end of the seven years and deliver those saints still alive. He will preserve His own in the midst of their suffering, and those Tribulation Saints who were martyred will be resurrected. (Revelation 12:11)

4. <u>THE PRETRIB MID-WEEK RAPTURE OF THE CHURCH.</u> — Christ will come for His Church right before the midpoint of the seven years, and this will be before the "tribulation" described in Matthew 24:21 has started. This may be at the sounding of the "last trumpet" of Revelation 11:15.

5. <u>THE PREWRATH RAPTURE OF THE CHURCH.</u> — Christ will come sometime near the middle of the seven years, right before the opening of the sixth seal of the Book of Revelation (Rev. 6:12), when God's wrath begins to be poured out upon the world (Rev. 6:12–17). The Church will enter the final seven years and begin to suffer Satan's wrath (compare Rev. 12:11), but it will not experience God's wrath but rather be raptured out before this point (1 Thess. 5:9).

G. COHEN

3 DECISIVE WARS

War	Participants	Occurs	Reason for War	Outcome	Scripture References
1	Russia and Allies (Arab nations, Iran, Germany) vs. Israel	Before or during first 3-1/2 years of Tribulation Period (This could happen at any time!)	Russia desires Israel's vast mineral wealth.	God will intervene and through an earthquake in Israel plus rain and hail, the Russian army will be wiped out. It will take the Israelites 7 years to collect the debris. It will also take them 7 months to bury the dead!	Ezekiel 38:1-39:16
2 Battle of Armageddon	Armies from All Nations vs. God at Jerusalem	At End of 7-year Tribulation Period	Flushed with power Antichrist will defy God, seek to destroy the 144,000 witnessing Jews and Jerusalem.	The Lord Jesus Christ comes down from heaven and wipes out the combined armies of more than 200 million men. The blood bath covers over 185 miles of Israel and is "even unto the horse bridles." (Revelation 14:20) Antichrist and the False Prophet are cast alive into the Lake of Fire. (Revelation 19:20) Satan is bound in the bottomless pit for 1000 years. (Revelation 20:1-3)	Joel 3:9, 12 Zechariah 14:1-4 Revelation 16:13-16 Revelation 19:11-21 Ezekiel 39:17-29
3 The Final Rebellion	Satan vs. God	At End of 1000 year Millennium Period	God allows Satan one more opportunity on earth to preach his deceiving message.	Satan will be successful in deceiving vast multitudes (out of those born during the millennial period) to turn away from Christ. This horde of perhaps millions of people will completely circle the Believers in Jerusalem in a state of siege. When this occurs, God brings FIRE down from Heaven killing the millions in Satan's army. Satan is then cast into the Lake of Fire, where the False Prophet and Antichrist are, and they will be tormented day and night for ever and ever.	Revelation 20:7-10

515

MODERN ELECTRONICS AND END-TIME PROPHECY

15 And he had power to give life unto the image of the beast, that the image of the beast should both speak, and cause that as many as would not worship the image of the beast should be killed.

16 And he causeth all, both small and great, rich and poor, free and bond, to receive a mark in their right hand, or in their foreheads:

17 And that no man might buy or sell, save he that had the mark, or the name of the beast, or the number of his name.

18 Here is wisdom. Let him that hath understanding count the number of the beast: for it is the number of a man; and his number is Six hundred three score and six. Revelation 13:15–18

For centuries believers have wondered at reading the above words. How could the image of the beast be made to speak? How would the followers of this Antichrist be marked? And what would be the nature and code of this 666 symbol?

Let us first note that "the Beast" here is usually thought to be the Antichrist, "the man of sin" of 2 Thessalonians 2:3, the one who would commit the future "Abomination of Desolation" blasphemy at the Temple site in Jerusalem (Matthew 24:15; 2 Thess. 2:3). He would be the leader of the ten member end-time confederation of European nations— revived Rome (Revelation 17:12).

The modern electronics age is supplying us with suggested answers. At the same time that Israel is back in the land and facing seemingly insoluble dilemmas involving peace, Jerusalem, and the possibility of rebuilding the Temple, the electronics world of microcircuitry seems on the verge of bringing the 666 technology onto the prophetic stage.

Today, flat semiconductor chips or wafers, only millimeters in length made of silicon or germanium, can hold countless electronic components of microscopic size. By 1980 a chip could hold 30,000 transistors; by 1990 the number was over a million per chip. The results of such technological breakthroughs have been seen in the explosions of the personal computer industry, the credit card and moneyless banking industries, as well as in the crime/top secret surveillance and identification fields.

In an Atlanta, Georgia, toll road motorists no longer need to stop to pay highway road tolls. Rather an ID tab is fastened upon the front windshields of participating cars and modern electronic devices electronically and correctly bill the accounts of participants as they drive by the cameras at a cool 50 miles per hour! At some intersections in Germany, similar electronically activated surveillance cameras photograph the license plates of cars that illegally go through red lights, and then issue the traffic citations!

Then if you move to West Palm Beach, Florida, if certain people get their way, you soon may have to have a tiny microchip placed underneath the skin of your dog—which could tell the city fathers if you have a paid up license and which could also locate your dog if lost! Add to this the bankcards, credit cards, and cash cards which are fast racing us towards a cashless society. Then too, rampant crime not only reflects a world of changing values—getting ready to accept Antichrist—but also is causing almost daily demands that we need a method (1) to keep track of criminals; and (2) to keep track of children who may get lost or abducted. So enter the microchip implant! If tiny security devices can help police police locate your stolen car, or your dog or cat, how much more are such devices needed to locate lost children?

All of this fits the world scene of Revelation 13:15–18, quoted above, wherein in verse 15 the Image of the Beast is given life and made to speak. This could mean that, just as the Church in a sense is the "body of Christ," so too the organization of the followers of Antichrist may be that "image of the Beast" which speaks for Satan in the last days. These words, however, may also prophetically speak of an actual mannequin image which electronically moves like a person and utters prerecorded political speeches!

Verses 15–16 seem to portray a world in which the followers of "the Leader," will have microscopically tiny identification implants placed on their right hands or foreheads. Already many today are looking ahead to such devices to replace credit cards in the future cashless society. With such devices, anyone out of "fellowship" with "the Leader" could have his card number flagged at the master computer headquarters and he or she would literally no longer be able "to buy or sell," nor to secure gasoline, nor to eat...nor to hide.

This badge, verse 18 informs us, will somehow be connected with the number 666, which is often taken to be the number of Satan's counterfeit trinity, 6 being the number of man, made on the 6th day, and short of the divine number 7, used so often in the Book of Revelation. Verse 18 says, "Here is wisdom...it is the number of a man," thus telling us that when the Antichrist issues his numbering system, or when he takes over the existing system, his identity will be linked to and revealed by this 666 number (or set of numbers, or number grid). God said it, not some inventive numerologist. He gave it to the future tribulation saints so that they would have this clue so as not to be deceived by this coming Leader who will be Satan's false saviour on earth.

G. COHEN

517

EARTHQUAKES PROPHESIED FOR THE FINAL DAYS

The Bible connects the judgments at the end of this age with signs and wonders, including earthquakes. In the Old Testament Korah, Dathan, and Abiram who rebelled against Moses were swallowed by an earthquake that split open the ground before them (Numbers 16:28–34). That an earthquake occurred two years after Amos began to preach judgment to the Northern Kingdom was taken as a sign of God's endorsement of the prophet and of His soon destruction of Samaria (Amos 1:1–2).

Likewise, the end of this present age and the events before the final judgment are portrayed as coming after an increase of earthquakes on the earth. In the New Testament, earthquakes are mentioned as precursors of the events surrounding the Second Coming of Christ.

What is so remarkable to the Bible student is that in those ancient times no one had the means to know whether or not earthquake activity would decrease or increase. The ancient "geologists" might well have reasoned that, like a new large house, the earth was still in the process of settling, and that in the coming years as the earth aged, earthquakes would all but vanish. Instead, the Bible made the right choice thousands of years ago. God's Word said that earthquakes would not only, continue but that they would even increase in frequency toward the end of this age, and they have.

Zechariah 14:4–5 prophesies an endtime earthquake which will split the Mount of Olives in a north-south direction at the Second Coming of Christ. Christ himself declared in the Olivet Discourse, "And there shall be ... earthquakes, in divers places" (Matt. 24:7; Mark 13:8; Luke 21:11).

The Book of Revelation tells us, "And the same hour was there a great earthquake, and the tenth part of the city fell, and in the earthquake were slain of men seven thousand" (Rev. 11:13). Revelation 16:18 further speaks of a coming great earthquake in connection with the pouring out of the seventh and last Bowl of Wrath upon end-time Babylon, "And there was a great earthquake, such as was not since men were upon the earth, so mighty an earthquake and so great."

EARTHQUAKES MENTIONED IN THE BIBLE:

Exod. 19:18	At Sinai, before the giving of the ten commandments
Numb. 16:32	At the rebellion of Korah
I Sam. 14:15	At Jonathan's defeat of the Philistines
I Kg. 19:11	As a revelation of God's power
Psa. 46:3	As a natural calamity
Psa. 104:32	As a sign of God's power
Isa. 13:13	Speaking of God's future power
Isa. 24:20	Of the Lord's future judgments
Amos 1:1	As a sign of coming judgment
Nah. 1:5	As a sign of God's power
Hag. 2:6	Speaking of God's power

Zech. 14:5	At the Messiah's coming upon the Mt. of Olives
Matt. 24:7	Christ speaking of the end of this age
Matt. 27:51,54	At the death of Christ
Mark 13:8	Christ speaking of the end of this age
Luke 21:11	Christ speaking of the end of this age
Acts 16:26	Releasing Paul from prison at Philippi
Heb. 12:26	Quoting Hag. 2:6, speaking of the future
Rev. 16:18,20	Endtime judgment of modern Babylon

FREQUENCY OF MODERN EARTHQUAKES: (*Prophecy in the News*, Feb. 94)

1890 – 1900	1	1930 – 1940	5	1970 – 1980	46
1900 – 1910	3	1940 – 1950	4	1980 – 1990	52
1910 – 1920	2	1950 – 1960	9	1990 – 2000	——
1920 – 1930	2	1960 – 1970	13		

FREQUENCY OF LARGE EARTHQUAKES BY THE CENTURIES

10th	32	14th	137	18th	640
11th	53	15th	174	19th	2119
12th	84	16th	253	20th	——
13th	115	17th	378		

(These numbers, prior to the 19th and 20th centuries, are of course before modern measuring devices and global reporting.)

SOME MODERN DAY EARTHQUAKES: Severity/Magnitude

Jan. 24, 1556	Shensi Province, China	830,000 killed
Nov. 1, 1755	Lisbon, Portugal	15,000 killed
Apr. 19, 1906	San Francisco & 3 day fire	1,000 killed
Dec. 16, 1920	Kansu Province, China	200,000 killed
Jan. 13, 1915	Avezzano, Italy	30,000 killed
Sept. 1, 1923	Kwanto Plain (Shinsai), Japan	140,000 killed
Mar. 2, 1933	100 miles S of Honshu, Japan	8.9 magnitude
May 31, 1935	Quetta, India	50,000 killed
Jan. 24, 1939	Chile	30,000 killed
Dec. 27, 1939	Northern Turkey	100,000 injured
Nov. 4, 1952	Kamchatka, USSR	8.8 magnitude
May 22, 1960	Concepcion, Chile	8.8 magnitude
Mar. 28, 1964	Prince William Sound	8.9 magnitude
Feb. 4, 1976	Guatemala	23,000 killed
Jul 28, 1976	Tangshan, China	240,000 killed
Aug. 17, 1976	Mindanao, Philippines	8,000 killed
Sept. 19, 1985	Central Mexico	25,000 killed
Nov. 14, 1985	North of Bogota, Columbia	25,000 killed
Dec. 7, 1988	Soviet Armenia	25,000 killed
Oct. 17, 1989	San Francisco and N. Calif.	7.1 magnitude
Jun. 21, 1990	Northwest Iran	50,000 killed
Jan. 17, 1994	Los Angeles, California	6.7 magnitude

[Source: *1991 Information Please Almanac* & other works.]

G. COHEN

END TIME FLOODS PROPHESIED

"Thou carriest them away as with a flood.
They are as a sleep" (Psalm 90:5a)

As the Days of Noah

Our Savior also referred to Noah's flood when He spoke of the future Tribulation Period:

"But as the days of Noah were, so shall also the coming of the Son of man be.

"For as in the days that were before the flood they were eating and drinking, marrying and giving in marriage, until the day that Noah entered into the ark,

"And knew not until the flood came, and took them all away; so shall also the coming of the Son of man be" (Matthew 24:37-39).

Even though God promised that He would never again destroy the world by a flood, it is possible that the Tribulation will be introduced with a series of widespread flooding in various parts of the world. Psalm 93 paints the picture all the more vividly:

"The floods have lifted up, O LORD, the floods have lifted up their voice; the floods lift up their waves" (Psalm 93:3).

Since 1993, flooding has increased dramatically all over the world. Perhaps we are presently witnessing the fulfillment of the prophecies leading up to the beginning of the Tribulation period.

Here is a partial list of floods since the autumn of 1992:

August 24, 1992 - Hurricane Andrew slammed across Florida.

March 12-15, 1993 - Upwards to 50 inches of snow covered the eastern seaboard of North America from Cuba to Canada.

June 27, 1993 - The upper Mississippi and Missouri rivers overflowed, creating another (although temporary) great lake.

August 1-10, 1993 - Two typhoons and a tidal wave swept over Japan.

August, 1993 - Tropical Storm Bret flooded Caracas, Venezuela.

October, 1993 - Europe suffered spectacular flooding through the entire month.

August 21, 1993 - Flooding in Nepal, Malaysia, Bangladesh, and China. Floods covered over half of the land mass of the Himalayan kingdom of Nepal. Over 1,100 were drowned. China coined a new phrase to describe flooding—"black rain."

December 25, 1993 - The second time around Europe—over 50,000 homeless.

December 26, 1993 - Algiers, Algeria suffered rain-soaked mudslides—12 killed, 46 injured.

January through March, 1994 - Several snow and ice storms destroyed millions of trees across the United States from Arkansas to the east coast.

March 27, 1994 - Devastating tornadoes hit Alabama and adjoining states.

July 6, 1994 - Tropical storm Alberto dumped 21 inches of rain in Georgia. It was the worst flooding in 100 years.

October 15, 1994 - North Houston, Texas under as much as 15 feet of water.

October 15, 1994 - Greece flooded.

October 16, 1994 - Typhoon swept across Indonesia.

November 1-15, 1994 - Egypt flooded for the first time since Noah's flood.

November 8-11, 1994 - France and Italy suffer intense flooding again.

November 8-21, 1994 - Hurricane Gordon killed 829 people in Haiti, Jamaica, Cuba, and Florida.

These are just a partial listing that rocked the world in 1992-94 with devastating floods. Indeed, the floods of Psalm 93 appear to have become the "floods of '93" and more!

The Flood as a Metaphor

The term *"flood"* used in Psalm 90 may be symbolic as well. Moses writes that God will carry the wicked away *"as with a flood."* The word *"as"* in forms us of the symbolic nature of this descriptive term.

The *"flood"* in this passage was considered by Radak (a twelfth century rabbi) as a "rushing stream." Mankind will be judged with the speed and fury of a mighty torrent. Such will be the case when God throws this unbelieving world into great tribulation.

Daniel uses the symbol of a flood as he writes about the antichrist:

"And in his estate shall stand up a vile person, to whom they shall not give the honor of the kingdom: but he shall come in peaceably, and obtain the kingdom by flatteries.

"And with the arms of a flood shall they be overflown from before him, and shall be broken; yea, also the prince of the covenant" (Daniel 11:21-22).

John uses a similar application in Revelations:

"And the serpent cast out of his mouth water as a flood after the woman, that he might cause her to be carried away of the flood.

"And the earth helped the woman, and the earth opened her mouth, and swallowed up the flood which the dragon cast out of his mouth" (Revelation 12:15-16).

Reprinted from January 1995 issue of "PROPHECY IN THE NEWS" by permission of J.R. Church.

FAVORITE BIBLE STORIES

God's Work of Creation	Genesis, Ch. 1	Wisdom and Her Rewards	Proverbs, Ch. 8
Adam and Eve	Genesis, Ch. 2	The Soft Answer	Proverbs, Ch. 15
Noah and the Ark	Genesis, Ch. 6	A Good Name is Better Than Riches	Proverbs, Ch. 22
God's Covenant with Noah	Genesis, Ch. 9	The Prince of Peace	Isaiah, Ch. 9
Tower of Babel	Genesis, Ch. 11	Ezekiel's Vision of Cherubim and	
God's Call to Abram	Genesis, Ch. 12	Wheels	Ezekiel, Ch. 10
The Story of Lot	Genesis, Ch. 19	The Parable of the	
Abraham and Isaac	Genesis, Ch. 22	Dry Bones	Ezekiel, Ch. 37
Isaac and Rebekah	Genesis, Ch. 24	The Fiery Furnace	Daniel, Ch. 3
Jacob's Vision of a Ladder	Genesis, Ch. 28	The Writing on the Wall	Daniel, Ch. 5
Jacob Wrestles with an Angel	Genesis, Ch. 32	Daniel in the Lion's Den	Daniel, Ch. 6
Joseph and His Brothers	Genesis, Ch. 37	Jonah and the Big Fish	Jonah, Ch. 1
Joseph Interprets Pharaoh's Dream	Genesis, Ch. 41	The Temptation of Jesus	Matthew, Ch. 4
The Baby Moses	Exodus, Ch. 2	Jesus Calls Peter and Andrew	Matthew, Ch. 4
The Burning Bush	Exodus, Ch. 3	The Lord's Prayer	Matthew, Ch. 6
The First Passover	Exodus, Ch. 12	The Golden Rule	Matthew, Ch. 7
The Crossing of the Red Sea	Exodus, Ch. 14	The Transfiguration of Jesus	Matthew, Ch. 17
The Quails and Manna	Exodus, Ch. 16	The Last Supper	Matthew, Ch. 26
The Ten Commandments	Exodus, Ch. 20	Jesus Stills the Storm	Mark, Ch. 4
The Battle of Jericho	Joshua, Ch. 6	Jesus and the Children	Mark, Ch. 10
Joshua's Long Day	Joshua, Ch. 10	Jesus Clears the Temple	Mark, Ch. 11
The Sword of the Lord and Gideon	Judges, Ch. 7	The Birth of Jesus	Luke, Ch. 2
The Exploits of Samson	Judges, Ch. 15	The Feeding of Five-thousand	Luke, Ch. 9
Samson and Delilah	Judges, Ch. 16	The Good Samaritan	Luke, Ch. 10
Ruth and Naomi	Ruth, Ch. 1	Seventy Disciples	Luke, Ch. 10
Ruth Gleans in the Field	Ruth, Ch. 2	The Prodigal Son	Luke, Ch. 15
Samuel and Eli	I Samuel, Ch. 3	The Story of Zaccheus	Luke, Ch. 19
David and Goliath	I Samuel, Ch. 17	Peter's Denial	Luke, Ch. 22
David and Jonathan	I Samuel, Ch. 19	Resurrection of Jesus	Luke, Ch. 24
Saul Consults the Witch of Endor	I Samuel, Ch. 28	The Miracle of Water into Wine	John, Ch. 2
David's Psalm of Thanksgiving	II Samuel, Ch. 22	Jesus Talks with Nicodemus	John, Ch. 3
Solomon's Wisdom	I Kings, Ch. 3	The Woman at the Well	John, Ch. 4
Solomon Builds the Temple	I Kings, Ch. 6	Jesus Walks on the Sea	John, Ch. 6
The Queen of Sheba Visits Solomon	I Kings, Ch. 10	Lazarus Raised from the Dead	John, Ch. 11
Elijah and the Prophets of Baal	I Kings, Ch. 18	Triumphal Entry into Jerusalem	John, Ch. 12
Job's Prosperity Restored	Job, Ch. 42	The Ascension of Jesus	Acts, Ch. 1
The Shepherd Psalm	Psalm 23	Coming of the Holy Spirit	Acts, Ch. 2

Peter's Sermon	Acts, Ch. 3	Conversion of Saul	Acts, Ch. 9
Philip Talks with an		Faith and Work	James, Ch. 2
Ethiopian	Acts, Ch. 8	The Bridled Tongue	James, Ch. 3

FAVORITE READINGS

The Ten Commandments	Exodus 20:3-17	The Promise of the Gospel	Isaiah 40
The Lord's Prayer	Matthew 6:9-13	A Prayer for Forgiveness	Psalm 51
The Shepherd Psalm	Psalm 23	The Heroes of the Faith	Hebrews 11
The Birth of Jesus	Luke 2		
The Crucifixion	John 19	The Value of the Scriptures	2 Timothy 3
The Resurrection	Matthew 28		
Resurrection through Jesus	1 Corinthians 15	Living Successfully with Others	Romans 12
The Beatitudes	Matthew 5:3-12	Banishing Fear of Death	John 11:25
The Sermon on the Mount	Matthew 5-7	Spiritual Peace	John 14
The Great Commandments	Matthew 22:35-40	Hope in Time of Trouble	Psalm 42
Jesus' New Commandment	John 13:34	Assurance of God's Mercy	Psalm 40:1-5
The Golden Rule	Matthew 7:12	The Christian's Hope	Romans 8:31-39
The Last Judgment	Matthew 25:31-46	Confidence in God	Psalm 37
The Great Commission	Matthew 28:19-20	The Christian's Armor	Ephesians 5:11-17
The Good Samaritan	Luke 10:30-37	God's Eternal Mercy	Psalm 103
The Prodigal Son	Luke 15:11-32	Christ Teaches Forgiveness	Matthew 18:21-35
The House Built upon a Rock	Matthew 7:24-27	Two Types of Prayer	Luke 18:9-14
The Abiding Chapter	John 15	The Love of Christ	Ephesians 3:14-21
The Praises of Charity	1 Corinthians 13	A Promise for Faithfulness	Proverbs 3:1-6
Wise and Foolish Virgins	Matthew 25:1-13	Jesus' Mission	Luke 19:10
God is Our Refuge and Strength	Psalm 46	Promise of Eternal Life	John 3:16
The Choice of Treasure	Matthew 6:19-34	The Way to Salvation	Romans 10:9
When God Seems Far Away	Psalm 139	The Crown of Life	Revelation 2:10
Withstanding Temptation	Psalm 1	What We Shall Reap	Galatians 6:7
From Death unto Life	John 5:24	Opening the Door to Jesus	Revelation 3:20
Setting a Good Example	Matthew 5:16	Seaching the Scriptures	John 5:39
The Return for Good Deeds	Luke 6:38	Treatment of Others	Ephesians 4:32
		Gospel of Christ	Romans 1:16
		Duties of Children	Ephesians 6:1, 2

READINGS FOR LIFE'S EXPERIENCES

When Things Look Blue .... Isaiah 40
When Tempted to Do Wrong .... Psalm 139
If You Are Facing a Crisis .... Psalm 46
When You Are Discouraged .... Psalm 23
If You Are Bored .... Psalms 103 and 104 or Job 38-40
When Business Is Poor .... Psalm 37
When You Are Lonely or Fearful .... Psalm 27
When You Are Anxious for Dear Ones .... Psalm 107
When You Plan Your Budget .... Luke 19
To Live Successfully with Your Fellowmen ...... Romans 12
If You Are Sick or in Pain .... Psalm 91
When You Leave Home for Labor or Travel ..... Psalm 121
When You Are Very Weary .... Matthew 11:28-30
     Romans 8:31-39

When Everything Seems to Be Going
  from Bad to Worse .... 2 Timothy 3
The Best Investment Is Described .... Matthew 6
Does God Figure in Our National Life? .... Deuteronomy 8
When Your Friends Seem to Go Back on You .... I Corinthians 13
For Inward Peace .... John 14
When You Have Been Placed in a
  Position of Great Responsibility .... Joshua 1
If You Have Been Bereaved .... 1 Corinthians 15   Revelation 21
For a Stirring Record of What
  Trust in God Can Do .... Hebrews 11
If You Are Satisfied with Being Well-to-Do...... Luke 15 and 16
If You Have Experienced Severe Losses .... Romans 8
If You Are Having to Put Up a Stiff Fight .... Ephesians
When You Have Sinned .... 1 John 1   John 3:1-21
  Isaiah 53   Psalm 51
For the Way of Prayer .... 1 Kings 8   Psalms 42, 51
  Luke 11:1-3; 18:1-14   John 17
If You Have a Fear of Death .... John 11, 17, 20   2 Corinthians 4, 5
  Revelation 21

BIBLICAL GENEALOGICAL CHART
(LINE OF REDEMPTION)

Symbols
Number after name .... Bible reference
( ) .... Wife
[ ] .... Other Name
♀ .... Daughter

The date of Adam is uncertain.

c. before a date means, circa [Latin, "around"], and denotes an approximate date or set of dates.

NOTE: Early dates, especially those prior to 200 BC, are provided for general guidance, but cannot be regarded as exact.

Chart names: ADAM[1] – (EVE)[2], SETH[3], ABEL[4], CAIN[5], ENOCH[6], IRAD[7], MEHUJAEL[8], METHUSAEL[9], LAMECH[10], (ADAH)[11], (ZILLAH)[12], JABAL[13], JUBAL[14], TUBAL – CAIN[15], NAAMAH♀[16], ENOSH[17], KENAN[18], MAHALALEEL[19], JARED[20], ENOCH[21], METHUSELAH[22], LAMECH[23], NOAH[24], SHEM[25]

LUD, ARAM (Syria), ASSHUR (Assyria), ELAM (Persia), [27], [28], UZ, HUL, GETHER, MESHECH

Prophets:
Enoch
Jude 14
Pre-deluvian

The date of Noah and the Flood is uncertain.

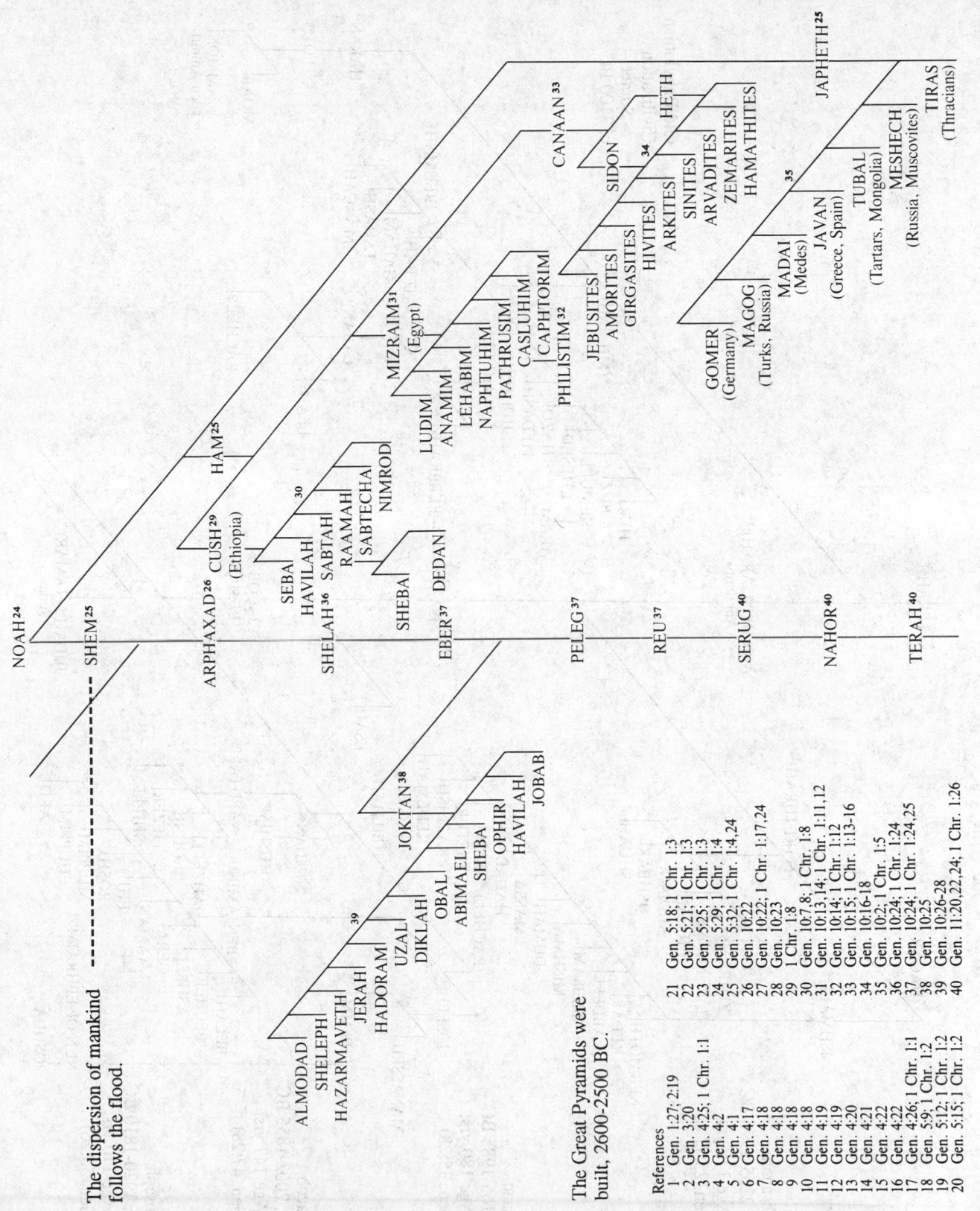

The dispersion of mankind
follows the flood.

The Great Pyramids were
built, 2600-2500 BC.

References
1   Gen. 1:27; 2:19
2   Gen. 3:20
3   Gen. 4:25; 1 Chr. 1:1
4   Gen. 4:2
5   Gen. 4:1
6   Gen. 4:17
7   Gen. 4:18
8   Gen. 4:18
9   1 Chr. 1:8
10 Gen. 10:7,8; 1 Chr. 1:8
11 Gen. 10:13,14; 1 Chr. 1:11,12
12 Gen. 10:14; 1 Chr. 1:12
13 Gen. 10:15; 1 Chr. 1:13-16
14 Gen. 10:16-18
15 Gen. 10:2; 1 Chr. 1:5
16 Gen. 10:24; 1 Chr. 1:24
17 Gen. 4:26; 1 Chr. 1:1
18 Gen. 5:9; 1 Chr. 1:2
19 Gen. 5:12; 1 Chr. 1:2
20 Gen. 5:15; 1 Chr. 1:2
21 Gen. 5:18; 1 Chr. 1:3
22 Gen. 5:21; 1 Chr. 1:3
23 Gen. 5:25; 1 Chr. 1:3
24 Gen. 5:29; 1 Chr. 1:4
25 Gen. 5:32; 1 Chr. 1:4,24
26 Gen. 10:22
27 Gen. 10:22; 1 Chr. 1:17,24
28 Gen. 10:23
29 1 Chr. 1:8
30 Gen. 10:7,8; 1 Chr. 1:8
31 Gen. 10:13,14; 1 Chr. 1:11,12
32 Gen. 10:14; 1 Chr. 1:12
33 Gen. 10:15; 1 Chr. 1:13-16
34 Gen. 10:16-18
35 Gen. 10:2; 1 Chr. 1:5
36 Gen. 10:24; 1 Chr. 1:24
37 Gen. 10:24,25; 1 Chr. 1:24,25
38 Gen. 10:25
39 Gen. 10:26-28
40 Gen. 11:20,22,24; 1 Chr. 1:26

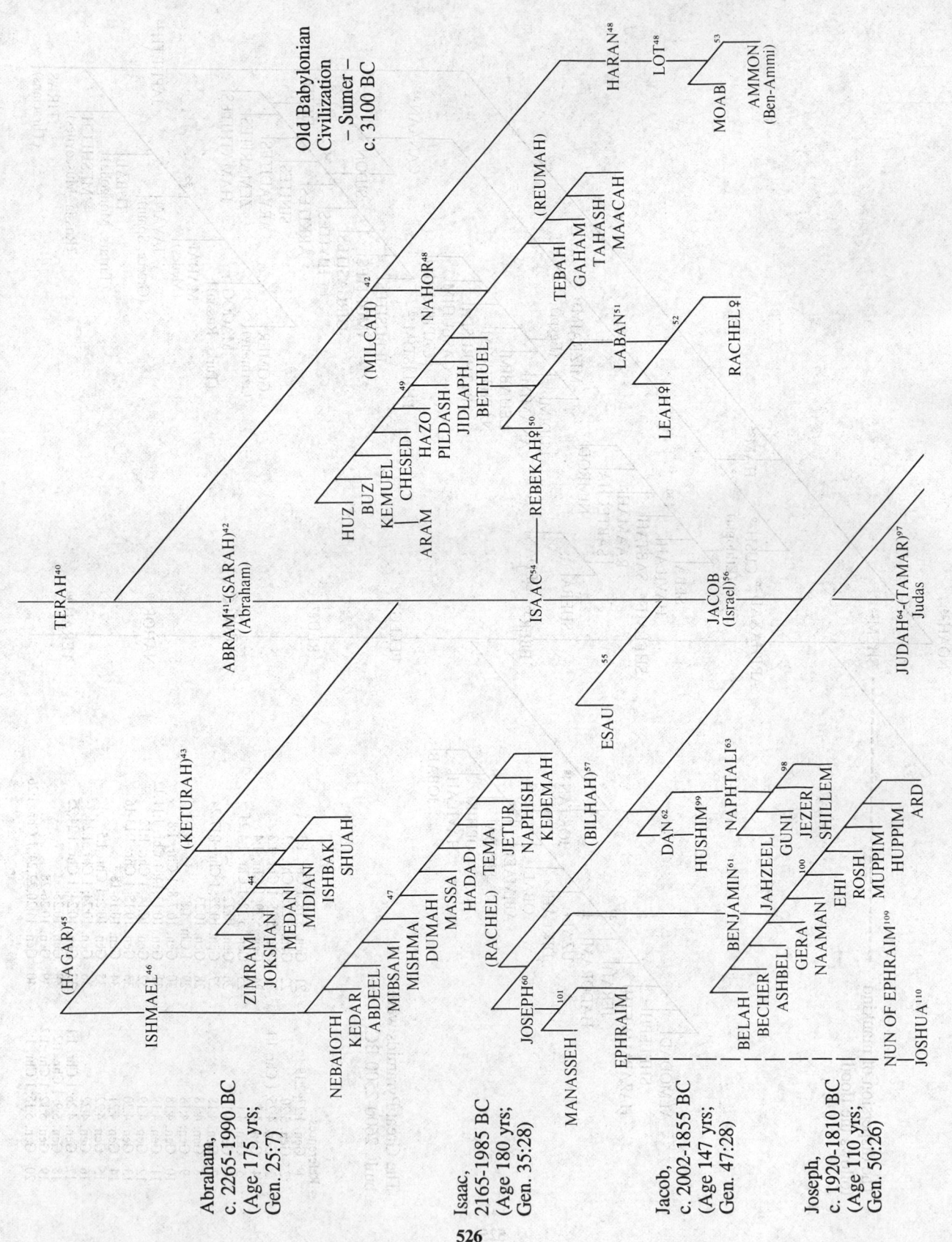

Old Babylonian
Civilization
– Sumer –
c. 3100 BC

TERAH[40]

ABRAM[41]–(SARAH)[42]
(Abraham)

HARAN[48]

LOT[48]

MOAB
AMMON (Ben-Ammi)[53]

(MILCAH)[42]

NAHOR[48]

(REUMAH)

HUZ
BUZ
KEMUEL
CHESED
ARAM
HAZO[49]
PILDASH
JIDLAPH
BETHUEL
REBEKAH♀[50]

TEBAH
GAHAM
TAHASH
MAACAH

LABAN[51]
LEAH♀
RACHEL♀[52]

ISAAC[54]——REBEKAH♀

JACOB
(Israel)[56]

ESAU[55]

JUDAH[64]–(TAMAR)[97]
Judas

Abraham,
c. 2265-1990 BC
(Age 175 yrs;
Gen. 25:7)

(HAGAR)[45]

(KETURAH)[43]

ISHMAEL[46]

NEBAIOTH
KEDAR
ABDEEL
MIBSAM
MISHMA
DUMAH
MASSA
HADAD
TEMA
JETUR
NAPHISH
KEDEMAH

ZIMRAM
JOKSHAN
MEDAN[44]
MIDIAN
ISHBAK
SHUAH[47]

Isaac,
2165-1985 BC
(Age 180 yrs;
Gen. 35:28)

(BILHAH)[57]

(RACHEL)

DAN[62]
NAPHTALI[63]
HUSHIM[99]

JOSEPH[60]

MANASSEH
EPHRAIM[101]

Jacob,
c. 2002-1855 BC
(Age 147 yrs;
Gen. 47:28)

BENJAMIN[61]

BELAH
BECHER
ASHBEL
GERA
NAAMAN
EHI
ROSH
MUPPIM
HUPPIM
ARD

JAHZEEL
GUNI
JEZER
SHILLEM[98]

NAAMAN[100]

NUN OF EPHRAIM[109]

JOSHUA[110]

Joseph,
c. 1920-1810 BC
(Age 110 yrs;
Gen. 50:26)

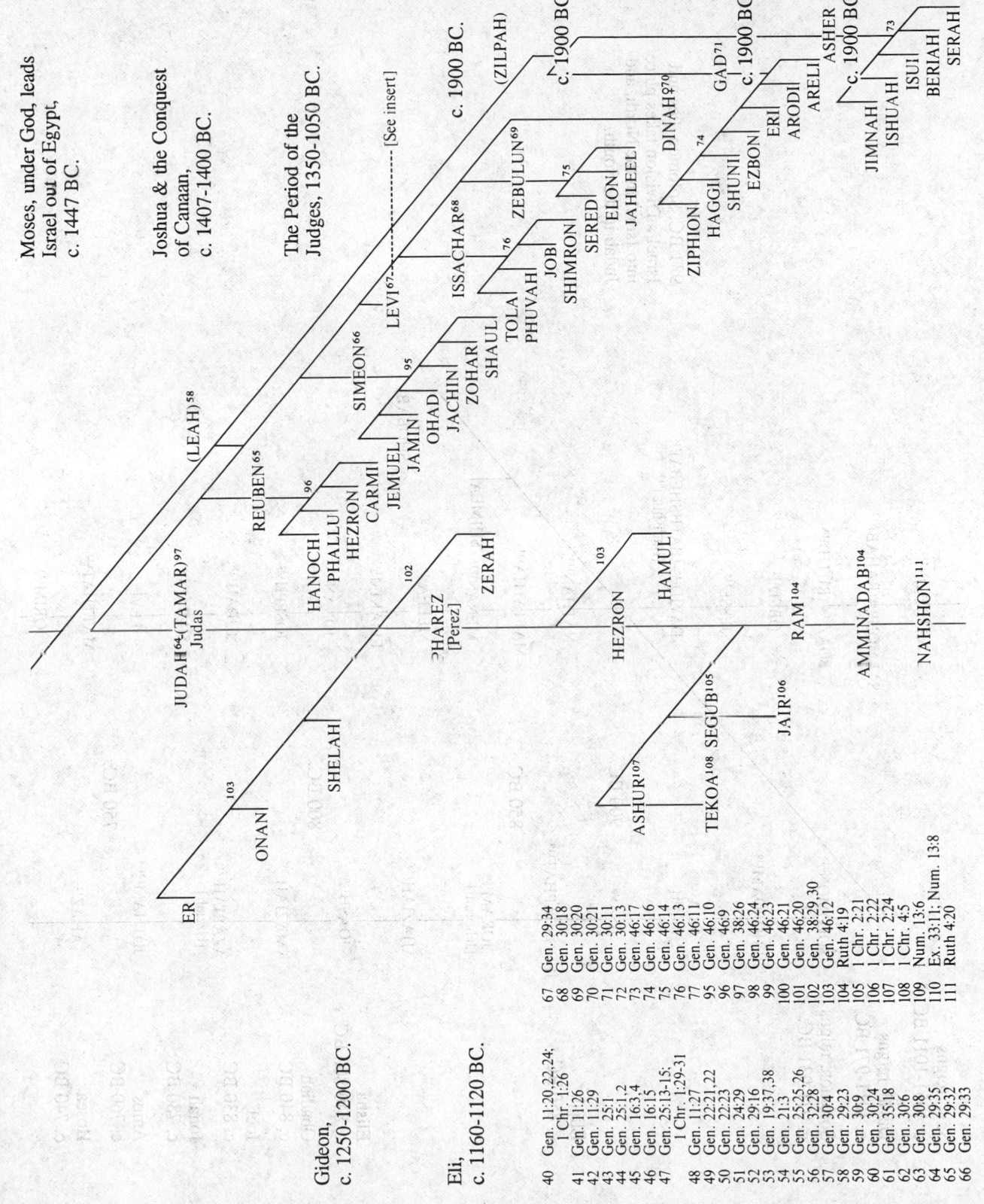

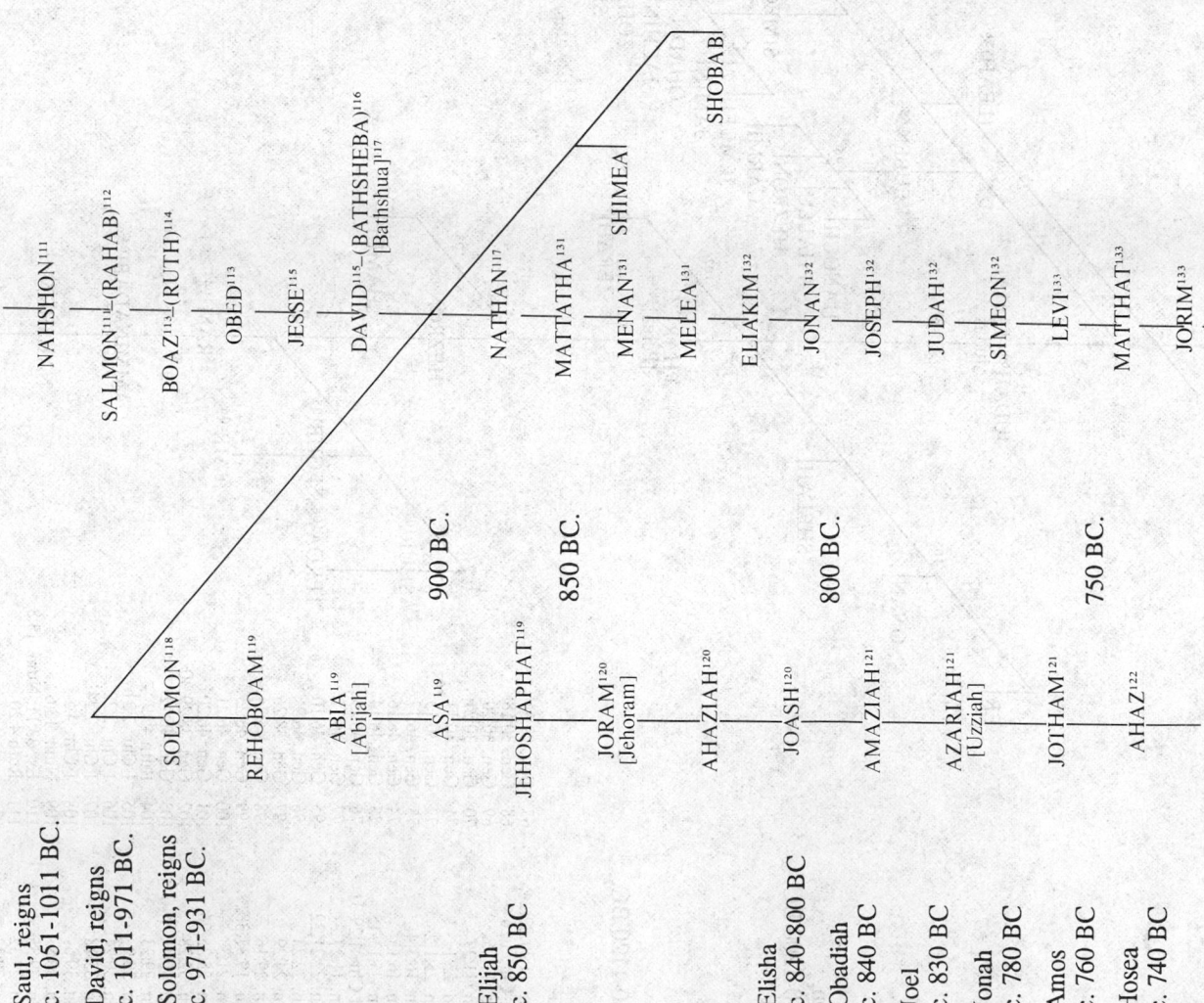

26036 AP.

721 BC, Northern Kingdom (Capital Samaria) falls to Assyria

The Assyrian Empire 1100-600 BC.

612 BC, Nineveh destroyed; Assyrian capital moves to Assher

The Babylonian (Chaldean) Empire 625-359 BC.

Nebunezzar invades Jerusalem, 605, 597, 586 BC.

Solomon's Temple destroyed, 586 BC;

Southern Kingdom (Judah; capital, Jerusalem) falls.

The Persian Empire, 550-330 BC.

539 BC, Persia conquers the city of Babylon.

536-516 BC, First Return of the Jews out of Babylon. Second Temple completed 516 BC.

454 BC, Ezra leads Second Return.

444 BC, Nehemiah leads Third Return; rebuilds walls.

111	Ruth 4:20
112	Matt. 1:5
113	Ruth 4:21
114	Ruth 4:10
115	Ruth 4:22
116	2 Sam. 12:24
117	1 Chr. 3:5
118	2 Sam. 12:24
119	1 Chr. 3:10
120	1 Chr. 3:11
121	1 Chr. 3:12
122	1 Chr. 3:13
123	1 Chr. 3:14
124	1 Chr. 3:15
125	1 Chr. 3:16; Jer. 37:1
126	Matt. 1:12
127	Matt. 1:13
128	Matt. 1:14
129	Matt. 1:15
130	Matt. 1:16
131	Luke 3:31
132	Luke 3:30
133	Luke 3:29
134	Luke 3:28
135	Luke 3:27
136	Luke 3:26
137	Luke 3:25

JORIM[133]
ELIEZER[133]
JOSE[133]
ER[134]
ELMODAM[134]
COSAM[134]
ADDI[134]
MELCHI[134]
NERI[135]
SALATHIEL[135]
ZERUBBABEL[135]
RHESA[135]
JOANNA[135]
JUDAH[136]
JOSEPH[136]
SEMEI[136]
MATTATHIAS[136]
MAATH[136]
NAGGE[137]

700 BC.

650 BC.

600 BC.

586 BC. Judah Falls

AHAZ[122]
HEZEKIAH[122]
MANASSEH[122]
AMON[123]
JOSIAH[123]
JEHOIAKIM[124]
JEHOIACHIN[125] [Jeconiah, Coniah]
ZEDEKIAH[125]
SALATHIEL[126]
ZERUBBABEL[126]
ABIUD[127]

Isaiah 740-690 BC

Micah 730-700 BC

Nahum 640 BC

Zephaniah c. 630 BC

Jeremiah 630-580 BC

Habakkuk c. 610 BC

Daniel 605-530 BC

Ezekiel 595-550 BC

Zechariah 520-490 BC

Haggai 520-490 BC

Malachi 440-420 BC

Malachi
440-420 BC

127 Matt. 1:13
128 Matt. 1:14
129 Matt. 1:15
130 Matt. 1:16
131 Luke 3:31
132 Luke 3:30
133 Luke 3:29
134 Luke 3:28
135 Luke 3:27
136 Luke 3:26
137 Luke 3:25
138 Luke 3:24
139 Luke 3:23
140 Luke 1:27; Matt. 1:16
141 Matt. 1:21.25

336-323 BC, Alexander the Great conquers Egypt, Israel and the entire Persian Empire.

323-200 BC, Alexander's Generals divide the Mediterranean world and fight one another. Ptolemy line takes Egypt; Selucid line takes Syria and Israel.

168-165 BC, Antiochus IV of Syria persecutes Israel.

165-63 BC, Hasmonean (Maccabee-Jewish of the tribe of Levi) rule of Israel for Rome.

37-4 BC, Herod the Great, King of Israel.

Augustus Caesar, 29 BC - 14 AP.

Pontius Pilate, Procurator of Judeau, 26036 AP.

ABIUD[127]
ELIAKIM[127]
AZOR[127]
SADOC[128]
ACHIM[128]
ELIUD[128]
ELEAZAR[129]
MATTHAN[129]
JACOB[129]
JOSEPH[130]

NAGGE[137]
ESLI[137]
NAUM[137]
AMOS[137]
MATTATHIAS[137]
JOSEPH[138]
JANNA[138]
MELCHI[138]
LEVI[138]
MATTHAT[138]
HELI[139]
MARY♀[140]
JESUS[141]

530

UNUSUAL ITEMS IN THE BIBLE

THE WORM OF MARK 9:44-48

The Bible speaks occasionally of worms, such as in Jonah 4:7, wherein the worm prepared by God ate through the stem of the gourd plant that was shading Jonah, which process disturbed the prophet. In Psalm 22:6, a Messianic psalm, we read in prophetic foreknowledge the words, "But I am a worm, and no man." In Acts 12:23 we read, "Herod was eaten of worms," speaking of the lowly end of the proud and shrewd Herod Agrippa I, who slew James the apostle in 44 AD.

In Mark 9:44, 46, 48, however, we read of our Lord speaking of a "worm" in a very unusual sense. He says, "Where their worm dieth not, and the fire is not quenched." The Greek word here is skolax, which is the normal word for worm. The question is what did the Lord mean when he spoke of those whose worm would never die? The context of the account is that the Lord is speaking of future rewards and judgment, and warning against "hell" (Mark 9:43). The word for hell in the Greek is usually hades, literally, the "unseen" world of the lost. Here it is gehenna, the name of the valley southwest of Jerusalem where the fires to burn garbage are kept burning day and night. It is the portrait of final judgment and separation from God.

Two qualities of "Gehenna," or hell, are mentioned by the Lord in vs 44, "Where their worm dieth not, and the fire is not quenched." This refers to the everlasting nature of the final punishment of the lost—the fire is never stopped or put out, and the worm which might devour the carcass of a human, and which itself eventually dies, here lives on. The portrait is clearly of an eternally lasting situation, rather than to something which occurs and is then over and has no continuance.

Realizing that God's judgment is eternal—whatever might be the arguments comparing it to burning, the chemical process of rapid oxidation with heat and light, which destroys or changes the thing burned by chemical oxidation—should cause every sinner to flee to Christ for salvation. John 3:16. Mankind is urged to come to faith in Christ for many reasons, including a deep love and appreciation of His death on the cross for us, as well as for the rewards promised to the faithful believer. But here in Mark 9, hearers are also urged to flee from the wrath to come, from "the worm" that "dieth not."

GGC

"Servant"

Person employed to perform services for another
Working for a master
Helper
Slave
Assistant
Waits on others
Meets the needs of another
Prepares and offers food
Provides guests with something to eat
Owned by and wholly subject to the will of another, by purchase or birth
One who surrenders himself to another
One who hears the call to duty for another
One who obeys the call to duty for another

Scripture References

Genesis 26:24; 4-5	Exodus 14:26-31	Numbers 12:1-8	1 Samuel 3:10
2 Samuel 3:17-18	2 Kings 9:35-36	Isaiah 41:8-10	Romans 1:1-3
1 Corinthians 3:5	Philippians 1:1	James 1:1	Jude 1
Philippians 2:5-11	Matthew 20:20-24, 26-28	1 Corinthians 9:19	

BODY, SOUL AND SPIRIT

The Bible clearly teaches the unity of the entire human race, and we note that biologically humans of any race can reproduce with those of any other (Gen 1:27-28; 2:7,22; Acts 17:26).

On the words body, soul, and spirit there have been endless discussions throughout the years. Some interpret the Bible as teaching that man [man and woman] has two parts, a visible body and an invisible soul. This is known as the dichotomous (two part) view of man's nature, wherein man is viewed as having (1) a physical body, and (2) a soul-spirit, the unseen part of man, which houses the mind, self-consciousness, the conscience, the emotions, the will, and the spirit. Plato, 5th/4th century BC, suggested that while the body was perishable, the soul was part of deity and lived on. Aristotle, 4th century BC, divided the soul into two portions, that which controlled the body and that which was rational. Genesis 2:7 says, upon man's creation, "and man became a living soul." The Hebrew here for "living soul" is nephesh chayah, "soul living," and this same expression is also used in Genesis 1:20, when speaking of the sea animals. In Luke 1:46, "My soul doeth magnify the Lord," we see reflected a spiritual capacity within the soul. Ezekiel 18:20 declares, "The soul that sinneth, it shall die."

Others interpret the scriptures as teaching that man is composed of three parts, as part of the image of God who is a Trinity. This is the trichotomous view. Man is seen here as having (1) a physical body, (2) a soul (nephesh in Hebrew; psyuche in Greek), which is the mind, self-consciousness, emotions, and will, and (3) a spirit (ruach in Hebrew; pneuma in Greek), which is the God consciousness portion of man, which may also hold the conscience, and the part, along with all or part of the soul, which lives on after death. When Jesus told Nicodemus that he must be born again, he said, "That which is born of the flesh is flesh; and that which is born of the spirit is spirit." Paul in the Bible says, "...I pray God your whole spirit and soul and body be preserved blameless unto the coming of our Lord Jesus Christ" (1 Thess 5:23).

Amid these views there are those who hold the creationist view of the soul, i.e., that God creates each individual soul at conception or at some time in the gestation process. This was the view of Thomas Aquinas, 13th century AD. Others adhere to the traducionist view, that the soul, like the traits passed on with the genes of the body, is passed on from the parents to the child. Mormons hold to a pre-existence of all souls, while some Eastern religions advocate that the soul is a result of reincarnation from one life to another. The naturalistic view, held chiefly by those who do not give credence to the scriptures, sees the soul as a naturalistic development of the self-consciousness chiefly from environmental stimuli and causes.

When mankind fell into sin, it is understood that all of the parts of man, body, soul/spirit, were affected. Man as a totality became guilty before God, and he was now in bondage to sin and could not cease from being a sinner, nor could he live a holy life any longer to merit salvation by good works. Every facet of man was affected, so that the body now died, the soul was no longer innocent or pure in its thoughts and the deeds which it guided, and the spirit lost its communion with God and was now separated from God, and in this sense dead, and headed for everlasting separation from God—except for His salvation intervention through the work of Christ on the cross. This was Calvin and Luther's "total depravity," sometimes also called "total inability." The sin-nature being passed on from generation to generation is known as the result and effect of the first couples' "original sin."

The process of the transmission of original sin and the sin nature from one generation to another is explained by the creationist, in that a clean sinless created soul is made by God, but it becomes defiled when it enters the body. The traducianist explains that the soul is rather defiled as it is passed on from one sinful generation to the new born generation. While unbelieving naturalists may deny the transmittal of the sin nature from one generation to another—with some even denying the concept, entity, and existence of sin—what is evident from the history of the world as well as from the teaching of scriptures, is that every human has a nature marred by sin, and those no nation, no period, no era has ever been free from crime, wars, and suffering brought about directly by (a) selfish and wicked deeds of other humans, (b) wicked deeds of ourselves, and (c) by our lack of doing all of our duty toward our fellow man, or showing him total self-negating kindness and sacrifice.

GGC

USAGE OF THE COLOR BLACK

Some have asked the meaning of the woman's words in the Song of Solomon, who said, "I am black, but comely, O ye daughters of Jerusalem, as the tents of Kedar, as the curtains of Solomon. Look not upon me, because I am black, because the sun hath looked upon me..."

Song of Solomon 1:5-6

What was her meaning? We may note that it could mean:

a. The speaker was indeed a black person, an Ethiopian, who had migrated into Israel—this would fit with her perhaps being perceived as somewhat unusual in Jerusalem, even though she was attractive ("comely"), and would explain why the "daughters of Jerusalem" might be looking at her;

b. The speaker was very dark with sunburn from being out doors in the summer—this would fit in with the rest of verse 6 which says that she was made by her mother to work out of doors in the vineyards, although she confesses that she did not do as much work as she might have; or

c. The speaker uses the color as a metaphor for sadness—in that she is sick at heart over her perhaps unrequited love.

The "tents of Kedar," mentioned in verse 5 refer to Ishmaelites who were generally wealthy Bedouins who lived in black tents made from the hair and skins of black goats. Solomon probably had some expensive tents or curtains also made of this material, or of this color, which is also alluded to in the same verse.

Jeremiah 8:21, "I am black," (*kdar-ti*), however, was said in a context of great sadness, as the prophet stood in his beloved Jerusalem in the wake of the oncoming Babylonian invasion. Thus here black would refer to his state of depression rather than to the color of his skin. The word in Hebrew, *kdar* with the -*ti* at the end meaning "I," is defined by Gesenius' Lexicon, as, "to be foul, to be turbid...dirty, to be blackish in color, to cause to mourn, to cause to be dark as the sun or stars." The Jay Green *Interlinear Bible* (AP&A, 1984), for example, simply translates it as, "I mourn." This is clearly the meaning here. Joel 2:6 (*paarur*) and Nahum 2:10 (*paarur*) both use "blackness" in the same way.

It may be noted that the skin colors of the predominant races—white, black, yellow, red, green (i.e., olive)—all may find pejorative uses in human language, e.g., the white of leprosy, the black of depression, the yellow of fearfulness, the red of blood-guiltiness, and the green of envy. The blueness of a wound could also be added, as well as being blue, meaning sad, to show that all colors may be given sad, as well as more cheerful, applications.

Some have argued heatedly over the color of Jesus' skin, just as others have debated his hair length and whether or not he had a beard. Some say that he was white with blond hair, while others claim him to have been of olive green mediterranean complexion, with still others arguing that he was black, from an Ethiopian line of Jews. Is this really to be debated? Truly we love Christ as the Savior for His moral perfections, for His perfect life and sacrificial love for us, and for His being our divine Savior, and our love for Him does not await our personal inspection of his skin color at His glorious return. Then too, at that return there shall be, "a great multitude, which no man could number, of all nations, and kindreds, and people, and tongues" standing "before the Lamb, clothed with white robes, and palms in their hands" (Rev 7:9).

GGC

THE TIME OF THE PATRIARCHS

Adam and Eve created/Cain
Gen. 2

Seth born/Enoch's translation/Noah's birth
Gen. 5

The flood
Gen. 7

Babel
Gen. 11

Abraham
Gen. 12 (b.c. 2000-1850)

Isaac
Gen. 21 (b.c. 1900-1750)

Jacob
Gen. 25 (b.c. 1800-1700)

Joseph
Gen. 37 (b.c. 1750-1650)

Moses born
Ex. 2

The Exodus
Gen. 12-14 (b.c. 1290-1260)

Giving of the Law
Gen. 19-31

Wilderness wanderings
Ex. 15–Josh. 3

Crossing Jordan
Josh. 3 (b.c. 1240)

Death of Joshua
Josh. 24

THE
TIME
OF THE
JUDGES

There are two views on the dating of the period of the Judges:
Earlier—1380-1050; Later—1220-1050. Several of the judges were
contemporaries, hence ruling years cannot be counted tandem.

Othniel Mesopotamian Oppression
Judges 3   8 yrs.

Ehud   Shamgar Moabite Oppression
Judges 3   18 yrs.

Deborah Philistine Canaanite Oppression
Judges 4   20 yrs.

Gideon Midianite Oppression
Judges 6-8   7 yrs.

Abimelech
Judges 9

Tola   Jair
Judges 10

Samson Philistine Ammonite Oppression
Judges 13-16   18 yrs.

Jephthah   Ibzan   Elon   Abdon
Judges 10-11-12

Eli Ark Taken
1 Sam. 1-4

20 yrs. without leader Philistine Oppression
1 Sam. 7   40 yrs.

Samuel and Saul
1 Sam. 7-9   10-16, 19, 25

THE
TIME
OF THE
KINGS

The United Kingdom

Saul   40 yrs. 1050 b.c. I Kings 9-11

David   40 yrs. 1010 b.c. I Kings 9-11

Solomon   40 yrs.   971 b.c. I Chron. 10 and

II Chron. 9

The Kingdom Divided 931 b.c.

Israel			Judah		
I Dynasty	I Kings 12 to II Kings 9				
Jeroboam	22 yrs.		**Rehoboam**	17 yrs.	
Nadab	2 yrs.	910 b.c.	**Abijah**	3 yrs.	913 b.c. 911 b.c.
II Dynasty	II Chron. 10-22				
Baasha	24 yrs.				
Elah	2 yrs.		**Asa**	41 yrs.	
Zimri	7 days	886 b.c.			
III Dynasty	War	885 b.c.			
Omri	8 yrs.	881 b.c.			875 b.c.
Ahab	22 yrs.	874 b.c.	**Jehoshaphat**	25 yrs.	
Ahaziah	2 yrs.	853 b.c.	jointly	4 yrs.	849 b.c.
			Joram	8 yrs.	
Joram	12 yrs.	841 b.c.	**Ahaziah**	1 yr.	847 b.c.

Jehu slays the Kings of Israel and Judah

THE TIME OF THE KINGS (cont.)

The Kingdom Divided   841 b.c.

Israel			Judah		
IV Dynasty	II Kings 9-18		**Athaliah Queen**	6 yrs.	
					835 b.c.
Jehu	28 yrs.	814 b.c.	**Joash**	40 yrs.	
Jehoahaz	17 yrs.	799 b.c.			
					797 b.c.
Jehoash	16 yrs.	782 b.c.	**Amaziah**	29 yrs.	
	II Chron. 22-29			about	
			jointly	17 yrs.	
Jeroboam II	41 yrs.				
		753 b.c.			
Zachariah	6 mos.				
			Uzziah	52 yrs.	
Shallum	1 mo.	751 b.c.			
V Dynasty				about	
			jointly	15 yrs.	740 b.c.
Menahem	10 yrs.				
		741 b.c.			
Pekahiah	2 yrs.		**Jotham**	16 yrs.	
VI Dynasty	740 b.c.			about	
Pekah	20 yrs.		jointly	8 yrs.	735 b.c.
East and West of Jordon			**Ahaz**	16 yrs.	
	731 b.c.				
VII Dynasty	731 b.c.				
			jointly	1 yr.	
Hoshea	9 yrs.		**Hezekiah**		
	722 b.c.				
Samaria taken captive by Assyria			(cont.)		

End of Israel's Kingdom

THE
TIME
OF THE
KINGS (cont.)

Later Kingdom of Judah

	II Kings 18-25
Hezekiah	29 yrs. 701 b.c.
	II Chron. 28-36
Manasseh	55 yrs.
Amon	2 yrs. 642 b.c.
	640 b.c.
Josiah	31 yrs.
Jehoahaz	3 mos. 609 b.c.
Jehoiachim	11 yrs. Jerusalem taken great captivity
Jehoiachin	3 mos. 597 b.c.
Zedekiah	11 yrs. (Jer. 52)
	587 b.c.

Jerusalem Destroyed

End of Kingdom of Judah

CAPTIVITY & RESTORATION

Jerusalem Destroyed 587 b.c.

II Chron. 36 Isaiah
Jeremiah Ezekiel
Daniel

Captivity

Cyrus restores Jews under Zerubbabel 536 b.c.

Rebuilding Temple stopped by Samaritans 535 b.c.

Haggai 522 b.c.

Temple dedicated

Zechariah 515 b.c.

Xerxes (Ahasuerus of Esther)

Esther 486 b.c.

Commission of Ezra 458 b.c.

Reformation in Jerusalem 457 b.c.

Commission of Nehemiah 445 b.c.

The Walls rebuilt

to

Opposition of Sanballat 432 b.c.

Second commission of Nehemiah

about

Malachi Malachi 430 b.c.

THE CAPTIVITY TO THE END OF THE OLD TESTAMENT

Period about 200 years

PROPHETS	JEWISH EVENTS	DATE B.C.	CONTEMPORARY HISTORY
Jer. 36-39, 46	First captivity (Daniel et al.)	605	Battle of Carchemish
Jer. 39:1-10, 2 Kgs. 25:1-21	Second captivity (Jerusalem captured)	597	
Jer. 43, 44	Third captivity (Temple destroyed)	586	Nebuchadrezzar beseiges Tyre
Ezek. 17-21	Last of Ezekiel's prophecies	571	Evil Merodach, Babylon, 562
2 Kgs. 25:28	Jehoiachin released	562	Temple of Diana, Ephesus, 552 (?)
			Public library at Athens, 544
			Babylon taken by Cyrus, 539
Dan. 5	Belshazzar's feast	539	First year of Cyrus, 538
Dan. 6	Daniel in den of lions	538	Pythagoras, c.582-c.507
2 Chr. 36:22, 23 Ezr. 1:1	The decree for the return	538	
	End of first reckoning of 70 years	538	Pisistratus, Athens, 605?-527
Ezr. 1:5-2:70	*First return,* 50,000 under Zerubbabel	538	Nabonidus, Babylon, 556
Ezr. 3-6	Foundation of Temple laid Long delay	537-6	Darius in Babylon, 521
Ezr. 4:24	Building of Temple resumed	520	Beginning of Roman Republic, 510
Ezr. 6:15	Temple dedicated	516	Marathon, 490
	End of second reckoning of 70 years	516	Xerxes I (Ahasuerus), 486-465/64
	No knowledge of events until		Invasion of Greece, 480
Es. 1	Feast of Ahasuerus (Xerxes I)	483	Herodotus, Socrates
Es. 2	Esther becomes queen	479	Xenophon, Plato
Es. 3-7	Haman's plot	474	First decemvirate, Rome, 451
Ezr. 7:1, 8, 9	*Second return* under Ezra	458	Pericles, Athens, 444
Neh. 2:1	Return under Nehemiah	445	Parthenon, Athens, 443-438
Neh. 6:15	Wall of Jerusalem	444	First Peloponnesian War, 431
Neh. 10	Reforms		Xenophon's retreat, 401
	Death of Nehemiah	400(?)	

Note: The 70 years of exile prophesied by Jeremiah begin with the destruction of the Temple in 586 and Second Temple completed in 516.

HOUSE OF BREAD
"RESTAURANT"

def. – WEBSTER'S NEW WORLD DICTIONARY:
"AN ESTABLISHMENT WHERE MEALS ARE PREPARED AND SERVED"

By definition therefore, the act of gathering in a Christian Church "To Be Fed." This might be thought of as meeting in a unit of the world's finest *"Restaurant"* chain called...

"THE HOUSE OF BREAD"
(Hebrew = "Bethlehem")

Family Owned: Father, Son and Holy Spirit

Executive Offices: Heaven

General Manager: God the Father — a co-founder

MasterChef: Jesus the Son — co-authored the Cookbook (Bible) which contains all required recipes to transform raw ingredients to a finished product.   (natural man)   (disciples).

Maitre'd: Holy Spirit — He guides the operation and oversees quality control

Head Waiter: Local Pastor

Table Captains: Deacons

Waiters: Guests who have become members (see membership rules below)

Busboy: The Owner(s) — He is always willing to pick up after us
(forgive)

Membership: This is an "invitation only" establishment but the membership (yoke) is *easy*. Through the good *graces* of the Owner guests are offered membership as a free gift; however, while it's for life, ongoing renewal (fruitfulness) is necessary to give evidence of being active.

Capacity: All humanity

Market Size: 5 Billion plus

Marketing: Strictly word of mouth (personal testimony)

Market Share: All invited and welcome but most go elsewhere.

Dress Code: Come just as you are but a suit is available when you leave.
(Christian armor)

Reservations:	Made *after* you arrive because there is *always* room for one more — these reservations are unique because once made they are forever.
Best Table Location:	The Upper Room
Ambience:	Illuminated by a Bright Morning Star
Music:	Lyrics By David
Etiquette:	The MasterChef provided for a *white as snow washing* when He founded the establishment; so washing up (baptism) after arrival (salvation), is highly desirable and strongly recommended.
Menu:	The food (burden) is *light*:

- The pure milk of the Word, the Bread of Life and the Cup of Salvation
- Salt is beneficial here, please use plenty
- Water served only once because after you drink you'll not thirst again
- Desserts (treasures) stored up for later use

Quality:	The *only* thing that's not *sacrificed* even though it is surely the only restaurant around where the expected result of being fed is to *die*. But not to worry, the MasterChef is also the "doctor in the house" (Great Physician) who heals every time.
Complaint Department:	See the Maitre'd — His job is to help all by interceding with the other Owners.
Directions:	How to get there is found in the Cookbook; also provided is a lamp to guide your steps along with a map to make straight your path.
Lost and Found:	All are lost but only some are found. (guests) (members)
Security:	Provided by Angelic Protective Services, Inc.
Price Range:	Expensive, but your tab was picked up by the ever-gracious Owner. (debt) (paid)
In Appreciation:	For life's best dining experience a *Tithe* is expected. (no tipping please)

Final Note:

Optional dining facility available courtesy of Lucifer's House of Flesh Restaurant Company. Here is where those who don't like the menu at The House of Bread prefer to be patrons.   (the lost)

Used by Permission
W. Lawrence LeNeve
Copyright Pending (rev.)
1994

THE PROMISED LAND

The exact boundaries of the Promised Land are difficult to determine due to: (1) the difficulty of being certain of the modern identification of then-well-known locations: (2) the uncertainty if named places and rivers were to be "points" or "extended lines", and (3) uncertainties as to the exact directions in which these lines were to be extended. Nevertheless, this map is offered as a good general picture of the future promised territory.

GENERAL REFERENCES

Due. 1:1-8	Gen. 12:7
Jos. 1:4	Gen. 13:14-17
Due. 11:24	Gen. 24:7
	Exo. 23:31

BY TRIBES:

Num. 34:1-12	Eze. 47:13-21
Jos. 15:1-12	Eze. 48:1-9
Jos. 15:21-63	

542

What many of us seem to forget is that: God created

	The Heavens	NO CHARGE!
	The Earth	NO CHARGE!
	The Universe	NO CHARGE!
	The Waters	NO CHARGE!
	The Plants and Fruit Trees	NO CHARGE!
	The Sun	NO CHARGE!
	The Moon	NO CHARGE!
	The Birds	NO CHARGE!
	Every Living Creature	NO CHARGE!

Then He brought forth Man . . . . .NO CHARGE!

And for man He gave him Woman . . . . .NO CHARGE!

Then God sent His Son to tell us of His
Father and to die for our sins . . . . .NO CHARGE!

And all we have to do is to believe and
He promises to Give us Eternal Life at . . . . .NO CHARGE!

And, now, for His saints, Christ is
preparing a mansion in Heaven for us at . . . . .NO CHARGE!

How can I do less than give Him my best . . . and live for Him completely
AFTER ALL HE'S DONE FOR ME!

2000 Years

2000 Years
A Time of Law

2000 Years
A Time of Grace

ETERNITY PAST

Gen. 1:1 In the Beginning

Gen. 1:2 Without Form — Void   Isa. 14:12 Satan?

Gen. 7:2-4   Gen. 8 and 9   2 Peter 2:5   NOAH

Pyramids   2500 BC

ABRAM — ABRAHAM   2000 BC

7 weeks – 49 years Dan. 9:25 Rebuild Jerusalem   453 BC

EZRA   NEHEMIAH

62 weeks 434 years Dan. 9:25-26   Messiah Cut Off-Crucified   404 BC – AD 30

1 week 7 years Dan. 9:27   (Soon Rev. 22:20)

70   490

Matt. 27:50-53

Matt. 1:25   Luke 1:27-35   John 1:14 (1-2-13)   Birth of Christ   4 BC AD 1

Luke 23:43   Acts 1:9-11   1 Cor. 15:51   Gal. 1:4   Death-Crucified   AD 30-34

Ephesus 30-100 AD   Syyrna 100-313   Permagos 313-600   Thyatira 600-1517

Sardis 1517-1648   Philadelphia 1648-1900   Laodicea 1900

Romans 10 – Israel set aside A nation – Israel Reborn   May 14, 1948

Return of Jerusalem to Israel – 1967

Rapture Pre-Rapture "Belief" Meet Christ   Matt. 24:37   I Cor. 15:51-52   1 Thes. 4:13-18

Luke 21:25-28   Titus 2:13   I Thes. 1:2,9

"Dead" in Christ – Past Believers

Before Tribulation – Wrath   Luke 17:26-36   2 Peter 3:4   Rev. 20:6

Noah   Gen. 7:1-4 (1-24)   Lot   Gen. 19:21-22   Gen (19-)   Romans 5:9   I Thes. 5:9   Rev. 3:10

PARADISE	JEW	Luke 16:22-26	Psa. 30:3
	CHURCH	Luke 23:43	Psa. 49:15
	BELIEVERS	Acts 2:31	Psa. 86:13

HELL	Dead	Psa. 16:10	Psa. 86:13
HADES	Unbelievers	Psa. 22:19	Psa. 115:17
SHEOL		Psa. 49:17,19	Psa. 139:8
BOTTOMLESS PIT		Psa. 63:9	Prov. 15:11
ABYSS		Psa. 69:28	Prov. 23:14

544

3-1/2 Years	"70th Week" Dan. 9:27	3-1/2 Years	1000 Years
42 Mon Rev. 13:5	1 Week 7 Years	42 Mon Rev. 11:2	(7 days as a 1000)
1260 Days Rev. 12:6		1260 Days Rev. 12:6	2 Peter 3:8
1/2 Week Dan. 9:27		1/2 Week	
PEACE		**WRATH**	

Matt. 24:15-21   Dan. 9:27   Hab. 2:2-3

7 Seals Rev. 1-14   7 Trumpets   7 Bowls-Vials

Rev. 7:2-11 Living
Rev. 6:12 Earthquakes
Rev. 6:9 Martyrs
Rev. 6:8 Pale Horse Power To Kill
Rev. 6:5 Black Horse Economic
Rev. 6:4 Red Horse War
Rev. 6:2 White Horse Anti-Christ

Romans 11 Zec. 14 — **Israel Restored**
12000 Each Tribe Rev. 7:2-9 (Perhaps to Petra)
Isa. 13:6 Joel 2:1,11 Matt. 24:21-22

144000 Rev. 12:13-17
Rev. 14:1-7 **Day of the Lord**
2 Peter 3:10 Acts 2:20

Rev. 9:14-21 Slay 1/3 Men 200,000,000 Army
Rev. 9:1-11 Pit Torment
Rev. 8:12 Sun-Moon 1/3 Stars
Rev. 8:10-11 Bitter Waters Wormwood
Rev. 8:8-9 1/3 Sea-Blood
Rev. 8:7 1/3 Earth

Rev. 10:1-11 Rainbow **Little Book**
Rev. 16:21-28 Done
Rev. 16:10 Darkness
Rev. 16:8-9 Scorch Fire
Rev. 16:4 Water to Blood
Rev. 16:3 Died in Sea
Rev. 16:2 Sores
Rev. 16:1

2 Cor. 5:8-10 — "JSC" **Judgement Seat of Christ**
Rom. 14:10 Tribulation Saints Believers
Dan. 12:1-4

Rev. 13:8 — **Book of Life**
Rev. 20:12-15
Rev. 19:7-8 — **Marriage of Lamb**
Zec. 11:4 Rev. 3:4,8-11 **Two Witnesses**

Acts 17:31 **War Armageddon**
Rev. 19:14-21 Rev. 16:12-17 War
Rev. 14:14-20
Matt. 24:21-22
Eze. 38:1-9 7 years to bury dead
Zec. 14:1-4 Joel 3:9-12 Eze. 39:17-29
Rev. 20:4 1000 Year **Millennium**

Jude 6 Rev. 20:11-13-15 — "GWT" **Great White Throne**
Rev. 19:20 Rev. 20:1-3,7-10,14-15 Rev. 21:8 **Lake of Fire**
Satan Loosed — Then Destroyed
Rev. 20:2-3,7
Rev. 20:1-7 Rev. 21

New Heaven—New Earth
Isa. 65:17 Isa. 66:22 Rev. 22
Rev. 21:1,10
ETERNITY FUTURE

LAKE OF FIRE

Deu. 32:22	Amos 9:2	Matt. 5:29-30,46	Luke 3:17	Jude 6:7,9
Job 26:6	Hab. 2:5	Matt. 13:42,49-50	Luke 16:23-24,26,30	Rev. 1:18
Eze. 31:16	2 Sam. 22:6	Matt. 16:18	Acts 2:27-31	Rev. 14:10
Eze. 32:18,21,27	Isa. 33:14	Matt. 25:46	2 Pet. 2:4	Rev. 21:8
	Isa. 38:18			

<u>DID YOU REALIZE THAT</u>

CHRIST IS IN THE

OLD CONCEALED   NEW REVEALED

Testament   Testament

CHRIST IS OUR

PROPHET,   PRIEST   and   KING

THE CHURCH IS THE

BRIDE OF CHRIST

According to Ecclesiastes 1:9-10

IF IT IS NEW...IT IS NOT TRUE

IF IT IS TRUE...IT IS NOT NEW

You should pay careful attention when you see
these special words in your Bible:

I	IF	WHY	LOVE	FAITH
1	2	3	4	5

Little words but so meaningful

MOUNTAINS OF THE BIBLE

Abarim, east of Jordan	Nu 27.12	Horeb, See Sinai	Ex 3.1
Ararat, in eastern part of mod. Turkey	Gn 8.4	Lebanon, in mod. Lebanon	Dt 3.25
Bashan, north of Gilead	Ps 68.15	Mizar, not positively identified	Ps 42.6
Carmel, on seacoast of Palestine	I K 18.19	Moriah, in Jerusalem	Gn 22.2
Ebal, in Samaria	Dt 11.29	Nebo, opposite Jericho, 12 miles W. of Dead Sea	Dt 32.49
Ephraim, central Palestine	Jsh 17.15	Olives or Olivet, east of Jerusalem	Mt 21.1
Gerizim, in Samaria	Dt 11.29		
Gilboa, where Saul died	1 S 28.4	Pisgah, in Moabite plateau	Nu 21.20
Gilead, north of Dead Sea	Gn 31.21	Seir, S W of Dead Sea	Gn 14.6
Halak, 30 miles S W of Dead Sea	Jsh 11.17; 12.7	Sinai, where Moses received Law	Ex 16.1
Hermon, in Anti-Lebanon range	Dt 3.8	Tabor, in Plain of Jezreel	Jg 4.6
Hor, Aaron's burial place	Nu 20.22	Zion or Sion, where Jerusalem is located	2 S 5.7

COINS IN THE BIBLE

In the Old Testament

The earliest reference in the Bible to coinage is the word "dram" found in 1Ch. 29:7. (The NASB employs the word "daric.") This is the only reference to this coin before the captivity of the Jews in the 7th century B.C. Apparently the historian was incorporating the equivalent term for the amount given "for the service of the house of God" in David's time, (c.1000B.C.) when the Hebrews had not yet used coins as currency. There is another reference to "dram" in Ezr. 8:27.

Another Hebrew word translated "dram" (NASB "drachma") is found in Ezr. 2:69 and Ne. 7:70,71,72. These are the only direct references to coins in the O.T.

Any hint of money in pre-exilic Jewish life must be understood as references to bars, ingots and jewelry made of precious metals and used in trading. A man's wealth could be estimated by the number of herds he possessed.

Old Testament references to the "shekel" meant a piece of silver or gold, not a coin. No coins minted before 600 B.C. have yet been discovered in Bible lands. The exact worth and weight of a shekel fluctuated from place to place and from time to time. Various evaluations concerning their purchasing power have been suggested in this last quarter of the twentieth century. The dram was known to the Jews during their captivity as the Persian (or golden) daric, introduced by Darius at the end of the 6th century B.C. The coin was oval shaped, rather thick, and portrayed the king on the obverse (inscription) side, kneeling with bow and arrow. Its weight was 130 gr. and is worth approximately $5.60.

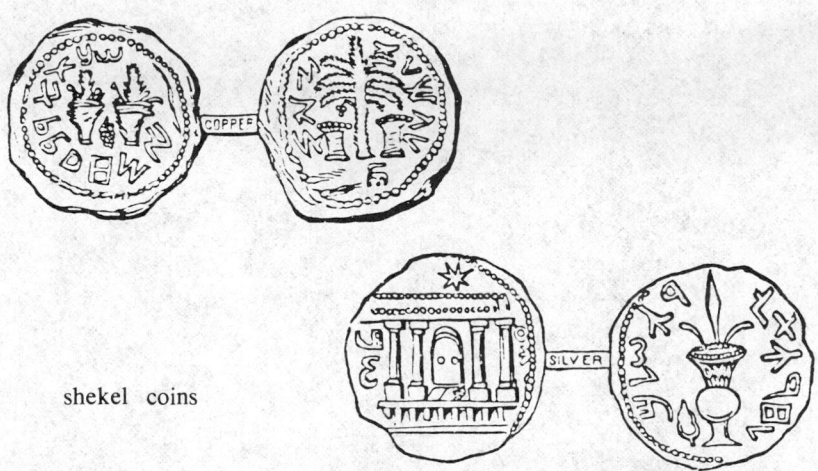

shekel coins

There are various general references to money, e.g. tribute money. The pound and the talent represent large measures of money rather than coins. Certain words are used both for definite and indefinite sums of money. The following coins are listed according to their first occurrences in the N.T.:

1. FARTHING (NASB cent) Mt. 5:26; Mk. 12:42: A quadrans, i.e. the fourth part of an asserius; a Roman bronze coin worth one-fourth cent.

2. GOLD, SILVER, AND BRASS Mt. 19:9: The more common general term for money in the N.T. is silver. The aureus was a Roman gold coin, then in use, but not recorded in the N.T. It may be implied in the word "gold". The chalkon was the copper coin mentioned here; a very small coin worth one-half cent. The same word is used for money in Mk. 6:8; 12:4.

3. FARTHING (NASB cent) Mt. 10:29; Lk. 12:6: Gr. *assarion,* the smallest copper coin, sometimes called as; worth one cent.

4. TRIBUTE (NASB two drachma) Mt. 17:24: Gr. didrachma, a double drachma. This coin was used as tribute money for payment of the Temple tax. It was a silver coin equal to two Greek drachmas; value 32 cents.

5. PIECE OF MONEY (NASB stater or shekel worth four drachmas). Mt. 17:27: This Greek silver coin was found by Peter in the mouth of the fish to pay the appropriate tax for Jesus and Peter; worth 64 cents.

6. PENCE (NASB denarii). Mt. 18:28: This was the basic Roman silver coin worth 16 cents, commonly known as the denarius and used as the ordinary day's wages for a laborer. It is found 16 times in the N.T., including all of the gospels and Revelation. It is generally plural and twice rendered pennyworth.

7. PIECES OF SILVER. Mt. 26:15; 27:3,5,6,9: Gr. arguria. Thayer refers to these as tetradrachmas, worth 64 cents. Judas sold the Lord for 30 'pieces', less than twenty dollars.

NOTE: Matthew, the tax collector, gives us more information concerning coins than any other writer in the Bible.

8. MITES (NASB small copper coins). Mk. 12:42: This is the only Jewish coin in the N.T., bronze, and the smallest of all coins in circulation; worth about one-eighth cent.

9. PIECES OF SILVER (NASB silver coins). Lk. 15:8: This was the Greek drachma worth 16 cents, equivalent to the Roman denarius; a silver penny.

10. PIECES OF SILVER. Ac. 19:19: Probably fifty thousand Greek Drachmas.

chalkon

WEIGHTS AND MEASURES

The Jewish law (Lv. 19:35,36) contained precepts respecting just weights and measures. The potential for fraud was enormous. Metal was valued according to its purity and weight. This accounts for the practice of carrying weights in a bag (Deut. 25:13-15). In order to aid the biblical student, only those words which are actually used in the KJV are included in this listing.

I. WEIGHTS

In early times the common weight was the shekel which means a weight. There were parts of a shekel such as the fourth, third, and half. The shekel was the basis of all calculations of weight.

1. Bekah: (Ex. 38:26) half a shekel; e.g., a golden ring of half a shekel weight, Gen. 24:22.

2. Gerah: (Ex. 30:13) one-twentieth of a shekel and the smallest of Hebrew weights.

3. Maneh (mina): (Ez. 45:12 only). In weighing silver and gold, this was equal to 50 shekels; other commodities used 60 shekels.

4. Pound

(1). The Hebrew word maneh (1 Ki. 10:17; Ezr. 2:69; Ne. 7:71,72) is employed in weighing silver and gold.

(2). Gr. mna used in Lk. 19 nine times.

(3). Gr. litra (Jn. 12:3; 19:39).

5. Shekel, a piece of silver. There is the shekel of the sanctuary (Ex. 30:13) and the shekel of the king (2 S. 14:26).

6. Talent or circle (Ex. 25:39). Usually a round weight of gold, silver, iron, or bronze (1 Ch. 29:7). This was the largest weight for metals. Rv. 16:21 refers to hailstones "about the weight of a talent."

II. MEASURES (LINEAR)

The cubit, derived from the human frame, was the basic unit of linear measurement in Israel. The Hebrews used the forearm as the cubit.

1. Cubit (Dt. 3:11): The Hebrews had the common cubit of 17.72 inches and the longer cubit with the handbreadth added, 20.67 inches.

2. Finger (Jr. 52:21 only): This was the smallest Israelite linear measure.

3. Handbreadth (Ex. 25:25): The width of the hand (palm) at the base of the four fingers.

4. Span (Ex. 28:16): One-half cubit, the space between the extended thumb and the little finger—about 8¾ inches.

5. Reed (Rv. 11:1): Similar to our yardstick. Ezekiel's temple was to be measured by six long cubits (Ezk.40:5).

6. Pace (2 S. 6:13): Just a step—between three and four feet.

III. MEASURES (DISTANCE)

1. Furlong (Lk. 14:13): One-eighth Roman mile, or 600 feet.

2. Mile (Mt. 5:41): The Roman mile was equivalent to 1,000 paces, or 4,850 feet.

3. A day's journey (Nu. 11:31): On foot, 20-25 miles.

4. A sabbath day's journey (Acts 1:12): About ⅞ mile.

IV. MEASURES (AREA)

1. Acre (I Sam. 14:44): The only unit of area referred to in the Bible. It is possibly the amount of land a pair of yoked oxen could plow in a day—3,200 sq. yds. or ¾ of an acre. This is equivalent to 0.45 km.

V. MEASURES (CAPACITY - DRY)

The Unit of measure was the ephah.

1. Ephah (Ezk. 45:10) of Egyptian origin: Equal in capacity to the bath, a liquid measure. 10 omers equals one ephah.

2. Handful (Lv. 2:2): The amount the hand could hold. An inexact quantity.

3. Homer (Lv. 27:16)—also called cor (Ezk. 45:14) due to its being a circular measure. 10 ephahs equal one homer. The half homer (Heb. lethek) for barley is found in Ho. 3:2 only.

4. Cab (2 K. 6:25 only) is equivalent to 1/6 seah. Rabbinical sources suggest 2.3 pints.

5. Omer, a small bowl (Ex. 16:16): An ancient Hebrew measure which contained the portion of manna assigned each individual for his daily food (Ex. 16:16-20).

6. Measure—Heb. seah (Gn. 18:6): A measure used in a common household, ⅓ ephah.

7. Bushel (Mt. 5:15): A small grain measure.

8. Measure (Rv. 6:6 only): A Greek measure.

9. Measure—Gr. koros (Lk. 16:7): Derived from Hebrew cor. A large measure.

10. Measure—Gr. saton (Mt. 13:33): Derived from Hebrew seah.

VI. MEASURES (CAPACITY - LIQUID)

The unit of measure was the bath.

1. Bath (1 K. 7:26) equal to ephah, a dry measure. This was the largest of the liquid measures.

2. Log (Lv. 14:10) hollow, originally called a basin. It was the smallest biblical measurement. A log of oil was used in the rites of purification for lepers; 1/12 hin.

3. Hin (Ex. 29:40) of Egyptian origin. This measure was associated with the offerings and anointing oil.

4. Firkin (Jn. 2:6). A Greek liquid measure used at the wedding feast in Cana.

5. Pot (Mk. 7:4 only). Pitcher or jar; a small vessel with no Hebrew equivalent.

6. Measures—Gr. batos (Lk. 16:8 only). A Jewish measure, supposedly 9 gals.

BIBLICAL SYMBOLISM

The following are a representation of the many symbols and symbolic words used in the Bible, along with their common interpretations. Some symbols have more than one meaning, depending on the context. The Biblical prophets used symbols, parables, and examples more frequently than modern writers and so those that follow are only a sample of the many that could be presented. Nevertheless, a knowledge of these will unlock the meaning of many passages and upon meditation prove to be a great blessing to the Biblical student. Also, the reader must be aware that some symbols are real items, but they at the same time also represent spiritual truths or future events, while others are only figures of speech.

SYMBOL:	MEANING:	EXAMPLE:
Alpha and Omega	Christ, the First & Last	Rev 1:11
Amalek	fighting against sin	Exod 17:16
bear	Media Persia	
beasts, animals	nations (in visions)	Dan 7:3; 8:20, 21
charity KJV	love demonstrated	1 Cor 13:1-13
circumcision	sign of God's covenant	Gen 17:10
clothing	Holy Spirit	Luke 24:49
dove	Holy Spirit	Matt 3:16, Mark 1:10 Luke 3:22, John 1:32
dragnet	final judgment	Matt 13:47
dragon	Satan; wicked and powerful	Rev 12:9
feasts of the Lord	God's eternal plan	Lev 23
Sabbath	God's heavenly rest	Deut 5:12-15
the 7 special feasts:		
Passover	Christ's death for us	Luke 22:15-20
Unleavened bread	the holy life	Luke 12:1
First fruits	Christ in resurrection	1 Cor 15:20
Pentecost	Fullness of the Church	Acts 2:1-6
Trumpets	Christ's 2nd Coming	1 Thess 4:16
Day of Atonement	Israel's conversion	Zech 12:10-14
Tabernacles	God Provides for our needs; he gathers all into His heavenly barn in the end	John 7:37, 38
fig tree	outward profession; Israel	Matt 21:19
fire	Holy Spirit	Acts 2:3
fisherman	soul winner	Mark 1:17
flock	God's people; the church	1 Pet 5:2
forty (number)	a period of testing	Numb 14:33-34
fox	a cunning, crafty person	Luke 13:32
goat	Greece	Dan 8:21
heads	nations or geographical areas	Dan 7:6
horns	kings or national leaders	Rev 17:12
horses (4)	conditions that spread rapidly	Rev 6:2-8
hour	key moment or period	John 2:4; Rev 17:1
Jezebel	Evil system or person	1 Kg 16:31; Rev 2:20
Jordan River	entrance into promised land	Josh 3:13
lamb	innocent one; Christ	Isa 53:7; Rev 5:6
leaven	evil teachings	Matt 16:6

BIBLICAL SYMBOLISM

SYMBOL:	MEANING:	EXAMPLE:
leopard	Greece	Dan 7:6
leper, leprosy	sinner, sin	Numb 5:2
A linen girdle	Judah in Jeremiah's day	Jer 13:10
lion	a powerful person	1 Pet 5:8; Rev 5:5
manna	God's Provision	Exod 16:15
mystery, mysteries	secrets	1 Cor 15:51
nakedness	sinfulness without defense	Rev 3:17, 18
oil	Holy Spirit	Luke 4:18; Acts 10:38; 2 Cor 1:21; 1 John 2:20
Passover	sacrificial blood covering sin	Exod 12:3
pearl	the truth in the gospel; Christ	Matt 13:45-46
pillar of cloud	God's guidance	Exod 13:21
plumbline	judgment coming soon	Amos 7:7-8
rainbow	God's mercy	Gen 9:12
Ram	Media Persia	Dan 8:20
rent veil of Temple	(i.e. torn) barrier removed by Christ's death	Matt 27:51
rest, the promised	heaven; promised land	Heb 3:11,18
rock, smitten	Christ struck for us	Exod 17:6
rod, Aaron's budded	God's sovereign choice	Numb 17:6-10
rod, Moses'	symbol of God's ability to give power to the weak	Exod 4:1,2; 7:20
sack cloth	sign of mourning or repentance	Rev 11:3
sea	people, nations	Dan 7:3
seal	Holy Spirit	2 Cor 1:22; Eph 1:13-4:30
seed	offspring	Gen 13:15,16
seed (in parable)	Word of God & witness	Matt 13:19,20
serpent	Satan	Rev 12:9
servant	Holy Spirit	Gen 24
seven (number	a complete cycle	Gen 7:2; Rev 1:11
sheep	people needing guidance	Matt 15:24
shepherd	Caretaker; Christ	1 Pet 5:4
sickle	judgment, end times	Rev 14:14
tabernacle	God's Presence	Exod 25:8-9
tares	counterfeit believers	Matt 13
ten (number)	completeness	Exod 20:1-17
30 pieces of silver	betrayal of Christ	Zech 11:12; Matt 27:9
Throne (white)	final judgment	Rev 20:11
tongues	languages; special communication	1 Cor 14:21; Isa 28:11
twelve (number)	Governmental number	Rev 21:12,14
two sticks tied together	Ephriam & Judah, bound in unity	Ezek 37:16-17
valley of dry bones	Israel	Ezek 37:1-2
water	salvation; that which gives life	John 4:14; 7:38-39
wedding garment	salvation given by God	Matt 22:11
wheels (King, Servant, Man, God)	four facets of Christ	Ezek 1:15
wind	Holy Spirit	John 3:8; Acts 2:1-2
wine of the Last Supper	Christ's atoning blood	Matt 26:27
wine press	Judgment	Isa 63:3
wolf, wolves	cruel & evil persons	Acts 20:29
wolves in sheep's clothing	false religious teachers	Matt 7:15

GUIDE TO THE LAWS OF THE BIBLE

In order to make available the light which the Bible throws upon the problems of human conduct and responsibility, the following compilation of the laws of the Bible is offered. Since the Bible is the foundation of the legal systems of all civilized nations it is highly important that those matters be made accessible.

A. Forms of Government

	BOOK	CHAP.	VERSE

I. Patriarchal. The family being the unit of life, the father as head of the family was the authoritative ruler. He had power of life and death.

	BOOK	CHAP.	VERSE
	Ex.	12	26, 27
	Deut.	6	7
	Job	1	5

II. Theocracy. God was the direct ruler of His people.

	Ex.	19	3-8

III. Government by Judges.

	Judges	2	13-18

The people forgot God. God chastised them by selling them into slavery to their enemies. Upon repentance God raised up military chieftains as deliverers. This form of government continued for about 300 years.

(Also entire book of Judges and I Sam. to 10th Chapter.)

IV. Monarchy

	I Sam.	10	24

This was begun by the coronation of Saul, reached its height in David and Solomon and ended with the Babylonian captivity.

(Books of Samuel, Kings, and Chronicles)

B. Qualification for Citizenship under the Monarchy

1. Those of Israel who ratified the covenant at Sinai and later children born into their homes were entitled to the rights of citizenship.

	Ex.	19	5, 8
	Deut.	23	2

2. Moabites and Ammonites excluded.

	Deut.	23	3

3. Edomites and Egyptians in the third generation were eligible.

	Deut.	23	8

C. Laws of the Theocracy

I. PERTAINING TO FOREIGNERS.

(1) Law applied equally to aliens as to citizens.

	Ex.	12	49
	Lev.	24	22

(2) Jew not to marry a foreigner.

	Gen.	34	14

(3) Forbidden to own slaves of own people.

	Lev.	25	47, 48

(4) Interest on money charged.

	Deut.	23	20

II. PERTAINING TO SLAVERY.

(1) Obtained by (a) Captives in War.
(b) Inherited.
(c) Bought.
(d) Sold for debt or theft.

	BOOK	CHAP.	VERSE
(a)	Num.	31	9
(b)	Lev.	25	46
(c)	Ex.	21	2
(d)	Deut.	15	12
	Ex.	22	3

(2) How treated.
(a) Jewish slaves to be set free in Sabbatical year.

	Lev.	25	40

(b) Regarded as part of owner's household and possession.

	Ex.	20	17
	Gen.	12	16
	Gen.	14	4

(c) Could be smitten by master.

	Ex.	21	20

(d) Fugitive not to be returned.

	Deut.	23	15, 16

III. PERTAINING TO TAXATION.

(1) Census taken.

	Num.	1	1-3
	Num.	4	1-3
	Num.	26	2

(1) Sons inherited father's estate.	Deut.	21	16, 17
(2) Double portion to firstborn.	Deut.	21	16, 17
(3) Willing to one son prohibited.	Deut.	21	15-17
(4) Wife not heir, but descended with property to next of kin.	Ruth	4	1-12
(5) Daughters heirs when no sons.	Num.	27	7, 8
(6) When no sons or daughters, inheritance by nearest of kin.	Num.	27	8-11

2. Kinds of Property.
   (1) Real Estate.

(a) Land allotted among tribes.	Num.	26	52-56
(b) Title not transferable.	Num.	36	4-7
(c) Not permanently sold.	Lev.	25	23-28
(d) Year of Jubilee lands returned to heirs.	Lev.	25	15, 16, 34
(e) Release of land proclaimed by sound of trumpet.	Lev.	25	8-34
(f) Mode of transfer.			
(1) Deed made.	Jer.	32	9-14
(2) Drawing off shoe, sign of relinquishing right.	Ruth	4	3-11
(3) Deed delivered in presence of witnesses.	Jer.	32	12
(4) Deed recorded.	Jer.	32	14
(5) Mortgages given.	Neh.	5	2-5

   (2) Personal Property.

This includes all property which is moveable, as against real property such as houses and lands.

(a) Sale recognized.	Lev.	25	14
(b) Pledges of personal property.			
(1) Children given as pledge.	II Ki.	4	1-7
(2) Mill of millstone prohibited.	Deut.	24	6
(3) Pledges not retained overnight.	{Deut.	24	13
	{Ex.	22	26, 27
(4) Pledges voluntary.	Deut.	24	10, 11

   (3) Interest on Money.

Interest was called usury in Bible times. Now usury means excess interest.

(a) Taking of interest forbidden among Jews.	{Ex.	22	25
	{Deut.	23	19, 20

Money then was not loaned for purpose of trade, but for the relief of poor.

(b) Allowed to be taken from foreigners.	Deut.	23	20
(c) Penalty for charging interest.	Neh.	5	11

Restoration of pledges, plus 1%.

(d) Weights and Measures.			
Divers weights and measures forbidden.	Deut.	25	13-16

Perfect and just weights and measures only tolerated by God.

VII. CRIMINAL LAWS.

In a theocracy crime was considered as against God instead of against fellow man or the state.

1. Crimes against the public.
Penalty.

	Deut.	27	25
(1) Bribery.	Ex.	23	8

Reservations:	Made *after* you arrive because there is *always* room for one more — these reservations are unique because once made they are forever.
Best Table Location:	The Upper Room
Ambience:	Illuminated by a Bright Morning Star
Music:	Lyrics By David
Etiquette:	The MasterChef provided for a *white as snow washing* when He founded the establishment; so washing up (baptism) after arrival (salvation), is highly desirable and strongly recommended.
Menu:	The food (burden) is *light*:

- The pure milk of the Word, the Bread of Life and the Cup of Salvation
- Salt is beneficial here, please use plenty
- Water served only once because after you drink you'll not thirst again
- Desserts (treasures) stored up for later use

Quality:	The *only* thing that's not *sacrificed* even though it is surely the only restaurant around where the expected result of being fed is to *die*. But not to worry, the MasterChef is also the "doctor in the house" (Great Physician) who heals every time.
Complaint Department:	See the Maitre'd — His job is to help all by interceding with the other Owners.
Directions:	How to get there is found in the Cookbook; also provided is a lamp to guide your steps along with a map to make straight your path.
Lost and Found:	All are lost but only some are found. (guests) (members)
Security:	Provided by Angelic Protective Services, Inc.
Price Range:	Expensive, but your tab was picked up by the ever-gracious Owner. (debt) (paid)
In Appreciation:	For life's best dining experience a *Tithe* is expected. (no tipping please)

Final Note:

Optional dining facility available courtesy of Lucifer's House of Flesh Restaurant Company. Here is where those who don't like the menu at The House of Bread prefer to be patrons. (the lost)

Used by Permission
W. Lawrence LeNeve
Copyright Pending (rev.)
1994

THE PROMISED LAND

The exact boundaries of the Promised Land are difficult to determine due to: (1) the difficulty of being certain of the modern identification of then-well-known locations: (2) the uncertainty if named places and rivers were to be "points" or "extended lines", and (3) uncertainties as to the exact directions in which these lines were to be extended. Nevertheless, this map is offered as a good general picture of the future promised territory.

GENERAL REFERENCES

Due. 1:1-8	Gen. 12:7
Jos. 1:4	Gen. 13:14-17
Due. 11:24	Gen. 24:7
	Exo. 23:31

BY TRIBES:

Num. 34:1-12	Eze. 47:13-21
Jos. 15:1-12	Eze. 48:1-9
Jos. 15:21-63	

Beirut
LEBANON
Damascus
Mediterranean Sea
Sea of Galilee
ISRAEL
Amman
Jerusalem
Dead Sea
River of Egypt (Wadi) (El Arish)
Perhaps
Elath
Gulf of Aqaba
Red Sea

SYRIA
PROMISED LAND BOUNDARY
Euphrates River
IRAQ
JORDAN

ISRAEL OF THE 12 TRIBES
Tigris
Euphrates
Future
River of Eg/Wadi El Arish
Perhaps

Z	EZE. 47:13-22	Z – – – Z	
O	EX. 23:31	O - - - - O	
X	GEN. 15:18	X —— X	

542

(2) Perjury.	{	Lev.	19	12
	{	Ex.	20	16
Penalty attached.		Deut.	19	16-20
(3) Defiance of Law.		Num.	15	30, 31
Penalty attached.		Deut.	17	12, 13
(4) Perverting or obstructing justice.		Ex.	23	1, 2, 6 & 7
Penalty.		Deut.	16	19, 20
		Ex.	22	19

2. Crimes of Immorality.

(1) Adultery.		Ex.	20	14
Penalty.		Deut.	22	20-25
(2) Rape.		Deut.	22	25, 26
Penalty.		Deut.	22	25, 26
(3) Prostitution.		Deut.	23	17
Penalty.		Lev.	21	9
(4) Seduction.		Ex.	22	16, 17
Penalty.		Deut.	22	28, 29
(5) Incest.		Deut.	22	30
Penalty.		Lev.	20	11-21
(6) Sodomy.	{	Deut.	23	17
	{	Lev.	18	22
Penalty.	{	Lev.	20	13
	{	Ex.	22	19

3. Crimes against Persons.

(1) Murder.		Ex.	20	13
Penalty.	{	Gen.	9	5, 6
	{	Ex.	21	12, 14
(2) Manslaughter.	{	Ex.	21	13
Penalty.	{	Num.	35	6, 15
(3) Assault.	{	Ex.	21	18, 26 & 27
Penalty.	{	Ex.	21	19
(4) Kidnaping.	{	Ex.	21	16
Penalty.	{	Ex.	21	16
(5) Slander.		Lev.	19	16

4. Crimes against God.

(1) Worshipping other Gods.	{	Ex.	20	1
Penalty.	{	Ex.	22	20
(2) Sorcery.	{	Lev.	20	27
Penalty.	{	Ex.	22	18
(3) Blasphemy.	{	Lev.	24	16
Penalty.	{	Lev.	24	16

5. Crimes against Property.

(1) Theft.	{	Ex.	20	15
	{	Ex.	22	1-4
(2) Arson.		Ex.	22	6
(3) Removing a landmark.		Deut.	19	14

VIII. HUMANE LAWS.

1. Duties toward persons.

(1) Widows and orphans.	Ex.	22	22, 23
(2) Neighbors.	Lev.	19	13
(3) The poor.	Lev.	19	9, 10
(4) Strangers.	Lev.	19	33, 34
(5) Needy and helpless.	Lev.	19	14
(6) Servants.	Deut.	24	14, 15

        2. Duties toward animals.
            (1) Beasts of burden.   { Ex.   23   12
                                                                             { Deut.   25   4
            (2) Wild animals.   { Ex.   23   11
                                                                             { Lev.   25   5-7
            (3) Mother and young.   { Deut.   22   6, 7
                                                                             { Lev.   22   28
            (4) Enemy's Ass.   Ex.   23   5
        3. Keeping the Sabbath.   Ex.   20   8-11

IX. CEREMONIAL LAWS.
        1. Clean and unclean food.   { Lev.   11   2-31
                                                                             { Deut.   14   3-20
        2. Eating of blood forbidden.   Lev.   3   17
        3. Flesh torn of beasts, not to be eaten.   Ex.   22   31
        4. Fruit of young trees, not to be eaten.   Lev.   19   23-25
        5. Sacred obligations.
            (1) Firstborn.   { Ex.   34   19, 20
                                                                             { Ex.   13   2, 3
            (2) Firstfruits.   { Ex.   34   26
                                                                             { Deut.   18   4
            (3) Tithes.   Lev.   27   30-33
            (4) Poll tax.   Ex.   30   12-16
            (5) Freewill offering.   Lev.   22   17-20
        6. Sacred calendar.
            (1) Sabbath.   Deut.   5   12-15
            (2) Passover.   Deut.   16   1-7
            (3) Feast of Unleavened bread.   Ex.   34   18
            (4) Feast of weeks.   Deut.   16   9-11
            (5) Feast of Tabernacles.   Deut.   16   13-17
            (6) Sabbatical year.   Deut.   15   1-3
            (7) Day of Atonement.   Lev.   23   26-32

D. Legal Procedure

I. JUDGES APPOINTED.   { Ex.   18   13-26
                                                                            { 2 Chr.   19   4-12
        1. Moses, first judge.   Ex.   18   13-27
        2. Priests judges in small matters.   Ex.   18   22
        3. King as judge.   I Ki.   7   7

II. SUBMISSION OF CASES.
        1. Ordinary cases submitted to Judges.   Deut.   25   1, 2
        2. Exceptional cases taken to Supreme Court.   Deut.   17   9-11
        3. Extreme cases submitted to the Lord for decision.   { Num.   5   12-31
                                                                            { Deut.   21   1-9
                                                                            { Deut.   19   17-19
        4. Judges must decide righteously.   Ex.   23   6-8
        5. Bribery forbidden.   Deut.   16   18-20

III. WHERE COURTS WERE HELD.
        1. At city gates.   { Deut.   21   19
                                                                            { Deut.   25   7
        2. In Porch of Judgment.   I Ki.   7   7

IV. JUDGMENTS.

1. Regarded as from God.	Deut.	1	17
2. Righteous to be justified and wicked condemned.	Deut.	25	1
3. Sentence to be executed.	{ Deut.	25	2, 3
	{ Deut.	17	7

V. APPEALS.

1. To Moses.	Ex.	18	26
2. To Priests.	Deut.	17	8-11
3. To the King.	I Ki.	3	16-27

VI. DAMAGES.

1. For maiming a person.	Lev.	24	10, 19, 20
2. For stealing.	Ex.	22	4, 5
3. Kindling a fire which damages property.	Ex.	22	6
4. Breach of trust.	Lev.	6	1-5
5. Killing an animal.	{ Lev.	24	18-21
	{ Ex.	21	35, 36
6. Loss of animal falling into pit.	Ex.	21	33, 34
7. Loss of borrowed property.	Ex.	22	14

E. Methods of Punishment

1. By infliction in kind.	{ Gen.	9	6
	{ Ex.	21	24, 25
2. By burning.	Lev.	20	14
3. By mutilation.	Deut.	25	11, 12
4. By hanging.	Deut.	21	22, 23
5. By stoning.	Lev.	24	16
6. By scourging or beating.	Deut.	25	2, 3
7. By excommunication.	Ezra	10	8
8. By imprisonment.	Ezra	7	26
9. By compensation for damages.	Ex.	21	19, 32, 36
10. By restitution for stolen or borrowed property.	Ex.	22	12, 14 & 15

F. Method of Protection

1. Cities of Refuge Appointed.	Num.	35	6-15
2. Protection till trial could be had.	Num.	35	12
3. Murderer not protected.	Num.	35	31-32
4. Unintentional man slayer remained in city till death of high priest.	Josh.	20	4, 6

MIRACLES AND MIRACULOUS EVENTS OF THE OLD TESTAMENT

Creation	Gen.	1	2	Miriam's leprosy cured	Num.	12	10, 15
The flood	Gen.	7		Fire from heaven on Aaron's offering	Lev.	9	24
Multiplication of languages	Gen.	11	7, 9	Jordan divided	Josh.	3	
Men of Sodom smitten with blindness	Gen.	19	11	Jericho taken	Josh.	6	
Sodom and Gomorrah destroyed	Gen.	19	24, 25	Sun and moon stayed	Josh.	10	12
Lot's wife turned into a pillar of salt	Gen.	19	26	Lion slain	Jgs.	14	6
The burning bush not consumed	Ex.	3	2	Philistines killed	Jgs.	14	19
Rod made serpent	Ex.	4	3	Water supplied for Samson	Jgs.	15	19
Rod restored	Ex.	4	4	Gates carried away	Jgs.	16	3
Hand made leprous	Ex.	4	6, 7	Dragon's house pulled down	Jgs.	16	30
Water turned into blood	Ex.	4	9, 30	Dragon and Philistines smitten	1 Sam	5	
River into blood	Ex.	7	20	Beth-Shemethites smitten	1 Sam	6	19
Frogs	Ex.	8	6, 13	Thunder and rain	1 Sam	12	18
Lice	Ex.	8	17	Uzzah struck dead	2 Sam	6	7
Flies	Ex.	8	21, 31	Jeroboam's hand withered	1 Ki.	13	4
Murrain	Ex.	9	3	Altar rent	1 Ki.	13	5
Boils	Ex.	9	10	Hand restored	1 Ki.	13	6
Hail	Ex.	9	23	Drought { 1 Ki. / Jas.	1 Ki. / Jas.	17 / 5	1 / 17
Locusts	Ex.	10	13, 19				
Darkness	Ex.	10	22	Meal and oil multiplied	1 Ki.	17	14
First-born destroyed	Ex.	12	29	Child restored to life	1 Ki.	17	22
Pillar of Cloud	Ex.	13	21, 22	Sacrifice consumed by fire	1 Ki.	18	38
Pillar of fire	Ex.	13	21, 22	Captains and men slain by fire	2 Ki.	1	10
Sea divided	Ex.	14	21	Rain brought	1 Ki.	18	41
Egyptians overwhelmed	Ex.	14	26, 28	Waters of Jordan divided	2 Ki.	2	8
Water sweetened	Ex.	15	25	Elijah carried into heaven by chariot of fire	2 Ki.	2	11
Quails for food	Ex.	16	13	Jordan divided	2 Ki.	2	14
Manna	Ex.	16	14, 35	Waters healed	2 Ki.	2	21
Water from rock	Ex.	17	6	Mocking children torn by bears	2 Ki.	2	24
Amalek vanquished	Ex.	17	11	Water supplied	2 Ki.	3	16
Destruction of Korah	Num.	16	32	Widow's oil multiplied	2 Ki.	4	5
Plague and its removal	Num.	16	41, 50	Loaves multiplied	2 Ki.	4	43
Water from rock in Kadesh	Num.	20	11				
Brazen serpent	Num.	21	8				
Aaron's rod blossoms	Num.	17	8				
Baalam's ass speaks	Num.	22	28, 31				
Aaron's sons destroyed	Lev.	10	1, 2				

Pottage rendered harmless	2 Ki.	4	41
Child raised to life	2 Ki.	4	35
Naaman healed	2 Ki.	5	14
Gehazi struck with leprosy	2 Ki.	5	27
Iron caused to swim	2 Ki.	6	6
Syrians smitten	2 Ki.	6	18
Syrian army put to flight	2 Ki.	7	6
Resurrection of a man	2 Ki.	13	21
Shadow put back	2 Ki.	20	11
Sennacherib's army destroyed	2 Ki.	19	35
Fire from heaven on Solomon's offering	2 Chr.	7	1
Hezekiah healed	2 Ki.	20	7
Uzziah made leprous	2 Chr.	26	19, 21
Three saved from fiery furnace	Dan.	3	19, 27
Daniel saved from lions	Dan.	6	16, 23
Jonah delivered from whale's belly	Jonah	2	

PARABLES OF THE OLD TESTAMENT

Concerning the Moabites and Israelites	Num.	23	24
Trees making a king	Jgs.	9	7, 15
Strong bringing forth sweetness	Jgs.	14	14
Poor man's ewe lamb	2 Sam.	12	1, 4
Two brothers striving	2 Sam.	14	1
The escaped prisoner	1 Ki.	20	35, 40
The thistle and cedar	2 Ki.	14	9
Israel compared to a vine	Ps.	80	8, 16
Vineyard yielding wild grapes	Is.	5	1, 6
The vine tree	Ezek.	15	
The great eagles and the vine	Ezek.	17	3, 10
Lion's whelps	Ezek.	19	2, 9
The wasted vine	Ezek.	19	10, 14
The boiling pot	Ezek.	24	3, 5
Holy flesh	Hag.	2	12-14

For the Miracles and Parables of our Lord,
see pages 573 and 574

FEELING FAITH AND FACT

Three men were walking on a wall
Feeling, Faith and Fact
Feeling took an awful fall
and Faith was taken back
But Fact remained both strong and true
and that brought back Faith and then Feeling too!

LIFE AND TEACHINGS OF JESUS CHRIST

ANGELS

The word for angel in the O.T. is <u>Malach</u>, and hence Malachi's name means, "My messenger," or "My angel," with the - -i at the end signifying "my" in Hebrew. In the New Testament it is <u>aggelos</u> in the Greek, with the double gg being always pronounced as "ng." In both the O.T. and the N.T. it signifies either or both an earthly "messenger" or a heavenly one, which we then call an "angel."

We conclude from the Bible that the angels were individually created spirits, and are not a reproducing race. They do not marry, Mark 12:25. They are spiritual beings, incorporeal (without a physical body), but they apparently can assume temporarily the appearance of a human or look like a human.

There are various types of angels, with the Bible revealing the names of two archangels: Michael is <u>Mi cha El</u>, "Who-is Like God!" and Gabriel is <u>Gabor El</u>, "A-Mighty-One is-God!" Dan 12:1; Rev 12:7; Jude 1:9; Dan 8:16; 9:21; Luke 1:19,26.

There are, in addition to the normal and regular angels, also <u>cherubim</u> (Gen 3:24); <u>Seraphim</u>, or "Burners" (Isa 6:2-3), and Living Creatures ["Beasts" KJV]. The -im is the Hebrew plural.

The primary division is between the good angels and the evil, or fallen angels. Satan is the name given to the chief evil spirit, and he is also called, Lucifer or "morning star" (Isa 14:12), seeming to allude to the fact that he once shone brightly as the morning planet Venus—but that he fell. He is also called the Devil, "<u>diabolos</u>," which is the Greek word for "accuser," which function we see him do in Job 1:8-12; 2:4-7. In the prophetic denunciations of the King of Babylon in Isaiah 14:4-18 and of the King of Tyre in Ezekiel 28:11-19, we may be hearing the Lord's denunciation of the Satanic spiritual person behind these tyrants—one who originally had great power and authority, but who sinned in pride and fell. Many think Satan to have been an archangel. Revelation 12:9 calls him "the Old Serpent" reflecting back to his deceptive work in the garden of Eden. Satan is ubiquitous (seemingly very busy and appearing here and there); but he is not omnipresent, as is God only.

Revelation 12:4 seems to indicate that one-third of the angels fell with Satan. Genesis 6:2—("The sons of God saw the daughters of men . . .")—may be a passage indicating an attempt by fallen angels to corrupt the human race, much as the demons in Christ's day wished to enter human bodies to do their harm. Revelation 12:13-17 shows that Satan will play a leading part in persecuting Israel and the tribulation saints at the end of the age.

The Bible speaks of evil angels, demons (<u>diamonia</u> in the Greek, "devils" in the KJV), and of fallen angels held in "everlasting chains" awaiting the judgment (Jude 6). Whether these are the same is debated. The demons were active at the time of Christ, and seemed to desire to enter a body in order to

carry out their evil desires. Yet in the epistles we see that believers are never warned to beware of demon possession. Apparently, so that Christ might have triumphed over all of the fury of evil, there was a permissive liberty given to the demons at that time, but not afterwards.

The Bible clearly teaches that Christ was and is superior to the angels (Hebrews chapters 1 & 2; 1 Peter 3:22).

In harmony with 2 Timothy 2:23 telling us to "avoid" "foolish and unlearned questions" we hesitate to join certain angel debates, which some scream over as if they had already been in heaven and have first hand knowledge—i.e., Can angels sing? Do they appear as men only, or as women also?

Angels are very powerful (Rev 20:1-3), but they are not omniscient, and do not know the time of the Second Coming of Christ, Matt 24:36.

Angels do so many wonderful things, including.—

witness to creation,	Job 38:7
serve in God's heavenly court,	Isa 6:2-4
praise God,	Psa 103:20-21
minister to believers,	Heb 1:14; Acts 12:7
bring messages from God,	Zech 1:14
guarded Israel in the wilderness,	Ex 23:20
protect God's people,	Dan 3:28
destroyed Sodom,	Gen 19:1
pour out endtime judgments,	Rev 16:1
oppose evil angels,	Dan 12:1
found Isaac a wife,	Gen 24:7,40
announced the birth of John and Jesus,	Luke 1:11; 1:26
ministered to Christ,	Matt 4:11—Christ said that He could call 12 Legions of angels to defend Him, Matt 26:53, had such been in God's plan.
have a special relationship/assignment to children,	Matt 18:10—which some have labeled as "Guardian angels."

An angel-like appearance of God is called a "theophany" and a Christ appearance is known as a "Christophany." Some urge that the "Angel of the LORD" is often/always a Christophany, but such must be shown in each case. See Genesis 22:11-18; 31:11; Exodus 3; Judges 6 and 13.

Believers are warned not to worship angels, Col 1:18; and hypothetically not to receive a message from even an angel if it is contrary to the gospel, Gal 1:8.

This study should end with the admonition: "Let brotherly love continue. Be not forgetful to entertain strangers: for thereby some have entertained angels unawares" (Hebrews 13:1-2).

GGC

CHART OF THE LIFE OF JESUS CHRIST.

Ancestry	On one side God himself. On the other every phase of character, every human tendency represented in his genealogy.
Preparations for his coming	Universal peace. One empire. One language generally known. The Jews with the Scriptures in all lands. A general awakening.
Birth of Jesus about December, B.C. 5 Childhood and Youth	Home training. Bible study. Schooling. Different languages. Travel to Jerusalem. Great religious meetings. Village life. Work at a trade. Knowledge of his country's history and hopes. A perfect and beautiful character.
Preparations for his ministry	John the Baptist. Baptism. The Holy Spirit: The Voice from God. Temptation.
A.D. 27 Judea First Year – Year of Beginnings	**John's ministry of preparation began six months before Jesus began to preach, continued through the first year and three months into the second year.** First disciples. First miracle. First reform. First discourse. First tour. First Samaritan disciple. Healing of the nobleman's son.
A.D. 28 Galilee Second Year – Year of Principles	**Imprisonment of John the Baptist, March.** The Pool of Bethesda. Organization. Choosing apostles. Sermon on the Mount. Miracles proving his authority and illustrating his work. Forgiveness of Sins. Seeking the lost. Life from the dead. The light of the world. Warnings and invitations. Parables. The year in which Jesus laid down and worked out many of the fundamental principles and truths of his kingdom.
A.D. 29 Galilee / Perea 2 - 3 months Third Year – Year of Development	**The Death of John the Baptist in March. Increasing opposition.** Feeding the five thousand. Miracles: The dropsical man, the ten lepers, blind Bartimeus. The transfiguration. At the feast of tabernacles. Discourses in the Temple. Healing of one born blind. The good shepherd. Parables: The great supper, the lost sheep, the lost coin, the prodigal son, the unjust steward, the rich man and Lazarus, the pounds.
A.D. 30 Perea Last three months Jan. Feb. March	Raising of Lazarus. Miracles. Parables. Instructions. Children. Zaccheus.
Saturday April 1 – Saturday April 8 Last Week	Anointed at Bethany. Triumphal entry. Cleansing the Temple. Last great day of public teaching. Rest at Bethany. Passover/The Lord's Supper. The trial. The crucifixion. The burial. In the tomb.
Sunday April 9 – Thursday May 18 Resurrection Days	Forty days. Eleven appearances, between April 9 and May 18. A.D. 30 The Ascension. Thursday, May 18 from Mount of Olives.
The Ever-Living Saviour	Return through the Holy Spirit. A Saviour in heaven. Ever abiding with his people. Coming again in his kingdom. A universal king, the world redeemed.

THE HARMONY OF THE GOSPELS

THE HARMONY OF THE GOSPELS

Jesus Institutes "The Lord's Supper" . . . . Matthew 26:26 Mark 22 Luke 22:19

Peter's Three Denials Foretold . . . . Matthew 26:34 Mark 14:30
Luke 22:34 John 13:38

Jesus' Agony in Gethsemane . . . . Matthew 26:36 Mark 14:32 Luke 22:39 John 18:1

The Betrayal and Arrest . . . . Matthew 26:47 Mark 14:43 Luke 22:47 John 18:2

Jesus Taken to Annas . . . . John 18:13

Before Caiaphas the High Priest . . . . Matthew 26:57 Mark 14:53
Luke 22:54 John 18:19

Peter's Three Denials . . . . Matthew 26:69 Mark 14:66 Luke 22:54 John 18:15

Jesus before the Council . . . . Matthew 27:1 Mark 15:1 Luke 22:66

Jesus before Pilate . . . . Matthew 27:2, 11 Mark 15:1 Luke 23:1 John 18:28

Pilate Declares Jesus Innocent . . . . Luke 23:4 John 19:4

Pilate Sends Jesus to Herod . . . . Luke 23:7

The Jews Reject Jesus . . . . Matthew 27:21, 25 Mark 15:6 Luke 23:18
John 18:40 John 19:15

Pilate Condemns Jesus to Death . . . . Matthew 27:26 Mark 15:15
Luke 23:24 John 19:16

Jesus Mocked by the Soldiers . . . . Matthew 27:27 Mark 15:16 John 19:2

Jesus Led Away to be Crucified . . . . Matthew 27:31 Mark 15:20
Luke 23:33 John 19:18

The Crucifixion of Jesus . . . . Matthew 27:35 Mark 15:24 Luke 23:33 John 19:18

Jesus on the Cross . . . . Matthew 27:36 Mark 15:25 Luke 23:34 John 19:19

The Death of Jesus . . . . Matthew 27:50 Mark 15:37 Luke 23:46 John 19:30

The Centurion's Witness . . . . Matthew 27:54 Mark 15:39 Luke 23:47

The Burial of Jesus . . . . Matthew 27:57 Mark 15:42 Luke 23:50 John 19:38

The Resurrection of Jesus . . . . Matthew 28:1 Mark 16:1 Luke 24:1 John 20:1

Appearances of Jesus After the Resurrection:

To Mary Magdalene . . . . Matthew 16:9 John 20:11

To the Women . . . . Matthew 28:1

To the Eleven . . . . Mark 16:14 John 20:19

To Two Going to Emmaus . . . . Mark 16:12 Luke 24:13

To the Eleven (a week later) . . . . John 20:26

To the Apostles in Galilee . . . . Mark 16:14 John 21:1

To Peter . . . . Luke 24:34 1 Corinthians 15:5

To Five Hundred Brethren in Galilee . . . . 1 Corinthians 15:6

To James . . . . 1 Corinthians 15:7

To Paul . . . . 1 Corinthians 15:8

Jesus' Commission to the Apostles . . . . Matthew 28:19 Mark 16:15 Luke 24:44

Jesus Talks with Peter . . . . John 21:15

The Ascension of Jesus . . . . Mark 16:19 Luke 24:50 Acts 1:4

The Descent of God the Holy Ghost . . . . Acts 2:1

Abasement	Matt.	11	23, 24	Bigotry	Luke	18	10-12
Abel	Matt.	23	34, 35	Birds	Matt.	8	20
Abiding in Christ	John	15	4-10	Blasphemy	Matt.	12	31, 32
Ability	Matt.	25	14, 15	Blessings, spiritual	Matt.	5	3-11
Ablution	Matt.	6	17, 18	Blessings, temporal	Luke	12	22-31
Abomination	Luke	16	15	Blind leaders	Matt.	15	14
Abraham	John	8	56, 58	Borrowing	Matt.	5	42
Abraham's bosom	Luke	16	22, 23	Bottles	Mark	2	22
Abstinence	Luke	21	34	Breach of trust	Luke	16	10-12
Abundant life	John	10	10	Bread	Matt.	4	4
Access to God	John	10	7, 9	Bread of life	John	6	48-51
Accountability	Luke	12	47, 48	Brethren	Matt.	23	8
Accusation, false	Matt.	5	11	Builders	Luke	6	47-49
Ado	Mark	5	39	Burdens	Luke	11	46
Adulteress forgiven	John	8	10, 11	Burial	Matt.	8	22
Adultery	Matt.	5	32	Burning bush	Mark	12	26
Adversary	Matt.	5	25	Bushel	Luke	11	33
Adversity	John	16	33	Business, God's	Luke	2	49
Affliction	Matt.	24	7-12	Caesar	Matt.	22	21
Agreement	Matt.	18	19	Call of God	Matt.	20	16
Almsgiving	Luke	12	33	Camel	Matt.	23	24
Altar	Matt.	23	18, 19	Candle	Luke	8	16
Ambition	Luke	22	25-30	Capital and labor	Matt.	20	1-15
Amen	Matt.	6	13	Capital punishment	Matt.	26	52
Angels	Matt.	13	39, 41	Careless hearing	Matt.	13	19
Anger	Matt.	5	22	Care of God	Matt.	6	30, 33
Antediluvians	Luke	17	26, 27	Cares of the world	Matt.	13	22
Anxiety	Luke	12	22-31	Caution	Mark	4	24
Apostasy	Luke	8	13	Cephas (Peter)	John	1	42
Apostles	Luke	11	49	Ceremonialism	Mark	7	6-13
Apostles, sent forth	Mark	16	15, 16	Character	John	1	47
Appearance, outward	Matt.	23	27, 28	Charity	Luke	6	30
Ark, Noah's	Matt.	24	37, 38	Chastity in thought	Matt.	5	27, 28
Ass	Luke	14	5	Cheating	Mark	10	19
Atonement	Matt.	20	28	Cheek, smitten	Matt.	5	39
Authority of Christ	John	5	25-27	Chickens	Matt.	23	37
Avarice	Luke	12	16-21	Childlikeness	Mark	10	15
Backsliding	Luke	9	62	Children	Matt.	19	14
Bank	Luke	19	23	Choice	Luke	10	41, 42
Baptism, Holy Ghost	Acts	1	5	Christ, ascension of	John	6	61, 62
Baptism, water	Matt.	28	19	Christ, as bridegroom	Matt.	9	15
Baptism, of John	Mark	11	30	Christ, as king	John	18	37
Baptism, of suffering	Matt.	20	22, 23	Christ, betrayal of	Matt.	26	21, 23
Barn	Matt.	6	26	Christ, blood of	Luke	22	20
Barrenness	Luke	23	28-30	Christ, exalted	Luke	22	69
Beam	Luke	6	41, 42	Christ, lifted up	John	3	14, 15
Beatitudes	Matt.	5	3-11	Christ, resurrection	Luke	9	22
Bed	Mark	2	8-11	Christ, second coming	John	14	2, 3
Beelzebub	Luke	11	17-19	Christ, the way	John	14	6
Begging	Luke	16	3	Christs, false	Matt.	24	24
Belly	Matt.	15	17	Church	Matt.	16	18
Beneficence	Matt.	5	42	Circumcision	John	7	22, 23
Beware	Matt.	7	15	Cleansing, spiritual	John	15	3

570

THE MIRACLES OF OUR LORD

The First Miracle: Water Made Wine ....John 2:1
Many Healings ....Matthew 4:23   Matthew 8:16   Matthew 15:30
                                                  Mark 1:32   Luke 4:40 etc.
A Leper ....Matthew 8:1–4   Mark 1:40   Luke 5:12
The Centurion's Servant ....Matthew 8:5   Luke 7:1
Peter's Wife's Mother ....Matthew 8:14   Mark 1:29   Luke 4:38
The Tempest Stilled ....Matthew 8:23   Mark 4:35   Luke 8:22
Two Demoniacs ....Matthew 8:28   Mark 5:1   Luke 8:26
A Palsied Man ....Matthew 9:1   Mark 2:1   Luke 5:18
The Twelve-Year Afflicted Woman ....Matthew 9:20   Mark 5:25   Luke 8:43
Raising of Jairus' Daughter ....Matthew 9:23   Mark 5:22   Luke 8:41
Two Blind Men ....Matthew 9:27
A Dumb Demoniac ....Matthew 9:32   Matthew 12:22   Luke 11:14
A Man with a Withered Hand ....Matthew 12:10   Mark 3:1   Luke 6:6
Five Thousand Fed ....Matthew 14:15   Mark 6:35   Luke 9:12   John 6:1
Jesus Walks on the Sea ....Matthew 14:22   Mark 6:47   John 6:16
The Syrophenician's Daughter ....Matthew 15:21   Mark 7:24
Four Thousand Fed ....Matthew 15:32   Mark 8:1
The Epileptic Boy ....Matthew 17:14   Mark 9:14   Luke 9:37
Two Blind Men (Jericho) ....Matthew 20:30
A Man with an Unclean Spirit ....Mark 1:23   Luke 4:33
A Deaf Mute ....Mark 7:31
A Blind Man (Bethesda) ....Mark 8:22
Blind Bartimaeus ....Mark 10:46   Luke 18:35   Matthew 20:30
Draught of Fishes ....Luke 5:4
Raising of Widow's Son ....Luke 7:11
An Infirm Woman ....Luke 13:11
A Dropsical Man ....Luke 14:1
Ten Lepers ....Luke 17:11
Malchus' Ear Healed ....Luke 22:50
A Nobleman's Son ....John 4:46
A Cripple (Bethesda) ....John 5:1
A Man Born Blind ....John 9:1
Raising of Lazarus ....John 11:38
A Great Haul of Fishes ....John 21:1

For the Old Testament Miracles,
see pages 560 and 561.

573

THE PARABLES OF OUR LORD

Candle Under a Bushel . . . . Matthew 5:15   Mark 4:21   Luke 8:16; 11:33
The Builders . . . . Matthew 7:24–27   Luke 6:47–49
New Cloth on Old Garment . . . . Matthew 9:16   Mark 2:21   Luke 5:36
New Wine in Old Bottles . . . . Matthew 9:17   Mark 2:22   Luke 5:37
The Sower . . . . Matthew 13:3   Mark 4:1   Luke 8:4
The Wheat and the Tares . . . . Matthew 13:24–30
The Mustard Seed . . . . Matthew 13:31   Mark 4:30   Luke 13:18
The Leaven . . . . Matthew 13:33   Luke 13:20
The Hidden Treasure . . . . Matthew 13:44
The Pearl of Great Price . . . . Matthew 13:45
The Net . . . . Matthew 13:47
The Unmerciful Servant . . . . Matthew 18:23–35
The Laborers in the Vineyard . . . . Matthew 20:1–16
The Two Sons . . . . Matthew 21:28–32
The Wicked Husbandmen . . . . Matthew 21:33–46   Luke 20:9–18
The Marriage Feast . . . . Matthew 22:1–14
The Fig Tree . . . . Matthew 24:32
The Ten Virgins . . . . Matthew 25:1–13
The Talents . . . . Matthew 25:14–30
The Sheep and the Goats . . . . Matthew 25:31
The Seed Growing Secretly . . . . Mark 4:26–29
The Householder . . . . Mark 13:34
The Two Debtors . . . . Luke 7:41
The Good Samaritan . . . . Luke 10:25–37
The Importunate Friend . . . . Luke 11:5
The Rich Fool . . . . Luke 12:13–21
Servants Watching . . . . Luke 12:35
The Wise Steward . . . . Luke 12:42
The Fruitless Fig Tree . . . . Luke 13:6–9
The Great Supper . . . . Luke 14:16–24
On Counting the Cost . . . . Luke 14:25–33
The Lost Sheep . . . . Luke 15:3–7
The Lost Coin . . . . Luke 15:8–10
The Lost Son . . . . Luke 15:11–32
The Dishonest Steward . . . . Luke 16:1–14
The Rich Man and Lazarus . . . . Luke 16:19–31
Unprofitable Servants . . . . Luke 17:7
The Importunate Widow and Unjust Judge . . . . Luke 18:1–8
The Pharisee and Publican . . . . Luke 18:8–14
The Pounds . . . . Luke 19:11–27

For the Old Testament Parables,
see page 561.

NAMES AND TITLES OF JESUS CHRIST

SUBJECT	BOOK	CHAP.	VERSE
Adam	1 Cor.	15	45
Advocate	1 Jno.	2	1
Almighty	Rev.	1	8
Alpha and Omega	Rev.	1	8, 11
	Rev.	22	13
Altogether lovely	Sol.	5	16
Amen	Rev.	3	14
Ancient of Days	Dan.	7	22
Angel	Gen.	48	16
Angel of God's presence	Is.	63	9
Anointed	Jno.	1	41
Anointed One, the Prince	Dan.	9	25
Anointed above His Fellows	Ps.	45	7
Anointed of the Lord	Ps.	2	2
Anointed with the Holy Ghost	Acts	10	38
Apostle of our Profession	Heb.	3	1
Apple tree	Sol.	2	3
Arm of the Lord	Is.	51	9, 10
Author and Finisher of Faith	Heb.	12	2
Author of Eternal Salvation	Heb.	5	9
Babe	Luke	2	12, 16
Beginning and End	Rev.	1	8, 11
Beginning of Creation of God	Rev.	3	14
Begotten of the Father	Jno.	1	14
Beloved	Song	5	16
	Eph.	1	6
Beloved of God	Matt.	12	18
Beloved Son	Matt.	3	17
	2 Pet.	1	17
Bishop of Souls	1 Pet.	2	25
Blessed and only Potentate	1 Tim.	6	15
Branch of Righteousness	Jer.	33	15
Branch of the root of Jesse	Is.	11	1
Brazen Serpent	Jno.	3	14
Bread from Heaven	Jno.	6	51
Bread of Life	Jno.	6	48
Bridegroom	Matt.	9	15
Bright and Morning Star	Rev.	22	16
Brightness of Father's Glory	Heb.	1	3
Brother	Mark	3	35
	Heb.	2	11
Builder	Zech.	6	13
Bundle of Myrrh	Sol.	1	13
Camphire	Sol.	1	14
Captain	Josh.	5	14
	Heb.	2	10
Carpenter	Mark	6	3
Carpenter's Son	Matt.	13	55
Chief Shepherd	1 Pet.	5	4
Chiefest among ten thousand	Sol.	5	10
Child	Is.	9	6
Chosen of God	Matt.	12	18
Christ	Matt.	1	16
	Matt.	2	4
	Jno.	1	41
Christ, The	Matt.	16	20
	Mark	14	61
Christ, a King	Luke	23	2
Christ Jesus	Acts	19	4
	Rom.	3	24
Christ Jesus our Lord	1 Tim.	1	12
	Rom.	8	39
Christ of God	Luke	9	20
Christ the chosen of God	Luke	23	35
Christ the Lord	Luke	2	11
Christ the power of God	1 Cor.	1	24
Christ the wisdom of God	1 Cor.	1	24
Christ the Son of God	Acts	9	20
Christ, Son of the Blessed	Mark	14	61
Commander	Is.	55	4
Consolation of Israel	Luke	2	25
Corner-stone	Eph.	2	20
	1 Pet.	2	6
Counsellor	Is.	9	6
Covenant of the People	Is.	42	6
Covert from the Tempest	Is.	32	2
Creator of Israel	Is.	43	15
Creditor	Luke	7	41
David	Jer.	30	9
	Ezek.	37	24, 25
	Hos.	3	5
Days-Man	Job	9	33
Day-Spring from on High	Luke	1	78
Day-Star	2 Pet.	1	19
Deliverer	Rom.	11	26
Desire of all Nations	Hag.	2	7
Dew	Hos.	14	5

577

SUBJECT	BOOK	CHAP.	VERSE
Nazarene	Matt.	2	23
Offspring of David	Rev.	22	16
Ointment	Sol.	1	3
Only Begotten	Jno.	1	14
Only wise God, our Saviour	Jude		25
Passover of the Saints	1 Cor.	5	7
Peace, Our	Eph.	2	14
Pearl of great Price	Matt.	13	46
Physician	Matt.	9	12
Plant of Renown	Ezek.	34	29
Polished Shaft	Is.	49	2
Potentate	1 Tim.	6	15
Power of God	1 Cor.	1	24
Precious Corner Stone	Is.	28	16
	1 Pet.	2	7
Priest	Heb.	5	6
Prince and Saviour	Acts	5	31
Prince of Life	Acts	3	15
Prince of Peace	Is.	9	6
Prince of the Kings of the Earth	Rev.	1	5
Prophet	Luke	24	19
	Acts	3	22, 23
Propitiation	1 Jno.	2	2
	1 Jno.	4	10
Power of God	1 Cor.	1	24
Purifier and Refiner	Mal.	3	3
Quickening Spirit	1 Cor.	15	45
Rabbi	Matt.	26	25, 49
	Mark	9	5
	Jno.	1	38, 49
Rabboni	Mark	10	51
	Jno.	20	16
Rain and Showers	Ps.	72	6
Ransom for All	1 Tim.	2	6
Redeemer	Job	19	25
	Is.	59	20
	Is.	60	16
Redemption	1 Cor.	1	30
Resurrection and the Life	Jno.	11	25
Righteous Branch	Jer.	23	5
Righteous Judge	2 Tim.	4	8
Righteous Servant	Is.	53	11
Righteousness	Jer.	23	6
Rivers of Water	Is.	32	2
Rock	Is.	32	2
Rock of Offence	Is.	8	14
	1 Pet.	2	8
Rod and Branch	Is.	11	1
Roe and Hart	Sol.	2	9
Root of David	Rev.	5	5
Root of Jesse	Is.	11	10
	Rom.	15	12
Rose of Sharon	Sol.	2	1
Ruler in Israel	Mic.	5	2
Ruler of the Kings of the Earth	Rev.	1	5
Sacrifice and Offering	Eph.	5	2
Salvation	Luke	2	30
Samaritan	Luke	10	33
Sanctification	1 Cor.	1	30
Sanctuary	Is.	8	14
Saviour	Is.	19	20
	Luke	2	11
	Acts	5	31
	Phil.	3	20
Saviour, Jesus Christ	2 Tim.	1	10
	Titus	2	13
	2 Pet.	1	1
Saviour, God Our	1 Tim.	2	3, 7
Saviour of the Body	Eph.	5	23
Saviour of the World	Jno.	4	42
	1 Jno.	4	14
Sceptre out of Israel	Num.	24	17
Second Man	1 Cor.	15	47
Seed of David	2 Tim.	2	8
Seed of the Woman	Gen.	3	15
Servant	Is.	42	1, 19
Servant of Rulers	Is.	49	7
Sharp Sword	Is.	49	2
Shepherd	Jno.	10	11
	Heb.	13	20
Shepherd of Israel	Ps.	80	1
Shepherd of Souls	1 Pet.	2	25
Shiloh	Gen.	49	10
Shoot	Is.	11	1
Solomon	Sol.	3	7
	Sol.	8	11, 12
Son of the Blessed	Mark	14	61
Son of David	Matt.	9	27
	Mark	10	47, 48
	Luke	18	38
Son of the Father	2 Jno.		3
Son of God	Matt.	4	3
	Matt.	8	29
Son of Man	Matt.	8	20
Son of Mary	Mark	6	3
Son of the Most High	Luke	1	32
Son of God	Dan.	3	25
Sower	Matt.	13	3
Spiritual Drink	1 Cor.	10	4
Spiritual Meat	1 Cor.	10	3
Spiritual Rock	1 Cor.	10	4

SUBJECT	BOOK	CHAP.	VERSE	SUBJECT	BOOK	CHAP.	VERSE
Staff or Supporter	Sol.	8	5	True Vine	Jno.	15	1
Star Out of Israel	Num.	24	17	Truth	Jno.	14	6
Stone Rejected	Matt.	21	42	Unspeakable Gift	2 Cor.	9	15
Stone of Stumbling	Is.	8	14	Very Christ	Acts	9	22
	1 Pet.	2	8	Vine	Jno.	15	1
Sun of Righteousness	Mal.	4	2	Wall of Fire	Zech.	2	5
Sure Foundation	Is.	28	16	Way	Is.	35	8
Surety	Heb.	7	22		Jno.	14	6
Teacher	Matt.	26	18	Wedding Garment	Matt.	22	12
	Mark	14	14	Well-Beloved	Sol.	1	13
	Luke	22	11	Well of Living Water	Sol.	4	15
	Jno.	11	28	Which Is, Which Was,			
Teacher come				Which Is to Come	Rev.	1	4
from God	Jno.	3	2	Wisdom	Prov.	8	1, 22
Testator	Heb.	9	16	Wisdom of God	Luke	11	49
Treasure Hid in a Field	Matt.	13	44		1 Cor.	1	24
Treasury or				Witness	Rev.	1	5
Storehouse	Col.	2	3	Wonderful	Is.	9	6
Tree of Life	Rev.	2	7	Word	Jno.	1	1, 14
Tried Stone	Is.	28	16	Word of God	Heb.	11	3
True Light	Jno.	1	9	Word of Life	1 Jno.	1	1
	1 Jno.	2	8	Worthy to receive			
True God	1 Jno.	5	20	Power, etc.	Rev.	5	12

THE HOLY SPIRIT: TITLES, DEITY AND WORK

SUBJECT	BOOK	CHAP.	VERSE	SUBJECT	BOOK	CHAP.	VERSE
Titles of:				Spirit of the Father	Matt.	10	20
Comforter	Jno.	14	16	Spirit of the Lord	Is.	11	2
Eternal Spirit	Heb.	9	14	Spirit of the Son	Ga.	4	6
Free Spirit	Ps.	51	12	Spirit of Understanding	Is.	11	2
Holy Spirit	Ps.	51	11	Spirit of Wisdom	Is.	11	2
Power of the Highest	Luke	1	35	**Diety of:**			
Spirit of Adoption	Rom.	8	15	Eternal	Heb.	9	14
Spirit of Christ	1 Pet.	1	11	Omnipotent	Rom.	8	11
Spirit of Counsel	Is.	11	2	Omniscient	1 Cor.	2	10, 11
Spirit of Glory	1 Pet.	4	14	Omnipresent	Ps.	139	11
Spirit of God	Gen.	1	2	**Work of:**			
Spirit of Grace	Zech.	12	10	Assisted in Creation	Gen.	1	2
Spirit of Holiness	Rom.	1	4	Inspires Scriptures	2 Tim.	3	16
Spirit of Judgment	Is.	4	4	Agent in Christ's	Luke	1	35
Spirit of Knowledge	Is.	11	2	incarnation	Matt.	1	18
Spirit of Life	Rom.	8	2	Convicts the world	Jno.	16	8, 11
Spirit of Lord God	Is.	61	1	Regenerates believers	Jno.	3	3, 5
Spirit of Might	Is.	11	2	Sets believers free	Rom.	8	2
Spirit of Prophecy	Rev.	19	10				

DETAILED CHRONOLOGY OF THE ACTS

ACTS.	EVENTS.	PLACE.	DATE A.D.*	CONTEMPORARY HISTORY.
1: 1-3	Resurrection days	Galilee	30. April, May	Tiberius, emperor, 14-37 A.D.
1: 4-12	Commission to Apostles and Ascension	Bethany	30. May 18	Pontius Pilate, procurator, 26-36.
1:13, 14	Waiting for the promise of the Father	Jerusalem, in an upper room.	30	PAUL enters public life, A.D. 29, aged 30.
1:15-26	Election of Matthias to take the place of Judas .	"	....	
2: 1-13	Pentecost: the Gift of Tongues	Jerusalem	....	Seneca. 4 B.C.-65 A.D.
2:14-36	Peter's address	"	....	Essays and Tragedies.
2:37-41	The first converts: 3000 .	"	....	
2:42-47	The early church	"	....	
3: 1-10	The lame man healed ...	Temple courts	....	Gamaliel. 30-40
3:11-26	Second address by Peter .	"	....	A.D.
4: 1-22	The first persecution: Peter and John imprisoned	Jerusalem	....	Philo Judaeus. 20 B.C.- after 40 A.D.
4:23-37	A fresh baptism of the Spirit	"	....	
5: 1-11	Ananias and Sapphira ...	"	30	
5:12-16	Spread of Gospel in Jerusalem	"	to	
5:17-42	Second persecution: Sanhedrin	"	34	
6: 1-7	Appointment of deacons .	"	35	
6: 8-15	Preaching of Stephen ...	"	35 to 36	Deposition of Pontius Pilate.
7: 1-60	Martyrdom of Stephen ..	"	36	36.
8: 1-4	General persecution	....		Sent to Rome for trial.
8: 5-25	Philip the Evangelist in ..	Samaria		Vitellius takes his place as
8:26-40	Philip and the Ethiopian .	Road to Gaza	....	governor.
9: 1-22	Conversion of Saul of Tarsus	Near Damascus	....	PAUL, aged 37.
(Gal. 1:17)	Saul in Arabia			Death of Tiberius, 16 March, 37.
9:23-27	St. Paul persecuted; escapes	Damascus ...	38	
9:28-29	St. Paul preaches in Jerusalem	Jerusalem	....	Accession of Caligula.
9:30	St. Paul goes to Cilicia ...	Tarsus, etc. ..	38-40	Release of Herod
9:31-35	St. Peter cures Eneas ...	Lydda		Agrippa I.
9:36-42	Dorcas restored to life ..	Joppa		Banishment of Antipas, 39.
10: 1-48	Cornelius the Centurion converted	Caesarea	41	Caligula orders his statue to be set up at Jerusalem.
11: 1-18	The question of admitting the Gentiles	Jerusalem	....	Claudius Emperor.

580

ACTS.	EVENTS.	PLACE.	DATE A.D.*	CONTEMPORARY HISTORY.
11:19-21	First Gentile church	Antioch	38-41	Jan. 24, 41, to Oct. 13, 54.
	Herod Agrippa I, King of Judea		41	Seneca in exile, 41-49.
11:22, 23	Barnabas at Antioch	Antioch	42, 43	
11:25, 26	Paul called from Tarsus to Antioch	"	42, 43	Romans in Britain, 43.
12: 1, 2	Martyrdom of St. James .	Jerusalem ...	44. Spring	
12: 3-18	Imprisonment and deliverance of St. Peter	" ...	44. Spring	Death of Herod Agrippa I, 44.
12:19-23	Death of Herod Agrippa I	Caesarea	44. Early Summer	London founded, 47.
11:27-30	Famine. Relief sent to Jerusalem by Barnabas and Saul		44-46	
12:24, 25	Return of Saul and Barnabas with John Mark to	Antioch	46	Expulsion of Jews from Rome, 48 (?)
13:1-14:28	First Missionary Journey by Saul and Barnabas.	Asia Minor ..	March 47 to 49	
13: 1-3	Ordained as missionaries .	Antioch		
13: 4-52	In Cyprus and Antioch of Pisidia	Asia Minor		
14: 1-20	In Iconium, Lystra, Derbe	"		
14:21-25	Revisiting the churches ..	" ..	49	
14:26-28	Report to home church ..	Antioch	49	Caractacus defeated in Britain.
15: 1-35	Council at Jerusalem	Jerusalem ...	50	
15:40-18:22	Second Missonary Journey by St. Paul and Silas	Asia Minor and Greece .	50-52	
16: 1-5	Revisiting the churches ..	Asia Minor ..	50-52	
16: 6-11	St. Paul enters Europe ..	Macedonia ..	50-52	
16:12-40	St. Paul at Philippi; Lydia, conversion of jailer	Philippi	50-52	
17: 1-14	St. Paul in Thessalonica and Berea	Macedonia		Gallio pro-consul at Corinth.
17:15-34	St. Paul at Athens	Greece	51-52	
18: 1-18	St. Paul at Corinth. Crispus	Greece	51-52	
	1 and 2 Thessalonians			
18:18-22	Returns home via Ephesus and Caesarea to	Antioch	51-52	Felix, procurator, 52-59.
18:22	Brief visit to Jerusalem ..	Jerusalem		
18:22, 23	St. Paul in Antioch	Syria	52	Nero, emperor, 54-68.
	Galatians			
18:23-21:16	Third Missionary Journey by Paul.	Asia Minor and Greece .	53-57	Birth of Tacitus, 55.
18:24-28	Apollos at Ephesus	Asia Minor		St. Peter at Corinth, 55 or 56.
19: 1-11	St. Paul nearly three years at	Ephesus	53-56	
	1 Corinthians	.....	56	
19:12-20	Sceva the Exorcist	"		
19:21-41	Riot at Ephesus. Diana .	"		
20: 1-5	St. Paul revisits Macedonia	Macedonia ...	57	
	2 Corinthians	....		

Acts.	Events.	Place.	Date A.D.*	Contemporary History.
	St. Paul three months at Corinth .... *Romans*	Greece		
20: 6-12	St. Paul at Troas. Eutychus	Troas		
20:13-16	Sails to Miletus			
20:17-38	Address to Ephesian elders at	Miletus	57	
21: 1-16	Journey by Tyre and Caesarea to	Jerusalem		
21:17-20	St. Paul's reception by church	Jerusalem		
21:21-40	St. Paul's arrest in Temple	"		
22:1-23:11	St. Paul a prisoner in Castle of Antonia	"		
23:12-22	The conspiracy against Paul's life	"		
23:23-35	St. Paul sent secretly to ..	Caesarea		
24: 1-22	St. Paul's trial before Felix	"		
24:23-27	St. Paul in prison two years at	"	57	Festus, procurator, 59-63.
25: 1-12	St. Paul accused to Festus. He appeals to Caesar ...	"	59	*St. Luke's Gospel* probably written.
25:13-26:32	St. Paul before Festus and Agrippa	"		
27: 1-44	St. Paul's voyage and shipwreck	Mediterranean	Sept. 59	
28: 1-10	St. Paul on the Island of Malta	"	60	Nero murders Agrippina.
28:11-29	St. Paul at Rome: Conference with the Jews	Rome		
28:30, 31	Paul a prisoner in his own hired house at .... *Colossians, Philemon, Ephesians*	" "	61, 62	Rebellion of Boadicea in Britain.
	Philippians .... Close of the history in the *Acts*	"		Boadicea defeated by Suetonius about 62.
	Probable composition of Acts	Rome	62-68	
	First trial. Release	"	63	
	James		62 or earlier	Great earthquake at Pompeii.
	Hebrews (?)			
	Goes to Asia by way of Macedonia			
	Sails with Titus to Crete and returns to Ephesus			Great Fire of Rome, ascribed by Nero to the Christians, July 19, 64.
	Leaving Timothy goes by Philippi to Corinth			
	1, 2, Peter		58-64	
	1 Timothy. Titus			
	Journey to Spain (?)			

	Winters at Nicopolis			
	Journey to Dalmatia (?) and through Macedonia to Troas			
	Martyrdom of St. Peter		65	
	St. Paul's second arrest. Sent to Rome		66	
	Trial before Emperor		....	Jewish war begins.
	2 Timothy .... Rome			Massacre by Florus at
	Martyrdom of St. Paul .. "		66 or 67	Jerusalem.
	Destruction of Jerusalem		Aug. 70	Repulse of Cestius
	Jude. 1, 2, 3, John			Gallus.

MIRACLES OF THE EARLY CHURCH
IN THE BOOK OF ACTS

Gift of tongues at Pentecost	Acts 2: 1-14
Healing of the lame man at the Temple gate by Peter and John	" 3: 1-11
Death of Ananias and Sapphira at the word of Peter........................	" 5: 1-11
Numerous acts of healing at Jerusalem by all the apostles..................	" 5:12-16
Opening of the prison doors to the apostles................................	" 5:17-25
Cases of healing in Samaria by Philip the Deacon..........................	" 8:6,7,13
Cure of Aeneas at Lydda by Peter...	" 9:32-35
Raising of Dorcas at Joppa by Peter......................................	" 9:36-41
Deliverance of Peter from prison in Jerusalem..............................	" 12: 5-17
Blindness of Elymas, at Cyprus, at the word of Paul.......................	" 13: 9-11
Healing of impotent man at Lystra by Paul.................................	" 14: 8-12
Cure of possessed girl at Philippi by Paul..................................	" 16:16-18
Numerous miracles of healing by Paul.....................................	" 19:11,12
Raising of Eutychus at Troas by Paul.....................................	" 20: 7-12
Cure of Pubilus and others at Malta by Paul................................	" 28: 7-10

MOUNTAINS OF THE BIBLE

Abrim, east of Jordan	Nu 27:12	Horeb,See Sinai	Ex 3:1
Ararat, in eastern part of mod. Turkey	Gn 8:4	Lebanon, in mod. Lebanon	Dt 3:25
Bashan, north of Gilead	Ps 68:15	Mizar, not positively identified	Ps 42:6
Carmel, on seacoast of Palestine	I K 18:19	Moriah, in Jerusalem	Gn 22:2
Ebal, in Samaria	Dt 11:29	Nebo, opposite Jericho, 12 miles W. of Dead Sea	Dt 32:49
Ephriam, central Palestine	Jsh 17:15	Olives or Olivet, east of Jerusalem	Mt 21:1
Gerizim, in Samaria	Dt 11:29		
Gilboa, where Saul died	I S 28:4	Pigsgah, in Moabite plateau	Nu 21:20
Gilead, north of Dead Sea	Gn 31:21	Seir, S W of Dead Sea	Gn 14:6
Halak, 30 miles S W of Dead Sea	Jsh 11:17; 12:7	Sinai, where Moses received Law	Ex 16:1
Hermon, in Anti-Lebanon range	Dt 3:8	Tabor, in Plain of Jezreel	Jg 4:6
		Zion or Sion, where	
Hor, Aaron's burial place	Nu 20:22	Jerusalem is located	2 S 5:7

MESSIANIC PROPHECIES OF THE OLD TESTAMENT
AND THEIR NEW TESTAMENT FULFILLMENT IN CHRIST

PROPHECY	O.T. REF.	N.T. FULFILLMENT
Seed of the woman	Gn 3.15	Gl 4.4 He 2.14
Through Noah's sons	Gn 9.27	Lk 6:36
Seed of Abraham	Gn 12.3	Mt 1.1 Gl 3.8 Gl 3.16
Seed of Isaac	Gn 17.19	Ro 9.7 He 11.18
Blessing to nations	Gn 18.18	Gl 3.8
Seed of Isaac	Gn 21.12	Ro 9.7 He 11.18
Blessing to Gentiles	Gn 22.18	Gl 3.8 Gl 3.16 He 6.14
Blessing to Gentiles	Gn 26.4	Gl 3.8 Gl 3.16 He 6.14
Blessing through Abraham	Gn 28.14	Gl 3.8 Gl 3.16 He 6.14
Of the tribe of Judah	Gn 49.10	Rv 5.5
No bone broken	Ex 12.46	Jn 19.36
Blessing to firstborn son	Ex 13.2	Lk 2.23
No bone broken	Nu 9.12	Jn 19.36
Serpent in wilderness	Nu 21.8,9	Jn 3.14,15
A star out of Jacob	Nu 24.17-19	Mt 2.2 Lk 1.33,78 Rv 22.16
As a prophet	Dt 18.15,18,19	Jn 6.14 Jn 7.40 Ac 3.22,23
Cursed on the tree	Dt 21.13	Gl 3.13
The throne of David established forever	2 S 7.12,13,16,25,26 1 Ch 17-11-14,23-27 2 Ch 21.7	Mt 19.28 Mt 21.4 Mt 25.31 Mk 12.37 Lk 1.32 Jn 7.4 Ac 2.30 Ac 13.23 Ro 1.3,2 Tm 2.8 He 1.5,8 He 8.1 He 12.2 Rv 22.1
A promised redeemer	Jb 19.25-27	Jn 5.28,29 Gl 4.4 Ep 1.7,11,14
Declared to be the Son of God	Ps 2.1-12	Mt 3.17 Mk 1.11 Ac 4.25,26 Ac 13.33 He 1.5 He 5.5 Rv 2.26,27 Rv 19.15,16
His resurrection	Ps 16.8-10	Ac 2.27 Ac 13.35 Ac 26.23
Hands and feet pierced	Ps 22.1-31	Mt 27.31 Mt 27.35,36
Mocked and insulted		Mt 27.39-43 Mt 27.45-49
Soldiers cast lots for coat		Mk 15.20,24,25,34 Lk 19.24 Lk 23.35 Jn 19.15-18,23,24,34 Ac 2.23,24
Accused by false witnesses	Ps 27.12	Mt 26.60,61
He commits His spirit	Ps 31.5	Lk 23.46
No bone broken	Ps 34.20	Jn 19.36
Accused by false witnesses	Ps 35.11	Mt 26.59-61 Mk 14.57,58
Hated without reason	Ps 35.19	Jn 15.24,25
Friends stand afar off	Ps 38.11	Mt 27.55 Mk 15.40 Lk 23.49
"I come to do thy will"	Ps 40.6-8	He 10.5-9
Betrayed by a friend	Ps 41.9	Mt 26.14-16,47,50 Mk 14.17-21 Lk 22.19-23 Jn 13.18,19
Known for righteousness	Ps 45.2,6,7	He 1.8,9
His resurrection	Ps 49.15	Mk 16.6
Betrayed by a friend	Ps 55.12-14	Jn 13.18
His ascension	Ps 68.18	Ep 4.8
Hated without reason	Ps 69.4	Jn 15.25
Stung by reproaches	Ps 69.9	Jn 2.17 Ro 15.3
Given gall and vinegar	Ps 69.21	Mt 27.34,48 Mk 15.23 Lk 23.36 Jn 19.29
Exalted by God	Ps 72-1-19	Mt 2.2 Php 2.9-11 He 1.8

MESSIANIC PROPHECIES OF THE OLD TESTAMENT
AND THEIR NEW TESTAMENT FULFILLMENT IN CHRIST

PROPHECY	O.T. REF.	N.T. FULFILLMENT
He speaks in parables	Ps 78.2	Mt 13.34,35
Seed of David exalted	Ps 89.3,4,19,27-29, 35-37	Lk 1.32 Ac 2.30 Ac 13.23 Ro 1.3 2 Tm 2.8
Son of Man comes in glory	Ps 102.16	Lk 21.24,27 Rv 12.5-10
"Thou remainest"	Ps 102.24-27	He 1.10-12
Prays for His enemies	Ps 109.4	Lk 23.34
Another to succeed Judas	Ps 109,7,8	Ac 1.16-20
A priest like Melchizedek	Ps 110.1-7	Mt 22.41-45 Mt 26.64 Mk 12.35-37 Mk 16.19 Ac 7.56 Ep 1.20 Cl 1.20 He 1.13 He 2.8 He 5.6 He 6.20 He 7.21 He 8.1 He 10.11-13 He 12.2
The chief corner stone	Ps 118.22,23	Mt 21.42 Mk 12.10,11 Lk 20.17 Jn 1.11 Ac 4.11 Ep 2.20 1 P 2.4
The King comes in the name of the Lord	Ps 118.26	Mt 21.9 Mt 23.39 Mk 11.9 Lk 13.35 Lk 19.38 Jn 12.13
David's seed to reign	Ps 132.11 c.f. 2 S 7.12,13,16, 25,26,29	
Declared to be the Son of God	Pr 30.4	Mt 3.17 Mk 14.61,62 Lk 1.35 Jn 3.13 Jn 9.35-38 Jn 11.21 Ro 1.2-4 Ro 10.6-9 2 P 1.17
Repentance for the nations	Is 2.2-4	Lk 24.47
Hearts are hardened	Is 6.9,10	Mt 13.14,15 Jn 12.39,40 Ac 28.25-27
Born of a virgin	Is 7.14	Mt 1.22,23
A rock of offense	Is 8.14,15	Ro 9.33 1 P 2.8
Light out of darkness	Is 9.1,2	Mt 4.14-16 Lk 2.32
God with us	Is 9.6,7	Mt 1.21,23 Lk 1.32,33 Jn 8.58 Jn 10.30 Jn 14.19 2 Co 5.19 Cl 2.9
Full of wisdom and power	Is 11.1-10	Mt 3.16 Jn 3.34 Ro 15.12 He 1.9
Reigning in mercy	Is 16.4,5	Lk 1.31-33
Nail in a sure place	Is 22.21-25	Rv 3.7
Death swallowed up in victory	Is 25.6-12	1 Co 15.54
A stone in Zion	Is 28.16	Ro 9.33 1 P 2.6
The deaf hear, the blind see	Is 29.18,19	Mt 5.3 Mt 11.5 Jn 9.39
King of kings, Lord of lords	Is 32.1-4	Rv 19.16 Rv 20.6
Son of the Highest	Is 33.22	Lk 1.32 1 Tm 1.17 1 Tm 6.15
Healing for the needy	Is 35.4-10	Mt 9.30 Mt 11.5 Mt 12.22 Mt 20.34 Mt 21.14 Mk 7.30 Jn 5.9
Prepare ye the way of the Lord	Is 40.3-5	Mt 3.3 Mk 1.3 Lk 3.4,5 Jn 1.23
The Shepherd dies for His Sheep	Is 40.10,11	Jn 10.11 He 13.20 1 P 2.24,25
The Meek Servant	Is 42.1-16	Mt 12.17-21 Lk 2.32
A light to the Gentiles	Is 49.6-12	Ac 13.47 2 Co 6.2

585

MESSIANIC PROPHECIES OF THE OLD TESTAMENT
AND THEIR NEW TESTAMENT FULFILLMENT IN CHRIST

PROPHECY	O.T. REF.	N.T. FULFILLMENT
Scorged and spat upon	Is 50.6	Mt 26,67 Mt 27.26,30
		Mk 14.65 Mk 15.15,19
		Lk 22.63-65 Jn 19.1
Rejected by His people	Is 52.13-53.1-12	Mt 8.17 Mt 27.1,2,12-14,38
Suffered vicariously		Mk 15.3,4,27,28 Lk 23.1-25,
Silent when accused		32-34 Jn 1.29 Jn 11.49-52
Crucified with transgressors		Jn 12.37,38 Ac 8.28-35
Buried with the rich		Ac 10.43 Ac 13.38,39
		1 Co 15.3 Ep 1.7 1 P 2.21-25
		1 Jn 1.7,9
Calling of those "not a people"	Is 55.4,5	Jn 18.37 Ro 9.25,26 Rv 1.5
Deliverer out of Zion	Is 59.16-20	Ro 11.26,27
Nations walk in the light	Is 60.1-3	Lk 2.32
Annoited to preach liberty	Is 61.1-3	Lk 4.17-19 Ac 10.38
Called by a new name	Is 62.1,2	Lk 2.32 Rv 3.12
Thy King cometh	Is 62.11	Mt 21.5
A vesture dipped in blood	Is 63.1-3	Rv 19.13
Afflicted with the afflicted	Is 63.8,9	Mt 25.34-40
The elect shall inherit	Is 65.9	Ro 11.5,7 He 7.14 Rv 5.5
New heavens and new earth	Is 65.17-25	2 P 3.13 Rv 21.1
The Lord our righteousness	Jr 23.5,6	Jn 2.19-21 Ro 1.3,4 Ep 2.20,21
		1 P 2.5
Born a King	Jr 30.9	Jn 18.37 Rv 1.5
Massacre of infants	Jr 31.15	Mt 2.17,18
Conceived by the Holy Spirit	Jr 31.22	Mt 1.20 Lk 1.35
A New Covenant	Jr 31.31-34	Mt 26.27-29 Mk 14.22-24
		Lk 22.15-20 1 Co 11.25
		He 8.8-12 He 10.15-17
		He 12.24 He 13.20
A spiritual house	Jr 33.15-17	Jn 2.19-21 Ep 2.20,21
		1 P 2.5
A tree planted by God	Ezk 17.22-24	Mt 13.31,32
The humble exalted	Ezk 21.26,27	Lk 1.52
The good Shepherd	Ezk 34.23,24	Jn 10.11
Stone cut without hands	Dn 2.34,35	Ac 4.10-12
His Kingdom triumphant	Dn 2.44,45	Lk 1.33 1 Co 15.24 Rv 11.15
An everlasting dominion	Dn 7.13,14	Mt 24.30 Mt 25.31 Mt 26.64
		Mk 14.61,62 Ac 1.9-11 Rv 1.7
Kingdom for the saints	Dn 7.27	Lk 1.33 1 Co 15.24 Rv 11.15
Time of His birth	Dn 9.24-27	Mt 24.15-21 Mt 27.30
		Lk 3.1
Israel restored	Ho 3.5	Jn 18.37 Ro 11.25-27
Flight into Egypt	Ho 11.1	Mt 2.15
Promise of the Spirit	Jl 2.28-32	Ac 2.17-21 Ro 10.13
The sun darkened	Am 8.9	Mt 24.29 Ac 2.20 Rv 6.12
Restoration of Tabernacle	Am 9.11,12	Ac 15.16-18
Israel regathered	Mi 2.12,13	Jn 10.14,26
The Kingdom established	Mi 4.1-8	Lk 1.33
Born in Bethlehem	Mi 5.1-5	Mt 2.1 Lk 2.4,10,11
Earth filled with knowledge of the glory of the Lord	Hk 2.14	Ro 11.26 Rv 21.23-26

MESSIANIC PROPHECIES OF THE OLD TESTAMENT
AND THEIR NEW TESTAMENT FULFILLMENT IN CHRIST

PROPHECY	O.T. REF.	N.T. FULFILLMENT
The Lamb on the Throne	Zc 2.10-13	Rv 5.13 Rv 6.9 Rv 21.24 Rv 22.1-5
A holy priesthood	Zc 3.8	Jn 2.19-21 Ep 2.20,21 1 P 2.5
A heavenly High Priest	Zc 6.12,13	He 4.4 He 8.1,2
Triumphal entry	Zc 9.9,10	Mt 21.4,5 Mk 11.9,10 Lk 20.38 Jn 12.13-15
Sold for 30 pieces of silver Money buys potter's field	Zc 11.12,13	Mt 26.14,15 Mt 27.9
Piercing of his body	Zc 12.10	Jn 19.34,37
Shepherd smitten—sheep scattered	Zc 13.1,6,7	Mt 26.31 Jn 16.32
Preceded by forerunner	Ml 3.1	Mt 11.10 Mk 1.2 Lk 7.27
Our sins purged	Ml 3.3	He 1.3
The light of the world	Ml 4.2,3	Lk 1.78 Jn 1.9 Jn 12.46 2 P 1.19 Rv 2.28 Rv 19.11-16 Rv 22.16
The coming of Elijah	Ml 4.5,6	Mt 11.14 Mt 17.10-12

Heaven and Earth
Light
Firmament
Sun, Moon and Stars
Fish
Fowl
Beast
Cattle
Creeping Things
Man
Man's Dominion
—Genesis 1.

Garden of Eden
Tree of Knowledge
Making of Woman
—Genesis 2.

The Ten Commandments.
—Exodus 20:3
—Deuteronomy 5:7
—Deuteronomy 6:5
—Deuteronomy 10:12

Jesus' Commandments.
—Matthew 22:37
—Mark 12:28
—John 13:34
—John 14:15
—John 15:12
—Luke 10:27

The Fall of Man.
—Genesis 3:6

The Serpent Deceives Eve.
—Genesis 3:1

Mankind's Punishment and Loss of
Paradise.
—Genesis 3:16

Cain Slays Abel.
—Genesis 4:8

Genealogy.
—Genesis 5:1

Noah's Ark.
—Genesis 6:14

The Flood.
—Genesis 7:17

The Rainbow.
—Genesis 9:13

Tower of Babel.
—Genesis 11:3

Confusion of Tongues.
—Genesis 11:5

Abram Goes into Egypt.
—Genesis 12:1

Hagar.
—Genesis 16:1

Abram's Name Changed to Abraham.
—Genesis 17:5

Sodom and Gomorrah Destroyed.
—Genesis 19:24

Lot's Wife.
—Genesis 19:26

Abraham Asked to Offer Isaac.
—Genesis 22:1

Esau Sells Birthright to Jacob.
—Genesis 25:29

Jacob's Ladder.
—Genesis 28:12

Jacob Works Seven Years Each for Rachel
and Leah.
—Genesis 29:18

Jacob's Scheme to Become Rich.
—Genesis 30:37

Jacob's Name Changed to Israel.
—Genesis 35:10

Joseph's Coat of Many Colors.
—Genesis 37:3

Joseph Sold into Egypt.
—Genesis 37:28

Joseph Cast in Prison.
—Genesis 39:20

Joseph Interprets Pharaoh's Dream.
—Genesis 41:25

Joseph's Brothers Come to Buy Corn in Egypt.
—Genesis—Chaps. 42, 43, 44, 45, 46

Enoch Walks with God.
—Genesis 5:24

Methuselah—Oldest Man.
—Genesis 5:27

Birth of Moses.
—Exodus 2:1

God Appears in Burning Bush.
—Exodus 3:2

God Sends Moses to Deliver Israel out of Egypt.
—Exodus 3:9

Rod Turned into Serpent.
—Exodus 4:3

Moses Slow of Speech.
—Exodus 4:10

Moses Smites Rock and Water Flows.
—Exodus 17:5

The Plagues upon Pharaoh.
—Exodus 7, 8, 9, 10, 11

The Passover is Instituted.
—Exodus 12:3

Passage of the Red Sea.
—Exodus 14:22

Pharaoh's Army Drowned.
—Exodus 14:26

God Feeds Children of Israel with Manna.
—Exodus 16:14

God Appeared to Moses on the Mount.
—Exodus 19:3

Thunders and Lightnings upon the Mount.
—Exodus 19:16

The Lord Descends on Mount Sinai in Fire.
—Exodus 19:18

Moses' Law and Ordinances Clean Meat, Fowl, Fish, etc.
Leviticus
—Chapters 11, 17, 18, 19, 20, 21, 22, 23, 24, 25
Exodus—Chapters 21, 22, 23
Deuteronomy—Chapters 14, 22, 23, 24, 25

Laws of Body Purification.
—Leviticus 12, 13, 14, 15

Golden Calf.
—Exodus 32:1

Scape Goat.
—Leviticus 16:20

"I have trodden the winepress alone . . ."
—Isaiah 63:3

Balaam.
—Numbers 10:1

Silver Trumpet.
—Numbers 10:1

Tithing.
—Deuteronomy 14:22

God Gives Moses Two Tables of Testimony.
—Exodus 31:18

Moses Breaks the Two Tables.
—Exodus 32:15

The Two Tables Renewed.
—Exodus 34:1
—Deuteronomy 10:1

Songs of Moses.
—Deuteronomy—Chapters 32-33

Moses' Death and Burial.
—Deuteronomy 34:5

Joshua Succeeds Moses.
—Joshua 1:1

Waters of Jordan Divided.
—Joshua 3:14

Stones Taken from Midst of Jordan.
—Joshua 4:1

Manna Ceaseth.

—Joshua 5:12

"For the place whereon Thou Standest is Holy."

—Joshua 5:15

—Exodus 3:5

Sun and Moon Stand Still.

—Joshua 10:12

Joshua's Death and Burial.

—Joshua 24:29

The Song of Deborah and Barak.

—Judges 5:1

Birth of Samson.

—Judges 13:24

Samson's Riddle.

—Judges—Chapter 14

Samson Slays Philistines.

—Judges 15:15

Delilah Entices Samson.

—Judges 16:4

Samson's Death.

—Judges 16:30

Ruth and Naomi.

—Ruth 1:16

How the Word of the Lord was First Revealed to Samuel.

—I Samuel 3:1

An Angel Destroys the Host of the Assyrians.

—II Chronicles 32:21

Rebuilding the Wall of Jerusalem.

—Nehemiah—Chapters 2, 3, 4, 5, 6

David Slays Goliath.

—I Samuel 17:12

David and Jonathan.

—I Samuel 20:1

David Spares Saul's Life.

—I Samuel 24:7

David's Lamentation.

—II Samuel 1:17

Uriah's Wife.

—II Samuel 11:2

Parable of Ewe Lamb.

—II Samuel 12:1

Solomon is Born.

—II Samuel 12:24

Absalom Slays Amnon.

—II Samuel 13:29

Seven of Saul's Sons Hanged.

—II Samuel 21:1

Solomon Succeeds David.

—I Kings 2:1

Solomon's Prayer for Wisdom.

—I Kings 3:5

Solomon's Temple.

—I Kings—Chapters 6, 7, 8

God's Covenant with Solomon.

—I Kings 9:1

Queen of Sheba Visits Solomon.

—I Kings 10

—II Chronicles 9

Solomon's Wives and Concubines.

—I Kings 11:1

Solomon's Death.

—I Kings 11:41

Elijah Fed by Ravens.

—I Kings 17:4

Elijah Raises Widow's Son from Dead.

—I Kings 17:17

Elijah Proves the True God.

—I Kings 18:19

God Appears to Elijah under Juniper Tree.

—I Kings 19:4

Baal's Prophets Slain.

—I Kings 18:40

Elijah Twice Orders Fire from Heaven.
—II Kings 1:5

Elijah Divides Jordan.
—II Kings 2:8

Elijah Taken up by a Fiery Chariot.
—II Kings 2:11

Elisha Divides Jordan.
—II Kings 2:14

Elisha Heals the Waters.
—II Kings 2:21

Elisha Obtains Water.
—II Kings 3:16

Elisha Multiplies the Widow's Oil.
—II Kings 4:1

Elisha Raises the Shunammite's Son.
—II Kings 4:34

Elisha Heals Deadly Pottage and Feeds a Multitude.
—II Kings 4:38

Elisha's Death.
—II Kings 13:20

Jehoshaphat's Prayer and Overthrow of his Enemies.
—II Chronicles 20

Queen Vashti and Queen Esther.
—Esther 1

Haman's Treason and Hanging.
—Esther 3, 4, 5, 6, 7

Job and his Afflictions.
—Book of Job

The Resurrection of Dry Bones.
—Ezekiel 37

Jonah Swallowed by the Great Fish.
—Jonah—Chapters 1, 2

Nebuchadnezzar's Dream Revealed to Daniel and Interpreted.
—Daniel—Chapters 1, 2, 3, 4

The Three Hebrew Children Cast into the Fiery Furnace.
—Daniel 3:21

Belshazzar's Feast; the Handwriting on the Wall, etc.
—Daniel—Chapter 5

Daniel Cast into Lion's Den.
—Daniel 6:16

Daniel's Prayer.
—Daniel 9:15

"Delight thyself also in the Lord; and He shall give thee the desires of thine heart."
—Psalm 37:4

"Trust in the Lord with all thine heart; and lean not unto thine own understanding."
—Proverbs 3:5

"In all thy ways acknowledge Him, and He shall direct thy paths."
—Proverbs 3:6

"Wisdom is the principal thing; therefore get wisdom; and with all thy getting get understanding."
—Proverbs 4:7

Genealogy of Jesus.
—Matthew 1:1
—Luke 3:23

Birth of Jesus.
—Matthew 1:18
—Luke 2:6

Jesus Wrapped in Swaddling Clothes and Laid in a Manger.
—Luke 2:7, 12

The Wise Men Directed by Star.
—Matthew 2:1

Jesus Baptized.
—Matthew 3:13
—Mark 1:9
—Luke 3:21

Jesus' Coat without Seam.
—John 19:23

Soldiers Cast Lots for Jesus Garments.
—Matthew 27:35
—Mark 15:24
—John 19:24
—Luke 23:34

Pool of Siloam.
—John 9:7

Pool of Bethesda.
—John 5:3

Jesus Tempted by Satan.
—Matthew 4:3
—Mark 1:13
—Luke 4:3

Jesus Begins to Preach and Heal.
—Matthew 4:17
—Luke 4:14

Jesus' Teachings

The Beatitudes.
—Matthew 5:1

The Lord's Prayer.
—Matthew 6:9
—Luke 11:2

The Sermon on the Mount.
—Matthew—Chapters 5, 6, 7
—Luke 6:20

Jesus' Commandments.
—Matthew 22:37
—Mark 12:28
—John 13:34
—John 14:15
—John 15:12
—Luke 10:27

"God is a Spirit. . . ."
—John 4:24

Jesus' First Miracle.
—John 2:1

Jesus at the Age of Twelve Astonishes all Hearers.
—Luke 2:47

Nicodemus Visits Jesus at Night.
—John 3:2

"Remember Lot's Wife".
—Luke 17:32

Of Divorcement and Marriage.
—Matthew 19:3
—Mark 10:2

Widow's Mite.
—Mark 12:42
—Luke 21:2

The Unmerciful Servant.
—Matthew 18:23

How to Attain Eternal Life.
—Matthew 19:16

Jesus Foretells His Death and Resurrection.
—John 2:19

Conspiracy Against Jesus.
—Matthew 26:1
—Mark 14:1
—Luke 22:1

Gives Sight to Blind.
—Matthew 9:28
—Matthew 20:30
—Mark 10:46
—Luke 18:35
—Mark 8:22

Overthrows Tables of Money Changers.
—Matthew 21:12
—Luke 19:45
—John 2:15

Tribute to be Paid to Caesar.
—Matthew 22:15
—Mark 12:13
—Luke 20:20

Signs of Christ's Coming to Judgment.
—Matthew 24:29
—Mark 13:26
—Revelation 1:7

Cleanses the Leper.
—Matthew 8:1
—Mark 1:40
—Luke 5:12

Heals Palsy.
—Matthew 9:2
—Mark 2:3
—Luke 5:18

Stills the Sea Tempest.

    —Matthew 8:24

    —Mark 4:35

    —Luke 8:23

Casts out Devils.

    —Matthew 8:28

    —Mark 5:1

    —Luke 8:27

Raises Jairus' Daughter from Dead.

    —Matthew 9:23

    —Mark 5:35

    —Luke 8:49

Heals Blind and Dumb.

    —Matthew 12:22

    —Mark 3:11

    —Luke 11:14

Heals Sick by Touch of Hem of Garment.

    —Matthew 14:34

    —Mark 6:56

    —Luke 8:44

Heals Canaanite's Daughter also Lame, Blind, Dumb.

    —Matthew 15:21

    —Mark 7:24

Lunatic Healed.

    —Matthew 17:14

    —Mark 9:14

    —Luke 9:37

Jesus Feeds Five Thousand with Five Loaves and Two Fishes.

    —Matthew 14:15

    —Mark 6:36

    —Luke 9:12

    —John 6:5

Feeds Four Thousand with Seven Loaves and a Few Fish.

    —Matthew 15:32

    —Mark 8:1

Pays Tribute with Money Taken from Mouth of Fish.

    —Matthew 17:27

How Often to Forgive.

    —Matthew 18:21

Jesus Names Twelve Apostles and Sends Them out to Do Miracles.

    —Matthew 10:1

    —Luke 6:12

    — Mark 3:13

    —Luke 9:1

Description of the Last Judgment.

    —Matthew 25:31

Judas Betrays Jesus.

    —Matthew 26:14

    —Mark 14:10

    —Luke 22:3

    —John 13:2

    —John 18:1

Jesus Denied by Peter.

    —Matthew 26:69

    —Luke 22:55

    —Mark 14:66

    —John 18:16

Parables

Parable of the Prodigal Son.

    —Luke 15:11

Parable of Pieces of Silver.

    —Luke 15:8

Parable of the Marriage of the King's Son.

    —Matthew 22:2

    —Luke 14:16

Parable of the Ten Virgins.

    —Matthew 25:1

Parable of the Talents.

    —Matthew 25:14

    —Luke 19:12

Parable of the Sower and the Seed.

    —Matthew 13:1

    —Mark 4:14

    —Luke 8:11

Parable of the Tares.

    —Matthew 13:24

Parable of the Mustard Seed.

    —Matthew 13:31

    —Mark 4:30

    —Luke 13:18

Parable of the Lost Sheep.

—Luke 15:4

—Matthew 18:12

John the Baptist Born.

—Luke 1:57

John the Baptist Sends his Disciples to Jesus.

—Matthew 11:2

—Luke 7:18

John the Baptist Beheaded.

—Matthew 14:10

—Mark 6:27

People's Opinion of Jesus.

—Matthew 16:13

Jesus Foretells His Death and Betrayal.

—Mark 10:32

—Luke 18:31

—Matthew 20:17

Jesus' Transfiguration.

—Matthew 17:1

—Mark 9:2

—Luke 9:28

Miraculous Draught of Fish.

—Luke 5:4

—John 21:6

Heals Centurion's Servant.

—Luke 7:1

Raises Widow's Son.

—Luke 7:11

Infirm Woman Healed.

—Luke 13:11

Heals Dropsy.

—Luke 14:2

Heals Ten Lepers.

—Luke 17:11

Jesus Restores Sight to Man Born Blind.

—John 9:1

Jesus Raises Lazarus.

—John 11:1

Delivers the Woman Taken in Adultery.

—John 8:1

Mary Anoints Jesus' Feet.

—John 12:3

Jesus Washes His Disciples' Feet.

—John 13:5

Jesus Eats the Passover.

—Matthew 26:17

—Mark 14:12

—Luke 22:7

Jesus Prays in the Garden.

—Matthew 26:36

—Luke 22:39

—John 18:1

—Mark 14:32

Jesus Delivered to Pilate.

—Matthew 27:2

—Mark 15:1

—Luke 23:1

—John 18:28

Jesus Gives Apostles Power over Unclean Spirits.

—Luke 9:1

—Mark 6:7

—Mark 3:14

—Matthew 10:1

Jesus Sends Seventy Disciples out to Heal.

—Luke 10:1

Story of the Rich Man and Lazarus.

—Luke 16:19

Zacchaeus Climbed Sycamore Tree.

—Luke 19:4

Jesus Turns Water into Wine.

(*His First Miracle*).—John 2:1

Jesus Talks with a Woman of Samaria.

—John 4:7

Jesus Walks on the Sea.

—John 6:19

"Jesus Wept."

—John 11:35

Jesus Heals the Withered Hand.

  —Luke 6:6
  —Mark 3:1
—Matthew 12:9

Issue of Blood Healed.

  —Mark 5:25
  —Luke 8:43
—Matthew 9:20

Legions of Devils Cast Out.

  —Mark 5:9
  —Luke 8:26
—Matthew 8:28

Bartimaeus Receives Sight.

  —Mark 10:46

Heals One Diseased for Thirty-Eight Years.
  —John 5:5

Judas Hangs Himself.

  —Matthew 27:5

Potter's Field Bought with Thirty Pieces of Silver for which Judas Betrayed Jesus.
  —Matthew 27:7

Peter Cuts off Malchus' Ear.

  —John 18:10
—Matthew 26:51
  —Luke 22:49

Jesus Crucified, Buried, etc.

  —Matthew 27
  —Mark 15
  —Luke 23
  —John 19

Jesus' Resurrection.

  —Matthew 28
  —Luke 24
  —Mark 16
  —John 20

Jesus' Legs Not Broken.

  —John 19:33

Jesus' Garments Divided.

  —John 19:23
—Matthew 27:35
  —Mark 15:24
  —Luke 23:34

Jesus Appears Thru Closed Doors.
  —John 20:26
  —John 20:19

Jesus Appears to Women After Death.
  —Matthew 28:9
  —Mark 16:9
  —John 20:14

Jesus Appears to Disciples After Death.
  —Matthew 28:16
  —Mark 16:14
  —Luke 24:36
  —John 20:19

Jesus Appears to Two Disciples After Death.
  —Mark 16:12
  —Luke 24:13

Jesus Appears to Disciples Third Time and Ascends.
  —John 21:14
  —Luke 24:51

Doubting Thomas.

  —John 20:24

Lame Man Healed by Peter.

  —Acts 3:6

The Apostles Imprisoned.

  —Acts 5:18

Saul's Conversion.

  —Acts 9:4

Peter Heals Aeneas.

  —Acts 9:34

Peter Raises the Dead.

  —Acts 9:40

Peter Delivered from Prison by an Angel.
  —Acts 12:7

Ananias and Sapphira.

  —Acts 5:1

Saul Called Paul.

  —Acts 13:9

Paul Heals a Cripple.

  —Acts 14:8

Paul Stoned.

—Acts 14:19

Paul and Silas Imprisoned.

—Acts 16:19

Paul Pleads his Cause.

—Acts 23:1

Law of Marriage.

—I Corinthians 7

Spiritual Gifts, etc.

—I Corinthians 12

"O death, where is thy sting. . . ."

—I Corinthians 15:55

"God is love. . . ."

—I John 4:16

LAST THINGS

AT TIMES BELIEVERS CAN DIFFER

Even believing Christians have often differed over the interpretation of verses which prophesy of events which will end this age. This should not surprise us, as such a situation is itself indicated in Scripture. Thus Christ, in speaking of the time of His second coming, says, ". . . knoweth no man . . ." (Matt. 24:36), "ye know not" (v. 42), and "an hour as ye think not" (v. 44; 25:13). The emphases of the Bible are that (1) God's prophetic plan for the ages will indeed come true; (2) people should make certain that they are prepared for Christ's return.

SIX APPROACHES TO THE BOOK OF REVELATION

One of the basic items of controversy has been the mode of interpretation of the Book of Revelation. The following are the major schemes which have been applied to it: (1) *Modernistic Approach*—here unbelievers have outright denied either that John the apostle wrote the book, or that predictive knowledge of the future is even possible; (2) *Allegorical Approach*—some have said that it is a hidden mystery book of symbols—a partial truth—and that buried beneath its words are secret coded messages about Greek philosophy; (3) *Preterite Approach*—advocates here see the Beast of Revelation chapter 13 as Nero and the entire book John's secret way of criticizing the Roman Empire of the first century A.D.; (4) *Historical Approach*—this view lines up the seven seals, seven trumpets, and seven bowls, and all events of chapters 6-19 into World History from A.D. 30 to the end of this age. Revelation becomes a history book of THIS AGE penned in advance. This is a grand scheme, but has been abandoned by almost every living believer simply because the events of past history do not fit Revelation's descriptions, either literally or figuratively; (5) *Topical Approach*—As in the previous view, here it is again maintained that the Book of Revelation is a history book of THIS AGE. Here, however, it is urged that only a "moderate concordance" be pressed, i.e., don't try to push hard to line up historic events with Bible chapters, rather see the various episodes of the Revelation as merely indicating in general terms that God's good will triumph over evil during this age; (6) *Futuristic Approach*—This view, held by the majority of believers today, sees the Book of Revelation as describing a yet future final period of world struggle, wherein Antichrist and his empire (the "Beast" of chapter 13) dominates the world for 3½ years out of a 7 year final period (Rev. 13:5; Dan. 9:27). Christ, at His glorious second coming, destroys the Antichrist at Armageddon and takes over at last the reign of His world (Rev. 16:16; 19:11f).

THREE MILLENNIAL VIEWS

Long debates have been held on the millennial question. *Millennium* means "thousand years" and refers to the six references in Revelation 20 which describe the period when Satan is bound and Christ and His saints rule on earth. The major views on this question are three: (1) *Postmillennial View*—There are only a few alive who hold this today; but the writer did himself recently hear a most learned believer defend it. It advocates that the second coming of Christ to earth will occur *post*, after, the blessed 1000 years described in Revelation 20. *The gospel message will convert the masses of this world* before the end of this age, and as a result of this world conversion to Christianity the 1000 golden years of the earth will take place. At the close of this the King will arrive to a waiting and worshipping redeemed world of saints. (2) *Amillennial View*—This view is especially popular in certain sections of the U.S. and among certain denominations. In Greek "A" as a prefix means "no," and thus "a-millennial" means "no millennium in the future." This view denies any future golden age of 1000 years, but rather asserts that *the millennium is taking place now in this present age within the church.* Some of its followers thus prefer to label it as "Realized Millennialism," arguing that the promises of Satan being bound and of the wolf and the lamb dwelling together (Rev. 20; Isa. 11:6) are being realized today. The fallacy here, however, is that Rev. 20:3 describes the millennial age as a period when Satan shall "deceive the nations no more." This simply is not in harmony with either the present condition of the world or with the history of this entire age, despite whatsoever lengthy and erudite defenses are marshalled to the contrary. (3) *The Premillennial View*—holds that indeed Christ must come "before," *pre*, the 1000 years of blessedness and peace because *it is the event of His coming which at last brings about world peace* with Satan's binding (Rev. 19:11f; 20:1f). The events of Revelation 19 and 20, taken in the simple order in which they occur, here yield Christ destroying Antichrist and his armies at Armageddon and then binding Satan and subduing the world to Himself. This accords perfectly with Matt. 24-25, and is thus the view held by the majority of believing prophetic teachers of today.

FOUR RAPTURE VIEWS

The Rapture Question is another subject of controversy. 1 Thess. 4:17 speaks of Christ coming again to "catch up" His church, the believers. The modern word for this taking up of the "bride" (the church) by the "groom" (Christ) is "rapture," from the Latin *rapturo* used in the Latin Vulgate, 430 A.D., to translate the Greek, "*harpadzo*," "caught up" in I Thess. 4:17. The major views as to the time of Christ's coming for his church are: (1) *Post-Tribulation Rapture*—Christ will take His church out of this world at the end of their suffering through, and being martyred in, the final seven year period at the close of this age which will be dominated by Antichrist's persecution (Dan. 9:27; Rev. 13:5). (2) *Mid-Tribulation Rapture*—Christ will arrive at the mid-point of the seven years of tribulation to rescue His church. (3) *Mid-Week Pre-Trib View*—Here it is asserted that Christ does come in the middle of the final seven years of Dan. 9:27, but it is argued that the "tribulation" described in Matt. 24:21, when believers shall suffer, does not begin until the second half of the seven years! (4) *Pre-Tribu-*

lation Rapture—"God hath not appointed us to wrath" (I Thess. 5:9) and the coming of Christ for His Church will be to rescue them before, *pre,* He unlooses His wrath on a sinful world during the final seven years of this age. This is the dominant view of Bible-believing churches today. In any event do note: (a) the biblical emphasis is to be ready, not to figure out dates. "Watch . . . for ye know not what hour your Lord doth come," Matt. 24:42.

FOUR PHASES OF THE SECOND COMING

It may be of assistance to some readers to understand the following suggestion. There is only one Second Coming of Christ. This second coming, however, will embrace many events which I choose to classify into four major sub-events, namely: (1) *the rapture,* or "catching up" of the believers, I Thess. 4:13-18; (2) *the tribulation* seven year period on earth wherein Antichrist rises to a position of world leadership and ruthlessly persecutes all who would believe in Christ and Israel, Dan. 9:27; Rev. 13:5; Rev. 12; (3) *the*

Battle of Armageddon which sees Antichrist's armies assembled in northern Israel to destroy that nation and which battle is ended by the coming of Christ with His saints to (a) destroy the Antichrist "beast," (b) to destroy the False Prophet, and (c) to bind Satan. Rev. 19:11, 14, 20; 20:1-3. And (4) *Christ's setting up of His Millennial Kingdom* described in Rev. 20:1-6; Matt. 25:31-46; Isaiah 11:4-13; Zech. 14.

THINGS NOT REVEALED

One should remember that some things are simply not yet revealed in God's Word . . . "The secret things belong unto the Lord our God: but those things which are revealed belong unto us . . ." (Deut. 29:29). If something is not revealed, then no amount of prayer will show one the answer, except that it is not for our knowing at present. Such details are absent because God chose not to communicate them to us for His good and wise reasons, just as a wise parent withholds information from a child. See John 16:12.

STUDYING BIBLE PROPHECY—
A PREMILLENNIAL, PRETRIBULATION VIEW

SO YOU WANT TO KNOW WHAT THE BIBLE TEACHES ABOUT THE FUTURE!

There is nothing more fascinating than Bible Prophecy! But you must follow the rules of the game!

(1) BE SURE YOU ARE BORN AGAIN (John 3:3; 1 Peter 1:23) through faith in Christ as personal Savior (John 3:16; 1:12; Acts 16:31). We cannot understand the "deep things of God" (1 Cor. 2:9-10) until we enter the Family of God (2 Cor. 6:18). The unsaved man can only view spiritual trust as "foolishness" (1 Cor. 2:14).

(2) NEXT, STUDY YOUR BIBLE IN THE RIGHT ORDER, simple things before difficult, "milk" (1 Pet. 2:2) before "meat" (Heb. 5:12-14). Begin with the Gospel of John (John 20:31) and not with the Book of Revelation. (3) JOIN A GOOD BIBLE CLASS UNDER A COMPETENT TEACHER, for this is God's order (Acts 8:30-31; 2 Tim. 2:2). (4) NEVER FORGET THAT THE HOLY SPIRIT WHO LIVES WITHIN YOU (1 Cor. 3:16) IS YOUR FINAL TEACHER (John 16:12-15). If you are yielded to His control (Eph. 5:18), He will "guide you into all truth" and even "show you things to come." (5) REALIZE THAT, UNLIKE BIBLE HISTORY, THESE EVENTS HAVE NOT YET OCCURRED, so be merciful to those who differ on details or on the order of events (1 Cor. 13:2).

HERE IS THE GENERAL SEQUENCE OF NEW TESTAMENT PROPHECY:

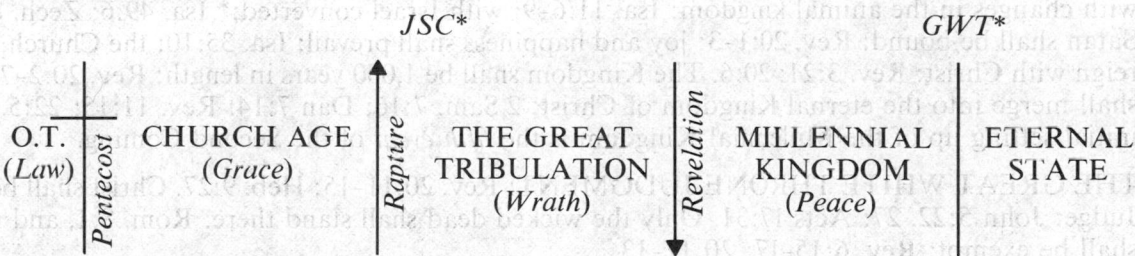

| O.T. (Law) | | CHURCH AGE (Grace) | | JSC* — Rapture | THE GREAT TRIBULATION (Wrath) | Revelation | MILLENNIAL KINGDOM (Peace) | GWT* | ETERNAL STATE |

TO HELP YOUR STUDY, HERE ARE SOME OF THE PRIMARY SCRIPTURES:

1. THE BEGINNING OF THE CHURCH: Matt. 16:18; Acts 2:41-47.

2. SIGNS OF THE END OF THE PRESENT AGE: Matt. 24:3-8; 16:1-3; Apostasy: 2 Pet. 2:1-2; 1 Tim. 4:1-2, Indifference: 2 Pet. 3:3-4. Perplexity of Nations: Luke 21:25. The regathering of Israel: Jer. 30:3; Isa. 43:5-6; Zech. 8:7-8 etc. Immorality and other sins increase: 2 Tim. 3:1-5. Plus other "shadows of the Tribulation" falling across this age: Trend to world government; federation of religious bodies; computerized society, etc.

3. THE RAPTURE ("TAKING UP") OF THE CHURCH: 1 Thes. 4:13-18; 1 Cor. 15:51-52; John 15:3; Titus 2:13 etc. Followed by the *Judgment Seat of Christ:* 2 Cor. 5:10; Rom. 14:10; 1 Cor. 3:12-15; 4:5 and the Marriage Supper of the Lamb: Rev. 19:7-9.
(*The "taking up" of the church—i.e., believers—is actually the *first event* in the Second Coming of Christ program.)

4. THE GREAT TRIBULATION: Its various *names:* Deut. 4:30; Jer. 30:7; Dan. 12:1; Joel 2:1–2; 3:12–14; Zech. 14:1–3; Matt. 24:21; Luke 21:34–36; 1 Thess. 5:1–3; Rev. 3:10; 6:15–16
    Its *duration:* Dan. 9:27 ("week" of years); 12:7; Rev. 12:6, 14; 13:5.
    Its *characteristics:* Church already removed by Rapture: 1 Thes. 1:10; 5:9; Rev. 3:10. The restraining Holy Spirit gone: 2 Thes. 2:7–8 with John 14:16. Satan cast down to earth: Rev. 12:7–10, with great wrath: Rev. 12:12. He will achieve worship: Rev. 13:4. Antichrist to sieze governmental control: Rev. 13:1–9; Dan. 7:24; 8:23–25; 9:27. He will also be worshiped: Rev. 13:14–15. He will be identified by his mark and his number: Rev. 13:16–18. He will be supported by a confederation of ten kings: Rev. 17:12–14. He will be destroyed by Christ at His second coming: Rev. 19:19–20. This is the *second event* in the Second Coming of Christ.

5. THE BATTLE OF ARMAGEDDON: Rev. 16:13–16; 14:14–20; 19:17–18; Zech. 12:11; Joel 3:2. Kings of the Sun Rising march to Armageddon: Rev. 16:12; 9:14–16. Russia's invasion of Israel: Ezek. 38:1–39:24. Note her allies: Ezek. 38:5–6, and the intervention of the Lord God: 38:18–23. This is the *third event* in the Second Coming.

6. THE REVELATION OF CHRIST, coming to judge in power and glory. Isa. 11:11; Zech. 14:4, 9; Matt. 24:27–30; Mark 13:24–26; Luke 21:25–28; Acts 1:11; Col. 3:4; 1 Thess. 3:13; 2 Thess. 1:10; 2:8 Jude 1:14; Rev. 1:7; 11:15; 16:15; 19:11–16; 22:7, 12, 20. This is the *fourth event* in the Second Coming.

7. THE MILLENNIAL KINGDOM: Always linked with the rule of Christ: Dan. 7:13–14; Isa. 9:6–7; Luke 1:30–33. He shall reign over the earth: Zech. 14:9; Matt 6:10; with peace: Isa. 2:3–4; and righteousness: Isa. 11:4–5; Jer. 33:14–17; reigning from Jerusalem: Micah 4:1–2; with changes in the animal kingdom: Isa. 11:6–9; with Israel converted:* Isa. 49:6; Zech. 8:23. Satan shall be bound: Rev. 20:1–3; joy and happiness shall prevail: Isa. 35:10; the Church shall reign with Christ: Rev. 3:21; 20:6. The Kingdom shall be 1,000 years in length: Rev. 20:2–7, but shall merge into the eternal Kingdom of Christ: 2 Sam. 7:16; Dan 7:14; Rev. 11:15; 22:5. The initial setting up of the Millennial Kingdom is the *fifth event* of the Second Coming.

8. THE GREAT WHITE THRONE JUDGMENT: Rev. 20:11–15; Heb. 9:27. Christ shall be the Judge: John 5:22, 27; Acts 17:31. Only the wicked dead shall stand there: Rom. 8:1, and none shall be exempt: Rev. 6:15–17; 20:12–13.
    (*Jer. 33:33–34, the Gentiles gathered: Matt. 25:31–32; and those converted entering the Kingdom.)

9. THE ETERNAL STATE: A new heaven and a new earth: Rev. 21:1. For the saints, the New Jerusalem: Rev. 21:9–27. Heaven a place of rest: Rev. 14:13, and reunion: 2 Sam. 12:23; a place of indescribable beauty: 2 Cor. 12:4; John 14:2–3; Rev. 22:1–6; of service: Rev. 7:15; where all limitations are removed: 1 Cor. 15:54–55; Rev. 7:16–17; 21:25.
    The final Hell is the Lake of Fire: Rev. 20:14–15, from which Christ died to save us: 1 Cor. 15:3–4; 2 Cor. 5:20; 2 Pet. 3:9.

    GOD'S COMMAND is to *STUDY*: 2 Tim. 2:15; to pay *HEED* to Doctrine: 1 Tim. 4:13–16; to *OBEY* that which is written: John 14:21. (Basic outline by Dr. G. Stanton.)

GUIDE TO PERSONAL WITNESSING

If you are a Christian, the Bible challenges you to be a witness for Jesus Christ.

Some are frightened by the thought of witnessing to others. They feel that such vital work requires great ability, when as a matter of fact, consecration of merely what we are and what we have, be it little or much, will be used by the Holy Spirit to bring surprising results. Indeed, the lack of natural skill and training will actually prove to be an asset, if if causes the would-be witness to rely entirely upon the power of the Holy Spirit to do that which only the Holy Spirit can. Only in this way can one be "fishers of men." (Matt. 4:19)

The purpose here is to describe the simple steps to take. And they are simple. Simplicity is a strong characteristic of the Gospel. It is best received in the simple directness of a childlike faith, and it should be passed on to others in the same way. True, the Gospel is the profound Word of God, full of power and action. Its scope is limitless in affairs human and divine; but God takes care of that. The marvel is that it can be handled by unskilled hands.

A little child cannot understand the intricate construction of a television set, but he can turn it on and release pictures being made on the other side of the world. This is but a faint illustration of what a child of God can do with the Gospel. The Christian who really desires to be a witness can by the simplest of words and the simplest of actions bring the very power of God into a needy life and lead such a person to accept Jesus Christ as his Savior.

Another important thing to recognize at the outset is that a person must first be convicted of sin and therefore realize the need of a Savior. Only the Holy Spirit can bring that conviction. He alone can regenerate the human heart. But the Holy Spirit uses the simple effort of the witnessing Christian to that definite end.

There are often other factors in "fishing for men", but these two are of prime importance to start with: simple directness on your part and reliance upon God to do His part.

You cannot repeat these facts to yourself too often.

I. THE CALL TO PERSONAL WORK

Christ Commands It

"And ye shall be witnesses unto me unto the uttermost part of the earth." (Acts 1:8)

Gratitude Demands It

"Go home to thy friends, and tell them how great things the Lord hath done for thee, and hath had compassion on thee." (Mark 5:19)

The World Needs It

"For God so loved the world, that he gave his only begotten Son, that whosoever believeth in him should not perish, but have everlasting life." (John 3:16)

"For even the Son of man came not to be ministered unto, but to minister, and to give his life a ransom for many." (Mark 10:45)

The Church Needs It

"As we have therefore opportunity, let us do good unto all men, especially unto them who are of the household of faith." (Galatians 6:10)

The Christian Grows by It

"But unto every one of us is given grace according to the measure of the gift of Christ ... Till we all come in the unity of the faith, and of the knowledge of the Son of God, unto a perfect man, unto the measure of the stature of the fulness of Christ. But speaking the truth in love, may grow up into him in all things, which is the head, even Christ." (Ephesians 4:7, 13, 15)

Experience Abundantly Warrants It

It has been stated that 85 per cent of commercial business is accomplished by personal solicitation. Modern technology has tremendously increased production in the industrial world, so that a machine now does the work of a hundred men. At the same time, the demand for individual salesmanship is greater than ever before in the world's history. Advertising cannot take the place of a face-to-face interview. Goods may be produced by

machines, but it takes personal work to sell goods and to make contracts. Personal work is also the means God uses to extend and expand His Kingdom.

II. EQUIPMENT FOR PERSONAL WORK

The Tools Are at Hand

You have the Bible—God's Word—"The sword of the Spirit."

"For the word of God is quick, and powerful, and sharper than any two-edged sword . . . and is a discerner of the thoughts and intents of the heart." (Hebrews 4:12)

In addition to this, you have, in some degree at least, the power of language, of personality, of influence, and various faculties and characteristics by which you make your impression upon those around you. In most persons (perhaps in your case) there is some individual gift which can be consecrated to this work with special effectiveness.

The Power Is Promised

No matter how great your natural endowments, divine power must accompany your efforts to make them successful. That power is clearly and emphatically promised.

"And Jesus came and spake unto them, saying, All power is given unto me in heaven and in earth. Go ye therefore, and teach all nations . . . Teaching them to observe all things whatsoever I have commanded you:

and, lo, I am with you always, even unto the end of the world." (Matthew 28:18-20)

Both Tools and Power Must Be Used

Remember: In this work, God has a part, and you have a part. They are distinct and separate, but they work together. Do not confuse them. Your part is to use the tools; God supplies the power. You can never convert a person; only the Holy Spirit can do that. You simply tell the story, and back it up with consistent living. God will do the rest.

Many have failed in this work by trying to do God's part instead of their own. They forgot to invoke the power. "Work as though all depended upon you, and pray as though all depended upon God."

Tools and power: both must be engaged.

Take a Step Forward

Staying where you are and merely wishing you might be an effective witness will get you nowhere. Demanding to see your way through, before starting, will bring only disappointment. This is a spiritual achievement, and is a step-by-step process. It is predicated upon faith in God—faith in His Plan, His Promise, His Power, and His Presence.

Your first step is to ask in faith for His power and guidance; then the way opens up for the next step. Take one step at a time.

"In all thy ways acknowledge him, and he shall direct thy paths." (Proverbs 3:6)

You want God's guidance and power every step of the way in this; therefore, stay close and keep in intimate touch with Him.

'Fishers of Men'

This is our Lord's own term. Jesus, standing upon the shore of Galilee, called some fishermen from their boats and nets to follow Him and be His disciples. He told them He would make them "fishers of men."

Matthew (4:19) and Mark (1:17) so record the incident, and Luke (5:10) states it, "Henceforth thou shalt catch men." The fishermen clearly understood what Jesus meant, and promptly laid down their tackle, left their boats, and entered the great School of Fishing, under the tutelage of the Master.

Thus the suggestions of methods offered in these "Helps" are grouped about the thought of fishing, while the great objective is the winning of people to Jesus Christ.

Again-warning: In both the Matthew and Mark accounts, Jesus said: "I will make you fishers of men." Only as we are taught and guided by Him can we hope to be successful "fishermen."

III. THREE ESSENTIAL LESSONS IN FISHING

The Desire to Fish

A successful fisherman may fish from pure love of the sport, or he may fish to make a living; but in any event he must be intent upon catching fish.

Here at the outset, examine your motives. Only one object is worthy in a "fisher of men": to bring persons to the Master. If that is not the consuming desire of your heart urging you to this effort, pray for it. Ask Jesus, first of all, to fill you with a longing to induce others to accept Him as their Savior. He will give this desire if it is earnestly asked for. Proof: Luke (11:13). Let it be part of your daily prayer that He will quicken and nourish the desire.

Tackle and Bait

Think of it as if you are preparing for a fishing trip. Any successful fisherman will tell you that the more thorough the preparation, the more likely you are to bring fish home.

Prayer and Bible study are the two most important items of preparation in Christian witnessing. If you are not diligent here, you cannot succeed as a "fisher of men."

This does not mean that one must be familiar with the whole Bible. A few plain statements from the Word of God are sufficient to begin with; but it is well always to have your New Testament at hand. Let the "salvation" texts be your daily Bible study until you are familiar with their content and location and can easily refer to them. Better still, commit them to memory.

Along with prayer, God's Word is your most important equipment. Turn to Hebrews 4:12 and see how sufficient and how necessary it is. Look also at Isaiah 55:10-13 and see how sure it is. Your own words may fail, but God's Word cannot return to Him void.

You have no absolute assurance that your own or anybody else's well-turned phrases will hit the mark; but you work with God's guarantee behind you when you use His Word. It is "the sword of the Spirit—quick and powerful."

A Place to Fish

Sometimes fish are scarce and sometimes plentiful, varying with the seasons and other conditions. But there are spiritually needy people all around us—and at all times.

There is no "closed season" on this kind of fishing.

Of all Christian work, personal witnessing is perhaps most neglected; yet, of all work it is the most vital to the extension of God's Kingdom.

Places of fishing for souls are all about us: men and women and young people, working beside us in store, office, factory, field, and on the road; living with us in our homes and in our neighborhoods. Some are little children quite competent to understand the need and plan of salvation through Christ. If we are "fishers of men," we will be continually on the lookout for those whom we can win to Jesus; and, being on the lookout, we cannot fail to find some at almost every turn.

As soon as we seriously interest ourselves in this fishing, we will find our hands gloriously full of the King's Business. Every place will be a fishing place, and at all places there will be opportunities for witnessing.

"In the morning sow thy seed, and in the evening withhold not thine hand: for thou knowest not whether shall prosper, either this or that, or whether they both shall be alike good." (Ecclesiastes 11:6)

IV. THE METHOD

No doubt there would be more personal workers if would-be "fishers of men" were given some clear and workable method.

Jesus' use of the word "fishing" suggests a simple method. Simple does not always mean easy. A simple method may call out the best that is in us, but it will be one that anybody can understand. In recognizing the value of a method, we are not forgetting that the Holy Spirit is the power that turns men to Christ; but since the Holy Spirit operates through individuals, it is important that individuals use all the tact, wisdom, and skill at their command—with method.

In Christian witnessing, the method may be divided into three movements: the approach, presentation and the follow-up.

The Approach

Fishing in streams requires cautious approach, lest the fish be frightened away. Some who fish in the mountains, where trout are very wary, crawl upon hands and knees to the brink, and cast the hook ever so quietly. It is done as noiselessly as the falling of a leaf from an overhanging tree.

The Christian witness approaches tactfully. Not with stealth, but with tact—and tact is simply putting yourself in the other fellow's place and considering his need or his taste. Tact quickly discovers and corrects a wrong approach. Be tactful. Be earnest. Be frank. Be courageous. Be considerate.

Sometimes the circumstances in which you find a man give a clue as to the best method of approaching him. Your approach as an angler is more apt to be effective if you know the fish—its habitat, its habits, its likes, its dislikes. A good fisherman, therefore, studies the fish.

Just so, your approach to a man on this—regarded by many as a delicate subject—will be more effective if you have learned about his attitude toward life and toward things in general. Seek to get on common ground with him first. Show a keen interest (sincerely) in what he talks to you about. Try to be of some help in solving the problems he is battling with—not necessarily spiritual problems. These are sometimes obvious and do not have to be told; but avoid offending him in offering help that is not desired. Love is the key to success in the Christian life, and you will find it is also the key to your success as a witness for Christ.

If you are interested only in "making a sale" you will find your results are short-lived. Sincere love is something God can give you as you make each contact.

Approach him with the firm purpose of making a permanent friend of him, not as a transient, and not ostentatiously as a strong one to a weak one, but as, yourself, a poor sinner saved by grace. It may be stated somewhat in this way: "We are both sinners in the sight of God; the only difference between us is that I have a Savior, and you have not, but that difference is wiped out the moment you accept Jesus Christ." Keep yourself reminded of the fact that you have for him something he needs more than anything else in the world—and that is Christ.

Study Jesus' method with individuals, as for instance, with Nicodemus (John 3:1-21), with Zacchaeus (Luke 19:1-10), and with the woman of Samaria (John 4:6-48).

Presentation

Successful angling is attracting the fish to accept the bait. As a "fisher of men," it is your business so to present Christ's claims and the sinner's need that one will be moved to accept Christ as his Savior and to enter at once upon the program of a Christian. The particular excuses men give for not doing this will indicate to you the best passages of Scripture to use in talking to them.

Do not argue. "If you permit yourself to be drawn into an argument, you will likely lose the business," is a maxim of salesmanship. If you win the point of argument, you irritate your man; if he wins the point, your case is lost. Arguing is poor angling.

The woman of Samaria tried to sidetrack Jesus on an argument as to the relative merits of Mount Moriah and Mount Gerizim (John 4:19-24) but He brought her promptly back to the main issue—and won her.

Simply, quietly, confidently, accurately, give out the Word of God. That is, tell what God says. No need to go behind that—nor beside, nor around it. Do not allow the discussion to shift to some other premise. If it does, shift it back. Answer all with God's Word. You recognize no higher, no earlier, no later authority.

This is the only angling that is guaranteed not to fail. (See Isaiah 55:10-11)

Follow-Up

Much too often efforts turn out poorly because "fishers of men" fail to follow-up with their new convert. Vast numbers of people are induced to join the church, only to lapse into the old life, although continuing to be nominal church members. This is largely because the church often fails to give new converts personal attention and something to do.

When you have brought one to a decision for Christ, see to it that he makes his public confession (Matthew 10:32) and becomes a member of some church. But remember, this is only the beginning of his Christian experience and growth, and, though mature in years, he is "a babe in Christ" and will need friendly assistance for some time.

Encourage your convert to give his testimony, as occasion suggests. This will help him to break with the old life and line up with the new. Show him how to go now and win

another. He, too, must become a "fisher of men" if he would grow in grace and become strong in his new faith.

Encourage your convert by seeing him if possible at frequent intervals and helping him to get nourishment. Show him how to gain strength by a daily schedule of prayer and Bible study. You will yourself grow stronger while you are helping him to grow. Get your pastor interested in finding something for him to do, be it ever so simple—something that will identify him with his new life in Christ and with the church. If your church does not have an organization for Bible study and Christian service, start one. One of the happy things about God's Vineyard is that there is work for all.

After all is said about methods, it should be noted that no plan can be used for everyone. It is said that no two leaves on a tree, or in a forest, are exactly alike. No two people are exactly alike. God is a Creator of infinite variety. No two fishermen are alike. No two fish are the same. No two days in one person's experience are exactly alike. That is why we should not give up when the first effort seems to fail. Circumstances overnight often change one's outlook, and the reaction to your next effort will doubtless be very different. So continue to fish.

Thus we are thrown back in every case absolutely upon the discriminating and infinite wisdom of God who has promised the Holy Spirit to those who seek His guidance.

In all the holy service you may perform for God, perhaps none will demand such instant and unremitting prayer as fishing for men. God must guide and make effective from start to finish. Therefore, keep consciously in touch with Him at all times.

THE GOSPEL PLAN
OF SALVATION

In your work as a fisher of men, you will find that most of those you talk with respond to a clear, logical presentation of the Gospel plan. Here, as an aid to Christian witnessing we have provided questions and answers in a fashion that will show the means to Salvation according to the words of Scripture. It may help you to be more effective if you memorize these verses as they are the very heart of the Bible message.

How can I find joy and contentment?

"Then said Jesus unto them . . . I am come that they might have life, and that they might have it more abundantly." (John 10:7, 10)

Who will have this abundant life?

"God hath given to us eternal life, and this life is in his Son. He that hath the Son hath life; and he that hath not the Son of God hath not life." (I John 5:11, 12)

Won't I be saved by keeping the Golden Rule and by doing good deeds?

"Not by works of righteousness which we have done, but according to his mercy he saved us, by the washing of regeneration, and renewing of the Holy Ghost." (Titus 3:5)

But I am not really bad; I don't consider myself to be a great sinner.

"For all have sinned, and come short of the glory of God." (Rom. 3:23)

"For whosoever shall keep the whole law, and yet offend in one point, he is guilty of all." (James 2:10)

Maybe I sin once in a while, but God won't turn me down if I only sin a little.

"The wages of sin is death." (Rom. 6:23)

It seems as if God is more interested in punishment than anything else. How do I know God cares for me at all?

"For God so loved the world, that he gave his only begotten Son, that whosoever believeth in him should not perish, but have everlasting life." (John 3:16)

What must I do?

"Believe on the Lord Jesus Christ, and thou shalt be saved, and thy house." (Acts 16:31)

Is that the only way?

"Jesus saith unto him, I am the way, the truth, and the life: no man cometh unto the Father, but by me." (John 14:6)

605

Won't my good works have any importance?

"For by grace are ye saved through faith; and that not of yourselves: It is the gift of God: Not of works, lest any man should boast." (Eph. 2:8, 9)

For what purpose did Christ come?

"Christ Jesus came into the world to save sinners." (I Tim. 1:15)

Explain a little more about believing in Jesus.

"If thou shalt confess with thy mouth the Lord Jesus, and shalt believe in thine heart that God hath raised him from the dead, thou shalt be saved." (Rom. 10:9)

What is the extent of Christ's power?

"He is able also to save them to the uttermost that come unto God by him, seeing he ever liveth to make intercession for them." (Heb. 7:25)

Who may receive this great gift?

"Behold, I stand at the door, and knock: if any man hear my voice, and open the door, I will come in to him, and will sup with him, and he with me." (Rev. 3:20)

What does Christ say in this matter?

"Without me ye can do nothing." (John 15:5)

Is there no other way?

"Neither is there salvation in any other: for there is none other name under heaven given among men, whereby we must be saved." (Acts 4:12)

How do we receive our faith?

"God hath dealt to every man the measure of faith." (Rom. 12:3)

From what does it come?

"Faith cometh by hearing, and hearing by the word of God." (Rom. 10:17)

May we act without faith?

"Whatsoever is not of faith is sin." (Rom. 14:23)

Is it too late for me to become a Christian? Won't I be condemned by my past sins?

"If any man be in Christ, he is a new creature: old things are passed away; behold, all things are become new." (II Cor. 5:17)

Are sinners welcomed in heaven?

"I say unto you, that likewise joy shall be in heaven over one sinner that repenteth, more than over ninety and nine just persons, which need no repentance." (Luke 15:7)

What are we to remember in connection with God's forgiveness of us?

"Forgive us our debts, as we forgive our debtors . . . For if ye forgive men their trespasses, your heavenly Father will also forgive you: But if ye forgive not men their trespasses, neither will your Father forgive your trespasses." (Matt. 6:12, 14, 15)

How does Jesus explain this?

"For this my son was dead, and is alive again; he was lost, and is found." (Luke 15:24)

How are we assured of God's great power of redemption?

"If the spirit of him that raised up Jesus from the dead dwell in you, he that raised up Christ from the dead shall also quicken your mortal bodies by his Spirit that dwelleth in you." (Rom. 8:11) "As Christ was raised up from the dead by the glory of the Father, even so we also should walk in newness of life." (Rom. 6:4)

Do you really think I could last as a Christian?

"Being confident of this very thing, that he which hath begun a good work in you will perform it until the day of Jesus Christ." (Phil. 1:6)

Will God support me?

"Be of good courage, and he shall strengthen your heart, all ye that hope in the Lord." (Ps. 31:24)

How do I get God's help?

"In every thing by prayer and supplication with thanksgiving let your requests be made known unto God. And the peace of God, which passeth all understanding, shall keep your hearts and minds through Christ Jesus." (Phil. 4:6, 7)

What protection will faith give me?

"Taking the shield of faith, wherewith ye shall be able to quench all the fiery darts of the wicked." (Eph. 6:16)

How great is God's mercy?

"As the heaven is high above the earth, so great is his mercy toward them that fear him." (Ps. 103:11)

I would like to be a Christian, but I don't have time. I'm very busy with my job right now.

"Ye cannot serve God and mammon. Therefore I say unto you, take no thought for your life, what ye shall eat, or what ye shall drink; nor yet for your body, what ye shall put on . . . for your heavenly Father knoweth that ye have need of these things. But seek ye first the Kingdom of God, and his righteousness; and all these things shall be added unto you. Take therefore no thought for the morrow; for the morrow shall take thought for the things of itself. Sufficient unto the day is the evil thereof." (Matt. 6:24-34)

How does Jesus ask us to live?

"And Jesus answered him, The first of all the commandments is, Hear, O Israel; The Lord our God is one Lord: And thou shalt love the Lord thy God with all thy heart, and with all thy soul, and with all thy mind, and with all thy strength: this is the first commandment. And the second is like, namely this, Thou shalt love thy neighbor as thyself. There is none other commandment greater than these." (Mark 12:29-31)

How should we serve God?

"I beseech you therefore, brethren, by the mercies of God, that ye present your bodies a living sacrifice, holy, acceptable unto God, which is your reasonable service." (Rom. 12:1)

How did Jesus set an example?

"Whosoever will be chief among you, let him be your servant: Even as the Son of man came not to be ministered unto, but to minister, and to give his life a ransom for many." (Matt. 20:27, 28)

What else must I do?

"Whereby are given unto us exceeding great and precious promises: that by these ye might be partakers of the divine nature, having escaped the corruption that is in the world through lust. And beside this, giving all diligence, add to your faith virtue; and to virtue knowledge; and to knowledge temperance; and to temperance patience; and to patience godliness; and to godliness brotherly kindness; and to brotherly kindness charity. For if these things be in you, and abound, they make you that ye shall neither be barren nor unfruitful in the knowledge of our Lord Jesus Christ." (II Pet. 1:4-8)

What, again, is the first step?

"Believe on the Lord Jesus Christ, and thou shalt be saved." (Acts 16:31)

MASSAH AND MERIBAH

Some Bible students have seen the words "*Massah*" and "*Meribah*" periodically used in the Bible and have wondered to what do they refer and what spiritual lesson might be found in them? The occasion for these words uttered by Moses was the events described in Exodus 17:1-7. Late in the second month after the children of Israel had been led out of Egypt by God's power, the host arrived at Rephidim and there the new nation pitched its extended camp. There was no water and soon, rather than go to prayer in faith, the murmuring and complaining began. Accusations were made against Moses, and Moses cried unto the Lord. God commanded Moses to take his rod and to smite the rock at Horeb, and water came out of the rock. Moses called that place, "Massah and Meribah" (Exo 17:7). *Massah* means "trial, temptation, testing," and *meribah* means "contention."

Exodus 17:1-7 thus reminds us of the internal complaining of the newly freed Children of Israel that did not see water when they camped, and of God's supplying the life sustaining liquid in the desert through the smiting of the rock, typical of Christ being smitten at the cross. Then Exodus 17:8-16 follows, describing Israel's continual struggle against the outside threat of Amalek, typical of the world. Psalm 81:7 says, "... I proved thee [tested you] at the waters of Meribah. .." Lessons for the Christian include a warning against complaining and faithlessness; let us rather come to God in prayer trusting for His supply.

At a time some years later, the Children of Israel again found themselves without water in the same general region of Kadesh, Numbers 20:1-13. Again the complainers murmured against Moses, and bitterly confronted God's faithful prophet. This time God commanded Moses to go and speak to the rock. Moses lost his temper at the complainers and struck the rock two times—and the water gushed forth (Numb 20:7-11). God rebuked Moses for striking the rock. Why? Not simply because he had lost his temper, but because he had not followed God's instructions precisely—and spoke to the rock. Moses broke the type! The type of the rock was Christ. Paul said, "And [they, i.e., the Children of Israel] did all drink the same spiritual drink: for they drank of that spiritual Rock that followed them: and that Rock was Christ" (1 Cor 10:4). The imagery that was being set was that the rock (Christ) was to be struck once, and once only, for our sins (at the cross), and then after that by faith the unbeliever or believer need only to call out to him, to speak the words, and the water of life and the blessings of God would gush forth! Moses by striking the rock a second time, and actually he even hit it twice the second time, had broken the type and this could not be repaired.

Massah and Meribah speaks of a place where the Israelites complained in the desert for water. The Feast of Tabernacles commemorates annually God's provision for Israel in the desert. On the final day of this eight day feast, the High Priest would go through a ceremony of pouring water from the Pool of Siloam from a golden pitcher into a golden bowl, and prayer was given thanking God for providing water in the desert for the Children of Israel, as well as for those of that day who depended upon God for the rains to nourish their lands. The Gospel of John in 7:1-3,37-40, tells us of a teaching that Jesus gave on this very day, *viz.*, "In the last day, that great day of the feast, Jesus stood and cried, saying, If any man thirst, let him come unto Me and drink" (John 7:37). He was proclaiming that He was indeed that rock in the desert to be smitten of God, and from which water would flow out to the blessing of all who would believe.

GGC

A

Aaron *enlightened*

Lineage:

Son of Amram and Jochebed	Ex.	6	20
Descendant of Merari	Ex.	6	19
Descendant of Levi	Ex.	6	16
Brother of Moses and Miriam	Ex.	6	20
	Ex.	15	20
Husband of Elisheba	Ex.	6	23
Father of Nadab, Abihu, Eleazar and Ithamar	Ex.	6	23
	I Chr.	6	3
Grandfather of Phinehas	I Chr.	6	25
Geneology of	I Chr.	6	3–15

History:

Meets Moses in the wilderness	Ex.	4	14
Spokesman for Moses	Ex.	4	14–16
	Ex.	7	1
Prophet for Moses	Ex.	7	1
People murmur against	Ex.	5	20
	Ex.	16	2
	Num.	14, 16	
Inspired	Ex.	12	1
	Lev.	10	8
	Num.	2	1
His rod becomes a serpent	Ex.	7	10
Involved in announcing plagues in Egypt	Ex.	8	5, 17, 24
	Ex.	9	10
Helped in delivering Israel from Egypt	Ex.	6	13, 26
	Mic.	6	4
	Josh.	24	5
Goes with elders up to Sinai	Ex.	59	24
	Ex.	24	1, 9
Hur holds up Moses' hands	Ex.	17	12
Was chosen by God	Ps.	105	26
	Heb.	5	4
Sin at Sinai (golden calf)	Ex.	32	
	Acts	7	40
Spared by Moses' intercession	Deut.	9	20
Judges Israel	Ex.	24	14
Puts pot of manna in ark	Ex.	16	34
Sedition against Moses	Num.	12	
Intercession for Miriam	Num.	12	
Forbidden to mourn for death of his sons	Lev.	10	6, 19
Spoken against by Korah	Num.	16	3
Makes atonement and plague is stayed	Num.	16	46–48
Budding rod	Num.	17	8
Excluded from the promised land	Num.	20	12
Dies on Mt. Hor	Num.	20	28
123 years old at death	Num.	33	39
Succeeded by Eleazar	Deut.	10	6
Character	Ps.	106	16

Priesthood of:

Consecrated	Ex.	29	
	Lev.	8	
Duties to offer sacrifice	Ex.	30	7
	Lev.	9	
Enters priestly office	Lev.	9	
Descendants ordained priests perpetually	Num.	3	3
	Num.	18	1
	II Chr.	26	18
Anointed	Ex.	30	25, 30
Role as a teacher of divine things	Lev.	10	8, 11
To enter holy of holies on Day of Atonement	Ex.	30	10
	Heb.	9	7
His priesthood inferior to Christ's	Heb.	5	7

Sins:

Allows idolatry	Ex.	32	
Speaks against Moses	Num.	12	1–16
Presumption when rock is smitten	Num.	20	10–12

Ab *the fifth Hebrew month (July–August)*
See Months
Means "father" in Hebrew. Often used in names (Abimelech, Abner, Abijah)

Aramaic: Abba	Rom.	8	15
	Mark	14	36

Abaddon *destruction*

Apollyon—angel of the bottomless pit	Job	26	6
	Job	28	22
	Rev.	9	11

Abana *see Amana and Pharpar*

Rivers of Damascus, flow eastwards from the Anti-Lebanon and from Hermon respectively	II Ki.	5	12
The former rises in a deep pool, and is a rapid stream, passing by Abila of Lysanias and through Damascus and being lost, about twenty miles to the east, in the swampy lake (Bahret el Ateibeh) at the edge of the desert (it is now called Nahr Barada, "cold river.")	Luke	3	1

abandon *forsake*

Sinful city	Gen.	19	
Sinful pride of works	Phil.	3	7–10
Home	Gen.	12	
Wicked ways	II Chr.	7	14
Jerusalem	Mat.	23	37, 38
God of depraved sinners	Rom.	1	
Incestuous church member	I Cor.	5	1–5

Abarim *regions beyond; mountains of Nebo, Pisgah*

Of Mt. Nebo	Num.	27	12
In Transjordan	Deut.	32	49
Area around Nebo	Num.	33	47
Place of Moses' death	Deut.	32	49
Reubenite territory	Num.	32	2–7
Israelites camped there just prior to entering promised land	Num.	21	11

abase *degrade*

Behold proud and *a* him	Job	40	11
Lion will not *a* him	Is.	31	4
And *a* him that is high	Ezek.	21	26
Exalt himself shall be *a*	Mat.	23	12
	Luke	14	11
	Luke	18	14
I know how to be *a*	Phil.	4	12
Offence in *a* myself	II Cor.	11	7
God will *a* sinners	II Ki.	14	8–14
	Is.	14	12–17
	Dan.	4	33, 37

abated *become less*

Waters were *a*	Gen.	8	3, 11
Be *a* from thy estimation	Lev.	27	18
Nor was Moses' force *a*	Deut.	34	7
Then their anger was *a*	Judg.	8	3

Abba *Aramaic for "Father"*

	Mark	14	36
	Rom.	8	15
	Gal.	4	6

Abdon *servile*

A judge of Israel	Judg.	12	13
A town of Asher	Josh.	21	30
	I Chr.	6	74
The Benjamite	I Chr.	8	23, 30
	I Chr.	9	36
Son of Jeiel	I Chr.	8	30
Messenger of king Josiah	II Chr.	34	20

Abednego *servant or worshipper of Nego, Nebo, a Babylonian god*

Saved from fiery furnace	Dan.	1	7
	Dan.	3	12

Abel *breath, vapor*

Second son of Adam and Eve	Gen.	4	2
A shepherd	Gen.	4	2
Killed by his brother Cain	Gen.	4	8
Replaced by Seth	Gen.	4	25
Righteous	Mat.	23	35
	I John	3	12
Blood of	Luke	11	51
	Heb.	12	24
Faith of	Heb.	11	4

Abel-beth-Maachah *meadow by the house of oppression*

In extreme north of Israel	I Ki.	15	20
	II Sam.	20	14, 15

Abhor *loathe*

I *a* them	Lev.	20	23
Soul shall not *a* you	Lev.	26	11
Soul *a* my judgements	Lev.	26	15
Soul shall *a* you	Lev.	26	30
Soul *a* my statutes	Lev.	26	43
Utterly *a* it	Deut.	7	26
Not *a* an Edomite	Deut.	23	7
He *a* them	Deut.	32	19
Men *a* the offering	I Sam.	22	19
They *a* me	Job	30	10
I *a* myself and repent	Job	42	6
Lord will *a* bloody	Ps.	5	6
Whom the Lord *a*	Ps.	10	3

Abhor —continued

He *a* not evil	Ps.	36	4
He *a* his own	Ps.	106	40
Hate and *a* lying	Ps.	119	163
Nations shall *a* him	Prov.	24	24
Land that thou *a*	Is.	7	16
Whom the nation *a*	Is.	49	7
Do not *a* us	Jer.	14	21
I *a* the excellency	Amos	6	8
That *a* idols	Rom.	2	22
A that is evil	Rom.	12	9
Savior to be *a*	Ex.	5	21
Friends *a* me	Job	19	19
Cast off and *a*	Ps.	89	38
A of the Lord	Prov.	22	14
Beauty to be *a*	Ezek.	16	25
An *a* to all flesh	Is.	66	24
Soul also *a* me	Zech.	11	8

Abiathar *father of abundance*

Excellent father, the priest	I Sam.	23	9
Escapes Saul's vengeance	I Sam.	22	20
Faithful to David	I Sam.	23	6
	I Sam.	30	7
	II Sam.	15	24
Follows Adonijah	I Ki.	1	7
Deposed by Solomon	I Ki.	2	26

Abib *ears of corn*

Name of the first Hebrew month, the passover month	Ex.	13	4
	Ex.	23	15
	Ex.	34	18

abide *continue to stay*

Servant *a* instead	Gen.	44	33
A every men	Ex.	16	29
He saw Israel *a*	Num.	24	2
A without camp	Num.	31	19
A in city of refuge	Num.	35	25
A here by maidens	Ruth	2	8
There *a* forever	I Sam.	1	22
Ark shall not *a*	I Sam.	5	7
Nor *a* in paths	Job	24	13
Shall *a* in tabernacle	Ps.	15	1
Shall *a* under shadow	Ps.	91	1
Earth and it *a*	Ps.	119	90
Her feet *a* not	Prov.	7	11
Ear heareth reproof *a*	Prov.	15	31
The earth *a* forever	Eccl.	1	4
Eat, drink, merry, *a*	Eccl.	8	15
Will *a* in this land	Jer.	42	10
No man *a*	Jer.	49	18, 33
Shall *a* many days	Hosea	3	3
Sword shall *a*	Hosea	11	6
Who can *a* it	Joel	2	11
Who can *a* the fierceness	Nah.	1	6
May *a* the day	Mal.	3	2
There *a*	Mat.	10	11
There *a*	Mark	6	10
Shepherds *a*	Luke	2	8
There *a*	Luke	9	4
I must *a* at thy house	Luke	19	5
A with us	Luke	24	29
Wrath of God *a*	John	3	36
Have not his word *a* in	John	5	38
And die, it *a* alone	John	12	24
That Christ *a* forever	John	12	34
Another Comforter, he may *a*	John	14	16
A in and I in you	John	15	4
A in the vine	John	15	4
He that *a* in me	John	15	5
If a man *a* not in me	John	15	6
A in me, my words *a* in you	John	15	7
A my love, *a* his love	John	15	10
To my house and *a*	Acts	16	15
A not still in unbelief	Rom.	11	23
Any man work *a*	I Cor.	3	14
Now *a* faith, hope, charity	I Cor.	13	13
Yet he *a* faithful	II Tim.	2	13
That saith he *a* in him	I John	2	6
A in the light	I John	2	10
Word of God *a* in you	I John	2	14
Doeth the will of God *a*	I John	2	17
Whosoever *a* in him	I John	3	6
Know that he *a* in us	I John	3	24
A not in doctrine	II John	1	9
He that *a* in doctrine	II John	1	9

Abiel *My father is God*

Grandfather of Saul	I Sam.	9	1, 2
Grandfather of Abner	I Sam.	14	51
One of David's mighty men	I Chr.	11	32

Abiezer, Abi-ezer *father of help*

Named Jeezer	Num.	26	30
Son of Manasseh	Josh.	17	2
Ancestor of Gideon	Judg.	6	11
One of David's mighty men	II Sam.	23	27
One of the twelve captains	I Chr.	27	12

Abigail *father's joy*

Wife of Nabal	I Sam.	25	3
Pacifies David	I Sam.	25	14–35
Marries David	I Sam.	25	39–42
Captured by Amalekites	I Sam.	30	5
Mother of Chileab	II Sam.	3	3
Mother of Amasa	II Sam.	17	25

Abihail *father of strength*

A Merari Levite	Num.	3	35
Wife of Abishur	I Chr.	2	29
A man of Gad	I Chr.	5	14
Wife of Rehoboam	II Chr.	11	18
Father of Esther	Esth.	9	29

Abihu *he is my father*

Son of Aaron	Ex.	6	23
Offers strange fire	Lev.	10	1, 2

Abihud *father of honor*

Son of Bela	I Chr.	8	3

Abijah, *my father is Jehovah (Abia, Abiah)*

A son of Jeroboam	I Ki.	14	1
Death foretold	I Ki.	14	12
A son of Rehoboam; also called Abijam; defeats Jeroboam	I Ki.	15	1–8
	II Chr.	11	20–23
	II Chr.	13	13–20
Wars with Jeroboam	II Chr.	13	
Mother of Hezikiah	II Chr.	29	1
Priest of David	I Chr.	24	10
Priest in time of Nehemiah	Neh.	10	7
Priest with Zerubbabel	Neh.	12	4, 17

ability

According to his *a*	Lev.	27	8
They gave after their *a*	Ezra	2	69
We after our *a*	Neh.	5	8
Had *a* to stand in the palace.	Dan.	1	4
To every man according to *a*	Mat.	25	15
According to *a* to send	Acts	11	29
As of the *a* God giveth	I Pet.	4	11
See able			

God's ability

To save	Heb.	7	27
To keep	Jude	1	24, 25
To comfort	Heb.	2	18
To subdue	Phil.	3	21
To give grace	II Cor.	9	8
Keep promises	Rom.	4	21
Raise the dead	Heb.	11	19

Abimelech *father of the king*

With Abraham's wife	Gen.	20	2
Restores Sarah	Gen.	20	14
Healed at Abraham's prayer	Gen.	20	17, 18
King of Philistines	Gen.	26	8
Rebukes Isaac	Gen.	26	10
Covenant with Isaac	Gen.	26	28
King at Shechem	Judg.	9	6
Son of Gideon	Judg.	8	31
Murders his brethren	Judg.	9	5
Jotham's parable	Judg.	9	7–20
His death	Judg.	9	53
A priest of Israel	I Chr.	18	16

Abinadab *father of a vow*

Son of Jesse and a soldier of Saul	I Sam.	17	13
Saul's son slain in battle	I Sam.	31	2
Receives the ark	II Sam.	6	3
Father of one of Solomon's twelve officers	I Ki.	4	11

Abiram *father is exalted*

In rebellion against Moses	Num.	16	1–3
His punishment	Num.	16	31–34
Example of God's power	Deut.	11	6
The foundation of Jericho	I Ki.	16	34

Abishag *ignorance of the father*

Ministers to David	I Ki.	1	3, 4
Sought by Adonijah	I Ki.	2	21
Causes break with Solomon	I Ki.	2	22

Abishai *gift of the father*
Brother of Joab	I Sam.	26	6
Wants to slay Saul	I Sam.	26	7–9
Son of Zeruiah	II Sam.	2	18
Pursues Abner	II Sam.	2	24
Aids in slaying Abner	II Sam.	3	30
Leads army against Ammon	II Sam.	10	10
Officer of David	II Sam.	18	2
Seeks to slay Shimei	II Sam.	19	21
Slays 18,000 Edomites	I Chr.	18	12

Abishalom *my father is peace*
Father of Maachah	I Ki.	15	2, 10
Called Absalom	II Chr.	11	20

Abishua *father of salvation*
Descendant of Aaron	I Chr.	6	4
Ancestor of Ezra	Ezra	7	5
A son of Bela	I Chr.	8	3, 4

able
Provide out of people *a* men	Ex.	18	21
Moses chose *a* men	Ex.	18	25
Every man as he is *a*	Deut.	16	17
No man been *a* to stand	Josh.	23	9
Who is *a* to stand before God	I Sam.	6	20
Who is *a* to judge?	I Ki.	3	9
Who is *a* to build?	II Chr.	2	6
Who is *a* to stand before envy?	Prov.	27	4
God is *a* to deliver.	Dan.	3	17
	Dan.	6	20
Land not *a* to bear his words.	Amos	7	10
God is *a* of these stones	Mat.	3	9
Believe ye that I am *a*?	Mat.	9	28
Are ye *a* to drink of cup?	Mat.	20	22
No man was *a* to answer.	Mat.	22	46
Not *a* to do least.	Luke	12	26
None is *a* to pluck.	John	10	29
Not *a* to resist wisdom.	Acts	6	10
A to separate us from love of God	Rom.	8	39
Tempted above that ye are *a*	I Cor.	10	13
A ministers of New Testament	II Cor.	3	6
A to comprehend with all saints.	Eph.	3	18
A to subdue all things.	Phil.	3	21
A to succour them that are tempted.	Heb.	2	18
A to save to the uttermost.	Heb.	7	25
A to save and destroy	James	4	12
A to keep you from falling.	Jude	24	
No man *a* to open book.	Rev.	5	3
Who shall be *a* to stand?	Rev.	6	17

ablution *see purification*

Abner *father of light*
Commander of Saul's army	I Sam.	14	50
Brings David and Saul together	I Sam.	17	54–58
Reproved by David	I Sam.	26	14–16
Makes Ish-bosheth king	II Sam.	2	8–9
Kills Asahel, Joab's brother	II Sam.	2	18–23
Goes over to David	II Sam.	3	8–12
Slain by Joab	II Sam.	3	27–30
Mourned by David	II Sam.	3	31–34

abode *dwell*
The people *a* there before God	Judg.	21	2
Mary *a* with her about three months	Luke	1	56
The Spirit, and it *a* on him	John	1	32
A murderer, and *a* not in truth	John	8	44
Long time *a*, speaking loudly	Acts	14	3
Paul *a* with them, and wrought	Acts	18	3
(See I Sam. 7:2; Ezra 8:15)			

abolish
The end of that *a*	II Cor.	3	13
A in his flesh the enmity	Eph.	2	15
Christ who hath a death	II Tim.	1	10
(See Isa. 2:18; 51:6; Ezek. 6:6)			

abominable *detestable*
Ahab *a* in following idols	I Ki.	21	26
How much more *a* is man?	Job	15	16
They have done *a* works.	Ps.	14	1
	Ps.	53	1
Cast out like *a* branch.	Is.	14	19
Broth of *a* things.	Is.	65	4
	Jer.	16	18
This *a* thing that I hate.	Jer.	44	4
In works they deny him, being *a*	Tit.	1	16
Walked in *a* idolatries	I Pet.	4	3
(See Lev. 11:43; Deut. 14:3; Rev. 21:8)			

abomination
Of offerings	Lev.	7	18
	Deut.	17	1
	Deut.	23	18
Defilement	Prov.	15	8
	Is.	1	13
	Is.	41	24
	Deut.	24	4
	Prov.	16	12
	Is.	66	17
	Ezek.	16	
	Rev.	21	27
Idolatry	Deut.	7	25
	Deut.	26	27
	Deut.	15	
	I Ki.	11	5
	II Ki.	23	13
	Ezek.	18	12
	Mal.	2	11
Pride and falsity	Prov.	3	32
	Prov.	6	16
	Prov.	11	1, 20
	Prov.	16	5
	Prov.	17	15
	Prov.	20	10, 23
Of the heathen censured	Lev.	18	26
	Deut.	18	9
	I Ki.	14	24
	Rom.	1	18
	Col.	5	3
Of Jerusalem described	Is.	1	3
	Jer.	2	
	Ezek.	5	11
	Ezek.	7	
	Ezek.	8	
	Ezek.	11	
	Ezek.	16	
	Ezek.	23	
	Hosea	1	
Prayer of the wicked	Prov.	28	9
Of desolation foretold	Dan.	11	31
	Dan.	12	11
	Mat.	24	15
	Mark	13	14
Egyptians eating with Hebrews	Gen.	43	
Blood marriages	Lev.	18	
Improper clothing	Deut.	22	
Divers weights and measures	Deut.	25	1
Promiscuity	Ezek.	22	
A to Egyptians	Gen.	43	32
	Gen.	46	34
Be an *a* to you.	Lev.	11	10
It is *a* to the Lord	Deut.	7	25
All that do unrighteously are *a*	Deut.	25	16
The forward *a* to the Lord.	Prov.	3	32
	Prov.	11	20
Wickedness an *a* to my lips.	Prov.	8	7
Sacrifice, etc. of wicked *a*	Prov.	15	8, 9, 26
Even his prayer shall be *a*	Prov.	28	9
The residue thereof an *a*	Is.	44	19
Land desolate because of *a*	Ezek.	33	29
A of Desolation.	Dan.	11	31
	Mat.	24	15
	Mark	13	14
Esteemed among men, *a* in sight of God.	Luke	16	15
Not enter that worketh *a*	Rev.	21	27

Abomination of Desolation
Predicted by Daniel	Dan.	12	11
Predicted by Christ	Mark	13	14
	Mat.	24	15

abortion *premature birth*
Laws regarding	Ex.	21	22–25
Job curses his birth	Job	10	18, 19
Jeremiah curses his birth	Jer.	20	15–17
A curse for Israel's sins	Hosea	9	14

Not To Do
Slay thee not	Ex.	23	7
Out of mothers womb	Num.	12	12
God who makes all	Eccl.	11	5

abound *be plentiful*
That ye may *a* in hope.	Rom.	15	13
Always *a* in work of the Lord.	I Cor.	15	58
As suffering *a*, so consolation *a*	II Cor.	1	5
(See Rom. 3:7; 5:15; Phil. 4:12)			

above
Portion of God from *a*	Job	31	2
Way of life *a* to wise	Prov.	15	24
Disciple not *a* master	Mat.	10	24
	Luke	6	40

above —*continued*

He that cometh from *a* is *a* all.	John	3	31
I am from *a*	John	8	23
A that which is written	I Cor.	4	6
Jerusalem *a* is free	Gal.	4	26
(*See* Gen. 48:22; Ps. 138:2; Jas. 1:17)			

Abraham, Abram *father of a great multitude*

Family history	Gen.	11	27–31
God calls him	Gen.	12	1–3
He goes into Canaan	Gen.	12	4–6
Denies his wife	Gen.	12	10–20
Separates from Lot	Gen.	13	7–12
Canaan promised to	Gen.	13	12–15
Rescues Lot	Gen.	14	14
Blessed by Melchizedek	Gen.	14	19
	Heb.	7	1
Father of Ishmael	Gen.	16	15
God renews the covenant	Gen.	17	2–7
His name changed	Gen.	17	5
Institutes circumcision	Gen.	17	10–14
Entertains angels	Gen.	18	1–33
Pleads for Sodom	Gen.	18	23–32
Father of Isaac	Gen.	21	2–5
Sends away Hagar	Gen.	21	14
Tested in offering Isaac	Gen.	22	2–10
His faith rewarded	Gen.	22	11–14
Death and burial	Gen.	25	7–10
Children by Keturah	I Chr.	1	32, 33
An example of faith	Rom.	4	1–25
Faithful inherit his blessing	Gal.	3	8–11
Christ, the seed of	Heb.	2	16
Called the "Friend of God"	James	2	23
Men of faith	Heb.	11	8
	Rom.	4	

Characteristics:

Friend of God	II Chr.	20	7
Obedient	Gen.	22	1–18
Tither	Gen.	14	20
	Heb.	7	1, 2, 4
Unselfish	Gen.	13	8, 9
Courageous	Gen.	14	13–16
Independent	Gen.	14	21–23
Hospitable	Gen.	18	1–8
Prayer	Gen.	18	23–33
Faith	Gen.	15	6
Rich man	Gen.	13	2
Mighty prince	Gen.	23	5, 6
Good provider	Gen.	25	5, 6
Peacemaker	Gen.	13	8

Absalom *father of peace*

Son of David	II Sam.	3	3
He kills Amnon	II Sam.	13	28, 19
Flees to Geshur	II Sam.	13	37, 38
Brought back by Joab	II Sam.	14	23
His great beauty	II Sam.	14	25, 26
Plots against David	II Sam.	15	2–6
Vow at Hebron	II Sam.	15	7–9
His conspiracy	II Sam.	15	10–12
Commits incest	II Sam.	16	21, 22
Fights against David	II Sam.	17	24–26
His death	II Sam.	18	9–15
David mourns him	II Sam.	18	33

abstain *cease*

From Sin:

Idols	Acts	15	20
Fornication	I Thes.	4	3
Lusts of the flesh	I Pet.	2	11
Appearance of evil	I Thes.	5	22

Foods:

Nazarites, no wine	Num.	6	1–3
Kings not to take strong drink	Prov.	31	4
Women in pregnancy	Judg.	13	3, 4
Meats	Rom.	14	1–23
	I Cor.	8	1–13
Levites	Lev.	10	9
Samson's mother	Judg.	35	5, 6
John the Baptist	Luke	1	13–15

abuse *mistreat*

Use world as not *a*	I Cor.	7	31
That I *a* not my power	I Cor.	9	18

acacia see shittim wood

accept *to receive*

Shalt thou not be *a*?	Gen.	4	7
A before the Lord	Ex.	28	38
	Lev.	10	19
A the work of his hands	Deut.	33	11
A in sight of all the people	I Sam.	18	5

The Lord thy God *a* thee	II Sam.	24	23
Will ye *a* his person?	Job	13	8
	Job	32	21
Not good to *a* wicked	Prov.	18	5
I will not *a* them	Jer.	14	12
	Amos	5	22
Supplication be *a*	Jer.	37	20
	Jer.	42	2
I will *a*	Ezek.	20	40
	Ezek.	43	27
No prophet is *a*	Luke	4	24
Worketh righteousness is *a*	Acts	10	35
My service be *a* of saints.	Rom.	15	31
Present or absent, we may be *a*	II Cor.	5	9
(*See* Ps. 119:108; Eccl. 12:10; Mal. 1:8)			

access to God *right to approach*

Its blessedness	Ps.	65	4
In prayer	Mat.	6	6
Is by Christ	Rom.	5	1–2
Is by Holy Ghost	Eph.	2	18
Obtained through faith	Heb.	11	6

accomplish

A as a hireling	Job	14	6
They *a* diligent search	Ps.	64	6
Desire *a* is sweet	Prov.	13	19
Her warfare is *a*	Is.	40	2
Straitened till it be *a*	Luke	12	50
Afflictions are *a* in brethren	I Pet.	5	9
(*See* Is. 55:11; Luke 18:31; 22:37)			

accord *harmony*

Spontaneous	Acts	12	10, 20
Voluntary	II Cor.	8	17
Single-mindedness	Josh.	9	2
Unity	Acts	1	14
Reflective of the mind of Christ	Phil.	2	2

according

A as he promised	Ex.	12	25
A as God hath blessed thee	Deut.	16	10
A to ways	Job	34	11
	Jer.	17	10
	Jer.	25	14
	Jer.	32	19
A to works	Mat.	16	27
	Rom.	2	6
A to the appearance	John	7	24
The called *a* to his purpose	Rom.	8	28
Gifts differing *a* to grace	Rom.	12	6
A to that a man hath	II Cor.	8	12
(*See* Matt. 9:29; Tit. 3:5)			

accountable to God

On judgment day	Mat.	12	36
Not to each other	Rom.	14	10–12

account *report*

Give *a* of stewardship	Luke	16	2
A worthy of obtain	Luke	20	35
Every one give *a* to God	Rom.	14	12
A to him for righteousness	Gal.	3	6
Watch as they that give *a*	Heb.	13	17
(*See* Job 33:13; Ps. 144:3; Matt 12:36)			

accursed *detestable*

A thing	Josh.	22	20
Hanged is *a* of God	Deut.	21	23
Keep yourselves from the *a* thing	Josh.	6	18
Wish myself *a* from Christ	Rom.	9	3
No man called Jesus *a*	I Cor.	12	3
Preach other gospel, let him be *a*	Gal.	1	8, 9
(*See* Deut. 21:23; Josh. 6:17; Is. 65:20)			

accusation

By false *a*	Luke	19	8
Against elder receive not *a*	I Tim.	5	19
Railing *a*	II Pet.	2	11
	Jude	9	
(*See* Matt. 27:37; Mark 15:26; Luke 6:7)			

accuse

A not a servant to master	Prov.	30	10
When *a* he answered nothing	Mat.	27	12
Was *a* that he had wasted	Luke	16	1
That I will *a* you to the Father	John	5	45
Not *a* of riot or unruly	Tit.	1	6

accusations, false see false accusations

Aceldama, potter's field *field of blood*

Bought with betrayal money	Mat.	27	6–10
	Acts	1	16–19

Achaia *grief*

Visited by Paul	Acts	18	12, 27
Contribution for poor	Rom.	15	26

Achan, Achar *he that troubleth*

Takes the accursed thing	Josh.	7	1
	I Chr.	2	7
Is stoned	Josh.	7	20–25

Achaz *see Ahaz*

Achish *only a man*

King of Gath	I Sam.	21	10
Feared by David	I Sam.	21	12
Helps David	I Sam.	27	5, 6
Sends David away	I Sam.	29	6–11
Receives Shimei	I Ki.	2	39, 40
Called Abimelech	Ps.	34	title

Achor, valley of *trouble*

Achan slain here	Josh.	7	24–26
A door of hope	Hosea	2	15

acknowledge *admit*

I *a* my sin	Ps.	32	5
	Ps.	51	3
In all thy ways *a* him	Prov.	3	6
Though Israel *a* us not	Is.	63	16
He that *a* the son	I John	2	23
(See Dan. 11:39; Hos. 5:15)			

acquaint *inform*

A thyself with him	Job	22	21
A with my ways	Ps.	139	3
A with grief	Is.	53	3

acquit *set free*

Not *a* me from mine iniquity	Job	10	14
Lord will not at all *a* wicked	Nah.	1	3

Acrabbim *see Akrabbim*

actions, God

God weighs our *a*	I Sam.	2	3
Sees wickedness	Job	11	11
Knows our works	Job	34	21

Adah *ornament*

Wife of Lamech	Gen.	4	19–21
Wife of Esau	Gen.	36	2

Adaiah *witness of Jehovah; adorned of Jehovah*

Grandfather of Josiah	II Ki.	22	1
A Levite	I Chr.	6	41
Son of Shimei	I Chr.	8	21
Son of Jeroham	I Chr.	9	12
Father of Maaseiah	II Chr.	23	1
A son of Bani who took a strange wife	Ezra	10	18, 39
Descendant of Judah	Neh.	11	4, 5

Adam *from red-earth*

The first man created	Gen.	1	26, 27
Blessed	Gen.	1	28
Placed in Eden	Gen.	2	8
Test of obedience	Gen.	2	16, 17
First called Adam	Gen.	2	19
Creatures named by	Gen.	2	19
His fall and punishment	Gen.	3	1–24
Hides from God	Gen.	3	8
Calls his wife Eve	Gen.	3	20
His death	Gen.	5	5
His transgression	Job	31	33
Called son of God	Luke	3	38
Head of fallen race	Rom.	5	14
In, all die	I Cor.	15	22
Christ, the second	I Cor.	15	45–47
Eve fell before Adam	I Tim.	2	13, 14
A town near Jordan	Josh.	3	16

adamant *hard*

Translated diamond	Ex.	28	18
Of sin	Jer.	17	1
Of a heart	Zech.	7	12
Of strength	Ezek.	3	9

Adan *see Nebuzar-adan*

Adar, Addar, Hazar-addar *glorious*

A town of Judah	Josh.	15	3
Son of Bela	I Chr.	8	3
Month for feast of Purim	Esth.	9	21, 22

Adbeel *disciplined of God*

Son of Ishmael	Gen.	25	13

add

Not to add to word of God	Deut.	4	2
	Rev.	22	18
Of children	Gen.	30	24
Of sacrifices	Lev.	5	16
Of cities	Deut.	19	9
Of years	Is.	38	5

Of grief	Jer.	45	3
Of burdens	II Chr.	10	14
Of length of days	Prov.	3	2
Of learning	Prov.	16	23

adder *any of various poisonous snakes*

Dan compared to	Gen.	49	17
Likened to the wicked	Ps.	58	3, 4
Like an evil man	Ps.	140	3
Likened to wine	Prov.	23	31, 32

Ader *see Edar*

Adin *adorned*

Sons return from captivity	Ezra	2	15
A covenant-sealer	Neh.	10	16

adjuration *charging solemnly*

Joshua at Jericho	Josh.	6	26
Saul at Bethaven	I Sam.	14	24
Ahab to Micaiah	II Chr.	18	15
Caiaphas to Jesus	Mat.	26	63
Unclean spirit to Jesus	Mark	5	7
Exorcists to evil spirits	Acts	19	13

Admah *earth*

City near Sodom	Gen.	10	19
Destroyed with Sodom and Gomorrah	Deut.	29	23

administration of law

Impartial justice demanded	Lev.	19	15
Not accept gifts	Deut.	16	19, 20
One witness insufficient	Deut.	19	15
Instructions to king of Judah	Jer.	22	1–4
Speak the truth	Zech.	8	16
Trial for every man	John	7	51
See courts			

admonition *a mild rebuke*

Paul to the mariners	Acts	27	9
Of one another	Rom.	15	14
	Col.	3	16
Against idolatry	I Cor.	10	11
Duty of parents	Eph.	6	4
To erring brethren	II Thes.	3	15
Of Moses by God	Heb.	8	5

Adna, Adnah *pleasure*

Comes to David	I Chr.	12	20
Chief of Judah	II Chr.	17	14
Took strange wife	Ezra	10	30
Post-exilic priest	Neh.	12	15

Adoni-bezek *lord of lightning (Bezek)*

Thumbs cut off	Judg.	1	5–7

Adonijah *Jehovah is my Lord*

Son of David	II Sam.	3	4
Usurps kingdom	I Ki.	1	5–49
Pardoned by Solomon	I Ki.	1	53
Is slain	I Ki.	2	24, 25
Seeks Abishag	I Ki.	2	13–23
A Levite teacher	II Chr.	17	3
A covenant sealer	Neh.	10	16

Adoniram, Adoram *my Lord is exalted*

Called Adoram	II Sam.	20	24
Son of Abda	I Ki.	4	6
Officer of the levy	I Ki.	5	14
Stoned to death	I Ki.	12	18

Adoni-zedek *lord of righteousness*

King of Jerusalem	Josh.	10	1–3
His death	Josh.	10	26

adoption by God

Of the Israelites	Ex.	4	22
Is of God's grace	Ezek.	16	8
Privilege of saints	John	1	12
Of the Gentiles	Acts	15	3–4
Through the Spirit	Rom.	8	14
Of sinners	II Cor.	6	17–18
Is by faith	Gal.	3	23–26
Is through Christ	Gal.	4	1–7
Heir of God, through Christ	Tit.	3	1–7

Blessings of:

Confers a new name	Num.	6	27
Love of peace	Mat.	5	9
Produces a likeness to God	Mat.	5	44–48
A forgiving spirit	Mat.	6	14
Become joint heirs	Mat.	6	25–34
Gives new birth	John	1	12, 13
An eternal home	John	14	1–3
Leads to holiness	I John	3	1–3

adoption of children

Of Eliezer by Abram	Gen.	15	1–3

adoption of children —*continued*

Joseph's sons by Jacob	Gen.	48	5, 6
Of Moses	Ex.	2	3–10
Esther by Mordecai	Esth.	2	7

adoration *a worshiping*

Majesty of God	Ps.	104	1–6
Vision of the Lord's glory	Is.	6	1–3
Of angels prohibited	Col.	2	18

advancement *act of advancing*

Of Moses	I Sam.	12	6
Of Joseph	Gen.	41	38–46
Of Levites	Ex.	32	26–28
Of Phinehas	Num.	25	7–14
Of Haman	Esth.	3	1
Of Mordecai	Esth.	10	2
Of Daniel	Dan.	2	48
First last	Mat.	20	16

advantage *opportunity*

What *a* will it be?	Job	35	3
What is a man *a*?	Luke	9	25
What *a* hath the Jew?	Rom.	3	1
What *a* if the dead?	I Cor.	15	32
Lest Satan get *a* of us.	II Cor.	2	11
In admiration because of *a*	Jude	16	

Advent of Christ *see* Second Coming

adversaries *opposers*

As a result of sin	Lev.	26	16
Abimelech and men of Shechem	Judg.	9	22, 23
Of the Lord to be destroyed	I Sam.	2	10
Of Solomon	I Ki.	11	14
Zedekiah and king of Babylon	II Ki.	24	20
Of Judah to be cut off	Is.	11	13
Punished by adversary	Ezek.	20	
Of Christ made ashamed	Luke	13	17
Christians not to fear	Phil.	1	28
The devil	I Pet.	5	8

adversity *calamity*

Result of sin	Lev.	26	14–20
Friends in	II Sam.	17	27–29
Result of forsaking God	II Chr.	15	3–7
Comfort in	Job	29	12–16
Prayer will overcome	Ps.	119	81–88
Fainting under	Prov.	24	10
Mercy to the faithful	Is.	30	20–23

advise *give opinion*

Jethro to Moses	Ex.	18	12–25
Rejected by Rehoboam	I Ki.	12	6–8
Accepted	Acts	5	34–41
Foolish	Job	2	9

advice *opinion*

Give your *a* and counsel	Judg.	20	7
Blessed be thy *a*	I Sam.	25	33
Our *a* not be first	II Sam.	19	43
With good *a* make war	Prov.	20	18
Herein I give my *a*	II Cor.	8	10

advocate *defender of a cause*

An office of Christ	I John	2	1

Aenon *springs*

John baptizes at	John	3	23

affairs *action*

Guide *a* with discretion	Ps.	112	5
A of the king.	I Chr.	26	32
Thou hast set over the *a*	Dan.	3	12
I may hear of your *a*	Phil.	1	27
Now my *a*	Eph.	6	21
Entangleth himself with *a*	II Tim.	2	4

affection *tender feeling*

Maternal	Gen.	21	15, 16
Fraternal	Gen.	43	30–35
Should be set on God	Deut.	6	5
Paternal	II Sam.	13	37
Should not grow cold	Ps.	106	12, 13
	Mat.	24	12
Christ first in	Mat.	10	37
	Luke	14	26
Of wicked are unnatural	Rom.	1	24
Rejection of carnal	Rom.	8	13
False teachers seek	Gal.	1	10
Set on heavenly things	Col.	3	1, 2

afflict *distress*

Taskmasters to *a* them	Ex.	1	11
Almighty have *a* me.	Ruth	1	21
I will *a* seed of David	I Ki.	11	39
How thou didst *a* the people	Ps.	44	2
Do justice to the *a*	Ps.	82	3

The days wherein thou hast *a*	Ps.	90	15
I was greatly *a*	Ps.	116	10
Lord will maintain cause of *a*	Ps.	140	12
Neither oppress the *a*	Prov.	22	22
Furnace of *a*	Prov.	48	10
Refuge in day of *a*	Jer.	16	19
In *a* will seek me early	Hosea	5	15
A ariseth for the word's sake	Mark	4	17
Out of much *a* I wrote.	II Cor.	2	4
Great trial of *a*	II Cor.	8	2
Add *a* to my bonds	Phil.	1	16
Received word in much *a*	I Thes.	1	6

afflicted, duties toward the *see* duties

affliction *distress or grief*

Continuance determined by God	Gen.	15	13, 14
Sometimes ends in good	Gen.	50	20
	Ex.	1	11, 12
Turns us to God	Deut.	4	30
Endurance of	I Sam.	3	18
	Luke	21	19
	James	5	13
God appoints	II Ki.	6	33
Man is born to	Job	5	6, 7
God dispenses	Job	11	10
Sin produces	Job	20	12–14
Exhibits love of God	Prov.	3	12
	I Cor.	11	32
Tempered with mercy	Is.	30	18–21
Supplication under	Dan.	9	3
	Mat.	26	39
Promotes glory of God	John	9	1–3
Christ, our example in	Heb.	12	1–3

ages, extraordinary

Adam, 930 years	Gen.	5	5
Seth, 912 years	Gen.	5	8
Enos, 905 years	Gen.	5	9–11
Cainan, 910 years	Gen.	5	14
Mahalaleel, 895 years	Gen.	5	17
Enoch, 365 years	Gen.	5	23
Methuselah, 969 years	Gen.	5	27
Lamech, 777 years	Gen.	5	31
Noah, 950 years	Gen.	9	29

agony *suffering*

Jesus on the cross	Mark	15	34–37
Christ, before betrayed	Luke	22	44
Paul's	II Cor.	1	8, 9

agreement *covenant*

Between true believers and idolatry	II Cor.	6	16
	Is.	52	11
Israel and heathen	Ex.	34	12–16
Jacob and Laban			
	Gen.	31	
Between David and Jonathan	I Sam.	20	4–17
With hell	Is.	28	15
Paul's, for worship	II Cor.	6	16

agriculture *earth cultivation*

Man placed in garden of Eden	Gen.	2	15
Ground cursed	Gen.	3	17, 19
Cultivation of the earth	Gen.	3	23
Not to be engaged in on sabbath	Ex.	23	12
Promises of God's blessings on	Lev.	26	4
	Deut.	7	13
	Deut.	11	14, 15
And the tithe	Lev.	27	30, 32
God's commandments concerning methods of	Lev.	19	19
	Lev.	19	23–25
	Lev.	23	22
	Deut.	22	10
Diligence	Prov.	27	23–27
Profit to all	Eccl.	5	9
In peace	Is.	2	4
Knowledge	Is.	28	24–26
In war	Jer.	51	23
Fertility and barrenness are from God	Heb.	6	7, 8

Agrippa *a wild olive*

Hears Festus' appeal for Paul	Acts	25	13–27
Refuses conversion	Acts	26	28, 29
Declares Paul innocent	Acts	26	31, 32
See Herod			

ague *a fever*

A curse of disobedience	Lev.	26	16

Ahab *uncle*

King of Israel	I Ki.	16	29
Marries Jezebel and turns to idolatry	I Ki.	16	31

Introduces Baal worship	I Ki.	16	31–33
Defeats Syrians	I Ki.	20	
Takes Naboth's vineyard	I Ki.	21	
Notorious for his wickedness	I Ki.	21	
His repentance	I Ki.	21	
He is wounded and dies	I Ki.	22	
Dogs licks his blood	I Ki.	22	
Seventy sons beheaded	II Ki.	10	
Formal alliance with Jehoshaphat	II Chr.	18	
A false prophet at Babylon	Jer.	29	

Ahasuerus *mighty man, Xerxes 486–465 BC*

King of Persia	Esth.	1	1
He marries Esther, and she becomes queen	Esth.	2	16, 17
Advances Haman	Esth.	3	1, 2
A decree against the Jews	Esth.	3	12, 13
Hangs Haman	Esth.	7	9, 10
Jews allowed to defend themselves	Esth.	8	11–13
Rewards Mordecai's loyalty	Esth.	9	4
Father of Darius	Dan.	9	1

Ahaz, Achaz *he hath seized*

Son of Jotham	II Ki.	15	38
Fight, Rezin and Pekah	II Ki.	16	5, 6
Wicked king of Judah	II Ki.	16	1–4
Tributary of Assyria	II Ki.	16	7–9
Spoils the temple	II Ki.	16	10–18
Father of Hezekiah	II Ki.	16	20
Makes a sun dial	II Ki.	20	1
Descendant of Benjamin	I Chr.	8	35
His wickedness punished	II Chr.	28	5
His idolatry	II Chr.	28	22–25
Comforted by Isaiah	Is.	7	1–12
Ancestor of Christ	Mat.	1	9

Ahaziah, Jehoahaz *Jehovah hath seized*

King of Israel, son of Ahab	I Ki.	22	51
His sickness and idolatry	I Ki.	22	51–53
	II Ki.	1	2–4
Reprimanded by Elijah	II Ki.	1	3–18
Makes alliance with Jehoshaphat	II Chr.	20	35–37
King of Judah, son of Jehoram	II Ki.	8	25
	II Chr.	22	1
His wicked reign	II Ki.	8	27
Goes with Joram to meet Jehu	II Ki.	9	21
Smitten by Jehu	II Chr.	22	9
Also called Jehoahaz	II Chr.	21	17
Also called Azariah	II Chr.	22	6

Ahiah *brother of Jehovah*

A son of Ahitub	I Sam.	14	3
One of Solomon's princes	I Ki.	4	3
A chief of the Benjamites	I Chr.	8	7

Ahiam *brother of a nation; brother of mother*

One of David's mighty men	II Sam.	23	33

Ahiezer *my brother is help*

A Danite prince	Num.	2	25
His offering at the dedication of the altar	Num.	7	66–71
A hero of David	I Chr.	12	3

Ahihud *brother of unity*

A prince of the Ashurites	Num.	34	27
A son of Ehud	I Chr.	8	7

Ahijah *brother of Jehovah*

A prophet who predicts the division of the kingdom	I Ki.	11	29–39
	I Ki.	12	15
Visted by Jeroboam's wife	I Ki.	14	2–6
Prophesies curse on Jeroboam	I Ki.	14	7–16
Father of Baasha	I Ki.	15	33
A son of Jerahmeel	I Chr.	2	25
One of David's mighty men	I Chr.	11	36
A Levite keeper of the treasures	I Chr.	26	20
A covenant-sealer	Neh.	10	26

Ahikam *my brother has risen*

Sent to Huldah for interpretation of book of law	II Ki.	22	12–14
He aids Jeremiah	Jer.	26	24
Father of Gedaliah	II Ki.	25	22

Ahilud *child's brother*

Recorder of David	II Sam.	8	16
Father of Jehoshaphat	I Chr.	18	15
Father of Baana	I Ki.	4	12

Ahimaaz *my brother is anger*

Father-in-law of Saul	I Sam.	14	50
Son of Zadok	II Sam.	15	27
Warns David of danger	II Sam.	17	15–22
One of Solomon's twelve officers	I Ki.	4	15

Ahimelech *brother of the king*

High priest at Nob	I Sam.	21	1
Gives David hallowed bread and Goliath's sword	I Sam.	21	2–9
Slain by Saul's order, for assisting David	I Sam.	22	11–18
David's captain	I Sam.	26	6
Son of Abiathar	II Sam.	8	17
Also called Abimelech	I Chr.	18	16

Ahinadab *my brother is noble*

One of Solomon's twelve officers	I Ki.	4	14

Ahinoam *my brother is pleasant*

Wife of Saul	I Sam.	14	50
Wife of David	I Sam.	25	43
With David at Gath	I Sam.	27	3
Taken prisoner by Amalekites and later rescued by David	I Sam.	30	5–18
Mother of Amnon	I Chr.	3	1

Ahio *brotherly*

Son of Abinadab	II Sam.	6	3
Descendant of Benjamin	I Chr.	8	14
Son of Jehiel	I Chr.	9	35–37
Accompanies the ark to Zion	I Chr.	13	7

Ahithophel *my brother is folly*

His treachery with Absalom	II Sam.	15	12, 31
Highly esteemed for his wisdom	II Sam.	16	23
Disgrace and suicide	II Sam.	17	23
Counsellor of David	I Chr.	27	33

Aholibah *my tent is in her*

Symbolic name of Jerusalem and Judah	Ezek.	23	4, 11, 22, 36, 44

Aholibamath *tent of the high place*

A wife of Esau	Gen.	36	2, 18, 25
Called Judith	Gen.	26	34
Edomite duke	Gen.	36	41

Aholah and Aholibah *her own tent*

Symbolic of Samaria and Jerusalem	Ezek.	23	4
Parable concerning their wickedness	Ezek.	23	5–35

Ai, Hai *ruin, a heap of stones*

City near the site of Abram's first altar, near Bethel	Gen.	12	3
The Israelites smitten at	Josh.	7	2–5
The city taken by stratagem	Josh.	8	1–29
King of, hanged	Josh.	8	29
Royal City in Palestine	Josh.	10	1
Occupied by the exiles who return	Ezra	2	28
Called Aija	Neh.	11	31
An Ammonite city	Jer.	49	3

Aijalon, Ajalon *a place of gazelles*

A valley in Dan where Joshua commands the sun and the moon to stand still	Josh.	10	12
	Josh.	19	42
A Levitical city of the Kohathites	Josh.	21	24
Refuge city	I Chr.	6	66–69
Given to Benjamin	I Chr.	8	13
Fortified by Rehoboam	II Chr.	11	10
Invaded by the Philistines	II Chr.	28	18
A city in the country of Zebulun	Judg.	12	12

Ain *a fountain*

A well to the west of Riblah	Num.	34	11
A city of Judah	Josh.	15	32
Given to the tribe of Simeon	Josh.	19	7
Made a city of the Levites	Josh.	21	16
Also called Ashan	I Chr.	6	59
Sixteenth letter of Hebrew alphabet	Ps.	119	121

air *atmosphere*

Fowl that flieth in the	Deut.	4	17
Birds of the	II Sam.	21	10
The way of an eagle in the	Prov.	30	19
A bird of the, shall carry the voice	Eccl.	10	20
Birds of the, have nests	Mat.	8	20
Not as one that beateth the	I Cor.	9	26
For ye shall speak into the	I Cor.	14	9
Satan called the prince of power of the	Eph.	2	2
Meet the Lord in the	I Thes.	4	17
The sun and the, darkened	Rev.	9	2
The seventh angel pours out his vial into the	Rev.	16	17

airplane

Prophecies suggesting modern air vehicles	Is.	31	5
	Is.	60	8
	Jer.	48	40
	Ezek.	1	19

Ajalon *see Aijalon*

Akkub *subtle, to grab by the heel*

A son of Elioenai	I Chr.	3	24

Akkub —*continued*

A child of the porters and aide to the priest	Ezra	2	42
	Neh.	8	7
	Neh.	12	25
A chief of Nethinims	Ezra	2	43, 45

Akrabbim, Acrabbim, Maaleh-acrabbim *land of scorpions*

A pass through the mountains SW of the Dead Sea, border of Judah	Num.	34	4
	Josh.	15	3
	Judg.	1	36

alabaster

It is a variety of gypsum largely used in Egypt in early times for carving into boxes and vases for holding ointment and perfumes. "Breaking the Box" meant breaking the seal only.	Mat.	26	7
	Mark	14	3
	Luke	7	37

alarm *a trumpet signal*

Judah challenges Israel	II Chr.	13	12
To announce the day of the Lord	Joel	2	1
	Zeph.	1	14–16
By Death	Ex.	12	29–33
By Attack	Judg.	7	20–23
By preaching	Acts	24	24–36

alas

A my master	II Ki.	6	5, 15
Stamp, and say *a*	Ezek.	6	11
A for the day of the Lord	Joel	1	15
Say in highways *a a*	Amos	5	16
A a that great city	Rev.	18	10

almond *tropical tree*

A gift from Jacob to Pharaoh	Gen.	43	11
Used as a motif for candlesticks	Ex.	25	33, 34
Wood used in Aaron's rod	Num.	17	8
Symbol of old age	Eccl.	12	5
Vision of Jeremiah	Jer.	1	11

Almon-diblathaim *see* Beth-diblathaim

almsgiving *relief of the poor*

Should be in secret	Mat.	6	1–4
Give such as you have	Luke	11	41
Will be rewarded	Luke	12	33
Of Zacchaeus	Luke	19	8
Practiced by early Christians	Acts	2	44, 45
Of Dorcas	Acts	9	36
Cornelius commended for	Acts	10	2–4
With simplicity	Rom.	12	8
Macedonian churches	Rom.	15	6
Inspired by love	I Cor.	13	3
God loveth a cheerful giver	II Cor.	9	7
A Christian duty	I Tim.	6	17, 18

aloes, lign-aloes *an aromatic tree*

Likened to the tents of Israel	Num.	24	6
Used as perfume	Ps.	45	8
Used to anoint the church	S. of S.	4	14
Nicodemus embalms Jesus	John	19	39

alone

Not good man should be *a*	Gen.	2	18
Bear all these people *a*	Num.	11	14
	Deut.	1	9
Lord *a* did lead him	Deut.	32	12
Who *a* doeth great wonders	Ps.	136	4
Ephraim joined to idols, let him *a*	Hosea	4	17
Not live by bread *a*	Mat.	4	4
	Luke	4	4
Jesus was alone	Mat.	14	23
	Luke	9	18
I am not *a*	John	8	16
	John	16	32
Went high priest *a* once	Heb.	9	7
Faith is dead, being *a*	James	2	17

Alpha *first letter of Greek alphabet; beginning*

Christ, and Omega	Rev.	21	6

Alphaeus, Alpheus *successor*

Father of Matthew, the Levite	Mark	2	14
Father of James the Less	Luke	6	15

altar *place of sacrifice*

Designed for sacrifice	Ex.	20	24
To be made of earth or unhewn stone	Ex.	20	24, 25
	Deut.	27	5, 6
Are not to have steps up to them	Ex.	20	26
For idolatrous worship to be destroyed	Ex.	34	13
	Deut.	7	5

Fires to burn perpetually	Lev.	6	12, 13
Probable origin of inscriptions on	Deut.	27	8
Natural rocks sometimes used as	Judg.	6	19–21
Of brick, hateful to God	Esth.	65	3

Mentioned in scriptures:

Of Noah	Gen.	8	20
Of Abraham	Gen.	12	7, 8
	Gen.	13	18
	Gen.	22	9
Of Isaac	Gen.	26	25
Of Jacob	Gen.	33	18–20
Of Moses	Ex.	17	15
	Ex.	24	4
Of Balaam	Num.	23	1, 29
Of Joshua in mount Ebal	Josh.	8	30, 31
Of transjordanic tribes	Josh.	22	10–29
Of Gideon	Judg.	6	24
Of Samuel	I Sam.	7	17
Of David	II Sam.	24	21, 25
Of Jeroboam at Bethel	I Ki.	12	33
Of Baal destroyed by Jehoiada	II Ki.	11	17, 18
Of Ahaz	II Ki.	16	10–12
Of Judah destroyed by Hezekiah	II Ki.	18	4
Of Manasseh and Ahaz destroyed by Josiah	II Ki.	23	12
Of the temple of Solomon	II Chr.	4	1, 19
Of Judah destroyed by King Asa	II Chr.	14	2, 3
Of the second temple	Ezra	3	2, 3
Of Ezekiel's vision	Ezek.	41	15–22
Of the Athenians	Acts	17	23

altar of burnt offerings

Dimensions and construction of	Ex.	27	1–9
Cleansed and purified with blood	Ex.	29	36, 37
All sacrifices to be offered on	Ex.	29	38–42
Sanctified by God	Ex.	29	44

Called by various names:

The brasen altar	Ex.	39	39
The altar of God	Ps.	43	4
The altar of the Lord	Mal.	2	13
Placed in court outside the tabernacle	Ex.	40	6, 29
Anointed and sanctified with holy oil	Ex.	40	10
	Lev.	8	10, 11
The fire upon it	Lev.	1	8, 9
	Lev.	6	13
	Lev.	9	24
Offerings at the dedication of	Num.	7	1–89
The priests alone to serve	Num.	18	3, 7
The Jews condemned for swearing lightly by	Mat.	23	18, 19
A type of Christ	Heb.	13	10

Mentioned in scriptures:

Built by Moses	Ex.	27	1
Built by Solomon	I Ki.	8	63, 64
Built by Jeroboam	I Ki.	12	32, 33
Removed and profaned by Ahaz	II Ki.	16	10–16
Renewed by Asa	II Chr.	15	8
Cleansed by Hezekiah	II Chr.	29	18
Rebuilt by Manasseh	II Chr.	33	1, 16
Polluted by Israel	Mal.	1	7, 10

altar, golden *see* altar of incense

altar of incense

Built by Moses	Ex.	30	1
Dimensions and construction of	Ex.	30	1–5
Placed before the vail in the outer sanctuary	Ex.	30	6
Anointed with holy oil	Ex.	30	26, 27
Called the golden altar	Ex.	39	38
Punishment for offering strange fire on	Lev.	10	1, 2
Atonement made for, by the high priest once every year	Lev.	16	18, 19
Solomon also builds	I Ki.	6	22
	I Ki.	7	48
A type of Christ	Rev.	8	3
	Rev.	9	13

alter *make different*

Not *a* thing gone out	Ps.	89	34
Law of Medes and Persians, which *a* not	Dan.	6	8
Fashion of countenance *a*	Luke	9	29

altogether

A become filthy	Ps.	14	3
A such an one as thyself	Ps.	50	21
He is *A* lovely	S. of S.	5	16
(*See* Ps. 19:9; 39:5; 139:4)			

always

I would not live *a*	Job	7	16

Not *a* chide	Ps.	103	9
I am with you *a*	Mat.	28	20
Me ye have not *a*	Mark	14	7
	John	12	8
Rejoice in Lord *a*	Phil.	4	4
(*See* Ps. 16:8; Is. 57:16; John 11:42)			

Amalek *warlike*
Son of Eliphaz	Gen.	36	11, 12
Fights with Israel and is overcome	Ex.	17	8–13

Amalekites *warlike people*
The scene of ancient warfare	Gen.	14	7
Descent of Esau	Gen.	36	12
The first to oppose Israel	Ex.	17	8
Located in the south of Canaan	Num.	13	29
A powerful and influential nation	Num.	24	7
Their utter destruction foretold	Num.	24	20
Unite with Eglon to defeat Israel	Judg.	3	13
Part of their possessions taken by Ephraim	Judg.	5	14
	Judg.	6	3–5
Overcome by Gideon	Judg.	6	33, 34
Saul overcomes, and delivers Israel	I Sam.	14	47, 48
Saul commissioned to destroy Amalek	I Sam.	15	1–3
Massacred by Saul	I Sam.	15	4–8
Agag, king of, slain by Samuel	I Sam.	15	32, 33
Invaded by David	I Sam.	27	8, 9
Pillage and burn Ziklag	I Sam.	30	1, 2
Pursued and slain by David	I Sam.	30	10–20
Remnant of, completely destroyed	I Chr.	4	41–43
Confederate against Israel	Ps.	83	7

Amariah *Jehovah has said*
Father of Ahitub, ancestor of Zadok	I Chr.	6	7
Son of Azariah	I Chr.	6	11
Second son of Hebron, a Levite	I Chr.	23	19
A chief priest of Jerusalem	II Chr.	19	11
A tithe-gatherer	II Chr.	31	15
A son of Bani, who took a strange wife	Ezra	10	42
A covenant-sealer	Neh.	10	3
One of the children of Judah at Jerusalem	Neh.	11	4
Ancestor of Zephaniah	Zeph.	1	1

Amaziah *Jehovah has been mighty*
King of Judah	II Ki.	14	1
Slain at Lachish	II Ki.	14	19
Quarrels with Jehoash	II Ki.	14	8–11
	II Chr.	25	17–20
Conforms to Mosaic law	II Chr.	25	1–4
Assembles an army	II Chr.	25	5–9
Uses Israelite soldiers	II Chr.	25	6
Defeats Edom	II Chr.	25	11
Worships idols	II Chr.	25	14–16
Reprimanded by prophet	II Chr.	25	7-10, 15
Defeated by Joash	II Chr.	25	21–24
A Simeonite, father of Joshah	I Chr.	4	34
A Levite of the family of Merari	I Chr.	6	45
Priest who tries to silence Amos	Amos	7	10

ambassador *messenger*
Jacob to Esau	Gen.	32	3
Moses to king of Edom	Num.	20	14
Gibeonites to Joshua	Josh.	9	4
Jephthah to Ammon	Judg.	11	12–28
Babylon to Hezekiah	II Chr.	32	31
Of Necho, king of Egypt	II Chr.	35	21, 22
Faithful rewarded	Prov.	13	17
King of Judah to Pharaoh	Is.	30	4
Hezekiah to Sennacherib	Is.	33	7
For Christ	II Cor.	5	20
Paul and Barnabas	Acts	13	3
Paul, in bonds	Eph.	6	20
Apostles	I Cor.	4	9

ambidextrous men *able to use both hands with ease*
David's mighty men	I Chr.	12	1, 2

ambition *a strong desire to achieve something*
Vanity of	Job	20	5–9
Punishment of	Prov.	17	19
	Is.	14	12–15
	Ezek.	31	10, 11
	Obad.		3, 4
Condemned	Is.	5	8
	Mat.	16	26
	Mat.	20	25, 26
	Mat.	23	11, 12
The devil tempts Christ	Mat.	4	8–10
Approved	Rom.	15	19, 20
	I Cor.	12	31
	I Tim.	3	1
Leads to strife and contention	James	4	1, 2

Exemplified:
Adam and Eve	Gen.	3	5, 6
Builders of Babel	Gen.	11	4
Miriam and Aaron	Num.	12	1–12
Abimelech	Judg.	9	1–6
Absalom	II Sam.	15	4
	II Sam.	18	18
Adonijah	I Ki.	1	5
Sennacherib	II Ki.	19	23
Haman	Esth.	5	9–13
Lucifer	Is.	14	12–15
Sons of Zebedee	Mat.	20	20–22
Simon Magus	Acts	8	18–23
Diotrephes	III John		9–10

ambush *concealed place*
Used to capture Ai	Josh.	8	2, 4
Men of Shechem	Judg.	9	25
Israel against Gibeah	Judg.	20	29
David uses against Philistines	II Sam.	5	23–25
Against Jehoshaphat's enemies	II Chr.	20	22
Against Babylon	Jer.	51	12

amen *so be it*
For emphasis, sometimes doubled, affirmation	Num.	5	22
	Ps.	41	13
An interjection	Deut.	27	15–26
	Mat.	6	13
	II Cor.	1	20
Let all the people say	Ps.	106	48
A title of Christ	Rev.	3	14
Used at the conclusion of a prayer	Mat.	6	13
Frequently translated "verily"	John	1	51
	John	3	3, 5, 11
	John	5	19, 24, 25

amend *change*
A your ways	Jer.	7	3
	Jer.	26	13
	Jer.	35	15
Hour when he began to *a*	John	4	52
To repair and *a* the house	II Chr.	34	10

amerce *to fine*
Punishment by fine	Deut.	22	19

amethyst *a semi-precious stone*
Found in the high priest's breastplate	Ex.	28	19
Part of the foundation of the new Jerusalem	Rev.	21	20

Ami *see* Amon

Aminadab *see* Amminadah

amiss *wrongly*
We have done *a*	II Chr.	6	37
Speak anything *a*	Dan.	3	29
Hath done nothing *a*	Luke	23	41
Because ye ask *a*	James	4	3

Amittai *true*
Father of the prophet Jonah	II Ki.	14	25
	Jonah	1	1

Ammi *my people*
Symbolic of Israel in the restoration Hosea's son	Hosea	2	1

Ammiel *people of God*
One of the twelve spies	Num.	13	12
Father of Machir	II Sam.	9	4, 5
Father of Bath-sheba, who is also called Eliam	II Sam.	11	3
	I Chr.	3	5
A Levite Son of Obededom	I Chr.	26	5

Ammihud *kinsman is glory*
Father of Elishama Ephraimite	Num.	1	10
A Simeonite	Num.	34	20
A Naphtalite	Num.	34	28
Father of Talmai	II Sam.	13	37
A descendant of Judah	I Chr.	9	4

Amminadab, Aminadab *my people is generous*
Father-in-law of Aaron	Ex.	6	23
Father of Nahshon	Num.	1	7
A man of Judah	I Chr.	2	10
Ancestor of Jesus	Mat.	1	4
	Luke	3	33
A son of Kohath, perhaps the same as Izhar	I Chr.	6	22
A Levite who helps bring the ark to Jerusalem	I Chr.	15	10, 11

Ammi-nadib *my people is noble*
Famous for his chariots	S. of S.	6	12

Ammon, Ammonites *sons of my people*

Descent of: Lot's son by incest	Gen.	19	38
	Deut.	2	19
	Jer.	25	21

Physical characteristics of the country:

Well-fortified	Num.	21	24
Half given to the Gadites	Josh.	13	25
Fertile	Jer.	49	4

Character of:

Idolatrous	Judg.	10	6
	I Ki.	11	7, 33
	II Ki.	23	13
Fond of ornaments	II Chr.	20	25
Superstitious	Jer.	27	3, 9
Vindictive	Ezek.	25	3, 6
Cruel and covetous	Amos	1	13
Proud and reproachful	Zeph.	2	10

Chief cities of:

Rabbah	II Sam.	12	26, 27
Ai	Jer.	49	3

Jewish laws respecting:

Not to be distressed	Deut.	2	19
	II Chr.	20	10
Perpetual exclusion from the congregation	Deut.	23	3
	Neh.	13	1
No covenant to be made with	Deut.	2	19
	II Chr.	20	10

History of:

Assist Eglon against Israel	Judg.	3	12, 13
With Philistines oppress Israel	Judg.	10	6–9
Jepthah delivers Israel from	Judg.	10	15–18
	Judg.	11	4–33
Saul's victories over	I Sam.	11	11
	I Sam.	14	47
Spoil of, consecrated to God	II Sam.	8	11, 12
Ill-treat David's ambassadors	II Sam.	10	1–4
Victories over Joab	II Sam.	10	7–14
	II Sam.	12	26–29
The royal treasure of, taken	II Sam.	12	30
People of Rabbah reduced to hard bondage	II Sam.	1	31
Defeated by Jotham	II Chr.	27	5
Miraculous defeat of	II Chr.	20	5–24
Submit to Uzziah	II Chr.	26	8
Jews reprobated for intermarrying with	Ezra	9	1–3
	Neh.	13	23–28
Vex the Jews after captivity	Neh.	4	3, 7, 8

Predictions respecting:

Subjection to the Jews	Is.	11	14
Subjection to Babylon	Jer.	25	9–21
	Jer.	27	3, 6
	Jer.	49	1–5
Punishment for oppressive cruelty	Amos	1	13–15
Restoration	Jer.	49	6
Destruction for hatred to Israel	Ezra	25	2–10
	Zeph.	2	8, 9

amnesty *a pardon*

To Shimei	II Sam.	19	16–23
To Amasa	II Sam.	17	25
To Absalom	II Sam.	14	23–24

Amnon *faithful*

David's eldest son by Ahinoam	II Sam.	3	2, 13
His scandalous treatment of Tamar	II Sam.	13	1–14
Slain by Absalom	II Sam.	13	20–29
A descendant of Judah	I Chr.	4	20

Amon, Ami *skilled workmen*

Governor of the city of Samaria under Ahab	I Ki.	22	10, 26
King of Judah, son and successor of Manasseh	II Ki.	21	18, 19
Murdered by palace intrigue	II Ki.	21	23–26
Father of Josiah	II Chr.	33	21–25
Ancestor of Jesus	Mat.	1	10
A family of temple servants, also called Ami	Ezra	2	57
	Neh.	7	59

Amorites *mountaineers*

Descent of: Canaan, the son of Ham	Gen.	10	15, 16
	I Chr.	1	13, 14
People profane, wicked and idolatrous	Gen.	15	16
	Josh.	24	15
One of the seven nations of Canaan	Gen.	15	21
	Ex.	3	8, 17
Originally inhabit mountain district in the south	Num.	13	29
	Deut.	1	7, 20
	Judg.	1	36

Refuse passage to Israel	Num.	21	21–23
Deprived of territory by Israel	Num.	21	24–35
Acquire land from Moab	Num.	21	26, 30
Have many strong cities	Num.	32	17, 33
Great Kings	Ps.	136	18, 19
Doomed to utter destruction	Deut.	20	17, 18
Governed by many independent kings	Josh.	5	1
	Josh.	9	10
Western kings of, confederated against Israel	Josh.	10	1–5
Miraculous overthrow of	Josh.	10	11–14
Kings of, degraded and slain	Josh.	10	24–27
Land of, given to Reubenites, etc.	Josh.	13	15–31
Not destroyed by Israel	Judg.	1	34–36
Intermarriage	Judg.	3	5, 6
Peace with Israel in the days of Samuel	I Sam.	7	14
Brought into bondage by Solomon	I Ki.	9	20, 21
The Jews after the captivity condemned for intermarrying with	Ezra	9	1, 2

Amos *burden bearer*

A herdman, a native of Tekoa	Amos	1	1
His divine call to prophesy	Amos	7	14, 15
Announces the doom of Amaziah and his family	Amos	7	10–17
Condemns the sins of Israel	Amos	4	1–7, 9
Prophecy of Christ	Amos	9	11–15
An ancestor of Jesus	Luke	3	25

Amoz *powerful*

Father of Isaiah	Is.	1	1

Amphipolis *about the city*

A city of Thrace visited by Paul	Acts	17	1

Amram *exalted people*

Father of Miriam, Aaron and Moses	Ex.	6	18–20
	Num.	26	59
His descendants called Kohathites, Levites or Amramites	Num.	3	19–20, 27
An Edomite called Hemdan	Gen.	36	26
A Jew who married a strange wife	Ezra	10	34

amusements *worldly pleasures*

In idolatrous worship	Ex.	32	6, 19
	I Cor.	10	7
Samson made sport of	Judg.	16	25
Lead to rejection of God	Job	21	11–14
	Luke	8	13, 14
Terminate in sorrow	Prov.	14	13
Lead to poverty	Prov.	21	17
Vanity of	Eccl.	2	1–14
A gift of God	Eccl.	3	11–13
	Eccl.	9	7-9
Wisdom of abstaining from	Eccl.	7	2–6
Judgment of	Eccl.	11	9
	II Pet.	2	13, 14
Denounced by God	Is.	5	11, 12
	Is.	47	8–10
	Eph.	4	17, 19
A characteristic of the wicked	II Tim.	3	4
	Tit.	3	3
	I Pet.	4	3
Music	I Sam.	18	6, 7
Salome dances	Mat.	14	6–8
Belong to the world of the flesh	Gal.	5	19, 21
Renunciation of, exemplified by Moses	Heb.	11	25
Dominate in the end times	II Tim.	3	1, 4
	Rev.	18	21–24
	Mat.	24	38, 39

Anaiah *Jehovah hath covered; Jehovah answers*

A priest who is present when Ezra reads the law	Neh.	8	4
Seals the covenant	Neh.	10	22

Anak, Anakims *a race of long necked giants*

Descent of Arba	Num.	13	22
	Deut.	9	2
Israel terrified by	Num.	13	33
	Num.	14	1
Great stature of	Deut.	2	10, 11
Driven out by Joshua	Josh.	10	36, 39
	Josh.	11	21
Inhabitants of the mountains of Judah	Josh.	11	21
Almost annihilated	Josh.	11	21, 22
Allies with the Philistines	Josh.	11	22
Seat of habitation at Hebron	Josh.	14	15
Reknowned for strength in the ancient world	Josh.	14	12
Hebron given to Caleb	Josh.	15	13, 19
Divided into three tribes	Josh.	15	14

Ananias *Jehovah hath favored*

Husband of Sapphira, smitten by God	Acts	5	1–6
A disciple who instructs and baptizes Saul of Tarsus after his conversion	Acts	9	10–18
	Acts	22	12–16
A priest at Jerusalem	Acts	23	2
Presses the prosecution against Paul at Caesarea	Acts	24	1

anarchy *lawlessness*

Kadesh	Num.	14	1–10
Against civil leaders	Ezra	10	8
	Jude	1	8
At Ephesus	Acts	19	28–34
In the end times	II Thes.	2	3–12
Prediction against Israel	Is.	3	5–8
Of wicked men	II Pet.	2	10–19

Anathema Maran-atha

Signifying one accursed until the coming of the Lord	I Cor.	16	22

Anathoth *answer to prayer*

A city of priests in the tribe of Benjamin	Josh.	21	18
	I Chr.	6	60
Home of Abiezer	II Sam.	23	27
Abiathar lives here	I Ki.	2	26
A son of Becher	I Chr.	7	8
Occupied by returned exiles	Ezra	2	23
Home of Jeremiah	Jer.	1	1
	Jer.	11	21, 23
Jeremiah buys field there	Jer.	32	7–9
Prediction of evil on men of Anathoth	Jer.	11	23
A chief who signs the covenant	Neh.	7	27
	Neh.	10	19
A Benjamite	I Chr.	7	8

ancestors *see* genealogy

anchor

An instrument for holding a boat in position	Acts	27	29, 40
Anchor of the soul	Heb.	6	19

ancient

A is wisdom	Job	12	12
I understand more than *a*	Ps.	119	100
The *a* of days did sit	Dan.	7	9
Prudent, and the *a*	Is.	3	2
Judgment with the *a*	Is.	3	14
Priest, and counsel from the ancients	Ezek.	7	26
With the *a* is wisdom	Job	12	12

Ancient of days

Term referring to God	Dan.	7	9, 22

Andrew *manliness*

Called to be apostle	Mat.	4	18–20
Brother of Simon Peter	Mark	1	16
Named an apostle	Mark	3	14, 18
Leaves John the Baptist to follow Jesus	John	1	37, 40
Fisherman, disciple of John	John	1	40
Brings Peter to Jesus	John	1	41
Finds lad with fishes	John	6	8, 9
Inquisitive	Mark	13	3, 4

angel of light

A name applied to Satan	II Cor.	11	14

angels *messengers, envoys*
Nature of:

Sometimes represented in form of man	Gen.	18	1–9
	Gen.	19	1–16
Are wise	II Sam.	14	20
Created by God and Christ	Neh.	9	6
	Col.	1	16
Called sons of God	Job	1	6
	Job	38	7
The holy ones	Job	5	1
	Ps.	89	5, 7
Are numerable	Job	25	3
	Heb.	12	22
Are mighty	Ps.	103	20
Glorious in appearance	Is.	6	2
	Ezek.	1	1–28
	Luke	24	1
Immortal	Heb.	12	22
Never marry or are given in marriage	Mat.	22	30
Are holy	Mat.	25	31
Are not to be worshiped	Col.	2	18
	Rev.	19	10
	Rev.	22	9
Are elect	I Tim.	5	21
Spiritual beings	Heb.	1	13, 14
Examples of meekness	II Pet.	2	11
	Jude		9

Invisible	Num.	22	22–31
Emotional	Luke	15	10

Rank and dignity:

Are of different orders	Is.	6	2
	I Thes.	4	16
	I Pet.	3	22
	Jude		9
	Rev.	12	7
Differ in rank and dignity	I Thes.	4	16
	Jude		9
Are ministering spirits	I Ki.	19	5
	Acts	12	7–11
Surround the throne of God	I Ki.	22	19
Intermediaries between man and God	Ps.	8	5
	Heb.	2	7
Have charge over the children of God	Ps.	34	7
	Dan.	6	22
	Mat.	18	10
Obey and execute the will of God	II Sam.	24	16
	Ps.	103	20
	Mat.	6	10
	Num.	22	22
	Mat.	28	2
	Acts	12	23
	Rev.	16	1–17
Communicate the will of God and Christ	Dan.	8	16, 17
	Dan.	12	6, 7
	Luke	1	19, 28
	Acts	8	26
	Rev.	1	1
Minister to Christ	Mat.	4	11
	Luke	22	43
	John	1	51
Execute the purposes of Christ	Mat.	13	41
	Mat.	24	31
Shall attend Christ in His second coming	Mat.	16	27
	II Thes.	1	7
Ministration of, obtained by prayer	Mat.	26	53
	Acts	12	5, 7
Shall worship Christ	Heb.	1	6, 7

Announcing important events:

Resurrection	Mark	16	5–7
Conception of Christ	Luke	1	30–35
Conception of John the Baptist	Luke	1	36
Birth of Christ	Luke	2	8–12

Named in scriptures:

Gabriel	Dan.	8	16
	Dan.	9	21
	Luke	1	19, 26
Michael	Dan.	10	13, 21
	Dan.	12	1
	Jude		9
	Rev.	12	7

Appearances to man:

Hagar	Gen.	16	7
	Gen.	21	17, 18
Abraham	Gen.	18	1–33
Lot	Gen.	19	1–3
	Gen.	19	15–22
Jacob	Gen.	28	12
Moses	Ex.	3	2
Balaam	Num.	22	23
Joshua	Josh.	5	13–15
Israelites	Judg.	2	1–5
Gideon	Judg.	6	11–23
Manoah's wife	Judg.	13	3–5
Manoah	Judg.	13	11
David	II Sam.	24	17
	I Chr.	21	16
Elijah	I Ki.	19	5–15
Daniel	Dan.	8	16
	Dan.	9	21
	Dan.	10	11
	Dan.	12	1–13
Zechariah	Zech.		3
Zechariah	Luke	1	11–20
Joseph	Mat.	1	20
Mary Magdalene	Mat.	28	2–7
Zacharias	Luke	1	11, 13
Mary	Luke	1	26–38
Shepherds	Luke	2	8–12
The apostles	Acts	1	10, 11
Peter	Acts	5	19
Philip	Acts	8	26
Cornelius	Acts	10	3–32

angels —continued

Paul	Acts	27	23, 24
John	Rev.	1	1
A which redeemed me	Gen.	48	16
A of Lord encampeth	Ps.	34	7
Man did eat *a* food	Ps.	78	25
Neither say before *a* it was error	Eccl.	5	6
A of his presence saved them	Is.	63	9
He had power over the *a*	Hosea	12	4
The reapers are the *a*	Mat.	13	39
Are as *a* in heaven	Mark	12	25
	Luke	20	36
An *a* strengthening him	Luke	22	43
A went down at a certain season	John	5	4
We shall judge *a*	I Cor.	6	3
Transformed into *a* of light	II Cor.	11	14
Word spoken by *a*	Heb.	2	2
Not nature of *a*	Heb.	2	16
Entertained *a* unawares	Heb.	13	2

(See Gen. 19:1; Ps. 8:5; Mat. 25:41)

angels, fallen; apostates

Charged with folly	Job	4	18
Satan their leader	Eph.	2	2
	Eph.	6	12
Delivered into chains of darkness	II Pet.	2	4
	Jude		6
Cast out	Rev.	12	9–11

angels of churches

Refers to ministers	Rev.	2	1–29
	Rev.	3	1–22

anger *fury, indignation*

Brings its own punishment	Job	5	2
	Prov.	19	19
	Prov.	25	28
Should not betray us into sin	Ps.	37	8
	Eph.	4	26
A characteristic of fools	Prov.	12	16
	Prov.	14	29
	Eccl.	7	9
May be averted by wisdom	Prov.	29	8
Meekness pacifies	Prov.	15	1
	Eccl.	10	4
Be slow to	Prov.	15	18
	Prov.	16	32
	Tit.	1	7
	James	1	19
Forbidden	Mat.	5	22
	Rom.	12	19
A work of the flesh	Gal.	5	20
Children should not be provoked to	Eph.	6	4
	Col.	3	21
Anger without sin	Eph.	4	31

Justifiable, exemplified:

Jacob	Gen.	31	36
Moses	Ex.	11	8
	Ex.	32	19
	Lev.	10	16
Samuel	I Sam.	15	16–31
Jonathan	I Sam.	20	34
Nehemiah	Neh.	5	6
	Neh.	13	17, 25
Our Lord	Mark	3	5

Sinful, exemplified:

Cain	Gen.	4	5
Esau	Gen.	27	45
Simeon and Levi	Gen.	49	5–7
Potiphar	Gen.	39	1, 19
Moses	Num.	20	10, 11
Balaam	Num.	22	27
Saul	I Sam.	20	30
Ahab	I Ki.	21	4
Naaman	II Ki.	5	11
Asa	II Chr.	16	10
Uzziah	II Chr.	26	19
Haman	Esth.	3	5
Nebuchadnezzar	Dan.	3	13
Jonah	Jonah	4	4
Herod	Mat.	2	16
Jews	Luke	4	28
High priest, etc.	Acts	5	17
	Acts	7	54

anger of God

Prayers to avert	Ex.	32	11
	Ps.	38	1
	Ps.	74	1, 2
	Ps.	80	4
	Dan.	9	16
	Hab.	3	2
To be endured	II Sam.	24	17
	Mic.	7	9
Cannot be resisted	Job	9	13
	Ps.	76	7
	Nah.	1	6
Tempered with mercy	Ps.	30	5
	Is.	54	8
Is righteous	Ps.	58	10, 11
	Rom.	2	6, 8
	Rom.	9	20–22
Manifested in terror	Ps.	76	6–8
	Jer.	10	10
To be dreaded	Ps.	76	7
	Ps.	90	11
	Mat.	10	28
Manifested in judgments and afflictions	Ps.	78	49–51
	Is.	9	19
	Jer.	7	20
Is slow	Ps.	103	8
	Is.	48	9
	Nah.	1	3
Is averted upon confession of sin and repentance	Jer.	3	12, 13
	Joel	2	12–14
	Luke	15	18–20
Folly of provoking	Jer.	7	19
	I Cor.	10	22
Reserved for the day of wrath	Zeph.	1	14–18
	Rev.	19	15
Is averted from them that believe	John	3	14–18
	Rom.	5	1
Averted by Christ	II Cor.	5	18, 19
	Eph.	2	14–17
	Col.	1	20

Provoked by:

Idolatry	Josh.	23	16
	II Ki.	22	17
	Ps.	78	58, 59
	Jer.	44	3
Those who forsake him	Ezra	8	22
	Is.	1	4
The wicked	Ps.	7	11
	Is.	3	8
	Nah.	1	2, 3
	Rom.	1	18
	Eph.	5	6
Unbelief	Ps.	78	21, 22
	John	3	36
	Heb.	3	18, 19
Iniquity	Ps.	89	30–32
	Ps.	102	9, 10
	Is.	47	6
Impenitence	Prov.	1	30, 31
	Rom.	2	5

Exemplified against:

The world of Noah	Gen.	7	21–23
Builders of Babel	Gen.	11	8
Sodom and Gomorrah	Gen.	19	24, 25
Egyptians	Ex.	7	20
	Ex.	8	6, 16
	Ex.	9	3, 9, 23
	Ex.	10	13, 22
	Ex.	12	29
Israelites	Ex.	14	27
	Ex.	32	35
	Num.	14	40–45
	Num.	21	6
	Num.	25	9
	II Sam.	24	1, 15
Sons of Aaron	Lev.	10	2
Aaron and Miriam	Num.	12	9, 10
The spies	Num.	14	37
Five kings	Josh.	10	25
Abimelech	Judg.	9	56
Men of Beth-shemesh	I Sam.	6	19
Enemies of Israel	I Sam.	7	10
Saul	I Sam.	31	6
Uzzah	II Sam.	6	7
Assyrians	II Ki.	19	35, 37

anger

Cursed be their *a*	Gen.	49	7
Slow to *a*	Num.	9	17
Rebuke me not in *a*	Ps.	6	1
	Jer.	10	24

Endureth but a moment	Ps.	30	5
Grievous words stir up *a*	Prov.	15	1
Discretion deferreth *a*	Prov.	19	11
A resteth in bosom of fools	Eccl.	7	9
He looked on them with *a*	Mark	3	5
Put off *a*, wrath, malice	Col.	3	8
(*See* Ps. 37:8; 85:3; 90:7; Prov. 16:32)			

angry

God is *a* with the wicked	Ps.	7	11
He that is soon *a*	Prov.	14	17
Make no friendship with *a* man	Prov.	22	24
Doest thou well to be *a*?	Jonah	4	4
Whosoever is *a* with brother	Mat.	5	22
Are ye *a* at me?	John	7	23
Be ye *a*, and sin not	Eph.	4	26
Bishop not soon *a*	Tit.	1	7
(*See* Gen. 18:30; Prov. 21:19; Eccl. 5:6)			

anguish *great pain, sorrow*

Of soul	Gen.	42	21
Of the spirit	Ex.	6	9
	Job	7	11
Of Saul	II Sam.	1	9
Of the wicked man	Job	15	24
	Is.	8	22
	Is.	30	6
Upon the soul of evil man	Rom.	2	9
Of a woman in childbirth	John	16	21
Judgment of wicked	Luke	16	23, 24
Of the heart	II Cor.	2	4
Hearkened not for *a*	Ex.	6	9
I will speak in *a* of spirit	Job	7	11
Tribulation and *a* on every soul	Rom.	2	9
Out of much *a* of heart	II Cor.	2	4
See	Gen.	42	21
	Is.	8	22
	John	16	21

animals

Food for men	Gen.	9	2, 3
God's care of	Gen.	9	9, 10
	Ps.	104	11, 21
Under the curse	Gen.	3	14
	Gen.	7	17
Possessed of devils	Mat.	8	31, 32
Clean and Unclean	Gen.	8	20
	Lev.	7	21
	Deut.	14	3–20
	Acts	10	11–15
Offered in sacrifice	Gen.	4	4
Instruments of God's will	Ex.	8	11

Animals of the Bible

Antelope	Deut.	14	5
Apes	I Ki.	10	22
Asses	Gen.	22	3
Badgers	Ex.	25	5
Bears	I Sam.	17	34
Bats	Deut.	14	18
Behemoth	Job	40	15
Boars	Ps.	80	13
Bullocks	Ex.	29	11
Calves	Gen.	18	7
Camels	Gen.	12	16
Cattle	Gen.	1	25
Chameleon	Lev.	11	30
Chamois	Deut.	14	5
Colts	Zech.	9	9
Conies, rock rabbits	Lev.	11	5
Deer	Deut.	14	5
Dogs	Deut.	23	18
Dragons	Deut.	32	33
Dromedaries	I Ki.	4	28
Elephants (margin)	I Ki.	10	22
Ewe lambs	Gen.	21	30
Ferret	Lev.	11	30
Foxes	Judg.	15	4
Goats	Gen.	15	9
Greyhound	Prov.	30	31
Hare	Lev.	11	6
Hart	Deut.	14	5
Heifers	Gen.	15	9
Hind	Gen.	49	21
Horses	Deut.	17	16
Kine (cows)	Gen.	32	15
Lambs	Ex.	29	39
Leopards	S. of S.	4	8
Leviathan	Ps.	104	26
Lions	Judg.	14	5

Lizard	Lev.	11	30
Mice	Lev.	11	29
Moles	Is.	2	20
Oxen	Ex.	21	28
Pygarg	Deut.	14	5
Rams	Gen.	15	9
Roe (roebuck)	Deut.	12	15, 22
Scorpions	Deut.	8	15
Sheep	Gen.	4	2
Snail	Lev.	11	30
Spiders	Prov.	30	28
Swine	Lev.	11	7
Unicorn (wild ox)	Num.	23	22
Weasels	Lev.	11	29
Whale	Mat.	12	40
Wolves	Hab.	1	8

anise *dill*

Seeds used in cooking and medicine, seasoning	Mat.	23	23

Anna *gracious*

A prophetess in Jerusalem who recognizes the baby Jesus as the Messiah	Luke	2	36–38

Annas *mercy of Jehovah*

High priest with Caiaphas	Luke	3	2
Jesus led before	John	18	13
Sends Jesus to Caiaphas	John	18	24
Peter's trial before	Acts	4	6

Anointed, The *see* Jesus Christ

anointing *applying oil or ointment*

Ceremonial, of persons (of priests, prophets, and kings)	Ex.	29	7, 29
	Num.	35	25
	I Ki.	19	16
	Is.	61	1
Of things	Ex.	29	36
	Ex.	30	26, 27
	Ex.	40	9–11
	Lev.	8	10, 11
Of the body	Deut.	28	40
	Ruth	3	3
	Esth.	2	12
	Ps.	92	10
Healing the sick	Mark	6	13
	Luke	10	34
Spiritual	Luke	4	18
	II Cor.	1	21, 22
	Heb.	1	8, 9
	I John	2	20, 27

Examples of:

Aaron and his sons	Ex.	28	41
Saul	I Sam.	9	16
David	I Sam.	16	1, 12
Solomon	I Ki.	1	34
Elisha	I Ki.	19	16
Christ, by several women as proof of their love and reverence	Mat.	26	6, 7
	Mark	14	3
	Luke	7	37–46
Name "Christ" means "Anointed One"	Is.	61	1
	Ps.	45	7

anoint *rub on, consecrate*

Arise, and *a* shield	Deut.	28	40
	II Sam.	14	2
	Is.	21	5
A to preach	Is.	61	1
	Luke	4	18
A my body to burying	Mark	14	8
My head thou didst not *a*	Luke	7	46
A eyes of blind man	John	9	6
Mary *a* feet of Jesus	John	12	3
He which *a* us is God	II Cor.	1	21
A thine eyes with eyesalve	Rev.	3	18
(*See* Judg. 9:8; Ps. 2:2; 84.9, Jas. 5:14)			

anon *soon, presently*

	Mat.	13	20
	Mark	1	30

another

A seed	Gen.	4	25
Glean in *a* field	Ruth	2	8
Let *a* praise thee	Prov.	27	2
My glory not give to *a*	Is.	42	8
	Is.	48	11
A gospel	II Cor.	11	4
	Gal.	1	6, 7
Bear one *a* burdens	Gal.	6	2
Pray one for *a*	James	5	16

another —*continued*

A Book	Rev.	20	12
(*See* I Sam. 10:6; Job 19:27; Esther 9:19, 22; Mal. 3:16)			

answer (n.) *reply*

No *a*	Job	19	16
	Job	32	3
	John	19	9
A soft *a* turneth	Prov.	15	1
A of tongue from the Lord	Prov.	16	1
Be ready to give A	I Pet.	3	15
A of good conscience	I Pet.	3	21
(*See* Job 35:12; Luke 2:47; II Tim. 4:16)			

answer (v.)

By terrible things wilt thou *a*	Ps.	65	5
I will not *a*	Prov.	1	28
A a matter before he heareth	Prov.	18	13
A not a fool	Prov.	26	4, 5
Money *a* all things	Eccl.	10	19
Not to meditate what ye shall *a*	Luke	21	14
Somewhat to *a*	II Cor.	5	12
How ye ought to *a*	Col.	4	6
(*See* I Ki. 18:29; Ps. 138:3; Is. 65:12, 24)			

answers by fire

Moses and Aaron in the tabernacle	Lev.	9	24
Elijah and the prophets of Baal	I Ki.	18	24–29
On the altar of David	I Chr.	21	16
Solomon's prayer	II Cor.	7	1

ant *a small insect*

Example of industry	Prov.	6	6

Antediluvians *very old*

Worship	Gen.	4	3, 4, 26
Occupations	Gen.	4	2, 3, 20–22
Art	Gen.	4	20–22
Prophets	Jude	14	15
	II Pet.	2	5
Great age	Gen.	5	3–32
Great size	Gen.	6	4
Great sinners	Gen.	6	1–5
Warned by God	I Pet.	3	19, 20
	II Pet.	2	5
Mentioned by Christ	Mat.	24	37–39

Anthropomorphisms: *Describing God in human terms*
God:

Resting	Gen.	2	2–4
Repenting	Gen.	6	6
	Ex.	32	14
Looking	Gen.	9	16
	Gen.	11	5
Moving	Gen.	11	7
	Gen.	35	13
Remembering	Gen.	19	29
Learning	Gen.	22	12
Hearing	Ex.	2	24
	Ps.	94	9
Jealous	Ex.	20	5
Having wings	Ps.	36	7
	Ps.	57	1
Hands	Is.	1	15
Eyes	Hab.	1	13
	I Pet.	3	12
Laughing	Prov.	1	26
	Ps.	2	4

antichrist *against or instead of Christ*

Warning against	Mat.	24	24
Man of perdition	II Thes.	2	1–4
The Beast	Rev.	11	7
People who deny Jesus	I John	2	18, 22
	I John	4	3
	II John		7

Character:

Against Christ	II Thes.	2	4
Miraculous	II Thes.	2	9
Deceptive	Rev.	19	20
Desires worship	II Thes.	2	4
Persecutes Christians	Rev.	13	7
Lawless	II Thes.	2	3–10
Rejects the deity of Christ	I John	4	3
	II John	7	
Many	I John	2	18–22
Will be defeated by Christ	II Thes.	2	8
	Rev.	19	20
Thrown into hell	Rev.	20	10
Destruction of	Dan.	11	36–45

antidote *a remedy against poison*

For plague of sin	Num.	21	8–9
	John	3	14–15

For deadly pottage	II Ki.	4	38, 41
For strife	Phil.	2	3

Antioch *the capital city of Syria*

Nicolas, the deacon of	Acts	6	5
Christians flee persecution	Acts	11	19
Barnabas and Paul settle in	Acts	11	22, 26
Disciples first called Christians	Acts	11	26
Agabus prophesies	Acts	11	28
Paul rebukes Peter at	Gal.	2	11
Sent Paul on missionary journies	Acts	13	1–4

Pisidian Antioch is in Asia Minor

Paul preaches at	Acts	13	14
Paul stoned	Acts	14	19
Paul returns	Acts	14	21
Paul recalls persecution at	II Tim.	3	11

Antipas *like his father*

Christian martyr of Pergamos	Rev.	2	13
See Herod (Herod Antipas)			

Antipatris *city of Antipater*

Town Paul is taken to as he travels from Jerusalem to Caesarea	Acts	23	31

Antitype *fulfillment of a type*

Translated "figure"	Heb.	9	24
	I Pet.	3	21

anxiety *uneasiness of mind*

Avoiding worldly care	Mat.	6	25–34
Seek kingdom of God	Mat.	13	22
For material things	Luke	12	22–31
Cares of married life	I Cor.	7	32
Prayer alleviates	Phil.	4	6, 7
Contentment from	I Tim.	6	8
Christian soldier is free from	II Tim.	2	4
Casting out	I Pet.	5	7

Conquered by:

Faith	Ps.	37	1–5
God's control	Rom.	8	28, 29
Prayer	Phil.	4	6

apes *monkeys from Ophir*

Imported by Solomon	I Ki.	10	22
	I Chr.	9	21

Aphek, Aphik *fortress*

City in Sharon	Josh.	12	18
City of Asher	Judg.	1	31
City near Eben-ezer	I Sam.	4	1
Site of Philistine camp before battle of Gilboa	I Sam.	29	1
Scene of Ben-hadad's defeat	I Ki.	20	26

Aphik *See Aphek*

Apocalypse *Unveiling*

Title of Revelation "revelation"	Rom.	16	25
	Gal.	1	12

Apocrypha *"hidden"*

Writings from the period between the N.T. and O.T. (400 B.C.—A.D. 40) which are rejected by Protestants. (Ex. Books of Maccabees, Tobit, Judith, Susanna, Bel and the Dragon)

Apollos *belonging to Apollo; destroyer*

A Jew of Alexandria	Acts	18	24, 25
Eloquent man taught by Aquila	Acts	18	25–28
Taught by Aquila and Priscilla	Acts	18	26
Causes division of the church	I Cor.	3	4–6
Preached in Achaia	Acts	18	27, 28
Friend of Paul	I Cor.	16	12
Paul tells Titus of	Tit.	3	13

Apollyon *see Abaddon*

apostasy *falling away*

From God	Heb.	3	12
	Deut.	32	15
From Faith	I Tim.	4	1, 2
Result of forgetting	Is.	65	11, 12
God will judge	Is.	65	13–15
	Jer.	17	5
Result of cares of this world	Mat.	13	20
Result of sin	Heb.	4	9–11
	I Tim.	3	6
Result of false teaching	Acts	20	29
Result of persecution	Mat.	13	21
Common in the end times	Mat.	24	10
	II Thes.	2	3
	II Tim.	3	1–7
Of Israel in the wilderness	Acts	7	39–43
Opposed to sound doctrine	II Tim.	4	3, 4
Impossible to be reinstated	Heb.	6	4–6

Examples

Saul	I Sam.	15	11
Solomon	I Ki.	11	1–10
Judas	Acts	1	25
Hymeneus	II Tim.	2	17, 18
Demas	II Tim.	4	10

apostles *persons sent forth*

Empowered to work miracles	Mat.	10	18–20
	Mark	16	20
	Luke	9	1
	Acts	2	43
Sent first to the house of Israel	Mat.	10	5, 6
	Luke	24	47
	Acts	13	46
Persecutions and sufferings of	Mat.	10	16, 18
	Mark	13	9–13
	Luke	21	16
	John	15	20
	Acts	4	1–22
	I Cor.	4	9
Hated by the world	Mat.	10	22
	John	15	18, 19
Urged to be humble	Mat.	20	26, 27
	Mark	9	33–35
	John	13	12–16
Sent to preach the gospel to all nations	Mat.	28	19, 20
	Mark	16	15
Christ always with them	Mat.	28	20
Twelve ordained by Christ	Mark	3	14
	John	15	16
Witness the resurrection of Christ	Luke	24	33, 51
	Acts	10	40, 41
Commanded to love one another	John	15	17
The Holy Ghost given to	John	14	26
	John	20	22
	Acts	2	1–4
	Acts	9	17
Not of the world	John	17	16
Unlearned men	Acts	4	13
Married men	I Cor.	9	5
Title for Christ	Heb.	3	1

Called by:

Christ	Mat.	10	1
	Acts	20	24
	Rom.	1	5
The Holy Ghost	Acts	13	2, 4
God	I Cor.	1	1
	I Cor.	12	28
	Gal.	1	15, 16

apparel *anything that clothes or adorns*

Micah's offering to the Levite	Judg.	17	10
Changes to enter the house of the Lord	II Sam.	12	20
Used as a disguise	II Sam.	14	2
Elegant, worn by princes and kings	Esth.	6	8, 9
	Esth.	8	15
Gaudy, not to be worn by devout women	I Tim.	2	9
	I Pet.	3	3
Symbol of pride	Is.	3	16–24
Indicates worldliness	Ezek.	27	24–27
	I Pet.	3	3
Symbol of royalty	Esth.	8	15
Priestly garments	Ezra	3	10
	Ex.	28	29
Harlot	Gen.	38	14
Virgin	II Sam.	13	18
May indicate mourning	II Sam.	12	20
Modesty desired	I Tim.	2	9

apart

Desert place *a*	Mat.	14	13
Mountain *a*	Mat.	23	17
	Luke	9	28
	Mark	6	31

(*See* Ps. 4:3; Zech. 12:12; Jas. 1:21)

appear

When shall I *a* before God?	Ps.	42	2
Let thy work *a*	Ps.	90	16
A unto men to fast	Mat.	6	16
Outwardly *a* righteous	Mat.	23	28
That it might *a* sin	Rom.	7	13
We all *a* before judgment seat	II Cor.	5	10
Glory in a	II Cor.	5	12
A of Christ	Heb.	9	28
	I Pet.	1	7
Abstain from all *a* of evil	I Thes.	5	22
Profiting may *a*	I Tim.	4	15

appeasement *alleviation*

By use of gifts	Gen.	32	20
By being slow to anger	Prov.	15	18

appetite *a desire or craving*

Taken away by sorrow	I Sam.	1	6–8
	II Sam.	3	35
	Job	6	6, 7
	Ps.	102	4, 9
Lost because of sin	Ps.	107	17, 18
For knowledge of God should be encouraged	Prov.	2	3–5
	I Pet.	2	2
Consider diligently the food before thee	Prov.	23	1–8
Of the soul	Eccl.	6	7
Of nations that fight against Israel	Is.	29	8
Jesus, tempted by Satan	Mat.	4	1–3
For righteousness shall be satisfied	Mat.	5	6
For food	Prov.	23	1, 2
Physical	I Sam.	14	31–33
	I Cor.	7	1–9
	Prov.	6	24–29
For wine	Prov.	23	29–35
For onions	Num.	11	4, 5

apple of the eye *the pupil, symbolic of something cherished*

God's people are precious to him	Deut.	32	10
	Zech.	2	8
A prayer of David	Ps.	17	8
God's law should be	Prov.	7	2
	Lam.	2	18

apples of gold *symbolizing great value*

Words well spoken	Prov.	25	11

appoint *choose*

Thou has *a* his bounds	Job	14	5
Days of my *a* time	Job	14	4
House *a* for all living	Job	30	23
Preserve those *a* to die	Ps.	79	11
	Ps.	102	20
A feasts	Is.	1	14
A him his portion	Mat.	24	51
	Luke	12	46
They *a* two	Acts	1	23
Seven men whom we may *a*	Acts	6	3
Hath *a* a day	Acts	17	31
God hath not *a* to wrath	I Thes.	5	9
A to men once to die	Heb.	9	27

(*See* Heb. 3:2; I Pet. 2:8)

appointment *a naming or selecting*

Service of Gershonites	Num.	4	27
Darius' decree	Ezra	6	9
To comfort Job	Job	2	11

appreciation *grateful recognition*

Of a good name	Eccl.	7	1
Of John the Baptist	Mat.	11	11
Of men	Ps.	107	8–21

apprehension *understanding*

Of knowledge of God	Acts	17	11
	Rom.	15	4
	Eph.	1	17–19
Of Christ	Phil.	3	12–14

approach *come near*

They *a* unto the most holy	Num.	4	19
Days *a* that thou must die	Deut.	31	41
His sword to *a* unto him	Job	40	19
Blessed whom thou causest to *a*	Ps.	65	4
Take delight in *a* God	Is.	58	2
Where no thief *a*	Luke	12	33
Light no man can *a*	I Tim.	6	16
As ye see the day *a*	Heb.	10	25

approval *sanction*

Of all good things	Phil.	1	10
To be sought from God	II Tim.	2	15
Of Christ	Rom.	14	18
	II Tim.	2	15
Result of study	II Cor.	6	4
Result of faithfulness	II Cor.	7	11
Result of a clear conscience	Rom.	2	18
Result of a knowledge of the law	Acts	2	22
Christ *a* by God	II Cor.	10	18
Self-approval			

aprons *garments to protect clothing*

First clothing of Adam and Eve	Gen.	3	7
Used by Paul to heal diseased	Acts	19	12

Aquila *an eagle*

Meets Paul at Corinth	Acts	18	1, 2
Tentmaker	Acts	18	2, 3

Aquila —continued
Settles with his wife, Priscilla, in Ephesus	Acts	18	18, 19
Teaches Apollos	Acts	18	24–26
Works in church at Rome and Corinth	Rom.	16	3
	I Cor.	16	19

Arabah a plain
Border city of the tribe of Benjamin	Josh.	18	18
Translated "desert"	Ezek.	47	8
	Is.	35	1

Arabia, Arabians desert
Referred to as the east country	Gen.	25	6
	Judg.	6	3
	Ezek.	25	4
Kings and governors bring tributes to Solomon	II Chr.	9	14
With the Philistines, slay the sons of Jehoram	II Chr.	21	16, 17
Later defeated by Uzziah	II Chr.	26	7
Oppose the rebuilding of the walls of Jerusalem	Neh.	2	19
Judgments against	Is.	21	13
To be destroyed by God's wrath	Jer.	25	24
Merchants in lambs, rams and goats	Ezek.	27	21
Jews at time of Pentecost	Acts	2	11
Paul withdraws here for contemplation after his conversion	Gal.	1	17
Mount Sinai located here	Gal.	4	25

Arad wild ass
Canaanite king	Num.	21	1
	Num.	33	40
A Benjamite	I Chr.	8	15
A town conquered by Joshua and given to Judah	Josh.	12	14
	Judg.	1	16
Belonging to the Kenites	Judg.	1	16

Arah wandering
A son of Ulla, of the house of Asher	I Chr.	7	39
Head of a family returning from exile	Ezra	2	5
Father of Shechaniah	Neh.	6	18

Aram height
Son of Shem	Gen.	10	22
	I Chr.	1	17
Father of Uz, Hul, Gether and Mash	Gen.	10	23
Son of Kemuel	Gen.	22	21
A city from which a concubine of Manasseh comes	I Chr.	7	14
A son of Shamer	I Chr.	7	34
Ancestor of Jesus	Mat.	1	3, 4
Hebrew name for Syria	II Sam.	8	5, 6

Aramea see Syria

Aramaic A North Semitic Language
O. T. Passages	Dan.	2	4–7, 28
	Ezra	4	8–16, 18
	Ezra	7	12–26
	Jer.	10	11
	Gen.	31	47
N. T. Passages	Mat.	27	46
	Mark	5	41
	Mark	7	34
Probably spoken language of Jesus.			

Ararat, Armenia high mountain
The ark rests here after the flood	Gen.	8	4
Called Armenia	II Ki.	19	37
Adrammelech and his sons seek refuge	Is.	37	38
Kingdom of Ararat to help destroy Babylon	Jer.	51	27

Araunah, Ornan strong is Jehovah
His threshingfloor becomes the place of the temple	II Sam.	24	16–18
	I Chr.	21	15
	II Chr.	3	1

Arba, Arbah four
City where Abraham and Isaac sojourn	Gen.	35	27
Also called Hebron	Josh.	15	13
A great man among the Anakims	Josh.	14	15

arbitrator a judge of a dispute
Solomon, a wise	I Ki.	3	16–28
Christ	Mat.	22	17–33
Moses	Ex.	18	18–27

archangel chief angel
Lord shall descend with voice of the archangel	I Thes.	4	16
Michael, contends with the devil over the body of Moses	Jude		9
Fights against the devil	Rev.	12	7–9

archers shooters with bows
Ishmael	Gen.	21	20
Wound Saul	I Sam.	31	3
Jonathan is an expert	I Sam.	20	34–39
David has Judaeans taught use of the bow	II Sam.	1	18
Ahab and Josiah killed by	I Ki.	22	34
	II Chr.	35	22
Figurative usage	Is.	21	17
	Jer.	50	29
	Job	16	13
	Gen.	49	23

architect a specialist in architecture
Bezaleel inspired by God	Ex.	31	1–5
Hiram of Tyre	I Ki.	7	13–46

Areopagite belonging to the council held on Areopagus
Dionysius, follows Paul	Acts	17	34

Areopagus, Mars' hill hill of Mars
Paul gives his memorable speech here	Acts	17	19,22

Aretas pleasing
King of Damascus who tries to apprehend Paul	II Cor.	11	32

Argob stony
A district in the kingdom of Og, subdued by Israel	Deut.	3	4
	I Ki.	4	13
Helps Pekah slay Pekahiah	II Ki.	15	25

arguments reasons offered for or against something
Job will plead his cause before God	Job	23	4

Ariel lion of God
Chief man of Ezra	Ezra	8	16
A name given Jerusalem by Isaiah	Is.	29	1,2

Arimathaea high place
A city of the Jews, home of Joseph	Mat.	27	57
	Mark	15	43
	Luke	23	50–53
	John	19	38

Arioch great; lion-like
King of Ellasar	Gen.	14	1
King Nebuchadnezzar's captain	Dan.	2	14,15
Ordered to destroy the wise men	Dan.	2	24
Brings Daniel before Nebuchadnezzar	Dan.	2	25

arise
A, go over this Jordan	Josh.	1	2
There a a little cloud	I Ki.	18	44
Let God a	Ps.	68	1
Shall the dead a and praise thee?	Ps.	88	10
A and have mercy on Zion	Ps.	102	13
To upright a light	Ps.	112	4
A, shine, thy light is come	Is.	60	1
Sun of righteousness a	Mal.	4	2
Damsel, a	Mark	5	41
	Luke	8	54
Young man, a	Luke	7	14
I will a and go to my father	Luke	15	18
A from the dead, and Christ	Eph.	5	14
Till the day star a	II Pet.	1	19

Aristarchus best ruler
Accompanies Paul to Asia	Acts	19	29
	Acts	20	4
Accompanies Paul to Rome	Acts	27	2
Fellowprisoner of Paul	Col.	4	10
	Philem.		24

Aristobulus best counsellor
Some of his servants are converted and greeted by Paul	Rom.	16	10

ark of bulrushes
Moses' mother hides him	Ex.	2	3
	Heb.	11	23

ark of Noah
Size and construction of	Gen.	6	14–16
Noah to put his family, animals and food inside	Gen.	6	18–22
Noah embarks	Gen.	7	1,7
	Mat.	24	37–39
Travels on flood waters	Gen.	7	18
Only those within remain alive	Gen.	7	23
Comes to rest on the mountains of Ararat	Gen.	8	1–16
Symbol of Noah's faith	Heb.	11	7
A figure of baptism	I Pet.	3	20

ark of the covenant
God gives directions to Moses for its construction	Ex.	25	10–21
To be covered with a vail	Num.	4	5, 20
Kohathites to bear the ark on their shoulders	Num.	7	9
	Num.	10	21

Joshua orders the peoples' behavior regarding its passage through Jordan	Josh.	3	1–17
The Israelites and the ark pass safely over	Josh.	4	1–18
Israelites fetch the ark from Shiloh when defeated by the Philistines	I Sam.	4	3–10
Taken by Philistines after second defeat	I Sam.	4	11, 17–22
Brings plagues to the Philistines	I Sam.	5	1–12
The Philistines send back the ark	I Sam.	6	1–21
Brought to the house of Abinadab	I Sam.	7	1
David sends for the ark	II Sam.	6	2–4
Brought to Zion and placed in the tabernacle	II Sam.	6	12–17
	I Chr.	15	1–29
Solomon brings the ark to the temple	I Ki.	8	1–9, 21
In heaven	Heb.	9	4
	Rev.	11	19

Contains:

Ten Commandments	Deut.	10	4
Aaron's Rod	Neh.	17	10
Pot of Manna	Ex.	16	33
	Heb.	9	4

arm

A of his hands made	Gen.	49	24
By greatness of thine *a*	Ex.	15	16
Underneath everlasting *a*	Deut.	33	27
An *a* of flesh	II Chr.	32	8
Own *a* did not save them	Ps.	44	3
Hast a mighty *a*	Ps.	89	13
Be thou their *a*	Is.	33	2
Mine *a* shall judge; on my *a*	Is.	51	5
Put on strength, O *a* of the Lord	Is.	51	9
The Lord made bare his holy	Is.	52	10
A of the Lord revealed	Is.	53	1
	John	12	38
Lord hath sworn by the *a*	Is.	62	8
Led them by his glorious *a*	Is.	63	12
Strong man *a* keepeth	Luke	1	51
	Luke	11	21
High *a* brought he them	Acts	13	17
A yourselves with same	I Pet.	4	1
See	Ps.	77	15
	Ps.	98	1
	Is.	40	10–11
	Is.	59	16
	Jer.	17	5
	Ezek.	31	17
	Zech.	11	17

arm of God *represents power*

Extended for redemption	Ex.	6	6
	Deut.	4	34
	Ps.	77	15
Protects Israelites passing through Canaan	Ex.	15	16
Extended for justice and judgment	Ps.	89	10, 13

Armageddon *height of Megiddo*

Scene of great battle against evil	Rev.	16	16
Also called the valley of Jezreel	Hosea	2	22
Good place for battles	Judg.	5	19

armies *bodies of men prepared for war*

Notable armies:

Of God	Ex.	7	4
	Ex.	12	17
	Num.	33	1
	Job	25	3
Of Moses	Num.	1	3
	Num.	2	2–16
Levites not included	Num.	1	47–54
Of Saul	I Sam.	13	2
	I Sam.	17	10
Of the Philistines and Goliath	I Sam.	17	26, 45
Of David	I Sam.	22	2
	II Sam.	23	8–39
Of Nebuchadnezzar	II Ki.	25	4, 5
Of Uzziah	II Chr.	26	11–15
Organization of	Num.	31	14
	Deut.	20	9
	Ps.	44	9
Weakened by God's disfavour	Ps.	68	12
	Ps.	108	11
Destroyed by God's wrath	Is.	34	2
	Mat.	22	7
In parables	Luke	21	20

Spirtual armies:

Disciples should teach all nations	Mat.	28	18–20
Christians must be soldiers	I Tim.	1	18
	I Tim.	6	12

	II Tim.	2	3
	Heb.	2	10
Faith defeats enemies' armies	Heb.	11	34
In heaven	Rev.	19	14

Religious ceremonies accompanying:

Counsel of God	Num.	27	21
	Judg.	1	1
Sacrifices	I Sam.	13	11, 12
Prophets prophesy	II Chr.	20	14–17
Songs	II Chr.	20	21, 22
Ark taken to battle	I Sam.	4	4–11

armour *defensive arms used in battle*

Stones and swords	Judg.	20	15, 16
Helmets of brass, coats of mail, spears and shield	I Sam.	17	5–7
Javelin	I Sam.	18	10, 11
Stripped from Saul	I Sam.	31	9, 10
Bow and arrows	II Ki.	13	15
Spear	Is.	2	4
Sword	Eph.	6	17
Helmet	I Sam.	17	38
Hezekiah shows his	II Ki.	20	13
Various types of	I Chr.	5	18
	II Chr.	26	14
	II Chr.	26	15
Can be taken from strong man by stronger	Luke	11	22

armour, spiritual

Righteous, compassed with favour	Ps.	5	12
Of light	Rom.	13	12
Paul wears armour of righteousness	II Cor.	6	7
To withstand wiles of the devil	Eph.	6	11–17

armourbearer

Abimelech commands his, to slay him	Judg.	9	54
David is Saul's	I Sam.	16	21
Goliath's	I Sam.	17	7, 41

army— *body of men armed for war*

organization	Num.	1	3
of Moses	Num.	2	2–16
of David	II Sam.	23	8–39
Exemption of Levites	Num.	1	47–54

Used:

Chariots	I Ki.	4	26
Archers	I Chr.	5	18
Slingers	II Chr.	26	14
Infantry	II Chr.	25	5
organizations	Num.	31	14
Saul's army	I Sam.	13	2
Israel's army without God	Ps.	44	9
	Ps.	108	11
Host of God	Job	25	3
Christ is our Captain	Heb.	2	10

Army:

Chief captain of his *a*	Gen.	26	26
Brought your *a* out of Egypt	Ex.	12	17
He that came out of the *a*	I Sam.	4	16
The *a* which followed them	I Ki.	20	19
The *a* of the Chaldees	II Ki.	25	5
Given to the *a* of Israel	II Chr.	25	9
Goest not forth with our *a*	Ps.	44	9
That were in his *a*	Dan.	3	20
Sent forth his *a*	Mat.	22	7
Then came I with an *a*	Acts	23	27
Turned to flight the *a*	Heb.	11	34
A which were in heaven	Rev.	19	14
Against his *a*	Rev.	19	19

Arnon *swift*

Border river of Moab	Num.	21	13, 14
	Josh.	12	1, 2
Moses instructed to cross	Deut.	2	24
Inheritance of Reuben	Josh.	13	8, 9, 16

Aroer *naked*

City built by children of Gad	Num.	32	34
Given to Reuben	Deut.	3	12
On the bank of Arnon	Deut.	2	36
	Josh.	12	2
	Josh.	13	16
Inhabitants send spoils by David	I Sam.	30	28
Conquered by Hazael	II Ki.	10	32, 33
Desolation prophesied	Is.	17	2
Taken by Moab	Jer.	48	19

Arphad, Arpad *camp*

A fortified city of Assyria	II Ki.	18	34
	II Ki.	19	13
Denunciations of Assyria	Is.	10	9
	Is.	36	19
	Is.	37	13

arrogance, arrogancy *haughtiness*

Should be avoided	I Sam.	2	3
	Prov.	8	13
Of the proud to cease	Is.	13	11
The pride of Moab	Jer.	48	29

arrows *weapons shot from a bow*

Of Israel shall pierce their enemies	Num.	24	8
	Ps.	45	5
Of God threatened	Deut.	32	23, 42
	Zech.	9	14
Which Jonathan shot	I Sam.	20	37
Sent by God against David's enemies	II Sam.	22	15
Of the Lord's deliverance	II Ki.	13	15–19
Of the Almighty, plague Job	Job	6	4
That flieth by day	Ps.	91	5
False witness likened to	Prov.	25	18
A deceitful tongue like	Jer.	9	8
Used against Babylon	Jer.	50	9
Evil, of famine	Ezek.	5	16
Of the Lord, as lightning	Zech.	9	14

arson *purposely burning*

Restitution to be made for	Ex.	22	6
Jephthah threatened by the men of Ephraim	Judg.	12	1
Samson	Judg.	15	4, 5
Absalom	II Sam.	14	30

art

Carving	Ex.	31	5
Smiths	II Tim.	4	14
	II Chr.	2	7
Engraving	Ex.	28	11
Jewelers	Ex.	28	17–21
Needlework	Ex.	26	36
	Ezek.	13	18
Stonecutters	Ex.	31	5
Potter	Jer.	18	3
Painting	Jer.	22	14
Armorer	I Sam.	8	12
Brickmaker	Ex.	5	7
Musician	I Sam.	18	6
Tailor	Ex.	28	3
Tanner	Acts	9	43
Weaver	Ex.	35	35

Famous Artists:

Jubal	Gen.	4	21
Tubal-Cain	Gen.	4	22
Bezaleel and Aholiab	Ex.	31	2–14
Hiram	I Ki.	7	13–51

Artaxerxes *honoured king*

King of Persia	Ezra	4	7
Commissions Ezra to rebuild the temple	Ezra	7	11–26
Nehemiah permitted to rebuild Jerusalem	Neh.	2	1–10

Artemas *gift of Artemis; safe and sound*

Sent to Titus by Paul	Tit.	3	12

artificer *a skilled craftsman*

Tubal-cain, an instructor in brass and iron	Gen.	4	22
All things in temple of David made by	I Chr.	29	5
Judged	Is.	3	1–3

artillery *implements of war*

Bows and arrows of Jonathan called	I Sam.	20	40

Arza *earth*

Elah, king of Isreal, is assassinated in this house	I Ki.	16	9,10

Asa *physician*

Third king of Judah			
His good reign	I Ki.	15	8–24
Wars with Baasha	I Ki.	15	16
Right in the eyes of the Lord	II Chr.	14	2–8
Fortified Judah	II Chr.	14	6–8
Defeat of Ethiopians	II Chr.	14	9–15
Destroys his mother's idol	II Chr.	15	16
Seeks aid from Syrians	II Chr.	16	2
Seeks physician's help	II Chr.	16	12
Rebuked by Hanani	II Chr.	16	7–10
Death	II Chr.	16	14
Buried in Jerusalem	II Chr.	16	13, 14
Ancestor of Jesus	Mat.	1	7
Levite son of Elkanah and father of Berechiah	I Chr.	9	16

Asahel *God hath made*

Son of Zeruiah, David's sister	I Chr.	2	16
Pursues Abner	II Sam.	2	19
Warned by Abner	II Sam.	2	20
Slain by Abner	II Sam.	2	23
Avenged by Joab	II Sam.	3	27

A levite appointed by Jehoshaphat to give instruction in the law	II Chr.	17	8
A Levite in Hezekiah's time in charge of tithes	II Chr.	31	13
A priest, father of Jonathan	Ezra	10	15

Asahiah, Asaiah *Jehovah hath made*

A member sent by Josiah to consult with the prophetess Huldah	II Ki.	22	12–14
	II Chr.	34	20
Descendant of Simeon	I Chr.	4	36
Levite who brings the ark from the home of Obededom	I Chr.	6	30
	I Chr.	15	6, 11
Firstborn of the Shilonites, called Masseiah	I Chr.	9	5
	Neh.	11	5

Asaph *collector, gatherer*

Father of Joah	II Ki.	18	18
Levite, son of Berachian Chief chorister	I Chr.	6	39
	I Chr.	16	5, 7
A seer	II Chr.	24	30
Appointed by the king	I Chr.	25	6
Official at dedications	II Chr.	5	12
	II Chr.	29	30
	II Chr.	35	15
Writer of Psalms	Ps.	50	73–83
Family of singers	Ezra	2	41
Keeper of forest	Neh.	2	8

ascend

Angels of God *a*	John	1	51
No man hath *a* to heaven	John	3	13
I am not yet *a*	John	20	17
Smoke of incense *a*	Rev.	8	4
They *a* up to heaven	Rev.	11	12
(*See* Ps. 24:3; 139:8)			

ascension of Christ *Jesus Christ*

ascension

Of Enoch	Gen.	5	24
Of Elijah	II Ki.	2	11
Of Christians	I Thes.	4	13–18

asceticism *self denial*

Nazarites	Num.	6	1–21
Samson	Judg.	16	16, 17
John the Baptist	Mat.	3	4
Extremes rejected	Luke	7	33–36
	Col.	2	20–23
	I Thes.	4	3, 4

Asenath *of the goddess Neith*

Wife of Joseph	Gen.	41	45
Mother of Manasseh and Ephraim	Gen.	41	50–52
Daughter of Potipherah, priest of On	Gen.	46	20

Aser see Asher

Ash *a tree*

From which idols are carved	Is.	44	14

ashamed

Let none that wait on thee be *a*	Ps.	25	3
Let me never be *a*	Ps.	31	1
Not be *a*, world without end	Is.	45	17
As the thief is *a*	Jer.	2	26
Were they *a*?	Jer.	6	15
	Jer.	8	12
A of your revenues	Jer.	12	13
Plowmen were *a*	Jer.	14	4
To beg I am *a*	Luke	16	3
Not *a* of gospel	Rom.	1	16
Hope maketh not *a*	Rom.	5	5
Not *a* of testimony	II Tim.	1	8
Not *a* to call them brethren	Heb.	2	11
Not *a* to be called their God	Heb.	11	16
Suffer as Christian, not be *a*	I Pet.	4	16
(*See* Gen. 2:25; II Tim. 1:12)			

Ashdod *stronghold*

Fortified town, one of the five chief cities of the Philistines	Josh.	11	22
	Josh.	13	3
Assigned to Judah	Josh.	15	46, 47
Ark brought here by Philistines	I Sam.	5	1–3
Home of Dagon	I Sam.	5	1–8
Subdued by Uzziah	II Chr.	26	6
Opposes Nehemiah	Neh.	4	7
Intermarriage of citizens with Jews	Neh.	13	23, 24
Conquered by Tartan	Is.	20	1
Prophecies concerning	Jer.	25	20
	Amos	1	8
	Amos	3	9

| | | Zeph. | 2 | 4 |
| | | Zech. | 9 | 6 |

Asher, Aser *happy*

	Ref.	Ch.	Vs.
The eighth son of Jacob	Gen.	30	13
His blessing	Gen.	49	20
Descendants	Num.	1	40, 41
	Num.	2	27
	Num.	26	44
	I Chr.	7	30
	Luke	2	36
	Rev.	7	6
Mixed with Canaanites	Judg.	1	31, 32
Their inheritance	Josh.	19	24
	Judg.	5	17
A town near Shechem	Josh.	17	7

Asherah *female counterpart of Baal*

Translated "groves"	II Ki.	23	6
	Ex.	34	13
Idol worship	I Ki.	15	13
	I Ki.	16	32, 33
	II Ki.	21	7

ashes *a powder*

Man likened to dust and	Gen.	18	27
	Job	30	19
Their removal from the altar after sacrifice	Lev.	6	10, 11
Purification	Num.	19	1–10
Used as a token of humility and mourning	II Sam.	13	19
	Esth.	4	1, 3
	Job	42	6
	Ps.	102	9
	Is.	58	5
	Jonah	3	6
	Mat.	11	21
Purifying the flesh	Heb.	9	13
Cities turned into	II Pet.	2	6

Ashkelon, Askelon *weighing*

Captured by Judah	Judg.	1	18
Samson slays 30 men	Judg.	14	19
Chief city of the Philistines	I Sam.	6	17
Prophecies concerning	Jer.	25	20
	Jer.	47	5
	Amos	1	8
	Zeph.	2	4
	Zech.	9	5

Ashriel *see Asriel*

Ashtaroth

A city held by Og, king of Bashan	Deut.	1	4
	Josh.	9	10
Smitten by Israel	Josh.	12	4
Given to Manasseh	Josh.	13	31
Awarded to the Gershonites	I Chr.	6	71

Ashtoreth *wife*

(See Asherah)

Divinity worshiped by Israel	Judg.	2	13
Goddess of the Zidonians	I Ki.	11	5
Goddess of Philistines	I Sam.	31	10
Idols in Israel	Judg.	2	13
	Judg.	10	6
	I Ki.	11	5
Removed by Josiah	II Ki.	23	13

Ashur, Asshur *(blackness?)*

Son of Shem	Gen.	10	22
Son of Hezron, father of Tekoa	I Chr.	2	24
	I Chr.	4	5

See Assyria

Asia *orient*

Represented at Pentecost	Acts	2	9
Disputing with Stephen	Acts	6	9
Paul forbidden to go there	Acts	16	6
Christian converts in	Acts	19	27
Worship Diana	I Pet.	1	1
Roman province where the seven churches are situated	Rev.	1	4

ask

In **a** you a king	I Sam.	12	17
Thou hast **a**	I Ki.	3	11
A of me, and I shall give	Ps.	2	8
A for the old paths	Jer.	6	16
They shall **a** way to Zion	Jer.	50	5
Give him that **a**	Mat.	5	42
A and it shall be given	Mat.	7	7
	Luke	11	9
Know not what ye **a**	Mark	10	38
Pilate **a** him	Mark	15	2
Every one that **a**	Luke	11	10
A in my name	John	14	13
	John	15	16

A no questions	I Cor.	10	25
Above all we **a**	Eph.	3	20
Lack wisdom, let him **a** of God	James	1	5
Have not, because you **a** not	James	4	2
A reason of hope	I Pet.	3	15
Whatsoever we **a**	I John	3	22
	I John	5	14

Askelon *see Ashkelon*

asp *a poisonous serpent*

Venomous snake, probably a cobra	Deut.	32	33
Curse of the wicked	Job	20	14, 16
Made harmless	Is.	11	8
Their poison likened to the deceitful tongue	Rom.	3	13

aspiration *strong wish*

The way of the upright	Prov.	22	29
Closer fellowship with God	Is.	26	8, 9
Serving the Lord	Rom.	12	10, 11
For things above	Col.	3	1, 2

ass *domesticated animal of Palestine*

Used for riding	Gen.	22	3
Beast of burden	Gen.	42	26, 27
	I Sam.	16	20
Mosaic law concerning	Ex.	13	13
	Ex.	23	4
	Ex.	23	12
	Deut.	22	10
Of Balaam talks	Num.	22	22–30
Saul seeks the lost, of Kish	I Sam.	9	3, 20
Sold for food	II Ki.	6	25
Drawing chariots	Is.	21	7
Wild	Job	24	5
	Job	39	5
	Dan.	5	21
Stubbornness	Hosea	8	9
Stupidity of	Prov.	26	3
	Is.	1	3
Jawbone used to slay Philistines	Judg.	15	15–17
Ridden by Jesus	Mat.	21	2, 5, 7
	John	12	14
Cared for on sabbath	Luke	13	15

assassination *see murder*

Assault:

Of parent	Ex.	21	15
Laws of	Ex.	21	18–25
General rule	Mat.	5	38, 39
Of Jesus	Is.	50	6
	Mat.	26	67
	Mat.	27	30

assembly *appointed body*

Solemn assembly established	Lev.	23	36
	Num.	10	3
	Num.	29	35
	Neh.	8	18
To voice complaint	Num.	20	2–6
For war	I Sam.	17	47
Of saints	Ps.	89	7
Praise in	Ps.	107	32
God's disapproval	Is.	1	13
Of upright	Ps.	111	1
Of treacherous men	Jer.	9	2
Of the early disciples	Acts	1	4
On Pentecost	Acts	2	1–21
Matters to be determined in	Acts	19	39
Should not be forsaken	Heb.	10	25
Condemned Christ	Mat.	26	3, 4
To worship	Heb.	10	25

See congregation

Asshur *see Ashur, Assyria*

Asshurim *steps*

People of Arabia descended from Abraham	Gen.	25	3

Assir *captive, prisoner*

Son of Korah	Ex.	6	24
Son of Jeconiah	I Chr.	3	17
A son of Ebiasath	I Chr.	6	22, 23

assistance, divine

Acknowledgments of:

Abraham	Gen.	24	1
Hannah	I Sam.	1	2, 20
Hezekiah	II Ki.	19	20
Job	Job	42	10
Psalmist	Ps.	120	1

Promised:

To our soul	Ps.	33	20

assistance, divine —*continued*			
Desires of heart	Ps.	37	4, 5
Help from hills	Ps.	121	1
When we call	Is.	58	9
Good gifts	Mat.	7	11
Whatsoever ye ask	Mat.	21	22
Upon request	Luke	11	5–13
	John	15	7
Wisdom	James	1	5
To asker	I John	3	22
	I John	5	14, 15
Necessary in all our undertakings	John	15	5
	I Cor.	15	10
	Phil.	2	13
	I Tim.	1	12
Assur *see* Assyria			
assurance *full conviction*			
Effect of righteousness	Is.	32	17
Election	Ps.	4	3
Of eternal life	John	10	28, 29
	Acts	17	31
	I John	5	13
Love of God is constant	Rom.	8	38, 39
Of understanding God	Col.	2	2
Changed life	II Cor.	5	17
	I John	3	14–22
Of hope	Heb.	6	11
Result of faith	Heb.	10	22
Redemption	Job	19	25
Preservation	Ps.	27	3–5
Continuance in grace	Phil.	1	6
Assyria, Asshur, Assur *name derived from Asshur*			
An ancient empire situated along the Tigris or Hiddekel river	Gen.	2	14
	Ezra	4	2
Nineveh, chief city of	Gen.	10	11
	II Ki.	19	36
Known to the Hebrews in time of Abraham	Gen.	25	18
Called Asshur	Num.	24	22
	Hosea	14	3
Army miraculously destroyed	II Ki.	19	35
	Is.	37	36
Idolatry the religion of	II Ki.	19	37
Celebrated for:			
Fertility	II Ki.	18	31–32
	Is.	36	16–17
Extent of conquests	II Ki.	18	33–35
	II Ki.	19	11–13
	Is.	10	9–14
Extensive commerce	Ezek.	27	23, 24
Called Assur	Ps.	83	8
Prophecies concerning	Is.	8	1–22
	Is.	10	5, 6
	Is.	14	24–27
	Is.	30	31
	Is.	31	8
	Mic.	5	6
	Nah.	3	18
	Zeph.	2	13
	Zech.	10	10, 11
Departed glory and fall of	Ezek.	31	3–17
Ephraim makes covenant with	Hosea	12	1
The land of Nimrod	Mic.	5	6
Kings of:			
Pul or Tiglath-pileser, who carries Israel captive	II Ki.	15	19, 29
	II Ki.	16	10
Shalmaneser resettles Samaria	II Ki.	17	3, 24
Sennacherib takes cities of Judah	II Ki.	18	13
Esarhaddon reigns	II Ki.	19	37
Asnapper completes the repeopling of Samaria	Ezra	4	10
astonished *surprised*			
Pillars of heaven are *a*	Job	26	11
As many were *a* at thee	Is.	52	14
Be *a* O ye heavens	Jer.	2	12
Was *a* at the vision	Dan.	8	27
	Mat.	7	28
	Mat.	22	33
	Mark	1	22
	Mark	11	18
A at his doctrine	Luke	4	32
A at his understanding and answers	Luke	2	47
A at draught of fishes	Luke	5	9
Women made us *a*	Luke	24	22

Saul trembling and *a*	Acts	9	6
Saw Peter, they were *a*	Acts	12	16
Deputy believed, being *a*	Acts	13	12
Astonishment:			
Become an *a* and a proverb	Deut.	28	37
Drink wine of *a*	Ps.	60	3
A hath taken hold	Jer.	8	21
Filled with cup of *a*	Ezek.	23	33
astrologers *star gazers*			
Practice in Babylon	Is.	47	1, 13, 14
Inferior to counsel of wise men	Dan.	1	20
Nebuchadnezzar seeks their counsel	Dan.	2	2
Daniel denounces them	Dan.	2	27
Asuppim *stores; gatherings*			
Storage places near the southern gates of the temple	I Chr.	26	15
Translated "thresholds"	Neh.	12	25
Atad *thorn*			
Threshingfloor where funeral party bearing Jacob's body halts seven days	Gen.	50	10
Called Abel-mizraim	Gen.	50	11
Ater *shut*			
Member of Hezekiah's family, who returns from exile	Ezra	2	16
	Neh.	7	21
A porter at the temple	Ezra	2	42
	Neh.	7	45
A covenant-sealer	Neh.	10	17
Athaliah *Jehovah is great*			
Daughter of Ahab and wife of Jehoram	II Ki.	8	16–18
Slays the royal seed of Judah	II Chr.	22	10
Slain by order of Jehoiada	II Ki.	11	13–16
	II Chr.	23	12–15
Mother of Ahaziah	II Chr.	22	2
Seizes the throne and reigns six years	II Chr.	22	10–12
A Benjamite, the son of Jeroham	I Chr.	8	26
The father of Jeshaiah	Ezra	8	7
atheism *the belief that there is no God*			
Arguments against	Job	12	7–25
	Rom.	1	19, 20
Only the wicked and the fool denies God	Job	34	9
	Ps.	10	4, 11
	Ps.	14	1
atonement *reconciliation*			
Explained	Rom.	5	8–11
	II Cor.	5	18–19
	Gal.	4	
	I John	2	2
	I John	4	10
Foretold	Dan.	9	24–27
Ministers should fully set forth	Acts	5	29–31, 42
	I Cor.	15	3
	II Cor.	5	21
Necessity for	Is.	59	16
	Luke	19	10
	Heb.	9	22
Saints glorify God for	I Cor.	6	20
	Gal.	2	20
	Phil.	1	20–21
Saints praise God for	Rev.	5	9–13
Saints rejoice in God for	Rom.	5	11
By priests alone	I Chr.	6	49
	II Chr.	29	24
Extraordinary	Ex.	32	30–34
	Num.	16	47
	Num.	25	10–13
Made by sacrifice	Lev.	1	4, 5
Typical of Christ's atonement	Rom.	5	6–11
Moses seeks, for sin of people	Ex.	32	30
Individual offering made for	Lev.	1	2–4
For all the people	Lev.	9	7
To the Gibeonites	II Sam.	21	3
Offerings for, reinstituted	Neh.	10	30
Day of *a*	Lev.	23	28
	Lev.	25	9
Wherewith shall I make *a*?	II Sam.	21	3
By whom we received *a*	Rom.	5	11
Necessary for:			
Propitiating God	Ex.	32	30
Purifying	Ex.	29	36
Ransoming	Ex.	30	15–17
	Job	33	24
Ordered for:			
Altar	Ex.	29	36–37
	Lev.	16	18–19
Congregation	Num.	15	25
	II Chr.	29	24

Healed lepers	Lev.	14	18
Holy place	Lev.	16	16–17
Leprous house healed	Lev.	14	53
Persons sinning ignorantly	Lev.	4	20
Persons sinning willfully	Lev.	6	7
Persons unclean	Lev.	5	2–3, 6
Persons withholding evidence	Lev.	5	1, 6
Priests	Ex.	29	31–33
	Lev.	8	34
Women after childbirth	Lev.	12	8

Exhibits the:

Grace and mercy of God	Eph.	2	4–5, 7
	I Tim.	2	4
	Rom.	8	28–39
Love of Christ	John	15	13
	Gal.	2	20
	Eph.	5	2, 25
	Rev.	1	5
Love of God	Rom.	5	8
	I John	4	9–10

Has delivered saints from the:

Power of the devil	Col.	2	15
	Heb.	2	14–15
Power of sin	Rom.	8	3
	I Pet.	1	18–19
Power of the world	Gal.	1	4
	Gal.	6	14

atonement of Christ *see* Jesus Christ

attain

I cannot *a* to it	II Sam.	23	19
	I Chr.	11	21
	Ps.	139	6
Gentiles *a* to righteousness	Rom.	9	30
That I might *a*	Phil.	3	11, 12 and 16

   (*See* Gen. 47:9; Prov. 1:5; Ezek. 46:7; I Tim. 4:6)

attendance, church

Early example by disciples	Acts	2	46
Sabbath observed at Antioch	Acts	13	14
Not to be neglected	Heb.	10	25

attitude

Compassion	Ps.	119	136
Obedience	John	14	15, 23
Transformed	Rom.	12	1, 2
Jesus	Luke	19	41
Paul	Rom.	9	1–3

Augustus *see* Caesar Augustus

Augustus' band *Roman soldiers*

Paul taken to Rome by	Acts	27	1

aul *see* awl

authority *the right to command*

God-given, of man in the world	Gen.	1	26–30
Obedience to	Josh.	1	16
People rejoice when, is in hands of righteous	Esth.	8	15
	Prov.	29	2
	Acts	8	27, 28
Jesus is given all authority in heaven and in earth	Is.	9	5–7
	Mat.	28	18
Christ teaches with	Mat.	7	28–29
Christ's compared to centurion's	Mat.	8	8–9
Exercised by the great	Mat.	20	25
Of Christ over unclean spirits	Mark	1	27
Jesus' authority questioned	Mark	11	27, 28
To forgive sins	Luke	5	24
Power of the centurion	Luke	7	8
Of Christ to execute judgment	John	5	22–27
Christ uses, to deliver an adulteress	John	8	3–11
Of Apostles	II Cor.	10	8
Civil authority should be obeyed	Rom.	13	1–7
	Tit.	3	1
Of husband	I Tim.	2	12

avarice *greediness*

Achan takes spoils of war	Josh.	7	20, 21
Causes of family trouble	Prov.	15	27
Abundance does not satisfy	Eccl.	5	10
Leaders become corrupt	Is.	56	11
Of Ahab	I Ki.	21	1–4
Judas Iscariot plans betrayal	Mat.	26	15, 16
The parable of the rich man	Luke	12	16–21
Of Ananias and Sapphira	Acts	5	1–10
Felix hopes for a bribe	Acts	24	26–27
Root of evil	I Tim.	6	10
Cause of misery	James	5	3
Balaam forsakes the right way	II Pet.	2	15

Aven *emptiness*

A city of Egypt	Ezek.	30	17
Bethel, the idolatrous city	Hosea	10	8
A valley in Damascus	Amos	1	5

avenge

Thou shalt not *a*	Lev.	19	18
A blood of his servants	Deut.	32	43
Sun stood still till people *a*	Josh.	10	13
The Lord judge, and *a*	I Sam.	24	12
God *a* me.	II Sam.	22	48
	Ps.	18	47
I will *a* me of mine enemies.	Is.	1	24
A me of mine adversary.	Luke	18	3
A not yourselves	Rom.	12	19
God hath *a* blood of his servants.	Rev.	19	2

   (*See* Gen. 4:24; Judg. 15:7; I Sam. 25:26)

avenger of blood

Capital punishment sanctioned	Gen.	9	5, 6
	Num.	35	19
	Deut.	19	12
Cities of refuge from the avenger	Num.	35	11–15
Kill not in anger or enmity	Num.	35	20, 21

awake

As a dream when one *a*	Ps.	73	20
When shall I *a*?	Prov.	23	35
A, *A*, put on strength	Is.	51	9
	Is.	52	1
A, ye drunkards.	Joel	1	5
A, O sword	Zech.	13	7
When *a*, they saw his glory.	Luke	9	32
A to righteousness	I Cor.	15	34
A thou that sleepest.	Eph.	5	14

   (*See* Jer. 51:57; John 11:11)

awakening, spiritual

Israel is called to	Is.	26	19–21
	Is.	52	1–3
The church is called to	Rom.	13	11
	I Cor.	15	34
	Eph.	5	14
Called for by Joshua	Josh.	24	1–31

Exemplified:

Led by Samuel	I Sam.	7	3–6
Led by Elijah	I Ki.	18	21–40
Led by Hezekiah	II Chr.	30	1–27
Led by Ezra	Ezra	10	1–17
John the Baptist	Luke	3	2–14
Jesus in Samaria	John	4	28–42
Pentecost in Jerusalem	Acts	2	1–47
Philip in Samaria	Acts	8	5–12
Peter at Lydda	Acts	9	32–35
Paul and Barnabas	Acts	13	14–52

awe *a feeling of reverence and fear*

Reverence for God	Ps.	4	4
The world's inhabitants called to stand in	Ps.	33	8
The attitude of the heart for God's word	Ps.	119	161

awl, aul *a small pointed tool for making holes*

Used to mark a servant by boring a hole in his ear	Ex.	21	6
	Deut.	15	17

axe *a tool used for hewing and chopping*

For cutting trees	Deut.	19	5
	Ps.	74	5
Sharpened by Philistines	I Sam.	13	20
Not used in the building of the temple	I Ki.	6	7
Made to swim by Elisha	II Ki.	6	5–7
Figurative of divine judgment	Is.	10	15
	Jer.	10	3
	Jer.	46	22
	Jer.	51	20
	Ezek.	26	9
	Mat.	3	10
	Luke	3	9

axletree *the bar connecting the wheels of a carriage*

Hiram uses in the bases of temple	I Ki.	7	32, 33

Azariah *Jehovah is keeper*

A descendant of David's high priest, Zadok	I Ki.	4	2
Son of Nathan	I Ki.	4	5
King of Judah, son of Amaziah	II Ki.	14	21
Rebuilds Elath	II Ki.	14	22
Also called Uzziah, which see	II Chr.	26	1–5
Son of Ethan	I Chr.	2	8
A man of Judah, who has Egyptian blood in his veins	I Chr.	2	34, 38, 39
A son of Ahimaaz	I Chr.	6	9
Father of Amariah, who is high priest under Jehoshaphat	I Chr.	6	10
	Ezra	7	3

Azariah —continued

A son of Hilkiah, the high priest	I Chr.	6	13
	I Chr.	9	11
Grandfather of Ezra	Ezra	7	1
A descendant of Kohath	I Chr.	6	36
A prophet sent to encourage Asa to destroy the idols in Judah	II Chr.	15	1, 2
A son of King Jehoshaphat	II Chr.	21	2
Another son of Jehoshaphat	II Chr.	21	2
King of Judah, son of Jehoram	II Chr.	22	6
A captain who aids in elevating Joash to the throne of Judah	II Chr.	23	1
The high priest who hinders Uzziah from burning incense on the altar	II Chr.	26	17–20
A chief of the tribe of Ephraim	II Chr.	28	12
A Kohathite Levite	II Chr.	29	12
A Merarite	II Chr.	29	12
A priest of the family of Zadok, who becomes chief priest in Hezekiah's time	II Chr.	31	10–13
One of those who repairs the wall of Jerusalem	Neh.	3	23, 24
Name given to Seraiah, who comes up to Jerusalem with Jerubbabel	Ezra	2	2
	Neh.	7	7
One who explains the law to the people while Ezra is reading it	Neh.	8	7
A priest who seals Nehemiah's covenant	Neh.	10	2
The Hebrew name of Abednego	Dan.	1	6, 7
	Dan.	2	17

Azaziah *Jehovah hath strengthened*

A singer of David	I Chr.	15	21
Father of Hoshea	I Chr.	27	20
An overseer of the temple	II Chr.	31	13

Azekah *dug over*

A town of Judah	Josh.	10	10, 11
Philistine territory	I Sam.	17	1
Rehoboam fortifies	II Chr.	11	9
Assaulted by Nebuchadnezzar	Jer.	34	7
Post-exilic occupation	Neh.	11	30

Azel *noble*

Descendant of Jonathan	I Chr.	8	37, 38
	I Chr.	9	43, 44
Unidentified site in the neighbourhood of Jerusalem	Zech.	14	5

Azmaveth, Beth-azmaveth *death is strong*

One of David's mighty men	II Sam.	23	31
David's treasurer	I Chr.	27	25
A descendant of Saul	I Chr.	8	36
Father of Jeziel	I Chr.	12	3
A village near Jerusalem	Ezra	2	24
	Neh.	12	29

Aznoth-tabor *ears of Tabor*

The lower slopes of mount Tabor in Naphtali	Josh.	19	34

Azor *helper*

An ancestor of Jesus	Mat.	1	13, 14

Azotus *stronghold*

Visited by Philip	Acts	8	40

Azriel *God is my help*

Prince of Manasseh	I Chr.	5	24
A Naphtalite	I Chr.	27	19
Father of Seraiah	Jer.	36	26

Azrikam *my help has arisen*

Son of Neariah	I Chr.	3	23
A descendant of Jonathan	I Chr.	8	38
A Levite	I Chr.	9	14
	Neh.	11	15
Ruler of the house under Ahaz	II Chr.	28	7

Azubah *desolation*

Mother of Jehoshaphat	I Ki.	22	42
Wife of Caleb	I Chr.	2	18, 19

Azur, Azzur *helper*

A sealer of Nehemiah's covenant	Neh.	10	17
Father of the false prophet, Hananiah	Jer.	28	1
Father of Jaazaniah	Ezek.	11	1

Azzah *see Gaza*   Deut.   2   23

B

Baal *owner, possessor*

God of the Moabites	Num.	22	41
Phoenician god	Judg.	10	6
Worship conducted in high places	I Ki.	16	32
	II Ki.	21	3
Many priests of	I Ki.	18	19
Worship held under form of bull and images	I Ki.	18	25, 26
	II Ki.	17	16
	II Chr.	28	2
Altars built for	Judg.	2	11–14
	Jer.	11	13
Worshiped by Israel	Judg.	2	13
	Jer.	2	8
	Jer.	11	13
	Jer.	12	16
	Hosea	13	1, 2

Sinful rites:

Self-mutilation	I Ki.	18	28
Human sacrifice	II Chr.	28	3, 4
	Jer.	19	5
Fornication	Jer.	7	9
Prophecy	Jer.	23	13

Altars and priests destroyed by:

Gideon	Judg.	6	25–35
Elijah	I Ki.	18	40
Jehu	II Ki.	10	18–29
Jehoiada	II Ki.	11	18
Hezekiah	II Ki.	18	4
Josiah	II Ki.	23	4, 5
Town of Simeon	I Chr.	4	33
Father of Reubenite who is taken prisoner by Tilgath-pilneser	I Chr.	5	5
Benjamite, son of Jehiel	I Chr.	8	30

Baalah, Balah *mistress*

A town also known as Kirjath-jearim in northern Judah	Josh.	15	9, 10
A ridge on the northern boundary	Josh.	15	11
A city in south Judah	Josh.	15	29
Also called Balah	Josh.	19	3

Baalath-beer *mistress of the well*

Border city of Simeon	Josh.	19	8
Also called Baal	I Chr.	4	33

Baale *lord of Judah*

Town from which David brings the ark to Jerusalem	II Sam.	6	2
Called Baalah and Kirjath-jearim	Josh.	15	9, 10

Baal-gad *lord of fortune*

Northerly extent of Joshua's victories	Josh.	11	17

Baal-hamon *lord of multitude*

Site of Solomon's vineyard	S. of S.	8	11

Baali *my master*

Title refused by God	Hosea	2	16

Baalim *lords Canaanite*

Gods	Judg.	10	10–14
Troubled Israel	Judg.	2	11
	Judg.	3	7

Baal-peor *lord of the opening*

Israel punished for idolatrous worship of	Num.	25	1–5
	Ps.	106	28
	Hosea	9	10
24,000 die	Num.	25	1–5

Baal-perazim, Perazim *lord of breach of waters*

Place where David defeats Philistines	II Sam.	5	20
Also called Perazim	Is.	28	21

Baal-shalisha *lord of Shalisha*

A man of, brings food to Elisha	II Ki.	4	42
Remembered in the N.T.	I Cor.	10	8

Baal-zebub *see Beelzebub*

"lord of flies" said of power of Christ	Mat.	10	25
	Mat.	12	24
God of Ekron	II Ki.	1	2

Baanah *son of affliction*

One of the murderers of Ish-bosheth	II Sam.	4	2–9
Father of one of David's valiant men	II Sam.	23	29
	I Chr.	11	30
Son of Hushai, one of Solomon's officials charged with providing food	I Ki.	4	16
One who returns after captivity	Ezra	2	2

Baasha *wicked*

Evil king of Israel	I Ki.	15	16–21
Slays house of Jeroboam	I Ki.	15	27–29
Downfall foretold	I Ki.	16	1–7
Builds Ramah	II Chr.	16	1
War with Asa	I Ki.	15	16, 32

babbling *talking unwisely or inadvisedly*

Of drunkards	Prov.	23	29, 30
Likened to the bite of a serpent	Eccl.	10	11
Paul accused of	Acts	17	18
Timothy told to avoid	I Tim.	6	20
	II Tim.	2	16

babe

Famous:

Moses	Ex.	2	6
John the Baptist	Luke	1	41, 44
Christ	Luke	2	12, 16

Figurative:

Young christians	I Pet.	2	2
Carnal	Heb.	5	13
Behold the *b* wept.	Ex.	2	6
Out of mouth of *b*	Ps.	8	2
	Mat.	21	16
Leave their substance to *b*	Ps.	17	14
B shall rule over them.	Is.	3	4
Revealed to *b*	Mat.	11	25
	Luke	10	21
The *b* wrapped in swaddling clothes.	Luke	2	12
Teacher of *b*	Rom.	2	20
B in Christ.	I Cor.	3	1
As newborn *b*	I Pet.	2	2

Babel *confusion*

Nimrod, king of	Gen.	10	10
Confusion of tongues at the building of the tower of	Gen.	11	4–9

Babylon *the gate of god; confusion*

Also see Chaldea

Origin of	Gen.	10	10
Origin of the name	Gen.	11	8, 9
Founded by the Assyrians, and a part of their empire	II Ki.	17	24
Ambassadors of, sent to Hezekiah	II Ki.	20	12
Governed by kings	II Ki.	20	12
	Dan.	5	1
Treatment of the Jews in	II Ki.	25	27–30
	Dan.	1	3–7
Watered by the rivers	Ps.	137	1
	Jer.	51	13
Grief of the Jews in	Ps.	137	1–6
The Jews exhorted to be subject to and settle in	Jer.	27	8–17
	Jer.	29	1–7
Revolt of the Jews from, and their punishment illustrated	Ezra	17	11–21
Presidents placed over	Dan.	2	48
	Dan.	6	1–3
Babylon the chief province of	Dan.	3	1
	Dan.	4	29, 30
Composed of many nations	Dan.	3	2, 3
	Dan.	4	30
With Media and Persia divided by Darius into 120 provinces	Dan.	6	1
Formerly a part of Mesopotamia	Acts	7	2
The gospel preached in	I Pet.	5	13
Destruction foretold because of its sins	Rev.	16	19

As a power was:

Oppressive	Is.	14	4
Arrogant, proud	Is.	14	13, 14
	Jer.	50	29, 31, 32
Cruel and destructive	Is.	14	17
	Jer.	51	24, 25
Grand and stately	Is.	47	1, 5
Instrument of God's vengeance on other nations	Is.	47	6
	Jer.	51	7
Secure and self-confident	Is.	47	7, 8
Covetous	Jer.	51	13

Babylon the capital of:

Its antiquity	Gen.	11	4, 9
Called the glory of kingdoms	Is.	13	19
Called the beauty of Chaldees	Is.	13	19
Called the golden city	Is.	14	4
Surrounded with a great wall	Jer.	51	53, 58
Called Babylon the great	Dan.	4	30
Enlarged by Nebuchadnezzar	Dan.	4	30
Called the city of merchants	Ezek.	17	4

Inhabitants of:

Addicted to magic	Is.	47	9, 12, 13
	Dan.	2	1, 2
Wicked	Is.	47	10
Idolatrous	Jer.	50	38
	Dan.	3	18
Profane and sacrilegious	Dan.	5	1–3

Predictions respecting:

Destruction of	Is.	13	1–22
	Is.	21	1–10
	Jer.	25	12
	Jer.	51	1–64
Restoration of the Jews from	Is.	14	1–4
	Is.	48	20
	Jer.	29	10
	Jer.	50	4, 8, 19
Perpetual desolation of	Is.	13	19–22
	Is.	14	22, 23
	Jer.	50	13, 39
	Jer.	51	37, 43
Captivity of the Jews by	Jer.	20	4–6
	Jer.	22	20–26
	Jer.	25	9–11
	Mic.	4	10
Conquests by	Jer.	21	3–10
	Jer.	27	2–6
	Ezek.	21	19–32
	Ezek.	29	18–20

Remarkable for:

Manufacture of garments	Josh.	7	21
National greatness	Is.	13	19
	Jer.	51	41
Naval power	Is.	43	14
Antiquity	Jer.	5	15
Military power	Jer.	5	16
	Jer.	50	22
Wealth	Jer.	51	13
Commerce	Ezek.	17	4

Represented by:

A great eagle	Ezek.	17	3
A head of gold	Dan.	2	3
A lion with eagle's wings	Dan.	7	4

Also see Nebuchadnezzar

Babylonian Captivity *see* captivity

Baca, valley of *weeping, valley of misery*

Probably figurative of sorrow	Ps.	84	6

bachelorhood *state of unmarried man*

Paul's advice to the unmarried	I Cor.	7	7–9, 32

back

Shalt make them turn their *b*	Ps.	21	12
Plowers plowed on my *b*	Ps.	129	3
Rod for the fool's *b*	Prov.	26	3
Cast my sins behind thy *b*	Is.	38	17
I gave my *b* to the smiters	Is.	50	6
Turned their *b* unto me.	Jer.	2	27
	Jer.	32	33
Rolled *b* the stone.	Mat.	28	2
Looking *b* is fit for the kingdom.	Luke	9	62
Bow down their *b* always.	Rom.	11	10
Not of them who draw *b*	Heb.	10	39

backbiting *speaking maliciously*

David describes a citizen of Zion	Ps.	15	3
Solomon's advice on avoiding quarrels	Prov.	25	23
God's judgment impartial	Rom.	1	30
Paul admonishes the people of Corinth against	II Cor.	12	20

backsliding *becoming less virtuous*

Punishment of	Deut.	11	28
	Prov.	14	14
	Jer.	2	19
	Jer.	5	6
God's displeasure at	I Ki.	11	9
	Ps.	78	56–58
	II Cor.	11	3
	Gal.	3	1
	Rev.	2	4
Promise of pardon	II Chr.	7	14
	Jer.	3	12
	Jer.	31	20
	Jer.	36	3
	Hosea	14	4
Warnings against	Ps.	85	8
	I Cor.	10	12
	Heb.	10	38, 39
Return from	Jer.	3	22
	Lam.	5	21

backsliding —continued
Examples of:

Israel	Ex.	32	8
	Jer.	3	6–11
	Hosea	4	16
	Hosea	11	7
Saul	I Sam.	15	11
Solomon	I Ki.	11	3, 4
Peter	Mat.	26	70–74

backward

Shadow return *b*	II Ki.	20	10
	Is.	38	8
B I cannot perceive.	Job	23	8
Driven *b*	Ps.	40	14
	Ps.	70	2
Judgment is returned *b*	Is.	59	14
They went *b* and not forward.	Jer.	7	24
They went *b* and fell to the ground.	John	18	6

bad company *see companions, evil*

badger, rock *see coney*

badgers' skins *probably skins of sea-cow or dugong*

Used for covering the tabernacle	Ex.	36	19
	Ex.	39	34
Used for making sandals	Ezek.	16	10

bag *container*

In thy *b* divers weights.	Deut.	25	13
Smooth stones in a *b*	I Sam.	17	40
Transgression sealed in a *b*	Job	14	17
Taken a *b* of money	Prov.	7	20
Lavish gold out of *b*	Is.	46	6
B of deceitful weights.	Mic.	6	11
B with holes.	Hag.	1	6
B that wax not old	Luke	12	33
Judas a thief, and had the *b*	John	12	6
	John	13	29

Bahurim *low grounds*

Place where Phaltiel, son of Laish is ordered to relinquish Michal	II Sam.	3	15, 16
Where Shimei dwells	II Sam.	16	5
Where Ahimaaz and Jonathan hide in the well from Absalom	II Sam.	17	18, 19
A village between the Jordan and Jerusalem	I Chr.	11	33

baker *one who bakes bread*

Offends the king of Egypt and is placed in the guard's house			
	Gen.	40	1
	Gen.	41	10
Samuel describes what a king will have the daughters of Israel do	I Sam.	8	13
Hosea compares adulterers with a baker's oven	Hosea	7	4

Balaam *lord of the people*

Son of Beor	Num.	22	5
Requested by Balak to curse Israel			
	Num.	22	5, 6
	Josh.	24	9
His ass speaks	Num.	22	22–35
Blesses Israel	Num.	23	5, 20
His parables	Num.	23	7–10
	Num.	23	18–24
His prophecies	Num.	24	5–9
	Num.	24	16–24
His wicked counsel	Num.	24	17
Slain	Num.	31	8
	Josh.	13	22
Other references to this episode	Deut.	23	4
	Josh.	24	9
	Mic.	6	5
	II Pet.	2	15, 16

Balac *see Balak*

Baladan *see Merodach-baladan*

Balah *see Baalah*

Balak, Balac *he destroys*

King of Moab who wants Balaam to curse Israel			
	Num.	22	1–6
	Josh.	24	9
	Judg.	11	25
Also called Balac	Rev.	2	14

balance *an instrument for weighing*

Just	Lev.	19	36
	Ezek.	45	10
Symbolic	Job	31	6
	Ps.	62	9
	Dan.	5	27
	Rev.	6	5

False, condemned	Prov.	11	1
	Prov.	20	23
	Hosea	12	7
	Amos	8	5
	Mic.	6	11
God's justice	Job	31	6
Nations as the small dust of	Is.	40	12, 15
For weighing money	Is.	46	6
Judgment of the third seal	Rev.	6	5

baldness *absence of hair*

As a sign of leprosy	Lev.	13	40–43
Priests forbidden to make themselves bald	Lev.	21	5
	Ezek.	44	20
Conclusion of Nazarite vow	Num.	6	9
A token of mourning	Deut.	14	1
	Is.	22	12
	Ezek.	7	18
	Mic.	1	16
Bald head, a cry of contempt	II Ki.	2	23
A curse on haughty women	Is.	3	24
Pagan practice	Lev.	21	5
	Deut.	14	1

Examples:

Job	Job	1	20
Moab	Is.	15	2
	Jer.	48	37
Israel	Jer.	16	6
	Amos	8	10
Philistines	Jer.	47	5
Tyrus	Ezek.	27	31
	Ezek.	29	18

balm *balsam*

Article having commercial value	Gen.	37	25
	Ezek.	27	17
Sent to Joseph	Gen.	43	11
Used for healing	Jer.	46	11
From Gilead	Jer.	8	22

band

Break their *b* asunder.	Ps.	2	3
	Ps.	107	14
There are no *b* in their death.	Ps.	73	4
To loose the *b* of wickedness.	Is.	58	6
Drew them with *b* of love.	Hosea	11	4
Two staves, beauty and *b*	Zech.	11	7
He brake *b*, and was driven.	Luke	8	29
Every one's *b* were loosed.	Acts	16	26
All the body by *b*	Col.	2	19
Gathered to him whole *b*	Mat.	27	27
	Mark	15	16
B called the Italian *b*	Acts	10	1
Certain of the Jews *b*	Acts	23	12

Bani *built*

One of David's captains	II Sam.	23	36
A Levite	I Chr.	6	46
A Judahite	I Chr.	9	4
His children return from capitivity	Ezra	2	10
He and his sons married strange wives	Ezra	10	29, 34, 38
Father of Rehum, a Levite	Neh.	3	17
A covenant-sealer	Neh.	10	14
Progeny of Asaph	Neh.	11	22

banishment *enforced absence*

End of, requested for Absalom	II Sam.	14	13, 14
Punishment for those who ignore God's law	Ezra	7	26
Of Adam	Gen.	3	22–24
Of Cain	Gen.	4	12, 14
Of Jesus, by his townsmen	Luke	4	16, 29
Of Paul and Barnabas	Acts	13	50
Of Jews, by Claudius	Acts	18	2
Of John to Patmos	Rev.	1	9

bank *rising land at river's edge, a money exchange*

In Abel	II Sam.	20	15
A vision of holy waters	Ezek.	47	7
Daniel's vision	Dan.	8	16
Money deposited in, gains interest	Mat.	25	27
	Luke	19	23
Moneychangers in the temple	John	2	15

banker *see moneychanger*

bankrupt

Parable	Mat.	18	25
Gentiles	Eph.	2	12
Laodicea	Rev.	3	14, 17

banner *ensign*

Used in rejoicing	Ps.	20	5
Used in describing the church	S. of S.	2	5
	S. of S.	6	4, 10

Used in mustering host	Is.	13	2
banquet *a ceremonious feast*			
Honouring Isaac	Gen.	21	8
Pharaoh's birthday	Gen.	40	20
In honour of the law of Moses	Neh.	8	10, 12
A mark of excess	Eccl.	10	16, 19
	Is.	5	11, 12
In the mountain	Is.	25	6
For wedding guests	Mat.	22	4
Who should be invited	Luke	14	13
For the prodigal son	Luke	15	23–27
baptism *a cleansing*			
As administered by John	Mat.	3	1–12
	John	3	23
Sanctioned by Christ's submission to it	Mat.	3	13–15
	Luke	3	21
A commandment of Christ to His followers	Mat.	28	19, 20
	Mark	16	15, 16
With the Holy Ghost	Mark	1	8
	Luke	3	16
	John	1	33
	Acts	2	1–4
Pharisees and lawyers reject	Luke	7	30
Necessity for	John	3	5
	Acts	19	2–6
Jesus does not baptize	John	4	1, 2
Baptized added to church	Acts	2	41–47
Spiritual grace received by baptism	Acts	2	38
	Acts	22	16
	Rom.	6	3, 4
	I Pet.	3	21
Water, the visible sign	Acts	8	36
	Acts	10	47
One in Christ	I Cor.	12	13
	Gal.	3	23–28
For the dead	I Cor.	15	29
There is but one	Eph.	4	5
Requisites for:			
Confession of sin	Mat.	3	6
Faith	Mat.	20	20–23
	Acts	8	12, 37
	Acts	16	30–34
	Acts	18	8
Repentance	Acts	2	38
	Acts	19	4
Administered to:			
Jesus	Mat.	3	13–17
Multitude of Judaea	Luke	3	7
People of Samaria	Acts	8	5–12
Simon	Acts	8	13
The Ethiopian eunuch	Acts	8	26, 39
Saul	Acts	9	18
Lydia and her household	Acts	16	14, 15
Keeper of the prison	Acts	16	27–33
Corinthians	Acts	18	8
Ephesians	Acts	19	5
Crispus and Gaius	I Cor.	1	14
Israelites in Red sea	I Cor.	10	1, 2
Baptism, John's			
At Aenon	Mat.	3	16
Of repentance	Luke	3	3
Preparation	Mat.	3	11, 12
	Acts	19	4
Of Jesus	Mat.	3	13–17
Baptist *see* John the Baptist			
bar			
The middle *b*	Ex.	26	28
	Ex.	36	33
High walls, gates and *b*	Deut.	3	5
Go down to the *b* of the pit.	Job	17	16
His bones are like *b* of iron.	Job	40	18
The earth with her *b*	Jonah	2	6
Barabbas, Abbas *son of Abba or father*			
A robber released instead of Jesus	Mat.	27	16, 17
	Mark	15	6–8
	Luke	23	18
	John	18	40
Barachel *God hath blessed*			
Father of Elihu	Job	32	2, 6
Barachias			
Father of Zacharias	Mat.	23	35
Barak *lightning*			
Son of Abinoam	Judg.	4	6
Incited by Deborah to deliver Israel from Sisera	Judg.	4	6–16

Paul uses him as an example of faith	Heb.	11	32
barbarian *a rude, uncivilized foreigner*			
Paul is kindly entertained by them	Acts	28	1–6
Paul ministers to them	Rom.	1	14
barefoot *with the feet bare*			
David goes, to worship God on mount Olivet	II Sam.	15	30
Isaiah prophesies the shameful captivity	Is.	20	2–4
Expresses reverence	Ex.	3	5
Bariah *a fugitive*			
Descendant of David, son of Shemaiah	I Chr.	3	22
Bar-jesus *see* Elymas			
Bar-jona, Simon *see* Peter			
	Mat.	16	17
barley *a cereal grass, type of food*			
Crop smitten by the plague of hail	Ex.	9	31
Estimation of vows	Lev.	27	16
A cake of, used as weapon	Judg.	7	13
Ruth gleans	Ruth	2	17
Food for animals	I Ki.	4	28
Gift to Elisha	II Ki.	4	42
Used to make bread	Ezek.	4	9
Item of trade	II Chr.	2	10
Feeding of 5,000	John	6	9, 13
Barnabas *son of consolation*			
A Levite of Cyprus also called Joses	Acts	4	36, 37
Donates property	Acts	4	36, 37
Introduces Saul of Tarsus	Acts	9	27
Preaches at Antioch	Acts	11	22–30
Returns from Jerusalem with Paul and Mark	Acts	12	25
Dedicated to missionary service at Antioch	Acts	13	1–7
Persecution at Iconium	Acts	13	50–52
People of Lystra think he and Paul are gods	Acts	14	12–14
Return to Antioch	Acts	14	20–28
Goes with Paul to church council at Jerusalem	Acts	15	1–5, 12
Disagrees with Paul	Acts	15	36–41
Paul's friend	I Cor.	9	6
	Gal.	2	1, 9
Leans toward Judaism	Gal.	2	13
barns *ancient granaries of Palestine*			
Used for the storing of seed	Job	39	12
	Hag.	2	19
Used in parable	Mat.	6	26
	Mat.	13	30
	Luke	12	18, 24
barrel *a storage cask*			
Used to store meal	I Ki.	17	12, 14
Used to store liquid	I Ki.	18	33
barrenness *incapacity to produce offspring*			
Reproach	Gen.	30	22–24
Sent as punishment	II Sam.	6	23
God can cure	Ps.	113	9
Used in allegory	Gal.	4	27
Examples of:			
Sarah	Gen.	11	30
	Gen.	16	1
Rebekah	Gen.	25	21
Rachel	Gen.	29	31
	Gen.	30	1
Manoah's wife	Judg.	13	2
Hannah	I Sam.	1	2
The Shunammite	II Ki.	4	14
Elisabeth	Luke	1	7
Barsabas, Joseph *see* Joseph			
Barsabas, Judas *see* Judas			
Bartholomew *son of Tolmai*			
An apostle	Mat.	10	3
	Acts	1	13
Probably the same as Nathaniel	John	1	45
Bartimaeus *son of Timaeus*			
Blind beggar regains sight	Mark	10	46–52
Baruch *blessed*			
Son of Zabbai	Neh.	3	20
A post-exilic priest	Neh.	11	5
Son of Neriah	Jer.	32	12, 16
Secretary of Jeremiah	Jer.	36	4–19
Taken into Egypt	Jer.	43	1–7
base (baser sort—the rabble) *of humble rank.*			
Children of *b* men	Job	30	8
Kingdom might be *b*	Ezek.	17	14
Set there upon her own *b*	Zech.	5	11

base (baser sort—the rabble) —continued

I have made you *b*	Mal.	2	9
Fellows of *b* sort	Acts	17	5
B things of the world.	I Cor.	1	28
Who in presence am *b*	II Cor.	10	1

Bashan *fruitful*

Conquered by Moses	Num.	21	33–35
	Deut.	3	1–4
Land of Gilead, east of Jordan	Deut.	3	10, 14
Habitation of Gad	I Chr.	5	11
Notable for its fertile land	Ezek.	39	18
Captured by Hazael	II Ki.	10	32
Famous for cattle	Ezek.	39	18

Bashemath, Basmath *sweet-smelling*

Marriage to Esau	Gen.	26	34
	Gen.	36	3
Also called Mahalath	Gen.	28	9
Mother of Reuel	Gen.	36	4
Daughter of Solomon	I Ki.	4	15

basket *a vessel interwoven of flexible material*

The baker's dream	Gen.	40	16–18
Container for bread	Ex.	29	3, 23
	Lev.	8	2, 26, 31
	Num.	6	15, 17, 19
Container for fruit	Deut.	26	2, 4
	Amos	8	1, 2
Container for meat	Judg.	6	19
Beheading of Ahab's sons	II Ki.	10	7
For carrying bulky items	Ps.	81	6
Container for grapes	Jer.	6	9
Container for figs	Jer.	24	1, 2
As a food container	Mat.	14	20
	Mark	8	8, 19
	John	6	13
Escape of Paul	II Cor.	11	33

bastard *an illegitimate child*

May not enter into the congregation	Deut.	23	2
	Zech.	9	6
Ishmael	Gen.	16	3
Moab and Ammon	Gen.	19	36
Jephthah	Judg.	11	1

bat *a flying mammal*

Named as unclean meat in dietary laws	Lev.	11	13, 19
	Deut.	14	18

bath *a Hebrew measure*

Measure of capacity of liquids	I Ki.	7	26
	II Chr.	2	10
	Is.	5	10

bathing *act of washing one's body*

Pharaoh's daughter finds Moses	Ex.	2	5
Moses consecrates Aaron and his sons	Lev.	8	6
Uncleanliness of issues	Lev.	15	5–27
Aaron's preparation for sin offering for the people	Lev.	16	4, 24
After burning the offering	Lev.	16	26, 28
After touching unclean things	Lev.	22	6
Law and use of water of separation	Num.	19	19
Preparation of Ruth to meet Boaz	Ruth	3	3
David sees Bath-sheba	II Sam.	11	2, 4
In preparation for worship	II Sam.	12	20
Naaman cured of leprosy	II Ki.	5	10
Jesus cures a blind man	John	9	7
Washing feet	John	13	10

Also see purification

Bath-sheba, Bath-shua *daughter of the oath*

Daughter of Eliam, wife of Uriah	II Sam.	11	3
Commits adultery with David	II Sam.	11	4, 5
Mother of Solomon	II Sam.	12	24
	I Ki.	1	15–22
Intercedes with Solomon for Adonijah	I Ki.	2	13–22
Also called Bath-shua	I Chr.	3	5

battering ram

Used to beat down walls	Ezek.	4	2
	Ezek.	21	22

battle axe *broad axe formerly used as offensive weapon*

Allegorical of Israel	Jer.	51	20

battles *prolonged combats between armies*

Four kings against five kings	Gen.	14	1–11
Joshua and Israelites fight Amalek and his hordes	Ex.	17	8–16
Israelites against Midianites	Num.	31	1–12
Laws concerning	Deut.	20	1–20
Joshua against king of Ai	Josh.	8	1–28
Five kings' war against Gibeon	Josh.	10	1–20
Barak delivers Israel	Judg.	4	10–24

Gideon and the Midianites	Judg.	7	12–25
Israelites defend against Amorites	Judg.	11	19–23
Israelites overcome by Philistines	I Sam.	4	1, 2, 10
Saul defeats the Ammonites	I Sam.	11	11
Jonathan smites the Philistines	I Sam.	14	11–14
	I Sam.	14	28–31
Saul wars against his enemies	I Sam.	14	47, 48
Philistines victorious over Saul	I Sam.	31	1, 2, 7
Abner beaten by David	II Sam.	2	17, 30, 31
David smites the Philistines	II Sam.	5	20, 24, 25
Ammonites are overcome by David	II Sam.	10	6–19
Israelites are smitten in wood of Ephraim	II Sam.	18	6–8
David again fights against Philistines	II Sam.	21	17–21
Syrians are smitten by Israelites	I Ki.	20	19–21
	I Ki.	20	26–30
Ahab slain at Ramoth-gilead	I Ki.	22	30–35
The Moabites are overcome	II Ki.	3	24, 25
David smites Moabites	I Chr.	18	2
David smites king of Zobah	I Chr.	18	3
David defeats Syrians	I Chr.	18	5
Ammonites are overcome	I Chr.	19	7–18
Abijah wars with Jeroboam	II Chr.	13	2, 3
	II Chr.	13	13–19
Asa defeats Ethiopians	II Chr.	14	9–15
Amaziah overthrows Edomites	II Chr.	25	11–14

bdellium *a gum resin similar to myrrh*

As a resin	Gen.	2	12
Used in description of manna	Num.	11	7

beacon *a signal for guidance or warning*

God's mercies	Is.	30	17

beam *large or long piece of wood or metal*

Elisha causes iron to float	II Ki.	6	6
The providence of God	Ps.	103–104	3
Rash judgment	Mat.	7	3
Jesus contrasts with a mote	Luke	6	42

bear *large mammal with long, shaggy hair*

David slays a lion and a bear near Bethlehem	I Sam.	17	34–36
Destroys Elisha's mockers	II Ki.	2	24
One of the empires in Daniel's vision is represented by a	Dan.	7	5
Figurative fierceness	II Sam.	17	8
Folly	Prov.	17	12

bear *to carry or suffer*

Punishment of mankind	Gen.	4	13
Simon carries the cross	Mat.	27	32
	Mark	15	21
Witness	John	15	27
	Acts	23	11
Of subjection	Rom.	13	4
Christ, the sins of many	Heb.	9	28

beard *hair that grows on or around chin and lips*

Shaved as a sign of respect	Gen.	41	14
Discerning leprosy	Lev.	13	29
Law of mourning of the priests	Lev.	21	5
Aaron's	Ps.	133	2
Neglect of, regarded as weakness	I Sam.	21	13
Shaved as humiliating punishment	II Sam.	10	4, 5
	I Chr.	19	4, 5
Grasped in greeting	II Sam.	20	9
Cut off in time of mourning	Ezra	9	3

beasts *four-footed animals*

Creation	Gen.	1	24
Named by Adam	Gen.	2	20
Taken on the ark by Noah	Gen.	7	2
Belong to God	Ex.	13	12
Man forbidden to lie with	Ex.	22	19
Clean and unclean	Lev.	11	2–47
Used in offerings	Lev.	27	9–11
Often used symbolically in visions	Dan.	7	1–28
	Acts	10	10–17
	Rev.	4	6–9
	Rev.	14	3
Serpent more subtil than any *b*	Gen.	3	1
Like *b* that perish.	Ps.	49	12
As a *b* before thee.	Ps.	73	22
Regardeth life of *b*	Prov.	12	10
Fought with *b*	I Cor.	15	32
Every kind of *b* is tamed.	James	3	7
As natural brute *b*	II Pet.	2	12

beatings *form of punishment*

Mosaic law concerning	Deut.	25	2, 3
For correcting children	Prov.	23	13, 14

In the days of Christ	Mark	13	9
	Luke	20	10, 11
Of apostles	Acts	5	40
	Acts	16	19–24
	II Cor.	11	25

Beatitudes *blessedness*
Christ's sermon on the mount	Mat.	5	3–12
	Luke	6	20–22

beautiful women
Sarah	Gen.	12	11
Rachel	Gen.	29	17
Abigail	I Sam.	25	3
Bath-sheba	II Sam.	11	2, 3
Esther	Esth.	2	7
Job's daughters	Job	42	15
Tamar	II Sam.	13	1
Abishag	I Ki.	1	4

beauty *charm, grace*
Vanity of	Ps.	39	11
	Prov.	6	25
	Prov.	31	30
	Ezek.	16	14
Floral	Mat.	6	28, 29
Of Israel	Ps.	45	8–11
S. of S.	Ps.	1	8
Gift of God	Ezek.	16	14

Instances of:
Rebekah	Gen.	24	16
Joseph	Gen.	39	6
Moses	Ex.	2	2
	Heb.	11	23
David	I Sam.	16	12, 18
Absalom	II Sam.	14	25
Vashti	Esth.	1	11

Bechorath, Becorath *first-born*
Ancestor of King Saul	I Sam.	9	1

bed *used for sleeping or resting*
Supplied with pillows	I Sam.	19	13
	I Sam.	26	7
Reclined on by day	II Sam.	4	5
	II Sam.	11	2
Comfort in time of grief	I Ki.	21	4
	Job	7	13
Illustrative of the grave	Job	17	13
	Is.	57	2
Used for meditation and praise	Ps.	4	4
	Ps.	149	5
	S. of S.	3	1
Used for evil contrivings	Ps.	36	4
	Mic.	2	1
Covered with tapestry and linen	Prov.	7	16
Perfumed by lustful women	Prov.	7	17
Sold for debt	Prov.	22	27

Materials used for a bed:
Clothing	Ex.	22	26, 27
Earth	II Sam.	12	16
	II Sam.	13	31
Couch	Ps.	6	6
Mats or rugs	Mat.	9	6
	Mark	2	9
Ivory	Amos	6	4
Gold and Silver	Esth.	1	6

Bedan *according to judgment*
He delivers Israel	I Sam.	12	11
A descendant of Gilead	I Chr.	7	17

bedchamber *a bedroom*
Place of rest	II Sam.	4	7
Invaded by frogs	Ex.	8	3
Prepared for Elisha	II Ki.	4	8–10
Places for private conversations	II Ki.	6	12
	Eccl.	10	20

bedstead
Made of iron	Deut.	3	11
Made of gold and silver	Esth.	1	6
Made of ivory	Amos	6	4

bee *an insect*
Of Amorites	Deut.	1	44
Hosts of Assyria compared to	Ps.	118	12
	Is.	7	18
Swarms in carcase of lion	Judg.	14	8

Beeliada *the Lord hath known*
Also called Eliada	II Sam.	5	16
A son of David	I Chr.	14	7

Beelzebub, Baal-zebub *lord of the fly*
God of Ekron	II Ki.	1	2, 3, 6
Christ's miracles ascribed to	Mat.	9	34
Prince of devils	Mat.	12	24
	Mark	3	22
	Luke	11	15, 18, 19

Beer *a well*
Well dug at the direction of Moses	Num.	21	16–18
The place to which Jotham runs after uttering his parable	Judg.	9	21

Beeri *man of a well*
Father of Judith, wife of Esau	Gen.	26	34
Father of Hosea, the prophet	Hosea	1	1

Beer-lahai-roi, Lahai-roi *well of living one*
Hagar meets the angel	Gen.	16	14
Isaac dwells beside	Gen.	25	11

Beeroth *wells*
A Gibeonite city, now called Bireh	Josh.	9	17
Home of Rechab and of Naharai	II Sam.	4	2
	II Sam.	23	37
In Edom	Deut.	10	6

Beer-sheba *well of an oath*
Hagar finds refuge	Gen.	21	14
Where Abraham makes a covenant with Abimelech	Gen.	21	31
God appears to Hagar	Gen.	21	14, 17
Home of Abraham	Gen.	22	19
Home of Isaac	Gen.	26	23, 33
	Gen.	28	10
Home of Jacob	Gen.	46	1, 5
Inheritance of Judah	Josh.	15	28
	Josh.	19	2
Possessed by Simeon	Josh.	19	1, 2
A center of government	I Sam.	8	2
Elijah flees to	I Ki.	19	3
Occupied by exiles	Neh.	11	27, 30
Boundary of Israel	II Sam.	17	11

Beesh-terah *a burning; house of Ashterah*
One of two cities allotted to the Gershonites	Josh.	21	27
Same as Ashtaroth	I Chr.	6	71

befall
Mischief *b* him.	Gen.	42	4
	Gen.	44	29
Why is all this *b* us?	Judg.	6	13
No evil *b* thee.	Ps.	91	10
B men *b* beasts; one thing *b*	Eccl.	3	19

beggar *one who lives by asking alms*
Lifted up by God	I Sam.	2	8
Outcome of indolence	Prov.	20	4
A shameful condition	Luke	16	3
Lazarus	Luke	16	20–22
Common in Israel	Josh.	9	8
God's special care	I Sam.	2	8
Lazarus	Luke	16	20–22
Bartimaeus	Mark	10	46

beginning
Though *b* was small	Job	8	7
B of wisdom	Ps.	111	10
	Prov.	1	7
	Prov.	9	10
Word true from *b*	Ps.	119	160
Better end of a thing than *b*	Eccl.	7	8
From *b* not so	Mat.	19	8
B at Jerusalem	Luke	24	47
Hold *b* of our confidence	Heb.	3	14

(See I Chr. 17:9; Prov. 8:22, 23; Col. 1:18)

begotten
	Ps.	2	7
	Acts	13	33
	Heb.	1	5
This day have I *b* thee.	Heb.	5	5
As of the only *b* of the Father.	John	1	14
God gave only *b* son	John	3	16
B us again to a lively hope.	I Pet.	1	3
When he bringeth in first *b*	Heb.	1	6

beguile *to deceive*
The serpent corrupts Eve	Gen.	3	13
	II Cor.	11	3
Laban deceives Jacob	Gen.	29	21–28
Joshua beguiled	Josh.	9	22
Exhortation to constancy	Col.	2	4
	Col.	2	18
False teachers beguile unstable souls	II Pet.	2	14

behave

David *b* wisely	I Sam.	18	5, 14
B ourselves valiantly.	I Chr.	19	13
I will *b* wisely	Ps.	101	2
Child shall *b* proudly	Is.	3	5
bishop must be of good *b*	I Tim.	3	2
(See Ps. 131:2; 1 Cor. 13:5; Tit. 2:3)			

behaviour, behavior *conduct, deportment*

Deceptive	I Sam.	21	13
Valiant	I Chr.	19	13
Wise	Ps.	101	2
Child shall be proud	Is.	3	5
Charitable	I Cor.	13	4–8
Rules for unblamable	I Thes.	2	10–12
Orderly	II Thes.	3	7
In the house of God	I Tim.	3	15
Holy	Tit.	2	3

beheading *cutting off the head*

Ish-bosheth	II Sam.	4	7, 8
John the Baptist	Mat.	14	8–12
	Mark	6	16, 27
	Luke	9	9
James	Acts	12	12
Of the righteous	Rev.	20	4

behemoth

Believed to be either a hippopotamus or an elephant	Job	40	15

behind

Not hoof be left *b*	Ex.	10	26
Things which are *b*	Phil.	3	13
Fill up that which is *b*	Col.	1	24
(See I Ki. 14:9; Neh. 9:26; II Cor. 11:5)			

behold

B the upright	Ps.	37	37
Their angels do always *b*	Mat.	18	10
That they may *b* my glory	John	17	24
B as in a glass	II Cor.	3	18
(See Num. 24:17; Ps. 91:8; 119:37; Jas. 1:23)			

Bel *lord*

Patron god of Babylon	Is.	46	1
	Jer.	50	2
	Jer.	51	44

Bela, Belah *devouring*

Same as Zoar, a city of the plain	Gen.	14	8
An Edomite king, son of Beor	Gen.	36	32
A son of Benjamin	Gen.	46	21
	Num.	26	38
Chief of the Reubenites	I Chr.	5	8

Belial *worthlessness, wickedness*

Symbolic of wicked people	Deut.	13	13
	Judg.	19	22
	I Sam.	10	27
Seducers of Israel	Deut.	15	9
Eli's son called	I Sam.	2	12
Of a fool	I Sam.	25	25
Of wicked	I Sam.	30	22
Evil disease	Ps.	41	8
Ungodly witness	Prov.	19	28
Applied to Satan	II Cor.	6	15

believe *see also faith*

that they may *b*	Ex.	4	5
if ye will not *b*	Is.	7	9
which ye will not *b*	Hab.	1	5
Lord I *b* help mine	Mark	9	24
if ye *b* not	John	8	24
I *b* thou art Christ	John	11	27
b on the Lord Jesus	Acts	16	31
b in thy heart that God	Rom.	10	9
to you that *b*	I John	3	23
b not every spirit	I John	4	1
B in Lord, *b* his prophets	II Chr.	20	20
They *b* not in God	Ps.	78	22
Simple *b* every word	Prov.	14	15
As thou hast *b*, so be it	Mat.	8	13
B ye that I am able?	Mat.	9	28
Why then did ye not *b*?	Mat.	21	25
	Mark	11	31
Come down from the cross, we will *b*	Mark	27	42
Only *b*	Mark	5	36
	Luke	8	50
If thou canst *b*, all things possible	Luke	9	23
B that ye receive	Mark	11	24
Things must surely *b*	Luke	1	1
Which for a while *b*	Luke	8	13
Slow of heart to *b*	Luke	24	25
B not for joy	Luke	41	

All men through him might *b*	John	1	7
They *b* the scripture	John	2	22
B heavenly things	John	3	12
How can ye *b* which receive honour?	John	5	44
How shall ye *b* my words?	John	47	
Seen me, and *b* not	John	6	36
Neither did his brethren *b*	John	7	5
Have any of the rulers *b*?	John	48	
B the works	John	10	38
To intent ye may *b*	John	11	15
Never die, *b* thou this?	John	26	
All men will *b*	John	48	
B in the light	John	12	36
The world may *b*	John	17	21
Have not seen, yet have *b*	John	29	
Multitude of them that *b*	Acts	4	32
All that *b* are justified	Acts	13	39
Ordained to eternal life *b*	Acts	48	
B with all his house	Acts	16	34
Father of all that *b*	Rom.	4	11
Against hope *b* in hope	Rom.	18	
B on him shall not be ashamed	Rom.	9	33
Wife that *b* not	I Cor.	7	12
We *b*, and therefore speak	II Cor.	4	13
Promise to them that *b*	Gal.	3	22
Admired in all that *b*	II Thes.	1	10
B to saving of soul	Heb.	10	39
Devils *b* and tremble	James	2	19

believers *title of Christians*

Used twice in the New Testament	Acts	5	14
	I Tim.	4	12

believing *trusting, accepting*

Necessary in prayer	Mat.	21	22
Faithlessness of Thomas	John	20	27
All things written in the law	Acts	24	14
Peace in	Rom.	15	13
Though ye see not Christ	I Pet.	1	7, 8

bells

Golden bells on the priest's ephod	Ex.	28	33–35
	Ex.	39	25
Ornamental use on horses	Zech.	14	20

belly

The serpent is cursed	Gen.	3	14
Full of wind	Job	15	2
Jonah in, of whale	Jonah	1	17
	Mat.	12	40

beloved *dearly loved*

Of a wife	Deut.	21	15
Of a husband	S. of S.	6	1–3
B dwell in safety	Deut.	33	12
Giveth his *b* sleep	Ps.	127	2
Greatly *b*	Dan.	9	23
	Dan.	10	11, 19
B son	Mat.	3	17
	Mat.	17	5
	Mark	1	11
	Luke	3	22
	Luke	9	35
	II Pet.	1	17
B for fathers' sake	Rom.	11	28
Accepted in the *b*	Eph.	1	6
B brother	Col.	4	9
	Phil.	16	
(See Neh. 13:26; Rom. 16:9; Col. 4:14)			
Christ called	Mat.	3	17
	Eph.	1	6
Applied to Christians	Col.	4	9
	Philem.	16	
	I John	4	1

Belshazzar *prince of Bel*

A king of Babylon	Dan.	5	1
His impious feast and death	Dan.	5	1–31
Son of Nebuchadnezzar	Dan.	5	2

Belteshazzar *preferred of Bel*

Name given to Daniel by Babylonians	Dan.	1	7

Ben *son*

A Levite appointed by David for service to the ark	I Chr.	15	18

Benaiah *Jehovah has built*

The son of Jehoiada	II Sam.	8	18
Commands David's body guards	II Sam.	23	20–23
Later becomes a partisan for Solomon	I Ki.	1	8, 38, 44

Slays:

Joab	I Ki.	2	29–34
Adonijah	I Ki.	2	25

Shimei	I Ki.	2	46
By order of David, slays Joab	I Ki.	2	28–34
One of David's mighty men	II Sam.	23	30
A Levite who plays with a psaltery on Alamoth	I Chr.	15	20
A priest appointed to blow trumpet before ark	I Chr.	16	5, 6
A Levite of the sons of Asaph	II Chr.	20	14
An overseer under Hezekiah	II Chr.	31	13
Post-exilic Jews	Ezra	10	25–43
The father of Pelatiah	Ezek.	11	1, 13

Ben-ammi *son of my people*

Son of the youngest daughter of Lot	Gen.	19	38

benediction *a blessing*

Moses and Aaron bless their people	Lev.	9	22
Aaron's	Num.	6	23–26
Joshua blesses tribe	Josh.	22	6, 7
David grants blessing	II Sam.	6	18, 20
Solomon blesses congregation of Israel	I Ki.	8	54–61
Paul's	II Cor.	13	14
Blessing God's name	Jude	1	24, 25
Congregational	Heb.	13	20, 21

benedictus *a short canticle of praise*

The song of Zacharias at the birth of John the Baptist	Luke	1	68–79

benefactor *one who gives benefits*

Christ admonishes disciples	Luke	22	25
Of God	Ps.	68	19

benevolence

To poor	Lev.	19	9, 10
To relatives	Lev.	23	35
To enemies	Prov.	25	21
To giver	Is.	58	10, 11

Ben-hadad *son of Hadad*

Son of Hadad, king of Syria	I Ki.	15	18–20
In league with Asa	II Chr.	16	1–6
King of Syria who makes a covenant with Ahab	I Ki.	20	1–34
Fails in siege against Samaria	II Ki.	6	24
Hazael slays him	II Ki.	8	7–15
Son of Hazael, king of Syria	II Ki.	13	24
Israel delivered into hands of	II Ki.	13	3
Jehoash defeats him	II Ki.	13	25
Destruction of his palaces foretold	Jer.	49	27
	Amos	1	4

Benjamin *son of right hand*

Son of Jacob and Rachel	Gen.	35	18, 24
	Gen.	46	19
	Gen.	42	4
Taken into Egypt	Gen.	42–45	
Judah's plea for	Gen.	44	18–34
Descendants of	Gen.	46	21
	Num.	26	38–41
Prophecy concerning	Gen.	49	27
Grandson of Benjamin	I Chr.	7	10
A son of Harim, who took a strange wife	Ezra	10	32
A Jew who helps purify the wall of Jerusalem	Neh.	12	34
A gate of Jerusalem	Jer.	20	2
	Jer.	37	13
	Zech.	14	10

Tribe of:

Numbered	Num.	1	37
	Num.	26	41
Moses' benediction upon	Deut.	33	12
Land allotted to	Josh.	18	11–28
	Ezek.	48	23
Joins Deborah in war against Sisera	Judg.	5	14
Tribal rebellion	Judg.	20	13–25
Defeated by Israel	Judg.	20	26–48
Almost annihilated	Judg.	21	6–15
Saul, the first king of Israel from	I Sam.	9	1–17
Return from exile	Ezra	1	5
Mordecai, a member of	Esth.	2	5
Jerusalem within the territory of	Jer.	6	1
Paul, a member of	Rom.	11	1

Ben-oni *son of my sorrow*

Benjamin, so called by his dying mother	Gen.	35	18

Beor *torch or light*

Father of Bela	Gen.	36	32
Father of Balaam	Num.	22	5
Called Bosor	II Pet.	2	15

Berachiah *see* Berechiah

Berea, Beroea *a city of Macedonia*

Paul preaches here	Acts	17	10, 13

bereavement *loss of loved one*

Forbidden as a judgment of sin	Lev.	10	6
God comforts in	II Sam.	12	22, 23
	Is.	38	1–5
Judgment of God	Jer.	15	7
	Jer.	18	21
Punishment for sin	Lam.	1	20
Christian	I Thes.	4	13–18
Future hope	John	11	20–27

Instances of:

Abraham for Sarah	Gen.	23	2
Jacob for Joseph	Gen.	37	33–35
Joseph for Jacob	Gen.	50	1
Egyptians for firstborn	Ex.	12	29–33
David for Absalom	II Sam.	18	33
Job for his sons	Job	1	18–22
Mary and Martha for Lazarus	John	11	14–38

Berechiah, Berachiah *Jehovah hath blessed*

Son of Jerubbabel	I Chr.	3	20
Father of Asaph	I Chr.	6	39
Son of Asa	I Chr.	9	16
Doorkeeper of the ark	I Chr.	15	23, 24
An Ephraimite chief	II Chr.	28	12
Father of Meshullam, one of Nehemiah's chiefs	Neh.	3	4
Father of the prophet Zechariah	Zech.	1	1

Beriah *son of evil*

A son of Asher	Gen.	46	17
A son of Ephraim	I Chr.	7	22, 23
A son of Shimei	I Chr.	23	10

Berith *covenant*

An idol in Shechem	Judg.	9	46

Baal-berith

	Judg.	8	33
	Judg.	9	4

Bernice *one that brings victory*

Daughter of Agrippa	Acts	12	1
Sister of Agrippa II, married to her uncle, Herod	Acts	25	13
Paul preaches to	Acts	26	1–30

Berodach-baladan *see* Merodach-baladan

Beroea *see* Berea

Berothah *wells*

Seaport on the Mediterranean	Ezek.	47	16
Color of	Ezek.	1	16
Color of angel's body	Dan.	10	5, 6

beryl *a precious stone*

Adorns the breastplate of the high priests	Ex.	28	20
	Ex.	39	13
Gem of the Egyptians	Ezek.	28	13
John's vision	Rev.	21	20

beseech

B the Lord	Ex.	32	11
	Deut.	3	23
	I Ki.	13	6
	Jer.	26	19
I *b* show me thy glory	Ex.	33	18
Return, we *b*, O God	Ps.	80	14
B God, he be gracious	Mal.	1	9
Centurion, *b* him	Mat.	8	5
Devils *b* him	Mat.	8	31
	Luke	8	31
Fell on his face and *b*	Luke	5	12
B him that he would come	Luke	7	3
B him to depart from them	Luke	8	37
B That he would tarry	John	4	40
Paul *b* them all	Acts	27	33
B you by the mercies of God	Rom.	12	1
Wherefore I *b* you	I Cor.	4	16
As though God did *b* you	II Cor.	5	20
B the Lord Thrice	II Cor.	12	8
I *b*, be as I am.	Gal.	4	12
For love's sake *b* thee	Phil.	9	
As I *b* thee	I Tim.	1	3

besom *a broom*

Symbol of destruction	Is.	14	23

Besor *cool*

A brook visited by David	I Sam.	30	9

besought

B the Lord	Ex.	32	11
	Deut.	3	23
	Jer.	26	19
Devils *b* him	Mat.	8	31
	Mark	5	10

besought—*continued*

B him to depart	Luke	8	37
B that he would tarry	John	4	40
I *b* the Lord thrice	II Cor.	12	8
(*See* Gen. 42:21; Esth. 8:3)			

best

Spared *b* of sheep	I Sam.	15	9, 15
At his *b* state is vanity	Ps.	39	5
B robe	Luke	15	22
B gifts	I Cor.	12	31
(*See* Gen. 43:11; Deut. 23:16; II Sam. 18:4)			

bestiality *beastly nature*

Prohibited by Mosaic law	Lev.	18	23
Penalty for	Lev.	20	15

bestow

B upon you a blessing	Ex.	32	29
The Lord hath *b* on us	Is.	63	7
No room to *b* my fruits	Luke	12	17
Though I *b* all my goods	I Cor.	13	3
Grace *b* on me not in vain	I Cor.	15	10
Lest I have *b* labour in vain	Gal.	4	11
Manner of love the Father hath *b*	I John	3	1

Beth *a house*

Second letter of Hebrew alphabet	Ps.	119	Title

Beth-abara *house of passage*

Where John baptizes	John	1	28

Bethany *house of dates*

Lodging-place of Christ when in Jerusalem	Mat.	21	17
Home of Simon, the leper	Mat.	26	6
Near mount of Olives	Luke	19	29
Christ ascends from	Luke	24	50
Home of Lazarus, Martha and Mary	John	11	1
Lazarus raised from the dead	John	11	1-44

Beth-aven *house of vanity*

City near Ai	Josh.	7	2
Philistines defeated by Israel	I Sam.	13	5
	I Sam.	14	23
Disapproved for impiety and idolatry	Hosea	4	15
	Hosea	5	8
	Hosea	10	5

Beth-diblathaim, Almon-diblathaim *house of the two cakes*

Israelites encamp here	Num.	33	46
Despoiled for contempt of God	Jer.	48	22

Beth-el *house of God*

Where Abraham camps	Gen.	12	8
Makes altar here	Gen.	13	3, 4
Vision of Jacob's ladder	Gen.	28	16-22
Previously called Luz	Gen.	28	19
Jacob settles here	Gen.	35	1-15
In the inheritance of the Benjamites	Judg.	21	19
Samuel judges here	I Sam.	7	16
Idols placed by Jeroboam	I Ki.	12	28-33
Elijah and sons of prophets live here	II Ki.	2	2, 3
Mocking of Elisha	II Ki.	2	23, 24
Altars and idols destroyed	II Ki.	23	4, 15-20
Captured by Abijah	II Chr.	13	19
Its idolatry brings shame	Jer.	48	13
Amos prophesies here	Amos	7	10-13
Jeremiah announces judgment of	Jer.	48	13
Opposed by Hosea	Hosea	10	15
Called Bethul	Josh.	19	4

Bethesda *house of mercy*

A pool in Jerusalem with five porches	John	5	2

Beth-horon *house of the hollow*

Where kings of Amorites are defeated by God	Josh.	10	10, 11
City of Joseph	Josh.	16	3, 5
Allotted to Levites	Josh.	21	20, 22
Rebuilt by Solomon	II Chr.	8	5
Built by a woman	I Chr.	7	24
Strategic location	Josh.	10	10-14
	I Sam.	13	18

Bethlehem, Beth-lehem Judah or **Ephratah** *house of bread*

Rachel dies here	Gen.	35	16-20
	Gen.	48	7
Called Ephratah	Mic.	5	2
Home of Levite, disciple of Micah	Judg.	17	7, 8
Home of Naomi and Ruth	Ruth	1	19
Home of Boaz	Ruth	2	4
Home of Joab	I Chr.	2	15, 16
Home of David's father, Jesse	I Sam.	16	1
Samuel sent by God	I Sam.	16	4
Fortified by Rehoboam	II Chr.	11	6
Suggested as a place for the tabernacle	Ps.	132	6
City founded by Salma	I Chr.	2	51

Inhabitants numbered among those returning from Babylon	Ezra	2	21
	Neh.	7	26
Birthplace of the Messiah predicted	Mic.	5	2
	Mat.	2	5, 6
	John	7	42
Jesus born here	Mat.	2	1
	Luke	2	4-7
Herod slays children of	Mat.	2	16
Town allotted to Zebulun	Josh.	19	15
Home of Ibzan, the judge	Judg.	12	8-10

Beth-nimrah, Nimrah *house of sweet water*

Reubenites and Gadites vie for cattle land	Num.	32	3
Allotted to Gad by Moses	Num.	32	36
	Josh.	13	27

Beth-peor *house of Peor*

A Moabite town where Moses last speaks	Deut.	3	29
	Deut.	4	46
Moses is buried near	Deut.	34	6
Given to Reuben	Josh.	13	15, 20

Beth-phage *house of figs*

A place near Bethany, where Christ sends His disciples to fetch an ass	Mat.	21	1, 2
	Mark	11	1, 2
	Luke	19	29, 30
On the backside of Mount of Olives	Mat.	21	1

Bethsaida *house of fishing*

Condemned by Christ for unbelief	Mat.	11	21
	Luke	10	13
A place on the shore of the sea of Galilee, to which Christ goes after feeding the five thousand	Mark	6	45
	Luke	9	10
Where He restores the sight of a blind man	Mark	8	22
The home of Philip, Andrew and Peter	John	1	44
	John	12	21

Beth-shan, Beth-shean *house of quiet*

A stronghold allotted to Manasseh	Josh.	17	11
	Judg.	1	27
Possessed by Manasseh	I Chr.	7	29
Known for chariots	Josh.	19	41
Philistines dishonour the bodies of Saul and his sons	I Sam.	21	7-13

Beth-shemesh *house of the sun, a high place*

A city of Judah	Josh.	15	10
Allotted to the children of Aaron	Josh.	21	16
Many are smitten for looking into the returning ark	I Sam.	6	19
Where Jehoash defeats Amaziah	II Ki.	14	11-14
Invaded by the Philistines	II Chr.	28	18
Also called Ir-Shemesh	Josh.	19	41
A town of Issachar	Josh.	19	22, 23
A town of Naphtali	Josh.	19	38
	Judg.	1	33
An Egyptian city	Jer.	43	13

betray

Shall *b* one another	Mat.	24	10
Opportunity to *b*	Mat.	26	16
	Mark	14	11
	Luke	22	6
B me	Mat.	26	21, 23, 46
B innocent blood	Mat.	27	4
He that *b* me is at hand	Mark	14	42
B thou the Son of man?	Luke	22	48
Ye have been now the *b*	Acts	7	52
Same night he was *b*	I Cor.	11	23

betrayal *a breaking of faith*

Unfaithfulness in one's own household	Job	19	15
The cost of treachery	Zech.	11	10-14
Prophecy of last days	Mat.	10	21

Persons betrayed:

Samson by Delilah	Judg.	16	18-20
Of Jesus Christ foretold	Ps.	41	9
David by Doeg	I Sam.	22	9, 10
Bethel by one of its inhabitants	Judg.	1	24, 25
Disciples	Mat.	10	21
By Judas Iscariot	Mat.	26	47-50
	Mark	14	42-46
	Luke	22	47, 48
	John	18	2-5
By Israel	Mat.	27	9, 10

betrothal *mutual pledge to marry*

Rebekah and Isaac	Gen.	24	51, 67
Parents' consent required	Gen.	29	18-20
	Ex.	22	16, 17

Hebrew laws of	Ex.	21	9
	Lev.	19	20
	Deut.	20	7
	Deut.	22	22–30
	Hosea	2	19, 20
Mary and Joseph	Luke	1	26, 27

better

To obey *b* than sacrifice	I Sam.	15	22
I am no *b* than my fathers	I Ki.	19	4
Loving kindness *b* than life.	Ps.	63	3
B to get wisdom than gold	Prov.	16	16
Two are *b* than one	Eccl.	4	9
B a good name than	Eccl.	7	1
Former days *b* than these	Eccl.	7	10
Are ye not much *b* than they?	Mat.	6	26
Man *b* than a sheep?	Mat.	12	12
Nothing *b*, but rather grew worse	Mark	5	26
Old wine *b*	Luke	5	39
With Christ far *b*	Phil.	1	23
Esteem other *b* than themselves	Phil.	2	3
B than the angels	Heb.	1	4
The Mediator of a *b* covenant	Heb.	8	6
Speaketh *b* things than that of Abel	Heb.	12	24
B not have known the way	II Pet.	2	21

betting *see gambling*

Beulah *married*

A name given the land of Israel, symbolic of its future prosperity	Is.	62	4

bewail

All wept and *b* her	Luke	8	52
Of women, which also *b*	Luke	23	27
B many which have sinned	II Cor.	12	21
(*See* Deut. 21:13; Judg. 11:37; Rev. 18:9)			

beware

B, and drink not wine	Judg.	13	4
B lest he take thee away	Job	36	18
B of leaven	Mat.	16	6
	Mark	8	15
	Luke	12	1
B of scribes	Mark	12	38
	Luke	20	46
B of covetousness	Luke	12	15
B of dogs, *b* of evil workers	Phil.	3	2
(*See* Deut. 6:12; 8:11; 15:9)			

bewitched *cast a spell over*

Simon, the sorcerer	Acts	8	9, 125
The foolish Galatians	Gal.	3	1, 186

beyond

B the word of the Lord	Num.	22	18
Amazed *b* measure	Mark	6	51
	Mark	7	37
B their power	II Cor.	8	3
B measure I persecuted	Gal.	1	13
That no man go *b*	I Thes.	4	6

Bezaleel *the shadow of God*

The chief builder of the tabernacle	Ex.	31	1–11, 81
Son of Uri	I Chr.	2	20, 375
Married a foreign wife	Ezra	10	30, 446

Bezek *sowing*

A town captured in Judah in the invasion of Canaan	Judg.	1	4, 226
The place where Saul mobilizes the Israelites	I Sam.	11	8, 264

bier *a coffin*

Used for Abner	II Sam.	3	31, 290
The widow's son raised from	Luke	7	14, 65

bigamy *having more than one wife*

Lamech, the first to practice	Gen.	4	19, 4
Prohibited by law	Deut.	17	17, 184
	Lev.	18	18
	I Tim.	3	2, 12

Practiced:

Abraham	Gen.	16	
Esau	Gen.	26	34
Jacob	Gen.	29	30
David	I Sam.	25	39–44
Solomon	I Ki.	11	1–8

Evil results:

Favoritism	Deut.	21	15–17
Strife	I Sam.	1	5
Jealousy	Gen.	16	
	Gen.	21	9–16
Apostasy	I Ki.	11	4–8

bigotry *religious intolerance*

Shows disrespect for work of others	Num.	11	27–29
	Mark	12	38–40
Denounced by God	Is.	65	5
In judging the actions of Christ	Mat.	11	18, 19
	Mark	2	16
	John	5	18
Jesus' teaching against, rejected	Luke	4	28
Of the Pharisee	Luke	18	9–14
Peter cured of	Acts	10	28
Of Saul of Tarsus	Acts	22	3, 4
	Gal.	1	13, 14
Paul's argument against	Rom.	3	1–23
	Rom.	4	1–13
Unhappiness of	Mat.	21	15
Samaritan woman's error	John	4	9
Results in blindness	John	8	48, 49

Bildad *son of contention*

A friend of Job	Job	2	11
	Job	8	1–22
	Job	18	1–21
	Job	25	1–6

Bilhah *modesty*

Rachel's maid	Gen.	29	29
Given as Jacob's concubine	Gen.	30	3, 4
Mother of Dan and Naphtali	Gen.	30	5–8
Incest with Reuben	Gen.	35	22
Town of Simeon	I Chr.	4	29

binding of Satan

For a thousand years	Rev.	20	2

Binea *foundation; wanderer*

A descendant of Jonathan	I Chr.	8	37

birds

Created by God	Gen.	1	20
Taken in the ark	Gen.	7	3
Used for a sacrifice	Gen.	15	9
	Lev.	14	4
	Luke	2	24
Some shall not be eaten	Lev.	11	13
	Deut.	14	11–18
Some are eaten	Gen.	9	2, 3
Protected by Mosaic law	Deut.	22	6
Snare used to capture	Ps.	124	7
Where they nest	Ps.	104	17
Praise God for	Ps.	148	10
Mentioned figuratively	Prov.	1	17
	Prov.	6	5
	Eccl.	10	20
	Amos	3	5
	Mat.	8	20
Known for singing	Ps.	104	12
A sign of spring	S. of S.	2	12
Also see individual species of birds			

Types of Birds:

Bittern	Zeph.	2	14
Cock	Mark	14	30
Cuckow	Lev.	11	16
Cormorant	Lev.	11	17
Crane	Is.	38	14
Dove	Ps.	68	13
Eagle	Ex.	19	4
Glede	Deut.	14	13
Hawk	Lev.	11	16
Hen	Luke	13	34
Heron	Lev.	11	19
Kite	Lev.	11	14
Lapwing	Lev.	11	19
Ospray	Lev.	11	13
Ostrich	Job	39	13
Owls	Is.	34	13
	Ps.	102	6
	Is.	34	15
	Lev.	11	17
	Is.	34	14
Partridge	Jer.	17	11
Peacock	I Ki.	10	22
Pelican	Lev.	11	18
Pigeon	Lev.	12	6
Quail	Ex.	16	13
Raven	Gen.	8	7
Sparrow	Ps.	84	3
Stork	Lev.	11	19
Swallow	Ps.	84	3
Swan	Lev.	11	18
Turtledove	Gen.	15	9
Vulture	Lev.	11	14

Birsha *son of wickedness*			
King of Gomorrah	Gen.	14	2
birth *beginning of life*			
Pain of, a punishment for sin	Gen.	3	16
Cursed	Job	3	1–11
	Jer.	20	14, 15
Day of death better than	Eccl.	7	1
Spiritual birth	John	3	5
Blind from birth	John	9	1
Causing ceremonial uncleanness	Lev.	12	2, 5
Time of joy	John	16	21
Births foretold:			
Ishmael	Gen.	16	11
Isaac	Gen.	18	10
Samson	Judg.	13	3, 24
Samuel	I Sam.	1	11, 20
Josiah	I Ki.	13	2
Shunammite's son	II Ki.	4	16
Cyrus	Is.	45	1–4
Jesus	Is.	9	6–8
	Mic.	5	1–3
	Luke	1	30, 31
John the Baptist	Luke	1	13
Birth control	Gen.	38	8–10
birthday			
A festive occasion	Gen.	40	20
	Mat.	14	6
	Mark	6	21
birth, new *see* regeneration			
birthright *any right acquired by birth*			
Sold by Esau	Gen.	25	31–34
	Heb.	12	16
Inheritance of the firstborn	Gen.	43	33
	II Chr.	21	3
Law concerning	Deut.	21	15
Lost by Reuben	I Chr.	5	1
Manasseh	Gen.	48	15–20
Solomon	I Chr.	28	5–7
Of royal succession	II Chr.	21	3
Hosah's son	I Chr.	26	10
bishop *a spiritual overseer*			
Elders in the church	Acts	20	17
	Phil.	1	1
Qualifications for	I Tim.	3	1–8
	Tit.	1	7–10
Christ, the	I Pet.	2	25
Ordained	Tit.	1	5, 7
Multiplicity	Phil.	1	1
Interchangeable with elder	Acts	20	17, 28
To oversee the church	Acts	20	17, 28–31
To protect the sheep	Heb.	13	17
Of Christ	I Pet.	2	25
bishopric *charge, office*			
Referring to discipleship	Acts	1	20
Bithnyia *a province of Asia Minor*			
Paul not allowed to go here	Acts	16	7
Peter writes to	I Pet.	1	1
bitter			
Exceeding ***b*** cry	Gen.	27	34
With ***b*** herbs.	Ex.	12	8
	Num.	9	11
Waters were ***b***	Ex.	15	23
Devoured with ***b*** destruction	Deut.	32	24
Writest ***b*** things	Job	13	26
That put ***b*** for sweet	Is.	5	20
I will weep ***b***	Is.	22	4
An evil thing and ***b***	Jer.	2	19
bitter herbs			
Eaten with the passover feast	Ex.	12	8
	Num.	9	11
bitter waters			
Marah	Ex.	15	23
Water of the ordeal	Num.	5	18–27
bittern *a heron*			
Figure of speech in prophecy	Is.	14	23
	Is.	34	11
	Zeph.	2	14
bitterness *inner hatred*			
Against being childless	I Sam.	1	10
Of one's own soul	Job	10	1
	Job	21	25
	Prov.	14	10
	Is.	38	15
Against a foolish son	Prov.	17	25

Must be put aside for a Christian life	Acts	8	22, 23
	Eph.	4	31
	Heb.	12	15
Of death	I Sam.	15	32
bitterness			
Surely the ***b*** of death is past	I Sam.	15	32
In ***b*** of soul	Job	10	1
	Job	21	25
	Is.	38	15
Heart knoweth own ***b***	Prov.	14	10
Be in ***b*** for him as one that is in ***b***	Zech.	12	10
In the gall of ***b***	Acts	8	23
Let all ***b*** be put away	Eph.	4	31
Lest any root of ***b***	Heb.	12	15
bitumen, pitch, slime *a mineral resembling asphalt*			
Noah used in Ark	Gen.	6	14
Found by the Dead Sea	Gen.	14	10
Used in making bricks	Gen.	11	3
Used in making basket for baby Moses	Ex.	2	3
black *devoid of light*			
Test of leprosy	Lev.	13	31, 37
Color of stormy sky	I Ki.	18	45
Skin	Job	30	30
	S. of S.	1	5
Night	Prov.	7	9
Hair	Mat.	5	36
Color of a burnt oven	Lam.	5	10
Horse of second chariot	Zech.	6	2
Horse	Rev.	6	5
Color of sackcloth	Rev.	6	12
Sun	Joel	2	10
Of evil	Joel	2	6
Of Hell	Jude		13
blacksmith *one who works with iron*			
Tubal-cain, the first	Gen.	4	22
Israel has none	I Sam.	13	19
Should not make graven images	Is.	44	9, 12
blains *blisters accompanying boils*			
Sixth plague of Egypt	Ex.	9	9, 10
blamelessness *freedom from fault*			
Unto the laws of the Lord	Luke	1	6
	Phil.	2	14, 15
	Phil.	3	6
Of faith will be rewarded	I Cor.	1	8
	I Thes.	5	23
	II Pet.	3	14
Bishops should be	I Tim.	3	2
	Tit.	1	6, 7
blameless			
Ye shall be ***b***	Gen.	44	10
Now shall I be more ***b***	Judg.	15	3
Profane sabbath, are ***b***	Mat.	12	5
Ordinances of the Lord ***b***	Luke	1	6
Ye may be ***b***, in the day	I Cor.	1	8
B and harmless	Phil.	2	15
Touching righteousness of law ***b***	Phil.	3	6
Spirit, soul, and body, ***b***	I Thes.	5	23
Bishop must be ***b***	I Tim.	3	2
	Tit.	1	7
Office of a deacon, found ***b***	I Tim.	3	10
In charge, that they may be ***b***	I Tim.	5	7
If any be ***b*** the husband of	Tit.	1	6
Without spot and ***b***	II Pet.	3	14
blasphemy *contempt for God*			
Forbidden in Ten Commandments	Ex.	20	7
Taking the name of the Lord in vain	Lev.	19	12
	Deut.	5	11
	Ps.	74	18
	Ezek.	20	27
	Ezek.	36	20
Stoning, a punishment for	Lev.	24	16, 23
	I Ki.	21	10, 13
	Acts	7	58, 59
Proceeds from the heart	Mat.	15	19
	Mark	7	21, 22
	Col.	3	8
Antichrist	Dan.	11	36, 37
	II Thes.	2	4
Result of Pride	Ps.	73	9, 11
	Ezek.	35	12, 13
Falsely accused:			
Naboth	I Ki.	21	12, 13
Stephen	Acts	6	9–13
Jesus	Mat.	9	2, 3
	Mat.	26	65
	Luke	5	21

	Luke	22	65
	John	10	33, 36

Instances of:

Israelites	Lev.	24	10–14
	Num.	21	5, 6
Sennacherib	II Ki.	19	20–22
Job's wife	Job	2	9
Babylonians	Is.	52	5
Edom or Seir	Ezek.	35	12
Jews at Corinth	Acts	18	5, 6
The beast	Rev.	13	1, 5
Against the Holy Spirit	Mat.	12	31, 32
	Mark	3	28, 29
	Luke	12	10

Alleged of:

Jesus	Mat.	9	3
Stephen	Acts	6	11, 13
Judgment of God against	Ezek.	35	7–12
	I Tim.	3	1, 2

Blastus *sprout*

Herod's chamberlain	Acts	12	20

blemish *defect, deformity*

Animals used as an offering should be without	Ex.	12	5
	Ex.	29	1
	Lev.	1	3
	Lev.	22	19–25
	Deut.	17	1
Priest without	Lev.	21	17–24
Absalom has no	II Sam.	14	25
Israelite children without, trained by Nebuchadnezzar	Dan.	1	4
Church of Christ without	Eph.	5	27
Christ as a lamb without	I Pet.	1	19

blessed *hallowed, holy*

Those chastened by the Lord endure chastisement	Job	5	17–19
	Ps.	94	12
	Heb.	12	5–9
Whose sins are forgiven	Ps.	32	1, 2
	Rom.	4	7
Who hear and obey	Ps.	119	1, 2
	Mat.	13	16
	Luke	11	28
	James	1	25
	Rev.	1	3
	Rev.	22	7, 14
Who fear the Lord	Ps.	128	1–6
Who believe and suffer for Christ	Mat.	11	6
	Mat.	16	16, 17
	Luke	6	20–22
	Gal.	3	9
More blessed to give than to receive	Acts	20	35
Who endures temptation	James	1	12
Who die in the Lord	Rev.	14	13
Others pronounced blessed	Deut.	15	10
	Ps.	5	12
	Ps.	41	1
	Ps.	106	3
	Ps.	112	2
	Ps.	119	1
	Prov.	20	7
	Prov.	22	9
	Luke	14	13, 14
	Rev.	16	15

Persons blessed:

Jacob by Isaac	Gen.	27	27
Jacob by God	Gen.	48	3
Joseph and his sons by Jacob	Gen.	48	9, 15
Twelve tribes by Moses	Deut.	33	1–29

blessings

Form of	Num.	6	22–26
For obedience	Deut.	11	26–28
	Deut.	20	1–20
Blessings and curses	Deut.	28	1–68
	Lev.	26	1–46
Spiritual joys, in worship	Ps.	24	5
	Eph.	1	3
Temporal blessings	Gen.	22	17
	Mat.	6	26
	Phil.	4	19
Rendering good for evil	I Pet.	3	9

Exemplified:

To Noah at the time of the flood	Gen.	7	1
Abraham	Gen.	24	1
Isaac	Gen.	26	12, 24, 29

Jacob	Gen.	35	9–15
Israelites in Egypt	Ex.	11	3
Manna	Ex.	16	14, 31
Quails	Num.	11	31–33
For the twelve tribes	Deut.	33	6–25
David	II Sam.	5	10
	I Chr.	14	17
Solomon	I Ki.	3	13
	I Chr.	29	25
Elijah fed by ravens	I Ki.	17	2–7
Job	Job	1	10
Daniel	Dan.	1	9

blindfold *a covering for the eyes*

Put on Jesus at His trial	Luke	22	64

blindness *lack of sight*

Of Isaac in old age	Gen.	27	1
Ill-treatment of the blind forbidden	Lev.	19	14
	Deut.	27	18
	Mal.	1	8
Improper sacrifice	Lev.	26	16
Inflicted for disobedience	Deut.	28	28, 29
Prayer for deliverance	Ps.	13	3
	Ps.	119	18
Condition of war	I Sam.	11	2

Inflicted on:

Men of Sodom	Gen.	19	11
Samson by captors	Judg.	16	20, 21
Syrian army	II Ki.	6	18
Saul of Tarsus	Acts	9	8, 9
Elymas	Acts	13	11
As judgment on the wicked	Ps.	69	23
	Is.	6	10
	II Cor.	4	4

Healed by Christ:

Two men in Galilee	Mat.	9	27–30
Blind and dumb man	Mat.	12	22
Two men by the way side	Mat.	20	30–34
Man in Bethsaida	Mark	8	22–26
Bartimaeus, the beggar	Mark	10	46–52
	Luke	18	35–43
Blind in Nain	Luke	7	21
Man in Jerusalem	John	9	1–7

blindness, spiritual

Caused by:

Bribery	Deut.	16	19
Blind leaders	Is.	56	10
	Mat.	15	14
	Mat.	23	16
Refusal to see the truth	Jer.	5	21
	Mat.	6	22, 23
Refusing to believe	John	1	5
	John	12	40
	II Cor.	4	4
Evil deeds	John	3	19
Love of material things	I Cor.	2	14
Lack of Christian graces	II Pet.	1	3, 9
	I John	2	11
Self-satisfaction	Rev.	3	17

Removed by:

Missionaries, called "A light unto the Gentiles	Is.	42	6, 7
	Acts	28	17, 18
By Christ	Is.	9	2
	Is.	29	18
	Luke	4	18
	John	8	12
	John	9	39
	II Cor.	3	14
	II Cor.	4	6
	I Pet.	2	9

blood

Of covenant	Ex.	24	8
	Heb.	13	20
Forbidden as food	Gen.	9	4
	Lev.	3	17
	Deut.	12	16, 23
	Acts	15	20, 29
Life is in the blood	Gen.	9	4
Plague of	Ex.	7	17–25
	Ps.	78	44
	Ps.	105	29
Sprinkled on door posts	Ex.	12	7–23
	Heb.	11	28
Of the covenant	Ex.	24	5–8
	Mat.	26	28
	Heb.	9	18–22
	Ex.	24	6–8

blood—*continued*

Sprinkled on altar and people	Ezek.	43	18, 20
Shedding of blood	Heb.	9	22
Of sin offering	Ex.	29	12
	Ex.	30	10
	Lev.	4	5, 6, 17
	Lev.	8	15
Causing uncleanness	Lev.	15	19
Of peace offering	Lev.	3	2, 8, 13
Of trespass offering	Lev.	7	2
Of burnt offering	Lev.	8	19
	Deut.	12	27
Used for cleansing leprosy	Lev.	14	7, 51
Of atonement	Lev.	16	14–19
	Lev.	17	11
To be avenged	Deut.	32	43

Figurative of:

Of color red	II Ki.	3	22
Guilt	Lev.	20	9
	II Sam.	1	16
	Ezek.	18	13
Sin	Is.	59	2, 3
Victories	Ps.	58	10
Judgment	Ezek.	16	38
	Rev.	16	6
Destruction	Ezek.	35	6
Oppression and cruelty	Hab.	2	12

Well-known scriptures mentioning:

Water turned into	Ex.	7	20
Blood on door posts	Ex.	12	13
Sweating blood	Luke	22	44
Field of blood	Acts	1	19
Drinking enemies'	I Chr.	11	19
Shed like water	Ps.	79	3
Land soaked with	Is.	34	7
Moon turned to	Joel	2	31
	Acts	2	16, 20

Christ's blood:

Everlasting covenant	Heb.	13	20
Lord's supper	I Cor.	11	25
Cleansing power	I John	1	7
Redemptive power	Eph.	1	7
	Col.	1	14
	I Pet.	1	18, 19
Bought church with	Acts	20	28
As a sacrifice	I Pet.	1	19
Washes robes in	Rev.	7	14
Powerful	Rev.	12	11

bloodguiltiness *responsibility for death of others*

Prayer for deliverance from	Ps.	51	14
For murder	Ex.	21	14
David after murder of Uriah	Ps.	51	4
Judas after betrayal	Mat.	27	4
Blood of the innocent	Jer.	2	34
	Mat.	27	4
For themselves—rejectors of Christ	Ezek.	33	4
	Acts	18	6

blood, issue of *see* issue of blood

blood money

Received by Judas	Mat.	26	14–16
Predicted	Zech.	11	12

blood of Christ, the *see* Jesus Christ

bloody sweat *see* sweat

blossom

The desert shall blossom	Is.	35	1
Aaron's rod	Num.	17	8
Israel shall	Is.	27	6
Fig tree	Hab.	3	17
Figurative of pride	Ezek.	7	10

blot

B out of book	Ex.	32	32
	Ps.	69	28
B out his name	Deut.	29	20
B out thy transgressions	Is.	43	25
B out, as a thick cloud	Is.	44	22
Neither *b* out their sins	Jer.	18	23
That your sins be *b* out	Acts	3	19
B out the handwriting	Col.	2	14

blow

B an alarm	Num.	10	5, 6
B with the trumpets	Josh.	6	9, 13
Causeth his wind to *b*	Ps.	147	18
The great trumpet shall be *b*	Is.	27	13
See the south wind *b*	Luke	12	55
Wind shall not *b* on the earth	Rev.	7	1

blue

Used in tabernacle	Ex.	25	4
Priest's robe	Ex.	28	31
Royalty	Esth.	1	6
	Esth.	8	15
Fringes of Israelite's garments	Num.	15	38

Boanerges *sons of thunder*

Surname of the sons of Zebedee	Mark	3	17

boar, wild *male of swine*

Wild beast of woods	Ps.	80	13
Also see swine			

boasting *bragging, extolling*

The folly of	Prov.	20	14
	Prov.	27	1
	Is.	10	15
Of evil	Ps.	52	1
Spiritual	Ps.	94	4
	Rom.	11	17
	II Cor.	10	12
	Eph.	2	8, 9
Opposed to grace	Rom.	3	27

Instances of:

Goliath	I Sam.	17	44
Ben-hadad	I Ki.	20	10, 11
Sennacherib	Is.	10	8–15
The disciples	Luke	10	17, 20
Theudas	Acts	5	36
Paul, in a good sense	II Cor.	8	24

boats *sea vessels*

Shimei and men of Judah go on ferry boat	II Sam.	19	18
In days of Christ	John	6	22, 23
Life boat	Acts	27	16, 30
Paul to Rome in	Acts	27	16
Life boats	Acts	27	32
Jonah	Jonah	1	5

Boaz, Booz *strength*

Wealthy man of Bethlehem	Ruth	2	1
Kindness toward Ruth	Ruth	2	3, 8–18
Marries Ruth	Ruth	4	10–13
Ancestor of David and Jesus	Ruth	4	17
	Mat.	1	5
	Luke	3	23, 32
A pillar of the temple	I Ki.	7	21
	II Chr.	3	17

body, human

Created out of dust	Gen.	2	7
Wonderfully made	Ps.	139	14
Not to be disfigured	Lev.	19	28
	Lev.	21	5
	Deut.	14	1
	Lev.	21	11
Laws concerning the dead body	Num.	9	6
	Deut.	21	23
	Hag.	2	13
Corruptible	Job	17	14
Its resurrection	Mat.	22	30
	I Cor.	15	12
	Phil.	3	21
As a living sacrifice to God	Rom.	12	1
Must not sin against	I Cor.	6	13
	I Thes.	4	4
Of Christians called "the temple of the Holy Ghost"	I Cor.	3	16
	I Cor.	6	19
Heavenly body	II Cor.	5	1
The Church is Christ's	I Cor.	12	12–27
Christ magnified in	Phil.	1	20
Defiled by the tongue	James	3	6
Mortal	I Cor.	15	53
Blameless	I Thes.	5	23
Tool of sin	Rom.	1	24–32
	I John	2	16, 17
Composed of parts	I Cor.	12	12–20
Eaten by worms	Job	19	26

Body of Christ:

Made by God	Heb.	10	5
Denial by antichrist	I John	4	2, 3
Necessary for salvation	Heb.	2	14
For atonement	Heb.	10	20
Communion bread	I Cor.	11	24
Grew	Luke	2	52
Became tired	John	4	6
Suffered pain	Heb.	2	14, 18
The Church	I Cor.	10	16, 17
	I Cor.	12	12
	Eph.	1	23

After the resurrection	Luke	24	39
Different after resurrection	John	20	19
Did not experience decay	Acts	2	31

boiling *state of agitation*

Method of cooking	Lev.	8	31
Of own son	II Ki.	6	29
Figurative, of bowels	Job	30	27
Figurative, of God's power	Job	41	31

boils *swelling of the skin, localized sores*

Sixth Egyptian plague	Ex.	9	8, 11
	Rev.	16	2
A sign of leprosy	Lev.	13	18–20
Remedy	II Ki.	20	7
	Is.	38	21
An affliction of Job	Job	2	7

boldness *dauntlessness, fearlessness*

A characteristic of saints	Prov.	28	1

Produced by:

Trust in God	Is.	50	6, 7
The fear of God	Acts	5	29
Faithfulness to God	I Tim.	3	13
Christ sets an example of	John	7	26
Is through faith in Christ	Eph.	3	11, 12
	Heb.	10	19
Pray for	Eph.	6	19, 20
Have, in prayer	Heb.	4	16
Express your trust in God with	Heb.	13	6
Saints shall have, in judgment	I John	4	17

Ministers should exhibit, in:

Reproving sin	Is.	58	1
	Mic.	3	8
Preaching	Acts	4	31
	Phil.	1	14
The face of opposition	Acts	13	46
	I Thes.	2	2
Faithfulness to their people	II Cor.	7	4
	II Cor.	10	1

Exemplified:

David	I Sam.	17	40–50
Nehemiah	Neh.	6	11
Shadrach	Dan.	3	17, 18
Daniel	Dan.	6	10–20
Joseph of Arimathea	Mark	15	43
Peter and John	Acts	4	13
	Acts	5	29
Stephen	Acts	7	51–57
Paul	Acts	9	27
	Acts	19	8
	II Cor.	7	4
	Gal.	2	11
Barnabas and Paul	Acts	14	3
Apollos	Acts	18	26–28

Also see courage

bond *(or vow)*

Law of	Num.	30	
Of peace	Eph.	4	3
In *b* of iniquity	Acts	8	23
B of peach	Eph.	4	3
B of perfectness	Col.	3	14
Thou hast loosed my *b*	Ps.	116	16
B abide me	Acts	20	23
Worthy of death or *b*	Acts	23	29
	Acts	26	31
Others had trial of *b*	Heb.	11	36

bondage *see slavery*

bondage, spiritual *slavery*

Typified by Israel in Egypt	Ex.	1	13, 14
Deliverance from, illustrated	Deut.	4	20
Deliverance from, promised	Is.	42	6, 7
Christ delivers from	Luke	4	18, 21
	John	8	36
	Rom.	7	24, 25
	Eph.	4	8
Obedience as means of deliverance	Rom.	6	17–20

The gospel, the instrument of deliverance

from	John	8	32
	Rom.	8	2
Saints are delivered from	Rom.	6	18, 22
To the devil	I Tim.	3	7
	II Tim.	2	26
To corruption	II Pet.	2	19
Through fear of death	Heb.	2	14, 15

bondservant *a slave*

Hagar, the bondwoman	Gen.	21	10
	Gal.	4	22, 23

In Egypt	Deut.	6	21
Laws concerning bondmen	Lev.	19	20
	Lev.	25	39
	Deut.	15	12
Solomon's	I Ki.	9	20–22
During the exile	Ezra	9	9

bones *parts of the skeleton*

Of Adam and Eve	Gen.	2	23
Joseph's	Gen.	50	25
	Ex.	13	19
	Heb.	11	22
Of kinship	Judg.	9	2
	II Sam.	19	13
Scattered as a judgment	II Ki.	23	14
	Ps.	53	5
	Ps.	141	7
	Jer.	8	1, 2
	Ezek.	6	5
Vision of dry	Ezek.	37	1–11
Passover lamb	Ex.	12	46
	John	19	36
Christ's	John	19	36
	Luke	24	39
Saul and Jonathan's	II Sam.	21	12, 14
Of Elisha	II Ki.	13	21

bonfire *a fire built outdoors*

Kindled by God's breath	Is.	30	33

bonnet *a man's headdress*

Worn by Aaron's sons	Ex.	28	40
	Ex.	29	9
Directions for making	Ex.	39	28
Taken from women	Is.	3	20
Worn by the sons of Zadok	Ezek.	44	18

Book of Law

Referred to by Moses	Deut.	28	61
	Deut.	29	27
Referred to by Paul	Gal.	3	10
Referred to in Joshua	Josh.	1	8
To be copied for King	Deut.	17	18
Placed beside the ark	Deut.	31	26
Read to the returned exiles	Neh.	8	8
Josiah's reforms	II Ki.	23	2–14

books *rolls of dressed skins*

First mention	Gen.	5	1
Divine communications recorded	Ex.	17	14
	Is.	30	8
	Jer.	36	2
	Rev.	1	19
Erasures in, alluded to	Ex.	32	33
	Num.	5	23
Important events recorded in	Ezra	4	15
	Ezra	6	1, 2
	Esth.	2	23
Probable origin of	Job	19	23, 24
The ancients fond of making	Eccl.	12	12

Made of:

Papyrus or paper reed	Is.	19	7
Parchment	II Tim.	4	13
Often sealed	Is.	29	11
	Dan.	12	4
	Rev.	5	1
Made in a roll	Is.	34	4
	Jer.	36	2
	Ezek.	2	9
Written with pen and ink	Jer.	36	18
	III John		13
Often written on both sides	Ezek.	2	10
Often dedicated to persons of distinction	Luke	1	3
	Acts	1	1

Lost Books

Book of Jasher	Josh.	10	13
Book of Gad	I Chr.	29	29
Book of Nathan	I Chr.	29	29
Book of Iddo	II Chr.	13	22
Book of wars of the Lord	Num.	21	14
Book of Samuel	I Sam.	10	25
Chronicles of David	I Chr.	27	24
Are numerous and most expensive	Acts	19	19

Book of Life

Moses aware of	Ex.	32	32
Possibility of being blotted out	Ps.	69	28
	Rev.	3	5
People in it delivered from the tribulation	Dan.	12	1
Christian's names are there recorded	Phil.	4	3
Followers of antichrist not written in it	Rev.	13	8
	Rev.	17	8

books—*continued*

Opened on judgment day	Rev.	20	12
	Dan.	7	10
Causes Christians to rejoice	Luke	10	20
Curse	Rev.	22	19
Also identified with the Book of Remembrance	Ps.	139	16
	Mal.	3	16
	Rev.	20	12

books of judgment

Seen in visions	Dan.	7	10
	Rev.	20	12

booth: *hut*

Made of branches	Jonah	4	5
For cattle	Gen.	33	17
For watchmen	Is.	1	8
	Is.	24	20
Feast of Tabernacles (Booths)	Lev.	23	40–43
	Neh.	8	15, 16

booty *plunder*

Spoils of war	Gen.	34	27–29
	Num.	31	26
Camels become	Jer.	49	32
Retribution on the Chaldeans	Hab.	2	7, 8
Judgment against Judah	Zeph.	1	13
All booty destroyed for the Lord	Deut.	20	14, 16
	Josh.	6	17–19
	I Sam.	15	2, 3
Divided among soldiers	I Sam.	30	24, 25
Isaiah's son Mahershalalhashbaz (Hasten the booty hurry the spoil)	Is.	8	3
Also see spoils			

Booz *see* Boaz

Born

Man *b* to trouble	Job	5	7
B of woman	Job	14	1
	Job	25	4
	Mat.	11	11
This man was *b* there	Ps.	87	4
Unto us a child is *b*	Is.	9	6
Shall a nation be *b* at once?	Is.	66	8
B of God	John	1	13
	I John	4	7
	I John	5	1, 4, 18
B again	I John	3	3
	I Pet.	1	23
B of Spirit	I Pet.	3	8
As one *b* out of due time	I Cor.	15	8
As new *b* babes	I Pet.	2	2

(*See* Job 3:3; Prov. 17:17; Eccl. 3:2; Mat. 19:12; John 8:41)

born again *see* regeneration

borne

B our griefs, carried our sorrows	Is.	53	4
Grievous to be *b*	Mat.	23	4
	Luke	11	46

(*See* Job 34:31; Lam. 5:7; Mat. 20:12)

borrowing *receiving with intention of returning*

From Egyptians	Ex.	3	22
	Ex.	12	35
Law concerning	Ex.	22	14
	Deut.	15	2–6
Elisha multiplies the widow's oil	II Ki.	4	3
Prophets axe	II Ki.	6	5
Its consequences	II Ki.	6	5
	Neh.	5	4, 5
	Prov.	22	7
Of the wicked	Ps.	37	21
Teachings of Jesus	Mat.	5	42
Donkey on which Christ rode	Mat.	21	2, 3

bosom *seat of the passions, affections*

Job protesting his integrity	Job	31	33
David prays for safety	Ps.	35	13
Illustrating the blessings of obedience	Prov.	6	27
Admonitions concerning anger	Eccl.	7	9
Foretelling the coming of the Lord	Is.	40	11
Figuratively, paradise	Luke	16	22
Implies great intimacy	John	1	18
	John	13	23
Stomach	Ex.	4	6
Of marriage	Deut.	28	54, 56
	Gen.	16	5
Abraham's bosom (of heaven)	Luke	16	22, 23

Bosor *a lamp*

Father of Balaam	II Pet.	2	15

botany *the science of plants*

Solomon an authority	I Ki.	4	30, 33
Laws of nature	Mat.	7	16–18, 20

botch *a swelling*

A curse for disobedience	Deut.	28	27, 35
See blains			

bottle

Primitive bottles either of earthenware or of skins	Gen.	21	14
	Jer.	19	1
Tear bottles used	Ps.	56	8
Of wine	I Sam.	25	18
	Hosea	7	5
Of milk	Judg.	4	19
Of water	Gen.	21	14
Old and new	Job	32	19
	Mat.	9	17
Breakable	Job	32	19
	Jer.	48	12

bottomless pit

The angel Apollyon has charge of	Rev.	9	1, 2, 11
	Rev.	20	1, 2
A beast in	Rev.	11	7
	Rev.	17	8
Satan bound there	Rev.	20	1, 2
Key to	Rev.	9	1
	Rev.	20	1

bound

He set the *b* of the people	Deut.	32	8
If they be *b* in fetters	Job	36	8
Being *b* in affliction	Ps.	107	10
Foolishness is *b* in heart of child	Prov.	22	15
Opening of prison to them that are *b*	Is.	61	1
I go *b* in spirit	Acts	20	22
Word of God is not *b*	II Tim.	2	9
In bonds, as *b* with them	Heb.	13	3

bountiful

Lord hath dealth *b*	Ps.	13	6
Deal *b* with thy servant	Ps.	119	17
A *b* eye shall be blessed	Prov.	22	9
Nor churl said to be *b*	Is.	32	5
He that soweth *b* shall reap *b*	II Cor.	9	6
Enrich to all *b*	II Cor.	9	11

bounty *blessing*

Gifts to the queen of Sheba	I Ki.	10	13
Paul exhorts the brethren concerning	II Cor.	9	5

bow

In the cloud, sign of God's mercy	Gen.	9	13
	Ezek.	1	28
Weapon	Gen.	48	22
	Josh.	24	12
	I Sam.	18	4
	II Sam.	1	18, 22
	II Ki.	9	24
	Ps.	44	6
	Ps.	78	57
	Jer.	49	35
	Hosea	7	16
	Rev.	6	2
B the head and worshipped	Ex.	12	27
Thou shalt not *b* down thyself	Ex.	20	5
Every one that *b* down	Judg.	7	5
B down thine ear and hear	Prov.	22	17
Unto me every knee shall *b*	Is.	45	23
B their knees	Mark	15	19
B my knees unto the Father	Eph.	3	14

bowels *various meanings*

Of mercy	Gen.	43	30
	Is.	63	15
	Luke	1	78
	Phil.	1	8
	Phil.	2	1
	Col.	3	12
Intestinal organ	Num.	5	22
	II Sam.	20	10
	II Chr.	21	14–20
Gushed out	Acts	1	18
Involved in procreation	Gen.	15	4
	Gen.	25	23
Of compassion	I John	3	17
	Gen.	43	30

bowing (the knee) *eastern mode of salutation*

Foretold in Joseph's dream	Gen.	37	10
In the Ten Commandments	Ex.	20	5
Gideon's army	Judg.	7	5, 6
To Solomon	I Ki.	1	53

To Bath-sheba	I Ki.	2	19
To the only God	Is.	45	23
In mockery	Mat.	27	29
	Mark	15	19
To Christ	Rom.	14	11, 12
	Phil.	2	10
To God	Eph.	3	14

box *a receptacle of firm material*

Used for oil	II Ki.	9	1
Made of alabaster	Mat.	26	7
	Mark	14	3

box tree *an evergreen*

Planted by God	Is.	41	19
In Lebanon	Is.	60	13

boy: *male child*

Of Jacob and Esau	Gen.	25	27
Traded for a harlot	Joel	3	3
Streets full of	Zech.	8	5

Bozrah *stronghold*

Ancient capital of Edom	Gen.	36	33
Prophecies concerning	Is.	34	6
	Is.	63	1
	Jer.	49	13, 22
Sheep of	Mic.	2	12
A city of Moab	Jer.	48	24

bracelet *a wrist and arm ornament*

Worn by Rebekah	Gen.	24	30
Children of Israel give in offering	Ex.	35	22
Worn by Saul	II Sam.	1	10
Of women	Is.	3	19
Taken as spoil	Num.	31	50
	II Sam.	1	10

brambles *see thorns*

branch *a member or part of any body*

Family descendants	Gen.	49	22
Title applied to Christ as offspring of David	Is.	11	1
	Jer.	23	5
	Zech.	3	8
Waved on day of triumphal entry	Mat.	21	8
	Mark	11	8
	John	12	13
Title applied to followers of Christ	John	15	5
Of Israel	Rom.	11	16, 21
Pruning of	Is.	18	5
	John	15	6

brasen, brazen serpent

Made by Moses for the healing of the Israelites	Num.	21	8, 9
Destroyed by Hezekiah	II Ki.	18	4
Called Nehushtan	II Ki.	18	4
Symbolic of Christ's crucifixion	John	3	14, 15

brass, copper

Workers in	Gen.	4	22
	I Ki.	7	14
Offerings of, for the tabernacle	Ex.	38	29
Found in mountains of Canaan	Deut.	8	9
Collected by David for the temple	I Chr.	22	3, 14, 16
Inferior in value to gold and silver	Is.	60	17
Coined for money	Mat.	10	9

Figurative of:

Obstinate sinners	Is.	48	4
Macedonian Empire	Dan.	2	39
The strength of Christ	Rev.	1	15

Used for:

Altars	Ex.	27	2
Sacred vessels	Ex.	27	3
Lavers	Ex.	30	18
Mirrors	Ex.	38	8
Fetters	Judg.	16	27
Helmets	I Sam.	17	5
Pillars	I Ki.	7	15, 16
Shields	I Ki.	14	27
Musical instruments	I Chr.	15	19
Gates	Ps.	107	16
Idols	Dan.	5	4
Household vessels	Mark	7	4

bravery

Showy appearance and fine dress	Is.	3	18
Opposing apostasy	Gal.	1	8
David	I Sam.	17	26, 37
Jonathan	I Sam.	14	6
David's mighty men	II Sam.	23	8–39

Jesus	Mat.	23	
	John	2	15

Also see courage

brawler *one who quarrels*

Brawling woman	Prov.	25	24
Disqualification for a bishop	I Tim.	3	1, 3

brazen sea *see* molten sea

brazen serpent *see* brasen serpent

breach *break through*

In temple	II Ki.	12	5
	II Ki.	22	5
In walls	Neh.	4	7
	II Ki.	14	13
	II Ki.	25	10
Between God and people	Ex.	32	32
	Is.	59	2
Of promise	Num.	14	34
Breach on Uzzah	II Sam.	6	8
As a judgment	Amos	6	11
Repaired by God	Amos	9	11
	Is.	58	11

bread

Principle food used by ancients	Gen.	18	5
	Gen.	21	14
Served at passover feast	Ex.	12	8
	Ex.	23	15
Plenty promised to obedient	Lev.	26	5
Given by God	Num.	11	6–9
	Ruth	1	6
	Mat.	6	11
Offered with sacrifices	Num.	28	2
Offered to Idols	Jer.	7	18
With water, the food of prisons	I Ki.	22	27
Yielded by the earth	Job	28	5
	Is.	55	10
Strengthening	Ps.	104	15
Scarceness of, a punishment	Ps.	105	16
	Ezek.	5	16
Cast upon water	Eccl.	11	1

Made of:

Wheat	Ex.	29	2
Barley	Judg.	7	13
	John	6	9
Possibly of manna	Num.	11	8
Grain ("corn")	Is.	28	28
Mixed with oil	Ex.	29	2
Mixed with honey	Ex.	16	31
Kneaded	Gen.	18	6

Formed into:

Wafers	Ex.	16	31
Cakes	Ex.	29	23
Loaves	I Sam.	10	3, 4

Baked:

On hearths	Gen.	18	6
On coals of fire	John	21	9
In ovens	Lev.	26	26
Of affliction	I Ki.	22	27
Made by men	Gen.	40	2
Made by women	Lev.	26	26
Sold at bakeries	Jer.	37	21
As the staff of life	Ezek.	4	16
	Ezek.	5	16

Different varieties:

Leavened	Lev.	23	17
	Mat.	13	33
Unleavened	Ex.	12	18
Common	I Sam.	21	4
Hallowed or shewbread	I Sam.	21	4–6
Multitudes miraculously fed	Mat.	14	19–21
	Mat.	15	34–37
Served at the last supper	Luke	22	7–19

bread of life

Christ is the bread of life	John	6	33–35
	John	6	48–51
Manna	Ex.	16	4
Body of Christ	I Cor.	11	23, 24
	Mat.	26	26

break

Day *b* and shadows flee	S. of S.	2	17
	S. of S.	4	6
Bruised reed shall be not *b*	Is.	42	3
	Mat.	12	20
B up your fallow ground	Jer.	4	3
	Hosea	10	12
B one of these least commandments	Mat.	5	19
To weep and *b* my heart	Acts	21	13

breaking the sabbath *see* sabbath			
breastplate *armour for the breast*			
Part of a high priest's dress	Ex.	28	15–20
Fastened to the ephod	Ex.	28	22–26
Skillfully made	Ex.	39	8
Symbolic of righteousness	Is.	59	17
	Eph.	6	14
Symbolic of faith	I Thes.	5	8
John's vision	Rev.	9	9
breast			
Used figuratively	Job	21	24
	Is.	66	11
	Ezek.	16	7
Of marriage partner	S. of S.	1	13
	S. of S.	4	5
	Prov.	5	19
For baby	Ps.	22	9
Of animals	Lam.	4	3
Punishment for defilement	Ezek.	23	3–10
Publican smites his breast	Luke	18	13
Smitten after crucifixion	Luke	23	48
Peter leans on Jesus'	John	13	25
John's vision	Rev.	15	6
breath of God			
Gives life to man	Gen.	2	7
	Job	33	4
	Ps.	33	6
Power to destroy	Gen.	7	22
	Job	4	9
	Is.	30	33
Creates the earth	Ex.	15	8
	II Sam.	22	16
Controls the elements	Job	37	10
Slays the wicked	Is.	11	4
brethren *plural of brother*			
Duty toward each other	Gen.	13	8
	Deut.	15	7
	Ps.	133	1
	Mat.	5	22
	Mat.	18	15–17
Joseph reveals himself to his	Gen.	45	1–5
Disciples called	Mat.	12	48–50
Needy are Christ's	Mat.	25	40
Should not speak evil of	James	4	11
Commanded to love one another	I Pet.	1	22
brethren of the Lord			
James, Joses, Simon and Judas	Mat.	13	55
	Mark	6	3
Journey with Jesus to Capernaum	John	2	12
Do not believe in Jesus	John	7	1–10
United with Mary after the resurrection	Acts	1	14
Ranked with the apostles	I Cor.	9	5
James, a leader of the church	Gal.	1	19
Author of James	James	1	1
Possibly the author of Jude	Jude		1
brevity of life—			
Few days	Job	14	1
Soon cut off	Ps.	90	10
Prolonged by prayer	Is.	38	2–5
Prolonged by Obedience	Ex.	20	12
Days flee away quickly	Job	9	25, 26
Fades as a leaf	Is.	64	6
Cut off like a weaver	Is.	38	12
Shortly put off tabernacle	II Pet.	1	13, 14
70 years	Ps.	90	10
Compared to:			
A flower	Job	14	2
A tale that is told	Ps.	90	9
A pilgrimage	Gen.	47	9
A weaver's shuttle	Job	7	6
Grass	I Pet.	1	24
Vapor	James	4	14
A moment	II Cor.	4	17
A shadow	Job	14	1, 2
A handbreadth	Ps.	39	5
A wind	Ps.	78	39
bribery *gift given for influence*			
Forbidden	Deut.	16	19
Will be punished	Job	15	34
Denounced	Prov.	17	23
	Prov.	29	4
	Eccl.	7	7
	Is.	33	15
	Ezek.	13	19
	Amos	2	6
	Amos	5	12
Sign of greed	Prov.	15	27
Blindeth the wise	Ex.	23	8
Instances of:			
Delilah	Judg.	16	5
Samuel's sons	I Sam.	8	3
Shemaiah	Neh.	6	10–13
Benhadad	I Ki.	15	19
Felix seeks bribe of Paul	Acts	24	26
brick *a building material*			
Used to build the tower of Babel	Gen.	11	3
Made by Israelites in Egypt	Ex.	1	14
	Ex.	5	7–19
Used for altars	Is.	65	3
Made in a kiln	Jer.	43	9
Used for houses	Is.	9	10
brick-kiln *oven for hardening bricks*			
David punishes Rabbah	II Sam.	12	31
Made for burning clay	Jer.	43	9
Used in fortifying a city	Nah.	3	14
bride			
Gifts presented to	Gen.	24	53
Maids of	Gen.	24	59
	Gen.	29	29
Receives dowry	Gen.	24	53
Wears jewels	Is.	49	18
	Is.	61	10
Brings joy to husband	Is.	62	5
Special attire of	Jer.	2	32
Of Christ, the church	John	3	29
	Rev.	21	2
	Rev.	22	17
Of Israel	Ezek.	16	8–14
bridegroom			
Exempt from military duty	Deut.	24	5
Symbolic of Jehovah	Ps.	19	5
Decked with ornaments	Is.	61	10
Parable of	Mat.	25	1–13
Christ, the bridegroom of the church	Mat.	9	15
	Mat.	25	1
	John	3	29
Companions of	Judg.	14	11
Song of	S. of S.	4	7–16
Receives a crown	S. of S.	3	11
Of God	Ezek.	16	8–14
bridle *harness*			
Used on animals	Ps.	32	9
	Prov.	26	3
Figurative of:			
Control of tongue	Ps.	39	1
	James	1	26
	James	3	2
Restraint	Is.	30	28
	Is.	37	29
briers *see* thorns			
brigandines *light armour*			
Worn by Israelites	Jer.	46	4
brimstone *sulphur*			
Rains upon Sodom and Gomorrah	Gen.	19	24
Symbolic of destruction	Job	18	15
	Luke	17	29
Figurative of torment	Rev.	9	17
	Rev.	14	10
	Rev.	19	20
bring, to carry			
Earth *b* forth grass	Gen.	1	11
The waters *b* forth	Gen.	20	
In sorrow . . . *b* forth	Gen.	3	16
I, do *b* a flood of	Gen.	6	17
B me unto thy holy	Ps.	43	3
Mountains shall *b*	Ps.	72	3
What a day may *b*	Prov.	27	1
B every work into	Eccl.	12	14
B no more vain	Is.	1	13
B thy sons from far	Is.	60	9
B ye all the tithes	Mal.	3	10
B thy gift to the	Mat.	5	23
B me a penny	Mark	12	15
I *b* you good tidings	Luke	2	10
B forth fruit with	Luke	8	15
B all things to	John	14	26
B forth more fruit	John	15	2
B this man's blood	Acts	5	28
B to naught things	I Cor.	1	28
B it into subjection	I Cor.	9	27

To *b* us unto Christ	Gal.	3	24
Will God *b* with	I Thes.	4	14
Might *b* us to God	I Pet.	3	18
They shall *b* the	Rev.	21	26

broken, *destroyed into pieces*

Of a *b* heart	Ps.	34	18
A *b* and a contrite	Ps.	51	17
Reproach has *b* my	Ps.	69	20
Like a *b* tooth	Prov.	25	19
B cisterns, that can	Jer.	2	13
Had *b* the sabbath	John	5	18
Scripture cannot be *b*	John	10	35
Of him shall not be *b*	John	19	36
On *b* pieces of	Acts	27	44
Which is *b* for you	I Cor.	11	24
B down the middle	Eph.	2	14

brooks *small streams of water*

Many in Canaan	Deut.	8	7
Protection to a country	Is.	19	6
Abound with fish	Is.	19	8

Found along the banks:

Willows	Lev.	23	40
Grass	I Ki.	18	5
Reeds	Is.	19	7
Stones	Job	22	24

Named in the Bible:

Eschol	Num.	13	23, 24
Arnon	Num.	21	14, 15
Zered	Deut.	2	13
Besor	I Sam.	30	9
Kidron	I Ki.	15	13
Cherith	I Ki.	17	3, 5
Gaash	I Chr.	11	32
Kison	Judg.	5	21

brother

Signifies a relative	Gen.	14	16
Signifies a neighbour	Deut.	23	7
	Judg.	21	6
Common parentage	Gen.	42	6
Of an ally	Amos	1	9
Laws concerning his widow	Deut.	25	5–10
	Mat.	22	24–29
Signifies a companion	II Sam.	1	26
	I Ki.	13	30
Ten brothers hanged on same gallows	Esth.	9	13, 14
Signifies mankind	Mat.	18	35
Lawsuits between, forbidden	I Cor.	6	6

A fraternal epithet:

Used by Israelites	Deut.	22	1–4
Instituted by Christ	Mat.	12	50
Used by disciples	Acts	9	17
	Acts	21	20
	II Cor.	2	13
Of Christians	Mat.	23	8, 9
	Mat.	5	23, 24
	James	2	15
	James	4	11
	II Thes.	3	15

brotherhood of man

All have one father	Gen.	1	27, 28
	Prov.	22	2
	Mal.	2	10
Between Judah and Israel	Zech.	11	14
All are one blood	Acts	17	26
Love between all men	I Pet.	2	17
Mutual aid enjoined	Mat.	25	34–40
	Heb.	13	3

brotherly kindness

A sign of affection	Rom.	12	10
A Christian virtue	Eph.	4	32
Commanded by Peter	II Pet.	1	5–7

brotherly love

A commandment of Jesus	John	13	24
Commanded by Paul	Rom.	13	8–10
	Heb.	13	1
Lack of, a sin	I John	3	10
Defined	I John	4	11–21

bruise: *damage*

Head of Satan	Gen.	3	15
Of Christ	Is.	53	10
Power of iron	Dan.	2	40
Unacceptable in sacrifices	Lev.	22	24
Of Israel	Is.	1	6
Satan's defeat	Rom.	16	20
Of a demoniac	Luke	9	39

bruised reed *weak*

Pharaoh called a	II Ki.	18	21
Symbolic of weakness	Is.	42	3
	Mat.	12	20

bucket *a vessel for drawing water*

Used figuratively	Num.	24	7
	Is.	40	15

buckler *a kind of shield*

To those who trust God	II Sam.	22	31
God is my	Ps.	18	2
	Ps.	91	4
	Prov.	2	7
Of a soldier	I Chr.	5	18

bud *undeveloped shoot or stem*

The rod of Aaron	Num.	17	8
The destruction of Ethiopia foretold	Is.	18	5
Figurative of the blessing of the faithful	Is.	61	11
Destruction is threatened	Hosea	8	7

build

Go to, let us *b* a city	Gen.	11	4
B walls of Jerusalem	Ps.	51	18
Except the Lord *b* the house	Ps.	127	1
A time to *b* up	Eccl.	3	3
B old waste places	Is.	58	12
	Is.	61	4
Wise man *b* on rock	Mat.	7	24
	Luke	6	48
Began to *b*, not able to finish	Luke	14	30
Able to *b* you up	Acts	20	32
B on another man's foundation	Rom.	15	20
If any *b* on this foundation	I Cor.	3	12
In whom ye are *b* together	Eph.	2	22
Every house is *b* by some man	Heb.	3	4

builder

Stone which *b* refused	Ps.	118	22
	Mat.	21	42
	Mark	12	10
	Luke	20	17
	Acts	4	11
	I Pet.	2	7
As a wise master-*b*	I Cor.	3	10
Whose *b* and maker is God	Heb.	11	10

building

The Church compared to	I Cor.	3	9
	Eph.	2	21
	Col.	2	7
Ye are God's *b*	I Cor.	3	9
We have a *b* of God	II Cor.	5	1
In whom *b* fitly framed	Eph.	2	21

Bul *growth*

The Hebrew eighth month	I Ki.	6	38

bull *mature male of bovine species*

Given sabbath to rest	Ex.	23	12
Clean meat	Deut.	14	4, 5
Of Bashan	Ps.	22	12, 13
Wild and trapped	Is.	51	20
The spoils of battle	Jer.	52	20
Used in sacrifice	Heb.	9	13, 14
	Heb.	10	4
Of strength	Ps.	68	30

bullock *a young bull*

For use in sacrifice	Ex.	29	3
	Ezra	7	17
Brought to door of tabernacle	Lev.	4	4
God refuses to accept	Ps.	50	9
Used for plowing	I Sam.	14	14
Figurative use describing the peaceable kingdom	Is.	65	25

bulrush, flag *a marsh reed*

Used as fodder	Gen.	41	2–4
Moses found in	Ex.	2	3,5
Called flags	Ex.	2	5
Used to build ships	Is.	18	2
As a measuring device	Ezek.	40	3–8

bulwark(s) *ramparts*

As a fortification	Deut.	20	20
In war	Eccl.	9	14
A turret used for engines of war	II Chr.	26	15
An ornament of the church	Ps.	48	13
Figurative of salvation	Is.	26	1

burden *load, responsibility*

A heavy load	Ex.	23	5
Moses complains of his	Num.	11	11–15
Sins as	Job	7	20
	Ps.	38	4

burden—*continued*

Lifted by the Lord	Ps.	55	22
	Mat.	8	17
God's severe judgment	Is.	15	1–9
	Is.	17	1–14
	Is.	19	1–25
Meaning "a prophecy"	Nah.	1	1
	Hab.	1	1
Amos means "burden"	Amos	1	1
Of the Lord is light	Mat.	11	30
The bearing of another's	Gal.	6	2

burdensome *onerous*

Jerusalem to her adversaries	Zech.	12	3
Paul keeps from being	II Cor.	11	9
The recompense	I Thes.	1	5–7

burglarizing *rifling by forced entry*

Penalty for	Ex.	22	2–4

burial *interment*

Non-burial a judgment for disobedience	Deut.	28	25, 26
	Ps.	79	2
	Eccl.	6	3
Of Saul by men of Jabesh-gilead	II Sam.	2	4–6
Places of:			
For criminals, marked by heaps	Josh.	7	26
Frequently prepared and pointed out during life	Gen.	50	5
	II Chr.	16	14
	Mat.	27	60
Held in high veneration	Neh.	2	3, 5
Members of a family interred in the same	Gen.	49	31
	II Sam.	2	32
Desecrated by idolatry	Is.	65	3–4
Pillars erected on	Gen.	35	20
Provided for aliens and strangers	Mat.	27	7
Provided for the common people	Jer.	26	23
Sometimes had inscriptions	II Ki.	23	17
Sometimes not apparent	Luke	11	44
Tombs erected over	Mat.	23	27–29
Visited by sorrowing friends	John	11	31
Were ceremonially unclean	Num.	19	16, 18
Places used for:			
Caves cut out	Mat.	27	60
Gardens	II Ki.	22	16
Natural caves	Gen.	23	19
Top of hill	Josh.	24	33
Under trees	Gen.	35	8
Places of:			
In cave	Gen.	23	11
On hills	II Ki.	23	6
In valleys	Jer.	7	32
In houses	I Sam.	25	1
Sealed with stones	Mat.	27	60
Preparation for:			
Embalming	Gen.	50	26
Wrapping in linen	Mat.	27	59
Anointing	John	19	38–40
Washing	Acts	9	37
Mourning	John	11	19

burial grounds, cemetery *places for interment*

Of Sarah	Gen.	23	19
Of Abraham	Gen.	25	9
Of Deborah	Gen.	35	8
Of Rachel	Gen.	35	19
Of Isaac	Gen.	35	29
Of Jacob	Gen.	50	13
Of Miriam	Num.	20	1
Of Moses	Deut.	34	6
Of Abner	II Sam.	3	32
Of David	I Ki.	2	10
Of Solomon	I Ki.	11	43
Potter's field	Mat.	27	3–10
Of Christ	Luke	23	53
Of Stephen	Acts	8	2
Of Lazarus	John	11	17, 18
Kings of Judah	I Ki.	14	31
	I Ki.	15	24
	II Ki.	21	18
	II Ki.	21	23–27
	II Chr.	35	23, 24

burial of Christ *see* Jesus Christ

burial sepulchres *tombs*

Strong family feeling concerning	Gen.	49	29–33
Only kings and prophets within the city	I Sam.	25	1
	I Ki.	2	10
Sweet-smelling	II Chr.	16	14
Given by God	Ezek.	39	11–16

burn

Let not thine anger *b*	Gen.	44	18
I would *b* them together	Is.	27	4
While musing the fire *b*	Ps.	39	3
Shall thy wrath *b* like fire?	Ps.	89	46
B lips and wicked heart	Prov.	26	23
Wickedness *b* as the fire	Is.	9	18
Dwell with everlasting *b*	Is.	33	14
Day that shall *b* as oven	Mal.	4	1
Bind tares to *b* them	Mat.	13	30
Chaff he will *b*	Luke	3	17
Loins girded and lights *b*	Luke	12	35
Did not our heart *b*	Luke	24	32
He was a *b* and shining light	John	5	35
Give body to be *b*	I Cor.	13	3
Whose end is to be *b*	Heb.	6	8
Not to come to mount that *b*	Heb.	12	18
Cast into a lake *b*	Rev.	19	20

burning bush *see* bush

burnt offering *see* offerings

burst

Presses shall *b* out	Prov.	3	10
Not be found in the *b*	Is.	30	14
Will *b* thy bonds	Jer.	30	8
	Nah.	1	13
Doth *b* the bottles	Mark	2	22
	Luke	5	37
B asunder in the midst	Acts	1	18

bush, burning bush *thorny acacia of the Arabian peninsula*

The Lord speaks to Moses	Ex.	3	1–4
	Mark	12	26
	Luke	20	37
	Acts	7	35

bushel *a dry measure*

Neither light a candle and hide it under a	Mat.	5	15, 16
	Mark	4	21
	Luke	11	33

business *employment, means of livelihood*

Joseph is well-favoured in	Gen.	39	11
Of spying	Josh.	2	14, 20
	Judg.	18	2
Secret	I Sam.	21	1, 2
Of the Levites	Neh.	13	30
Of sailing	Ps.	107	23–30
Christ among the doctors	Luke	2	46–49
Abandoned by Levi	Luke	5	27, 28
Instructions for:			
Diligence in	Gen.	24	32, 33
	Prov.	22	29
Excessive interest	Ex.	22	25–27
Honesty in	Lev.	19	35, 36
Haste sometimes required	I Sam.	21	8
Guard against neglect	I Ki.	20	39, 40
Be industrious, not slothful	Prov.	6	1–11
	Rom.	12	11
Value of hard work	Eccl.	5	12
Righteousness commended	Jer.	22	13
Should be free from corruption	Ezek.	22	12
Selfishness to be avoided	Luke	12	16–21
Compassion in	I Thes.	4	10–18
Faithfulness	Heb.	3	1–6
Success is according to God's will	James	4	13–15

busybodies *officious persons*

Commanded against	Lev.	19	16
Only fools are	Prov.	20	3
	Prov.	26	17
Abstain from being	I Thes.	4	11
Products of sloth	II Thes.	3	11
	I Tim.	5	13
Sinful	I Pet.	4	15

butler *a manservant*

Offends Pharaoh and is imprisoned	Gen.	40	1–3
Also called cupbearer	Neh.	1	11

butter *solidified or churned milk fat*

As food	Deut.	32	14
	Judg.	5	25
Indicative of prosperity	Deut.	32	14
Steps washed with	Job	29	6
Words smoother than	Ps.	55	21
Churning of milk brings	Prov.	30	33
Given to visitors	Gen.	18	8
	II Sam.	17	29
And honey, the food of the Messiah	Is.	7	14, 15, 22

buy

B any soul with money	Lev.	22	11

B meat for money	Deut.	2	6
B the truth	Prov.	23	23
B and eat, *b* wine and milk	Is.	55	1
B victuals	Mat.	14	15
	Mark	6	36
Go to them that sell, and *b*	Mat.	25	9
Disciples were gone to *b* meat	John	4	8
Whence shall we *b* bread	John	6	5
B things we have need of	John	13	29
B as though they possessed not	I Cor.	7	30
B and sell, and get gain	James	4	13
B of me gold tried	Rev.	3	18
No man might *b* or sell	Rev.	13	17
No man *b* their merchandise	Rev.	18	11

Buzi *contempt*

Father of Ezekiel	Ezek.	1	3

by-word: *a derogatory saying*

Judgment on Israel	Deut.	28	37
	I Ki.	9	7
Suffering of Job	Job	17	6
A song	Job	30	9

C

cab

A unit of dry measure	II Ki.	6	25

Caesar *the title of Roman emperors*

Augustus	Luke	2	1
Paul appeals to	Acts	25	10–12
Tiberius	Luke	3	1
Tribute to	Mat.	22	17–21
	Mark	12	14–17
Claudius	Acts	11	28
Expels Jews from Rome	Acts	18	2
Nero	Acts	25	11, 12
Paul's appeal to	Acts	26	32
Saints of his household	Phil.	4	22
Paul before	II Tim.	4	16–18

Caesarea *a seaport named for Augustus Caesar*

Philip visits	Acts	8	40
Refuge for Paul	Acts	9	30
Home of Cornelius	Acts	10	1, 24
Peter makes his defense	Acts	11	11
The capital of Herod	Acts	12	19
Paul lands at	Acts	18	22
Home of Philip	Acts	21	8
Disciples from	Acts	21	16
Soldiers go to	Acts	23	23
Felix, governor, resides at	Acts	23	23
Paul imprisoned at	Acts	25	4, 13

Caesarea Philippi *named after Philip the tetrarch*

Visited by Jesus	Mat.	16	13
	Mark	8	27

Caiaphas *depressed*

High priest, son-in-law of Annas	Luke	3	2
	John	18	13
Demands Christ's death	Luke	22	71
	John	11	49–53
Orders apostles not to preach	Acts	4	1–22

Cain *acquired*

The firstborn, son of Adam	Gen.	4	1
A tiller of the soil	Gen.	4	2
He slays Abel	Gen.	4	3–8
He is exiled	Gen.	4	9–16
He builds a city	Gen.	4	17
An example of evil	Heb.	11	4
	I John	3	12
Apostate	Jude		11
A city of Judah	Josh.	15	57

Cainan, Kenan *fixed*

Son of Enos	Gen.	5	9–14
Father of Mahalaleel	Gen.	5	12
	I Chr.	1	2
Ancestor of Christ	Luke	3	36

cake

A *c* tumbled into host	Judg.	7	13
To every man a *c*	II Sam.	6	19
I have not a *c*	I Ki.	17	12
A *c* baked on coals	I Ki.	19	6
Ephraim is a *c* not turned	Hosea	7	8

calamities *misfortunes, catastrophes*

God's judgment for ingratitude	Deut.	32	35
	Jer.	46	21
Befall Benjamin	Judg.	20	30–40
Befall Israel	I Sam.	4	15–22
David's day of	II Sam.	22	19
	Ps.	18	18
Job faces many	Job	1	13–22
	Job	6	2
God's protection against	Ps.	57	1
A time for prayer	Ps.	141	5
Of the wicked, scorned	Prov.	1	26
Sudden, for the sinner	Prov.	6	15
	Prov.	24	22
Punishment to them who find joy in	Prov.	17	5
The value of friends in	Prov.	27	10
Should bring us back to God	Amos	4	1–13
End times	Mat.	24	29–34

calamus *a plant*

Used in anointing oil	Ex.	30	23
Sweet-smelling	S. of S.	4	14
An article of trade	Ezek.	27	19

caldron, cauldron *a kettle or boiler*

Used as container for sacrifice	I Sam.	2	14
	Jer.	52	18, 19
Used figuratively	Job	41	20
	Ezek.	11	3, 7
As an instrument of judgment	Mic.	3	3

Caleb *impetuous, dog*

Son of Jephunneh	Num.	13	6
Investigates Canaan	Num.	13	2, 6
Reports favourably of Canaan	Num.	13	30
	Num.	14	6–9
God rewards	Num.	14	24–30
	Num.	14	38
Assists in dividing Canaan	Num.	34	19
Recipient of a part of Canaan	Num.	34	17–19
Asks for and receives Hebron	Josh.	14	6–14
	Josh.	15	13–19
He rewards Othniel	Judg.	1	12–15
Of the posterity of Jabez	I Chr.	4	15
Wholly followed the Lord	Deut.	1	36
	Josh.	14	8, 9, 14
An ancestor of Nabal	I Sam.	25	3
The son of Hezron	I Chr.	2	18
Son of Hur	I Chr.	2	50

calf *young cow*

As food	Gen.	18	7, 8
As a sin offering	Lev.	9	2
Used figuratively	Ps.	29	6
	Is.	11	6
Kill the fatted calf	Luke	15	11–31
Of Samaria	Hosea	8	5, 6
Second beast before God's throne	Rev.	4	7

calf, golden *golden image of young cow*

Aaron fashions golden idol	Ex.	32	3, 4
	Acts	7	41
Represented visibly the God of Israel	Ex.	32	4, 5
Moses destroys the idol	Ex.	32	19, 20
	Deut.	9	12, 21
Jeroboam sets up idols	I Ki.	12	28, 29
	Hosea	8	5, 6
Worshipped by Jehu	II Ki.	10	29
Prophecies against	I Ki.	13	1–5
Altars destroyed	II Ki.	23	4, 15–20

call *distinct order, appeal*
Of helpers of God:

Noah	Gen.	6	13–22
Abraham	Gen.	12	1–3
Jacob	Gen.	28	12–15
Moses	Ex.	3	1–22
Gideon	Judg.	6	11–23
Samuel	I Sam.	3	4–21
Elijah	I Ki.	17	2–14
Elisha	I Ki.	19	16, 19
Isaiah	Is.	6	
Jeremiah	Jer.	1	
Ezekiel	Ezek.	2	3
Hosea	Hosea	1	1–11
Amos	Amos	7	14, 15
Jonah	Jonah	3	1–3
Peter, Andrew, James and John	Mat.	4	18–22
	Mark	1	16–20
Paul	Acts	9	1–9
	Rom.	1	1
	Gal.	1	1

call—*continued*			
To a definite work	Ex.	31	1–11
To praise the Lord	Ps.	33	1–22
By another name	Is.	62	2, 12
Basis for Christian hope	Rom.	8	28–30

calling, the Christian

Reward of	Rom.	11	29
	Eph.	1	18
Few are chosen for	I Cor.	1	26
The worthiness of	Eph.	4	1
The constancy of	Phil.	3	14
	II Thes.	1	11
	II Pet.	1	10
Not shameful	II Tim.	1	9
A chosen generation	I Pet.	2	9
Blessed are they who receive	Rev.	19	9
High	Phil.	3	14
Holy	II Tim.	1	9
Heavenly	Heb.	3	1
Hope of	Eph.	4	4
	Eph.	1	18

call of God *divine calling*

To repentance and salvation	Ps.	50	1–23
	Prov.	1	24–33
	Jer.	35	13–17
Not to admire worldly property	Ps.	49	1–20
Folly of rejecting	Prov.	1	24–30
	Mat.	22	2–14
Prophets receive	Is.	6	1–13
	Jer.	7	1–34
	Hosea	6	1–11

callousness *coarseness, harshness*

Of Gallio	Acts	18	17
Of Pharaoh	Ex.	7	13
	Ex.	8	15
Of wicked	I Tim.	4	2

calumny *see* slander

Calvary *skull*

The place of the crucifixion of Christ	Luke	23	33
The Hebrew term is Golgotha	John	19	17

camel *a large, ruminant mammal*

Gifts to Abraham	Gen.	12	16
As transportation	Gen.	24	64
The wealth of Jacob	Gen.	30	43
A beast of burden	Gen.	37	25
	I Ki.	10	2
God's threat to Pharaoh	Ex.	9	3
As unclean meat	Lev.	11	4
	Deut.	14	7
Swift	I Sam.	30	17
Ornamented	Judg.	8	21, 26
Used in war	I Sam.	30	17
Spoils of battle	I Chr.	5	21
The wealth of Job	Job	1	3
Hair made into clothing	Mat.	3	4
Description of Pharisees	Mat.	23	24
Very large	Mat.	19	24

camel's hair *cloth made from mixture of hair and wool*

The raiment of John the Baptist	Mat.	3	4

camp *a collection of tents or shelters*

Protection by an angel of God	Ex.	14	19, 20
Covered by quail	Ex.	16	13
The unclean not allowed in	Lev.	13	46
	Num.	5	2
Tabernacle in the midst of it	Num.	2	17
Of the Israelites in the wilderness	Num.	1	52
	Num.	33	7–50
The order of the tribes in	Num.	2	1–34
The eternal presence of God in	Deut.	23	14
Activities outside the camp	Lev.	24	23
	Heb.	13	13
The Lord smites the Assyrians'	II Ki.	19	35

Cana *reeds*

A town of Galilee where Jesus performs His first miracle	John	2	1
Nobleman visits Christ at	John	4	46, 47
Nathanael's birthplace	John	21	2

Canaan *low land*

Patriarchs dwell in	Gen.	12	6
	Gen.	28	1–22
	Gen.	36	1–43
Promised to Abraham	Gen.	12	7
	Gen.	13	14–18
	Gen.	17	8
Promised to Isaac	Gen.	26	2, 3

Promised to Jacob	Gen.	28	13
Inhabitants of	Ex.	15	15
Land of	Ex.	23	31
	Josh.	1	4
	Zeph.	2	5
Israelites not to walk in their ways	Lev.	18	3
	Lev.	20	23
The spies visit, and their report	Num.	13	1–33
Murmurers forbidden to enter	Num.	14	22, 23
Moses and Aaron not allowed to enter	Num.	20	12
	Deut.	3	27
	Deut.	32	48–52
Allotted to the children of Israel	Num.	26	52–56
	Josh.	14	1–15
Partial occupation	Judg.	1	21–36
Moses views from Pisgah	Num.	27	12
	Deut.	3	27
	Deut.	34	1
Conquered by Joshua	Josh.	9	10

Names for:

Land of Hebrews	Gen.	40	15
Palestina	Ex.	15	14
Land of Israel	I Sam.	13	19
Immanuel's land	Is.	8	8
Beulah	Is.	62	4
Pleasant land	Dan.	8	9
The Lord's land	Hosea	9	3
Holy land	Zech.	2	12
Land of Jews	Acts	10	39
Land of promise	Heb.	11	9
A son of Ham, cursed on account of his father's mockery of Noah	Gen.	9	25

Canaanites

A name given to the pre-Israelitish inhabitants of Palestine	Gen.	15	19–21
Members of a Jewish political party	Mat.	10	4
	Acts	1	13

Canaanite, -s

C was then in land	Gen.	12	6
	Gen.	13	7
The Amorites, C, Girgashites	Gen.	15	21
	Ex.	3	8, 17
	Ex.	23	23
	Deut.	7	1
	Deut.	12	8
	Judg.	3	5
	Neh.	9	8
Shalt not take a wife of C	Gen.	24	3
Make me to stink amongst C	Gen.	34	30
Daughter of a certain C	Gen.	38	2
Drive out the C	Ex.	23	28
	Ex.	33	2
Lord delivered up the C	Num.	21	3
	Neh.	9	24
C would dwell in land	Josh.	17	12
	Judg.	1	27
Shalt drive out the C	Josh.	17	18
Up against the C first	Judg.	1	1
To fight against the C	Judg.	9	10
Pharaoh had slain the C	I Ki.	9	16
To abominations of C	Ezra	9	1
Shall possess that of C	Obad.	20	
No more C in house of	Zech.	14	21
Simon the C	Mat.	10	4
	Mark	3	18

Candace *prince of servants*

Queen of Ethiopia	Acts	8	27

candle

Figurative	Job	18	6
	Job	21	17
	Ps.	18	28
	Prov.	20	27
Not to be hidden	Mat.	5	15
	Luke	8	16
Used to give light	Luke	15	8
Not needed in heaven	Rev.	22	5
Used in searching	Zeph.	1	12

candlestick

In the tabernacle (menorah)	Ex.	25	31
	Ex.	37	17
	Lev.	24	4
	Num.	8	2–4
Description of golden	Ex.	25	31–40
Placed in holy place	Heb.	9	2
Burns constantly	Ex.	27	20, 21

Charge of the Levites	Num.	3	31
In visions	Zech.	4	2
	Rev.	1	12
Woman's preparation for Elisha	II Ki.	4	10
Symbol of the two witnesses	Rev.	11	4

cankerworm
Judgment on crops	Joel	1	4
	Joel	2	25
Renowned for powers of multiplication and appetite	Nah.	3	15, 16

cannibalism *eating human flesh*
Curse for disobedience	Lev.	26	29
	Deut.	28	53
By woman of Samaria	II Ki.	6	28, 29

Capernaum *village of comfort*
Headquarters of Christ in His Galilean ministry	Mat.	4	13
	John	2	12
Denounced for unbelief	Mat.	11	23
	Luke	10	15
Home of Simon Peter	Mark	1	21, 29

Works of Jesus performed here:
Heals the centurion's palsied servant	Mat.	8	5–13
Provides the half-shekel for the temple tribute	Mat.	17	24
Teaches in the synagogue	Mark	1	21
	Luke	4	31
	John	6	59
Performs many miracles	Mark	1	23–45
	Mark	2	1–12
	Luke	4	33–41
Teaches humility to disciples	Mark	9	33–37
Heals a nobleman's son by word from Cana	John	4	46
Bread of life sermon	John	6	24–71

capital punishment *death penalty for crime*
For murder	Gen.	9	6
	Ex.	21	12–15
	Mat.	26	52
For an ox	Ex.	21	28
Confirmed by Paul	Rom.	13	1–7

Reasons:
Adultery	Lev.	20	10
Incest	Lev.	20	11
Bestiality	Ex.	22	19
Sodomy	Lev.	18	22
Rape	Deut.	22	25
Perjury	Zech.	5	4
Kidnapping	Ex.	21	16
Witchcraft	Ex.	22	18
Offering human sacrifice	Lev.	20	2–5
Striking or cursing father	Ex.	21	15, 17
Disobedience to parents	Deut.	21	18–21
Blasphemy	Lev.	24	11–14
Breaking Sabbath	Ex.	35	2
False prophet	Deut.	13	1–10
Idolatry	Ex.	22	20
Treason	I Ki.	2	25

Cappadocia *large district in Asia Minor*
Represented on day of Pentecost	Acts	2	9
Visited by Peter	I Pet.	1	1

captain *military commander*
Of the guard	Gen.	37	36
	Acts	28	16
Of heads of tribes	Num.	2	3, 5
Of the temple	Luke	22	4, 52
Roman officer in charge of garrison of Jerusalem	John	18	12
	Acts	22	28
Jesus, of salvation	Heb.	2	10
Of angel of the Lord	Josh.	5	14
Of God	II Chr.	13	12
Of Jephthah	Judg.	11	6, 11
Of David	I Sam.	22	2
Of Naaman	II Ki.	5	1
Frequently conspire against the king	I Ki.	16	16
	II Ki.	15	25

captivity *state of bondage*
Of Israelites foretold	Lev.	26	33
	Deut.	28	36
Prophecy fulfilled	II Ki.	17	20
	I Chr.	5	26
Of Judah foretold	Is.	39	6
	Jer.	13	19
	Jer.	20	4
	Jer.	32	28

Prophecy fulfilled	II Ki.	25	1–30
	II Chr.	36	1–23
	Ps.	137	1–9
	Jer.	39	1–18
	Dan.	1	1–21
Of ten tribes foretold	Amos	6	7
	Amos	7	11
Return of Israelites from	Ezra	1	1–11
	Ezra	2	1–70
	Neh.	2–7	
	Ps.	126	1–6

Three great captivities:
By Assyria	I Chr.	5	26
Again by Assyria	II Ki.	17	3, 6
By Babylon	II Ki.	25	1–30

caravan *group traveling together*
Of Ishmeelites, buys Joseph	Gen.	37	25
Of Jacob and his sons to Egypt	Gen.	46	5, 6
Jacob's return from Egypt	Gen.	50	7–15
Of the queen of Sheba to Solomon	I Ki.	10	1, 2
Of the Jews to Jerusalem	Ezra	8	30

carbuncle *a precious stone*
Used in the breastplate of judgment	Ex.	28	17
Gates made of	Is.	54	12
Jewel of Tyre	Ezek.	28	13

carcass, carcase *a dead body*
Of animal	Judg.	14	8
Of a man	Josh.	8	29
Considered untouchable	Lev.	5	2
	Deut.	14	8
Curse for disobedience	Deut.	28	26
Of Jezebel to be defiled	II Ki.	9	36, 37
Of the transgressor	Is.	66	24
Signs of Christ's coming	Mat.	24	28
Of non-believers	Heb.	3	17

Carchemish, Charchemish *stronghold of Chemiosh*
A city on the Euphrates	II Chr.	35	20
King of Egypt defeated here	Jer.	46	2
Conquered by the Assyrians	Is.	10	9

care, divine *heavenly solicitude*
Of animals	Deut.	25	4
	I Cor.	9	9
Of birds	Mat.	6	26
	Luke	12	24
Of His children	Mat.	6	25–31
	Luke	12	7, 24
	I Pet.	5	7
Of vegetation	Mat.	6	28, 30
The parable of the sower	Mat.	13	18–23
For the church	John	10	13
	John	21	15–16
	I Pet.	5	
God's care	Ps.	104	

care, worldly *earthly anxiety*
Of David for his people	II Sam.	18	2, 3
Christ preaches freedom from	Mat.	6	25
	Luke	12	22
	John	6	27
Parable of the good Samaritan	Luke	10	30–36
Martha's complaint	Luke	10	40–42
Christ's, for His mother	John	19	26, 27
Of the married man	I Cor.	7	23
Of apostles for the churches	II Cor.	7	12
	II Cor.	8	16
	II Cor.	11	28
Of Martha	Luke	10	40, 41
Should be few	I Tim.	6	8
	II Tim.	2	4
Avoid covetousness	Heb.	13	5

Remedy:
Trust God	Ps.	37	5
	Jer.	17	7
Commit it to the Lord	Prov.	16	3
Prayer	Phil.	4	6
Casting cares on God	I Pet.	5	7

Careah *see Kareah*

careless *indifferent*
People of Dan	Judg.	18	7
Connected with pleasures	Is.	47	8
Of drunkenness	Is.	32	9, 10
Sinful Israel	Amos	6	1
World before Christ's return	Mat.	24	37–39

Carmel *gardenland; fruitful place*
One of the cities of Judah, smitten by Joshua	Josh.	12	22
	Josh.	15	55

Carmel—*continued*

Saul erects a memorial at	I Sam.	15	12
Home of Nabal	I Sam.	25	2–7
King Uzziah's vineyards at	II Chr.	26	10
A fertile picturesque mountain range in Palestine	S. of S.	7	5
	Is.	33	9
	Amos	1	2
Elijah builds an altar upon and confounds the worshippers of Baal	I Ki.	18	17–46
Elisha's abode in	II Ki.	2	25
	II Ki.	4	25
Known for its forests	Is.	37	42
	II Ki.	19	23
Well watered	Amos	1	2
Caves of	Amos	9	3
	Mic.	7	14

carnal *opposed to spiritual*

Israelites murmur because of want	Ex.	16	3
God's law is spiritual, but not man's	Rom.	7	14
Warnings against	Rom.	8	5, 6
Enemy of God	Rom.	8	7
Paul accuses the Corinthians	I Cor.	3	1, 3, 4
The reaping of, things	I Cor.	9	11
God's weapons are spiritual	II Cor.	10	4
Of money	Rom.	15	27
Carnal commandment	Heb.	7	16
Constant in belief	Col.	2	18
Ordinances proper for this time	Heb.	9	10

carpenter(s) *worker and builder in wood*

Builds a house for David	II Sam.	5	11
Makes a graven image	Is.	44	13–15
Captives of Nebuchadnezzar	Jer.	24	1
Freed from Nebuchadnezzar	Jer.	29	2
Four, shown to Zechariah by God	Zech.	1	20
Jesus, the son of	Mat.	13	55
Jesus called a	Mark	6	3

Carpus *fruit*

Keeps Paul's cloak at Troas	II Tim.	4	13

carriage *that which is carried, goods*

Put in front by the Danites	Judg.	18	21
Sometimes left behind	I Sam.	17	22
	Is.	10	28
Heavy-laden	Is.	46	1
David left his *c* in the hands of the keeper of the *c*	I Sam.	17	22
Cattle and *c* before them.	Judg.	18	21
Your *c* were heavy laden.	Is.	46	1
We took up our *c*	Acts	21	15

carry

C us not up hence	Ex.	33	15
C lambs in his bosom	Is.	40	11
Our sorrows	Is.	53	4
C them all days of old	Is.	63	9
Began to *c* in beds	Mark	6	55
C neither purse nor scrip	Luke	10	4
Not lawful to *c* thy bed	John	5	10
C thee whither wouldst not	John	21	18
Can *c* nothing out of world	I Tim.	6	7

cart: *a small wheeled vehicle*

Pulled by kine	I Sam.	6	7
Made by wood	I Sam.	6	14
David uses to transport the ark	II Sam.	6	3
Used by threshing	Is.	28	27
Used for pulling heavy loads	Amos	2	13
Used to transport the tabernacle	Num.	7	3

carving *cutting and decorating wood or stone*

Knowledge of, given to Bezaleel	Ex.	31	1–7
	Ex.	35	30–33
In cedar of Solomon's temple	I Ki.	6	18
Need for a man skilled in	II Chr.	2	7
Works decking the bed	Prov.	7	16

cassia *a spice-bearing tree or its oil*

Oil used for making ointment	Ex.	30	24, 25
Fragrance used to scent clothing	Ps.	45	8
Traded in the market at Tyre	Ezek.	27	19

cast

I was *c* on thee from womb	Ps.	22	10
The lot is *c* into lap	Prov.	16	33
Covering *c* over all people	Is.	25	7
Whole body *c* into hell.	Mat.	5	29
	Mark	9	45
Say to mountain, be *c* into sea	Mat.	21	21
One *c* out devils	Mark	9	38
	Luke	9	49

C gifts into treasury	Luke	21	1
C down imaginations	II Cor.	10	5
C all care upon him	I Pet.	5	7
Love *c* out fear	I John	4	18

castaway *outcast*

The unprofitable servant becomes a	Mat.	25	30
Avoid being a	I Cor.	9	27

caste *a rigid class distinction*

Distinction between Jews and Samaritans	John	4	9
Distinction abolished by God	Acts	10	28, 34, 35
Abolished	Acts	10	28–35
	Gal.	3	28
Religious	Mark	9	38
Among Prophets	Amos	7	14
Among tribes	I Sam.	9	21

castle(s) *a fortified dwelling*

David takes and lives in the, of Zion	I Chr.	11	5, 7
Supervised by Jehonathan	I Chr.	27	25
Built in Judah by Jehoshaphat	II Chr.	17	12
Paul imprisoned in	Acts	21	34, 37
A tower	Gen.	25	16
Bars of	Prov.	18	19
A man's house is his castle	Deut.	24	10, 11

castration *being gelded or emasculated*

Cannot enter the congregation of the Lord	Deut.	23	1
Demonstrating loyalty	Mat.	19	12
Eunuch	Is.	56	4
Of Daniel	Dan.	1	8

catch

To *c* the poor	Ps.	10	9
Devil *c* away that which was sown	Mat.	13	19
To *c* him in his words	Mark	12	13
C men	Luke	5	10
Wolf *c* and scattereth sheep	John	10	12

caterpillar

Solomon asks God to destroy	I Ki.	8	37
As judgment	Joel	2	25
	Jer.	51	27
Tremendous eaters	Ps.	78	46

cattle *domestic animals collectively*

On the ark	Gen.	8	1
Measure of riches	Gen.	13	2
Jacob makes Laban's herd increase	Gen.	30	39–43
The trade of shepherds is to feed	Gen.	46	32
Of the Israelites, spared by God	Ex.	9	3, 4
Taken for prey or spoils	Deut.	2	35
	Deut.	3	7
	Josh.	8	2
Gilead known for	Num.	32	1
Bashan known for	Ps.	22	12
Of Job, listed as part of his wealth	Job	1	3
Of God, on a thousand hills	Ps.	50	10
Used figuratively	Ezek.	34	17, 20, 22
Jesus speaks of saving	Mat.	12	11
	Luke	14	5
Drink from Jacob's well	John	4	12

Caught

Ram *c* by horns	Gen.	22	13
They *c* the servant	Mark	12	3
That night they *c* nothing	John	21	3
The Spirit *c* away Philip	Acts	8	39
A man *c* up to third heaven.	II Cor.	12	2
Be *c* up together with them	I Thes.	4	17

caul *a kind of cap or covering*

Removed during sacrificial ceremony	Lev.	3	4
Taken away by the Lord	Is.	3	18
Rent by the Lord	Hosea	13	8

cave *hollow place in earth, as on a hill*

Place of burial	Gen.	19	30
	Gen.	23	19
	Gen.	49	29, 30
	John	11	38
People hide themselves in	Josh.	10	16
	I Sam.	13	6
David escapes to a, at Adullam	I Sam.	22	1
David spares Saul in	I Sam.	24	3, 10
At Engedi	I Sam.	24	1, 3
Place of thieves	Mat.	21	13
Prophets hidden by Obadiah in	I Ki.	18	4
Elijah lodges in	I Ki.	19	9
Wicked shall hide from the Lord in	Is.	2	19, 21

cedar *to be firm*

Used in purifications	Lev.	14	4–6
	Num.	19	6
Chief source in Lebanon	Judg.	9	15
	Is.	2	13

Used in David's palace	II Sam.	5	11
	I Chr.	17	1
Furnished by Hiram for Solomon's temple	I Ki.	5	6–10
	I Ki.	9	11
For the second temple	Ezra	3	7
For building masts of ships	Ezek.	27	5
Merchants carry goods in chests of	Ezek.	27	23, 24
Used in making Idols	Is.	44	14
Figuratively of height	Amos	2	9

Cedron *see* Kidron

celebrate *rest*
The sabbath by the Jews	Lev.	23	32
From evening to evening	Lev.	23	32
Feast of tabernacles	Lev.	23	41

celestial *of heaven, divine*
Bodies	I Cor.	15	40

celibacy *the state of being unmarried*
Under certain circumstances it is recommended	Mat.	19	9–12
	I Cor.	7	1, 26–33
	Rev.	14	1, 4
Of Paul	I Cor.	9	5
Demanded by apostates	I Tim.	4	1–3

cellar
Of wine	I Chr.	27	27
Of oil	I Chr.	27	28

cemetery *see* burial grounds

Cenchrea *millet*
A harbor in city of Corinth	Acts	18	18
A church established here	Rom.	16	1

censer *portable dish used for offering incense*
Of Korah	Num.	16	6, 7
Used for offering incense	Lev.	16	12
	Num.	16	35–39
Made of gold	I Ki.	7	50
	Heb.	9	4
	Rev.	8	3
Made of Brass	Num.	16	39
Used in idolatrous rites	Ezek.	8	10–12

censoriousness *faultfinding, criticism*
Jesus reproves	Mat.	7	1–5
Unbrotherly	James	4	11
Of Michal	II Sam.	6	20, 23
Of Diotrephes	III John		9

census *any official count of the population*
A poll tax to be levied at each	Ex.	30	12
	Ex.	38	26
Of Israel in the desert	Num.	26	1–64
By David	II Sam.	24	1–9
Satan provokes a	I Chr.	21	1–7
Solomon completes	II Chr.	2	17
Of returned exiles	Ezra	2	1–70
Caesar's	Luke	2	1

centurion *commander of a hundred men*
Servant of, healed	Mat.	8	5–8
	Luke	7	2, 10
At crucifixion, acknowledges Christ	Mat.	27	54
	Mark	15	39
	Luke	23	47
Cornelius	Acts	10	1
Intercedes on Paul's behalf	Acts	22	25–30
In charge of Paul	Acts	27	43

Cephas *see* Peter

ceremonialism *vain following of ritual*
Jesus condemns the following of tradition	Mark	7	6–9
Discussion of, by Paul and Barnabas	Acts	15	1–29
Old Testament condemns	Is.	1	11–15
	Hosea	6	6
False religion	Col.	2	14–23

ceremonies *formal acts or rites*
Passover, observed by Israelites	Num.	9	3
In the first covenant	Heb.	9	1, 10
Also see feasts and festivals			

chaff *threshed or winnowed husks of grain*
Wicked carried away like	Job	21	18
	Ps.	1	4
	Ps.	35	5
	Is.	29	5
	Hosea	13	3
False prophecies like	Jer.	23	28
Figurative use for worthlessness	Is.	41	15
	Jer.	23	28
Will be burned by Jesus	Mat.	3	12
	Luke	3	17

Blown away by the wind	Ps.	35	5

chain *linked metal, used for necklace or shackles*
Given by Pharaoh to Joseph	Gen.	41	42
Given to Ezekiel by the Lord	Ezek.	16	11
Given to those who can read certain handwriting	Dan.	5	7
Proclaiming Daniel as ruler	Dan.	5	29
Put about the necks of camels	Judg.	8	21, 26
Burst by man with unclean spirit	Mark	5	3
Peter delivered from Herod's	Acts	12	7
Paul bound with, for the hope of Israel	Acts	21	33
	Acts	28	20
	II Tim.	1	16
Binding fallen angels in everlasting darkness	II Pet.	2	4
	Jude		6
A great, used to bind Satan	Rev.	20	1, 2

chalcedony *a kind of grayish or milky quartz*
Garnishes the third foundation of the holy city	Rev.	21	19

Chaldea *a region on the Euphrates River and the Persian Gulf*
Terah and his family leave Ur of	Gen.	11	31
Abraham originally from Ur of	Gen.	15	7
	Neh.	9	7
Later name of Babylon	Is.	13	19
Home of wise men	Dan.	1	4
Men characterized as bitter and nasty	Hab.	1	6
Also see Babylon			

chamber
Little *c* on wall	II Ki.	4	10
As bridegroom coming out of *c*	Ps.	19	5
Beams of *c* in the waters	Ps.	104	3
Enter into thy *c*	Is.	26	20
C of imagery	Ezek.	8	12
In secret *c*	Mat.	24	26
In upper *c*	Acts	9	37
	Acts	20	8

chamberlain *a steward or bedchamber attendant of a ruler*
Nathan-melech, of the house of the Lord	II Ki.	23	11
The seven, that serve Ahasuerus, the king	Esth.	1	10
Two, seek to lay hand on Ahasuerus	Esth.	6	2
Blastus, Herod's, makes friends with Herod's enemies	Acts	12	20
Erastus, at Corinth	Rom.	16	23

chameleon *any lizard that changes colour*
Not to be eaten	Lev.	11	29, 30

chamois *a small goat-like antelope*
A type of antelope, listed as clean meat	Deut.	14	5

champaign *a broad expanse of plain*
A level country	Deut.	11	30

championship *defending or supporting*
David and Goliath	I Sam.	17	4–53
Young men of David's and Abner's armies	II Sam.	2	14–17
Representatives of the Philistines' and David's armies	II Sam.	21	15–22

chance
It was a *c* that happened	I Sam.	6	9
Happened by *c*	II Sam.	1	6
It may *c* of wheat	I Cor.	15	37
(See Deut. 22:6; Eccl. 9:11)			
No second	Luke	16	20–30
	Heb.	9	27

chancellor *a high official*
A state officer	Ezra	4	8, 9, 17

change
Till my *c* come	Job	14	14
Thou *c* his countenance	Job	14	20
Sweareth, and *c* not	Ps.	15	4
As a vesture shalt thou *c* them	Ps.	102	26
I am the Lord, I *c* not	Mal.	3	6
C glory of uncorruptible God	Rom.	1	23
We shall all be *c*	I Cor.	15	51
C from glory to glory	II Cor.	3	18
C our vile body	Phil.	3	21

changers *see* moneychangers

Chanoch *see* Enoch

chapiter *cornice crowning a pillar*
On tabernacle posts	Ex.	38	17, 19
On temple pillars	I Ki.	7	16

character
Tested	Gen.	2	15–17
An assumed	Gen.	42	7, 8
Defamation of, punished	Deut.	22	13–19
Good	Prov.	22	1
	Eccl.	7	1

character—*continued*

Revealed in countenance	Is.	3	9
Decision of	Dan.	1	8
Strength of	Dan.	3	14–18
Disguised	Luke	20	20
Deeds reflect	John	9	33

Of saints:

Blameless	Phil.	2	15
Bold	Prov.	28	1
Contrite	Is.	57	15
Devout	Acts	8	2
Faithful	Rev.	17	14
Godly	Ps.	4	3
Humble	Ps.	34	2
Holy	Col.	3	12
Loving	Col.	1	4
Meek	Is.	29	19
Obedient	Rom.	16	19
Merciful	Mat.	25	31–40
Pure in heart	Mat.	5	8
Stedfast	Acts	2	42
Undefiled	Ps.	119	1
Zealous	Tit.	2	14

Of wicked:

Abominable	Rev.	21	8
Blasphemous	Luke	22	65
Blind	II Cor.	4	4
Boastful	Ps.	10	3
Corrupt	Mat.	7	17
Deceitful	Rom.	3	13
Disobedient	Neh.	9	26
Foolish	Deut.	32	6
Forgetting God	Job	8	13
Hating the light	Job	24	13
Hypocritical	Is.	29	13
Lying	Ps.	58	3
Prayerless	Job	21	15
Selfish	II Tim.	3	2
Unclean	Is.	64	6
Sensual	II Pet.	2	21–22

Charchemish *see* Carchemish

charge

To Moses and Aaron	Ex.	6	13
Of Moses to Joshua	Deut.	31	7
Of David to Solomon	I Ki.	2	1, 3
	I Chr.	22	5, 6
Of Jehoshaphat to the judges	II Chr.	19	4–7
Of Paul to the elders of Ephesus	Acts	20	16, 17, 32
Of Paul to Timothy	I Tim.	5	21
	II Tim.	4	1–22
Of Peter to the elders	I Pet.	5	1–14

charger *a large dish*

Used in offering	Num.	7	13
John Baptist's head carried on	Mat.	14	8, 11

chariot(s)

For war	Ex.	14	7
Made of iron	Josh.	17	18
David introduced to Israel	II Sam.	8	4
Drawn by camels	Mic.	1	13
Pharaoh's troops	Ex.	14	7
Jabin's	Judg.	4	3
Philistine troops	I Sam.	13	5
Solomon has many	I Ki.	10	26
Sent by the king of Syria to take Elisha	II Ki.	6	11, 14
Of fire sent to defend Elisha	II Ki.	6	17
Of God	Ps.	68	17

charity *affection, high regard*

How to manifest	Lev.	19	17
	Lev.	25	35
	Is.	58	7
	John	13	35
Exhortations to	Deut.	10	19
	Mat.	5	44
	Gal.	5	14
	Gal.	6	10
Almsgiving	Prov.	19	17
	Mat.	19	21
	Acts	10	2, 4
Love to our neighbour	Mat.	22	39
	Mark	12	33
	James	2	8
Exemplified by Christ	John	13	34
	John	15	12, 13
	Eph.	5	2, 25
	Rev.	1	5

Commended	I Cor.	8	1
	Gal.	5	6, 22
	Eph.	3	17
	Col.	3	14
The excellence of charity	I Cor.	13	1–13
An active principle	I Thes.	1	3
	Heb.	6	10
All things should be done with	I Cor.	16	14
A bond of union	Col.	2	2
Commanded by God	I John	4	21
The end of the commandment	I Tim.	1	5
Explained	I Cor.	13	4–7
Good and pleasant	Ps.	133	1–2
Greatest sacrifices are nothing without	I Cor.	13	3
Love of God is a motive to	John	13	34
	I John	3	11
Necessary to true happiness	Prov.	15	17
Should be connected with brotherly kindness	Rom.	12	10
	II Pet.	1	7

Exhibited in:

Clothing the naked	Is.	58	7
	Mat.	25	36
Covering the faults of others	I Pet.	4	8
Forbearing	Eph.	4	2
Forgiving injuries	Eph.	4	32
	Col.	3	13
Loving each other	Gal.	5	13
Ministering to the wants to others	Mat.	25	35
	Heb.	6	10
Rebuking	Lev.	19	17
	Mat.	18	15
Relieving strangers	Lev.	25	35
	Mat.	25	35
Supporting the weak	Gal.	6	2
	I Thes.	5	14
Sympathizing	Rom.	12	15
	I Cor.	12	26
Visiting the sick	James	1	27
Also see love			

charmer *magicians*

Illegal in Israel	Deut.	18	11
Connected with idolatry	Is.	19	3
Of the wicked	Ps.	58	5

Charran *see* Haran

chase

Ye shall *c* your enemies	Lev.	26	7
One man of you shall *c* a thousand	Josh.	23	10
Israel returned from *c*	I Sam.	17	53
C away his mother	Prov.	19	26
Shall be *c* as the chaff	Is.	17	13

chastisement *punishment*

Sign of God's love	Deut.	8	5
Is to be endured	Prov.	3	11, 12
By us upon Christ	Is.	53	5
Purging power	John	15	2
Sign of sonship	Heb.	12	6
Of Israel	Is.	1	5–9
To repentance	Hag.	2	17
Use of natural calamities	II Chr.	7	13
Not to be despised	Job	5	17

chastity *abstention from illicit sexual relations*

Joseph resists temptation	Gen.	39	7–20
One of the Ten Commandments	Ex.	20	14
	Deut.	5	21
Practiced by Ruth and Boaz	Ruth	3	6–14
Controlled by the mind	Job	31	1
	Mat.	5	27, 28
Solomon exhorts	Prov.	2	16
	Prov.	5	20
	Prov.	7	5
Paul exhorts Christians to	I Cor.	7	1–9
Christian principle	Acts	15	20
	Eph.	5	3
Part of sanctification	I Thes.	4	3
First fruits of the tribulation	Rev.	14	4

cheating *tricking or deceiving*

Forbidden by the Ten Commandments	Ex.	20	15, 16
	Deut.	5	19, 20
	Mat.	19	18
	Mark	10	19
	Rom.	13	9
The Lord	Mal.	3	8, 9
(*See* dishonesty)			

Chebar *great*

River where visions seen	Ezek.	1	1, 3
Israelites captive here	Ezek.	3	15, 23

cheek

Place frequently smitten:			
Micaiah	II Chr.	18	13
Job	Job	16	10
Christ	Is.	50	6
To turn the other	Luke	6	29
Of beauty	S. of S.	5	13

cheerfulness *gladness, heartiness*

Haman's hanging provokes	Esth.	5	14
To be desired	Prov.	15	13, 15
	Prov.	17	22
Christ exhorts followers to	John	16	33
Paul recommends, under duress	Acts	27	25, 26
Loved by God	II Cor.	9	6, 7
Of a husband to his wife	Deut.	24	5
Of countenance	Prov.	15	13
Of heart	Eccl.	11	9
Food causes	Zech.	9	17

cheese *milk curd pressed into cake*

Brought by David to Saul's soldiers	I Sam.	17	18
Food for David	II Sam.	17	29
Likened to afflictions	Job	10	10

Chemosh *one who subdues*

National deity of the Moabites	Num.	21	29
	I Ki.	11	33
Also deity of the Amorites	Judg.	11	24
Altar built by Solomon	I Ki.	11	7
Sacrifice children	II Ki.	3	27
Altars destroyed	II Ki.	23	13, 14
Moabites punished for worship of	Jer.	48	7, 13, 46

Cherethims, Cherethites *from land of Philistines*

Attacked by Egyptians	I Sam.	30	14
David's servants	II Sam.	8	18
	II Sam.	15	18
Seek Sheba in Jerusalem	II Sam.	20	7, 23
Associated with the Philistines	Ezek.	25	16
Escort Solomon to Gihon	I Ki.	1	38, 44
Commanded by Benaiah	I Chr.	18	17
Destroyed by God	Ezek.	25	16

Cherith *gorge*

Elijah hidden here	I Ki.	17	3, 5

cherub, cherubims *angels*

Guarding tree of life in Eden	Gen.	3	24
Suspended above mercy seat	Ex.	25	18–20, 22
Woven into the veil of the temple	Ex.	26	31
Embroidered on curtains	Ex.	36	8
Adorn the temple	I Ki.	6	23–29, 32, 35
	I Ki.	8	6, 7
Part of Ezekiel's vision	Ezek.	10	1–22
Described	Ezek.	1	5–10

chestnut, chesnut *see plane tree*

chiding *rebuking*

Cain chides God	Gen.	4	13
Between Jacob and Laban	Gen.	31	26–42
Israel with Moses	Ex.	17	7
Jesus of disciples:			
For unbelief	Mat.	8	26
For slowness of heart	Mat.	15	16
For forbidding children	Mat.	19	14
Of disbelievers	Mat.	16	8–11
	Mat.	17	14–21
Of Peter for sleeping	Mat.	26	40
Of disciples, for criticizing	Mark	10	13–16

Chidon *javelin*

Threshingfloor where Uzzah is stricken	I Chr.	13	9
Called Nahon	II Sam.	6	6

chief *most important*

Should be servant	Mat.	20	27
Butler	Gen.	40	9
Tribal leaders	Deut.	1	15
Shepherd	I Pet.	5	4
Captain	Acts	21	31
Priest	I Chr.	29	22
	Mat.	26	47

childbirth

First command of God	Gen.	1	28
Curse of Eve	Gen.	3	16
By servant, at Rachel's request	Gen.	30	3–7
By Leah's servant	Gen.	30	9–11
Duty of young married women	I Tim.	5	14
Salvation of women	I Tim.	2	15
Virgin	Mat.	1	23
Woman	Rev.	12	2

childlessness *see* barrenness

children

The gift of God	Gen.	33	5
Wicked	Ex.	21	15
	I Sam.	2	12
Slain by she-bears	II Ki.	2	23
A blessing	Prov.	10	1
Of Bethlehem, slain by Herod	Mat.	2	16
Blessed by Christ	Mat.	19	13
Of light	Luke	16	8
	Eph.	5	8
Of the devil	Acts	13	10
Of God	Eph.	5	1
	Heb.	12	5
Correction of	Prov.	13	24
	Prov.	19	18
	Prov.	22	15
	Prov.	29	15
	Eph.	6	4
	Col.	3	24
Commandments to	Ex.	20	12
	Lev.	19	3
	Ps.	119	9
	Eccl.	12	1
A blessing	Ps.	127	3–5
	Prov.	17	6
Obedient:			
Isaac	Gen.	22	6
Jephthah's daughter	Judg.	11	36
Samuel	I Sam.	2	26
Christ	Luke	2	51
In answer to prayer:			
Of Abraham	Gen.	15	2–5
Of Isaac	Gen.	25	21
Of Leah	Gen.	30	17–22
Of Hannah	I Sam.	1	9–20
Of Zacharias	Luke	1	13
Dedicated to God:			
Samson	Judg.	13	5, 7
Samuel	I Sam.	1	24–28
Partiality of parents	Gen.	27	6–17
	Deut.	21	15–17
Sacrificed	II Ki.	17	31
Sold	II Ki.	4	1
Murdered	Ex.	1	22
Miracles involving	I Ki.	17	17–23
	II Ki.	4	17–36
	Mat.	9	18–26
Instruction of	Ex.	18	8–16
	Deut.	6	6–9
	Ps.	78	1–8
	Prov.	22	6
Good:			
Shem and Jepheth	Gen.	9	23
Josiah	II Chr.	34	3
Isaac	Gen.	22	6–12
Joseph	Gen.	45	9–13
Moses	Ex.	18	7
Jephthah's daughter	Judg.	11	36
Ruth	Ruth	1	15–17
Samuel	I Sam.	2	26
David	I Sam.	22	3, 4
Jehoshaphat	I Ki.	22	43
Esther	Esth.	2	20
Daniel	Dan.	1	6
Jesus	Luke	2	52
Timothy	II Tim.	3	15
Evil:			
Canaan	Gen.	9	25
Lot's daughters	Gen.	19	30–38
Ishmael	Gen.	21	9
Esau	Gen.	26	34
Eli's sons	I Sam.	2	12, 22–25
Samuel's sons	I Sam.	8	3
Absalom	II Sam.	15	
Adonijah	I Ki.	1	5
Children who mocked Elisha	II Ki.	2	23
Amon	II Ki.	21	21
Adrammelech	II Ki.	19	37
Gift of God	Gen.	4	25
	Gen.	28	3
	Ruth	4	13
	Job	1	21
	Ps.	113	9
God's special care of	Deut.	10	18
	Ps.	27	10
	Mal.	3	5

children, duties of *see* duties			
Chileab *restraint*			
David's second son	II Sam.	3	3
Also called Daniel	I Chr.	3	1
Chilion *wasting away*			
Son of Naomi	Ruth	1	2–5
Husband of Orpah	Ruth	1	4
Property bought by Boaz	Ruth	4	1–9
Chlnnereth, Chinneroth, Cinneroth *lyre*			
A district north of Palestine	Josh.	11	2
	I Ki.	15	20
Plain of Gennesaret	Mat.	14	34
The sea of	Josh.	12	3
	Josh.	13	27
Sea of Galilee	Num.	34	11
A city of Naphtali	Josh.	19	35
Chios *snowy*			
Island on Paul's way to Macedonia	Acts	20	15
Chisleu *the hunter*			
Ninth month of the Jewish year	Neh.	1	1
	Zech.	7	1
Chittim, Kittim *giants*			
Cyprus Island settled by sons of Javan	Gen.	10	4
	Num.	24	24
	Jer.	2	10
Part of Tyre	Is.	23	1–12
Source of ivory	Ezek.	27	6
Its ships fight Persian king	Dan.	11	30
choice *selection*			
To follow God's commandments or not	Deut.	11	26–28
	Is.	48	18
David's	II Sam.	24	10–14
To lead idolatrous life	Jer.	2	11–13
	Jer.	44	15–20
To sacrifice riches	Mat.	19	20–23
Mary's, commended	Luke	10	42
A wife	Gen.	24	13–21
Land	Josh.	14	2
Soldiers	Judg.	7	
Deacons	Acts	6	5
Disciple	Acts	1	26
King	I Sam.	12	13
Gods	Judg.	5	8
God of an individual	II Sam.	6	21
	I Chr.	28	4
	II Tim.	2	4
A tribe	Ps.	78	67
A nation	Ezek.	20	5
A city	I Ki.	8	44
Injunction of God:			
Between life and death	Deut.	30	19
Between God and Baal	I Ki.	18	21
Those who choose God:			
Jacob	Gen.	28	20, 21
Moses	Ex.	2	11
	Heb.	11	24, 25
Levites	Ex.	32	26
Israel's covenant	Deut.	26	17, 18
Joshua's command	Josh.	24	14–16
Ruth	Ruth	1	16
Naaman	II Ki.	5	15, 17
Those who choose evil:			
Lot	Gen.	13	10, 11
Israel	Is.	65	12
Jesus' crucifiers	Mat.	27	21
chosen of God			
Christ	Luke	23	35
A place to put his name	Deut.	12	21
Priests	Deut.	21	5
Solomon	I Chr.	29	1
Weak things	I Cor.	1	27
Despised things	I Cor.	1	28
Poor	James	2	5
Jeshurun (Israel)	Is.	44	1, 2
A fast	Is.	58	5, 6
Believer	John	15	16
Chorazin *city near sea of Galilee*			
Mighty works rebuffed	Mat.	11	21
	Luke	10	13
Christ, *see* Jesus			
Altogether lovely	S. of S.	5	16
Resigned	Luke	22	42
Resisting temptation	Mat.	4	1–10
Saints are conformed to	Rom.	8	29
Zealous	John	2	17
	John	8	29

Creator	John	1	3
	Col.	1	17
	Heb.	1	2
First begotten	Heb.	1	6
First-born	Col.	1	15, 18
The foundation of the church	Is.	28	16
As God	John	1	1–5
	Phil.	2	6, 9–10
The image of God	Col.	1	15
	Heb.	1	3
Incarnate	John	1	14
The Judge	Mat.	16	27
	Mat.	25	31, 33
Lord of lords	Rev.	17	14
The Mediator	I Tim.	2	5
	Heb.	8	6
The Shepherd	Is.	40	10–11
	John	10	11, 14
The true Light	Luke	1	78–79
	John	1	4, 9
The truth	I John	5	20
	Rev.	3	7
The way	John	14	6
	Heb.	10	19–20
Celebrated by the redeemed	Rev.	5	8–14
	Rev.	7	9–12
Imparted to saints	John	17	22
	II Cor.	3	18
In the calling of the Gentiles	Ps.	72	17
	John	12	21, 23
His grace and truth	John	1	14
His exaltation	Acts	7	55–56
	Eph.	1	21
Sinless perfection	Heb.	7	26–28
His transfiguration	Mat.	17	2
His triumph	Rev.	19	11, 16
Words	Luke	4	22
	John	7	46
Works	Mat.	13	54
	John	2	11
Is incomparable	S. of S.	5	10
	Phil.	2	9
Is unchangeable	Heb.	1	10–12
Revealed in the gospel	Is.	40	4
Saints shall behold, in heaven	John	17	24
Saints shall rejoice at the revelation of	I Pet.	4	13
Acknowledged by his apostles	John	20	28
Creator of all things	Is.	40	28
	John	1	3
	Heb.	1	2
Discerning the thoughts of the heart	Luke	5	22
	Ezek.	11	5
	John	2	24–25
Entitled to equal honor with the Father	John	5	23
As eternal	Mic.	5	2
	John	1	1
	Col.	1	17
	Heb.	1	8–10
	Rev.	1	8
The Eternal God and Creator	Heb.	1	8, 10–12
He presents the church to himself	Eph.	5	27
He redeems and purifies the church unto himself	Rev.	5	9
	Tit.	2	14
God over all	Ps.	45	6–7
	Rom.	9	5
God the Judge	Eccl.	12	14
	II Cor.	5	10
	II Tim.	4	1
God the Word	John	1	1
Having power to forgive sins	Col.	3	13
	Mark	2	7, 10
Husband of the church	Is.	54	5
	Eph.	5	25–32
	Rev.	21	2, 9
King of kings and Lord of lords	Rev.	17	14
The Lord from heaven	I Cor.	15	47
Lord of all	Acts	10	36
	Rom.	10	11–13
Lord of the sabbath	Gen.	2	3
	Mat.	12	8
The object of divine worship	II Cor.	12	8–9
	Heb.	1	6
	Rev.	5	12
The object of faith	I Pet.	2	6
	Jer.	17	7
	John	14	1

Omnipotent	Ps.	45	3
	Phil.	3	21
	Rev.	1	8
Omnipresent	Mat.	18	20
	Mat.	28	30
	John	3	13
Omniscient	John	16	30
	John	21	17
One with the Father	John	10	30, 38
	John	12	45
The only begotten Son of the Father	John	1	14, 18
	I John	4	9
Possessed of the fullness of the Godhead	Col.	2	9
	Heb.	1	3
Raising the dead	John	5	21
	John	6	40, 54
Sending the Spirit equally with the Father	John	14	16
	John	15	26
Son of God	Mat.	26	63–67
The source of grace equally with the Father	I Thes.	3	11
	II Thes.	2	16–17
Supporter and preserver of all things	Neh.	9	6
	Col.	1	17
The true God	Jer.	10	10
	I John	5	20
Unchangeable	Mal.	3	6
	Heb.	1	12
	Heb.	13	8
Unsearchable	I Thes.	3	11
	II Thes.	2	16–17
Saints live unto him as	II Cor.	5	15
Appointed by God	Eph.	1	22
Mystical body	Eph.	4	12, 15
	Eph.	5	23
Commissioned his apostles	Mat.	10	1, 7
	Mat.	28	19
	John	20	21
Declared by himself	Mat.	21	42
Preeminence in all things	I Cor.	11	3
	Eph.	1	22
	Col.	1	18
Imparts gifts	Eph.	4	8
Instituted the sacraments	Mat.	28	19
	Luke	22	19–20
Predicted	Ps.	118	22
	Mat.	21	42
Saints are complete in	Col.	2	10

Christian *believer in Christ*

Daily life	Mat.	5	46–48
	Eph.	4	17
Name first used in Antioch	Acts	11	26
Agrippa almost persuaded to become	Acts	26	28, 29
Endure hardships	II Tim.	2	3, 4
Suffering, of, glorified	I Pet.	4	16

Christian attributes

Purity of heart	Mat.	5	8
Acceptance of persecution	Mat.	5	11, 12
Love of enemies	Mat.	5	44
Not judging others	Mat.	7	1, 2
Regard for others	Mat.	7	12
Obedience	Mat.	7	21
	Tit.	3	1
Self-denial	Mat.	16	24
Love of God	Mat.	22	36, 37
Faithfulness	Mat.	25	14–23
	I Tim.	6	12
Faith in God	Mark	11	22
Lack of covetousness	Luke	12	15
Forgiveness	Luke	17	3, 4
Productiveness	John	15	1–6
Generosity	Acts	4	34–37
	Rom.	12	13
Obedience to God	Acts	5	27–29
Hatred of evil	Rom.	12	9
Fervour of spirit	Rom.	12	11
Hospitality	Rom.	12	13
	Heb.	13	2
Blessing of persecutors	Rom.	12	14
Sympathy	Rom.	12	15
Content with the lowly	Rom.	12	16
Honesty	Rom.	12	17
Lacking vengeance	Rom.	12	19
Subjection to authority	Rom.	13	1–7
Rejection of lust	Rom.	13	14
Hopefulness	Rom.	15	4–13
Avoidance of envy	I Cor.	3	3
Eschewing fornication and uncleanness	I Cor.	6	18
	Eph.	5	3, 4
	James	1	21
Temperance	I Cor.	9	25
Constancy	I Cor.	15	58
Accepting burdens	Gal.	6	2
Determination	Gal.	6	9
Meekness, forbearance	Eph.	4	2
	Tit.	3	2
Truthfulness	Eph.	4	25
	I John	1	8, 9
Lacking bitterness and malice	Eph.	4	31
Kindness	Eph.	4	32
Utilizing time	Eph.	5	16
Understanding	Eph.	5	17
Gratefulness	Eph.	5	20
Sincerity	Phil.	2	15
Joyousness	Phil.	4	4
Absence of anger, malice	Col.	3	8
Edification	I Thes.	5	11
Prayerfulness	I Thes.	5	17
Righteousness	I Tim.	6	11
Avoidance of worldly entanglements	II Tim.	2	4
Study of God's law	II Tim.	2	15
Patience	II Tim.	2	24
	Heb.	10	36
Uncorruptness	Tit.	2	7, 8
Zeal	Tit.	2	14
Discerning good from evil	Heb.	5	14
Attending church	Heb.	10	25
Peacefulness	Heb.	12	14
Contentment	Heb.	13	5
Holiness	I Pet.	1	15, 16
Guilelessness	I Pet.	2	1
Humility	I Pet.	5	5
Dependence on God	I Pet.	5	6, 7
Godliness	II Pet.	1	5–7
Diligence	II Pet.	1	10
Grace	II Pet.	3	18

Christian living

Exalted life	Rom.	8	31–39
Subjection of the body	I Cor.	9	27
By the grace of God	I Cor.	15	10
Life of suffering	II Cor.	11	23–28
Explained by Paul	Gal.	2	20

Christ-likeness *similarity to Christ*

Predestined by God	Rom.	8	29
How to attain	II Cor.	3	16–18
Attained in heaven	I John	3	2

christs, false

Warning	Mat.	7	15
	Mark	13	22
	Acts	20	29

chrysolite, chrysolyte *precious stone*

Wall of new Jerusalem encrusted with	Rev.	21	19, 20

chrysoprasus, chrysoprase *precious stone*

Wall of new Jerusalem encrusted with	Rev.	21	19, 20

church *assembly*

God provides ministers for	Jer.	3	15
	Eph.	4	11, 12
God defends	Mat.	16	18
Authority of	Mat.	18	15–17
Believers continually added to	Acts	2	47
	Acts	11	24–26
The wicked persecute	Acts	8	1–3
	I Thes.	2	14, 15
Teaching of	Acts	11	26
	I Cor.	12	28
	I Cor.	14	4, 5
Members meet together the first day of the week	Acts	20	7
	I Cor.	16	1, 2
Ministers commanded to feed	Acts	20	28
Saluted	Acts	18	22
	I Cor.	16	19
Purchased by the blood of Christ	Acts	20	28
	Eph.	5	25
	Heb.	9	12
Subject to Christ	Rom.	7	4
	Eph.	5	24
Unity of	Rom.	12	5
	I Cor.	10	17
	I Cor.	12	13
Defiling of, will be punished	I Cor.	3	17
Not to be despised	I Cor.	11	22

church—continued			
Is edified by the word	I Cor.	14	4, 13
	Eph.	4	15–16
The object of the grace of God	II Cor.	8	1
	Is.	27	3
Christ, the head of	Eph.	1	22
	Eph.	5	23
The body of Christ	Eph.	1	23
	Col.	1	24
Displays the wisdom of God	Eph.	3	10
Loved by Christ	Eph.	5	25, 29
	S. of S.	7	10
Glorious	Eph.	5	27
Belongs to God	I Tim.	3	15
Seven churches, in Asia	Rev.	1	4, 11, 20
The church:			
Christ, the foundation stone of	I Cor.	3	11
	Eph.	2	20
	I Pet.	2	4, 6
Clothed in righteousness	Rev.	19	8
Elect	I Pet.	5	13
Extent of, predicted	Is.	2	2
	Ezek.	17	22–24
	Dan.	2	34–35
	Hab.	2	14
Glory to be ascribed to God by	Eph.	3	21
Sanctified and cleansed by Christ	I Cor.	6	11
	Eph.	5	26–27
Shows forth the praises of God	Is.	60	6
Unity of	Gal.	3	28
Being established	Ps.	48	8
	Is.	33	20
Being the seat of God's worship	Ps.	96	6
Eminent position	Ps.	48	2
	Is.	2	2
Derived from Christ	Is.	60	7
	Luke	2	34
Derived from God	Is.	28	5
God delights in	Ps.	45	11
	Is.	62	3–5
Is abundant	Is.	66	11
Result from the favor of God	Is.	43	4
Saints delight in	Is.	66	11
Sin obscures	Lam.	2	14–15
Local congregations mentioned:			
Jerusalem	Acts	11	22
Antioch	Acts	13	1
Caesarea	Acts	18	22
Cenchrea	Rom.	16	1
Corinth	I Cor.	1	1
Macedonia	II Cor.	8	1
Galatia	Gal.	1	2
Ephesus	Eph.	1	1
Philippi	Phil.	1	1
	Phil.	4	15
Colosse	Col.	1	2
Thessalonica	I Thes.	1	1
Babylon	I Pet.	5	13
Called:			
Bride of Christ	John	3	29
	Rev.	21	2
Flock	Acts	20	28
One body	Rom.	12	4, 5
	I Cor.	10	17
Church of God	I Cor.	1	2
Temple of God	I Cor.	3	16
God's husbandry	I Cor.	3	9
God's building	I Cor.	3	9
Israel of God	Gal.	6	16
Household of God	Eph.	2	19
The body	Eph.	4	12
Children of light	Eph.	5	8
The wife of the Lamb	Rev.	19	7
	Rev.	21	9
Members called:			
Believers	Acts	5	14
Disciples	Acts	6	1
	Acts	20	7
Christians	Acts	11	26
Saints	Rom.	8	27
	Eph.	1	1
Brethren	Rom.	12	1
	Gal.	6	1
	Col.	1	2
The faithful	Eph.	1	1
Kings	Rev.	1	6
Priests	Rev.	1	6

church attendance *see* attendance, church			
church, discipline			
Decency and order, the objects of	I Cor.	14	40
Exercise, in a spirit of charity	II Cor.	2	6–8
Ministers authorized to establish	Mat.	16	19
	Mat.	18	18
Prohibits women preaching	I Cor.	14	34
	I Tim.	2	12
Should be submitted	Heb.	13	17
Deals with:			
Doctrine	I Tim.	1	3
	Tit.	1	13
Ordering its affairs	I Cor.	11	34
	Tit.	1	5
Rebuking offenders	I Tim.	5	20
	II Tim.	4	2
Removing obstinate offenders	I Cor.	5	3–5, 13
	I Tim.	1	20
church, growth of			
3,000 on day of Pentecost	Acts	2	41
Steady growth of the church in apostolic times	Acts	5	14
	Acts	6	1, 2
	Acts	9	31
Many conversions from missionary labours among Gentiles	Acts	11	21, 24
	Acts	16	5
	Acts	17	4
	Acts	18	8
church sleeper			
Falls during long sermon	Acts	20	9
churlishness *meanness*			
In Nabal	I Sam.	25	3
Devises wickedness	Is.	32	5, 7
Cilicia *Roman province in Asia Minor*			
Visited by Paul	Acts	15	23, 41
Native country of Paul	Acts	21	39
	Acts	22	3
	Gal.	1	21
Disputed with Stephen	Acts	6	9
cinnamon *an import from the East*			
Used in ointment	Ex.	30	23
Used for perfuming beds	Prov.	7	16, 17
Raise in a garden	S. of S.	4	14
Item of trade	Rev.	18	13
Cinneroth *see* Chinnereth			
circuit			
From year to year in *c*	I Sam.	7	16
Walketh in *c* of heaven	Job	22	14
His *c* unto the ends of it	Ps.	19	6
Returneth according to his *c*	Eccl.	1	6
circumcision *a Hebrew religious rite*			
Instituted by God	Gen.	17	9, 10
	Lev.	12	3
	John	7	22
Described as painful and bloody	Gen.	17	11
	Ex.	4	26
	Josh.	5	8
Punishment for neglecting	Gen.	17	14
	Ex.	4	24, 26
Child named at the time of	Gen.	21	3, 4
	Luke	1	59
	Luke	2	21
Not performed in the wilderness	Josh.	5	5
Sometimes performed on slain enemies	I Sam.	18	25–27
	II Sam.	3	14
A prerequisite of the privileges of the Jewish church	Ezek.	44	7
Abolished in Christ	Gal.	2	3–5
	Gal.	5	2, 6
	Eph.	2	11, 15
	Col.	3	11
Paul denounced for opposing	Acts	21	21
Performed:			
On all males on the eighth day	Gen.	17	12, 13
	Lev.	12	3
By the heads of families	Gen.	17	23
With knives or sharp stones	Ex.	4	25
	Josh.	5	3
By persons in authority	Josh.	5	3
In the presence of the family	Luke	1	58, 59
Even on the sabbath day	John	7	22, 23
Called the:			
Convenant of circumcision	Acts	7	8
Circumcision in the flesh	Eph.	2	11
Concision	Phil.	3	2

Instances of:			
Abraham	Gen.	17	23-27
Shechemites	Gen.	34	24
Moses	Ex.	4	25
Israelites at Gilgal	Josh.	5	2-9
John the Baptist	Luke	1	59
Jesus	Luke	2	21
Timothy	Acts	16	3
Paul	Phil.	3	5
Figurative use	Ex.	6	12
	Jer.	4	4
	Jer.	9	26
	Rom.	2	28, 29
	Col.	2	11

Cis *see* Kish

cistern *a pit for storing water*

Synonymous with pits or wells	II Sam.	17	18
	Eccl.	12	6
Common in Palestine Figurative	Is.	36	16
	Jer.	2	13
Of prosperity	II Ki.	18	31
Of personal property	Prov.	5	15
Sometimes empty	Ex.	21	33
	Gen.	37	22

cities

First mention of	Gen.	4	17
Often of great antiquity	Gen.	10	11, 12
Often built to perpetuate a name	Gen.	11	4
Sodom, a wicked	Gen.	13	13
Often insignificant	Gen.	19	20
	Eccl.	9	14
Entered through gates	Gen.	34	24
	Neh.	13	19, 22
Treasure cities of Pharaoh	Ex.	1	11, 14
Arranged in streets and lanes	Num.	22	39
	Zech.	8	5
	Luke	14	21
Sometimes with suburbs	Num.	35	2
	Josh.	21	3
Surrounded with walls	Deut.	1	28
	Deut.	3	5
Provided with judges	Deut.	16	18
	II Chr.	19	5
Often with citadels	Judg.	9	51
Often deserted on the approach of an			
enemy	I Sam.	31	7
	Jer.	4	29
Jerusalem, an excited	Mat.	21	10, 11
Athens, an idolatrous	Acts	17	16
Built:			
In plains	Gen.	11	2, 4
	Gen.	13	12
Of brick and slime	Gen.	11	3
In desert places	II Chr.	8	4
	Ps.	107	35, 36
Often beside rivers	Ps.	46	4
	Ps.	137	1
Of stone and wood	Ps.	102	14
	Ezek.	26	12
With compactness	Ps.	122	3
On hills	Mat.	5	14
	Luke	4	29
	Rev.	17	9
Often in a square form	Rev.	21	16
Famous cities:			
Sodom and Gomorrah	Gen.	19	24
Jerusalem	Josh.	18	28
Babylon	Rev.	18	2
Nineveh	Jonah	1	2
Hebron	Gen.	23	2
Shechem	Gen.	34	2
Bethlehem	Mic.	5	2
Megiddo	II Ki.	23	29
Hazor	Judg.	4	2
Antioch	Acts	11	26
Athens	Acts	17	15
Rome	Rom.	1	7

cities of refuge *asylum*

Persons responsible for accidental			
manslaughter	Num.	35	6
	Josh.	20	1-9

cities of the plain

Five cities in the vale of Siddim	Gen.	14	1-3

citizen, duties of *see* duties

citizenship

Paul's	Acts	16	37
	Acts	21	39
	Acts	22	25
Duties of:			
Not to curse ruler	Acts	23	5
Pray for king	Ezra	6	10
	I Tim.	2	1, 2
Fear king	Prov.	24	21
Pay taxes	Mat.	17	24
	Mat.	22	17-20
Strive for peace	Jer.	29	7
To obey rulers	Rom.	13	1-7
	Tit.	3	1
	I Pet.	2	13-17
Protection from injustice	Acts	16	37
	Acts	22	25
Loyal citizens:			
Hushai	II Sam.	17	15, 16
Barzillai	II Sam.	19	32
Mordecai	Esth.	2	21-23

city, holy

Jerusalem called	Neh.	11	1, 18
Zion	Is.	60	14
Heavenly Jerusalem	Heb.	12	22
	Rev.	21	10

City of David

Stronghold of Zion renamed by David	II Sam.	5	6-9
	I Chr.	11	5, 7
David brings the ark here	II Sam.	6	16
David buried here	I Ki.	2	10
Bethlehem	Luke	2	4, 11

City of God

Made glad	Ps.	46	4
Heavenly Jerusalem	Heb.	12	22

City of Salt

Town in the wilderness of Judah	Josh.	15	62

City of waters

A place of Ammon	II Sam.	12	26, 27

civil service

Daniel trained for	Dan.	1	3-5
Joseph	Gen.	39	1-6
	Gen.	41	38
Jeroboam	I Ki.	11	38
Nehemiah	Neh.	2	1-8
Mordecai	Esth.	6	2
Parable	Mat.	25	14-30
Jealousy in	Dan.	6	4
Political pressure	Mark	15	15
Bribery of	Acts	24	26
Perversion of	Mic.	7	14

civility *politeness*

At wedding	Luke	14	8-10
Required of brethren	Rom.	12	10
	I Pet.	2	17
Of Timothy	Phil.	2	19-23
Of Gaius	III John		1-6

class struggles

Jews-Philistines	Gen.	26	16
Jews-Egyptians	Gen.	43	32
Jews-Canaanites	Judg.	1	28
Jews-Samaritans	John	4	9
Jews-Gentiles	Acts	6	1
Rich-poor	I Ki.	12	11-18
Unlawful	Ex.	12	48, 49

Claudia *lame*

A Christian lady at Rome	II Tim.	4	21

Claudius *see* Caesar

Claudius Lysias *dissolving*

Sends Paul to Felix	Acts	23	24-26
Saves Paul from mob	Acts	24	7
Felix awaits arrival	Acts	24	22

clay *an earthy substance*

Man formed of	Gen.	2	7
	Job	33	6
Pottery	Is.	29	16
Figuratively, of man's relationship to God	Is.	45	9
	Is.	64	8
Houses made of	Job	4	19
Used in healing	John	9	6
Used in bricks	II Sam.	12	31
Roman Empire	Dan.	2	33-35

clean

Wash and be *c*	II Ki.	5	12
C thing out of an unclean?	Job	14	4
Heavens not *c* in his sight	Job	15	15
Fear of the Lord is *c*	Ps.	19	9
He that hath *c* hands	Ps.	24	4
Create in me a *c* heart	Ps.	51	10
Is his mercy *c* gone for ever?	Ps.	77	8
Ways *c* in his own eyes	Prov.	16	2
Wash you, make you *c*	Is.	1	16
Be *c* that bear vessels of the Lord	Is.	52	11
Then will I sprinkle *c* water on you	Ezek.	36	25
Thou canst make me *c*	Mat.	8	2
	Mark	1	40
	Luke	5	12
Make *c* the outside	Mat.	23	25
	Luke	11	39
All things *c* unto you	Luke	11	41
Ye are not all *c*	John	13	11
C through the word	John	15	3
I am *c*	Acts	18	6
Arrayed in fine linen *c* and white	Rev.	19	8

cleanliness *state of being clean*

Literal sense	Lev.	4	12
	Mat.	27	59
Legalistic or ceremonial sense	Gen.	7	2, 8
	Lev.	11	1–47
	Acts	10	14, 28
Spiritual sense	Ps.	19	9
	John	15	3

cleanse

C from secret faults	Ps.	19	12
I have *c* my heart in vain	Ps.	73	13
A young man *c* his way	Ps.	119	9
His leprosy was *c*	Mat.	8	3
C lepers	Mat.	10	8
	Mat.	11	5
	Luke	7	22
C first that which is within	Mat.	23	26
None was *c* saving Naaman	Luke	4	27
Were not ten *c*?	Luke	17	17
What God hath *c*	Acts	10	15
	Acts	11	9
Let us *c* ourselves	II Cor.	7	1
Might *c* it with washing	Eph.	5	26
C your hands, ye sinners	James	4	8
C us from all sin	I John	1	7

clear

How shall we *c* ourselves?	Gen.	44	16
By no means *c* the guilty	Ex.	34	7
C shining after rain	II Sam.	23	4
Thine age be *c* than noonday	Job	11	17
C when thou judgest	Ps.	51	4
As the sun	S. of S.	6	10
Light shall not be *c*	Zech.	14	6
See c to pull out mote	Mat.	7	5
	Luke	6	42
Saw every man *c*	Mark	8	25
Things from creation *c* seen	Rom.	1	20
Approved yourselves to be *c*	II Cor.	7	11
C as crystal	Rev.	21	11
	Rev.	22	1

cleave

C unto his wife	Gen.	2	24
C to the Lord your God	Josh.	23	8
Tongue *c* to roof of mouth	Job	29	10
	Ps.	137	6
	Ezek.	3	26
Hath *c* to my hands	Job	31	7
My soul *c* to dust	Ps.	119	25
With purposes of heart *c*	Acts	11	23
C to that which is good	Rom.	12	9

Clement *kind, merciful*

A Christian of Philippi who labours with Paul	Phil.	4	3

Cleopas *of a renowned father*

One who meets the resurrected Jesus on the road to Emmaus	Luke	24	13–35

Cleophas *of a renowned father*

Husband of Mary	John	19	25

cloak *outer garment*

To be given with coat	Mat.	5	40
For sin	John	15	22
Of covetousness	I Thes.	2	5
Paul's	II Tim.	4	13
Of Maliciousness	I Pet.	2	16

close

Earth *c* upon them	Num.	16	33
Lord hath *c* your eyes	Is.	29	10
Friend sticketh *c* than a brother	Prov.	18	24
They kept it *c*	Luke	9	36

closet *inner chamber*

A place where one may pray alone	Mat.	6	6

clothing

Man in the beginning goes naked	Gen.	2	25
Made of leaves	Gen.	3	7
The first clothing is skins of animals	Gen.	3	21
Israelite's did not wax old	Deut.	8	4
Renting of as a sign of sorrow	I Ki.	21	27
	Josh.	7	6
Washing of	Num.	19	7
Not gaudy	Is.	3	16–24
	I Pet.	3	3
	I Tim.	2	9
Not unisex	Deut.	22	5
Materials used later:			
Wool	Gen.	31	19
	Lev.	13	47
	Job	31	20
Fine linen	Gen.	41	42
	Luke	16	19
Linen	Ex.	9	31
	Lev.	16	4
Silk	Ezek.	16	10, 13
	Rev.	18	12
Camels' and goats' hair Also see garments	Mat.	3	4

cloud *a mass of vapour*

Descriptive of	Prov.	16	15
	Is.	5	6
	Hosea	6	4
Son of man shall come in	Mat.	24	30
	Luke	21	27
	Rev.	1	7
	Rev.	14	14
Appearance of the Lord in:			
To Moses	Ex.	24	15–18
	Ex.	34	5
	Lev.	16	2
	Num.	11	25
	Num.	12	5
Over the tabernacle	Ex.	40	34–38
In the tabernacle	I Ki.	8	10
In temple	II Chr.	5	13
Vision of Ezekiel	Ezek.	10	4
At the baptism of Jesus	Mat.	17	5

cloudburst *a sudden heavy rainfall*

Brought upon the people because of their transgressions	Ezra	10	9–13

cloud, pillar of

A miraculous cloud, like a pillar, which moves in front of the Israelites in the wilderness. By night it shines with light	Ex.	13	21, 22
	Ex.	14	19, 20
	Ps.	78	14
	Ps.	105	39
	I Cor.	10	1
God manifests Himself in the	Ex.	14	24
	Num.	12	5
	Deut.	31	15
To come again	Is.	4	5

clovenfooted *having the foot divided*

Animals that shall be eaten	Lev.	11	3–8

Cnidus *a city of Asia Minor*

Seen by Paul on his voyage to Italy	Acts	27	7

coal *charcoal or embers of a fire of wood*

Used for cooking	I Ki.	19	6
	John	21	9
Used for warmth	Is.	47	14
	John	18	18
Used by smiths	Is.	44	12
Improper use of coal	Prov.	6	28
Used figuratively:			
As offspring	II Sam.	14	7
For kindness to an enemy	Prov.	25	21, 22
	Rom.	12	20, 21
For purifying	Is.	6	6, 7
Of immorality	Prov.	6	28

coasts

Locusts rested in all the *c*	Ex.	10	14

No leavened bread seen in thy *c*	Deut.	16	4
Sent concubine into all the *c*	Judg.	19	29
Send messengers into all *c*	I Sam.	11	3–7
Lice in all their *c*	Ps.	105	31
Whirlwind raised from *c*	Jer.	25	32
Slew children in all *c*	Mat.	2	16
Depart out of their *c*	Mark	8	34
	Mark	5	17
Jesus departed into *c* of Tyre	Mat.	15	21
And Barnabas out of *c*	Acts	13	50

coat of mail *see armour*

coat

Adam's	Gen.	3	21
Joseph's	Gen.	37	3
Anron's	Ex.	28	4
Samuel's	I Sam.	2	19
Peter's	John	21	7
Made by Dorcas	Acts	9	30
Christ's	John	19	23
Rent in sorrow	II Sam.	15	32

cock, crowing of the

Peter to deny Jesus before	Mat.	26	34, 74, 75
	John	18	25–27
Sign of dawn	Mark	13	35

cockatrice *a venomous serpent*
Used figuratively:

A kingdom of peace	Is.	11	8
God's judgment upon the Jews	Jer.	8	17

Also see adder

cockle *a noxious weed found in grain fields*

Grows with barley	Job	31	40

coffer *a chest*

The Philistines return the ark and an offering of jewelry in a	I Sam.	6	8, 11, 15

coffin *a chest or case for a corpse*

Joseph put in a	Gen.	50	26

cold

Of winter	Gen.	8	22
Cometh from the north	Job	37	9
Regulated by God	Ps.	147	17
Of water refreshing	Prov.	25	25
	Mat.	10	42
	Rev.	3	15–16
Of apostasy	Mat.	24	12
Of snow	Prov.	25	13

collection *offering*

King Joash commands a	II Chr.	24	6–9
For the saints at Jerusalem	Rom.	15	26
Paul gives instructions for a	I Cor.	16	1

college

Section of Jerusalem where prophetess Huldah lives	II Ki.	22	14
	II Chr.	34	22

color

Joseph's coat	Gen.	37	3, 23, 32
Several kinds used	Ex.	25	4, 5
Purple, associated with power	Ex.	28	5, 6
	Judg.	8	26
	John	19	2
Blue, associated with royalty	Ex.	28	28
	Esth.	8	15

cloths covering vessels of tabernacle

Of God	Num.	4	6
	Ex.	24	10

Red, associated with:

Purification	Num.	19	2
Prosperity	II Sam.	1	24
Sin	Is.	1	18
Royalty	Mat.	27	28
Conquest	Rev.	12	3
Judgment	Is.	63	1–3
	Joel	2	6
Black, associated with death and curse	Job	3	5
	Is.	50	3
Day of the Lord as darkness	Zeph.	1	14–15
Of Hell	II Pet.	2	4
Of outer space	Jude		13
Wine that sparkles	Prov.	23	31
White, associated with purity	Eccl.	9	8
Future prosperity	Is.	54	11
Of purification	Ps.	51	7
	Is.	1	18
	Dan.	12	10
Of aged hair	Rev.	1	14

Colosse *city in Asia Minor*

Paul addresses the Christians of	Col.	1	2

colt *young donkey, ass or camel*

Part of Jacob's gift to Esau	Gen.	32	15
Jacob's blessing upon Judah	Gen.	49	11
Jesus rides into Jerusalem	Mat.	21	2, 5, 7
	Mark	11	1–7
	Luke	19	29–35
	John	12	14, 15

come

c and let us sell him	Gen.	37	27
c on, let us deal wisely	Ex.	1	10
Joy *c* in the morning	Ps.	30	5
He that *c* after me	Mat.	3	11
c unto me, all ye	Mat.	11	28
c one mightier than I	Mark	1	7
Suffer little children to *c*	Mark	10	14
Son of man	Luke	12	40
c unto the Father	John	14	6
Father the hour is *c*	John	17	1
Then *c* the end	I Cor.	15	24
Fulness of time was *c*	Gal.	4	4
So *c* as a thief	I Thes.	5	2
Let us *c* boldly	Heb.	4	16
Down from Father of lights	James	1	17
Spirit and bride say, *c*	Rev.	22	17
Even so *c* Lord Jesus	Rev.	22	20

comeliness *beauty*

Messiah will not have	Is.	53	2
Tyrus is described	Ezek.	27	10
Members of the body of Christ	I Cor.	12	23

comfort *relief from distress, encouragement*

From affliction	Job	10	20
	Ps.	77	2
	Ps.	119	50, 52
	Luke	16	25
	II Cor.	1	4
Thy rod and thy staff	Ps.	23	4
In spite of mistakes	Is.	12	1
Comfort ye, comfort ye	Is.	40	1
For Zion	Is.	51	3
	Is.	66	13
For those who mourn	Is.	61	2, 3
	Mat.	2	18
	Mat.	5	4
	John	11	19
Used in a blessing	Mat.	9	22
	Mark	10	49
	Luke	8	48
	II Cor.	13	11
	II Thes.	2	17
Through the Holy Ghost	Acts	9	31
Through faith	Rom.	1	12
Through scriptures	Rom.	15	4
Through God	II Cor.	1	3
	II Cor.	7	6
Through each other	II Cor.	2	7
	II Cor.	7	7, 13
	I Thes.	4	18

comforter

One who reinforces or strengthens	Job	16	2
	Ps.	69	20
	Lam.	1	9, 16
	Nah.	3	7
Jesus speaks of the Holy Spirit or the Holy Ghost	John	14	16, 26
	John	15	26
	John	16	7, 8, 13

command

Of God to Adam	Gen.	2	16
To Moses	Ex.	3	14
To Joshua	Josh.	1	9
Of Moses to the sons of Levi	Deut.	31	10
Of Christ to the twelve	Mat.	10	5
	Mark	16	15
To Peter	John	21	15
He will *c* his children	Gen.	18	19
Lord shall *c* the blessing	Deut.	28	8
All that thou *c* us	Josh.	1	16
He *c* and it stood fast	Ps.	33	9
Lord will *c* his lovingkindness	Ps.	42	8
He *c* even the winds	Luke	8	25
Fire from heaven	Luke	9	54
If ye do whatsoever I *c*	John	15	14
c all men everywhere	Acts	17	30
c to abstain from meats	I Tim.	4	3
Could not endure that *c*	Heb.	12	20

commandments(s) *act of commanding*

Should be taught	Deut.	6	1–6
Children should observe	Deut.	32	46
	Prov.	6	20, 23
	Prov.	7	1
	Eph.	6	2
Faithful	Ps.	119	86
Broad	Ps.	119	96
Law is read to all the congregation	Josh.	8	34, 35
	I Chr.	28	8
Obedience enjoined	Deut.	11	27–28
Of God are dependable, broad and wise	Ps.	119	86, 96, 98
Of King Nebuchadnezzar	Dan.	3	22
Of God broken by men	Mat.	15	1–9
	Mark	7	7–9
Of Jesus to the rich man	Mat.	19	17–21
	Mark	10	17–21
	Luke	18	18–22
Of love	John	15	12
Two great	Mat.	22	36–40
	Mark	12	28–31
Of love	John	13	34
Is holy	Rom.	7	12
Paul writes not by	I Cor.	7	6
	II Cor.	8	8
Of men	Col.	2	22
Of God to Paul	I Tim.	1	1
Intention of the	I Tim.	1	5
Carnal	Heb.	7	16–18
Observing the	I John	2	3, 4
Old and new	I John	2	7, 8
	II John		5

Commandments, Ten *see* Ten Commandments

commendation *praise*

At the judgment	Mat.	25	20, 21
Of John the Baptist	Luke	7	28
Of great sacrifices	Luke	21	3
Letters of	II Cor.	3	1

commerce *business, trade*

Spices and nuts have a place in trade	Gen.	43	11
In Egypt	Gen.	47	13, 17
Babylonian imports	Josh.	7	21
Trade in Solomon's time	I Ki.	5	10, 11
	I Ki.	10	22
	II Chr.	9	21
Traveling merchants, called chapmen	II Chr.	9	14
A rich international commerce implied	Ezek.	16	10–13
Made with Tyre	Ezek.	27	17–25
	Ezek.	28	2–5
Oil exported to Egypt	Hosea	12	1
On the Sabbath	Neh.	13	15–22
At the Temple	John	2	13–16

commission

Faithfulness in performing	Gen.	24	33
	Ezra	8	36
	Acts	26	12, 19, 20
To prophesy	Amos	7	15
	Jonah	1	1, 2
To make Christians of all the nations	Mat.	28	19, 20
Of seventy disciples	Luke	10	1–16

commit

c thy way to the Lord	Ps.	37	5
Jesus did not *c* himself	John	2	24
Hath *c* judgment to Son	John	5	22
Sin is the servant of sin	John	8	34
c oracles of God	Rom.	3	2
c to us word of reconciliation	II Cor.	5	19
Charge I *c* unto thee	I Tim.	1	18
Keep that which is *c* to thee	I Tim.	6	20
c himself to him that judgeth	I Pet.	2	23
Whsoever *c* sin	I John	3	4

common

c people sin through ignorance	Lev.	4	27
evil, and it is *c* among men	Eccl.	6	1
is *c* reported	Mat.	28	15
The *c* people heard him gladly	Mark	12	37
All things *c*	Acts	2	44
	Acts	4	32
In the *c* prison	Acts	5	18
Never eaten anything *c*	Acts	10	14
	Acts	11	8
Temptation *c* to men	I Cor.	10	13
Write of *c* salvation	Jude		3

communion

Instituted by Christ	Mat.	26	26–30
Proper manner of observance	I Cor.	11	20–34
Both bread and wine are necessary to be received in	Mat.	26	27
	I Cor.	11	26
Continually partaken of, by the primitive church	Acts	2	42
	Acts	20	7
Is the communion of the body and blood of Christ	I Cor.	10	16
Newness of heart and life necessary to the worthy partaking of	I Cor.	5	7–8
Object of	Luke	22	19
	I Cor.	11	24, 26
Partakers of	I Cor.	10	21
Prefigured	Ex.	12	21–28
	I Cor.	5	7–8
Self-examination commanded	I Cor.	11	28, 31

Unworthy Partakers of

Are guilty of the body and blood of Christ	I Cor.	11	27
Are visited with judgments	I Cor.	11	30
Discern not the Lord's body	I Cor.	11	29

communion with God

Insures power	Ex.	25	22
Secured in worship	Mat.	18	20
Only through Christ	I Cor.	10	16
	Gal.	4	6
	Heb.	4	14–16
Comes from within	II Cor.	6	16
Requires repentance	James	4	8
Requires obedience	John	14	23
Is communion with the Father	I John	1	3
Is communion with the Holy Ghost	I Cor.	12	13
	II Cor.	13	14
	Phil.	2	1
Is communion with the Son	I Cor.	1	9
	I John	1	3
	Rev.	3	20
Promised to the obedient	John	14	23
Reconciliation must precede	Amos	3	3

Saints

Desire	Ps.	42	1
	Phil.	1	23
Have, in the Lord's supper	I Cor.	10	16
Have, in meditation	Ps.	63	5–6
Have, in prayer	Phil.	4	6
Should always enjoy	Ps.	16	8
	John	14	16–18

Instances of:

Enoch	Gen.	5	22, 24
Noah	Gen.	6	9, 13–22
Abraham	Gen.	12	1–3, 7
	Gen.	18	1–33
Hagar	Gen.	16	8–12
Isaac	Gen.	26	2, 24
	Gen.	28	13, 15
Moses	Ex.	4	1–17
	Ex.	34	28
Joshua	Josh.	1	1–9
	Josh.	6	2–5
Gideon	Judg.	6	11–24
Solomon	I Ki.	3	5–14
	II Chr.	1	7–12

companion

Best man	Judg.	14	20
Wife	Mal.	2	14
Fellow worker	Phil.	2	25
Friend	I Chr.	27	33
Common suffering	Rev.	1	9

companions, evil

To be avoided	Ex.	23	2, 32, 33
	Num.	16	26
	Ps.	1	1
	Ps.	26	4
	Prov.	1	10–15
	Prov.	4	14, 15
	I Cor.	5	9–11
	Eph.	5	7

compare

Who in heaven *c* to Lord?	Ps.	89	6
Not to be *c* to wisdom	Prov.	3	15
	Prov.	8	11
What likeness will ye *c* unto him?	Is.	40	18
To whom will ye *c* me	Is.	46	5

c to find gold	Lam.	4	2
Not worthy to be *c* with the glory	Rom.	8	18
c spiritual things with spiritual	I Cor.	2	13

comparison
I done in *c* of you?	Judg.	8	2
In your eyes in *c* of it	Hag.	2	3
With what *c* shall we	Mark	4	30

compass *(spread endeavours all over)*
Waves of death *c* me	II Sam.	22	5
Fetched a *c*	II Ki.	3	9
	Acts	28	13
Sorrows of death *c* me	Ps.	18	4
	Ps.	116	3
c thine altar	Ps.	26	6
c with songs of deliverance	Ps.	32	7
c on face of the deep	Prov.	8	27
c yourselves with sparks	Is.	50	11
c sea and land	Mat.	23	15
Jerusalem *c* with armies	Luke	21	20
Himself *c* with infirmity	Heb.	5	2
c about with cloud of witness	Heb.	12	1

compassion *sympathy, mercy*
For the lowly	Ex.	2	23–25
On repentant Israel	Deut.	13	17
	Deut.	30	3
A good example	II Chr.	28	15
For the afflicted	Job	6	14
Of God	Ps.	78	38
Conqueror has none	II Chr.	36	17
Manifested in mercy	Hosea	11	4
Of Christ	Mat.	9	36
A father's appeal to	Mark	9	17–27
On Widow of Nain	Luke	7	13
Of the good Samaritan commended by God	Luke	10	33–37
For the penitent	Luke	15	17–20

complicity *acting as an accomplice*
In evil, denounced	Ps.	50	18
Partner of a thief	Prov.	29	24
One who aids evil	John	2	10

composure *calmness, settled state*
Stephen's holy	Acts	7	59, 60
Peter's undisturbed	Acts	12	3–6
Jesus	John	19	11
Three Hebrews	Dan.	3	17–18
Lack of	I Ki.	19	3–14

Conaniah *see Cononiah*

concealment *hiding*
Of evil deeds a great mistake	Gen.	37	26
	Job	27	11
	Ps.	40	10
	Prov.	28	13
Example of Achan	Josh.	7	20, 21
Commended	Prov.	11	13
	Prov.	12	23
	Prov.	25	2

conceit *personal vanity*
Warnings against	Prov.	3	7
	Rom.	12	16
	Is.	5	21
Folly of	Prov.	6	12–15
	Prov.	12	15
	Prov.	26	5
Of wealth	Prov.	18	11
	Prov.	28	11
Should be avoided by Christians	Rom.	12	16
	I Cor.	8	2

conception *beginning*
By Sarah	Gen.	21	1–3
Of Christ foretold	Is.	7	14
By Mary	Mat.	1	18–21
By Elisabeth	Luke	1	36

concerning
Things *c* himself	Luke	24	27
As *c* the flesh Christ came	Rom.	9	5
Simple *c* evil	Rom.	16	19
c giving and receiving	Phil.	4	15
Will of God *c* you	I Thes.	5	18
c fiery trial	I Pet.	4	12

concubine *slave girl*
Called wives	Gen.	37	2
	Judg.	21	3–5
May be dismissed	Gen.	21	9–14

Abraham's	Gen.	16	1–3
Jacob's	Gen.	30	4
Nahor's	Gen.	22	24
Eliphaz's	Gen.	36	12
Caleb's	I Chr.	2	46–48
Gideon's	Judg.	8	30, 31
Saul's	II Sam.	3	7
David's	II Sam.	5	13
Solomon's	I Ki.	11	3
Rehoboam's	II Chr.	11	21
Abijah's	II Chr.	13	21
Belshazzar's	Dan.	5	2, 3
Laws concerning	Ex.	21	7–11
	Deut.	21	10–17
Jealousy of	Gen.	21	10–14
Children not heirs	Gen.	15	4
Children made heirs	Gen.	30	10–13

concupiscence *sinful desire*
Must be brought under control	Rom.	7	8
	Col.	3	5
	I Thes.	4	5
Results in sin	James	1	14
Also see lasciviousness			

condemnation *declaring guilt, censure*
Universal sin	Ps.	14	3
	Rom.	3	12, 19
	Rom.	5	12
	Rom.	6	23
For unbelief	Mat.	7	1–5
	Mat.	11	20
	Mat.	23	14
	Luke	23	40
	John	3	18, 19
	Rev.	20	15
Of the innocent	John	19	6
Freed from, by Christ	Rom.	8	1, 33
According to works	II Cor.	11	15
Judgment of oneself	I Tim.	3	6
Of false teachers	II Pet.	2	1

condescend *to humble oneself*
Of God to Moses	Ex.	4	2–17
	Ex.	33	18–23
Of God to sinners	Is.	1	18–20
	Ps.	113	5–6
Christ	Phil.	2	5–10
Of God to Christians	I John	4	10

condolence *expression of sympathy*
For grief	Job	5	19
Complete assurance	Ps.	23	1–6
When in deep despair	Ps.	27	5
Divine aid	Is.	61	3
Doubters	John	14	1–4
Hope for the future	I Thes.	4	13–18
Instances of:			
David to Hanun	II Sam.	10	2
King of Babylon to Hezekiah	II Ki.	20	12, 13
Friends of Job	Job	2	11
Jesus to Mary	John	11	23–35
A Christian duty	James	1	27

coney *small animal, rock badger*
Unclean to eat	Lev.	11	5
Live in the hills	Ps.	104	18
Symbol of weakness	Prov.	30	26

confectionaries *perfumers*
Women's profession	Ex.	30	35
	I Sam.	8	13

confession of Christ
As test of being saints	I John	2	23
Consequences of not	Mat.	10	33
Fear of man prevents	John	7	13
	John	12	42, 43
Influences of the Holy Spirit necessary to	I Cor.	12	3
	I John	4	2
Connected with faith	Rom.	10	9
Necessary to salvation	Rom.	10	9–10
Persecution should not prevent us from	Mark	8	35
	II Tim.	2	12
False confession	Mat.	7	21–23
Made before men	Mat.	10	32
By John the Baptist	John	1	15
Of the blind man	John	9	25–33
Chief rulers did not	John	12	42
For salvation	Rom.	10	9
All in the future	Phil.		
Used to discern false prophets	I John	4	2–3
Necessary for the indwelling	I John	4	15

confession of sin

By Moses for his people	Ex.	32	31–33
	Num.	12	11
	Num.	21	7
By a sin offering	Lev.	5	5
By Joshua	Josh.	7	19, 20
In adversity	Judg.	10	13–16
By Samuel for his people	I Sam.	7	1–17
Ezra's prayer	Ezra	9	6
	Ezra	10	11
Nehemiah, for the children of Israel	Neh.	1	6
Of Daniel	Dan.	9	4
By Judas	Mat.	27	3, 4
By Simon Peter	Luke	5	8
Should be with humility	Luke	18	10–13
To one another	James	5	16
Brings forgiveness	I John	1	9
	Ps.	32	5
Exhortation to	Josh.	7	19
	Jer.	3	13
	James	5	16
God regards	Job	33	27, 28
	Dan.	9	20
God requires	Lev.	5	5
	Hosea	5	15
Illustrated	Luke	15	21
	Luke	18	13
Promises to	Lev.	26	40–42
	Prov.	28	13
Should be full and unreserved	Ps.	32	5
	Ps.	51	3
	Ps.	106	6

Should be accompanied with

Forsaking sin	Prov.	28	13
Godly sorrow	Ps.	38	18
	Lam.	1	20
Prayer for forgiveness	II Sam.	24	10
	Ps.	25	11
	Ps.	51	1
	Jer.	14	7–9, 20
Restitution	Num.	5	6–7
Self-abasement	Is.	64	5–6
	Jer.	3	25
Submission to punishment	Lev.	26	41
	Neh.	9	33
	Ezra	9	13

confidence *assurance, state of feeling sure*

Strong	Num.	14	6–9
Disappointed	I Sam.	4	5–11
Warrant	II Sam.	22	1–7
Of the faithful	Ps.	23	1–6
Joyful	Ps.	31	14–21
Triumphant	Hab.	3	17–19
For the future	II Cor.	1	8–10

confidence, betrayed

Joshua by the Gibeonites	Josh.	9	3–15
Eglon by Ehud	Judg.	3	15–23
Ahimelech by David	I Sam.	21	1–9
Abner by Joab	II Sam.	3	27
Amasa by Joab	II Sam.	20	9, 10
Worshippers of Baal by Jehu	II Ki.	10	18–28
In other god's	Deut.	29	18–19
Of Benhadad	I Ki.	20	11
In foreign nations	II Ki.	18	21
In wealth	Ps.	49	6–7
In their own wisdom	Is.	5	21
In lying words	Jer.	7	8
In himself	Mark	14	29

confirmation *strengthening*

An old ceremony	Ruth	4	7
Work of apostles	Acts	14	22
Of the gospel	Phil.	1	7
The work of God	I Pet.	5	10
To strengthen	Is.	35	3
	I Chr.	14	2
Give assurance	I Ki.	1	14
	II Cor.	2	8
A kingdom	II Ki.	15	19
A letter	Esth.	9	29–31
A convenant	Dan.	9	27

conformity *in agreement, harmony*

With God	Rom.	8	29
Condemned	Rom.	12	2

confusion *state of great disorder*

Of tongues	Gen.	11	4–9

Because of trepasses	Dan.	9	7
City filled with	Acts	19	29
	Acts	21	30–34
God not the author of	I Cor.	14	33
Causes of	James	3	16

congregation *meeting of, assembly of persons*

All Israel	Ex.	12	6–11
	I Ki.	8	65
A meeting place	Ex.	27	21
Sin offering for	Lev.	4	13, 14
	Lev.	16	17–33
Want to stone offenders	Lev.	24	14
	Num.	15	35
	Deut.	23	1–4
Of the dead	Prov.	21	16
Of the righteous	Ps.	1	5
	Ps.	22	22
Of Jews and Gentiles at Antioch	Acts	13	42–49
Also see assembly			

connivance *to cooperate secretly*

A winking eye	Prov.	10	10
Against Eli	I Sam.	3	11
Korah's	Num.	16	1–3
Pilate's	Mat.	27	17–26

Coniah *see Jehoiachin*

Cononiah, Conaniah *Jehovah hath established*

A Levite, supervisor of Hezekiah	II Chr.	31	12, 13
A Levite of Josiah	II Chr.	35	9

conscience *sense of right and wrong*

Accuses of sin	II Sam.	24	10
	Acts	2	37
Blood of Christ alone can purify	Heb.	9	14
	Heb.	10	2–10, 22
Keep the faith in purity of	I Tim.	3	9
Ministers should commend themselves to that of their people	II Cor.	4	2
	II Cor.	5	11
Of others, not to be offended	Rom.	14	21
Of saints, pure and good	Heb.	13	18
	I Pet.	3	16, 21
Testimony of, a source of joy	I John	3	21
We should have the approval of	Job	27	6
	Rom.	14	22
Punishment of sinners	Gen.	3	10
	Gen.	4	13
	Gen.	42	21
	Mat.	27	3
	Luke	9	7
	John	8	9
Called the candle of the Lord	Prov.	20	27
A result of faith	Acts	24	16
	Rom.	13	5
	II Cor.	1	12
	I Tim.	1	5, 19
	I Pet.	2	19
Evil, bears witness	Rom.	2	15, 16
	Rom.	9	1
	II Cor.	1	12
Of the weak cannot resist sin	I Cor.	8	7–13
	I Cor.	10	28
May be seared	I Tim.	4	2
May be defiled	Tit.	1	15

consecration *dedication for holy purpose*

Of firstborn	Ex.	13	2, 12
	Deut.	15	19
Of Israel	Ex.	19	6
Ceremony of	Ex.	29	1–46
For personal	Ex.	32	29
	Lev.	8	1–13
	Num.	8	5, 6
Of Samuel	I Sam.	1	11
Of the body	Rom.	6	13
	Rom.	12	1
	II Cor.	8	5
Of Christ	Heb.	10	20
From the world	II Cor.	6	14–18

conservatism *opposition to change*

A parable	Luke	5	36, 38
Of food	Mat.	16	9–10
Of money	Mat.	25	14–30
Of oil	II Ki.	4	1–7

consider

Wise to **c** latter end	Deut.	32	29
When I **c** thy heavens	Ps.	8	3
Blessed is he that **c** the poor	Ps.	41	1

c mine affliction	Ps.	119	153
Go to ant, *c* her ways	Prov.	6	6
c diligently what is before thee	Prov.	23	1
They *c* not that they do evil	Eccl.	5	1
My people doth not *c*	Is.	1	3
In latter days ye shall *c*	Jer.	23	20
	Jer.	30	24
It may be they will *c*	Ezek.	12	3
C your ways	Hag.	1	5–7
C the lilies	Mat.	6	28
	Luke	12	27
C not the beam	Mat.	7	3
C the ravens	Luke	12	24
Nor *c* it is expedient	John	11	50
C thyself, lest thou also be tempted	Gal.	6	1
C the Apostle and High Priest	Heb.	3	1
C him that endured	Heb.	12	3
C the end of their conversation	Heb.	13	7

consolation *comfort*

By casting one's burden on the Lord	Deut.	33	27
	Ps.	55	22
	Mat.	11	28
	Luke	4	18
	II Cor.	1	1–11
By keeping the commandments and gaining the love of Christ	Luke	2	25
	John	14	15
	Rom.	15	4, 5
God-given	II Cor.	1	3–5
	II Cor.	5	1
	II Cor.	7	6, 7
	Heb.	4	9
	James	4	7
For enduring temptation	James	1	12
	Rev.	2	10
For the dying	Rev.	14	13

conspiracy *plot*

Joseph's brothers against him	Gen.	37	18
Against Moses	Num.	16	1–3
Against Joash	II Ki.	12	20
Of the prophets	Ezek.	22	25
Against Jesus	Mat.	26	3–5
	Mark	3	6
	Mark	14	1
	Luke	22	2
	John	11	55–57
	John	13	18
Against Stephen	Acts	6	8–15
Against Paul	Acts	23	12–14

constancy *faithfulness*

Of Ruth to Naomi	Ruth	1	16
Of Jonathan to David	I Sam.	20	17
Of women to Jesus	Mat.	27	55
Of Priscilla and Aquila	Rom.	16	3, 4

constellation *a group of stars*

Shall not give light	Is.	13	10
Orion	Job	9	9

constraint *restriction*

The spirit in me	Job	32	18
Disciples by Jesus	Mat.	14	22
	Mark	6	45
Jesus by men at Emmaus	Luke	24	29
The love of Christ causes	II Cor.	5	14
Converts made not by	I Pet.	5	2

consultation *a meeting to discuss*

With a witch or fortuneteller	I Sam.	28	7
Chief priests hold	Mat.	26	3, 4
	Mark	15	1
To put Lazarus to death	John	12	10
With wisemen	Mat.	2	7
	I Ki.	12	6

consuming *perishing*

The burning bush is not consumed	Ex.	3	2
God like a, fire	Deut.	4	24
	Deut.	9	3
	Heb.	12	29
A, fire out of rock	Judg.	6	21
The fire, burnt offering	I Ki.	18	38
	II Chr.	7	1

consumption *a disease*

As a curse for disobedience	Lev.	26	16
	Deut.	28	22
God's judgment and promise	Is.	10	22
	Is.	28	22

contempt *disrespect*

An enemy's	I Sam.	17	42
Saul's daughter, Michal, for David	II Sam.	6	16
Nehemiah's plea disregarded	Neh.	2	17–20
Upon princes	Job	12	21
	Ps.	107	40
Against the righteous	Ps.	31	18
For those at ease, and the proud	Ps.	123	3, 4
Comes with the wicked	Prov.	18	3
Of parents	Prov.	23	22
Is promised for some at the end of time	Dan.	12	2
Shown in the parable of the wedding feast	Mat.	22	2–6
Shown for Jesus by the crowd	Mat.	26	67, 68
For other men, shown by a Pharisee	Luke	18	11, 12
For Christ by Moses' disciples	John	9	28, 29
For Paul's speech	II Cor.	10	10
Of the poor	James	2	1–3

contend

I will *c* with him that *c*	Is.	49	25
Who will *c* with me?	Is.	50	8
How canst thou *c* with horses?	Jer.	12	5
Earnestly *c* for the faith	Jude		3

contention *dispute, strife*

Between the herdsmen of Abram and Lot	Gen.	13	8
Caused by pride	Prov.	13	10
Should be avoided	Prov.	17	14
By fool's lips	Prov.	18	6
Without cause	Prov.	23	29
Caused by meddling	Prov.	26	17
Is annoying	Prov.	27	15
Between Paul and Barnabas	Acts	15	39
In the church at Corinth	I Cor.	1	11
Can be destructive	Gal.	5	15
Not sincere	Phil.	1	16
Is unprofitable and vain	Tit.	3	9

contentment *satisfaction*

With your wages	Luke	3	14
With your work	I Cor.	7	20
With what you have	Phil.	4	11
	Heb.	13	5
Characteristic of a good man	Prov.	14	14
	Prov.	16	18
With divine presence	Heb.	13	5
With having food and clothing	I Tim.	6	8

Instances of:

Esau refuses Jacob's present	Gen.	33	9
Barzillai refuses to go to Jerusalem	II Sam.	19	33–37
The Shunammite refuses Elisha's request	II Ki.	4	13

continual

Imagination evil *c*	Gen.	6	5
Praise *c* in my mouth	Ps.	34	1
	Ps.	71	6
Bind them *c* on thine heart	Prov.	6	21
My name is blasphemed	Is.	52	5
Lest by her *c* coming	Luke	18	5
Were *c* in the temple	Luke	24	53
Give ourselves *c* to prayer	Acts	6	4
Abideth a priest *c*	Heb.	7	3

continue

Thy lovingkindness	Ps.	36	10
Name shall *c* as long as the sun	Ps.	72	17
He *c* all night in prayer	Luke	6	12
If ye *c* in my word	John	8	31
C ye in my love	John	15	9
C with one accord	Acts	1	14
	Acts	2	46
Shall we *c* in sin?	Rom.	6	1
C in prayer	Rom.	12	12
	Col.	4	2
That *c* not in all things	Gal.	3	10
If ye *c* in faith	Col.	1	23
	I Tim.	2	15
Here have we no *c* city	Heb.	13	14
C there a year, and buy	James	4	13
All things *c* as they were	II Pet.	3	4
No doubt have *c* with us	I John	2	19

contract, *see* **covenant**

contrary

Wind was *c*	Mat.	15	24
C to the law	Acts	18	13
C to name of Jesus	Acts	26	9
C the one to the other	Gal.	5	17
Handwriting *c* to us	Col.	2	14
C to all men	I Thes.	2	15
C to sound doctrine	I Tim.	1	10

contribution *gift to aid another*

"Is more blessed to give than to receive"	Acts	20	35
For the poor	Rom.	15	26
For the poor saints at Jerusalem	II Cor.	8	1, 2

contrition *sorrow for sin*

Is of the heart	Ps.	34	18
	Ps.	51	17
Leads to a high place in eternity	Is.	57	15
Will bring the return to God	Mal.	3	7
By Peter, for denying Christ	Mat.	26	75

controversy *a dispute*

Is sometimes fatal	Gen.	4	1–8
Can be settled by going to God	Deut.	17	8
To be settled by the priests	Deut.	21	5
Between God and Israel	Mic.	6	2
Of Jesus and the Jews	John	8	33–59

conversation *talking together*

Of the Lord with Moses	Ex.	33	9
On the walk to Emmaus	Luke	24	13–29
Of Jesus with Nicodemus	John	3	1–21
Of Jesus with the woman of Samaria	John	4	7–26
Of Peter and Cornelius	Acts	10	27
Of King Agrippa and Paul	Acts	26	27–31
Of Agrippa and Festus	Acts	26	32
Of the old man, corrupt	Eph.	4	22
As becomes the gospel of Christ	Phil.	1	27
Should be without covetousness	Heb.	13	5
Can show wisdom	James	3	13
Should be holy	I Pet.	1	15

converts *those who are changed*

The law of the Lord regarding	Ps.	19	7
Transgressors may become	Ps.	51	13
The obstinate may be	Is.	6	10
Jesus promises to heal all	Mat.	13	15
	Mark	4	12
	John	12	40
Only enter into the kingdom of heaven	Mat.	18	3
Strengthen thy brethren	Luke	22	32

Instances of:

Ruth	Ruth	1	16
Nebuchadnezzar	Dan.	4	1–37
The mariners with Jonah	Jonah	1	5, 6, 9
Ninevites	Jonah	3	1–9
Gadarenes	Luke	8	35–39
Thief on the cross	Luke	23	39–43
Samaritans	John	4	28–42
Three thousand at Pentecost	Acts	2	41
The eunuch	Acts	8	35–38
Saul of Tarsus	Acts	9	3–18
Cornelius	Acts	10	1–48
Sergius Paulus	Acts	13	7, 12
	Acts	26	12–23
Jews and Greeks at Antioch	Acts	13	43
Lydia	Acts	16	14, 15
Jailer	Acts	16	27–34
Greeks	Acts	17	4, 12

conviction *opinion*

Leads to spiritual belief	John	8	9
	John	8	46
	John	16	8
Must not be delayed	Heb.	3	7, 8
Work of conscience	Rom.	2	15
Work of the Law	James	2	9

Examples of:

Adam	Gen.	3	8–10
Joseph's brethren	Gen.	42	21–22
Pharaoh	Ex.	9	27
Israel	Num.	21	7
David	I Chr.	21	30
Belshazzar	Dan.	5	6
Jonah	Jonah	2	1–10
Judas	Mat.	27	3–5
Paul	Acts	9	4–18
Philippian jailor	Acts	16	30

convocation *calling together*

Shall be held on the first and seventh days	Ex.	12	16
On the sabbath	Lev.	23	2, 4
For the passover	Lev.	23	4, 5
For the feast of the pentecost	Lev.	23	16
On the day of atonement	Lev.	23	28
On the first day of the feast of the tabernacles	Lev.	23	34, 35
As holy	Num.	29	7
At Sheclem	Deut.	27	12–13
For Jushua	Josh.	23	2
For instruction	Neh.	13	1–14

cooking *the preparation of food*

Of Sarah	Gen.	18	6
Of Rebekah	Gen.	27	3–10
Forbidden on the sabbath	Ex.	35	3
Frying with oil	Lev.	2	7
Done by Gideon	Judg.	6	18–20
To be done by the daughters	I Sam.	8	13
For Saul and Samuel	I Sam.	9	22–24
With spice, on a wood fire	Ezek.	24	10
By the priests	Ezek.	46	20

co-operation *acting together*

In building	Gen.	11	2–3
In helping fallen	Eccl.	4	10
In prayer	Mat.	18	19
To sustain Moses in his weakness	Ex.	17	12
In labour brings success	Neh.	4	16, 17
In prayer, is asked by Jesus	Mat.	18	19

Coos *island near Greece*

Paul stops here	Acts	21	1

copper *see brass*

coppersmith *one who works with brass*

Alexander, a, does Paul evil	II Tim.	4	14

cor *a measure for liquids and solids*

Equal to one homer	Ezek.	45	14

coral *a hard substance made up of shells of marine animals*

Value compared to wisdom	Job	28	18
Sold in Syria as a valuable sea stone	Ezek.	27	16

corban *a gift*

In fulfillment of a vow	Mark	7	11

cord

Let spies down by a *c*	Josh.	2	15
Let us cast away their *c*	Ps.	2	3
Holden with the *c* of sins	Prov.	5	22
A threefold *c*	Eccl.	4	12
Silver *c* loosed	Eccl.	12	6
Draw iniquity with *c*	Is.	5	18
Lengthen thy *c*	Is.	54	2
C of a man	Hosea	11	4
Scourge of small *c*	John	2	15

cordiality *friendly feeling*

Lacking in Simon	Luke	7	44–46
Of Abraham	Gen.	18	1–8
Of lot	Gen.	19	2–3
Barzillai	II Sam.	17	27–28
Lacking in Nabal	I Sam.	25	9–15

Core *see Korah*

corlander *cutting furrow*

The seed of, compared to	Ex.	16	31
	Num.	11	7

Corinth *a city of Greece*

Where an early church is built	Acts	18	1–4
	I Cor.	1	2
Visited by Apollos	Acts	19	1
Home of Erastus	II Tim.	4	20

cormorant

A bird forbidden as food	Deut.	14	17
	Is.	34	11

corn *applied to all grains*

Joseph gathers an abundance	Gen.	41	42–49
Offering	Lev.	2	14, 15
Burned	Judg.	15	5
Grown in the valleys	Ps.	65	13
Sign of prosperity	Deut.	7	13
Mosaic law concerning	Deut.	23	25
Parched	Ruth	2	14
	I Sam.	17	17
Blasted	II Ki.	19	26

Cornelius *of a horn*

A Roman centurion convert	Acts	10	48

cornerstone *main stone of a building*

"Stone which builders refused"	Ps.	118	22
	Mat.	21	42–44
	Acts	4	11
Daughters of Israel compared to	Ps.	144	12
Christ, the sure foundation	Is.	28	16
	Eph.	2	20

cornet *musical instrument*

Used in praise	II Sam.	6	5
Calls people to worship	I Chr.	15	28
	Dan.	3	5, 7, 10
Played by David	Ps.	98	
Call to repentance	Hosea	5	8
Used in war	Josh.	6	16

corpse *dead body*

Isaiah's prophecy against Assyria	II Ki.	19	35
Ruin of Nineveh	Nah.	3	3
Of John the Baptist	Mark	6	29
Nazarites not to touch	Num.	6	6

correction *punishment, chastisement*

For breaking God's commandments	Ps.	89	30–32
Withhold not the rod of	Prov.	10	13
	Prov.	13	24
	Prov.	22	15
	Prov.	23	13
Children smitten in vain	Jer.	2	30
Scripture is given for	II Tim.	3	16
Brings happiness	Job	5	17
Wickedness shall	Jer.	2	19

corruption *decay, depravity, impurity*

Depravity of man	Gen.	6	5
	Ps.	14	1–3
Concerning food	Lev.	22	25
By association	I Ki.	11	1–11
Of sin	Is.	38	17
	Gal.	6	8
Apostasy	Jude		10
	II Pet.	2	12

corruption, mount of

Solomon builds idols upon	I Ki.	11	7, 8
Destroyed by Josiah	II Ki.	23	13

corruption of body *deterioration of flesh*

Physical decomposition	Job	17	14
	Job	19	26
Of Lazarus	John	11	39
None in body of Jesus	Acts	13	37
Result of fall	Rom.	8	21
No in heaven	I Cor.	15	50–54

Cosam *a fortuneteller*

Ancestor of Christ	Luke	3	28

cosmetics

Extensively used, including eye shadow	II Ki.	9	30
Unguents and perfumes	Ezek.	23	40
	Ps.	45	8
	S. of S.	3	6
	Is.	3	24
False hair	Is.	3	18
	I Tim.	2	9
	I Pet.	3	3

cotes *see* sheepcotes

coulter *a knife*

Weapon used by Israelites	I Sam.	13	20, 21

council *assembly*

A court in Jerusalem	Mat.	5	22
	Mat.	10	17
Jesus tried before	Mat.	26	57–59
	Mark	15	1–15
	Luke	22	66–71
Unable to exercise death penalty	John	18	31
Apostles tried before	Acts	4	5–30
Stephen charged before	Acts	6	12–15
Paul pleads before	Acts	23	1–5

counsel *advice*

Given by Moses to Israelites	Ex.	18	19
Consequences of evil	Num.	31	16
God's counsel not sought	Josh.	9	14
Hushais	II Sam.	17	14
Rejected by Rehoboam	I Ki.	12	8–16
Of the ungodly	Ps.	1	1
Advantage of	Ps.	73	24
	Prov.	11	14
To a wise man	Prov.	9	9
Fool rejects	Prov.	12	15
Not heeded	Prov.	1	25, 26
Should be listened to	Prov.	12	15
Ashamed of his own	Hosea	10	6
Jesus' to the rich young ruler	Mat.	19	22
Pharisees with Herodians	Mark	3	6

Asked of God:

By Israel	Judg.	20	18
By Saul	I Sam.	14	37
By David	I Sam.	23	2
	Ps.	73	24

counsellor *adviser*

Many are desirable	Prov.	11	14
A title of Christ	Is.	9	6
God, the supreme counsellor	Rom.	11	34

Instances of:

Jonathan, David's uncle	I Chr.	27	32
Ahaziah's mother	II Chr.	22	3
Joseph of Arimathea	Luke	23	50
Ahithophel	I Chr.	27	33

count

C for righteousness	Gen.	15	6
	Ps.	106	31
	Rom.	4	3
	Gal.	3	6
C as sheep for the slaughter	Ps.	44	22
Field be *c* for a forest	Is.	32	15
C him as a prophet	Mat.	14	5
	Mark	11	32
C worthy	Luke	21	36
	Acts	5	41
	I Tim.	5	17
Neither *c* I my life dear	Acts	20	24
I *c* loss for Christ	Phil.	3	8
C not myself to have apprehended	Phil.	3	13
C blood an unholy thing	Heb.	10	29
C it all joy	James	1	2
As some men *c* slackness	II Pet.	3	9

countenace *facial expression*

Can be interpreted	Gen.	31	2, 5
Moses' transfigured	Ex.	34	29–35
	II Cor.	3	7
"Lord lift up His countenance upon thee"	Num.	6	26
Should not be used for deception	Mat.	6	16
Fierce	Deut.	28	50

Affected by:

Guilt	Gen.	4	5
	Is.	3	9
Sorrow	I Sam.	1	18
	Neh.	2	2, 3
Laughter	Job	29	24
Wickedness	Ps.	10	4
God's grace	Ps.	21	6
	Ps.	44	3
	Acts	2	28
A merry heart	Prov.	15	13
Anger	Prov.	25	23
Fear	Ezek.	27	35
	Dan.	5	6
Food	Dan.	1	15
Prayer	Luke	9	29

country

A custom of	Gen.	29	26
Love for own	Gen.	30	25
Pleasure in good news of a far country	Prov.	25	25
Prophet not accepted in own	Mat.	13	57
	Luke	4	24
Desire for a better country	Heb.	11	14–16

counterfeit *False imitation*

Christs	Mat.	24	4, 5, 24
Preachers	II Cor.	11	14, 15
Christians	Gal.	2	3, 4
Apostles	II Cor.	11	13
Teachers	II Pet.	2	1
Prophets	I John	4	4
Gospels	Gal.	1	6–12
Doctrines	Heb.	13	9
Commandments	Tit.	1	13, 14
Miracle	II Thes.	2	7–12
Science	I Tim.	6	20
Religion	James	1	26
Worship	Mat.	15	8, 9
Prayers	James	4	3

countrymen

Of the same nation	II Cor.	11	22–26
Of the same tribe	I Thes.	2	14

courage *a cardinal virtue*

In one's old age	Josh.	14	10–12
Samson prays for	Judg.	16	28
Through faith	I Sam.	14	6
	I Sam.	17	37, 45
	Dan.	6	10–23
	Heb.	13	6
Moral	Is.	51	7
	Ezek.	2	6
	Mark	13	9–13
Spiritual	Acts	5	29
	Acts	28	15
Exhortations to	Num.	13	20
	Josh.	1	6
	Josh.	10	25
	II Sam.	10	12
	Ps.	31	24

courage—*continued*			
Enjoined upon:			
Joshua	Deut.	31	7, 23
	Josh.	1	6–9
	I Chr.	22	13
Solomon	I Chr.	28	20
Asa	II Chr.	15	1–7
Jehoshaphat to officers	II Chr.	19	11
Israelites	II Chr.	32	7, 8
course *a planned movement*			
Of life	Acts	13	20–24
	Acts	13	25
Of a voyage	Acts	21	7
An order of priests	Luke	1	5
An evil	Jer.	23	10
Of the race of life	II Tim.	4	7
Pattern of nature	James	3	6
courtesy *politeness*			
Encouraged	Col.	4	6
	I Pet.	3	8
Ancient customs	Gen.	18	8
Rules for guests	Prov.	23	1, 2
	I Cor.	10	27
Rising before superiors	Gen.	31	35
Rising before aged	Lev.	19	32
Examples of:			
Julius to Paul	Acts	27	3
Publius to Paul	Acts	28	7
courts			
Held by Moses in the wilderness	Ex.	18	13–20
Sanhedrin:			
Probably derived from the seventy elders	Num.	11	24–30
Composed of chief priests	Mat.	26	57, 59
Mentioned in Christ's time	Luke	22	66
Decisions of, conclusive	Deut.	1	17
In all cities	Deut.	6	18
Evidence of witnesses in	Deut.	17	6
Corruption and bribery in	Amos	5	12
Held in hall of judgment	John	18	28, 33
Generally held in the morning	Acts	5	21
Have authority from God	Rom.	13	1–5
Accused plead own cause	Acts	24	10
courtship *wooing*			
Of Isaac and Rebekah	Gen.	1	67
Of Rachel and Jacob	Gen.	29	9–11
Of Samson	Judg.	14	7
Of Ruth and Boaz	Ruth	3	9–13
Of Esther	Esth.	2	17
courtyard			
Around the tabernacle	Ex.	38	9
Some have wells	II Sam.	17	18
Built of stone and cedar beams	II Ki.	6	36
Within a porch	I Ki.	7	8
Of the temple	II Chr.	4	9
Of Palace	II Ki.	20	4
cousin *kinsman or kinswoman*			
Elisabeth, cousin of Mary	Luke	1	36, 58
covenant, ark of the *see* ark of the covenant			
covenant-breakers *shatterers of a compact*			
Cursed by the Lord	Is.	24	5, 6
The priests	Ezek.	44	7
covenant-keepers *observers of a compact*			
Are treasured	Ex.	19	5, 6
Are rewarded forever	Ps.	103	17–20
covenant, new			
Promised	Jer.	31	31
Christ, the covenant between God and His people	I Cor.	11	25
covenant of salt *purity and perpetuity*			
With Aaron	Num.	18	19
With David	II Chr.	13	5
covenant, the *agreement of God*			
God is faithful to	Deut.	7	9
	I Ki.	8	23
Be mindful of	I Chr.	16	15
Is unchangeable	Ps.	89	34
	Is.	54	10
	Gal.	3	17
Is everlasting	Ps.	111	9
	Is.	55	3
Christ, the substance of	Is.	42	6
	Is.	49	8
Renewed	Jer.	31	31–33
Christ, the messenger of	Mal.	3	1
Fulfilled in Christ	Luke	1	68–79
Confirmed	Gal.	3	17
Ratified by the blood of Christ	Heb.	9	11–14
Made with:			
Moses . . . land	Ex.	6	4
	Ex.	23	31
	Num.	34	3–12
Noah	Gen.	8	16
	Gen.	9	8–17
Abraham	Gen.	17	2–14
	Luke	1	72–75
	Acts	3	25
Abraham . . . land	Gen.	15	18
	Gen.	17	8
Isaac . . . land	Gen.	17	19, 21
	Gen.	26	3, 4
Jacob . . . land	Gen.	28	13, 14
Israel	Ex.	6	4
Phinehas	Num.	25	12, 13
David	II Sam.	23	5
	Ps.	89	3, 4
Between men:			
Abraham-Abimelech	Gen.	21	22–32
Jacob-Laban	Gen.	31	44–54
Jonathan-David	I Sam.	18	3–4
Ahab-Benhadad	I Ki.	20	34
Zedekiah-his subjects	Jer.	34	8
Joshua-people	Josh.	24	1–28
Hezekiah-people	II Chr.	29	10
Josiah-people	II Ki.	23	3
covenants *agreements between two parties*			
Confirmed by oath	Gen.	21	23, 31
God a witness to	Gen.	31	50, 53
Violated by the wicked	Rom.	1	31
Should not be broken	Gal.	3	15
Designed for:			
Selling land	Gen.	23	14–16
Mutual protection	Gen.	31	50–52
Preserving peace	Josh.	9	15, 16
Establishing friendship	I Sam.	18	3
Assistance in war	I Ki.	15	18, 19
Ratified by:			
Giving presents	Gen.	21	27–30
Making a feast	Gen.	26	30
Salting	Num.	18	19
Loosing the shoe	Ruth	4	7–11
Writing and sealing	Neh.	9	38
Giving the hand	Lam.	5	6
	Ezek.	17	18
A monument	Gen.	31	45–53
A sacrifice	Gen.	15	9–17
covering *wrapper*			
A protection for the ark	Gen.	8	13
For the leper	Lev.	13	45
For a hiding place	II Sam.	17	19
Clouds	Job	22	14
Stripped from the poor	Job	24	7
Destruction is without	Job	26	6
covetousness *avarice*			
Described:			
Is idolatry	Ps.	10	3
Is persistent	Prov.	21	26
Is of the heart	Ezek.	33	31
	II Pet.	2	14
False security	Hab.	2	9
Defiles man	Mark	7	22
Causes loss of inheritance	Eph.	5	5
Forbidden:			
By the tenth commandment	Ex.	20	17
	Deut.	5	21
Beware of	Luke	12	15
Paul reminds the Romans	Rom.	13	9
Consequence of:			
Shall perish	Job	20	1–29
The righteous are delivered	Prov.	11	8
Troubles own house	Prov.	15	27
Shall have no peace	Is.	57	17–21
Leads to dishonest gains	Ezek.	22	12, 13
Mortification	Col.	3	5
Leads to destruction	I Tim.	6	9, 10
Examples of:			
Eve, in desiring the forbidden fruit	Gen.	3	6
Laban, in deceiving Jacob in wages	Gen.	31	7, 15, 41
Balaam, in loving wages of unrighteousness	Num.	22	1
	II Pet.	2	15
Achan, in hiding the treasure	Josh.	7	21
Saul, in sparing Agag and the booty	I Sam.	15	8, 9

David, of Bath-sheba	II Sam.	11	2–5
Ahab, in desiring Naboth's vineyard	I Ki.	21	2–16
Judas, in betraying Jesus for silver	Mat.	26	15, 16
Ananias and Sapphira	Acts	5	1–11
Felix, in hoping for a bribe from Paul	Acts	24	26

cow *mature female of any bovine*

Found in Egypt	Gen.	41	2
Offered as sacrifice	Lev.	3	1
Rules for offering	Lev.	22	28
As a beast of burden	I Sam.	6	7
Milk used as food	II Sam.	17	29
Used figuratively in describing the peaceable kingdom	Is.	11	7

cowardice, spiritual *devoutness influenced by timidity*
Caused by:

Fear of man	Prov.	29	25
	Is.	51	12
Fear of the Jews	John	7	13
Fear of the Pharisees	John	12	42
The covenantal curse	Lev.	26	36
Defeat	Josh.	7	5
Wickedness	Prov.	28	1

Examples:

Abraham	Gen.	12	11–19
Isaac	Gen.	26	7–9
Jacob	Gen.	31	31
Spies	Num.	13	28
Israel	I Sam.	17	24
Joseph of Arimathaea	John	19	38
Peter	Mat.	26	69–74

cracknels *brittle biscuits*

A food	I Ki.	14	3

craftiness *cunning*

Perceived by Christ	Luke	20	23
Paul accused of	II Cor.	12	16
Warning against	Eph.	4	14

Instances of:

Satan, in the temptation of Eve	Gen.	3	1–5
Jacob, in purchasing Esau's birthright	Gen.	25	31–33
Gibeonites, in their treaty with Joshua	Josh.	9	3–15

craftsman

Of idols	Deut.	27	15
	Acts	19	24
Destroyed with Babylon	Rev.	18	22
Located in a certain district	Neh.	11	35

creation *causing to exist*

Of heaven and earth	Gen.	1	1
Of light	Gen.	1	3, 4
Of firmament	Gen.	1	6, 7
Of land	Gen.	1	9, 10
Of vegetation	Gen.	1	11, 12
Of sun, moon and stars	Gen.	1	14–18
Of fish and birds	Gen.	1	20–22
Of beasts	Gen.	1	24, 25
Of man	Gen.	1	26–28
Praise for	Ps.	148	1–14
Of wind	Amos	4	13
By God	John	1	1–3
Christ's oneness with God	Eph.	3	9
	Col.	1	16
Involvement of Holy Spirit	Ps.	104	30
	Gen.	1	2
By faith	Heb.	11	3, 223
By his word	Ps.	33	9
Exhibits God's power	Rom.	1	20
Declares His glory	Ps.	19	1

Creator *one who creates, the supreme being*

God, so named	Is.	40	28
	John	1	1–3
To be served	Rom.	1	25
To be remembered	Eccl.	12	1

creature

Living	Gen.	1	21
Looking for redemption	Rom.	8	19–21
New creature in Christ	II Cor.	5	17
Christ, first born	Col.	1	15
Worshipped by apostles	Rom.	1	25

creditor *one to whom money is due*

Laws concerning	Ex.	21	2–5
	Deut.	15	1–18
	Deut.	23	19
Should be treated with fairness	II Ki.	4	1–7
	Rom.	13	8
Selling of others to pay	Is.	50	1
A parable of forgiving	Mat.	18	23–35
	Luke	7	41–43

cremation *incineration of a corpse*

Of Saul and his sons	I Sam.	31	12, 13
Zimri, by his own hand	I Ki.	16	15–19
Judgment on idolators	Num.	16	35
	II Ki.	23	20

Crescens *growing*

A companion of Paul	II Tim.	4	10

Crete *an island in the Mediterranean*

Represented on the day of Pentecost	Acts	2	1, 11
Passed by Paul on his way to Rome	Acts	27	7
Titus sent here	Tit.	1	5
Inhabitants noted for lying	Tit.	1	12

crib *a stall*

Used figuratively	Job	39	9
	Is.	1	3
Christ born in	Luke	2	7

cried

C unto the Lord	Ps.	3	4
Needy when he *c*	Ps.	72	12
Wisdom *c* without	Prov.	1	20
C after knowledge	Prov.	2	3
Jesus *c* with loud voice	Mark	15	34–37

crime *sin, vice, iniquity*

Partial lists of	Ezek.	22	8–30
	Hosea	4	1, 2
	Mat.	15	19
	Rom.	1	24–32
	Rom.	13	9
	Gal.	5	19–21
Must be proven	Acts	25	16

(*See* adultery, arson, murder, etc.)

criminal *a felon*

Confined in prisons	Gen.	39	20–23
	Ezra	7	26
	Acts	16	19–40
Release of Barabbas	Mat.	27	26
Two thieves mentioned	Mark	15	27

(*See* adultery, arson, murder, etc.)

crimson *red*

Used in the temple	II Chr.	2	7
Symbol of iniquity	Is.	1	18
	Jer.	4	30

cripple *one who creeps or limps*

Mephibosheth	II Sam.	4	4
Healed by Christ	Mat.	11	5
Healed by Paul	Acts	14	8–10

crisping pins *pins used in curling*

A means of beautification	Is.	3	22

Crispus *curled*

Chief ruler of synagogue at Corinth	Acts	18	8
Baptized by Paul	I Cor.	1	14

cross *an instrument for execution*

Borne by disciples	Mat.	16	24
	Luke	14	27
Simon compelled to carry	Mat.	27	32
Jesus crucified on	Mark	15	21
	Acts	2	23, 36
Borne by Jesus	John	19	17
Symbolic of redemption	Gal.	5	11
	Col.	2	14
Glorying in the	Gal.	6	14
Shameful death	Phil.	2	8

crow *see* cock, crowing of

crown *garland*

Part of the tabernacle	Ex.	25	25
Worn by priests	Ex.	29	6
Worn by kings	II Sam.	1	10
	II Sam.	12	30
	II Ki.	11	12
	Esth.	6	8
Worn by queens	Esth.	1	11
	Esth.	2	17
Made of gold	Ps.	21	3
	Zech.	6	11
An ornament	Ezek.	23	42
Of thorns	Mat.	27	29
Figurative	I Cor.	9	25
	I Thes.	2	19
	II Tim.	4	8
	James	1	12
Of victory	II Tim.	2	5
Symbolic	Rev.	4	10
	Rev.	9	7
	Rev.	12	3
	Rev.	19	12

crowns of Christians

Of glory	Prov.	4	9
	I Pet.	5	4
Of righteousness	II Tim.	4	8
Of life	James	1	12
Of faith	Rev.	4	10

crucifixion *death on a cross*

The reproach of	Gal.	3	13
	Gal.	5	11
Figurative	Rom.	6	6
	Gal.	2	20
	Gal.	6	14
Demanded by the crowds	Mat.	27	22
Title over Jesus	John	19	19
At Golgotha	John	19	17
Of the world	Gal.	6	14
Christ's predicted	Mat.	20	19

Examples of:

Of disciples foretold	Mat.	23	34
Jesus	Mat.	27	33, 35
Of two malefactors	Mat.	27	38

cruelty *brutality*

Of Sarah to Hagar	Gen.	16	6
	Gen.	21	9–14
Of Simeon and Levi	Gen.	34	25–29
Of Pharaoh	Ex.	1	8–22
	Ex.	5	6–18
Of Abimelech	Judg.	9	5
Of the king of Moab	II Ki.	3	27
Of Jehu	II Ki.	10	1–28
In war	Is.	13	16, 18
Of Jews to Jesus	Mat.	26	67
	Mat.	27	28–31
Of soldiers to Jesus	Luke	22	64
	John	19	3

crumbs

Fall under the table	Mat.	15	27
Begged for	Luke	16	20, 21

1399A cruse *a jar*

For carrying water	I Sam.	26	11
For honey	I Ki.	14	3
For holding oil	I Ki.	17	12
For salt	II Ki.	2	20

cry

I have heard their *c*	Ex.	3	7
C of the city went up to heaven	I Sam.	5	12
He hearth the *c* of the afflicted	Job	34	28
Forgetteth not *c* of humble	Ps.	9	12
His ears open to their *c*	Ps.	34	15
Incline thine ear to my *c*	Ps.	88	2
Righteous *c*, Lord heareth	Ps.	34	17
Food to young ravens which *c*	Ps.	147	9
Doth not wisdom *c*?	Prov.	8	1
Stoppeth his ears at *c* of the poor	Prov.	21	13
C aloud, spare not	Is.	58	1
Shall *c* for sorrow of heart	Is.	65	14
He shall not strive nor *c*	Mat.	12	19
C the more.	Mat.	20	31
	Mark	10	48
	Luke	18	39
Elect, who *c* day and night	Luke	18	7
Jesus *c*, if any man thirst	John	7	37
Some *c* one thing, and some another	Acts	19	32
	Acts	21	34
Whereby we *c*, Abba, Father	Rom.	8	15
Hire of labourers *c*	James	5	4

cubit *a measure of length, about 18 inches*

Measure of distance	Gen.	6	16, 6
	Deut.	3	11, 169
Who can add to his height	Mat.	6	27, 8
	Luke	12	25, 74

cuckoo, cuckow *leanness*

An unclean bird	Lev.	11	16, 102

cucumber *to be hard*

Eaten in Egypt	Num.	11	5, 136
Cultivated	Is.	1	8, 590

cummin *to preserve*

A plant bearing small aromatic seed	Is.	28	25, 27, 609
	Mat.	23	23, 27

cunning *crafty, skillful*

Of the hunter	Gen.	25	27, 23
Of a workman	Ex.	38	23, 89
Musician sought by Saul	I Sam.	16	16, 270
Of a lewd woman	Prov.	7	6–27, 561

cup *a vessel*

Of Pharaoh	Gen.	40	11, 39
Of silver	Gen.	44	2, 43
Used for drinking	II Sam.	12	3, 297
Of gold	I Chr.	28	16, 17, 401
"My cup runneth over"	Ps.	23	5, 503
Of salvation	Ps.	116	13, 544
Of fury	Jer.	25	15, 661
Of the Lord	Mat.	20	22, 23
At the last supper	Mat.	26	27, 31
Of the father	Mat.	26	39, 31
	John	18	11, 112
	I Cor.	10	16, 170

cupbearer *official of kings*

Pharaoh's	Gen.	40	13, 39
Solomon's	I Ki.	10	5, 327
Nehemiah	Neh.	1	11, 447

cures *see miracles, disease and physician*

curiosity seekers *searchers for the unusual*

Eve	Gen.	3	6, 7, 3
Jacob	Gen.	32	29
Israel	Ex.	19	21–24
Manoah	Judg.	13	17–18
People of Bethshemesh	I Sam.	16	19
Prophets	I Pet.	1	12
Peter	Mat.	26	58, 32
At the crucifixion	Mat.	27	47, 49, 34
Herod	Luke	9	9, 69
Zaccheus	Luke	19	1–6, 82
To see Lazarus	John	12	9, 106
The Greeks	John	12	20, 21, 106
The Athenians	Acts	17	21, 136

curse *retribution*

Upon the earth	Gen.	3	17–19
Upon Cain	Gen.	4	11, 12
Upon Canaan	Gen.	9	25
Upon the disobedient	Lev.	26	14–39
	Deut.	28	15–68
Job of his birth	Job	3	1
Baloam	Num.	23	8
From mount Ebal	Deut.	27	15–26
Christ redeems from	Gal.	3	13
Fig tree	Mark	11	21
Those not knowing the Law	John	7	49

cursing *calling evil down upon*

Of parents	Ex.	21	17
	Mat.	15	4
	Mark	7	10
Shimei curses David	II Sam.	16	5–8
Precepts of Jesus concerning	Mat.	5	44
	Luke	6	28
Not against rulers	Ex.	22	28
Not against deaf	Lev.	19	14
Bless instead of	Rom.	12	14
Out of the same mouth	James	3	10

curtain

Tabernacle	Ex.	26–27	9–18
In palace of Ahasuerus	Esth.	1	6
The heavens as	Ps.	104	2

Cush *black*

A country, probably Ethiopia	Gen.	2	13
	Is.	11	11
Son of Ham	Gen.	10	6
Father of Nimrod	Gen.	10	8

Cushi *an Ethopian*

Messenger who informs David of death of Absalom	II Sam.	18	21–32
Father of Shelemiah	Jer.	36	14
Father of Zephaniah	Zeph.	1	1

custom *established practice*

Observance of	Gen.	29	26
Mode of worship	Luke	4	16
Clemency at feast	John	18	39
Attachment to	Acts	6	14
Of sabbath worship	Luke	4	16

custom *taxes*

Matthew, a collector of	Mat.	9	9
Duty paid the king	Rom.	13	6, 7
Priests exempt	Ezra	7	24

cymbal *to curve*

A musical instrument used in worship	II Sam.	6	5
	I Chr.	15	16
	I Chr.	16	5
	Ps.	150	5
Words without charity, as tinkling	I Cor.	13	1

cypress *a hardwood tree*			
Used in the making of idols	Is.	44	14
Cyprus *a large island in the Mediterranean*			
Home of Barnabas	Acts	4	36
The gospel is spread here by the disciples	Acts	11	19
Paul and Barnabas preach here	Acts	13	4
Barnabas and Mark sail here	Acts	15	39
Mnason, a disciple of	Acts	21	16
Cyrene *colony of North Africa*			
Simon of, who carries Jesus' cross	Mat.	27	32
Men from, receive the gospel	Acts	11	20
Niger and Lucius from	Acts	13	1
Cyrenius *see Quirinius*			
Cyrus *the sun*			
King of Persia	II Chr.	36	22
His proclamation	Ezra	1	1–4
Commands to rebuild temple	Ezra	4	3
Contemporary with Daniel	Dan.	6	28
Prophecy concerning	Is.	44	28
	Is.	45	1
	Is.	13	17–22

D

Dagon *fish; grain-god*			
National god of the Philistines	Judg.	16	23
Smitten in the temple at Ashdod	I Sam.	5	3–5
Saul's head fastened in house of	I Chr.	10	10
Dalmatia *see Illyricum*			
Dalphon *dripping*			
A son of Haman slain by the Jews	Esth.	9	7–10
dam *mother*			
Of birds, not to be taken	Deut.	22	6–7
Of cattle	Ex.	22	30
	Lev.	22	27
damages *injury*			
Disability	Ex.	21	18–22
	Ex.	21	28–32
Done by an ox	Deut.	22	8
Negligence	Ex.	21	33–34
Shechem	Gen.	34	12
Zachaeus	Luke	19	8
To animals	Ex.	21	33–36
Liable	Deut.	22	13–14
Rape	Deut.	22	28
Murder	Deut.	21	1–4
Abimelech	Gen.	20	15–16
Damaris *a little woman*			
An Athenian woman converted by Paul	Acts	17	34
Damascus *city of Syria*			
Visited by Abram	Gen.	14	15
Subjugated by David	II Sam.	8	6
	I Chr.	18	6
Elisha's prophecy at	II Ki.	8	7
Clean rivers	II Ki.	5	12
Recaptured by Jeroboam	II Ki.	14	28
Taken by Assyria	II Ki.	16	9
King Ahaz copies an altar here	II Ki.	16	10
Prophecies concerning	Is.	7	8
	Is.	8	4
	Is.	17	1
	Jer.	49	23
	Ezek.	27	18
	Amos	1	3
	Amos	3	12
Paul's journey to	Acts	9	2–16
Paul baptized here	Acts	17	22
Paul revisits	Gal.	1	17
damnation *condemnation*			
For hypocrites	Mat.	23	14
	II Pet.	2	1
For blasphemy against the Holy Ghost	Mark	3	29
For long prayers and unconcern for widows	Mark	12	40
	Luke	20	47
For the unbeliever	Mark	16	16
For the evil-doer	John	5	29
	Rom.	3	8
For those that resist the power of God	Rom.	13	2

For the doubtful and faithless	Rom.	14	23
	I Tim.	5	12
For the unrighteous and untruthful	II Thes.	2	12
damsel *young woman*			
Of Rebekah	Gen.	24	55
Of Dinah	Gen.	34	3
Of a wife	Deut.	22	15
Of Ruth	Ruth	2	5
Of Abishag	I Ki.	1	4
Herodias daughter	Mat.	14	11
Recognizes Peter	Mat.	26	69
Demon possessed	Acts	16	16
Dan *judge*			
Son of Jacob and Bilhah	Gen.	30	6
Blessed by Jacob	Gen.	49	16
Tribe of, numbered	Num.	1	38
	Num.	26	42
Blessed by Moses	Deut.	33	22
Their inheritance	Josh.	19	40
Take the town Laish for their capital	Judg.	18	27, 28
A town at the northern boundary of Israel	Judg.	20	1
	I Chr.	21	2
Set up idolatry here	Judg.	18	30
	I Ki.	12	29
Condemned by prophet	Amos	8	14
Commercial center	Ezek.	27	19
	Judg.	5	17
Destroyed by Ben-hadad	I Ki.	15	20
	II Chr.	16	4
dancing *moving the body in rhythm*			
To praise God	Ex.	15	20
	II Sam.	6	14
	Ps.	30	11
	Ps.	149	3
	Ps.	150	4
Practiced in idol-worship	Ex.	32	19
Celebrating military victories	Judg.	11	34
	I Sam.	18	6
	I Sam.	21	11
	I Sam.	30	16
For pleasure	Eccl.	3	4
	Is.	13	21
	Jer.	31	4, 13
	Mat.	11	17
	Mat.	14	6
	Mark	6	22
Daniel, Belteshazzar *God is my judge*			
Called Chileab	II Sam.	3	2, 3
A son of David	I Chr.	3	1
A priest who accompanies Ezra from Babylon	Ezra	8	1, 2
One of the captives in Babylon	Dan.	1	3, 6
Also called Belteshazzar	Dan.	1	7
Abstinence of	Dan.	1	8
Interprets and understands dreams	Dan.	1	17
	Dan.	2	36–45
	Dan.	4	24–28
Devoutness of	Ezek.	14	14, 20
	Dan.	2	18
The handwriting on the wall	Dan.	5	17–29
Promoted by Darius	Dan.	6	2
Conspired against by the princes	Rom.	6	4
Disregards the idolatrous decree	Dan.	6	10
Cast into the lion's den	Dan.	6	16
His deliverance from the lion's den	Dan.	6	22
His vision of the four beasts	Dan.	7	1–12
His vision of the ram and the goat	Dan.	8	1–14
His vision of 70 weeks	Dan.	9	20–27
Promise given of return from captivity	Dan.	10	10
	Dan.	12	13
Darius *preserver*			
King of Persia	Ezra	4	5
Renews building of the temple	Ezra	6	1–15
Feast of the passover observed under	Ezra	6	16–22
Probably Darius Codomannus, last king of Persia	Neh.	12	22
Captured Babylon	Dan.	5	31
Son of Ahasuerus	Dan.	9	1
Darius I son of Hystaspes			
Allowed Jews to rebuild temple	Zech.	1	1
	Ezra	4	5
	Hab.	1	1
Darius II			
The Persian	Neh.	12	22

darkness *devoid of light*

Divided from light	Gen.	1	1–18
Instances of supernatural	Gen.	15	12
	Ex.	10	21–23
	Ex.	14	20
	Josh.	24	7
	Is.	45	3
Caused by locusts	Ex.	10	14, 15
A great voice out of	Deut.	5	22
Of the mind	Job	37	19
	Prov.	2	13
	Is.	9	2
	John	8	12
	I Cor.	4	5
God's power to overcome	Job	5	14
	Mat.	25	30
	Acts	13	8–11
	II Cor.	4	6
Christ's coming takes away	Prov.	2	13
	Is.	42	7
	John	8	12
	Rom.	13	12
	II Cor.	6	14
Figurative of punishment	Mat.	22	13
	Jude		6
At the time of betrayal and crucifixion	Mat.	27	45
	Luke	22	53
Hate and evil deeds bring	John	3	19
	I John	2	9
Of Hell	Mat.	22	13

dart *arrow or spear*

Absalom slain by a	II Sam.	18	14
God's power likened to	Job	41	26
The temptress' cunning likened to	Prov.	7	23
Used as a symbol of evil	Eph.	6	16

dash

In pieces	Ps.	2	9
	Is.	13	16
	Hosea	13	16
Thy foot	Ps.	91	12
	Mat.	4	6
	Luke	4	11
Little ones against stones	Ps.	137	9

Dathan *son of Eliab*

Son of Eliab, the Reubenite	Num.	16	1
	Deut.	11	6
Cause of dissension among the Israelites	Num.	16	1–25
God's punishment of	Num.	16	26–34
	Ps.	106	17

daughter

Female of particular race or country	Gen.	28	1–3
Feminine offspring	Gen.	31	43
Subject to slavery	Ex.	21	7–11
Forbidden incest	Lev.	20	14
Given in marriage by parents	Judg.	1	12–13
Jephthah's	Judg.	11	35
Property rights	Num.	27	1–11
Pharaoh's	Ruth	4	3
	Heb.	11	24
Guide lines	Prov.	31	29
Their inheritance determined	Num.	27	1–9
As applied to cities and dwellers of a town	Ps.	137	8
	Is.	10	32
	Zech.	2	10

David *beloved*

Son of Jesse, born in Bethlehem	Ruth	4	22
	I Sam.	17	12
Genealogy	I Chr.	2	3–15
Shepherd	I Sam.	16	11
Kills lion and bear	I Sam.	17	34–36
Chosen by God	Ps.	78	70
Anointed by Samuel	I Sam.	16	13
Soothes Saul with a harp	I Sam.	16	23
Armourbearer	I Sam.	16	21–23
Kills Goliath of Gath	I Sam.	17	49–51
Is honoured by Saul	I Sam.	18	5
Saul jealous and tries to kill him	I Sam.	18	8–11
Loved by Jonathan and by Michal	I Sam.	18	1, 28
	I Sam.	19	2, 11
	I Sam.	20	1–42
	I Sam.	23	16
Overcomes the Philistines	I Sam.	18	27
	I Sam.	19	8
Flees to Naioth	I Sam.	19	18
Eats of the shewbread	I Sam.	21	5, 6
	Mat.	12	4

Flees to Gath and feigns madness	I Sam.	21	10, 13
Dwells in the caves of Adullam	I Sam.	22	1
Escapes Saul's pursuit	I Sam.	23	1–29
	Ps.	57	1–11
	Ps.	59	1–17
Twice spares Saul's life	I Sam.	24	4
	I Sam.	26	8, 9
Saves Keilah	I Sam.	23	1–13
Takes parents to Moab	I Sam.	22	
His wrath against Nabal appeased by Abigail	I Sam.	25	23
Dwells at Ziph	I Sam.	26	
Dwells at Ziklag	I Sam.	27	1–12
Dismissed from army by Achish	I Sam.	29	6, 7
Destroys the Amalekites	I Sam.	30	17
Kills messenger who brings news of Saul's death	II Sam.	1	15
Laments the death of Saul and Jonathan	II Sam.	1	17
Dwells at Ziklag for over a year	I Sam.	27	7
Becomes king of Judah	II Sam.	2	4
Has capital at Hebron for seven years	II Sam.	5	5
Forms a league with Abner	II Sam.	3	13
Laments the death of Abner	II Sam.	3	31
Avenges the murder of Ishbosheth	II Sam.	4	12
Becomes king of all Israel	II Sam.	5	3
	I Chr.	11	3
Takes Jerusalem	II Sam.	29	27
Builds a palace	II Sam.	5	11
His victories	II Sam.	5–10	
	II Sam.	12	29
	II Sam.	21	15
	I Chr.	18–20	
	Ps.	60	1–12
Brings the ark to Zion	II Sam.	6	1–23
	I Chr.	13	1–14
	I Chr.	15	1–29
Reproves Michal for despising his religious joy	II Sam.	6	21
Desires to build God a house and is forbidden by Nathan	II Sam.	7	2–5
	I Chr.	17	4
God's promises to him	II Sam.	7	10–12
	I Chr.	17	16
Fulfilled	Acts	13	22–23
His prayer and thanksgiving	II Sam.	7	18–23
	I Chr.	17	16–20
His kindness to Mephibosheth	II Sam.	9	6–13
His sin concerning Bath-sheba and Uriah	II Sam.	11	2–27
His repentance at Nathan's parable	II Sam.	12	1–31
Troubles in his family	II Sam.	13	1–39
	II Sam.	14	1–33
Absalom's conspiracy	II Sam.	15	1–31
Cursed by Shimei	II Sam.	16	5
Barzillai's kindness to	II Sam.	17	27–29
His grief at Absalom's death	II Sam.	18	33
	II Sam.	19	1
Returns to Jerusalem	II Sam.	19	15
Pardons Shimei	II Sam.	19	16
Sheba's conspiracy against	II Sam.	20	1–26
Renders justice to the Gibeonites	II Sam.	21	1–22
His psalms of thanksgiving	II Sam.	22	1–51
	I Chr.	16	7
	Ps.	18	1–50
	Ps.	103	1–22
	Ps.	105	1–45
His mighty men	II Sam.	23	8–11
	I Chr.	11	10
His offense in numbering the people	II Sam.	24	1–25
	I Chr.	21	1–30
Abishag to give him heat	I Ki.	1	2–3
Appoints Solomon his successor	I Ki.	1	30
	Ps.	72	1–20
His charge to Solomon	I Ki.	2	1–46
	I Chr.	22	6
	I Chr.	28	9–21
His death	I Ki.	2	46
	I Chr.	29	28
Regulates the service of the tabernacle	I Chr.	23–26	
Sons of	I Chr.	3	1–9
The forefather of Christ	Mat.	9	27
Jesus called son of	Mat.	9	27
	Mat.	12	23
Tomb of, in Jerusalem	Acts	2	29
Chronicles written by Samuel, Nathan, and God	I Chr.	29	29–30
Wrote at least seventy-three of the psalms.			

David, city of *see* city of David

day *a period of time*

Twelve hours	John	11	9
Creative period	Gen.	1	5–8
Six days for work	Mark	15	42
Lord's day	Rev.	1	10
As a thousand years	II Pet.	3	8
General word for time	I Sam.	3	2
Sabbath day's journey	Acts	1	12
Twenty-four hours	Luke	13	14
Eschatological, day of the Lord	Joel	1	15
Even unto even	Lev.	23	32
Choose a God this	Josh.	24	15
Of four parts	Neh.	9	3
Of joy and gladness	Esth.	8	17
Work, for the night is coming	John	9	4.
Serve God constantly	Acts	26	7

day of atonement

Commanded by God	Ex.	30	20
Only entry of high priest into the holy of holies	Lev.	16	2, 3
	Heb.	9	7
A day of humiliation and cleansing	Lev.	16	29, 31
	Lev.	23	27
Tenth day of seventh month	Lev.	23	26, 27
A solemn day of fasting and prayer	Lev.	23	26–32
Year of jubilee commenced on	Lev.	25	9
Offerings to be made on	Lev.	16	3, 5–15
Punishment for not observing	Lev.	23	29–30
Called "the fast"	Acts	27	9
Typical	Heb.	9	8, 24

Atonement made on, for The:

High priest	Lev.	16	11
	Heb.	9	7
Holy place	Ex.	30	10
	Lev.	16	15–16
Whole congregation	Lev.	16	17, 24
	Lev.	23	28
	Heb.	9	7

day of judgment *see* judgment, the last

day star *see* Lucifer

deacon *appointed servant of the church*

Also signifies servant or minister	Mat.	23	11
	Mark	10	43
Ordained by the apostles	Acts	6	1–6
Qualification of	Acts	6	3
	I Tim.	3	8

deaconess *woman appointed to serve the church*

To help poor and sick of parish	Rom.	16	1

dead *no longer living, without life*
Figurative use for:

Unregenerate	Eph.	2	1
Pleasure lovers	I Tim.	5	6
Decadent church	Rev.	3	1
Cuttings for the *d*	Lev.	19	28
As ye have dealt with *d*	Ruth	1	8
D dog	I Sam.	24	14
	II Sam.	9	8
	II Sam.	16	9
Forgotten as a *d* man	Ps.	31	12
D praise not the Lord	Ps.	115	17
Living dog better than *d* lion	Eccl.	9	4
D know not any thing	Eccl.	5	
Thy *d* men shall live	Is.	26	19
Weep not for the *d*	Jer.	22	10
Let the *d* bury their *d*	Mat.	8	22
Deaf hear, *d* raised	Mat.	9	24
	Mark	5	39
	Luke	7	22
	Luke	8	52
	Luke	11	5
Not God of the *d*	Luke	22	32
Full of *d* men's bones	Luke	23	27
Rising from *d* should mean	Mark	9	10
Though one rose from the *d*	Luke	15	24–32
	Rev.	1	18
	Rev.	16	31
Though *d* shall he live	John	11	25
He that was *d* came forth	John	44	
Judge of quick and *d*	Acts	10	42
	II Tim.	4	1
D to sin	Rom.	6	2–11
	I Pet.	2	24
Lord both of *d* and living	I Pet.	14	9
If the *d* rise not	I Cor.	15	15
How are the *d* raised?	I Cor.	35	

Trust in God who raiseth *d*	II Cor.	1	9
Arise from the *d*	II Cor.	5	14
Firstborn from the *d*	Col.	1	18
D with Christ	Col.	2	20
	II Tim.	2	11
D in Christ shall rise first	I Thes.	4	16
D while she liveth	I Tim.	5	6
From *d* works	Heb.	6	1
	Heb.	9	14
Being *d* yet speaketh	Heb.	11	4
Brought again from the *d*	Heb.	13	20
Faith *d*	James	2	17–20–26
Preached to them that are *d*	I Pet.	4	6
First-begotten of the *d*	Rev.	1	5
Blessed are the *d*	Rev.	14	13

Dead sea *lies southeast of Jerusalem*

Called Salt sea	Gen.	14	3
Sea of the plain	Deut.	3	17
East sea	Joel	2	20
Former sea	Zech.	14	8

deaf

Like *d* adder that stoppeth	Ps.	58	4
Shall the *d* hear the words	Is.	29	18
The *d* hear	Mat.	11	5
	Luke	7	22
He maketh the *d* to hear	Mark	7	37
Thou *d* spirit, come out	Mark	9	25
(See Ex. 4:11; Lev. 19:14; Is. 42:18; 43:8)			

deal

Nor *d* falsely	Lev.	19	11
D not foolishly	Ps.	75	4
They that *d* truly are his delight	Prov.	12	22
In land of uprightness *d* unjustly	Is.	26	10
Every one *d* falsely	Jer.	6	13
	Jer.	8	10
D treacherously against the Lord	Hosea	5	7
Why hast thou thus *d* with us?	Luke	2	48
According as God hath *d*	Rom.	12	3

dearth *scarcity of food supply, famine*

In Egypt for seven years	Gen.	41	54
	Acts	7	11
Agabus foretells	Acts	11	28

death *the act or fact of dying*

All shall be raised from	Acts	24	15
Ordered by God	Deut.	32	39
	Job	14	5
Pray to be prepared for	Ps.	39	4
Prepare for	II Ki.	20	1
Shall finally be destroyed by Christ	Hosea	13	14
	I Cor.	15	26
The consequence of Adam's sin	Gen.	3	19–24
	Rom.	5	14
Inflicted as a punishment	Gen.	9	6
	Ex.	21	12
	Lev.	20	2
	Lev.	21	9
	I Ki.	21	10
	Mat.	15	4
Characterized	Deut.	31	16, 17
	Job	1	21
	Job	14	2
Prayers and exhortations concerning	II Ki.	20	2, 3
	Eccl.	9	10
Of saints	II Ki.	22	20
	Ps.	23	4
	Dan.	12	2
	John	11	11
Universal	Job	1	21
	Job	3	17
	Job	21	13
	Ps.	49	19
	Ps.	89	48
	Eccl.	5	15
	Heb.	9	27
Of the wicked	Prov.	10	7
	Is.	14	19, 20
	Ezek.	3	19
	Luke	16	22, 23
	John	8	21
Eternal	Prov.	14	12
	Dan.	12	2
	Mat.	7	13
	Mat.	23	33
	Mat.	25	30, 41
	Mark	9	44
	Rom.	2	7

death—*continued*

Fear of	Heb.	2	15
Earthly tabernacle dissolved	II Cor.	5	1
Spiritual	Is.	9	2
	Mat.	4	16
	Luke	1	79
	Rom.	6	13
	Rom.	8	6
	Col.	2	13
	Heb.	6	1
	Heb.	9	14
	I John	3	14
	Rev.	3	1
Of Christ foretold	Is.	53	1–12
	Dan.	9	26
Its object	Is.	53	1–12
	I Cor.	5	7
	I Tim.	2	6
	Tit.	2	14
	Heb.	9	26
	Rev.	1	5
Excluded from heaven	Luke	20	36
	Rev.	21	4
Salvation from, by Christ	John	3	16
	John	5	24
	John	8	51
	James	5	20
Voluntary	John	10	11, 18
	Heb.	10	7
Vanquished by Christ	Rom.	6	9
	II Tim.	1	10
	Heb.	2	15
	Rev.	1	18
The second death	Rev.	2	11
	Rev.	20	14
	Rev.	21	8

Described as:

Departing	Phil.	1	23
Gathering to our people	Gen.	49	33
God requiring the soul	Luke	12	20
Going down into silence	Ps.	115	17
Going the way whence there is no return	Job	16	22
Putting off this tabernacle	II Pet.	1	14
Returning to dust	Gen.	3	19
	Ps.	104	29
Yielding up the ghost	Acts	5	10

Embalming:

Of Jacob	Gen.	50	2, 3
Of Joseph	Gen.	50	26
Of Asa	II Chr.	16	14
Of Jesus	Mark	15	46
	Mark	16	1
	John	19	39, 40

debate

D cause with neighbour	Prov.	25	9
Ye fast for strife and *d*	Is.	58	4
Full of envy, *d*	Rom.	1	29
I fear lest there be *d*	II Cor.	12	20

Debir, Kirjath-sannah, Kirjath-sepher

King of Eglon	Josh.	10	3–27
A city of Judah	Josh.	15	15, 16
Taken by Joshua	Josh.	10	38
Same as Kirjath-sepher	Josh.	15	15
Anakims driven out of	Josh.	11	21
Captured by Othniel	Josh.	15	15–17
A Levitical city	Josh.	21	15
A place near the valley of Achor, in North Judah	Josh.	15	7
In Transjordon	Josh.	13	26

Deborah *a bee*

Nurse to Rebekah	Gen.	24	59
	Gen.	35	8
Judges and delivers Israel	Judg.	4	4–14
Her song	Judg.	5	1–31

debt *an obligation or liability*

Released at the end of seven years	Deut.	15	1–4
Censured	Ps.	37	21
	Prov.	3	27
	Luke	16	5
	Rom.	13	8
Forgive us our	Mat.	6	12
Compassion on poor	Ex.	22	25–27
Rules for repossession	Deut.	24	10–13
Mortgaged land	Neh.	5	3–4
Of David's men	I Sam.	22	2

Related to love	Luke	7	41–42
Parable of	Mat.	18	23–35
Interest forbidden	Ezek.	18	8–17
Not of the flesh	Rom.	8	12

debtor *a person who owes to another*

Could be enslaved	II Ki.	4	1
Imprisoned	Mat.	18	30

Decalogue *see Ten Commandments*

Decapolis *league of ten cities*

Jesus makes many disciples here	Mat.	4	25
	Mark	5	20

deceit *trick, fraud*

God abhors	Ps.	5	6
Punishment of	Ps.	55	23
Is falsehood	Ps.	119	118
Forbidden	Prov.	24	28
Comes from the heart	Jer.	17	9
	Mark	7	22
Hinders knowledge of God	Jer.	9	6
Hypocrites practice	Hosea	11	12
Wicked are full of	Rom.	1	29
The tongue an instrument of	Rom.	3	13
False teachers are workers of	Rom.	16	18
	II Cor.	11	13
	Eph.	4	14
Folly of fools is	Prov.	14	8
Hatred covered by	Prov.	26	26
Prophets of	Jer.	23	26
A characteristic of antichrist	II John		7
Hinders knowledge of God	Jer.	9	6
Accompanied by a kiss	Prov.	27	6

Deceitful things:

The heart	Jer.	17	9
Weights	Mic.	6	11
Workers	II Cor.	11	13
Lusts	Eph.	4	22

Instances of deception:

By Satan	Gen.	3	4
Abraham	Gen.	12	13
	Gen.	20	2
Isaac	Gen.	26	7
Jacob	Gen.	27	6–23
Jacob's sons	Gen.	34	13–31
	Gen.	37	29–32
Joseph	Gen.	42–44	
The Gibeonites	Josh.	9	3–15
Ehud	Judg.	3	15–30
Delilah	Judg.	16	4–20
David	I Sam.	21	10–15
Hushai	II Sam.	16	15–19
Amnon	II Sam.	13	6–14
Herod	Mat.	2	8
Pharisees	Mat.	22	16
Ananias and Sapphira	Acts	5	1–10

decision

Of Levi choosing the Lord	Ex.	32	26
Not to turn to right or left	Josh.	1	7
To serve the Lord	I Sam.	12	20
Demanded by Elijah	I Ki.	18	21
Determined by God	Prov.	16	33
	II Chr.	19	11

Examples:

Abel	Heb.	11	4
Jacob	Gen.	28	20
Joseph	Gen.	39	9
Moses	Heb.	11	24–25
Israel	Ex.	19	7
Caleb	Num.	14	24
Balaam	Num.	22	15–18
Phinehas	Num.	25	7–13
Joshua	Josh.	24	15
Ruth	Ruth	1	16
A prophet	I Ki.	13	8
Matthew	Mat.	9	9
Paul	II Tim.	4	7

declaration *announcement*

Of the glory of God	I Chr.	16	24
	Ps.	19	1
	Is.	66	19
Of His wondrous works	Ps.	26	7
	Ps.	145	4
Of liberty to the captives	Is.	61	1
Of Christ as the Son of God	Luke	1	31, 32
	Rom.	1	4

declare

D glory among heathen	I Chr.	16	24
	Ps.	96	3

D his way to his face	Job	21	31
D if thou hast understanding	Job	38	4
I will *d* decree	Ps.	2	7
D among the people his doings	Ps.	9	11
Heavens *d* glory of God	Ps.	19	1
I have *d* thy faithfulness	Ps.	40	10
I WILL *d* what he hath done	Ps.	66	16
Live and *d* the works of the Lord	Ps.	118	17
Shall *d* thy mighty acts	Ps.	145	4
D his doings among people	Is.	12	4
Who hath *d* from beginning?	Is.	41	26
	Is.	45	21
D things that are right	Is.	45	19
Who shall *d* his generation?	Is.	53	8
	Acts	8	33
D my glory among Gentiles	Is.	66	19
Have *d* thy name, and will *d* it	John	17	26
We *d* glad tidings	Acts	13	32
D the counsel of God	Acts	20	27
D to be Son of God with power	Rom.	1	4
The day shall *d* it	I Cor.	3	13
Have seen *d* we to you	I John	1	3

decline

Thou shalt not *d* from sentence	Deut.	17	11
D neither to right nor left	II Chr.	34	2
Days like a shadow that *d*	Ps.	102	11
	Ps.	109	23
Not *d* from thy law	Ps.	119	51
Neither *d* from words of my mouth	Prov.	4	5

dedication *consecration*

Of the tabernacle	Ex.	40	1–38
	Lev.	8	1–36
	Num.	7	84
	II Chr.	5	6
	II Chr.	7	5
Of the body to God	Judg.	5	2
	Rom.	12	1
	Heb.	10	20
Of the wall of Jerusalem	Neh.	12	27

dedication, feast of *see* feasts and festivals

deed *document for transfer of land*

For property of Jeremiah	Jer.	32	6–12

deeds *acts*

A sign of strength	Joel	2	11
An evil	Judg.	19	30
Jesus mighty in	Luke	24	19
Moses mighty in	Acts	7	22
God's judgment according to	Rom.	2	5, 6
	Rev.	20	12
A good doer is blessed	Col.	3	17
	Heb.	13	16
	James	1	25
To love in	I John	3	18

deep

Darkness on face of *d*	Gen.	1	2
Fountains of *d*	Gen.	7	11
	Gen.	8	2
The *d* that coucheth beneath	Deut.	33	13
Face of *d* is frozen	Job	38	30
Thy judgments are a great *d*	Ps.	36	6
D calleth to *d*	Ps.	42	7
See his wonders in the *d*	Ps.	107	24
Led them through *d*	Is.	63	13
No *d* of earth	Mat.	13	5
Launch out into *d*	Luke	5	4
Digged *d* and laid foundation	Luke	6	48
Command to go into the *d*	Luke	8	31
The well is *d*	John	4	11
Searcheth *d* things of God	I Cor.	2	10

deer *see* fallowdeer

defeat *failure to win*

In battle	I Sam.	4	3
	II Sam.	1	4, 19
	Is.	5	25
	Hosea	14	3
Spiritual	Is.	49	4
	Luke	14	30
	II Tim.	2	3
	Heb.	4	1

defence *guard against attack*

God is, to His people	Deut.	33	29
	Job	22	25
	Ps.	5	11
	Ps.	7	10
	Ps.	59	9

	Is.	31	5
	Zech.	12	8
Of Paul before the courts	Acts	21–26	
The shield of faith	Eph.	6	16

deference *a yielding*

Courteous, to elders	Job	32	4
To an evil request	Mat.	14	6–10

defiance *bold resistance*

Balaam urged to	Num.	23	7, 8
In battle	I Sam.	17	10
	II Sam.	23	9
Of God	Is.	31	1
Of Nebuchadnezzar's golden image	Dan.	3	16–18

defilement *corruption, depravity*

Breaking the sabbath	Ex.	31	14
	Ezek.	23	38
Caused by childbirth	Lev.	12	2–8
From touching dead	Num.	9	11–22
A leprous man	Lev.	13	45, 46
Of the promised land	Num.	35	33
	Jer.	2	7
Hides God from us	Is.	59	2, 3
The Lord	Jer.	2	7
	Jer.	16	18
The sanctuary	Ezek.	23	38
By eating corrupt food	Dan.	1	8
	I Cor.	8	7
Comes from within	Mat.	15	11
	Mark	7	15
	James	3	6
Of the temple of God	I Cor.	3	17

defraud

Shalt not *d* neighbour	Lev.	19	13
Whom have I *d*?	I Sam.	12	3
D not	Mark	10	19
	I Cor.	7	5
Rather suffer yourselves to be *d*	I Cor.	6	7
We have *d* no man	II Cor.	7	2
No man *d* his brother	I Thes.	4	6

degrees *elevation*

Markings on a sun dial	II Ki.	20	9–11
Classes of the Levites	I Chr.	15	18
Made equal by God	Ps.	62	9
	Luke	1	52
Title of Psalms	Ps.	120–134	
Of rank	Luke	1	52
	Ps.	62	9

Dekar *pierce*

Father of one of Solomon's officers	I Ki.	4	9

Delaiah *Jehovah has drawn*

A descendant of Aaron and leader of the priests in David's time	I Chr.	24	18
Descendants return from captivity	Ezra	2	59, 60
	Neh.	7	61, 62
Son of Shemaiah, who advises King Jehoiakim	Jer.	36	12, 25

deliberation *considering carefully*

Necessary for wise judgment	Deut.	1	16
	I Ki.	3	9
	Ezra	10	16
	Prov.	18	13
	Eccl.	8	5
Before becoming a disciple	Luke	14	28–32
Self-examination	I Cor.	11	28
	II Cor.	13	5

delicate *dainty*

"With my delicates,"	Jer.	51	34
He that *d* bringeth up his servant	Prov.	29	21
I no more called tender and *d*	Is.	47	1
That did feed *d* are desolate	Lam.	4	5
That live *d* are in king's courts	Luke	7	25

delight *great satisfaction*

In the Lord:

Commanded	Ps.	37	4
Blessedness of	Ps.	112	1
Hypocrites pretend to	Is.	58	2
	Jer.	6	10
Observing the sabbath leads to	Is.	58	13, 14
The reward is great in heaven	Luke	6	23
Of God for man	Mic.	7	18
	Luke	6	23
	Rom.	15	13

Delilah *delicate, lustful, languishing*

Philistine woman loved by Samson	Judg.	16	4

Delilah—*continued*

Induces Samson to disclose the secret of his strength	Judg.	16	5–20

deliver

Come down to *d* them	Ex.	3	8
	Acts	7	34
Any *d* out of my hand	Deut.	32	39
	Is.	43	13
D our lives from death	Josh.	2	13
Which cannot profit nor *d*	I Sam.	12	21
Were gods able to *d* their lands?	II Chr.	32	13
D thee in six troubles	Job	5	19
Great ransom cannot *d*	Job	36	18
To *d* their soul from death	Ps.	33	19
D my feet from falling	Ps.	56	13
D thee from snare of fowler	Ps.	91	3
Forbear to *d* them	Prov.	24	11
Shall wickedness *d* those	Eccl.	8	8
Have I no power to *d*?	Is.	50	2
I am with thee to *d* thee	Jer.	1	8
D such as are for death to death	Jer.	43	11
God is able to *d* and will *d*	Dan.	3	17
Neither mighty *d* himself	Amos	2	14
D us from evil	Mat.	6	13
	Luke	11	4
All things *d* to me of my Father	Mat.	11	27
	Luke	10	22
Let him *d* now	Mat.	27	43
Being *d* by counsel of God.	Acts	2	23
Was *d* for our offences	Rom.	4	25
D to death for Jesus' sake	II Cor.	4	11
D us from the wrath to come	I Thes.	1	10
Faith once *d* to the saints	Jude		3

deliverance *rescue or release*

Promised to the faithful	Ps.	91	1–3
	Mat.	10	22
	Luke	4	18
Sought in prayer	Mat.	6	13
	James	5	15

Exemplified:

Lot from destruction at Sodom	Gen.	19	15–25
City of refuge	Josh.	20	5
By judges	Judg.	13	5
Demonstrates God's uniqueness	Dan.	3	29
Moses	Ex.	2	
Of Israel	Ex.	14	
David	I Sam.	17	37
From the fiery furnace	Dan.	3	26, 27
Daniel in the lion's den	Dan.	6	22
Jonah, from the belly of the whale	Jonah	2	1–10
The apostles from prison	Acts	5	18, 19
Peter from chains	Acts	12	7
Paul and Silas	Acts	16	25, 26

deluge, the *the great flood*

Sent as punishment for the extreme wickedness of man	Gen.	6	5–7
	Gen.	6	11–13, 17
Noah forewarned of	Gen.	6	13
	Heb.	11	7
Noah and companions saved from	Gen.	6	18–22
	Gen.	7	13, 14
Date of its commencement	Gen.	7	11
Extreme height of	Gen.	7	19, 20
Decrease of	Gen.	8	3, 5
Date of its complete removal	Gen.	8	13
The wicked warned of	I Pet.	3	19, 20
	II Pet.	2	5

Called the:

Flood	Gen.	9	28
Waters of Noah	Is.	54	9

Produced by:

Forty days incessant rain	Gen.	7	4, 12, 17
Opening of the fountains	Gen.	7	11

That it shall never occur again:

Promised	Gen.	8	21, 22
Confirmed by covenant	Gen.	9	9–11
The rainbow a token	Gen.	9	12–17
A pledge of God's faithfulness	Is.	54	9, 10

Illustrative:

Of the destruction of sinners	Ps.	32	6
	Is.	28	2, 18
Of baptism	I Pet.	3	20, 21
The end times	II Pet.	3	5–15
	Mat.	24	36–39

delusion *deception*

Characteristic of the wicked	Ps.	49	18
Result of prosperity	Ps.	30	6
	Hosea	12	8
	Rev.	3	17
Given up to	II Thes.	2	10–11
God will not punish sin	Jer.	5	12
Christ will not come	II Pet.	3	4
Consequences	Mat.	7	23
	I Thes.	5	3
Church of Laodicea	Rev.	3	17

demagogue *a leader of the people*

Absalom, an artful	II Sam.	15	2–6
Pilate	Mat.	27	17–26
Felix	Acts	24	27
Herod	Acts	12	3

Demas *governor of the people*

A fellow labourer of Paul	Col.	4	14
	Philem.		24
He later deserts Paul	II Tim.	4	10

Demetrius *of Demeter*

A silversmith at Ephesus who made models of the temple of Diana	Acts	19	24
Stirs up a riot because of Paul's preaching	Acts	19	25–41
A Christian highly commended by John	III John		12

demon(s) *spiritual being at enmity with God*

Dread approach of final judgment	Mat.	8	29
Beelzebub is their chief	Mat.	12	24–28
Angels of the devil destined for ultimate destruction	Mat.	25	41
	Rev.	12	7, 9
Recognize their true status before God	James	2	19
Worship of	Deut.	32	17
	Lev.	17	7
Possession by	Mat.	8	28–34
Possess swine	Mat.	8	30–32
Power over	Mat.	10	1
	Mark	9	18–28
Believe	James	2	19
Judgment	Jude		6
Acknowledge Christ's deity	Mark	1	23–24
Possessed Mary Magdalene	Mark	16	9
Dumb man	Mat.	9	32
Blind and dumb	Mat.	12	22
Causing insanity	Mat.	17	14–18
Christ has power over	Mat.	4	24
	Mat.	8	16
Comfort	John	4	4

den *pit or cave*

Used as place of refuge	Judg.	6	2
	Heb.	11	38
Inhabited by beasts	Job	37	8
Used figuratively	Jer.	7	11
	Mark	11	17

denial

Of Christ, deprecated	II Tim.	1	8
	Tit.	1	16
	II Pet.	2	1
	Jude		4
Its punishment	Mat.	10	33
	II Tim.	2	12
	II Pet.	2	1
	Jude		4
By Peter	Mat.	26	69
By the Jews	John	18	40
	John	19	15
	Acts	3	13

deny

Lest ye *d* your God	Josh.	24	27
Lest I be full, and *d* thee	Prov.	30	9
Shall *d* me before men	Mat.	10	33
Let him *d* himself and take	Mat.	16	24
Which *d* resurrection	Luke	20	27
He cannot *d* himself	II Tim.	2	13
In works they *d* himself	Tit.	1	16

depart

Sceptre shalt not *d* from Judah	Gen.	49	10
Have not *d* from my God	II Sam.	22	22
They say to God *d*	Job	21	14
	Job	22	17
To *d* from evil is understanding	Job	28	28
D from evil, and do good	Ps.	34	14
	Ps.	37	27
When old, he will not *d* from it	Prov.	22	6
They need not *d*	Mat.	14	16
D from me ye cursed	Mat.	25	41

Lettest thy servant *d* in peace	Luke	2	29
Devil *d* for a season	Luke	4	13
D from me, I am a sinful man, O Lord	Luke	5	8
When Jesus knew he should *d*	John	13	1
Besought that it might *d* from me	II Cor.	12	8
Having a desire to *d*	Phil.	1	23
Some shall *d* from faith	I Tim.	4	1
Nameth Christ *d* from iniquity	II Tim.	2	19

depravity of man *corrupt act or practice*

In time of Noah	Gen.	6	5, 13
All are susceptible	Eccl.	9	3
	Is.	53	6

Caused by:

Idolatry	Ps.	14	1–3
Deceitfulness	Jer.	17	9
Unrighteousness	Rom.	1	18
Nature of man	Gen.	8	21
Universal	Ps.	130	3
	Rom.	3	23
	Rom.	7	18–25
	Rom.	1	18–32
	Gal.	3	11–22
Opposed to the spirit	I Cor.	2	14
Dead in sin	Eph.	2	1
	Col.	2	13

deputy *acting for another*

Serves as a king	I Ki.	22	47
Converted by Paul	Acts	13	7, 8
Gallio of Achaia	Acts	18	12
Of the law	Acts	19	38

Derbe *a city of Lycaonia*

Paul visits	Acts	14	6, 20
Timothy found here	Acts	16	1
Probably the birthplace of Gaius	Acts	20	4

derision *reproach*

Of Hezekiah	II Chr.	30	1–10
Of Job	Job	30	1
God holds the wicked in	Ps.	2	4
	Prov.	1	26
Of Jeremiah	Jer.	20	7
Upon Jesus	Luke	16	14
Endured until death	Luke	23	35

descent *to come down*

Fall of the wicked	Ps.	49	17
Punishment of Tyrus	Ezek.	26	20
Punishment of Assyria	Ezek.	31	16
Holy Spirit upon Jesus	Mark	1	10
The earthly body	Eph.	4	10

desert *arid plains, wilderness*

David flees to	I Sam.	23	14
A terrible land	Is.	21	1

Described as:

Dry and without water	Ex.	17	1
Uncultivated	Num.	20	5
Waste and howling	Deut.	32	10
Tractless	Is.	43	19
Uninhabited and lonesome	Jer.	2	6

Infested with:

Serpents	Deut.	8	15
Robbers	Lam.	4	19
Beasts	Mark	1	13

desertion *abandonment*

In doubt	John	6	52–66
Prevented by shipmen	Acts	27	30–32
In ignorance	II Tim.	4	16
By disciples	Mat.	26	56

desire *wish*

For work of the hands	Job	14	15
Granted by God	Ps.	21	2
	Ps.	145	16
	Hag.	2	7
All known by God	Ps.	38	9
Of the wicked shall not be fulfilled	Ps.	92	11
	Ps.	112	10
Shall be granted to the righteous	Prov.	10	24
	Prov.	11	23
Not accomplished without labour	Prov.	21	25
For salvation of Israel	Rom.	10	1
Of the flesh	Eph.	2	3

desire, spiritual

Of seeking hearts	Ps.	27	4
	Ps.	42	
	Is.	26	9
God's promise	Ps.	37	4
For righteousness	Mat.	5	6
	I Cor.	14	1

To grow spiritually	I Pet.	2	2

desolation, abomination of *see* abomination of desolation

despair *hopelessness*

Overcome by trust in God	Ps.	42	5, 11
	II Cor.	4	8, 9
From a heavy responsibility	Num.	11	10–15
Leads to blasphemy	Is.	8	21
	Rev.	16	11
Of the young	Is.	40	30
Leads to sin	Jer.	18	12
In doing good	Gal.	6	9
	II Thes.	3	13
	Heb.	12	3
Solution	I Pet.	5	7

Examples of:

Cain	Gen.	4	13
Hagar	Gen.	21	14–16
Israel	Ex.	6	9
Moses	Num.	11	11–15
David	I Sam.	27	1
Judas	Mat.	27	5

despise *condemn, scorn*

A cause for rebuke	Lev.	26	15
	I Sam.	2	30
	Ezek.	20	13
	I Cor.	11	22
The folly of unbelievers	Ps.	51	17
	Ps.	73	20
Instrument of a fool	Prov.	1	7
Not your aged parents	Prov.	23	22
Not man, but God	I Thes.	4	8

despondency *loss of hope*

In mourning	Gen.	37	34, 35
Difficult journey	Num.	21	4
A prayer	Ps.	13	1–3
Homesickness	Ps.	137	1–3
During sickness	Is.	38	9–12
In trouble	II Cor.	7	5–6

Instances of:

Hagar	Gen.	21	15, 16
Moses	Num.	11	11, 15
Israelites	Num.	17	12
Joshua	Josh.	7	7
Elijah	I Ki.	19	2, 4
David	Ps.	42	6
Jonah	Jonah	4	3–8
Two disciples	Luke	24	13–17
The mariners with Paul	Acts	27	20

destitute *condition of extreme want*

The prayer of	Ps.	102	17
Leave not my soul	Ps.	141	8
Minds, of the truth	I Tim.	6	5
Brother or sister	James	2	14–17

destroy

Righteous with the wicked	Gen.	18	23
D Lord's anointed	II Sam.	1	14
He hath *d* me on every side	Job	19	10
Though worm's *d* this body	Job	19	26
Seek my soul to *d* it	Ps.	40	14
	Ps.	63	9
I will *d* all wicked of the land	Ps.	101	8
Prosperity of fools shall *d* them	Prov.	1	32
One sinner *d* much good	Eccl.	9	18
Not *d* in all my holy mountain	Is.	11	9
	Is.	65	25
D them with double destruction	Jer.	17	18
Thou hast *d* thyself	Hosea	13	9
Not come to *d* but to fulfill	Mat.	5	17
Fear him that is able to *d*	Mat.	10	28
Miserably *d* those wicked men	Mat.	21	41
Art thou come to *d* us?	Mark	1	24
	Luke	4	34
D the husbandmen	Mark	12	9
	Luke	20	16
Say, I will *d* this temple	Mark	14	58
Is it lawful to save life, or to *d* it?	Luke	6	9
Not come to *d* men's lives	Luke	9	56
Flood came, and *d* them all	Luke	17	27
D this temple, and I will raise	John	2	19
D not him with thy meat	Rom.		15
Preacheth the faith he once *d*	Gal.	1	23
D with brightness of His coming	II Thes.	2	8
Able to save and to *d*	James	4	12
D the works of the devil	I John	3	8

destruction

Be devoured with bitter *d*	Deut.	32	24
His counsellors to his *d*	II Chr.	22	4
Heart lifted up to his *d*	II Chr.	26	16
Endure to see *d* of my kindred	Esth.	8	6
Neither be afraid of *d*	Job	5	21
D is ready at his side	Job	18	12
D from God was a terror to me	Job	31	23
Thou turnest man to *d*	Ps.	90	3
Redeemeth thy life from *d*	Ps.	103	4
D shall be to workers of iniquity	Prov.	10	29
Pride goeth before *d*	Prov.	16	18
A fool's mouth is his *d*	Prov.	18	7
Hell and *d* are never full	Prov.	27	20
Wasting and *d* in their paths	Is.	59	7
Destroy them with double *d*	Jer.	17	18
Of the daughter of my people	Lam.	2	11
O grave, I will be thy *d*	Hosea	13	14
Broad is way that leadeth to *d*	Mat.	7	13
D and misery are in their ways	Rom.	3	16
Vessels of wrath fitted to *d*	Rom.	9	22
Many walk, whose end is *d*	Phil.	3	19
Then sudden *d* cometh	I Thes.	5	3
Punished with everlasting *d*	II Thes.	1	9
Bring on themselves swift *d*	II Pet.	2	1
Wrest Scriptures to their own *d*	II Pet.	3	16

determine

Seeing his days are *d*	Job	14	5
That is *d* shall be done	Dan.	11	36
Son of man goeth, as it was *d*	Luke	22	22
Pilate was *d* to let him go	Acts	3	13
Hath *d* the times appointed	Acts	17	26
I *d* not to know any thing	I Cor.	2	2

(See II Chr. 2:1; 25:16; Is. 19:17; Dan. 9:24)

device

D return on his own head	Esth.	9	25
Let them be taken in the *d*	Ps.	10	2
Maketh *d* of the people of none effect	Ps.	33	10
Bringeth wicked *d* to pass	Ps.	37	7
Be filled with their own *d*	Prov.	1	31
Man of wicked *d* will he condemn	Prov.	12	2
Many *d* in a man's heart	Prov.	19	21
No work nor *d* in grave	Eccl.	9	10
Will walk after our own *d*	Jer.	18	12
He shall forecast *d*	Dan.	11	24
Like stone graven by man's *d*	Acts	17	29
Not ignorant of his *d*	II Chr.	2	11

(See II Chr. 2:14; Esth. 8:3; Job 5:12)

Devil see Satan

devils

Sacrifices offered to	Lev.	17	7
Cast out by Christ	Mat.	4	24
	Mat.	8	31
Confess Jesus to be Christ	Mat.	8	29
	Acts	19	15
Cast out by His apostles	Luke	9	1
	Acts	5	16
Believe and tremble	James	2	19

devise

D works in gold	Ex.	31	4
	Ex.	35	32–35
To confusion that *d* my hurt	Ps.	35	4
He *d* mischief on his bed	Ps.	36	4
D not evil against thy neighbor	Prov.	3	29
He *d* mischief continually	Prov.	6	14
A heart that *d* wicked imaginations	Prov.	18	
Err that *d* evil, a good	Prov.	14	22
Man's heart *d* his way	Prov.	16	9
D wicked devices to destroy the poor	Is.	32	7
The liberal *d* liberal things	Is.	8	
Cunningly *d* fables	II Pet.	1	16

devotions, morning *religious worship, prayers*

Jacob's vision	Gen.	28	12, 18–22
Hannah and Elkanah	I Sam.	1	19
Job offers devotions for his sons	Job	1	5
Jesus	Mark	1	35

devour

D fire	Ex.	24	17
	Is.	29	6
	Is.	30	27–30
	Is.	33	14
Fire from Lord *d* them	Lev.	10	2
D with burning heat	Deut.	32	24
Sword *d* one as well as another	II Sam.	11	25
Wood *d* more than sword *d*	II Sam.	18	8
Fire out of his mouth *d*	II Sam.	22	9
	Ps.	18	8

Death shall *d* his strength	Job	18	13
Beasts of field *d* it	Ps.	80	13
Man who *d* that when is holy	Prov.	20	25
Jaw teeth as knives, to *d*	Prov.	30	14
Strangers *d* it in your presence	Is.	1	7
If ye rebel, ye shall be *d* with sword	Is.	20	
Your sword hath *d* prophets	Jer.	2	30
Fire shall *d* them	Ezek.	15	7
Pass through fire to *d* them	Ezek.	23	37
A fire *d* before them	Joel	2	3
Fig trees, Palmerworm *d* them	Amos	4	9
D by fire of jealousy	Zeph.	1	18
Will rebuke the *d* for your sakes	Mal.	3	11
Fowls *d* them	Mat.	13	4
	Mark	4	4
	Luke	8	5
D widows' houses	Luke	23	14
	Mark	12	40
Thy son hath *d* thy living	Luke	15	30
If a man *d* you	II Cor.	11	20
Ye bite and *d* one another	Gal.	5	15
Which shall *d* adversaries	Heb.	10	27
Seeking whom he may *d*	I Pet.	5	8

(See Gen. 31:15; II Sam. 2:26; Ps. 50:3; 52:4)

devout *pious, showing reverence*
Persons so called:

Simon	Luke	2	25
Jews in Jerusalem	Acts	2	5
Cornelius	Acts	10	2
Women of Antioch	Acts	13	50
Ananias	Acts	22	12

dew *refreshing small drops, make moist*

A blessing	Gen.	27	28
	Deut.	33	13
A sign of plenty	Gen.	28	16, 18
Manna given with	Ex.	16	13–15
Figurative	Deut.	32	2
	Ps.	110	3
	Ps.	133	3
	Prov.	19	12
	Is.	26	19
Temporary	Hosea	6	4
Gideon's test	Judg.	6	37–40

dexterity *skillfulness, handiness*

700 chosen men	Judg.	20	16
Benaiah	II Sam.	24	20

diadem *an ornamental cloth headband worn as a crown, dignity*

Used figuratively	Job	29	14
Ornament denoting royalty	Is.	62	3
Of the Lord	Is.	28	5
Removal of judgment	Ezek.	21	26

dial, sun dial

Moves ten degrees backward	II Ki.	20	11

diamond *hard, nearly pure carbon*

A precious stone in the breastplate of judgment	Ex.	28	18
	Ex.	39	11
Used as a cutting tool	Jer.	17	1
Precious	Ezek.	28	13

Dibon, Dibon-gad, Dimonah *mope, pine*

An Amorite town	Num.	21	30
Israel takes	Num.	32	3
Children of Gad rebuild	Num.	32	34
Called Dibon-gad	Num.	33	45, 46
A high place	Is.	15	2
Given to Reuben	Josh.	13	17
Destruction predicted	Jer.	48	18–22
Village in Judah	Neh.	11	25
Also called Dimonah	Josh.	15	22

Didymus see Thomas

die see death

diet *habitual food*

Code of the Jews	Lev.	11	1–47
Given to Jehoiachin	Jer.	52	31–34
Of John the Baptist	Mat.	3	4

difficulty *hardship*

Nothing is too hard for God to overcome	Gen.	18	14
	Jer.	32	17
Removed by faith	Num.	14	7–9
The way of the transgressors	Prov.	13	15
Of understanding	II Pet.	3	16
The teachings of Jesus	John	6	48–60
Childbirth	I Sam.	4	19–21
Despondency from	I Ki.	19	14

By faith	Num.	14	7–9
None with God	Gen.	18	13–14
Trails	Gen.	22	1–15
Magnified by spies	Num.	13	31
From peril	Neh.	4	14–23
By prayer	Mark	11	23–24
A seekers	Luke	19	1–5
Zeal greater than	Mark	2	1–4
Christian work	II Tim.	2	3–4

dig

Wells *d* which thou *d* not	Deut.	6	11
Out of hills mayest *d* brass	Deut.	8	9
D a pit and is fallen	Ps.	7	15
	Ps.	57	6
D a winepress	Mat.	21	33
D in the earth, and his Lord's money	Mat.	25	18
Let it alone, till I *d* about it	Luke	13	8
I cannot *d*, to beg I am ashamed	Luke	16	3
And *d* down thine altars	Rom.	11	3

dignity

Excellence of	Gen.	49	3
Folly in great	Eccl.	10	6
Of the Chaldeans	Hab.	1	7

diligence *perseverance*

God rewards	Deut.	11	13, 14
	Heb.	11	6
Christ an example	Mark	1	35
	Luke	2	49
Saints should abound in	II Cor.	8	7

Required by God in:

Obeying Him	Deut.	6	17
	Deut.	11	13
Seeking Him	I Chr.	22	19
	Heb.	11	6
Lawful business	Prov.	27	23
	Eccl.	9	10
Striving after perfection	Phil.	3	13, 14
Guarding against defilement	Heb.	12	15
Cultivating Christian graces	II Pet.	1	5

Exemplified:

Jacob	Gen.	31	40–43
Hezekiah	II Chr.	31	21
Apostles	Acts	5	42
Paul	I Thes.	2	9
Onesiphorus	II Tim.	1	16, 17

dill *see* anise

Dinah *vindicated*

A daughter of Jacob and Leah	Gen.	30	19, 21
	Gen.	34	1
Her outrage by Shechem	Gen.	34	2–31

dinner *the noon meal*

Better where love is	Prov.	15	17
Served at marriages	Mat.	22	4
Customary to wash before	Luke	11	37, 38
Guests at	Luke	14	12–14

Dionysius *reveller*

An Areopagite converted by Paul	Acts	17	22, 34

diplomacy *skill in dealing with people*

Joseph	Gen.	41	33–46
Solomon	I Ki.	3	1
	I Ki.	5	1–18
	I Ki.	10	1–6
Pilate	Luke	23	12
Daniel	Dan.	1	8–16
Paul practices	I Cor.	9	20–23

direction *guidance, instruction*

Divine	Ex.	13	21
	Prov.	3	6
	Is.	30	21
	I Thes.	3	11
Of ungodly should be rejected	Ps.	1	1
Strait is the gate and narrow the way	Mat.	7	14

disappointment *failure of one's hopes*

In realizing material wealth	Lev.	26	16
	Deut.	28	39
	Amos	5	11
	Hag.	1	6
Of the crafty	Job	5	12
Of purposes	Prov.	15	22
In battle	Is.	31	1
Esau	Gen.	26	34–35
Of Eli	I Sam.	2	12
Jacob with Leah	Gen.	29	25

disarmament *to reduce armaments*

Prophesied	Is.	2	4
	Mic.	4	3

disaster *serious or sudden misfortune*

Caused by God	Gen.	6	17
	Jer.	46	8
	Mat.	24	6–8
Punishment of sin	Prov.	24	20–22
	Is.	17	10, 11
	Ezek.	25	7

discern

Can I *d* between good and evil?	II Sam.	19	35
That I may *d* between good and bad	I Ki.	3	9
Understanding to *d* judgment	I Ki.	3	11
I *d* among the youths	Prov.	7	7
Wise *d* time and judgment	Eccl.	8	5
Not *d* between right and left	Jonah	4	11
D between righteous and wicked	Mal.	3	18
D face of sky	Mat.	16	3
	Luke	12	56
Because they are spiritually *d*	I Cor.	2	14
Not *d* the Lord's body	I Cor.	11	29

disciples *pupils or learners*

Used in Old Testament	Is.	8	16
Includes the twelve apostles	Mat.	10	1–4
Of John	John	1	29, 37
	Acts	19	1–7
Called Christians	Acts	11	26

Character traits of:

Self-denial	Mat.	16	24
Renunciation	Luke	14	26, 33
Perseverance	John	8	31
Brotherly love	John	13	35

Rewarded with:

The light of life	John	8	12
Honour in heaven	John	12	26
Divine guidance	John	16	13

discipleship: *Prerequisites*

Forsaking all	Luke	14	33
Obedience	John	14	15
Love	John	13	35
Taking up the cross	Mat.	16	24
Continuance	John	8	31
Fruit	John	15	8
Ability to suffer	Mat.	10	25

discipline *see* correction

As correction	Ps.	39	11
For righteousness of life	Heb.	12	11
From government	I Pet.	2	14
From scripture	II Tim.	3	16
In love	Heb.	12	5–7
Of children	Prov.	13	24
	Prov.	19	15

Within the church:

Maintaining sound doctrine	I Tim.	1	3
	Tit.	1	13
Ordering its affairs	I Cor.	11	34
	Tit.	1	5
Rebuking offenders	I Tim.	5	20
	II Tim.	4	2
Removing obstinate offenders	I Cor.	5	3, 5, 13
	I Tim.	1	20
Decency and order, the objects of	I Cor.	14	40
Exercise, in a spirit of charity	II Cor.	2	6–8
Ministers authorized to establish	Mat.	16	19
	Mat.	18	18
Prohibits women preaching	I Cor.	14	34
	I Tim.	2	12
Should be submitted	Heb.	13	17

discouragement *loss of confidence*

Of Israelites in the wilderness	Num.	21	4, 5
	Num.	32	7
	Deut.	1	21
Of the builders of the wall	Neh.	4	10
Apostles without	II Cor.	4	8–10
Faith wipes away	Col.	3	23–25

discourtesy *impoliteness*

Of Nabal	I Sam.	25	3, 14
Of Simon	Luke	7	44

discover *find, identity*

We will *d* ourselves to them	I Sam.	14	8
The Foundations of the worlds were *d*	II Sam.	22	16
	Ps.	18	15
He *d* deep things	Job	12	22
And *d* the forests	Ps.	29	9
D not a secret to another	Prov.	25	9
Your transgressions are *d*	Ezek.	21	24
D the foundation	Hab.	3	13
D a certain creek	Acts	27	39

discretion *caution, prudence*

David makes a good name because of	I Sam.	18	30
Success by	I Sam.	25	23–28
A woman without	Prov.	11	22
A woman with	Tit.	2	5
In time of war	Luke	14	31, 32
Safety by	Acts	23	6, 7

diseases

Sometimes sent as punishment	Deut.	28	21
	John	5	14
Sometimes through Satan	I Sam.	16	14–16
	Job	2	7
Medicine used for curing	Prov.	17	22
	Is.	1	6
Illustrative of sin	Is.	1	5
Physicians attempt to cure	Jer.	8	22
	Mat.	9	12
	Luke	4	23
Many and divers	Mat.	4	24

Mentioned in Bible:

Ague	Lev.	26	16
Abscess	II Ki.	20	7
Boils and blains	Ex.	9	10
Blindness	John	9	1
Consumption	Lev.	26	16
	Deut.	28	22
Deafness	Mat.	11	5
Dropsy	Luke	14	2
Dysentery	II Chr.	21	18, 19
	Acts	28	8
Emerods	Deut.	28	27
Epilepsy	Mat.	4	24
Fever	Deut.	28	22
Insanity	Mat.	15	22
	Mark	5	15
Issue of blood	Mat.	9	20
Itch	Deut.	28	27
Leprosy	Lev.	13	2
Palsy	Mat.	8	6
Scab	Deut.	28	27
Sunstroke	II Ki.	4	18–20
Ulcers	Is.	1	6
Worms	Acts	12	23

disguise *conceal one's identity*

Of Saul	I Sam.	28	8
With ashes on the face	I Ki.	20	38
Aided by darkness	Job	24	15

dishonesty *lack of integrity*

Forbidden by Mosaic law	Lev.	6	2–7
	Lev.	19	13
Just measures and weights must be used	Lev.	19	35, 36
	Deut.	25	13–16
A grievous sin	Prov.	21	6
	Jer.	7	8, 9
Renounced by Paul	II Cor.	4	2

Instances of:

Jacob	Gen.	25	29–33
Rebekah	Gen.	27	6–29
Rachel	Gen.	31	19
Micah	Judg.	17	2
Joab	II Sam.	14	2–20
Jezebel	I Ki.	21	5–16
Judas	John	12	4–6
Peter	John	18	25–27

dishonor

Clothed with shame and *d*	Ps.	35	26
	Ps.	71	13
And *d* shall he get	Prov.	6	33
Son *d* father	Mic.	7	6
I honour my father, ye do *d* me	John	8	49
To *d* their own bodies	Rom.	1	24
d thou God?	Rom.	2	23
One vessel to honour, another to *d*	Rom.	9	21
It is sown in *d*	I Cor.	15	43
By honour and *d*	II Cor.	6	8
Are vessels, some to honour, some to *d*	II Tim.	2	20
(*See* I Cor. 11:4, 5)			

disinherit *to cut off*

A threat to Israel	Num.	14	12

disobedience *refusal to obey*

Brings a curse	Deut.	11	28
	Deut.	28	15
Forfeits God's blessing	James	5	6
Provokes God's anger	I Sam.	13	14
	Ps.	78	40
	Is.	3	8

Shall be punished	Is.	42	24, 25
	Jer.	12	17
	Heb.	2	2
	Jer.	22	21
A characteristic of the wicked	Tit.	1	16
	Tit.	3	3

Instances of:

Adam and Eve	Gen.	3	6–11
Moses	Ex.	4	13, 14
	Num.	20	11, 23, 24
Pharaoh	Ex.	5	2
	Ex.	9	12
Children of Israel	Ex.	16	17–20
	Num.	14	1–10
	Deut.	1	26
Saul	I Sam.	13	13
David	II Sam.	12	9
The blind man	Mat.	9	30, 31
The leper	Mark	1	43–45

disorderly *unruly*

Not to associate with	II Thes.	3	6
Paul was not	II Thes.	3	7
Busybodies	II Thes.	3	11

Dispensation *a period of uniform divine working*

Of the gospel	I Cor.	9	17
Of the fulness of time	Eph.	1	10
Of grace	Eph.	3	2
Of God	Col.	1	25

dispersion *scattered*

Judgment on sheep of Israel	Jer.	25	34
Future regathering	Is.	11	12
Jews in Persian empire	Esth.	3	8
Jews among the Gentiles	John	7	35
	James	1	1
A curse on a disobedient Israel	Deut.	28	36

display *show; ostentation*

By Solomon	I Ki.	10	1–10
By Ahasuerus	Esth.	1	2–7
By Haman	Esth.	5	11
By Hezekiah	Is.	39	2
By Agrippa	Acts	25	23
Of false religion	Mat.	6	1–4

displeasure *discomfort*

Moses fears God's displeasure	Deut.	9	19
With rulers of the land	Ps.	2	5
With wickedness of Israel	Amos	5	21–27
Jesus with the moneychangers	Mat.	21	12, 13

dispossess *to put out*

Israelites, the people of Canaan	Num.	33	53
	Deut.	7	17
The Amorites by Israel	Judg.	11	23

disputing *arguing pro and con*

With God	Job	23	7
	Rom.	9	20
With men	Mark	9	33, 34
	Rom.	14	1
	Phil.	2	14
	I Tim.	6	20
	Tit.	3	9
In the synagogue, by Paul	Acts	17	17

dissension *disagreement in opinion*

Concerning circumcision	Acts	15	1, 2
Concerning resurrection	Acts	23	7

distraction *that which diverts attention*

Of affliction	Ps.	88	15
Of marriage	I Cor.	7	35

distress

Answered by God	Gen.	35	3
	II Sam.	22	7
	Ps.	18	6
	Ps.	120	1
Caused by negligence	Gen.	42	21
Helped by own desire	Neh.	2	17
A plea for God's help	Ps.	4	1
	Ps.	25	17
Praise for God's help	Is.	25	4
Endured for love of Christ	II Cor.	12	10

distribute *divide among several*

To the brethren	Neh.	13	13
	John	6	11
	II Cor.	9	13
To the poor	Luke	18	22
Duties required of us	Rom.	12	13
As possessing	I Cor.	7	17

ditch *a trench dug in the earth*

	Book	Ch.	V.
Valley full of	II Ki.	3	16
Fallen into	Ps.	7	15
Leaders fall into	Mat.	15	14
	Luke	6	39

divers

	Book	Ch.	V.
Not sow with *d* seeds	Deut.	22	9
Not wear garment of *d* sorts	Deut.	22	11
Not have in bag *d* weights	Deut.	25	13
D measures, great and small	Deut.	25	14
D weights and measures abomination	Prov.	20	10–23
Sick with *d* diseases	Mat.	4	24
	Mark	1	34
	Luke	4	40
Earthquakes in *d* places	Mat.	24	7
	Mark	13	8
	Luke	21	11
D of them came from far	Mark	8	3
D kinds of tongues	I Cor.	12	10
God, who in *d* manners, spake	Heb.	1	1
D lusts	II Tim.	3	6
	Tit.	3	3
Joy when ye fall into *d* temptations	James	1	2

divination *foretelling future events*

	Book	Ch.	V.
Forbidden	Lev.	19	26–28, 31
	Lev.	20	6
An abominable practice	Deut.	18	9–15
	I Sam.	15	23
By Israel	II Ki.	17	17
	Is.	2	6
Denounced	Is.	8	19
	Mal.	3	5
Messages of, false	Jer.	29	8
	Ezek.	21	29
Healed by Paul	Acts	16	16–19
Work of the flesh	Gal.	5	19, 20
Practiced by:			
Magicians	Gen.	41	8
Charmers	I Sam.	28	3
Witches	I Sam.	28	7–25
Soothsayers	Is.	2	6
Astrologers	Is.	47	13
Sorcerers	Jer.	27	9
Necromancers	Deut.	18	11
Wizards	Deut.	18	11

division *discord, dissension*

	Book	Ch.	V.
Evil of, illustrated	Mat.	12	25
Contrary to the purpose of Christ	John	10	16
Contrary to the desire of Christ	John	17	21–23
Avoid those who cause	Rom.	16	17
Condemned	I Cor.	1	10–13
Between Israel and Egypt	Ex.	8	23
Characteristic of carnal	I Cor.	3	3
Diotrephes	III John		9, 10

divorce *legal separation*

	Book	Ch.	V.
Not allowed to those who accuse falsely	Deut.	22	18, 19
Permitted by Mosaic law	Deut.	24	1–4
	Mat.	19	8
To a maidservant	Ex.	21	7–11
To a captive of war	Deut.	21	10–14
Putting away foreign wives	Ezra	10	1–16
	Neh.	13	23–30
Cannot remarry same person	Jer.	3	1
Hated by God	Mal.	2	14–16
Separation-reconciliation	I Cor.	7	10–17
Figurative	Hosea	1	3
Women can remarry	Deut.	24	2
Symbolic of God's casting off Israel	Is.	50	1
Adultery, only valid reason	Mat.	5	32
Condemned by Jesus	Mark	10	4–12

doctors *teachers*

	Book	Ch.	V.
Teacher of the law of Moses	Luke	2	46
	Luke	5	17
Gamaliel, the Pharisee	Acts	5	34

doctrine

	Book	Ch.	V.
False	Jer.	10	8
	Mat.	16	12
Of Christ	Mat.	7	28, 29
	Acts	2	42
	I Tim.	3	16
	Heb.	6	2
Adorned by obedience	Rom.	16	17
	Tit.	2	7, 10
Those opposed to, to be avoided	Rom.	16	17
No other to be taught	I Tim.	1	3
Of devils	I Tim.	4	1

	Book	Ch.	V.
Not to be blasphemed	I Tim.	6	1
Verbal inspiration	II Tim.	3	16
	II Pet.	1	21
Of God	I Tim.	1	17
	John	4	24
Of man	Gen.	1	27–28
	Gen.	3	15–19
	Rom.	1	
	Rom.	3	23
	Rom.	5	8
Of salvation	Rom.	6	23
	John	3	16
	Rom.	10	9
Of the church	Mat.	16	18
	Col.	1	18
	Acts	2	47
Of the end times	I Thes.	4	16–18
	II Thes.	2	2–10
	Mat.	24	25
	Rev.		
Perverting	Gal.	1	6–7
	I John	4	1–6
False teaching	Mat.	5	19
Falsely accepting the commandments of men	Mat.	15	9
Deceivers	Rom.	16	17–18
	Col.	2	4
	Col.	18	23
Preaching another Jesus	II Cor.	11	3
Not known by children	Eph.	4	14
Jewish fables	Tit.	1	10–14
Of stability	Heb.	13	9
Of false prophets	II Pet.	2	1–3
Apostate	Jude	4	11

dog

	Book	Ch.	V.
An unclean animal	Ex.	22	31
	Deut.	23	18
Regarded with contempt	I Sam.	17	43
	II Ki.	8	13
	Mat.	7	6
	Rev.	22	15
Domesticated	Mat.	15	26–27
Scavengers	I Ki.	14	11
	I Ki.	21	19, 23, 24
Guard of the sheep	Job	30	1
Figurative:			
Of enemies	Ps.	22	16–20
Of impenitence	Prov.	26	11
	II Pet.	2	22
False teachers	Phil.	3	2
Of the lost	Rev.	22	15

dominion *rule, authority*

	Book	Ch.	V.
Of man	Gen.	1	26, 28
	Gen.	2	19, 20
	Ps.	8	6
	Ps.	72	8
	Dan.	2	38
	Heb.	2	7
Of Esau	Gen.	27	40
Of Joseph foretold	Gen.	37	8
Of Christ foretold	Num.	24	19
Of kings, rulers	Neh.	9	37
	Is.	26	13
Of God	Job	25	2
	Ps.	103	22
	Ps.	145	13
	Dan.	4	3
	Dan.	4	34
	Dan.	7	14
	Dan.	7	27
	Col.	1	16
Of sin	Ps.	19	13
	Ps.	119	133
	Rom.	6	14
Of Nebuchadnezzar	Jer.	27	6
	Jer.	28	14
Of death	Rom.	6	9
Of Jesus Christ	Eph.	1	21

door *way of entrance*

	Book	Ch.	V.
Posts of, sprinkled with blood	Ex.	12	22, 23
Of tabernacle	Num.	12	5
	Num.	16	18
Law to be written on posts	Deut.	11	20
Of temple	I Ki.	6	31–35
	I Ki.	7	50
Hinges for	I Ki.	7	50
	Prov.	26	14

door—*continued*

Shut, waiting on God	Is.	26	20
	Mat.	6	6
Of sepulchre	Mat.	27	60
	Mat.	28	2
	Mark	15	46
Peter at	John	18	16
Prison, opened	Acts	5	19
"I stand at the door"	Rev.	3	20
Figurative:			
Death	Job	38	17
Everlasting	Ps.	24	7, 9
Lips	Ps.	141	3
Of hope	Hosea	2	15
Of Jesus' coming	Mat.	25	10
	Luke	13	25
	Rev.	3	20
Representing Christ	John	10	1, 7, 9
Of faith	Acts	14	27
Of opportunity	I Cor.	16	9
	II Cor.	2	12
	Col.	4	3
	Rev.	3	8

doorkeeper

For the ark	I Chr.	15	23, 24
Position preferred	Ps.	84	10

Dorcas, Tabitha *gazelle*

Raised from death by Peter	Acts	9	36–42

Dothan *two wells or double feast*

Where Joseph is sold	Gen.	37	17
Elisha's home	II Ki.	6	13

double *twofold*

Money for Joseph	Gen.	43	12
Restitution for thievery	Ex.	22	4
Elijah's spirit	II Ki.	2	9
With a double heart	I Chr.	12	33
	Ps.	12	2
Payment for sins	Is.	40	2
	Jer.	16	18
	Jer.	17	18
Double-mindedness	Luke	16	13
	James	1	8
	James	4	8
Should not be double-tongued	I Tim.	3	8

doubt *to question*

Brings trouble	Deut.	28	66–68
Rebuked by Jesus	Mat.	8	26
	Mat.	14	31
	Mat.	21	21
	Mark	4	40
	Mark	11	23
	Luke	8	25
	Luke	12	29
Of Jews concerning Jesus	John	10	24
Of authorities concerning apostles' escape from prison	Acts	5	24
Of Peter concerning vision	Acts	10	17, 20
	Acts	11	8–12
Of those weak in faith	Rom.	14	1, 23
Paul perplexed concerning Galatians	Gal.	4	20
Without, in prayer	I Tim.	2	8
Examples among believers:			
Abraham	Gen.	15	8
Sarah and Abraham	Gen.	18	12–15
Moses	Ex.	3	11
	Ex.	4	1, 10, 13
	Ex.	5	22, 23
	Ex.	6	12
	Num.	11	21, 22
Children of Israel	Ex.	14	11, 12
Gideon	Judg.	6	13, 15
Samuel	I Sam.	16	1, 2
Elijah	I Ki.	18	7–14
Job	Job	10	1–5
Jeremiah	Jer.	8	18–22
John the Baptist	Mat.	11	2, 3
Zacharias	Luke	1	18–20
Thomas	John	20	24, 25
Ananias	Acts	9	13

dough *wet flour thick enough to roll*

Offering of	Num.	15	20
	Neh.	10	37
Kneaded	Jer.	7	18
	Hosea	7	4

dove *a bird, white pigeon*

Sent from the ark by Noah	Gen.	8	10, 12
Why considered the emblem of peace	Gen.	8	11
Offered in sacrifice	Gen.	15	9
Clean and used as food	Deut.	14	11–18
Sold in the temple	Mat.	21	5
Symbolic of:			
Beauty	S. of S.	2	14
The meekness of Christ	S. of S.	5	12
Simplicity	Mat.	10	16
The Holy Ghost	John	1	32
Of Israel	Hosea	11	1
Silly	Hosea	7	11

down

Take root *d*	II Ki.	19	30
Let them wander up and *d*	Ps.	59	15
Thou knowest my *d* sitting	Ps.	139	2
I am tossed up and *d*	Ps.	109	23
Spirit of the beast that goeth *d*	Eccl.	3	21
Walk up and *d* in his name	Zech.	10	12
Were driven up and *d*	Acts	27	27

dowry *gift or endowment*

Money paid to bride's father	Gen.	30	20
	Ex.	22	17
50 shekels of silver	Deut.	22	29
Present for daughter	I Ki.	9	16
For a violated virgin	Ex.	22	16–17
Shechem for Dinah	Gen.	34	12
Isaac for Rebekah	Gen.	24	22, 47, 53
Jacob for Rachel	Gen.	29	27–20
David for Michael	I Sam.	18	20–25

doxologies *see benediction*

dragon *a huge serpent*

A terrible creature	Deut.	32	33
	Jer.	51	34
	Rev.	12	4
Found in the wilderness, desert and seas	Ps.	74	13
	Is.	34	13
	Mal.	1	3
Seen in John's vision	Rev.	12	3
Symbolic of:			
Wicked men	Ps.	44	19
Enemies of the church	Ps.	91	13
Cruel and evil kings	Ezek.	29	3
The Devil	Rev.	13	2
The antichrist	Rev.	12	3

dragon well

A well within the gates of Jerusalem	Neh.	2	13

dram

A Persian coin	I Chr.	29	7
	Ezra	8	27
	Neh.	7	70

draught

Drain for sewage	Mat.	15	17
	Mark	7	19
A catch of fish	Luke	5	4, 9

dreams *thoughts during sleep*

The Israelites often perplexed by	Gen.	40	6
	Job	7	14
	Dan.	2	1
Interpreted by Joseph	Gen.	40	12–19
	Gen.	41	25–32
God's will revealed in	Num.	12	6
	Job	33	1–5
False prophets pretend to receive revelations through	Deut.	31	1–5
	Jer.	23	25–32
Tell of the future	Gen.	41	1–7
Sometimes without meaning	Job	20	8
	Is.	29	8
Mentioned in scripture:			
Abimelech	Gen.	20	3–7
Jacob	Gen.	28	12
Laban	Gen.	31	24
Joseph	Gen.	37	5–9
Pharaoh's butler and baker	Gen.	40	5–19
Pharaoh	Gen.	41	1–7
Solomon	I Ki.	3	5–15
Nebuchadnezzar	Dan.	2	1, 31
	Dan.	4	5, 8
Daniel	Dan.	7	1–28
Joseph	Mat.	1	20, 21
	Mat.	2	13, 19, 20
Wise men	Mat.	2	11, 12
Pilate's wife	Mat.	27	19

dregs *the most worthless part of anything*

Wicked of the earth shall drink	Ps.	75	8
Jerusalem drank	Is.	51	17, 22

dress *see* garment

drew

Time *d* nigh that Israel must die	Gen.	47	29
Because I *d* him out of the water	Ex.	2	10
Joshua *d* not his hand back	Josh.	8	26
D off his shoes	Ruth	4	8
Man *d* a bow	I Ki.	22	34
	II Chr.	18	33
Jehu *d* bow with full strength	II Ki.	9	24
D up with cords	Jer.	38	13
D them with cords of a man	Hosea	11	4
She *d* not near to her God	Zeph.	3	2
When time of fruit *d* near	Mat.	21	34
Elder son *d* nigh to house	Luke	15	25
Jesus himself *d* near	Luke	24	15
D away much people	Acts	5	37
Time of the promise *d* near	Acts	7	17

drink *any liquid for drinking*

Water	Gen.	21	14
Bitter water	Num.	5	24
Milk	Judg.	5	25
Strong	Prov.	20	1
	Is.	5	11
	Is.	28	7
The blood of Christ	John	6	53–56
Do not drink strong *d* when ye go	Lev.	10	9
Nazarite separate from strong *d*	Num.	6	3
Give congregation *d*	Num.	20	8
Bestow money for strong *d*	Deut.	14	26
Nor drunk strong *d* forty years	Deut.	29	6
Strong *d* is raging	Prov.	20	1
May follow strong *d*	Is.	5	11
Erred through strong *d*	Is.	28	7
I will prophesy of strong *d*	Mic.	2	11
That giveth his neighbour *d*	Hab.	2	15
Thirsty, and ye gave me *d*	Mat.	25	35
A Jew, askest *d* of me	John	4	9
My blood is *d* indeed	John	6	55
If thine enemy thirst give him *d*	Rom.	12	20
The kingdom of God is not meat and *d*	Rom.	14	17
Drink same spiritual *d*	I Cor.	10	4
Judge you in meat or *d*	Col.	2	16
What shall we *d*	Ex.	15	24
No water for people to *d*	Ex.	17	1
D bitter water	Num.	5	24
Water to *d* for I am thirsty	Judg.	4	19
Every one water of his cistern	II Ki.	18	31
	Is.	36	16
	Prov.	5	15
D of the river of thy pleasures	Ps.	36	8
D the wine of astonishment	Ps.	60	3
Givest them tears to *d*	Ps.	80	5
He shall *d* of the brook in the way	Ps.	110	7
It is not for kings to *d* wine	Prov.	31	4
d yea *d* abundantly	S. of S.	5	1
Let us eat and *d*	Is.	22	13
My servants shall *d*, but ye shall be thirsty	Is.	65	13
We will *d* no wine	Jer.	35	6
They shall *d* and make a noise	Zech.	9	15
Whosoever shall give to *d*	Mat.	10	42
Are ye able to *d*?	Mat.	20	22
	Mark	10	38
Saying, *d* ye all of it	Mat.	26	27
When I *d* it new	Mat.	26	29
	Mark	14	25
	Luke	22	18
May not pass except I *d* it	Mat.	26	42
Shall give you cup of water to *d*	Mark	9	41
If they *d* any deadly thing	Mark	16	18
Let him come to me and *d*	John	7	37
Not good to *d* wine	Rom.	14	21
As oft as ye *d* it	I Cor.	11	25

drink offerings *see* offerings

drink, strong *see* wine

dromedary *one-humped camel of unusual speed*

Used for war	I Ki.	4	28
Used to post letters	Esth.	8	10
As a carrier	Is.	60	6
Swift	Jer.	2	23

drop

My doctrine *d* as the rain	Deut.	32	2
Heavens *d* dew	Deut.	33	28
	Prov.	3	20

Which the clouds do *d*	Job	36	28
Thy paths *d* fatness	Ps.	65	11
Heavens *d* at presence of God	Ps.	68	8
As a *d* of a bucket	Is.	40	15
Down ye heavens	Is.	45	8
The mountains shall *d* down new wine	Joel	3	18
	Amos	9	13
Sweat as it were great *d* of blood	Luke	22	44

dropsy *a disease causing excess fluid in the body*

Christ heals	Luke	14	2–4

dross *refuse, slag*

Disposed of	Ps.	119	119
Pollutes	Prov.	25	4
	Ezek.	22	18
Mistaken for the pure	Prov.	26	23

drought *aridness*

As a curse	Deut.	28	23
	I Ki.	17	1
Satisfaction during	Is.	58	11
Longest	James	5	17
Consuming	Gen.	31	40
Characteristic of the wilderness	Deut.	8	15
	Jer.	2	6
Of summer	Ps.	32	4
Overcome by a river	Jer.	50	38
Caused by the Lord as a judgment	Hag.	1	11

drown *suffocation by water*

Pharaoh's army	Ex.	15	4
	Heb.	11	29
As a punishment	Mat.	18	6
Of lusts	I Tim.	6	9
Of love	S. of S.	8	7
Jonah almost	Jonah	1	15–17

drowsiness *sleepiness*

Leads to poverty	Prov.	23	21
Disciples	Mat.	26	43
Boy during a sermon	Acts	20	9

drunkard

Forbidden by Mosaic law	Deut.	21	20
A singer of obscene songs	Ps.	69	12
Produces poverty	Prov.	23	20, 21
Without feeling	Prov.	26	9
Sorrow will come to	Is.	5	11
Sways	Is.	24	20
Lacks judgment	Is.	28	7, 8
Woe unto the maker	Hab.	2	15
Should be avoided	I Cor.	5	11
Classed with the wicked	I Cor.	6	10
Punishment of	Deut.	21	20, 21
	Amos	6	6, 7
	Mat.	24	49–51
The folly of	Prov.	20	1
Forbidden	Is.	5	11
	Eph.	5	18
Is debasing	Is.	28	7, 8
The wicked addicted to	Dan.	5	1–4
Overcharges the heart	Luke	21	34
Cautioned against	Luke	21	34
	Gal.	5	21
Excludes from kingdom of God	I Cor.	6	10
	Gal.	5	21

Leads to:

Poverty	Prov.	23	21
Strife	Prov.	23	29, 30
Sorrow	Prov.	23	29, 30
Error	Is.	28	7

Instances of:

Noah	Gen.	9	21
Uriah	II Sam.	11	13
Belshazzar	Dan.	5	4

dulcimer *a musical instrument*

As a signal for worship	Dan.	3	5, 10

dumb *mute*

Made by the Lord	Ex.	4	11
Speak for	Prov.	31	8
Produced by fear	Is.	53	7
	Acts	8	32
Struck by the Lord	Ezek.	3	26
Daniel becomes, after speaking to angel	Dan.	10	15
Of idols	Hab.	2	18–19
Of a donkey	II Pet.	2	16
Caused by a spirit	Mark	9	17
Healed by Jesus	Mat.	9	32, 33
	Mat.	12	22
	Mat.	15	30

dumb—*continued*			
Struck, by Gabriel	Luke	1	20–22
dung *mature*			
The beggar sits upon a hill of	I Sam.	2	8
Sold for food	II Ki.	6	25
The price of sin	II Ki.	9	37
Eating of one's own	II Ki.	18	27
Saved for fertilizer	Neh.	2	13
	Luke	13	8
Symbolic of destruction	Lam.	4	5
	Ezek.	4	12, 15
	Dan.	2	5
Of human righteousness	Phil.	3	8
dungeon *subterranean prison*			
Joseph imprisoned in	Gen.	40	8, 15
Jeremiah imprisoned in	Jer.	38	6, 11
dust *powdery earth*			
Man formed from	Gen.	2	7
Serpent shall eat	Gen.	3	14
Man to return to, at death	Gen.	3	19
	Eccl.	3	20
Of great number	Gen.	13	16
Dust storms to destroy	Deut.	28	24
On head, symbol of mourning	Josh.	7	6
	Job	2	12
Of death	Ps.	22	15
Living in, symbol of low situation	I Sam.	2	8
	Nah.	3	18
Sitting in, symbol of afflictions	Is.	47	1
	Lam.	3	29
To shake off, symbol of rejection	Mat.	10	14
	Luke	9	5
God remembers that man is	Ps.	103	14
duties *obligations*			
Of parents:			
Teach the way of the Lord	Gen.	18	19
Train children well and they won't fail	Prov.	22	6
Provoke not to wrath	Eph.	6	4
	Col.	3	21
Set a good example	Tit.	2	2–4
Of children:			
Honour thy father and thy mother	Ex.	20	12
	Lev.	19	3
	Jer.	35	18, 19
	Col.	3	20
Be respectful	I Ki.	2	19
Hear their instruction	Prov.	1	8
Of man to man:			
Love thy neighbour as thyself	Lev.	19	18
	Mat.	22	39
Be kind to the poor	Lev.	25	25–28
	Deut.	24	12–21
The golden rule	Mat.	7	12
Help one another	Mat.	25	34–46
Learn true religion	James	1	27
Of man to God:			
Love and serve Him	Deut.	6	5
	Deut.	10	12
	Josh.	22	5
	Mat.	22	21, 36–38
Of ministers:			
To meditate the law of God	Josh.	1	8
Prepare the way of the Lord	Is.	40	1–11
Show the people their transgressions	Is.	58	1
Teach right from wrong	Ezek.	44	23
Christ's charge to His apostles	Mat.	10	7–28
Teach all nations	Mat.	28	19, 20
"Feed my lambs"	John	21	15–17
A witness unto men	Acts	22	15
Edifying the body of Christ	Eph.	4	11, 12
Of citizens:			
Show reverence to the king	I Ki.	1	31
	Eccl.	10	20
Obey the law	Ezra	7	26
	I Pet.	2	13, 14
"Render unto Caesar"	Mat.	22	21
Be subject to rulers	Rom.	13	1–6
Toward the afflicted:			
Show pity	Job	6	14
Do justice to	Ps.	82	3
Do not oppress	Prov.	22	22
Comfort them	I Tim.	5	10
Visit them	James	1	27
Show them the way of prayer	James	5	13
Of husbands and wives:			
Continue loving each other	Prov.	5	18, 19

Live joyfully together	Eccl.	9	9
Don't deal treacherously	Mal.	2	15
Bound by law unto death	Rom.	7	2
Virtues of the married state	I Cor.	7	3–13, 39
	I Pet.	3	1–7
Wives should be subject to their husbands	Eph.	5	22–25
	Col.	3	18, 19
Things a wife should learn	Tit.	2	4, 5
dwell			
Cause his name to *d* there	Deut.	12	11
Which *d* between cherubims	II Ki.	19	15
	Ps.	80	1
	Is.	37	16
D in the house of the Lord	Ps.	23	6
Than to *d* in tents of wickedness	Ps.	84	10
Good for brethren to *d* together	Ps.	133	1
D in the high and holy place	Is.	57	15
D in me, and I in him	John	6	56
He *d* with you, and shall be in you	John	14	17
God *d* not in temples	Acts	7	48
	Acts	17	24
Sin that *d* in me	Rom.	7	17
By his Spirit that *d* in you	Rom.	8	11
In him, *d* all; the fulness of the Godhead	Col.	2	9
Word of Christ *d* in you richly	Col.	3	16
D in the light	I Tim.	6	16
Holy Ghost who *d* in us	II Tim.	1	14
How *d* the love of God in him	I John	3	17
God *d* in us	I John	4	12
dwelling *residence*			
Of God:			
In Zion	Ps.	76	2
In Jesus	John	1	14
In the spirit of truth	John	14	17
Among men in future	Rev.	21	3
dyeing: *artificial coloring*			
Of tabernacle skins	Ex.	26	14
Of garments	Is.	63	1
Of hats	Ezek.	23	15
dysentery, flux *illness of the intestines*			
Paul heals	Acts	28	8
dyspepsia *indigestion*			
Paul recommends wine	I Tim.	5	23

E

eagle *a large bird*			
Forbidden as food	Lev.	11	13
	Deut.	14	12
Carries her young on her wings	Deut.	32	11
Swift	Deut.	28	49
A bird of prey	Job	9	26
	Mat.	24	28
Dwells in the high rocks	Job	39	27, 28
Greatness of	Ezek.	17	1–7
Bald	Mic.	1	16
Symbolic of:			
God's care	Deut.	32	11
Strength	Ps.	103	5
Great and powerful kings	Ezek.	17	3
ear *organ of hearing*			
Of priests, anointed with blood	Ex.	29	20
Of lepers, anointed with blood for healing	Lev.	14	14
Deaf	Is.	35	5
Stopped	Is.	33	15
Itching	II Tim.	4	3
Opened by Christ	Mark	7	33
God opens and closes	Job	33	16
	Is.	6	10
Made by God	Prov.	20	12
Christ will open	Is.	35	5
Should at all times:			
Hear the will of God	Ex.	15	26
	Jer.	9	20
	Mat.	13	16
Seek knowledge and understanding	Prov.	5	1
	Prov.	18	15
Be receptive to reproof	Prov.	15	31
	Prov.	25	12

Listen to the cry of the poor	Prov.	21	13
Seek the spiritual	Eccl.	1	8

early rising

Neglect of, leads to poverty	Prov.	6	9–11
Practiced by the wicked for evil purposes	Prov.	27	14
	Mic.	2	1

Essential for:

Executing God's commands	Gen.	22	3
Devotion	Ps.	5	3
	Ps.	59	16
Discharge of daily duties	Prov.	31	15

Exemplified by:

Abraham	Gen.	19	27
Isaac	Gen.	26	31
Jacob	Gen.	28	18
Moses	Ex.	34	4–5
Hannah	I Sam.	1	19–28
Joshua	Josh.	8	10
David	I Sam.	17	20
Jesus	Mark	1	35
	Luke	21	38
	John	8	2
Mary and others	Mark	16	2
Apostles	Acts	5	21

earnest *pledge*

Of the Spirit	II Cor.	5	5
	II Cor.	1	22
Of our inheritance	Eph.	1	14

earnestness *sincerity*

In seeking God	Jer.	24	7
	Jer.	29	13
Servant for rest	Job	7	2
Of expectations	Rom.	8	19
	Phil.	1	20
Of looking	Luke	22	56
	Acts	3	12
Elias in prayer	James	5	17
In penitence	Joel	2	12
Important	Luke	11	5–9
Jesus', in prayer	Luke	22	44
Paul's efforts characterized by	Phil.	3	13, 14

earrings *ear adornment*

Given Rebekah	Gen.	24	22
Given to Jacob	Gen.	35	4
Melted to form golden calf	Ex.	32	2–4
Symbols of worldly pride	Is.	3	19–21
	Ezek.	16	11, 12
	Hosea	2	13
	I Pet.	3	3

ears of corn

In Pharaoh's dream	Gen.	41	5–7
Symbolizing feasting	Lev.	23	14
Laws for harvesting	Lev.	23	22
Gathered by Ruth	Ruth	2	2
Simile to wickedness	Job	24	24
Plucked on sabbath	Mat.	12	1
	Mark	2	23

earth

Man given dominion over	Gen.	1	26
	Ps.	115	16
Man formed out of	Gen.	2	7
Man shall return to	Gen.	3	19
Corrupted by sin	Gen.	6	11, 12
	Is.	24	5
Once inundated	Gen.	7	17–24
Not to be inundated again	Gen.	9	11
Is the Lord's	Ex.	9	29
	I Cor.	10	26
Full of minerals	Deut.	8	9
	Job	28	1–5
Satan goes to and fro in	Job	1	7
	I Pet.	5	8
Saints shall inherit	Ps.	25	13
	Mat.	5	5
God shall be exalted in	Ps.	46	10
God reigns in	Ps.	46	8, 9
	Ps.	97	1
	Is.	11	4
To be destroyed by fire	II Pet.	3	10–12

God has:

Created	Gen.	1	1
	Neh.	9	6
	Job	38	4
	Ps.	9	2
Made fruitful	Gen.	1	11
Enlightened	Gen.	1	14–16
Suspended in space	Job	26	7
Watered	Ps.	65	9
Established forever	Ps.	78	69

Described as:

Full of God's goodness	Ps.	33	5
Full of God's riches	Ps.	104	24
Full of God's mercies	Ps.	119	64
Full of God's glory	Is.	6	3
Full of God's knowledge	Is.	11	9
	Hab.	2	14
God's footstool	Is.	66	1
	Mat.	5	35

earthquake

At mount Sinai	Ex.	19	18
Opens the earth	Num.	16	31, 32
Man always terrified by	Num.	16	34
	Zech.	14	5
	Mat.	27	54
Makes waters roar	Ps.	46	3
Accompanied by fire	Ps.	104	32
	Nah.	1	5
At Christ's death	Mat.	27	51

Examples:

In Jonathan's day	I Sam.	14	15
For Elijah	I Ki.	19	11
	Amos	1	1
In Uzziah's day	Zech.	14	5
For Paul and Silas	Acts	16	26

Visible token of:

God's power	Job	9	6
	Heb.	12	26
God's anger	Ps.	60	2
	Is.	13	13
God's presence	Ps.	68	7, 8
	Ps.	114	7

ease

Shalt thou find no *e*	Deut.	28	65
Thought of him that is at *e*	Job	12	5
Dieth, being wholly at *e*	Job	21	23
His soul shall dwell at *e*	Ps.	25	13
Rise up, ye women at *e*	Is.	32	9
Woe to them that are at *e*	Amos	6	1
Whether is *e* to say	Mat.	9	5
	Mark	2	9
	Luke	5	23
My yoke is *e* and burden light	Mat.	11	30
E for camel	Mat.	19	24
	Mark	10	25
	Luke	18	25
Take thine *e* and be merry	Luke	12	19
Charity is not *e* provoked	Luke	12	19
	I Cor.	13	5
Sin which doth so *e* beset us	Heb.	12	1

East

Men of the	Job	1	3
Glory of God proceeding from etc.	Ezek.	43	2
	Ezek.	47	8
Wise men from, worship Christ	Mat.	2	1
E of the garden of Eden	Gen.	3	24
Land of the people of the *e*	Gen.	29	1
Thin ears blasted with *e* wind	Gen.	41	23, 27
Lord brought an *e* wind	Ex.	10	13
	Ex.	14	21
Greatest of all the men of the *e*	Job	1	3
Scattereth *e* wind on the earth	Job	38	24
Breakest ships with *e* wind	Ps.	48	7
Promotion cometh not from *e*	Ps.	75	6
As far as *e* from west	Ps.	103	12
Stayeth rough wind in day of *e* wind	Is.	27	8
Bring thy seed from the *e*	Is.	43	5
	Zech.	8	7
Faces toward the *e*	Ezek.	8	16
Ephram followeth *e* wind	Hosea	12	1
An *e* wind shall come	Hosea	13	15
Sat on *e* side of city	Jonah	4	5
Wise men from the *e*	Mat.	2	1
Many come from *e*	Mat.	8	11
	Luke	13	29
As lighting out of the *e*	Luke	24	27

eating *partaking of food*

In Eden, limited	Gen.	2	16, 17
Not allowed with unbelievers, strangers	Gen.	43	32
	Ex.	8	26
	Acts	11	3

eating—*continued*

Rules formulated	Lev.	10	12–20
	Lev.	11	1–47
On tables	Judg.	1	7
	Ezek.	23	41
In field at noon	Ruth	2	14
Heavier meal at night	Ruth	3	7
Hannah unable to eat for grief	I Sam.	1	5–8
With manners	Prov.	23	1–3
Not with evil persons or sinners	Prov.	23	6–8
	Mat.	9	11
	Luke	15	2
	I Cor.	5	11
Excessiveness discouraged	Eccl.	10	16, 17
Ezekiel eats a book	Ezek.	2	9
	Ezek.	3	3
With unwashed hands	Mat.	15	2
Disciples too busy	Mark	6	31
A special celebration	Luke	15	23, 27
Jesus' body represented by bread	John	6	53–58
Bread sopped, given Judas	John	13	26
Without offending	I Cor.	8	7, 13
	I Cor.	10	31, 32
Without question	I Cor.	10	25–27
Only for those who work	II Thes.	3	10

Eben-ezer *stone of help*

Israelites defeated here	I Sam.	4	1
Ark taken by Philistines	I Sam.	5	1
Stone commemorating God's aid	I Sam.	7	12

Eber, Heber *region beyond*

Descendant of Shem	Gen.	10	21, 24
Father of Peleg and Joktan	Gen.	10	25–30
Ancestor of Abraham	Gen.	11	16–26
To perish, predicted	Num.	24	24
Gadite, called Heber	I Chr.	5	13
Son of Elpaal	I Chr.	8	12
Son of Shashak	I Chr.	8	22, 25
Levite priest	Neh.	12	20

ebony *hard wood*

Important into Tyre	Ezek.	27	15

eclipse of sun *darkening of sun by moon*

Moses creates at God's command	Ex.	10	21–23
Prophesied	Amos	8	9

economy *frugality*

Sometimes unwise	Prov.	11	24
Jesus instructs His disciples	John	6	12, 13
Of a goodman	Prov.	13	22
Not of he who loves pleasure	Prov.	21	17–20
Of Jesus	Mat.	14	20

Eden *pleasantness*

Extremely fertile first home of man	Gen.	2	8
Adam and Eve expelled for disobedience	Gen.	3	1–24
Of paradise	Joel	2	3
Garden of God	Ezek.	31	8–9
Wilderness made like	Is.	51	3
A section of Mesopotamia	II Ki.	19	12
Active in trade	Ezek.	27	23
A son of Joah	II Chr.	29	12

edification *instruction*

Object of ministry	Rom.	14	19
Paul's example	II Cor.	12	19
Of a neighbor	Rom.	15	2
Purpose of prophecy	I Cor.	14	3
Purpose of Paul's writing	II Cor.	13	10
Love	I Cor.	8	1
Purpose of church leaders	Eph.	4	11–12
Contrasted to contentious questions	I Tim.	1	4

Edom, Idumaea, Idumea *red*

Esau named	Gen.	25	30
The country of Esau	Gen.	32	3
Idumea, Greek name	Is.	34	5
Land destroyed for Esau's wrongdoing	Jer.	49	7–22
	Obad.		1, 6–21
People of, come to hear Jesus	Mark	3	8

Edomites

The descendants of Esau	Gen.	36	1
Deny the Israelites passage	Num.	20	18
Their possessions	Deut.	2	5
Not to be abhorred	Deut.	23	7
Subdued by David	II Sam.	8	14
Revolt	II Ki.	8	20
Subdued by Amaziah	II Ki.	14	7
Proud	Obad.	1	9
Cruel	I Sam.	18	18
	Ps.	137	7

To be judged	Lam.	4	21–22
Prophecies against	Is.	34	
	Jer.	49	7–22
	Ezek.	25	12–14
	Ezek.	35	
	Mal.	1	2–5

Edrei *strong; good pasture*

Battleground of Og and Israelites	Num.	21	33
City in Bashan	Deut.	3	10
Og defeated by Moses	Josh.	13	12
Allotted to Naphtalites	Josh.	19	37

education *process of developing knowledge*

Of God's word, compulsory	Deut.	6	6, 7
	Deut.	11	18–21
	Deut.	31	11–13
By parent's	Eph.	6	4
Slow process	Is.	28	10
Monuments to assist	Josh.	4	19–24
Neglected, reformed by Nehemiah	Neh.	13	23–30
Fools despise	Prov.	1	7
Likened to ornament	Prov.	1	8, 9
Of children, important	Prov.	22	6
Daniel's from God	Dan.	1	17
Moses' from Egyptians	Acts	7	22
Paul's by Gamaliel	Acts	22	3
By all who know	Gal.	6	6
Timothy's	II Tim.	3	15–16

effect

Devices of people of none *e*	Ps.	33	10
The *e* of righteousness, quietness	Is.	32	17
Command of God of none *e*	Mat.	15	6
	Mark	7	13
Promise of none *e*	Rom.	4	14
	Gal.	3	17
Let cross of Christ be of none *e*	I Cor.	1	7
Christ has become of no *e*	Gal.	5	4

effectual

A great door and *e*	I Cor.	16	9
The *e* working	Eph.	3	7
	Eph.	4	16
The *e* prayer of a righteous man	James	5	16

effeminacy *unmanliness*

Egypt's lot for erring	Is.	19	16
Babylon's lot for erring	Jer.	50	35, 37
	Jer.	51	30
Ruin of Nineveh	Nah.	3	13
Shall not attain heaven	I Cor.	6	9

Eglon *like a heifer*

Town near Lachish	Josh.	10	3–23
	Josh.	10	34–37
King deposed by Moses	Josh.	12	12
Allotted to Judah	Josh.	15	39
King of Moab	Judg.	3	12–30

egotism *vanity, self-love*

of Goliath	I Sam.	17	4–11
Of Simon	Acts	8	9–11
Not approved	Rom.	12	3, 16
	I Cor.	4	6, 7
	Gal.	5	26
Of Satan	Mat.	4	3–10
Of Haman	Esth.	6	6–12
Of the end times	II Tim.	3	1–7
Of Diotrephes	III John		9, 10
See conceit			

Egypt *black*

Abram goes down into	Gen.	12	10
Joseph sold into	Gen.	37	36
Joseph's advancement in	Gen.	39–41	
Jacob's sons go here to buy corn	Gen.	41	1–57
Jacob and his family go here	Gen.	46	6
Israelites' bondage here	Ex.	1	12
Their departure from	Ex.	13	17
Army of, pursue and perish in the Red sea	Ex.	14	1–31
"Remnant of Judah" taken here	Jer.	43	7
Jesus taken to	Mat.	2	13
Prophecies concerning	Gen.	15	13
	Is.	11	11
	Ezek.	29	2
	Hosea	9	3
	Zech.	10	10
Future conversion of	Is.	9	18–25

Ekron *eradication*

Philistine city	Josh.	13	3
Allotted to Dan	Josh.	19	43
Captured by Judah	Judg.	1	18

Ark brought here	I Sam.	5	10
To be destroyed	Jer.	25	9, 20
Denounced	Amos	1	8
	Zech.	9	5, 7

Elah *strong; oak*

A duke of Edom	Gen.	36	41
	I Chr.	1	52
Valley where Israelites camp	I Sam.	17	2
	I Sam.	21	9
Father of Shimei	I Ki.	4	18
Son of Baasha, king of Israel	I Ki.	16	6–14
Father of Hoshea	II Ki.	15	30
	II Ki.	17	1
	II Ki.	18	1
Son of Caleb	I Chr.	4	15
Benjamite, son of Uzzi	I Chr.	9	8

Elam *eternal; youth*

A son of Shem	Gen.	10	22
	I Chr.	1	17
A country	Gen.	14	1, 9
	Is.	11	11
In Isaiah's vision	Is.	21	2
Destruction foretold	Is.	22	6
	Jer.	49	34–39
In Daniel's vision	Dan.	8	2
A Benjamite	I Chr.	8	24
Korhite Levite	I Chr.	26	3
Returns from exile	Ezra	2	7
	Ezra	8	7
	Neh.	7	12
Another family of returned exiles	Ezra	2	31
	Neh.	7	34
A priest	Neh.	12	42

Elamites: *people from Elam*

Semites	Gen.	10	22
Powerful nation	Gen.	14	1
In Persian empire	Ezra	4	9
Come to pentecost	Acts	2	9

Elath, Eloth *grove*

Edomite town	Deut.	2	8
On shore of Red sea	I Ki.	9	26
Rebuilt by Amaziah, restored to Judah	II Ki.	14	22
	II Chr.	26	2
Jews driven out by Syrians	II Ki.	16	6
	II Chr.	26	2

El-bethel *house of God*

God appears to Jacob	Gen.	35	7, 9

elders *wise men, family and tribal chiefs*

Attend Jacob's funeral	Gen.	50	7
Gathered together by Moses	Ex.	3	16, 18
	Num.	11	16, 24
Commandments revealed to	Ex.	19	7
Seventy to aid Moses	Ex.	24	1
Prophesy	Num.	11	25
Moabite and Midianite	Num.	22	4, 7
Help Moses command	Deut.	27	1
Exhorted by Joshua	Josh.	23	2
Leaders, teachers	Judg.	8	14, 16
Select Jephthah to lead	Judg.	11	5–11
Represent people to king	I Sam.	8	4
Serve David	II Sam.	12	17
Assembled by Solomon	I Ki.	8	1–3
Hold counsel with princes	Ezra	10	8
Wise men	Ezek.	27	9
Disciples transgress traditions of	Mat.	15	2
	Mark	7	3
Question Jesus' authority	Mat.	21	23
False witnesses against Jesus	Mat.	26	59
Mock Jesus	Mat.	27	41
Deliver Jesus to Pilate	Mark	15	1
Sent to Christ by centurion	Luke	7	3
Stir up against Jesus	Acts	6	12
Sent aid by disciples	Acts	11	29, 30
Ordained in church	Acts	14	23
Cooperate with apostles	Acts	15	22, 23
	Acts	16	4
Called by Paul as overseers of church	Acts	20	17–38
Required abilities of	I Tim.	3	1–7
	Tit.	1	5–14
	I Pet.	5	1–4
Called presbytery	I Tim.	4	14
To be shown respect	I Tim.	5	1
Worthy, to be honoured	I Tim.	5	17
Accuse before witnesses only	I Tim.	5	19
Ordained to teach	Tit.	1	5, 9

To be obeyed	Heb.	13	7, 17
Pray for the sick	James	5	14, 15
Exhorted to care for followers	I Pet.	5	1–5

Eleazar *whom God aids*

Third son of Aaron, father of Phinehas	Ex.	6	23, 25
	Ex.	28	1
	Num.	3	2
Consecrated priest, chief Levite	Ex.	6	23
	Ex.	28	1
	Lev.	10	6–20
	Num.	3	32
Succeeds Aaron	Lev.	10	1, 2
	Num.	20	25–28
Aids Moses in numbering people	Num.	26	63
Helps Joshua divide Canaan	Josh.	14	1
A son of Abinadab	I Sam.	7	1, 2
Son of Dodo, one of David's heroes	II Sam.	23	9
	I Chr.	11	12
A Levite, son of Mahli	I Chr.	23	21
	I Chr.	24	28
A son of Phinehas	Ezra	8	33
A son of Parosh, renounces his wife	Ezra	10	25
A Levite priest	Neh.	12	42
Son of Eliud, ancestor of Joseph and Jesus	Mat.	1	15

elect *choice, chosen*

Christ so called	Is.	42	1
	I Pet.	2	6
God's chosen	Is.	45	1
By God	John	15	16
	John	17	6
Before the foundation of the world	Eph.	1	4
Unto good works	Eph.	2	10
To salvation	II Thes.	2	13
Of Christ	Is.	42	1
Jacob	Mal.	1	2–3
Lady	II John	1	
Under the gospel	Mat.	24	22
	Col.	3	12
	Tit.	1	1
Angels	I Tim.	5	21
Lady	II John	1	

election

Of rulers by lot	Neh.	11	1
According to foreknowledge	I Pet.	1	2
Before birth	Rom.	9	11
Of Israel	Rom.	11	28
Its privileges and duties	Mark	13	20
	Rom.	8	29
	I Cor.	1	27
	II Pet.	1	10
According to the purpose of God	Rom.	9	11
	Eph.	1	11
Of God	I Thes.	1	4
Of Christ, as Messiah	I Pet.	2	6
Of churches	I Pet.	5	13
Of Israel	Deut.	7	6
	Is.	45	4
Of ministers	Luke	6	13
	Acts	9	15

Ensures to Saints:

Acceptance with God	Rom.	11	7
Belief in Christ	Acts	13	48
Blessedness	Ps.	33	12
	Ps.	65	4
Effectual calling	Rom.	8	30
The inheritance	Is.	65	9
	I Pet.	1	4–5
Vindication of their wrongs	Luke	18	7
Working of all things for good	Rom.	8	28

Of Saints:

According to the foreknowledge of God	Rom.	8	29
By Christ	John	13	18
For the glory of God	Eph.	1	6
Irrespective of merit	Rom.	9	11
By God	Tit.	1	1
By grace	Rom.	11	5
Personal	Mat.	20	16
	John	6	44
	Acts	22	14
	II John	1	13
Recorded in heaven	Luke	10	20
Sovereign	Rom.	9	15–16
	I Cor.	1	27
To adoption	Eph.	1	5
To conformity with Christ	Rom.	8	29
To eternal glory	Rom.	9	23
To spiritual warfare	II Tim.	2	4

El-elohe-Israel *God the God of Israel*

Name of Jacob's altar	Gen.	33	20

elements: *basic parts*

Under God's control	Job	37	5-6
Used in judgments	Deut.	11	17
Melted	II Pet.	3	10-12
Beggarly	Gal.	4	9

elephant *large mammal with ivory tusks*

Ivory mentioned	I Ki.	10	22
	II Chr.	9	21

Eli, Eli, lama sabachthani

Words of Jesus on the cross	Mat.	27	46
	Mark	15	34
My God, my God, why have you forsaken me?	Ps.	22	1

Eli, Eloi *my God: height*

High priest	I Sam.	1	9
	I Sam.	2	11
Judge of Israel	I Sam.	4	18
Prophecies concerning his sons	I Sam.	2	27-36
Misjudges, rebukes, then blesses Hannah	I Sam.	1	14-17
Rebuked for indulgence of his evil sons	I Sam.	2	23-25
	I Sam.	3	13
Death of	I Sam.	4	18
Concern for ark	I Sam.	4	11-18
Teaches Samuel	I Sam.	3	1-18

Eliab *my God is a father*

Son of Helon	Num.	1	9
	Num.	10	16
Forefather of Dathan and Abiram, a Reubenite	Num.	26	8, 9
	Deut.	11	6
Called Elihu	I Sam.	1	1
Ancestor of Samuel	I Chr.	6	27
Called Eliel	I Chr.	6	34
Son of Jesse, oldest brother of David	I Sam.	16	6
	I Chr.	27	18
A hero of the tribe of Gad	I Chr.	12	8, 9
A Levite, a musician	I Chr.	15	18, 20
	I Chr.	16	5

Eliada, Eliadah *my God is knowing*

A son of David	II Sam.	5	16
	I Chr.	3	8, 9
Called Beeliada	I Chr.	14	7
Father of Rezon	I Ki.	11	23
One of the warriors of Benjamin	II Chr.	17	17

Eliah *see* Elijah

Eliakim, Jehoiakim *my God is raising*

Son of Hilkiah	II Ki.	18	18
Confers with commander of Assyria	II Ki.	18	26, 37
Brings reply to Isaiah	Is.	37	2
Original name of Jehoiakim, king of Judah	II Ki.	23	34
	II Chr.	36	4
A priest	Neh.	12	41
A son of Abiud	Mat.	1	13
A son of Melea	Luke	3	30

Eliam *God of the people*

Father of Bath-sheba	II Sam.	11	3
Called Ammiel	I Chr.	3	5
One of David's valiant men	II Sam.	23	34
Called Ahijah	I Chr.	11	36

Elias *see* Elijah

Eliel *God is God*

A chief of Manasseh	I Chr.	5	24
Ancestor of Samuel	I Chr.	6	34
Son of Shimhi	I Chr.	8	20, 21
Son of Shashak	I Chr.	8	22, 25
A Mahavite, one of David's heroes	I Chr.	11	46
Another of David's heroes	I Chr.	11	47
A Gadite, one of David's heroes	I Chr.	12	11
A son of Hebron	I Chr.	15	9, 11
A Levite, in charge of the offerings	II Chr.	31	13

Eliezer *my God is a helper*

Abraham's steward	Gen.	15	2
Son of Moses	Ex.	18	4
	I Chr.	23	15
Son of Becher	I Chr.	7	8
Priest of David	I Chr.	15	24
Son of Zichri	I Chr.	27	16
A prophet	II Chr.	20	37
Servant of Ezra	Ezra	8	16
Three men who married foreign wives	Ezra	10	18, 23, 31
Ancestor of Jesus	Luke	3	23, 29

Elihu *my God is He*

Son of Tohu	I Sam.	1	1

A Manassite warrior, who joins David at Ziklag	I Chr.	12	20
A temple porter	I Chr.	26	1, 7
A chief of the tribe of Judah	I Chr.	27	18
One of Job's three friends	Job	32	2

Elijah, Elias *my God is Jehovah*

The Tishbite, and prophet	I Ki.	18	36
Predicts a great drought	I Ki.	17	1
Persecuted by Ahab	I Ki.	17	2-7
Fed by ravens	I Ki.	17	6
Multiplies widow's oil and meal	I Ki.	17	8-16
Raises widow's son	I Ki.	17	21, 22
Returns, meeting Obadiah	I Ki.	18	1-16
Slays the priests of Baal	I Ki.	18	40
Flees into the wilderness of Beer-sheba	I Ki.	19	3
Travels to Horeb	I Ki.	19	8
Fasts forty days	I Ki.	19	8
Still small voice	I Ki.	19	12
Anoints Elisha	I Ki.	19	19
Denounces Ahab	I Ki.	21	19-21
Calls down fire from heaven	II Ki.	1	10-12
Divides Jordan	II Ki.	2	8
Carried up to heaven in a chariot of fire	II Ki.	2	11
His mantle taken by Elisha	II Ki.	2	13
Also called Elias, when he appears at Christ's transfiguration	Mat.	17	3
Piety spoken of	I Ki.	19	10-14
	Luke	1	17
	James	5	17
Antitype of John the Baptist	Mat.	11	14
	Mat.	16	14
	Mat.	17	10-12
Son of Harim who took a foreign wife	Ezra	10	21

Elimelech *my God is my king*

Emigrates to Moab with his wife Naomi and his two sons	Ruth	1	2, 3
	Ruth	2	1, 3
	Ruth	4	3, 9

Eliphalet, Eliphelet, Elpalet *my God is deliverance*

One of David's mighty men	II Sam.	23	34
A son of David	II Sam.	5	16
	I Chr.	3	6
A descendant of Saul	I Chr.	8	39
A companion of Ezra	Ezra	8	13
A son of Hashum	Ezra	10	33

Eliphaz *to whom God is strength*

The son of Esau	Gen.	36	4
A friend of Job	Job	2	11
Reproves Job	Job	4	1-5
Job prays for him	Job	42	7, 8, 10

Eliphelet *see* Eliphalet

Elisabeth *Greek form for Hebrew: God of the oath*

Wife of Zacharias and mother of John the Baptist	Luke	1	5, 13
Cousin of Mary	Luke	1	36
Barren	Luke	1	7-13
Greets Mary	Luke	1	39-45

Elisha *to whom God is salvation*

Appointed to succeed Elijah	I Ki.	19	16
Called by Elijah	I Ki.	19	14
Witnesses Elijah's translation	II Ki.	2	
Receives his mantle	II Ki.	2	13
Heals the waters with salt	II Ki.	2	21, 22
Destroys children who mock him	II Ki.	2	24
Shunamite's land is restored	II Ki.	8	1-6
Instructs Jehu	II Ki.	9	1-3
Jehoram desires to kill	II Ki.	6	31-33
His death	II Ki.	13	20, 21
Called Eliseus	Luke	4	27

His miracles:

Divides the Jordan	II Ki.	2	14
Oil for woman whose sons were to be sold	II Ki.	4	4-7
Raises dead boy	II Ki.	4	34
Neutralizes poison	II Ki.	4	40, 41
Increases bread to feed one hundred men	II Ki.	4	43, 44
Heals Naaman's leprosy	II Ki.	5	14
The iron swims	II Ki.	6	6
Reveals counsels of Syrian king	II Ki.	6	12
Syrians struck blind	II Ki.	6	18

His prophecies:

Foretells Shunammite woman's son	II Ki.	4	16
Death of the unbelieving prince	II Ki.	7	2
Prophesies plenty to the starving in Samaria	II Ki.	7	1
Seven years famine in Canaan	II Ki.	8	1
The victory of Jehoash over Syria	II Ki.	13	19

Elishah *God is salvation*

Descendant of Noah	Gen.	10	4
Islands of the Mediterranean	Ezek.	27	7

Elishama, Elishua *God hath heard*

Son of Ammihud	Num.	1	10
	Num.	2	18
A son of David	II Sam.	5	13, 16
	I Chr.	3	8
A descendant of Judah	I Chr.	2	41
Another son of David, also called Elishua	I Chr.	3	6
A priest	II Chr.	17	8
Secretary to Jehoiakim	Jer.	36	12, 20, 21

Elisheba *God of the oath*

Wife of Aaron	Ex.	6	23

Elishua *see* Elishama

Eliud *God of majesty*

Father of Eleazar and ancestor of Jesus	Mat.	1	14, 15

Elkanah *whom God possessed*

A son of Korah	Ex.	6	24
Father of Samuel	I Sam.	1	1
A Levite, father of Zophai	I Chr.	6	25, 36
A Levite	I Chr.	9	16
One who joins David at Ziklag	I Chr.	12	6
Doorkeeper of the ark	I Chr.	15	23
A prince of Ahaz	II Chr.	28	7

Elmodam *measure*

Ancestor of Jesus	Luke	3	23, 28

Eloi *see* Eli

Eloquent: *gifted in speaking*

Moses denies	Ex.	4	10
Listed with the upper class	Is.	3	3
Of Apollos	Acts	18	24
Not of Paul	I Cor.	2	1, 4, 5
	II Cor.	11	6

Elpalet *see* Eliphalet

Elul *vine*

Sixth month of the Jewish year	Neh.	6	15
	Hag.	1	14, 15

Elymas, Bar-jesus *wise man*

Opposes Paul	Acts	13	6–8

emancipation *setting free*

Of all Jewish slaves	Ex.	21	2
	Lev.	25	39–41
Spiritual	Is.	61	1
By following Jesus	John	8	31, 32
By Cyrus	II Chr.	36	23
	Ezra	1	1–4

embroider *to ornament with needlework*

The ephod	Ex.	28	6–8
Aaron's coat	Ex.	28	38, 39
By Bezaleel for the tabernacle	Ex.	35	30, 35
Garments for rich	Judg.	5	30

emerald *green, transparent precious stone*

Set in breastplate	Ex.	28	18
Exported from Tyre and used for ornaments	Ezek.	27	16
	Ezek.	28	13
Colour of the rainbow	Rev.	4	3
Foundation of heavenly Jerusalem	Rev.	21	19

emerods *see* hemorrhoids

Emmanuel, Immanuel *God with us*

Prophecy of Messiah	Is.	7	14
Name given to Jesus	Mat.	1	23

Emmaus *hot springs*

A village near Jerusalem where Jesus appears after resurrection	Luke	24	13

Emmor *see* Hamor

emotion *mental agitation*

By Josiah	II Ki.	22	11
Mixed	Ezra	3	11–13
In Jewish worship	Neh.	8	6, 9
Of the disciples	John	20	1–10
Envy	Prov.	27	4
Hatred	Amos	5	15
	Prov.	8	13
Joy	Neh.	12	43
Fear	Ex.	15	16
Anger	Gen.	27	45
Sorrow	Gen.	3	16
Regret	Luke	16	27–30
Despair	Eccl.	2	20

employee *one who works for wages*

Shall not work on sabbath	Ex.	20	10
Should be paid	Lev.	19	13
	Mat.	10	10
Expects to be rewarded	Job	7	2
Should abide by agreements	Mat.	20	1–13
Payment owed	Rom.	4	4
Shall not muzzle	I Tim.	5	18
Wicked	Mat.	21	33–41
Not loyal	John	10	12
Kindness to	Ruth	2	4
Oppression of	Mal.	3	5
	James	5	4

employer *a person who hires people to work for wages*

Forbidden to oppress	Deut.	24	14
Required to be considerate	Job	31	13
Required to pay fair wages	Col.	4	1
To forbear threatening	Eph.	6	9
To give a fair wage	Col.	4	1

employment *work, occupation, job*

Of Adam	Gen.	2	15
Day and night	I Chr.	9	33
Of a woman	Prov.	31	10–31
For food	II Thes.	3	7–10
Amos	Amos	7	14
Gideon	Judg.	6	11
Elisha	I Ki.	19	19
Matthew	Mat.	9	9
Peter	Mat.	4	18

emulation *jealousy*

May be beneficial	Rom.	11	14
Work of the flesh	Gal.	5	20

encamp *make camp*

In the wilderness	Ex.	13	20
	Num.	33	
In war	Judg.	6	4
Of the angel of the Lord	Ps.	34	7

enchanter *one who casts a spell*

Condemned by God	Deut.	18	10, 12
Magic	Ex.	7	11
Sorcery	Acts	8	9, 11

enchantment *a magic spell or charm*

Forbidden	Lev.	19	26
Punishment	Is.	47	9
None against Israel	Num.	23	23
Used by Balaam	Num.	24	1
Practiced in Israel in Hoshea's days	II Ki.	17	17
Used by Manasseh	II Ki.	21	6
Rebuked by Isaiah	Is.	47	9, 12

encouragement *giving hope*

Israel receives	Ex.	14	13
In the wilderness	Ex.	19	3–6
Good example of	Josh.	1	1–9
From fear	Is.	41	13
Given by Christ	Mat.	14	27
Given to Paul	Acts	23	11
In affliction	Rom.	8	16–18
David	I Sam.	30	6
Priests and Levites	II Chr.	31	4
Joshua	Deut.	1	38
	Deut.	3	28
Josiah	II Chr.	35	2
Given by an angel	Gen.	32	12
Given by God	Josh.	1	1–8
Given by Barnabas	Acts	4	36
Given by example	Acts	27	33–36

end of the world

Time of harvest	Mat.	13	39–43
Time of, is unknown	Mat.	24	3–44
Rejected by many	II Pet.	3	3–5
Lawlessness	Mat.	24	12
No warning	Mat.	24	37–42
By fire	II Pet.	3	10
Christ's return	I Thes.	4	16–18
Time of trouble	Jer.	30	7
Time of judgment	Rev.	20	1–15
Antichrist	Rev.	13	2–5
Multiplied natural calamity	Mat.	24	7
Apostasy, prior to	Mat.	24	36–39
Numerous wars	Mat.	24	6–7
Increased learning	Dan.	12	4
Increased travel	Dan.	12	4

En-dor *fountain of Dor*

A city south of mount Tabor	Josh.	17	11
Home of witch whom Saul consults	I Sam.	28	7

endurance *ability to last, or ability to stand pain*

In disciples	Mat.	10	22
Reward of	II Tim.	4	7, 8
Of chastening	Heb.	12	7
Of wrongful suffering	I Pet.	2	19

endure

As children be able to *e*.	Gen.	33	14
Can I *e* to see the evil?	Esth.	8	6
Lord shall *e* for ever.	Ps.	9	7
	Ps.	102	12
	Ps.	104	31
Weeping may *e* for a night	Ps.	30	5
Fear thee as long as the sun and moon *e*	Ps.	72	5
His name shall *e* for ever	Ps.	72	17
His mercy *e* for ever	Ps.	106	1
	Ps.	107	1
	Ps.	118	1
	Ps.	136	1
	Ps.	138	8
	Jer.	33	11
His righteousness *e* for ever	Ps.	111	3
	Ps.	112	3, 9
Doth crown *e* to every generation?	Prov.	27	24
Can thy heart *e*?	Ezek.	22	14
He that shall *e* to the end	Mat.	24	13
	Mark	13	13
E but for a time	Mark	4	17
Charity *e* all things	I Cor.	13	7
E hardness as a good soldier	II Tim.	2	3
In heaven a better and *e* substance	Job	10	34
If ye *e* chastening	Heb.	12	7
Blessed is man that *e* temptation	James	1	12
We count them happy who *e*	James	5	11
The word of the Lord *e* for ever	I Pet.	1	25
For conscience *e* grief	I Pet.	2	19

enemies *foes*

The property of, to be protected	Ex.	23	4, 5
The friendship of, deceitful	II Sam.	20	9, 10
	Prov.	27	6
	Mat.	26	48, 49
Desire not the death of	I Ki.	3	11
God delivers from	Ezra	8	31
	Ps.	18	48
	Ps.	60	12
	Ps.	136	24
Should not be cursed	Job	31	30
Pray to be delivered from	Ps.	17	9
	Ps.	59	1
Do not rejoice in their failings	Prov.	24	17
Christ prays for His	Luke	23	34
Satan	Mat.	13	39
Of the cross	Phil.	3	18
Should be:			
Helped	Prov.	25	21
	Rom.	12	20
Won by kindness	I Sam.	24	9–20
	II Ki.	6	21–23
Loved	Mat.	5	44
Prayed for	Acts	7	60

En-gedi *fountain of the kid*

Called Hazezon-tamar	Gen.	14	7
A town of Judah	Josh.	15	62
David dwells here	I Sam.	23	29
Saul's plight	I Sam.	24	1–22
Famous vineyards	S. of S.	1	14

engine *mechanical tool*

Used to shoot arrows	II Chr.	26	15
For war	Ezek.	26	9

engraving *a marking*

Of stones in the priest's breastplate	Ex.	28	9–11, 21, 36
	Ex.	39	8–14
Of idols	Ex.	32	4
Of the priest's girdle	Ex.	39	6
Of the priest's crown	Ex.	39	30

En-hakkore *fountain of him that calleth*

A spring, miraculously supplied to Samson	Judg.	15	19

enjoyment *pleasure*

Of one's inheritance	Num.	36	8
Of man's labour	Eccl.	2	24
	Eccl.	3	13
	Eccl.	5	18
Of the word of one's hands	Is.	65	22
Of the living God	I Tim.	6	17
Of sin, not lasting	Heb.	11	25
Dependent on obedience	Deut.	7	9–15
Aided by unity	Ps.	133	1

enlargement

Of Japheth	Gen.	9	27
Of troubles	Ps.	25	17
Broders of garments	Mat.	23	15
Of heart	II Cor.	6	11
God's promise to Israel	Ex.	34	24
Spiritual, given to Solomon	I Ki.	4	29
Requested by Jabez	I Chr.	4	10
Commanded by God	Is.	54	2

enmity *hostility, hatred*

Caused by sin	Gen.	3	15
Forbidden by Mosaic law	Num.	35	21, 22
Between Pilate and Herod	Luke	23	12
Carnal mind enmity against God	Rom.	8	7
	James	4	4
Abolished by Christ	Eph.	2	15

Enoch, Henoch, Hanoch *dedication*

Eldest son of Cain	Gen.	4	17
A city built by Cain	Gen.	4	17
Father of Methuselah	Gen.	5	18–24
His faith	Heb.	11	5
His prophecy	Jude		14
Translated	Gen.	5	22

Enon *a place*

John baptized here	John	3	23

Enos, Enosh *man*

Son of Seth	Gen.	4	26
Grandson of Adam	Gen.	5	6–11

enough

I have *e*	Gen.	33	9
It is *e*, Joseph is yet alive	Gen.	45	28
People bring more than *e*	Ex.	36	5
It is *e*	II Sam.	24	16
	I Ki.	19	4
	I Chr.	21	15
	Mark	14	41
	Luke	22	38
Four things say not, it is *e*	Prov.	30	15
Eat, and have not *e*	Hosea	4	10
	Hag.	1	6
Not room *e* to receive it.	Mal.	3	10
It is *e* for disciple	Mat.	10	25
Lest there be not *e*	Mat.	25	9
Bread *e* and to spare	Luke	15	17

enquire

People come to *e* of God	Ex.	18	15
As if a man *e* at oracle of God	II Sam.	16	23
To *e* in his temple	Ps.	27	4
Returned and *e* early after God	Ps.	78	34
Thou dost not *e* wisely	Eccl.	7	10
If ye will *e*, *e* ye	Is.	21	12
Should I be *e* of at all by them?	Ezek.	14	3
I will yet for this be *e* of	Ezek.	36	37
E who in it is worthy.	Mat.	10	11
To *e* among themselves	Luke	22	23
Of which salvation the prophets *e*	I Pet.	1	10

enrich *make rich*

Promised to David	I Sam.	17	25
Through God's kindness	Ps.	65	9
	Ezek.	27	33
	II Cor.	9	11
By following Jesus	I Cor.	1	5

En-rogel *fountain of the fuller*

Fountain near Jerusalem	Josh.	15	7
Jonathan and Ahimaaz stationed here	II Sam.	17	17
Adonijah feasts here	I Ki.	1	9

ensign *banner, signal*

Of tribes of Israel	Num.	2	2
Of enemies of God	Ps.	74	4
Of nations from afar	Is.	5	26
Crown used as	Zech.	9	16
Causing fear	Is.	31	9
Figurative of Jesus	Is.	11	10
Warning of Ethiopia	Is.	18	3

entertainment *see amusement*

enthusiasm *zeal*

Not always lasting	Mat.	13	20, 21
Instances of:			
Caleb	Num.	13	30–33
Gideon	Judg.	6, 7	
David	II Sam.	6	15, 16
Jehu	II Ki.	9	1–14
	II Ki.	10	1–28
Paul	Phil.	3	7–14

enticement *temptation, seduction*

Forbidden by Mosaic law	Ex.	22	16
	Deut.	13	6
Should be rejected	Prov.	1	10
By friends	Prov.	1	10
By lust	James	1	14
Fall into a pit	Prov.	28	10
Brought on by violence	Prov.	16	29
By one's own lust	James	1	14

Examples:

Samson	Judg.	16	5
Ahab	II Chr.	18	19–21

envy *resentful begrudging*

Harmful to him who envies	Job	5	2
	Prov.	14	30
	Prov.	27	4
Forbidden	Prov.	3	31
	Rom.	13	13
Provoked by good works of others	Eccl.	4	4
Punishment of	Is.	26	11
The wicked are fuel of	Rom.	1	29
Proof of a carnal mind	I Cor.	3	1, 3
Charity envieth not	I Cor.	13	4
Produced by foolish arguments	I Tim.	6	4
Inconsistent with the gospel	James	3	14

Instances of:

Cain, of Abel	Gen.	4	4–8
Philistines, of Isaac	Gen.	26	14
Rachel	Gen.	30	1
Joseph's brothers	Gen.	37	11
Aaron and Miriam, of Moses	Num.	12	1–10
Saul, of David	I Sam.	18	8, 9, 29
Priests, of Jesus	Mat.	27	18
	John	11	47
Jews, of Paul and Barnabas	Acts	13	45
	Acts	17	5

Epaenetus *laudable*

A convert to Christianity	Rom.	16	5

Epaphras *lovely*

Founder of Colossian church	Col.	1	7
Fellow prisoner of Paul	Philem.		23

Epaphroditus *lovely one*

A messenger of the Philippians	Phil.	4	18
Friend of Paul	Phil.	2	25–30

Ephah *measure, about a bushel*

A tenth of used for sin offering	Lev.	5	11
Measure of flour	Judg.	6	19
Product of an homer of seed	Is.	5	10
Made smaller by false merchants	Amos	8	5

Ephes-dammin, Pas-damin *boundary of blood*

Where Daivd slays Goliath	I Sam.	17	1

Ephesus *city of Asia Minor*

Apollos, Aquila and Priscilla labour here	Acts	18	24–28
Paul baptized here	Acts	19	1–7
Paul preaches here	Acts	19	8–10
Result of Paul's labours	Acts	19	19
Location of temple of Diana	Acts	19	24–32
Riot incited by Demetrius	Acts	19	24–41
Letter to	Eph.	1	1
Addressed by John in Revelation	Rev.	1	11
Paul's second visit	Acts	20	17–31
Paul directs Timothy to remain	I Tim.	1	3

ephod *a garment*

Emblem of the priestly office	Ex.	28	4
Used by idolatrous priests	Judg.	17	5
Used as an oracle	I Sam.	23	9–12

Description:

Made of gold, blue, purple and scarlet	Ex.	28	6
Set with precious stones	Ex.	28	9–11
Fastened to the breastplate	Ex.	28	25–28
Made of linen	II Sam.	6	14

Worn by:

Aaron	Ex.	39	5
Samuel	I Sam.	2	18
The high priest	I Sam.	2	28
	I Sam.	14	3
Ordinary priests	I Sam.	22	18
David	II Sam.	6	14
Father of Hanniel	Num.	34	23

Ephphatha *be opened*

Word spoken by Christ	Mark	7	34

Ephraim *doubly fruitful*

Absalom slain here	II Sam.	18	6–9

Ephraim, gate of

A gate of Jerusalem	II Ki.	14	13
	Neh.	8	16

Ephraim, tribe of

Descended from	Gen.	41	52
	Gen.	48	5
Strength of, on leaving Egypt	Num.	1	32, 33
Encamp west of the tabernacle	Num.	2	18
Strength of, on entering Canaan	Num.	26	37
Bounds of its territory	Josh.	16	4–9
Canaanites made captive	Josh.	16	10

Remarkable persons of:

Joshua	Num.	13	8
	Josh.	1	1
Abdon	Judg.	12	13–15
Zichri	II Chr.	28	7

Assisted:

Manasseh in taking Bethel	Judg.	1	22–25
Deborah and Barak	Judg.	5	14
Gideon	Judg.	7	24, 25
Town near Jerusalem visited by Christ	John	11	54
Term used to describe Israel	Hosea	4	16, 17
A mountain range	I Sam.	1	1

Ephratah, Ephrath *fruitful*

Ancient name for Bethlehem	Gen.	35	16, 19
	Gen.	48	7
	Ruth	4	11
	Mic.	5	2
Wife of Caleb	I Chr.	2	19, 50
Mother of Hur	I Chr.	4	4

Ephron, Ephrain *belonging to a calf*

Son of Zohar, the Hittite	Gen.	23	8
Sold burial ground to Abraham	Gen.	25	9, 10
A mountain	Josh.	15	9

Epicureans *sect of philosophers*

Dispute with Paul	Acts	17	18

epilepsy *a nervous disease*

Cured by Jesus	Mark	9	17–27

epistles *letters*

First epistle mentioned in Bible	II Sam.	11	14
Huram to Solomon	II Chr.	2	11
Elijah to Jehoram	II Chr.	21	12–15
Mordecai to the Jews	Esth.	8	9–14
Jeremiah to the exiles in Babylon	Jer.	29	1, 3
Luke to Theophilus	Luke	1	1–4
Tertius was Paul's secretary in writing Romans	Rom.	16	22
Lost epistles	I Cor.	5	9
	Col.	4	16

Of Paul, see books of Romans,
  Corinthians, Galatians, Ephesians,
  Philippians, Colossians, Thessalonians,
  Timothy, Titus and Philemon
Of James, Peter, John and Jude, see books
  of New Testament bearing their names

equality of man

Ordained by God	Job	31	13–15
	Ps.	33	13
Taught by Jesus	Mat.	20	25
	Mat.	23	8
	Mark	10	42
Discovered by Peter	Acts	10	28
Taught by Paul	Rom.	10	12
	Gal.	3	28
Complaint against	Mat.	20	12

equity *uprightness*

The Lord judges with	Ps.	98	9
A prophecy concerning Jesus	Is.	11	4
Only through God	Is.	59	14
See justice			

Er *watchful*

Son of Judah	Gen.	46	12
Son of Shelah	I Chr.	4	21
Ancestor of Jesus	Luke	3	28

Erastus *beloved*

Sent to Macedonia by Paul	Acts	19	22
	II Tim.	4	20
A chamberlain of Corinth	Rom.	16	23

error *mistake*

Uzzah smitten for	II Sam.	6	7
Remorse for	Job	19	4
Should be truthful about	Eccl.	5	6
None found in Daniel	Dan.	6	4
Recompense for	Rom.	1	27
Love of money	I Tim.	6	10
An error not to listen to God	I John	4	6

error—*continued*
Instances:

Saul	I Sam.	26	21
Israelites	Is.	3	12
	Is.	28	7
	Amos	2	4

Esaias *see* Isaiah

Esar-haddon *victor*

King of Assyria, son of Sennacherib	II Ki.	19	37

Esau *hairy*

Eldest of twin sons born to Isaac and Rebekah	Gen.	25	19–26
Beloved by Isaac	Gen.	25	28
Sells his birthright	Gen.	25	29–34
Marries a Hittite	Gen.	26	34
Marriage, a grief to Isaac and Rebekah	Gen.	26	35
Many wives	Gen.	26	34
	Gen.	28	9
Defrauded of blessing	Gen.	27	38–41
Reconciliation	Gen.	33	1–15
Buries his father	Gen.	35	29
Called Edom	Gen.	36	1
Settles at Seir	Gen.	36	6–8
	Deut.	2	5
Hated of God	Mal.	1	2
	Rom.	9	13
A profane person	Heb.	12	16

escape *to flee*

Of Noah	Gen.	7	7, 8
Of Lot from Sodom	Gen.	19	15–30
Of David from Saul	I Sam.	19	10
David from Absalom	II Sam.	15	14–16
Joash	I Ki.	11	2
Wicked shall not	Job	11	20
"With the skin of my teeth"	Job	19	20
From inner torment	Ps.	55	8
	Ps.	71	2
Liars will not	Prov.	19	5
None, from judgment of God	Mat.	23	33
	Rom.	2	3
From life's temptations	Luke	21	36
Of Jesus from the Jews	John	10	39
Of the apostles from prison	Acts	5	16–20
Of Paul and prisoners from shipwreck	Acts	27	42–44
Youthful lusts	II Tim.	2	22

Esh-baal *see* Ish-bosheth

Eshek *strife*

A Benjamite	I Chr.	8	39

Eshtaol *treaty*

A town of Judah	Josh.	15	33
Allotted to Dan	Josh.	19	41
	Judg.	18	2
Samson born near here	Judg.	13	25
Samson buried here	Judg.	16	31

Esli *at my side is God*

Ancestor of Jesus	Luke	3	25

Esrom *enclosed*

In genealogy of Christ	Mat.	1	3
Greek for Hezron	I Chr.	2	5

establish

I will *e* my covenant	Gen.	17	19
E my goings	Ps.	40	2
Faithfulness shalt *e* in heavens	Ps.	89	2
E work of our hands	Ps.	90	17
Lord hath *e* the heavens	Prov.	3	19
Throne is *e* by righteousness	Prov.	16	12
Every purpose is *e* by counsel	Prov.	20	18
In mercy shall throne be *e*	Is.	16	5
He *e* world by wisdom	Jer.	10	12
	Jer.	51	15
Two witnesses, every word *e*	Mat.	18	16
Yea, we *e* the law	Rom.	3	31
Going about to *e* their own righteousness	Rom.	10	3
E upon better promises	Heb.	8	6
The heart be *e* with grace	Heb.	13	9
God of all grace *e* you	I Pet.	5	10

esteem *value, respect*

Rock of salvation, lightly esteemed	Deut.	32	15
Those who forsake God shall not be	I Sam.	2	30
A poor man, lightly esteemed	I Sam.	18	23
Who controls his speech shall be	Prov.	17	28
A prophecy of Christ	Is.	53	3, 4
Esteem for others desirable	Phil.	2	3
	I Thes.	5	13

Esther *Greek star; her Hebrew name was Hadassah, Myrtle tree*

Daughter of Abihail	Esth.	2	15
Niece of Mordecai	Esth.	2	7, 15
Also called Hadassah	Esth.	2	7, 15
Chosen queen	Esth.	2	17
Reveals plot against the king's life	Esth.	2	22
Fasts against decree to destroy Israelites	Esth.	4	16, 17
Gains a hearing from Ahasuerus	Esth.	5	1–5
Accuses Haman to the king	Esth.	7	4–6
Intercedes for her people	Esth.	8	5, 6
Edict of reversal	Esth.	8	3–6
Institutes Purim	Esth.	9	29–32

eternal *everlasting*

God is thy refuge	Deut.	33	27
Promises of eternal life	Ps.	121	8
	Luke	23	43
	John	6	54
	II Cor.	5	1
Eternal punishment	Dan.	12	2
	Mat.	10	28
	Mark	3	29
	Jude		7
Eternal life through Christ	John	3	14–16
	Rom.	6	23
	Heb.	5	9
	Heb.	9	12
Things not seen	II Chr.	4	18

eternity *infinite duration*

Only mentioned in	Is.	57	15
Of praise to God	Ps.	30	12
	Ps.	41	13
God exists from eternity past	Ps.	90	2
	I Tim.	1	17
Christ's priesthood	Ps.	110	4
Kingdom of God	Mat.	6	13
Hell	Mat.	18	8
	Jude		6
God's righteousness	II Chr.	9	9
God's mercy	Ps.	119	142
God's habitation	Ps.	100	5
	Is.	57	15

Etham *bounded by the sea*

Wilderness camp of the Israelites	Ex.	13	20
	Num.	33	6, 7

Ethan *enduring*

A renowned sage	I Ki.	4	31
	Ps.	89	
A son of Zerah	I Chr.	2	6, 8
Descendant of Merari	I Chr.	15	17
A singer for David	I Chr.	15	19

Ethanim *incessant rains*

Seventh month of the Jewish year	I Ki.	8	2

Ethbaal *with Baal*

King of Sidon and father of Jezebel	I Ki.	16	31

ethics *system of moral duty*

Jews	Ex.	20	
Christians	Rom.	12	

Ethiopia *burnt faces*

Moses marries a woman of	Num.	12	1
Defeated by Asa	II Chr.	14	9–15
	II Chr.	16	8
Warriors of	II Chr.	12	3
	Jer.	46	9
Within the Babylonian Empire	Esth.	1	1
Prophecy concerning the conversion of	Ps.	68	31
	Is.	45	14
	Dan.	11	43
Wealth of	Is.	43	3
Called the land of Cush	Is.	11	11
Desolation of	Is.	20	2–6
	Ezek.	30	4–9
	Hab.	3	7
People tall and black	Is.	45	14
	Jer.	13	23
Ebed-melech, an Ethiopian, treats Jeremiah kindly	Jer.	38	7–13
	Jer.	39	15–18
Eunuch becomes a believer	Acts	8	27–39

Eubulus *prudent*

A friend of Paul	II Tim.	4	21

Eucharist *see* Communion

Eunice *victorious*

Mother of Timothy	II Tim.	1	5
A converted Jewess	Acts	16	1

eunuch *a castrated male*

Prohibited from certain privileges	Deut.	23	1
Influential court officials	Jer.	38	7–13
	Jer.	52	25
Daniel	Dan.	1	10
Those who voluntarily become	Mat.	19	12
Converted by Philip	Acts	8	26–29

Euodias *success*

A Christian woman of Philippi	Phil.	4	2

Euphrates *the good and abounding river*

A river in the garden of Eden	Gen.	2	14
Called the great river	Gen.	15	18
	Deut.	1	7
Eastern boundary of the promised land	Deut.	11	24
Called the flood	Josh.	24	2
Assyria bounded by	II Ki.	23	29
	Is.	7	20
Captivity of Judah represented by	Jer.	13	3–9
Egyptian army destroyed at	Jer.	46	2, 6, 10
Babylon situated on	Jer.	51	13, 36
Boundary of Persian Empire	Ezra	4	10, 11

Euroclydon *east wind*

A tempestuous wind	Acts	27	14

Eutychus *fortunate*

Falls asleep during Paul's sermon	Acts	20	9
A young man of Troas restored to life by Paul	Acts	20	9–12

evangelist *messenger of good tidings*

Philip called one	Acts	21	8
A calling by Christ	Eph.	4	11
Paul exhorts Timothy to be one	II Tim.	4	5

Eve *life*

Creation of	Gen.	1	26–28
	Gen.	2	21–24
Beguiled by Satan	Gen.	3	
Clothed with fig leaves	Gen.	3	7
Cursed denounced against	Gen.	3	16
Clothed with skins	Gen.	3	21
Children of	Gen.	4	1, 2
Deceived by Satan	I Tim.	2	13–15

even

I, *e* I, do bring a flood	Gen.	6	17
Angels to Sodom at *e*	Gen.	19	1
Bless me, *e* me	Gen.	27	34, 38
From *e* unto *e*	Lev.	23	32
Unto the entering of the gate	Judg.	9	40
E praise unto our God.	Ps.	40	3
Guide *e* unto death.	Ps.	48	14
E in laughter the heart.	Prov.	14	13
Will *e* forsake you.	Jer.	23	33
E so, Father.	Mat.	11	26
E the very dust of your city	Luke	10	11
Not of the world, *e* as I.	John	17	16
E Christ pleased not himself.	Rom.	15	3
E so, come, Lord Jesus	Rev.	22	20

evening

The day originally begins with	Gen.	1	5
Paschal lamb killed in	Ex.	12	6, 18
Golden candlesticks lighted in	Ex.	27	20, 21
	Ex.	30	8
Man ceases from labour in	Ruth	2	17
	Ps.	104	23
Wild beasts come forth in	Jer.	5	6
Called:			
Cool of the day	Gen.	3	8
Even	Gen.	19	1
	Deut.	28	67
Eventide	Josh.	8	29
	Acts	4	3
A time for:			
Meditation	Gen.	24	63
Prayer	Ps.	55	17
	Mat.	14	15, 23
Taking food	Mark	14	17, 18

evermore

Pleasures for *e*	Ps.	16	11
Will glorify thy name for *e*	Ps.	86	12
Blessed be name of Lord for *e*	Ps.	113	2
Lord preserve thy going out *e*	Ps.	121	8
Lord, *e* give us this bread.	John	6	34
Rejoice *e*	I Thes.	5	16
Son, who is consecrated for *e*	Heb.	7	28
I am alive for *e*	Rev.	1	18

every

E imagination of heart evil.	Gen.	6	5
Alive *e* one of you this day.	Deut.	4	4

For this shall *e* one that is godly.	Ps.	32	6
Refrained from *e* evil way	Ps.	119	101
Simple beneath *e* word	Prov.	14	15
E word of God is pure	Prov.	30	5
A time to *e* purpose	Eccl.	3	1
E knee shall bow.	Is.	45	23
	Rom.	14	11
By *e* word that proceedeth	Mat.	4	4
To *e* one which hath	Luke	19	26
Bringing into captivity *e* thought	II Cor.	10	5
Far above *e* name	Eph.	1	21
	Phil.	2	9
E creature of God is good.	I Tim.	4	4
Prepared to *e* good work	II Tim.	2	1
Lay aside *e* weight	Heb.	12	1
E good and perfect gift.	James	1	17
Believe not *e* spirit.	I John	4	1

evidence *proof*

False not allowed	Ex.	20	16
	Mat.	19	18
Rumours not acceptable	Lev.	5	1
For capitol offence two witnesses required.	Deut.	17	6
Requested by judges	Deut.	19	18
In church procedures	Mat.	18	16
Verified	John	4	39–42
Rejected	John	9	24–28
Of Satan	II Thes.	2	9, 10
For purpose of belief	John	20	30, 31

evil *the antithesis of good*

The knowledge of good and evil	Gen.	2	17
Spreading of	Gen.	6	5
Source of	Gen.	3	1–7
	I Sam.	24	13
	Mark	7	23
	John	3	19
	I Tim.	6	10
Of the heart	James	1	14
	Ps.	7	14
Provokes the Lord to anger	Judg.	2	11, 13
	Judg.	4	1
Evil spirits sent by God	I Sam.	19	9
Not of charity	I Cor.	13	4, 5
Avoid the appearance of	I Thes.	5	22
"Deliver us from evil"	Amos	5	14
	Mat.	6	13
	III John		11
Redemption through Christ	Gal.	1	4
God not subject to	James	1	13
Of money	I Tim.	6	10
The Lord said unto Satan	Job	1	12
Wickedness shall be broken as a tree	Job	24	20
I will fear no *e*	Ps.	23	4
Tents of wickedness	Ps.	84	10
Ye that love the Lord, hate *e*	Ps.	97	10
He shall not be afraid of *e* tidings	Ps.	112	7
Woe unto them	Is.	5	20
Their works are in the dark	Is.	29	15
If thine eye be *e*	Mat.	6	23
Cast the bad away	Mat.	13	48
Abhor *e*	Rom.	12	9
Be not overcome of *e*	Rom.	12	21
Redeeming the time	Eph.	5	16
Withstand in the *e* day	Eph.	6	13
Abstain from all appearance	I Thes.	5	22
Evil kings:			
Solomon	I Ki.	11	6
Jehoaz	II Ki.	13	1, 2, 11
Jeroboam	II Ki.	14	24
Zechariah	II Ki.	15	9
Ahaz	II Ki.	16	2
Of natural calamity	Is.	45	7
	Mic.	1	12

evil companions *see* companions, evil

evildoers

Fret not thyself because of *e*	Ps.	37	1
E shall be cut off	Ps.	37	9
Depart ye *e*	Ps.	119	115
A seed of *e*	Is.	1	4
Hypocrite and an *e*	Is.	9	17
Speak evil of you, as of *e*	I Pet.	3	16
E or as a busybody	I Pet.	4	15

evil eye

Selfish, covetous observations	Prov.	23	6
	Mat.	20	15
Sign of an evil heart	Mark	7	21, 22

Evil-merodach *man of Merodach*			
King of Babylon who restores Jehoiachin	II Ki.	25	27
	Jer.	52	31
evil spirits			
Sometimes sent by God	I Sam.	19	9
Cast out by Jesus	Luke	7	21
Cast out by Paul	Acts	19	11, 12
evil-speaking			
Against a ruler	Ex.	22	28
Against Job	Job	19	18
Lord shall cut off	Ps.	12	3
Of enemies	Ps.	41	5
Of drunkards	Ps.	69	12
Like a sharp razor	Ps.	52	2
Like a sword	Ps.	64	2
Hated by God	Prov.	6	16
Judged	Mat.	12	34–37
Must be stopped	Tit.	1	10, 11
Against religion	James	1	26
Extremely destructive	James	3	5–10
Condemned	Eph.	4	25
	James	4	11
exalt			
My father's God, I will *e* him	Ex.	15	2
Shall *e* horn of anointed	I Sam.	2	10
Thou art *e* as head above all.	I Chr.	29	11
Let us *e* his name together	Ps.	34	3
In righteousness shall they be *e*	Ps.	89	16
My horn shall thou *e*	Ps.	92	10
Art *e* far above all gods.	Ps.	97	9
Be thou *e* above the heavens	Ps.	108	5
E her, and she shall promote thee	Prov.	4	8
By blessing of upright the city is *e*	Prov.	11	11
Righteousness *e* a nation	Prov.	14	34
Mountain of Lord's house be *e* above the hills	Is.	2	2
	Mic.	4	1
Every valley shall be *e*	Is.	40	4
My servant shall *e*	Is.	52	13
E him that is low	Ezek.	21	26
E to heaven.	Mat.	11	23
	Luke	10	15
E himself shall be abased.	Mat.	23	12
	Luke	14	11
	Luke	18	14
Him hath God *e*	Acts	5	31
Be *e* above measure	II Cor.	12	7
God hath highly *e* him	Phil.	2	9
E himself above all called God	II Thes.	2	4
May *e* you in due time	I Pet.	5	6
examine			
Sat down to *e* matter	Ezra	10	16
E me, O Lord, prove me.	Ps.	26	2
If we this day be *e*	Acts	4	9
Be *e* by scourging	Acts	22	24
Let a man *e* himself	I Cor.	11	28
E yourselves, prove	II Cor.	13	5
example *a pattern*			
God, our example	Lev.	11	44
	Mat.	5	48
Abstain from the bad	Deut.	18	9
	II Chr.	30	7
	Ezek.	20	18
	III John		11
Power of evil	Deut.	18	9
Following evil fathers	Jer.	16	12
	Jer.	17	1, 2
	Ezek.	20	18
Of an evil priest	Hosea	4	9
Evil of Pharisees	Mat.	23	1–3
Of the Old Testament saints	I Cor.	10	6
To follow good	III John		11
Paul, our example	I Cor.	11	1
	Phil.	3	17
	II Thes.	3	7
Follow the good	Phil.	4	9
	James	5	10
	I Pet.	2	12, 13
Advice to the young	I Tim.	4	12
To Titus	Tit.	2	7
To women	I Pet.	3	5
example of Christ			
Servant	Mark	10	45
	Luke	22	27
In washing feet	John	13	13–17
Glorifying God	Rom.	15	2–7

Of humility	Phil.	2	5–8
Of forgiving	Col.	3	13
Of endurance	Heb.	12	2
Of suffering	I Pet.	2	21
	I Pet.	3	17, 18
	I Pet.	4	1
How to walk	I John	2	6
Laying down his life	I John	3	16
In heaven	Rev.	3	21
exceeding			
Thy *e* great reward	Gen.	15	1
An *e* bitter cry	Gen.	27	34
Land is *e* good	Num.	14	7
E glad with thy countenance	Ps.	21	6
God, my *e* joy	Ps.	43	4
Thy commandment is *e* broad	Ps.	119	96
Four things are *e* wise	Prov.	30	24
Which is *e* deep	Eccl.	7	24
Men feared the Lord *e*	Jonah	1	16
An *e* great city.	Jonah	3	3
E glad of the gourd	Jonah	4	6
Rejoiced with *e* great joy	Mat.	2	10
An *e* high mountain	Mat.	4	8
Rejoice and be *e* glad	Mat.	5	12
They were *e* amazed	Mat.	19	25
My soul is *e* sorrowful	Mat.	26	38
	Mark	14	34
King was *e* sorry	Mark	6	26
His raiment *e* white	Mark	9	3
Herod was *e* glad	Luke	23	8
Moses was *e* fair	Acts	7	20
Being *e* mad against them	Acts	26	11
Sin might become *e* sinful	Rom.	7	13
E weight of glory	II Cor.	4	17
E joyful in tribulation	II Cor.	7	4
E zealous of traditions	Gal.	1	14
E greatness of his power	Eph.	1	19
The *e* riches of his grace	Eph.	2	7
Able to do *e* abundantly	Eph.	3	20
Praying *e* earnestly	I Thes.	3	10
Your faith groweth *e*	II Thes.	1	3
Be glad with *e* joy	I Pet.	4	13
E great and precious promises	II Pet.	1	4
Present you faultless with *e* joy	Jude		24
excel			
Unstable as water, shalt not *e*	Gen.	49	4
Angels that *e* in strength	Ps.	103	20
Thou *e* them all	Prov.	31	29
Wisdom *e* folly	Eccl.	2	13
The glory that *e*	II Cor.	3	10
excellency			
E of dignity	Gen.	49	3
The greatness of thine *e*	Ex.	15	7
Doth not their *e* go away?	Job	4	21
Thundereth with voice of his *e*	Job	37	4
Deck with majesty and *e*	Job	40	10
Cast him down from his *e*	Ps.	62	4
I will make thee an eternal *e*	Is.	60	15
I came not with *e* of speech	I Cor.	2	1
That the *e* of the power may be of God	II Cor.	4	7
Count all things but loss for the *e*	Phil.	3	8
excellent			
Almighty is *e* in power	Job	37	23
How *e* is thy name in earth!	Ps.	8	1, 9
E in whom is all my delight	Ps.	16	3
How *e* is thy lovingkindness!	Ps.	36	7
I will speak of *e* things	Prov.	8	6
Righteous more *e* than neighbour	Prov.	12	26
Of an *e* spirit	Prov.	17	27
Lord hath done *e* things	Is.	12	5
E in working	Is.	28	29
E spirit in Daniel	Dan.	5	12
	Dan.	6	3
Things that are *e*	Rom.	2	18
	Phil.	1	10
A more *e* way	I Cor.	12	31
Obtained a more *e* name	Heb.	1	4
A voice from the *e* glory	II Pet.	1	17
except			
Not let go, *e* thou bless me.	Gen.	32	26
E their Rock and sold them	Deut.	32	30
E the Lord build the house	Ps.	127	1
E Lord had left remnant	Is.	1	9
	Rom.	9	29
Can two walk, *e* agreed?	Amos	3	3

E your righteousness exceed that of the scribes	Mat.	5	20
E ye be converted	Mat.	18	3
E days be shortened	Mat.	24	22
	Mark	13	20
Pharisees *e* they wash oft	Mark	7	3
E ye repent, ye shall perish	Luke	13	3
Do miracles *e* God be with him?	John	3	2
E a man be born again	John	3	3
E ye see signs and wonders	John	4	48
E ye eat flesh of the Son of man	John	6	53
No power, *e* it were given from above	John	19	11
E I see print of the nails	John	20	25
E ye be circumcised, ye cannot	Acts	15	1
As I am, *e* these bonds	Acts	26	29
How preach *e* they be sent?	Rom.	10	15
Not quickened, *e* it die	I Cor.	15	36
E there come a falling away	II Thes.	2	3
Not crowned, *e* he strive lawfully	II Tim.	2	5

excitement *agitation, commotion*

Over guests	Gen.	18	2
Over Jews leaving Egypt	Ex.	12	35
Over defeat of Philistines	I Sam.	17	52
Over the golden calf	Ex.	32	6
In battle	Josh.	6	20
In Jerusalem	Mat.	21	10, 11
By the glory of the Lord	Luke	9	28–35
Mob rule	Luke	23	20–25
Caused by the evil	Acts	6	9–15
Caused by fear	Acts	16	26–30
Caused by Paul	Acts	21	27–40

exclusiveness *selectivity*

Of the Jews	John	4	9, 10
	Acts	10	28
Abolished by Christ	Gal.	3	26–29
Of Doctrine	Gal.	1	8
	Acts	4	12
	John	14	6

excommunication *ecclesiastical censure*

A reason for	Mat.	18	15–18
From society	Luke	6	22, 23
From the synagogue	John	9	22
	John	9	34, 35
	John	12	42, 43
Comfort for	II Cor.	2	6–10
For Diotrephes	III John		9, 10

excuse *a reason for a failure*

Of Adam, for his sin	Gen.	3	8–13
By Aaron	Ex.	32	22–24
By Saul	I Sam.	15	20–24
Of the slothful	Prov.	22	13
Parable of the talents	Mat.	25	14–30
A feeble one	Luke	11	5–7
Parable of the supper	Luke	14	16–24
Those that are without	Rom.	1	20
A reason for	II Cor.	12	19

execration *a detested act*

The price for disobedience	Jer.	42	18
	Jer.	44	12

execute *to perform*

The justice of the Lord	Deut.	33	21
The priest's office	I Chr.	6	10
	I Chr.	24	2
The judgments of the Lord	Ps.	9	16
	Ps.	103	6
	Joel	2	11
Mercy	Hosea	11	9
Vengeance	Mic.	5	15
Wrath upon the evil	Rom.	13	4

exhibition *display*

The refusal of Vashti	Esth.	1	11, 12
Solomon	I Ki.	1	33

exhortation *language intended to incite and encourage*

To obeisance	Deut.	4	1–6
To give thanks	Ps.	136	1–26
For wisdom	Prov.	1	1–9
To repentance	Luke	3	3–18
	Acts	2	38
To fidelity	Acts	11	23
To fear the Lord	Acts	13	16–41
To conformity	Rom.	12	1–21
To firmness	I Cor.	15	58
	Col.	2	1–7
To sanctity	II Cor.	7	1–7
	I Thes.	4	1–10

To liberality of spirit	II Cor.	8	1–15
To generosity	II Cor.	9	1–15
To singleness of purpose	Eph.	4	1–23
Of spiritual love	Eph.	5	1–10
To meekness	Phil.	2	3–11
By Paul	Phil.	4	1–23
To faith	Heb.	11	1–40

exile *banishment*

The curse of Cain	Gen.	4	11, 12
Ittai, the Gittite	II Sam.	15	19–22
Adam	Gen.	3	22–24
Jacob	Gen.	27	43
Absalom	II Sam.	14	13, 14
David	II Sam.	15	23
Jeroboam	I Ki.	11	40
Jesus	Mat.	2	13–15
John, the apostle	Rev.	1	9

exodus *departure*

From Egypt	Ex.	12	41, 42

exorcism *casting out spirits by magic*

Jesus accused of	Mat.	12	24
By the seven sons of Sceva	Acts	19	13–16

expectation *anticipation*

Of the poor	Ps.	9	18
Through wisdom	Ps.	62	1–7
	Prov.	24	13, 14
Denied to the wicked	Prov.	10	28
	Prov.	11	7
Of captivity	Is.	20	5
Of freedom	Is.	20	6
Of peace	Jer.	29	11
Of the lame man	Acts	3	2–6
Waits for manifestation	Rom.	8	19
Of hope	Phil.	1	20
For sacrifice	Heb.	10	13

expedient

E for us that one man die	John	11	50
E for you that I go away	John	16	7
All things not *e*	I Cor.	6	12
	I Cor.	10	23
This is *e* for you	II Cor.	8	10
It is not *e* for me to glory	II Cor.	12	1

experience

By *e* the Lord blessed me	Gen.	30	27
My heart had *e* of wisdom	Eccl.	1	16
Patience worketh *e*, and *e* hope	Rom.	5	4

expulsion *see* exile

externals *visible form*

Prominence by scribes and Pharisees	Mat.	23	2–7
	Luke	11	39–44

extortion *exaction*

The penalty for	Ps.	109	11–16
Outcast	Is.	16	3, 4
An abomination	Ezek.	22	12
Practiced by the Pharisees	Mat.	23	25
A parable	Luke	18	9–14
Brings damnation	I Cor.	5	9, 10
	I Cor.	6	9, 10

eyebrows

Lepers shave off	Lev.	14	2, 9
Not to be plucked	Deut.	14	1

eyes *organ of sight*

Grow dim with age	Gen.	27	1
Made red by wine	Gen.	49	12
"The apple of his eye"	Deut.	32	10
Often put out as punishment	Judg.	16	21
	II Ki.	25	7
Of the Lord are everywhere	II Chr.	16	9
	Job	28	10
	Prov.	15	3
Lifted up in prayer	Ps.	121	1
	Ps.	123	1
Opened by the Lord	Ps.	146	8
Are never satisfied	Prov.	27	20
Light of the body	Mat.	6	22
Cast out the mote	Mat.	7	5

eye

E of both were opened	Gen.	3	7
His *e* were dim	Gen.	27	1
E for *e*	Deut.	19	21
	Mat.	5	38
Lest thou lift up *e* to heaven	Deut.	4	19
Gift doth blind *e* of wise	Deut.	16	19
Kept him as apple of his *e*	Deut.	32	10

eye—*continued*

E of all Israel upon thee	I Ki.	1	20
Lord opened *e* of young man	II Ki.	6	17
E of Lord run to and fro	II Chr.	16	9
	Zech.	4	10
And no *e* had seen me.	Job	10	18
Mine *e* shall behold, and not another	Job	19	27
Commandment enlightening the *e*	Ps.	19	8
E of Lord on them that fear him	Ps.	33	18
E of Lord on the righteous	Ps.	34	15
	I Pet.	3	12
Formed *e* shall he not see?	I Pet.	94	9
Lift up mine *e* to hills	I Pet.	121	1
E of all wait upon thee	I Pet.	145	15
E of man are never satisfied	Prov.	27	20
E not satisfied with seeing	Eccl.	1	8
Wise man's *e* are in his head	Eccl.	2	14
I will hide mine *e* from you	Is.	1	15
To open the blind *e* to bring	Is.	42	7
They shall see *e* to *e*	Is.	52	8
Neither hath *e* seen	Is.	64	4
	I Cor.	2	9
Mine *e* a fountain of tears	Jer.	9	1
Mine *e* shall weep sore	Jer.	13	17
Mine *e* run down with tears	Jer.	14	17
Of purer *e* than to behold evil	Hab.	1	13
Light of the body is the *e*	Mat.	6	22
	Luke	11	34
Blessed are your *e*	Mat.	13	16
If *e* offend thee, pluck it out.	Mat.	18	9
E were fastened on him.	Luke	4	20
Their *e* were holden	Luke	24	16
Anointed *e* of blind man	John	9	6
Could not this man, which opened *e*?	John	11	37
Before whose *e* Christ has been set.	Gal.	3	1
E of your understanding enlightened	Eph.	1	18
All things are opened unto *e* of him	Heb.	4	13
The lust of the *e*	I John	2	16

eyeservice *regard*

The pleasing of man	Eph.	6	6, 7
	Col.	3	22

Ezar, Ezer *help*

A duke of the Horites	Gen.	36	21
A son of Seir	I Chr.	1	38
Father of Bilhan, Zavan and Jakan	I Chr.	1	42
Father of Hushah	I Chr.	4	4
Son of Hur	I Chr.	4	4
Grandson of Ephratah	I Chr.	4	4
Son of Ephraim	I Chr.	7	21
Slain by men of Gath	I Chr.	7	21
A Gadite warrior	I Chr.	12	9
A son of Jeshua	Neh.	3	19
A priest	Neh.	12	42

Ezekias *see* Hezekiah

Ezekiel *God strengthens*

A son of Buzi, and one of the greater Jewish prophets during the exilic period	Ezek.	1	1–3
His vision as a priest	Ezek.	1	4–28
Is deeply moved by his visions	Ezek.	1	28
	Ezek.	3	12–15
	Ezek.	8	1–4
	Ezek.	11	13, 22–25
Commanded to speak to Israel	Ezek.	3	1–11
	Ezek.	33	7
Elders seek his advice	Ezek.	8	1
	Ezek.	20	1
An eloquent and popular speaker	Ezek.	33	30–33
Performs symbolical actions as object lessons	Ezek.	4	1–5
	Ezek.	6	11
	Ezek.	12	3–7, 18
	Ezek.	21	6, 12, 14
Intercedes for Israel	Ezek.	9	8
Warns people against worshipping idols	Ezek.	14	1–11
Predicts judgments upon Jerusalem	Ezek.	14	12–23
Speaks in riddles and parables	Ezek.	17	1–24
	Ezek.	20	49
	Ezek.	23	1–49
	Ezek.	24	3–14

Visions of hope:

Dry bones resurrected	Ezek.	37	1–14
New temple	Ezek.	40–42	

Ezion-gaber, Ezion-geber *backbone of the mighty*

Place on Red sea where the Israelites camp on their wilderness journey	Num.	33	35
	Deut.	2	8

A seaport during the reigns of Solomon and Jehoshaphat	I Ki.	9	26
	I Ki.	22	48
	II Chr.	8	17

Ezra *help*

A Judahite	I Chr.	4	17
A scribe, priest, reformer	Ezra	7	1–9
	Ezra	8	1
Had prepared himself to teach Israel	Ezra	7	10
Commissioned by Artaxerxes	Ezra	7	13–26
Reads the law and commands the people to rejoice	Neh.	8	1–18
Orders a fast	Ezra	8	21
Prays	Ezra	9	5–15
People repent and reforms are made	Ezra	10	1–44
	Neh.	9, 10	
Ancestor of a priestly family who return from exile	Neh.	12	1, 13, 33

F

fable *fictitious narrative*

With a moral, in the tale of the trees and of the thistle	Judg.	9	8–15
	II Ki.	14	9
False, invented tales	I Tim.	1	4
	I Tim.	4	7
	II Tim.	4	4
	Tit.	1	14
	II Pet.	1	16

face *front part of the head*

Of God hidden from the disobedient	Gen.	4	14
	Deut.	31	18
	Ezek.	39	23
Lord speaks to Moses face to face	Ex.	33	11

Transfigured:

Of Moses	Ex.	34	29–35
Jesus	Mat.	17	2
	Luke	9	29

Of the Lord:

Beholds evil	Gen.	19	13
Entreated	I Ki.	13	6
Against evil	Ps.	34	16
Christ goes before	Luke	1	76
Painted, to enhance	II Ki.	9	30
Character revealed in	Is.	3	9
Covering of	Is.	6	2
In fasting	Mat.	6	16

factions *see* division

fade

Whose leaf *f*	Is.	1	30
Grass withereth, flower *f*	Is.	40	7
We all *f* as a leaf	Is.	64	6
The leaf shall *f*	Jer.	8	13
Whose leaf shall not *f*	Ezek.	47	12
Rich man shall *f* away	James	1	11
Inheritance that *f* not away	I Pet.	1	4
	I Pet.	5	4

failure *a deficiency or lack*

Caused by God	Gen.	11	3–8
Of spies caused by fear	Num.	13	31–33
Because of hearing and not doing	Mat.	7	26, 27
Early disciples could not heal	Mat.	17	15–17
	Mark	9	24–28
Because of no oil	Mat.	25	8–13
Disciples fish all night	Luke	5	5
Lack of forethought	Luke	14	28–32
Because of unbelief	Heb.	4	6

faintheartedness *cowardice, timidity*

Sent by the Lord for diobedience	Lev.	26	36
Makes men unfit for battle	Deut.	20	8
Isaiah comforts Ahaz	Is.	7	4
People of Damascus	Jer.	49	23
Always pray	Luke	18	1
In preaching the gospel	II Cor.	4	1, 16
In rebuke	Heb.	12	5
Patience in labour	Rev.	2	3

fainting *lacking strength*

Of Jacob	Gen.	45	26
Of David	II Sam.	21	15
Of trees in the field	Ezek.	31	15
Of Daniel	Dan.	8	27
Because of thirst	Amos	8	13
Of Jonah	Jonah	4	8
For lack of food	Mat.	15	32

Fair Havens, The

A harbor in Crete, passed by Paul on journey to Rome	Acts	27	8

faith *belief of testimony*

Miracles performed through	Mat.	9	22
	Luke	8	50
	Acts	3	16
Power of	Mat.	17	20
	Mark	9	23
	Luke	17	6
Object of	Mark	11	22
	John	6	29
	Acts	20	21
In Christ	Acts	8	12
	II Tim.	3	15
Evidenced in confessing Christ	Rom.	10	9–12
	II Tim.	1	12
	I John	4	15
The gift of God	Rom.	12	3
	I Cor.	2	5
	I Cor.	12	9
	Eph.	2	8
Works by love	I Cor.	13	1–13
	Col.	1	4
	Heb.	10	23
	I John	3	14, 23
Exhortations to continue in	I Cor.	16	13
	Eph.	6	16
	Col.	2	7
	I Tim.	4	12
	Heb.	10	22
Unity of	Eph.	4	5, 13
	Jude		3
Trial of	II Thes.	1	4
	Heb.	11	17
	James	1	3, 13
	I Pet.	1	7
Definition of	Heb.	11	1–40
Jesus, the author of	Heb.	12	2
Without works is dead	James	2	17, 20, 26
All things should be done in	Rom.	14	22
Christ dwells in the heart by	Eph.	3	17
Christ precious to those having	I Pet.	2	7
Commanded	Mark	11	22
	I John	3	23
Essential to the profitable reception of the gospel	Heb.	4	2
Evidence of the new birth	I John	5	1
Evidence of things not seen	Heb.	11	1
Examine whether you be in	II Cor.	13	5
Excludes boasting	Rom.	3	27
Excludes self-justification	Rom.	10	3–4
A gift of the Holy Ghost	I Cor.	12	9
The gospel effectual in those who have	I Thes.	2	13
Impossible to please God without	Heb.	11	6
Accompanied by repentence	Mark	1	15
	Luke	24	47
Followed by conversion	Acts	11	21
Fruitful	I Thes.	1	3
Most holy	Jude		20
The work of God	Acts	11	21
	I Cor.	2	5
Justification is by	Rom.	4	16
Necessary in prayer	Mat.	21	22
	James	1	6
Necessary in the Christian warfare	I Tim.	1	18–19
	I Tim.	6	12
Often tried by affliction	I Pet.	1	6–7
Preaching designed to produce	John	17	20
	Acts	8	12
	Rom.	10	14–15, 17
	I Cor.	3	5
Saints die in	Heb.	11	13
The scriptures designed to produce	John	20	31
	II Tim.	3	15
The substance of things hoped for	Heb.	11	1
Those who are not Christ's have not	John	10	26–27
Whatsoever is not of, is sin	Rom.	14	23
The wicked destitute of	John	10	25

	John	12	37
	Acts	19	9
	II Thes.	3	2
The wicked often profess	Acts	8	13, 21

Objects of:

Christ	John	6	29
	Acts	20	21
God	John	14	1
The Gospel	Mark	1	15
Promises of God	Rom.	4	21
	Heb.	11	13
Writings of Moses	John	5	46
	Acts	24	14
Writings of the prophets	II Chr.	20	20
	Acts	26	27

By It, Saints:

Are supported	Ps.	27	13
	I Tim.	4	10
Live	Gal.	2	20
Obtain a good report	Heb.	11	2
Overcome the devil	Eph.	6	16
Overcome the world	I John	5	4–5
Resist the devil	I Pet.	5	9
Stand	Rom.	11	20
	II Cor.	1	24
Walk	Rom.	4	12
	II Cor.	5	7

Produces:

Boldness in preaching	II Cor.	4	13
Confidence	I Pet.	2	6
Hope	Rom.	5	2
Joy	Acts	16	34
	I Pet.	2	6
Peace	Rom.	15	13

Through It Is:

Access to God	Eph.	3	12
Adoption	John	1	12
	Gal.	3	26
Edification	I Tim.	1	4
	Jude		20
Eternal life	John	3	15–16
	John	6	40, 47
The gift of the Holy Ghost	Acts	11	15–17
	Gal.	3	14
	Eph.	1	13
Inheritance of the promises	Gal.	3	22
	Heb.	6	12
Justification	Acts	13	39
	Rom.	3	21–22, 30
	Rom.	5	1
Preservation	I Pet.	1	5
Remission of sins	Acts	10	43
	Rom.	3	25
Rest in heaven	Heb.	4	3
Salvation	Mark	16	16
	Acts	16	31
Sanctification	Acts	15	9
Spiritual life	John	20	31
	Gal.	2	20
Spiritual light	John	12	36, 46

Different kinds of:

Great	Mat.	8	10
Little	Mat.	8	26
	Mat.	14	28–31
	Mat.	17	20
Humble	Luke	7	6, 7
Rootless	Luke	8	13
Boundless	John	11	21–27
Timid	John	12	42, 43
Mutual	Rom.	1	12
Vain	I Cor.	15	14, 17
Unfeigned	I Tim.	1	5
Common	Tit.	1	4
Dead	James	2	17, 20
Of devils	James	2	19
Perfect	James	2	22
Precious	II Pet.	1	1

Blessings of:

Leads to salvation	Mark	16	16
	John	3	16, 36
	Acts	16	31
	Heb.	11	6
	I John	5	10
Purification	Acts	15	9
Sanctification	Acts	26	18
Justification	Rom.	3	28
	Rom.	5	1
	Gal.	2	16

faith—*continued*

Topic	Book	Ch.	Verse
Produces peace, joy, hope, etc.	Rom.	5	1
	Rom.	15	13
	II Cor.	4	13
	I Pet.	1	8
Gives access to God	Rom.	5	2
Shield of the Christian	Eph.	6	16
	I Thes.	5	8
Overcometh the world	I John	5	4
Instances of:			
Noah	Gen.	6	14–22
	Heb.	11	7
Abraham	Gen.	12	1–4, 7
	Gen.	22	1–10
	Rom.	4	8–21
	Heb.	11	8–19
Joseph	Gen.	50	20
	Heb.	11	22
Caleb	Num.	13	30
Moses	Num.	16	28, 29
	Heb.	11	24–28
David	I Sam.	17	37, 46, 47
Shadrach, Meshach, Abednego	Dan.	3	17
Daniel	Dan.	6	10
Ninevites	Jonah	3	5
Joseph	Mat.	1	18–24
	Mat.	2	13, 14
Peter	Mat.	16	16
Nathanael	John	1	49
Martha	John	11	27
Stephen	Acts	6	5
Barnabas	Acts	11	24
Paul	Acts	27	23–25
	Gal.	1	23
	II Tim.	4	7

faithfulness *steadfastness, sincerity*

Topic	Book	Ch.	Verse
Towards men	Deut.	1	16
	Prov.	14	5
	Luke	16	10
	I Cor.	4	2
	Tit.	2	10
	Rev.	2	10
Commended in the service of God	II Ki.	12	15
	Mat.	24	45
	II Cor.	2	17
	III John		5
Illustrated in parables	Mat.	25	14–23
	Luke	19	12–19
Will be rewarded	Luke	12	42–44
Instances of:			
Abraham	Gen.	22	1–18
Joseph	Gen.	39	4, 22
Moses	Num.	12	7
David	I Sam.	22	14
Daniel	Dan.	6	4
Paul	Acts	20	20
Timothy	I Cor.	4	17

fall of man

Topic	Book	Ch.	Verse
All men partake of the effects of	I Ki.	8	46
	Gal.	3	22
	I John	1	8
	I John	5	19
By the disobedience of Adam	Gen.	3	11–12
	Rom.	5	12, 15, 19
Cannot be remedied by men	Prov.	20	9
	Jer.	2	22
	Jer.	13	23
Abominable	Job	15	16
	Ps.	14	3
Blinded in heart	Eph.	4	18
Born in sin	Job	15	14
	Job	25	4
	Ps.	51	5
	Is.	48	8
	John	3	6
A child of wrath	Eph.	2	3
Conscious of guilt	Gen.	3	7–8, 10
Constant in evil	Ps.	10	5
	II Pet.	2	14
Corrupt and perverse in his ways	Gen.	6	12
	Ps.	10	5
	Rom.	3	12–16
Defiled in conscience	Tit.	1	15
	Heb.	10	22
Depraved in mind	Rom.	8	5–7
	Eph.	4	17
	Col.	1	21

Topic	Book	Ch.	Verse
Devoid of the fear of God	Rom.	3	18
Estranged from God	Gen.	3	8
	Ps.	58	3
	Eph.	4	18
	Col.	1	21
Evil in heart	Gen.	6	5
	Gen.	8	21
	Jer.	16	12
	Mat.	15	19
	II Tim.	2	26
In bondage to the devil	Heb.	2	14–15
In bondage to sin	Rom.	6	19
	Rom.	7	5, 23
	Gal.	5	17
	Tit.	3	3
Intractable	Job	11	12
Loves darkness	John	3	19
Receives not the things of God	I Cor.	2	14
Short of God's glory	Rom.	3	23
Totally depraved	Gen.	6	5
	Rom.	7	18
Turned to his own way	Is.	53	6
Unrighteous	Eccl.	7	20
	Rom.	3	10
Without understanding	Ps.	14	2–3
	Rom.	3	11
Banishment from paradise	Gen.	3	24
Condemnation to labor and sorrow	Gen.	3	16, 19
	Job	5	6–7
Eternal death	Job	21	30
	Rom.	5	18, 21
	Rom.	6	23
Temporal death	Gen.	3	19
	Rom.	5	12
	I Cor.	15	22
Remedy for, provided by God	Gen.	3	15
	John	3	16
Through temptation of the devil	Gen.	3	1–5
	II Cor.	11	3
	I Tim.	2	14
Story of	Gen.	3	1–24
Pattern of temptation	Gen.	3	1–5
	I John	2	16, 17
Eve: Beguiled	I Cor.	11	3
	II Tim.	2	12–14
Adam covered his transgression	Job	31	33
Originating in man	Eccl.	7	29
As first father sinned	Is.	43	27
Broke covenant	Hosea	6	7
Death in sin	Eph.	2	1
Its consequences, sin and death	Gen.	3	19
	Rom.	5	12
	I Cor.	15	21

fall

Topic	Book	Ch.	Verse
Let none of his words *f*	I Sam.	3	19
How are the mighty *f*!	II Sam.	1	19, 25, 27
F into hands of God	II Sam.	24	14
	I Chr.	21	13
Deep sleep *f* on men	Job	4	13
Let them *f* by their own counsels	Job	33	15
	Ps.	5	10
Is *f* into ditch	Ps.	7	15
Though he *f* not utterly cast down	Ps.	37	24
A thousand shall *f* at thy side	Ps.	91	7
Where no counsel is, the people *f*	Prov.	11	14
He that trusteth in riches shall *f*	Prov.	28	
Just man *f* seven times	Prov.	24	16
Rejoice not when thine enemy *f*	Prov.	17	
Diggeth a pit shall *f* there in	Prov.	26	27
Woe to him alone when he *f*	Eccl.	4	10
How art thou *f*!	Is.	14	12
Let no lot *f* on it.	Ezek.	24	6
F down and worship	Dan.	3	5
	Mat.	4	9
Say to hills, *f*	Hosea	10	8
	Luke	23	30
Sparrow *f* to ground	Mat.	10	29
F into pit on sabbath day	Mat.	12	11
Both *f* into the ditch	Mat.	15	14
	Luke	6	39
Stars *f* from heaven	Mat.	24	29
	Mark	13	25
To his master he standeth or *f*	Rom.	14	4
Occasion to *f*	Rom.	13	

Take heed lest he *f*	I Cor.	10	12
Some are *f* asleep	I Cor.	15	6, 18
F into the condemnation	I Tim.	3	6
Lest he *f* into reproach	I Tim.	3	7
Rich *f* into temptation	I Tim.	6	9
If they fall away	Heb.	6	6
To *f* into hands of living God	Heb.	10	31
Joy when ye *f* into temptation	James	1	2
Flower thereof *f*	James	11	
	I Pet.	1	24

fallowdeer
Deer of pale yellow which Hebrews were allowed to eat	Deut.	14	5
	I Ki.	4	23

fallow ground
Ground untilled	Jer.	4	3
	Hosea	10	12

false accusations *untrue statements*
Against a neighbor	Ex.	20	16
	Deut.	5	20
	Prov.	25	18
	Mat.	19	18
	Luke	18	20
Of gluttony and winebibbing	Mat.	11	19
Come out of the heart	Mat.	15	19
Council seeks witness against Jesus	Mark	14	55–60
Zacchaeus promises to restore goods	Luke	19	8
Against Paul	Acts	16	20, 21

Of Jesus:
Gluttony	Mat.	11	19
Blasphemy	Mat.	26	64, 65
Insanity	Mark	3	21
Demon possession	John	7	20
Breaking the sabbath	John	9	16
Treason	John	19	12

false confidence
In self	Deut.	29	19
	I Ki.	20	11
	Prov.	3	5
	Prov.	23	4
	Is.	5	21
	II Cor.	9	9
In outward resources	Ps.	20	7
	Ps.	33	17
	Prov.	11	28
	Is.	22	11
	Is.	31	1–3
	Jer.	48	7
In man	Ps.	33	16
	Ps.	118	8
	Is.	2	22
	Jer.	17	5
	Hosea	5	13

Examples:
Babel	Gen.	11	4
Sennacherib	II Ki.	19	23
Hezekiah	Is.	22	11
Peter	Mat.	26	35

falsehood *untruth*
Not to be made	Ex.	23	1
A talebearer	Lev.	19	11
Told to the man of God	I Ki.	13	17, 18
Gives no comfort	Job	21	34
Job will not speak	Job	27	4
	Job	36	4
Abhorred by the Lord	Ps.	5	6
By the wicked	Ps.	7	14
Deceitful and evil tongues	Ps.	34	13
	Ps.	52	2
	I Pet.	3	10
Vow against slandering	Ps.	101	5
Disliked by the Lord	Prov.	6	16–19
People scorned for	Is.	28	15
	Is.	57	4
	Is.	59	13
Not profitable	Jer.	7	8
One of many sins	Hosea	7	1
Bribe given to soldiers	Mat.	28	11–15
Jesus calls the devil father of	John	8	44
Ananias lies to Peter	Acts	5	1–10
Paul wants the people to speak the truth	Eph.	4	25
	Col.	3	9
The fate of liars	Rev.	21	8
	Rev.	22	15

false prophet(s) *one who falsely pretends to be inspired to God*
Speaks without God's command	Deut.	18	20
Signs but wrong message	Deut.	13	1–5
Of peace	Jer.	23	17
In end times	Mat.	24	11
Speaks of wine	Mic.	2	11
In sheep's clothing	Mat.	7	15, 16
Christ foretells rise of	Mat.	24	11, 24
	Mark	13	21–23
Peter foretells of	II Pet.	2	1
Is condemned	Rev.	19	20

false teacher(s)
Teach traditions of men	Mat.	15	9
Uses deceiving speech	Rom.	16	17, 18
People will turn to	II Tim.	4	3, 4
Will deny the Lord	II Pet.	2	1
Change the gospel	Gal.	1	6–8
People pleasers	II Tim.	4	3
Bring damnable heresies	II Pet.	2	1
Of Jannes and Jambres	II Tim.	3	8

false weights *incorrect weights or balances*
The law requires just weights	Deut.	25	13–15
Abominable to the Lord	Prov.	11	1
	Prov.	20	23

false witnesses *false testifiers*
One of ten commandments	Ex.	20	16
Forbidden	Ex.	23	1
To be investigated by judges	Deut.	19	16–20
Cause cruelty	Ps.	27	12
Accuse falsely	Ps.	35	11
Disliked by the Lord	Prov.	6	19
Contrasted with a good witness	Prov.	12	17
	Prov.	14	5
	Prov.	21	28
Shall be punished	Prov.	19	5
Shall perish	Prov.	21	28
Against Naboth	I Ki.	21	13
Against Jesus at His trial	Mat.	27	59–61
Against Stephen	Acts	6	13
Against Paul	Acts	17	5–7
Of God	I Cor.	15	15

fame
Have heard *f* of thee	Num.	14	15
We heard the *f* of God	Josh.	9	9
F of Solomon	I Ki.	10	1
	II Chr.	9	1
We have heard *f* with ears	Job	28	22
Isles that have not heard *f*	Is.	66	19
Get them *f* in every land.	Zeph.	3	19
F of Jesus	Mat.	4	24
	Mark	1	28
	Luke	4	14, 37
	Luke	5	15
The *f* thereof went abroad	Mat.	9	26
Herod heard of the *f* of Jesus	Mat.	14	1

familiar spirits *spirit called up for consultation*
Not to be sought after	Lev.	19	31
Law against	Lev.	20	6, 27
Abomination to the Lord	Deut.	18	11, 12
Counsel sought by Saul	I Sam.	28	3, 7–9
	I Chr.	10	13
Dealt with by King Manasseh	II Ki.	21	6
Destroyed by King Josiah	II Ki.	23	24
God should be sought	Is.	8	19
Egyptians will seek	Is.	19	3
Voice like a	Is.	29	4

family
Warned against departing from God	Deut.	29	18
	Jer.	10	25
Blessed	Ps.	128	3–6

Should:
Live in mutual forgiveness	Gen.	50	17–21
	Mat.	18	21, 22
Be taught the scriptures	Deut.	4	9, 10
Worship God together	I Cor.	16	19
Be disciplined	I Tim.	3	4, 5, 12

Examples of devout:
Abraham	Gen.	18	19
Jacob	Gen.	35	2
Joshua	Josh.	24	15
Job	Job	1	5
Lazarus	John	11	1–5
Lydia	Acts	16	15

Government of:
Husband head of home	Eph.	5	23
Wives to submit	Eph.	5	22
	Col.	3	18

family—*continued*

Rebellious wives	Esth.	1	20
Abraham-Sarah	I Pet.	3	1
Children in obedience	Eph.	6	1, 2

Unhappiness of:

Hatred	Prov.	15	17
A foolish son	Prov.	21	9
A contentious woman	Prov.	21	9, 19
Jacob-Esau	Gen.	27	4–46
Jacob-Rachel-Leah	Gen.	29	30–34
Abraham-Hagar	Gen.	16	5
	Gen.	21	10, 11

famine *extreme scarcity*

In time of:

Abraham	Gen.	12	10
Isaac	Gen.	26	1
Joseph	Gen.	41	27–57
The judges	Ruth	1	1
David	II Sam.	21	1
Elijah	I Ki.	17, 18	
Elisha	II Ki.	4	38
	II Ki.	8	1
The seige of Samaria	II Ki.	6	24, 25
Predicted in reign of Claudius	Acts	11	28
Sent as judgment	Lev.	26	19–29
	Ezek.	4	16, 17
	Amos	4	6–9
	Mat.	24	7
	Rev.	6	5–8
Described	Deut.	28	53–57
	Is.	9	18–21
	Joel	1	17–20
Cannibalism in	Deut.	28	53
	II Ki.	6	28
Righteous delivered from	Job	5	20
Caused emigration	Ruth	1	1
	Gen.	12	10
Future	Mat.	24	7
	Rev.	6	5–8

fanaticism- *enthusiasm for a cause*

Examples:

Prophets of Baal	I Ki.	18	22–29
Enemies of Christ	John	19	15
Stephen's	Acts	7	
Jews	Acts	7	57
Saul	Acts	9	1, 2
Peter's	Acts	5	28, 29
Demetrius	Acts	19	24–30

fan *a fork for pitching grain*

Provender winnowed for oxen	Is.	30	24
Figure of judgment	Jer.	15	7
	Jer.	51	2
	Mat.	3	12
	Luke	3	17

farewell addresses

Moses	Deut.	33	
Joshua	Josh.	24	
David	I Ki.	2	
Naomi	Ruth	1	6–16
Paul	Acts	20	17–38
	II Tim.	4	1–8
John	Rev.		

farmer *one who farms*

Cain, brother of Abel	Gen.	4	2
Elisha	I Ki.	19	19, 20
Uzziah	II Chr.	26	9, 10
A rich and selfish	Luke	12	16–21
Amos	Amos	7	14
Gideon	Judg.	6	11

farthing *a copper coin*

A payment	Mat.	5	26
Two sparrows sold for a	Mat.	10	29
	Luke	12	6
Widow's two mites	Mark	12	42

fasting *abstaining from food*

Turned into gladness	Zech.	8	19
Christ defends His disciples for not	Mat.	9	14–17
Recommended	I Cor.	7	5

Observed on occasions of:

Bereavement	I Sam.	31	7–13
	II Sam.	1	12
	II Sam.	3	35
Private afflictions	II Sam.	12	16
Confession of sin	Neh.	9	1, 2
Approaching danger	Esth.	4	16
Anxiety	Dan.	6	18–20
Ordination of ministers	Acts	13	3

Accompanied by:

Confession of sin	I Sam.	7	6
Humiliation	Neh.	9	1
Reading of the scriptures	Jer.	36	6
Prayer	Dan.	9	3

Habitual:

By John's disciples	Mat.	9	14
By Pharisees	Mark	2	18
By Anna	Luke	2	37
By Cornelius	Acts	10	30
By Paul	II Cor.	6	5

Prolonged:

Moses	Ex.	24	18
	Ex.	34	28
Samuel	I Sam.	7	5, 6
Elijah	I Ki.	19	8
Men of Nineveh	Jonah	3	5–8
Daniel	Dan.	10	2, 3
Jesus	Mat.	4	2
John's disciples	Mat.	9	14
Anna	Luke	2	37
Pharisees	Mat.	9	14

fat

Offered in sacrifice	Ex.	23	18
	Lev.	3	3–16
	Is.	43	24
Belongs to the Lord	Lev.	3	16
Forbidden as food	Lev.	3	16, 17
	Lev.	7	23
Idolatrous sacrifices of	Deut.	32	38
Figurative	Ps.	37	20
	Is.	25	6

father *a parent*

Should be honoured	Deut.	5	16
Has compassion upon his children	Ps.	103	13
Children should obey	Eph.	6	1–3
Fatherhood of God	I Chr.	29	10
	Is.	9	6
	Mat.	6	9
	John	20	17
Title of idolatrous priests	Judg.	17	10
Forbidden as a title	Mat.	23	9
Duties of	Deut.	21	18
	Prov.	3	12
	Prov.	13	24
	Eph.	6	4
	Heb.	12	9
Of nations	Gen.	17	4
	Rom.	4	17
Passing iniquity to children	Ex.	20	5
	Num.	14	18
Of a master teacher	II Ki.	2	12
Title of Christ	Is.	9	6
Of Israel	Jer.	31	9
To whom honor is due	Mal.	1	6
Abba	Rom.	8	15
Abraham	Rom.	4	11
Of mercies	II Cor.	1	3
Of spirits	Heb.	12	9
Of lights	James	1	17
Of the trinity	I John	5	7

fatherless *without a living father*

Duty toward	Ex.	22	22
	Deut.	14	29
	Prov.	23	10
	James	1	27
Protected by God	Deut.	10	18
The wicked oppress	Job	6	27
	Is.	1	23
	Jer.	5	28
Not to be afflicted	Ex.	22	22
Of judgment	Jer.	49	11
To receive part of the tithe	Deut.	14	28
Treat justly	Deut.	24	17–22
God's special care	Ps.	10	14–18
	Ps.	27	10
	Ps.	68	5
	Mal.	3	5

fathom *a nautical measure, 6 feet*

Paul's shipwreck	Acts	27	28

fatigue *weariness*

Overcomes David's men	I Sam.	30	9, 10
Indifference as to offering for the Lord	Mal.	2	11–13
Disciples sleep	Mat.	26	45
Jesus and disciples rest in desert	Mark	6	31
Jesus rests at the well	John	4	5, 6

fault

How to deal with	Mat.	18	15
	Gal.	6	1
Exhortation of confess	James	5	16
I remember my *f* this day	Gen.	41	9
I found no *f* in him.	I Sam.	29	3
Cleanse me from secret *f*	Ps.	19	12
Find no occasion or *f* in him	Dan.	6	4
Tell him his *f*	Mat.	18	15
I find no *f* in this man.	Luke	23	4
	John	18	38
	John	19	4
Why doth he yet find *f*?			
	Rom.	9	19
Utterly a *f* among you.	I Cor.	6	7
If a man be overtaken in a *f*	Gal.	6	1
Finding *f* with them	Heb.	8	8
Confess your *f* one to another	James	5	16
If, when buffeted for your *f*	I Pet.	2	20
Without *f* before throne	Rev.	14	5

faultfinding

Is condemned	Is.	29	20, 21
Mote in brother's eye	Mat.	7	3–5
Equal pay to the last hired labourers	Mat.	20	9–12
Eating with publicans	Luke	5	29, 30
Association with a sinner	Luke	7	34, 39
Mary using oil on Jesus' feet	John	12	3–6

favoritism *manifestation of partiality*

Shown by Rebekah to Jacob	Gen.	27	6–46
Shown by Jacob for Rachel	Gen.	29	30, 34
Shown by Jacob for Joseph	Gen.	37	3, 4
Shown by Joseph for Benjamin	Gen.	43	33
Forbidden	Lev.	19	15
	Deut.	21	15–17
Shown by Elkanah for Hannah	I Sam.	1	4, 5
Requested by a mother for her two sons	Mat.	20	20, 21
Denied by Jesus	Mat.	20	22–24

favor of God

Shown to Abraham	Gen.	18	17
On the righteous	Job	33	26
	Prov.	3	4
On Job	Job	42	10
On the Israelites	Ps.	44	3
	Ps.	85	1
Bestowed on Christ	Mat.	3	16
Bestowed on Mary	Luke	1	30
Shown to David	Acts	7	46

fear

Neither *f* ye the people	Num.	14	9
they may learn to *f* me	Deut.	4	10
Thou shalt *f* day and night	Deut.	66	
Of heart wherewith thou shalt *f*	Deut.	67	
If thou *f* to go down	Judg.	7	10
That they may *f* thee	I Ki.	8	40
Neither *f* other gods	II Ki.	17	38
Servants who desire to *f*	Neh.	1	11
Did I *f* a great multitude?	Job	31	34
I will *f* no evil	Ps.	23	4
Whom shall I *f*?	Ps.	27	1
Laid up for them that *f*	Ps.	31	19
Wherefore should I *f* in days?	Ps.	49	5
Righteous also shall see, and *f*	Ps.	52	6
Shall *f* and declare the work	Ps.	64	9
Heathen shall *f* thy name	Ps.	102	15
My reproach which I *f*	Ps.	119	39
A companion of them that *f*	Ps.	63	
Men should *f* before him.	Eccl.	3	14
Neither *f* ye their fear.	Is.	8	12
Like to women, afraid and *f*	Is.	19	16
City of terrrible nations shall *f*	Is.	25	3
The workmen shall *f* and be	Is.	44	11
And they shall *f* no more	Jer.	23	4
Them one heart that may *f*	Jer.	32	39
They shall *f* and tremble for	Jer.	33	9
Your heart faint, and ye *f* for	Jer.	51	46
Inhabitants of Samaria *f*	Hosea	10	5
Move as worms, and *f*	Mic.	7	17
The people did *f* before	Hag.	1	12
Ashkelon shall see it and *f*	Zech.	9	5
Say, of men, we *f* the	Mat.	21	26
Forewarn you whom ye shall *f*	Luke	12	5
Of bondage again to *f*	Rom.	8	15
Be not highminded, but *f*	Rom.	11	20
I *f* lest as the serpent	II Cor.	11	3

I *f* lest I shall not find you	II Cor.	12	20
Rebuke that others may *f*	I Tim.	5	20
Let us *f* lest promise	Heb.	4	1
I exceedingly *f* and quake	Heb.	12	21
F none of those things	Rev.	2	10

fear of God

Of punishment	Gen.	3	8
	Is.	2	19
	Heb.	10	27
Commanded	Lev.	19	14
	Is.	8	13
	Rom.	11	20
	Rev.	14	7
Enjoined	Deut.	10	12
	Jer.	10	7
	Mat.	10	28
Advantages of	Ps.	31	19
	Prov.	10	27
	Mal.	3	16
	II Cor.	7	1

Examples:

Noah	Heb.	11	7
Abraham	Gen.	22	12
Midwives	Ex.	1	17, 21
Phinehas	Num.	25	11
Nehemiah	Neh.	5	15
Job	Job	1	8
David	Ps.	5	7
Cronelius	Acts	10	2

fearless *without fear*

Caleb	Num.	14	6–10
Moses	Ex.	2	11, 12
Jonathan	I Sam.	14	6–14
David	I Sam.	17	34–37
Shadrach	Dan.	3	16–18
Daniel	Dan.	6	16, 17
Peter and apostles	Acts	5	29
Paul	Acts	21	10–14

feasts and festivals

Covenants ratified by	Gen.	26	28–30
Birthdays celebrated	Gen.	40	20
Guests arranged according to age and rank	Gen.	43	33
	I Sam.	9	22
Divine protection given during a	Ex.	34	24
Marriage feasts provided by bridegroom	Judg.	14	10, 17
Coronations celebrated by	I Ki.	1	25
	I Chr.	12	38–40
Music and dancing	Is.	5	12
	Mat.	14	6

Feast of dedication, the:

To commemorate the cleansing of the temple	Dan.	11	31
Held in the winter	John	10	22

Feast of jubilee:

Held every fiftieth year	Lev.	25	8, 10
Begins upon the day of atonement	Lev.	25	9
All field labour ceases	Lev.	25	11
Is especially holy	Lev.	25	12
Hebrew servants released	Lev.	25	40, 41, 54
All inheritances restored	Lev.	27	24

Feast of the new moon:

Held first day of the month	Num.	10	10
Offerings made during	Num.	28	11–15
Observed with great solemnity	I Chr.	23	31
	II Chr.	2	4
Restored after captivity	Ezra	3	5
Celebrated with blowing of trumpets	Ps.	81	3, 4
A time for worship in God's house	Ezek.	46	1
Disliked by the wicked	Amos	8	5

Feast of passover or unleavened bread:

Paschal lamb eaten first day	Ex.	12	6, 8
To commemorate passing over firstborn	Ex.	12	12, 13
Lasts seven days	Ex.	12	15
Nothing leavened to be eaten	Ex.	12	20
Celebrated on leaving Egypt	Ex.	12	28, 50
To commemorate deliverance of Israel from bondage	Ex.	13	5–10
Commences the fourteenth of the first month at eve	Lev.	23	5
	Num.	9	3
First and last days are holy convocations	Num.	28	18
Sacrifices offered	Num.	28	19–24
All males to attend	Deut.	16	16
Celebrated on entering land of promise	Josh.	5	10, 11
Purification necessary to attend	II Chr.	30	15–19
Punishment for improper keeping	II Chr.	30	18, 20

feasts and festivals—*continued*

Lord's supper instituted at	Mat.	26	26–28
	Luke	22	15
Called the feast of unleavened bread	Mark	14	1
	Luke	22	1

Feast of pentecost, weeks, harvest, firstfruits:

Called the feast of harvest	Ex.	23	16
Called the feast of weeks	Ex.	34	22
Held fiftieth day after offering first sheaf of barley harvest	Lev.	23	15, 16
To be perpetually observed	Lev.	23	21
A time of holy rejoicing	Deut.	16	11
All males to attend	Deut.	16	16
Holy Ghost given to apostles	Acts	2	1–4
Observed by early Christians	Acts	20	16
	I Cor.	16	8

Feast of Purim or Pur:

To commemorate the defeat of Haman's wicked plan	Esth.	3	7–15
Begins on fourteenth of twelfth month	Esth.	9	17
Instituted by Mordecai	Esth.	9	20
Jews bind themselves to keep	Esth.	9	27, 28

Feast of sabbatical year:

Kept every seventh year	Lev.	25	4
All field labour ceases	Lev.	25	4, 5
All fruits of the earth to be common property	Lev.	25	6, 7
Surplus of sixth year to provide for	Lev.	25	20–22
Jews threatened for neglecting	Lev.	26	34, 35, 43
Cancellation of debts	Deut.	15	1–3

Feast of tabernacles, ingathering, booths:

All males compelled to attend	Ex.	23	16, 17
Called the feast of the ingathering	Ex.	34	22
Begins fifteenth of seventh month	Lev.	23	34, 39
Waving of palm branches	Lev.	23	40
To be perpetually observed	Lev.	23	41
First and last days are holy convocations	Num.	29	12, 35
Sacrifices offered	Num.	29	13–39
Held after harvest and vintage	Deut.	16	13
Lasts seven days	Deut.	16	15
Law publicly read every seventh year	Deut.	31	10–12
Celebrated at the dedication of Solomon's temple	I Ki.	8	2, 65

Feast of trumpets:

Held the first day of seventh month	Lev.	23	24
A memorial of blowing of trumpets	Lev.	23	24
A holy convocation and rest	Lev.	23	24, 25
Sacrifices offered	Num.	29	2–6

fed

God who *f* me all my life	Gen.	48	15
He *f* thee with manna	Deut.	8	3
Verily thou shalt be *f*	Ps.	37	3
F them with finest of wheat	Ps.	81	16
I am full of fat of *f* beasts	Is.	1	11
When I *f* them to the full	Jer.	5	7
Shepherds *f* themselves, not flock	Ezek.	34	8

feeble *weakness*

Enemies mock the Jews	Neh.	4	2
Job has helped the weak	Job	4	4
Not a weak person in the tribes	Ps.	105	37
Shall be strengthened	Is.	35	3
Of hands and knees	Jer.	6	24
	Ezek.	7	17
	Ezek.	21	7
Feebleminded are to be comforted	I Thes.	5	14
Lift up the hands	Heb.	12	12

feed

to *f* their father's flock	Gen.	37	12
Their trade to *f* cattle	Gen.	46	32
Commanded ravens to *f* thee	I Ki.	17	4
F him with bread and water of affliction	I Ki.	22	27
	II Chr.	18	26
F them, and lift them up	Ps.	28	9
Death shall *f* on them	Ps.	49	14
Lips of righteous *f* many	Prov.	10	21
F me with food convenient	Prov.	30	8
Lambs shall *f* after their manner.	Is.	5	17
Cow and bear shall *f*	Is.	11	7
He shall *f* his flock like a shepherd	Is.	40	11
Strangers shall *f* your flocks	Is.	61	5
The wolf and lamb shall *f* together	Is.	65	25
Pastors, *f* you with knowledge	Jer.	3	15
F every one in his place	Jer.	6	3
F delicately are desolate	Lam.	4	5
Ephraim *f* on wind	Hosea	12	1
F flock of the slaughter	Zech.	11	4
Your heavenly Father *f* them	Mat.	6	26

Sow not, yet God *f* them	Luke	12	24
F my lambs	John	21	15
If enemy hunger, *f* him	Rom.	12	20
F the flock of God	I Pet.	5	2
Lamb shall *f* and lead them	Rev.	7	17

feet

Sitting at	Deut.	33	3
	Luke	10	39
	Acts	22	3
Shoes	Ex.	3	5
	Josh.	9	5
Land on which	Josh.	14	9
Covered	I Sam.	24	3
Fetters of	II Sam.	3	34
Lame in	II Sam.	19	24
Sure footed	II Sam.	22	37
Diseased	II Chr.	16	12
Sound of	II Ki.	6	32
	I Ki.	14	6
Bells worn on	Is.	3	16, 18

foot-washing

A custom of courtesy performed by Abraham and Lot for guests	Gen.	18	4
	Gen.	19	2
Done by Abigail for David's servants	I Sam.	25	40, 41
Of Jesus, with tears	Luke	7	44
Done by Jesus for His disciples	John	13	4–14
Duty to saints	I Tim.	5	10

feigning *pretending*

By David in fear of King Achish	I Sam.	21	13
By wife of Jeroboam	I Ki.	14	5
Of Judah towards the Lord	Jer.	3	10
Of scribes and priests	Luke	20	20
Of false teachers	II Pet.	2	3

Felix *happy*

Procurator of Judaea	Acts	23	26
Paul sent to	Acts	23	24, 26–35
Paul tried and convicted before	Acts	24	1–27

fell

His countenance *f*	Gen.	4	5
Joseph's brethren *f* before him	Gen.	44	14
The wall *f* down	Josh.	6	20
	Heb.	11	30
Fire of Lord *f* and consumed sacrifice	I Ki.	18	38
Their priests *f* by sword	Ps.	78	64
There *f* a voice from heaven	Dan.	4	31
Lot *f* on Jonah	Jonah	1	7
Wise men *f* down and worshipped	Mat.	2	11
House *f* not	Mat.	7	25
	Luke	6	48
Servant *f* down, saying	Mat.	18	29
Peter *f* down at Jesus' knees	Luke	5	8
F among thieves	Luke	10	30, 36
On whom tower *f*	Luke	13	4
His father *f* on his neck	Luke	15	20
Went backwards and *f*	John	18	6
Judas by transgression *f*	Acts	1	25
Lot *f* on Matthias	Acts	1	26
Said this, he *f* asleep	Acts	7	60
Saul *f* and heard a voice	Acts	9	4
Since fathers *f* asleep	II Pet.	3	4

fellow *companion, associate*

Citizens	Eph.	2	19
Workers	Phil.	4	13
	Col.	4	11
Helpers	III John		8
Servants	Rev.	19	10
	Rev.	22	9

fellowship *communion, comradeship*

Communion of saints	Ps.	55	14
	Luke	22	32
	I Cor.	12	12, 13
	II Cor.	6	14–18
Commended	Eccl.	4	9–12
With Christ	Mat.	18	20
Continued stedfastly by converts	Acts	2	42
Ministering to the saints	II Cor.	8	4
Right hand of, given to Paul and Barnabas	Gal.	2	9
With the wicked forbidden	Eph.	5	11
	II Pet.	3	17
In the gospel	Phil.	1	5
One with another and God	I John	1	3, 7
With God	Gen.	5	22–24
	Ex.	29	45
	Lev.	26	12
	Is.	57	15

With Christ	Mat.	18	20
	John	6	53
	John	17	21–23
	Rev.	3	20

fellowship of Christ
God is faithful	I Cor.	1	9
Is declared	I John	1	3

fenced cities *places fortified by walls*
Spies report about, of Canaan	Num.	23	28
Of Bashan	Deut.	3	5
Shall be besieged	Deut.	28	52
David's servants pursue a traitor	II Sam.	20	6
Of Judah	II Ki.	18	13
Destruction is predicted by Isaiah	II Ki.	19	25
Manasseh guards, of Judah	II Chr.	33	14

fens *low lands, marshes*
God talks with Job	Job	40	21

ferret *kind of lizard*
An unclean animal	Lev.	11	29, 30

Festus, Porcius *joyful*
Succeeds Felix as governor of Judaea	Acts	24	27
Paul is brought before him	Acts	25	1–27
Paul's defense before him and Agrippa	Acts	26	1–32

fetters *shackles for the feet*
Samson is bound by Philistines with	Judg.	16	6–21
David mourns death of Abner	II Sam.	3	34
Zedekiah, Manasseh and Jehoiakim bound			
with, and taken to Babylon	II Ki.	25	7
	II Chr.	33	11
	II Chr.	36	6
Heathen kings to be bound with	Ps.	149	8
Broken by man with unclean spirit	Mark	5	3, 4
	Luke	8	29

fever *to be on fire*
For those who disobey God's commands	Lev.	26	16
	Deut.	28	22
Of Peter's mother-in-law healed by Jesus	Mat.	8	14, 15
	Mark	1	30, 31
Of nobleman's son healed by Jesus	John	4	52
Of Publius' father healed by Paul	Acts	28	8

few
They seemed but a *f* days	Gen.	29	20
F and evil have the days of my life have			
been	Gen.	47	9
To save by many or *f*	I Sam.	14	6
City large, but people *f*	Neh.	7	4
Man is of *f* days	Job	14	1
When a *f* years are come	Job	16	22
Let thy words be *f*	Eccl.	5	2
Grinders cease because *f*	Eccl.	12	3
F there be that find it	Mat.	7	14
The labourers are *f*	Mat.	9	37
	Luke	10	2
Many called, *f* chosen	Mat.	20	16
	Mat.	22	14
Faithful in a *f* things	Mat.	25	21
Are there *f* that be saved?	Luke	13	23
For a *f* days chastened us	Heb.	12	10
A *f* things against thee	Rev.	2	14, 20

fidelity *loyalty*
To be shown by servants	Tit.	2	9, 10

See **faithfulness**

field *cleared land*
Money paid for	Gen.	23	13
Place of meditation	Gen.	24	63
Every man sells his	Gen.	47	20
Ruth gleans in	Ruth	2	8, 17
Consider the lilies of	Mat.	6	28
Potter's	Mat.	27	7, 8
Of corn	Mark	2	23
Swine fed in	Luke	15	15, 16
Plowed	Mic.	3	12
	Jer.	26	18
Of the world	Mat.	13	38
Of blood	Acts	1	19
Harvest of	John	4	35

fierce
Their anger, for it was *f*	Gen.	49	7
Nation of a *f* countenance	Deut.	28	50
A king of *f* countenance	Dan.	8	23
Devils, exceeding *f*	Mat.	8	28
They were more *f*	Luke	23	5
Men shall be incontinent, *f*	II Tim.	3	3
Ships driven of *f* winds	James	3	4

fiery serpents
Bite the Israelites	Num.	21	6
Of brass made by Moses	Num.	21	8, 9
Found in the wilderness	Deut.	8	15
Used figuratively	Is.	14	29
	Is.	30	6
Jesus will be lifted up, like the brass			
serpent of Moses	John	3	14, 15

fig tree
Sign of prosperity	I Ki.	4	25
Smitten by God	Ps.	105	33
Symbol of plenty	Mic.	4	4
Barren cursed	Mat.	21	19
Parable of	Mat.	24	32
	Luke	13	6–9
Nathanael under a	John	1	49, 50
Common in Palestine	Num.	13	23
	Deut.	8	8
Of Egypt	Ps.	105	33
As a remedy	II Ki.	20	7
	Is.	38	21
Adam uses fig leaves	Gen.	3	7
Made into cakes	I Sam.	25	18–35

fight
Lord *f* for you	Ex.	14	14
	Deut.	1	30
	Deut.	3	22
	Deut.	20	4
We will go up and *f*	Deut.	1	41
Lord God that *f* for you	Josh.	23	10
Quit like men, and *f*	I Sam.	4	9
Give me a man that we may *f*	I Sam.	17	10
The battles of the Lord	I Sam.	25	28
F against them that *f* against me	Ps.	35	1
Teacheth my fingers to *f*	Ps.	144	1
Then would my servants *f*	John	18	36
F against God	Acts	5	39
	Acts	23	9
So *f* I, not as one that	I Cor.	9	26
Without were *f*	II Cor.	7	5
Wars and *f* among you	James	4	1
Of faith	I Tim.	6	12
	II Tim.	4	7
	Heb.	10	32
	Heb.	11	34

figure *a form or likeness*
Of any likeness shall not be made	Deut.	4	16
Of cherubim carved on walls of temple	I Ki.	6	29
Of gods worshipped by Israelites	Acts	7	43
Of Adam	Rom.	5	14
Of Paul	I Cor.	4	6
Of time and holy places	Heb.	9	9, 24
Of Isaac	Heb.	11	19
Of baptism	I Pet.	3	21

filial honour *respect shown by a son or daughter for father and mother*
Of Joseph	Gen.	47	12
Of David	I Sam.	22	3
Of Solomon	I Ki.	2	19
Of Elisha	I Ki.	19	19, 20
Lack of, shall bring a curse	Prov.	30	17
Commanded by God	Mat.	15	4

filial obedience *act of obeying by son or daughter*
Instruction and law of parents not to be			
forsaken	Prov.	1	8
Of Jesus as a boy	Luke	2	51
Pleasing to the Lord	Col.	3	20
Continually	Prov.	6	20–22
Enjoined	Eph.	6	1–3
Timothy	II Tim.	1	5
John	Mat.	4	21

fill
F waters in the seas	Gen.	1	22
Earth *f* with glory of Lord	Num.	14	21
	Ps.	72	19
	Hab.	2	14
Open mouth, I will *f* it	Ps.	81	10
Openest hand, are *f* with good	Ps.	104	28
Be *f* with own devices	Prov.	1	31
Barns be *f* with plenty	Prov.	3	10
F with his own ways	Prov.	14	14
Mouth be *f* with gravel	Prov.	20	17
Hunger, shall be *f*	Mat.	5	6
Let the children first be *f*	Mark	7	27
F with Holy Ghost	Luke	1	15
	Acts	4	8
	Acts	9	17
	Acts	13	9

fill—continued

Hath *f* hungry with good	Luke	1	53
Sorrow hath *f* your heart	John	16	6
F our hearts with food and gladness	Acts	14	17
F with all knowledge	Rom.	15	14
Fulness of him that *f* all in all	Eph.	1	23
Be *f* with fulness of God	Eph.	3	19
Be *f* with the Spirit	Eph.	5	18
F with fruits of righteousness	Phil.	1	11
F up what is behind	Col.	1	24
In them is *f* up wrath of God	Rev.	15	1

fillet *an ornamental band*

Of silver and gold for the pillars of the tabernacle	Ex.	27	10, 11
	Ex.	36	38
	Ex.	38	10, 19
On pillars of temple in Jerusalem	Jer.	52	21

filthy *dirty, foul, corrupt*

Man who drinks iniquity	Job	15	16
Corrupt men have become	Ps.	14	3
	Ps.	53	3
Righteousness of wicked likened to, rags	Is.	64	6
Garments worn by Joshua as he stands before an angel	Zech.	3	3, 4
Communication shall be done with	Col.	3	8
Lucre should not be sought by bishops and elders	I Tim.	3	3
	Tit.	1	7
	I Pet.	5	2
Conversation of wicked disliked by Lot	II Pet.	2	7

financial planning:

Of Paul	I Cor.	16	1–3
For building	Luke	14	26–33
False	James	4	13–16
	Luke	12	18

find

Be sure your sin will *f* you out.	Num.	32	23
To *f* out every device.	II Chr.	2	14
Things past *f* out.	Job	9	10
Where I might *f* him.	Job	23	3
Shalt *f* knowledge of God.	Prov.	2	5
My words life to those that *f* them.	Prov.	4	22
Seek me early shall *f* me.	Prov.	8	17
	Jer.	29	13
Whoso *f* me *f* life	Prov.	8	35
Whose *f* a wife, *f* a good thing	Prov.	18	22
What thy hand *f* to do, do it.	Eccl.	9	10
Shalt *f* it after many days.	Eccl.	11	1
Not *f* thine own pleasure.	Is.	58	13
F rest to your souls	Jer.	6	16
	Mat.	11	29
Seek, and ye shall *f*	Mat.	7	7
	Luke	11	9
Loseth life, shall *f* it.	Mat.	10	39
Lest he *f* you sleeping	Mark	13	36
They might *f* accusation.	Luke	6	7
Seeking fruit, and *f* none.	Luke	13	7
Seek diligently till she *f* it.	Luke	15	8
I *f* a law that when I would do good.	Rom.	7	21
His ways past *f* out	Rom.	11	33
May *f* mercy in that day.	II Tim.	1	18
F grace to help	Heb.	4	16
See death, and shall not *f* it.	Rev.	9	6

fine

Place for gold where they *f* it	Job	28	1
More to be desired than *f* gold	Ps.	19	10
	Ps.	81	16
The *f* of the wheat.	Ps.	147	14
Wisdom better than fine gold	Prov.	8	19
As an ornament of *f* gold	Prov.	25	12
Man more precious than *f* gold	Is.	13	12
Joseph bought *f* linen	Mark	15	46
Granted to be arrayed in *f* linen	Rev.	19	8

finger *a digit of the hand*

Of God	Ex.	8	19
	Ex.	31	18
	Luke	11	20
Part of ceremony for consecrating priests	Ex.	29	12
A man with six fingers on each hand	II Sam.	21	20
Writes upon the wall	Dan.	5	5
Used by Jesus to write on the ground	John	8	1, 6
Thomas touches Jesus with his	John	20	25, 27

fir *a pinaceous tree*

Used for musical instruments	II Sam.	6	5
Given by Hiram of Tyre to Solomon	I Ki.	5	8, 10
Used for building the temple	I Ki.	6	15, 34

Storks build their nests in	Ps.	104	17
Used for rafters	S. of S.	1	17
Used for ships	Ezek.	27	5

fire

God appears by	Ex.	19	18
	Dan.	7	10
	Mat.	3	11
Not to be kindled on the sabbath	Ex.	35	3
For consuming sacrifices	Lev.	9	24
Instrument of judgment	Lev.	10	1
Emblem of God's word	Jer.	23	29
Everlasting	Mark	9	44
Tongues as of	Acts	2	3
God is consuming	Heb.	12	29
As a signal	Jer.	6	1
Furnaces of	Dan.	3	6
Children passed through	II Ki.	16	3
	II Ki.	17	17

Miracles with:

Abraham's sacrifice	Gen.	15	17
David	I Chr.	21	26
Elijah	I Ki.	18	38
In Plagues of Egypt	Ex.	9	24
Consumes Korah	Num.	16	35
Captains against Elijah	II Ki.	1	9–12

Figurative of:

Cleansing	Is.	6	6, 7
	Ps.	104	4
	Mat.	3	11
Spiritual power	Is.	33	14
Of Hell	Mat.	18	8
	Ex.	3	2
God's presence	Acts	2	3

firebrand *a piece of burning substance*

Used by Samson for destroying crops	Judg.	15	4, 5
Used figuratively	Prov.	26	18
	Is.	7	4
	Amos	4	11
	Zech.	3	2

firepan

A pan of brass, gold or silver used about the altar of burnt offering	Ex.	27	3
	Ex.	38	3
To hold live coals for burning incense	Lev.	10	1
	Lev.	16	12
	I Ki.	7	50
Taken to Babylon when Jerusalem is besieged	II Ki.	25	15

fire, pillar of

Lord leads Israelites by night in a	Ex.	13	21, 22
	Ex.	40	38
Lord looks toward the Egyptians through a	Ex.	14	24
Over the tabernacle	Num.	9	15–23
Levites recall God's goodness in	Neh.	9	12

fire, strange see strange

firkin *a liquid measure*

Water turned to wine measured by	John	2	6

firmament *the heavens*

God creates the	Gen.	1	6–8
Shows God's handywork	Ps.	19	1

first

I fell before the Lord as at the *f*	Deut.	9	18, 25
The glory of the *f* house	Ezra	3	12
	Hag.	2	3
Art thou the *f* man born?	Job	15	7
Honour the Lord with *f* fruits	Prov.	3	9
F in his own cause	Prov.	18	17
Thy *f* father hath sinned	Is.	43	27
F be reconciled to thy brother	Mat.	5	24
Seek ye *f* the kingdom of God	Mat.	6	33
F cast beam out of own eye	Mat.	7	5
	Luke	6	42
F to go and bury my father	Mat.	8	21
	Luke	9	59
Last state of that man worse than *f* Elias must *f* come	Mat.	12	45
	Mat.	17	10
	Mark	9	12
The *f* commandment	Mat.	22	38
	Mark	12	28
F the blade, then the ear	Mark	4	28
If any desire to be *f*, same shall be last	Mark	9	35
Gospel must *f* be published	Mark	13	10
That he had not *f* washed	Luke	11	38
Sitteth not down *f*	Luke	14	28

But *f* must he suffer many things	Luke	17	25
He *f* findeth his own brother	John	1	41
Whosoever *f* stepped in	John	5	4
Called Christians *f* at Antioch	Acts	11	26
Christ *f* that should rise from the dead	Acts	26	23
Of the Jew *f*	Rom.	2	9
The *f* fruits of the Spirit	Rom.	8	23
F born among many brethren	Rom.	8	29
If the *f* fruit be holy	Rom.	11	16
F apostles, secondarily prophets	I Cor.	12	28
Christ the *f* fruits of them that slept	I Cor.	15	20, 23
The *f* man was made a living soul	I Cor.	15	45
The *f* man is of the earth	I Cor.	15	47
F gave own selves to the Lord	II Cor.	8	5
If there be *f* a willing mind	II Cor.	8	12
Who *f* trusted in Christ	Eph.	1	12
F commandment with promise	Eph.	6	2
F-born of every creature	Col.	1	15
Dead in Christ shall rise *f*	I Thes.	4	16
A falling away *f*	II Thes.	2	3
In me *f* Christ might shew	I Tim.	1	16
Learn *f* to shew piety at home	I Tim.	5	4
Husbandman must be *f* partaker	II Tim.	2	6
After *f* and second admonition	Tit.	3	10
Which be the *f* principles	Heb.	5	12
Offer *f* for his own sins	Heb.	7	27
He taketh away the *f*	Heb.	10	9
Wisdom from above is *f* pure	James	3	17
If judgment *f* begin at us	I Pet.	4	17
Because he *f* loved us	I John	4	19
Angels who kept not *f* estate	Jude	6	
Thou hast left thy *f* love	Rev.	2	4
This is the *f* resurrection	Rev.	20	5
F heaven and *f* earth passed away	Rev.	21	1

firstborn

Privileges of	Gen.	43	33
	Deut.	21	15
	Col.	1	15
Esau	Gen.	27	19
Leah	Gen.	29	26
Reuben	I Chr.	5	1
Manasseh	Gen.	48	18
Levites taken instead	Num.	3	12
Not to be disinherited	Deut.	21	15
Not given for transgression	Mic.	6	7
	Mat.	1	25
Jesus	Luke	2	7
Of the dead	Col.	1	18
In Egypt slain	Ex.	11	4
Dedicated to God	Ex.	13	2, 12
Redemption of	Ex.	34	20

firstfruits

To be given to God	Ex.	22	29
Of resurrection	I Cor.	15	20
Offerings of	Num.	18	12
Presented at tabernacle	Ex.	22	29
	Ex.	23	19
Given to prophets	II Ki.	4	42
As a wave offering	Lev.	23	10-14
As a leave offering	Num.	15	20

fish

Created by God	Gen.	1	20-22
Appointed for food	Gen.	9	2, 3
Clean and unclean	Lev.	11	9-12
In Heshbon	S. of S.	7	4
In Egypt	Is.	19	10
Figurative	Ezek.	47	9, 10
Broiled	John	21	9-13
Miracles connected with:			
Jonah swallowed by	Jonah	1	17
	Jonah	2	1-10
Loaves and fishes	Mat.	14	19
	Luke	5	6
Coin obtained from mouth of	Mat.	17	27
Great draught of	Luke	5	4-7
Furnished to disciples by Jesus	Luke	24	42

fisherman, fisher

Simon and Andrew	Mark	1	16
"Fishers of men"	Mark	1	17

fish gate *one of the gates of Jerusalem*

Manasseh builds a wall about Jerusalem	II Chr.	33	14
Built by sons of Hassenaah	Neh.	3	3
People stand above it to give thanks	Neh.	12	39

fishhooks *hooks for catching fish*

Figuratively, leading away of captives	Amos	4	2

fist fighting

Punishment for	Ex.	21	18, 19

fitches *an annual plant*

Cultivated for its aromatic seeds	Is.	28	25, 27
Used in making bread	Ezek.	4	9

flag *see bulrush*

flagon

A receptacle for liquids	II Sam.	6	19
	Is.	22	24

flattery *false praise*

Warnings against	Ps.	12	3
	Prov.	20	19
	Acts	12	21-23
Results of	Prov.	26	28
	Prov.	28	23
	Dan.	11	21, 22
Of titles	Job	32	21
By evil men	Ps.	5	8-9
By self	Ps.	36	2
By a strange woman	Prov.	7	5
When spreading a trap	Prov.	29	5
Instances of:			
Widow of Tekoah	II Sam.	14	4-20
Certain spies	Luke	20	20, 21
Jacob	Gen.	33	10
Gideon	Judg.	8	1-3
Absalom	II Sam.	15	2-6
False prophets	I Ki.	22	13

flax *a plant, fiber of which is used for making linen*

Damaged by hail	Ex.	9	31
Spies hidden on roof among stalks of	Josh.	2	6
Fine flax weavers in Egypt	Is.	19	9
Used for smoking	Is.	42	3
Man in vision holds	Ezek.	40	3
Possessions to be taken away	Hosea	2	5, 9

flea *insect common in Palestine*

Used by David in speaking to Saul of himself as something insignificant	I Sam.	24	14
	I Sam.	26	20

flee

This city is near to *f* unto	Gen.	19	20
Shall *f* when none pursueth	Lev.	26	17, 36
That hate thee, *f* before thee	Num.	10	35
	Ps.	68	1
Should such a man as I *f*	Neh.	6	11
He *f* as a shadow	Job	14	2
Would fain *f* out of his hand	Job	27	22
How say ye to my soul, *f* as	Ps.	11	1
Whither shall I *f* from presence?	Ps.	139	7
The wicked *f* when no man pursueth	Prov.	28	1
Till shadows *f* away	Ps.	2	17
	Ps.	4	6
Sighing shall *f* away	Is.	35	10
	Is.	51	11
As if a man did *f* from a lion	Amos	5	19
To *f* from wrath to come	Mat.	3	7
	Luke	3	7
When persecuted in one city, *f* to another	Mat.	10	23
F to mountains	Mat.	24	16
	Mark	13	14
	Luke	21	21
Stranger not follow him	John	10	5
The hireling *f*	John	10	13
f these things	I Tim.	6	11
f youthful lusts	II Tim.	2	22
Resist the devil, he will *f*	James	4	7
Death shall *f* from them	Rev.	9	6

fleece *wool of sheep*

Shall be given to priests	Deut.	18	4
Used as a sign by Gideon	Judg.	6	37-40
Job clothes the poor with	Job	31	20

flesh *various meanings*

Corrupted	Gen.	6	12
Destroyed in flood	Gen.	7	21
Living creatures	Gen.	6	13, 19
Of lamb eaten before the Exodus	Ex.	12	8
Of priests shall not be cut	Lev.	21	5
Life in blood	Lev.	17	14
Not to be defaced	Lev.	19	28
Ravens bring, to Elijah	I Ki.	17	6
Wearied	Eccl.	12	12
Troubled	Prov.	11	17
As grass	Is.	40	6
Spirit poured on	Joel	2	28
	Acts	2	17

flesh—*continued*

Unprofitable	John	17	2
Cannot inherit the kingdom	I Cor.	15	50
Christ	Heb.	2	14
	I Pet.	4	1
Husband and wife shall be one	Mat.	19	5
Is weak	Mat.	26	41
Jesus was made	John	1	14
Those who seek flesh are flesh	Rom.	7	5
	Rom.	8	5
Works of the	Gal.	5	16–24

fleshhook

Shall be made of brass for the tabernacle	Ex.	27	3
	Ex.	38	3
Shall be put on the altar	Num.	4	14
Custom for using	I Sam.	2	13, 14
Of gold for the temple of Solomon	I Chr.	28	17
Made by Huram for the temple	II Chr.	4	16

flies *two-winged insects*

In swarms plague Egypt	Ex.	8	21–31
Folly likened to smell of dead	Eccl.	10	1

flint *hardness*

Water obtained from rock of, in wilderness	Deut.	8	15
Moses sings of oil from	Deut.	32	13

flirtation *coquetry*

Of evil women is dangerous	Prov.	7	6–27

flock *a company of sheep or people*

Of Jacob and his songs	Gen.	47	1
Offer the firstlings of	Deut.	12	6
Pastures clothed with	Ps.	65	13
He shall feed his	Is.	40	11
Carried away captive	Jer.	13	17
God's people, Israel	Ezek.	34	31
Shepherds keeping watch over	Luke	2	8
Figuratively used	Luke	12	32
The church	Acts	20	28
Pastors to feed	I Pet.	5	2

flood, the *see* deluge, the

flood

Threatened	Gen.	6	17
Sent	Gen.	7	11
	Mat.	24	38
	II Pet.	2	5
Asswaged	Gen.	8	
Even I, bring a *f* of waters	Gen.	6	17
Foundation overflown with *f*	Job	22	16
He bindeth *f* from overflowing	Job	28	11
Lord sitteth upon the *f*	Ps.	29	10
In *f* of great waters	Ps.	32	6
They went through *f* on foot	Ps.	66	6
Carriest them away as with a *f*	Ps.	90	5
Neither can *f* drown love	Ps.	8	7
I will pour *f* on dry ground	Is.	44	3
Enemy come in like a *f*	Is.	59	19
The *f* came, and the winds blew	Mat.	7	25
In days before the *f*	Mat.	24	38
Knew not till *f* came	Mat.	24	39
	Luke	17	27
Bringing in *f* on world of ungodly	II Pet.	2	5
The river Euphrates "The other side of the flood,"	Josh.	24	3

floor

To buy the threshing *f* of thee	II Sam.	24	21
Overlaid *f* of house with gold	I Ki.	6	30
Loved a reward on every corn-*f*	Hosea	9	1
Gather as sheaves into the *f*	Mic.	4	12
Purge his *f*	Mat.	3	12
	Luke	3	17

flour *ground meal of barley or wheat*

Wheat, used for bread	Ex.	29	2, 40
Fine, used as offering	Lev.	2	1
As a sin offering	Lev.	5	11–13
Part of the meat offering	Lev.	6	15
To be sold for a shekel	II Ki.	7	1

flow

Wind to blow and waters *f*	Ps.	147	18
That the spices may *f* out	Ps.	4	16
All nations shall *f* unto it	Is.	2	2
Caused waters to *f* out of rock	Is.	48	21
Shalt see, and *f* together	Is.	60	5
Shall *f* to the goodness of the Lord	Jer.	31	12
People shall *f* to mountain of Lord	Mic.	4	1
Shall *f* living water	John	7	38

flowers

Appear in spring	S. of S.	2	12
Cultivated in gardens	S. of S.	6	2–3

Used in worship of idols	Acts	14	13
Wild in fields	Ps.	103	15
Symbolic of the brevity of life	Job	14	2
	Is.	40	6–8
Beauty of	Mat.	6	28, 29
	Luke	12	27

Illustrative of:

Glory of Man	I Pet.	1	24
Graces of Christ	S. of S.	5	13
Kingdom of Israel	Is.	28	1
Rich men	James	1	10–11

Representations of:

On the golden candlestick	Ex.	25	31, 33
	II Chr.	4	21
Sea of brass	I Ki.	7	26
	II Chr.	4	5
Woodwork of the temple	I Ki.	6	33, 35

Those mentioned in scripture:

Flower of grass	I Pet.	1	24
Lily	Hosea	14	5
	Mat.	6	28
Lily of the valley	S. of S.	2	1
Rose	Is.	35	1
Rose of Sharon	S. of S.	2	1

flute

A musical instrument	Dan.	3	5

flux *see* dysentery

folly *foolishness*

Wickedness of Shechem	Gen.	34	7
Of adultery shall bring punishment	Deut.	22	21
Of Achan in keeping silver	Josh.	7	15
Of Nabal in refusing to give food to David	I Sam.	25	25
Of Amnon to his sister	II Sam.	13	12
Will lead a son astray	Prov.	5	23
Of a fool is open	Prov.	13	16
Of fools is deceit	Prov.	14	8
A fool returns to his folly	Prov.	26	4, 11
Wisdom excels	Eccl.	2	13
Warning against	Eccl.	10	6
Of prophets in Samaria	Jer.	23	13
Paul speaks of his	II Cor.	11	1

food

Prepared by females	Gen.	27	9
	I Sam.	8	13
The first control of	Gen.	41	25–57
Things prohibited as	Ex.	22	31
	Lev.	17	10–16
	Deut.	14	9, 10
	I Cor.	8	8–13
Regulations concerning	Lev.	11	1–47
Trees planted for	Lev.	19	23
A gift of God	Ps.	136	1, 25
	Eccl.	3	13
Jesus tempted with	Mat.	4	1–3
Miraculous supply of	Mat.	14	15–21
Gives physical strength	Acts	9	19
Thanks given for	Acts	27	35
Given to the hungry	James	2	15, 16

Articles of:

Barley	Ruth	1	22
Bread	Gen.	18	5
Milk	Gen.	49	12
Vinegar	Num.	6	3
Oil	Deut.	12	17
Butter	Deut.	32	14
Parched corn	Ruth	2	14
Cheese	I Sam.	17	18
Wine	II Sam.	6	19
Flesh	II Sam.	6	19
Fruit	II Sam.	16	2
Herbs	Prov.	9	2
Honey	S. of S.	5	1
Fish	Mat.	7	10
Eggs	Deut.	22	6
Cucumbers	Num.	11	5
Grapes	Lev.	25	5
Pomegranates	Num.	13	23
Butter	Deut.	32	14
Vinegar	Num.	6	3

fool *(one wickedly blind)*

Their character and conduct	Ps.	14	1
	Ps.	49	13
	Ps.	53	1
	Ps.	92	6
	Prov.	10	8, 23

	Prov.	12	15, 16
	Prov.	13	16
	Prov.	14	16
	Prov.	15	5
	Prov.	17	7, 10, 12, 16, 21, 28
	Prov.	18	2, 6, 7
	Prov.	19	1
	Prov.	20	3
	Prov.	26	4
	Prov.	27	3, 22
	Eccl.	4	5
	Eccl.	5	1, 3
	Eccl.	7	4, 9
	Eccl.	10	2, 14
	Is.	44	25
	Mat.	7	26
	Mat.	23	17
	Mat.	25	2
	Luke	12	20
	Rom.	1	22
I have played the *f*	I Sam.	26	21
Died Abner as a *f* dieth?	II Sam.	3	33
F said in his heart	Ps.	14	1
	Ps.	53	1
Neither doth *f* understand this	Ps.	92	6
F despise wisdom	Prov.	1	7
A prating *f* shall fall	Prov.	10	8, 10
F die for want of wisdom	Prov.	10	21
The *f* shall be servant to the wise	Prov.	11	29
Way of *f* right in own eyes	Prov.	12	15
Companion of *f* shall be destroyed	Prov.	13	20
F make a mock at sin	Prov.	14	9
A *f* despiseth his father's instruction	Prov.	15	5
The instruction of *f* is folly	Prov.	16	22
A *f*, when he holdeth his peace, is counted wise	Prov.	17	28
A *f* hath no delight in understanding	Prov.	18	2
Every *f* will be meddling	Prov.	20	3
A *f* uttereth all his mind	Prov.	29	11
F walketh in darkness	Eccl.	2	14
No remembrance of wise more than	Eccl.	2	16
A *f* voice known by multitude of words	Eccl.	5	3
Heart of *f* in house of mirth	Eccl.	7	4
Wayfaring men, though *f*	Is.	35	8
At his end he shall be a *f*	Jer.	17	11
Who so shall say, thou	Mat.	5	22
Ye *f* and blind	Mat.	23	17
	Luke	11	40
Thou *f* this night	Luke	12	20
O *f*, and slow of heart	Luke	24	25
Let him become a *f*	I Cor.	3	18
Thou *f* that thou sowest	I Cor.	15	36
Let no man think me a *f*	II Cor.	11	16
I am become a *f* in glorying	II Cor.	12	11
Walk not as *f*, but as wise	Eph.	5	15

foolish

O *f* people	Deut.	32	6
I have done very *f*	II Sam.	24	10
	I Chr.	21	8
Nor charged God *f*	Job	1	22
As one of the *f* women	Job	2	10
I have seen the *f* taking root	Job	5	3
F not stand in thy sight	Ps.	5	5
I was envious at the *f*	Ps.	73	3
Forsake the *f*, and live	Prov.	9	6
A *f* son is grief	Prov.	17	25
	Prov.	19	13
Neither be thou *f*	Eccl.	7	17
My people are *f*	Jer.	4	22
Be likened unto a *f* man	Mat.	7	26
Five were wise, and five *f*	Mat.	25	2
Their *f* heart was darkened	Rom.	1	21
An instructor of the *f*	Rom.	2	20
Made *f* wisdom of this world	I Cor.	1	20
O *f* Galatians	Gal.	3	1
Nor *f* talking	Eph.	5	4
F questions avoid	II Tim.	2	23
	Tit.	3	9
We were sometimes *f*	Tit.	3	3

foolishness *lack of sense*

Brings sorrow	Ps.	38	4–10
A synonym for sin	Ps.	38	5
Mark of wickedness	Eccl.	7	25
The gospel so designated	I Cor.	1	18
	I Cor.	2	14
Worldly wisdom is, with God	I Cor.	1	20
Originates in the heart	Mark	7	21–23
Counsel into *f*	II Sam.	15	31
O God, thou knowest my *f*	Ps.	69	5
F is bound in heart of child	Prov.	22	15
Thought of *f* is sin	Prov.	24	9
The beginning of words is *f*	Eccl.	10	13
To them that perish *f*	I Cor.	1	18
The *f* of preaching	I Cor.	1	21
Christ crucified, to Greeks *f*	I Cor.	1	23
The *f* of God is wiser than men	I Cor.	1	25
Things of Spirit are *f* to him	I Cor.	2	14
Wisdom of world *f* with God	I Cor.	3	19

foot

Without thee no man lift *f*	Gen.	41	44
Nor did thy *f* swell	Deut.	8	4
Shoe is not waxen old on *f*	Deut.	29	5
My *f* standeth in an even place	Ps.	26	12
When my *f* slippeth	Ps.	38	16
Went through the flood on *f*	Ps.	66	6
Dash *f* against a stone	Ps.	91	12
	Mat.	4	6
	Luke	4	11
Not suffer *f* to be moved	Ps.	121	3
Thy *f* shall not stumble	Prov.	3	23
Remove thy *f* from evil	Prov.	4	27
Withdraw *f* from neighbour's house	Prov.	25	17
Keep thy *f* when thou goest	Eccl.	5	1
From sole of *f* to head no soundness	Is.	1	6
Salt trodden under *f*	Mat.	5	13
People followed on *f*	Mat.	14	13
If thy *f* offend thee	Mat.	18	8
	Mark	9	45
Dead, bound hand and *f*	John	11	44
If the *f* say, because I am not	I Cor.	12	15
Trodden under *f* the Son of God	Heb.	10	29

footman *infantry soldier*

Philistines slay 30,000	I Sam.	4	10
Runners or couriers	I Sam.	22	17
	Jer.	12	5
All but 10,000 slain by Syria	II Ki.	13	7
David captures 20,000	I Chr.	18	4

footstool *rest for feet*

Of Solomon's throne, made of gold	II Chr.	9	18
Enemies will become	Ps.	110	1
	Mat.	22	44
	Heb.	10	13
Not condoned as seat for lowly	James	2	3
Of God:			
David wishes to build house as	I Chr.	28	2
Worship at God's	Ps.	99	5
	Ps.	132	7
Earth is God's	Is.	66	1
	Mat.	5	35

forbearance *abstention*

Sinful to meddle with God's will	II Chr.	35	21
Virtue and duty	Eph.	4	2
	Col.	3	13
Of masters for servants	Eph.	6	9
Of God:			
Abraham entreats	Gen.	18	23–32
For sinful Israel	Neh.	9	30, 31
For Nineveh	Jonah	4	10, 11
Parable of the vineyard, example	Mark	12	1–11
Sinful to despise	Rom.	2	4
Foundation of redemption	Rom.	3	25

forbid

Joshua said *f* them	Num.	11	28
F him not	Mark	9	39
	Luke	9	50
Suffer little children and *f* them not	Mark	10	14
	Luke	18	16
F not to take coat	Luke	6	29
F to give tribute	Luke	23	2
Can any *f* water?	Acts	10	47
F not to speak with tongues	I Cor.	14	39
F us to speak to Gentiles	I Thes.	2	16

force

Nor natural *f* abated	Deut.	34	7
Made them cease by *f*	Ezra	4	23
The violent take it by *f*	Mat.	11	12
Perceived they would take him by *f*	John	6	15
A testament is of *f* after	Heb.	9	17

ford *shallow place for crossing waterway*

Jacob crosses at Jabbok	Gen.	32	22

ford—continued

Spies cross the Jordan	Josh.	2	7
Ehud leads Israelites across Jordan	Judg.	3	28
Moabites at Arnon	Is.	16	2

forehead brow

Appearance of leprosy	Lev.	13	41, 42
David's sling hits Goliath's	I Sam.	17	49
Ezekiel's made strong	Ezek.	3	8, 9
Worthy are marked	Ezek.	9	4
Jewels for	Ezek.	16	12
Followers of the Lamb marked	Rev.	14	1, 9

foreigner see alien

foreign missionaries teachers abroad

Some from Antioch	Acts	13	1–3
Meet at Jerusalem	Acts	21	15–20

foreknowledge prescience

Of God:

All events	Is.	42	9
	Acts	15	18
Of possibilities	I Sam.	23	11
Of the coming of Jesus	Mat.	24	36
Concerning Christ's death	Acts	2	23
Peter's election as a disciple	I Pet.	1	2

Of Jesus:

Concerning His betrayal	John	6	64
His impending death	John	13	1
All events of His life	John	18	4
Of men's hearts	John	1	47, 48

forerunner herald

John the Baptist, for Jesus	Mat.	3	1, 3
	Mat.	11	10, 11
	Mark	1	2
	Luke	7	27
Jesus, for followers	John	14	2
	Heb.	6	20

foresaw to see before

David of Christ	Acts	2	25
Scripture	Gal.	3	8
Prudent man	Prov.	22	3

foreskin prepuce

Removed during circumcision	Gen.	17	7–14
	Lev.	12	2, 3
Zipporah uses sharp stone	Ex.	4	25
Joshua uses sharp knives	Josh.	5	2, 3
David gives Saul 200 as dowry	I Sam.	18	22–27

Symbolic:

Of the heart	Deut.	10	16
	Jer.	4	4
In admonishment	Heb.	2	16

forest land densely covered with trees

Abounds with wild honey	I Sam.	14	25, 26
	Is.	44	14
Place of refuge	I Sam.	22	5
Supplies timber for building	I Ki.	5	6–8
Power of God extends over	Ps.	29	9
Infested with wild beasts	Ps.	50	10
	Jer.	5	6

Mentioned in scripture:

Ephraim	II Sam.	18	6, 8
Lebanon	I Ki.	7	2
Carmel	II Ki.	19	23
Bashan	Is.	2	13
Arabia	Is.	21	13

forethought thinking in advance

Of Adam	Gen.	3	7
Of Abraham	Gen.	12	12, 13
Of Lot	Gen.	19	19
Of Jacob	Gen.	32	11
Coming evil	Prov.	22	3
Of David	I Sam.	27	1
Of an ant	Prov.	6	6–8

foretold tell before

Of Christ	Mic.	5	2
	Is.	9	6
	Is.	7	14
	Ps.	22	2
	Zech.	9	9
Of Paul	Acts	21	11
Of Jerusalem	Mat.	24	2

forgery fabrication

Jezebel sends letters	I Ki.	21	7, 8
Job reproves his friends	Job	13	4
Lies by proud	Ps.	119	69

forewarn

Will f whom ye shall fear	Luke	12	5
As we also have f your	I Thes.	4	6

forget: do not remember

Jerusalem	Ps.	137	5
God cannot	Heb.	6	10
Paul tries to	Phil.	3	13
Man before a mirror	James	1	24

forgetting God

Warnings against	Deut.	6	12
Prosperity often leads to	Deut.	8	12–14
Punishment of	Job	8	13
	Hosea	8	14
Troubles should not lead to	Ps.	44	17
Characteristic of the wicked	Prov.	2	17
	Jer.	3	21
Encouraged by false teachers	Jer.	23	27

forgiveness pardon

Joseph and his brothers	Gen.	50	17
Pharaoh begs Moses' intercession	Ex.	10	17
Moses entreats God	Ex.	32	32
Through purging blood	Lev.	4	13–21
	Heb.	9	22
Through prayer	I Ki.	8	30
	Ps.	130	4
For confessing sins	Ps.	25	18
	Ps.	32	5
	I John	1	9
Transgressor blessed	Ps.	32	1
Readily of God	Ps.	86	5
God's mercy	Ps.	103	3
Of Ephraim	Jer.	31	34
Power of God to	Dan.	9	9
	Mark	2	7
Of debts, trespassing	Mat.	6	12, 16
Only if in heart for others	Mat.	6	15
	Mark	11	25, 26
	Luke	6	37
For speakers against Christ	Mat.	12	32
Of all offenders	Mat.	18	21, 22
	Mat.	18	35
Not for blasphemers against Holy Ghost	Mark	3	29
Through repentance	Luke	17	3
	Acts	3	19
Through acceptance of Christ	Acts	26	18
Christian virtue	Rom.	12	8
	Eph.	4	32
	Col.	3	13
Of excommunicated persons	II Cor.	2	6–10
Through Christ	Eph.	1	7
Of children's sins	I John	2	12

Examples:

Esau	Gen.	33	4, 11
Joseph	Gen.	45	5–15
David	I Sam.	24	10–12
Solomon	I Ki.	1	53
Jesus	Luke	23	24

form pattern

Worship:

Worship rejected if not proper	I Chr.	15	13, 14
Improper	Lev.	10	1
In religious service	II Chr.	29	34
Heart condition important	Mat.	12	3, 4

Physical material:

Earth	Gen.	1	2
Of Samuel	I Sam.	28	14
Of Christ	Is.	53	2
	Phil.	2	7
Of Doctrine	II Tim.	1	13
Of godliness	II Tim.	3	5
Of knowledge	Rom.	2	20

formalism strictly observing stated forms

False security of	I Sam.	15	22
	Hosea	6	6
	Ps.	51	16, 17
	Is.	1	11
Of fasting	Jer.	14	12
	Mat.	6	16
Of circumcision	I Cor.	7	19
Rejected by Paul	Phil.	3	4–7
End times	II Tim.	3	5

formula fixed set of words

Joshua's success as leader	Josh.	1	8
For friendship	Prov.	18	24
Used in baptism	Mat.	28	19

fornication illicit intercourse

Rules against	Lev.	20	6–21
Solomon exhorts against	Prov.	7	1–27
Only reason for divorce	Mat.	5	32

Defiles man	Mat.	15	19, 20
Jews not born of	John	8	41
Strictly forbidden	Acts	15	20
	I Cor.	5	1–9
	Eph.	5	3
Marriage is solution	I Cor.	7	1, 2
Work of the flesh	Gal.	5	19
Abstinence from, will of God	I Thes.	4	3
Figurative	II Chr.	21	11
	Rev.	14	8
	Rev.	19	2

forsaking God

Wicked guilty of	Deut.	28	20
Resolve against	Josh.	24	16
Warnings against	Josh.	24	20
	I Chr.	28	9
Provokes God to forsake	Judg.	10	13
	II Chr.	15	2
Idolaters guilty of	I Sam.	8	8
Ingratitude of	Jer.	2	5, 6
Trusting in man is	Jer.	17	5
Followed by remorse	Jer.	17	13
	Ezek.	6	9
Is forsaking His covenant	Jer.	22	9

Instances of:

Children of Israel	I Sam.	12	10
Saul	I Sam.	15	10, 11
Kingdom of Judah	II Chr.	12	1, 5
Disciples	John	6	66

fort *strong hold*

David hides there	II Sam.	5	9
Nebuchadnezzar builds against Jerusalem	II Ki.	25	1

forth

Earth bring *f* grass	Gen.	1	11, 12
Sent *f* his dove	Gen.	8	10
Stretch *f* thine hand	Ex.	8	5
Arise, go *f*	II Sam.	19	7
Cometh *f* like a flower	Job	14	2
His going *f* is from the end	Ps.	19	6
This time *f* and for evermore	Ps.	113	2
	Ps.	115	18
Knowest not what a day may bring *f*	Prov.	27	1
There shall come *f* a rod	Is.	11	1
Break *f* into singing	Is.	49	13
	Is.	54	1
Sower went *f* to sow	Mat.	13	3
Arose and stood *f*	Luke	6	8
Bring *f* fruit	Rom.	7	4, 5

fortress *a fortified place*

Defended against enemies	Judg.	6	2
	Is.	33	16
Cities used as	Judg.	9	31
"My rock and my fortress"	II Sam.	22	2
Strong towers built for	II Chr.	26	9
Symbolic of God's protection	Ps.	18	2
Often deserted	Is.	34	13
Ministers likened to	Jer.	6	27

forty days

Duration of flood	Gen.	7	17
Jacob embalmed	Gen.	50	2, 3
Moses on mount Sinai	Ex.	24	18
Moses' spies stay in Canaan	Num.	13	25
Moses fasts and prays	Deut.	9	18, 25, 26
Goliath challenges Israel	I Sam.	17	16
Elijah fasts in Horeb	I Ki.	19	2, 8
Trial for Nineveh	Jonah	3	4
Jesus tempted by devil	Luke	4	1, 2
Jesus seen after resurrection	Acts	1	3

forty stripes

Quota of lashes allowed	Deut.	25	3
Paul beaten five times	II Cor.	11	23, 24

forty years

Israel's wanderings in wilderness	Num.	14	33
Clothing still good	Deut.	29	5
Time of rest and peace	Judg.	3	11
Duration of David's reign	I Ki.	2	11
Duration of Salomon's reign	I Ki.	11	42
Egypt's desolation	Ezek.	29	11
Duration of Saul's reign	Acts	13	21

forward

I go *f*, but he is not there	Job	23	8
Backward, and not *f*	Jer.	7	24
Every one straight *f*	Ezek.	1	9
	Ezek.	10	22
Went *f* a little	Mark	14	35

I also was *f* to do	Gal.	2	10

forwardness

Know the *f* of your mind	II Cor.	9	2

fought

The Lord *f* for Israel	Josh.	10	14
He that *f* for you	Josh.	23	3
Have *f* with beasts	I Cor.	15	32
I have *f* a good fight	II Tim.	4	7

foul

My face is *f* with weeping	Job	16	16
It will be *f* weather	Mat.	16	3
He rebuked the *f* spirit	Mark	9	25
Babylon, hold of every *f* spirit	Rev.	18	2

found

Noah *f* grace in eyes of the Lord	Gen.	6	8
The dove *f* no rest	Gen.	8	9
How hast thou *f* it so quickly?	Gen.	27	20
God hath *f* out the iniquity	Gen.	44	16
F a man gathering sticks	Num.	15	32
Hast thou *f* me, mine enemy?	I Ki.	21	20
I *f* book of the law	II Ki.	22	8
Good things *f* in thee	II Chr.	19	3
I have *f* a ransom	Job	33	24
When thou mayest be *f*	Ps.	32	6
Comforters, but *f* none	Ps.	69	20
Sparrow hath *f* an house	Ps.	84	3
F no city to dwell in	Ps.	107	4
One man among a thousand have I *f*	Eccl.	7	28
I *f* him whom my soul loveth	S. of S.	3	4
F of them that sought me not	Is.	65	1
	Rom.	10	20
I sought for a man, but *f* none	Ezek.	22	30
Weighed, and *f* wanting	Dan.	5	27
Not *f* so great faith	Mat.	8	10
	Luke	7	9
F one pearl of great price	Mat.	13	46
F others standing idle	Mat.	20	6
F nothing thereon	Mat.	21	19
	Mark	11	13
	Luke	13	6
He *f* them asleep	Mat.	26	43
	Mark	14	40
	Luke	22	45
They *f* fault	Mark	7	2
They *f* him in the temple	Luke	2	46
They *f* the servant whole	Luke	7	10
I have *f* the sheep	Luke	15	6
I have *f* the piece of money	Luke	15	9
Was lost, and is *f*	Luke	15	32
I have *f* no fault	Luke	23	14
F the stone rolled away	Luke	24	2
We have *f* the Messias	John	1	41, 45
Our fathers *f* no sustenance	Acts	7	11
If he *f* any of this way	Acts	9	2
I *f* an altar with inscription	Acts	17	23
F this man a pestilent fellow	Acts	24	5
To life, I *f* to be unto death	Rom.	7	10
We are *f* false witnesses	I Cor.	15	15
F in fashion as a man	Phil.	2	8
Enoch was not *f*	Heb.	11	5
He *f* no place of repentance	Heb.	12	17
Not *f* thy works perfect	Rev.	3	2

foundation *base*

Laid for temples	I Ki.	6	37
Security afforded by	Mat.	7	25
Laid for houses	Luke	6	48

Figuratively applied to:

The heavens	II Sam.	22	8
The earth	Job	38	4
The world	Ps.	18	15

Illustrative of:

The righteous	Prov.	10	25
Christ and His church	Is.	28	16
	I Cor.	3	11
Teachings of the apostles	Eph.	2	20
God's power	Heb.	11	10

fountain gate

A gate in the wall of Jerusalem	Neh.	2	14
	Neh.	12	37

fountains and springs

A haven for travelers	Gen.	16	7
Found in valleys and hills	Deut.	8	7
Add fertility to the earth	I Ki.	18	5
Stopped, to defeat enemies	II Chr.	32	3, 4
Created by God	Ps.	74	15
	Ps.	104	10

fountains and springs—*continued*

Provide water for beasts and birds	Ps.	104	11, 12

Symbolic of:

God	Ps.	36	9
	Jer.	2	13
A good wife	Prov.	5	18
Wisdom	Prov.	13	14
	Prov.	16	22
	Prov.	18	4
Christ	Zech.	13	1
Holy Ghost	John	7	38, 39

four square *sides all equal*

Altar	Ex.	27	1
Breastplate	Ex.	28	16
Court of Ezekiel's temple	Ezek.	40	47
Heavenly Jerusalem	Rev.	21	16

fowl *birds*

Driven away by Abram	Gen.	15	11
Some an abomination	Lev.	11	13–20
Solomon's daily fare	I Ki.	4	23
People better than	Luke	12	24

fowler

Deliver thee from snare of *f*	Ps.	91	3
A bird from hand of the *f*	Prov.	6	5
Prophet is a snare of a *f*	Hosea	9	8

fowlers

Escaped out of snare of *f*	Ps.	124	7

fox

Used by Samson against Philistines	Judg.	15	4–6
Found in deserts	Ezek.	13	4
Dwells in holes	Mat.	8	20

Figurative of:

Enemies of the church	S. of S.	2	15
False prophets	Ezek.	13	4
Craftiness	Luke	12	32
Of desolation	Lam.	5	18

frankincense *gum resin*

Perfume, placed before tabernacle	Ex.	30	34–36
Placed on meat offerings	Lev.	2	1, 2
An overseer appointed by Solomon	I Chr.	9	29
Portion given to priests	Neh.	13	5
From Arabia	Is.	60	6
Sweet-smelling perfume	S. of S.	3	6
Precious gift to Jesus	Mat.	2	11

fratricide *act of killing one's brother or sister*

Cain slays Abel	Gen.	4	8
Abimelech slays Jerubbaal's sons	Judg.	9	1–5
Absalom has Amnon killed	II Sam.	13	28, 29
Jehoram slays all his brothers	II Chr.	21	4
Prevalence of wickedness	Mic.	7	6
	Mat.	10	21
Solomon-Adonijah	I Ki.	2	23–25

fraud *deception*

Sinful	Lev.	19	13
Gibeonites condemned for	Josh.	9	3–27
Characteristic of the wicked	Ps.	10	7
Herod	Mat.	2	8
Jacob	Gen.	27	19
Judas' betrayal	Mat.	26	47–50
Simon attempts to buy holiness	Acts	8	18, 20
Rich men, upon labourers	James	5	4

freedom *liberty*

Laws governing	Ex.	21	2, 5, 6
Killer of Goliath wins	I Sam.	17	25
In death	Job	3	19
Of oppressed	Is.	58	6
From worldly cares	Mat.	6	25, 34
Through truth	John	8	32
Jews always had	John	8	33
Through Jesus	John	8	36
Chief Roman buys his	Acts	22	28
From sin	Rom.	6	16–18
	Rom.	8	2
State of Paul	I Cor.	9	1, 19
Where the spirit of the Lord is	II Cor.	3	17
From Jewish law	Gal.	5	1–6
For serving God	I Pet.	2	16

freeman *person not in bondage*

Servant of Lord	I Cor.	7	22

fret *worry*

Not to	Ps.	37	1, 7, 8
	Prov.	24	19
Accompanies hunger	Is.	8	21
Foolish	Prov.	19	3
Martha	Luke	10	41

freewill offering *see offerings*

friendship *fondness, attachment*

Lord and Moses	Ex.	33	11
David and Jonathan	I Sam.	20	16, 17
	II Sam.	1	26
Deceitful	II Sam.	20	9, 10
	Ps.	41	9
Elijah and Elisha	II Ki.	2	1, 2
Jehoshaphat and Ahab	II Chr.	18	1–34
Unfaithful	Ps.	55	12, 13
Destroyed by tail-bearing	Prov.	17	9
Constant	Prov.	17	17
Friendliness begets	Prov.	18	24
True friends invaluable	Prov.	27	9, 10
	Eccl.	4	9–12
	Luke	10	30–35
Not always trustworthy	Mic.	7	5
Jesus with sinners	Mat.	11	19
Judas' betrayal of Jesus	Mat.	26	47–50
Jesus' with Mary, Martha and Lazarus	John	11	5, 7
Commandment of Jesus	John	15	12–14
Joseph's with Christ, undisclosed	John	19	38
Abraham-God	James	2	23
Abraham-Lot	Gen.	14	14–16
Ruth-Naomi	Ruth	1	16
David-Jonathan	I Sam.	18	1–4
David-Hiram	I Ki.	5	1
Job-friends	Job	2	11–13
Paul and Titus	II Cor.	2	12, 13
Paul and Onesiphorus	II Tim.	1	16–18
God and Abraham	James	2	23
With worldly matters	James	4	4
Paul forsaken by	II Tim.	4	16

frog *amphibian animal*

Egypt plagued	Ex.	8	2–14
	Ps.	78	45
Spirits of devils	Rev.	16	13, 14

frontlet *safeguard*

A jewel or amulet worn between the eyes	Ex.	13	16
	Deut.	6	8
	Deut.	11	18

frost *frozen moisture*

Falls at night	Gen.	31	40
Breath of God	Job	37	10
From whence?	Job	38	29, 30
Destroys trees	Ps.	78	47
Scattered like ashes	Ps.	147	16
Jehoiakim cast out	Jer.	36	30

froward *disobedient*

Israel to be punished	Deut.	32	20
Not favoured by God	Job	5	13
Abomination to God	Prov.	3	32
	Prov.	11	20
Man provokes strife	Prov.	16	28
Peter advocates gentleness	I Pet.	2	18

frugality *careful economy*

Advocated by Jesus	John	6	11–13
A fool is not	Prov.	21	17
A good man is	Prov.	13	22
Widow of Zarephth	I Ki.	17	5–13

fruit

First three years not to be touched	Lev.	19	23
Blessed to the obedient	Deut.	7	13
	Deut.	28	4
Of faith meet for repentance, etc.	Mat.	3	8
	Mat.	7	16
	John	4	36
	James	3	17
Every tree in the which is *f*	Gen.	1	29
Shewed them the *f* of the land	Num.	13	26
Take the first of all *f*	Deut.	26	2
Of *f* of thy body will I set upon thy throne	Ps.	132	11
My *f* is better than gold	Prov.	8	19
F of the righteous a tree of life	Prov.	11	30
Satisfied by the *f* of mouth	Prov.	12	14
	Prov.	18	20
His *f* was sweet to my taste	S. of S.	2	3
F of their doings	Is.	3	10
	Mic.	7	13
I create the *f* of the lips	Is.	57	19
Ye have eaten the *f* of lies	Hosea	10	13
A basket of the summer *f*	Amos	8	1
F of body for sin of soul	Mic.	6	7
Neither shall *f* be in the vines	Hab.	3	17
Earth is stayed from her *f*	Hag.	1	10
F meet for repentance	Mat.	3	8
	Luke	3	8

Make tree good, and his *f* good	Luke	12	33
Let no *f* grow on thee	Luke	21	19
Drink of *f* of the vine	Luke	26	29
	Mark	14	25
Earth bringeth forth *f* of herself	Mark	4	28
I come seeking *f* on this fig tree	Luke	13	7
F to life eternal	John	4	36
Branch cannot bear *f* of itself	John	15	4
What *f* had ye in those things?	Rom.	6	21
Bring forth *f* unto God	Rom.	7	4
The *f* of the Spirit	Gal.	5	22
	Eph.	5	9
I desire *f* that may abound	Phil.	4	17
First partaker of the *f*	II Tim.	2	6
Peaceable *f* of righteousness	Heb.	12	11
Offer *f* of our lips	Heb.	13	15
Waiteth for the precious *f*	James	5	7
Trees whose *f* withereth, without *f*	Jude		12

fryingpan *low, flat pan*
Used in cooking	Lev.	7	9

fugitive *deserter, runaway*
Curse of Cain	Gen.	4	12
Gileadites taunted by Ephraim	Judg.	12	4
Captured by Nebuzar-adan	II Ki.	25	11
Moabites threatened	Is.	15	5
Judgment on Pharaoh	Ezek.	17	21

fulfil
The Lord *f* all thy counsel	Ps.	20	4
F desire of them that fear him	Ps.	145	19
To *f* all righteousness	Mat.	3	15
Not come to destroy but to *f*	Mat.	5	17
Till all be *f*	Mat.	5	18
	Mat.	24	34
What sign when all shall be *f*?	Mark	13	4
All written may be *f*	Luke	21	22
Till it be *f* in kingdom of God	Luke	22	16
My joy is *f*	John	3	29
	John	17	13
Who shall *f* all my will	Acts	13	22
God hath *f* the same unto us	Acts	13	33
Righteousness of law be *f* in us	Rom.	8	4
Love is the *f* of the law	Rom.	13	10
All the law is *f* in one word	Gal.	5	14
So *f* the law of Christ	Gal.	6	2
F ye my joy	Phil.	2	2
To *f* the Word of God	Col.	1	25
F good pleasure of his goodness	II Thes.	1	11
If ye *f* the royal law	James	2	8
Till the thousand years be *f*	Rev.	20	3

fulfilling
Stormy wind *f* his word	Ps.	148	8
Love is the *f* of the law	Rom.	13	10
F desires of flesh and mind	Eph.	2	3

full
Give house *f* of silver	Num.	22	18
	Num.	24	13
Houses *f* of good things	Deut.	6	11
Joshua was *f* of spirit of wisdom	Deut.	34	9
I went out *f*	Ruth	1	21
The mountain was *f* of horses	II Ki.	6	17
Come to grave in *f* age	Job	5	26
Of few days and *f* of trouble	Job	14	1
His mouth is *f* of cursing	Ps.	10	7
	Rom.	3	14
Waters of a *f* cup	Ps.	73	10
F of habitations of cruelty	Ps.	74	20
The earth is *f* of thy mercy	Ps.	119	64
Hell and destruction are never *f*	Prov.	27	20
Lest I be *f*, and deny thee	Prov.	30	9
Yet the sea is not *f*	Eccl.	1	7
I am *f* of burnt offerings	Is.	1	11
Earth shall be *f* of knowledge of the Lord	Is.	11	9
I am *f* of the fury of the Lord	Jer.	6	11
Earth *f* of his praise	Hab.	3	3
Streets *f* of boys and girls	Zech.	8	5
Body *f* of light	Mat.	6	22
	Luke	11	36
Woe unto you that are *f*	Luke	6	25
F of grace and truth	John	1	14
That your joy might be *f*	John	15	11
	John	16	24
F of Holy Ghost	Acts	6	3
	Acts	7	55
Now ye are *f*	I Cor.	4	8
I am instructed to be *f*	Phil.	4	12

Make *f* proof of thy ministry	II Tim.	4	5
Meat to them of *f* age	Heb.	5	14
Joy unspeakable and *f* of glory	I Pet.	1	8

fuller *one who whitens garments*
Messiah likened to	Mal.	3	2
Bleacher of cloth	Mark	9	3

fuller's field
A field near Jerusalem where cleansed garments were spread out to dry	II Ki.	18	17
	Is.	7	3
	Is.	36	2

funerals *ceremonies for disposing of deceased*
Interrupted by Jesus' miracle	Luke	7	11–17
Jacob's	Gen.	50	3–7

furlongs *measure of distance; 220 yards, 1/8 mile*
Disciples row 20 or 30	John	6	19
Bethany 15 from Jerusalem	John	11	18
Blood from Babylonian winepresses flows 600	Rev.	14	20

furnace *enclosed chamber for producing heat*
Smoking, in Abram's vision	Gen.	15	17
Egypt likened to	Deut.	4	20
	I Ki.	8	51
For gold	Prov.	17	3
Shadrach, Meshach and Abednego delivered from	Dan.	3	1–30
Damnation for wicked	Mat.	13	42

Symbolic:
Words of Lord like silver	Ps.	12	6
God's wrath upon Israel	Ezek.	22	18, 22

furrow *trench made by plow*
Rained upon by God's bounty	Ps.	65	10

Symbolic:
Of great inflictions	Ps.	129	3
Judgments against Israel like hemlock in	Hosea	10	4

fury *wrath, frenzy*
Jacob flees Esau's	Gen.	27	44
God's against wicked	Job	20	23
	Is.	59	18
God's against Babylon	Jer.	21	5
Wine cup of God's	Jer.	25	15
Lord's will rest	Ezek.	21	17
Lord's for Zion	Zech.	8	2
See anger of God			

future *that which is to come*
Unknown by man	Prov.	27	1
	Luke	19	41–44
Humility in kingdom of God	Luke	9	61, 62
Uncertain	Luke	12	16–20
	James	4	13–15

G

Gaash *earthquake*
Mountain in Ephraim	Josh.	24	30
Burial place of Joshua	Judg.	2	9
Home of Hiddai, one of David's men	II Sam.	23	30

Gaba *see Geba*

Gabbatha *height*
Judgement seat of Pilate set up in	John	19	13

Gabriel *man of God*
One of seven archangels	Dan.	8	16
Appears to Daniel in prayer	Dan.	9	21
Announces birth of John the Baptist	Luke	1	18–20
Appears to Mary to tell her of Jesus' birth	Luke	1	26–28

Gad *good fortune*
Eldest son of Zilphah and Jacob	Gen.	30	11
	Gen.	35	26
He becomes the head of one of the twelve tribes	Num.	2	14
Territory granted to	Num.	32	1
	Deut.	3	16–20
A seer or prophet in the reign of David	I Sam.	22	5
	I Chr.	21	9

Gadarenes, Gergesenes
Home of demoniac	Luke	8	28
By sea of Galilee, east	Mark	5	1

Gaddiel *God is my fortune*

A chief of Zebulun, one of the twelve spies	Num.	13	2, 10

Gadi *fortunate*

Father of Menahem	II Ki.	15	14, 17

Gaham *a flame, burning*

Son of Nahor	Gen.	22	23, 24

Gahar *hiding place*

Post-exilic Nethinim	Ezra	2	43, 47
	Neh.	7	46, 39

gain

Is is *g* to make ways perfect?	Job	22	3
Greedy of *g*	Prov.	1	19
	Prov.	15	27
The *g* thereof better than gold	Prov.	3	14
By usury an unjust *g*	Prov.	28	8
Dishonest *g*	Ezek.	22	13, 27
He shall divide the land for *g*	Dan.	11	39
Consecrate their *g* to the Lord	Mic.	4	13
If he *g* the world	Mat.	16	26
	Mark	8	36
	Luke	9	25
Have *g* other two talents	Mat.	25	22
Had *g* by trading	Luke	19	15
Brought masters much *g*	Acts	16	16
No small *g* to craftsman	Acts	19	24
That I might *g* the more	I Cor.	9	19
Did I make a *g* of you?	II Cor.	12	17
To die is *g*	Phil.	1	21
What things were *g* to me	Phil.	3	7
Supposing that *g* is godliness	I Tim.	6	5
Buy and sell, and get *g*	James	4	13

gains, unjustly gotten

By lying	Prov.	21	6
By oppression	Prov.	22	16
Of no permanence	Jer.	17	11
Wicked deeds	Jer.	22	13
Inadequate wages	James	5	4

gainsay

Adversaries not able to *g*	Luke	21	15
Came without *g*	Acts	10	29
Stretched hands to a *g* people.	Rom.	10	21
Perished in the *g* of Core.	Jude	11	

gainsayers

Able to convince *g*	Tit.	1	9

Gaius *commended*

Paul's companion	Acts	19	29
Accompanies Paul to Derbe	Acts	20	4
A Corinthian who is baptized by Paul	Rom.	16	23
	I Cor.	1	14
Commended by John	III John		1–11

Galatia *an ancient kingdom in central Asia Minor*

Visited twice by Paul	Acts	16	3, 6
	Acts	18	18, 23
Collection taken of them	I Cor.	16	1
Peter speaks to	I Pet.	1	1
Churches of	Gal.	1	1, 2
Tend toward apostasy	Gal.	1	7, 8
Disobedient	Gal.	3	1
Confused about the law.	Gal.	3	11–17

Galbanum *Asiatic gum resin*

Used in sacred oil	Ex.	30	34, 35

Galilee *circuit, the circle*

A city of refuge in	Josh.	20	7
Prophecy concerning	Is.	9	1
	Mat.	4	14, 15
Scene of most of Christ's life	Mat.	2	22
	Mat.	4	23
	Mark	1	9
	Luke	4	14
	Luke	24	6
	Acts	10	37
People of, receive Jesus	John	4	45, 53
Jesus appears here after His resurrection	John	21	1–25
Churches in	Acts	9	31
Sea of			
Also called:			
Sea of Chinnereth	Num.	34	11
Sea of Gennesaret	Luke	5	1
Sea of Tiberias	John	6	1
Jesus calls His disciples on the shore of	Mat.	4	18–22
Miracles of Jesus from	Mat.	8	24–32
	Mat.	14	22–23
	Mat.	17	27

gall *bitter substance*

Gall	Job	16	13
Used figuratively	Deut.	29	18
	Acts	8	18–23
A bitter herb	Jer.	8	14
Given to Jesus on the cross	Mat.	27	30–34
	Ps.	69	21
From snakes	Job	20	14

Gallio *a Roman proconsul, deputy of Achaia*

Dismisses complaint against Paul	Acts	18	12–17

gallows *an upright frame with a crossbeam*

Used for execution of criminals	Esth.	5	14
	Esth.	6	4
	Esth.	7	9, 10
	Esth.	9	13, 25
Shame of being hanged upon	Gal.	3	13

Gamaliel *recompense of God*

A chief of Manasseh	Num.	1	10
	Num.	2	20
A teacher who speaks before the Sanhedrin	Acts	5	33–40
Teaches Paul	Acts	22	3

gambling

Forbidden	Ex.	20	15
	Lev.	19	11
See lots			

games *any test of skill*

Foot races	I Cor.	9	24, 26
Gladatorial	I Cor.	15	32
Figurative	Gal.	5	7
	Heb.	12	1
Run in rain	Gal.	2	2
	Phil.	2	16
Encouraged by crowds	Heb.	12	1
Receiving crown	II Tim.	4	7, 8
See amusement			

gaoler, jailer

Of Philippi, converted	Acts	16	27–34

garden *a well-cultivated region*

Of Eden	Gen.	2	8
Of the Lord	Gen.	13	10
Symbolic of plenty	Is.	58	11
Of Gethsemane	John	18	1
As a place of burial	John	19	41
Adam expelled from	Gen.	3	23
Guarded by a lodge	Is.	1	8
Necessity of water	Is.	1	30
Must be planted	Jer.	29	5
Eden-like garden will be restored	Ezek.	36	35
Of Sushan	Esth.	1	5
For idols	Is.	65	3

gardener *a person who works in a garden*

Adam	Gen.	2	15
Jesus mistaken for	John	20	15

garlick *a clove from a bulb of the lily family*

Mentioned among the good things in Egypt	Num.	11	5

garment, raiment *any article of clothing*

Of the priests	Ex.	28	1–42
	Ex.	39	1–29
Manner of purifying	Lev.	13	47–59
	Zech.	3	3, 4
Of righteousness	Is.	61	10
	Mat.	22	11, 12
	II Cor.	5	2–4
	Rev.	3	18
	Rev.	7	14
	Rev.	16	15
	Rev.	19	8
Of Christ, lots cast for	Mat.	27	35
	John	19	23, 24

garner *a granary*

David prays for a full	Ps.	144	13
Laid desolate	Joel	1	17
Symbolic	Mat.	3	12

garnish

He *g* the house	II Chr.	3	6
By Spirit he *g* the heavens	Job	26	13
Swept and *g*	Mat.	12	44
	Luke	11	25
Foundations of the walls were *g*	Rev.	21	19

Garrison

Jonathan smote *g* of Philistines.	I Sam.	13	3
David put *g* in Syria.	II Sam.	8	6
	I Chr.	18	6
Thy strong *g* shall go down.	Ezek.	26	11
Kept the city with a *g*	II Cor.	11	32

gates *openings providing passageway*

Of heaven	Gen.	28	17
	Ps.	24	7
	Is.	26	1, 2
Wood	Neh.	1	3
Of death and hell	Ps.	9	13
	Mat.	16	18
Brass	Ps.	107	16
	Is.	45	2
Of the grave	Is.	38	10
Double doors	Is.	45	1
	Ezek.	41	24
The strait	Mat.	7	13
	Luke	13	24
Iron	Acts	12	10

Gath *a wine press*

Men of, smitten with emerods	I Sam.	5	8, 9
David flees to	I Sam.	27	4
One of five Philistine cities	II Sam.	1	20
Taken by Hazael	II Ki.	12	17
Taken by David	I Chr.	18	1
Uzziah breaks down the wall of	II Chr.	26	3–6
Anakim lived there	Josh.	11	22
Home of Obed-edom	II Sam.	6	10
Ark taken there	I Sam.	5	8
Inhabitants called Gittites	Josh.	13	3
David takes refuge	I Sam.	27	2–7
Shimei's servants flee there	I Ki.	2	39–41
Fortified by Rehoboam	II Chr.	11	8

Gath-hepher, Gittah-hepher *wine press of the well*

A city of Zebulun	Josh.	19	13
Home of the prophet Jonah	II Ki.	14	25

Gaza, Azzah *strong*

One of the five main Philistine cities	Josh.	13	3
	Jer.	25	20
Allotted to Judah	Josh.	15	47
City of Anakim	Deut.	2	23
Temple of Dagon	Judg.	16	23
Samson carries away gates of	Judg.	16	1–3
Samson dies at	Judg.	16	21–31
Destruction of, foretold	Jer.	47	1–5
	Amos	1	6, 7
	Zeph.	2	4
	Zech.	9	5
Desert of	Acts	8	26–39
A city of Ephraim	Judg.	6	4
	I Chr.	7	28

Gazer *see* Gezer

Gazez *shearer*

Son of Caleb	I Chr.	2	46
A grandson of Caleb	I Chr.	2	46

Geba, Gaba *a hill*

Also called Gaba	Josh.	18	24
A frontier city of Benjamin	Josh.	21	17
Near it Jonathan fights the Philistines	I Sam.	14	4–14
Asa rebuilds the city	I Ki.	15	22
	II Chr.	16	6
Inhabitants return after exile	Neh.	11	31

Gedaliah *great is Jehovah*

Governor of the remnant of Judah	II Ki.	25	22
Treacherously slain by Ishmael	II Ki.	25	25
Friend of Jeremiah	Jer.	40	5, 6
A musician	I Chr.	25	3, 9
A post-exilic priest, who took a strange wife	Ezra	10	18
A prince who causes imprisonment of Jeremiah	Jer.	38	1
Ancestor of Zephaniah	Zeph.	1	1

Gedeon *see* Gideon

Gedor *a fortress*

A hill town of Judah near Hebron	Josh.	15	58
	I Chr.	12	7
Ancestor of two Judahite families	I Chr.	4	4, 18
Valley of, taken by Simeonites	I Chr.	4	39, 40
Ancestor of King Saul	I Chr.	8	31
	I Chr.	9	37

Gehazi *valley of vision*

Servant of Elisha	II Ki.	4	12
His covetousness and his punishment	II Ki.	5	20–27
Afflicted with leprosy	II Ki.	5	27
Told Elisha of desire	II Ki.	4	14
Got king to return Shunamite's land	II Ki.	8	4–6

genealogy *a recorded history of lineage*

Generations of Adam	Gen.	5	1–32
	I Chr.	1	1–3
	Luke	3	23, 38

Of Noah	Gen.	10	1–32
	I Chr.	1	4
Of Shem	Gen.	11	10–27
Of Terah	Gen.	11	27–32
Of Abraham	Gen.	25	1–18
	I Chr.	1	28
Of Isaac	Gen.	25	19–28
Of Jacob	Gen.	29	31–35
	Gen.	30	1–25
	Gen.	46	8–27
	Ex.	1	1–4
	Num.	26	37–50
Of Esau	Gen.	36	1–43
	I Chr.	1	35
Of the tribes	I Chr.	2	1–55
	I Chr.	4	1–37
	I Chr.	5	1–15
	I Chr.	6	1–53
	I Chr.	7	1–40
Of David	I Chr.	3	1–24
A Saul	I Chr.	8	33
	I Chr.	9	39
Of Christ	Mat.	1	1–25
	Luke	3	23–38
Endless	I Tim.	1	4

generation

History of origins	Gen.	2	4
Race	Mat.	24	34
Characterized as evil	Deut.	32	5
Characterized as good	Gen.	7	1
Period or age	Gen.	7	1
Families	Job	42	16

Gennesaret *Greek for Chinnereth, a harp*

District of Galilee	Mark	6	53
A lake of Palestine, miracles wrought here	Luke	5	1–6
Also called Tiberias	John	21	1
See Galilee			

Gentiles, heathen *pagan, in opposition to Jew and Christian*

Origin of	Gen.	10	4, 5
Their conversion predicted	Is.	11	10
	Gen.	22	18
	Deut.	32	21
	Ps.	2	8
	Ps.	22	27–31
	Is.	2	2–4
	Jer.	16	19
	Mal.	1	11
	Mat.	12	18
Prediction fulfilled	Acts	8	36, 37
	Acts	10	45–48
	Acts	15	3, 4
	Eph.	2	11
Their state by nature	I Cor.	12	2
	Eph.	2	11
	Eph.	4	17
	I Thes.	4	5
	I Pet.	4	3, 4
Christ made known to	Col.	1	27
Used repetitive prayers	Mat.	6	7, 8
Suppress the revelation of God in nature	Rom.	1	18–32
Have law written in their heart	Rom.	2	14, 15
Sacrificed to devils	I Cor.	10	20
Sinners	Gal.	2	15
Practiced evil	Eph.	5	12

gentleness *kindness*

Of Christ	Mat.	11	29
	II Cor.	10	1
Of God	II Sam.	22	36
The fruit of the spirit	Gal.	5	22
Of Paul and Timothy	I Thes.	2	7
Exhortations to	II Tim.	2	24
	Tit.	3	2

Gera *bean*

Son of Bela	Gen.	46	21
Father of Ehud	Judg.	3	15
Father of Shimei	II Sam.	16	5
Descendant of Bela	I Chr.	8	6–8

gerah *the smallest weight*

The twentieth part of a shekel	Ex.	30	13
	Lev.	27	25

Gerar *rolling country*

City near Gaza	Gen.	10	19
Visited by Abraham	Gen.	20	1
Abimelech rules	Gen.	20	2

Gerar—continued
Visited by Isaac	Gen.	26	1
A valley	Gen.	26	17

Gergesenes *see* Gadarenes

Gerizim *rocky*
The scene of ceremonial blessing	Deut.	11	29
	Deut.	27	12
	Josh.	8	33
Jotham makes a speech here	Judg.	9	7
Samaritans worship here	John	4	20

Gershom, Gershon *driving away*
Son of Levi, called Gershon	Gen.	46	11
Son of Moses	Ex.	2	21, 22
Father of Jonathan	Judg.	18	30
Son of Phinehas	Ezra	8	2

Geshur, Geshuri *bridge*
District in Bashan	Deut.	3	14
Not subdued by Israel	Deut.	3	14
	Josh.	13	2–13
David marries princess of	II Sam.	3	3
Absalom dwells here after murder of Amnon	II Sam.	13	38

get
G thee out of thy country	Gen.	12	1
	Acts	7	3
Through thy precepts I *g* understanding	Ps.	119	104
G wisdom, *g* understanding	Prov.	4	5
With all thy *g*, *g* understanding	Prov.	4	7
G of treasures by a lying tongue	Prov.	21	6
He that *g* riches, and not by right	Jer.	17	11
G thee behind me, Satan	Mat.	16	23
	Mark	8	33
	Luke	4	8

Gethsemane *oil press*
Our Lord's agony here	Mat.	26	36, 50
	Mark	14	32, 53, 57
Jesus betrayed here	John	18	1, 2

Gezer, Gazer, Gob *a precipice*
Joshua crushes the kingdom of	Josh.	10	33
Pharaoh burns it	I Ki.	9	16
Given to Levites	Josh.	2	21
Smitten by David	I Sam.	27	8
Fortified by Solomon	I Ki.	9	17
A war with the Philistines	II Sam.	5	25
	I Chr.	20	4
	II Sam.	22	19

ghost *soul, spirit*
Signifies death	Gen.	35	29
	Mark	15	37
	Acts	5	5, 10

giants
Before the flood	Gen.	6	4
Men of violence	Gen.	6	4, 13
In Canaan they terrify the spies	Num.	13	33
	Deut.	1	28
Og	Deut.	3	11
Anakim	Num.	13	28–33
Rephaim	Gen.	14	5
Emim	Gen.	14	5
Zamzummim	Deut.	2	20
David kills Goliath	I Sam.	17	40–51
Many slain	II Sam.	21	15–22
One who is six-fingered	II Sam.	21	20
Joshua destroys all but those of Gath, Gaza and Ashdod	Josh.	11	21
	Josh.	11	22
	Josh.	14	12

Gibbethon *high place*
A city of Dan	Josh.	19	40, 44
Given to the Levites	Josh.	21	20, 23
While held by the Philistines, besieged by Israel	I Ki.	15	27
	I Ki.	16	15, 17

Gibeah, Gibeath *hill*
A town of Judah	Josh.	15	1, 57
A town of Benjamin	Josh.	18	28
A city of Benjamin	Judg.	19	16, 22–29
The people's wickedness	Judg.	20	10, 13, 35
Philistines take the ark to	I Sam.	7	1, 2
Home of Saul	I Sam.	10	26

Gibeon *hill*
A city in Benjamin	Josh.	18	21, 25
Is given to the priests	Josh.	21	13, 17
Amasa slain at	II Sam.	20	8, 10
Joab slain at	I Ki.	2	28–34
Solomon's dream at	I Ki.	3	5

Tabernacle of the Lord kept at	I Chr.	16	39
	I Chr.	21	29
	II Chr.	1	1–5
Reoccupied in the post-exilic period	Neh.	3	7
Pool of	II Sam.	2	13

Gibeonites *dwellers of Gibeon*
Joshua deceived by	Josh.	9	3–15
Labourers	Josh.	9	17–27
Rescued in war	Josh.	10	1–43
Saul mistreats, and is punished	II Sam.	21	1
David makes atonement for	II Sam.	21	3–9

Giddel *very great*
The head of the Nethinims	Ezra	2	43, 47
A servant of Solomon	Ezra	2	55, 56
Children of	Neh.	7	49
	Neh.	7	58

Gideon, Gedeon, Jerubbaal *tree-feller*
Son of Joash	Judg.	6	11
Angel of the Lord appears to	Judg.	6	11, 12
Destroys the altar and grove of Baal	Judg.	6	25, 27
Named Jerubbaal	Judg.	6	32
God gives him two signs	Judg.	6	36–40
His army reduced	Judg.	7	2–7
His stratagem	Judg.	7	16–20
Subdues the Midianites	Judg.	7	25
	Judg.	8	11, 12
Makes an ephod of the spoil	Judg.	8	24–27
Had 71 sons	Judg.	8	30, 31
His death	Judg.	8	32
Called Gedeon	Heb.	11	32

gier eagle *the Egyptian vulture*
Included among the unclean birds	Lev.	11	13
	Deut.	14	12, 17

gift
Of God	John	4	10
Unspeakable	II Cor.	9	15
The Holy Ghost	Acts	2	38
	Acts	8	20
	Acts	10	45
Spiritual	Ps.	29	11
	Ps.	68	18, 35
	Ps.	84	11
	Prov.	2	6
	Ezek.	11	19
	Acts	11	17
	Rom.	12	6
	I Cor.	12	1–31
	Eph.	2	8
	James	1	5
Temporal	Gen.	1	26, 27
	Gen.	9	3
	Gen.	27	28
	Lev.	26	4
	Ps.	34	10
	Ps.	65	9
	Ps.	136	25
	Ps.	145	15
	Is.	30	23
	Acts	14	17

Various:
Gladness	Ps.	4	7
Heart's desire	Ps.	21	2
Good things	Ps.	34	10
To sinners travail	Eccl.	2	26
Rest	Mat.	11	28
Eternal life	John	6	27
	Rom.	6	23
Grace	Eph.	4	7
Every good gift from God	James	1	17
Things necessary for godliness	II Pet.	1	3

Gihon *bursting forth*
A river in Armenia	Gen.	2	13
Pools and valleys of, near Jerusalem	I Ki.	1	45
	II Chr.	32	30
	II Chr.	33	14

Gilboa *bubbling fountain*
A mountain near Jezreel	I Sam.	28	4
Saul is killed here	I Sam.	31	1–6
Jonathan and his brothers are slain here	I Sam.	31	1, 2
	II Sam.	1	4
Barren and cursed	II Sam.	1	21

Gilead *hard, rough country*
Land of, east of Jordan granted to Reuben, Gad and Manasseh	Num.	32	1, 33
	Deut.	3	13

Invaded by the Ammonites	Judg.	10	9, 17
	Judg.	11	5
Inherited by Machir	Deut.	3	15
Jephthah, leader of	Judg.	11	1
Ish-bosheth king over	II Sam.	2	9
Battle between David and Absalom	II Sam.	17	26
Home of Elijah	I Ki.	17	1
Goats from	S. of S.	4	1
Balm	Jer.	8	22
Iniquity	Hosea	6	8
	Hosea	12	11
Captured by Damascus	Amos	1	3
Benjamin shall inherit	Obad.	19	
Good grazing land	Mic.	7	14
Father of Jephthah	Judg.	11	1–6

Gilgal *circle of stones*

Where Israel's twelve symbolic stones are set up	Josh.	4	1–9, 20
Site of first Israelite encampment after crossing the Jordan	Josh.	4	19
	Josh.	5	10
Saul anointed king here	I Sam.	11	15
Saul forfeits the kingdom	I Sam.	13	4–15
	I Sam.	15	20–23
Idolatry denounced	Hosea	4	15
	Hosea	9	15
	Amos	4	2–4
David welcomed after Absalom's death	II Sam.	19	15, 40
Royal city of Canaan, conquered by Joshua	Josh.	12	23
Important town in Samaria, the location of Elijah's school of prophets	II Ki.	2	1–4
	II Ki.	4	38–40

gin *a snare or trap*

Used for catching animals	Job	18	9
	Ps.	140	5
	Is.	8	14
	Amos	3	5

girdle

Of the high priest	Ex.	28	39
Of leather	II Ki.	1	8
Made of linen	Prov.	31	24
Of women	Is.	3	24
Of John	Mat.	3	4
Jesus wears towel as	John	13	2, 4
Symbol of truth	Eph.	6	14

girl

Sold for wine	Joel	3	3
Plays in the streets	Zech.	8	5

Gittah-hepher *see* Gath-hepher

Gittites *inhabitants of Gath*

David's men called	II Sam.	15	18–23

gittith *set to*

A musical term	Ps.	81	title

giving

A good example	II Chr.	31	5
A tithe	Mal.	3	10
All the time	I Cor.	16	2
Happily	II Cor.	8	11, 12
Not before men	Mat.	6	1–4
For equality	II Cor.	8	11–14
Cheerfully	II Cor.	9	6–7
Widow's mite	Luke	21	2–4
Israelite chiefs	Num.	7	

gladness *cheerfulness*

In God's service	II Chr.	30	21
Imperative privilege	Mat.	5	11, 12
In the first church	Acts	2	46
Brought ark to Jerusalem	II Sam.	6	12
In God's presence	I Chr.	16	27
Passover feast	II Chr.	30	21, 23
Post-exilic feast of booths	Neh.	8	17
Over Haman's deliverance	Esth.	8	16, 17
David	Ps.	51	8
To serve the Lord with	Ps.	100	2

glass *mirror*

Luxury	Is.	3	18–23
See through, darkly	I Cor.	13	12
Sea of	Rev.	4	6
	Rev.	15	2

gleaning *gathering*

Laws concerning	Lev.	19	9, 10
	Lev.	23	22
	Deut.	24	21
Liberality of Boaz concerning	Ruth	2	15

Gideon's proverb	Judg.	7	24
	Judg.	8	2

glede *bird of prey*

Among unclean birds	Deut.	14	12, 13

glorifying God

Ordered to	I Chr.	16	28
	Ps.	22	23
	Is.	42	12
Due Him for His holiness	I Chr.	16	29
	Ps.	99	9
	Rev.	15	4
Instances of deliverance	Ps.	50	15
Universal	Ps.	86	9
	Rev.	5	13
For His faithfulness and truth	Is.	25	1
For His judgments	Is.	25	3
	Ezek.	28	22
	Rev.	14	7
Punishment for not	Dan.	5	23, 30
	Mal.	2	2
	Acts	12	23
	Rom.	1	21
Miraculous works	Mat.	15	31
	Acts	4	21, 22
His grace to others	Acts	11	17, 18
	II Cor.	9	13
	Gal.	1	24

Examples of:

David	Ps.	57	5
Mary	Luke	1	46
Angels	Luke	2	14
Woman with an infirmity	Luke	13	13
Leper	Luke	17	15
Centurion	Luke	23	47
Paul	Rom.	11	36
Gentiles	Acts	13	48

glory *worship, adoration, praise*

God is to his people	Ps.	3	3
Christ is	Is.	60	1
Joy of saints	I Pet.	1	8
Of nature	Luke	12	27
By doing good deeds	John	15	8
Not in men	I Cor.	3	21
In transformation	II Cor.	3	18
By trial	II Cor.	11	30
On the cross	Gal.	6	14
Of man, transient	I Pet.	1	24
Exhibited in Christ	John	1	14

Of God:

Great	Ps.	138	5
Eternal	Ps.	104	31
Rich	Eph.	3	16
To Moses	Ex.	34	5–7
	Ex.	33	18–23
To Stephen	Acts	7	55

gluttony *the act of eating too much*

Esau sells birthright because of	Gen.	25	30–34
Israel is example of	Num.	11	32, 33
Sons of Eli	I Sam.	2	12–17
Warned against	Prov.	23	1–3
	Prov.	23	21
Belshazzar	Dan.	5	1
Jesus is accused of	Mat.	11	19

go

Let me *g*	Gen.	32	26
Angel shall *g* before	Ex.	23	23
	Ex.	32	34
My presence shall *g* with thee	Ex.	33	14
Thy God, he it is that doth *g*	Deut.	31	6
Wither thou *g*, I will go	Ruth	1	16
I shall *g* to him, he shall not return	II Sam.	12	23
I *g* the way of all the earth	I Ki.	2	2
Teach thee in way thou shalt *g*	Ps.	32	8
Whither shall I *g* from thy spirit?	Ps.	139	7
Train child in way he should *g*	Prov.	22	6
Three things which *g* well	Prov.	30	29
To *g* a mile, *g* twain	Mat.	5	41
I say *g*, and he *g*	Mat.	8	9
G rather to lost sheep of Israel	Mat.	10	6
G ye, and teach all nations	Mat.	28	19
G and do likewise	Luke	10	37
Lord, to whom shall we *g*?	John	6	68
I *g* to prepare a place for you	John	14	2
If thou let this man *g*	John	19	12

goad *a sharp, pointed stick*

Shamgai slays 600 men with a	Judg.	3	31
An instrument of torture	I Sam.	13	21
Words of wise	Eccl.	12	11

goat *a cud-chewing mammal*

Abraham sacrifices a	Gen.	15	9
Used for food	Gen.	27	9
	I Sam.	16	20
For passover dinner feast	Ex.	12	2, 5
	II Chr.	35	7
Not to be cooked in its mother's milk	Ex.	23	19
Hair used in curtains of the tabernacle	Ex.	26	7
	Ex.	35	21, 23
	Ex.	36	14
Eight days old before killed	Lev.	22	27
Hair used for clothing	Num.	31	20
One of the clean animals	Deut.	14	4
	Lev.	11	1–8
Many	Deut.	32	14
	S. of S.	4	1
	S. of S.	6	5
	I Sam.	25	2
	II Chr.	17	11
Gideon's sacrifice	Judg.	6	19
Manoah's sacrifice	Judg.	13	19
Hair of, used in pillows	I Sam.	19	13
Wild, in Palestine	I Sam.	24	2
	Ps.	104	18
Milk of	Prov.	27	27

Gob *see* Gezer

God *The Supreme Being*

His names:

Almighty God	Gen.	17	1
Creator	Gen.	1, 2	
Deliverer	II Sam.	22	2
Eternal God	Deut.	33	27
Everlasting God	Gen.	21	33
Father	Mat.	11	25
	Acts	1	4
	Gal.	1	1
Father of lights	James	1	17
Fortress	II Sam.	22	2
God of heaven	Jonah	1	9
God of hosts	Is.	1	24
God of Israel	Num.	16	9
Heavenly Father	Mat.	6	26
Holy Ghost	Mat.	28	19
	John	15	26
	Acts	1	2
	Rev.	3	1
Holy One of Israel	Ps.	71	22
I Am	Ex.	3	14
Jehovah	Ex.	6	3
Judge	Gen.	18	25
King eternal	I Tim.	1	17
Living God	Deut.	5	26
Lord of hosts	Is.	1	24
Lord of sabaoth	James	5	4
Mighty God	Is.	9	6
Most high God	Gen.	14	18
Son	Mat.	11	27
	Mark	13	32
	Acts	9	20
	Heb.	4	14
The Lord God	Ex.	34	6

Emblems of:

Fire	Ex.	13	21
	Ps.	78	14
	Mat.	3	11
	Heb.	12	29
Wind	I Ki.	19	11
	John	3	8
	Acts	2	2
Rain and dew	Ps.	68	9
	Hosea	6	3
	Hosea	10	12
	Hosea	14	5
A voice	Is.	6	8
	John	16	13
	Heb.	3	7
Oil	Is.	61	1, 3
	Heb.	1	9
	I John	2	20, 27
A dove	Mat.	3	16
	John	3	5
Water	John	3	5
	Eph.	5	26

	Heb.	10	22
	Rev.	22	17
Cloven tongues	Acts	2	3, 6–11
Seal	II Cor.	1	22
	Eph.	1	13, 14
	Rev.	7	2

Unity of:

A trinity	Deut.	6	4
	Is.	44	6
Confirmed by Jesus	Mat.	28	19, 20
	John	10	30
Confirmed by Paul	Acts	11	15–18
	I Cor.	8	4

His attributes:

Knowledge, wisdom, power	Gen.	1	3, 6–9
	Ex.	14	1–31
	Josh.	23	9
	Prov.	5	21
	Dan.	2	20
	Mat.	5	48
	Luke	1	49
	I Tim.	1	12, 17
	Rev.	19	6
Just	Gen.	2	16, 17
	Job	8	3, 20
	Is.	45	21
	Nah.	1	3
	Mat.	20	13
Goodness, mercy and love	Gen.	21	12
	Num.	14	18
	II Sam.	12	13
	Ezra	8	18
	Prov.	8	30
	Ezek.	20	17
	Joel	2	13
	Mat.	5	45
	John	3	16
Eternal	Gen.	21	33
	Ps.	104	31
	Is.	9	6
	Rom.	1	20
Jealous	Ex.	20	5
	Josh.	24	19
	I Cor.	10	22
Invisible	Ex.	33	20
	Job	23	8
	John	1	18
	I Tim.	6	16
	Heb.	11	27
Holiness	Ex.	34	5–7
	Lev.	21	8
	I Sam.	2	2
	Is.	6	3
	Rom.	7	12
Immutable	Num.	23	19
	Mal.	3	6
	Acts	4	28
	James	1	17
Faithfulness and truth	Num.	23	19
	I Ki.	8	56
	John	7	28
	II Thes.	3	3
	Heb.	6	18
	Rev.	15	3
Incomprehensible	Job	5	9
	Ps.	36	6
	Is.	40	12
	I Tim.	6	16
Unsearchable	Job	11	7
	Job	37	15
	Eccl.	8	17
	Rom.	11	33
Omnipresent	Job	28	1–28
	Acts	17	27
Omniscient	Prov.	15	3
	Ezek.	11	5
	Rom.	1	20

His characters:

Disposer of events	Gen.	11	8
	Ex.	9	16
	II Sam.	7	8
	Jer.	10	10
	Dan.	4	1–37
	Luke	10	21
Judge of all	Gen.	18	25
	Judg.	11	27
	Eccl.	12	14

	Acts	10	42
	Rom.	2	16
	Heb.	12	23
	Jude		6
	Rev.	18	8
Sanctuary and refuge	Deut.	33	27
	II Sam.	22	3
	Ps.	46	1
	Ezek.	11	16
	Heb.	6	18
Saviour	Ps.	106	21
	Is.	43	3–11
	Jer.	14	8
	Luke	1	47
Searcher of hearts	Prov.	17	3
	Jer.	17	10
	Acts	1	24
	Rom.	8	27
	Rev.	2	23
His law:			
Given to Adam	Gen.	2	16, 17
	Rom.	5	12–14
To Noah	Gen.	9	6
To the Israelites	Ex.	20	2
	Ps.	78	5
Through Moses	Ex.	31	18
	John	7	19
Requires perfect obedience	Deut.	27	26
	Mat.	22	37
	Gal.	3	10
	James	2	10
Man cannot render perfect obedience to	I Ki.	8	46
	Eccl.	7	20
	Rom.	3	10
The wicked forsake	II Chr.	12	1
	Ps.	78	10
	Is.	5	24
	Hosea	4	6
Punishment for disobeying	Neh.	9	26, 27
	Is.	65	11–13
	Jer.	9	13–16
Described	Ps.	19	7, 8
	Ps.	119	142
	Rom.	7	12, 14,fh
	Rom.	12	2
	I John	5	3
Blessedness of keeping	Ps.	119	1
	Mat.	5	19
	I John	3	22, 24
	Rev.	22	14
Explained by Christ	Mat.	7	12
	Mat.	22	37–40
Through the ministration of angels	Acts	7	53
	Gal.	3	19
	Heb.	2	2
Man cannot be justified by	Acts	13	39
	Rom.	3	20, 28
	Gal.	2	16
	Gal.	3	11
All men have transgressed	Rom.	3	9, 19
Gives the knowledge of sin	Rom.	3	20
	Rom.	7	7
Love is the fulfilling of	Rom.	13	8, 10
	Gal.	5	14
	James	2	8
Designed to lead to Christ	Gal.	3	24
His ways:			
Perfect	Ps.	18	30
Not like man's	Is.	55	8, 9
Sinners falter at	Hosea	14	9
Everlasting	Heb.	3	6
Just and true	Rev.	15	3
Wisdom	Prov.	2	6
	James	1	5
Dispensed according to His will	Eccl.	2	26
	Dan.	2	21
	Rom.	12	6
	I Cor.	7	7
Christ, the chief of	Is.	42	6
	John	3	16
	John	4	10
	John	6	32, 33
To be prayed for	Mat.	7	7, 11
	John	16	23, 24
Rest	Mat.	11	28
	II Thes.	1	7
The Holy Ghost	Luke	11	13
	Acts	8	20

Eternal life	John	6	27
	Rom.	6	23
Repentance	Acts	11	8
Righteousness	Rom.	5	16, 17
Faith	Eph.	2	8
	Phil.	1	29
To be used for mutual profit	I Pet.	4	10
His spiritual gifts:			
Are through Christ	Ps.	68	18
	Eph.	4	7, 8
Glory	Ps.	84	11
	John	17	22
Grace	Ps.	84	11
	James	4	6
His temporal gifts:			
Rain and fruitful seasons	Gen.	27	28
	Lev.	26	4, 5
	Is.	30	23
	Acts	14	17
All good things	Ps.	34	10
	I Tim.	6	17
To be prayed for	Zech.	10	1
	Mat.	6	11
Food and raiment	Mat.	6	25–33
gods *see idolatry*			
goddess *female divinity*			
Ashtoreth	I Ki.	11	5
Diana of the Ephesians	Acts	19	27
	Acts	19	35
	Acts	19	37
Godhead *the Deity, God*			
Not material	Acts	17	29
Is invisible but present	Rom.	1	20
Dwells in Christ	Col.	2	6, 9
godliness *see holiness*			
The mystery of *g*	I Tim.	3	16
G is profitable unto all things.	I Tim.	4	8
Supposing that gain is *g*	I Tim.	6	5
A form of *g*	II Tim.	3	5
The truth which is after *g*	Tit.	1	1
Pertain to life and *g*	II Pet.	1	3
In all holy conversation and *g*	II Pet.	3	11
godly			
The *g* man ceaseth	Ps.	12	1
In *g* sincerity	II Cor.	1	12
G sorrow worketh repentance	II Cor.	7	10
All that will live *g* in Christ	II Tim.	3	12
Live *g* in this world.	Tit.	2	12
Reverence and *g* fear	Heb.	12	28
Lord knoweth how to deliver *g*	II Pet.	2	9
Bring forward after a *g* sort	III John	6	
Gog *mountain*			
Son of Shemaiah, a Reubenite	I Chr.	5	4
A Scythian prince, prophecy against	Ezek.	38	3–9
Symbolic personage	Rev.	20	8
Golan *captive*			
A town in Bashan	Deut.	4	43
	Josh.	20	2, 8
A city given to the Levites	Josh.	21	27
	I Chr.	6	71
gold *a precious metal*			
Solomon rich in	I Ki.	10	2, 14, 21
Refined	Job	28	19
	Job	31	24
	Prov.	8	19
Belongs to God	Ezek.	16	3, 17
	Hag.	2	8
Of the rich	James	5	1–3
Is perishable	I Pet.	1	7
Warning concerning	I Pet.	3	1, 3
Streets of	Rev.	21	21
Early sources:			
Havilah	Gen.	2	11, 12
Ophir	I Ki.	9	28
	I Ki.	10	11
	I Chr.	29	4
	II Chr.	8	18
Sheba	I Ki.	10	10
	II Chr.	9	9
	Ps.	72	15
Tarshish	I Ki.	22	48
Parvaim	II Chr.	3	6
Uphaz	Jer.	10	9
Used for:			
Ornaments	Gen.	24	22
	Ex.	3	22
	S. of S.	1	10

gold—continued

As money	Gen.	44	8
	I Chr.	21	25
	Ezra	8	25–28
	Acts	20	33
	I Pet.	1	18
Overlaying	Ex.	25	11, 13
	I Ki.	6	20–22
Vessels and utensils	Ex.	25	29, 38, 39
	Ex.	37	16
	I Chr.	18	11
	I Chr.	22	14, 16
Candlesticks for the tabernacle	Ex.	25	31–38
	Ex.	37	17–24
Ornamenting the priests' garb	Ex.	39	1–31
Woven into embroidered tapestry	Ex.	39	3
Wedge of	Josh.	7	21
	Is.	13	12
Altar lamps and other articles	I Ki.	7	49–51
	II Ki.	25	15
	Jer.	52	19
	Dan.	5	3
Shields	I Ki.	10	17
Hammered work	II Chr.	9	15
Bedsteads	Esth.	1	6
Crowns	Ps.	21	3
	Zech.	6	11
Clothing	Ps.	45	9, 13
Artificial fruit	Prov.	25	11

golden calf

Made by Aaron	Ex.	32	2–4
Jeroboam makes two	I Ki.	12	26–30

golden candlestick see candlestick

golden city

Babylon	Is.	14	4

golden rule

Old Testament version	Lev.	19	18
	Rom.	13	9
Jesus	Mat.	7	12

goldsmith a skilled worker in gold

Of bezaleel	Ex.	31	2–3
Refiner	Mal.	3	3
Israelite workman in gold	Neh.	3	8
Makes idols	Is.	46	6
	Is.	40	19
	Is.	41	7

Golgotha place of a skull

Place where Jesus is crucified, Hebrew name	Mat.	27	33
	Mark	15	22
	John	19	17

Goliath shining

A giant of Gath	I Sam.	17	4
Is slain by David	I Sam.	17	50
	I Sam.	21	9
	I Sam.	22	10
His sons	II Sam.	21	15–22
	I Chr.	20	4–8

Gomer completion

A son of Japheth	Gen.	10	2, 3
	I Chr.	1	5, 6
	Ezek.	38	6
The wife of Hosea	Hosea	1	3

Gomorrah submersion

One of the cities of the plain	Gen.	10	19
	Gen.	13	10
Defeated by Chedorlaomer	Gen.	14	2, 8–11
Wickedness of	Gen.	18	20
Destroyed	Gen.	19	24–28

gone

Wrath g out from the Lord.	Num.	16	46
That which is g out of thy lips.	Deut.	23	23
I had g with the multitude.	Ps.	42	4
My feet were almost g	Ps.	73	2
Is his mercy clean g for ever?	Ps.	77	8
Wind passeth over, it is g	Ps.	103	16
I am g like the shadow	Ps.	109	23
The rain is over and g	S. of S.	2	11
All we like sheep have g astray.	Is.	53	6
Virtue had g out of him.	Mark	5	30
	Luke	8	46
The world is g. after him.	John	12	19
Hope of their gains was g	Acts	16	19
They are all g out ofthe way.	Rom.	3	12
In the way of Cain.	Jude		11

good and evil

Adam and Eve choose between	Gen.	3	1–24
Plea to choose between	Josh.	24	15
Subjective conflict between	Rom.	7	9–25
Conflict between	Rev.	16	13–21

gopher wood a pine or fir

Noah's ark made of	Gen.	6	14

Goshen a land of plenty

An area in Egypt good for herds and flocks	Gen.	45	10
	Gen.	46	28
Also called Rameses	Gen.	47	11
Exempted from plagues	Ex.	8	22
	Ex.	9	26
Region in Canaan	Josh.	10	41
A town in Judah	Josh.	15	51

gospel glad tidings

Preached to the poor and others	Mat.	11	5
Its effects	Mark	1	14
	Rom.	1	16
	Eph.	4–6	
Of God	Rom.	1	1
Desired of prophets	Mat.	13	17
To be preached in all the world.	Mat.	24	14
Goal of Paul	Acts	20	24
To be obeyed	Rom.	10	15–17
Established according to	Rom.	16	25
Foolish to the world	I Cor.	1	18–25
Necessity of Preaching	I Cor.	9	16–18
Of the resurrection	I Cor.	15	1, 2
Hid by the god of this world	II Cor.	4	3–6
Reached among the gentiles	Gal.	2	2
Unto Abraham	Gal.	3	8
Bring forth fruit	Col.	1	5–6
Comes in power	I Thes.	1	5
Called by means of	II Thes.	2	10
Must be mixed with faith	Heb.	4	2
Rejected by the Jews	Acts	13	46
Awful consequences of not obeying	II Thes.	1	8–9
Be careful not to hinder	I Cor.	9	12
Brings peace	Luke	2	10, 14
Everlasting	I Pet.	1	25
Exhibits the grace of God	Acts	14	3
	Acts	20	32
Foretold	Is.	41	27
	Is.	52	7
	Is.	61	1–3
	Mark	1	15
Good tidings of great joy for all people	Luke	2	10–11, 31–32
Let him who preaches another be accursed	Gal.	1	8
Life and immortality brought to light by Jesus through	II Tim.	1	10
Must be believed	Mark	1	15
Preached by Christ	Mat.	4	23
Produces hope	Col.	1	23
Profession of, attended by afflictions	II Tim.	3	12
Promises to sufferers for	Mark	8	35
	Mark	10	30
Rejection of, by many, foretold	Is.	53	1
A blessing to the Gentiles	Rom.	11	28
Saints have fellowship in	Phil.	1	5
Testifies to the final judgment	Rom.	2	16
There is fullness of blessing in	Rom.	15	29

Called the:

Doctrine according to godliness	I Tim.	6	3
Gospel of Christ	Rom.	1	9, 16
	II Cor.	2	12
	I Thes.	3	2
Gospel of God	I Thes.	2	8
	I Pet.	4	17
Word of Christ	Col.	13	16
Word of God	I Thes.	2	13
Word of Grace	Acts	14	3
	Acts	20	32
Word of Salvation	Acts	13	26
Word of Truth	James	1	18

Preached to:

Every creature	Mark	16	15
The Gentiles	Mark	13	10
	Gal.	2	9
The Jews	Luke	24	47
The poor	Luke	4	18

Those who receieve, should:

Adhere to the truth of	Gal.	1	6–7
	Gal.	2	14
Earnestly contend for the faith of	Phil.	1	17, 27
	Jude		3

Have their conversation becoming	Phil.	1	27
Live in subjection to	II Cor.	9	13
Not be ashamed of	II Tim.	1	8
Sacrifice friends and property for	Mat.	10	37
Sacrifice life itself for	Mark	8	35
Of Christ, characterized:			
A treasure of great price	Mat.	13	44–46
	Luke	13	20, 21
Is like a mustard seed	Mat.	13	31, 32
	Luke	13	18, 19
The kingdom of God	Luke	16	16
Of faith	Rom.	10	8
Glorious	II Cor.	4	4
Of reconciliation	II Cor.	5	19
Concerning salvation	Eph.	1	13
Dispensation of the grace of God	Eph.	3	2
Concerning peace	Eph.	6	15
Mystery of	Eph.	6	19
Of life	Phil.	2	16
Of truth	Eph.	1	13
Of ministration of the Spirit	II Cor.	3	8
Of sound words	II Tim.	1	13
Everlasting	Rev.	14	6
Prophecies of:	Is.	2	3–5
	Is.	55	1–5
	Joel	2	28–32

gossip *idle talk*

Forbidden	Lev.	19	16
Separates friends	Prov.	16	28

gourd *a wild vine*

A plant like a cucumber	II Ki.	4	39
A vine, God uses to shelter Jonah	Jonah	4	6

government *system of governing*
Earliest:

Ruled by head of clan	Gen.	22	1
	Deut.	21	18
Moses becomes chief of nation, appointed by God	Ex.	3	13–18
Heads of clans later form elders	Num.	22	7
Appoints Joshua successor	Num.	27	18–23

Period of judges:

Theocracy, God as king, each man does what is right in his own eyes	Judg.	17	6

Hebrew monarchy:

King, the center of unity; hereditary succession	I Sam.	10	1
	II Sam.	5	1–25
	I Ki.	14	21
City elders influential	II Sam.	9	11
Bureaucracy under David and Solomon	I Ki.	4	21–34
	I Chr.	11	12–47
Forced labour	I Ki.	5	13
Heavy tributes	I Ki.	12	3–14
Prestige of priestly courts	II Ki.	10	1, 5

governor *chief ruler*

Authoritative ruler	Gen.	42	6
The title of Christ	Mat.	2	6
To be honoured	I Pet.	2	13, 14
Joseph	Gen.	42	6
Special revenue	Neh.	5	18
God is of the nations	Ps.	22	28

Gozan *quarry*

A river in the district of Mesopotamia	II Ki.	17	6
Israel taken into capitivty by the king of Assyria to	II Ki.	17	6
	II Ki.	18	11
	II Ki.	19	12
	I Chr.	5	26

grace

Of God and Jesus Christ	Ps.	84	11
	Zech.	4	7
	Luke	2	40
	John	1	16
	I Cor.	15	10
Salvation through	Acts	15	11
	Rom.	3	24
	Eph.	2	5
Effects of	II Cor.	1	12
	Tit.	2	11
Prayer for	Rom.	16	20
	Heb.	4	16
Danger of departing from	Gal.	5	4
Exhortations concerning	II Tim.	1	9
	Heb.	12	15, 28

	II Pet.	3	18
Danger of abusing	Jude		4
Christ is full of	John	1	14
Christ as author	John	1	17
Salutary grace	Rom.	1	7
Abounding	Rom.	5	20
Election of	Rom.	11	5
Sufficient	II Cor.	12	9
Forgiven according to	Eph.	1	7
Minister of	Eph.	4	29
Benediction	Eph.	6	24
Heirs of	I Pet.	3	7
To the humble	I Pet.	5	5

grace before meals

Offered by Samuel	I Sam.	9	11–13
Offered by Jesus	Mat.	14	19
Offered by Paul	Acts	27	35

gracious *merciful, kindly*

God be *g* to thee	Gen.	43	29
I will hear, for I am *g*	Ex.	22	27
I will be *g* to whom I will be *g*	Ex.	33	19
Lord be *g* unto thee	Num.	6	25
Tell whether God will be *g*	II Sam.	12	22
A God *g*, merciful	Neh.	9	17, 31
Hath God forgotten to be *g*	Ps.	77	9
Lord will wait that he may be *g*	Is.	30	18
May be the Lord will be *g*	Amos	5	15
I knew that thou art a *g* God	Jonah	4	2
Beseech God, he will be *g* to us	Mal.	1	9
Wondered at the *g* words	Luke	4	22
Tasted that the Lord is *g*	I Pet.	2	3

graciously

Children which God hath *g* given	Gen.	33	5
God hath dealt *g* with me	Gen.	33	11
And grant me thy law *g*	Ps.	119	29
Receive us *g*	Hosea	14	2

graft *attach branches*

Wild olive tree	Rom.	11	17, 23, 24

grafting *to insert, to transplant*

Contrary to nature	Rom.	11	17–24

grandchildren

Jacob's	Gen.	48	5
Heritage to	Ex.	20	5, 6

grandmother *mother of one's father or mother*

Unfeigned faith	II Tim.	1	5

grant *give, admit*

God *g* thee thy petition	I Sam.	1	17
God *g* what he requested	I Chr.	4	10
God *g* the thing I long for	Job	6	8
Desire of righteous shall be *g*	Prov.	10	24
G that my two sons may sit	Mat.	20	21
	Mark	10	37

grape *fruit of the grapevine*
Cultivated by:

Noah	Gen.	9	20
The Canaanites	Num.	13	24
	Deut.	6	11
	Josh.	24	13
The Edomites	Num.	20	14, 17
The Amorites	Num.	21	21, 22
	Is.	16	8, 9
The Philistines	Judg.	15	5

Grown at:

Shechem	Judg.	9	26, 27
Abel	Judg.	11	33
Timnath	Judg.	14	5
Shiloh	Judg.	21	20, 21
En-gedi	S. of S.	1	14
Baal-hamon	S. of S.	8	11
Jezreel	I Ki.	21	1
Carmel	II Chr.	26	10
Samaria	Jer.	31	5
Lebanon	Hosea	14	6, 7
Sour	Ezek.	18	2
The culture of	Lev.	25	3, 11
	Deut.	28	39
	II Chr.	26	10
	S. of S.	6	11
	Is.	5	1
	Jer.	31	5
Wine made of	Jer.	25	30
The wine of, forbidden to the Nazarites	Num.	6	1–4

grass

Created on the third day	Gen.	1	11
Is mown	Ps.	72	6

grass—continued

Man's life is like	Ps.	90	5, 6
On the roofs of houses	Ps.	129	6
God's care of	Mat.	6	30
	Luke	12	28
The rich are as	James	1	10, 11

grass-eating king

Nebuchadnezzar	Dan.	4	33

grasshopper locust

Is eaten	Lev.	11	22
Figurative	Num.	13	33
Destroys fields	Amos	7	1, 2
Israel when compared to the Canaanites	Num.	13	33
Multitudes of	Judg.	6	5
Small size	Is.	40	22

grate a frame of metal bars

For the altar	Ex.	27	4, 5
	Ex.	38	4

gratitude thankfulness

King of Sodom to Abraham	Gen.	14	22–24
Chief butler to Joseph	Gen.	14	10–12
Nabal is not	I Sam.	25	10
David to Barzillai	II Sam.	19	31–35
Ruth to Boaz	Ruth	2	8–17
The people to Jonathan	I Sam.	14	45
David to Jonathan	II Sam.	9	1
David to Hanun	II Sam.	10	2
Elisha for kindness	II Ki.	4	8–17
Pagans to Paul	Acts	28	1–10

grave tomb, burial place

Jews buried in caves	Gen.	23	9
Jacob prepares his own	Gen.	50	5
Defiled by touching	Num.	19	16, 18
Weeping at	II Sam.	3	32
	John	11	31
	John	20	11
Of parents	II Sam.	19	37
Welcomed	Job	3	20–22
None return from the	Job	16	21, 22
Everyone equal here	Job	21	23–26
No wisdom in	Eccl.	9	10
Is cruel	S. of S.	8	6
Ransomed from the	Hosea	13	14

Resurrection from the:

Of Jesus	Mat.	28	5, 6
	I Cor.	15	12–20
The saints after the resurrection of Jesus	Mat.	27	52, 53
Of Lazarus	John	11	43, 44
	John	12	17
Of all dead foretold	John	5	28, 29
	I Cor.	15	22–54

graveclothes burial dress

Of Jesus	Luke	24	12
Worn by Lazarus	John	11	43, 44

gravel small stones

Mouth filled with	Prov.	20	17
Offspring like	Is.	48	19
Teeth broken with	Lam.	3	16

graven image an idol

A sin to make	Ex.	20	4
The Canaanites make	Deut.	7	1, 5
Made by the heathens	Jer.	50	38

great big, large in size

Famine	II Ki.	6	24, 25
Reward in heaven	Mat.	5	12
Faith	Mat.	8	10
Earthly possessions	Mat.	19	22
Commandment	Mat.	22	36–38
Commission	Mat.	28	19, 20
Stone	Mark	16	4
Fever	Luke	4	38
Supper	Luke	14	16–28
Wonders and miracles	Acts	6	8
Mystery	Eph.	5	32
God	Tit.	2	13
High priest	Heb.	4	14
Shepherd	Heb.	13	20
Fish	Jonah	1	17
Man	Job	32	9
Woman	II Ki.	4	8
Tribulation	Rev.	7	14
Voice	Rev.	1	10
Invitation	Rev.	22	17

greatness

In teaching the truth	Mat.	5	19
In service	Mat.	23	11
Ascribed to God	Deut.	32	3
Of God's power	Eph.	1	19

greaves armour for the legs

Of brass	I Sam.	17	6

Greece, Grecia a country in the southern Balkan peninsula

Prophecies of	Dan.	8	21–23
	Dan.	10	20
	Dan.	11	2
	Zech.	9	13
Israelites sold to	Joel	3	16
The inhabitants of, called Gentiles	Mark	7	26
	Rom.	2	10
	Rom.	3	9
	I Cor.	10	32
	I Cor.	12	13
People desire to see Jesus	John	12	20–23
Early Christians persecuted in	Acts	6	9–14
	Acts	9	29
	Acts	18	17
Many converts in	Acts	14	1
Intermarriage with Jews	Acts	16	1
Accept the Messiah	Acts	17	2–4, 12
Paul preaches in	Acts	17	16–31
Speak Greek	John	12	20

greed avarice

Of Samuel's sons	I Sam.	8	1, 3
Warned against	Prov.	1	13–19
Causes trouble	Prov.	15	27
Of false ministers	Is.	56	10, 11
Root of all evil	I Tim.	6	10
Of filthy lucre	I Tim.	3	3
Of a lion	Ps.	17	12

grief sorrow, affliction

Divine	Gen.	6	5, 6
From marriage	Gen.	26	34, 35
Barrenness	I Sam.	1	11
Anger and shame	I Sam.	20	34
Weeping	I Sam.	30	1–4
Of a husband	II Sam.	3	15, 16
Abstinence in	II Sam.	12	16, 17
Effect of	II Sam.	19	1–8
Of David	II Sam.	19	24–28
Transgression	Ezra	9	1–6
Silence in	Job	2	11–13
In affliction	Mark	5	22, 23
In bereavement	John	11	31–33
From distrust	John	21	17
Of Christ	Is.	53	

grind

The faces of the poor	Is.	3	15
Took young men to g	Lam.	5	13
I will g him to powder	Mat.	21	44
	Luke	20	18
Two women shall be g	Mat.	24	41
	Luke	17	35

See Eccl. 12:3, 4

groan

Men g from out of the city	Job	24	12
How do the beasts g	Joel	1	18
We ourselves g within	Rom.	8	23
We g desiring to be clothed	II Cor.	5	2

ground earth, field

Cursed	Gen.	3	17
	Gen.	5	29
Vegetables from the	Gen.	2	9
Animals from	Gen.	2	19
Man made from	Gen.	2	7
	Gen.	3	19, 23
	Job	4	19
	Job	33	6

groves

Places for worship	Gen.	21	33
	Deut.	16	21
	I Ki.	15	13
Forbidden	Deut.	16	21
	Judg.	6	25
	I Ki.	14	15
To be destroyed	Ex.	34	13

grow

Let them g into a multitude	Gen.	48	16
Though he make it not to g	II Sam.	23	5
G like cedar on Lebanon	Ps.	92	12
Grass to g for cattle	Ps.	104	14
	Ps.	147	8

He shall *g* up before him	Is.	53	2
He shall *g* as the lily.	Hosea	14	5
Ye shall *g* up as calves	Mal.	4	2
Consider the lilies how they *g*	Mat.	6	28
	Luke	12	27
Let both *g* together	Mat.	13	30
No fruit *g* on thee henceforward	Mat.	21	19
Seed *g* up, he knoweth not how	Mark	4	27
Doubted whereunto this would *g*	Acts	5	24
G unto a holy temple	Eph.	2	21
Your faith *g* exceedingly	II Thes.	1	3
Milk of word that ye may *g*	I Pet.	2	2
G in grace	II Pet.	3	18

growth, spiritual

Of Jesus	Luke	2	40
Of Saul	Acts	9	22
In righteousness	II Cor.	9	10
In Christ	Eph.	4	15
Through the word	I Pet.	2	2
By adding graces	II Pet.	1	4–11
In grace	II Pet.	3	18

grudge *give with ill will*

Forbidden	Lev.	19	18

guard *bodyguard*

Royal officer of importance	Gen.	37	36
	II Sam.	23	23
	II Ki.	10	25
	II Ki.	25	8
Includes runners	I Sam.	22	17
Foreign mercenaries	II Sam.	20	23
	II Sam.	23	22, 23
Praetorian guard of the Roman emperors	Acts	28	16

guest *visitor*

Pharaoh to Abram	Gen.	12	15, 16
Salutation to	Gen.	18	2, 3
Abraham's hospitality to the angels	Gen.	18	1–8
Angel, of Lot	Gen.	19	1–11
Shown consideration	Ex.	2	16–21
	II Ki.	4	8–10
Many entertained	Mat.	22	10
Rooms provided for	Mark	14	14
Rules for the conduct of	Prov.	23	1–3, 6–8
	Prov.	25	6, 7, 17
	Luke	10	5–7
	Luke	14	7–11
	I Cor.	10	27

guestchamber

A room for guests	Mark	14	14
	Luke	22	11

guidance

Of meek	Ps.	25	9
God will	Ps.	48	14
Guarantee	Ps.	37	5, 7
	Prov.	3	4–7
By counsel	Ps.	73	24
Inner voice	Is.	30	21
In way of peace	Luke	1	79
Into truth	John	16	13
Examples of	Ps.	5	8
	Ps.	27	11
	Ps.	143	10

guile *sly tricks*

If a man slay with *g*	Ex.	21	14
In whose spirit is no *g*	Ps.	32	2
Keep lips from speaking *g*	Ps.	34	13
	I Pet.	3	10
An Israelite, in whom is no *g*	John	1	47
I caught you with *g*	II Cor.	12	16
Laying aside malice and *g*	I Pet.	2	1
Nor was *g* found in his mouth	I Pet.	2	22
In mouth was found no *g*	Rev.	14	5

guilt *done wrong*

Put away the *g*	Deut.	19	13
	Deut.	21	9

guiltiness

Have brought *g* upon us	Gen.	26	10
Deliver me from blood *g*	Ps.	51	14

guiltless

Lord will not hold him *g*	Ex.	20	7
	Deut.	5	11
We will be *g*	Josh.	2	19
G of blood	II Sam.	3	28
Ye would not have condemned the *g*	Mat.	12	7

guilty

Verily *g* concerning our brother	Gen.	42	21
By no means clear the *g*	Ex.	34	7
	Num.	14	18
All the world becomes *g* before God	Rom.	3	19
G of the body and blood	I Cor.	11	27
Offend in one point, he is *g* of all	James	2	10

gutter

At watering troughs	Gen.	30	38, 41
On the stronghold of Zion	II Sam.	5	8

H

Habakkuk *the embraced one*

A poet and prophet after the destruction of Nineveh	Hab.	1	1
	Hab.	3	1
Prophetic burden	Hab.	1	1–4
God's response	Hab.	1	5–11
His problem	Hab.	1	12–17
God's answer	Hab.	2	1–20
His hymn of praise to God	Hab.	3	1–19

habergeon *sleeveless coat of armour*

For neck and shoulders	Ex.	28	32
Breastplate	Neh.	4	16
	Eph.	6	14

habit *a custom*

Of sin difficult to break	Jer.	13	23
	Jer.	22	21
Of prayer	Acts	10	1, 2

habitation *place to live*

I will prepare him an *h*	Ex.	15	2
Guided them to thy holy *h*	Ex.	15	13
Have built an house of *h*	II Chr.	6	2
I have loved *h* of thy house	Ps.	26	8
From the place of his *h*	Ps.	33	14
Let their *h* be desolate	Ps.	69	25
Be thou my strong *h*	Ps.	71	3
Full of *h* of cruelty	Ps.	74	20
Justice and judgment the *h* of thy throne	Ps.	89	14
Made the Most High thy *h*	Ps.	91	9
Might go to a city of *h*	Ps.	107	7, 36
Lord hath desired it for his *h*	Ps.	132	13
He blesseth the *h* of the just	Prov.	3	33
Dwell in a peaceable *h*	Is.	32	18
Receive you in everlasting *h*	Luke	16	9
Hath determined bounds of *h*	Acts	17	26
An *h* of God through the Spirit	Eph.	2	22
Angels which left their own *h*	Jude		6

Hachaliah *Jehovah saddens*

The father of Nehemiah	Neh.	1	1
	Neh.	10	1

Hachilah *dark*

A hill in Judah	I Sam.	23	19
David hides from Saul here	I Sam.	26	1–3

Hadad, Hadar *fierce*

Son of Ishmael	I Chr.	1	30
	Gen.	25	15, 16
Son of Bedad, an Edomite king	I Chr.	1	46
	Gen.	36	35
An adversary of David	I Ki.	11	14, 17–22
King of Pai	I Chr.	1	50

Hadadezer, Hadarezer *Hadad is help*

King of Zobah	II Sam.	8	3
Slain by David	II Sam.	8	10
Here called Hadarezer	II Sam.	10	16

Hadarezer *see Hadadzer*

Hadassah *a myrtle*

The Hebrew name for Esther	Esth.	2	7

Hades *see hell*

Hadoram *noble honour*

A son of Joktan	Gen.	10	27
Called Joram	II Sam.	8	10
Son of Tou or Toi	I Chr.	18	10
Here called Adoram	II Sam.	20	24
Also called Adoniram	I Ki.	4	6
Keeper of the king's tribute	II Chr.	10	18
Stoned while collecting taxes	I Ki.	12	18

Hagar, Agar *flight*

A handmaid of Sarai	Gen.	16	1
Given to Abram to be his wife	Gen.	16	2
Comforted by an angel	Gen.	16	7–11
Mother of Ishmael	Gen.	16	15
Sent away by Abraham	Gen.	21	14–21
Called Agar	Gal.	4	22–26

Haggai *my feast*

A prophet	Ezra	5	1
	Ezra	6	14
Rebuked	Hag.	1	1–13
Encouraged	Hag.	2	1–23

Haggith, *festive*

Wife of David, mother of Adonijah	II Sam.	3	2, 4
	I Ki.	1	5

Hai *see* Ai

hail *a salute*

Of Judas	Mat.	26	47–49
Of the soldiers	Mat.	27	27–29
Of Gabriel	Luke	1	26–28
Of Christ	Mat.	28	9

hail, hailstones *small, roundish pellets of ice*

Upon Egypt	Ex.	9	18–29
Upon the enemies of Israel	Josh.	10	11
	Hab.	2	17
Destruction of vines	Ps.	78	47
For rain	Ps.	105	32
One of God's wonders	Job	38	22
Usually accompanied by a storm	Is.	28	2

hair

Of old age	Gen.	42	38
Of Absalom	II Sam.	14	26
The raiment of John	Mat.	3	4
Inability to make black hair white	Mat.	5	36
Numbered	Mat.	10	30
Worn short by men	I Cor.	11	14
Worn long by women	I Cor.	11	15
	I Tim.	2	9
As white as snow	Rev.	1	14
Used as evidence of leprosy	Lev.	13	3
Of a Nazarite	Num.	6	19
Plucked off, sign of defeat	Neh.	13	25
Careful setting of	Is.	3	24
Esau	Gen.	25	25
	Gen.	27	11
Elijah	II Ki.	1	8

half-hearted *lacking in interest*

Jehu	II Ki.	10	31
Joash	II Ki.	13	18, 19
The Israelites	II Chr.	20	33
Amaziah	II Chr.	25	1, 2
Judah	Jer.	3	10
Ahab and Israel	I Ki.	18	21
Northern Kingdom	Hosea	10	1, 2

half-homer *five ephahs*

A dry measure	Hosea	3	2

hall *an assembly room, a passage*

Of judgment	John	18	28

Hallelujah *praise Jehovah*

See Alleluia	Ps.	104–106	
	Ps.	146–150	

hallow *consecrate*

Israelites hallowed by God	Lev.	22	32
The jubilee	Lev.	25	10
The lot of the priest	Num.	5	10
Solomon's temple	I Ki.	9	3
The sabbath	Jer.	17	22
	Ezek.	44	24
The Lord's prayer	Mat.	6	9–13

hallowed bread *see* showbread

halt *stop, lame*

How long *h* ye between two opinions	I Ki.	18	21
I am ready to *h*	Ps.	38	17
My families watched for my *h* (lame)	Jer.	20	10
Better to enter into life *h*	Mat.	18	8
	Mark	9	45
Bring hither *h* and blind	Luke	14	21
Blind, *h*, waiting for moving of the water	John	5	3

Ham *hot*

Son of Noah	Gen.	5	32
Father of Canaan	Gen.	9	18
Canaan cursed	Gen.	9	22–27
Tribe of	Gen.	10	6–20

Place where Chedorlaomer smites the

Zuzims	Gen.	14	5
Land of	I Chr.	4	40

Haman *magnificent*

Advancement	Esth.	3	1
Wrathful	Esth.	3	5
Plots against the Jews	Esth.	3	8–13
Hanged	Esth.	7	10
Sons slain and hanged	Esth.	9	10, 14

Hamath, Hemath *fortress*

Inhabited by Canaanites	Gen.	10	18
Visited by spies	Num.	13	21
Of the north border	Num.	34	8
Toi, king of	II Sam.	8	9, 10
Recovered by Jeroboam	II Ki.	14	25, 28
Conquered by Chaldeans	II Ki.	25	20, 21
Solomon builds in	II Chr.	8	4
The remnant left from	Is.	11	11
Weak-hearted	Jer.	49	23
Prosperous	Amos	6	2
Future northern border of Israel	Ezek.	47	16–20

Hammedatha *double*

Father of Haman	Esth.	3	1

hammer *a tool*

Used to kill Sisera	Judg.	4	21
None heard	I Ki.	6	7
Used by carpenters and smiths	Is.	41	7
Used in making idols	Jer.	10	4
Used to break rocks	Jer.	23	29
Figurative	Jer.	50	23

Hamor, Emmor *an ass,* prince of Shechem

Sells a land parcel to Jacob	Gen.	33	19
Father of Shechem	Gen.	34	2
Slain	Gen.	34	26
Here called Emmor	Acts	7	16

Hanameel *God hath favoured*

Cousin of Jeremiah	Jer.	32	7
Sells a field to Jeremiah	Jer.	32	9

Hanan *gracious, merciful*

Son of Shashak	I Chr.	8	23, 25
Son of Azel	I Chr.	8	38
One of David's valiant men	I Chr.	11	26
Son of Maachah	I Chr.	11	43
A Nethinim	Ezra	2	46
A Levite	Neh.	8	7
Seals covenant	Neh.	10	10
Two chiefs, sealers of the covenant	Neh.	10	22, 26
Treasurer of the congregation	Neh.	13	13
Son of Zaccur	Neh.	13	13
An officer of the temple	Jer.	35	4

Hananeel *God is gracious*

A tower of the wall of Jerusalem	Neh.	3	1
	Zech.	14	10

Hanani *gracious*

Father of Jehu	I Ki.	16	1, 7
Son of Heman	I Chr.	25	4
A musician in the temple	I Chr.	25	25
A prophet	II Chr.	16	7
Son of Immer	Ezra	10	20
Brother of Nehemiah	Neh.	1	2
Keeper of the gates of Jerusalem	Neh.	7	2, 3
A priest and musician	Neh.	12	36

Hananiah *Jehovah is gracious*

Son of Zerubbabel	I Chr.	3	19
Father of Pelatiah and Jesaiah	I Chr.	3	21
Son of Shashak	I Chr.	8	24
Son of Heman	I Chr.	25	4
A musician in the temple	I Chr.	25	23
A captain of Uzziah	II Chr.	26	11
Son of Bebai	Ezra	10	28
Son of an apothecary	Neh.	3	8
Son of Shelemiah	Neh.	3	30
A keeper of the gates of Jerusalem	Neh.	7	2
A sealer of the covenant	Neh.	10	23
A priest	Neh.	12	12, 41
Son of Azur, a prophet	Jer.	28	1, 5
Prophesies falsely	Jer.	28	15
Dies	Jer.	28	17
Father of Zedekiah	Jer.	36	12
Grandfather of Irijah	Jer.	37	13
A child of Judah	Dan.	1	6
Called Shadrach	Dan.	1	7

hand *terminal part of the arm*

In a promise	Gen.	14	22–24
In consecration	Ezra	29	10

In benediction	Lev.	9	22
In solemnizing testimony	Lev.	24	14
In ordination	Num.	8	10, 11
In friendship	II Ki.	10	15
In a contract	Ezra	10	19
Of righteousness	Job	17	9
Of honour	Ps.	45	9
Of power	Is.	23	11
Of clapping	II Ki.	11	12
In ceremony	Mat.	15	2
In blessing	Mat.	19	13
In innocency	Mat.	27	24
In healing	Mark	6	5
Imposition of	Heb.	6	2
Figuratively	Mat.	5	30
	Mat.	18	8
	Mark	9	43

Laying of:

On sacrificial animal	Lev.	16	21
	Num.	8	12
For violence	Neh.	13	21
	Mat.	21	46
For an office	I Tim.	5	22
For healing	Mat.	9	18
For ordination	Acts	6	6
For the Holy Spirit	Acts	8	17, 18

hand breadth *a measure, about four inches*

Linear measure	Ex.	25	25
Thickness	I Ki.	7	26
The shortening of life	Ps.	39	5
The vision	Ezek.	40	5

handmaid, handmaiden *a female servant*

Of Sarai	Gen.	16	1
Mercy	Ps.	86	16
Heir to her mistress	Prov.	30	23
Mary	Luke	1	38

hand of God

Is against them	Deut.	2	15
Against Naomi	Ruth	1	13
Gives one heart	II Chr.	30	12
The good work	Neh.	2	18
The curse	Job	2	10, 11
The persecution	Job	19	21
The mighty	I Pet.	5	6

handful

Earth brought forth by *h*	Gen.	41	47
H of ashes	Ex.	9	8
Let fall also some of the *h*	Ruth	2	16
H of meal in a barrel	I Ki.	17	12
Be an *h* of corn	Ps.	72	16
Better is an *h* with quietness	Eccl.	4	6
As the *h* after the harvestman	Jer.	9	22

handwriting *writing peculiar to a person*

Upon the wall	Dan.	5	5
Blotted out	Col.	2	14

hanging *suspending*

Curtains for the tabernacle	Ex.	27	9–18
A form of punishment	Num.	25	4
Curtains of the palace of Ahasuerus	Esth.	1	6
Cursed is everyone hanged on a tree	Deut.	21	22, 23

Instances of:

Chief baker of Pharaoh	Gen.	40	22
King of Ai	Josh.	8	28, 29
The five kings	Josh.	10	22–27
Ahithophel	II Sam.	17	23
Absalom	II Sam.	18	9–17
Sons of Saul	II Sam.	21	3–9
Haman	Esth.	7	10
Sons of Haman	Esth.	9	14
Suicide of Judas	Mat.	27	3–5

Haniel *see Hanniel*

Hannah *gracious*

Wife of Elkanah	I Sam.	1	5
Rival of Peninnah	I Sam.	1	6, 7
A son of Ulla, of Asher	I Chr.	7	39

Hanoch *see Enoch*

Hanun *whom God pities*

King of Ammonites	II Sam.	10	1
Dishonours David's servants	II Sam.	10	2–5
Conquered by David	II Sam.	10	6–14
A builder of the wall	Neh.	3	13
Son of Zalaph	Neh.	3	30

happiness *a state of well-being*

Is abundant and satisfying	Ps.	36	8
	Ps.	63	5
Is in God	Ps.	73	25, 26
Not lasting in earthly things	Eccl.	2	10, 11
A formula for	Mat.	5	1–12

May be obtained by:

Obedience to God	Ps.	40	8
Aiding the poor	Prov.	14	21
Trust in God	Prov.	16	20
	Phil.	4	6, 7
Following Christ	John	13	15–17
	II Cor.	12	10
Speaking no evil	I Pet.	3	10–14

Often marred by:

Jealousy	Esth.	5	13
Wealth	Job	21	13
Envy	Ps.	37	1
Power	Ps.	37	35
Drunkenness	Is.	5	11, 12

Haran, Charran *a mountaineer*

Son of Terah	Gen.	11	26
Father of Lot	Gen.	11	26–29
A place in Mesopotamia	Gen.	11	31
	Ezek.	27	23
Terah dies here	Gen.	11	32
Departed from by divine command	Gen.	12	1–5
Jacob flees to	Gen.	27	43
Jacob departs	Gen.	31	17–21
Land of idolatry	Josh.	24	2, 14
	Is.	37	12
Son of Caleb	I Chr.	2	46
Father of Gazez	I Chr.	2	46
Son of Shimei	I Chr.	23	9

harden *become hard*

I will *h* Pharaoh's heart	Ex.	4	21
	Ex.	7	3
	Ex.	14	4
H hearts of Egyptians	Ex.	14	17
Shalt not *h* thy heart	Deut.	15	7
H their necks	II Ki.	17	14
	Neh.	9	16
I would *h* myself in sorrow	Job	6	10
Who hath *h* himself against him	Job	9	4
H not your hearts	Ps.	95	8
	Heb.	3	8, 15
	Heb.	4	7
A wicked man *h* his face	Prov.	21	29
He that *h* his heart	Prov.	28	14
He that, being often reproved, *h* his neck	Prov.	29	1
Why hast thou *h* our heart	Is.	63	17
His mind was *h* in pride	Dan.	5	20
Their heart *h*	Mark	6	52
	Mark	8	17
He hath *h* their heart	John	12	40
Whom he will he *h*	Rom.	9	18
Lest any of you be *h*	Heb.	3	13

hardness *harshness*

Of labour	Ex.	1	11–14
	Josh.	9	27
	Judg.	16	21
Of heart	Ex.	7	13
	I Sam.	6	6
	II Chr.	36	11–13

Examples of:

Pharaoh	Ex.	4	21
Job, in sorrow	Job	6	10
Zedekiah	II Chr.	36	13
Fathers	Neh.	9	16
Israel	Is.	63	17
	Jer.	7	26
Nebuchadnezzar	Dan.	5	20
Jews	Mark	3	5
Disciples	Mark	8	17

hare *a rodent, not a rabbit*

Forbidden as meat	Lev.	11	6

Hareph *to pull off*

Son of Caleb	I Chr.	2	50, 51

Hareth *forest*

A forest in Judah where David finds refuge	I Sam.	22	5

Harim *snub nose*

A priest	I Chr.	24	8
Two who return from captivity	Ezra	2	32, 39
Their sons took strange wives	Ezra	10	21, 31
Sealers of the covenant	Neh.	10	5, 27

harlot *prostitute*

Wicked	Lev.	19	29
Forbidden	Lev.	21	1, 7

harlot—*continued*

An abomination	Deut.	23	18
Rahab	Josh.	2	1
Solomon and the two harlots	I Ki.	3	16–28
Shamelessness of	Prov.	2	16
Description of	Prov.	7	11–21
	Prov.	9	13–18
To be shunned	Prov.	5	3–20
	Prov.	7	25–27
Tamar	Gen.	38	24
Samson	Judg.	16	1
Of idolatry	Ezek.	23	5
Of Babylon	Rev.	17	5
Jephthah's mother	Judg.	11	1
Figuratively	Ezek.	23	1–49
	Hosea	2	13
	Joel	3	3

harp *a musical instrument*

Originates with Jubal	Gen.	4	21
Used in worship	I Sam.	10	5
	I Chr.	25	1, 3
	Ps.	43	4
Played by David	I Sam.	16	17, 18
Used at national jubilees	I Sam.	18	6
	Neh.	12	27, 36
Used in festive entertainment	Job	21	12
	Is.	23	15, 16
Used by Jews in Babylon	Ps.	137	2
With ten strings	Ps.	33	2
Discordant	I Cor.	14	6, 7

harrow *an agricultural implement*

As an instrument of torture	II Sam.	12	31
	I Chr.	20	3
Pulled by oxen	Job	39	10

hart, hind *male and female red deer*

Designated a clean animal	Deut.	12	15
	Deut.	14	5
Sure-footed	II Sam.	22	34
Provision for Solomon's household	I Ki.	4	23
Used in allegory	Ps.	42	1
Gentle	Prov.	5	19
Beautiful	S. of S.	2	7

harvest *a crop, to reap*

Shall not cease	Gen.	8	22
The sabbath to be observed in	Ex.	34	21
	Neh.	13	15
The feasts of	Ex.	34	22
	Lev.	23	15–17
Rules of	Lev.	23	22
	Lev.	26	5
Celebrated joy	Judg.	9	27
	Is.	9	3
	Jer.	48	33
	Job	24	6
Figurative	Prov.	10	5
	Jer.	8	20
	Joel	3	13
	Mat.	13	39
	II Cor.	9	6
Of judgment	Rev.	14	15

Hasadiah *Jehovah has favoured*

Son of Zerubbabel	I Chr.	3	19, 20

Hashabiah *Jehovah hath regarded*

A Levite, son of Amaziah	I Chr.	6	45
A musician, son of Jeduthan	I Chr.	25	3, 19
A Hebronite warrior	I Chr.	26	30
Son of Kemuel	I Chr.	27	17
A prince of Josiah	II Chr.	35	9
A Merarite Levite	Ezra	8	19
A chief of the priests	Ezra	8	24
	Neh.	12	21
Seals covenant	Neh.	10	11
At the dedication of the walls	Neh.	12	24
A son of Bunni	Neh.	11	15
Son of Mattaniah, a Levite	Neh.	11	22

Hashub, Hasshub *intelligent*

A Levite, also called Hasshub	I Chr.	9	14
	Neh.	11	15
Son of Pahath-moab	Neh.	3	11
A builder of the wall	Neh.	3	23
Sealer of the covenant	Neh.	10	23

Hashubah *esteemed*

Son of Zerubbabel	I Chr.	3	19, 20

Hashum *wealthy*

Head of a family who returns from captivity	Ezra	2	19

	Ezra	10	33
	Neh.	7	22
Companion of Ezra	Neh.	8	4
Seals covenant	Neh.	10	18

Hassenaah *see Senaah*

hast *have*

Sell all thou *h*	Mat.	19	21
	Mark	10	21
	Luke	18	22
There thou *h* that is thine	Mat.	25	25
But this thou *h*, that	Rev.	2	6
Hold that fast which thou *h*	Rev.	3	11

haste *hurry*

Shall eat it in *h*	Ex.	12	11
King's business required *h*	I Sam.	21	8
I said in my *h*	Ps.	31	22
	Ps.	116	11
He that *h* with feet sinneth	Prov.	19	2
He that *h* to be rich	Prov.	28	22
Ye shall not go out with *h*	Is.	52	12
The Lord will *h* it	Is.	60	22
Day of the Lord *h* greatly	Zeph.	1	14
Came in *h* to the king	Mark	6	25

hasty

He that is *h* of spirit exalteth folly	Prov.	14	29
Seest thou a man *h* in words	Prov.	29	20
Let not thy heart be *h*	Eccl.	5	2
Be not *h* in thy spirit	Eccl.	7	9
As *h* fruit before summer	Is.	28	4
Why is the decree so *h*	Dan.	2	15

hate *see hatred*

In the sense of loving less	Gen.	29	31
	Luke	14	26
By enemies	Ps.	25	19
	Ps.	35	19

hatred *abhorrence*

Forbidden	Lev.	19	17
Work of the flesh	Gal.	5	19, 20
To be put away	Eph.	4	31
Christian requirement	I John	4	20
Divine	Prov.	6	16–19
Causes strife	Prov.	10	12
Hidden	Prov.	10	18
Causes unhappiness	Prov.	15	17
Repay with good	Mat.	5	43, 44
Of the light	John	3	20
Of a brother	I John	2	9
	I John	3	15
	John	7	7
Christ experienced			
Leads to deceit	Prov.	26	24–25
Liars prone to	Prov.	26	28
Punishment of	Ps.	34	21
	Ps.	44	7
	Amos	1	11

Inconsistent with:

The knowledge of God	I John	2	9, 11
The love of God	I John	4	20

Saints should:

Expect	Mat.	10	22
	John	15	8–19
Give no cause for	Prov.	25	17
Not marvel at	I John	3	13
Not rejoice in the calamities of those who exhibit	Job	31	29–30
	Ps.	35	13–14

Examples:

Of Esau for Jacob	Gen.	27	41
Of Joseph's brothers	Gen.	37	4–8
Of Shimei for David	II Sam.	16	5–13
Of Herodias for John	Mat.	14	3–11
Of the Jews for Christ	Mat.	27	20–25
Of the followers of Christ	John	15	18, 19

Hattush *gathered together*

Son of Shemaiah	I Chr.	3	22
Descendant of David	Ezra	8	2
The son of Hashabniah	Neh.	3	10
A sealer of the covenant	Neh.	10	4
A priest	Neh.	12	2

haughtiness *arrogance*

A cruel	Esth.	3	1–6
Humbled	Is.	3	16–26
Condemned	Jer.	48	29
Of Moab	Jer.	48	29
Will be brought low by God	Is.	13	11
Will fall	Prov.	16	18
See pride			

haunt			
Of David	I Sam.	23	22
havens, fair *see* fair havens			
Havilah *circular*			
An unknown region	Gen.	2	11
A son of Cush	Gen.	10	7
A son of Joktan	Gen.	10	29
	I Chr.	1	23
A dwelling place of the Ishmaelites	Gen.	25	18
Amalekites here defeated by Saul	I Sam.	15	7
hawk *a bird of prey*			
Unclean fowl	Lev.	11	16
Ability to fly	Job	39	26
Hazael *whom God watches over*			
Anointed by Elijah as king of Syria	I Ki.	19	15
Murders Ben-hadad	II Ki.	8	8–15
Conquests of Israel	II Ki.	10	32, 33
	II Ki.	8	28, 29
	II Ki.	12	17, 18
	II Ki.	13	3, 22
His death	II Ki.	13	24
Hazar-addar *village of Addar*			
In the land of Canaan	Num.	34	4
Called Adar	Josh.	15	3
Hazar-enan *village of springs*			
Boundary of the promised land	Num.	34	9
	Ezek.	47	17
Hazeroth *encampment*			
A place between Sinai and Kadesh where the Israelites encamp	Num.	11	35
	Num.	12	1–16
	Num.	33	17, 18
	Deut.	1	1
Hazezon-tamar *see* En-gedi			
Hazor *enclosure*			
Fortified capital of Jabin's kingdom	Josh.	11	1, 10, 11, 13
Taken by Joshua	Josh.	12	7, 19
Given to children of Naphtali	Josh.	19	32, 36
Israelites forget the Lord and are oppressed by Jabin here	Judg.	4	2, 17
	I Sam.	12	9
Taken by Assyria	II Ki.	15	29
Rebuilt by Solomon	I Ki.	9	15
A city of Judah	Josh.	15	21, 23, 25
A town of Benjamin	Neh.	11	33
A region in the Arabian desert	Jer.	49	28–33
Another town in South Judah	Josh.	15	25
He *fifth letter of Hebrew alphabet. Used to designate the fifth part of Ps. 119, each verse of which part begins with this letter.*			
I, even I, am *h*	Deut.	32	39
They said, *h* is not here	Luke	24	6
Is not this *h*	John	7	25
head			
Bowing of	Gen.	24	26
Of responsibility	Josh.	2	19
Not shaved	Judg.	13	5
Pain of	II Ki.	4	19
Lifted as a sign of favour	Ps.	27	6
Of gold	Dan.	2	38
Baldness of	Amos	8	10
Husband	Eph.	5	23
Place of crowns	Rev.	19	12
Shaved	Num.	6	9
Hallowed	Num.	6	11
Sisera's, smitten off	Judg.	5	26
Not to swear by	Mat.	5	36
Anointed	Mat.	6	17
Of John cut off	Mat.	14	6–11
Christ smitten on	Mat.	27	30
Coals of fire upon	Rom.	12	20
Of woman uncovered	I Cor.	11	5
Christ, of the church	Col.	1	18
Not holding the	Col.	2	19
headband *article of female attire*			
To be taken away by the Lord	Is.	3	20
head-tone *cornerstone*			
Foundation of Zerubbabel	Zech.	4	7
Of Christ	Acts	4	11
	I Pet.	2	7
healing			
A gift of the spirit	I Cor.	12	9, 28
Is answer to prayer	James	5	14, 15
Of physical disease:			
Lord heals Hezekiah	II Ki.	20	5

Who heals?	Ps.	103	3
The apostles heal	Acts	5	16
Paul heals a cripple	Acts	14	8–11
Of the spirit:			
God tells Moses he heals Israel	Ex.	15	26
Lord heals people who have not been cleansed properly for the passover	II Chr.	30	20
From sin	Ps.	41	4
	Is.	6	10
Brings rejoicing	Ps.	30	2–4
Broken heart is healed	Ps.	147	3
Lord will smite and heal Egypt	Is.	19	22
Hosea wants people to repent and be healed	Hosea	6	1
Denied to Nineveh	Nah.	3	19
Son of righteousness shall come with	Mal.	4	2
By the tree of life	Rev.	22	2
Ministry of Jesus:			
By His stripes	Is.	53	5
	I Pet.	2	24
Of many sicknesses	Mat.	4	23, 24
Of the centurion's servant	Mat.	8	7
In the cities and villages	Mat.	9	35
Power given to disciples	Mat.	10	1
	Mark	3	13–15
	Luke	9	1–6
In Judaea	Mat.	19	2
In the desert near Bethsaida	Luke	9	11
Of man with dropsy	Luke	14	2
Of ear of high priest's servant in garden of Gethsemane	Luke	22	51
See miracles			
health *state of being sound in body, mind or soul*			
Promised to the obedient	Ex.	15	26
	Deut.	7	15
Praise to God who is	Ps.	42	11
	Ps.	43	5
For all nations	Ps.	67	2
Found in God's word	Prov.	4	20–22
A reward of godliness	Is.	58	8
Will be restored by the Lord	Jer.	30	17
For those who return from captivity	Jer.	33	6
Paul persuades those on ship to eat for their	Acts	27	34
Temperate	I Cor.	9	25, 27
Object of brotherly concern	III John		1, 2
heap *pile of*			
Shall be an *h* forever	Deut.	13	16
Over him a *h* of stones	Josh.	7	26
I could *h* up words	Job	16	4
Though he *h* up silver	Job	27	16
H coals of fire	Prov.	25	22
	Rom.	12	20
To gather and to *h* up	Eccl.	2	26
Harvest shall be an *h*	Is.	17	11
Thou hast made of a city an *h*	Is.	25	2
City shall be builded on own *h*	Jer.	30	18
H on wood	Ezek.	24	10
Samaria as an *h* of the field	Mic.	1	6
Jerusalem shall become *h*	Mic.	3	12
They shall *h* dust	Hab.	1	10
H to themselves teachers	II Tim.	4	3
Ye have *h* treasures for last days	James	5	3
hear			
H and fear the Lord	Deut.	31	12
I *h* your evil doings	I Sam.	2	23
Lowing of oxen which I *h*	I Sam.	15	14
They shall *h* of thy great name	I Ki.	8	42
Saying, O Baal, *h* us	I Ki.	18	26
H a noise of chariots	II Ki.	7	6
All that could *h* with understanding	Neh.	8	2
H it, and know thou it	Job	5	27
H my words, ye wise men	Job	34	2
H my prayer	Ps.	4	1
	Ps.	143	1
Lord, *h* thee in day of trouble	Ps.	20	1
H, O Lord, when I cry	Ps.	27	7
Make me *h* joy and gladness	Ps.	51	8
I will *h* what God the Lord will speak	Ps.	85	8
To *h* thy loving-kindness	Ps.	143	8
H instruction and be wise	Prov.	8	33
H the words of the wise	Prov.	22	17
H conclusion of the whole matter	Eccl.	12	13
H O heavens, and give ear	Is.	1	2
H, but understand not	Is.	6	9
	Mark	4	12

hear—*continued*

H, ye that are afar off	Is.	33	13
H, and your soul shall live	Is.	55	3
	John	5	25
He that *h*, let him *h*	Ezek.	3	27
H prayer of thy servant	Dan.	9	17
The deaf *h*	Mat.	11	5
My beloved Son, *h* him	Mat.	17	5
	Mark	9	7
Take heed what ye *h*	Mark	4	24
	Luke	8	18
Came to *h* him and be healed	Luke	6	17
He that *h* you *h* me	Luke	10	16
How is it I *h* this of thee	Luke	16	2
Dead shall *h* voice of Son of God	John	5	25
An hard saying, who can *h* it	John	6	60
He that is of God, *h* God's words	John	8	47
God *h* not sinners	John	9	31
How *h* we every man in our own tongue	Acts	2	8
To tell or *h* some new thing	Acts	17	21
How shall they *h* without a preacher	Rom.	10	14
I *h* there be divisions	I Chr.	11	18
We *h* that some walk disorderly	II Thes.	3	11
Save thyself, and them that *h* thee	I Tim.	4	16
Swift to *h*	James	1	19
We know that he *h* us	I John	5	15
Than to *h* that children walk in truth	III John	4	
If any man *h* my voice	Rev.	3	20
Neither see, nor *h*, nor walk	Rev.	9	20

heart

Of man	Gen.	6	5
	Mat.	12	34
Searched and tried by God	I Chr.	28	9
	Prov.	21	2
	Jer.	12	3
	Rev.	2	23
Enlightened	Ps.	27	14
	II Cor.	4	6
	I Thes.	3	13
Breastplate on Aaron's	Ex.	28	30
Talking in, silently	I Sam.	1	13
Looked on by God	I Sam.	16	7
Lord turns heart of King	Ezra	6	22
Devises man's way	Prov.	16	9
Teacheth the mouth	Prov.	16	23
A new, promised	Jer.	24	7
	Ezek.	11	19
Center of man's actions	Mat.	9	4
	Luke	6	45

Types of:

Faint	Gen.	45	26
Willing	Ex.	35	5
Wise	Ex.	35	35
	Job	9	4
Sorrowful	Lev.	26	16
Discouraged	Deut.	5	29
Astonished	Deut.	28	28
Glad	Deut.	28	47
Trembling	Deut.	28	65
Melted	Josh.	14	18
Smitten	I Sam.	24	5
Despising	II Sam.	6	16
Understanding	I Ki.	3	9
Large	I Ki.	4	29
Double	Ps.	12	2
Broken	Ps.	44	21
Froward	Ps.	101	4
Proud	Ps.	101	5
Subtle	Prov.	7	10
Perverse	Prov.	12	8
Heavy	Prov.	12	25
Merry	Prov.	15	13
	Prov.	17	22
Foolish	Prov.	22	15
Wicked	Prov.	26	23
Fat	Is.	6	10
Stout	Is.	10	12
Fearful	Is.	35	4
Deceitful	Jer.	17	9
Whorish	Ezek.	6	9
Stony	Ezek.	13	22

hearth

Fireplace of stones	Gen.	18	6
Figuratively	Ps.	102	3
	Is.	30	14
	Zech.	12	6
Jehoiakim sits before the	Jer.	36	22, 23

heartlessness *mercilessness*

Of robbers who leave Samaritan wounded on road to Jericho	Luke	10	30
Of the unjust judge	Luke	18	2
Of those who rebuke the blind man	Luke	18	39
In refusing aid to the needy	James	2	15, 16
Joseph's brethren	Gen.	37	28
Levi and Simeon	Gen.	34	25
Haman	Esth.	3	8, 9
Laban	Gen.	31	7

heat *warmth*

Is eternal	Gen.	8	22
Jonah overcome with	Jonah	4	8
Cold and *h*, summer and winter	Gen.	8	22
In *h* of the day	Gen.	18	1
The *h* of this great anger	Deut.	29	24
Nothing hid from *h* thereof	Ps.	19	6
Shadow from *h*	Is.	4	6
	Is.	25	4
Cloud of dew in *h* of harvest	Is.	18	4
Neither shall *h* smite them	Is.	49	10
Borne burden and *h* of the day	Mat.	20	12
Came viper out of the *h*	Acts	28	3
Sun risen with burning *h*	James	1	11
Elements melt with fervent *h*	II Pet.	3	10
Seven times more than wont to be *h*	Dan.	3	19
As an oven *h* by the baker	Hosea	7	4

heath *variety of juniper tree*

In the desert or wilderness	Jer.	17	6
	Jer.	48	6

heathen *see* Gentiles

heave offering, *see* offerings

heaven

The firmament created	Gen.	1	1, 8
God's dwelling place	I Ki.	8	30
	Is.	6	1
	Deut.	26	15
	Job	22	12
	Eccl.	5	2
	Is.	57	15
	Mat.	6	9
Our prayers heard in	II Chr.	30	27
Its happiness	Is.	49	10
	Mat.	5	12
	I Cor.	13	12
	Rev.	7	16
Who enter	Mat.	5	3
	Mat.	25	34
	Rom.	8	17
	Heb.	12	23
Who excluded from	Mat.	7	21
	Mat.	25	46
	Luke	13	27
	I Cor.	6	9
	Gal.	5	21
	Rev.	21	8
Angels are in	Mat.	18	10
	John	14	1, 2
	Ps.	23	6
	Ps.	73	24
	Mat.	5	12
	Mat.	6	20
	II Cor.	5	1
	Rev.	5	9
Future home of saints	Heb.	11	16
	Rev.	7	13–17
Christ ascends to	Acts	1	9–11
The new	Rev.	21	1
Cannot contain God	II Chr.	2	6
Temple of	Ps.	11	4
God's awareness in	Ps.	20	6
	Ps.	33	13
	Ps.	102	19
Elijah ascends to	II Ki.	2	11
Space	Ps.	19	1
	Ps.	115	16
	Ps.	8	3
	Neh.	9	6
	II Pet.	3	10
	Rev.	21	1–4
	II Pet.	3	13
Created by God	Rev.	10	6
Enoch translated into	Gen.	5	24
Everlasting	Ps.	89	29
Flesh and blood cannot inherit	I Cor.	15	50

God's throne	Acts	7	49
High	Ps.	103	11
Immeasurable	Jer.	31	37
Lay up treasure in	Luke	12	33
Names of saints are written in	Luke	10	20
	Heb.	12	23
Repentance occasions joy in	Luke	15	7
Saints rewarded in	I Pet.	1	4

Christ:

As mediator, entered into	Acts	3	21
	Heb.	6	20
	Heb.	9	12, 24
Is all-powerful in	Mat.	28	18
	I Pet.	3	22

God:

Answers his people from	I Chr.	21	26
	II Chr.	7	14
	Neh.	9	27
Fills	I Ki.	8	27
	Jer.	23	24
Is the Lord of	Dan.	5	23
	Mat.	11	25
Reigns in	Ps.	135	6
	Dan.	4	35
Sends his judgments from	Gen.	19	24
	I Sam.	2	10
	Dan.	4	13
	Rom.	1	18

Is called:

The kingdom of Christ and of God	Eph.	5	5
Paradise	II Cor.	12	2, 4
A rest	Heb.	4	9

Heavenly Father *see* God

heaviness

Full of *h*	Ps.	69	20
My soul melteth for *h*	Ps.	119	28
H in the heart maketh it stoop	Prov.	12	25
The end of that mirth is *h*	Prov.	14	13
Garment of praise for spirit of *h*	Is.	61	3
Have great *h* and sorrow	Rom.	9	2
Let your joy be turned to *h*	James	4	9
If need be, ye are in *h*	I Pet.	1	6

heavy

Moses's hands were *h*	Ex.	17	12
This thing is too *h* for thee	Ex.	18	18
Sent with *h* tidings	I Ki.	14	6
The bondage was *h*	Neh.	5	18
Thy hand was *h* upon me	Ps.	32	4
Songs to a *h* heart	Prov.	25	20
Wine to those of *h* hearts	Prov.	31	6
And make their ears *h*	Is.	6	10
To undo the *h* burdens	Is.	58	6
All ye that are *h* laden	Mat.	11	28
They bind *h* burdens	Mat.	23	4
He began to be very *h*	Mat.	26	37
Their eyes were *h*	Mat.	26	43
	Mark	14	40

Heber *union*

Son of Beriah and head of family of Heberites	Gen.	46	17
	Num.	26	45
	I Chr.	7	31, 32
A Kenite, husband of Jael	Judg.	4	11–24
	Judg.	5	24
A Judahite, son Ezra	I Chr.	4	18
A Gadite	I Chr.	5	13
A Benjamite, son of Elpaal	I Chr.	8	17, 18
Another Benjamite	I Chr.	8	22
Christ's ancestor	Luke	3	35
	Gen.	10	24

Hebrew *on the other side, from beyond*

Abraham's descendants	Gen.	14	13
Name for the Israelites	Gen.	40	15
	Deut.	15	12
Paul, a devout	Phil.	3	5
Distinctive language of the Israelites	John	19	13, 20
	Acts	21	40
	II Ki.	18	26, 28

Hebron *union*

Son of Kohath, a Levite and founder of family	Ex.	6	18
	Num.	3	19
	I Chr.	6	2, 18
Town in hill country of Judah	Josh.	15	48, 54
An altar built by Abram at	Gen.	13	18

Sarah dies in, and a burialplace is purchased	Gen.	23	1–20
Isaac and Jacob live here	Gen.	35	27
	Gen.	37	14
Spies come to	Num.	13	22
Conquered by Joshua	Josh.	12	10
	Josh.	10	3–39
Joshua destroys the Anakim at	Josh.	11	21
Given to Caleb for an inheritance	Josh.	14	12–14
Originally called Kirjath-arba	Josh.	14	15
Becomes city of refuge	Josh.	20	1–7
David reigns over Judah in	II Sam.	2	1–4, 11
David's sons born at	II Sam.	3	1–5
Burial place of Abner and Ish-bosheth	II Sam.	3	32
	II Sam.	4	12
Conspirators hanged over pool in	II Sam.	4	12
Elders come to, to ask David to rule over Israel	II Sam.	5	1–5
Absalom made king at	II Sam.	15	7, 9, 10
Again inhabited after captivity	Neh.	11	25
Boundary town of Asher	Josh.	19	24, 28
Son of Mareshah	I Chr.	2	42, 43

hedge *enclosure of thorn bushes or small trees*

A protection	Job	1	10
	Ps.	80	12
Of thorns	Prov.	15	19
Used figuratively in judgments for sin	Is.	5	5
	Jer.	49	3
	Ezek.	13	5
	Ezek.	22	30
People sheltered in	Luke	14	23

heed *attention, notice*

Took no *h* to the sword	II Sam.	20	10
Jehu took no *h*	II Ki.	10	31
By taking *h* to thy word	Ps.	119	9
Preacher gave good *h*	Eccl.	12	9
Let us not give *h* to any words	Jer.	18	18
He gave *h* unto them	Acts	3	5
Neither gave *h* to fables	I Tim.	1	4
	Tit.	1	14
Giving *h* to seducing spirits	I Tim.	4	1
We ought to give the more earnest *h*	Heb.	2	1

heel *hind part of human foot*

Jacob holds Esau's	Gen.	25	26
	Hosea	12	3
Used figuratively	Gen.	3	15
	Gen.	49	17
	Job	13	27
	Job	18	9
	Ps.	49	5
	John	13	18

heifer *a young cow*

Used as a sign in Lord's covenant with Abram	Gen	15	9
For peace offering	Lev.	3	1
Red, used in sacrifice	Num.	19	2–10
Used for atonement of murder	Deut.	21	1–9
Used figuratively by Samson when men answer his riddle	Judg.	14	18
Egypt compared to fair	Jer.	46	20
Continually eating	Jer.	50	11
Israel compared to backsliding	Hosea	4	16
Used for treading grain	Hosea	10	11
Used for sanctifying the flesh	Heb.	9	13

heirs *those who inherit*

Lord tells Abram he shall have an	Gen.	15	3–5
Sarah does not want son of Hagar to be, with Isaac	Gen.	21	10
Isaac becomes	Gen.	25	5, 6
Laws for sons and daughters	Num.	27	1–8
	Deut.	21	15–17
Daughters of Zelophehad	Num.	36	1–8
Duty of levir	Ruth	4	1–12
Uncertain	Eccl.	2	18–19
Woman of Tekoah tells David her, will be destroyed	II Sam.	14	7
Handmain, to mistress	Prov.	30	23
Husbandmen plot to kill, of householder	Mat.	21	38
With God and joint-heirs with Christ	Rom.	8	17
Of promise	Gal.	3	29
	Heb.	6	17
Of God through Christ	Gal.	4	7
Fellow, in Christ	Eph.	3	6
In hope of eternal life	Tit.	3	7
Christ of all things	Heb.	1	1, 2

heirs—*continued*			
Of salvation	Heb.	1	14
Of the kingdom	James	2	5
Includes women	I Pet.	3	7
Young, same status as servant	Gal.	4	1
Helam *their rampart*			
a town of Syria, east of Jordan			
Place where David defeats Hadarezer	II Sam.	10	16–19
Heli *Greek form of Eli*			
Father of Joseph	Luke	3	23
hell			
Wicked shall be turned into	Ps.	9	17
	Prov.	5	5
Human power can not save from	Ezek.	32	27
The body suffers in	Mat.	5	29
The soul suffers in	Mat.	10	28
Powers of, can not prevail against the church	Mat.	16	18
Degrees of punishment in	Mat.	23	14
	Luke	12	47, 48
Prepared for the devil	Mat.	25	41
Destiny of beast and false prophet	Rev.	19	20
Visited by Christ	Acts	2	31
	I Pet.	3	19
Devils confined in, until judgment day	II Pet.	2	4
	Jude		6
Finality	Luke	16	22–31
Endeavor to keep others from	Prov.	23	14
	Jude		23
Illustrated	Is.	30	33
A place of torment	Luke	16	23
Destruction from the presence of God	II Thes.	1	9
Eternal	Is.	33	14
	Rev.	20	10
The wise avoid	Prov.	15	24
Described as:			
Devouring fire	Is.	33	14
Unquenchable fire	Mat.	3	12
A furnace of fire	Mat.	13	42, 50
Everlasting fire	Mat.	25	41
Everlasting punishment	Mat.	25	46
A place of torment	Luke	16	23
Fire and brimstone	Rev.	14	10
A lake of fire	Rev.	20	15
Darkness	Mat.	8	12
helmet *protective headpiece worn by soldiers*			
Of brass worn by Goliath	I Sam.	17	5
Of brass worn by David	I Sam.	17	38
Made for Uzziah's armies	II Chr.	26	14
Symbol of salvation	Is.	59	17
	Eph.	6	17
	I Thes.	5	8
Used figuratively in	Jer.	46	4
	Ezek.	23	24
	Ezek.	27	10
help			
An *h* meet for him	Gen.	2	18
The shield of thy *h*	Deut.	33	29
Is not my *h* in me	Job	6	13
Lord send *h* from sanctuary	Ps.	20	2
He is our *h* and our shield	Ps.	33	20
God a very present *h* in trouble	Ps.	46	1
Vain is the *h* of man	Ps.	60	11
	Ps.	108	12
Thou hast been my *h*	Ps.	63	7
Unless the Lord had been my *h*	Ps.	94	17
The hills, from whence cometh my *h*	Ps.	121	1
Our *h* is in the name of the Lord	Ps.	124	8
Trust not in man, in whom is no *h*	Ps.	146	3
To whom will you flee for *h*	Is.	10	3
Nor be an *h* nor profit	Is.	30	5
Having obtained *h* of God	Acts	26	22
Haste to *h* me	Ps.	22	19
	Ps.	38	22
H thou mine unbelief	Mark	9	24
Men of Israel, *h*	Acts	21	28
Spirit also *h* our infirmities	Rom.	8	26
H together by prayer	II Cor.	1	11
Grace to *h* in time of need	Heb.	4	16
help meet *wife*			
God makes help meet for Adam	Gen.	2	18
hem *edge or border of a garment*			
Of high priest's robe is described	Ex.	28	33, 34
	Ex.	39	24–26
Woman touches, of Jesus' garment	Mat.	9	20
People touch, of Jesus' garment and are made whole	Mat.	14	36
Jews to put on their garments	Num.	15	38
hemlock *a bitter, poisonous plant*			
Used figuratively	Hosea	10	4
	Amos	6	12
hemorrhoids, emerods			
Threatened as a punishment	Deut.	28	27
Sent as judgment on the Philistines	I Sam.	5	6
hen *female of domestic fowl*			
Son of Zephaniah	Zech.	6	14
Figurative	Mat.	23	37
	Luke	13	34
Henoch *see* Enoch			
Hephzi-bah *my delight is in her*			
Wife of Hezekiah	II Ki.	21	1, 3
Prophetic name for Jerusalem when restored	Is.	62	4
herbs			
Creation of	Gen.	1	11, 12
Smitten in Egypt	Ex.	9	22
Eaten by locusts	Ex.	10	12
Green	II Ki.	19	26
Tender	Job	38	27
Garden plants	I Ki.	21	2
Mustard	Mat.	13	32
Vegetarians	Rom.	14	2
Given for food	Gen.	1	29, 30
	Prov.	15	17
herbs, bitter			
Part of meal eaten by Israelites on night before leaving Egypt	Ex.	12	8
herdsmen			
Strife among	Gen.	13	7, 8
Despised by Egyptians	Gen.	46	34
Honoured by Hebrews	I Sam.	21	7
Amos' occupation	Amos	7	14
	Amos	1	1
here			
Said, *h* am I	Ex.	3	4
	I Sam.	3	5, 6
He is not *h*; for he is risen	Mat.	28	6
Good for us to be *h*	Luke	9	33
H is thy pound	Luke	19	20
Lord, if thou had been *h*	John	11	21, 32
H have we no continuing city	Heb.	13	14
heredity- *transmission of traits*			
Adam	Gen.	5	3
Moral character	Ex.	20	5, 6
	Num.	14	33
	Job	21	19
Judgment passed on	Ps.	37	28
	Is.	65	6, 7
Personal responsibility	Jer.	31	29
	Ezek.	18	19, 20
Spiritually in Adam	I Cor.	15	22
heresy *an opinion tending to promote dissension*			
Propagandism of, forbidden	Deut.	13	1–15
	Tit.	3	10, 11
	II John		10, 11
Teachers of, among early Christians	Acts	15	24
	II Cor.	11	4
	Gal.	1	7
	Gal.	2	4
	II Pet.	2	1–22
	Jude		4–16
	Rev.	2	2
Paul and Silas accused of	Acts	16	20, 21
Paul accused of	Acts	18	13
Disavowed by Paul	Acts	24	13–16
See false teachers			
heritage *inheritance*			
Fate of the wicked	Job	20	29
A goodly	Ps.	16	6
	Jer.	3	19
	Ps.	61	5
Promised land	Gen.	12	1
Of the heathen	Ps.	111	6
Children as	Ps.	127	3
Shall be protected	Is.	54	17
	Mic.	7	14
God's	I Pet.	5	3
Hermas, Hermes *Mercury*			
Two friends of Paul	Rom.	16	14

Hermogenes *born of Mercury*
One who deserts Paul ... II Tim. 1 15
Hermon *lofty, rugged, 9100 feet*
A mountain in the north of Palestine ... Josh. 11 17
... Josh. 12 5
... Josh. 13 5
... Ps. 89 12
... Ps. 133 3
Also called Sirion or Sion ... Deut. 3 8
... Deut. 4 48
hero *person of distinguished fortitude*
Joel ... Judg. 5 24–27
Jonathan ... I Sam. 14 6–15
David's mighty men ... I Sam. 23 8–39
Daniel ... Ezek. 14 14
David, after war with Philistines ... I Sam. 18 5–7
Jesus, riding into Jerusalem ... Mat. 21 1–9
... Mark 11 1–10
Paul, in going to Jerusalem ... Acts 21 13–20
Herod *heroic*
The Great, tetrarch of Judaea; issues murderous edict against children of Bethlehem ... Mat. 2 16
Antipas, son of former; murderer of John the Baptist ... Mat. 14 1, 2
... Luke 3 19
Tetrarch of Galilee ... Luke 23 7–15
... Acts 13 1
Philip, son of the Great; marries Herodias ... Mat. 14 3
... Mark 6 17
... Luke 3 19
Philip II, son of the Great; tetrarch of Batanea, Ituraea, etc. ... Luke 3 1
Agrippa I, grandson of the Great; tetrarch of Galilee; king of his grandfather's realm ... Acts 12 1–19
Agrippa II, son of former; king of consolidated tetrarchies ... Acts 25 13–27
... Acts 26 1–28
Herodians *valiant a Jewish faction*
Seek to entangle Jesus ... Mat. 22 16–22
... Mark 12 13–17
Conspire to slay Jesus ... Mark 3 6
... Mark 12 13
Herodias *valiant daughter of Aristobulus*
Requests head of John the Baptist ... Mat. 14 3–6
... Mark 6 17
... Luke 3 19
Herodion *valiant*
A Roman Christian ... Rom. 16 11
heron *a large bird*
Called unclean ... Lev. 11 13, 19
... Deut. 14 12, 18
Heshbon *device*
An Amorite capital ... Num. 21 25–30, 34
... Deut. 1 4
Built by Reuben's children ... Num. 32 37
Alloted to Gad ... Josh. 21 38, 39
Fishpools at ... S. of S. 7 4
Prophecy concerning ... Is. 16 8, 9
... Jer. 48 2, 34
... Jer. 49 1–3
Levitical city ... Josh. 21 39
Occupied by Moabites ... Is. 15 1–4
Heth *fear*
Son of Canaan ... Gen. 10 15
Sons of, show kindness ... Gen. 23 5–7
Ancestor of the Hittites ... Gen. 23 10
Esau marries his daughters ... Gen. 27 46
... Gen. 36 1, 2
hew *cut*
H two tables of stone ... Ex. 34 4
H them out cisterns ... Jer. 2 13
H down and cast into the fire ... Mat. 3 10
... Luke 3 9
Sepulchre which was *h* out ... Mark 15 46
hewer *one who hews, cuts with blows*
Moses, of stone ... Ex. 34 1, 4
Gibeonites, of wood ... Josh. 9 21, 23, 27
Jews, of cisterns ... Jer. 2 13
Of trees bearing bad fruit ... Mat. 3 10
... Luke 3 9
Sepulchre hewn out of rock ... Mark 15 46
Hezekiah, Ezekias *strength of Jehovah*
King of Judah ... II Ki. 16 20

... II Ki. 18 1, 2
... I Chr. 3 13
... II Chr. 29 1
... Mat. 1 9
His piety ... II Ki. 18 3, 5, 6
... II Chr. 29 2
... II Chr. 31 20, 21
... II Chr. 32 32
... Jer. 26 19
Purges nation of idolatry ... II Ki. 18 4
... II Chr. 31 1
... II Chr. 33 3
Prospered of God ... II Ki. 18 7
... II Chr. 32 27–30
Brings water of brook of Gihon into Jerusalem ... II Ki. 20 20
... II Chr. 32 4, 30
Prophecies concerning ... II Ki. 19 20–34
... II Ki. 20 16–18
... Is. 38 5–8
... Is. 39 5–7
... Jer. 26 18, 19
Sickness and restoration of ... II Ki. 20 1–11
... II Chr. 32 24
... Is. 38 1–8
His lack of wisdom with Babylon ... II Ki. 20 12–19
... II Chr. 32 25, 26, 31
... Is. 39 1–8
Death and burial of ... II Ki. 20 21
... II Chr. 32 33
Military operation of ... I Chr. 4 39–43
... II Chr. 32 1–30
... Is. 36, 37
Religious zeal of ... I Chr. 29–31
Restores true forms of worship ... II Chr. 31 2–21
Scribes of ... Prov. 25 1
His psalm of thankgiving ... Is. 38 9–20
Son of Neariah ... I Chr. 3 23
... Ezra 2 16
One of the exiles ... Neh. 7 21
Called Hizkijah ... Neh. 10 17
hezron *surrounded*
A Reubenite ... Gen. 46 9
... Ex. 6 14
... I Chr. 4 1
... I Chr. 5 3
Son of Pharez ... Gen. 46 12
... Ruth 4 18
Ancestor of Hezronites ... Num. 26 6, 21
... I Chr. 2 5, 9, 18
hid *out of sight*
The Lord hath *h* it from me ... II Ki. 4 27
More than for *h* treasures ... Job 3 21
Mine iniquity have I not *h* ... Ps. 32 5
My sins are not *h* ... Ps. 69 5
Thy word have I *h* in mine heart ... Ps. 119 11
It may be ye shall be *h* ... Zeph. 2 3
There is nothing *h* ... Mat. 10 26
... Mark 4 22
They are *h* from thine eyes ... Luke 19 42
Even the *h* wisdom ... I Chr. 2 7
If our gospel be *h* ... II Chr. 4 3
Your life is *h* with Christ ... Col. 3 3
The *h* man of the heart ... I Pet. 3 4
To eat of the *h* manna ... Rev. 2 17
Hiddekel *rapid*
Ancient name of river Tigris ... Gen. 2 14
... Dan. 10 4
hide *out of sight*
Shall I be *h* from Abraham ... Gen. 18 17
H me in the grave ... Job 14 13
He *h* his face ... Ps. 10 11
H me under the shadow of thy wings ... Ps. 17 8
H me in pavilion ... Ps. 27 5
H them in secret of thy presence ... Ps. 31 20
How long wilt thou *h* thyself ... Ps. 89 46
Darkness *h* not from thee ... Ps. 139 12
I will *h* mine eyes from you ... Is. 1 15
H thyself for a little moment ... Is. 26 20
A man shall be as an *h* place ... Is. 32 2
Thou art a God that *h* thyself ... Is. 45 15
No secret they can *h* from thee ... Ezek. 28 3
H a multitude of sins ... James 5 20
H us from the face of him ... Rev. 6 16
(See ...

Hiel *God lives*			
Rebuilder of Jericho	I Ki.	16	34
In him is fulfilled curse pronounced by			
Joshua	Josh.	6	26
Hierapolis *holy city*			
City of Phrygia	Col.	4	13
high			
It is as *h* as heaven	Job	11	8
Behold stars, how *h* they are	Job	22	12
Men of *h* degree are a lie	Ps.	62	9
As the heaven is *h* above the earth	Ps.	103	11
Though the Lord by *h*	Ps.	138	6
It is *h*, I cannot attain unto it	Ps.	139	6
Afraid of that which is *h*	Eccl.	12	5
Spirit poured on us from on *h*	Is.	32	15
Though thou make thy nest *h*	Jer.	49	16
Go into the *h*-ways	Mat.	22	9
	Luke	14	23
Dayspring from on *h*	Luke	1	78
Power from on *h*	Luke	24	49
Mind not *h* things	Rom.	12	16
For prize of the *h* calling	Phil.	3	14
(See . . .	Is.	57	15
	Acts	13	17
	II Chr.	10	5
high places			
A term used to describe places of worship	Gen.	12	8
Forbidden	Deut.	12	2
	I Ki.	12	31
	Jer.	3	6
To be destroyed	Lev.	26	30
Idolatrous worship at	I Ki.	11	7
	II Ki.	17	9, 29
	Jer.	7	31
Destroyed by:			
Hezekiah	II Ki.	18	4
Josiah	II Ki.	23	8
Asa	II Chr.	14	3
Jehoshaphat	II Chr.	17	6
high priest			
Divinely instituted	Ex.	28	1
	Lev.	21	10
His garments	Lev.	8	7
Duties of	Lev.	24	8
	Num.	18	2, 5, 7
	I Sam.	2	28
	II Ki.	12	10
	II Chr.	24	6, 14
Christ is our	Heb.	2	17
To offer sacrifices	Heb.	5	1
To designate duties of lower priests	Num.	4	19
	I Sam.	2	36
To consecrate levites	Num.	8	11–21
Had charge of treasury	II Ki.	22	4
To burn incense	Ex.	30	7, 8
To offer for his own sins	Lev.	4	3–12
Enters holy of holies on Day of Atonement	Lev.	16	
highways *main roads*			
Of the king	Num.	20	17
To cities of refuge	Deut.	19	2, 3
Of holiness	Is.	35	8
To destruction	Mat.	7	13, 14
Beggard by side of	Mark	10	46
Infested with robbers	Luke	10	30
Of the upright	Prov.	16	17
Of return from Assyria	Is.	11	16
For God in the desert	Is.	40	3, 4
Around Gibeah	Judg.	20	31
Near Bethshemesh	I Sam.	6	12
Clean up	Is.	62	10
Place Bartimaeous sat	Mark	10	46
Hilkiah *Jehovah my portion*			
Father of Eliakim	II Ki.	18	37
A high priest	II Ki.	22	8
Four Levites	I Chr.	6	45
	I Chr.	26	11
	Neh.	8	4
	Neh.	12	8, 21
Father of Jeremiah	Jer.	1	1
Father of an ambassador	Jer.	29	3
hill *elevation of land*			
The everlasting *h*	Gen.	49	26
A land of *h* and valleys	Deut.	11	11
Set my king on holy *h*	Ps.	2	6
Who shall ascend the *h* of the Lord	Ps.	24	3

Bring to me thy holy *h*	Ps.	43	3
Cattle on a thousand *h* are mine	Ps.	50	10
Strength of the *h* is his	Ps.	95	4
Let the *h* be joyful together	Ps.	98	8
I will lift up mine eyes to the *h*	Ps.	121	1
Before the *h* was I brought forth	Prov.	8	25
Shall be exalted above *h*	Is.	2	2
Weighed the *h* in balance	Is.	40	12
To the *h*, Fall on us	Hosea	10	8
	Luke	23	30
City set on an *h*	Mat.	5	14
Every *h* be brought low	Luke	3	5
Paul stood in Mars' *h*	Acts	17	22
hills *natural elevation of land*			
Perpetual	Gen.	49	26
	Hab.	3	6
hin *about 1¼ gallons*			
A Hebrew liquid measure	Ex.	29	40
	Lev.	19	36
	Lev.	23	13
hind *see* hart			
hinder			
H me not	Gen.	24	56
H the building	Neh.	4	8
Who can *h* him	Job	9	12
	Job	11	10
Them entering in ye *h*	Luke	11	52
What doth *h* me to be baptized	Acts	8	36
Lest we should *h* the gospel of Christ	I Cor.	9	12
Ye did run well; who did *h* you	Gal.	5	7
Satan *h* us	I Thes.	2	18
That your prayers be not *h*	I Pet.	3	7
Hinnom, valley of *wailing*			
South and west of Jerusalem	Josh.	15	8
	Josh.	18	16
Where Molech is worshipped	I Ki.	11	7
Defiled	II Ki.	23	10
Place of sacrifice	II Chr.	28	3
	II Chr.	33	6
Called Tophet	Is.	30	33
Called "the valley"	Neh.	2	13, 15
Jeremiah gives message	Jer.	19	1–5
Hiram, Huram *noble*			
King of Tyre builds a house for David	II Sam.	5	11
	I Chr.	14	1
	II Chr.	2	3, 11
Aids Solomon in building the temple	I Ki.	5	1–18
	II Chr.	2	3–16
Dissatisfied with cities given by Solomon	I Ki.	9	11–13
Makes presents to Solomon	I Ki.	9	14, 26–28
	I Ki.	10	11
Chief architect	I Ki.	7	13–45
	II Chr.	2	13
	II Chr.	4	11–16
A Benjamite	I Chr.	8	1, 5
hire *wages*			
Law concerning, hired property	Ex.	22	14, 15
Not to be withheld	Lev.	19	13
	Deut.	24	15
	James	5	4
In the vineyard	Mat.	20	1, 7–9
Labourer worthy of	Luke	10	7
Father's servants	Luke	15	17
God giving	Gen.	30	18
Of prostitution	Deut.	23	18
	Mic.	1	7
Solomon to Hiram	I Ki.	5	6
Do not muzzle the ox	I Tim.	5	18
hireling *one who is hired*			
Symbolic of life	Job	7	1, 2
Oppressed	Mal.	3	5
Compared with shepherd	John	10	12, 13
hiss *expressing hatred or disapproval*			
Astonished	I Ki.	9	8
Portion of wicked man	Job	27	23
Contempt	Jer.	25	18
	Lam.	2	15, 16
history *account of past*			
Tyre:			
City 14th century B.C. near Sidon and			
Mount Carmel captured by Israel			
assigned to Asher	Josh.	19	29
David formed an alliance	II Sam.	5	11
	I Ki.	5	1
Ezekiel predicted downfall	Ezek.	28	

Citizens heard Jesus preach	Mark	3	8
Jesus visited that area	Mark	7	24
Paul landed at *T*	Acts	21	3, 7

Books:
Genesis-Esther			

Dating Systems:
Religious	Deut.	15, 16	
	Hag.	1	1
Secular: by Kings	Zech.	1	1
	Is.	6	1
	Amos	1	1
Learning from history	I Chr.	10	1–11
	Rom.	15	4
Summaries of	Acts	7	
	Heb.	12	

Hittites *people of Heth*
Children of Heth	Gen.	10	15
	Gen.	23	10
Sell burying ground to Abraham	Gen.	23	3–20
Esau intermarries with	Gen.	26	34
	Gen.	36	2
Land given to Israelites	Ex.	3	8
	Deut.	7	1, 2
	Josh.	1	4
Dwelling place of	Num.	13	29
	Josh.	1	4
Conquered by Joshua	Josh.	9	1, 11
Intermarry with Israelites	Judg.	3	5–7
	Ezra	9	1
Pay tribute to Solomon	I Ki.	9	20, 21
Retain own kings	I Ki.	10	29
	II Ki.	7	6
	II Chr.	1	17
Officers from, in David's army	I Sam.	26	6
	II Sam.	11	3
	II Sam.	23	39

Hivites *villagers*
A tribe of Canaanites	Gen.	10	17
Located at Shechem	Gen.	34	2
Dwelling place of	Josh.	11	3
	Judg.	3	3
	II Sam.	24	7
Land given to Israelites	Ex.	23	23, 28
	Deut.	20	16, 17
	Judg.	3	5
Conquered by Joshua	Josh.	9	1, 11
	Josh.	12	7, 8
	Josh.	24	11
Pay tribute to Solomon	I Ki.	9	20, 21
	II Chr.	8	7, 8

Hizkijah *see* Hezekiah

hoar frost *white*
On the ground	Ex.	16	14
Scattered	Ps.	147	16

hoary head *white*
Joab's	I Ki.	2	6, 9
A virtue	Prov.	16	31

Hobab *beloved see* Jethro
Son of Raguel	Num.	10	29
	Judg.	4	11

Hodaviah, Hodevah *praise ye*
A Manassite	I Chr.	5	24
A Benjamite	I Chr.	9	7
A Levite	Ezra	2	40
Called Judah	Ezra	2	40
Called Hodevah	Neh.	7	43

Hodiah *my splendor is Jehovah*
Wife of Ezra	I Chr.	4	19
Also called Jehudijah	I Chr.	4	18

hold
Lord will not *h* him guiltless	Ex.	20	7
	Deut.	5	11
King *h* out golden scepter	Esth.	4	11
Thou wilt not *h* me innocent	Job	9	28
Thy right hand hath *h* me up	Ps.	18	35
H me up, and I shall be safe	Ps.	119	117
Man of understanding *h* his peace	Prov.	11	12
A fool when he *h* his peace	Prov.	17	28
Lord will *h* thy hand	Is.	41	13
Never *h* their peace day nor night	Is.	62	6
I cannot *h* my peace	Jer.	4	19
He will *h* to the one	Mat.	6	24
	Luke	16	13
H thy peace, come out	Mark	1	25
	Luke	4	35

H the truth in unrighteousness	Rom.	1	18
H forth the word	Phil.	2	16
H such in reputation	Phil.	2	29
Not *h* the Head	Col.	2	19
H fast that which is good	I Thes.	5	21
H faith and a good conscience	I Tim.	1	19
H fast form of sound words	II Tim.	1	13
H beginning of confidence	Heb.	3	14
H fast our profession	Heb.	4	14
	Heb.	10	23
H fast till I come	Rev.	2	25
H that fast which thou hast	Rev.	3	11
(*See . . .*	Judg.	9	46
	I Sam.	22	4
	Jer.	51	30
	Ezek.	19	9
	Acts	4	3
	Rev.	18	2

hole
Be an *h* in the top of it	Ex.	28	32
Child shall play on *h* of asp	Is.	11	8
H of pit whence you are digged	Is.	51	1
A *h* in the wall	Ezek.	8	7
To put it into a bag with *h*	Hag.	1	6
Foxes have *h*	Mat.	8	20
	Luke	9	58

holiday *for rest*
One year in seven	Lev.	25	2–7

holiness
Becoming in the church	Ps.	93	5
Behavior of aged women should be as becomes	Tit.	2	3
Character of Christ, the standard of	Rom.	8	29
	I John	2	6
	Phil.	2	5
Character of God, the standard of	I Pet.	1	15–16
Chastisements are intended to produce, in saints	Heb.	12	10
	James	1	2–3
Commanded	Lev.	20	7
	Eph.	5	8
	Col.	3	12
None shall see God without	Eph.	5	5
	Heb.	12	14
Promised to the church	Obad.	1	17
	Is.	35	8
Required by God	Lev.	11	45
The church is the beauty of	I Chr.	16	29
	Ps.	29	2
Necessary to inherit God's kingdom	Ps.	24	3, 4
	Heb.	12	14
Promised to the church	Is.	35	8
	Zech.	14	20, 21
Blessed are they who seek	Mat.	5	8
Of John the Baptist	Mark	6	20
Commanded by Paul	Rom.	12	1
	II Cor.	7	1
	Heb.	12	14
Required in prayer	I Tim.	2	8
Ministers should possess	Tit.	1	8
Christ, an example of	Heb.	7	26
	I Pet.	2	21, 22
A nation	Ex.	19	6
"Holiness to the Lord" mitre engraving	Ex.	39	30
In diet	Lev.	10	8–10
Based on election	Deut.	14	2
Connected with keeping commandments	Deut.	28	9
Personal responsibility	Josh.	7	12–13
Holy mountain	Zech.	8	3
Christ called the "Holy One"	Mark	1	24
	Acts	2	27
	I John	2	20
Image of God	Eph.	4	24

Christ:
An example of	Heb.	7	26
	I Pet.	2	21–22
Desires for his people	John	17	17
Effects in his people	Eph.	5	25–27

Ministers should:
Avoid everything inconsistent with	Lev.	21	6
	Is.	52	11
Be examples of	I Tim.	4	12
Exhort to	I Pet.	1	14–16
	Heb.	12	14
Possess	Tit.	1	8

Motives to:
The dissolution of all things	II Pet.	3	11

holiness—*continued*			
The glory of God	John	15	8
	Phil.	1	11
The love of Christ	II Cor.	5	14–15
The mercies of God	Rom.	12	1–2
Obtained through:			
Union with Christ	John	15	4, 5
The word of God	John	17	17
Obedience to God	Rom.	6	22
	Tit.	2	11, 12
Saints:			
Called to	I Thes.	4	7
	II Tim.	1	9
Elected to	Rom.	8	29
	Eph.	1	4
Possess	I Cor.	3	17
	Heb.	3	1
Shall be presented to God in	Col.	1	22
	I Thes.	3	13
Shall continue in, forever	Rev.	22	11
Should continue in	Luke	1	75
Should have their conversation in	I Pet.	1	15
	II Pet.	3	11
Should serve God in	Luke	1	74–75
Should yield their members as instruments			
of	Rom.	6	13, 19
Should lead to separation from the wicked	Num.	16	21, 26
	II Cor.	6	17–18
The wicked are without	I Tim.	1	9
	II Tim.	3	2
holiness of God, the			
Is incomparable	Ex.	15	11
	I Sam.	2	2
To be imitated	Lev.	11	44
	Lev.	20	26
	I Pet.	1	15, 16
Should be magnified	Ps.	48	1
	Ps.	99	3, 5
Pledged to fulfill His promises	Ps.	89	35
Heavenly hosts adore	Is.	6	3
	Rev.	4	8
Requires holy service	Josh.	24	19
	Ps.	93	5
Saints should praise	Ps.	30	4
Should be magnified	I Chr.	16	10
	Rev.	15	4
Should produce reverential fear	Rev.	15	4
Exhibited in His:			
Character	John	17	11
	Ps.	22	3
Kingdom	Ps.	47	8
	Mat.	13	41
	Rev.	21	27
	I Cor.	6	9–10
Words	Ps.	60	6
	Jer.	23	9
Works	Ps.	145	17
Name	Is.	57	15
	Luke	1	49
holy city *see* city, holy			
holy day *see* sabbath			
Holy Ghost, Holy Spirit *third person of the Trinity*			
Titles of:			
Spirit of God	Gen.	1	2
Holy spirit	Ps.	51	11
Free spirit	Ps.	51	12
Spirit of judgment	Is.	4	4
Spirit of Wisdom	Is.	11	2
Spirit of the Lord	Is.	11	2
Spirit of counsel	Is.	11	2
Spirit of the Father	Mat.	10	20
Power of the Highest	Luke	1	35
The Comforter	John	14	16, 26
Spirit of life	Rom.	8	2
Spirit of adoption	Rom.	8	15
Spirit of the Son	Gal.	4	6
Eternal Spirit	Heb.	9	14
Spirit of Christ	I Pet.	1	11
Spirit of prophecy	Rev.	19	10
Description:			
Omnipresent	Ps.	139	7–13
Omnipotent	Luke	1	35
The world cannot receive	John	14	17
Proceeds from the Father	John	15	26
Omniscient	I Cor.	2	10

Eternal	Heb.	9	14
Spirit of glory and of God	I Pet.	4	14
Duties:			
Creates and gives light	Job	33	4
The source of wisdom	Is.	11	2
	I Cor.	12	8
Sanctifying the church	Ezek.	37	28
	Rom.	15	16
The source of miraculous power	Mat.	12	28
	Luke	11	20
Author of the new birth	John	3	5, 6
	I John	5	4
Abiding with the saints forever	John	14	16
Dwelling in saints	John	14	17
	I Cor.	14	25
Teaching	John	14	26
To testify of Christ	John	15	26
Convincing of sin, righteousness and			
judgment	John	16	8–11
Speaking in and by the prophets	Acts	1	16
Comforter of the church	Acts	9	31
	II Cor.	1	3
Directing where the gospel should be			
preached	Acts	16	6, 7, 10
Appointing and sending ministers	Acts	20	28
Imparting the love of God	Rom.	5	3–5
Imparts hope	Rom.	15	13
	Gal.	5	5
Inspiring scripture	II Tim.	3	16
	II Pet.	1	21
Emblems of:			
A dove	Mat.	3	16
Fire	Ex.	13	21
	Is.	4	4
	Mat.	3	11
Oil	Ex.	29	7
	Is.	61	3
	Mat.	25	3, 4
	Luke	10	34
Rain and dew	Ps.	68	9
	Ps.	72	6
	Ps.	133	3
	Ezek.	34	26, 27
A seal	John	6	27
	Eph.	4	30
	Rev.	7	2
A voice	Is.	6	8
	Mat.	10	20
	Heb.	3	7–11
Water	Ps.	1	3
	Is.	41	17, 18
	Is.	55	1
	John	3	5
	John	7	37, 38
	I Ki.	19	11
Wind	Ezek.	37	9, 10, 14
	John	3	8
Gift of:			
By the Father	Neh.	9	20
	Luke	11	13
Is abundant	Ps.	68	9
	John	7	38, 39
Given	Ps.	68	18
	Luke	11	13
	John	14	16
	Acts	2	38
	Acts	5	32
Is permanent	Is.	59	21
The pledge of continued favour of God	Ezek.	39	29
To Christ without measure	John	3	34
By the Son	John	20	22
Taken away from incorrigible sinners	Rom.	1	24–28
Received through faith	Gal.	3	14
Evidence of union with Christ	I John	3	24
Sin against	Is.	63	10
	Mat.	12	31, 32
	Acts	8	18–22
Instances of inspiration:			
Joseph	Gen.	41	38
Bezaleel	Ex.	31	3
Seventy elders	Num.	11	17
Balaam	Num.	24	2
Joshua	Num.	27	18
The judges	Judg.	3	10
	Judg.	6	34
	Judg.	13	25

King David	I Chr.	28	11, 12
The prophets	II Chr.	15	1
	Zech.	1	1
	Luke	1	41
The disciples	Acts	6	3

holy place *see* tabernacle
holy of holies, *see* tabernacle
Holy Spirit *see* Holy Ghost
holy things

Laws respecting	Ex.	28	38
	Lev.	5	15
	Lev.	22	2
	Neh.	10	33
Office of Levites	I Chr.	23	28
Sin of Jerusalem	Ezek.	22	8

home *dwelling*

Joseph's	Gen.	43	16
Law concerning new wife	Deut.	24	5
Naomi comes	Ruth	1	1
Jeroboam invites man of God	I Ki.	13	7
Reaping	Job	39	12
Creator to be remembered	Eccl.	12	5
Visited by Jesus	Luke	10	38
The church in the	Rom.	16	5
Heavenly	II Cor.	5	1, 2, 6
Religion at	I Tim.	5	4
Directions to wives	Tit.	2	5

See houses and family

homeborn

Law concerning	Ex.	12	49
Israel	Jer.	2	14

homeless *without a home*

Jesus	Luke	9	58
The apostles	I Cor.	4	11

homer, cor *a Hebrew measure*

Ordinances	Ezek.	45	11, 14
Purchased for	Hosea	3	2

homesick

Jacob	Gen.	30	25
Hadad	I Ki.	11	21, 22
Jeroboam	I Ki.	11	40
	I Ki.	12	2, 3
	Ruth	1	6
Israel in exile	Ps.	137	
Prodigal son	Luke	15	11–19
Epaphroditus, possible Timothy	Acts	13	13

homicide *see* murder
honesty *fair dealing*

In business	Lev.	19	35, 36
Brings happiness	Prov.	16	7, 8
Guarantees success	Is.	33	15, 16
Rare in Jerusalem	Jer.	5	1
Trained in	Mark	10	17–20
Of employee	Luke	3	13
In restitution	Luke	19	8
Essential in Christian character	Rom.	12	17
	II Cor.	8	21
Requires diligence	I Thes.	4	11, 12

Examples of:

Jacob, returning money	Gen.	43	12
Samuel	I Sam.	12	1–4
Overseers of the temple repairs	II Ki.	12	15
Treasurers of the temple	Neh.	13	13

honey *liquid from bees*

Not to be offered with any sacrifice	Lev.	2	11
Abundant in Egypt	Num.	16	13
Often sent as a gift	I Ki.	14	3
A good food	Prov.	24	13
Given by the Lord	Ezek.	16	19

Found in:

Rocks	Deut.	32	
	Ps.	81	16
Carcases	Judg.	14	8
Woods	I Sam.	14	25

honeycomb *container for honey*

Pleasant words as	Prov.	16	24
Sweet to the taste	Prov.	24	13
Full soul loathes	Prov.	27	7
Figurative	S. of S.	4	11

honor *esteem due to worth*

Due to parents	Ex.	20	12
	Mat.	15	4
	Eph.	6	2
To the aged	Lev.	19	32
	I Tim.	5	1

Granted by God	I Ki.	3	13
	Esth.	8	16
Due to God	Ps.	29	2
	Is.	58	13
	Rev.	4	11
Judas sells his	Mat.	26	14–16
A posthumous	Acts	9	36–41
To the king	I Pet.	2	17
God over Pharaoh	Ex.	14	17, 18
Promised to Balaam	Num.	22	17, 37
Of Israel	Deut.	26	19
Not for Barak	Judg.	4	9
Given to Solomon	I Ki.	3	13
Of Hezekiah	II Chr.	32	33
Wives give to husbands	Esth.	1	20
Christ crowned with	Heb.	2	7, 9
Wisdom giveth	Prov.	4	8
Humility is before	Prov.	15	33

hoof

None left behind	Ex.	10	26
Of horses	Jer.	47	3
	Ezek.	26	11
Brass	Mic.	4	13
Divided in clean animals	Lev.	11	3–8

hook

For curtains	Ex.	26	32
For pruning	Is.	18	5
Hanging meats	Ezek.	40	43
For fishing	Mat.	17	27
	Amos	4	2
Symbol of peace	Is.	2	4
Beaten into swords	Joel	3	10

hope *trust, reliance*

In God	Ps.	39	7
	I Pet.	1	21
Encouragement to hope	Ps.	130	7
	Zech.	9	12
Brings happiness	Ps.	146	5
Of the wicked shall perish	Prov.	10	28
Comfort in death	Prov.	14	32
Possessed by Paul	Acts	24	15
	II Cor.	3	12
In God's promises	Acts	26	6, 7
	Tit.	1	2
Hope against hope	Rom.	4	18
In Christ	Rom.	5	2
	I Tim.	1	1
Makes not ashamed	Rom.	5	5
Brings salvation	Rom.	8	24
Cannot be seen	Rom.	8	24, 25
Leads to patience	Rom.	8	25
Faith, hope, charity	I Cor.	13	13
In eternal life	I Cor.	15	19
	Tit.	3	7
In the midst of trouble	II Cor.	4	8
A gift from God	II Thes.	2	16
Leads to purity	I John	3	3

Obtained through:

The gospel	Rom.	15	4
	Col.	1	5, 23
Power of the Holy Ghost	Rom.	15	13
Faith	Gal.	5	5
Grace	II Thes.	2	16

hopeless

Naomi of having children for Ruth	Ruth	1	12
Of Job	Job	7	6
	Job	41	9

House of Israel

Wicked	Ezek.	37	11
	Eph.	2	12

Hophni *fighter*

Son of Eli	I Sam.	1	3
A priest	I Sam.	1	3
Sons of worthlessness	I Sam.	2	12
Improper sacrifice	I Sam.	2	16, 17
Rebuked by Eli	I Sam.	2	23
Predicted death	I Sam.	2	34
Came with the ark against the Philistines	I Sam.	4	4
Killed by the Philistines	I Sam.	4	11

hopper *see* grasshopper
Hor *mountain*

Mountain on which Aaron dies	Num.	20	25–28
Mountain in Lebanon	Num.	34	7, 8

Horam *hill*

King of Gezer	Josh.	10	33

Horeb *desert, a range of mountains*

"Mountain of God"	Ex.	3	1
	Ex.	33	6
	Deut.	1	6
Moses gets water out of rock	Ex.	17	6
Moses here forty days	Ex.	24	18
	Ex.	34	28
	Deut.	9	9
Law given on	Deut.	4	10
	Deut.	5	2
	Deut.	18	16
	I Ki.	8	9
	Mal.	4	4
Elijah here forty days	I Ki.	19	8
See Sinai			

Hormah *laid waste*

A Canaanite town in southern Judah	Num.	14	45
	Num.	21	1–3
	Deut.	1	44
Formerly called Zephath	Judg.	1	17
Taken by Judah and Simeon	Josh.	12	14
	Judg.	1	17
Within territory allotted to Judah	Josh.	15	30
	I Sam.	30	30
Near Ziklag	I Sam.	30	30
Allotted to Simeon	Josh.	19	4
	I Chr.	4	30

hornet *wasp*

Destructive	Ex.	23	28
	Deut.	7	20
	Josh.	24	12

horns

Carvings of, used on altar	Ex.	27	2
Figurative of power	Deut.	33	17
	I Ki.	22	11
Musical instruments	Josh.	6	4, 5
	I Chr.	25	5
Used to hold the anointing oil	I Sam.	16	1
	I Ki.	1	39
Figurative of divine protection	II Sam.	22	3
	Ps.	18	2
Made of ivory and ebony	Ezek.	27	15
Natural weapons on heads of animals	Dan.	7	20
Of honour	Lam.	2	3
	I Sam.	2	1, 10
Of an ox	Ex.	21	29
Of Moab	Jer.	48	25
Of Israel	Lam.	2	3
Of a goat	Dan.	8	5
Of the altar	Ex.	30	3
Of iron	I Ki.	22	11
Of a bullock	Ps.	69	31
Of a unicorn	Ps.	92	10
Fourth beast had ten	Dan.	7	7, 20
Represent kings	Dan.	7	24
Of a ram	Dan.	8	6
Of a lamb	Rev.	5	6
Of the beast	Rev.	13	1
For trumpets	Josh.	6	13, 14

horror

Of darkness	Gen.	15	12
Overwhelmed by	Ps.	55	5
	Ps.	119	53

horse

Exchanged for bread	Gen.	47	17
Forbidden to increase	Deut.	17	16
Fed on grain and grass	I Ki.	4	23
	I Ki.	18	5
Many found in Egypt	I Ki.	10	29
	Is.	31	1
Endued with strength	Job	39	19
Trained for war	Prov.	21	31
	Jer.	51	27
Swifter than leopards	Hab.	1	8
Colours of	Zech.	1	8
	Zech.	6	2, 3
Bells on the neck	Zech.	14	20
Controlled by bit and bridle	James	3	3

Used for:

Drawing chariots	Ex.	14	9
Cavalry	I Sam.	13	5
Bearing burdens	Neh.	7	68
Riding	Esth.	6	8–10

horseleach *adherer*

Common in Palestine	Prov.	30	15

horsemen

Pharaoh's	Ex.	14	9
Run from	Joel	2	4
Slain by	Nah.	3	3
Zechariah's	Zech.	1	8
To go to Caesarea to keep Paul safe	Acts	23	23, 32

horsetraders

Tyrus noted for	Ezek.	27	14

hosanna *save, we pray*

The cry when Jesus enters Jerusalem	Mat.	21	9, 15
	Mark	11	9
	John	12	13
Taken from	Ps.	118	25

Hosea *save*

One of minor prophets	Hosea	1	1
Called Osee	Rom.	9	25
Marries Gomer	Hosea	1	3
Three children: Jezreel, Loruhamah, Loammi	Hosea	1	4, 6, 9

hosen

A garment, exact meaning of the Hebrew word is uncertain	Dan.	3	21

Hoshea *salvation*

Called Oshea; original name of Joshua	Num.	13	8, 16
	Deut.	32	44
King of Israel assassinates Pekah and usurps throne	II Ki.	15	30
Evil reign of	II Ki.	17	1, 2
Becomes subject to Assyria	II Ki.	17	3
Conspires against Assyria and is imprisoned	II Ki.	17	4
Last king of Israel	II Ki.	17	6
	II Ki.	18	9–12
A chief of Ephraim	I Chr.	27	20
A Jewish exile	Neh.	10	23

hospitality *hospitable treatment*

Commanded	Rom.	12	13
	I Pet.	4	9
Required of ministers	I Tim.	3	2
	Tit.	1	8
A test of Christian character	I Tim.	5	10
Not to oppress stranger	Ex.	23	9
	Lev.	19	10, 33, 34
Justice to stranger	Deut.	10	18

Should be shown to:

Fatherless and widows	Deut.	26	12
Enemies	II Ki.	6	22, 23
	Rom.	12	20
The poor	Is.	58	7
	Luke	14	13
Strangers	Heb.	13	2

Instances of:

Melchizedek to Abraham	Gen.	14	18
Abimelech to Abraham	Gen.	20	14, 15
Lot to angel	Gen.	19	1–11
Laban to Abraham's servant	Gen.	24	31
Joseph to his brethren	Gen.	43	31–34
Pharaoh to Jacob	Gen.	45	16–20
Martha to Jesus	Luke	10	38
Lydia to Paul and Silas	Acts	16	15
Publius to Paul	Acts	28	8
Wisdom shows	Prov.	9	1–5
Parable	Mat.	22	2–10
Necessary to enter the Kingdom	Mat.	25	34–46

host *multitude*

Army	Gen.	21	22
Angels	Gen.	32	2
	Josh.	5	14
Of the Lord	I Chr.	9	19
Heavenly	Luke	2	13

hostage *one held as security*

Of Jehoash	II Ki.	14	14
	II Chr.	25	24

host of heaven

Object of idolatrous worship	Deut.	4	19
	Jer.	19	13
	II Ki.	17	16
	II Ki.	21	5
	II Ki.	23	4
Angels	I Ki.	22	19
Of stars, sun and moon	Gen.	2	1

hot

Anger and *h* displeasure	Deut.	9	19
Forefront of the *h* battle	II Sam.	11	15
Neither chasten in thy *h* displeasure	Ps.	6	1
	Ps.	38	1

Can one go upon *h* coals	Prov.	6	28
Conscience seared with *h* iron	I Tim.	4	2
Art neither cold nor *h*	Rev.	3	15

hough *cut the leg tendons*
Joshua commanded to do it	Josh.	11	6
David of the captured chariot horses	II Sam.	8	4

hour
One	Dan.	4	19
	Mat.	20	12
	Mark	14	37
	Luke	22	59
Appointed time	Mat.	24	36
	Mark	13	32
	Mark	14	35
	John	2	4
	John	12	27
	John	16	32
Of Christ	John	13	1
	John	7	30
	John	12	23
Of prayer	Acts	3	1
Of temptation	Rev.	3	10
Of judgment	Rev.	14	7
	Rev.	18	10
The third (9 a.m.)	Mat.	20	3
	Mark	15	25
	Acts	2	15
	Acts	23	23
The sixth (12 noon)	Mat.	27	45
	Mark	15	33
	Luke	23	44
	John	4	6
The ninth (3 p.m.)	Mark	15	34
	Acts	3	1
	Acts	10	3, 30
The tenth (4 p.m.)	John	1	39
The eleventh (5 p.m.)	Mat.	20	6
Of prayer	Dan.	6	10
	Acts	2	15

houses
Not to be coveted	Ex.	20	17
Mosaic law regarding sale	Lev.	25	29–33
Dedicated	Deut.	20	5
Built on city walls	Josh.	2	15
Mortgaged	Neh.	5	3
Ceiled and plastered	Dan.	5	5
Sometimes built without foundations	Mat.	7	26
	Luke	6	49
Used for worship	Acts	1	13, 14
	Rom.	16	5
	I Cor.	16	19
Rented	Acts	28	30
Figurative of the body	II Cor.	5	1–5

Built of:
Brick	Ex.	1	11–14
Stone	Lev.	14	40–45
Ivory	I Ki.	22	39
Clay	Job	4	19
Wood	Is.	9	10

Included:
Summer apartments	Judg.	3	20
Porches	Judg.	3	23
Inner chambers	I Ki.	22	25
Courts	Esth.	1	5
Guest chambers	Mark	14	14

Flat roofs:
Surrounded with battlements	Deut.	22	8
Used for drying flax	Josh.	2	6
Used for exercise	II Sam.	11	2
A tent on	II Sam.	16	22
Idolatrous altars on	Jer.	19	13

Of God:
Bethel	Gen.	28	17, 22
Tabernacle	Josh.	9	23
Temple	II Chr.	5	14
Second Temple	Ezra	6	7
Of the church	I Tim.	3	15
Of Israel	II Sam.	12	8
	Ps.	135	19
	Is.	5	7

household
Jacob commands	Gen.	35	2
Jacob's to Egypt	Ex.	1	1
Rahab's delivered	Josh.	6	25

Put in order	II Sam.	17	23
Provided for	Prov.	31	15, 21
Baptized	Acts	16	15
	I Cor.	1	16
Caesar's	Phil.	4	22

Hul *circle*
Grandson of Shem	Gen.	10	23
	I Chr.	1	17

Huldah *weasel*
A prophetess	II Ki.	22	14
	II Chr.	34	22
Wife of Shallum	II Ki.	22	14
Predictions	II Ki.	22	15–20

human sacrifice *see* sacrifice

humiliation
Atonement for	Lev.	16	29–31
Especially of Day of Atonement	Lev.	23	26–33
Because of pride	Dan.	4	29–33
Because of blasphemy	I Sam.	17	42–50
	II Ki.	18	32, 33
Experienced by Joshua	Josh.	7	6–8
Abolished by God	II Chr.	7	14
Acknowledged by Ezra	Ezra	9	1–10
Displayed by Job	Job	2	7–10
Brought about by sin	Luke	15	11–19
Use of	II Cor.	12	6–10

humility *humbleness*
Produced by afflictions	Lev.	26	41
Necessary in prayer	II Chr.	7	14
Lack of, condemned	II Chr.	36	12
	Jer.	44	10
Comes before honour	Prov.	15	33
Excellency of	Prov.	16	19
Leads to riches and honour	Prov.	22	4
A command of God	Mic.	6	8
Blessed	Mat.	5	3
Useful in social life	Luke	14	8–10
Should be cultivated	Col.	3	12

Those who possess are:
Heard by God	Ps.	10	17
Esteemed by God	Is.	66	2
Greatest in Christ's kingdom	Mat.	18	4
	Mat.	20	26–28
Exalted by God	Luke	14	11

Examples of:
Abraham	Gen.	18	27
Jacob	Gen.	32	10
Joseph	Gen.	41	16
Moses	Ex.	3	11
David	I Chr.	29	14
Mephibosheth	II Sam.	9	8
Ahab	I Ki.	21	29
Josiah	II Chr.	34	27
Isiah	Is.	6	5
Job	Job	40	4
John the Baptist	Mat.	3	15, 16
Elisabeth	Luke	1	43
Peter	Luke	5	8
Paul	Acts	20	19
Cornelius	Acts	10	33
John	Rev.	1	9

Of Christ shown in:
Associating with the despised	Mat.	9	10–11
	Luke	15	1–2
Becoming a servant	Mat.	20	28
Birth	Luke	2	4–7
Death	John	10	15, 17–18
	Phil.	2	8
	Heb.	12	2
Entry into Jerusalem	Zech.	9	9
	Mat.	21	5, 7
Exposing himself to reproach and contempt	Ps.	22	6
	Ps.	69	9
	Rom.	15	3
	Is.	53	3
Obedience	John	6	38
	Heb.	10	9
Partaking of our infirmities	Heb.	4	15
	Heb.	5	7
Poverty	Luke	9	58
	II Cor.	8	9
Refusing honors	John	5	41
	John	6	15
Station in life	Mat.	13	55
	John	9	29

humility—*continued*

Subjection to his parents	Luke	2	51
Submitting to sufferings	Is.	50	6
	Is.	53	7
	Acts	8	32
	Mat.	27	37–39
Submitting to ordinances	Mat.	3	13–15
Taking our nature	Phil.	2	7
	Heb.	2	16
Washing his disciples' feet	John	13	5

hunger, physical

Causes discontent among Israelites	Ex.	16	2, 3
Appeased by a miracle	Ex.	16	8–16
A stimulus to work	Prov.	16	26
Endured by Jesus	Mat.	4	1–4
	Mark	11	12
May be appeased on the sabbath	Mat.	12	1–8
Suffered by Peter	Acts	10	9, 10
Suffered by Paul	II Cor.	11	27
None in heaven	Rev.	7	16, 17
Curse	Deut.	28	48
Suffered by the idle	Prov.	19	15
Jeremiah	Jer.	38	9
Slain by	Lam.	4	9
	Rev.	6	8
Test from God	Deut.	8	3
Of an enemy	Rom.	12	20
Of apostles	I Cor.	4	11
Poor	Mat.	25	35
David	Luke	6	3

hunger, spiritual

Promises godliness	Prov.	2	3–5
Buy without money	Is.	55	1, 2
Famine of the word of God	Amos	8	11, 12
Milk of the word	I Pet.	2	2
Is blessed	Mat.	5	6
	Luke	6	21
Taken away by Jesus	John	6	35

hunter, hunting

Nimrod	Gen.	10	9
Ishmael	Gen.	21	20
Esau	Gen.	25	27
	Gen.	27	3, 5, 30
Authorized in Mosaic law	Lev.	17	13
Fowling	I Sam.	26	20
Birds by net, snare	Prov.	1	17
	Amos	3	5
Men snared like birds	Eccl.	9	12
	Lam.	3	52
Figurative	Jer.	16	16
Of Nimrod	Gen.	10	8, 9
Of Ishmael	Gen.	21	20
Of Esau	Gen.	27	3
Of an adulteress	Prov.	6	26

Hur *hole*

An Israelite	Ex.	17	10, 12
	Ex.	24	14
A son of Caleb	Ex.	31	2
	Ex.	35	30
A king of Midian	Num.	31	8
	Josh.	13	21
Called Ben Hur, an officer of Solomon's commissary	I Ki.	4	8
Father of Caleb	I Chr.	2	50
	I Chr.	4	4
A son of Judah	I Chr.	4	1
A ruler	Neh.	3	9

Huram *see* Hiram

hurt *pain*

Slain young man to my *h*	Gen.	4	23
That thou wilt do us no *h*	Gen.	26	29
That sweareth to his own *h*	Ps.	15	4
In power of my hand to do *h*	Gen.	31	29
Ruleth over another to his own *h*	Eccl.	8	9
They shall not *h* nor destroy	Is.	11	9
Have healed *h* slightly	Jer.	6	14
	Jer.	8	11
For the *h* of my people	Jer.	8	21
Ye provoke me to your own *h*	Jer.	25	7
No manner of *h* found upon him	Dan.	6	23
Deadly thing, it shall not *h*	Mark	16	18
Nothing shall by any means *h* you	Luke	10	19
No man set on thee to *h* thee	Acts	18	10
This voyage be with *h*	Acts	27	10
H not earth, neither sea	Rev.	7	3

husband

Duty of, to wives:

Be faithful to them	Prov.	5	19
	Mal.	2	14–15
Consult with them	Gen.	31	4–7
Dwell with them for life	Mat.	19	3–9
Love them	Col.	3	19
Not to leave them, though unbelieving	I Cor.	7	14, 16
Regard them as themselves	Gen.	2	23
	Mat.	19	5
Not to interfere with their duties to Christ	Luke	14	26
	Mat.	19	29
Should have but one wife	Gen.	2	24
	I Cor.	7	2–4
	Mark	10	6–8
Has authority over their wives	Gen.	3	16
	Eph.	5	22, 23
	I Cor.	11	3
Should love and comfort his wife	I Sam.	1	8
	Eph.	5	25
Should be content with one wife	Prov.	5	18
	Eccl.	9	9
Honest	Deut.	22	13–21
Cheering	Deut.	24	5
Shall cleave to his wife	Mat.	19	5
Must accept wife's weaknesses	I Cor.	7	10–13
Duty of wife to	Col.	3	18
Should respect his wife	I Pet.	3	7

Good husbands, exemplified:

Adam	Gen.	3	20
Job	Job	2	7–10
Isaac	Gen.	24	67
Elkanah	I Sam.	1	4–8
Joseph	Mat.	1	19

Bad husbands, exemplified:

Solomon	I Ki.	11	1–4
Ahasuerus	Esth.	1	10–22
Nabal	I Sam.	25	3, 4

husbandman *agriculturist*

Wicked	Mat.	21	33–42
	Mark	12	1–9
Parable of the vine	John	15	1

husbandry *wise management, farming*

For Uzziah	II Chr.	26	10
God's fellow workmen	I Cor.	3	9

husk *hull*

A pod	Num.	6	4
Corn in, brought to priest	II Ki.	4	42
Eaten by prodigal son	Luke	15	16

hyacinth, jacinth *zircon*

A precious stone	Rev.	9	17
	Rev.	21	20

Hymenaeus *a wedding song*

A false teacher	I Tim.	1	20
	II Tim.	2	17

hymn *song of praise*

Spiritual song	Mat.	26	30
	Acts	16	25
	Eph.	5	19
	Col.	3	16
Of Moses	Ex.	15	
Of Deborah	Judg.	5	
Of Hannah	I Sam.	2	1–10
Of Mary	Luke	1	46–55

hypocrisy *feigning to be what one is not*

Denounced by the prophets	Is.	29	13
	Jer.	7	4
Of the Israelites	Is.	48	1
	Is.	58	2–4
Is fault finding	Mat.	7	3–5
Denounced by Jesus	Luke	16	15
Condemned by Paul	I Tim.	4	2
	Tit.	1	16
Hinders spiritual growth	I Pet.	2	1–3

Instances of:

Jacob	Gen.	27	
Delilah	Judg.	16	
Absalom	II Sam.	15	7, 8
Pharisees	Mat.	16	5
Judas	Mat.	26	49
Ananias	Acts	5	1–8
Simon Magus	Acts	8	13–23

hypocrite *pretender, cheat*

Hopes of, shall perish	Job	8	13
Opposed by the upright	Job	17	8

Will be punished	Job	15	34
	Mat.	23	13, 14
	Mat.	24	51
Their worship, not acceptable to God	Is.	1	11
	Mat.	15	7–9
God knows and detects	Is.	29	15, 16
Likes publicity	Mat.	6	2
Christ knows and detects	Mat.	22	18
Characteristics of:			
Destroys others by slander	Prov.	11	9
Vile	Is.	32	6
Holier than thou	Is.	65	5
Professing but not practicing	Ezek.	33	31, 32
	Mat.	23	1–3
Critical of others	Mat.	7	3–5
Regards tradition more than truth	Mat.	15	1–9
Gives lip service	Mat.	15	8
Pretentious	Mat.	23	5
Self-righteous	Luke	18	11
hyssop *aromatic plant*			
Used by Israelites	Ex.	12	22
	Lev.	14	4, 6, 51
A bushy herb of the mint family	I Ki.	4	33
Used in giving Jesus vinegar on the cross	John	19	29
Figurative of spiritual cleansing	Ps.	51	7

I

I AM- *God's title of self-existence*			
To Moses	Ex.	3	14
Of Christ	John	8	57, 58
Ibhar *God's choice*			
Son of David	II Sam.	5	15
Ibleam *destroying*			
City of Manasseh	Josh.	17	11
	Judg.	1	27
	II Ki.	9	27
ice			
Brooks blackish because of	Job	6	16
Like morsels	Ps.	147	17
Iconium *image*			
A city of Asia Minor	Acts	13	51
Paul preaches in	Acts	14	21, 22
Reputation of Timothy there	Acts	16	2
Paul is persecuted by people of	Acts	14	1–6
	II Tim.	3	11
Iconoclasm *image breaking*			
Idols destroyed	Ex.	23	24
	Deut.	7	5
By Jacob	Gen.	35	2–4
My Moses	Ex.	32	19, 20
By Gideon	Judg.	6	28–32
By David	II Sam.	5	21
By Jehu	II Ki.	10	26–28
By Jehoiada	II Ki.	23	4–20
By Jehoshaphat	II Chr.	17	6
Iddo, Jadau *timely*			
Father of Ahinadab	I Ki.	4	14
A descendant of Gershom	I Chr.	6	21
A son of Zechariah	I Chr.	27	21
A prophet	II Chr.	9	29
	II Chr.	12	15
	II Chr.	13	22
Father of Zechariah	Ezra	5	1
	Ezra	6	14
The chief of Jews at Casiphia	Ezra	8	17
Man with a foreign wife	Ezra	10	43
A priest	Neh.	12	4, 16
identification *establish the identity of*			
Of babies	Gen.	38	28
Of a man	Mark	1	6
	II Ki.	1	8
	Gen.	38	25
Of a woman	Gen.	38	15
Hidden	I Ki.	20	38
	I Sam.	28	8
Spiritual	John	1	31–34
	Gal.	2	20
Of the followers of the beast	Rev.	13	16

idleness *slothfulness*			
Accusation of	Ex.	5	6–9
Reproved	Prov.	6	6
	Rom.	12	11
	Heb.	6	12
Leads to:			
Poverty	Prov.	10	4
Hunger	Prov.	19	15
Want	Prov.	20	4
Ruin	Prov.	24	30, 31
Tattling	I Tim.	5	13
idol, image *statue*			
Manufacture of	Ex.	20	4
	Ex.	32	4, 20
	Deut.	4	23
	Is.	40	19, 20
	Is.	44	9–12, 17
	Hab.	2	18
	Acts	19	24, 25
Manufacture of, forbidden	Ex.	20	4
	Ex.	34	17
	Lev.	26	1
Made of gold and silver	Ex.	32	3, 4
	Ps.	115	4
	Ps.	135	15–17
	Is.	2	20
	Is.	30	22
	Is.	31	7
	Hosea	8	4
Things offered to, not to be eaten	Ex.	34	15
Made of wood and stone	Lev.	26	1
	Deut.	4	28
	II Ki.	19	18
	Is.	37	19
	Is.	44	13–19
	Ezek.	20	32
Coverings of	Is.	30	22
idolatry *worship of an image*			
Forbidden	Ex.	20	3–5
	Deut.	4	15–19
To be destroyed	Ex.	23	24
	Deut.	7	5
Punishment of	Deut.	7	16
	Jer.	8	1–3
	I Cor.	6	9
	Eph.	5	5
	Rev.	14	9–11
Folly of	I Ki.	18	26
	Ps.	115	4–8
	Is.	40	19
	Jer.	2	26–28
Consists of:			
Ancestral worship	Ps.	106	28
Worshipping images	Is.	44	17
Worshipping angel	Col.	2	18
Examples of:			
Laban's household	Gen.	31	32–35
Israelites	Ex.	32	1
	Judg.	18	30
Canaanites	Deut.	29	17
Micah	Judg.	17	1–13
Solomon	I Ki.	11	5
Jeroboam	I Ki.	12	28
Ahab	I Ki.	16	30, 31
Manasseh	II Ki.	21	4
Ahaz	II Chr.	28	2
Nebuchadnezzar	Dan.	3	5
Inhabitants of Lystra	Acts	14	11
Athenians	Acts	17	16
Ephesians	Acts	19	28
Galatians	Gal.	4	8
Destroyed by:			
Asa	I Ki.	15	12
Jehoshaphat	II Chr.	17	6
Hezekiah	II Chr.	30	14
Josiah	II Chr.	34	1–7
Idumaea, Idumea *see Edom*			
ignorance *destitute of knowledge*			
Sin offerings for	Num.	15	22–29
Of the Sadducees	Mat.	22	23–33
Effects of	Rom.	10	3
	II Pet.	3	5
Man's condition before God	Job	28	12
	Ps.	139	6
Of youths	Prov.	7	6–23

ignorance—*continued*

Of the future	Eccl.	8	6, 7
Of how to live	Jer.	10	23
Paul's deprecation of	I Cor.	10	1
	I Cor.	12	1–31
Caused by sin	Eph.	4	18
A cure for	II Tim.	2	15

Examples of:

Sinners	Mat.	13	15
Soldiers at the cross	Luke	23	34
Nicodemus	John	3	9, 10
Samaritan woman	John	4	9, 10
Philip	John	14	8, 9
Abimelech	Gen.	20	1–18

illumination *insight*

Spiritual	I Cor.	2	10
Remember when	Heb.	10	32
General call	John	1	9

illustration *an example*

Use of the Old Testament	I Cor.	10	6
Men's lives	Heb.	12	
	Acts	7	
Allegory	Gal.	4	22–27

Illyricum, Dalmatia *joy*

Visited by Paul	Rom.	15	19
Visited by Titus	II Tim.	4	10

image *likeness*

Man created in, of God	Gen.	1	26, 27
	Gen.	5	1
	Gen.	9	6
	James	3	9
Man regenerated into	Rom.	8	29
	II Cor.	3	18
	Col.	3	10
Christ, of God	Col.	1	15
	Heb.	1	3
Of jealousy	Ezek.	8	3, 5

See idol

imagination

Of man, evil	Gen.	6	5
	Deut.	31	21
	Gen.	8	21
	Jer.	23	17
I of heart evil	Gen.	8	21
Walk in *i* of heart	Deut.	29	19
Lord understandeth all *i* of the thoughts	I Chr.	28	9
Scattered the proud in *i* of their hearts	Luke	1	51
Became vain in their *i*	Rom.	1	21
Casting down *i*	II Cor.	10	5

imagine *mind picture*

Why do people *i* vain things	Ps.	2	1
	Acts	4	25
How long will ye *i* mischief	Ps.	62	3
What do ye *i* against the Lord	Nah.	1	9
Let none *i* evil	Zech.	7	10
	Zech.	8	17

Immauel *see* Emmanuel

Immer *loquacious*

A family of priests	I Chr.	9	12
	Ezra	2	37
	Ezra	10	20
	Neh.	7	40
	Neh.	11	13
Head of a division of priests	I Chr.	24	14
Name of a man or town	Ezra	2	59
	Neh.	7	61
Father of Zadok	Neh.	3	29
Father of Pashur	Jer.	20	1, 2

immortality *deathlessness*

David's faith in	II Sam.	12	19–23
The spirit of man	Eccl.	12	7
Ascribed to God and Christ	I Tim.	1	17
	I Tim.	6	13–16
	Ps.	102	24–28
	Ex.	3	14

Proofs of:

Testimony of David	Ps.	49	15
The transfiguration	Mat.	17	1–6
The dead shall live	John	5	25, 28, 29
Believers to be raised up	John	6	40
"This mortal must put on immortality"	I Cor.	15	51–54
Teachings of the gospel	II Tim.	1	10
Testimony of Peter	I Pet.	1	3, 4
Promised by God	I John	2	17, 25
Enoch	Gen.	5	24
Elijah	II Ki.	2	11

Eternal inheritance	Ps.	37	18
Victory over death	Ps.	49	14, 15
Pharaoh	Ezek.	32	31
Future blessings	Mark	10	30
	John	14	1–4

immutability *unchangeable*

Claimed by God	Mat.	3	6
By his attributes	Tit.	1	2
Of his counsel	Heb.	6	17, 18
Compared to earth	Heb.	1	11, 12
Does not vary	James	1	17
Constant at beginning and end	Rev.	1	8–18
Christ: unchangeable priesthood	Heb.	7	24
Christ: yesterday, today, forever	Heb.	13	8

impartiality *fairness*

Of God	Acts	10	34
	Eph.	6	9
	Col.	3	25
In regard to wealth of people	James	2	1–9
In judgment	I Pet.	1	17

impenitence *not penitent*

Of Pharaoh	Ex.	9	30, 34
	Ex.	10	27
	Ex.	14	5, 8
Of Israelites	Num.	14	22, 23
	II Ki.	17	14
	II Chr.	24	19
	II Chr.	36	16, 17
	Neh.	9	16, 17, 29, 30
	Jer.	36	31
Of Eli's sons	I Sam.	2	25
Of Amaziah	II Chr.	25	16
Of Manasseh	II Chr.	33	10
Of Amon	II Chr.	33	23
Zedekiah	II Chr.	36	12, 13
	Jer.	37	2
Belshazzar	Dan.	5	22, 23
The rich young man	Mat.	19	22
In the synagogue	Mark	3	5
Before judgment	Rom.	2	5

impetuous *acting thoughtlessly*

Esau	Gen.	25	29–30
Vashti	Esth.	1	10–12
Nabal	I Sam.	25	10–11
Joab	II Sam.	18	14

impossible

Nothing shall be *i* unto you	Mat.	17	20
With men it is *i*	Mat.	19	26
	Mark	10	27
	Luke	18	27
With God nothing *i*	Luke	1	37
	Luke	18	27
It is *i* but that offences will come	Luke	17	1
I for those enlightened	Heb.	6	4
Without faith it is *i* to please God	Heb.	11	6

imposter *disguised*

Saul	I Sam.	28	8
David	I Sam.	21	13, 14
Ahab	I Ki.	22	30
Josiah	II Chr.	35	22
Gibeonites	Josh.	9	3–14
Antichrist	II Thes.	2	1–4

impotence *weakness*

Of folk at pool of Bethesda	John	5	3, 7
Of man healed by Peter	Acts	4	9
Of man healed by Paul	Acts	14	8

imprisonment *confinement*

Of Joseph	Gen.	39	20
Of Jeremiah	Jer.	38	6
Of debtors	Mat.	5	25, 26
	Mat.	18	30
Of John the Baptist	Mat.	11	2
	Mat.	14	3
Of apostles	Acts	5	18
Of Peter	Acts	12	4
Of Paul and Silas	Acts	16	24

Incarnation *see* Christ

incense *sweet smell*

Formula for compounding	Ex.	30	34, 35
Uses of	Ex.	30	36–38
	Lev.	16	12
	Num.	16	17, 40, 46
	Deut.	33	10

Compounded:

By Bezaleel	Ex.	37	29
By priests	I Chr.	9	30

Offered:			
Morning and evening	Ex.	30	7, 8
	II Chr.	13	11
On the altar	Ex.	30	1, 7
	Ex.	40	5, 27
	II Chr.	2	4
	II Chr.	32	12
In making atonement	Lev.	16	12, 13
	Num.	16	46, 47
	Luke	1	10
In idolatrous worship	I Ki.	12	33
	Jer.	41	5
	Ezek.	8	11
Presented by wise men to Jesus	Mat.	2	11
Figurative:			
Of prayer	Ps.	141	2
Of praise	Mal.	1	11
Of an acceptable sacrifice	Eph.	5	2
Symbolic:			
Of the prayers of saint	Rev.	5	8
	Rev.	8	3, 4
incest *an unnatural vice*			
Defined and forbidden	Lev.	18	6–18
	Lev.	20	11, 12, 17, 19–21
	Deut.	22	30
	Deut.	27	20, 22, 23
	Ezek.	22	11
	I Cor.	5	1
Instances of:			
Lot with his daughters	Gen.	19	31–36
Abraham	Gen.	20	12
Reuben	Gen.	35	22
	Gen.	49	4
Judah	Gen.	38	16–18
	I Chr.	2	4
Amram	Ex.	6	20
Amnon	II Sam.	13	14
Absalom	II Sam.	16	21, 22
Israel	Amos	2	7
Herod	Mat.	14	3, 4
	Mark	6	17, 18
Marriage of near of kin:			
Isaac with Rebekah	Gen.	24	15, 67
Jacob with Leah and Rachel	Gen.	29	23, 30
Rehoboam	II Chr.	11	18
incline *lean*			
I your heart to the Lord	Josh.	24	23
That he may *i* our hearts to keep the law	I Ki.	8	58
I your ears to the words of my mouth	Ps.	78	1
I his ear unto me	Ps.	116	2
I my heart to thy testimonies	Ps.	119	36
Her house *i* unto death	Prov.	2	18
Nor *i* ear	Jer.	7	24
	Jer.	11	8
	Jer.	17	23
	Jer.	34	14
incorruptible *not corrupted*			
To obtain an *i* crown	I Cor.	9	25
The dead shall be raised *i*	I Cor.	15	52
An inheritance *i*	I Pet.	1	4
increase			
The land shall yield her *i*	Lev.	26	4
Tithe all *i* of thy seed	Deut.	14	22
Thy latter end greatly *i*	Job	8	7
That scattereth and yet *i*	Job	11	24
If riches *i*, set not heart on them	Ps.	62	10
Earth shall yield her *i*	Ps.	67	6
	Ezek.	34	27
Lord shall *i* you more and more	Ezek.	115	14
With the *i* of his lips	Prov.	18	20
A wise man will *i* learning	Prov.	1	5
	Prov.	9	9
He that *i* knowledge, *i* sorrow	Eccl.	1	18
Not be satisfied with *i*	Eccl.	5	10
Of *i* of his government shall be no end	Is.	9	7
He *i* strength	Is.	40	29
Knowledge shall be *i*	Dan.	12	4
He daily *i* lies	Hosea	12	1
Jesus *i* in wisdom	Luke	2	52
Lord, *i* our faith	Luke	17	5
He must *i*, I decrease	John	3	30
Word of God *i*	Acts	6	7
Churches *i* daily	Acts	16	5

God gave the *i*	I Cor.	3	6
I in the knowledge of God	Col.	1	10
Body *i* with *i* of God	Col.	2	19
That ye *i* more and more	I Thes.	4	10
I am rich, and *i* with goods	Rev.	3	17
(ar.), interest	Lev.	25	36
Offspring	I Sam.	2	33
indeed			
Shalt thou *i* reign over us	Gen.	37	8
Will God *i* dwell on the earth	I Ki.	8	27
Thou wouldest bless me *i*	I Chr.	4	10
Hear ye *i*, see ye *i*	Is.	6	9
A prophet *i*	Mark	11	32
The Lord is risen *i*	Luke	24	34
An Israelite *i*	John	1	47
That this is *i* the Christ	John	4	42
My flesh is meat *i*, and my blood is drink *i*	John	6	55
Ye shall be free *i*	John	8	36
indecision *unable to decide*			
Israel before Elijah	I Ki.	18	21
Faulty	Hosea	10	2
Cannot serve two masters	Mat.	6	24
Spirit-flesh	Mat.	26	41
	James	4	17
Double minded	James	1	8
Moses	Ex.	14	15
Joshua	Josh.	7	10
Esther	Esth.	5	8
Believing rulers	John	12	42
Felix	Acts	24	25
India			
Eastern boundary of Persian Empire	Esth.	1	1
	Esth.	8	9
indictments *formal accusations*			
Naboth	I Ki.	21	13
Jeremiah	Jer.	26	1–24
	Jer.	37	13–15
Daniel	Dan.	6	13
Jesus:			
Of blasphemy	Mat.	26	61, 63–65
	Mark	14	58, 61–64
	Luke	22	67–71
	John	19	7
Of treason	Mat.	27	11, 37
	Mark	15	2, 26
	Luke	23	2, 3, 38
	John	18	30, 33
	John	19	12, 19–22
Stephen	Acts	6	11, 13
Paul	Acts	17	7
	Acts	18	13
	Acts	24	5
	Acts	25	18, 19, 26, 27
Paul and Silas	Acts	16	20, 21
indifference *uncaring*			
Denounced	Amos	6	1
To be destroyed	Is.	47	8, 9
Inhabitants of Laish	Judg.	18	7
Admonished	Is.	32	9, 10, 11
Merciless	Luke	10	30–36
Laodicea	Rev.	3	14–17
Gallio	Acts	18	12, 17
indignation *anger*			
Pour out thine *i* upon them	Ps.	69	24
Wrath, *i*, and trouble	Ps.	78	49
Till the *i* be overpast	Is.	26	20
Who can stand before his *i*	Nah.	1	6
Moved with *i*	Mat.	20	24
They had *i*	Mat.	26	8
They were filled with *i*	Acts	5	17
Yea, what *i*	II Cor.	7	11
Fearful looking for of fiery *i*	Heb.	10	27
The cup of his *i*	Rev.	14	10
indiscrimination *lack of distinction*			
Calamities	Is.	24	1–4
God	Mat.	5	45
Peter was not	Gal.	2	12–14
Needed in church	James	2	2, 3
industry *earnest application to work*			
Commanded	Gen.	2	15
	Prov.	6	6
	Prov.	13	4
	Eph.	4	28
	Tit.	3	14
Rewarded	Prov.	13	13
	Prov.	31	31

infant *young child*

Slay man, woman, *i*	I Sam.	15	3
No more thence an *i* of	Is.	65	20

infants

As *i* which never saw light	Job	3	16
I shall be dashed in	Hosea	13	16
Brought also *i* to him	Luke	18	15

infanticide *child murder*

Ordered by Pharaoh	Ex.	1	15, 16
Ordered by Herod	Mat.	2	16–18

inferior *lower position, quality*

I am not *i* to you	Job	12	3
	Job	13	2
Another kingdom *i* to thee	Dan.	2	39
Ye *i* to other churches	II Cor.	12	13

infidelity *not believing or faithful*

By Satan	II Cor.	4	4
By lusts	James	1	13
By pride	John	5	44
To be avoided	II Cor.	6	15–17
One not supporting his family	I Tim.	5	8
Examples:			
Cain	Gen.	4	6, 7
Balaam	Num.	24	
Korah	Num.	16	1–3, 33
Simon Magus	Acts	8	18, 20

infinite *without limit, endless*

Not thine iniquities *i*	Job	22	5
His understanding is *i*	Ps.	147	5
Her strength, and it was *i*	Nah.	3	9

infirmity *weakness*

This is mine *i*	Ps.	77	10
Spirit of man will sustain his *i*	Prov.	18	14
Himself took our *i*	Mat.	8	17
The *i* of your flesh	Rom.	6	19
The Spirit also helpeth our *i*	Rom.	8	26
Strong bear the *i* of the weak	Rom.	15	1
Take pleasure in *i*	II Cor.	12	10
Touched with the feeling of our *i*	Heb.	4	15

ingathering, feast of *see* feasts and festivals

ingratitude *ill return for kindnesses*

Of man to God	Num.	16	9, 10
	Deut.	8	12–14
	Deut.	28	47, 48
	Judg.	2	10–12
	I Sam.	8	7, 8
	I Ki.	16	1–3
	Rom.	1	21
Examples of:			
Israel	Deut.	32	18
	Judg.	8	34, 35
	Judg.	10	11–14
Saul	I Sam.	15	11, 16–23
David	II Sam.	12	7, 9
Nebuchadnezzar	Dan.	5	2, 3, 19–23
The lepers	Luke	17	12–18
Punishment of	Prov.	17	13
	Jer.	18	20
Of man to man	II Tim.	3	2
Examples of:			
Laban to Jacob	Gen.	31	1–43
Pharaoh's butler to Joseph	Gen.	40	23
Israelites to Moses	Ex.	16	3
	Ex.	17	2–4
	Num.	16	12–14
Israelites to Gideon	Judg.	8	35
Men of Keilah to David	I Sam.	23	5–12
Saul to David	I Sam.	24	17
David to Uriah	II Sam.	11	6–17, 27
David to Joab	I Ki.	2	5, 6

inheritance *right of receiving*

Of the meek	Ps.	37	11, 12
Of those who trust in God	Is.	57	13
Of property	Luke	15	11, 12
Of Israel:			
The land of Canaan	Lev.	20	24
Law of	Num.	27	6–11
	Deut.	21	15
None to priests	Num.	18	20
Land allotted to various tribes	Josh.	14	1–5
Spiritual:			
In Christ	Eph.	1	11
	Col.	3	24
	I Pet.	1	4
Those excluded from	Eph.	5	5
Among the saints	Col.	1	12

iniquity *see* sin

The *i* of the Amorites	Gen.	15	16
Visiting the *i* of the fathers	Ex.	20	5
	Ex.	34	7
	Num.	14	18
	Deut.	5	9
Forgiving *i* and transgression	Ex.	34	7
	Num.	14	18
A God of truth without *i*	Deut.	32	4
They that plow *i* reap the same	Job	4	8
I stoppeth her mouth	Job	5	16
If I have done *i*, I will do no more	Job	34	32
Pardon mine *i*, for it is great	Ps.	25	11
Blessed to whom Lord imputeth not *i*	Ps.	32	2
I was shapen in *i*	Ps.	51	5
If I regard *i* in my heart	Ps.	66	18
Add *i* to their *i*	Ps.	69	27
Thou hast set our *i* before thee	Ps.	90	8
Who forgiveth all thine *i*	Ps.	103	3
If thou shouldest mark *i*	Ps.	130	3
He that soweth *i* shall reap vanity	Prov.	22	8
A people laden with *i*	Is.	1	4
Woe to them that draw *i*	Is.	5	18
Thine *i* is taken away	Is.	6	7
Her *i* is pardoned	Is.	40	2
He was bruised for our *i*	Is.	53	5
Make reconciliation for *i*	Dan.	9	24
Take away *i*, receive us graciously	Hosea	14	2
Canst not look on *i*	Hab.	1	13
I shall abound	Mat.	24	12
Purchased field with reward of *i*	Acts	1	18
In bond of *i*	Acts	8	23
Servants to *i* unto *i*	Rom.	6	19
The mystery of *i* doth work	II Thes.	2	7
Depart from *i*	II Tim.	2	19
Redeem us from *i*	Tit.	2	14
Tongue is a world of *i*	James	3	6
God hath remembered *i*	Rev.	18	5
Injured	Gal.	4	12

injustice *wrong*

Forbidden	Ex.	22	21
	Ex.	23	6
	Lev.	19	15
	Deut.	16	19
	Deut.	24	17
	Job	31	16, 21, 28
	Ps.	82	2
	Prov.	29	7
	Jer.	22	3
	Luke	16	10, 11
Results of	Prov.	11	7
	Prov.	22	16
	Prov.	28	8
	Amos	5	11
	Amos	8	4–7
	Mic.	6	10, 13–15

ink

Used in book	Jer.	36	18
For writing	II Cor.	3	3
	II John		12
	III John		13

inkhorn

Used by writers	Ezek.	9	2, 3, 11

inn *halting place for caravans*

Joseph's brothers stop at	Gen.	42	27
	Gen.	43	21
Zipporah circumcises son at	Ex.	4	24
Bethlehem, crowded	Luke	2	7
Samaritan taken to	Luke	10	34

inner circle

Jesus' close companions	Mat.	26	36, 37
	Mark	5	37–42
	Mark	9	2

innocence *guiltlessness*

Signified by washing hands	Deut.	21	6
	Ps.	26	6
	Mat.	27	24
Found in Jeremiah	Jer.	2	35
Found in Daniel	Dan.	6	22
Professed by Pilate	Mat.	27	24
Contrasted with guilt	Gen.	2	25
	Gen.	3	7–11
Of Christ	Is.	53	7–9
	Acts	13	28
Believers before God	II Cor.	5	21

innumerable *without number*

Sand	Gen.	22	17
Stars	Gen.	15	5
Hair of your head	Mat.	10	30
Angels	Heb.	12	22
People that followed Christ	Luke	12	1
Grasshoppers	Jer.	46	23
Evils	Ps.	40	12

insanity *madness*

A judgment from God	Deut.	28	28
	Zech.	12	4
Feigned by David	I Sam.	21	13–15
Nebuchadnezzar's	Dan.	4	32–34
Cured by Jesus	Mat.	4	24
	Mat.	17	15
Jesus accused of	Mark	3	21
	John	10	20
Paul accused of	Acts	26	24, 25
See demons			

inscription *writing*

On gravestones	II Ki.	23	17
On cross	Mat.	27	37
	Mark	15	26
	Luke	23	38
	John	19	19
Found by Paul in Athens	Acts	17	23

insects

Clean and unclean	Lev.	11	21–25
	Deut.	14	19
Ant	Prov.	6	6
Bee	Is.	7	18
Beetle	Lev.	11	22
Cankerworm	Joel	2	25
Caterpillar	Jer.	51	14
Flea	I Sam.	26	20
Flies	Ex.	8	21
Gnat	Mat.	23	24
Grasshopper	Amos	7	1
Moth	Luke	12	33
Lice	Ex.	8	16
Palmerworm	Joel	2	25
Scorpion	I Ki.	12	11
Snail	Lev.	11	30
Spider	Prov.	30	28
Worm	Mark	9	44

insincerity *see hypocrisy*

insomnia *sleeplessness*
Instances of:

Ahasuerus	Esth.	6	1
Job	Job	7	4
Nebuchadnezzar	Dan.	2	1
Darius	Dan.	6	9, 18
Paul and Silas	Acts	16	25

inspiration

For works of art	Ex.	31	2–5
All scripture given by	II Sam.	23	2
	II Tim.	3	16
	II Pet.	1	21
The words	Jer.	1	9
	I Ki.	16	1
	Deut.	18	18
	Ex.	4	10–15
	Jer.	1	9
By a voice	Is.	6	8
	Acts	8	28
Given to the prophets	Is.	51	16
	Jer.	1	9, 10
Directs ministers	Ezek.	3	24–27
	Acts	11	12
Of the Holy Ghost, foretold	Joel	2	28
By incarnation	John	1	1, 14, 18
	Heb.	1	1, 2
By visions	Ezek.	1	1
	Ezek.	40	1, 2
In a trance	Acts	10	9–16
By dreams	Gen.	28	10–17
	Mat.	1	18–21
Purpose of	John	20	30, 31
Written	Ex.	17	24
	Num.	33	2
	Jer.	36	1, 2
Necessity	Rom.	10	17
Inerrant	John	10	35
Claims of Old Testament	Ex.	34	27
Unchangeable	Mat.	5	18, 19
	Deut.	4	2
	Rev.	22	18, 19

Records God's words	Ex.	32	16
	Mat.	17	5
	I Chr.	28	19

instability *fickleness*
Instances of:

Lot's wife	Gen.	19	17, 26
Reuben	Gen.	49	4
Saul toward David	I Sam.	18	19
David in yielding to lust	II Sam.	11	2–9
Solomon in yielding to wives	I Ki.	11	1–8
Ephraim and Judah	Hosea	6	4
Disciples	John	6	66
Mark	Acts	15	38
Denounced	James	1	6, 8
	II Pet.	2	14

instant

It shall be at an *i* suddenly	Is.	29	5
They besought him *i*	Luke	7	4
Twelve tribes *i* serving God (ar.), urgent, importunate	Acts	26	7
Continuing *i* in prayer	Rom.	12	12
Be *i* in season, out of season	II Tim.	4	2

instruction

From nature	Prov.	24	30–34
From study of human nature	Eccl.	3–12	
By object lessons:			
The pot of manna	Ex.	16	32
The pillar of twelve stones	Josh.	4	19–24
Wearing sackcloth, going barefoot	Is.	20	2, 3
Potter's vessel	Jer.	19	1–12
Illustrations on a tile	Ezek.	4	1–3
Eating and drinking sparingly	Ezek.	12	18–20
The boiling pot	Ezek.	24	1–14
Widowhood	Ezek.	24	16–27
See symbols and parables			

instrument

I of cruelty in habitations	Gen.	49	5
Prepared the *i* of death	Ps.	7	13
Sing with *i* of ten strings	Ps.	33	2
	Ps.	92	3
My songs to the stringed *i*	Is.	38	20
Sharp threshing *i*	Is.	41	15
One that can play on an *i*	Ezek.	33	32
Members *i* of unrighteousness	Rom.	6	13

insult *gross indignity*

Ignored by Saul	I Sam.	10	26, 27
Inflicted on Jesus	Luke	4	16, 28, 29
Inflicted on Paul	Acts	23	1–5
Of David	II Sam.	16	5–11
Of Elijah	II Ki.	2	24

insurrection *revolt*

Led by Sheba	II Sam.	20	1–22
Described by David	Ps.	55	1–23
Barabbas	Mark	15	7

integrity *uprightness*

Commanded by God	Gen.	18	19
	Ex.	18	21
	Deut.	16	19
Of David	I Sam.	24	16–22
	Ps.	26	1
Maintained by Job	Job	27	4
	Job	31	6, 7
Brings a reward	Ps.	18	20
	Ps.	24	3, 4
	Prov.	28	20
Provides guidance	Prov.	11	3
Yields contentment	Prov.	14	30
	Prov.	21	3, 15
A man of, described	Ezek.	18	5–9
Explained by Christ	Mat.	7	12
	Luke	6	31
Apostles, men of	II Cor.	7	2
	I Tim.	1	5
	Heb.	13	18

intemperance *lack of control, moderation*

Punishment of	Deut.	21	20
	Is.	28	1
	Nah.	1	10
	I Cor.	6	10
Dangers of	Prov.	23	21, 29–32
Not for kings	Prov.	31	4, 5
Warning against	Luke	12	45
	Rom.	13	13
In the church	I Cor.	11	20–22

intemperance—*continued*
Instances of:

Noah	Gen.	9	21
Lot	Gen.	19	32
Joseph and his brethren	Gen.	43	34
Israel	Num.	11	4, 18, 20, 33
Sons of Eli	I Sam.	2	12–17
Nabal	I Sam.	25	36
Ammon	II Sam.	13	28, 29
Ahasuerus	Esth.	1	10
Belshazzar	Dan.	5	1
King of Israel	Hosea	7	5

Falsely accused of:

Hannah	I Sam.	1	12–16
Jesus	Mat.	11	19
The disciples	Acts	2	13–15

See drunkard, drunkenness, gluttony

intend *plan*

Did not *i* to go up	Josh.	22	23
Ye *i* to add more to	II Chr.	28	13
Ye *i* to bring this man's	Acts	5	28
What ye *i* to do as touching	Acts	5	35

intended

For they *i* evil against	Ps.	21	11

intendest

I thou to kill me, as the	Ex.	2	14

intending

Which of you *i* to build	Luke	14	28
I after Easter to bring	Acts	12	4
Sailed to Assos, there *i* to	Acts	20	13

intent *purpose*

To the *i* the Lord might	II Sam.	17	14
To *i* he might destroy	II Ki.	10	19
To the *i* he might let	II Chr.	16	1
To the *i* that I might	Ezek.	40	4
To the *i* that the living	Dan.	4	17
Not there to the *i* ye	John	11	15
For what *i* he spake this to	John	13	28
And came hither for that *i*	Acts	9	21
I ask for what *i* ye have	Acts	10	29
To the *i* we should not	I Cor.	10	6
To the *i* that now to the	Eph.	3	10

intercession *petition in behalf of another*

Of Moses for the Israelites	Ex.	32	9–14
	Num.	14	19
Of Samuel	I Sam.	7	5–7
Of David for Solomon	I Chr.	29	18, 19
Of Job for his sons	Job	1	1–5
Asked by Paul	Rom.	15	30
Of the elders of the church for the sick	James	5	14

Of Christ:

For weak	Luke	22	32
In behalf of sinners	Luke	23	34
For His followers	John	17	9, 11

Of man with man:

Reuben in behalf of Joseph	Gen.	37	21, 22
Jonathan in behalf of David	I Sam.	19	1–6
David in behalf of Saul	I Sam.	24	4–12
Bath-sheba in behalf of Solomon	I Ki.	1	15–20
Festus in behalf of Paul	Acts	25	4–21

interest *usury*

not to a poor brother	Ex.	22	25
	Lev.	25	36
May unto a stranger	Deut.	23	20
Cry of the poor because of	Neh.	5	1–13
Promise	Ps.	15	5
Prophetic commendation	Ezek.	18	8, 9
Parable about	Luke	19	12–27

intermediate state *pre-resurrect state of the dead*

Conscious	Rev.	6	9–12
	Luke	16	19–31
Presence with the Lord	II Cor.	5	6–9
Better than life	Phil.	1	23, 24
No communication with the living	Ex.	22	18
	Deut.	18	10–12
	Luke	16	19–31
Samuel	I Sam.	28	7–25
Transfiguration	Mat.	16	28
	Mat.	17	13
Immediately in paradise	Luke	23	43
	Eccl.	12	7
Bodies buried in earth	Mat.	27	51–53
	Rom.	1	4

interpreter *translator*

Of dreams	Gen.	40	8
	Dan.	2	18–30

Of language	Gen.	42	23
	Neh.	8	8
In Christian churches	I Cor.	12	10
	I Cor.	14	5, 13

intolerance *bigotry*

Of idolatrous religions	Ex.	22	20
	Deut.	17	1–7
Of the Jews, in persecuting Jesus	Mat.	27	27–31
	Mark	14	43–58
	John	19	15, 16
Denounced by Jesus	Mark	9	38, 39
Suffered by the disciples	Acts	4	1–3
	Acts	7	57–60
	Acts	21	30–40
Elijah	I Ki.	18	40
Jehu	II Ki.	10	18–31
Jews under Azariah	II Chr.	15	12, 13

inventions

Use of metals	Gen.	4	22
Engines of war	II Chr.	26	15
Of musical instruments by David	I Chr.	23	5
	Amos	6	5
Provoke God	Ps.	106	29
Many are sought	Eccl.	7	29

invisible *cannot be seen*

May be seen through creation	Rom.	1	20
God is	I Tim.	1	17
May be seen through faith	Heb.	11	27

inward *Wisdom in the i parts*

Truth in the *i* parts	Job	38	36
	Ps.	51	6
I thought of every one is deep	Ps.	64	6
I will put my law in their *i* parts	Jer.	31	33
I part is full of ravening	Luke	11	39
Law of God after the *i* man	Rom.	7	22
The *i* man is renewed	II Cor.	4	16

Irad *fugitive*

Son of Enoch	Gen.	4	18

Irijah *Jehovah sees*

A captain who imprisons Jeremiah	Jer.	37	13, 14

iron *the most common and useful of all metals*

First recorded use of	Gen.	4	22
Ore	Deut.	8	9
	Job	28	2
Axe head of, swims	II Ki.	6	5, 6
Barbed	Job	41	7
Melted	Ezek.	22	20

Uses:

In temple	I Chr.	22	3
	I Chr.	29	2, 7
Axes	II Ki.	6	5
	Is.	10	34
Bedstead	Deut.	3	11
Breastplate	Rev.	9	9
Chariot	Josh.	17	16, 18
	Judg.	1	19
Fetters	Ps.	149	8
Furnace	Deut.	4	20
Gate	Acts	12	10
Harrow	II Sam.	12	31
Idols	Dan.	2	33
	Dan.	5	4
Yokes	Jer.	28	13
Armor	II Sam.	23	7
Spear head of Goliath	I Sam.	17	7
Threshing instruments	Amos	1	3
Weapons	Num.	35	16

irony *expressing the opposite*

Michal	II Sam.	6	20
Elijah	I Ki.	18	27
Job	Job	12	2
Ezekiel	Ezek.	28	3–5
Amos	Amos	4	4
Pilate	Mark	15	19
	Mat.	27	37
Jesus	Mark	2	17

Iru *city wise*

Eldest son of Caleb	I Chr.	4	15

Isaac *laughter*

Son of Abraham and Sarah promised	Gen.	17	15–19
God's covenant with	Gen.	17	21
Born	Gen.	21	1–8
Offered in sacrifice by his father	Gen.	22	1–19
	Heb.	11	17
Husband of Rebekah	Gen.	24	67
	Gen.	25	20

Covenant reaffirmed	Gen.	26	2–5
Dwells in southern Palestine	Gen.	24	62
A peaceful and devout man	Gen.	24	63
	Gen.	26	14–22
Buries his father	Gen.	25	9
Father of Esau and Jacob	Gen.	25	24–26
Possesses large flocks and herds	Gen.	26	12–14
Lies about Rebekah	Gen.	26	7–11
Strife over wells	Gen.	26	15, 21
Deceived by Rebekah and Jacob	Gen.	27	1–25
Blesses Jacob	Gen.	27	19–29
Blesses Esau	Gen.	27	38–40
His death and burial	Gen.	35	27–29
Ancestor of Jesus	Mat.	1	1, 2
Obedience	Gen.	22	9
Peaceableness	Gen.	26	14–22
A prophet	Neh.	11	20
Devout	Gen.	24	63
	Gen.	25	21

Isaiah, Esaias *the salvation of Jah*

Prophet, son of Amoz	Is.	1	1
His call	Is.	6	1–13
Sent to Ahaz	Is.	7	1–9
Contemporary of Amos and Hosea	Amos	1	1
	Hosea	1	1
Special sons	Is.	8	1–4, 18
Acts out message	Is.	20	2, 3
Writes about Uzziah and Hezekiah	II Chr.	26	22
	II Chr.	32	32
Prophesies concerning various nations	Is.	7–10	
	Is.	13–23	
	Is.	45–47	
Sent to Hezekiah	Is.	37	1–7
	Is.	38	4–22
	Is.	39	3–8
Fulfillment of prophecies	Mat.	3	3
	Mat.	4	14
	Mark	1	2
	Luke	4	17
	Rom.	9	29

Important prophecies:

The kingdom of Christ	Is.	2	1–5
	Is.	32	1–5
Birth of Christ	Is.	7	14
Assyrian invasion	Is.	8	1–4
Calls Christ, the root of Jesse	Is.	11	1–9
Destruction by Babylon	Is.	13	1–22
Babylonian captivity	Is.	39	3–7
Preaching of John the Baptist	Is.	40	3–8
Sufferings of Christ	Is.	53	1–2
Of Moab	Is.	16	1–14
Of Tyre and Sidon	Is.	23	1–18
Of Sennacherib	Is.	37	14–38

Iscariot *see* Judas

Ishbak *leaving*

Son of Abraham and Keturah	Gen.	25	2
	I Chr.	1	32

Ish-bosheth, Esh-baal *man of shame*

Youngest son of Saul	II Sam.	2	8
Rival of David for the throne of Israel	II Sam.	2	8–10
Beheaded	II Sam.	4	5–12
Called Esh-baal	I Chr.	8	33

Ishi *my man*

Son of Appaim	I Chr.	2	31
A Judahite chief	I Chr.	4	20
A Simeonite	I Chr.	4	42
A chief of the tribe of Manasseh	I Chr.	5	24
A substitute name for God	Hosea	2	16, 17

Ishiah, Isshiah, Jesiah *Jehovah exists*

An Issacharite	I Chr.	7	3
A warrior of David	I Chr.	12	6
A Levite	I Chr.	24	21
A Kohathite Levite, son of Uzziel	I Chr.	24	25

Ishmael *may God hear*

The son of Abraham by Hagar	Gen.	16	15, 16
	I Chr.	1	28
Promised a nation	Gen.	17	20
	Gen.	21	18
Sent away by Abraham to wander in wilderness	Gen.	21	14–20
Takes an Egyptian wife	Gen.	21	21
Helps bury his father	Gen.	25	9
Children of	Gen.	25	12–16
	I Chr.	1	29–31
His daughter marries Esau	Gen.	28	9
	Gen.	36	3

Dies at age 137	Gen.	25	17, 18
The crafty son of Nethaniah, a member of the royal house of David	II Ki.	25	23
	Jer.	40	8
Assassinates Gedaliah	II Ki.	25	25
	Jer.	41	1–11
Takes man Jews captive	Jer.	41	10
A son of Azel	I Chr.	8	38
	I Chr.	9	44
Father of Zebadiah	II Chr.	19	11
A military officer	II Chr.	23	1
A priest who divorces his foreign wife	Ezra	10	22

Ishmaelites

Region of Havilah	Gen.	25	18
Merchants buy Joseph	Gen.	37	25–36
Related to Midianites	Gen.	37	28, 36
Israel's enemies	Ps.	83	6

Ishuai, Ishui, Isui *he will justify*

Third son of Asher	Gen.	46	17
	I Chr.	7	30
Son of Saul	I Sam.	14	49

island

He shall deliver the *i* of	Job	22	30
The wild beasts of the *i*	Is.	34	14
Under a certain *i* Claudia	Acts	27	16
Must be cast on a certain *i*	Acts	27	26
The *i* was called Melita	Acts	28	1
Of the chief man of the *i*	Acts	28	7
Others who had diseases in the *i*	Acts	28	9
Every *i* was moved out	Rev.	6	14
Every *i* fled away, mountains	Rev.	16	20

isles *borders, distant lands*

The *i* of the Gentiles	Gen.	10	5
Laid a tribute on the *i*	Esth.	10	1
The kings of the *i* shall	Ps.	72	10
Let the multitude of the *i* be	Ps.	97	1
Ye the Lord in the *i* of	Is.	24	15
He taketh up the *i* as a very	Is.	40	15
The *i* saw it and feared, the	Is.	41	5
The *i* shall wait for his law	Is.	42	4
The *i* and the inhabitants thereof	Is.	42	10
Listen, O *i* unto me, and	Is.	49	1
The *i* shall wait upon me	Is.	51	5
	Is.	60	9
The *i* afar off that have not	Is.	66	19
Over the *i* of Chittim	Jer.	2	10
The kings of the *i* shall drink	Jer.	25	22
Hear and declare it in the *i*	Jer.	31	10
Shall not *i* shake at	Ezek.	26	15
The *i* tremble, the *i* shall	Ezek.	26	18
Of the people for many *i*	Ezek.	27	3
Benches of ivory, brought out of *i*	Ezek.	27	6
Blue and purple from the *i* of	Ezek.	27	7
Many *i* were the merchandise	Ezek.	27	15
Inhabitants of the *i* shall be	Ezek.	27	35
Dwell carelessly in the *i*	Ezek.	39	6
Turn his face to the *i*	Dan.	11	18
The *i* of the heathen	Zeph.	2	11

Israel *prince of God*

A name given to Jacob	Gen.	32	24–32
The collective name for the twelve tribes	Ex.	1	15
	I Sam.	4	6
Gospel preached to	Mat.	10	6, 7
Name of the ten tribes as distinguished from Judah	II Sam.	2	9
A name of Christ in prophecy	Is.	49	3
Figuratively, the church or true Christians collectively	Rom.	9	6
	Gal.	6	16

Israelites *descendants of Israel*
Tribes of:

Named after the sons of Jacob	Num.	26	1–51

In Egypt:

Dwell in Goshen	Gen.	46	28–34
Enslaved and oppressed by Egyptians	Ex.	1, 2, 5	
Moses commissioned as deliverer	Ex.	3	2–22
Exempt from plagues	Ex.	8	22, 23
Institute the passover	Ex.	12	1–28
Flight from Egypt	Ex.	12	31
Pass through the Red Sea	Ex.	14	19–22

In the wilderness:

Guided by a pillar of cloud	Ex.	14	19
	Num.	9	15
Fed by manna and water	Ex.	16	4
	Ex.	17	1–6

Israelites—*continued*

Covenant at Sinai	Ex.	19	1–8
Their idolatry	Ex.	32	1–35
Moses breaks the tablets	Ex.	32	19–35
Tables renewed	Ex.	34	1–35
Removed from Sinai	Num.	10	1–13
Their journeys	Num.	33	1–56
Conquer and divide Canaan under Joshua	Josh.	1–13	
The land allotted	Josh.	15–21	
Governed by judges	Judg.	2	1–23
Governed by kings	I Sam.	10	1–27

Revolt of the ten tribes:

Disagreement after Saul's death	II Sam.	2	1–32
Absalom's rebellion	II Sam.	15	10–37
Rebellion of Sheba	II Sam.	20	1–19
Under Rehoboam	I Ki.	12	1–33
Samaria besieged	II Ki.	6	24–33
Able-bodied carried to captivity in Assyria	II Ki.	17	1–41
The remnant join the kingdom of Judah	II Chr.	30	18–26

Judah:

Ruled by a series of predomiantly evil kings	I Ki.	15–22	
	II Ki.	8–24	
Captivity in Babylon	II Ki.	25	1–21
Their return	Ezra	2	1–70
God's wrath against	Ps.	78	1–72
	Ps.	106	1–48
Their deliverance	Ps.	105	1–45
Their sufferings our example	I Cor.	10	6

Prophecies concerning:

Of captivity	Deut.	28	41
Of war and other judgments	Deut.	28	49–57
	II Ki.	20	17, 18
	Jer.	1	11–16
	Ezek.	11	7–12
	Mat.	23	35–38
To have no permanent home	Deut.	28	65
Of blessing and restoration	Is.	1	25–27
	Is.	33	13–24
	Jer.	3	14–18
	Dan.	11	30–45
	Rom.	11	1–36
Of their rejection of the Messiah	Is.	8	14, 15
	Mat.	21	33–44
Dispersion of	Is.	24	1
	Ezek.	5	10, 12
	Dan.	9	7
Chosen peculiar	Deut.	14	2
	Deut.	7	6–8
	Gen.	49	10
	Josh.	1	11
	Is.	7	14
	Is.	43	21
	Is.	49	15–16
	Jer.	31	3
Disobedient	Is.	1	4
	Is.	59	3
	Jer.	2	19
	Jer.	5	21–26
Scattered	Deut.	28	25, 43, 64–65
	I Ki.	9	7
	Luke	21	24
Regathered	Jer.	31	31–40
	Ezek.	37	19–22
	Zech.	12	7
	Zech.	13	1

Issachar *there is hire*

The ninth son of Jacob, fifth by Leah	Gen.	30	17, 18
Prophetic benedictions upon	Gen.	49	14, 15
A tribe of Israel	Num.	1	28, 29
Place in march and camp	Num.	2	3–5
	Num.	10	14, 15
Strength of, on leaving Egypt	Num.	2	6
Place on Gerizim	Deut.	27	12
Some of his territory taken by Manasseh	Josh.	10	11
Tola was from	Judg.	10	1
Moses' blessing upon	Deut.	33	18, 19
Bounds of their inheritance	Josh.	17	10, 11
Assists Deborah against Sisera	Judg.	5	15
A Korhite doorkeeper in the time of David	I Chr.	26	5

Isshiah *see Ishiah*

issue of blood

The menstruous flow of blood	Mat.	9	20

Isuah *see Ishuah*

Isui *see Ishuai*

Italy

Soldiers from	Acts	10	1
Jews expelled from	Acts	18	2
Visited by Paul	Acts	27	1–6

itching ears

Denotes strong desire to hear new things	II Tim.	4	3

Ithamar *island of palms*

Youngest son of Aaron	Ex.	6	23
Ordained to priesthood	Ex.	28	1
Exercises direction over the tabernacle	Ex.	38	21
	Num.	4	28
Descendants	I Chr.	24	4–6

ivory *animal tusk*

Used on Solomon's throne	II Chr.	9	17
An item of trade	II Chr.	9	21
Exported from Tarshish	I Ki.	10	22
From Chittim	Ezek.	27	6
Ahab's palace	I Ki.	22	39
Houses made of	Amos	3	15
Thrones of	I Ki.	10	18
Beds of	Amos	6	4
Implies exotic beauty	Ps.	45	8
	S. of S.	5	14
Used for dishes and vessels	Rev.	18	12

J

Jaalam *occult*

A son of Esau	Gen.	36	5

Jaasiel, Jasiel *made of God*

One of David's mighty men	I Chr.	11	47
Son of Abner	I Chr.	27	21

Jaazaniah, Jezaniah *Jehovah hears*

A military commander	II Ki.	25	23
	Jer.	40	7, 8
A Rechabite who Jeremiah tests	Jer.	35	3–7
A son of Shaphan	Ezek.	8	11
A son of Azur	Ezek.	11	1–4

Jaazer, Jazer *helpful*

An Amorite town	Num.	21	32
	I Chr.	26	31
In Gilead	II Sam.	24	5
Given to Gad	Josh.	13	24
Levitical city	Josh.	21	34

Jabal *wanderer*

Son of Lamech and Adah	Gen.	4	20

Jabbok *pouring out*

One of the tributaries of the Jordan	Gen.	32	22–31
Mentioned as a boundary	Num.	21	24
	Judg.	11	13, 22

Jabesh-gilead *in the region of Gilead*

Town allotted to Manasseh	Num.	32	39, 40
Defended by Saul	I Sam.	11	1–11
Saul and his sons buried here	I Sam.	31	11–13

Jabneel, Jabneh *God causes to build*

A town in northern Judah	Josh.	15	11
A town near the sea of Galilee	Josh.	19	33
	II Chr.	26	6

Jachin *he doth establish*

Fourth son of Simeon	Gen.	46	10
Head of a family	Num.	26	12
One of the pillars in front of Solomons's temple	I Ki.	7	21
Head of a course of priests	I Chr.	24	17
Post-exilic priest	Neh.	1	10

jacinth *see hyacinth*

jackal *a dog-like animal*

Called a dragon	Is.	34	13
	Jer.	49	33
Howling animal	Mic.	1	8
Of desolation	Is.	13	22
	Jer.	9	10
Sniff up the wind	Jer.	14	6
Giving suck	Lam.	4	3

Jacob *supplanter*

Son of Isaac and Rebekah, brother of Esau	Gen.	25	26

Birth	Gen.	25	26
Obtains Esau's birthright	Gen.	25	29–34
	Heb.	12	16
Receives father's blessing by deceit	Gen.	27	1 29
	Heb.	11	20
Escapes to Pandam-aram	Gen.	27	43
	Gen.	28	1–5
His vision of the ladder	Gen.	28	10–22
Serves fourteen years for Leah and Rachel	Gen.	29	15–35
	Hosea	12	12
Dealings with Laban	Gen.	31	1–55
Vision of God's host	Gen.	32	1, 2
Wrestles with an angel	Gen.	32	24
	Hosea	12	4
Name changed to Israel	Gen.	32	28
	Gen.	35	10
Reconciliation with Esau	Gen.	33	4
Builds an altar at Bethel	Gen.	35	1–3
His twelve sons	Gen.	35	23–26
Dwells in Canaan	Gen.	37	1
His grief over loss of Joseph	Gen.	37	34, 35
Sends into Egypt to buy corn	Gen.	42	1, 2
	Gen.	43	1–14
His love for Benjamin	Gen.	43	14
	Gen.	44	29
Goes down to Egypt	Gen.	46	1–7
	I Sam.	12	8
	Acts	7	14, 15
Brought before Pharaoh	Gen.	47	1–10
Land of Goshen assigned to	Gen.	47	11, 12, 27
Benediction upon his sons	Gen.	48, 49	
His death and burial	Gen.	49	33
	Gen.	50	2–13
Ancestor of Jesus	Mat.	1	2
Noted for faith	Heb.	11	21
Prophecies concerning	Gen.	25	23
	Gen.	27	28, 29
	Gen.	28	10–15
	Gen.	35	9–14
	Gen.	46	3
Father of Joseph	Mat.	1	16

Jacob's well
Jesus and the Samaritan woman at	John	4	5–12

Jadau *see* Iddo

Jah *see also* Jehovah
Shortened form for Jehovah
Extol Him by His name *J*	Ps.	68	4

Jahath *unity*
A descendant of Judah	I Chr.	4	2
A Gershomite Levite	I Chr.	6	20
Son of Shimei	I Chr.	23	11
Son of Shelomoth	I Chr.	24	22
A Merarite Levite	II Chr.	34	12

Jahaz, Jahaza, Jahazah, Jahzah *lowland*
Here Sihon is defeated	Num.	21	23
	Deut.	2	32
Allotted to Reuben	Josh.	13	18
Later given to Levites	Josh.	21	36
	I Chr.	6	78
Recaptured by Moab	Is.	15	4

Jahaziel *God sees*
A warrior at Ziklag	I Chr.	12	24
The priest who sounds the trumpet	I Chr.	16	6
Third son of Hebron	I Chr.	23	19
A prophet, son of Zechariah	II Chr.	20	14
A returned exile	Ezra	8	5

Jahzah *see* Jahaz

jailer *see* gaoler
Philippian	Acts	16	19–34

Jair *he enlightens*
Founder of twenty-three cities in Gilead, of Manasseh	Num.	32	41
	I Chr.	2	22
A judge of Israel	Judg.	10	3, 4
Father of Elhanan	I Chr.	20	5
Father of Mordecai	Esth.	2	5

Jairus *Greek form of Jair*
Ruler of the synagogue	Mark	5	22
Daughter raised from the dead	Mark	5	35–42
	Luke	8	49–55

Jakim *he sets up*
A Benjamite	I Chr.	8	19
Descendant of Aaron	I Chr.	24	12

Jambres *see* Jannes
James *form of Jacob*
Son of Zebedee, brother of John	Mat.	4	21
	Mat.	27	56
Called to be an apostle	Mat.	4	21, 22
	Mark	1	19, 20
Civil ambitions of	Mat.	20	20–23
	Mark	10	35–41
Closely associated with Jesus	Mark	1	29
	Mark	5	37
	Mark	14	33
	Luke	8	51
Surnamed Boanerges by Jesus	Mark	3	17
Rebuked by Jesus	Luke	9	54
Martyred	Acts	12	2
Son of Alphaeus, an apostle	Mat.	10	3
	Mark	3	18
Called "the less"	Mark	15	40
Brother of Jesus	Mat.	13	55
	Mark	6	3
	Gal.	1	19
Opposes Jesus' work	Mat.	12	46–50
	Mark	3	31–35
	John	7	3–5
Presides over the church council	Acts	15	13–34
Won to faith after resurrection	I Cor.	15	7
Head of the church at Jerusalem	Gal.	1	19

Janna
Ancestor of Joseph	Luke	3	24

Jannes and Jambres
Two Egyptian magicians	Ex.	7	11, 12
	II Tim.	3	8

Japheth *enlarges*
A son of Noah	Gen.	6	10
Migrates to Asia Minor	Gen.	10	2–5

Japhia *splendid*
King of Lachish	Josh.	10	3
A town of Zebulun	Josh.	19	12
Son of David	I Chr.	14	6

Japho *see* Joppa

Jarah *honey*
Called Jehoadah	I Chr.	8	36
Descendant of Saul	I Chr.	9	42

Jared *see* Jered

Jarha *the month of sweeping away(?)*
An Egyptian servant	I Chr.	2	35

Jarib *he will contend*
Son of Simeon	I Chr.	4	24
Companion of Ezra	Ezra	8	16
Priest who married a foreign wife	Ezra	10	18

Jasher *of the upright*
An ancient book of Hebrew poems	II Sam.	1	18
	Josh.	10	13

Jashub *he will return*
A son of Issachar, also called Job	Gen.	46	13
	Num.	26	24
A son of Bani	Ezra	10	29

Jasiel *see* Jaasiel
Jason *Greek hero; healing*
A Christian at Thessalonica	Acts	17	5

jasper *to polish*
A precious stone	Ex.	28	20
In heaven	Rev.	4	3

Jattir *excelling*
City in southern Judah	Josh.	15	48
Levitical city	Josh.	21	14
David sends spoil to	I Sam.	30	27

javelin
A heavy spearlike weapon	Num.	25	7

jawbone, jaw
Used as a weapon	Judg.	15	15
Bridled	Is.	30	28
	Hosea	11	4

Jazer *see* Jaazer

jealousy *feeling*
Divine jealousy	Ex.	20	5
	Deut.	29	20
	Zeph.	1	18
Mosaic law concerning	Num.	5	12–31
Is cruel as death	S. of S.	8	6
Provoked by envy	Rom.	10	19
	Rom.	11	11
Forbidden	Rom.	13	13

jealousy—*continued*
Instances of:

Cain of Abel	Gen.	4	5
Sarah of Hagar	Gen.	16	5
Joseph's brethren	Gen.	37	4–11
Saul of David	I Sam.	18	8–30
Brother of prodigal son	Luke	15	25–32

Jeberechiah *Jehovah is blessing*

Father of Zechariah	Is.	8	2

Jebus, Jebusi *trodden down*

One of the ancient names of Jerusalem	Josh.	18	16
	Judg.	19	10
Captured by Joab	I Chr.	11	4
Called Zion	II Sam.	5	7, 9

Jebusites *belonging to Jebus*

The tribe which lives in Jerusalem	Josh.	15	63
	Judg.	1	21
Canaanite tribe	Deut.	7	1
Land given to Abraham	Gen.	15	21
Conquered by Joshua	Josh.	24	11
Conquered by David	II Sam.	5	6–9
Intermarriage with Israel	Judg.	3	5, 6
	Ezra	9	1, 2
Paid tribute to Solomon	I Ki.	9	20, 21

Jecholiah, Jecoliah *Jehovah will prevail*

Mother of Azariah and Uzziah	II Ki.	15	2
	II Chr.	26	3

Jechonias, Jeconiah *see* Jehoiachin

Jedaiah *Jehovah is praise; Jehovah knows*

Descendant of Simeon	I Chr.	4	37
Head of a family of priests	I Chr.	24	7
Helps repair the wall	Neh.	3	10
Priest who returns from captivity	Neh.	12	6
Another chief priest	Neh.	12	7, 21
A crown maker	Zech.	6	10–15

Jediael *known of God*

Son of Benjamin	I Chr.	7	6
Son of Shimri	I Chr.	11	45
	I Chr.	12	20
A porter in the temple	I Chr.	26	2

Jedidiah *darling of the Lord*

A name given to Solomon	II Sam.	12	25

Jeduthun *praising*

Chief musician of the temple service	I Chr.	16	41
Probably called Ethan	I Chr.	25	1
Psalm titles	Ps.	39	
	Ps.	62	
	Ps.	77	
Father of one of the returnees	Neh.	11	17

Jeezer *see* Abiezer

Jegar-sahadutha *heap of witness*

A memorial erected by Laban and Jacob	Gen.	31	47

Jehiah *Jehovah lives*

Doorkeeper for the ark	I Chr.	15	24

Jehiel, Jehiah *carried away with God; Jehovah lives*

Levite who plays psaltery	I Chr.	15	18, 24
A Gershonite Levite	I Chr.	23	8
Companion of David's sons	I Chr.	27	32
Son of Jehoshaphat	II Chr.	21	2
Son of Heman	II Chr.	29	14
An overseer in the house of God	II Chr.	31	13
A priest who presides at the solemn passover	II Chr.	35	8
Father of Obadiah	Ezra	8	9
Father of Shechaniah	Ezra	10	2
Priest who married a foreign wife	Ezra	10	21
Father of Gibeon	I Chr.	9	35
David's mighty man	I Chr.	11	44

Jehoadah *Jehovah adorns*

A descendant of Saul, through Jonathan	I Chr.	8	36

Jehoahaz *Jehovah lays hold of*

King of Israel, son of Jehu	II Ki.	13	2–7
King of Judah, son of Josiah	II Ki.	23	33
Called Shallum	Jer.	22	11, 12
Variant form of Ahaziah	II Chr.	21	17

Jehoash *see* Joash

Jehohanan *Jehovah is gracious*

A porter of the tabernacle	I Chr.	26	3
A military chief under Jehoshaphat	II Chr.	17	15
Son of Bebai, renounces foreign wife	Ezra	10	28
A high priest	Neh.	12	13
A singer in the temple	Neh.	12	42
Father of Ishmael	II Chr.	23	1
Son of Tobiah the Ammonite	Neh.	6	18

Jehoiachin, Jechonias, Jeconiah, Coniah *Jehovah will establish*

King of Judah	II Ki.	24	6–8
Wicked reign of	II Ki.	24	9
Taken captive by Nebuchadnezzar	II Ki.	24	10–16
In prison 37 years	II Ki.	25	27
Released and honoured until death	Jer.	52	31–34
Ancestor of Jesus	Mat.	1	12

Jehoiada *Jehovah knows*

Father of Benaiah	II Sam.	8	18
High priest of Judah, who anoints Joash king	II Ki.	11	12
Overthrows and kills wicked queen	II Ki.	11	16
Instructs king in repairing temple	II Ki.	12	2–11
Dies	II Chr.	24	15
Counsellor to King David	I Chr.	27	34
Son of Paseah, repairs the gate	Neh.	3	6
One of the captive priests	Jer.	29	26
Son of Benaiah	I Chr.	27	34

Jehoiakim *Jehovah sets up*

Second son of Josiah, also called Eliakim	II Ki.	23	34
	I Chr.	3	15
Wicked reign over Judah	II Chr.	36	4–8
Denounced	Jer.	22	18, 19
Burns the sacred roll	Jer.	36	1–32
Captured by Nebuchadnezzar	II Chr.	36	6
Killed Urijah, a prophet	Jer.	26	20–23

Jehoram *Jehovah is exalted*

Eldest son of Jehoshaphat	I Ki.	22	50
Evil reign of Judah	II Chr.	21	1–11
Brother-in-law of Jehoram of Israel	II Ki.	8	18
Prophecy of terrible disease	II Chr.	21	12–15
Death of	II Chr.	21	19
A wicked king of Israel	II Ki.	3	1–5
Also called Joram	II Ki.	9	23
Second eldest son of Ahab	II Ki.	1	17
Breaks with foreign cult	II Ki.	3	2
Unsuccessful at taking Moab	II Ki.	3	
Killed by Jehu	II Ki.	9	24–26
A priest who teaches in Judah	II Chr.	17	8, 9

Jehoshaphat, Josaphat *Jehovah is judge*

Son of Ahilud	II Sam.	8	16
Recorder under David and Solomon	II Sam.	20	24
	I Ki.	4	3
Son of Asa	I Ki.	15	24
King of Judah	I Ki.	22	1–4
Fortifies Judah	II Chr.	17	2
Begins public education program	II Chr.	17	7, 9
A good and just king	II Chr.	17	1–13
Alliance with Ahab	II Chr.	18	1–3
Reprimanded	II Chr.	19	1–8
Defeats Moabites	II Chr.	20	14–31
Navy destroyed	II Chr.	20	35–37
In genealogy of Christ	Mat.	1	8
Father of Jehu	II Ki.	9	2
A priest who serves as trumpeter	I Chr.	15	24
A valley near Jerusalem	Joel	3	2

Jehoshua, Jehoshuah *see* Joshua

Jehovah *see* God

Name *J* was not known to them	Ex.	6	3
Thou whose name alone is *J*	Ps.	83	18
J is my strength and my song	Is.	12	2
The Lord *J* is everlasting strength	Is.	26	4

Jehovah-jireh *Jehovah will see or provide*

Abraham sacrifices a ram instead of Isaac	Gen.	22	14

Jehovah-nissi *Jehovah is my banner*

An altar erected by Moses	Ex.	17	15

Jehovah-rophi *Jehovah who heals*

That healeth thee	Ex.	15	26

Jehovah-rohi *Jehovah my shepherd*

My shepherd	Ps.	23	1

Jehovah-shalom *Jehovah is peace*

An altar built by Gideon	Judg.	6	24

Jehovah tsidkenu *Jehovah our righteousness*

He shall be called	Jer.	23	6

Jehozabad *Jehovah has bestowed*

Son of a Moabitess	II Ki.	12	21
Assassin of Joash	II Chr.	24	26
Son of Obed-edom	I Chr.	26	4
A Benjamite captain	II Chr.	17	18

Jehozadak *see* Jozadak

Jehu *Jehovah is He*

Son of Hanani	I Ki.	16	1
A prophet	II Chr.	19	2
Announces judgment on Baasha	I Ki.	16	1, 7, 12

Son of Nimshi	II Ki.	9	2
Anointed king of Israel	II Ki.	9	3
Slays Jezebel	II Ki.	9	30–33
Destroys house of Ahab	II Ki.	10	11–14
Slays idolators	II Ki.	9	14–37
Confronts Hazael of Syria	II Ki.	10	32
Prophecies concerning	II Ki.	10	30
	II Ki.	15	12
	Hosea	1	4
Worships idols	II Ki.	10	29–31
Son of Obed	I Chr.	2	38
Son of Josibiah	I Chr.	4	35
One of David's mighty men	I Chr.	12	3

Jehucal, Jucal *Jehovah is able*
Sent by the king to the prophet Jeremiah	Jer.	37	3
Also called Jucal	Jer.	38	1

Jehudi *a Jew*
He burns the roll in the king's court	Jer.	36	23

Jehudijah see Hodiah

Jehush see Jeush

Jeiel *Jehovah has gathered*
A Reubenite chief	I Chr.	5	7
A Benjamite	I Chr.	35	9
One of David's heroes, called Jehiel	I Chr.	11	44
A Levite porter and musician	I Chr.	15	18
	I Chr.	16	5
A Levite who encourages Judah against enemies	II Chr.	20	14
A scribe for King Uzziah	II Chr.	26	11
A Levite who cleanses the temple	II Chr.	29	13
A chief Levite who offers passover	II Chr.	35	9
A returned exile	Ezra	8	13
A priest who married a foreign wife	Ezra	10	43

Jekuthiel *obedience of Jehovah*
Son of Ezra	I Chr.	4	18

Jemima *affectionate*
Job's eldest daughter	Job	42	14

Jemuel *day of God*
Son of Simeon, also called Nemuel	Gen.	46	10
	Ex.	6	15

Jephthae, Jephthah *he will open*
Son of a harlot	Judg.	11	1
A judge of Israel	Judg.	11	1–3
Made captain of Israel	Judg.	11	1–3
His rash vow	Judg.	11	30, 31
Defeats the Ammonites	Judg.	11	32, 33
Its fulfillment	Judg.	11	34–40
Smites Ephraimites	Judg.	12	1–5
Death of	Judg.	12	7
Called deliverer	I Sam.	12	11
Faith of	Heb.	11	32

Jephunneh *it will be prepared*
Father of Caleb	Num.	13	6
An Asherite	I Chr.	7	38

Jered, Jerod *descent*
Son of Mahalaleel	I Chr.	1	2
Son of Ezra	I Chr.	4	18

Jeremiah, Jeremy *Jehovah doth establish*
A prophet, son of Hilkiah	Jer.	1	1
His call	Jer.	1	4–19
Conspiracy against	Jer.	11	21–23
Rejected by his family and friends	Jer.	12	6–8
	Jer.	20	10
His prayers	Jer.	14	7–9
	Jer.	15	15–18
	Jer.	32	17–25
Tells of seventy years captivity	Jer.	25	
Writes prophecy in a book	Jer.	36	1, 2
Rewritten by Baruch, his secretary	Jer.	36	27–32
Freed by Zedekiah	Jer.	37	17–21
Imprisoned again	Jer.	38	1–10
Aided by an Ethiopian	Jer.	38	10–28
Carried to Egypt	Jer.	43	6, 7
Sorrow under persecution	Jer.	15	10, 15
Foretells desolation of Jerusalem	Jer.	19	1–15
Cast into prison	Jer.	20	3–6
Letter to the captives of Babylon	Jer.	29	1–32
Released by Nebuchadnezzar	Jer.	39	11–14

Lamentations of:
Over Josiah	II Chr.	35	25
Over good fortune of the wicked	Jer.	12	1–6
Over Jerusalem	Jer.	18	11–13
Jesus refers to	Mat.	2	17
Grandfather of Jehoahaz	II Ki.	23	31

A chief of Manasseh	I Chr.	5	24
An Israelite who joins David at Ziklag	I Chr.	12	4
Two Gadites who join David at Ziklag	I Chr.	12	10, 13
Post-exilic priest	Neh.	12	1, 7, 12
Signer of covenant	Neh.	10	2

Jeremoth, Jerimoth *elevation*
Son of Bela	I Chr.	7	7
Son of Becher	I Chr.	7	8
A Benjamite	I Chr.	8	14
An archer who joins David	I Chr.	12	5
A Merarite Levite	I Chr.	23	23
A musician, son of Heman	I Chr.	25	22
Son of Azriel	I Chr.	27	19
Son of David	II Chr.	11	18
Levitical overseers	II Chr.	31	13
Post-exilic man who divorces his wife	Ezra	10	26, 27

Jeremy see Jeremiah

Jericho *a fragrant place*
A city near the Jordan	Num.	22	1
	Deut.	34	1
Home of Rahab, the harlot	Josh.	2	1
	Heb.	11	31
Besieged by Joshua	Josh.	6	1–15
Destroyed by Joshua	Josh.	6	15–27
Joshua curses it	Josh.	6	26
Allotted to Benjamites	Josh.	18	12, 21
Rebuilt by Hiel	I Ki.	16	34
Prophetic school located in	II Ki.	2	5–7
Waters purified by Elisha	II Ki.	2	18–22
Captives of Judah released	II Chr.	28	7–15
Help build walls of Jerusalem	Neh.	3	2
Babylonian captives return	Neh.	7	36
Blind man healed in	Mat.	20	29–34
Home of Zacchaeus	Luke	19	1–10

Jerimoth see Jeremoth

Jerioth *curtains*
Wife of Caleb	I Chr.	2	18

Jeroboam *he will defend the people*
Son of Nebat	I Ki.	11	26
Promoted by Solomon	I Ki.	11	28
Flees to Egypt	I Ki.	11	30–40
Recalled and made king	I Ki.	12	1–20
Turns to idolatry	I Ki.	12	26–33
His hand withers	I Ki.	13	1–10
Wife consults prophet	I Ki.	14	1–18
King of Israel, successor to Jehoash	II Ki.	14	16, 23
A wicked reign	II Ki.	14	24
Conquest of Hamath and Damascus	II Ki.	14	25–28
Denounced by Amos	Amos	7	9, 10

Jeroham *compassionate*
Father of Elkanah	I Chr.	6	27
Father of three priests	I Chr.	8	27
Father of Ibneiah	I Chr.	9	8
Father of Adaiah	I Chr.	9	12
A Benjamite of Gedor	I Chr.	12	7
Father of a Danite chief	I Chr.	27	22
Father of Azariah	II Chr.	23	1

Jerubbaal see Gideon

Jeruel *founded by God*
A wilderness south of Judah	II Chr.	20	16

Jerusalem *the habitation of peace*
The ancient Salem	Gen.	14	18
The ancient Jebusi or Jebus	Josh.	15	8
	Judg.	19	10
Allotted to the tribe of Benjamin	Josh.	18	28
Enlarged by David	II Sam.	5	9
Ark brought to	II Sam.	6	12–17
God's care and protection	II Sam.	24	16
	II Chr.	6	6
	II Chr.	12	7
	Is.	31	5
Water supply brought within the walls	II Ki.	18	17
	II Ki.	20	20
Captives return	Ezra	2	
Walls rebuilt and dedicated	Neh.	12	38–47
Wickedness of	Is.	1	4
	Jer.	5	1–5
	Ezek.	5	5–8
Christ's triumphal entry	Mat.	21	1–11
Christ laments over	Mat.	23	37
	Luke	19	41
Seat of Roman government	Mat.	27	2–19
Christ crucified in	Luke	9	31
Christ first preaches in	Luke	21	37, 38
Gospel first preached in	Luke	24	47

Jerusalem—continued

Holy Ghost first given in	Acts	2	1–5
Persecution of Christians begins	Acts	8	1

Gates of:

old gate, fish gate, sheep gate, prison gate	Neh.	3	1, 3, 32
	Neh.	12	39
Ephraim gate	II Chr.	25	23
Benjamin gate	Jer.	37	13
Corner gate	Zech.	14	10
Valley gate	Neh.	2	13
Dung gate	Neh.	2	13
Water gate	Neh.	3	26
Horse gate	Neh.	3	28
King's gate	I Chr.	9	18
East gate	Neh.	3	29

Called:

City of David	II Sam.	5	7
Holy city	Neh.	11	1
	Mat.	4	5
City of God	Ps.	46	4
City of the great king	Ps.	48	2
Zion	Ps.	48	12
	Is.	33	20
Ariel	Is.	29	1, 2
Throne of the Lord	Jer.	3	17
City of truth	Zech.	8	3

Streets of:

East street	II Chr.	29	4
Of the house of God	Ezra	10	9
Of the water gate	Neh.	8	16
Baker's street	Jer.	37	21

Captured and pillaged:

By Shishak, king of Egypt	I Ki.	14	25, 26
By Jehoash, king of Israel	II Ki.	14	13, 14
By Pekah	II Ki.	16	5
By Nebuchadnezzar	II Ki.	24	8–16
By Sennacherib	II Ki.	18	13–37
By the Philistines	II Chr.	21	16

Prophecies concerning:

A quiet place of abode	Is.	33	20
To be rebuilt by Cyrus	Is.	44	26–28
Fall to king of Babylon	Jer.	20	5
A heap of ruin	Jer.	26	18
Christ to enter as king	Zech.	9	9
Great distress	Mat.	24	21, 29
	Luke	21	23, 24
The heavenly Jerusalem	Heb.	12	22
New Jerusalem	Rev.	21	2

Jesher *uprightness*

Son of Caleb	I Chr.	2	18

Jeshimon *the desert waste*

Probably the wilderness or wasteland to the west of the Dead sea	Num.	21	20
	I Sam.	23	24

Jeshua, Jeshuah *Jehovah is salvation*

An Aaronite, head of ninth order	I Chr.	24	11
Descendants return from Babylon	Ezra	2	36
	Neh.	7	39
A Levite in charge of tithes	II Chr.	31	15
Descendants return from captivity	Ezra	2	40
	Neh.	7	43
A priest who accompanies Zerubbabel	Ezra	2	2
Son of Jozadak	Ezra	3	2
Rebuilds temple	Ezra	3	8–13
Contends with those who seek to defeat the rebuilding	Ezra	4	1–3
	Ezra	5	1, 2
Son of Pahath-moab	Ezra	2	6
	Neh.	7	11
A Levite, interprets the law	Neh.	8	7
In charge of thanksgiving	Neh.	12	8
A town of Judah	Neh.	11	26
See also Joshua			

Jesiah *see* Ishiah

Jesimiel *God will place*

A descendant of Simeon	I Chr.	4	36

Jesse *gifts*

Descendant of Ruth and Boaz	Ruth	4	17–22
Son of Obed, father of David	Ruth	4	17, 22
	I Sam.	17	12
By divine command, Samuel visits, to choose a king	I Sam.	16	1–13
Saul sends messengers to	I Sam.	16	19–23
Sons join Saul's army	I Sam.	17	13
Dwells with David at Moab	I Sam.	22	3, 4
Descendants	I Chr.	2	12–17
An ancestor of Jesus	Mat.	1	5, 6, 16

Jesurun *see* Jeshurun

Jesus *Jehovah saves*

Name given Christ	Mat.	1	21
Joshua, military leader called	Acts	7	45
	Heb.	4	8
Friend of Paul	Col.	4	11
Obedient to God the Father	Ps.	40	8
	John	4	34
Faithful	Is.	11	5
	I Thes.	5	24
Compassionate	Is.	40	11
	Mat.	15	32
	Luke	7	13
Patient	Is.	53	7
	Mat.	27	14
Meek	Is.	53	7
	Zech.	9	9
	Mat.	11	29
Guileless	Is.	53	9
	I Pet.	2	22
Righteous	Is.	53	11
	Heb.	1	9
Just	Zech.	9	9
	John	5	30
	Acts	22	14
Benevolent	Mat.	4	23, 24
	Mat.	9	35
	Acts	10	38
Self-denying	Mat.	8	20
	II Chr.	8	9
Lowly in heart	Mat.	11	29
Good	Mat.	19	16
Holy	Luke	1	35
	Acts	4	27
	Rev.	3	7
Zealous	Luke	2	49
Subject to His parents	Luke	2	51
Humble	Luke	22	27
	Phil.	2	8
Forgiving	Luke	23	34
True	John	1	14
	I John	5	20
Sinless	John	8	46
	II Chr.	5	21
Loving	John	13	1
	John	15	13
Long-suffering	I Tim.	1	16
Merciful	Heb.	2	17
Harmless	Heb.	7	26
Spotless	I Pet.	1	19

As a prophet:

Abounds in wisdom	Luke	2	40, 47, 52
	Col.	2	3
Alone knows and reveals God	Mat.	11	27
	John	3	2, 13, 34
	John	17	6, 14, 26
	Heb.	1	1–2
Anointed with the Holy Ghost	Luke	4	18
	John	3	34
Declared his doctrine to be that of the Father	John	8	26, 28
	John	12	49–50
	John	14	10, 24
Faithful to his trust	Luke	4	32
	John	17	8
	Heb.	3	2
	Rev.	1	5
	Rev.	3	14
Foretold	Deut.	18	15, 18
	Is.	52	7
	Nah.	1	15
God commands us to hear	Deut.	18	15
	Mat.	17	25
	Acts	3	22
	Acts	7	37
God will severely visit our neglect of	Deut.	18	19
	Acts	3	23
	Heb.	2	3
Meek in his teaching	Is.	42	2
	Mat.	12	17–20
Mighty in deed and word	Mat.	13	54
	Mark	1	27
	Luke	4	32
	John	7	46
Preached the gospel and worked miracles	Mat.	4	23
	Mat.	11	5
	Luke	4	43

Prediction of His office	Acts	3	22, 23
	Deut.	18	15
Calls Himself	Luke	13	33
Foretells future	Mat.	24	3–35
Recognized by people as such	Mat.	21	11, 46
Speaks with authority	Mat.	7	29
As a priest:			
After the order of Melchizedek	Heb.	5	6
	Heb.	6	20
Appointed and called by God	Heb.	3	2
	Heb.	5	4
Appointment of, and encouragement to steadfastness	Heb.	4	14
Consecrated with an oath	Heb.	7	20, 21
Entered into heaven	Heb.	4	14
	Heb.	10	12
Faithful	Heb.	3	2
Has an unchangeable priesthood	Heb.	7	23, 28
His sacrifice superior to all others	Heb.	9	13–14, 23
Intercedes	Heb.	7	25
	Heb.	9	24
Is of unblemished purity	Heb.	7	26, 28
Made reconciliation	Heb.	2	17
Needed no sacrifice for himself	Heb.	7	27
Obtained redemption for us	Heb.	9	12
Offered himself a sacrifice	Heb.	9	14, 26
Offered sacrifice but once	Heb.	7	27
	Heb.	9	25–26
On his throne	Zech.	6	13
Superior to Aaron and the Levitical priests	Heb.	7	11, 16, 22
	Heb.	8	1, 2, 6
Sympathizes with those who are tempted	Heb.	2	18
	Heb.	4	15
Predicted	Ps.	110	4
	Zech.	6	13
Applied to Him by Hebrews	Heb.	3	1
	Heb.	5	5
	Heb.	6	20
	Heb.	9	11–15
Priestly work	Mark	10	45
	Rom.	3	24, 25
	I John	2	2
As a king:			
Acknowledged by His followers	Luke	19	38
	John	12	13
Declared by himself	Mat.	25	34
	John	18	37
Glorious	Ps.	24	7–10
	I Cor.	2	8
	James	2	1
Has an everlasting kingdom	Dan.	2	44
	Dan.	7	14
	Luke	1	33
Has a righteous kingdom	Ps.	45	6
	Heb.	1	8–9
Has an universal kingdom	Ps.	2	8
	Ps.	72	8
	Zech.	14	9
	Rev.	11	15
Not of this world	John	18	36
Jews shall seek unto	Hosea	3	5
Of Zion	Ps.	2	6
	Is.	52	7
	Zech.	9	9
	Mat.	21	5
	John	12	12–15
Kings shall do homage to	Ps.	72	10
	Is.	49	7
On the throne of David	Is.	9	7
	Ezek.	27	24–25
	Luke	1	32
	Acts	2	30
Saints, the subjects of	Col.	1	13
	Rev.	15	3
Saints receive a kingdom from	Luke	22	29–30
	Heb.	12	28
Saints shall behold	Is.	33	17
	Rev.	22	3–4
Shall overcome all his enemies	Ps.	110	1
	Mark	12	36
	I Cor.	15	25
	Rev.	17	14
Supreme	Ps.	89	27
	Rev.	1	5
	Rev.	19	16
Predicted	Is.	9	6, 7
	Heb.	1	8, 9

As head	Eph.	1	20–22
Future aspect	Eph.	1	5
Power as a	Mat.	28	18
As the shepherd:			
Chief	I Pet.	5	4
Good	John	10	11, 14
Great	Mic.	5	4
	Heb.	13	20
Foretold	Gen.	49	24
	Is.	40	11
	Ezek.	34	23
	Ezek.	37	24
	John	10	3
Calls	Is.	40	11
Cherishes	Ps.	23	1–2
Feeds	John	10	9
Gathers	Is.	40	11
	John	10	16
Gives eternal life to	John	10	28
Guides	Ps.	23	3
	John	10	3–4
Knows	John	10	14, 27
Laid down his life for	Mat.	26	31
	John	10	11, 15
	Acts	20	28
Protects and preserves	Ezek.	34	10
	Zech.	9	16
	John	10	28
His human nature:			
Man of sorrows	Is.	53	3, 4
	Luke	22	44
Born of woman	Mat.	1	18
	Luke	1	31
	Gal.	4	4
Having human feelings	Mat.	8	24
	Luke	19	41
	John	4	6, 7
	John	11	35
Called son of David	Mat.	22	42
	Mark	10	47
	Rom.	1	3
Having a human soul	Mat.	26	38
	Acts	2	31
Enduring indignities	Mat.	26	67
	Luke	22	64
Buried	Mat.	27	59, 60
	Mark	15	46
Has four brothers	Mark	6	3
Circumcision	Luke	2	21
Increasing in wisdom and stature	Luke	2	52
Nailed to the cross	Luke	23	33
Partaking of our flesh and blood	John	1	14
	Heb.	2	14
Without sin	John	8	46
	Heb.	4	15
	I John	3	5
Like us in all things	Acts	3	22
	Heb.	2	17
The seed of Abraham	Gal.	3	16
	Heb.	2	16
His divine nature:			
Son of God	Mat.	3	17
	Mat.	26	63, 64
	John	1	14, 18
	John	3	16
	I John	4	9
Manifested in His words and works	Mat.	13	54
	Luke	4	22
	John	5	21
Acknowledged by His disciples	Mat.	16	16
	John	1	49
	John	20	28
The eternal God and Creator	John	1	1–5
	Col.	1	16, 17
	Heb.	1	2, 3
Equality with God	John	5	17–23
	John	16	15
	I Thes.	3	11
One with the Father	John	12	45
	John	17	10
Image of God and firstborn	Col.	1	15
	Heb.	1	3
King of Kings and Lord of Lords	Rev.	19	16
Types of:			
Scapegoat	Lev.	16	20–26

Jesus—*continued*

Moses	Deut.	18	15
Brazen serpent	John	3	14
Manna	John	6	32
Adam	Rom.	5	14
Passover	I Cor.	5	7
Abel	Heb.	12	24

Jesus Christ, atonement of

Acceptable to God	Eph.	5	2
Effect by Christ alone	John	1	29, 36
	Acts	4	10, 12
	I Thes.	1	10
	I Tim.	2	5–6
	Heb.	2	9
	I Pet.	2	24
Faith in, indispensable	Rom.	3	25
	Gal.	3	13–14
Foreordained	I Pet.	1	20
	Rev.	13	8
Justification by	Rom.	5	9
	II Cor.	5	21
Reconciles the justice and mercy of God	Is.	45	21
	Rom.	3	25–26
Reconciliation to God effected by	II Cor.	5	18–20
	Eph.	2	13–16
	Col.	1	20–22
	Heb.	2	17
	I Pet.	3	18
Redemption by	Mat.	20	28
	I Tim.	2	6
	Heb.	9	12
	Rev.	5	9
Remission of sins by	Rom.	3	25
	Eph.	1	7
	I John	1	7
	Rev.	1	5
Sanctification by	II Cor.	5	15
	Eph.	5	26–27
	Tit.	2	14
	Heb.	10	10
	Heb.	13	12
Was voluntary	Heb.	10	5–9
	John	10	11, 15
Foretold	Is.	53	4–6
	Is.	53	8–12
	Zech.	13	1, 7
	John	11	50, 51
Commemorated in the Lord's supper	Mat.	26	17–30
	I Cor.	11	26
The necessity of	Luke	24	44–47
For sins of all people	John	1	29
Relation to the church	Acts	20	28
Reconciliation by Christ	Rom.	5	10
Exhibits the grace and mercy of God	Rom.	8	28–39
	Eph.	2	8
	I Tim.	2	5, 6
	Heb.	2	9–18
Purpose of	Tit.	2	11–15
Made but once	Heb.	7	27
Access to God by	Heb.	10	19–22
Punishment by rejection	Heb.	10	29
Divinely ordained	I Pet.	1	3–12
Saved through His blood	I John	1	7
	Rev.	1	5
Evidence of God's love	I John	3	1–3
	I John	4	7
Heavenly interpretation	Rev.	7	9–17
	Rev.	12	10–12

Jesus Christ, confessing

Accepted	John	6	68
Confessed	Phil.	2	11
Named	Luke	2	11
Seen	John	20	25
Sovereign	I Tim.	6	15
	Mat.	12	8
Healer	Acts	9	34
Liberator	Is.	61	1
	Rom.	8	2
Our redemption	I Cor.	1	30
	II Cor.	5	21
Sin bearer	John	1	29
Preached by disciples	Acts	2	21
	Acts	3	6
	Acts	8	4
Divinely approved	Mat.	10	32, 33
A notable example	Mat.	16	17–19
Prevented by fear	John	12	42, 43

Before baptism	Acts	8	37
A universal demand	Rom.	10	9
	Phil.	2	11
Evidence new life	I John	4	2

Jesus, different titles of

Adam, the second	I Cor.	15	45–47
Advocate	I John	2	1
Alpha and Omega	Rev.	1	11
Amen	Rev.	3	14
Apostle of our profession	Heb.	3	1
Author and finisher of our faith	Heb.	12	2
Beginning of the creation of God	Rev.	3	14
Blessed and only Potentate	I Tim.	6	15
Captain of salvation	Heb.	2	10
Chief corner stone	Eph.	2	20
Chief Shepherd	I Pet.	5	4
Counsellor	Is.	9	6
Dayspring	Luke	1	78
Desire of all nations	Hag.	2	7
Emmanuel	Is.	7	14
	Mat.	1	23
Everlasting Father	Is.	9	6
Faithful witness	Rev.	1	5
First and last	Rev.	1	11
Good shepherd	John	10	11
Governor	Mat.	2	6
Great High Priest	Heb.	3	1
	Heb.	4	14
Head of the church	Eph.	4	15
	Eph.	5	23
	Col.	1	18
Heir of all things	Heb.	1	2
Holy One	Mark	1	24
	Acts	2	27
Horn of salvation	Luke	1	35
I Am	John	8	58
Just One	Acts	7	52
King of the Jews	Mat.	2	2
Lamb of God	John	1	36
	Rev.	5	12
	Rev.	13	8
	Rev.	22	1
Life, the	John	14	6
Life, bread of	John	6	35
Light of the world	John	8	12
	John	9	5
Light, true	John	1	9
Lion of the tribe of Judah	Rev.	5	5
Lord God Almighty	Rev.	15	3
Lord our righteousness	Jer.	23	6
	Acts	17	31
	Heb.	7	2
Mediator	Gal.	3	19
	I Tim.	2	5
	Heb.	9	15
Messiah	Dan.	9	25
	John	1	41
Morning star	Rev.	22	16
Prince of life	Acts	3	15
Prince of Peace	Is.	9	6
Prophet, Priest and King	Mat.	2	2
	John	18	37
	Heb.	1	8
Redeemer	Job	19	25
	Is.	59	20
Resurrection and life	John	11	25
Root of David	Rev.	22	16
Saviour	II Pet.	2	20
	II Pet.	3	18
Son of the Blessed	Mark	14	61
Son of God	Mat.	2	15
	Luke	4	34, 41
	John	3	16
	John	16	27, 30
	Rom.	1	9
Son of the Highest	Luke	1	32
Son of man	Ezek.	2	1
	Mat.	16	13
	Luke	5	24
	Acts	7	56
Son of righteousness	Mal.	4	2
Truth, the	John	14	6
Way, the	John	14	6
Wonderful	Is.	9	6
Word of God	Rev.	19	13
Word of life	I John	1	1

Jesus, life and works on earth of

Genealogy	Mat.	1	1–17
	Luke	3	23–38
Facts before birth	Mat.	1	18–25
	Luke	1	26–38
	Luke	1	39–56
Birth of	Luke	2	1–20
Magi visit	Mat.	2	1–12
Circumcision of	Luke	2	21–38
Flight into, and return from Egypt	Mat.	2	13–23
With doctors in the temple	Luke	2	41–52
Baptized by John	Mat.	3	13–17
	Mark	1	9–11
	Luke	3	21–23
Temptation of	Mat.	4	1–11
	Luke	4	1–13
Baptizes	John	3	22
	John	4	2
Begins to preach and heal	Mat.	4	12
	Mark	1	14
	Luke	4	16
His selection of disciples	Mat.	4	18
Sermon on the mount	Mat.	5–7	
Lord's prayer	Mat.	6	9–13
Cleanses the temple	John	2	14
Transfiguration on the mount	Mat.	17	1
	Mark	9	1
Blesses little children	Mat.	19	13
	Mark	10	13
	Luke	18	15
Rides into Jerusalem	Mat.	21	1
	Luke	19	29
Drives moneychangers out of temple	Mat.	21	12
	Mark	11	15
	Luke	19	45
Washes disciples' feet	John	13	5
Anointed by Mary at Bethany	Mat.	26	6–13
Institutes the Lord's supper	Mat.	26	26
	Mark	14	22
	Luke	22	19
His agony	Mat.	26	36
	Mark	14	32
	Luke	22	39
Betrayed by Judas	Mat.	26	47
Deserted by disciples	Mat.	26	31, 56
	John	18	15
His trials	Mat.	26	57
	Mat.	27	2
	Mat.	27	23
	Mark	15	15
His crucifixion	Mat.	27	33–54
	Mark	15	21–39
	Luke	23	33–47
	John	19	17–30
Buried by Joseph and Nicodemus	Mat.	27	57–66
	Mark	15	42
	Luke	23	50
	John	19	38
His resurrection	Mat.	28	1–10
	Mark	16	1–8
	Luke	24	1–12
	John	20	1–18

Appearances after resurrection:

To Mary Magdalene	Mat.	28	9
To disciples	Mat.	28	16
	Mark	16	12
Thomas	John	20	27
Peter	John	21	15

Ascension:

Described	Mark	16	19
	Luke	24	51
	Acts	1	9–11
	I Pet.	3	22
Prophecies respecting	Ps.	24	7–10
	Ps.	68	18
	John	6	62
	John	7	33
	John	14	2, 28
	John	16	5
	John	20	17

Purpose of:

To prepare a place for you	John	14	2
Intercession	Rom.	8	34
For us	Heb.	9	24
	Eph.	4	8–15
Appears after His ascension	Acts	7	55
	Acts	9	4

	Rev.	1	13
	Job	19	25
Second coming prophesied	Ps.	50	3–6
	Dan.	7	13, 14
	Mat.	24	3, 27–31
	Heb.	9	28
	Rev.	22	12

Also see Messianic prophecies, parables and miracles

Jesus Christ, types of:

Aaron	Heb.	5	4–5
Ark	I Pet.	3	20–21
Atonement	Lev.	16	15–16
Bronze altar	Ex.	27	1–2
Burnt offering	Lev.	1	2, 4
Cities of refuge	Num.	35	6
	Heb.	6	18
David	II Sam.	8	15
	Ps.	89	19–20
Eliakim	Is.	22	20–22
Golden altar	Ex.	40	26–27
Isaac	Heb.	11	17–19
Jacob	Gen.	32	28
Jonah	Mat.	12	40
Joseph	Gen.	50	19–20
Joshua	Josh.	1	5–6
Laver of brass	Ex.	30	18–20
Melchizedek	Heb.	7	1–17
Mercy seat	Ex.	25	17–22
Noah	Gen.	5	29
	II Cor.	1	5
Peace offering	Lev.	3	1
	Eph.	2	14, 16
Red heifer	Num.	19	2–6
Rock of Horeb	Ex.	17	6
	I Cor.	10	4
Sin offering	Lev.	4	2–3, 12
Solomon	II Sam.	7	12–13
Tabernacle	Ex.	40	34
Tree of life	Gen.	2	9
	John	1	4
Trespass offering	Lev.	6	1–7
Veil of the tabernacle and temple	Heb.	10	20
Zerubbabel	Zech.	4	7–9

Jether *abundance*

Eldest son of Gideon	Judg.	8	20
Father of Amasa	I Ki.	2	5, 32
Husband of Abigail, David's sister	I Chr.	2	15–17
Son of Jada	I Chr.	2	32
Son of Ezra	I Chr.	4	17
An Asherite	I Chr.	7	30, 38

Jethro *His excellence*

Moses dwells with	Ex.	2	15–22
Here called Reuel	Ex.	2	18
Father-in-law of Moses	Ex.	3	1
Moses asks his permission to return to Egypt	Ex.	4	18
Visits Moses	Ex.	18	1–7
Advises Moses	Ex.	18	8–27
Here called Raguel	Num.	10	29

Jetur *encircled*

Son of Ishmael	Gen.	25	15
	I Chr.	1	31

Jeush, Jehush *collector; hasty*

Son of Esau	Gen.	36	5, 14
A Benjamite, son of Bilhan	I Chr.	7	10
Son of Shimei	I Chr.	23	10, 11
Son of Rehoboam	II Chr.	11	19

jewels *costly ornaments*

Of Rebekah	Gen.	24	30
Precious	Gen.	24	53
Buried	Gen.	35	4
Borrowed	Ex.	11	2
In the breastplate of judgment	Ex.	28	17–21
For the calf	Ex.	32	2, 3
For the tabernacle	Ex.	35	22
As an offering	Num.	31	50, 51
	I Sam.	6	8, 15
In the crown of the king of Ammon	II Sam.	12	30
The gift of the queen of Sheba	I Ki.	10	2, 10
Sign of office	Esth.	3	10, 12
Of wisdom	Job	28	13–20
Discretion in use of	Prov.	11	22
Symbol of spiritual adornment	Is.	3	18–21
	Ezek.	16	12, 17, 39

jewels—*continued*

Attire of males	Ezek.	23	42
Of Eden	Ezek.	28	13
Of great price	Mat.	13	45, 46
In the new Jerusalem	Rev.	21	1–27

Jewish alphabet

All letters listed in titles of	Ps.	119	1–176

Jewish calendar

Abib or Nisan (April)	Ex.	13	4
Zif (May)	I Ki.	6	1
Sivan (June)	Esth.	8	9
Tammuz (July)	Jer.	39	2
Ab (August)	Num.	33	38
Elul (September)	Neh.	6	15
Ethanim or Tisri (October)	I Ki.	8	2
Bul (November)	I Ki.	6	38
Chisleu (December)	Ezra	10	9
Tebeth (January)	Esth.	2	16
Sebat (February)	Zech.	1	7
Adar (March)	Esth.	3	7
See also Feasts			

Jews

A form of Judah, applied to the people of the praise of Judah, and in later periods to all Israelites	II Ki.	16	6
	II Ki.	25	25
	II Chr.	32	18
Smite their enemies	Esth.	9	5
A wealthy people	Esth.	10	3
Christ sent to	Mat.	15	24
Christ, a Jew	John	4	9, 22
Called for Christ's crucifixion	Mat.	27	21–23
	John	18	39, 40
Stir up Gentiles	Acts	14	2
Banished from Rome	Acts	18	2
Conspire to kill Paul	Acts	23	11–22
Kill Jesus	I Thes.	2	14, 15
Self-righteous	Rom.	10	1–3
See Israelites			

Jezaniah *see* Jaazaniah

Jezebel *chaste*

Daughter of Ethbaal, wife of Ahab	I Ki.	16	30, 31
Persecutes prophets	I Ki.	18	4, 13, 19
	II Ki.	9	7, 22
Vows to kill Elijah	I Ki.	19	1–3
Plots and succeeds in having Naboth slain	I Ki.	21	5–16
Her death foretold	I Ki.	21	23
	II Ki.	9	10
Her death	II Ki.	9	30–37
Symbolizes evil	Rev.	2	20

Jezoar *see* Zoar

Jezreel *God sows*

A city of Judah	Josh.	15	56
City at mount Gilboa	Josh.	19	18
A valley	Josh.	17	16
	Judg.	6	33
Ruled by Ish-bosheth	II Sam.	2	9
Residence of Ahab	I Ki.	18	45, 46
Place of Naboth's vineyard	I Ki.	21	1
Joram returns to be healed	II Ki.	8	29
Jezebel slain here	II Ki.	9	30, 33
Ahab's heirs slain	II Ki.	10	11
A man of Judah	I Chr.	4	3
Son of Hosea	Hosea	1	4
Figurative of Israel	Hosea	1	4, 5, 11

Jiphthah-el *God will open*

A valley in the land of Zebulun	Josh.	19	10, 14

Joab *Jehovah is Father*

Son of Zeruiah, nephew of David	II Sam.	8	16
	I Chr.	2	15, 16
Commander of David's army	II Sam.	8	16
	II Sam.	20	23
Leads capture of Jebus	II Sam.	5	8–10
Slays Abner	II Sam.	3	27
Defeats the Ammonites	II Sam.	10	7–14
Brings Absalom home	II Sam.	14	23
Slays Absalom	II Sam.	18	14
Censures David	II Sam.	19	1–9
Slays Amasa	II Sam.	20	8–13
Causes Sheba's death	II Sam.	20	20–22
Opposes David on census	II Sam.	24	3
Aids in census	II Sam.	24	4–9
Supports Adonijah	I Ki.	1	7
David's analysis of	I Ki.	2	1–6
Slain by order of Solomon	I Ki.	2	29–34
Destroys Edom	I Ki.	11	16

Son of Seraiah	I Chr.	4	14
Descendents return from Babylon	Ezra	2	6
	Ezra	8	9

Joanna, Joanan *Jehovah is gracious*

Ancestor of Jesus	Luke	3	23, 27
Wife of Chuza	Luke	8	3
Reports Christ's resurrection	Luke	24	10

Joash, Jehoash *whom Jehovah supports*

Father of Gideon	Judg.	6	11
Defends his son	Judg.	6	29–32
Buried at Ophrah	Judg.	8	32
Son of King Ahab	I Ki.	22	26
Son of Ahaziah	II Ki.	11	2
Saved from death by his aunt	II Ki.	11	2, 3
Anointed king	II Ki.	11	12
Begins his reign when seven	II Ki.	11	21
Lives in righteousness	II Ki.	12	2
Repairs the temple	II Ki.	12	4–16
Turns to idolatry	II Chr.	24	17–22
Bargains with Syrians	II Chr.	24	23, 24
Diseased	II Chr.	24	25
Conspired against and slain	II Chr.	24	25, 26
Son of Jehoahaz, a king of Israel	II Ki.	13	9
Israel	II Ki.	13	9
An idolator	II Ki.	13	11
Defeats Ben-hadad	II Ki.	13	25
Defeats Amaziah	II Ki.	14	11–14
A descendant of Shelah	I Chr.	4	21, 22
Son of Becher	I Chr.	7	8
Son of Shemaah	I Chr.	12	3
Officer of David, in charge of oil stores	I Chr.	27	28

Joatham *Jehovah is perfect*

Ancestor of Christ	Mat.	1	9, 16

Job *howler*

A son of Issachar	Gen.	46	13
Ancient saint of the land of Uz	Job	1	1
His character	Job	1	1–8
	Job	2	3
	Ezek.	14	14, 20
His afflictions and patience	Job	1	13, 20
	Job	2	7, 10
	James	5	11
Complains of his life	Job	3	1
Reproves his friends	Job	6	1
	Job	26–30	
Solemnly protests his integrity	Job	31	1
Humbles himslef	Job	40	3
	Job	42	1
God accepts and doubly blesses	Job	42	10

Jobab *howler*

Son of Joktan	Gen.	10	29
Son of Zerah	Gen.	36	33, 34
King of Madon	Josh.	11	1
Son of Shaharaim	I Chr.	8	9
Son of Elpaal	I Chr.	8	18

Jochebed *Jehovah is gracious*

Mother of Moses and Aaron	Ex.	6	20
Wife of Amram	Ex.	6	20
Mother of Miriam	Num.	26	59

Joed *appointer*

A Benjamite	Neh.	11	7

Joel *Jehovah is God*

Son of Samuel	I Sam.	8	1, 2
A Simeonite	I Chr.	4	35
A Reubenite, father of Shemaiah	I Chr.	5	4, 8
Chief of the Gadites	I Chr.	5	12
A Kohathite Levite, son of Azariah	I Chr.	6	36
	II Chr.	29	12
Son of Uzzi	I Chr.	7	3
One of David's valiant men	I Chr.	11	38
A Gershomite	I Chr.	15	7
Son of Laadan	I Chr.	23	8
Over the treasures of the house of the Lord	I Chr.	26	22
A Levite	I Chr.	15	11
Son of Pedaiah	I Chr.	27	20
Son of Nebo	Ezra	10	43
Son of Zichri	Neh.	11	9
Son of Pethuel, a prophet	Joel	1	1
	Acts	2	16
Proclaims God's judgments	Joel	1	1–14
	Joel	2	1–11
Exhorts to repentance	Joel	2	12–32
Sets forth blessings	Joel	3	18–21

Johanan *Jehovah is gracious*

Captain, son of Careah	II Ki.	25	23

Warns Gedaliah	Jer.	40	13–16
Defeats Ishmael	Jer.	41	11–15
Seeks prayers of Jeremiah	Jer.	42	2, 3
Jewish refugees taken to Egypt	Jer.	41	16–18
Disobeys	Jer.	43	1–7
Son of Josiah	I Chr.	3	15
Son of Elioenai	I Chr.	3	24
A Levite, son of Azariah	I Chr.	6	9
Father of Azariah, a priest	I Chr.	6	10
Benjamite warrior who joins David at Ziklag	I Chr.	12	4
A Gadite captain	I Chr.	12	12
An Ephraimite leader	II Chr.	28	12
Son of Hakkatan	Ezra	8	12
Son of Eliashib	Ezra	10	6
Son of Tobiah	Neh.	6	18
A Levite, son of Joiada	Neh.	12	11, 22

John *short form of Jonathan meaning gift of Jehovah*

The apostle	Mark	1	19, 20
Son of Zebedee	Mat.	4	21
Chosen an apostle	Mat.	10	2
Member of the inner circle	Mat.	17	1
	Mark	14	33–38
	Luke	8	51
Fisherman	Luke	5	1–11
Sent to prepare the passover	Luke	22	8
Sat next to Jesus at the Last Supper	John	13	23–25
Declares divinity of Christ	John	1	1
Christ's love for	John	13	23
	John	19	26
His care for the Lord's mother	John	19	27
Sees ascension	Acts	1	9–13
Heals man	Acts	3	1–11
Imprisoned	Acts	8	14 25
Sees Christ's glory in heaven	Rev.	1	13
Writes the Revelation	Rev.	1	19
Writes three epistles I, II, III, John			
The Baptist, son of Zacharias	Luke	1	5–23
	Luke	1	57–67
His coming foretold	Is.	40	3
	Luke	1	13–17
Nazarite vow	Luke	1	15
Shows Jesus to be the Messiah	John	1	29–36
Beheaded	Mark	6	14
His birth and circumcision	Luke	1	57
Office, preaching and baptism	Luke	3	1
	John	1	6
	Acts	1	5
Imprisoned by Herod	Luke	3	20
Sends his disciples to Christ	Luke	7	18
Christ's testimony	Luke	7	27
Baptizes Christ	John	1	32
	John	3	26
His disciples receive the Holy Ghost	Acts	18	24

Johonadab *see Jonadab*

Joiada *Jehovah knows*

Son of Paseah	Neh.	3	6
Son of Eliashib	Neh.	12	10, 22
Father of Jonathan	Neh.	12	11
Son married strange wife	Neh.	13	28

Joiarib *Jehovah will contend*

Adviser of Ezra, sent to Iddo	Ezra	8	16
Father of Adaiah	Neh.	11	5
A chief priest	Neh.	12	6, 19
Father of Jedaiah	Neh.	11	10

join *put together*

Hand *j* in hand	Prov.	11	21
	Prov.	16	5
That *j* house to house	Is.	5	8
Let us *j* ourselves to the Lord	Jer.	50	5
Ephraim is *j* to idols	Hosea	4	17
What God hath *j*	Mat.	19	6
	Mark	10	9
Durst no man *j* himself	Acts	5	13
Go near, and *j* thyself to this chariot	Acts	8	29
Perfectly *j* in the same mind	I Cor.	1	10
J to the Lord	I Cor.	6	17
The whole body fitly *j*	Eph.	4	16

joining

	I Chr.	22	3

joint

Thigh out of *j*	Gen.	32	25
All my bones are out of *j*	Ps.	22	14
Like foot out of *j*	Prov.	25	19
Which every *j* supplieth	Eph.	4	16
Body by *j* and bands knit together	Col.	2	19
Dividing of *j* and marrow	Heb.	4	12

joint heirs	Rom.	8	17

Jokdeam *burning of the people*

A city of Judah	Josh.	15	56

Jokmeam *people will be raised*

A city of Kohathites	I Chr.	6	68
Same as Jokneam	I Ki.	4	12

Jokneam *people will be lamented or possessed*

Ruled by a king	Josh.	12	22
Allotted to Zebulun	Josh.	19	11
A Levitical city	Josh.	21	34
Town of Ephraim	I Chr.	6	68
	I Ki.	4	12

Jona *see Jonas*

Jonadab, Jehonadab *Jehovah is bounteous*

Son of Rechab, companion of Jehu	II Ki.	10	15
Commands his sons not to drink wine	Jer.	35	5–10
	Jer.	35	16–19
Opposed idolatry	II Ki.	10	15–27
Son of Shimea	II Sam.	13	3
His complicity	II Sam.	13	3–5
Comforts David	II Sam.	13	32–36

Jonah, Jonas *dove*

A prophet, son of Amittai	II Ki.	14	25
Commanded to go to Nineveh	Jonah	1	1, 2
Flees	Jonah	1	3
Punishment	Jonah	1	4–17
Prays for salvation	Jonah	2	1–10
Obeys command	Jonah	3	3
Successful	Jonah	3	5–9
Grieves	Jonah	4	1
Bigot	Jonah	4	2, 3
Cured	Jonah	4	4–11
Called Jonas	Mat.	12	41
Sign	Luke	11	29, 30

Jonan *Jehovah hath been gracious*

An ancestor of Jesus	Luke	3	30

Jonas, Jona *Greek form of Jonah*

Father of Simon	John	1	42
Here called Jona	John	21	15–17

Jonathan *Jehovah's gift*

A Levite, son of Gershom	Judg.	18	30
Becomes priest for Danites	Judg.	18	3–31
Defeats garrison at Geba	I Sam.	13	3
Son of Saul	I Sam.	13	16
Victorious at Michmash	I Sam.	14	1–18
Innocently breaks Saul's oath	I Sam.	14	24–39
Saved by the people	I Sam.	14	43–45
Saul's eldest son	I Sam.	14	49
Warns David with bow	I Sam.	20	1–42
Loves David	I Sam.	19	1–7
	I Sam.	23	16–18
Two covenants with David	I Sam.	18	1–4
	I Sam.	23	15–18
Killed	I Sam.	31	2, 6
Buried by men of Jabeshgilead	I Sam.	31	11–13
Lamented by David	II Sam.	1	12, 17–27
David cares for his son	II Sam.	4	4
Son of Abiathar	II Sam.	15	27
Acts as spy for David	II Sam.	15	28
	II Sam.	17	17–22
Informs Adonijah	I Ki.	1	42–48
Son of Shimeah, slays giant	II Sam.	21	20, 21
Father of a hero	II Sam.	23	32
Son of Jada	I Chr.	2	32
Son of Shage	I Chr.	11	34
Uncle of David	I Chr.	27	32
Father of Ebed	Ezra	8	6
Son of Asahel	Ezra	10	15
Son of Joiada and a chief priest	Neh.	12	11, 22
Son of Melicu	Neh.	12	14
Father of Zechariah	Neh.	12	35
Son of Kareah	Jer.	40	8

Joppa, Japho *to shine, beautiful*

A city of Dan	Josh.	19	46
Exports	II Chr.	2	16
	Ezra	3	7
Passenger traffic from	Jonah	1	3
The miracle of Peter	Acts	9	36–42
The vision of Peter	Acts	10	9–18

Joram, Jehoram *Jehovah raised*

Son of Toi	II Sam.	8	9, 10
Here called Hadoram	I Chr.	18	9, 10
Son of Ahab	II Ki.	3	1
Slain by Jehu	II Ki.	9	14–26
Son of Eliezer	I Chr.	29	25

Joram, Jehoram *Jehovah raised*

A priest	II Chr.	17	8
Son of Jehoshaphat, king of Judah	II Chr.	21	1
Slays brothers	II Chr.	21	2
Idolator	II Ki.	8	17, 18
Edom revolts	II Chr.	21	8–10
Married to daughter of Ahab	II Chr.	21	6
Subdues Edom	II Chr.	21	8, 9
Dies of plague	II Chr.	21	19
Father of Ahaziah	II Chr.	22	1
Slain by Jehu	II Ki.	9	14–26

Jordan *descender*

River of Canaan	Gen.	13	10
Jacob crosses over	Gen.	32	9, 10
Waters of, divided	Josh.	3	1–17
Divided by Elijah	II Ki.	2	6–8
Divided by Elisha	II Ki.	2	13, 14
Its waters heal	II Ki.	5	10
John baptizes here	Mat.	3	1–6
Jesus baptised in	Mark	1	9

Jorim *Jehovah exalts*

Father of Eliezer	Luke	3	29

Jorkoam *people will be poured forth*

Descendant of Caleb	I Chr.	2	42
Son of Raham	I Chr.	2	44

Josabad *see Jozabad*

Josaphat *see Jehoshaphat*

Jose *let him add*

Ancestor of Jesus Christ	Luke	3	28, 29

Josedech *see Jozadak*

Joseph *he shall add*

Son of Jacob and Rachel	Gen.	30	24
His father's favourite child	Gen.	33	2
	Gen.	48	21, 22
His dreams and the jealousy of his brothers	Gen.	37	5–11
	Ps.	105	17
	Acts	7	9
Sold into Egypt	Gen.	37	29–35
Servant to Potiphar	Gen.	39	1–4
Resists temptation, placed into prison	Gen.	39	7–20
Interprets dreams	Gen.	40	1–23
	Gen.	41	1–36
Made governor of Egypt	Gen.	41	39–43
Prepares for the famine	Gen.	41	48
Receives his brothers	Gen.	42	1–25
Brings brothers and father to Egypt	Gen.	46	1–34
	Gen.	50	1–26
Buys land of Egypt for Pharaoh	Gen.	47	13–26
Sons Ephraim and Manasseh	Gen.	48	1
Dies at 110 years	Gen.	50	26
Father of Igal	Num.	13	7
A son of Asaph	I Chr.	25	2
A returned exile	Ezra	10	42
A priest	Neh.	12	14
Husband of Mary	Mat.	1	18–25
	Mark	6	3
Descendant of David	Mat.	1	20
Hears angel in dream	Mat.	1	20–24
Takes family to Egypt	Mat.	2	13–15
A carpenter by trade	Mat.	13	55
Dwells at Nazareth	Luke	2	4
Travels to Bethlehem	Luke	2	4, 5
Jesus born	Luke	2	7
Returns to Nazareth	Luke	2	39
Joseph of Arimathaea	Mark	15	42
	Luke	23	50–54
Secret disciple	John	19	38
Requests Christ's body	Mark	15	43
Supplies tomb for Christ's burial	Luke	23	53
Three ancestors of Jesus	Luke	3	24, 26, 30
Surnamed Barsabas	Acts	1	21–23

Joses *adding*

Brother of Jesus	Mark	6	3
Son of Eliezer	Luke	3	29
A Levite, called Barnabas	Acts	4	36

Joshua, Jehoshua, Jehoshuah, Oshea *Jehovah is salvation*

A minister or servant of Moses	Ex.	24	13
	Ex.	33	11
Son of Nun	Num.	13	8
	I Chr.	7	27
Defeated Amalek	Ex.	17	8–16
Sent to view the promised land	Num.	13	8
Makes a favourable report	Num.	14	6–10
Ordained and charged as successor of Moses	Num.	27	18–23
	Deut.	31	3, 7, 23
Filled with the Spirit	Num.	27	18
Leads the people into the land of Canaan	Josh.	1–4	
Esteem in which he is held	Josh.	1	16–18
Renews circumcision	Josh.	5	2–9
Re-establishes the passover	Josh.	5	10, 11
Besieges and takes Jericho	Josh.	6	
His faith	Josh.	6	16
Captures Ai	Josh.	7	8
Conquers all Canaan	Josh.	11	23
Allots land of Canaan	Josh.	13–19	
Reviews the covenant	Josh.	23	1–16
Death and burial	Josh.	24	29, 30
Called Jeshua	Neh.	8	17
Called Jesus	Acts	7	45
	Heb.	4	8
Called Oshea	Num.	13	8
A Beth-shemite	I Sam.	6	14
A governor of Jerusalem	II Ki.	23	8

See Jeshua, Jesus

Josiah, Josias *healed by Jehovah*

Prophecy of his birth	I Ki.	13	1,2
Son of Amon	II Ki.	21	25, 26
A reformer	II Ki.	22	1–20
Repairs temple	II Ki.	22	3–9
Finds Book of the Law	II Ki.	22	10–17
Keeps passover	II Ki.	23	21–23
Destroys high places	II Ki.	23	3–20, 24
Jeremiah laments	II Chr.	35	25–27
In the genealogy of Christ	Mat.	1	10, 11
Suppresses idolatry	II Ki.	23	1–20
Slain	II Ki.	23	29, 30
Father of Jehoahaz	II Ki.	23	30
Husband of Hamutal	II Ki.	23	31
Father of Eliakim	II Ki.	23	34
Here called Josias	Mat.	1	10, 11
Son of Zephaniah	Zech.	6	10

Jotham *Jehovah is perfect*

Youngest son of Jerubbaal	Judg.	9	5
Rebukes men of Shechem	Judg.	9	7–20
Flees from Abimelech	Judg.	9	21
Son of Jahdai	I Chr.	2	47
Son of Uzziah	II Chr.	26	21
King of Judah	II Ki.	15	5, 7
Captures Ammon	II Chr.	27	5–9
Isaiah and Hosea prophesy in his reign	Is.	1	1
	Hosea	1	1
In genealogy of Christ	Mat.	1	9

journey *trip or travels*

Lord made *j* prosperous	Gen.	24	21
Take the victuals for your *j*	Josh.	9	11
Or he is in a *j*	I Ki.	18	27
How long shall thy *j* be	Neh.	2	6
Nor scrip for your *j*	Mat.	10	10
	Mark	6	8
	Luke	9	3
A friend in his *j*	Luke	11	6
Took his *j* into a far country	Luke	15	13
Jesus, wearied with his *j*	John	4	6
In *j* often	II Cor.	11	26

joy *mirth, gladness*

God's word affords	Neh.	8	12
	Jer.	15	16
Of the wicked is short-lived	Job	20	5
	Eccl.	7	6
In worshipping God	Ps.	21	1
	Ps.	89	16
	Ps.	149	2
Follows weeping	Ps.	30	5
	Ps.	126	5
	John	16	20
Serve God with	Ps.	100	2
Promised to saints	Ps.	132	11
Of the wicked is derived from folly	Prov.	15	21
Not in earthly things	Eccl.	2	10, 11
Given by God	Eccl.	2	26
In times of stress	Hab.	3	17, 18
	Luke	6	22, 23
	James	1	2
The gospel, good tidings of	Luke	2	10, 11
In conversion of sinners	Luke	15	7–10
	Acts	15	3
Through belief in Christ	John	15	10, 11
	Phil.	3	3
Through answers to prayer	John	16	24

In Christ's victory over death	John	16	33
In the Holy Ghost	Rom.	14	17
Coming of Christ will afford	I Pet.	4	13
Experienced by:			
Believers	Luke	24	52
	Acts	16	34
Peace-makers	Prov.	12	20
The just	Prov.	21	15
Parents of good children	Prov.	23	24
Exemplified:			
Hannah	I Sam.	2	1
David	I Chr.	29	9
Wise men	Mat.	2	10
Virgin Mary	Luke	1	47
Converts	Acts	2	46

Jozabad, Josabad *Jehovah endowed*

A warrior of David	I Chr.	12	4
Two captains of Manasseh	I Chr.	12	20
An overseer of tithes	II Chr.	31	13
A Levite	II Chr.	35	9
Son of Jehsua, a Levite	Ezra	8	33
Expounds law	Neh.	8	7
Chief Levite	Neh.	8	7
Son of Pashur	Ezra	10	22

Jozachar *Jehovah has remembered*

A servant who helps slay Joash	II Ki.	12	20, 21
Here called Zabad	II Chr.	24	26

Jozadak, Jehozadak, Josedech *Jehovah is just*

Son of Seraiah, a priest	I Chr.	6	14
Goes into captivity	I Chr.	6	15
Father of Jeshua	Ezra	3	2
Here called Josedech	Hag.	1	1, 12

Jubal *a stream*

The father of musicians	Gen.	4	21

Jubile year, jubilee year *see* feasts and festivals

Jucal *see* Jehucal

Judaea, Judea *land of praise*

Comprises the whole of the ancient kingdom of Judah	I Ki.	12	21–24
Roman district ruled by Pontius Pilate	Luke	3	1
Jesus born in	Mat.	2	1, 5, 6
Called the land of Judah	Mat.	2	6
John the Baptist preaches in	Mat.	3	1
Jesus tempted in the wilderness of	Mat.	4	1
A mountainous country	Luke	1	39, 65
One of the divisions of the holy land under the Romans	Luke	3	1
Churches started there	I Thes.	2	14
Principal towns:			
Bethlehem	Mat.	2	1, 6, 16
Jerusalem	Mat.	4	25
Arimathaea	Mat.	27	57
Jericho	Luke	10	30
Emmaus	Luke	24	13
Bethany	John	11	1, 18

Judah *praised*

Fourth son of Jacob by Leah	Gen.	35	23
Intercedes for Joseph	Gen.	37	26, 27
Takes two wives	Gen.	38	1–6
Incest with his daughter-in-law	Gen.	38	12–26
Father of Pharez and Zarah	Gen.	38	29, 30
Prophetic benediction of his father	Gen.	49	8–12
Messianic prophecy	Gen.	49	10
Ancestor of Jesus	Mat.	1	2, 3
Land of Judah, called Judea after the exile	Ezra	5	8
A Levite who married a foreign wife	Ezra	10	23
Son of Senuah	Neh.	11	9
A Levite who comes to Jerusalem	Neh.	12	8
Son of priest who helps dedicate wall	Neh.	12	36
Levite workman on temple	Ezra	3	9

Judah, tribe of

Descended from Jacob's fourth son	Gen.	29	35
Prophecies concerning	Gen.	49	10
Strength of, when leaving Egypt	Num.	1	26, 27
Place of, in camp and march	Num.	2	3, 9
	Num.	10	14
Strength of, on entering Canaan	Num.	26	22
Moses' benediction upon	Deut.	33	7
Bounds of inheritance	Josh.	15	1–12
Chosen by God to lead in conquest of the promised land	Judg.	1	1–4
Fights against Benjaminites	Judg.	20	18, 19
Makes David king	II Sam.	2	1–11
Rebuked by David	II Sam.	19	11–15
Loyalty to David	II Sam.	20	1, 2

Faithful to Rehoboam	I Ki.	12	21
Last tribe carried into captivity	II Ki.	25	21
Jesus descended from	Mat.	1	3–16
	Luke	3	23–33

Judas *celebrated*

Surnamed Iscariot	Mat.	10	4
Chosen as an apostle	Mat.	10	4
	Mark	3	19
Prophecies concerning	Mat.	26	21–25
	Mark	14	18–21
Plots to betray Jesus	Mat.	26	14–16
	Luke	22	3–6
	John	13	2
Betrays Jesus with a kiss	Mat.	26	47–50
	Acts	1	16–25
Returns money	Mat.	27	3–10
Hangs himself	Mat.	27	5
	Acts	1	18
Protests use of ointment	John	12	4–6
Treasurer of the disciples	John	12	6
	John	13	29
A brother of Jesus	Mat.	13	55
	Mark	6	3
An apostle, also called Thaddaeus	Mark	3	18
	Luke	6	16
Inquisitive	John	14	22
An instigator from Galilee	Acts	5	37
A Jew of Damascus who entertains Paul	Acts	9	11
Barsabas, a Christian sent to Antioch with Paul	Acts	15	22–32
Judah in Greek	Mat.	1	2, 3
In genealogy of Christ	Luke	3	30

Jude *praise*

Author of the epistle	Jude		1
Brother of James, some believe him to be Judas, the brother of Jesus	Mat.	13	55

Judea *see* Judaea

judge *a civil magistrate*

Moses instructs tribes to appoint	Ex.	18	13–26
	Deut.	1	12–16
Not to take bribes	Deut.	16	18
Israel does not always heed	Judg.	2	17, 18
To be in righteousness	Deut.	1	16
Particularly to judge sin	I Sam.	2	25
Becomes job of king	I Sam.	8	5, 6, 20
Requires wisdom	I Ki.	3	9
Particular care of poor and fatherless	Prov.	3	9
	Jer.	5	28
Upheld and strengthened by God	Judg.	2	18
Corrupt judges	I Sam.	2	12
	I Sam.	8	1–5
Judges of Israel:			
Othniel	Judg.	3	9
Ehud	Judg.	3	15
Shamgar	Judg.	3	31
Deborah	Judg.	4	4
Gideon	Judg.	6	36
Abimelech	Judg.	9	22
Tola	Judg.	10	1, 2
Jair	Judg.	10	3
Jephthah	Judg.	12	7
Ibzan	Judg.	12	8
Elon	Judg.	12	11
Abdon	Judg.	12	13
Samson	Judg.	16	30, 31
Eli	I Sam.	4	15, 18
Samuel	I Sam.	7	15

judgment *decision given*

Cautions concerning	Mat.	7	1
	Luke	6	37
	Luke	12	57
	John	7	24
	Rom.	2	1
	James	4	11
Described	Ps.	50	
	Dan.	7	9
	Mat.	25	31
	II Thes.	1	8
	Rev.	6	12
	Rev.	20	11
Hope of Christians respecting	Rom.	8	33
	I Cor.	4	5
	II Tim.	4	8
	I John	2	28
	I John	4	17
The books shall be opened at	Dan.	7	10

judgment—*continued*

Christ will acknowledge saints at	Mat.	25	34–40
	Rev.	3	5
Devils shall be condemned at	II Pet.	2	4
	Jude		6
Final punishment of the wicked will succeed	Mat.	13	40–42
	Mat.	25	46
A first principle of the gospel	Heb.	6	2
Neglected advantages increase condemnation at	Mat.	11	20–24
	Luke	11	31–32
None, by nature can stand in	Ps.	130	3
	Ps.	143	2
	Rom.	3	19
Of Christians, by the gospel	James	2	12
Of heathens, by the law of conscience	Rom.	2	12, 14–15
Of Jews by the law of Moses	Rom.	2	12
Predicted in the Old Testament	I Chr.	16	33
	Ps.	96	13
Saints shall be rewarded at	Rev.	11	18
Saints shall sit with Christ in	I Cor.	6	2
	Rev.	20	4
Shall be administered by Christ	John	5	27
	Acts	10	42
Shall be in Righteousness	Ps.	98	9
Warn the wicked of	II Cor.	5	11
The wicked shall be condemned in	Mat.	7	22–23
	Mat.	25	41
The word of Christ shall be a witness against the wicked in	John	12	48

Certainty of, a motive to:

Faith	Is.	28	16–17
Holiness	II Cor.	5	9–10
	II Pet.	3	11, 14
Prayer and watchfulness	Mark	13	33

Shall be of all:

Actions	Eccl.	11	9
	Rev.	20	13
Thoughts	Eccl.	12	14
	I Cor.	4	5
Words	Mat.	12	36–37
	Jude		15
Against the gods execute *j*	Ex.	12	12
The *j* is God's	Deut.	1	17
Judge people with just *j*	Deut.	16	18
All his ways are *j*	Deut.	32	4
Executed *j* and justice	II Sam.	8	15
	I Chr.	18	14
Ungodly shall not stand in *j*	Ps.	1	5
Prepared his throne for *j*	Ps.	9	7
The meek will he guide in *j*	Ps.	25	9
Bring forth thy *j* as the noon-day	Ps.	37	6
Justice and *j* are habitation of throne	Ps.	89	14
	Ps.	97	2
I will sing of mercy and *j*	Ps.	101	1
Then shalt thou understand *j*	Prov.	2	9
J cometh from the Lord	Prov.	29	26
To every purpose there is time and *j*	Eccl.	8	6
When thy *j* are in the earth	Is.	26	9
Taken from prison and from *j*	Is.	53	8
Keep mercy and *j*	Hosea	12	6
In danger of the *j*	Mat.	5	21
Pass over *j* and the love of God	Luke	11	42
Committed all *j* to the Son	John	5	22
For *j* I am come	John	9	39
Now is the *j* of this world	John	12	31
Reprove the world of *j*	John	16	8
His *j* was taken away	Acts	8	33
J came on all to condemnation	Rom.	5	18
We shall all stand before *j* seat	Rom.	14	10
After this is the *j*	Heb.	9	27
Certain fearful looking for of *j*	Heb.	10	27
J begin at house of God	I Pet.	4	17

Judgments:

Are frequently tempered with mercy	Jer.	4	27
	Jer.	5	10, 15–18
	Amos	9	8
Are from God	Deut.	32	39
	Job	12	23
	Amos	3	6
	Mic.	6	9
Are in all the earth	I Chr.	16	14

Received for:

Despising the warnings of God	II Chr.	36	16
	Prov.	1	24–31
	Jer.	44	4–6
Disobedience to God	Lev.	26	14–16
	II Cor.	7	19–20
Idolatry	II Ki.	22	17
	Jer.	16	18
Iniquity	Is.	26	21
	Ezek.	24	13–14
Murmuring against God	Num.	14	29
Persecuting saints	Deut.	32	43
Sins of rulers	I Chr.	21	2, 12

Types of:

Abandonment by God	Hosea	4	17
Blotting out the name	Deut.	29	20
Captivity	Deut.	28	41
	Ezek.	29	23
Continued sorrows	Ps.	32	10
	Ps.	78	32–33
Cursing men's blessings	Mal.	2	22
Enemies	II Sam.	24	13
Famine	Deut.	28	38–40
	Amos	4	7–9
Pestilence	Deut.	28	21–22
	Amos	4	10
The sword	Ex.	22	24
	Jer.	19	7

Inflicted upon:

All enemies of saints	Jer.	30	16
False gods	Num.	33	4
Individuals	Deut.	29	20
	Jer.	30	16
Nations	Gen.	15	14
	Jer.	51	20–21
Posterity of sinners	Ex.	20	5
	Ps.	37	28
	Lam.	5	7

Saints:

Acknowledge the justice of	II Sam.	24	17
	Ezra	9	13
	Neh.	9	33
	Jer.	14	7
Pray for those under	Ex.	32	11–13
	Num.	11	2
	Dan.	9	3
Preserved during	Job	5	19–20
	Ps.	91	7
	Is.	26	20
	Ezek.	9	6
	Rev.	7	3
Provided for, during	Gen.	47	12
	Ps.	35	19
	Ps.	37	19
Sympathize with those under	Jer.	9	1
	Jer.	13	17
	Lam.	3	48
Sent for correction	Job	37	13
	Jer.	30	11
Sent for the deliverance of saints	Ex.	6	6
Should be a warning to others	Luke	13	3, 5

Should lead to:

Contrition	Neh.	1	4
	Esth.	4	3
	Is.	22	12
Humiliation	Josh.	7	6
	II Chr.	12	6
	Lam.	3	1–20
	John	3	5–6
Learning righteousness	Is.	26	9
Prayer	II Chr.	20	9

judgment hall *see pretorium*

judgment seat *seat of justice*

Used to denote trial for crime committed	Mat.	27	19
	Acts	18	12
	Acts	25	10
Of Christ	Rom.	14	10

judgment, the last

The righteous and wicked	Eccl.	3	17
Small and great	Rev.	20	12
Time of, unknown to us	Mark	13	32
Motive to repentance	Acts	17	30, 31
A day appointed for	Acts	17	31
The wicked dread	Acts	24	25
Of heathens	Rom.	2	12–15
Of the quick and the dead	II Tim.	4	1
Upon all men	Heb.	9	27

Judith *Jewess*

Wife of Esau	Gen.	26	34
Here called Aholibamah	Gen.	36	2

Julia *feminine form of Julius*

A Christian woman of Rome	Rom.	16	15

Julius *downy*

A centurion	Acts	27	1
Saves Paul	Acts	27	41–44

Junia *belonging to Juno*

A kinsman of Paul	Rom.	16	7

juniper *a shrub*

Shelters Elijah in the wilderness	I Ki.	19	4, 5
Its roots used for food	Job	30	4
Used for fuel for fires	Ps.	120	4

Jupiter *chief Roman god*

People of Lystra call Barnabas	Acts	14	12, 13

Jushab-hesed *whose love is returned*

Son of Zerubbabel	I Chr.	3	20

justice *fair dealing*

In business	Lev.	19	36
Commanded	Deut.	16	20
	Is.	56	1
Gifts impede	Ex.	23	8
Christ, an example of	Ps.	98	9
	Is.	11	4
	Jer.	23	5
Reward of	Jer.	22	15
To servants	Col.	4	1
Promises to	Is.	33	15–16
	Jer.	7	5, 7
Specially required in rulers	II Sam.	23	3
	Ezek.	45	9

God:

Delights in	Prov.	11	1
Displeased with the want of	Eccl.	5	8
Gives wisdom to execute	I Ki.	3	11–12
	Prov.	2	6, 9
Requires	Mic.	6	8
Sets the highest value on	Prov.	21	3

Saints should:

Always do	Ps.	119	121
	Ezek.	18	8–9
Pray for wisdom to execute	I Ki.	3	9
Receive instruction in	Prov.	1	3
Study the principles of	Phil.	4	8
Take pleasure in doing	Prov.	21	15
Teach others to do	Gen.	18	19

To be done:

In executing judgment	Deut.	16	18
	Jer.	21	12
To the fatherless and widows	Is.	1	17
To the poor	Prov.	29	14
	Prov.	31	9

The wicked:

Abhor	Mic.	3	9
Afflict those who act with	Job	12	4
	Amos	5	12
Banish	Is.	59	14
Call not for	Is.	59	4
Pass over	Luke	11	42
Scorn	Prov.	19	28

Exemplified:

Moses	Num.	16	15
David	II Sam.	8	15
Solomon	I Ki.	3	16–27
Josiah	Jer.	22	15
Joseph	Luke	23	50, 51
Apostles	I Thes.	2	10

Of God:

Acknowledge	Ps.	51	4
The habitation of his throne	Ps.	89	14
Impartial	II Chr.	19	7
	Jer.	32	19
Incomparable	Job	4	1
Incorruptible	Deut.	10	17
	II Chr.	19	7
Plenteous	Job	37	23
Undeviating	Job	8	3
	Job	34	12
Unfailing	Zeph.	3	5
Without respect of persons	Rom.	2	11
	Col.	3	25
	I Pet.	1	17
Denied by the ungodly	Ezek.	33	17, 20
Magnify	Ps.	99	3–4

Not to be sinned against	Jer.	50	7
A part of his character	Deut.	32	4
	Is.	45	21

justification *state of being justified*

Wicked will not receive	Ex.	23	7
Requires perfect obedience under the law	Lev.	18	5
	James	2	10
Man cannot attain under the law	Ps.	143	2
	Rom.	9	31, 32
An act of God	Is.	50	8
	Rom.	8	33
Promised in Christ	Is.	53	11
Is by faith alone	Acts	13	39
	Rom.	3	30
Not be hearing only	Rom.	2	13
By grace	Rom.	5	17–21
	Tit.	3	7
Work of the servant	Is.	53	11
Men justifying themselves	Luke	10	29
	Luke	16	15
In the Spirit	I Tim.	3	16
By the resurrection of Christ	Rom.	4	25
	I Cor.	15	17
By the blood of Christ	Rom.	5	9
Assures salvation	Rom.	8	30
Is not of works	Gal.	2	16

Exemplified:

Abraham	Gen.	15	6
The publican	Luke	18	14
Paul	Phil.	3	8, 9

Justus *righteous*

The surname of Joseph	Acts	1	23
A godly man in Corinth	Acts	18	7
A converted Jew	Col.	4	11

juvenile delinquency *youthful failure of duty*

Means of prevention	Prov.	13	24
	Prov.	19	18
Brings reproach	Prov.	19	26
Description of	Prov.	30	11–14
Eli's sons	I Sam.	2	22–25
Samuel's sons	I Sam.	8	3
Those who mocked Elisha	II Ki.	2	22–24
Absalom	I Sam.	14	30

K

Kadesh, Kadesh-barnea *consecrated, sanctuary*

In the wilderness of Zin	Num.	27	14
Called En-mishpat	Gen.	14	7
Hagar flees hither	Gen.	16	7, 14
Dwelling of Abraham	Gen.	20	1
Return of the spies to	Num.	13	26
Unbelief here	Num.	14	1–38
Rebellion of Korah, Dathan and Abiram	Num.	16	
Miriam dies here	Num.	20	1
Moses smites the rock	Num.	20	1–12
Part of southern border of Canaan	Num.	34	4
A distance from Horeb	Deut.	1	2

Kadmiel *God is of old*

A father of Levites	Ezra	2	40
Father of Jeshua	Neh.	12	24
Seals convenant	Neh.	10	9

Kanah *place of reeds*

A river in the land of Ephraim	Josh.	16	8
	Josh.	17	9
A city in the land of Asher	Josh.	19	28

Kareah, Careah *bald*

Father of Johanan and Jonathan	II Ki.	25	23
	Jer.	40	8

Karniam *see Ashtaroth*

Kedar *black skinned*

A son of Ishmael	Gen.	25	13
Descendants wealthy	Jer.	49	28, 29
	Ezek.	27	21
Sheep-breeders	Is.	60	7
Traders	Ezek.	27	21
Skillful archers	Is.	21	16, 17
Barbarous people	Ps.	120	5
Tents are beautifully black	S. of S.	1	5
Dwelt in villages	Is.	42	11

Kedemah *eastern*			
A son of Ishamael	Gen.	25	15
	I Chr.	1	31
Kedesh *sacred place*			
A city of Judah	Josh.	15	23
A city of Naphtali	Josh.	19	37
Called Kedesh-naphtali	Judg.	4	6
A city of refuge	Josh.	21	32
Home of Barak	Judg.	4	6
Taken captive	II Ki.	15	29
Here called Kishon	Josh.	21	28
A city of Issachar	I Chr.	6	72
keep *obey, care for*			
They shall *k* the way of the Lord	Gen.	18	19
I am with thee, and will *k* thee	Gen.	28	15, 20
The Lord bless thee and *k* thee	Num.	6	24
He will *k* the feet of his saints	I Sam.	2	9
O that thou wouldst *k* me	Job	14	13
K me as the apple of the eye	Ps.	17	8
K me from presumptuous sins	Ps.	19	13
K thy tongue from evil	Ps.	34	13
His angels charge to *k* thee	Ps.	91	11
Neither will he *k* his anger for ever	Ps.	103	9
He that *k* thee will not slumber	Ps.	121	3
Except the Lord *k* the city	Ps.	127	1
Love wisdom, she will *k* thee	Prov.	4	6
K thy heart with all diligence	Prov.	4	23
Fear God, and *k* his commandments	Eccl.	12	13
Thou wilk *k* him in perfect peace	Is.	26	3
Will he *k* his anger?	Jer.	3	5, 12
K the doors of thy mouth	Mic.	7	5
Let the earth *k* silence	Hab.	2	20
Blessed are they that hear the word and *k* it	Luke	11	28
He that hateth his life shall *k* it	John	12	25
If a man love me, he will *k* my words	John	14	23
K them from the evil	John	17	15
To *k* back part of the price	Acts	5	3
Delivered the decrees to *k*	Acts	16	4
Let us *k* the feast	I Cor.	5	8
I *k* under my body	I Cor.	9	27
K in memory what I preached	I Cor.	15	2
K the unity of the Spirit	Eph.	4	3
The peace of God shall *k* your heart	Phil.	4	7
K thyself pure	I Thes.	5	22
K that committed to thy trust	I Thes.	6	20
To *K* himself unspotted	Josh.	1	27
K yourselves from idols	I John	5	21
To him that is able to *k* you	Jude	24	
I will *k* thee from hour of temptation	Rev.	3	10
Keeper, the Divine			
Faithful companion	Gen.	28	13, 15
Shall neither slumber nor sleep	Ps.	121	4
A protecting father	John	17	11
Guards and keeps us	II Thes.	1	12
Keilah *insignificant*			
A city of Judah	Josh.	15	44
Saved by David	I Sam.	23	1-5
David escapes from Saul	I Sam.	23	13
Has two rulers at time	Neh.	3	17, 18
Kelaiah, Kelita *maiming, dwarf*			
Divorced a strange wife	Ezra	10	23
A Levite, who explains law	Neh.	8	7
Seals convenant	Neh.	10	10
Kemuel *raised of God*			
Son of Nahor and Milcah	Gen.	22	20, 21
Prince of Ephraim	Num.	34	24
Father of Hashabiah	I Chr.	27	17
Kenan *see* Cainan			
Kenaz *hunter*			
Son of Eliphaz	Gen.	36	11
An Edomite duke	Gen.	36	15, 42
Father of Othniel	Judg.	1	13
Grandson of Caleb	I Chr.	4	13-15
Brother of Caleb	Josh.	15	17
Father of Othniel	Judg.	1	13
Keren-happuch *horn of paint*			
Youngest daughter of Job	Job	42	14
Kerioth *buildings, cities*			
A city of Judah	Josh.	15	21, 25
A town of Moab	Jer.	48	24
A place of stronghold	Jer.	48	41
Destroyed	Amos	2	2

Keturah *perfumed*			
Wife of Abraham	Gen.	25	1
Sons of	I Chr.	1	32
Sons do not receive the inheritance	Gen.	25	6
key			
Open doors	Judg.	3	25
Symbol of:			
Authority	Is.	22	22
Hell and death	Rev.	1	18
Of the bottomless pit	Rev.	20	1
keys of the kingdom			
Of heaven	Mat.	16	19
Kezia *cassia*			
The second daughter of Job	Job	42	14
Kibroth-hattaavah *graves of lust*			
A burial ground	Num.	11	33-35
An encampment of Israelites	Num.	33	16, 17
A place of wrath	Deut.	9	22
kid *a young goat*			
For festive occasions	Ex.	23	19
	Luke	15	29
For sacrifice	Num.	7	16
For food	Judg.	6	19
Used for payment of debt	Gen.	38	17
Not to be cooked in it's mother's milk	Ex.	23	19
For a sin offering	Lev.	5	6
Used as a present	Judg.	15	1
Peaceful	Is.	11	6
kidnapping *carrying away by force*			
Penalty for, is death	Ex.	21	16
	Deut.	24	7
Examples:			
Of Joseph	Gen.	37	23-28
Of Joash	II Ki.	11	1-12
Of Jeremiah	Jer.	43	1-8
kidneys *vital organs*			
An inner organ	Lev.	3	4
Used in burnt offering	Ex.	29	13, 22
A kernel of wheat	Deut.	32	14
Kidron, Cedron *raging brook*			
Called the King's Dale	II Sam.	18	18
Valley and stream between Jerusalem and mount of Olives	I Ki.	2	37
	Neh.	2	15
David flees across	II Sam.	15	23
Idols destroyed here	I Ki.	15	13
	II Chr.	29	16
Crossed by Jesus	John	18	1
kill *cause death, destroy*			
Thou shalt not *k*	Ex.	20	13
	Deut.	5	17
	Mat.	5	21
	Rom.	13	9
To *k* us in the wilderness	Num.	16	13
I *k* and I make alive	Deut.	32	39
Am I God, to *k*	II Ki.	5	7
If they *k* us, we shall but die	II Ki.	7	4
For thy sake are we *k*	Ps.	44	22
A time to *k*	Eccl.	3	3
Fear not them that *k* the body	Mat.	10	28
	Luke	12	4
Is it lawful to save life, or to *k*?	Mark	3	4
The Jews sought to *k* him	John	7	19
	John	7	1
Why go ye about to *k* me?	John	7	19
Will he *k* himself?	John	8	22
Thief cometh to steal and *k*	John	10	10
For thy sake we are *k* all the day	Rom.	8	36
The letter *k*, spirit giveth life	II Cor.	3	6
As chastened and not *k*	II Cor.	6	9
Ye *k* and desire to have	James	4	2
Ye condemned and *k* the just	James	5	6
He that *k* with sword must be *k*	Rev.	13	10
kind			
If thou be *k* to this people	II Chr.	10	7
Garnered of every *k*	Mat.	13	47
This *k* goeth not out	Mat.	17	21
	Mark	9	29
God is *k* to unthankful and evil	Luke	6	35
Charity suffereth long and is *k*	I Cor.	13	4
A *k* of first-fruits	James	1	18
kindle			
Wrath of the Lord was *k*	Num.	11	33
	Deut.	11	17
	II Ki.	22	13
	Ps.	106	40

His wrath is **k** but a little	Ps.	2	12
A contentious man to **k** strife	Prov.	26	21
My repentings are **k** together	Hosea	11	8
What will I, if it be already **k**	Luke	12	49
How great a matter a little fire **k**	James	3	5

kindness

Exhortations to	Prov.	19	22
	Prov.	31	26
	Rom.	12	10
	I Cor.	13	4
	Eph.	4	32
	Col.	3	12
Show **k** to my father's house	Josh.	2	12
Showed more **k** in latter end	Ruth	3	10
I will requite you this **k**	II Sam.	2	6
God gracious, of great **k**	Neh.	9	17
His merciful **k** is great	Ps.	117	2
Let the righteous smite me, it shall be a **k**	Ps.	141	5
With everlasting **k**	Is.	54	8
I remember the **k** of thy youth	Jer.	2	2
Lord is of great **k**	Joel	2	13
	Jonah	4	2
By long-suffering, by **k**	II Cor.	6	6
Brotherly **k** to **k** charity	II Pet.	1	7

kine *cattle*

Stalls for	Gen.	33	17
Pharaoh's dream	Gen.	41	2–7
In Gilead	Num.	32	1–4
For sacrifice	I Ki.	8	63
Of Bashan	Ezek.	39	18
Symbolic	Amos	4	1

kingdom of heaven

Likened to:

A man who sowed good seed	Mat.	13	24–30
A grain of mustard seed	Mat.	13	31, 32
Leaven	Mat.	13	33
A treasure	Mat.	13	44
A pearl	Mat.	13	45
A net	Mat.	13	47–50
A king who called his servants to a reckoning	Mat.	18	23–35
A householder	Mat.	20	1–16
A king's marriage feast	Mat.	22	2–14
Ten virgins	Mat.	25	1–13
A traveling man	Mat.	25	14–30
Keys of	Mat.	16	19
Children of the	Mat.	18	3
	Mark	10	14
To be sought	Mat.	6	33
Rich cannot enter	Mark	10	23–25
Glad tidings of	Luke	8	1
Mysteries of	Luke	8	10
"My kingdom is not of this world"	John	18	36
Of Christ	Mat.	16	28
Of God	Rev.	12	10
	Mark	4	26

     See heaven

kingdom of Satan

Mentioned by Christ	Mat.	12	26

kings *male ruler*

God reserves the choice of	Deut.	17	14, 15
	I Sam.	9	16, 17
Of Israel not to be foreigners	Deut.	17	15
Israel warned against seeking	I Sam.	8	9–18
Have power to make war and peace	I Sam.	11	5–7
Attended by a bodyguard	I Sam.	13	2
	I Chr.	11	25
Called the Lord's anointed	I Sam.	16	6
Approached with greatest reverence	I Sam.	24	8
	II Sam.	14	22
Dwell in royal palaces	II Chr.	9	11
Under of power of God	Dan.	4	25
	Dan.	2	21
God gives rulers their power	John	19	10, 11
Requested by people	I Sam.	8	5, 6
Ordained of God	Rom.	13	1
To pray for	I Thes.	2	1–4

Duties of good king:

Fear God	Deut.	17	19
Keep the law of God	I Ki.	2	3
Promote the interests of the church	Ezra	1	2–4
Serve Christ	Ps.	2	10–12
Abhor wickedness	Prov.	16	12
Investigate all matters	Prov.	25	2

Be understanding	Prov.	28	16
Not pervert judgment	Prov.	31	3–5
Maintain the cause of the poor	Prov.	31	8, 9

Good, exemplified:

David	II Sam.	8	15
Asa	I Ki.	15	11
Jehoshaphat	I Ki.	22	43
Amaziah	II Ki.	15	3
Uzziah	II Ki.	15	34
Hezekiah	II Ki.	18	3
Josiah	II Ki.	22	2

Who rule the United Kingdom:

Saul (1050–1010)	I Sam.	11	15
David (1010–970)	II Sam.	2	4
Solomon (970–931)	I Ki.	1	39
Rehoboam	I Ki.	12	1–20

Who rule Judah:

Rehoboam (930–913 BC)	I Ki.	12	21–24
Abijam or Abijah (913–910)	I Ki.	15	1–8
Asa (910–869)	I Ki.	15	9–24
Jehoshaphat (872–848)	I Ki.	22	41–50
Jehoram or Joram (853–841)	II Ki.	8	16–24
Ahaziah (841)	II Ki.	8	25–29
Athaliah (841–835)	II Ki.	11	1–3
Joash or Jehoash (835–796)	II Ki.	11	4
Amaziah (796–767)	II Ki.	14	1–20
Azariah or Uzziah (792–740)	II Ki.	14	21, 22,
Jotham (750–732)	II Ki.	15	32–38
Ahaz (732–715)	II Ki.	16	1
Hezekiah (715–686)	II Ki.	18	1
Manasseh (697–642)	II Ki.	21	1–18
Amon (642–640)	II Ki.	21	19–26
Josiah (640–609)	II Ki.	22	1–20
Jehoahaz (609)	II Ki.	23	31–33
Jehoiakim (609–598)	II Ki.	23	34–37
Jehoiachin (598–597)	II Ki.	24	8–16
Zedekiah (597–586)	II Ki.	24	17–20

Who rule Israel:

Jeroboam (930–909)	I Ki.	12	20, 25
Nadab (909–908)	I Ki.	15	25–27, 31
Baasha (908–886)	I Ki.	15	28–34
Elah (886–885)	I Ki.	16	8–14
Zimri (885)	I Ki.	16	11, 12, 15–20
Omri (885–874)	I Ki.	16	29
Ahab (874–853)	I Ki.	16	29
Ahaziah (853–852)	I Ki.	22	51–53
Jehoram or Joram (852–841)	II Ki.	3	1
Jehu (841–814)	II Ki.	9	2–37
Jehoahaz (814–798)	II Ki.	13	1–9
Jehoash or Joash (798–782)	II Ki.	13	10–25
Jeroboam, the Second (793–753)	II Ki.	14	29
Zachariah (753)	II Ki.	15	8–12
Shallum (752)	II Ki.	15	13–15
Menahem (725–742)	II Ki.	15	16–22
Pekahiah (742–740)	II Ki.	15	23–26
Pekah (725–732)	II Ki.	15	27–31
Hosheah (732–723)	II Ki.	17	1–6
Melchizedek, **k** of Salem	Gen.	14	18
	Heb.	7	1
The shout of a **k** is among them	Num.	23	21
Resembled children	Judg.	8	18
Trees went forth to anoint a **k**	Judg.	9	8
Now make us a **k**	I Sam.	8	5
God save the **k**	I Sam.	10	24
I set my **K** upon a holy hill	Ps.	2	6
My **K** and my God	Ps.	5	2
	Ps.	84	3
The Lord is **k** for ever	Ps.	10	16
	Ps.	29	10
Lord of hosts is **k** of glory	Ps.	24	10
Give the **k** thy judgments	Ps.	72	1
God is my **K** of old	Ps.	74	12
By me **k** reign	Prov.	8	15
The diligent shall stand before **k**	Prov.	22	29
Fear the Lord and the **k**	Prov.	24	21
Woe to thee when thy **k** is a child	Eccl.	10	16
Curse not the **k**	Eccl.	10	20
Mine eyes have seen the **k**	Is.	6	5
A **k** shall reign in righteousness	Is.	32	1
Thine eyes shall see the **k** in his beauty	Is.	33	17
The Lord is an everlasting **k**	Jer.	10	10
A **k** shall reign and prosper	Jer.	23	5
When the **k** came in to see the guests	Mat.	22	11
What **k** going to war?	Luke	14	31
Blessed be the **k** that cometh	Luke	19	38
Saying that he is Christ a **k**	Luke	23	2
By force, to make him a **k**	John	6	15

kings—continued

Behold your *k*	John	19	14
There is another *k*, one Jesus	Acts	17	7
Now to the *k* eternal	I Thes.	1	17
K and priests unto God	Rev.	1	6
	Rev.	5	10
Thou *k* of saints	Rev.	15	5

king's dale

The valley of Shaveh	Gen.	14	17
Memorial of Absalom	II Sam.	18	18

Kir *wall, fortress*

A city subject to Assyria	II Ki.	16	9
Place of Exile	Amos	1	5
City of Moab	Is.	15	1

Kir-hareseth, Kir-haresh *an earthern wall*

Place in Moab	Is.	16	7, 11
Destroyed by Joram	Jer.	48	31

Kiriathaim, Kirjathaim *twin cities*

A city of the Reubenites	Num.	32	37
Defeated by Chedor-laomer	Gen.	14	5
Moabite town	Deut.	2	9, 10
A city on the frontier of Moab	Ezek.	25	9
Called Kartan	Josh.	21	32
A city of Naphtali	I Chr.	6	76

Kirjathaim *see* Kiriathaim

Kirjath-arba *city of Arba*

An ancient name for Hebron, a city	Gen.	23	2
	Josh.	14	15
In the hill country of Judah	Josh.	20	7
City of refuge	Josh.	20	7
Named after Arba	Josh.	15	54

Kirjath-arim *see* Kirjath-jearim

Kirjath-baal *see* Kirjath-jearim

Kirjath-jearim, Kirjath-arim, Kirjath-baal *city of forests*

Inhabited by Gibeonites	Josh.	9	17
Called Baalah	Josh.	15	9
Called Kirjath-baal	Josh.	18	14
A city of Judah	Josh.	18	14, 15
Prophecy against	Jer.	26	20
Ark there for a time	I Sam.	7	1, 2
Home of Urijah	Jer.	26	20

Kirjath-sannah *see* Debir

Kirjath-sepher *see* Debir

Kish, Cis *bow*

Father of Saul	I Sam.	9	1–3
Uncle of Abner	I Sam.	14	51
Here called Cis	Acts	13	21
Son of Jehiel	I Chr.	9	35, 36
Son of Mahli	I Chr.	23	21
Father of Jerahmeel	II Chr.	24	29
Son of Abdi	II Chr.	29	12
Ancestor of Mordecai	Esth.	2	5

Kishon, Kishion *bending, tortuous*

A river of Palestine	Judg.	4	7
Sisera defeated here	Judg.	4	13–17
Prophets of Baal slain	I Ki.	18	40
A town of Issachar	Josh.	19	17, 20
Here called Kishon	Josh.	21	28

kiss

Of affection	Gen.	33	4
	Gen.	27	26, 27
Of greeting	II Sam.	19	39
	II Cor.	13	12
	I Pet.	5	14
Of deceit	II Sam.	20	9, 10
	Prov.	27	6
Of love	Prov.	7	13
	S. of S.	1	2
Of death	Mat.	26	48, 49
Of penitence	Luke	7	37, 38
Holy	Rom.	16	16
	I Cor.	16	20
Of submission	II Sam.	15	5
	I Ki.	19	18

kite *a bird*

May not be eaten	Deut.	14	13

Kittim *see* Chittim

knead *to mix by pressure*

Of Sarah	Gen.	18	6
Of women	Jer.	7	18
Of a baker	Hosea	7	4

kneading trough *a receptacle for working dough*

For mixing dough	Ex.	8	3
	Ex.	12	34
	Hosea	7	4

kneeling *resting on knees*

Before Jesus	Mat.	17	14
	Mark	1	40
In mockery of Jesus	Mat.	27	29
In acknowledgment of Almighty God	Rom.	14	11

In prayer:

Solomon	II Chr.	6	13, 14
Jesus	Luke	22	41
Stephen	Acts	7	59, 60
Peter	Acts	10	40
Paul	Acts	20	36, 37

knees *leg joints*

Strengthened by word of God	Job	4	4
Shall bow unto God	Is.	45	23
	Eph.	3	14
Grow weak with fright	Ezra	7	17
Knock together in fear	Dan.	5	6

knew

The Lord is in this Place and I *k* it not	Gen.	28	16
K where I might find him	Job	23	3
Before I formed thee I *k* thee	Jer.	1	5
I never *k* you, depart	Mat.	7	23
I *k* thee, thou art an hard man	Mat.	25	24
Jesus *k* what was in man	John	2	25
If thou *k* the gift of God	John	4	10
World by wisdom *k* not God	I Cor.	1	21
None of princes of world *k*	I Cor.	2	8
Who *k* no sin	II Cor.	5	21
Name written no man *k*	Rev.	19	12

knock *rap*

"It shall be open	Mat.	7	7, 8
"Behold I stand at the door and"	Rev.	3	20
Waiting for	Luke	12	36
Not opened at night	Luke	13	25
Peter came from prison	Acts	12	13, 16

knop *knob*

On the golden candlesticks	Ex.	25	33–36
On temple	I Ki.	7	24
An ornament	I Ki.	6	18
	I Ki.	7	24

know

To *k* good and evil	Gen.	3	22
Samuel did not yet *k* the Lord	I Sam.	3	7
K thou it is for thy good	Job	5	27
We are but of yesterday, and *k* nothing	Job	8	9
I *k* that my Redeemer liveth	Job	19	25
Make me to *k* mine end	Ps.	39	4
Be still, and *k* that I am God	Ps.	46	10
K my heart	Ps.	139	23
To *k* way wherein I should walk	Ps.	143	8
Gave my heart to *k* wisdom	Eccl.	1	17
K that God will bring judgment	Eccl.	11	9
The ox *k* his owner	Is.	1	3
My people shall *k* my name	Is.	52	6
The heart is deceitful, who can *k* it?	Jer.	17	9
Thou shalt *k* the Lord	Hosea	2	20
Let not thy left hand *k* what	Mat.	6	3
If ye *k* how to give good gifts	Mat.	7	11
It is given to you to *k*	Mat.	13	11
	Mark	4	11
	Luke	8	10
If thou hadst *k*	Luke	19	42
I *k* him not	Luke	22	57
He shall *k* of the doctrine	John	7	17
I *k* my sheep, and am *k* of mine	John	10	14
Not for you to *k* the times	Acts	1	7
We *k* that all things work for good	Rom.	8	28
Neither can he *k*	I Cor.	2	14
We *k* in part	I Cor.	13	9
K the love of Christ	Eph.	3	19
I *k* whom I have believed	II Tim.	1	12
Thou hast *k* the scriptures	II Tim.	3	15
We *k* that when he shall appear	I John	3	2
I *k* thy works	Rev.	2	2
	Rev.	3	1, 8
Make them *k* I have loved thee	Rev.	3	9

knowledge *acquaintance with fact*

Tree of knowledge	Gen.	2	9, 17
Requested of God	I Ki.	3	9
	Ps.	119	66
God has all	Job	21	22
Words without knowledge	Job	35	16
For the young	Prov.	1	4
Pleasant	Prov.	2	10

Causes sorrow	Eccl.	1	18
Daniel	Dan.	1	4
Solomon	Eccl.	1	16
False	Rom.	2	20
Love of Christ passes it	Eph.	3	19
Hid in Christ	Col.	2	3
To be added to virtue	II Pet.	1	5
Fear of the Lord, a beginning of	Prov.	1	7
Fools hate	Prov.	1	22, 29
Is power	Prov.	3	20
	Prov.	24	5
More valuable than gold	Prov.	8	10
Sought by the wise	Prov.	15	14
	Prov.	18	15
Attained by instruction	Prov.	21	11
Increases sorrow	Eccl.	1	18
None in the grave	Eccl.	9	10
Earth shall be full of	Is.	11	9
Shall be increased	Dan.	12	4
Those who reject are destroyed	Hosea	4	6
Ministers should possess	Mal.	2	7
Of salvation	Luke	1	77
Of truth, makes free	John	8	32
May cause conceit	I Cor.	8	1
Given by the Holy Ghost	I Cor.	12	8
Christians should grow in	II Pet.	3	18

Kohath *assembly*

Son of Levi	Gen.	46	11
A father of four sons	Ex.	6	18

Kohathites— *descendants of Kohath*

Formed divisions of Levites	Num.	3	27
	Ex.	6	18-20
Special duties given	Num.	4	15-20
Numberings of Kohathite males	Num.	3	27, 28
	Num.	4	34-37
Cities allotted	Josh.	21	4
Heman the Kohathite	I Chr.	6	31-38
Moses and Aaron	Ex.	6	20

Kolaiah *voice of Jehovah*

A Benjamite, father of Pedaiah	Neh.	11	7
Father of false prophet, Ahab	Jer.	29	21

Korah *bald*

Son of Esau	Gen.	36	5, 14
Son of Eliphaz	Gen.	36	16
Son of Izhar	Ex.	6	21
Rebels against Moses	Num.	16	1-3
Buried alive	Num.	16	23-35
Called core	Jude		11
Son of Hebron	I Chr.	2	43
Son of Kohath	I Chr.	6	22

Kore *a partridge*

A Levite of the house of Korah	I Chr.	9	19
	I Chr.	26	1
A Levite, keeper of the east gate	II Chr.	31	14

Korhites, Korathites, Korahites

Family of Korah	Ex.	6	24
One of the families of the Levites	Num.	26	58
Keepers of the entry of the tabernacle	I Chr.	9	19
Shallum's son overseer of the pans	I Chr.	9	31
Writers of	Ps.	42	
	Ps.	44	
	Ps.	46	
	Ps.	47	
	Ps.	49	
	Ps.	84	
	Ps.	48	
	Ps.	87	
	Ps.	88	
Musicians	I Chr.	6	22-32

L

Laban *white*

Brother of Rebekah	Gen.	24	29
Son of Bethuel	Gen.	28	5
Father of Leah and Rachel	Gen.	29	16
Father-in-law of Jacob	Gen.	29	23, 28
Tricks Jacob	Gen.	29	15-30
Makes deals to keep Jacob	Gen.	30	25-43

His covenant with Jacob	Gen.	31	44-55
A place of unidentified site	Deut.	1	1

labor *to work*

Appointed to man	Gen.	3	19
	Ex.	20	9
Is beneficial to man	Prov.	10	16
Is blessed by God	Prov.	11	13
	Eccl.	5	12
	I Cor.	4	12
An example	Acts	20	33-35
	II Thes.	3	8-12
Is honourable and good	Eph.	4	28
Encouraged by Paul	I Thes.	4	11
Rest offered to those who	Mat.	11	28
Not for perishable values	John	6	27
Trouble over wages	Mat.	20	1-16

laborer

Shall not be oppressed or defrauded	Lev.	19	13
	Deut.	24	14
	Mal.	3	5
Shall not be exploited	Jer.	22	13
	James	5	4
For the Lord's harvest, are few	Mat.	9	37-38
Parable of	Mat.	20	1-15
Is worthy of his reward	Luke	10	7
	I Tim.	5	18
Spiritual	I Cor.	3	9

labor trouble

Complaint over wages	Mat.	20	1-15
Workers mistreated	Mat.	21	33-36

Lachish *impregnable*

A city destroyed by Joshua	Josh.	10	31-35
Assigned to Judah	Josh.	15	39
Amaziah slain	II Ki.	14	19
Fortified city of Rehoboam	II Chr.	11	5, 9
Amaziah murdered	II Ki.	14	19
Sennacherib captures	II Ki.	18	13-17
Resettled after the exile	Neh.	11	30
Besieged by Nebuchadnezzar	Jer.	34	7
Sin city	Mic.	1	13

lack *not enough*

People destroyed for *l* of knowledge	Hosea	4	6
Young lions do *l*?	Ps.	34	10
What *l* I yet?	Mat.	19	20
One thing thou *l*	Mark	10	21
But ye *l* opportunity	Phil.	4	10
If any *l* wisdom, ask of God	James	1	5

lad *young boy*

Grievous because of the *l*	Gen.	21	12
God heard the voice of the *l*	Gen.	17	
I and the *l* will go yonder	Gen.	22	5
L was with the sons of Bilhah	Gen.	37	2
Send the *l* with me and we	Gen.	43	8
We said, The *l* cannot leave	Gen.	44	22
The *l* be not with us, his life is bound up in the *l*'s life	Gen.	30	
	Gen.	31	
	Gen.	34	
Who redeemed me, bless the *l*	Gen.	48	16
Samson said to the *l*	Judg.	16	26
Behold I will send a *l*	I Sam.	20	21
Unto the *l* Run, and as the *l* ran	I Sam.	20	36
A *l* saw them and told	II Sam.	17	18
A *l* here hath five barley	John	6	9

ladder *a climbing device*

The vision of Jacob	Gen.	28	10-16

lady *a woman of social standing*

Of Persia and Media	Esth.	1	18
Term applied to Babylon	Is.	47	5, 7
The elect	II John		1, 5
Of women of the court	Judg.	5	29

Lahai-roi *see Beer-lahai-roi*

Lahmi *foodful(?)*

A giant, brother of Goliath	I Chr.	20	5

lamb *a young sheep*

Covenants confirmed by gift of	Gen.	21	28-30
Used for food	Deut.	32	14
	Amos	6	4
Shepherds care for	I Sam.	17	34
	Is.	40	11
Tribute often paid by	II Ki.	3	4
Item of trade	Ezra	7	17
Disciples called lambs	Luke	10	3
	John	21	15
Christ, the lamb of God	John	1	29-36
	Is.	53	7

lamb—*continued*
Offered in sacrifice:

At the passover	Ex.	12	3, 6, 7
Under a year old	Ex.	12	5
	Num.	6	14
Every morning and evening	Ex.	29	38, 39
After birth of a child	Lev.	12	6

Symbolic of:

Patience	Is.	53	7
Innocence	Jer.	11	9
Purity of Christ	I Pet.	1	19

lame *crippled*

Not allowed office of high priest	Lev.	21	18
Smitten by David	II Sam.	5	8
Mephibosheth	II Sam.	4	4
Healed in millennium	Is.	35	6
Not to be offered as a sacrifice	Mal.	1	8, 13
Legs not equal length	Prov.	26	7
Healed by Christ	Luke	7	22
Should be cared for	Luke	14	13
Healed by apostles	Acts	3	1–9
	Acts	8	5–7

Lamech *destroyer*

Descendant of Cain	Gen.	4	17, 18
First to take more than one wife	Gen.	4	19
Father of Noah	Gen.	5	28, 29
Age and death	Gen.	5	31

lamentation *audible expression of sorrow*

For Jacob	Gen.	50	10
Of David over Saul and Jonathan	II Sam.	1	17
For Israel	Ps.	60	1–4
	Ps.	74	1–3
	Lam.	1	5
	Amos	5	1–4
Of Rachel for her children	Jer.	31	15
	Mat.	2	18
For Jesus	Luke	23	25–27
Isaiah for Babylon	Is.	14	1–32
People for Babylon	Rev.	18	11

lamp *gives light*

Seen in visions	Gen.	15	17
	Zech.	4	2
	Rev.	4	5
Burns olive oil	Ex.	27	20
Put in empty pitchers	Judg.	7	16
Parable concerning	Mat.	25	1

Used for lighting:

The tabernacle	Ex.	25	37
	Ex.	27	20, 21
Chariots of war	Nah.	2	3, 4
Marriage processions	Mat.	25	1
Travelers at night	John	18	3
Private apartments	Acts	20	8

Symbolic of:

God's guidance	II Sam.	22	29
	Ps.	18	28
The word of God	Ps.	119	105
Ministers	John	5	35

lance *something to strike with*

A javelin	Jer.	50	42

lancet *to hurl*

A spear or javelin	I Ki.	18	28

land

Appears on third day of Creation	Gen.	1	9
Bought and sold	Gen.	23	3–18
	Acts	4	34
	Acts	5	1–8
Laws concerning sale of	Gen.	23	3–20
	Lev.	25	15, 16, 23–33
	Ruth	4	9–11
To rest every seventh year	Ex.	23	11
Sold for debt	Neh.	5	3–5

Promised by God

Moses	Ex.	6	4
	Ex.	23	31
	Num.	34	3–12
Abram	Gen.	15	18
	Gen.	17	19
Isaac	Gen.	26	3–4
Jacob	Gen.	28	13–14
Bought by Joseph in famine	Gen.	47	20
Iniquities upon	Lev.	16	22
	Lev.	18	25
	Gen.	4	10
	Num.	35	33
	Ezek.	8	17

Cared for by God	Deut.	11	12
Taken by Joshua	Josh.	11	16
Rest of	Josh.	14	15
	Judg.	3	11
	Ex.	23	11
Pagans viewed gods as owning land	II Ki.	18	33
Lord is jealous of	Joel	2	18
Women's rights	Num.	27	1–11
	Ruth	4	3–9

landmarks

Protected from fraudulent removal	Deut.	19	14

language *speech*

Unity	Gen.	11	1–6
Confusion of	Gen.	11	1–9
Gift of	Mark	16	17
Many spoken at Jerusalem	John	19	20

Mentioned in scripture:

Of Ashdod	Neh.	13	24
Hebrew	II Ki.	18	28
Syriac	II Ki.	18	26
Chaldea	Dan.	1	4
Greek	Luke	23	38
Many tongues	Acts	2	8–11
Lycaonia	Acts	14	11
Latin	Luke	23	28
In heaven	Rev.	5	9

lantern *a shielded lamp*

Used by men who capture Jesus	John	18	3

Laodicea *Asian city*

Paul's concern for	Col.	2	1
Epaphras' zeal for	Col.	4	12, 13
Message to, through John	Rev.	1	11
Lukewarm	Rev.	3	14–22

lap

Those who lap the water are saved	Judg.	7	5–7
Child dies on his mother's lap	II Ki.	4	18–20
Nehemiah's shook	Neh.	5	13

lapidary

One who cuts precious stones	Ex.	31	5
	Ex.	35	33

Lapidoth *torches*

Husband of Deborah	Judg.	4	4

lapwing *a bird*

Classed as unclean food	Lev.	11	19

lasciviousness *wantonness*

Source of	Mark	7	21
	Gal.	5	19
Censured	II Cor.	12	21
	Eph.	4	19
	I Pet.	4	3
	Jude		4

Instances of:

Sodomites	Gen.	19	5
Lot's daughters	Gen.	19	30–38
Eli's sons	I Sam.	2	22
David	II Sam.	5	13
	II Sam.	11	2–27
Solomon	I Ki.	11	1–3
Persian kings	Esth.	2	3, 13–19

Lasharon *plain of Sharon*

King of, killed by Joshua	Josh.	12	18

last

Let my *l* end be like his	Num.	23	10
At the *l* it biteth like a serpent	Prov.	23	32
She remembereth not her *l* end	Lam.	1	9
State of that man worse	Mat.	12	45
	Luke	11	26
First shall be *l*	Mat.	19	30
	Mat.	20	16
	Mark	10	31
	Luke	13	30
L error worse than first	Mat.	27	64
The *l* day	John	6	39
	John	11	24
Spoken in *l* days by his Son	Heb.	1	2

latchet

Not broken	Is.	5	27
John Baptist not worthy to loose Christ's	Mark	1	7

Latin *the language of Rome*

Inscription on the cross written in	Luke	23	38
	John	19	20

laugh

At famine thou shalt *l*	Job	5	22

That sitteth in heaven shall *l*	Ps.	2	4
I will *l* at your calamity	Prov.	1	26
A time to weep, a time to *l*	Eccl.	3	4
Woe unto you that *l*	Luke	6	25

laughter
Attributed to God	Ps.	37	13
A time for	Eccl.	3	4
Sometimes sorrow better than	Eccl.	7	3
Of a fool is vanity	Eccl.	7	6
Sorrow in	Prov.	14	13
Of Abraham	Gen.	17	17
Of Sarah	Gen.	18	12
To scorn	II Chr.	30	10
See happiness			

laver *a wash basin*
Directions for making	Ex.	30	18–20
Used in the tabernacle	Ex.	40	7
Used for washing	Ex.	40	30–32
Sanctified	Lev.	8	11
Brazen, made by Solomon	I Ki.	7	23–26
Carried to Babylon	II Ki.	25	13, 16
Figurative	Rev.	4	6
	Rev.	15	2

law *a rule of conduct*
Of God, given to Adam	Gen.	2	16
Given to Noah	Gen.	9	3
Promulgated through Moses	Ex.	19	20
Of Moses ordained	Ex.	21	1–36
	Lev.	1	1–17
	Num.	3	1–51
	Deut.	12	1–32
Given at Sinai	Ex.	19	
	Hab.	3	3
Received by angels	Deut.	33	2
Found by Hilkiah	II Ki.	22	8
Written on door posts	Deut.	6	9
Expounded by Levites	Lev.	10	11
Taught in synagogues	Luke	4	16–32
Temporary	Jer.	3	16
	Mat.	5	17, 18
Ratified by blood	Heb.	9	18–22
Schoolmaster to lead to Christ	Gal.	3	24, 25
To be remembered	Mal.	3	4
Preserved on stone	Deut.	27	1–26
	Josh.	8	32
Requires perfect obedience	Deut.	27	26
	James	2	10
Read every seventh year	Deut.	31	9–13
Book of, discovered by Hilkiah	II Ki.	22	8
Described	Ps.	19	7
	Rom.	7	12
Abolished in Christ	Acts	15	24
	Gal.	2–6	
	Heb.	7	1–28
Paul's appeal to	Acts	22	24–30
All guilty under	Rom.	3	20
Fulfilled by Christ	Rom.	5	18
Read by:			
Joshua	Josh.	8	34
Josiah	II Ki.	23	2
Ezra	Neh.	8	1–18

lawgiver *maker of laws*
God	Is.	33	22
	James	4	12

lawsuits *application for justice*
Censured	Prov.	25	8–10
	I Cor.	6	1

lawyer *one versed in Mosaic law*
Test Jesus with questions	Mat.	22	35
	Luke	10	25–37
Jesus' satire against	Luke	11	45–52
Zenas, a Christian	Tit.	3	13

laying on of hands
As a blessing	Gen.	48	14
	Mat.	19	13
	Luke	4	40
A burden of guilt	Lev.	1	4
See hands			

Lazarus *Greek for Eleazer, whom God helps;*
A beggar	Luke	16	20
Brother of Mary and Martha	John	11	1, 2
Sickness and death of	John	11	1–14
Resurrection of	John	11	38–44
Sups with Jesus	John	12	1, 2, 9
Threatened	John	12	10, 11

laziness *slothfulness*
Reproved	Prov.	6	6–10
Described	Prov.	19	24
Great waster	Prov.	18	9
Characterized by sleep	Prov.	19	15
	Prov.	10	5
Commanded against	II Thes.	3	10–12
	Heb.	6	12
	Rom.	12	11
Leads to begging	Prov.	20	4
Leads to poverty	Prov.	24	33, 34

lead *a metal*
A mineral	Ex.	15	10
Purified by fire	Num.	31	22, 23
	Jer.	6	29
Used in making inscriptions on stone	Job	19	24
An article of trade	Ezek.	27	12
Used for weights	Zech.	5	7, 8

lead
Pillar of cloud to *l* them	Ex.	13	21
Lord alone did *l* him	Deut.	32	12
He *l* me beside still waters	Ps.	23	2
Send light and truth let them *l* me	Ps.	43	3
L me to Rock higher than I	Ps.	61	2
L me in the way everlasting	Ps.	139	24
L me to land of uprightness	Ps.	143	10
A little child shall *l* them	Is.	11	6
Gently *l* those with young	Is.	40	11
L them in paths not known	Is.	42	16
L us not into temptation	Mat.	6	13
	Luke	11	4
Way, which *l* unto life	Mat.	7	14
If the blind *l* the blind	Mat.	15	14
	Luke	6	39
We may *l* a quiet life	I Tim.	2	2
Lamb feed and *l* them	Rev.	7	17

leader *a guide*
Moses' request for	Num.	27	15–17
Ehud, a bold	Judg.	3	15–29
Jesus, a great	Is.	55	4
Of the blind	Mat.	15	14

leaf
Foliage of a tree	Gen.	3	7
Of a folding door	I Ki.	6	34
Page of a roll	Jer.	36	23

league *an agreement or covenant*
A fraudulent	Josh.	9	3–16
A fraternal	I Sam.	20	16, 17
Examples:			
Abraham and Mamre	Gen.	14	13
Joshua and the Gibeonites	Josh.	9	
Moabites, Amalekites and Ammonites	Judg.	3	12, 13
Asa and Benhadad	I Ki.	15	18
Forbidden	Ex.	23	32, 33
	Deut.	7	2
See alliances			

Leah *wearied*
Daughter of Laban	Gen.	29	16
Married to Jacob	Gen.	29	23–26
Children of	Gen.	29	31–35
Flees with Jacob	Gen.	33	2–7
"Builder of the house of Israel"	Ruth	4	11
Buried in Hebron	Gen.	49	31

leap *jump*
Lame man *l* as an hart	Is.	35	6
And *l* for joy	Luke	6	23
He *l* up, stood, and walked	Acts	3	8
Man in whom the evil spirit was *l* on them	Acts	19	16

learning *receiving instruction*
By experience	Gen.	30	27
Increased by wise man	Prov.	1	5
Daniel, a man of	Dan.	1	17
Of war	Mic.	4	3
To be content	Phil.	4	11
Jesus' from God	John	7	14–16
Moses, a man of	Acts	7	22
Paul accused of madness from	Acts	26	24
Scriptures written for our	Rom.	15	4
Not always constructive	I Tim.	5	13
Obedience, part of Christ's	Heb.	5	8

leather *tanned skins*
Tanning and dyeing known to early			
Hebrews	Ex.	25	5
	Acts	9	43
Tent coverings	Ex.	26	14

leather—*continued*
Apparel:

Clothing of all types	Lev.	13	48, 49
Girdles	II Ki.	1	8
	Mat.	3	4
Sandals	Ezek.	16	10

leaven *fermenting dough*

Forbidden during passover	Ex.	12	15
Excluded from burnt offerings	Lev.	2	11
Sacrificed at feast of weeks	Lev.	23	17
Used in breadmaking	Hosea	7	4
Spreading to all parts	Gal.	5	9

Symbolic of:

Kingdom of heaven	Mat.	13	33
Doctrines of Pharisees and Sadducees	Mat.	16	6, 11, 12
Herod's wickedness	Mark	8	15
Of malice	I Cor.	5	6, 8

Lebanon *white mountain*

One boundary of promise land	Deut.	1	7
Mountain and forest area	Deut.	3	25
Allotted to Israel	Josh.	13	5
Not conquered by Israelites	Judg.	3	1–3
Cedar and fir trees grow	Judg.	9	15
	I Ki.	5	8, 10
Dwelling place of wild beasts	II Ki.	14	9
Place of beauty	Is.	35	2
Distinct aroma of	S. of S.	4	11
Land of streams	S. of S.	4	15
Prophecies against	Is.	10	34
	Is.	33	9

Lebbaeus *dry*

Apostle	Mat.	10	3

leek

Onion-like plant	Num.	11	5

lees *dregs of wine*

Wine sediment	Is.	25	6
Symbolic of indifference and laziness	Jer.	48	11
	Zeph.	1	12

left

In her *l* hand riches and honour	Prov.	3	16
To the right hand nor to the *l*	Prov.	4	27
The goats on the *l*	Mat.	25	33
One taken, the other *l*	Mat.	24	40, 41
L all, and have followed thee	Mat.	10	28
Not be *l* one stone	Mat.	13	2

lefthanded

Ehud	Judg.	3	15
700 of Benjamin's warriors	Judg.	20	16
David's men use both hands	I Chr.	12	1, 2

legacy *bequest*

David leaves to Solomon	I Ki.	2	1–7
Elijah to Elisha	II Ki.	2	13, 9
Abraham	Gen.	25	5, 6

legion *considerable number*

Of angels	Mat.	26	53
Roman soldiers, called bands	Mat.	27	27
Of devils	Mark	5	9–15

Lehi, Ramath-lehi *jawbone*

Scene of slaughter of Philistines	Judg.	15	9, 14
	Judg.	15	17, 19

leisure *unoccupied, free time*

Apostles have none	Mark	6	31

Lemuel *devoted to God*

Author of proverbs	Prov.	31	1–13

lending *allow the use of*

Not for usury	Ex.	22	25
To needy	Deut.	15	7, 8
Debt released after seven years	Deut.	15	1–9
To many nations	Deut.	28	12
Samuel, to God	I Sam.	1	20, 28
Pity for poor is loan to the Lord	Prov.	19	17
Sign of a good man	Ps.	112	5
Without selfish motives	Luke	6	34–35

length of life *see* longevity

lentils *plant with pod*

Served as pottage	Gen.	25	34
Brought for David	II Sam.	17	28
Philistines amass over	II Sam.	23	11
Made into bread	Ezek.	4	9

leopard *cat-like animal*

"Can a leopard change its spots?"	Jer.	13	23
Symbol of Grecian power	Dan.	7	6
Ephraim emulates	Hosea	13	7
Swift	Hab.	1	8
Fierceness	Jer.	5	6
	Hosea	13	7

Taming during millennium	Is.	11	6

leper *sufferer from leprosy*

Moses becomes	Ex.	4	6
Miriam stricken and healed	Num.	12	10–16
Naaman sent to Samaria for cure	II Ki.	5	1–27
Azariah smitten by Lord	II Ki.	15	5
Uzziah smitten	II Chr.	26	19
Gehazi	II Ki.	5	27
Separate burial of	II Chr.	26	23
Lepers of Samaria	II Ki.	7	3

leprosy *chronic, infectious disease*

Laws concerning	Lev.	13	1–46
Unclean	Lev.	13	44–46
Thought to infect clothes and walls	Lev.	13	47–59
Rules for cleansing	Lev.	14	1–32
Cured by Jesus	Mat.	8	3

letters *written messages*

Jezebel forges some	I Ki.	21	7, 8
David to Joab	II Sam.	11	14
Rabshakeh to Hezekiah	Is.	37	9–14
King of Babylon to Hezekiah	Is.	39	1
Sanballat to Nehemiah	Neh.	6	5
Saul receives, for Damascus	Acts	9	1, 2
Of greeting from apostles	Acts	15	23
Called epistles	Rom.	16	22
Of approval	I Cor.	16	3
Of commendation	II Cor.	3	1, 2
Paul's weighty and powerful	II Cor.	10	10

Levi *attached*

Third son of Jacob by Leah	Gen.	29	34
Massacres Shechem	Gen.	34	25–30
Founds Levites	Gen.	46	11
Receives no inheritance in Israel	Josh.	13	33
Dies in Egypt	Ex.	6	16
Son of Alphaeus	Mark	2	14
Son of Melchi	Luke	3	24
Son of Simeon	Luke	3	29

leviathan *huge*

Fierce, strong	Job	41	1–31
Meat in wilderness	Ps.	74	14
Made by God	Ps.	104	26
Symbol of Israel's enemies	Is.	27	1

Levite *descendant of Levi*

Consecrated in service of Lord	Ex.	3	5–13
Genealogies	Ex.	6	16–20
	I Chr.	6	16–48
Aaron and Moses	Ex.	28	1
In charge of the tabernacle	Num.	1	50
Chosen as reward for faith	Num.	3	1–37
Serve from age thirty to fifty	Num.	4	3
Age lowered	Num.	8	24
	I Chr.	23	24
Portion of land set aside for	Num.	35	2–8
Should not be forsaken	Deut.	12	19
The Lord is their inheritance	Deut.	18	1, 2
No land inheritance	Josh.	14	3
Shall be purified	Mal.	3	3
Sent to question John	John	1	19
Taken in place of firstborn	Num.	3	12, 41–45
Sedition of	Num.	16	1–5
Three divisions	Num.	3	17
Cities assigned to	Josh.	21	
Villages near Jerusalem	Neh.	12	29
Bore the ark	Deut.	10	8
Prepared the shewbread	I Chr.	23	28, 29
Assisted priests	II Chr.	29	12–36
Taught law	Deut.	33	10
	Neh.	8	7–13
Intermarriage	Ezra	9	1, 2
Exempt from military duties	Num.	1	47–54

levy *imposed payment or tax*

King Solomon's, of men	I Ki.	5	13–18
Of bondservice	I Ki.	9	20–23

lewdness *base conduct*

Committed in Israel	Judg.	20	6
God shall deliver Israel from	Ezek.	23	27–29
Revealed	Hosea	2	10
Committed by priests	Hosea	6	9
Unclean	Jer.	13	27
Of the men of Israel	Ezek.	22	9
Will cease when God judges	Ezek.	23	27
Of Hosea's wife	Hosea	2	10

liars *tellers of untruths*

All men are	Ps.	116	11

Poor man better than	Prov.	19	22
Sword upon	Jer.	50	36
Devil, father of	John	8	44
Against God	Acts	5	4
Law written for	I Tim.	1	9, 10
Cretians known as	Tit.	1	12
Sword upon	I John	2	4
Fire and brimstone await	Rev.	21	8
Examples of some:			
Cain	Gen.	4	9
Jacob	Gen.	27	19
Joseph's brothers	Gen.	37	31, 32
Gibeonites	Josh.	9	3–15
Saul	I Sam.	15	13–24
Gehazi, servant of Naaman	II Ki.	5	20, 21
Peter	Mat.	26	72
Christ, through us	I John	1	10
One who denies Christ	I John	2	22
False apostles	Rev.	2	1, 2

liberality *bounteous generosity*

To the Lord	Ex.	25	1–6
	Ex.	35	
	Ex.	36	6
Of Araunah	II Sam.	24	24
Of a good man	Ps.	112	5
Promise of blessing	Prov.	11	24
	Mal.	3	10
Winning of friends by	Prov.	19	6
Of the virtuous woman	Prov.	31	20
Toward strangers	Lev.	25	35
Toward the poor	Deut.	15	11
Rewarded	Prov.	11	25
Without boasting	Mat.	6	1–4
Jesus stresses	Mat.	25	34–40
Toward the needy and helpless	Luke	10	30–35
Toward saints	Rom.	12	13
Practiced by Christ	II Cor.	8	9
Pleasing to God	II Cor.	9	7
Toward all men, especially believers	Gal.	6	10
Sign of true faith	I John	3	17, 18

Libertines *freed men*

Oppose Stephen	Acts	6	9

liberty, Christian *freedom of Christians*

Declared by Jesus	Luke	4	18
Through truth	John	8	32
Through Jesus	John	8	36
From laws of Moses	Rom.	7	6
State of God's children	Rom.	8	21
From civil law	I Cor.	6	12
Not to be abused	I Cor.	8	9–11
Enables one to serve with love	Gal.	5	13
False promises a danger to	II Pet.	2	19

Libnah *whiteness*

Campsite of Israelites	Num.	33	20, 21
Captured by Joshua	Josh.	10	29–31
Allotted to Judah	Josh.	15	42
Given to Aaron	Josh.	21	13
Revolts from Judah	II Ki.	8	22
Home of Hamutal	II Ki.	23	31

Libni *white*

A son of Gershon	Ex.	6	17
A Levite	Num.	26	58
Called Laadan	I Chr.	23	7
Son of Mahli	I Chr.	6	29

Libya *land west of Egypt*

Desolation foretold	Ezek.	30	4, 5
Jews come from at Pentecost	Acts	2	10

lice *small insect*

In third plague against Egypt	Ex.	8	16–18
	Ps.	105	31

lieutenants *viceroys*

Receive king's commissions	Ezra	8	36
Commanded by Haman	Esth.	3	12
Called princes	Dan.	3	2

life *animation*

Created by God	Gen.	2	7–9
Rebekah weary of	Gen.	27	46
Referred to as pilgrimage	Gen.	47	9
By Divine guidance	Deut.	8	2, 3
By God's will	I Sam.	2	5, 6
God can lengthen for obedience	I Ki.	3	14
Elijah weary of	I Ki.	19	2–4
God can lengthen for prayer	II Ki.	20	5, 6
Job curses his	Job	3	1–11
Job's without hope	Job	7	16

Short and troublesome	Job	14	1, 2
Attended to by righteous	Prov.	11	19
Disappointing	Eccl.	2	17
To be enjoyed as a gift	Eccl.	5	18, 19
Jonah wishes his over	Jonah	4	8
Be not overanxious to provide for the wants of	Mat.	6	25
Not only material matters	Luke	12	15
Must be appreciated	John	12	25
Eternal, gift of God	Rom.	6	23
Prolonged for honouring parents	Eph.	6	2, 3
Immortality brought by Jesus	II Tim.	1	10
Revealed in love	I John	3	14
Artificial ones	Rev.	3	1
Cares and pleasures of, dangerous	Luke	8	14
	Luke	21	34
	II Tim.	2	4
Limited	Job	7	1
	Job	14	5
Short	Ps.	89	47
Uncertain	James	4	13–15
Vain	Eccl.	6	12
Forfeited by sin	Gen.	2	17
	Gen.	3	17–19
God as the author of	Acts	17	28
God preserves	Ps.	36	6
	Ps.	66	9
God's loving-kindness better than	Ps.	63	3
In the hand of God	Job	12	10
	Dan.	5	23
Miraculously restored by Christ	Mat.	9	18, 25
	Luke	7	15, 22
	John	11	43
Obedience to God tends to prolong	Deut.	30	20
Of others, not to be taken away	Ex.	20	13
Of saints, specially protected by God	Job	2	6
	Acts	18	10
	I Pet.	3	13
Of the wicked, not specially protected by God	Job	36	6
	Ps.	78	50
Preserved by discretion	Prov.	13	3
Saints have true enjoyment of	Ps.	128	2
	I Tim.	4	8
Shortness of, should lead to spiritual improvement	Deut.	32	29
	Ps.	90	12
Should be laid down, if necessary, for Christ	Mat.	10	39
	Luke	14	26
	Acts	20	24
Should be laid down, if necessary, for the brethren	Rom.	16	4
	I John	3	16
Value of	Job	2	4
	Mat.	6	25
We know not what is good for us in	Eccl.	6	12
The wicked have their portion of good during	Ps.	17	14
	Luke	6	24
	Luke	16	25
Be thankful for:			
Its preservation	Ps.	103	4
	John	2	6
The supply of its wants	Gen.	48	15
Life, spiritual:			
All saints have	Eph.	2	1, 5
	Col.	2	13
Christ the author of	John	5	21, 25
	John	14	6
	I John	4	9
A life unto God	Rom.	6	11
	Gal.	2	19
Living in the Spirit	Gal.	5	25
Newness of life	Rom.	6	4
Fear of God is	Prov.	14	27
	Prov.	19	23
God the author of	Ps.	36	9
	Col.	2	13
Has its infancy	Luke	10	21
	I Cor.	3	1–2
	I John	2	12
Has its maturity	Eph.	4	13
	I John	2	13–14
Hidden with Christ	Col.	3	3
The Holy Ghost the author of	Rom.	8	9–13
Hypocrites destitute of	Jude		12

life—continued			
Illustrated	Ezek.	37	9–10
	Luke	15	24
Lovers of pleasure destitute of	I Tim.	5	6
Maintained by:			
Christ	John	6	57
	I Cor.	10	3–4
Faith	Gal.	2	20
Prayer	Ps.	69	32
The word of God	Mat.	4	4
Pray for the increase of	Ps.	119	25
	Ps.	143	11
Revived by God	Ps.	85	6
	Hosea	6	2
Saints praise God for	Ps.	119	175
Seek to grow in	Eph.	4	15
	I Pet.	2	2
Should animate the services of saints	Rom.	12	1
	I Cor.	14	15
Life, eternal:			
Cannot be inherited by works	Rom.	3	10–19
Christ is	I John	1	2
	I John	5	20
Exhortation to seek	John	6	27
Revealed by Christ	John	6	68
Revealed in the scriptures	John	5	39
The self-righteous think to inherit, by works	Mark	10	17
They who are ordained to, believe the gospel	Acts	13	48
To know God and Christ is	John	17	3
Given:			
By Christ	John	6	27
	John	10	28
By God	Ps.	113	3
In answer to prayer	Ps.	21	4
In Christ	I John	5	11
Through Christ	Rom.	5	21
To all given to Christ	John	17	2
To those who believe in God	John	5	24
Saints:			
Are preserved unto	John	10	28–29
Have hope of	Tit.	1	2
	Tit.	3	7
Have promises of	I Tim.	4	8
	II Tim.	1	1
	Tit.	1	2
	I John	2	25
Look for the mercy of God unto	Jude		21
May have assurance of	II Cor.	5	1
	I John	5	13
Shall go into	Mat.	25	46
Shall inherit	Mat.	19	29
Shall reap, through the Spirit	Gal.	6	8
Shall reign in	Dan.	7	18
	Rom.	5	17
Shall rise unto	John	5	29
Should lay hold of	I Tim.	6	12, 19
The wicked:			
Have not	I John	3	15
Judge themselves unworthy of	Acts	13	46

lift *raise up*

L up your hands, O ye gates	Ps.	24	7
Lord *l* up the meek	Ps.	147	6
L up their voices	Luke	17	13
Son of man be *l* up	John	3	14
L up holy hands	I Tim.	2	8
He shall *l* you up	James	4	10

light *illumination*

Sun, moon, and stars appointed to communicate to the earth	Gen.	1	14–17
	Jer.	31	35
Theory of, beyond man's comprehension	Job	38	19–20, 24
Communicated to the body through the eye	Prov.	15	30
Created by God	Gen.	1	2–5
	Is.	45	7
Divided from darkness	Gen.	1	4
Only for children of Israel	Ex.	10	21–23
Of morning, steady	II Sam.	23	4
Darkness in death	Job	10	22
O wicked, extinguished	Job	18	5, 6
Of Lord's countenance	Ps.	4	6
Lord is	Ps.	27	1
Lord's, for all	Ps.	36	9
Blindness, lack of	Ps.	38	10
Sown for righteous	Ps.	97	11

Garment of God's	Ps.	104	2
God's word	Ps.	119	105
Path of just, like	Prov.	4	18
Law is	Prov.	6	23
Sweet to behold	Eccl.	11	7
Not to be confused by evil persons	Is.	5	20
Messiah is a light unto the Gentiles	Is.	49	6
Reward for godliness	Is.	58	7, 8
Lord, everlasting	Is.	60	20
"Ye are the light of the world"	Mat.	5	14–16
Goodness creates	Mat.	6	22, 23
Life of men is	John	1	4, 5
John sent to interpret	John	1	7–9
	John	5	35
Hated by evil-doers	John	3	19–21
Of life, through Jesus	John	8	12
For believers	John	12	35
Believers, children of	John	12	36
From heaven, blinds Saul	Acts	9	3
Jesus' purpose	Acts	13	47
Brought by the Lord	I Cor.	4	5
Gospel of Christ	II Cor.	4	4
God the only source of	James	1	17
Believers walk in	I John	1	7
Perpetual in city of God	Rev.	22	5
Described as:			
Bright	Job	37	21
Manifesting objects	John	3	20–21
	Eph.	5	13
Shining	Job	41	18
Useful and precious	Eccl.	2	13
Illustrative of:			
Christ the source of all wisdom	Luke	2	32
	John	1	4, 9
	John	12	46
Favor of God	Is.	2	5
Future glory of saints	Col.	1	12
Glory of Christ	Acts	9	3, 5
	Acts	26	13
Glory of God	I Tim.	6	16
Glory of the church	Is.	60	1–3
Gospel	II Cor.	4	4
	I Pet.	2	9
Purity of Christ	Mat.	17	2
Purity of God	I John	1	5
Saints	Luke	16	8
	Eph.	5	8
	Phil.	2	15
The soul of man	Job	18	5–6
Whatever makes manifest	John	3	21
	Eph.	5	13
Wisdom of God	Dan.	2	22
Wise rulers	II Sam.	21	17
	II Sam.	23	4
Word of God	II Pet.	1	19
lightning flash of light			
Announces God's presence on mount Sinai	Ex.	19	16
Symbol of God's wrath	Ps.	18	14
Symbol of Christ's advent	Mat.	24	27
Symbol of Satan's fall	Luke	10	18

lign-aloes *see aloes*

ligure *precious stone*

On third row of breastplate of judgment	Ex.	28	19

likeness

Make man after our *l*	Gen.	1	26
Not make *l* of anything	Ex.	20	4
When I awake, with thy *l*	Ps.	17	15
What *l* will ye compare?	Is.	40	18
L of his death, *l* of his resurrection	Rom.	6	5
In the *l* of sinful flesh	Rom.	8	3
Was made in the *l* of men	Phil.	2	7

lily *white*

Valley flower	S. of S.	2	1
Found in gardens	S. of S.	6	2
More glorious than humans	Mat.	6	28, 29

lily work

Decoration of pillars	I Ki.	7	19, 22

lime *calcium oxide*

Ingredient of plaster	Deut.	27	2, 4
Kilns used	Is.	33	12
King's bones burned in	Amos	2	1

line

Their *l* is gone through the earth	Ps.	19	4
L upon *l*; here a little	Is.	28	10
Judgment will I lay to the *l*	Is.	28	17
Boast in another man's *l*	II Cor.	10	16
(See Amos 7:17, Josh. 2:18, 21)			

lineage *see genealogy*

line *yarn made of flax*

Joseph dressed in	Gen.	41	42
Worn by Aaron's sons	Ex.	28	5
Angels clothed in	Rev.	15	6
Not to mix with wood	Deut.	22	11
Embalming wrappings	Mark	15	46
Samuel's ephod	I Sam.	2	18
Imported	I Ki.	10	28
Left in tomb by Christ	John	20	5

lintel *upper part of door frame*

Smitten with blood	Ex.	12	22, 23
To be smitten	Amos	9	1

Linus *net*

A Christian from Rome	II Tim.	4	21

lion

Conquered by:

Samson	Judg.	14	5–9
David	I Sam.	17	34, 36
Benaiah	II Sam.	23	20
Saints	Heb.	11	33
Samson's riddle concerning	Judg.	14	14, 18
Used in ornamenting the temple	I Ki.	7	29, 36
Statues on Solomon's throne	I Ki.	10	19, 20
Disobedient prophet slain by	I Ki.	13	24–28
An unnamed person slain by	I Ki.	20	36
Sent as judgment upon the Samaritans	II Ki.	17	25, 26
Fierceness of	Job	4	10
	Job	28	8
Instincts of	Ps.	10	9
	Amos	3	4
The roaring of	Prov.	20	2
Strength of	Prov.	30	30
Proverb of	Eccl.	9	4
Lair of, in the jungles	Jer.	4	7
Parable of	Ezek.	19	1–9
Daniel in the lion's den	Dan.	6	16–24
Used for torture of criminals	Dan.	6	16–24
	II Tim.	4	17
King of beasts	Mic.	5	8

Figurative:

Of a ruler's wrath	Prov.	19	12
Of divine judgments	Is.	15	9
Of Satan	I Pet.	5	8

Lion of the tribe of Judah

A title for Christ	Rev.	5	5

lips *language*

Uncircumcised	Ex.	6	12, 30
Of Hannah	I Sam.	1	13
Flattering	Ps.	12	2, 3
Lying	Ps.	31	18
As swords	Ps.	59	7
To praise God	Ps.	63	5
Perverse	Prov.	4	24
Of a strange woman	Prov.	5	3
Of the righteous	Prov.	10	21, 32
Of the wise	Prov.	15	7
Sweet	Prov.	16	21
Fool's	Prov.	18	6
	Eccl.	10	12
Unclean	Is.	6	5
Stammering	Is.	28	11
Poison of	Rom.	3	13

Symbolic of:

Scorn	Ps.	22	7
Wisdom	Prov.	10	19
Shame	Mic.	3	7

liquor *alcoholic drink*

"Offer the first of thy"	Ex.	22	29
Forbidden to the Nazarites	Num.	6	3

litigation *going to law*

To be avoided	Mat.	5	25
	Luke	12	58
	I Cor.	6	1–8

litter

A contrivance for carrying persons	Is.	66	20

little

It was *l* thou hadst	Gen.	30	30
A *l* lower than the angels	Ps.	8	5
	Heb.	2	7
A *l* that a righteous man hath	Ps.	37	16
Better is *l* with the fear of the Lord	Prov.	15	16
Four things *l* of earth	Prov.	30	24
Hide thyself for a *l* moment	Is.	26	20
Here a *l*, and there a *l*	Is.	28	10

Taketh up isles as a little thing	Is.	40	15
To whom *l* is forgiven	Luke	7	47
Been faithful in a very *l*	Luke	19	17
Bodily exercise profiteth *l*	I Tim.	4	8
Life a vapour that appeareth for a *l* time.	James	4	14

live

Take of tree of life, and *l* for ever	Gen.	3	22
This do, and *l*	Gen.	42	18
Shall no man see me and *l*	Ex.	33	20
He shall *l* in them	Lev.	18	5
	Neh.	9	29
	Ezek.	20	11
Not *l* by bread alone	Deut.	8	3
	Mat.	4	4
	Luke	4	4
If a man die, shall he *l* again?	Job	14	14
Heart shall *l* that seek God	Ps.	69	32
Dead men shall *l*	Is.	26	19
Hear, and your soul shall *l*	Is.	55	3
He shall surely *l*	Ezek.	3	21
	Ezek.	18	9
	Ezek.	33	13
We shall *l* in his sight	Hosea	6	2
The just shall *l* by faith	Hab.	2	4
	Rom.	1	17
This do, and thou shalt *l*	Luke	10	28
Hear voice of God, and *l*	John	5	25
Though he were dead, yet shall he *l*	John	11	25
In him we *l* and move	Acts	17	28
We believe we shall *l* with him	Rom.	6	8
Not to *l* after the flesh	Rom.	8	12
Whether we *l*, we *l* unto the Lord	Rom.	14	8
Should *l* of the Gospel	I Cor.	9	14
As dying, and behold we *l*	II Cor.	6	9
L with him by power of God	II Cor.	13	4
I *l* by faith of Son of God	Gal.	2	20
If we *l* in the Spirit	Gal.	5	25
To me to *l* is Christ	Phil.	1	21
If the Lord will, we shall *l*	James	4	15
I am he that *l*, and was dead	Rev.	1	18
A name that thou *l*	Rev.	3	1
L with Christ	Rev.	20	4

liver *an organ of the body*

In a sacrifice	Lev.	3	4, 10
Of pain	Prov.	7	23
Of suffering	Lam.	2	11
	Job	16	13
Superstitious rites with	Ezek.	21	21

living water

Given by Christ	John	4	10
	Rev.	7	17

lizard *small reptile*

Classed as unclean food	Lev.	11	29, 30

Lo-ammi *not my people*

A symbolic name given to a son of Hosea	Hosea	1	9

loan *see lending*

loaves

Miraculous multiplication of	Mat.	14	15–21
	Mat.	15	34–38
	Luke	9	12–17

lock

For door	Judg.	3	23
On city gates	Neh.	3	13, 14
Forelock of hair	Ezek.	8	3

locust *an insect*

Plague of	Ex.	10	1–19
Authorized as food	Lev.	11	22
Devastation by	Deut.	28	38
A judgment	Deut.	28	42
	Joel	1	4
	Joel	2	25
Eaten by John the Baptist	Mat.	3	4
Sun obscured by	Joel	2	2, 10
Used as food	Mat.	3	4

Lod, Lydda *fissure, opening*

A city of Benjamin	I Chr.	8	12
	Neh.	7	37
Called Lydda	Acts	9	38

Lo-debar *"not a word"*

A city of Manasseh	II Sam.	9	4, 5
Home of Mephibosheth	II Sam.	9	3–6

lodge

A hut	Is.	1	8
Spending the night	Gen.	24	23
	Judg.	19	13

lodge—*continued*

Dwell, Ruth with Naomi	Ruth	1	16
Nehemiah does not allow	Neh.	13	21
Of birds in trees	Mat.	13	32
Of a cave	I Ki.	19	9
Christ at Bethany	Mat.	21	17

loft *upper room*

Corpse place in	I Ki.	17	17–19
Third story	Acts	20	9

lofty *exalted, high*

Heart not haughty, nor eyes *l*	Ps.	131	1
L looks be humbled	Is.	2	11
	Is.	5	15
The *l* city he layeth low	Is.	26	5
The high and *l* One	Is.	57	15

log

A liquid measure	Lev.	14	10

Lois *agreeable*

Grandmother of Timothy	II Tim.	1	5

loneliness *solitude*

Consolation in times of loneliness	Ps.	23	1–6
Of Jacob	Gen.	32	23–30
Of David	Ps.	38	11
Of Jeremiah	Jer.	15	17
Of Paul	II Tim.	4	6

longevity *length of life*

Promised to the good	Job	5	26
Allotted 70 years	Ps.	90	10
See ages, extraordinary			

long-suffering *patient endurance*
Of God:

For His own glory	Is.	48	9
In the days of Noah	I Pet.	3	20
Toward all men	II Pet.	3	9

Of Christians:

An attribute of love	I Cor.	13	4
Fruit of the spirit	Gal.	5	22
Duty toward one another	Eph.	4	1, 2
In preaching the word	II Tim.	4	2
As a worker for Christ	II Cor.	6	4
By Christ's power	Col.	1	11
Accompanied with forgiving	Col.	3	12, 13

look *see, seek*

L not behind thee	Gen.	19	17
L for light, but have none	Job	3	9
He *l* on men	Job	33	27
They *l* to him and were lightened	Ps.	34	5
That I am not able to *l* up	Ps.	40	12
L upon the face of thine anointed	Ps.	84	9
As eyes of servants *l* to masters	Ps.	123	2
At that day shall a man *l* to his Maker	Is.	17	7
L unto me, and be ye saved	Is.	45	22
To this man will I *l*	Is.	66	2
We *l* for peace	Jer.	8	15
	Jer.	14	19
I will *l* well to thee	Jer.	40	4
I *l* to the Lord	Mic.	7	7
Do we *l* for another?	Mat.	11	3
	Luke	7	19
In a day he *l* not for	Mat.	24	50
No man *l* back is fit for the kingdom	Luke	9	62
Then *l* up	Luke	21	28
Disciples *l* one on another	John	13	22
Said, *l* on us	Acts	3	4, 12
L ye out seven men	Acts	6	3
We *l* not at things seen	II Cor.	4	18
L not every man on his own things	Phil.	2	4
We *l* for the Saviour	Phil.	3	20
L for that blessed hope	Tit.	2	13
To them that *l* shall he appear	Heb.	9	28
He *l* for a city	Heb.	11	10
L unto Jesus	Heb.	12	2
Angels desire to *l* into	I Pet.	1	12
We *l* for new heavens	II Pet.	3	13

looking backward

Lot's wife	Gen.	19	15, 26
Warning against	Gen.	19	17
Israel's example	Num.	11	4, 5
Makes man unfit for service	Luke	9	62

looking-glass *see* mirror

loose

L thy shoe from off thy foot	Josh.	5	15
Canst thou *l* the bands of Orion?	Job	38	31
L those appointed to death	Ps.	102	20

Thou hast *l* my bonds	Ps.	116	16
Or ever the silver cord be *l*	Eccl.	12	6
To *l* the bands of wickedness	Is.	58	6
L on earth, be *l* in heaven	Mat.	16	19
	Mat.	18	18
L him, and let him go	John	11	44
Having *l* the pains of death	Acts	2	24

Lord

Is any thing too hard for the *L*?	Gen.	18	14
Then shall the *L* be my God	Gen.	28	21
The *L*, the *L* God, merciful and gracious	Ex.	34	6
The *L* is God	Deut.	4	35
	I Ki.	18	39
The *L* our God is one *L*	Deut.	6	4
L do so to me, and more	Ruth	1	17
	I Sam.	20	13
It is the *L*	I Sam.	3	18
	John	21	7
That art *L* alone	Neh.	9	6
	Is.	37	20
Blessed is the nation whose God is the *L*	Ps.	33	12
The *L* is God	Ps.	100	3
	Ps.	118	27
One *L*, and his name one	Zech.	14	9
Not every one that saith, *L*, *L*	Mat.	7	21
The joy of the *L*	Mat.	25	21
Son of man is *L* of the Sabbath	Mark	2	28
	Luke	6	5
Why call ye me *L*, *L*?	Luke	6	46
L to whom shall we go?	John	6	68
Ye call me Master and *L*	John	13	13
Crucified, both *L* and Christ	Acts	2	36
Who art thou, *L*?	Acts	9	5
	Acts	26	15
Same *L* over all	Rom.	10	12
L of the dead and of the living	Rom.	14	9
L of glory	I Cor.	2	8
L from heaven	I Cor.	15	47
One *L*, one faith	Eph.	4	5
Confess Jesus Christ is *L*	Phil.	2	11
King of kings, *L* of *l*	I Tim.	6	15

Lord *see* God

lord *ruler*

A prince	Josh.	13	3
	Judg.	3	3
	I Sam.	5	8

Lord's day *see* sabbath

Lord's prayer

Jesus teaches the disciples to pray	Mat.	6	9–13
	Luke	11	2–4

Lord's supper *see* Communion

Lo-ruhamah *not pitied*

Daughter of Hosea	Hosea	1	6, 8

lose

A time to get, and a time to *l*	Eccl.	3	6
He that findeth his life shall *l* it	Mat.	10	39
	Mat.	16	25
	Mark	8	35
	Luke	9	24
L his own soul	Mat.	16	26
	Mark	8	36
	Luke	9	25
If he *l* one sheep	Luke	15	4
That loveth his life shall *l* it	John	12	25

loss

Gained this harm and *l*	Acts	27	21
He shall suffer *l*	I Cor.	3	15
I count all things but *l* for Christ	Phil.	3	8

lost

Gone astray like *l* sheep	Ps.	119	176
L sheep of the house of Israel	Mat.	10	6
	Mat.	15	24
To save that which was *l*	Mat.	18	11
	Luke	19	10
Son was *l*	Luke	15	24
Gather fragments, that nothing be *l*	John	6	12
None is *l* but son of perdition	John	17	12
Gospel hid to them that are *l*	II Chr.	4	3

lost sheep *sinners*

Psalmist says he is like a	Ps.	119	176
Jesus instructs His disciples to preach to the, of Israel	Mat.	10	6
Jesus uses parable of	Mat.	18	11–14
	Luke	15	4–7

Lot *veil*

Son of Haran	Gen.	11	27–31
Moves with Abram to land of Canaan	Gen.	12	5
Returns from Egypt with Abram to Bethel	Gen.	13	1–3
Separates from Abram and settles in Sodom	Gen.	13	5–13
Taken captive by Chedorlaomer and rescued by Abram	Gen.	14	1–16
Saved from destruction in Sodom	Gen.	19	1–11
Protests against going to the mountains	Gen.	19	15–23
His wife looks back and is changed to a pillar of salt	Gen.	19	26
Commits incest with his daughters	Gen.	19	30–38

lots

The scapegoat chosen by	Lev.	16	8–10
Land of Canaan divided by	Num.	26	55
Bickering over	Josh.	17	14
Fighting order selected by	Judg.	1	3
Feast of Purim	Esth.	3	7
God's guidance by means of	Prov.	16	33
Saul chosen king by	I Sam.	10	20, 21
Priests designated for service by	I Chr.	24	5
Used to decide a doubtful question	Jonah	1	7
Garments of Jesus divided by	Mat.	27	35
An apostle chosen by	Acts	1	26

Lot's wife

Turned to pillar of salt	Gen.	19	26

love for fellowmen

Should be universal	Deut.	10	19
Necessary to true happiness	Prov.	15	17
Shown toward enemies	Mat.	5	44
The second great commandment	Mat.	22	37–39
Love of God is a motive to	John	13	34
Commanded	John	15	12

Exemplified:

Joseph	Gen.	45	15
Ruth	Ruth	1	16, 17
Jonathan and David	I Sam.	20	17, 41, 42
Obadiah	I Ki.	18	4
Lydia	Acts	16	15
Aquilla and Priscilla	Rom.	16	3, 4
Paul	II Cor.	6	11, 12

love of Christ

Shown towards Peter	Luke	22	32, 61
For Lazarus	John	11	5, 36
Unchangeable	John	13	1
Exemplified towards John	John	13	23
To those who love Him	John	14	21
To the Father	John	14	31
To be imitated	John	15	12

love of God

Irrespective of merit	Deut.	7	7
Shown to the destitute	Deut.	10	18
Is everlasting	Jer.	31	3
Manifested towards sinners	John	3	16
Shown in the giving of Christ	John	3	16
For the cheerful giver	II Cor.	9	7
Part of His character	II Cor.	13	11
To be sought in prayer	II Cor.	13	14
Basis for redemption	Eph.	2	4, 5
	I John	3	1

love to Christ

Characteristic of saints	S. of S.	1	4
Should be unquenchable	S. of S.	8	7
Exhibited by God	Mat.	17	5
Means of communion with God	John	14	23
Even unto death	Acts	21	13
Should be unquestioning	I Pet.	1	8

Exemplified:

Joseph of Arimathaea	Mat.	27	57–60
Penitent woman	Luke	7	47
Thomas	John	11	16
Mary Magdalene	John	20	11
Peter	John	21	15–17
Paul	Acts	21	13

love to God

God faithful to those who have	Deut.	7	9
Commanded	Deut.	11	1

Should produce:

Obedience to God	Deut.	30	20
Joy	Ps.	5	11
Hatred of sin	Ps.	97	10
Characteristic of saints	Ps.	5	11
With all the heart	Mat.	22	37
First great commandment	Mat.	22	37, 38

Hypocrites without	Luke	11	42
Exhibited by Christ	John	14	31

lovers

Isaac and Rebekah	Gen.	24	67
Jacob and Rachel	Gen.	29	20–30
Shechem and Dinah	Gen.	34	1–4
Samson and Delilah	Judg.	16	4
Boaz and Ruth	Ruth	2	4–12
David and Michal	I Sam.	18	20, 21
Ahasuerus and Ester	Esth.	2	16, 17

lovingkindness

David implores Lord to show to those that trust Him	Ps.	17	7
Of God is praised	Ps.	36	7
Asked for by David, who has sinned	Ps.	51	1
Is good to make known the Lord's	Ps.	92	2
David wants to hear God's	Ps.	143	8
Isaiah will speak of the Lord's	Is.	63	7
Israel will be restored through	Jer.	31	3

Loving-kindness of God:

Gives a knowledge of	Ps.	107	43
Former manifestations of, to be pleaded in prayer	Ps.	25	6
	Ps.	89	49
Never utterly taken from saints	Ps.	89	33
	Is.	54	10
Praise God for	Ps.	138	2
Proclaim to others	Ps.	40	10
Through Christ	Eph.	2	7
	Tit.	3	4–6

Described as:

Better than life	Ps.	63	3
Everlasting	Is.	54	8
Good	Ps.	69	16
Great	Neh.	9	17
Marvelous	Ps.	31	21
Merciful	Ps.	117	2
Multitudinous	Is.	63	7

Pray for its:

Continuance	Ps.	36	10
Extension	Gen.	24	12
	II Sam.	2	6

Saints:

Are ever mindful of	Ps.	26	3
	Ps.	48	9
Are heard according to	Ps.	119	149
Betrothed in	Hosea	2	19
Comforted by	Ps.	119	76
Crowned with	Ps.	103	4
Preserved by	Ps.	40	11
Quickened after	Ps.	119	88
Receive mercy through	Is.	54	8
Should expect, in affliction	Ps.	42	7–8

low

The Lord bringeth *l*	I Sam.	2	7
Set on high those that be *l*	Job	5	11
High and *l*, rich and poor	Ps.	49	2
Men of *l* degree are vanity	Ps.	62	9
Remembered us in *l* estate	Ps.	136	23
The lofty city he layeth *l*	Is.	26	5
Exalted them of *l* degree	Luke	1	52
Men of *l* estate	Rom.	12	16
Rich in that he is made *l*	James	1	10

lower

L than the angels	Ps.	8	5
	Heb.	2	7
Go into *l* parts of the earth	Ps.	63	9
Descended into *l* parts	Eph.	4	9

loyalty *allegiance, devotion*

Enjoined	Ex.	22	28
Enforced	Ezra	10	8
David	I Sam.	24	6–10
Uriah	II Sam.	11	9
Hushai	II Sam.	17	15, 16
Jehoiada	II Ki.	11	4–12
To be given Joshua as Moses' successor	Num.	27	20
Darius decrees loyalty to God	Ezra	6	10
Artaxerxes decrees people shall observe law of God	Ezra	7	26
Psalmist promises	Ps.	119	16, 30
Son should respect the Lord	Prov.	24	21
A wise man will be loyal to king and God	Eccl.	8	2
The highest	Mat.	22	37–39
To friends	John	15	13
Every person should be subject to God	Rom.	13	1

Lucas *see Luke*

Lucifer, day star *light-bearer or -bringer*

Name applied to king of Babylon by Isaiah	Is.	14	12

Lucius *illumination*

A teacher of Cyrene in the church at Antioch	Acts	13	1
Paul and his kinsman, salute the Romans	Rom.	16	21

lucre, filthy *dishonest gain or profit*

Samuel's sons guilty of	I Sam.	8	3
A good bishop does not seek	I Tim.	3	3, 8
	Tit.	1	7, 11
An elder should serve willingly and not for	I Pet.	5	2

Lud, Ludim *strife*

Son of Mizraim and descendant of Ham	Gen.	10	13
	I Chr.	1	11
Descendant known for their archery	Is.	66	19
	Jer.	46	9
One of five sons of Shem	Gen.	10	22
Province of Tyre	Ezek.	27	10

Luke, Lucas *light-giving*

A Greek author	Luke	1	1–4
	Acts	1	1, 2
Companion of Paul on various journeys	Acts	16	10–17
	Acts	21	1–18
	II Tim.	4	11
A physician, well-loved	Col.	4	14
Paul's fellowworker	Phil.		24

lukewarm *indifferent*

Applied to church of Laodicea	Rev.	3	16

lump *mass*

Of figs used by Hezekiah for healing boil	II Ki.	20	7
Of clay	Rom.	9	21
Of dough	I Cor.	5	6, 7

lunatic *insane*

David pretends	I Sam.	21	13–15
Covenantal curse	Deut.	28	28
Nebuchadnezzar	Dan.	4	32–34
Brought to Jesus for healing	Mat.	4	24
Child uncured by disciples is brought to Jesus	Mat.	17	14–18
Accusation against Jesus	John	10	20

lust *any kind of intense desire*

Sin of Eve	Gen.	3	6
Commanded against	Ex.	20	17
God gives up evil person unto	Ps.	81	12
After beauty	Prov.	6	25
Devil characterized as having	John	8	44
Of youths	II Tim.	2	22
Of the old man	Eph.	4	22
Causes wars and strife	James	4	1–3
Heart must be free of	Prov.	6	24, 25
	I Cor.	10	6
Called adultery	Mat.	5	27, 28
The word is choked out by thorns of	Mark	4	19
Punishment of	I Tim.	6	9
Leads to temptation	James	1	14
Should be avoided	I John	2	16

luxuries *pleasant but not necessary*

Israel sinful in	Amos	6	1–7
Of Babylon	Rev.	18	10–13
Moses overcomes desires for	Heb.	11	24–27

Luz *almond tree; bending*

A Canaanite city, renamed Bethel after Jacob's dream	Gen.	28	19
Jacob and his family build an altar here	Gen.	35	6
	Gen.	48	3
On border of land given to Joseph's children	Josh.	16	2
On border of land given to tribe of Benjamin	Josh.	18	13
Town of Hittites	Judg.	1	26

Lycaonia *wolf-like(?)*

A province of Asia Minor visited by Paul	Acts	14	6, 11

Lycia *a wolf*

A province in Asia, visited by Paul	Acts	27	5, 6

Lydda *strife*

A village where Peter heals Aeneas	Acts	9	32–35

Lydia *from Ludos*

Country in league with Egypt	Ezek.	30	5
Woman of Thyatira, baptized by Paul	Acts	16	12–15
Entertains Paul and Silas at her home	Acts	16	14, 15

lying *deceiving*

Forbidden by the Lord	Lev.	19	11, 12
David prays for lying lips to be quieted	Ps.	31	18
David's enemies take pleasure in	Ps.	62	4
Hated by David	Ps.	119	163
Is abhorred by the Lord	Prov.	6	16–19
	Prov.	12	22
Punishment is due the liar	Prov.	19	5
A lying tongue despises its victim	Prov.	26	28
Jeremiah laments over such sins as	Jer.	9	3–6
Jesus calls the devil a liar	John	8	44
Anania and his wife lie about sale of a possession	Acts	5	1–9
Fate of liars and other sinners is described	Rev.	21	8

Lystra *ransoming*

City of Asia where Paul heals a cripple	Acts	14	6–18
Paul is stoned and left for dead	Acts	14	19–21
	II Tim.	3	11
Home of Timotheus, Paul's helper	Acts	16	1, 2

M

Maacah, Maachah *pushing, pressing*

Son of Nahor, the brother of Abram	Gen.	22	24
Father of Achish and king of Gath, called also Maoch	I Sam.	27	2
	I Ki.	2	39
Daughter of Talmai and mother of Absalom	II Sam.	3	3
District in Syria, called also Syria-maachah	II Sam.	10	6–8
	I Chr.	19	6, 7
Favorite wife of Rehoboam and mother of Abijah	I Ki.	15	2
	II Chr.	11	20–23
Called Michaiah	II Chr.	13	2
One of Caleb's concubines	I Chr.	2	48
Wife of Machir	I Chr.	7	15, 16
Wife of Jehiel, a chief man of tribe of Benjamin	I Chr.	9	35
Father of one of David's mighty men	I Chr.	11	43
Father of Shephatiah	I Chr.	27	16

Maachathites: *patronymic of Maacah*

In Gilead	Deut.	3	14
Not expelled by Israel	Josh.	13	13
Jezaniah, a descendant of	Jer.	40	8

Maaleh–acrabbim *see Akrabbim*

Maaseiah *work of Jehovah*

A Levite musician in time of David	I Chr.	15	16, 18–20
Captain who assists in making Joash king of Judah	II Chr.	23	1
Officer in army of King Uzziah	II Chr.	26	11
Son of King Ahaz, slain by Zichri of Ephraim	II Chr.	28	7
Governor of Jerusalem during reign of Josiah	II Chr.	34	1, 8
Four exiles who had taken foreign wives during captivity	Ezra	10	18, 21
	Ezra	10	22, 30
Father of Azariah	Neh.	3	23
A priest who stands by Ezra as he reads the law to his people	Neh.	8	4
Probably same as 1	Neh.	8	7
One who seals the covenant	Neh.	10	1, 25
A descendant of Perez who lives in Jerusalem	Neh.	11	5, 6
A Benjamite	Neh.	11	7
Probably same as 1	Neh.	12	41
Priest who assists at dedication of wall	Neh.	12	42
Father of Zephaniah	Jer.	21	1
Father of false prophet Zedekiah	Jer.	29	21
Grandfather of Baruch	Jer.	32	12–16
Doorkeeper in the temple	Jer.	35	4

Maath *small*

Ancestor of Jesus	Luke	3	26

Macedonia *province in Asia*

Referred to in prophecy	Dan.	2	39
Paul has a vision of going to	Acts	16	9, 10
Paul goes to Thessalonica in	Acts	17	1–14
Silas and Timothy minister there	Acts	18	5
First country in Europe evangelized	Acts	19	21, 22
	Acts	20	1–6
Church of, sends contribution to Jerusalem	Rom.	15	26

Know for liberality	II Cor.	8	1–3
Thessalonica located there	I Thes.	1	7
	I Thes.	4	10

Machir *sold*

Son of Manasseh and grandson of Joseph	Gen.	50	23
Father of the Macherites	Num.	26	29
Inherits Gilead	Num.	32	40
Governors help Deborah and Barak	Judg.	5	14
A man of Lodebar	II Sam.	9	4, 5
Provides David with food	II Sam.	17	27–29

Machpelah, the cave of *double cave*

Purchased by Abraham when his wife Sarah dies	Gen.	23	1–20
Abraham is buried in	Gen.	25	10
Burial place of Isaac and Rebekah, Jacob and Leah	Gen.	49	30, 31
	Gen.	50	12, 13

mad, madness *insanity, temporary rage*

David pretends to be	I Sam.	21	13–15
In idolatry	Jer.	50	38
Festus declares Paul's education has made him	Acts	26	24
People speaking in tongues at church may be considered, by unbelievers	I Cor.	14	23
Pharisees are, because Jesus heals on the sabbath	Luke	6	11
Paul tells of his former	Acts	26	11

made

Who *m* thee a prince over us?	Ex.	2	14
Thy works in wisdom hast thou *m*	Ps.	104	24
This is the day the Lord hath *m*	Ps.	118	24
I am wonderfully *m*	Ps.	139	14
Lord *m* all things for himself	Prov.	16	4
He hath *m* everything beautiful	Eccl.	3	11
God hath *m* man upright	Eccl.	7	29
All things were *m* by him	John	1	3
Hath not my hand *m* all these things?	Acts	7	50
Understood by the things that are *m*	Rom.	1	20
M all things to all men	I Cor.	9	22
He hath *m* him to be sin for us	II Cor.	5	21
M of a woman, *m* under the law	Gal.	4	4
I was *m* a minister	Eph.	3	7
	Col.	1	23
M in the likeness of men	Phil.	2	7
M a little lower than the angels	Heb.	2	9
To be *m* like unto his brethren	Heb.	2	17
That they might be *m* manifest	I John	2	19

Madian *see* Midian

Magdala *tower*

A town or district visited by Jesus	Mat.	15	39

Magdalene *see* Mary

Magi *a religious caste or order*

Wise men who come to worship the baby Jesus	Mat.	2	1–14

magicians *those who claim to understand magic*

Fail to interpret Pharaoh's dream	Gen.	41	8
Claim special powers	Ex.	7	11, 12
Recognized Moses' power from God	Ex.	8	19
Daniel better than	Dan.	1	20
Simon Magus	Acts	8	9
Elymas	Acts	13	6, 8
Hebrews are forbidden to deal with	Lev.	19	31
	Deut.	18	9–14
Can't interpret dream of Nebuchadnezzar	Dan.	1	20
Jannes and Jambres	II Tim.	3	8

magistrates *officers of civil law*

Spies find none in Laish	Judg.	18	7
Ezra is commissioned by Artaxerxes to appoint	Ezra	7	25
Disciples appear before	Luke	12	11, 12
Paul and Silas appear before	Acts	16	19–22
	Acts	16	35–38
Should be obeyed	Tit.	3	1

magnanimity *nobleness of soul*

Of Abram to Lot in choosing land	Gen.	13	7–9
Of Judah for his brother, Benjamin	Gen.	44	32–34
Of David to Saul in sparing his life	I Sam.	24	2–11
Of Paul for Agrippa	Acts	26	27–29
Of Paul for Israel	Rom.	9	1–3

magnify *to make larger*

This day will I begin to *m* thee	Josh.	3	7
What is man, that thou shouldest *m* him	Job	7	17
M the Lord with me	Ps.	34	3
Say, Lord be *m*	Ps.	40	16
	Ps.	70	4
	Ps.	70	4

Thou hast *m* thy word above all	Ps.	138	2
He will *m* the law	Is.	42	21
My soul doth *m* the Lord	Luke	1	46
Speak with tongues, and *m* God	Acts	10	46
I *m* mine office	Rom.	11	13

Magog *land of Gog*

Son of Japheth	Gen.	10	2
Ezekiel prophesies concerning descendants	Ezek.	38	2, 14–23
Symbolizes enemies of God	Rev.	20	8, 9

Mahalath *sickness, grief*

Daughter of Ishmael and wife of Esau	Gen.	28	9
Called Bashemath	Gen.	36	2, 3
Granddaughter of David and wife of Rehoboam	II Chr.	11	18
Musical term	Ps.	53	title

Mahanaim *two camps*

Where angels meet Jacob	Gen.	32	1, 2
Located on border between Manasseh and Gad	Josh.	13	26, 30
Assigned to Merari Levites	Josh.	21	34, 38
Ish-bosheth establishes his capital here	II Sam.	2	8, 12
David lodges at	II Sam.	17	24, 27–29
Overseen by Abinadab	I Ki.	4	14

Maher-shalal-hash-baz *spoil speedeth, prey hasteth*
(Longest name in Bible)

Isaiah's son	Is.	8	1–4

Mahli, Mahali *weak*

Merari Levite who founded family of Mahlites	Ex.	6	19
Appointed to do service in the tabernacle	Num.	3	20, 33
Levites who are numbered in the plains of Moab	Num.	26	58
Ministers in house of God	Ezra	8	18
Son of Mushi	I Chr.	6	47
	I Chr.	23	23

Mahlon *sickly*

Elder son of Naomi and first husband of Ruth	Ruth	1	2, 5
	Ruth	4	3, 10

maid, maiden *young, unmarried woman*

Servant	Gen.	16	2
Of Rachel and Leah	Gen.	30	3–12
Of Pharaoh's daughter	Ex.	2	5
Young girl	Ex.	2	8
Punishment for killing a	Ex.	21	20, 21
Daughter of old man	Judg.	19	24
Of Naaman	II Ki.	5	1–3
Of great beauty, Esther	Esth.	2	7, 8
Jesus raises daughter of ruler from dead	Mat.	9	24, 25
Recognizes Peter	Mat.	26	71
Jesus describes fate of servant who beats his	Luke	12	45, 46

maidservant *handmaid*

Of Abimelech are healed	Gen.	20	17
Shall not work on the sabbath	Ex.	20	10
Law concerning sale of a daughter as	Ex.	21	7
Law concerning freeing of a	Deut.	15	17

mail, coat of *armour for upper portion of body*

Worn by Goliath	I Sam.	17	5

majesty *greatness, grandeur*

David gives praise to the Lord	I Chr.	29	11
Of God is fearsome	Job	37	22
Of Christ	II Pet.	1	16
Ascribed to God	Jude		25

majesty *grand, noble*

Of God (see God)	I Chr.	29	11
	Ps.	93	
	Ps.	96	
	Is.	24	14
	Nah.	1	
	Hab.	3	
Of Christ (see Christ)	II Pet.	1	16
With God is terrible *m*	John	37	22
Voice of the Lord is full of *m*	Ps.	29	4
Honour and *m* are before him	Ps.	96	6
Thou art clothed with *m*	Ps.	104	1
Glorious *m* of his kingdom	Ps.	145	12
On right hand of *m*	Heb.	1	3
	Heb.	8	1
To God be glory and *m*	Jude		25

maker

Shall a man be more pure than his *m*	Job	4	17
My *m* would soon take me away	Job	32	22
None saith, Where is God my *m*	Job	35	10

maker—*continued*

Ascribe righteousness to my *m*	Job	36	3
Kneel before the Lord our *m*	Ps.	95	6
Reproacheth his *m*	Prov.	14	31
	Prov.	17	5
The Lord is *m* of them all	Prov.	22	2
Shall a man look to his *m*	Is.	17	7
Woe to him that striveth with his *m*	Is.	45	9
Forgetteth the Lord thy *m*	Is.	51	13
Thy *m* is thine husband	Is.	54	5
Israel hath forgotten his *m*	Hosea	8	14
Imagine the *M* hath graven	Hab.	2	18
Whose builder and *m* is God	Heb.	11	10

Maktesh *a trough*

Valley in the city of Jerusalem	Zeph.	1	11

Malachi *my messenger*

Last of the minor prophets	Mal.	1	1

Malchiah, Malchijah *Jehovah is King*

A Gershomite Levite	I Chr.	6	40
Aaronite priest, father of Pashur	I Chr.	9	12
Called Melchiah	Jer.	21	1
An Aaronite, head of fifth course of priests	I Chr.	24	9
Three men who divorce their foreign wives after the exile	Ezra	10	25, 31
	Neh.	3	11
Son of Rechab	Neh.	3	14
A goldsmith's son who assists in repairing the wall	Neh.	3	31
One who is with Ezra when he reads the law	Neh.	8	4
A priest who seals the covenant	Neh.	10	3
A musician, priest who assists in dedicating the wall	Neh.	12	42
Jail keeper	Jer.	38	6

Malchiel *God is king*

Son of Beriah and head of clan of Asher	Gen.	46	17
	Num.	26	45

Malchi-shua, Melchi-shua *king is noble*

Son of King Saul	I Sam.	14	49
Slain by Philistines in battle of Gilboa	I Sam.	31	2

Malchus *king or kingdom*

High priest's servant whose ear is cut off by Peter	Mat.	26	51
Healed by Jesus	Luke	22	50, 51

malefactor *a criminal*

Two crucified with Jesus	Mat.	27	38–44
Jesus accused before Pilate as a	John	18	29, 30

malformation *wrong formation*

Of a Philistine giant	II Sam.	21	20

malice *premeditated hate*

For children	I Cor.	14	20
The new person in Christ will put aside	Eph.	4	31
Not at communion	I Cor.	5	8
To be put off	Col.	3	8
	I Pet.	2	1
Paul once lived in	Tit.	3	3
Diotrephes speaks maliciously against Christians	III John		10
See hatred, jealousy, revenge			

mallows *shrubs growing on salt marshes*

Men eat, in the widerness	Job	30	4

Malluch, Melicu *reigning as counselor*

A Merarite Levite	I Chr.	6	44
Two Jews who divorce their foreign wives	Ezra	10	29, 32
Two men who seal the covenant	Neh.	10	4, 27
A priest who goes with Jerubbabel	Neh.	12	2, 7

Mammon *personification of wealth*

Man can't give allegiance both to God and	Mat.	6	24

Mamre *fatness, strength*

District of Hebron where Abraham builds an altar	Gen.	13	18
Lord appears to Abraham at	Gen.	18	1–5
Dwelling place of Isaac	Gen.	35	27
Chieftain of Amorites	Gen.	14	13, 24

man

Created by God	Gen.	1	26
In the image of God	Gen.	1	27
	I Cor.	11	7
Male and female	Gen.	1	27
	Gen.	5	2
For God's pleasure	Rev.	4	11
Blessed by God	Gen.	1	28
Given dominion over all creatures	Gen.	1	28
	Ps.	8	6–8
Created on the sixth day	Gen.	1	31

Made a living soul by the breath of God	Gen.	2	7
	Job	33	4
Placed in the garden of Eden	Gen.	2	15
Woman formed to be a help to	Gen.	2	18–25
Every herb and tree given to, for food	Gen.	1	29
Filled with shame after the fall	Gen.	3	10
Gave names to other creatures	Gen.	2	19–20
His disobedience and punishment	Gen.	3	1–12
	Gen.	3	16–24
Allowed to eat flesh after the flood	Gen.	9	3
Spiritually dead	Eph.	2	1
Days of, compared to a shadow	I Chr.	29	15
Soul life continues after death of body	II Sam.	12	23
	Eccl.	12	7
Born to labor	Job	5	7
Has a limited time on earth	Job	7	1
	Ps.	90	10
Unworthy of God's favor	Job	7	17
God preserves and provides for	Job	7	20
	Ps.	36	6
	Ps.	145	15, 16
Cannot be just with God	Job	9	12
	Job	25	2
	Ps.	143	2
	Rom.	3	20
Cannot cleanse himself	Job	15	14
	Jer.	2	22
Cannot profit God	Job	22	2
	Ps.	16	2
Shall return to dust	Job	34	15
Inferior to angels	Ps.	8	5
Born in sin	Ps.	51	5
Shall be rewarded according to his work	Ps.	62	12
	Rom.	2	6
Must die	Ps.	89	48
	Eccl.	8	8
Wonderfully made	Ps.	139	14
God enables him to speak	Prov.	16	1
All the ways of, clean in his own eyes	Prov.	16	2
Fails under mental stress	Prov.	18	14
"As he thinketh, so is he"	Prov.	23	7
Ignorant of the future	Eccl.	8	7
	Eccl.	10	14
God's purpose in creation completed by making	Gen.	2	5, 7
Has but few days	Job	14	1
Has sought out many inventions	Eccl.	7	29
Help of, vain	Ps.	60	11
Ignorant of what is good for him	Eccl.	6	12
Ignorant of what is to come after him	Eccl.	10	14
Intellect of, matured by age	I Cor.	13	11
Involved posterity in his ruin	Rom.	5	12–19
Made by God in his successive generations	Job	10	8–11
	Job	31	15
Made for God	Rev.	4	11
Made wise by the inspiration of the Almighty	Job	32	8–9
Unprofited by all his labor and travail	Eccl.	2	22
	Eccl.	6	12
Unworthy of God's favor	Ps.	8	4
Walks in a vain show	Ps.	39	6
Whole duty of	Eccl.	12	13
Wiser than other creatures	Job	35	11
Would give all his possessions for the preservation of life	Job	2	4
Loved by God	John	3	16
The whole duty of	Eccl.	12	13
	Mic.	6	8
Cannot determine his own destiny	Jer.	10	23
More valuable than other creatures	Mat.	6	26
	Mat.	10	21
Redemption through Christ	Luke	20	36–38
	John	11	23–26
	I Cor.	15	51–58
Christ takes on the nature of	John	1	14
Of every nation, all of one blood	Acts	17	26
Nature and constitution different from other creatures	I Cor.	15	39
No trust to be placed in	Ps.	118	8
	Is.	2	22
Of the earth earthy	I Cor.	15	47
Possessed of:			
Affections	I Chr.	29	3
	Col.	3	2
Conscience	I Tim.	4	2
Soul	Acts	14	22
	I Pet.	4	19

Spirit	Prov.	18	14
	Prov.	20	17
	I Cor.	2	11
Will	II Pet.	1	21
Memory	Gen.	41	9
	I Cor.	15	2
A body	Mat.	6	25
A soul	Luke	12	20
Conscience	Rom.	2	15
Will	I Cor.	9	17
Understanding	Eph.	1	18
	Eph.	4	18

Called:

Flesh	Gen.	6	12
	Joel	2	28
The potsherd of the earth	Is.	45	9
Vain man	Job	11	12
	James	2	20
A worm	Job	25	6

Compared to:

Clay in the potter's hands	Is.	64	8
	Jer.	18	2, 6
Grass	Is.	40	6–7
	I Pet.	1	24
A sleep	Ps.	90	5
Vanity	Ps.	144	4
A wild ass's colt	Job	11	12

Created:

By Christ	John	1	3
	Col.	1	16
By the Holy Ghost	Job	33	4
From the dust	Job	33	6
In knowledge (inferred)	Col.	3	10
In the image of God	James	3	9
In uprightness	Eccl.	7	29
On the sixth day	Gen.	1	31
A type of Christ	Rom.	5	14
Under obligations to obedience	Gen.	2	16–17
Upon the earth	Deut.	4	32
	Job	20	4

God:

Destroys the hopes of	Job	14	19
Instructs	Ps.	94	10
Makes his beauty consume away	Ps.	39	11
Makes the wrath of, to praise him	Ps.	76	10
Orders the going of	Prov.	5	21
	Prov.	20	24
Prepares the heart of	Prov.	16	1
Turns, to destruction	Ps.	90	3

Christ:

Approved of God as	Acts	2	22
As such, the cause of the resurrection	I Cor.	15	21–22
Called the second, as covenant head of the church	I Cor.	15	47
Head of every	I Cor.	11	3
Knew what was in	John	2	25
Made in the likeness of	Phil.	2	7
A refuge, to sinners	Is.	32	2
Was found in fashion as	Phil.	2	8

Manaen *consoler, comforter*

A Christian prophet in the church at Antioch	Acts	13	1

Manasseh *causing to forget*

Elder son of Joseph	Gen.	41	50, 51
Receives special blessing from Jacob	Gen.	48	1–22
Children of, visit Joseph	Gen.	50	23
Jacob prophesies concerning the tribe	Gen.	49	22–26
Enumeration of tribe	Num.	1	34, 35
Place in camp and march	Num.	2	18, 20
Inheritance of half of tribe east of Jordan	Num.	32	33, 39–42
Mosaic blessing	Deut.	33	13–17
Territory given to	Josh.	17	1, 2
Daughters of Zelophehad	Josh.	17	3
Joins other tribes in building an altar	Josh.	22	1–34
Inheritance of half of tribe west of Jordan	Josh.	22	7
Smitten by Hazael	II Ki.	10	33
Returns from captivity	I Chr.	9	3
Many of tribe join David	I Chr.	12	19, 31
Gathers in Jerusalem during reign of Asa	II Chr.	15	9–13
Allotment in Ezekiel	Ezek.	48	4
Modification of the name Moses	Judg.	18	30
Son of Hezekiah, king of Judah	II Ki.	20	21
Builds altars for Baal	II Ki.	21	1–20
Taken captive to Babylon	II Chr.	33	1–12
Returns home and rebuilds altar for God	II Chr.	33	13–20
Two men who divorce their foreign wives	Ezra	10	30, 33

mandrake *a plant (sometimes called May apple)*

Used as a magic love potion	Gen.	30	14–16
Has a pleasant smell	S. of S.	7	13

manch *a Hebrew weight equal to sixty shekels or about two pounds*

The Lord tells Ezekiel there shall be just weights	Ezek.	45	12

manger *a feeding trough or stall for cattle*

Mary lays the baby Jesus in a	Luke	2	7, 12, 16

manifest *obvious, self-evident*

Things hidden which eventually come out into the open	Mark	4	22
Jesus' glory	John	2	11
Jesus makes Himself clear to only the disciples	John	14	21, 22
The toughts of the Lord's heart	I Cor.	4	5
Saviour is	II Cor.	2	14
Sins of the flesh are self-evident	Gal.	5	19
God becomes visible in the flesh	I Tim.	3	16
	I John	1	2
	I John	3	5
Nothing is hidden from God	Heb.	4	13
Love is shown by God through His Son	I John	4	9

manna *food miraculously supplied to the Israelites in the wilderness*

Provided by God	Ex.	16	4
	Num.	11	1–9
Israel ate for forty years	Ex.	16	35
Is specifically described	Ex.	16	31
Portion preserved as a testimony	Ex.	16	32–34
Ceases when Israelites camp at Gilgal	Josh.	5	10–12
Chirst is the bread of life	John	6	30–35
	John	6	48, 58
Church at Pergamos promised	Rev.	2	17

manner *way, kind*

Ye shall do no *m* of work	Lev.	23	31
Is this the *m* of man	II Sam.	7	19
All *m* of meat	Ps.	107	18
All *m* of pleasant fruits	S. of S.	7	13
Lambs shall feed after their *m*	Is.	5	17
Say all *m* of evil against you	Mat.	5	11
What *m* of man is this	Mat.	8	27
	Mark	4	41
	Luke	8	25
M of Jews to bury	John	19	40
Evil communications corrupt good *m*	I Cor.	15	33
My *m* of life	II Tim.	3	10
As the *m* of some	Heb.	10	25
Forgetteth what *m* of man	James	1	24
Holy in all *m* of conversation	I Pet.	1	15
What *m* of persons ought ye to be	II Pet.	3	11
What *m* of love	I John	3	1

manners *social rules of conduct, customs*

Obeisance shown to strangers	Gen.	18	2
	Gen.	19	1
Displayed by Abraham	Gen.	18	8
Used as a ruse	Gen.	31	35
Respect for the aged and for superiors	Lev.	19	32
	Job	29	8
Rules for guests	Prov.	23	1, 2
	I Cor.	10	27

Manoah *rest, quiet*

A Danite of Zorah and father of Samson	Judg.	13	2–24
	Judg.	16	31

manslayer *one who has slain a human being*

Protected in cities of refuge	Num.	35	6, 12, 28
See murder			

mantle *covering*

Coarse cloth for making beds in tents	Judg.	4	18
Large sleeveless outer garment	I Sam.	15	27
Elijah covers his face with	I Ki.	19	13
Worn by Elijah	II Ki.	2	8
Elisha picks up Elijah's	II Ki.	2	11–14
Ezra rents his, in grief	Ezra	9	3
Job tears his	Job	1	20
Female apparel	Is.	3	22

Maon *abode*

Town in the hill country of Judah	Josh.	15	55
David takes refuge from Saul near	I Sam.	23	24, 25
Place where Nabal, the rich man, lives	I Sam.	25	2
Place of a people that oppress Israel	Judg.	10	10–12
See Mehunim			
Son of Shammai and father of Beth-zur	I Chr.	2	45

Mara *bitter*

Name Naomi applies to herself	Ruth	1	20

Marah *bitter*

First camp of the Israelites	Ex.	15	22–25
Moses makes the water sweet	Num.	33	8, 9

Maranatha *see* Anathema

marble *limestone capable of taking a polish*

Used by Solomon to build the temple	I Chr.	29	2
Pillars made of	Esth.	1	6
Beloved's legs as	S. of S.	5	15
Merchants trade for	Rev.	18	12

Marcus *see* Mark

Mareshah *summit*

Fortified city of Judah	Josh.	15	44
Battle fought near here	II Chr.	14	9, 10
Birthplace of Eliezer, the prophet	II Chr.	20	37
Micah prophesies concerning	Mic.	1	15
Father of Hebron	I Chr.	2	42
Son of Laadah or possibly a city founded by Laadah	I Chr.	4	21

mariners *seamen, sailors*

Carry gold to Solomon	I Ki.	9	27
Should look to the Lord in their distress	Ps.	107	23–30
	Is.	42	10
Are afraid and pray to their gods	Jonah	1	4, 5
Are shipwrecked with Paul	Acts	27	1–44
Show cowardice	Acts	27	30

mark *sign*

Target	I Sam.	20	20
Circumcision	Gen.	17	14
For the dead forbidden	Lev.	19	28
Cain's	Gen.	4	15
Beast's	Rev.	13	18

Mark, Marcus *hammer or mallet*

Evangelist and author of the gospel of Mark	Mark	14	51, 52
Son of Mary	Acts	12	12
A follower of Jesus who accompanies Paul	Acts	12	25
Turns back at Perga	Acts	13	13
Causes contention between Paul and Barnabas	Acts	15	36–38
Paul reevaluates his opinion of John Mark	II Tim.	4	11
Nephew or cousin of Barnabas	Col.	4	10
Fellowworker and labourer of Paul	Col.	4	11
	Philem.		24
Probably converted by Peter	I Pet.	5	13

market *a place for general merchandise*

Located near city gate	II Ki.	7	17, 18
Great variety of merchandise in	Ezek.	27	13–25
Pharisees like to be heard in the	Mat.	23	7
Pharisees must wash after being in	Mark	7	4
Children play here	Luke	7	32
Judgment seat at	Acts	16	19
Paul preaches in the market in Athens	Acts	17	17

marriage *joining together*

Divinely instituted	Gen.	2	24
Polygamy of patriarchs	Gen.	4	19
Contracted for by parents	Gen.	21	21
	Judg.	14	2
Contracted by brother	Gen.	24	50
Dowry	Gen.	24	53
Should be with parental consent	Gen.	28	8

Wives obtained by:

Purchase	Gen.	29	20
Kidnapping	Judg.	21	21–23
Given as reward for valour	I Sam.	17	25
Given by kings	I Sam.	17	25

Celebrated with:

Feasting	Gen.	29	22
	John	2	1–10
For seven days	Judg.	14	12
Great rejoicing	Jer.	33	11
Denied to priests	Lev.	21	7
Forbidden with near relations	Deut.	7	3, 4
Polygamy forbidden	Deut.	17	17
Preceded by betrothal period	Deut.	20	7
	Mat.	1	18
Of brother's widow	Deut.	25	5
Examples of Levirate marriage	Gen.	38	8, 11
	Ruth	4	5
	Mat.	22	24
Military exemption	Deut.	24	5
Herald preceded bridegroom	Mat.	25	6
Celibacy not advised	Judg.	11	38
	Is.	4	1
	Jer.	16	9
	I Tim.	5	14

Divorce only in case of fornication	Mat.	5	31, 32
Requirements for bishop	I Tim.	3	2
Intermarriage with foreigners	Neh.	13	23
Figurative use	Is.	54	5
	Rev.	19	7
Wedding robes adorned with jewels	Is.	61	10
May be dissolved because of adultery	Mat.	19	3–9
"Let no man put asunder"	Mat.	19	6
Parables of	Mat.	22	2
	Mat.	25	1–10
Miracle of Jesus at	John	2	1–10
Is honorable	Heb.	13	4

marrow

Soul satisfied as with *m*	Ps.	63	5
Health and *m* to the bones	Prov.	3	8
Feast of fat things full of *m*	Is.	25	6
To the dividing asunder of joints and *m*	Heb.	4	12

Marsena *worthy*

One of the seven princes of Persia	Esth.	1	14

Mar's hill *see* Areopagus

mart *a market or trading place*

Tyre, for many countries	Is.	23	3

Martha *lady, mistress*

Entertains Jesus in her home	Luke	10	38–42
Troubled about many things	Luke	10	41
Sister of Mary and Lazarus	John	11	1, 2, 39
Beloved by Jesus	John	11	5
Sincere believer	John	11	21
Serves supper to Jesus and his disciples	John	12	2

martyr *one whose death testifies his faith*

Abel	Gen.	4	3–8
Prophets killed by Jezebel	I Ki.	18	4, 13
Zechariah	II Chr.	24	21, 22
John the Baptist	Mark	6	18–28
Stephen is the first Christian	Acts	7	59, 60
James, the apostle	Acts	12	2
Antipas	Rev.	2	13
Jesus	Rev.	17	6
Believers in all ages	Rom.	8	36
Children delivering up parents	Mat.	10	21, 22
Prophets	Mat.	23	24
Souls under the altar	Rev.	6	9
The two witnesses	Rev.	11	7–12
Result of evil	I John	3	12

marvel

M not at the matter	Eccl.	5	8
Jesus *m*	Mat.	8	10
	Mark	6	6
	Luke	7	9
All men did *m*	Mark	5	20
M not at this	John	5	28
Why *m* ye at this	Acts	3	12
M not if world hate you	I John	3	13

marvellous

M things without number	Job	5	9
Show *m* loving kindness	Ps.	17	7
He hath done *m* things	Ps.	98	1
M in our eyes	Ps.	118	23
	Mat.	21	42
	Mark	12	11
Herein is a *m* thing	John	9	30
Called you into his *m* light	I Pet.	2	9

marvellously

God thundereth *m*	Job	37	5

Mary *rebellion*

The mother of Jesus and wife of Joseph	Mat.	1	16, 18, 25
	Luke	1	26–28
Prophecy concerning	Is.	7	14
Cousin of Elisabeth, mother of John the Baptist	Luke	1	36
Visits Elizabeth	Luke	1	39–41
Magnificat	Luke	1	46–55
Gives birth to Jesus	Luke	2	5–7
Flees with her family to Egypt	Mat.	2	13–15
Goes to Jerusalem with Joseph to present Jesus	Luke	2	22
Wonders at the prophecy of Simeon	Luke	2	33–35
Takes the boy Jesus to the temple in Jerusalem	Luke	2	41–50
Seeks Jesus while He is teaching	Mat.	12	46, 47
Present at the wedding feast when Jesus turns water into wine	John	2	1–12
Present at the cross and is committed to the care of John	John	19	25–27
Dwells with disciples in Jerusalem	Acts	1	14

Mary Magdalene

Released of demons and supports the work of Jesus	Luke	8	1–3
One of those who stands near the cross of Jesus	Mat.	27	56
Sits at the sepulchre after Jesus' death	Mat.	27	61
Sees the empty tomb and runs to tell the disciples	Mat.	28	1–7
Recognizes Jesus after the resurrection	Mat.	28	8–10

Mary of Bethany

Anoints Jesus and is commended by Him	Mat.	26	10–13
Is eager to learn from Jesus	Luke	10	38–42
Sister of Lazarus and Martha	Luke	10	39
Deeply loved by Jesus	John	11	5
Comes to Jesus when her brother dies	John	11	28–32
Wife of Cleophas	John	19	25
Mother of James the less	Mat.	27	56
Watches near sepulchre of Jesus	Mat.	27	61
Mother of Mark	Acts	12	12
Sister of Barnabas	Col.	4	10
A Christian at Rome to whom Paul sends greetings	Rom.	16	6

masons *builders with stone*

From Tyre, help build house for David	II Sam.	5	11
	I Chr.	14	1
Are paid for repairing the temple	II Ki.	12	12
	II Chr.	24	12
Hired to help rebuild the temple after exile	Ezra	3	7

Massa *a burden*

Son of Ishmael and grandson of Abraham	Gen.	25	12–14
	I Chr.	1	30

massacre *merciless slaughter*
Authorized by:

Moses through the law of the Lord	Deut.	20	13
Samuel to destroy Amalek	I Sam.	15	1–3
Jehu to destroy worshipers of Baal	II Ki.	10	20–25
Decree to destroy the Jews	Esth.	3	8–15
God in Ezekiel's vision	Ezek.	9	4–9
Herod after Jesus is born	Mat.	2	16

Examples:

Heshbon	Deut.	2	34
Bashan	Deut.	3	6
Ai	Josh.	8	24–26
Hazor	Josh.	11	11, 12
Royal seed	II Ki.	11	1

Massah *testing*

Camp where Israelites murmur against the Lord	Ex.	17	7
	Deut.	6	16
Place Israel tempted God	Deut.	9	22
	Deut.	6	16
Proved God there	Deut.	33	8

Master

Name by which Jesus is addressed	Mark	4	38

master *leader, head*

A patriarchal head of a house	Gen.	24	7–9
An owner of slaves	Ex.	21	4–8
A political leader or king	II Sam.	12	8
A leader of sacred song	I Chr.	15	27
One in charge of eunuchs	Dan.	1	3
Duty of	Ex.	20	10
	Lev.	19	13
	Lev.	25	40
	Deut.	24	14
	Job	31	13
	Jer.	22	13
	Col.	4	1
	James	5	4
If I be a *m* where is my fear	Mal.	1	6
The Lord will cut off the *m* and the scholar	Mal.	2	12
No man can serve two *m*	Mat.	6	24
	Luke	16	13
Disciple is not above his *m*	Mat.	10	24
	Luke	6	40
One is your *M*, even Christ	Mat.	23	8, 10
Why troublest thou the *M*	Mark	5	35
	Luke	8	49
M, it is good for us to be here	Mark	9	5
	Luke	9	33
Good *M*, what shall I do	Mark	10	17
	Luke	10	25
	Luke	18	18
When the *m* of the house is risen	Luke	13	25
Art thou a *m* of Israel	John	3	10

The *M* is come, and calleth for thee	John	11	28
Ye call me *M* and ye say well	John	13	13
To his own *m* he standeth or falleth	Rom.	14	4
M is in heaven	Eph.	6	9
Count *m* worthy of honour	I Tim.	6	1
Be not many *m*	James	3	1

Mathusala *see* Methuselah

Mattaniah *gift of Jehovah*

Original name of Zedekiah, king of Judah	II Ki.	24	17
A Levite of sons of Asaph	I Chr.	9	15
	Neh.	11	22
Leader of the singers	Neh.	11	17
Comes with Zerubbabel to Jerusalem	Neh.	12	8
Son of Heman	I Chr.	25	4, 16
An Asaphite in time of Hezekiah	II Chr.	29	13
Four men who divorce their foreign wives	Ezra	10	26, 27
	Ezra	10	30, 37
Doorkeeper in the temple	Neh.	12	25
An Asaphite who takes part in dedication of the walls	Neh.	12	35
A Levite, father of Zaccur	Neh.	13	13

Mattatha *gift*

Son of Nathan and grandson of David	Luke	3	31

Mattathias *gift of Jehovah*

Two ancestors of Jesus, several generations apart	Luke	3	25, 26

matter

If there arise a *m* too hard	Deut.	17	8
The root of the *m* is found in me	Job	19	28
I am full of *m*	Job	32	18
My heart is inditing a good *m*	Ps.	45	1
That handleth a *m* wisely	Prov.	16	20
Answereth a *m* before he heareth it	Prov.	18	13
That which hath wings shall tell the *m*	Eccl.	10	20
Hear conclusion of the whole *m*	Eccl.	12	13
Omitted the weightier *m*	Mat.	23	23
If it were a *m* of wrong	Acts	18	14
I will know uttermost of the *m*	Acts	24	22
Dare any having a *m* go to law	I Cor.	6	1
Ready as a *m* of bounty	II Cor.	9	5
How great a *m* a little fire kindleth	James	3	5

Matthan *gift*

Joseph's grandfather	Mat.	1	15, 16

Matthat *gift*

Two ancestors of Jesus	Luke	3	24, 29

Matthew *gift of Jehovah*

The publican called by Jesus to be His disciple	Mat.	9	9, 10
	Mat.	10	1–5
Called Levi	Mark	2	14, 15
Gives feast to Jesus	Luke	5	29
At Pentecost	Acts	1	13

mean

What *m* ye by this service	Ex.	12	26
What *m* the testimonies	Deut.	6	20
What *m* these stones	Josh.	4	6, 21
Not stand before *m* men	Prov.	22	29
The *m* man	Is.	2	9
	Is.	5	15
What the rising from the dead should *m*	Mark	9	10
A citizen of no *m* city	Acts	21	39

means

By no *m* clear the guilty	Ex.	34	7
	Num.	14	18
None can by any *m* redeem his brother	Ps.	49	7
Shalt by no *m* come out	Mat.	5	26
Sought *m* to bring him	Luke	5	18
Nothing shall by any *m* hurt you	Luke	10	19
By what *m* he now seeth	John	9	21
By what *m* he is made whole	Acts	4	9
That I might by all *m* save some	I Cor.	9	22
Lest by any *m*, as the serpent	II Cor.	11	3
Lest by any *m* I should run in vain	Gal.	2	2
By any *m* attain	Phil.	3	11
No man deceive you by any *m*	II Thes.	2	3

Mearah *cave*

Part of region yet unconquered by Israelites	Josh.	13	4

measure

Ye shall *m* from without the city	Num.	35	5
A just *m* shalt thou have	Deut.	25	15
The *m* is longer than the earth	Job	11	9
He weigheth the waters by *m*	Job	28	25
To know the *m* of my days	Ps.	39	4
Tears to drink in great *m*	Ps.	80	5

measure—*continued*

Who hath ***m*** the waters	Is.	40	12
Comprehended dust of earth in a ***m***	Is.	40	12
I will ***m*** former work into bosom	Is.	65	7
Correct thee in ***m***	Jer.	30	11
	Jer.	46	28
If heaven can be ***m***	Jer.	31	37
Sand of the sea cannot be ***m***	Jer.	33	22
	Hosea	1	10
Thou shalt drink water by ***m***	Ezek.	4	11
With what ***m*** ye mete	Mat.	7	2
	Mark	4	24
	Luke	6	38
Three ***m*** of meal	Mat.	13	33
	Luke	13	21
Fill up ***m*** of your fathers	Mat.	23	32
Were amazed beyond ***m***	Mark	6	51
Good ***m***, pressed down	Luke	6	38
God giveth not the Spirit by ***m***	John	3	34
To every man the ***m*** of faith	Rom.	12	3
Exalted above ***m***	Rom.	12	7
M themselves by themselves	II Cor.	10	12
Not boast of things without our ***m***	II Cor.	10	13
Beyond ***m*** I persecuted	Gal.	1	13
The ***m*** of the gift of Christ	Eph.	4	7
To the ***m*** of the stature	Eph.	4	13
A ***m*** of wheat for a penny	Rev.	6	6
Rise, and ***m*** the temple of God	Rev.	11	1
A golden reed to ***m*** the city	Rev.	21	15
According to the ***m*** of man	Rev.	21	17

measures of capacity

Assuming aniephah to contain 8 gallons, we obtain the following fairly accurate measures:

1 Log = 7/8 pint	Lev.	14	10–21
1 Cab = 4 Logs = 3 1/2 pints	II Ki.	6	25
1 Hin = 3 Cabs = 1 1/8 gallons	Ex.	29	40
1 Omer = 1 4/5 Cabs = 6 pints	Ex.	16	36
	Lev.	5	11
	Lev.	14	10
1 Seah = 3 1/2 Omers = 2 Hins = 2 2/3 gallons			
1 Ephah or Bath = 3 Seahs = 8 gallons	Is.	5	10
	Ezek.	45	11
1 Lethech = 5 Ephahs = 40 gallons			
1 Homer = 10 Ephahs = 80 gallons	Is.	5	10
	Ezek.	45	14

measures of length

The Royal System measures 1 4/25 for every 1 unit in the Common System. We give approximate measures of the Common System:

1 Digit or fingerbreadth = 3/4 inch			
1 Palm = 4 Digits = 3 inches	Ex.	25	25
	Ps.	39	5
1 Span = 3 Palms = 9 inches	Ex.	28	16
	I Sam.	17	4
1 Cubit = 2 Spans = 1 1/2 feet	Gen.	6	15f.
	Deut.	3	11
1 Reed = 6 Cubits = 9 feet			
1 Fathom = 6 feet 1 inch	Acts	27	28
1 Furlong = 202 yards	Luke	24	13

meat *food in general*

God provides herbs and fruit as	Gen.	1	29, 30
Isaac requests Esau to prepare vension before blessing him	Gen.	27	4
Clean and unclean	Lev.	11	34
	Deut.	14	4–21
Gives Elijah much strength	I Ki.	19	8
A good wife provides, for her household	Prov.	31	15
Of an ant	Prov.	6	8
Ezekiel is instructed to eat	Ezek.	4	10
Daniel refuses to eat king's	Dan.	1	5, 8–16
Life is more important than	Mat.	6	25
The will of God	John	4	34
Figuratively used	Mat.	24	45
	I Cor.	3	2
	Heb.	5	14
Food to poor	Mat.	25	35
Christ appears to disciples and asks for	Luke	24	41
Problems with idol meat	I Cor.	8	13

meat offerings *see* offerings

Medan *discord*

Son of Abraham and Keturah	Gen.	25	2
	I Chr.	1	32

meddle

Why ***m*** to thy hurt	II Ki.	14	10
	II Chr.	25	19
M not with him that flattereth	Prov.	20	19
M not with them given to change	Prov.	24	21
That ***m*** with strife	Prov.	26	17

Mede (-s)

Cities of the ***M***	II Ki.	17	6
	II Ki.	18	11
The province of the ***M***	Ezra	6	2
Among the laws of the ***M***	Esth.	1	19
I will stir up ***M*** against them	Is.	13	17
	Jer.	51	11
All the kings of the ***M***	Jer.	25	25
Kingdom is given to the ***M***	Dan.	5	28
The law of the ***M***	Dan.	6	8, 12, 15
Ahasuerus of the seed of the ***M***	Dan.	9	1
Year of Darius the ***M***	Dan.	11	1

Medeba *gently flowing waters*

A city of Moab	Num.	21	30
Allotted to Reuben	Josh.	13	9, 16
David defeats enemies at	I Chr.	19	7–15

Media *land of the Medes*

Captive Israelites placed here	II Ki.	17	6
	II Ki.	18	11
Prophecies concerning	Is.	13	17, 18
	Is.	21	2
A country, located in Asia	Dan.	8	20

Media

Power of Persia and ***M***	Esth.	1	3
Seven princes of Persia and ***M***	Esth.	14	
The ladies of ***M*** shall say this	Esth.	18	
Book of the kings of ***M***	Esth.	10	2
O ***M*** all the sighing	Is.	21	2
Two horns are kings of ***M***	Dan.	8	20

mediation *intervention*

A double	Ex.	7	1, 2
By Moses, for Israel	Ex.	20	19–21
For transgressors	Ex.	32	30–33
An effectual	Num.	16	46–48
Job longs for	Job	9	33
By Jesus for us	I Tim.	2	5
	Heb.	12	24
Abraham for Sodom	Gen.	18	23–32
Moses for Pharaoh	Ex.	8	12, 13, 30
Ezra for Israel	Ezra	9	5–15
Nehemiah for Judah	Neh.	1	4–9
By Israel requested	Deut.	5	5

medicine *cure, remedy*

In connection with midwifery	Gen.	25	24–26
For barrenness	Gen.	30	14–16
Elisha's antidotes for poisons	II Ki.	2	21
	II Ki.	4	39–41
Egyptians noted for	Jer.	46	11
In Christ's time	Mark	5	26
Made from:			
Figs	Is.	38	21
Roots and leaves	Ezek.	47	12
Wine	I Tim.	5	23
Oil	James	5	14

meditation *reflection*

Evening	Gen.	24	63
A prayerful	Ps.	19	14
Peter awakened by	Mark	14	72
A poorly-timed	Luke	12	16–20
On the word of God:			
Divine summons	Josh.	1	8
In the quiet of night	Ps.	4	4
All the day	Ps.	119	97
A ministerial duty	I Tim.	4	15
A source of delight:			
For the righteous	Ps.	1	1, 2
In anxiety	Ps.	39	3
Source of strength	Ps.	119	15, 99

Mediterranean sea

Sea of the Philistines	Ex.	23	31
Called the great sea	Num.	34	6, 7
	Josh.	15	12, 47
The uttermost sea	Deut.	11	24
Sea of Joppa	Ezra	3	7
The utmost sea	Joel	2	20
The hinder sea	Zech.	14	8

meekness *humility*

"The meek shall inherit the earth"	Ps.	37	11
	Mat.	5	5
Shall be exalted	Ps.	147	6
In adversity	Is.	39	5–8
With courage	Jer.	26	12–15

Commended	Zeph.	2	3
Fruit of the Spirit	Gal.	5	22, 23
Essential	II Tim.	2	25
	James	1	21
Under injury	I Pet.	2	18, 19
The glory of	I Pet.	2	19, 20
A divine	I Pet.	2	21–23
Instances of:			
Abraham	Gen.	13	8
Isaac	Gen.	26	20–22
Moses	Ex.	2	13
Gideon	Judg.	8	2, 3
Hannah	I Sam.	1	13–16
David	I Sam.	17	29
Jesus	Is.	42	1–4
	Mat.	26	47–54
Stephen	Acts	7	59, 60
Paul	Acts	21	20–26
Job	James	5	11

meet

An help *m* for him	Gen.	2	18
The rich and poor *m* together	Prov.	22	2
Hell is moved to *m* thee	Is.	14	9
Prepare to *m* thy God	Amos	4	12
Fruits *m* for repentance	Mat.	3	8
City came to *m* Jesus	Mat.	8	34
Not *m* to take children's bread	Mat.	15	26
	Mark	7	27
Went forth to *m* the bridegroom	Mat.	25	1
Works *m* for repentance	Acts	26	20
Not *m* to be called an apostle	I Cor.	15	9
Made us *m* to be partakers	Col.	1	12
In the clouds, to *m* the Lord	I Thes.	4	17
Herbs *m* for them by whom it is dressed	Heb.	6	7

Megiddo, Megiddon *place of troops*

A city in Issachar	Josh.	17	1
Conquest of, by Joshua	Josh.	12	21
Deborah defeats Sisera in valley of	Judg.	5	19
Enslaved by Israel	Judg.	1	27, 28
One of Solomon's storehouse districts	I Ki.	4	12
Walled by Solomon	I Ki.	9	15
Ahaziah dies at	II Ki.	9	27
Josiah slain at	II Ki.	23	29, 30
Prophecy concerning	Zech.	12	11
Battle of Armageddon	Rev.	16	16

Mehetabeel *God's best*

Wife of Hadar	Gen.	36	39
Father of Delaiah	Neh.	6	10

Mehunim, Meunim *habitations*

Makes war on Uzziah	II Chr.	26	7
Descendants return from exile	Ezra	2	50
	Neh.	7	52

Melchi *my king*

Two ancestors of Mary	Luke	3	24, 28

Melchisedec, Melchizedek *king of righteousness*

King of Salem	Gen.	14	18–20
A priest and type of Christ	Heb.	7	1–21

Melchi-shua *see* Malchi-shua

Melea *my dear friend*

Ancestor of the family of Jesus	Luke	3	31

Melech *king*

Descendant of Saul	I Chr.	8	35
	I Chr.	9	41

Melicu *see* Malluch

Melita *escaping an island in the Mediterranean*

Paul shipwrecked on the coast of	Acts	28	1–10

melon *a succulent plant*

Grown in Egypt	Num.	11	5

melt *change condition*

Hearts of Canaanites	Josh.	2	11
	Josh.	14	8
Of rebellious Israelites	II Sam.	17	10
Melting of waters	Ps.	58	7
Heart of Egypt	Is.	19	1
The land by the Lord's touch	Amos	9	5
Hills	Nah.	1	5
Elements	II Pet.	3	10
Manna by the heat of the sun	Ex.	16	21
Christ's heart	Ps.	22	14
Silver	Ezek.	22	22

Melzar *butler*

One who has charge of Daniel	Dan.	1	11–16

members

Of the body, types of the church	Rom.	12	4
	I Cor.	12	12
In thy book all my *m* written	Ps.	139	16
One of thy *m* should perish	Mat.	5	29
Another law in *m* warring	Rom.	7	23
Your bodies are *m* of Christ	I Cor.	6	15
The body is not one *m*	I Cor.	12	14
We are *m* of another	Eph.	4	25
M of his body	Eph.	5	30
The tongue is a little *m*	James	3	5
Lusts that war in your *m*	James	4	1

memorials *serving to preserve remembrance*

Passover	Ex.	12	14
Firstborn set apart as	Ex.	13	12–16
Pot of manna	Ex.	16	32–34
Shoulder stones of ephod	Ex.	28	12
Feast of tabernacles	Lev.	23	41–43
Twelve stones	Josh.	4	7
Stone of Joshua	Josh.	24	26, 27
Lord's supper	Luke	22	19

memory

Of the just, blessed	Prov.	10	7
Of the wicked, cut off	Ps.	109	15
	Is.	26	14
Utter the *m* of thy goodness	Ps.	145	7
The *m* of them is forgotten	Eccl.	9	5
Made their *m* to perish	Is.	26	14
Keep in *m* what I preached	I Cor.	15	2

Memphis, Noph *haven of good*

Prophecies concerning	Is.	19	13
	Jer.	2	16
	Ezek.	30	16
Exiled Jews settle here	Jer.	44	1
	Jer.	46	19
A celebrated city in Egypt	Hosea	9	6

Menan *soothsayer*

An ancestor of Jesus	Luke	3	31

mene *numbered*

The handwriting on the wall	Dan.	5	25, 26

men-pleasers

In public officers	Acts	12	1–3
	Acts	24	27
With eyeservice	Eph.	6	6
Warning against	Col.	3	22

menstruation *menstrual flow*

Cessation of, in old age	Gen.	18	11
Immunities of women during	Gen.	31	35
Laws relating to	Lev.	15	19–30
	Lev.	20	18
	Ezek.	18	6
Uncleanness of	Is.	30	22
Of animals	Jer.	2	24
Protracted—12 years	Mark	5	25

mention

Make no *m* of other gods	Ex.	23	13
	Josh.	23	7
I will make *m* of thy righteousness	Ps.	71	16
Make *m* that his name is exalted	Is.	12	4
We will make *m* of thy name	Is.	26	13
I will *m* the loving kindness of the Lord	Is.	63	7
May not *m* name of Lord	Amos	6	10
M of you in my prayers	Rom.	1	9
	Eph.	1	16
	I Thes.	1	2
Made *m* of departing of Israel	Heb.	11	22

Mephibosheth *destroying shame*

Lame son of Jonathan	II Sam.	4	4
David entertains him	II Sam.	9	1–7
Property restored to	II Sam.	9	9, 10
Trick of Ziba his servant	II Sam.	16	1–4
His ingratitude to David	II Sam.	19	24–27
Property of, confiscated	II Sam.	19	29, 30
Called Merib-baal	I Chr.	8	34
Son of Saul	II Sam.	21	8, 9

Merab *see* Michal

Merari *unhappy*

Son of Levi	Gen.	46	11
Head of the Merari Levites	Num.	3	33–35
	Num.	26	57
Duties	Num.	3	35–37
Receive cities	Josh.	21	7, 34–40
Courses of	I Chr.	23	6–23
Postexilic	Ezra	8	18, 19

Merathaim *double rebellion*

A symbolic name, apparently for Babylonia	Jer.	50	21

merchandise *see* commerce

merchants *traders, storekeepers*

Of Midian	Gen.	37	28
Of Solomon	I Ki.	10	28
Defile the sabbath	Neh.	13	19–21
Prince of Tyre	Is.	23	8
Of Ethiopia	Is.	45	14
Deceitful	Hosea	12	7
Many in Nineveh	Nah.	3	16
Parable of the goodly pearl	Mat.	13	45
Without customers	Rev.	18	11

Mercurius *Roman and Greek god*

Paul taken for	Acts	14	11, 12

mercy *compassion*

Commanded by God	II Ki.	6	21–23
	Mic.	6	8
A characteristic of the godly	Ps.	37	26
	Is.	57	1
Beneficial to the giver	Prov.	11	17
	Prov.	14	21
	Mat.	5	7
Should be shown to the poor	Prov.	14	31
	Dan.	4	27
Lack of, a sin	Hosea	4	1
	Mat.	23	23
	James	2	13
Commanded by Christ	Luke	6	36
Should be manifested to those in distress	Luke	10	37
Must be shown with cheerfulness	Rom.	12	8

mercy of God

Typified by	Ex.	25	17
Is part of His character	Ex.	34	6
	Ps.	62	12
	Neh.	9	17
	John	4	2, 10–11
	II Cor.	1	3
Is great and manifold	Num.	14	18
	Neh.	9	27
	Is.	54	7
Manifested to repentant sinners	II Chr.	30	9
	Prov.	28	13
	Is.	55	7
	Ps.	32	5
	Luke	15	18–20
Is plenteous and abundant	Ps.	86	5
	I Pet.	1	3
Is everlasting	Ps.	89	28
	Ps.	118	1–4
	I Chr.	16	34
	Ps.	106	1
	Ps.	107	1
The earth is full of	Ps.	119	64
Given to the afflicted	Is.	49	13
	Is.	54	7
Is new every morning	Lam.	3	23
Shown to those who fear Him	Luke	1	50
	Ps.	103	17
Manifested in the sending of Christ	Luke	1	78
The publican prays for	Luke	18	13
High as heaven	Ps.	36	5
	Ps.	103	11
Manifold	Lam.	3	32
Over all his works	Ps.	145	9
Plenteous	Ps.	86	5, 15
	Ps.	103	8
Rich	Eph.	2	4
Sure	Is.	55	3
	Mic.	7	20
Tender	Ps.	25	6
	Ps.	103	4
God's delight	Mic.	7	18
A ground of hope	Ps.	130	7
	Ps.	147	11
A ground of trust	Ps.	52	8

Manifested:

In long-suffering	Lam.	3	22
	Dan.	9	9
In salvation	Tit.	3	5
To his people	Deut.	32	43
	I Ki.	8	23
To returning backsliders	Jer.	3	12
	Hosea	14	4
	Joel	2	13
To the fatherless	Hosea	14	3
To whom he will	Hosea	2	23
	Rom.	9	15, 18

With everlasting kindness	Is.	54	8

Should be:

Magnified	I Chr.	16	34
	Ps.	115	1
	Ps.	118	29
	Jer.	33	11
Pleaded in prayer	Ps.	6	4
	Ps.	25	6
	Ps.	51	1
Rejoiced in	Ps.	31	7
Sought for others	Gal.	6	16
	I Tim.	1	2
	II Tim.	1	18
Sought for ourselves	Ps.	6	2

mercy seat *the golden lid of the ark of the covenant*

Described	Ex.	25	17–22
Placed on the ark	Ex.	26	34
Made by Bezaleel	Ex.	37	1, 6–9
Sprinkeld with blood	Lev.	16	14, 15
In Solomon's temple	I Chr.	28	11
Contained the tablets, a pot of manna, Aaron's budding rod	Heb.	9	5
Type of Christ	Heb.	9	5–12

Mered *rebellion*

Son of Ezra	I Chr.	4	17

Meremoth *heights*

Son of Uriah	Ezra	8	33
	Neh.	3	4–21
Descendant of Bani	Ezra	10	36
A post-exilic priest	Neh.	10	5

Meribaal *see* Mephibosheth

Meribah *contention*

A place where Moses strikes the rock and brings forth water	Ex.	17	1–7
Place near Kadesh	Num.	27	14
The sin of Moses here	Deut.	32	48–51
Called "waters of strife"	Ps.	81	7
	Ps.	106	32

Merodach *thy rebellion*

A Babylonian idol	Jer.	50	2

Merodach-baladan, Berodach-baladan *thy rebellion: Baal is lord*

King of Persia	II Ki.	20	12
Sends messengers to Hezekiah	Is.	39	1–8

merriment *gaiety, mirth*

Attribute of the heart	Judg.	19	6, 9
	I Ki.	21	7
Like medicine	Prov.	17	22
Caused by wine	Eccl.	10	19
An evil	Luke	12	16–19
Commended	Luke	15	32
Reflected in singing	James	5	13

Instances of:

Sons of Jacob	Gen.	43	15–34
Boaz	Ruth	3	7
Nabal	I Sam.	25	36
Judah and Israel	I Ki.	4	20
Ahasuerus	Esth.	1	2, 10

Mesha *freedom*

A place in possession of the Jokanites	Gen.	10	30
King of Moab	II Ki.	3	4, 5
Son of Caleb	I Chr.	2	42
A Benjamite	I Chr.	8	9

Meshach *guest of a king*

Name given by chief eunuch to Mishael	Dan.	1	7
Made an overseer at Daniel's request	Dan.	2	49
In the fiery furnace	Dan.	3	13–30

Meshech *tall*

Son of Japheth	Gen.	10	2
Also called Mesech	I Chr.	1	5
Son of Shem	I Chr.	1	17
A tribe	Ps.	120	5
Settled in Gog	Ezek.	38	2
	Ezek.	39	1
The Moschi, slave traders	Ezek.	27	13

Meshezabeel *God delivers*

Father of Berechiah	Neh.	3	4
A Judahite	Neh.	10	21
	Neh.	11	24

Meshillemith, Meshillemoth *recompense*

Priest of Jerusalem	I Chr.	9	12
Also called Meshillemoth	Neh.	11	13
Father of Berechiah	II Chr.	28	12

Meshullam *friend*

Grandfather of Shaphan	II Ki.	22	3
A son of Zerubbabel	I Chr.	3	19
A Gadite of Bashan	I Chr.	5	13
Three Benjamites	I Chr.	8	17
	I Chr.	9	7, 8
An Aaronite	I Chr.	9	11
A priest	I Chr.	9	12
A Kohathite, overseer of the temple repairs	II Chr.	34	12
A companion of Ezra	Ezra	8	16
A returned exile	Ezra	10	15
Son of Bani	Ezra	10	29
Two persons who rebuild the wall	Neh.	3	4, 6
Assistant to Ezra	Neh.	8	4
Two priests who sign the covenant	Neh.	10	7, 20
A Benjamite	Neh.	11	7
Two priests of Ezra	Neh.	12	13, 16, 33
A Levite	Neh.	12	25

Mesopotamia *Greek: Between the rivers extension*

Nahor dwells in	Gen.	24	10
Balaam from	Deut.	23	4
Home of Cushan-rishathaim	Judg.	3	8
Mercenary chariots	I Chr.	19	6
Israelites subjected to	Judg.	3	8
Delivered from, by Othniel	Judg.	3	9, 10
Represented at Pentecost	Acts	2	9
Abraham a native of	Acts	7	2

mess *a quantity of food*

Given to Joseph's brothers	Gen.	43	34

messenger *courier*

Uriah, a fated	II Sam.	11	14–17
Isaiah	Is.	6	5–8
Figurative	Mal.	2	7
	Mat.	11	10
Of the covenant	Mal.	3	1
Of Satan	II Cor.	12	7
Sent to Joseph by his brethren	Gen.	50	16
Came to warn David of Absalom	II Sam.	15	13
Sent from Jezebel to threaten Elijah	I Ki.	19	2
To summon Micaiah to the court	I Ki.	22	13
Brought Job the bad news	Job	1	14
Not to be a fool	Prov.	25	13
Prophet as from the Lord	Hag.	1	13
Of the spies	Josh.	6	17
Rabshakeh	II Ki.	19	9

Messiah, Messias *anointed one*

Prophecies of His coming	Is.	7	14–17
	Jer.	23	5–8
	Dan.	9	25–27
Jesus acknowledges Himself as	Mark	14	61, 62
	John	4	25, 26

See Jesus

Messianic Prophecies and Their Fulfillment:

Of the seed of a woman	Gen.	3	15
	Gal.	4	4
To overcome the serpent	Gen.	3	15
	Heb.	2	14, 15
Of Abraham	Gen.	12	1–3
	Gal.	3	16
A star out of Jacob	Num.	24	17
	Luke	3	34
Of the tribe of Judah	Gen.	49	10
	Heb.	7	14
Of the seed of David	Is.	11	1, 2, 10
	Acts	13	22, 23
Born in the city of Bethlehem	Mic.	5	2
	Luke	2	4–7
Called Immanuel	Mat.	1	22, 23
	Is.	7	14
Born of a virgin	Mat.	1	18–25
	Is.	7	14
Slaying of infants in Bethlehem	Jer.	31	15
	Mat.	2	16–18
Fled into land of Egypt	Hosea	11	1
	Mat.	2	13–15
Ministry preceded by forerunner	Mal.	3	1
	Mark	1	1–8
Ministry confined largely to Galilee	Is.	9	1, 2
	Mat.	4	12–16
Great zeal for God's house	Ps.	69	9
	John	2	17
Prophet of God	Deut.	18	15–18
	Acts	3	20–23
A man of sorrows	Is.	53	3
	Mat.	8	20
Rejected by his own nation	Is.	53	3
	John	1	11

Rejected as chief cornerstone	Ps.	118	22
	I Pet.	2	4, 7
A priest after order of Melchisedec	Heb.	6	20
	Ps.	110	4
Triumphal entry into Jerusalem	Zech.	9	9
	Mat.	21	1–11
Betrayal by a professed friend	Mark	14	10
	Ps.	41	9
Forsaken by his disciples	Zech.	13	7
	Mat.	26	31
Sold for thirty pieces of silver	Zech.	11	12
	Mat.	26	15
Traitor's money used for potter's field	Zech.	11	13
	Mat.	27	6, 7
Silent before his accusers	Is.	53	7
	Mat.	26	62, 63
Smitten and spit upon by enemies	Is.	50	6
	Mark	14	65
Suffered vicariously for others	Is.	53	4–6
	Mat.	8	17
Crucified with sinners	Is.	53	12
	Mat.	27	38
Hands and feet, pierced	Ps.	22	16
	John	19	36, 37
Mocked and insulted in his death	Ps.	22	6–8
	Mat.	27	39–44
Given gall and vinegar while dying	Ps.	69	21
	John	19	29
The piercing of his side	Zech.	12	10
	John	19	34
Lots cast for his garments	Ps.	22	18
	Mark	15	24
Died without having bones broken	Ps.	34	20
	John	19	33
Buried in a rich man's tomb	Is.	53	9
	Mat.	27	57–60
Raised from the grave	Ps.	16	10
	Mat.	28	1–9

metals

Brass, bronze	Ex.	38	8
Copper	Ezra	8	27
Gold	I Ki.	9	28
Iron	Gen.	4	22
Lead	Ex.	15	10
Silver	Gen.	23	15
Steel	II Sam.	22	35
Tin	Num.	31	22

metaphor *word pictures*

God as a rock	Deut.	32	4
	I Sam.	2	2

Christ as:

A door	John	10	9
A vine	John	15	1
Christians as salt	Mat.	5	13
Jesus speaks in	Mark	4	11

See parables

meteyard

A measuring rod	Lev.	19	35

Methusael *man of God*

Father of Lamech	Gen.	4	18

Methuselah, Mathusala *man of a dart*

Son of Enoch, grandfather of Noah	Gen.	5	21
	Luke	3	37
His great age	Gen.	5	27

Meunim *see* Mehunim

Miamin *see* Mijamin

Micah, Michah *who is like unto Jehovah*

An Ephraimite	Judg.	18	18
Head of a family of Reuben	I Chr.	5	5
Son of Merib-baal	I Chr.	8	34, 35
	I Chr.	9	40, 41
A Kohathite, called Michah	I Chr.	23	20
	I Chr.	24	24, 25
Father of Abdon	II Chr.	34	20
One of the minor prophets	Jer.	26	18, 19
	Mic.	1	1, 14, 15
Denounces idolatry of people	Mic.	1	1–10
Predicts Messiah's kingdom	Mic.	4	1–8
	Mic.	5	1–3

Micaiah *who is like Jehovah*

A prophet reproved by King Ahab	I Ki.	22	8–28
	II Chr.	18	4–27

mice *see* mouse			
Micha *who is like Jehovah*			
A covenant-signer	Neh.	10	11
Father of Mattaniah	Neh.	11	17
Called Michaiah	Neh.	12	35
Michael *who is like unto God*			
An Asherite	Num.	13	13
Two Gadites	I Chr.	5	13, 14
A Gershonite Levite	I Chr.	6	40
A descendant of Issachar	I Chr.	7	3
A Benjamite	I Chr.	8	16
Captain of Manasseh	I Chr.	12	20
Father of Omri	I Chr.	27	18
Son of Jehoshaphat, slain by his brother, Jehoram	II Chr.	21	2-4
Father of Zebadiah	Ezra	8	8
The archangel, his message to Daniel	Dan.	10	13, 21
	Dan.	12	1
Disputes with Satan	Jude		9
Wars against the dragon	Rev.	12	7
Michaiah *who is like Jehovah*			
Father of Achbor	II Ki.	22	12
Mother of Abijah	II Chr.	13	1, 2
A teacher-prince	II Chr.	17	7
A priest-musician	Neh.	12	35
Another priest	Neh.	12	41
Son of Gemariah	Jer.	36	11
Michal, Merab *a brook*			
Saul's youngest daughter	I Sam.	14	49
Won by David	I Sam.	18	22-28
Rescues David from death	I Sam.	19	9-17
Separated; marries Phalti	I Sam.	25	44
Restored to David	II Sam.	3	13-16
Ridicules husband's great zeal	II Sam.	6	16-23
middle wall *dividing line*			
A partition in the temple	Eph.	2	14
Midian, Madian *strife*			
Son of Abraham by Keturah	Gen.	25	2, 4
Land of, probably east of gulf of Akabah	Ex.	2	15
Called Madian	Acts	7	29
Midianites *descendants of Midian*			
Merchantmen who buy Joseph	Gen.	37	25-28
Enemy of the children of Israel	Num.	22	3-6
Moses victorious over them	Num.	31	1-18
Defeated by Gideon	Judg.	7	1-23
Prophecies concerning	Is.	60	6
	Hab.	3	7
midnight *middle of the night*			
Lord smites firstborn in Egypt	Ex.	12	29
Samson takes the gates of Gaza	Judg.	16	3
Raises to give thanks	Ps.	119	62
Bridegroom cometh	Mat.	25	6
"Ye know not when"	Mark	13	35
Go to a friend at	Luke	11	5
Paul and Silas pray at	Acts	16	25
Paul preaches until	Acts	20	7
midwife *a woman who helps women in childbirth*			
With Rachel	Gen.	35	17
A command of the king of Egypt to	Ex.	1	15-21
might *power, force*			
Do according to thy *m*	Deut.	3	24
Love thy God with all thy *m*	Deut.	6	5
The *m* of mine hand hath gotten wealth	Deut.	8	17
Go in thy *m*	Judg.	6	14
David danced with all his *m*	II Sam.	6	14
In thine hand is power and *m*	I Chr.	29	12
	II Chr.	20	6
Speak of the *m* of thy terrible acts	Ps.	145	6
Do it with thy *m*	Eccl.	9	10
To them that have no *m*	Is.	40	29
Let not mighty man glory in his *m*	Jer.	9	23
Not by *m* nor by power	Zech.	4	6
Strengthened with *m*	Eph.	3	16
	Col.	1	11
Glory and *m* be unto God	Rev.	7	12
mighty			
He was a *m* hunter	Gen.	10	9
Become a *m* nation	Gen.	18	18
To the help of the Lord against the *m*	Judg.	5	23
How are the *m* fallen	II Sam.	1	19
God is wise in heart and *m* in strength	Job	9	4
The *m* shall be taken away	Job	34	20
Lord strong and *m*, the Lord *m* in battle	Ps.	24	8
Gird thy sword, O Most *M*	Ps.	45	3

His voice, a *m* voice	Ps.	68	33
Thou hast a *m* arm	Ps.	89	13
Laid help upon one that is *m*	Ps.	89	19
Lord mightier than *m* waves	Obad.	93	4
His seed shall be *m* on earth	Ps.	112	2
That is slow to anger better than *m*	Prov.	16	32
Their Redeemer is *m*	Prov.	23	11
The *m* One of Israel	Is.	1	24
	Is.	30	29
	Is.	49	26
	Is.	60	16
M to save	Is.	63	1
M in work	Jer.	32	19
Neither shall *m* deliver himself	Amos	2	14
M works	Mat.	11	20
	Mat.	13	54
	Mat.	14	2
	Mark	6	2
He hath put down the *m*	Luke	1	52
The *m* power of God	Luke	9	43
A prophet *m* in deed and word	Luke	24	19
M in the Scriptures	Acts	18	24
Not many *m*	I Cor.	1	26
Weapons of warfare *m* through God	II Cor.	10	4
The working of his *m* power	Eph.	1	19
Migron *precipice*			
Saul encamps near	I Sam.	14	2
Prophecy concerning	Is.	10	28, 29
Mijamin, Miamin *from the right hand; fortunate*			
A priest in the time of David	I Chr.	24	9
Son of Parosh who married a foreign wife	Ezra	10	25
A priest who seals the covenant with Nehemiah	Neh.	10	7
A chief of the priests	Neh.	12	5, 7
Milcah *counsel*			
Wife of Nahor	Gen.	11	29
Grandmother of Rebekah	Gen.	22	20-23
	Gen.	24	15, 24, 47
Daughter of Zelophehad	Num.	26	33
Given inheritance	Num.	36	1-12
	Josh.	17	3, 4
Milcom *see* Molech			
mildew *a fungus*			
Curse for disobedience	Deut.	28	22
Destroys crops	Amos	4	9
	Hab.	2	17
mile *a thousand paces*			
Used figuratively	Mat.	5	41
Miletus, Miletum *seaport in Asia Minor*			
Visited by Paul	Acts	20	15
Paul meets the elders here	Acts	20	17-38
Trophimus left sick at	II Tim.	4	20
milk			
Used for food	Gen.	18	8
From cows, goats, sheep and camels	Gen.	32	15
	Deut.	32	14
	I Sam.	6	7-10
	Prov.	27	27
Canaan, a land of milk and honey	Ex.	3	8
	Josh.	5	6
In bottles	Judg.	4	19
Churned into butter	Prov.	30	33
Used figuratively	Heb.	5	12, 13
	I Pet.	2	2
mill *a grinder*			
Used by women	Ex.	11	5
	Mat.	24	41
Manna ground in	Num.	11	8
Made of two stones	Deut.	25	6
millennium			
Thousand year reign of Christ after the Great Tribulation	Rev.	20	1-10
Time of peace	Is.	11	6
Longevity	Is.	65	17-25
Worship	Zech.	14	16-21
millet *a grain*			
Used to make bread	Ezek.	4	9
Millo *fullness; terrace*			
A clan near Shechem	Judg.	9	6, 20
A citadel near Jerusalem	II Sam.	5	9
Repaired by Solomon	I Ki.	9	15
Joash slain here	II Ki.	12	20
Hezekiah slain here	II Chr.	32	5

millstone

Abimelech killed by	Judg.	9	53
Figurative of a hard heart	Job	41	24
Probably used in executions by drowning	Mat.	18	6

mincing *affectedly nice*

Sign of haughtiness	Is.	3	16

mind

Serve God with willing *m*	I Chr.	28	9
	Neh.	4	6
	Acts	20	19
	II Cor.	8	12
Love the Lord with all your *m*	Mat.	22	37
Devoted to God	Mark	12	30
	Rom.	7	25
Carnal mind is hostile to God	Rom.	8	7
Christians should have united *m*	I Cor.	1	10, 11
	II Cor.	13	11
	I Pet.	3	8
Given by God	I Tim.	1	7

Is sometimes:

Grieving	Gen.	26	35
Sorrowful	Deut.	28	65
Wicked	Prov.	21	27
Ready	Acts	17	11
Reprobate	Rom.	1	28
Of Christ	Phil.	2	3, 5
Despiteful	Ezek.	36	5
Hardened	Dan.	5	20
Changed	Hab.	1	11
Doubtful	Luke	12	29
Blinded	II Cor.	3	14
Corrupted	II Cor.	11	3
Defiled	Tit.	1	15
Faint	Heb.	12	3

mine

All the earth is *m*	Ex.	19	5
	Ps.	50	12
Silver is *m*, and gold is *m*	Hag.	2	8
They shall be *m*, saith the Lord	Mal.	3	17
Is not *m* to give	Mat.	20	23
	Mark	10	40
All *m* are thine, and thine are *m*	John	17	10

mingle, mix

Fire and hail	Ex.	9	24
	Rev.	8	7
Seeds not to be	Lev.	19	19
Of intermarriage	Ezra	9	2
Israel with the nations	Ps.	106	35
Of wine	Prov.	9	2
	Mark	15	23
Vinegar and gall	Mat.	27	34

Miniamin *from the right hand; fortunate*

A Levite who helps distribute offerings	II Chr.	31	15
A priest who returns from Babylon	Neh.	12	17

mining *taking minerals from the earth*

Of iron and brass	Deut.	8	9
Of gold and silver	Job	28	1
Of oil	Job	29	6

ministers

Teachers, appointed by God	Ex.	28	1
	Heb.	5	4
Marriage of	Lev.	21	7–15
	I Cor.	9	5
	I Tim.	3	2, 12
When unfaithful, shall be punished	Ezek.	33	6–8
	Mat.	24	48–51
Beautiful description of	Mal.	2	5–7
Necessity for	Mat.	9	37, 38
When faithful, are rewarded	Mat.	24	46, 47
	I Cor.	3	14
Commissioned by Christ	Mat.	28	19
Paul's ideals for	II Cor.	6	1–10
	I Tim.	4	1–10

Called:

Preachers	Rom.	10	14
Ambassadors for Christ	II Cor.	5	20
Defenders of the faith	Phil.	1	7
Men of God	Deut.	33	1
Servants of God	Tit.	1	1
Pastors	Jer.	3	15

Qualifications of:

Pure and holy	Ex.	28	36
	Is.	52	11
Sober, just and temperate	Lev.	10	9
	Tit.	1	8
Humble and patient	Acts	20	19
	II Cor.	6	4

Devoted	Acts	20	24
Prayerful	Eph.	3	14
Examples to their people	Phil.	3	17
	I Tim.	4	12
Studious and meditative	I Tim.	4	13, 15
Impartial	I Tim.	5	21

Are obligated to:

Pray for their people	Joel	2	17
Preach the gospel to all people	Mark	16	15
Comfort	II Cor.	1	4–6
Build up the church	II Cor.	12	19
Teach	II Tim.	2	2

Should preach:

With boldness	Ezek.	2	6
	Mat.	10	27
Everywhere	Mark	16	20
With zeal and constancy	Acts	6	4
	I Thes.	2	8, 9
Christ crucified	Acts	8	5, 35
Repentance and faith	Acts	20	21

Their people should:

Pray for them	Rom.	15	30
Follow their instructions	Mat.	23	3
Help them	Rom.	16	9
Regard them as God's messengers	I Cor.	4	1
Support them	I Cor.	9	7–11
Personal attendant	Gen.	39	4
Joshua	Josh.	1	1

minority

Joshua and Caleb	Num.	14	1–10
Christians	Mat.	7	13, 14

minstrel *musical entertainer*

Plays for Elisha	II Ki.	3	14, 15
Plays at funerals	Mat.	9	23

mint *a garden herb*

Used by Pharisees to pay tithes	Mat.	23	23
	Luke	11	42

Miphkad *assignment*

A gate at Jerusalem	Neh.	3	31

miracles *impossible happenings*

Convincing effect of	Ex.	4	28–31
	Judg.	6	17–40
	Dan.	4	2, 3
	John	4	48–53
Of the Holy Ghost	Mat.	12	28
	I Cor.	12	9
Demanded by unbelievers	Mat.	12	38, 39
Faith required to perform	Mat.	17	20
In the name of Christ	Mark	16	17
Performed through the power of God	John	3	2
	Acts	15	12

Purpose of:

To strengthen faith	Ex.	4	3–5
	John	11	15
For deliverance from evil	Ex.	6	5–7
	Mat.	9	6
As proof of God's power	I Ki.	18	37–39
	John	10	38
Proof of the Messiahship of Jesus	Mat.	11	4–6
	John	2	11
	John	20	30, 31
To confirm the word	Mark	16	15–18
	Heb.	2	3, 4
To lead believers to Christ	John	7	31
	Acts	8	6

Of the Old Testament:

Creation	Gen.	1	1–27
Flood	Gen.	7	
Confusion of languages	Gen.	11	1–10
Destruction of Sodom and Gomorrah	Gen.	19	24
Lot's wife turned to a pillar of salt	Gen.	19	26
Birth of Isaac	Gen.	21	1–3
Burning bush not consumed	Ex.	3	2
Aaron's rod changed into a serpent	Ex.	7	10–12
The plagues of Egypt	Ex.	7–12	
The Red sea divided to give Israelites passage	Ex.	14	21–31
Pillar of cloud and fire	Ex.	13	21
The waters of Marah sweetened	Ex.	15	23–25
The manna sent	Ex.	16	14–35
Water from the smitten rock	Ex.	17	5–7
	Num.	20	7–11
Nadab and Abihu consumed for offering strange fire	Lev.	10	1, 2
Fire of judgment	Num.	11	1–3

miracles—*continued*

Leprosy on Miriam	Num.	12	10–15
The earth swallows Korah	Num.	16	32
Aaron's rod buds	Num.	17	1–13
The brazen serpent	Num.	21	8, 9
Balaam's ass speaks	Num.	22	21–30
River Jordan divided	Josh.	3	14–17
	II Ki.	2	7, 8, 14
The walls of Jericho fall down	Josh.	6	6–20
Sun and moon stand still	Josh.	10	11–14
Gideon's fleece	Judg.	6	37–40
Water flows from the hollow place	Judg.	15	19
Emerods on the Philistines	I Sam.	5	1–12
Thunder and rain in harvest	I Sam.	12	17, 18
The sound in the mulberry trees	II Sam.	5	23–25
Uzzah struck dead for touching the ark	II Sam.	6	7
Jeroboam's hand withered	I Ki.	13	4–6
Altar rent	I Ki.	13	5
The widow's son raised from death	I Ki.	17	17–24
Fire from heaven	I Ki.	18	38
Elijah's wondrous feeding	I Ki.	19	4–8
Ahaziah's men consumed by fire	II Ki.	1	10–12
Jordan divided	II Ki.	2	8, 14
Elijah translated to heaven	II Ki.	2	11
Waters of Jericho healed with salt	II Ki.	2	21, 22
Bears destroy mocking young men	II Ki.	2	24
The widow's oil multiplied	II Ki.	4	2–7
The son of the Shunammite	II Ki.	4	14–37
Deadly pottage cured	II Ki.	4	38–41
Hundred men fed with twenty loaves	II Ki.	4	42–44
Naaman's leprosy	II Ki.	5	10–27
Iron axe head made to swim	II Ki.	6	5–7
Syrian army smitten with blindness	II Ki.	6	18–20
Elisha's bones revive the dead	II Ki.	13	21
Sennacherib's army destroyed	II Ki.	19	35
The shadow of the sundial goes back ten degrees	II Ki.	20	9–11
Uzziah struck with leprosy	II Chr.	26	16–21
Shadrach, Meshach and Abednego	Dan.	3	19–27
Daniel in the lion's den	Dan.	6	16–23
Deliverance of Jonah	Jonah	2	1–10

Of the New Testament:

The incarnation of Jesus	Mat.	1	18–25
The star of Bethlehem	Mat.	2	1–9
The deliverance of Jesus	Mat.	2	13–23
Conception by Elisabeth	Luke	1	18, 24, 25

Of Jesus, in chronological order:

Water made wine	John	2	1–11
Heals the nobleman's son	John	4	46–54
Draught of fishes	Luke	5	1–11
Heals the demoniac	Mark	1	23–26
Heals Peter's mother-in-law	Mat.	8	14–17
Cleanses the leper	Mat.	8	1–4
Heals the paralytic	Mat.	9	1–8
Healing the impotent man	John	5	1–16
Restoring the withered hand	Mat.	12	9–13
Restores the centurion's servant	Mat.	8	5–13
Raises the widow's son to life	Luke	7	11–16
Heals a demoniac	Mat.	12	22–37
Stills the tempest	Mat.	8	23–27
Casts devils out of two men	Mat.	8	28–34
The daughter of Jairus resurrected	Mark	5	22–24
Cures the woman with the issue of blood	Mat.	9	20–22
Restores two blind men to sight	Mat.	9	27–31
Heals a demoniac	Mat.	9	32, 33
Feeds five thousand people	Mat.	14	15–21
Walks on the sea	Mat.	14	22–33
Feeds four thousand people	Mat.	15	32–39
Restores one deaf and dumb	Mark	7	31–37
Restores a blind man	Mark	8	22–26
Restores lunatic child	Mat.	17	14–21
Tribute money from a fish's mouth	Mat.	17	24–27
Heals ten lepers	Luke	17	11–19
Cures a man born blind	John	9	1–7
Raises Lazarus from the dead	John	11	1–46
Heals the woman with the spirit of infirmity	Luke	13	10–17
Cures a man with dropsy	Luke	14	1–6
Restores two blind men near Jericho	Mat.	20	29–34
Curses the fig tree	Mat.	21	17–22
Heals he ear of Malchus	Luke	22	49–51
Second draught of fishes	John	21	6

Of the disciples:

By other disciples	Mark	9	39
	John	14	12
By the seventy	Luke	10	17–20

Peter and John cure a lame son	Acts	3	2–11
By the apostles	Acts	3	6–16
	Acts	4	10, 30
	Acts	9	34, 35
	Acts	16	18
Death of Ananias and Sapphira	Acts	5	5–10
Peter cures the sick	Acts	5	15, 16
Peter and others delivered from prison	Acts	5	19–23
Philip carried away by the Spirit	Acts	8	39
Aeneas	Acts	9	34
Dorcas raised	Acts	9	40

Paul:

Cured of blindness	Acts	9	3–6
	Acts	9	17, 18
Strikes Elymas blind	Acts	13	11
Heals a cripple	Acts	14	10
Cures sick	Acts	16	18
Raises Eutychus to life	Acts	20	9–12
Shakes a viper off his hand	Acts	28	5
False miracles	Ex.	8	18, 19
	Deut.	13	1–3
	II Thes.	2	3, 9

Miriam *rebellion; thick, strong*

Sister of Moses and Aaron	Ex.	2	2–4
	Num.	26	59
Watches over baby Moses	Ex.	2	4–9
Becomes prophetess and leader of women during the exodus	Ex.	15	20, 21
	Mic.	6	4
Rebels against Moses and stricken with leprosy	Num.	12	1–10
Healed by Moses' prayer	Num.	12	11–16
Dies; is buried in Kadesh	Num.	20	1
A descendant of Caleb	I Chr.	4	15–17

mirror *reflecting surface*

Used for grooming	James	1	23, 24
Called a looking glass	Job	37	18
Melted for the laver	Ex.	8	8

mirth *gladness or gaiety*

An expression of thanks	Neh.	8	12
	Jer.	30	19
End is sometimes grief	Prov.	14	13
Vanity of	Eccl.	2	1, 2
Good for the soul	Eccl.	8	15
In work well done	Eccl.	10	7

mischief *action that annoys*

Of calamity	Gen.	42	4
Work of a fool	Prov.	10	23
Of children of the devil	Acts	13	10
Practiced by Saul	I Sam.	23	9
Conceived by hypocrites	Job	15	34
Punishment of	Ps.	7	14–16
	Prov.	26	27
Devised by the wicked	Ps.	36	1, 4
Wicked shall fall into	Prov.	25	16
	Prov.	28	14

miser *a covetous person*

Described	Eccl.	4	8, 9
Is friendless	Eccl.	4	10

misery *distress*

Consequence of wickedness	Deut.	28	66, 67
	Job	15	20
Forgotten through drink	Prov.	31	7
Caused by great wealth	James	5	1
Great upon man	Eccl.	8	6

misfortune

Of Job	Job	1	13–22
Of Joseph	Gen.	37	23–25
Of Israel in Egypt	Ex.	2	23–25
Result of sin	Is.	59	1, 2
Works for good	Rom.	8	28

Mishael *who is of God*

A son of Uzziel	Ex.	6	22
Helps carry the bodies out of camp	Lev.	10	4
An associate of Ezra	Neh.	8	4
Son of Judah, companion of Daniel	Dan.	1	6
Given name of Meshach	Dan.	1	7
Assists in interpreting dream	Dan.	2	17–23

Mishma *report*

Son of Ishmael	Gen.	25	13, 14
Descendant of Simeon	I Chr.	4	25

missionary *one sent to propagate religion*

Noah	Gen.	9	9, 10
	II Pet.	2	5
Jonah	Jonah	3	2, 3

Early Christians	Acts	8	4
Philip	Acts	8	5
Paul and Barnabas	Acts	13	
Peter	Acts	15	7–11
Titus	Tit.	1	5

missions *organized efforts*

World wide	Is.	2	2–5
	Mal.	1	11
Prior to the end times	Mark	13	10
Commanded by Christ	Mat.	24	14
	Mark	16	15–18
	Luke	24	47

mist *fog*

Waters the ground	Gen.	2	6
Causes blindness	Acts	13	8–11

mistake *see error*

mistress *a woman of authority*

Of Elijah's house	I Ki.	17	17
Sarah	Gen.	16	8
Of Nineveh	Nah.	3	4

mite *smallest Jewish coin*

The widow's	Mark	12	42
	Luke	21	2

mitre, miter *high priest's headdress*

Inscribed "Holiness to the Lord"	Ex.	28	36–39
Worn by Aaron	Lev.	16	4
On the day of atonement	Lev.	16	4
Priest in Zechariah's vision	Zech.	3	5

Mitylene *mutilated*

Capital of Lesbos, visited by Paul	Acts	20	14, 15

mixed

That go to seek *m* wine	Prov.	23	30
Thy wine *m* with water	Is.	1	22
Not being *m* with faith	Heb.	4	2

Mizpah, Mizpeh *a watch-tower*

Where Jacob and Laban make covenant	Gen.	31	44–53
"The Lord watch between me and thee"	Gen.	31	49
A valley near Lebanon	Josh.	11	3
A town in Judah	Josh.	15	38
A town allotted to Benjamin	Josh.	18	26
Samuel calls people to prayer	I Sam.	7	5–7
Saul crowned king at	I Sam.	10	17–25
Fortified by Asa	I Ki.	15	22
Residence of governor	II Ki.	25	23
Inhabited after exile	Neh.	3	7, 15
Encampment in Gilead	Judg.	10	17
A place in Moab	I Sam.	22	3

Mizraim *limits*

Son of Ham	Gen.	10	6
Semitic name for upper Egypt	Gen.	50	11

Mnason *remembering*

Christian of Cyprus who entertains Paul	Acts	21	16

Moab *from father*

A son of Lot	Gen.	19	37
Land occupied by Moabites	Num.	21	13
Military forces numbered in	Num.	26	3, 63
Israelites renew covenant	Deut.	29	1
Moses dies and is buried	Deut.	34	5, 6

Moabites *descendants of Moab*

Descendants of Lot	Gen.	19	37
East of the Dead Sea between Wadi Arnon and Zered	Num.	21	13
	Judg.	11	18
Conquered by Amorites	Num.	21	25–27
Called the people of Chemosh	Num.	21	29
Balak, king of	Num.	22	4
A snare to the Israelites	Num.	25	1–5
Moses commanded not to distress	Deut.	2	9
Ruth, a Moabitess	Ruth	2	2
David takes refuge among	I Sam.	22	3, 4
Conquered by David	II Sam.	8	2
Israelites married daughters	Ezra	9	1–3
	Neh.	13	23
Prophecies concerning	Jer.	48	
Trouble with Jephtah	Judg.	11	17, 18
Land not given to Israel	Deut.	2	9, 29
War with	II Ki.	3	5–27
Denounced by Amos	Amos	2	1–3
Burden of Moab	Is.	15	

mob *an unruly crowd*

Stephen tried by	Acts	7	54–60
At Thessalonica	Acts	17	5
At Ephesus	Acts	19	29–40
At Jerusalem	Acts	21	27, 30

mocking *scoffing*

Ishmael mocks Sarah	Gen.	21	9
Elijah mocks priests of Baal	I Ki.	18	27
Of Elisha, by children	II Ki.	2	23–25
Of Hezekiah's postmen	II Chr.	30	6–10
Of God's messengers	II Chr.	36	16, 17
By fools	Prov.	14	9
Condemned	Prov.	17	5
	Prov.	30	17
	Jude		18
Of Christ, by his enemies	Mat.	27	29
	Luke	23	11
Of Paul at Athens	Acts	17	32
Zedekiah mocks Micaiah	I Ki.	22	24
Job's tormentors	Job	15	12
Ammonites mock at God	Ezek.	25	3
Tyre mocks Jerusalem	Ezek.	26	2
God is not	Gal.	6	7

moderation

Should be known to all men	Phil.	4	5

modest *unpretentious*

Woman should wear modest dress	I Tim.	2	9

modesty *see humility*

molding

Of images	Ex.	32	4, 8
Of pillars	I Ki.	7	15
Of laver	I Ki.	7	23
Of mirrors	Job	37	18

mole *a burrowing animal*

An unclean animal	Lev.	11	29, 30

Molech, Moloch, Milcom *king*

Children sacrificed to	Lev.	18	21
	Lev.	20	1–5
	Jer.	32	35
Worshipped by Solomon and his wives	I Ki.	11	1–8
Idol of the Ammonites	I Ki.	11	5–7
	Acts	7	43
Found in Israel	Amos	5	6

molten *melted*

After he had made *m* calf	Ex.	32	4, 8
	Deut.	9	12, 16
	Neh.	9	18
Shalt make thee no *m* gods	Ex.	34	17
	Lev.	19	4
Chapters of *m* brass	I Ki.	7	16
He made a *m* sea	I Ki.	7	23
Undersetters *m*	I Ki.	7	30
Their spokes were all *m*	I Ki.	7	33
And brass is *m* out of	Job	28	2
Sky is strong, and as a *m*	Job	37	18
Filthiness of it may be *m*	Ezek.	24	11
The mountains shall be *m*	Mic.	1	4

molten image *see idol*

molten sea, brasen sea, brazen sea

Basin or tank in the court of Solomon's temple	I Ki.	7	23–26
Destroyed by Nebuchadnezzar	II Ki.	25	13, 16
	Jer.	27	19–22

moment *short space of time*

Into midst of thee in a *m*	Ex.	33	5
Consume them in a *m*	Num.	16	21
Try him every *m*	Job	7	18
In a *m* shall they die	Job	34	20
His anger endureth but a *m*	Ps.	30	5
Hide thyself as it were for a *m*	Is.	26	20
I will water it every *m*	Is.	27	3
I hid my face from thee for a *m*	Is.	54	8
Kingdoms of world in a *m*	Luke	4	5
All be changed in a *m*	I Cor.	15	52
Affliction, which is but for a *m*	II Cor.	4	17

monarchy

Described by Samuel	I Sam.	8	11–18

money *a medium of exchange*

Gold and silver used as	Gen.	13	2
	Num.	22	18
Jews forbidden to take usury for	Lev.	25	37
Power and usefulness of	Eccl.	7	12
Value determined by weight	Jer.	32	10
Brass used as	Mat.	10	9
Of the Romans, stamped with the image of Caesar	Mat.	22	20, 21
Often brings misery	Acts	1	16–19
Cannot buy spiritual power	Acts	8	18–20
"Love of, the root of all evil"	I Tim.	6	10

money—continued			
Gold and silver used as	Gen.	13	
Is given:			
For land	Gen.	23	9
For slaves	Gen.	37	28
For merchandise	Gen.	43	12
As alms	I Sam.	2	36
As offerings	II Ki.	12	7–9
For tribute	II Ki.	23	33
As wages	Ezra	3	7

moneychangers

Driven out of the temple	Mat.	21	12
	Mark	11	15
	John	2	15

monster

A sea animal	Lam.	4	3

months *see Jewish calendar*

moon *heavenly body*

Created by God	Gen.	1	14
	Ps.	8	3
Light of the night	Gen.	1	16
Worship of, forbidden	Deut.	4	19
	Deut.	17	3–6
	Jer.	8	1–3
New moon, a time of festivity	I Sam.	20	5, 6
Appointed for signs and seasons	Ps.	104	19
Lunacy attributed to	Ps.	121	6
Symbolic of the glory of Christ	Is.	60	20
In last days, shall give no light and turn to blood	Mat.	24	29
	Rev.	6	12
Has a glory of its own	I Cor.	15	41

Mordecai *bitterness of my oppressed*

A Jewish captive	Esth.	2	5, 6
Foster father of Esther	Esth.	2	7
Informs Ahasuerus	Esth.	2	21–23
Does not bow before Haman	Esth.	3	1–6
Is rewarded	Esth.	6	1–11
Promoted in Haman's place	Esth.	8	1, 2, 15
Intercedes for Jews	Esth.	8	9
Establishes festival of Purim	Esth.	8	17
A returned exile	Ezra	2	2

Moresheth-gath *possession of Gath*

Birthplace of Micah	Mic.	1	14

Moriah *my teacher is Jehovah*

Where Abraham offers his son	Gen.	22	1–13
Site of Solomon's temple	II Chr.	3	1

morning

Evening and the *m*	Gen.	1	5, 8, 13
M stars sang together	Job	38	7
Joy cometh in the *m*	Ps.	30	5
In the *m* it flourisheth	Ps.	90	6
They that watch for the *m*	Ps.	130	6
In the *m* sow thy seed	Eccl.	11	6
Goodness is a *m* cloud	Hosea	6	4
Very early in the *m*	Mark	16	2
The bright and *m* star	Rev.	22	16

morning star *pertains to the dawn*

A title of Christ	Rev.	22	16

morrow

Boast not thyself of to-*m*	Prov.	27	1
To-*m* we die	Is.	22	13
	I Cor.	15	32
To-*m* shall be as this day	Is.	56	12
Take no thought for the *m*	Mat.	6	34
Ye know not what shall be on the *m*	James	4	14

morsel *small bit*

Given by Abraham	Gen.	18	5
Offered by Levite's father-in-law	Judg.	19	5
Ruth eats from Boaz	Ruth	2	14
Job in regard to the poor	Job	31	17
For which Esau sold his birthright	Heb.	12	16
Better than a house of sacrifices with strife	Prov.	17	1

mortality *see man*

mortar, morter

Used in the building of the tower of Babel	Gen.	11	3, 9
A cement	Ex.	1	14
Used in plastering houses	Lev.	14	42, 45
Untempered	Ezek.	13	10–15
	Ezek.	22	28
To be trodden	Nah.	3	14
An instrument for grinding grain	Num.	11	8
	Prov.	27	22

mortgage *give as security for a loan*

Property mortgaged for food	Neh.	5	1–3

mortify

If ye *m* deeds of body	Rom.	8	13
M your members which	Col.	3	5

Mosera, Moseroth *correction, bond*

An encampment of the Israelites near mount Hor	Num.	33	30, 31
Aaron dies here	Deut.	10	6

Moses *drawn out*

A Levite and son of Amram	Ex.	2	1–4
Hidden in the ark	Ex.	2	3
Discovered and adopted by Pharaoh's daughter	Ex.	2	5–10
Takes the life of an Egyptian, flees to Midian	Ex.	2	11–22
Joins Jethro, marries his daughter	Ex.	2	19, 20
Has two sons	Ex.	2	22
	Ex.	18	3
Is herdman for Jethro	Ex.	3	1
Has the vision of the burning bush	Ex.	3	2–6
Idea of one God manifested to him	Ex.	3	4–15
God reveals to him his purpose	Ex.	3	7–10
Commissioned as leader of the Israelites	Ex.	3	10
Given divine aid and power	Ex.	3	12–14
	Ex.	4	1–7
Meets Aaron in the wilderness	Ex.	4	27, 28
With Aaron assembles the leaders of Israel	Ex.	4	29–31
Goes before Pharaoh, demands the liberties of his people	Ex.	5	1
Rejected by Pharaoh, hardships endured	Ex.	5	1–23
People murmur against Moses and Aaron	Ex.	5	20, 21
	Ex.	17	2, 3
Receives comfort and assurance from the Lord	Ex.	6	1–8
Unbelief of the people	Ex.	6	9
Renews his appeal to Pharaoh	Ex.	6	11
Under God's direction, brings plagues upon Israel	Ex.	7	12
Secures deliverance of his people, leads them from Egypt	Ex.	13	
Crosses the Red sea	Ex.	14	
Composes a song for the Israelites	Ex.	15	
Joined by his family in the wilderness	Ex.	18	1–12
Institutes a system of government	Ex.	18	13–26
Arrives at Sinai	Ex.	19	1, 2
Talks with God on mount Sinai	Ex.	19	3–6
	Acts	7	38
Receives the law of God	Ex.	20	1–26
Instructed to build tabernacle	Ex.	31	
Breaks law tables	Ex.	32	15–19
Destroys golden calf	Ex.	32	30–29
Second forty days on mount Sinai	Ex.	34	1–28
Given tables of the law	Ex.	34	1–10
Face radiant with glory of God	Ex.	34	29–33
	II Cor.	3	13–17
Gives divers laws	Num.	2	9
Discouraged by Israel's murmurings	Num.	11	10–15
Marries an Ethiopian	Num.	12	1
Jealousy of Aaron and Miriam	Num.	12	
Spies sent to Canaan	Num.	13	1–33
Not permitted to enter Canaan	Num.	27	12–14
Appoints Joshua as his successor	Num.	27	22, 23
Wanderings	Num.	33	1–49
Delivers farewell address	Deut.	32	1–52
Dies, buried by God	Deut.	34	5, 6
Greatest of Israel's prophets	Deut.	34	10
A prayer of Moses	Ps.	90	
Present with Jesus on mount of transfiguration	Mat.	17	3, 4
Learned in all the wisdom of Egypt	Acts	7	22
His loyalty to his people	Heb.	11	24–26

moth

An insect	Job	4	19
	Job	27	18
	Ps.	39	11
Destructive to garments	Job	13	28
	Is.	50	9
	Is.	51	8

moth-eaten *gnawed away, decayed*

Garments	Job	13	28
	James	5	2

mother *female parent*

Of all living, Eve	Gen.	3	20
Should be honoured	Ex.	20	12
	Mat.	15	4
	Eph.	6	2

Death penalty for killing of	Ex.	21	15
Indignities toward, forbidden	Lev.	18	7
	Lev.	20	11
Should be feared	Lev.	19	3
Son will be put to death for cursing	Lev.	20	9
	Prov.	20	20
Hannah, a devoted	I Sam.	1	22–28
Maacah, an idolatrous	I Ki.	15	13
Farewell kiss of a	I Ki.	19	20
A brutal	II Ki.	6	28, 30
Athaliah, a cruel	II Ki.	11	1
Law of thy	Prov.	1	8
	Prov.	6	20
Respected in age	Prov.	23	22
A symbol of God's love	Is.	49	15
	Is.	66	13
An ambitious	Mat.	20	20, 21
Herodias, a revengeful	Mark	6	21–25
See duties			

mother-in-law *mother of one's husband or wife*

Rebekah, an unhappy	Gen.	26	34, 35
Not to be defiled	Lev.	20	14
	Deut.	27	23
Naomi, beloved by Ruth	Ruth	1	14–17
Peter's, healed by Jesus	Mat.	8	14, 15
	Mark	1	30, 31

mouldy

Bread	Josh.	9	5, 12

Mountains in the Bible

Abarim	Num.	27	12
Ararat	Gen.	8	4
Bashan	Ps.	68	15
Bethel	I Sam.	13	2
Carmel	I Ki.	18	19
Ebal	Deut.	11	29
Ephraim	Josh.	17	15
Gerizim	Deut.	11	29
Gilboa	I Sam.	31	1
Gilead	Gen.	31	21
Hermon	Deut.	3	8
Hor	Num.	20	22
Horeb	Ex.	3	1
Lebanon	Deut.	3	25
Mizar	Ps.	42	6
Moriah	Gen.	22	2
Nebo	Deut.	32	49
Olives or Olivet	Mat.	21	1
Pisgah	Num.	21	20
Seir	Gen.	14	6
Sinai	Num.	3	1
Tabor	Judg.	4	6
Zion, or Sion	Is.	4	5
Place of escape	Gen.	19	17
Mountain of God	Ex.	3	1, 12
Mountain of the Lord's house	Is.	2	2
Divided	Zech.	14	4
Transfiguration	Mat.	17	1
Temptation of Christ	Mat.	4	4

Mourning *expression of grief*

Attire of	Gen.	38	14
	II Sam.	14	2
Rending the garments in	Gen.	37	29, 34
	Num.	14	6
	Mat.	26	65
Lamentations in	Gen.	50	10
	Ex.	12	30
	Jer.	22	18
	Mat.	2	17, 18
Laying aside all ornaments	Ex.	33	4, 6
Causes ceremonial defilement	Lev.	21	1
	Num.	19	11, 16
	Num.	31	19
Head uncovered	Lev.	10	6
	Lev.	21	10
For Nadab and Abihu, forbidden	Lev.	10	6
Covering the upper lip	Lev.	13	45
Cutting the flesh	Lev.	19	28
	Lev.	21	5
	Deut.	14	1
	Jer.	16	6, 7
Forbidden to priests, except for close relatives	Lev.	21	1–11
Prevents offerings from being accepted	Deut.	26	14
	Hosea	9	4
Dust on the head	Josh.	7	6

Fasting	I Sam.	31	13
Personal appearance neglected	II Sam.	14	2
Covering the head and face	II Sam.	19	4
	Jer.	14	3, 4
Walking barefoot	II Sam.	15	30
	Is.	20	2
Hired mourners	II Chr.	35	25
	Eccl.	12	5
	Mat.	9	23, 24
Cutting off the hair or beard	Ezra	9	3
Sitting on the ground	Is.	3	26
Dressing in black	Jer.	14	2
Ashes on the head	Ezek.	27	30
Sexes separated in	Zech.	12	12, 14

Examples of:

Abraham for Sarah	Gen.	23	2
The Egyptians for Jacob	Gen.	50	1–3
Israelites for Aaron	Num.	20	29
David over Saul and his sons	II Sam.	1	17–27
David for Abner	II Sam.	3	33, 34
David for Absalom	II Sam.	18	33
Jeremiah for Josiah	II Chr.	35	25

mouse, mice *a small animal*

Forbidden to use as food	Lev.	11	29
	Is.	66	17
Images of	I Sam.	6	4, 5, 11, 18

mouth

Of God	Deut.	8	3
	Mat.	4	4
Of babes	Ps.	8	2
Of fools	Prov.	14	3
	Prov.	15	2
	Prov.	18	7
	Prov.	26	7
Of the righteous, etc.	Ps.	37	30
	Prov.	10	31
	Eccl.	10	12
Of the wicked	Ps.	32	9
	Ps.	107	42
	Ps.	109	2
	Ps.	144	8
	Prov.	4	24
	Prov.	5	3
	Prov.	6	12
	Prov.	19	28
	Rom.	3	14
	Rev.	13	5
m that speaketh lies	Ps.	63	11
Satisfieth thy *m* with good things	Ps.	103	5
A fool's *m* is his destruction	Prov.	18	7
Labour of man is for his *m*	Eccl.	6	7
People draw near me with *m*	Is.	29	13
	Mat.	15	8
The law of truth was in his *m*	Mal.	2	6
Of abundance of heart the *m* speaketh	Mat.	12	34
	Luke	6	45
Out of the *m* of babes	Mat.	21	16
I will give you a *m* and wisdom	Luke	21	15
With the *m* confession is made unto salvation	Rom.	10	10
Not muzzle *m* of ox	I Cor.	9	9
Out of the same *m* proceedeth	James	3	10

move

M them to jealousy	Deut.	32	21
I shall not be *m*	Ps.	10	6
	Ps.	16	8
	Ps.	30	6
	Ps.	62	2
The city was *m*	Mat.	21	10
	Acts	21	30
They will not *m* them	Mat.	23	4
In him we live and *m*	Acts	17	28
None of these things *m* me	Acts	20	24
(*See* John 5:3; Heb. 12:28.)			

Moza *going forth*

A son of Caleb	I Chr.	2	46
Son of Zimri, a Benjamite	I Chr.	8	36, 37
	I Chr.	9	42, 43

muffler *a long veil*

Female dress	Is.	3	16, 19

mulberry tree *weeping*

A sign for battle	II Sam.	5	23, 24
	I Chr.	14	14, 15

mule *a cross between a horse and ass*

Royal riders	II Sam.	13	29
	II Sam.	18	9
	I Ki.	1	33, 38

mule—*continued*

Tribute paid in	I Ki.	10	25
As pack animals	II Ki.	5	17
	I Chr.	12	40
For carrying mail	Esth.	8	10, 14
Carry those who return from captivity	Ezra	2	66
	Neh.	7	68
By saints in Isaiah's vision	Is.	66	20
Used as trade	Ezek.	27	14
In war	Zech.	14	14, 15

multiply *increase*

Be fruitful and **m**	Gen.	1	22
	Gen.	8	17
	Gen.	35	11
Their sorrows shall be **m**	Ps.	16	4
Thou hast **m** the nation	Is.	9	3
Peace be **m**	Dan.	4	1
	Dan.	6	25
	I Pet.	1	2
	II Pet.	1	2
	Jude		2
Word of God grew and **m**	Acts	12	24
M your seed sown	II Cor.	9	10

multitude *great number*
Fed miraculously by:

Moses	Num.	11	30–32
Elisha	II Ki.	4	38–44
Jesus	Mat.	14	13–21
Follows Jesus	Mat.	14	13–15
	Luke	8	37
God Almighty make thee a **m**	Gen.	28	3
Not follow a **m** to do evil	Ex.	23	2
As the stars for **m**	Deut.	1	10
	Deut.	10	22
	Deut.	28	62
	Heb.	11	12
As sand on seashore for **m**	Josh.	11	4
	Judg.	7	12
	I Sam.	13	5
	II Sam.	17	11
	I Ki.	4	20
M of years should teach wisdom	Job	32	7
M of thy mercy	Ps.	5	7
	Ps.	51	1
	Ps.	69	13
No king saved by the **m** of an host	Ps.	33	16
In the **m** of my thoughts	Ps.	94	19
In the **m** of words there wanteth not sin	Prov.	10	19
In the **m** of counsellors	Prov.	11	14
	Prov.	15	22
	Prov.	24	6
Through the **m** of business	Eccl.	5	3
Hide a **m** of sins	James	5	20
Charity shall cover the **m** of sins	I Pet.	4	8

munitions *military supplies*

Fortifications, used in war	Nah.	2	1

Muppim, Shuppim *wavings*

The head of the Benjamites	Gen.	46	21
Also called Shupham and Shephuphan	Num.	26	39
	I Chr.	8	5
Called Shuppim	I Chr.	7	12, 15
	I Chr.	26	16

murder *premeditated killing of one human by another*

Forbidden	Gen.	9	6
	Lev.	24	17
	Mat.	5	21
Its penalty	Gen.	4	12
	Num.	35	30
	Gal.	5	21
Comes from the heart	Mat.	15	19

Examples of:

Cain	Gen.	4	13, 14
Eglon	Judg.	3	21
Sisera	Judg.	4	17–21
Sons of Jerubbaal	Judg.	9	1–5
Abner	II Sam.	3	27
Ish-bosheth	II Sam.	4	5–8
Amnon	II Sam.	13	28, 29
Absalom	II Sam.	18	14
Amasa	II Sam.	20	10
Elah	I Ki.	16	10
Ben-hadad	II Ki.	8	7, 15
Jehoram	II Ki.	9	24
Ahaziah	II Ki.	9	27
Jezebel	II Ki.	9	30–37

Joash	II Ki.	12	20, 21
Zachariah	II Ki.	15	10
	II Chr.	24	21, 22
Shallum	II Ki.	15	14
Pekahiah	II Ki.	15	25
Pekah	II Ki.	15	30
Amon	II Ki.	21	23
Gedaliah	II Ki.	25	25

murmuring *a mumbled or muttered complaint*
Of Israel:

From fear	Ex.	14	10–12
From thirst	Ex.	15	24
	Ex.	17	1–4
From lack of food	Num.	11	1–6
From disappointment	Num.	20	1–5
From discouragement	Num.	21	4–6

Rebuked:

Foolish and vain	Prov.	19	3
Against punishment	Lam.	3	39
Of labourers	Mat.	20	1–13
Of Martha	Luke	10	40–42
Not for Christians	John	6	43
Warned against	I Cor.	10	10

murrain *a pestilence*

A plague of Egypt	Ex.	9	3
	Ps.	78	50

muse *think, meditate*

While I was **m**, the fire burned	Ps.	39	3
I **m** on work of thy hands	Ps.	143	5
All men **m** in their hearts	Luke	3	15

music

Instrumental	Gen.	4	21
	Dan.	6	18
An aid to prophets	I Sam.	10	5, 6
	II Ki.	3	15
Beneficial in mental disorders	I Sam.	16	14–23
Vocal	II Sam.	19	35
	Acts	16	25
David invents instruments	I Chr.	23	5
Sacred songs of praise	Ps.	66	
	Ps.	89	
	Ps.	95	
Promotes joy	Eccl.	2	8

Used:

To celebrate victories	Ex.	15	20
In worshiping God	II Sam.	6	4, 5
	II Chr.	7	6
At consecration of temples	II Chr.	5	11–13
At feasts and festivals	II Chr.	30	21
	Is.	5	12
In idol worship	Dan.	3	5
For entertainments and dances	Amos	6	5
	Mat.	11	17
At funerals	Mat.	9	18, 23
On occasions of great joy	Luke	15	25

Instruments made of:

Silver	Num.	10	2
Horns of animals	Josh.	6	8
Wood	II Sam.	6	5
Brass	I Cor.	13	1

Instruments mentioned in Bible:

Organ	Gen.	4	21
Timbrel	Ex.	15	20
Psaltery	I Sam.	10	5
Pipe	I Ki.	1	40
Trumpet	II Ki.	11	14
Cymbals	I Chr.	16	5
Cornet	Ps.	98	6
Harp	Ps.	137	2
Viol	Is.	5	12
Dulcimer	Dan.	3	5
Flute	Dan.	3	5

must

M I needs bring thy son?	Gen.	24	5
It **m** not be so done in our	Gen.	29	26
He **m** do after the law	Num.	6	21
M we fetch you water out of?	Num.	20	10
M I not take heed to speak?	Num.	23	12
Lord speaketh that I **m** do	Num.	23	26
By what way we **m** go	Deut.	1	22
I **m** die in this land I **m**	Deut.	4	22
Way by which we **m** go	Josh.	3	4
A little, and lo I **m** die	I Sam.	14	43
Ruleth over men **m**	II Sam.	23	3
Hast said, so **m** we do	Ezra	10	12
They must needs be borne	Jer.	10	5

Fulfilled, that thus it *m*?	Mat.	26	54
New wine *m* be put into new bottles	Mat.	2	22
	Luke	5	38
Son of man *m* suffer many things	Mark	8	31
	Mark	9	12
Say the scribes that Elias *m*?	Mark	9	11
Of wars be ye not troubled, for such things *m* be	Mark	13	7
	Luke	21	9
Gospel *m* first be published	Mark	13	10
M be about my Father's	Luke	2	49
Zacchaeus, to-day I *m* abide	Luke	19	5
The things written *m* be	Luke	24	44
He *m* release one to them	Luke	23	17
Son of man *m* be delivered	Luke	24	7
Ye *m* be born again	John	3	7
The serpent, so *m* the Son of	John	3	14
M increase, but I *m* decrease	John	3	30
And he *m* needs go through.	John	4	4
God is a spirit, *m* worship him	John	4	24
I *m* work the works of him	John	9	4
Knew not that he *m* rise again	John	20	9
M have been fulfilled	Acts	1	16
Other name whereby we *m*	Acts	4	12
Told thee what thou *m* do	Acts	9	6
Ye *m* be circumcised and	Acts	15	24
Said, Sirs, what *m* I do to?	Acts	16	30
Fear not, thou *m* be brought	Acts	27	24
We *m* be cast on a certain island	Acts	27	26
Wherefore ye *m* needs	Rom.	13	5
There *m* also be heresies	I Cor.	11	19
For he *m* reign till he hath	I Cor.	15	25
For we *m* all appear	II Cor.	5	10
I *m* needs glory, I will glory	II Cor.	11	30
A bishop then *m* be blameless	I Tim.	3	2
	Tit.	1	7
He *m* have a good report	I Tim.	3	7
Likewise *m* deacons be grave	I Tim.	3	8
It remaineth that some *m*	Heb.	4	6
There *m* be the death of the	Heb.	9	16
Cometh to God, *m* believe that	Heb.	11	6
As they that *m* give account	Heb.	13	17
Shew thee things which *m*	Rev.	4	1
That he *m* be loosed a little	Rev.	20	3
To shew things which *m* shortly	Rev.	22	6

mustard seed

Parable of	Mat.	13	31
	Mark	4	30–32
	Luke	13	19
Faith as	Luke	17	6

mutilation *maiming*

Of human body forbidden	Lev.	19	28
Forbidden in the priesthood	Lev.	21	18
A non-Christian practice	I Ki.	18	24–28

mutiny *revolt*

Among the people of Israel	Num.	14	1–4

mutual

Of Faith	Rom.	1	12

muzzle

The ox which treadeth	Deut.	25	4
Of Christian workers	I Tim.	5	18
	I Cor.	9	9

Myra *myrtle juice*

An inland city of Lycia	Acts	27	5

myrrh *a resin of several species*

Used as oil for anointing	Ex.	30	23, 25
Used for perfume	Prov.	7	17
	S. of S.	3	16
For Jesus at the crucifixion	Mark	15	23
For embalming	John	19	39

myrtle *a shrub of great beauty*

Branches used for booths made during the feast of the tabernacle	Neh.	8	15
Planted in the wilderness	Is.	41	19
As an everlasting sign	Is.	55	13

Mysia *in northwest Asia Minor*

Paul visits	Acts	16	7, 8
Assos and Pergamos in	Rev.	2	12–17

mysteries *that which cannot be explained*

Secret things belong to God	Deut.	29	29
Unsolved	Deut.	34	5, 6
Of God's handiwork	Eccl.	4	11
Of the kingdom known to the disciples	Mat.	13	11
Of the kingdom of God, made known by Christ	Rom.	16	25, 26
	Eph.	1	9

Fruitless without love	I Cor.	13	2
Of the resurrection	I Cor.	15	51–54
Spiritual union with Christ	Eph.	5	30–33
Of Jesus' incarnation	I Tim.	3	16
Fellowship of	Eph.	3	9
Of the gospel	Eph.	6	19
	Col.	1	26
Of God	Col.	2	2
Of iniquity	II Thes.	2	7
Of faith	I Tim.	3	9
Of Babylon	Rev.	17	5

N

Naam *agreeable*

Son of Caleb	I Chr.	4	15

Naamah *pleasant; sweet*

the daughter of Lamech and Zillah	Gen.	4	22
A city in Judah	Josh.	15	41
A foreign wife of Solomon and the mother of Rehoboam	I Ki.	14	21, 31
	II Chr.	12	13

Naaman *pleasantness*

Son of Benjamin	Gen.	46	21
Grandson of Benjamin	Num.	26	40
A Syrian general, healed of leprosy by Elijah	II Ki.	5	1–23
Mentioned by Jesus	Luke	4	27

Naashon *enchanter*

A captain of the tribe of Judah	Num.	1	7
	Num.	7	12, 17
	Num.	10	14
Mentioned in the lineage of Christ	Mat.	1	1, 4
	Luke	3	23, 32

Nabal *fool*

A sheepmaster	I Sam.	25	3–5
His conduct toward David	I Sam.	25	10, 11
Abigail's intercession for	I Sam.	25	18, 24, 25
His death	I Sam.	25	38
Abigail later marries David.	I Sam.	25	39–42

Naboth *fruits*

Slain by Jezebel	I Ki.	21	1–19
His murder avenged	II Ki.	9	25, 26

Nachon *ready; established*

Threshingfloor where Uzzah is slain	II Sam.	6	6, 7
	I Chr.	13	9, 10

Nachor *see Nahor*

Nadab *liberal; willing*

Son of Aaron	Ex.	6	23
Offers strange fire and dies	Lev.	10	1, 2
Is buried	Lev.	10	4, 5
Family is forbidden to mourn him	Lev.	10	6, 7
The successor and son of Jeroboam	I Ki.	14	20
He reigns wickedly and is murdered by Baasha	I Ki.	15	25–30
Descendant of Jerahmeel	I Chr.	2	25, 28, 30
Son of Gibeon, a Benjamite	I Chr.	8	29, 30
	I Chr.	9	35, 36

Nagge *bright*

Ancestor of Jesus	Luke	3	23, 25

nagging woman

Samson's wife	Judg.	16	13–17
Better to dwell in a corner	Prov.	25	24

Nahash *serpent*

The Ammonite, subdued by Saul	I Sam.	11	1–11
His kindness to David	II Sam.	10	1, 2
His death	I Chr.	19	1
Could possibly be Jesse, father of David	II Sam.	17	25
	I Chr.	2	13, 15

Nahath *rest; descent*

Son of Reuel, grandson of Esau	Gen.	36	13, 17
A Levite, also called Tohu and Toah	I Chr.	6	26, 34
A Levite, overseer of offerings	II Chr.	31	12, 13

Nahor, Nachor *snoring*

Son of Serug	Gen.	11	22–26
In the ancestry of Jesus	Luke	3	23, 34
Abraham's brother	Gen.	11	26

Nahor, Nachor—*continued*			
Marriages and descendants of	Gen.	11	27, 29
	Gen.	22	20–24
	Gen.	24	15, 24
Called Nachor	Josh.	24	2
Nahshon *diviner*			
The brother-in-law of Aaron, son of Amminadab	Ex.	6	23
Captain of Judah	Num.	2	3
Forefather of Boaz and David	Ruth	4	20–22
Ancestor of Jesus	Mat.	1	1, 4
Nahum *comforting*			
A prophet of Judah	Nah.	1	1
His vision	Nah.	2	1–13
	Nah.	3	1–19
nail			
Finger	Deut.	21	12
	Dan.	4	33
Made of:			
Wood	Judg.	4	21
Iron	I Chr.	22	3
Gold	II Chr.	3	9
Jael murders Sisera with	Judg.	4	18, 21
Pierces Jesus' hands and feet	John	20	25
Used figuratively	Eccl.	12	11
Of a position	Neh.	9	8
Surety of coming Kingdom	Is.	22	23, 25
On fingers	Deut.	21	12
Used in idol construction	Is.	41	7
Nain *beauty*			
A town of Galilee where a widow's son is raised	Luke	7	11–15
naked *not covered*			
They were **n** and were	Gen.	2	25
Knew that they were **n**	Gen.	3	7, 10, 11
People were **n** for Aaron had made them **n** to their	Ex.	32	25
Saul lay down **n** all	I Sam.	19	24
Spoiled clothed all the **n**	II Chr.	28	15
Ahaz made Judah **n** and	II Chr.	28	19
N came I out of my mother's womb, and nude shall I return	Job	1	21
Thou hast stripped the **n** of	Job	22	6
They cause the **n** to lodge	Job	24	7, 10
Hell, is **n** before him and	Job	26	6
No shall he return, to go	Eccl.	5	15
When thou seest the **n**	Is.	58	7
Shalt make thyself **n**	Lam.	4	21
Hath covered the **n**	Ezek.	18	7, 16
Lest I strip her **n** and set	Hosea	2	3
Shall flee away **n** in	Amos	2	16
I will go stripped and **n**	Mic.	1	8
Having thy shame **n**	Mic.	1	11
Bow was made quite **n**	Hab.	3	9
I was **n** and ye clothed	Mat.	25	43
When saw we thee **n** and?	Mat.	38	44
Linen cloth about his **n**	Mark	14	51
Linen cloth, fled from them **n**	Mark	14	52
Peter was **n** and cast	John	21	7
Fled out of that house **n**	Acts	19	16
Present hour we are **n**	I Cor.	4	11
We shall not be found **n**	II Cor.	5	3
But all things are **n** to	Heb.	4	13
If a brother or sister be **n**	James	2	15
Poor, and blind, and **n**	Rev.	3	17
Garments, lest he walk **n**	Rev.	16	15
Make her desolate and **n**	Rev.	17	16
(*See* bare)			
nakedness *unclothed*			
Adam and Eve	Gen.	3	7–13
Shall not distract from love of Christ	Rom.	8	35
Part of Paul's tribulations	II Cor.	11	27
Figurative use	James	2	15
name *authority, character*			
Given by the mother at birth	Gen.	4	1, 25
Given by the father at circumcision	Luke	1	59–63
Of God, to be reverenced	Ex.	20	7
	I Tim.	6	1
Value of a good	Prov.	21	22
	Eccl.	7	1
Of Christ:			
Prayer offered in	John	16	23
Miracles performed in	Acts	3	6
Baptized in	Acts	2	38
Of Christ:			
Give thanks in	Eph.	5	20
To be universally exalted	Phil.	2	9–11

Miracles performed in	Acts	3	6
To be honoured	II Tim.	2	19
Names *that are changed:*			
Abram to Abraham	Gen.	17	5
Sarai to Sarah	Gen.	17	5
Jacob to Israel	Gen.	32	28
Joseph to Zophnath-paaneah	Gen.	41	45
Three Hebrew princes	Dan.	1	7
Saul to Paul	Acts	13	9
Why ask after my **n**?	Gen.	32	29
Let my **n** be named on them	Gen.	48	16
This is my **n** forever	Ex.	3	15
Where I record my **n**	Ex.	20	24
Blot out **n** from under heaven	Deut.	9	14
N of God of Jacob	Ps.	20	1
If we forget **n** of our God.	Ps.	44	20
The **n** of the wicked shall rot	Prov.	10	7
The **n** of the Lord is a strong tower	Prov.	18	10
Thy **n** is an ointment poured forth	S. of S.	1	3
It shall be to the Lord for a **n**	Is.	55	13
Whose **n** is Holy	Is.	57	15
Thou art great, and thy **n** is great	Jer.	10	6
Sworn by my great **n**	Jer.	44	26
One Lord, and his **n** one	Zech.	14	9
Wherein have we despised thy **n**?	Mal.	1	6
To you that fear my **n**	Mal.	4	2
Hallowed by thy **n**	Mat.	6	9
	Luke	11	2
Receiveth prophet in **n** of a prophet	Mat.	10	41
Gathered together in my **n**	Mat.	18	20
Many shall come in my **n**	Mat.	24	5
	Mark	13	6
	Luke	21	8
Cast out your **n** as evil	Luke	6	22
N written in heaven	Luke	10	20
Remission of sins in his **n**	Luke	24	47
If another shall come in his own **n**	John	5	43
Whatsoever ye ask in my **n**	John	15	16
Ye might have life through his **n**	John	20	31
None other **n** under heaven	Acts	4	12
Far above every **n** that is named	Eph.	1	21
At **n** of Jesus every knee should bow	Phil.	2	10
Whose **n** are in the book of life	Phil.	4	3
Do all in the **n** of the Lord Jesus	Col.	3	17
Obtained a more excellent **n**	Heb.	1	4
That worthy **n**	James	2	7
Reproached for **n** of Christ	I Pet.	4	14
A **n** written, which no man knoweth.	Rev.	2	17
Hast a **n** that thou livest	Rev.	3	1
Father's **n** in their foreheads	Rev.	14	1
	Rev.	22	4
Naomi *my pleasantness*			
Wife of Elimelech	Ruth	1	1, 2
Changes name to Mara	Ruth	1	20
Ruth's mother-in-law	Ruth	1	1–4
Relative of Boaz	Ruth	4	1–13
Naphish *refreshed*			
A son of Ishmael	Gen.	25	13, 15
Also called Nephish	I Chr.	1	31
Naphtali *my struggle for*			
Son of Jacob	Gen.	30	8
One of the twelve spies	Num.	13	2, 14
Tribe of, numbered	Num.	26	48
Tribe of Barak	Judg.	4	6
Subdues the Canaanites	Judg.	6	35
	Judg.	7	23
Kills some captives	I Ki.	15	29
	II Chr.	16	4
Loyal to David	I Chr.	12	23, 34
Christ ministers there	Mat.	4	12–16
Nathan *gift*			
A son of David and Bathsheba	II Sam.	5	14
Ancestor of Jesus	Luke	3	31
Prophet in the reign of David and Solomon	II Sam.	7	1–17
Chastises David for his adultery	II Sam.	12	1–15
Anoints Solomon	II Sam.	12	25
Calls Solomon Jedidiah	II Sam.	12	24, 25
Wrote book of Solomon's works	II Chr.	9	29
Father of Igar	II Sam.	23	36
A son of Attai	I Chr.	2	36
A companion of Ezra	Ezra	8	16
A son of Bani	Ezra	10	39
Nathanael *God gave*			
Commended by Christ	John	1	45–51
Could be same as Bartholomew	Mark	4	18

nations *tribes*

The origin of	Gen.	11	1–9
Abraham, father of all	Gen.	17	1–4
Sins of	Is.	30	1, 2
Chastised	Is.	14	26, 27
	Jer.	25	12–33
	Dan.	7	9–12
	Zeph.	3	6, 8
Will perish	Ps.	9	17
	Is.	60	12
Lamented	Ezra	9	1–15
	Neh.	1	4–11
	Jer.	6	14
	Jer.	9	1, 2
Prayer of	Ps.	85	1–7
	Lam.	2	20–22
	Dan.	9	3–21
Prayer for peace of	Jer.	29	7
Peace given by God	Josh.	21	44
	I Chr.	22	18
	I Chr.	23	25
	Eccl.	3	8
	Is.	45	7
Promises of peace to	I Ki.	2	33
	Ps.	46	9
	Is.	60	17, 18
	Jer.	50	34
	Mic.	4	3, 4
Will be judged	Mat.	25	31–46
Will be taught	Mat.	28	19
Of one blood	Acts	17	26

nature

Do by *n* the things in the law	Rom.	2	14
Olive tree which is wild by *n*	Rom.	11	24
Doth not *n* teach you?	I Cor.	11	14
Which by *n* are no gods	Gal.	4	8
By *n* the children of wrath	Eph.	2	3
Took not the *n* of angels	Heb.	2	16
The course of *n*	James	3	6
Partakers of the divine *n*	II Pet.	1	4

naught

Water *n*, and the ground	II Ki.	2	19

naughtiness *state of being naughty*

Of the heart	I Sam.	17	28
Taken in by own	Prov.	11	6
Lay aside and receive the word	James	1	21

Naum *Greek for Nahum*

A forefather of Jesus	Luke	3	23, 25

navel *a depression in the middle of the abdomen*

Fear of God shall be health to	Prov.	3	8
Used figuratively	S. of S.	7	2
How to treat at birth	Ezek.	16	4

navy *a fleet of ships*

Of Solomon	I Ki.	9	26
Of Hiram	I Ki.	10	11
Of Jehoshaphat	I Ki.	22	48
Of Chittim	Dan.	11	30, 40

Nazarene *man of Nazareth*

Jesus called the	Mat.	2	23
Followers of Jesus called	Acts	24	5

Nazareth *branch*

A town of Galilee	Mat.	2	22, 23
Jesus lives here	Mat.	21	11
The home of Joseph and Mary	Luke	1	26, 27
	Luke	2	4, 5
Jesus not accepted in	Luke	4	16–29
Had an evil reputation	John	1	46

Nazarite *an ascetic order*

Law of the	Num.	6	1–21
	Judg.	13	5
The character of	Lam.	4	7
	Amos	2	11, 12

Examples of:

Samson	Judg.	13	5, 7, 24
Samuel	I Sam.	1	11, 20
The Rechabites	Jer.	35	1–19
John the Baptist	Luke	7	33

Neapolis *new city*

A seaport of Philippi, visited by Paul	Acts	16	10–12

near

This city is *n* to flee to	Gen.	19	20
Knew not evil was *n*	Judg.	20	34
Trouble is *n*	Ps.	22	11
Better a neighbour that is *n*	Prov.	27	10

Call upon the Lord while he is *n*	Is.	55	6
The day of the Lord is *n*	Obad.		15
	Zeph.	1	14
It is *n* even at the doors	Mat.	24	33
Ye know that summer is *n*	Mat.	13	18
Our salvation is *n*	Rom.	13	11
Draw *n* with a true heart	Heb.	10	22

Nebat *a look*

The father of Jeroboam	I Ki.	12	2

Nebo *speaker; height*

A city allotted to Reuben	Num.	32	1, 3, 33, 38
A mountain in the land of Moab and the scene of Moses' death	Deut.	32	49
	Deut.	34	1, 5–7
A city of Judah	Ezra	2	29
The ancestor of certain Jews	Ezra	10	43
The planet Mercury, worshipped by the Babylonians	Is.	46	1

Nebuchadnezzar, Nebuchadrezzar, *Nebo protect the boundary*

Conquest of Egypt	II Ki.	24	7
Conquest of Jerusalem	II Chr.	36	5–21
Conquest of Tyre	Ezek.	29	18
Instrument of God's judgment	Jer.	27	8
Founder of Babylonian Empire	Jer.	21	2
Prophecy concerning	Jer.	21	7–10
	Ezek.	26	7–12
His dream	Dan.	2	

Nebuzar-adan *Nebo has given seed*

Captain of the Chaldeans	II Ki.	25	8
He shows kindness towards Jeremiah	Jer.	39	11, 12

necromancy *a form of magic*

Condemned	Deut.	18	10, 11
	Deut.	26	14
Speaking to dead spirits	I Sam.	28	7, 11–20

need

Lend sufficient for his *n*	Deut.	15	8
He shall have no *n* of spoil	Prov.	31	11
What things ye have *n* of	Mat.	6	8
	Luke	12	30
What further *n* of witnesses?	Mat.	26	65
	Mark	14	63
	Luke	22	71
Buy things we have *n* of	John	13	29
As every man had *n*	Acts	2	45
	Acts	4	35
Cannot say, I have no *n* of thee	I Cor.	12	21
To abound and to suffer *n*	Phil.	4	12
God shall supply all your *n*	Phil.	4	19
Grace to help in time of *n*	Heb.	4	16
Ye have *n* that one teach you	Heb.	5	12
What *n* that another priest rise?	Heb.	7	11
Seeth his brother have *n*	I John	3	17
Rich, and have *n* of nothing	Rev.	3	17
City had no *n* of the sun	Rev.	21	23
Whole *n* not a physician	Mat.	9	12
	Mark	2	17
	Luke	5	31
They *n* not depart	Mat.	14	16
Just persons, which *n* no repentance	Luke	15	7
N we epistles of commendation?	II Cor.	3	1
Workman that *n* not to be ashamed	II Tim.	2	15
They *n* no candle	Rev.	22	5

needful

One things is *n*	Luke	10	42
Things *n* to the body	James	2	16

needle

Used for sewing	Eccl.	3	7
Jesus uses as a comparison	Mat.	19	24

needlework *embroidery, sewing*

A hanging for the temple	Ex.	26	36
Part of welcome of heroes	Judg.	5	30
The king's daughter	Ps.	45	14

needy *not having enough to live on, poor*

Give to the	Deut.	15	11
The wicked turn away the	Job	24	4
Not always forgotten	Ps.	9	18
God spares the	Ps.	72	13
God lifts the	Ps.	113	7
To be defended	Ps.	82	3, 4
Plead the cause of	Prov.	31	9
Be strength to	Is.	25	4
Oppressors warned	Amos	8	4–10
Special care by God	Jer.	22	16

See also poor

neglect *disregard*

Of children	I Sam.	3	14–17
Of dress	II Sam.	19	24
Of important virtues	Mat.	23	23
Brings regret	Mat.	25	1–9
Punished	Mat.	25	27–30
Of one in need	Luke	10	30–35
Of salvation	Heb.	2	1–3
Of good deeds	James	4	17

negro *black person*

Moses marries a	Num.	12	1
A prophet's life is saved by a	Jer.	38	6–13
Servant spared	Jer.	39	15–18
A convert to Christianity	Acts	8	26–39

Nehemiah *Jah comforts*

Son of Hachaliah	Neh.	1	1
His grief and prayer for Jerusalem	Neh.	1	3–11
Cup bearer to Artaxerxes	Neh.	1	11
His visit at Jerusalem	Neh.	2	9
His conduct here	Neh.	4	1–23
	Neh.	9	1–38
	Neh.	10	1–39
Reforms	Neh.	5	1–19
	Neh.	13	1–31
Jewish exile who returns to Jerusalem	Ezra	2	2
	Neh.	7	7
Son of Azbuk	Neh.	3	16

Nehushta *bronze*

Wife of Jehoiakim	II Ki.	24	6, 8

Nehushtan *brasen*

The brasen serpent destroyed by Hezekiah	II Ki.	18	4

neighbor *a fellow man*

Do not bear false witness against	Ex.	20	16
Duty towards one's	Ex.	22	26
	Ex.	23	4
	Lev.	19	13
	Deut.	15	2
Love thy *n* as thyself	Lev.	19	18
	Mat.	19	19
Do not despise a	Prov.	14	21
Debate with	Prov.	25	9
Do not flatter	Prov.	29	5
Do not steal words from	Jer.	23	30
Be truthful to	Zech.	8	16
Help	Luke	10	30–36
Helpful	Prov.	27	10
To be truthful with	Eph.	4	25

neighing *sound*

Of horses	Jer.	8	16
Of lewdness	Jer.	13	27
	Jer.	5	8

Nekeb *cavern*

A place near the sea of Galilee	Josh.	19	33

Nemuel *day of God; God spreads*

Son of Simeon	Gen.	46	10
	Num.	26	12
Son of Eliab	Num.	26	9

Nepheg *sprout*

Son of Izhar	Ex.	6	21
Son of David	II Sam.	5	15

nephew *grandchild*

Not to have is a curse	Job	18	19
To be cut off from Babylon	Is.	14	22
Of Abdon	Judg.	12	14
Of a widow	I Tim.	5	4

nepotism *bestowal of patronage by relationship*

By Joseph	Gen.	47	10–13
By Saul	I Sam.	14	50
By David	II Sam.	8	16
	II Sam.	9	3
By Nehemiah	Neh.	7	2

Ner *lamp*

Father of Abner	I Sam.	14	50, 51
Grandfather of Saul	I Chr.	8	33

Nereus *wet; sea god*

A Christian of Rome	Rom.	16	15

Neri *light of Jehovah; Greek for Neriah*

Ancestor of Jesus	Luke	3	27

Neriah *lamp of the Lord*

Father of Baruch	Jer.	32	12
Father of Seraiah	Jer.	51	59

Nero *Roman emperor*

Paul's appeal to	Acts	25	10–12
Paul's salute to	Phil.	4	22

nest

Thou puttest thy *n* in a rock	Num.	24	21
As an eagle stirreth up her *n*	Deut.	32	11
I shall die in my *n*	Job	29	18
The swallow hath found a *n*	Ps.	84	3
As a bird that wandereth from her *n*	Prov.	27	8
Birds of the air have *n*	Mat.	8	20
	Luke	9	58

net *snare*

Figurative of a moral snare	Ps.	9	15
	Prov.	29	5
Used to catch birds	Prov.	1	17
Used in hunting animals	Is.	51	20
Figurative of God's kingdom	Mat.	13	47, 48
Used for fishing	Luke	5	4–6
Evil hunt their brothers with	Mic.	7	2
Job compassed in God's	Job	19	6
Flatterer spreads it	Prov.	29	5

Nethaneel *God has given*

Son of Zuar	Num.	1	8
Prince of Issachar	Num.	2	5
Offering at the altar built by Moses	Num.	7	18–23
Son of Jesse	I Chr.	2	13, 14
A Levite musician	I Chr.	15	24
A scribe, father of Shemaiah	I Chr.	24	6
Son of Obed-edom	I Chr.	26	4
A teacher in Judah	II Chr.	17	7
A priest	II Chr.	35	9
Son of Pashur	Ezra	10	22
Son of Jedaiah	Neh.	12	21
A musician	Neh.	12	36

Nethaniah *given of the Lord*

Father of Ishmael	II Ki.	25	25
Son of Asaph	I Chr.	25	22
Sent to teach in Judah	II Chr.	17	8
Father of Jehudi	Jer.	36	14

Nethinims *given ones*

Bondmen	Josh.	9	23, 27
Return from Babylon	Ezra	2	43–58, 70
Grouped with Solomon's servants	Ezra	2	58
Returned to Jerusalem	Ezra	7	7
Ministered in the house of God	Ezra	8	17
Appointed to serve the Levites	Ezra	8	20
Separated to do God's law	Neh.	10	28, 29
Travel with Ezra	Ezra	7	7
Not taxed	Ezra	7	24
Dwell in Ophel	Neh.	3	26

nettle *a coarse herb armend with stinging hairs*

Sign of indolence	Prov.	24	30, 31
Symbolic of desolation	Zeph.	2	9

network

In the altar	Ex.	27	4
Design on capital of pillars	I Ki.	7	18
	Jer.	52	22
Particularly of designs of pomegranates	Jer.	52	23
Of weaving	Is.	19	9

never

Poor cease	Deut.	15	11
God break the covenant	Judg.	2	1
Sword depart from David's house	II Sam.	12	10
Lord let the righteous be moved	Ps.	55	22
Forget God's precepts	Ps.	119	93
Babylon inhabited	Is.	13	20
Peter deny Christ	Mat.	26	33
Fire of hell quenched	Mark	9	43

new

Sing a new song to the Lord	Ps.	33	3
"No new thing under the sun"	Eccl.	1	9
God bringeth new things	Is.	42	9
	Is.	43	19
A new heaven and earth	Is.	66	22
	Rev.	21	1–4
God's mercies are new every morning	Lam.	3	23
N heart, spirit	Ezek.	11	19
Christians shall speak with new tongues	Mark	16	17
A new commandment	John	13	34
A new creature in Christ	II Cor.	5	17
N name	I John	3	1

new birth *see* regeneration

new covenant *see* covenant

new Jerusalem *see* Jerusalem

new moon, feast of the *see* feasts and festivals

Nicodemus *victor over the people*

A Pharisee	John	3	1

Visits Jesus	John	3	2–13
Defends Jesus	John	7	50–52
Brings spices for burial of Jesus	John	19	39

Nicolaitanes, Nicolaitans *conqueror of the people*
A sect; doctrine hated by God	Rev.	2	6, 15
Doctrine likened to that of Balaam	Rev.	2	14, 15

Nicopolis *city of victory*
A city visited by Paul	Tit.	3	12

Niger *black*
Surname of Simeon	Acts	13	1

nigh *near*
The word is *n* thee	Deut.	30	14
	Rom.	10	8
Lord is *n* to them of broken heart	Ps.	34	18
His salvation *n* them that fear him	Ps.	85	9
Lord is *n* unto all them that call upon him	Ps.	145	18
Day of the Lord is *n* at hand	Joel	2	1
Made *n* by the blood of Christ	Eph.	2	13
Is *n* unto cursing	Heb.	6	8

night *a period when no light of the sun is visible*
Named by God	Gen.	1	5
Ruled by moon and stars	Gen.	1	16, 18
Heavenly bodies designed to separate day from	Gen.	1	14
Time of meditation	Ps.	77	6
Spent in prayer	Luke	6	12
None in heaven	Rev.	21	25
	Rev.	22	5
Belongs to God	Ps.	74	16
Caused by God	Ps.	104	20
Commenced at sunset	Gen.	28	11
Designed for rest	Ps.	104	23
Divided into four watches by the Romans	Mark	13	35
Favorable to the purposes of the wicked	Gen.	31	39
	Job	24	14–15
	Obad.	1	5
The darkness God called *n*	Gen.	1	5
A *n* to be much observed	Ex.	12	42
When shall the *n* be gone?	Job	7	4
N unto *n* sheweth knowledge	Ps.	19	2
Weeping may endure for a *n*	Ps.	30	5
Moon to rule by *n*	Ps.	136	9
The *n* shall be light about me	Ps.	139	11
Watchman, what of the *n*?	Is.	21	11
Came up in a *n* perished in a *n*	Jonah	4	10
He continued all *n* in prayer	Luke	6	12
This *n* thy soul shall be required	Luke	12	20
The *n* cometh, when no man can work	John	9	4
If a man walk in the *n*, he stumbleth	John	11	10
The *n* is far spent	Rom.	13	12
The same *n* he was betrayed	I Cor.	11	23
Cometh as a thief in the *n*	I Thes.	5	2
	II Pet.	3	10
Shall be no *n* there	Rev.	21	25
	Rev.	22	5

Can be:
Accompanied by heavy dews	Num.	11	9
	Judg.	6	38, 40
	Job	29	19
Cold and frosty	Gen.	31	40
	Jer.	36	30
Very dark	Prov.	7	9

God frequently:
Executed his judgments in	Ex.	12	12
	II Ki.	19	35
	Job	27	20
	Deut.	5	30
Revealed his will in	Gen.	31	24
	Gen.	46	2
	Num.	22	20
	Dan.	7	2
Visited his people in	I Ki.	3	5
	Ps.	17	3

Illustrative of:
Death	John	9	4
Seasons of severe calamities	Is.	21	12
	Amos	5	8
Seasons of spiritual desertion	S. of S.	3	1
Spiritual darkness	Rom.	13	12

The Jews:
Forbidden to allow malefactors to hang during	Deut.	21	23
Forbidden to keep the wages of servants during	Lev.	19	13
In affliction, spent in prayer	Ps.	22	2
In affliction, spent in sorrow and humiliation	Ps.	6	6
	Joel	1	13
Often kept lamps burning during	Prov.	31	18

Nile *the great river of Egypt*
Called Sihor	Is.	23	3

Nimrah *see* Beth-nimrah

Nimrod *valiant; rebellion*
Son of Cush	Gen.	10	8
A mighty hunter	Gen.	10	9
Founds Babylon	Gen.	10	10
Founds Assyria	Gen.	10	11
Founds Nineveh	Gen.	10	11

Nimshi *extricated*
Father of Jehu	I Ki.	19	16
Descendant of Jehoshaphat	II Ki.	9	2

Nineve, Nineveh *dwelling*
Founded by Nimrod	Gen.	10	9–11
A city of Assyria	II Ki.	19	36
Jonah commanded to preach at	Jonah	1	2
It repents	Jonah	3	1–10
Spared	Jonah	4	11
Destroyed	Nah.	2	8–13

Nisan *beginning*
Called Abib	Ex.	13	4
Hebrew month	Neh.	2	1

nitre, niter *a nitrate*
Compared to the heavy heart	Prov.	25	20
For washing	Jer.	2	22

Noadiah *convened of Jehovah; meeting of Jehovah*
A Levite, son of Binnui	Ezra	8	33
A prophetess	Neh.	6	14

Noah, Noe *rest*
Son of Lamech	Gen.	5	28, 29
Father of Shem, Ham and Japheth	Gen.	5	32
Commissioned to build ark	Gen.	6	15–22
Establishes covenant	Gen.	9	9–17
Curses Canaan	Gen.	9	25, 26
Blesses Shem and Japheth	Gen.	9	26, 27
Dies	Gen.	9	29
Preacher of righteousness	II Pet.	2	5
Example of faith	Heb.	11	7
Daughter of Zelophehad	Num.	26	33
Receives inheritance	Num.	27	1–7
Marries cousin	Num.	36	11

Nob *height*
Refuge of David	I Sam.	22	9–11
A city of priests	I Sam.	22	19
A city of Benjamin	Neh.	11	32

noble
The *n* put not their necks to work	Neh.	3	5
The *n* held their peace	Job	29	10
Brought down all the *n*	Is.	43	14
A *n* vine	Jer.	2	21
Bereans were more *n*	Acts	17	11
Not many *n* are called	I Cor.	1	26

nobleman *a peer*
A parable concerning	Luke	19	12–27
Son of, healed	John	4	46–53

Nod *wandering*
A land east of Eden	Gen.	4	16

Noe *see* Noah

noise *clamor*
Of the trumpet	Ex.	20	18
Of war	Ex.	32	17, 18
Silence commanded	Josh.	6	10
Of a shout	I Sam.	4	6
Of coronation	I Ki.	1	41
	II Ki.	11	13
Of a dog	Ps.	59	6
Of the sea	Ps.	65	7
Joyful to the Lord	Ps.	100	1
Army frightened by	II Ki.	7	6–8
When the temple foundations are laid	Ezra	3	13
Of a multitude in the mountains	Is.	13	4
Of wings in Ezekiel's vision	Ezek.	1	24

noisome *harmful*
Of pestilence	Ps.	91	3
Of beasts	Ezek.	14	21
Of sores on man	Rev.	16	2

Non *see* Nun

Noph *see* Memphis

nose, nostrils *organ of smell*

The breath of life in	Gen.	7	22
Smoke through	Job	41	20
Smell of apples	S. of S.	7	8
Mutilation of	Ezek.	23	25
Flat	Lev.	21	8
A hook in	II Ki.	19	28
Pierced	Job	41	2
Smoke in	Is.	65	5

nose jewels *ornaments worn in the nose*

In swine's snout	Prov.	11	22
Ornamental	Is.	3	21

nothing

Gathered much had *n* over	Ex.	16	18
	II Cor.	8	15
Neither offer of that which costs *n*	II Sam.	24	24
It is *n* with thee to help	II Chr.	14	11
Portions to them for whom *n* is prepared	Neh.	8	10
We are of yesterday, and know *n*	Job	8	9
It profiteth a man *n*	Job	34	9
Mine age is as *n* before thee	Ps.	39	5
Dieth, he shall carry *n* away	Ps.	49	17
N shall offend them	Ps.	119	165
The sluggard desireth and hath *n*	Prov.	13	4
That maketh himself rich, yet hath *n*	Prov.	13	7
He shall take *n* of his labour	Eccl.	5	15
All nations before him are as *n*	Is.	40	17
Is it *n* to you?	Lam.	1	12
Inhabitants of earth as *n*	Dan.	4	35
N shall be impossible	Mat.	17	20
	Luke	1	37
N but leaves	Mat.	21	19
	Mark	11	13
They had *n* to pay	Luke	7	42
This man hath done *n* amiss	Luke	23	41
Prince of this world hath *n* in me	John	14	30
Without me ye can do *n*	John	15	5
Bring to *n* the understanding of prudent	I Cor.	1	19
Judge *n* before the time	I Cor.	4	5
Having *n*, yet possessing all things	II Cor.	6	10
Can do *n* against the truth	II Cor.	13	8
Christ shall profit you *n*	Gal.	5	2
N to be refused	I Tim.	4	4
We brought *n* into this world	I Tim.	6	7
The law made *n* perfect	Heb.	7	19
Perfect and entire, wanting *n*	James	1	4

nought *nothing, no value*

Set at *n* my counsel	Prov.	1	25
Spent strength for *n*	Is.	49	4
Ye have sold yourselves for *n*	Is.	52	3
Stone which was set at *n*	Acts	4	11
It will come to *n*	Acts	5	38
Why set at *n* thy brother?	Rom.	14	10
To bring to *n* things that are	I Cor.	1	28
Riches is come to *n*	Rev.	18	17

nourish *feed, keep alive*

N and brought up children	Is.	1	2
Was *n* by the king's country	Acts	12	20
N in words of faith	I Tim.	4	6
Have *n* your hearts	James	5	5

number, numeral *figure, count*

The dust of the earth	Gen.	13	16
The stars	Gen.	15	5
David numbers Israel	I Chr.	21	1
Our days	Ps.	90	12
With the transgressor	Is.	53	12
By the hair of the head	Mat.	10	30
Things without *n*	Job	5	9
	Job	9	10
More in *n* than the sand	Ps.	139	18
He telleth the *n* of the stars	Ps.	147	4
Bringeth out their hosts by *n*	Is.	40	26
N of Israel shall be as the sand	Hosea	1	10
	Rom.	9	27
Men sat down, in *n* about five thousand	John	6	10
N of disciples was multiplied	Acts	6	1
The churches increased in *n*	Acts	16	5
Not make ourselves of the *n*	II Cor.	10	12
The *n* of his name	Rev.	13	17

(verb)

If a man can *n* the dust	Gen.	13	16
Tell stars, if able to *n* them	Gen.	15	5
N the people	II Sam.	24	2
	I Chr.	21	2

Who can *n* the clouds?	Job	38	37
More than can be *n*	Ps.	40	5
So teach us to *n* our days	Ps.	90	12
That which is wanting cannot be *n*	Eccl.	1	15
He was *n* with the transgressors	Is.	53	12
	Mark	15	28
Hairs of head are all *n*	Mat.	10	30
	Luke	12	7
He was *n* with us	Acts	1	17
A multitude which no made could *n*	Rev.	7	9

numbering

Of the People	Num.	1	26
By Moses	II Sam.	24	
By David	I Chr.	21	
Of the Levites	Num.	3	14
	Num.	4	34

Nun, Non *fish*

Father of Joshua	Ex.	33	11
Called Non	I Chr.	7	27

nurse *cares for the sick, suckle*

Deborah takes care of Rebekah	Gen.	24	59
	Gen.	35	8
Employed to care for infants	Ex.	2	7–9
	II Ki.	11	2
Naomi of Ruth's child	Ruth	4	16
Figurative	Num.	11	12
Causes lameness of child	II Sam.	4	4
Gentle	I Thes.	2	7

Nymphas *bridegroom; sacred to nymphs*

A Christian of Laodicea	Col.	4	15

O

oak *a hardwood tree*

Hiding place under	Gen.	35	4
Burialplace of Deborah	Gen.	35	8
By the sanctuary	Josh.	24	26
Absalom hanged in	II Sam.	18	10
Place of holy men	Judg.	6	11
	I Ki.	13	14
In Jabesh	I Chr.	10	12
Of Bashan	Is.	2	13
Oars made of	Ezek.	27	6
Symbol of strength	Amos	2	9
	Zech.	11	2

oath *affirmation of a promise*

Confirmed by raising the hand	Gen.	14	22
Confirmed by placing hand under thigh	Gen.	24	2, 9
Not to be taken in name of idols	Josh.	23	7
Sworn in fear and reverence	Eccl.	9	2
Condemned for profane	Jer.	23	10
Condemned for false	Zech.	5	3, 4
Forbidden to take in name of any created thing	Mat.	5	33–37
Purpose of, explained	Heb.	6	16

Used for:

Confirming covenants	Gen.	26	28
Deciding controversies in court	Ex.	22	11
	Num.	5	19
Pledging allegiance	II Ki.	11	4
Binding to performance of duties	II Chr.	15	14, 15

Expressions used:

By the fear of Isaac	Gen.	31	53
As the Lord liveth	Judg.	8	19
The Lord do so to me	Ruth	1	17
As my soul liveth	I Sam.	1	26
By the Lord	II Sam.	19	7
Before God I lie not	Gal.	1	20
God is witness	I Thes.	2	5
The Lord witness	Jer.	42	5
Lord make thee	Ruth	4	11

Obadiah *servant of the Lord*

Governor of Ahab's house	I Ki.	18	3
Conceals prophets	I Ki.	18	4, 13
A descendant of Zerubbabel	I Chr.	3	19, 21
Son of Izrahiah	I Chr.	7	3
Son of Azel	I Chr.	8	38
A Levite, son of Shemaiah	I Chr.	9	16
A Gadite warrior	I Chr.	12	9
Father of Ishmaiah	I Chr.	27	19

A teacher of the law in Judah	II Chr.	17	7–9
A Merarite Levite	II Chr.	34	12
Son of Jehiel	Ezra	8	9
Sealer of the covenant	Neh.	10	5
A porter of the gates	Neh.	12	25
A prophet	Obad.		1

obduracy: *Stubbornly resistant*

Against the prophets	II Chr.	36	15, 16
Israel in the wilderness	Ps.	95	8–11
Against the Lord	Prov.	1	24–29
At reproof	Prov.	29	1

Examples:

Antediluvians	Gen.	6	3, 5, 7
Sodomites	Gen.	19	9, 14
Pharaoh	Ex.	7	14, 22
Israelites	Num.	14	22
Sons of Eli	I Sam.	2	22–25

Obed *serving*

Son of Boaz and Ruth	Ruth	4	13, 17
Father of Jesse	Ruth	4	22
An ancestor of Jesus	Mat.	1	5
Son of Ephlal	I Chr.	2	37
Father of Jehu	I Chr.	2	38
One of David's valiant men	I Chr.	11	47
Son of Shemaiah	I Chr.	26	7
Father of Azariah	II Chr.	23	1

obedience *compliance with the laws*

Enjoined	Ex.	19	5
	Jer.	26	13
	James	1	25
Brings a reward	Ex.	23	22
	Deut.	28	10
	Luke	11	28
Preferred to sacrifice	I Sam.	15	22
	Ps.	50	8
Lengthens life	Deut.	3	14
Pray to be taught	Ps.	119	35
Apostles obedient to the voice of God	Acts	26	19
	I Pet.	1	2
Children to parents	Eph.	6	1–3
Wives to husbands	Tit.	2	4, 5
To civil law	I Pet.	2	13, 14

To God:

Angels engaged in	Ps.	103	20
Blessedness of	Deut.	11	27
	Deut.	28	1–13
	James	1	25
A characteristic of saints	I Pet.	1	14
Christ an example of	Mat.	3	15
	Phil.	2	5–8
Commanded	Deut.	13	4
Confess your failure in	Dan.	9	10
Exhortations to	Jer.	38	20
Impossible without faith	Heb.	11	6
Justification obtained by that of Christ	Rom.	5	19
Obligations to	Acts	4	19–20
	Acts	5	29
Pray to be taught	Ps.	143	10
Promises to	I Sam.	12	14
	Is.	1	19
	Jer.	7	23
Punishment of refusing	Deut.	11	28
Resolve upon	Ex.	24	7
	Josh.	24	24
Jesus made perfect through	Heb.	5	8
To be universal in the latter days	Dan.	7	27
The wicked refuse	Ex.	5	2
	Neh.	9	17
Should be from the heart	Deut.	11	13
	Rom.	6	17

Includes:

Keeping his commandments	Eccl.	12	13
Obeying his voice	Ex.	19	5
	Jer.	7	23
Obeying the gospel	Rom.	1	5
	Rom.	10	16–17
By obeying His law	Is.	42	24
	Deut.	11	27
By obeying Christ	II Cor.	10	5
	Ex.	23	21
Submission to higher powers	Rom.	13	1

Should Be:

Undeviating	Deut.	28	14
Unreserved	Josh.	22	2–3
With willingness	Is.	1	19
	Ps.	18	44
	Phil.	2	12

Exemplified:

Noah	Gen.	6	22
Abraham	Gen.	12	1–4
Caleb	Num.	14	24
Elijah	I Ki.	17	5
David	Ps.	119	106
Hezekiah	II Chr.	31	20
Ezra	Ezra	7	10
Job	Job	1	8
Joseph	Mat.	1	24
Jesus	John	15	10
Paul	Acts	26	19

obeisance *homage*

To Joseph by his brothers	Gen.	43	28
To the father-in-law	Ex.	18	7
Of kings	Ps.	72	11
To the baby Jesus	Mat.	2	11
Of Jairus to Jesus	Luke	8	41
To kings	II Sam.	14	4
	II Chr.	24	17

obey *yield*

Who is the Lord, that I should *o* his voice?	Ex.	5	2
A blessing, if ye *o* commandments	Deut.	11	27
Lord's voice will we *o*	Josh.	24	24
To *o* is better than sacrifice	I Sam.	15	22
O my voice, and I will be your God	Jer.	7	23
Amend ways, and *o* voice of the Lord	Zech.	6	15
We ought to *o* God rather than men	Acts	5	29
His servants ye are to whom ye *o*	Rom.	6	16
Children, *o* your parents in the Lord	Eph.	6	1
That *o* not the gospel	II Thes.	1	8
	I Pet.	4	17
Salvation to all that *o* him	Heb.	5	9
O them that have rule over you	Heb.	13	17
Purified souls in *o* the truth	I Pet.	1	22
If any *o* not the word	I Pet.	1	1

oblations *see offerings*

observe *to conform, to watch*

The sabbath	Ex.	31	16
The wise	Ps.	107	43
The ways of God	Prov.	23	26
All things commanded by God	Mat.	28	20
Lawful customs	Acts	16	21
Feast of passover	Ex.	12	17
Feast of pentecost	Ex.	34	22
Not to observe times	Lev.	19	26
Feast of tabernacles	Deut.	16	13
Of lying vanities	Jonah	2	8
Of days and months	Gal.	4	10

observer of times *celebrator of time*

Banned	Lev.	19	26
An abomination	Deut.	18	10, 14
Idolatrous	Gal.	4	10

obstinancy *unreasonably determined*

The hardened heart	Ex.	8	19
A provoking	Ex.	32	7–10
Of Balaam, rebuked	Num.	22	21–35
The hardened spirit	Deut.	2	30
A rebellious	I Sam.	8	18–20
Figurative	Is.	48	4

obtain *procure, acquire*

Favor of God	Prov.	8	35
Eternal joy and gladness	Is.	35	10
Mercy	Hosea	2	23
Freedom	Acts	22	28
"Run that ye may"	I Cor.	9	24
Salvation	I Thes.	5	9
A better resurrection	Heb.	11	35
Lusts cannot obtain	James	4	2
Children	Gen.	16	2
A corruptible crown	I Cor.	9	25

occupations *vocations*

Minister	Josh.	1	1
Prophet	I Sam.	3	20
Soldier	II Ki.	5	1
Treasurer	I Chr.	27	25
Supervisor	I Chr.	27	26
Counsellor	I Chr.	27	33
The priest	Neh.	3	1
Fishermen	Mat.	4	18
Shepherd	Mat.	9	36
Carpenter	Mark	6	3
Tentmaker	Acts	18	3
Silversmith	Acts	19	24

odors *smells*

Sweet	Lev.	26	31
	Esth.	2	12
Burning of incense	Jer.	34	5
Of prayers	Rev.	5	8
Item of trade of Babylon	Rev.	18	13

offence *trespass, insult*

Blessedness of not taking, at Christ	Mat.	11	6
Be cautious of giving	II Cor.	6	3
Remove that which causes	Is.	57	14
Occasions of, forbidden	I Cor.	10	32
	II Cor.	6	3
Satan an	Mat.	16	23
Inevitable	Mat.	18	7
Stumblingstone	Rom.	9	33
Give none	I Cor.	10	32
We should be without	Phil.	1	10

Saints should:

Avoid those who cause	Rom.	16	17
Be cautious of giving	Ps.	73	15
	Rom.	14	13
	I Cor.	8	9
Have a conscience void of	Acts	24	16
Not let their liberty occasion	I Cor.	8	9
Not take	John	16	1
Reprove those who cause	Ex.	32	21
	I Sam.	2	24
Use self-denial rather than occasion	Rom.	14	21
	I Cor.	8	13

The wicked take, at:

Christ as the bread of life	John	6	58-61
Christ as the cornerstone	I Pet.	2	8
Christ crucified	I Cor.	1	23
	Gal.	5	11
The low station of Christ	Mat.	15	11-12
The righteousness of faith	Rom.	9	32

offend *displease*

I will not *o* any more	Job	34	31
Nothing shall *o* them	Ps.	119	165
A brother *o* is harder to be won	Prov.	18	19
He shall pass over and *o*	Hab.	1	11
Gather all things that *o*	Mat.	13	41
Whose *o* one of these	Mat.	18	16
	Mark	9	42
	Luke	17	2
If thine eye *o* thee	Mat.	18	9
	Mark	9	47
Be *o* because of me	Mat.	26	31
Whereby thy brother is *o*	Rom.	14	21
Yet *o* in one point	James	2	10

offender *transgressor*

Manasseh	II Ki.	21	1-9
For a word	Is.	29	20, 21
Worthy of death	Acts	25	11

offer

To *o* the first of thy ripe fruits	Ex.	22	29
People willingly *o* themselves	Judg.	5	2
Who so *o* praise	Ps.	50	23
O sacrifice of thanksgiving	Ps.	116	17
Then come and *o* thy gift	Mat.	5	24
O the gift that Moses commanded	Mat.	8	4
One cheek, *o* also the other	Luke	6	29
O in the service of your faith	Phil.	2	17
Now ready to be *o*	II Tim.	4	6
Christ was once *o* to bear the sins of many	Heb.	9	28
(See Mal. 1:10; Eph. 5:2; Heb. 10:18.)			

offerings *things presented to God in worship*

Antiquity of	Gen.	4	3, 4
To be made to God alone	Ex.	22	20
Unacceptable without gratitude	Ps.	50	8, 14
Not a substitute for righteousness	Hosea	6	6

Required to be:

Perfect	Lev.	22	19, 21
Brought to place appointed by God	Deut.	12	6
	Mat.	5	23
In a clean vessel	Is.	66	20
The best of their kind	Mal.	1	14
Offered in righteousness	Mal.	3	3
Presented by the priest	Heb.	5	1

Different kinds of:

Burnt	Lev.	1	3-17
Drink	Gen.	35	14
Firstfruits	Ex.	23	16
Freewill	Lev.	23	38
Gifts	Ex.	35	22

Heave	Ex.	29	27, 28
Incense	Ex.	30	8-10
Jealousy	Num.	5	15
Meat	Lev.	2	1-16
Peace	Lev.	3	1-17
Personal, for redemption	Ex.	30	13, 15
Sin	Lev.	4	3-35
Thank	Lev.	7	12
Tithe	Lev.	27	30
Trespass	Lev.	5	6-19
Wave	Ex.	29	26

Illustrative of:

The conversion of the Jews	Is.	66	20
The conversion of the Gentiles	Rom.	15	16
Christ's offering of Himself	Eph.	5	2

office

Me he restored to *o*	Gen.	41	13
Put me into priest's *o*	I Sam.	2	36
Their *o* was to distribute	Neh.	13	13
Let another take his *o*	Ps.	109	8
I magnify mine *o*	Rom.	11	13
The *o* of a bishop	I Tim.	3	1
The *o* of the priesthood	Heb.	7	5

officers *agents*

Dukes	Gen.	36	15
The priest	Ex.	28	1-3
Princes	Num.	1	16
The Levites	Num.	1	47-54
Captains	Deut.	1	13-15
Judges	Deut.	1	16, 17
Ministers	Josh.	1	1
Appointed	II Sam.	8	15-18
	I Ki.	4	1-21
	Ezra	7	24, 25
Apostles	Luke	6	13
Deacons	Acts	6	1-6
Bishops	Acts	20	28

offscouring *refuse*

Apostles called	I Cor.	4	13

offspring *progeny*

Many	Job	5	25
Established	Job	21	8
Blessings received	Is.	44	3
Number as stones	Is.	48	19
Fame of	Is.	61	9
Of David	Rev.	22	16
Of the Lord	Acts	17	28, 29

Og *giant*

Defeated by Moses	Num.	21	33-35
Land given away	Deut.	3	8-10, 12-17
Of gigantic stature	Deut.	3	11
King of Bashan	Deut.	3	11

oil *an unctuous liquid*

For illumination of tabernacle	Ex.	27	20
Sacred	Ex.	30	23-25
Not to be profaned	Ex.	30	31-33
In meat offerings	Lev.	2	1, 4-7
Preparation of pure	Lev.	24	2-4
Harvest of olives	Deut.	24	20
Anointing	II Sam.	10	1
Item of trade	II Ki.	4	1-7
Of myrrh, for purification	Esth.	2	12
Job has plenty	Job	29	6
Cosmetic	Is.	61	3
Tribute	Hosea	12	1
Used figuratively	Zech.	4	12
To heal the sick	Luke	10	34
For food	Lev.	2	4, 5
	Deut.	12	17
Of the Holy Spirit	I John	2	20, 27

ointment *an unguent*

Sacred:

Formula prepared by apothecary	Ex.	30	23-25
Uses	Ex.	30	26-33
Compounded by Bezaleel	Ex.	37	1, 29

Not sacred:

As a cosmetic	Ruth	3	3
Precious	II Ki.	20	13
For the head	Eccl.	9	8
Better than all spices	S. of S.	4	10
For healing	Is.	1	6
Anointing	Amos	6	6
In connection with burial	John	12	3, 7, 8
On Christ	Mat.	26	7
Precious	Mark	14	3
For embalming	Luke	23	55, 56

old age *see age, old*

Old Testament
Called by Paul	II Cor.	3	6, 14
Provides examples for learning	I Cor.	10	6
Written to give hope	Rom.	15	4
Inspired	II Tim.	3	16
Cannot be broken	John	10	34, 35
Fulfilled in Christ	Mat.	5	17, 18
Methods of communication	Heb.	1	1
Messianic character	Luke	24	44, 45

olive, oil tree *a fruit, a tree*
Leaf brought to Noah	Gen.	8	11
Common in land of Canaan	Ex.	23	11
Oil extracted from fruit	Lev.	24	2
Command to cultivate	Deut.	28	40
In building	I Ki.	6	23, 31–35
Branches for booths	Neh.	8	15
Flowers of	Job	15	33
Fruitful	Ps.	128	3
Beautiful	Jer.	11	16
	Hosea	14	6
Wild and cultured	Rom.	11	24
Used figuratively	James	3	12

Olivet, Olives, mount of *hill east of Jerusalem*
Called mount of corruption	II Ki.	23	13
David crosses barefoot	II Sam.	15	30
Shall split	Zech.	14	4
Jesus' triumphal entry by way of	Mat.	21	1
Jesus retires to	Mat.	24	3
Jesus makes His ascension from	Acts	1	12

Olympas *heavenly*
A Christian at Rome	Rom.	16	15

Omar *talkative*
Son of Eliphaz	Gen.	36	11
Duke of Esau	Gen.	36	15

Omega *the last letter of the Greek alphabet*
The end, the last	Rev.	1	8, 11
	Rev.	22	13

omer *a dry measure*
Used in measurement of manna	Ex.	16	16, 18, 22
One tenth part of an ephah	Ex.	16	36

Omri *my sheaf*
King of Israel	I Ki.	16	16
Establishes himself	I Ki.	16	21, 22
Father of Ahab	I Ki.	16	29
Father of Athaliah	II Ki.	8	26
Denounced	Mic.	6	16
Son of Becher	I Chr.	17	8
A Judahite	I Chr.	9	4
Son of Michael	I Chr.	27	18

Onan *strong*
Son of Judah	Gen.	38	2,4
Takes the widow of his brother	Gen.	38	8, 9
Slain	Gen.	38	10

once
I will speak but this *o*	Gen.	18	32
	Judg.	6	35
He saved himself not *o*	II Ki.	6	10
God speaks *o*	Job	33	14
	Ps.	62	11
Shall a nation be born at *o*?	Is.	66	8
He died unto sin *o*	Rom.	6	10
I was alive without the law *o*	Rom.	7	9
Now *o* in end of the world	Heb.	9	26
Contend for faith *o* delivered unto the saints	Jude		3

one
Hast thou but *o* blessing?	Gen.	27	38
O of a thousand	Job	9	3
	Job	33	23
Help on *o* that is mighty	Ps.	89	19
Two are better than *o*	Eccl.	4	9
Ye shall be gathered *o* by *o*	Is.	27	12
O jot or *o* tittle shall in no wise pass from law	Mat.	5	18
None good but *o*	Mat.	19	17
	Mark	10	18
	Luke	18	19
O thing thou lackest	Mark	10	21
	Luke	18	22
O thing is needful	Luke	10	42
O thing I know	John	9	25
O Lord, *o* faith, *o* baptism	Eph.	4	5
This *o* thing I do	Phil.	3	13

Onesimus *profitable*
Carries epistle	Col.	4	7–9
A servant of Paul, a convert	Philem.		10

Onesiphorus *profit bearing*
A Christian of Ephesus	II Tim.	1	16–18

onion *a liliaceous plant*
An article of food in Egypt	Num.	11	3–5

onycha *a shell*
An ingredient of perfume	Ex.	30	34

onyx *nail, claw*
Mineral found in land of Havilah	Gen.	2	11, 12
Used in ephod and breastplate	Ex.	25	7
	Ex.	28	9–12
Donated for garments	Ex.	35	4–9
Precious	Job	28	16
In foundation of new Jerusalem	Rev.	21	20

open
If the earth *o* her mouth	Num.	16	30
I will *o* my dark saying	Ps.	49	4
I will *o* my mouth in a parable	Ps.	78	2
O thy mouth wide	Ps.	81	10
Thou *o* thine hand	Ps.	104	28
O to me the gates of righteousness	Ps.	118	19
O thou mine eyes	Ps.	119	18
O thy mouth for the dumb	Prov.	31	8
He shall *o*, and none shall shut	Is.	22	22
O gates, that righteous may enter	Is.	26	2
To *o* the blind eyes	Is.	42	7
Thy gates shall be *o* continually	Is.	60	11
O the windows of heaven	Mal.	3	10
Lord *o* to us	Mat.	25	11
	Luke	13	25
While he *o* to us the scriptures	Luke	24	32
To *o* their eyes	Acts	26	18
That God would *o* to us a door of utterance	Col.	4	3
All things are *o* to him	Heb.	4	13
And no man *o*	Rev.	3	7
Who is worthy to *o* the book?	Rev.	5	2

openly
Shall reward thee *o*	Mat.	6	4
	Mat.	6	18
Seeketh to be known *o*	John	7	14
Have beaten us *o*	Acts	16	37

Ophel *a hill, bulge*
A tower in the wall of Jerusalem	II Chr.	27	3
Very high	II Chr.	33	14
Inhabited by Nethinims	Neh.	3	26, 27

opinion *ones thought*
Public:
Jesus inquires of	Mat.	16	13
Feared by Nicodemus	John	3	2
Joseph of Arimathaea	John	19	38
Parents of blind man fear	John	9	21, 22
Rulers feared	John	12	42, 43
Chief priests fear	Mat.	21	26
Concessions to:
Paul	Acts	16	3
James	Acts	21	18–26
Those wanting circumcision	Gal.	6	12
Peter	Gal.	2	11–14
Halting between	I Ki.	18	21
Elihu's	Job	32	6, 10, 17

opportunity *a good chance*
Readiness for	Ex.	2	7–10
Lost	Jer.	8	20
To attain the kingdom of heaven	Mat.	25	1–30
Judas seeks, for betrayal	Mat.	26	16
For salvation	Luke	19	41–44
To preach the word	Acts	8	35–39
To do good	Gal.	6	10
Be mindful of	Heb.	11	15

oppression *cruel exercise of authority*
Forbidden	Lev.	25	14
Hearkened to by God	Deut.	26	7
Of the hired servant	Deut.	24	14
Called bondage	Neh.	5	1–5
Of the poor	Ps.	12	5
The effect of	Ps.	107	39
	Eccl.	7	7
Despise the gains of	Is.	33	15
By the greedy	Amos	8	4–6
Examples of oppressors:
Pharaoh	Ex.	6	5–14
Rehoboam of people	I Ki.	12	14
King of Syria	II Ki.	13	4

oppression—*continued*			
The deceitful	Hosea	12	7
The Pharisees	Mat.	23	4
The devil	Acts	10	38
Rich men	James	2	6
God is refuge from	Ps.	9	9
Prayers against	Ps.	17	9
God's judgment	Ps.	103	6
National implications	Acts	7	7
Oppressor not to be envied	Prov.	3	31
oracle *a wise answer, place of*			
As the counsel of Ahithophel	II Sam.	16	23
Of God to be taught	Heb.	5	12
The holy of holies	II Chr.	4	20
	I Ki.	6	16–23
Of Moses	Acts	7	38
Of God	Rom.	3	2
orator *a public speaker*			
Eloquent	Is.	3	3
The accuser	Acts	24	1–8
Examples of:			
Joshua	Josh.	23	2–16
Paul	Acts	17	22–31
ordained *invested with authority*			
A place for God's people	I Chr.	9	9
Idolatrous priests	II Ki.	23	5
Porters by David	I Chr.	9	22
Peace by God	Is.	26	12
Paul in the churches	I Cor.	7	17
Elders by Titus	Tit.	1	5
Feast of Purim	Esth.	9	27
God's ordering the universe	Ps.	8	3
Jesus ordains His disciples	Mark	3	14
Elders in the churches	Acts	14	23
Civil servants	Rom.	13	1–7
Ungodly to condemnation	Jude		4
Ministers ordained to:			
Preach and to heal	Mark	3	15
Be a witness	Acts	1	22
Do good works	Eph.	2	10
Offer gifts and sacrifices	I Chr.	9	9
order			
Necessary in the churches	I Cor.	14	40
	Tit.	1	5
Set thine house in *o*	II Ki.	20	1
	Is.	38	1
A land without *o*	Job	10	22
Would *o* my cause	Job	23	4
Steps of a good man are *o* by the Lord	Ps.	37	23
I will set them in *o*	Ps.	50	21
The *o* of Melchizedek	Ps.	110	4
	Heb.	5	6
	Heb.	6	20
	Heb.	7	11
Every man shall rise in his *o*	I Cor.	15	23
ordinance			
Made a statute and an *o*	Ex.	15	25
The *o* of God	Is.	58	2
	Rom.	13	2
Gone away from mine *o*	Mal.	3	7
Commandments contained in *o*	Eph.	2	15
Handwriting of *o*	Col.	2	14
In carnal *o*	Heb.	9	10
Submit to every *o* of man	I Pet.	2	13
organ *a wind instrument*			
Jubal, the father of all who handle	Gen.	4	21
Used for festive occasions	Job	21	12
Praise the Lord with	Ps.	150	4
Orion *a fool*			
A constellation	Job	9	9
Divinely made	Amos	5	8
ornaments *decorations*			
Of apparel, used as gifts	Gen.	24	22
Useful as well as ornamental	Gen.	38	18
	II Sam.	1	10
Symbol of an office of high rank	Gen.	41	42
	Dan.	5	7
Not worn in mourning	Ex.	33	4
Brought as offerings	Ex.	35	22
Used in the temple	I Ki.	7	48–50
Worn profusely	Is.	3	18–23
Of the spirit	I Pet.	3	4
Ornan *see* Araunah			
Orpah *neck*			
Daughter-in-law of Naomi	Ruth	1	4, 14

orphans *children who lose their parents*			
Shall not afflict	Ex.	22	22–24
Shall rejoice and keep the law	Deut.	16	11, 14
Should be helped	Deut.	24	17–22
Cruelty to	Job	22	9
	Job	24	3, 9
Lord protects	Ps.	27	10
James' injunction	James	1	27
Osee *see* Hosea			
Oshea *see* Joshua			
osprey *a hawk*			
Unclean	Lev.	11	13
ossifrage *the eagle*			
Unclean	Lev.	11	13
ostentation *pretentions show*			
For a purpose	II Sam.	15	1–6
False pride	Esth.	1	3, 4
Causes self-exaltation	Esth.	5	11, 12
Boastfulness a form of	Prov.	25	14
Improper in sacrifice	Mat.	6	2, 16
Of hypocrites	Mat.	23	1–7
Humility better than	Luke	18	10–14
Blasphemous	Acts	12	20–23
ostrich			
God deprives of wisdom	Job	39	13–17
Noted for its speed	Job	39	18
Cruel	Lam.	4	3
Othneil *power of God*			
Brother of Caleb	Josh.	15	16, 17
Takes niece to wife	Judg.	1	11–15
First judge of Israel	Judg.	3	9–11
Father of Hathath	I Chr.	4	13
ouches *jewels, ornaments*			
Setting for precious stones	Ex.	28	11, 12
To fasten materials	Ex.	39	18
ought			
That *o* not to be done	Gen.	20	9
No such thing *o* to be	II Sam.	13	12
To know what Israel *o*	I Chr.	12	32
None *o* to carry the ark but	I Chr.	15	2
O ye not to walk in the?	Neh.	5	9
To him who *o* to be feared	Ps.	76	11
These *o* ye to have done	Mat.	23	23
	Luke	11	42
Desolation standing where it *o* not	Mark	13	14
Hour what ye *o* to say	Luke	12	12
That men *o* always to pray	Luke	18	1
O fools, *o* not Christ to?	Luke	24	26
The place where men *o*	John	4	20
O to wash one another's feet	John	13	14
And by our law he *o* to die	John	19	7
We *o* to obey God	Acts	5	29
O not to think the Godhead	Acts	17	29
Ye *o* to be quiet, and to do	Acts	19	36
How so labouring ye *o* to	Acts	20	35
That they *o* not to circumcise	Acts	21	21
Who *o* to have been here	Acts	24	19
Judgement seat, where do I *o* to	Acts	25	10
That I *o* to do many things	Acts	26	9
What to pray for as we *o*	Rom.	8	26
More highly than he *o*	Rom.	12	3
We *o* to bear the infirmities of	Rom.	15	1
Nothing as he *o* to know	I Cor.	8	2
O not to cover his head	I Cor.	11	7
The woman *o* to have power	I Cor.	11	10
Of whom I *o* to rejoice	II Cor.	2	3
I *o* to have been commended	II Cor.	12	11
So *o* men to love their	Eph.	5	28
May speak boldly, as I *o* to speak	Eph.	6	20
	Col.	4	4
Know how ye *o* to answer	Col.	4	6
How ye *o* to walk	I Thes.	4	1
Know how ye *o* to follow	II Thes.	3	7
Speaking things which they *o* not	I Tim.	5	13
Teaching things which they *o* not	Tit.	1	11
We *o* to give the more	Heb.	2	1
He *o* for people and for himself	Heb.	5	3
These things *o* not so to be	James	3	10
For that ye *o* to say, If the	James	4	15
Persons *o* ye to be?	II Pet.	3	11
O himself also to walk	I John	2	6
O to lay down our lives for	I John	3	16
If God loved us, we *o* also	I John	4	11
We therefore *o* to receive	III John		8

outcasts

Of Israel gathered together	Ps.	147	2
	Is.	11	12
Jews in Egypt	Is.	27	13
Jews in Elam	Jer.	49	36
To be protected	Is.	16	3, 4
Received by Christ	Mat.	8	2, 3

outlandish *foreign*

Sins of Solomon caused by outlandish women	I Ki.	11	4
	Neh.	13	26

outlaw *the lawless*

Barabbas called	Mark	15	7

oven *a chamber for baking*

Preparation of meat in	Lev.	2	4
Unclean should be destroyed	Lev.	11	35
Bread made in	Lev.	26	26
Figurative	Ps.	21	9
	Hosea	7	4, 6, 7
	Mal.	4	1
	Mat.	6	30
Black	Lam.	5	10

overcome

A troop shall *o* him	Gen.	49	19
A man whom wine hath *o*	Jer.	23	9
A stronger shall *o*	Luke	11	22
I have *o* the world	John	16	33
Be not *o* of evil, but *o* evil with good	Rom.	12	21
Victory that *o* the world	I John	5	4
To him that *o* will I give to eat of tree of life	Rev.	2	7
	Rev.	2	11, 26
	Rev.	3	5, 12, 21

overseer *supervisor*

Of a household	Gen.	39	4
Of the vineyards	I Chr.	27	27
Of the herds	I Chr.	27	29
Of the flocks	I Chr.	27	31
Solomon has many	II Chr.	2	18
The bishop	Acts	20	17, 28

oversight

Peradventure it was an *o*	Gen.	43	12
The *o* of the house of God	Neh.	13	4
Taking the *o*, not by constraint	I Pet.	5	2

overtake

Up, when thou dost *o*	Gen.	44	4
I will pursue, I will *o*	Ex.	15	9
Lest avenger of blood *o*	Deut.	19	6
Shall come and *o* thee	Deut.	28	2
These curses shall *o* thee	Deut.	15	45
Them, for ye shall *o* them	Josh.	2	5
Shall I *o* them?			
Pursue: for thou shalt surely *o* them	I Sam.	30	8
Lest Absalom *o* us	II Sam.	15	14
Neither doth justice *o* us	Is.	59	9
Ye feared shall *o* you	Jer.	42	16
She shall not *o* her lovers	Hosea	2	7
Gibeah did not *o* them	Hosea	10	9
Not *o* nor prevent us	Amos	9	10
Behold, the plowman shall *o*	Amos	9	13
Should *o* you as a thief	I Thes.	5	4

overthrow

I will not *o* this city	Gen.	19	21
Thou shalt *o* their gods	Ex.	23	24
Purposed to *o* my goings	Ps.	140	4
Yet forty days, and Nineveh shall be *o*	Jonah	3	4
If it be of God, ye cannot *o* it	Acts	5	39
O the faith of some	II Tim.	2	18

overwhelm

Ye *o* the fatherless	Job	6	27
Horror hath *o* me	Ps.	55	5
When my heart is *o*	Ps.	61	2
My spirit was *o*	Ps.	77	3
	Ps.	142	3
	Ps.	143	4
Then the water had *o* us	Ps.	124	4

owe

Pay me that thou *o*	Mat.	18	28
How much *o* thou?	Luke	16	5, 7
O no man any thing (See Philem. 18, f.)	Rom.	13	8

owl *a nocturnal bird of prey*

Unclean	Lev.	11	11, 16
Nocturnal	Ps.	102	2, 6
Figuratively	Is.	34	14, 15

own

Of thine *o* have we given thee	I Chr.	29	14
Our lips are our *o*	Ps.	12	4
Do what I will with mine *o*	Mat.	20	15
He came to his *o*, and his *o* received him not	John	1	11
Having loved his *o*	John	13	1
World would love his *o*	John	15	19
Ye are not your *o*	I Cor.	6	19
Let no man seek his *o*	I Cor.	10	24
Charity seeketh not her *o*	I Cor.	13	5
All seek their *o* things	Phil.	2	21

ox

Not to be coveted	Ex.	20	17
Stealing of	Ex.	22	1
Going astray	Ex.	23	4
Canaanite's to be killed	I Sam.	12	3
Eat grass	Job	40	15
Knoweth his owner	Is.	1	3
Face on Ezekiel's creature	Ezek.	1	10
Used for sacrifice	Ex.	20	24
Used for drawing wagons	Num.	7	3
A clean animal	Deut.	14	4
Not to be yoked with an ass	Deut.	22	10
Not to be muzzled	Deut.	25	4
Used for plowing	I Ki.	19	19
A strong animal	Ps.	144	14
Sold in the temple	John	2	15
See bull, bullock			

ox goad *a pointed rod*

Used in battle	Judg.	3	31
	I Sam.	13	21
Symbolic of mental incentive	Eccl.	12	11
For the unruly	Acts	9	5
	Acts	26	14

Ozem *strength*

Son of Jesse	I Chr.	2	13, 15
Son of Jerahmeel	I Chr.	2	25

Ozias *see* Uzziah

P

pacify *tranquilize*

Esau of Jacob	Gen.	32	10–20
Wise man	Prov.	16	14
Anger and wrath	Prov.	21	14
By yielding	Eccl.	10	4

Padan-aram *tableland of Aram*

A region, home of Rebekah	Gen.	25	20
Jacob goes to	Gen.	28	6, 7

paddle *a tool*

Used to dig	Deut.	23	13

Pahath-moab *pit of Moab*

Descendants return from Babylon	Ezra	2	6
Sons took strange wives	Ezra	10	17, 30
Father of Hashub	Neh.	3	11
Seals covenant	Neh.	10	14

pain *suffering*

Of childbirth	I Sam.	4	19, 20
	Is.	21	3
Of the flesh	Job	14	22
All the days of the wicked	Job	15	20
God chastens with	Job	33	19
Of hell	Ps.	116	3
At the very heart	Jer.	4	19
Perpetual	Jer.	15	18
Affliction of exile	Lam.	3	5
Of death	Acts	2	24
Fifth vial	Rev.	16	10
None in heaven	Rev.	21	4

paint *pigment, portray*

The face	II Ki.	9	30
The eyes	Jer.	4	30
	Ezek.	23	40
Rooms	Jer.	22	14
Murals	Ezek.	8	7–12
Portraiture	Ezek.	23	14

palace *official residence of a sovereign*

Of Solomon	I Ki.	7	1–12
A place for archives	Ezra	6	2
Of Babylon	Dan.	4	29
Proclamations issued in	Amos	3	9
For kings	I Ki.	21	1
	Amos	1	12
Of David	II Sam.	7	2
At Shushan	Esth.	1	2
Proclamations from	Amos	3	9

Palestine, Palenstina *land of strangers*

Judgment of	Ex.	15	14
	Is.	14	29, 31
Land of Israel	I Sam.	13	19
Holy land	Zech.	2	12
Land of promise	Heb.	11	9

palm *various meanings*

Cut off	I Sam.	5	4
Engraved	Is.	49	16
Of priest	Lev.	14	15
Of Idol	I Sam.	5	4
Officer strikes Jesus with	John	18	22
Found in oasis	Ex.	15	27
At the feast of the tabernacles	Lev.	23	40
	Neh.	8	15
City of palm trees	Deut.	34	3
A judge dwells under	Judg.	4	5
Carvings of	I Ki.	6	29, 32
Symbol of prosperity	Ps.	92	12
In Ezekiel's vision	Ezek.	40	16
	Ezek.	41	18
Symbolic of triumph	John	12	12, 13
	Rev.	7	9

palmerworm *a larva destructive to fruit trees*

Voracious	Joel	1	4
Devours gardens	Amos	4	9

palsy *paralysis*

Healed by Jesus	Mat.	8	5–13
Healed by Philip	Acts	8	7
Healed by Peter	Acts	9	33–35

Pamphylia *southern Asia Minor*

A region in Egypt	Acts	2	10
Paul preaches here	Acts	14	24, 25
John Mark turns back	Acts	13	13

pan

Flat plate for baking, and a deeper vessel for holding liquids	Lev.	2	5

panic *unreasoning fear*

Of Army	Lev.	26	17
	Josh.	23	10
From God	Gen.	35	5
	Ex.	14	10–12
	Judg.	7	22
	I Sam.	14	15–20

paper *papyrus*

Used in apostolic times	II John		12
Made of reeds	Is.	19	7

Paphos *hot*

A city of Cyprus visited by Paul	Acts	13	6, 13

paps *breasts of a woman*

Abuse of, denounced	Ezek.	23	21
Of Mary blessed	Luke	11	27
Of a harlot	Ezek.	23	21

parables *story pictures*
Remarkable, of the Old Testament:

Trees addressed by Jotham	Judg.	9	8–15
David's sin told in	II Sam.	12	1–14
Woman of Tekoah	II Sam.	14	6–11
The escaped prisoner	I Ki.	20	35–40
The unfruitful vineyard	Is.	5	1–6
The plowman	Is.	28	24–28

Of Christ:

Wise and foolish builders	Mat.	7	24–27
Children of the bride-chamber	Mat.	9	15
New cloth and old garment	Mat.	9	16
New wine and old bottles	Mat.	9	17
Unclean spirit	Mat.	12	43
Sower	Mat.	13	3, 18
Tares	Mat.	13	24–30
	Mat.	13	36–43
Mustard seed	Mat.	13	31, 32
Leaven	Mat.	13	33
Treasure hid in a field	Mat.	13	44
Pearl of great price	Mat.	13	45, 46

Net cast into the sea	Mat.	13	46–50
Meats defiling pot	Mat.	15	10–15
Unmerciful servant	Mat.	18	23–25
Labourers hired	Mat.	20	1–16
Two sons	Mat.	21	28–32
Wicked husbandmen	Mat.	21	33–45
Marriage feast	Mat.	22	2–14
Fig tree leafing	Mat.	24	32–34
Man of the house watching	Mat.	24	43
Faithful and evil servants	Mat.	24	45–51
Ten virgins	Mat.	25	1–13
Talents	Mat.	25	14–30
Kingdom divided against itself	Mark	3	24, 25
Strong man armed	Mark	3	27
Lighted candle	Mark	4	21
Seed growing secretly	Mark	4	26–29
Man taking a far journey	Mark	13	34–37
Blind leading the blind	Luke	6	39
Beam and mote	Luke	6	41, 42
Tree and its fruit	Luke	6	43–45
Creditor and debtors	Luke	7	41–47
Good Samaritan	Luke	10	30–37
Importunate friend	Luke	11	5–9
Rich fool	Luke	12	16–21
Cloud and wind	Luke	12	54–57
Barren fig tree	Luke	13	6–9
Men bidden to a feast	Luke	14	7–11
Builder of a tower	Luke	14	28–30, 33
King going to war	Luke	14	31–33
Savour of salt	Luke	14	34, 35
Lost sheep	Luke	15	3–7
Lost piece of silver	Luke	15	8–10
Prodigal son	Luke	15	11–32
Unjust steward	Luke	16	1–8
Rich man and Lazarus	Luke	16	19–31
Importunate widow	Luke	18	1–8
Pharisee and Publican	Luke	18	9–14
Pounds	Luke	19	12–27
Good shepherd	John	10	1–6
Vine and branches	John	15	1–5
Purpose of	Mat.	13	10–16, 34, 35

paradise *pleasure ground*

Place of glorified spirits	Luke	23	43
	II Cor.	12	4
	Rev.	2	7

See Eden and heaven

paradox *two meanings*

Rich-poor	Prov.	13	7
Findeth-loses	Mat.	10	39
	Mark	8	35
Love life-loses it	John	12	25
Wiseman-fool	I Cor.	3	18
Honor-dishonor	II Cor.	6	4
Weak-strong	II Cor.	12	4
Gain-loss	Phil.	3	7
Answer a fool-do not	Prov.	26	4, 5

Paran, El-paran *place of caves, in Sinai*

A place in Canaan	Gen.	14	6
Desert or wilderness of	Gen.	21	21
	Num.	10	12
	Num.	12	16
	Num.	13	3, 26
	Deut.	1	1
Israelites encamp in	Num.	12	16
David takes refuge in	I Sam.	25	1
Hadad flees to	I Ki.	11	17, 18
Mountain of	Deut.	33	2
	Heb.	3	3

Parbar *suburb*

Place between wall of temple and the city beyond	I Chr.	26	18

parcel *portion, fragment*

Of ground	Gen.	33	19
	I Chr.	11	13

parched *dry and hot*

Corn	Lev.	23	14
	Ruth	2	14
Ground	Is.	35	7

parchments *skins of animals prepared for writing on*

Paul requests	II Tim.	4	13

pardon *set free*

Of sin	Job	7	21
	Ps.	25	11
	Jer.	33	8
	Jer.	50	20

Not *p* your transgressions	Ex.	23	21
P our iniquity	Ex.	34	9
The Lord *p* thy servant	II Ki.	5	18
The good Lord *p* every one	II Chr.	30	18
A God ready to *p*	Neh.	9	17
He will abundantly *p*	Is.	55	7
Who is a God like unto thee that *p* iniquity?	Mic.	7	18

parent *a father or mother*

Covenant benefits for children also	Gen.	6	18
Involved in children's wickedness	I Sam.	2	27–36
	I Sam.	4	10–22

Partiality of:

Isaac for Esau	Gen.	25	28
Rebekah for Jacob	Gen.	25	28
	Gen.	27	6–17
Jacob for Joseph	Gen.	33	2
	Gen.	37	3
Jacob for Benjamin	Gen.	42	4
	Gen.	48	22

Parental affection exemplified:

By Hagar	Gen.	21	15, 16
Rebekah's mother	Gen.	24	55
Isaac and Rebekah	Gen.	25	28
Isaac	Gen.	27	26, 27
Laban	Gen.	31	26–28
Jacob	Gen.	37	3, 4
	Gen.	42	4, 38
	Gen.	45	26–28
Moses' mother	Ex.	2	1–10
Naomi	Ruth	1	8, 9
Hannah	I Sam.	2	19
David	II Sam.	12	18–23
	II Sam.	18	5, 12, 13, 33
Rizpah	II Sam.	21	10
Mother of infant brought to Solomon	I Ki.	3	22–28
Mary	Mat.	12	46
	Luke	2	48
	John	2	5
	John	19	25
Jairus	Mark	5	22, 23
Father of demoniac	Mark	9	17, 22, 24
Nobleman	John	4	49

Indulgent:

Eli	I Sam.	2	27–29
	I Sam.	3	13, 14
David	I Ki.	1	6

Paternal blessings:

Of Noah	Gen.	9	24, 26, 27
Of Abraham	Gen.	17	18
Of Isaac	Gen.	27	10–40
	Gen.	28	3, 4
Of Jacob	Gen.	48	15–20
	Gen.	49	1–28

Paternal reproaches:

Of Noah	Gen.	9	24, 25
Of Jacob	Gen.	49	4, 5, 7

Prayers in behalf of children:

Of Hannah	I Sam.	1	27
Of David	II Sam.	7	25–29
	II Sam.	12	16
	I Chr.	17	16–27
	I Chr.	29	19
Of Job	Job	1	5
See duties			

parlor *speaking chamber*

King's audience chamber	Judg.	3	20, 23–25
Samuel entertains Saul	I Sam.	9	22
In the sanctuary	I Chr.	28	11

Parmenas *steadfast*

One of first seven deacons	Acts	6	5

Parosh, Pharosh *flea*

His children return from captivity	Ezra	2	3
	Ezra	8	3
Ones who had taken strange wives	Ezra	10	25
Father of Pedaiah who helped build the wall	Neh.	3	25
Family that signed the covenant	Neh.	10	14

Parshandatha *prayer-given*

Son of Haman	Esth.	9	7

part *fraction of the whole*

Mary chooses the good	Luke	10	42
Prophesy in	I Cor.	13	9
Ye have no *p* in the Lord	Josh.	22	25
If ought but death *p* thee and me	Ruth	1	17

We have no *p* in David	II Sam.	20	1
Their inward *p* is very wickedness	Ps.	5	9
They *p* my garments	Ps.	22	18
In hidden *p* make me know wisdom	Ps.	51	6
The Lord taketh my *p*	Ps.	118	7
He that is not against us is on our *p*	Mark	9	40
Mary hath chosen that good *p*	Luke	10	42
While he blessed them, he was *p* from them	Luke	24	51
Thou hast no *p* with me	John	13	8
Four *p*, to every soldier a *p*	John	19	23
P them to all men	Acts	2	45
Thou hast neither *p* nor lot in this matter	Acts	8	21
We know in *p*, and we prophesy in *p*	I Cor.	13	9
What *p* hath he that believeth with an infidel?	II Cor.	6	15
Himself took *p* of the same	Heb.	2	14

partaker *one sharing*

P with adulters	Ps.	50	18
Not be *p* in blood of prophets	Mat.	23	30
P of their spiritual things	Rom.	15	27
P with the altar?	I Cor.	9	13
P of that one bread	I Cor.	10	17
P of the Lord's table	I Cor.	10	21
P of the heavenly calling	Heb.	3	1
P of Christ's suffering	I Pet.	4	13
A *p* of the glory	I Pet.	5	1
Be *p* of the divine nature	II Pet.	1	4

Parthians *inhabitants of Parthis*

At Pentecost	Acts	2	9

partial *not complete*

But have been *p* in law	Mal.	2	9
Are ye not then *p* in?	James	2	4

partiality

Observe these things, doing nothing by *p*	I Tim.	5	21
Without *p* and without	James	3	17

partner *one who shares*

Simon, James and John	Luke	5	10
Paul and Titus	II Cor.	8	23
Paul and Philemon	Phil.		17
For help	Eccl.	4	9, 10

partridge

Esteemed as food	I Sam.	26	20
Used figuratively	Jer.	17	11

Paruah *blooming*

Father of Jehoshaphat	I Ki.	4	17

paschal lamb

A male of the first year, without blemish	Ex.	12	5
Instructions regarding slaughter and preparation	Ex.	12	5–11
Blood of, sprinkled on lintel and door posts	Ex.	12	22
	Heb.	9	13, 14
Always eaten with unleavened bread at the passover	Ex.	12	39
A type of Christ	I Cor.	5	7
See feasts and festivals			

Pas-dammim *see Ephes-dammim*

Pashur *freedom*

Descendants return from captivity	Ezra	2	38
A priest, son of Malchaiah	Neh.	11	12
A covenant-signer	Neh.	10	1, 3
Son of Immer and governor of the temple	Jer.	20	1–3, 6
Father of Gedaliah	Jer.	38	1

pass

God will bring it to *p*	Gen.	41	32
When I see the flood, I will *p* over	Ex.	12	13
Cover thee while I *p* by	Ex.	33	22
When thou *p* through waters	Is.	43	2
Till heaven and earth *p*	Mat.	5	18
Let this cup *p*	Mat.	26	39
	Mark	14	36
Neither can they *p* to us	Luke	16	26
Is *p* from death to life	John	5	24
	I John	3	14
Fashion of this world *p* away	I Cor.	7	31
Old things are *p*	II Cor.	5	17
Love of Christ, which *p* knowledge	Eph.	3	19
Peace of God, which *p* all understanding	Phil.	4	7
The heavens shall *p* away	II Pet.	3	10

passenger

Foolish woman calls to	Prov.	9	15
Valley of	Ezek.	39	11
Witnesses of great death	Ezek.	39	14, 15

passion *suffering*

Last sufferings of Jesus	Acts	1	3
Kindred feelings	Acts	14	15
	James	5	17

passover *see* feasts and festivals

past

Bitterness of death is *p*	I Sam.	15	32
God requireth that which is *p*	Eccl.	3	15
The harvest is *p*	Jer.	8	20
Ways *p* finding out	Rom.	11	33
Being *p* feeling	Eph.	4	19

pastor *shepherd*

Unfaithful punished	Jer.	23	2
Keeper of the Lord's flocks	Eph.	4	11
	Jer.	2	8

pasture

Thy servants have no *p*	Gen.	47	4
They went to seek *p*	I Chr.	4	39
They found fat *p*	I Chr.	4	40
Because there was *p*	I Chr.	4	41
Of the mountains is his *p*	Job	39	8
Why doth thine anger smoke against sheep of they *p*?	Ps.	74	1
So we sheep of thy *p* will	Ps.	79	13
People of his *p*	Ps.	95	7
	Ps.	100	3
Wild asses, a *p* of flocks	Is.	32	14
Scatter sheep of my *p*	Jer.	23	1
Hath spoiled their *p*	Jer.	25	36
Like harts that find no *p*	Lam.	1	6
Them in a good *p*, a fat *p*	Ezek.	34	14
Small thing to have eaten good *p*	Ezek.	34	18
Ye my flock of my *p* are	Ezek.	34	31
According to their *p* so	Hosea	13	6
Because they have no *p*	Joel	1	18
Go in and out an find *p*	John	10	9

patara

A Lycian city, visited by Paul	Acts	21	1, 2

path

Angel of Lord stood in *p*	Num.	22	24
A *p* which no fowl knoweth	Job	28	7
Show me the *p* of life	Ps.	16	11
Lead me in a plain *p*	Ps.	27	11
Thy *p* is in the great waters	Ps.	77	19
Thy word is a light unto my *p*	Ps.	119	105
Thou compassest my *p*	Ps.	139	3
The *p* of the just	Prov.	4	18
We will walk in his *p*	Is.	2	3
	Mic.	4	2
In *p* they have not known	Is.	42	16
Ask for the old *p*	Jer.	6	16
Make his *p* straight	Mat.	3	3
	Mark	1	3
	Luke	3	4
Make straight *p* for feet	Heb.	12	13

Pathros *land in southern Egypt*

Descendant of Mizraim	Gen.	10	14
	I Chr.	1	12
Jewish captives in	Is.	11	11
	Jer.	44	1, 15
	Ezek.	29	14
Prophecy against	Ezek.	30	14

patience *endurance*
Instances of:

Isaac toward people	Gen.	26	15–22
Moses	Ex.	16	7, 8
Job	Job	1	21
	James	5	11
David	Ps.	40	1
Simeon	Luke	2	25
The Thessalonians	II Thes.	1	4
Paul	II Tim.	3	10
Prophets	James	5	10
John	Rev.	1	9
The church at Ephesus	Rev.	2	2, 3
The church at Thyatira	Rev.	2	18, 19
Commended	Eccl.	7	8
	Is.	40	31
	Rom.	12	12
	II Thes.	3	5
	I Tim.	6	11
	James	5	7
Blessings resulting from	Rom.	15	4
	Rev.	2	2
	Rev.	3	10

Patmos *an island in the Aegean Sea*

John an exile on	Rev.	1	9

patriarch *father*

Head of the family	Acts	2	29
	Acts	7	8, 9
	Heb.	7	4

patriotism

Pledge of allegiance	Deut.	26	1–11
Beseeching God for blessing on the land	Ps.	85	1–13
Pray for peace of Jerusalem	Ps.	122	6
In exile	Ps.	137	1–6
Moses	Heb.	11	24–26
Uriah	II Sam.	11	11
Nehemiah	Neh.	1	2, 4–11

Patrobas *paternal*

Roman Christian	Rom.	16	14

pattern *arrangement*

Of the tabernacle, etc.	Ex.	25	9, 40
	Ezek.	43	10
	Heb.	8	5
P which the Lord had showed	Num.	8	4
In me Christ might show *p*	I Tim.	1	16
Showing thyself a *p* of good works	Tit.	2	7
Was necessary that *p* of things	Heb.	9	23

Paul *little*

Consents to stoning of Stephen	Acts	7	58
Also called Saul	Acts	8	1
Persecutes the Christians	Acts	8	3
	Acts	9	1, 2
His vision and conversion	Acts	9	3–22
	Acts	22	4–19
	I Tim.	1	12, 13
Born in Tarsus	Acts	9	11
A tentmaker, by trade	Acts	18	3
Steadfast and faithful	Acts	20	24
	II Tim.	4	7, 8
A strict religious heritage	Acts	21	40
	Gal.	1	14
Educated at Jerusalem, taught by Gamaliel	Acts	22	3
Courageous	Acts	22	25
Called to be an apostle	Acts	22	14–21
	II Tim.	1	1, 11
A Roman citizen	Acts	22	25–28
Of the tribe of Benjamin	Rom.	11	1
Parisee	Phil.	3	5
Patient and loving	II Cor.	2	4
A fully dedicated man	Phil.	3	7, 8
Possibly a widower	I Cor.	9	5

Preparation for missionary journeys:

Instructed by Ananias	Acts	9	6
Preaches in Damascus	Acts	9	20, 22
Presecuted by the Jews	Acts	9	23
Received by the disciples in Jerusalem	Acts	9	26–29
Befriended by Barnabas	Acts	11	25, 26
Teaches in Antioch	Acts	11	26
Directed by a vision	Acts	22	17–22
Let down the wall in a basket	Gal.	1	17
Goes to Arabia, then returns to Damascus	Gal.	1	17
Interviews Peter and James	Gal.	1	18

His first missionary journey:

Accompanied by Barnabas	Acts	13	1–4
Sails to Cyprus	Acts	13	4
Assisted by John Mark	Acts	13	5–13
Name changed to Paul	Acts	13	9
Visits Perga in Pamphylia	Acts	13	13
Preaches in the synagogue at Antioch in Pisidia	Acts	13	14–41
Persecuted and expelled	Acts	13	50, 51
Stoned at Lystra	Acts	14	8–19
Went to Derbe	Acts	14	20, 21
Returns to Antioch	Acts	14	26
Attends council at Jerusalem	Acts	15	1–35
Argues against circumcision of Gentiles	Acts	15	1, 2
Reports to the apostles of work among the Gentiles	Acts	15	12
Returns to Antioch with letters to the Gentiles	Acts	15	22, 25

His second missionary journey:

Rejects John Mark	Acts	15	36–40
Accompanied by Silas	Acts	15	40
Travels through Syria and Cilicia	Acts	15	41
Joined by Timothy	Acts	16	1–4
Revisits churches in Galatia	Acts	16	1–6
Called to Macedonia in vision	Acts	16	9, 10
Luke accompanies	Acts	16	10

At Philippi, Lydia becomes first European Christian convert	Acts	16	13-15
Persecuted and imprisoned	Acts	16	19-34
Travels to Thessalonica	Acts	17	1-9
Accepted by Bereans	Acts	17	10-13
Visits Athens and disputes with Grecians on Mars' hill	Acts	17	16-34
Writes I and II Thessalonians	I Thes.	1	1
	II Thes.	1	1
Established church in Corinth	Acts	18	7-11
Stopped at Ephesus	Acts	18	19-21

His third missionary journey:

Establishes church in Ephesus	Acts	19	1-8
Writes Galatians	Gal.	1	1, 2
	I Cor.		
Proceeds to Macedonia	Acts	20	1-6
Performs miracles	Acts	20	6-12
Sails by Ephesus to Jerusalem	Acts	20	16, 17
Charge to the elders at Ephesus	Acts	20	17-38
Warned not to go to Jerusalem, but proceeds	Acts	21	11
Received by the church in Jerusalem	Acts	21	15-19
Seized by the Jews	Acts	21	27-40
His defense	Acts	22	1-29
Escorted to Caesarea	Acts	23	23-33
His trial before Felix	Acts	24	1-27
In prison two years	Acts	24	27
His examination before Agrippa	Acts	25	13-27
Taken of Rome in custody of Julius	Acts	27	1-5
Overtaken by storm	Acts	27	14-20
Shipwrecked, spends 3 months on island of Melita	Acts	27	14-44
In Rome, no case against him	Acts	28	17-29
Preaches here two years	Acts	28	30, 31
His farewell words	II Tim.	4	6-22

Paulus, Sergius see Sergius Paulus

pauper *poor, beggar*

Lazarus	Luke	16	19-23

pavement *beaten floor*

Of stones	II Ki.	16	17
At the temple	II Cor.	7	3
In the palace at Sushan	Esth.	1	6
In vision of a city	Ezek.	40	17, 18
Place of judgment	John	19	13

pavilion *canopy, shelter*

Of the king of Syria	I Ki.	20	12
Of the Lord	II Sam.	22	12
	Ps.	27	5
	Ps.	31	20

pawn *pledge, guaranty*

Ordinances concerning	Ex.	22	26
	Deut.	24	10-13, 17
From the widow	Job	24	3
Bed	Prov.	22	27
Should be returned	Ezek.	18	5, 7, 12
	Ezek.	33	15
Clothes by altar	Amos	2	8

pawnbroker *one who loans money*

Ordinance concerning	Deut.	24	10-13

paws *feet of an animal*

David delivered from	I Sam.	17	37

pay

Shalt not slack to **p** vow	Deut.	23	21
Will **p** my vows	Ps.	22	25
	Ps.	66	13
	Ps.	116	14
Vow, and **p** to the Lord	Ps.	76	11
Defer not to **p** it	Eccl.	5	4
I will **p** thee all	Mat.	18	26
P that thou owest	Mat.	18	28
Ye **p** tithe of mint, arise	Mat.	23	23
For this cause **p** tribute	Rom.	13	6

peace, spirtual

Christ is the prince of	Is.	9	6
God ordains	Is.	26	12
Denied to the wicked	Is.	48	22
Through the atonement of Christ	Is.	53	5
Established by covenant	Is.	54	10
Announced by angels	Luke	2	14
Gift of God	Acts	10	36
Christ gives	John	14	27
	John	16	33
	II Thes.	3	16
Christ is our peace	Eph.	2	14

Accompanies:

Acquaintance with God	Job	22	21
The love of God's law	Ps.	119	165
Righteousness	Is.	32	17
Faith	Rom.	15	13

peace, military

Of a city	Jer.	29	7
	Deut.	20	10
Millennial	Hosea	2	18
	Is.	2	4
Jabin and Heber	Judg.	4	17
Israel and Amorites	I Sam.	7	14
Of Solomon	I Ki.	4	24

peacemakers

Job promised to	Prov.	12	20
Happy are the	Mat.	5	9

peace offering see offerings

peacock *eye-feathered cock*

Imported from Tarshish	II Chr.	9	21

pearl

Wisdom of greater value	Job	28	18
Parable of	Mat.	13	45, 46
Ornaments made of	I Tim.	2	9
	Rev.	17	4
Merchants have	Rev.	18	12, 16
Figurative	Mat.	7	6
	Rev.	21	21

Pedaiah *God saved*

Grandfather of King Jehoiakim	II Ki.	23	36
Father of Zerubbabel	I Chr.	3	18, 19
Father of Joel	I Chr.	27	20
Son of Parosh	Neh.	3	25
Levite treasurer	Neh.	8	4
	Neh.	13	13
A Benjamite	Neh.	11	7

pedigrees *ancestral line*

Numbering of the tribe	Num.	1	18
Not having	Heb.	7	3, 6
Priests rejected for not having	Neh.	7	64

peevishness *fretfulness, churlishness*

Of Saul	I Sam.	18	8
Of Nabal	I Sam.	25	3

Pekah *open-eyed*

Son of Remaliah and captain of Israel's army	II Ki.	15	25
Conspires against King Pekahiah	II Ki.	15	25
Made king of Israel	II Ki.	15	27
Victorious in war	II Chr.	28	6
Slain by Hoshea	II Ki.	15	30, 31
Prophecies against	Is.	7	1, 4-9
	Is.	8	6-8

Pekahiah *God opens eyes*

King of Israel	II Ki.	15	22-26
Plotted against and slain by Pekah	II Ki.	15	25

Pelatiah *saved of Jehovah*

Son of Hananiah	I Chr.	3	21
A Simeonite warrior	I Chr.	4	42
A covenant-signer	Neh.	10	22
Struck dead for defying Ezekiel	Ezek.	11	1, 13

Peleg, Phalec *division*

Son of Eber	Gen.	10	25
	Gen.	11	16-19
	I Chr.	1	19, 25
	Luke	3	35

Peleth *freedom, separation*

A Reubenite	Num.	16	1
Son of Jonathan	I Chr.	2	33

Pelethites

David's faithful bodyguards	I Ki.	1	38
	II Sam.	8	18
Flee with David from Absalom	II Sam.	15	18

pelicans

Not to be eaten	Lev.	11	18
	Deut.	14	17
Symbol of desolation	Ps.	102	6

Peor see Baal-peor

pen

An iron instrument used for engraving	Job	19	24
	Jer.	17	1
A reed used for writing	III John		13

pence *see* penny
Peniel *see* Penuel
Peninnah *pearl*

Wife of Elkanah	I Sam.	1	2, 4

penitence *see* repentance
penknife *small knife*

Used by Jehudi	Jer.	36	23

penny, pence *a small coin*

A day's pay	Mat.	20	2–13
Bears Caesar's image	Mat.	22	19–21
Inflation of	Rev.	6	6
Worth of bread	Mark	6	37
Debt of one hundred	Mat.	18	28

Pentecost *see* feasts and festivals
Pentecost, day of

Holy Ghost given to the apostles	Acts	2	1–4
	Acts	20	16
Feast of weeks	Deut.	16	10
Feast of harvest	Ex.	23	16
First fruits	Num.	28	26
Institution of	Ex.	23	16
	Lev.	23	15–21
Paul wants to attend in Jerusalem	Acts	20	16

Penuel, Peniel *face of God*

Here Jacob wrestles with an angel	Gen.	32	30
A city	Judg.	8	17
	I Ki.	12	25
Chief of Gedor	I Chr.	4	4
A Benjamite	I Chr.	8	25

penury *poverty*

Contrasted with labour	Prov.	14	23
Widow's	Luke	21	4

people

Of God, their blessing and privileges,	Deut.	7	6
	Deut.	32	9
I will take you for a *p*	Ex.	6	7
	Deut.	4	20
	II Sam.	7	24
	Jer.	13	11
Did ever *p* hear voice of God and live?	Deut.	4	33
Who is like unto thee, O *p*	Deut.	33	29
P I knew not shall serve me.	II Sam.	22	44
	Ps.	18	43
Ye *p* pour out your heart.	Ps.	62	8
Happy is that *p*	Ps.	144	15
Sin is a reproach to any *p*	Prov.	14	34
The ants are a *p* not strong.	Prov.	30	25
A *p* laden with iniquity	Is.	1	4
This is a rebellious *p*	Is.	30	9
	Is.	65	2
A *p* cometh from the north.	Jer.	6	22
	Jer.	50	41
Of what *p* art thou?	Jonah	1	8
P shall flow unto it.	Mic.	4	1
A *p* prepared for the Lord.	Luke	1	17
By them that are no *p*	Rom.	10	19
Purify to himself a peculiar *p*	Tit.	2	14
Remaineth a rest to *p* of God.	Heb.	4	9
Redeemed us out of every *p*	Rev.	5	9

Peor *a cleft, opening*

Mountain of Moab	Num.	23	28
A Moabite deity	Josh.	22	17

Perazim *see* Baal-perazim
perceive *to see, feel*

A heart to *p*	Deut.	29	4
We *p* that the Lord is among us.	Josh.	22	31
I cannot *p* him.	Job	23	8
P that there is nothing better.	Eccl.	3	22
See ye indeed, but *p* not.	Is.	6	9
Deeper speech than thou canst *p*	Is.	33	19
Nor *p* what God hath prepared.	Is.	64	4
Ye shall see, and not *p*	Mat.	13	14
	Mark	4	12
	Acts	28	26
P ye not, neither understand?	Mark	8	17
P not the beam.	Luke	6	41
I *p* that virtue is gone out of me.	Luke	8	46
I *p* that thou art a prophet.	John	4	19
P ye how ye prevail nothing?	John	12	19
P that God is no respecter of persons.	Acts	10	34
P that he had faith.	Acts	14	9
Hereby *p* we the love of God.	I John	3	16

perdition *damnation*

What leads to	Phil.	1	28
	I Tim.	6	9

	Heb.	10	39
	II Pet.	3	7
	Rev.	17	8
Son of	John	17	12
	II Thes.	2	3

Perez, Phares, Pharez *breach*

A Judahite	Gen.	38	29
Father of Pharzites	Num.	26	20
Called Perez	Neh.	11	4, 6
In lineage of Jesus	Mat.	1	3

Perez-uzza, Perez-uzzah *breach of Uzzah*

Name given place where Uzzah dies	II Sam.	6	8
	I Chr.	13	10, 11

perfection *highest degree of excellence*

Of God	Deut.	32	4
	II Sam.	22	31
	Job	36	4
Of God's law	Ps.	19	7
	James	1	25
Of Christ	John	19	4
	Heb.	5	9
	Heb.	7	28
Of saints	Eph.	4	12
	Col.	3	14
	II Tim.	3	17
Sacrifices to be	Lev.	22	21
Commanded to be	Deut.	18	13
	Gen.	17	1
Of peace	Is.	26	3
Of beauty	Ezek.	27	3
Of understanding	Luke	1	3
Of knowledge	Acts	24	22
Of Love	I John	4	18

Ascribed to:

Noah	Gen.	6	8, 9
Jacob	Num.	23	21
David	I Ki.	11	4, 6
Asa	I Ki.	15	14
Job	Job	1	1
Zacharias and Elisabeth	Luke	1	5
Nathanael	John	1	47

perform *to carry out*

P oath I sware to Abraham.	Gen.	26	3
	Deut.	9	5
	Luke	1	72
Not able to *p* it thyself.	Ex.	18	18
Hands cannot *p* their enterprise.	Job	5	12
Unto thee shall the vow be *p*	Ps.	65	1
I have sworn, and I will *p* it.	Ps.	119	106
Zeal of the Lord will *p* this.	Is.	9	7
I will *p* my good word.	Jer.	29	10
	Jer.	33	14
P unto the Lord thine oaths.	Mat.	5	33
Was able also to *p*	Rom.	4	21
How to *p* that which is good I find not.	Rom.	7	18
P it until day of Christ.	Phil.	1	6

performance *a deed, feat*

Blessed	Luke	1	45
Expedient	II Cor.	8	11

perfume

Used in religious rites	Ex.	30	7
	Ex.	35	28
Beds perfumed	Prov.	7	17
Applied to the person	Prov.	27	9
	S. of S.	3	6
	Is.	57	9

Perga *earthy*

A city of Pamphylia	Acts	13	13, 14
Paul preaches in	Acts	14	25

Pergamos *heights, origin of "parchment"*

A city of Mysia	Rev.	1	11
	Rev.	2	12, 13

peril *danger*

Cannot keep us from Christ	Rom.	8	35
Suffered by Paul	II Cor.	11	26
Promised	II Tim.	3	1
Of Christ	Mat.	2	10–15
Of disciples	Mat.	10	22, 23

perish *to die*

If they touch the mountain.	Ex.	19	21
Of beasts	Ps.	12	20
Wicked	Ps.	68	2
	Prov.	11	10
Man shall perish but God will endure	Ps.	102	26
Joy when the wicked	Prov.	11	10
People perish where there is no vision	Prov.	29	18

Those who would perish should call upon God	Jonah	1	6
With the sword	Mat.	26	52
With hunger	Luke	15	17
Believe in Christ should not	John	3	16
The Lord not willing that any	II Pet.	3	9
Disciples thought they would.	Mark	4	38
Christian shall not	John	3	15, 16
Of money	Acts	8	20

Perizzites *villagers*

Tribe of ancient Canaanites	Gen.	13	7
	Gen.	15	20
	Judg.	1	4
Israel given their land.	Ex.	3	8
Dwelt in a woodland area.	Josh.	17	15
Israel dwelt among	Judg.	3	5
Solomon taxed	II Chr.	8	7
Intermarriage with	Ezra	9	1

perjury *false swearing*

Forbidden	Ex.	20	16
	Ezek.	17	16
	I Tim.	1	10

Instances of:

Witnesses against Naboth	I Ki.	21	8–13
Witnesses against David	Ps.	35	11
Witnesses against Jesus	Mat.	26	59
	Mark	14	56, 57
Peter	Mat.	26	74
	Mark	14	71
Stephen	Acts	6	11, 13, 14

pernicious *deadly*

Ways of false teachers	II Pet.	2	2

perpetual *lasting forever*

Priest's office be for *p* statute	Ex.	29	9
Keep sabbath for *p* covenant	Ex.	31	16
Destructions are come to a *p* end	Ps.	9	6
P desolation	Ps.	74	3
	Jer.	25	9
	Ezek.	35	9
	Zeph.	2	9
A *p* backsliding	Jer.	8	5
Why is my pain *p*	Jer.	15	18
Join the Lord in a *p* covenant	Jer.	50	5
The *p* hills	Hab.	3	6

persecution *affliction, harassment*

Of the righteous	Gen.	49	23
	Job	12	4
	Ps.	37	32
	Jer.	26	11–14
Deliverance from	Ps.	124	2–7
Divine chastisement	Lam.	1	3
Results of	Mat.	5	10–12
	Luke	6	22, 23
	I Pet.	4	14
	Rev.	6	9, 11
	Rev.	7	13–17
Conduct under	Mat.	5	44
	Mat.	10	16–23, 28
	Acts	5	41
	Phil.	1	28
	Heb.	10	33, 34
	I Pet.	4	13–19
Foretold	Mat.	13	21
Diffuses the gospel	Acts	8	1, 4

Instances of:

Of Moses	Ex.	2	15
Of Gideon	Judg.	6	28–30
Of Elijah	I Ki.	19	10
Of Elisha	II Ki.	6	31, 32
Of the Jews	Neh.	4	1–3
Of Job	Job	16	1–4
Of David	Ps.	31	13
Of Jeremiah	Jer.	17	15, 18
Of Daniel	Dan.	6	11–13, 16, 17
Of John the Baptist	Mat.	14	3–12
Of the disciples	John	9	22, 34
Of Stephen	Acts	6	9–15
Of James and Peter	Acts	12	2–6

perseverance *persistence*

Blessedness of	James	1	25
A characteristic of saints	Prov.	4	18
An evidence of reconciliation with God	Col.	1	21–23
Is not in vain	I Cor.	15	58
In seeking God	I Chr.	16	11

Promised by God	Ps.	37	24
Maintained through the fear of God	Jer.	32	40
An evidence of discipleship	John	8	31
	Heb.	3	6–14
Exhortations to	Acts	14	22
	Heb.	12	2, 3
In prayer	Rom.	12	12
	Eph.	6	18
In well doing	Gal.	6	9
Leads to success	II Tim.	4	6–8
	II Pet.	1	10–12
Leads to assurance of hope	Heb.	6	10–11
Promised to saints	Job	17	9
Promises to	Mat.	10	22
	Mat.	24	13
	Rev.	2	26–28
Continuing in the faith	Col.	1	23
	II Tim.	4	7
Holding fast hope	Heb.	3	6
Waiting upon God	Hosea	12	6
Well-doing	Rom.	2	7
	II Thes.	3	13

Maintained through:

The intercession of Christ	Luke	22	31–32
	John	17	11
The power of Christ	John	10	28
The power of God	Phil.	1	6

Want of:

Excludes from the benefits of the gospel	Heb.	6	4–6
Illustrated	Mark	4	5, 17
Punished	John	15	6
	Rom.	11	22

Persia *land of Perses*

Israel captive in	II Chr.	36	20
An empire	Esth.	1	1–3
Government of	Esth.	8	8
Advisory princes in	Dan.	6	1–7

Persis *Persian*

A Christian woman at Rome	Rom.	16	12

persistence

The early Christians' example	Acts	2	42
Paul's example	II Cor.	12	7–8
	Acts	20	18–35
The psalmist's example	Ps.	55	17
Christ persisted with Peter	Mat.	26	32–33
	Luke	22	61
	John	21	1–17
God loves and calls with everlasting love	Jer.	31	3
The Lord called Samuel three times	I Sam.	3	8
The Lord reveals himself repeatedly	Heb.	1	1
	Luke	20	9–15
	II Pet.	3	9
Grace abounds	Rom.	5	20
In good things	I Thes.	5	21
	Gal.	6	9
	II Thes.	3	13
The just man's resilience	Prov.	24	16
Peter's continued knocking	Acts	12	16

persons

God no respecter of	Deut.	10	17
	II Chr.	19	7
	Job	34	19
	Acts	10	34
	Rom.	2	11
	Gal.	2	6
	Eph.	6	9
	Col.	3	25
	I Pet.	1	17
Nor honour *p* of mighty	Lev.	19	15
Neither doth God respect any *p*	II Sam.	14	14
Shall save the humble *p*	Job	22	29
Vile *p*	Ps.	15	4
	Is.	32	5
Vain *p*	Ps.	26	4
	Prov.	12	11
	Prov.	28	19
I will not know wicked *p*	Ps.	101	4
Regardest not *p* of men	Mat.	22	16
	Mark	12	14
Innocent of blood of this just *p*	Mat.	27	24
Forgave it in the *p* of Christ	II Cor.	2	10
The express image of his *p*	Heb.	1	3
What manner of *p* ought ye to be	II Pet.	3	11
Having men's *p* in admiration	Jude		16

persuade *try to convince*

We will *p* him, and secure you	Mat.	28	14
Will not be *p* though one rose from dead	Luke	16	31
Almost thou *p* me to be a Christian	Acts	26	28
P them concerning Jesus	Acts	28	23
Let every man be fully *p*	Rom.	14	5
We *p* men	II Cor.	5	11
Do I now *p* men or God	Gal.	1	10
Am *p* that he is able to keep	II Tim.	1	12
Are *p* better things of you	Heb.	6	9

pertain

Things which *p* to God	Rom.	15	17
Things that *p* to this life	I Cor.	6	3
Things *p* to God	Heb.	5	1
All things that *p* to life	II Pet.	1	3

perverse *contrary, stubborn*

A *p* generation	Deut.	32	5
Cannot my taste discern *p* things	Job	6	30
P lips put far from thee	Prov.	4	24
P tongue falleth into mischief	Prov.	17	20
Thine heart shall utter *p* things	Prov.	23	33
O *p* generation	Mat.	17	17
	Luke	9	41
In the midst of a *p* nation	Phil.	2	15
P disputings	I Tim.	6	5

pervert *turn from right way*

A gift doth *p* words of righteous	Deut.	16	19
Thou shalt not *p* judgment of stranger	Deut.	24	17
Doth God *p* judgment	Job	8	3
He that *p* his ways shall be known	Prov.	10	9
Ye have *p* the words of God	Jer.	23	36
Ye that *p* equity	Mic.	3	9
Wilt thou not cease to *p* right ways	Acts	13	10
Would *p* the gospel of Christ	Gal.	1	7

pestilence *the plague*

Sent as a judgment	Lev.	26	16, 25
Threatened for disobedience	Lev.	26	25
	Num.	14	12
	Deut.	28	21
	Jer.	14	12
	Jer.	27	13
	Ezek.	5	12
	Ezek.	6	11
	Ezek.	7	15
	Luke	21	11
Inflicted	Num.	14	37
	Num.	16	46
	Num.	25	9
	II Sam.	24	15
	Ps.	78	50
Removed	Num.	16	47
	II Sam.	24	16
Smite thee with *p*	Ex.	9	15
Deliver thee from noisome *p*	Ps.	91	3
Before him went *p*	Hab.	3	5
There shall be *p*	Mat.	24	7
See plague			

pestle *threshing instrument*

Used symbolically	Prov.	27	22

Peter *stone*

Called as a disciple	Mat.	4	18, 19
	Mark	1	16, 17
Sent forth into service	Mat.	10	2
Walks upon the water	Mat.	14	28–31
Also called Simon Bar-jona and Cephas	Mat.	16	16, 17
	John	1	42
Confesses Jesus to be the Christ	Mat.	16	16
	Mark	8	29
Perfidy foretold by Jesus	Mat.	26	33–35
	Luke	22	31–34
His denial of Jesus and his repentance	Mat.	26	69–75
	Mark	14	66–72
	John	18	17, 18, 25–27
Married	Mark	1	30
Brother of Andrew	Mark	1	16
Questions Jesus concerning His second coming	Mark	13	3, 4
A fisherman	Luke	5	2–6
A favourite apostle	Luke	9	28
Uneducated	Acts	4	13
Cuts off Malchus' ear and is rebuked by Jesus	Luke	22	50–54
Commissioned to feed the flock	John	21	1–23
Son of Jonas	John	21	15
His death foretold	John	21	18, 19

After the resurrection:

Visits the sepulchre	Luke	24	12
Jesus appears to	Luke	24	34
Addresses the disciples	Acts	1	15–22
Preaches at Pentecost	Acts	2	14–40
Heals the lame man	Acts	3	1–6
Accused by the council and his defense	Acts	4	1–23
Foretells the death of Ananias and Sapphira	Acts	5	1–11
Imprisoned; his defense before council	Acts	5	17–42
Gives a courageous answer	Acts	5	29
Is fearless and undaunted	Acts	5	40, 41
Prays for baptism of the Holy Ghost	Acts	8	15–18
Rebukes Simon the sorcerer	Acts	8	18–24
Raises Dorcas from the dead	Acts	9	36–43
Advocates preaching the gospel to the Gentiles	Acts	11	1–18
Imprisoned and liberated by an angel	Acts	12	3–8
His decision regarding circumcision	Acts	15	7–11
Visited by Paul	Gal.	1	18

Pethor *prophet*

Balaam's residence	Num.	22	5

Pethuel *enlarged of God*

Father of Joel	Joel	1	1

petition *formal request*

God grant thee thy *p*	I Sam.	1	17
I desire one small *p*	I Ki.	2	20
What is thy *p*?	Esth.	5	6
	Esth.	7	2
	Esth.	9	12
The Lord fulfil all thy *p*	Ps.	20	5
Maketh his *p* three times a day.	Dan.	6	13
We have the *p* that we desired	I John	5	15

Phalec *see* Peleg

Phanuel *face of God*

Father of Anna	Luke	2	36

Pharaoh *great house*

King of Egypt at the time of Abraham	Gen.	12	14–20
King of Egypt in Joseph's time	Gen.	41	1
King of Egypt at time of exodus	Ex.	3	11
Father-in-law of Solomon	I Ki.	3	1
Ruler of Egypt at time of David	I Ki.	11	17–22
King of Egypt during time of Hezekiah	II Ki.	18	21
Pharaoh-nechoh	II Ki.	23	29
Father-in-law of Mered	I Chr.	4	18
Pharaoh-hophra	Jer.	37	4–7
Shishak	I Ki.	14	25, 26
Tirhakah	II Ki.	19	9

Phares, Pharez *see* Perez

pharisee *separated*

Take counsel against Christ	Mat.	12	14
Seek a sign from Christ	Mat.	12	38
	Mat.	16	1
Christ's controversies with	Mat.	19	3
	Mark	2	18
	Luke	5	30
	Luke	16	14
Fasting	Mat.	9	14
Washing of hands	Mat.	15	1–3
View of sabbath	Mat.	12	2–8
Censured by Christ	Mat.	23	2, 13
People cautioned against	Mark	8	15
Christ entertained by	Luke	11	37
Send officers to take Him	John	7	32
Nicodemus remonstrates with	John	7	50, 51
Contend about circumcision	Acts	15	5
Their belief in the resurrection	Acts	23	8

Celebrated ones:

Simon	Mat.	26	6
Nicodemus	John	3	1
Gamaliel	Acts	5	34
Saul of Tarsus	Acts	23	6

Pharpar *rapid*

A river of Damascus	II Ki.	5	12

Phebe *radiant*

A deaconess of the church at Cenchrea	Rom.	16	1

Phenice, Phenicia *see* Phoenicia

Philadelphia *brotherly love*

A city of Lydia	Rev.	1	11
Church here commended	Rev.	3	7

philanthropy *love of mankind*

Practical	Ex.	2	1–10
Creditable	Jer.	38	6–13

Divine	Mat.	4	23, 24
Noble	Luke	10	30, 33
Pious	Acts	4	34–37
Preference in	Gal.	6	10

Philemon *affectionate*
One of Paul's converts	Phil.	1	1

Philetus *beloved*
A false teacher of Rome	II Tim.	2	17, 18

Philip *lover of horses*
Brother of Herod Antipas and husband of Herodias	Mat.	14	3
	Mark	6	17
	Luke	3	1, 19
One of the twelve apostles	Mark	3	18
Tells Nathaniel of Christ	John	1	43–48
Feeding of the five thousand	John	6	5–7
From Bethsaida	John	1	44
Assists in caring for the multitude	John	6	5–7
Reproved by Christ	John	14	8, 9
Present in the upper room	Acts	1	13
Tetrarch of Ituraea	Luke	3	1
Made deacon	Acts	6	5
Preaches in Samaria	Acts	8	5
Baptizes the eunuch	Acts	8	38
His daughters' prophecies	Acts	21	8, 9

Philippi *pertains to Philip*
A city of Macedonia where Paul is persecuted	Acts	16	12–40
	Acts	20	1–6

Philistia *migration*
A sea coast in the land of the Philistines	Ps.	60	8
Same as Palestina	Is.	14	29

Philistines *wanderers*
Fill up Isaac's wells	Gen.	26	15
Territory of	Ex.	13	17
	Ex.	23	31
Lords of	Josh.	13	3
	Judg.	3	3
	Judg.	16	5, 30
	I Sam.	5	8, 11
	I Sam.	6	5, 12
Their wars with Israel	I Sam.	4	1
	I Sam.	28	1, 4
	I Sam.	29	1, 2
	I Sam.	31	1–3
	II Chr.	21	16
Mentioned in	Ps.	83	7
	Is.	2	6
	Is.	9	12
	Is.	11	14
	Jer.	25	20
Their destruction foretold	Jer.	47	1–7
	Ezek.	25	15
	Zech.	9	6

Also called:
Casluim	Gen.	10	14
Caphtorim	Deut.	2	23
Cherethites	I Sam.	30	14–16

Kings of:
Abimelech I	Gen.	20	2
Abimelech II	Gen.	26	8
Achish	I Sam.	21	10–15

Contend with:
Joshua	Josh.	13	2, 3
Shamgar	Judg.	3	31
Samson	Judg.	14	1–20
	Judg.	16	1–31
Samuel	I Sam.	4	1, 2
Jonathan	I Sam.	14	1–51
Saul	I Sam.	17	46–49
David	I Sam.	17	38–51
Jehoram	II Chr.	21	16
Uzziah	II Chr.	26	6
Hezekiah	II Ki.	18	8

Philologus *fond of words*
A Christian and disciple in Rome	Rom.	16	15

philosophy *love of wisdom or knowledge*
Two classes of	Acts	17	18
Vanity of	Col.	2	8

Phinehas *oracle*
Son of Eleazar, high priest	Ex.	6	25
Slays Zimri and Cozbi	Num.	25	7, 8
	Num.	25	14, 15
Sent against the Midianites	Num.	31	6, 7
Famous in Israel's history	Ps.	106	30

Son of Eli	I Sam.	1	3
His sin	I Sam.	2	12–17
His death	I Sam.	4	4–11
Father of Eleazar	Ezra	8	33

Phlegon *burning*
A Christian of the Roman church	Rom.	16	14

Phoenice, Phenice, Phoenicia *date palm*
A strip of coastland on the Mediterranean, great city of Tyre	Ezek.	27	3
	Ezek.	28	2
Jesus preaches here	Mat.	15	21
Visited by Paul	Acts	15	3

Phoenix *date palm*
A harbor on the coast of Crete	Acts	27	12

Phrygia *a province of Asia Minor*
Represented at Pentecost	Acts	2	10
Paul in	Acts	16	3, 6
	Acts	18	23

Phut, Put *a bow*
Son of Ham	Gen.	10	6
Country occupied by the descendants of	Ezek.	27	10
	Nah.	3	9

Phuvah *see Puah*

Phygellus *fugitive*
A Christian in Asia who deserts Paul	II Tim.	1	15

phylactery *frontlets*
A box containing the ten portions of the law	Ex.	13	9, 16
	Deut.	6	4–9
	Deut.	11	18
Worn by the Jews, for prayer, on the head and left arm	Mat.	23	5

physician *a person who heals, relieves, or comforts*
Also embalms	Gen.	50	2
Treats diseases	II Chr.	16	12
Some are not good	Job	13	4
A symbol	Jer.	8	22
	Mat.	9	12
Not for healthy people	Mark	2	17
Some are unsuccessful	Mark	5	25, 26
"Heal thyself"	Luke	4	23
"Luke, the Beloved"	Col.	4	14

picture *likeness, image*
Against the law	Lev.	26	1
To be destroyed	Num.	33	52
Of gold and silver	Prov.	25	11
Pleasant	Is.	2	16

pieces *parts*
Of bread	I Sam.	2	36
	Prov.	6	26
	Prov.	28	21
Break rocks into	Jer.	23	29
Thirty pieces of silver	Zech.	11	13
	Mat.	27	6, 9
Of ground	Luke	14	18

pierce *go through*
P them with arrows	Num.	24	8
It will go into his hand and *p* it	II Ki.	18	21
	Is.	36	6
P my hands and my feet	Ps.	22	16
They shall look on me whom thy have *p*	Zech.	12	10
	John	19	37
P themselves with many sorrows	I Tim.	6	10
P to the dividing asunder	Heb.	4	12
They also which *p* him	Rev.	1	7

piety *respect, sanctity*
Examples of:
Enoch	Gen.	5	24
Noah	Gen.	6	9
Obadiah	I Ki.	18	3, 4
Josiah	II Ki.	22	1, 2
Hezekiah	II Chr.	31	20
Job	Job	1	1
Daniel	Dan.	6	10
Simeon	Luke	2	25
Anna	Luke	2	36, 37
Barnabas	Acts	11	22, 24
Ananias	Acts	22	12
Helping widows	James	1	27

pigeon *dove*
Used as offering	Lev.	1	14
	Lev.	12	6
	Num.	6	10, 11
	Luke	2	24

Pi-hahiroth *place of meadows*

Last stop before crossing the Red sea	Ex.	14	2, 9
	Num.	33	7, 8

Pilate, Pontius *armed with a dart*

Governor of Judaea	Luke	3	1
Destroys the Galileans	Luke	13	1
Made friends with Herod	Luke	23	12
Declares Christ's innocence, but delivers			
Him to be crucified	Mat.	27	1–26
	Mark	15	1–15
	Luke	23	13, 14, 25
Put title on cross	John	19	19
Grants the request of Joseph of Arimathea	Mark	15	43–45
	John	19	38

pilgrim *wanderer*

Life compared to a pilgrimage	Gen.	47	9
In land of Palestine	Ex.	6	4
House of	Ps.	119	54
Applied to patriarchs	Heb.	11	13
Title of Christians	I Pet.	2	11

pillage *plundering*

Of the house of the Lord by Babylon	II Ki.	25	8–13

pillar *upright column*

Of salt	Gen.	19	26
A memorial stone	Gen.	31	45
Of cloud	Ex.	13	21
As a boundary	Josh.	15	6
Pulled down by Samson	Judg.	16	25–30
Of Solomon's palaces	I Ki.	7	6
Of Solomon's temple	I Ki.	7	13–22
Broken and carried to Babylon	II Ki.	25	13
Used to mark roads	Jer.	31	21
Church so-called	I Tim.	3	15
Of Absalom	II Sam.	18	18
Of the earth	I Sam.	2	8
To mark a grave	Gen.	35	20
Of iron	Jer.	1	18

pillar of cloud *see* cloud, pillar of

pillar of fire *see* fire, pillar of

pillow *any object used as a headrest*

Jacob uses stones as	Gen.	28	11
Of goats' hair	I Sam.	19	13, 16
Woe to women who sew	Ezek.	13	18
Jesus sleeps on a	Mark	4	38

pin *a peg*

Holds ropes	Ex.	27	19
Of a loom	Judg.	16	14
Hang a vessel from a	Ezek.	15	3

pine *a variety of evergreen*

A tree of Lebanon	Is.	41	19
	Is.	60	13
A wild olive tree	Neh.	8	15

pine *waste away*

P away, in iniquities of their fathers shall			
they *p* away	Lev.	26	39
Fetch olive and *p*	Neh.	8	15
These *p* away, stricken	Lam.	4	9
Ye shall *p* away for	Ezek.	24	23
If sins be upon us, and we *p*	Ezek.	33	10

pinnacle *the highest point*

Satan directs Jesus to	Mat.	4	5
	Luke	4	9

pipe *flute*

A woodwind instrument	I Sam.	10	5, 2
	Is.	30	29, 6
Persons playing on the	Mat.	9	23
At Solomon's coronation	I Ki.	1	40
Played at feasts	Is.	5	12
In paradise	Ezek.	28	13
Seven in Zechariah's vision	Zech.	4	2
Depart from Babylon	Rev.	18	22

Piram *wild*

King of Jarmuth	Josh.	10	3
Overcome by Joshua	Josh.	10	16–18
Slain by Joshua	Josh.	10	24–27

Pisgah *piece, peak*

Balaam prophesies on	Num.	23	14–30
Moses sees promised land from	Deut.	3	27
Called Nebo	Deut.	32	49

Pisidia *a province in Asia Minor*

Paul visits	Acts	13	9, 14
	Acts	14	24

Pison *dispersive*

One of the four rivers of Eden	Gen.	2	10, 11

pit *a hole in the ground*

Benaiah slays a lion in a	II Sam.	23	20
Refers to the grave or death	Job	17	16
	Ps.	88	4
	Is.	14	15
	Ezek.	26	20
As a prison	Is.	24	22
	Zech.	9	11
The bottomless pit	Rev.	9	1, 2, 11
	Rev.	11	7
	Rev.	17	8
	Rev.	20	1, 3

pitch *see* bitumen

pitcher *a jar used for liquids or foods*

Vessel used for water	Gen.	24	16–20
Gideon's use of	Judg.	7	10–20
As a meal jar	I Ki.	17	12
Earthenware	Lam.	4	2

Pithon *harmless*

Son of Micah, descendant of Saul	I Chr.	8	35
	I Chr.	9	41

pity *sorrow felt for another's misfortune*

Do not show, to offenders	Deut.	19	13, 21
Job seeks	Job	19	21
Man who took prized lamb	II Sam.	12	6
On the poor	Prov.	19	17
Cast off by Edom	Amos	1	11
Parable of unmerciful debtor	Mat.	18	33
Of God	Is.	63	9
	James	5	11
Of Jesus	Mark	6	34

place

Idolatrous

	I Ki.	11	7
	I Ki.	12	31
	I Ki.	13	22
	Ps.	78	58
	Ezek.	16	24
Destruction of	Lev.	26	30
	II Ki.	18	4
	II Ki.	23	5
	II Chr.	14	3
	II Chr.	17	6
	II Chr.	34	3
	Ezek.	6	3
The *p* whereon thou standest is holy	Ex.	3	5
	Josh.	5	15
Thine eyes may be open toward this *p*	I Ki.	8	29
The *p* is too strait	II Ki.	6	1
	Is.	49	20
The *p* where thine honour dwelleth	Ps.	26	8
Thou art my hiding-*p*	Ps.	32	7
	Ps.	119	114
From the *p* of his habitation	Ps.	33	14
The *p* thereof shall know it no more	Ps.	103	16
The eyes of the Lord are in every *p*	Prov.	15	3
All go to one *p*	Eccl.	3	20
The *p* of my feet glorious	Is.	60	13
Where is the *p* of my rest	Is.	66	1
The Lord cometh out of his *p*	Mic.	1	3
Incense be offered in every *p*	Mal.	1	11
See the *p* where the Lord lay	Mat.	28	6
	Mark	16	6
In what *p* soever	Mark	6	10
Two and two into every *p*	Luke	10	1
Give this man *p*	Luke	14	9
My word hath no *p* in you	John	8	37
With one accord in one *p*	Acts	2	1
The *p* was shaken	Acts	4	31
The *p* of the scripture	Acts	8	32
Rather give *p* unto wrath	Rom.	12	19
Neither give *p* to the devil	Eph.	4	27
No *p* of repentance	Heb.	12	17

plague *affliction*

On the Egyptians:

Of blood	Ex.	7	14–25
Of frogs	Ex.	8	1–15
Of lice	Ex.	8	16–19
Of flies	Ex.	8	20–24
Of cattle	Ex.	9	1–7
Of boils and blains	Ex.	9	8–12

plain *common, ordinary*

Jacob was a *p* man	Gen.	25	27
Lead me in a *p* path	Ps.	27	11
They are *p* to him that understandeth	Prov.	8	9
The way of righteous is made *p*	Prov.	15	19

Rough places made *p*	Is.	40	4
He spake *p*	Mark	7	35

plainly

If the servant *p* say	Ex.	21	5
Write this law very *p*	Deut.	27	8
Stammerers shall speak *p*	Is.	32	4
If thou be Christ, tell us *p*	John	10	24
Now speakest thou *p*	John	16	29
Declare *p*	Heb.	11	14

plaister, plaster *to cover*

On houses	Lev.	14	42
On stones	Deut.	27	2
On the wall of the king's palace	Dan.	5	5

plane tree, chestnut, chesnut

A tree similar to a sycamore maple	Gen.	30	37
	Ezek.	31	8

planets *heavenly bodies*

Worshiped by some priests	II Ki.	23	5

planks *long, thick broad boards*

Made of fir	I Ki.	6	15
Used in the building of the temple	Ezek.	41	25, 26

plant

Figuratively mentioned	Ps.	128	3
	S. of S.	4	13
	Jer.	2	21
Bring forth boughs like a *p*	Job	14	9
Sons as *p* grown up	Ps.	144	12
His pleasant *p*	Is.	5	7
As a tender *p*	Is.	53	2
A *p* of renown	Ezek.	34	29
Ever *p* my Father hath not planted	Mat.	15	13
I will *p* thcm	II Sam.	7	10
	I Chr.	17	9
Like a tree *p*	Ps.	1	3
	Jer.	17	8
P in the house of the Lord	Ps.	92	13
He that *p* the ear	Ps.	94	9
They shall not be *p*	Is.	40	24
Be thou *p* in the sea	Luke	17	6
If we have been *p* together	Rom.	6	5
I have *p*	I Cor.	3	6

plants of the Bible

Anise	Mat.	23	23
Bramble	Judg.	9	14, 15
Brier	Judg.	8	7, 16
Bulrush	Ex.	2	3
Calamus	S. of S.	4	13, 14
Camphire	S. of S.	1	14
Cummin	Is.	28	25, 27
Fitch	Ezek.	4	9
Garlic	Num.	11	5
Gourd	II Ki.	4	39
Grass	Ps.	103	15
Hyssop	Ex.	12	22
Lily	S. of S.	2	2
Mallows	Job	30	4
Mandrake	Gen.	30	14–16
Mint	Mat.	23	23
Mustard	Luke	13	19
Rose	S. of S.	2	1
Rue	Luke	11	42
Saffron	S. of S.	4	13, 14
Spikenard	S. of S.	4	13, 14
Vine of Sodom	Deut.	32	32
Wormwood	Deut.	29	18

plaster

On the Egyptians:

Of hail	Ex.	9	18–34
Of locusts	Ex.	10	1–20
Of darkness	Ex.	10	21–23
Death of the firstborn	Ex.	11	4–7
	Ex.	12	17, 29, 30

On the Israelites:

For idolatry	Ex.	32	35
For eating quail	Num.	11	31–33
For refusing to enter the promised land	Num.	14	37
For murmuring about the destruction of Korah	Num.	16	41–50
Of serpents	Num.	21	6
For the sin of Peor	Josh.	22	17
For David's sin	II Sam.	24	10–25
As judgment	Lev.	26	21
	Deut.	28	59
On the Philistines	I Sam.	6	4, 5
Foretold	Rev.	11	6
	Rev.	15	1, 6–8

	Rev.	16	1–21
	Rev.	22	18, 19

See plaister

play

People rose up to *p*	Ex.	32	6
	I Cor.	10	7
A man that can *p* well	I Sam.	16	14
I will *p* before the Lord	II Sam.	6	21
Let us *p* the men	II Sam.	10	12
Where beasts of field *p*	Job	40	20
Wilt thou *p* with him	Job	41	5
P skillfully with a loud noise	Ps.	33	3
Sucking child shall *p*	Is.	11	8
Can *p* well on an instrument	Ezek.	33	32
Boys and girls *p* in the street	Zech.	8	5

player

A cunning *p*	I Sam.	16	16
The *p* on instruments	Ps.	68	25

plea *argument*

Esther, for the Jews	Esth.	7	1–4
	Esth.	8	4–8

plead *ask earnestly*

Will ye *p* for Baal	Judg.	6	31
Who shall set me a time to *p*	Job	9	19
Who will *p* with me	Job	13	19
Might *p* for a man with God	Job	16	21
P for the widow	Is.	1	17
The Lord standeth up to *p*	Is.	3	13
Let us *p* together	Is.	43	26
I will yet *p* with you	Jer.	2	9
O Lord, thou hast *p*	Lam.	3	58
P with your mother, *p*	Hosea	2	2

pleading

Of God with Israel	Is.	1	11–31
	Is.	3	13
	Jer.	2–6	
	Jer.	13	
	Ezek.	17	20
	Ezek.	20	36
	Ezek.	22	
	Joel	3	2
	Mic.		
Of Job with God	Job	16	21

pleasant

P to the eyes	Gen.	3	6
Were *p* in their lives	II Sam.	1	23
Lines have fallen in *p* places	Ps.	16	6
They despised the *p* land	Ps.	106	24
How *p* for brethren to dwell together	Ps.	133	1
Knowledge is *p* to thy soul	Prov.	2	10
Bread eaten in secret is *p*	Prov.	9	17
The words of the pure are *p* words	Prov.	15	26
P words are as honeycomb	Prov.	16	24
It is *p* to behold the sun	Eccl.	11	7
Lament for *p* fields	Is.	32	12
Our *p* things are laid waste	Is.	64	11
Is Ephraim a *p* child	Jer.	31	20
Song of one that hath a *p* voice	Ezek.	33	32
I ate no *p* bread	Dan.	10	3

pleasing God

Characteristic of Jesus	Mat.	3	17
	John	8	29
A Christian duty	I Thes.	4	1
Benevolences	Heb.	13	16

Examples of:

The apostles	I Thes.	2	4
Enoch	Heb.	11	5

pleasure

Vanity of wordly	Eccl.	2	1–26
Effects of	Luke	8	14
	James	5	1–20
	II Pet.	2	13
Exhortations against	II Tim.	3	4
	Tit.	3	3
	Heb.	11	25
	I Pet.	4	1–19
Hard in old age	Gen.	18	12
Of the King	Ezra	10	11
	Ezra	5	17
Of God	Job	22	13
	Eph.	1	5, 9
	Rev.	4	11

pledges *securities for debt*

Limitations of	Ex.	22	26
	Deut.	24	6
	Job	24	3

pledges—*continued*

The wicked do not fulfill	Job	22	6
	Amos	2	8
The just man restores	Ezek.	18	7

Pleiades *seven stars*

A constellation made by God	Job	9	9

plenty *prosperity*

Of corn and wine	Gen.	27	28
Seven years of, before famine	Gen.	41	29
Canaan, a land of	Deut.	8	7–10
A gift of God	Deut.	16	10
	Ps.	144	13–15
	Acts	14	17
Of food	II Chr.	31	10
Justice of God	Job	37	23
Barns filled with	Prov.	3	10
A reward for working	Prov.	28	19
Taken away in judgment	Luke	16	19, 22

plough, plow *to cultivate*

Mosaic law concerning mixed team	Deut.	22	10
Twenty-four oxen, used by Elisha	I Ki.	19	19
Used by Job's servants	Job	1	14
Man using, and looking back	Luke	9	62
Used to measure land	I Sam.	4	14
Plowing iniquity	Job	4	8
Sluggard will not	Prov.	20	4
Breaks clods	Is.	28	24
Plowing the sea	Amos	6	12
Zion	Jer.	26	18

plowshares *cutting blade*

Beaten into swords	Joel	3	10
Swords to be beaten into	Is.	2	4
	Mic.	4	3

pluck *pull*

Thou mayest *p* the ears	Deut.	23	25
Then will I *p* them up	II Chr.	7	20
They *p* the fatherless from the breast	Job	24	9
He shall *p* my feet out of the net	Ps.	25	15
P thee out of thy place	Ps.	52	5
They which pass *p* her	Ps.	80	12
A time to *p* up	Eccl.	3	2
A firebrand *p* out of the burning	Amos	4	11
	Zech.	3	2
If eye offend thee, *p* it out	Mat.	5	29
	Mat.	18	9
	Mark	9	47
Began to *p* ears of corn	Mat.	12	1
	Mark	2	23
Nor shall any *p* them out of my hand	John	10	28
Twice dead, *p* up by the roots	Jude		12

plumbline *a line*

Used in building	Amos	7	7, 8

poetry *style of writing*
Epic:

Moses' song	Ex.	15	1–19
Miriam's song	Ex.	15	21
Song of Deborah	Judg.	5	2–31

Sacred lyrics:

Moses' and Miriam's song	Ex.	15	
Hannah's song	I Sam.	2	1–10
Song of Elisabeth	Luke	1	42–45
Song of Mary	Luke	1	46–55

Didactic:

Moses' song	Deut.	32	

Elegy:

On the death of Saul	II Sam.	1	19–27
Of Abner	II Sam.	3	33, 34

Acrostic:

Praise to the Lord	Ps.	112	

poison *a harmful substance*

Of serpents	Deut.	32	24
Pottage made safe by Elisha	II Ki.	4	40, 41
Of adders	Ps.	140	3
Of the tongue	James	3	8
Of dragons	Deut.	32	33
Of asps	Job	20	16

politeness *having good manners*

A tender	Gen.	43	26–29
False	II Sam.	20	9, 10
An example of humility	Luke	14	8–10

politicians *persons actively engaged in politics*
Some are deceitful:

Absalom	II Sam.	15	2–6
Darius	Dan.	6	4–15
Pilate	Mat.	27	23–27

Women:

Abigail	I Sam.	25	5–33
Wise woman of Abel	II Sam.	20	15–22
Bath-sheba	I Ki.	1	15–21

poll *head, cut the hair*

Of the men of Israel	Num.	1	2
Of hair on Absalom's head	II Sam.	14	25, 26
Of the priests' hair	Ezek.	44	20

pollutions *impurities*

Of God's house	Ex.	20	25
	II Chr.	33	7
	Ezek.	8	6
	Ezek.	44	7
	John	2	14–17
Under Mosaic law	Lev.	15	11
	Num.	5	2, 3
	Ezek.	22	26
Of the heathen	Lev.	18	24
	Lev.	20	3
Of the sabbath	Neh.	13	15
	Is.	56	2
	Ezek.	20	13

Pollux *see* Castor and Pollux

polygamy *plural marriage*

Forbidden by Mosaic law	Deut.	17	17
	Mat.	19	4, 5
Denied to bishops	I Tim.	3	2

Evil effects of:

On Jacob	Gen.	29	30
	Gen.	30	15
Husband's favouritism	Deut.	21	15–17
On Elkanah	I Sam.	1	4, 5
On Rehoboam	II Chr.	11	21

Some of those who practice:

Lamech	Gen.	4	19
Abraham	Gen.	16	1, 2
Jacob	Gen.	29	28, 30
Gideon	Judg.	8	30
David	II Sam.	3	2–5
Solomon	I Ki.	11	1–8
Ahab	II Ki.	10	1

pomegranate

Figures of the fruit sewed on the ephod	Ex.	28	31, 33
	Ex.	39	22, 24
Grown in Canaan	Num.	13	23
Carved on the pillars of the temple	I Ki.	7	18, 20, 42
	Jer.	52	22, 23
Wine made of	S. of S.	8	2

pommel *bowl*

A round ornament on temple column	I Ki.	7	41, 42
	II Chr.	4	12, 13

Pontius *see* Pilate, Pontius

Pontus *the sea, North Asia Minro*

Home of Jews following dispersion	Acts	2	9
	I Pet.	1	1
Aquila lives	Acts	18	2

pool *reservoir*

Water brought to	II Ki.	20	20

Well-known pools of scripture:

Gibeon	II Sam.	2	13
Hebron	II Sam.	4	12
Samaria	I Ki.	22	38
Upper pool of Jerusalem	II Ki.	18	17
Siloah	Neh.	3	15
Lower pool of Jerusalem	Is.	22	9
Bethesda	John	5	2
Siloam	John	9	7
King's	Neh.	2	14
Wilderness as	Is.	41	18
Of Nineveh	Nah.	2	8

poor *needy*

Will always be with us	Deut.	15	11
	Zeph.	3	12
	Mat.	26	11
God hears and forgets not	Ps.	9	18
	Ps.	69	33
Should commit themselves to God	Ps.	10	14
God protects and provides for	Ps.	12	5
	Ps.	68	10
Are often wise and upright	Prov.	28	11
Should give to, without ostentation	Mat.	6	1
Neglect of, a neglect of Christ	Mat.	26	41–46
Offering of, acceptable to God	Mark	12	42–44
Jesus preaches to	Luke	4	18
Christians should give to, cheerfully	II Cor.	8	12
	II Cor.	9	7

Cared for by the church	Gal.	2	10
May be rich in faith	James	2	5
Jewish law provides for:			
By exempting from usury	Ex.	22	25–27
By gleanings from the harvest	Lev.	19	9, 10
By jubilee year legislation	Lev.	25	8–10
By paying wages promptly	Deut.	24	14, 15
Caused by:			
Laziness	Prov.	11	4, 5
Drunkenness and gluttony	Prov.	23	21
Bad company	Prov.	28	19

poplar *tree or shrub*

Green poplar	Gen.	30	37
Burn incense under	Hosea	4	13

popularity *being well-liked*

Sought by hypocrites	John	12	42, 43
By use of sorcery	Acts	8	9–11
By acts of cruelty to others	Acts	12	1–3
	Acts	24	27
A cause of envy	Acts	13	44, 45
Caution regarding	Col.	3	22
Of Jesus:			
Not sought by Him	Mark	1	40–45
By His ministry of mercy	Mark	2	2
A burden	Mark	6	31–34
From His preaching	Luke	5	1
Instances:			
David	II Sam.	3	36
Absalom	II Sam.	15	2–6
Job	Job	29	

population *number of people*

Increased in Egypt	Ex.	1	7
Recorded during the wilderness wandering	Num.	1	46
By David	II Sam.	24	1–10
Of Nineveh	Jonah	4	11

Poratha *fruitfulness*

One of Haman's sons	Esth.	9	8, 10

porch *roof supported by columns*

Part of the temple	I Ki.	6	3
On Solomon's palaces	I Ki.	7	6–21
In Ezekiel's vision	Ezek.	40	7–49
A covered runway	Mat.	26	71
	Mark	14	68

Porcius *see* Festus

pork *flesh of a pig*

The Jews forbidden to eat	Lev.	11	7, 8

porters *doorkeepers*

At the city gates	I Chr.	9	17–32
Must be at the temple	I Chr.	9	27
Post determined by lots	I Chr.	26	13–19
One third of the tribe of Levi to be, of the temple	II Chr.	23	4
Levites act as	II Chr.	23	5
At the king's palace	II Chr.	34	13
At the doors of the temple	II Chr.	35	15

Postexilic

	Neh.	7	73
Open door	John	10	3

portion *a share*

Of food	Gen.	47	22
Of the wicked	Ps.	11	6
	Mat.	24	51
Of saints	Ps.	73	26
	Lam.	3	24
Inheritance	Luke	15	12

portion *part, share*

Is there yet any *p* for us	Gen.	31	14
The Lord's *p* is his people	Deut.	32	9
A double *p* of thy spirit	II Ki.	2	9
This is the *p* of a wicked man	Job	20	29
What *p* of God is there from above	Job	31	2
The Lord is the *p* of mine inheritance	Ps.	16	5
They shall be a *p* for foxes	Ps.	63	10
Thou art my *p*, O Lord	Ps.	119	57
	Ps.	142	5
Giveth a *p* to her maidens	Prov.	31	15
This was my *p* of all my labour	Eccl.	2	10
For that is his *p*	Eccl.	3	22
	Eccl.	5	18
	Eccl.	9	9
Neither have they any more *p* for ever	Eccl.	9	6
Give a *p* to seven	Eccl.	11	2
Divide him a *p* with the great	Is.	53	12
They shall rejoice in their *p*	Is.	61	7
Made my pleasant *p* a desolate wilderness	Jer.	12	10

The Lord is my *p*	Lam.	3	24
With *p* of king's meat	Dan.	1	8
Changed the *p* of my people	Mic.	2	4
Their *p* in due season	Luke	12	42

possess *own, control*

Thy seed shall *p* the gate	Gen.	22	17
	Gen.	24	60
Made to *p* months of vanity	Job	7	3
To *p* iniquities of youth	Job	13	26
Thou hast *p* my reins	Ps.	139	13
The Lord *p* me in the beginning	Prov.	8	22
I give tithes of all I *p*	Luke	18	12
In patience *p* ye your souls	Luke	21	19
As though they *p* not	I Cor.	7	30
Yet *p* all things	II Cor.	6	10

possession

For an everlasting *p*	Gen.	17	8
	Gen.	48	4
Uttermost parts of the earth for thy *p*	Ps.	2	8
Good things in *p*	Prov.	28	10
Had great *p*	Mat.	19	22
	Mark	10	22
Sold thier *p*	Acts	2	45
Redemption of purchased *p*	Eph.	1	14

possessor

	Gen.	14	19
	Acts	4	34

possible

With God all things are *p*	Mat.	19	26
	Mark	10	27
If *p* deceive the very elect	Mat.	24	24
	Mark	13	22
If *p*, let this cup pass from me	Mat.	26	39
	Mark	14	35
All things are *p* to him that believeth	Mark	9	23
All things are *p* to thee	Mark	14	36
	Luke	18	27
Not *p* he should be holden	Acts	2	24
If *p*, live peaceably	Rom.	12	18
Not *p* that the blood of bulls	Heb.	10	4

post

The columns at the side of a door opening	Ex.	21	6
	Ezek.	41	21
A messenger	Esth.	3	13
A messenger	Job	9	25
Of Hezekiah	II Chr.	30	1, 6, 10
Of Ahasuerus	Esth.	8	10, 14

pot *a round vessel*

Of brass	Ex.	38	3
Golden	Heb.	9	4
Death in a	II Ki.	4	40, 41
For cooking	II Chr.	35	13
For washing	Ps.	60	8
For refining	Prov.	27	21
For storing oil	II Ki.	4	2
For water	John	4	28

Potiphar *belonging to the sun god (Ra)*

Officer of Pharaoh, who buys Joseph as a slave	Gen.	37	36
	Gen.	39	1

Poti-pherah *belonging to Ra, the sun god*

Joseph's father-in-law, priest of On	Gen.	41	45, 50
	Gen.	46	20

potsherd *a piece of broken pottery*

A piece of a broken vessel, earthenware	Job	2	8
Rendered sherd	Is.	30	14

pottage *a thick soup, stew*

Esau's birthright sold for	Gen.	25	29–34
Elisha purifies unwholesome	II Ki.	4	38–41

potter *a molder of clay*

In posterity of Shelah	I Chr.	4	22, 23
Makes vessels of clay	Jer.	18	3–6
Symbolic of God's power	Rom.	9	21, 22
Use of hands	Lam.	4	2
Work broken	Ps.	2	9
	Is.	30	14

potter's field *see* Aceldama

pound *unit of weight*

Weight for money	Ezra	2	69
Parable of	Luke	19	12–27
About twelve ounces	John	12	3

pour

P water on the dry land	Ex.	4	9
My soul is *p* out	Job	30	16
P rain according to vapour	Job	36	27
I *p* out my soul	Ps.	42	4

pour —continued

Grace is *p* into thy lips	Ps.	45	2
P out your heart before him	Ps.	62	8
I will *p* out my Spirit	Prov.	1	23
	Is.	44	3
	Joel	2	28
	Acts	2	17
Name is as ointment *p* forth	S. of S.	1	3
I will *p* water on him that is thirsty	Is.	44	3
P out his soul to death	Is.	53	12
P out thine heart like water	Lam.	2	19
Fury is *p* out like fire	Nah.	1	6
I will *p* on house of David	Zech.	12	10
If I will not *p* out a blessing	Mal.	3	10
P ointment on his head	Mat.	26	7
	Mark	14	3
He *p* out the changers' money	John	2	15
Wine of wrath of God which is *p* out	Rev.	14	10

poverty *condition of being poor*

David speaks of his	I Sam.	18	22, 23
Because of dearth	Neh.	5	1–5
Is the destruction of the poor	Prov.	10	15
Wealth in	Prov.	13	7
Consolation in	Prov.	19	22
Leads to stealing	Prov.	30	8, 9
Giving to God in	Mark	12	41–44
Paul experiences	II Cor.	11	25–27

Causes of:

Indolence	Prov.	6	10, 11
Love of pleasure	Prov.	21	17
Drunkenness	Prov.	23	21
Bad associations	Prov.	28	19

power *strength, ability to act*

Physical power to do harm	Gen.	31	29
To engage in international politics	Ex.	32	11–14
	I Ki.	14	25–28
	Jer.	34	
To expend accrued resources	I Sam.	9	1–4
Belongs to God	Ps.	62	11

power of Christ

Is unlimited	Mat.	28	18
Shall be manifested at His second coming	Mark	13	26
A comfort in time of trouble	II Cor.	12	9
Is supreme	Eph.	1	20, 21
Is able to subdue all things	Phil.	3	21
Christians are strengthened by	Phil.	4	13
	II Tim.	4	18
Ministers should make known	II Pet.	1	16

Exhibited in:

His teaching	Mat.	7	28, 29
	Luke	4	32
Performing miracles	Mat.	8	27
	Luke	5	17
Forgiving sins	Mat.	9	6
Extending power to His disciples	Mark	16	17, 18
Raising Himself from the dead	John	2	19–22
	John	10	18
Overcoming the world	John	16	33
Giving eternal life	John	17	2

power of God

Should be acknowledged	I Chr.	29	11
	Mat.	6	13
Is the source of all strength	I Chr.	29	12
	Ps.	68	35
Should be magnified	Ps.	21	13
	Jude		25
Controls all nature	Job	26	12
	Ps.	65	5, 6
Must be feared	Jer.	5	22
	Mat.	10	28
Is infinite	Mat.	19	26
The wicked know not	Mat.	22	29
Christians are strengthened by	Eph.	6	10
	Col.	1	11

Expressed by the:

Finger of God	Ex.	8	19
Hand of God	Ex.	9	3, 15
Thunder of His power	Job	26	14
Arm of God	Job	40	9
Voice of God	Ps.	29	3, 5

Exemplified in:

Destruction of the wicked	Ex.	9	16
	Rom.	9	22
Governing all things	Ps.	66	7
Creation	Ps.	102	25
	Jer.	10	12

Miracles of Christ	Luke	11	20
Resurrection of Christ	II Cor.	13	4

power of the Holy Ghost

Is the power of God	Mat.	12	28
	Luke	11	20
Christ begins His ministry in	Luke	4	14
Promised by God	Luke	24	49
Endowed upon ministers	Luke	24	49
	Acts	1	8
Promised by Christ	Acts	1	8

praetorium *see pretorium*

praise *glorify, extol*

God is worthy of	Deut.	10	21
	II Sam.	22	4
	Luke	1	46, 68
Accompanied with musical instruments	I Chr.	16	42, 43
	Ps.	150	3, 5
Is due God for His mercy	II Chr.	20	21
	Ps.	89	1
Should be offered with joy and gladness	II Chr.	29	30
	Ps.	63	5
Should be offered with the whole heart	Ps.	9	1
	Ps.	111	1
Evident in nature	Ps.	65	13
	Is.	55	12
Is obligatory upon all men	Ps.	107	8
	Ps.	145	21
Is due God for His lovingkindness and truth	Ps.	138	2
For ever and ever	Ps.	145	1, 2
Some reasons for	Ps.	147	1–12
Of self, forbidden	Prov.	27	2
Praise of man, censured	John	12	42, 43
Acceptable through Christ	Job	13	15
Christ is worthy of	Rev.	5	12

Exemplified:

Moses	Ex.	15	1–19
Miriam	Ex.	15	21
Deborah	Judg.	5	
David	II Sam.	22	
	I Chr.	16	8–36
Israelites	I Chr.	16	36
Mary	Luke	1	46–54
Shepherds	Luke	2	20
Disciples	Luke	19	37
Lame man	Acts	3	8

prayer *earnest, humble request*

Of the hypocrite condemned	Ps.	109	7
	Prov.	1	28
Commanded	Is.	55	7
	Mat.	7	7
Christ commands secret prayer	Mat.	6	6
Of sinners, not heard	John	9	31
To be offered in Christ's name	John	16	24, 26
A duty of Christians	Eph.	6	18
Brings access to God	Phil.	4	6

Form of:

Uttering of vows	Gen.	28	18–22
Unspoken desires	I Sam.	1	12–15
Petition	Ps.	25	1–22
Confession	Ps.	51	1–19
Mere ejaculations	Mat.	8	25
Simple communion with God	Mark	1	35–45
Praise and thanksgiving	Luke	1	46–55
Prolonged utterance	John	17	1–26

Posture in:

Falling on the face	Num.	16	22
Standing	I Ki.	8	22
Kneeling	II Chr.	6	13
Lifting up hands	Ps.	28	2
	I Tim.	2	8
Bowing down	Ps.	95	6
Spreading forth hands	Is.	1	15

Accompanied with:

Self-abasement	Gen.	18	27
Repentance	I Ki.	8	33
Humility	II Chr.	7	14
Fasting	Neh.	1	4
Confession	Neh.	1	4, 7
Praise	Ps.	66	17
Weeping	Jer.	31	9
Faith	Mat.	21	22
Watchfulness	Luke	21	36
Thanksgiving	Phil.	4	6

A true heart	Heb.	10	22
Correct attitude of heart	I Pet.	1	17–23

Answers to:

God gives	Ps.	99	6
Through the grace of God	Is.	30	19
Promised	Is.	58	9
	I John	5	15
Christ gives	John	4	10, 14

Causes for unanswered:

Hypocrisy	Job	27	8, 9
Neglect of God's laws	Prov.	28	9
Living in sin	Is.	59	2
Forsaking God	Jer.	14	10, 12
Idolatry	Ezek.	8	15–18
Self-righteousness	Luke	18	11, 12, 14
Wavering in faith	James	1	5–7
Asking amiss	James	4	3

Great prayers of the Old Testament:

Abraham's intercession for Sodom and Gomorrah	Gen.	18	22–33
Moses' intercession for his people	Ex.	32	11–14
	Ex.	32	30–32
David's thanksgiving	II Sam.	7	18–29
Solomon's prayer for wisdom	I Ki.	3	4–15
At the installation of the ark in the temple	I Ki.	8	12–53
Upon Isaiah's vision and call	Is.	6	11
Isaiah's prayer of confession and petition	Is.	63	15–19
	Is.	64	1–12
Jeremiah's prayer when purchasing Anathoth	Jer.	32	16–25
Of Habakkuk	Job	3	1–19

Examples of public prayer:

Joshua	Josh.	7	6 9
David	I Chr.	29	10–19
Solomon	II Chr.	6	1–42
Jews	Luke	1	10
Early Christians	Acts	2	46
Peter	Acts	3	1
Paul	Acts	16	16

Of Jesus:

The Lord's	Mat.	6	9
After the miracle of the feeding	Mat.	14	23
When He is baptized	Luke	3	21
Before choosing the disciples	Luke	6	12, 13
At the transfiguration	Luke	9	28, 29
In Gethsemane	Luke	22	44
His last words	Luke	23	46
At the grave of Lazarus	John	11	41, 42
Following the triumphal entry	John	12	27, 28

preacher *one who delivers a sermon*

Strikes a rival	I Ki.	22	24
Fed bread and water	I Ki.	22	26–28
A successful one	Jonah	4	1–5
One who is poor	Acts	3	6
Paul is a powerful	I Cor.	2	4
Is given wages	II Cor.	11	8
The duties of a	II Tim.	4	2–5
Noah is the first	II Pet.	2	5

preaching

Of Jonah	Jonah	3	1–10
	Mat.	12	41
Of John the Baptist	Mat.	3	1, 2
	Mark	1	4, 15
	Luke	3	2, 3
Of Noah	II Pet.	2	5
Of Christ	Mat.	4	17
	Mark	1	15
Of the gospel commanded	Mat.	28	19
Of the apostles	Mark	6	7, 12
Christ crucified for	I Cor.	1	17, 23
The purpose of	Col.	1	25–29
A solemn charge	II Tim.	4	2

precious *worth much*

P things	Gen.	24	53
	Deut.	33	13
The word of the Lord was *p*	I Sam.	3	1
My soul was *p* in thine eyes	I Sam.	26	21
Let my life be *p*	II Ki.	1	13
It cannot be valued with *p* onyx	Job	28	16
The redemption of their souls is *p*	Ps.	49	8
P shall their blood be in his sight	Ps.	72	14
P in sight of Lord is death of saints	Ps.	116	15
Bearing *p* seed	Ps.	126	6
Like *p* ointment upon the head	Ps.	133	2
How *p* are thy thoughts, O God	Ps.	139	17
Wisdom is more *p* than rubies	Prov.	3	15
Lips of knowledge are a *p* jewel	Prov.	20	15

Good name better than *p* ointment	Eccl.	7	1
A man more *p* than gold	Is.	13	12
A *p* corner stone	Is.	28	16
	I Pet.	2	6
Thou wast *p* in my sight	Is.	43	4
Take the *p* from the vile	Jer.	15	19
The *p* sons of Zion	Lam.	4	2
Husbandman waiteth for *p* fruit of earth	James	5	7
Trial of your faith more *p* than of gold	I Pet.	1	7
The *p* blood of Christ	I Pet.	1	19
To you which believe he is *p*	I Pet.	2	7
Obtained like *p* faith	II Pet.	1	1
Exceeding great and *p* promises	II Pet.	1	4

precept *a rule of moral conduct*

Commanded by God at mount Sinai	Neh.	9	14
Keep diligently	Ps.	119	4
Established for a purpose	Ps.	119	104
	Mark	10	4, 5
"Precept upon precept"	Is.	28	10, 13
Given through Moses	Heb.	9	10

predestinate *foreordain*

Of believers	Rom.	8	29, 30
	Eph.	1	4, 5
Of Isaac	Gen.	21	12
For a purpose	Ex.	9	16
Based in God's love	Deut.	7	7, 8
	Deut.	10	15
	Deut.	32	8
Hardening of hearts	Josh.	11	20
Based in God's pleasure	I Sam.	12	22
Decision of the king	I Ki.	12	15
Human involvement and responsibility	I Ki.	20	42
Planned before the event	II Ki.	19	25
Choosing of Jerusalem	II Chr.	6	6
Based in His desire	Job	23	13
Judah chosen	Ps.	78	67, 68
Israel chosen	Ps.	135	4
	Is.	44	1, 2
Jacob before birth	Mal.	1	2
Few chosen	Mat.	20	16, 23
Elect	Mat.	24	22
Given by the Father to the Son	John	6	37, 39, 44
To destruction	Jude		4

pre-eminence *excelling all others*

In death	Eccl.	3	19
Of Jesus	Col.	1	18
A caution	I Tim.	5	21
Diotrephes loves	III John		9, 10

pregnancy *period of being pregnant*

Protect oneself during	Ex.	21	22–25

prejudice *judgment or opinion*

Against Jesus:

Because of His origin	Mark	6	3
Because of Jewish loyalty	Luke	9	51–53
Because He comes from Nazareth	John	1	46

Racial:

Denounced by Christ	Acts	10	28
Shown against Paul	Acts	19	30, 34
Strong in early church	Gal.	2	11–14
Miriam against Moses' wife	Num.	12	1

premeditation *think before*

Disciples not to	Mark	13	11
Prodigal son	Luke	15	18, 19
Foolish if secular	James	4	13–17
David at Keilah	I Sam.	23	10, 11

preparation *preparing for*

P of the heart of man	Prov.	16	1
The day of *p*	Mat.	27	62
	Mark	15	42
	Luke	23	54
	John	19	14
Feet shod with *p* of the gospel of peace	Eph.	6	15

prepare *make ready*

I will *p* him an habitation	Ex.	15	2
P your hearts unto the Lord	I Sam.	7	3
O *p* mercy and truth	Ps.	61	7
Thou hast *p* of thy goodness for the poor	Ps.	68	10
They may *p* a city	Ps.	107	36
When he *p* the heavens	Prov.	8	27
They *p* their meat in summer	Prov.	30	25
P the table, watch in the watch tower	Is.	21	5
P the way of the Lord	Is.	40	3
	Mal.	3	1
	Mat.	3	3
	Mark	1	3
	Luke	1	76

prepare—*continued*

P the way of the people	Is.	62	10
P to meet thy God	Amos	4	12
Shall *p* way before thee	Mat.	11	10
Given to them for whom it is *p*	Mat.	20	23
	Mark	10	40
Where wilt thou that we *p*	Mat.	26	17
	Mark	14	12
	Luke	22	9
I go to *p* a place for you	John	14	2
Vessels of mercy afore *p*	Rom.	9	23
Things God hath *p*	I Cor.	2	9
Who shall *p* to battle	I Cor.	14	8
A body hast thou *p* me	Heb.	10	5
Hath *p* for them a city	Heb.	11	16
presbytery	I Tim.	4	14

presence of God *nearness*

With the obedient	Gen.	28	15
At the exodus	Ex.	13	21
Strength in battle	Deut.	20	1
"Lo, I am with you alway"	Mat.	28	20
Angels and elders stand in	Luke	1	19
	Rev.	5	8, 11
Christ enters	Heb.	9	24

present

Brought every man his *p*	I Ki.	10	25
	II Chr.	9	24
God is a very *p* help in trouble	Ps.	46	1
Power of the Lord was *p*	Luke	5	17
Being yet *p* with you	John	14	25
All here *p* before God	Acts	10	33
Do good, evil is *p* with me	Rom.	7	21
The sufferings of this *p* time	Rom.	8	18
The be *p* with the Lord	II Cor.	5	8
Deliver us from this *p* evil world	Gal.	1	4
Having loved this *p* world	II Tim.	4	10
Live godly in this *p* world	Tit.	2	12
No chastening for the *p* seemeth joyous	Heb.	12	11
Established in the *p* truth	II Pet.	1	12
P your bodies a living sacrifice	Rom.	12	1
To *p* you holy, unblameable	Col.	1	22

presents *see gifts*

preserve *keep, save, defend*

A miraculous	Deut.	8	4
By hiding	Josh.	2	1–7
By associaton	II Ki.	3	14, 15
Of saints	Ps.	37	28
Even to the end	Is.	46	3, 4
Of believers	II Tim.	4	18

preserve *keep safe*

I have seen God, and life is *p*	Gen.	32	30
God sent me to *p* you a posterity	Gen.	45	7
That he might *p* us alive	Deut.	6	24
In the days when God *p* me	Job	29	2
Let uprightness *p* me	Ps.	25	21
Thou *p* man and beast	Ps.	36	6
P thou those that are to die	Ps.	79	11
Lord shall *p* thy going out, and thy coming in	Ps.	121	8
Discretion shall *p* thee	Prov.	2	11
Mercy and truth *p* the king	Prov.	20	28
Eyes of the Lord *p* knowledge	Prov.	22	12
I will *p* thee	Is.	49	8
Whosoever shall lose his life shall *p* it	Luke	17	33

press

Could not come nigh for the *p*	Mark	2	4
	Luke	8	19
Jesus turned about in the *p*	Mark	5	30
Thy hand *p* me sore	Ps.	38	2
I am *p* under you, as a cart is *p*	Amos	2	13
They *p* on him to touch him	Mark	3	10
Good measure, *p* down	Luke	6	38
Every man *p* into it	Luke	16	16
Were *p* out of measure	II Cor.	1	8
I *p* toward the mark	Phil.	3	14

presumption *taking for granted*

Should guard against	Ps.	19	13
	James	4	13, 14
Israel's sin	Is.	14	13, 14
On how long life is	Is.	56	12
	Luke	12	19
On the goodness of God	Amos	6	1–3
	Rom.	2	4

Examples of:

Builders of Babel	Gen.	11	4
Israelites	Num.	14	44
	Deut.	1	43

Korah	Num.	16	1–33
Prophets	Deut.	18	20
Beth-shemites	I Sam.	6	19
Uzzah	II Sam.	6	6
Uzziah	II Chr.	26	14, 16
Vagabond Jews	Ps.	19	13
	James	4	13, 14

pretorium, praetorium

Also called:

Common hall	Mat.	27	27
Judgement hall	Mark	15	16
	Acts	23	35
Palace	Phil.	1	13

prevail *succeed*

Power with God, and hast *p*	Gen.	32	28
When Moses held up his hand, Israel *p*	Ex.	17	11
By strength shall no man *p*	I Sam.	2	9
Let not man *p*	II Chr.	14	11
	Ps.	9	19
Iniquities *p* against me	Ps.	65	3
If one *p* against him	Eccl.	4	12
Gates of hell shall not *p*	Mat.	16	18
Perceive ye how ye *p* nothing	John	12	19
So mightly grew the word of God and *p*	Acts	19	20

prevarication *lying*

Speak the truth	Eph.	4	25
Warning against	Col.	3	9
Of Ananias and Sapphira	Acts	5	1–10

prevent *(anticipate, come before, precede)*

Snares of death *p* me	II Sam.	22	6
	Ps.	18	5
God of mercy shall *p* me	Ps.	59	10
In morning shall my prayer *p* thee	Ps.	88	13
I *p* the dawning of the morning	Ps.	119	147
Jesus *p* him	Mat.	17	25
Shall not *p* them which are asleep	I Thes.	4	15

prey *victim*

In morning he shall devour the *p*	Gen.	49	27
Like a lion greedy of *p*	Ps.	17	12
Who hath not given us as a *p*	Ps.	124	6
Shall the *p* be taken from the mighty	Is.	49	24
My flock shall no more be a *p*	Ezek.	34	22

price

Of redemption, the blood of Christ	I Cor.	6	20
	I Cor.	7	23
	I Pet.	1	19
Pearl of great	Mat.	13	46
Ornament of	I Pet.	3	4
I will buy it at a *p*	II Sam.	24	24
	I Chr.	21	22
P of wisdom above rubies	Job	28	18
Buy wine and milk without *p*	Is.	55	1
One pearl of great *p*	Mat.	13	46
It is the *p* of blood	Mat.	27	6
Kept back part of the *p*	Acts	5	2
	Job	28	13
	Prov.	31	10
	Zech.	11	12
	Mat.	26	15
P of Christ	Zech.	11	13

pride *conceit, overhigh opinion of oneself*

Instances of	II Ki.	20	13
	Zeph.	3	11
	I Cor.	8	1
Evil results of	Ps.	10	2
	Prov.	21	24
	Prov.	28	25
	Jer.	43	2
Followed by shame	Prov.	11	2
	Prov.	18	12
	Prov.	29	23
	Is.	28	3

Examples of:

Eli	I Sam.	2	3
David	I Sam.	17	28
King Uzziah	II Chr.	26	14
King Hezekiah	II Chr.	32	25
Nebuchadnezzar	Dan.	4	28, 30
Belshazzar	Dan.	5	20
Herod	Acts	12	20–23

priesthood *the office of a priest*

Of believers:

Israelites promised	Ex.	19	6
Prophecy concerning	Is.	61	6

Fulfilled in Jesus	I Pet.	2	5
Will be with Jesus	Rev.	20	6
Of Christ:			
Intercedes	Rom.	8	34
Human and divine	Heb.	2	17
Sympathetic	Heb.	4	14, 15
Eternal	Heb.	6	20
Completely sinless	Heb.	7	26
Supreme in heaven	Heb.	8	1
Offers His blood	Heb.	9	11–14
priests *officers in religion*			
High	Ex.	28	1–43
	Lev.	8	2, 34–36
Son of Aaron	Ex.	29	9
Levitical	Ex.	28	1
	Lev.	8	2
Conspire to destroy Jesus	Luke	22	1–6
	Luke	22	66–71
Try and condemn Jesus	John	18	15–32
Persecute the disciples	Acts	22	5
Try, condemn and destroy Stephen	Acts	6	8, 12–15
Many converts among	Acts	6	7
Laws governing:			
Consecration	Ex.	29	1–37
Forbidden to drink and shave	Lev.	10	8–20
	Lev.	21	5
Rules for marriage	Lev.	21	13–15
No inheritance	Num.	26	62
Exempted from taxes	Ezra	7	24
Their duties:			
To offer sacrifices	Lev.	1	4–17
Teach law	Lev.	10	11
Purify the unclean	Lev.	15	31
Responsible for the inner temple	Num.	4	5–15
To act as judges	Num.	5	14–31
Pronounces blessings	Num.	6	22–27
Bear the ark through the Jordan	Josh.	4	15–18
Officiate in the holy place	Heb.	9	6
Examples of evil:			
The sons of Micah	Judg.	17	5
Eli's sons	I Sam.	2	12–17, 22
Heathens	I Sam.	5	5
Jeroboam	I Ki.	12	26–31
Prince of Peace			
Christ is called	Is.	9	6
prince			
Of Peace	Is.	9	6
Of life	Acts	3	15
Of this world	John	14	30
	John	16	11
Of the power of the air	Eph.	2	2
Of devils, Christ's miracles ascribed to	Mat.	12	24
	Mark	3	22
	Luke	11	15
	Num.	1	5
Princes of the Tribes	Num.	1	5–15
Their offerings	Num.	7	12–88
As a *p* hast thou power with God	Gen.	32	28
Who made thee a *p* over us	Ex.	2	14
A *p* is fallen in Israel	II Sam.	3	38
He poureth contempt on *p*	Job	12	21
	Ps.	107	40
Where is the house of the *p*	Job	21	28
That accepteth not the person of *p*	Job	34	19
P in all the earth	Ps.	45	16
Than to put confidence in *p*	Ps.	118	9
Put not your trust in *p*	Ps.	146	3
By me *p* decree justice	Prov.	8	15
A *p* that wanteth understanding	Prov.	28	16
It is not for *p* to drink strong drink	Prov.	31	4
P walking as servants	Eccl.	10	7
Are not my *p* altogether kings	Is.	10	8
Whose merchants are *p*	Is.	23	8
P shall rule in judgment	Is.	32	1
All her *p* shall be nothing	Is.	34	12
Israel shall abide many days without a *p*	Hosea	3	4
The *p* and judge asketh for reward	Mic.	7	3
Casteth out devils by *p* of devils	Mat.	9	34
P of this world	John	12	31
Him hath God exalted to be a *P*	Acts	5	31
Nor the wisdom of the *p* of this world	I Cor.	2	6
princes			
Leaders of the tribes	Num.	1	16
Give offerings	Num.	7	2
Royal	I Ki.	4	2

princess *female member of a royal family*			
Taught in household duties	II Sam.	13	8, 9
Solomon's wife is a	I Ki.	11	3
One who is a widow	Lam.	1	1
principalities			
And powers	Eph.	3	10
	Col.	2	15
Christ the head of all	Col.	1	16
	Col.	2	10
Nor *p*, nor powers, shall be able to separate	Rom.	8	38
Far above all *p*	Eph.	1	21
We wrestle against *p*, against powers	Eph.	6	12
To be subject to *p*	Tit.	3	1
print *mark*			
On the heels of the feet	Job	13	27
On the pages of a book	Job	19	23
Of nails	John	20	25
Prisca, Priscilla *little old woman*			
Wife of Aquila, ardent Christians	Acts	18	1–3
	Acts	18	18, 26
Accompanies Paul	Rom.	16	3
Highly regarded by Paul	II Tim.	4	19
prison			
Put butler and baker in *p*	Gen.	40	3
Bring my soul out of *p*	Ps.	142	7
Out of *p* he cometh to reign	Eccl.	4	14
He was taken from *p* and from judgment	Is.	53	8
Opening of the *p*	Is.	61	1
Thou be cast into *p*	Mat.	5	25
In *p* and ye came unto me	Mat.	25	36
To go with thee to *p* and to death	Luke	22	33
Put apostles in common *p*	Acts	5	18
The spirits in *p*	I Pet.	3	19
prisoner *one put in prison*			
Required to work	Judg.	16	21
Fed bread and water	I Ki.	22	27
Consolations for	Ps.	69	33
	Ps.	102	19, 20
Kept in stocks and chains	Prov.	7	22
	Acts	16	24
In visited	Mat.	25	35–46
Released for festivals	Mark	15	6
Severe hardships of:			
Cruelty	Jer.	38	6
Scourged	Mat.	27	26
	II Cor.	11	23, 24
Responsible to keepers	Acts	12	18, 19
Tortured	Acts	22	24
Allowed to defend themselves	Acts	24	10
Kindness to:			
Jeremiah, by the prison keeper	Jer.	38	7–28
Paul, by the jailor	Acts	16	33
Paul, by Felix	Acts	24	23–27
Paul, by Julius, the centurion	Acts	28	16, 30, 31
Of war:			
By the command of God	Num.	31	9, 17
Put to death	Josh.	10	16–27
Thumbs and toes cut off	Judg.	1	6, 7
Blinded	II Ki.	25	7
Examples of:			
Joseph	Gen.	39	20–23
Jeremiah	Jer.	38	6–28
John the Baptist	Mat.	14	3–12
Jesus	Mat.	26	47–75
Apostles	Acts	5	17–40
Peter	Acts	12	3–19
Paul	Acts	16	19–40
Silas	Acts	16	19–40
privileges *rights not enjoyed by all people equally*			
Given the disciples through Jesus Christ	Mat.	13	11
	Col.	1	26, 27
Withdrawn from the unbelievers	Mat.	21	43
	Mat.	25	28
Taken away as punishment	Luke	19	41, 42
	Heb.	3	16, 17
Granted those who love God	I Cor.	2	9, 10
prize *reward*			
A reward for merit	I Cor.	9	24
Eager for the	Phil.	3	14
probation *moral trial*			
Adam is on	Gen.	2	15–17
Amorites	Gen.	15	16
Solomon	I Ki.	9	4–9
None after death	Mat.	25	10–13

probation—continued
Is taught in parables:

Of Israel	Deut.	8	1–20
Talents and pounds	Mat.	25	14–30
The fig tree	Luke	13	6–9
The embezzling steward	Luke	16	1–12
Of Paul	Heb.	6	1–20

proceed *to go on*

The thing *p* from the Lord	Gen.	24	50
Every word that *p* out of mouth of God	Deut.	8	3
	Mat.	4	4
I will *p* no further	Job	40	5
I will *p* to do a marvellous work	Is.	29	14
A law shall *p* from me	Is.	51	4
They *p* from evil to evil	Jer.	9	3
Things which *p* out of the mouth	Mat.	15	18
I *p* forth from God	John	8	42
Let no corrupt communication *p*	Eph.	4	29
Out of same mouth *p* blessing and cursing	James	3	10

procession *an orderly moving group*

A sorrowful	Luke	23	24–28

proclaim *declare publicly*

I will *p* the name of	Ex.	33	19
Feast of the Lord ye shall *p*	Lev.	23	2, 4, 21
P liberty	Lev.	25	10
P peace unto it	Deut.	20	10
Go to *p* in the ears of	Judg.	7	3
P a fast, and set Naboth	I Ki.	21	9
Jehu said, *P* a solemn	II Ki.	10	20
P that they fetch pine	Neh.	8	15
P before him, Thus shall	Esth.	6	9
Most men *p* their own	Prov.	20	6
He hath sent me to *p* liberty	Is.	61	1
To *p* the acceptable year	Is.	61	2
Go and *p* these words	Jer.	3	12
	Jer.	11	6
	Jer.	19	2
Stand in gate of the Lord, and *p*	Jer.	7	2
A covenant to *p* liberty	Jer.	34	8
I *p* a liberty for you to sword	Jer.	34	17
P ye this among Gentiles	Joel	3	9
And *p* and publish the	Amos	4	5

procrastination *act of delaying*

Must not apply to offerings	Ex.	22	29
Denounced	Prov.	3	27, 28
Offensive of God	Ezek.	12	22–28
An example	Mat.	25	2–13
Condemned by Jesus	Luke	9	59–62
Lord will come and judge	Mat.	24	48–51
Felix	Acts	24	25

prodigal son *son who lived in reckless extravagance*

The parable of	Luke	15	11–32

profane *irreverent*

Idolatry is	Lev.	18	21
Breaking the sabbath is	Neh.	13	17
Prophets and priests are sometimes	Jer.	23	11
Law is made for the	I Tim.	1	9
Not the name of God	Lev.	20	3
	Lev.	21	6
Priest on Sabbath	Mat.	12	5
The temple	Acts	24	6
Babblings	II Tim.	2	16
	I Tim.	6	20
Esau	Heb.	12	16

profanity *irreverence, blasphemy*

Forbidden by Mosaic law	Lev.	20	3
	Lev.	21	6
Shall be punished	Lev.	21	9
Priests should teach evils of	Ezek.	44	23
Paul accused of	Acts	24	6
Christians should avoid	I Tim.	4	7
	II Tim.	2	16

profess *declare openly*

Will I *p*, I never knew you	Mat.	7	23
P themselves to be wise	Rom.	1	22
Hast *p* a good profession	I Tim.	6	12
They *p* that they know God	Tit.	1	16

profession

Of Christ, to hold fast	Heb.	3	1
	Heb.	4	14
	Heb.	10	23

profit *gain*

What *p* shall birthright do to me	Gen.	25	32
What *p* is it if we slay our brother	Gen.	37	26
What *p*, if pray unto him	Job	21	15

What *p* is in my blood	Ps.	30	9
In all labour there is *p*	Prov.	14	23
What *p* hath a man of his labour	Eccl.	1	3
	Eccl.	3	9
	Eccl.	5	16
There was no *p* under the sun	Eccl.	2	11
The *p* of the earth is for all	Eccl.	5	9
By wisdom there is *p*	Eccl.	7	11
Things wherein is no *p*	Jer.	16	19
What *p* that we have kept his ordinance	Mal.	3	14
What *p* of circumcision	Rom.	3	1
Not seeking mine own *p*	I Cor.	10	33
About words to no *p*	II Tim.	2	14
He chasteneth us for our *p*	Heb.	12	10
It *p* nothing to delight in God	Job	34	9
Vain things which cannot *p*	I Sam.	12	21
Treasures of wickedness *p* nothing	Prov.	10	2
Riches *p* not in the day of wrath	Prov.	11	4
A people that could not *p*	Is.	30	5
Changed for that which doth not *p*	Jer.	2	11
Lying words that cannot *p*	Jer.	7	8
What is a man *p* if he gain the world	Mat.	16	26
	Mark	8	36
Given to every man to *p* withal	I Cor.	12	7
Charity, it *p* me nothing	I Cor.	13	3
Christ shall *p* you nothing	Gal.	5	2
Bodily exercise shall *p* little	I Tim.	4	8
The word preached did not *p*	Heb.	4	2
What doth it *p*	James	2	14

profitable

Can a man be *p* to God	Job	22	2
Wisdom is *p* to direct	Eccl.	10	10
P that one of thy members perish	Mat.	5	29
Godliness is *p* to all things	I Tim.	4	8
Scripture is *p* for doctrine	II Tim.	3	16

progenitors *see genealogy*

prognosticators *foretellers*

Cannot save	Is.	47	13
The Holy Spirit prophesies	I Pet.	1	9–12
False prophet	Deut.	18	22

prohibition *use of strong drink forbidden*

For priests	Lev.	10	8–11
For Nazarites	Num.	6	3, 4
For the wife of Manoah	Judg.	13	4, 14
By a father	Jer.	35	6–8, 14
By John the Baptist	Luke	1	15

promises of God

Confirmed by an oath	Ps.	89	3–4
	Heb.	6	17
Exceeding great and precious	II Pet.	1	4
Given to those who believe	Gal.	3	22
Good	I Ki.	8	56
Holy	Ps.	105	42
Inherited through faith and patience	Heb.	10	36
Made in Christ	Eph.	3	6
	II Tim.	1	1
Man, by nature, has no interest in	Eph.	2	12
Not one shall fail	I Ki.	8	56
Performed in due season	Acts	7	17
	Gal.	4	4
Through the righteousness of faith	Rom.	4	13, 16
Yea and amen in Christ	II Cor.	1	20
Fear, lest ye come short of	Heb.	4	1
Gentiles shall be partakers of	Eph.	3	6
God faithful to	Tit.	1	2
	Heb.	10	23
God remembers	Ps.	105	42
	Luke	1	54–55
Inheritance of the saints is	Rom.	4	13
	Gal.	3	18
The law could not annul	Gal.	3	18
The law not against	Gal.	13	21
Of pardon and reconciliation	Ex.	34	7
	Jer.	31	34
	II Cor.	6	16–18
Are inviolable and precious	Num.	23	19
	Josh.	23	14
	II Pet.	1	4
Of strength and help	Ps.	23	
	Ps.	84	11
	Zeph.	3	17
Performed in due time	Jer.	33	14
Of temporal blessing	Ex.	23	25
	Lev.	26	6
	Ps.	34	9
	Phil.	4	19
	I Tim.	4	8

Fulfilled in Christ	Luke	1	69–73
	Acts	13	23
	Eph.	3	6
	II Sam.	7, 12	
Contained in the scriptures	Rom.	1	2
Confirmed by Christ	Rom.	15	8
Should inspire holiness	II Cor.	7	1
Scoffers despise	II Pet.	3	3–4
Should wait for the performance of	Acts	1	4
Obtained through faith	Heb.	6	12, 15
	Heb.	11	33
The covenant established upon	Heb.	8	6
Made to:			
Adam	Gen.	3	15
Noah	Gen.	8	21, 22
	Gen.	9	11
Abraham	Gen.	12	7
	Gal.	3	16
Hagar	Gen.	16	10
Isaac	Gen.	26	3, 4
Jacob	Gen.	28	14
David	II Sam.	7	12
Solomon	I Ki.	19	
The poor and fatherless	Ps.	10	14
	Ps.	12	5
	Jer.	49	11
Christ	Gal.	3	16, 19
Those who love Him	James	1	12
	James	2	5
All who are called of God	Acts	2	39
David	Ps.	89	3–4
The fathers	Acts	13	32
	Acts	26	6–7
The Israelites	Rom.	9	4
Saints:			
Children of	Rom.	9	8
	Gal.	4	28
Expect the performance of	Luke	1	38, 45
	II Pet.	3	13
Have implicit confidence in	Heb.	11	11
Heirs of	Gal.	3	29
	Heb.	6	17
	Heb.	11	9
Plead, in prayer	Gen.	32	9, 12
	I Chr.	17	23, 26
	Is.	43	26
Sometimes tempted to doubt	Ps.	77	8, 10
Stagger not at	Rom.	4	20
Subjects of:			
Adoption	II Cor.	6	18
Blessing	Deut.	1	11
Christ	Acts	13	22–23
A crown of life	James	1	12
Entering into rest	Heb.	4	1–3
Eternal life	Tit.	1	2
	I John	2	25
Forgiveness of sins	Is.	1	18
	Heb.	8	12
The gospel	Rom.	1	1–2
The Holy Spirit	Acts	2	33
	Eph.	1	13
Life in Christ	II Tim.	1	1
The life that now is	I Tim.	4	8
New heavens and earth	II Pet.	3	13
Preservation in affliction	Is.	43	2
Putting the law into the heart	Jer.	31	33
	Heb.	8	10
Second coming of Christ	II Pet.	3	4

promotion *advancement, exaltation*

Of Joseph	Gen.	41	38–42
Of Haman	Esth.	3	1
Comes from God	Ps.	75	6, 7
Of fools	Prov.	3	35
Aprostles seek	Mark	10	35–37

property *ownership*

Taken violently	Gen.	21	25
Bought	Gen.	23	16–20
Fought for	Gen.	26	18–22
For Pharaoh	Gen.	47	20
Of priests not to be sold	Gen.	47	22
Rules concerning sale of	Lev.	25	23–34
	Lev.	27	14–25
Landmarks not to be removed	Deut.	19	14
Confiscated	I Ki.	21	15, 16
Loss by absence	II Ki.	8	1–6
Inherited	Eccl.	2	21

Personal property:

To covet is forbidden	Ex.	20	17
Servants considered	Ex.	21	2–11
Responsibility for actions of animals	Ex.	21	28–36
	Ex.	22	5–15
Punishment for damage of	Lev.	6	2–5
Dedicated to God	Lev.	27	9–13
Strayed or lost	Deut.	22	1–4
Sold for debt	Prov.	22	26, 27

prophecies respecting Christ and their fulfillment

As the seed of woman	Gen.	3	15
	Gal.	4	4
As the seed of Abraham	Gen.	17	7
	Gal.	3	16
As the seed of Isaac	Gen.	21	12
	Heb.	11	17–19
The time of His coming	Gen.	49	10
	Luke	2	1
No bone shall be broken	Ex.	12	46
	John	19	33, 36
As the Son of God	Ps.	2	7
	Luke	1	32, 35
His flesh not seeing corruption	Ps.	16	10
	Acts	2	31
Lots cast for His garments	Ps.	22	18
	Mat.	27	35
Betrayal by a friend	Ps.	41	9
	John	13	18, 21
His ascension	Ps.	68	18
	Luke	24	51
Gall and vinegar given Him to drink	Ps.	69	21
	Mat.	27	34
Great men to adore Him	Ps.	72	10
	Mat.	2	1–11
Born of a virgin	Is.	7	14
	Mat.	1	18
To be called Immanuel	Is.	7	14
	Mat.	1	22, 23
His ministry to commence in Galilee	Is.	9	1, 2
	Mat.	4	12–16
Conversion of the Gentiles	Is.	11	10
	Acts	10	45, 47
His resurrection	Is.	26	19
	Luke	24	6, 31, 34
Preceded by John the Baptist	Is.	40	3
	Mat.	3	1, 3
His death	Is.	53	12
	Mat.	27	50
Entering the public ministry	Is.	61	1, 2
	Luke	4	16–21
Slaying of children of Bethlehem	Jer.	31	15
	Mat.	2	16–18
His being called out of Egypt	Hosea	11	1
	Mat.	2	15
His being smitten on the cheek	Mic.	5	1
	Mat.	27	30
Place of birth	Mic.	5	2
	Mat.	2	1
Triumphal entry into Jerusalem	Zech.	9	9
	Mat.	21	1–5
Sold for 30 pieces of silver	Zech.	11	12
	Mat.	26	15
Coming into the temple	Mal.	3	1
	Mat.	21	12

prophecy *foretelling of future events*

God is the author of	Is.	44	7
	Is.	45	21
God accomplishes	Is.	44	26
	Acts	3	18
Will be fulfilled	Ezek.	12	22–25
A gift of the Holy Ghost	I Cor.	12	10
	II Pet.	1	21
Tests of	Deut.	13	1
	Deut.	18	20
	Jer.	14	15
	Jer.	23	16
	Ezek.	13	3
Blessedness of reading, hearing, and keeping	Rev.	1	3
	Rev.	22	7
Christ the great subject of	Acts	3	22–24
	Acts	10	43
	I Pet.	1	10–11
Despise not	I Thes.	5	20
Foretelling future events	Gen.	49	1
	Num.	24	14

prophecy—*continued*			
For the benefit of after ages	I Pet.	1	12
Fulfilled respecting Christ	Luke	24	44
A gift of Christ	Eph.	4	11
	Rev.	11	3
Gift of, promised	Acts	2	16–17
Give heed to	II Pet.	1	19
Receive in faith	II Chr.	20	20
	Luke	24	25
A sure word	II Pet.	1	19
Given from the beginning	Luke	1	70
God gives through Christ	Rev.	1	1
Guilt of pretending to the gift of	Jer.	14	14
	Jer.	23	13–14
	Ezek.	13	2–3
A light in a dark place	II Pet.	1	19
Not of private interpretation	II Pet.	1	20
Punishment for:			
Adding to, or taking from	Rev.	22	18–19
Not giving ear to	Neh.	9	30
Of important events:			
Birth of Jesus	Is.	11	1–10
Fall of Babylon	Is.	13	19–22
Jewish captivity	Is.	39	7
Return of the Jews	Jer.	24	6
Destruction of Jerusalem	Lam.	1	1, 2
Betrayal of Jesus	John	13	18

prophetess *a female prophet*			
Miriam	Ex.	15	20
Deborah	Judg.	4	4
Huldah	II Ki.	22	14
Noadiah	Neh.	6	14
Anna	Luke	2	36
Four daughters of Philip	Acts	21	9
Jezebel	Rev.	2	20

prophets *men who speak for God*			
Raised up on occasions of emergency	I Sam.	3	19–21
Called seer and messengers of God	I Sam.	9	19
	II Chr.	36	15
Sometimes speak in parables	II Sam.	12	1–6
Denounce the wickedness of kings	II Sam.	12	7–12
	I Ki.	21	17–22
Imprisoned and persecuted	I Ki.	19	10
	I Ki.	22	27
	Jer.	32	2
	Mat.	23	34–37
Frequently rise from the ranks of the people	I Ki.	19	19–21
	Amos	1	1
Trained in schools	II Ki.	2	3, 5
Reprove the wicked and urge repentance	II Ki.	17	13
	Jer.	25	4, 5
Have pity for the penitent	Is.	1	18
Plead for righteousness, mercy and justice	Is.	1	10–20
	Amos	4	4–6
	Mic.	6	6–9
Predict the birth of Christ	Is.	11	1–10
	Zech.	6	12
Counsellors to kings	Is.	37	2, 3
Oppose animal sacrifices	Jer.	7	22
False prophets denounced	Jer.	14	15
Bold and undaunted	Ezek.	2	6
Vigilant and faithful	Ezek.	3	17–21
Women sometimes endowed as	Joel	2	28
Condemn the selfish rich	Amos	4	1
Oppose overemphasis of temple ritual	Mat.	12	6
Not honoured in their own country	Mat.	13	57
	Luke	4	24–27
Christ, a prophet	Mat.	21	11
John the Baptist, a prophet	Luke	7	28
Mighty through faith	Heb.	11	32–40
They who uttered:			
Filled with the Holy Ghost	Luke	1	67
Moved by the Holy Ghost	II Pet.	1	21
Ordained by God	I Sam.	3	20
	Jer.	1	5
Raised up by God	Amos	2	11
Sent by Christ	Mat.	23	34
Sent by God	II Chr.	36	15
	Jer.	7	25
Spoke by the Holy Ghost	Acts	1	16
	Acts	11	28
	Acts	28	25
Spoke in the name of the Lord	II Chr.	33	18
	James	5	10
Spoke with authority	I Ki.	17	1

Major prophets of the Old Testament:			
Isaiah	Is.	1	1
Jeremiah	Jer.	1	1, 5
Ezekiel	Ezek.	1	3
Daniel	Mat.	24	15
Minor prophets of the Old Testament:			
Jonah	II Ki.	14	25
Haggai	Ezra	5	1
Hosea	Hosea	1	1
Joel	Joel	1	1
Amos	Amos	1	1
Obadiah	Obad.		1
Micah	Mic.	1	1
Nahum	Nah.	1	1
Habakkuk	Hab.	1	1
Zephaniah	Zeph.	1	1
Zechariah	Zech.	1	1
Malachi	Mal.	1	1

prophets, false *see* false prophets

prophets, Names of—			
Aaron	Ex.	7	1
Abraham	Gen.	20	1, 7
Agabus	Acts	21	10
Ahijah	I Ki.	11	29
Amos	Amos	7	14, 15
Balaam	Num.	22	5–41
David	Acts	2	29, 30
Eldad	Num.	11	26
Elijah	I Ki.	18	36
Elisha	I Ki.	19	16
Gad	I Sam.	22	5
Hananiah	Jer.	28	17
Iddo	II Chr.	13	22
Jehu	I Ki.	16	7
John the Baptist	Luke	7	28
Joshua	I Ki.	16	34
Medad	Num.	11	26
Micaiah	I Ki.	22	8
Moses	Deut.	34	10
Nathan	II Sam.	7	2
Oded	II Chr.	28	9
Samuel	I Sam.	3	20
Shemaiah	II Chr.	12	5
Zacharias	Luke	1	67

propitiation, appeasement			
Christ through faith in His blood	Rom.	3	25
For our sins	I John	2	2
Rooted in love	I John	4	10

proselyte *convert to another faith*			
Mosaic law regarding	Ex.	12	48, 49
Entitled to all the privileges	Is.	56	3–7
Present at Pentecost	Acts	2	10
Many follow Paul	Acts	13	43
Are required:			
To be circumcised	Gen.	17	13
To observe the law of Moses	Num.	10	14
To enter into a covenant with God	Deut.	29	10–13
To give up all heathen practices	Ruth	2	11
	Ps.	45	10

prosper			
If now thou do *p* my way	Gen.	24	42
The Lord made all Joseph did to *p*	Gen.	39	3
Transgress, but it shall not *p*	Num.	14	41
Thou shalt not *p* in thy ways	Deut.	28	29
Shalt *p*, if thou takest heed	I Chr.	22	13
Believe his prophets so shall ye *p*	II Chr.	20	20
God of heaven will *p* us	Neh.	2	20
Whatsoever he doeth shall *p*	Ps.	1	3
Ungodly who *p* in the world	Ps.	73	12
They shall *p* that love thee	Ps.	122	6
He that covereth sins shall not *p*	Prov.	28	13
Knowest not whether shall *p*	Eccl.	11	6
Pleasure of Lord shall *p*	Is.	53	10
No weapon that is found against thee shall *p*	Is.	54	17
It shall *p* in the thing whereto I sent it	Is.	55	11
Wherefore doth way of wicked *p*	Jer.	12	1
A king shall reign and *p*	Jer.	23	5
Speak lies, but it shall not *p*	Dan.	11	27
As God hath *p* him	I Cor.	16	2

prosperity *success*			
Through deception	Jer.	6	28
A warning against	Luke	12	16–28
	Luke	16	19–26
Promised to the righteous	Ps.	36	8
	Prov.	3	1, 2

Dangers of:			
Forgetting God	Deut.	6	10–12
Self-destruction	Prov.	1	32
Denying God	Prov.	30	8, 9
Of the wicked:			
Not understood	Job	12	6
Is of short duration	Job	20	5
	Ps.	92	7

prostitution

Forbidden	Lev.	19	29
Punishment of	Lev.	21	9
Wages received for	Deut.	23	18
Description of	Prov.	5	3–5
	Prov.	7	6–27
	Prov.	9	13–18
Warning against	Prov.	6	24–35

protection

Withdrawn from the disobedient	Lev.	26	14–17
Of God, is unfailing and perpetual	Deut.	31	6
	Ps.	121	3
Not to be found in idols or riches	Deut.	32	37–39
	Prov.	11	28
God will provide	II Thes.	3	3
	I Pet.	1	5
Of Joshua	Josh.	1	5
Of Gideon	Judg.	6	16
Is given to:			
Repentant sinners	Job	22	23, 25
The oppressed	Ps.	9	9
The poor	Ps.	72	12
Those who hearken to God	Prov.	1	33
Is promised by God:			
In all places	Gen.	28	15
In sleep	Ps.	4	8
In death	Ps.	23	4
In all dangers	Ps.	91	3–7
In persecution	Luke	21	18
In temptation	I Cor.	10	13

proud *thinking well of oneself*

He smiteth through the *p*	Job	26	12
Behold every one that is *p*	Job	40	11
Rewardeth the *p* doer	Ps.	31	23
Blessed is the man that respecteth not the *p*	Ps.	40	4
Render a reward to the *p*	Ps.	94	2
Him that hath a *p* heart	Ps.	101	5
Thou hast rebuked the *p*	Ps.	119	21
Soul filled with contempt of the *p*	Ps.	123	4
The *p* he knoweth afar off	Ps.	138	6
Lord hateth a *p* look	Prov.	6	17
The Lord will destroy the house of the *p*	Prov.	15	25
High look and a *p* heart is sin	Prov.	21	4
Patient in spirit better than the *p*	Eccl.	7	8
He is a *p* man	Heb.	2	5
We call the *p* happy	Mal.	3	15
He hath scattered the *p*	Luke	1	51
He is *p*, knowing nothing	I Tim.	6	4
God resisteth the *p*	James	4	6
	I Pet.	5	5

prove *test*

I may *p* them	Ex.	16	4
God is come to *p* you	Ex.	20	20
Humble thee, and *p* thee	Deut.	8	2, 16
Let me *p* thee but this once	Judg.	6	39
I have not *p* them	I Sam.	17	39
She came to *p* Solomon	I Ki.	10	1
	II Chr.	9	1
Thou hast *p* my heart	Ps.	17	3
Examine me, O Lord, and *p* me	Ps.	26	2
When you fathers *p* me	Ps.	95	9
	Heb.	3	9
I will *p* thee with mirth	Eccl.	2	1
P me now herewith	Mal.	3	10
I go to *p* them	Luke	14	19
This he said to *p* him	John	6	6
P that this is very Christ	Acts	9	22
P what is that good will of God	Rom.	12	2
P your own selves	II Cor.	13	5
P all things	I Thes.	5	21

proverbs *short sayings that convey a familiar truth*

Express finality of human judgment	Deut.	28	37
	Jer.	24	9
Sometimes take inquisitive form	I Sam.	10	12
Solomon spoke 3000	I Ki.	4	32

Design of	Prov.	1	1, 4
Fulfilled	II Pet.	2	22
Use picturesque phrases from:			
The physical world	Job	14	19
Agriculture	Prov.	15	17
Home life	Prov.	21	9
Examples of well-known:			
The tree is known by its fruit	Mat.	12	33
Physician, heal thyself	Luke	4	23
If the salt has lost its savour	Luke	14	34
Evil communications corrupt good manners	I Chr.	15	33
Whatsoever a man soweth	Gal.	6	7

providence *divine care or guidance*

All pervading	Ps.	139	1–5
Man's efforts are vain without	Prov.	21	31
Result of depending upon	Luke	22	35
Righteous	Ps.	145	17
	Dan.	4	37
For good to saints	Rom.	8	28
For his glory	Is.	63	14
Cannot be defeated	I Ki.	22	30, 34
	Prov.	21	30
Care over his works	Ps.	145	9
Danger of denying	Is.	10	13–17
	Ezek.	28	2–10
	Dan.	4	29–31
	Hosea	2	8–9
Ever watchful	Ps.	121	4
	Is.	27	3
Sometimes dark and mysterious	Ps.	36	6
	Ps.	73	16–17
	Ps.	77	19
	Rom.	11	33
The wicked	Is.	10	5–12
	Acts	3	17–18
Pray to guided by	Gen.	24	12
	Acts	1	24
Rules the elements	Ps.	104	5–9
	Is.	50	2
Man's efforts are futile without	Ps.	127	1, 2
Directs all events	Prov.	16	33
Christians should trust	Mat.	6	33, 34
	Mat.	10	28–31
Provision for Adam	Gen.	1	29
	Gen.	2	16
To blessing for obedient	Ex.	23	22
	Deut.	5	29
Rain and fruitfulness	Lev.	26	4–10
The land of Israel	Deut.	11	12
Over all things	I Chr.	29	12–16
World affairs	Acts	17	26, 27
Exercised in:			
Bringing his words to pass	Num.	26	65
	Josh.	21	45
	Luke	21	32–33
Defeating wicked designs	Ex.	15	9–19
	II Sam.	17	14, 15
	Ps.	33	10
Delivering saints	Ps.	91	3
	Is.	31	5
Determining the period of human life	Ps.	31	15
	Ps.	39	5
	Acts	17	26
Leading saints	Deut.	8	2, 15
	Is.	63	12
Ordaining the conditions and circumstances of men	I Sam.	2	7–8
	Ps.	75	6–7
Ordering the minutest matters	Luke	21	18
Ordering the ways of men	Prov.	16	9
	Prov.	19	21
	Prov.	20	24
Overruling wicked designs for good	Gen.	45	5–7
	Gen.	50	20
	Phil.	1	12
Preserving his creatures	Neh.	9	6
	Ps.	36	6
	Mat.	10	29
Preserving the course of nature	Gen.	8	22
	Job	26	10
Prospering saints	Gen.	24	48, 56
Protecting saints	Ps.	91	4
	Ps.	140	7
Providing for his creatures	Ps.	104	27–28
	Ps.	136	25
	Ps.	147	9
	Mat.	6	26

providence—*continued*

Ruling the elements	Job	37	9–13
	John	1	4, 15
	Nah.	1	4
Special preservation of saints	Ps.	37	28
	Ps.	91	11
	Mat.	10	30

Saints should:

Commit their works unto	Prov.	16	3
Encourage themselves in	I Sam.	30	6
Have full confidence in	Ps.	16	8
	Ps.	139	10
Pray in dependence upon	Acts	12	5

Should be acknowledged:

In adversity	Job	1	21
	Ps.	119	75
In all things	Prov.	3	6
In our daily support	Gen.	48	15
In prosperity	Deut.	8	18
	I Chr.	29	12
In public calamities	Amos	3	6

province *an administrative district*

Of Judea	Ezra	5	8
Of the Medes	Ezra	6	2
Of Babylon	Ezra	7	16
Of Elam	Dan.	8	2
Of Cilicia	Acts	23	34
Of Jerusalem	Neh.	11	3
Of Ahasuerus	Esth.	1	1
Officers of	Esth.	2	3
Release of	Esth.	2	18
Daniel ruler of	Dan.	2	48
Of Achaia	Acts	18	12
Of Asia	Acts	19	10
Of Galatia	Acts	16	6

provision

P for the way	Gen.	42	25
	Gen.	45	21
I will bless her *p*	Ps.	132	15
King appointed a daily *p*	Dan.	1	5
Make not *p* for the flesh	Rom.	13	14

provoke *make angry, vex*

Obey his voice, *p* him not	Ex.	23	21
How long will this people *p* me	Num.	14	11
P me, and break my covenant	Deut.	31	20
They that *p* God are secure	Job	12	6
How oft did they *p* him	Ps.	78	40
They *p* him with their inventions	Ps.	106	29
Began to urge, and *p* him to speak	Luke	11	53
P to jealousy	Rom.	10	19
	Rom.	11	11
Charity is not easily *p*	I Cor.	13	5
P not your children to wrath	Eph.	6	4
When they heard, did *p*	Heb.	3	16
P to love and good works	Heb.	10	24

provoking God *see* anger of God

prudence *ability to discipline oneself*

The young should cultivate	Prov.	3	21
Connected with wisdom	Prov.	8	12
	Prov.	16	21
In control of speech	Prov.	10	19
	James	1	19
Of the wicked, denounced by God	Is.	5	21
Given by God	Eph.	1	8

Those who have:

Suppress anger	Prov.	12	16
Understand their own way	Prov.	14	8
Accept reproof	Prov.	15	5
Receive knowledge	Prov.	18	15
Foresee and avoid evil	Prov.	22	3
Understand the ways of God	Hosea	14	9

Exemplified by:

Jacob	Gen.	32	3–23
David	I Sam.	16	18
Abigail	I Sam.	25	23–31
Joseph	Mat.	1	19
Christ	Mat.	21	24–27
Paul	Acts	23	6

psalm *a sacred song or poem*

Make a joyful noise with	Ps.	95	2
Sing, unto the Lord	Ps.	105	2
Christ fulfills prophecies of	Luke	24	44
	Acts	13	33
For the merry	James	5	13
David wrote many	Luke	20	42

Prophecy in	Luke	24	44
For Christians	Eph.	5	19
	Col.	3	16

psaltery *an ancient musical stringed instrument*

Used in religious services	II Chr.	29	25
Played at dedication of walls	Neh.	12	27
Played for praise of God	Ps.	33	2
Used in idolatrous worship	Dan.	3	5
In worship	Ps.	150	3

Ptolemais *Accho*

A seaport near Haifa	Acts	21	7

Pua, Puah, Phuvah *utterance*

Son of Issachar	Gen.	46	13
Founds family of Punites	Num.	26	23
A Hebrew midwife	Ex.	1	15
Father of Tola, son of Dodo	Judg.	10	1

public opinion *popular sentiment*

A power of evil	Ex.	32	22–24
Accepts code	Deut.	5	27
Accepts leader	Josh.	1	16, 17
Rejects a king	I Ki.	12	16
Fear not	Ps.	27	1
Jesus concerned with	Mat.	16	13
Feared	Mark	11	18, 30–32
	Luke	22	2
Effect of	John	9	22

publicans *Roman tax collectors*

Disreputable	Mat.	5	46, 47
Matthew, a publican	Mat.	9	9
Many embrace the gospel	Mat.	21	31
Repent under the preaching of John the Baptist	Luke	3	2–12
Parable concerning	Luke	18	9–14
Despised by the Jews	Luke	18	11
Jesus dines with	Luke	19	2–8
Paralleled with heathen	Mat.	18	17
Seek to hear Jesus	Luke	15	1

publish *make known*

I will *p* the name of the Lord	Deut.	32	3
P it not in Askelon	II Sam.	1	20
May *p* it with the voice of thanksgiving	Ps.	26	7
Great was the company that *p* it	Ps.	68	11
That *p* peace	Is.	52	7
	Nah.	1	15
He caused it to be *p*	Jonah	3	7
He began to *p* it much	Mark	1	45
	Mark	5	20
P throughout whole city	Luke	8	39
Word of the Lord was *p*	Acts	13	49

Publius *popular, common*

Chief of the island of Melita	Acts	28	7
Paul heals his father	Acts	28	8

Pudens *modest, bashful*

A Christian at Rome	II Tim.	4	21

pulpit *an elevated stage for a clergyman*

Of bronze	II Chr.	6	13
Of wood	Neh.	8	4

punishment

Of the wicked, is from God	Lev.	26	18
Not inflicted on testimony of less than two witnesses	Num.	35	30
Not to be remitted for murder	Num.	35	31
A warning to others	Deut.	13	11
Is the reward of sin	Ps.	91	8
	Is.	3	11
	Rom.	6	23
Often commences in this life	Prov.	11	31
Should be accompanied by remorse	Is.	66	24
Shall be according to deed	Mat.	16	27
Consummated at the day of judgment	Mat.	25	31, 46
	II Pet.	2	9

In this life by:

Bringing down their pride	Is.	13	11
Cutting off	Ps.	94	23
Deliverance unto enemies	Neh.	9	27
Famine	Lev.	26	19–20
	Ps.	107	34
Fear	Lev.	26	36–37
	Job	18	11
Noisome beasts	Lev.	26	22
Put in slippery places	Ps.	73	3–19
Reprobate mind	Rom.	1	28
Sickness	Lev.	26	16
	Ps.	78	50
Trouble and distress	Is.	8	22
	Zeph.	1	15

War	Lev.	26	25, 32–33
	Jer.	6	4
Brought on by:			
Covetousness	Jer.	51	13
	Is.	57	17
Disobeying God	Neh.	9	26–27
	Neh.	9	2
	Eph.	5	6
Disobeying the gospel	II Thes.	1	8
Evil ways and doings	Jer.	21	14
	Hosea	4	9
	Hosea	12	2
Idolatry	Is.	10	10–11
	Lev.	26	30
Ignorance of God	II Thes.	1	8
Iniquity	Ezek.	3	17–18
	Ezek.	18	4, 13, 20
	Jer.	36	31
	Amos	3	2
Oppressing	Is.	49	26
	Jer.	30	16, 20
Persecuting	Jer.	11	21–22
	Mat.	23	34–36
Rejection of the law of God	I Sam.	15	23
	Hosea	4	6–9
Sin	Lam.	3	39
Pride	Is.	10	12
	Luke	14	11
Unbelief	Mark	16	16
Minor offences punished by:			
Fines	Ex.	21	22
Scourging	Deut.	25	2, 3
Mutilating	Judg.	1	5–7
	Ezek.	23	25
Torturing	Judg.	16	21
	Mat.	18	34
Imprisonment	Ezra	7	26
	Mat.	5	25
Binding in chains	Ps.	105	18
Confinement in stocks	Jer.	20	2
Future, described as:			
Blackness of darkness	II Pet.	2	17
	Jude		13
Damnation of hell	Mat.	23	33
Darkness	Mat.	8	12
	II Pet.	2	17
Death	Rom.	5	12–17
	Rom.	6	23
Eternal damnation	Mark	3	29
Everlasting burnings	Is.	33	14
Everlasting destruction	Ps.	52	5
	Ps.	92	7
	II Thes.	1	9
Everlasting fire	Mat.	25	41
	Jude		7
Hell	Ps.	9	17
	Mat.	5	29
	Luke	12	5
	Luke	16	23
Often sudden and unexpected	Ps.	35	8
	Ps.	64	7
	Prov.	29	1
	Luke	12	20
	I Thes.	5	3
Resurrection of damnation	John	5	29
The righteousness of God requires	II Thes.	1	6
Rising to shame and everlasting contempt	Dan.	12	2
Second death	Rev.	2	11
	Rev.	21	8
Torment forever and ever	Rev.	14	11
Torment with fire	Rev.	14	10
Wine of the wrath of God	Rev.	14	10
The wrath of God	John	3	36
Mosaic law demands death penalty for:			
Murder	Gen.	9	5, 6
Disobedience to parents	Ex.	21	15, 17
Kidnapping	Ex.	21	16
Witchcraft	Ex.	22	18
Sodomy	Lev.	18	22
Adultery	Lev.	20	10
Incest	Lev.	20	15, 16
Blasphemy	Lev.	24	11
Rape	Deut.	22	25
Treason	I Ki.	2	25
Perjury	Zech.	5	4

Modes of death penalty:			
Burning	Gen.	38	24
Beheading	Gen.	40	19
Hanging	Num.	25	4
Cutting in pieces	Dan.	2	5
Exposing to wild beasts	Dan.	6	16, 24
Drowning	Mat.	18	6
Crucifying	Mat.	27	35
Pur, Purim *see* feasts and festivals			
purchase			
Abraham *p* of sons of Heth	Gen.	25	10
I *p* to be my wife	Ruth	4	10
Congregation thou hast *p*	Ps.	74	2
This man *p* a field	Acts	1	18
Thought that the gift of God may be *p* with money	Acts	8	20
He hath *p* with his own blood	Acts	20	28
Redemption of *p* possession	Eph.	1	14
P to themselves a good degree	I Tim.	3	13
pure			
With the *p* thou wilt show thyself *p*	II Sam.	22	27
	Ps.	18	26
Shall a man be more *p* than his Maker	Job	4	17
If thou wert *p* and upright	Job	8	6
My doctrine is *p*	Job	11	4
May prayer is *p*	Job	16	17
Stars are not *p* in his sight	Job	25	5
Words of the Lord are *p*	Ps.	12	6
Commandment of Lord is *p*	Ps.	19	8
Words of the *p* are pleasant	Prov.	15	26
Who can say, I am *p* from sin	Prov.	20	29
Shall I count them *p*	Mic.	6	11
A *p* language	Zeph.	3	9
I am *p* from blood of all men	Acts	20	26
All things indeed are *p*	Rom.	14	20
Whatsoever things are *p*	Phil.	4	8
A *p* conscience	I Tim.	3	9
	II Tim.	1	3
Keep thyself *p*	I Tim.	5	22
To the *p* all things are *p*	Tit.	1	15
Bodies washed with *p* water	Heb.	10	22
P religion	James	1	27
Wisdom from above is first *p*	James	3	17
I stir up your *p* minds	II Pet.	3	1
Purifieth himself even as he is *p*	I John	3	3
purge			
P me with hyssop	Ps.	51	7
Transgressions, thou shalt *p*	Ps.	65	3
Purely *p* away thy dross	Is.	1	25
Thy sin is *p*	Is.	6	7
I have *p* thee, and thou wast not *p*	Ezek.	24	13
P them as gold	Mal.	3	3
He will throughly *p* his floor	Mat.	3	12
	Luke	3	17
Branch that beareth fruit, he *p*	John	15	2
P out the old leaven	I Cor.	5	7
If a man *p* himself from these	II Tim.	2	21
P your conscience	Heb.	9	14
Worshippers once *p*	Heb.	10	2
Hath forgotten he was *p*	II Pet.	1	9
purification			
Laws concerning	Lev.	13–16	
Of women	Esth.	2	12
	Luke	2	22
Of the heart, by faith	Acts	15	9
At passover	John	11	55
Those killed in battle	Num.	31	19–24
By blood	Ex.	24	5–8
Washing with water	Lev.	1	9
As a penalty	Lev.	7	20, 21
Hands in water	Deut.	21	6
Traditons of Jews	Mat.	15	2
Of Paul	Acts	21	24, 26
Figurative	Ps.	26	6
	Ezek.	36	25
	Heb.	10	22
purity			
Of God's word and law	Ps.	12	6
	Prov.	30	5
Moral, enjoined	Gal.	5	16
purple *a colour between violet and crimson*			
Tabernacle curtains	Ex.	26	1
The temple vail	Ex.	26	36
	II Chr.	3	14
Hangings for the gate	Ex.	27	16

purple—*continued*

In the ephod	Ex.	28	6
In the breastplate	Ex.	28	15
In the holy garments	Ex.	39	1, 2
Symbolic of royalty	Judg.	8	26
Christ's robe	Mark	15	17

purpose *intention*

Every *p* is established by counsel	Prov.	20	18
A time to every *p*	Eccl.	3	1, 17
	Eccl.	8	6
To what *p* are your sacrifices	Is.	1	11
Lord hath *p*, who shall disannul it	Is.	14	27
With the *p* of heart	Acts	11	23
Called according to his *p*	Rom.	8	28
That *p* of God might stand	Rom.	9	11
Do I *p* according to the flesh	II Cor.	1	17
Every man as he *p* in heart	II Cor.	9	7
According to the *p* of him who worketh	Eph.	1	11
Eternal *p* in Christ	Eph.	3	11
For this *p* the Son of God	I John	3	8

purse *bag*

To hold money	Prov.	7	20
Not carried by disciples	Luke	10	4

pursue *follow after*

Lest avenge *p*	Deut.	19	6
	Josh.	20	5
Terrors *p* my soul	Job	30	15
Seek peace, and *p* it	Ps.	34	14
He that *p* evil *p* death	Prov.	11	19
Wicked flee when no man *p*	Prov.	28	1

put

I will *p* enmity	Gen.	3	15
P not thine hand with the wicked	Ex.	23	1
P ten thousand to flight	Lev.	26	8
	Deut.	32	30
Lord *p* word in Balaam's mouth	Num.	23	5
I *p* my life in my hands	Judg.	12	3
	I Sam.	28	21
P me into one of the priest's offices	I Sam.	2	36
To *p* my name there	I Ki.	9	3
	I Ki.	11	36
	I Ki.	14	21
P their lives in jeopardy	I Chr.	11	19
What God *p* in my heart	Neh.	2	12
Hath *p* my brethren far from me	Job	19	13
Thou hast *p* gladness in my heart	Ps.	4	7
Thou hast *p* all things under his feet	Ps.	8	6
	Eph.	1	22
	Heb.	2	8
Lover and friend hast thou *p* far from me	Ps.	88	18
That *p* darkness for light	Is.	5	20
I have *p* my Spirit upon him	Is.	42	1
	Mat.	12	18
Let not man *p* asunder	Mat.	19	6
	Mark	10	9
He *p* his hands on them	Mark	10	16
No man to *p* me into the pool	John	5	7
P all his enemies under his feet	I Cor.	15	25
P off old man	Eph.	4	22
	Col.	3	9
P that on my account	Phil.		18
P him to an open shame	Heb.	6	6
To *p* away sin by the sacrifice of himself	Heb.	9	26
I must *p* off this my tabernacle	II Pet.	1	14
Will *p* you in remembrance	Jude		5
P on you none other burden	Rev.	2	24

Put *see* Phut

Pygarg *the leaper, type of antelope*

A clean animal	Deut.	14	5

Q

quail *partridge or bobwhite*

Israel fed with	Ex.	16	13
People punished for eating	Num.	11	31–33

quake *see* earthquake

quarantine *restraint due to contagion*

For leprosy	Lev.	13	2–5
	Lev.	13	31–33
Of the unclean woman	Lev.	15	19

quarreling *angry disputing*

Cause of	Prov.	13	10
A brawling woman	Prov.	21	9
To be avoided	Tit.	3	2
Avenged by sword	Lev.	26	25
King of Syria	II Ki.	5	7
Herodias against John	Mark	6	9
To forgive	Col.	3	13
See strife			

quarries *open excavations*

Near Gilgal	Judg.	3	19

Quartus *fourth*

A Christian of Corinth	Rom.	16	23

Quaternion

A squad of four soldiers	Acts	12	4

queen *a female monarch*

Deference due	I Ki.	2	19
Of Sheba	I Ki.	10	1–13
Maachah, mother of Asa	I Ki.	15	13
Jezebel	I Ki.	21	1, 5
Athaliah usurps throne	II Ki.	11	1–3
Sits on a throne	Neh.	2	6
Makes a feast	Esth.	1	9
Vashti dethroned	Esth.	1	12–21
Esther crowned	Esth.	2	17
Of heaven	Jer.	44	17, 25
Candace	Acts	8	27

quench *put out*

The fire was *q*	Num.	11	2
They shall *q* my coal	II Sam.	14	7
Q not the light of Israel	II Sam.	21	17
Many waters cannot *q* love	S. of S.	8	7
Shall not be *q* night or day	Is.	34	10
Smoking flax shall he not *q*	Is.	42	3
	Mat.	12	20
Neither shall their fire be *q*	Is.	66	24
Where fire is not *q*	Mark	9	44, 46, 48
Able to *q* fiery darts of wicked	Eph.	6	16
Q not the Spirit	I Thes.	5	19
Q the violence of fire	Heb.	11	34

question

To prove him with a *q*	I Ki.	10	1
	II Chr.	9	1
Neighter durst ask any more *q*	Mat.	22	46
What *q* ye with them	Mark	9	16
I will ask of you one *q*	Mark	11	29
If it be a *q* of words	Acts	18	15
In danger to be called in *q*	Acts	19	40
Asking no *q* for conscience' sake	I Cor.	10	25
Doting about *q*	I Tim.	6	4
Unlearned *q* avoid	II Tim.	2	23
	Tit.	3	9

quick *sudden, fast*

They go down *q*	Num.	16	30
	Ps.	55	15
They had swallowed us up *q*	Ps.	124	3
Make him of *q* understanding	Is.	11	3
The word of God is *q* and powerful	Heb.	4	12
Judge the *q* and the dead	Acts	10	42
	II Tim.	4	1
	I Pet.	4	5

quicken *make alive*

Thou shalt *q* me again	Ps.	71	20
Q us, and we will call on thy name	Ps.	80	18
Q me according to thy word	Ps.	119	25
Q me, O Lord, for thy name's sake	Ps.	143	11
Shall *q* your mortal bodies	Rom.	8	11
That which thou sowest is not *q*	I Cor.	15	36
You hath he *q*, who were dead	Eph.	2	1
Q us together with Christ	Eph.	2	5
	Col.	2	13
Q by thy Spirit	I Pet.	3	10

quickening

Spiritual	John	5	21
	John	6	63
	Rom.	4	17
	I Cor.	15	45
	II Cor.	3	6
	I Tim.	6	13

quickly

How hast thou found it so *q*	Gen.	27	20
Have turned *q* out of the way	Ex.	32	8
	Deut.	9	12
Go *q* to congregation	Num.	16	46
During *q*, overtake them	Josh.	2	5

Threefold cord not *q* broken	Eccl.	4	12
Agree with thine adversary *q*	Mat.	5	25
That thou doest, do *q*	John	13	27
Repent, else I come *q*	Rev.	2	5, 16
Behold I come *q*	Rev.	3	11
	Rev.	22	7, 12, 20

quicksand *sand deposit which easily engulfs objects*

Paul in danger of	Acts	27	17

quiet

The faithful shall dwell in	Prov.	1	33
	Is.	30	15
	Is.	32	17, 18
To be enjoined	I Thes.	4	11
	I Tim.	2	2
One dieth, being at ease and *q*	Job	21	23
Glad, because they be *q*	Ps.	107	30
Words of wise men are heard in *q*	Eccl.	9	17
Take heed, and be *q*	Is.	7	4
The earth is at rest, and is *q*	Is.	14	7
In *q* resting places	Is.	32	18
Sorrow on the sea; it cannot be *q*	Jer.	49	23
I will be *q*	Ezek.	16	42
Ye ought to be *q*	Acts	19	36
Ornament of a meek and *q* spirit	I Pet.	3	4

quietness *tranquility*

Applied to peace	Judg.	8	28
Commended	Job	34	29
	Prov.	17	1
Strength of	Is.	30	15
Work in	II Thes.	3	12

Quirinius, Cyrenius *warrior*

Governor of Syria	Luke	2	2

quiver *a case for carrying arrows*

Slung across shoulder	Gen.	27	3
On side of chariot	Lam.	3	13

R

Raamses *see* Rameses

Rabbah, Rabbath *great*

Bedstead of Og, the giant	Deut.	3	11
A city of Gad	Josh.	13	25
Besieged	II Sam.	11	1
	II Sam.	12	26
Capital city of Ammon	II Sam.	12	27 30
Falls to David	II Sam.	12	31
Destruction foretold	Ezek.	25	5
A city of Judah	Josh.	15	50

Rabbi, Rabboni *master (Aramaic)*

Applied to scribes and Pharisees	Mat.	23	2, 7
Title loved	Mat.	23	7
Title of Jesus	John	1	38
The teacher	John	3	2
Title of John the Baptist	John	3	26
Title given by Mary	John	20	16
Forbidden	Mat.	23	8

rabble *mob, riffraff*

Lusts	Num.	11	4
Captures Jesus	Mat.	26	47, 50
Calls for crucifixion	Mat.	27	20–24
Rousers	Acts	17	1–14
	John	20	16

Rabboni *see* Rabbi

Rab-shakeh *chief cupbearer*

Officer of Sennacherib	Is.	36	1–22
	II Ki.	18	17
	II Ki.	19	4

raca *vain fellow (Aramaic)*

Term used in defamation	Mat.	5	22

race

Unity of the human	Gen.	3	20
	Job	31	15
	Mal.	2	10
No man is common or unclean	Acts	10	28
See prejudice			
For the strong	Ps.	19	5
Not necessarily won by the swift	Eccl.	9	11
Only one prize	I Chr.	9	24
Compared to Christian life	Phil.	2	16
	Heb.	12	1, 2

Rachab *see* Rahab

Rachel *lamb*

Daughter of Laban	Gen.	29	5, 6
Second wife of Jacob	Gen.	29	28
Gives maid in order to secure children	Gen.	30	3, 4
Mother of Joseph	Gen.	30	25
Steals images of father	Gen.	31	19
Labour and death	Gen.	35	16–20
Mother of Benjamin	Gen.	35	24
Name used in blessing	Ruth	4	11
Weeping for slain children	Mat.	2	18

Ragau *see* Reu

rage *fit of fury*

Of Naaman	II Ki.	5	12
Of a fool	Prov.	14	16
Of the heathen	Acts	4	25
Of the sea	Ps.	89	9
Of Sennacherib against God	II Ki.	19	27–28
Of the heathen	Ps.	2	1
Of enemies	Ps.	7	6
Jealousy	Prov.	6	34
Of the tongue	Hosea	7	16

rags *tatters*

Clothed in	Prov.	23	21
Filthy	Is.	64	6
Rotten	Jer.	28	11, 12

Raguel *see* Reuel

Rahab, Rachab *broad, tumult*

A harlot of Jericho	Josh.	2	1
Hides spies	Josh.	2	3, 4, 6
Life spared	Josh.	6	22–25
Ancestress of Jesus	Mat.	1	5
An example of faith	Heb.	11	31
Justified by works	James	2	25
Poetic name for Egypt	Ps.	87	4
	Is.	51	9

railer *scoffer, reviler*

Nabal	I Sam.	25	14
Shimei	II Sam.	16	7
At the crucifixion	Mark	15	29
Ostracized	I Cor.	5	11
Knows nothing	I Tim.	6	4
Contrariwise	I Pet.	3	8, 9
Not against angels	II Pet.	2	11
Against the devil	Jude		9

raiment *see* garments

raiment *clothing*

Goodly *r*	Gen.	27	15
If the Lord will give me *r*	Gen.	28	20
Thy *r* waxed not old	Deut.	8	4
Nor take a widow's *r* to pledge	Deut.	24	17
Though he prepare *r* as clay	Job	27	16
Ten changes of *r*	II Ki.	5	5
Be brought to the king in *r* of needlework	Ps.	45	14
I will stain all my *r*	Is.	63	3
I will clothe thee with *r*	Zech.	3	4
His *r* of camel's hair	Mat.	3	4
The body more than *r*	Mat.	6	25
	Luke	12	23
A man clothed in soft *r*	Mat.	11	8
	Luke	7	25
His *r* white as light	Mat.	17	2
	Mark	9	3
	Luke	9	29
They parted his *r*	Luke	23	34
	John	19	24
Having food and *r*, let us be content	I Tim.	6	8
A poor man in vile *r*	James	2	2
Buy white *r*	Rev.	3	18

rain *water falling in drops*

Withheld because of iniquity	Deut.	11	17
	Jer.	5	25
God exhibits greatness and goodness in giving	Job	36	26, 27
	Acts	14	17
Designed for:			
Refreshing the earth	Ps.	72	6
Replenishing springs	Ps.	104	8
Making the earth fruitful	Heb.	6	7
Instances of extraordinary:			
Time of flood	Gen.	7	4, 12
Plague of, upon Egypt	Ex.	9	18, 23
In days of Samuel	I Sam.	12	17, 18
After drought	I Ki.	18	45

rain—*continued*

After the captivity	Ezra	10	9, 13

Illustrative of:

Doctrine of faithful ministers	Deut.	32	2
God's judgments	Job	20	23
Spiritual blessings	Ps.	84	6
Impiety	Prov.	28	3
Word of God	Is.	55	10, 11
Righteousness	Hosea	10	12

rainbow *a phenomenon*

Token of the covenant	Gen.	9	8–17
Glorious	Ezek.	1	28
Surrounds the throne of God	Rev.	4	3
Worn by angels	Rev.	10	1

raise

Lord will *r* up a prophet	Deut.	18	15
	Acts	3	22
He *r* poor out of the dust	I Sam.	2	8
	Ps.	113	7
He *r* those that be bowed down	Ps.	145	14
	Ps.	146	8
I will *r* up decayed places	Is.	44	26
In the third day he will *r* us up	Hosea	6	2
Dead are *r* up	Mat.	11	5
	Luke	7	22
In three days I will *r* it up	John	2	19
I will *r* him up at the last day	John	6	40
Why incredible that God should *r* the dead	Acts	26	8
Was *r* again for our justification	Rom.	4	25
As Christ was *r* from the dead	Rom.	6	4
God will *r* up us by his power	I Cor.	6	14
Trust in God which *r* the dead	II Cor.	1	9
He shall *r* up us by Jesus	II Cor.	4	14
R us up together	Eph.	2	6
Accounting that God was able to *r* him	Heb.	11	19
The Lord shall *r* him up	James	5	15
Believe in God that *r* him	I Pet.	1	21

raisins *dried grapes*

Clusters of	I Sam.	25	18
As food	I Sam.	30	11, 12
Bunches of	II Sam.	16	1
Render a flagon of wine	I Chr.	16	3
	Hosea	3	1

ram *a male sheep*

ram, battering *see battering-ram*

Used in the covenant	Gen.	15	9
The burnt offering	Gen.	22	13
As food	Gen.	31	38
Skins dyed red	Ex.	26	14
Trespass offering	Lev.	5	15
Of consecration	Lev.	8	22
The breast for a wave offering	Lev.	8	29
Blood mixed with anointing oil	Lev.	8	30
Horns used as trumpets	Josh.	6	4–6, 8, 13
Used symbolically	Dan.	8	3–7, 20

Ram *high, exalted*

Son of Hezron	Ruth	4	19
Called Aram, ancestor of Jesus	Mat.	1	3, 4
Son of Jerahmeel	I Chr.	2	25
Father of Maaz, Jamin and Eker	I Chr.	2	27
Ancestor of Elihu	Job	32	2

Rama, Ramah *elevation*

A city of Benjamin	Josh.	18	25
Near mount Ephraim	Judg.	4	5
Fortified	I Ki.	15	17, 21, 22
Inhabitants return from captivity	Ezra	2	26
A gathering place for captives	Jer.	40	1
Burialplace of Rachel	Mat.	2	18
A city of Asher	Josh.	19	29
City of Naphtali	Josh.	19	36
Residence of Samuel	I Sam.	1	19
	I Sam.	7	17
David flees to	I Sam.	19	18
Samuel buried here	I Sam.	25	1
A city, called Ramoth-gilead	II Ki.	8	28, 29

Ramath *see* Ramoth

Ramathaim-zophim *see* Rama

Ramath-lehi *see* Lehi

Rameses, Raamses, Ramses *son of Ra (the sun god)*

A district, the best land of Egypt	Gen.	47	11
A treasure city	Ex.	1	11
Starting point of the exodus	Ex.	12	37
	Num.	33	3, 5

Ramoth, Ramath *heights*

A city of Gilead	Deut.	4	43
East of the Jordan	Josh.	20	8
Called Ramath	Josh.	19	8
Of the south	I Sam.	30	27
City of Issachar	I Chr.	6	72, 73
Son of Bani	Ezra	10	29

Ramoth *gilead*

Given to Gad	Josh.	20	8
Claimed by king of Israel	I Ki.	22	3
Ahab shot there	II Chr.	18	3
Joram slain fighting Syrians	II Chr.	22	5
Levitical city	I Chr.	6	80

rampart *wall of defense*

A protective barrier	Lam.	2	8
	Nah.	3	8

ransom *see* redemption

Christ our	Mat.	20	28
	I Tim.	2	6
He shall give for the *r* of his life	Ex.	21	30
Give every man a *r* for his soul	Ex.	30	12
I have found a *r*	Job	33	24
A great *r* cannot deliver thee	Job	36	18
Nor give to God a *r* for him	Ps.	49	7
He will not regard any *r*	Prov.	6	35
R of a man's life are his riches	Prov.	13	8
R of the Lord shall return	Is.	35	10
I gave Egypt for thy *r*	Is.	43	3
To give his life a *r* for many	Mark	10	45
I will *r* them from grave	Hosea	13	14

rape *to ravish*

Brings death penalty	Deut.	22	25–27
Causes the death of a concubine	Judg.	19	24–29
	Judg.	20	3–5
Of Tamar	II Sam.	13	1–14

Rapha, Raphah *he has healed*

Fifth son of Benjamin	I Chr.	8	2
A descendant of Saul and Jonathan	I Chr.	8	37

rash *hasty action*

In speaking	Ps.	116	11
	Prov.	29	20
	Eccl.	5	2
In spirit	Prov.	14	29
	Eccl.	7	9
Leads to want	Prov.	21	5

Examples:

Moses	Ex.	2	11, 12
	Num.	20	10–12
Jephtha	Judg.	11	31–39
Uzzah	II Sam.	6	6, 7
Josiah	II Chr.	35	20–24
James and John	Luke	9	54

rasor *see* razor

rationing *fixed allowance*

Of food, clothing, luxuries	Gen.	41	35, 54
	Is.	3	18–26

raven *a black bird*

Released from the ark by Noah	Gen.	8	7
Unfit for food	Lev.	11	15
Feeds Elijah	I Ki.	17	4, 6
God cares for	Job	38	41
	Ps.	147	9
	Luke	12	24
Feeds on carrion	Prov.	30	17
Fine glossy black plumage	S. of S.	5	11
Associated with plundered cities	Is.	34	11

razor *sharp-edged instrument*

Never used by Samson	Judg.	16	17
The Lord shaves with	Is.	7	20
Barber's razor	Ezek.	5	1

reading

Of the Bible	Deut.	17	18, 19
	Luke	4	16–22
	Acts	17	10, 11
Of the law	Josh.	8	34
	Neh.	8	9
Of the prophets	Luke	4	16
Of the epistles	Col.	4	16

ready

A Syrian *r* to perish	Deut.	26	5
A God *r* to pardon	Neh.	9	17
Blessing of him *r* to perish	Job	29	13
I am *r* to halt	Ps.	38	17
Pen of a *r* writer	Ps.	45	1

Lord good, and *r* to forgive	Ps.	86	5
Strong drink unto him *r* to perish	Prov.	31	6
Be more *r* to hear	Eccl.	5	1
Shall come which were *r* to perish	Is.	27	13
Tongue of stammerers *r* to speak plainly	Is.	32	4
All things are *r*	Mat.	22	4
	Luke	14	17
Be ye also *r*	Mat.	24	44
	Luke	12	40
They that were *r* went in	Mat.	25	10
The spirit is *r*, but the flesh is weak	Mark	14	38
R to go with thee	Luke	22	33
Your time is always *r*	John	7	6
I am *r* not to be bound only	Acts	21	13
Declaration of your *r* mind	II Cor.	8	19
R to distribute	I Tim.	6	18
I am now *r* to be offered	II Tim.	4	6
R to every good work	Tit.	3	1
Old is *r* to vanish	Heb.	8	13
R to be revealed in last time	I Pet.	1	5
Be *r* always to give an answer	I Pet.	3	15
But of a *r* mind	I Pet.	5	2
The things that are *r* to die	Rev.	3	2
I am *r* to preach the gospel at Rome	Rom.	1	15
Declaration of your *r* mind	II Cor.	8	19
R to distribute	I Tim.	6	18
I am now *r* to be offered	II Tim.	4	6
R to every good work	Tit.	3	1
Old is *r* to vanish	Heb.	8	13
R to be revealed in last time	I Pet.	1	5
Be *r* always to give an answer	I Pet.	3	15
But of a *r* mind	I Pet.	5	2

reaping *gathering, as a harvest*

Provision for poor	Lev.	19	9, 10
Spiritual, its reward	John	4	35–38
Promise to the faithful	Gal.	6	9
Used symbolically	Ps.	126	5
	Amos	9	13
	Mat.	6	26
	I Cor.	9	11

reason

Seven men that can render a *r*	Prov.	26	16
To search out the *r* of things	Eccl.	7	25
By *r* of him who hath subjected	Rom.	8	20
A *r* of the hope that is in you	I Pet.	3	15
That I may *r* with you	I Sam.	12	7
Choose words to *r* with him	Job	9	14
I desire to *r* with God	Job	13	3
Let us *r* together	Is.	1	18
Why *r* ye among yourselves	Mat.	16	8
	Mark	2	8
What *r* ye in your hearts	Luke	5	22
While they *r*, Jesus drew near	Luke	24	15
As he *r* of righteousness	Acts	24	25

Rebekah, Rebecca *noose, tying*

Daughter of Milcah and Bethuel	Gen.	24	15, 47
Wife of Isaac	Gen.	24	57–67
Sister of Laban	Gen.	25	20
Mother of Jacob and Esau	Gen.	25	21–26
Aids Jacob in fraud	Gen.	27	1–33
Buried in cave at Machpelah	Gen.	49	31

rebellion *revolt*

Against God	I Sam.	13	14
An act of treason	Prov.	17	11
Caused by envy	Num.	16	1–24
Against civil law	Rom.	13	2, 3

Instances:

Absalom	II Sam.	15	18
Sheba	II Sam.	20	1–22
The ten tribes	I Ki.	12	16–20

rebellion against God

Man is prone to	Deut.	31	27
God forgives	Neh.	9	26, 27
Heart is seat of	Mat.	15	18, 19

Exemplified:

Pharaoh	Ex.	5	1, 2
Moses and Aaron	Num.	20	12, 24
Israelites	Deut.	9	23, 24
Saul	I Sam.	15	9, 23
Jeroboam	I Ki.	12	28–33
Zedekiah	II Chr.	36	13
Kingdoms of Israel	Hosea	7	14
	Hosea	13	16

Exhibited in:

Unbelief and refusal to hearken	Deut.	9	23
	Ezek.	20	8
	Zech.	7	11

Rejecting His government	I Sam.	8	7
	I Sam.	15	23
Despising His law and counsels	Neh.	9	29
Revolting from Him	Is.	31	6
Departing from Him and His precepts	Is.	59	13
	Dan.	9	5
Distrusting His power	Ezek.	17	15

Connected with:

Stubbornness	Deut.	31	27
Contempt of God	Ps.	107	11
Injustice and corruption	Is.	1	23

rebuke *to reprimand sharply*

Of a brother	I Sam.	17	28
A wife's	II Sam.	6	20
Better than flattery	Prov.	28	23
Of disciples, by Jesus	Mark	10	13–16
Request God not	Ps.	6	1
A wise man	Prov.	9	8
A delight	Prov.	24	25
Of nations	Is.	2	4
Not an elder	I Tim.	5	1
A solemn duty	Luke	17	3, 4
For past deeds	Acts	13	9–11
With authority	Tit.	2	15
Moderation in	Jude		9

Examples of:

Saul by Samuel	I Sam.	13	13
Ahab by Elijah	I Ki.	21	20
Judah by Zachariah	II Chr.	24	20
Israel by Ezra	Ezra	10	10, 11
The Lord by Peter	Mat.	16	22

receive

Shall we *r* good, and not *r* evil	Job	2	10
R the law from his mouth	Job	22	22
The Lord will *r* my prayer	Ps.	6	9
He shall *r* blessing from the Lord	Ps.	24	5
God shall *r* me	Ps.	49	15
Hast *r* gifts for men	Ps.	68	18
Afterward *r* me to glory	Ps.	73	24
If thou wilt *r* my words	Prov.	2	1
She hath *r* of the Lord's hand double	Is.	40	2
R us graciously	Hosea	14	2
If ye will *r* it, this is Elias	Mat.	11	14
He that is able to *r* it, let him *r* it	Mat.	19	12
Whatsoever ye ask, believing ye shall *r*	Mat.	21	22
R the word with joy	Mark	4	16
	Luke	8	13
When ye pray, believe that ye *r*	Mark	11	24
He was *r* up into heaven	Mark	16	19
	Acts	1	9
May *r* you into everlasting habitations	Luke	16	9
R reward of our deeds	Luke	23	41
As many as *r* him	John	1	12
A man can *r* nothing, except it be given him	John	3	27
Come in his own name, him ye will *r*	John	5	43
Ask, and ye shall *r*	John	16	24
Ye shall *r* the gift of the Holy Ghost	Acts	2	38
Shall *r* remission of sins	Acts	10	43
More blessed to give than to *r*	Acts	20	35
By whom we have *r* atonement	Rom.	5	11
Him that is weak in faith *r* ye	Rom.	14	1
Every man shall *r* his own reward	I Cor.	3	8
R of the Lord that which I delivered	I Cor.	11	23
Every one may *r* things done in his body	II Cor.	5	10
He shall *r* for the wrong done	Col.	3	25

reciprocation *a return in kind*

Duty to each other	Rom.	15	27
Ministers to people	Gal.	6	6

reckon

He shall *r* with him that bought him	Lev.	25	50
Thy thoughts cannot be *r* up	Ps.	40	5
When he had begun to *r*	Mat.	18	24
Lord of those servants cometh, and *r* with them	Mat.	25	19
The reward is not *r* of grace	Rom.	4	4
R yourselves dead to sin	Rom.	6	11
I *r* that the sufferings of this present time	Rom.	8	18

recompense *pay, reward*

He shall *r* his trespass	Num.	5	7
To me belongeth *r*	Deut.	32	35
The Lord *r* thy work	Ruth	2	12
Why should the king *r* me	II Sam.	19	36
Vanity shall be his *r*	Job	15	31
He will *r* it whether	Job	43	33

recompense—continued

Say not, I will *r* evil	Prov.	20	22
R shall be rendered	Prov.	12	14
God will come with a *r*	Is.	35	4
I will *r*, even *r* into their bosom	Is.	65	6
I will *r* their iniquity	Jer.	16	18
I will *r* them according to their deeds	Jer.	25	14
	Hosea	12	2
The days of *r* are come	Hosea	9	7
Will ye render me a *r*	Joel	3	4
And a *r* be made thee	Luke	14	12
For they cannot *r* thee	Luke	14	14
Let their table be made a *r*	Rom.	11	9
R to no man evil of evil	Rom.	12	17
Now for a *r*, be ye also enlarged	II Cor.	6	13
That hath said, I will *r*	Heb.	10	30
Great *r* of reward	Heb.	10	35

reconcile *agreement*

Should he *r* himself	I Sam.	29	4
First be *r* to thy brother	Mat.	5	24
If when enemies we were *r* to God	Rom.	5	10
Be ye *r* to God	II Cor.	5	20
That he might *r* both to God	Eph.	2	16
To *r* all things to himself	Col.	1	20
	II Cor.	5	18
	Heb.	2	17

reconciliation *an overcoming of an estrangement*

Necessity for, illustrated	Mat.	5	21–24
	Mat.	6	12
	Mat.	18	21–35
A pledge of final salvation	Rom.	5	10
Of man and man:			
Jacob and Esau:	Gen.	32	1–32
	Gen.	33	1–17
In cities of refuge	Deut.	19	4–10
Saul and David	I Sam.	24	1–22
With God:			
Through Christ	Rom.	5	10
A coming to peace with God	Eph.	2	13–22
A power to transfrom men	Col.	1	21
Effects of:			
Peace of God	Rom.	5	1
Access to God	Rom.	5	2
Union of Jews and Gentiles	Eph.	2	14
Union of things in heaven and earth	Col.	1	20

recorder *historian*

High ranking official	II Sam.	8	16
Adviser of the king	II Ki.	18	18, 37

recover

Enquire whether shall *r*	II Ki.	1	2
The prophet would *r* him	II Ki.	5	3
That I may *r* strength	Ps.	39	13
R me, and make me live	Is.	38	16
Why is not my people *r*	Jer.	8	22
Lay hands on sick, and they shall *r*	Mark	16	18
R of sight to the blind	Luke	4	18
They may *r* themselves	II Tim.	2	26

recreation *see amusements*

red

Colour of Esau	Gen.	25	25
Colour of the pottage	Gen.	25	30
Judah's eyes	Gen.	49	12
The rams' skins in the tabernacle	Ex.	26	14
Heifer of purification	Num.	19	1–22
Symbolic of sin	Is.	1	18
Apparel	Is.	63	2
Vision of the red horse	Zech.	1	8
	Rev.	6	4
Sky	Mat.	16	2
Vision of the red dragon	Rev.	12	3–17

redeem *buy back, set free*

I will *r* you.	Ex.	6	6
People whom thou hast *r*	Ex.	15	13
What nation like Israel whom God went to *r*?	II Sam.	7	23
Nor is it in our power to *r* them	Neh.	5	5
In famine he shall *r* thee	Job	5	20
R me from hand of mighty	Job	6	23
R Israel out of all his troubles	Ps.	25	22
R me and be merciful to me	Ps.	26	11
The Lord *r* the soul of his servants	Ps.	34	22
God will *r* my soul from he grave	Ps.	49	15
He shall *r* their soul from deceit	Ps.	72	14
He shall *r* Israel	Ps.	130	8
The *r* shall walk there	Is.	35	9
Return to me, I have *r* thee	Is.	44	22

Is my hand shortened, that it cannot *r*?	Is.	50	2
The *r* of Lord shall return	Is.	51	11
Ye shall be *r* without money	Is.	52	3
I will *r* them from death	Hosea	13	14
Lord hath visited and *r* his people	Luke	1	68
He who should have *r* Israel	Luke	24	21
R us from curse of the law	Gal.	3	13
To *r* them that were under law	Gal.	4	5
That he might *r* us from all iniquity	Tit.	2	14
Not *r* with corruptible things	I Pet.	1	18
Thou hast *r* us to God	Rev.	5	9

redeemer *one who saves*

Of Israel	Is.	41	14
Title of Christ	Is.	59	20

redemption *deliverance*

Of property:			
Laws concerning	Lev.	25, 27	
Of Ruth by Boaz	Ruth	4	1–6
By Jeremiah	Jer.	32	1–15
Of slaves:			
Laws concerning	Lev.	25	47–55
For the soul:			
God, the author of	Ps.	31	5
Through Christ	Rom.	3	24
	Gal.	4	4, 5
By Christ's death	I Pet.	1	18, 19
Is precious	Ps.	49	8
Of his people	Ps.	111	9
Those looking for	Luke	2	38
	Luke	21	28
Of our body	Rom.	8	23
Through Christ's blood	Eph.	1	7
	Col.	1	14
The day of	Eph.	4	30
Eternal	Heb.	9	12

Red sea *sea of reeds*

Waters divided	Ex.	14	26–31
Egyptians perish in	Deut.	11	3, 4
Jehoshaphat's ships wrecked on	I Ki.	22	48
Solomon's navy on	II Chr.	9	21

reed, cane

Easily broken	II Ki.	18	21
Abundant along the Nile	Job	40	21
Used for measuring	Ezek.	40	5
A symbol of weakness	Mat.	11	7
Various uses at the crucifixion	Mat.	27	29, 30, 48

refining *taking away impurities*

Of silver and gold	Prov.	17	3
Symbolic of purification	Is.	48	10
	Zech.	13	9
	Mal.	3	2
Spiritual:			
By chastening	Job	15	2
By trials	I Pet.	1	7

refrain *hold back*

Joseph could not *r* himself	Gen.	45	1
I will not *r* my mouth	Job	7	11
I have not *r* my lips	Ps.	40	9
I *r* my feet from every evil way	Ps.	119	101
R thy foot from their pants	Prov.	1	15
He that *r* his lips is wise	Prov.	10	19
Wilt thou *r* thyself, O Lord?	Is.	64	12
R from these men	Acts	5	38
R his tongue from evil	I Pet.	3	10

refresh

On the seventh day He rested and was *r*	Ex.	31	17
Come home, and *r* thyself	I Ki.	13	7
I will speak that I may be *r*	Job	32	20
When times of *r* shall come	Acts	3	19
I may with you be *r*	Rom.	15	32

refuge, cities of *see cities of refuge*

refuge, divine

In God	Deut.	33	27
For the oppressed	Ps.	9	9
In trouble	Ps.	27	5
From enemies	Ps.	31	20
From the avenger of blood	Josh.	20	3
In the day of trouble	Ps.	59	16
Flee to	Heb.	6	18

refugee *one who flees for safety*

Jacob	Gen.	31	18
David	I Sam.	23	25, 26
Absalom	II Sam.	13	37, 38
Hadad	I Ki.	11	14–18

Jesus	Mat.	2	13–15

refuse *reject*

How long *r* ye to keep my commandments?	Ex.	16	28
Whether thou *r* or choose	Job	34	33
The stone which the builders *r*	Ps.	118	22
I have called, and ye *r*	Prov.	1	24
Be wise, and *r* it not	Prov.	8	33
He that *r* instruction despiseth his soul	Prov.	15	32
His hands *r* to labour	Prov.	21	25
May know to *r* the evil	Is.	7	15, 16
They *r* to return	Jer.	8	5
People *r* to hear my words	Jer.	13	10
Rachel *r* to be comforted	Jer.	31	15
If thou *r* to go forth	Jer.	38	21
Because they *r* to return	Hosea	11	5
They *r* to hearken	Zech.	7	11
This Moses whom they *r*	Acts	7	35
I *r* not to die	Acts	25	11
Nothing to be *r*	I Tim.	4	4
R profane fables	I Tim.	4	7
See that ye *r* not him that speaketh	Heb.	12	25
(See Lam. 3:45; Amos 8:6)			

regeneration, new birth, rebirth *re-creation, born again*

Transformation from self-centered to God-centered	Is.	1	16
	Jer.	31	33
For the glory of God	Is.	43	7
Manner of effecting illustrated	John	3	8
None can enter heaven without	John	3	3
Of the mercy of God	Tit.	3	5
Of the will of God	James	1	18
Preserves from Satan's devices	I John	5	18
Is of the spirit	John	3	1–12
	I Pet.	1	23
Found through Christ	Rom.	8	29
All saints partake of	Rom.	8	16–17
	I Pet.	2	2
	I John	5	1
Connected with adoption	Is.	43	6–7
	John	1	12–13
Corruption of human nature requires	John	3	6
	Rom.	8	7–8
Through the instrumentality of the ministry of the gospel	I Cor.	4	15
The resurrection of Christ	I Pet.	1	3
The word of God	James	1	18
	I Pet.	1	23

Described as:

Circumcision of the heart	Dcut.	30	6
	Rom.	2	29
	Col.	2	11
The inward man	Rom.	7	22
	II Cor.	4	16
A new creation	II Cor.	5	17
	Gal.	6	15
	Eph.	2	10
A new heart	Ezek.	36	26
A new spirit	Ezek.	11	19
	Rom.	6	6
Newness of life	Rom.	6	4
Partaking of the divine nature	II Pet.	1	4
Putting on the new man	Eph.	4	24
A spiritual resurrection	Rom.	6	4–6
	Eph.	2	1, 5
	Col.	2	12
	Col.	3	1
The washing of regeneration	Tit.	3	5

Effected by:

Christ	I John	2	29
God	John	1	13
	I Pet.	1	3
The Holy Ghost	John	3	6
	Tit.	3	5

Evidenced by:

Brotherly love	I John	4	7
Faith in Christ	I John	5	1
Righteousness	I John	2	29

Produces:

Delight in God's law	Rom.	7	22
Hatred of sin	I John	3	9
	I John	5	18
Knowledge of God	Jer.	24	7
	Col.	3	10
Likeness to Christ	Rom.	8	29
	II Cor.	3	18
	I John	3	2
Likeness to God	Eph.	4	24
Victory over the world	I John	5	4

Examples of:

Jacob at Jabbok	Gen.	32	22–32
Saul	I Sam.	10	9
Josiah on hearing second law	II Ki.	22	8–13
Isaiah in temple	Is.	6	1–8
Saul of Tarsus	Acts	9	3–18

As taught by:

Jesus	Mat.	18	1–4
Paul	Rom.	8	12–17

register *genealogical record*

Prepared by Ezra	Ezra	2	62
	Neh.	7	5, 64

Rehabiah *the Lord enlarges*

Grandson of Moses	I Chr.	23	17
	I Chr.	26	25

Rehoboam, Roboam *enlargement of the people*

Successor to Solomon as king	I Ki.	11	43
Refuses to reform abuses	I Ki.	12	1–15
Ten tribes revolt from	I Ki.	12	16–24
Builds fortified cities	II Chr.	11	5–23
Invades and despoils	I Ki.	14	25–28
Idolatry	I Ki.	14	21–24
Death of	I Ki.	14	31
Called Roboam	Mat.	1	7

Rehoboth *open spaces, streets*

City of Asshur	Gen.	10	11
Town on site of well dug by Isaac	Gen.	26	22
Home of Saul, an Edomite chief	Gen.	36	37

Rehum *merciful*

A chief who returns from exile	Ezra	2	2
Called Nehum	Neh.	7	7
A Persian chancellor	Ezra	4	8, 9, 17
A Levite	Neh.	3	17
One who seals the covenant	Neh.	10	25
A priest who returns from exile	Neh.	12	3, 7

reign

Shalt thou indeed *r* over us?	Gen.	37	8
The Lord shall *r* for ever	Ex.	15	18
	Ps.	146	10
They that hate you shall *r* over you	Lev.	26	17
Thou shalt *r* over many nations	Deut.	15	6
Trees said, *r* thou over us	Judg.	9	8
A king shall *r* over us	I Sam.	12	12
Thou mayest *r* over all	II Sam.	3	21
That the hypocrite *r* not	Job	34	30
God *r* over the heathen	Ps.	47	8
The Lord *r*	Ps.	93	1
	Ps.	96	10
	Ps.	97	1
	Ps.	99	1
By me kings *r*	Prov.	8	15
A servant when he *r*	Prov.	30	22
Out of prison he cometh to *r*	Eccl.	4	14
Lord of hosts shall *r* in Zion	Is.	24	23
A king shall *r* in righteousness	Is.	32	1
Saith unto Zion, thy God *r*	Is.	52	7
Shalt thou *r* because?	Jer.	22	15
A king shall *r* and prosper	Jer.	23	5
The Lord shall *r* over them	Mic.	4	7
We will not have this man *r* over us	Luke	19	14
Shall *r* in life by Jesus Christ	Rom.	5	17
Let not sin *r* in your bodies	Rom.	6	12
I would to God ye did *r*	I Cor.	4	8
He must *r* till	I Cor.	15	25
If we suffer, we shall also *r* with him	II Tim.	2	12
We shall *r* on the earth	Rev.	5	10
He shall *r* for ever and ever	Rev.	11	15
The Lord God omnipotent *r*	Rev.	19	6
Shall *r* with him a thousand years	Rev.	20	6
They shall *r* for ever and ever	Rev.	22	5

reins *guidance, controls*

He cleaveth my *r* asunder	Job	16	13
Though my *r* be consumed	Job	19	27
God trieth the hearts and *r*	Ps.	7	9
My *r* instruct me in night	Ps.	16	7
Examine me, try my *r*	Ps.	26	2
Thus was I pricked in my *r*	Ps.	73	21
Thou hast possessed my *r*	Ps.	139	13
My *r* shall rejoice	Prov.	23	16
Faithfulness shall be the girdle of his *r*	Is.	11	5
Of Lord, that triest the *r*	Jer.	11	20
Thou art far from their *r*	Jer.	12	2
Seest the *r*	Jer.	20	12

reins—*continued*

Arrows to enter into my *r*	Lam.	3	13
I am he who searcheth the *r*	Rev.	2	23

rejection *state of being rejected*

Of God's word	Acts	13	46
For lack of repentance	Heb.	12	17

Of God:

By Israel	I Sam.	8	7, 8
By Saul	I Sam.	15	26
Counsel of, by Pharisees	Luke	7	30
By Jerusalem	Luke	13	34

Of Jesus:

Likened to house built on sand	Mat.	7	26, 27
After swine perish	Mat.	8	34
Shall be denied before God	Mat.	10	33
As an excessive drinker	Mat.	11	16–19
In parable of vineyard and wicked husbandmen	Mat.	21	38–45
By Peter	Mat.	26	33–35, 69–75
By folk of own community	Mark	6	3–6
By some disciples	John	6	60–66
By Pharisees	John	8	13, 45–47
Shall be judged	John	12	48

rejoice *be glad*

Shall *r* in all ye put your hand to	Deut.	12	7
Thou shalt *r* in every good thing	Deut.	26	11
The Lord will *r* over you	Deut.	28	63
	Deut.	30	9
I *r* in thy salvation	I Sam.	2	1
Let the heart of them *r* that seek the Lord	I Chr.	16	10
	Ps.	105	3
Let thy saints *r* in goodness	II Chr.	6	41
The Lord had made them to *r*	II Chr.	20	27
	Neh.	12	43
If I *r* because my wealth was great	Job	31	25
The horse *r* in his strength	Job	39	21
R with trembling	Ps.	2	11
Let all that trust in thee *r*	Ps.	5	11
I will *r* in thy salvation	Ps.	9	14
Jacob shall *r*	Ps.	14	7
R as a strong man to run a race	Ps.	19	5
Our heart shall *r* in him	Ps.	33	21
Let not mine enemies *r* over me	Ps.	35	19
Hear me, lest they should *r* over me	Ps.	38	16
The bones which thou has broken may *r*	Ps.	51	8
In shadow of thy wings will I *r*	Ps.	63	7
Let the righteous *r*	Ps.	68	3
That thy people may *r* in thee	Ps.	85	6
In thy name shall they *r* all the day	Ps.	89	16
Let the heavens *r*	Ps.	96	11
Let the earth *r*	Ps.	97	1
The Lord shall *r* in his works	Ps.	104	31
Righteous shall see it, and *r*	Ps.	107	42
I *r* at thy word	Ps.	119	162
Let Israel *r* in him that made him	Ps.	149	2
Who *r* to do evil	Prov.	2	14
R with the wife of thy youth	Prov.	5	18
If thine heart be wise, my heart shall *r*	Prov.	23	15
R not when thine enemy falleth	Prov.	24	17
When the righteous are in authority people *r*	Prov.	29	2
My heart *r* in all my labour	Eccl.	2	10
For a man to *r* and do good	Eccl.	3	12
Than that a man should *r*	Eccl.	3	22
	Eccl.	5	19
R, O young man, in thy youth	Eccl.	11	9
As men *r* when they divide the spoil	Is.	9	3
Noise of them that *r* endeth	Is.	24	8
Poor among men shall *r*	Is.	29	19
The desert shall *r*	Is.	35	1
As the bridegroom *r* over the bride	Is.	62	5
My servants shall *r*, but ye	Is.	65	13
When ye see this, your heart shall *r*	Is.	66	14
I will *r* over them to do them good	Jer.	32	41
Let not the buyer *r*	Ezek.	7	12
R not, O Israel, for joy	Hosea	9	1
R in a thing of nought	Amos	6	13
R not against me, O enemy	Mic.	7	8
Yet I will *r* in the Lord	Hab.	3	18
The Lord will *r* over thee	Zeph.	3	17
R greatly, O duaghter of Zion	Zech.	9	9
He *r* more of that sheep	Mat.	18	13
Many shall *r* at his birth	Luke	1	14
R ye in that day, and leap for joy	Luke	6	23
In this *r* not, but rather *r* because	Luke	10	20
R with me	Luke	15	6, 9

And he that reapeth may *r*	John	4	36
Willing for a season to *r*	John	5	35
If ye loved me, ye would *r*	John	14	28
Ye shall weep, but he world shall *r*	John	16	20
Therefore did my heart *r*	Acts	2	26
R in hope of glory of God	Rom.	5	2
R with them that do *r*	Rom.	12	15
They that *r* as though they *r* not	I Cor.	7	30
R not in iniquity, but *r* in the truth	I Cor.	13	6
I do *r*, yea, and will *r*	Phil.	1	18
I joy and *r* with you all	Phil.	2	17
R in the Lord	Phil.	3	1
	Phil.		4
R evermore	I Thes.	5	16
Let brother of low degree *r*	James	1	9
Ye *r* with job unspeakable	I Pet.	1	8

rejoicing *see* joy

Rekem *variegated, friendship*

Midianite king slain by the Israelites	Num.	31	8
	Josh.	13	21
A city in Benjamin	Josh.	18	21, 27
Son of Hebron	I Chr.	2	43, 44
A Manassite	I Chr.	7	16

relatives *persons connected by blood or marriage*

The interference of	Num.	12	1, 2
Gideon is afraid of his	Judg.	6	25–27
Of Jesus	Mat.	13	55, 56
Persecution from	Mark	13	12
A hindrance to some	Luke	9	59–62
Often helpful	John	1	40–42

relief agency

In the early Christian church	Acts	4	31–37

relieve *assist, aid*

Poor brother	Lev.	25	35
Fatherless and widows	Ps.	146	9
	I Tim.	5	16
The oppressed	Is.	1	17
The soul	Lam.	1	11
The afflicted	I Tim.	5	10

religion *see* worship

religion

Straitest sect of our *r*	Acts	26	5
Conversation in Jews' *r*	Gal.	1	13
Profited in the Jews' *r* above	Gal.	1	14
Heart, this man's *r* is vain	James	1	26
Pure *r* and undefiled before God	James	1	27

remain

While earth *r*	Gen.	8	22
Let nothing *r* until the morning	Ex.	12	10
His body shall not *r* on tree	Deut.	21	23
R, yet much land to be possessed	Josh.	13	1
I, even I, only, *r* a prophet	I Ki.	18	22
Ark *r* in the family of Obededom	I Chr.	13	14
Yet shall he *r* in the tomb	Job	21	32
The perfect shall *r* in the land	Prov.	2	21
My wisdom *r* with me	Eccl.	2	9
It would have *r* until this day	Mat.	11	23
Gather up the fragments that *r*	John	6	12
Whiles it *r*, was it not thine own?	Acts	5	4
We who *r* unto coming of the Lord	I Thes.	4	15
There *r* a rest to the people of God	Heb.	4	9
There *r* no more sacrifice for sins	Heb.	10	26
Strengthen things which *r*	Rev.	3	2

remedy *a cure*

Broken and destroyed without	Prov.	6	15
	Prov.	29	1
For sin	I John	1	7

remembrance *memory*

Of Amalek, to be blotted out	Deut.	25	19
None in death	Ps.	6	5
Of holiness	Ps.	30	4
Of iniquity	Ezek.	21	23
Of sins of youth	Ezek.	23	19
Peter, of the fig tree	Mark	11	21
Occasioned by sacrifice	Heb.	10	3
By way of a letter	II Pet.	3	1

remission of sin *pardon of sin*

Jesus' blood shed for	Mat.	26	28
To be preached	Luke	24	47
Baptism for	Mark	1	4
Belief necessary	Acts	10	43
Of sins	Rom.	3	25
Necessity of shedding blood	Heb.	9	22

Remmon *see* Rimmon

Remmon-methoar *see* Rimmon

remnant of Israel

Restoration promised	Is.	11	16
From all nations	Jer.	23	3, 4
Prayed for	Is.	37	4
	II Ki.	19	4
Lord left	Is.	1	9
	Ezek.	6	8
Very small	Is.	16	14
Sins forgiven	Mic.	7	18
To be regathered	Is.	10	20–23

remorse *guilt felt for one's actions*

Because of iniquity	Ps.	31	10
For treachery	Mat.	27	3–5
A fitting	Luke	23	46–48
Examples of:			
David	Ps.	51	1–19
Peter	Mat.	26	75
Judas	Mat.	27	3–5

render *give*

I will *r* vengeance	Deut.	32	41
The Lord *r* to every man his faithfulness	I Sam.	26	32
He will *r* to man his righteousness	Job	33	26
The work of a man shall be *r* to him	Job	34	11
What shall I *r* to the Lord?	Ps.	116	12
R to every man according to his works	Prov.	24	12
	Rom.	2	6
Seven men who can *r* a reason	Prov.	26	16
So will we *r* the calves of our lips	Hosea	14	2
I will *r* double	Zech.	9	12
R to him fruits in their seasons	Mat.	21	41
R unto Caesar	Mat.	22	21
	Mark	12	17
	Luke	20	25
R to all their dues	Rom.	13	7
What thanks can we *r* to God?	I Thes.	3	9
Not *r* evil for evil	I Thes.	5	15
	I Pet.	3	9

rending *tearing*

The clothes	Gen.	37	34
	II Sam.	13	19
	Ezra	9	5
By the high priest	Mat.	26	65
	Mark	14	63

renew *restore*

R a right spirit within me	Ps.	51	10
Thy youth is *r* like the eagle's	Ps.	103	5
Thou *r* the face of the earth	Ps.	104	30
They that wait on the Lord shall *r* their strength	Is.	40	31
R our days as of old	Lam.	5	21
The inward man is *r* day by day	II Cor.	4	16
Be *r* in the spirit of your mind	Eph.	4	23
New man, which is *r* in knowledge	Col.	3	10
If they fall away, to *r* them again	Heb.	6	6

rent *torn, broken*

Old bottles	Josh.	9	4
The altar	I Ki.	13	3
May be made worse	Mat.	9	16
"Veil of the temple was rent"	Mark	15	38

renunciation *a sacrifice*

Of home and friends	Mark	10	28–31
Of business	Luke	5	27, 28
Required of Jesus' disciples	Luke	14	33
Promises a reward	Luke	18	29, 30
Paul, an example of	Phil.	3	8

repentance *contrition for sins*

What it is	Is.	45	22
	Mat.	6	19–21
	Acts	14	15
	II Cor.	5	17
	Col.	3	2
	I Thes.	1	9
	Heb.	12	1–2
The present time, the proper time	Ps.	95	7, 8
	Prov.	27	1
	Heb.	3	7, 8
Danger of neglecting	Prov.	1	23–33
	Mat.	11	20
	Luke	13	3, 5
Exhortations to	Ezek.	14	6
	Ezek.	18	30
Commanded to all by God	Ezek.	18	30–32
	Acts	17	30
Followed by a new life	Mat.	3	8
	Acts	26	20

Christ calls sinners to	Mat.	9	13
Joy in heaven over	Luke	15	7, 10
Precedes baptism	Acts	2	38
Necessary to the pardon of sin	Acts	2	38
	Acts	3	19
Given by God	Acts	11	18
	II Tim.	2	25
Commanded by Christ	Rev.	2	5, 16
By the operation of the Holy Ghost	Zech.	12	10
Called repentance unto life	Acts	11	18
Called repentance unto salvation	II Cor.	7	10
Christ came to call sinners to	Mat.	9	13
Christ exalted to give	Acts	5	31
Conviction of sin necessary to	I Ki.	8	38
	Prov.	28	13
	Acts	2	37–38
	Acts	19	18
Denied to apostates	Heb.	6	4–6
Ministers should rejoice over their people on their	II Cor.	7	9
Should be evidenced by fruits	Is.	1	16–17
	Dan.	4	27

Should be accompanied by:

Confession	Lev.	26	40
	Job	33	27
Conversion	Acts	3	19
	Acts	26	20
Faith	Mark	1	15
	Acts	20	21
Prayer	Acts	8	22
Self-abhorrence	Job	42	6
Turning from idolatry	Ezek.	14	6
	I Thes.	1	9
Turning from sin	II Chr.	6	26
Humility	II Chr.	7	14
	James	4	9–10
Shame and confusion	Ezra	9	6
	Jer.	31	19
	Ezek.	16	61, 63
	Dan.	9	7–8
Faith	Mat.	21	32
Greater zeal in duty	II Cor.	7	8–11
Prayer	I Ki.	8	33

We should be led to, by:

The chastisements of God	I Ki.	8	47
	Rev.	3	19
The goodness of God	Rom.	2	4
The long-suffering of God	II Pet.	3	9

The wicked:

Averse to	Jer.	8	6
	Mat.	21	32
Neglect the time given for	Rev.	2	21
Not led to, by the judgments of God	Rev.	9	20–21
	Rev.	16	9
Not led to, by miraculous interference	Luke	16	30–31

Preached:

By John the Baptist	Mat.	3	2
By Christ	Mat.	4	17
By the apostles	Mark	6	12
	Acts	20	21
In the name of Christ	Luke	24	47

Instances of:

Peter	Mat.	26	75
Prodigal son	Luke	15	17–19
Theif on the cross	Luke	23	40, 41
Corinthians	II Cor.	7	9, 10
Paul	Gal.	1	23
Israelites	Judg.	10	15, 16
David	II Sam.	12	13

Rephah *support, healing*

Ancestor of Joshua	I Chr.	7	25

Rephaiah *healed by God*

A descendant of David	I Chr.	3	9, 21
A captain of Simeon	I Chr.	4	42
Son of Tola	I Chr.	7	1, 2
Called Rapha	I Chr.	8	37
A descendant of Saul	I Chr.	9	39, 43
The governor of half of Jerusalem	Neh.	3	8, 9

Rephaim *giants*

A race in Palestine	Gen.	14	5
Giants of	Deut.	2	11, 20
A valley on the boundary of Judah and Benjamin	II Sam.	5	18
	II Sam.	23	13

Rephidim *expanse*

Receives water by miracle here	Ex.	17	1–6
Amalek's defeat	Ex.	17	8–16
An encampment of the Israelites	Num.	33	14, 15

report

Their evil *r*	Gen.	37	2
Thou shalt not raise a false *r*	Ex.	23	1
An evil *r* of the land	Num.	13	32
Nations who shall hear *r* of thee	Deut.	2	25
It is no good *r* I hear	I Sam.	2	24
It was a true *r*	I Ki.	10	6
	II Chr.	9	5
A good *r*	Prov.	15	30
Who hath believed our *r*?	Is.	53	1
Men of honest *r*	Acts	6	3
Of good *r* among the Jews	Acts	10	22
By evil *r* and good *r*	II Cor.	6	8
Whatsoever things are of good *r*	Phil.	4	8
A bishop must have a good *r*	I Tim.	3	7
These having obtained a good *r*	Heb.	11	39
It is *r* among the heathen	Neh.	6	6
R, say they, and we will *r* it	Jer.	20	10
This saying is commonly *r*	Mat.	28	15
Well *r* of	Acts	16	2
He will *r* that God is in you	I Cor.	14	25
Well *r* for good works	I Tim.	5	10

reproach *disgrace*

Caused by neglect	Neh.	2	17, 18
Caused by affliction	Ps.	31	9–11
Borne by David	Ps.	69	7
Breaks the heart	Ps.	69	20
Of idol worshippers	Ezek.	22	4
Joy in	Mat.	5	11, 12
Fear of	John	12	42, 43
On cause of Christ	Rom.	2	23, 24
Welcomed by Moses	Heb.	11	24, 25

reprobate *wicked, corrupt person*

Curses the result of not listening to the Lord	Deut.	28	15–20
Judged divinely	Jer.	15	1–5
Rejects Christ	Mat.	13	14, 15
Rejects God	Rom.	1	28
Doomed	II Thes.	2	11, 12

reproof *reprimand*

God gives to His children	II Sam.	7	14
	Heb.	12	6, 7
Is for correction	Ps.	39	11
God gives to the wicked	Ps.	50	21
An excellent oil	Ps.	141	5
Rejection of, leads to error	Prov.	10	17
Leads to wisdom and honour	Prov.	15	31
	Prov.	29	15
Leads to understanding and knowledge	Prov.	15	32
	Prov.	19	25
Valuable when wisely given	Prov.	25	12
A proof of friendship	Prov.	27	5, 6
Better than flattery	Prov.	28	23
Better than the praise of fools	Eccl.	7	5
Christ sent to give	Is.	2	4

Reasons for:

Impenitence	Mat.	11	20–24
Hypocrisy	Mat.	15	7
Unbelief	Mat.	17	17, 20
Hardness of heart	Mark	8	17
Vain boasting	Luke	22	34

Ministers should give:

Unreservedly	Is.	58	1
Fearlessly	Ezek.	2	3–7
With Christian love	II Thes.	3	15
Openly	I Tim.	5	20
Sharply, if necessary	Tit.	1	13

reptiles

Frogs	Ex.	8	2
Tortoises	Lev.	11	29
Chameleons, ferrets and lizards	Lev.	11	30
Crocodiles	Job	41	1, 2
Serpents	Ps.	58	4
Adders	Prov.	23	32
Asps	Is.	11	8
Vipers	Is.	30	6
Cockatrices	Is.	59	5
Dragons	Ezek.	29	3
Lizard	Lev.	11	30
Unclean	Lev.	11	31–40
Worshipped	II Ki.	18	4

reputation *public esteem*

Of Daniel	Dan.	6	4
Of John the Baptist	Mark	6	20
Of Jesus	Luke	9	18–20
Of Gamaliel	Acts	5	34
Of Saul	Acts	9	11–13
Of Cornelius	Acts	10	22
Of the church at Rome	Rom.	1	7, 8
Of Job	Ezek.	14	14
Of Anak	Deut.	9	2
Of Israel	Josh.	2	8–11
Disciples at Jerusalem	Gal.	2	2

require *need, want*

Blood of your lives will I *r*	Gen.	9	5
Of my hand didst thou *r* it	Gen.	31	39
What doth the Lord *r*?	Deut.	10	12
	Mic.	6	8
Let the Lord *r* it	Josh.	22	23
	I Sam.	20	16
The king's business *r* haste	I Sam.	21	8
One thing I *r* of thee	II Sam.	3	13
Whatsoever thou shalt *r* I will do	II Sam.	19	38
The Lord look upon it, and *r* it	II Chr.	24	22
We will restore, and *r* nothing	Neh.	5	12
He hath said, thou wilt not *r* it	Ps.	10	13
Sin offering hast thou not *r*	Ps.	40	6
Two things have I *r* of thee	Prov.	30	7
God *r* that which is past	Eccl.	3	15
Who hath *r* this at your hand?	Is.	1	12
His blood will I *r* at thine hand	Ezek.	3	18
	Ezek.	33	6
Be *r* of this generation	Luke	11	50
This night thy soul shall be *r*	Luke	12	20
Of him shall much be *r*	Luke	12	48
I might have *r* mine own with usury	Luke	19	23
Gave sentence that it should be as *r*	Luke	23	24
The Jews *r* a sign	I Cor.	1	22
It is *r* in stewards that they be faithful	I Cor.	4	2

rescue *save*

No one to	Deut.	28	31
Of Jonathan	II Sam.	14	45
The soul	Ps.	35	17

reserve *keep back*

Hast thou not *r* a blessing?	Gen.	27	36
Wicked *r* to day of destruction	Job	21	30
Will he *r* his anger for ever?	Jer.	3	5
He *r* the appointed weeks of harvest	Jer.	5	24
The Lord *r* wrath for his enemies	Nah.	1	2
An inheritance *r* in heaven	I Pet.	1	4
Mist of darkness *r* for ever	II Pet.	2	17
Heavens and earth are *r* unto fire	II Pet.	3	7
To whom is *r* the blackness of darkness	Jude		13

residue *remainder*

I am deprived of the *r* of my years	Is.	38	10
The *r* of the Spirit	Mal.	2	15
That the *r* might seek the Lord	Acts	15	17

resignation *patient submission*

To judgment of God	I Sam.	3	17, 18
To loss by death	II Sam.	12	18–23
To misfortune	Job	1	21
To the will of God	Mark	14	36
To persecution	Acts	21	11–14

resist *strive against*

Satan at his right hand to *r*	Zech.	3	1
I say, that ye *r* not evil	Mat.	5	39
Your adversaries shall not be able to *r*	Luke	21	15
Ye do always *r* the Holy Ghost	Acts	7	51
Who hath *r* his will?	Rom.	9	19
Whosoever *r* the power *r* ordinance of God	Rom.	13	2
God *r* the proud	James	4	6
	I Pet.	5	5
R the devil, and he will flee	James	4	7
Whom *r* stedfast in the faith	I Pet.	5	9

respect

The Lord had *r* to Abel	Gen.	4	4
God had *r* unto them	Ex.	2	25
Thou shalt not *r* person of poor	Lev.	19	15
I will have *r* unto you	Lev.	26	9
Ye shall not *r* persons in judgment	Deut.	1	17
Have *r* to the prayer of thy servant	I Ki.	8	28
	II Chr.	6	19
The Lord had *r* to them	II Ki.	13	23
No *r* of persons with God	II Chr.	19	7
	Rom.	2	11
	Eph.	6	9
	Col.	3	25

He *r* not wise of heart	Job	37	24
Blessed is the man that *r* not proud	Ps.	40	4
R unto thy covenant	Ps.	74	20
I will have *r* to thy statutes	Ps.	119	117
Yet hath he *r* unto the lowly	Ps.	138	6
Not good to have *r* of persons	Prov.	24	23
	Prov.	28	21
His eyes shall have *r* to the Holy One	Is.	17	7
Nor had *r* to him that fashioned it	Is.	22	11
Had no glory in this *r*	II Cor.	3	10
Not that I speak in *r* of want	Phil.	4	11
Who without *r* of persons	I Pet.	1	17

responsibility *accountability*

Parental	I Sam.	3	12-14
Of Jews for death of Jesus	Mat.	27	25
According to privilege	Rom.	12	3, 6-8
Of bishops	Heb.	13	17
Personal:			
For sins	Ezek.	18	20, 30
For our own words	Mat.	12	37
For denial of truth	John	15	22-24
Final judgment	I Cor.	3	8, 13-15
To bear our own burden	Gal.	6	4, 5
Attempts to shift:			
Adam	Gen.	3	12
Eve	Gen.	3	13
Sarah	Gen.	16	5
Esau	Gen.	27	36
Aaron	Ex.	32	22-24
Saul	II Sam.	15	20, 21
Pilate	Mat.	27	25

rest

Cessation from labour of God	Gen.	2	2
On the sabbath	Ex.	31	15
Sabbatical year	Lev.	25	4, 5
For harvesters	Ruth	3	1
Enjoined by Jesus	Mark	6	31
As the end of Israel's wanderings	Deut.	12	9
	Heb.	4	1
Lost through disobedience to God	Num.	14	23
Freedom from war	Judg.	3	11, 30
	Judg.	5	31
Solomon a "man of rest"	I Chr.	22	9
Spiritual:			
Rewards of	Ps.	37	7
	Is.	30	15
Man yearns for	Ps.	55	6
Promised by God	Ps.	116	7-18
To the righteous man	Ps.	132	14
Promised by Christ	Mat.	6	34
	Mat.	11	28-30
Received by faith	Heb.	4	3
Eternal in heaven	Rev.	14	13

restitution *reparation*

In Mosaic law	Lev.	6	1-7
	Lev.	24	17-24
	Num.	5	7
	Prov.	6	30, 31
Brings forgiveness	Ezek.	33	15, 16
Proof of repentance	Luke	19	8, 9

restore

To *r* every man's money	Gen.	42	25
He shall *r* double	Ex.	22	4
He shall *r* it in the principal	Lev.	6	5
Things strayed thou shalt *r* again	Deut.	22	2
He *r* my soul	Ps.	23	3
R to me the joy of thy salvation	Ps.	51	12
I will *r* thy judges	Is.	1	26
I will *r* health to thee	Jer.	30	17
Elias shall *r* all things	Mat.	17	11
	Mark	9	12
I *r* him fourfold	Luke	19	8
Wilt thou *r* the kingdom?	Acts	1	6
R such an one in meekness	Gal.	6	1

Restrain

Rain from heaven was *r*	Gen.	8	2
Nothing will be *r* from them	Gen.	11	6
People were *r* from bringing	Ex.	36	6
He *r* them not.	I Sam.	3	13
Thou *r* prayer before God	Job	15	4
Dost thou *r* wisdom?	Job	15	8
Wrath shalt thou *r*	Ps.	76	10
Scarce *r* they the people	Acts	14	18

resurrection *return to life of the dead*

Of the body foretold	Job	19	25, 26
	Is.	26	19
Change	Job	14	12-15
In God's likeness	Ps.	17	15
Redeemed from the grave	Ps.	49	15
Valley of dry bones	Ezek.	37	
Ransomed from the grave	Hosea	13	14
David's prophecy	Ps.	16	10
Typified	Ezek.	37	1
Proclaimed by Christ	Mat.	22	31
	Luke	14	14
	John	5	28, 29
	John	11	23, 25
Preached by the apostles	Acts	4	2
	Rom.	6	5
	II Cor.	4	17
	I John	3	2
Basis of future hope	I Thes.	4	14-18
Examples of:			
The son of a widow	I Ki.	17	17-22
Son of the Shunammite	II Ki.	4	32-35
An unidentified man	II Ki.	13	20, 21
Jairus' daughter	Mat.	9	23-25
Only son of a widow	Luke	7	11-15
Lazarus	John	11	43, 44
Dorcas	Acts	9	36-40
Foretold	Ps.	16	10, 11
	Mat.	16	21
Announced by an angel	Mat.	28	5, 6
A fundamental doctrine	Acts	2	22-32
	Acts	4	33
	I Thes.	4	14-18
Raised by God	II Cor.	4	14
	Heb.	11	19
New body	II Cor.	5	1-5
Power of	Phil.	3	10, 21
Basic doctrine	Heb.	6	2
Proved by appearances to:			
Several women	Mat.	28	9
The apostles at Galilee	Mat.	28	16, 17
Mary Magdalene	Mark	16	9
Disciples on the road to Emmaus	Luke	24	13-15
Peter	Luke	24	35
Those at the ascension	Luke	24	50, 51
Ten apostles	John	20	19
Eleven apostles	John	20	26
To five hundred	I Cor.	15	6
To brother, James	I Cor.	15	7
To Paul	I Cor.	15	8
Appearance to John	Rev.	1	18

retain

Dost thou *r* thine integrity?	Job	2	9
Let thine heart *r* my words	Prov.	4	4
A gracious woman *r* honour	Prov.	11	16
No man hath power to *r* the spirit	Eccl.	8	8
Whosoever sins he *r*, they are *r*	John	20	23
Did not like to *r* God	Rom.	1	28

retaliation *reprisal*

An eye for an eye	Ex.	21	24
Forbidden	Prov.	24	29
Rebuked by Christ	Mat.	5	38-42
	Luke	9	54-56

return

To dust shalt thou *r*	Gen.	3	19
R to the Lord	I Sam.	7	3
	Is.	19	22
	Is.	55	7
	Hosea	6	1
R to thee with all their heart	I Ki.	8	48
Let the shadow *r* backward	II Ki.	20	10
Naked shall I *r* thither	Job	1	21
He shall *r* no more	Job	7	10
Believeth not he shall *r* out of darkness	Job	15	22
If thou *r* to the Almighty	Job	22	23
Shall *r* to the days of his youth	Job	33	25
My prayer *r* into mine own bosom	Ps.	35	13
His people *r* hither	Ps.	73	10
Thou sayest, *r*, ye children of men	Ps.	90	3
They die, and *r* to the dust	Ps.	104	29
R to thy rest, O my soul	Ps.	116	7
None that go to her *r* again	Prov.	2	19
As a dog *r* to his vomit	Prov.	26	11
Naked shall he *r* to go as he came	Eccl.	5	15
Dust *r* to earth, and spirit *r* to God	Eccl.	12	7
If ye will enquire, enquire ye, *r*, come	Is.	21	12
The ransomed of the Lord shall *r*	Is.	35	10
	Is.	51	11
It shall not *r* to me void	Is.	55	11

return—*continued*

If thou wilt *r*, saith the Lord, *r* unto me	Jer.	4	1
They shall *r* with their whole heart	Jer.	24	7
That the wicked *r*, and live	Ezek.	18	23
I will *r* to my place	Hosea	5	15
They *r*, but not the Most High	Hosea	7	16
Who knoweth if he will *r* and repent?	Joel	2	14
R to me, and I will *r* to you	Mal.	3	7
Then shall ye *r* and discern	Mal.	3	18
I will *r* into my house	Mat.	12	44
	Luke	11	24
Neither let him in field *r* back	Mat.	24	18
R to thine own house	Luke	8	39
Not found that *r* to give glory to God	Luke	17	18

Reu, Ragau *friend*

Ancestor of Abraham	Gen.	11	18–26
Called Ragau	Luke	3	35

Reuben *behold a son*

Eldest son of Jacob and Leah	Gen.	29	32
Gathers mandrakes for his mother	Gen.	30	14
Commits incest with Bilhah	Gen.	35	22
Offers his sons as pledge to Joseph	Gen.	42	37
Has four sons	Gen.	46	9
His descendants	Num.	26	5–9
Tribe of, decreased	Num.	1	21
	Num.	2	10, 11
	Num.	26	7
Settles in rich pasture lands east of Jordan	Num.	32	1–32
Rebuked by Deborah	Hag.	5	15, 16
Honoured in future glory of Israel	Ezek.	48	6, 7
	Rev.	7	5

Reuel, Ragau, Raguel *friend of God*

Son of Esau and Bashemath	Gen.	36	4, 10
	Gen.	36	13, 17
Another name for Jethro	Ex.	2	18
Called Raguel	Num.	10	29
A Gadite	Num.	2	14
A Benjamite	I Chr.	9	8

revelations from God *divine manifestations*

To His people and to prophets	Deut.	29	29
	Job	33	16
	Is.	40	5
	Is.	53	1
	Jer.	33	6
	Dan.	2	22
	Amos	3	7
To Samuel	I Sam.	15	22
Predicted by Joel	Joel	2	28–32
Hidden from wise men	Mat.	11	25
In Christ	John	1	14
	John	14	9
By the Holy Spirit	John	14	26
	John	16	13
Fulfillment in Pentecost	Acts	2	16, 47
Fulfillment of Christ's promise	Acts	2	33–36
Of spiritual things	I Cor.	2	10
To Paul	II Cor.	12	1–9
	Gal.	1	12
To Isaiah	Is.	6	1–6
To prophets	Deut.	18	18
	I Pet.	1	12
	Jer.	1	5–10
To Moses	Ex.	3	14
To Joshua	Josh.	5	14
To Jacob	Gen.	32	30
To Abraham	Gen.	15	15–20
In nature	Ps.	19	1–6
	Rom.	1	20
	Acts	14	15–17
In visions	Ezek.	1	1
In a trance	Acts	10	9–16
In dreams	Gen.	28	10–17
By Urim	Ex.	28	30
	Num.	27	21
By lot	I Chr.	24	1–19
By miracles	Deut.	4	32–35
By incarnation	Heb.	1	1
By inspiration	II Tim.	3	16

revenge *vengeance*

Forbidden	Lev.	19	18
	Prov.	24	29
	Rom.	12	17, 19
Overcome by kindness	Prov.	25	21, 22
	Rom.	12	20
Comes from a spiteful heart	Ezek.	25	15

Punishment for	Amos	1	11, 12
Should be overcome with love	Luke	6	35–38
Rebuked by Jesus	Luke	9	54
Inconsistent with Christianity	Luke	9	55
Jesus an example of forebearing	I Pet.	2	23

Examples:

Simeon and Levi	Gen.	34	25
Samson	Judg.	15	7, 8
Joab	II Sam.	3	27
Absalom	II Sam.	13	23–29
Jezebel	I Ki.	19	2
Ahab	I Ki.	22	27
Haman	Esth.	3	8–15
Edomites	Ezek.	25	12
Herodias	Mark	6	19–24

reverence *profound respect*

Should be shown to God and His possessions	Lev.	19	30
	Deut.	28	58
	Ps.	89	7
	Rev.	22	18, 19
Attitudes of	Neh.	8	4–6
An affectionate	Luke	7	36–39
Shown to Christ	Phil.	2	9, 11

revile

Thou shalt not *r* the gods	Ex.	22	28
Blessed when men shall *r* you	Mat.	5	11
They that passed by *r* him	Mat.	27	39
They that were crucified *r* him	Mark	15	32
Being *r*, we bless	I Cor.	4	12
When he was *r*, *r* not again	I Pet.	2	23
(*See* Isa. 51:7; I Cor. 6:10)			

revive

Will they *r* stones?	Neh.	4	2
Whilt thou not *r* us again?	Ps.	85	6
Thou wilt *r* me	Ps.	138	7
To *r* the spirit of the humble	Is.	57	15
After two days will he *r* us	Hosea	6	2
They shall *r* as corn	Hosea	14	7
R thy work in midst of years	Heb.	3	2
When the commandment came, sin *r*	Rom.	7	9
Christ both died, rose, and *r*	Rom.	14	9

revolution *see rebellion*

reward *compensation*

Given at second coming of Christ	Mat.	16	27
	Rev.	22	12
Is of God's good pleasure	Mat.	20	14, 15
	Luke	12	32
Prepared by Christ	John	14	2
Not on account of merit	Rom.	4	4, 5
Is of grace	Rom.	4	4, 5, 16
	Rom.	11	6
Hope of, a cause of rejoicing	Rom.	5	2
Present afflictions not to be compared with	Rom.	8	18
	II Cor.	5	17
Is from God	Col.	3	24
	Heb.	11	6
Prepared by God	Heb.	11	16

Prospect of, leads to:

Enduring suffering for Christ	II Chr.	4	16–18
	Heb.	11	25, 26
Pressing forward	Phil.	3	14
Diligence	II John		8
Faithfulness unto death	Rev.	2	10

Described as:

Beholding face of God	Ps.	17	15
	Mat.	5	8
	Rev.	22	4
Treasure in heaven	Mat.	19	21
	Luke	12	33
Being with Christ	John	12	26
	Phil.	1	23
Beholding glory of Christ	John	17	24
Joint heirship with Christ	Rom.	8	17
Being glorified with Christ	Rom.	8	17, 18
	Col.	3	4

Rhegium *breach*

On coast of Italy	Acts	28	13

Rhesa *head*

Ancestor of Christ	Luke	3	27

Rhoda *a rose*

Maid in Mary's home	Acts	12	12, 13

Rhodes *island near Asia*

Passed by Paul	Acts	21	1

rib *bone*

Eve formed of Adam's	Gen.	2	22

Riblah *fertility*

A place on eastern boundary of Israel	Num.	34	11
A town of Hamath	II Ki.	23	33
Zedekiah blinded here	II Ki.	25	6, 7, 21
Pharaoh-necho	II Ki.	23	31-34

rich

Lest thou shouldest say, I have made Abraham *r*	Gen.	14	23
The *r* shall not give more	Ex.	30	15
If a stranger wax *r*	Lev.	25	47
The Lord maketh poor and maketh *r*	I Sam.	2	7
Two men in city, one *r*, the other poor	II Sam.	12	1
He shall not be *r*	Job	15	29
The *r* shall entreat thy favour	Ps.	45	12
Be not afraid when one is made *r*	Ps.	49	16
Hand of diligent maketh *r*	Prov.	10	4
The blessing of the Lord maketh *r*	Prov.	10	22
The *r* hath many friends	Prov.	14	20
The *r* answereth roughly	Prov.	18	23
He that loveth wine shall not be *r*	Prov.	21	17
The *r* and poor meet together	Prov.	22	2
Labour not be *r*	Prov.	23	4
The *r* man is wise in his own conceit	Prov.	28	11
Curse not the *r* in thy bedchamber	Eccl.	10	20
With the *r* in his death	Is.	53	9
Let not the *r* man glory	Jer.	9	23
Ephraim said, I am *r*	Hosea	12	8
Blessed be the Lord, for I am *r*	Zech.	11	5
Many that were *r* cast in much	Mark	12	41
The *r* he hath sent empty away	Luke	1	53
Woe to you *r*, for	Luke	6	24
That is not *r* toward God	Luke	12	21
Call not thy *r* neighbours	Luke	14	12
Sorrowful, for he was very *r*	Luke	18	23
The Lord is *r* to all	Rom.	10	12
Now ye are full, now ye are *r*	I Cor.	4	8
Poor, yet making many *r*	II Cor.	6	10
Yet for your sakes he became poor	II Cor.	8	9
God who is *r* in mercy	Eph.	2	4
He in good works	I Tim.	6	18
Hath not God chosen the poor *r* in faith?	James	2	5
Because thou sayest, I am *r*	Rev.	3	17

riches *wealth*

Given by God	Deut.	8	17, 18
	I Sam.	2	7
	Prov.	10	22
	Eccl.	5	19
Dangers of	Deut.	32	15
	Prov.	15	6
	Hosea	12	8
	Mat.	13	22
	I Tim.	6	10
	James	2	6
Proper use of	I Chr.	29	3
	Job	31	16
	Ps.	62	10
	Jer.	9	23
	Luke	16	9
	I John	3	17
Evil use of	Job	20	15
	Ps.	73	12
	Prov.	11	28
	Prov.	15	6
	Eccl.	5	10
	James	5	3
End of the wicked rich	Job	20	16
	Prov.	11	4
	Luke	6	24
	James	5	1-6
Earthly	Ps.	49	6-8
	Prov.	19	14
	Ezek.	7	19
	Mat.	6	19
	James	1	9-11
The true	Luke	16	11

riddle *puzzling statement*

Of Samson	Judg.	14	12-20
By Agur	Prov.	30	15, 16
By Queen of Sheba	I Ki.	10	1

ride

Who *r* upon the heaven	Deut.	33	26
In majesty *r* properously	Ps.	45	4
Hast caused men to *r* over our heads	Ps.	66	12
Extol him that *r* on the heavens	Ps.	68	4, 33
The Lord *r* on a swift cloud	Is.	19	1
Thy king cometh unto thee *r*	Zech.	9	9

ridicule *mockery*

An insulting	II Sam.	10	1-5
Punishment for	II Ki.	2	23-25
Of the builders of the wall	Neh.	2	17-20
Of Nehemiah	Neh.	4	1-6
Of Jesus	Mat.	27	39-44
For failure	Luke	14	28-30
Of Paul at Athens	Acts	17	32
Of the faithful	Heb.	11	36

right

Shall not the Judge of all do *r*?	Gen.	18	25
Lord who led me in *r* way	Gen.	24	48
Thou shalt do that is *r*	Deut.	6	18
	Deut.	12	25
	Deut.	21	9
The *r* of the first-born is his	Deut.	21	17
God of truth, just and *r* is he	Deut.	32	4
Redeem thou my *r*	Ruth	4	6
I will teach you good and *r* way	I Sam.	12	23
Thy matters are good and *r*	II Sam.	15	3
Thou hast done *r*	Neh.	9	33
How forcible are *r* words	Job	6	25
Should I lie against my *r*?	Job	34	6
He will not lay on man more than *r*	Job	34	23
Thinkest thou this to be *r*?	Job	35	2
He giveth *r* to the poor	Job	36	6
Thou hast maintained my *r*	Ps.	9	4
Hear the *r*, O Lord	Ps.	17	1
Statutes of the Lord are *r*	Ps.	19	8
Sceptre of thy kingdom is a *r* sceptre	Ps.	45	6
Renew a *r* spirit within me	Ps.	51	10
Thy judgments are *r*	Ps.	119	75
The Lord will maintain the *r* of the poor	Ps.	140	12
I have led thee in *r* paths	Prov.	4	11
Opening of my lips shall be *r* things	Prov.	8	6
Thoughts of righteous are *r*	Prov.	12	5
There is a way that seemeth *r*	Prov.	14	12
	Prov.	16	25
They love him that speaketh *r*	Prov.	16	13
Every way of a man is *r* in his own eyes	Prov.	21	2
Prophesy not *r* things	Is.	30	10
That getteth riches, and not be *r*	Jer.	17	11
Till he comes whose *r* it is	Ezek.	21	27
Ways of the Lord are *r*	Hosea	14	9
They know not to do *r*	Amos	3	10
Whatsoever is *r* I will give you	Mat.	20	4
In his *r* mind	Mark	5	15
	Luke	8	35
Why judge ye not what is *r*?	Luke	12	57
Obey your parents, this is *r*	Eph.	6	1
Forsaken the *r* way	II Pet.	2	15

righteousness

Is obedience to God's law	Deut.	6	25
	Rom.	10	5
None, by nature have	Job	15	14
God loves	Ps.	11	7
The wicked are far from	Ps.	119	150
Brings its own reward	Prov.	11	18
Nations exalted by	Prov.	14	34
Thrones of kings established by	Prov.	16	12
God delights in the exercise of	Jer.	9	24
Heavens shall declare	Ps.	50	6
	Ps.	97	6
His care and defense teaches	Mic.	6	4-5
Illustrated	Ps.	36	6
Leads him to love righteousness	Ps.	11	7
Part of his character	Ps.	116	5
	Ps.	119	137
God looks for	Is.	5	7
Christ is the Sun of	Mal.	4	2
Exhortation to seek	Mat.	6	33
The kingdom of God is	Rom.	14	17
No salvation by works of	Eph.	2	8, 9
Christ brings in an everlasting righteousness	Dan.	9	24
Christ called the Lord our righteousness	Jer.	23	6
Christ the end of the law for	Rom.	10	4
Christ being made righteousness unto us	I Cor.	1	30
Our being made the righteousness of God, in Christ	II Cor.	5	21
The righteousness of faith	Rom.	4	13
	Rom.	9	30
	Rom.	10	6
The righteousness of God by faith in Christ	Rom.	3	22
The righteousness of God, without the law	Rom.	3	21
A free gift	Rom.	5	17
The Gentiles attained to	Rom.	9	30

righteousness—*continued*

God's righteousness never to be abolished	Is.	51	6
Of the Lord	Is.	54	17
Predicted	Is.	56	1
	Ezek.	16	14
Promises made through	Rom.	4	13
Revealed in the gospel	Rom.	1	17
Shown openly before the heathen	Ps.	98	2
Shown to the posterity of saints	Ps.	103	17
The wicked have no interest in	Ps.	69	27

Saints:

Clothed with the robe of righteousness	Is.	61	10
Desire to be found in	Phil.	3	9
Exalted in righteousness	Ps.	89	16
Glory in having	Is.	45	24–25
Have, on believing	Rom.	4	5, 11, 24

Of God:

Part of His character	Ps.	7	9
Abundant	Ps.	48	10
Everlasting	Ps.	119	142
Angels acknowledge	Rev.	16	5
Christ acknowledged	John	17	25
Christ committed his cause to	I Pet.	2	23

Described as:

Beyond computation	Ps.	71	15
Enduring forever	Ps.	111	3
The habitation of his throne	Ps.	97	2
Very high	Ps.	71	19

Exhibited in:

His acts	Judg.	5	11
	I Sam.	12	7
His commandments	Deut.	4	8
	Ps.	119	172
His government	Ps.	96	13
	Ps.	98	9
His judgments	Ps.	19	9
	Ps.	119	7, 62
His testimonies	Ps.	119	138, 144
His ways	Ps.	145	17
His word	Ps.	119	123
The final judgment	Acts	17	31
The gospel	Rom.	3	25–26
The punishment of the wicked	Rom.	2	5
	II Thes.	1	6
	Rev.	16	7
	Rev.	19	2

Saints:

Acknowledge in his dealings	Ezra	9	15
Acknowledge though the wicked prosper	Jer.	12	1
	Ps.	73	12–17
Ascribe to him	Job	36	3
	Dan.	9	7
Confident of beholding	Mic.	7	9
Declare to others	Ps.	22	31
Do not conceal	Ps.	40	10
Magnify	Ps.	7	17
	Ps.	51	14
	Ps.	145	7
Mention, only	Ps.	71	16
Plead, in prayer	Ps.	143	11
	Dan.	9	16
Recognize in the fulfillment of his promises	Neh.	9	8
Talk of	Ps.	35	28
	Ps.	71	15, 24
Upheld by	Is.	41	10

We should pray:

For its continued manifestation	Ps.	36	10
To be answered in	Ps.	143	1
To be delivered in	Ps.	31	1
	Ps.	71	2
To be judged according to	Ps.	35	24
To be led in	Ps.	5	8
To be quickened in	Ps.	119	40

Blessedness of:

Turning others to	Dan.	12	3
Bestowed without works	Rom.	4	6
Hungering and thirsting after	Mat.	5	6
Suffering for	I Pet.	3	14

Exemplified:

Jacob	Gen.	30	33
David	II Sam.	22	21
Zacharias	Luke	1	6
Abel	Heb.	11	4
Lot	II Pet.	2	8

Rimmon, Remmon, Remmon-methoar *pomegranate*

Town given to Simeon	Josh.	19	1–7
	I Chr.	6	77
A prominent Zebulunite town	Josh.	19	13
A rock in Benjamin	Hag.	20	45–47
A Benjamite	II Sam.	4	2, 5, 9
Influential deity in Syria	II Ki.	5	17, 18

rings *seals or signets*

Symbol of authority	Gen.	41	42
	Esth.	3	10, 12
Of the tabernacle	Ex.	25	12, 14, 15
Hands as	S. of S.	5	14
Of Ezekiel's creatures	Ezek.	1	18
On the breastplate of the high priests	Ex.	28	26–28
Worn as jewelry, by women	Is.	3	21
Given to the prodigal son	Luke	15	22
Worn by gentlemen	James	2	2

riot *tumultuous disturbance*

Quieted by town clerk	Acts	19	20–41

ripe *full grown*

Brought forth *r* grapes	Gen.	40	10
Offer the first of thy *r* fruits	Ex.	22	29
Whatsoever is first *r* shall be thine	Num.	18	13
Put in sickle, for harvest is *r*	Joel	3	13
Harvest of earth is *r*	Rev.	14	15

rise

A sceptre shall *r* out of Israel	Num.	24	17
Ye are *r* up in your fathers' stead	Num.	32	14
Commandeth the sun, and it *r* not	Job	9	7
Man lieth down, and *r* not	Job	14	12
What shall I do when God *r* up?	Job	31	14
Though war should *r* against me	Ps.	27	3
It is vain to *r* up early	Ps.	127	2
He shall *r* at the voice of the bird	Eccl.	12	4
Earth shall fall, and not *r*	Is.	24	20
Now will I *r*, saith the Lord	Is.	33	10
The glory of the Lord is *r* upon thee	Is.	60	1
I spake unto you, *r* early	Jer.	7	13
	Jer.	25	3
	Jer.	35	14
R early and protesting	Jer.	11	7
Sitting down and *r* up	Lam.	3	63
He maketh sun to *r* on evil and good	Mat.	5	45
The third day he shall *r* again	Mat.	20	19
	Mark	9	31
	Mark	10	34
	Luke	18	33
	Luke	24	7
R, let us be going	Mat.	26	46
R, he calleth thee	Mark	10	49
I cannot *r* and give thee	Luke	11	7
The Lord is *r* indeed	Luke	24	34
Thy brother shall *r* again	John	11	23
R, Peter, kill and eat	Acts	10	13
The first that should *r* from the dead	Acts	26	23
Christ that died, yea rather that is *r* again.	Rom.	8	34
He that shall *r* to reign	Rom.	15	12
If the dead *r* not	I Cor.	15	15
If ye then be *r* with Christ	Col.	3	1
The dead in Christ shall *r* first	I Thes.	4	16

rivers

God's power over, unlimited	Is.	50	2
	Nah.	1	4
Banks of, planted with trees	Ezek.	47	7

Illustrative:

Of salvation	Is.	32	2
	Rev.	22	1, 2
Of gifts of Holy Spirit	Is.	41	18
	John	7	38, 39
Of heavy afflictions	Is.	43	2
Of grief	Lam.	3	48
Of God's judgments	Is.	8	7, 8
	Jer.	47	2
	Zech.	10	11

rivers of the Bible

Abana	II Ki.	5	12
Arnon	Deut.	2	36
Chebar	Ezek.	1	1
Euphrates	Gen.	2	14
Gihon	Gen.	2	13
Gozan	II Ki.	17	6
Jabbok	Deut.	2	37
Jordan	Mark	1	5
Kanah	Josh.	16	8
Kishon	Judg.	5	21
Nile (Sihor)	Jer.	2	18
Pharpar	II Ki.	5	12

Pison	Gen.	2	10, 11
Tigris (Hiddekel)	Gen.	2	14
Ulai	Dan.	8	2
Rizpah *hot coal, floor*			
Concubine of Saul	II Sam.	3	6–8
Her sons hanged by Gibeonites	II Sam.	21	8–11
roar *deep sound*			
The sea *r*	I Chr.	16	32
	Ps.	96	11
	Ps.	98	7
Not fear, though waters *r*	Ps.	46	3
Young lions *r* after their prey	Ps.	104	21
King's wrath is as the *r* of a lion	Prov.	19	12
We *r* all like bears	Is.	59	11
Their voice *r* like the sea	Jer.	6	23
The Lord shall *r* from on high	Jer.	25	30
Divideth sea, when waves *r*	Jer.	31	35
He shall *r* like a lion	Hosea	11	10
The Lord shall *r* out of Zion	Joel	3	16
	Amos	1	2
Will a lion *r* if he hath no prey?	Amos	3	4
The sea and waves *r*	Luke	21	25
The devil as a *r* lion	I Pet.	5	8
robbery *taking away by force*			
Forbidden	Lev.	19	13
	Is.	10	2
	Ezek.	39	10
Of caravans	Judg.	9	25
Of the poor, deplored	Prov.	22	22
Of God	Mal.	3	8
Denounced by Jesus	Mat.	6	20
	Luke	10	30–37
	John	10	7–10
Punishment	John	18	40
Experienced by Paul	II Cor.	11	26
robe			
Figurative	Job	29	14
	Is.	61	10
Article of clothing	Luke	20	46
	Luke	23	11
	Rev.	7	9
Roboam *see* Rehoboam			
rock			
Smitten by Moses	Deut.	8	15
Name of deity	Deut.	32	4
Oil from	Deut.	32	13
Houses on	Jer.	49	16
	Mat.	7	24, 25
Figurative:			
Of God's care	Is.	32	2
Of Peter	Mat.	16	18
Of Christ	I Cor.	10	4
Of God	I Sam.	2	12
	II Sam.	22	32, 47
	Ps.	18	2
	Ps.	71	3
Writing upon	Job	19	24
Houses in	Prov.	30	26
Cleft of	S. of S.	2	14
	Ex.	33	22
Broken by hammers	Jer.	23	29
Wise man's house	Mat.	7	25
Of offense	Rom.	9	33
	I Pet.	2	8
rod			
Of Moses	Ex.	4	2, 4, 17
Of Aaron buds	Num.	17	8
Of God, brings affliction	Job	9	34
Denoting authority	Ps.	2	9
	Ezek.	20	37
As support	Ps.	23	4
Figurative of Christ	Is.	11	1
Of strength	Ps.	110	2
For backs of fools	Prov.	10	13
	Prov.	26	3
For children	Prov.	13	24
	Prov.	29	15
Paul beaten with	II Cor.	11	25
roe, roebuck *deer*			
A fast runner	II Sam.	2	18
	I Chr.	12	8
	S. of S.	2	17

Roi *see* Beer-lahai-roi			
roll *see* books			
Rome *strength*			
Jews excluded from	Acts	18	2
Letters to Christians in	Rom.	1	7
Christians in	Rom.	16	5–15
Paul's visit to— *see* Paul	Acts	28	16
roof			
Under the shadow of my *r*	Gen.	19	8
Make a battlement for thy *r*	Deut.	22	8
Tongue cleaveth to *r* of mouth	Job	29	10
	Ps.	137	6
	Ezek.	3	26
I am not worthy thou shouldest come under *r*	Mat.	8	8
	Luke	7	6
They uncovered the *r*	Mark	2	4
room			
Is there *r* for us?	Gen.	24	23
The Lord hath made *r* for us	Gen.	26	22
Hast set my feet in a large *r*	Ps.	31	8
Thou preparedst *r* before it	Ps.	80	9
A man's gift maketh *r* for him	Prov.	18	16
There shall not be *r* enough	Mal.	3	10
Love the uppermost *r*	Mat.	23	6
	Mark	12	39
	Luke	20	46
There was no *r* to receive them	Mark	2	2
A large upper *r*	Mark	14	15
	Luke	22	12
No *r* for them in the inn	Luke	2	7
No *r* to bestow my fruits	Luke	12	17
How they chose out the chief *r*	Luke	14	7
Yet there is *r*	Luke	14	22
That occupieth the *r* of the unlearned	I Cor.	14	16
root *source*			
Used figuratively	II Ki.	19	30
	Is.	5	24
"Root of the matter"	Job	19	28
A good beginning meets with success	Prov.	12	12
Jesse, root of Jesus	Is.	11	1
A good root necessary for proper growth	Mat.	13	6
	Rom.	11	16
"Root of all evil"	I Tim.	6	10
Root up	I Ki.	14	15
	Job	18	14
Root of the matter	Job	19	28
Out of dry ground	Is.	53	2
Axe laid to	Mat.	3	10
ropes *large, stout cords*			
Emblem of servitude	I Ki.	20	31, 32
Threefold	Eccl.	4	12
Used in casting lots	Mic.	2	5
rose *a flower*			
Of Sharon	S. of S.	2	1
Flourishing of Christ's kingdom	Is.	35	1
rose *to rise*			
Cain *r* up against Abel	Gen.	4	8
The sun *r* upon him	Gen.	32	31
Waters *r* up upon an heap	Josh.	3	16
When men *r* up against us	Ps.	124	2
Not be persuaded, though one *r* from the dead	Luke	16	31
Christ both died and *r*	Rom.	14	9
People *r* up to play	I Cor.	10	7
He was buried, and *r* again	I Cor.	15	4
Him who died and *r* again	II Cor.	5	15
rotten rags			
Used in rescuing Jeremiah	Jer.	38	11–13
rough			
He stayeth his *r* wind	Is.	27	8
R places be made plain	Is.	40	4
R ways be made smooth (*See* Gen. 42:7; Prov. 18:23)	Luke	3	5
royal			
Yield *r* dainties	Gen.	49	20
Why should I dwell in the *r* city?	I Sam.	27	5
R wine	Esth.	1	7
R apparel	Esth.	5	1
	Esth.	6	8
	Esth.	8	15
	Acts	12	21
If ye fulfil the *r* law	James	2	8
Ye are a *r* priesthood	I Pet.	2	9

rubies *red*

Precious gems	Job	28	18
	Prov.	20	15
	Prov.	31	10
Compared with Nazarites	Lam.	4	7

rudder *helm*

For steering ships	Acts	27	40
Compared to the tongue	James	3	4

rudiments *basic principles*

Elements of the world	Col.	2	8, 20

rue *a plant*

Tithed	Luke	11	42

Rufus *red*

Son of Simon	Mark	15	21
Probably the same	Rom.	16	13

ruin *destruction*

They were the *r* of him	II Chr.	28	23
Hast brought his strongholds to *r*	Ps.	89	40
A flattering mouth worketh *r*	Prov.	26	28
Made of a defenced city a *r*	Is.	25	2
Iniquity shall not be your *r*	Ezek.	18	30
The *r* of that house was great	Luke	6	49
Build again the *r* thereof	Acts	15	16

rule *govern*

To *r* the day	Gen.	1	16
Thy husband shall *r* over thee	Gen.	3	16
I will not *r* over you	Judg.	8	23
He that *r* over men must be just	II Sam.	23	3
Jews had *r* over them	Esth.	9	1
He *r* by his power for ever	Ps.	66	7
Thou *r* the raging of the sea	Ps.	89	9
His kingdom *r* over all	Ps.	103	19
R in midst of enemies	Ps.	110	2
That *r* his spirit	Prov.	16	32
A wise servant shall have *r*	Prov.	17	2
A servant to have *r* over princes	Prov.	19	10
No *r* over his own spirit	Prov.	25	28
One man *r* over another	Eccl.	8	9
Babes shall *r* over them	Is.	3	4
Princes shall *r* in judgment	Is.	32	1
His arm shall *r* for him	Is.	40	10
Thou never barest *r* over them	Is.	63	19
No more *r* over nations	Ezek.	29	15
Heathen should *r* over them	Joel	2	17
Who are accounted to *r*	Mark	10	42
He that *r*, with diligence	Rom.	12	8
Put down all *r*	I Cor.	15	24
Measure of the *r*	II Cor.	10	13
As many as walk to this *r*	Gal.	6	16
Let us walk by the same *r*	Phil.	3	16
Let the peace of God *r* in your hearts	Col.	3	15
How to *r* his house	I Tim.	3	5
Elders that *r* well	I Tim.	5	17
That have the *r* over you	Heb.	13	7, 17

rulers *see kings*

rumor *story with proof*

Heard a *r* from the Lord	Jer.	49	14
R shall be upon *r*	Ezek.	7	26
Wars and *r* of wars	Mat.	24	6
	Mark	13	7
This *r* went forth	Luke	7	17

run

I have *r* through a troop	II Sam.	22	30
	Ps.	18	29
The eyes of the Lord *r* to and fro	II Chr.	16	9
	Zech.	4	10
As a strong man to *r* a race	Ps.	19	5
My cup *r* over	Ps.	23	5
I will *r* the way of thy commandments	Ps.	119	32
His word *r* very swiftly	Ps.	147	15
Their feet *r* to evil	Prov.	1	16
	Is.	59	7
We will *r* after thee	S. of S.	1	4
They shall *r*, and not be weary	Is.	40	31
Nations shall *r* to thee	Is.	55	5
If thou hast *r* with the footmen	Jer.	12	5
One post shall *r* to meet another	Jer.	51	31
That he may *r* that readeth	Hab.	2	2
R, speak to this young man	Zech.	2	4
Nor of him that *r*	Rom.	9	16
They which *r* in a race, *r* all	I Cor.	9	24
Lest I should *r*, or had *r* in vain	Gal.	2	2
Ye did *r* well	Gal.	5	7
Let us *r* with patience	Heb.	12	1
That ye *r* not to the same excess	I Pet.	4	4

rush *see bulrush*

rust *corrosion*

Is corrupting	Mat.	6	19, 20
Of gold and silver	James	5	3

Ruth *friendship*

Moabitess	Ruth	4	5
Ancestor of Jesus	Ruth	4	13, 21, 22
	Mat.	1	5

S

Sabacthani *see Eli, Eli*

Sabaoth *hosts*

The Lord of	Rom.	9	29

sabbath, the Lord's day

Instituted by God	Gen.	2	3
The seventh day	Ex.	20	9–11
A sign of the covenant	Ex.	31	13, 17
The fourth commandment	Deut.	5	12–16
During the Babylonian exile	Neh.	13	15–22
Necessary wants may be supplied on	Mat.	12	1
Deeds of mercy lawful on	Mat.	12	12
	Luke	13	16
Made for man	Mark	2	27
Christ, the Lord of	Mark	2	28
Observed by Christ	Luke	4	16
Christ teaches on	Luke	4	31
Word of God to be preached on	Acts	13	14, 15, 44
Paul preaches on	Acts	17	2
First day of the week observed	Acts	20	7

Mosiac law concerning:

People to remain indoors on	Ex.	16	29
Servants and cattle to rest on	Ex.	20	10
Forbidden to kindle fire on	Ex.	35	3
No manner of work to be done on	Lev.	23	3
No purchases to be made on	Neh.	10	31
No burdens to be carried on	Jer.	17	21

Observed by:

Moses	Num.	15	32–34
Women caring for body of Christ	Luke	23	56
Paul	Acts	13	14
Disciples	Acts	16	13

Violations of:

Gathering manna	Ex.	16	27
Gathering sticks	Num.	15	32
Inhabitants of Jerusalem	Jer.	17	21–23

sabbatical year *a rest every seventh year*

The servant set free	Ex.	21	2–6
The land to remain fallow	Ex.	23	11
	Lev.	25	2–7
Debtors released	Deut.	15	2, 12
Exaction	Neh.	10	31
Judgment for violation	Jer.	34	12–22
See feasts and festivals			

Sabeans *inhabitants of Seba or Sheba*

Invade Uz	Job	1	14
Slay servants	Job	1	15
A ransom	Is.	43	3
Noted merchants	Is.	45	14
Judgment of	Joel	3	8

sabotage *malicious destruction*

By Paul, of the church	Acts	26	9–11
	Gal.	1	13

sack *bag*

Holds corn and money	Gen.	42	25
Old	Josh.	9	4

sackbut *a kind of harp*

A musical instrument	Dan.	3	5, 7

sackcloth *a coarse garment*

Worn in mourning	Gen.	37	34
Worn by captives	I Ki.	20	31
Cloth of repentance	I Ki.	21	27
Worn next to skin	II Ki.	6	30
Banned in king's presence	Esth.	4	2
Worn in fasting	Ps.	35	13
Cloth of prophets	Is.	20	2
Symbol of darkness	Is.	50	3
	Rev.	6	12

sacraments *religious ceremonies*

Olive oil used in consecration of priests and kings	Ex.	29	7
	II Sam	5	3
Use of holy anointing oil	Ex.	30	22–33
Circumcision signifies admission into the people of God	Deut.	14	2

Instituted by Christ:

The Lord's supper	Mark	14	22–25
Baptism	John	3	22

sacrifice *offering*

A test for Abraham	Gen.	22	1–13
Of Jacob	Gen.	31	54
Of humans, forbidden	Deut.	12	31
Obedience better than	I Sam.	15	22
Beneficial	Prov.	3	9, 10
	Luke	18	20–24
Justice more acceptable to God	Prov.	21	3
Of the poor widow	Mark	12	41–44
Our bodies are a living	Rom.	12	1
Of the church of Macedonia	II Cor.	8	1–4
Christ, a sacrifice for us	Heb.	9	24–26
Jacob offered *s*	Gen.	31	54
Do *s* to the Lord	Ex.	5	17
	Ex.	8	8
Thou shalt *s* burnt offerings	Ex.	20	24
Offer *s* of thanksgiving	Lev.	7	12
	Ps.	116	17
Wherefore kick ye at my *s*?	I Sam.	2	29
To obey is better than *s*	I Sam.	15	22
We seek your God, and do *s* to him	Ezra	4	2
Will they *s*?	Neh.	4	2
Offer *s* of righteousness	Ps.	4	5
S thou didst not desire	Ps.	40	6
	Ps.	51	16
The *s* of God are a broken spirit	Ps.	51	17
I will freely *s* to thee	Ps.	54	6
Bind the *s* to horns of the altar	Ps.	118	27
Lifting up of my hands as the evening *s*	Ps.	141	2
S sacrifices of thanksgiving	Ps.	107	22
S of wicked an abomination	Prov.	15	8
A house full of *s* with strife	Prov.	17	1
To do justice is more acceptable than *s*	Prov.	21	3
The *s* of fools	Eccl.	5	1
To him that *s* and that *s* not	Eccl.	9	2
To what purpose the multitude of your *s*?	Is.	1	11
Nor your *s* sweet unto me	Jer.	6	20
That bring *s* of praise	Jer.	33	11
Gather to my *s*, a great *s*	Ezek.	39	17
Daily *s* taken away	Dan.	8	11
	Dan.	9	27
	Dan.	11	31
I desired mercy, not *s*	Hosea	6	6
	Mat.	9	13
	Mat.	12	7
They *s*, but the Lord accepteth not	Mat.	8	13
Have ye offered unto me *s*?	Amos	5	25
They *s* unto their net	Hab.	1	16
The Lord hath prepared a *s*	Zeph.	1	7
Every *s* shall be salted	Mark	9	49
To love the Lord is more than *s*	Mark	12	33
Have ye offered *s* forty years?	Acts	7	42
Would have done *s*	Acts	14	13
I present your bodies a living *s*	Rom.	12	1
Christ our passover is *s* for us	I Cor.	5	7
Offered in *s* to idols	I Cor.	8	4
	I Cor.	10	19, 28
Things Gentiles *s*, they *s* to devils	I Cor.	10	20
A *s* to God for a sweet-smelling savour	Eph.	5	2
Offered on *s* of your faith	Phil.	2	17
A *s* acceptable, well-pleasing to God	Phil.	4	18
Put away sin by the *s* of himself	Heb.	9	26
There remaineth no more *s* for sin	Heb.	10	26
Let us offer the *s* of praise	Heb.	13	15
To offer up spiritual *s*	I Pet.	2	5
Things *s* to idols	Rev.	2	14, 20

sacrilege *profanation*

Condemned	Lev.	19	8
Abhorred	I Sam.	2	12–17
Questions concerning	Rom.	2	22
Punishment for	I Cor.	3	17
For filthy lucre	Tit.	1	11
Constraint of	I Pet.	5	2

Instances of:

A birthright	Gen.	25	31–34
Strange fire	Lev.	10	1–7

Not of the seed	Num.	126	40
Looking upon the ark	I Sam.	6	19
Taking hold of the ark	II Sam.	6	6, 7
Idolatry	II Chr.	28	22–25
Of the vessels	Dan.	5	1–4
The den of thieves	Mat.	21	12, 13
Of the Eucharist	I Cor.	11	29

Sadducees *followers of Zadok, righteous*

Jesus tempted by	Mat.	16	1
Christ cautions His disciples against	Mat.	16	1–5
Deny the resurrection	Mat.	22	23
Silenced by Jesus	Mat.	22	23–34
Persecute the early Christians	Acts	4	1–3
	Acts	5	17, 18, 40
Dispute with the Pharisees	Acts	23	5–10

safe

Is the young man *s*?	II Sam.	18	29
Houses are *s* from fear	Job	21	9
Hold me up, and I shall be *s*	Ps.	119	117
Righteous runneth into it, and is *s*	Prov.	18	10
Who so trusteth in the Lord shall be *s*	Prov.	29	25
Received him *s*	Luke	15	27
They escaped all *s* to land	Acts	27	44
For you it is *s*	Phil.	3	1

safety

In the Lord	Deut.	33	12
	Job	11	18
In hiding	Judg.	9	5
Children of the foolish are without	Job	5	4
Promised by God	Ps.	12	5
Comes from God	Ps.	33	17–19
	Prov.	21	31
In numbers	Prov.	11	14
	Prov.	24	6
Promised to the needy	Is.	14	30

saffron *a species of crocus*

Cultivated in gardens	S. of S.	4	14

saints *godly persons*

God will protect	I Sam.	2	9
	Ps.	97	10
Duties of	II Chr.	6	41
	Ps.	30	4
	Heb.	6	10
Their blessings and privileges	Dan.	7	18
	Zech.	14	5
	Col.	1	12
True followers of Christ	Eph.	2	13–20
Christians	Acts	9	32, 41
Prayer and intercession for	Rom.	8	27
	Eph.	6	18

Compared to:

The sun	Judg.	5	31
A fruitful tree	Ps.	1	3
	Jer.	17	8
Doves	Ps.	68	13
Cedars in Lebanon	Ps.	92	12
Lambs	Is.	40	11
Unfailing springs	Is.	58	11
Stars	Dan.	12	3
Jewels	Mal.	3	17
Salt	Mat.	5	13
Babes	Mat.	11	25
Vessels of gold and silver	II Tim.	2	20

Sala, Salah *sprout*

Son of Arphaxad	Gen.	10	24
Life span of	Gen.	11	14, 15
Called Shelah	I Chr.	1	18, 24
Ancestor of Jesus	Luke	3	35

Salamis *ancient city of Cyprus*

Visited by Paul	Acts	13	4, 5

Salathiel, Shealtiel *I asked from God*

Son of Jeconiah	I Chr.	3	17
Father to Zerubbabel	Ezra	3	2, 8
Ancestor of Jesus	Mat.	1	12
	Luke	3	27

Salem *peace*

Shortened form of Jerusalem	Gen.	14	18
Place of tabernacle	Ps.	76	2
Melchizedek king of	Heb.	7	1

salesmen *sellers*

Lodge without	Neh.	13	20
In the temple	Mat.	21	12

Salim *completeness, tossing*

A city near Enon	John	3	23

saliva *spittle*

Swallowed	Job	7	19
Form of contempt	Job	30	10
Upon the Lord	Mat.	26	67
In healing	John	9	6, 7

Salma *clothing, strength*

Son of Caleb	I Chr.	2	50, 51

Salmon *clothing*

A wooded mountain	Judg.	9	48
Son of Nahshon	Ruth	4	20
Father of Boaz	Ruth	4	21
Called Salma	I Chr.	2	11
Ancestor of Jesus	Mat.	1	4, 5

Salmone *peaceful*

A promontory of Crete	Acts	27	7

Salome *peaceful*

Daughter of Herodias	Mark	6	22
Asks for head of John the Baptist	Mark	6	28
A woman who watches the crucifixion	Mark	15	40
Visits sepulchre after resurrection	Mark	16	1–8

salt

Lot's wife turned into a pillar of	Gen.	19	26
Elisha purifies the water with	I Ki.	2	19–22
Symbolic of God's eternal covenant	Mat.	5	13
Figurative of wisdom in speech	Col.	4	6
For destruction	Mark	9	49

Used for:

Seasoning animal sacrifices	Lev.	2	13
Ratifying convenants	Num.	18	19
	II Chr.	13	5
To kill vegetation	Judg.	9	45
Seasoning food	Job	6	6
Newborn babies	Ezek.	16	4

Salt, city of *see* city of Salt

salt, covenant of *see* covenant of salt

salt, pillar of

The price of curiosity	Gen.	19	26

Salt, sea of *see* Dead sea

salt, valley of

Syrians slain by David in	II Sam.	8	13
Edomites slain in	II Ki.	14	7
Children of Seir slain in	II Chr.	25	11

salutation *greeting*

Bowing	Gen.	18	2
Prostration	Gen.	19	1
Kissing	Gen.	33	4
Inquiry of peace	Gen.	43	27, 28
Blessing	Gen.	43	19
From the master	Ruth	2	4
From the servant	Ruth	2	4
Inquiry of health	II Sam.	20	9
To a ruler	I Chr.	12	18
To a king	Neh.	2	3
Hail	Mat.	26	49
All hail	Mat.	28	9
In a letter	Rom.	1	1–7
	I Thes.	1	1
"My Lords"	Gen.	19	2
"God be gracious unto thee"	Gen.	43	29
"Peace"	I Sam.	25	6
"Hail master"	Mat.	26	49
"The Lord be with you"	Ruth	2	4

salvation *redemption*

All the earth shall see	Is.	52	10
	Luke	3	6
Announced after the fall	Gen.	3	15
Confession of Christ necessary to	Rom.	10	10
Came to the Gentiles through the fall of the Jews	Rom.	11	11
From sin, to be worked out with fear and trembling	Phil.	2	12
God is willing to give	I Tim.	2	4
Godly sorrow produces repentance unto	II Cor.	7	10
The gospel is the power of God unto	I Cor.	1	18
The heavenly host ascribe to God	Rev.	7	10
	Rev.	19	1
Is of God	Ps.	37	39
	Ps.	3	8
	Jer.	3	23
By Christ alone	Is.	45	21–22
	Is.	59	16
Far off from the wicked	Ps.	119	155
	Is.	59	11
Not by works	Rom.	11	6
	Eph.	2	9
	Tit.	3	5

Of the appointment of God	I Thes.	5	9
Of the long-suffering of God	II Pet.	3	15
Of love	Rom.	5	8
Of mercy	Ps.	6	4
Of the purpose of God	II Tim.	1	9
Through faith in Christ	Acts	16	31
	Eph.	2	8
	I Pet.	1	5
Sought in vain from idols	Is.	45	20
Now is the time for	Is.	49	8
	II Cor.	6	2
Is by Christ	Is.	63	9
	Acts	4	12
Perseverance necessary to	Mat.	10	22
Is through faith in Christ	Mark	16	16
	Rom.	10	9
Repentance necessary for	Luke	13	2–5
Many shall not obtain	Luke	13	23–30
Regeneration necessary to	John	3	3
Christ crucified for	John	3	14, 15
	Gal.	1	4
The scriptures a means of	Rom.	1	16
	II Tim.	3	15
	James	1	21
No by our works	Rom.	11	6
	II Tim.	1	9
Is of grace	Eph.	2	5, 8
Available to all	Tit.	2	11
Is of love and mercy	Tit.	3	5
	I John	4	9, 10
Danger in neglecting	Heb.	2	3

Christ:

Appointed for	Is.	49	6
The author of	Heb.	5	9
Brings, with him	Is.	62	11
	Luke	19	9
Came to effect	Mat.	18	11
	I Tim.	1	9
The Captain of	Heb.	2	10
Exalted to give	Acts	5	31
Has	Zech.	9	9
Mighty to effect	Is.	63	1
	Heb.	7	25
Raised up for	Luke	1	69

Deliverance from:

The devil	Col.	2	15
	Heb.	2	14–15
Enemies	Luke	1	71, 74
Eternal death	John	3	16–17
Sin	Mat.	1	21
	I John	3	5
This present evil world	Gal.	1	4
Uncleanness	Ezek.	36	29
Wrath	Rom.	5	9
	I Thes.	1	10

Described as:

Common	Jude		3
Eternal	Is.	45	17
	Is.	51	6
	Heb.	5	9
From generation to generation	Is.	51	8
Glorious	II Tim.	2	10
To the uttermost	Heb.	7	25

Illustrated by:

Chariots	Hab.	3	8
Clothing	II Chr.	6	41
	Ps.	132	16
	Ps.	149	4
	Is.	61	10
A horn	Luke	1	69
A rock	Deut.	32	15
	II Sam.	22	47
A shield	II Sam.	22	36
A victory	I Cor.	15	57
Walls and bulwarks	Is.	26	1
	Is.	60	18
Wells	Is.	12	13
Tower	II Sam.	22	51
Horn	Ps.	18	2
Rock	Ps.	95	1
Cup	Ps.	116	13
Helmet	Is.	59	17
Lamp	Is.	62	1

Ministers:

Are a sweet savor of Christ	II Cor.	2	15
Should be clothed with	II Chr.	6	41
	Ps.	132	16

Should endure suffering	II Tim.	2	10
Should exhort to	Ezek.	3	18–19
	Acts	2	40
Should labor to lead others to	Rom.	11	14
Should use self-denial to lead others to	I Cor.	9	22
Show the way of	Acts	16	17
Of the Gentiles, predicted	Is.	45	22
	Is.	49	6
	Is.	52	10
Of Israel, predicted	Is.	35	4
	Is.	45	17
	Zech.	9	16
	Rom.	11	26
Preaching the word	I Cor.	1	21
Reconciliation to God, a pledge of	Rom.	5	10
Revealed in the gospel	Eph.	1	13
	II Tim.	1	10

Saints:

Appointed to obtain	I Thes.	5	9
Are heirs of	Heb.	1	14
Ascribe, to God	Ps.	25	5
	Is.	12	2
Beautified with	Ps.	149	4
Chosen to	II Thes.	2	13
	II Tim.	1	9
Clothed with	Is.	61	10
Daily approach nearer to	Rom.	13	11
Declare	Ps.	40	10
	Ps.	71	15
Earnestly look for	Ps.	119	123
Evidence, by works	Heb.	6	9–10
Glory in	I Cor.	1	31
	Gal.	6	14
Have a token of	Phil.	1	28–29
Have, through grace	Acts	15	11
Hope for	Lam.	3	26
	Rom.	8	24
Kept by the power of God unto	I Pet.	1	5
Long for	Ps.	119	81, 174
Love	Ps.	40	16
Praise God for	I Chr.	16	23
	Ps.	96	2
Pray for assurance of	Ps.	35	3
Pray for a joyful sense of	Ps.	51	12
Pray to be visited with	Ps.	85	7
	Ps.	106	4
	Ps.	119	41
Rejoice in	Ps.	9	14
	Ps.	21	1
	Is.	25	9
Receive, as the end of their faith	I Pet.	1	9
Satisfied by	Luke	2	30
Wait for	Gen.	49	18
	Lam.	3	26
Welcome the tidings of	Is.	52	7

Conditions of:

Repent	Mat.	3	2
	Mark	1	4
	Luke	3	8
	Acts	3	19
Believe	John	5	24
	John	3	15, 16
	John	20	31
Confess	Acts	2	21
	Rom.	10	9

Samaria *watch mountain*

Capital of the northern kingdom	I Ki.	16	23–29
Besieged by Ben-hadad	I Ki.	20	1–4
The prophet Elisha dwells in	II Ki.	2	25
Besieged a second time	II Ki.	6	24
Saved by a miracle	II Ki.	7	1–16
Seized by the Assyrians	II Ki.	17	5, 6
A corrupt and wicked city	Ezek.	16	46
	Amos	3	9, 10
The entire northern kingdom at times so designated	I Ki.	21	1
District of, subdivision of a Persian province	Neh.	4	2
Jesus journeys through	John	4	1–42
No dealings between the Jews and inhabitants of	John	4	9
Expects the Messiah	John	4	25
Philip preaches in	Acts	8	5
Churches founded	Acts	9	31
Visited by Paul	Acts	15	3

Samaritans *inhabitants of Samaria*

Worship idols	II Ki.	17	29
Idols destroyed	II Ki.	23	19
Seek alliance	Ezra	4	1–3
Strongly oppose building the walls	Neh.	4	1–23
Come to Jerusalem to worship	Jer.	41	5
Parable of	Luke	10	30–37
Jews do not deal with	John	4	9
Worship where temple once stood	John	4	20, 21
Believe in a Messiah	John	4	25
Converted by Jesus	John	4	39–42
Receive Holy Ghost	Acts	8	14–17
Receive gospel	Acts	8	25

Samson *like the sun*

His birth divinely announced	Judg.	1	14
Son of Manoah	Judg.	13	22–24
Marries a Philistine woman	Judg.	14	1–4
His riddle propounded	Judg.	14	8–19
Avenged for the estrangement of his wife	Judg.	15	3–8
His great strength	Judg.	15	7–14
	Heb.	11	32
Slays a thousand Philistines	Judg.	15	13–17
His immorality	Judg.	14	1–4
Physically strong, morally weak	Judg.	16	3, 12
	Judg.	16	15–17
Betrayed by Delilah	Judg.	16	4–19
Triumphs in death	Judg.	16	23, 31
A judge of Israel	Judg.	16	31
Man of faith	Heb.	11	32

Samuel *asked of God*

His miraculous birth	I Sam.	1	7–20
Consecrated to God	I Sam.	1	11, 22 28
His mother's song	I Sam.	2	1–10
Serves in the temple	I Sam.	2	11, 18, 19
His vision	I Sam.	3	1–18
Defeats Philistines through prayer and sacrifice	I Sam.	7	7–14
A judge of Israel	I Sam.	7	15–17
His circuit	I Sam.	7	15–17
His sons corrupt	I Sam.	8	1–3
A prophet	I Sam.	9	7–9
Anoints Saul	I Sam.	10	1–13
His integrity as judge and ruler	I Sam.	12	1–5
Rebukes Saul	I Sam.	13	11 15
Anoints David	I Sam.	16	
His death	I Sam.	25	11
A man prayer	Ps.	99	6
Model of holiness	Jer.	15	1
A man of faith	Heb.	11	32, 33

Sanballat *strength*

Opponent of Nehemiah	Neh.	2	10, 19
Opposes building of walls	Neh.	4	1–8
Father-in-law of Joiada	Neh.	13	28

sanctification *state of being holy*

Set apart for the service of God	Ps.	4	3
	II Cor.	6	7
Possessed by ministers	Jer.	1	5
Through the word of God	John	17	17, 19
Should lead to holiness	Rom.	6	22
Is in Christ	I Cor.	1	2
	I Cor.	1	30
	Heb.	13	12
Christians receive salvation through	I Cor.	1	30
	II Thes.	2	13
Necessary to inherit the kingdom of God	I Cor.	6	9–11
Ministers should pray that their people possess	I Thes.	5	23
Qualifies for service	II Thes.	2	21

Effected by:

God	Ezek.	37	28
The Holy Ghost	Rom.	15	16
Christ	Heb.	2	11

sanctify

The Lord that doth *s* you	Ex.	31	13
S yourselves	Lev.	11	44
	Lev.	20	7
	Josh.	7	13
	I Sam.	16	5
S the Lord of hosts	Is.	8	13
They shall *s* the Holy One	Is.	29	23
That *s* themselves in gardens	Is.	66	17
I *s* and ordained thee a prophet	Jer.	1	5
I will *s* my great name	Ezek.	36	23
S ye a fast	Joel	1	14
	Joel	2	15
Him whom the Father hath *s*	John	10	36

sanctify—*continued*

S them through thy truth	John	17	17
Inheritance among them which are *s*	Acts	20	32
	Acts	26	18
Being *s* by the Holy Ghost	Rom.	15	16
But ye are *s*	I Cor.	6	11
Unbelieving husband is *s* by the wife	I Cor.	7	14
The very God of Peace *s* you	I Thes.	5	23
It is *s* by the word of God	I Tim.	4	5
A vessel *s* for the Master's use	II Tim.	2	21
He that *s* and they who are *s*	Heb.	2	11
He perfected for ever them that are *s*	Heb.	10	14
That he might *s* the people	Heb.	13	12
S the Lord God in your hearts	I Pet.	3	15

sanctimony *hypocritical piety*

In prayer	Mat.	6	5
In fast	Mat.	6	16
Condemned	Mat.	23	2–39

sanctuary *a consecrated place*

Established by the Lord	Ex.	15	17
To be reverenced	Lev.	19	30
See tabernacle			
Plant them in the *s*	Ex.	15	17
Let them make me a *s*	Ex.	25	8
As I have seen thee in the *s*	Ps.	63	2
Till I went into the *s* of God	Ps.	73	17
Beautify the place of my *s*	Is.	60	13
First covenant had a worldly *s*	Heb.	9	1
(See Ps. 20:2; 68:24; 77:13; 78:54; 96:6; 134; 150; Heb. 8:9)			

sand *disintegrated rock*

Upon the seashore	Gen.	22	17
Body hidden in	Ex.	2	12
Numberless	Ps.	139	18
House built upon	Mat.	7	26

sandals *a kind of shoe*

Worn by apostles	Mark	6	7–9
Bound on	Acts	12	8

Sanhedrin *supreme council of Jews*

Composed of Pharisees	Mat.	12	14
Question Jesus	Luke	22	66–71
Condemn Jesus	John	11	47–53
Condemn Peter	Acts	5	21–33
Judge Stephen	Acts	6	12–15

sanitation

Of dead	Lev.	5	2
	Lev.	11	24–40
	Num.	19	11–16
At childbirth	Lev.	12	3
	Ezek.	16	4
Of leprosy	Lev.	13	2–59
	Num.	5	2–4
Disinfection:			
By washing	Lev.	11	24, 25
By fire	Lev.	7	19
Shaving hair off	Lev.	14	8
Of Food	Lev.	7	15–27
	Lev.	11	2–47
Quarantine	Lev.	13	2–5
	Lev.	15	19

Sapphira *beautiful*

Wife of Ananias	Acts	5	1
Withholds money from the church	Acts	5	2, 8
Struck dead	Acts	5	10

sapphire *a precious stone*

Set in breastplate	Ex.	28	15, 18
Found in earth	Job	28	6
Precious stone	Job	28	16
Coloured like the firmament	Ezek.	1	26
In the foundation of the new Jerusalem	Rev.	21	19

Sarah, Sara, Sarai, Serah *princess*

Wife of Abraham	Gen.	11	29
Barren	Gen.	11	30
Noted for beauty	Gen.	12	11
Taken as a wife by Pharaoh	Gen.	12	15–20
Advises concubinage	Gen.	16	2, 3
Skeptical of God's promise	Gen.	18	12–15
Bears Isaac	Gen.	21	3
Asks Hagar's exile	Gen.	21	10
Dies	Gen.	23	1, 2
Buried at Machpelah	Gen.	23	19
Stong in faith	Rom.	4	19
	Heb.	11	11
Daughter of Asher	Num.	26	46

sarcasm *bitter taunt*

Jotham's parable	Judg.	9	7–15

Of Samson	Judg.	14	18
Eliab to David	I Sam.	17	28
Of David	II Sam.	6	21
Of Elijah	I Ki.	18	27
Of Ahab	I Ki.	20	11
Of Jehoash	II Ki.	14	9
Of Rabshakeh	II Ki.	18	23, 24
Of Sanballat	Neh.	4	1, 2
Of God	Jer.	25	27, 28
Of Jesus	Mark	7	6–9
Of the priests	Mark	15	31, 32
To Ananias	Acts	23	1–5
Of Jesus	Mat.	27	28, 29
Of Agrippa	Acts	26	28

sarcophagus *see burial*

Sardis *an ancient city*

Location of the church in Asia Minor	Rev.	1	11
Receive instructions	Rev.	3	1–6

sardius *a precious stone, may be modern ruby*

Set in breastplate	Ex.	28	17
A precious stone	Ezek.	28	13
In foundation of new Jerusalem	Rev.	21	20

sardonyx *a kind of onyx*

A foundation stone	Rev.	21	20

Saron *see Sharon*

Saruch, Serug *tendril*

Son of Reu	Gen.	11	20
Father of Nahor	Gen.	11	22
Ancestor of Jesus	Luke	3	35

sat

I have not *s* with vain persons	Ps.	26	4
The people who *s* in darkness	Mat.	4	16
He *s* on the right hand of God	Mark	16	19
He that was dead *s* up	Luke	7	15
Mary *s* at Jesus' feet	Luke	10	39
A colt whereon never man *s*	Luke	19	30
Jesus *s* on the well	John	4	6
S for alms at gate of the temple	Acts	3	10

Satan, the devil *evil spirit*

In the form of a serpent	Gen.	3	4, 5
David provoked by	I Cor.	21	1
Upholds the wicked	Ps.	109	6
Hinders God's work	Zech.	3	1
	Mat.	13	19
	I Thes.	2	18
Christ tempted by	Mat.	4	3–10
Leads men to evil	John	13	2
The wicked deceived by	II Cor.	4	4
	II Tim.	2	26
Must be resisted	Eph.	6	1–18
	James	4	7
Apostates delivered unto	I Tim.	1	20
Cast down to hell	II Pet.	2	4
Overcome by saints	I John	2	13
Sins against God	I John	3	8
Condemned on the judgment day	Jude		6
	Rev.	20	10
	Mat.	25	41
Triumph over, by Christ:			
In resisting his temptation	Mat.	4	11
In empowering His disciples	Mat.	10	1
In casting out evil spirits	Luke	11	20
Completed by the resurrection	Col.	2	15

satisfaction *contentment*

Depart in peace	Luke	2	25–35
Of redemption	Luke	2	36–38
Sword shall be *s* with blood	Luke	46	10

satisfy

To *s* the desolate ground	Job	38	27
I shall be *s* with thy likeness	Ps.	17	15
The meek shall eat and be *s*	Ps.	22	26
In days of famine be *s*	Ps.	37	19
My soul shall be *s*	Ps.	63	5
O *s* us early with thy mercy	Ps.	90	14
With long life will I *s* him	Ps.	91	16
Who *s* thy mouth with good things	Ps.	103	5
He *s* them with bread from heaven	Ps.	105	40
He *s* the longing soul	Ps.	107	9
I will *s* her poor with bread	Ps.	132	15
Thou *s* every living thing	Ps.	145	16
If he steal to *s* his soul	Prov.	6	30
He that tilleth his land shall be *s*	Prov.	12	11
A good man shall be *s* from himself	Prov.	14	14
Open thine eyes, and thou shalt be *s*	Prov.	20	13
Three things are never *s*	Prov.	30	15

The eye is not *s* with seeing	Eccl.	1	8
Shall not be *s* with silver	Eccl.	5	10
Shall eat, and not be *s*	Is.	9	20
	Mic.	6	14
See of travail of his soul and be *s*	Mic.	53	11
The Lord shall *s* thy soul	Is.	58	11
People be *s* with my goodness	Jer.	31	14
He is as death and cannot be *s*	Hab.	2	5
Whence *s* these with bread?	Mark	8	4

satyr *a sylvan deity, he-goat, hairy one*

Worship forbidden	Lev.	17	7
Shall dance at fall of Babylon	Is.	13	21
	Is.	34	14

Saul *asked for*

A king of Edom	Gen.	36	37, 38
A Benjamite, son of Kish	I Sam.	9	1, 2
Made king of Israel	I Sam.	9–10	
Defeats Amalekites	I Sam.	15	
His disobedience and rejection by God	I Sam.	15	
Sends messenger to Jesse	I Sam.	16	17–23
His jealousy of David	I Sam.	18	
David spares his life	I Sam.	24	5–8
His confession and blessing upon David	I Sam.	26	
His kingdom invaded	I Sam.	28	1–5
Seeks counsel of the witch	I Sam.	28	6–14
Is defeated, three of his sons slain	I Sam.	31	2
Commits suicide	I Sam.	31	4
His death a judgment	I Chr.	10	13
Saul of Tarsus *see* Paul			

save *rescue*

To *s* your lives	Gen.	45	7
The Lord goeth to *s* you	Deut.	20	4
Wherewith shall I *s* Israel?	Judg.	6	15
No restraint to *s* by many or few	I Sam.	14	6
He is in thine hand, but *s* his life	Job	2	6
He shall *s* the humble	Job	22	29
God, who *s* the upright	Ps.	7	10
He *s* such as he of contrite spirit	Ps.	34	18
Neither did their own arms *s* them	Ps.	44	3
S with thy right hand	Ps.	60	5
God will *s* Zion	Ps.	69	35
He shall *s* the children of the needy	Ps.	72	4
S thy servant	Ps.	86	2
To *s* him from those that condemn	Ps.	109	31
S now, I beseech thee	Ps.	118	25
Thy right hand shall *s* me	Ps.	138	7
Hear their cry, and *s* them	Ps.	145	19
Wait on the Lord, and he shall *s* thee	Prov.	20	22
Your God, will come and *s* you	Is.	35	4
Pray unto a God that cannot *s*	Is.	45	20
Look unto me, and be ye *s*	Is.	45	22
Lord's hand is not shortened, that it cannot *s*	Is.	59	1
Mighty to *s*	Is.	63	1
Let them arise, if they can *s* thee	Jer.	2	28
Summer is ended, and we are not *s*	Jer.	8	20
I am with thee to *s* thee	Jer.	15	20
	Jer.	30	11
	Jer.	42	11
S me and I shall be *s*	Jer.	17	14
I will *s* them by the Lord	Hosea	1	7
Is there any other that may *s* thee?	Hosea	13	10
Cry unto thee, and thou wilt not *s*	Hab.	1	2
He will *s*	Zeph.	3	17
S his people from their sins	Mat.	1	21
Whosoever will *s* his life	Mat.	16	25
	Mark	8	35
	Luke	9	24
To seek and to *s* that which was lost	Mat.	18	11
	Luke	19	10
Who then can be *s*?	Mat.	19	25
	Mark	10	26
	Luke	18	26
He *s* others himself he cannot *s*	Mat.	27	42
	Mark	15	31
Is it lawful to *s* life?	Mark	3	4
	Luke	6	9
Not to destroy but to *s*	Luke	9	56
He let him *s* himself	Luke	23	35
These things I say that ye might be *s*	John	5	34
I came not to judge, but to *s*	John	12	47
S yourselves from this generation	Acts	2	40
None other name whereby we must be *s*	Acts	4	12
What must I do to be *s*?	Acts	16	30
We are *s* by hope	Rom.	8	24
If I might *s* some	Rom.	11	14
	I Cor.	9	22

By foolishness of preaching to *s* some	I Cor.	1	21
S as by fire	I Cor.	3	15
Christ came to *s* sinners	I Tim.	1	15
Thou shalt *s* thyself and them	I Tim.	4	16
Able to *s* him from death	Heb.	5	7
Able to *s* to the uttermost	Heb.	7	25
Word which is able to *s* your souls	James	1	21
Can faith *s* him?	James	2	14
Able to *s* and destroy	James	4	12
Prayer of faith shall *s* the sick	James	5	15
Shall *s* a soul from death	James	5	20
If the righteous scarcely be *s*	I Pet.	4	18
Others *s* with fear	Jude	23	

savior *deliverer*

Othniel, the judge as	Judg.	3	9
A king as a	II Ki.	13	5
God, our Saviour	Is.	43	3
	Is.	45	15
	I Tim.	1	1
	I Tim.	4	10
	II Sam.	22	3
	Ps.	106	21
	Is.	60	16
	Luke	1	47
	Tit.	1	3
Jesus, our Saviour	Luke	2	11
	John	4	42
	II Pet.	2	20

saw *a tool*

Used figuratively	II Sam.	12	31
Fro cutting stone	I Ki.	7	9

scall *see* leprosy

scandal *defamation*

Transgression of Eli's sons	I Sam.	2	22–24
Lechery	II Sam.	16	21, 22

scapegoat

Part of the sin offering on day of atonement	Lev.	16	5–10
Bears sin of the people	Lev.	16	20–22

scarlet *crimson*

The offering	Ex.	25	3
The curtains of the tabernacle	Ex.	26	1
The vail	Ex.	26	31
The hanging	Ex.	26	36
The ephod	Ex.	28	6
The girdle	Ex.	28	8
The breastplate	Ex.	28	15
A cloth for the shewbread	Num.	4	8

Symbolic of:

Prosperity	Prov.	31	21
Iniquity	Is.	1	18
Royalty	Dan.	5	7
Battle	Nah.	2	3

scatter

Thence did the Lord *s* them	Gen.	11	9
I will *s* you among the heathen	Lev.	26	33
Let thine enemies be *s*	Num.	10	35
	Ps.	68	1
He *s* his bright cloud	Job	37	11
Which *s* the east wind	Job	38	24
S the people that delight in war	Ps.	68	30
Workers of iniquity shall be *s*	Ps.	92	9
Lifted up hand to *s* them	Ps.	106	26
He *s* the hoar frost	Ps.	147	16
There is that *s*, and yet increaseth	Prov.	11	24
Woe to pastors that *s* the sheep	Jer.	23	1
Sheep shall be *s*	Zech.	13	7
	Mat.	26	31
	Mark	14	27
S as sheep having no shepherd	Mat.	9	36
He that gathereth not *s*	Mat.	12	30
	Luke	11	23
Wolf *s* the sheep	John	10	12

scent *odour*

Of water	Job	14	9
Not changed	Jer.	48	11
Of wine	Hosea	14	7

sceptre *a rod or staff indicating authority*

Figure of sovereignty	Gen.	49	10
Shall rise	Num.	24	17
Made of gold	Esth.	4	11
Held out in favour	Esth.	5	2
Made of iron	Ps.	2	9
	Rev.	2	27
Symbol of justice	Ps.	45	6

sceptre—*continued*

Oppression under	Is.	9	4
Of rulers	Is.	14	5
Rod of authority	Amos	1	5
Of righteousness	Heb.	1	8

Sceva *left-handed*

An Ephesian Jew	Acts	19	14

schism *formal division in a church*

Condemned	I Cor.	12	25

scholar *pupil*

Casts lots	I Chr.	25	8
Profaned	Mal.	2	12

school *an institution for teaching*

Instruction from parents	Deut.	4	9, 10
Instruction to all	Deut.	31	10–13
Instruction of adults	I Sam.	19	20
	Jer.	7	1–34
For prophets	II Ki.	2	3, 5, 15
	II Ki.	4	38
Well attended	II Ki.	6	1, 2
State sponsored	II Chr.	17	7–9
At Jerusalem	II Chr.	34	22
Do not forsake	Prov.	1	8
Provides tutors	Dan.	1	3, 4
Taught by Jesus	Luke	5	17
Of Tyrannus	Acts	19	9

schoolmaster *instructs in education and governs scholars*

The law called	Gal.	3	24, 25

science *learning, knowledge*

Cannot understand	Job	26	7–14
Understood by Daniel	Dan.	1	4
False	I Tim.	6	20

scoffers *scorners*

Like their fathers	II Chr.	30	6–10
Victims of wraths	II Chr.	36	16
Not blessed	Ps.	1	1
Fools	Prov.	1	22, 25
An abomination	Prov.	24	9
Ishmael	Gen.	21	9
Children of Bethel	II Ki.	2	23
Sanballat	Neh.	4	1
Soldiers at the crucifixion	Mat.	27	28–31
Pharisees	Luke	16	14
Herod	Luke	23	11
Athenians	Acts	17	32

scorning *taunting*

Of Christ, predicted	Ps.	22	6, 8
	Is.	53	3
Judgment against	Prov.	19	29
Drunkards addicted to	Ps.	69	12
	Hosea	7	5
Idolaters addicted to	Is.	57	3–6
Endured by Christ	Mat.	9	24
	Mat.	27	29
Endured through faith	Heb.	11	17–39

Those who indulge:

Delight in	Prov.	1	22
Hear no rebuke	Prov.	13	1
Hate those who reprove	Prov.	15	12
Are proud and haughty	Prov.	21	24
Are contentious	Prov.	22	10
Are hated by men	Prov.	24	9
See mocking			

scorpion *spider-like insect*

Inhabits desert areas	Deut.	8	15
A lash likened to	I Ki.	12	11
Enemies likened to	Ezek.	2	6
Apostles given power over	Luke	10	19
Not to be used for food	Luke	11	12
Sting in tail	Rev.	9	10

scourging *lashing*

Retribution for	Ex.	21	20
Punishment for fornication	Lev.	19	20
Forty stripes	Deut.	25	1–3
As severe chastisement	I Ki.	12	11
Predicted for apostles	Mat.	10	17
Of Jesus foretold	Mat.	27	26
Of Sosthenes	Acts	18	17
Suffered by Paul	II Cor.	11	24, 25

screech owl *an owl whose cry sounds lide a shriek*

Called the night-monster	Is.	34	14

scribes *writers*

Writers and transcribers of the law	II Sam.	8	17
The king's secretary	II Ki.	12	10–12

Mustering officer of the army	II Ki.	25	19
Generally men of great wisdom	I Chr.	27	32
Shebna	II Ki.	18	18
	Is.	36	3
Witnessing legal transactions	Jer.	32	12
In copying the law	Neh.	12	26, 36
Ezra	Neh.	8	4
Jeremiah's secretary Baruch	Jer.	36	26
Members of the council	Mat.	2	4
Hypocrisy of, reproved by Jesus	Mat.	5	20
Instructors in the law	Mat.	7	29
Jesus falsely accused by	Mat.	9	3
Censured by Christ	Mat.	15	1–3
Conspire against Jesus	Mat.	26	3, 57
Denounced by Jesus	Mark	12	38
Test Jesus with questions	John	8	3–9
Persecute the early Christian	Acts	4	4–21
	Acts	6	9–12

scrip *a wallet or bag*

The shepherd's bag	I Sam.	17	40
Not used by apostles	Mat.	10	10

scriptures *writings*

To be kept unaltered	Deut.	4	2
	Prov.	30	6
Called the law of the Lord	Ps.	1	2
Pray to be taught	Ps.	119	12, 13
Encourage faith and hope	Ps.	119	49
	John	20	21
Bring comfort	Ps.	119	82
	Rom.	15	4
Are a dependable guide	Prov.	6	23
	II Pet.	1	19
Destruction of, punished	Jer.	36	29–31
Everything should be tried by	Is.	9	20
	Acts	17	11
Given by inspiration of God	II Tim.	3	16
Given by inspiration of the Holy Ghost	Acts	1	16
	Heb.	3	7
	I Pet.	1	21
The Holy Ghost enables us to understand	John	16	13
	I Cor.	2	10–14
Ignorance of, a source of error	Mat.	22	29
	Acts	13	27
Intended for the use of all men	Rom.	16	26
The letter of, without the spirit, killeth	John	6	63
	II Cor.	3	6
Let them dwell richly in you	Col.	3	16
Mere hearers of, deceive themselves	James	1	22
No prophecy of, is of any private interpretation	II Pet.	1	20
One portion of, to be compared with another	I Cor.	2	13
Reveal the laws, statutes, and judgments of God	Ex.	24	3–4
Work effectually in them that believe	I Thes.	2	13
Written for our instruction	Rom.	15	4
Referred to and expounded by Chirst	Mat.	4	4
	Mark	12	10
The wicked know not	Mat.	22	29
Fulfilled in Christ	Mat.	26	54, 56
Blessed are those who hear	Luke	11	28
Christ teaches from	Luke	24	27
Testify of Christ	John	5	39
	Acts	10	43
Given by inspiration of God	Acts	1	16
	II Tim.	3	16
Proves the divinity of Christ	Acts	18	28
Basis of Paul's preachings	I Cor.	15	1–8
Good for doctrine and practice	II Tim.	3	16, 17
Called the word of God	Heb.	4	12
Will endure forever	I Pet.	1	25
Apollos might in	Acts	18	24
Rejected by some	II Pet.	3	16
Infallible	John	10	35
To be inquired of	Rom.	4	3
	Rom.	11	2
Did not originate in man	II Pet.	1	20
The wicked reject	Jer.	8	9
Advantage of possessing	Rom.	3	2
Able to make wise unto salvation through faith in Christ	II Tim.	3	15
Full and sufficient	Luke	16	29, 31
Blessedness of hearing and obeying	James	1	25
Christ enables us to understand	Luke	24	45
Christ sanctioned, by appealing to them	John	7	42
Testify of Christ	Acts	18	28
	I Cor.	15	3

Contain the promises of the gospel	Rom.	1	2
Denunciations against those who add to or take from	Rev.	22	18–19

Described as:

Perfect	Ps.	19	7
Precious	Ps.	19	10
Pure	Ps.	12	6
	Ps.	119	140
	Prov.	30	5
Quick and powerful	Heb.	4	12
True	Ps.	119	160
	John	17	17

Designed for:

Admonishing	Ps.	19	11
	I Cor.	10	11
Building up in the faith	Acts	20	32
Cleansing the heart	John	15	3
	Eph.	5	26
Cleansing the ways	Ps.	119	9
Converting the soul	Ps.	19	9
Illuminating	Ps.	119	130
Keeping from destructive paths	Ps.	17	4
Making wise the simple	Ps.	19	7
Producing obedience	Deut.	17	19–20
Promoting growth in grace	I Pet.	2	2
Quickening	Ps.	119	50, 93
Regenerating	James	1	18
	I Pet.	1	23
Rejoicing the heart	Ps.	19	8
	Ps.	119	111
Sanctifying	John	17	17
	Eph.	5	26
Supporting life	Mat.	4	4

Saints:

Delight in	Ps.	1	2
Esteem above all things	Job	23	12
Esteem as a light	Ps.	119	105
Grieve when men disobey	Ps.	119	158
Hide in their hearts	Ps.	119	11
Hope in	Ps.	119	74, 81, 147
Keep in remembrance	Ps.	119	16
Long after	Ps.	119	82
Love exceedingly	Ps.	119	86, 113
Meditate in	Ps.	1	2
	Ps.	119	99, 148
Obey	Ps.	119	67
	Luke	8	21
	John	17	6
Plead the promises of, in prayer	Ps.	119	25, 28, 41
Pray to be conformed to	Ps.	119	133
Regard as sweet	Ps.	119	103
Rejoice in	Ps.	119	162
	Jer.	15	16
Speak of	Ps.	119	172
Stand in awe of	Ps.	119	161
	Is.	66	2
Trust in	Ps.	119	42

The wicked:

Corrupt	II Cor.	2	17
Frequently wrest, to their own destruction	II Pet.	3	16
Make, of none effect through their traditions	Mark	7	9–13
Obey not	Ps.	119	158
Stumble at	I Pet.	2	8

Called the:

Book	Ps.	40	7
	Rev.	22	19
Book of the law	Neh.	8	3
	Gal.	3	10
Book of the Lord	Is.	34	16
Holy Scriptures	Rom.	1	2
	II Tim.	3	15
Law of the Lord	Is.	30	9
Oracles of God	Rom.	3	2
	I Pet.	4	11
Scripture of truth	Dan.	10	21
Sword of the Spirit	Eph.	6	17
Word	James	1	21–23
	I Pet.	2	2
Word of Christ	Col.	3	16
Word of God	Luke	11	28
	Heb.	4	12
Word of truth	James	1	18

Should be:

Appealed to	I Cor.	1	31
	I Pet.	1	16

Laid up in the heart	Deut.	6	6
	Deut.	11	18
Not handled deceitfully	II Cor.	4	2
Received with meekness	James	1	21
The standard of teaching	I Pet.	4	11
Used against our spiritual enemies	Mat.	4	4
	Eph.	6	11, 17
Taught to children	Deut.	6	7
	II Tim.	3	15
Read	Deut.	17	19
	Is.	34	16
Read publicly to all	Deut.	31	11–13
	Neh.	8	1
	Acts	13	15
	Jer.	36	6
Taught to every one	II Chr.	17	7–9
	Neh.	8	7–8
Not only heard but obeyed	Mat.	7	24
	Luke	11	28
Believed	John	2	22
Searched daily	Acts	17	11
	John	5	39
	John	7	52
Received as the word of God	I Thes.	2	13

scroll *written roll of parchment*

The heavens rolled	Is.	34	4
	Rev.	6	14

sea, molten *see* molten sea
sea of Galilee *see* Galilee, sea of
sea of glass

Around God's throne	Rev.	4	6

sea:

S to go back, made the s dry.	Ex.	14	21
Didst blow, the s covered	Ex.	15	10
Lord made the s and all	Ex.	20	11
	Ps.	95	5
	Jonah	1	9
	Acts	4	24
	Acts	14	15
Quails from the s	Num.	11	31
You came unto the s	Josh.	24	6
At s a navy of Tharshish	I Ki.	10	22
Look toward the s	I Ki.	18	3
Coast to the s of plain	II Ki.	14	25
Let the s roar	I Chr.	16	32
	Ps.	96	11
	Ps.	98	7
Divide the s, went through the s	Neh.	9	11
	Job	26	12
	Ps.	74	13
	Ps.	78	13
	Jer.	31	35
Am I a s or a whale?	Job	7	12
Is broader than the s	Job	11	9
Or who shut up the s?	Job	38	8
He maketh the s like a pot	Job	41	31
The s into dry land	Ps.	66	6
Dominion from s to s	Ps.	72	8
But the s overwhelmed their	Ps.	78	53
So is this great and wide s	Ps.	104	25
Down to the s in ships	Ps.	107	23
The s saw it and fled	Ps.	114	3
Gave to the s his decree	Prov.	8	29
As the waters cover the s	Is.	11	9
	Hab.	2	14
Stretched and gone over s	Is.	16	8
The waters shall fail from the s	Is.	19	5
Zidon that pass over s	Is.	23	2
Shall cry aloud from the s	Is.	24	14
Ye that go down to the s	Is.	42	10
My rebuke, I dry up the s	Is.	50	2
Are like the troubled s	Is.	57	20
Their voice roareth like the s	Jer.	6	23
Voice shall roar like the s	Jer.	50	42
I will dry up her s and make	Jer.	51	26
Breach is great like the s	Lam.	2	13
As the s causeth his waves to	Ezek.	26	3
Came up from the s	Dan.	7	3
Wander from s to s	Amos	8	12
Shall we do, that the s?	Jonah	1	11
That day he shall come from s to s	Mic.	7	12
He rebuketh the s and	Nah.	1	4
Thou didst walk through the s	Hab.	3	15
Heavens, earth, and s	Hag.	2	6
Shall be from s to s	Zech.	9	10
Through the s with affliction	Zech.	10	11

sea:—*continued*			
And rebuked the *s*	Mat.	8	26
Even winds and *s* obey him	Mat.	8	27
	Mark	4	39, 41
Go thou to the *s* and cast an	Mat.	17	27
For ye compass *s* and land	Mat.	23	15
The *s* and the waves	Luke	21	25
Themselves to the *s*	Acts	27	40
He hath escaped the *s*	Acts	28	4
Passed through the *s*	I Cor.	10	1
Throne was a *s* of glass	Rev.	4	6
To hurt the earth and *s*	Rev.	7	2
Who created the *s* and the	Rev.	10	6
Worship him that made the *s*	Rev.	14	7
I saw a *s* of glass, mingled	Rev.	15	2
And the *s* gave up the dead	Rev.	20	13
And there was no more *s*	Rev.	21	1
(*See* coast, great, red, salt)			
seal *the signet ring*			
Given as a pledge	Gen.	38	18–25
Engraved	Ex.	28	11, 21, 36
Treasures secured by	Deut.	32	34
Attached to all royal decrees	I Ki.	21	8
	Esth.	3	12
Documents secured by	I Ki.	21	8
Covenants secured by	Neh.	9	38
Used on deeds	Jer.	32	10
Sepulchre of Jesus, made sure by	Mat.	27	66
Book with seven seals	Rev.	5	1
Servants of God sealed	Rev.	7	3, 4
Figurative of:			
Restraint	Job	37	7
Secrecy	Dan.	12	4
Full approval	John	3	33
Security	II Tim.	2	19
seamstress *a needlewoman*			
Dorcas is one	Acts	9	36–42
search *inquire after, seek*			
Of the spies	Num.	14	7, 38
	Josh.	2	2
By God	Ps.	139	23
Honour of kings	Prov.	25	2
For wisdom	Eccl.	1	13
The heart	Jer.	17	10
With candles	Zeph.	1	12
"For the young child"	Mat.	2	8
The scriptures	John	5	39
The deep things	I Cor.	2	10
seasons *natural occasions*			
Established by God	Gen.	8	22
Bring forth fruit	Ps.	1	3
Changed by God	Dan.	2	20, 21
Figurative use	I Pet.	1	6
Of corn	Job	5	26
Word spoken in due	Prov.	15	23
To everything there is	Ex.	3	1
Of the latter rain	Jer.	5	24
Of day and night	Jer.	33	20
Of the moon	Ps.	104	19
A little one, Satan loosed	Rev.	20	3
Pleasures of sin for	Heb.	11	25
seat			
Thy *s* will be empty	I Sam.	20	18
That I might come even to his *s*	Job	23	3
When I prepared my *s* in the street	Job	29	7
The *s* of the scornful	Ps.	1	1
Cause *s* of violence to come near	Amos	6	3
S of them that sold doves	Mat.	21	12
Scribes sit in Moses's	Mat.	23	2
Chief *s* in synagogues	Mat.	23	6
	Mark	12	39

(*See* Ezek. 8:3; 28:2; Luke 1:52; Rev. 2:13)

Sebat, Shebat *a rod*			
Eleventh Hebrew month	Zech.	1	7
seclusion *isolation*			
For prayer	Mat.	14	23
Needed for leisure	Mark	6	31
For a miracle	Mark	7	31–37
second coming of Christ, the			
Announced by Christ	Mat.	25	30, 31
	John	14	3
Signs preceding	Mat.	24	3–51
Time of, unknown	Mat.	24	26
Announced by the angels	Acts	1	10, 11
Preached by the apostles	Acts	3	20
	I Tim.	6	14

Always should be considered as at hand	Rom.	13	12
	I Pet.	4	7
The wicked scoff at	II Pet.	3	3, 4
Foretold by the prophets	Jude		14
	Dan.	7	13
Every eye shall see Him	Rev.	1	7
Caught up to meet him	I Thes.	4	13–18
Connected with rise of Antichrist	II Thes.	2	2, 3
Bodily changes of believers	I Cor.	15	51, 52
Christians:			
Should be ready for	Luke	12	40
Await patiently	I Cor.	1	7
	I Thes.	1	10
Will receive a crown of glory	I Pet.	5	4
Shall be like Him	I John	3	2
Purpose of:			
To execute judgment	John	5	22
	II Tim.	4	1
	Jude		15
Bring to light the hidden things of darkness	I Cor.	4	5
To destroy death	I Cor.	15	25, 26
To complete the salvation of His followers	Heb.	9	28
Manner of:			
Accompanied by angels	Mat.	16	27
With power and great glory	Mat.	24	30
As the lightning	Mat.	24	27
Unexpectedly	Mat.	24	44
In His own glory	Mat.	25	31
In the clouds	Mat.	26	64
Suddenly	Mark	13	36
In flaming fire	II Thes.	1	8
secret *hidden from others*			
Things, belong to God	Deut.	29	29
All known to God	Ps.	44	21
	Ps.	90	8
Of others, not to be divulged	Prov.	25	9
Revealed by God	Dan.	2	28
	Amos	3	7
	Mat.	11	25
Alms to be offered in	Mat.	6	4
Prayer to be offered in	Mat.	6	6
	Mark	1	35
Name of the Angel of the Lord	Judg.	13	18
Of sin	Ps.	19	12
	Ps.	90	8
	Deut.	27	15
Of love	Prov.	27	5
secretary *a confidential clerk*			
To a prophet	Jer.	36	10, 17
sects *orders, followings*			
Herodians	Mat.	22	16
Sadducees	Acts	5	17
Pharisees	Acts	15	5
Nazarenes	Acts	24	5
Christians called	Acts	28	22
Secundus *secondary*			
A Thessalonian Christian	Acts	20	4
	Acts	20	4
security *shelter, guarantee*			
For debt	Deut.	24	10–13
False	Job	29	18
Against evil	Ps.	112	7
In sleep	Prov.	3	24
Deceived by pride	Obad.		3
The reward of Christian diligence	II Pet.	1	5–10
False	Ps.	50	21
	Is.	28	15
	Rev.	3	17
	Obad.		3
sedition *resistance to lawful authority*			
Against Moses	Num.	12	1–13
Barabbas guilty of	Luke	23	18, 19
Punishment for	Acts	5	36, 37
Charge against Paul	Acts	24	5
A work of the flesh	Gal.	5	19, 20
seducers *inducers of evil*			
Of Dinah	Gen.	34	2
Of a maid	Ex.	22	16, 17
Of the betrothed	Deut.	22	23, 24
Of the father's wife	Deut.	22	30
Of Tamar	II Sam.	13	1–14
Manasseh	II Ki.	21	9
Fall into own pits	Prov.	28	10
False prophets as	Ezek.	13	8–10
Rely on deception	Mat.	24	11
Warnings against	Mark	13	21, 22

see

Lord came down to *s* the city	Gen.	11	5
You shall *s* my face no more	Gen.	44	23
When I *s* the blood	Ex.	12	13
There shall no man *s* me and live	Ex.	33	20
I shall *s* him, but not now	Num.	24	17
Let me *s* the good land	Deut.	3	25
Open his eyes, that he may *s*	II Ki.	6	17
Mine eye shall *s* no more *s* good	Job	7	7
In my flesh shall I *s* God	Job	19	26
God looked to *s* if any did understand	Ps.	14	2
	Ps.	53	2
O Taste and *s* that the Lord is good	Ps.	34	8
Many shall *s* it, and trust in the Lord	Ps.	40	3
Come and *s* the works of God	Ps.	66	5
He that formed the eye, shall he not *s*?	Ps.	94	9
Lest they *s* with their eyes	Is.	6	10
Thine eyes shall *s* thy teachers	Is.	30	20
The eyes of them that *s* shall not be dim	Is.	32	3
Thine eyes shall *s* the King in his beauty	Is.	33	17
They shall *s* eye to eye	Is.	52	8
When we shall *s* him	Is.	53	2
Pure in heart shall *s* God	Mat.	5	8
Show John the things ye *s* and hear	Mat.	11	4
We would *s* a sign	Mat.	12	38
S ye shall *s*	Mat.	13	14
	Mark	4	12
	Acts	28	26
S thou to that	Mat.	27	4
Come *s* the place where the Lord lay	Mat.	28	6
Having eyes, *s* yet not?	Mark	8	18
Desire to *s*, and ye shall not *s*	Luke	17	22
Come and *s*	John	1	39
	John	11	34
	Rev.	6	1
He shall not *s* life	John	3	36
I was blind, now I *s*	John	9	25
That they who *s* not, might *s*	John	9	39
We *s* through a glass	I Cor.	13	12
We *s* not yet all things put under him	Heb.	2	8
Though now ye *s* him not	I Pet.	1	8
We shall *s* him as he is	I John	3	2

seed

Every herb, tree and grass yields its own	Gen.	1	11, 12, 29
Sowing time secured by the covenant	Gen.	8	21, 22
Conception is by	Lev.	12	2
Not to be mingled in sowing	Lev.	19	19
Tithe of, to be given to God	Lev.	27	30
Ground carefully prepared for	Is.	28	24, 25
Each has its own body	I Cor.	15	38
Parables concerning	Mat.	13	
	Luke	8	
Of descendants	Gen.	12	7
	Gen.	21	12
	Gal.	3	16, 29

The Jews punished by:

Its increase consumed by locusts	Deut.	28	38
Its yielding but little increase	Is.	5	10
its berry choked by thorns	Jer.	12	13
Its rotting in the ground	Joel	1	17

Illustrative of:

The word of God	Luke	8	11
Spiritual life	I John	3	9

seeking God

None, by nature, are found to be engaged in	Ps.	14	2
	Rom.	3	11
Promise connected with	Ps.	69	32
Afflictions designed to lead to	Hosea	5	15
Blessedness of	Ps.	119	2
By prayer	Job	8	5
	Dan.	9	3
Ends in praise	Ps.	22	26
They who neglect denounced	Is.	31	1
In His house	Deut.	12	5
	Ps.	27	4
By keeping His commandments	I Chr.	28	8
	Mal.	2	7
Ensures His protection	Ezra	8	22
By prayer	Job	8	5
Leads to joy	Ps.	70	4
	Ps.	105	3
In the day of trouble	Ps.	77	2
	Ps.	78	33, 34
Brings understanding	Prov.	28	5
Imperative upon all	Is.	8	19

By His word	Is.	34	16
Is never in vain	Is.	45	19
Commanded	Is.	55	6
	Mat.	7	7
While He may be found	Is.	55	6
Punishment for neglect of	Zeph.	1	4–6
Through Jesus	Mal.	3	1
	Heb.	14	9, 10
Shall bring reward	Heb.	11	6
Heaven	Mat.	6	33

Ensures:

Being heard of him	Ps.	34	4
Gifts of righteousness	Hosea	10	12
His being found	Deut.	4	29
	I Chr.	28	9
	Prov.	8	17
	Jer.	29	13
His favor	Lam.	3	25
His not forsaking us	Ps.	9	10
Life	Ps.	69	32
	Amos	5	4, 6
Prosperity	Job	8	5–6
	Ps.	34	10

Includes seeking:

Christ	Luke	2	15–16
The city which God has prepared	Heb.	11	10
	Heb.	16	13–14
His face	Ps.	27	8
	Ps.	105	4
His kingdom	Luke	12	31
His name	Ps.	83	16
His precepts	Ps.	119	45, 94
His righteousness	Mat.	6	33
His strength	I Chr.	16	11
	Ps.	105	4
Honor which comes from him	John	5	44
Justification by Christ	Gal.	2	16–17

Should be:

Evermore	Ps.	105	4
Immediate	Hosea	10	12
While he may be found	Is.	55	6
With diligence	Heb.	11	6
With the heart and soul	Deut.	4	29
	I Chr.	22	19

The wicked:

Not led to, by affliction	Is.	9	13
Prepare not their hearts for	II Chr.	12	14
Refuse, through pride	Ps.	10	4
Rejected, when too late in	Prov.	1	28
Sometimes pretend to	Ezra	4	2
	Is.	58	2

Saints:

Characterized by	Ps.	24	6
Desirous of	Job	5	8
Early in	Job	8	5
	Ps.	63	1
	Is.	26	9
Earnest in	S. of S.	3	2, 4
Engage in, with the whole heart	II Chr.	15	2
	Ps.	119	10
Prepare their hearts for	II Chr.	30	19
Purpose, in heart	Ps.	27	8
Set their hearts to	II Chr.	11	16
Specially exhorted to	Zeph.	2	3

Exemplified:

Asa	II Chr.	14	7
Uzziah	II Chr.	26	5
David	Ps.	34	4
Daniel	Dan.	9	3, 4
Abraham	Neh.	11	14

seem

I shall *s* as a deceiver	Gen.	27	12
S it but a small thing?	Num.	16	9
There is a way that *s* right	Prov.	14	12
Taken that which he *s* to have	Luke	8	18
If any *s* to be wise	I Cor.	3	18
Lest any *s* to come short	Heb.	4	1
No chastening *s* to be joyous	Heb.	12	11
If any man *s* to be religious	James	1	26

seen

I have *s* God face to face	Gen.	32	20
Ye have *s* what I did to Egyptians	Ex.	19	4
Ye have *s* that I talked with you	Ex.	20	22
Die, because we have *s* God	Judg.	13	22
What have they *s*?	II Ki.	20	15
Mine eye hath *s* all this	Job	13	1
They have *s* thy goings, O God	Ps.	68	24

seen—*continued*

He hath not **s** the sun	Eccl.	6	5
Mine eyes have **s** the Lord	Is.	6	5
Neither hath eye **s**	Is.	64	4
	I Chr.	2	9
Who hath **s** such things?	Is.	66	8
Thou hast **s** me, tried heart	Jer.	12	3
To be **s** of men	Mat.	6	1
	Mat.	23	5
Never so **s** in Israel	Mat.	9	33
Tell no man what they had **s**	Mark	9	9
We have **s** strange things	Luke	5	26
They had **s** a vision of angels	Luke	24	23
No man hath **s** God	John	1	18
We testify that we have **s**	John	3	11
Hast thou **s** Abraham?	John	8	57
He that hath **s** me, hath **s** the Father	John	14	9
Because thou hast **s**, thou hast believed	John	20	29
Speak things we have **s**	Acts	4	20
Have I not **s** Jesus Christ?	I Cor.	9	1
Whom no man hath **s**	I Tim.	6	16
Evidence of the things not **s**	Heb.	11	1
Whom having not **s**, ye love	I Pet.	1	8
Can he love God who he hath not **s**?	I John	4	20

seers *prophets*

Not to accept bribes	Num.	22	18
Counsel king	I Sam.	9	19
Schooled	II Ki.	2	3–5
Keep chronicles	I Chr.	29	29
Martyred	Jer.	2	30
Persecuted	Amos	2	12
	Acts	7	52
Inspired by angels	Acts	7	53
Gad	II Sam.	24	11
Heman	I Chr.	25	5

Seir *hairy*

A mount of the Horites	Gen.	14	6
Settled by Edomites	Gen.	32	3
Prophecy of Balaam	Num.	24	18
Its desolation	Ezek.	35	15
The conquest of Joshua	Josh.	11	15–18
Remnant of Amalekite slain	I Chr.	4	42
Called the Mount of Esau	Obad.	19	
Town on the border of Judah	Josh.	15	10

seize *to take possession by force*

From ambush	Josh.	8	7
By darkness	Job	3	6
By death	Ps.	55	15
The inheritance	Mat.	21	38

Sela, Selah *rock*

A city of Edom	II Ki.	14	7
In judgment	Is.	16	1

selah *pause, suspension*

A musical direction	Ps.	3	2, 4
	Hab.	3	3, 9, 13

Seleucia *white light*

A seaport city of Syria	Acts	13	4

self-condemnation

Recognizes wickedness	II Sam.	24	17
By justification	Job	9	20
By realization	Prov.	5	12
By judgment of others	Rom.	2	1

self-confidence

Makes one boastful	I Ki.	20	11
A result of prosperity	Ps.	30	6
	Ps.	49	6
Not to be trusted	Prov.	16	25
Warnings against	Is.	5	21
	Luke	11	35
Of the Pharisee	Luke	18	9–14

self-control

For a clear conscience	Acts	24	16
The fruit of the Holy Spirit	Gal.	5	22, 23
Over our bodies	Rom.	6	12
Over our lips	Ps.	141	3
	James	1	26
Over our spirits	Prov.	16	32
Reward of	Rev.	21	7
Through divine help	Jer.	10	23
Value of	Prov.	16	32
	Prov.	25	28
Displayed by Saul	I Sam.	10	27
Gives strength	Prov.	25	28
Of the tongue	Eccl.	5	3–7
	James	3	1–12

Shown by Jesus	Mat.	27	12–14
Of David	I Sam.	24	1–15
Of the body	I Chr.	9	27

self-defense

Help from the sanctuary	Ps.	20	1, 2
By silence	Mat.	27	12–14
The wise answer	Luke	23	3
Happiness in	Acts	26	1, 2

self-delusion

A characteristic of the wicked	Ps.	49	18
Sinners often give up to	Ps.	81	11, 12
	II Thes.	2	10, 11
Prosperity frequently leads to	Hosea	12	8
	Luke	12	17–20
	Ps.	30	6
Fatal consequences of	Mat.	7	23
	I Thes.	5	3
	Mat.	24	48–51
	Luke	12	20
Frequently persevered in, to the last	Mat.	7	22
	Mat.	25	11–12
	Luke	13	24–25
Obstinate sinners often given up to	Hosea	4	17

Exhibited in thinking that:

Our lives shall be prolonged	Is.	56	12
	Luke	12	19
Privileges entitle us to heaven	Mat.	3	9
	Luke	13	25–26
We are above adversity	Ps.	10	6
We are rich in spiritual things	Rev.	3	17
We should adhere to established wicked practices	Jer.	44	17
We may have peace while in sin	Deut.	29	19
Our own way is right	Prov.	14	12
We are pure	Prov.	30	12
God will not punish our sins	Jer.	5	12
Gifts entitle us to heaven	Mat.	7	21, 22
We are better than others	Luke	18	11
Our lives will be prolonged	James	4	13–16
Christ will not come to judge	II Pet.	3	4

self-denial

Christ sets an example of	Mat.	4	8–10
	Phil.	2	6–8
Danger of neglecting	Mat.	16	25
Reward of	Mat.	19	28, 29
Often not easy	Mark	10	17–22
Necessary in following Christ	Luke	14	27–33
Ministers especially called to possess	II Cor.	6	4, 5

Includes:

Controlling the appetite	Prov.	23	2
Assisting others	Luke	3	11
Forsaking all	Luke	14	33
Abstaining from lusts	Rom.	6	12
	I Pet.	2	11
Not pleasing ourselves	Rom.	15	1–3

self-exaltation

By Haman	Esth.	5	11, 12
By Job	Job	12	3
Seeks destruction	Prov.	17	19
Wicked	Ezek.	31	10–14
Through deception	Obad.		3, 4
Ends in abasement	Mat.	23	12
Of Herod	Acts	12	20–23
Contends with God	II Cor.	10	5, 17, 18
	II Thes.	2	4

self-examination

Should be with prayer	Ps.	26	2
With diligent searching	Ps.	77	6
To be followed with repentance	Ps.	119	59
	Lam.	3	40
Necessary before communion	I Cor.	11	28
Commanded by Paul	II Cor.	13	5
By the word of God	Heb.	4	12

self-indulgence

Leads to poverty	Prov.	23	21
Not withheld	Eccl.	2	10
Carnal	Amos	6	3–6
Of the rich fool	Luke	12	16–21
Causes torment	Luke	16	19–31
Not for the Christian	Rom.	13	13

selfishness *caring too much for self*

Contrary to the will of God	Lev.	19	18
	Mat.	22	29
Jesus condemns by example	John	4	34
	Rom.	15	3
Inconsistent with Christian love	Rom.	12	4, 5
	I Cor.	12	12–27

Ministers must not possess	I Cor.	9	19–23
All men addicted to	Eph.	2	3
Exhibited in:			
Hoarding	Prov.	11	26
	James	2	15, 16
Greed	Is.	56	11
	Mic.	3	11
Serving God for reward	Mal.	1	10
Pleasing ourselves	Rom.	15	1
Neglect of the poor	I John	3	17
Examples:			
Cain	Gen.	4	9
James and John	Mark	10	37
Multitude	John	6	26

self-righteousness

A warning against	Deut.	9	4
Folly of	Job	9	20
Man is prone to	Prov.	20	6
Abomination in the sight of God	Is.	65	5
	Luke	16	15
Prohibits submission to God	Rom.	10	3
Is not wise	II Cor.	10	12
Zophar	Job	11	4–6
A fool's way	Prov.	12	15
The way of a man	Prov.	14	12
	Prov.	16	2
Woe to them	Is.	5	21
Cursed	Jer.	17	5
Of Edom	Jer.	49	4, 16
Of pseudo-Christians	Mat.	7	22, 23
Pharisees	Luke	11	39

self-will

Caused by unbelief	II Ki.	17	14
Caused by pride	Neh.	9	16, 29
Characteristic of the wicked	Prov.	7	11
Leads to destruction	Prov.	29	1
Known by God	Is.	48	4
Exhibited in:			
Refusing to listen to parents	Deut.	21	18, 19
Refusing to hearken to God	Prov.	1	24
Refusing to receive correction	Jer.	5	3
Forbidden	II Chr.	30	8
Caused by an evil heart	Jer.	7	24
Refusing to hear prophets	I Sam.	8	19
	Jer.	44	16
Resisting Holy Ghost	Acts	7	51

sell

S me thy birthright	Gen.	25	31
Let us *s* him to the Ishmaelites	Gen.	37	27
Ahab did *s* himself to work wickedness	I Ki.	21	25
Will ye even *s* your brethren?	Neh.	5	8
Victuals on sabbath day to *s*	Neh.	10	31
Buy the truth, and *s* it not	Prov.	23	23
I will *s* your sons and daughters	Joel	3	8
S the refuse of the wheat	Amos	8	6
Go and *s* that thou hast	Mat.	19	21
	Mark	10	21
	Luke	18	22
Let me *s* his garment	Luke	22	36
We will buy and *s*	James	4	13
See Isa. 24:2; Acts 16:14			

Semei *Greek form of Shimei*

An ancestor of Jesus	Luke	3	26

senators *elders*

Taught by Joseph	Ps.	105	17–22

send

Shall *s* his angel	Gen.	24	7
S me good speed	Gen.	24	12
God did *s* me to preserve life	Gen.	45	5
S by hand of him whom thou wilt *s*	Ex.	4	13
S him away by a fit man	Lev.	16	21
Man of God thou didst *s*	Judg.	13	8
S out thy light and thy truth	Ps.	43	3
Lord, *s* not prosperity	Ps.	118	25
Whom shall I *s*?	Is.	6	8
He shall *s* them a saviour	Is.	19	20
S labourers	Mat.	9	38
	Luke	10	2
S her away	Mat.	15	23
That he might *s* them to preach	Mark	3	14
Whom the Father will *s* in my name	John	14	26
Believed that thou didst *s* me	John	17	8

Senir, Shenir *peak, mount of snow*

Name of mount Hermon	Deut.	3	9

Dwelling place for tribe of Manasseh	I Chr.	5	23
A place of fir trees	Ezek.	27	5

Sennacherib *Moon god (sin) multiplied brothers*

King of Assyria	II Ki.	18	13–16
Sends Rab-shakeh to demand surrender	II Ki.	18	17–37
His death foretold	II Ki.	19	7
His death	II Ki.	19	35–37

sensual *bodily senses*

Good of	Eccl.	2	24
	Eccl.	8	15
Eat, drink and be merry	Is.	22	13
	I Chr.	15	32
Rich fool	Luke	12	19–20
Fruitlessness of	James	5	5
In the end times	Jude	18	19

sent

God *s* me before you	Gen.	45	7
I AM hath *s* me unto you	Ex.	3	14
I am not *s* but to lost sheep of Israel	Mat.	15	24
Last of all he *s* unto them his son	Mat.	21	37
	Mark	12	6
The will of him that *s* me	John	4	34
Work the works of him that *s* me	John	9	4
May believe that thou hast *s* me.	John	11	42
Eternal life to know him whom thou hast *s*	John	17	3
How shall they preach except thy be *s*?	Rom.	10	15
The Holy Ghost *s* from heaven	I Pet.	1	12
God *s* his only begotten Son	I John	4	9

Senuah, Hasenuah *thorny, hatred*

A Benjamite	I Chr.	9	7
Father of Judah	Neh.	11	9

separate *to set apart*

"The sheep from the goats"	Mat.	25	32
From bad company	Luke	6	22
From the love of Christ	Rom.	8	35
From the love of God	Rom.	8	39

separation *severance*

Declined	Ruth	1	14–18
Desired	Jer.	9	2
Of the blessed and the cursed	Mat.	25	31–46
From the wicked	I Cor.	5	9–13
From idolatry	II Cor.	6	15–18
From the disorderly	II Thes.	3	6

sepulchre, sepulcher, tomb *a burial vault*

A cave	Gen.	23	9
For family	Gen.	25	8, 9
Under an oak tree	Gen.	35	8
Marked by a pillar	Gen.	35	20
Touching is unclean	Num.	19	16
In a house	I Sam.	25	1
In the mount	II Ki.	23	16
Writings upon	II Ki.	23	17
For a king	II Ki.	23	30
	II Chr.	24	16
In hell	Is.	14	15
Hewn in rock	Is.	22	16
In a valley	Jer.	7	32
Robbed	Jer.	8	1
Of the common people	Jer.	26	23
Inhabited by demoniacs	Mat.	8	28
Whited	Mat.	23	27
Garnished	Mat.	23	29
Potter's field	Mat.	27	7
Closed with a stone	Mat.	27	60
Sealed	Mat.	27	66
Visited	Mat.	28	1
Denied to dead	Rev.	11	9

Serah *see* Sarah

Seraiah *Jehovah has prevailed*

Scribe to David	II Sam.	8	17
Called Sheva	II Sam.	20	25
A chief priest	II Ki.	25	18
Slain	II Ki.	25	19–21
Captain of army	II Ki.	25	23
Advised to surrender	II Ki.	25	24
Son of Kenaz	I Chr.	4	13
Father of Joab	I Chr.	4	14
Son of Asiel	I Chr.	4	35
A priest, returns from Babylon	Ezra		
Helps to dedicate walls	Neh.	12	1, 12
A priest who seals the covenant	Neh.	10	2
Son of Hilkiah	Neh.	11	11
Son of Azriel	Jer.	36	26
Son of Neriah, a prince	Jer.	51	59
Casts book into Euphrates	Jer.	51	61–64

seraphim *celestial beings*

Stand above throne of God	Is.	6	2
Praise God	Is.	6	3
Purify Isaiah	Is.	6	6, 7

Sergius Paulus *little, small*

Proconsul of Cyprus	Acts	13	7
Converted by Paul	Acts	13	12

sermon *a discourse of religious instruction*

Of repentance	Mat.	3	1, 2
	Mat.	4	17
On the mount	Mat.	5	
	Mat.	6	
	Mat.	7	1-27
By the seaside	Mat.	13	1-52
In the synagogue	Luke	4	16-30
By Peter	Acts	2	14-36
Of Paul	Acts	9	20
Subject of	Acts	17	2, 3
Too long	Acts	20	9-12

serpent *a snake*

Cursed by God	Gen.	3	14, 15
Rod becomes	Ex.	4	2-4
Poisonous	Deut.	32	24
Used as a judgment	Num.	21	6
Bite	Prov.	23	32
	Eccl.	10	8
Live among rocks	Prov.	30	19
Moses lifted up	John	3	14
Deal adder	Ps.	58	4
Shall eat dust	Is.	65	25
Of the sea	Amos	9	3
Not for food	Mat.	7	10
Power over	Mark	16	18
	Luke	10	19
Called the devil	Rev.	12	9

serpents, fiery *see* fiery serpents

Serug *tendril branch see* Saruch

servant *one who serves*

Bought and sold	Gen.	17	13, 27
Figurative of humility	Gen.	18	3
Given as a dowry	Gen.	29	24
Thieves punished by being made	Gen.	43	18
Mosaic law concerning	Ex.	21	1-11
	Lev.	25	40-55
Defaulting debtors made	Lev.	25	39
	Mat.	18	25
Captives of war made	Deut.	20	14
Manstealing forbidden	Deut.	24	7
	I Tim.	1	10
To be paid promptly	Deut.	24	15
	Col.	4	1
Children of debtors sold for	II Ki.	4	1-7
Emancipation of	Ezra	1	1-4
Sometimes rises to rank and station	Eccl.	10	7
Christ condescends to the status of	Mat.	20	25-28
	Luke	22	27
	John	13	5
Worthy of his hire	Luke	10	7
To be faithful to his master	I Cor.	4	2
Servants of Christ do the will of God	Eph.	6	6, 7
Illustrative of Christ	Phil.	2	7, 8
Shall honour their master	I Tim.	6	1
Paul intercedes for	Philem.		10-21
Should follow Christ's example	I Pet.	2	21

serve

Nation they *s* will I judge	Gen.	15	14
The elder shall *s* the younger	Gen.	25	23
	Rom.	9	12
Not bow down to them nor *s* them	Ex.	20	5
	Deut.	5	9
Thou shalt fear the Lord, and *s* him	Deut.	6	13
	Deut.	10	12
	Deut.	11	13
	Deut.	13	4
	Josh.	22	5
	Josh.	24	14
	I Sam.	7	3
	I Sam.	12	14
Choose you whom ye will *s*	Josh.	24	15
People I knew not shall *s* me	II Sam.	22	44
S him with a perfect heart	I Chr.	28	9
What is the Almighty, that we should *s* him?	Job	21	15
A seed shall *s* him	Ps.	22	30
All nations shall *s* him	Ps.	72	11

Confounded that *s* graven images	Ps.	97	7
Made me to *s* with thy sins	Is.	43	24
Join themselves to the Lord, to *s* him	Is.	56	6
Thy God whom thou *s* will deliver	Dan.	6	16
To *s* him with one consent	Zeph.	3	9
Said, It is vain to *s* God	Mal.	3	14
No man can *s* two masters	Mat.	6	24
	Luke	16	13
Left me to *s* alone	Luke	10	40
These many years do I *s* thee	Luke	15	29
He that is chief, as he that doth *s*	Luke	22	26
If any man *s* me, let him follow me	John	12	26
Leave word of God, and *s* tables	Acts	6	2
Should *s* in newness of spirit	Rom.	7	6
By love *s* one another	Gal.	5	13
Ye *s* the Lord Christ	Col.	3	24
Turned from idols to *s* the living god	I Thes.	1	9
We may *s* god God acceptably	Heb.	12	28
They *s* him day and night	Rev.	7	15

service *useful to others*

Commanded by God	Deut.	10	12
Commanded by Christ	Mat.	7	21
	John	21	17
A sign of greatness	Mark	10	43, 44
Brings joy	Luke	10	1-17
Jesus gives an example of	John	13	12-14
Involves suffering	Acts	20	18, 19
A Christian duty	Acts	20	33-35
	Gal.	6	2

service tests

Established	Deut.	10	12, 13
Failed by Saul	I Sam.	15	20-25
Shall determine who will inherit kingdom of God	Mat.	25	31-40
	Luke	12	47, 48
Given to Peter	John	21	15-17

set

I do *s* my bow in the cloud	Gen.	9	13
Lord did not *s* his love on you	Deut.	7	7
I *s* before you a blessing and curse	Deut.	11	26
I *s* before thee life and death	Deut.	30	15
S thy words in order before me	Job	33	5
Lord hath *s* apart him that is godly	Ps.	4	3
I *s* the Lord always before me	Ps.	16	8
We will *s* up our banners	Ps.	20	5
S my feet upon a rock	Ps.	40	2
He hath *s* his love upon me	Ps.	91	14
S me in a largely place	Ps.	118	5
God hath *s* one against the other	Eccl.	7	14
I *s* before you the way of life	Jer.	21	8
A city *s* on a hill	Mat.	5	14
Nothing to *s* before thee	Luke	11	6
Herod *s* him at nought	Luke	23	11
S to his seal that God is true	John	3	33
No man shall *s* on thee	Acts	18	10
Lay hold on hope *s* before us	Heb.	6	18
S before thee an open door	Rev.	3	8

Seth, Sheth *appointed*

Son of Adam and Eve	Gen.	4	25
Father of Enos	Gen.	4	26
Called Sheth	I Chr.	1	1
Ancestor of Jesus	Luke	3	38
With reference to Moab	Num.	24	17

seven

Clean beasts taken into the ark	Gen.	7	2
Blood sprinkled	Lev.	4	6
Jericho encompassed	Josh.	6	4
Chamberlains	Esth.	1	10
Worship seven times a day	Ps.	119	164
Things hateful to God	Prov.	6	16-19
Women wanting one man	Is.	4	1
Steps in the temple	Ezek.	40	22, 26
Seven lamps and pipes	Zech.	4	2
Devils cast out	Mat.	16	9
Churches in Asia	Rev.	1	
Golden candlesticks	Rev.	1	243

Days:

Week consists of	Gen.	2	3
Noah remains in the ark	Gen.	8	10, 12
Mourning for Jacob lasts	Gen.	50	10
Passover lasts	Ex.	12	15
Dedication of temple lasts	I Ki.	8	65

Weeks:

Period between passover and pentecost	Lev.	23	15

Months:

Holy convocations	Lev.	23	24-44

Years:

Jacob serves	Gen.	29	18–30
Of plenty	Gen.	41	1–32
Of famine	Gen.	41	54–56
	II Sam.	24	13
Insanity of Nebuchadnezzar lasts	Dan.	4	32
Altars of Balaam	Num.	23	1, 29
Nations in Palestine	Deut.	7	1
Ways to flee under the curse	Deut.	28	7, 25
Trumpets	Josh.	6	4, 6
Locks of Samson's hair	Judg.	16	13
Sons of Jesse	I Sam.	16	10
Abominations	Prov.	26	25
Weeks of Daniel	Dan.	9	25
Loaves	Mat.	15	34
Stars	Rev.	1	20

seven sayings of Christ

"Why hast thou forsaken me"	Mat.	27	46
"Father forgive them"	Luke	23	32
"Thou shalt be with me in paradise"	Luke	23	43
"Into thy hands I commend my spirit"	Luke	23	46
"Woman, behold thy son"	John	19	26
"I thirst"	John	19	28
"It is finished"	John	19	30

seventy

Elders worship	Ex.	24	1, 9
Years in captivity	Jer.	25	11, 12
Weeks for reconciliation	Dan.	9	24
Times seven	Mat.	18	22
Disciples	Luke	10	1
Return with joy	Luke	10	17

sew

They *s* fig leaves together	Gen.	3	7
A time to rend, a time to *s*	Eccl.	3	7
Woe to the women that *s* pillows	Ezek.	13	18
No man *s* new cloth on old garments	Mark	2	21

sexes *males and females*

Creation of	Gen.	1	27
Separate tents for	Gen.	31	33
Different clothing	Deut.	22	5
One flesh	Mat.	19	4–6
Rules in worship	I Cor.	11	3–16

sexual perversion *maladjustment in sex life*

An abomination	Lev.	18	22
Not with beasts	Lev.	18	23
Brings death	Lev.	20	13–16
Cursed	Deut.	27	20–23
Homosexuality	Rom.	1	26, 27

Shaaph *friendship*

Son of Jahdai	I Chr.	2	47
Son of Caleb	I Chr.	2	48, 49

shadow *shade within defined limits*

Symbolic of divine protection	Job	7	2
	Ps.	17	8
Of the evening	Jer.	6	4
Of things to come	Col.	2	17
Of heavenly things	Heb.	8	5
Reverse direction of	II Ki.	20	9
Of man's life	Job	14	2
	Ps.	102	11
	Eccl.	8	13
Of a rock	Is.	32	2
Of a tree	Mark	4	32

shadow of death

Brought to light	Job	12	22
Shows on eyelids	Job	16	16
"The valley of the"	Ps.	23	4
Bond of affliction	Ps.	107	10–12
Lighted by Christ	Mat.	4	16

Shadrach *royal or great scribe*

Name changed from Hananiah	Dan.	1	7
Friend of Daniel in Babylon	Dan.	2	17
Over affairs of Babylon	Dan.	2	49
Does not worship idols	Dan.	3	18
Passes through fiery furnace	Dan.	3	19–28
Promoted	Dan.	3	30

shake

I will *s* myself	Judg.	16	20
S the earth out of her place	Job	9	6
Though the mountains *s*	Ps.	46	3
The fruit thereof shall *s* like Lebanon	Ps.	72	16
When he ariseth to *s* the earth	Is.	2	19
I will *s* the heavens	Is.	13	13
	Hag.	2	6, 21

Foundations of earth do *s*	Is.	24	18
S thyself from the dust	Is.	52	2
I will *s* all nations	Hab.	2	7
S dust off your feet	Mat.	10	14
	Mark	6	11
	Luke	9	5
For fear the keepers did *s*	Mat.	28	4
Good measure, *s* together	Luke	6	38
Be not soon *s* in mind	II Thes.	2	2
I *s* not the earth only	Heb.	12	26

Shallecheth *casting out*

Western gate of David's temple	I Chr.	26	16

Shallum *retribution*

Called Shillem	Gen.	46	24
Son of Naphtali	I Chr.	7	32
Son of Jabesh	II Ki.	15	10
Slays King Zachariah	II Ki.	15	10
Becomes king of Israel	II Ki.	15	13
Slain by Menahem	II Ki.	15	14
Husband of Huldah	II Ki.	22	14
Son of Tikvah	II Chr.	34	22
Head of a Jerahmeelite family	I Chr.	2	40
Son of Josiah, an alternate name of Jehoahaz	I Chr.	3	15
	Jer.	22	11
Head of a group of Simeonites	I Chr.	4	25
Son of Zadok, a priest	I Chr.	6	12
Father of Hilkiah	I Chr.	6	13
Called Meshullam	I Chr.	9	11
Ancestor of Ezra	Ezra	7	2
A porter at the Jerusalem temple	I Chr.	9	17
Son of Kore	I Chr.	9	19
Father of Mattithiah	I Chr.	9	31
Father of Jehizkiah	II Chr.	28	12
A porter who took a strange wife	Ezra	10	24, 42
Official who helps repair the city wall	Neh.	3	12
Father of Hanameel, uncle of Jeremiah	Jer.	32	7–12

Shalmaneser *Shulman is chief*

An Assyrian king	II Ki.	17	3
Besieges Samaria	II Ki.	18	9–11

shame *disgrace*

Of Adam and Eve	Gen.	3	10
Of God's enemies	Ps.	40	14
	Ezek.	7	18
Some are hardened to	Jer.	8	12
Apostles willing to suffer	Acts	5	41
Subdued by hope	Rom.	5	5
Of the cross	Heb.	6	6
	Heb.	12	2
Clothed with	Job	8	22
	Ps.	35	26
Glory changed into	Ps.	4	2
Of face	Ps.	69	7
	Ps.	83	16
Promotion of fools	Prov.	3	35
To the scorner	Prov.	9	7
Comes with pride	Prov.	11	2
A prudent man covers	Prov.	12	16
Caused by a son	Prov.	17	2
	Prov.	29	15
Chariots of Israel	Is.	22	18
Of their glory	Phil.	3	19
Of Christ	Heb.	6	6
	Heb.	12	2

Sometimes caused by:

Nudity	Ex.	32	25
Laziness	Prov.	10	5
Ignorance	Prov.	13	18
Sin	Ezek.	16	52
Quarreling	I Cor.	6	1–5
Men wearing long hair	I Cor.	11	14
Women talking in church	I Cor.	14	34, 35

Shamir *thorn*

A town of Judah	Josh.	15	48
A city in mount Ephraim	Judg.	10	1
Son of Micah	I Chr.	24	24

Shammah, Shammoth *consternation, waste*

A duke of Edom	Gen.	36	13, 17
Son of Jesse	I Sam.	17	13
Called by various names	II Sam.	13	3
	I Chr.	2	13
	I Chr.	20	7
Son of Agee	II Sam.	23	11
A valiant warrior	II Sam.	23	33
Called Shammoth	I Chr.	11	27

Shammua, Shammuah *fame*

A Reubenite spy	Num.	13	4
Son of David	II Sam.	5	14
Called Shimea	I Chr.	3	5
Father of Obadiah, called Shemaiah	I Chr.	9	16
A Levite, father of Abda	Neh.	11	17
A priest, son of Bilgah	Neh.	12	18

Shaphat *judge*

A Simeonite spy	Num.	13	5
Father of the prophet Elisha	I Ki.	19	16
Son of Shemaiah	I Chr.	3	22
A Gadite chief	I Chr.	5	12
Son of Adlai	I Chr.	27	29

Sharezer, Sherezer *protect the king*

Son of Sennacherib	II Ki.	19	37
A delegate to priests	Zech.	7	1-3

Sharon *a plain*

A Gadite dwelling place	I Chr.	5	16
A pasture land	I Chr.	27	29
Beautiful and fertile	S. of S.	2	1
	Is.	33	9

sharp *keen, harsh*

Stone	Ex.	4	25
Rock	I Sam.	14	4
Eyes	Job	16	9
Razor	Ps.	52	2
Tongue	Ps.	140	3
The two-edged sword	Prov.	5	4
A threshing instrument	Is.	41	15
Knife	Ezek.	5	1
Contention	Acts	15	39
Knives for cutting	Josh.	5	2, 3
Arrows	Ps.	45	5
	Ps.	120	4
Sword, tongue as	Ps.	57	4
Sickle	Rev.	14	14, 18
Out of his mouth	Rev.	1	16
	Rev.	19	15

Shaul *asked*

Called Saul	Gen.	36	37
An Edomite king	I Chr.	1	48
Son of Simeon	Gen.	46	10
Founds Shaulites	Num.	26	13
Son of Kohath	I Chr.	6	22, 24

shaving *removing hair*

Of leprosy	Lev.	13	33
Not to round corners of beards	Lev.	21	5
Forbidden to Nazarites	Num.	6	5
Preparation for offering	Num.	8	7
Samson's locks	Judg.	16	19
As humiliation	II Sam.	10	4
To show penitence	Job	1	20
With a razor	Is.	7	20
Forbidden to priests	Ezek.	44	20

Shavsha *see Sheva*

Shealtiel *see Salathiel*

shearing house *a place for clipping wool*

Amnon slain in	II Sam.	13	28, 29
Scene of massacre	II Ki.	10	12-14

Shear-jashub *the remnant shall return*

Son of Isaiah	Is.	7	3

sheaves

Joseph's dream concerning	Gen.	37	7
Of the firstfruits	Lev.	23	10
To be left in the field	Deut.	24	19
	Job	24	10
Typical	Ps.	126	6
	Mic.	4	12
	Mat.	13	30

Sheba *seven, or an oath*

A son of Raamah	Gen.	10	7
A son of Joktan	Gen.	10	28, 29
A son of Jokshan	Gen.	25	3
A city of Simeon	Josh.	19	2
Son of Bichri	II Sam.	20	1
Leads insurrection	II Sam.	20	2-22
Queen of, visits Solomon	I Ki.	10	1-13
Kings bring gifts	Ps.	72	10
Noted for incense	Is.	60	6
Noted for gold	Ps.	72	15
Noted for precious stones	Ezek.	27	22
Chief of Gad	I Chr.	5	13

Shebah *oath*

A well, named by Isaac	Gen.	26	32, 33

Shebat *see Sebat*

Shebna, Shebnah *growth, short for Shebaniah*

Scribe of King Hezekiah	II Ki.	18	18
Self-exalted	Is.	22	15-19

Shebuel, Shubael *God is renown*

Son of Gershom	I Chr.	23	16
Called Shubael	I Chr.	24	20
Ruler of the treasures	I Chr.	26	24
Son of Heman	I Chr.	25	4
A singer	I Chr.	25	20

Shecaniah *Jehovah has dwelt*

A priest of David's time	I Chr.	24	11
A priest in Hezekiah's time	II Chr.	31	15
Descendant of David	I Chr.	8	21, 22
Two men whose descendants are companions of Ezra	Ezra	8	3, 5
One who took a strange wife	Ezra	10	2
Father of Shemaiah	Neh.	3	29
Father-in-law of Tobiah	Nah.	6	18
A priest who returns from exile	Neh.	12	3

Shechem, Sichem, Sychem, Sychar *shoulder*

Abraham dwells in	Gen.	12	6
Jacob's altar built here	Gen.	33	18-20
Jacob buried here	Gen.	50	13
	Acts	7	16
Burialplace of Joseph	Josh.	24	32
Son of Hamor	Gen.	33	19
Slain by Jacob's sons	Josh.	24	32
Ancestor of Shechemites	Num.	26	31
City of refuge	Josh.	20	7
Tribes assembled at	Josh.	24	1-28
Joshua buried at	Josh.	24	30-32
Abimelech crowned at	Judg.	8	31
Destroyed	Judg.	9	39, 45
Rehoboam made king at	Judg.	9	39, 45
Jeroboam made king	I Ki.	12	20
Rebuilt	I Ki.	12	25
Visited by Jesus	John	4	1-42

shed

By man shall his blood be *s*	Gen.	9	6
Is *s* for many for remission of sins	Mat.	26	28
Love of God is *s* abroad in our hearts	Rom.	5	5
Which he *s* on us through Jesus Christ	Tit.	3	6
Without *s* of blood is no remission	Heb.	9	22

sheep

Under man's care from the earliest ages	Gen.	4	4
Offered in sacrifice	Gen.	8	20
Tended by Rachel	Gen.	29	6, 9
Plague upon	Ex.	9	3
Stealing of	Ex.	22	1
Firstling	Lev.	27	26
Lord's blessing upon	Deut.	7	13
	Deut.	28	4
Stray	Deut.	22	1
To be slain	I Sam.	15	3, 14
Part of the spoil	I Sam.	15	21
David tens	I Sam.	16	9
	II Sam.	7	8
Scattered as	Jer.	50	17
Fed on the mountains and in the valleys	Ex.	3	1
	Is.	65	10
A clean animal and used as food	Deut.	14	4
Milk of, used as food	Deut.	32	14
Given as tribute	II Ki.	3	4
Wool and skin made into clothing	Job	31	20
	Heb.	11	37
Meek and submissive	Is.	53	7
Parable of the lost	Mat.	18	11-13

Figurative:

Of the Jews	Ps.	74	1
Of backsliders	Jer.	50	6
Of lost sinners	Mat.	9	36
	Is.	53	6
Of the defenselessness of ministers	Mat.	10	16
Of the righteous	Mat.	25	32, 33
Of Christians	John	10	7-26
Of Christ	Is.	53	7
Clothing of false prophets	Mat.	7	15

sheepcote, sheepfold *a pen*

Built by Israelites	Num.	32	16
Provides defense	Ezek.	34	10-15
Robbed	John	10	1

sheep gate *a city gate*

Built by priests	Neh.	3	1
Place of merchants	Neh.	3	32
Dedication of	Neh.	12	39

shekel *weight equal to twenty gerahs*

As offering	Ex.	30	13
Fines paid in	Deut.	22	19, 29
For fees	Neh.	10	32
For taxes	Mat.	17	24–27
Measure of weight	Josh.	7	21

shekinah *a visible sign of God's presence*

In the ark of testimony	Ex.	25	22
The cloud upon the mercy seat	Lev.	16	2
Dwells between the cherubims	II Sam.	6	2
Cloud filled with	I Ki.	8	10
To the threshold	Ezek.	9	3

Shelah *prayer, peace*

Son of Arphaxad	Gen.	10	24
Called Salah	Luke	3	35
Son of Judah	Gen.	38	2, 5
Promised to Tamar	Gen.	38	11

Shelemiah *Jehovah's thank offering*

Father of Zechariah, a porter	I Chr.	26	14
Two men who took strange wives	Ezra	10	39, 41
Father of Hananiah	Neh.	3	30
A priest and treasurer	Neh.	13	13
Son of Cushi	Jer.	36	14
Son of Abdeel	Jer.	36	26
Father of Jehucal	Jer.	37	3
Father of Irijah	Jer.	37	13

Shelomith, Shelomoth *peaceful*

Daughter of Dibri	Lev.	24	11
Daughter of Zerubbabel	I Chr.	3	19
Son of Shimei	I Chr.	23	9
Son of Izhar	I Chr.	23	18
Called Shelmoth	I Chr.	24	22
A treasurer of dedicated things	I Chr.	26	26, 28
A child of Rehoboam	II Chr.	11	20
Companion of Ezra	Ezra	8	10

Shem, Sem *name*

Son of Noah	Gen.	5	32
Preserved in ark	Gen.	7	13
His filial conduct	Gen.	9	21–23
Blessed by Noah	Gen.	9	26, 27
Sons of	Gen.	10	1, 22
Ancestor of Jesus	Luke	3	36

Shema *report, rumour*

A city of Judah	Josh.	15	26
Son of Hebron	I Chr.	2	43
Called Shemaiah	I Chr.	5	4
Father of Azaz	I Chr.	5	8
Son of Elpaal	I Chr.	8	12, 13
Stands by Ezra at reading of the law	Neh.	8	4
Passage recited by Jews	Deut.	6	4

Shemaiah *Jehovah hath heard*

A prophet of Judah	I Ki.	12	22
Prevents war	II Chr.	11	2–4
Prophesies punishment of Rehoboam	II Chr.	12	5, 7
Writes chronicles	II Chr.	12	15
A descendant of David	I Chr.	3	22
Father of Shimri	I Chr.	4	37
A son of Joel	I Chr.	5	4
A son of Hasshub	I Chr.	9	14
A chief Levite in time of David, assists in moving the ark	I Chr.	15	8, 11
Son of Nethaneel	I Chr.	24	6
A porter of the temple in time of David	I Chr.	26	4, 6, 7
A Levite teacher	II Chr.	17	8
A Levite, son of Jeduthun	II Chr.	29	14
A Levite treasurer	II Chr.	31	14, 15
A chief Levite	II Chr.	35	9
A Jew who returns from Babylon	Ezra	8	13
An aide to Ezra	Ezra	8	16
A priest who puts away his Gentile wife	Ezra	10	21
A son of Harim	Ezra	10	31
Keeper of the east gate	Neh.	3	29
A false prophet	Neh.	6	10
A priest, signer of the covenant	Neh.	10	8
A priest with Zerubbabel	Neh.	12	6, 18
A Levite exile	Neh.	12	35
Three men who celebrate dedication of the wall	Neh.	12	34, 36, 42
Father of Urijah	Jer.	26	20
A false prophet	Jer.	29	24–32
Father of Delaiah	Jer.	36	12

Shemariah, Shamariah *Jehovah has guarded*

A mighty man of David	I Chr.	12	5
Son of Rehoboam	II Chr.	11	18, 19
One who took a strange wife	Ezra	10	32
Son of Bani, who took a strange wife	Ezra	10	41

sheminith *eighth*

A musical term	I Chr.	15	21

Shenir, Senir *a peak, snow*

Amorites call mount Hermon	Deut.	3	9
Called Senir	I Chr.	5	23

Shepham *a bare spot*

Place on eastern boundary of Canaan	Num.	34	10, 11

Shephatiah *Jehovah is judge*

Son of David	II Sam.	3	2, 4
Father of Meshullam	I Chr.	9	8
A mighty man of David	I Chr.	12	5
A Simeonite ruler	I Chr.	27	16
Son of King Jehoshaphat	II Chr.	21	2
Descendants return from Babylon	Ezra	2	4
Descendant of Perez	Neh.	11	4
One who opposes Jeremiah	Jer.	38	1, 4

shepherd *one who cares for flocks*

Abel, the first	Gen.	4	2
Both male and female	Gen.	29	6
	I Sam.	17	15
Abomination to the Egyptians	Gen.	46	34
Responsibilities of	Gen.	29	2–10
	I Chr.	4	39, 40
	Jer.	33	12
	Mat.	25	32
	John	10	3–5
Abomination to Egyptians	Gen.	46	34
David, a shepherd	I Sam.	16	11–13
Aided by dogs	Job	30	1
Feeds flock	Is.	40	11
Of Cyrus	Is.	44	28
Raiment of	Jer.	43	12
Seeketh his flock	Ezek.	34	12
A foolish and idle	Zech.	11	15–17
Cottages of	Zeph.	2	6
Angels appear to	Luke	2	8–20
Illustrative:			
Of God's care	Ps.	23	
Of God, as leader of Israel	Ps.	77	20
Of kings, as leaders	Is.	44	28
Of ministers of the gospel	Jer.	23	4
Of Christ seeking the lost	Luke	15	2–7
Of Christ, the good shepherd	John	10	14
Christ the great one	Heb.	13	20

sheriffs *chief executive officers*

Administrative officers	Dan.	3	2, 3

Sheshbazzar *worshiper of fire*

Prince of Judah	Ezra	1	8
Persian name for Zerubbabel	Ezra	5	14
Governor of Judah	Hag.	2	2, 21

Sheth *compensation see Seth*

A tribe of Moab	Num.	24	17

Sheva, Shavsha *self-satisfying*

Called Seraiah	II Sam.	8	17
Scribe of David	II Sam.	20	25
Called Shavsha	I Chr.	18	16
Son of Caleb			
Father of Machbenah and Gibea	I Chr.	2	49

shewbread *see showbread*

Shibboleth, Sibboleth *a stream*

A pass word	Judg.	12	5, 6

shield *defensive armour*

Used by Saul	II Sam.	1	21
Made of gold and brass	II Sam.	8	7
	I Ki.	14	27
Stored in the tabernacle	II Ki.	11	10
Used by the Benjamites	II Chr.	14	8
Uzziah equips the children of Israel with	II Chr.	26	14
Painted red	Nah.	2	3
Symbolic of:			
God's protection	Ps.	33	20
God's truth	Ps.	91	4
Faith	Eph.	6	6
God as	Gen.	15	1
	Ps.	59	11
	Ps.	91	4
Of salvation	Ps.	18	35

Shihor, Sihor *dark, turbid*

A river in Egypt	Josh.	13	3
Provides drinking water	Jer.	2	18

Shilhi *massive, armed*

Father of Azubah	I Ki.	22	41
Father-in-law of King Asa	I Ki.	22	42

Shiloah *see* Siloam

Shiloh *rest, he whose it is*

Title of the Messiah	Gen.	49	10
Location of tabernacle	Josh.	18	8–10
Seat of government	Josh.	21	1, 2
A meeting place	Josh.	22	9, 12
A town in Canaan	Judg.	21	12
Sanctuary destroyed	Jer.	7	12

Shiloni

Father of Zechariah	Neh.	11	5

Shimea, Shimeah, Shimeam *fame*

Son of David	I Chr.	3	1, 5
Called Shammua	I Chr.	14	4
Brother of David	I Chr.	20	7
Called Shimeah	II Sam.	13	3
A Merarite Levite	I Chr.	6	30
A Gershomite Levite	I Chr.	6	39
Son of Mikloth	I Chr.	8	32
Called Shimeam	I Chr.	9	38

Shimei, Shimi, Shimhi *my fame*

A son of Gershon	Ex.	6	17
A Benjamite	II Sam.	16	5–13
One of David's mighty men	I Ki.	1	8
One of Solomon's officers	I Ki.	4	18
Grandson of Jeconiah	I Chr.	3	19
Son of Zacchur	I Chr.	4	26, 27
A Reubenite, son of Gog	I Chr.	5	4
A Merarite, son of Libni	I Chr.	6	29
A Gershonite, son of Johath	I Chr.	6	42
Father of a family in Benjamin	I Chr.	8	21
A Levite	I Chr.	23	9
A singer in time of David	I Chr.	25	17
Overseer of David's vineyards	I Chr.	27	27
A son of Heman	II Chr.	29	14
Treasurer of tithes	II Chr.	31	12, 13
A Levite who puts away his Gentile wife	Ezra	10	23
Two Israelites who married strange wives	Ezra	10	33, 38
Grandfather of Mordecai	Esth.	2	5

Shimma *fame*

Son of Jesse	I Chr.	2	13
Called Shimea	I Chr.	20	7

Shinar *plain of Babylonia*

A land, kingdom of Nimrod	Gen.	10	9, 10
Site of the tower of Babel	Gen.	11	2
Amraphel, once king of	Gen.	14	1, 9
Captives return from	Is.	11	11

shine *to glow*

"The Lord make His face to"	Num.	6	25
Wisdom makes a face	Eccl.	8	1
The righteous shine as the stars	Dan.	12	3
"Let your light so"	Mat.	5	16
Of Jesus' face at transfiguration	Mat.	17	2
Of raiment	Mark	9	3
	Luke	24	4
Manifest	Job	10	3
Recover	Job	11	17
Upon thy ways	Job	22	28
Cloud cover	Job	36	32
Of a face (favour)	Ps.	31	16
	Ps.	67	1
	Ps.	80	3
	Ps.	119	135
Of the moon	Is.	13	10
Of the sun	Rev.	21	23
Of the stars	Joel	3	15
The gospel	II Cor.	4	4
Of a candle	Rev.	18	23

ship *seagoing vessel*

Probably originates from the ark	Gen.	7	17, 18
Used in war	Num.	24	24
Solomon builds a navy of	I Ki.	9	26
Wonderful	Prov.	30	19
Jonah flees in	Jonah	1	3
Generally made from the fir tree	Ezek.	27	5
Used for fishing	Mat.	4	21
Used for carrying passengers	Mark	4	38
Often impelled by oars	John	6	19
Of Zebedee	Mat.	4	21, 22
Jesus rides in	Mark	4	38
Often sent to Tarshish	Is.	60	9
	II Chr.	9	21
	II Chr.	20	37
Of Babylon	Rev.	18	17, 19
Used in commerce	Acts	21	3
Commanded by a master	Acts	27	11
Course directed by the elements	Acts	27	20

Shiprah *splendid*

A Hebrew midwife	Ex.	1	15
Ordered to kill male children	Ex.	1	16

shipwreck *destruction of a vessel*

At Ezion-geber	I Ki.	22	48
Voyage abandoned	II Chr.	20	35–37
Suffered three times by Paul	Acts	27	40–44
	II Cor.	11	25
Symbolic of ruin	I Tim.	1	19

shipyard *a place where ships are built*

In the land of Edom	I Ki.	9	26

Shittim *the thorny, acacia*

A city in the plains of Moab	Num.	25	1
Called Abel-shittim	Num.	33	49
Joshua sends spies	Josh.	2	1
To be watered	Joel	3	18
Balaam's work	Mic.	6	5

shittim wood *from the acacia tree*

Used as an offering	Ex.	25	5
Ark of the covenant made from	Ex.	25	10
A table made of	Ex.	25	23
Used in building the tabernacle	Ex.	26	15, 26
Altars made of	Ex.	38	1

Shobab *rebellious, returning*

Son of David	II Sam.	5	13, 14
Son of Caleb	I Chr.	2	18

Shobal *wandering*

Son of Seir	Gen.	36	20, 23
Son of Caleb	I Chr.	2	50, 52
Son of Judah	I Chr.	4	1, 2

shoes

Taken off on holy ground	Ex.	3	5
	Josh.	5	15
Loose shoe	Deut.	25	9
	Ruth	4	7, 8
Worn out	Josh.	9	5, 13
Beautiful	S. of S.	7	1
Of a bride	Amos	8	6
Given to the prodigal son	Luke	15	22
Made of iron	Deut.	33	25
Made of badgers' skins	Ezek.	16	10
Not worn in mourning	Ezek.	24	17
Poor sold for a pair of	Amos	2	6
Called sandals	Mark	6	9
Loosing of, a humble service	John	1	27
	Mat.	3	11

shoelatchet *a thong for fastening a shoe or sandal*

Not taken by Abram	Gen.	14	23
Loosening of, a humble service	Mark	1	7

short

Lord's hand waxed *s*?	Num.	11	23
The light is *s* because	Job	17	12
Triumphing of the wicked is *s*	Job	20	5
How *s* my time is	Ps.	89	47
Come *s* of glory of God	Rom.	3	23
Because a *s* work will Lord	Rom.	9	28
Brethren, the time is *s*	I Cor.	7	29
From you for a *s* time	I Thes.	2	17
He hath but a *s* time	Rev.	12	12
He must continue a *s* space	Rev.	17	10
(*See* come, cut)			

shot

Her blossoms *s* forth	Gen.	40	10
The archers *s* at him, and	Gen.	49	23
Shall surely be stoned, or *s* through	Ex.	19	13
We have *s* at them	Num.	21	30
The arrow which Jonathan had *s*	I Sam.	20	37
The shooters *s* from	II Sam.	11	24
Said, Shoot, and he *s*	II Ki.	13	17
Archers *s* at king Josiah	II Chr.	35	23
S out lightnings, and	Ps.	18	14
Tongue is an arrow *s* out	Jer.	9	8
It became a vine, and *s*	Ezek.	17	6
This vine *s* forth her branches	Ezek.	17	7
Waters when he *s* forth	Ezek.	31	5
He hath *s* up his top among	Ezek.	31	10

shoulder *part of the body*

Supports water jug	Gen.	21	14
Bowed in tribute	Gen.	49	15
Of the ram, used as offering	Num.	6	19
Weapons carried upon	Josh.	4	5
Withdrawing, a sign of rebuke	Neh.	9	29
Used for carrying burdens	Job	31	36
Shepherds carry their sheep on	Luke	15	5

Government upon	Is.	9	6
For carrying things	Is.	22	22
	Gen.	21	14
	Ezek.	12	7
Heave	Lev.	7	34
	Lev.	10	14
Right shoulder	Ex.	29	22

shouting *a sudden and loud outcry*

In victory	Josh.	6	16, 20
The earth rings with	I Sam.	4	5
In praising God	Ezra	3	11
	Ps.	47	1
In rejoicing	Zeph.	3	14
In thanksgiving	Luke	17	15
In wonder	Acts	12	22
Of joy	Ezra	3	13
Of God	Ps.	47	5
	Jer.	25	30
Against Babylon	Jer.	51	14
At Christ's coming	I Thes.	4	16
In idolatry	Ex.	32	18

shovel *an implement*

Made of brass	Ex.	27	3
Used in temple	Ex.	38	3
Covered with badger skins	Num.	4	14

show

Every man walketh in a vain *s*	Ps.	39	6
For a *s* make long prayers	Luke	20	47
To make a fair *s* in the flesh	Gal.	6	12
Made a *s* of them openly	Col.	2	15
Who will *s* us any good?	Ps.	4	6
Thou wilt *s* me the path of life	Ps.	16	11
S forth the praises of the Lord	Is.	60	6
Father, *s* the Son all things	John	5	20
Ye do *s* the Lord's death	I Cor.	11	26
S unto you eternal life	I John	1	2

showbread, shewbread, hallowed bread

Required to be kept before the Lord always	Ex.	25	30
Mosaic law concerning	Lev.	24	5–9
Called hallowed bread	I Sam.	21	6
Unlawfully eaten by David	I Sam.	21	6
	Mat.	12	3, 4
Kohathites to prepare	I Chr.	9	32
Continual	II Chr.	2	4
Set in order	II Chr.	13	11
Cleansed	II Chr.	29	18
Put in the tabernacle	Heb.	9	2
Prepared by Levites	I Chr.	9	32
Provided by a yearly tax	Neh.	10	32, 33

Table of:

Described	Ex.	25	23–29
Consecrated	Ex.	30	26, 27
Placed on the north side of the tabernacle	Ex.	40	22
How it is removed	Num.	4	7, 15

showers

Distil as *s* on the grass	Deut.	32	2
The poor are wet with *s*	Job	24	8
The earth soft with *s*	Ps.	65	10
He shall come down as *s*	Ps.	72	6
Therefore the *s* have been	Jer.	3	3
Can the heavens give *s*?	Jer.	14	22
Shall be *s* of blessing	Ezek.	34	26
Shall be as *s* on grass	Mic.	5	7
The Lord shall give them *s* of rain (*See* rain)	Zech.	10	1

showers of blessings

Promised by God	Ezek.	34	26

shroud *a garment*

Used figuratively	Ezek.	31	3

Shua, Shuah, Shuhah *riches*

Son of Abraham	Gen.	25	2
Father-in-law of Judah	I Chr.	2	3
Brother of Chelub	I Chr.	4	11
Daughter of Heber	I Chr.	7	32

Shunammite *resident of Shunem*

Cherishes David	I Ki.	1	3, 4
Sought by Adonijah	I Ki.	2	13–25
A woman who shows hospitality to Elisha	II Ki.	4	8
Her son raised from dead	II Ki.	4	32–36

Shur *fortification*

Where Hagar fled	Gen.	16	7
Saul smites the Amalekites unto	I Sam.	15	7
David chases Amalekites	I Sam.	27	8
A desert east of Egypt	Gen.	25	18
	Ex.	15	22

Shushan *lily*

Capital of Medo-persian Empire	Esth.	1	1–3
King's palace located here	Esth.	2	5, 8
In province of Elam	Dan.	8	2

shut

The Lord *s* him in	Gen.	7	16
Wilderness hath *s* them in	Ex.	14	3
Let her be *s* out from camp	Num.	12	14
Miriam was *s* out from the camp	Num.	12	15
S the gate of Jericho	Josh.	2	7
They *s* the tower to them	Judg.	9	51
For he is *s* in, by entering into	I Sam.	23	7
Not the pit *s* her mouth	Ps.	69	15
S their eyes, lest they	Is.	6	10
So he shall open and none shall *s* he shall *s* and none shall	Is.	22	22
For he hath *s* their eyes	Is.	44	18
And gates shall not be *s*	Is.	45	1
Kings shall *s* their mouths	Is.	52	15
Thy gates shall not be *s* day	Is.	60	11
Shall I *s* the womb? saith	Is.	66	9
Spirit said, Go *s* thyself	Ezek.	3	24
Looked toward the east was *s*	Ezek.	44	1
This gate shall be *s*, it shall not be opened, god . . . it shall be *s*	Ezek.	44	2
The gate shall be *s* the six	Ezek.	46	1
The gate shall not be *s* till the	Ezek.	46	2
After his going forth, one shall *s*	Ezek.	46	12
My God hath *s* the lions'	Dan.	6	22
Prison truly found we *s*	Acts	5	23
Power to *s* heaven	Rev.	11	6
Gates shall not be *s* by day	Rev.	21	25

Sibboleth *see* Shibboleth

Sichem *see* Shechem

sickle *an agricultural implement*

Shall not use on neighbour's grain	Deut.	23	25
Used in time of harvest	Jer.	50	16
Harvest in the end times	Joel	3	13
	Rev.	14	14, 15

sickness *diseased condition*

Sent as a punishment for sin	Lev.	26	14–16
	Ps.	107	17, 18
	I Cor.	11	30
Sent by God	Deut.	28	22, 59–61
	II Sam.	12	15
Often incurable by human means	Deut.	28	27
God heals	Deut.	32	39
	Ps.	103	3
Medicines used in healing	II Ki.	20	7
	Jer.	46	11
	I Tim.	5	23
God's help should be sought in	II Chr.	16	12, 13
Suffered by the godly	Job	2	3–10
Satan permitted to inflict	Job	2	6–8
	Luke	13	16
God hears the prayers of those in	Ps.	30	2
	Ps.	107	18–20
God comforts His people in	Ps.	41	3
Praise God for recovery from	Ps.	103	1–3
	Luke	17	15
Brought on by intemperance	Hosea	7	5
Healed by Christ and His disciples	Mat.	8	16
	Mat.	10	8
	John	11	1–44
	Acts	9	37
Faith required of those healed by Christ	Mat.	9	28, 29
	Mark	5	34
Healing of, lawful on the sabbath	Luke	13	14–16
Healing by prayer	James	5	13–15

Siddim *plains, furrows*

A valley near the Dead sea	Gen.	14	3
Full of slime pits	Gen.	14	10

side

Delivered on every	Judg.	8	34
	I Sam.	14	47
Rest on every	I Ki.	5	4
	I Chr.	22	18
	II Chr.	14	7
River	Ex.	2	5
	Num.	24	6
Door posts	Ex.	12	7, 22
Lord's	Ex.	32	26
Sword girded on	Neh.	4	18
Raised on one	Dan.	7	5
Crucified with thieves on	John	19	18
Put hands in his	John	20	20, 25
Angel smote Peter on	Acts	12	7

Sidon, Zidon *fishery*

Son of Canaan	Gen.	10	15
A border city of the Canaanites	Gen.	10	19
On the border of Zebulun	Gen.	49	13
The lot of Asher	Josh.	19	28
People are careless	Judg.	18	7
Jews exiled to	Joel	3	4
Inhabitants contribute cedar for the temple	I Ki.	5	6
Visited by Jesus	Mat.	15	21
Inhabitants come to hear Jesus	Mark	3	8
Visited by Paul	Acts	27	3

siege *act of war*

Preceded by offer of peace	Deut.	20	10–12
By use of embankments	Deut.	20	19, 20
Of Jericho	Josh.	6	
Of Jerusalem, by David	II Sam.	5	6, 9
Brings distress upon the inhabitants	II Ki.	6	24–29
Of Jerusalem, by Nebuchadnezzar	II Ki.	24	10, 11
Trees not cut in	Deut.	20	19
Children eaten in	Deut.	28	53
Of Ezekiel	Ezek.	4	2, 3
Waters of	Nah.	3	14
Of Jerusalem	Zech.	12	2

sift *to separate*

S the nations with the sieve of vanity	Is.	30	28
Will *s* Israel as corn is *s*	Amos	9	9
Satan hath desired to *s* you	Luke	22	31

sigh

Merryhearted *s*	Is.	24	7
Sorrow and *s* shall flee away	Is.	35	10
Looking up to heaven he *s*	Mark	7	34

sight

See this great *s*	Ex.	3	3
Better is *s* of eyes	Eccl.	6	9
Blind receive their *s*	Mat.	11	5
	Luke	7	21
Recovering of *s* to the blind	Luke	4	18
Receive thy *s*	Luke	18	42
	Acts	22	13
He vanished out of their *s*	Luke	24	31
We walk by faith, not by *s*	II Cor.	5	7
In *s* of God of great price	I Pet.	3	4

sign *a token*

The rainbow, a sign of the convenant	Gen.	9	13
Asked for, to confirm faith	Mat.	12	38, 39
	Mark	8	11, 12
Of a traitor	Mat.	26	47, 48
Given to the shepherds	Luke	2	12, 13
Of the last days	Luke	21	25–36
Sign seekers rebuked by Jesus	John	4	48

Asked for and given to:

Abraham	Gen.	15	8–17
Moses	Ex.	4	1–9

Asked for and given to:

Gideon	Judg.	6	17, 36–40
Hezekiah	II Ki.	20	8–11
On thy hand	Ex.	13	9
Sabbath as	Ex.	31	13, 17
Censers as	Num.	16	38
Destruction of Korah	Num.	26	10
Law upon the hand	Deut.	6	8
False prophet	Deut.	13	1, 2
Stones marking the crossing of the Jordan	Josh.	4	6
Smoke as	Judg.	20	38
A prophecy as	I Sam.	2	34
	Is.	7	11
Of Jonathan	I Sam.	14	10
Renting on the altar	I Ki.	13	3, 5
Virgin birth	Is.	7	14
Prophet as a sign	Is.	20	3
Ezekiel as	Ezek.	24	24

signet *see seal*

Sihon *bold, great*

King of the Amorites	Num.	21	21
His capital at Heshbon	Deut.	2	26
Defeated by Israelites	Deut.	2	32–36

Sihor *see Shihor*

Silas, Silvanus *wooded*

A disciple	Acts	15	22
A prophet	Acts	15	32
Travels in Syria and Cilicia	Acts	15	41
Cast into prison	Acts	16	22, 23
Preaches at Corinth	II Cor.	1	19

Receives epistle	I Pet.	5	12
Called Silvanus	I Thes.	1	1

silence *stillness*

In grief	Job	2	11–13
Sign of respect	Job	29	21
Lying lips put to	Ps.	31	18
As a result of sorrow	Ps.	39	2
Of the dead	Ps.	115	17
	Ps.	31	17
Of desolation	Is.	15	1
Of Judgment	Jer.	8	14
	Amos	8	3
A sign of wisdom	Prov.	17	28
Avoids trouble	Prov.	21	23
There is a proper time for	Eccl.	3	7
Of Jesus, foretold	Is.	53	7
Sometimes difficult	Jer.	20	9
"Let the earth keep"	Hab.	2	20
Of Jesus, before Pilate	Mat.	27	14
Not kept by the apostles	Acts	5	26–42
In the churches	I Cor.	14	34
Women to learn in	I Tim.	2	11, 12
Crowd during Paul's defense	Acts	22	2
In heaven	Rev.	8	1

silk *a fine material*

Worn by the prosperous	Prov.	31	22
	Ezek.	16	13
Covered with	Ezek.	16	10
Bought and sold	Rev.	18	12

silla *a high way*

A place of uncertain location	II Ki.	12	20

silly

Of a dove	Hosea	7	11
Of a woman	II Tim.	3	6

Siloam, Shiloah, Siloah *sent*

A pool near Jerusalem	II Ki.	20	20
Supplies Jerusalem with water	II Chr.	32	30
Wall rebuilt	Neh.	3	15
Blind man washes in	John	9	6–11
The tower	Luke	13	4

Silvanus *see Silas*

silver *a precious metal*

Used for money	Gen.	23	15, 16
	I Ki.	16	24
Made into household utensils	Gen.	44	2
	Num.	7	13
Used for jewelry	Ex.	3	22
Made into decorations for the tabernacle	Ex.	26	19, 25
	Ex.	27	17
Often given as a gift	I Ki.	10	25
Abundant in Solomon's time	I Ki.	10	21, 22
Found in the earth	Job	28	1
Used for idols	Ps.	115	4
Purified by fire	Prov.	17	3
Traded for	Ezek.	27	12
Jesus sold for thirty pieces of	Mat.	26	15
Peter had none	Acts	3	6
working in, a trade	Acts	19	24

silversmith *a worker in silver*

Incites labour riot	Acts	19	24–29

Simeon *a hearkening*

Son of Jacob and Leah	Gen.	29	33
Slays Shechemites	Gen.	34	25
Conspires against Joseph	Gen.	37	18–20
Held as hostage	Gen.	42	24
Father of six sons	Gen.	46	10
Condemned	Gen.	49	5–7
The tribe of	Num.	1	22, 23
Order in camp	Num.	2	2, 12, 13
Upon mount Gerizim	Deut.	27	11, 12
Its inheritance	Josh.	19	1–9
Joins in renewal of the passover	II Chr.	15	9–14
Idolatrous	II Chr.	34	1–7
A devout man	Luke	2	25–35
An ancestor of Jesus	Luke	3	30
A disciple, also called Niger	Acts	13	1
Name given to Peter	Acts	15	14

similitude

The *s* of the Lord	Num.	12	8
Saw no *s*	Deut.	4	12
After the *s* of a palace	Ps.	144	12
After the *s* of Adam's transgression	Rom.	5	14
After *s* of Melchisedec	Heb.	7	15
Men made after *s* of God	James	3	9

Simon *hearing, hearkening*

An apostle, the Canaanite	Mat.	10	4
A brother of Jesus	Mat.	13	55
Called Bar-jona	Mat.	16	16–19
An apostle, surnamed Peter	Mark	3	14, 16
See Peter			
A leper	Mat.	26	6
A man of Cyrene	Mat.	27	32
A Pharisee	Luke	7	36–44
Father of Judas Iscariot	John	6	71
A sorcerer	Acts	8	9–13
Admonished by Peter	Acts	8	18–24
A tanner	Acts	9	43

simony *ecclesiastical corruption*

Condemned by Peter	Acts	8	18, 19

simpleton *fool*

Loves simplicity	Prov.	1	22
Good description	Prov.	7	7–23
Lacks wisdom	Prov.	8	5
Knows nothing	Prov.	9	13
Believes every word	Prov.	14	15
Inherits folly	Prov.	14	18
Cunning	Prov.	19	25
Learns by example	Prov.	21	11
Is punished	Prov.	22	3
Offering taken for	Ezek.	45	19, 20
Like a silly dove	Hosea	7	11
Easily deceived	Rom.	16	18

simplicity *lack of duplicity*

Loved	Prov.	1	22
Necessity for	Mat.	18	2, 3
In our giving	Rom.	12	8
Exhortation to	Rom.	16	19
In writing	II Cor.	1	12

sin *breaking law of God*

Originates with Adam and Eve	Gen.	3	6, 7
Fear of God restrains	Ex.	20	20
Only God can forgive	Ex.	34	7
	Dan.	9	9
	Mark	2	7
Children bear the consequences of	Ex.	34	7
	Is.	14	21
"Your sin will find you out"	Num.	32	23
No man is without	I Ki.	8	46
	Eccl.	7	20
God is angered by	I Ki.	16	2
God marks and remembers	Job	10	14
	Rev.	18	5
Known to God	Job	11	11
	Job	14	16
	Ps.	69	5
All men are conceived and born in	Job	15	14
Guilt of concealing	Job	31	33
Must be guarded against	Ps.	4	4
Prayer hindered by	Ps.	66	18
	Is.	59	2
Must be confessed	Prov.	28	13
	I John	1	9
Like scarlet and crimson	Is.	1	18
God will punish	Is.	13	11
Responsibility rests solely upon the individual	Jer.	31	29, 30
	Ezek.	18	2–4
Christ redeems from	Mat.	1	21
	Eph.	1	7
	I John	1	7
The unpardonable	Mat.	12	31, 32
	Mark	3	29
	Luke	12	10
Out of the heart	Mat.	15	18, 19
Forgiven are not to return to	John	5	14
	Rom.	6	12–22
Suffering not necessarily a result of	John	9	2, 3
Death, the wages of	Rom.	6	23
Christ alone is without	II Cor.	5	21
	Heb.	4	15
The law is made to restrain	I Tim.	1	9, 10

Defined:

Whatever conflicts with faith is	Rom.	14	23
Failure to do good works is	James	4	17
Is transgression of the law	I John	3	4
Is of the devil	I John	3	8
All unrighteousness is	I John	5	17

Some causes of:

Jealousy	Gen.	37	4
Idolatry	Ex.	20	3–6
Rebellion against God	Deut.	9	7
Prosperity	Job	21	7–15
An evil tongue	Ps.	109	20
Hatred	Prov.	10	12
Greed and oppression	Is.	3	15
	Mic.	2	2
Pride	Mark	7	22
Lust	James	1	15

Often leads to:

Murder	Gen.	37	20
Separation from God	Deut.	31	17, 18
	Mic.	3	4
Misery	Job	15	20
Disease	Job	20	11
Unrest	Ps.	38	3
Destruction	Prov.	10	29
Disgrace	Prov.	14	34
Adultery	Mark	7	21
Theft	Mark	7	22
Poverty and ruin	Luke	15	11–16
Shame	Rom.	6	21
Exclusion from heaven	I Cor.	6	9
	Gal.	5	19–21

Sin *(a locality)*

A wilderness between Elim and Sinai	Ex.	16	1
A fortress in Egypt	Ezek.	30	15
Destroyed	Ezek.	30	16

Sinai, Sina *pertaining to moon god (Sina)*

A mountain in the peninsula east of the Red sea	Ex.	16	1
Moses given law on	Ex.	19	3–25
Called Horeb	Deut.	1	2
Called Sina	Acts	7	30, 38
Desert wilderness	Ex.	19	2

sincerity *honesty of intention*

God to be served in	Josh.	24	14
The wicked devoid of	Ps.	5	9
	Ps.	55	21
Worship in	John	4	24
Should characterize our love for one another	Rom.	12	9
Of the apostles	II Cor.	1	12
In the preaching of the gospel	II Cor.	2	17
In our love for Jesus	Eph.	6	24
Prayer for	Phil.	1	10
The gospel sometimes preached without	Phil.	1	16
Ministers should be examples of	Tit.	2	7
Jesus, an example of	I Pet.	2	22

singers *people who produce musical tones with the voice*

Use psalteries	I Ki.	10	12
Work day and night	I Chr.	9	33
Levites at David's festival	I Chr.	15	16
Accompanied with cymbals of brass	I Chr.	15	19
Clothed in fine linen	I Chr.	15	27
Sing in praise of God	II Chr.	5	13
Use harps	II Chr.	9	11
Go before the army	II Chr.	20	21
Precede in the instrumentalists	Ps.	68	25
Men and women	Eccl.	2	8
Chambers for	Ezek.	40	44

singing *producing harmonious sounds*

Greeting returning soldiers	I Sam.	18	6
At the building of the temple	I Chr.	6	32
Instruction given in	I Chr.	25	7
Accompany burnt offerings	II Chr.	23	18
At the passover feast	II Chr.	30	21
In lamentation	II Chr.	35	25
At the dedication of the wall	Neh.	12	27
In gladness	Ps.	100	2
Of birds	S. of S.	2	12
Heaven and earth	Is.	49	13
Hills	Is.	55	12
Unto Zion	Is.	51	11
Of hymns	Mark	14	26
With the spirit	I Cor.	14	15
In thanksgiving	Eph.	5	19
In worship	Col.	3	16
When merry	James	5	13
A new song	Rev.	5	4

sink

I *s* in deep mire where	Ps.	69	2
Out of the mire, and let me not *s*	Ps.	14	
Thus shall Babylon *s* and	Jer.	51	64
Beginning to *s* he cried	Mat.	14	30
So that they began to *s*	Luke	5	7
Let these sayings *s* down	Luke	9	44

sinlessness *freedom from transgression*

Possessed by no man	Eccl.	7	20
Can be obtained by no man	Prov.	20	9
Christ only is	I John	3	9

sinner *one who sins*

Men of Sodom were s	Gen.	13	13
Standeth not in way of s	Ps.	1	1
Gather not my soul with s	Ps.	26	9
S shall be converted to thee	Ps.	51	13
If s entice thee	Prov.	1	10
Evil pursueth s	Prov.	13	21
One s destroyeth much good	Eccl.	9	18
Came not to call righteous but s	Mat.	9	13
	Mark	2	17
A friend of s	Mat.	11	19
	Luke	7	34
Woman who was a s	Luke	7	37
Joy in heaven over one s	Luke	15	7
Be merciful to me a s	Luke	18	13
How can a man that is a s do such miracles?	John	9	16
While we were yet s	Rom.	5	8
Converteth s, shall save a soul	James	5	20

sin offering *see* offerings

Sion *peak, elevation*

A name for mount Hermon	Deut.	4	48
See Zion			

Sirion *coat of mail*

Sidonians call mount Hermon	Deut.	3	9
Figurative	Ps.	29	6

Sisera *battle array*

Captain of Canaanite army	Judg.	4	2
His army defeated	Judg.	4	15, 16
Slain by Jael	Judg.	4	17–21
A Nethinim, family returns from Babylon	Ezra	2	53

sister

A half sister	Gen.	20	12
A woman of same tribe	Num.	25	18
Law concerning	Deut.	27	22
Lying about	Gen.	12	13
	Gen.	26	7
Rehab asks for salvation for	Josh.	2	13
Job's daughters	Job	1	4
Christ's	Mat.	19	29
Used figuratively	Ezek.	16	46
	Ezek.	16	49
	Mat.	12	50
A Christian woman	Rom.	16	1

sit

Ye that s in judgment	Judg.	5	10
Why s we here till we die?	II Ki.	7	3
Will not s with wicked	Ps.	26	5
They that s in the gate	Ps.	69	12
S thou at my right hand	Ps.	110	1
Their strength is to s still	Is.	30	7
Why do we s still?	Jer.	8	14
S every man under his vine	Mic.	4	4
To s on my right hand	Mat.	20	23
	Mark	10	37
S thou here in a good place	James	2	3
To s with me in my throne	Rev.	3	21

Sitnah *opposition*

A well dug by Isaac	Gen.	26	21

Sivan

The third month in the Hebrew calendar	Esth.	8	9

skeleton *bony framework of the body*

Burned into lime	Amos	2	1

skepticism *unbelief in*

Of Pharaoh	Ex.	5	2
Answered by Job	Job	21	15
Practiced by fools	Ps.	14	1
Profitless	Mal.	3	14
Of Thomas	John	20	24–29

skill *proficiency*

At hewing	I Ki.	5	6
Of engraving	II Chr.	2	7
At instruments of music	II Chr.	34	12
In learning and wisdom	Dan.	1	17
Given by God	Dan.	9	22
Given instruction	I Chr.	15	22
To destroy	Ezek.	21	31
In wailing	Amos	5	16

skin

Raiment for	Ex.	22	27
Used in offerings	Ex.	29	14
	Ex.	35	7
Diseases of	Lev.	13	38, 39
	Job	7	5
	Job	30	30
"Skin for skin"	Job	2	4
"Skin of my teeth"	Job	19	20
Cannot be changed	Jer.	13	23
Grown old and withered	Lam.	3	4
	Lam.	4	8
Girdle made of	Mark	1	6

skull, place of a *see* Golgotha

sky

Let the s pour down righteousness	Is.	45	8
Is lifted up even to s	Jer.	51	9
For the s is red	Mat.	16	2, 3
Many as stars of s	Heb.	11	12
(Often translated "heaven")			

slack

He will not be s to him that hateth	Deut.	7	10
Poor that dealeth with s hand	Prov.	10	4
Lord is not s concerning his promise	II Pet.	3	9

slain *put to death by violence*

By Lamech	Gen.	4	23
Rescue those that are ready to be	Prov.	24	11
By fire and sword	Is.	60	16
With hunger	Lam.	4	9

slander, calumny *malicious talk*

Forbidden	Ex.	23	1
Punishment for	Deut.	19	16–21
Should not be listened to	I Sam.	24	9
The wicked addicted to	Ps.	50	20
Often arises from hatred	Ps.	109	3
An abomination to God	Prov.	6	16, 19
Those who indulge in, are fools	Prov.	10	18
Separates friends	Prov.	16	28
Those who indulge in, not to be trusted	Jer.	9	4
Men shall give account for	Mat.	12	36
Comes from an evil heart	Luke	6	45
Suffered by ministers	Rom.	3	8
	II Cor.	6	8
Christians should return good for	I Cor.	4	12, 13
Ministers' wives should avoid	I Tim.	3	11
Idleness leads to	I Tim.	5	13
Women warned against	Tit.	2	3
Christians should give no occasion for	I Pet.	2	12
	I Pet.	3	16

Instances of:

Joseph, by Potiphar's wife	Gen.	39	14–18
David, by his enemies	Ps.	31	13
Jeremiah, by the Jews	Jer.	18	18
Jesus, by the Jews	Mat.	11	19
	Mark	14	64
	Luke	23	2
Paul, by the Jews	Acts	17	5–10

slave, slavery *bondman, bondage*

Position of trust	Gen.	15	2–4
Acquired by purchase	Gen.	17	27
Mosaic law pertaining to	Ex.	21	1–11, 32
	Lev.	25	39–55
Foreign	Deut.	29	11
Given military subjugation	Josh.	9	23, 27
Master seeks counsel of	I Sam.	9	7, 8
Public control	I Ki.	9	21
Sold for triviality	Amos	8	6
Made ruler over household	Mat.	24	45
See servant			
Manstealing forbidden	Deut.	21	10–14
Fugitive not to be returned	Deut.	23	15, 16
Of Hagar	Gen.	16	1
Paul intercedes for	Phil.		10–21
Captives of war	Deut.	20	14
	Deut.	21	10–14
Thieves punished by	Gen.	43	18
Defaulting debtors	Mat.	18	25
Children of defaulting debtors	II Ki.	4	1–7
Voluntary	Lev.	25	47
As a dowry	Gen.	29	24
Owned by priests	Lev.	22	11
Slaves owning slaves	II Sam.	9	10
May marry master	Ex.	21	7–10
To be circumcised	Gen.	17	13, 27
Religious rights	Deut.	12	12
Rest on Sabbath	Ex.	20	10

Kindness to	Lev.	25	43
	Mat.	8	8–13
Joseph	Gen.	37	26–28
Israel	Ex.	1	10–22
Canaanites	I Ki.	9	21

slave traders *traffickers of slaves*

Men of Tyre	Ezek.	27	2, 13
In Babylon	Rev.	18	10, 11, 13

sleep *slumber*

Jacob at Bethel	Gen.	28	11
Not with a poor mans goods	Deut.	24	12, 13
Samson's	Judg.	16	19
Samuel's	I Sam.	3	3
Of David's death	I Ki.	1	6
King could not	Esth.	6	1
God shall not	Ps.	121	4
Characteristic of a sluggard	Prov.	24	33
Perpetual	Jer.	51	39
Lazarus, of death	John	11	12
From communion	I Cor.	11	30
Sent by God	I Sam.	26	12
In peace	Ps.	4	8
A symbol of death	Ps.	13	3
Shall be sweet	Prov.	3	24
Excessive, makes sluggards	Prov.	6	10
During the harvest, condemned	Prov.	10	5
Hindered by wealth	Eccl.	5	12
"Not dead, but sleepeth"	Mat.	9	24
Heavy with	Luke	9	32
Time to awake out of	Rom.	13	11
Will arise from, in resurrection	Eph.	5	14

slime *see bitumen*

sling *an instrument that hurls stones*

Stones are hurled by	Judg.	20	16
Used by shepherds	I Sam.	17	40
David kills Goliath with	I Sam.	17	40–50
Used in war	II Ki.	3	25
Used in hunting	Job	41	28

slothful, the *lazy*

Lead a thorny life	Prov.	15	19
Are great wasters	Prov.	18	9
Are single-minded	Prov.	19	24
Refuse to labour	Prov.	21	25
Alibi	Prov.	22	13
Cause poverty	Prov.	24	30, 31
Paul cautions against	Rom.	12	11

slow

I am *s* of speech	Ex.	4	10
A God *s* to anger	Neh.	9	17
That is *s* to wrath	Prov.	14	29
S of heart	Luke	24	25
S to speak, *s* to wrath	James	1	19

sluggard *a drone*

Is not wise	Prov.	6	6
Sleeps too much	Prov.	6	9
Shall experience poverty	Prov.	6	11
Harmful to others	Prov.	10	25
Desires nothing	Prov.	13	4
Alibies	Prov.	20	4
Is conceited	Prov.	26	16

slumber

He that keepeth thee will not *s*	Ps.	121	3
None shall *s* nor sleep	Is.	5	27
Thy shepherds *s*	Nah.	3	18
While bridegroom tarried, they *s*	Mat.	25	5
Give not *s* to thine eyelids	Prov.	6	4
God hath given them the spirit of *s*	Rom.	11	8

small

S round thing, *s* as hoar frost	Ex.	16	14
Is it a *s* thing that thou hast brought us?	Num.	16	13
A *s* thing in thy sight	II Sam.	7	19
	I Chr.	17	17
After the fire a still *s* voice	I Ki.	19	12
Is it a *s* thing to weary men?	Is.	7	13
For a *s* moment	Is.	54	7
A *s* one shall become a strong nation	Is.	60	22
The day of *s* things	Zech.	4	10
No *s* dissension	Acts	15	2

smell

As *s* of a field	Gen.	27	27
Where were the *s*?	I Cor.	12	17
An odour of a sweet *s*	Phil.	4	18
He *s* the battle afar	Job	39	25
Thy garments *s* of myrrh	Ps.	45	8
Noses have they, but *s* not	Ps.	115	6

smite *strike, hit hard*

He that *s* a man	Ex.	21	12
Shall I *s* them?	II Ki.	6	21
The sun shall not *s* thee by day	Ps.	121	6
S a scorner	Prov.	19	25
Neither shall heat *s* thee	Is.	49	10
Giveth his cheek to him that *s* thee	Lam.	3	30
Knees *s* together	Nah.	2	10
S the Shepherd	Zech.	13	7
	Mat.	26	31
	Mark	14	27
Lest I *s* the earth with a curse	Mal.	4	6
S thee on right cheek	Mat.	5	39
Begin to *s* his fellow-servants	Mat.	24	49
Why *s* thou me?	John	18	23

smith *a worker in metals*

An instructor	Gen.	4	22
Clever in his work	Ex.	31	3–5
Works on the temple	Ex.	31	6–11
Not in all Israel	I Sam.	13	19
Works for Solomon	I Ki.	7	13, 14
Taken into captivity	II Ki.	24	14
Of gold	Neh.	3	8, 31
Works in coals	Is.	44	12
Created by God	Is.	54	16
Of silver idols	Acts	19	24
Of copper	II Tim.	4	14

smiting of cheek *a form of assault*

A reproach	Job	16	10, 4
A prophecy of Christ	Lam.	3	30, 6
"Turn the other cheek"	Mat.	5	38, 39
Suffered by Jesus	Mat.	26	67

smoke

Of burning land	Gen.	19	28
Of Ai	Josh.	8	20
Of Gibeah	Judg.	20	38
Out of His nostrils	II Sam.	22	9
	Job	41	20
Wonders of God's judgment	Joel	2	30
Of incense	Rev.	8	4
Of God's anger and jealousy	Deut.	29	20
	Ps.	74	1
Pillar of, as a symbol	Judg.	20	38, 40
Of the seething caldron	Job	41	20
Driven away	Ps.	68	2
Hurts the eyes	Prov.	10	26
Out of the chimney	Hosea	13	3
Darkens the sun	Rev.	9	2
Of torment	Rev.	14	11

Smyrna *myrrh*

An Ionian city where there is a church	Rev.	1	11

snail *a gastropod mollusk*

Forbidden as food	Lev.	11	30

snake, *see serpent*

snare *a trap, gin*

Of Moses	Ex.	10	7
Inhabitants of the land	Ex.	34	12
Gideon's ephod	Judg.	8	27
Set by the proud	Ps.	140	5
Fool's lips	Prov.	18	7
False prophet	Hosea	9	8
Rich fall into	I Tim.	6	9
Serving false gods a	Deut.	7	16
Set by the wicked	Ps.	119	110
Used for birds	Ps.	124	7
A fool's lips are a	Prov.	18	7
Of the evil	Prov.	29	6
Of the scornful	Prov.	29	8
Of unrighteousness	Luke	21	34, 35
Of the devil	I Tim.	3	7

sneezings *spasmodic expirations of breath*

Seven times	II Ki.	4	35

snow *frozen water vapour*

Time of	II Sam.	23	20
Melts	Job	6	16, 17
Forms water	Job	9	30
A treasure	Job	38	22
"Whiter than snow"	Ps.	51	7
Used figuratively	Prov.	26	1
Irrigates earth	Is.	55	10
Symbol of purity	Lam.	4	7
As white	Ex.	4	6
	Num.	12	10
	Is.	1	18
Consumed by heat	Job	24	19
In summer	Prov.	26	1

snow—*continued*

Ideal wife not afraid of	Prov.	31	21
Hair as white as	Rev.	1	14

snuffdishes *utensils*

Used in the temple	Ex.	25	38
Of pure gold	Ex.	37	23

snuffers *used to extinguish candles*

Of pure gold	Ex.	37	23
Used in the temple	I Ki.	7	50

So

King of Egypt	II Ki.	17	4
Possibly a title "vizier"			
Possibly a place name			

soap, sope *a cleansing agent*

Fails to clean	Jer.	2	22

sober

S for your cause	II Cor.	5	13
Let us watch and be s	I Thes.	5	6
A bishop must be s	I Tim.	3	2
	Tit.	1	8
That aged men be s	Tit.	2	2
Be s, and watch unto prayer	I Pet.	4	7
Be s, be vigilant	I Pet.	5	8
(*See Acts 26:25; Titus 2:12.*)			

sobriety *temperance*

In self praise	Rom.	12	3
Required of Christians	I Thes.	5	6, 8
Required of ministers and their wives	I Tim.	3	2, 3, 11
The gospel designed to teach	Tit.	2	12
Commanded	I Pet.	1	13

Socoh *thorns*

A city of Judah	Josh.	15	35
A commissary city	I Ki.	4	10
Captured by Philistines	II Chr.	28	18
A city in mountains of Judah	Josh.	15	48
Son of Heber	I Chr.	4	18

sociability *friendliness*

Created by fear	Mal.	3	16
Rather than enmity	John	4	7–9
Of the early church	Acts	2	46

social duties *obligations to society*

Consideration of others	Prov.	31	26
Interest in others	Luke	10	30–34
Honesty	Rom.	12	17
Forgiveness	Eph.	4	32
Graciousness	Col.	4	6
Righteousness	I Thes.	5	15

Sodom, Sodoma *burning*

City on southeast border of Canaan	Gen.	10	19
Wickedness	Gen.	13	13
Resists invasion	Gen.	14	1–12
Intercession for	Gen.	18	16–33
Destroyed because of wickedness	Gen.	19	1–29
Figurative of wickedness	Is.	1	10
Remains uninhabitable	Jer.	49	18
More tolerable than for those that reject			
Christ	Mat.	10	15
	Mark	6	11
Apostates	II Pet.	2	6
	Jude		7
Witness shall lie in streets of	Rev.	11	8

sodomy *unnatural sexual intercourse*

Forbidden by Mosaic law	Ex.	22	19
A vile thing	Judg.	19	22–24
In the days of the Kings	I Ki.	14	24
	I Ki.	15	11, 12
	I Ki.	22	46
	II Ki.	23	7
Is dishonourable	Rom.	1	24, 26, 27
Unrighteous	I Cor.	6	9

soil conservation

Year of rest	Lev.	25	1–5

sojourn *stay for a time*

Down into Egypt to s	Gen.	12	10
This one fellow came in to s	Gen.	19	9
S in this land, and I will be	Gen.	26	3
They said, For to s in the land	Gen.	47	4
Will s with thee and keep	Ex.	12	48
Which s that offereth sacrifice	Lev.	17	8
Of strangers that s, that giveth.	Lev.	20	2
Of strangers that s of them	Lev.	25	45
A Levite went to s	Judg.	17	8
Said to Micah, I go to s where	Judg.	17	9
Elimelech went to s	Ruth	1	1

Widow with whom I s	I Ki.	17	20
S wheresoever thou canst s	II Ki.	8	1
Woe is me, that I s in Meshech	Ps.	120	5
Carry her afar off to s	Is.	23	7
Went down into Egypt to s	Is.	52	4
Faces to enter into Egypt and go to s	Jer.	42	15, 17
	Jer.	44	12, 14, 28
Place whither ye desire to s	Jer.	42	22
Shall no more s there	Lam.	4	15
Them from where they s	Ezek.	20	38
And strangers who s among	Ezek.	47	22
That his seed should s	Acts	7	6

sold *disposed of for a consideration*

A birthright	Gen.	25	33
Into slavery	Ps.	105	17
For nothing	Is.	52	3
A girl for wine	Joel	3	3
"All that he had"	Mat.	13	46
Five sparrows	Luke	12	6
Possessions sold by early Christians	Acts	2	45

soldiers *skilled warriors*

Military enrollment	Num.	1	1–46
Those exempted by Mosaic law	Deut.	20	5–7, 9
Fearful	Judg.	7	2, 3
Ratio of those subject to duty	Judg.	20	10
Some are hired	II Chr.	25	5, 6
Dressed in scarlet	Nah.	2	3
A commander of authority	Mat.	8	8, 9
Mock Jesus	Mat.	27	27–31
Crucify Jesus	Mat.	27	31–37
Accept bribes	Mat.	28	11–15
Cast lots for Jesus' garments	John	19	23, 24
Guard Peter in prison	Acts	12	4–6
Rescue Paul from mob	Acts	21	31–35
For Christ	II Tim.	2	3
Christian's armour	Eph.	6	11–18

solemn assembly *see* feasts and festivals

solitude *isolation*

Not good for man	Gen.	2	18
For prayer	Mat.	14	23
For leisure	Mark	6	30, 31

Solomon *peaceable*

Son of David	II Sam.	12	24
Called Jedidiah	II Sam.	12	24, 25
Succeeds David as king	I Ki.	1	11–48
Marries Pharaoh's daughter	I Ki.	3	1
His prayer for wisdom	I Ki.	3	5–14
Widsom and fame of	I Ki.	3	16–28
	I Ki.	4	29–34
Builds the temple	I Ki.	5, 6	
Builds his palace	I Ki.	7	1–12
Dedicates the temple	I Ki.	8	
God's covenant with	I Ki.	9	1–9
Visited by the queen of Sheba	I Ki.	10	1–13
His idolatry	I Ki.	11	1–8
Rebuked by God	I Ki.	11	9–25
Becomes very wealthy	II Chr.	9	13–28
Cruel and oppressive	II Chr.	10	4
Writer of many proverbs	I Ki.	4	32

son

Created by God	Gen.	6	2
A male child	Gen.	27	1
Denotes grandson	Gen.	29	5
Moses, a foster	Ex.	2	10
Figurative of man's relation to God	Ex.	4	22
Of a virgin	Mat.	1	23
Save s of thine handmaid	Ps.	86	16
A wise s maketh a glad father	Prov.	10	1
	Prov.	15	20
Unto us a s is given	Is.	9	6
S of the morning	Is.	14	12
The S of God	Dan.	3	25
	Luke	3	38
	John	1	34
	Acts	9	20
As a man spareth his own s	Mal.	3	17
No man knoweth the s	Mat.	11	27
The carpenter's s	Mat.	13	55
This is my beloved S	Mat.	17	5
Christ? whose s is he?	Mat.	22	42
Art thou the Christ, the S of the Blessed?	Mark	14	61
Only s of his mother	Luke	7	12
Father divided against the s	Luke	12	53
Only begotten S	John	1	18
	John	3	18

Men should honour the *S*	John	5	23
If the *S* shall make you free	John	8	36
The *s* of perdition	John	17	12
	II Thes.	2	3
The *s* of consolation	Acts	4	36
The *s* of a Pharisee	Acts	23	6
God, sending his own *S*	Rom.	8	3
Spared not his own *S*	Rom.	8	32
If a *s*, then an heir	Gal.	4	7
God hath spoken to us by His *S*	Heb.	1	2
Though he were a *S*, yet learned he obedience	Heb.	5	8
Scourgeth every *s* whom he receiveth	Heb.	12	6
He that hath the *S* hath life	I John	5	12
The Messiah	Mat.	3	17
Of man, Jesus	Mat.	12	8

Son of God

Fourth is like *S* of God	Dan.	3	25
If thou be the *S* of God, command	Mat.	4	3
Do with thee, Jesus thou *S* of God?	Mat.	8	29
Truth thou are *S* of God	Mat.	14	33
Thou be Christ the *S* of God	Mat.	26	63
I am the *S* of God	Mat.	27	43
Truly this was the *S* of God	Mat.	27	54
Jesus Christ the *S* of God	Mark	1	1
Saying, Thou art the *S* of God	Mark	3	11
	John	1	49
Shall be called *S* of God	Luke	1	35
Son of Adam, which was the *S* of God	Luke	3	38
The *S* of God?	Luke	22	70
This is the *S* of God	John	1	34
The only begotten *S* of God	John	3	18
Hear the voice of the *S* of God	John	5	25
Thou believe on the *S* of God?	John	9	35
I said, I am the *S* of God	John	10	36
S of God might be glorified	John	11	4
Made himself the *S* of God	John	19	7
Jesus is Christ, the *S* of God	John	20	31
He said, I believe that Jesus Christ is the *S* of God	Acts	8	37
That he is the *S* of God	Acts	9	20
Declared to be the *S* of God with	Rom.	1	4
For the *S* of God was not yea and nay	II Cor.	1	19
Faith of the *S* of God	Gal.	2	20
Of knowledge of *S* of God	Eph.	4	13
High priest, Jesus the *S* of God	Heb.	4	14
Themselves the *S* of God afresh	Heb.	6	6
Like to the *S* of God abideth	Heb.	7	3
Trodden under foot *S* of God	Heb.	10	29
For this purpose the *S* of God was	I John	3	8
Confess Jesus is the *S* of God	I John	4	15
Believeth Jesus is the *S* of God	I John	5	5
He that believeth on the *S* of God	I John	5	10
Believe on the name of *S* of God	I John	5	13
We know that the *S* of God is	I John	5	20
Things saith the *S* of God	Rev.	2	18

Song of degrees *for going up to Jerusalem*

A title given to fifteen psalms	Ps.	120–134	

songs *tunes*

Of salvation	Ex.	15	2
Solomon wrote many	I Ki.	4	32
Given by God	Job	35	10
Of praise to God	Ps.	28	7
	Ps.	96	1
Of thanksgiving	Ps.	69	30
To a well-beloved	Is.	5	1
Sung at the last supper	Mat.	26	30
Sung by Paul and Silas	Acts	16	25
Of Moses	Deut.	31	19, 21
Of Deborah	Judg.	5	12
Organized by David	I Chr.	6	31
Of the Lord, sang with offerings	II Chr.	29	27
A byword	Job	30	9
New	Ps.	33	3
	Ps.	40	3
In the night	Ps.	77	6
In captivity	Ps.	137	3, 4
Of fools	Eccl.	7	5
Book of the Bible	S. of S.	1	1

song writer *composer*

Solomon, a celebrated	I Ki.	4	32

son-in-law *husband of one's daughter*

The unjust	Gen.	30	37–42
An angry one	Judg.	15	6

An honourable one	I Sam.	22	14
Peter, a faithful	Mark	1	29, 30

soothsayer *see* sorcerers

sop *food steeped in a liquid*

Jesus gives some to Judas	John	13	25–30

Sopater *see* Sosipater

sope *see* soap

Sophereth *scribe*

Families of Solomon's servants	Ezra	2	55
	Neh.	7	57

sorcerers *magicians*

Utilized by Pharaoh	Ex.	7	11
Should be destroyed	Ex.	22	18
To be stoned	Lev.	20	27
Forbidden	Deut.	18	10–12
God judges against	Mal.	3	5
Simon bewitches Samaritans	Acts	8	9–11
Bar-jesus in Paphos	Acts	13	6–8
Consigned to eternal damnation	Rev.	21	8
Not among redeemed	Rev.	22	15

sore

Maketh *s* and bindeth up	Job	5	18
Thou hast thrust *s* at me	Ps.	118	13
They were *s* displeased	Mat.	21	15
Wept *s*	Acts	20	37
(*See* Is. 1:6; Heb. 10:29)			

sorrow *grief, affliction*

In childbirth	Gen.	3	16
Of Jacob for his sons	Gen.	42	38
Hannah's, relieved by prayer	I Sam.	1	1–18
Of David	II Sam.	15	30
Of David for Absalom	II Sam.	18	32, 33
Turns into joy	Job	41	22
	John	16	20
Of heathens, multiplied	Ps.	16	4
Many, for wicked	Ps.	32	10
Experience of life	Ps.	90	10
Even in laughter	Prov.	14	13
Spirit is broken	Prov.	15	13
Improves heart	Eccl.	7	3
Will be eliminated	Is.	25	8
	Is.	35	10
Messiah, a man of	Is.	53	3
Messiah carries our	Is.	53	4
Misery of Jerusalem	Lam.	1	12
Beginning of	Mat.	24	8
Of Jesus	Mat.	27	46
Of King Herod	Mark	6	21–27
Of Jesus' disciples	Mark	14	18, 19
	John	16	6
Healed by Jesus	Luke	4	18
Of Jesus for Lazarus' death	John	11	33–35
Continuous in Paul's heart	Rom.	9	2
Penitence is beneficial	II Cor.	7	9, 11
Godly, opposed to worldly	II Cor.	7	10
Eliminated by God	Rev.	21	4

Sosipater, Sopater *saving father*

Accompanies Paul	Acts	20	4
Kinsman of Paul	Rom.	16	21

Sosthenes *good strength*

Ruler of synagogue	Acts	18	17
Christian convert	I Cor.	1	1

soul *person, inner feelings*

Man endowed with	Gen.	2	7
Departs the body at death	Gen.	35	18
Atonement for	Lev.	17	11
Redemption of	Ps.	34	22
	Ps.	49	8, 15
Rest promised for	Mat.	11	28–30
Worth of	Mat.	16	26
	Mark	8	37

Characteristics of:

Seeks God with all its might	Deut.	10	12
Humbled by fasting	Ps.	35	13
Can be healed of sin	Ps.	41	4
Can be cast down in despair	Ps.	42	5
Human forces unable to kill	Mat.	10	28
Serve him with all your *s*	Deut.	11	13
Love the Lord with all your *s*	Deut.	13	3
	Josh.	22	5
The *s* of Jonathan was knit with *s* of David	I Sam.	18	1
Return with all their *s*	I Ki.	8	48
Set your *s* to seek the Lord	I Chr.	22	19

soul—continued

Life unto the bitter in *s*	Job	3	20
In whose hand is the *s* of every living thing	Job	12	10
If your *s* were in my *s* stead	Job	16	4
To deliver their *s* from death	Job	33	19
Redemption of their *s* is precious	Job	49	8
My *s* thirsteth for God	Job	63	1
Bless the Lord, O my *s*	Job	103	1
	Job	104	1
Return unto thy rest, O my *s*	Job	116	7
No man cared for my *s*	Ps.	142	4
Liberal *s* shall be made fat	Prov.	11	25
That the *s* be without knowledge, it is not good	Prov.	19	2
Hear, and your *s* shall live	Is.	55	3
If thou satisfy the afflicted *s*	Is.	58	10
Their *s* shall be as a garden	Jer.	31	12
Lord that made this *s*	Jer.	38	16
All *s* are mine	Ezek.	18	4
Sinned against thy *s*	Heb.	2	10
To destroy both *s* and body	Mat.	10	28
Lose his own *s*	Mark	8	36
In patience possess ye your *s*	Luke	21	19
Of one *s*	Acts	4	32
Let every *s* be subject unto higher power	Rom.	13	1
Your *s* and body be preserved	I Thes.	5	23
An anchor of the *s*	Heb.	6	19
Believe to saving of *s*	Heb.	10	39
Shall save a *s* from death	James	5	20
Lusts which war against the *s*	I Pet.	2	11
Commit the keeping of their *s* to him	I Pet.	4	19

sound
A noise:

Of a trumpet	Josh.	6	5, 20
Of shouting	II Sam.	6	15
Of feet	II Ki.	6	32
Of a harp	Ps.	92	3
Of waters	Rev.	1	15

Whole, correct:

Sound wisdom	Prov.	2	7
A heart	Prov.	14	30
Of doctrine	I Tim.	1	10
	I Tim.	4	3
	Tit.	1	9
	Tit.	2	1
Of mind	II Tim.	1	7
Of words	II Tim.	1	13
In faith	Tit.	2	2

sour grapes *spoiled, acid grapes*

Used figuratively	Is.	18	5
Eaten, teeth set on edge	Jer.	31	29, 30

sow: *to plant*

They that *s* wickedness, reap the same	Job	4	8
That *s* in tears shall reap in joy	Ps.	126	5
He that observeth the wind shall not *s*	Eccl.	11	4
In the morning *s* thy seed	Eccl.	11	6
That *s* beside all waters	Is.	32	20
S not among thorns	Jer.	4	3
S in righteousness, reap in mercy	Hosea	10	12
Thou shalt *s*, but not reap	Mic.	6	15
Ye have *s* much, and bring in little	Hag.	1	6
They *s* not	Mat.	6	26
Sower went forth to *s*	Mat.	13	3
	Mark	4	3
	Luke	8	5
Reapest that thou didst not *s*	Luke	19	21
He that *s* and he that reapeth	John	4	36
That which thou *s* is not quickened	I Cor.	15	36
He which *s* sparingly	II Cor.	9	6
Whatsoever a man *s*, that shall he also reap	Gal.	6	7

sowing wild oats

Punished in later life	Job	20	11
Lack of honour to parents	Prov.	30	11
Revelry and corruption	Is.	56	12
Reaps eternal damnation	Gal.	6	7, 8
Deprives of kingdom of heaven	Phil.	3	19

Spain *European country*

Paul wishes to visit	Rom.	15	24-28

spake

He *s*, and it was done	Ps.	33	9
They *s* against God	Ps.	78	19
I *s* unto you, rising up early	Jer.	7	13
Feared the Lord *s* often one to another	Mat.	3	16
Never man *s* like this man	John	7	46
God *s* to Moses	John	9	29

God *s* on this wise	Acts	7	6
I *s* as a child	I Cor.	13	11
God, who *s* in time past	Heb.	1	1
Refused him that *s* on earth	Heb.	12	25
Men of God *s* as they were moved	II Pet.	1	21

span *approximately nine inches*

Size of breastplate	Ex.	28	16
	Ex.	39	9
Measure of height	I Sam.	17	4
Of children	Lam.	2	20

spare *show mercy, set free*

I will *s* the place for their sakes	Gen.	18	26
S me according to thy mercy	Neh.	13	22
S me, that I may recover strength	Ps.	39	13
He shall *s* poor and needy	Ps.	72	13
He that *s* the rod	Prov.	13	24
Let not thy soul *s* for his crying	Prov.	19	18
S not, lift up thy voice	Is.	58	1
Should not I *s* Nineveh?	Jonah	4	11
I will *s* them, as a man *s* his own son	Mal.	3	17
Have bread enough and to *s*	Luke	15	17
He that *s* not his own Son	Rom.	8	32
Lest he also *s* not thee	Rom.	11	21
If God *s* not angels	II Pet.	2	4
(See II Cor. 9:6)			

speak

Taken upon me to *s* unto the Lord	Gen.	18	27
We cannot *s* bad or good	Gen.	24	50
He can *s* well	Ex.	4	14
As a man *s* to his friend	Ex.	33	11
Went in to *s*, with the Lord	Ex.	34	34
S, Lord, thy servant heareth	I Sam.	3	9
God *s* once, yea twice	Job	33	14
Yet to *s* on God's behalf	Job	36	2
I will hear what the Lord will *s*	Ps.	85	8
My mouth shall *s* the praise of the Lord	Ps.	145	21
S not in the ears of a fool	Prov.	23	9
A time to *s*	Eccl.	3	7
To *s* a word in season	Is.	50	4
I that *s* in righteousness	Is.	63	1
At the end it shall *s*	Hab.	2	3
S every man the truth	Zech.	8	16
	Eph.	4	25
How ye shall *s*	Mat.	10	19
	Mark	13	11
Every idle word that men shall *s*	Mat.	12	36
When all men *s* well of you	Luke	6	26
We *s* that we do know	John	3	11
We cannot but *s*	Acts	4	20
Permitted to *s* for thyself	Acts	26	1
That ye all *s* the same thing	I Cor.	1	10
In sight of God *s* we in Christ	II Cor.	2	17
We believe, and therefore *s*	II Cor.	4	13
We *s* not as pleasing men	I Thes.	2	4
To *s* evil of no man	Tit.	3	2
See that ye refuse not him that *s*	Heb.	12	25
Slow to *s*	James	1	19

speaking evil

Separates friends	Prov.	16	28
Must be accounted for	Mat.	12	36
To be discarded	Eph.	4	31
	I Pet.	2	1
Of no man	Tit.	3	2

spear *a weapon*

Used in war	II Sam.	23	8, 18
Stored in the tabernacle	II Chr.	23	9
Shall be beaten into pruninghooks	Is.	2	4
	Mic.	4	3
Thrust into Jesus' side	John	19	34

speckled

Israel's heritage is likened to	Jer.	12	9
Goats	Gen.	30	32-39

speech

Whole earth was of one *s*	Gen.	11	1
I am slow of *s*	Ex.	4	10
My *s* shall distil as dew	Deut.	32	2
Solomon's *s* pleased the Lord	I Ki.	3	10
Day unto day uttereth *s*	Ps.	19	2
Excellent *s* becometh not a fool	Prov.	17	7
Thy *s* is comely	S. of S.	4	3
Thy *s* shall be low out of the dust	Is.	29	4
Of deeper *s* than thou canst perceive	Is.	33	19
They *s* bewrayeth thee	Mat.	26	73
Not with excellency of *s*	I Cor.	2	1
His *s* is contemptible	II Cor.	10	10

Let your *s* be alway with grace	Col.	4	6
Sound *s*, that cannot be condemned	Tit.	2	8

speeder *one who races*

Jehu cited	II Ki.	9	20

spend *pay out, wear out*

They *s* their days in wealth	Job	21	13
They shall *s* their days in prosperity	Job	36	11
We *s* our years as a tale that is told	Ps.	90	9
Why *s* money for that which is not bread?	Is.	55	2
Very gladly *s* and be *s* for you	II Cor.	12	15

spent *used up, worn out*

The water was *s*	Gen.	21	15
Our money is *s*	Gen.	47	18
Your strength be *s* in vain	Lev.	26	20
My days are *s* without hope	Job	7	6
My life is *s* with grief	Ps.	31	10
I have *s* my strength for nought	Is.	49	4
Had *s* all that she had	Mark	5	26
	Luke	8	43
S their time to tell some new thing	Acts	17	21
The night is far *s*	Rom.	13	12

spices *aromatic vegetable substances*

Used as ointment	Ex.	30	23, 24
Used in temple	I Chr.	9	29
From Gilead	Gen.	37	25
Queen of Sheba	I Ki.	10	2
Tithed	Mat.	23	23
Scent Asa's tomb	II Chr.	16	14
Used as perfume	Ps.	45	8
	Prov.	7	17
Used for embalming	John	19	38–40

spider *web-spinning creature*

Housed in fragile web	Job	8	14
Exists even in palaces	Prov.	30	28
Web likened to evil-doing	Is.	59	5, 6

spies *secret agents*

Jacob accuses his brothers	Gen.	42	9
Sent to Canaan by Moses	Num.	13	1–3
Sent to Jericho by Joshua	Josh.	2	1–4
Sent throughout Israel by Absalom	II Sam.	15	10–12
Sent to watch Christ by priests	Luke	20	20
Exist in the church	Gal.	2	4
Received by Rahab	Heb.	11	31

spikenard *aromatic oil from herb*

Pleasant odour for king	S. of S.	1	12
Pleasant fruit and spice	S. of S.	4	13, 14
Christ anointed by a woman	Mark	14	3
Mary anoints Christ with	John	12	3

spirit

Of jealousy	Num.	5	14
Broken	Prov.	15	13
Of man	Eccl.	12	7
	Zech.	12	1
	I Cor.	2	11
Born of	John	3	5
Of truth	John	14	17
Of divination	Acts	16	16
Of Christ	Rom.	8	9
	I Pet.	1	11
Of bondage	Rom.	8	15
Of slumber	Rom.	11	8
Fruit of	Gal.	5	22
Of fear	II Tim.	1	7
Of antichrist	I John	4	3
Of angels	Heb.	1	7, 14
Evil	I Sam.	16	14–20
Dumb	Mark	9	17
Of error	I John	4	6
Of grace	Heb.	10	29
Humble	Prov.	16	19
	Is.	57	15
Of jealousy	Num.	5	14, 30
Of wisdom	Deut.	34	9
	Is.	11	2
Wounded	Prov.	18	14

Spirit, Holy *see* Holy Ghost

spiritual awakening *see* awakening, spiritual

spirituality *spiritual character*

Recommended mode of life	Mark	9	39–50
Samaritan woman perceives	John	4	10–14
	John	4	24–26
Comprises life and peace	Rom.	8	6
In Jesus' mind	Phil.	2	5
Produces salvation and godliness	Tit.	2	11–13

Falsely said to be mad	Hosea	9	7
Paul longs to impart	Rom.	1	11
Of the law	Rom.	7	14
Comparing	I Cor.	2	13
Judges all	I Cor.	2	15
Gifts	I Cor.	14	12
To restore the weak	Gal.	6	1
Of songs	Eph.	5	19
	Col.	3	16

spit *to eject from within mouth*

Humiliating insult	Num.	12	14
To heap shame	Deut.	25	9
Job suffers contempt of	Job	30	10
Inflicted on Jesus	Mat.	26	67

spoil *things taken, destroy*

At night he shall divide the *s*	Gen.	49	27
Necks of them that take *s*	Judg.	5	30
The people flew upon the *s*	I Sam.	14	32
They offered to the Lord of the *s*	II Chr.	15	11
Take the *s* of them for a prey	Esth.	3	13
	Esth.	8	11
That tarried at home divided the *s*	Ps.	68	12
Rejoice as one that findeth great *s*	Ps.	119	162
Than to divide the *s* with the proud	Prov.	16	19
Have no need of *s*	Prov.	31	11
Who gave Jacob for a *s*?	Is.	42	24
He shall divide the *s* with the strong	Is.	53	12
S of silver, *s* of gold	Nah.	2	9
Ye shall *s* the Egyptians	Ex.	3	22
All that pass by the way *s* him	Ps.	89	41
The little foxes, that *s* the vines	S. of S.	2	15
Woe to thee that *s*, and thou wast not *s*	Is.	33	1
When thou art *s*, what wilt thou do?	Jer.	4	30
S his goods	Mat.	12	29
	Mark	3	27
Beware lest any man *s* you	Col.	2	8
Having *s* principalities	Col.	2	15

spokesman *speaker for another*

Aaron, for Moses	Ex.	4	14–17

spot *mark, moral stain*

Lambs without *s*	Num.	28	3
	Num.	29	17
Their *s* is not the *s* of his children	Deut.	32	5
There is no *s* in thee	S. of S.	4	7
Can the leopard change his *s*?	Jer.	13	23
A glorious church, not having *s*	Eph.	5	27
Keep commandment without *s*	I Tim.	6	14
Offered himself without *s*	Heb.	9	14
As a lamb without *s*	I Pet.	1	19
That ye may found without *s*	II Pet.	3	14
These are *s* in your feasts	Jude		12

spring *season of*

Promised annual return of	Gen.	8	22
Described	Prov.	27	25
	S. of S.	2	11–13

spring

All my *s* are in thee	Ps.	87	7
He sendeth the *s* into valleys	Ps.	104	10
He turneth dry ground into water *s*	Ps.	107	35
Troubled fountain, and a corrupt *s*	Prov.	25	26
S up, O well	Num.	21	17
Neither doth trouble *s* out of the ground	Job	5	6
Truth shall *s* out of the earth	Ps.	85	11
Thine health shall *s* forth	Is.	58	8
The pastures do *s*	Joel	2	22
Seed should *s*, he knoweth not how	Mark	4	27
Well of water *s* up	John	4	14

Springs *see* Palestine Springs

sprinkling *a religious ceremony*

Oxen blood, by Moses	Ex.	24	6, 8
Blood of a bullock	Lev.	4	6
To cleanse lepers	Lev.	14	7
Of the house	Lev.	14	51
Of water	Ezek.	36	25
Of oil	Lev.	14	16
Of Christ's blood	Heb.	10	22
	I Pet.	1	2
Our hearts	Heb.	10	22
Blood of, speaks of better things	Heb.	12	24

spy *see* spies

stab *to wound with knife*

Asahel by Abner	II Sam.	2	22, 23
Abner by Joab	II Sam.	3	27
Ish-bosheth by Rechab and Baanah	II Sam.	4	5, 6
Amasa by Joab	II Sam.	20	10

stacte *drop*

Spice used for incense	Ex.	30	34

staff *pole*

With my *s* I passed over	Gen.	32	10
Eat it with *s* in hand	Ex.	12	11
The angel put forth end of his *s*	Judg.	6	21
Lay my *s* upon face of the child	II Ki.	4	29
Thou trustest upon the *s*	II Ki.	18	21
	Is.	36	6
Thy rod and *s* comfort me	Ps.	23	4
Lord doth take away the stay and *s*	Is.	3	1
Thou hast broken the *s* of his shoulder	Is.	9	4
As if the *s* should lift up itself	Is.	10	15
Lord hath broken the *s* of the wicked	Is.	14	5
Fitches are beaten out with a *s*	Is.	28	27
Where the grounded *s* shall pass	Is.	30	32
How is the strong *s* broken	Jer.	48	17
Took my *s*, even Beauty	Zech.	11	10
Taken nothing, save a *s* only	Mark	6	8
Leaning on the top of his *s*	Heb.	11	21

stairs

Went up with winding *s*	I Ki.	6	8
In secret places of the *s*	S. of S.	2	14
Paul stood on the *s*	Acts	21	40

stall *place in stable*

Out of the midst of the *s*	Amos	6	4
Be no herd in the *s*	Hab.	3	17
Grow up as calves of the *s*	Mal.	4	2
Loose his ox from the *s*	Luke	13	15

stammerers *people who stumble in speech*

Messiah will speak as	Is.	28	11
Will speak plainly	Is.	32	4
Cannot be understood	Is.	33	19

stand

S still, and see the salvation of the Lord	Ex.	14	13
	II Chr.	20	17
Ye *s* this day all of you before the Lord	Deut.	29	10
The Lord, before whom I *s*	I Ki.	17	1
	I Ki.	18	15
	II Ki.	3	14
	II Ki.	5	16
Two kings *s* not: how then shall we *s*?	II Ki.	10	4
To *s* for their life	Esth.	8	11
He shall *s* at latter day upon the earth	Job	19	25
The ungodly shall not *s* in judgment	Ps.	1	5
S in awe, and sin not	Ps.	4	4
Who shall *s* in his holy place?	Ps.	24	3
The counsel of the Lord *s* for ever	Ps.	33	11
Who may *s* in thy sight?	Ps.	76	7
Our feet shall *s* within thy gates	Ps.	122	2
If thou shouldest mark iniquities who shall *s*?	Ps.	130	3
Counsel of the Lord shall *s*	Prov.	19	21
A man diligent shall *s* before kings	Prov.	22	29
Who is able to *s* before envy?	Prov.	27	4
S not in an evil thing	Eccl.	8	3
Word of our God shall *s* for ever	Is.	40	8
S by thyself; I am holier than thou	Is.	65	5
S in the ways, ask for the old paths	Jer.	6	16
S in thy lot at end of days	Dan.	12	13
S, *s*, shall they cry	Nah.	2	8
Who shall *s* when he appeareth?	Mal.	3	2
House divided shall not *s*	Mat.	12	25
	Mark	3	25
Why *s* ye all the day idle?	Mat.	20	6
Why *s* ye gazing up into heaven?	Acts	1	11
This grace where in we *s*	Rom.	5	2
God is able to make him *s*	Rom.	14	4
S fast in the faith	I Cor.	16	13
S fast in the liberty	Gal.	5	1
S fast in one spirit	Phil.	1	27
Having done all, to *s*	Eph.	6	13
S fast in the Lord	Phil.	4	1
	I Thes.	3	8
The foundation of God *s* sure	II Tim.	2	19
The Judge *s* before the door	James	5	9
True grace of God wherein ye *s*	I Pet.	5	12
I *s* at the door and knock	Rev.	3	20
Who shall be able to *s*?	Rev.	6	17
The dead, small and great, *s* before God	Rev.	20	12

standard-bearer *man to carry banner*

Faints	Is.	10	18

star-gazers *astrologers*

Called upon to save Babylon	Is.	47	13

stars *lights in the sky*

Created by God	Gen.	1	16
Infinite in number	Gen.	15	5
	Jer.	33	22
Represent Joseph's brothers	Gen.	37	9
In their courses	Judg.	5	20
Morning	Job	38	7
	Rev.	2	28
Along with the moon rules the night	Ps.	136	9
For light	Jer.	31	35
Cast down	Dan.	8	10
Shine forever	Dan.	12	3
Of self-exaltation	Obad.		4
Signs in	Luke	21	25
Wandering	Jude		13
Crown of	Rev.	12	1
Planets	II Ki.	23	5
Orion	Job	9	9

stature *size of body*

Canaanites, of great	Num.	13	32
Saul tall of	I Sam.	9	1, 2
Philistine of Gath, a giant	II Sam.	21	20
Like a palm tree	S. of S.	7	7
Of cedar trees	Ezek.	19	11
Cannot change	Mat.	6	27
	Luke	12	25
Christian maturity	Eph.	4	13
Jesus' increased	Luke	2	52
Zacchaeus, of very small	Luke	19	1–3

statutes

Of the Lord	I Chr.	29	19
	Ps.	119	12, 16
He made a *s* and an ordinance	Ex.	15	25
Make them know the *s* of God	Ex.	18	16
A perepetual *s*	Lev.	3	17
	Lev.	16	34
	Lev.	24	9
The *s* of the Lord are right	Ps.	19	8
Hath changed my *s*	Ezek.	5	6
Walk in the *s* of life	Ezek.	33	15

stay *a support*

Lord was David's	II Sam.	22	19
Of bread and water	Is.	3	1
Of the tribes of Egypt	Is.	19	13

stead

He closed up the flesh in *s*	Gen.	2	21
Me another seed in *s* of Abel	Gen.	4	25
Abraham offered the ram in *s*	Gen.	22	13
Abide in *s* of the lad	Gen.	44	33
He shall be to thee in *s* of a mouth, thou shalt be to him in *s*	Ex.	4	16
That son that is priest in his *s*	Ex.	29	30
	Lev.	16	32
I have taken the Levites in *s* of all firstborn	Num.	3	12, 41, 45
	Num.	8	16
Mayest be to us in *s* of eyes	Num.	10	31
Risen up in your father's *s*	Num.	32	14
Esau dwelt in their *s*	Deut.	2	12
Dwelt in their *s*	Deut.	2	21–23
Whom he raised in their *s*	Josh.	5	7
I pray, her sister in *s*	Judg.	15	2
Saul, in whose *s* thou	II Sam.	16	8
He made Amasa captain in *s*	II Sam.	17	25
Sit on my throne in my *s*	I Ki.	1	30
Made me king in *s* of David	I Ki.	3	7
Rehoboam made in their *s*	I Ki.	14	27
Placed in cities of Samaria in *s* of Israel	II Ki.	17	24
Queen in *s* of Vashti	Esth.	2	4, 17
Were in my soul's *s*	Job	16	4
To thy wish in God's *s*	Job	33	6
Shall set others in their *s*	Job	34	24
In *s* of thy fathers shall	Ps.	45	16
Wicked cometh in his *s*	Prov.	11	8
Shall stand up in his *s*	Eccl.	4	15
In *s* of sweet smell there shall be stink, in *s* of	Is.	3	24
In *s* of the thorn shall come up fir tree, and in *s* of the brier	Is.	55	13
Who taketh strangers in *s* of her	Ezek.	16	32
Pray you in Christ's *s*	II Cor.	5	20
In thy *s* might have	Philem.		13
See reigned			

stealing *theft*

Forbidden	Ex.	20	15

Punishable by death	Deut.	24	7
Judgments against Israelites for	Hosea	4	2
Stealers shall not inherit the kingdom of heaven	I Cor.	6	9, 10
Should be ended	Eph.	4	28
Teach servants against	Tit.	2	9, 10

stedfastness *firmness*

Exhibited by God	Num.	23	19
	James	1	17
Exhortations to	Deut.	10	20
	I Cor.	15	58
	Phil.	4	1
	II Thes.	2	15
Under affliction	Job	2	10
	Ps.	44	17–19
	Rom.	8	35–37
A characteristic of the godly	Job	17	9
	John	8	31
Secured by the power of God	Ps.	55	22
	Ps.	62	2
The wicked devoid of	Ps.	78	8, 37
In keeping the faith	I Cor.	16	13
	I Pet.	5	9
In maintaining Christian liberty	Gal.	5	1
In well doing	Gal.	6	9

Exemplified:

Joshua	Josh.	24	15
Job	Job	2	3
David	Ps.	18	21, 22
Early Christians	Acts	2	42

Stephanas *crown*

Corinthian convert	I Cor.	1	16
	I Cor.	16	15, 17

Stephen *crowned*

One of seven deacons	Acts	6	1–8
Accused of blasphemy	Acts	6	9–15
Makes great defense for himself	Acts	7	1–53
Stoned to death	Acts	7	58
First Christian martyr	Acts	7	59, 60

steps

Neither go up by *s*	Ex.	20	26
But a *s* between me and death	I Sam.	20	3
Thou hast enlarged my *s*	II Sam.	22	37
	Ps.	18	36
Thou numberest my *s*	Job	14	16
Doth not he count my *s*?	Job	31	4
If my *s* hath turned out of the way	Job	31	7
The *s* of a good man are ordered by the Lord	Ps.	37	23
Nor have our *s* declined	Ps.	44	18
My *s* had well nigh slipped	Ps.	73	2
Order my *s* in thy word	Ps.	119	133
Thy *s* shall not be straitened	Prov.	4	12
The Lord directeth his *s*	Prov.	16	9
Not in man to direct his *s*	Jer.	10	23
Walk in *s* of that faith	Rom.	4	12
Walked we not in the same *s*?	II Cor.	12	18
That ye should follow his *s*	I Pet.	2	21

stewardship

Of silver and gold	Hag.	2	8
Faithful, rewarded	Mat.	16	27
Parable of the talents	Mat.	25	14–30
Of fellow man	Luke	10	30-37
The faithful, described	Luke	12	35–38
Sharing goods with the poor	Luke	19	8, 9
Of man's life	Rom.	14	8

stiff *excuse, sorry*

A *s*-necked people	Ex.	32	9
	Ex.	34	9
	Deut.	9	13
	Deut.	10	16
Speak not with a *s* neck	Ps.	75	5
Impudent children and *s*-hearted	Ezek.	2	4
Ye *s*-necked, ye always resist the Holy Ghost	Acts	7	51

still *without motion, quiet*

As *s* as a stone	Ex.	15	16
If we sit *s* here, we die	II Ki.	7	4
Beside the *s* waters	Ps.	23	2
Be *s*, and know that I am God	Ps.	46	10
Be not *s*, O God	Ps.	83	1
So that the waves thereof are *s*	Ps.	107	29
Their strength is to sit *s*	Is.	30	7
I have been *s*	Is.	42	14
Why do we sit *s*?	Jer.	8	14

Said to sea, Peace, be *s*	Mark	4	39
Good to have been there *s*	II Sam.	14	32
Dost thou *s* retain thine integrity	Job	2	9
He that is unjust, let him be unjust *s*	Rev.	22	11

stink *offensive odour*

River shall, of dead fish	Ex.	7	18
Bread does not	Ex.	16	23, 24
David's wounds	Ps.	38	5
Ointment, because of dead flies	Eccl.	10	1
Carcases of slain	Is.	34	3
Northern army shall	Joel	2	20
Lazarus' body	John	11	39, 43

stir *move about, arouse*

He lay down as a lion, who shall *s* him up?	Num.	24	9
Innocent *s* up himself	Job	17	8
Is so fierce that dare *s* him	Job	41	10
S up thyself, and awake	Ps.	35	23
And he did not *s* up all his	Ps.	78	38
S up thy strength, and come	Ps.	80	2
But grievous words *s*	Prov.	15	1
That ye *s* not up my love	S. of S.	2	7
	S. of S.	3	5
	S. of S.	8	4
The Lord shall *s* up a	Is.	10	26
Behold, I will *s* up the Medes	Is.	13	17
He shall *s* up jealousy like	Is.	42	13
He shall *s* up all against	Dan.	11	2
Shall *s* up his power against	Dan.	25	
That thou *s* up the gift	II Tim.	1	6
Meet to *s* you up	II Pet.	1	13
	II Pet.	3	1

stocks *wooden frame for punishment*

Job's feet tied in	Job	13	27
	Job	33	11
Jeremiah placed in	Jer.	20	2, 3
Mad prophets should be put in	Jer.	29	26
Paul and Silas placed in	Acts	16	19, 24

Stoicks *of the porch*

Group of philosophers	Acts	17	18

stomacher *ornamented girdle*

To be replaced by sackcloth	Is.	3	24

stone

Commandments engraved upon	Ex.	24	12
Precious stones in the breastplate and ephod	Ex.	28	9–21
Idols are made of	Deut.	4	28
Used in building altars	Josh.	8	31
Law of Moses written on	Josh.	8	32
Used as a witness	Josh.	24	26, 27
Used for a landmark	I Sam.	6	18
David slays Goliath with a	I Sam.	17	48, 49
Precious stones in the king's crown	II Sam.	12	30
Temple built of	I Ki.	5	17, 18
City wall built of	Neh.	4	3
Jesus' tomb sealed by	Mat.	27	60
To build houses	Is.	9	10
	Amos	5	11
Gotten from quarries	I Ki.	6	7
Hewers of	I Ki.	5	18
	II Ki.	12	12
Memorial pillars	Gen.	28	18–22
For closing sepulchers	Mat.	27	60
Throwing of	Judg.	20	16
In breastplate	Ex.	28	9–21
David kills Goliath with	I Sam.	17	49, 50
Of a dead man	I Sam.	25	37
Shall cry out	Hab.	2	11
Waterpots of	John	2	6

Figurative:

Of temptation	Is.	8	14
Of Christ	Is.	28	16
Of the impenitent heart	Ezek.	36	26
Of true believers	Mat.	16	18
Of Christ's rejection	Mat.	21	42–44

stones, precious *gems*

Adamant	Ezek.	3	9
Agate	Is.	54	12
Amethyst	Ex.	28	19
Beryl	Ex.	28	20
Carbuncle	Ezek.	28	13
Chalcedony	Rev.	21	19
Chrysolyte	Rev.	21	20
Chrysoprasus	Rev.	21	20
Coral	Job	28	18
Crystal	Rev.	22	1

stones, precious—*continued*

Diamond	Ex.	28	18
Emerald	Ex.	28	18
Jacinth	Rev.	21	20
Jasper	Rev.	21	11
Ligure	Ex.	39	12
Onyx	Gen.	2	12
Pearl	I Tim.	2	9
Ruby	Job	28	18
Sapphire	Ex.	28	18
Sardius	Ex.	28	17
Sardonyx	Rev.	21	20
Topaz	Ex.	28	17

stoning

Of wizards	Lev.	20	7
Witnesses lay hands on victim's head	Lev.	24	14
Of blasphemers	Lev.	24	16
A sabbath-breaker	Num.	15	32–36
Outside city gates	Deut.	17	2–5
	Acts	7	58
Achan, by Israelites	Josh.	7	20, 25
King David, by Shimei	II Sam.	16	5, 6
Adoram by all Israel	I Ki.	12	18
Naboth, by Belialites	I Ki.	21	13
Zechariah, for forsaking the Lord	II Chr.	24	20, 21
By one without sin	John	8	7
Jesus, for blasphemy	John	10	31, 33
Stephen	Acts	7	59
Paul	Acts	14	19
Prophets	Heb.	11	37

store *supply*

Blessed be thy basket and *s*	Deut.	28	5
All this *s* cometh of thine hand	I Chr.	29	16
Our garners affording all manner of *s*	Ps.	144	13
None end of the *s*	Nah.	2	9
Let every one lay by him in *s*	I Cor.	16	2
Laying up in *s* a good foundation	I Tim.	6	19
By the same word are kept in *s*	II Pet.	3	7

store cities *for military supplies*

Built by Solomon	I Ki.	9	19
	II Chr.	8	4, 6
Conquered by Ben-hadad	II Chr.	16	4
Built by Jehoshaphat	II Chr.	17	12

storehouse *place for storing things*

Opened by Joseph	Gen.	41	56
Hezekiah builds, for his riches	II Chr.	32	27, 28
Bring tithes to	Mal.	3	10

stork *a long-legged bird*

Unclean bird	Lev.	11	19
Nests in fir trees	Ps.	104	17
Regular in migration	Jer.	8	7
Large wingspread	Zech.	5	9

storm *atmospheric disturbance*

Thunder and hail	Ex.	9	23–25
Hailstones	Josh.	10	11
Windy	Ps.	55	8
Made calm	Ps.	107	29
At sea	Is.	25	4
Difficulties likened to	Jonah	1	4–14
Calmed by Jesus	Mark	4	37, 39
	Luke	8	23
While Paul is at sea	Acts	27	14–22

straight

Make thy way *s*	Ps.	5	8
Crooked cannot be made *s*	Eccl.	1	15
	Eccl.	7	13
Make *s* in the desert a highway	Is.	40	3
Crooked shall be made *s*	Is.	40	4
	Is.	42	16
	Is.	45	2
	Luke	3	5
Cause them to walk in a *s* way	Jer.	31	9
Make his paths *s*	Mat.	3	3
	Mark	1	3
	Luke	3	4
	John	1	23
Street which is called *s*	Acts	9	11
Make *s* paths for your feet	Heb.	12	13

(*See* Mark 1:21; Luke 12:54; Jas. 1:24)

straightforwardness *directness*

Divine instruction	Prov.	4	27

strait *difficulty, narrow*

I am in a great *s*	II Sam.	24	14
He shall be in *s*	Job	20	22
I am in a *s* betwixt two	Phil.	1	23
Place where we dwell is too *s*	II Ki.	6	1

Place is too *s* for me	Is.	49	20
Enter in at the *s* gate	Mat.	7	13
	Luke	13	24

(*See* Mic. 2:7; Luke 12:50; Acts 26:5; II Cor. 6:12)

strange *foreign, different*

Fire	Lev.	10	1
Way of man is	Prov.	21	8
Lord's act of judgment	Is.	28	21
Miracles performed	Luke	5	26
Behaviour of Christians	I Pet.	4	4

stranger *a foreigner, an unknown person*

Loved by God	Deut.	10	18
To be treated kindly	I Ki.	8	41, 43
Numerous in Solomon's time	II Chr.	2	17
Oppression of, condemned	Ps.	94	6
Under God's protection	Ps.	146	9
Used figuratively	Mat.	25	35
Buried in separate places	Mat.	27	7
One who gives thanks to God	Luke	17	18
To be entertained	Heb.	13	2

Mosaic law concerning:

Not to eat of the passover while uncircumcised	Ex.	12	43, 48
Not to work on the sabbath	Ex.	20	10
To be loved	Lev.	19	34
	Deut.	10	19
Not to practice idolatry	Lev.	20	2
Not to blaspheme God	Lev.	24	16
Subject to civil law	Lev.	24	22
May be purchased as servants	Lev.	25	44
Not to be chosen as kings	Deut.	17	15
Marriage to, forbidden	Deut.	25	5
To have the law read to them	Deut.	31	12
To be judged righteously	Deut.	1	16

stratagem *device for deception*

By Joshua, in battle	Josh.	8	1–22
By Absalom, successful	II Sam.	14	28–33

straw, stubble *grain stalks*

Rebekah has enough	Gen.	24	25
Used with brick	Ex.	5	7–16
Consumed	Ex.	15	7
Levite has sufficient	Judg.	19	19
Food for horses	I Ki.	4	28
Carried away by wind	Job	21	18
Lion shall eat	Is.	11	7
Burned by fire	Is.	47	14
	Mal.	4	1
Scattered by wind	Jer.	13	24
Wicked devoured like	Nah.	1	10
Foundation of	I Cor.	3	12

street *paved road*

In Damascus named after Ahab	I Ki.	20	34
Used by wicked women	Prov.	7	6–23
"Lion is in"	Prov.	26	13
Doors shut on	Eccl.	12	4
Mourners go about in	Eccl.	12	5
Carcases torn in	Is.	5	25
Crying for wine in	Is.	24	11
People act idolatrous	Jer.	7	17, 18
For bakers	Jer.	37	21
Incense burned in	Jer.	44	21
Children swoon in	Lam.	2	11
Filled with slain	Ezek.	11	6
"Wailing shall be in"	Amos	5	16
Chariots shall rage in	Nah.	2	4
Made waste	Zeph.	3	6
Old people shall dwell in	Zech.	8	4
Playground for children	Zech.	8	5
People pray in	Mat.	6	5
Named Straight	Acts	9	11
Of pure gold	Rev.	21	21

strength *power, force*

Lord is our	Ex.	15	2
	Ps.	27	1
Man shall not gain through	I Sam.	2	9
Given Elijah	I Ki.	19	2–8
Power of God	Job	12	13
	Ps.	68	34
For upright, way of Lord is	Prov.	10	29
Wisdom better than	Eccl.	9	16
God is, for poor	Is.	25	4
Isaiah, exhorts God's	Is.	51	9
God shows His	Luke	1	51
Man is without	Rom.	5	6
In weakness	II Cor.	12	9, 10

Spiritual, from God	Eph.	3	16
The Lord is my	Ps.	18	2
	Is.	12	2
The way of the Lord is	Prov.	10	29
Wisdom is better than	Eccl.	9	16
Of the ground	Gen.	4	12
Of a unicorn	Num.	23	22
Food gives	I Sam.	28	22
To be ascribed to God	Ps.	68	34
Of an ox	Prov.	14	4
Knowledge increases	Prov.	24	5
The Lamb is worthy to receive	Rev.	5	12

strife *conflict*

Punishment for	Ps.	55	9
Forbidden	Prov.	3	30
Appeased by slowness to anger	Prov.	15	18
Fools engage in	Prov.	18	6
Seek God's protection from	Jer.	18	19
Avoided by Jesus	Luke	9	52-56
Exists in the early church	I Cor.	1	11
Leads to mutual destruction	Gal.	5	15
Excludes from heaven	Gal.	5	20, 21
Warning against	Phil.	2	3
Avoid questions that lead to	II Tim.	2	14

Caused by:

Hatred	Prov.	10	12
Pride	Prov.	13	10
Wrath	Prov.	15	18
Scorning	Prov.	22	10
Drunkenness	Prov.	23	29, 30
Gossiping	Prov.	26	20
Foolish talk	I Tim.	6	4
Lust	James	4	1
Anger	Prov.	29	22

strike

S hands	Job	17	3
	Prov.	22	26
He shall *s* through kings	Ps.	110	5
Till a dart *s* through	Prov.	7	23
Did *s* Jesus with their hands	Mark	14	65

striker *argumentative person*

Unqualified for bishopric	I Tim.	3	3

stripes *strokes of a whip*

Limited to forty for punishment	Deut.	25	3
Punishment for children	II Sam.	7	14
Punishment for wickedness	Ps.	89	32
Sometimes futile	Prov.	17	10
For fools	Prov.	19	26
Healed through Messiah's	Is.	53	5
For dishonest servants	Luke	12	47
To be endured	I Cor.	6	5
Paul abundant in	II Cor.	11	23

stripes, forty *see* forty stripes

stripling *youth*

David, when he slays Goliath	I Sam.	17	55, 56

strive

Spirit shall not always *s*	Gen.	6	3
If men *s* together and	Ex.	21	18
Plead with them that *s* with me	Ps.	35	1
S not without cause	Prov.	3	30
He shall not *s* nor cry	Mat.	12	19
S to enter in at strait gate	Luke	13	24
S with me in your prayers	Rom.	15	20
The servant of the Lord must	II Tim.	2	24

strong

If I speak of strength, he is *s*	Job	9	19
As a *s* man to run a race	Ps.	19	5
The Lord *s* and mighty	Ps.	24	8
Be thou my *s* rock	Ps.	31	2
Thou art my *s* refuge	Ps.	71	7
Who is a *s* Lord like unto thee?	Ps.	89	8
Name of the Lord is a *s* tower	Prov.	18	10
The battle is not to the *s*	Eccl.	9	11
Love is *s* as death	S. of S.	8	6
We have a *s* city	Is.	26	1
For that he is *s* in power	Is.	40	26
He shall divide the spoil with the *s*	Is.	53	12
Their Redeemer is *s*	Jer.	50	34
Let the weak say, I am *s*	Joel	3	10
A *s* man armed keepeth his palace	Luke	11	21
S in faith	Rom.	4	20
We that are *s* ought to bear infirmities of weak	Rom.	15	1
We are weak, but ye are *s*	I Cor.	4	10
Need of milk, and not of *s* meat	Heb.	5	12

Out of weakness were made *s*	Heb.	11	34
(*See* Job 17:9; Jer. 20:7; I Cor. 1:25; 10:22)			

strong drink *see* wine

strong hold *secure refuge, fortress*

Spies to uncover	Num.	13	19
Israelites make	Judg.	6	2
David lives in, in wilderness	I Sam.	23	14, 19, 29
David captures Zion	II Sam.	5	7
Tyre is	II Sam.	24	7
Set on fire	II Ki.	8	12
Fortified by Rehoboam	II Chr.	11	11
Tyre overthrown	Is.	23	11
Assyrian seeks refuge	Is.	31	9
Dibon's to be destroyed	Jer.	48	18
Kerioth's surprised	Jer.	48	41
Israel's, destroyed in Jerusalem	Lam.	2	2, 5
Conquering king shall take over	Dan.	11	24, 39
Jerusalem is Zion's	Mic.	4	8
Lord is, in day of trouble	Nah.	1	7
Like fig trees	Nah.	3	12
Must be fortified	Nah.	3	14
Shall be derided	Hab.	1	10
Tyrus builds one	Zech.	9	3
God is our	Zech.	9	12

stubble *see* straw

Wrath consumed them as *s*	Ex.	15	7
As *s* before the wind	Job	21	18
	Ps.	83	13
Conceive chaff, bring forth *s*	Is.	33	11
As driven *s*	Is.	41	2
I will scatter them as *s*	Jer.	13	24
Upon this foundation, hay, *s*	I Cor.	3	12

stubbornness *obstinacy*

Of son, punishable by stoning	Deut.	21	18-21
Of wicked	Judg.	2	19
A rebellious generation	Ps.	78	8
Loses salvation	Prov.	1	24-32
Characteristic of lewd women	Prov.	7	11
Israelites show	Is.	48	4-8
	Jer.	32	33
Of Jews against Egypt	Jer.	46	16, 17

study *applying oneself*

Of God's law, richly rewarded	Josh.	1	8
In hearts of righteous	Prov.	15	28
Of destruction by evil men	Prov.	24	2
Of scriptures	Acts	17	10, 11
To be quiet	I Thes.	4	11
To prove God's approval	II Tim.	2	15

stuff *household goods, belongings*

Jacob's, searched	Gen.	31	37
Joseph tells brothers not to consider	Gen.	45	20
Mosaic law concerning	Ex.	22	7
Israelites have sufficient	Ex.	36	7
Stolen goods hidden among	Josh.	7	11
Saul hides among	I Sam.	10	22
Two hundred of David's men guard	I Sam.	25	13
	I Sam.	30	24
Ezekiel prepares for moving	Ezek.	12	3, 4, 7
Sometimes must be left behind	Luke	17	31

stumble *falter*

Foot shall not *s*	Prov.	3	23
Know not at what they *s*	Prov.	4	19
None shall be weary nor *s*	Is.	5	27
They *s* in judgment	Is.	28	7
We *s* at noonday	Is.	59	10
S and fall	Jer.	46	6
	Dan.	11	19
Ye have caused many to *s*	Mal.	2	8
They *s* at that stumblingstone	Rom.	9	32
Whereby thy brother *s*	Rom.	14	21
Which *s* at the word	I Pet.	2	8

stumblingblock

Must be taken away	Is.	57	14
Do not put in brother's path	Rom.	14	13, 21
Christ, to the Jews	I Cor.	1	23

subject *submissive*

And was *s* to them	Luke	2	51
Even the devils are *s* to us	Luke	10	17
Is not *s* to the law of	Rom.	8	7
Creature was made *s* to vanity	Rom.	8	20
Let every soul be *s* to the	Rom.	13	1
Spirits of prophets are *s*	I Cor.	14	32
Son also himself be *s* to him	I Cor.	15	28
Church is *s* to Christ	Eph.	5	24
As though living in the world, are ye *s*?	Col.	2	20

subject—*continued*

Put them in mind to be *s*	Tit.	3	1
Lifetime *s* to bondage	Heb.	2	15
Elias was *s* to like	James	5	17
Servants, be *s* to your	I Pet.	2	18
And powers being made *s*	I Pet.	3	22
All of you be *s* one to another	I Pet.	5	5

subjugation *bringing under a yoke*

Total	I Sam.	13	9–23
Of Saul, through blindness	Acts	9	1–9

submission *yielding, surrendering*

Eli, to Lord's punishment	I Sam.	3	11–18
David, to tragic loss	II Sam.	12	15–23
Christ, to will of God	Luke	22	42
All souls, to God	Rom.	13	1–7
	James	4	7
	I Pet.	5	6
Wives, to husbands	Eph.	5	22
Younger people, to elders	I Pet.	5	5

substance *material, wealth*

Shall they come with great *s*	Gen.	15	14
Bless, Lord, his *s*	Deut.	33	11
Nor shall his *s* continue	Job	15	29
Thou dissolvest my *s*	Job	30	22
They leave their *s* to babes	Ps.	17	14
My *s* was not hid from thee	Ps.	139	15
Honour the Lord with thy *s*	Prov.	3	9
He that be usury increaseth his *s*	Prov.	28	8
I have found me out *s*	Hosea	12	8
I will consecrate their *s*	Mic.	4	13
Ministered to him of their *s*	Luke	8	3
Wasted his *s*	Luke	15	13
In heaven a better *s*	Heb.	10	34
Faith is the *s* of things hoped for	Heb.	11	1

substitution

The offering for the one giving it	Lev.	1	4
	Lev.	16	21, 22
Levites for the firstborn	Num.	3	12, 41
Life of Ahab for Benhadad	I Ki.	20	42
Christ for sinner	Is.	53	4–6

subtilty *craft, cunning*

Of serpent	Gen.	3	1
Of Jacob	Gen.	27	35
Of Joseph's brothers	Gen.	37	29–32
Jonadab uses	II Sam.	13	3
Wish to take Jesus by	Mat.	26	4
Elymas accused by Paul	Acts	13	10

success *prosperity*

Of Jacob	Gen.	30	40, 43
Through God's law	Josh.	1	7–9
Pitfalls of	Judg.	7	1–3
Wisdom and humility in	I Sam.	18	3–16
Of Jotham, in his rule	II Chr.	27	1–6
Material, opposed to spiritual	Mat.	16	26
Comes from God	I Cor.	3	4–7

Succoth *booths*

Jacob builds home here	Gen.	33	17
Israelites encamp at	Ex.	12	37
	Ex.	13	20
	Num.	33	5, 6
Valley town allotted to Gad	Josh.	13	27
Elders refuse to aid Gideon	Judg.	8	5–17

suffering *enduring pain*

Of Messiah, predicted	Is.	53	3–9
Persecution of Christians	Mat.	5	11
Of Christ, great	Mat.	26	38
	Mark	15	34
Of apostles	Acts	5	41
	I Cor.	4	10
In death	II Cor.	4	11
To reign with Christ	II Tim.	2	12
Moses prefers	Heb.	11	24, 25

For Christ:

As joint-heirs	Rom.	8	17–26
Consolation in	II Cor.	1	7
Paul's duty	Phil.	1	29
Filling up the afflictions of Christ	Col.	1	24
All godly will	II Tim.	3	12
To perfect church	I Pet.	5	10

Of Christ:

Made perfect by	Heb.	2	9–18
Learned obedience by	Heb.	5	8, 9
For sins	I Pet.	3	18
	I Pet.	4	1

suicide *self-murder*

Of Samson	Judg.	16	21–30

Of Saul	I Sam.	31	4
Of Saul's armourbearer	I Sam.	31	5
Of Ahithophel	II Sam.	17	23
Of Zimri	I Ki.	16	18
Of Judas	Mat.	27	3–5
Paul prevents	Acts	16	25–28
Contemplated	Job	3	
Elijah	I Ki.	19	4
Jonah	Jonah	4	8

summer *warmest season*

Promised	Gen.	8	22
Period of drought	Ps.	32	4
Made by God	Ps.	74	17
No snow during	Prov.	26	1
Fruit ripens	Is.	28	4
	Amos	8	1, 2
Fig tree sprouts leaves before	Mat.	24	32

sun

Created by God	Gen.	1	14, 16
Appointed to rule the day	Gen.	1	16
	Ps.	136	8
Not to be worshipped	Deut.	4	19
	Deut.	17	3
Illustrative of God's power	Ps.	84	11
Produces and ripens fruit	Deut.	33	14
Destructive to human life	Ps.	121	6
	Is.	49	10
Made to praise and glorify God	Ps.	148	3
"Nothing new under the"	Eccl.	1	9
Rising and setting of	Eccl.	1	5
Darkens colour of the skin	S. of S.	1	6
"Shines on the evil and the good"	Mat.	5	45
Symbolic of the glory of Christ	Mat.	17	2

Miracles connected with:

Stands still for a day	Josh.	10	12, 13
Shadow put back on the dial	II Ki.	20	11
Darkened at the crucifixion	Luke	23	44, 45
Darkened as a judgment	Ex.	10	21–23
	Joel	2	10, 31
	Mic.	3	6

Sunday *see sabbath*

sun dial *time indicator dependent on sun*

Shows receding of sun	Is.	38	8

sundry *various, many*

God's revelation	Heb.	1	1

sunstroke *illness due to excessive exposure to sun*

Cause of child's death	II Ki.	4	18–20

sup

Make ready wherewith I may *s*	Luke	17	8
Took the cup, when he had *s*	I Cor.	11	25
I will *s* with him, and he with me	Rev.	3	20

superscription *inscription*

On money	Mat.	22	19, 20
On the cross	Mat.	27	37, 38
	Luke	23	38

superstition *excessive fear of gods*

Romans question Festus	Acts	25	19

Examples of:

Elders of Israel	I Sam.	4	3
Syrian soldiers	I Ki.	20	23
Heathen	Jer.	10	2
Seafarers	Jonah	1	4–16
People of Lystra	Acts	14	11
People of Athens	Acts	17	22
Barbarians	Acts	28	4

supper *evening meal*

Banquets for celebration	Mark	6	21
Lord's instituted	Luke	22	20
Prepared for Jesus at Bethany	John	12	2
Jesus washes disciples' feet at	John	13	2–5

supplication *petition*

To God directly	Job	8	5
	Ps.	119	170
	Phil.	4	6
Heard by Lord	Ps.	6	9
Should be acceptable to God	Jer.	37	20
Jacob's, to angel	Hosea	12	4
Of Jesus' disciples	Acts	1	14
In the Spirit	Eph.	6	18

Sur *turning aside*

Temple gate	II Ki.	11	6
Called "gate of the foundation"	II Chr.	23	5

sure *certain*

Be *s* your sin will find you out	Num.	32	23

Covenant ordered and **s**	II Sam.	23	5
No man is **s** of life	Job	24	22
His commandments are **s**	Ps.	111	7
Make **s** thy friend	Prov.	6	3
His waters shall be **s**	Is.	33	16
The **s** mercies of David	Is.	55	3
	Acts	13	34
The foundation of God standeth **s**	II Tim.	2	19
Your calling and election **s**	II Pet.	1	10
A more **s** word of prophecy	II Pet.	1	19

surety *security for a loan*

Judah will be, for Benjamin	Gen.	43	9
Should be, for one's servant	Ps.	119	122
For strangers, unwise	Prov.	11	15
For debts, discouraged	Prov.	22	26
Of Jesus	Heb.	7	22
Of a	Gen.	15	13
	Gen.	18	13

surfeiting *overindulging*

Undesirable	Luke	21	34

surgery *removal of diseased parts*

Of froward tongue	Prov.	10	31
Of offending hand	Mat.	5	30
Task of the Spirit	Rom.	8	13

surname *family name*

Jacob called Israel	Is.	45	4
Lebbaeus called Thaddaeus	Mat.	10	3
James and John called Boanerges	Mark	3	17
Judas called Iscariot	Luke	22	3
Joseph called Justus	Acts	1	23
Joses called Barnabas	Acts	4	36
Simon called Peter	Acts	10	5
John called Mark	Acts	12	12
Judas called Barsabas	Acts	15	22

surrender *yield*

Of bodies	Dan.	3	28
Complete, to Jesus	Mark	10	21, 22
A widow's money	Mark	12	41–44
Of power	I Cor.	9	12
Of Paul, complete	Phil.	3	8

Susanna *lily*

Ministers to Jesus	Luke	8	3

suspicion *believing something is bad*

A feigned	Gen.	42	7–12
Joseph's brothers fearful	Gen.	50	14, 15
Saul's, of David and Ahimelech	I Sam.	22	13–16
Joab's, unjustified	II Sam.	3	20–25
Joseph's, allayed	Mat.	1	18–25

swaddling clothes *bands of cloth wrapped around newborn*

Cloud likened to	Job	38	9
Baby Jesus wrapped in	Luke	2	7, 12

swallow *long-winged bird*

Builds nests	Ps.	84	3
Flies about	Prov.	26	2
Chatters	Is.	38	14
Migratory	Jer.	8	7

swallow

Earth	Num.	16	30, 34
	Rev.	12	16
Joab of the inheritance of the Lord	II Sam.	20	19, 20
The Lord of them that hate Him	Ps.	21	9
Oppressions of man	Ps.	56	1, 2
The innocent by sinners	Prov.	1	12
Lips of the fool will	Eccl.	10	12
Death by victory	Is.	25	8
	I Cor.	15	54
Jonah by a fish	Jonah	1	17
A camel by hypocrites	Mat.	23	24
By captivity	Hosea	8	7, 8

swan *web-footed water bird*

Not to be eaten	Lev.	11	13, 18
	Deut.	14	16

swear *take oath*

Ye shall not **s** by my name falsely	Lev.	19	12
That **s** to his hurt	Ps.	15	4
He that **s**, as he that feareth an oath	Eccl.	9	2
Unto me every tongue shall **s**	Is.	45	23
Shall **s** by the God of truth	Is.	65	16
Thou shalt **s**, The Lord liveth	Jer.	4	2
Every one that **s** shall be cut off	Zech.	5	3
S not	Mat.	5	34
	James	5	12
Because of **s** the land mourneth	Jer.	23	10
By **s**, and lying, they break out	Hosea	4	2

swearing *using profanity*

Blasphemy prohibited	Ex.	20	7
Condemned by Jesus	Mat.	5	34–37
	James	5	12
Peter guilty of	Mat.	26	73, 74
See oaths			

swearing falsely

Punishment for	Lev.	6	1–5
Forbidden	Lev.	19	12
	Mat.	5	33
Will bring a curse upon the house	Zech.	5	1–4
Hateful to God	Zech.	8	17

sweat *perspiration*

Sign of labour	Gen.	3	19
Of Jesus, bloody	Luke	22	44
Priests shall not wear clothes causing	Ezek.	44	18

sweet *pleasant to taste*

Waters made	Ex.	15	25
David as a psalmist	II Sam.	23	1
Counsel	Ps.	55	14
Meditation of Lord	Ps.	104	34
Words of Lord	Ps.	119	103
Sleep is	Prov.	3	24
	Eccl.	5	12
Pleasant words	Prov.	16	24
Stolen waters are	Prov.	9	17
Bitter things to hungry	Prov.	27	7
Bitter confused with	Is.	5	20
Melody	Is.	23	16
Wine is	Mic.	6	15
Of honey	Rev.	10	9, 10

swift *fast*

Feet **s** in running to mischief	Prov.	6	18
The race is not to the **s**	Eccl.	9	11
The Lord rideth upon a **s** cloud	Is.	19	1
Feet are **s** to shed blood	Rom.	3	15
(See Job 7:6; 9:25; Ps. 147:15)			

swim

The iron did **s**	II Ki.	6	6
Spread forth hands to **s**	Is.	25	11
Waters to **s** in	Ezek.	47	5

swine *hogs, pigs*

Unclean, not to be eaten	Lev.	11	7
	Deut.	14	8
Unworthy	Prov.	11	22
	Mat.	7	6
Abomination to God	Is.	65	4
Blood also abomination	Is.	66	3, 17
Run into sea	Mat.	8	28–32
Wallow in mire	II Pet.	2	22

sword *a weapon*

Used in war	Num.	21	24
Ehud's worn on his leg	Judg.	3	21
Used for punishing criminals	I Sam.	13	33
Frequently has two edges	Ps.	149	6
Will be made into plowshares	Is.	2	4
	Mic.	4	3
Is one of God's four sore judgments	Ezek.	14	21
Plowshares made into, in time of war	Joel	3	10
Used in self-defense	Luke	22	36
Sometimes used for self-destruction	Acts	16	27

Figurative:

Of judgment	Deut.	32	41
Of deep mental anguish	Ps.	42	10
	Luke	2	35
Of a malicious tongue	Ps.	57	4
	Prov.	25	18
Of God's word	Eph.	6	17
	Heb.	4	12

Sychar *drunken*

Town in Samaria where Jesus teaches	John	4	5–39

Sychem, Shechem *shoulder*

Camp of Abraham	Gen.	12	6
Land purchased by Abraham	Gen.	33	18, 19
	Josh.	24	32
Religious center	Josh.	24	1
Town of Ephraim	Josh.	20	7
Capital of Jeroboam	I Ki.	12	1–20
Son of Hamor	Gen.	34	1–31
Son of Gilead	Num.	26	30, 31
Son of Shemida	I Chr.	7	19

sycomore, sycamore *shade tree*

Massive in size	I Ki.	10	27
Destroyed by frost	Ps.	78	47
Changed into cedars	Is.	9	10

sycomore, sycamore—*continued*

Bears figs	Amos	7	14
Zacchaeus greets Jesus from	Luke	19	1–5

Syene *low*

City of Egypt	Ezek.	29	10
	Ezek.	30	6

symbols *signs or marks*

Rainbow	Gen.	9	12, 13
Circumcision	Gen.	17	11
Passover	Ex.	12	3–28
The pillar of cloud	Ex.	13	21, 22
Darkness-God's inscrutability	Ex.	20	21
The smitten rock	Ex.	17	6
	I Cor.	10	4
The brasen serpent	Num.	21	8, 9
Star in the east	Mat.	2	2
Manna	John	6	31–58
Wine-of Christ's blood	Mat.	26	27–29
Tabernacle	Heb.	8	2, 5
	Heb.	9	1–12
Canaan-of rest	Heb.	3	11, 12
Bow-shot by Jonathan	I Sam.	20	21–37
Men meeting Saul	I Sam.	10	2–7
Rain and thunder	I Sam.	12	16–18
Rent altar	I Ki.	13	3, 5
Rent vail	Mat.	27	51
Nakedness	Is.	20	2–4
Almond rod	Jer.	1	11
Sticks	Ezek.	37	16
Shadow on dial	II Ki.	20	8–11
Fruit basket	Amos	8	1, 2
Book cast into the Euphrates	Jer.	51	63
Ezekiel's beard	Ezek.	5	1–4
Plumb line	Amos	7	7, 8

sympathy *sharing another's feelings*

Not for murderer	Deut.	19	11–13
Job's friends silent	Job	2	11–13
Job's in his prosperity	Job	29	12–17
Should be sensible	Is.	58	7
Of the Lord for all of us	Is.	63	9
Jeremiah's, for the Jews	Jer.	9	1
Of Jesus for bereaved	Luke	7	11–13
Of Samaritan	Luke	10	30–35
Of women for Jesus	Luke	23	25–28
For the weak	Acts	20	35
For Paul	Acts	21	10–14
For the excommunicated	II Cor.	2	6–8
Christian responsibility	Gal.	6	2
For the unfortunate	Heb.	13	3

synagogue

Place of assembly	Acts	13	43
	James	2	2
A place for worship	Ps.	74	8
	Acts	13	5, 14
Christ preaches and teaches in	Mat.	4	23
	Mark	1	39
Christ performs miracles in	Mat.	12	9, 10
Offenders are punished in	Mat.	23	34
Each sect has its own	Acts	6	9
The apostles preach and teach in	Acts	9	20
	Acts	13	5
As a court	Luke	12	11
	Mat.	10	17
	Acts	22	19
Law expounded	Mat.	4	23
	Mark	1	39
Of Satan	Rev.	2	9
	Rev.	3	9

Syntyche *fortunate*

Christian woman of Philippi	Phil.	4	2

Syracuse

City on island of Sicily, visited by Paul	Acts	28	12

Syria, Aramaea

The country around Damascus	II Sam.	8	5
Conquest by David	II Sam.	8	5–13
Includes the city of Damascus	II Sam.	8	6
Inhabited by warlike people	I Ki.	20	23, 25
Conquest by Jeroboam	II Ki.	14	25, 28
Besieged by king of Assyria	II Ki.	16	7–9
Fame of Jesus extends through	Mat.	4	24
Paul journeys to	Acts	9	1–3
Paul converted near Damascus	Acts	9	3–19
Paul preaches in	Acts	15	41
Prophecies concerning	Is.	7	8–16
	Amos	1	3–5
Subject by the Romans	Luke	2	2
Letters of the church sent to	Acts	15	23

Syrophenician *native of Stria*

Healed by Jesus	Mark	7	26–30

T

Taanach, Tanach *sandy*

King of, conquered by Joshua	Josh.	12	21
Allotted to Manasseh	Josh.	17	11
Given to Levites	Josh.	21	25
Canaanites not driven out	Judg.	1	27
Site of battle	Judg.	5	19–22
City of Joseph's descendants	I Chr.	7	29

tabering *drumming*

Beating of breasts in bereavement	Nah.	2	7

tabernacle *dwelling, tent*

Purpose of	Ex.	25	8
Pattern of, revealed to Moses	Ex.	25	9
All males made to visit three times each year	Ex.	30	11–16
Made of offerings of the people	Ex.	35	4–29
Completed	Ex.	39	32
Filled with glory	Ex.	40	34–38
Bezaleel and Aholiab gifted in building	Ex.	31	2–6
Dedicated	Lev.	8	10, 11
Punishment for defiling	Lev.	15	31
Offerings brought to	Lev.	17	4
A movable tent	II Sam.	7	6, 7
Brought to the temple by Solomon	I Ki.	8	1, 4, 5
	II Chr.	5	5

Description of:

Furniture of	Ex.	25	10
	Ex.	27	1
	Ex.	38	1
Most holy place of	Ex.	26	34
Curtains of	Ex.	27	9
Court of	Ex.	27	18
Outer covering	Ex.	36	14
Frame	Ex.	36	20
Holy place of	Ex.	38	1
Second covering	Ex.	39	34

Is set up at:

Mount Sinai	Ex.	40	18, 19
Gilgal	Josh.	5	10, 11
Shiloh	Josh.	18	1
Nob	I Sam.	21	1–6
Mount Zion	I Chr.	15	1
	I Chr.	16	1, 2
Gibeon	I Chr.	16	39

New Testament explanation of:

Altar	Rom.	3	25
	I John	2	2
	Heb.	7	25
Veil	Heb.	10	20
Holy place	Heb.	9	2–7, 23, 24

Titles of:

Sanctuary	Ex.	25	8
Tabernacle of the congregation	Ex.	27	21
	Ex.	33	7
Tabernacle of testimony	Ex.	38	21
Tabernacle of witness	Num.	17	7, 8
House of the Lord	Josh.	6	24
Temple of the Lord	I Sam.	1	9
	I Sam.	3	3

Tabitha *see Dorcas*

table

Richly spread	I Ki.	10	5
Prophets eat at Jezebel's	I Ki.	18	19
Prepared by God	Ps.	23	5
Wisdom furnishes	Prov.	9	2
Dogs eat crumbs from	Mat.	15	27
Idolators cannot share Lord's	I Cor.	10	21

Of shewbread:

Of shittim wood	Ex.	37	10–16
In tent of congregation	Ex.	40	22

table *tablet, writing surface*

Of the law:

Broken by Moses	Ex.	32	15–19
Renewed	Ex.	34	1–5

Of the heart	Jer.	17	1
	II Cor.	3	3
Zacharias uses to write	Luke	1	63
Tables of stone			
Containing the law	Ex.	24	12
	Ex.	31	18
Broken by Moses	Ex.	32	19
	Deut.	9	17
	Ex.	34	1
	Deut.	10	1
(*See* II Cor. 3:3)			
Tabor *height*			
Mountain border of Issachar	Josh.	19	12, 22
	Ps.	89	12
Site of war between Canaanites and Barak	Judg.	4	6–14
Town of Zebulun	I Chr.	6	77
Oak of, near Bethel	I Sam.	10	3
tabret *a musical instrument*			
Possessed by prophets	I Sam.	10	5
Played at feasts	Is.	5	12
taches *buckles or clasps*			
Of gold	Ex.	26	6
Of brass	Ex.	26	11
Holds vail	Ex.	26	33
tact *discernment*			
Of Jacob	Gen.	32	4, 5
Of Gideon	Judg.	8	1–3
Turns away wrath	Prov.	15	1
In management of malcontents	I Sam.	11	7, 12–15
In conciliation	II Sam.	2	5–7
In arbitration	I Ki.	3	24–28
In organizing the temple music	I Chr.	15	16–24
Exemplified by Jesus	John	4	7–14
Of the church council at Jerusalem	Acts	21	20–25
In arraying factions against each other	Acts	23	6–10
In preaching	I Cor.	9	19–22
In stimulating benevolent giving	II Cor.	8	1–9
Tadmor *city of palms*			
A city in the wilderness	I Ki.	9	18
Tahapanes, Tahpanhes			
A city in Egypt	Jer.	2	16
Location of Pharaoh's house	Jer.	43	9
Destroyed	Jer.	43	10–13
Called Tehaphnehes	Ezek.	30	18
Tahath *beneath, humility*			
A camp in the wilderness	Num.	33	26, 27
Son of Kohath	I Chr.	6	24
Two Ephraimites	I Chr.	7	20
Tahpenes *grandeur*			
Queen of Egypt	I Ki.	11	18–20
tailoring *workmanship of a tailor*			
A priest's garments	Ex.	39	1–29
take			
I will *t* you for a people	Ex.	6	7
Not *t* the name of Lord in vain	Ex.	20	7
	Deut.	5	11
T us for thine inheritance	Ex.	34	9
He knoweth the way that I *t*	Job	23	10
Then the Lord will *t* me up	Ps.	27	10
T not thy Holy Spirit from me	Ps.	51	11
I will *t* the cup of salvation	Ps.	116	13
T with you words	Hosea	14	2
T with thee one or two more	Mat.	18	16
T that thine is, and go thy way	Mat.	20	14
T, eat	Mat.	26	26
	Mark	14	22
	I Cor.	11	24
Soul, *t* thine ease	Luke	12	19
He shall *t* of mine	John	16	15
Why not rather *t* wrong?	I Cor.	6	7
If ye *t* it patiently	I Pet.	2	20
That no man *t* thy crown	Rev.	3	11
If any man *t* away from this prophecy	Rev.	22	19
tale			
We spend our years as a *t*	Ps.	90	9
That carry *t* to shed blood	Ezek.	22	9
Their words seemed as *t*	Luke	24	11
(ar.) number, Ex. 5:18; I Chr. 9:28.			
talebearers *spreaders of gossip*			
Forbidden	Lev.	19	16
No truth in their hearts	Ps.	15	1–3
Reveal secrets	Prov.	11	13
Separate friends	Prov.	17	4
Their words are wounds	Prov.	18	8
Use flattery	Prov.	20	19
Causes strife	Prov.	26	20

talent *ancient weight and money unit*			
A weight for metals	Ex.	25	39
	I Chr.	29	7
A monetary unit	I Ki.	16	24
	II Ki.	23	33
The parable of	Mat.	25	14–29
"Talitha cumi" *"maiden arise"*			
Spoken by Jesus	Mark	5	41
talk			
God doth *t* with man	Deut.	5	24
T of them when thou sittest	Deut.	6	7
Will ye *t* deceitfully for him?	Job	13	7
T of thy righteousness	Ps.	71	24
I will *t* of thy doings	Ps.	77	12
T of thy power	Ps.	145	11
It shall *t* with thee	Prov.	6	22
Let me *t* with thee of thy judgments	Jer.	12	1
While he *t* with us by the way	Luke	24	32
It is he that *t* with thee	John	9	37
I will not *t* much with you	John	14	39
A man full of *t*	Job	11	2
Might entangle him in his *t*	Mat.	22	15
Nor foolish *t*	Eph.	5	4
Talmai *bold*			
A giant, son of Anak	Num.	13	22, 33
King of Geshur	II Sam.	3	3
Talmon *oppressive*			
A porter	I Chr.	9	17
Descendants return from captivity	Ezra	2	42
Tamah, Thamah *laughter*			
Called Thamah	Ezra	2	53
Descendants return from Babylon	Neh.	7	55
Tamar, Thamar *palm tree*			
Wife of Er	Gen.	38	6–30
	Mat.	1	3
Daughter of David	II Sam.	13	1
Daughter of Absalom	II Sam.	14	1
A city on southern border of Palestine	Ezek.	47	19
Tammuz *son of life*			
A Babylonian god	Ezek.	8	14
Tanach *see* Taanach			
tanner *one who tans hides*			
A man in Joppa	Acts	9	43
tapestry *heavy, handwoven textile*			
Hung in the tabernacle	Ex.	26	1
Woven with gold thread	Ex.	39	3
Used for idolatrous worship	II Ki.	23	7
Used in the palace of kings	Esth.	1	6
Used to cover beds	Prov.	7	16
A sign of prosperity	Prov.	31	22
tares *weeds*			
Parable of	Mat.	13	24–43
target *article of armour*			
Made of brass	I Sam.	17	6
Made of beaten gold	I Ki.	10	16
Worn by spearman	II Chr.	14	8
tarry *stay, delay, wait*			
T all night	Gen.	19	2
Why *t* the wheels of his chariots?	Judg.	5	28
If we *t* till morning light	II Ki.	7	9
She that *t* at home	Ps.	68	12
He that telleth lies shall not *t* in my sight	Ps.	101	7
They that *t* long at the wine	Prov.	23	30
My salvation shall not *t*	Is.	46	13
Though it *t*, wait for it	Hab.	2	3
The bridegroom *t*	Mat.	25	6
T ye here, and watch	Mat.	26	38
	Mark	14	34
He went in to *t* with them	Luke	24	29
If I will that he *t*	John	21	22
Why *t* thou? Arise and be baptized	Acts	22	16
T one for another	I Cor.	11	33
Will come, and will not *t*	Heb.	10	37
(*See* Ps. 40:17; 70:5)			
Tarshish, Tharshish *established*			
Son of Javan	Gen.	10	4
A trading center of importance	I Ki.	10	22
	Ezek.	27	12
Visited by Jonah	Jonah	1	3
Son of Bilhan	I Chr.	7	10
A Persian prince	Esth.	1	14
Tarsus			
A city of Cilicia	Acts	21	39
Birthplace of Paul	Acts	22	3

taste

T of manna like wafers	Ex.	16	31
The *t* of it as *t* of fresh oil	Num.	11	8
Is there any *t* in the white of an egg?	Job	6	6
How sweet are thy words to my *t*	Ps.	119	103
Fruit was sweet to my *t*	S. of S.	2	3
His *t* remained in him	Jer.	48	11
Doth not mouth *t* meat?	Job	12	11
O *t* and see that the Lord is good	Ps.	34	8
Some which shall not *t* of death	Mat.	16	28
	Mark	9	1
	Luke	9	27
None bidden shall *t* of my supper	Luke	14	24
Keep my saying, he shall never *t* of death	John	8	52
Touch not, *t* not	Col.	2	21
Should *t* death for every man	Heb.	2	9
Have *t* of the heavenly gift	Heb.	6	4
Have *t* that the Lord is gracious	I Pet.	2	3

tattooing *indelibly marking the skin*

Forbidden	Lev.	19	28

taught

Thou hast *t* them the good way	II Chr.	6	27
He *t* the people knowledge	Eccl.	12	9
Their fear is *t* by precept of men	Is.	29	13
Thy children shall be *t* of the Lord	Is.	54	13
Though I *t* them, rising up early	Jer.	32	33
He *t* as one having authority	Mat.	7	29
	Mark	1	22
Thou hast *t* in our streets	Luke	13	26
They shall be all *t* of God	John	6	45
Him *t* in the word	Gal.	6	6
If ye have been *t* by him	Eph.	4	21
As anointing hath *t* you	I John	2	27

taunt *reproach, insulting remark*

Will deliver them to be a *t*	Jer.	24	9
A reproach and a *t*	Ezek.	5	15

taverns, The three

A place near Rome	Acts	28	15

tax collector *a gatherer of revenue*

An overseer of tribute	II Sam.	20	24
One who is stoned to death	II Chr.	10	18
Unpopular	Mat.	9	11
Matthew, a former	Luke	3	12, 13
Zaccheus is one	Luke	19	2–10

taxes *revenue*

Paid in provisions	I Ki.	4	7–28
Personal	II Ki.	15	20
On land	II Ki.	23	35
Priests exempted from	Ezra	7	24
Paid in wheat	Amos	5	11
Paid by Jesus	Mat.	17	24–27
"Render unto Caesar"	Mat.	22	17
Decree of Caesar, all to pay	Luke	2	1

teachers *instructors*

Not obeyed	Prov.	5	13
Are improtant	Is.	30	20
Shine as the firmament	Dan.	12	3
In the early church	Acts	13	1
Talent given by God	Eph.	4	11
Of the law	I Tim.	1	7
Women as	Tit.	2	3
Should be trained	Heb.	5	12

teachers, false *see* false teachers

teaching *giving instruction*

Of art and crafts	Ex.	35	30–35
Commanded	Lev.	10	11
Jesus teaches with authority	Mark	1	21, 22
Is necessary	Acts	8	27–35
One to another	Col.	3	16
Ministers should be prepared for	II Tim.	2	24
Of Moses	Ex.	4	15
Responsibility of Levites	Lev.	10	11
	Deut.	24	8
Responsibility of parents	Deut.	6	1–8
Moses of Israel	Deut.	6	1
Ezra of Israel	Ezra	7	10
Of Sinners	Ps.	25	8, 9
	Ps.	51	13
The fear of the Lord	Ps.	34	11
To pray	Luke	11	1
Job of the Holy Ghost	Luke	12	12
	John	14	26
Old women to teach young	Tit.	2	4
Needed by Christians	Heb.	5	12

tears

Observed by God	Ps.	56	8
	Is.	38	3–5
Wiped away	Rev.	7	17
None in heaven	Rev.	21	4
Mine eye poureth out *t*	Job	16	20
I water my couch with *t*	Ps.	6	6
My *t* have been my meat	Ps.	42	3
Put my *t* into bottle	Ps.	56	8
The bread of *t*	Ps.	80	5
They that sow in *t*	Ps.	126	5
I will water thee with my *t*	Is.	16	9
Lord will wipe away *t*	Is.	25	8
Oh that mine eyes were a fountain of *t*	Jer.	9	1
Refrain thine eyes from *t*	Jer.	31	16
Mine eyes do fail with *t*	Lam.	2	11
Neither shall thy *t* run down	Ezek.	24	16
Covering altar of Lord with *t*	Mal.	2	13
To wash his feet with *t*	Luke	7	38
Ceased not to warn with *t*	Acts	20	31
Offered up supplications with *t*	Heb.	5	7
He sought it carefully with *t*	Heb.	12	17
God shall wipe away *t*	Rev.	7	17
	Rev.	21	4

Tebeth

The tenth month of the Jewish year	Esth.	2	16

teeth

White with milk	Gen.	49	12
"Skin of my"	Job	19	20
Broken by God	Ps.	3	7
Of the wicked are as swords	Prov.	30	14
Of the threshing instrument	Is.	41	15
Set on edge	Jer.	31	29
Flesh in	Num.	11	33
Of beasts	Deut.	32	24
Of lions	Job	4	10
	Rev.	9	8
Of Leviathan	Job	41	14
As swords	Prov.	30	14
Set on edge	Jer.	31	29
Of iron	Dan.	7	19

Tekel *see* Mene

Tekoah *trumpet*

A fortified city of Judah	II Chr.	11	5, 6
Wise woman of, intercedes	II Sam.	14	2–20
Fortress	II Chr.	20	20
A victim of enemies	Jer.	6	1
Residence of Amos	Amos	1	1

tell *to speak*

T the stars	Gen.	15	5
T it not in Gath	II Sam.	1	20
T the towers thereof	Ps.	48	12
If I were hungry, I would not *t* thee	Ps.	50	12
Who can *t* what shall be after?	Eccl.	6	12
That which hath wings shall *t*	Eccl.	10	20
Who can *t* if God will turn?	Jonah	3	9
T him his fault	Mat.	18	15
T it unto the church	Mat.	17	
Neither *t* I you	Mat.	21	27
	Luke	20	8
T how great things	Mark	5	19
We cannot *t*	Mark	11	33
	Luke	20	7
T that fox	Luke	13	32
Canst not *t* whence	John	3	8
He will *t* us all things	John	4	25
To *t* or hear some new thing	Acts	17	21

Tema *a desert*

A prince, son of Ishmael	Gen.	25	15, 16
A people of Arabia	Job	6	19
Land of	Is.	21	14
Judgment of	Jer.	25	23

Teman, Temani *the south*

Son of Eliphaz	Gen.	36	11, 15
A tribe	Gen.	36	34
Noted for wisdom	Jer.	49	7, 20
Condemnation of	Amos	1	12
God's presence there	Hab.	3	3
A duke of Edom	Gen.	36	42

temperance *self-control*

In eating	Prov.	23	1–3
Approved	Dan.	1	11–16
Exhortations	Rom.	14	21
	I Pet.	2	11, 12
In all things	I Cor.	9	25
Fruit of the Spirit	II Pet.	1	6

tempest *a furious storm*

Will be sent upon the wicked	Ps.	11	6
Calmed by God	Ps.	107	29
Jonah's ship caught in	Jonah	1	4
Calmed by Jesus	Mat.	8	24–26
Paul's ship caught in	Acts	27	18
Job broken by	Job	9	17
Rain of, on the wicked	Ps.	11	6
With wind	Ps.	55	8
Of hail	Is.	28	2
A covert from	Is.	32	2
Judgment upon Ammon	Amos	1	14
Figurative of apostates	II Pet.	2	17

temple, Herod's

Jesus drives moneychangers from the	Mat.	21	12, 13
Miracles performed in	Mat.	21	14, 15
Destruction foretold	Mat.	24	1, 2
Veil of, rent at time of crucifixion	Mat.	27	51
Jesus teaches in	Mark	11	27–33
Zacharias' vision here	Luke	1	5–23
	Luke	1	57–64
Jesus brought to	Luke	2	21–39
Jesus in, when a youth	Luke	2	46
Forty-six years in building	John	2	20
Solomon's porch	John	10	23
Paul's vision in	Acts	22	17–21

temple, idolatrous

Of Dagon	I Sam.	5	2
At Bethel	I Ki.	12	31, 33
Of Rimmon	II Ki.	5	18
Of Baal	II Ki.	10	21, 27
At Babylon	II Chr.	36	7
Of Diana, at Ephesus	Acts	19	27

temple, Solomon's

David forbidden to build	II Sam.	7	2–12
Solomon commissioned to build	II Sam.	7	13
On threshingfloor of Araunah	II Sam.	24	18–24
Materials for, furnished by Hiram	I Ki.	5	8–18
Built by Solomon	I Ki.	6	1–38
Dedication of	I Ki.	8	1–66
Holiness of	I Ki.	8	10
Destroyed by Nebuchadnezzar	II Ki.	25	9–17
Site of	I Chr.	21	28–30
Greatness of	II Chr.	2	5, 6
Restoration of, ordered by Cyrus	Ezra	1	7–11
Beauty of	Is.	64	11
Destruction of, foretold	Is.	66	6

Pillaged by:

Shishak	I Ki.	14	25–28
Jehoash	II Ki.	12	18
Hezekiah	II Ki.	18	16
Asa	II Chr.	16	2
Joash	II Chr.	25	23, 24
Ahaz	II Chr.	28	21, 24

Repaired by:

Jehoash	II Ki.	12	4–14
Hezekiah	II Chr.	29	3–30
Josiah	II Ki.	23	5–10

temple, spiritual

Of the body of Jesus	Mat.	26	61
Of the indwelling of God	I Cor.	3	16, 17
Must be kept holy	II Cor.	6	6–18
Of the kingdom of Christ	Rev.	14	15, 17

temple, the second

Restored by Zerubbabel	Ezra	1	1–11
Building of, suspended	Ezra	4	1–24
Resumed	Ezra	4	24
Completed	Ezra	6	14, 15
Dedicated	Ezra	6	15–18
Inferior to Solomon's	Ezra	3	12

temporal blessings *earthly blessings*

Given to every beast and fowl	Gen.	1	30
Unceasing	Gen.	8	22
Promised by God to Abraham	Gen.	22	17
A gift of God	Lev.	26	4–10
A promise of	Is.	30	23–26
To those who seek	Mat.	6	25–34

temporal blessings *see* blessings

tempt *to try, test*

God did *t* Abraham	Gen.	22	1
Wherefore do ye *t* the Lord?	Ex.	17	2
Shall not *t* the Lord	Deut.	6	16
	Mat.	4	7
	Luke	4	12
I will not ask, neither will I *t* he Lord	Is.	7	12

They that *t* God are even delivered	Mal.	3	15
Why *t* ye me?	Mat.	22	18
	Mark	12	15
	Luke	20	23
Agreed together to *t* the Spirit	Acts	5	9
Why *t* ye God?	Acts	15	10
Will not suffer you to be *t*	I Cor.	10	13
Lest thou also be *t*	Gal.	6	1
Lest the tempter *t* you	I Thes.	3	5
Hath suffered, being *t*	Heb.	2	18
In all points *t* like as we are	Heb.	4	15
God cannot be *t*, neither *t* he any man	James	1	13

temptation *enticement*

Often arises from:

Appetite	Gen.	25	29–33
Evil associates	Prov.	1	10
Covetousness	Prov.	28	20
The devil	Mat.	4	1–11
Poverty	Mat.	4	2, 3
Prosperity	Mat.	4	8
Lusts	James	1	14
Of Christ	Mat.	4	1–11
A concealed	Mat.	22	15–22
Is a trial of faith	James	1	2, 3
Deliverance promised	II Pet.	2	9

Exemplified:

Eve	Gen.	3	1, 4, 5
Joseph	Gen.	39	7
Balaam	Num.	22	15
Achan	Josh.	7	21
David	II Sam.	11	2
Jeroboam	I Ki.	15	30
Peter	Mark	14	67–71
Paul	II Cor.	12	7
	Gal.	4	14
By Satan	I Chr.	21	1
Hezekiah	II Chr.	32	30
By false prophets	Deut.	13	3
Of Nazarites	Amos	2	12
Pray not to be led into	Luke	11	4
Victory over	I Cor.	10	13
To rejoice in	I Pet.	1	6
Resistance to	Gen.	39	7–10
	Job	31	1
	Job	5	12
	James	4	7
	Ps.	73	

tempters *enticers*

Will be destroyed	Deut.	13	6–16
Should be resisted	Prov.	1	10–19
"Shall fall into own pit"	Prov.	28	10
Against Jesus	Mat.	4	3
Fail	I Thes.	3	4–8

temptress *a female enticer*

Eve	Gen.	3	1–6
Potiphar's wife	Gen.	39	7–19
Delilah	Judg.	16	5–20
Jezebel	I Ki.	21	7
Zeresh	Esth.	5	14
Job's wife	Job	2	9, 10
Harlots	Prov.	5	3–6

ten

Years	Gen.	16	3
Curtains	Ex.	26	1
Women	Lev.	26	26
Shekels of gold	Num.	7	14
Portions	Josh.	17	5
Pieces of silver	Luke	15	8

Ten Commandments, Decalogue

Enumerated	Ex.	20	3–17
Written on two tablets of stone	Ex.	31	18
A covenant with God	Deut.	4	13
Copied by Joshua	Josh.	8	30, 32
Quoted by Jesus	Mat.	19	18, 19
Law of, is spiritual	Mat.	5	28
	Rom.	7	14
Spoken by God	Ex.	20	1
	Deut.	5	4, 22
Written by God	Ex.	32	16
	Ex.	34	1, 28
	Deut.	4	13
	Deut.	10	4
Conscience testifies to	Rom.	2	15
Designed to lead to Christ	Gal.	3	24
Established by faith	Rom.	3	31

Ten Commandments, Decalogue—*continued*

Gives the knowledge of sin	Rom.	3	20
	Rom.	7	7
Man by nature	Rom.	7	5
	Rom.	8	7
Man cannot be justified by	Acts	13	39
	Rom.	3	20, 28
	Gal.	2	16
	Gal.	3	11
Man's duty to keep	Eccl.	12	13
Sin is a transgression of	I John	3	4
To be used lawfully	I Tim.	1	8
Summed up by Christ	Mat.	22	35–40
All men have transgressed	Rom.	3	9, 19
Believers:			
Delight in	Ps.	119	77
	Rom.	7	22
Freed from the bondage of	Rom.	6	14
	Rom.	7	4, 6
	Gal.	3	13
Freed from the curse of	Gal.	13	13
Have written on their hearts	Jer.	31	33
Keep	Ps.	119	55
Lament over the violation of by others	Ps.	119	136
Love	Ps.	119	97, 113
Pledge themselves to walk in	Neh.	10	29
Pray for power to keep	Ps.	119	34
Pray to understand	Ps.	119	18
Prepare their hearts to seek	Ezra	7	10
Should make the subject of their conversation	Ex.	13	9
Should remember	Mal.	4	4
Christ:			
Came to fulfill	Mat.	5	17
Explained	Mat.	7	12
	Mat.	22	37–40
Magnified	Is.	42	21
Given:			
Through Moses	Ex.	31	18
	John	7	19
To the Israelites	Ex.	20	2
	Ps.	78	5
Obedience to:			
A characteristic of saints	Rev.	12	17
Of prime importance	I Cor.	7	19
A test of love	I John	5	3
Requires:			
Obedience of the heart	Ps.	51	6
	Mat.	5	28
	Mat.	23	37
Perfect obedience	Deut.	27	26
	Gal.	3	10
	James	2	10

tender *kind, loving*

Thine heart was *t*	II Ki.	22	19
	II Chr.	34	27
Cause the *t* herb to spring	Job	38	27
No more be called *t*	Is.	47	1
Grow up as a *t* plant	Is.	53	2
Through the *t* mercy of our God	Luke	1	78
Lord is pitiful and of *t* mercy	James	5	11

tents

Origin and antiquity	Gen.	4	20
Used by patriarchs	Gen.	13	5
Separate, for females of family	Gen.	24	67
Separate, for servants	Gen.	31	33
Pitched when cloud remained	Num.	9	17, 18
Of Israelites in the desert	Ex.	33	8
Used by the Arabs	Is.	13	20
Figurative use	Is.	40	22
	Is.	54	2
Fastened by cords and stakes	Is.	54	2
Inquiry about the Canaanites	Num.	13	19
Door of	Num.	16	27
Murmuring in	Deut.	1	27
Of Philistines	I Sam.	17	53
Spoiled	II Ki.	7	16
Of Kedar	S. of S.	1	5

Terah *station*

The father of Abraham, dies at Haran	Gen.	11	24–32
	I Chr.	1	26
	Luke	3	34
Worships idols	Josh.	24	2
An Israelite camp in the wilderness	Num.	33	1, 27, 28

teraphim *images of household gods*

Stolen by Rachel	Gen.	31	19
Searched for	Gen.	31	30–35

In the house of Micah	Judg.	17	5
Taken by Danites	Judg.	18	17–20
A part of heathen worship	Hosea	3	4

terror *dread*

By night	Ps.	91	5
Of the Lord	II Cor.	5	11
Removed by faith	I Pet.	3	14
The *t* of God	Gen.	35	5
The sword without and *t* within	Deut.	32	25
T shall make him afraid	Job	18	11
In the *t* of the shadow of death	Job	24	17
Destruction was a *t* to me	Job	31	23
The *t* of death are fallen upon me	Ps.	55	4
Not afraid for *t* by night	Ps.	91	5
Thine heart shall meditate *t*	Is.	33	18
Thou shalt be far from *t*	Is.	54	14
Be not a *t* unto me	Jer.	17	17
I will make thee a *t*	Jer.	20	4
	Ezek.	26	21
Thou shalt be a *t*	Ezek.	27	36
	Ezek.	28	19
Rulers are not a *t* to good works	Rom.	13	3
Knowing *t* of the Lord	II Cor.	5	11
Be not afraid of their *t*	I Pet.	3	14

Tertius *third*

Secretary to Paul	Rom.	16	22

Tertullus *triple-hardened*

An orator	Acts	24	1
Accuses Paul	Acts	24	2–8

test

Of Abraham	Gen.	22	1
The wilderness wanderings	Deut.	8	2
By false prophets	Deut.	13	1–3
Of Hezekiah	II Chr.	32	31
Of Job	Job	1	8–21
Of Israel	Ps.	66	10, 11
	Zech.	13	9
Worketh patience	James	1	2–5, 12
Of faith	I Pet.	1	6, 7
For Israelites	Judg.	3	1–7
A password used as	Judg.	12	5, 6
Of armour	I Sam.	17	38, 39
Of intelligence	I Ki.	10	1–3
Of fire	I Ki.	18	22–39
By diet	Dan.	1	12–16

testament *a solemn covenant*

In the blood of Christ	Mat.	26	28
Explanation of the new	Heb.	9	15
Ark of, in heaven	Rev.	11	19
New testament	II Cor.	3	6

testimony *affirmation or declaration*

Ark of, *see* ark
Legal, *see* witnesses

Altar of	Josh.	22	26–28
Makes known God's deeds	I Chr.	16	8, 9
	Is.	12	4, 5
A constant duty	Mal.	3	16
In the home	Mark	5	18, 19
Inspired by miracles	Luke	8	38, 39
Before God	Luke	12	8, 9
Of the disciples	John	15	27
He established a *t* in Jacob	Ps.	78	5
Thy *t* are very sure	Ps.	93	5
Thy *t* are my delight	Ps.	119	24
I turned my feet to thy *t*	Ps.	119	59
Thy *t* are wonderful	Ps.	119	129
Bind up that *t*	Is.	8	16
To the law and to the *t*	Is.	8	20
For a *t* against them	Mat.	10	18
	Mark	13	9
No man receiveth his *t*	John	3	32
We know that his *t* is true	John	21	24
Gave *t* to the word of his grace	Acts	14	3
Declaring the *t* of God	I Cor.	2	1
The *t* of our conscience	II Cor.	1	12
Enoch had this *t*	Heb.	11	5
The *t* of Jesus	Rev.	1	2
	Rev.	19	10

(*See* Ex. 25:16, 21)

tetrarch *a Roman ruler*

Puts John in prison	Mat.	14	1–3
Officer of Caesar	Luke	3	1

Thaddaeus *breast*

Called Lebbaeus	Mat.	10	3
An apostle	Mark	3	14, 18

thanks *express gratitude*

He prayed, and gave *t*	Dan.	6	10
He took the cup, and gave *t*	Mat.	26	27
	Luke	22	17
He giveth God *t*	Rom.	14	6
T be to God, who giveth us the victory	I Cor.	15	57
T be to God for his unspeakable gift	II Cor.	9	15
Giving *t* always for all things	Eph.	5	20
What *t* can we render?	I Thes.	3	9

thanksgiving

Commanded	Ps.	50	14
Is a good thing	Ps.	92	1

Should be offered:

For God's goodness and mercy	Ps.	106	1
Before taking food	John	6	11
For victory over death	I Cor.	15	57
For the gift of Christ	II Cor.	9	15
Through Christ	Eph.	5	20
In everything	I Thes.	5	18
Christ sets an example of	Mat.	11	25
The wicked averse to	Rom.	1	21
Should always accompany prayer	Col.	4	2

Exemplified:

David	I Chr.	29	13
Levites	II Chr.	5	12, 13
Daniel	Dan.	2	23
Jonah	Jonah	2	9
Simeon	Luke	2	28
Anna	Luke	2	38
Paul	Acts	28	15

Tharshish *see* Tarshish

theatre *an auditorium*

Paul not allowed to enter	Acts	19	29

Thebez *whiteness*

A city besieged by Abimelech	Judg.	9	50–56
Abimelech killed here	II Sam.	11	21

theft

Forbidden	Ex.	20	15
Mosaic law respecting	Ex.	22	1–8
Man stealers put to death	Ex.	21	16
In a vineyard	Deut.	23	24
Hated by God	Is.	61	8
Ashamed when caught	Jer.	2	26
Negates worship	Jer.	7	9, 10
Includes all types of fraud	Lev.	19	13
Punishment	Ezek.	22	29, 31
	I Cor.	6	10
Proceeds from the heart	Mat.	15	19

Exemplified:

Rachel	Gen.	31	19
Achan	Josh.	7	21
Shechemites	Judg.	9	25
Micah	Judg.	17	2
Spies of Laish	Judg.	18	14–27
Judas	John	12	6

Theophilus *friend of God*

One of the first Christians and a friend of Luke	Luke	1	3
	Acts	1	1

Thessalonica *a city of Asia*

Paul visits	Acts	17	1–13
Two famous Christians of	Acts	20	4
	Acts	27	2
Paul writes two epistles to the residents of	I Thes.	1	1
	II Thes.	1	1

thief *one guilty of theft or larceny*

Punishment of	Ex.	22	2
His conduct described	Jer.	49	9
Christ's second coming typified by	Luke	12	39
(*See* theft)			

think

T on me when it shall be well	Gen.	40	14
T upon me, my God, for good	Neh.	5	19
The Lord *t* upon me	Ps.	40	17
As he *t* in his heart	Prov.	23	7
If God will *t* upon us	Jonah	1	6
T not to say within yourselves	Mat.	3	9
T not I am come to destroy	Mat.	5	17
T they shall be heard	Mat.	6	7
Why *t* ye evil in your hearts?	Mat.	9	4
What *t* thou?	Mat.	17	25
	Mat.	22	17
What *t* ye of Christ?	Mat.	22	42
Will *t* that he doeth God service	John	16	2
Not to *t* more highly than he ought to *t*	Rom.	12	3

Let him that *t* he standeth	I Cor.	10	12
To *t* any thing as of ourselves	II Cor.	3	5
If a man *t* himself to be something	Gal.	6	3
Able to do above all we ask or *t*	Eph.	3	20
T on these things	Phil.	4	8
Let not that man *t* he shall receive	James	1	7
Do ye *t* that the scripture saith in vain?	James	4	5

thirst *desire for drink*

Relief from	Ex.	17	1–6
Dying of, and revived	Judg.	15	18, 19
Of Jesus	John	19	28–30
Of enemy	Rom.	12	20
Result of judgment	Deut.	28	48
Water quenches	Neh.	9	15, 20
Vinegar for, in scorn	Ps.	69	21
Of fish	Is.	50	2
Of Hosea's wife	Hosea	2	3
For hearing God's word	Amos	8	11

thistle *a plant with prickly leaves*

A noxious plant	Gen.	3	18
Parables of	II Ki.	14	9
	II Chr.	25	18
	Mat.	7	16

Thomas, Didymus *twin*

One of the twelve apostles	Mat.	10	1, 3
His zeal	John	11	16
Has no apprehension	John	14	1–6
His unbelief and confession	John	20	24–26
Is convinced	John	20	27, 28
	John	21	1, 2
At the upper room	Acts	1	13

thongs *narrow strips of leather*

Paul bound in	Acts	22	25

thorns, brambles, briers *prickly plants*

Ground cursed with	Gen.	3	18
Used as an awl	Job	41	2
Used for fuel	Ps.	58	9
Hedges of	Hosea	2	6
Crown of, placed on Christ	Mark	15	17
In Paul's flesh	II Cor.	12	1–9

thought *what one thinks*

T of his heart only evil	Gen.	6	5
The Lord understandeth the *t*	I Chr.	28	9
In *t* from the visions of the night	Job	4	13
No *t* can be withholden from thee	Job	42	2
God is not in all his *t*	Ps.	10	4
Thy *t* cannot be reckoned	Ps.	40	5
Thy *t* are very deep	Ps.	92	5
The Lord knoweth the *t* of man	Ps.	94	11
How precious are thy *t* to me	Ps.	139	17
Try me, and know my *t*	Ps.	139	23
The *t* of the righteous are right	Prov.	12	5
The *t* of the wicked are abomination	Prov.	15	26
Thy *t* shall be established	Prov.	16	3
Let the unrighteous forsake his *t*	Is.	55	7
My *t* are not your *t*	Is.	55	8
They know not the *t* of the Lord	Mic.	4	12
Jesus knowing their *t*	Mat.	9	4
	Mat.	12	25
	Luke	5	22
	Luke	6	8
	Luke	11	17
Out of the heart proceed evil *t*	Mat.	15	19
	Mark	7	21
Jesus, perceiving the *t* of their heart	Luke	9	47
Why do *t* arise in your hearts?	Luke	24	38
The Lord knoweth the *t* of the wise	I Cor.	3	20
Bringing into captivity every *t*	II Cor.	10	5
The word of God is a discerner of the *t*	Heb.	4	12
Are become judges of evil *t*	James	2	4
Yet *t* evil against me	Gen.	50	20
I *t* He will surely come out	II Ki.	5	11
We have *t* of thy lovingkindness	Ps.	48	9
Thou *t* I was such an one as thyself	Ps.	50	21
When I *t* to know this	Ps.	73	16
I *t* on my ways	Ps.	119	59
I will repent of the evil I *t* to do	Jer.	18	8
I *t* to do well	Zech.	8	15
For them that *t* upon his name	Mal.	3	16
When he *t* thereon, he wept	Mark	14	72
He *t* within himself, What shall I do?	Luke	12	17
They *t* the kingdom of God should appear	Luke	19	11
They *t* he had spoken of taking of rest	John	11	13
T not good to take him	Acts	15	38
Why should it be *t* a thing incredible?	Acts	26	8

thought—*continued*

I *t* as a child	I Cor.	13	11
T it not robbery to be equal with God	Phil.	2	6

thousand

Covenant to generations	Deut.	7	9
Samson slew	Judg.	15	15
Captain over	I Sam.	18	13
Bullocks offered	I Ki.	3	4
Years	Rev.	20	1–7
	II Pet.	3	8

threaten

Disciples were	Acts	4	17, 21, 29
Christ did not	I Pet.	2	23
Saul	Acts	9	1
Forbearing	Eph.	6	9
Of Jezebel	I Ki.	19	1, 2

three taverns *see* taverns, The three

threshing *separating grain*

Floors for	Gen.	50	10, 11
By beating	Ruth	2	17
By treading	Is.	25	10

threshingfloor

For threshing grain	Num.	18	27
Of Araunah, bought by David for sacrifices	II Sam.	24	16–25

thrice *three times*

T in the year shall	Ex.	34	23, 24
And Joash smote *t*	II Ki.	13	18
Thou shalt smite Syria but *t*	II Ki.	13	19
Thou shalt deny me *t*	Mat.	26	34
	Mat.	26	75
	John	13	38
This was done *t*	Acts	10	16
T was I beaten with rods, once was I stoned, *t* I suffered	II Cor.	11	25
I besought the Lord *t*	II Cor.	12	8

throne *a raised seat used by royalty*
Examples of:

Of Pharaoh	Gen.	41	39, 40
O David	I Ki.	2	12, 24
Of Israel	I Ki.	8	20
Of Solomon called "Throne of the Lord"	I Chr.	29	23
Of Solomon	II Chr.	9	15–19
Of Herod	Acts	12	21
Symbol of power	I Sam.	1	9
	Mat.	19	28
Used for state functions	I Ki.	10	18–20
	Acts	12	21
In heaven	Ps.	11	4
In holiness	Ps.	47	8
In justice	Ps.	89	14
Of Iniquity	Ps.	94	20
Like a fiery flame	Dan.	7	9
Promised to the overcomer	Rev.	3	21

thumb

Of Aaron anointed	Lev.	8	23
In cleansing of worshiper	Lev.	14	11, 14, 25
Oil put on	Lev.	14	17, 28
Cut from prisoners' hands	Judg.	1	6, 7

Thummim *see* Urim

thunder

One of the afflictions sent by God on the Egyptians	Ex.	9	23
Shows presence of God on Sinai	Ex.	19	16–18
A plague on the Philistines	I Sam.	7	10
A sign of God's anger	I Sam.	12	17, 18
A sign of God's power	Job	26	14
Sent as a judgment	Is.	29	6
James and John, called "sons of"	Mark	3	17
Likened to the voice of God	Rev.	6	1

Thyatira *a city of Asia Minor*

Home of Lydia, an early convert	Acts	16	14
Church of Revelation	Rev.	2	18–24

thyine wood *aromatic wood*

Sold in the marketplaces	Rev.	18	12

Tiberias, sea of

A second name given to the sea of Galilee	John	6	1

Tiberius Caesar

The Roman emperor	Luke	3	1

tidings

Said *t*, my lord the king	II Sam.	18	31
Not be afraid of evil *t*	Ps.	112	7
T out of the east	Dan.	11	44
Showing glad *t* of kingdom of God	Luke	8	1
Glad *t* of good things	Rom.	10	15

Tiglath-pileser, Tilgath-pileser, Tilgath-pilneser *Lord of the Tigris*

A king of Assyria who invades Israel and carries captives to his country	II Ki.	15	29
	I Chr.	5	6, 26
Forms a pact with Ahaz	II Ki.	16	7–10
He captures Damascus	II Chr.	28	19–21

Tigris *see* Hiddekel

tile *a rectangular piece of stone, concrete or clay*

A soft, clay brick	Ezek.	4	1
Used on Palestinian houses	Mark	2	4
Used in roofing	Luke	5	19

till *cultivate, plow*

To *t* the ground	Gen.	2	5
	Gen.	3	23
He that *t* his hand	Prov.	12	11
	Prov.	28	19
Desolate land shall be *t*	Ezek.	36	34

Timaeus *honoured*

Father of Bartimaeus	Mark	10	46

timber *wood*

Used in building	I Ki.	5	18
Used in repairing	II Ki.	22	6
Used in the building of the temple	II Chr.	2	9
For the gates of the palace	Neh.	2	8

timbrel *a musical instrument like a tambourine*
Used by:

Miriam	Ex.	15	20
By Jephthah's daughter	Judg.	11	34
Used in temple services	II Sam.	6	5
Used in dancing	Job	21	12

time

Beginning of	Gen.	1	1, 14
Division into watches	Ex.	14	24
Indicated by a sun dial	II Ki.	20	9–11
End of	Job	26	10
Fullness of	Gal.	4	4
In a *t* when thou mayest be found	Ps.	32	6
Not be ashamed in the evil *t*	Ps.	37	19
Deliver him in *t* of trouble	Ps.	41	1
What *t* I am afraid	Ps.	56	3
In an acceptable *t*	Ps.	69	13
	Is.	49	8
Remember how short my *t* is	Ps.	89	47
There is a *t* to every purpose	Eccl.	3	1
T and chance happeneth to all	Eccl.	9	11
I will hasten it in his *t*	Is.	60	22
Thy *t* was the *t* of love	Ezek.	16	8
A *t* and *t* and the dividing of *t*	Dan.	7	25
It is *t* to seek the Lord	Hosea	10	12
Is it *t* to dwell in houses?	Hag.	1	4
Neither shall vine cast fruit before the *t*	Mal.	3	11
Endure but for a *t*	Mark	4	17
Now the *t* is far passed	Mark	6	35
Knewest not the *t* of thy visitation	Luke	19	44
My *t* is not yet come	John	7	6
Spent their *t* in nothing else	Acts	17	21
High *t* to awake	Rom.	13	11
The *t* is short	I Cor.	7	29
Redeeming the *t*	Col.	4	5
The *t* of my departure is at hand	II Tim.	4	6
Grace to help in *t* of need	Heb.	4	16
That appeareth for a little *t*	James	4	14
Pass the *t* of sojourning in fear	I Pet.	1	17

Timma *restraint*

Concubine of Eliphaz	Gen.	36	12
Daughter of Seir, sister of Lotan	Gen.	36	22
	I Chr.	1	39
Son of Eliphaz	I Chr.	1	36

Timnah *allotment*

A duke of Edom	Gen.	36	40
A town of Judah	Josh.	15	10
A city in the hill country of Judah	Josh.	15	21

Timnath *assigned portion*

A city where Tamar meets Judah	Gen.	38	12–14
Home of Samson's wife	Judg.	14	1, 2, 5

Timnath-serah *extra portion*

A city of Ephraim, given to Joshua	Josh.	19	50
Joshua buried in	Josh.	24	29, 30

Timon *deeming worthy*

One of the seven deacons of the church at Jerusalem	Acts	6	5

Timothy, Timotheus *honouring God*

His parents	Acts	16	1
Faith of	Acts	16	2

Is circumcised	Acts	16	3
Paul leaves him at Berea	Acts	17	14
Meets Paul at Corinth	Acts	17	15
Is sent by Paul to Macedonia	Acts	19	22
Paul rejoins him and they go to Asia	Acts	20	1–4
Sends greetings to the Romans	Rom.	16	21
Paul's regard for	I Cor.	4	17

Preaches to the:

Corinthians	II Cor.	1	19
Philippians	Phil.	2	19
Thessalonians	I Thes.	3	2, 6
The zeal of	Phil.	2	19–22
Is Paul's companion	I Thes.	3	2
Paul writes to	I Tim.	1	1, 2
	II Tim.	1	1, 2
The power of	I Tim.	4	14
Knows the scripture	II Tim.	3	15–17
Spiritual heritage	II Tim.	1	5

tin *a soft, silver-white metal*

An ordinary metal	Num.	31	22
Made in Tarsish	Ezek.	27	12
Symbolic of evil	Is.	1	25

tire *embellishment*

A headdress used for ornamental purposes	Ezek.	24	17
	II Ki.	9	30
A pendant, worn by women	Is.	3	18

Tirshatha *his excellency*

A Persian title	Ezra	2	63
Carried by Zerubbabel and Nehemiah	Neh.	7	65, 70

Tirzah *delight*

A daughter of Zelophehad	Num.	26	33
Special rules regarding her inheritance	Num.	27	1–11
A city of Canaan	Josh.	12	24
Home of Jeroboam	I Ki.	14	17
The capital of Israel at one time	I Ki.	15	21, 33
Kings move from	I Ki.	16	23, 24
Beauty of	S. of S.	6	4

tithe *the tenth of anything*

Jacob promised	Gen.	28	20
	Heb.	7	6
Probable beginning first fruits	Deut.	26	2, 10
Provided sacrificial meal	Deut.	14	22–27
Used for charity	Deut.	14	28
	Deut.	26	12–15
Paid by Abraham	Gen.	14	20
Considered a just return for God's blessings	Gen.	28	22
Belongs to God	Lev.	27	30–33
To Levites for their services	Num.	18	21, 24
Brought to the temple	Deut.	12	6–20
Stored in temple	Neh.	12	44
During Hezekiah's reign	II Chr.	31	5, 10
Customs relating to	Neh.	10	37, 38
The Jews slow in giving	Neh.	13	10
Demanded by God	Mal.	3	8
Customary in later times	Mat.	23	23

Titus *honourable*

Paul's love for	II Cor.	2	13
A Greek, companion to Paul	Gal.	2	3
Sent by Paul to Dalmatia	II Tim.	4	10
Left by Paul in Crete	Tit.	1	5

Tobiah, Tobijah *Jehovah is good*

Levite sent to teach in Judah	II Chr.	17	8
A Jew who gives gold and silver for the crown of Joshua	Zech.	6	10–14
A Jew returned from exile	Ezra	2	60
The Ammonite, vexes the Jews	Neh.	6	1, 12

toe *part of the foot*

Of Aaron and his sons anointed	Ex.	29	20
In purification	Lev.	14	14, 17
Of prisioners cut off	Judg.	1	6, 7
A man with six on each foot	II Sam.	21	20

toil *work, labor*

T of our hands	Gen.	5	29
They *t* not, neither	Mat.	6	28
Them *t* in rowing	Mark	6	48
Have *t* all the night	Luke	5	5

token *a sign*

Sun and moon, sign of the seasons	Gen.	1	14
The mark of Cain	Gen.	4	15
A rainbow, of God's covenant	Gen.	9	12–17
Circumcision, of the covenant of Abraham	Gen.	17	11
A sign	Ex.	3	12
Miracles of Moses	Ex.	4	1–9
Blood of the passover lamb	Ex.	12	13

The passover	Ex.	13	9
The firstborn	Ex.	13	14–16
Cover of the altar	Num.	16	38–40
Scarlet thread	Josh.	2	18, 21
Dew on Gideon's coat	Judg.	6	36–40

tolerance *tolerating beliefs*

Religious	Mark	9	38–40
	Rom.	14	1–23
	I Cor.	10	28–32
Of sin	I Cor.	5	1–10
	II Cor.	6	14–18
Taught by Jesus	Luke	9	49, 50
Practiced by Paul	Philem.		17, 18

toll *tax or fee paid*

Then will they not pay *t*	Ezra	4	13
T, tribute, and custom, was paid	Ezra	4	20
Lawful to impose *t* on them	Ezra	7	24

tomb *see sepulchre*

tongue

Unruly	James	3	1–12
To be bridled	Ps.	39	1
	Prov.	4	24
	Prov.	10	19
	Prov.	14	23
	Prov.	17	20
	Prov.	18	6
	Eccl.	3	7
	Eccl.	10	12
	Mat.	5	22
	Mat.	12	36
	Eph.	4	29
	Eph.	5	4
	Col.	3	8
	Col.	4	6
	Tit.	1	10
	Tit.	2	8
	Tit.	3	2
	I Pet.	3	10
	Jude		16
Tongues, confusion of	Gen.	11	7–9
Gifts of	Acts	2	3
	Acts	10	46
	Acts	19	6
	I Cor.	12	10
	I Cor	13	1
	I Cor.	14	2
Hid from scourge of *t*	Job	5	21
Hide wickedness under his *t*	Job	20	12
T cleaved to roof of mouth	Job	29	10
They flatter with their *t*	Ps	5	9
Keep thy *t* from evil	Ps.	34	13
	I Pet.	3	10
T of the just as choice silver	Prov.	10	20
T of the wise is health	Prov.	12	18
A lying *t* is but for a moment	Prov.	12	19
A wholesome *t* is a tree of life	Prov.	15	4
Death and life are in the power of the *t*	Prov.	18	21
Whoso keepeth his *t* keepeth his soul	Prov.	21	23
A soft *t* breaketh the bone	Prov.	25	15
His *t* as a devouring fire	Is.	30	27
Given me the *t* of the learned	Is.	50	4
Taught their *t* to speak lies	Jer.	9	5
Let us smite him with the *t*	Jer.	18	18
And bridleth not his *t*	James	1	26
The *t* is a little member	James	3	5

tongues *languages, ecstatic utterance*

A linguistic miracle at Pentecost	Acts	10	46
Characteristic of early Christianity	I Cor.	12–14	
Must be interpreted	I Cor.	14	27

tooth, broken

Unfaithful man like a	Prov.	25	19

topaz *a precious stone*

Used in breastplate	Ex.	39	10
Found in Ethiopia	Job	28	19

Tophet, Topheth *contempt, altar*

A place in Hinnom where Jewish children pass through the fire	II Ki.	23	10
	Jer.	19	6, 11–14
Destroyed by Josiah	II Ki.	23	10
Horror of	Is.	30	33

torment *infliction of extreme pain*

Of fatal diseases	Mat.	4	24
Of the wicked	Luke	16	23–28
	Rev.	14	10, 11
Without end	Rev.	20	10

tortoise

Not to be eaten	Lev.	11	29

toss

I am *t* up and down	Ps.	109	23
He will *t* thee like a ball	Is.	22	18
T with tempest	Is.	54	11
Children *t* to and fro	Eph.	4	14
He that wavereth is like a wave *t*	James	1	6

touch

Nor shall ye *t* it, lest ye die	Gen.	3	3
T not mine anointed	I Chr.	16	22
	Ps.	105	15
There shall no evil *t* thee	Job	5	19
Lo, this hath *t* thy lips	Is.	6	7
T no unclean thing	Is.	52	11
	II Cor.	6	17
The Lord *t* my mouth	Jer.	1	9
He that *t* you *t* the apple of his eye	Zech.	2	8
If I may but *t* his garment	Mat.	9	21
	Mark	5	28
Children, that he should *t* them	Mark	10	13
	Luke	18	15
Ye yourselves *t* not the burdens	Luke	11	46
T me not	John	20	17
T not, taste not	Col.	2	21
Wicked one *t* him not	I John	5	18

towel *a cloth for wiping*

Used by Jesus	John	13	4, 5

tower

Watchmen posted on	II Ki.	9	17
Used as armouries	S. of S.	4	4
Frequently very high	Is.	2	15

Mentioned in scriptures:

Babel	Gen.	11	9
Edar	Gen.	35	21
Penuel	Judg.	8	17
Shechem	Judg.	9	46
Thebez	Judg.	9	50, 51
Jezreel	II Ki.	9	17
David	S. of S.	4	4
Lebanon	S. of S.	7	4
Meah	Neh.	12	39
Hananeel	Jer.	31	38
Syene	Ezek.	29	10
Siloam	Luke	13	4

Trachonitis *rugged tract*

A region south of Damascus	Luke	3	1

trade *business*

A beneficial	Gen.	34	20–23
Forbidden to use trickery in	Deut.	25	13–16
Forbidden to deal in, on the sabbath	Neh.	13	16, 17
Dishonesty in, condemned	Amos	8	4–8
Of cattle	Gen.	46	32
Of gold	I Ki.	9	28
Of silver	Rev.	18	12
Of pearls	Rev.	18	12
Of ivory	Rev.	18	12
Of silk	Rev.	18	12
Of scarlet	Rev.	18	12
Of brass	Rev.	18	12

tradition *an unwritten code*

Does not always follow God's law	Mat.	15	3
Of the Jewish elders	Mark	7	3
Paul believes in	I Cor.	11	2
Warned against	Col.	2	8
Makes the law of God of none effect	Mat.	15	6
Traditions of Paul	II Thes.	3	6
	II Thes.	2	15
Not redeemed by	I Pet.	1	18
Paul zealous of	Gal.	1	14

traffic *buying and selling*

Of merchants	I Ki.	10	15
Land of	Ezek.	17	4
Led to prosperity	Ezek.	28	5
Of iniquity	Ezek.	28	18
Of Tyre	Is.	23	8

train *various meanings*

Servants and children	Gen.	14	14
A group of attendants	I Ki.	10	2
Flowing clothing	Is.	6	1

traitor *a betrayer*

Judas Iscariot	Mat.	26	14–16
	Mat.	26	46–50
A very wicked person	II Tim.	3	1–5

trance *a state of abstraction, as of the mind or body*

Examples of:

Balaam	Num.	24	3, 4, 15, 16
Peter	Acts	10	9, 10
Paul	Acts	22	17

transfiguration *changing appearance*

Examples of:

Moses	Ex.	34	29–35
Christ	Mat.	17	1–9
	Mark	9	2–10
	Luke	9	29–36
	II Pet.	1	16–18
Stephen	Acts	6	8, 15

transgressions *see sin*

transgress

Wherefore do ye *t* commandments of Lord?	Num.	14	41
	II Chr.	24	20
Ye make the Lord's people to *t*	I Sam.	2	24
If ye *t*, I will scatter you	Neh.	1	8
My mouth shall not *t*	Ps.	17	3
Ashamed which *t* without cause	Ps.	35	3
For a piece of bread that man will *t*	Prov.	28	21
Come to Bethel and *t*	Amos	4	4
He *t* by wine	Hab.	2	5
Whosoever committeth sin *t* the law	I John	3	4

transgression *offense*

Forgiving *t*	Ex.	34	7
	Num.	14	18
There is no *t* in my hand	I Sam.	24	11
Saul died for his *t*	I Chr.	10	13
He mourned because of their *t*	Ezra	10	6
Why dost thou not pardon my *t*?	Job	7	21
Make me to know my *t*	Job	13	23
Innocent from the great *t*	Ps.	19	13
Blessed is he whose *t* is forgiven	Ps.	32	1
As for our *t*, thou shalt purge them away	Ps.	65	3
I will visit their *t*	Ps.	89	32
Fools because of their *t* are afflicted	Ps.	107	17
He that covereth *t*	Prov.	17	9
Blotted out thy *t*	Is.	44	22
For the *t* of my people was he stricken	Is.	53	8
Show my people their *t*	Is.	58	1
Not deliver in day of his *t*	Ezek.	33	12
What is the *t* of Jacob?	Mic.	1	5
That passeth by *t* of remnant	Mic.	7	18
Where no law is, is not *t*	Rom.	4	15
After similitude of Adam's *t*	Rom.	5	14

transgressor

Then will I teach *t* thy ways	Ps.	51	13
Way of *t* is hard	Prov.	13	15
The *t* shall be ransom for the upright	Prov.	21	18
Thou wast called a *t* from the womb	Is.	48	8
He was numbered with the *t*	Is.	53	12
	Mark	15	28
	Luke	22	37
Thou art become a *t* of the law	James	2	11

transitory *fleeting*

Examples of:

Power on earth	Ps.	37	34–36
Man's life	Ps.	39	5
Possessions on earth	Ps.	102	25, 26
Pleasures of the world	Is.	47	8, 9
Glory on earth	I Pet.	1	24

translations *without earthly death*

Examples of:

Enoch	Gen.	5	24
Elijah	II Ki.	2	1–12
Jesus	Mark	16	19
Paul desirous of	II Cor.	5	4
Believers	I Thes.	4	16, 17

transportation *a way of traveling*

Wagons	Gen.	46	5
Oxen	I Sam.	6	7, 8
Rafts	I Ki.	5	7–9
Camels	I Ki.	10	1, 2
Asses	I Ki.	13	13
Horses	I Ki.	20	20
Ships	I Ki.	5	7–9

travail *labour*

A curse on Eve	Gen.	3	16
Of Rachel	Gen.	35	16–19
Christ's death	Is.	53	11
In leaving Egypt	Ex.	18	8
Of a woman	Ps.	48	6
	Jer.	6	24
	Mic.	4	9

Life of man	Eccl.	2	23
God hath given to men	Eccl.	3	10
Of Paul	Gal.	4	19
	I Thes.	2	9

treachery *betrayal of trust or faith*
Examples of:

Rahab	Josh.	2	1–16
A man of Bethel	Judg.	1	24, 25
Jael	Judg.	4	18–21
Shechemites	Judg.	9	23
Delilah	Judg.	16	18, 19
Saul	I Sam.	18	17, 19
Joab	II Sam.	3	26, 27
Baanah and Rechab	II Sam.	4	6
David	II Sam.	11	14, 15
Jehu	II Ki.	10	18–28
Enemies of Nehemiah	Neh.	6	1–19
Haman	Esth.	3	8–15
Judas	Mat.	26	47–49

tread

Whereon your feet *t*	Deut.	11	24
Muzzle ox when he *t* corn	Deut.	25	4
	I Cor.	9	9
	I Tim.	5	18
T down wicked in their place	Job	40	12
Let him *t* down my life	Ps.	7	5
Through thy name will we *t* them under	Ps.	44	5
Shall *t* down our enemies	Ps.	60	12
	Ps.	108	13
Thou shalt *t* upon lion and adder	Ps.	91	13
To *t* my courts	Is.	1	12
To *t* them down like mire	Is.	10	6
Treaders shall *t* out no wine	Is.	16	10
I will *t* them in mine anger	Is.	63	3
As they that *t* grapes	Jer.	25	30
None shall *t* with shouting	Jer.	48	33
Loveth to *t* out corn	Hosea	10	11
Power to *t* on scorpions	Luke	10	19
City shall they *t* under foot	Rev.	11	2
He *t* wine-press of wrath	Rev.	19	15

treason *disloyalty*
Instances of:

Against Moses	Num.	12	1–11
Against Jericho	Josh.	2	1–16
Against Succoth	Judg.	8	14
Against Abimelech	Judg.	9	22–25
Against Jephthah	Judg.	12	1–4
Against David	II Sam.	15	1–14
Against Rehoboam	I Ki.	12	16–20
Done by Zimri	I Ki.	16	15–20
Against Athaliah	II Ki.	11	14–16
Death penalty for	Esth.	2	23
Jesus and Paul falsely accused of	Luke	23	2, 3, 38
	Acts	17	7

treasure *anything of high value*

Money	Gen.	42	25–38
Precious stones	I Chr.	29	8
Uncertain	Prov.	27	24
Forbidden to hoard	Mat.	6	19
Hidden	Mat.	13	44
Of wisdom and knowledge	Col.	2	3

treasure cities and houses *places where treasure is stored*
Cities that are built for the storage of the

king's treasures	Ex.	1	11
	I Ki.	9	19
	II Chr.	8	4, 6
Houses of kings	II Ki.	20	13
	Ezra	1	7, 8
	Esth.	3	9
The preservation of records in	Ezra	5	17
Treasurers in charge of	Ezra	7	20, 21

treasury *a place where treasure is kept*

Watched by Jesus	Mark	12	41
Chests in the temple for the offerings	Luke	21	1

tree of life

In the garden of Eden	Gen.	2	8–14
Man excluded from	Gen.	3	22–24
Wisdom called	Prov.	3	13, 18
In God's paradise	Rev.	2	7

trees

Created	Gen.	1	11, 12
Give welcome shade during the heat of day	Gen.	18	4
Often considered sacred	Gen.	21	33
Used as a marker for burial	Gen.	35	4, 8

In parables:

Jotham's	Judg.	9	7–15
Jehoash's	II Ki.	14	9
The corrupt tree	Mat.	7	17–20
Made for the glory of God	Ps.	148	9

Illustrative:

Of wisdom	Prov.	3	18
Of useless persons	Is.	56	3
Of Christ	Rom.	11	24

trees of the Bible

Almond	Jer.	1	11
Almug	I Ki.	10	11
Aloes	Ps.	45	8
Apple	S. of S.	2	3
Ash	Is.	44	14
Cedars of Lebanon	II Ki.	14	9
Chestnut	Ezek.	31	8
Cypress	Is.	44	14
Elm	Hosea	4	13
Fig	Judg.	9	11
Fir	I Ki.	5	10
Hazel	Gen.	30	37
Juniper	I Ki.	19	5
Lign aloes	Num.	24	6
Mulberry	II Sam.	5	23
Myrrh	S. of S.	4	14
Myrtle	Neh.	8	15
Oak	Is.	2	13
Oil	Is.	41	19
Olive	Judg.	9	9
Palm	Ex.	15	27
Pine	Is.	41	19
Pomegranate	Deut.	8	8
Poplar	Hosea	4	13
Shittah	Is.	41	19
Sycamore	I Ki.	10	27
Teil	Is.	6	13
Willow	Is.	44	4

tremble

Nations shall *t* because	Deut.	2	25
Fear not and do not *t*	Deut.	20	3
Of those that *t* at the	Ezra	10	3
Earth, the pillars thereof *t*	Job	9	6
The pillars of heaven *t* and	Job	26	11
Hast made the earth to *t*	Ps.	60	2
Lord reigneth, let the people *t*	Ps.	99	1
Of the house shall *t*	Eccl.	12	3
Hills did *t*, their carcases	Is.	5	25
Man that made the earth to *t*	Is.	14	16
T ye women that are at ease	Is.	32	11
That the nations may *t* at thy	Is.	64	2
Hear word of Lord, ye that *t*	Is.	66	5
Will ye not *t* at my presence?	Jer.	5	22
At his wrath the earth shall *t*	Jer.	10	10
And they shall *t* for all the	Jer.	33	9
And they shall *t* for all the	Jer.	33	9
The land of Babylon shall *t*	Jer.	51	29
They shall *t* at every moment	Ezek.	26	16
	Ezek.	32	10
Now shall isles *t* in the day	Ezek.	26	18
Men *t* before the God	Dan.	6	26
Then the children shall *t*	Hosea	11	10
T as a bird out of Egypt	Hosea	11	11
Inhabitants of the land *t*	Joel	2	1
Quake, the heavens shall *t*	Joel	2	10
Shall not the land *t* for Amos	Amos	8	8
The land of Midian did *t*	Hab.	3	7
Devils also believe and *t*	James	2	19

trespass offerings *see* offerings

trials *the acts of trying, testing*

Of Abram	Gen.	22	1–13
In business	Gen.	31	36–41
Form character	Ex.	14	27–31
Before courts	Lev.	24	10–14
Stubbornness in	II Chr.	28	21–23
Of faith	Job	23	10
	Heb.	11	17
	James	1	3
Of the heart, God's prerogative	Ps.	26	2
	I Thes.	2	4
Can be a blessing	Mat.	5	10–12
Right of	John	7	51
	Acts	16	37–39
Paul has confidence in	Rom.	8	35–39

tribes of Israel *see* Israelites

tribulation *severe affliction*

Turn to God in times of	Deut.	4	30
In the last days	Mat.	24	21
Prophesied for disciples	John	16	33
Prepares us for the kingdom of God	Acts	14	22
Works patience	Rom.	5	3
God comforts in	II Cor.	1	4
Rewarded	Rev.	7	13–17
Seed on stony ground endures	Mat.	13	21
Upon evil doers	Rom.	2	9
Patient in	Rom.	12	12
Joyful in	II Cor.	7	4
Church of Smyrna endured	Rev.	2	19

tribute *a tax levied for protection from invasion*

From conquered nations	Josh.	16	10
	Judg.	1	30–33
	Mat.	17	24–27
By the Arabians to Solomon	II Chr.	9	14
To Jehoshaphat	II Chr.	17	11
On Israel	II Ki.	23	33

Trinity *Tri-unity of God-Three in One*

Doctrine of, proved from scripture	Mat.	3	16–17
	Mat.	28	19
	I Cor.	12	3–6
	II Cor.	13	14
	Eph.	4	4–6
	I Pet.	1	2
Manifest at the baptism of Jesus	Mat.	3	16, 17
	I Cor.	12	3–6
Baptism administered in the name of	Mat.	28	19
Benediction given in the name of	II Cor.	13	14
Salvation the work of	II Thes.	2	13, 14
	Tit.	3	4–6
	I Pet.	1	2
In creation	Gen.	1	26
	Gen.	3	22
In Isaiah's vision	Is.	6	3
In Christ's birth	Mat.	1	18
In Christ's ministry	John	3	34, 35
Christ's prayer for comforter	John	14	16, 17, 26

Each person in, described as:

Author of all spiritual operations	Heb.	13	21
	Col.	1	29
	I Cor.	12	11
Creator	Gen.	1	1
	Col.	1	16
	John	1	3
	Job	26	13
	Job	33	4
Eternal	Rev.	22	13
	Heb.	9	14
Holy	Rev.	15	4
Inspiring the prophets	Heb.	1	1
	Mark	13	11
Omnipotent	Rev.	1	8
	Rom.	15	19
	Jer.	32	17
	Heb.	1	3
Omnipresent	Jer.	23	24
	Ps.	139	7
Omniscient	Acts	15	18
	I Cor.	2	10–11
Raising Christ from the dead	I Cor.	6	14
	I Pet.	3	18
Sanctifier	Heb.	2	11
Source of eternal life	Rom.	6	23
	John	10	28
Supplying ministers to the church	Eph.	4	11
	Acts	13	2
	Acts	20	28
Teacher	Luke	21	15
	John	14	26
	Gal.	1	12
True	John	7	28

Troas *a seaport of Mysia*

Paul's vision at	Acts	16	8
Visited by Paul	Acts	20	5, 6
	II Tim.	4	13

trodden

Hast *t* down strength	Judg.	5	21
Old way which wicked men have *t*	Job	22	15
Thou hast *t* down all that err	Ps.	119	118
I have *t* the winepress alone	Is.	63	3
Now shall she be *t* as mire	Mic.	7	10

Salt to be *t* under foot	Mat.	5	13
Fell by wayside, and was *t*	Luke	8	5
Jerusalem shall be *t* of Gentiles	Luke	21	24
Hath *t* under foot the Son of God	Heb.	10	29

Trogyllium *a town in Caria, Asia Minor*

Paul visits here	Acts	20	15

Trophimus *nourishing*

A Gentile Christian	Acts	20	4
Accompanies Paul to Jerusalem	Acts	21	27–29
Is sick in Miletus	II Tim.	4	20

trouble *worry*

Israelites at the Red Sea	Ex.	14	10–12
About water	Ex.	15	23–25
About food	Ex.	16	2, 3
When Moses tarries in the mount	Ex.	32	1
When spies bring their report	Num.	13	28–33
Elijah	I Ki.	19	4–15
Disciples, how to fed multitude	Mat.	14	15
Disciples, in the tempest	Mat.	8	23–26
Disciples, when Jesus is risen	Luke	24	4–9
Mary at the sepulchre	John	20	11–17
People in shipwreck	Acts	27	22–23
See affliction and suffering			
Turn to the Lord in	II Chr.	15	4
Came upon the returnees	Neh.	9	32
Job's	Job	3	26
Few days and full of	Job	14	1
Times of	Ps.	9	9
	Ps.	27	5
Considered by the Lord	Ps.	9	13
Preserved from	Ps.	32	7
Help in	Ps.	46	1
Righteous is delivered from	Prov.	11	8
Of sickness	Jer.	8	15
	Jer.	14	19
Jacob's	Jer.	30	7

true *real, faithful*

We are *t* men	Gen.	42	11
Tell me nothing but that which is *t*	I Ki.	22	16
Israel hath been without the *t* God	II Chr.	15	3
Thou gavest them *t* laws	Neh.	9	13
Judgments of the Lord are *t*	Ps.	19	9
Thy word is *t* from the beginning	Ps.	119	160
The Lord is the *t* God	Jer.	10	10
The Lord be a *t* witness	Jer.	42	5
We know that thou art *t*	Mat.	22	16
	Mark	12	14
The *t* riches	Luke	16	11
That was the *t* light	John	1	9
Herein is that saying *t*	John	4	37
If I bear witness of myself, my witness is not *t*	John	5	31
The *t* bread	John	6	32
All things that John spake were *t*	John	10	41
The *t* vine	John	15	1
To know thee the only *t* God	John	17	3
	I John	5	20

trumpet *a wind instrument*

Made of:

Ram's horn	Josh.	6	4–6, 8, 13
Silver	Num.	10	2
Their uses	Num.	10	1–10
	Josh.	6	4
	Ps.	81	3
	Ezek.	7	14
	Ezek.	33	3
	Joel	2	1
Employed in worship	I Chr.	13	8
The seven	Rev.	8	1–13
Giving uncertain sounds	I Cor.	14	8
In battle	Judg.	7	16, 18
Of alarm	Jer.	6	1
For the regathering	Is.	27	13
To call attention to sin	Is.	58	1
Heard no more in Babylon	Rev.	18	22
At the rapture	I Thes.	4	16

trumpets, feast of *see* feasts and festivals

trust *see* faith

trust

In God	Ps.	4	5
	Ps.	40	3
	Ps.	64	10
	Prov.	3	5
	Is.	51	5
	Jer.	17	7

Exemplified	I Sam.	17	45
	II Ki.	18	5
	Dan.	3	28
	II Tim.	1	12
	II Tim.	4	18
Blessings resulting from	Ps.	5	11
	Ps.	32	10
	Prov.	16	20
	Prov.	28	25
	Prov.	29	25
	Is.	26	3
	Is.	57	13
	Heb.	13	6
In man, riches, etc., vain	Job	31	24
	Ps.	20	7
	Prov.	11	28
	Prov.	28	26
	Is.	30	3
	Jer.	7	4
	Jer.	17	5
	Jer.	46	25
	Jer.	49	4
	Ezek.	33	13
	I Tim.	6	17
He putteth no *t* in his saints	Job	15	15
Maketh the Lord his *t*	Ps.	40	4
In thee is my *t*	Ps.	141	8
In him will I *t*	II Sam.	22	3
	Ps.	18	2
	Ps.	91	2
Though he slay me, yet will I *t* in him	Job	13	15
I *t* in thee	Ps.	25	2
	Ps.	55	23
	Ps.	56	3
	Ps.	143	8
T in the Lord	Ps.	37	3
	Ps.	62	8
	Is.	26	4
It is better to *t* in the Lord	Ps.	118	8
I will *t*, and not be afraid	Is.	12	2
Let him *t* in the name of the Lord	Is.	50	10
T not in any brother	Jer.	9	4
Let thy widows *t* in me	Jer.	49	11
T ye not in a friend	Mic.	7	5
The Lord knoweth them that *t* in him	Nah.	1	7
In his name shall Gentiles *t*	Mat.	12	21
	Rom.	15	12
Them that *t* in riches	Mark	10	24

truth
Of God:

Always goes before his face	Ps.	89	14
Is abundant	Ex.	34	6
One of His attributes	Deut.	32	4
Exhibited in His ways	Rev.	15	3
Serve God in	Josh.	24	14
Kings are preserved by	Prov.	20	28
Wicked are without	Hosea	4	1
Characteristic of saints	John	4	24
John bears witness to	John	5	33
Makes men free	John	8	31, 32
The devil is devoid of	John	8	44
Ministers should speak	II Cor.	12	6
The fruit of the Spirit is	Eph.	5	9
Is part of the Christian armour	Eph.	6	14
Is in Christ	I Tim.	2	7
Men of	Ex.	18	21
Evidence searched out to establish	Deut.	13	14
Speaking	Ps.	15	2
Often coupled with mercy	Ps.	25	10
	II Sam.	15	20
	Ps.	61	7
	Ps.	57	3
	Prov.	3	3
He keeps, forever	Ps.	146	6
Remembered toward saints	Ps.	98	3
United with mercy in redemption	Ps.	85	10
In the inward parts	Ps.	51	6
A shield	Ps.	91	4
Judgment in	Ps.	96	13
To all generations	Ps.	100	5
The way of	Ps.	119	30
Of God's law	Ps.	119	142
Christ full of	John	1	14, 17
Christ the truth	John	14	6

Denied by:

The devil	Gen.	3	4–5
The self-righteous	I John	1	10
	I John	5	10

Described as:

Great	Ps.	57	10
Inviolable	Num.	23	19
	Tit.	1	2
Plenteous	Ps.	86	15
Reaching to the clouds	Ps.	57	10

Exhibited in His:

Counsels of old	Is.	25	1
Fulfillment of his covenant	Mic.	7	20
Fulfillment of promises in Christ	II Cor.	1	20
Judicial statutes	Ps.	19	9
Punishment of the wicked	Rev.	16	7
Word	Ps.	119	160
	John	17	17
Works	Ps.	33	4
	Ps.	111	7
	Dan.	4	37

We should:

Confide in	Ps.	31	5
	Tit.	1	2
Magnify	Ps.	71	22
	Ps.	138	2
Make known to others	Is.	38	19
Plead, in prayer	Ps.	89	49
Pray for its exhibition to others	II Sam.	2	6
Pray for its manifestation to ourselves	II Chr.	6	17

Tubal-cain *hammer blow of the smith*

Son of Lamech	Gen.	4	19, 22

tumult *uproar*

Under David	II Sam.	20	1
Rehoboam	I Ki.	12	16, 17
Against Christ	Mat.	27	24
Against Paul	Acts	19	24–29
Caused by envy	James	3	16
Should be avoided by Christians	II Cor.	12	20

turtle, turtledove *a wild dove*

Voice of the	S. of S.	2	12
	Jer.	8	7
Used for offerings	Gen.	15	9
	Lev.	12	6
	Luke	2	24

tutors *private teachers*

Overseers of children	Gal.	4	2

twain

With *t* he covered his face	Is.	6	2
To go a mile, to with him *t*	Mat.	5	41
They are no more *t*	Mat.	19	6
	Mark	10	8
Veil of temple was rent in *t*	Mat.	27	51
	Mark	15	38
To make in himself of *t* one new man	Eph.	2	15

twelve

Years	Gen.	14	4
Princes	Gen.	17	20
Sons of Jacob	Gen.	35	22
Brethren	Gen.	42	13
Tribes of Israel	Gen.	49	28
Wells of water	Ex.	15	27
Pillars	Ex.	24	4
Cakes	Lev.	24	5
Silver spoons and bowls	Num.	7	84
Golden spoons	Num.	7	86
Spies	Num.	13	3–16
Rods	Num.	17	2
Fountains of water	Num.	33	9
Men	Deut.	1	23
Memorial stones	Josh.	4	1–9
Cities	Josh.	18	24
Thousand	II Sam.	17	1
Officers	I Ki.	4	7
Thousands	I Ki.	4	26
Oxen	I Ki.	7	44
Lions	II Chr.	9	19
He-goats	Ezra	6	17
Months	Esth.	2	12
Brasen bulls	Jer.	52	20
Cubits	Jer.	52	21
Apostles	Mat.	10	2–4
Baskets	Mat.	14	20
Thrones	Mat.	19	28
Legions of angels	Mat.	26	53
Hours	John	11	9
Patriarchs	Acts	7	8
Stars	Rev.	12	1

twelve—*continued*			
Angels	Rev.	21	12
Foundations	Rev.	21	14
Gates of pearl	Rev.	21	21
Manner of fruits	Rev.	22	2
twins *a pair*			
Jacob and Esau	Gen.	25	24–26
Zarah and Pharez	Gen.	38	27–30
two			
Lights	Gen.	1	16
Wives	Gen.	4	19
	I Sam.	1	2
Unclean animals	Gen.	6	19
Bands	Gen.	32	10
Burdens	Gen.	49	14
Omers	Ex.	16	22
Days	Ex.	21	21
Weeks	Lev.	12	5
Trumpets	Num.	10	2
Servants	Num.	22	22
Rams	Num.	29	14
Kings	Deut.	3	8
Captains	I Ki.	2	5
Calves	I Ki.	12	28
She bears	II Ki.	2	24
Armies	S. of S.	6	13
Olive trees	Amos	3	3
Masters	Mat.	6	24
Mites	Mark	12	42
Prophets	Rev.	11	10
Tychicus *fortuitous*			
Accompanies Paul to Greece	Acts	20	4
Carries the epistle to the Colossians	Col.	4	7
Promised a mission to Crete	Eph.	6	21
Sent to Ephesus	II Tim.	4	12
Tyrannus *tyrant*			
An Ephesian, in whose school Paul teaches	Acts	19	9, 10
tyranny *see oppression*			
Tyre, Tyrus *rock, seaport of Phoenicia*			
Stronghold on border of Asher	Josh.	19	29
Hiram, king of	I Ki.	5	1
David and Solomon form alliances with	I Ki.	5	1
	II Chr.	2	3
Celebrated for:			
Its commerce	Is.	23	2, 3
Its beauty	Ezek.	27	3, 4
Its wealth	Ezek.	27	33
Inhabitants of:			
Proud and haughty	Is.	23	9
Seafaring men	Ezek.	26	17
Wicked	Ezek.	28	18
Its fall predicted	Ezek.	26	7
Christ visits the coasts of	Mat.	15	21
Depends on Galilee for provision	Acts	12	20
Paul finds disciples at	Acts	21	3, 4

U

unawares			
Destruction come upon him at *u*	Ps.	35	8
That day come upon you *u*	Luke	21	34
Entertained angels *u*	Heb.	13	2
Certain men crept in *u*	Jude		4
unbelief *withholding of belief*			
Rebuked by Christ	Mat.	17	17
Leads to damnation	Mark	16	16
Miracles designed to remove	John	10	37, 38
Is sin	John	16	9
The Jews rejected for	Rom.	11	20
Comes from the devil	II Cor.	4	4
From an evil heart	Heb.	3	12
Warning against	Heb.	3	12
Of Israel in Egypt	Ex.	4	1
Israel in the wilderness	Ps.	78	19–22
Isaiah asks	Is.	53	1
Did not believe prophets	Jer.	5	12–14
Nobleman	John	4	48
Council	Luke	22	67
Even if one should rise from the dead	Luke	16	31
Examples of:			
Eve	Gen.	3	4–6

Moses and Aaron	Num.	20	12
Israelites	Deut.	9	23
Naaman	II Ki.	5	11, 12
Disciples	Mat.	17	17
Zacharias	Luke	1	20
Thomas	John	20	25
Saul	I Tim.	1	13
People of Jericho	Heb.	11	31
Abraham did not	Rom.	4	20
Israel concerning Christ	Rom.	9	31, 32
Of the truth	II Thes.	2	11, 12
unbelievers *skeptics*			
Fate of			
	Mark	16	16
	James	5	1–20
	Rev.	21	8
Christians forbidden to marry	II Cor.	6	14
unblemished *without blemish*			
Offerings required to be	Ex.	12	5
The church must be	Eph.	5	27
Christ is	I Pet.	1	19
uncertainties *things indeterminate*			
Earthly beauty	Ps.	39	11
Earthly riches	Prov.	23	5
The future	Prov.	27	1
Of life	James	4	14
Earthly glory	I Pet.	1	24
unchangeable *cannot be changed*			
Persian laws are	Dan.	6	15
God	Mal.	3	6
Christ's priesthood	Heb.	7	22–24
Jesus is	Heb.	13	8
uncharitable *censorious*			
In:			
Finding fault	Is.	29	20, 21
Harsh judgments	Mat.	7	3, 4
Prejudices	John	1	46
Superstitions	Acts	28	1–4
Doubtful disputations	Rom.	14	1, 2
Examples of:			
Toward Moses	Ex.	5	21
Toward the two and a half tribes	Num.	32	1–33
	Josh.	22	11–31
Toward Hannah	I Sam.	1	14–17
Toward David	I Sam.	17	28
Toward Job	Job	8	1–22
Toward Paul	Acts	21	28
uncircumcised			
Found in the non-Jewish	Gen.	34	14
Lips	Ex.	6	12, 30
Fruit	Lev.	19	23
A sign of impurity	Lev.	26	41
In the heart	Ezek.	44	7
Ears	Acts	7	51
Not to eat passover	Ex.	12	48
Israel at Gilgal	Josh.	5	7
Philistines	Josh.	5	7
	I Sam.	14	6
Israel in Jeremiah's time	Jer.	9	26
Abraham when he had faith	Rom.	4	11, 12
Gospel of committed to Paul	Gal.	2	7
Does not avail	Gal.	5	6
uncle *a male relative*			
Abraham	Gen.	13	7–9
Laban	Gen.	29	12, 13
Mordecai of Esther	Esth.	2	7
unclean *impure*			
Animals	Lev.	11	1–47
	Lev.	20	25
	Deut.	14	3
Spirits	Mat.	10	1
	Mat.	12	43, 45
	Acts	5	16
	Rev.	16	13
Sharp difference between	Lev.	10	10
Of a person until evening	Lev.	11	24
A woman seven days	Lev.	12	2, 5
To be cried by leper	Lev.	13	45
Of a place	Lev.	14	40
Nazarite shall not for the dead	Num.	6	7
Peter would not eat	Acts	10	28
Paul's teachings on	Rom.	14	14
uncleanliness *filth*			
Leprosy is	Lev.	13	9–17
Causes of	Lev.	15	1–33

uncorruptible			
God	Rom.	1	23
unction see anointing			
undefiled *pure, without evil*			
Christ is	Heb.	7	26
The marriage bed	Heb.	13	4
Religion	James	1	27
Inheritance	I Pet.	1	4
understanding *wisdom*			
Given by God	I Chr.	22	12
By God's word	Ps.	119	104
Imparts forbearance	Prov.	14	29
Mature	I Cor.	14	20
understanding			
Wisdom and *u*	Ex.	31	3
	Deut.	4	6
Hast asked *u*	I Ki.	3	11
God gave Solomon wisdom and *u*	I Ki.	4	29
Filled with wisdom and *u*	I Ki.	7	14
Men that had *u* of the times	I Chr.	12	32
Had *u* in visions	II Chr.	26	5
He hath counsel and *u*	Job	12	13
Thou hast hid their heart from *u*	Job	17	4
Where is the place of *u*?	Job	28	12
To depart from evil is *u*	Job	28	28
The Almighty giveth them *u*	Job	32	8
Who hath given *u* to the heart?	Job	38	36
Neither imparted to her *u*	Job	39	17
Sing ye praises with *u*	Ps.	47	7
Meditation of my heart shall be of *u*	Ps.	49	3
Give me *u*	Ps.	119	34
I have more *u* than my teachers	Ps.	119	99
His *u* is infinite	Ps.	147	5
Apply thine heart to *u*	Prov.	2	2
U shall keep thee	Prov.	2	11
Lean not to thine own *u*	Prov.	3	5
Happy is the man that getteth *u*	Prov.	3	13
By *u* hath he established the heavens	Prov.	3	19
Get wisdom, get *u*	Prov.	4	5, 7
Doth not *u* put forth her voice?	Prov.	8	1
Go in the way of *u*	Prov.	9	6
The knowledge of the holy is *u*	Prov.	9	10
He that is slow to wrath is of great *u*	Prov.	14	29
U is a wellspring of life	Prov.	16	22
He that keepeth *u* shall find good	Prov.	19	8
There is no *u* against the Lord	Prov.	21	30
By instruction and *u*	Prov.	23	23
By *u* an house is established	Prov.	24	3
Prince that wanteth *u*	Prov.	28	16
Have not the *u* of a man	Prov.	30	2
Nor riches to men of *u*	Eccl.	9	11
The spirit of *u* shall rest on him	Is.	11	2
Make him of quick *u*	Is.	11	3
A people of no *u*	Is.	27	11
The *u* of prudent men shall be hid	Is.	29	14
There is no searching of his *u*	Is.	40	28
He stretched out the heaven by *u*	Jer.	51	15
Mine *u* returned unto me	Dan.	4	34
Are ye without *u*?	Mat.	15	16
	Mark	7	18
To love him with all the *u*	Mark	12	33
Astonished at his *u*	Luke	2	47
Then opened he their *u*	Luke	24	45
Without *u*	Rom.	1	31
Bring to nothing *u* of prudent	I Cor.	1	19
Pray with the *u* also	I Cor.	14	15
In *u* be men	I Cor.	14	20
Eyes of *u* being enlightened	Eph.	1	18
Having the *u* darkened	Eph.	4	18
Peace of God, which passeth all *u*	Phil.	4	7
Filled with all spiritual *u*	Col.	1	9
Riches of full assurance of *u*	Col.	2	2
God hath given us an *u*	I John	5	20
unfaithfulness *not faithful*			
Of Israel	Jer.	11	9, 10
Judgment against	Mat.	21	42, 43
Of wife	Hosea	1	2
unfortunates *unsuccessful people*			
Army of	I Sam.	22	1, 2
unfruitfulness *without fruit*			
Vineyard, Israel	Is.	5	2, 3
Hewn down	Mat.	7	19
Pruned from the vine	John	15	2–6
The causes of:			
Worldliness	Mat.	13	22
Negligence	Luke	19	20–27

Results of:			
God's judgment	Mat.	3	10
Disappointment	Luke	13	6–9
Rejection	Heb.	6	8
ungodliness *state of being ungodly*			
God angry at	Rom.	1	18
Should avoid	Tit.	2	12
In men	II Pet.	3	7
ungodly *wicked, sinful*			
U men made me afraid	II Sam.	22	5
	Ps.	18	4
Shouldest thou help the *u*?	II Chr.	19	2
God hath delivered me to the *u*	Job	16	11
Is it fit to say, ye are *u*?	Job	34	18
The counsel of the *u*	Ps.	1	1
The way of the *u* shall perish	Ps.	1	6
Plead my cause against an *u* nation	Ps.	43	1
These *u* who prosper	Ps.	73	12
An *u* man diggeth up evil	Prov.	16	27
An *u* witness scorneth judgment	Prov.	19	28
Christ died for the *u*	Rom.	5	6
Where shall the *u* appear?	I Pet.	4	18
Ensample unto those that live *u*	II Pet.	2	6
Perdition of *u* men	II Pet.	3	7
U men, turning grace of God into lasciviousness	Jude		4
(*See* Rom. 1:18; II Tim. 2:16; Tit. 2:12)			
unicorn *a horned beast, wild ox*			
Has great strength	Num.	23	22
	Job	39	9–12
Agile of foot	Ps.	29	6
Figurative of the judgments of God	Is.	34	7
union with Christ			
Advantages of	Eccl.	4	9–12
Assurance of	John	14	20
Is of God	I Cor.	1	30
In the Lord's supper	I Cor.	10	16, 17
Maintained by faith	Gal.	2	20
Ends distinction	Eph.	2	10–14
As marriage	Eph.	5	20–25
As body	I Cor.	12	10–20
As vine	John	15	4, 5
unity *oneness*			
Of the church	John	10	16
	Rom.	12	5
	I Cor.	10	17
	I Cor.	12	13
	Gal.	3	28
	Eph.	1	10
	Eph.	2	19
	Eph.	3	4
	Eph.	5	23, 30
Of brethren	Ps.	133	1
	John	17	21
	Acts	4	42
Enjoined	Rom.	12	16
	Rom.	15	5
	I Cor.	1	10
	II Cor.	13	11
	Phil.	1	27
	Phil.	2	2
	I Pet.	3	8
For brethren to dwell together in *u*	Ps.	133	1
Endeavouring to keep *u* of the Spirit	Eph.	4	3
Till we come in *u* of the faith	Eph.	4	13
(*See* Gen. 49:6; Ps. 86:11)			
unjust *not fair*			
Deliver me from *u* man	Ps.	43	1
Hope of *u* man perisheth	Prov.	11	7
He that *u* gain	Prov.	28	8
An *u* man is an abomination	Prov.	29	27
The *u* knoweth no shame	Zeph.	3	5
He sendeth rain on just an *u*	Mat.	5	45
He that is *u* in least is *u* in much	Luke	16	10
Hear what the *u* judge saith	Luke	18	6
Not as other men, *u*	Luke	18	11
Resurrection of just and *u*	Acts	24	15
Go to law before the *u*	I Cor.	6	1
Christ suffered, the just for the *u*	I Pet.	3	18
Reserve *u* to day of judgment	II Pet.	2	9
He that is *u*, let him be *u* still	Rev.	22	11
unknown			
To the *u* God	Acts	17	23
Speaketh in *u* tongue	I Cor.	14	2
As *u* and yet well known	II Cor.	6	9

unlawful

An *u* thing for a Jew	Acts	10	28
Vexed his soul with their *u* deeds	II Pet.	2	8

unleavened bread

Used at passover	Ex.	12	18
Used as an offering	Lev.	7	12
Feast of	Lev.	23	6
Typical	I Cor.	5	7

unmercifulness *having no mercy*

Simeon and Levi	Gen.	34	
Refusal to pardon is	Mat.	6	15
In business	Mat.	18	28
God has	Mat.	18	35
Harsh judgment because of	James	2	13

Unni *answering is with Jehovah*

A musician who lived in David's time	I Chr.	15	16, 18, 20
A Levite during Nehemiah's time	Neh.	12	1, 9

unpardonable sin

Blasphemy of the Holy Ghost	Mat.	12	31, 32
	Luke	12	10

unprofitable

Reason with *u* talk	Job	15	3
Cast *u* servant into darkness	Mat.	25	30
Say, We are *u* servants	Luke	17	10
Together become *u*	Rom.	3	12
In time past *u*	Philem.		11
Not with grief: for that is *u*	Heb.	13	17
(See Heb. 7:18)			

unrighteous

An *u* witness	Ex.	23	1
Deliver me out of hand of *u*	Ps.	71	4
Decree *u* decrees	Is.	10	1
Let *u* man forsake his thoughts	Is.	55	7
Not faithful in *u* mammon	Luke	16	11
Is God *u* who taketh vengeance?	Rom.	3	5
U shall not inherit the kingdom	I Cor.	6	9
God not *u* to forget	Heb.	6	10

unrighteousness *wickedness*

Should be avoided by Christians	Rom.	6	13
Some find pleasure in	II Thes.	2	12
The blood of Christ cleanses	I John	1	7
Do no *u* in judgment	Lev.	19	15
There is no *u* in him	Ps.	92	15
Mammon of *u*	Luke	16	9
True, and no *u* in him	John	7	18
Hold the truth in *u*	Rom.	1	18
Them that obey *u*	Rom.	2	8
If our *u* commend righteousness	Rom.	3	5
Instruments of *u*	Rom.	6	13
Is there *u* with God?	Rom.	9	14
What fellowship with *u*?	II Cor.	6	14
Pleasure in *u*	II Thes.	2	12
Be merciful to their *u*	Heb.	8	12
Receive the reward of *u*	II Pet.	2	13
To cleanse us from all *u*	I John	1	9
All *u* is sin	I John	5	17

unselfishness *not selfish*
Examples of:

Abraham	Gen.	13	9
King of Sodom	Gen.	14	21
Judah	Gen.	44	33, 34
Moses	Num.	11	29
Gideon	Judg.	8	22, 23
Saul	I Sam.	11	12, 13
Jonathan	I Sam.	23	17, 18
David	II Sam.	23	16, 17
Nehemiah	Neh.	5	14–18
Daniel	Dan.	5	17
Jonah	Jonah	1	12, 13
Joseph	Mat.	1	19
The disciples	Acts	4	34, 35
Christ	I Cor.	8	9
Paul	I Cor.	10	33
Philemon	Philem.		13, 14
Priscilla and Aquila	Rom.	16	3, 4
Onesiphorus	II Tim.	1	16–18
Shows true love	Mat.	22	39
In the ministry	John	3	27, 30
Christians must be	Phil.	2	3

unworldliness *state of being unworldly*

Has divine purpose	John	15	19
In consecration	Rom.	12	1, 2
In the ministry	II Tim.		
Moses has	Heb.	11	24, 25
In true love for God	I John	2	15
Mind things above	Col.	3	1–3

unworthiness *being unworthy*
Examples of:

John the Baptist	Mat.	3	1, 11
The centurion	Mat.	8	8
The saints	Mat.	25	37–39
Peter	Luke	5	8
Paul	I Cor.	15	9
Corinthians	I Cor.	6	2
Jews	Acts	13	46

Upharsin *divided*

One of the words written on the wall	Dan.	5	25, 28

Uphaz *desire of fine gold*

A country known for its gold	Jer.	10	9

uphold *sustain, approve*

U me with thy free spirit	Ps.	51	12
Lord is with them that *u* my soul	Ps.	54	4
U me according to thy word	Ps.	119	116
The Lord *u* all that fall	Ps.	145	14
Honour shall *u* humble	Prov.	29	23
I will *u* thee with the right hand	Is.	41	10
My servant, whom I *u*	Is.	42	1
Wondered that there was none to *u*	Is.	63	5
U all things by word of his power	Heb.	1	3

upright

With *u* show thyself *u*	II Sam.	22	26
	Ps.	18	25
The *u* man is laughed to scorn	Job	12	4
U men shall be astonied	Job	17	8
Good and *u* is the Lord	Ps.	25	8
	Ps.	92	15
Mark the perfect man, and behold the *u*	Ps.	37	37
The *u* shall have dominion	Ps.	49	14
The assembly of the *u*	Ps.	111	1
To the *u* ariseth light	Ps.	112	4
That are *u* in their hearts	Ps.	125	4
The *u* shall dwell in thy presence	Ps.	140	13
The *u* shall dwell in the land	Prov.	2	21
Way of Lord is strength to the *u*	Prov.	10	29
The integrity of the *u*	Prov.	11	3
U in their way are his delight	Prov.	11	20
Tabernacle of the *u* shall flourish	Prov.	14	11
The prayer of the *u* is his delight	Prov.	15	8
The *u* shall have good things	Prov.	28	10
God hath made man *u*	Eccl.	7	29
His soul is not *u* in him	Hab.	2	4

uprightness *being honest and just*

God's pleasure in	I Chr.	29	17
In the heart	II Chr.	29	34
Can secure peace	Ps.	37	37
In speech	Is.	33	15

uprising *see rebellion*

Ur *fiery*

A city of Chaldees, home of Abraham	Gen.	11	28, 31
	Gen.	15	7
	Neh.	9	7
Father of Eliphal	I Chr.	11	35

Urbane *polite*

A Christian at Rome	Rom.	16	9

Uriah, Urijah, Urias *Jehovah is my light*

One of the mighty men of David	II Sam.	23	39
	I Chr.	11	41
David commits adultery with the wife of	II Sam.	11	2–5
	I Ki.	15	5
David summons him from war	II Sam.	11	6–13
David plans death of	II Sam.	11	14–25
David marries his widow	II Sam.	11	26, 27
Also called Urias	Mat.	1	6
A priest, Meremoth's father	Ezra	8	33
Also called Urijah	Neh.	3	4, 21
A priest who witnesses one of Isaiah's predictions	Is.	8	2
Also called Urijah	II Ki.	16	10
A prophet	Jer.	26	20

Uriel *God is light*

A Levite of the family of Kohath	I Chr.	6	1, 24
	I Chr.	15	5, 11
Father of Michaiah	II Chr.	13	2

Urijah *see Uriah*

Urim and Thummim *lights and perfections*

Sacred objects in the breastplate	Ex.	28	30
	Lev.	8	8
After judgment of	Num.	27	21
Only priests are allowed to interpret	Deut.	33	8
	Ezra	2	63
	Neh.	7	65

Answer of the, not given to King Saul	I Sam.	28	6
Israel consults	Judg.	1	1
	Judg.	20	18, 23
Not found in postexilic period	Ezra	2	63

use

Good to *u* of edifying	Eph.	4	29
Meet for master's *u*	II Tim.	2	21
Works for necessary *u*	Tit.	3	14
U not vain repetitions	Mat.	6	7
That *u* this world, as not abusing it	I Cor.	7	31
U not liberty for an occasion to the flesh	Gal.	5	13
If a man *u* it lawfully	I Tim.	1	8
Not *u* liberty for a cloak	I Pet.	2	16

usurpation *taking place or power of another*

Political:

Absalom	II Sam.	15	1-12
Adonijah	I Ki.	1	5-9
Baasha	I Ki.	15	27
Zimri	I Ki.	16	9
Jehu	II Ki.	9	11-37
Athaliah	II Ki.	11	1-16
Shallum	II Ki.	15	10

Religious:

Saul	I Sam.	13	8-14
Solomon	I Ki.	2	26, 27
Uzziah	II Chr.	26	16-21
Ahaz	II Ki.	16	12, 13

usury *excessive interest from loans*

Forbidden	Lev.	25	35-37
	Deut.	23	19
Some Jews guilty of	Neh.	5	1-13
(See interest)			

utmost sea *see Galilee*

utter

My lips shall *u* knowledge	Job	33	3
Day unto day *u* speech	Ps.	19	2
I will *u* dark sayings	Ps.	78	2
Who can *u* the mighty acts of the Lord	Ps.	106	2
Shall *u* memory of goodness	Ps.	145	7
Wisdom *u* her voice	Prov.	1	20
False witness will *u* lies	Prov.	14	5
Thine heart shall *u* perverse things	Prov.	23	33
A fool *u* all his mind	Prov.	29	11
Let not thine heart be hasty to *u* before God	Eccl.	5	2
Lord shall *u* his voice	Joel	2	11
Groanings that cannot be *u*	Rom.	8	26
Not lawful for a man to *u*	II Cor.	12	4
Things hard to be *u*	Heb.	5	11

uttermost *extreme, furtherest*

Give *u* parts of earth for possession	Ps.	2	8
Till thou hast paid the *u* farthing	Mat.	5	26
Came from *u* parts to hear	Mat.	12	42
Wrath is come to the *u*	I Thes.	2	16
Save them to the *u* that come	Heb.	7	25

Uz *counsel, firmness*

Descendant of Shem	Gen.	10	23
Son of Nahor and Milcah	Gen.	22	20, 21
Descendant of Seir	Gen.	36	28
The home of Job	Job	1	1

Uzza, Uzzah *strength*

The driver of the cart which carries the ark to Jerusalem	II Sam.	6	3-11
The owner of a garden	II Ki.	21	18, 26
Descendant of Merari	I Chr.	6	29
A Benjamite	I Chr.	8	1, 6, 7
An ancestor of a family of the Nethinim	Ezra	2	43, 49

Uzzi *Jehovah is strength*

A priest, son of Bukki	I Chr.	6	5, 6, 51
Grandson of Issachar	I Chr.	7	2, 3
Grandson of Benjamin	I Chr.	7	6, 7
Son of Michri	I Chr.	9	8
An overseer of the Levites at Jerusalem	Neh.	11	22
Head of the priests of Jedaiah	Neh.	12	19, 42

Uzziah, Ozias *Jehovah is my strength*

King of Judah, son of Amaziah	II Ki.	15	1-3
	Mat.	1	8
Burns incense and is stricken with leprosy	II Chr.	26	16-21
A long reign	II Ki.	15	1, 2
During life of Isaiah	Is.	1	1
Death of	II Chr.	26	23
Son of Uriel, a Levite	I Chr.	6	24
Father of Jehonathan	I Chr.	27	25
A priest who puts away his foreign wife	Ezra	10	18, 19, 21
Father of Athaiah	Neh.	11	4

Uzziel *God is my strength*

The son of Kohath	Num.	3	19, 27, 30
A captain of the tribe of Simeon	I Chr.	4	41-43
Son of Bela	I Chr.	7	7
The head of David's musicians	I Chr.	25	1, 4
Son of Jeduthun	II Chr.	29	14
A goldsmith who helps repair the walls of Jerusalem	Neh.	3	8

V

vagabond *wanderer*

Cain is called a	Gen.	4	9, 12
Wandering exorcists	Acts	19	13
Children of the wicked	Ps.	109	10

vagrancy *shiftlessness*

The law regarding	Deut.	21	18-21

vail, veil *a covering*

A token of modesty	Gen.	24	65
Worn by women for concealment	Gen.	38	14
Removing of, considered rude	S. of S.	5	7
Shows subjection	I Cor.	11	3-10
Used figuratively	II Cor.	3	14-16
	Heb.	10	20

The sacred:

Moses commanded to make	Ex.	26	31-33
Made by Bezaleel	Ex.	36	35
Designed to conceal the holy of holies	Ex.	40	3
Rent at the death of Jesus	Mat.	27	51

vain *empty, worthless*

Not regard *v* words	Ex.	5	9
Not take the name of the Lord in *v*	Ex.	20	7
	Deut.	5	11
It is not a *v* thing for you	Deut.	32	47
Turn not after *v* things	I Sam.	12	21
They are but *v* words	II Ki.	18	20
	Is.	36	5
V man would be wise	Job	11	12
Shall *v* words have an end?	Job	16	3
The people imagine a *v* thing	Ps.	2	1
	Acts	4	25
Not sat with *v* persons	Ps.	26	4
Horse is a *v* thing for safety	Ps.	33	17
Every man walketh in a *v* show	Ps.	39	6
V is the help of man	Ps.	60	11
	Ps.	108	12
Wherefore hast thou made all men in *v*?	Ps.	89	47
It is *v* for you to rise early	Ps.	127	2
Followeth *v* persons	Prov.	12	11
	Prov.	28	19
Beauty is *v*	Prov.	31	30
All the days of his *v* life	Eccl.	6	12
Bring no more *v* oblations	Is.	1	13
I said not, Seek ye me in *v*	Is.	45	19
Laboured in *v*, spent strength in *v*	Is.	49	4
In *v* is salvation hoped for	Jer.	3	23
How long shall thy *v* thoughts lodge?	Jer.	4	14
In *v* shalt thou use medicines	Jer.	46	11
Ye have said, It is *v* to serve God	Mal.	3	14
V repetitions	Mat.	6	7
In *v* do they worship me	Mat.	15	9
	Mark	7	7
Became *v* in their imaginations	Rom.	1	21
He beareth not the sword in *v*	Rom.	13	4
Your labour is not in *v*	I Cor.	15	58
Receive not the grace of God in *v*	II Cor.	6	1
Lest I should run in *v*	Gal.	2	2
Philosophy and *v* deceit	Col.	2	8
V babblings	I Tim.	6	20
	II Tim.	2	16
This man's religion is *v*	James	1	26
Redeemed from *v* conversation	I Pet.	1	18

vainglory *self-pride, vanity*

Is certain to lead to strife	Gal.	5	26
	Phil.	2	3

Vajezatha *strong as the wind*

One of Haman's sons	Esth.	9	9

valley *land between mountains*

Plentiful with fountains and springs	Deut.	8	7

valley—continued

Canaan abounds in	Deut.	11	11
Used figuratively	Ps.	23	4
	Luke	3	5
Often the scene of idolatrous rites	Is.	57	5

Mentioned in the Bible:

Hebron	Gen.	37	14
Jericho	Deut.	34	3
Moab	Deut.	34	6
Achor	Josh.	7	24
Ajalon	Josh.	10	12
Lebanon	Josh.	11	17
Salt	II Sam.	8	13
Succoth	Ps.	60	6
Baca	Ps.	84	6
Vision	Is.	22	1
Gibeon	Is.	28	21
Slaughter	Jer.	7	32
Decision, Jehoshaphat	Joel	3	2, 14
Hinnom	Josh.	15	8
Kidron	II Chr.	30	14
Jezreel	Judg.	6	33

valley gate

One of the gates of Jerusalem	Neh.	2	13

valley of dry bones

In Ezekiel's dream	Ezek.	37	1–14

value worth

Physicians of no v	Job	13	4
Ye are of more v than many sparrows	Mat.	10	31
	Luke	12	7
Whom they of Israel did v	Mat.	27	9

vanish disappear

Heavens shall v away	Is.	51	6
He v out of their sight	Luke	24	31
Knowledge, it shall v	I Cor.	13	8
Waxeth old, ready to v	Heb.	8	13
Life is a vapour that v	James	4	14

vanity emptiness

Idolatry	II Ki.	17	15
Beauty of man	Ps.	39	11
Man's thoughts	Ps.	94	11
Shows the transitory nature of man	Ps.	144	4
Childhood and youth	Eccl.	1	10
Worldly pleasure	Eccl.	2	1
Worldly possessions	Eccl.	2	4–11
Worldly wisdom	Eccl.	2	15, 21
Love of riches	Eccl.	5	10
Self-righteousness	Is.	57	12
A consequence of the fall	Rom.	8	20
Religion of hypocrites	James	1	26
Faith without works	James	2	14

Vashni Jehovah is strong

Son of Samuel	I Chr.	6	28
Probably same as Joel	I Chr.	6	33

Vashti the best

The wife of King Ahasuerus	Esth.	1	9
Refuses to dance and is divorced	Esth.	1	19–22

veal flesh of calves

King Saul receives	I Sam.	28	21–25

veil see vail

Of Rebekah	Gen.	24	65
Of Tamar	Gen.	38	14, 19
Of Moses	Ex.	34	33, 35

vengeance revenge

Belongs to God	Deut.	32	35
	Ps.	99	8
	Is.	34	8
	Jer.	50	15
	Ezek.	24	25
	Nah.	1	2
	II Thes.	1	8
Rejoice when he seeth v	Ps.	58	10
To me belongeth v	Ps.	94	1
	Heb.	10	30
The day of v	Prov.	6	34
	Is.	34	8
	Is.	61	2
	Jer.	51	6
Your God will come with v	Is.	35	4
Garments of v for clothing	Is.	59	17
For these be days of v	Luke	21	22
Whom v suffereth not to live	Acts	28	4
V is mine, saith the Lord	Rom.	12	19
The v of eternal fire	Jude		7

veneration respect

For parents	Gen.	48	15, 16
For leaders	Ex.	33	8
For God	Ps.	33	8
For God's possessions	Eccl.	5	1

vengeance revenge

On Hamor and Shechem	Gen.	34	20–31
Belongs to God	Deut.	32	35

venison flesh of game animal

Eaten by Isaac	Gen.	25	28

venom poison of snakes

Of asps	Deut.	32	33

verdict a decision, judgment

A sentence of the law	Deut.	17	9–12
Against Jesus	Mat.	26	63–66

verily truly

Are v guilty concerning	Gen.	42	21
Saying, v my sabbaths	Ex.	31	13
I v thought thou hadst hated her	Judg.	15	2
V our Lord hath made	I Ki.	1	43
V she hath no child, her	II Ki.	4	14
Do good, and v thou	Ps.	37	3
V every man at his best state	Ps.	39	5
V there is a reward for the righteous, v he is a God that	Ps.	58	11
But v God hath heard me	Ps.	66	19
V I have cleansed my heart	Ps.	73	13
V thou art a God that hidest thyself	Is.	45	15
V it shall be well with thy remnant, v I will cause the	Jer.	15	11
V I say unto you	Mat.	5	18
	Mat.	5	2, 5, 16
	Mat.	8	10
	Mat.	10	15, 23, 42
	Mark	3	28
	Luke	4	24
	Luke	11	51
V I say unto thee	Mat.	5	26
	Mat.	26	34
Elias v cometh first	Mark	9	12
Nay v let them come	Acts	16	37
John v baptized with baptism	Acts	19	4
Am v a man which am a Jew	Acts	22	3
I v though I ought to do	Acts	26	9
For circumcision v profiteth if thou	Rom.	2	25
V their sound went into all	Rom.	10	18
Pleased them v; debtors they	Rom.	15	27
I v as absent in body	I Cor.	5	3
V righteousness had been	Gal.	3	21
For v he took not on him the nature of angels	Heb.	2	16
For men v swear by the greater	Heb.	6	16

vessel utensil

Of the temple	I Ki.	7	40
Carried to Babylon	II Ki.	25	13, 14
Restored	Ezra	1	7
Profaned	Dan.	5	2
A potter's	Ps.	2	9
	Ps.	31	12
Clean	Is.	66	20
Marred	Jer.	18	4
Moab broken as	Jer.	48	38
Empty	Jer.	51	34
In Peter's vision	Acts	10	11
Of God's election	Rom.	9	21, 23
Wife as weaker	I Pet.	3	7

vestment see garment

vestry a room where garments are kept

In the temple of Baal	II Ki.	10	22

vex annoy

Thou shalt not v a stranger	Ex.	22	21
	Lev.	19	33
How will he v himself?	II Sam.	12	18
How long will ye v my soul?	Job	19	2
Shall v them in his displeasure	Ps.	2	5
Judah shall not v Ephraim	Is.	11	13
They rebelled, and v his Holy Spirit	Is.	63	10
V his righteous soul	II Pet.	2	8

vial cruet, flask

Full of odours	Rev.	5	8
The seven	Rev.	15	7
Samuel's	I Sam.	10	1

vices evil conduct, faults in character

Mental	Gal.	5	20
Physical	Gal.	5	19, 21

victory
Celebrated by women	I Sam.	18	6, 7
In battle comes from God	Ps.	55	18
Over death	I Cor.	15	52–57
Of Christ	Rev.	17	14
Lord's	II Sam.	23	10
Over the beast	Rev.	15	2

victuals *food*
Forbidden to sell on the sabbath day	Neh.	10	31
Complaining for	Jer.	44	17
For the multitude	Mat.	14	15

vile *very bad*
Thy brother should seem *v*	Deut.	25	3
Sons made themselves *v*	I Sam.	3	13
Wherefore are we reputed *v*?	Job	18	3
I am *v*; what shall I answer thee?	Job	40	4
A *v* person	Ps.	15	4
	Is.	32	5
	Dan.	11	21
Take forth the precious from the *v*	Jer.	15	19
God gave them up to *v* affections	Rom.	1	26
Who shall change our *v* body	Phil.	3	21
A poor man in *v* raiment	James	2	2

vindictiveness *being revengeful*
Elisha forbids	II Ki.	6	21, 22
Jesus condemns	Luke	9	54, 55

vine
Fable of	Judg.	9	12, 13
Parables of Israel	Ps.	80	8–14
	Ezek.	17	6–10
	Ezek.	19	10–14
Laid waste	Is.	5	6
Jesus called a	John	15	1–7
Of earth	Rev.	14	18, 19
In a dream	Gen.	40	9, 10
Of Sodom	Deut.	32	32
Of peace	I Ki.	4	25
	Zech.	3	10
A wild	II Ki.	4	39
Of a wife	Ps.	128	3
Fruitful	Is.	32	12
Of Israel	Hosea	10	1

vine dresser
Of Israel	II Ki.	25	12

vinegar *a sour wine*
Forbidden	Num.	6	3
Used as spice with food	Ruth	2	14
Given to Jesus on the cross	Mat.	27	34, 48

vineyards
Damage to, forbidden	Ex.	22	5
Frequently walled or fenced	Num.	22	24
Of Naboth	I Ki.	21	1–16
Of the kings of Israel	I Chr.	27	26–28
Leased	S. of S.	8	11, 12
Cottages built in, for keepers	Is.	1	8
Winepress in	Is.	5	2
Towers in	Is.	5	2
	Mat.	21	33
Of red grapes particularly esteemed	Is.	27	2
Rechabites forbidden to plant	Jer.	35	7–9
Parable of	Mark	12	1–12

vintage *harvest of grapes*
Of the wicked	Job	24	6
Gathered in baskets	Jer.	6	9

viol
An instrument of music	Is.	5	12

violence *harmful action*
Earth was filled with *v*	Gen.	6	11
Him that loveth *v*	Ps.	11	5
Redeem their soul from *v*	Ps.	72	14
V covereth them as a garment	Ps.	73	6
They drink the wine of *v*	Prov.	4	17
Because he had done no *v*	Is.	53	9
V shall no more be heard	Is.	60	18
They have filled the land with *v*	Ezek.	8	17
	Ezek.	28	16
Cry to thee of *v*	Hab.	1	2
Covereth *v* with garment	Mal.	2	16
Kingdom of heaven suffereth *v*	Mat.	11	12
Do *v* to no man	Luke	3	14
Quenched *v* of fire	Heb.	11	34

viper *small snake*
A serpent	Job	20	16
Bites Paul on the hand	Acts	28	3–5

virgins *young women*
A penalty for seducing	Deut.	22	28, 29
Apparel of	II Sam.	13	18
Christ born of	Mat.	1	18
Parable of ten	Mat.	25	1–13
Care for things of God	I Cor.	7	34

virtuous women *pure women*
Pleasure to husbands	Prov.	12	4
Described	Prov.	31	10–31
Apparel of	I Tim.	2	9, 10

visage *countenance*
Marred	Is.	52	14
Form of, changed	Dan.	3	19

visions *mental sight*
In answer to prayer	II Ki.	6	17
God's will made known by	Ps.	89	19
False prophets pretend to have	Jer.	14	14
Frequently difficult to interpret	Dan.	7	15
Lack of	I Sam.	3	1
In the night	Job	20	8
If none the people perish	Prov.	29	18
Valley of	Is.	22	1
False	Jer.	14	14
	Jer.	23	16

Given to:
Abraham	Gen.	15	1
Jacob	Gen.	46	2
Moses	Ex.	3	2, 3
Samuel	I Sam.	3	2–15
Nathan	II Sam.	7	4, 17
Eliphaz	Job	4	13–16
Isaiah	Is.	6	1–8
Ezekiel	Ezek.	1	4–14
Nebuchadnezzar	Dan.	2	28
Daniel	Dan.	7, 8	
Peter	Acts	10	9–17
Paul	II Cor.	12	1–11
John	Rev.	1	1
Balaam	Num.	24	4
Nahum	Nah.	1	1

visit
God will *v* you	Gen.	50	24
	Ex.	13	19
V iniquity of fathers	Ex.	20	5
	Ex.	34	7
	Num.	14	18
	Deut.	5	9
When I *v* I will *v* their sin upon them	Ex.	32	34
That thou shouldest *v* him	Job	7	18
The son of man, that thou *v* him	Ps.	8	4
	Heb.	2	6
Look down, and *v* this vine	Ps.	80	14
V me with thy salvation	Ps.	106	4
Shall I not *v* for these things?	Jer.	5	9
	Jer.	9	9
I was sick, and ye *v* me	Mat.	25	36
God hath *v* and redeemed his people	Luke	1	68
To *v* his brethren	Acts	7	23
God did *v* Gentiles	Acts	15	14
To *v* fatherless and widows	James	1	27

visitation of sick
Ahaziah visits Joram	II Ki.	8	29
Joash visits Elisha	II Ki.	13	14
Job is visited by friends	Job	2	11
Approved by God	Mat.	25	36
A duty	James	5	14

voice of God
Proclaims the law	Ex.	20	1–17
Its majesty and power	Ps.	18	13

Heard by:
Adam	Gen.	3	9, 10
Moses	Ex.	3	14
Samuel	I Sam.	3	4
Elijah	I Ki.	19	12, 13
Ezekiel	Ezek.	1	24
Christ at His baptism	Mat.	3	17
The disciples	Mat.	17	5
Saul of Tarsus	Acts	9	4
John	Rev.	1	10

voice
The *v* of thy brother's blood	Gen.	4	10
The *v* is Jacob's *v*	Gen.	27	22
Beware of him, and obey his *v*	Ex.	23	21
All the people answered with one *v*	Ex.	24	3
Did ever people hear *v* of God, and live?	Deut.	4	33

voice—*continued*

After the fire a still small *v*	I Ki.	19	12
There was neither *v* nor hearing	II Ki.	4	31
The *v* of them that weep	Job	30	31
Canst thou thunder with a *v* like him?	Job	40	9
The *v* of my supplications	Ps.	31	22
	Ps.	86	6
With the *v* of joy	Ps.	42	4
The floods have lifted up their *v*	Ps.	93	3
To-day if ye will hear his *v*	Ps.	95	7
	Heb.	3	7, 15
Hearkening to *v* of his word	Ps.	103	20
My *v* is to sons of man	Prov.	8	4
Rise up at the *v* of the bird	Eccl.	12	4
The *v* of the turtle is heard	S. of S.	2	12
Gracious at *v* of thy cry	Is.	30	19
The *v* of him that crieth	Is.	40	3
A *v* of singing	Is.	48	20
With the *v* together shall they sing	Is.	52	8
The *v* of weeping shall be no more heard	Is.	65	19
The *v* of them that make merry	Jer.	30	19
A *v* of a multitude at ease	Ezek.	23	42
One that hath a pleasant *v*	Ezek.	33	32
V like a noise of many waters	Ezek.	43	2
	Rev.	1	15
With *v* of thanksgiving	Jonah	2	9
The *v* of one crying in the wilderness	Mat.	3	3
	Mark	1	3
	Luke	3	4
	John	1	23
Neither shall any man hear his *v*	Mat.	12	19
A *v* from heaven	Mark	1	11
	Luke	3	22
The dead shall hear the *v* of the Son of God	John	5	25
The sheep know his *v*	John	10	4
This *v* came not because of me	John	12	30
Every one that is of the truth heareth my *v*	John	18	37
Except it be for this one *v*	Acts	24	21
I gave my *v* against them	Acts	26	10
By my *v* I might teach others	I Cor.	14	19
I desire to change my *v*	Gal.	4	20
Descend with *v* of archangel	I Thes.	4	16
Any man hear my *v*	Rev.	3	20

void *empty*

Earth without form and *v*	Gen.	1	2
	Jer.	4	23
A nation *v* of counsel	Deut.	32	28
Made *v* the covenant	Ps.	89	39
They have made *v* thy law	Ps.	119	126
He that is *v* of wisdom	Prov.	11	12
Word shall not return unto me *v*	Is.	55	11
A conscience *v* of offence	Acts	24	16
Do we make *v* the law?	Rom.	3	31
Faith is made *v*	Rom.	4	14

vomit *eject from stomach*

The wicked	Job	20	15
The dog returns to	Prov.	26	11

vows *solemn promises to God*

Mosaic laws concerning	Lev.	27	1–25
Of a Nazarite	Num.	6	1–21
To be performed faithfully	Num.	30	2–16
To be voluntary	Deut.	23	21, 22

Examples of:

Jacob	Gen.	28	20–22
Israelites	Num.	21	2
Jephthah	Judg.	11	30, 31
Hannah	I Sam.	1	11
Elkanah	I Sam.	1	21
Mother of Micah	Judg.	17	2, 3
Job	Job	31	1
David	Ps.	132	1–5
Pagan sailors	Jonah	1	16
Jonah	Jonah	2	9
Paul	Acts	18	18
Jews with Paul	Acts	21	23–26

voyage *journey*

Of Paul	Acts	27	8, 10

vulture *a carnivorous bird*

Classified as one of the unclean birds	Lev.	11	14
Possibly the falcon	Job	28	7
Used figuratively	Is.	34	15

W

wafers *cakes of bread*

Eaten with honey	Ex.	16	31
Used as offerings	Ex.	29	2, 23

wages *payment for personal labour*

Of Jacob	Gen.	29	15–30
For child-care	Ex.	2	9
To be duly paid	Lev.	19	13
Paid in food	II Chr.	2	10
Parable concerning	Mat.	20	1–15
To be paid promptly	Lev.	19	13
Not muzzle the ox	Deut.	25	4
Woe, if not paid	Jer.	22	13
Oppressor of hireling the Lord will judge	Mal.	3	5
Labourer is worthy of	Luke	10	7

wages of sin

Trouble	Job	15	20–31
Losses on earth	Job	27	13–23
Spiritual death	Rom.	6	23

wagon *a four-wheeled vehicle*

Pharaoh sends a	Gen.	45	19, 21
Oxen pull	Num.	7	3

wailing *lamentation*

A sign of grief	Esth.	4	3
Of the wicked	Mat.	13	42
At the second coming of Jesus	Rev.	1	7
For the destruction of Zion	Jer.	9	10, 18, 19
None for the wicked	Ezek.	7	11
For Israel	Amos	5	16, 17
Of prophet	Mic.	1	8

wait

Should I *w* for the Lord any longer?	II Ki.	6	33
I will *w* till my change come	Job	14	14
If I *w*, the grave is my house	Job	17	13
They *w* for me as for rain	Job	29	23
Let none that *w* be ashamed	Ps.	25	3
	Ps.	69	6
W on the Lord	Ps.	27	14
	Ps.	37	34
	Prov.	20	22
I *w* patiently for the Lord	Ps.	40	1
My soul *w* upon God	Ps.	62	1
Praise *w* for thee, O God, in Zion	Ps.	130	6
	Ps.	65	1
These *w* upon thee	Ps.	145	15
He that *w* on his master	Prov.	27	18
Our God, we *w* for him	Is.	25	9
The Lord *w* to be gracious	Is.	30	18
The isles shall *w* for his law	Is.	42	4
We *w* for light	Is.	59	9
Good that a man hope and quietly *w*	Lam.	3	26
W on thy God continually	Hosea	12	6
I will *w* for the God of my salvation	Mic.	7	7
Though the vision tarry, *w* for it	Hab.	2	3
Who *w* for the kingdom of God	Mark	15	43
W for the consolation of Israel	Luke	2	25
Like men that *w* for their Lord	Luke	12	36
Then do we with patience *w* for it	Rom.	8	25
Let us *w* on our ministering	Rom.	12	7
We *w* for the hope of righteousness	Gal.	5	5

waiting on God

God of providence	Jer.	14	22
Exhortations and encouragements to	Ps.	27	14
	Ps.	37	7
All the day	Ps.	25	5
In the way of his judgments	Is.	26	8
Specially in adversity	Ps.	59	1–9
	Is.	8	17
With hope in his word	Ps.	130	5
With resignation	Lam.	3	26
With the soul	Ps.	62	1, 5
Should be done with patience	Ps.	37	7
As the giver of all good things	Ps.	104	27, 28
For mercy	Ps.	123	2
With earnest desire	Ps.	130	6
Will bring salvation	Prov.	20	22
Those who do, are blessed	Is.	30	18
Provides strength	Is.	40	31
Should be continual	Hosea	12	6
In full confidence	Mic.	7	7
God calls us to	Zeph.	3	8

For the fulfillment of His promises	Acts	1	4
For the coming of Christ	I Cor.	1	7
	I Thes.	1	10
Illustrated	Ps.	123	2
	Luke	12	36
	James	5	7
Is good	Ps.	52	9
The patience of saints often tried in	Ps.	69	3
Predicted of the Gentiles	Is.	42	4
	Is.	60	9

For:

The consolation of Israel	Luke	2	25
The fulfillment of his word	Hab.	2	3
Hope of righteousness by faith	Gal.	5	5
Pardon	Ps.	39	7–8
For guidance and teaching	Ps.	25	5
For protection	Ps.	33	20
	Ps.	59	9–10
Salvation	Gen.	49	18
	Ps.	62	1–2

Saints:

Have expectation from	Ps.	62	5
Plead, in prayer	Ps.	25	21
	Is.	33	2
Resolve on	Ps.	52	9

They who engage in:

Are blessed	Dan.	12	12
Are heard	Ps.	40	1
Experience his goodness	Lam.	3	25
Shall be saved	Is.	25	9
Shall inherit the earth	Ps.	37	9
Shall not be ashamed	Ps.	25	3
	Is.	49	23
Shall receive the glorious things prepared by God for them	Is.	64	4
Shall rejoice in salvation	Is.	25	9
Wait upon him only	Ps.	62	5

wakefulness *alertness*

God asks for	Is.	52	1
To righteousness	I Cor.	15	34
A duty	Eph.	5	14

walk

W before me, and be perfect	Gen.	17	1
The Lord, before whom I *w*	Gen.	24	40
Whether they will *w* in my law	Ex.	16	4
I will *w* among you	Lev.	26	12
Though I *w* in imagination of heart	Deut.	29	19
He *w* in the circuit of heaven	Job	22	14
Though I *w* through valley of shadow of death	Ps.	23	4
I will *w* in mine integrity	Ps.	26	11
W about Zion	Ps.	48	12
We *w* to house of God in company	Ps.	55	14
That I may *w* before God in light of living	Ps.	56	13
From them that *w* uprightly	Ps.	84	11
Shall *w* in light of thy countenance	Ps.	89	15
The pestilence that *w* in darkness	Ps.	91	6
Feet have they, but *w* not	Ps.	115	7
I will *w* before the Lord	Ps.	116	9
I will *w* at liberty	Ps.	119	45
Though I *w* in midst of trouble	Ps.	138	7
Cause me to know wherein I should *w*	Ps.	143	8
Mayest *w* in way of good men	Prov.	2	20
He that *w* uprightly	Prov.	10	9
	Prov.	28	18
He that *w* with wise men shall be wise	Prov.	13	20
The poor that *w* in integrity	Prov.	19	1
	Prov.	28	6
Let us *w* in the light of the Lord	Is.	2	5
The people that *w* in darkness	Is.	9	2
This is the way, *w* in it	Is.	30	21
The redeemed shall *w* there	Is.	35	9
Shall *w* and not faint	Is.	40	31
The good way, and *w* therein	Jer.	6	16
It is not in man that *w* to direct his steps	Jer.	10	23
Those that *w* in pride	Dan.	4	37
The just shall *w* in them	Hosea	14	9
Can two *w* together, except they be agreed?	Amos	3	3
To *w* humbly with thy God	Mic.	6	8
They shall *w* up and down	Zech.	10	12
Jesus appeared to two of them, as they *w*	Mark	16	12
I must *w* to-day and tomorrow	Luke	13	33
Shall not *w* in darkness	John	8	12
If any man *w* in the day	John	11	9
W in newness of life	Rom.	6	4
Who *w* not after the flesh, but after the Spirit	Rom.	8	1
We *w* by faith	II Cor.	5	7
As many as *w* according to this rule	Gal.	6	16
Ordained that we should *w* in them	Eph.	2	10
W worthy of the vocation	Eph.	4	1
See that ye *w* circumspectly	Eph.	5	15
Many *w*, of whom I told you	Phil.	3	18
That ye might *w* worthy of the Lord	Col.	1	10
How ye ought to *w*	I Thes.	4	1
Brother that *w* disorderly	II Thes.	3	6
W about seeking whom he may devour	I Pet.	5	8
If we *w* in the light	I John	1	7
Ought so to *w* as he *w*	I John	2	6

walk with God

We are not to walk:

According to the flesh	Rom.	8	4
Craftily	II Cor.	4	2
In darkness	John	8	12
	I John	1	6
In disorder	II Thes.	3	6
In our own ways	Acts	14	16
In the way of Cain	Jude		11

We are to walk:

As children of light	Eph.	5	8
As Christ walked	I John	2	6
Circumspectly	Eph.	5	15
In the Spirit	Gal.	5	16, 25
According to His command	Deut.	5	33
Uprightly	Prov.	2	7
In the old paths	Jer.	6	16
Humbly with God	Mic.	6	8
In newness of life	Rom.	6	4
"Not after the flesh, but after the spirit"	Rom.	8	1
Honestly	Rom.	13	13
By faith, not by sight	II Cor.	5	7
In love	Eph.	5	2
Worthy of the Lord	Col.	1	10
By the gospel rule	Phil.	3	16
In the light	I John	1	7

Instances of:

Enoch	Gen.	5	24
Noah	Gen.	6	9

wall

Whose branches run over the *w*	Gen.	49	22
The waters were a *w* to them	Ex.	14	22
A *w* being on this side and a *w* on that	Num.	22	24
A *w* by night and day	I Sam.	25	16
I have leaped over a *w*	II Sam.	22	30
	Ps.	18	29
Hyssop that springeth out of *w*	I Ki.	4	33
Turned his face to the *w*	II Ki.	20	2
	Is.	38	2
So built we the *w*	Neh.	4	6
As a bowing *w* shall ye be	Ps.	62	3
Peace be within thy *w*	Ps.	122	7
As high *w* in his own conceit	Prov.	18	11
Stone *w* was broken down	Prov.	24	31
Like a city without *w*	Prov.	25	28
As a storm against the *w*	Is.	25	4
Salvation will God appoint for *w*	Is.	26	1
We grope for the *w*	Is.	59	10
Thou shalt call thy *w* Salvation	Is.	60	18
Will make thee fenced *w*	Jer.	15	20
A hole in the *w*	Ezek.	8	7
Fingers wrote upon the *w*	Dan.	5	5
They shall climb the *w*	Joel	2	7
Leaned hand on *w* and serpent bit him	Amos	5	19
The stone shall cry out of the *w*	Hab.	2	11
Thou whited *w*	Acts	23	3
The middle *w* of partition	Eph.	2	14
The *w* of the city had twelve foundations	Rev.	21	14

walls *defense, rampart*

Of Bashan	Deut.	3	4–6
Of Jericho	Josh.	2	1, 15
Of Beth-shan	I Sam.	31	10
Of Rabbah	II Sam.	11	20
Of Abel	II Sam.	20	15, 21
Of Jerusalem	Neh.	4	1–6
Of Babylon	Jer.	51	44
Handwriting on	Dan.	5	5

wander *go aimlessly*

God caused me to *w*	Gen.	20	13

wander—*continued*

W in wilderness	Num.	14	33
	Ps.	107	4
Cursed be he that maketh blind to *w*	Deut.	27	18
He causeth them to *w*	Job	12	24
He *w* abroad for bread	Job	15	23
Ravens *w* for lack of meat	Job	38	41
Then would I *w* far off	Ps.	55	7
Let them *w* up and down	Ps.	59	15
As a bird that *w* from nest	Prov.	27	8
Shall *w* every one to his quarter	Is.	47	15
They loved to *w*	Jer.	14	10
Shall *w* from sea to sea	Amos	8	12
They *w* about in sheepskins	Heb.	11	37

want *need*

From sin	Deut.	28	48
Of the wicked	Job	15	20, 23
Because of idleness	Prov.	19	15
Made a blessing	Luke	15	11–24
Contentment in	Phil.	4	11, 12
Serve thine enemies in *w*	Deut.	28	48
A place where there is no *w*	Judg.	18	10
Let all thy *w* lie on me	Judg.	19	20
If I have seen any perish for *w*	Job	31	19
There is no *w* to them that fear him	Ps.	34	9
W as an armed man	Prov.	6	11
	Prov.	24	34
I have given *w* of bread	Amos	4	6
She of her *w* cast in all	Mark	12	44
He began to be in *w*	Luke	15	14
Not that I speak of *w*	Phil.	4	11
I shall not *w*	Ps.	23	1
That seek the Lord shall not *w* any good thing	Ps.	34	10
Him that *w* understanding	Prov.	9	4
The wicked shall *w*	Prov.	13	25
None shall *w* her mate	Is.	34	16
That they may *w* bread and water	Ezek.	4	17
When they *w* wine	John	2	3
When I *w*, I was chargeable to no man	II Cor.	11	9
Perfect and entire, *w* nothing	James	1	4

war *armed conflict*

God determines the victor in	Num.	21	2, 3
God frequently orders	Num.	30	1, 2
Armies raised by conscription	Num.	31	2–4
Of extermination	Num.	31	7–17
Portions of booty dedicated to the Lord	Num.	31	37–41
Averted	Josh.	22	11–34
Sent as a punishment for sin	Judg.	5	8
	I Chr.	5	22–26
Returning soldiers greeted with festivities	Judg.	11	34
Booty distributed among victors	I Sam.	30	22–24
Mercenaries employed	II Sam.	10	6–8
Started in the spring	II Sam.	11	1
Tribute demanded	II Ki.	14	14
Repulsive to God	I Chr.	22	8, 9
Forbidden	II Chr.	11	4
God will cause to cease	Ps.	46	9
	Is.	2	7
	Mic.	4	3
God scatters the people who delight in	Ps.	68	30
"A time of war, a time of peace"	Eccl.	3	8
Wisdom required in	Eccl.	9	14–18
	Luke	14	31, 32
Slain often neglected	Is.	14	19
	Is.	18	6
"Wars and rumours of wars"	Mat.	24	6
"All who take the sword, shall perish by the sword"	Mat.	26	52
Originates in the lusts of men	James	4	1

Mosaic laws concerning:

Minimum age	Num.	1	45
New home owners exempt	Deut.	20	5
Betrothed men exempt	Deut.	20	7
Cowards exempt	Deut.	20	8
Fruit trees not to be destroyed	Deut.	20	19
Newly wed husbands exempt	Deut.	24	5

Preceded by:

Dedication	Deut.	20	1–4
Blaring of trumpets	Judg.	7	18
Sacrifice and fasting	I Sam.	7	8, 9
	II Chr.	20	3–13
Consulting the prophets	I Ki.	22	6
Singing to the Lord	II Chr.	20	21
Wise counsel	Prov.	24	6
	Luke	14	31
Great preparation	Joel	3	9

Weapons used in:

Dagger	Judg.	3	16–22
Chariots	Judg.	4	3
Armour	I Sam.	17	38, 39
Stones	I Sam.	17	49
Swords	I Sam.	18	14
Arrows	I Sam.	20	20
Spears	I Sam.	26	7
Battering rams	Ezek.	4	2

Tactics:

Ambush	Josh.	8	12
Dividing companies	Judg.	7	16
Night attacks	Judg.	7	16, 19
Adapted to terrain of country	I Ki.	20	23
Scorched earth policy	II Ki.	3	24, 25

Often attended by:

Desolation	Ps.	46	8
Devastation	Is.	1	7
Oppression	Is.	3	5
Famine	Is.	51	19
Cruelty	Jer.	18	21
Pestilence	Jer.	27	13

wardrobe *one's clothes*

A lady's	Is.	3	17–23

warfare, spiritual

Is against the devil	Gen.	3	15
	Eph.	6	12
Thank God for victory in	Rom.	7	25
Comfort by God in	II Cor.	7	5, 6
Is not of the flesh	II Cor.	10	3
Christians must stand firm in	Eph.	6	13, 14
To be conducted through faith	I Tim.	1	18, 19
Against the world	I John	5	4, 5
Ultimate victory predicted	Rev.	17	14

To be carried on:

With confidence in God	Ps.	27	1–3
With prayer	Ps.	35	1–3
Under the Lord's banner	Ps.	60	4
With stedfastness in the faith	I Cor.	16	13

warning *the act of telling of danger*

Types of:

Despised	Gen.	19	14
Disobedience	Deut.	30	17, 18
Danger	II Ki.	6	8–10
Sorrowful	Mat.	26	21, 22
Solemn	Mat.	26	31
A dream	Mat.	27	19
From hell	Luke	16	23–28
Faithful	Acts	20	31

Examples of:

Asahel	II Sam.	2	20–23
Jesus	Mat.	2	13–15
Noah	Heb.	11	7
Paul	I Cor.	4	14
Saved by	Ezek.	33	1–5
Duty of the guard	Ezek.	33	18–21
Duty to give	Is.	58	1
From history	I Cor.	10	1–11
By example	Jude		7

wash

Go, *w* in Jordan	II Ki.	5	10
If I *w* myself with snow water	Job	9	30
Thou *w* away things which grow	Job	14	19
When I *w* my steps with butter	Job	29	6
I will *w* my hands in innocency	Ps.	26	6
W me throughly from mine iniquity	Ps.	51	2
W me, and I shall be whiter than snow	Ps.	51	7
W you, make you clean	Is.	1	16
Though thou *w* thee with nitre	Jer.	2	22
W thy heart from wickedness	Jer.	4	14
Nor wast *w* in water	Ezek.	16	4
When thou fastest, *w* thy face	Mat.	6	17
Except they *w*, they eat not	Mark	7	4
Began to *w* his feet with tears	Luke	7	38
Go, *w* in the pool of Siloam	John	9	7
Jesus began to *w* disciples' feet	John	13	5
W away thy sins	Acts	22	16
Having our bodies *w* with pure water	Heb.	10	22
W us from our sins	Rev.	1	5
Have *w* their robes	Rev.	7	14

washings *cleansings*

Of the feet	Gen.	18	4
Enjoined by the law	Ex.	29	4
Of the hands	Deut.	21	6
Used figuratively	Is.	4	4
	Eph.	5	26

Traditional, censured	Mark	7	3
Christ washes disciples' feet	John	13	1–15
Through the blood of Christ	I Cor.	6	11

washpot

Moab called, of God	Ps.	60	6–8

waste *devastate*

Of children	Prov.	19	26
A complaint made	Mark	14	3–5
Leads to want	Luke	15	11–32
Jesus discourages	John	6	12
Of the ground	Job	38	27
Land made by lions	Jer.	2	15
Of Bozrah	Jer.	49	13
Of Jerusalem	Ezek.	5	14
Of Egypt	Ezek.	29	9
Of Nineveh	Nah.	2	10
Streets	Zeph.	3	6
Houses	Hag.	1	9

watch *guard*

As a *w* in the night	Ps.	90	4
Set a *w* before my mouth	Ps.	141	3
Make the *w* strong	Jer.	51	12
I will stand upon my *w*	Hab.	2	1
Sealing the stone, and setting a *w*	Mat.	27	66
The Lord *w* between me and thee	Gen.	31	49
Dost thou not *w* over my sin?	Job	14	16
I *w*, and am as a sparrow	Ps.	102	7
More than they that *w* for morning	Ps.	130	6
W in the *w*-tower	Is.	21	5
All that *w* for iniquity are cut off	Is.	29	20
I will *w* over them for evil	Jer.	44	27
W therefore	Mat.	24	42
	Luke	21	36
	Acts	20	31
W and pray	Mat.	26	41
	Mark	13	33
	Mark	14	38
W ye, stand fast in the faith	I Cor.	16	13
Let us *w* and be sober	I Thes.	5	6
	I Pet.	4	7

watchfulness *vigilance*

For the advent of Christ	Mat.	25	13
Is required	Mark	13	33
Is commanded	Mark	13	37
A reward for	Luke	12	37
Against temptation	I Pet.	5	8

watchman *see guard*

water

Of creation	Gen.	1	6–10
In Noah's time	Gen.	6	17
	Gen.	7	6
Turned into blood	Ex.	7	20
Of the Red Sea, divided	Ex.	14	21, 22
Miraculously supplied to the Israelites	Ex.	17	1–6
Longed for, by David	II Sam.	23	15
Of affliction	I Ki.	22	27
Purified by Elisha	II Ki.	2	19–22
The sick healed in	II Ki.	5	6–10
	John	5	2–9
Supplied to a city	II Ki.	20	20
A blessing from God	Job	38	25–30
"Cast thy bread upon"	Eccl.	11	1
A daily allowance of	Ezek.	4	11
Used in baptism	Mat.	3	11
Jesus walks upon	Mat.	14	25–27
Peter walks upon	Mat.	14	28–32
Changed to wine	John	2	8–10
City waterworks	II Ki.	20	20
Separation of	Num.	19	2–22
Supplied to Jehoshaphat's army	II Ki.	3	16–20
To be turned into blood	Rev.	16	3–5

Figurative of:

Life	John	4	14
	John	7	37–39
Affliction	II Sam.	22	17
	Ps.	69	1
Salvation	John	4	10
	Is.	12	3
Love	Prov.	5	15

water basin *a vessel for holding water*

Used by Jesus when He washes the disciples' feet	John	13	5

water cure

At the pool of Bethesda	John	5	2–4

water of life

Forsaken by the Jews	Jer.	2	13
Given constantly	Zech.	14	8
Promised by Christ	John	4	10
Symbolic of everlasing life	John	7	37, 38

waterproofing *to make impervious to water*

Noah's ark covered with pitch	Gen.	6	14
Basket for baby Moses is covered with slime and pitch	Ex.	2	3

water test

Used by Gideon in selecting his army	Judg.	7	4–7
Test of adultery	Num.	5	21–23

waters parted

Moses	Ex.	14	21–22
Elijah	II Ki.	2	8
Elisha	II Ki.	2	14

waterworks system

Built by King Hezekiah	II Ki.	20	20

wave offerings *see offerings*

waves

All thy *w* are gone over me	Ps.	42	7
Stilleth the *w*	Ps.	65	7
	Ps.	89	9
	Ps.	107	29
Lord is mightier than mighty *w*	Ps.	93	4
Thy righteousness as *w* of the sea	Is.	48	18
Ship was covered with *w*	Mat.	8	24
Tossed with *w*	Mat.	14	24
	Mark	4	37
Raging *w* of the sea	Jude		13

wax

My heart is like *w*	Ps.	22	14
As *w* melteth, wicked perish	Ps.	68	2
Hills melted like *w* at presence of Lord	Ps.	97	5
Cleft as *w* before the fire	Mic.	1	4
My wrath shall *w* hot	Ex.	22	24
	Ex.	32	10
Is the Lord's hand *w* short?	Num.	11	23
Raiment *w* not old	Deut.	8	4
	Deut.	29	5
	Neh.	9	21
W fat and kicked	Deut.	32	15
Eyes began to *w* dim	I Sam.	3	2
Shall *w* old as a garment	Ps.	102	26
	Is.	50	9
	Is.	51	6
	Heb.	1	11
People's heart *w* gross	Mat.	13	15
	Acts	28	27
Love of many shall *w* cold	Mat.	24	12
Bags which *w* not old	Luke	12	33

way

If thou prosper my *w*	Gen.	24	42
Pillar of cloud to lead the *w*	Ex.	13	21
The *w* of all the earth	Josh.	23	14
	I Ki.	2	2
I will teach you the good and right *w*	I Sam.	12	23
As for God, his *w* is perfect	II Sam.	22	31
	Ps.	18	30
When thou hast taught them the good *w*	II Chr.	6	27
Seek of him a right *w*	Ezra	8	21
To a man whose *w* is hid	Job	3	23
To wander where there is no *w*	Job	12	24
	Ps.	107	40
I go the *w* whence I shall not return	Job	16	22
Hast thou marked the old *w*?	Job	22	15
He knoweth the *w* that I take	Job	23	10
Where is the *w* where light dwelleth?	Job	38	19
The Lord knoweth the *w* of the righteous	Ps.	1	6
Lest ye perish from the *w*	Ps.	2	12
The meek will he teach his *w*	Ps.	25	9
Commit thy *w* unto the Lord	Ps.	37	5
I will take heed to my *w*	Ps.	29	1
This their *w* is their folly	Ps.	49	13
That thy *w* may be known	Ps.	67	2
He made a *w* to his anger	Ps.	78	50
Behave wisely in a perfect *w*	Ps.	101	2
I will run the *w* of thy commandments	Ps.	119	32
Lead me in the *w* everlasting	Ps.	139	24
Lord preserveth the *w* of his saints	Prov.	2	8
In all thy *w* acknowledge him	Prov.	3	6
Her *w* are *w* of pleasantness	Prov.	3	17
Consider her *w* and be wise	Prov.	6	6
The *w* of life	Prov.	6	23
	Prov.	15	24
	Jer.	21	8

way—continued

The *w* of the Lord is strength	Jer.	10	29
Train up a child in the *w* he should go	Jer.	22	6
The *w* of the spirit	Eccl.	11	5
This is the *w*, walk ye in it	Is.	30	21
A *w*, called The *w* of holiness	Is.	35	8
Prepare the *w* of the Lord	Is.	40	3
	Luke	3	4
My *w* is hid from the Lord	Is.	40	27
Neither are your *w* my *w*	Is.	55	8
The *w* of peace they know not	Is.	59	8
	Rom.	3	17
Where is the good *w*?	Jer.	6	16
The *w* of man is not in himself	Jer.	10	23
I will give them one heart and one *w*	Jer.	32	39
They shall ask the *w* to Zion	Jer.	50	5
Are not my *w* equal	Ezek.	18	29
Turn aside *w* of the meek	Amos	2	7
The Lord hath his *w* in the whirlwind	Nah.	1	3
Consider your *w*	Hag.	1	5
He shall prepare the *w* before me	Mal.	3	1
Broad is the *w* that leadeth to destruction	Mat.	7	13
Teachest the *w* of God in truth	Mat.	22	16
	Mark	12	14
	Luke	20	21
When he was a great *w* off	Luke	15	20
But climbeth up some other *w*	John	10	1
The *w* ye know	John	14	4
I am the *w*, the truth, and the life	John	14	6
Show unto us the *w* of salvation	Acts	16	17
Expounded the *w* of God more perfectly	Acts	18	26
After the *w* which they call heresy	Acts	24	14
They are all gone out of the *w*	Rom.	3	12
His *w* are past finding out	Rom.	11	33
Make a *w* to escape	I Cor.	10	13
A more excellent *w*	I Cor.	12	31
Took handwriting out of *w*	Col.	2	14
Compassion on them out of the *w*	Heb.	5	2
The *w* into the holiest	Heb.	9	8
By a new and living *w*	Heb.	10	20
The *w* of truth be evil spoken	II Pet.	2	2
Have forsaken the right *w*	II Pet.	2	15
They have gone in the *w* of Cain	Jude		11
Just and true are thy *w*	Rev.	15	3

ways, God's

Are perfect	II Sam.	22	31
Are far above man's	Is.	55	8, 9
Are taught by Jesus	Mat.	22	16
Are perverted by sorcerer	Acts	13	10
Taught by Aquila and Priscilla	Acts	18	26
Are not always understandable to man	Rom.	11	33
Are just and true	Rev.	15	3

weak, the

Our duty to help	Acts	20	35
The strong ought to be patient with	Rom.	15	1
Warning concerning	I Cor.	8	8–13
Paul sets an example for	I Cor.	9	22

weakness, spiritual

Paul overcomes his	II Cor.	12	9, 10
Patriarchs grow out of, through faith	Heb.	11	34

wealth *riches, possessions*

A blessing for Abraham	Gen.	24	34, 35
Taken from Hamor and Shechem	Gen.	34	29
God gives the ability to acquire	Deut.	8	11–18
God gives Solomon great	II Chr.	1	11, 12
The wicked often have	Job	21	13
Does not matter after death	Ps.	49	6, 10
The God-fearing man shall have	Ps.	112	3
Makes friends	Prov.	19	4
Ill-gotten	Acts	19	25
Each man should seek to aid another man attain	I Cor.	10	24
Of Boaz	Ruth	2	1
Taxed by Menahem	II Ki.	15	20
Mordecai sought for Jews	Esth.	10	3
Diminished if ill-gotten	Prov.	13	11
See riches			

weapon

He shall flee from iron *w*	Job	20	24
The *w* of his indignation	Is.	13	5
	Jer.	50	25
No *w* formed against thee shall prosper	Is.	54	17
With destroying *w* in his hand	Ezek.	9	1
W of our warfare	II Cor.	10	4

weary

I am *w* of my life	Gen.	27	46
There the *w* be at rest	Job	3	17
My soul is *w* of life	Job	10	1
Not given water to the *w* to drink	Job	22	7
I am *w* with groaning	Ps.	6	6
Be not *w* of Lord's correction	Prov.	3	11
Lest he be *w* of thee	Prov.	25	17
None shall be *w* among them	Is.	5	27
Cause the *w* to rest	Is.	28	12
As shadow of a great rock in a *w* land	Is.	32	2
God fainteth not, neither is *w*	Is.	40	28
They shall run, and not be *w*	Is.	40	31
A word in season to him that is *w*	Is.	50	4
I am *w* of repenting	Jer.	15	6
I was *w* of forbearing	Jer.	20	9
I have satiated the *w* soul	Jer.	31	25
Let us not be *w* in welldoing	Gal.	6	9
	II Thes.	3	13
Will ye *w* God also?	Is.	7	13
They *w* themselves to commit iniquity	Jer.	9	5
Lest by continual coming she *w* me	Luke	18	5

weasel

Animal classed as unclean	Lev.	11	29

weather

Changed by Samuel's prayer	I Sam.	12	16–19
Sayings about the	Job	37	9, 17, 22
Forecast by signs	Luke	12	54–57

weaving *making of cloth*

Of the ephod for the priests	Ex.	28	32
One of the skills of Bezaleel and Aholiab	Ex.	35	35
Of coats for Aaron and his sons	Ex.	39	27
Of Samson's hair by Delilah	Judg.	16	14
In idolatrous worship	II Ki.	23	7
Life compared to shuttle	Job	7	6

wedding *nuptial ceremony*

Guests are bidden to come to	Mat.	22	3, 8
Special garments to be worn	Mat.	22	11
Instructions to guests	Luke	14	8
See marriage			

wedge of gold

Stolen by Achan	Josh.	7	20, 21
Mentioned in prophecy	Is.	13	12

weeds *seaweeds*

Around Jonah's head	Jonah	2	5

weeks

Introduced	Gen.	2	1–4
Regulated by law	Ex.	20	9–11
The feast of	Deut.	16	9, 10
Gabriel explains prophecy of	Dan.	9	24–27

weeping *shedding tears*

For the dead	Gen.	23	2
In sympathy	Job	30	25
Followed by joy	Ps.	30	5
In doing good	Ps.	126	5, 6
"A time to weep"	Eccl.	3	4
On account of sin	Jer.	9	1
In time of trouble	Jer.	50	4
"And gnashing of teeth"	Mat.	8	12
By Jesus	John	11	35
Instances of:			
Abraham for Sarah	Gen.	23	2
Jacob and Esau	Gen.	33	4
Hannah	I Sam.	1	7
Jonathan and David	I Sam.	20	41
Mary	Luke	7	38
Jesus	Luke	19	41
Mary Magdalene	John	20	11
Paul	Acts	20	19

weights *a system of measures*

Must be just	Lev.	19	35
	Deut.	25	13–15
	Prov.	11	1
Jewish weights:			
Shekel	Gen.	24	22
Talent	Ex.	25	39
	Mat.	25	15, 16
Gerah	Ex.	30	13
Bekah	Ex.	38	26
Maneh	Ezek.	45	12

weights, false *see false weights*

welcome *a cordial greeting*

David is given a hero's	I Sam.	18	6, 7
Extended to Jesus	Luke	8	40
Abraham to angels	Gen.	18	1–10

well *a source of water*			
A cause of quarrels	Gen.	21	25–30
	Gen.	26	15–22
Destroyed in war	II Ki.	3	19
Used for irrigation	Eccl.	2	6
Jesus rests by	John	4	6
Of Jacob	John	4	6
Of Solomon	Eccl.	2	6
Of Uzziah	II Chr.	26	10
Of Hezekiah	II Chr.	32	4
Of Bethlehem	II Sam.	23	15
At Haran	Gen.	24	16
Of salvation	Is.	12	3
Without water	Jer.	15	18
Mouth of a righteous man	Prov.	10	11
Private property	Prov.	5	15
Of living water	S. of S.	4	15
	John	4	14

wen *a cyst*			
Animal not to be used for sacrifice	Lev.	22	22

wench *maidservant*			
Used as a messenger	II Sam.	17	17

wept			
The people *w* very sore	Ezra	10	1
	Neh.	8	9
I *w* before God	Neh.	1	4
By rivers of Babylon we *w*	Ps.	137	1
We mourned, ye have not *w*	Luke	7	32
He beheld the city, and *w* over it	Luke	19	41
Jesus *w*	John	11	35
They that weep, as though they *w* not	I Cor.	7	30

wet			
They are *w*	Job	24	8
Let grass be *w* with dew	Dan.	4	15

whale *large fish or sea monster*			
Created by God	Gen.	1	21
Pharaoh is compared to	Ezek.	32	2
Jonah is swallowed by	Jonah	1	17
	Mat.	12	40

wheat *cereal grain*			
Grown in Mesopotamia	Gen.	30	14
Grown in Egypt	Ex.	9	32
Ground for bread	Ex.	29	2
First fruits of, brought to the Lord	Ex.	34	22, 26
Moses' song refers to the finest	Deut.	32	14
Ruth gleans	Ruth	2	23
Ground in a mortar	Prov.	27	22
Used figuratively	Luke	3	17
Shall be separated from the tares	Mat.	13	30
Thistles grow instead	Job	31	40
	Jer.	12	13
Chaff of	Jer.	23	28
Sifted	Luke	22	31
From death to life	John	12	24
Sold for a penny	Rev.	6	6

wheel *disk, circular frame*			
Figuratively used	Prov.	20	26
Water from cistern raised by	Eccl.	12	6
Potter's work is done on	Jer.	18	3
Ezekiel's visions	Ezek.	1	15–21
Of a chariot	Ex.	14	25
	Judg.	5	28
Of a cart	Is.	28	28
Rattling of	Nah.	3	2

whelp *cub, young of beasts*			
Of lions	Gen.	49	9
Of bear	II Sam.	17	8
Parable of lion's	Ezek.	19	1–9

whirlwind *a severe storm*			
Elijah translated in	II Ki.	2	1, 11
God talks to Job in	Job	38	1
Symbolic of destruction	Prov.	1	27
Figurative of divine judgment	Jer.	23	19
	Ezek.	1	4
Figurative of fruits of sin	Hosea	8	7

white *colour of pure snow*			
A royal colour worn by Mordecai	Esth.	8	15
Symbolizes purification from sin	Is.	1	18
Raiment of Christ	Mat.	17	1, 2
Raiment of angels	Mat.	28	2, 3
Raiment of the redeemed	Rev.	3	4, 5
Horse	Rev.	6	2
Cloud	Rev.	14	14
Throne	Rev.	20	11

whole			
Made	Mat.	12	13
	Mark	3	5
	Luke	6	10
(*See* Miracles.)			
My life is yet *w* in me	II Sam.	1	9
The *w* need not a physician	Mat.	9	12
W have no need of physician	Mark	2	17
	Luke	5	31
Faith hath made thee *w*	Mark	5	34
	Luke	8	48
	Luke	17	19
Wilt thou be made *w*?	John	5	6
Jesus Christ maketh thee *w*	Acts	9	34
If the *w* body were an eye	I Cor.	12	17

whore *prostitute or harlot*			
Laws concerning	Deut.	22	21
	Deut.	23	17, 18
An example of	Judg.	19	2
Vision of great	Rev.	17	1–18

whoredom *practice of harlotry*			
Wickedness of	Lev.	19	29
Severely denounced	Num.	25	1–5
Idolatrous worship	Deut.	31	16
Of Jezebel	II Ki.	9	22
Warning against	Prov.	6	24–35
Figuratively used in judgments	Jer.	3	

whoremonger *a whoremaster*			
Not an heir to God's kingdom	Eph.	5	5
Laws must be made for	I Tim.	1	10
Will be judged by God	Heb.	13	4
Punishment of	Rev.	21	8
	Rev.	22	15

wicked *morally bad*			
Punishment of	Ex.	20	5
	Lev.	26	14–17
	Job	27	13–23
	Mat.	18	35
God will show mercy to	Deut.	5	29
	I John	3	16
Prayers of	II Sam.	22	42
	Is.	59	2
	James	1	6, 7
Hate reproof	I Ki.	22	8
Suffer physical pain	Job	15	20–23
Are insecure	Job	18	5–8
	Is.	57	20
Their triumphs are short	Job	20	5
Provoke God's wrath	Ps.	5	5, 6
	I Cor.	10	5
Are corrupt in character	Ps.	5	9
A good description	Ps.	10	2–11
Contrasted with the righteous	Ps.	11	5
	Ps.	32	10
	Prov.	15	9
	Rom.	2	9, 10
Their prosperity not long lasting	Ps.	37	1, 2
	Prov.	24	19, 20
Do not pay debts	Ps.	37	21
Their worship offensive to God	Ps.	50	16, 17
	Is.	1	10–15
Hate the righteous	Ps.	64	2–6
	Luke	6	22, 23
Lack courage	Prov.	28	1
"There is no peace unto"	Is.	48	22
Will be pardoned upon repentance	Is.	55	7
	II Pet.	2	9
Warned	Jer.	7	13–15
	Ezek.	33	8
	Luke	3	7–9
Saved through Christ	Mat.	18	11–14
	Luke	19	10
Shall not inherit the kingdom of God	I Cor.	6	9, 10
	Eph.	5	5

wickedness *evil*			
God saw *w* was great	Gen.	6	5
This great *w*	Gen.	39	9
W proceedeth from the wicked	I Sam.	24	13
They that sow *w* reap the same	Job	4	8
Though *w* be sweet	Job	20	12
Is not thy *w* great?	Job	22	5
W is in their dwellings	Ps.	55	15
Than to dwell in tents of *w*	Ps.	84	10
They eat the bread of *w*	Prov.	4	17
W is abomination to my lips	Prov.	8	7

wickedness—continued

Treasures of *w* profit nothing	Prov.	10	2
W overthroweth the sinner	Prov.	13	6
The *w* of folly	Eccl.	7	25
Neither shall *w* deliver	Eccl.	8	8
W burneth as the fire	Is.	9	18
To loose the bands of *w*	Is.	58	6
Thine own *w* shall correct thee	Jer.	2	19
No man repented of his *w*	Jer.	8	6
We acknowledge our *w*	Jer.	14	20
If he turn not from his *w*	Ezek.	3	19
In the day that he turneth from his *w*	Ezek.	33	12
For the *w* of their doings	Hosea	9	15
Ye have plowed *w*	Hosea	10	13
Treasures of *w* in house of wicked	Mic.	6	10
Out of the heart proceed *w*	Mark	7	22
Inward part is full of *w*	Luke	11	39
Repent of this thy *w*	Acts	8	22
Being filled with all *w*	Rom.	1	29
The leaven of *w*	I Cor.	5	8
Spiritual *w* in high places	Eph.	6	12
Whole world lieth in *w*	I John	5	19

widow

Mosaic laws concerning	Lev.	21	14
	Deut.	25	5
Vows of, binding	Num.	30	9
Under God's protection	Deut.	10	18
	Ps.	68	5
	Prov.	15	25
To be honoured	Deut.	14	29
	I Tim.	5	3–6
Oppressors of, condemned	Deut.	27	19
	Mat.	23	14
Sorrow of	Ruth	1	20, 21
Elijah sustained by	I Ki.	17	8–16
"Widow's mite"	Mark	12	42
Paul advises	Rom.	7	3
	I Cor.	7	8, 9

Examples:

Naomi	Ruth	1	3
Widow of Zarephath	I Ki.	17	8–16
Anna	Luke	2	36, 37
Widow of Nain	Luke	7	11–15
Widow from Tekoah	II Sam.	14	4, 5

wife, wives

Duties to husband	Gen.	3	16
	Eph.	5	22, 23
	Tit.	2	4
Domestic duties	Gen.	18	6
	Prov.	31	13–27
More than one	Gen.	26	34
Unfaithful	Gen.	39	7
	II Sam.	11	2–5
Mosaic law concerning	Ex.	21	3, 22
	Num.	30	2–15
	Deut.	24	1–5
Tactful, Abigail	I Sam.	25	3, 14, 42
Taken as part of spoils of war	I Sam.	30	3–5
Solomon has seven hundred	I Ki.	11	3
Wicked, Jezebel	I Ki.	21	5–16
Incorruptible, Vashti	Esth.	1	10–22
A brawling, condemned	Prov.	21	9
Portrait of a good	Prov.	31	10–29
Should not separate from husband	Rom.	7	2
	I Cor.	7	13
Has much influence	I Cor.	7	14
To keep silent in church	I Cor.	14	34
Husband to love	Eph.	5	25, 28
	Col.	3	18
To dress modestly	I Pet.	3	3, 4
Beloved by her husband	Gen.	24	67
	Gen.	29	30
	I Sam.	1	8
Hated	Gen.	29	31–33

Called:

Help meet	Gen.	2	18, 20
Fruitful vine	Ps.	128	3
Crown to her husband	Prov.	12	4
Desire of thine eyes	Ezek.	24	16
Weaker vessel	I Pet.	3	7

Examples:

Potiphar's	Gen.	39	7
Bathsheba	II Sam.	11	2–5
Zipporah	Ex.	4	25
Solomon's	I Ki.	11	4–8
Jezebel	I Ki.	21	5–16
Vashti	Esth.	1	10–22

Abigail	I Sam.	25	3
Michal	II Sam.	6	16
Sarah	Gen.	17	15
	I Pet.	3	6
Rebekah	Gen.	24	62–67

wilderness *desert*

Hagar's flight to	Gen.	16	7
Elijah's flight to	I Ki.	19	4
David's flight to	I Sam.	23	14, 15
Shur, where Israelites find no water	Ex.	15	22
Zin, an encampment of the Israelites	Num.	33	36
Moab	Deut.	2	8
Given to families of Judah	Josh.	15	1, 61, 62
Maon, hiding place of David	I Sam.	23	24, 25
Paran, another hiding place of David	I Sam.	25	1
Ziph, where Saul tries to find David	I Sam.	26	2
Kadesh	Ps.	29	8
Used figuratively	Is.	5	17
Jesus feeds people in the	Mat.	14	13, 15
John the Baptist lives in	Luke	1	80
Called terrible	Deut.	1	19
	Deut.	8	15
A solitary place	Is.	35	1
To be made a pool	Is.	41	18
Cities to be made	Is.	50	2
Desolate	Ezek.	6	14
	Jer.	12	10
	Joel	2	3
	Joel	3	19

wiles

They vex you with *w*	Num.	25	18
Able to stand against *w* of devil	Eph.	6	11

will *last testament*

Of Abraham	Gen.	25	5–8
Of Jacob	Gen.	49	
Of David	I Ki.	2	1–9
Of Jehoshaphat	II Chr.	21	3
Cannot be annulled	Gal.	3	15
In force after death	Heb.	9	16, 17
See testament			

will of God

Is irresistible	Dan.	4	17, 35
Must be performed	Mat.	7	21
To be sought in prayer	Mat.	26	39, 42
Jesus' work is	John	4	34
Knowledge comes with doing	John	7	17
Man cannot defy the	Rom.	9	19
Sincere desire to do	Eph.	6	6
Giving thanks is the	I Thes.	5	18
Fulfilled by Christ	Heb.	10	7
Should be submitted to	James	4	15
Benefit from doing	I Pet.	2	15
Eternal life the reward for doing	I John	2	17

willing

Whosoever is of a *w* heart	Ex.	35	5
Serve God with a *w* mind	I Chr.	28	9
People shall be *w* in day of thy power	Ps.	110	3
The spirit is *w*	Mat.	26	41
If thou be *w*, remove this cup	Luke	22	42
Ye were *w* for a season to rejoice	John	5	35
If God, *w* to show wrath	Rom.	9	22
W rather to be absent	II Cor.	5	8
If there be first a *w* mind	II Cor.	8	12
W to communicate	I Tim.	6	18
Not *w* that any should perish	II Pet.	3	9

willingly

People *w* offered themselves	Judg.	5	2, 9
Lord doth not afflict *w*	Lam.	3	33
Creature was made subject to vanity, not *w*	Rom.	8	20
Not as of necessity, but *w*	Philem.		14
	I Pet.	5	2
They *w* are ignorant	II Pet.	3	5

willow *tree growing in marshy places*

Used for booths at feast of tabernacles	Lev.	23	40
Jews hang their harps on	Ps.	137	2
Parable of eagle who plants a	Ezek.	17	5

wind *movement of air*

Takes away plague of locusts	Ex.	10	19
Brings quails for food	Num.	11	31
Brings rain	I Ki.	18	45
Wreaks havoc	Job	1	19
Job likens speeches and life to	Job	6	26
	Job	7	7
	Job	8	2
Part of God's great works	Job	27	21
	Job	37	9, 17, 21

Controlled by God	Ps.	147	18
	Ps.	148	7, 8
	Prov.	30	4
Figuratively used for God's care	Is.	26	18
Created by God	Amos	4	13
East:			
Hot	Gen.	41	6
On the Euphrates	Ezek.	19	12
In Canaan	Hosea	13	15
At Ninevah	Jonah	4	8
West:	Ex.	10	19
North:	Prov.	25	23
South:	Job	37	9, 21
Helped dry the earth	Gen.	8	1
God does not speak to Elijah in	I Ki.	19	11
Invisible	II Ki.	3	17
	John	3	8
Used to blow chaff away	Ps.	1	4
He that causes trouble in the home shall inherit	Prov.	11	29

windows of heaven *sign of abundance*

Opened and the rain pours down	Gen.	7	11
Opened and many blessings are given	Mal.	3	10

wine *an alcoholic beverage*

Made by Noah	Gen.	9	20, 21
Given to Abraham	Gen.	14	18
Made from grapes	Gen.	40	11
Inflames the eyes	Gen.	49	12
Offered with sacrifices	Ex.	29	40
Forbidden to priests while officiating	Lev.	10	9
Used to relieve depression	Ps.	104	15
	Prov.	31	6, 7
Is a mocker	Prov.	20	1
A cause of poverty	Prov.	21	17
Excessive use causes much sorrow	Prov.	23	29, 30
Sacramental use of	Mat.	26	27–29
Given to Jesus at the crucifixion	Mark	15	23
Water made into	John	2	1–10
Warning against excessive use	Eph.	5	18
Recommended by Paul as medicine	I Tim.	5	23
From pomegranates	S. of S.	8	2
Kept in jars	Jer.	13	12
Kept in skins	Josh.	9	4, 13
Kept in bottles	Jer.	48	12
	Mat.	9	17
Cellars for	I Chr.	27	27
New	Hag.	1	11
Old	Luke	5	39
Forbidden to practicing priests	Lev.	10	9
Forbidden to Nazarites	Num.	6	2, 3
Abstinence of Daniel	Dan.	1	5, 8
Forbidden to kings	Prov.	31	4
Given by Melchizedek to Abraham	Gen.	14	18
Commerce of	Rev.	18	13
At a banquet	Esth.	5	6
Lot	Gen.	19	32
Nabal	I Sam.	25	36

winebibber *one who drinks excessively of wine*

Admonition not to be a	Prov.	23	20
Christ is falsely accused of being a	Mat.	11	19

winepress *vat for treading out juice from grapes*

Built in vineyards	Is.	5	2
Symbol of sufferings	Is.	63	3
Figurative of judgments of God	Lam.	1	15
Common in Palestine	Mat.	21	33

wings

Bare you on eagles' *w*	Ex.	19	4
The shadow of thy *w*	Ps.	17	8
	Is.	36	7
	Is.	57	1
	Is.	61	4
	Ps.	91	4
W of the wind	Ps.	18	10
	Ps.	104	3
Oh that I had *w* like a dove	Ps.	55	6
W of the morning	Ps.	139	9
Riches make themselves *w*	Prov.	23	5
Mount with *w* as eagles	Is.	40	31
With healing in his *w*	Mal.	4	2
As a hen gathereth chickens under *w*	Mat.	23	37
	Luke	13	34

winter

Time for, shall never cease	Gen.	8	22
Rainy season in Canaan	S. of S.	2	11
Winter houses	Jer.	36	22

Shipping suspended in the Mediterranean	Acts	27	12
	Acts	28	11
Paul spends one in Nicopolis	Tit.	3	12

wisdom *Godly knowledge*

Characteristic of elders	Deut.	1	15
Chosen by Solomon	I Ki.	3	5–12
Shared with other nations	I Ki.	4	30, 31
Not confined to rank or sex	II Sam.	20	22
	I Ki.	10	23
"Better than rubies"	Prov.	8	11
The beginning of	Prov.	9	10
Superior to strength	Eccl.	9	16
"Jesus increased in"	Luke	2	52
Christ, of God	I Cor.	1	24
Commanded to walk in	Col.	4	5
A gift of God	James	1	5

Of God:

All human wisdom derived from	Ezra	7	25
Beyond human comprehension	Ps.	139	6
Incomparable	Is.	44	7
	Jer.	10	7
Infinite	Ps.	147	5
Mighty	Job	36	5
Perfect	Job	36	4
	Job	37	16
Underived	Job	21	22
	Is.	40	44
Universal	Job	28	24
	Dan.	2	22
	Acts	15	18
Unsearchable	Is.	40	28
	Rom.	11	33
Wonderful	Ps.	139	6
His counsels	Is.	28	29
	Jer.	32	19
His foreshowing events	Is.	42	9
	Is.	46	10
His works	Job	37	16
	Ps.	104	24
	Ps.	136	5
	Prov.	3	19
	Jer.	10	12
Redemption	I Cor.	1	24
	Eph.	1	8
	Eph.	3	10
Searching the heart	I Chr.	28	9
	Rev.	2	23
Understanding the thoughts	I Chr.	28	9
	Ps.	139	2
His saints	II Sam.	7	20
	II Tim.	2	19
Actions	Job	34	21
	Ps.	139	2–3
Afflictions of saints	Ex.	3	7
	Ps.	142	3
The heart	Ps.	44	21
	Prov.	15	11
	Luke	16	15
Infirmities of saints	Ps.	103	14
Minutest matters	Mat.	10	29–30
Most secret things	Mat.	6	18
Time of judgment	Mat.	24	36
Wants of saints	Mat.	6	8
Way of saints	Job	23	10
	Ps.	1	6
Wicked	Neh.	9	10
	Job	11	11
Words	Ps.	130	4
Works of the wicked	Is.	66	18
The gospel contains treasures of	I Cor.	2	7
Nothing concealed from	Ps.	139	12
One of his attributes	I Sam.	2	3
	Job	9	4
Saints ascribe to him	Dan.	2	20
Should be magnified	Rom.	16	27
	Jude		25
The wicked question	Ps.	73	11
	Is.	47	10
Wisdom of saints derived from	Ezra	7	25

Types of:

Piety	Deut.	4	6
Prophetic	I Sam.	10	12
	Is.	28	23–29
Common sense and tact	II Sam.	20	14–22
Learning	I Ki.	3	16–28

wisdom—*continued*

Statecraft	I Ki.	5	12
Mechanical skill	I Ki.	7	14
Military skill	Is.	10	13

Wise men mentioned:

Joseph	Gen.	41	16, 25–39
Bezaleel	Ex.	31	3–5
Aholiab	Ex.	31	6
Ethan, Herman, Chalcol, Darda	I Ki.	4	31
Hiram	I Ki.	7	14
Ezra	Ezra	7	25
Daniel	Dan.	1	17
The Magi	Mat.	2	1–12
Stephen	Acts	6	9, 10
Moses	Acts	7	22

wise

A tree to make one *w*	Gen.	3	6
The gift blindeth the *w*	Ex.	23	8
	Deut.	16	19
Oh that they were *w*	Deut.	32	29
Taketh the *w* in their own craftiness	Job	5	13
Vain man would be *w*	Job	11	12
Great men are not always *w*	Job	32	9
He respecteth not any *w* of heart	Job	37	24
Be *w* now, O kings	Ps.	2	10
Making *w* the simple	Ps.	19	7
Ye fools, when will ye be *w*?	Ps.	94	8
Whoso is *w*, and will observe	Ps.	107	43
A *w* man shall attain *w* counsels	Prov.	1	5
Be not *w* in thine own eyes	Prov.	3	7
The *w* shall inherit glory	Prov.	3	35
Thou shalt be *w* for thyself	Prov.	9	12
He that winneth souls is *w*	Prov.	11	30
He that walketh with *w* men shall be *w*	Prov.	13	20
Whosoever is deceived thereby is not *w*	Prov.	20	1
A man *w* in his own conceit	Prov.	26	12
What hath the *w* more than the fool?	Eccl.	6	8
Heart of *w* is in house of mourning	Eccl.	7	4
The *w* are in the hand of God	Eccl.	9	1
The words of the *w* are as goads	Eccl.	12	11
Woe unto them that are *w* in their own eyes	Is.	5	21
They are *w* to do evil	Jer.	4	22
They that be *w* shall shine	Dan.	12	3
Be ye *w* as serpents	Mat.	10	16
Thou hast hid these things from the *w*	Mat.	11	25
Professing themselves to be *w*	Rom.	1	22
Be not *w* in your own conceits	Rom.	12	16
Where is the *w*?	I Cor.	1	20
Lord knoweth thoughts of the *w*	I Cor.	3	20
Ye are *w* in Christ	I Cor.	4	10
To make *w* unto salvation	II Tim.	3	15
Wise men	Mat.	2	1, 2

witch

Law requires, to be put to death	Ex.	22	18
Forbidden	Deut.	18	10, 12
Is consulted by Saul	I Sam.	28	7–25

witchcraft *practice of divination or sorcery*

Practiced by Jezebel	II Ki.	9	22
Abolished by Josiah	II Ki.	23	24
To be abolished by God	Mic.	5	12
Used by Simon in Samaria	Acts	8	9
One of the sins of the flesh	Gal.	5	19, 20

withered hand

Of Jeroboam healed	I Ki.	13	1–6
Healed by Jesus on the sabbath	Mat.	12	10–13

witness, false *see* false witnesses

witness

God invoked as	Gen.	31	50
	Judg.	11	10
	I Sam.	12	5
	Mic.	1	2
	Rom.	1	9
	I Thes.	2	5
Borne to Christ, by the Father	Mat.	3	16
	Luke	3	22
	John	12	28
	Heb.	2	4
	I John	5	7
To be implicitly received	I John	5	6, 9
By the apostles	Acts	1	8
	Acts	2	32
	Acts	4	33
	Acts	5	32
	Acts	10	41
	Acts	22	15
	Acts	26	16

	I Pet.	5	1
	Rev.	20	4
By the prophets	Acts	10	43
	I Pet.	1	10
Christ the faithful and true	Rev.	1	5
	Rev.	3	14
False	Ex.	20	16
	Ex.	23	1
	Lev.	19	11
	Deut.	5	20
	Deut.	19	16
	Prov.	6	16, 19
	Prov.	12	17
	Prov.	19	5, 9, 28
	Prov.	21	28
	Prov.	25	18
	Jer.	7	9
	Zech.	5	4
	Luke	3	14
Against Christ	Mat.	26	60
	Mark	14	56
Witnesses, two or three required	Num.	35	30
	Deut.	17	6
	Deut.	19	15
	Mat.	18	16
	II Cor.	13	1
	I Tim.	5	19
The two, vision of	Rev.	11	1–13
Covenant be a *w* between us	Gen.	31	44
God is *w* betwixt me and thee	Gen.	31	50
This stone shall be a *w*	Josh.	24	27
My *w* is in heaven	Job	16	19
A faithful *w* in heaven	Ps.	89	37
A faithful *w* will not lie	Prov.	14	5
A true *w* delivereth souls	Prov.	14	25
Be not *w* against thy neighbour without cause	Prov.	24	18
I have given him for a *w* to the people	Is.	55	4
The Lord be a faithful *w* between us	Jer.	42	5
A swift *w* against the sorcerers	Mal.	3	5
For a *w* to all nations	Mat.	24	14
Sought *w* against Jesus	Mark	14	55
The same came for *w*	John	1	7
Ye receive not our *w*	John	3	11
The Father hath borne *w* of me	John	5	37
He left not himself without *w*	Acts	14	17
Conscience bearing *w*	Rom.	2	15
	Rom.	9	1
Compassed with cloud of *w*	Heb.	12	1
We receive *w* of men	I John	5	9
Hath the *w* in himself	I John	5	10
Jesus Christ the faithful *w*	Rev.	1	5
I call heaven and earth to *w*	Deut.	4	26
W against me	I Sam.	12	3
Their countenance doth *w* against them	Is.	3	9
What is it which these *w* against thee?	Mat.	26	62
	Mark	14	60
Holy Ghost *w* in every city	Acts	20	23
W both to small and great	Acts	26	22
Being *w* by the Law and the Prophets	Rom.	3	21
Before Pilate *w* a good confession	I Tim.	6	31
Of whom it is *w* that he liveth	Heb.	7	8

By the Holy Ghost:

Borne against all unbelievers	Neh.	9	30
	Acts	28	25–27
Faithful preaching of the apostles accompanied by	I Cor.	2	4
	I Thes.	1	5
First preaching of the gospel confirmed by	Acts	14	3
	Heb.	2	4
Is truth	I John	5	6

Borne to Christ:

As coming to redeem and sanctify	I John	5	6
As foretold by himself	John	15	26
As Messiah	Luke	3	22
	John	1	32–33
As perfecting saints	Heb.	10	14–15
In heaven	I John	5	7, 11
On earth	I John	5	8

Given to saints:

As an evidence of adoption	Rom.	8	16
As an evidence of Christ in them	I John	3	24
As an evidence of God in them	I John	4	13
On believing	Acts	15	8
	I John	5	10
To testify to them of Christ	John	15	26

wives

Duties of, to their husbands:

To be faithful to them	I Cor.	7	3–5, 10
To be subject to them	Gen.	3	16
	Eph.	5	22, 24
	I Pet.	3	1
To love them	Tit.	2	4
To obey them	I Cor.	14	34
	Tit.	2	5
To remain with them for life	Rom.	7	2–3
To reverence them	Eph.	5	33

Good:

Are benevolent to the poor	Prov.	31	20
Are a blessing to husbands	Prov.	12	4
	Prov.	31	10, 12
Are diligent and prudent	Prov.	31	13–27
Are from the Lord	Prov.	19	14
Are praised by husbands	Prov.	31	28
Are a token of the favor of God	Prov.	18	22
Bring honor on husbands	Prov.	31	23
Duty of, to unbelieving husbands	I Cor.	7	13–14, 16
	I Pet.	3	1–2
Secure confidence of husbands	Prov.	31	11

wizard *see* witchcraft

wolf

Wolves, unjust judges and false teachers so called	Zeph.	3	3
	Mat.	10	16
	Luke	10	3
The *w* shall dwell with the lamb	Is.	11	6
The *w* and the lamb shall feed together	Is.	65	25
Inwardly they are *w*	Mat.	7	15
Hireling seeth the *w* coming	John	10	12
W shall enter among you	Acts	20	29

woman

Creation of	Gen.	1	27
First to sin	Gen.	3	6
A curse upon	Gen.	3	1–16
Can not marry without consent of parents	Gen.	24	3, 4
Vails the face	Gen.	24	65
Takes part in ancient worship	Ex.	15	20
	I Chr.	25	5, 6
Worships in separate congregations	Ex.	38	8
Holds right to hold property	Num.	27	6–11
Holds right to make contracts	Num.	30	3–9
Forbidden to wear men's costume	Deut.	22	5
Required to attend the reading of the law	Deut.	31	12
Treated with cruelty in war	Deut.	32	25
Virtuous, held in high esteem	Ruth	3	11
A good woman described	Prov.	31	10–31
Sold for husband's debts	Mat.	18	25
Last at the cross	Mat.	27	55, 56
First to visit the sepulchre	Mark	16	1–6
First to whom the risen Lord appears	Mark	16	9
Active in early church	Acts	1	14
	Acts	12	12, 13
Long hair, her glory	I Cor.	11	5–15
Christian, to dress modestly	I Tim.	2	9, 10

Described as:

Courteous to strangers	Gen.	24	17
Patriotic	Ex.	15	20
Active in instigating iniquity	Num.	31	15, 16
Gay and happy	Judg.	11	34
Affectionate	II Sam.	1	26
Shrewd	II Sam.	20	16–22
Subtle and deceitful	Prov.	6	24–29
Timid	Is.	19	16
Fond of self-indulgence	Is.	32	9–11
Tender to her offspring	Is.	49	15
Fond of ornaments	Jer.	2	32
Silly and easily led to error	II Tim.	3	6
Weaker than men	I Pet.	3	7

Domestic duties of:

Cooking	Gen.	18	6
Tending flock	Gen.	24	19, 20
Drawing water	Gen.	29	9
Spinning	Ex.	35	25, 26
Gleaning in the fields	Ruth	2	8
Sewing	I Sam.	2	19
Keeping vineyards	S. of S.	1	6
Doorkeeper	Mat.	26	69

As rulers:

Deborah	Judg.	4	4
Queen of Sheba	I Ki.	10	1–13
Athaliah	II Ki.	11	1–16
Candace	Acts	8	27

As poets:

Miriam	Ex.	15	21
Deborah	Judg.	4	4
Hannah	I Sam.	2	1–10
Elisabeth	Luke	1	42–45
Mary	Luke	1	46–55

As prophets:

Miriam	Ex.	15	21
Deborah	Judg.	4	4–6
Huldah	II Ki.	22	12–20
Anna	Luke	2	36–38
Philip's daughters	Acts	21	9

Instances of good:

Mother of Samson	Judg.	13	23
Naomi	Ruth	1	2–12
Ruth	Ruth	1	16, 17
Hannah	I Sam.	1	9–18
Vashti	Esth.	1	11, 12
Esther	Esth.	4	15–17
Pilate's wife	Mat.	27	19
Elisabeth	Luke	1	41–45
Mary	Luke	1	26–28
Mary and Martha	Luke	10	38–42
Lydia	Acts	16	14
Lois and Eunice	II Tim.	1	5

Evil acts of:

Eve, in seducing her husband	Gen.	3	6
Lot's wife, for disobedience	Gen.	19	26
Sarah, in her malice toward Hagar	Gen.	21	9–11
Rebekah, in her partiality	Gen.	27	11–17
Rachel, in her jealousy of Leah	Gen.	30	1
Potiphar's wife, in her lust	Gen.	39	7–20
Delilah, in her conspiracy	Judg.	16	4–20
Bath-sheba, in her adultery	II Sam.	11	4, 5, 27
Jezebel, in her persecution of the prophets	I Ki.	18	4, 13
Job's wife, in her counsel	Job	2	9
Herodias, causing death of John the Baptist	Mat.	14	8

womb *uterus*

Of Sarah, closed by the Lord	Gen.	20	18
Of Rebekah, holds two nations	Gen.	25	21–24
Of Rachel, gives birth to Joseph	Gen.	30	22
Of Hannah, shut	I Sam.	1	5
Conception in the	Luke	1	30, 31
Fruit of	Deut.	7	13
Of Naomi	Ruth	1	11
Of Birth	Job	3	11
	Job	10	18
	Ps.	22	9
	Jer.	1	5
Bones grow in	Eccl.	11	5
Lord forming a person in	Is.	44	2, 24
Miscarrying	Hosea	9	14
Leaping in	Luke	1	41, 44
Grasping brother's heel in	Hosea	12	3

wonder

A sign and *w*	Deut.	13	1
	Deut.	28	46
I am as a *w* unto many	Ps.	71	7
Thou art the God that doest *w*	Ps.	77	14
Wilt thou show *w* to the dead?	Ps.	88	10
Declare his *w* among all people	Ps.	96	3
Who alone doeth great *w*	Ps.	136	4
Walked barefoot for a sign and a *w*	Is.	20	3
I will do a marvellous work and a *w*	Is.	29	14
How long to the end of these *w*?	Dan.	12	6
I will show *w*	Joel	2	30
	Acts	2	19
They were filled with *w*	Acts	3	10
Stay yourselves, and *w*	Is.	29	9
He *w* that there was no intercessor	Is.	59	16
Regard, and *w* marvellously	Hab.	1	5
They *w* at the gracious words	Luke	4	22
That dwell on the earth shall *w*	Rev.	17	8
(*See* Ex. 3:20; Deut. 6:22; Ps. 89:5.)			

wonderful

Thy love was *w*	II Sam.	1	26
Things too *w* for me	Job	42	3
Thy testimonies are *w*	Ps.	119	129
Such knowledge is too *w* for me	Ps.	139	6
His name shall be called *W*	Is.	9	6
Thou hast done *w* things	Is.	25	1
Lord, which is *w* in counsel	Is.	28	29
When they saw the *w* things that he did	Mat.	21	15

wood

Gibeonites are made hewers of	Josh.	9	21-27
Figuratively used	Jer.	46	22
For sacrifice	Gen.	22	6, 7
Spies were asked about	Num.	13	20
Ark made of	Deut.	10	1
A mountain of	Josh.	17	18
She bears come out of	II Ki.	2	24
For fires	Prov.	26	21
	Jer.	5	14
Gathered	Jer.	7	18
Yokes of	Jer.	28	13
Solitary place	Mic.	7	14
Foundations of	I Cor.	3	12
Idols of	Is.	37	19
Pulpit of	Neh.	8	4

wool

Used for clothing	Lev.	13	47-59
Used for a sign	Judg.	6	37
Symbol for purification of sins	Is.	1	18
Moths destroy	Is.	51	8
Traded in Damascus	Ezek.	27	18
Prohibited in priests' dress	Ezek.	44	17

word

Men to be judged for words	Eccl.	5	2
	Ezek.	35	13
	Mat.	2	17
	Mat.	3	13
	Mat.	12	37
Not add unto the w which I command you	Deut.	4	2
Every w of God	Deut.	8	3
	Mat.	4	4
The w is nigh	Deut.	30	14
	Rom.	10	8
Doth not the ear try w	Job	12	11
Darkened counsel by w	John	38	2
Let the w of my mouth be acceptable	Ps.	19	14
The Lord gave the w	Ps.	68	11
There is not a w, but thou knowest it	Ps.	139	4
A w spoken in due season	Prov.	15	23
A w fitly spoken	Prov.	25	11
Make a man an offender for a w	Is.	29	21
Thine ears shall hear a w behind thee	Is.	30	21
The w is gone out of my mouth	Is.	45	23
To speak a w in season	Is.	50	4
The w is not in them	Jer.	5	13
Nor shall the w perish	Jer.	18	18
The w thou hast spoken	Jer.	44	16
Speak great w against the Most high	Dan.	7	25
Take with you	Hosea	14	2
Speak the w only	Mat.	8	8
Every idle w that men shall speak	Mat.	12	36
My w shall not pass away	Mat.	24	35
The sower soweth the w	Mark	4	14
What a w is this?	Luke	4	36
A prophet mighty in deed and w	Luke	24	19
In the beginning was the W	John	1	1
The W was made flesh	John	1	14
Thou hast the w of eternal life	John	6	68
W ye hear is not mine	John	14	24
Ye are clean through the w I have spoken	John	15	3
I have given them the w thou gavest me	John	17	8
Any w of exhortation	Acts	13	15
To you is w of salvation sent	Acts	13	26
Received the w with readiness	Acts	17	11
The w of his grace	Acts	20	32
The w of truth and soberness	Acts	26	25
Kingdom of God is not in w, but in power	I Cor.	4	20
Our w was not yea and nay	II Cor.	1	18
The w of reconciliation	II Cor.	5	19
All the law is fulfilled in one w	Gal.	5	14
Him that is taught in the w	Gal.	6	6
Holding forth the w of life	Phil.	2	16
Whatsoever ye do in w or deed	Col.	3	17
Our gospel came not in w only	I Thes.	1	5
Comfort one another with these w	I Thes.	4	18
Labour in the w and doctrine	I Tim.	5	17
Preach the w	II Tim.	4	2
Holding fast the faithful w	Tit.	1	9
If the w spoken by angels was stedfast	Heb.	2	2
The w preached did not profit	Heb.	4	2
The w of God is quick and powerful	Heb.	4	12
Is unskilful in the w of righteousness	Heb.	5	13
Have tasted the good w of God	Heb.	6	5

word of God, the

Not to be added to or taken from	Deut.	4	2
To be taught to children	Deut.	6	7
A source of spiritual knowledge	Deut.	8	3
	John	17	8
	John	20	31
Belongs to us and our children	Deut.	29	29
To be read publicly	Deut.	31	11-13
To be read and studied diligently	Deut.	32	24-30
Is pure and holy	Ps.	12	6
	Rom.	8	12
A source of delight and joy	Ps.	19	8
	Ps.	119	16
Brings understanding	Ps.	119	104
"A lamp unto my feet"	Ps.	119	105
A way of life	Prov.	6	20-23
Written under God's command	Is.	8	1
	Hab.	2	2
Will endure forever	Is.	40	8
	I Pet.	1	25
Fulfilled by Jesus	Mat.	5	17
	John	19	24
Likened to seed	Mat.	13	3-8
	Mark	4	26-32
Not to know, is to err	Mat.	22	29
Explained by Jesus	Luke	4	17-31
Testifies of Jesus	John	5	39
Taught by the apostles	Acts	2	3, 4
	Acts	18	24, 25
A source of hope	Rom.	15	4
To be truthfully taught	II Cor.	4	2
	II Tim.	2	15
Comes from inspiration of God	II Tim.	3	16
Quick and powerful	Heb.	4	12
Equated with scripture	John	10	35

Called:

Book of the law	Neh.	8	3
Law of the Lord	Ps.	1	2
Book	Ps.	40	7
Book of the Lord	Is.	34	16
Scripture of truth	Dan.	10	21
Word of truth	Luke	11	28
Holy scriptures	Rom.	1	2
Oracles of God	Rom.	3	2
Word of Christ	Col.	3	16

work effort, labor

Rest from, on the seventh day	Gen.	2	2
Commanded by God	Gen.	3	19
	Deut.	4	28
Should be done faithfully	II Chr.	34	2
Of hands, blessed by God	Job	1	10
Sometimes disappointing	Eccl.	2	11
A time for every	Eccl.	3	17
"Be strong and work"	Hag.	2	4
Christian work required of all	Mark	13	34
Some to be done on the sabbath	John	5	17
"The night cometh, when no man can work"	John	9	4
No good will come of evil	Acts	5	38
"All things work together"	Rom.	8	28
Of God, not to be destroyed	Rom.	14	20
Shall be made manifest	I Cor.	3	13
For Christ, should be constant	I Cor.	15	58
Every man should prove his own	Gal.	6	4
Commanded by Paul	II Tim.	4	5
Patience required in perfect	James	1	4

works, good

Remembered by God	Neh.	13	14
	Heb.	6	9, 10
Many, are those from God	Ps.	40	5
Wrought by God in us	Is.	26	12
All known to God	Is.	66	18
Christ, an example of	John	10	32
Salvation unattainable by, without faith	Eph.	2	8, 9
Are to the glory of God	Phil.	1	11
Do, in the name of Christ	Col.	3	17
Scripture will lead us to	II Tim.	3	16, 17
Commanded by Paul	Heb.	13	16
Bring a blessing	James	1	25
"Without faith, is dead"	James	2	17

works of God

In creation	Gen.	1, 2	
Tables	Ex.	32	16
Wondrous	Job	37	14
To be declared	Ps.	64	9
To be remembered	Ps.	78	7
To be considered	Eccl.	7	13
Spoken	Acts	2	11

Not to destroy	Rom.	14	20
Not believed	Acts	13	41
works of Satan			
Incite men to sin	John	8	37–47
	John	13	2
Will be destroyed	I John	3	8
world			
Created by God	Gen.	1	1, 2
Early ideas of:			
Set upon pillars	I Sam.	2	8
Remains in place	I Chr.	16	30
Cannot be moved	Ps.	93	1
Is controlled by God	Is.	66	1
Followers of Jesus, light of the	Mat.	5	14
The end of	Mat.	13	49
God's love for	John	3	16
To be burned up	II Pet.	3	10, 11
See earth			
He set the *w* upon them	I Sam.	2	8
The *w* shall be stable	I Chr.	16	30
Chased out of the *w*	Job	18	18
Who hath disposed the whole *w*	Job	34	13
Upon the face of the *w*	Job	37	12
From men of the *w*	Ps.	17	14
The *w* and they that dwell therein	Ps.	24	1
	Ps.	98	7
	Nah.	1	5
The *w* is mine	Ps.	50	12
The ungodly, who prosper in the *w*	Ps.	73	12
W is established	Ps.	93	1
	Ps.	96	10
He hath set the *w* in their heart	Eccl.	3	11
Nor fill the face of the *w* with cities	Is.	14	21
The *w* languisheth	Is.	24	4
Let the *w* hear	Is.	34	1
Not confounded, *w* without end	Is.	45	17
All the kingdoms of the *w*	Mat.	4	8
	Luke	4	5
The light of the *w*	Mat.	5	14
The cares of this *w*	Mat.	13	22
	Mark	4	19
The field is the *w*	Mat.	13	38
In the end of this *w*	Mat.	13	40
Gain the whole *w*	Mat.	16	26
	Mark	8	36
	Luke	9	25
Woe to the *w* because of offences	Mat.	18	7
Shall be preached in all the *w*	Mat.	24	14
	Mark	14	9
In the *w* to come eternal life	Mark	10	30
	Luke	18	30
Since the *w* began	Luke	1	70
	Acts	3	21
Worthy to obtain that *w*	Luke	20	35
Taketh away the sin of the *w*	John	1	29
God so loved the *w*	John	3	16
The Saviour of the *w*	John	4	42
	I John	4	14
Bread of God giveth life to the *w*	John	6	33
Jesus said, I am the light of the *w*	John	8	12
	John	9	5
I came not to judge the *w*, but to save the *w*	John	12	47
Not as the *w* giveth, give I unto you	John	14	27
The prince of this *w* cometh	John	14	30
If the *w* hate you	John	15	18
	I John	3	13
I leave the *w*, and go to the Father	John	16	28
I pray not for the *w*	John	17	9
That the *w* may believe thou hast sent me	John	17	21, 23
The *w* could not contain the books	John	21	25
Turned the *w* upside down	Acts	17	6
That all the *w* may become guilty	Rom.	3	19
And be not conformed to this *w*	Rom.	12	2
The *w* by wisdom knew not God	I Cor.	1	21
They that use this *w*, as not abusing it	I Cor.	7	31
The god of this *w* hath blinded	II Cor.	4	4
Deliver us from this present evil *w*	Gal.	1	4
Without God in the *w*	Eph.	2	12
We brought nothing into this *w*	I Tim.	6	7
Love not the *w*	I John	2	15
worms			
Consume excess manna	Ex.	16	20, 24
Job's mother and sister are	Job	17	14
Shall eat the wicked	Job	24	20
Figurative	Is.	14	11

Do not die in hell	Mark	9	43–50
Herod eaten by	Acts	12	23
wormwood *a bitter plant*			
Symbol of evil	Deut.	29	18
Fate of sinful woman is like	Prov.	5	4
Symbol of punishment and suffering	Jer.	9	15
Denotes offensiveness	Amos	5	7
Star called	Rev.	8	11
worry *anxiety*			
Cure for	Mat.	6	19–34
worship *religious reverence and homage*			
Of Abraham	Gen.	12	7, 8
Of Jacob	Gen.	35	1–3
To be rendered only to God	Ex.	20	3
Cleansing prior to	Ex.	28	41
	Lev.	14	9
Sacrifices offered in	Lev.	12	6
	Lev.	15	13–15
God's presence in	Lev.	19	30
Family	Deut.	16	11, 14
David's ordinances for	I Chr.	23–26	
Of Job	Job	1	5
Public, in the temple	Jer.	26	2
Idolatrous	Jer.	44	19
Paid to man	Luke	14	10
Of man, forbidden	Acts	10	25, 26
Of angels, forbidden	Rev.	19	10
Attitudes in:			
Prostration	Gen.	17	3
Sandals removed	Ex.	3	5
Bowing	Ex.	34	8
Covering the face	I Ki.	19	13
Covering the head	I Cor.	11	10
Places of:			
Springs	Gen.	16	7–14
In the desert	Gen.	28	10–12
Mountains	Ex.	3	1
Solomon's temple	I Ki.	3	2
Jerusalem temple	II Ki.	23	4
Times of:			
Sabbath as a holy day	Ex.	20	8–11
Of Christ:			
By the wise men	Mat.	2	1, 11
By His disciples	Mat.	14	33
By angels	Heb.	1	6
In heaven	Rev.	5	8–14
worthy			
I am not *w* of thy mercies	Gen.	32	10
Show himself a *w* man	I Ki.	1	52
Whose shoes I am not *w* to bear	Mat.	3	11
I am not *w* thou shouldest come under my roof	Mat.	8	8
	Luke	7	6
The workman is *w* of his meat	Mat.	10	10
That loveth father more than me is not *w* of me	Mat.	10	37
They which were bidden were not *w*	Mat.	22	8
I am not *w* unloose	Mark	1	7
	Luke	3	16
	John	1	27
Fruits *w* of repentance	Luke	3	8
Neither thought I myself *w*	Luke	7	7
The labourer is *w* of his hire	Luke	10	7
	I Tim.	5	18
wounds *injuries*			
Lies are like	Prov.	18	8
Figuratively used in judgments	Is.	1	6
Of man bandaged by Samaritan	Luke	10	34
Judgment for	Ex.	21	25
Incurable	Job	34	6
	Jer.	15	18
Self-inflicted by adulterer	Prov.	6	33
The Messiah	Is.	53	5
Healed	Rev.	13	3
By a sword	Joel	2	8
By stones	Mark	12	4
By archers	I Sam.	31	3
Words of a talebearer	Prov.	18	8
	Prov.	26	2
Accidental	Deut.	23	1
wrath *anger*			
Cursed be their *w*	Gen.	49	7
There is *w* gone out from the Lord	Num.	16	46
Were it not I feared the *w* of the enemy	Deut.	32	27
W killeth the foolish man	Job	5	2

wrath—*continued*

Drink of *w* of the Almighty	Job	21	20
Because there is *w*, beware	Job	36	18
The *w* of man shall praise thee	Ps.	76	10
By thy *w* are we troubled	Ps.	90	7
To whom I sware in my *w*	Ps.	95	11
Soft answer turneth away *w*	Prov.	15	1
W of a king is as messengers of death	Prov.	16	14
W is cruel, and anger outrageous	Prov.	27	4
Much *w* with his sickness	Eccl.	5	17
In a little *w* I hid my face	Is.	54	8
In *w* remember mercy	Heb.	3	2
From the *w* to come	Mat.	3	7
	Luke	3	7
Treasurest up *w* against the day of *w*	Rom.	2	5
Rather give place to *w*	Rom.	12	19
Let not the sun go down on your *w*	Eph.	4	26
Father, provoke not your children to *w*	Eph.	6	4
Put off these, *w*, malice	Col.	3	8
Delivered us from *w* to come	I Thes.	1	10
God hath not appointed us to *w*	I Thes.	5	9
Lifting up holy hands without *w*	I Tim.	2	8
Slow to speak, slow to *w*	James	1	19
Hide us from *w* of the Lamb	Rev.	6	16

wrathful

Let thy *w* anger take	Ps.	69	24

wrestling

Of Jacob with an angel	Gen.	32	24–32

write

W them on posts of thy house	Deut.	6	9
	Deut.	11	20
W them upon the table of thine heart	Prov.	3	3
	Prov.	7	3
A child may *w* them	Is.	10	19
W ye this man childless	Jer.	22	30
I will *w* law in their hearts	Jer.	31	33
	Heb.	8	10
W the vision on tables	Hab.	2	2
W not, The King of the Jews	John	19	21
I will *w* on him my new name	Rev.	3	12

writings

Of commandments	Ex.	32	15–19
Book of law by Moses	Deut.	31	24
Of law by Joshua before the people	Josh.	8	32
About building the temple given to David	I Chr.	28	19
Of Cyrus' decree	II Chr.	36	22, 23
Interpreted by Daniel	Dan.	5	24
Of Jesus on the ground	John	8	6
In hearts	II Cor.	3	2

wrong

To him that did the *w*	Ex.	2	13
To testify what is *w*	Deut.	19	16
There is no *w* in mine hands	I Chr.	12	17
He suffered no man to do them *w*	I Chr.	16	21
	Ps.	105	14
I cry out of *w*, but am not heard	Job	19	7
Do no *w*, do no violence	Jer.	22	3
Friend, I do thee no *w*	Mat.	20	13
A matter of *w*	Acts	18	14
Why do ye not take *w*?	I Cor.	6	7
He that doeth *w* shall receive for the *w*	Col.	3	25
The king was *w*	Col.	22	7

wrought *fashioned, work*

What hath God *w*	Num.	23	23
God hath *w* wonderfully	I Sam.	6	6
Lord *w* salvation in Israel	I Sam.	11	13
	I Sam.	19	5
Every one *w* in the work	Neh.	4	17
This work was *w* of God	Neh.	6	16
The hand of the Lord hath *w* this	Job	12	9
Who can say, Thou hast *w* iniquity?	Job	36	23
Hast *w* for them that trust in thee	Ps.	31	19
Strengthen that which thou hast *w* for us	Ps.	68	28
Curiously *w* in lowest parts of the earth	Ps.	139	15
Work *w* under the sun	Eccl.	2	17
Thou hast *w* all our works in us	Is.	26	12
Who hath *w* and done it?	Is.	41	4
I *w* for my name's sake	Ezek.	20	9
The wonders God hath *w* toward me	Dan.	4	2
The sea *w*, and was tempestuous	Jonah	1	11
These last have *w* but one hour	Mat.	20	12
She hath *w* a good work on me	Mat.	26	10
	Mark	14	6
Manifest, that they are *w* in God	John	3	21
What wonders God had *w*	Acts	15	12
He abode with them, and *w*	Acts	18	3
Things which Christ hath not *w* by me	Rom.	15	18

He that hath *w* us for the selfsame thing is God	II Cor.	5	5
He that *w* effectually	Gal.	2	8
Which he *w* in Christ	Eph.	1	20
Through faith *w* righteousness	Heb.	11	33
How faith *w* with his works	James	2	22
To have *w* the will of the Gentiles	I Pet.	4	3
Lose not those things which we have *w*	II John		8

Y

year

Beginning of, changed	Ex.	12	1
	Lev.	23	5
For seasons, and for days, and *y*	Gen.	1	14
Few and evil have the *y* of my life been	Gen.	47	9
Keep this ordinance from *y* to *y*	Ex.	13	10
Make atonement once a *y*	Lev.	16	34
A *y* of rest	Lev.	25	5
Thou shalt tithe the increase *y* by *y*	Deut.	14	22
Consider the *y* of many generations	Deut.	32	7
When from *y* to *y* in circuit	I Sam.	7	16
Are thy *y* as man's days?	Job	10	5
When a few *y* are come	Job	16	22
Multitude of *y* should teach wisdom	Job	32	7
Neither can the number of his *y* be searched out	Job	36	26
My *y* are spent with sighing	Ps.	31	10
Prolong his *y* as many generations	Ps.	61	6
Thou crownest the *y* with thy goodness	Ps.	65	11
The *y* of the right hand of the Most High	Ps.	77	10
Their *y* did he consume in trouble	Ps.	78	33
A thousand *y* in thy sight	Ps.	90	4
	II Pet.	3	8
We spend our *y* as a tale that is told	Ps.	90	9
The days of our *y* are threescore *y* and ten	Ps.	90	10
Thy *y* are throughout all generations	Ps.	102	24
Thy *y* shall have no end	Ps.	102	27
The *y* of thy life shall be many	Prov.	4	10
The *y* of the wicked shall be shortened	Prov.	10	27
Nor the *y* draw nigh	Eccl.	12	1
According to the *y* of an hireling	Is.	21	16
Add ye *y* to *y*	Is.	29	1
The acceptable *y* of the Lord	Is.	61	2
	Luke	4	19
The *y* of my redeemed is come	Is.	63	4
The *y* of their visitation	Jer.	11	23
	Jer.	23	12
	Jer.	48	44
Not be careful in *y* of drought	Jer.	17	8
This *y* thou shalt die	Jer.	28	16
Thou art come unto thy *y*	Ezek.	22	4
It shall be his to the *y* of liberty	Ezek.	46	17
The *y* of many generations	Joel	2	2
Revive thy work in midst of the *y*	Hab.	3	2
Let is alone this *y*	Luke	13	8
Ye observe months and *y*	Gal.	4	10
Thy *y* shall not fail	Heb.	1	12
Continue there a *y*, and buy	James	4	13

years, thousand

"As one day"	II Pet.	3	8
Satan is chained for	Rev.	20	2–7

yield *give*

Ground not *y* her strength	Gen.	4	12
That it may *y* the increase	Lev.	19	25
The land shall *y* her increase	Lev.	26	4
	Ps.	67	6
	Ps.	85	12
Y ourselves unto the Lord	II Chr.	30	8
Vineyards, which may *y* fruits	Ps.	107	37
The bud shall *y* no meal	Hosea	8	7
Fig tree and vine *y* their strength	Joel	2	22
Though fields shall *y* no meat	Hab.	3	17
Jesus *y* up the ghost	Mat.	27	50
Do not thou *y* unto them	Acts	23	21
Y yourselves unto God	Rom.	6	13
Y your members servants to righteousness	Rom.	6	19
It *y* the peaceable fruit of righteousness	Heb.	12	11
No fountain can *y* salt water and fresh	James	3	12

yoke *frame for joining oxen to plow*

Symbol of oppression	Gen.	27	40
Symbol of authority of Jesus	Mat.	11	29, 30
Of oxen	Luke	14	19
Peter does not want, on disciples	Acts	15	5–10
Of believers and unbelievers	II Cor.	6	14
Lifted by Christ	Gal.	5	1
Of servants	I Tim.	6	1

young

Exhortations to	Lev.	19	32
	Prov.	1	8
	Eccl.	12	1
Christ's example	Luke	2	46, 51
Not show favour to the *y*	Deut.	28	50
As an eagle fluttereth over her *y*	Deut.	32	11
When his *y* ones cry to God	Job	38	41
I have been *y*, and now am old	Ps.	37	25
A nest where she may lay her *y*	Ps.	84	3
He giveth food to the *y* ravens	Ps.	147	9
Their *y* ones shall lie down together	Is.	11	7
Gently lead those that are with *y*	Is.	40	11
When *y*, thou girdedst thyself	John	21	18
Teach *y* women to be sober	Tit.	2	4

youth

Sins of	Job	20	11
Should resist temptations	Prov.	1	10–16
"Remember thy creator in"	Eccl.	12	1
Teaches the scriptures	II Tim.	3	15
Examples of religious:			
Joseph	Gen.	37	9–12
David	Ps.	71	17
Rich young man	Mark	10	17–22

Z

Zabad *bestowed*

Called Jozachar	II Ki.	12	21
A Judahite, son of Nathan	I Chr.	2	34–37
An Ephraimite	I Chr.	7	20, 21
Son of Ahlai and one of David's mighty men	I Chr.	11	41
Conspiracy against Joash	II Chr.	24	26
Three men who put away their foreign wives	Ezra	10	27, 33, 43

Zabbai *God has given*

One who puts away a foreign wife	Ezra	10	28
Father of Baruch	Neh.	3	20

Zabud *endowed*

Son of Nathan, officer of Solomon	I Ki.	4	5

Zabulon, *see Zebulun*

Zacchaeus *pure*

A tax collector who becomes a follower of Jesus	Luke	19	1–10

Zaccur, Zacchur *remembered*

A Reubenite, father of Shammua	Num.	13	1, 2, 4
A Simeonite	I Chr.	4	26
A Merarite Levite	I Chr.	24	27
A Levite, one of David's leaders of music	I Chr.	25	2, 10
Son of Imri who helps rebuild the wall	Neh.	3	2
A Levite who seals the covenant	Neh.	10	1, 12
Father of Hanan	Neh.	13	13

Zachariah *Jehovah has remembered*

Son of Jeroboam	II Ki.	14	29
Last of the house of Jehu	II Ki.	10	30
Grandfather of Hezekiah	II Ki.	18	2

Zacharias *whom Jehovah remembers*

Father of John the Baptist	Luke	1	5–80
A priest, slain in the temple	Luke	11	51

Zadok *righteous*

A high priest in David's reign	II Sam.	19	11
Removes ark from Jerusalem and later returns with it	II Sam.	15	24–36
	II Sam.	17	15, 17–21
Refuses to help Adonijah usurp the throne	I Ki.	1	8, 26
Anoints Solomon	I Ki.	1	32–45
Father of Jerusha	II Ki.	15	33
Son of Ahitub, and priest	I Chr.	6	12
A man of valour, who helps David	I Chr.	12	28

Son of Baana, who helps repair the wall	Neh.	3	4
Son of Immer, who helps repair the wall	Neh.	3	29
Son of Meraioth	Neh.	11	11
A treasurer of the temple	Neh.	13	13

Zamzummims *murmurers*

Called Zuzims	Gen.	14	5
A race of giants	Deut.	2	20, 21

Zanoah *rejected*

A town in lowland of Judah	Josh.	15	1, 34
Occupied after exile	Neh.	11	30
A town in hill country of Judah	Josh.	15	56
Descendant of Caleb	I Chr.	4	18

Zaphnath-paaneah *God speaks*

Name given to Joseph by Pharaoh	Gen.	41	45

Zarephath *smelting place*

City where Elijah revives the widow's son	I Ki.	17	8–24
Called Sarepta by Jesus	Luke	4	26

zeal *active interest*

Of Phinehas	Num.	25	7, 11
In old age	Josh.	14	10–12
Of Jehu	II Ki.	10	16
Lack of, a sin	Amos	6	1–6
Christ an example of	John	2	17
Of the Jews for the law	Acts	21	20
Of Paul for the Jewish religion	Acts	22	3
In good works	Gal.	4	18
	Tit.	2	14
	Rev.	3	19
Of Moses	Ex.	2	12
Of Joshua	Num.	11	27–29
Of Gideon	Judg.	6	11–32
Of Jephthah	Judg.	11	30, 31
Of Samuel	I Sam.	12	23
Of Saul	I Sam.	14	38–44
Of David	II Sam.	6	
Of Elijah	I Ki.	19	10
Of Asa	I Ki.	15	11–15
Of Jehoshaphat	II Chr.	17	3–10
Of Hezekiah	II Chr.	30	31
Of Anna	Luke	2	38
Of Paul for Christianity	Rom.	1	8, 9
Of Isaiah	Is.	6	8
In business	Rom.	12	11
Without love profitless	I Cor.	13	3
Of spiritual gifts	I Cor.	14	12
In the work of the Lord	I Cor.	15	58
In the millennium	Is.	2	3–5

Zebadiah *Jehovah has given*

A son of Elpaal, a Benjamite	I Chr.	8	15
Another named as son of Elpaal	I Chr.	8	17
A Benjamite who joins David at Ziklag	I Chr.	12	2, 7
A Korhite gatekeeper	I Chr.	26	2, 13
An officer of David	I Chr.	27	7
A Levite	II Chr.	17	8
A Judahite officer	II Chr.	19	11
Head of a family which returns with Ezra	Ezra	8	8
A priest who puts away a foreign wife	Ezra	10	20

Zebedee *gift of Jehovah*

Father of James and John	Mat.	4	21

Zebulun, Zabulun *habitation*

Son of Jacob and Leah	Gen.	30	20
Descendants of	Gen.	46	14
Tribe of:			
Moses' benediction upon	Deut.	33	18, 19
Land allotted to	Josh.	19	10–16
Levitical cities of	Josh.	21	34, 35
Loyalty in resisting Israelites' enemies	Judg.	4	10
	Judg.	6	35
	I Chr.	12	33, 38–40
Conquest of Tiglath-pileser	II Ki.	15	29
Joins in renewing the passover	II Chr.	30	11, 18
Jesus dwells in the land of	Mat.	4	15
Distinguished in the new Jerusalem	Rev.	7	8

Zechariah, Zachariah *Jehovah hath remembered*

Son of Jeroboam	II Ki.	14	29
Grandfather of King Hezekiah	II Ki.	18	2
Reubenite chieftain	I Chr.	5	7
Son of Meshelemiah	I Chr.	9	21
Brother of Kish, uncle of Saul	I Chr.	9	37
A Levite musician	I Chr.	15	18, 20
A priest	I Chr.	15	24
A Kohathite Levite	I Chr.	24	25
A Merarite Levite	I Chr.	26	11
Father of Iddo	I Chr.	27	21
Prince of Judah who assists Jehoshaphat	II Chr.	17	7

Zechariah, Zachariah—*continued*

An Asaphite Levite	II Chr.	20	14
Son of Jehoshaphat	II Chr.	21	2
A priest, son of Jehoiada	II Chr.	24	20
A prophet and adviser of King Uzziah	II Chr.	26	5
An overseer for repairing the temple	II Chr.	34	12
A ruler of the temple	II Chr.	35	8
A prophet, descendant of Iddo	Ezra	5	1
	Zech.	1	1
Two men who return from exile	Ezra	8	3, 11
Summoned by Ezra	Ezra	8	15, 16
Descendant of Elam	Ezra	10	26
One who stands by Ezra at the reading of the law	Neh.	8	4
A descendant of Perez	Neh.	11	4
Son of Shiloni	Neh.	11	5
A son of Pashur	Neh.	11	12
Son of Jonathan	Neh.	12	35
A priest and trumpeter	Neh.	12	41
A highly esteemed contemporary of Isaiah	Is.	8	2

Zedekiah *righteousness of Jehovah*

King of Judah	II Ki.	24	17, 18
Wicked reign of	II Ki.	24	19, 20
Rejects Nebuchadnezzar	II Ki.	24	20
Imprisons Jeremiah	Jer.	37	15–21
Seeks intercession with God	Jer.	38	14–27
Taken captive by Nebuchadnezzar	Jer.	39	1–5
Sees his sons murdered and then is blinded	Jer.	39	6–14
Imprisoned until his death	Jer.	52	11
Grandson of Jehoiakim	I Chr.	3	16
A false prophet	II Chr.	18	10
Smites Micaiah	II Chr.	18	23
A false prophet	Jer.	29	21–23
A prince of Judah	Jer.	36	12
Signer of the covenant	Nah.	10	1

Zelah *limping, slope*

A city in Benjamin	Josh.	18	21, 28
Saul buried here	II Sam.	21	14

Zelotes *zealot*

Surname of Simon	Luke	6	15

Zenas *gift of Zeus*

A Christian lawyer	Tit.	3	13

Zephaniah *God's secret*

A Kohathite	I Chr.	6	36
A priest in the reign of Zedekiah	Jer.	21	1
Reads letter to Jeremiah	Jer.	29	25–29
Slain	Jer.	52	24–27
Ninth of the minor prophets	Zeph.	1	1
Father of Josiah	Zech.	6	10, 14

Zerah, Zarah *eastern, sprout*

Son of Reuel	Gen.	36	13, 17
Father of Jobab	Gen.	36	33
Son of Judah	Gen.	38	30
	Gen.	46	12
	Neh.	11	24
Son of Simeon	Num.	26	13
	I Chr.	4	24
A Gershonite	I Chr.	6	21
A Levite	I Chr.	6	41
King of Ethiopia	II Chr.	14	9–15

Zerahiah *rising of God*

An ancestor of Ezra	I Chr.	6	6, 51
	Ezra	7	4
Father of Elihoenai	Ezra	8	4

Zerubbabel, Zorobabel *seed of Babylon*

Leads Jews back from Babylon	Ezra	2	1, 2
Directs rebuilding of altar and temple	Ezra	3	2, 8
	Ezra	4	2, 3
Prophecies relating to	Hag.	2	21–23
	Zech.	4	6–10
Ancestor of Jesus	Luke	3	27

Zeruiah *bruised, balm*

Mother of three soldiers	II Sam.	2	18
	I Chr.	2	16
Abigail's sister	II Sam.	17	25
Sister of David	I Chr.	2	16

Ziba *statue, plantation*

Saul's servant	II Sam.	9	2–4
Becomes Mephibosheth's servant	II Sam.	9	9–12
	II Sam.	16	1–4

Zichri *remembered*

Son of Izhar	Ex.	6	21
Three Benjamites	I Chr.	8	19, 23, 27
A Levite	I Chr.	9	15

Two chiefs in days of David	I Chr.	26	25
	I Chr.	27	16
Father of Amasiah	II Chr.	17	16
Father of Elishaphat	II Chr.	23	1
An Ephraimite	II Chr.	28	7
Father of Joel	Neh.	11	9
A priest	Neh.	12	17

Zidon, *see* Sidon

Zif, Ziz *bloom*

Second month (May)	I Ki.	6	1, 37

Ziklag *flowing, winding*

A city of Judah	Josh.	15	31
Allotted to Simeon	Josh.	19	5
David dwells at	I Sam.	27	5, 6
Invaded and robbed	I Sam.	30	1–31
Inhabited after exile	Neh.	11	28

Zilpah *dropping*

Leah's handmaid	Gen.	29	24
A wife of Jacob	Gen.	30	9
Mother of Gad and Asher	Gen.	30	9–13

Zimri *sung*

A chief of Simeon	Num.	25	14
King of Israel	I Ki.	16	9–20
Son of Zerah	II Ki.	9	31
A Benjamite	I Chr.	8	36
	I Chr.	9	42
An unknown place	Jer.	25	25

Zin *shrub, low land*

A desert south of Judah	Num.	13	21
Children of Israel in	Num.	20	1
A border of Canaan	Num.	34	3, 4
	Josh.	15	1, 3

Zion, Sion *citadel, fortress*

Fortress captured by David	II Sam.	5	7
Ark placed here	II Sam.	6	10–12
Symbolic name for Jerusalem and Israel	Is.	4	3
In reference to the temple	Is.	8	18
Figurative of heaven	Rev.	14	1

Ziph *melting*

Two cities of Judah	Josh.	15	24, 55
David in	I Sam.	23	14, 15, 24
	I Sam.	26	2
Built by Rehoboam	II Chr.	11	8
Grandson of Caleb	I Chr.	2	42
Son of Jehaleleel	I Chr.	4	16

Zipporah *a little bird*

Wife of Moses	Ex.	2	16–22
Moses upbraided concerning	Num.	12	1

Ziz *see* Zif

Ziza, Zina *plenty, shining*

A Simeonite	I Chr.	4	37
A Gershonite	I Chr.	23	10, 11
Son of Rehoboam	II Chr.	11	20

Zoan *departure*

A city in Egypt	Num.	13	22
Counsellors of Pharaoh from	Is.	19	11, 13
Princes of	Is.	30	4
Prophecies concerning	Ezek.	30	14

Zoar *little*

A city of Moabites	Gen.	13	10
Not destroyed with Sodom and Gomorrah	Gen.	19	20, 23, 30
Territory of	Deut.	34	3
	Is.	15	5

Zoba, Zobah *encampment*

A kingdom in northern Palestine	I Sam.	14	47
Conquered by David	II Sam.	8	3–8, 12
	I Ki.	11	23, 24
Invaded by Solomon	II Chr.	8	3

Zohar *white*

Father of Ephron	Gen.	23	8
	Gen.	25	9
Son of Simeon	Ex.	6	15

Zophar *little bird*

A Naamathite, a friend of Job	Job	2	11
Does as commanded	Job	42	7–9

Zorah, Zareah, Zoreah *hornet*

A city of Dan	Josh.	15	33
	Josh.	19	41
City of Samson	Judg.	13	2, 24, 25
	Judg.	16	31
Men of, as spies, warriors	Judg.	18	1–31
Fortified by Rehoboam	II Chr.	11	10
Repeopled after captivity	Neh.	11	29

Zorobabel *see* Zerubbabel

THE MIDDLE EAST BEFORE THE FLOOD
(GENESIS 2:4-17)

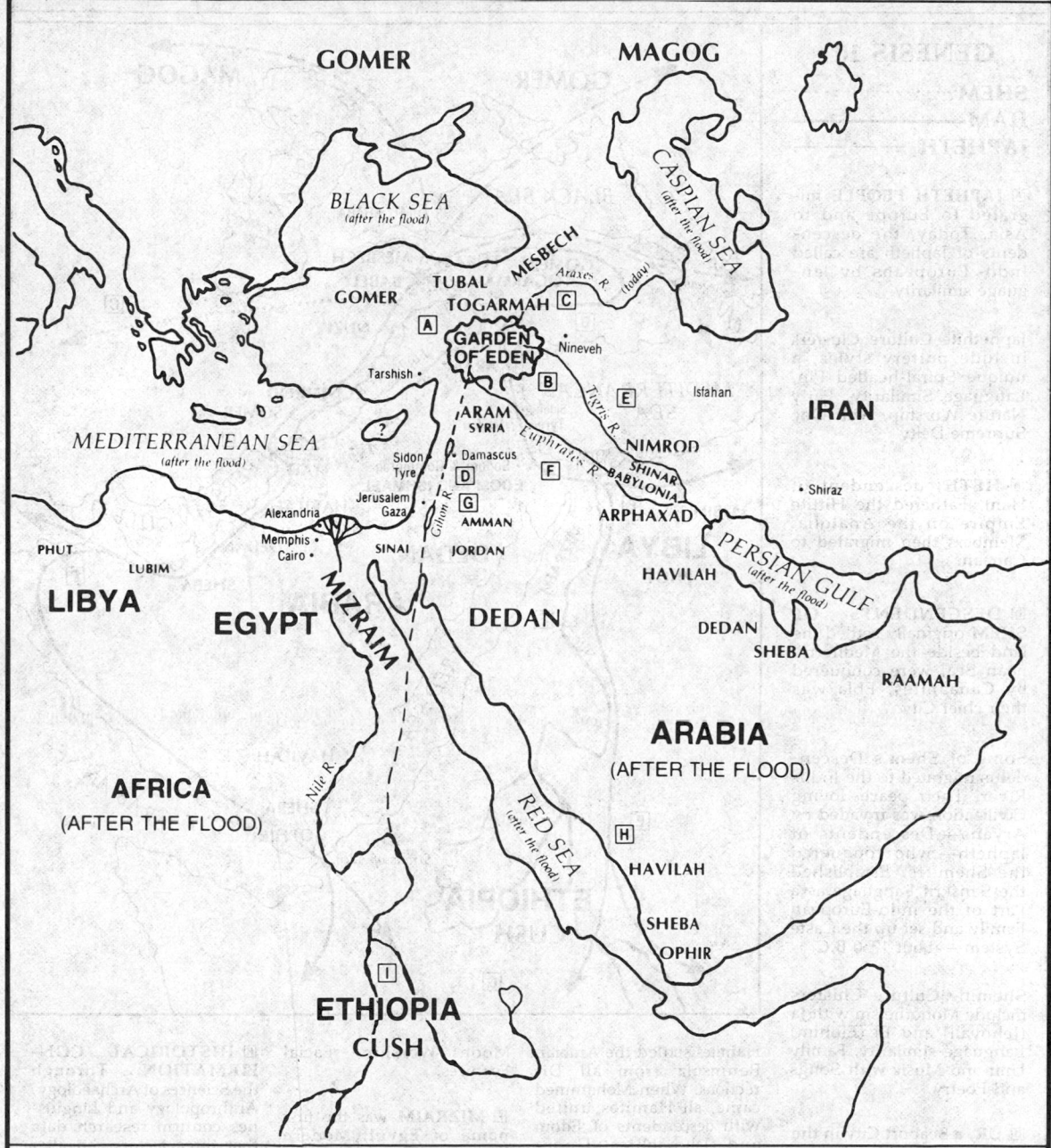

Ⓐ **AREA OF EDEN** Genesis 2:8, 10, 3:23; Isaiah 57:3; Ezekiel 28:13; 31:9; 36:33.

Ⓑ **TREE OF LIFE** Gen. 2:17; 3:3.

Ⓒ **PISON RIVER** traditional. Gen. 2:11, 12.

Ⓓ **PISON RIVER** probable.

Ⓔ **TIGRIS RIVER** known also as Hiddekel. Gen. 2:14; Dan. 10:4.

Ⓕ **EUPHRATES RIVER** Gen. 2:14; 15:18; Deut. 11:24; 1 Chronicles 5:9.

Ⓖ **GIHON RIVER** now the Great Rift Valley and includes the Jordan River.

Gen. 2:13. The Gihon Spring persists east of Jerusalem. 2 Chron. 32:30.

Ⓗ **HAVILAH** is identified with Shur: Gen. 25:18; with gold: Gen. 2:11; with Ishmaelites.

Ⓘ **ETHIOPIA** Gen. 2:13; Job 28:19; Ps. 68:31; Isaiah 43:3, 45:14; Acts 8:27.

ORIGINS OF NATIONS
FROM DESCENDANTS OF NOAH

GENESIS 10

SHEM ·············
HAM ————————
JAPHETH — — — —

A JAPHETH PEOPLE migrated to Europe and to Asia. Today, the descendents of Japheth are called Indo- Europeans by language similarity.

Japhethite Culture Clusters include pottery styles, a unique Spiral-headed Pin, Language Similarity, Early Nature Worship, with One Supreme Deity.

B HETH, descendent of Ham, Fathered the Hittite Empire on the Anatolia. Members then migrated to Canaan.

C DESCENDENTS OF SHEM originally settled the land beside the Mediterranean Sea; were conquered by Canaanites. Ebla was their chief City.

Some of Shem's Descendents migrated to the Indus River. Their peace- loving Civilization was invaded by Aryans— Descendents of Japheth— who conquered the Shemites. Established the Sanskrit Language as a Part of the Indo-European Family and set up the Caste System—about 1750 B.C.

Shemitic Culture Clusters include Monotheism with Ja (Jehovah) and El (Elohim) Language similarity; Family Unit and Music with Songs and Poetry.

D UR, a Seaport City in the Province of Chaldee, Sumer

E DESCENDENTS OF HAM crossed the Straits of Aden to Ethiopia.

Some Hamites migrated to India and South.

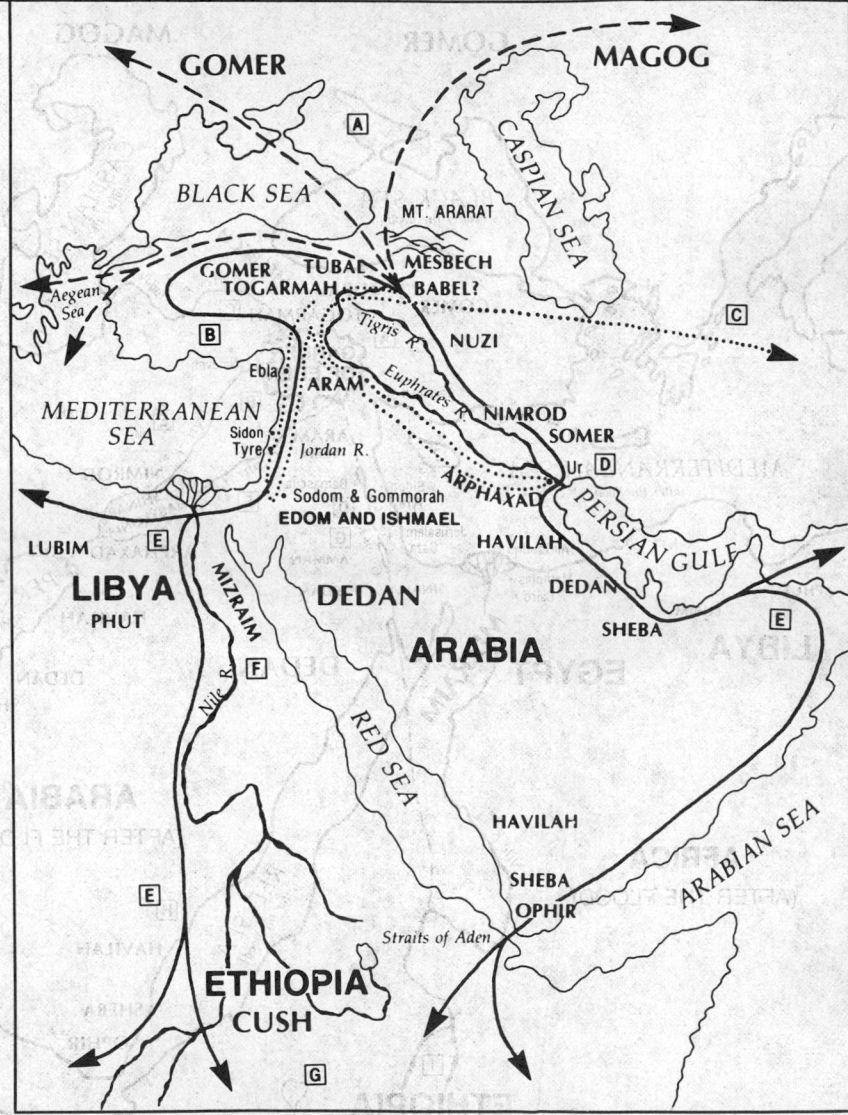

Hamites settled the Arabian Peninsula from all Directions. When Mohammed came, all Hamites united with descendents of Edom and Ishmaelites Under Islam's Authority — 650 A.D.

Hamitic Culture Clusters include the Ziggurat-Step Pyramid — Great Pyramids; Early Sex-Image Idolatry, Moon Worship, Facial Features.

F MIZRAIM was the first name of Egypt; Modern Egyptian planes bear that name. Gen. 10: 6

G AFRICANS today are grouped into three families. Nilotic and North Africans — Central Africans -- Mixed — East and Southern.

H HISTORICAL CONFIRMATION... Through the Sciences of Archaeology, Anthropology and Linguistics confirm research data that three factors can alter Genetic Coding in small populations. They are: Excessive Climate Change, Excessive Diet Change and Extreme Stress. The Sovereignty of God Implanted Latent Genes; this change is not through Mutations.

FROM THE EXODUS TO THE JUDGES

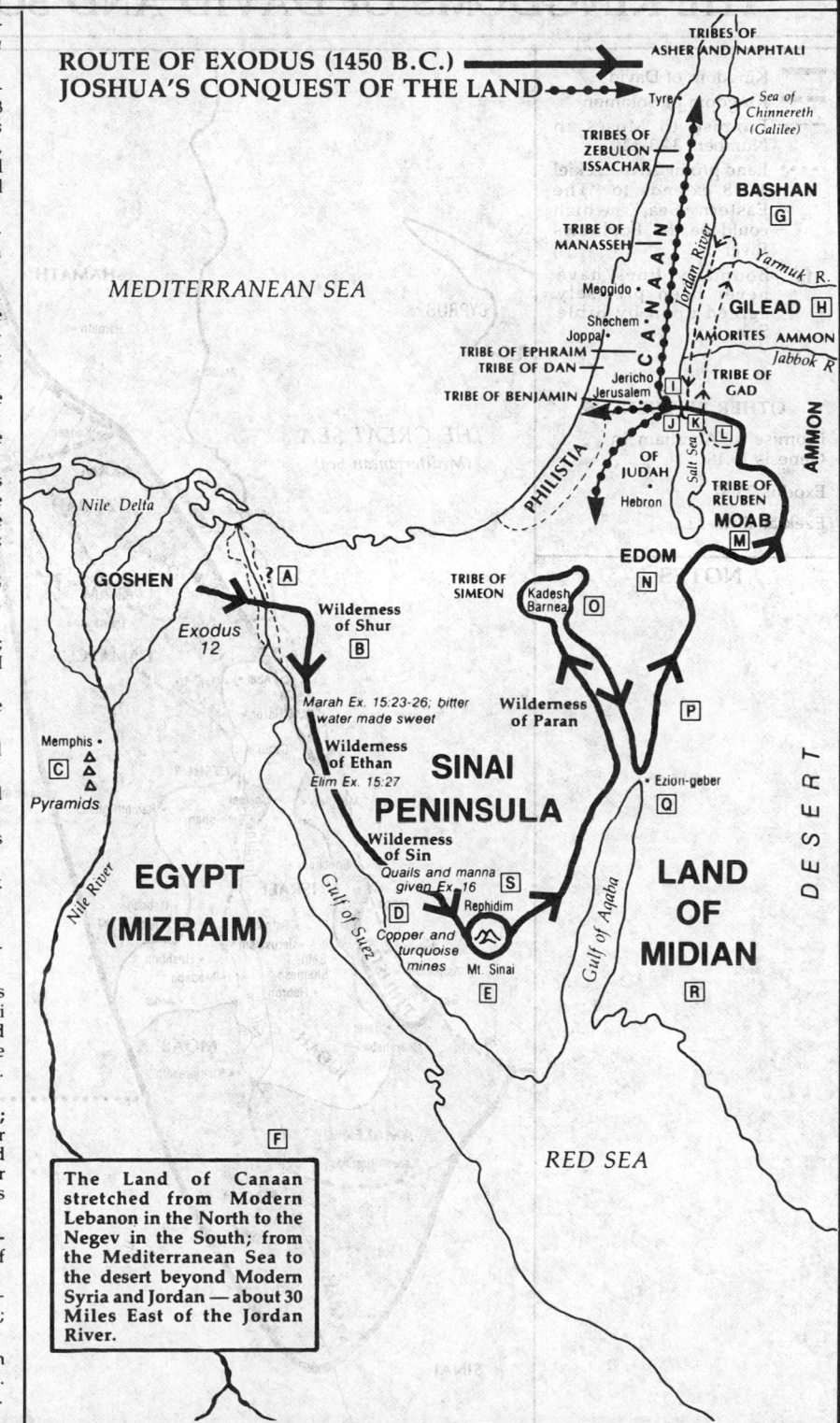

A **The ?** Indicates the Uncertain Extent of the *Red Sea* 3500 Years Ago.

B **Ex. 15:22 & Deut. 1:40** Indicate Israel wandered 3 Days' Journey into *Shur's Wilderness;* Needing Water, They Turned Back to the Red Sea Highway and Found Water at Marah.

C **MEMPHIS,** Egypt's Capital in the Days of Abraham — Joseph.

D **Moses'** Queen-Mother, Hatshepsut, May Have Taken him Here; He Met Jehovah-Worshiping Midianites.

E **Most of the Laws** Were Given On and Around *Mt. Sinai,* Ex. 19 through the Leviticus.

F **About 60 Miles South** Is Karnak-Thebes-Luxor, Where Moses Was Reared to be the Next Pharaoh, Acts 7:21-23; Heb. 11:24-27.

G **LAND OF KING OG** Num. 34:11; Josh. 11:2, 13:27.

H **GILEAD,** Land of cattle; Tribe of Reuben Num. 32:1; I Chron. 5:9.

I **JERICHO,** Josh. 2:6 The spies & Rahab.

J **GILGAL** where Israel camped in Canaan. Josh. 4:5.

K **MT. NEBO**— Moses died & Was buried. Deut. 34.

L **5 Towns** served as Israel's base to fight.

M **MOAB'S** king Balak hired Balaam to curse Israel. Num. 22-24.

N **EDOM,** from Easu's descendents. Num. 20:14-22.

O **KADESH BARNEA:** spies searched the Land; Israeli Rejected the Offer and Had to Wander 40 Yrs. In the Wilderness. Num. 13; Num. 32:8.

P **PETRA & ALN MUSA;** Moses Struck the Rock for Water a Second Time and Therefore Could Not Enter the Land for That Rock Was Christ. Num. 20:7-13.

Q **ISRAEL'S LAST ENCAMPMENT** was north of *Ezion-geber.* Num. 33:35, 36.

R **MIDIAN,** son of Abraham & Keturah, Gen. 25:2; Moses' wife, Ex. 2:11-23.

S **REPHIDIM,** Battle with the Amalekites Ex. 17:8-16. Jethro advises Moses, Ex. 18.

ROUTE OF EXODUS (1450 B.C.) ➜
JOSHUA'S CONQUEST OF THE LAND ····▸

The Land of Canaan stretched from Modern Lebanon in the North to the Negev in the South; from the Mediterranean Sea to the desert beyond Modern Syria and Jordan — about 30 Miles East of the Jordan River.

903

THE LAND PROMISED TO ISRAEL; THE KINGDOMS OF DAVID AND SOLOMON.

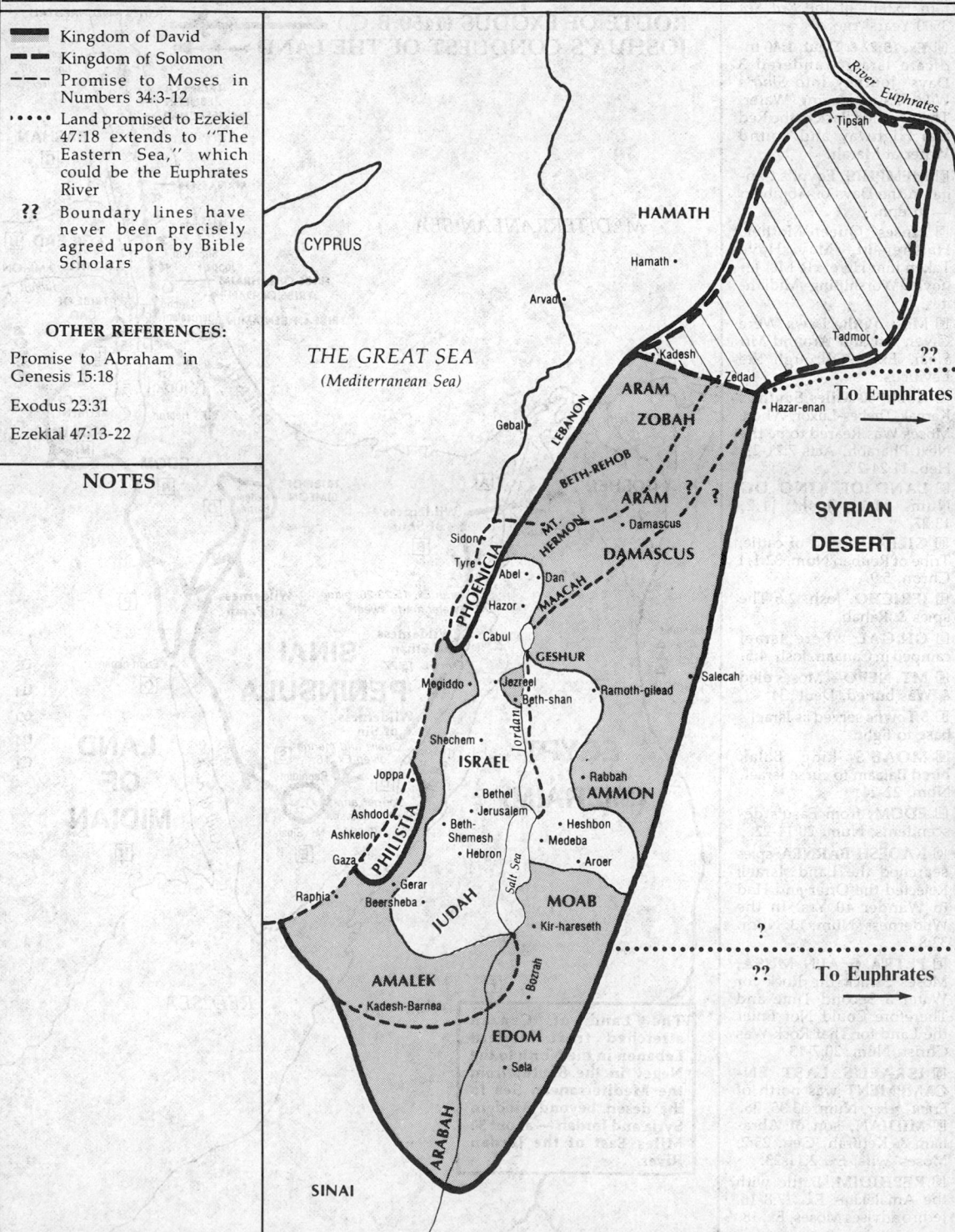

	Kingdom of David
— — —	Kingdom of Solomon
– – –	Promise to Moses in Numbers 34:3-12
· · · · ·	Land promised to Ezekiel 47:18 extends to "The Eastern Sea," which could be the Euphrates River
??	Boundary lines have never been precisely agreed upon by Bible Scholars

OTHER REFERENCES:

Promise to Abraham in Genesis 15:18

Exodus 23:31

Ezekial 47:13-22

NOTES

River Euphrates

HAMATH

CYPRUS

Tipsah

Hamath

Arvad

THE GREAT SEA
(Mediterranean Sea)

Kadesh

Zedad

Tadmor

??

To Euphrates

Hazar-enan

Gebal

ARAM ZOBAH

SYRIAN DESERT

BETH-REHOB

ARAM

? ?

Sidon

MT. HERMON

Damascus

DAMASCUS

Tyre

Abel • Dan

LEBANON

Hazor

MAACAH

PHOENICIA

Cabul

GESHUR

Salecah

Megiddo

Jezreel

Ramoth-gilead

Beth-shan

Jordan

Shechem

ISRAEL

Joppa

Bethel

Rabbah

AMMON

Jerusalem

Ashdod

Beth-Shemesh

Heshbon

Ashkelon

Hebron

Medeba

Gaza

PHILISTIA

Aroer

Raphia

Gerar

Salt Sea

Beersheba

JUDAH

MOAB

Kir-hareseth

?

??

To Euphrates

AMALEK

Bozrah

Kadesh-Barnea

EDOM

Sela

ARABAH

SINAI

904

SIXTH CENTURY B.C. EMPIRES

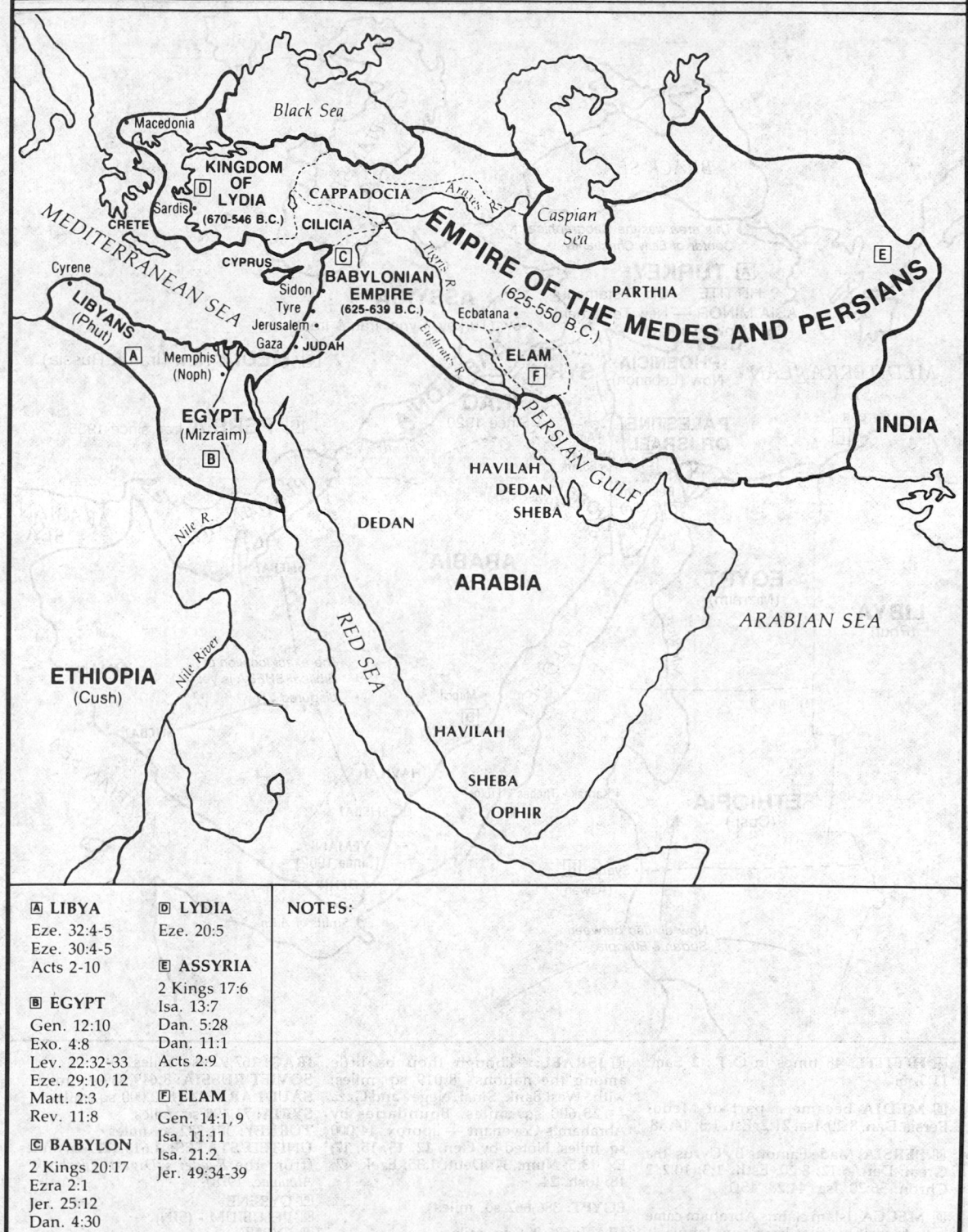

Black Sea

Macedonia

KINGDOM OF LYDIA
(670-546 B.C.)

Sardis

CRETE

CAPPADOCIA

Araxes R.

Caspian Sea

CILICIA

CYPRUS

EMPIRE OF THE MEDES AND PERSIANS
(625-550 B.C.)

PARTHIA

MEDITERRANEAN SEA

Sidon

Tyre

Jerusalem

Gaza

BABYLONIAN EMPIRE
(625-639 B.C.)

Tigris R.

Ecbatana

Euphrates R.

JUDAH

Cyrene

LIBYANS
(Phut)

Memphis (Noph)

EGYPT
(Mizraim)

ELAM

INDIA

HAVILAH
DEDAN
SHEBA

Nile R.

DEDAN

PERSIAN GULF

RED SEA

ARABIA

ARABIAN SEA

ETHIOPIA
(Cush)

Nile River

HAVILAH

SHEBA

OPHIR

A LIBYA	D LYDIA	NOTES:
Eze. 32:4-5	Eze. 20:5	
Eze. 30:4-5		
Acts 2-10	E ASSYRIA	
	2 Kings 17:6	
B EGYPT	Isa. 13:7	
Gen. 12:10	Dan. 5:28	
Exo. 4:8	Dan. 11:1	
Lev. 22:32-33	Acts 2:9	
Eze. 29:10, 12		
Matt. 2:3	F ELAM	
Rev. 11:8	Gen. 14:1, 9	
	Isa. 11:11	
C BABYLON	Isa. 21:2	
2 Kings 20:17	Jer. 49:34-39	
Ezra 2:1		
Jer. 25:12		
Dan. 4:30		

MAJOR NATIONS OF THE BIBLE THEN AND NOW

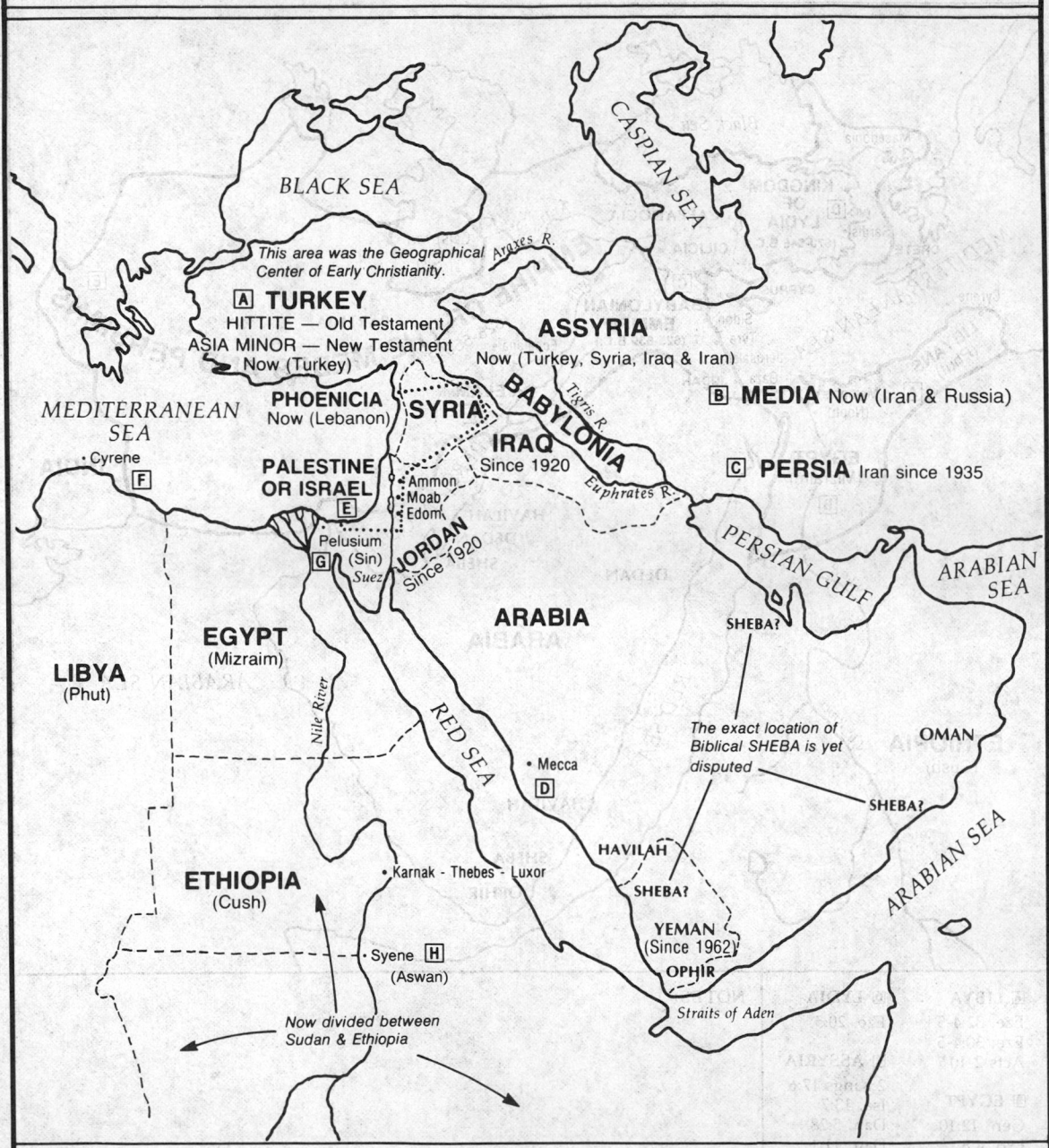

BLACK SEA

This area was the Geographical Center of Early Christianity.

Araxes R.

CASPIAN SEA

Ⓐ **TURKEY**
HITTITE — Old Testament
ASIA MINOR — New Testament
Now (Turkey)

ASSYRIA
Now (Turkey, Syria, Iraq & Iran)

MEDITERRANEAN SEA

PHOENICIA
Now (Lebanon)

SYRIA

BABYLONIA

Tigris R.

Ⓑ **MEDIA** Now (Iran & Russia)

IRAQ
Since 1920

Euphrates R.

Ⓒ **PERSIA** Iran since 1935

• Cyrene
Ⓕ

PALESTINE OR ISRAEL
Ⓔ

Ammon
Moab
Edom

JORDAN
Since 1920

Pelusium (Sin)
Ⓖ
Suez

PERSIAN GULF

ARABIAN SEA

EGYPT
(Mizraim)

LIBYA
(Phut)

Nile River

RED SEA

ARABIA

SHEBA?

The exact location of Biblical SHEBA is yet disputed

OMAN

SHEBA?

• Mecca
Ⓓ

HAVILAH

SHEBA?

ARABIAN SEA

ETHIOPIA
(Cush)

• Karnak - Thebes - Luxor

YEMAN
(Since 1962)

OPHIR

• Syene Ⓗ
(Aswan)

Now divided between Sudan & Ethiopia

Straits of Aden

Ⓐ **HITTITE:** 48 times in O.T.; 2 Sam. 11:3, 6.

Ⓑ **MEDIA** became a part of Medo-Persia:Dan. 8:20; Isa. 21:2; Est. 1:3, 14, 18

Ⓒ **PERSIA,** Made Famous By Cyrus, the Great: Dan. 6:12; 8:20; Esth. 1:3; 10:2; 2 Chron. 36:20; Isa. 44:28; 45:1

Ⓓ **MECCA** (Islam claims Abraham came here to visit his first-born son, Ishmael)

Ⓔ **ISRAEL:** "Though thou be little among the nations" 8,019 sq. miles; with West Bank, Sinai, Negev and Gaza — 25,600 sq. miles. Boundaries by Abraham's Covenant — approx. 14,000 sq. miles. Noted by Gen. 12, 13, 15, 17; Ex. 13:5; Num. 34; Deut. 1:35; Ezek. 47, 48; Josh. 24.

EGYPT: 386,662 sq. miles

IRAN: 636,296 sq. miles

IRAQ: 167,925 sq. miles
SOVIET RUSSIA: 8,649,539 sq. miles
SAUDI ARABIA: 830,000 sq. miles
SYRIA: 71,498 sq. miles
TURKEY: 301,382 sq. miles
UNITED STATES: 3,615,122 sq. miles
(from the *Reader's Digest Yearbook - Almanac,* 1978).

Ⓕ **CYRENE**
Ⓖ **PELUSIUM - (SIN)**
Ⓗ **SYENE**

PALESTINE — OLD AND NEW TESTAMENT

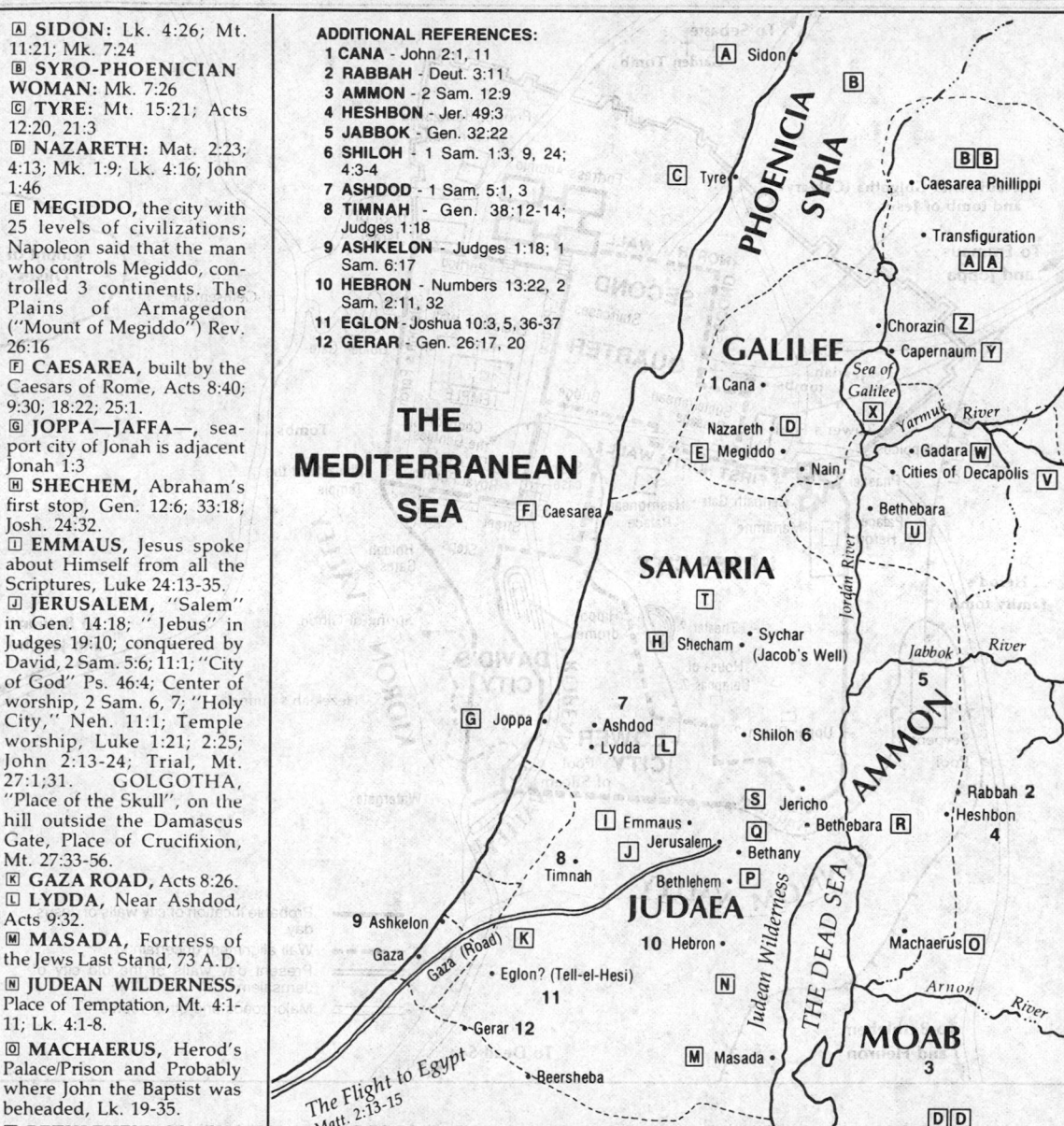

A SIDON: Lk. 4:26; Mt. 11:21; Mk. 7:24

B SYRO-PHOENICIAN WOMAN: Mk. 7:26

C TYRE: Mt. 15:21; Acts 12:20, 21:3

D NAZARETH: Mat. 2:23; 4:13; Mk. 1:9; Lk. 4:16; John 1:46

E MEGIDDO, the city with 25 levels of civilizations; Napoleon said that the man who controls Megiddo, controlled 3 continents. The Plains of Armagedon ("Mount of Megiddo") Rev. 26:16

F CAESAREA, built by the Caesars of Rome, Acts 8:40; 9:30; 18:22; 25:1.

G JOPPA—JAFFA—, seaport city of Jonah is adjacent Jonah 1:3

H SHECHEM, Abraham's first stop, Gen. 12:6; 33:18; Josh. 24:32.

I EMMAUS, Jesus spoke about Himself from all the Scriptures, Luke 24:13-35.

J JERUSALEM, "Salem" in Gen. 14:18; " Jebus" in Judges 19:10; conquered by David, 2 Sam. 5:6; 11:1; "City of God" Ps. 46:4; Center of worship, 2 Sam. 6, 7; "Holy City," Neh. 11:1; Temple worship, Luke 1:21; 2:25; John 2:13-24; Trial, Mt. 27:1;31. GOLGOTHA, "Place of the Skull", on the hill outside the Damascus Gate, Place of Crucifixion, Mt. 27:33-56.

K GAZA ROAD, Acts 8:26.

L LYDDA, Near Ashdod, Acts 9:32.

M MASADA, Fortress of the Jews Last Stand, 73 A.D.

N JUDEAN WILDERNESS, Place of Temptation, Mt. 4:1-11; Lk. 4:1-8.

O MACHAERUS, Herod's Palace/Prison and Probably where John the Baptist was beheaded, Lk. 19-35.

P BETHLEHEM: Mt. 2:5, 16; Lk. 2:4; John 7:42.

Q BETHANY: Mt. 21:17; 26:6; Lk. 10:38; 24:50; Jn. 11:18; 12:1.

R BETHABARA, Beyond Bethany, the place of Jesus' Baptism, Mt. 3:13-17; Mk. 1:3; Lk. 3:2.

S JERICHO: Mt. 20:29; Mk. 10:46; Lk. 10:30.

T SAMARIA, Capital of the Northern Kingdom; 1 Kngs. 16:24, 29; 2 Kngs. 6:19; Jews

ADDITIONAL REFERENCES:
1. **CANA** - John 2:1, 11
2. **RABBAH** - Deut. 3:11
3. **AMMON** - 2 Sam. 12:9
4. **HESHBON** - Jer. 49:3
5. **JABBOK** - Gen. 32:22
6. **SHILOH** - 1 Sam. 1:3, 9, 24; 4:3-4
7. **ASHDOD** - 1 Sam. 5:1, 3
8. **TIMNAH** - Gen. 38:12-14; Judges 1:18
9. **ASHKELON** - Judges 1:18; 1 Sam. 6:17
10. **HEBRON** - Numbers 13:22, 2 Sam. 2:11, 32
11. **EGLON** - Joshua 10:3, 5, 36-37
12. **GERAR** - Gen. 26:17, 20

in Jesus' day refrained from going thru Samaria; But Jesus "must needs go through . . ." John 4:4-42; Acts 8:5-25.

U BETHABARA, a probable place of baptism, John 1:28; 10:40. The road through Bethabara was usually taken to prevent going thru Samaria

V "TEN CITIES" of the Decapolis Mt. 4:25; Mk. 5:20; 7:31.

W GADARA: Mk. 5:1; Lk. 8:26, 37.

X SEA OF GALILEE: Mt. 2:22; 21:11; John 6:1; 21:1.

Y CAPERNAUM: Mt. 4:13; 8:5, 11:17; Mk. 1:21; John 4:46; 6:17, 24.

Z CHORAZIM: Mt. 1:21.

AA TRANSFIGURATION: the exact location is uncertain, Mt. 17:1-21; Lk. 9:18-62.

BB CAESAREA PHILLIPPI: Mt. 16:13; Mk. 8:27.

CC NABATAEANS—Atetas, King of the Nabataeans, 2 Corinthians 11:32.

DD ARABIANS — Paul went to Arabia, Galatians 1:17; 4:25.

JERUSALEM IN 66 A.D.

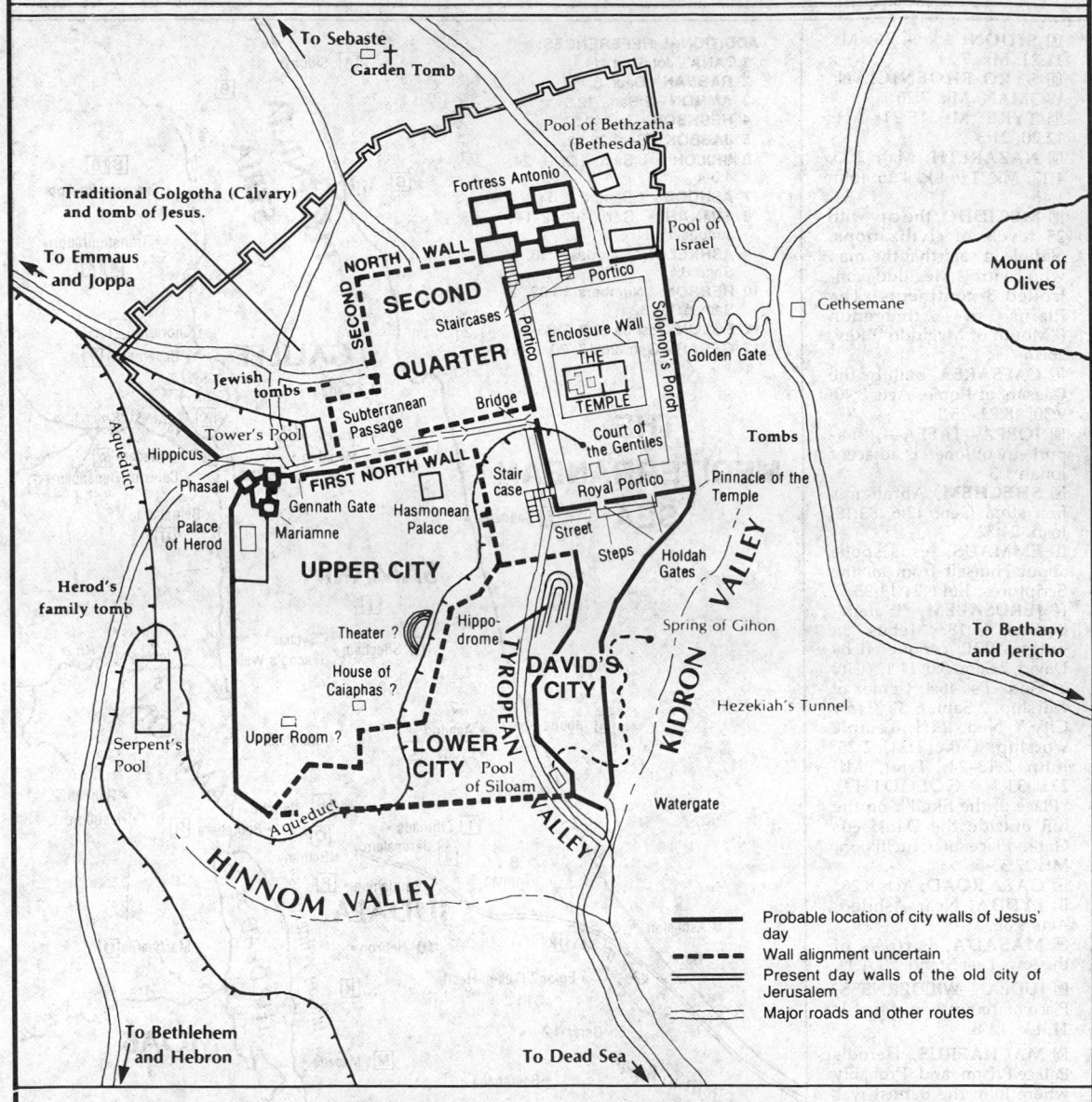

To Sebaste
Garden Tomb

Pool of Bethzatha
(Bethesda)

Traditional Golgotha (Calvary)
and tomb of Jesus.

Fortress Antonio

Pool of
Israel

To Emmaus
and Joppa

NORTH   WALL

SECOND

Portico

Mount of
Olives

Staircases

Enclosure Wall

SECOND

Gethsemane

Jewish
tombs

QUARTER

Portico

THE
TEMPLE

Solomon's Porch

Golden Gate

Tower's Pool

Subterranean
Passage

Bridge

Court of
the Gentiles

Tombs

Hippicus

FIRST NORTH WALL

Stair
case

Royal Portico

Pinnacle of the
Temple

Phasael

Gennath Gate

Hasmonean
Palace

Street

Palace
of Herod

Mariamne

UPPER CITY

Steps

Holdah
Gates

KIDRON

Aqueduct

Herod's
family tomb

Theater ?

Hippo-
drome

Spring of Gihon

VALLEY

To Bethany
and Jericho

House of
Caiaphas ?

TYROPEAN

DAVID'S
CITY

Hezekiah's Tunnel

Serpent's
Pool

Upper Room ?

LOWER
CITY

Pool
of Siloam

VALLEY

Watergate

Aqueduct

HINNOM VALLEY

Probable location of city walls of Jesus'
day

Wall alignment uncertain

Present day walls of the old city of
Jerusalem

Major roads and other routes

To Bethlehem
and Hebron

To Dead Sea

"UPPER ROOM" Mt. 26:17-25; Mk. 14:15; Acts 1:13.
"DAVID'S TOWERS", made Roman Headquarters,
The Praetorium, where "The Pavement" was Jn. 19:13.
PALACE OF HASMONEANS Luke 23:7.
GOLGOTHA, "Place of the Skull & the Crucifixion, Mt.
27:33; Jn. 19:17.
GARDEN TOMB, Jn. 19:38-42; Mt. 27:61, 62; 28:1.
HEROD'S GATE
BETHESDA POOL, John 5:2.
SHEEP GATE, John 5:2.
ANTONIA'S TOWER, Acts 21:34.

VIA DOLOROSA, Mt. 27:32; Mk. 15:20, 21.
THE TEMPLE GATE BEAUTIFUL Acts 3:2.
COURT OF THE GENTILES, Jn. 8:2.
SOLOMON'S PORCH, Jn. 10:32; Acts 3:11; 5:12.
HOLY PLACE Ex. 26:33, 28; Lev. 6:16; Heb. 9, 10; Mt.
27:50, 51.
HOLY OF HOLIES, Lk. 1:2, 5-12; Heb. 9:14.
THE POOL OF GIHON, Gen. 2; II Chron. 32:30.
AKELDAMA, "Field of Blood", Mt. 27:4-8.
POOL OF SILOAM John 9:7.
THE GARDEN OF GETHSEMANE.